letter history	Illustrated orthographic history on the first page of each letter of the alphabet.
manual alphabet	Illustration at the entry.
maps	Locator map at the entry for the country or territory; half-page maps at **United States of America** and **Canada**.
Morse code	Table at the entry.
musical notes	Time values for musical notes at **note**.
proofreaders' marks	Table at **proofread**.
punctuation and grammar	Refer to the relevant entry; for example, see **comma, split infinitive.**
Roman numerals	Table at **Roman numeral.**
signs and symbols	Table at **symbol.**
subatomic particles	Table at **particle.**
synonyms	Refer to the relevant entry; for example, see **flock.**
taxonomy	Taxonomic table of living organisms at **taxonomy.**
usage	Usage notes appear with the relevant entries; for example, see **ain't, like.**
weights and measures	Table of common and scientific units at **measurement.**

THE AMERICAN HERITAGE
DICTIONARY
OF THE ENGLISH LANGUAGE

DICTI

THE AMERICAN HERITAGE

ONARY

OF THE ENGLISH LANGUAGE

WILLIAM MORRIS, Editor

Published by

AMERICAN HERITAGE PUBLISHING CO., INC.

and

HOUGHTON MIFFLIN COMPANY

BOSTON/NEW YORK/ATLANTA/GENEVA, ILLINOIS/DALLAS/PALO ALTO

©1969 by American Heritage Publishing Co., Inc.
551 Fifth Avenue, New York, New York 10017

All rights reserved under Bern and Pan-American Copyright Conventions

Standard Book Numbers: 395–09064–4 (deluxe edition);
395–09065–2 (plain edges); 395–09066–0 (thumb-indexed)

Library of Congress Catalog Card Number 76–86995

Manufactured in the United States of America

Computer composed by Inforonics, Inc.
in Maynard, Massachusetts

Contents

Introduction

by William Morris

This Dictionary of the English language is an entirely new work. It has been produced by the American Heritage Publishing Company, publishers of *American Heritage,* the magazine of history; of *Horizon,* a quarterly devoted to culture and the arts; and of a wide spectrum of books. Since these enterprises were established in 1954, their editors have felt a deep sense of responsibility as custodians of the American tradition in language as well as history. Consequently, at a time when the language, already a historical melting pot, is under constant challenge—from the scientist, the bureaucrat, the broadcaster, the innovator of every stripe, even the voyager in space—they undertook to prepare a new dictionary. It would faithfully record our language, the duty of any lexicographer, but it would not, like so many others in these permissive times, rest there. On the contrary, it would add the essential dimension of guidance, that sensible guidance toward grace and precision which intelligent people seek in a dictionary. They will find it here, in a dictionary that is in many respects a notable departure from previous British and American lexicographical practice.

To many people a dictionary is a forbidding volume, a useful but bleak compendium, to be referred to hastily for needed information, such as spelling and pronunciation. Yet what a dictionary ought to be is a treasury of information about every aspect of words, our most essential tools of communication. It should be an agreeable companion. By knowledgeable use of the dictionary we should learn where a word has come from, precisely what its various shades of meaning are today, and its social status.

In the five years of preparation of this work, many of the leading scholars and scientists of the English-speaking world have collaborated with our permanent editorial staff in the enterprise of recording with accuracy and authority those ele-ments of our language which are of concern to literate people. The vocabulary recorded here, ranging from the language of Shakespeare to the idiom of the present day, is that of the educated adult. The "educated adult" referred to is, of course, a kind of ideal person, for he has at his fingertips a most comprehensive lexicon, not only for the conduct and discussion of everyday affairs, but also for all of the arts and all of the sciences.

We have had the enthusiastic cooperation of many distinguished linguists, several of whom have contributed articles on their areas of special interest in the pages following. Morris Bishop, poet and past president of the Modern Language Association, comments with wit and keen perception on the levels of usage to be found in our society today and the contributions of our Usage Panelists (described below) in resolving controversial questions of linguistic propriety. Morton Bloomfield, Professor of English at Harvard University, records the story of the evolution of the English language from its Germanic origins to the present day. Calvert Watkins, Professor of Linguistics and the Classics at Harvard University, contributes a fascinating account of the Indo-European origins of English. Henry Lee Smith, Jr., one of the nation's best-known linguistic scholars, Professor of Linguistics and English at the State University of New York at Buffalo, analyzes the relationships among the diverse American dialects. Richard Ohmann, Professor of English at Wesleyan University and editor of *College English,* the journal of the National Council of Teachers of English, analyzes grammar and meaning in light of the most recent research. Wayne O'Neil, Professor of Humanities at Massachusetts Institute of Technology, explicates new insights into the relationship of spelling to pronunciation in English. Henry Kučera, Professor of Linguistics and of Slavic Languages at Brown University, describes the application of computers to linguistic analysis and lexicography. Taken together, these introductory articles bring layman and student alike abreast of the latest important developments in language study.

We have engaged the services of hundreds of authorities in every range of human endeavor and scholarship, from archaeology to space research, from Indo-European to computer programming. Over a four-year period, many thousands of definitions were sent to these specialists for emendation or approval.

To furnish the guidance which we believe to be an essential responsibility of a good dictionary, we have frequently employed usage-context indicators such as "slang," "nonstandard," or "regional." But going beyond that, we asked a panel of 100 outstanding speakers and writers a wide range of questions about how the language is used today, especially with regard to dubious or controversial locutions. After careful tabulation and analysis of their replies, we have prepared several hundred usage notes to guide readers to effectiveness in speech and writing. As a consequence, this Dictionary can claim to be more precisely descriptive, in terms of current usage levels, than any heretofore published—especially in offering the reader the lexical opinions of a large group of highly sophisticated fellow citizens.

In order to acquaint the reader with the history of our language, we engaged a special staff of more than a score of linguistic scholars, working under the direction of Professor Watkins at Harvard. With the help of the Dictionary's own staff of etymologists, they conducted a five-year research program amounting to a re-evaluation of the histories of all the words in the Dictionary. The etymologies are written in plain language with no abbreviations or symbols. In addition, an innovation was made in presenting more fully than ever before the *prehistoric* origins of the language; following the main body of the Dictionary is an Appendix of Indo-European roots, giving detailed and fascinating information about the ancient interrelationships of thousands of widely different words.

A major concern of the editors has been the language used in the word definitions themselves. Our aim has been to phrase definitions in concise, lucid prose. Here, too, we have undertaken to eliminate "dictionary shorthand"—the frustrating signs, symbols, and abbreviations that are commonplace in other dictionaries. Except for a few obvious abbreviations (*n.* for *noun, v.* for *verb,* and the like), we have followed a policy of spelling out all definitions. Where necessary to clarify a meaning or idiomatic usage, the editors have included an example, either quoted from literature or staff-written. We have also eliminated the meaningless lists of undefined compound forms which serve, in many American dictionaries, merely the purpose of inflating the so-called "entry count."

Simplicity and clarity have been sought in the system of representing the pronunciations. American speech takes many forms. The aim here is not to represent all or even most of its variations, but to provide one or more pronunciations for each word that can be easily reproduced from familiar symbols by the reader untrained in phonetics. The pronunciations are those that would be regarded as standard even by those who may themselves have regional "accents."

One important aspect of the fresh approach taken by the editors of *The American Heritage Dictionary of the English Language* is obvious at a glance. Utilizing the most recent advances in typographic design and printing, we have created what we believe to be a most attractive dictionary. The page, with its large, readable type and wide margins, was expressly designed to invite *reading*. The inclusion of several thousand illustrations, both in line drawings and photography, represents another notable advance in dictionary design. The pictures have been chosen as much as possible in an attempt to add genuine meaning to the subjects they illustrate. Though the pictures are in many cases attractive in themselves, the aim has been less to add beauty to the book than to give the reader fuller information than would be possible in a dictionary of traditional design.

As has been implied above, a primary aim of our staff has been to make this Dictionary as readable as we possibly could. We editors know that dictionaries can be fascinating. Working closely with them day by day, we see the vast amounts of interesting information that many users are not aware of, usually because it is hard to work one's way through the thorny underbrush of conventional sign language to find the treasure that lies buried in the entries. It is our earnest hope that, by presenting our Dictionary in inviting and readily readable fashion, without any lessening of authority, we will encourage the reader to explore and enjoy the riches of our remarkable tongue.

In the preparation of a work of this magnitude the cooperation of many hands and minds is essential. Of greatest significance, perhaps, has been the generous contribution of the members of our Usage Panel, who borrowed many hours from their busy pursuits to the end of creating what one panelist calls "a dictionary put together with deep respect for people who have an eye and ear and tongue for what is still the richest, most rewarding language in the world."

Thanks, too, are due to our many consultants and advisors in the various scholarly, scientific, and technological disciplines. Our publishing colleagues at Houghton Mifflin Company have also made many valued suggestions from the earliest planning stages through final review of extended sections of manuscript and proof. To the scores of our editorial staff associates involved in the day-to-day tasks of creating and editing this Dictionary, we extend our unstinting thanks and appreciation.

Editorial Staff

Usage Panel

J. Donald Adams
Literary critic; formerly Editor,
The New York Times Book Review

Cleveland Amory
Columnist, *Saturday Review, TV Guide,* and *Holiday;*
commentator, Group W Radio

Isaac Asimov
Writer; Associate Professor of Biochemistry,
Boston University School of Medicine

John Bainbridge
Staff writer, *The New Yorker*

Russell Baker
Columnist, *The New York Times*

Sheridan Baker
Professor of English, University of Michigan;
Editor, *The Michigan Quarterly Review*

Lincoln Barnett
Writer; formerly Associate Editor, *Life*

Jacques Barzun
Writer; University Professor, Columbia University

Stewart Beach
Writer; formerly Executive Editor, *This Week*

Charles F. Berlitz
Author and editor of language instruction books

Theodore M. Bernstein
Assistant Managing Editor, *The New York Times*

Morris Bishop
Writer; Professor Emeritus of Romance Languages,
Cornell University; past President,
Modern Language Association

Alton Blakeslee
Science writer, The Associated Press

Morton W. Bloomfield
Professor of English, Harvard University

Ben Zion Bokser
Rabbi, Forest Hills Jewish Center;
Visiting Associate Professor, Jewish Theological
Seminary

Arna Bontemps
Writer; Professor of English, University of Illinois,
Chicago Circle; formerly Librarian, Fisk University

Charles P. Boren
Managing Editor, *Lewiston* (Idaho) *Morning Tribune*

Catherine Drinker Bowen
Biographer; historian

Joseph A. Brandt
Professor Emeritus of Journalism, University of
California, Los Angeles; formerly President,
University of Oklahoma, Director, University of
Oklahoma Press, Princeton University Press, and
University of Chicago Press

Herbert Brucker
Writer; formerly Editor, *Hartford Courant;*
past President, American Society of Newspaper
Editors

Erwin D. Canham
Editor in Chief, *The Christian Science Monitor;*
past President, American Society of Newspaper
Editors; past Chairman of the Board, United States
Chamber of Commerce

Carl Carmer
Writer; poet; member of Advisory Board, *American
Heritage;* past President, International Association
of Poets, Playwrights, Editors, Essayists, and
Novelists (P.E.N.), Poetry Society of America, and
Authors Guild of Authors League of America

Gerald Carson
Writer; member of Advisory Board, *American
Heritage;* formerly Vice President, Benton & Bowles,
Inc., and Director, Kenyon & Eckhardt, Inc.

Hodding Carter
Editor and Publisher, *Delta Democrat-Times,*
Greenville, Miss.; winner of Pulitzer Prize (1946)
for editorial writing

Claudia Cassidy
Writer; formerly music and drama critic, *Chicago
Tribune*

Bruce Catton
Historian; Senior Editor, *American Heritage;*
winner of Pulitzer Prize (1954) for historical writing

John Ciardi
Poet; writer; Poetry Editor, *Saturday Review;*
past President, National College English Association

Arthur A. Cohen
Writer; formerly Editor in Chief and Vice President,
General Book Division, Holt, Rinehart and Winston,
Inc.; co-founder, Meridian Books

Marc Connelly
Playwright; formerly Professor of Playwriting,
Yale University; past President, Authors League of
America and National Institute of Arts and Letters

Alistair Cooke
Chief American correspondent, *The Guardian*
(England); commentator, British Broadcasting
Corporation

Roy H. Copperud
Professor of Journalism, University of Southern
California; columnist, *Editor & Publisher*

George A. Cornish
Editor in Chief, *Encyclopedia Americana;*
formerly Managing Editor and Executive Editor,
New York Herald Tribune

Robert Coughlan
Staff writer, *Life*

Malcolm Cowley
Writer; literary advisor, Viking Press, Inc.;
formerly Associate Editor, *The New Republic*

Basil Davenport
Writer; formerly member of Editorial Board,
Book-of-the-Month Club

Donald Davidson
Writer; poet; Professor Emeritus of English,
Vanderbilt University

Marshall B. Davidson
Writer; Senior Editor, *Horizon;*
formerly Editor of Publications,
The Metropolitan Museum of Art, New York

René Dubos
Professor of Pathology, Rockefeller University;
winner of Pulitzer Prize (1969) for general nonfiction

Luther Evans
Librarian of International Affairs, Columbia
University; formerly Librarian of Congress

John Fischer
Contributing Editor and
formerly Editor in Chief, *Harper's Magazine*

George Gamow
Professor of Physics, University of Colorado

Lewis Gannett
Editor, *Mainstream of America* Series;
formerly columnist, *New York Herald Tribune*

Brendan Gill
Drama critic, *The New Yorker*

Eric F. Goldman
Rollins Professor of History, Princeton University;
President, Society of American Historians;
member of Advisory Board, *American Heritage;*
formerly Special Consultant to the President
of the United States

Sydney Harris
Drama critic and columnist, *Chicago Daily News*

Mark O. Hatfield
U.S. Senator from Oregon

Gilbert Highet
Writer; Anthon Professor of the Latin Language and Literature, Columbia University; Chairman of Advisory Board, *Horizon;* member of the Editorial Board, Book-of-the-Month Club

Paul Horgan
Writer; Director, Center for Advanced Studies, Wesleyan University; winner of Pulitzer Prize (1955) for historical writing

Langston Hughes
Writer; poet; formerly columnist, *Chicago Defender* and *New York Post*

Peter Hurd
Painter; cattle-rancher

John K. Hutchens
Literary critic; member of Editorial Board, Book-of-the-Month Club; formerly book reviewer, *New York Herald Tribune*

William F. Johnston
Publisher and Editorial Advisor, Student Publications, University of Washington

Lewis Webster Jones
Formerly President, Rutgers University, University of Arkansas, and Bennington College; past Chairman, Board of Trustees, Educational Testing Service

Walter Kerr
Sunday drama critic, *The New York Times;* formerly drama critic, *New York Herald Tribune;* past President, New York Critics' Circle

John Kieran
Writer; naturalist; formerly member of Board of Experts, "Information, Please" radio program and sports columnist, *The New York Times*

James Kraft
Assistant Professor of English, Wesleyan University

Louis Kronenberger
Professor of Theatre Arts, Brandeis University; contributor, *Atlantic Monthly;* formerly drama critic, *Time*

Milton I. Levine, M.D.
Professor of Clinical Pediatrics, New York Hospital-Cornell Medical Center; radio commentator, Columbia Broadcasting System; formerly syndicated newspaper columnist

Walter Lippmann
Syndicated newspaper columnist; winner of Pulitzer Prize in 1958 (special citation) and in 1962 (international reporting)

Russell Lynes
Contributing Editor and formerly Managing Editor, *Harper's Magazine*

Eugene McCarthy
U.S. Senator from Minnesota

Dwight Macdonald
Contributor, *The New Yorker;* columnist, *Esquire*

David McCord
Poet; essayist; Honorary Curator of the Poetry and Farnsworth Rooms, Harvard College Library

Margaret Mead
Writer; Curator of Ethnology, American Museum of Natural History, New York; past President, American Anthropological Association

Rhoda Métraux
Anthropologist, Institute for Intercultural Studies, New York

William J. Miller
Vice President for Public Relations, Federated Department Stores, Inc.; formerly chief editorial writer, *New York Herald Tribune*

Marianne Moore
Writer; winner of Pulitzer Prize (1952) for poetry

Lewis Mumford
Writer; past President, American Academy of Arts and Letters; formerly Professor of Humanities, Stanford University, and Professor of City and Regional Planning, University of Pennsylvania

John Courtney Murray, S.J.
Professor of Theology, Woodstock College, Maryland; formerly Editor, *Theological Studies,* and Associate Editor, *America*

Maurine Neuberger
Formerly U.S. Senator from Oregon

James Newman
Writer; member, Board of Editors, *Scientific American;* Honorary Consultant to Library of Congress in literature of mathematics

Margaret Nicholson
Writer; Editor of Contract and Copyright Dept., Farrar, Straus & Giroux, Inc.; formerly Head of Publishing Dept., Oxford University Press

David Ogilvy
Advertising copywriter; Chairman and Chief Executive Officer, Ogilvy & Mather International, Inc.

Mario Pei
Professor of Romance Philology, Columbia University

James A. Pike
Staff member, Center for the Study of Democratic Institutions; formerly Episcopal Bishop of California

Katherine Anne Porter
Writer; winner of Pulitzer Prize (1966) for fiction

Orville Prescott
Writer; formerly co-editor, "Books of The Times" in *The New York Times*

Charles D. Rice
Columnist, *This Week*

Berton Roueché
Staff writer, *The New Yorker*

Richard Rovere
Washington correspondent, *The New Yorker*

Vermont Royster
Editor, *The Wall Street Journal;* winner of Pulitzer Prize (1953) for editorial writing

Winthrop Sargeant
Music critic, *The New Yorker*

Robert Saudek
Television producer; Director, The Institute of Film and Television, New York University

Glenn T. Seaborg
Chairman, U.S. Atomic Energy Commission; winner of Nobel Prize (1951) for chemistry

Harlow Shapley
Director Emeritus, Harvard College Observatory; past President, American Academy of Arts and Sciences and American Association for the Advancement of Science

John K. Sherman
Book and Arts Editor, *Minneapolis Star*

Walter W. (Red) Smith
Syndicated sports columnist

Theodore Sorensen
Lawyer; Editor at Large and Director, *Saturday Review;* formerly Special Counsel to the President of the United States

Wallace Stegner
Writer; Professor of English, Stanford University; Editor at Large, *Saturday Review*

George R. Stewart
Writer; Professor Emeritus of English, University of California, Berkeley

Allen Tate
Poet; critic; Regents' Professor of English, University of Minnesota

Henry F. Thoma
Editor in Chief and Head, College Department, Houghton Mifflin Company

Virgil Thomson
Composer; formerly music critic, *New York Herald Tribune;* winner of Pulitzer Prize (1949) for music

Barbara W. Tuchman
Historian; winner of Pulitzer Prize (1963) for general nonfiction

Stewart Udall
    Chairman, Overview Corporation;
    formerly U.S. Secretary of the Interior
    and U.S. Representative from Arizona

Irita Van Doren
    Formerly Literary Editor, *New York Herald Tribune*

Mark Van Doren
    Writer; Professor Emeritus of English, Columbia
    University; winner of Pulitzer Prize (1940) for poetry

William Vaughan
    Associate Editor, *Kansas City Star;*
    syndicated newspaper columnist

Calvert Watkins
    Professor of Linguistics and the Classics,
    Harvard University

Richard Watts, Jr.
    Drama critic, *New York Post*

Hobart G. Weekes
    Associate Editor, *The New Yorker*

Anthony West
    Literary critic, *The New Yorker*

Rogers Whitaker
    Associate Editor and sports writer, *The New Yorker*

Oscar Williams
    Poet; editor

William Zinsser
    Columnist, *Life;* formerly columnist, *Look,*
    and drama editor, movie critic, and editorial writer,
    New York Herald Tribune

Consultants

ARTS AND HUMANITIES

Richard D. Altick
    Regents' Professor of English, Ohio State University

Willi Apel
    Professor Emeritus of Musicology, Indiana University

Charles F. Berlitz
    Author and editor of language instruction books

James Marston Fitch
    Professor of Architecture, Columbia University

Ignace J. Gelb
    Frank P. Hixon Distinguished Service Professor
    of Assyriology, University of Chicago

Harold F. Harding
    Benedict Professor of Speech, University of Texas,
    El Paso

James Humphry III
    Vice President, The H.W. Wilson Company;
    formerly Chief Librarian,
    The Metropolitan Museum of Art, New York

Bernard M.W. Knox
    Director, The Center for Hellenic Studies,
    Washington, D.C.

Burt Korall
    Popular Music and Entertainment Critic,
    Saturday Review

Wayne C. Minnick
    Professor of Speech and Associate Dean,
    College of Arts and Sciences, Florida State University

Beaumont Newhall
    Director, George Eastman House, Rochester, N.Y.

Allardyce Nicoll
    Formerly Chairman of Drama Department,
    Yale University; Professor Emeritus, English,
    The Shakespeare Institute,
    University of Birmingham (England)

George Kimball Plochmann
    Professor of Philosophy, Southern Illinois University

Maurice F. Tauber
    Melvil Dewey Professor of Library Service,
    Columbia University

Walter Terry
    Dance critic, *Saturday Review*

John Walker
    Director, The National Gallery of Art,
    Washington, D.C.

Calvert Watkins
    Professor of Linguistics and the Classics,
    Harvard University

LIFE SCIENCES

Isaac Asimov
    Associate Professor of Biochemistry,
    Boston University School of Medicine

Jesse F. Bone
    Professor of Veterinary Medicine,
    Oregon State University

Ralph Buchsbaum
    Professor of Biology, University of Pittsburgh

William H. Burt
    Professor of Zoology and Curator of Mammals,
    University of Michigan

Spencer H. Davis, Jr.
    Professor of Plant Pathology, Rutgers University

Frederick C. Fink
    Manager, Microbiological Services,
    Pfizer Diagnostics Department,
    Chas. Pfizer & Co., Inc.

Garrett Hardin
    Professor of Biology, University of California,
    Santa Barbara

Adrian Lambert, M.D.
    Associate Professor of Clinical Surgery,
    College of Physicians and Surgeons,
    Columbia University

Douglas A. Lancaster
    Assistant Professor of Ecology and Systematics,
    Cornell University

R.H. Nelson
    Executive Secretary, Entomological Society of America

James A. Peters
    Curator, Reptiles and Amphibians,
    United States National Museum, Washington, D.C.

Joseph L. Peterson
    Mycologist, Department of Plant Biology,
    Rutgers University

Olin Sewall Pettingill, Jr.
    Director, Laboratory of Ornithology,
    Cornell University

Timothy Prout
    Professor of Zoology, University of California,
    Riverside

Donn E. Rosen
    Associate Curator, Department of Ichthyology,
    American Museum of Natural History,
    New York

Frederick E. Smith
    Professor of Natural Resources,
    University of Michigan

William C. Steere
Director, The New York Botanical Garden;
Professor of Botany, Columbia University

Norman Taylor
Formerly Curator of Plants,
Brooklyn Botanic Garden, New York

Georg Zappler
Formerly Curator of Research,
New Jersey State Museum, Trenton

PHYSICAL SCIENCES AND MATHEMATICS

Peter M. Bernays
Senior Associate Editor, Chemical Abstracts Service

Edward J. Cogan
Professor of Mathematics, Sarah Lawrence College

Richard Hanau
Professor of Physics, University of Kentucky

Paul J. Kliauga
Assistant to the Director of Publications,
American Institute of Physics, New York

James E. Miller
Professor of Meteorology, New York University

Lloyd Motz
Professor of Astronomy, Columbia University

Frederick H. Pough
Contributing Editor, *Lapidary Journal;* formerly
Director, Santa Barbara Museum of Natural History,
Santa Barbara, Calif.

John A. Shimer
Professor of Geology, Brooklyn College

M.J. Sienko
Professor of Chemistry, Cornell University

Thaddeus L. Smith
Mathematical Statistician, National Insurance
Actuarial and Statistical Association

George L. Trigg
Editor, *Physical Review Letters*

William C. Vergara
Director of Advanced Research, Bendix Corporation

PRACTICAL AND APPLIED SCIENCES

Frank O. Braynard
Editor, *Tow Line*

Col. Elbridge Colby, USA (retired)
Professor Emeritus of Journalism,
George Washington University

Frederick C. Durant III
Assistant Director, National Air and Space Museum,
Smithsonian Institution, Washington, D.C.

Dorothy Fey
Executive Director,
The United States Trademark Association

Clayton Knight
Aviation historian

N. Dan Larsen
Staff architect, Rutgers University

Dorothy Nickerson
Past President, Inter-Society Color Council

Frank K. Perkins
Formerly bridge and games columnist,
The Boston Herald

J. Lowell Pratt
Co-author, *The Official Encyclopedia of Sports*

Virginia L. Robertson
Home economics consultant,
Encyclopedia International

Col. Milton Seaman, USAFR
Liaison Office Coordinator, U.S. Air Force Academy

Milton A. Sprague
Professor of Soils and Crops, Rutgers University

Victor Strauss
Printing consultant

RELIGION

Walter J. Burghardt, S.J.
Professor of Historical Theology, Woodstock College,
Maryland; Editor, *Theological Studies*

Klaus J. Hansen
Associate Professor, Department of History,
Queen's University, Kingston, Ont. (Canada)

Harry M. Orlinsky
Professor of Bible, Hebrew Union College-
Jewish Institute of Religion, New York

Jaroslav Pelikan
Titus Street Professor of Ecclesiastical History,
Yale University

Allison W. Phinney
Supervisor, Editorial Division,
The First Church of Christ, Scientist, Boston, Mass.

The Rev. Canon Edward N. West
Sub-Dean of the Cathedral Church of St. John
the Divine, New York

SOCIAL SCIENCES

Harold E. Driver
Professor of Anthropology, Indiana University

Thomas F. Dwyer, M.D.
Assistant Professor in Clinical Psychiatry,
Harvard University; Associate in Psychiatry,
Massachusetts General Hospital

John Flynn
Vice President, Perera Fifth Avenue, Inc.

Charles Fried
Professor of Law, Harvard Law School

Carl J. Friedrich
Eaton Professor of Government, Harvard University

N.L. Gage
Professor of Education and Psychology,
Stanford University

John A. Garraty
Professor of History, Columbia University

William N. Kinnard, Jr.
Professor of Finance and Real Estate,
University of Connecticut

Jesse William Markham
Professor of Business Administration,
Harvard Graduate School of Business Administration

Wilbert E. Moore
Sociologist, Russell Sage Foundation

Hallam L. Movius, Jr.
Professor of Anthropology, Harvard University

Edwin B. Newman
Lecturer on Psychology, Harvard University;
co-editor, *American Journal of Psychology*

J.H. Plumb
Professor of Modern English History,
Christ's College, Cambridge University (England)

Norman J.G. Pounds
Professor of History and Geography,
Indiana University

Bernard Wailes
Professor of Anthropology,
University of Pennsylvania

A Brief History of the English Language

by Morton W. Bloomfield

Language, like other important patterns of human behavior, slowly but constantly evolves from older forms into newer ones. When different groups of people speaking one language become separated by geographical, political, or social barriers, each group gradually develops its own variety of the language, which we call a dialect. So long as the differences between two varieties do not make mutual comprehension impossible (though they may make it difficult), and so long as the speakers of each do not consider themselves to be speaking a different language, we may say that these varieties are dialects of the same language.

However, the tendency of language throughout the early centuries of human civilization, as tribal groups broke up into subdivisions and migrated, was to split again and again into dialects that in time became mutually incomprehensible. At that point they are recognized as separate languages. Most of the languages spoken today in western Asia and Europe can be traced back to a remote "ancestor" language which we call Indo-European. It was an unwritten language and therefore, of course, no records of it survive. Yet, as the Appendix devoted to Indo-European in this Dictionary demonstrates, it can be reconstructed. The character of its words and phrases and of its grammatical structure can be inferred by comparative study of the many languages which are its descendants.

As a matter of fact, the early history of any given descendant has to be reconstructed too, by essentially the same method, for written records are a relatively recent development. In the case of English, which is our subject here, we have no written records surviving from earlier than the eighth century A.D., and they do not become common before the tenth and eleventh centuries. But by studying the written records of other languages that clearly show a common ancestry with English —Dutch and German, for example—and by assuming that evolutionary changes before the existence of writing were generally similar in kind to observable changes since, we can make a reasonable guess as to the vocabulary and structure of the earlier forms of the three sister languages, as well as of their common parent. Thus, for instance, the Modern English *blue eyes* and the modern German *blaue Augen* are both traced back to a presumed parent language which we designate as West Germanic; this in turn is considered to be a major dialect of Primitive or Common Germanic, in which language the phrase is reconstructed as *blaewō augona*. All the steps from *blaewō augona* to *blue eyes* can be traced or reasonably assumed.

Various kinds of historical evidence indicate that about 1,500 years ago three closely related tribes, the Angles, the Saxons, and the Jutes, dwelt beside each other on the North Sea shore in what is today northern Germany and southern Denmark. Their language was a variety of West Germanic; and when it began to show significant differences from the other West Germanic dialects spoken around them, we may say that the English language was born. The speakers of this language were probably not aware for some time that it was different, but ultimately political and geographical circumstances created such an awareness. For many decades, however, Old English (as we call it) must have been very similar to other West Germanic dialects, and especially to the other North Sea dialects of Old Saxon and Old Frisian. A modern variant of Old Frisian is still spoken in the northern Netherlands and the extreme northeast of Germany. Old Frisian and Old English uniquely share certain sound developments. But gradually Old English became a distinctively different language, even though it continued to bear, as its modern form still bears, marks of its Germanic ancestry.

The chief political events that tended toward the development of Old English as a separate language were no doubt the effects of the invasion of England by the Angles and the Saxons, which began around the middle of the fifth century. We do not know exactly what pressures caused the Germanic invaders to cross the channel, but it seems clear that the ease with which they overcame the native Britons encouraged further invasion and settlement. Britain, of course, had already been subdued by Caesar's Roman legions in the first century, and only the gradual collapse of the Roman Empire, including Roman withdrawal from Britain, made the success of the Germanic tribes possible.

During the next two or three centuries these tribes conquered most of England and parts of Scotland. They drove back the British inhabitants into Wales and Cumberland, killing many and enslaving others. They developed kingdoms and a settled form of life. So complete was their domination of their new land that almost no words have come down to us from the older forms of Celtic, the language of the ancient Britons. Welsh, the language of Wales, is a modern descendant of Celtic, and in more recent centuries there have been borrowings from Welsh. Meanwhile, even as Old English continued to evolve away from its West Germanic sister languages on the continent, it began to develop regional dialects of its own. The evidence indicates that the four main dialects, identified as West Saxon, Kentish, Mercian, and Northumbrian, differed mostly in pronunciation, their syntax and vocabularies remaining more or less similar.

The West Saxon dialect occupies an especially important role in Old English. It is the dialect of most of the documents that have come down to us, and was the basis of a kind of standard language which by the tenth century was widely used as the cultural linguistic norm of England. The political dominance of Wessex among the various Anglo-Saxon kingdoms assured the victory of its dialect. A standard language meant that there was a prestigious, relatively fixed form of Old English which was widely understood, and that the scribes who wrote down literary, political, and legal documents were learned in the use of it. Anglo-Saxon England is remarkable in Europe, after the fall of Rome, in having developed a standard literary and official language centuries before all the other European countries. However, as we shall see, this standardization was to be violently upset by political events.

As a Germanic language, Old English had inflectional endings resembling those of modern German. New words were largely formed by compounding and derivation; borrowing from other languages was not frequent, although some Latin and Greek words and a few from other tongues did enter Old English. The language had a much freer word order than Modern English because the inflectional endings indicated grammatical relations which are shown by function words and word order in the language as we speak it today. However, Old English is by no means as free in its word order as Latin, various constraints of linguistic custom operating to restrict its freedom. There is a kind of compression in its style that gives Old English prose a special kind of dignity. Old English poetry had a very rich vocabulary, probably partly archaic at the time of its use. The verse was composed in great measure by formulas, using phrases of fixed metrical pattern which could be repeated in endless and fascinating variation. As we have noted, grammatical forms were much like those of modern German, with a number of noun declensions (although in later Old English these tend to fall together), strong and weak adjectives (two sets of declensions for all adjectives, depending on degree of particularity wished for), and strong and weak verbs rather like the same categories in Modern English. Nouns were of the masculine, feminine, or neuter gender, which determined the form of accompanying adjectives and the gender (and form) of referential pronouns. One cannot understand Old English without special study, yet even the most untutored reader of Modern English can grasp the meaning of some words or phrases. Here is Mark 12:1 in Old English:

> *Sum monn him plantode wingeard and betynde hine ond dealf anne seath and getimbrode anne stiepel and gesette hine mid eorthtilium and ferde on eltheodignesse.*

Here is a fairly literal translation of it:

> A certain man planted a vineyard for himself and enclosed it (him) and dug a pit and built a tower (steeple) and peopled (set) it (him) with farmers (earth-tillers) and went into a foreign country.

Old English is preserved in a rich literature, the oldest of any produced by the Germanic peoples, and in legal documents, inscriptions, and glosses. Much of this must be credited to the conversion of the Anglo-Saxon people to Christianity in the seventh and eighth centuries. The clerical scribes learned Latin, the language of their church, and then began to represent the vernacular language, Old English, with adaptations of the Roman alphabet. A few early inscriptions are preserved in the runic alphabet, which is an older form of the Roman alphabet borrowed by the Germanic peoples from the Romans much earlier. It is largely because we know rather precisely what sounds the Latin letters stand for that we can reconstruct the pronunciation of Old English with considerable certainty.

Some Old English literature is in the form of translations from religious classics; some of it consists of paraphrases and reworkings of religious stories. There are also original meditations, saints' lives, epics, practical work like collections of charms, and entertaining moralistic works like gnomes and riddles. It is an impressive body of work, and owes much to King Alfred (849–899), who actively encouraged the widespread literary use of Old English. He was himself a writer and translator, and he employed many other scholars at his court.

During much of King Alfred's reign, and again early in the 11th century, England was under invasion by Danes and Norwegians—or, as they are often called, the Vikings. The linguistic result of extended Viking occupation of parts of the country was a good deal of exchange and assimilation between the languages of the rival peoples. Since, however, the two were still quite closely related Germanic tongues at this point in their development, this interchange produced no striking shift in the history of English, despite the introduction of some Scandinavian (Old Norse) words and, to a lesser extent, grammatical forms.

A much more drastic change was brought about by the invasion and conquest of England by the Normans from northwestern France in 1066. Originally of Viking ancestry, the Normans had, by the middle of the 11th century, become Frenchified in language and culture; their language is designated as Norman French—a dialect of Old French. The effects of the Norman Conquest were profound in the field of language no less than in other fields. So immense were the changes this event brought about that we give a special name to the period of English after they begin to show themselves, from about 1100: we call the language, from then to about 1500, Middle English.

The replacement of the Anglo-Saxon upper classes by a French-speaking group led to the disappearance of the standard Old English language. As it lost its cultural linguistic center, English fell back completely onto its various dialects and became a language of peasants and laborers —and therefore, largely, unwritten. The early Middle English manuscripts that we have inherited simply represent late Old English, spelled in whatever way seemed to the local scribe (who was likely to be a Norman) to duplicate the sounds of the language as he heard it. This at least has the advantage of giving us clues to the changes that had been taking place in spoken Old English for many decades—changes that to some extent were concealed as long as the scribes used the standardized and relatively fixed literary language.

William the Conqueror and his successors ruled not only England but Normandy, across the English Channel, until 1204. Then France won back the Duchy of Normandy, and the Anglo-Normans, politically detached from the continent, began to regard England as their permanent homeland. One result was the gradual adoption of English as their ordinary form of speech, rather than Norman French. But they brought to English, of course, the influence of Norman French, with its Latin background. Not only did French words come into the English vocabulary in large numbers, but English speech and literary style began to be receptive to borrowings from other languages, particularly Latin.

Middle English, then, comprises the various dialects of late Old English, modified both by evolutionary changes that were already in process and that continued for centuries, and by influences from Norman French. It is clear that English had been steadily losing or reducing its inflections, and consequently was becoming less free in word order; it was also losing its grammatical gender. By the later Middle English period, regardless of the many changes in sound and syntax yet to come, the essentials of Modern English had been created through these evolutionary changes and through the mingling of French and English, with an injection of Scandinavian.

The resurrection of English, in the 13th and 14th centuries, as the universal language of England once again made a standard dialect inevitable. Because London became the capital, its dialect won out over the other dialects of Middle English. Normally we recognize five of these: Northern (descended in the main from Northumbrian), spoken north of the Humber; Midland (descended from Mercian), spoken between the Thames and the Humber and usually divided into East and West Midland; Southern, or South Western (descended from West Saxon), spoken south of the Thames except in Kent; and Kentish, or South Eastern (descended from Kentish), spoken in Kent and its environs.

London was in the East Midland area, and its variety of East Midland as spoken by the court, governmental officials, and university men (both Oxford and Cambridge are in the East Midland area) became the basis for standard English. By the end of the Middle Ages it was victorious and was gradually depressing the other dialects, except for Scottish, which has continued a lively existence as a literary and standard language down to today, though not uninfluenced by the London dialect.

It should be noted that the proper Old English ancestor of standard English is not the Wessex dialect, in which practically all our Old English documents are written, but the Mercian (for London was in Mercia), in which little is preserved. However, in spite of this break, we can still trace our English vocabulary back to Old English with confidence.

The position of the London dialect was further strengthened, though not determined, because it was the language in which Chaucer, Gower, and Lydgate, the major writers of England in the later Middle Ages, wrote. After a lapse of some 350 years, England again had a standard language; but the battle of the vernacular was not yet won.

Middle English in its later forms is recognizably English, and a modern speaker could certainly understand a fair amount of it, although there are traps to be avoided. Some words still used today no longer have the same meaning—for example, *hope* meant "expect," and *edify* meant "build"— and some words have disappeared. Yet the vocabulary is basically familiar. The following passage from Chaucer's Prologue to *The Canterbury Tales*, written about 1387, is not unrepresentative and is clearly English:

> Ther was also a Nonne, a Prioresse,
> That of hir smylyng was ful symple and coy;
> Hir gretteste ooth was but by Seinte Loy;
> And she was cleped [called] madame Eglentyne.
> Ful weel she soong the service dyvyne.

The spelling of Middle English is much more phonetic than that of Modern English, so that the strange orthography often indicates differences in pronunciation from the way we speak today. A final *e*, when not before a vowel, was sounded as a separate syllable, the phonetic value being that of the *a* in Modern English *sofa*. All the consonants were pronounced; for example, the *k* and *gh* in *knight*, and the *l* in *walked*. Yet almost any passage from Chaucer is felt as English, as Old English is not.

A series of major vowel changes from about 1350 to 1550 marks the shift from Middle English to Modern English, and is usually termed the Great Vowel Shift. It is the demarcation between the older stages of the language, strange to modern ears, and the later, which are recognizable as essentially what we speak today. Readers of Shakespeare are aware that his English is not the same as ours, but feel that it is close to our kind of English. The Great Vowel Shift in effect moved the long stressed vowels forward in the mouth and diphthongized long *i* and long *u* to (aī) and (au) respectively, so that Middle English *I*, pronounced (ē), became the Modern English pronunciation of the first person singular pronoun, and Middle English *hous*, pronounced (hōōs), became Modern English *house*. Printing, introduced into England by William Caxton in the midst of this shift, tended to preserve the old Middle English spelling and thus helped to put our orthography into the rather disorganized state from which it has suffered down to our day.

As English was called upon to perform a wider and wider variety of functions, and above all to increase its vocabulary to cope with tasks formerly left to Latin, it modified itself to fit the new needs. The Renaissance period is noted for its great influx of vocabulary, especially from the classical languages, and from French and Italian. Englishmen adopted words right and left; and although some words did not survive, enough did to make the vocabulary of English perhaps the largest of any language. This has created certain difficulties. For example, adjectives and nouns referring to the same thing may be unrelated in root to each other (*oral/mouth; ocular/eye*). But the wide borrowing has produced a rich store of synonyms from different linguistic sources (for example, *royal, kingly,* and *regal*).

A good example of this lexical movement may be seen in Andrew Borde's prologue to his *Breviary of Healthe*, written in 1552: "Egregious doctours and maysters of the Eximiouse and Archane

Science of physicke, of your Urbanitie Exasperate not your selfe agaynste me for makyinge of this lytle volume of Phisycke." These "inkhorn" terms, as they were called, provoked some indignation, yet the demands made upon English led to the adoption of many of these words. *Eximiouse* (which meant "excellent") has disappeared, but *exasperate* is a word heard every day, and *egregious* is not rare, although its meaning has shifted from "distinguished" to "flagrant." We now have thousands of long and short, hard and easy, Germanic and Romance (that is, derived from Latin) words in our language, each with its particular powers. Shakespeare can be as moving when he writes "the multitudinous seas incarnadine" as when he writes "to be or not to be." English has extensive resources, both concrete and abstract, everyday and elegant or academic, to satisfy various kinds of users and various goals.

American English is descended from that variety of English brought over to the colonies in the 17th century. It developed on its own to some extent—obviously in the matter of names for new objects, peoples, and flora and fauna—without ever losing contact with its base in England. The American and British varieties of the language have persisted, and seem in this era of mass communications and easy travel to be getting closer to each other. The fate of a language is closely bound up with the political fate of its speakers, and the world role of the United States in the past 30 years has strengthened the position of American English.

The regional dialects of English in America have traditionally been called New England, General American, and Southern; and although there has been some questioning of this categorization in recent years, it still seems more useful than the Northern, Midland, and Southern division some favor. In any event, the mobility of modern life and communication devices such as radio and television are profoundly affecting regional dialects, and they seem on the way to merging with each other. Social dialects, on the other hand, are extremely persistent, especially in England and to some extent in America. We are very much aware of the problem of ghetto and urban dialects today, and consequently of the value of bidialectism as well as of bilingualism. It is sufficient merely to mention the other major dialects of English: Canadian English, Irish English, Australian English, Scottish, Indian English—each, it must be emphasized, with its own subdialects.

In spite of some differences, there has been a basic stability in the rules or inner regulations of English over the centuries. As Professor Ian Gordon has written in *The Movement of English Prose*: "The segmented English sentence, stressed in word-groups, each word-group separated from its neighbour by a boundary-marker, the major stress of each group falling on the semantically important word in the group, the groups occurring in a relatively fixed order, the words in each group generally falling in a precisely fixed order—all this, plus the continuity of the original vocabulary and the preservation of the original structural words, has ensured an underlying stability in English speech, and in the prose which is based upon it."

With the establishment of a standard dialect in the late 14th century and the acquisition of an adequate vocabulary in the 16th and 17th centuries, it was left to the 18th and 19th centuries to create adequate grammars and dictionaries, so that by about 1800 English was fully ready to assume the international responsibility that the cultural, scientific, and political importance of England and America was to thrust upon it. English in 1750 was a language of more or less minor importance in the world; by 1850 it was a world language. Since then it has spread all over the globe and is the international language par excellence. If there are more speakers of some varieties of Chinese than English, a fact not completely established, Chinese does not have the world authority, the geographic spread, the important literature and scientific writings, or the commercial significance of English. English opens gates to great literature and philosophy and makes possible the universality of science. Although this high eminence is not fundamentally because of its innate superiority, it is certainly well fitted for its eminence and for the task of bringing various peoples together and establishing ties rather than severing them.

We have seen, then, how Modern English has developed a vocabulary of great extent and richness, drawn from many languages of the world. Its inflections are few, but its syntactic rules are probably as intricate as those of any language. Its verbal system presents great complexities, making for subtle distinctions. It is both a very concrete and an abstract language. It favors sibilants over other sounds, and yet possesses a wide phoneme repertory. Its spelling is fairly irregular, although not without some patterns and rules. Above all it is a supple and variegated language, which its native speakers should cherish and which provides them with their hold on the past, their contact with the present, and their claim on the future. Finally, it makes possible their view of the world and of themselves.

The Indo-European Origin of English

by Calvert Watkins

Speaking to the Asiatick Society in Calcutta on February 2, 1786, the English orientalist and jurist Sir William Jones uttered his famous pronouncement:

> ... the Sanskrit language, whatever be its antiquity, is of a wonderful structure; more perfect than the Greek, more copious than the Latin, and more exquisitely refined than either, yet bearing to both of them a stronger affinity, both in the roots of verbs and in the forms of grammar, than could possibly have been produced by accident; so strong, indeed, that no philologer could examine them all three, without believing them to have sprung from some common source, which, perhaps, no longer exists.

Jones was content with the assertion of a common original language, without exploring the details. Others took up the cause, notably the German philosopher Friedrich von Schlegel, to whom is principally due the popular diffusion of the long-lived misconception that the European languages were in some sense derived from Sanskrit. But it remained for another German, Franz Bopp, to found the new science of comparative grammar, with the publication in 1816 of his work *On the conjugational system of the Sanskrit language, in comparison with that of the Greek, Latin, Persian, and Germanic languages.* He was twenty-five when it appeared.

It has been rightly said that the comparatist has one fact and one hypothesis. His one fact is that certain languages present similarities among themselves which are so numerous and so precise that they cannot be attributed to chance, and which are such that they cannot be explained as borrowings or as universal features. His one hypothesis is that these languages must then be the result of descent from a common original. Certain similarities may be accidental: the Greek verb "to breathe," "blow," has a root *pneu-*, and in the language of the Klamath Indians of Oregon the verb "to blow" is *pniw-*. Other similarities may

reflect universal or near-universal features of human language: in the languages of most countries where the bird is known, the *cuckoo* has a name derived from the noise it makes. A vast number of languages around the globe have "baby-talk" words like *mama* and *papa*. Finally, languages commonly borrow words and other features from each other, in a whole gamut of ways ranging from casual or chance contact to learned coinages of the kind that English systematically makes from Latin and Greek.

But where all of these possibilities must be excluded, the comparatist assumes genetic filiation: descent from a common ancestor, which, in the case of Indo-European, as Sir William Jones surmised almost two centuries ago, no longer exists.

In the early part of the 19th century, scholars set about exploring systematically the similarities observable among the principal languages spoken now or formerly in the regions from Iceland and Ireland in the west to India in the east, and from Scandinavia in the north to Italy and Greece in the south. They were able to group these languages into a *family* which they called *Indo-European* (the term first occurs in English in 1813, though in a sense slightly different from today's). The similarities among the different Indo-European languages require us to assume that they are the continuation of a single prehistoric language (called *Indo-European* or *Proto-Indo-European*). In the words of the greatest Indo-Europeanist, the French scholar Antoine Meillet, "we will term *Indo-European language* every language which at any time whatever, in any place whatever, and however altered, is a form taken by this ancestor language, and which thus continues by an uninterrupted tradition the usage of Indo-European."

Those dialects or branches of Indo-European still represented today by one or more languages are: Indic and Iranian, Greek, Armenian, Slavic, Baltic, Albanian, Celtic, Italic, and Germanic,

The present century has seen the addition of two branches to the family, neither of which has left any living trace: Hittite and other Anatolian languages, the earliest attested in the Indo-European family, spoken in what is now Turkey in the second millennium B.C.; and the two Tocharian languages, the easternmost of Indo-European dialects, spoken in Chinese Turkestan in the first millennium A.D.

It should be pointed out that the Indo-European family is only one of many language families that have been identified around the world, comprising several thousand different languages. We have good reason, however, to be especially interested in the history of the Indo-European family. Our own language, English, is the most prevalent member of that family, being spoken as a native language by nearly 300 million people, and being the most important second language in the world. The total number of speakers of all Indo-European languages amounts to approximately half the population of the earth.

English is thus one of many direct descendants of Indo-European; one of the dialects of the parent language became prehistoric Common Germanic, which subdivided into dialects of which one was West Germanic; this in turn broke up into further dialects, one of which emerged into documentary attestation as Old English. From Old English we can follow the development of the language directly, in texts, down to the present day. (See Professor Bloomfield's article "A Brief History of the English Language.") This history is our linguistic heritage; our ancestors, in a real cultural sense, are our linguistic ancestors. Only a small proportion of people in the United States can trace their biological ancestry back more than a century or two; and certainly large segments of the population had languages other than English in their backgrounds only a few generations ago. But every individual is part of a culture, with language its external expression. That language, our language, has an ancestry, a history; indeed, languages have perhaps the longest uninterrupted histories of all the cultural phenomena that we can study.

But it must be stressed that linguistic heritage, while it may well tend to correspond with cultural continuity, does not imply genetic or biological descent. That is, there is no more reason to suppose that we, as speakers of an Indo-European language, are descended biologically from the speakers of Proto-Indo-European, than that the English-speaking population of Nigeria is Anglo-Saxon. The transmission of language by conquest, assimilation, migration, or any other ethnic movement is a complex and enigmatic process which this discussion does not propose to examine—beyond the general proposition that in the case of Indo-European no genetic conclusions can or should be drawn.

The comparative method remains today the most powerful device for elucidating linguistic history. When it is carried to a successful conclusion, the comparative method leads not merely to the assumption of the previous existence of an antecedent common language, but to a reconstruction of all the salient features of that language. In the best circumstances, as with Indo-European, we can reconstruct the sounds, forms, words, even the structure of sentences—in short, both grammar and lexicon—of a language spoken before the human race had invented the art of writing. It is worth reflecting on this accomplishment. A reconstructed grammar and dictionary cannot claim any sort of completeness, to be sure, and the reconstruction may be changed because of new data or better analysis. But it remains true, as one distinguished scholar has put it, that a reconstructed protolanguage is "a glorious artifact, one which is far more precious than anything an archaeologist can ever hope to unearth."

English, genetically a member of the Germanic branch of Indo-European, and retaining much of the basic structure of its origin, has an exceptionally mixed lexicon. During the millennium of its documented history, it has borrowed very extensively from its Germanic and Romance neighbors and from Latin and Greek. At the same time it has lost the great bulk of its original Old English vocabulary. However, the inherited vocabulary, though now numerically a small proportion of the total, remains the genuine core of the language; all of the 100 words shown to be the most frequent in the Brown University *Standard Corpus of Present-Day Edited American English* (see Professor Kučera's article "Computers in Language Analysis and in Lexicography"), are native, inherited words; and of the second 100, 83 are native. Precisely because of its propensity to borrow from ancient and modern Indo-European languages, especially those mentioned above but including nearly every other member of the family, English has in a way replaced much of the Indo-European lexicon it lost. Thus, while the distinction between native and borrowed vocabulary remains fundamentally important, more than 50 per cent of the basic roots of Indo-European as represented in Julius Pokorny's *Indogermanisches Etymologisches Worterbuch* (Bern, 1959) are represented in modern English by one means or the other. Indo-European therefore looms doubly large in the background of our language.

Note: At the end of the Dictionary is an exhaustive Appendix listing every Indo-European root ancestral to at least one English word, with descriptions of the details of its descent, cross-referred throughout to the individual etymologies in the body of the Dictionary. As preface to the Appendix is a longer article by Professor Watkins entitled "Indo-European and the Indo-Europeans," containing a description of the reconstructed language and a series of observations of the cultural inferences that can be drawn from it.

Good Usage, Bad Usage, and Usage

by Morris Bishop

The words of a living language are like creatures: they are alive. Each word has a physical character, a look and a personality, an ancestry, an expectation of life and death, a hope of posterity. Some words strike us as beautiful, some ugly, some evil. The word *glory* seems to shine; the common word for excrement seems to smell. There are holy words, like the proper name of God, pronounced only once a year in the innermost court of Jerusalem's Temple. There are magic words, spells to open gates and safes, summon spirits, put an end to the world. What are magic spells but magic spellings? Words sing to us, frighten us, impel us to self-immolation and murder. They belong to us; they couple at our order, to make what have well been called the aureate words of poets and the inkhorn words of pedants. We can keep our words alive, or at our caprice we can kill them—though some escape and prosper in our despite.

Thought makes the word; also the word makes thought. Some psychologists allege that explicit thought does not exist without verbalization. Thought, they say, emerges from our silent secret speech, from the tiny quivers of the speech organs, from the interior monologue we all carry on endlessly. Let us pause a moment and reflect on our thought; we reflect in words, on a surge of hurrying words.

Much of our formless, secret thought is, to be sure, idiotic. "We find it hard to believe that other people's thoughts are as silly as our own, but they probably are," said the American scholar James Harvey Robinson. Before we permit silent speech to emerge as spoken language, we must make choices and arrange words in patterns of sense and form, accessible to other people. These choices and patterns are usage. And usage is the ruler, the governor, the judge of language. Horace said it nearly two thousand years ago in his *Ars Poetica: "usus, Quem penes arbitrium est, et jus,*

et norma loquendi." Or, in an old translation of the passage:

> Yes, words long faded may again revive;
> And words may fade now blooming and alive,
> If USAGE wills it so, to whom belongs
> The rule and law, the government of tongues.

Deferring to the rule and law of usage, we may yet order our words well or ill, thus creating Good Usage and Bad Usage.

Now the trouble begins. Whose usage is good, whose bad? Is not my usage good for me? May I not tell my own words what to do? Do you have authority over my usage? Does anyone have authority? And if authority exists, is it helpful or hurtful to usage?

We tend to demand freedom for our own usage, authority for others'. Yet we are not above seeking comfort and support from authority. One of our commonest phrases is "look it up in the dictionary." (Not any particular dictionary; just "the dictionary.") Every court of law has its big dictionary; the law settles cases, awards millions, rates crimes and misdemeanors, by quoting the definitions of some poor attic lexicographer, "a harmless drudge," as defined by lexicographer Samuel Johnson. We acclaim freedom, but we love the word *freedom* more than the fact. Most people most of the time would rather be secure than free; they cry for law and order. In the matter of usage, we suspect that complete freedom might outbabble Babel; without common agreement on the meaning of most words, communication would cease.

Who, then, shall wield authority? The King, perhaps? The phrase *the King's English* came in, we are told, with Henry VIII, who ruled from 1509 to 1547. He was a poet and a man of letters when he had the time. The King's English remained standard, even under George I, who could not speak English. Recent Kings and Queens of England have not been noteworthy for an ex emplary style. In America the President's English has never ruled the citizenry. The one notorious Presidential venture into lexicography was Harding's use of *normalcy*. But he said that he had looked it up in the dictionary.

The King's English was naturally identified with the spoken style of gentlemen and ladies of the English court. Similarly in France, the grammarian Vaugelas defined (in 1647) good usage as the speech habits of the sounder members of the court, in conformity with the practice in writing of the sounder contemporary authors. Good usage, then, would represent the practice of an elite of breeding, station, and intellect.

The idea of an elite with authority over language clearly needed delimitation. In France, Cardinal Richelieu, who piqued himself on his style in verse and prose, authorized in 1635 the formation of an *Académie française*, composed of writers, bookish nobles and magistrates, and amateurs of letters. The *Académie*, the supreme court of the French literary world, set itself the task of preparing a dictionary. It has been working at its dictionary, off and on, for over three hundred years. But England and America have always refused to constitute government-sponsored academies with power to regulate citizens' words.

Lacking an academy, Englishmen appealed to the practice of good writers to preserve or "fix" general usage. Thence more trouble. Who are the good writers? Shakespeare, no doubt. But Shakespeare, with his wild and carefree coinages, his cheery disregard for grammatical agreements, demands our admiration more than our imitation. In Latin, a fossilized tongue, the rule is simple: if a locution is in Cicero, it is correct. In English we have no Cicero. The only writers whom all critics would accept as "best" have been so long dead that their works are uncertain models for the living language of our times.

We should, perhaps, make the authority of the best writers defer to that of professional judges of language, the critics and grammarians. Quintilian, rhetorician of the first century A.D., appealed to the consensus of the *eruditi*, the scholarly, the well-informed. Ben Jonson said: "Custom is the most certain mistress of language, as the public stamp makes the current money . . . That I call custom of speech, which is the consent of the learned; as custom of life, which is the consent of the good." In the 17th and 18th centuries, the English grammarians appeared, devoting themselves to "refining, ascertaining, and fixing" the language. They were scholars. Aware of linguistic history, they conceived of English usage as a development from primitive barbarism to the harmonious perfection of their own times. They regarded the past as a preparation, the present as a glorious achievement, the future as a threatening decadence. Jonathan Swift was terrified of the coming corruption and invoked governmental authority to "fix" the language; else, he feared, within two centuries the literary works of his time, including his own, would be unreadable.

The grammarians justified their judgments by appealing not only to history but to reason. They strengthened the concepts of Good and Bad to become Right and Wrong. They regarded language as something existing mysteriously apart from man, governed by a universal grammar waiting to be discovered by intrepid scholars. No doubt they were sympathetically fascinated by the story Herodotus tells of the king who isolated two small children with a deaf-and-dumb shepherd to find out what language they would learn to speak, thus to identify the original speech of mankind. (It was Phrygian.) Rightness was to be achieved by logical analysis of form and meaning, with much use of analogy. Popular usage was scouted, as of its nature corrupt. The grammarians made great play with Purity and Impurity. Pure English lived in perpetual danger of defloration by the impure.

The grammarians did some useful work in rationalizing the language. However, their precepts were often overlogical or based on faulty logic. From them, derive many of the distinctions that have ever since tortured scholars young and old. The *shall/will, should/would* rules are said to be an invention of the 17th-century John Wallis. John Lowth, in 1762, first laid it down that two negatives are equivalent to an affirmative. It was Lowth who banned the use of the superlative to indicate one of two, as in Jane Austen's "the youngest of the two daughters of a most affectionate, indulgent father."

Samuel Johnson, whose epoch-making *A Dictionary of the English Language* appeared in 1755, shared many of the convictions of the grammarians. He was concerned to fix the language against lowering corruption, for, he said in his Preface, "Tongues, like governments, have a natural tendency to degeneration; we have long preserved our constitution, let us make some struggle for our language." He foresaw linguistic calamity. "The tropes of poetry will make hourly encroachments, and the metaphorical will become the current sense; pronunciation will be varied by levity or ignorance, and the pen must at length comply with the tongue; illiterate writers will at one time or other, by publick infatuation, rise into renown, who, not knowing the original import of words, will use them with colloquial licentiousness, confound distinction, and forget propriety." Those who knew better must fight on in the hopeless war: "we retard what we cannot repel, we palliate what we cannot cure."

One will have noticed, amid the funeral music of Dr. Johnson's Preface, the startling phrase: "the pen must at length comply with the tongue." This was a view already accepted more cheerfully by some other distinguished writers. Malherbe, 17th-century scholar-poet-critic and "legislator of Parnassus," said that he learned proper French by listening to the porters at the haymarket. Though Dr. Johnson deplored the fact, he recognized that speech, not writing, not grammatical logic, must in the end command usage. This idea took shape and found fuller expression in the work of Noah Webster (1758–1843).

Webster was a Connecticut farm boy with a Yale education, in a day when colleges did not teach English as a course. His series of spelling books and dictionaries actually went far toward "fixing" the American language. His standard of correctness, however, was the usage of the enlightened members of each community, not just that of the "polite part" of city society, which he believed consisted largely of coxcombs. "General custom must be the rule of speaking," he said; and "it is always better to be *vulgarly* right than *politely* wrong." He was astonishingly liberal, even radical, in his acceptance of popular usage, giving his approval to *It is me, Who is she married to?* and *Them horses are mine.*

Thus, common usage began to assume dominance at the expense of formal grammar. The scholarly Irish archbishop Richard C. Trench in 1857 defined a dictionary as an inventory of the language: "It is no task of the maker of it to select the *good* words of a language . . . He is an historian of it, not a critic."

This view of language and its use has prevailed in the 20th century and seems unlikely to fade. A school of linguistic scientists constituted itself, and in time found a place on most college faculties, ousting the old-fashioned philologists of the English and foreign-language departments. The descriptive or structural linguists, as they called themselves, would no more criticize a locution than a physicist would criticize an atom or an entomologist a cockroach.

The principles of descriptive linguistics have thus been simply put: (1) Language changes constantly; (2) Change is normal; (3) Spoken language is *the* language; (4) Correctness rests upon usage; (5) All usage is relative. This creed arouses indignation if not wrath in many people, including highly educated ones. But with the exception of number 3, which has been felt even by some linguists to be an overstatement on the part of gentlemen whose livelihood requires the written word, dispute about these principles seems to be nearly over among those who profess the study of English. The underlying assumption is that language, by its very nature, is a growing, evolving thing; and that whereas it may be cultivated, it cannot be "fixed" without killing it. Like any other fundamental social activity, it will undergo vicissitudes that to the older generation often seem regrettable; and indeed, some changes in language turn out to be empty fads that are soon forgotten, like some changes in women's fashions. Others are found to be enduringly useful, so that a generation later it becomes hard to imagine how we got along without them.

A descriptive linguist's lexicon can be expected to refrain from value judgments, from imposed pronunciations and spellings. It may classify usages as standard or nonstandard, formal, informal, or slang; but not right or wrong. It describes usage; it piously avoids prescribing it. Yet

surely there is the possibility of self-deception here, of an objectivity more imaginary than real. By the very act of leaving *alrite* out of a dictionary, the lexicographer implies that that spelling— which does, after all, exist—is not all right. On the other hand, if he exhibits his scientific disinterest by reporting that "*ain't* is used orally in most parts of the United States by many cultivated speakers," the truth is that he is being inadequately descriptive with respect to contexts of usage. A reader who takes that description seriously is likely to lay an egg *(slang)* at his next cocktail party unless he has the charm of Eliza Doolittle.

The makers of *The American Heritage Dictionary of the English Language* accept usage as the authority for correctness, but they have eschewed the "scientific" delusion that a dictionary should contain no value judgments. Some, to be sure, they have made merely implicit: the arrant solecisms of the ignoramus are here often omitted entirely, "irregardless" of how he may feel about this neglect. What is desirable is that when value judgments are explicit, they should be clearly attributed. Thus good usage can usually be distinguished from bad usage, even as good books can be distinguished from bad books. The present editors maintain that those best fitted to make such distinctions are, as Noah Webster said, the enlightened members of the community; not the scholarly theoreticians, not the instinctive verbalizers of the unlettered mass. The best authorities, at least for cultivated usage, are those professional speakers and writers who have demonstrated their sensitiveness to the language and their power to wield it effectively and beautifully.

The lexicographers of this Dictionary therefore commissioned a Usage Panel of about a hundred members—novelists, essayists, poets, journalists, writers on science and sports, public officials, professors. (Their names and credentials are to be found in a list preceding this section of special articles.) The panelists have in common only a recognized ability to speak and write good English. They accepted their task and turned to it with gusto. They revealed, often with passion, their likes and dislikes, their principles, and also their whims and crotchets. "We all get self-righteous in our judgments on language," Malcolm Cowley observes. As a matter of fact, many of them revealed, on particular questions, an attitude more reminiscent of Dr. Johnson than of the modern linguistic view: they tend to feel that the English language is going to hell if "we" don't do something to stop it, and they tend to feel that their own usage preferences are clearly *right*.

This does not mean for a moment that their preferences are invalid or negligible. Where this Dictionary differs notably from those that have preceded it, with regard to usage, is in exposing the lexical opinions of a larger group of recognized leaders than has heretofore been consulted, so that the ordinary user, looking up an expression whose social status is uncertain, can discover just how and to what extent his presumed betters agree on what he ought to say or write. Thus, he is not turned away uncounseled and uncomforted: he has before him an authoritative statement on a disputed issue; yet, he is left one of the most valuable of human freedoms, the freedom to say what he pleases.

It is significant that on specific questions, the Usage Panel disagreed more than they agreed, revealing a fact often conveniently ignored—that among those best qualified to know, there is a very considerable diversity of usage. Anyone surveying the panelists' various opinions is likely to conclude that good usage is indeed an elusive nymph, well worth pursuing but inconstant in shape and dress, and rather hard to back into a corner. In only one case did they agree 100 per cent—in disfavor of *simultaneous* as an adverb ("the referendum was conducted *simultaneous* with the election"). Some other scores approached unanimity, as in the following:

Expression	Approved by	Disapproved by
ain't I? in writing		99%
between you and I in writing		99%
dropout used as a noun	97%	
thusly		97%
debut as a verb ("the company will debut its new models")		97%
slow as an adverb ("Drive Slow")	96%	
medias as a plural (instead of *media*)		95%
their own referring to the singular ("nobody thinks the criticism applies to their own work")		95%
but what ("There is no doubt but what he will try")		95%
myself instead of *me* in compound objects, in writing ("He invited Mary and myself to dinner")		95%
anxious in the sense of *eager*	94%	
type for *type of* ("that type shrub")		94%
rather unique; most unique		94%

While the panelists tend toward conservatism, they try to avoid overniceness, prissiness. (*Was graduated*, says John Bainbridge contemptuously, is preferred "by all who write with a quill pen.") Sixty-one per cent of them feel bad about the expression *I feel badly* when they see it in writing; only 45 per cent object when they hear it in speech. More than most people, they know the history of words and have tested the value of idioms. More than most, they have grown tired of overused vogue words. They dislike *senior citizen* ("I'd as soon use *underprivileged* for *poor*—or any other social science Choctaw"—Berton Roueché). They are not concerned that senior citizens themselves seem to rejoice in the term

and recoil at *old folks* and even at *old*. *Enthuse* finds little favor, and stirs preservative zeal in some: "By God, let's hold the line on this one!" cries Dwight Macdonald. *Finalize*, says Isaac Asimov, "is nothing more than bureaucratic illiteracy." But for the consensus, the reader is referred to the entries **enthuse** and **finalize**, each of which, like many other neologisms, is discussed in a Usage note.

The panelists are by no means opposed to all coinages. "I have great admiration," says Gilbert Highet, "for the American genius for creating short vivid words (often disyllabic) to express complex ideas, for example, a collision between a vehicle and another object which is not direct but lateral or oblique, *sideswipe*." In general, the jurymen are more cordial toward popular, low-level inventions than toward the pomposities of professional jargons. John K. Sherman welcomes *rambunctious* as a "tangy Americanism." Forty per cent of the Panel are ready to accept the expression *not about*, used to express determination not to do something; but the other 60 per cent are not about to do so. None of them, however, likes Business English; and they betray a particular spite against the language of Madison Avenue, once a very respectable street, now an avenue of ill fame. Yet the advertisers are, after all, fecund creators languagewise.

It would seem that the panelists are often more attentive to the practice of their own social group than to grammatical logic or etymological precision. They are antipedantic, scornful of the grammarians' effort to ban *it's me*. Some, like Theodore C. Sorenson, would throw away the rule that the relative *that* must introduce restrictive clauses, *which* nonrestrictive. One or two would drop *whom* altogether, as a needless refinement. Ninety-one per cent of the panelists accept the use of *internecine* to mean "pertaining to civil war or to a struggle within a family, group, organization, nation, or the like." They know, of course, that the Latin *internecinus* just means mutually deadly, but they do not seem to care.

The Usage Panel has given us the enlightened judgments of a cultivated elite on a great many interesting and troublesome expressions. The very diversity of their response attests that language is alive and well in the United States, and that even the most descriptive of dictionaries could not succeed in reporting all of its shifting nuances.

Within their field, the determination of good current usage, the counselors found, as we have observed, no absolute standard of rightness. Though naturally believing in their own superiority, they do not presume to dictate. They seem to conclude, without explicit statement, that usage is our own affair, with due regard to the usage of other good writers and speakers. Let that be our conclusion. The duty of determination falls upon us all. By our choices we make usage, good or bad. Let us then try to make good choices, and guard and praise our lovely language and try to be worthy of her.

Dialects of English

by Henry Lee Smith, Jr.

I t is obvious to all of us that people differ in the way they speak the same language. These differences, which are always patterned and systematic, can be correlated with geographical regions and with socioeconomic status, and constitute the *dialects* of a language. Each of us individually also has a unique way of talking, since we may have been exposed to the influence of more than one dialect, regional or social, in addition to having personal idiosyncrasies. This unique set of speech habits constitutes one's *idiolect.* No regional or social dialect can be singled out as the only correct form of a language, but since language is a social phenomenon, certain dialects, generally those used by the educated and by those holding high status in the society, will inevitably be accorded higher prestige, and, conversely, the speech forms of the poor and uneducated will often be looked down upon or used as "proof" of their shiftlessness and inability to learn. Thus, "correct pronunciation" is a relative matter, and the "best" form of any language, from the standpoint of communication, is that which distracts least from what is being said.

How is it possible for speakers of two distinctly different dialects to understand each other? Examination indicates that all linguistic systems are so structured that the listener has to respond to many linguistic events in two or more ways simultaneously. He must recognize that the sound or combination of sounds he hears may have several different meanings or significances, depending on linguistic context; he must instantly (and, usually, unconsciously) select the significance intended by the speaker and reject the nonapplicable ones. (In the case of a pun, the listener must of course consciously grasp *both* intended meanings.) The situation exists without regard to dialects, since even in the same dialect a given linguistic item may have several possible meanings. *Bear* and *bare,* which in most American dialects are pronounced

identically, offer an obvious example. But when two dialects are involved, the question is whether the listener will be able to recognize a word that he himself pronounces differently—especially when it is spoken in such a way that it resembles or reproduces, in sound, an entirely different word in his own dialect. Let us say, for example, that a speaker of dialect X "drops his *r*'s" so that when he pronounces the word *sore,* it sounds like the word *saw* as it is pronounced by a speaker of the more widespread dialect Y. To confuse matters further, let us suppose that the speaker of dialect X who drops his *r*'s also adds—and this does occur—an "excrescent *r*" in certain positions, so that he pronounces the word *saw* to rhyme with dialect Y's pronunciation of *sore.* In a conversation between speakers of these two dialects, such an expression as *I saw an eyesore* might be expected to produce ridiculous confusions; yet ordinarily it will not. This is because the total linguistic context, and particularly the grammatical context, "cues" the listener so that he can distinguish differences of pronunciation that are truly *contrastive* (that is, that indicate a difference in meaning) and those that are *noncontrastive* or *equivalent* (that is, that indicate the same meaning regardless of the difference in pronunciation). Only human languages among communication systems show this paradoxical ambivalence between *phonology* (sound structure) and *grammar;* no other means of human or animal communication is so structured; and to learn what is significant and what is not significant, what constitutes *contrast* and what constitutes *equivalence* at the various levels of organization of language, requires a kind of learning that is uniquely human, differing in kind, not just in degree, from all other learning.

Complexly structured as languages are, and uniquely equipped as human beings are to learn them, language behavior is essentially habitual, and great pressure is exerted on the individual to conform to the linguistic norms of his speech community. Yet, at the same time, he learns to understand the dialects of other regions and classes. It is almost as though we were partners to an agreement to consider certain aspects of our language inviolate, but to permit quite a wide range of diversity in other areas. For instance, such contrasts as that between the initial sounds in *pen* and *ten* are not to be tampered with, but whether the speaker pronounces *pen* so as to rhyme with his pronunciation of *pin,* as happens in some American dialects, is seen as a matter of far less consequence. When human beings, by virtue of their unique intelligence and their unique conditioning, learn their native languages, they not only learn the structuring of their own dialects, but they also internalize, so to speak, the overall pattern of the language, within which, by a sort of mental calibration, linguistic forms different in certain features from those they have learned are seen to be equivalent to the ones they are accustomed to. *Contrast* versus *equivalence,* then, lies at the center of the study of dialect.

In discussing dialects we are, of course, dealing with the language as it is spoken and heard, not as it is written and read. In order to write about sounds we need visual symbols to stand for them. One such set of symbols is used to represent pronunciations in this Dictionary. This is a simplified system, which, as explained in the "Guide to the Dictionary," is designed to lead each reader to supply the sounds of his own dialect for many of the symbols. Obviously this system cannot be used to point out differences among dialects.

There are no unnecessary complications introduced in the symbols used in this article. They are the minimum necessary for any discussion of the dialects of English, and they are derived from theory that is intended to be, as all good theory should be, the simplest possible accounting for the facts.

Nevertheless, experience has shown that many readers—often including those most concerned with language, such as writers and editors—boggle at any set of symbols that look like "funny spelling." If the reader will *sound out the symbols as they are introduced and speak aloud the example words,* a discussion that may look forbidding will be found quite simple once it is heard, not merely seen. In fact, unless one is experienced with phonological symbols, it is probably *essential* to try to pronounce each example word aloud until the contrast indicated can be heard.

When one considers the number of distinguishable dialects of English, to say nothing of the variations among individual idiolects, it might seem impossible to supply an analysis that would provide symbols to account for every significant speech sound made by any native speaker at any time. But such an analysis has been made, and the result—perhaps surprisingly, considering the mass of data involved—is not complicated. Actually, this should not be surprising, for despite the many sounds involved we do understand one another's speech with a high degree of accuracy. The principle that simplifies the analysis—both the unconscious analysis of the English speaker and the study of the linguist—is the fundamental distinction already cited between speech differences that are significant in communicating and those that are not, that is, the distinction between contrastive and noncontrastive events in speech.

Traditionally, the linguist first considers the smallest segments of sound that can be identified in the stream of speech. These are called *phones.* Just as the atom has subatomic particles, so even these segments can be seen as bundles of *articulation features,* that is, as distinct movements or positions of the speech organs. For example, the initial sounds in the pairs *pen, ten; pin, tin* are alike in exhibiting the same manner of articulation; they are *stops,* so called because they are formed by a momentary stoppage of the passage of air through the vocal tract. They differ, however, in the place where the stoppage occurs; the *p*-sounds are made by stopping the air by a coming together of both lips *(bilabial),* while the stoppage of the *t*-sounds is made by contact between the tip *(apex)* of the tongue and the ridge behind the teeth *(alveolar ridge).* Initial *p*-sounds and *t*-sounds share other features in common. To take only one feature, for example, both are articulated without vibration of the vocal cords and are called *voiceless.* In contrast, the initial *b*-sounds and *d*-sounds in *Ben, den; bin, din,* though also characterized, respectively, as bilabial and alveolar stops, are *voiced* (at least partially). Through these different initial sounds *contrasts* are established, and sounds we react to as being the same as these sounds in word-initial position also furnish the basis of contrasts in positions other than the initial position in the word, for example in the pairs *pip, pit; bib, bid; latter, ladder; flappy, flabby.* Careful listening can establish the fact that though the *p*-sounds and *t*-sounds when they occur initially and when they follow an *s* are *phonetically similar,* they are by no means identical. To take a noticeable feature, the puff of air that accompanies the initial sound of *peek* is missing in the word *speak.* The differences, however, between these two sounds are not contrastive. Such differences are never used to distinguish one word from another as is, for example, the difference between voiced and voiceless that distinguishes *bin* from *pin.*

The analysis of language is simplified by the fact that contrasts are actually established, not by individual phones, but by families or *classes* of sounds whose members are phonetically similar, noncontrastively distributed, and congruently patterned, that is, having the same kinds of variants. The linguist calls these classes of sounds *phonemes,* and the members of a class are referred to as the *allophones* of the phoneme. Though from one point of view the phoneme is an abstraction, a fiction, a *construct* of the analyst of language, from another point of view it is a psychological reality, since every native speaker identifies phones occurring in the stream of speech and *assigns* them to a phoneme class of his language. This identification and assignment process takes place below the level of awareness for allophones of a phoneme, but not for *diaphones* of a phoneme. Diaphones are phones seen as members of a phoneme that are characteristic of one dialect but not necessarily of another. For example, the alveolar phone one hears medially in many pronunciations of *latter, waiter, water, butter, bottle*, etc., is often voiced (like a *d*-sound) rather than voiceless; but the native speaker, having internalized the phonemic pattern of the language as a whole—the *phonemic inventory*—identifies diaphones of the *t*-phoneme that may be different from his own as equivalent to those in his dialect.

The inventory of consonant phonemes for English as a whole follows. Phonemes are conventionally enclosed between a pair of slanted bars.

Table I

/p/	/t/	/k/
/b/	/d/	/g/
	/č/ *ch* in *church*	
	/j/ *j* and *dge* in *judge*	
/f/ /θ/ *th* in *thin*	/s/	/š/ *sh* in *shin*
/v/ /ð/ *th* in *then*	/z/	/ž/ *s* in *measure*
/m/	/n/	/ŋ/ *ng* in *sing*, but *ng* spells ŋg in *finger*
	/l/ /r/	

In addition to the 21 consonant phonemes, there are three "glidelike" phonemes, /y/, /w/, and /h/, which are called *semivowels* and which do double duty. That is, their allophones function like those of consonant phonemes when they precede vowels—for example, *ye, yea; we, way; he, hay; you, yo-yo; woo, woe; who, hoe; hah, haw*—but when they follow a short or simple vowel phoneme, they furnish the second element or segment of what is generally known as a long vowel, or diphthong, more technically known as a complex vocalic nucleus. To see how this works, we must first look at the short vowels, again, more technically, simple vocalic nuclei.

To begin with, nearly all speakers use contrasting simple vowel phonemes in *pit, pet, pat, put, putt, pot*, and, in addition to these six, Northern Middle Western speakers show a seventh contrasting simple vowel in *caught* versus *cot, taut* versus *tot, wrought* versus *rot*, etc. Though the tongue is low in the mouth in the pronunciation of all these words, the back rather than the center portion is slightly tensed for the vowels in *caught, taught,*

etc., and their articulation is accompanied by a slight but clearly perceptible rounding of the lips. In contrast, the vowels in *pot, tot, cot*, etc., are completely unrounded, and the tongue is considerably more forward. An eighth simple vowel must be placed in the inventory since the majority of English speakers *at times* make a four-way contrast between the vowels in *gist* (as in *pit*), *jest* (as in *pet*), *just* (pronounced, for the adjective, as in *putt*), and *just* (for the adverb when not stressed as in *I'd just as soon*). The contrast-making vowel in the last word is also heard as the first vowel in many pronunciations of *children*, and under *weak* stress it occurs as the vowel in the plural ending in such words as *matches, horses, judges*. It can be heard quite clearly in these dialects in such *minimal pairs* as *roses* versus *Rosa's*, where the latter word has, under weak stress, a *mid-central* vowel, like that of *putt* or *but*, rather than the vowel we have been identifying, which the linguist would describe as a *high central* vowel.

There is still one more simple vowel that must be added to the inventory, since, particularly in New England, many speakers use a "short *o*-sound" in *coat, wrote, home, whole,* so as to make these words sound to speakers of other dialects much like words with mid-central vowels in them, that is, like *cut, rut, hum, hull*. But the New Englander's vowel is pronounced with the tongue farther back and is accompanied by clearly perceptible lip-rounding. It is, therefore, in contrast with the mid-central vowels that he, too, has in *cut, rut, hum,* and *hull*. The New Englander also shows no regular occurrence of the low-central *unrounded* vowel as heard in most American and Canadian dialects in such words as *pot, cot,* and *lot*, but uses the low back *rounded* vowel, identified in the Chicagoan's pronunciation of *caught* and *thought,* for both *cot* and *caught, tot* and *taught, caller* and *collar*, etc., and thus makes no contrast between the two sets of words. This low back rounded vowel also occurs in most dialects in Great Britain in the words *pot, tot, cot*, etc.; unlike the New Englander, however, the British speaker contrasts these words with *taught, caught*, etc., but, as we shall see, with a complex rather than with a simple nucleus. Table II arranges all nine of the simple vowels in the inventory in terms of tongue position—whether high and to the front, low and to the center, etc.—and gives symbols for each of the phonemes:

Table II

	Front	Center	Back (with lip-rounding)
High	/i/ *pit*	/ɨ/ *just*, adv.	/u/ *put*
Mid	/e/ *pet*	/ə/ *putt, just*, adj.	/o/ *coat, home* [New England]
Low	/æ/ *pat*	/a/ *pot*	/ɔ/ *pot, cot* [New England and British] *caught* [Northern Middle West]

Now, as mentioned earlier, the semivowel glides /y/, /w/, and /h/ can follow each of the nine short vowels to form the so-called long vowels and diphthongs. Each of the three glides attaches to each of the nine simple nuclei to give a total of 27 complex nuclei. These are shown in Table III, which consists of the simple vowels of Table II with the glides added:

Table III

with /y/			with /w/			with /h/		
(iy)	iy	uy	iw	iw	(uw)	(ih)	ih	(uh)
(ey)	əy	(oy)	ew	əw	(ow)	(eh)	əh	(oh)
æy	(ay)	ɔy	(æw)	(aw)	ɔw	æh	(ah)	ɔh

The complex nuclei that are encircled are those most frequently used by most speakers of present-day English. For aid in identifying these symbols, in addition to the identifying words, the approximately corresponding symbols from the Dictionary pronunciation key are given below in parentheses; and those from the International Phonetic Alphabet appear in brackets. It must be emphasized, however, that the other systems of symbols do not represent the precise level of the phoneme as developed in this article and, therefore, do not match perfectly.

The following words exemplify the complex vocalic nuclei encircled above:

see	/iy/	(ē) [i]
say, they	/ey/	(ā) [e] or [ei]
I, ride	/ay/	(ī) [aɪ]
boy	/oy/	(oi) [ɔɪ]
do, choose	/uw/	(o͞o) [u]
go, rode	/ow/	(ō) [o]
out, loud	/aw/ or /æw/	(ou) [aʊ]
Pa, ah	/ah/	(ä) [ɑ:]
paw, law	/oh/ or /ɔh/	(ô) [ɔ]

A little practice will show that in the /y/ glide the tongue moves forward and higher, for the /w/ the tongue moves higher and back and the lips are somewhat rounded, and for the /h/ the tongue moves toward a central position without concomitant lip-rounding. The position of the tongue for the simple nucleus will determine where it ends up in the complex nucleus. If it is high to start, it finishes higher, and so forth.

Table III introduces no new symbols. Thus, with the 21 consonants of Table I and the 9 vowels of Table II, plus the three glide semivowels, all the significant (segmental) sounds used by any speaker of English can be represented. (It is necessary to specify "segmental" because there are also 12 "suprasegmental" phonemes of pitch, stress, and juncture that are not incorporated in this article.)

But as far as communication goes, the situation is not even that complicated. The 36 vowel nuclei of Tables II and III combine on the next higher level of response to produce only half as many

units. We noted that by a kind of mental calibration, linguistic forms other than those one has learned are seen to be equivalent to those one is accustomed to. This calibration that enables a native speaker to recognize phonemes that contain varying phones operates at a higher level to produce from phonemes a broader grouping termed the *morphophone*. The full explication of this recent concept can be found in a paper by the author in the March 1967 issue of *Language*, the journal of the Linguistic Society of America. It will be possible here only to suggest how the concept is derived out of dialect variations and may be applied to their study.

To understand the morphophone it is necessary to go back and examine in some detail the kinds of contrast established by phonemes in different dialects. The words *paw* and *Pa,* and others like them, show /oh/ in contrast with /ah/ in the Central Atlantic Seaboard, but /ɔ/ versus /ah/ in the Northern Middle West. In most Canadian dialects and in the northern United States west of Nebraska and the Dakotas, there is no contrast between *paw* and *Pa,* /ah/ occurring in both words. In the Central Atlantic Seaboard, /ih/ occurs before /r/ in *peer, fear,* etc., /uh/ before /r/ in *poor,* /oh/ before /r/ in *pour,* and /eh/ before /r/ in *pair.* Regularly in this dialect, complex nuclei with /h/ occur in monosyllabic words when /r/ or /r/ plus a consonant follows a stressed vowel, so we hear *girl, first, fur; Carl, parsed, far,* as /gəhrl/, /fəhrst/, /fəhr/; /kahrl/, /pahrst/, /fahr/. In the case of dissyllabic words with /r/, /ah/ contrasts with /a/ in such pairs as *sari* /sahriy/ versus *sorry* /sariy/, and /ah/ versus /a/ furnishes the basis for the contrast in monosyllabic words with /m/ as in *bomb* /bam/ versus *balm* /bahm/. The simple versus complex nucleus contrast is heard in *bother* /baðɨr/ versus *father* /fahðɨr/, though *rather* may be pronounced with four different nuclei, two simple and two complex—/raðɨr/, /ræðɨr/, /rahðɨr/, /ræhðɨr/.

In contrast to the situation described above, /h/ almost never occurs before /r/ in Northern Middle Western dialects, and we hear /pir/, /pur/, /por/, /per/; /gərl/, /fərst/, /fər/; /karl/, /parst/, /far/; /sariy/, /sariy/. In addition, no simple versus complex nucleus distinction occurs in the other examples cited above, and we find /bam/ for both *bomb* and *balm,* and /baðɨr/ for *bother* and /faðɨr/ for *father.* In fact, the only place the /h/ glide *does* occur in these dialects is at the end of such words as *paw* and *Pa,* /pɔh/ and /pah/, since a *stressed* vowel in English must be followed either by a consonant or a semivowel, though under *weak* stress any one of the nine simple vowels may occur finally, as, for example, in /siti/ rather than /sitiy/ for *city,* as heard in Great Britain and in many dialects in the southeast of the United States. In Coastal New England, we find many speakers using complex nuclei with /y/ and /w/ followed by a syllable consisting of /ə/ in *peer,* /piyə/; *pair,*

/peyə/; *poor,* /puwə/; *pour,* /powə/; Southern Coastal speakers, on the other hand, frequently show /pihə/, /pehə/, /puhə/, /pohə/ for these words, with /pohə/ often occurring for both *poor* and *pour.* The dialects of quite an extended area in the southeastern part of the country, ranging from northwestern Mississippi through southern and eastern Tennessee (Chattanooga) and including northwestern and north-central Georgia (Carrollton-Atlanta), show interesting pronunciations of *fire* and *pyre,* with the four variant forms /fayɨr/, /fayə/, /fæyə/, /fæhə/ having been recorded for the first word of the pair, and /pahɨr/, /pæhr/, /pahr/, /pahə/ for the second. Quite often, more than one of the above forms occurs in the same idiolect. In Philadelphia, Baltimore, and Washington, *fire* and *pyre* rhyme, being heard as /fayɨr/, /payɨr/; /fayə/, /payə/; or /fahr/, /pahr/, with the last pair of pronunciations often regarded as nonstandard. In these cities, standard speakers often use either /ahr/ or /æwir/ for *our,* but only /æwir/ for *hour,* while nonstandard speakers may use /æhr/ for both *our* and *hour,* /pæhr/ for *power* versus the standard speaker's /pæwir/, etc. Also, standard and nonstandard speakers alike contrast *can* (verb), /kæn/, and *can* (noun), /kehn/; *bomb,* /bam/, and *balm,* /bahm/; *hurry,* /həriy/, and *furry,* /fəhriy/.

When we take these dialect variations into account and note further such strikingly different pronunciations as /lawst/ (northern Alabama), /lohst/ (New York City), /lɔst/ (Chicago), for *lost;* /haws/ (Cleveland), /hæws/ (Philadelphia), /həws/ (Toronto), /hews/ (Richmond), for *house,* and /meriy/ (Milwaukee), /mæriy/ (Gary, Indiana), /mehriy/ (Baltimore), /meyriy/ (Charlottesville, Virginia), for *Mary,* it becomes apparent that there must be some way in which speakers of different dialects immediately sense the equivalence between the occurrences of quite different phonemes in what they recognize to be the same words.

The level at which this calibration is achieved is called the level of the morphophone, and within this level there are to be seen different gradations, so to speak, at which speakers differentiate between contrast and equivalence. From one point of view, the morphophone can be seen as a sort of "holding company" or "super family" of different phonemes that are *noncontrasting in the same words;* but from another point of view it must be seen as a *unit* of the language *as a whole* which, *as a unit,* furnishes the basis for higher-order or higher-level *contrasts.* Again, like the phoneme, the morphophone is more than a mere construct of the analyst, since its psychological reality is simply demonstrated when we realize how quickly and unerringly speakers are enabled to suppress, so to speak, the contrast-making aspect of different phonemes in favor of reacting to these as noncontrasting *expressions* of units at a higher level covering the whole language. For example,

the words *house* and *out* contain the same morphophone unit for *all* speakers of *all* dialects of English even though the unit may be expressed by four different noncontrasting phoneme sequences or *variants,* for example, /aw/, /æw/, /əw/, /ew/. We can symbolize this unit by **aw.** (with a period rather than slant bars) and note how it contrasts with another unit, heard in *gross* and *oat,* which will be represented by **ow.** . This latter unit is expressed as /əw/ in Philadelphia, as /ew/ by some speakers in London, and as /ow/ generally in the northern United States and in Canada. Thus, /əw/ and /ew/ are members, or variants, of *two* contrasting morphophone units, **aw.** and **ow.** , with /əw/ occurring for **ow.** in *oat* in Philadelphia and contrasting in that dialect with /æw/ for **aw.** in *out,* while in Toronto /əw/ is the regular expression of **aw.** in *out,* and *oat* contrasts there through the /ow/ expression of **ow.** . In London all three expressions, or variants, of **ow.** occur, so we hear /owt/, /əwt/, /ewt/ for *oat* in contrast with either /aw/ or /æw/ representing **aw.** in *out.* Thus, though there may be overlapping variants of morphophonic units, each dialect always preserves the *morphophonic contrast,* and each morphophonic unit always has at least one variant that it shares with no other unit, as is the case with /ow/ expressing **ow.** and with /aw/ and /æw/ expressing **aw.** . Our present-day writing system is based principally on the graphic representation of morphophone units, not of phonemes, and hence the written forms (digraphs) *ou* and *oa* in *house* and *oat* stand, respectively, for the units **aw.** and **ow.** ; and each reader responds to the graphic symbolizations by giving the phonemic expressions of the morphophones that are characteristic of his dialect or idiolect.

Actual examination of dialects shows the maximum number of vowel morphophones to be 18. These may be expressed by various phonemes. The phonemes in the table are the ones by which the morphophones are expressed in my dialect. The 15 morphophones in the table are all that make contrasts when occurring before the consonants /p/, /t/, and /k/. This is known as *pristine environment,* and the contrasts are termed *primary.*

Table IV

1. **i.**	/pit/	*pit*				4. **u.**	/put/	*put*
2. **e.**	/pet/	*pet*	7. **ə.**	/pət/	*putt*	5. **o.**	/koht/	*caught*
3. **æ.**	/pæt/	*pat*				6. **a.**	/pat/	*pot*

8. **iy.**	/piyt/	*peat*	14. **yuw.**	/byuwt/	*beaut*	11. **uw.**	/buwt/	*boot*
9. **ey.**	/peyt/	*pate*	15. **oy.**	/hoyt/	*Hoyt*	12. **ow.**	/bowt/	*boat*
10. **ay.**	/bayt/	*bite*				13. **aw.**	/bæwt/	*bout*

The units are numbered and symbolized by letters followed by periods in order to minimize the confusion that may arise with the phoneme, which is shown between slant bars. The horizontal line separates the units that will be termed *short* from those that will be designated *long,* the difference being that the long units are always and only expressed by complex phonemic nuclei, though short units may be expressed by either complex or simple nuclei.

There are also 21 consonant morphophones whose phoneme variants are neither so numerous nor so interesting to the study of dialects, and there are morphophones for the three semivowels we have discussed. Since the morphophone is a mental phenomenon and not simply a physical sound, there can be a zero morphophone, but we need not be concerned with the concept here.

The concept of the morphophone permits analysis of dialect differences more extensive and sophisticated than is possible in this article. There are "free" or "pure" variants that contrast in the same kinds of words. These are the variants we have discussed in establishing the morphophone. There are conditioned variants that contrast only when preceded or followed by certain sounds. In Tidewater Virginia, for example, the noun *house* is pronounced /hews/ while the verb is pronounced /hæwz/.

In addition to variants that are analyzed as expressions of the same morphophone, there are dialect differences that involve the substitution of morphophones. For example, if the same speaker pronounces *get* as /git/, but in all similar words pronounces /e/ as in *wet, pep,* and *neck,* we have to say that the phoneme in /git/ is the morphophone **i.** and not a variant of the morphophone **e.** .

There are changes in morphophones, such as that between the word *divide* and the word *division,* that occur with all speakers of the language. These are called *alterations.* There are other changes called *replacements* that belong only to certain dialects. For example, most speakers have the morphophone **s.** in *house* and **z.** in *houses,* but in the speech of large numbers of residents of metropolitan areas along the eastern Great Lakes, the plural retains **s.** instead of shifting to **z.** . The replacement of **s.** by **z.** is almost universal in such pairs as *louse, lousy,* but in certain other words the replacement becomes quite a precise identification of the speaker's region. The 40th parallel of latitude, separating Philadelphia from Trenton, neatly divides eastern speakers into northern and southern by whether the **s.** of the word *grease* is replaced by **z.** in the word *greasy.* The **z.** is southern and the **s.** northern.

Just as the *"grease-greasy"* line forms the basis of a clear-cut division between northern and southern speakers, so the famous triad *merry, marry, Mary* distinguishes speakers east of the crest of the Allegheny Mountains from those to the west. In the southern part of the Central Atlantic Seaboard, for example, we hear *merry* as /meriy/, expressing the morphophones **m.e.r.iy.** ; *marry* as /mæriy/ to express **m.æ.r.iy.** ; and *Mary* as /mehriy/ to express **m.ey.r.iy.** . In Chicago, all three words show /meriy/ to express **m.e.r.iy.** . To account for the vowel in *marry,* we see the substitution of **e.** for **æ.** , and *Mary* shows the substitution (shortening) of **e.** for **ey.** . In Gary, Indiana, many speakers have the shortening **æ.** for **ey.** in *Mary,* to give /mæriy/, and some older-generation speakers in Virginia and New England still have the phonemes /ey/ for the morphophone **ey.** in *Mary, vary, fairy,* etc. In Philadelphia many speakers show the substitution **ə.** for **e.** in *merry,* to give /məriy/, and speakers in Buffalo give either /meriy/ or /mehriy/ for each of the three words. Their pronunciations of the three words as /meriy/ are accounted for as were the occurrences in the Chicago dialect, but the occurrences with /eh/ require separate explanations. Starting with /mehriy/ for *Mary,* we can assume the conditioning of **ey.** by the following /r/ phoneme, as is the case with the Central Atlantic Seaboard speakers, while the /eh/ in the pronunciation of *marry* can be taken simply as an occurrence of the principal variant of the morphophone **æ.** , which is regularly /eh/ for this dialect. Finally, the /eh/ in *merry* can be seen as a lengthened expression of the morphophone **e.** , since in this dialect, before /r/, /h/ varies freely with its absence, as in /sariy/, /sahriy/; /sɔriy/, /sɔhriy/, all for *sorry,* and with /sariy/ and /sahriy/ occurring as well for the word *sari.*

The two levels of phoneme and morphophone, finally, offer a refined and objective method of distinguishing *dialect* and *language,* that is, of designating two closely related speech forms as dialects of a single language or as constituting separate languages. Such knowledge cannot help being of immeasurable assistance in understanding the nature of numerous social problems stemming from language differences.

Grammar and Meaning

by Richard Ohmann

A grammar can set out to do any of a number of things. It can assert the propriety of certain forms of language, and urge them upon all speakers and writers; such, in intent, are many of the older school grammars. Or it can attempt a neutral description of the way members of a speech community actually talk; this is the aim of much grammatical scholarship in this century. Again, a descriptive grammar can look at the speech or writing of a specified group within the society—educated people, say, or professional writers. In short, the same conflicts in purpose that have troubled dictionary editors and their publics beset grammarians as well.

In the past two decades, a still different perspective on grammars and their use has developed, through the work of the linguist Noam Chomsky and many others. They refer to the grammars they build as *generative*. The rules of such a grammar must account for—or, to put it another way, must be capable of generating—every conceivable sentence of a language that is felt by native speakers of that language to be grammatical or, as it is usually put, well-formed. But in addition to describing the facts of language, a generative grammar tries to explain them; in this it differs from grammars of other kinds. To explain the facts of language is to link a description of them to what we know about human mental capacities. So a generative grammar is actually a theory of a particular language—more precisely, a theory of the knowledge that any fluent speaker has of that language. Herein is another sharp difference between generative and other grammars: what a generative grammar describes and explains is not merely the linguistic "output" of speakers, but their *understanding* of language. In brief, a grammar of this sort attempts to describe part of human mentality. In the view of generative grammarians, grammar is a part of human psychology.

Language, like the body, is so comfortable and familiar that we hardly notice its presence or its complexity. Yet once examined closely, the accomplishment of any ordinary speaker is rather astonishing. He can produce and understand an indefinite number of new sentences—sentences he has never encountered previously. Put before 25 speakers a fairly simple drawing, ask them to describe in a sentence the situation it portrays, and they will easily come up with such examples as:

> A bear is occupying a telephone booth, while a tourist impatiently waits in line.
>
> A man who was driving along the road has stopped and is waiting impatiently for a grizzly bear to finish using the public phone.
>
> A traveler waits impatiently as a bear chatters gaily in a highway phone booth.

Almost certainly, each of the 25 sentences will be different from all the others, yet each will adequately describe the drawing. Speech is creative; it is in no rigid way determined by given circumstances. Moreover, as the bear-and-telephone examples show, the ability to come up with a suitable sentence does not depend on having associated the sentence with the situation before: it is obviously unlikely that any speaker who produced one of these particular sentences had ever before encountered it, much less the situation it describes. The same is true of a speaker's ability to understand new sentences produced by other people. Probably all the sentences in this essay are new to the reader, yet if they are grammatical, he should have no trouble perceiving their structure and understanding them.

The number of possible sentences in English is enormous—for all practical purposes infinite. Using the vocabulary and structures supplied in any 25 typical sentences, and permuting them in all possible ways (so long as the resulting sentences are grammatical), one could usually construct billions of sentences. An analysis by computer shows that the 25 sentences about the bear in the phone booth yield the materials for 19.8 billion sentences, all describing just one situation. When one reflects that the number of seconds in a century is only 3.2 billion, it is clear that no speaker has heard, read, or spoken more than a tiny fraction of the sentences he *could* speak or understand, and that no one learns English by learning any particular sentences of English. What speakers *have* learned is a grammar. And the examples show one requirement we must make of a grammar: that it be capable of generating an infinite number of grammatical sentences. But the grammar itself must be finite, since the finite human brain must "contain" it.

A closely related ability, common to speakers of English, which our grammar must account for, is that of telling sentences from nonsentences—that is, of distinguishing the grammatical from the ungrammatical. Anyone to whom English is native can do this, not only in blatant cases ("Leave me" versus "Me leave"), but also in subtler pairings:

> Got he a chance?
> Has he a chance?
>
> The accident was seen by thousands.
> The accident was looked by thousands.

In each pair, the two members differ only slightly in their make-up, yet one is clearly an English sentence and one is not. We must, apparently, posit a "grammatical intuition" of some intricacy that allows such discriminations, without the speaker's consciously knowing how he makes them.

One may want to attribute this capacity to something other than a grammatical intuition, but no other explanation seems adequate. Speakers do not need to learn to create sentences, understand new sentences, and distinguish between English and non-English through formal instruction; preschool children, illiterates, and feeble-minded adults are capable of these acts. Nor is the grammatical sense based entirely on meaning. The meaning of many ungrammatical sentences can be grasped as, for instance, that of "Got he a chance?" and "The accident was looked by thousands." Conversely, meaningless (or at least mystifying) sentences may be grammatical, as is the case with:

> Fragile hippos cheat lucidly.
> The flat mountains multiply backwards.

Note that even these "nonsense" sentences can be paired with closely related nonsentences:

> Fragile hippos seem lucidly.
> Multiply backwards mountains flat the.

"Meaningful" is not identical with "grammatical." Speakers have a special grammatical knowledge, and that knowledge is what a grammar must explicate.

Here are a few more abilities that speakers of English have:

1. They can perceive more than one grammatical structure in the same sequence of words. Thus, "I had three books stolen" has at least three meanings, depending on which way its words are related to one another. This is evident if we expand the sentence three ways:

> I had three books stolen from me.
> I had three books stolen for me.
> I had three books stolen, when something interrupted my burglarizing.

2. Speakers can notice differences in structure among sentences that look alike:

> The cow was found by a stream.
> The cow was found by a farmer.

3. They can see likenesses in basic structure (and meaning) among sentences that look quite different:

> The cow was found by a farmer.
> A farmer found the cow.
> Was the cow found by a farmer?
> The farmer's finding the cow pleased everyone.

These three abilities suggest another requirement we must make of an English grammar: that it abstract considerably from the physical signals of speech, including word order, since often the way speakers understand sentences is related in no direct way to these overt characteristics.

Perhaps this brief discussion is enough to hint at the difficulty of explaining what speakers of English know. It is time to make an even more abbreviated sketch of a theory that could handle the task.

For purposes of illustration, let us pretend that we are dealing with an "English language" that includes only four known words, namely: *the, guard, saw,* and *someone.* What is required to start with is a set of analytical rules that will show how sentences are generated, or constructed, in this very limited language. Such rules we will call *phrase-structure* rules, meaning by "phrase structure" either a single word or two or more words that serve a particular grammatical function. By studying the way in which the four words in this "English language" are used, we can derive a fundamental phrase-structure rule: A sentence may consist of a noun phrase followed by a predicate. In a generative grammar, as compared with older-style grammars, it is found to be useful to express such rules in a more abstract, symbolic form than that used in traditional parsing, so that we get:

Sentence ⟶ Noun Phrase + Predicate

(The arrow means "may consist of.") Now let us add more rules:

Predicate ⟶ Verb + Noun Phrase
Noun Phrase ⟶ Article + Noun
Noun Phrase ⟶ Pronoun
Article ⟶ *the*
Noun ⟶ *guard*
Verb ⟶ *saw*
Pronoun ⟶ *someone*

This group of rules actually constitutes a very simple grammar, which is capable of generating four sentences:

The guard saw { the guard. / someone.

Someone saw { someone. / the guard.

But since English actually has infinitely more sentences than this, the grammar must be enlarged if it is to perform its task. We might try adding a word and expanding one rule accordingly:

Article ⟶ { *the* / *a*

This adds several sentences to the grammar's output. Here's another rule that might be expanded:

Noun ⟶ { *guard* / *light*

This adds sentences such as:

Someone saw the light.
The guard saw a light.

But it also introduces sequences like "The light saw a guard," which is not grammatical. Thus the rules will have to be modified in some way. For instance, we might try marking nouns as "animate" and "inanimate," and verbs as taking animate or inanimate subjects. This we could suggest by a simple notation like:

Verb ⟶ _____ *saw*
(animate)

and by assigning "features" to the nouns: "guard" would have the feature +animate, while "light" would have the feature −animate. Thus, the grammar would allow only "guard" to appear as subject of "saw."

There are clearly implications here for semantics—the science of meanings. Although the features +animate and −animate are purely syntactic—that is, based on syntactic compatibility—they evidently have their semantic analogues. That is to say, words like *someone, guard,* and *cow* have an element of meaning in common, just as they behave in some ways alike syntactically. Native speakers of English, like those of any language, must in some sense have words unconsciously "indexed" by syntactic and semantic features, so that they can capitalize on whatever is systematic about the English lexicon. A time may come when some dictionaries, too, will arrange words in such a way—thus, for instance, allowing the semantic information in a dictionary to be stored in and easily retrieved from a computer in many ways other than the alphabetical one which necessarily prevails today.

In any case, phrase-structure rules account for the basic structures of English, and for the main grammatical relationships such as subject-verb and verb-direct object. For a while, grammarians thought that a complete grammar of English might be composed of phrase-structure rules, but it now seems clear that such a grammar would be quite inadequate. Among other faults, it would have far too many separate rules and structures.

The 19 billion sentences about the bear in the phone booth would require many thousands of phrase-structure rules to account for the different patterns of word arrangement used. This is far too much apparatus, it would seem, to explain the speaker's accomplishment. Just as clearly, phrase-structure rules cannot explain the ambiguity of a sentence like "I had three books stolen," whose words can have any of three different structures. Again, a grammar constructed out of phrase-structure rules alone will have nothing to say about relationships such as that between:

A farmer found the cow.
and
The cow was found by a farmer.

Yet it would obviously be grammatically economical, as well as psychologically right, to explain such relationships.

For these and other reasons, it is necessary to add a second kind of rule to the grammar: the *transformation*. Transformations apply not to single units, but to whole structures; they may add to or subtract from those structures, or change the order of elements, or substitute one element for another. For example, a transformation changes the structure:

Noun Phrase^1 + Past Tense + Verb + Noun Phrase^2
to
Noun Phrase^2 + Past Tense + *be* + *by* + Noun Phrase^1

This (in crudely simplified form) is the *passive* transformation, the rule that accounts for the relationship between:

A farmer found the cow.
and
The cow was found by a farmer.

In addition to representing a similarity that every speaker of English is aware of, the passive transformation has the great advantage of economy. Rather than having passive forms generated by a whole separate set of phrase-structure rules, just one rule converts any active form (with a transitive verb and a direct object) into the corresponding passive. Savings like this begin to make the grammar manageable, just as, presumably, they make it possible for a speaker of English to understand without difficulty a large number of sentences he has never heard before.

Other transformations combine two or more structures to create complex ones. For instance, a sentence like "The farmer's finding the cow pleased everyone" would not be generated by phrase-structure rules alone. Rather, these rules would separately generate the structures:

The farmer + find + the cow
and
(Something) + please + everyone

Then a transformation would convert the first of these into:

The farmer's finding the cow

and another would substitute this structure for

something. Other combining transformations generate relative clauses, adverbial clauses, complement structures, and the like, and so build the more complex sentences of English.

There is one important thing to notice at this point. The basic grammatical relationships that are indicated in the simple sentences by word order often have a different representation in the complex sentences built up by transformation. Thus, in the simple structure:

The farmer + find + the cow

farmer is subject of the verb *find,* whereas in:

The farmer's finding the cow pleased everyone

farmer appears as an adjectival modifier and *find* as a noun. Yet any speaker knows that the "real" relationship between "farmer" and "find" is the one revealed in the simple structure, not in the final sentence. Otherwise he would not understand what the sentence said—would not notice that there was a subject-verb connection between "farmer" and "find" or, to put it another way, that the farmer indeed found the cow.

One way to interpret the native speaker's insight into more complicated sentences is to say that each sentence has a *deep structure,* built up by the application of phrase-structure rules; and this deep structure expresses all the basic content, or meaning, of a sentence. Another implication of such findings for semantics is that many words that are transformationally derived need not be separately defined. For example, the word *dismissal* often occurs in sentences such as:

His dismissal of the undersecretary caused alarm.

This has as part of its deep structure:

He + dismiss + the undersecretary

No meaning is added by the transformation; hence *dismissal* really need not be thought of as a separate word with the meaning "act of dismissing." All the necessary information is provided by a definition of *dismiss,* along with the relationship between *he* and *dismiss.* Notice that we also have sentences such as:

His dismissal by the undersecretary caused alarm.

Here the deep structure reveals a different relationship:

The undersecretary + dismiss + him

In other words, the phrase *his dismissal* is in itself ambiguous. However, the ambiguity results not from multiple meanings of the word *dismissal,* but rather from the possibility of tying *his dismissal* to either of the two deep structures cited. If dictionaries did not have to serve people other than native speakers, there would be no more point in having a second definition of *dismissal* ("condition of being dismissed") than in having the first. Both are unnecessary to a speaker who knows the word *dismiss* and the two transformations that can produce *his dismissal.* To generalize, there

is a great deal of syntax concealed in complex words, and to capitalize on that fact would be to bring out many regularities in the lexicon.

To return to the main theme: the part of a grammar that deals with syntax has two kinds of rules, which collaborate to produce deep structures and surface structures. Deep structures represent basic meaning, and surface structures are wholly responsible for the sound of a sentence —such features as stress, intonation, and the quality of the vowels.

Hence, a generative grammar with transformational rules mediates between sound and sense, and so provides a model of part of what every native speaker knows. Although there are many unsolved problems in grammar—indeed, many areas of confusion and open controversy—at least the assumptions outlined here have been and continue to be fruitful.

That being so, it may be well to add a few words of speculation on the implications of such a grammar for the study of mind. No grammar of a language, to repeat, is adequate unless it is compatible with the facts of language learning—for instance, the fact that the child hears an irregular scattering of sentences and nonsentences, and from that sample somehow builds an adequate theory of the language being spoken around him. How could he ever do that if his language has roughly the form described here? In the past, the standard answer has been "induction": The child generalizes from his sensory experience, groups sounds together, associates them with meanings.

But if what the child must learn is a grammar with deep structures—as seems quite certain— then this picture of language learning is impossible. There simply are no physical signs, no sensory representations, of many critical features of meaning which the child has to extract from the stream of speech—namely, most of the features represented in deep structure. Hence a child approaching the task of acquiring the language spoken around him would be utterly incapable of doing so if he were equipped only with a *tabula rasa.* He must have some initial presuppositions about what he is to find in the stream of speech; that is to say, he must have some innate mental structure that is peculiarly adapted to the creative and rapid learning of language.

Furthermore, since a child will learn with equal ease whatever language he is first exposed to, his innate assumptions must pertain equally well to all languages. It follows that all languages have some structure in common. If it has seemed implausible, for a long time, that this could be so —that there could be a universal grammar—perhaps that is because surface structures do vary wildly among the thousands of languages of the world. It may nonetheless be true that deep structures of all languages are much alike and are closely related to universal categories of human thought and perception. This exciting possibility today beckons on the horizon of generative-transformational grammar.

The Spelling and Pronunciation
of English

by Wayne O'Neil

It is unfortunate that our orthography bears so little relation to our phonology." Statements such as this are typical in discussions dealing with the adequacy of English spelling. What is meant is that the spelling does not directly *reflect* the way in which a word is pronounced. This, of course, is true; but the generally accepted corollary that English orthography bears little relation to English phonology is in fact quite false. One has only to look at the phonology of English with care to see the orthography-phonology relationship: The pronunciations of words are quite generally *predictable* from their spellings. In trying to prove the contrary, it is not sufficient to cite a random set of orthographic vagaries, a handful of letters indicating the same sound, a handful of sounds being indicated by the same letter, and so on. To analyze no further than this is only to raise a question, not to answer it.

The general problem we must deal with, then, is clear: What is the nature and extent of the correlation, in English, between spelling and pronunciation? In this Dictionary, as in dictionaries generally, words are assigned two spellings. One we call phonetic; through it we seek to represent, as accurately and as particularly as we reasonably can, the pronunciation or pronunciations associated with a given lexical item. This spelling appears in parentheses following the boldface entry. In the introductory section "Guide to the Dictionary," the reader is told exactly how to interpret this phonetic spelling. The other representation that we have for each word is that of the standard spelling system, shown in the boldface entry. But in most dictionaries the relationship of the standard spelling to the phonetic representation is not clarified; or, worse, it is ignored, felt to be beyond rational discussion, standard spelling being (in this view) a reflection of nothing natural in language. It is the purpose of the following paragraphs to summarize what can now be said

about the relationship of these two kinds of spelling, and about the phonological basis of standard orthography, as these matters have been clarified in recent work in English phonology and phonological theory, especially that of Noam Chomsky and Morris Halle in *The Sound Pattern of English* (New York, 1968).

In brief, we will argue that English orthography is nearly optimal, not at the level of phonetic or actual pronunciation, but at an abstract level, a psychologically significant level from which pronunciations can be predicted and to which they can be referred. Moreover, quite aside from pronunciation, this orthography preserves information about the history and the meaning of words that is of great value in human communication.

In a scientific grammar of a language, as in a dictionary, there will be two discrete representations or "spellings" for each lexical item, at two interesting levels. One we can call the phonetic spelling. The other, however, is not that of the standard spelling system, but that of the phonological level. The two levels of representation are related in grammar by a complicated set of rules. The grammarians' phonetic spelling will be similar to the phonetic spelling of the dictionary, though considerably more precise for reasons explained in the "Guide to the Dictionary." The phonological spelling represents a level at which a given item is assigned a single representation from which can be predicted by rule the various phonetic spellings that the item can assume. (It must be stressed that the phonological spelling is an abstraction, in somewhat the same sense in which a line drawn in a geometry text is an abstraction because it represents a one-dimensional concept. The phonological spelling likewise represents a concept and is not in itself a word.) The prediction is made on the basis of an item's phonological shape (length of vowels, number of syllables, and the like) and on the basis of other phonological and grammatical information. Specific values can thus be assigned to the various segments (letters) of the phonological spelling; stress is also so assigned.

For example, consider the item *telegraph-* (not the word *telegraph*, but the item *telegraph-* from which are derived the verb *telegraph*, the adjective *telegraphic*, the noun *telegraphy*). Let us assume that its phonological spelling is [tĕlĕgrăf]. Now, if the word derived from this item is simply a member of the category Verb, that is, if no derivational endings are added to it, its stresses are assigned (completely automatically, because of the way English is spoken) by virtue of its phonological structure (that it consists of a prefix [tĕlĕ-] and a stem [-grăf], that its stem is monosyllabic, its prefix disyllabic, etc.) and, by virtue of its grammatical category (Verb), the stress pattern then will be [tĕl′ĕ-grăf′]. Further, because the second vowel is unstressed it will be (automatically) reduced, so the phonetic spelling will be (tĕl′ə-grăf′). (To interpret the symbols, see the pronunciation key facing the first page of the letter A.) If, however, the item *telegraph-* is suffixed with *-ic*, that is, if it is a derived adjective, then the stresses are assigned differently, although the same vowel is reduced: (tĕl′ə-grăf′ĭk). If it is suffixed with *-y*, that is, if it is a derived noun, then its stress is assigned so that different vowels are reduced: (tə-lĕg′rə-fē). The complicated set of rules referred to above consists of just such generalizations, for example, about the assignment of stresses and the reduction of vowels.

The phonology of a language, then, contains rules or generalizations that perform such functions as assigning stress, reducing vowels, and under other conditions inserting vowels and shortening long vowels. Here are instances of the last two phenomena: (1) phonological [plăsm] is related to phonetic (plăz′əm) by a rule that inserts epenthetic vowels in such a situation—and, additionally, by a rule that voices [s] to (z) in voiced environments; and (2) the rule that shortens long vowels under certain conditions is seen in such a typical pair as *sublime, sublimity:* (a) stress is assigned to the final syllable of a word if that syllable is strong, for example, if it contains a long vowel followed by any number of consonants; the stress remains on that syllable even when certain suffixes, such as *-ity, -ify,* and *-ic,* are added to the word—thus: [sŭ-blīm′], [sŭ-blīm′ĭ-tē]; (b) long vowels are then shortened when they stand three syllables from the end of the word—thus: [sŭ-blĭm′], [sŭ-blĭm′ĭ-tē]; (c) all short vowels not under stress are then reduced to (ə). Thus the phonetic spellings are (sə-blīm′), (sə-blĭm′ə-tē), in which stress falls on the same syllable of the basic item but where the vowels on which the stress falls differ radically.

Irregular items and words are those that do not obey the general rules of the language. Their phonetic spellings must show either that they undergo rules that ordinarily would not be expected to af-

fect them or that, on the other hand, they do *not* undergo rules that ordinarily *would* be expected to affect them. Thus *man* must be so spelled when it is made plural that the (ă) is shown to undergo vowel shift (a rule generally restricted to long vowels) to the sound (ĕ). And so with the (ĭ) of *sit* when its past tense is given: (săt). *Obese* must be so spelled that its (ē) does *not* undergo the general shortening before *-ity*. Predictably, the plural of (măn) should be (mănz); the past of (sĭt) should be (sĭt′ĭd); the *-ity* form of (ō-bēs′) should be (ō-bĕs′ə-tē). It is not the generalizations that are wrong; it is rather that the items *man, sit,* and *obese* are irregular.

Consider now the relationships among the two spellings in phonology and the two in lexicography. Clearly, the phonetic representation in a dictionary more or less consistently approximates the phonetic representation given in phonology. As pointed out in the "Guide to the Dictionary," the dictionary system of symbols is simpler than the phonetician's, but it is firmly based phonetically. Just as clear but not nearly so well understood is the fact that for a wide range of languages, and most particularly for English, employing an alphabetic orthography, the standardized spelling of a word is quite an accurate, generally consistent, and therefore adequate representation of its phonological spelling in grammar, even though the standardized spelling does not reflect the phonetics of a given situation. This is true insofar as the phonetic spellings associated with a single phonological spelling are predictable by general rule, that is, are not irregular. But since there is no rule general to English by which to predict *men* from *man, oxen* from *ox, sat* from *sit,* or *rode* from *ride,* we would expect what is in fact true, that these irregularities would be indicated directly in the standard orthography; it is just these phonetic differences that need to be reflected in the spelling. The contrary kind of irregularity—such as *obese, obesity,* where an item fails to undergo a general rule—is predictably not captured in the spelling.

The point is that wherever the phonetic spelling is predictable by general rule from the phonological spelling plus grammatical information (for example, is the item a noun or a verb?), the orthography need not, probably should not, and indeed generally does not reflect the phonetics of the situation. Rather, it reflects the phonological consistency underlying these phonetic facts. For example, if we look back at our initial example, *telegraph-,* we see that in the standard spelling of the words *telegraph, telegraphic,* and *telegraphy,* the spelling *telegraph-* for the basic lexical item around which all are formed remains constant despite the fact that the phonetic shapes it assumes are quite various: (tĕl′ə-grăf′), (tĕl′ə-grăf′-) (before *-ic*), and (tə-lĕg′rəf-) (before *-y*). Presumably this is a virtue, not a vice, of the orthography, for in this way the etymological and semantic relationships among various words are made apparent. A standard orthography that sought to represent the phonetic shapes of all items would conceal these relationships in over-nice differentiations that would be of interest to individuals learning the language or the pronunciation of a new word but that would simply be in the way of one who already knows the language.

Moreover, a spelling system based on phonological, not phonetic, representations removes one of the steps that would otherwise be involved in reading. In receiving speech, or in reading a phonetically based orthography, one has to move from the pronunciation to the abstract phonological representation. But in reading an orthography based on phonological representations, the reader finds, without any intervening steps, the abstract representation. Reading can thus proceed at a rate unlimited by the rate at which speech can be received.

Once English orthography is considered from this point of view, the great extent to which it is characterized by phonological regularity becomes apparent. Many examples come to mind. See, for example, *reject* (verb), *reject* (noun), *rejection* (and compare *object, protect,* etc.), where again the spelling of the basic item remains constant for all three: *reject-,* despite the three rather different phonetic shapes it assumes: (rĭ-jĕkt′) for the first, (rē′jĕkt′) for the second, and (rĭ-jĕksh′-) the last. Anyone can multiply such examples ad infinitum.

To glimpse the value of our phonologically based orthography, consider the many spellings given to phonetic (ə). Take just those found in the second syllable of two-syllable words, such as *civil* (sĭv′əl), *solemn* (sŏl′əm), *moral* (môr′əl), *person* (pûr′sən), where (ə) is spelled in four different ways. This may seem unreasonable until we recognize that four meaningfully different pronunciations emerge for these same vowels in words derived from the four examples—*civility* (sə-vĭl′ə-tē), *solemnity* (sə-lĕm′nə-tē), *morality* (mə-răl′ə-tē), *personify* (pər-sŏn′ə-fī′)—and that the four different spellings capture the underlying difference among such items. Note also that the principled basis of the *mn* in *solemn* also emerges in such a word as *solemnity* (sə-lĕm′nə-tē).

As a final and different sort of example, consider the use of *s* and *ss* in English spelling, in particular their use surrounded by vowels or other voiced sounds. In such instances, *s* (for example,

in *resemble, resent,* and *music*) is interpreted as [z] and *ss* (for example, in *dissemble, dissent,* and *mussel*) as [s]. Now, one could easily argue for using the letter *z* in the former case and *s* in the latter. Would anything be lost by such a spelling reform? One thing that would be lost would be the unique representation of the item *-semble* central not only to *dissemble* and *resemble* but also to *semblance, assemble,* etc. Then, too, the unique representation of *dis-* with its useful negative denotation (as in *dislike* and *disprove*) would be lost if we reformed *dissemble* to *disemble* and *dissent* to *disent.* Still, the destructive ramifications of such a reform are even greater. For instance, the generalization whereby (yōō) is found preceding a single consonant followed by a vowel and never preceding a double consonant or consonant cluster followed by a vowel would be lost, as would the converse, whereby (ŭ) is never found preceding a single consonant followed by a vowel. In English (byōō′tə-nē) and (myōō′tə-fəl)—by analogy with *mutiny* and *beautiful*—are possible words that do not happen to exist. But (bŭt′ə-nē) and (mŭt′ə-fəl) cannot occur in English. The uniqueness of representations and the significant generalizations just mentioned are preserved by simply representing the consonants of *mussel, button,* and the like with two letters rather than one, so that the [ŭ] of mussel is followed by two consonants in just the way in which the [ŭ] of *mustard* is.

This is not to deny that there are quite a few (though not nearly so many as people have tended to argue) nonphonological, nonphonetic spellings in English. For example, there is no salvaging the *-gh*'s of *enough, rough,* etc. (though a good case, too complex to explore here, in phonology can be made for the *-gh*'s of *right, night,* and the like). Clearly, there is some orthography that is of no value. But just as clearly there is a great deal that is of value if only we look for its value in the right place. English orthography quite generally, especially in its representation of the Greco-Latin component of the English vocabulary, represents a natural level of language—the deepest level of phonology. Standard spelling persists over the decades and centuries. It is not simply because of man's reflex antagonism to change that spelling reforms fail. The resistance of standard spelling to change reflects, rather, an important fact of historical linguistics: The underlying phonological spellings of language that are represented by alphabetic writing systems are themselves quite resistant to change.

Computers in Language Analysis and in Lexicography

by Henry Kučera

At the time the editors of this Dictionary began their work the first contributions of computational linguistics to lexicography were becoming available. They have had at their disposal an analysis of a body of language data that would have cost many years of human labor to complete without the computer.

A lexicographer, contemplating the compilation of a new dictionary, is faced with a number of basic initial problems such as how many and which entries to include, which meanings to consider in defining a word, how to organize the definitions, and how to illustrate the usage of words. His decision will, of course, be based partly on such nonlinguistic considerations as the size of the dictionary, the audience that he has in mind for the book, and the amount of money the publisher wishes to invest. But one thing the lexicographer must consider most carefully is the current state of the language he is planning to describe. For this reason, he collects citations illustrating the current usage of words, and studies the lexical, grammatical, and semantic properties of the language in normal discourse.

At the same time, the lexicographer may find it useful to have some knowledge of the basic lexical properties of large bodies of language data, knowledge that cannot be obtained from editorially chosen individual citations. Given a reasonably representative selection of contemporary texts, he may wish to know, for example, how many different words there are in such a textual corpus, what words they are, and with what frequency each occurs. In many instances the lexicographer may also be interested in the textual context that could provide useful information about particular shades of meaning in word usage. Such lexicographic interests naturally overlap, to a considerable extent, those of a linguist engaged in theoretical research on language structures or those of a practical specialist working to develop a machine that will automatically translate from one language to another.

Since any useful analysis of language usage has to be based on a large body of textual material, even elementary information could be obtained, before the advent of computers, only with enormous labor. Let us imagine that one wished to determine some very basic lexical properties of a textual corpus containing a million running words. If this were to be done by hand (or, more accurately, by the human brain), the task would require an inordinate amount of time; each of the one million words would have to be inspected individually, and each new word recorded after first checking to make sure it had not already been noted. If the analysis were also to preserve information about the frequency of occurrence of individual words, or perhaps references to the pages or lines of the text where their occurrences were to be found, the assignment would become more formidable still. Dedicated linguists and lexicographers—and their graduate students—have done limited analyses in the past by this painful method. But not only are projects of this kind extremely time-consuming, the monotony of the task is also apt to lead to errors. The modern computer, which is incapable of boredom and which does not make mistakes (provided that it is correctly programmed and free from technical defect), is ideally suited to this assignment.

A computer, in spite of its name and in spite of the definitions of it in some dictionaries, is much more than a machine for performing calculations. Aside from their mathematical operations, computers can process, organize, compare, and manipulate data of a nonnumerical nature, including textual information. It is precisely this capacity of computers to deal with letters, words, sentences, or even whole texts that has made these machines of considerable importance in the study of language. Linguists and lexicographers alike have found in the computer a new and useful tool that has not only made the analysis of languages less laborious and less time-consuming but has also opened new insights into important problems of language usage.

As it happened, the editors of this Dictionary began their work shortly after the completion of a computer analysis especially useful to an American lexicographer. A collection of texts, known as the *Standard Corpus of Present-Day Edited American English*, had been chosen, punched on cards, and analyzed at Brown University. The Corpus contains a total of 1,014,232 running words and is divided into 500 samples, each approximately 2,000 words long. These 500 samples are distributed among 15 types, or genre categories, representing a wide range of subject matter and prose style (poetry and drama are not included), from the sports page of the newspaper to the scientific journal, and from popular romantic fiction to abstruse philosophical discussion. All of the selections constituting the Corpus were chosen by a random sampling procedure from texts first printed in the United States in a single calendar year. (A full description of the Corpus and its basic properties can be found in the book by Henry Kučera and W. Nelson Francis, *Computational Analysis of Present-Day American English*, Brown University Press, Providence, 1967.)

Once the Corpus had become available in a form suitable for computer processing (that is, on punched cards and/or magnetic tape), the analysis of its basic properties and the retrieval of lexicographically useful information could be performed relatively easily and quickly.

Among other things, the analysis showed that in the more than one million running words of the Corpus, there were exactly 50,406 *different* words. The ten most frequent words turned out to be *the* (69,971 occurrences), *of* (36,411), *and* (28,852), *to* (26,149), *a* (23,237), *in* (21,341), *that* (10,595), *is* (10,099), *was* (9,816), and *he* (9,543 occurrences). (There were only 2,859 occurrences of *she*, which is perhaps something for ladies to contemplate.)

This list does not contain many surprises in itself. What was also discovered, however, and what may well turn out to be of considerable interest to linguists and literary specialists, is that the relative frequencies of even these common words vary significantly in different types of writing. Separate word-frequency studies made for each genre of the Corpus show that *the* still retains its first rank in all 15 categories. But already at the next rank, the genre classification affects the relative frequency of usage: *of* is the second most frequent word in ten genres, *and* in four, and *to* in one. What is more interesting still is that *of* is regularly the second most frequent word in what we have called *informative prose* (newspaper selections, popular articles, learned and scientific writings, for example), while *and* or *to* occurs in second place in almost all the genres of *imaginative prose* (fiction of various kinds and humor).

Significantly, *of*, the second most frequent word (mostly by a large margin) in informative prose, usually ranks only fourth or even lower in imaginative prose. This simple analysis and other, more detailed results clearly indicate that the frequency of particular words is a partial but interesting determinant of writing style, affecting even the most common words of a language.

New equipment and more ambitious linguistic and computing procedures will undoubtedly make it possible in the future to develop more revealing approaches to questions of style. One such approach, which is being currently pursued at Brown University, attempts to characterize the stylistic properties of a text not only in terms of word frequencies but also by the relative frequency of occurrence of various grammatical structures utilized in sentence formation.

Computer-produced word-indexes and concordances are also being widely used by linguists, lexicographers, and literary scholars. A word-index is simply a list of all the different words that occur in a given textual corpus; each index entry is followed by a precise indication of the location (for example, volume, page, and line) where the occurrence of the word can be found. The context in which a particular word has been used can then be looked up in the original text. But a computer can make even this task far easier by constructing a concordance that not only gives the reference to each occurrence but also prints the context itself (for example, each line or sentence in which the word occurred), so that manual searching through the original text becomes unnecessary.

Given a reasonably large computer, it is relatively easy to produce word-indexes and simple concordances even for large bodies of text. Such a computer-produced concordance has recently been made at the University of Texas for the complete works of James Joyce; and at the University of Toronto one is being made for the whole of Middle Welsh literature. It is possible as well to have more complex information-retrieval procedures, for example, a concordance program that prints only those lines (or sentences) fulfilling several specific conditions; such conditions could include the requirement that two or three or even more particular words must occur within a certain span of each other in the text before the textual segment is to be retrieved. The sophistication and the complexity of such concordances is limited chiefly by the availability of programming skill and of a sufficiently large computer.

To give a simple illustration of the potential lexicographic usefulness of multiple-condition concordances, let us assume that we are interested in retrieving from a textual corpus all occurrences of the construction *run up*. We may wish to study the exact usage of the different senses, such as *run up the hill* and *run up the flag*, which suggest different structures as well as different meanings. We have to bear in mind, of course, that *run* can be represented in such constructions also by its other inflected forms (*runs, running, ran*); moreover, the various forms of *run* may be separated from *up* by a number of other words, as in *He ran the blue flag up*. What we thus need is a concordance program that allows us to specify, roughly, the following conditions: "Retrieve all sentences in which any one of the forms *run, runs, running,* or *ran* is followed by *up* within the same sentence." This approach assumes, of course, that we have a reliable automatic procedure for dividing our text into sentences (the *Standard Corpus of Present-Day Edited American English* has been mechanically segmented into sentences on the basis of the occurrence of initial capital letters, periods, etc.). Alternatively, we could specify that *run* (or any of its forms) and *up* can be separated from each other by ten words or less; we could then be reasonably certain to catch all occurrences of the construction but might also get some accidental combinations of *run* and *up* which do not belong together and which we would have to eliminate through an inspection of the printout.

All concordance programs described so far require the specification of the particular words or expressions whose occurrences are to be retrieved. But linguists and lexicographers frequently need to study the occurrences of certain *grammatical classes* of words (such as adjectives, nouns, or auxiliary verbs). A computer, of course, cannot understand such a command as "retrieve all nouns," because this instruction is not explicit enough; the machine knows no grammar. Instead, either the formal properties of the relevant grammatical category must be specified, or a semiautomatic grammatical analysis must be resorted to. The word-index is first grammatically annotated by the appropriate designations (nouns, adjectives, etc.). Some parts of this annotating can be done automatically—the computer can be instructed, for example, to mark all entries ending in -*ify* as verbs. In some cases the automatic grammatical annotation may be erroneous and must be corrected manually; in other cases, only a skilled human analyst can determine the proper grammatical classification in the first place.

Some of the newer computer-related equipment is of considerable help in this kind of semiautomatic grammatical analysis. Among the most useful tools is the cathode-ray-tube console, a computer-connected instrument resembling a television set, which can display on its screen textual information from the computer's memory in easily readable form, and which allows the linguist to transmit his corrections and additions directly back to the computer, without having to punch cards or to use other slow procedures of information input.

Once a word-index is grammatically annotated, it is possible to retrieve all occurrences of a desired grammatical class of words. Similarly, a grammatical version of a multiple-condition concordance (that is, the printout of lines in which several grammatical conditions are satisfied) can be prepared. A portion of the million-word *Standard Corpus of Present-Day Edited American English* has been grammatically annotated and is now being used in the analysis of "grammatical style." In this project, the individual sentences of the text are broken down to reveal the grammatical rules that are represented in these sentences, and the relative frequency of the various grammatical rules of different complexity is then utilized in the characterization of the overall grammatical complexity of a textual passage.

Computers are also playing a significant role in advanced theoretical linguistic research. Methods of the mathematical theory of communication, various word-frequency-distribution models, and other mathematical techniques have been used in the comparative study of language structures. Attempts have been made to determine, with the aid of computers, certain aspects of the similarity of languages and to investigate the correlation between such quantitative results and the degree of known genetic linguistic relationship.

The validity of individual grammatical rules, of partial grammars, and even of semantic theories has been tested by simulating sentence production by computers. And, naturally, much theoretical research and practical work has been done in the various machine-translation projects, including the compilation of computer-based bilingual dictionaries (Russian-English, German-English, and others), which, although still very limited in size, contain useful lexical and grammatical information.

Not all, and not even most, aspects of linguistic research or of lexicographic work are suitable for computer-oriented approaches. Some of the most important linguistic problems, such as the determination of the underlying "deep" structure of sentences or the study of the semantics of discourse, are and will undoubtedly remain largely dependent on human imagination and effort. In lexicography, too, it is primarily the knowledge and the skill of the editorial staff that determine the value and usefulness of a dictionary. It would thus be a serious mistake for linguists and lexicographers to rush to computers in the hope of being provided with a quick solution to all problems. It is imperative that computers be used in language analysis in an informed and judicious manner that takes the limitations of the machine fully into account. But—as I have tried to illustrate in this essay—it would be equally foolhardy for linguists and especially for lexicographers to disregard the potential of computers as research tools. Not only can computers save labor and increase accuracy, but they can also help to bring important new insights into crucial problems of language use.

Guide to the Dictionary

by Norman Hoss

The American Heritage Dictionary of the English Language is planned to provide the maximum information to the reader who consults it without any knowledge of its organization beyond its alphabetical order. To this end, it is made as explicit as possible. The reader is not expected to piece together information by inference, nor is he expected to know any special symbols, abbreviations, or other dictionary shorthand.

To make the Dictionary thus appear simple requires a complex structure. The enormous mass of information is shaped by rigorous rules to provide data on demand. The entire body of rules could be of interest only to a lexicographer, but a familiarity with the resulting pattern will enhance the value of the Dictionary for any reader. Anyone willing to peruse this summary should find that he can use the book more efficiently and that his insights into the language will be deepened. He may find—if he has such a turn of mind—that he will take a positive pleasure in reading, not merely consulting, the Dictionary.

The Entry

The word or phrase one looks up in the Dictionary is the main entry. It is printed in **boldface type** and is set out slightly from the margin of the column.

When two or more entries are identical, not only in spelling but in all other graphic features, such as capitalization, hyphenation, and accent marks, the entries bear superscript numbers.

As in most reference books, the alphabetical order takes account of each letter in turn through the full entry even if it consists of several words. Thus, the entry **orderly** falls between **order** and **order of magnitude**. (In some systems **orderly** would fall after **order of magnitude**.) Abbreviations are alphabetized in the same sequence as

words. When a phrase is inverted for alphabetizing, the letter sequence is considered up to the comma. Words after the comma come into alphabetizing only when the words are identical up to the comma. Thus **Marshall, Thurgood** comes before **Marshall Islands**, but after **Marshall, John**.

Syllabication

An entry word is divided into syllables by centered dots: **rep·re·sen·ta·tion**. In an entry that is a phrase, words that appear as separate entries are not syllabicated: **meth·a·done hydrochloride**. **Hydrochloride** is a separate entry; **methadone** is not. The syllabication of the entries is not intended to reflect any linguistic theory about the syllable. It represents the established practice of printers in breaking words at the ends of lines. Printers often impose additional limitations on breaking words, but in any system words are properly broken at one of the divisions shown.

Variants

Standardization of the spelling of American English is more nearly complete than at any earlier time, but the number of variant spellings in common use remains large. All variants presented in the Dictionary are acceptable in any context unless marked with a restrictive label, such as *Regional*. Variants are set in boldface type and are treated in two ways: (1) A variant may follow the main entry separated only by a comma. This indicates that the two forms are in almost equally frequent use in edited sources: **ax, axe**. (2) When there is a more distinct preference for one spelling, the variant is introduced by the word "Also": **e·soph·a·gus**. . . . Also **oo·soph·a·gus**.

A large class of variants consists of spellings that are preferred in British English and are sometimes used in American English. Such variants as **colour** and **centre** are labeled *Chiefly British*. The variant **-ise**, which occurs in many British spellings for which American has **-ize** (for example, **realize, realise**), is not given unless it is also a common American variant.

When a word that has a variant occurs in a compound, the variant is not repeated at the compound; for example, the chiefly British variant **colour** is given for **color**, but it is not repeated at **colorblind** and other compounds.

Apart from variant spellings, which are given at the beginning of an entry, there are often situations in which there are two or more distinct words or phrases that have identical meaning. These additional terms for the same thing are cited in quotation marks at the end of the definitions or at the end of the relevant sense. In such cases, the entry is the preferred term, but the other terms are to be regarded as fully acceptable unless they are introduced by a note or label indicating their status:

> **mountain lion**. . . . Also called "catamount," "cougar," "mountain cat," "panther," "puma."

The variant spelling or other less preferred term is entered at its alphabetical place and referred back to the defined entry thus:

> **oe·soph·a·gus**. Variant of **esophagus**.
> **pu·ma**. . . . The **mountain lion** *(see)*.

Inflected Forms

Because of possible spelling problems that occur with the addition of suffixes, all forms that an English verb may take are given, whether regular or irregular, in the following order: past tense, past participle (if different), present participle, third person singular present tense.

For adjectives and adverbs, the comparative and superlative degrees are given in that order when they are in common use:

> **base** . . . **baser, basest**
> **well** . . . **better, best**

Plurals of nouns other than those formed by suffixing **-s** or **-es** are shown and labeled *pl*. The regular **-s** plural is shown when there is a variant plural that is irregular or when any question might arise, as with words ending in **-o**:

> **cac·tus** . . . *pl*. **-ti** (**-tī**) or **-tuses**
> **to·ma·to** . . . *pl*. **-toes**
> **pi·a·no** . . . *pl*. **-os**

If a noun is defined chiefly or exclusively in its plural senses, the plural form is the main entry and is labeled *pl.n.* (plural noun).

Pronunciation

Pronunciation is given for all main entry words and for other forms as needed. It is indicated in parentheses following the form to which it applies. The key to the use of the pronunciation symbols extends across the bottom of each pair of facing pages. A fuller key appears on the page facing the beginning of the vocabulary.

The set of symbols used is designed to enable the reader to reproduce a satisfactory pronunciation with no more than quick reference to the key. All pronunciations given are acceptable in all circumstances. When more than one is given, the first is assumed to be the more common, but the difference in frequency may be insignificant.

It is a commonplace that Americans do not all speak alike. Indeed, if analysis were pressed far enough, it could be shown that no *two* Americans speak exactly alike. It is equally obvious, nevertheless, that Americans can understand each other —at least on the level of speech sounds. It is also a familiar observation that Americans in New Orleans speak more like each other than like Americans in Chicago.

IDIOLECT, DIALECT, AND LANGUAGE

Thus, the speech of an individual, called an *idiolect,* fits into the pattern of a group—a *dialect*— which, in turn, is one of many dialects in the overall pattern, the English *language*. All speakers of the language can understand each other—better, at any rate, than they can understand speakers of another language.

The word *dialect* is often used for the language pattern of a small, provincial, or nonliterate group and in this view is regarded as something outside the language proper. Linguists have found it more convenient for comparative studies to apply the term *dialect* to the language pattern of any group, no matter how large and influential (which does not mean that linguists are unaware of the social significance of dialects). To a linguist, then, Parisian French—to take an extreme example—is a dialect of the French language.

In America there are no such extremes among dialects. There is no dialect that occupies the position that Parisian French does in France, either in prestige or in the attention devoted to maintaining its "purity"; there is no American *Académie*. On the other hand, there are no American dialects of English that are not readily comprehensible to speakers of the major dialects.

PRONUNCIATION SYMBOLS

In fact, the differences among the major dialects of the United States are such that for most words a single set of symbols can represent the pronunciation found in each dialect, provided that the symbols are planned for the purpose stated above —to enable the reader to reproduce a satisfactory pronunciation—and are not required to fill the more demanding role of representing sounds for linguistic analysis. In this regard, Professor W. Freeman Twaddell has written: "The purposes of transcription [of pronunciation] and the study of phonetic relations within a language are not the same. It is not surprising that a unit defined for the one purpose should not be wholly applicable to the other."

Whatever the differences between the Dictionary's pronunciation key and a given set of symbols used in linguistic analysis, both are solidly based on a principle that has been at the heart of modern studies of phonology: Speech sounds fall into patterns such that a single symbol can represent more than one related sound.

When one listens to an unfamiliar language it becomes obvious that speech is a continuum, broken only by occasional pauses. It does not sound like the series of separate sounds that we think we hear in our own language because of familiarity with its written words. No analysis of speech represented by one symbol after another is a perfect picture of the total sound continuum.

Nevertheless, symbol-by-symbol analysis is successful in linguistic analysis; and use of the Dictionary will show that a native speaker can produce a natural pronunciation of an unfamiliar word from the symbols provided.

PHONES AND PHONEMES

Such a situation is possible because speech sounds (called *phones*) seem naturally to go together in significant "bundles" called *phonemes*. Linguists have spent a great deal of effort on definitions of the phoneme, but the notion appears so obvious to our intuition that there appears no need to add here to the extensive literature of the subject. The consonant sounds indicated by the letter *p* in the words *pit* and *speak* are not the same in all respects, although the lips are brought together and released to make both sounds. The same lip movement is involved in making the first consonant of the word *bit*, but our intuition confirms what the linguists tell us: The two sounds spelled *p* go together, belong to one phoneme, and the sound spelled *b* belongs to another phoneme. (It has been shown in other contexts that such intuition is not dependent on the fact that the same letter may be used in spelling the variant phones.) In the article "Dialects of English," Professor Smith shows how phonemes are rigorously determined.

The symbols of the Dictionary key are based on phonemes. However, in situations as cited below, a symbol may be interpreted to stand for different phonemes produced in the same word by different dialects as part of regular patterns of the dialects. When a single pronunciation is offered in the Dictionary, the reader will supply the features of his own dialect that are called forth by his reading of the key. Thus, two speakers from different dialect areas may produce phonetically quite different pronunciations from the same symbols, and both will be perfectly correct. Indeed, unless the two speakers are sophisticated about phonetics, they will feel that they have produced the same pronunciation. The features that are not specified by the symbols are such that they are automatically relegated to the general dialect patterns to which native speakers are conditioned.

REGULAR DIALECT VARIANTS

Some of those features that are not distinguished by the symbols are so similar phonetically that only a trained ear will notice the distinction, but others are plainly different sounds. Even in the latter case, neither of two such pronunciations will be heard as a mispronunciation. The difference between them is regular, applying to all similar words, and therefore it is heard as a general dialect difference rather than a "wrong" pronunciation of the specific word.

The most obvious example of such a regular dialect feature is known usually as *r*-dropping. In several important American dialects, the tongue is not retracted to account for an *r* after a vowel; for example, the two *r*'s in *quarter* would not be heard. Although this pronunciation feature in its several forms is obvious even to the untrained ear, the Dictionary's linguistic advisers unanimously agreed that it would be a waste of space to show the additional pronunciations for all the thousands of words affected. The reader whose dialect includes *r*-dropping will interpret the pronunciation symbol (r) according to his dialect pattern, just as he does the letter *r* in normal English spelling. He will be producing a perfectly correct pronunciation. Other regular dialect differences that are not shown are mentioned below along with those that are recorded because of their complex distribution among dialects and idiolects. The policies of treating variants are not intended to suggest any preference among the major dialects.

STYLES OF SPEECH

Apart from regional variations in pronunciation, there are variations among social groups. The pronunciations recorded in the Dictionary are exclusively those of educated speech. No pronunciation is given that could be regarded by any large group as a mispronunciation. Such a policy is necessary if the purpose is, as stated, to enable the reader to reproduce pronunciations satisfactory for all circumstances. The vastly more ambitious purpose of recording the whole of American speech could produce a work of great value, but one far beyond the scope of a general dictionary. In every community, educated speech is accepted and understood by everyone, including those who do not themselves use it.

Apart from both regional and social variations, there are different styles of speech used by a single educated person in different circumstances. Hurried speech in casual circumstances can produce sentences such as (mē′chə-bou-wŭn′) for "I'll meet you about one." This is intelligible in context, but hardly recordable. By its structure, the Dictionary must record words in isolation, yet it may not offer any pronunciation that does not actually occur in speech. The best solution is to record *careful natural* speech. On the one hand such a policy avoids slovenliness; on the other hand, affectation.

REDUCED VOWELS

The spelling of English is closely and interestingly related to pronunciation, as Professor O'Neil explains in the article "The Spelling and Pronunciation of English"; but spelling does not determine the correctness of a pronunciation. The chief problem that dictionary users have in interpreting a pronunciation key is with the linguistic fact of *reduced* vowels. When a vowel receives the weakest level of stress within an utterance, which may be thought of as no stress, it nearly always is changed in quality from what it would be if stressed. Thus between the words *telegraph* and *telegraphy* the stress shifts about on the first three vowels showing them as "full" and "reduced" (tĕl′ə-grăf′), (tə-lĕg′rə-fē).

The change in quality of these vowels has nothing to do with sloppy or hurried speech. The reduction of the vowels will occur even when the words are said carefully and in isolation, so long as the pronunciation is natural as well as careful.

Note that the reduced vowels are represented by a nonalphabetical symbol (ə), the only one in the key. It is called *schwa* (shwä *or* shvä). This character (which some linguists use in other ways) is used in the Dictionary only for reduced vowels; therefore, it will appear only in an unstressed syllable. The sound of the schwa is not here intended to be precise. Vowels are not reduced to a single exact vowel; the schwa sound will vary sometimes according to the "full" vowel it is representing and often according to its phonetic environment. Its sound always approaches the vowel produced by the tongue in a "neutral" position between forward and back and between high and low. This midcentral vowel when stressed is the vowel in *cut* (kŭt).

Vowels are not always reduced to a sound close enough to this tongue position to be represented by the schwa. Sometimes the tongue is higher and still central and sometimes it is higher and farther forward. These two sounds are not distinguished in the key, to avoid making it too complex. Both such reductions of vowels with the tongue higher are represented by the symbol for the more forward position of the tongue, (ĭ) as in *artist* (är′tĭst). The choice between schwa (ə) and "breve i" (ĭ) to represent reduced vowels is arrived at through a complex set of considerations. In nearly every case where (ĭ) appears there also is a variant pronunciation closer to (ə). Variation between the sounds occurs among and within dialects and idiolects and may occur even within a single utterance containing the same

word twice. Variants of (ə) and (ĭ) are not recorded, but variants involving either one and a "full" vowel may be. In reproducing a pronunciation, it is much less important for a reduced vowel that the sound be (ə) or (ĭ) than that the unstressed syllable be completely unstressed. Even a slight stress on a reduced vowel can make a pronunciation *sound* as absurd as the representation of reduced vowels *looks* to many readers who have strong visual images of words. For example, the pronunciation (măn′ĭj-mənt) for *management* looks odd and would sound odd if the second syllable were given stress. As long as reduced vowels receive no stress, the surrounding sounds will lead the reader to (ə) or (ĭ) according to his dialect.

ASSIMILATION

A conflict between spelling and sound also occurs with consonants in certain surroundings. The most familiar example is the ending syllable *-tion* (-shən). The linguistic fact it represents is called assimilation. Other assimilations occur in words such as *nature* (nā′chər), *mutual* (myōō′chōō-əl), *armature* (är′mə-chōōr′). Again, the conflict arises not out of slovenly speech. The pronunciation (fyōō′tyōōr′) for *future* does not happen in natural American speech. Here spelling is a bad guide to pronunciation. However, the pronunciation (ĕd′-yōō-kā′shən) for *education* does occur, though less commonly than (ĕj-ə-kā′shən), so assimilation is a strong tendency rather than a total rule.

R-COLORING

A problem of a different kind in symbolic representation has been called "*r*-coloring" of a vowel. As the tongue retracts to form an (r) after a vowel, the quality of the vowel is affected. The situation is complex because both the onset of the vowel (its "original" sound, so to speak) and the effect of the (r) retraction on the vowel vary with both dialect and idiolect. Consequently the symbols for some vowels before *r* are separately defined and are intentionally ambiguous in the Dictionary key in order to avoid representing confusing variants. The most complex situation involves the three (onset) sounds (ā), (ĕ), and (ă). The situation is traditionally exemplified by the three words *Mary, merry,* and *marry.* In some dialects all three are pronounced alike (mĕr′ē). In a broad range of idiolects cutting across some dialect boundaries the three words are distinguished. It is this pattern that the Dictionary represents, thus: Mary (mâr′ē), merry (mĕr′ē), marry (măr′ē). However, some words may be heard in all three pronunciations, indistinctly grading one into the other. For these words the Dictionary represents only (âr), for example *care* (kâr), *dairy* (dâr′ē).

Another vowel altered by a following *r* is that which is sounded with the tongue high and forward. It might be represented by (ē) were it not for the effect of the *r*. In words such as *hear, beer, dear,* the vowel is altered by the *r* so that it approaches (ĭ) in sound. In the Dictionary a special symbol (îr) for this combination is used as in (bîr) *beer*. The sound (îr) with a lower vowel also occurs as in (mĭr′ər) *mirror*.

There are dialect differences that are sometimes idiolectal in the distinctions among various pronunciations of the syllable *-or*. In pairs such as *for, four; horse, hoarse; morning, mourning,* the vowel varies between (ô) and (ō). They are represented in this Dictionary as follows: *for* (fôr), *four* (fôr, fōr); *horse* (hôrs), *hoarse* (hôrs, hōrs); *morning* (môr′nĭng), *mourning* (môr′nĭng, mōr′-). Other words for which both forms are shown include those such as *more* (môr, mōr), *glory* (glôr′ē, glōr′-), *historian* (hĭ-stôr′ē-ən, hĭ-stōr′-).

Another group of words with variations for the *-or* syllable includes words such as *forest, horrid, orange,* in which the pronunciation of *o* before *r* varies between (ô) and (ŏ). In these words, which roughly follow dialect lines, the (ôr) pronunciation is given first: *forest* (fôr′ĭst, fŏr′-).

The symbol (ûr) used in (hûr) *her*, (fûr) *fur*, etc., has a regular dialect variant that is not separately recorded. In one style the retraction for the *r* begins immediately after the onset of the vowel; in other dialects some but not all such syllables are heard with a vowel like (ŭ) extended before the retraction of the tongue for the (r).

SYLLABIC CONSONANTS

There are two consonants represented as complete syllables. These are *l* and *n* following stressed syllables ending in *d* or *t* in such words as *bottle* (bŏt′l), *fatal* (fāt′l), *button* (bŭt′n), *lighten* (līt′n), *riddle* (rĭd′l), *ladle* (lād′l), *hidden* (hĭd′n), *adenoidal* (ăd′n-oid′l). Syllabic *n* is not shown after a syllable ending in *nd* or *-nt: abandon* (ə-băn′dən), *mountain* (moun′tən), but syllabic *l* is shown in that environment: *spindle* (spĭnd′l).

A common and perfectly regular variant that is not recorded involves the lack of distinction between *which* and *witch, whale* and *wail.* The sound (hw) does not exist in the dialects that do not make a distinction in these pairs.

STRESS

Stress, the relative degree of loudness with which the syllables of a word (or phrase) are spoken, is as important as any other feature in reproducing a pronunciation from symbols. In the Dictionary, three levels of stress are indicated. An unmarked syllable has the weakest stress in the word. The strongest stress is marked with a bold mark (′). An in-between level of stress, here called secondary, is marked with a similar but lighter mark (′).

Linguists have suggested more levels of stress, but three appear adequate to produce a satisfactory pronunciation of single words from the symbols. Words of one syllable show no stress mark, since there is no other stress level to which the syllable is compared. In running speech, monosyllables most often carry primary stress. Long

words often have more than one secondary stress, and a word can have more than one primary stress, as in certain compounds; for example, *all-purpose* (ôl′pûr′pəs).

The pronunciations are syllabicated for clarity. The syllabication generally follows the familiar pattern of showing "short" vowels in syllables closed by a following consonant, and "long" vowels in syllables that end with the vowel. The pattern is not intended to exemplify a linguistic theory but to present a familiar pattern to make the symbols more easily readable. The pattern is modified in many complex ways that need not concern the reader, since their purpose is merely to make the pronunciations easy to read.

Syllabication is used functionally in two ways. It shows juncture. The syllabication in *nitrate* (nī′trāt′) shifts in *nightrider* (nīt′rī′dər) to show the natural break known to linguists as "plus juncture." Syllabication is used to distinguish the lengthened consonant in *misstep* (mĭs-stĕp′) from the sound in *mistake* (mĭ-stāk′).

Syllabication of the pronunciations does not necessarily match the syllabication of the boldface word being pronounced. The former follows strict, though not obvious, phonological rules; the latter represents the established practice of printers derived from an eclectic combination of phonological, morphological, and etymological considerations expressed in the "eye" of generations of proofreaders, that is, in their intuition of the shape a word assumes in the minds of American readers.

Parts of Speech

The traditional categories of parts of speech are used for identification. They are not to be regarded as perfectly exclusive categories. For example, a noun may be used with other nouns as an attributive, a function that has some of the aspects of an adjective, but lacks other essential aspects that would require classification as an adjective. Thus, the use of the word *cabbage* in *cabbage soup* does not justify entry of *cabbage* as an adjective. A transitive verb may appear without its object in a particular context without warranting the recording of an intransitive sense in the Dictionary. The possibility of a sentence such as, "He can construct without reference to the plans," does not establish *construct* as an intransitive verb.

The part-of-speech labels, because they are repeated thousands of times, are among the very few abbreviations used in the Dictionary. They are: *n.* (noun), *pron.* (pronoun), *adj.* (adjective), *v.* (verb), *tr.* (transitive), *intr.* (intransitive), *adv.* (adverb), *conj.* (conjunction), *prep.* (preposition), *interj.* (interjection).

When the same word is used as more than one part of speech, there is only one main entry. Definitions of the entry word used as an additional part of speech are introduced by a boldface dash and the new part-of-speech label:

fan·cy (făn′sē) *n., pl.* **-cies.** **1.** The light invention or play of the mind. . . —*adj.* **fancier, -ciest.** **1.** Appealing to the fancy. . . —*tr.v.* **fancied, -cying, -cies.** **1.** To visualize; imagine. . . —*interj.* Used to express surprise.

All the definitions in the numbered sequence following a part-of-speech label belong to that part of speech. When a new part of speech is introduced, the entry and its pronunciation are assumed to remain the same for the new part of speech, unless otherwise indicated. If spelling, capitalization, hyphenation, syllabication, or pronunciation changes with the change in part of speech, the new form is indicated thus:

rec·ord (rĕk′ərd) *n. Abbr.* **rec.** **1.** An account made in an enduring form. . . —*v.* **re·cord** (rĭ-kôrd′), **-corded, -cording, -cords.** —*tr.* **1.** To set down for preservation in writing. . . —*intr.* To record something. —*adj.* **rec·ord** (rĕk′ərd). *Abbr.* **rec.** Establishing a record.

Entries consisting of more than one word (hyphenated forms are considered one word) are not labeled as parts of speech.

Labels

In addition to the part of speech, three other kinds of information are given by labels:

1. A label *Plural* at the beginning of a definition indicates that the plural form of the entry word is used in the sense being defined; for example, one sense of **finding** is: "**2.** *Plural.* The tools and materials used by an artisan or workman." Less often the label *Singular* might appear if the entry word itself is in the plural form and the definition deals with the singular.

2. Many definitions are labeled according to the field of knowledge with which they are concerned. These labels are merely an aid to orientation; they are not to be interpreted as stating that the sense is not used outside the special field, but that the sense being defined is of primary concern within that field. Such labels are especially useful when a word has many senses; for example, *base*, where the *chemistry* sense is so labeled.

3. Most important among the labels are those that restrict a definition to some level or style of usage. All senses that are not labeled, or restricted by Usage notes, are to be regarded as suitable in all contexts (even though a particular word might be unlikely in a given context because of the subject it deals with).

The labels that indicate restricted usage in one way or another are: *Nonstandard, Informal, Slang, Vulgar, Obsolete, Archaic, Rare, Poetic, Regional* (plus labels indicating specific regions), *British*, and foreign-language labels such as *French*.

Nonstandard.

This label implies, of course, the existence of standard American English. While it cannot be said that standard language is uniform throughout America, it is clear that there are forms that do not belong to any standard, educated speech. Such words and expressions are recognized as nonstandard not only by those whose speech is standard, but even by most of those who regularly use nonstandard expressions. One application of the label *Nonstandard* is for forms that have resulted from error. The label also covers forms such as **ain't** and **nowheres** that have never been admitted to standard language, though they have long existed alongside equivalent standard forms.

Informal.

Among those whose speech is standard, there are always two levels of language, the language of formal discourse and the language of conversation. The great mass of words are the same in both, but there are many words perfectly acceptable in conversation that would not be suitable in formal writing; for example, the word **mad** in the sense: *mad about bagels.* Such words are here labeled *Informal.* The label must not be taken to imply ignorant or inferior usage. It describes what has been called the "cultivated colloquial," that is, the speech of educated persons when they are more interested in what they are saying than in how they are saying it. Informal terms may, of course, appear also in writing when the flavor of speech is being sought.

Slang.

The label *Slang* indicates a style of language rather than a level of formality or cultivation. The distinguishing feature of slang as understood in the Dictionary is the intention—however often unsuccessful—to produce rhetorical effect, such as incongruity, irreverence, or exaggeration; for example, an underworld informer **sings.** A word that is strictly denotative—simply points to a referent—is not slang. Slang always has strong connotations in addition to its denotation. It is frequently figurative and its figure is most often hyperbole. Its connotation is intentionally, often aggressively, informal. The label *Slang* is not applied to merely loose, slovenly, or illiterate usage; some forms of slang occur in the most cultivated speech, but not in discourse that is intended to be formal. A slang expression is usually transitory, either dying out or being incorporated in the standard vocabulary as its rhetorical aspect is lost. It may, however, survive for centuries and remain slang; for example, *bones* for *dice.*

Vulgar.

The label *Vulgar* warns of social taboo attached to a word. A straightforward denotative vulgar sense of a word is distinguished from a slang sense. The label *Vulgar* therefore appears both alone and as *Vulgar Slang;* for example **snot** is labeled *Vulgar,* **snotty,** *Vulgar Slang.* No word is omitted from the Dictionary merely because of taboo.

Obsolete.

A term labeled *Obsolete* is no longer used except in quotation or intentional archaism. The fact that an object or a situation to which a word refers may be obsolete does not make the word itself obsolete. For example, the entry **beaver²** (a part of armor) is not labeled, because its name is still *beaver,* but its description as "medieval" indicates that the object is no longer in use. The label is applied only to words that have themselves disappeared from current language; for example, Francis Bacon's use of **prevent** in: *"He had prevented* [come before] *the Houre, because* [so that] *we might have the whole day before us."*

Archaic. The label *Archaic* is applied to words that once were common, but are currently rare and are readily identifiable as belonging to a style of language no longer in general use; for example, **affright.**

Rare. Terms that are labeled *Rare* were never common. Rare does not necessarily imply archaic; a rare term may be of recent coinage. The label is not used for terms whose use is rare because of the limitation of their application, such as abstruse technical terms; it is confined to general terms for which more common synonyms exist; for example, **nocent,** the "lost positive" that turns up in the word *innocent.*

Poetic. The label *Poetic* is applied to locutions such as shortenings (*e'er, o'er*) which are or were common in poetry, but have never been common in prose.

Regional. When an expression is commonly used in one area and little used—even if known—in other areas, it bears in the Dictionary an area label, such as *Southwestern U.S., Southeastern U.S., New England, Northern England, Western England.* For example, the word **arroyo** is labeled *Southwestern U.S.* Often an expression may be common to several areas, and yet not be used in American speech in general. Such expressions are labeled *Regional;* for example, the use of **fair** as a verb in: *the weather will fair today.* If the expression is regarded as distinctly nonstandard *in its own area,* it is labeled *Nonstandard* and no information is given as to its regional character, since *Nonstandard* is the stronger (more restrictive) label; for example, **nowheres** is labeled *Nonstandard.*

British. Because the distinction between British and American vocabulary is seldom exclusive, and because British terms are often in use elsewhere in the world, as in Australia, this label usually appears as *Chiefly British;* for example, **lift** . . . *Chiefly British.* An **elevator** (*see*). The Dictionary makes no effort to record British English exhaustively, but most British terms deserve entry because of the shared literature.

Foreign-language labels. English has borrowed heavily from other languages, and this fact is normally indicated in the etymologies. Some expressions from other languages, though fairly common, are still felt by the native speaker as not belonging to English. Such words are represented in italic type by many publications. The language from which they come is indicated in the Dictionary by a label. Such entries do not have an etymology.

Many terms that appear to be foreign have been incorporated into the vocabulary of a special field such as law or medicine. These are given the label of the field rather than a language label. Thus **nolle prosequi** is labeled *Law* not *Latin.*

Cross-References

Many cross-references are used to expand the information given at any one entry. The cross-reference instructions are self-explanatory; the entry referred to is in boldface type. When one of two entries merely refers to the other, the entry that has the definition is the preferred form.

When a variant form is given at a defined entry, it is also entered at its alphabetical place unless it falls close (within a third of a column) to the defined entry.

Idioms

Many entry words are commonly used in phrases the meaning of which is not clear from the separate words. Except as noted, such phrases are defined within the entry for the most significant word. The phrase is introduced by a bold dash and is set in boldface type. Phrases, such as **dial tone,** made up of an attributive (adjective or noun) plus a noun are separate main entries. Verb phrases that form nouns are also separate main entries; for example, **make up** is a separate entry because of the noun **make-up.**

Order of Definitions

When an entry has multiple numbered definitions, they are ordered by a method of synchronic semantic analysis intended to serve the convenience of the general user of the Dictionary. The numerical order does not indicate the historical sequence by which the senses arose. The first definition, then, is not necessarily the earliest sense of the word, though it may be. The first definition is the central meaning about which the other senses may be most logically organized. The organization seeks to clarify that, despite its various meanings, the entry is a single "word" and not a number of separate words that happen to be spelled the same.

Etymologies

Etymologies appear in square brackets [ ] following the definitions. In accordance with the Dictionary's policy of eliminating special symbols and abbreviations, none have been used in the etymologies. The etymologies, like the definitions, have been written so that they speak for themselves, without the need for special explanation. Highly technical terms have not been used. The terminology used is the traditional, mostly familiar language of descriptive grammar, identifying parts of speech and the various grammatical and morphological forms and processes, such as *diminutive, frequentative, variant, stem, past participle, metathesis,* all of which are, of course, fully defined in their places in the Dictionary. Likewise, every language that is cited in an etymology is entered and described.

A special innovation is the systematic policy of tracing each word to its prehistoric Indo-European origin whenever possible. Every etymology pursues its story back to one of four possible conclusions:

1. Outside Indo-European. For example, a word from a Semitic language is traced as far into its historical origins as will conduce to illuminating the word or its relations to other words that are represented in English; it is not necessarily traced back to reconstructed Proto-Semitic. Likewise, words from Japanese, Korean, and Vietnamese that are early borrowings from Chinese are generally traced back to Ancient Chinese, while words taken directly into English from Chinese are not necessarily so traced; and American Indian words are often but not usually traced back into ancestral forms such as Proto-Algonquian.

2. Obscure origin. The origins of numerous English words are still obscure, either immediately or at some earlier historical stages. Many newly discovered origins are presented here, but many more will doubtless always remain obscure. In such cases, the earliest known form is marked with a dagger † referring to a footnote "†Of obscure origin" carried on every right-hand page through the Dictionary.

3. Proper names. If a word is taken from the name of a place or person, the story generally stops there, although sometimes a further etymology of the name itself is given if it seems sufficiently interesting or relevant. Such names are in any event identified with pertinent information as to time or place; and the reason for the coinage is stated if necessary.

4. Indo-European. It is remarkable that the great bulk of the now vast vocabulary of English can be traced back, either through its native origins in Old English and Proto-Germanic, or through borrowings from nearly every other Indo-European language (but chiefly from Germanic, Romance, Latin, and Greek), to the reconstructed ancestral language called Proto-Indo-European. In this Dictionary, for the first time, every word that can be so traced is taken back to its earliest ascertainable origins (either in Proto-Indo-European or in the prehistoric stage of one of its chief branches, such as Germanic or Celtic). It is also remarkable that the constantly ramifying nature of lexical creativity, descent, and borrowing is such that many tens of thousands of modern English words can be proved to be descended from a mere 1,500 Indo-European roots. Some such individual roots are represented in English by hundreds of English words. Each word so descended is traced in its own etymology in the body of the Dictionary back to its earliest documentary attestation. It is then cross-referred to the Appendix of Indo-European roots, with an asterisk referring to a footnote carried on each right-hand page guiding the reader to the Appendix at the end of the main vocabulary section. A description of the Indo-European language, with observations on the cultural inferences that can be drawn from it, by Professor Watkins, is carried at the beginning of the Appendix; there is also an explanatory Guide to the Appendix itself and, on the endpaper, a table of the Indo-European languages preceded by a chart of the principal sound changes. Along with its scholarly interest, the Appendix provides a rich source of curious information for the casually interested.

Certain details of style in the etymologies are worth describing. When a compound word is split into its component elements, an analytical gloss is given if necessary to explain the semantics of the compound, and then a boldface colon (:) is used. Each of the two components in turn is then traced to its further origins:

nepenthe. . . [Greek *nēpenthes (pharmakon),* "grief-banishing (drug)" : *nē,* not (see **ne** in Appendix*) + *penthos,* grief (see **kwenth-** in Appendix*).]

Quotation marks are used around certain glosses; these explain underlying meanings different from the effective meaning:

mediocre. . . [From Latin *mediocris,* "halfway up the mountain," in a middle state : *medius,* middle (see **medhyo-** in Appendix*) + *ocris,* mountain, peak (see **ak-** in Appendix*).]

The word "from" is used to indicate origin of any kind—by inheritance, borrowing, derivation, composition—with one exception. In order to stress the fact that the native core of English is a permanent unbroken continuum of its earlier forms, "from" is not used between Middle English and Old English, thus emphasizing that the forms given are earlier forms of *the same linguistic item* rather than their models or sources, as in the case of borrowings:

room. . . [Middle English *roum,* Old English *rūm.* See **rewǝ-** in Appendix.*]

Cross-references are indicated in two ways. If preceded by the word "see," as in the case of the references to the Appendix, and in some others, the words cited are in **boldface**. But *implicit* cross-references to the etymologies of other English words in the Dictionary are given in SMALL CAPITALS:

ritual. . . [Latin *rituālis*, from *ritus*, RITE.]

Obvious derivatives are not given etymologies. Thus, although *laxity* may be modeled on Latin *laxitās* (itself from *laxus*, lax), its relationship to *lax* is so obvious that to give it an etymology would be unreasonable in the limited space available.

The transliterations of various languages are standard and not innovative. Greek *kappa* is given as *K* and *chi* as *kh*; the Old English *thorn* and *edh* are both given as *th* (since they reflect only different scribal practices), while in Old Norse the *thorn* is given as *th* and the *edh* as *dh* (since here they do reflect different phonetic values); tone marks are given for Chinese and other tone languages; macrons are used for all long vowels in Latin, while in Greek only the graphically differentiated long vowels are so marked (long *a, i,* and *u* are not marked).

Undefined Forms

At the end of many entries will be found additional parts of speech formed from the entry word or obviously related to it and having the same essential meaning, but a different grammatical function as indicated by the part-of-speech label. These labeled forms avoid use of space for merely formulaic definitions that tell no more than the part-of-speech label does.

Sometimes different suffixes will produce words of different application but having the same part-of-speech label. These are separated by dashes and given separate labels:

—**ca·jol′er** *n.* —**ca·jol′er·y** *n.*

When different forms have the same applica-

tion, they are separated by commas and have a single part-of-speech label:

—**sto·lid′i·ty, stol′id·ness** *n.*

Stresses are indicated for all these undefined forms that have more than one syllable, and pronunciation is indicated as needed.

Sometimes the entry word may appear unchanged at the end of the entry, with a different part-of-speech label. This indicates that the word is used in exactly the same senses as those defined above, but with different grammatical function. Again this eliminates definitions that would not add any semantic information and would tell no more than is conveyed by the part-of-speech label.

Usage Notes

The Usage notes are a significant aspect of the Dictionary, as explained in the editor's introduction and the article "Good Usage, Bad Usage, and Usage" by Professor Bishop. The reader should find it useful to glance at the end of any entry he is consulting to see if it has such a note; if so, it is labeled simply **Usage**. The definitions may appear sometimes to contradict the Usage notes by recording a sense of a word that the Usage Panel finds unacceptable. This is not contradiction but basic policy of the Dictionary. All significant usages, regardless of status, are recorded in the definitions. Those that present usage problems are then pursued further in the notes.

Synonyms

Paragraphs that provide discrimination of related words also appear at the end of some entries and are headed **Synonyms**. The word *synonyms* should not be interpreted to indicate that the words treated together are of precisely the same meaning. It is their differences of meaning and usage that make the discrimination among them valuable.

Pronunciation Key

The system of indicating pronunciations in the Dictionary is explained in the section headed "Pronunciation" in the "Guide to the Dictionary." The column below headed AHD represents the pronunciation key used in the Dictionary. The symbols marked with an asterisk are discussed in the guide. Important insights into the theoretical basis of representing pronunciations as well as information on dialect variations may be obtained from the article "English Dialects" by Henry Lee Smith, Jr. The symbols in the right-hand column, labeled T-S, are from the system of phonemes described by Professor Smith and George L. Trager and are widely used by linguists. (The Trager-Smith symbols, however, are for phonemes of English only.) The symbols are explained in Professor Smith's article. The center column, labeled IPA, contains symbols from the International Phonetic Alphabet, also widely used by scholars. The three systems do not precisely correspond, because they were differently conceived for somewhat different purposes.

spellings	AHD	IPA	T-S
pat	ă	æ	æ
pay	ā	e	ey
care	*âr	ɛr, er	ehr, eyr, er
father	ä	ɑː, ɑ	ah
bib	b	b	b
church	ch	tʃ	č
deed, milled	d	d	d
pet	ĕ	ɛ	e
bee	ē	i	iy
fife, phase	f	f	f
gag	g	g	g
hat	h	h	h
which	*hw	hw (also ʍ)	hw
pit	*ĭ	ɪ	i
pie, by	ī	aɪ	ay
pier	*îr	ɪr, ir	ihr, iyr, ir
judge	j	dʒ	j
kick, cat, pique	k	k	k
lid, needle	*l (nēd′l)	l, ļ [ˈnidļ]	l (not syllabic)
mum	m	m	m
no, sudden	*n (sŭd′n)	n, ņ [ˈsʌdņ]	n (not syllabic)
thing	ng	ŋ	ŋ
pot, *horrid	ŏ	ɑ	a, o
toe, *hoarse	ō	o	ow
caught, paw, *for	ô	ɔ	oh, oh, ɔ
noise	oi	ɔɪ	oy
took	ŏŏ	ʊ	u
boot	ōō	u	uw
out	ou	aʊ	aw, æw
pop	p	p	p
roar	*r	r	r
sauce	s	s	s

spellings	AHD	IPA	T-S
ship, dish	sh	ʃ	š
tight, stopped	t	t	t
thin	th	θ	θ
this	*th*	ð	ð
cut	ŭ	ʌ	ə
urge, term, firm, word, heard	*ûr	ɝ, ɜr	ər, əhr
valve	v	v	v
with	w	w	w
yes	y	j	y
zebra, xylem	z	z	z
vision, pleasure, garage	zh	ʒ	ž
about, item, edible, gallop, circus	*ə	ə	ə, ɨ
butter	*ər	ɚ	ər

FOREIGN

	AHD	IPA
French ami	à	a
French feu, *German* schön	œ	œ
French tu, *German* über	ü	y
German ich, *Scottish* loch	KH	x
French bon	N	õ, æ̃, ã, œ̃
French compiègne	y' (kôN-pyĕn′y')	ɲ

STRESS

Primary stress	′	**bi·ol′o·gy** (bī-ŏl′ə-jē)
Secondary stress	′	**bi′o·log′i·cal** (bī′ə-lŏj′ĭ-kəl)

Note on Illustrations: Each illustration has been positioned as close as possible to the entry it illustrates. In those instances where close juxtaposition proved impossible, the illustration nevertheless always appears on the same page as the entry or on the page opposite.

Aa

К К Ҟ   Ƥ A A A   A A Ａ   a a   A *l* a a

1	2	3	4	5	6	7	8	9	10	11	12	13	14	15	16
Phoenician				Greek				Roman		Medieval			Modern		

Around 1000 B.C. *the Phoenicians and other Semites of Syria and Palestine began to use a graphic sign in the forms (1,2,3). They gave it the name* 'aleph, *meaning "ox," and used it to represent a laryngeal consonant ('), or glottal stop, such as is heard in one New York City pronunciation of English* bottle. *After 900* B.C. *the Greeks borrowed the sign from the Phoenicians in the reversed form (4). They also changed its name to* alpha, *and since they had no glottal stop in their language, they made the sign stand for the vowel a. Subsequently they developed two more forms (5,6), in which the middle bar slopes one way or the other, and finally the classical form (7), having the bar horizontal. The Greek forms passed unchanged via Etruscan into the Roman alphabet (8,9). The Roman Monumental Capital (10) is the prototype of our modern capital, printed (13) and written (14). The written Roman forms (8,9) developed into the late Roman and medieval Uncial (11) and Cursive (12), which are the bases of our modern small letter, printed (15) and written (16).*

a, A (ā) *n., pl.* **a's** or *rare* **as, A's** or **As.** **1.** The first letter of the modern English alphabet. See **alphabet.** **2.** Any of the speech sounds represented by this letter. **3.** Anything shaped like the letter **A.**

a, A, a., A. *Note:* As an abbreviation or symbol, *a* may be a small or a capital letter, with or without a period. Established forms or those generally preferred precede the definition. When no form is given, all four forms are in general use in that sense. **1. a.** about. **2. A.** academician; academy. **3. a.** acceleration. **4. a., A.** acid. **5. A, a., A.** acre. **6. a.** acreage. **7. a.** acting. **8. a.** adjective. **9. a.** afternoon. **10. A.** alto. **11. a., A.** amateur. **12. A.** America; American. **13. A** ammeter. **14. A** ampere. **15. a.** anonymous. **16. a., A.** answer. **17. a.** anterior. **18. a, a** are (measurement). **19. A** area. **20. a** *Physics.* atto-. **21. a.** before (Latin *ante*). **22. a.** in the year (Latin *annō*). **23. a.** year (Latin *annus*). **24. A** A human blood type of the ABO group. See **ABO. 25.** The first in a series. **26. A** The best or highest in quality or rank: *grade A milk.* **27. A a.** The sixth tone in the scale of C major, or the first note in the related minor scale. **b.** The scale based on this tone. **c.** A written or printed note representing this tone. **d.** A string, key, or pipe tuned to the pitch of this tone.

a¹ (ə; *emphatic* ā). Indefinite article functioning as an adjective. **1.** Used before nouns and noun phrases that denote a single, but unspecified, person or thing: *a region; a man.* **2.** Used before plural nouns modified by *few, good many,* or *great many: a few donations.* **3.** One kind of: *birds of a feather.* **4.** Any: *not a drop to drink.* See **an.** [Middle English *a(n),* from Old English *an, ān,* one. See **oino-** in Appendix.*]
Usage: A and *an* are redundant in, and should be omitted from, certain common constructions, such as: *no greater (an) honor could be won; no such (a) thing.*

a² (ə). Indefinite article functioning as a preposition. In every; to each; per: *once a month; one dollar a pound.* [Middle English *a, o,* reduced forms of *an, on,* in, at, ON.]

a³ (ə, ă). *Regional.* Have: *He'd a come if he could.* [Middle English *a, ha,* reduced forms of *haven, habben,* HAVE.]

a⁴, a' (ā, ô). *British Regional.* He, she, it, they, or I: *"And a' babbled of green fields."* (Shakespeare). [Middle English *a, ha,* reduced forms of *he,* he (it), *heo,* she (it), *hi(e),* they.]

a-¹. Indicates without, not, or opposite to; for example, **amoral, acotyledon.** See Usage note at **non-.** [Greek *a-, an-,* not. See **ne** in Appendix.*]

a-². Indicates: **1.** On or in; for example, **aboard, abed. 2.** In the act of; for example, *a-fishing, a-going.* **3.** In the direction of,

situated at, or toward; for example, **astern, abeam.** [Middle English *a-,* Old English *a-,* from *an, on,* in, at, ON.]

a-³. Indicates: **1.** Up, out, or away; for example, **arise, awake. 2.** Intensified action; for example, **abide, amaze.** [Middle English *a-,* up, out, away, Old English *ā-,* reduced form of *ar-, or-,* from Germanic.]

a-⁴. Indicates of or from; for example, **anew, afresh.** [Middle English *a-, o-,* reduced form of OF.]

AA 1. Alcoholics Anonymous. **2.** antiaircraft.

A.A. 1. antiaircraft. **2.** Associate in Arts.

AAA 1. Agricultural Adjustment Association. **2.** American Automobile Association. **3.** antiaircraft artillery.

A.A.A.L. American Academy of Arts and Letters.

A.A.A.S. American Association for the Advancement of Science.

Aa·chen (ä' кнən). *French* **Aix-la-Cha·pelle** (ĕks'là-shà-pĕl'). A city of North Rhine-Westphalia, Germany. It was the capital of Charlemagne's empire. Population, 176,000.

AACS, A.A.C.S. 1. Airways and Air Communications System. **2.** Army Air Communications System.

AAF, A.A.F. Army Air Forces.

Aa·land Islands. See Åland Islands.

Aal·borg (ôl'bôr'). A historic city and seaport of northern Denmark. Population, 86,000.

A.A.P.S.S. American Academy of Political and Social Science.

Aar (är). Also **Aa·re** (ä'rə). A river of Switzerland, rising in the Bernese Alps and flowing 183 miles northeast to the Rhine.

aard·vark (ärd'värk') *n.* A burrowing mammal, *Orycteropus afer,* of southern Africa, having a stocky, hairy body, large ears, a long, tubular snout, and powerful digging claws. [Obsolete Afrikaans, "earth-pig" : *aarde,* earth, from Dutch, from Middle Dutch *aerde* (see **er-³** in Appendix*) + *vark,* pig, from Middle Dutch *varken* (see **porko-** in Appendix*).]

aard·wolf (ärd'wŏolf') *n., pl.* **-wolves** (-wŏolvz'). A hyenalike mammal, *Proteles cristatus,* of southern and eastern Africa, having gray fur with black stripes, and feeding mainly on termites and insect larvae. [Afrikaans "earth-wolf" : *aarde,* earth (see **aardvark**) + *wolf,* wolf, from Middle Dutch (see **wlkwo-** in Appendix*).]

Aar·hus (ôr'hōōs'). A seaport in eastern Jutland. Population, 120,000.

Aar·on¹ (âr'ən, ăr'-). A masculine given name. [Late Latin, from Greek *Aarōn,* from Hebrew *'aharōn.*]

Aar·on² (âr'ən, ăr'-). The original high priest of the Hebrew nation, the older brother of Moses. Exodus 28:1–4; 40:12–13.

Aa·ron·ic (â-rŏn'ĭk, ă-rŏn'-) *adj.* Also **Aa·ron·i·cal** (-ĭ-kəl). **1.** Of, pertaining to, or characteristic of Aaron. **2.** Of, pertaining to, or characteristic of any high priest; priestly.

Aaron's rod. 1. Any of several flowering plants having tall, erect stems; especially, *Thermopsis caroliniana,* of the southeastern United States, having compound leaves and erect clusters of yellow flowers. **2.** *Architecture.* A rod-shaped molding decorated with a design of leaves, scrolls, or a twined serpent. [After the rod of the high priest Aaron which blossomed and produced almonds (Numbers 17:8).]

A.A.U.P. American Association of University Professors.

A.A.U.W. American Association of University Women.

Ab. Variant of **Av.**

ab-¹. *Zoology.* Indicates a part of the body opposite to or removed from another specified part; for example, **abomasum, aboral.** [Latin, from *ab,* away from. See **apo-** in Appendix.* In Latin compounds, *ab-* becomes *a-* before *m, p,* and *v; au-* before *f;* and *abs-* before *t.*]

aardvark

aardwolf

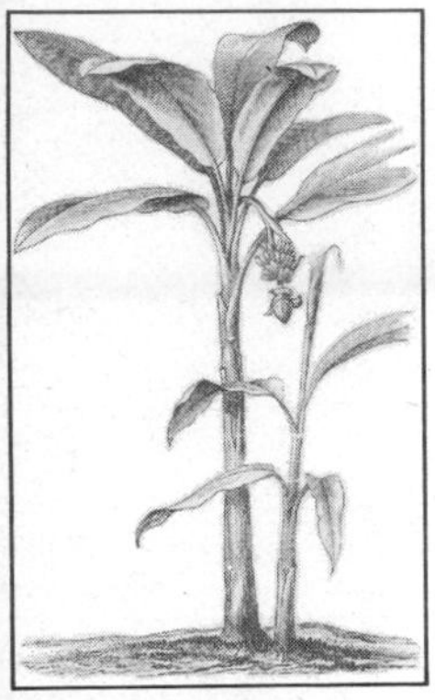
abaca

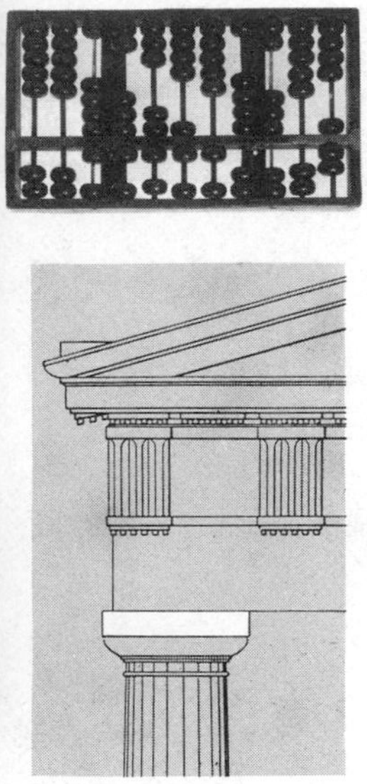
abacus
Above: Eleven-bar Chinese abacus for home use
Below: On a Doric column

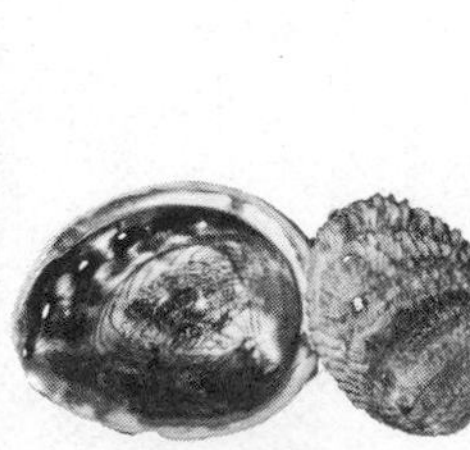
abalone
Left: Haliotis rufescens, red abalone, showing the inside of the shell
Right: Haliotis corrugata, pink abalone, showing the shell's exterior

ab–[2]. Indicates a centimeter-gram-second electromagnetic unit of measurement; for example, **abcoulomb.** [Short for ABSOLUTE.]

AB A human blood type of the ABO group. See **ABO.**

ab. about.

a.b. able-bodied seaman.

A.B. **1.** able-bodied seaman. **2.** Bachelor of Arts.

a·ba (ə-bä′) *n.* **1.** A light fabric woven of the hair of camels or goats. **2.** A loose-fitting sleeveless garment of this fabric worn by Arabs. [Arabic *'abā'.*]

A.B.A. **1.** American Bankers Association. **2.** American Bar Association.

ab·a·ca (ăb′ə-kä′) *n.* A Philippine plant, *Musa textilis,* related to the banana. Its leafstalks are the source of **Manila hemp** *(see).* [Spanish *abacá,* from Tagalog *abaká.*]

a·back (ə-băk′) *adv. Archaic.* Back; backward. **—taken aback.** Dumbfounded; startled. [Middle English *abak,* Old English *on bæc* : ON + *bæc,* BACK.]

ab·a·cus (ăb′ə-kəs) *n., pl.* **-cuses** or **-ci** (-sī′). **1.** A manual computing device consisting of a frame holding parallel rods strung with movable counters. **2.** A slab on the top of the capital of a column. [Latin *abacus,* from Greek *abax* (stem *abak-*), slab, mathematical table, originally a drawing board covered with dust, from Hebrew *'ābhāq,* dust.]

A·ba·dan (ä′bə-dän′, ăb′ə-dăn′). A port of southwestern Iran, on the Persian Gulf. Population, 302,000.

a·baft (ə-băft′, ə-bäft′) *adv.* Toward the stern. *—prep.* Toward the stern from. [Middle English *o(n) baft* : ON + *baft,* from Old English *beæftan,* behind : *be,* at, BY + *æftan,* behind (see **apo-** in Appendix*).]

A·ba·kan (ŭ-bŭ-kän′). A city in Soviet Central Asia, the capital of the Khakass Autonomous Region. Population, 56,000.

ab·a·lo·ne (ăb′ĕ-lō′nē) *n.* Any of the various large, edible marine gastropods of the genus *Haliotis,* having an ear-shaped shell with a row of holes and a colorful, pearly interior often used for making ornaments. [American Spanish *abulón*†.]

ab·amp (ăb′ămp′) *n.* An abampere.

ab·am·pere (ăb-ăm′pîr′) *n.* A centimeter-gram-second electromagnetic unit of current, equal to the current that produces a force of two dynes per centimeter of length on each of two infinitely long straight parallel wires one centimeter apart. It is equal to 10 amperes. [AB- (absolute) + AMPERE.]

a·ban·don (ə-băn′dən) *tr.v.* **-doned, -doning, -dons.** **1.** To forsake; desert. **2.** To surrender one's claim or right to; give up. **3.** To desist from. **4.** To yield (oneself) completely, as to emotion. —See Synonyms at **relinquish.** *—n.* A complete surrender of inhibitions. [Middle English *abandounen,* from Old French *abandoner,* from *(metre) a bandon,* "(to put) in one's power" : *a,* to, at, from Latin *ad,* to + *bandon,* power, from *ban,* jurisdiction, power, from (unattested) Frankish *ban* (see **bhā-**[2] in Appendix*).] **—a·ban′don·ment** *n.*

a·ban·doned (ə-băn′dənd) *adj.* Shameless; immoral.

a·base (ə-bās′) *tr.v.* **abased, abasing, abases.** To lower in rank, prestige, or esteem; humble; humiliate. See Synonyms at **degrade.** [Middle English *abassen,* from Old French *abaissier,* from Vulgar Latin *abbassiāre* (unattested) : *ad-,* to + *bassiāre* (unattested), to lower, from Late Latin *bassus,* low (see **bassus** in Appendix*).] **—a·base′ment** *n.*

a·bash (ə-băsh′) *tr.v.* **abashed, abashing, abashes.** To make ashamed or uneasy; disconcert. [Middle English *abaisen, abashen,* to gape with surprise, be dumbfounded, from Norman French *abaiss-,* variant of Old French *e(s)bass-,* present stem of *e(s)bahir* : *es-,* from Latin *ex-,* out of + *baer,* to gape, from Latin *batāre* (unattested), to yawn, gape (see **bat-** in Appendix*).] **—a·bash′ment** *n.*

a·bate (ə-bāt′) *v.* **abated, abating, abates.** *—tr.* **1.** To reduce in amount, degree, or intensity; lessen. **2.** To deduct from an amount; subtract. **3.** *Law.* **a.** To put an end to. **b.** To make void; annul. *—intr.* **1.** To subside; diminish. **2.** *Law.* To become void. —See Synonyms at **decrease.** [Middle English *abaten,* from Old French *abattre,* to beat down, from Vulgar Latin *abbattuere* (unattested) : *ad-,* at, to (used here to express completed action) + *battuere,* to beat (see **battuere** in Appendix*).] **—a·bat′er** *n.*

a·bate·ment (ə-bāt′mənt) *n.* **1.** Diminution in degree or intensity; moderation. **2.** The amount abated; reduction. **3.** *Law.* The act of abating; elimination or annulment.

ab·at·toir (ăb′ə-twär′) *n. French.* A slaughterhouse.

ab·ax·i·al (ăb-ăk′sē-əl) *adj.* Away from the axis.

abb. abbess; abbey; abbot.

Ab·ba (ăb′ə) *n.* **1.** In the New Testament, God. Mark 14:36. **2.** *Small* **a.** Father. Used as a title of honor in several Eastern churches. [Middle English, from Late Latin, from Greek, from Aramaic *abbā,* father.]

ab·ba·cy (ăb′ə-sē) *n., pl.* **-cies.** The office, term, or jurisdiction of an abbot. [Middle English *abbatie,* from Late Latin *abbātia,* from *abbās* (stem *abbāt-*), ABBOT.]

Ab·bas·side (ə-băs′īd) *n.* Also **Ab·bas·sid** (-ĭd). Any of the caliphs of the dynasty that ruled the Moslem empire from A.D. 750–1258 and claimed descent from Abbas, uncle of Mohammed. **—Ab·bas′side** *adj.*

ab·ba·tial (ə-bā′shəl) *adj.* Of or pertaining to an abbey, abbot, or abbess. [Middle English *abbacyal,* from Late Latin *abbātiālis,* from *abbās* (stem *abbāt-*), ABBOT.]

ab·bé (ăb′ā, ă-bā′) *n., pl.* **abbés.** In France, a title originally given to the superior of an abbey, now applied to any ecclesiastical figure. [French, from Old French, from Late Latin *abbās,* ABBOT.]

ab·bess (ăb′ĭs) *n., pl.* **-besses.** *Abbr.* **abb.** The female superior of a convent of nuns. [Middle English *abbesse,* from Old French, from Late Latin *abbātissa,* from *abbās* (stem *abbāt-*), ABBOT.]

Ab·be·vil·li·an (ăb′ə-vĭl′ē-ən) *adj.* Designating the earliest Paleolithic archaeological sites in Europe, characterized by bifacial stone hand axes. Also formerly called "Chellian." [After *Abbeville,* France, site of the archaeological finds.]

ab·bey (ăb′ē) *n., pl.* **-beys.** *Abbr.* **abb.** **1.** A monastery or convent. **2.** An abbey church. [Middle English, from Old French *abaie,* from Late Latin *abbātia,* from *abbās,* ABBOT.]

Ab·bey (ăb′ē), **Edwin Austin.** 1852–1911. American illustrator and muralist.

ab·bot (ăb′ət) *n. Abbr.* **abb.** The superior of a monastery. [Middle English *abbod,* Old English *abbod, abbad,* from Late Latin *abbās* (stem *abbāt-*), from Late Greek *abbās,* from Aramaic *abbā,* father, ABBA.]

abbr., abbrev. abbreviation.

ab·bre·vi·ate (ə-brē′vē-āt′) *tr.v.* **-ated, -ating, -ates.** **1.** To make shorter by removing or leaving out parts. **2.** To reduce (a word or phrase) to a shorter form intended to represent the full form. [Middle English *abbreviaten,* from Late Latin *abbreviāre,* to shorten : *ab-,* off, or *ad-,* toward + *brevis,* short (see **mreghu-** in Appendix*).] **—ab·bre′vi·a′tor** (-ā′tər) *n.*

ab·bre·vi·a·tion (ə-brē′vē-ā′shən) *n. Abbr.* **abbr., abbrev.** **1.** The act or product of abbreviating. **2.** A shortened form of a word or phrase used chiefly in writing to represent the complete form; for example, *Mass.* for *Massachusetts* or *USMC* for *United States Marine Corps.* **3.** *Music.* Any of various symbols used in musical notation to indicate that a series of notes is to be repeated.

ABC (ā′bē′sē′) *n., pl.* **ABC's.** **1.** *Usually plural.* The alphabet. **2.** *Plural.* The rudiments of reading and writing.

ab·cou·lomb (ăb′kōō-lŏm′) *n.* A centimeter-gram-second electromagnetic unit of charge, equal to the charge passing in one second through any cross section of a conductor carrying a steady current of one abampere. It is equal to ten coulombs. [AB- (absolute) + COULOMB.]

ABD Airport code for Abadan, Iran.

Ab·di·as (ăb-dī′əs). In the Douay Bible, **Obadiah** *(see).*

ab·di·cate (ăb′dĭ-kāt′) *v.* **-cated, -cating, -cates.** *—tr.* To relinquish (power or responsibility) formally. *—intr.* To relinquish formally high office or responsibility. [Latin *abdicāre,* to disclaim : *ab-,* away from + *dicāre,* to proclaim (see **deik-** in Appendix*).] **—ab′di·ca·ble** (-kə-bəl) *adj.* **—ab′di·ca′tion** *n.* **—ab′di·ca′tor** (-kā′tər) *n.*

ab·do·men (ăb′də-mən, ăb-dō′mən) *n.* **1.** The part of the body in mammals that lies between the thorax and the pelvis, and that encloses the viscera; belly. **2.** In arthropods, the major posterior part of the body. [Latin *abdōmen*†, belly.] **—ab·dom′i·nal** (-dŏm′ə-nəl) *adj.* **—ab·dom′i·nal·ly** *adv.*

ab·dom·i·nous (ăb-dŏm′ə-nəs) *adj.* Potbellied.

ab·duct (ăb-dŭkt′) *tr.v.* **-ducted, -ducting, -ducts.** **1.** To carry off by force; kidnap. **2.** *Physiology.* To draw away from the median line of a bone or muscle or from an adjacent part or limb. [Latin *abdūcere* (past participle *abductus*) : *ab-,* away + *dūcere,* to lead (see **deuk-** in Appendix*).] **—ab·duc′tion** *n.* **—ab·duc′tor** (-dŭk′tər) *n.*

a·beam (ə-bēm′) *adv.* At right angles to the keel of a ship. [A- (in the direction of) + BEAM (keel).]

a·be·ce·dar·i·an (ā′bē-sē-dâr′ē-ən) *n.* Also **a·be·ce·da·ry** (-sē′də-rē). **1.** One who teaches or studies the alphabet. **2.** One who is just learning; beginner; novice. *—adj.* **1.** Pertaining to the alphabet. **2.** Arranged alphabetically. **3.** Elementary; rudimentary. [Middle English, from Medieval Latin *abecedārium,* alphabet, from Late Latin *abecedārius,* pertaining to the alphabet, from the first four letters.]

a·bed (ə-bĕd′) *adv.* In bed.

A·bed·ne·go (ə-bĕd′nĭ-gō′). One of the three young men, the others being Meshach and Shadrach, who came unharmed out of the fiery furnace in Babylon. Daniel 3:12–30.

A·bel[1] (ā′bəl). A masculine given name. [From the Biblical character ABEL.]

A·bel[2] (ā′bəl). The second son of Adam, slain by his elder brother, Cain. Genesis 4:2. [Middle English, from Late Latin, from Greek, from Hebrew *Hebhel,* akin to Assyrian *ablu,* son.]

Ab·e·lard (ăb′ə-lärd′), **Peter.** French name, Pierre Abélard. 1079–1142. French philosopher and theologian.

a·bele (ə-bēl′) *n.* A tree, the **white poplar** *(see).* [Dutch *abeel,* from Old French *abel, aubel,* from Medieval Latin *albellus,* diminutive of Latin *albus,* white. See **albho-** in Appendix.*]

A·be·li·an group (ə-bē′lē-ən, ə-bēl′yən). *Algebra.* A **commutative group** *(see).* [After Niels Henrik *Abel* (1802–29), Norwegian mathematician.]

a·bel·mosk (ā′bəl-mŏsk′) *n.* A hairy plant, *Hibiscus abelmoschus,* of tropical Asia, having large yellow flowers and musk-scented seeds that are used in perfumery. Also called "musk mallow." [New Latin *Abelmoschus,* from Arabic *ḥabb-al-musk* (vulgar pronunciation *ḥabb-el-mosk*), "grain of musk" : *ḥabb,* grain + *mosk,* musk, from Persian *mushk,* MUSK.]

Ab·er·deen (ăb′ər-dēn′ *for senses 1, 2;* ăb′ər-dēn′ *for sense 3*). **1.** Also **Ab·er·deen·shire** (ăb′ər-dēn′shîr′). A county occupying 1,971 square miles in northeastern Scotland. Population, 321,000. **2.** The county seat of that county, on the North Sea at the mouth of the Dee. Population, 184,000. **3.** A city in northeastern South Dakota. Population, 23,000. **4.** A town in northeastern Maryland, site of the Aberdeen Proving Ground, a U.S. Army reservation.

Aberdeen An·gus (ăng′gəs). Any of a breed of black, hornless beef cattle that originated in Scotland.

ab·er·rant (ăb-ĕr′ənt) *adj.* **1.** Deviating from the proper or

ă pat/ā pay/âr care/ä father/b bib/ch church/d deed/ĕ pet/ē be/f fife/g gag/h hat/hw which/ĭ pit/ī pie/îr pier/j judge/k kick/l lid, needle/m mum/n no, sudden/ng thing/ŏ pot/ō toe/ô paw, for/oi noise/ou out/ŏŏ took/ōō boot/p pop/r roar/s sauce/sh ship, dish/

expected course. 2. Deviating from what is normal; untrue to type. —**ab·er′rance, ab·er′ran·cy** *n.*

ab·er·ra·tion (ăb′ə-rā′shən) *n.* 1. A deviation from the proper or expected course. 2. A departure from the normal or typical. 3. An abnormal alteration in one's mental state; lapse in mental capacities. 4. *Optics.* a. A defect of focus, as blurring or distortion, in an image. b. A physical defect in an optical element, as in a mirror or lens, that causes such an imperfection. See **chromatic aberration, spherical aberration.** 5. The apparent displacement of the position of a celestial body in the direction of motion of an observer on earth, caused by the motion of the earth and the finiteness of the velocity of light. [Latin *aberrātiō,* diversion, from *aberrāre,* to go astray : *ab-,* from + *errāre,* to stray (see **ers-**[1] in Appendix*).]

Ab·er·yst·wyth (ăb′ə-rĭst′wĭth). The county seat of Cardiganshire, Wales, on Cardigan Bay. Population, 10,000.

a·bet (ə-bĕt′) *tr.v.* **abetted, abetting, abets.** To encourage; incite. See Synonyms at **incite.** [Middle English *abetten,* from Old French *abeter,* to entice : *a-,* from Latin *ad-,* to + *beter,* to bait, from Germanic (see **bheid-** in Appendix*).] —**a·bet′ment** *n.*

a·bet·tor (ə-bĕt′ər) *n.* Also **a·bet·ter.** One who abets the commission of a crime and is present or nearby during the act.

ab ex·tra (ăb ĕk′strə). *Latin.* From without.

a·bey·ance (ə-bā′əns) *n.* 1. The condition of being temporarily set aside; suspension. 2. *Law.* A condition of undetermined ownership, as of an estate that has not yet been assigned. [Norman French *abeiance,* variant of Old French *abeance,* desire, from *abaer,* "to gape at," yearn for : *a-,* from Latin *ad-,* to + *baer,* to gape (see **abash**).] —**a·bey′ant** *adj.*

ab·far·ad (ăb-făr′ăd′, -făr′əd) *n.* A centimeter-gram-second electromagnetic unit of capacitance, equal to the capacitance of a capacitor having a charge of one abcoulomb and a potential difference of one abvolt. It is equal to one billion (10^9) farads. [AB- (absolute) + FARAD.]

ab·hen·ry (ăb-hĕn′rē) *n., pl.* **-ries.** A centimeter-gram-second electromagnetic unit of inductance, equal to the inductance resulting from a current variation of one abampere per second that produces an induced electromotive force of one abvolt. It is equal to one billionth (10^{-9}) henry. [AB- (absolute) + HENRY.]

ab·hor (ăb-hôr′) *tr.v.* **-horred, -horring, -hors.** 1. To regard with horror or loathing; abominate. 2. To reject vehemently; eschew; shun. [Middle English *abhorren,* from Latin *abhorrēre,* to shrink from : *ab-,* from + *horrēre,* to shudder (see **ghers-** in Appendix*).] —**ab·hor′rence** (-hôr′əns) *n.* —**ab·hor′rer** *n.*

ab·hor·rent (ăb-hôr′ənt, -hŏr′ənt) *adj.* 1. Disgusting; loathsome; repellent. 2. Feeling repugnance or loathing. 3. In opposition. —**ab·hor′rent·ly** *adv.*

A·bib (ä-vēv′) *n.* In the ancient Hebrew calendar, an earlier name for the month of **Nisan** *(see).* [Hebrew *'ābhībh,* "(month of) fresh barley," "spring."]

a·bid·ance (ə-bīd′əns) *n.* 1. Continuance. 2. Adherence; compliance. Usually used with *by.*

a·bide (ə-bīd′) *v.* **abode** (ə-bōd′) or **abided, abiding, abides.** —*tr.* 1. To wait patiently for. 2. To be in store for; await. 3. To withstand; persevere under. 4. To accept the consequences of; rest satisfied with. 5. To put up with; tolerate. —*intr.* 1. To remain in one place or state. 2. To continue; endure: *"who can abide in the fierceness of his anger?"* (Cotton Mather). 3. To dwell or sojourn. —See Synonyms at **bear, stay.** —**abide by.** To conform to; comply with. [Middle English *abiden,* Old English *ābīdan* : *a-* (intensive) + *bīdan,* to remain, await (see **bheidh-** in Appendix*).] —**a·bid′er** *n.*

a·bid·ing (ə-bī′dĭng) *adj.* Enduring. —**a·bid′ing·ly** *adj.*

Ab·i·djan (ăb′ĭ-jän′). The capital of the Ivory Coast, a seaport on the Gulf of Guinea. Population, 258,000.

ab·i·et·ic acid (ăb′ē-ĕt′ĭk). A yellowish resinous powder, $C_{19}H_{29}COOH$, isolated from rosin and used in lacquers, varnishes, and soaps. [From Latin *abiēs*† (stem *abiēt-*), silver fir.]

ab·i·gail (ăb′ə-gāl′) *n.* A lady's maid. [From the name of a serving maid in *The Scornful Lady* (1616), play by Beaumont and Fletcher.]

Ab·i·gail[1] (ăb′ə-gāl′). A feminine given name. [Hebrew *Abhīgayil,* "my father is joy."]

Ab·i·gail[2] (ăb′ə-gāl′). The wife of David. I Samuel 25:14–44.

A·bi·la. The ancient name for **Jebel Musa.**

Ab·i·lene (ăb′ə-lēn′). 1. A city in Kansas, 95 miles west of Topeka; boyhood home of Dwight D. Eisenhower. Population, 6,000. 2. A city in central Texas. Population, 90,000.

a·bil·i·ty (ə-bĭl′ə-tē) *n., pl.* **-ties.** 1. The quality of being able to do something; physical, mental, financial, or legal power to perform. 2. A natural or acquired skill or talent. [Middle English *abilite,* from Old French *habilite,* from Latin *habilitās,* from *habilis,* ABLE.]

Synonyms: *ability, capacity, faculty, talent, skill, competence, aptitude.* These nouns name qualities that enable a person to accomplish something. *Ability* is the power, mental or physical, to do something, and usually implies doing it well. *Capacity* refers to the condition that permits one to acquire that power. *Faculty* denotes an ability, inherent or acquired, in one area of achievement: *a faculty for mathematics. Talent* emphasizes inborn ability in a particular field, especially the arts. *Skill* implies recognized ability acquired or developed through experience. *Competence* suggests ability to do something satisfactorily but not outstandingly. *Aptitude* usually implies inherent capacity for, and interest in, a particular activity.

Usage: *Ability* is often followed by an infinitive: *ability to think* (not *ability of thinking*).

Ab·ing·ton (ăb′ĭng-tən). A city of southeastern Pennsylvania, near Philadelphia. Population, 56,000.

ab in·i·ti·o (ăb′ ĭ-nĭsh′ē-ō). *Abbr.* **ab init.** *Latin.* From the beginning.

ab in·tra (ăb′ ĭn′trə). *Latin.* From within.

ab·i·o·gen·e·sis (ăb′ē-ō-jĕn′ə-sĭs) *n.* The hypothetical development of living organisms from nonliving matter. Also called "autogenesis," "spontaneous generation." [A- (without) + BIO- + -GENESIS.]

Ab·i·ti·bi, Lake (ăb′ĭ-tĭb′ĭ). A lake of Canada, occupying 356 square miles in eastern Ontario and western Quebec.

Ab·i·ti·bi River (ăb′ĭ-tĭb′ĭ). A river of Canada, flowing 230 miles generally north from Lake Abitibi to James Bay.

ab·ject (ăb′jĕkt′, ăb-jĕkt′) *adj.* 1. Of the most contemptible kind. 2. Of the most miserable kind; wretched. —See Synonyms at **mean** (base). [Middle English, "rejected," from Latin *abjectus,* cast away, from the past participle of *abjicere,* to cast away : *ab-,* away from + *jacere,* to throw (see **yē-** in Appendix*).] —**ab′ject′ly** *adv.* —**ab′jec′tion** *n.*

ab·ju·ra·tion (ăb′jŏŏ-rā′shən) *n.* An abjuring; the state of being abjured; a renunciation.

ab·jure (ăb-jŏŏr′) *tr.v.* **-jured, -juring, -jures.** 1. To repudiate, or recant solemnly. 2. To renounce under oath; forswear. [Middle English *abjuren,* from Old French *abjurer,* from Latin *abjūrāre* : *ab-,* away + *jūrāre,* to swear (see **yewo-**[1] in Appendix*).] —**ab·jur′er** *n.*

Ab·kha·zi·an Autonomous Soviet Socialist Republic (ăb-kä′zhən). An administrative division, 3,320 square miles in area, of the northwestern Georgian S.S.R. Population, 456,000. Capital, Sukhumi. Also called "Abkhazia," "Abkhasia."

abl. ablative.

ab·la·tion (ă-blā′shən) *n.* 1. Surgical excision or amputation of any part of the body. 2. The totality of erosive processes by which a glacier is reduced. [Late Latin *ablātiō,* from *ablātus,* removed (past participle of *auferre,* to carry away) : *ab-,* away from + *-lātus,* "carried" (see **tel-**[1] in Appendix*).]

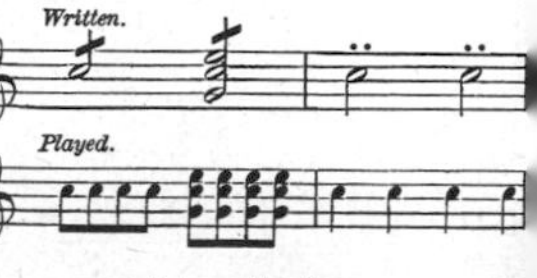

abbreviation
Abbreviation in musical notation

ab·la·tive (ăb′lə-tĭv) *adj.* Designating a grammatical case indicating separation, direction away from, and sometimes manner or agency, found in some Indo-European languages. —*n.* 1. The ablative case. 2. A word in the ablative case. [Middle English, from Old French *ablatif,* from Latin *ablātīvus,* "expressing removal," from *ablātus,* removed. See **ablation.**]

ablative absolute. In Latin grammar, an adverbial phrase syntactically independent from the rest of the sentence and containing two main elements both in the ablative case. It is usually used to express cause, circumstance, or time; for example, in the sentence *Regibus expulsis, leges respublica condit (The kings having been expelled, the republic sets up laws),* the phrase *Regibus expulsis* is the ablative absolute.

ab·laut (ăb′lout′; *German* äp′lout′) *n. Linguistics.* A patterned change in root vowels of verb forms, characteristic of Indo-European languages, indicating alteration of tense, aspect, or function; for example, *ring, rang, rung.* Also called "gradation." Compare **umlaut.** [German *Ablaut,* "off sound" : *ab,* off, away from, from Old High German *aba* (see **apo-** in Appendix*) + *Laut,* sound, from Middle High German *lūt,* from Old High German *hlūt* (see **kleu-**[1] in Appendix*).]

a·blaze (ə-blāz′) *adj.* 1. On fire. 2. Radiant with bright color.

a·ble (ā′bəl) *adj.* **abler, ablest.** 1. Having sufficient ability or resources. 2. Especially capable or talented. [Middle English, from Old French, from Latin *habilis,* manageable, apt, expert, from *habēre,* to hold, handle. See **ghabh-** in Appendix.*]

Usage: *Able* is regularly followed by an infinitive in the active voice *(able to hear),* but not in the passive. Thus, *he could be heard* (not *was able to be heard*).

-able, -ible. Indicates: 1. Susceptible, capable, or worthy of (the action of a verb or implied verb); for example, **debatable, eatable, adducible, collapsible.** 2. Inclined to (the nature of a noun or implied noun); for example, **knowledgeable, sizable, fashionable.** [Middle English, from Old French, from Latin *-ābilis, -ibilis,* forms (with different vowel stems) of the passive adjectival suffix *-bilis.*]

a·ble-bod·ied (ā′bəl-bŏd′ēd) *adj.* Physically strong and healthy.

able-bodied seaman. *Abbr.* **A.B., a.b.** A merchant seaman certified for all seaman's duties. Also called "able seaman." Compare **ordinary seaman.**

a·bloom (ə-blo͞om′) *adj.* In bloom; flowering.

ab·lu·tion (ă-blo͞o′shən) *n.* 1. A washing or cleansing of the body, especially with religious connotation. 2. The liquid used in such cleansing. [Middle English, from Latin *ablūtiō,* from *abluere,* to wash away : *ab-,* away from + *luere,* to wash (see **lou-** in Appendix*).] —**ab·lu′tion·ar′y** *adj.*

a·bly (ā′blē) *adv.* In an able manner; capably.

abn airborne.

Ab·na·ki (ăb-nä′kē) *n., pl.* **Abnaki** or **-kis.** 1. An Algonquian-speaking tribe of North American Indians of Maine, New Brunswick, and southern Quebec. 2. A member of this tribe. 3. The language of this tribe.

ab·ne·gate (ăb′nĭ-gāt′) *tr.v.* **-gated, -gating, -gates.** To deny to oneself; give up; renounce. [Latin *abnegāre,* to refuse, reject : *ab-,* away from + *negāre,* to deny (see **ne** in Appendix*).] —**ab′ne·ga′tor** (-gā′tər) *n.*

ab·ne·ga·tion (ăb′nĭ-gā′shən) *n.* Self-denial.

Ab·ner (ăb′nər). A masculine given name. [Hebrew *Abhnēr,* "my father is light" : *abh,* father + *nēr,* light.]

ab·nor·mal (ăb-nôr′məl) *adj.* Not normal; deviant. [Latin *abnormis,* departing from normal : *ab-,* away from + *norma,* rule, norm (see **gnō-** in Appendix*).] —**ab·nor′mal·ly** *adv.*

ab·nor·mal·i·ty (ăb′nôr-măl′ə-tē) *n., pl.* **-ties.** 1. The state or condition of not being normal. 2. An abnormal phenomenon.

Å·bo. The Swedish name for **Turku.**

ABO A classification of human blood types with regard to their compatability in transfusion. Bloods are typed as A, B, AB, or O.

a·board (ə-bôrd′, ə-bōrd′) *adv.* On board a ship or other passenger vehicle. **—all aboard.** Everybody get on (the train or boat). *—prep.* On board of; on; in. [Middle English : A- (on) + BOARD.]

a·bode (ə-bōd′). Past tense and past participle of **abide.** *—n.* **1.** A dwelling place or home. **2.** The act of abiding; a sojourn. [Middle English *abod,* from *abiden,* ABIDE.]

ab·ohm (ăb-ōm′) *n.* A centimeter-gram-second electromagnetic unit of resistance equal to one billionth (10^{-9}) of an ohm. [AB- (absolute) + OHM.]

a·bol·ish (ə-bŏl′ĭsh) *tr.v.* **-ished, -ishing, -ishes.** To do away with; put an end to. See Synonyms at **nullify.** [Middle English *abolysshen,* from Old French *abolire* (present stem *aboliss-*), from Latin *abolēre,* to destroy. See **al-**[3] in Appendix.*] **—a·bol′ish·a·ble** *adj.* **—a·bol′ish·er** *n.* **—a·bol′ish·ment** *n.*

Synonyms: *abolish, exterminate, extinguish, extirpate, eradicate, obliterate.* These verbs mean to get rid of. *Abolish* applies only to doing away with conditions or regulations, not material things or persons. *Exterminate* suggests destruction of living things by a deliberate, selective method. *Extinguish,* meaning to put out a flame or something likened to a flame, stresses the frailty of the object. *Extirpate* suggests effective destruction by getting at the roots or causes, while *eradicate* stresses the resistance to dislodgment posed by the object. *Obliterate* means to destroy so as to leave no trace, and applies principally to things.

ab·o·li·tion (ăb′ə-lĭsh′ən) *n.* **1.** An act of abolishing or state of being abolished; annulment; extinction. **2.** *Sometimes capital* **A.** The termination of slavery and the slave trade in the United States. [Latin *abolitiō,* from *abolitus,* past participle of *abolēre,* ABOLISH.] **—ab′o·li′tion·ar′y** *adj.*

ab·o·li·tion·ism (ăb′ə-lĭsh′ən-ĭz′əm) *n.* Advocacy of the abolition of slavery in the United States. **—ab′o·li′tion·ist** *n.*

ab·o·ma·sum (ăb′ō-mā′səm) *n., pl.* **-sa** (-sə). The fourth division of the stomach in ruminant animals, in which true digestion takes place. [New Latin : AB- (away from) + OMASUM.] **—ab′o·ma′sal** *adj.*

A-bomb (ā′bŏm′) *n.* An **atomic bomb** *(see).*

a·bom·i·na·ble (ə-bŏm′ə-nə-bəl) *adj.* **1.** Detestable; loathsome. **2.** Thoroughly unpleasant. [Middle English, from Old French, from Latin *abōminābilis,* from *abōminārī,* ABOMINATE.] **—a·bom′i·na·bly** *adv.*

abominable snowman. A hirsute manlike animal reportedly inhabiting the snows of the high Himalayas. Also called "yeti."

a·bom·i·nate (ə-bŏm′ə-nāt′) *tr.v.* **-nated, -nating, -nates.** To detest; abhor. [Latin *abōminārī,* "to shun as a bad omen" : *ab-,* away from + *ōmen* (stem *ōmin-*), omen (see **ō-** in Appendix*).] **—a·bom′i·na′tor** (-nā′tər) *n.*

a·bom·i·na·tion (ə-bŏm′ə-nā′shən) *n.* **1.** An abhorrence for someone or something; loathing. **2.** Something that elicits great dislike or abhorrence.

ab·o·ral (ăb-ôr′əl, -ōr′əl) *adj. Biology.* Opposite to or away from the mouth. [AB- (away from) + ORAL.] **—ab·o′ral·ly** *adv.*

ab·o·rig·i·nal (ăb′ə-rĭj′ə-nəl) *adj.* **1.** Autochthonous; native; indigenous. **2.** Of or pertaining to aborigines. —See Synonyms at **native.** *—n.* An aborigine. **—ab′o·rig′i·nal·ly** *adv.*

ab·o·rig·i·ne (ăb′ə-rĭj′ə-nē′) *n.* **1.** An autochthonous inhabitant of a region. **2.** *Plural.* The flora and fauna native to a geographical area. [From Latin *Aborīginēs,* pre-Roman tribes inhabiting Latium, probably an alteration of some tribal name, reshaped by folk etymology as if derived from *ab orīgine,* "from the beginning."]

a·born·ing (ə-bôr′nĭng, -bōr′nĭng) *adv.* While coming into being or getting under way: *"our own revolutionary war almost died aborning through lack of popular support"* (W.R. Hearst, Jr.). [A- (in the act of) + BORN + -ING.]

a·bort (ə-bôrt′) *v.* **aborted, aborting, aborts.** *—intr.* **1.** To terminate pregnancy prematurely. **2.** To cease organic growth before full development or maturation. **3.** To terminate an operation or procedure with a missile or a space vehicle before completion, especially because of equipment failure. *—tr.* **1.** To cause to terminate pregnancy prematurely. **2.** To interfere with the development of; conclude prematurely. [Latin *abortāre,* frequentative of *aborīrī* (past participle *abortus*), to die, disappear, miscarry : *ab,* off, away, hence, badly + *orīrī,* to arise, appear, be born (see **er-**[1] in Appendix*).]

a·bor·ti·fa·cient (ə-bôr′tə-fā′shənt) *adj.* Causing abortion. *—n.* Anything used to induce abortion. [ABORT(ION) + -FACIENT.]

a·bor·tion (ə-bôr′shən) *n.* **1.** Induced termination of pregnancy before the fetus is capable of survival as an individual. **2.** Any fatally premature expulsion of an embryo or fetus from the womb. **3.** Cessation of normal growth, especially of an organ, prior to full development or maturation. **4.** An aborted organism. **5.** Anything malformed or incompletely developed.

a·bor·tion·ist (ə-bôr′shən-ĭst) *n.* One who performs illegal abortions.

a·bor·tive (ə-bôr′tĭv) *adj.* **1.** Failing to accomplish an intended objective; fruitless. **2.** Partially or imperfectly developed. **—a·bor′tive·ly** *adv.* **—a·bor′tive·ness n.**

a·bou·li·a. Variant of **abulia.**

a·bound (ə-bound′) *intr.v.* **abounded, abounding, abounds. 1.** To be great in number or amount. **2.** To have a large number or amount. **3.** To be fully supplied or filled; teem. [Middle English *abounden,* from Old French *abonder,* from Latin *abundāre,* to overflow : *ab-,* away from + *undāre,* to flow, from *unda,* wave (see **wed-**[1] in Appendix*).]

a·bout (ə-bout′) *adv. Abbr.* **a., ab., abt. 1.** Approximately; nearly. **2.** Almost. **3.** To a reversed position or direction. **4.** In no particular direction; with no particular destination. **5.** All around; on every side. **6.** In the area or vicinity. **7.** In succession; one after another: *Turn about is fair play.* *—prep.* **1.** On all sides of; surrounding. **2.** In the vicinity of; around: *somewhere about.* **3.** In and around; here and there in; through. **4.** Almost the same as; close to; near. **5.** In reference to; relating to. **6.** In the possession of: *He has his wits about him.* **7.** Ready or prepared to do something. Used with an infinitive: *The chorus is about to sing.* **8.** Involved with or engaged in: *He is about his job.* *—adj.* Moving here and there; astir. Used predicatively: *to be up and about.* [Middle English *about,* Old English *abūtan, onbūtan* : ON + *būtan,* outside of (see **ud-** in Appendix*).]

Synonyms: *about, around, round.* These terms are sometimes interchangeable, as adverbs and prepositions. However, *around* either specifies or suggests complete encirclement of something, whereas *about* and *round* are less exact and indicate, more or less, semiencirclement: *The children gathered about* (or *round*) *the fireplace; then they danced around the table. Around* also is more specific than *about* in indicating a course: *goes around* (or *round*) *the sun; travel around the country* (implying a full, or nearly full, circuit); *travel about the country* (suggesting no regular course).

a·bout-face (ə-bout′fās′) *n.* **1.** A reversal of orientation, accomplished by a pivotal movement from a halt. **2.** A total change of attitude or standpoint. *—intr.v.* (ə-bout′fās′) **about-faced, -facing, -faces.** To reverse direction.

a·bout-ship (ə-bout′shĭp′) *intr.v.* **-shipped, -shipping, -ships.** To put a ship on the opposite course by changing its tack.

a·bove (ə-bŭv′) *adv.* **1.** Overhead; on high: *the clouds above.* **2.** In heaven; heavenward. **3.** Upstairs: *a table in the dining room above.* **4.** In a higher place. **5.** In an earlier part of a given text: *figures quoted above.* **6.** In or to a higher rank or position: *the ranks of major and above.* *—prep.* **1.** Over: *a spring above timberline.* **2.** Superior to in rank, position, or number; greater than: *principles above expediency.* **3.** Beyond the level or reach of: *a shot heard above the music.* **4.** In preference to. **5.** Too honorable to bend to: *above petty intrigue.* **6.** More than: *somewhat above normal temperature.* **—above all.** First of all. **—above and beyond.** In addition to. **—above measure.** In excess of what is proper; immoderately. *—n.* Something that is above: *as the above should make clear; an above and a below.* See Usage note below. *—adj.* Appearing earlier in the same text: *flaws in the above interpretation.* See Usage note. [Middle English *aboven, abuven,* Old English *abufan* : A- (on) + *bufan,* above (see **upo** in Appendix*).]

Usage: *Above* (adjective), in the sense of "appearing or stated earlier" or "above-mentioned," is acceptable in all writing to 72 per cent of the Usage Panel, though it is especially appropriate for business and legal matters. But only 44 per cent accept *above* as a noun in the same sense: *Read the above.*

a·bove·board (ə-bŭv′bôrd′, -bōrd′) *adv.* Without deceit or trickery. *—adj.* Honest; not concealed. [Originally a gambling term, "above the gambling table, not changing cards under the table."]

abp., Abp. archbishop.

ABQ Airport code for Albuquerque, New Mexico.

abr. abridged; abridgment.

ab·ra·ca·dab·ra (ăb′rə-kə-dăb′rə) *n.* **1.** A cabalistic word held to possess supernatural powers to ward off disease or disaster. **2.** Jargon; mumbo jumbo; gibberish. [Late Latin from Late Greek *abrasadabra,* a magic word used by a Gnostic sect, probably derived from *Abrasax,* name of a Gnostic deity.]

ABRACADABRA
ABRACADABR
ABRACADAB
ABRACADA
ABRACAD
ABRACA
ABRAC
ABRA
ABR
AB
A

abracadabra
The letters of the word *abracadabra* arranged in an inverted pyramid to be worn as an amulet

a·brade (ə-brād′) *tr.v.* **abraded, abrading, abrades.** To rub off or wear away by friction; erode. [Latin *abrādere,* to scrape off : *ab-,* off + *rādere,* to scrape (see **rēd-** in Appendix*).]

A·bra·ham[1] (ā′brə-hăm′). A masculine given name. [Middle English, from Late Latin, from Late Greek, from Hebrew *Abhrāhām,* "father of a multitude," altered from *Abram,* "high father."]

A·bra·ham[2] (ā′brə-hăm′). The first patriarch and progenitor of the Hebrew people; father of Isaac. Genesis 11–25.

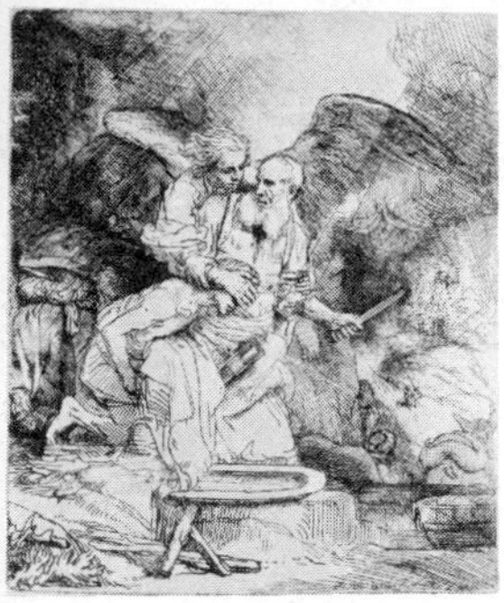

Abraham[2]
"Abraham's Sacrifice," an etching by Rembrandt

a·bran·chi·ate (ā-brăng′kē-ĭt, -āt′) *adj.* Also **a·bran·chi·al** (-əl), **a·bran·chi·ous** (-əs). *Zoology.* Having no gills. [A- (without) + Greek *brankhia,* gills. See **branchia.**]

ab·ra·sion (ə-brā′zhən) *n.* **1.** The process of wearing down or rubbing away by means of friction. **2.** A scraped or worn area. [Medieval Latin *abrāsiō,* from Latin *abrādere,* ABRADE.]

ab·ra·sive (ə-brā′sĭv, -zĭv) *adj.* Causing abrasion; harsh; rough. *—n.* A substance that abrades.

ab·re·act (ăb′rē-ăkt′) *tr.v.* **-acted, -acting, -acts.** *Psychoanalysis.* To release repressed emotions by abreaction. [Translation of German *abreagieren* : AB- (away from) + *reagieren,* to react.]

ab·re·ac·tion (ăb′rē-ăk′shən) *n. Psychoanalysis.* The release of the tension resulting from conflict or from repressed emotion through conscious examination and acting out, in imagination, words, or action, the situation causing the conflict.

a·breast (ə-brĕst′) *adv.* Side by side. **—abreast of** (or **with**). Keeping up with; aware of. [Middle English *abrest* : A- (on) + BREAST.]

a·bridge (ə-brĭj′) *tr.v.* **abridged, abridging, abridges. 1.** To reduce the length of (a written text); condense. **2.** To curtail; cut short. [Middle English *abregen,* from Old French *abregier,* from Late Latin *abbreviāre,* ABBREVIATE.] **—a·bridg′er** *n.*

a·bridg·ment (ə-brĭj′mənt) *n.* Also *chiefly British* **a·bridge·ment.** *Abbr.* **abr. 1. a.** The action of abridging. **b.** The state of being abridged. **2.** Condensation of a book.

a·broach (ə-brōch′) *adj.* **1.** Tapped; broached. **2.** Moving

ă pat/ā pay/âr care/ä father/b bib/ch church/d deed/ĕ pet/ē be/f fife/g gag/h hat/hw which/ĭ pit/ī pie/îr pier/j judge/k kick/l lid, needle/m mum/n no, sudden/ng thing/ŏ pot/ō toe/ô paw, for/oi noise/ou out/ŏŏ took/ōō boot/p pop/r roar/s sauce/sh ship, dish/

about; astir. [Middle English *abroche,* from Norman French : Old French *a-,* from Latin *ad-,* to + *broche,* BROACH (spigot).]

a·broad (ə-brôd′) *adv.* **1.** Out of one's own country. **2.** In a foreign country or countries. **3.** Away from one's place of residence; out of doors. **4.** On the move; at large; circulating. **5.** Broadly; widely. **6.** Not on target; astray; in error. —*n.* A foreign country; foreign countries collectively. Preceded by *from: a student from abroad.* [Middle English *abro(o)d,* "broadly, widely scattered" : A- (on, in) + *brood,* BROAD.]

ab·ro·gate (ăb′rō-gāt′) *tr.v.* **-gated, -gating, -gates.** To abolish or annul by authority. See Synonyms at **nullify.** [Latin *abrogāre* : *ab-,* away + *rogāre,* to ask, propose (see **reg-**¹ in Appendix*).] —**ab′ro·ga′tion** *n.*

a·brupt (ə-brŭpt′) *adj.* **1.** Unexpectedly sudden. **2.** Curt; brusque. **3.** Touching on one subject after another with sudden transitions: *abrupt, nervous prose.* **4.** Steeply inclined. **5.** *Biology.* Appearing to be cut or broken off short; truncate. [Latin *abruptus,* past participle of *abrumpere,* to break off : *ab-,* off + *rumpere,* to break (see **reup-** in Appendix*).] —**a·brupt′ly** *adv.* —**a·brupt′ness** *n.*

A·bruz·zi e Mo·li·se (ä-bro͞ot′tsē ā mô′lē-zā). A mountainous region of south-central Italy, occupying 5,880 square miles between the Apennines and the Adriatic. Population, 1,585,000.

abs absolute temperature.

abs. **1.** absence; absent. **2.** absolute; absolutely. **3.** abstract.

Ab·sa·lom (ăb′sə-ləm). In the Old Testament, David's favorite son, killed for rebelling against his father. II Samuel 13–19.

Ab·sa·ro·ka Range (ăb-sär′ə-kə). A section of the Rocky Mountains, extending about 175 miles from southern Montana into northwestern Wyoming. Highest elevation, Franks Peak (13,140 feet).

ab·scess (ăb′sĕs′) *n.* A localized collection of pus in any part of the body, formed by tissue disintegration and surrounded by an inflamed area. —*intr.v.* **abscessed, -scessing, -scesses.** To form an abscess. [Latin *abscēssus,* "a going away," hence, collection of pus, from *abscēdere,* to go away : *abs-, ab-,* away from + *cēdere,* to go (see **ked-**¹ in Appendix*).]

ab·scise (ăb-sīz′) *v.* **-scised, -scising, -scises.** —*tr.* To remove; cut off. —*intr.* To shed by abscission. [Latin *abscindere* (past participle *abscissus*) : *abs-, ab-,* away + *caedere,* to cut (see **skhai-** in Appendix*).]

ab·scis·sa (ăb-sĭs′ə) *n., pl.* **-sas** or **-scissae** (-sĭs′ē′). *Mathematics.* The coordinate representing the distance of a point from the *y*-axis in a plane Cartesian coordinate system, measured along a line parallel to the *x*-axis. [New Latin *(linea) abscissa,* "cut-off (line)," from Latin *abscissus,* past participle of *abscindere,* to cut off, ABSCISE.]

ab·scis·sion (ăb-sĭzh′ən) *n.* **1.** The act of cutting off. **2.** The process by which plant parts, such as leaves and petals, are shed.

ab·scond (ăb-skŏnd′) *intr.v.* **-sconded, -sconding, -sconds.** To leave quickly and secretly and hide oneself; especially, to avoid arrest or prosecution. [Latin *abscondere* : *abs-, ab-,* away + *condere,* to hide (see **dhē-**¹ in Appendix*).] —**ab·scond′er** *n.*

ab·sence (ăb′səns) *n. Abbr.* **abs. 1.** The state of being away. **2.** The time during which one is away. **3.** Lack: *an absence of curiosity.*

ab·sent (ăb′sənt) *adj. Abbr.* **abs. 1.** Missing or not present. **2.** Not existent; lacking. **3.** Inattentive. —*tr.v.* (ăb-sĕnt′) **absented, -senting, -sents.** To keep (oneself) away. [Middle English, from Old French, from Latin *absēns,* present participle of *abesse,* to be away : *abs-, ab-,* away from + *esse,* to be (see **es-** in Appendix*).] —**ab′sent·ly** *adv.*

ab·sen·tee (ăb′sən-tē′) *n.* One who is absent. —*adj.* **1.** Of or pertaining to one that is absent. **2.** Not in residence.

absentee ballot. A ballot marked and mailed in advance by a voter away from the place where he is registered.

ab·sen·tee·ism (ăb′sən-tē′ĭz′əm) *n.* Habitual failure to appear, especially for work or other regular duty.

ab·sent-mind·ed (ăb′sənt-mīn′dĭd) *adj.* Heedless of one's immediate surroundings or activity because of preoccupation with unrelated matters. —See Synonyms at **abstracted, forgetful.** —**ab′sent-mind′ed·ly** *adv.* —**ab′sent-mind′ed·ness** *n.*

absent without leave. *Abbr.* **awol, AWOL, a.w.o.l., A.W.O.L.** Absent from one's assigned military post or duties without official permission but without the intention to desert.

ab·sinthe (ăb′sĭnth) *n.* Also **ab·sinth. 1.** A green liqueur having a bitter licorice flavor and a high alcoholic content. It is prepared from wormwood and other herbs. **2.** A plant, **wormwood** *(see).* [French, from Latin *absinthium,* wormwood, from Greek *apsinthion,* of Mediterranean origin.]

ab·so·lute (ăb′sə-lo͞ot) *adj. Abbr.* **abs. 1.** Perfect in quality or nature; complete. **2.** Not mixed; pure; unadulterated. **3. a.** Not limited by restrictions or exceptions; unconditional. **b.** Unqualified in extent or degree; total. **4.** Not limited by constitutional provisions or other restraints. **5.** Unrelated to and independent of anything else. **6.** Not to be doubted or questioned; positive; certain. **7.** *Grammar.* **a.** Denoting a construction in a sentence that is syntactically independent of the main clause. For example, in *Their ship having sailed, we went home, Their ship having sailed* is an absolute phrase. **b.** Pertaining to a transitive verb when its object is implied but not stated. For example, *inspires* in *We have a teacher who inspires.* **c.** Pertaining to an adjective or pronoun that stands alone, the noun it modifies being implied but not stated. For example, *Theirs* and *best* in *Theirs were the best.* **8.** *Physics.* **a.** Pertaining to measurements or units of measurement derived from fundamental relationships of space, mass, and time. **b.** Pertaining to absolute temperature. **9.** *Law.* Complete and unconditional; having no encumbrances; final. —*n.* Something that is absolute. —**the Absolute.** *Philosophy.* **1.** Something regarded as the ultimate basis of all thought and being. **2.** Something regarded as independent of and unrelated to anything else. [Middle English *absolut,* from Latin *absolūtus,* completed, unfettered, unconditional, from the past participle of *absolvere,* to free from, complete : *ab-,* away from + *solvere,* to loose (see **leu-**¹ in Appendix*).] —**ab′so·lute′ness** *n.*

absolute alcohol. Ethyl alcohol containing no more than one per cent of water.

absolute ceiling. The maximum altitude above sea level at which an aircraft or missile can maintain horizontal flight under standard atmospheric conditions.

ab·so·lute·ly (ăb′sə-lo͞ot′lē, ăb′sə-lo͞ot′lē) *adv. Abbr.* **abs. 1.** Definitely and completely; positively; unquestionably. **2.** *Grammar.* In a manner that does not take an object: *He used that transitive verb absolutely.*

Usage: *Absolutely* and *positively* are unconditional terms, not to be used as mere intensives equivalent to *very, indeed,* or *yes.*

absolute magnitude. *Astronomy.* The intrinsic magnitude of a star computed as if viewed from a distance of 10 parsecs or 32.6 light-years.

absolute music. Instrumental music having an intellectual and affective content that depends solely on its rhythmic, melodic, and contrapuntal structures. Compare **program music.**

absolute pitch. 1. The precise pitch of an isolated tone, as established by its rate of vibration measured on a standard scale. **2.** The ability to identify the pitch of any tone heard, or to reproduce a tone without reference to another previously sounded. Also called "perfect pitch." Compare **relative pitch.**

absolute scale. A scale of temperature with absolute zero as the minimum and scale units equal in magnitude to centigrade degrees.

absolute temperature. *Abbr.* **abs** Temperature measured or calculated on the absolute scale.

absolute value. *Mathematics.* **1.** The numerical value or magnitude of a quantity, as of a vector or of a negative integer, without regard to its sign. **2.** The modulus of a complex number, equal to the square root of the sum of the squares of the real and imaginary parts of the number.

absolute zero. *Physics.* The temperature at which substances possess minimal energy, equal to −273.15°C or −459.67°F.

ab·so·lu·tion (ăb′sə-lo͞o′shən) *n. Roman Catholic Church.* The formal remission of sin imparted by a priest as part of the sacrament of penance.

ab·so·lut·ism (ăb′sə-lo͞o′tĭz′əm) *n.* **1.** A form of state in which all power is vested in the monarch and his advisers. **2.** The political theory reflecting this form. —**ab′so·lut′ist** *n.* & *adj.* —**ab′so·lu·tis′tic** *adj.*

ab·solve (ăb-zŏlv′, -sŏlv′) *tr.v.* **-solved, -solving, -solves. 1.** To pronounce clear of blame or guilt. **2.** To relieve of a requirement or obligation. **3. a.** To grant a remission of sin to. **b.** To pardon or remit (a sin). [Middle English *absolven,* from Latin *absolvere,* to free from : *ab-,* away from + *solvere,* to loose, free (see **leu-**¹ in Appendix*).] —**ab·solv′a·ble** *adj.* —**ab·solv′er** *n.*

ab·sorb (ăb-sôrb′, -zôrb′) *tr.v.* **-sorbed, -sorbing, -sorbs. 1.** To take in through or as through pores or interstices; soak in or up. **2.** To occupy the full attention, interest, or time of; engross. **3.** *Chemistry & Physics.* To retain wholly, without reflection or transmission, that which is taken in. Compare **adsorb. 4.** To take in; assimilate; incorporate. **5.** To receive the impact of without recoil or echo. **6.** To defray (costs). **7.** To take in and use up: *The market could not absorb the sugar production.* [Old French *absorber,* from Latin *absorbēre* : *ab-,* away from + *sorbēre,* to suck (see **srebh-** in Appendix*).] —**ab·sorb′a·bil′i·ty** *n.* —**ab·sorb′a·ble** *adj.* —**ab·sorb′er** *n.* —**ab·sorb′ing·ly** *adv.*

ab·sorbed (ăb-sôrbd′, -zôrbd′) *adj.* **1.** Engrossed. **2.** Sucked up or in. **3.** Assimilated. —See Synonyms at **abstracted.** —**ab·sorb′ed·ly** (ăb-sôr′bĭd-lē, ăb-zôr′-) *adv.* —**ab·sorb′ed·ness** *n.*

ab·sor·be·fa·cient (ăb-sôr′bə-fā′shənt, ăb-zôr′-) *adj.* Inducing or causing absorption. —*n.* A medicine that induces absorption. [ABSORB + -FACIENT.]

ab·sorb·ent (ăb-sôr′bənt, ăb-zôr′-) *adj.* Capable of absorbing something: *absorbent cotton.* —*n.* A substance having this capability. —**ab·sorb′en·cy** *n.*

ab·sorp·tance (ăb-sôrp′təns, ăb-zôrp′-) *n.* The ratio of absorbed to incident radiation. Compare **reflectance, transmittance.** [ABSORPT(ION) + -ANCE.]

ab·sorp·tion (ăb-sôrp′shən, ăb-zôrp′-) *n.* **1.** The act or process of absorbing, or the state of being absorbed. **2.** A state of mental concentration. [Latin *absorptiō,* from *absorbēre,* ABSORB.] —**ab·sorp′tive** *adj.*

absorption nebula. *Astronomy.* A dark **nebula** *(see).*

absorption spectrum. *Physics.* The spectrum of dark lines and bands observed when radiation traverses an absorbing medium. Compare **emission spectrum.**

ab·squat·u·late (ăb-skwŏch′o͞o-lāt′) *intr.v.* **-lated, -lating, -lates.** *Slang.* To move off hastily; depart quickly and secretively to avoid apprehension. [Mock-Latinate formation, purporting to mean "to go off and squat elsewhere."] —**ab·squat′u·la′ter** (-lā′tər) *n.* —**ab·squat′u·la′tion** *n.*

ab·stain (ăb-stān′) *intr.v.* **-stained, -staining, -stains.** To refrain from something by one's own choice. [Middle English *absteinen, abstenen,* from Old French *abstenir,* from Latin *abstinēre,* to hold (oneself) back : *abs-, ab-,* away from + *tenēre,* to hold (see **ten-** in Appendix*).] —**ab·stain′er** *n.*

ab·ste·mi·ous (ăb-stē′mē-əs) *adj.* **1.** Eating and drinking in moderation. **2.** Restricted to bare necessities; marked by moderation; sparing. [Latin *abstēmius* : *abs-, ab-,* away from +

-*tēmus*, from *tēmētum*†, liquor, mead, wine.] **—ab·ste′mi·ous·ly** *adv.* **—ab·ste′mi·ous·ness** *n.*

ab·sten·tion (ăb-stĕn′shən) *n.* The act or habit of abstaining. [Late Latin *abstentiō*, from Latin *abstinēre*, ABSTAIN.]

ab·sti·nence (ăb′stə-nəns) *n.* **1. a.** Denial of the appetites; abstention. **b.** Abstention from alcoholic beverages. **2.** *Roman Catholic Church.* Abstention from specified foods on days of penitential observance. [Middle English, from Old French, from Latin *abstinentia*, from *abstinēns*, present participle of *abstinēre*, ABSTAIN.] **—ab′sti·nent** *adj.* **—ab′sti·nent·ly** *adv.*

Synonyms: *abstinence, self-denial, temperance, sobriety, continence.* These nouns express restraint of one's appetites or desires. *Abstinence* implies the willful avoidance of pleasures, especially of food and drink, thought to be harmful. *Self-denial* suggests resisting one's desires for some higher, moral goal. *Temperance* and *sobriety* both stress avoidance of alcohol, but *temperance* is more often associated with the mere curtailment of drinking, while *sobriety* additionally suggests conservative action or manner. *Continence* specifically refers to restraint of sexual activity.

ab·stract (ăb-străkt′, ăb′străkt′) *adj. Abbr.* **abs., abstr. 1.** Considered apart from concrete existence or a specification thereof. **2.** Theoretical; not applied or practical. **3.** Not easily understood; abstruse. **4.** Thought of or stated without reference to a specific instance. **5.** Designating a genre of painting whose intellectual and affective content depends solely on intrinsic form. —*n.* (ăb′străkt′). *Abbr.* **abs., abstr. 1.** A statement summarizing the important points of a given text. **2.** The concentrated essence of a larger whole. **3.** Something abstract, as a term. **—in the abstract.** Apart from actual substance or experience. —*tr.v.* (ăb-străkt′ *for senses 1, 2, 3;* ăb′străkt′ *for sense 4*) **abstracted, -stracting, -stracts. 1.** To take away; remove. **2.** To remove without permission; filch. **3.** To consider theoretically; think of (a quality or attribute) without reference to a particular example or object. **4.** To summarize. [Middle English, from Latin *abstractus*, "removed from (concrete reality)," past participle of *abstrahere*, to pull away, remove : *abs-, ab-*, away from + *trahere*, to pull (see **tragh-** in Appendix*).] **—ab·stract′er** *n.* **—ab·stract′ly** *adv.* **—ab·stract′ness** *n.*

ab·stract·ed (ăb-străk′tĭd) *adj.* **1.** Removed or separated from something; apart. **2.** Lost or deep in thought; preoccupied; meditative. —See Synonyms at **forgetful. —ab·stract′ed·ly** *adv.* **—ab·stract′ed·ness** *n.*

Synonyms: *abstracted, absorbed, distraught, absent-minded.* These adjectives apply to absence of normal awareness of one's surroundings. *Abstracted* implies being so deep in thought as to be mentally elsewhere. *Absorbed* implies complete and pleasureable mental involvement in the object of thought. *Distraught* implies mental anxiety that makes concentration extremely difficult. *Absent-minded* suggests the making of trivial errors because the mind is straying from the matter at hand.

abstract expressionism. A school of painting that flourished after World War II until the early 1960's, characterized by its emancipation from traditional brushwork in freely developing shape and design and by its exclusion of representational content.

ab·strac·tion (ăb-străk′shən) *n.* **1.** The act or process of removing or separating. **2. a.** The act or process of separating the inherent qualities or properties of something from the actual physical object or concept to which they belong. **b.** A product of this process; a general idea or word representing a physical concept. **3.** Preoccupation. **4.** An abstract work of art.

ab·strac·tion·ism (ăb-străk′shən-ĭz′əm) *n.* The theory and practice of abstract art. **—ab·strac′tion·ist** *n. & adj.*

ab·strac·tive (ăb-străk′tĭv) *adj.* Of or derived by abstraction. **—ab·strac′tive·ly** *adv.*

ab·struse (ăb-stro͞os′) *adj.* Difficult to understand; recondite. See Synonyms at **ambiguous, mysterious.** [Latin *abstrūsus*, past participle of *abstrūdere*, to hide : *abs-, ab-*, away + *trūdere*, to push (see **treud-** in Appendix*).] **—ab·struse′ly** *adv.* **—ab·struse′ness** *n.*

ab·surd (ăb-sûrd′, -zûrd′) *adj.* Ridiculously incongruous or unreasonable. See Synonyms at **foolish.** [French *absurde*, from Latin *absurdus*. See **swer-**[2] in Appendix.*] **—ab·surd′i·ty, ab·surd′ness** *n.* **—ab·surd′ly** *adv.*

abt. about.

a·bu·li·a (ə-bo͞o′lē-ə) *n.* Also **a·bou·li·a.** *Psychiatry.* Loss or impairment of the ability to decide or act independently. [New Latin, from Greek *aboulia*, irresolution : *a-*, without + *boulē*, will (see **gwel-**[1] in Appendix*).] **—a·bu′lic** *adj.*

A·bu·na (ä-bo͞o′nä). A river rising in northeastern Bolivia and flowing 200 miles northeast to the Madeira in Brazil, forming part of the Bolivian-Brazilian border on its course.

a·bun·dance (ə-bŭn′dəns) *n.* Also **a·bun·dan·cy** (-dən-sē). **1.** A great quantity; plentiful amount. **2.** Fullness to overflowing: *"My thoughts . . . are from the abundance of my heart."* (De Quincey). **3.** Affluence; wealth.

a·bun·dant (ə-bŭn′dənt) *adj.* **1.** In plentiful supply; more than sufficient; ample. **2.** Abounding with; rich. Used with *in.* [Middle English *abundaunt*, from Old French *abundant*, from Latin *abundāns*, present participle of *abundāre*, ABOUND.] **—a·bun′dant·ly** *adv.*

a·buse (ə-byo͞oz′) *tr.v.* **abused, abusing, abuses. 1.** To use wrongly or improperly; misuse. **2.** To hurt or injure by maltreatment. **3.** To assail with contemptuous, coarse, or insulting words; revile. —*n.* (ə-byo͞os′). **1.** Misuse. **2.** A corrupt practice or custom. **3.** Maltreatment. **4.** Insulting or coarse language. [Middle English *abusen*, from Old French *abuser*, from *abus*, improper use, from Latin *abūsus*, a using up, past participle of *abūtī*, to use up, make (improper) use of : *ab-*, away + *ūtī*, to USE.] **—a·bus′er** *n.*

Synonyms: *abuse, misuse, mistreat, ill-treat, maltreat.* These verbs mean to treat a person or thing wrongfully or harmfully. *Abuse* applies to wrongful or unreasonable treatment by deed or word. *Misuse* stresses incorrect or unknowledgeable handling; it implies but does not emphasize harm. *Mistreat, ill-treat,* and *maltreat* all have the sense of inflicting injury, usually physical and often with intent to do harm. *Mistreat* may imply only negligence or lack of knowledge on the offender's part, but more often refers to harm inflicted deliberately. *Ill-treat* more specifically applies to harmful treatment of persons or animals. *Maltreat* implies rough handling.

A·bu Sim·bel (ä′bo͞o sĭm′bəl). A village in the Aswan area of southern Egypt; site of a group of ancient Egyptian rock temples built by Rameses II.

a·bu·sive (ə-byo͞o′sĭv, -zĭv) *adj.* **1.** Of, pertaining to, or characterized by abuse. **2.** Wrongly or incorrectly used or treated. **3.** Serving for abuse; insulting; reviling. **—a·bu′sive·ly** *adv.* **—a·bu′sive·ness** *n.*

a·but (ə-bŭt′) *v.* **abutted, abutting, abuts.** —*intr.* To touch at one end or side of something; lie adjacent. Used with *on, upon,* or *against.* —*tr.* To border upon; be next to. [Middle English *abutten*, from Old French *abuter*, to buttress, put an end to : *a*, to + *buter*, to strike, finish, from Common Romance *bottāre* (unattested) (see **bhau-** in Appendix*).] **—a·but′ter** *n.*

a·bu·ti·lon (ə-byo͞o′tə-lŏn′) *n.* Any of various shrubs or plants of the genus *Abutilon;* especially, the **flowering maple** *(see).* [New Latin, from Arabic *aubūṭīlūn.*]

a·but·ment (ə-bŭt′mənt) *n.* **1.** The act or process of abutting. **2. a.** Something that abuts. **b.** That on which something abuts. **c.** The point of contact of two abutting objects or parts. **3.** *Architecture.* That element which shares a common boundary or surface with its neighbor. **4.** *Engineering.* **a.** A structure that supports the end of a bridge. **b.** A structure that anchors the cables of a suspension bridge.

a·but·tal (ə-bŭt′l) *n.* **1.** An abutment. **2.** *Plural.* The parts, especially of a piece of land, that abut against other property; boundaries.

ab·volt (ăb-vōlt′) *n. Abbr.* **abv.** A centimeter-gram-second electromagnetic unit of potential difference, equal to the potential difference between two points such that one erg of work must be performed to move a one-abcoulomb charge from one of the points to the other. It is equal to one hundred-millionth (10^{-8}) of a volt. [AB- (absolute) + VOLT.]

A·by·dos (ə-bī′dəs). **1.** An ancient town in Asia Minor at the narrowest point of the Hellespont. **2.** An ancient city near the Nile, in east-central Egypt.

a·bysm (ə-bĭz′əm) *n.* An abyss. [Middle English *abi(s)me*, from Old French, irregularly from Late Latin *abyssus*, ABYSS.]

a·bys·mal (ə-bĭz′məl) *adj.* **1.** Unfathomable; extreme. **2.** Of or resembling an abyss. **—a·bys′mal·ly** *adv.*

a·byss (ə-bĭs′) *n.* **1. a.** The primeval chaos. **b.** The bottomless pit; hell. **2.** An unfathomable chasm; a yawning gulf. **3.** Any immeasurably profound depth or void: *"lost in the vast abysses of space and time"* (Loren Eiseley). [Late Latin *abyssus*, from Greek *abussos (limnē)*, "bottomless (lake)" : *a-*, not + *bussos*, bottom (see **gwadh-** in Appendix*).]

a·byss·al (ə-bĭs′əl) *adj.* **1.** Abysmal. **2.** Of or pertaining to the great depths of the oceans.

Ab·ys·sin·i·a. The former name for **Ethiopia.** [New Latin, from Arabic *Ḥabashah*, from *Ḥabash*, Abyssinians.]

Ab·ys·sin·i·an (ăb′ə-sĭn′ē-ən) *adj.* Of or pertaining to Ethiopia or its inhabitants. —*n.* An inhabitant of Ethiopia.

Abyssinian cat. A short-haired cat of a breed developed from Near Eastern stocks, having a reddish-brown coat tipped with small black markings.

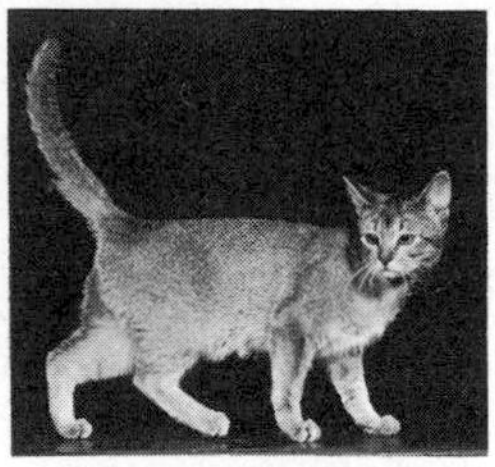

Abyssinian cat

ac alternating current.

Ac The symbol for the element actinium.

a.c. *Medicine.* before meals (New Latin *ante cibum*).

A.C. 1. Air Corps. **2.** alternating current. **3.** athletic club. **4.** before Christ (New Latin *ante Christum*).

a/c, A/C. account; account current.

a·ca·cia (ə-kā′shə) *n.* **1.** Any of various chiefly tropical trees of the genus *Acacia*, having compound leaves and tight clusters of small yellow or white flowers. Some species yield gums having a wide variety of uses. **2.** Loosely, any of several related trees, such as the locust. **3.** A substance, **gum arabic** *(see).* [Latin, from Greek *akakia*, probably from Egyptian.]

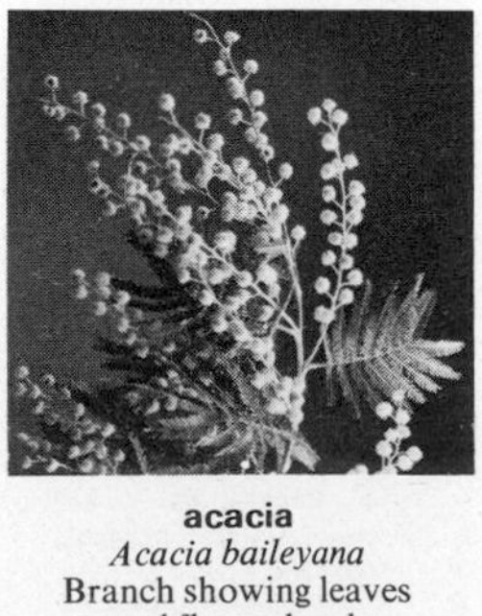

acacia
Acacia baileyana
Branch showing leaves and flower heads

acad. academic; academy.

Ac·a·deme (ăk′ə-dēm′) *n.* Also **ac·a·deme.** The world of scholarship and higher education; scholastic life or environment. [Pseudo-Greek form of Greek *Akadēmia*, ACADEMY.]

ac·a·dem·ic (ăk′ə-dĕm′ĭk) *adj. Abbr.* **acad. 1.** Of, pertaining to, or characteristic of a school. **2.** Relating to studies that are liberal or classical rather than technical or vocational. **3.** Pertaining or belonging to a scholarly society or organization. **4.** Scholarly to the point of being unaware of the outside world. **5.** Based on formal education. **6.** Formalistic; conventional. **7.** Theoretical; speculative: *"I took an academic interest in the thought of stealing the car"* (John Knowles). —*n.* A student or teacher. **—ac′a·dem′i·cal·ly** *adv.*

ac·a·dem·i·cals (ăk′ə-dĕm′ĭ-kəlz) *pl.n.* The cap and gown traditionally worn at academic ceremonies.

academic freedom. Liberty to pursue and teach relevant knowledge and to discuss it freely without restriction from school or public officials or from other sources of influence.

ac·a·de·mi·cian (ăk′ə-də-mĭsh′ən) *n. Abbr.* **A.** A member of an art, literary, or scientific academy or society.

ă pat/ā pay/âr care/ä father/b bib/ch church/d deed/ĕ pet/ē be/f fife/g gag/h hat/hw which/ĭ pit/ī pie/îr pier/j judge/k kick/l lid, needle/m mum/n no, sudden/ng thing/ŏ pot/ō toe/ô paw, for/oi noise/ou out/o͝o took/o͞o boot/p pop/r roar/s sauce/sh ship, dish/

ac·a·dem·i·cism (ăk′ə-dĕm′ə-sĭz′əm) *n.* Also **a·cad·e·mism** (ə-kăd′ə-mĭz′əm). Traditional formalism, especially when reflected in art.

a·cad·e·my (ə-kăd′ə-mē) *n., pl.* **-mies.** *Abbr.* **A., acad. 1.** An association of scholars. **2.** A school for special instruction. **3.** A secondary or college-preparatory school, especially a private one. [From ACADEMY.]

A·cad·e·my (ə-kăd′ə-mē) *n.* **1.** A specified society of scholars or artists. **2.** Platonism. **3.** The disciples of Plato. [Latin *Acadēmia,* from Greek *Akadēmia,* the Platonic school of philosophy, from *Akadēmia, Akadēmeia,* name of the place in Athens where Plato taught, after *Akadēmos,* legendary Attic hero.] **—Ac′a·dem′ic** *n.* & *adj.*

A·ca·di·a (ə-kā′dē-ə). **1.** A former name for a French colony of eastern Canada, that included Nova Scotia and New Brunswick. **2.** A parish in southern Louisiana settled by Acadian exiles.

A·ca·di·an (ə-kā′dē-ən) *adj.* Of or pertaining to Acadia or its inhabitants. *—n.* One of the early French settlers or their descendants. See **Cajun.**

A·ca·di·a National Park (ə-kā′dē-ə). A scenic recreation park, 44 square miles in area, on Mount Desert Island off the southern coast of Maine.

a·ca·jou (à-kà-zhōō′) *n.* Mahogany. [French, "cashew," from Portuguese *(a)caju,* from Tupi, "mahogany," probably by confusion with Tupi *agapú.*]

acantho–, acanth–. Indicates thorns; for example, **acanthocephalid.** [New Latin, from Greek *akanthos,* thorn plant, from *akantha,* thorn. See **ak-** in Appendix.*]

a·can·tho·ceph·a·lid (ə-kăn′thō-sĕf′ə-lĭd) *n.* Also **a·can·tho·ceph·a·lan** (-lən). Any of various parasitic worms of the phylum Acanthocephala, having a proboscis armed with hooked spines. [From New Latin *Acanthocephala,* "thornheads" (from the spiky proboscis) : ACANTHO- + *-cephala,* neuter plural of *-cephalus,* -CEPHALOUS.]

a·can·thoid (ə-kăn′thoid′) *adj.* Resembling a thorn or spine. [ACANTH(O)- + -OID.]

ac·an·thop·ter·yg·i·an (ăk′ăn-thŏp′tə-rĭj′ē-ən) *n.* Any fish of the superorder Acanthopterygii, which includes fishes having spiny fins, such as bass, perch, and mackerel. [New Latin *Acanthopterygii* : ACANTHO- + Greek *pterugion,* diminutive of *pterux,* wing, fin, from *pteron,* feather, wing (see **pet-**[1] in Appendix*).] **—ac′an·thop′ter·yg′i·an** *adj.*

a·can·thus (ə-kăn′thəs) *n., pl.* **-thuses** or **-thi** (-thī′). **1.** Any of various plants of the genus *Acanthus,* native to the Mediterranean region, having large, segmented, thistlelike leaves. **2.** An architectural ornament patterned after the leaves of the acanthus, used especially on capitals of Corinthian columns. [New Latin, from Greek *akanthos,* thorn plant, from *akantha,* thorn. See **ak-** in Appendix.*]

a cap·pel·la (ä kə-pĕl′ə). Without instrumental accompaniment. [Italian, "in the manner of the chapel (or **choir**)."]

a ca·pric·cio (ä kä-prēt′chō). *Music.* At whatever tempo and with whatever expression the performer or conductor desires. Used as a direction. [Italian, "capriciously."]

A·ca·pul·co (ä′kə-pōōl′kō). In full, Acapulco de Juaréz. A port on the Pacific coast of southern Mexico. Population, 49,000.

ac·a·ri·a·sis (ăk′ə-rī′ə-sĭs) *n.* Infestation with mites. [New Latin : ACAR(ID) + -IASIS.]

a·car·i·cide (ə-kăr′ə-sīd′) *n.* A substance lethal to ticks and mites; miticide. [ACARI(D) + -CIDE.] **—a·car′i·ci′dal** *adj.*

ac·a·rid (ăk′ə-rĭd) *n.* Any arachnid of the order Acarina, which includes the mites and ticks. [From New Latin *Acaridae* (family), from *Acarus* (genus), from Greek *akari*†, a kind of mite.] **—ac′a·rid** *adj.*

acaroid resin. A yellow or reddish gum obtained from various Australian grass trees, and used in varnishes, lacquers, and the manufacture of paper. Also called "acaroid gum." [From New Latin *acaroides,* from Greek *akari,* a kind of mite that was bred in wax or resin. See **acarid.**]

a·car·pous (ā-kär′pəs) *adj. Botany.* Producing no fruit; sterile. [A- (not) + -CARPOUS.]

ac·a·rus (ăk′ə-rəs) *n., pl.* **-ri** (-rī′). A mite, especially one of the genus *Acarus.* [New Latin *Acarus.* See **acarid.**]

a·cat·a·lec·tic (ā′kăt′ə-lĕk′tĭk) *adj.* Designating a line of verse having the required number of syllables in the last foot. *—n.* An acatalectic line. [Late Latin *acatalēcticus,* from Greek *akatalēktikos* : *a-,* not + *katalēktikos,* CATALECTIC.]

a·cau·date (ā-kô′dāt′) *adj.* Also **a·cau·dal** (ā-kôd′l). *Zoology.* Having no tail. [A- (not) + CAUDATE.]

ac·au·les·cent (ăk′ô-lĕs′ənt) *adj. Botany.* Stemless, or nearly so. [A- (not) + CAULESCENT.]

ACC 1. Airport code for Accra, Ghana. **2.** Air Coordinating Committee.

acc. 1. acceleration. **2.** accompanied. **3.** account; accountant. **4.** accusative.

Ac·cad. See **Akkad.**

ac·cede (ăk-sēd′) *intr.v.* **-ceded, -ceding, -cedes. 1.** To give one's assent; to consent; agree. Used with *to.* **2.** To arrive at or come into an office or dignity. Used with *to.* **3.** To become a party to an agreement or treaty. Used with *to.* —See Synonyms at **assent.** [Middle English *acceden,* from Latin *accēdere,* to go near, agree : *ad-,* to + *cēdere,* to go (see **ked-**[1] in Appendix*).] **—ac·ced′ence** (-sēd′əns) *n.* **—ac·ced′er** *n.*

ac·cel·er·an·do (ä-chĕl′ə-rän′dō) *adj. Music.* Gradually accelerating or quickening in time. Used as a direction. [Italian, from Latin *accelerandum,* gerund of *accelerāre,* ACCELERATE.] **—ac·cel′er·an′do** *adv.*

ac·cel·er·ate (ăk-sĕl′ə-rāt′) *v.* **-ated, -ating, -ates.** *—tr.* **1.** To increase the speed of. **2.** To cause to occur sooner than expected. **3.** *Physics.* To cause a change of velocity. *—intr.* To move or act faster. —See Synonyms at **speed.** [Latin *accelerāre* : *ad-* (intensive) + *celerāre,* to hasten, from *celer,* swift (see **kel-**[5] in Appendix*).] **—ac·cel′er·a′tive** *adj.*

ac·cel·er·a·tion (ăk-sĕl′ə-rā′shən) *n.* **1.** *Abbr.* **acc. a.** The act of accelerating. **b.** The process of being accelerated. **2.** *Physics. Symbol* **a** The rate of change of velocity with respect to time.

acceleration of gravity. *Symbol* **g** The acceleration of freely falling bodies under the influence of terrestrial gravity, equal to 980.665 cm/sec^2 or approximately 32 ft/sec^2 at sea level.

ac·cel·er·a·tor (ăk-sĕl′ə-rā′tər) *n.* **1.** One that accelerates. **2.** *Machinery.* A device, especially the gas pedal of an automobile, for increasing the speed of a machine. **3.** *Chemistry.* A substance that increases the speed of a chemical reaction. **4.** *Photography.* A chemical that reduces development time. **5.** *Physics.* Any device, such as an electrostatic generator, cyclotron, or linear accelerator, that accelerates charged subatomic particles or nuclei to energies useful for research. Also called "particle accelerator" and, loosely, "atom smasher."

ac·cel·er·om·e·ter (ăk-sĕl′ə-rŏm′ə-tər) *n.* Any of various devices used to measure acceleration. [ACCELER(ATION) + -METER.]

ac·cent (ăk′sĕnt′) *n.* **1.** *Linguistics.* The relative prominence of a particular syllable of a word by greater intensity *(stress accent),* or by variation or modulation of pitch or tone *(pitch accent).* **2.** Vocal prominence or emphasis given to a particular syllable, word, or phrase. **3.** A characteristic pronunciation: **a.** One determined by the regional or social background of the speaker. **b.** One determined by the phonetic habits of the speaker's native language carried over to his use of another language. **4.** A mark or symbol used in printing and writing of certain languages to indicate the vocal quality to be given to a particular letter: *an acute accent.* **5.** A mark or symbol used in printing and writing to indicate the stressed syllables of a spoken word. **6.** Rhythmically significant stress in a line of verse. **7. a.** Special stress given to a musical note within a phrase. **b.** A mark representing this stress. **8.** *Mathematics.* **a.** A mark, or one of several marks, used as a superscript to distinguish among variables represented by the same symbol. See **prime. b.** A mark used as a superscript to indicate the first derivative of a variable. **9.** A mark or one of several marks used as a superscript to indicate a unit, such as feet (′) and inches (″) in linear measurement. **10.** A distinctive feature or quality. *—tr.v.* (ăk′sĕnt′, ăk-sĕnt′) **accented, -centing, -cents. 1.** To stress or emphasize the pronunciation of. **2.** To mark with a printed accent. **3.** To accentuate; call attention to: *"the effect of appropriate drapery in accenting feminine graces"* (Edward Bellamy). [Middle English, from Old French, from Latin *accentus,* accentuation, originally "song added to (speech)" (translation of Greek *prosōidia,* PROSODY) : *ad-,* to + *cantus,* song, from the past participle of *canere,* to sing (see **kan-** in Appendix*).]

ac·cen·tor (ăk-sĕn′tər) *n.* Any of various sparrowlike songbirds of the family Prunellidae, that frequent mountainous regions. [Late Latin, "one who sings with another" : Latin *ad-,* to + *cantor,* singer, from *cantus,* song (see **accent**).]

ac·cen·tu·al (ăk-sĕn′chōō-əl) *adj.* **1.** Of or pertaining to accent. **2.** Designating verse rhythm based on stress accents. **—ac·cen′tu·al·ly** *adv.*

ac·cen·tu·ate (ăk-sĕn′chōō-āt′) *tr.v.* **-ated, -ating, -ates. 1.** To pronounce with a stress or accent. **2.** To mark (a letter, syllable, or word, for example) with an accent. **3.** To stress; emphasize: *"War is the most obvious human experience which accentuates the instability of the world."* (Wallace Fowlie). [Medieval Latin *accentuāre,* from Latin *accentus,* ACCENT.] **—ac·cen′tu·a′tion** *n.*

ac·cept (ăk-sĕpt′) *v.* **-cepted, -cepting, -cepts.** *—tr.* **1.** To receive (something offered) gladly; take willingly. **2.** To receive as adequate or satisfactory. **3.** To admit to a group or place. **4.** To be favorably disposed toward. **5. a.** To regard as usual, proper, or right. **b.** To regard as true; believe in. **6.** To bear up under resignedly or patiently: *accept one's fate.* **7. a.** To answer affirmatively: *accept an invitation.* **b.** To take upon oneself the duties or responsibilities of. **8.** To be able to hold (something applied or inserted): *This wood will not accept oil paints.* **9.** *Commerce.* To consent to pay, as by a signed agreement. *—intr.* To receive something willingly. —See Synonyms at **assent.** [Middle English *accepten,* from Old French *accepter,* from Latin *acceptāre,* frequentative of *accipere* (past participle *acceptus*), to receive, "take to oneself" : *ad-,* to + *capere,* to take (see **kap-** in Appendix*).]

ac·cept·a·ble (ăk-sĕp′tə-bəl) *adj.* Satisfactory; adequate. **—ac·cept′a·bil′i·ty, ac·cept′a·ble·ness** *n.* **—ac·cept′a·bly** *adv.*

ac·cep·tance (ăk-sĕp′təns) *n. Abbr.* **acpt. 1.** The act or process of accepting. **2.** The state or condition of being accepted or acceptable. **3.** Favorable reception; approval. **4.** Belief in something; agreement; assent. **5.** *Commerce.* **a.** A formal indication by a debtor of willingness to pay a time draft or bill of exchange, as by writing the word *accepted* and affixing his signature across the face of the instrument. **b.** A written instrument so endorsed. **6.** *Law.* Compliance by one party with the terms and conditions of offer of another so that a contract becomes legally binding between them.

ac·cep·tant (ăk-sĕp′tənt) *adj.* Accepting willingly.

ac·cep·ta·tion (ăk′sĕp-tā′shən) *n.* **1.** The usual or accepted meaning, as of a word or expression. **2.** Favorable reception. **3.** Ready belief. —See Synonyms at **meaning.**

Usage: Acceptation is now largely restricted to its primary sense of *accepted meaning.* It overlaps *acceptance* only in the

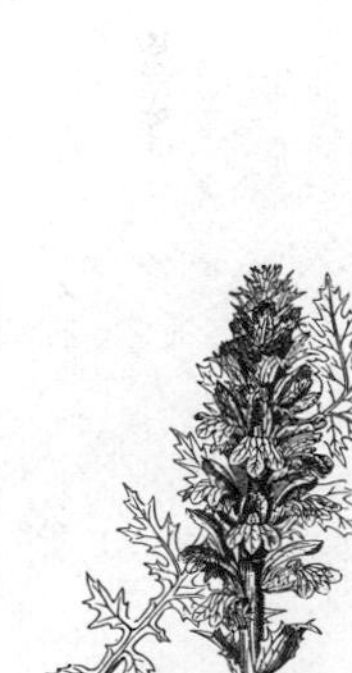

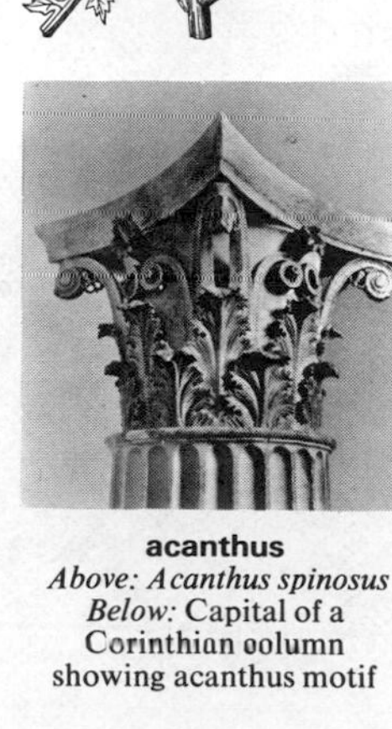

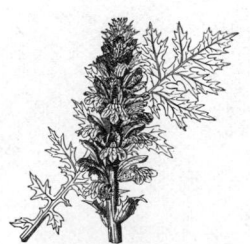

acanthus
Above: Acanthus spinosus
Below: Capital of a Corinthian column showing acanthus motif

secondary senses noted above, and is not to be used for *acceptance* otherwise.

ac·cept·ed (ăk-sĕp′tĭd) *adj.* Generally approved, believed, or recognized.

ac·cept·or (ăk-sĕp′tər) *n.* Also **ac·cept·er.** *Commerce.* One who signs a time draft or bill of exchange.

ac·cess (ăk′sĕs′) *n.* **1.** A means of approaching or nearing; passage. **2.** The act of approaching. **3.** The right to enter or make use of. **4.** The state or quality of being easy to approach or enter. **5.** A sudden outburst: *an access of rage.* [Middle English, from Old French *acces,* arrival, from Latin *accessus,* from the past participle of *accēdere,* to arrive : *ad-,* to + *cēdere,* to come (see **ked-**[1] in Appendix*).]

ac·ces·si·ble (ăk-sĕs′ə-bəl) *adj.* **1.** Easily approached or entered. **2.** Easily obtained. **3.** Open to: *accessible to flattery.* —**ac·ces′si·bil′i·ty, ac·ces′si·ble·ness** *n.* —**ac·ces′si·bly** *adv.*

ac·ces·sion (ăk-sĕsh′ən) *n.* **1.** The attainment of rank or dignity. **2. a.** An increase by means of something added: *an accession of property.* **b.** An addition. **3.** *Law.* **a.** The addition to or increase in value of property by means of improvements or natural growth. **b.** The right of a proprietor to ownership of such addition or increase. **4.** Agreement; assent. **5.** Access; admittance. **6.** A sudden outburst; an access. —*tr.v.* **accessioned, -sioning, -sions.** To record as acquired. —**ac·ces′sion·al** *adj.*

ac·ces·so·ry (ăk-sĕs′ər-ē) *n., pl.* **-ries.** Also **ac·ces·sa·ry.** **1.** Something supplementary; an adjunct. **2. a.** One who incites, aids, or abets a lawbreaker in the commission of a crime, but is not present at the time of the crime. Used in the phrase *accessory before the fact.* **b.** One who aids a criminal after the commission of a crime, but was not present at the time of the crime. Used in the phrase *accessory after the fact.* —See Synonyms at **appendage.** —*adj.* **1.** Having a secondary, supplementary, or subordinate function. **2.** Serving to aid or abet a lawbreaker, either before or after the commission of his crime, without being present at the time the crime was committed. [Middle English *accessorie,* from Medieval Latin *accessōrius,* from *accessor,* helper, accessory, subordinate, from Latin *accessus,* ACCESS.] —**ac′ces·so′ri·al** (ăk′sə-sôr′ē-əl, -sōr′ē-əl) *adj.* —**ac·ces′so·ri·ly** *adv.* —**ac·ces′so·ri·ness** *n.*

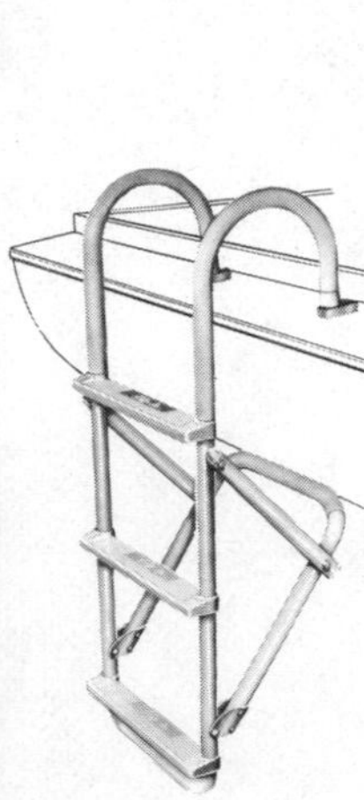

accommodation ladder

accessory fruit. *Botany.* A fruit, such as the pear, squash, or strawberry, that contains fleshy tissue developed from floral parts as well as the ovary. Also called "pseudocarp."

ac·ciac·ca·tu·ra (ä-chäk′ə-tŏŏr′ə) *n. Music.* A short grace note one half step below a principal note, sounded immediately before or at the same time as the principal note to add sustained dissonance. [Italian *acciaccatura,* "crushing sound," from *acciaccare*†, to crush.]

ac·ci·dence (ăk′sə-dəns, -dĕns′) *n.* **1.** *Grammar.* The section of morphology that deals with the inflections of words. **2.** The basic elements or rudimentary parts of any subject.

ac·ci·dent (ăk′sə-dənt, -dĕnt′) *n.* **1.** An unexpected and undesirable event; a mishap. **2.** Anything that occurs unexpectedly or unintentionally. **3.** Any circumstance or attribute that is not essential to the nature of something. **4.** Fortune; chance: *rich by accident of birth.* **5.** *Geology.* An irregular or unusual natural formation or occurrence. **6.** *Logic.* A predicable not essential to the definition of a class, but either essential (*inseparable accident*) or inessential (*separable accident*) to the nature of the individual. [Middle English, from Old French, from Latin (*rēs*) *accidēns,* "(a thing) happening," from *accidere,* to fall upon, happen : *ad-,* to + *cadere,* to fall (see **kad-** in Appendix*).]

ac·ci·den·tal (ăk′sə-dĕn′təl) *adj.* **1.** Occurring unexpectedly and unintentionally; by chance: *an accidental mistake.* **2.** Part of, but not essential; supplementary; incidental. **3.** *Music.* Of or denoting a sharp, flat, or natural not indicated in the key signature. —*n.* **1.** A factor or attribute that is not essential. **2.** *Music.* A chromatically altered note not belonging to the key signature. —**ac′ci·den′tal·ly** *adv.*

Synonyms: *accidental, fortuitous, contingent, incidental, adventitious.* These adjectives are related in a general way but are not always interchangeable. *Accidental* primarily refers to what occurs by chance or unexpectedly; it can also mean subordinate or nonessential. *Fortuitous* stresses chance or accident even more strongly, and inferentially minimizes cause. *Contingent,* in this context, describes what is possible but uncertain because of chance or unforeseen or uncontrollable factors. *Incidental* refers to what is an adjunct to something else, and does not necessarily imply the operation of chance. *Adventitious* applies to what is not inherent in something but added extrinsically, sometimes by accident or chance.

accident insurance. Insurance against injury or death because of accident.

ac·ci·die (ak′sə-dē) *n.* Also **a·ce·di·a** (ə-sē′dē-ə). Spiritual torpor; ennui. [Late Latin, from Greek *akēdia, akēdeia,* indifference, apathy : *a-,* not + *kēdos,* care (see **kād-** in Appendix*).]

ac·cip·i·ter (ăk-sĭp′ə-tər) *n.* Any hawk of the genus *Accipiter,* characterized by short wings and a long tail. [Latin, hawk. See **ōku-** in Appendix.*] —**ac·cip′i·trine′** (-trīn′, -trĭn) *adj.*

ac·claim (ə-klām′) *v.* **-claimed, -claiming, -claims.** —*tr.* To salute or hail; applaud. —*intr.* To shout approval. —See Synonyms at **praise.** —*n.* Enthusiastic applause; acclamation. [Latin *acclāmāre,* to shout at : *ad-,* to + *clāmāre,* to shout (see **kel-**[3] in Appendix*).] —**ac·claim′er** *n.*

ac·cla·ma·tion (ăk′lə-mā′shən) *n.* **1.** The act of acclaiming or being acclaimed. **2.** A shout or salute of enthusiastic approval; applause of acceptance or welcome. **3.** An oral vote, especially an enthusiastic vote of approval taken without formal ballot. Used especially in the phrase *by acclamation.* [Latin *acclāmātiō,* from *acclāmāre,* ACCLAIM.] —**ac·clam′a·to′ry** (ə-klăm′ə-tôr′ē, -tōr′ē) *adj.*

ac·cli·mate (ə-klī′mĭt, ăk′lə-māt′) *v.* **-mated, -mating, -mates.** —*tr.* To accustom (something or someone) to a new environment or situation; adapt; acclimatize. —*intr.* To become accustomed to a new environment. [French *acclimater* : *ac-,* from Latin *ad-,* to + *climat,* CLIMATE.]

ac·cli·ma·tion (ăk′lə-mā′shən) *n.* **1.** The process of acclimating or of becoming acclimated. **2.** The adaptation of an organism to its natural climatic environment, as distinguished from acclimatization.

ac·cli·ma·ti·za·tion (ə-klī′mə-tə-zā′shən) *n.* **1.** The process of acclimatizing; acclimation. **2.** The climatic adaptation of an organism, especially a plant, that has been moved to a new environment.

ac·cli·ma·tize (ə-klī′mə-tīz′) *v.* **-tized, -tizing, -tizes.** —*tr.* To acclimate (someone or something). —*intr.* To acclimate. —**ac·cli′ma·tiz′a·ble** *adj.* —**ac·cli′ma·tiz′er** *n.*

ac·cliv·i·ty (ə-klĭv′ə-tē) *n., pl.* **-ties.** An upward slope. [Latin *acclīvitās,* from *acclīvis,* uphill : *ad-,* to + *clīvus,* slope (see **klei-** in Appendix*).]

ac·co·lade (ăk′ə-lād′, ăk′ə-läd′) *n.* **1.** An embrace of greeting or salutation. **2.** Praise; approval: *critics' accolades.* **3.** The ceremonial bestowal of knighthood as by a tap on the shoulder with the flat of a sword. [French, from Provençal *acolada,* an embrace, from *acolar,* to embrace, from Vulgar Latin *accollāre* (unattested), to hug around the neck : *ad-,* to + *collum,* neck (see **kwel-**[1] in Appendix*).]

ac·com·mo·date (ə-kŏm′ə-dāt′) *v.* **-dated, -dating, -dates.** —*tr.* **1.** To do a favor or service for; oblige. See Usage note at **oblige.** **2.** To provide for; supply with. **3.** To contain comfortably or have space for. **4.** To make suitable; adapt; adjust. Often used reflexively: *He accommodates himself well to new surroundings.* **5.** To settle; reconcile. —*intr.* To become adjusted to, as the eye to focusing on objects at a distance. —See Synonyms at **contain.** [Latin *accommodāre,* to make fit : *ad-,* to + *commodus,* fit, "conforming with the (right) measure" : *con-,* with + *modus,* measure (see **med-** in Appendix*).] —**ac·com′mo·da′tive** *adj.* —**ac·com′mo·da′tive·ness** *n.*

ac·com·mo·dat·ing (ə-kŏm′ə-dā′tĭng) *adj.* Helpful and obliging. —**ac·com′mo·dat′ing·ly** *adv.*

ac·com·mo·da·tion (ə-kŏm′ə-dā′shən) *n.* **1.** The act or state of accommodating or being accommodated; adaptation; adjustment. **2.** Anything that meets a need; convenience. **3.** *Plural.* **a.** Lodgings; room and food. **b.** A seat, compartment, or room on a public vehicle. **4.** Reconciliation or settlement of opposing views; compromise. **5.** *Physiology.* Adaptation or adjustment in an organism, organ, or part, as in the lens of the eye to permit retinal focus of images of objects at different distances. **6.** *Commerce.* A loan or other financial favor.

accommodation ladder. A portable ladder or stairway hung from the side of a ship.

accommodation paper. A note or bill drawn, accepted, or endorsed by one or more parties to enable another party to obtain credit or raise money without consideration or collateral to the drawer, acceptor, or endorser, who guarantees the credit of the borrower.

accommodation train. A local railroad train that stops at all or nearly all stations and accommodates both passengers and freight.

ac·com·pa·ni·ment (ə-kŭm′pə-nē-mənt, ə-kŭmp′nē-) *n.* **1.** Something that accompanies; concomitant. **2.** Something added for embellishment, completeness, or symmetry; complement. **3.** A vocal or instrumental part that supports a solo part.

ac·com·pa·nist (ə-kŭm′pə-nĭst, ə-kŭmp′nĭst) *n.* A performer, as a pianist, who plays an accompaniment.

ac·com·pa·ny (ə-kŭm′pə-nē, ə-kŭmp′nē) *v.* **-nied, -nying, -nies.** —*tr.* **1.** To go along with; join in company. See Usage note below. **2.** To supplement with; add to. **3.** To coexist or occur with. **4.** To perform an accompaniment to. —*intr.* To play a musical accompaniment. [Middle English *accompanien,* from Old French *accompagner* : *ac-,* from Latin *ad-,* to + *compain(g),* companion, from Late Latin *compāniō,* COMPANION.]

Synonyms: *accompany, conduct, escort, chaperon* (or *chaperone*). These verbs are compared as they mean to be with or to go with another person or persons. *Accompany* suggests going with another on an equal basis. *Conduct* implies guidance of others. *Escort* stresses protective guidance. *Chaperon* (or *chaperone*) specifies adult supervision of young persons.

Usage: Persons are said to be *accompanied by* others. An inanimate object, state, or condition is usually said to be *accompanied with* (something else): *grief accompanied with remorse.*

ac·com·plice (ə-kŏm′plĭs) *n.* One who aids or abets a lawbreaker in a criminal act, either as a principal or an accessory. See Synonyms at **partner.** [Middle English, from *a complice,* a COMPLICE (influenced by ACCOMPLISH).]

ac·com·plish (ə-kŏm′plĭsh) *tr.v.* **-plished, -plishing, -plishes.** **1.** To succeed in doing; bring to pass. **2.** To reach the end of; to complete; finish. —See Synonyms at **perform, reach.** [Middle English *accomplissen,* from Old French *accomplir* (present stem *accompliss-*), to complete : *ac-,* from Latin *ad-,* to + *complir,* to complete, from Latin *complēre,* "to fill up," to finish : *com-* (intensive) + *plēre,* to fill (see **pel-**[8] in Appendix*).] —**ac·com′plish·a·ble** *adj.* —**ac·com′plish·er** *n.*

ac·com·plished (ə-kŏm′plĭsht) *adj.* **1.** Completed; done; finished. **2.** Skilled; expert. **3.** Sophisticated.

ac·com·plish·ment (ə-kŏm′plĭsh-mənt) *n.* **1.** The act of accomplishing or of being accomplished; completion. **2.** Something completed successfully; an achievement. **3.** Social poise.

ac·cord (ə-kôrd′) *v.* **-corded, -cording, -cords.** —*tr.* **1.** To make to conform or agree; bring into harmony. **2.** To grant; bestow upon: *I accord you my blessing.* —*intr.* To be in agreement, unity, or harmony. —See Synonyms at **agree.** —**according as. 1.** To the proportion or degree that. **2.** Depending on whether. —**according to. 1.** In accordance with. **2.** In proportion to. **3.** On the authority of. —*n.* **1.** Agreement; harmony. **2.** A settlement or compromise of conflicting opinions. **3.** A settlement of points at issue between nations. —**of one's own accord.** Voluntarily. [Middle English *acorden,* from Old French *acorder,* from Vulgar Latin *accordāre* (unattested), "to be heart-to-heart with" : Latin *ad-,* to + *cor* (stem *cord-*), heart (see **kerd-**[1] in Appendix*).]

ac·cord·ance (ə-kôrd′əns) *n.* **1.** Agreement; conformity. **2.** The act of granting.

ac·cord·ant (ə-kôrd′ənt) *adj.* In agreement or harmony; corresponding; consonant. Usually used with *to* or *with.* —**ac·cord′ant·ly** *adv.*

ac·cord·ing·ly (ə-kôr′dĭng-lē) *adv.* **1.** Correspondingly. **2.** Consequently.

ac·cor·di·on (ə-kôr′dē-ən) *n.* A portable musical instrument with a small keyboard and free metal reeds that sound when air is forced past them by pleated bellows operated by the player. —*adj.* Having folds or bends like the bellows of an accordion: *accordion pleats.* [German *Akkordion,* from *Akkord,* agreement, "harmony," from French *accord,* from Old French *acorder,* to ACCORD.] —**ac·cor′di·on·ist** *n.*

ac·cost (ə-kôst′, ə-kŏst′) *tr.v.* **-costed, -costing, -costs. 1.** To approach and speak to first. **2.** To solicit sexually. [Old French *accoster,* from Vulgar Latin *accostāre* (unattested), to come alongside someone : Latin *ad-,* near + *costa,* side, rib (see **kost-** in Appendix*).]

ac·couche·ment (ȧ-ko͞osh-mäN′) *n. French.* Parturition.

ac·count (ə-kount′) *n.* **1. a.** A narrative or record of events. **b.** A written or oral explanation, as of blame or cause. **2. a.** A precise list or enumeration of monetary transactions. **b.** Any detailed list or enumeration. **3.** *Abbr.* **A/C, a/c, acct., acc.** A business relationship involving the exchange of money or credit: *a charge account.* **4.** Worth, standing, or importance: *a man of some account.* **5.** Profit or advantage. —**call to account. 1.** To challenge or contest. **2.** To hold answerable for. —**give a good account of oneself.** To act in a creditable manner. —**on account. 1.** On credit. **2.** In part payment of. —**on account of. 1.** Because of. **2.** *Regional.* Because. —**on no account.** Under no circumstances. —**on one's own account. 1.** On one's own behalf. **2.** On one's own: *He wants to work on his own account.* —**on (someone's) account.** For (someone's) sake. —**take into account.** To take into consideration; allow for. —*tr.v.* **accounted, -counting, -counts.** To consider or esteem: *"Your honor is accounted a merciful man."* (Shakespeare). See Synonyms at **consider.** —**account for. 1.** To make or render a reckoning, as of funds received and paid out, or of persons or things: *Six survivors have been accounted for.* **2.** To be the explanation or cause of. **3.** To be answerable for. **4.** To kill, capture, or disable. [Middle English, from Old French *acont, acompt,* from *acunter, acompter,* "to count up to," reckon : *ac-,* from Latin *ad-,* to + *cunter, compter,* COUNT (compute).]

ac·count·a·ble (ə-koun′tə-bəl) *adj.* **1.** Answerable. **2.** Capable of being explained. —See Synonyms at **responsible.** —**ac·count′a·bil′i·ty, ac·count′a·ble·ness** *n.* —**ac·count′a·bly** *adv.*

ac·count·ant (ə-koun′tənt) *n. Abbr.* **acc.** One who keeps, audits, and inspects the financial records of individuals or business concerns and prepares financial and tax reports. See **certified public accountant.** —*adj.* Answerable. Used with *to: "His offense is so, as it appears, accountant to the law"* (Shakespeare). —**ac·count′an·cy** *n.*

account executive. An individual in an advertising firm who manages the account of one or more clients.

ac·count·ing (ə-koun′tĭng) *n.* The bookkeeping methods involved in making a financial record of business transactions and in the preparation of statements concerning the assets, liabilities, and operating results of a business.

account receivable *pl.* **accounts receivable.** *Abbr.* **A/R, AR** *Accounting.* An asset account in a balance sheet, showing amounts due from a firm's customers, usually maturing in less than a year.

ac·cou·ter (ə-ko͞o′tər) *tr.v.* **-tered, -tering, -ters.** Also *British* **ac·cou·tre** (-tər). To outfit and equip, as for military duty. See Synonyms at **furnish.** [French *accoutrer,* from Old French *acoustrer,* from Vulgar Latin *accons*ū*tūrāre* (unattested), to equip (with clothes) : Latin *ad-,* to + *consūtūra* (unattested), sewing, clothes, from Latin *consuere,* to sew together : *con-,* together + *suere,* to sew (see **syū-** in Appendix*).]

ac·cou·ter·ment (ə-ko͞o′tər-mənt) *n.* Also *British* **ac·cou·tre·ment** (-tər-mənt, -trə-mənt). **1.** The act of accoutering. **2.** *Plural.* The equipment other than arms and dress issued to a soldier. **3.** *Plural.* The outward forms whereby a thing may be recognized; trappings.

Ac·cra (ə-krä′, ăk′rə). The capital of Ghana, located on the Gulf of Guinea. Population, 338,000.

ac·cred·it (ə-krĕd′ĭt) *tr.v.* **-ited, -iting, -its. 1.** To ascribe or attribute to; credit with. **2. a.** To supply with credentials or authority; authorize. **b.** To appoint as an ambassador to a foreign government. **3.** To certify as meeting a prescribed standard. **4.** To believe. **5.** To enter on the credit side of an account book. —See Synonyms at **approve.** [French *accréditer,* from *(mettre) à crédit,* "(to put) to CREDIT."]

ac·cred·i·ta·tion (ə-krĕd′ə-tā′shən) *n.* The act of accrediting or the state of being accredited; specifically, the granting of approval to an institution of learning by an official review board after the school has met specific requirements.

ac·crete (ə-krēt′) *v.* **-creted, -creting, -cretes.** —*tr.* To make larger or more, as by increased growth. —*intr.* **1.** To grow together; fuse. Used with *to.* **2.** To grow or increase gradually, as by addition. [Back-formation from ACCRETION.]

ac·cre·tion (ə-krē′shən) *n.* **1.** Any growth or increase in size by gradual external addition, fusion, or inclusion. **2.** Something added externally to promote such growth or increase. **3.** *Biology.* Any growing together of plant or animal tissues that are normally separate. **4.** *Geology.* Slow addition to land by deposition of water-borne sediment. **5.** *Law.* An increase of land along the shores of a body of water, as by alluvial deposit. [From Latin *accrēscere* (past participle *accrētus*), ACCRUE.] —**ac·cre′tion·ar·y, ac·cre′tive** *adj.*

ac·cru·al (ə-kro͞o′əl) *n.* **1.** The act or process of accruing; increase. **2.** Something that increases or accrues.

ac·crue (ə-kro͞o′) *intr.v.* **-crued, -cruing, -crues. 1.** To come to someone or something as a gain, addition, or increment. **2.** To increase or accumulate, as by natural growth, or as interest on capital. **3.** *Law.* To become an enforceable or permanent right. [Middle English *acrewen,* probably from Old French *accreue,* growth, from the past participle of *accreistre,* to increase, from Latin *accrēscere* : *ad-,* in addition + *crēscere,* to grow (see **ker-**[3] in Appendix*).] —**ac·crue′ment** *n.*

acct. account.

ac·cul·tur·ate (ə-kŭl′chə-rāt′) *v.* **-ated, -ating, -ates.** —*tr.* To cause (a society) to change by the process of acculturation. —*intr.* To change or be modified by acculturation.

ac·cul·tur·a·tion (ə-kŭl′chə-rā′shən) *n.* The modification of a primitive culture by contact with an advanced culture. [AD- (toward) + CULTUR(E) + -ATION.]

ac·cum·bent (ə-kŭm′bənt) *adj.* **1.** Lying down; reclining. **2.** *Botany.* Resting against another part. Said especially of cotyledons. [Latin *accumbēns,* present participle of *accumbere,* to recline : *ad-,* near to + *-cumbere,* to recline (see **keu-**[2] in Appendix*).] —**ac·cum′ben·cy** *n.*

ac·cu·mu·late (ə-kyo͞om′yə-lāt′) *v.* **-lated, -lating, -lates.** —*tr.* To amass or gather; pile up; collect. —*intr.* To grow or increase; mount up. —See Synonyms at **gather.** [Latin *accumulāre* : *ad-,* in addition + *cumulāre,* to pile up, from *cumulus,* a heap (see **keu-**[3] in Appendix*).] —**ac·cu′mu·la·ble** (ə-kyo͞om′yə-lə-bəl) *adj.*

ac·cu·mu·la·tion (ə-kyo͞om′yə-lā′shən) *n.* **1.** The act of amassing or gathering, as into a heap or pile: *"Little things grew by continual accumulation"* (Samuel Johnson). **2.** The process of growing into a heap or large amount. **3.** A mass of something heaped up or collected: *an accumulation of rubbish.* **4. a.** The growth of a principal sum by retention of interest or profit. **b.** The gradual purchase of securities in a depressed market in anticipation of rising prices. **c.** In reckoning the yield on a bond, the difference between its face value and its cost if the bond is purchased at a discount. Compare **amortization.**

ac·cu·mu·la·tive (ə-kyo͞om′yə-lā′tĭv, -lə-tĭv) *adj.* **1.** Characterized by or showing the effects of accumulation; cumulative. **2.** Having a propensity to amass; acquisitive. —**ac·cu′mu·la·tive·ly** *adv.* —**ac·cu′mu·la·tive·ness** *n.*

ac·cu·mu·la·tor (ə-kyo͞om′yə-lā′tər) *n.* **1.** Someone or something that accumulates. **2.** A register or electric circuit in a calculator or computer that stores figures for computation. **3.** *British.* An automobile storage battery.

ac·cu·ra·cy (ăk′yər-ə-sē) *n.* Exactness; correctness.

ac·cu·rate (ăk′yər-ĭt) *adj.* **1.** Having no errors; correct. **2.** Deviating only slightly or within acceptable limits from a standard. [Latin *accūrātus,* done with care, past participle of *accūrāre,* to attend to carefully : *ad-,* to + *cūrāre,* to care for, attend to, from *cūra,* care (see **cūra** in Appendix*).] —**ac′cu·rate·ly** *adv.* —**ac′cu·rate·ness** *n.*

ac·curs·ed (ə-kûr′sĭd, ə-kûrst′) *adj.* Also **ac·curst** (ə-kûrst′). **1.** Under a curse; doomed. **2.** Abominable; hateful. [Middle English *acursed,* from *acursen,* to curse, Old English *ācursian* : *ā-* (intensive) + *cursian,* to curse, from *curs,* CURSE.] —**ac·curs′ed·ly** *adv.* —**ac·curs′ed·ness** *n.*

ac·cu·sa·tion (ăk′yo͞o-zā′shən) *n.* **1.** An act of accusing. **2.** An allegation. **3.** *Law.* A formal charge brought before a court against a person, stating that he is guilty of some punishable offense.

ac·cu·sa·tive (ə-kyo͞o′zə-tĭv) *adj. Abbr.* **acc.** Of or pertaining to the case of a noun, pronoun, adjective, or participle that is the direct object of a verb or the object of certain prepositions. —*n.* The accusative case. [Middle English, from Latin *(casus) accūsātīvus,* "(case) indicating accusation" (mistranslation of Greek *aitiatikos ptōsis,* "case of causation"), from *accūsāre,* to ACCUSE.] —**ac·cu′sa·tive·ly** *adv.*

ac·cu·sa·to·ri·al (ə-kyo͞o′zə-tôr′ē-əl, -tōr′ē-əl) *adj.* Also **ac·cu·sa·to·ry** (ə-kyo͞o′zə-tôr′ē, -tōr′ē). Containing or implying accusation.

ac·cuse (ə-kyo͞oz′) *v.* **-cused, -cusing, -cuses.** —*tr.* **1.** To charge (someone or something) with a shortcoming or error. **2.** To bring charges against (someone) for a misdeed. Used with *of.* —*intr.* To make an accusation against someone. [Middle English *acusen,* from Old French *acuser,* from Latin *accūsāre,* to accuse, "call to account" : *ad-,* to + *causa,* CAUSE.] —**ac·cus′er** *n.* —**ac·cus′ing·ly** *adv.*

ac·cused (ə-kyo͞ozd′) *sing. & pl.n. Law.* Preceded by *the.* The generic term for the defendant or defendants in a criminal case.

ac·cus·tom (ə-kŭs′təm) *tr.v.* **-tomed, -toming, -toms.** To famil-

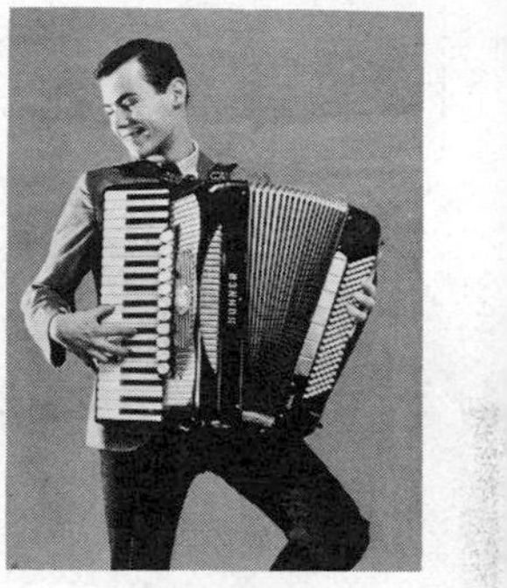

accordion

t tight/th thin, path/*th* this, bathe/ŭ cut/ûr urge/v valve/w with/y yes/z zebra, size/zh vision/ə about, item, edible, gallop, circus/ à *Fr.* ami/œ *Fr.* feu, *Ger.* schön/ü *Fr.* tu, *Ger.* über/KH *Ger.* ich, *Scot.* loch/N *Fr.* bon. ***Follows main vocabulary.** †**Of obscure origin.**

iarize, as by constant practice, use, or habit. Often used reflexively. [Middle English *accustomen*, from Old French *aco(u)stumer* : *a-*, from Latin *ad-*, to + *costume*, CUSTOM.]

ac·cus·tomed (ə-kŭs′təmd) *adj.* **1.** Usual, characteristic, or normal. **2.** In the habit of; used (to): *accustomed to sleeping late.* **3.** According to a custom: *"I hold an old accustomed feast"* (Shakespeare). —See Synonyms at **usual**.

ace (ās) *n.* **1. a.** A single pip or spot on a playing card, die, or domino. **b.** A playing card, die, or domino having one spot or pip. **2.** In racket games: **a.** A serve which one's opponent fails to return. **b.** A point scored by the failure of one's opponent to return a serve. **3.** *Informal.* A narrow margin. **4.** A military aircraft pilot who has destroyed five or more enemy aircraft. **5.** *Informal.* A person who is an expert in his field. **6.** *Physics.* A unit of matter, a **quark** *(see).* —*adj. Informal.* Topnotch; first-rate; expert. —*tr.v.* **aced, acing, aces.** *Slang.* **1.** To get the better of (someone). Often used with *out.* **2.** To receive a grade of A on (a test or examination): *He aced his term paper.* [Middle English *aas*, from Old French *as*, from Latin *ās*, unit. See **as** (Roman coin).]

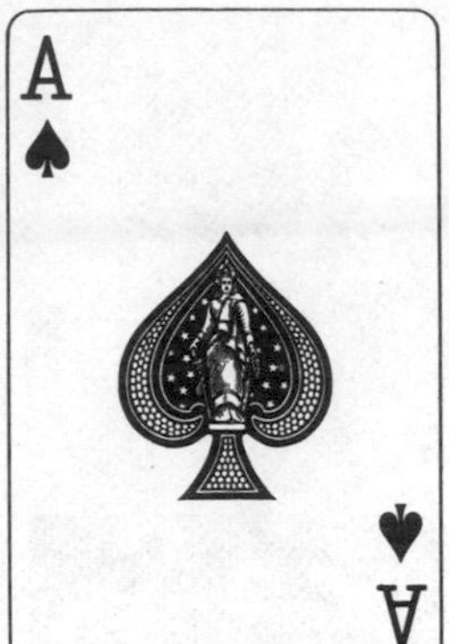

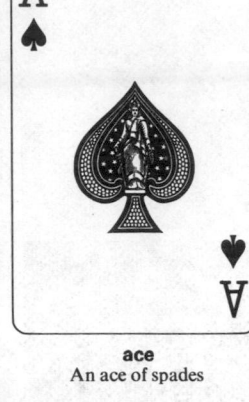

ace
An ace of spades

-acean. Indicates an organism belonging to a taxonomic group; for example, **cetacean.** [From New Latin *-acea* and *-aceae*, neuter and feminine plural of *-aceus*, -ACEOUS.]

a·ce·di·a. Variant of **accidie.**

ace in the hole. 1. A hidden advantage. **2.** *Golf.* A hole in one.

A·cel·da·ma[1] (ə-sĕl′də-mə). The potter's field near Jerusalem purchased by the priests as a burying ground for strangers with the reward Judas had received for betraying Jesus and which he had returned to them. Matthew 27:7. [From Greek *Akeldama*, from Aramaic *ḥăqēl, dĕmā*, "field of blood."]

A·cel·da·ma[2] (ə-sĕl′də-mə) *n.* Any place with dreadful associations. [From ACELDAMA.]

a·cel·lu·lar (ā-sĕl′yə-lər) *adj. Biology.* Containing no cells.

a·cen·tric (ā-sĕn′trĭk) *adj.* **1.** Having no center. **2.** Not centered; placed offcenter. [A- (not) + CENTRIC.]

-aceous. Indicates: **1.** Of or pertaining to; for example, **sebaceous. 2.** Resembling or of the nature of; for example, **farinaceous. 3.** Belonging to a taxonomic category, especially a botanical family; for example, **orchidaceous.** [New Latin *-aceus*, from Latin *-āceus*, "of a specific kind or group," originally an extension of an adjectival suffix *-āx, -āc-*.]

a·ceph·a·lous (ā-sĕf′ə-ləs) *adj.* **1.** Headless or lacking a clearly defined head. **2.** Having no leader. [Medieval Latin *acephalus*, headless, from Greek *akephalos* : *a-* (not) + -CEPHALOUS.]

a·ce·qui·a (ə-sā′kē-ə) *n. Southwestern U.S.* An irrigation canal. [Spanish, from Arabic *as-saqīyah*, irrigation ditch.]

ac·e·rate (ăs′ə-rāt′) *adj.* Also **ac·e·rat·ed** (-rā′tĭd). *Biology.* Pointed at one end; needle-shaped. [From Latin *ācer*, sharp. See **ak-** in Appendix.*]

a·cerb (ə-sûrb′) *adj.* **1.** Sour; bitter; astringent. **2.** Acid; sharp. [Latin *acerbus*, sharp, bitter. See **ak-** in Appendix.*]

ac·er·bate (ăs′ər-bāt′) *tr.v.* **-bated, -bating, -bates.** To vex; annoy. [Latin *acerbāre*, to make sour, from *acerbus*, ACERB.]

a·cer·bi·ty (ə-sûr′bə-tē) *n., pl.* **-ties. 1.** Sourness of taste. **2.** Acrimony.

ac·e·rose[1] (ăs′ə-rōs′) *adj. Botany.* Slender and sharp-pointed, as a pine needle is. [Incorrect use (by Linnaeus as if from Latin *ācer*, sharp, ACERATE) of Latin *acerōsus*, ACEROSE (chaffy).]

ac·e·rose[2] (ăs′ə-rōs′) *adj.* Resembling or mixed with chaff. [Latin *acerōsus*, chaffy, from *acus*, chaff. See **ak-** in Appendix.*]

a·cer·vate (ə-sûr′vĭt, ăs′ər-vāt′) *adj. Botany.* Growing in small heaps or compact clusters. [From Latin *acervāre*, to heap, from *acervus*, a heap. See **acervulus.**] —**a·cer′vate·ly** *adv.*

a·cer·vu·lus (ə-sûr′vyə-ləs) *n., pl.* **-li** (-lī′). In certain fungi, a fruiting body composed of a cushionlike mass of threads. [New Latin, "little heap," from Latin *acervus*†, heap.]

acet. acetone.

acet. a. acetic acid.

ac·e·tab·u·lum (ăs′ə-tăb′yə-ləm) *n., pl.* **-la** (-lə). **1.** *Anatomy.* The cup-shaped cavity in the hipbone into which the head of the thighbone fits. **2.** *Zoology.* A sucker, such as that of an octopus or cuttlefish. [Latin *acētābulum*, vinegar cup, from *acētum*, vinegar. See **ak-** in Appendix.*] —**ac′e·tab′u·lar** (-lər) *adj.*

ac·e·tal (ăs′ə-tăl′) *n.* **1.** A colorless, flammable, volatile liquid, $CH_3CH(OC_2H_5)_2$, used in cosmetics and as a solvent. **2.** Any of the class of compounds formed from aldehydes combined with alcohol. [German *Azetal* : ACET(O)- + AL(COHOL).]

ac·et·al·de·hyde (ăs′ĭt-ăl′də-hīd′) *n.* A colorless, flammable liquid, C_2H_4O, used to manufacture acetic acid, perfumes, and drugs. Also called "aldehyde." [ACET(O)- + ALDEHYDE.]

a·cet·a·mide (ə-sĕt′ə-mīd′, ăs′ĭt-ăm′īd′) *n.* Also **a·cet·a·mid** (ə-sĕt′ə-mĭd, ăs′ĭt-ăm′ĭd). The crystalline amide of acetic acid, CH_3CONH_2, used as a solvent and wetting agent and in lacquers and explosives. [German *Azetamid* : ACET(O)- + AMIDE.]

ac·et·an·i·lide (ăs′ĭt-ăn′ə-līd′) *n.* Also **ac·et·an·i·lid** (-lĭd). A white crystalline compound, $C_6H_5NH(COCH_3)$, used medicinally to relieve pain and reduce fever. [ACET(O)- + ANIL(INE) + -IDE.]

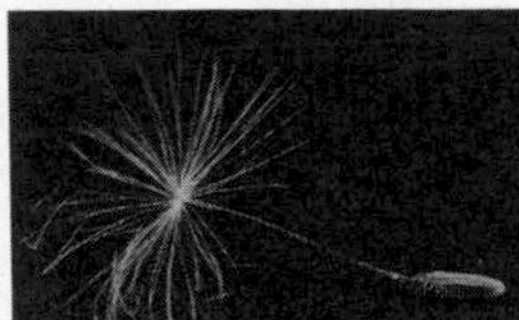

achene
Achene of dandelion, with pappus

ac·e·tate (ăs′ə-tāt′) *n.* **1.** A salt or ester of acetic acid. **2.** Cellulose acetate or any of various products, especially fibers, derived from it. [ACET(O)- + -ATE.] —**ac′e·tat′ed** *adj.*

a·ce·tic (ə-sē′tĭk) *adj.* Of, pertaining to, or containing acetic acid or vinegar. [From Latin *acētum*, vinegar. See **ak-** in Appendix.*]

acetic acid. *Abbr.* **acet. a.** A clear, colorless organic acid, CH_3COOH, with a distinctive pungent odor, used as a solvent and in the manufacture of rubber, plastics, acetate fibers, pharmaceuticals, and photographic chemicals. When at least 99.8 per cent pure, it is also called "glacial acetic acid."

acetic anhydride. An organic liquid, $(CH_3CO)_2O$, with a pungent odor, combining with water to produce acetic acid and used in the manufacture of various organic acetate derivatives.

a·cet·i·fy (ə-sĕt′ə-fī′) *v.* **-fied, -fying, -fies.** —*tr.* To convert (a neutral liquid) to acetic acid or vinegar. —*intr.* To become acetic; turn into acetic acid or vinegar. [ACET(O)- + -FY.] —**a·cet′i·fi·ca′tion** *n.* —**a·cet′i·fi·er** *n.*

aceto-, acet-. Indicates the presence of acetic acid or the acetyl radical; for example, **acetophenetidin, acetify.** [From Latin *acētum*, vinegar. See **ak-** in Appendix.*]

ac·e·to·a·ce·tic acid (ăs′ə-tō-ə-sē′tĭk, ə-sē′tō-). A syrupy, colorless acid, CH_3COCH_2COOH, excreted in the urine and found in abnormal quantities in the urine of diabetics.

ac·e·tone (ăs′ə-tōn′) *n. Abbr.* **acet.** A colorless, volatile, extremely flammable liquid, CH_3COCH_3, widely used as an organic solvent and, in especially pure grades, to clean and dry electronic component materials. [German *Azeton* : ACET(O)- + -ONE.] —**ac′e·ton′ic** (-tŏn′ĭk) *adj.*

acetone body. *Biochemistry.* A **ketone body** *(see).*

ac·e·to·phe·net·i·din (ăs′ə-tō-fə-nĕt′ə-dĭn) *n.* Also **ac·e·to·phe·net·i·dine** (-dēn′). A white powder or crystalline solid, $CH_3CONHC_6H_4OC_2H_5$, used in medicine to reduce fever and relieve pain. Also called "phenacetin." [ACETO- + PHEN(O)- + ET(HYL) + -ID(E) + -IN.]

ac·e·tous (ăs′ə-təs, ə-sē′təs) *adj.* Also **ac·e·tose** (ăs′ə-tōs′). **1.** Of, pertaining to, or producing acetic acid or vinegar. **2.** Having an acetic taste; sour-tasting. [Late Latin *acētōsus*, vinegary, from *acētum*, ACETUM.]

a·ce·tum (ə-sē′təm) *n.* **1.** Vinegar. **2.** An acetic acid solution of a drug. [Latin *acētum*. See **ak-** in Appendix.*]

ac·e·tyl (ăs′ə-tĭl, ə-sēt′l) *n.* The acetic acid radical CH_3CO. [ACET(O)- + -YL.] —**ac′e·tyl′ic** (ăs′ə-tĭl′ĭk) *adj.*

a·cet·y·late (ə-sĕt′l-āt′) *tr.v.* **-lated, -lating, -lates.** To bring an acetyl group into (an organic molecule), using a reagent such as acetic anhydride. —**a·cet′y·la′tion** *n.*

ac·e·tyl·cho·line (ăs′ə-tĭl-kō′lēn′, ə-sēt′l-) *n.* A white crystalline compound, $C_7H_{17}NO_3$, that transmits nerve impulses across intercellular gaps and forms salts used to lower blood pressure and increase peristalsis. [ACETYL + CHOLINE.]

ac·e·tyl·cho·lin·es·ter·ase (ăs′ə-tĭl-kō′lēn-ĕs-tə-rās′) *n.* **Cholinesterase** *(see).*

a·cet·y·lene (ə-sĕt′l-ēn′, -ən) *n.* A colorless, highly flammable or explosive gas, C_2H_2, used for metal welding and cutting and as an illuminant. [ACETYL + -ENE.] —**a·cet′y·len′ic** *adj.*

acetylene series. A series of unsaturated aliphatic hydrocarbons, each containing at least one triple carbon bond, having chemical properties resembling acetylene, and having the general formula C_nH_{2n-2} with acetylene being the simplest member.

a·ce·tyl·sal·i·cyl·ic acid (ə-sēt′l-săl′ə-sĭl′ĭk). A common drug, **aspirin** *(see).* [ACETYL + SALICYLIC ACID.]

ace·y·deuc·y (ā′sē-do͞o′sē, -dyo͞o′sē) *n.* A variation of backgammon. [ACE + DEUCE.]

A·chae·a (ə-kē′ə). Also **A·cha·ia** (ə-kī′ə, ə-kā′ə). **1.** In ancient Greece, a region in the northern Peloponnesus bounded on the north by the Gulfs of Corinth and Patras. **2.** A Roman senatorial province formed in 27 B.C. comprising all of Greece south of Thessaly. **3.** An administrative unit of Greece, on the northern Peloponnesus. Population, 237,000. Capital, Patras.

A·chae·an (ə-kē′ən) *adj.* Also **A·cha·ian** (ə-kī′ən, ə-kā′ən). Referring to Achaea or the Achaeans. —*n.* **1.** A member of one of the four principal tribes of ancient Greece believed to have created the Mycenaean civilization. **2.** A Greek, especially of the Mycenaean era.

Achaean League. Originally, a confederation of Achaean cities for the purpose of religious observances. Broken up by the Macedonians, the league was formed anew on political lines in 280 B.C.

A·chae·me·nid (ə-kē′mə-nĭd, ə-kĕm′ə-) *n.* A member of the ruling dynasty of Persia from the time of Cyrus the Great to the death of Darius III (533–330 B.C.). [Greek *Akhaimenidēs*, from *Akhaimenēs*, a Persian king, the eponymous founder of the dynasty.] —**A·chae′me·nid** *adj.*

A·cha·tes[1] (ə-kā′tēz). In the *Aeneid*, the faithful companion of Aeneas.

A·cha·tes[2] (ə-kā′tēz) *n.* A loyal friend. [From ACHATES.]

ache (āk) *intr.v.* **ached, aching, aches. 1.** To suffer a dull, sustained pain. **2.** *Informal.* To yearn painfully. —*n.* A dull, steady pain. [Middle English *aken*, Old English *ācan*. See **ages-** in Appendix.*]

a·chene (ā-kēn′) *n.* Also **a·kene.** *Botany.* A small, dry, thin-walled fruit, such as that of the buttercup and dandelion, that does not split open when ripe. [New Latin *achēnium*, "one that does not yawn or split open" : A- (not) + Greek *khainein*, to yawn (see **ghēi-** in Appendix*).] —**a·che′ni·al** (ā-kē′nē-əl) *adj.*

A·cher·nar (ā′kər-när′) *n.* A star in the constellation Eridanus that is one of the brightest stars in the sky and is 114 light-years from Earth. [From Arabic *ākhir al-nahr*, "the end of the river" (referring to the star's position in Eridanus).]

Ach·e·ron (ăk′ə-rŏn′) *n. Greek Mythology.* **1.** The river of woe over which Charon ferried the souls of the dead to Hades. **2.** Hades. [Greek *Akherōn*. See **eghero-** in Appendix.*]

A·cheu·li·an (ə-sho͞o′lē-ən) *adj.* Also **A·cheu·le·an.** *Archaeology.* Designating a stage of culture of the European Lower Paleolithic Age between the second and third interglacial periods, characterized by symmetrical stone hand axes. [French *acheuléen*, from *St. Acheul*, village in northern France and site of the archaeological finds from which the culture was classified.]

a·chieve (ə-chēv′) *v.* **achieved, achieving, achieves.** —*tr.* **1.** To

ă pat/ā pay/âr care/ä father/b bib/ch church/d deed/ĕ pet/ē be/f fife/g gag/h hat/hw which/ĭ pit/ī pie/îr pier/j judge/k kick/l lid, needle/m mum/n no, sudden/ng thing/ŏ pot/ō toe/ô paw, for/oi noise/ou out/o͝o took/o͞o boot/p pop/r roar/s sauce/sh ship, dish/

accomplish; do or finish with success. **2.** To attain or get with effort, as through exertion, skill, practice, or perseverance. —*intr.* To accomplish something successfully. —See Synonyms at **perform, reach.** [Middle English *acheven,* from Old French *achever,* "to bring to a head," from *a chef,* "to a head" : *a,* to, from Latin *ad-* + *chef,* head, from Latin *caput* (see **kaput-** in Appendix*).] —**a·chiev'a·ble** *adj.* —**a·chiev'er** *n.*

a·chieve·ment (ə-chēv'mənt) *n.* **1.** The act of accomplishing or finishing something. **2.** Something that has been accomplished successfully, especially by means of exertion, skill, practice, or perseverance.

achievement test. A test for the measurement and comparison of skills in various fields of vocational or academic study.

A·chil·les (ə-kĭl'ēz). The hero of Homer's *Iliad,* son of Peleus and Thetis.

Achilles' heel. A small but mortal weakness. [From the myth that Achilles was invulnerable except in the heel.]

Achilles' tendon. The large tendon running from the heel bone to the calf muscle of the leg. Also called "tendon of Achilles."

A·chin (ə-chēn'). A region of northern Sumatra, Indonesia.

a·chi·o·te (ä'chē-ō'tē) *n.* The seeds of the **annatto** *(see),* or a preparation made from them, used to flavor and impart a yellow or reddish color to various foods. [Spanish, from Nahuatl (Aztec) *achi(y)otl.*]

ach·la·myd·e·ous (ăk'lə-mĭd'ē-əs) *adj. Botany.* Having no floral envelope; without calyx or corolla. [A- (not) + CHLAMYDEOUS.]

a·chon·drite (ā-kŏn'drīt') *n.* A stony meteorite that contains no **chondrules** *(see).* —**a'chon·drit'ic** (ā'kŏn-drĭt'ĭk) *adj.*

a·chon·dro·pla·si·a (ā-kŏn'drō-plā'zhē-ə) *n.* Improper development of cartilage at the ends of the long bones, resulting in congenital dwarfism. [A- (not) + CHONDRO- + -PLASIA.] —**a·chon'dro·plas'tic** (-plăs'tĭk) *adj.*

ach·ro·mat·ic (ăk'rə-măt'ĭk) *adj.* **1.** Designating color perceived to have zero saturation, and therefore no hue, such as neutral grays, from black to white or black to colorless. **2.** *Optics.* Refracting light without spectral color separation. **3.** *Biology.* Staining poorly with standard dyes. **4.** *Music.* Having only the diatonic tones of the scale. [From Greek *akhrōmatos,* colorless : *a-,* not, without + *khrōma,* color (see **ghrēu-** in Appendix*).] —**ach'ro·mat'i·cal·ly** *adv.* —**a·chro'ma·tism'** (ā-krō'mə-tĭz'əm), **a·chro'ma·tic'i·ty** (-tĭs'ə-tē) *n.*

achromatic lens. A combination of lenses to produce images free of chromatic aberrations.

a·chro·ma·tin (ā-krō'mə-tĭn) *n.* The part of a cell nucleus that is relatively uncolored by stains or dyes. [Greek *akhrōmatos,* ACHROMATIC + -IN.] —**a'chro'ma·tin'ic** *adj.*

a·chro·ma·tize (ā-krō'mə-tīz') *tr.v.* **-tized, -tizing, -tizes.** To render achromatic; rid of color.

a·chro·ma·tous (ā-krō'mə-təs) *adj.* **1.** Without color. **2.** With less color than normal; having inadequate color. [Greek *akhrōmatos,* ACHROMATIC.]

a·chro·mic (ā-krō'mĭk) *adj.* Also **a·chro·mous** (-məs). Having no color; colorless. [A- (not) + CHROMIC.]

a·cic·u·la (ə-sĭk'yə-lə) *n., pl.* **-lae** (-lē'). A needlelike or needle-shaped object, part, or process, such as a bristle, spine, or crystal. [New Latin, from Latin *acicula,* hairpin, diminutive of *acus,* needle. See **ak-** in Appendix.*] —**a·cic'u·lar, a·cic'u·late** (-lĭt, -lāt'), **a·cic'u·lat'ed** (-lāt'ĭd) *adj.*

ac·id (ăs'ĭd) *n.* **1.** *Chemistry.* **a.** Any of a large class of substances, the aqueous solutions of which are capable of turning litmus indicators red, of reacting with and dissolving certain metals to form salts, of reacting with bases or alkalis to form salts, or have a sour taste. **b.** A substance that ionizes in solution to give the positive ion of the solvent. **c.** A substance capable of giving up a proton. **d.** Any molecule or ion that can combine with another by forming a covalent bond with two electrons of the other. **2.** A substance having a sour taste. **3.** *Slang.* A hallucinogen, **LSD** *(see).* —*adj.* **1.** *Chemistry.* **a.** Of or pertaining to an acid. **b.** Having a high concentration of acid. **2.** Having a sour taste. **3.** Biting; ill-tempered; sharp; caustic: *an acid wit.* [Latin *acidus,* sharp, sour, from *acēre,* to be sour. See **ak-** in Appendix.*] —**ac'id·ly** *adv.* —**ac'id·ness** *n.*

ac·id-fast (ăs'ĭd-făst', -fäst') *adj.* Not readily decolorized by acid. Said of bacteria. —**ac'id-fast'ness** *n.*

a·cid·ic (ə-sĭd'ĭk) *adj.* **1.** Acid. **2.** Tending to form an acid.

a·cid·i·fy (ə-sĭd'ə-fī') *v.* **-fied, -fying, -fies.** —*tr.* To make acid. —*intr.* To become acid. —**a·cid'i·fi'a·ble** *adj.* —**a·cid'i·fi·ca'tion** *n.* —**a·cid'i·fi'er** *n.*

ac·i·dim·e·ter (ăs'ĭ-dĭm'ə-tər) *n.* A hydrometer used to determine the specific gravity of acid solutions. —**ac'i·di·met'ric** (-dĭ-mĕt'rĭk) *adj.* —**ac'i·dim'e·try** *n.*

a·cid·i·ty (ə-sĭd'ə-tē) *n.* **1.** The state or quality of being acid. **2.** *Medicine.* **Hyperacidity** *(see).*

ac·i·do·phil·ic (ăs'ĭ-dō-fĭl'ĭk) *adj.* Also **ac·i·doph·i·lus** (-dŏf'ə-ləs). *Microbiology.* **1.** Growing well in an acid medium. **2.** Easily stained with acid dyes. [ACID + -PHILE + -IC.] —**a·cid'o·phil'** (ə-sĭd'ə-fĭl'), **a·cid'o·phile'** (-fīl') *n.*

ac·i·doph·i·lus milk (ăs'ĭ-dŏf'ə-ləs). Milk containing bacterial cultures that thrive in dilute acid, often used in treating gastrointestinal disorders. [New Latin *acidophilus,* "acid-loving" : Latin *acidus,* ACID + -PHILOUS.]

ac·i·do·sis (ăs'ĭ-dō'sĭs) *n.* A condition of pathologically high acidity of the blood. —**ac'i·dot'ic** (ăs'ĭ-dŏt'ĭk) *adj.*

acid test. A decisive, critical test of worth or quality. [From the test of gold in nitric acid.]

a·cid·u·late (ə-sĭj'ōō-lāt') *v.* **-lated, -lating, -lates.** —*tr.* To make slightly acid. —*intr.* To become slightly acid. [ACIDUL(OUS) + -ATE.] —**a·cid'u·la'tion** *n.*

a·cid·u·lous (ə-sĭj'ōō-ləs) *adj.* Sour in feeling or manner; biting; caustic. [Latin *acidulus,* sourish, diminutive of *acidus,* sour, ACID.]

ac·i·nac·i·form (ăs'ĭ-năs'ə-fôrm') *adj. Botany.* Resembling a scimitar in shape: *acinaciform leaves.* [Latin *acinācēs,* short saber, from Greek *akinakēs,* from Iranian + -FORM.]

ac·i·nar (ăs'ĭ-nər) *adj. Anatomy.* Of or pertaining to an acinus.

a·cin·i·form (ə-sĭn'ə-fôrm') *adj.* Having the shape of a cluster of grapes or a berry such as the raspberry. [ACIN(US) + -FORM.]

ac·i·nous (ăs'ĭ-nəs) *adj.* Consisting of small lobules or acini.

ac·i·nus (ăs'ĭ-nəs) *n., pl.* **-ni** (-nī'). **1.** *Botany.* One of the small divisions or drupelets of an aggregate fruit such as the raspberry. **2.** A grape or a bunch of grapes. **3.** *Anatomy.* One of the small saclike dilations composing a compound gland. [New Latin, from Latin *acinus,* berry (especially a grape), probably of Mediterranean origin.] —**a·cin'ic** (ə-sĭn'ĭk) *adj.*

-acious. Indicates a tendency toward or abundance of something; for example, **fallacious.** [French *-acieux,* from Latin *-ācius* and *-āx* (stem *-āc-*), adjectival suffixes.]

-acity. Indicates a quality or state of being; for example, **tenacity.** [French *acité,* from Latin *-ācitās,* from *-āx* (stem *-āc-*), -ACIOUS.]

ack. acknowledgment.

ack-ack (ăk'ăk') *n. Military Slang.* **1.** An antiaircraft gun. **2.** Antiaircraft fire. [British telephonic code for *AA,* abbreviation for ANTIAIRCRAFT.]

Ack·ia Battleground National Monument (ăk'yä). The site, in northeastern Mississippi, of the Battle of Ackia (1736), in which Chickasaw Indians supported by the British defeated a combined force of French soldiers and Chocktaw Indians, thus opening the region to English settlement.

ac·knowl·edge (ăk-nŏl'ĭj) *tr.v.* **-edged, -edging, -edges. 1. a.** To confess, avow, or admit the existence, reality, or truth of: *"he that acknowledgeth the Son hath the Father also"* (I John 2:23). **b.** To recognize as being valid or having force or power. **2. a.** To express recognition of. **b.** To express thanks or gratitude for. **3.** To report the receipt of. **4.** *Law.* To accept or certify as legally binding: *acknowledge a deed.* [Middle English, blend of *acknowen,* to recognize, acknowledge, Old English *oncnāwan* : *on,* ON + *cnāwan,* to KNOW and KNOWLEDGE.] —**ac·knowl'edge·a·ble** *adj.*

Synonyms: *acknowledge, admit, own, avow, confess, concede.* These verbs mean to make a disclosure, sometimes with reluctance or under pressure. To *acknowledge* is to accept responsibility for something one makes known or to give recognition to someone. *Admit* usually implies marked reluctance in acknowledging one's acts or accepting a different point of view as a result of pressure. *Own* stresses personal acceptance of, and responsibility for, one's deeds. *Avow,* a strong term, means to assert openly and boldly and implies the likelihood of opposition. *Confess* usually emphasizes disclosure of wrongdoing. To *concede* is to yield to a claim or demand, often with some reluctance.

ac·knowl·edg·ment (ăk-nŏl'ĭj-mənt) *n.* Also **ac·knowl·edge·ment** *Abbr.* **ack. 1.** The act of admitting, or owning to something. **2.** Recognition of someone's or something's existence, validity, authority, or right. **3.** An answer or response in return for something done. **4.** An expression or token of appreciation or thanks. **5.** A formal declaration made to authoritative witnesses to ensure legal validity.

a·clin·ic (ā-klĭn'ĭk) *adj. Geology.* Having no inclination or dip. [From Greek *aklinēs,* not inclining to either side : *a-,* not + *klinein,* to lean (see **klei-** in Appendix*).]

aclinic line. The **magnetic equator** *(see).*

ac·me (ăk'mē) *n.* The point of utmost attainment; peak. See Synonyms at **summit.** [Greek *akmē,* point, summit. See **ak-** in Appendix.*]

ac·ne (ăk'nē) *n.* An inflammatory disease of the oil glands, characterized by pimples on the face. [New Latin, misreading of Greek *akmē,* eruption on the face, point, ACME.]

a·cock (ə-kŏk') *adj.* In a cocked position. —**a·cock'** *adv.*

ac·o·lyte (ăk'ə-līt') *n.* **1.** One who assists a priest in the celebration of Mass. **2.** An attendant or follower. [Middle English *acolite,* from Old French, from Medieval Latin *acolytus,* variant of *acoluthus,* from Greek *akolouthos,* follower, following. See **anacoluthon.**]

A·con·ca·gua (ä'kōn-kä'gwä). The highest mountain (22,835 feet) in the Western Hemisphere, in the Andes of Argentina near the Chilean border.

ac·o·nite (ăk'ə-nīt') *n.* **1.** Any plant of the genus *Aconitum;* the **monkshood** *(see).* **2.** The dried, poisonous root of a species of monkshood, *A. Napellus,* sometimes used in medicine to relieve pain or to reduce fever. [Latin *aconitum,* from Greek *akoniton,* possibly from *akonitos,* "dustless," unconquerable (with reference to the deadly properties of the plant) : *a-,* without + *-konitos,* "dusty," from *konien,* to raise dust, struggle, from *konis,* dust (see **keni-** in Appendix*).]

A·ço·res. The Portuguese name for the **Azores.**

a·corn (ā'kôrn, ā'kərn) *n.* The fruit of the oak tree, consisting of a thick-walled nut usually set in a woody, cuplike base. [Middle English, variant of *akern,* from Old English *æcern.* See **ōg-** in Appendix.*]

acorn squash. A type of squash shaped somewhat like an acorn and having a longitudinally ridged rind.

acorn tube. A small, acorn-shaped vacuum tube used in very high frequency devices. Also *chiefly British* "acorn valve."

a·cot·y·le·don (ā'kŏt-ə-lēd'n) *n. Botany.* A plant having no cotyledons, or seed leaves, such as a moss or fern. —**a'cot·y·le'don·ous** (-lēd'ə-nəs) *adj.*

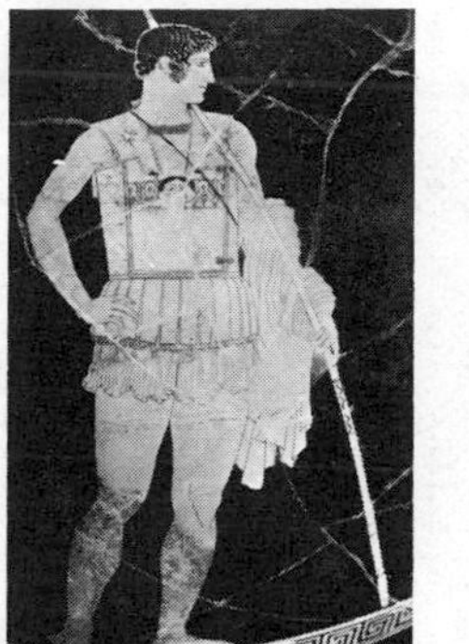

Achilles
Fifth-century B.C. vase painting

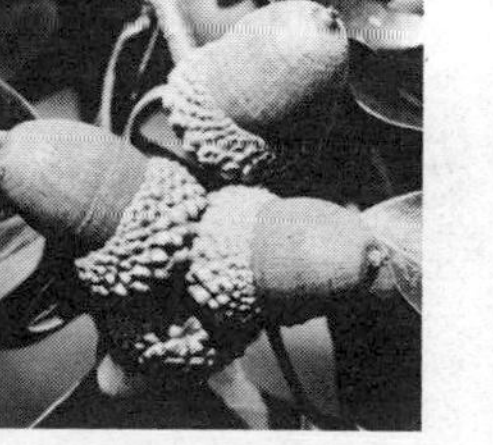

acorn
Acorns and leaves of the white oak

a·cous·tic (ə-ko͞o′stĭk) *adj.* Also **a·cous·ti·cal** (-stĭ-kəl). **1.** Of or pertaining to sound, the sense of hearing, or the science of sound. **2.** Designed to carry sound or to aid in hearing. [Greek *akoustikos,* pertaining to hearing, from *akouein,* to hear. See **keu-**[1] in Appendix.*] —**a·cous′ti·cal·ly** *adv.*

ac·ous·ti·cian (ă′ko͞o-stĭsh′ən) *n.* A specialist in acoustics.

acoustic nerve. The eighth cranial nerve, consisting of the *cochlear nerve,* which conducts acoustic stimuli to the brain, and the *vestibular nerve,* which conducts stimuli related to bodily equilibrium to the brain. Also called "auditory nerve."

a·cous·tics (ə-ko͞o′stĭks) *n.* **1.** The scientific study of sound, especially of its generation, propagation, perception, and interaction with materials and other forms of radiation. Used with a singular verb. **2.** The total effect of sound, especially as produced in an enclosed space. Used with a plural verb.

A.C.P. American College of Physicians.

acpt. acceptance.

ac·quaint (ə-kwānt′) *tr.v.* **-quainted, -quainting, -quaints. 1.** To make familiar. Used with *with* and used reflexively: *acquaint oneself with something.* **2.** To inform. Used with *with: acquaint someone with one's plans.* [Middle English *aqueynten, acointen,* from Old French *acointer,* from Medieval Latin *accognitāre,* from Latin *accognitus,* past participle of *accognōscere,* to know perfectly : *ad-* (intensive) + *cognōscere,* to know : *co-, com-,* completely + *gnōscere,* to know (see **gnō-** in Appendix*).]

ac·quain·tance (ə-kwān′təns) *n.* **1.** Knowledge or information about someone or something. **2.** Knowledge of a person acquired by a relationship less intimate than friendship. **3.** A person or persons whom one knows. —**ac·quain′tance·ship′** *n.*

ac·quaint·ed (ə-kwān′tĭd) *adj.* **1.** Known by or familiar with another. **2.** Informed; familiar: *acquainted with the facts.*

ac·qui·esce (ăk′wē-ĕs′) *intr.v.* **-esced, -escing, -esces.** To consent or comply passively or without protest. See Synonyms at **assent.** [Latin *acquiēscere,* to remain at rest, agree tacitly : *ad-,* at, to + *quiēscere,* to rest, from *quiēs,* rest (see **kweyə-** in Appendix*).]

Usage: *Acquiesce* is used with *in* when it takes a preposition: *to acquiesce in the ruling.*

ac·qui·es·cence (ăk′wē-ĕs′əns) *n.* **1.** Passive assent or agreement without protest. **2.** The state of being acquiescent. **3.** *Law.* Passive compliance, inaction, silence, or the like, construed as signifying acceptance or consent. —**ac′qui·es′cent** *adj.* —**ac′qui·es′cent·ly** *adv.*

ac·quire (ə-kwīr′) *tr.v.* **-quired, -quiring, -quires. 1.** To gain possession of. **2.** To get by one's own efforts. [Middle English *acqueren,* from Old French *acquerre,* from Latin *acquīrere,* to add to, get : *ad-,* in addition to + *quaerere,* to seek, obtain (see **quaerere** in Appendix*).]

ac·quire·ment (ə-kwīr′mənt) *n.* **1.** The act of acquiring. **2.** An attainment, as a skill or social accomplishment.

ac·qui·si·tion (ăk′wə-zĭsh′ən) *n.* **1.** The act of acquiring. **2.** Something acquired, especially as an addition to an established category or group. **3.** *Aerospace.* The process of locating a satellite, guided missile, or moving target so that its track or orbit can be determined. [Middle English *acquisicioun,* from Latin *acquīsītiō,* from *acquīrere,* ACQUIRE.]

ac·quis·i·tive (ə-kwĭz′ə-tĭv) *adj.* **1.** Grasping. **2.** Tending to acquire and retain ideas or information: *an acquisitive mind.* —**ac·quis′i·tive·ly** *adv.* —**ac·quis′i·tive·ness** *n.*

ac·quit (ə-kwĭt′) *tr.v.* **-quitted, -quitting, -quits. 1.** To free or clear from a charge or accusation. **2.** To release or discharge from duty or obligation. **3.** To repay (an obligation). **4.** To conduct (oneself). [Middle English *acquiten,* from Old French *aquiter,* from Vulgar Latin *acquitāre* (unattested), "to bring to rest," set free : *ad-,* to + *quitāre, quiētāre* (unattested), to put to rest, set free, from *quiēs,* quiet (see **kweyə-** in Appendix*).] —**ac·quit′ter** *n.*

ac·quit·tal (ə-kwĭt′l) *n. Law.* The judgment of a jury or judge that a person is not guilty of a crime as charged.

ac·quit·tance (ə-kwĭt′əns) *n.* A written release from an obligation.

a·cre (ā′kər) *n.* **1.** *Abbr.* **A., a., A.** A unit of area in the U.S. Customary System, used in land measurement and equal to 160 square rods, 4,840 square yards, or 43,560 square feet. See **measurement. 2.** *Plural.* Property in the form of land; estate. **3.** *Usually plural.* A wide expanse of land. **4.** *Archaic.* A field or plot of land. Now used only in the expression *God's acre* (a church graveyard). [Middle English *acre,* Old English *æcer,* field, acre. See **agro-** in Appendix.*]

A·cre (ä′kər, ā′kər, ä′krə *for sense 1;* ä′krə *for sense 2*). **1.** A seaport in northwestern Israel, the scene of much activity during the Crusades. **2.** A federal territory of Brazil, occupying 57,153 square miles in the northwest. Population, 160,000. Capital, Rio Branco.

Ac·re, Bay of (ä′kər, ā′kər, ä′krə). An inlet of the Mediterranean in northwestern Israel.

a·cre·age (ā′kər-ĭj, ā′krĭj) *n. Abbr.* **a. 1.** Area of land in acres. **2.** Acres collectively.

a·cred (ā′kərd) *adj.* Having or possessing many acres of land. Used chiefly in combination: *a many-acred estate.*

a·cre-foot (ā′kər-fo͝ot′) *n., pl.* **-feet** (-fēt′). The volume of water (43,560 cubic feet) that will cover an area of one acre to a depth of one foot.

a·cre-inch (ā′kər-ĭnch′) *n.* One-twelfth of an acre-foot, or 3,630 cubic feet.

ac·rid (ăk′rĭd) *adj.* **1.** Harsh to the taste or smell. **2.** Caustic in language or tone. [From Latin *ācer* (stem *ācr-*), sharp, bitter (probably influenced by ACID). See **ak-** in Appendix.*] —**a·crid′i·ty** (ə-krĭd′ə-tē), **ac′rid·ness** *n.* —**ac′rid·ly** *adv.*

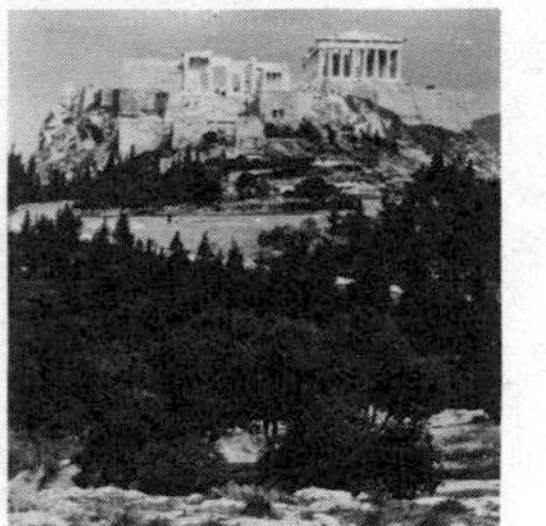

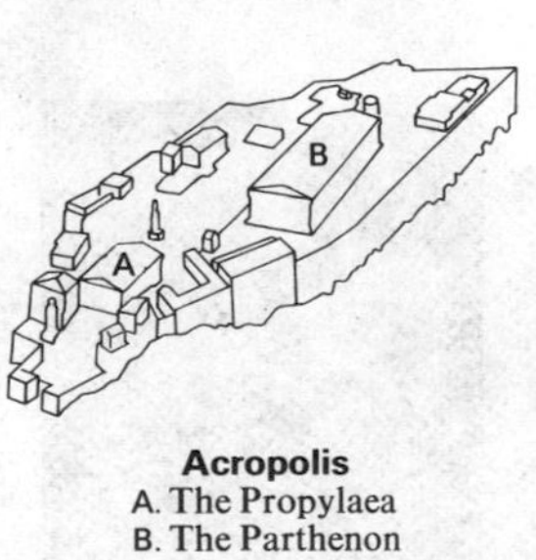

Acropolis
A. The Propylaea
B. The Parthenon

ac·ri·dine (ăk′rĭ-dēn′, -dĭn) *n.* A coal tar derivative, $C_{13}H_9N$, that has a strongly irritating odor and is used in the manufacture of dyes and synthetics. [ACRID + -INE.]

ac·ri·fla·vine (ăk′rĭ-flā′vēn′) *n.* A brown or orange powder, $C_{14}H_{14}N_3Cl$, derived from acridine and used as an antiseptic. [ACRI(DINE) + FLAVIN.]

ac·ri·mo·ni·ous (ăk′rə-mō′nē-əs) *adj.* Bitter in language or tone; rancorous. —**ac′ri·mo′ni·ous·ly** *adv.* —**ac′ri·mo′ni·ous·ness** *n.*

ac·ri·mo·ny (ăk′rə-mō′nē) *n.* Bitterness or ill-natured animosity, especially in speech or manner. [Latin *ācrimōnia,* sharpness, from *ācer,* sharp. See **ak-** in Appendix.*]

acro–. Indicates: **1.** A height or summit; for example, **acrophobia. 2.** An outer end, tip, or point; for example, **acrogen. 3.** An extremity of the body; for example, **acromegaly.** [From Greek *akros,* topmost, extreme. See **ak-** in Appendix.*]

ac·ro·bat (ăk′rə-băt′) *n.* **1.** One skilled in feats of agility and balance. **2.** One adept at quick changes of position. [French *acrobate,* from Greek *akrobatēs,* "one who walks on tiptoe," from *akrobatein,* to walk on tiptoe : ACRO- + *bat-,* stem of *bainein,* to walk (see **gwā-** in Appendix*).] —**ac′ro·bat′ic** *adj.* —**ac′ro·bat′i·cal·ly** *adv.*

ac·ro·bat·ics (ăk′rə-băt′ĭks) *pl.n.* **1.** The evolutions of an acrobat. **2.** The art of an acrobat. Used with a singular verb. **3.** Any manifestation of spectacular agility.

ac·ro·car·pous (ăk′rō-kär′pəs) *adj. Botany.* Having the spore-bearing capsule at the end or top of a leafy stem or stalk, as in many mosses. [New Latin *acrocarpus,* from Greek *akrokarpos,* bearing fruit at the top : ACRO- + -CARPOUS.]

ac·ro·dont (ăk′rə-dŏnt′) *adj. Zoology.* Having or designating teeth that lack roots and are fused to the bony ridge of the jaw, as in certain reptiles. [ACR(O)- + -ODONT.]

ac·ro·drome (ăk′rə-drōm′) *adj.* Also **a·crod·ro·mous** (ə-krŏd′rə-məs). Coming to a point and having the veins terminate at the tip. Said of leaves. [ACRO- + -DROME.]

ac·ro·gen (ăk′rə-jən) *n.* A flowerless plant, such as a fern or moss, having a stem from the tip of which all growth proceeds. [ACRO- + -GEN.] —**ac′ro·gen′ic** (ăk′rə-jĕn′ĭk), **a·crog′e·nous** (ə-krŏj′ə-nəs) *adj.* —**a·crog′e·nous·ly** *adv.*

a·cro·le·in (ə-krō′lē-ĭn) *n.* A colorless, flammable, poisonous liquid, CH_2CHCHO, having an acrid odor and vapors dangerous to the eyes. [ACR(ID) + OLEIN.]

ac·ro·me·gal·ic (ăk′rō-mĭ-găl′ĭk) *adj.* Exhibiting symptoms of acromegaly. —*n.* A person afflicted with acromegaly.

ac·ro·meg·a·ly (ăk′rō-mĕg′ə-lē) *n.* Pathological enlargement of the bones of the hands, feet, and face, resulting from chronic overactivity of the pituitary gland. [French *acromégalie,* "enlargement of extremities" : ACRO- + Greek *megal-,* stem of *megas,* big (see **meg-** in Appendix*).]

ac·ro·nym (ăk′rə-nĭm′) *n.* A word formed from the initial letters of a name, as *WAC* for *W*omen's *A*rmy *C*orps, or by combining initial letters or parts of a series of words, as *radar* for *ra*dio *d*etecting *a*nd *r*anging. [ACR(O)- + -ONYM.] —**ac′ro·nym′ic, a·cron′y·mous** (ə-krŏn′ə-məs) *adj.*

a·crop·e·tal (ə-krŏp′ə-təl) *adj. Botany.* Developing upward toward the apex from the base, as certain forms of inflorescence do. [ACRO- + -PETAL.] —**a·crop′e·tal·ly** *adv.*

ac·ro·pho·bi·a (ăk′rə-fō′bē-ə) *n.* Abnormally intense fear of being in high places. [ACRO- + -PHOBIA.]

a·crop·o·lis (ə-krŏp′ə-lĭs) *n.* **1.** The fortified height or citadel of an ancient Greek city. **2.** *Capital* **A.** The citadel of Athens. [Greek *akropolis,* "upper city," citadel : ACRO- + *polis,* city (see **pele-**[2] in Appendix*).]

ac·ro·spire (ăk′rə-spīr′) *n. Botany.* The first sprout from a germinating grain seed. [Variant (influenced by ACRO-) of dialectal *akerspire,* "ear-sprout" : *aker,* ear of grain, ultimately from Old English *æhher, ēar* (see **ak-** in Appendix*) + Middle English *spire,* Old English *spīr* (see **spei-** in Appendix*).]

a·cross (ə-krôs′, ə-krŏs′) *prep.* **1.** On, at, or from the other side of: *across the road.* **2.** So as to cross; over; through: *draw lines across the paper.* **3.** From one side of to the other: *a bridge across a river.* —*adv.* **1.** From one side to the other: *The bridge swayed when he ran across.* **2.** On or to the opposite side: *We came across by ferry.* **3.** Crossed; crosswise: *with arms across.* [Middle English *acros, on croice,* from Old French *a croix, en croix,* "in the form of a CROSS," hence "transversely."]

a·cross-the-board (ə-krôs′thə-bôrd′, -bōrd′, ə-krŏs′-) *adj.* **1.** Designating a racing wager whereby equal amounts are bet on the same contestant to win, place, or show. **2.** Including all categories or members, especially in an occupation or industry: *an across-the-board wage increase.*

a·cros·tic (ə-krôs′tĭk, ə-krŏs′-) *n.* **1.** A poem or series of lines in which certain letters, usually the first in each line, form a name, motto, or message read in sequence. **2.** A **word square** *(see).* [French *acrostiche,* from Old French, from Greek *akrostikhis,* "end-line" : ACRO- + *stikhos,* line of verse (see **steigh-** in Appendix*).] —**a·cros′tic** *adj.* —**a·cros′ti·cal·ly** *adv.*

ac·ry·late resin (ăk′rĭ-lāt′). Any of a class of acrylic resins used in emulsion paints, adhesives, plastics, and textile and paper finishes. Also called "acrylate."

a·cryl·ic acid (ə-krĭl′ĭk). An easily polymerized, colorless, corrosive liquid, $H_2C{:}CHCOOH$, used as a monomer for acrylate resins. [ACR(OLEIN) + -YL + -IC.]

acrylic fiber. Any of numerous synthetic fibers polymerized from acrylonitrile.

acrylic resin. Any of numerous thermoplastic or thermosetting polymers or copolymers of acrylic acid, methacrylic acid, esters of these acids, or acrylonitrile, used to produce synthetic rubbers, exceptionally clear, lightweight plastics resistant to weath-

ă pat/ā pay/âr care/ä father/b bib/ch church/d deed/ĕ pet/ē be/f fife/g gag/h hat/hw which/ĭ pit/ī pie/îr pier/j judge/k kick/l lid, needle/m mum/n no, sudden/ng thing/ŏ pot/ō toe/ô paw, for/oi noise/ou out/o͝o took/o͞o boot/p pop/r roar/s sauce/sh ship, dish/

er and corrosion, and other resin forms for many manufactured products including aircraft canopies and windows, contact lenses, refrigerator parts, protective coatings, and lubricant additives. Also called "acrylic."

ac·ry·lo·ni·trile (ăk′rĭ-lō-nī′trəl) *n.* A colorless, liquid organic compound, $H_2C{:}CHCN$, used in the manufacture of acrylic rubber and fibers. [ACRYL(IC RESIN) + NITRILE.]

A.C.S. **1.** American Chemical Society. **2.** American College of Surgeons.

act (ăkt) *n.* **1.** The process of doing or performing something; an action: *the act of thinking.* **2.** Something that is done or performed; a deed: *a charitable act.* See Usage note below. **3.** An enactment, edict, or decree, as of a judicial or legislative body. **4.** A formal written record of proceedings or transactions. **5.** One of the major divisions or sections of a play, drama, or opera. **6.** A theatrical performance that forms part of a longer presentation, as in vaudeville or a revue: *a juggling act.* **7.** *Informal.* A manifestation of intentional or unintentional insincerity; a pose: *put on an act.* —*v.* **acted, acting, acts.** —*tr.* **1.** To play the part of; assume the dramatic role of. **2.** To perform on the stage: *act a drama.* **3.** To behave like or pose as; impersonate: *act the fool.* **4.** To behave as suitable for: *Act your age.* **5.** *Obsolete.* To actuate; motivate. —*intr.* **1.** To behave or comport oneself: *She acts like a lady.* **2. a.** To perform in a dramatic role or roles; be an actor. **b.** To be suitable for theatrical performance: *This scene acts well.* **3.** To behave affectedly or unnaturally; pretend. **4.** To appear or seem to be: *The dog acts friendly.* **5.** To carry out an action; do something: *She acted immediately.* **6.** To operate or function in a specific way: *His mind acts quickly.* **7.** To serve or function as a substitute for someone or something: *A coin can act as a screwdriver.* —**act on** (or **upon**). **1.** To act according to: *He acted on my advice.* **2.** To produce an effect on. —**act out.** To enact; dramatize. —**act up.** *Informal.* To misbehave or malfunction. [Middle English *acte,* from Latin *āctus,* the process of action, and *āctum,* a thing done, both from *āctus,* past participle of *agere,* to drive, to do. See **ag-** in Appendix*.] —**ac′ta·bil′i·ty** *n.* —**act′a·ble** *adj.*

Usage: *Act* (noun) and *action* are sometimes interchangeable. *Act,* however, emphasizes what is done, rather than the process of doing, and is especially applicable to a specific, brief deed or performance by an individual. *Action* is the choice when process or function are stressed, and when performance is complex or long-range: *the action of machinery* or *of a chemical; one's actions* or *action* (that is, *acts* considered collectively or as a chain of events).

A.C.T. Australian Capital Territory.

Ac·tae·on (ăk-tē′ən). *Greek Mythology.* A young hunter who, having inadvertently observed Artemis while she was bathing, was turned by her into a stag and killed by his own dogs.

actg. acting.

ACTH A pituitary hormone synthesized or extracted from mammalian pituitaries for use in stimulating secretion of cortisone and other adrenal cortex hormones. Also called "corticotropin." [A(DRENO)C(ORTICO)T(ROPIC) H(ORMONE).]

ac·tin (ăk′tĭn) *n.* A muscle protein, active with myosin in muscular contraction. [Latin *āctus,* an ACT + -IN.]

ac·ti·nal (ăk′tĭ-nəl, ăk-tī′-) *adj. Zoology.* Of or designating the part of a sea anemone or similar animal from which the tentacles or rays radiate. [ACTIN(O)- + -AL.] —**ac′ti·nal·ly** *adv.*

act·ing (ăk′tĭng) *adj.* **1.** *Abbr.* **actg., a.** Temporarily assuming the duties or authority of another. **2.** Functioning; operating; working. **3.** Containing directions for use in a dramatic performance. —*n.* **1.** The occupation of an actor. **2.** Performance as an actor. **3.** Simulated behavior; pretense.

ac·tin·i·a (ăk-tĭn′ē-ə) *n., pl.* **-iae** (-ē-ē′). Also **ac·tin·i·an** (-ən). A sea anemone, or a related animal. [New Latin *actinia,* "the radially-structured ones," from Greek *aktis* (stem *aktin-*), ray. See **nekwt-** in Appendix.*]

ac·tin·ic (ăk-tĭn′ĭk) *adj.* Of or pertaining to actinism. [ACTIN(O)- + -IC.] —**ac·tin′i·cal·ly** *adv.*

actinic ray. Photochemically active radiation, as of the sun.

ac·ti·nide (ăk′tĭ-nīd′) *n.* Any of a series of chemically similar, mostly synthetic, radioactive elements with atomic numbers ranging from 89 (actinium) through 103 (lawrencium). Also called "actinoid." See **element.** [ACTIN(O)- + -IDE.]

ac·ti·nism (ăk′tĭn-ĭz′əm) *n. Rare.* The intrinsic property in radiation that produces photochemical activity. [ACTIN(O)- + -ISM.]

ac·tin·i·um (ăk-tĭn′ē-əm) *n. Symbol* **Ac** A radioactive element found in uranium ores and used, in equilibrium with its decay products, as a source of alpha rays. Its longest lived isotope is Ac 227 with a half-life of 21.7 years. Atomic number 89, melting point 1,050°C, boiling point (estimated) 3,200°C, specific gravity (calculated) 10.07, valence 3. See **element.** [New Latin : ACTIN(O)- + -IUM.]

actino-, actin-. Indicates: **1.** Radial or tentacled structure; for example, **actinoid. 2.** Radiation or radioactivity; for example, **actinometer.** [New Latin, from Greek *aktis* (stem *aktin-*), ray. See **nekwt-** in Appendix.*]

ac·ti·noid[1] (ăk′tĭ-noid′) *adj.* Having a radial form, as a starfish. [ACTIN(O)- + -OID.]

ac·ti·noid[2] (ăk′tĭ-noid′) *n. Chemistry.* An **actinide** *(see).* [ACTIN(O)- + -OID.]

ac·tin·o·lite (ăk-tĭn′ə-līt′) *n. Mineralogy.* A greenish variety of **amphibole** *(see).* [ACTINO- (from its radiated forms) + -LITE.]

ac·ti·nom·e·ter (ăk′tĭ-nŏm′ə-tər) *n.* Any of several radiometric instruments, such as a pyrheliometer, used chiefly for meteorological measurements of terrestrial and solar radiation. [ACTINO- + -METER.] —**ac′ti·no·met′ric** (-nō-mĕt′rĭk), **ac′ti·no·met′ri·cal** *adj.* —**ac′ti·nom′e·try** *n.*

ac·ti·no·mor·phic (ăk′tĭ-nō-môr′fĭk) *adj.* Also **ac·ti·no·mor·phous** (-fəs). *Biology.* Having radial symmetry; divisible vertically through two or more planes into similar halves. [ACTINO- + -MORPHIC.]

ac·ti·no·my·cete (ăk′tĭ-nō-mī′sēt′) *n.* Any of numerous generally filamentous and often pathogenic microorganisms of the family Actinomycetaceae, resembling both bacteria and fungi. [ACTINO- + -MYCETE.]

ac·ti·no·my·cin (ăk′tĭ-nō-mī′sĭn) *n.* Any of various often toxic antibiotic substances found in soil bacteria. [From New Latin *Actinomyces,* a genus of soil bacteria : ACTINO- + Greek *mukēs,* fungus (see **-mycete**).]

ac·ti·no·my·co·sis (ăk′tĭ-nō-mī′kō′sĭs) *n.* An inflammatory infection of cattle, hogs, and sometimes man, caused by microorganisms of the genus *Actinomyces,* and characterized by lumpy tumors of the neck, chest, and abdomen. Also called "lumpy jaw." [ACTINO- + MYCOSIS.] —**ac′ti·no·my·cot′ic** (ăk′tĭ-nō-mī-kŏt′ĭk) *adj.*

ac·ti·non (ăk′tĭ-nŏn′) *n. Symbol* **An** A radioactive inert gaseous isotope of radon, with a half-life of 3.92 seconds. [ACTIN(O)- + -ON.]

ac·ti·no·u·ra·ni·um (ăk′tĭ-nō-yŏŏ-rā′nē-əm) *n.* The isotope of uranium with mass number 235, fissionable with slow neutrons.

ac·ti·no·zo·an (ăk′tĭ-nō-zō′ən) *n. Zoology.* An **anthozoan** *(see).* [From New Latin *actinozoa,* "the radiated life-forms" : ACTINO- + -ZOA.]

ac·tion (ăk′shən) *n.* **1.** The state or process of acting or doing; condition of being active. **2.** An act or deed. **3.** A movement or a series of movements. **4.** The manner of movement: *a horse with good action.* **5.** Activity; energy. **6.** *Plural.* Behavior or conduct: *Actions speak louder than words.* **7.** The transmission of energy, force, or influence. **8.** The operating parts of a mechanism: *the action of a gun.* **9.** Any change that occurs in the body or in a bodily organ as a result of its functioning. **10.** The series of events and episodes that form the plot of a story or play. **11.** The appearance of animation of a figure in painting or sculpture. **12.** *Law.* **a.** A judicial process; lawsuit. **b.** The right of an individual to exercise his privilege to legal process. **13.** Armed encounter; combat: *troops sent into action.* —See Usage note at **act.**

ac·tion·a·ble (ăk′shən-ə-bəl) *adj.* Giving just cause for legal action. —**ac′tion·a·bly** *adv.*

action painting. A school of nonrepresentational painting that exploits the element of chance by such techniques as dribbling and splattering, often evoking dynamism through the interlaced directions of pigment impact. —**action painter.**

Ac·ti·um (ăk′tē-əm, ăk′shē-əm). A promontory and town of ancient Greece, located opposite modern Preveza; site of the naval victory by Octavian's forces under Agrippa over those of Mark Antony and Cleopatra (31 B.C.).

ac·ti·vate (ăk′tə-vāt′) *tr.v.* **-vated, -vating, -vates. 1.** To set in motion; make active. **2.** To create or organize (a military unit or post, for example). **3.** To purify (sewage) by aeration. **4.** *Chemistry.* To accelerate a reaction in, as by heat. **5.** *Physics.* To cause radiation. —**ac′ti·va′tion** *n.* —**ac′ti·va′tor** (-tər) *n.*

activated carbon. Highly absorbent carbon obtained by heating granulated charcoal to exhaust contained gases, used in gas absorption, solvent recovery, or deodorization, and as an antidote to certain poisons. Also called "activated charcoal."

ac·tive (ăk′tĭv) *adj.* **1.** In action; moving. **2.** Capable of functioning. **3.** Causing or initiating action or change. **4.** Engaged in activity; contributing; participating: *an active member of a club.* **5.** In a state of action; not passive or quiescent: *an active volcano.* **6.** Characterized by energetic action or activity; busy. **7. a.** Denoting a verb inflection or voice indicating that the subject of the sentence is performing or causing the action expressed by the verb. In the sentence *John bought a book, bought* is in the active voice. Compare **passive. b.** Expressing action rather than a state of being. Said of verbs such as *run, speak, move.* **8.** Producing profit, interest, or dividends: *active accounts.* **9.** *Military.* On full duty and full pay. —*n.* **1. a.** The active voice. **b.** A construction or form in the active voice. **2.** A participating member of an organization. [Middle English, from Old French *actif,* from Latin *āctīvus,* from *āctus,* to drive, ACT.] —**ac′tive·ly** *adv.* —**ac′tive·ness** *n.*

Synonyms: *active, energetic, dynamic, vigorous, lively.* These adjectives are compared as they qualify human activity. *Active* suggests a moving to and fro with little rest; *energetic,* sustained enthusiastic action with unflagging strength; and *dynamic,* exemplary forcefulness of activity inspiring to others. *Vigorous* implies manly capacity to act with healthy strength and firmness, while *lively* suggests brisk alertness and energy.

ac·tiv·ism (ăk′tĭv-ĭz′əm) *n.* A theory or practice based on militant action. —**ac′tiv·ist** *n.*

ac·tiv·i·ty (ăk-tĭv′ə-tē) *n., pl.* **-ties. 1.** The state or condition of being active. **2.** Energetic action or movement. **3.** A specified form of supervised action or field of action, especially one in the area of recreation. **4.** The intensity of a radioactive source.

act of God. *Law.* An unforeseeable or inevitable occurrence, such as a tornado, caused by nature and not by man.

ac·to·my·o·sin (ăk′tō-mī′ə-sĭn) *n.* A system of actin and myosin that with other substances constitutes muscle fiber and is responsible for muscular contraction and expansion. [ACT(IN) + MYOSIN.]

Ac·ton (ăk′tən). A former administrative division of London, England, now part of **Ealing** *(see).*

ac·tor (ăk′tər) *n.* **1.** A theatrical performer. **2.** One who takes

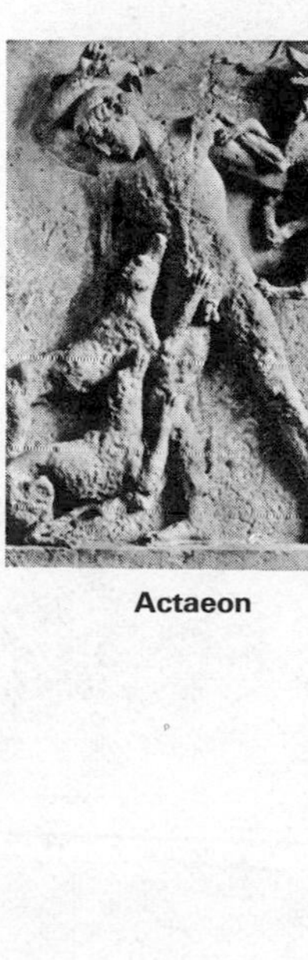

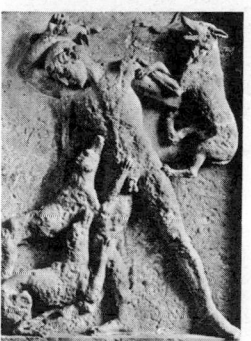

Actaeon

part; participant. —**bad actor.** *Slang.* An undesirable person. [Middle English, from Latin *āctor,* "a doer," from *āctus,* ACT.]

ac·tress (ăk′trĭs) *n.* A female theatrical performer.

Acts of the Apostles. The fifth book of the New Testament. Also called "Acts."

ac·tu·al (ăk′cho͞o-əl) *adj.* **1.** In existence; real; factual. **2.** Being, existing, or acting at the present moment. —See Synonyms at **real.** [Middle English *actuel,* from Old French, from Late Latin *āctuālis,* "pertaining to acts," from Latin *āctus,* an ACT.] —**ac′tu·al·ly** *adv.*

ac·tu·al·i·ty (ăk′cho͞o-ăl′ə-tē) *n., pl.* **-ties. 1.** The state or fact of being actual; reality. **2.** *Plural.* Actual conditions or facts.

ac·tu·al·ize (ăk′cho͞o-əl-īz′) *tr.v.* **-ized, -izing, -izes. 1.** To realize in action. **2.** To describe or portray realistically. —**ac′tu·al·i·za′tion** *n.*

ac·tu·ar·y (ăk′cho͞o-ĕr′ē) *n., pl.* **-ies.** A statistician who computes insurance risks and premiums. [Latin *āctuārius,* secretary of accounts, from *āctus,* public employment, state business, the process of action, ACT.]

ac·tu·ate (ăk′cho͞o-āt′) *tr.v.* **-ated, -ating, -ates. 1.** To put into action or motion: *actuate a mechanism.* **2.** To move to action. [Medieval Latin *āctuāre,* from Latin *āctus,* an ACT.] —**ac′tu·a′tion** *n.* —**ac′tu·a′tor** (-ā′tər) *n.*

ac·u·ate (ăk′yo͞o-ĭt, -āt′) *adj.* Pointed at the end; sharpened. [Middle English *acuat,* from Medieval Latin *acuātus,* from *acus,* needle. See **ak-** in Appendix.*]

a·cu·i·ty (ə-kyo͞o′ə-tē) *n.* Keenness; sharpness; acuteness: *visual acuity.* [Middle English *acuitie,* from Medieval Latin *acuitās,* from Latin *acuere,* to sharpen, from *acus,* needle. See **ak-** in Appendix.*]

a·cu·le·ate (ə-kyo͞o′lē-ĭt, -āt′) *adj. Biology.* Having a sting or prickles. [Latin *aculeātus,* from *aculeus,* diminutive of *acus,* needle, sting. See **acuity.**]

a·cu·men (ə-kyo͞o′mən) *n.* Quickness and accuracy of judgment; keenness of insight. [Latin *acūmen,* (mental) sharpness, from *acuere,* to sharpen, from *acus,* needle. See **ak-** in Appendix.*]

a·cu·mi·nate (ə-kyo͞o′mə-nĭt, -nāt′) *adj. Biology.* Tapering to a sharp point: *acuminate leaves.* —*tr.v.* (ə-kyo͞o′mə-nāt′) **acuminated, -nating, -nates.** To sharpen or taper. [Latin *acūminātus,* past participle of *acūmināre,* to sharpen, from *acūmen,* sharpness, ACUMEN.] —**a·cu′mi·na′tion** *n.*

ac·u·punc·ture (ăk′yo͞o-pŭngk′chər) *n.* A traditional Chinese therapeutic technique whereby the body is punctured with fine needles. [Latin *acū,* with a needle, from *acus,* needle (see **acuity**) + PUNCTURE.]

a·cute (ə-kyo͞ot′) *adj.* **1.** Having a sharp point or tip; not blunt. **2.** Keenly perceptive or discerning; shrewd; penetrating. **3.** Reacting readily to impressions; sensitive. **4.** Of great importance or consequence; crucial. **5.** Extremely severe or sharp; intense: *acute pain.* **6.** *Medicine.* Reaching a crisis rapidly. Said of a disease. Compare **chronic. 7.** *Music.* High in pitch; shrill. **8.** *Geometry.* Designating angles less than 90 degrees. —See Synonyms at **critical, sharp.** [Latin *acūtus,* sharp, from the past participle of *acuere,* to sharpen, from *acus,* needle. See **ak-** in Appendix.*] —**a·cute′ly** *adv.* —**a·cute′ness** *n.*

acute accent. A mark (´) indicating: **a.** A raised pitch, in certain languages such as Chinese and Ancient Greek. **b.** Primary stress of a spoken sound or syllable. **c.** Metrical stress in poetry. **d.** Sound quality or vowel length.

a·cy·clic (ā-sī′klĭk, ā-sĭk′lĭk) *adj.* **1.** *Botany.* Not having or forming whorls; not cyclic. **2.** *Chemistry.* Having an open-chain molecular structure rather than a ring-shaped structure.

ac·yl (ăs′əl) *n. Chemistry.* Any radical having the general formula RCO-, derived from an organic acid. [AC(ID) + -YL.]

ad[1] (ăd) *n. Informal.* An **advertisement** *(see).*

ad[2] (ăd) *n. Tennis.* An **advantage** *(see).*

ad-. Indicates motion toward; for example, **adsorb.** [Latin, from *ad,* to, toward, at. See **ad-** in Appendix.* In borrowed Latin compounds *ad-* indicates: 1. Motion toward, as in **advent.** 2. Proximity, as in **adjacent.** 3. Addition, increase, as in **accrue.** 4. Relationship, dependence, as in **adjunct.** 5. Intensified action, as in **accelerate.** Before *c, f, g, l, n, q, r, s,* and *t, ad-* is assimilated to *ac-, af-, ag-, al-, an-, acq-, ar-, as-,* and *at-;* before *sc, sp, st,* and *gn,* it is reduced to *a-.*]

-ad. *Biology.* Indicates direction toward; for example, **dorsad.** [Coined from Latin *ad,* toward. See **ad-** in Appendix.*]

ad. 1. adapter. **2.** advertisement.

A.D. 1. active duty. **2.** anno Domini (usually small capitals A.D.). See Usage note at **anno Domini.**

A·da (ā′də). A feminine given name. [Originally a pet form of ADELA, ADELAIDE; subsequently also representing Hebrew *Adah,* "adornment," "beauty."]

A.D.A. 1. American Dental Association. **2.** Americans for Democratic Action.

ad·age (ăd′ĭj) *n.* A short maxim or proverb. See Synonyms at **saying.** [French, from Old French, from Latin *adagium,* proverb. See **ēg-** in Appendix.*]

Usage: Adjectives such as *old, ancient,* and *time-tested* are redundant as modifiers of *adage.*

a·da·gio (ə-dä′jō, -jē-ō′) *adv. Music.* Slowly. Used as a direction. —*adj. Music.* Slow in tempo; slower than andante. —*n., pl.* **adagios. 1.** *Music.* A composition or movement played in this tempo. **2.** A section of a pas de deux, in which the ballerina and her partner perform steps requiring lyricism and great skill in lifting, balancing, and turning. [Italian *adagio,* "at ease" : *ad-,* at, from Latin, at, toward + *agio,* ease, from Old Provençal *aize,* from Vulgar Latin *adjacēs* (unattested), variant of Latin *adjacēns,* convenient, ADJACENT.]

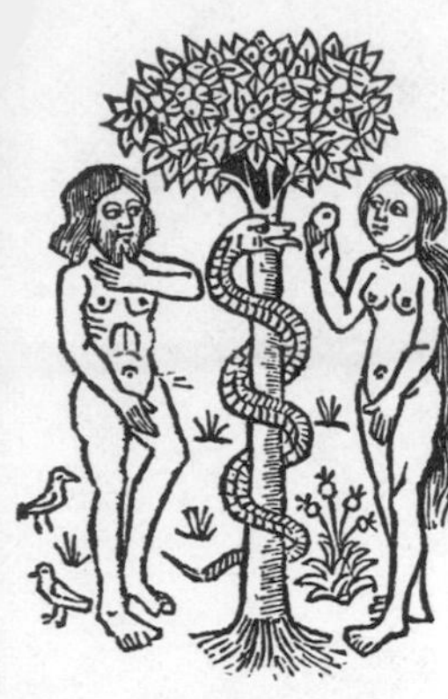

Adam[2]
Early 16th-century illustration of Adam and Eve being tempted by the serpent

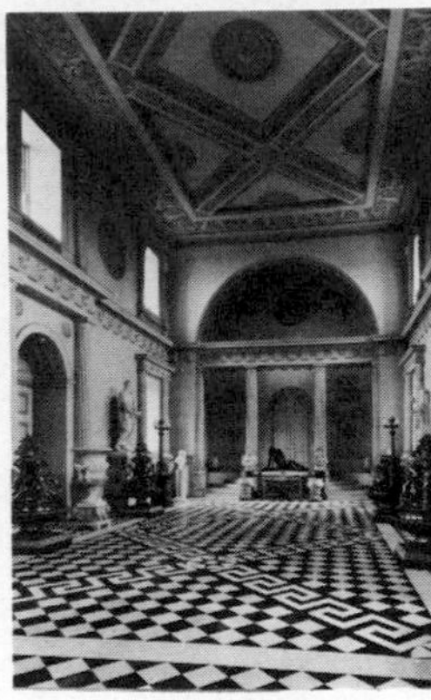

Adam[3]
Entrance hall of a British mansion designed by Robert Adam

A·dak (ā′dăk′). An island in the Andreanof group of islands in the Aleutians, site of important U.S. bases in World War II.

A·dal·ia. The former name for **Antalya.**

Ad·am[1] (ăd′əm). A masculine given name. [Late Latin, from Hebrew *'ādhām,* "man," from *'adhāmāh,* earth.]

Ad·am[2] (ăd′əm). **1.** The first man and progenitor of mankind. Genesis 2:7. **2.** The unregenerate side of human nature: *the old Adam.* —**A·dam′ic** (ə-dăm′ĭk) *adj.*

Ad·am[3] (ăd′əm) *adj.* Of or pertaining to the neoclassic style of furniture and architecture originated by Robert and James Adam.

Ad·am (ăd′əm), **Robert.** 1728–1792. British architect and furniture designer with his brother, **James** (1730–1794).

Ad·am-and-Eve (ăd′əm-ənd-ēv′) *n.* A plant, the **puttyroot** *(see).* [So called because the corms resemble human bodies.]

ad·a·mant (ăd′ə-mənt, -mănt′) *n.* **1.** A stone believed to be impenetrable. **2.** An extremely hard substance. —*adj.* **1.** Firm in purpose or opinion; unyielding. **2.** Adamantine. —See Synonyms at **inflexible.** [Middle English *adama(u)nt,* diamond, magnet, from Old French *adamaunt,* from Latin *adamās* (stem *adamant-*), from Greek *adamas,* hard metal, steel, diamond, possibly, "unbreakable" : *a-* not + *daman,* to tame, break down (see **deme-**[2] in Appendix*).]

ad·a·man·tine (ăd′ə-măn′tēn′, -tīn, -tĭn′) *adj.* **1.** Made of or resembling adamant. **2.** Having the hardness or luster of a diamond. **3.** Unyielding; inflexible.

Ad·am·ite (ăd′əm-īt′) *adj.* Descended from Adam. —*n.* **1.** A descendant of Adam; human being. **2.** *Rare.* A nudist.

Ad·ams (ăd′əmz), **Abigail (Smith).** 1744–1818. American writer of letters; wife of John Adams.

Ad·ams (ăd′əmz), **Charles Francis.** 1807–1886. American diplomat, lawyer, and political figure; son of John Quincy Adams.

Ad·ams (ăd′əmz), **Franklin Pierce.** Called "F.P.A." 1881–1960. American journalist, columnist, and author.

Ad·ams (ăd′əmz), **Henry Brooks.** 1838–1918. American historian and philosopher; son of Charles Francis Adams.

Ad·ams (ăd′əmz), **John.** 1735–1826. Second President of the United States (1797–1801).

Ad·ams (ăd′əmz), **John Quincy.** 1767–1848. Sixth President of the United States (1825–29); son of John Adams.

Ad·ams, Mount (ăd′əmz). **1.** A mountain, 12,470 feet high, in the Cascade Range of southern Washington. **2.** A mountain rising to 5,800 feet in the White Mountains of New Hampshire.

Ad·ams (ăd′əmz), **Samuel.** 1722–1803. American propagandist, political figure, and revolutionary leader.

Adam's apple. The projection of the largest laryngeal cartilage at the front of the throat, especially in men. [Translation of Hebrew *tappūah hāādām.*]

ad·ams·ite (ăd′əmz-īt′) *n. Symbol* **DM** A yellow crystalline compound, $(C_6H_4)_2(NH)AsCl$, used dispersed in air as a poison gas. [After Roger *Adams* (born 1889), American chemist.]

Adam's needle. A plant, the **Spanish bayonet** *(see).* [From the spines on its leaves and with allusion to Genesis 3:7.]

A·da·na (ä′də-nä′). A city and cotton-exporting center in southeastern Turkey on the Seyhan River. Population, 232,000.

a·dapt (ə-dăpt′) *v.* **adapted, adapting, adapts.** —*tr.* To adjust to a specified use or situation. —*intr.* To become adapted. [Latin *adaptāre,* to fit to : *ad-* to + *aptāre,* to fit, from *aptus,* APT.]

a·dapt·a·ble (ə-dăp′tə-bəl) *adj.* Capable of adapting or of being adapted. See Synonyms at **flexible.** —**a·dapt′a·bil′i·ty, a·dapt′a·ble·ness** *n.*

ad·ap·ta·tion (ăd′ăp-tā′shən) *n.* Also **a·dap·tion** (ə-dăp′shən). **1. a.** The state of being adapted. **b.** The act or process of adapting. **2.** Anything that is changed or changes so as to become suitable to a new or special use or situation. **3.** An alteration or adjustment, often hereditary, by which a species or individual improves its condition in relationship to its environment. **4.** The responsive alteration of a sense organ to repeated stimuli. **5.** Change in behavior of an individual or group in adjustment to new or modified cultural surroundings. —**ad′ap·ta′tion·al** *adj.* —**ad′ap·ta′tion·al·ly** *adv.*

a·dapt·er (ə-dăp′tər) *n.* Also **a·dap·tor.** *Abbr.* **ad. 1.** One that adapts. **2.** A device used to effect operative compatibility between different parts of one or more pieces of apparatus.

a·dap·tive (ə-dăp′tĭv) *adj.* Tending toward, fit for, or having a capacity for adaptation: *"Culture is man's adaptive system."* (James Deetz). —**a·dap′tive·ly** *adv.* —**a·dap′tive·ness** *n.*

adaptive radiation. The evolution of a relatively unspecialized species into several related species characterized by different specializations that fit them for life in various environments.

A·dar (ä-där′) *n.* The sixth month of the year in the Hebrew calendar. See **calendar.** [Hebrew *Adhār,* from Akkadian *ad(d)aru,* "the dark or cloudy month," from *adāru,* to be dark.]

Adar She·ni (shä-nē′). A Hebrew month, **Veadar** *(see).* [Hebrew *Adhār shēnī,* "second Adar."]

ADC, a.d.c., A.D.C. aide-de-camp.

add (ăd) *v.* **added, adding, adds.** —*tr.* **1.** To join or unite so as to increase in size, quantity, or scope. **2.** To combine (a column of figures, for example) to form a sum. **3.** To say or write further. —*intr.* **1.** To create or constitute an addition. Used with *to.* **2.** To find a sum in arithmetic. —**add up.** *Informal.* **1.** To come to a correct or desired total: *His figures don't add up.* **2.** To be reasonable, plausible, or consistent; make sense. —**add up to.** *Informal.* To mean; indicate. [Middle English *adden,* from Latin *addere,* to add, "to put to" : *ad-,* to + *dere,* to put, from *dare,* to do (see **dō-** in Appendix*).] —**add′a·ble, add′i·ble** *adj.*

ă pat/ā pay/âr care/ä father/b bib/ch church/d deed/ĕ pet/ē be/f fife/g gag/h hat/hw which/ĭ pit/ī pie/îr pier/j judge/k kick/l lid, needle/m mum/n no, sudden/ng thing/ŏ pot/ō toe/ô paw, for/oi noise/ou out/o͝o took/o͞o boot/p pop/r roar/s sauce/sh ship, dish/

add. 1. addendum. 2. addition; additional. 3. address.

Ad·dams (ăd′əmz), **Charles Samuel.** Born 1912. American cartoonist of the macabre.

Ad·dams (ăd′əmz), **Jane.** 1860–1935. American social worker.

ad·dax (ăd′ăks′) *n.* An antelope, *Addax nasomaculatus,* of northern Africa having long, spirally twisted horns. [Latin *addāx,* of African origin.]

ad·dend (ăd′ĕnd′, ə-dĕnd′) *n.* Any of a set of numbers to be added. [Shortened from ADDENDUM.]

ad·den·dum (ə-dĕn′dəm) *n., pl.* **-da** (-də). *Abbr.* **add.** Something added or to be added; especially, a supplement to a book. [Latin, neuter of *addendus,* gerundive of *addere,* to ADD.]

ad·der (ăd′ər) *n.* 1. Any of various venomous Old World snakes of the family Viperidae, especially the common viper, *Vipera berus,* of Eurasia. 2. Any of several nonvenomous snakes popularly believed to be harmful, such as the hognose snake, or puff adder, of North America. [Middle English *addre,* from *an addre,* mistaken from *a naddre,* Old English *nædre,* snake. See **nētr-** in Appendix.*]

ad·der's-mouth (ăd′ərz-mouth′) *n.* Any of various orchids of the genus *Malaxis,* having clusters of small, usually greenish flowers. [From the resemblance of the flowers to the opened mouths of snakes.]

ad·der's-tongue (ăd′ərz-tŭng′) *n.* 1. Any of several ferns of the genus *Ophioglossum;* especially, *O. vulgatum,* of the Northern Hemisphere, having a single sterile, leaflike frond, and a spore-bearing stalk. 2. Any of various plants of the genus *Erythronium,* such as the **dogtooth violet** *(see).* [From the spike sticking out from the base of the frond of the fern, suggesting a snake's tongue.]

ad·dict (ə-dĭkt′) *tr.v.* **-dicted, -dicting, -dicts.** To devote or give (oneself) habitually or compulsively. Used with *to.* See Usage note below. —*n.* (ăd′ĭkt). One who is addicted, especially to narcotics. [Latin *addictus,* "given over," one awarded to another as a slave, past participle of *addīcere,* to award to : *ad-,* to + *dīcere,* to say, pronounce, adjudge (see **deik-** in Appendix*).] —**ad·dic′tion** *n.* —**ad·dic′tive** *adj.* & *n.*

Usage: The past participle *addicted* is regularly followed by *to* plus noun (including the verbal noun ending in *-ing,* or gerund): *addicted to alcohol; addicted to lying.* It is not followed by the infinitive (not *addicted to lie).*

Ad·dis Ab·a·ba (ăd′ĭs ăb′ə-bə). The capital and largest city of Ethiopia, in the center of the country at an altitude of 8,000 feet. Population, 505,000.

Ad·di·son (ăd′ə-sən), **Joseph.** 1672–1719. English essayist and poet.

Addison's disease. A usually fatal disease caused by failure of the adrenal cortex to function and marked by a bronzelike skin pigmentation, anemia, and prostration. [Discovered by Thomas *Addison* (1793–1860), English physician.]

ad·di·tion (ə-dĭsh′ən) *n. Abbr.* **add.** 1. The act or process of adding. 2. The result of adding; something added; an annex. 3. The process of computing with sets of numbers so as to find their sum. —See Synonyms at **appendage.** —**in addition.** Besides; also; as well as. —**in addition to.** Over and above; besides. —**ad·di′tion·al** *adj.* —**ad·di′tion·al·ly** *adv.*

ad·di·tive (ăd′ə-tĭv) *adj.* Marked, produced by, or involving addition. —*n.* A substance added in small amounts to something else to improve, strengthen, or otherwise alter it.

ad·dle (ăd′l) *v.* **-dled, -dling, -dles.** —*tr.* To muddle; confuse: *"My brain is a bit addled by whiskey"* (O'Neill). —*intr.* 1. To become rotten; spoil, as an egg. 2. To become confused. —*adj.* 1. Mixed up; confused. Usually used in combination: *addle-brained.* 2. Spoiled; rotten. [From Middle English *adel,* rotten, putrid, Old English *adela,* filth, urine, akin to Middle Low German *adele*†.]

ad·dress (ə-drĕs′) *tr.v.* **-dressed, -dressing, -dresses.** 1. To speak to. 2. To make a formal speech to. 3. To direct (a spoken or written message) to the attention of. Used with *to: address a protest to the Council.* 4. To mark with a destination: *address a letter.* 5. a. To direct (oneself) in speech to. b. To direct the efforts or attention of (oneself): *address oneself to a task.* 6. To dispatch or consign (a ship, for example) to an agent or factor. 7. To adjust and aim the club at (a golf ball) in preparing for a stroke. —*n.* (ə-drĕs′; *also* ăd′rĕs *for senses 3, 4).* 1. A formal, spoken or written communication: *polite forms of address.* 2. A formal speech. 3. *Abbr.* **add.** The written or printed indication on mail or other deliverable items indicating destination. 4. *Abbr.* **add.** The location at which a particular organization or person may be found or reached. 5. *Usually plural.* Courteous attentions; wooing. 6. Manner or bearing of a person, especially in conversation. 7. Skillfulness or tact in handling a situation. 8. *Abbr.* **add.** The act of dispatching or consigning a ship, as to an agent or factor. 9. *Computers.* A number used in information storage or retrieval that is assigned to a specific memory location. —See Synonyms at **tact.** [Middle English *addressen,* from Old French *addresser,* from Vulgar Latin *addrictiāre* (unattested), to straighten, direct oneself toward : *ad-,* + *directiāre,* (unattested), to straighten, from Latin *dīrectus,* DIRECT.]

ad·dress·ee (ăd′rĕs-ē′, ə-drĕs′ē′) *n.* One to whom something is addressed.

ad·dress·er (ə-drĕs′ər) *n.* Also **ad·dres·sor.** A person who or a machine that addresses.

ad·duce (ə-do͞os′, ə-dyo͞os′, ă-) *tr.v.* **-duced, -ducing, -duces.** To cite as an example or means of proof in an argument; bring forward for consideration. [Latin *addūcere,* to bring to (someone) : *ad-,* toward + *dūcere,* to lead (see **deuk-** in Appendix*).] —**ad·duce′a·ble, ad·duc′i·ble** *adj.*

ad·du·cent (ə-do͞o′sənt, ə-dyo͞o′-, ă-) *adj. Physiology.* Drawing toward or together.

ad·duct (ə-dŭkt′, ă-) *tr.v.* **-ducted, -ducting, -ducts.** *Physiology.* To pull or draw toward the main axis. Used of muscles. [Back-formation from ADDUCTOR.] —**ad·duc′tion** *n.* —**ad·duc′tive** *adj.*

ad·duc·tor (ə-dŭk′tər, ă-) *n.* A muscle that adducts. [Latin *adductor,* "a bringer toward," from *addūcere,* ADDUCE.]

-ade. Indicates a sweetened drink of; for example, **lemonade.** [French *-ade,* from Provençal, Portuguese, and Spanish *-ada* and Italian *-ata,* all from Latin *-āta,* feminine of *-ātus,* "furnished with," past participial ending of verbs in *-āre.*]

Ade (ād), **George.** 1866–1944. American humorist.

Ad·e·la (ăd′ə-lə). A feminine given name. [Middle English, from Norman French and Medieval Latin *Adela,* from Old High German *adal,* nobility. See **athal-** in Appendix.*]

Ad·e·laide[1] (ăd′l-ād′). A feminine given name. [French, from German *Adalheid,* from Old High German *Adalhaid,* nobility : *adal,* nobility (see **athal-** in Appendix*) + *-heit,* -hood (see **skai-** in Appendix*).]

Ad·e·laide[2] (ăd′l-ād′). The capital of South Australia, an industrial city in the southeast and the oldest settlement in the state. Population, 640,000.

A·dé·lie Coast (ə-dā′lē). A region of Antarctica on the coast of Wilkes Land, under French sovereignty since 1938. Also called "Adélie Land."

A·dé·lie penguin (ə-dā′lē). A common Antarctic penguin, *Pygoscelis adeliae,* of medium size, with white underparts and black back and head. It lives and breeds in large exposed rookeries.

Ad·e·line (ăd′l-īn′). A feminine given name. [Middle English, from Norman French *Adeline,* probably diminutive of *Adela,* ADELA.]

-adelphous. *Botany.* Indicates possession of one or more groups of stamens; for example, **diadelphous.** [New Latin *-adelphus,* "having the stamens grouped together (in a 'brotherhood')," from Greek *adelphos,* brother. See **gwelbh-** in Appendix.*]

a·demp·tion (ə-dĕmp′shən) *n. Law.* The disposal by a testator of specific property bequeathed in his will so as to invalidate the bequest. [Latin *ademptiō,* a taking away, from *adimere* (past participle *ademptus),* to take to (oneself), take away : *ad-,* toward + *emere,* to buy, "take" (see **em-** in Appendix*).]

A·den (ăd′n, ād′n). Also **Aden Colony.** A former British colony, since 1968 part of the People's Republic of Southern Yemen.

Aden, Gulf of. The western arm of the Arabian Sea, bounded by Somalia on the south and Southern Yemen on the north.

A·den·au·er (ăd′n-ou′ər, äd′n-), **Konrad.** 1876–1967. German statesman; chancellor of West Germany (1949–63).

ad·en·ec·to·my (ăd′n-ĕk′tə-mē) *n., pl.* **-mies.** Surgical excision of a gland. [ADEN(O)- + -ECTOMY.]

ad·e·nine (ăd′n-ēn′, -ĭn) *n. Biochemistry.* A purine derivative, $C_5H_5N_5$, that is a constituent of nucleic acid in the pancreas, spleen, and other organs. [ADEN(O)- + -INE.]

ad·e·ni·tis (ăd′n-ī′tĭs) *n.* Inflammation of a lymph node or gland. [New Latin : ADEN(O)- + -ITIS.]

adeno-, aden-. Indicates a gland or glands; for example, **adenocarcinoma, adenoid.** [New Latin, from Greek *adēn,* gland. See **engw-** in Appendix.*]

ad·e·no·car·ci·no·ma (ăd′n-ō-kär′sə-nō′mə) *n., pl.* **-mata** (-mə-tə) or **-mas.** A malignant tumor originating in glandular tissue. —**ad′e·no·car′ci·nom′a·tous** (ăd′n-ō-kär′sə-nŏm′ə-təs, -nō′mə-təs) *adj.*

ad·e·noid (ăd′n-oid′) *adj.* Also **ad·e·noi·dal** (ăd′n-oid′l). 1. Glandlike; glandular. 2. Of or pertaining to the adenoids. —*n. Usually plural.* Lymphoid tissue growths in the nose above the throat that when swollen may obstruct nasal breathing, induce postnasal discharge, and make speech difficult. [Greek *adenoeidēs* : ADEN(O)- + -OID.]

ad·e·noi·dal (ăd′ə-noi′dəl) *adj.* 1. Variant of **adenoid.** 2. a. Having a nasal or constricted tone: *an adenoidal singer.* b. Mouth-breathing or gaping.

ad·e·no·ma (ăd′n-ō′mə) *n., pl.* **-mata** (-mə-tə) or **-mas.** An epithelial tumor of glandular origin and structure that is usually benign or of low-grade malignancy. [ADEN(O)- + -OMA.] —**ad′e·nom′a·tous** (ăd′n-ŏm′ə-təs) *adj.*

a·den·o·sine (ə-dĕn′ə-sēn′) *n.* An organic compound, $C_{10}H_{13}N_5O_4$, that is a structural component of nucleic acids. [Blend of ADENINE and RIBOSE.]

adenosine triphosphate. *Symbol* **ATP** An organic compound, $C_{10}H_{16}N_5O_{13}P_3$, that is an energy source in many metabolic reactions, especially those involving muscular activity.

a·dept (ə-dĕpt′) *adj.* Highly skilled. See Synonyms at **proficient.** —*n.* (ăd′ĕpt′). An initiate; expert. [Latin *adeptus,* "having attained (knowledge or skill)," past participle of *adipīscī,* to attain : *ad-,* toward + *apīscī,* to reach for (see **ap-**[1] in Appendix*).] —**a·dept′ly** *adv.* —**a·dept′ness** *n.*

ad·e·quate (ăd′ĭ-kwĭt) *adj.* 1. Able to satisfy a requirement; suitable. 2. Barely satisfactory or sufficient. —See Synonyms at **sufficient.** [Latin *adaequatus,* past participle of *adaequāre,* to make equal to : *ad-,* toward + *aequāre,* to make equal, from *aequus,* EQUAL.] —**ad′e·qua·cy** (-kwə-sē), **ad′e·quate·ness** *n.* —**ad′e·quate·ly** *adv.*

Ad·ha·ra (ăd-hä′rə) *n.* A bright star in the constellation Canis Major, approximately 652 light-years from Earth.

ad·here (ăd-hîr′) *intr.v.* **-hered, -hering, -heres.** 1. To stick fast or together by or as if by grasping, suction, or being glued. Used with *to.* 2. To be devoted as a follower or supporter. Used with *to: "to adhere to an enemy, is to become an enemy"*

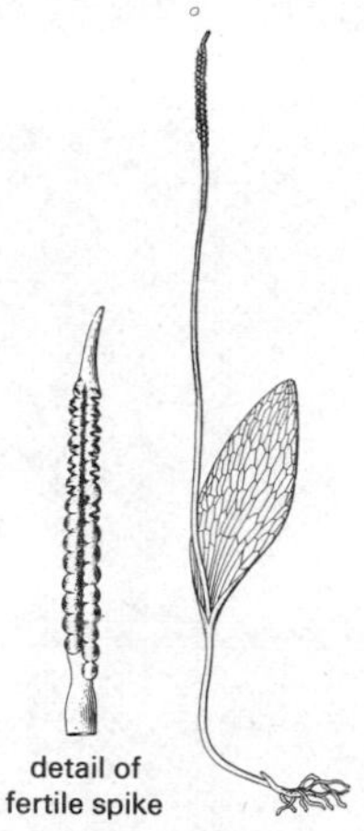
detail of
fertile spike

adder's-tongue
Ophioglossum vulgatum

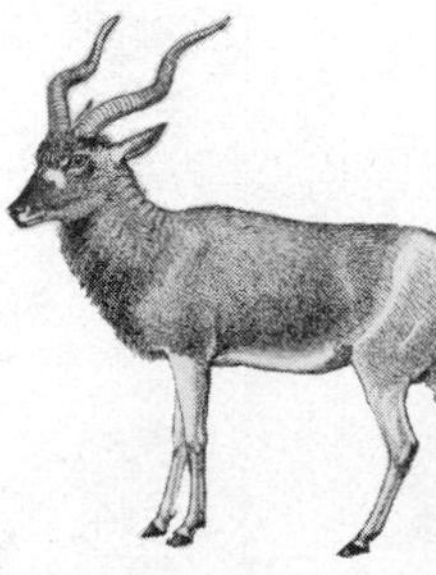

addax

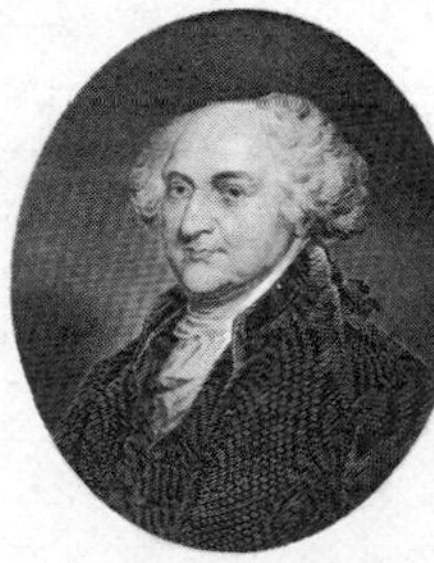

John Adams

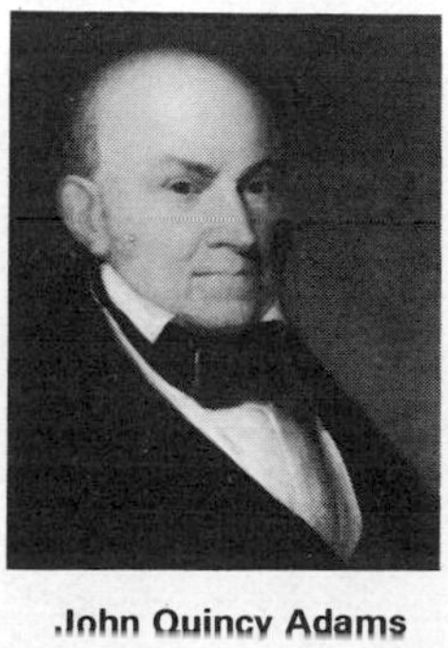

John Quincy Adams

t tight/th thin, path/*th* this, bathe/ŭ cut/ûr urge/v valve/w with/y yes/z zebra, size/zh vision/ə about, item, edible, gallop, circus/ à *Fr.* ami/œ *Fr.* feu, *Ger.* schön/ü *Fr.* tu, *Ger.* über/KH *Ger.* ich, *Scot.* loch/N *Fr.* bon. ***Follows main vocabulary. †Of obscure origin.**

(Donne). **3.** To follow closely; carry out without deviation. Used with *to: adhere to a plan.* [Latin *adhaerēre,* to stick to : *ad,* toward + *haerēre,* to stick (see **ghais-** in Appendix*).] —**ad·her′ence** *n.*

ad·her·ent (ăd-hîr′ənt) *adj.* **1.** Sticking or holding fast. **2.** *Botany.* Growing or fused together; adnate. —*n.* A supporter, as of a cause or individual: *"Rip's sole domestic adherent was his dog Wolf"* (Washington Irving). —**ad·her′ent·ly** *adv.*

ad·he·sion (ăd-hē′zhən) *n.* **1.** The act or state of adhering. **2.** Attachment or devotion, as to a cause or individual; loyalty. **3.** Assent or agreement, especially to join as a supporter. **4.** The physical attraction or joining of two substances, especially the macroscopically observable attraction of dissimilar substances. Compare **cohesion.** [Latin *adhaesiō,* from *adhaerēre,* ADHERE.]

ad·he·sive (ăd-hē′sĭv, -zĭv) *adj.* **1.** Tending to adhere; sticky. **2.** Gummed so as to adhere. —*n.* An adhesive substance, such as paste or cement. —**ad·he′sive·ly** *adv.* —**ad·he′sive·ness** *n.*

adhesive tape. A tape lined on one side with an adhesive.

ad hoc (ăd hŏk′). *Latin.* With respect to this (particular thing); for a specific purpose, case, or situation. [Latin, "toward this."]

ad ho·mi·nem (ăd hŏm′ĭ-nĕm). *Latin.* To the man; appealing to personal interests, prejudices, or emotions rather than to reason: *an argument ad hominem.*

ad·i·a·bat·ic (ăd′ē-ə-băt′ĭk, ā′dī-ə-) *adj. Physics.* Of, pertaining to, or designating a reversible thermodynamic process executed at constant entropy; loosely, occurring without gain or loss of heat. [Greek *adiabatos,* "impassable (to heat)" : *a-,* not + *diabatos,* passable, from *diabainein,* to go through : *dia,* through + *bainein,* to go (see **gwā-** in Appendix*).] —**ad′i·a·bat′i·cal·ly** *adv.*

a·dieu (ə-dyōō′, ə-dōō′; *French* à-dyœ′) *interj.* Good-by; farewell. —*n., pl.* **adieus** or *French* **adieux** (à-dyœ′). A farewell. [Middle English, from Old French, from *a dieu,* "(I commend you) to God" : *a,* to, from Latin *ad* + *dieu,* God, from Latin *deus,* god (see **deiw-** in Appendix*).]

A·di·ge (ä′dē-jā). The second-longest river in Italy, rising in the north and flowing southeast 225 miles to the Adriatic at the Gulf of Venice.

ad in·fi·ni·tum (ăd ĭn′fə-nī′təm). *Abbr.* **ad inf.** *Latin.* To infinity; without end; limitless.

ad in·ter·im (ăd ĭn′tə-rĭm). *Abbr.* **ad int.** *Latin.* In the meantime; meanwhile.

a·di·os (ä′dē-ōs′, ăd′ē-ōs′) *interj. Spanish.* Good-by; farewell. [Spanish *adios,* translation of French *adieu,* ADIEU.]

ad·i·pose (ăd′ə-pōs′) *adj.* Of or related to animal fat; fatty. —*n.* The fat found in adipose tissue. [New Latin *adiposus,* from Latin *adeps*† (stem *adip-*), fat.] —**ad′i·pose′ness, ad′i·pos′i·ty** (-pŏs′ə-tē) *n.*

adipose fin. An additional dorsal fin in certain fishes, such as the salmon, consisting mostly of fatty tissue and usually without supporting rays.

adipose tissue. Connective tissue in the body that contains stored cellular fat.

Ad·i·ron·dack Mountains (ăd′ə-rŏn′dăk′). A section of the Appalachian system in northeastern New York State. Highest elevation, Mount Marcy (5,344 feet). Also called "Adirondacks."

ad·it (ăd′ĭt) *n.* An almost horizontal entrance to a mine. [Latin *aditus,* access, from the past participle of *adīre,* to approach : *ad-,* toward + *īre,* to go (see **ei-¹** in Appendix*).]

adj. **1.** adjacent. **2.** adjective. **3.** adjourned. **4.** adjunct. **5.** adjustment. **6.** adjutant.

ad·ja·cen·cy (ə-jā′sən-sē) *n., pl.* **-cies. 1.** The state of being adjacent; contiguity. **2.** A thing that is adjacent.

ad·ja·cent (ə-jā′sənt) *adj. Abbr.* **adj.** Close to; next to; lying near; adjoining. [Middle English, from Latin *adjacēns,* present participle of *adjacēre,* to lie near : *ad-,* near to + *jacēre,* to lie, "be thrown down," intransitive of *jacere,* to lay, throw (see **yē-** in Appendix*).] —**ad·ja′cent·ly** *adv.*

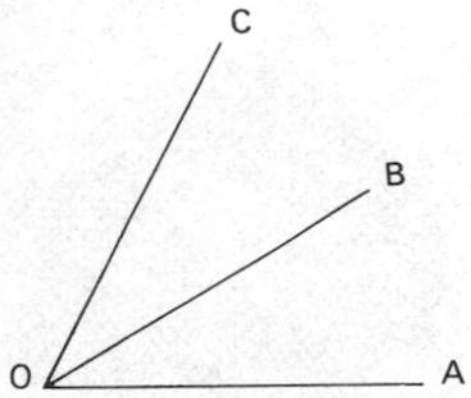

adjacent angle
AOB and BOC are adjacent angles

adjacent angle. Either of two angles having a common side and a common vertex and lying on opposite sides of the common side.

ad·jec·ti·val (ăj′ĭk-tī′vəl) *adj.* Of, pertaining to, or functioning as an adjective. —**ad′jec·ti′val·ly** *adv.*

ad·jec·tive (ăj′ĭk-tĭv) *n. Abbr.* **adj., a. 1.** *Grammar.* Any of a class of words used to modify a noun or other substantive by limiting, qualifying, or specifying. **2.** *Linguistics.* Any of a form class distinguished in English morphologically by one of several suffixes, such as *-able, -ous, -er,* and *-est,* or syntactically by position in a phrase or sentence, such as *brick* in *a brick house. Brick* becomes an adjective because it is between *a* and *house;* any word placed between these two would necessarily be an adjective. **3.** A dependent or subordinate. —*adj.* **1.** Pertaining to or acting as an adjective; adjectival. **2.** Dependent; subordinate. **3.** *Law.* Procedural. **4.** Requiring the use of a mordant: *adjective dyes.* [Middle English, from Old French *adjectif,* from Latin *adjectīvus,* "attributive," from *adjectus,* "attributed," added, from *adjicere,* to throw to, add : *ad-,* to + *jacere,* to throw (see **yē-** in Appendix*).] —**ad′jec·tive·ly** *adv.*

adjective pronoun. *Grammar.* A pronoun acting as an adjective; for example, *which* in *which dictionaries?* or *himself* in *he himself said so.*

ad·join (ə-join′) *v.* **-joined, -joining, -joins.** —*tr.* **1.** To be next to; be contiguous to. **2.** To attach to; unite. Used with *to.* —*intr.* To be contiguous. [Middle English *adjoinen,* from Old French *ajoindre,* from Latin *adjungere,* to join to : *ad-,* to + *jungere,* to join (see **yeug-** in Appendix*).]

ad·join·ing (ə-joi′nĭng) *adj.* Neighboring; contiguous; next to.

ad·journ (ə-jûrn′) *v.* **-journed, -journing, -journs.** —*tr.* To suspend until a later stated time. —*intr.* **1.** To suspend proceedings to another time or place. **2.** *Informal.* To move from one place to another: *We adjourned to the living room.* [Middle English *ajournen,* from Old French *ajourner,* "to put off to an appointed day" : *a-,* to, from Latin *ad-* + *jour,* day, from Late Latin *diurnum,* day, from *diurnus,* daily, from *diēs,* day (see **deiw-** in Appendix*).] —**ad·journ′ment** *n.*

adjt. adjutant.

ad·judge (ə-jŭj′) *tr.v.* **-judged, -judging, -judges. 1.** To determine or decide by judicial procedure; adjudicate. **2.** To order judicially; rule. **3.** To award (costs or damages, for example) by law. **4.** To regard, consider, or deem. [Middle English *ajugen,* from Old French *ajuger,* from Latin *adjūdicāre,* ADJUDICATE.]

ad·ju·di·cate (ə-jōō′dĭ-kāt′) *tr.v.* **-cated, -cating, -cates.** To hear and settle (a case) by judicial procedure. [Latin *adjūdicāre,* to award to (judicially) : *ad-,* to + *jūdicāre,* to be a judge, from *jūdex,* a judge (see **yewo-¹** in Appendix*).] —**ad·ju′di·ca′tion** *n.* —**ad·ju′di·ca′tive** *adj.* —**ad·ju′di·ca′tor** (-kā′tər) *n.*

ad·junct (ăj′ŭngkt′) *n. Abbr.* **adj. 1.** Something attached to another thing but in a dependent or subordinate position. **2.** A person associated with another in some duty or service in a subordinate or auxiliary capacity; helper; assistant. **3.** A word or words added in order to clarify, qualify, or modify other words. **4.** *Logic.* A nonessential attribute of a thing. —See Synonyms at **appendage.** —*adj.* **1.** Added or connected in a subordinate or auxiliary capacity: *an adjunct clause.* **2.** Attached to a faculty or staff in a temporary or auxiliary capacity. [Latin *adjunctum,* from *adjunctus,* past participle of *adjungere,* ADJOIN.] —**ad·junc′tion** *n.* —**ad·junc′tive** *adj.*

ad·ju·ra·tion (ăj′ōō-rā′shən) *n.* An earnest or solemn appeal: *"the tenderest adjurations of a dying friend"* (De Quincey). —**ad·jur′a·to′ry** (-ə-tôr′ē, -tōr′ē) *adj.*

ad·jure (ə-jŏŏr′) *tr.v.* **-jured, -juring, -jures. 1.** To command or enjoin solemnly, as under oath or penalty: *"and adjuring her in the name of God to declare the truth"* (Increase Mather). **2.** To appeal to or entreat earnestly. [Middle English *adjuren,* from Latin *adjūrāre,* to swear to : *ad-,* to + *jūrāre,* to swear (see **yewo-¹** in Appendix*).] —**ad·jur′er, ad·ju′ror** (ə-jŏŏr′ər) *n.*

ad·just (ə-jŭst′) *v.* **-justed, -justing, -justs.** —*tr.* **1.** To change so as to match or fit; make correspond. **2.** To bring into proper relationship; harmonize; settle. **3.** To adapt or conform, as to new conditions. Often used reflexively: *"unable to adjust themselves to their environment"* (Karl A. Menninger). **4.** To make accurate by regulation. **5.** *Insurance.* To decide how much is to be paid (on a claim). **6.** To correct (the range and direction of a gun) in firing. —*intr.* To adapt oneself; become suited or fit; conform. [Obsolete French *adjuster,* from Old French *ajoster,* from Vulgar Latin *adjuxtāre* (unattested), to put close to : Latin *ad-,* near to + *juxtā,* close by, near (see **yeug-** in Appendix*).] —**ad·just′a·ble** *adj.* —**ad·just′a·bly** *adv.* —**ad·just′er, ad·jus′tor** (-tər) *n.* —**ad·jus′tive** *adj.*

ad·just·ment (ə-jŭst′mənt) *n.* **1.** The act of making fit or conformable. **2.** A condition of adaptation. **3.** A means for adjusting. **4.** *Abbr.* **adj.** The settlement of a debt or claim.

ad·ju·tant (ăj′ōō-tənt) *n.* **1.** *Abbr.* **adj., adjt.** *Military.* A staff officer who helps a commanding officer with administrative affairs. **2.** An assistant. **3.** A stork, the **marabou** *(see).* [Latin *adjūtāns,* present participle of *adjūtāre,* to assist, AID.] —**ad′ju·tan·cy, ad′ju·tant·ship′** *n.*

adjutant general *pl.* **adjutants general.** *Abbr.* **AG, A.G. 1.** Adjutant of a unit having a general staff. **2.** An officer in charge of the National Guard of one of the states of the United States. **3.** *Capital* **A,** *capital* **G.** *Abbr.* **TAG** The chief administrative officer, a major general, of the U.S. Army. Preceded by *the.*

adjutant stork. The **marabou** *(see).*

Ad·ler (ăd′lər), **Alfred.** 1870–1937. Austrian psychiatrist.

Ad·ler (ăd′lər), **Felix.** 1851–1933. American educator and reformer; founder of the Society for Ethical Culture.

Ad·ler (ăd′lər), **Mortimer Jerome.** Born 1902. American educator and philosopher.

Ad·le·ri·an psychology (ăd-lîr′ē-ən). A psychological school or doctrine holding that behavior arises in subconscious efforts to compensate for inferiority or deficiency and that neurosis results from overcompensation. [After Alfred ADLER.]

ad lib (ăd lĭb′). In an unrestrained manner; freely; spontaneously. See Synonyms at **extemporaneous.**

ad-lib (ăd-lĭb′) *v.* **-libbed, -libbing, -libs.** *Informal.* —*tr.* To improvise and deliver extemporaneously. —*intr.* To improvise a speech, lines, or the like; extemporize. —*n.* Words, music, or actions ad-libbed. —*adj.* Spoken or performed spontaneously. [Shortened from AD LIBITUM.] —**ad-lib′ber** *n.*

ad lib·i·tum (ăd lĭb′ə-təm). *Abbr.* **ad lib., ad libit.** *Music.* Performed with freedom. Used as a direction. Compare **obbligato.** [Latin, "to the desire."]

ad loc. to (or at) the place (Latin *ad locum*).

adm. administrative; administrator.

Adm. admiral; admiralty.

ad·man (ăd′măn′) *n., pl.* **-men** (-mĕn′). *Informal.* A man employed in the advertising business.

ad·meas·ure (ăd-mĕzh′ər) *tr.v.* **-ured, -uring, -ures.** To divide and distribute proportionally; apportion. [Middle English *amesuren,* from Old French *amesurer,* to measure out to : *a,* to, from Latin *ad-* + *mesurer,* to MEASURE.] —**ad·meas′ure·ment** *n.* —**ad·meas′ur·er** *n.*

Ad·me·tus (ăd-mē′təs). *Greek Mythology.* A king of Thessaly and husband of Alcestis.

admin. administration; administrator.

ad·min·is·ter (ăd-mĭn′ĭs-tər) *v.* **-tered, -tering, -ters.** —*tr.* **1.** To have charge of; direct; manage. **2. a.** To give or apply in a formal way: *administer the last rites.* **b.** To apply as a remedy: *administer a sedative.* **3.** To mete out; dispense: *administer justice.* **4.** To manage or dispose of (trusts and estates) under a will or an official appointment. **5.** To impose, offer, or tender (an oath, for example). *—intr.* **1.** To manage as an administrator. **2.** To minister. Used with *to: administering to their pleasure.* [Middle English *administren,* from Old French *administrer,* from Latin *administrāre,* to be an aid to : *ad-,* to + *ministrāre,* to serve, from *minister,* servant (see **mei-**[2] in Appendix*).] **—ad·min'is·tra·ble** (-trə-bəl) *adj.* **—ad·min'is·trant** (-trənt) *adj.* & *n.*

ad·min·is·trate (ăd-mĭn'ĭs-trāt') *tr.v.* **-trated, -trating, -trates.** To administer.

ad·min·is·tra·tion (ăd-mĭn'ĭs-trā'shən) *n. Abbr.* **admin. 1.** The management of affairs. **2.** The activity of a sovereign state in the exercise of its powers or duties. **3.** *Often capital* **A.** The persons collectively who make up the executive branch of a government. Preceded by *the.* **4.** The management of any institution, public or private. Preceded by *the.* **5.** The term of office of an executive officer or body. **6.** *Law.* The management and disposal of a trust or estate. **7.** The dispensing, applying, or tendering of something, such as an oath, sacrament, or medicine. **—ad·min'is·tra'tive** *adj.* **—ad·min'is·tra'tive·ly** *adv.*

ad·min·is·tra·tor (ăd-mĭn'ĭs-trā'tər) *n. Abbr.* **adm., admin. 1.** One who administers, especially public affairs. **2.** A person appointed to administer an estate.

ad·mi·ra·ble (ăd'mər-ə-bəl) *adj.* Deserving admiration; excellent. **—ad'mi·ra·ble·ness** *n.* **—ad'mir·a·bly** *adv.*

ad·mi·ral (ăd'mər-əl) *n.* **1.** The commander in chief of a navy or fleet. **2.** *Abbr.* **Adm.** A naval officer, **Admiral of the Fleet** *(see).* **3.** In the U.S. Navy, U.S. Coast Guard, and Royal Canadian Navy: **a.** *Abbr.* **Adm.** An officer of the next-to-the-highest rank. **b.** A high-ranking naval officer; **rear admiral** or **vice admiral** *(both of which see).* **4.** The ship carrying an admiral; flagship. **5.** *Chiefly British.* The head of a fishing fleet. **6.** Any of various brightly colored butterflies of the genera *Limenitis* and *Vanessa.* [Middle English *a(d)miral,* from Medieval Latin *a(d)mīrālis* (reshaped as if from *admīrārī,* to ADMIRE), from Old French *amiral,* from Arabic *'amīr-al-,* "commander of" : *'amīr,* commander, EMIR + *al,* the.]

Admiral of the Fleet. The highest rank in the U.S. Navy and Royal Canadian Navy, equivalent to General of the Army or field marshal. Also "Admiral," "Fleet Admiral."

ad·mi·ral·ty (ăd'mər-əl-tē) *n., pl.* **-ties.** *Abbr.* **Adm. 1. a.** A court exercising jurisdiction over all maritime causes. **b.** Maritime law. **2.** *Capital* **A.** The department of the British government (Board of Admiralty) having control over naval affairs.

Admiralty Inlet. The northernmost section of Puget Sound, Washington.

Admiralty Island. An island with an area of 1,664 square miles, in the Alexander Archipelago of southeastern Alaska. Population, 19,000.

Admiralty Islands. A group of small volcanic islands, about 800 square miles in area, in the southwestern Pacific Ocean, part of the Bismarck Archipelago.

Admiralty Range. A mountain group in Victoria Land, Antarctica, northwest of the Ross Sea.

ad·mi·ra·tion (ăd'mə-rā'shən) *n.* **1.** A feeling of pleasure, wonder, and approval. **2.** An object of wonder; marvel: *"The young prince . . . is the admiration of the whole court."* (Lady Mary Wortley Montague). **3.** *Archaic.* Wonder. —See Synonyms at **regard.**

ad·mire (ăd-mīr') *v.* **-mired, -miring, -mires.** *—tr.* **1.** To regard with wonder, pleasure, and approval. **2.** To have a high opinion of; to esteem or respect. **3.** *Archaic.* To marvel or wonder at. *—intr.* **1.** To feel or express admiration. **2.** *Regional.* To feel pleasure; be pleased. Used with an infinitive: *"I admire to do it"* (Louisa May Alcott). [Latin *admīrārī,* to wonder at : *ad-,* to, at + *mīrārī,* to wonder, from *mīrus,* wonderful (see **smei-** in Appendix*).] **—ad·mir'er** *n.* **—ad·mir'ing·ly** *adv.*

ad·mis·si·ble (ăd-mĭs'ə-bəl) *adj.* **1.** Capable of being accepted; allowable. **2.** Worthy of being permitted to enter. **—ad·mis'si·bil'i·ty, ad·mis'si·ble·ness** *n.* **—ad·mis'si·bly** *adv.*

ad·mis·sion (ăd-mĭsh'ən) *n.* **1. a.** The act of admitting or allowing to enter. **b.** The state of being allowed to enter. See Usage note at **admittance. 2.** The right to enter; access. See Usage note at **admittance. 3.** The price required or paid for entering; entrance fee. See Usage note at **admittance. 4.** The act or process of acceptance and entry into a position or situation; appointment. **5.** A confession of crime or wrongdoing. **6.** A voluntary acknowledgment that something is true. **7.** A fact or statement granted or admitted; concession. [Middle English *admissioun,* from Latin *admissiō,* from *admittere* (past participle *admissus*), ADMIT.] **—ad·mis'sive** *adj.*

Admission Day. Any of several days celebrated by various states of the United States in commemoration of their respective admissions to the Union.

ad·mit (ăd-mĭt') *v.* **-mitted, -mitting, -mits.** *—tr.* **1.** To permit to enter. **2.** To serve as a means of entrance: *This ticket admits the whole group.* **3.** To permit to join or exercise certain rights, functions, or privileges. **4.** To have room for; be able to accommodate. **5.** To afford opportunity for; allow; permit. **6.** To acknowledge; confess: *admit the truth.* See Usage note below. **7.** To grant as true or valid, as for the sake of argument; concede. **8.** To accept or allow as true or valid. *—intr.* **1.** To afford possibility; permit; allow: Used with *of.* See Usage note below. **2.** To allow entrance; afford access. Used with *to: This door admits to the main hall.* —See Synonyms at **acknowledge.** [Middle English *admitten,* from Latin *admittere,* to send in to : *ad-,* to + *mittere,* to send (see **smeit-** in Appendix*).]

Usage: *Admit,* in the sense of *confess* or *acknowledge,* should not be used with *to: to admit an error* (not *admit to*), *to admit having erred* (not *admit to having*). The construction *admit of* properly expresses allowance or opportunity in *The problem admits of several approaches.* In such cases the subject is usually an abstraction; it is never a person.

ad·mit·tance (ăd-mĭt'əns) *n.* **1.** The act of admitting or entering. See Usage note below. **2.** Permission to enter; the power or right of entrance. See Usage note below. **3.** *Electricity.* The reciprocal of impedance. It is the ratio of a voltage to a current, is measured in mhos, and may be expressed as a complex quantity, the real part of which is conductance and the imaginary part susceptance.

Usage: *Admittance* applies largely to physical entry to a specific place *(admittance to the jury room).* In the corresponding sense of entry, *admission* is used figuratively *(admission of evidence to the court record)* or, when physical entry is involved, in the additional sense of right or privilege of participation *(admission to a club; price of admission to a theater).*

ad·mit·ted·ly (ăd-mĭt'ĭd-lē) *adv.* By general admission; confessedly.

ad·mix (ăd-mĭks') *v.* **-mixed, -mixing, -mixes.** *—tr.* To mix or blend. *—intr.* To be or become mixed or blended. [Back-formation from obsolete *admixt,* mixed into, from Latin *ad mixtus,* past participle of *admiscēre,* to mix into : *ad-,* to + *miscēre,* to mix (see **meik-** in Appendix*).]

ad·mix·ture (ăd-mĭks'chər) *n.* **1. a.** The act of mingling or mixing. **b.** The state of being mingled or mixed. **2.** That which is mingled or mixed; mixture; compound. **3.** Anything added in mixing. —See Synonyms at **mixture.**

ad·mon·ish (ăd-mŏn'ĭsh) *tr.v.* **-ished, -ishing, -ishes. 1.** To reprove mildly or kindly, but seriously. **2.** To counsel against something; caution; warn. **3.** To point out something forgotten or disregarded, by means of a warning, reproof, or exhortation. —See Synonyms at **warn.** [Middle English *admonissen,* back-formation from *admonesten* (the stem *admonest-* was mistaken for a past participle), from Old French *admonester,* from Vulgar Latin *admonestāre* (unattested), variant of Latin *admonēre,* to bring to (someone's) mind : *ad-,* to + *monēre,* to remind, advise (see **men-**[1] in Appendix*).] **—ad·mon'ish·er** *n.* **—ad·mon'ish·ing·ly** *adv.* **—ad·mon'ish·ment** *n.*

Synonyms: *admonish, reprove, rebuke, reprimand, reproach.* These verbs refer to adverse criticism intended as a corrective. *Admonish* stresses the act of advising or warning so that a fault may be rectified or a danger avoided. *Reprove* usually implies gentle criticism and constructive intent. *Rebuke* refers to sharp, usually angry, criticism, as does *reprimand,* which often also implies an official or otherwise formal act. *Reproach* usually refers to sharp criticism made regretfully or unhappily out of a sense of disappointment.

ad·mo·ni·tion (ăd'mə-nĭsh'ən) *n.* **1.** Mild censure. **2.** Cautionary advice. [Middle English *admonicioun,* from Old French *amonition,* from Latin *admonitiō,* from *admonēre,* ADMONISH.]

ad·mon·i·to·ry (ăd-mŏn'ə-tôr'ē, -tōr'ē) *adj.* Cautionary.

ad·nate (ăd'nāt') *adj. Biology.* Joined to or fused with another part or organ. Said of parts not usually united. [Latin *adnātus,* past participle of *adnāscī, agnāscī,* to be born in addition to. See **agnate.**] **—ad·na'tion** (ăd-nā'shən) *n.*

ad nau·se·am (ăd nô'zē-əm). *Latin.* To the point of nausea; to a disgusting or ridiculous degree.

ad·noun (ăd'noun') *n. Grammar.* An adjective, specifically when used as a noun, as in *the bold and the brave.* [AD- (additional) + NOUN (by analogy with ADVERB).] **—ad·nom'i·nal** (ăd-nŏm'ə-nəl) *adj.*

a·do (ə-do͞o') *n.* Bustle; fuss; trouble; bother. [Middle English, from the phrase *at do,* "to do" : *at,* from Old Norse *at* (used with infinitive), to (see **ad-** in Appendix*) + *don,* DO.]

a·do·be (ə-dō'bē) *n.* **1.** A sun-dried, unburned brick of clay and straw. **2.** Clay or soil from which such bricks are made. **3.** A structure built with such bricks. [Spanish *adobe,* from Arabic *aṭṭōba, al-ṭōba,* "the brick."] **—a·do'be** *adj.*

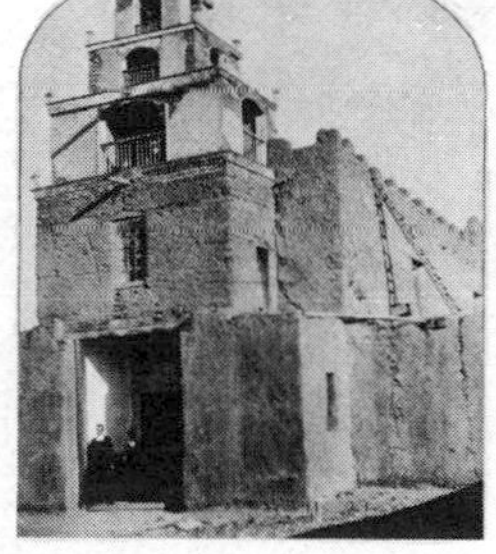

adobe
Church of San Miguel, Santa Fe, New Mexico, built of adobe

ad·o·les·cence (ăd'l-ĕs'əns) *n.* **1.** The period of physical and psychological development from the onset of puberty to maturity. **2.** The state or condition of being adolescent.

ad·o·les·cent (ăd'l-ĕs'ənt) *adj.* Of, pertaining to, or undergoing adolescence. *—n.* An adolescent person. See Synonyms at **young.** [Middle English, from Old French, from Latin *adolēscēns,* present participle of *adolēscere,* to grow up : *ad-,* toward + *alēscere,* to grow, "be nourished," inceptive of *alere,* to nourish (see **al-**[3] in Appendix*).]

Ad·olph (ăd'ŏlf', ā'dŏlf'). A masculine given name. [From German *Adolf* and Medieval Latin *Adolphus,* both from Old High German *Athalwolf, Adulf* : *adal, athal,* noble (see **athal-** in Appendix*) + *wolf,* wolf (see **wḷkwo-** in Appendix*).]

Ad·o·nai (ăd'ō-nī'). *Hebrew.* Lord. Used in Judaism as a spoken substitute for the ineffable name of God. See **Tetragrammaton.** [Hebrew *adōnāi,* "my lord(s)," from Phoenician *adōn,* lord.]

A·don·ic (ə-dŏn'ĭk) *adj. Prosody.* Indicating a measure consisting of a dactyl followed by a spondee. *—n.* An Adonic verse. [This meter was said to have been first used in verses lamenting Adonis' death.]

A·don·is[1] (ə-dŏn'ĭs, ə-dō'nĭs). *Greek Mythology.* A youth loved by Aphrodite for his striking beauty. [Greek *Adōnis,* from Phoenician *adōn,* lord. See also **Adonai.**]

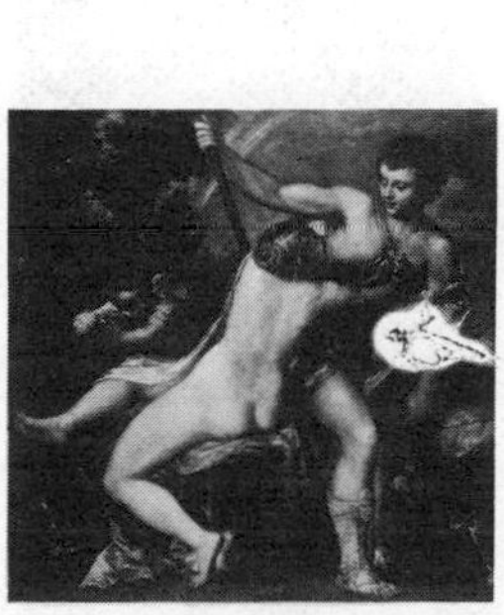

Adonis[1]
Detail of a painting, "Venus and Adonis," by Titian

A·don·is[2] (ə-dŏn'ĭs, ə-dō'nĭs) *n.* A young man of great physical beauty.

a·dopt (ə-dŏpt') *tr.v.* **adopted, adopting, adopts. 1.** To take into one's family through legal means and raise as one's own child. See Usage note below. **2.** To select and bring into a new relationship, as a friend, heir, or citizen. **3.** To take and follow (a course of action, for example) by choice or assent: *adopt a new technique.* **4.** To take up and use as one's own, as an idea, word, or the like. **5.** To take on or assume: *"He adopted the important air of a herald in red and gold"* (Stephen Crane). **6.** To vote to accept: *adopt a resolution.* **7.** To choose as a standard or required textbook or reference book in a course. [Latin *adoptāre,* to choose for oneself : *ad-,* to + *optāre,* to choose, desire (see **op-**² in Appendix*).] —**a·dopt′a·ble** *adj.* —**a·dopt′er** *n.* —**a·dop′tion** *n.*

Usage: In a foster home, one refers to *adopted* children and *adoptive* parents.

a·dop·tive (ə-dŏp′tĭv) *adj.* **1.** Tending to adopt or characteristic of adoption. **2.** Related by adoption. See Usage note at **adopt.** —**a·dop′tive·ly** *adv.*

a·dor·a·ble (ə-dôr′ə-bəl, ə-dōr′-) *adj.* **1.** *Archaic.* Worthy of or eliciting worship. **2.** *Informal.* Delightful; lovable; charming. —**a·dor′a·bil′i·ty, a·dor′a·ble·ness** *n.* —**a·dor′a·bly** *adv.*

ad·o·ra·tion (ăd′ə-rā′shən) *n.* **1.** The act of worship. **2.** Profound love or regard.

a·dore (ə-dôr′, ə-dōr′) *v.* **adored, adoring, adores.** —*tr.* **1.** To worship with divine honors. **2.** To love deeply. **3.** *Informal.* To like very much. —*intr.* To worship. —See Synonyms at **revere.** [Middle English *adoren,* from Old French *adorer,* from Latin *adōrāre,* to pray to : *ad-,* to + *ōrāre,* to speak, pray (see **or-** in Appendix*).] —**a·dor′er** *n.* —**a·dor′ing·ly** *adv.*

a·dorn (ə-dôrn′) *tr.v.* **adorned, adorning, adorns.** **1.** To be a decoration to; lend beauty to: *"the pale mimosas that adorned the favourite promenade"* (Ronald Firbank). **2.** To fit out or decorate with or as with ornaments: *"the sugar plantations were adorned with windmills"* (Alec Waugh). **3.** To enhance the distinction, beauty, splendor, or glory of; add luster to: *"Virtue adorned his mind"* (John Ford). [Middle English *adornen,* from Old French *adorner,* from Latin *adornāre,* to put ornament on : *ad-,* to + *ornāre,* to furnish, deck (see **ar-** in Appendix*).] —**a·dorn′er** *n.* —**a·dorn′ing·ly** *adv.* —**a·dorn′ment** *n.*

A·dou·la (ä-do͞o′lə), **Cyrille.** Born 1921. Congolese statesman; first premier of the Democratic Republic of the Congo.

A·do·wa. See **Aduwa.**

A·drar (ä-drär′). **1.** An oasis in west-central Algeria, located on the trans-Saharan motor route. **2.** A plateau region in Mali in the central Sahara.

ad rem (ăd rĕm′). *Latin.* To the point; pertinent.

ad·re·nal (ə-drē′nəl) *adj.* **1.** At, near, or on the kidneys. **2.** Of or pertaining to the adrenal glands or their secretions. —*n.* An adrenal gland. [AD- (toward, near) + RENAL.]

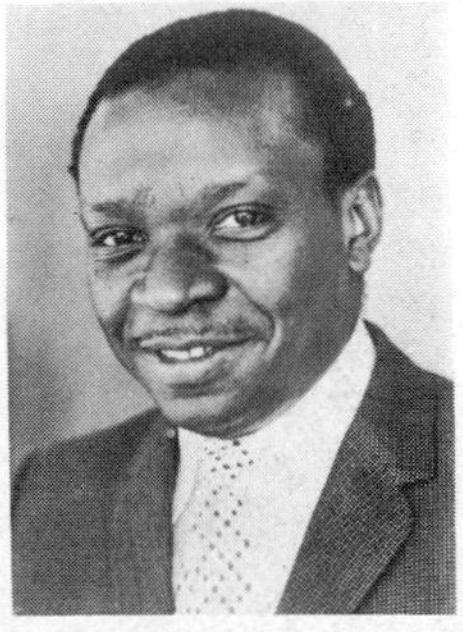

Cyrille Adoula

adrenal gland. Either of two small dissimilarly shaped endocrine glands, one located above each kidney, consisting of the cortex, which secretes hormones, and the medulla, which secretes epinephrine. Also called "suprarenal gland."

ad·ren·a·lin (ə-drĕn′əl-ĭn) *n.* Also **a·dren·a·line.** A secretion of the adrenal glands, **epinephrine** *(see).* Used in nontechnical contexts to denote the heightened emotion and sudden increase in physical strength associated with this substance: *"fear has its important uses, such as causing an outflow of adrenalin which helps one run away faster"* (Alan Paton). [ADRENAL + -IN.]

ad·ren·er·gic (ăd′rə-nûr′jĭk) *adj.* Of, pertaining to, or having chemical activity like that of epinephrine. Said of certain nerve fibers. [ADREN(ALIN) + Greek *ergon,* work, action (see **werg-**¹ in Appendix*).]

ad·re·no·cor·ti·co·trop·ic (ə-drē′nō-kôr′tĭ-kō-trŏp′ĭk, -trō′pĭk) *adj.* Also **ad·re·no·cor·ti·co·troph·ic** (-trŏf′ĭk, -trō′fĭk). Stimulating or otherwise acting upon the cortex of the adrenal gland. [ADREN(AL) + CORTICO- + -TROPIC.]

adrenocorticotropic hormone. A hormone, **ACTH** *(see).*

A·dri·an (ā′drē-ən). A masculine given name. [Middle English, from Latin *Ādriānus, Hādriānus,* "of the Adriatic Sea," Roman family name, from *Ādria, Hādria,* the Adriatic Sea.]

A·dri·an IV (ā′drē-ən). Original name, Nicholas Breakspear. 1100?–1159. Pope (1154–59).

A·dri·an (ā′drē-ən), **Edgar Douglas.** Born 1889. British physiologist; studied nerve cells.

A·dri·a·no·ple. The former name for **Edirne.**

A·dri·at·ic (ā′drē-ăt′ĭk) *adj.* Of or pertaining to the Adriatic Sea or to the peoples inhabiting its islands and coasts.

Adriatic Sea. An arm of the Mediterranean, 500 miles long and up to 140 miles wide, between Italy and the Balkan Peninsula. [Latin *Ādriāticus,* from *Ādria, Hādria.* See **Adrian.**]

a·drift (ə-drĭft′) *adv.* Without anchor or direction. —**a·drift′** *adj.*

a·droit (ə-droit′) *adj.* **1.** Dexterous; deft. **2.** Skillful and adept under pressing conditions. —See Synonyms at **dexterous.** [French, from *a droit,* "rightly" : *a,* to, at, from Latin *ad-* + *droit,* right, from Latin *dīrectus,* DIRECT.] —**a·droit′ly** *adv.* —**a·droit′ness** *n.*

ad·sci·ti·tious (ăd′sĭ-tĭsh′əs) *adj.* Not inherent or essential; derivative. [From Latin *adscītus,* derived, assumed, past participle of *adscīscere,* to approve, arrogate to oneself : *ad-,* to + *scīscere,* to seek to know, assume, inceptive of *scīre,* to know (see **skei-** in Appendix*).]

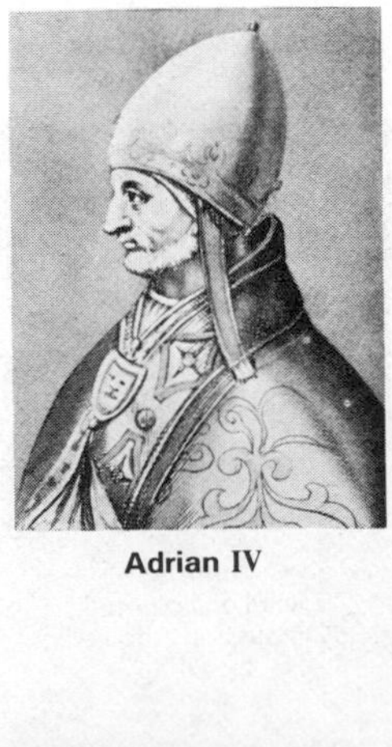

Adrian IV

ad·script (ăd′skrĭpt′) *adj.* Written after (a vowel), as distinguished from subscript: *iota adscript.* [Latin *adscrīptus,* past participle of *adscrībere,* to write after, ASCRIBE.]

ad·sorb (ăd-sôrb′, -zôrb′) *tr.v.* **-sorbed, -sorbing, -sorbs.** To take up by adsorption. Compare **absorb.** [AD- + Latin *sorbēre,* to drink in, suck (see **srebh-** in Appendix*).]

ad·sor·bate (ăd-sôr′bĭt, ăd-zôr′-) *n.* An adsorbed substance.

ad·sor·bent (ăd-sôr′bənt, ăd-zôr′-) *adj.* Capable of adsorption. —*n.* An adsorptive material, such as activated carbon.

ad·sorp·tion (ăd-sôrp′shən, ăd-zôrp′-) *n.* The assimilation of gas, vapor, or dissolved matter by the surface of a solid. [ADSORB + -TION.] —**ad·sorp′tive** *adj.*

ad·su·ki bean. Variant of **adzuki bean.**

ad·u·lar·i·a (ăj′o͞o-lâr′ē-ə) *n. Mineralogy.* A variety of **orthoclase** *(see).* [Italian, from French *adulaire,* after *Adula,* mountain group in Switzerland.]

ad·u·late (ăj′o͞o-lāt′) *tr.v.* **-lated, -lating, -lates.** To praise excessively or fawningly. [Back-formation from ADULATION.] —**ad′u·la′tor** (-tər) *n.* —**ad′u·la·to′ry** (-lə-tôr′ē, -tōr′ē) *adj.*

ad·u·la·tion (ăj′o͞o-lā′shən) *n.* Excessive praise or flattery. [Middle English *adulacioun,* from Old French *adulation,* from Latin *adulātiō,* from *adulārī*†, to flatter.]

a·dult (ə-dŭlt′, ăd′ŭlt′) *n.* **1.** One who has attained maturity or legal age. **2.** A fully grown, mature organism, such as an insect that has completed its final stage of metamorphosis. —*adj.* **1.** Fully developed and mature. **2.** Pertaining to, befitting, or intended for mature persons: *adult education.* [Latin *adultus,* past participle of *adolescere,* to grow up. See **adolescent.**] —**a·dult′hood′** *n.*

a·dul·ter·ant (ə-dŭl′tər-ənt) *n.* A substance that adulterates. —*adj.* Adulterating.

a·dul·ter·ate (ə-dŭl′tə-rāt′) *tr.v.* **-ated, -ating, -ates.** To make impure, spurious, or inferior by adding extraneous or improper ingredients. —*adj.* **1.** Spurious; adulterated; corrupt: *"prefer the adulterate enjoyments of the town to the genuine pleasures of a country"* (Smollett). **2.** Adulterous. [Latin *adulterāre,* to pollute, commit adultery. See **al-**¹ in Appendix.*] —**a·dul′ter·a′tion** *n.* —**a·dul′ter·a′tor** (-ā′tər) *n.*

a·dul·ter·er (ə-dŭl′tər-ər) *n.* One who commits adultery.

a·dul·ter·ess (ə-dŭl′trĭs, ə-dŭl′tər-ĭs) *n.* A woman who commits adultery.

a·dul·ter·ine (ə-dŭl′tə-rĭn′, -rīn) *adj.* **1.** Characterized by adulteration; spurious; fake. **2.** Unauthorized by law; illegal. **3.** Born of adultery: *adulterine offspring.* [Latin *adulterīnus* from *adulterāre,* to commit adultery, ADULTERATE.]

a·dul·ter·ous (ə-dŭl′tər-əs, -trəs) *adj.* Relating to, inclined to, or marked by adultery. —**a·dul′ter·ous·ly** *adv.*

a·dul·ter·y (ə-dŭl′tər-ē, -trē) *n., pl.* **-ries.** Voluntary sexual intercourse between a married person and a partner other than the lawful husband or wife. [Middle English *adulterie, a(d)vouterie,* from Old French *avoutrie, avoutire,* from Latin *adulterium,* from *adulter,* adulterer, from *adulterāre,* to ADULTERATE.]

ad·um·bral (ăd-ŭm′brəl) *adj.* In shadow. [From AD- (in) + Latin *umbra,* shadow (see **andho-** in Appendix*).]

ad·um·brate (ăd-ŭm′brāt′, ăd′əm-brāt′) *tr.v.* **-brated, -brating, -brates.** **1.** To give a sketchy outline. **2.** To prefigure indistinctly; to foreshadow. **3.** To disclose partially or guardedly. [Latin *adumbrāre,* overshadow : *ad-,* to + *umbra,* shadow (see **andho-** in Appendix*).] —**ad′um·bra′tion** (ăd′əm-brā′shən) *n.* —**ad·um′bra·tive** (ăd-ŭm′brə-tĭv) *adj.* —**ad·um′bra·tive·ly** *adv.*

a·dust (ə-dŭst′) *adj.* **1.** Burned; scorched. **2.** Melancholy; gloomy. [Middle English, from Latin *adūstus,* from the past participle of *adūrere,* to set fire to : *ad-,* to + *ūrere,* to burn (see **eus-** in Appendix*).]

A·du·wa (ä′də-wə). Also **A·do·wa.** A town in northern Ethiopia, the site of the victory of the Ethiopian Emperor Menelik II over the Italians (1896).

adv. 1. adverb; adverbial. **2.** advertisement.

ad va·lo·rem (ăd və-lôr′əm, və-lōr′əm). *Latin. Abbr.* **a.v., ad val.** In proportion to the value: *ad valorem duties on imported goods.*

ad·vance (ăd-văns′, -väns′) *v.* **-vanced, -vancing, -vances.** —*tr.* **1.** To move or bring forward in position. **2.** To put forward; propose; suggest. **3.** To aid the growth or progress of; to further. **4.** To raise in rank; promote. **5.** To cause to occur sooner; hasten. **6.** To raise in amount or rate; to increase. **7.** To pay (money or interest) before legally due. **8.** To supply or lend, especially on credit. —*intr.* **1.** To go or move forward or onward. **2.** To make progress; improve; grow. **3.** To rise in rank, position, or value. —*n.* **1.** The act or process of moving or going forward. See Usage note below. **2.** Improvement; progress. **3.** A rise or increase of price or value. **4.** *Plural.* Personal approaches made to secure acquaintance, favor, or an agreement; overtures. **5. a.** The furnishing of funds or goods on credit. **b.** The funds or goods so furnished; a loan. **6.** Payment of money before legally or normally due. —**in advance. 1.** In front. **2.** Ahead of time; beforehand; early. —*adj.* **1.** Made or given ahead of time; prior. **2.** Going before; in front; forward. See Usage note below. [Middle English *advancen,* from Old French *avancier,* from Vulgar Latin *abantiāre* (unattested), from Latin *abante,* "from before" : *ab-,* away from + *ante,* before (see **anti** in Appendix*).] —**ad·vance′ment** *n.* —**ad·vanc′er** *n.*

Synonyms: *advance, progress, promote, forward, further.* These verbs all refer to movement forward or upward, literally or figuratively; they vary widely in application, however. *Advance* alone is both transitive and intransitive. Intransitively it applies to forward movement (literal) and to enlargement of scope or importance, rise in status, or the like (figurative). *Progress,* which is only intransitive, also has both these senses, and differs principally in stressing the idea of steady and orderly movement toward a goal. Transitively, *advance* alone applies to forward movement with reference to time *(advance a deadline, advance money)* and to causing to rise in value *(advance prices). Advance* and *promote* are generally interchangeable when they mean to raise a person in rank or grade. *Advance, promote, forward,* and *further* all have the transitive sense of making something (such as a cause, a career, or a business venture) go forward, figur-

atively, by providing assistance. *Advance* and *forward* are nonspecific in this sense; *promote* and *further* stress active support and encouragement. *Forward* alone has the transitive sense of sending something onward or ahead, especially mail.
Usage: *Advance* (noun) is applicable to forward movement and to figurative progress in general. *Advancement* applies principally to figurative progress, as of persons being promoted or causes being furthered. *Advance* (adjective) emphasizes actual precedence in position *(advance guard)* or time *(advance warning)*, whereas *advanced* implies, figuratively, a forward position in relation to a norm *(advanced thought; advanced mathematics)*.

ad·vanced (ăd-vănst′, -vänst′) *adj.* **1. a.** Far on in course; at a late stage. **b.** Far on in life; very old. **2.** Ahead of contemporary thought or practice: *advanced ideas.* **3.** At the highest level of difficulty. See Usage note at **advance**.

advanced standing. The status of a college student granted credit, usually after passing a qualifying test, for courses omitted or taken elsewhere.

advance guard. A detachment of troops sent ahead of the main force to reconnoiter and provide protection.

ad·van·tage (ăd-văn′tĭj, ăd-vän′-) *n.* **1.** A factor favorable or conducive to success. **2.** Benefit or profit; gain. **3.** A relatively favorable position; superiority of means. **4.** *Tennis.* The first point scored after deuce, or the resulting score. Also called "ad," "vantage." **—take advantage of. 1.** To put to good use; avail oneself of. **2.** To profit selfishly by; exploit. **—to advantage.** To good effect; profitably; favorably. *—tr.v.* **advantaged, -taging, -tages.** To afford profit or gain to; to benefit. [Middle English *avantage,* from Old French, "the condition of being ahead," from *avant,* before, from Latin *abante,* (from) before. See **advance**.]

ad·van·ta·geous (ăd′văn-tā′jəs, ăd′vən-) *adj.* Affording benefit or gain; profitable; useful. See Synonyms at **beneficial**. **—ad′van·ta′geous·ly** *adv.* **—ad′van·ta′geous·ness** *n.*

ad·vec·tion (ăd-vĕk′shən) *n.* A local change in a property of a system, as of atmospheric temperature, caused by motion of the fluid in a gradient of the property. [Latin *advectiō,* conveyance, from *advehere* (past participle *advectus*), to carry to : *ad-,* to + *vehere,* to carry (see **wegh-** in Appendix*).]

ad·vent (ăd′vĕnt) *n.* The coming or arrival, especially of something awaited or momentous: *"a melodious tinkle of strings announced the advent of the minstrels"* (Ronald Firbank). [Middle English, from Latin *adventus,* from the past participle of *advenīre,* to come to : *ad,* to + *venīre,* to come (see **gwā-** in Appendix*).]

Ad·vent (ăd′vĕnt′) *n.* **1.** The birth of Christ. **2.** The **Second Advent** *(see).* **3.** The period including four Sundays before Christmas, the first of which is called **Advent Sunday** *(see).*

Ad·vent·ist (ăd′vĕn-tĭst) *n.* A member of any of several Christian denominations that believe Christ's second coming and the end of the world are near at hand. See **Seventh-Day Adventist**. **—Ad′vent·ism′** *n.*

ad·ven·ti·ti·a (ăd′vĕn-tĭsh′ē-ə) *n.* The outermost covering of an organ, especially of a blood vessel. [New Latin, from Latin *adventicius,* ADVENTITIOUS.]

ad·ven·ti·tious (ăd′vĕn-tĭsh′əs) *adj.* **1.** Acquired by accident; added by chance; not inherent. **2.** *Biology.* Appearing in an unusual place or in an irregular or sporadic manner: *adventitious shoots.* —See Synonyms at **accidental**. [Latin *adventicius,* "arriving (from outside)," from *adventus,* arrival, ADVENT.] **—ad′ven·ti′tious·ly** *adv.* **—ad′ven·ti′tious·ness** *n.*

ad·ven·tive (ăd-vĕn′tĭv) *adj. Biology.* Not native to, and not fully established in, a new habitat or environment; locally or temporarily naturalized: *an adventive weed.* *—n. Biology.* An adventive organism. [From Latin *adventus,* arrival, ADVENT.] **—ad·ven′tive·ly** *adv.*

Advent Sunday. The first Sunday of Advent; the Sunday nearest to St. Andrew's Day, the last day of November.

ad·ven·ture (ăd-vĕn′chər) *n.* **1.** An undertaking of a hazardous nature; a risky enterprise. **2.** An unusual experience or course of events marked by excitement and suspense. **3.** Participation in hazardous or exciting experiences. **4.** A financial speculation or business venture. *—v.* **adventured, -turing, -tures.** *—tr.* To venture; risk; dare. *—intr.* To take risks; engage in hazardous activities. [Middle English *aventure,* from Old French, from Vulgar Latin *(rēs) adventūra* (unattested), "(a thing) that will happen," from Latin *adventūrus,* future participle of *advenīre,* to arrive. See **advent**.]

ad·ven·tur·er (ăd-vĕn′chər-ər) *n.* **1.** One who adventures. **2.** A soldier of fortune. **3.** A heavy speculator. **4.** One who seeks wealth and social position by unscrupulous means.

ad·ven·tur·ess (ăd-vĕn′chər-ĭs) *n.* A woman who seeks social and financial advancement by dubious means.

ad·ven·tur·ous (ăd-vĕn′chər-əs) *adj.* **1.** Also **ad·ven·ture·some** (-səm). Inclined to undertake new and daring enterprises. **2.** Hazardous; risky. —See Synonyms at **reckless**. **—ad·ven′tur·ous·ly** *adv.* **—ad·ven′tur·ous·ness** *n.*

ad·verb (ăd′vûrb′) *n. Abbr.* **adv. 1.** A part of speech, comprising a class of words that modify a verb, adjective, or other adverb. **2.** A word belonging to this class, as *rapidly* in *He runs rapidly.* [Middle English, from Old French *adverbe,* from Latin *adverbium* (translation of Greek *epirrhēma,* "added word") : *ad-,* additional + *verbum,* word (see **wer-⁶** in Appendix*).] **—ad·ver′bi·al** *adj.* **—ad·ver′bi·al·ly** *adv.*

ad ver·bum (ăd vûr′bəm). *Latin.* Word for word; verbatim.

ad·ver·sar·y (ăd′vər-sĕr′ē) *n., pl.* **-ies.** An opponent; enemy. See Synonyms at **opponent**. **—the Adversary.** The Devil. [Middle English *adversarie,* from Latin *adversārius,* opponent, from *adversus,* ADVERSE.]

ad·ver·sa·tive (ăd-vûr′sə-tĭv) *adj.* Expressing antithesis or opposition. Said of words. *—n.* An adversative word, as *however* or *but.* [Latin *adversātivus,* from *adversāri,* to be opposed to, from *adversus,* ADVERSE.] **—ad·ver′sa·tive·ly** *adv.*

ad·verse (ăd-vûrs′, ăd′vûrs′) *adj.* **1.** Antagonistic in design or effect; hostile; opposed: *adverse criticism.* **2.** Contrary to one's interests or welfare; unfavorable; unpropitious: *adverse circumstances.* See Usage note at **averse**. **3.** In an opposite or opposing direction or position. **4.** *Botany.* Facing the axis or main stem. —See Synonyms at **contrary**. [Middle English, from Old French *advers,* from Latin *adversus,* past participle of *advertere,* to turn toward (with hostility) : *ad-,* toward + *vertere,* to turn (see **wer-³** in Appendix*).] **—ad·verse′ly** *adv.* **—ad·verse′ness** *n.*

ad·ver·si·ty (ăd-vûr′sə-tē) *n., pl.* **-ties. 1.** A state of hardship or affliction; misfortune. **2.** A calamitous event. —See Synonyms at **misfortune**.

ad·vert (ăd-vûrt′) *intr.v.* **-verted, -verting, -verts.** To call attention; refer: *advert to a problem.* [Middle English *a(d)verten,* from Old French *a(d)vertir,* from Vulgar Latin *advertīre* (unattested), from Latin *advertere,* to turn toward. See **adverse**.]

ad·ver·tise (ăd′vər-tīz′) *v.* **-tised, -tising, -tises.** Also **ad·ver·tize.** *—tr.* **1.** To make public announcement of; especially, to proclaim the qualities or advantages of (a product or business) so as to increase sales. **2.** *Archaic.* To warn or notify: *"This event advertises me that there is such a fact as death"* (Thoreau). *—intr.* **1.** To call the attention of the public to a product or business. **2.** To inquire in a public notice, as in a newspaper. Often used with *for: advertise for an apartment.* [Middle English *a(d)vertisen,* from Old French *a(d)vertir* (present participle *advertissant*), ADVERT.] **—ad′ver·tis′er** *n.*

ad·ver·tise·ment (ăd′vər-tīz′mənt, ăd-vûr′tĭs-mənt, -tĭz-mənt) *n. Abbr.* **ad., adv., advt.** A notice designed to attract public attention or patronage. Also informally called "ad."

ad·ver·tis·ing (ăd′vər-tī′zĭng) *n.* **1.** The action of attracting public attention to a product or business. **2.** The business of preparing and distributing advertisements. **3.** Printed or spoken advertisements, collectively.

ad·vice (ăd-vīs′) *n.* **1.** Opinion from one not immediately concerned as to what could or should be done about a problem; counsel. **2.** *Often plural.* Information or report, especially when communicated from a distance: *advices from an ambassador.* [Middle English *a(d)vise,* from Old French *a(d)vis,* opinion, from Vulgar Latin *advīsum* (unattested), opinion, probably from some such phrase as *ad (meum) vīsum,* "according to (my) view" : *ad,* to + *vīsum,* view, appearance, from the neuter past participle of *vidēre,* to see (see **weid-** in Appendix*).]

ad·vis·a·ble (ăd-vī′zə-bəl) *adj.* Worthy of being recommended or suggested; prudent; expedient. **—ad·vis′a·bil′i·ty, ad·vis′a·ble·ness** *n.* **—ad·vis′a·bly** *adv.*

ad·vise (ăd-vīz′) *v.* **-vised, -vising, -vises.** *—tr.* **1.** To offer advice to; to counsel. **2.** To recommend; suggest. **3.** To inform; notify: *advise a person of a decision.* *—intr.* **1.** To consult; take counsel. Used with *with: advise with one's associates.* **2.** To offer advice. [Middle English *a(d)visen,* from Old French *a(d)viser,* from Vulgar Latin *advīsāre* (unattested), to observe (influenced by Latin *advīsum,* ADVICE) : Latin *ad-,* to, at + *vīsere,* desiderative of *vidēre* (past participle *vīsus*), to see (see **weid-** in Appendix*).] **—ad·vi′so·ry** *adj.*
Usage: *Advise,* in the sense of *inform* or *notify,* is acceptable to 70 per cent of the Usage Panel. But many members would restrict such usage to business correspondence, as a genteelism.

ad·vised (ăd-vīzd′) *adj.* **1.** Considered; thought out. Used chiefly in the combinations *well-advised* and *ill-advised.* **2.** Informed: *be kept advised.*

ad·vis·ed·ly (ăd-vī′zĭd-lē) *adv.* With careful consideration; deliberately.

ad·vise·ment (ăd-vīz′mənt) *n.* Careful consideration.

ad·vis·er (ăd-vī′zər) *n.* Also **ad·vi·sor. 1.** A person who offers advice, especially in an official or professional capacity. **2.** A teacher who advises students in academic and personal matters.

ad·vo·ca·cy (ăd′və-kə-sē) *n.* Active support, as of a cause.

ad·vo·cate (ăd′və-kāt′) *tr.v.* **-cated, -cating, -cates.** To speak in favor of; recommend. See Synonyms at **support**. *—n.* (ăd′və-kĭt, -kāt′). **1.** A person who argues for a cause; supporter or defender. **2.** A person who pleads in another's behalf; an intercessor. **3.** *Scottish Law.* A lawyer. —See Synonyms at **lawyer**. [From Middle English *a(d)vocat,* a lawyer, from Old French, from Latin *advocātus,* "one summoned (to give evidence)," from *advocāre,* to call or summon to : *ad,* to + *vocāre,* to call (see **wekw-** in Appendix*).] **—ad′vo·ca′tor** (-kā′tər) *n.*

ad·vow·son (ăd-vou′zən) *n. English Ecclesiastical Law.* The right to present a vacant benefice. [Middle English *avoweson, advounson,* from Norman French *a(d)voeson,* variant of Old French *avoueson,* from Medieval Latin *advocātiō,* presentation, summoning, from Latin *advocāre,* to summon, ADVOCATE.]

advt. advertisement.

A·dy·gey Autonomous Region (ä′də-gā′). Also **A·dy·gei Autonomous Region.** An administrative division, 1,737 square miles in area, of the southwestern Russian S.F.S.R. Population, 353,000. Capital, Maikop.

ad·y·tum (ăd′ə-təm) *n., pl.* **-ta** (-tə). The sanctum in an ancient temple. [Latin, from Greek *aduton,* neuter of *adutos,* not to be entered : *a-,* not + *duein*†, to enter, sink.]

adz, adze (ădz) *n.* An axlike tool with an arched blade at right angles to the handle, used for dressing wood. [Middle English *adse,* Old English *adesa*†.]

A·dzhar Autonomous Soviet Socialist Republic (ä′jär′). An administrative division, 1,160 square miles in area, of the

adz

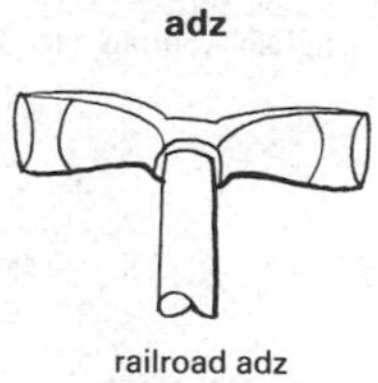

railroad adz

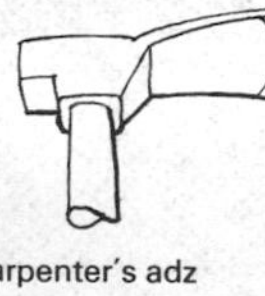

carpenter's adz

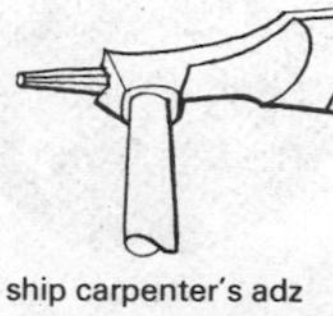

ship carpenter's adz

t tight/th thin, path/*th* this, bathe/ŭ cut/ûr urge/v valve/w with/y yes/z zebra, size/zh vision/ə about, item, edible, gallop, circus/ à *Fr.* ami/œ *Fr.* feu, *Ger.* schön/ü *Fr.* tu, *Ger.* über/KH *Ger.* ich, *Scot.* loch/N *Fr.* bon. ***Follows main vocabulary. †Of obscure origin.**

southwestern Georgian S.S.R. Population, 288,000. Capital, Batum. Also called "Adzharistan."

ad·zu·ki bean (ăd-zo͞o′kē). Also **ad·su·ki bean** (ăd-so͞o′kē, -zo͞o′kē). A plant, *Phaseolus angularis,* having yellow flowers and pods bearing edible seeds, widely cultivated as a food crop in the Orient. [Japanese *azuki,* "red bean."]

A.E.A. Actors' Equity Association.

A.E. and P. Ambassador Extraordinary and Plenipotentiary.

AEC, A.E.C. Atomic Energy Commission.

ae·ci·o·spore (ē′sē-ō-spôr′, -spōr′) *n. Botany.* A rust spore, formed in a chainlike series in an aecium. [AECI(UM) + SPORE.]

ae·ci·um (ē′sē-əm, ē′shē-əm) *n., pl.* **-cia** (-sē-ə, -shē-ə). Also **ae·cid·i·um** (ē-sĭd′ē-əm) *pl.* **-ia** (-ē-ə). *Botany.* A cuplike structure in rust fungi, containing chains of aeciospores. [New Latin, from Greek *aikia,* injury (rust fungi are destructive), from *aikēs,* unseemly. See **weik-**³ in Appendix.*] —**ae′ci·al** (ē′sē-əl, -shē-əl) *adj.*

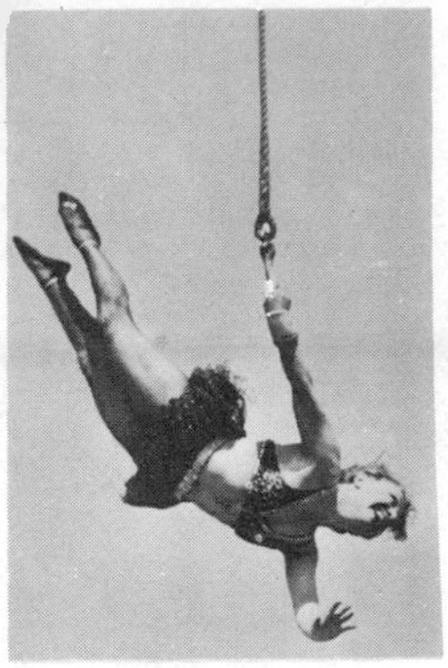

aerialist

a·e·des (ā-ē′dēz) *n., pl.* **aedes.** Any mosquito of the genus *Aëdes,* such as *A. aegypti,* which transmits yellow fever and dengue. [New Latin *Aedes,* from Greek *aēdēs,* unpleasant : *a-,* not + *ēdos,* pleasant (see **swād-** in Appendix*).]

ae·dile (ē′dīl′) *n.* In ancient Rome, a magistrate who had charge of public works, police, and the grain supply. [Latin *aedīlis,* "(one) concerned with buildings," from *aedēs,* house. See **aidh-** in Appendix.*]

Ae·ga·de·an Islands. Also **Ae·gá·di·an.** See **Egadi Islands.**

Ae·ga·tes. The ancient name for the **Egadi Islands.**

Ae·ge·an (ĭ-jē′ən) *adj.* **1.** Of or pertaining to the Aegean Sea or Aegean Islands. **2.** Of, pertaining to, or designating the prehistoric civilization that flourished in the Aegean area in the Bronze Age.

Ae·ge·an Islands (ĭ-jē′ən). **1.** The islands of the Aegean Sea. **2.** An administrative division of Greece that includes most of these islands.

Ae·ge·an Sea (ĭ-jē′ən). An arm of the Mediterranean, about 200 miles wide and 400 long, between Greece and Turkey, bounded in the south by Crete.

Ae·geus (ē′jo͞os, ē′jē-əs). *Greek Mythology.* A king of Athens and the father of Theseus.

Ae·gi·na (ē-jī′nə). **1.** An island off the southeastern coast of Greece. **2.** A town on this island, once an important city-state, and in the late 1820's the temporary capital of Greece.

Ae·gir (ăg′ər). *Norse Mythology.* The god of the sea.

ae·gis (ē′jĭs) *n.* Also **e·gis.** **1.** *Greek Mythology.* The shield of Zeus, lent by him to Athena. **2.** Protection. **3.** Sponsorship; patronage. [Latin, from Greek *aigis* (often depicted as a goatskin, and associated by folk etymology with *aix,* stem *aig-,* goat). See **aig-** in Appendix.*]

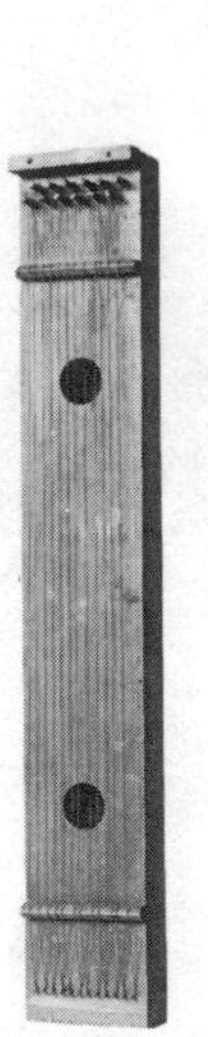

Aeolian harp
Nineteenth-century English Aeolian harp

Ae·gis·thus (ē-jĭs′thəs). *Greek Mythology.* The son of Thyestes and lover of Clytemnestra.

Ael·fric (ăl′frĭk). Called "Grammaticus." A.D.955?–1020? English abbot and writer.

–aemia. Variant of **-emia.**

Ae·ne·as (ĭ-nē′əs). The Trojan hero of the *Aeneid,* son of Anchises and Aphrodite, who escaped the sack of Troy and, after wandering seven years, settled in Italy.

Ae·ne·id (ĭ-nē′ĭd). An epic poem in Latin by Virgil, telling of the adventures of Aeneas after the destruction of Troy.

a·e·ne·ous, a·e·ne·us (ā-ē′nē-əs) *adj.* Having a brassy or golden-green color. [Latin *aēneus, aēnus,* of bronze or copper, from *aes,* bronze, copper. See **ayos-** in Appendix.*]

ae·o·li·an. Variant of **eolian.**

Ae·o·li·an (ē-ō′lē-ən) *adj.* **1.** Of or pertaining to Aeolis or its people. **2.** Of or pertaining to Aeolus, god of the winds. —*n.* **1.** A member of one of the major Greek tribes that settled in central Greece, Lesbos, and Aeolis. **2.** Aeolic.

Aeolian harp. A musical instrument consisting of an open box over which are stretched strings that sound when wind passes over them. Also called "wind harp."

Aeolian Islands. See **Lipari Islands.**

Ae·ol·ic (ē-ŏl′ĭk) *n.* A branch of East Greek that was spoken in Thessaly, Boeotia, and along the coast of Asia Minor north of Ionia, with adjacent islands.

ae·ol·i·pile (ē-ŏl′ə-pīl′) *n.* An ancient prototypal steam engine, consisting of a spherical or cylindrical vessel fitted with circumferential exhaust jets and mounted to permit free rotation about the steam inlet axis. [Latin *aeolipila,* from Greek *aioli-pulē,* "wind-vent" : *Aiolos,* AEOLUS + *pulē,* gate (see **pulē** in Appendix*).]

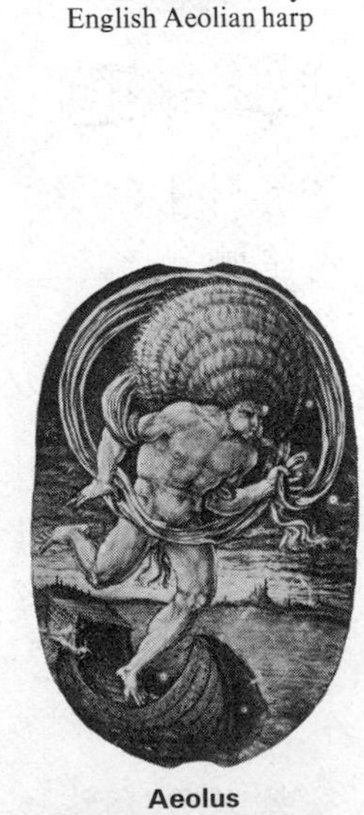

Aeolus
Illumination on folio of a chorale, in Piccolimini Library, Siena, Italy

Ae·o·lis (ē′ə-lĭs). Also **Ae·o·li·a** (ē-ō′lē-ə). A region of the west coast of Asia Minor settled in ancient times by the Aeolians.

Ae·o·lus (ē′ə-ləs). *Greek Mythology.* **1.** The god of the winds. **2.** A king of Thessaly and ancestor of the Aeolians. [Latin, from Greek *Aiolos,* from *aiolos*†, quick-moving.]

ae·on. Variant of **eon.**

ae·o·ni·an. Variant of **eonian.**

Ae·qui·an (ē′kwē-ən) *n.* A language belonging to the Sabellian branch of the Indo-European language family, spoken by the early Italic inhabitants of Latium. [From Latin *Aequi,* tribal name.]

aer·ate (âr′āt′) *tr.v.* **-ated, -ating, -ates.** **1.** To supply or charge (liquid) with a gas, especially carbon dioxide. **2.** To expose to the circulation of air for purification. **3.** To supply (blood) with oxygen. [AER(O)- + -ATE.] —**aer·a′tion** *n.*

aer·a·tor (âr′ā′tər) *n.* A device for aerating liquids.

aer·i·al (âr′ē-əl, ā-ĭr′ē-əl) *adj.* **1.** Of, in, or caused by the air. **2.** Living in the air. **3.** Reaching high into the air; lofty. **4.** Suggestive of air, as in lightness; airy. **5.** Unsubstantial; imaginary. **6.** Of, for, or by aircraft. **7.** *Botany.* Borne in the air rather than underground or under water: *aerial roots.* —*n.* (âr′ē-əl). *Electronics.* An **antenna** *(see).* [From Latin *āerius,* from Greek *aerios,* from *aēr,* air. See **wē-** in Appendix.*]

aer·i·al·ist (âr′ē-əl-ĭst) *n.* An acrobat who performs on a tightrope, trapeze, or similar apparatus.

aerial ladder. A ladder that can be extended to reach high places, especially one mounted on a fire engine.

aer·ie (âr′ē, ăr′ē, ĭr′ē) *n., pl.* **-ies.** Also **aer·y, eyr·ie, eyr·y.** **1.** The nest of an eagle or other predatory bird, built on a crag or other high place. **2.** A house or stronghold built on a height. [Medieval Latin *aeria, aerea,* from Old French *aire, aere,* from Latin *ārea,* open field, threshing floor, bird's nest (possibly influenced by Latin *ager,* native place, acre). See **area.**]

aero–, aer–. Indicates: **1.** Air, gas, or the atmosphere; for example, **aerogram, aerate.** **2.** Aircraft; for example, **aeronautics.** [Middle English, from Old French, from Latin, from Greek, from *aēr,* air. See **wē-** in Appendix.*]

aer·o·bal·lis·tics (âr′ō-bə-lĭs′tĭks) *n.* Ballistics, especially of missiles, in the atmosphere.

aer·o·bat·ics (âr′ō-băt′ĭks) *n.* Plural in form, used with a singular or plural verb. The performance of stunts, such as rolls and loops, with an airplane or glider. [AERO- + (ACRO)BATICS.]

aer·obe (âr′ōb′) *n.* An organism, such as a bacterium, requiring molecular oxygen or air to live. [French *aérobie,* "air-life" : AERO- + Greek *bios,* life (see **gwei-** in Appendix*).] —**aer·o′bic** (âr-ō′bĭk) *adj.*

aer·o·drome. *Chiefly British.* Variant of **airdrome.**

aer·o·dy·nam·ics (âr′ō-dī-năm′ĭks) *n.* Plural in form, used with a singular verb. The dynamics of gases, especially of atmospheric interactions with moving objects. —**aer′o·dy·nam′ic** *adj.*

aer·o·dyne (âr′ə-dīn′) *n.* Any heavier-than-air aircraft deriving lift from motion. [AERO- + -dyne, from Greek *dunamis,* power, from *dunasthai,* to be able (see **deu-**² in Appendix*).]

aer·o·em·bo·lism (âr′ō-ĕm′bə-lĭz′əm) *n.* **1.** The presence of air bubbles in the heart or blood vessels, often resulting from a wound in one of the large veins of the neck. Also called "air embolism." **2.** **Caisson disease** *(see).*

aer·o·foil. *Chiefly British.* Variant of **airfoil.**

aer·o·gram (âr′ə-grăm′) *n.* Also **aer·o·gramme** (for sense 2). **1.** A radiogram. **2.** An air-mail letter written on a standard, lightweight form that folds into the shape of an envelope and can be sent at a low postage rate. [AERO- + -GRAM.]

aer·o·lite (âr′ə-līt′) *n.* Also **aer·o·lith** (-lĭth′). A chiefly silicious meteorite. [AERO- + -LITE.] —**aer′o·lit′ic** (-lĭt′ĭk) *adj.*

aer·ol·o·gy (âr-ŏl′ə-jē) *n.* Total atmospheric meteorology as opposed to surface-based study. [AERO- + -LOGY.] —**aer′o·log′ic** (âr′ə-lŏj′ĭk), **aer′o·log′i·cal** *adj.* —**aer·ol′o·gist** *n.*

aer·o·me·chan·ics (âr′ō-mĭ-kăn′ĭks) *n.* Plural in form, used with a singular verb. The science of the motion and equilibrium of air and other gases, comprising aerodynamics and aerostatics. —**aer′o·me·chan′i·cal** *adj.* —**aer′o·me·chan′i·cal·ly** *adv.*

aer·o·med·i·cine (âr′ō-mĕd′ə-sĭn) *n.* The medical study and treatment of disturbances, disorders, and diseases resulting from or associated with atmospheric flight. Also called "aviation medicine." —**aer′o·med′i·cal** *adj.*

aer·o·me·te·or·o·graph (âr′ō-mē′tē-ôr′ə-grăf′, -gräf′) *n.* An aircraft instrument for simultaneously recording temperature, atmospheric pressure, and humidity.

aer·om·e·ter (âr-ŏm′ə-tər) *n.* A device for determining the weight and density of air or other gas. [French *aéromètre* : AERO- + -METER.]

aer·o·naut (âr′ə-nôt′) *n.* A pilot or navigator of a balloon or lighter-than-air craft. [AERO- + (ARGO)NAUT.]

aer·o·nau·tic (âr′ə-nô′tĭk) *adj.* Also **aer·o·nau·ti·cal** (-tĭ-kəl). Of or pertaining to aeronautics. —**aer′o·nau′ti·cal·ly** *adv.*

aer·o·nau·tics (âr′ə-nô′tĭks) *n.* Plural in form, used with a singular verb. **1.** The design and construction of aircraft. **2.** The theory and practice of aircraft navigation.

aer·o·neu·ro·sis (âr′ō-no͝o-rō′sĭs, âr′ō-nyo͝o-) *n.* A nervous exhaustion from prolonged piloting of aircraft. Also called "flying fatigue."

aer·on·o·my (âr-ŏn′ə-mē) *n.* The study of the upper atmosphere, especially of regions of ionized gas. [AERO- + -NOMY.]

aer·o·pause (âr′ō-pôz′) *n.* The region of the atmosphere above which aircraft cannot fly. [AERO- + -PAUSE.]

aer·o·phyte (âr′ə-fīt′) *n. Botany.* An **epiphyte** *(see).* [AERO- + -PHYTE.]

aer·o·plane. *Chiefly British.* Variant of **airplane.**

aer·o·sol (âr′ə-sôl′, -sŏl′, -sōl′) *n.* **1.** A gaseous suspension of fine solid or liquid particles. **2. a.** A substance, such as a detergent, insecticide, or paint, packaged under pressure with a gaseous propellant for release as an aerosol. **b.** An aerosol bomb. [AERO- + SOL(UTION).]

aerosol bomb. A usually hand-held container or dispenser from which an aerosol is released.

aer·o·space (âr′ō-spās′) *adj.* **1.** Of or designating the earth's atmosphere and the space beyond. **2.** Of or pertaining to the science or technology of flight. —**aer′o·space′** *n.*

aerospace vehicle. A vehicle capable of flight both within and outside the earth's atmosphere.

aer·o·sphere (âr′ō-sfĭr′) *n.* The lower portion of the atmosphere in which both unmanned and manned flight is possible. [French *aérosphère* : AERO- + -SPHERE.]

aer·o·stat (âr′ō-stăt′) *n.* An aircraft, especially a balloon or dirigible, deriving its lift from the buoyancy of surrounding air rather than from aerodynamic motion. [French *aérostat* : AERO- + -STAT.] —**aer′o·stat′ic, aer′o·stat′i·cal** *adj.*

aer·o·stat·ics (âr′ō-stăt′ĭks) *n.* Plural in form, used with a singular verb. The science of gases in equilibrium and of the equilibrium of balloons or aircraft under changing atmospheric flight conditions.

aer·o·ther·mo·dy·nam·ics (âr′ō-thûr′mō-dī-năm′ĭks) *n.* Plural in form, used with a singular verb. The study of the thermodynamics of gases, especially at high relative velocities.

ae·ru·go (ĭ-ro͞o′gō) *n.* Also **e·ru·go.** Green or blue-green copper rust; verdigris. [Latin *aerūgō,* from *aes* (stem **aer-**), copper, bronze. See **ayos-** in Appendix.*]

aer·y[1] (âr′ē, ā′ə-rē) *adj. Poetic.* Ethereal.

aer·y[2]. Variant of **aerie.**

Aes·chy·lus (ĕs′kə-ləs, ēs′-). 525–456 B.C. Greek poet; author of tragedies of which seven are extant.

Aes·cu·la·pi·an (ĕs′kyo͞o-lā′pē-ən) *adj.* Of or pertaining to the healing art; medical: *the Aesculapian art.*

Aes·cu·la·pi·us (ĕs′kyo͞o-lā′pē-əs). The Roman god of medicine and healing; identified with the Greek Asclepius.

Ae·sir (ā′sîr, ē′sîr) *pl.n.* The gods of Norse mythology. [Old Norse, plural of *āss,* a god. See **ansu-** in Appendix.*]

Ae·sop (ē′sŏp′, ē′səp). Greek fabulist of the late sixth century B.C.

Ae·so·pi·an (ē-sō′pē-ən) *adj.* Also **Ae·sop·ic** (ē-sŏp′ĭk). **1.** In the manner of Aesop's animal fables. **2.** Veiled in allegorical suggestions, hints, and euphemisms so as to elude political censorship: *"they could express their views only in a diluted form, resorting to Aesopian hints and allusions"* (Isaac Deutscher).

aes·thete, es·thete (ĕs′thēt′) *n.* **1.** One who cultivates a superior appreciation of the beautiful. **2.** An effete person; one whose pursuit and admiration of beauty is thought to be excessive or affected. [Back-formation from AESTHETIC.]

aes·thet·ic, es·thet·ic (ĕs-thĕt′ĭk) *adj.* **1.** Of or pertaining to the criticism of taste. **2. a.** Of or pertaining to the sense of the beautiful: *the aesthetic faculties.* **b.** Artistic: *an aesthetic success.* **3. a.** Having a love of beauty. **b.** *Informal.* In accordance with accepted notions of good taste. [French *esthetique,* from German *ästhetisch,* from New Latin *aestheticus,* from Greek *aisthētikos,* pertaining to sense perception, from *aisthēta,* perceptible things, from *aisthenasthai,* to perceive. See **aw-**[2] in Appendix.*] —**aes·thet′i·cal·ly** *adv.*

aes·the·ti·cian, es·the·ti·cian (ĕs′thə-tĭsh′ən) *n.* A critic concerned with the theory of beauty and the fine arts.

aes·thet·i·cism, es·thet·i·cism (ĕs-thĕt′ə-sĭz′əm) *n.* **1.** The pursuit of the sensuously beautiful; the cult of beauty and good taste. Often used disparagingly to characterize an excessive or affected cult of beauty. **2. a.** A doctrine affirming beauty as the basic principle from which all other principles are derived. **b.** A doctrine whereby art and artists are held to be free of any obligation or responsibility other than that of striving for beauty.

aes·thet·ics, es·thet·ics (ĕs-thĕt′ĭks) *n.* Plural in form, used with a singular verb. **1.** The branch of philosophy that provides a theory of the beautiful and of the fine arts. **2.** In the philosophy of Kant, the branch of metaphysics concerned with the laws of perception.

aes·ti·val (ĕs′tə-vəl, ĕs-tī′-) *adj.* Also **es·ti·val.** Of, pertaining to, or appearing in summer. [Middle English *estival,* from Old French, from Latin *aestīvālis,* from *aestīvus,* from *aestās,* summer. See **aidh-** in Appendix.*]

aes·ti·vate (ĕs′tə-vāt′) *intr.v.* **-vated, -vating, -vates.** Also **es·ti·vate.** To pass the summer, especially in a state of dormancy. [Latin *aestīvāre,* from *aestīvus,* AESTIVAL.]

aes·ti·va·tion (ĕs′tə-vā′shən) *n.* Also **es·ti·va·tion.** **1.** The act of spending or passing the summer: *"Intramural aestivation, or town-life in summer . . . is a peculiar form of suspended existence."* (Oliver Wendell Holmes). **2.** *Zoology.* A state of dormancy or torpor during the summer or periods of drought. Compare **hibernation.** **3.** *Botany.* The arrangement of petals, sepals, and other floral organs in the unopened bud.

ae·ta·tis su·ae (ē-tā′tĭs so͞o′ē). *Abbr.* **aetat., aet.** *Latin.* Of his (or her) age.

aeth·e·ling. Variant of **atheling.**

Aeth·el·red. See **Ethelred II.**

ae·ther (ē′thər) *n.* **1.** *Capital* **A.** *Greek Mythology.* The poetic personification of the clear upper air breathed by the Olympians. **2.** Variant of **ether.**

ae·the·re·al. Variant of **ethereal.**

Ae·thi·o·pi·a. See **Ethiopia.**

ae·ti·ol·o·gy. Variant of **etiology.**

Aet·na. See **Etna.**

Ae·to·li·a (ē-tō′lē-ə). A region of western Greece, on the Ionian Sea. —**Ae·to′li·an** *adj. & n.*

AF **1.** air force. **2.** Anglo-French. **3.** audio frequency.

Af. Africa; African.

a.f. audio frequency.

A.F. **1.** air force. **2.** Anglo-French. **3.** audio frequency.

A.F.A.M. Ancient Free and Accepted Masons.

a·far (ə-fär′) *adv.* **1.** From a distance. Usually preceded by *from: They come from afar.* **2.** At or to a distance; far away. Usually followed by *off: We saw it afar off.* [Middle English *afer,* from *on fer,* at a distance, and *of fer,* from a distance, from *fer,* FAR.]

a·feard (ə-fîrd′) *adj.* Also **a·feared.** *Regional & Archaic.* Afraid; frightened: *"Be not afeared; the isle is full of noises."* (Shakespeare). [Middle English *afered,* Old English *āfǣred,* past participle of *āfǣran,* to frighten : *ā-,* intensive prefix + *fǣran,* to frighten, from *fǣr,* fear (see **per-**[5] in Appendix*).]

af·fa·ble (ăf′ə-bəl) *adj.* **1.** Easy to speak to; approachable; amiable. **2.** Mild; gentle; benign. —See Synonyms at **amiable.** [Old French, from Latin *affābilis,* from *affārī,* to speak to : *ad-,* to + *fārī,* to speak (see **bhā-**[2] in Appendix*).] —**af′fa·bil′i·ty** *n.* —**af′fa·bly** *adv.*

af·fair (ə-fâr′) *n.* **1.** Anything done or to be done; concern; business. **2.** *Plural.* Transactions and other business matters, collectively specified: *man of affairs.* **3. a.** Any occurrence, event, or matter. **b.** Any object or contrivance, loosely specified: *Our first car was a ramshackle affair.* **c.** *Plural.* Personal effects. **4.** A private matter; personal concern. **5.** A matter causing scandal and controversy: *the Dreyfus affair.* **6.** A love affair; liaison. [Middle English *afere,* from Old French *afaire,* from the phrase *a faire,* "to do" : *a,* to, from Latin *ad-* + *faire,* to do, from Latin *facere* (see **dhē-**[1] in Appendix*).]

af·faire d'hon·neur (à-fâr′ dô-nœr′). *French.* An affair of honor; a duel.

af·fect[1] (ə-fĕkt′) *tr.v.* **-fected, -fecting, -fects.** **1.** To have an influence on; bring about a change in. **2.** To touch or move the emotions of. **3.** To attack or infect. Used of disease, pain, or the like. **4.** To allot or assign. Used only in the passive: *"One of the domestics was affected to his especial service."* (Thackeray). —*n.* (ăf′fĕct′). **1.** *Psychology.* **a.** A feeling or emotion as distinguished from cognition, thought, or action. **b.** A strong feeling having active consequences. See Usage note below. **2.** *Obsolete.* A disposition, feeling, or tendency. [Latin *afficere* (past participle *affectus*), to do something to, exert influence on : *ad-,* to + *facere,* to do (see **dhē-**[1] in Appendix*).]

Synonyms: *affect, influence, impress, touch, move, strike.* These verbs can all mean to produce a mental or emotional effect. To *affect* is to change a person's emotions in some usually specified way. *Influence* implies a degree of control over the thinking and actions, as well as the emotions, of another. To *impress* is to produce a marked, usually favorable, effect on the mind. *Touch* usually means to arouse a brief sense of pathos, whereas *move* suggests profound emotional effect capable of inciting action. *Strike* implies instantaneous mental response to a stimulus such as a sight or an idea.

Usage: *Affect* and *effect* have no senses in common; therefore the tendency to confuse the words must be guarded against closely. As verbs, *affect* (the more common) is used principally in the senses of influence (*how smoking affects health*) and pretense or imitation (*affecting nonchalance to hide fear*), whereas *effect* applies only to accomplishment or execution (*reductions designed to effect economy; means adopted to effect an end*). As nouns, the terms can be kept straight by remembering that *affect* is now confined to psychology.

af·fect[2] (ə-fĕkt′) *tr.v.* **-fected, -fecting, -fects.** **1.** To simulate or imitate in order to make some desired impression; assume; feign. **2. a.** To display a preference for. **b.** *Archaic.* To fancy; love. **c.** To tend to by nature; tend to assume: *affect crystalline form.* **3.** To imitate: *"Spenser, in affecting the ancients, writ no language."* (Jonson). [Middle English *affecter,* from Latin *affectāre,* to strive after, frequentative of *afficere* (past participle *affectus*). to AFFECT.] —**af·fect′er** *n.*

af·fec·ta·tion (ăf′ĕk-tā′shən) *n.* **1.** A show, pretense, or display. **2.** Any artificial behavior or mannerism adopted to impress others; affectedness. [Latin *affectātiō,* from *affectāre,* to strive after, AFFECT.]

Synonyms: *affectation, pose, air* (and *airs*), *mannerism.* These nouns refer largely to personal attributes acquired as adornments to human character. An *affectation* is a little habit of speech or dress that the wearer has borrowed from his ideal, hoping to pass it off as genuinely his own. *Pose* denotes an attitude adopted with the aim of calling favorable attention to oneself. *Air,* meaning a distinctive but intangible quality, does not usually imply sham: *air of authority; air of a professor.* In the plural, however, it suggests affectation and snobbishness: *put on airs. Mannerism* denotes a peculiar trait or quirk that others find obtrusive and distracting.

af·fect·ed[1] (ə-fĕk′tĭd) *adj.* **1.** Acted upon, influenced, or changed. **2.** Emotionally stirred or moved. **3.** Infected or attacked, as by disease or climate.

af·fect·ed[2] (ə-fĕk′tĭd) *adj.* **1.** Assumed or simulated to impress others. **2.** Speaking or behaving in an artificial way to make a particular impression. **3.** Disposed or inclined. —**af·fect′ed·ly** *adv.* —**af·fect′ed·ness** *n.*

af·fect·ing[1] (ə-fĕk′tĭng) *adj.* Full of pathos; touching; moving: *an affecting spectacle.* See Synonyms at **moving.** [From AFFECT (to influence).] —**af·fect′ing·ly** *adv.*

af·fect·ing[2] (ə-fĕk′tĭng) *adj. Obsolete.* **1.** Displaying love. **2.** Feigning or pretending: *"I never heard such a drawling, affecting rogue."* (Shakespeare). [From AFFECT (to simulate).]

af·fec·tion (ə-fĕk′shən) *n.* **1.** A fond or tender feeling toward another. **2.** *Often plural.* Feeling or emotion: *The state of his affections was unbalanced.* **3.** Any pathological condition of the mind or body. **4.** The act of influencing, affecting, or acting upon. **5.** The state of being influenced or acted upon. **6.** An attribute. **7.** Mental disposition or tendency. —See Synonyms at **love.** [Middle English *affeccioun,* from Old French *affection,* from Latin *affectiō,* (friendly) disposition, from *afficere,* to AFFECT.] —**af·fec′tion·al** *adj.* —**af·fec′tion·al·ly** *adv.*

af·fec·tion·ate (ə-fĕk′shən-ĭt) *adj.* **1.** Having or showing fond feelings or affection; loving; tender. **2.** *Obsolete.* Strongly or favorably disposed. Used with *to.* —**af·fec′tion·ate·ly** *adv.* —**af·fec′tion·ate·ness** *n.*

af·fec·tive (ə-fĕk′tĭv) *adj.* **1.** *Psychology.* Pertaining to or resulting from emotions or feelings rather than from thought. **2.** Pertaining to or arousing affection or emotion; emotional.

af·fen·pin·scher (ăf′ən-pĭn′chər, äf′ən-) *n.* Any of a breed of small dogs of European origin, having dark, wiry, shaggy hair and a tufted muzzle. [German *Affenpinscher,* "monkey-terrier" (so called because its face resembles a monkey's) : *Affe,* monkey, from Old High German *affo,* from Common Ger-

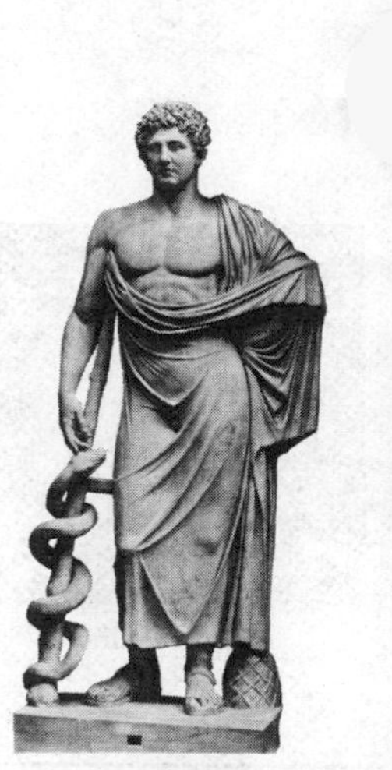

Aesculapius
Roman statue in the Vatican Museum

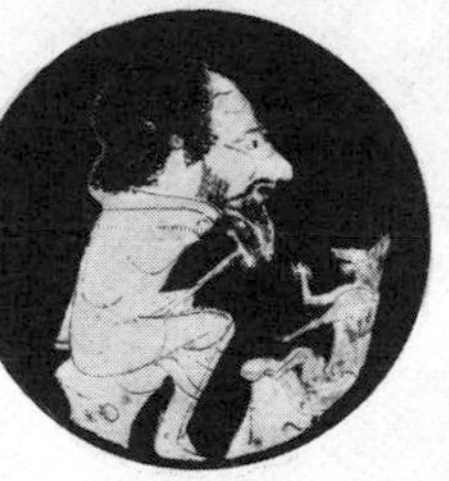

Aesop
The fabulist shown with a fox in central medallion of a fifth-century B.C. kylix

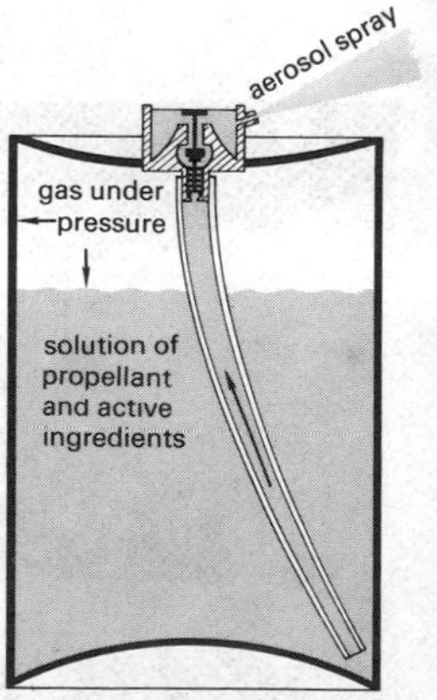
aerosol spray
gas under
pressure
solution of
propellant
and active
ingredients

aerosol bomb

manic *apan-* (unattested), APE + *Pinscher,* terrier (see **Doberman pinscher**).]

af·fer·ent (ăf′ər-ənt) *adj.* Directed toward a central organ or section, as nerves that conduct impulses from the periphery of the body inward to the spinal cord. Compare **efferent.** [Latin *afferēns,* present participle of *afferre,* to bring toward : *ad-,* toward + *ferre,* to bring (see **bher-**[1] in Appendix*).]

af·fet·tu·o·so (ăf′fĕt-to͞o-ō′zō) *adv. Music.* With warmth and tenderness. Used as a direction. [Italian, "emotional," from Late Latin *affectuōsus,* "tending to affect," from Latin *affectus,* past participle of *afficere,* to AFFECT.] —**af′fet·tu·o′so** *adj.*

af·fi·ance (ə-fī′əns) *tr.v.* **-anced, -ancing, -ances.** To bind in a pledge of marriage; betroth. [Middle English *affiaunce,* from Old French *affiance,* "trust," from *affier,* to trust to, from Medieval Latin *affīdāre* : Latin *ad-,* to + *fīdāre,* variant of Latin *fīdere,* to trust (see **bheidh-** in Appendix*).]

af·fi·ant (ə-fī′ənt) *n. Law.* One who makes an affidavit. [Old French, present participle of *affier,* to trust to. See **affiance.**]

af·fi·da·vit (ăf′ə-dā′vĭt) *n. Law.* A written declaration made under oath before a notary public or other authorized officer. [Medieval Latin *affīdāvit,* "he has pledged," from *affīdāre,* to trust to. See **affiance.**]

af·fil·i·ate (ə-fĭl′ē-āt′) *v.* **-ated, -ating, -ates.** —*tr.* **1.** To adopt as a subordinate associate. **2.** To associate (oneself) as a subordinate or subsidiary with. **3.** To admit as one's own child; adopt. **4.** *Law.* **a.** To determine the paternity of (an illegitimate child). Used with *upon.* **b.** To refer an illegitimate child to (its father). —*intr.* To associate or connect oneself: *We decided to affiliate.* —*n.* (ə-fĭl′ē-ĭt). A person or organization associated with another in subordinate relationship. [Medieval Latin *affīliāre,* "to take to oneself as a son" : *ad-,* to + *fīlius,* son (see **dhēi-** in Appendix*).] —**af·fil′i·a′tion** *n.*

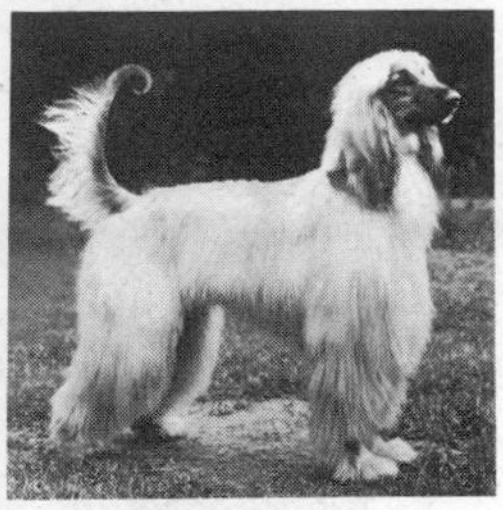

Afghan hound

af·fine (ə-fīn′) *adj.* **1.** Of or pertaining to a mathematical transformation of coordinates that is equivalent to a translation, contraction, or expansion with respect to a fixed origin and fixed coordinate system. **2.** Of or pertaining to the geometry of affine transformations. [Old French *affin,* AFFINED.]

af·fined (ə-fīnd′) *adj. Archaic.* **1.** Joined by kinship or affinity. **2.** Beholden; bound. [French *affiné,* from Old French *affin,* closely related, from Latin *affīnis,* neighboring, allied by marriage : *ad-,* near to + *fīnis,* border (see **final**).]

af·fin·i·ty (ə-fĭn′ə-tē) *n., pl.* **-ties. 1.** A natural personal attraction. **2.** Relationship by marriage. **3.** An inherent similarity between things. **4.** A chemical or physical attraction or attractive force. —See Synonyms at **likeness.** [Middle English *affinite,* from Old French *afinite,* from Latin *affīnitās,* from *affīnis,* AFFINED.]

Usage: *Affinity* may be followed by *of, between,* or *with.* Thus, *affinity of* persons (or things), *between* two persons (or things), *with* another person (or thing). It is not followed by *for,* nor should *affinity* be used, with *for,* to indicate a specific inclination. Thus, *skill in politics* (but not *affinity for politics*).

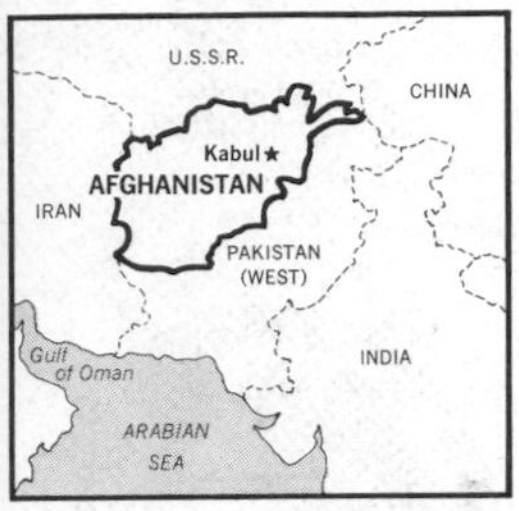

Afghanistan

af·firm (ə-fûrm′) *v.* **-firmed, -firming, -firms.** —*tr.* **1.** To declare positively or firmly; maintain to be true. **2.** To ratify or confirm. —*intr. Law.* To declare solemnly and formally, but not under oath. —See Synonyms at **assert.** [Middle English *affermen,* from Old French *afermer,* from Latin *affirmāre,* "to give firmness to," strengthen, assert : *ad-,* to + *firmāre,* to make firm, from *firmus,* firm (see **dher-**[2] in Appendix*).] —**af·firm′a·ble** *adj.* —**af·firm′a·bly** *adv.* —**af·firm′ant** *adj. & n.* —**af′fir·ma′tion** (ăf′ər-mā′shən) *n.* —**af·firm′er** *n.*

af·firm·a·tive (ə-fûr′mə-tĭv) *adj.* **1.** Giving assent; responding with the word *yes* or a phrase such as *We will.* **2.** Asserting that something is true as represented; confirming. **3.** *Logic.* Denoting a proposition in which the predicate states something about the subject to be true; for example, *Apples have seeds.* —*n.* **1.** A word or phrase signifying assent. **2.** The side in a debate that upholds a proposition. —**af·firm′a·tive·ly** *adv.*

af·fix (ə-fĭks′) *tr.v.* **-fixed, -fixing, -fixes. 1.** To secure (an object) to another; attach: *affix a label to a package.* **2.** To impute; attribute: *affix blame for the error to him.* **3.** To place at the end; append: *affix a postscript.* —*n.* (ăf′ĭks′). **1.** Something that is attached, joined, or added. **2.** A word element, such as a prefix or suffix, that is always attached to a base, stem, or root. [Medieval Latin *affīxāre* : Latin *ad-,* to + *fīxāre,* to fix, frequentative of *fīgere* (past participle *fīxus*), to fasten (see **dhīgw-** in Appendix*).] —**af·fix′er** *n.*

af·fla·tus (ə-flā′təs) *n.* A creative impulse; an inspiration. [Latin *afflātus,* inspiration, past participle of *afflāre,* to breathe on : *ad-,* toward + *flāre,* to blow (see **bhlē-**[2] in Appendix*).]

af·flict (ə-flĭkt′) *tr.v.* **-flicted, -flicting, -flicts.** To inflict physical or mental suffering upon; cause grievous distress to; trouble seriously: *"The second pain which will afflict the souls of the damned in hell is the pain of conscience."* (Joyce). [Middle English *afflicten,* from Latin *affligere* (past participle *afflīctus*), to dash against : *ad-,* to + *flīgere,* to strike (see **bhlig-** in Appendix*).] —**af·flict′er** *n.* —**af·flic′tive** *adj.* —**af·flic′tive·ly** *adv.*

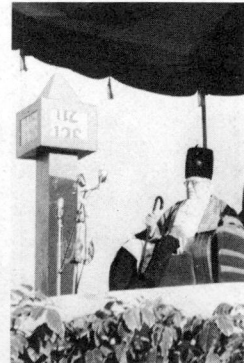

Aga Khan III
In 1954 at weighing-in ceremony, the traditional method of collecting tribute from Ismaili Shiite Moslems

af·flic·tion (ə-flĭk′shən) *n.* **1.** A condition of pain, suffering, or distress. **2.** A cause of pain, suffering, or distress.

af·flu·ence (ăf′lo͞o-əns) *n.* **1.** A plentiful supply of material goods; wealth. **2.** An abundance. **3.** A flowing toward.

af·flu·ent (ăf′lo͞o-ənt) *adj.* **1.** Rich; opulent: *"Living out in the suburbs, it is easy to assume that ours is, indeed, an affluent society."* (Michael Harrington). **2.** Copious; abundant. **3.** Flowing freely. —*n.* A stream or river that flows into another or other body of water; tributary. [Middle English, from Old French, from Latin *affluēns,* present participle of *affluere,* to flow to : *ad-,* toward + *fluere,* to flow (see **bhleu-** in Appendix*).] —**af′flu·ent·ly** *adv.*

af·flux (ăf′lŭks′) *n.* A flowing to or toward a particular area: *an afflux of blood to the head.* [Medieval Latin *affluxus,* from Latin, past participle of *affluere,* to flow to. See **affluent.**]

af·ford (ə-fôrd′, ə-fōrd′) *tr.v.* **-forded, -fording, -fords. 1.** To have the financial means for; be able to meet the expense of. **2.** To be able to spare or give up. Often preceded by *can* or *be able: He was able to afford one hour for lunch.* **3.** To be able to do or perform (something) without incurring harm or criticism, or with benefit to oneself. Often used with an infinitive or clause: *He can afford to take a tolerant attitude.* **4.** To provide: *Swimming affords good exercise.* [Middle English *aforthen,* Old English *geforthian,* to further, achieve, carry out, from *forthian,* to promote, from *forth,* forward. See **per**[1] in Appendix.*] —**af·ford′a·ble** *adj.*

af·for·est (ə-fôr′ĭst, ə-fŏr′-) *tr.v.* **-ested, -esting, -ests.** To convert (open land) into forest. [Medieval Latin *afforestāre* : *ad-,* to + *forestāre,* from Late Latin *forestis,* FOREST.] —**af·for′es·ta′tion** (ə-fôr′ĭs-tā′shən, ə-fŏr′-) *n.*

af·fran·chise (ə-frăn′chīz′) *tr.v.* **-chised, -chising, -chises.** To free from servitude; liberate from obligation or liabilities.

af·fray (ə-frā′) *n.* A quarrel or brawl noisy enough to disturb those not involved. See Synonyms at **conflict.** —*tr.v.* **affrayed, -fraying, -frays.** *Archaic.* To frighten. [Middle English, from Old French *effray, esfrei,* from *affreer, esfreer,* to fight in public, from Vulgar Latin *exfrīdāre* (unattested), "to break the peace" : Latin *ex,* out of + Frankish *frithuz* (unattested), peace (see **prī-** in Appendix*).]

af·fri·cate (ăf′rĭ-kĭt) *n. Phonetics.* A sound produced when the breath stream is completely stopped and then released at articulation; for example, the *t* plus *sh* sound in *churn* or *clutch* or the *j* sound in *judge.* Also called "affricative." [Latin *(vox) affricāta,* "rubbed" (sound), feminine past participle of *affricāre,* to rub against : *ad-,* to + *fricāre,* to rub (see **bhrei-** in Appendix*).]

af·fric·a·tive (ə-frĭk′ə-tĭv) *adj.* Of, pertaining to, or forming an affricate. —*n.* An **affricate** *(see).*

af·fright (ə-frīt′) *tr.v.* **-frighted, -frighting, -frights.** *Archaic.* To arouse fear in; terrify. —*n. Archaic.* **1.** Terror. **2.** A cause of terror. **3.** The act of frightening. —**af·fright′ment** *n.*

af·front (ə-frŭnt′) *tr.v.* **-fronted, -fronting, -fronts. 1.** To treat insolently or offensively; slight openly. **2.** To meet face to face defiantly; confront. —See Synonyms at **offend.** —*n.* **1.** An open or intentional offense, slight, or insult. **2.** *Obsolete.* An encounter or meeting. [Middle English *affronten,* from Old French *afronter,* from Vulgar Latin *affrontāre* (unattested) : Latin *ad-,* to + *frōns* (stem *front-*), forehead (see **front**).] —**af·front′er** *adj.* —**af·front′ing·ly** *adv.*

af·fu·sion (ə-fyo͞o′zhən) *n.* A pouring on of liquid, as in baptism. [Latin *affūsiō,* from *affūsus,* past participle of *affundere,* to pour on : *ad-,* to + *fundere,* to pour (see **gheu-**[1] in Appendix*).]

Afg. Afghanistan.

Af·ghan (ăf′găn′, -gən) *n.* **1.** A native of Afghanistan. **2. Pashto** *(see).* **3.** *Small* **a.** A coverlet of wool, knitted or crocheted in colorful geometric designs. —*adj.* Of or pertaining to Afghanistan, its people, or their language.

Afghan hound. A large, slender dog of an ancient breed, having long, thick hair, a pointed muzzle, and drooping ears.

af·ghan·i (ăf-găn′ē) *n.* The basic monetary unit of Afghanistan, equal to 100 puls. See table of exchange rates at **currency.**

Af·ghan·i·stan (ăf-găn′ə-stăn′). *Abbr.* **Afg.** A landlocked kingdom, 250,000 square miles in area, of southwestern Asia. Population, 13,800,000. Capital, Kabul.

a·fi·ci·o·na·do (ə-fē′sē-ə-nä′dō, ə-fĭs′ē-ə-) *n., pl.* **-dos.** An enthusiastic admirer or follower; devotee. [Spanish, from the past participle of *aficionar,* to incite affection, from *afición,* affection, from Latin *affectiō,* AFFECTION.]

a·field (ə-fēld′) *adv.* **1.** Off the usual or desired track. **2.** Away from one's home or usual environment. **3.** To or on a field.

a·fire (ə-fīr′) *adj.* **1.** Burning; on fire. **2.** Intensely interested and involved: *He was afire about the new project.* —**a·fire′** *adv.*

AFL, A.F.L, A.F. of L. American Federation of Labor.

a·flame (ə-flām′) *adj.* **1.** On fire; flaming. **2.** Keenly excited and interested: *aflame with a desire to learn.* —**a·flame′** *adv.*

AFL-CIO, A.F.L-C.I.O. The American Federation of Labor and Congress of Industrial Organizations.

a·float (ə-flōt′) *adj.* **1.** Floating. **2.** On a boat or ship away from the shore; at sea. **3.** In circulation; prevailing. **4.** Awash; flooded. **5.** Drifting about; moving without guidance: *Our plans are afloat.* —**a·float′** *adv.*

a·flut·ter (ə-flŭt′ər) *adj.* In a flutter; nervous and excited.

A·fog·nak (ə-fŏg′năk). An island of Alaska, about 43 miles long and up to 23 miles wide, lying north of Kodiak and east of the Alaska Peninsula.

a·foot (ə-fo͝ot′) *adj.* **1.** Walking; on foot. **2.** In the process of being carried out; astir. —**a·foot′** *adv.*

a·fore (ə-fôr′, ə-fōr′). *Archaic.* Before. [Middle English *afor(e)n,* Old English *onforan* : ON + *foran,* dative of *for,* FORE.]

a·fore·men·tioned (ə-fôr′mĕn′shənd, ə-fōr′-) *adj.* Mentioned previously or before.

a·fore·said (ə-fôr′sĕd′, ə-fōr′-) *adj.* Spoken of earlier.

a·fore·thought (ə-fôr′thôt′, ə-fōr′-) *adj.* Planned or intended beforehand; premeditated: *malice aforethought.*

a·fore·time (ə-fôr′tīm′, ə-fōr′-) *adv. Archaic.* At a former or past time; previously. —*adj. Archaic.* Earlier; former.

a for·ti·o·ri (ä fôr′shē-ôr′ē, ā fōr′shē-ō′rī′). *Latin.* For a stronger reason; all the more. Said of a conclusion arrived at with greater logical necessity than the one previously accepted.

a·foul (ə-foul′) *adv.* In a condition of entanglement, conflict, or

collision. **—run** (or **fall**) **afoul of.** To become entangled with; get into or have trouble with. **—a·foul′** *adj.*

Afr. Africa; African.

a·fraid (ə-frād′) *adj.* **1.** Filled with fear. **2.** Reluctant; averse: *not afraid of work.* **3.** Filled with regret. Often used to mitigate an unpleasant statement: *I'm afraid you're wrong.* [Middle English *af(f)raied,* past participle of *affraien,* to frighten, from Old French *affreer,* to AFFRAY.]

af·reet (ăf′rēt′, ə-frēt′) *n.* Also **af·rit.** *Arabic Mythology.* A powerful evil spirit or gigantic and monstrous demon. [Arabic *'ifrīt,* probably from Persian *āfrīda,* "a created being," from *āfrīdan,* to create.]

a·fresh (ə-frĕsh′) *adv.* Anew; once more; again.

Af·ri·ca (ăf′rĭ-kə). *Abbr.* **Afr., Af.** The second-largest continent (about 11,500,000 square miles) in the Eastern Hemisphere, south of Europe and between the Atlantic and Indian oceans.

Af·ri·can (ăf′rĭ-kən) *adj. Abbr.* **Afr., Af.** Of or pertaining to Africa, or any of its peoples or languages. *—n.* **1.** A person born or living in Africa. **2.** A member of one of the indigenous peoples of Africa.

African lily. A plant, *Agapanthus africanus,* native to southern Africa, having rounded clusters of blue, violet, or white flowers.

African mahogany. 1. Any of several African trees of the genus *Khaya;* especially, *K. ivorensis,* having wood similar to that of true mahogany. **2.** The wood of this tree, used for furniture, musical instruments, and boat interiors. **3.** Any of various other African woods resembling true mahogany.

African marigold. A widely cultivated plant, *Tagetes erecta,* native to Mexico, having finely divided foliage and showy, rounded, orange or yellow flowers.

African violet. Any of several plants of the genus *Saintpaulia,* native to tropical Africa and widely cultivated as house plants; especially, *S. ionantha,* having violet, white, or pink flowers.

Af·ri·kaans (ăf′rĭ-käns′, -känz′) *n.* A language developed from 17th-century Dutch among the Afrikaners. It now shares with English official-language status in the Republic of South Africa. Also called "Cape Dutch," "South African Dutch," "Taal."

Af·ri·kan·der (ăf′rĭ-kăn′dər) *n.* **1.** An Afrikaner. **2.** A breed of cattle with a humped back and large, spreading horns, originally developed in South Africa.

Af·ri·kan·er (ăf′rĭ-kä′nər) *n.* An Afrikaans-speaking descendant of the Dutch settlers of South Africa.

Afro–. Indicates Africa or African; for example, **Afro-American.** [From Latin *Āfr-,* stem of *Āfer,* an African.]

Af·ro-A·mer·i·can (ăf′rō-ə-mĕr′ə-kən) *adj.* Of or pertaining to American Negroes of African ancestry, their history, or their culture. *—n.* An American Negro of African ancestry.

Af·ro-A·si·at·ic (ăf′rō-ā′zhē-ăt′ĭk) *n.* A family of languages of southwestern Asia and northern Africa. Also called "Hamito-Semitic," "Semito-Hamitic." **—Af′ro-A′si·at′ic** *adj.*

aft (ăft, äft) *adv. Nautical.* At, in, toward, or close to the stern of a vessel. *—adj. Nautical.* Situated near or at the stern; after. [Probably shortening of ABAFT.]

aft. afternoon.

af·ter (ăf′tər, äf′-) *prep.* **1.** Behind in place or order. **2.** In quest or pursuit of: *seek after fame.* **3.** Concerning: *He asked after you.* **4.** Subsequent in time to; at a later time than: *come after dinner.* **5.** Subsequent to and because of or regardless of: *After all their differences, they remained friends.* **6.** Following continually: *year after year.* **7.** Next to or lower than in order or importance. **8.** In the style of; in imitation of: *satires after Horace.* **9.** With the same or close to the same name as; in honor or commemoration of: *named after her mother.* **10.** According to the nature or desires of; in conformity to: *a man after my own heart.* **11.** Past the hour of: *five minutes after three.* **—after all. 1.** When everything is considered. **2.** Eventually; ultimately. *—adv.* **1.** Behind; in the rear. **2.** At a later or subsequent time; afterward. *—adj.* **1.** Subsequent in time or place; later; following. Often used in combination, as in *afterglow.* **2.** *Nautical.* Nearer the stern of a vessel; farther aft. *—conj.* Following or subsequent to the time that: *I saw her after I arrived.* [Middle English *after,* Old English *æfter.* See **apo-** in Appendix.*]

af·ter·birth (ăf′tər-bûrth′, äf′-) *n.* The placenta and fetal membranes expelled from the uterus after childbirth. Also called "secundines."

af·ter·burn·er (ăf′tər-bûr′nər, äf′-) *n.* A device for augmenting the thrust of a jet engine by burning additional fuel with the uncombined oxygen in the exhaust gases.

af·ter·care (ăf′tər-kâr′, äf′-) *n.* Treatment or special care given to convalescent patients, especially after undergoing surgery.

af·ter·clap (ăf′tər-klăp′, äf′-) *n.* An unexpected, often unpleasant sequel to a matter that had been considered closed.

af·ter·damp (ăf′tər-dămp′, äf′-) *n.* An asphyxiating mixture of gases, primarily nitrogen and carbon dioxide, left in a mine after a fire or explosion.

af·ter·deck (ăf′tər-dĕk′, äf′-) *n. Nautical.* The part of a ship's deck past amidships toward the stern.

af·ter·ef·fect (ăf′tər-ə-fĕkt′, äf′-) *n.* An effect following its cause after some delay, especially a delayed or prolonged physiological or psychological response to a stimulus.

af·ter·glow (ăf′tər-glō′, äf′-) *n.* **1.** The light emitted or remaining after removal of a source of illumination, as: **a.** The atmospheric glow after sunset. **b.** The glow of an incandescent metal as it cools. **c.** Emission from a phosphor after removal of excitation. **2.** The comfortable feeling following a pleasant experience. **3.** A lingering impression of past brilliance.

af·ter·im·age (ăf′tər-ĭm′ĭj, äf′-) *n.* A visual image that persists after a visual stimulus ceases. Also called "photogene."

af·ter·life (ăf′tər-līf′, äf′-) *n.* **1.** A life believed to follow death. **2.** The part of one's life that follows a particular event.

af·ter·math (ăf′tər-măth′, äf′-) *n.* **1.** A consequence or result, especially of a disaster or misfortune. **2.** A second crop of grass in the same season: *"many a sweep of meadow smooth / from aftermath"* (Tennyson). [AFTER + obsolete *math,* mowing, Middle English *math* (unattested), Old English *mǣth* (see **me-**[4] in Appendix*).]

af·ter·most (ăf′tər-mōst′, äf′-) *adj.* Also **aft·most** (ăft′mōst′, äft′-) (for sense 1). **1.** *Nautical.* Nearest the stern; farthest aft. **2.** Nearest the end or rear; hindmost; last.

af·ter·noon (ăf′tər-no͞on′, äf′-) *n.* **1.** *Abbr.* **a., aft.** The part of the day from noon until sunset. **2.** The closing part. *—adj.* Of, pertaining to, or occurring in the afternoon.

af·ter·pains (ăf′tər-pānz′, äf′-) *pl.n.* The cramps or pains following childbirth, resulting from the contraction of the womb.

af·ter·piece (ăf′tər-pēs′, äf′-) *n.* A short comic piece performed after a play.

af·ter·sen·sa·tion (ăf′tər-sĕn-sā′shən, äf′-) *n.* A sensory impression, such as an afterimage or aftertaste, that persists or recurs after removal of a stimulus.

af·ter·shaft (ăf′tər-shăft′, äf′-) *n.* A feather or down growing from the underside of the shaft of another feather.

af·ter·taste (ăf′tər-tāst′, äf′-) *n.* **1.** A taste persisting in the mouth after the substance causing it is no longer present. **2.** A feeling that remains after an event or experience.

af·ter·thought (ăf′tər-thôt′, äf′-) *n.* An idea, response, or explanation that occurs to one after an event or decision.

af·ter·time (ăf′tər-tīm′, äf′-) *n.* The time to come; future.

af·ter·ward (ăf′tər-wərd, äf′-) *adv.* Also **af·ter·wards** (-wərdz). In or at a later time; subsequently.

af·ter·world (ăf′tər-wûrld′, äf′-) *n.* A world inhabited by the spirits of the dead.

Ag The symbol for the element silver (Latin *argentum*).

AG adjutant general.

A.G. 1. adjutant general. **2.** attorney general.

a·ga (ä′gə) *n.* Also **a·gha.** A high official of the Ottoman Empire. [Turkish *ağa,* "lord."]

A·ga·de. The original name for **Akkad.**

A·ga·dir (ä′gə-dĭr′, ăg′ə-). A port in southern Morocco, severely damaged by an earthquake in 1960. Population, 17,000.

a·gain (ə-gĕn′) *adv.* **1.** Once more; another time; anew. **2.** To a previous place, position, or state: *He left home, but went back again.* **3.** Furthermore; moreover. **4.** On the other hand: *He might go, and again he might not.* **5.** In return; in response; back. **—again and again.** Repeatedly; frequently. **—as much again. 1.** The same amount. **2.** Twice as much. [Middle English *again, ayen,* Old English *ongeagn,* in return, toward, against. See **gagina** in Appendix.*]

a·gainst (ə-gĕnst′) *prep.* **1.** In a direction or course opposite to: *row against the current.* **2.** So as to come into forcible contact with: *waves dashing against the shore.* **3.** In contact with so as to rest or press on: *He leaned against the tree.* **4.** In hostile opposition or resistance to: *struggle against fate.* **5.** Contrary to; opposed to: *against my better judgment.* **6.** In contrast or comparison with the setting or background of: *dark colors against a fair skin.* **7.** In preparation for; in anticipation of: *food stored against winter.* **8.** As a defense or safeguard from: *protection against the cold.* **9.** To the account or debt of: *draw a check against one's bank balance.* **10.** Directly opposite to; facing. Used chiefly in the phrase *over against: hang the mirror over against the fireplace.* [Middle English *against, ayenst,* alteration of *ayenes, againes,* from *again, ayen,* against, AGAIN.]

A·ga Khan (ä′gə kän′). A hereditary title of the religious and spiritual leader of the sect of Ismaili Moslems.

A·ga Khan III (ä′gə kän′). Title of Aga Sultan Sir Mahomed Shah. 1877–1957. Leader of Ismaili Moslems (1885–1957).

a·gal (ă-gäl′) *n.* A cord bound around the forehead and temples to hold in place the cloth head covering worn by Bedouins and other Arabs. [Arabic *'iqāl,* bond, rope.]

a·gal·loch (ə-găl′ək, ăg′ə-lŏk′) *n.* A wood, aloes. See **aloe.** [Greek *agallokhon,* of Oriental origin.]

ag·a·ma (ăg′ə-mə) *n.* Any of various small, long-tailed, insect-eating lizards of the family Agamidae, found in Old World tropics. [Carib.]

Ag·a·mem·non (ăg′ə-mĕm′nŏn′). *Greek Mythology.* The king of Mycenae, leader of the Greeks against Troy, husband of Clytemnestra, father of Orestes, Electra, and Iphigenia.

a·ga·mete (ā′gə-mēt′, ā-găm′ēt′) *n. Biology.* Any product of reproductive fission that is not a gamete.

a·gam·ic (ā-găm′ĭk) *adj.* Also **ag·a·mous** (ăg′ə-məs). *Biology.* Occurring or reproducing without the union of male and female cells; asexual or parthenogenetic. [From Late Latin *agamus,* unmarried, from Greek *agamos* : *a-,* not + -GAMOUS.] **—a·gam′i·cal·ly** *adv.*

ag·a·mo·gen·e·sis (ăg′ə-mō-jĕn′ə-sĭs, ā′găm-ō-) *n. Biology.* Asexual reproduction, as by budding, cell division, or parthenogenesis. [AGAM(IC) + GENESIS.] **—ag′a·mo·ge·net′ic** (-jə-nĕt′ĭk) *adj.* **—ag′a·mo·ge·net′i·cal·ly** *adv.*

A·ga·na (ä-gä′nyä). The capital of Guam, a town on the island's west coast. Population, 2,000.

Ag·a·nip·pe (ăg′ə-nĭp′ē) *n.* **1.** A spring on Mount Helicon, in Boeotia, sacred to the Muses. **2.** A source of inspiration.

ag·a·pan·thus (ăg′ə-păn′thəs) *n.* Any plant of the genus *Agapanthus,* which includes the **African lily** *(see).* [New Latin : Greek *agapē,* love, AGAPE + *anthos,* flower (see **andh-** in Appendix*).]

a·gape[1] (ə-gāp′, ə-găp′) *adv.* In a state of wonder or amazement, often with the mouth wide open. **—a·gape′** *adj.*

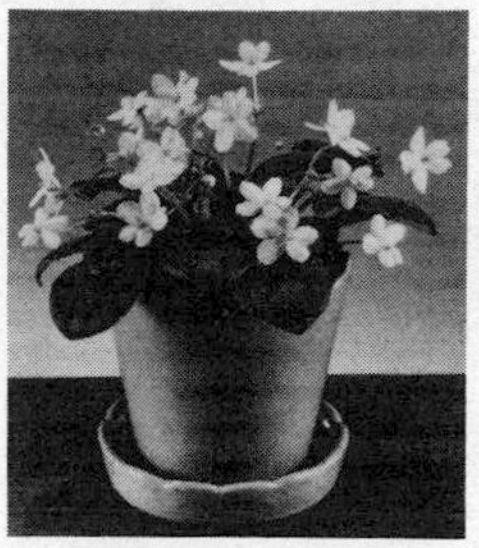

African violet
Saintpaulia ionantha

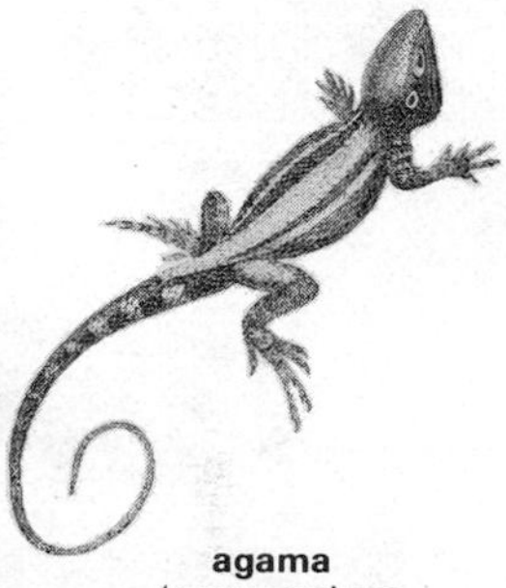

agama
Agama muricata

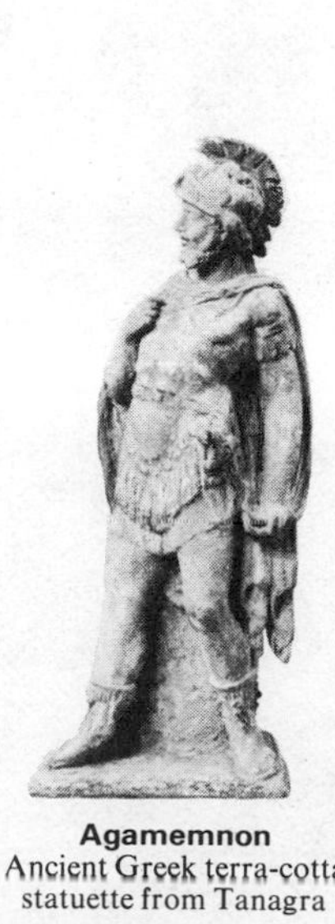

Agamemnon
Ancient Greek terra-cotta statuette from Tanagra

a·ga·pe[2] (ä′gə-pā′) *n., pl.* **-pae** (-pē′). **1.** Christian love. **2.** In the early Christian Church, the love feast accompanied by Eucharistic celebration. [Greek *agapē*†, love.]

a·gar (ā′gär, ä′gär) *n.* Also **a·gar-a·gar** (ā′gär′ā′gär′, ä′gär′-ä′-). A mucilaginous material prepared from certain marine algae and used as a base for bacterial culture media, as a laxative, and for thickening certain foods. [Malay, "jelly, gelatin."]

ag·a·ric (ăg′ə-rĭk, ə-găr′ĭk) *n.* **1.** Any fungus of the family Agaricacae, including the common cultivated mushroom, *Agaricus campestris.* **2.** The dried fruiting body of the fungus *Fomes laricis,* formerly used in medicine. [Latin *agaricum,* from Greek *agarikon,* after *Agaria,* city in Sarmatia.]

Ag·as·siz (ăg′ə-sē), **Alexander.** 1835–1910. Swiss-born American zoologist and author; son of Louis Agassiz.

Ag·as·siz (ăg′ə-sē), **(Jean) Louis (Rodolphe).** 1807–1873. Swiss-born American naturalist, author, and educator.

Ag·as·siz, Lake (ăg′ə-sē). A lake in North America that existed for about 1,000 years in the Pleistocene epoch, and extended some 700 miles in North Dakota and Minnesota and in Saskatchewan and Manitoba, Canada.

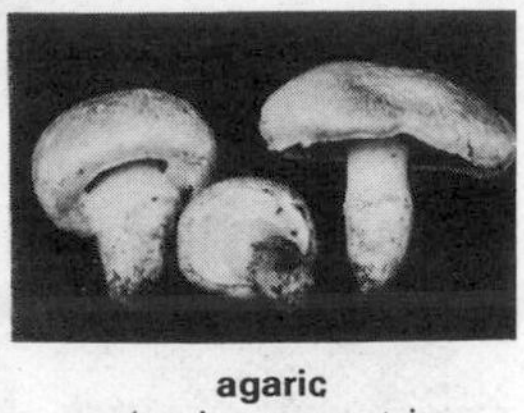

agaric
Agaricus campestris

ag·ate (ăg′ĭt) *n.* **1.** A fine-grained, fibrous variety of chalcedony with color banding or irregular clouding. **2.** A child's marble made of this material or a glass imitation of it. **3.** A tool with agate parts, as a burnisher tipped with agate. **4.** A printer's type size, approximately 5$\frac{1}{2}$ points. [Old French, from Latin *achātēs,* from Greek *akhātēs*†.] —**ag′a·toid** (-ə-toid) *adj.*

agate line. A measure of space used in estimating printed advertising, usually one column wide and $\frac{1}{14}$ of an inch deep.

Ag·a·tha (ăg′ə-thə). A feminine given name. [Middle English, from Latin, from Greek *Agathē,* from *agathē,* feminine of *agathos*†, good.]

a·ga·ve (ə-gā′vē, ə-gä′-) *n.* Any of numerous fleshy-leaved tropical American plants of the genus *Agave,* which includes the **century plant** *(see).* Some species are the source of commercially valuable fibers or of various beverages, such as pulque. [New Latin, "noble (plant)" (probably so named for its great height), from Greek *agauē,* feminine of *agauos*†, noble.]

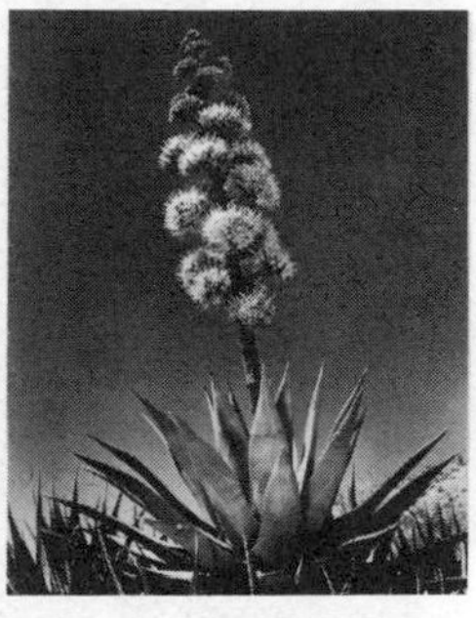

agave
Agave desertii

age (āj) *n.* **1.** The period of time during which someone or something exists. **2.** A lifetime. **3.** That time in life when a person becomes qualified to assume certain civil and personal rights and responsibilities, usually at eighteen or twenty-one years. Used chiefly in the phrases *of age* and *under age.* Also called "legal age." **4.** Any period of life denoted as differing from other periods; a stage: *the age of adolescence.* **5.** The latter portion of life; the state of being old. **6.** *Sometimes capital* **A.** Any period in history or geology designated by distinctive characteristics: *the age of enlightenment.* **7.** *Informal.* An extended period of time: *They left ages ago.* **8.** *Psychology.* **Mental age** *(see).* —See Synonyms at **period.** —*v.* **aged, aging, ages.** —*tr.* To cause to grow older or more mature. —*intr.* **1.** To become old. **2.** To manifest traits associated with old age. [Middle English, from Old French *age, aage,* from Vulgar Latin *aetāticum* (unattested), from Latin *aetās* (stem *aetāt-*) age. See **aiw-** in Appendix.*] —**ag′er** *n.*

-age. Indicates: **1.** Collectively; for example, **leafage. 2.** Relation to or connection with; for example, **parentage. 3.** Relationship to verb; for example, **cleavage. 4.** Condition or position; for example, **vagabondage, marriage. 5.** Charge or fee; for example, **postage, cartage. 6.** Residence or place; for example, **vicarage, orphanage.** [Middle English, from Old French, from Late Latin *-āticum,* from the neuter of *-āticus,* adjectival suffix : Latin *-ātus,* -ATE + -IC.]

a·ged (ā′jĭd *for senses 1, 2, 4;* ājd *for sense 3*) *adj.* **1.** Old; on in years. **2.** Of, pertaining to, or characteristic of old age. **3.** Of the age of: *aged three.* **4.** *Geology.* Near the base level of erosion. —See Synonyms at **old.** —**a′ged·ly** *adv.* —**a′ged·ness** *n.*

A·gee (ā′jē), **James.** 1909–1955. American author of poetry, novels, criticism, and screenplays.

age·ing. *British.* Variant of **aging.**

age·less (āj′lĭs) *adj.* **1.** Never seeming to grow old. **2.** Existing forever; eternal. —**age′less·ly** *adv.* —**age′less·ness** *n.*

a·gen·cy (ā′jən-sē) *n., pl.* **-cies. 1.** Action; operation; power: *"we cannot ignore human agency in history"* (Herbert J. Muller). **2.** A mode of action; means. **3.** A business or service authorized to act for others: *an employment agency.* [Latin *agentia,* from *agēns,* acting, AGENT.]

a·gen·da (ə-jĕn′də) *n.* Plural in form, used with a singular verb. **1.** A list of things to be done, especially the program for a meeting. **2.** Plural of **agendum.** See Usage note below. [Latin, plural of *agendum,* AGENDUM.]

Usage: *Agenda,* meaning "list" or "program," is well established as a collective noun with singular verb; 86 per cent of the Usage Panel accept such a combination. *Agendas,* a recent plural form of this collective, is acceptable to 59 per cent. The singular *agendum* denotes a single thing to be done or an individual item of such a program or list.

a·gen·dum (ə-jĕn′dəm) *n., pl.* **-da** (-də) or **-das.** Something to be done, especially an item on an agenda. See Usage note at **agenda.** [Latin *agendum,* neuter gerundive of *agere,* to act, do. See **ag-** in Appendix.*]

a·gen·e·sis (ā-jĕn′ə-sĭs) *n.* Also **ag·e·ne·sia** (ăj′ə-nē′zhə). *Biology.* Failure of an organism, organ, or part to develop.

a·gent (ā′jənt) *n. Abbr.* **agt. 1.** One that acts or has the power or authority to act. **2.** One that acts for or as the representative of another: *an insurance agent.* **3.** A means or mode by which something is done or caused; an instrument. **4.** A force or substance that causes some changes: *a chemical agent.* [Middle English, from Latin *agēns,* present participle of *agere,* to act, drive, do. See **ag-** in Appendix.*]

a·gen·tial (ā-jĕn′shəl) *adj.* Of, pertaining to, or acting as an agent or agency.

a·gent pro·vo·ca·teur (ȧ-zhäɴ′ prô-vô-kȧ-tœr′) *pl.* **agents provocateurs** (ȧ-zhäɴ′ prô-vô-kȧ-tœr′). *French.* A secret agent hired to penetrate some organization to incite trouble designed to make the organization or its members incur punishment.

age of consent. *Law.* The age at which a female may choose to have sexual intercourse. See **statutory rape.**

ag·e·ra·tum (ăj′ə-rā′təm) *n.* **1.** Any of various plants of the genus *Ageratum;* especially, *A. houstonianum,* a commonly cultivated species having clusters of usually violet-blue flowers. **2.** Loosely, any of several other plants having similar flower clusters. [New Latin *Ageratum,* from Latin *agēraton,* from Greek, neuter of *agēratos,* ageless : *a-,* not + *-gēratos,* from *gēras,* old age (see **ger-**[2] in Appendix*).]

ag·gior·na·men·to (äd-jôr′nä-mĕn′tō) *n., pl.* **-ti** (-tē). *Italian.* The process of modernizing an institution or organization.

ag·glom·er·ate (ə-glŏm′ə-rāt′) *v.* **-ated, -ating, -ates.** —*tr.* To make or form into a rounded mass. —*intr.* To take the shape of a rounded mass. —*adj.* (ə-glŏm′ər-ĭt). Gathered into a rounded mass. —*n.* (ə-glŏm′ər-ĭt). **1.** A confused or jumbled mass of things clustered together; a heap. **2.** A volcanic rock consisting of rounded and angular fragments. [Latin *agglomerāre* : *ad-,* to + *glomerāre,* to wind into a ball, from *glomus,* ball (see **gel-**[1] in Appendix*).] —**ag·glom′er·a′tive** (-rā′tĭv, -ər-ə-tĭv) *adj.* —**ag·glom′er·a′tor** (-ā′tər) *n.*

ag·glom·er·a·tion (ə-glŏm′ə-rā′shən) *n.* **1.** The process or act of agglomerating. **2.** The state of being agglomerated. **3.** A confused or jumbled mass; agglomerate.

ag·glu·ti·nate (ə-glo͞ot′n-āt′) *v.* **-nated, -nating, -nates.** —*tr.* **1.** To join together by causing adhesion, as with glue. **2.** *Linguistics.* To form (words) by combining words, or words and word elements. **3.** *Physiology.* To cause (red blood cells or microorganisms) to clump together. —*intr.* **1.** To join together into a group or mass. **2.** *Linguistics.* To form words by agglutination. **3.** To undergo agglutination. [Latin *agglūtināre* : *ad-,* to + *glūtināre,* to glue, from *glūten,* glue (see **gel-**[1] in Appendix*).] —**ag·glu′ti·nant** *adj.* & *n.*

ag·glu·ti·na·tion (ə-glo͞ot′n-ā′shən) *n.* **1.** The process of agglutinating; adhesion of distinct parts. **2.** A mass formed in this manner. **3.** *Linguistics.* The formation of words from morphemes that retain their original forms and meanings with little change during the combination process.

ag·glu·ti·na·tive (ə-glo͞ot′n-ā′tĭv) *adj.* **1.** Tending toward, concerning, or characteristic of agglutination. **2.** *Linguistics.* Designating a language in which words are formed primarily by means of agglutination.

ag·glu·ti·nin (ə-glo͞ot′n-ĭn) *n.* A substance that induces agglutination. [AGGLUTIN(ATION) + -IN.]

ag·grade (ə-grād′) *tr.v.* **-graded, -grading, -grades.** To fill and raise the level of (the bed of a stream) by deposition of sediment. [AD- (toward) + GRADE.] —**ag′gra·da′tion** (ăg′rə-dā′shən) *n.* —**ag′gra·da′tion·al** *adj.*

ag·gran·dize (ə-grăn′dīz′, ăg′rən-dīz′) *tr.v.* **-dized, -dizing, -dizes. 1.** To increase the scope of; enlarge; extend. **2.** To make greater in power, influence, stature, or reputation. **3.** To make (something) seem greater; exaggerate. [French *aggrandir* (present stem *aggrandiss-*) : *a,* to, from Latin *ad-* + *grandir,* to grow larger, from Latin *grandīre,* from *grandis,* great, GRAND.] —**ag·gran′dize·ment** (ə-grăn′dĭz-mənt, ə-grăn′dīz′-) *n.* —**ag·gran′diz′er** *n.*

ag·gra·vate (ăg′rə-vāt′) *tr.v.* **-vated, -vating, -vates. 1.** To make worse; make more of a burden; make more of a trouble. **2.** *Informal.* To annoy or exasperate; provoke; irritate; vex. —See Synonyms at **annoy.** [Latin *aggravāre,* to make heavier : *ad-,* in addition to + *gravāre,* to burden, from *gravis,* heavy (see **gwer-**[2] in Appendix*).] —**ag′gra·vat′ing·ly** *adv.* —**ag′gra·va′tive** *adj.* —**ag′gra·va′tor** (-vā′tər) *n.*

ag·gra·va·tion (ăg′rə-vā′shən) *n.* **1.** The act of aggravating. **2.** The state of being aggravated. **3.** A thing that irritates or makes worse, more troublesome, or more irritated. **4.** *Informal.* Exasperation; bothersomeness.

ag·gre·gate (ăg′rə-gĭt) *adj.* **1.** Gathered together into a mass or sum so as to constitute a whole; total. **2.** *Botany.* Crowded or massed into a dense cluster. **3.** Composed of a mixture of minerals separable by mechanical means. —*n.* (ăg′rə-gĭt). **1.** Any total or whole considered with reference to its constituent parts; an assemblage or group of distinct particulars massed together; a gross amount: *"an empire is the aggregate of many states under one common head"* (Burke). **2.** The mineral materials, such as sand or stone, used in making concrete. —*tr.v.* (ăg′rə-gāt′) **aggregated, -gating, -gates. 1.** To gather into a mass, sum, or whole. **2.** To total up to; amount to. [Middle English *aggregat,* from Latin *aggregātus,* past participle of *aggregāre,* to add to (the flock), attach to : *ad-,* to + *gregāre,* to herd, from *grex* (stem *greg-*), flock (see **ger-**[1] in Appendix*).] —**ag′gre·gate·ly** *adv.* —**ag′gre·ga′tion** *n.* —**ag′gre·ga′tive** *adj.* —**ag′gre·ga′tor** (-gā′tər) *n.*

aggregate fruit. *Botany.* A fruit, such as the raspberry, developed from the pistils of a single flower, and consisting of a coherent mass of drupelets. Compare **multiple fruit.**

ag·gress (ə-grĕs′) *intr.v.* **-gressed, -gressing, -gresses.** To start an attack or a quarrel. [Latin *aggredī* (past participle *aggressus*), to approach (with hostility), attack : *ad-,* toward + *gradī,* to step, go (see **ghredh-** in Appendix*).]

ag·gres·sion (ə-grĕsh′ən) *n.* **1.** The act of commencing hostilities or invasion; an assault. **2.** The habit or practice of launching attacks. **3.** *Psychoanalysis.* Hostile action or behavior.

ag·gres·sive (ə-grĕs′ĭv) *adj.* **1.** Inclined to move or act in a

ă pat/ā pay/âr care/ä father/b bib/ch church/d deed/ĕ pet/ē be/f fife/g gag/h hat/hw which/ĭ pit/ī pie/îr pier/j judge/k kick/l lid, needle/m mum/n no, sudden/ng thing/ŏ pot/ō toe/ô paw, for/oi noise/ou out/o͝o took/o͞o boot/p pop/r roar/s sauce/sh ship, dish/

hostile fashion. **2.** Assertive; bold; enterprising. —**ag·gres′sive·ly** *adv.* —**ag·gres′sive·ness** *n.*
ag·gres·sor (ə-grĕs′ər) *n.* One who starts a hostile action.
ag·grieve (ə-grēv′) *tr.v.* **-grieved, -grieving, -grieves. 1.** To distress or afflict. **2.** To injure unjustly; give reason for just complaint. [Middle English *agreven,* from Old French *agrever,* from Latin *aggravāre,* to make heavier, AGGRAVATE.]
ag·grieved (ə-grēvd′) *adj.* **1.** Feeling distress or affliction. **2.** Treated wrongly; offended. **3.** *Law.* Treated unjustly by a decision of the court or other legal authority. —**ag·griev′ed·ly** (ə-grē′vĭd-lē) *adv.* —**ag·griev′ed·ness** *n.*
a·gha. Variant of **aga.**
a·ghast (ə-găst′, ə-gäst′) *adj.* Shocked by something horrible; terrified. [Middle English *agast,* past participle of *agasten,* to frighten : *a-* (intensive) + *gasten,* to frighten, Old English *gæstan,* from *gāst,* ghost (see **gheis-** in Appendix*).]
ag·ile (ăj′əl, ăj′īl) *adj.* **1.** Able to move in a quick and easy fashion; active. **2.** Mentally alert. —See Synonyms at **nimble.** [Middle English, from Old French, from Latin *agilis,* easily moved, light, nimble, from *agere,* to drive (see **ag-** in Appendix*).] —**ag′ile·ly** *adv.* —**ag′ile·ness** *n.*
a·gil·i·ty (ə-jĭl′ə-tē) *n.* The state or quality of being agile; nimbleness; briskness.
Ag·in·court (ăj′ĭn-kôrt′). A village of northern France where in 1415 Henry V of England defeated the French.
ag·ing (ā′jĭng) *n.* Also *British* **ageing. 1.** The process of becoming old or mature. **2.** Any artificial process for imparting the characteristics and properties of age.
ag·i·o (ăj′ē-ō′) *n., pl.* **-os. 1.** A premium paid for changing one kind of money to another. **2.** An allowance or premium for the difference in value between two currencies being exchanged. [Italian *ag(g)io,* alteration of dialectal *lajjē,* from Medieval Greek *allagion,* exchange, from *allagē,* change, from *allos,* other. See **al-**[1] in Appendix.*]
ag·i·o·tage (ăj′ē-ə-tĭj, ăzh′ə-täzh′) *n.* **1.** The brokerage business; speculation in securities. **2.** Exchange transaction, especially of currencies. [French, from *agioter,* to practice stockjobbing, from *agio,* stockbrokering, from Italian *aggio,* AGIO.]
a·gist (ə-jĭst′) *tr.v.* **agisted, agisting, agists.** *Law.* To feed and take care of (cattle or horses belonging to others) for compensation. [Middle English *agisten,* to pasture, from Old French *agister,* "to provide lodging for" : *a-,* from Latin *ad-,* to + *gister,* to lodge, from Vulgar Latin *jacitāre* (unattested), to make lie down, frequentative of Latin *jacēre,* to lie, intransitive of *jacere,* to throw (see **yē-** in Appendix*).] —**a·gist′ment** *n.*
ag·i·tate (ăj′ə-tāt′) *v.* **-tated, -tating, -tates.** —*tr.* **1.** To move with violence or sudden forcefulness; excite physically: *a storm agitating the ocean.* **2.** To upset, disturb: *Grief agitated the widow.* **3.** To arouse interest in (a cause, for example) by the written or spoken word; discuss; debate. **4.** *Archaic.* To ponder over; plan. —*intr.* To stir up public interest in a cause. [Latin *agitāre,* frequentative of *agere,* to do, drive. See **ag-** in Appendix.*] —**ag′i·tat′ed·ly** *adv.* —**ag′i·ta′tive** *adj.*
ag·i·ta·tion (ăj′ə-tā′shən) *n.* **1.** The act of agitating. **2.** The state of being agitated; disturbance; commotion. **3.** Extreme emotional disturbance; perturbation. **4.** The stirring up of public interest on a matter of controversy, such as a political or social issue. —**ag′i·ta′tion·al** *adj.*
a·gi·ta·to (ä′jē-tä′tō) *adj. Music.* Agitated; fast and stirring. Used as a direction. [Italian, from Latin *agitātus,* past participle of *agitāre,* AGITATE.] —**a′gi·ta′to** *adv.*
ag·i·ta·tor (ăj′ə-tā′tər) *n.* **1.** A person who agitates, especially one who engages in political agitation. **2.** A machine for stirring or shaking. —**ag′i·ta·to′ri·al** (-tôr′ē-əl, -tōr′ē-əl) *adj.*
A·gla·ia (ə-glā′ə, ə-glī′ə). *Greek Mythology.* One of the three Graces. [Greek, personification of *aglaia,* splendor, from *aglaos,* bright, splendid. See **gel-**[2] in Appendix.*]
a·gleam (ə-glēm′) *adj.* Brightly shining. —**a·gleam′** *adv.*
ag·let (ăg′lĭt) *n.* Also **ai·glet** (ā′glĭt). **1.** A tag or metal sheath on the end of a lace, cord, or ribbon to facilitate its passing through eyelet holes. **2.** A similar device used for an ornament. [Middle English, from Old French *aguillette,* diminutive of *aguille,* needle, from Late Latin *acūcula,* pin, pine needle, diminutive of Latin *acus,* needle. See **ak-** in Appendix.*]
a·gley (ə-glī′, ə-glā′). Also **a·glee** (ə-glē′) *adv. Scottish.* Off to one side; awry. [Scottish, "squintingly" : *a-,* on + *gley,* to squint, from Middle English (Scottish dialect) *gleyen*†.]
a·glim·mer (ə-glĭm′ər) *adj.* Lighting up faintly; glimmering. —**a·glim′mer** *adv.*
a·glit·ter (ə-glĭt′ər) *adj.* Glittering; sparkling. —**a·glit′ter** *adv.*
a·glow (ə-glō′) *adj.* Glowing; in a glow. —**a·glow′** *adv.*
ag·mi·nate (ăg′mə-nĭt, -nāt′) *adj.* Also **ag·mi·nat·ed** (-nā′tĭd). Gathered in clusters. [From Latin *agmen* (stem *agmin-*), moving multitude, troop. See **ag-** in Appendix.*]
ag·nail (ăg′nāl′) *n.* **1.** A hangnail. **2.** A painful sore or swelling around a fingernail or toenail; a whitlow. [Middle English *agnail,* Old English *angnaegl,* "painful prick in the flesh." See **angh-** in Appendix.*]
ag·nate (ăg′nāt′) *adj.* **1.** Related on or descended from the father's or male side. **2.** From a common source; akin. —*n.* A relative on the male or father's side only. [Middle English, from Latin *agnātus,* "born in addition," past participle of *agnāscī,* to be born in addition to : *ad-,* in addition + *nāscī, gnāscī,* to be born (see **gene-** in Appendix*).] —**ag·nat′ic** (ăg-năt′ĭk) *adj.* —**ag·nat′i·cal·ly** *adv.* —**ag·na′tion** *n.*
Ag·ne·an (ăg′nē-ən) *n.* Tocharian A.
Ag·nes (ăg′nĭs). A feminine given name. [Middle English, from Medieval Latin *Agnēs, Hagnēs,* from Greek *hagnē,* feminine of *hagnos,* chaste, sacred. See **yag-** in Appendix.*]

Ag·new (ăg′no͞o), **Spiro Theodore.** Born 1918. Vice President of the United States under Richard Milhous Nixon (from 1969).
Ag·ni (ŭg′nē). The Vedic god of fire and guardian of man. [Sanskrit *agniḥ,* fire. See **egnis** in Appendix.*]
ag·no·men (ăg-nō′mən) *n., pl.* **-nomina** (-nŏm′ə-nə) **1.** An additional cognomen given to a Roman citizen, often in honor of military victories, as Publius Cornelius Scipio *Africanus.* **2.** A nickname. [Latin *agnōmen* : *ad-,* additional + *(g)nōmen,* name (see **nomen-** in Appendix*).]
ag·nos·tic (ăg-nŏs′tĭk) *n.* A thinker who disclaims any knowledge of God. —*adj.* Pertaining to the agnostics or their doctrines. [A- (not) + GNOSTIC.] —**ag·nos′ti·cal·ly** *adv.*
ag·nos·ti·cism (ăg-nŏs′tə-sĭz′əm) *n.* **1.** *Philosophy.* The doctrines of the agnostics, holding that certainty, first or absolute truths, are unattainable, and that only perceptual phenomena are objects of exact knowledge. **2.** *Theology.* A theory that does not deny God but denies the possibility of knowing Him.
Ag·nus De·i (ăg′nəs dē′ī, äg′no͞os dā′ē). **1.** The Lamb of God, an emblem of Christ, derived from John 1:29 and Isaiah 53:7. **2.** An iconographic representation of this. **3.** A liturgical prayer to Christ. [Latin.]
a·go (ə-gō′) *adj.* Gone by; past. Used after a noun: *two years ago.* —*adv.* In the past: *It happened long ago.* [Middle English *ago(n),* past participle of *agon,* to go away, be past, Old English *āgān* : *ā-* (intensive) + *gān,* to go (see **ghē-** in Appendix*).]
Usage: Ago is properly followed by *that,* not by *since,* in a construction such as *It was two years ago that she met him.* This can be restated *It is two years since she met him* (but not *two years ago since,* for *ago* would be redundant).
a·gog (ə-gŏg′) *adv.* In a state of keen anticipation; highly excited; astir. [Middle English, from Old French *en gogues,* "in merriments," from *gogue,* merriment, probably imitative of hubbub.] —**a·gog′** *adj.*
à go·go (ä gō-gō′). Also **à go-go.** In a fast and lively manner; freely. Chiefly used as an adverb: *dancing à gogo;* also used as an adjective: *an à gogo dance.* [French, "in a joyful manner," from *gogo,* probably reduplication of the first syllable of *gogue,* merriment, from Old French. See **agog.**]
-agogue, -agog. 1. Indicates a leader or inciter; for example, **demagogue. 2.** *Medicine.* Indicates something that stimulates the flow of; for example, **emmenagogue.** [Late Latin *-agōgus,* from Greek *-agōgos,* from *agōgos,* leading, drawing forth, from *agein,* to lead. See **ag-** in Appendix.*]
a·gone (ə-gôn′, ə-gŏn′) *adj. Archaic.* Gone; gone by; past. [Middle English *agon,* AGO.] —**a·gone′** *adv.*
a·gon·ic (ā-gŏn′ĭk, ə-gŏn′-) *adj.* Having no angle. [Greek *agōnos* : *a-,* not + *gōnia,* angle (see **genu-**[1] in Appendix*).]
agonic line. An imaginary line on the earth's surface connecting points where the magnetic declination is zero.
ag·o·nist (ăg′ə-nĭst) *n. Physiology.* A muscle that contracts and is opposed by contraction in another muscle, the antagonist. [Back-formation from ANTAGONIST.]
ag·o·nis·tic (ăg′ə-nĭs′tĭk) *adj.* Also **ag·o·nis·ti·cal** (-tĭ-kəl). **1.** Striving to overcome in argument; competitive; combative. **2.** Straining to achieve effect. **3.** Of or pertaining to contests, originally those of the ancient Greeks. [Late Latin *agōnisticus,* from Greek *agōnistikos,* from *agōnistēs,* contestant, from *agōn,* contest. See **ag-** in Appendix.*] —**ag′o·nis′ti·cal·ly** *adv.*
ag·o·nize (ăg′ə-nīz′) *v.* **-nized, -nizing, -nizes.** —*intr.* **1.** To be in extreme pain or suffer great anguish. **2.** To make a great or convulsive effort. —*tr.* To cause great pain or anguish to. [Old French *agoniser,* from Late Latin *agōnizāre,* from Greek *agōnizesthai,* to contend for a prize, to struggle, from *agōnia,* contest, AGONY.] —**ag′o·niz′ing·ly** *adv.*
ag·o·ny (ăg′ə-nē) *n., pl.* **-nies. 1.** The suffering of intense physical or mental pain. **2.** The struggle that precedes death. **3.** A sudden or intense emotion of a particular sort: *an agony of doubt.* **4.** A violent or intense struggle. [Middle English *agonie,* from Old French, from Late Latin *agōnia,* from Greek, contest, anguish, from *agōn,* contest, from *agein,* to drive. See **ag-** in Appendix.*]
agony column. A newspaper column containing advertisements chiefly about missing relatives or friends.
ag·o·ra[1] (ăg′ə-rə) *n., pl.* **-rae** (-rē′, -rī′) or **-ras.** A marketplace in ancient Greece, customarily used as a place of popular assembly. [Greek *agora,* from *ageirein,* to assemble. See **ger-**[1] in Appendix.*]
a·go·ra[2] (ä′gə-rä′) *n., pl.* **-rot** (-rōt′) or **-roth** (-rōt′). A coin equal to $\frac{1}{100}$ of the pound of Israel. See table of exchange rates at **currency.** [Hebrew *'agōrāh,* from *āgōr,* to collect.]
ag·o·ra·pho·bi·a (ăg′ə-rə-fō′bē-ə) *n.* Abnormal fear of open spaces. [New Latin : Greek *agora,* open space, AGORA + -PHOBIA.] —**ag′o·ra·pho′bic** (-fō′bĭk, -fŏb′ĭk) *adj.*
a·gou·ti (ə-go͞o′tē) *n., pl.* **-tis** or **-ties.** Also **a·gou·ty** *pl.* **-ties.** Any of several burrowing rodents of the genus *Dasyprocta,* of tropical America, having grizzled brownish or dark-gray fur. [French, from Spanish *agutí,* from Guarani *acutí.*]
agr. agricultural; agriculture.
A·gra (ä′grə). A city of the Republic of India, on the Jumna River in Uttar Pradesh State; the site of the Taj Mahal. Population, 505,000.
a·graffe (ə-grăf′) *n.* Also **a·grafe. 1.** A hook-and-loop arrangement used for a clasp on armor and clothing. **2.** *Masonry.* A cramp iron for holding stones together. [French *agrafe,* from Old French *agrafer,* to hook on to : *a-,* to, from Latin *ad-* + *grafer,* to hook, from *grafe,* hook, from Old High German *krāpfo* (see **ger-**[3] in Appendix*).]
a·gran·u·lo·cy·to·sis (ā-grăn′yə-lō-sī-tō′sĭs) *n.* A drug-induced

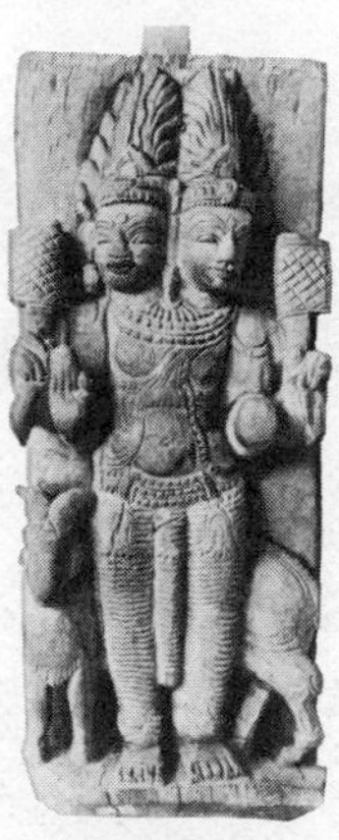

Agni
Indian relief carving in wood

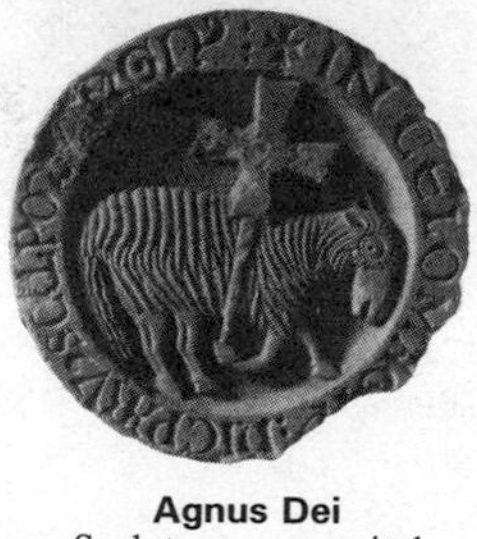

Agnus Dei
Sculpture on a capital of the basilica of the abbey at Cluny, France

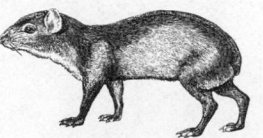

agouti
Dasyprocta cristata
Black agouti

disease marked by high fever, lesions of the mucous membranes, and a decrease in granular white blood corpuscles. [New Latin : A- (not) + GRANULE + -CYT(E) + -OSIS.]

a·gra·pha (ăg′rə-fə) *pl.n.* Also **A·gra·pha.** The sayings of Jesus not in the Bible. [Greek, neuter plural of *agraphos,* unwritten : *a-,* not + *graphein,* to write (see **gerebh-** in Appendix*).]

a·graph·i·a (ā-grăf′ē-ə) *n. Pathology.* A mental disorder marked by inability to write. [New Latin : A- (not) + Greek *graphein,* to write (see **gerebh-** in Appendix*).] —**a·graph′ic** *adj.*

a·grar·i·an (ə-grâr′ē-ən) *adj.* **1.** Relating to or concerning the land and its ownership, cultivation, and tenure. **2.** Pertaining to agricultural or rural matters. —*n.* A person who favors equitable distribution of land. [From Latin *agrārius,* from *ager,* land, field. See **agro-** in Appendix.*] —**a·grar′i·an·ly** *adv.*

a·grar·i·an·ism (ə-grâr′ē-ən-ĭz′əm) *n.* A movement for equitable distribution of land and for agrarian reform.

a·gree (ə-grē′) *v.* **agreed, agreeing, agrees.** —*intr.* **1.** To grant consent; accede. Used with the infinitive: *He agreed to accompany us.* **2.** To come into or be in accord: *The copy agrees with the original.* **3.** To be of one opinion. Often used with *with:* "*Didst thou not agree with me for a penny?*" (Matthew 20:13). **4.** To come to an understanding or to terms. Used with *about* or *on: Is it possible to agree on such great problems?* **5.** To be suitable; appropriate. Used with *with: Spicy food does not agree with him.* **6.** *Grammar.* To correspond in gender, number, case, or person. —*tr.* To grant or concede. Used with a noun clause: *He agreed that we should go.* —See Synonyms at **assent.** [Middle English *agreen,* from Old French *agreer,* from Vulgar Latin *aggrātāre* (unattested), to be pleasing to : *ad-,* to + *grātus,* pleasing, beloved, agreeable (see **gwerə-**[1] in Appendix*).]

Synonyms: *agree, conform, harmonize, accord, correspond, coincide.* These verbs all indicate compatible relationship between people or things. *Agree* may indicate mere lack of incongruity or discord, but often it suggests acceptance of ideas or actions and thus accommodation. *Conform* stresses close resemblance in form, thought, or basic characteristics, sometimes the result of accommodation to established standards. *Harmonize* implies a relationship of unlike things combined or arranged to make a pleasing whole. *Accord* implies close similarity between things or harmonious relationship or both. *Correspond* refers either to actual similarity in form or nature or to similarity in function of unlike things. *Coincide* stresses exact agreement in space, time, or thought.

a·gree·a·ble (ə-grē′ə-bəl) *adj.* **1.** Pleasing; pleasant; to one's liking. **2.** In accordance; conformable. **3.** Ready to consent or submit. —See Synonyms at **amiable.** —**a·gree′a·bil′i·ty, a·gree′a·ble·ness** *n.* —**a·gree′a·bly** *adv.*

a·greed (ə-grēd′) *adj.* **1.** Determined by common consent: *the agreed meeting place.* **2.** Of one opinion: *Both parties were agreed.* **3.** Allowed; granted. Used as a rejoinder.

a·gree·ment (ə-grē′mənt) *n. Abbr.* **agt. 1.** The act of agreeing. **2.** The state of being agreed; concord; harmony. **3.** An arrangement between parties regarding a method of action; covenant; treaty. **4.** *Law.* **a.** A properly executed and legally binding compact. **b.** The writing or document embodying this. **5.** *Grammar.* Correspondence in gender, number, case, or person between words. See Usage note at **number** (noun).

a·gres·tal (ə-grĕs′təl) *adj.* Also **a·gres·tial** (-chəl). Growing wild, especially in cultivated areas, as weeds do. [From Latin *agrestis,* rural, from *ager,* field, land. See **agro-** in Appendix.*]

a·gres·tic (ə-grĕs′tĭk) *adj.* Also **a·gres·ti·cal** (-tĭ-kəl). **1.** Rural; rustic. **2.** Unpolished; crude.

agric. agriculture; agriculturist.

A·gric·o·la (ə-grĭk′ə-lə), **Georgius.** Original name, Georg Bauer. 1494–1555. German mineralogist and author, regarded as father of mineralogy.

A·gric·o·la (ə-grĭk′ə-lə), **Gnaeus Julius.** A.D. 40–93. Roman general; legate of Britain; subdued much of the island.

ag·ri·cul·ture (ăg′rĭ-kŭl′chər) *n. Abbr.* **agr., agric.** The science, art, and business of cultivating the soil, producing crops, and raising livestock useful to man; farming. [Latin *agricultūra,* originally *agrī cultūra,* "cultivation of land" : *agrī,* genitive of *ager,* land (see **agro-** in Appendix*) + *cultūra,* cultivation, CULTURE.] —**ag′ri·cul′tur·al** *adj.* —**ag′ri·cul′tur·al·ly** *adv.* —**ag′ri·cul′tur·ist, ag′ri·cul′tur·al·ist** *n.*

A·gri·gen·to (ä′grē-jĕn′tō). A town of Italy on the southern coast of Sicily, site of the ruins of six fifth-century Doric temples. Population, 40,000.

ag·ri·mo·ny (ăg′rē-mō′nē) *n., pl.* **-nies. 1.** Any of various plants of the genus *Agrimonia,* having compound leaves, long clusters of small yellow flowers, and bristly fruits. **2.** Any of several other plants, such as the **hemp agrimony** *(see).* [Middle English *agrimonie,* from Old French *aigremoine,* from Latin *agrimōnia,* alteration of *argemōnia,* from Greek *argemōnē, argemōnia,* poppy, possibly from Hebrew *'argāmān,* red-purple.]

ag·ri·ol·o·gy (ăg′rē-ŏl′ə-jē) *n.* The study of primitive cultures. [Greek *agrios,* wild, from *agros,* open field (see **agro-** in Appendix*) + -LOGY.] —**ag′ri·o·log′i·cal** (-ə-lŏj′ĭ-kəl) *adj.*

A·grip·pa (ə-grĭp′ə), **Marcus Vipsanius.** 63–12 B.C. Roman general and statesman; chief colleague of Augustus.

Ag·rip·pi·na[1] (ăg′rĭ-pī′nə). Called "the Elder." 13 B.C.?–A.D. 33. Roman matron; daughter of Agrippa; wife of Germanicus Caesar; mother of Caligula and of Agrippina the Younger.

Ag·rip·pi·na[2] (ăg′rĭ-pī′nə). Called "the Younger." A.D. 15?–59. Roman empress; mother of Nero.

agro-. Indicates field, earth, or soil; for example, **agrology.** [From Greek *agros,* open field. See **agro-** in Appendix.*]

ag·ro·bi·ol·o·gy (ăg′rō-bī-ŏl′ə-jē) *n.* The science of plant and animal growth and nutrition as related to soil variation and crop yield. —**ag′ro·bi′o·log′ic** (-bī′ə-lŏj′ĭk), **ag′ro·bi′o·log′i·cal** *adj.* —**ag′ro·bi′o·log′i·cal·ly** *adv.* —**ag′ro·bi·ol′o·gist** *n.*

a·grol·o·gy (ə-grŏl′ə-jē) *n.* The applied science of soils in relation to crops. Compare **pedology.** [AGRO- + -LOGY.] —**ag′ro·log′ic** (ăg′rə-lŏj′ĭk), **ag′ro·log′i·cal** *adj.* —**ag′ro·log′i·cal·ly** *adv.* —**a·grol′o·gist** *n.*

a·gron·o·my (ə-grŏn′ə-mē) *n.* Also **ag·ro·nom·ics** (ăg′rə-nŏm′ĭks). The application of the various soil and plant sciences to soil management and the raising of crops; scientific agriculture. [French *agronomie* : AGRO- + -NOMY.] —**ag′ro·nom′ic** (ăg′rə-nŏm′ĭk), **ag′ro·nom′i·cal** *adj.* —**a·gron′o·mist** *n.*

ag·ros·tol·o·gy (ăg′rə-stŏl′ə-jē) *n.* The botanical study of grasses. [Greek *agrōstis,* a kind of wild grass, from *agros,* field (see **agro-** in Appendix*) + -LOGY.]

a·ground (ə-ground′) *adv.* On the ground or bottom; stranded, as in shallow water: *The ship ran aground.* —**a·ground′** *adj.*

agt. 1. agent. **2.** agreement.

A·guas·ca·lien·tes (ä′gwäs-kä-lyĕn′tās). **1.** A state occupying 2,500 square miles in central Mexico. Population, 263,000. **2.** The capital of this state. Population, 143,000.

a·gue (ā′gyo͞o) *n.* **1.** An attack of fever. **2.** A recurrent chill or fit of shivering. [Middle English, from Old French *ague,* from Medieval Latin *(fēbris) acūta,* "sharp (fever)," feminine of *acūtus,* sharp, past participle of *acuere,* to sharpen, from *acus,* needle. See **ak-** in Appendix.*] —**a′gu·ish** (ā′gyo͞o-ĭsh) *adj.* —**a′gu·ish·ly** *adv.* —**a′gu·ish·ness** *n.*

a·gue·weed (ā′gyo͞o-wēd′) *n.* **1.** A plant, *Gentiana quinquefolia,* of eastern North America, having clusters of pale blue-violet or white flowers. **2.** A plant, **boneset** *(see).*

A·gui·nal·do (ä′gē-näl′dō), **Emilio.** 1869–1964. Philippine revolutionary leader against Spain and the United States.

A·gul·has, Cape (ə-gŭl′əs). A group of rugged sea cliffs marking the divide between the Atlantic and Indian oceans at the southernmost point of Africa.

ah (ä) *interj.* Used to express various emotions, such as surprise, delight, pain, satisfaction, or dislike. [Middle English *a(h),* from Old French.]

A.h ampere-hour.

A.H. in the year of the Hegira (Latin *anno Hegirae*).

a·ha (ä-hä′) *interj.* Used to express surprise, triumph, or pleasure. [Middle English : AH + HA.]

A.H.A. 1. American Historical Association. **2.** American Hospital Association.

A·hab (ā′hăb′). A wicked king of Israel of the ninth century B.C., husband of Jezebel. I Kings 16:22.

A·hag·gar Mountains (ə-hăg′ər, ä′hə-gär′). Also **Hog·gar Mountains** (hŏg′ər). A mountainous upland region in southern Algeria. Highest elevation, Tahat (9,573 feet).

a·head (ə-hĕd′) *adv.* **1.** At or to the front or head. **2.** Before; in advance. **3.** Onward; forward; headlong. —**be ahead.** *Informal.* To be gaining or winning. —**get ahead.** To attain success.

a·hem (ə-hĕm′) *interj.* Used to attract attention or to express doubt or warning. [Expressive.]

a·him·sa (ə-hĭm′sä′) *n.* An Indian doctrine of nonviolence expressing belief in the sacredness of all living creatures and the possibility of reincarnation, strictly practiced by the Jains and affirmed by Buddhists and Hindus. [Sanskrit *ahiṁsā,* noninjury : *a-,* without (see **ne** in Appendix*) + *hiṁsā,* injury, from *hiṁsati,* he injures (see **ghei-**[1] in Appendix*).]

Ah·mad·a·bad (ä′məd-ə-bäd′). Also **Ah·med·a·bad.** The capital of Gujarat, Republic of India. Population, 1,254,000.

Ah·mad·na·gar (ä′məd-nŭg′ər). Also **Ah·med·na·gar.** The capital of Ahmadnagar district, in Maharashtra, Republic of India, about 65 miles northeast of Poona. Population, 119,000.

a·hoy (ə-hoi′) *interj. Nautical.* Used to hail a ship or person, or to attract attention. [AH + HOY.]

Ah·ri·man (ä′rĭ-mən) *n.* In Zoroastrianism, the spirit of evil, understood by some as the arch rival of **Ormazd** *(see).* [Persian *Ahrīman,* probably from Avestan *aṅra mainyu,* "the evil spirit" : *aṅra,* evil, hostile, probably from Iranian root *ans-*†, to hate + *mainyu,* spirit (see **men-**[1] in Appendix*).]

a·hue·hue·te (ä′wā-wā′tā) *n.* An evergreen tree, *Taxodium mucronatum,* native to Mexico. Some specimens have attained great age and girth. Also called "Montezuma cypress." [Spanish, from Nahuatl *ahuehueton,* "old man of the water" : *atl,* water + *huehueton,* old man, from *huehue,* old.]

A·hu·ra Maz·da (ä′ho͝o-rə măz′də). **Ormazd** *(see).*

Ah·ven·an·maa. The Finnish name for the **Åland Islands.**

Ah·waz (ä-wäz′). Also **Ah·vaz** (ä-väz′). A commercial center in southwestern Iran, on the Karun River. Population, 155,000.

ai (ī) *n., pl.* **ais.** A three-toed sloth of the genus *Bradypus.* See **sloth.** [Portuguese, from Tupi *ai, hai.*]

A.I.A. American Institute of Architects.

aid (ād) *v.* **aided, aiding, aids.** —*intr.* To help; assist. —*tr.* To give help or assistance to. —See Synonyms at **help.** —*n.* **1.** The act or result of helping; assistance; cooperation. **2.** One that helps; an assistant or helper. **3.** An aide-de-camp or aide. **4.** In medieval England: **a.** Any of several revenues or subsidies paid to the king. **b.** A money payment to a feudal lord by a vassal. [Middle English *eyden, aiden,* from Old French *aider,* from Latin *adjūtāre,* frequentative of *adjuvāre,* to give aid to, help : *ad,* to + *juvāre*†, to help.] —**aid′er** *n.*

aide (ād) *n.* **1.** An aide-de-camp. **2.** An assistant; helper: *a nurse's aide.* [French, from *aider,* to help, AID.]

aide-de-camp (ād′də-kămp′) *n., pl.* **aides-de-camp.** *Abbr.* **A.D.C., a.d.c., ADC.** A naval or military officer acting as secretary and confidential assistant to a superior officer of general or flag rank. [French, "camp assistant."]

ai·glet. Variant of **aglet.**

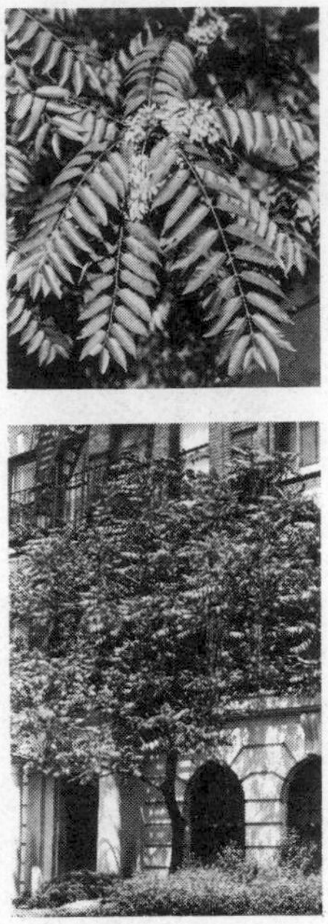

ailanthus
Above: Leaves and flowers
Below: Full tree

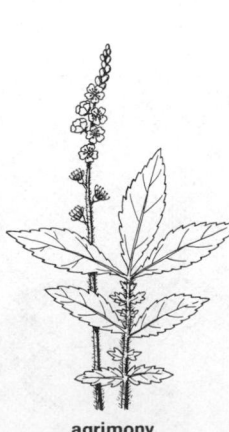

agrimony
Agrimonia gryposepala
Tall hairy agrimony

ă pat/ā pay/âr care/ä father/b bib/ch church/d deed/ĕ pet/ē be/f fife/g gag/h hat/hw which/ĭ pit/ī pie/îr pier/j judge/k kick/l lid, needle/m mum/n no, sudden/ng thing/ŏ pot/ō toe/ô paw, for/oi noise/ou out/o͝o took/o͞o boot/p pop/r roar/s sauce/sh ship, dish/

ai·grette, ai·gret (ā-grĕt′, ā′grĕt) *n.* **1.** An ornamental tuft of upright plumes, especially the tail feathers of an egret. **2.** An ornament, such as a spray of gems, resembling such a tuft. [French *aigrette,* "egret," from Old French. See **egret.**]

ai·guille (ā-gwēl′) *n.* **1.** A sharp, pointed mountain peak. **2.** A needle-shaped drill for boring holes in rock or masonry. [French, "needle," from Old French, AGLET.]

ai·guil·lette (ā′gwĭ-lĕt′) *n.* An ornamental cord or braid worn on the shoulder of a military uniform. [French, AGLET.]

Ai·ken (ā′kĭn), **Conrad (Potter).** Born 1889. American poet.

ail (āl) *v.* **ailed, ailing, ails.** —*intr.* To feel ill or have pain; be unwell. —*tr.* To cause pain; make ill or uneasy; trouble. [Middle English *eilen,* Old English *eglan.* See **agh-**[1] in Appendix.*]

ai·lan·thus (ā-lăn′thəs) *n.* A deciduous tree, *Ailanthus altissima,* native to China but naturalized in North America, especially in urban areas. It has compound leaves and clusters of greenish flowers with an unpleasant odor. Also called "tree of heaven." [New Latin, from Amboinese *ai lanto,* "tree (of) heaven."]

Ai·leen (ā-lēn′). A feminine given name. [Irish form of HELEN.]

ai·le·ron (ā′lə-rŏn′) *n.* A movable control surface on the trailing edge of an airplane wing. [French, diminutive of *aile,* wing, from Old French, from Latin *āla.* See **aks-** in Appendix.*]

ail·ment (āl′mənt) *n.* A physical or mental disorder; especially, a mild illness.

aim (ām) *v.* **aimed, aiming, aims.** —*tr.* **1.** To direct (a weapon, remark, or blow, for example) at someone or something. **2.** To propose; intend: *We aim to solve the problem.* —*intr.* **1.** To direct a weapon: *The gunner aimed carefully.* **2.** To determine a course: *aim at better education.* —*n.* **1.** The act of aiming or pointing. **2.** The sighting or line of fire of something aimed. **3.** *Obsolete.* The object or point aimed at; target; mark. **4.** Purpose; intention; plan. **5.** *Obsolete.* Conjecture; guess. —See Synonyms at **intention.** [Middle English *aimen,* to guess, aim, from Old French *aesmer,* to guess at : *a-,* at, to, from Latin *ad-* + *esmer,* to guess, from Latin *aestimāre,* to ESTIMATE.]

aim·less (ām′lĭs) *adj.* Without direction or purpose. —**aim′less·ly** *adv.* —**aim′less·ness** *n.*

ain[1] (ān) *adj. Scottish.* Own.

a·in[2]**.** Variant of **ayin.**

Ain (ăN). A river of eastern France, rising in the Jura Mountains and flowing about 120 miles south to the Rhône.

ain't (ānt). *Nonstandard.* Contraction of *am not.* Also extended in use to mean *are not, is not, has not,* and *have not.*

Usage: *Ain't,* with few exceptions, is strongly condemned by the Usage Panel when it occurs in writing and speech that is not deliberately colloquial or that does not employ the contraction to provide humor, shock, or other special effect. The first person singular interrogative form *ain't I* (for *am I not* or *amn't I*), considered as a special case, has somewhat more acceptance than *ain't* employed with other pronouns or with nouns. (*Ain't I* has at least the virtue of agreement between *am* and *I.* With other pronouns, or nouns, *ain't* takes the place of *isn't* and *aren't* and sometimes of *hasn't* and *haven't.*) But *ain't I* is unacceptable in writing other than that which is deliberately colloquial, according to 99 per cent of the Panel, and unacceptable in speech to 84 per cent. The example *It ain't likely* is unacceptable to 99 per cent in both writing and speech. *Aren't I* (as a variant of the interrogative *ain't I*) is acceptable in writing to only 27 per cent of the Panel, but approved in speech by 60 per cent. Louis Kronenberger has this typical reaction: "A genteelism, and much worse than *ain't I.*"

Ain·tab. The former name for **Gaziantep.**

Ai·nu (ī′no͞o) *n., pl.* **-nus. 1.** A member of an aboriginal Caucasian people inhabiting the northernmost islands of Japan. **2.** The language of the Ainu people. [Ainu, "man."]

air (âr) *n.* **1. a.** A colorless, odorless, tasteless gaseous mixture, mainly nitrogen (approximately 78 per cent) and oxygen (approximately 21 per cent) with lesser amounts of argon, carbon dioxide, neon, helium, and other gases. **b.** This mixture with varying amounts of moisture, low-altitude pollutants, and particulate matter, enveloping the earth; the atmosphere. **c.** The air or atmosphere in an enclosure: *The air in the conference room is invariably half cigar smoke.* **2.** The sky; firmament. **3.** An atmospheric movement; breeze; wind. **4.** *Archaic.* Breath. **5.** Utterance; publicity; circulation: *give air to one's grievances.* **6.** A peculiar or characteristic impression; appearance; aura: *The room had an air of loneliness.* **7.** Personal bearing, appearance, or manner; mien: *He has an air of gentility.* **8.** *Plural.* Affectation; haughty pose: *She gives herself aristocratic airs.* **9.** *Music.* A melody or tune, especially: **a.** The soprano or treble part in a harmonized composition. **b.** A solo with or without accompaniment. —See Synonyms at **affectation, bearing.** —**in the air. 1.** Abroad; prevalent. **2.** Uncertain; not settled; being thought out or formulated. —**on the air.** *Radio & Television.* Broadcast; being broadcast. —**take the air.** To go outdoors for fresh air; take a short walk or ride. —**up in the air. 1.** Not decided; uncertain; in suspense. **2.** Agitated or excited; upset; angry. —**walk on air.** To feel elated or extremely happy. —*tr.v.* **aired, airing, airs. 1.** To expose so that air can dry, cool, or freshen; ventilate. **2.** To give public utterance to; circulate. —See Synonyms at **vent.** [Blend of senses of several origins: 1. Atmosphere: Middle English *eir, ayr,* from Old French *air,* from Latin *āēr,* from Greek *aēr,* breath, atmospheric air (see **wē-** in Appendix*); 2. Manner, appearance: French *air,* from Old French *aire,* nature, quality, originally "place of origin," from Latin *ager,* place, field (see **agro-** in Appendix*) and Latin *ārea,* open space, threshing floor, AREA; 3. Melody: Italian *aria,* ARIA. In English these senses have interacted inextricably, with the first prevailing.]

air base. A base for military aircraft.

air bladder. *Biology.* **1.** An air-filled structure near the spinal column in many fishes, which functions to maintain buoyancy or, in some species, as an aid in respiration or hearing. Also called "swim bladder." **2.** Any air-filled saclike structure, such as one of the dilated parts of the thallus in certain seaweeds.

air·boat (âr′bōt′) *n.* A **swamp boat** *(see).*

air·borne (âr′bôrn′, -bōrn′) *adj. Abbr.* **abn 1.** Carried by or through the air: *airborne pollen.* **2.** Transported in aircraft: *airborne troops.* **3.** Flying; in flight.

air brake. A brake operated by compressed air.

air·brush (âr′brŭsh′) *n.* Also **air brush.** An atomizer using compressed air to spray paint or other liquids on a surface.

air·burst (âr′bûrst′) *n.* An explosion of a bomb or shell in the atmosphere.

air chamber. 1. Any enclosure filled with air for a special purpose. **2.** Such a compartment, especially in a hydraulic system, in which air elastically compresses and expands to regulate the flow of a fluid.

air command. A unit of the U.S. Air Force that is larger than an air force.

air-con·di·tion (âr′kən-dĭsh′ən) *tr.v.* **-tioned, -tioning, -tions.** To provide with or ventilate by air conditioning.

air conditioner. Any apparatus for controlling, especially lowering, the temperature and humidity of an enclosure.

air conditioning. 1. The state or condition produced by an air conditioner. **2.** A system of air conditioners.

air-cool (âr′ko͞ol′) *tr.v.* **-cooled, -cooling, -cools. 1.** To cool (an engine, for example) by a flow of air. **2.** To air-condition.

air corridor. An air route established by international agreement.

air cover. 1. Protective use of military aircraft during ground operations. **2.** The aircraft so employed.

air·craft (âr′krăft′, -kräft′) *n., pl.* **aircraft.** Any machine or device, including airplanes, helicopters, gliders, and dirigibles, capable of atmospheric flight.

aircraft carrier. A large naval ship designed as a mobile air base at sea, having a long flat deck to serve as a landing strip.

air·crafts·man (âr′krăfts′mən, -kräfts′mən) *n., pl.* **-men** (-mĭn). Also **air·craft·man.** A noncommissioned member of the British Royal Air Force or the Royal Canadian Air Force.

air cushion. 1. An inflatable cushion. **2.** An **air spring** *(see).*

air division. A unit of the U.S. Air Force larger than a wing and smaller than an air force.

air·drome (âr′drōm′) *n.* Also *chiefly British* **aer·o·drome** (âr′ə-drōm′). **1.** An airport. **2.** A landing field. **3.** An airplane hangar. [Earlier *aerodrome* : AERO- + -DROME.]

air·drop (âr′drŏp′) *n.* A delivery, such as of supplies or troops, by parachute from aircraft in flight. —*v.* **-dropped, -dropping, -drops.** —*tr.* To drop from an aircraft. —*intr.* To drop, as supplies or troops, from an aircraft.

air-dry (âr′drī′) *tr.v.* **-dried, -drying, -dries.** To dry by exposure to the air. —*adj.* Sufficiently dry so that further exposure to air will not evaporate moisture.

Aire (âr). A river in western Yorkshire, England, flowing 70 miles to the Ouse.

Aire·dale (âr′dāl′) *n.* A large terrier of a breed developed in England, having rather long legs and a wiry tan coat marked with black. [From *Airedale,* valley in Yorkshire, England.]

air embolism. *Pathology.* **Aeroembolism** *(see).*

air express. A system of transportation of packages by air.

air·field (âr′fēld′) *n.* **1.** An airport having hard-surfaced runways where aircraft can take off and land. **2.** A landing strip.

air·flow (âr′flō′) *n.* **1.** A flow of air. **2.** The air currents caused by the motion of an object such as an airplane or automobile.

air·foil (âr′foil′) *n.* Also *chiefly British* **aer·o·foil** (âr′ə-foil′). An aircraft part or surface, such as a wing, propeller blade, or rudder, the shape and orientation of which control stability, direction, lift, thrust, or propulsion.

air force. *Abbr.* **AF, A.F. 1.** The aviation branch of a country's armed forces, such as the United States Air Force. **2.** A unit of the U.S. Air Force larger than an air division and smaller than an air command.

air·frame (âr′frām′) *n.* An aircraft lacking only its power plant.

air freight. 1. A system of transporting freight by air. **2.** The amount charged for this service.

air gas. A manufactured gas, **producer gas** *(see).*

air·glow (âr′glō′) *n.* A low- or middle-latitude, more or less steady, faint photochemical luminescence in the upper atmosphere. Compare **aurora.**

air gun. A gun discharged by compressed air.

air·head (âr′hĕd′) *n.* An area of hostile or enemy-controlled territory secured by paratroops.

air hole. 1. A hole or opening through which gas or air may pass. **2.** An opening in the frozen surface of a body of water. **3.** *Aviation.* An **air pocket** *(see).*

air·i·ly (âr′ə-lē) *adv.* **1.** In a light spirit; gaily; jauntily. **2.** In a light manner; delicately; gently.

air·i·ness (âr′ē-nĭs) *n.* **1.** The quality or state of being light or airy. **2.** Delicacy; jauntiness.

air lane. A regular route of travel for aircraft; an airway.

air layering. A method of plant propagation in which a twig or shoot attached to the parent plant is wrapped in moist sphagnum moss or polyethylene plastic so that it will form roots and can later be removed and replanted.

air·less (âr′lĭs) *adj.* **1.** Without air. **2.** Lacking fresh air; stuffy. **3.** Without a breeze or wind; still.

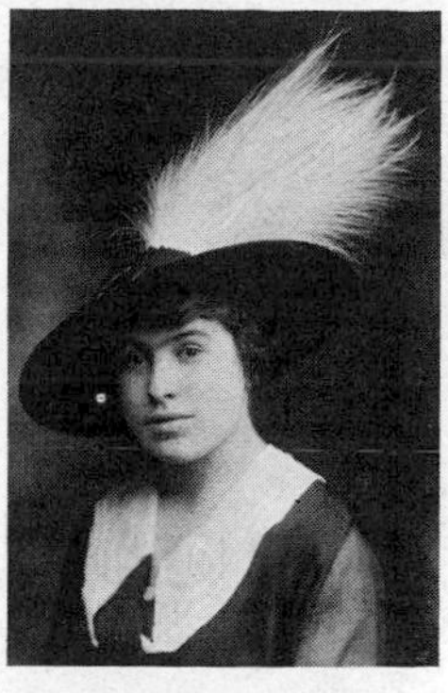

aigrette
Hat decorated with egret tail feathers

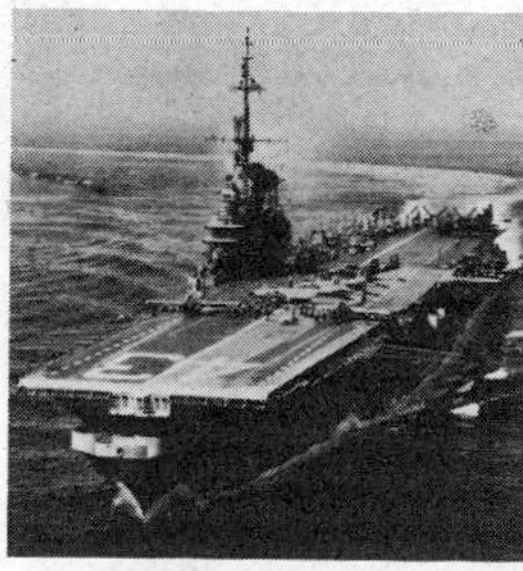

aircraft carrier
U.S.S. *Coral Sea*

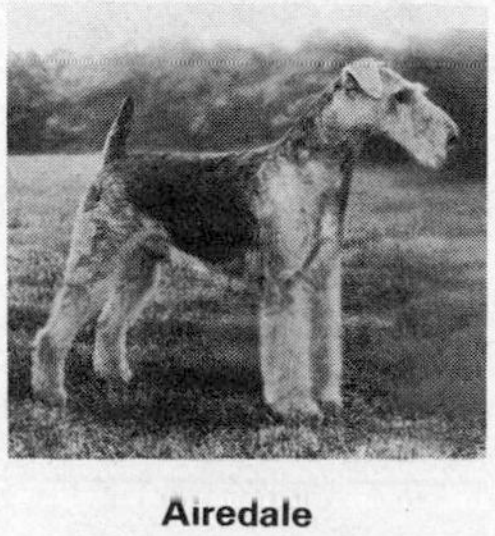

Airedale

Ajax¹
Greek vase painting of
Ajax and Achilles playing
game during siege of Troy

air letter. 1. An air-mail letter. **2.** A sheet of air-mail paper that can be folded as an envelope with a message inside.
air·lift (âr'lĭft') *n.* A system of transporting troops or supplies by air when surface routes are blocked. —*v.* airlifted, -lifting, -lifts. —*tr.* To transport by air, as when ground routes are blocked. —*intr.* To transport supplies or troops by air.
air·line (âr'līn') *n.* **1.** A system for scheduled transport of passengers and freight by air. **2.** A business organization providing such a system of air transport. **3.** An air route. **4.** The shortest distance between two geographical points; a direct line; beeline.
air·lin·er (âr'lī'nər) *n.* An airplane adapted for carrying passengers and operated by an airline.
air lock. 1. An airtight chamber, usually located between two regions of unequal pressure, in which air pressure can be regulated. **2.** A bubble or pocket of air or vapor, as in a pipe, that stops the normal flow of fluid through the conducting part.
air mail. Also **air·mail** (âr'māl'). **1.** The system of conveying mail by aircraft. **2.** Mail conveyed or to be conveyed by aircraft. —**air'-mail'** *adj.*
air·mail (âr'māl') *tr.v.* -mailed, -mailing, -mails. To send a letter, for example) by air mail.
air·man (âr'mən) *n., pl.* -men (-mĭn). **1.** An enlisted man or woman in the U.S. Air Force. **2.** An enlisted man in the U.S. Navy working with aircraft. **3.** An aviator.
airman basic. An enlisted man of the lowest rank in the U.S. Air Force.
air mass. *Meteorology.* A large body of air with only small horizontal variations of temperature, pressure, and moisture.
Air Medal. A decoration awarded by the U.S. Army, Air Force, or Navy for meritorious airborne conduct.
air mile. A unit of distance in air navigation. See **nautical mile.**
air·mind·ed (âr'mīn'dĭd) *adj.* Having enthusiasm for aviation or aircraft. —**air'·mind'ed·ness** *n.*
air·plane (âr'plān') *n.* Also *chiefly British* **aer·o·plane** (âr'ə-plān'). *Abbr.* **AP** Any of various winged vehicles capable of flight, generally heavier than air and propelled by jet engines or propellers. [French *aéroplane*, from Late Greek *aeroplanos*, wandering in the air : AERO- + *-planos*, wandering, from *planasthai*, to wander (see pele-¹ in Appendix*).]
air plant. *Botany.* An **epiphyte** (*see*).
air pocket. A downward air current that causes an aircraft to lose altitude abruptly. Also called "air hole."
air police. Military police of an air force.
air·port (âr'pôrt', -pōrt') *n.* **1.** A tract of leveled land where aircraft can take off and land, usually equipped with hard-surfaced landing strips, a control tower, hangars, and accommodations for passengers and cargo. **2.** A similar installation in which the landing area is on water.
air·proof (âr'prŏŏf') *adj.* Impermeable to air. —*tr.v.* airproofed, -proofing, -proofs. To make impermeable to air.
air pump. Equipment for compressing, removing, or forcing a flow of air.
air raid. An attack by hostile military aircraft, especially when armed with bombs. —**air'·raid'** *adj.* —**air raider.**
air rifle. A low-powered rifle, such as a BB gun, using manually compressed air to fire small pellets.
air sac. *Biology.* An air-filled space, such as one of the spaces in a bird's body that forms a connection between the lungs and the bone cavities, or a dilation in the trachea of many insects.
air·screw (âr'skrŏŏ') *n. British.* The propeller of an airplane.
air·ship (âr'shĭp') *n.* A self-propelled lighter-than-air craft with directional control surfaces; dirigible.
air·sick·ness (âr'sĭk'nĭs) *n.* Nausea resulting from nervous tension or changes in pressure or motion in an aircraft. —**air'·sick'** *adj.*
air sock. A windsock (*see*).
air·space (âr'spās') *n.* **1.** The portion of the atmosphere above a particular land area, especially a nation or other political subdivision. **2.** The space occupied by an aircraft formation or used in a maneuver.
air speed. Speed, especially of an aircraft, relative to the air.
air spray. 1. A device for spraying liquids, using compressed air. **2.** The liquid sprayed by such a device. —**air'-sprayed'** *adj.*
air spring. An enclosed volume of air which, by its resilience, acts as a spring or shock absorber. Also called "air cushion."
air·stream (âr'strēm') *n.* A flow of air, especially about an aircraft in flight, such as that caused by revolving propellers.
air·strip (âr'strĭp') *n.* A cleared area serving, usually temporarily or in emergency, as an airfield.
airt (ârt) *n. Scottish.* One of the cardinal points on the compass; a direction. [Middle English *art*, from Scottish Gaelic *aird*, probably from Old Irish *aird†*.]
air·tight (âr'tīt') *adj.* **1.** Impermeable by air or gas. **2.** Having no weak points; sound: *an airtight excuse.*
air-to-air missile (âr'tə-âr') *n.* A missile, usually guided, designed to be fired from aircraft at aircraft.
air-to-surface missile (âr'tə-sûr'fĭs). A missile, usually guided, designed to be fired from aircraft at targets on the ground. Also called "air-to-ground missile."
air·way (âr'wā') *n.* **1.** A passageway or shaft in which air circulates, as in ventilating a mine. **2.** A designated route of passage for an aircraft; an air lane.
air·wor·thy (âr'wûr'thē) *adj.* Prepared and in fit condition to fly. Said of aircraft. —**air'wor'thi·ness** *n.*
air·y (âr'ē) *adj.* -ier, -iest. **1.** Having the constitution or nature of air. **2.** High in the air; lofty; towering. **3.** Open to the air; breezy: *airy chambers.* **4.** Performed in the air; aerial. **5.** Resembling air; immaterial: *an airy apparition.* **6.** Insubstantial;

airship
U.S. Army, 1925

Alaric
Contemporary seal

irrational; unreal. **7.** Speculative; imaginative; visionary. **8.** Light as air; graceful or delicate: *an airy veil.* **9.** Displaying lofty nonchalance.
A·i·sha (ä'ē-shə). Also **A·ye·sha.** A.D. 611–678. Chief wife of Mohammed.
aisle (īl) *n.* **1.** A part of a church divided laterally from the nave by a row of pillars or columns. **2.** A passageway between rows of seats, such as in a church or auditorium. **3.** Any passageway, such as one between trees in an orchard. [Middle English *eile* (influenced by *ile, isle,* ISLE), from Old French *aile,* wing of a building, from Latin *ala,* wing. See aks- in Appendix.*]
Aisne (ān). A river of northeastern France, rising in the Argonne Forest and flowing about 175 miles westward to the Oise.
aitch (āch) *n.* The letter *h.* [Earlier *ache,* from French *hache,* probably from (unattested) Vulgar Latin *hacca†.*]
aitch·bone (āch'bōn') *n.* **1.** The rump bone in cattle. **2.** The cut of meat containing this bone. [Middle English *hachboon,* from phrase *an hach boon,* originally *a nachebon* : *nache, nage,* buttock, from Old French, from Late Latin *natica,* from Latin *natis,* buttock (see not in Appendix*) + *bon,* BONE.]
Aix-en-Pro·vence (ĕks'äN-prô-väNs'). A city of southern France, 17 miles north of Marseille. Population, 68,000.
Aix-la-Cha·pelle. The French name for **Aachen.**
A·jac·cio (ä-yät'chō). The capital of Corsica, on the western coast; birthplace of Napoleon Bonaparte. Population, 41,000.
a·jar¹ (ə-jär') *adv.* Partially opened: *Leave the door ajar.* [Middle English *on char,* "in the act of turning" : ON + *char,* a turn, Old English *cierr* (see **char**).] —**a·jar'** *adj.*
a·jar² (ə-jär') *adv.* Not harmonious; jarring: *ajar with the times.* [A- (on, in the act of) + JAR (discord).] —**a·jar'** *adj.*
A·jax¹ (ā'jăks'). *Greek Mythology.* A Greek warrior of great stature and prowess who fought against Troy; son of Telamon of Salamis.
A·jax² (ā'jăks). *Greek Mythology.* A Greek warrior of small stature and arrogant character who fought against Troy; son of Ileus of Locris.
Aj·mer (ŭj-mĭr'). A city of Rajasthan State, India. Population, 231,000.
AK Alaska (with Zip Code).
a.k.a. also known as.
A·ka·shi (ä-kä'shē). A city of Japan, on southwestern Honshu. Population, 120,000.
Ak·bar (ăk'bär'). Called "Akbar the Great." 1542–1605. Mogul emperor of India (1556–1605).
AKC American Kennel Club.
ak·ee (ăk'ē, ä-kē') *n.* **1.** A tropical tree, *Blighia sapida,* native to Africa, having fragrant flowers and capsules containing black seeds. **2.** The edible aril surrounding these seeds, used in tropical cooking. [Native name in Liberia.]
à Kempis, Thomas. See **Thomas à Kempis.**
a·kene. Variant of **achene.**
A·khe·na·ton, A·khe·na·ten (ä'kə-nä'tən). Also **Ikh·na·ton** (ĭk-nä'tən). Original name, Amenhotep IV. King of Egypt (1375–1358 B.C.) and religious reformer; husband of Nefertiti.
A·ki·ba ben Jo·seph (ä-kĭ'vä bĕn jō'zəf, -zĭf). A.D. 50?–132. Jewish teacher; martyred.
A·ki·hi·to (ä'kē-hē'tō). Born 1933. Crown prince of Japan.
a·kim·bo (ə-kĭm'bō) *adj.* With the hands on the hips and the elbows bowed outward. [Middle English *in kenebowe,* "in keen bow," "in a sharp curve," probably from Old Norse *i keng boginn* (unattested), "bent like a bow" : *keng,* accusative of *kengr†,* a curve, noun + *boginn,* accusative of *bogi,* a bow (see bheug-³ in Appendix*).] —**a·kim'bo** *adv.*
a·kin (ə-kĭn') *adj.* **1.** Of the same kin; related. **2.** Having a similar quality or character; analogous. **3.** *Linguistics.* Cognate. [A- (of) + KIN.] —**a·kin'** *adv.*
A·ki·ta (ä-kē-tä). A port city in northwestern Honshu, Japan. Population, 1,308,000.
Ak·kad (ăk'ăd', ä'käd'). Also **Ac·cad. 1.** A region of ancient Mesopotamia, comprising the northern part of later Babylonia. **2.** Original name **A·ga·de** (ä-gä'dĕ, ə-gä'dĕ). The capital of Babylonia, founded in 2300 B.C.
Ak·ka·di·an (ə-kā'dē-ən) *n.* **1.** A native or inhabitant of ancient Akkad. **2.** The Semitic language spoken in ancient Akkad. —*adj.* Of, pertaining to, or relating to the Akkadians or their Semitic language.
Ak·ron (ăk'rən). An industrial city of Ohio, 30 miles south of Cleveland. Population, 290,000.
Ak·tyu·binsk (ŭk-tyōō'bĭnsk). An industrial city of the Soviet Union, in west-central Kazakhstan. Population, 127,000.
–al¹. Indicates a pertinence to or connection with; for example, **adjectival.** [Middle English *-al, -el,* from Old French, from Latin *-ālis.*]
–al². Indicates the act or process of doing or experiencing the action indicated by the verb stem; for example, **denial.** [Middle English *-aille,* from Old French, from Latin *-ālia,* substantive neuter plural of *-ālis,* adjectival suffix.]
–al³. *Chemistry.* Indicates an aldehyde, an organic compound; for example, **citronellal.** [From AL(DEHYDE).]
Al 1. Alabama (with Zip Code). **2.** The symbol for the element aluminum.
al. alcohol; alcoholic.
A.L. American Legion.
a·la (ā'lə) *n., pl.* alae (ā'lē). *Biology.* A winglike structure or part, such as an ear lobe, the membranous border of some seeds, or one of the side petals of certain flowers, such as the sweet pea. [Latin *ala,* wing. See aks- in Appendix.*]
à la (ä'lä, ä'lə, ăl'ə). Also **a la.** In the style or manner of; in

accordance with: *a poem à la Ogden Nash.* [French, short for *à la mode de,* "in the manner of."]
ALA American Library Association.
Ala. Alabama.
A.L.A. American Library Association.
Al·a·bam·a (ăl′ə-băm′ə). *Abbr.* **Ala.** A southern state of the United States, 51,609 square miles in area, with its southern border on the Gulf of Mexico. It was admitted to the Union in 1819, as the 22nd state. Population, 3,267,000. Capital, Montgomery. See map at **United States of America.** —**Al′a·bam′i·an** (-ē-ən), **Al′a·bam′an** *adj.* & *n.*
Alabama River (ăl′ə-băm′ə). A river rising in central Alabama and flowing 315 miles south to the Gulf of Mexico at Mobile.
al·a·bas·ter (ăl′ə-băs′tər, -bäs′tər) *n.* **1.** A dense, translucent, white or tinted, fine-grained gypsum. **2.** A variety of hard calcite, translucent and sometimes banded. **3.** Pale yellowish pink to yellowish gray. See **color.** —*adj.* Also **al·a·bas·trine** (ăl′ə-băs′trĭn, -bäs′trĭn). Of or similar to alabaster; smooth, hard, and white. [Middle English *alabastre,* from Old French, from Latin *alabaster,* from Greek *alabastros, alabastos,* from Egyptian *'a-la-Baste,* "vessel of (the goddess) *Baste.*"]
à la carte (ä′ lä kärt′, ăl′ə). According to the bill of fare; with a separate price for each item on the menu. Compare **prix fixe.** [French, "by the menu" : *à,* by, to + *la,* the + *carte,* menu, from Old French, charter, CARD.]
a·lack (ə-lăk′) *interj. Archaic.* Used to express sorrow, regret, or alarm. Also "alackaday." [Middle English *alacke,* "ah, (what) loss!" : *a, ah,* AH + LACK.]
a·lac·ri·ty (ə-lăk′rə-tē) *n.* **1.** Cheerful willingness; eagerness. **2.** Lively action; sprightliness. [Latin *alacritās,* from *alacer,* lively, eager. See **al-²** in Appendix.*] —**a·lac′ri·tous** (-təs) *adj.*
A·la Dag (ä′lä däKH′). Also **A·la Dagh. 1.** A portion of the Taurus mountain range in southern Turkey. Highest elevation, Kaldi Dag (12,251 feet). **2.** A range in eastern Turkey. Highest elevation, 11,545 feet.
A·lad·din (ə-lăd′n). In the *Arabian Nights,* a boy who acquires a magic lamp and a magic ring with which he can summon two jinn to fulfill any desire.
A·la·gez, Mount (ä′lə-gĕz′). Also **Mount Ar·a·gats** (âr′ə-gäts). An extinct volcano, rising to 13,435 feet in northwestern Armenian S.S.R.
A·la·go·as (ä′lä-gō′əs). A state, 11,000 square miles in area, in northeastern Brazil. Population, 1,271,000. Capital, Maceió.
A·lai (ä-lī′). A mountain range of the Soviet Union, extending some 200 miles west from the China border into the southern Kirghiz S.S.R. Highest elevation, 19,500 feet.
à la king (ä′ lə kĭng′, ăl′ə). *Cooking.* Prepared in a cream sauce with green pepper or pimiento and mushrooms.
Al·a·man·ni·an, Al·a·man·nic. Variants of **Alemannic.**
al·a·me·da (ăl′ə-mē′də, -mā′də) *n. Southwestern U.S.* A promenade or shaded walk, especially one lined with poplars or other shade trees. [Spanish, from *álamo,* ALAMO.]
Al·a·me·da (ăl′ə-mē′də). A city in western California on an island in San Francisco Bay; site of a large naval air station. Population, 64,000.
A·la·mein, El (ĕl ăl′ə-mān′). A village in northern Egypt, 65 miles west of Alexandria; site of a major British victory over the Axis forces (1942) in World War II.
al·a·mo (ăl′ə-mō′) *n., pl.* **-mos.** *Southwestern U.S.* A poplar tree, especially a cottonwood. [Spanish *álamo*†.]
Al·a·mo, the (ăl′ə-mō′). A Franciscan mission in San Antonio, Texas; site of a massacre of Texans by Mexican forces (1836).
à la mode (ä′ lə mōd′, ăl′ə). **1.** According to or in style or fashion. **2.** *Cooking.* **a.** Served with ice cream. Said of certain desserts. **b.** Braised with vegetables and served in a rich, brown sauce. Said of meats. [French, "in the fashion."]
a·la·mode (ä′lə-mōd′, ăl′ə-mōd′) *n.* A lustrous plain-weave silk fabric for head coverings and scarfs. [From À LA MODE.]
Al·a·mo·gor·do (ăl′ə-mə-gôr′dō). A city in southern New Mexico, 50 miles southeast of the site of the first atomic bomb explosion (1945). Population, 22,000.
Al·an (ăl′ən). Also **Al·lan, Al·len.** A masculine given name. [Middle English *Alain, Aleyn,* from Breton *Alain,* from Common Celtic *Alun*†, probably "harmony."]
A·land Islands (ō′län). Also **Aa·land Islands.** *Finnish* **Ah·ve·nan·maa** (äKH′vĕ-nän-mä′). A strategic island group at the entrance to the Gulf of Bothnia, controlled by Finland since 1921. Population, 21,000. Capital, Mariehamn.
al·a·nine (ăl′ə-nēn′) *n.* An amino acid, $CH_3CH(NH_2)COOH$, a constituent of most proteins. [German *Alanin* : AL(DEHYDE) + *-an* (arbitrary infix) + -IN(E).]
a·lar (ā′lər) *adj.* **1.** Of, pertaining to, or having wings or alae. **2.** Shaped like or resembling a wing. **3.** *Anatomy.* Pertaining to the armpit; axillary. [Latin *ālāris,* from *āla,* wing. See **aks-** in Appendix.*]
Al·a·ric (ăl′ə-rĭk). A.D. 370?–410. King of the Visigoths; conqueror of Rome (410).
a·larm (ə-lärm′) *n.* **1.** A sudden fear caused by an apprehension of danger; fright. **2.** A warning of approaching or existing danger. **3.** An electrical or mechanical device that serves to warn of danger by means of a sound or signal. **4.** The sounding mechanism of an alarm clock. **5.** A call to arms. **6.** *Fencing.* A stamp on the ground with the advancing foot. —See Synonyms at **fear.** —*tr.v.* **alarmed, alarming, alarms. 1.** To frighten by a sudden revelation of danger. **2.** To warn of or indicate approaching or existing danger. —See Synonyms at **frighten.** [Middle English *alarme,* from Old French, from Old Italian *allarme,* from *all'arme,* "to arms!" : *alla,* to, from Latin *ad illam,* to that, from *ille,* that (see **al-¹** in Appendix*) + *arme,* arms, from Latin *arma* (see **ar-** in Appendix*).] —**a·larm′a·ble** *adj.* —**a·larm′ing·ly** *adv.*
alarm clock. A clock that can be set to sound a bell or buzzer at any desired hour.
a·larm·ist (ə-lär′mĭst) *n.* A person who needlessly alarms or attempts to alarm others, as by inventing or spreading frightening rumors and prophesying political or social calamities. —**a·larm′ism′** *n.*
alarm reaction. An innate mechanism in animals and man, providing a response to novel or threatening circumstances.
a·lar·um (ə-lär′əm, ə-lăr′-) *n. Archaic.* An alarm, especially a call to arms. [Middle English *alarom, alarme,* ALARM.]
a·la·ry (ā′lər-ē) *adj.* **1.** Of or pertaining to wings. **2.** Resembling a wing; wingshaped. [Latin *ālārius,* from *āla,* wing. See **aks-** in Appendix.*]
a·las (ə-lăs′, ə-läs′) *interj.* An exclamation expressing sorrow, regret, grief, compassion, or apprehension of danger or evil. [Middle English, from Old French : *a,* AH + *las,* wretched, from Latin *lassus,* weary (see **lēi-²** in Appendix*).]
Alas. Alaska (unofficial).
a·las·ka (ə-lăs′kə) *n.* **1.** A kind of heavy-duty rubberized overshoe. **2. a.** A heavy dress and coat fabric of cotton and wool. **b.** A yarn made of cotton and wool. [After ALASKA.]
A·las·ka (ə-lăs′kə). The largest state of the United States, occupying 586,400 square miles in extreme northwestern North America, separated from the other mainland states by British Columbia, Canada. It was admitted to the Union in 1959 as the 49th state. Population, 226,000. Capital, Juneau. See map at **United States of America.** —**A·las′kan** *adj.* & *n.*
A·las·ka, Gulf of (ə-lăs′kə). The northern inlet of the Pacific between the Alaska Peninsula and the Alexander Archipelago.
Alaska cedar. The **Nootka cypress** *(see).*
A·las·ka Highway (ə-lăs′kə). A strategic highway, 1,671 miles long, built by Canada and the United States in 1942–43 from Dawson Creek, British Columbia, to Fairbanks, Alaska. Also called "Alcan Highway."
Alaskan malamute. A dog, the **malamute** *(see).*
A·las·ka Peninsula (ə-lăs′kə). A continuation of the Aleutian Range of south-central Alaska, extending some 500 miles southwest between the Bering Sea and the Pacific Ocean.
A·las·ka Range (ə-lăs′kə). A mountain range extending about 400 miles in south-central Alaska. Highest elevation, Mount McKinley (20,320 feet).
a·las·tor (ə-lăs′tôr) *n.* Also **A·las·tor.** An avenging deity or spirit, masculine personification of Nemesis, frequently evoked in Greek tragedy. [Greek *alastōr,* "unforgetting one," from *alastos,* unforgettable : *a-,* not + *lathein, lanthanesthai* (stem *las-*), to forget (see **lādh-** in Appendix*).]
a·late (ā′lāt′) *adj.* Also **a·lat·ed** (ā′lā′tĭd). *Biology.* Having thin, winglike extensions or parts; winged. [Latin *ālātus,* from *āla,* wing. See **aks-** in Appendix.*]
Al·a·va, Cape (ăl′ə-və). A cape in northwestern Washington, the westernmost point of the continental United States, excluding Alaska.
alb (ălb) *n.* A long white linen robe with tapered sleeves worn by a priest as he celebrates Mass. [Middle English *albe, aube,* Old English *albe,* from Medieval Latin *(vestis) alba,* "white (garment)," from Latin *albus,* white. See **albho-** in Appendix.*]
Alb. People's Republic of Albania; Albanian.
Al·ba, Duke of. See **Alva.**
al·ba·core (ăl′bə-kôr′, -kōr′) *n., pl.* **albacore** or **-cores.** A large marine fish, *Thunnus alalunga,* of warm seas, having edible flesh that is a major source of canned tuna. [Portuguese *albacor,* from Arabic *al-bakrah* : *al,* the + *bakr,* young camel.]
Al·ba Lon·ga (ăl′bə lông′gə). A city of ancient Latium, southeast of Rome; the birthplace of Romulus and Remus.
Al·ba·ni·a¹ (ăl-bā′nē-ə, -bān′yə, ôl-). *Albanian* **Shqip·e·ri** (shkyĭp-ə-rē′). *Abbr.* **Alb.** Officially, People's Republic of Albania. A country occupying 10,629 square miles on the Adriatic coast of the Balkan Peninsula. Population, 2,000,000. Capital, Tirana.
Al·ba·ni·a² (ăl-bā′nē-ə, -bān′yə, ôl-). An ancient country of Asia corresponding roughly in area to the modern Azerbaijan S.S.R.
Al·ba·ni·an (ăl-bā′nē-ən, -bān′yən, ôl-) *adj. Abbr.* **Alb.** Of or pertaining to the People's Republic of Albania, its inhabitants, language, or properties. —*n.* **1.** A native or inhabitant of Albania. **2.** The Indo-European language of Albania.
Al·ba·ny (ôl′bə-nē). **1.** The capital of New York State since 1797, on the west bank of the Hudson at the head of deep-water navigation. Population, 130,000. **2.** A city of Georgia, in the southwest on the Flint River. Population, 58,000.
Al·ba·ny River (ôl′bə-nē). A river of Ontario, Canada, rising in the west and flowing 610 miles northeast to James Bay.
al·ba·tross (ăl′bə-trôs′, -trŏs′) *n., pl.* **-trosses** or **albatross. 1.** Any of various large, web-footed birds of the family Diomedeidae, chiefly of the oceans of the Southern Hemisphere, having a hooked beak and long, narrow wings. **2. Albatross cloth** *(see).* [Alteration of Portuguese *alcatraz,* pelican, from Arabic *al-ghaṭṭās* : *al,* the + *ghaṭṭās,* white-tailed sea eagle.]
albatross cloth. A lightweight woolen fabric used for making warm nightclothes and socks. Also called "albatross." [Origin obscure.]
Al Bay·da. The Arabic name for **Beida.**
al·be·do (ăl-bē′dō) *n., pl.* **-dos.** The fraction of incident electromagnetic radiation reflected by a surface. [Late Latin *albēdō,* whiteness, from Latin *albus,* white. See **albho-** in Appendix.*]
Al·bee (ăl′bē), **Edward.** Born 1928. American playwright.
al·be·it (ôl-bē′ĭt, ăl-) *conj.* Although; even though; though;

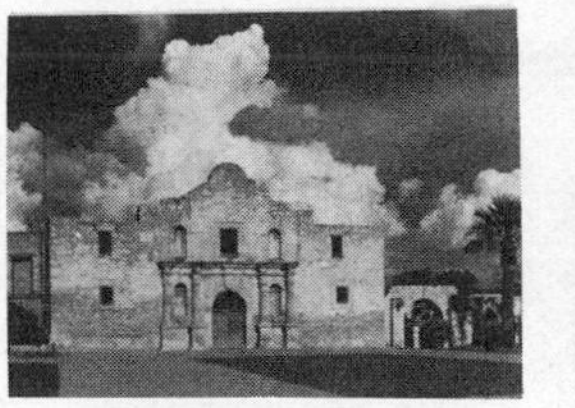
the Alamo
Facade of the mission

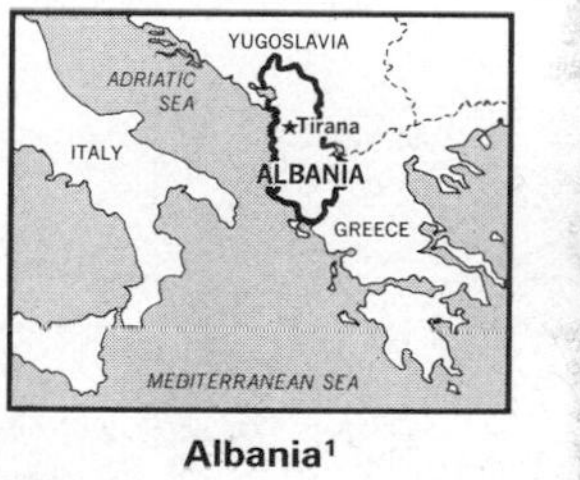

Albania¹

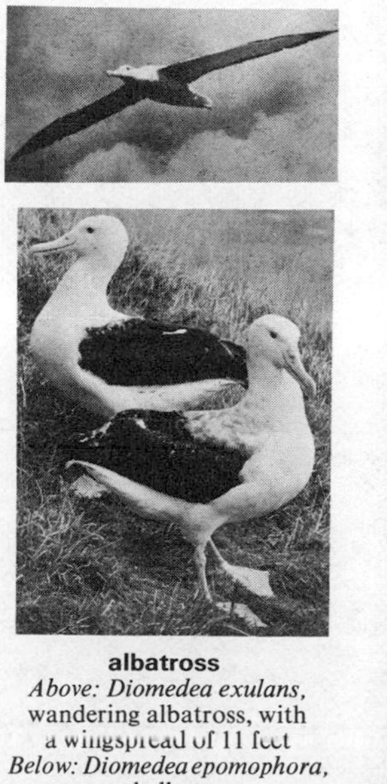
albatross
Above: Diomedea exulans, wandering albatross, with a wingspread of 11 feet
Below: Diomedea epomophora, royal albatross

notwithstanding. [Middle English *al be it*, "let it be entirely (that)" : *al*, ALL + *be*, subjunctive of *been*, to BE + IT.]

Al·be·marle, Duke of. See George **Monk.**

Al·be·marle Sound (ăl′bə-märl′). An arm of the Atlantic, penetrating 50 miles into northeastern North Carolina.

Al·bé·niz (äl-bā′nĕth, -nĕs), **Isaac.** 1860-1909. Spanish composer and pianist.

Al·bert (ăl′bərt). A masculine given name. [Middle English, from Old French *Aubert*, from Old High German *Adalbert* : *adal*, noble (see **athal**- in Appendix*) + *beraht*, bright (see **bhereg**- in Appendix*).]

Al·bert, Lake (ăl′bərt). The northernmost lake in the central African Rift Valley, occupying 2,064 square miles between the Democratic Republic of Congo (Kinshasa) and Uganda.

Al·bert (ăl′bərt), **Prince.** In full, Albert Francis Charles Augustus Emmanuel of Saxe-Coburg-Gotha. 1819-1861. Prince consort of Queen Victoria.

Al·ber·ta (ăl-bûr′tə). *Abbr.* **Alta.** A prairie province of Canada, 255,285 square miles in area. Population, 1,332,000. Capital, Edmonton. See map at **Canada.** —**Al′ber′tan** *n. & adj.*

Al·bert Ed·ward, Mount (ăl′bərt ĕd′wərd). A mountain rising to about 13,000 feet, in the Owen Stanley Range of southwestern New Guinea.

Al·bert Nile (ăl′bərt nīl). A name given to a section of the upper Nile running through northwestern Uganda.

Al·ber·tus Mag·nus (ăl-bûr′təs măg′nəs), **Saint.** Original name, Albert, Count von Bollstädt. 1206?-1280. German theologian and alchemist; canonized 1931.

al·bes·cent (ăl-bĕs′ənt) *adj.* Becoming white or moderately white; whitish. [Latin *albescēns*, from *albescere*, to become white, from *albus*, white. See **albho**- in Appendix.*]

Al·bi·gen·ses (ăl′bə-jĕn′sēz′) *pl.n.* A collective denomination for the members of a Catharist religious sect that flourished in southern France in the 12th and 13th centuries, and was exterminated by the Inquisition under Pope Innocent III, following the French conquest of Languedoc led by Simon de Montfort. [Medieval Latin, inhabitants of *Albiga*, Albi, town in southern France (where the sect was dominant).] —**Al′bi·gen′si·an** (-jĕn′sē-ən, -jĕn′shən) *adj.*

Al·bi·gen·si·an·ism (ăl′bə-jĕn′sē-ən-ĭz′əm, -jĕn′shən-ĭz′əm) *n.* The heretical teaching of the Albigenses, which espoused a form of Manichaean dualism.

al·bin·ism (ăl′bə-nĭz′əm) *n.* **1.** Absence of normal pigmentation in a person, animal, or plant. **2.** The state or condition of being an albino. [French *albinisme*, from German *Albinismus*, from *Albino*, albino, from Portuguese. See **albino.**]

al·bi·no (ăl-bī′nō) *n., pl.* **-nos.** An organism lacking normal pigmentation, such as a person having abnormally pale skin, very light hair, and lacking normal eye coloring, or an animal having white hair or fur and red eyes. [Portuguese, from *albo*, white, from Latin *albus*. See **albho**- in Appendix.*]

Al·bi·nus. See Alcuin.

Al·bi·on (ăl′bē-ən). A literary name for Britain. [Latin *Albiōn*, from Celtic *alb*- (unattested), high. See also **Alps.**]

al·bite (ăl′bīt′) *n.* A widely distributed white feldspar, NaAlSi₃O₈, one of the common rock-forming plagioclase group. [Swedish *albit*, from Latin *albus*, white. See **albho**- in Appendix.*] —**al·bit′ic** (ăl-bĭt′ĭk), **al·bit′i·cal** (-ə-kəl) *adj.*

Al·bo·rak (ăl′bə-răk′). *Moslem Legend.* The white mule upon which Mohammed visited the seven heavens.

al·bum (ăl′bəm) *n.* **1.** A book or binder with blank pages for the insertion and preservation of stamps, photographs, keepsakes, autographs, and the like. **2. a.** A set of phonograph records stored together in jackets under one binding. **b.** The holder for such records. **c.** One or more 12-inch long-playing records in a slip case. **3.** A printed collection of miscellaneous musical compositions, for home use. **4.** A tall, handsomely printed book, especially popular in the 19th century, often having a profusion of illustrations and short, sentimental texts. [Latin, blank tablet, neuter of *albus*, white. See **albho**- in Appendix.*]

al·bu·men (ăl-byōō′mən) *n.* **1.** A nutritive substance surrounding a developing embryo, such as the white of an egg or the material stored in a plant seed. **2.** Albumin. [Latin *albūmen*, from *albus*, white. See **albho**- in Appendix.*]

al·bu·min (ăl-byōō′mən) *n.* Any of several simple, water-soluble proteins that are coagulated by heat and are found in egg white, blood serum, milk, various animal tissues, and many plant juices and tissues. [ALBUM(EN) + -IN.]

al·bu·mi·noid (ăl-byōō′mə-noid′) *adj.* Also **al·bu·mi·noi·dal** (-byōō′mə-noid′l). Resembling albumin. —*n. Biochemistry.* Protein.

al·bu·mi·nous (ăl-byōō′mə-nəs) *adj.* Of, like, or pertaining to albumin or albumen.

al·bu·mi·nu·ri·a (ăl-byōō′mə-nŏōr′ē-ə, -nyŏōr′ē-ə) *n.* The presence of albumin in the urine, sometimes indicative of kidney disease. [ALBUMIN + -URIA.] —**al·bu′mi·nu′ric** *adj.*

al·bu·mose (ăl′byōō-mōs′, -mōz′) *n.* Any of a class of albuminous substances formed by enzymatic action on proteins during digestion. [French : *album(ine)*, ALBUMIN + -OSE.]

Al·bu·quer·que (ăl′bə-kûr′kē). A city and health resort in central New Mexico on the Rio Grande, established as a Spanish settlement in 1706. Population, 201,000.

Al·bu·quer·que (ăl′bōō-kĕr′kə), **Affonso de.** 1453-1515. Portuguese admiral; viceroy of Portuguese Indies.

al·bur·num (ăl-bûr′nəm) *n. Botany.* Sapwood (*see*). [Latin, from *albus*, white. See **albho**- in Appendix.*]

alc. alcohol; alcoholic.

Al·ca·ic (ăl-kā′ĭk) *adj. Prosody.* Of or designating a verse form

used in Greek and Latin poetry, consisting of strophes having four tetrametric lines. —*n. Prosody.* Verse composed in Alcaic strophes. Also used in the plural. [Late Latin *Alcaicus*, from Greek *Alkaīkos*, "of Alcaeus" (fl. 600 B.C.), Greek lyric poet.]

al·cai·de (ăl-kī′dē) *n.* Also **al·cay·de.** The commander or governor of a fortress as in Spain or Portugal. [Spanish, from Arabic *al-qā′id*, the commander, from *qād*, to command.]

al·cal·de (ăl-käl′dē) *n.* The mayor or chief judicial official of a Spanish or Spanish-American town. [Spanish, from Arabic *al-qādī* : *al*, the + *qādī*, judge, from *qadā*, to judge.]

Al·can Highway (ăl′kăn′). An unofficial name for the **Alaska Highway** (*see*).

Al·ca·traz (ăl′kə-trăz′). A small island in San Francisco Bay, California, the site of a former Federal prison.

al·caz·ar (ăl-kăz′ər, ăl′kə-zär′) *n.* **1.** A Spanish palace or fortress, originally one built by the Moors. **2.** *Capital* **A.** A palace in Seville, built and first used by the Moorish kings, and later used by the Spanish royalty. Preceded by *the.* [Spanish *alcázar*, from Arabic *al-qasr* : *al*, the + *qasr*, castle, from Latin *castra*, fort, plural of *castrum*, camp (see **kes**-² in Appendix*).]

Al·ces·tis (ăl-sĕs′tĭs). *Greek Mythology.* The wife of King Admetus of Thessaly. She agreed to die in place of her husband, and was later rescued from Hades by Hercules.

al·che·mist (ăl′kə-mĭst) *n.* A practitioner of alchemy. [Middle English *alkamist*, from Medieval Latin *alchymista*, from *alchymia*, ALCHEMY.] —**al′che·mis′tic, al′che·mis′ti·cal** *adj.*

al·che·mize (ăl′kə-mīz′) *tr.v.* **-mized, -mizing, -mizes.** To transform by or as if by alchemy: *"the remarkable ability to alchemize all bitter truths into an innocuous but piquant confection"* (James Baldwin).

al·che·my (ăl′kə-mē) *n.* **1.** A traditional chemical philosophy having as its asserted aims the transmutation of base metals into gold, the discovery of the panacea, and the preparation of the elixir of longevity. **2.** Any seemingly magical power or process of transmuting: *"that alchemy . . . by which women can concoct a subtle poison from ordinary trifles"* (Hawthorne). —See Synonyms at **magic.** [Middle English *alkamie*, from Old French *alquemie*, from Medieval Latin *alchymia*, from Arabic *al-kīmiyā′*, "the art of transmutation" : *al*, the + *kīmiyā′*, from Late Greek *khēm(e)ia*, "art of transmutation practiced by the Egyptians," from Greek *Khēmia*, "Black Land," Egypt, from Egyptian *Kh′mi*, from *khem*, black.] —**al·chem′i·cal** (-ĭ-kəl), **al·chem′ic** *adj.* —**al·chem′i·cal·ly** *adv.*

Al·ci·bi·a·des (ăl′sĭ-bī′ə-dēz′). 450?-404 B.C. Athenian general; protégé of Socrates; exiled and assassinated.

Al·cin·o·us (ăl-sĭn′ō-əs). *Greek Mythology.* A king of Phaeacia, father of Nausicaa, who entertained Odysseus.

Alc·me·ne (ălk-mē′nē). *Greek Mythology.* Amphitryon's wife, who gave birth to Hercules after being seduced by Zeus.

al·co·hol (ăl′kə-hôl′) *n.* **1.** *Abbr.* **al., alc.** A colorless volatile flammable liquid, C₂H₅OH, synthesized or obtained by fermentation of sugars and starches, and widely used, either pure or denatured, as a solvent, in drugs, cleaning solutions, explosives, and intoxicating beverages. Also called "ethanol," "ethyl alcohol," "grain alcohol." **2.** Intoxicating liquor containing alcohol. **3.** Any of a series of hydroxyl compounds, the simplest of which are derived from saturated hydrocarbons, have the general formula CₙH₂ₙ₊₁OH, and include ethanol and methanol. [New Latin *alcohol (vini)*, spirit (of wine), from Medieval Latin *alcohol*, fine powder of antimony used to tint the eyelids, any powder obtained by sublimation, quintessence, from Arabic *al-kohl, al-kuhl*, : *al*, the + *kohl, kuhl*, KOHL.]

al·co·hol·ic (ăl′kə-hôl′ĭk, -hŏl′ĭk) *adj. Abbr.* **al., alc. 1.** Of, pertaining to, or resulting from alcohol. **2.** Containing or preserved in alcohol. **3.** Suffering from alcoholism. —*n.* A person who drinks alcoholic liquors habitually and to excess, or who suffers from alcoholism.

al·co·hol·ic·i·ty (ăl′kə-hôl-ĭs′ə-tē) *n.* Alcoholic content.

al·co·hol·ism (ăl′kə-hôl-ĭz′əm) *n.* **1.** A chronic pathological condition, chiefly of the nervous and gastroenteric systems, caused by habitual excessive alcoholic consumption. **2.** Temporary mental disturbance, muscular incoordination, and paresis caused by excessive alcoholic consumption.

al·co·hol·ize (ăl′kə-hôl-īz′) *tr.v.* **-ized, -izing, -izes.** To saturate, mix, or treat with alcohol. —**al′co·hol′i·za′tion** *n.*

al·co·hol·om·e·ter (ăl′kə-hôl′ŏm′ə-tər) *n.* A hydrometer for determining the percentage of alcohol in liquids.

Al·co·ran (ăl′kô-răn′, -rän′) *n.* Also **Al·ko·ran.** The sacred book of the Moslems, the Koran (*see*).

Al·cott (ôl′kət, -kŏt′), **(Amos) Bronson.** 1799-1888. American educator and transcendentalist philosopher; father of L.M. Alcott.

Al·cott (ôl′kət, -kŏt′), **Louisa May.** 1832-1888. American author of popular novels for young people.

al·cove (ăl′kōv′) *n.* **1.** A recess or partly enclosed extension connected to or forming part of a room. **2.** A secluded bower or similar enclosed structure in a garden. [French *alcôve*, from Spanish *alcoba*, from Arabic *al-qubbah*, "the vault."]

Al·cuin (ăl′kwĭn). Also **Al·bi·nus** (ăl-bī′nəs). A.D. 735-804. English scholar and theologian; adviser of Charlemagne.

Al·cy·o·ne¹ (ăl-sī′ə-nē). *Greek Mythology.* Also **Hal·cy·o·ne** (hăl-sī′ə-nē) (for sense 1). **1.** The daughter of Aeolus who, in grief over the death of her husband Ceyx, threw herself into the sea and was changed into a kingfisher. **2.** A nymph, one of the Pleiades.

Al·cy·o·ne² (ăl-sī′ə-nē) *n. Astronomy.* The brightest star in the Pleiades, in the constellation Taurus.

Ald. alderman.

Al·dan (äl-dän′). A river of the Soviet Union, rising in southern

Yakutsk and flowing northward about 1,500 miles to the Lena.

Al·deb·a·ran (ăl-dĕb′ə-rən) *n.* A double star in the constellation Taurus, one of the brightest stars in the sky, 68 light-years from Earth. [Middle English, from Medieval Latin *Aldebaran,* from Arabic *al-dabarān,* "the follower (of the Pleiades)" : *al,* the + *dabarān,* following, from *dabar,* to follow.]

al·de·hyde (ăl′də-hīd′) *n.* **1.** Any of a class of highly reactive organic chemical compounds obtained by oxidation of primary alcohols, characterized by the common group CHO, and used in the manufacture of resins, dyes, and organic acids. **2.** Such a compound, **acetaldehyde** *(see).* [German *Aldehyd,* from New Latin, abbreviation of *al(cohol) dehyd(rogenatum),* "dehydrogenized alcohol."]

Al·den (ôl′dən), **John.** 1599?–1687. American Puritan colonist and political figure in New England; married Priscilla Mullens.

al·der (ôl′dər) *n.* **1.** Any of various deciduous shrubs or trees of the genus *Alnus,* growing in cool, moist places, and having reddish wood used in cabinet work. **2.** Any of several similar shrubs or trees. [Middle English *alder,* Old English *aler, alor.* See **el-**[2] in Appendix.*]

al·der·man (ôl′dər-mən) *n., pl.* **-men** (-mĭn). **1.** *Abbr.* **Ald., Aldm.** In many town and city governments, a member of the municipal legislative body. **2.** *Abbr.* **Ald., Aldm.** In England and Ireland, a member of the higher branch of the municipal or borough council. **3.** In Anglo-Saxon England: **a.** A lord or prince. **b.** The chief officer of a shire. [Middle English *alderman,* guild official, Old English *(e)aldormann,* viceroy : *(e)aldor,* chief, "elder," from *(e)ald,* old (see **al-**[3] in Appendix*) + MAN.] —**al′der·man·cy** (-sē) *n.* —**al′der·man′ic** (-măn′ĭk) *adj.*

Al·der·ney[1] (ôl′dər-nē). One of the Channel Islands, three square miles in area, in the English Channel, 28 miles west of Cherbourg, France. Population, 1,000.

Al·der·ney[2] (ôl′dər-nē) *n., pl.* **-neys.** One of a breed of small dairy cattle originally raised in the Channel Islands.

Al·der·shot (ôl′dər-shŏt). A town in Hampshire, England, 35 miles southwest of London; site of a large military training camp. Population, 31,000.

Al·dine (ôl′dīn′, -dēn′) *adj.* Of, pertaining to, or published by the press of Aldus **Manutius** *(see)* and his family. —*n.* A book printed by the Aldine press.

Aldm. alderman.

al·dol (ăl′dôl′, -dŏl′) *n.* A thick colorless to pale-yellow liquid, $C_4H_8O_2$, obtained from acetaldehyde and used to make perfumes and in ore flotation. [ALD(EHYDE) + -OL.]

al·dose (ăl′dōs′, -dōz′) *n. Chemistry.* Any of a class of monosaccharide sugars containing an aldehyde group. Also called "aldose sugar." [ALD(EHYDE) + -OSE.]

Al·dus Ma·nu·ti·us. See **Manutius.**

ale (āl) *n.* A fermented alcoholic beverage containing malt and hops, similar to but heavier than beer. [Middle English *ale,* Old English *alu, ealu.* See **alu-** in Appendix.*]

a·le·a·to·ry (ā′lē-ə-tôr′ē, -tōr′ē) *adj.* **1.** Dependent upon chance, luck, or an uncertain outcome. **2.** Of or pertaining to gambling. **3.** *Music.* Using or consisting of sound sequences played at random or arrived at by chance, as by throwing dice. [Latin *āleātōrius,* from *āleātor,* gambler, from *ālea*†, dice.]

A·lec·to (ə-lĕk′tō). *Greek Mythology.* One of the **Furies** *(see).*

a·lee (ə-lē′) *adv. Nautical.* At, on, or to the leeward side.

al·e·gar (ăl′ə-gər, ā′lə-) *n.* Vinegar produced by the fermentation of ale. [Middle English : ALE + (VINE)GAR.]

ale·house (āl′hous′) *n.* A place where ale is sold and drunk.

A·lei·chem, Sholem. See **Sholem Aleichem.**

A·lek·san·drovsk. The former name for **Zaporozhe.**

Al·ek·san·drovsk-Gru·shevsk·i. The former name for **Shakhty** *(see),* a city of the Soviet Union.

Al·e·man·ni (ăl′ə-măn′ī′) *pl.n.* A group of Germanic tribes that settled in Alsace and nearby areas during the fourth century A.D. and were defeated by the Franks in 496. [Latin, from Germanic *Alamanniz* (unattested). See **man-**[1] in Appendix.*]

Al·e·man·nic (ăl′ə-măn′ĭk) *n.* Also **Al·a·man·nic.** The High German dialect of the Alemanni, forms of which are now spoken in Alsace and parts of southern Germany and Switzerland. —*adj.* Also **Al·e·man·ni·an, Al·a·man·ni·an** (ăl′ə-măn′ē-ən). Of or pertaining to the Alemanni or their language.

A·lem·bert (dà-läN-bâr′), **Jean Le Rond d′.** 1717–1783. French philosopher, mathematician, and physicist.

a·lem·bic (ə-lĕm′bĭk) *n.* **1.** An apparatus formerly used for distilling. **2.** Something that purifies, alters, or transforms by a process comparable to distillation. [Middle English, from Old French *alambic,* from Medieval Latin *alambicum,* from Arabic *al-anbīq* : *al,* the + *anbīq,* still, from Greek *ambix*†, cup.]

a·leph (ä′lĭf) *n.* Also **a·lef.** The first letter of the Hebrew alphabet. See **alphabet.** [Hebrew *āleph,* "ox."]

a·leph-null (ä′lĭf-nŭl′) *n.* Also **a·leph-ze·ro** (-zîr′ō). *Mathematics.* The first **transfinite number** *(see).* [ALEPH (symbol for transfinite number) + NULL (smallest possible entity).]

A·lep·po (ə-lĕp′ō). A city and industrial center in northwestern Syria. Population, 496,000.

a·lert (ə-lûrt′) *adj.* **1.** Vigilantly attentive; watchful: *alert to danger.* **2.** Mentally responsive and perceptive; quick. **3.** Brisk; lively. —See Synonyms at **aware.** —*n.* **1.** A warning signal of attack or danger; especially, a siren warning of an air raid. **2.** The period of time during which such a warning is in effect. —**on the alert.** Watchful and prepared for danger or emergency. —*tr.v.* **alerted, alerting, alerts.** To notify of approaching danger or action; warn. [French *alerte,* from Italian *all′erta,* "on the watch" : *alla,* at the, from Latin *ad illam,* from *ille,* that (see **al-**[1] in Appendix*) + *erta,* watch, from *(torre)erta,* watchtower, "high (tower)," from Latin *ērectus,* raised, ERECT.]

a·leu·rone (ə-lo͝or′ōn′, ăl′yə-rōn′) *n.* Also **a·leu·ron.** Protein consisting of minute granules, forming the outermost layer of the endosperm in cereal grains. [German *Aleuron,* from Greek *aleuron,* flour. See **al-**[4] in Appendix.*] —**al′eu·ron′ic** (ăl′yə-rŏn′ĭk) *adj.*

Al·e·ut (ăl′ē-o͞ot′) *n., pl.* **Aleut** or **Aleuts.** Also **A·leu·tian** (ə-lo͞o′shən) (for sense 1). **1.** An Eskimo native of the Aleutian Islands. **2.** A subfamily of the Eskimo-Aleut family of languages, spoken in the Aleutian Islands. [Russian *aleút,* probably from Chukchi *aliuit,* "beyond the shore."]

A·leu·tian (ə-lo͞o′shən) *adj.* Of or pertaining to the Aleuts, their language, or their culture. —*n.* **1.** Variant of **Aleut.** **2.** *Plural.* See **Aleutian Islands.**

Aleutian Islands. A chain of volcanic islands, extending into the North Pacific for about 1,100 miles in a westward arc from Alaska, of which they are a part. Also called "Aleutians."

Aleutian Range. A volcanic mountain range extending about 600 miles along the Alaska Peninsula and into the Aleutian Islands; site of Katmai National Monument.

ale·wife[1] (āl′wīf′) *n., pl.* **-wives** (-wīvz′). A fish, *Alosa pseudoharengus,* closely related to the herrings, of North American Atlantic waters and some inland lakes. Sometimes called "oldwife." [Alteration (by association with ALEWIFE, alehouse keeper, "pot-bellied woman") of earlier *allowes* (plural), probably from French *alose,* from Gaulish Latin *alōsa*†.]

ale·wife[2] (āl′wīf′) *n., pl.* **-wives** (-wīvz′). A woman who keeps an alehouse.

Al·ex·an·der (ăl′ĭg-zăn′dər, -zän′dər). A masculine given name. [Middle English *Alysaundre,* from Old French, from Latin *Alexander,* from Greek *Alexandros,* "defender of men" : *alexein,* to defend, ward off (see **alek-** in Appendix*) + *anēr* (stem *andr-*), man (see **ner-**[2] in Appendix*).]

al·ex·an·der (ăl′ĭg-zăn′dər, -zän′dər) *n.* Also **Al·ex·an·der.** A cocktail made with crème de cacao, sweet cream, and brandy or gin. [From the name ALEXANDER.]

Al·ex·an·der I (ăl′ĭg-zăn′dər, -zän′dər). 1777–1825. Czar of Russia (1801–25).

Al·ex·an·der II (ăl′ĭg-zăn′dər, -zän′dər). 1818–1881. Czar of Russia (1855–81); emancipated serfs (1861).

Al·ex·an·der III[1] (ăl′ĭg-zăn′dər, -zän′dər). Original name, Orlando Bandinelli. Died 1181. Pope (1159–81); excommunicated Frederick I (Barbarossa).

Al·ex·an·der III[2] (ăl′ĭg-zăn′dər, -zän′dər). 1845–1894. Czar of Russia (1881–94).

Al·ex·an·der VI (ăl′ĭg-zăn′dər, -zän′dər). Original name, Rodrigo Borgia. 1431?–1503. Pope (1492–1503); patron of the arts; father of Cesare and Lucrezia Borgia.

Al·ex·an·der Archipelago (ăl′ĭg-zăn′dər, -zän′dər). A group of over 1,000 islands lying off the southeastern coast of Alaska, of which they are a part.

Al·ex·an·der I Island (ăl′ĭg-zăn′dər, -zän′dər). An island of Antarctica, about 235 miles long, in the Bellingshausen Sea off the west coast of the Antarctic Peninsula.

Al·ex·an·der Nev·ski (ăl′ĭg-zăn′dər, -zän′dər, nĕv′skē, nĕf′-). 1220?–1263. Russian saint; grand duke of Novgorod and Kiev.

Al·ex·an·ders (ăl′ĭg-zăn′dərz, -zän′dərz) *pl.n.* Any of several plants of the genus *Zizia* or related genera; especially, **golden Alexanders** *(see).* [Middle English *alysaunder,* Old English *alexandre,* from Latin *alexandrinum,* after Alexander the Great, from its brilliant color suggesting royalty.]

Al·ex·an·der the Great (ăl′ĭg-zăn′dər, -zän′dər). 356–323 B.C. King of Macedonia (336–323 B.C.); conqueror of Greece, the Persian Empire, and Egypt.

Al·ex·an·dret·ta. The former name for **İskenderun.**

Al·ex·an·dri·a (ăl′ĭg-zăn′drē-ə, -zän′drē-ə). **1.** *Arabic* **Al·Is·kan·da·ri·yah** (ăl-ĭs-kăn-dä-rē′yə, -yä). A city of Egypt, on the Mediterranean coast, west of the Nile delta, founded in 332 B.C. by Alexander the Great. Population, 1,513,000. **2.** A city of Virginia, on the Potomac, south of Washington, D.C.; the site of General George Washington's headquarters (established 1754). Population, 91,000.

Al·ex·an·dri·an (ăl′ĭg-zăn′drē-ən, -zän′drē-ən) *adj.* **1.** Of or pertaining to Alexander the Great. **2.** Of or pertaining to Alexandria, Egypt. **3.** Of, characteristic of, or designating a learned school of Hellenistic literature, science, and philosophy located at Alexandria in the last three centuries B.C. **4.** Marked by or concerned with the careful study, explication, or imitation of earlier forms and masterpieces. Said of writers and literary works. **5.** Of or designating a school of early Christian philosophy and theology located at Alexandria. —*n.* **1.** A native or inhabitant of Alexandria, Egypt, especially of Hellenistic times. **2.** A scholar or theologian of the Alexandrian school.

al·ex·an·drine (ăl′ĭg-zăn′drĭn, -zän′drĭn) *n.* Also **Al·ex·an·drine.** *Prosody.* **1.** The commonest French verse, consisting of a line of twelve syllables with a caesura usually falling after the sixth syllable. **2.** A line of English verse composed in iambic hexameter, usually with a caesura after the third foot, such as Pope's example: *"That like a wounded snake drags its slow length along."* —*adj.* Also **Al·ex·an·drine.** Of, pertaining to, or composed in alexandrines. [French *alexandrin,* from Old French, from *Alexandre,* title of a romance about Alexander the Great, written in this meter.]

al·ex·an·drite (ăl′ĭg-zăn′drīt′, -zän′drīt′) *n.* A greenish chrysoberyl that appears red in artificial light, used as a gemstone. [German *Alexandrit,* after ALEXANDER I.]

a·lex·i·a (ə-lĕk′sē-ə) *n.* A disorder in which cerebral lesions cause loss of the ability to read. Also called "word blindness." [New Latin : A- (without) + Greek *lexis,* speech, from *legein,* to speak (see **leg-**[1] in Appendix*).]

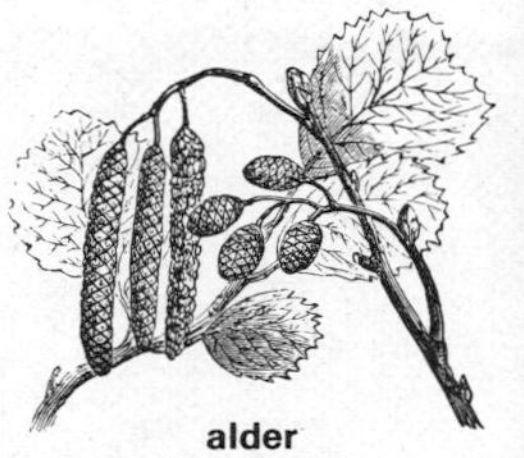

alder
Alnus glutinosa
Black alder

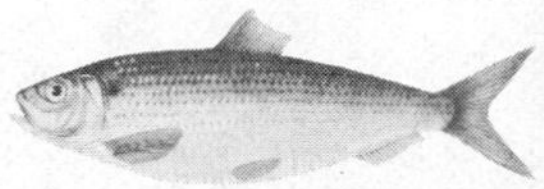

alewife[1]

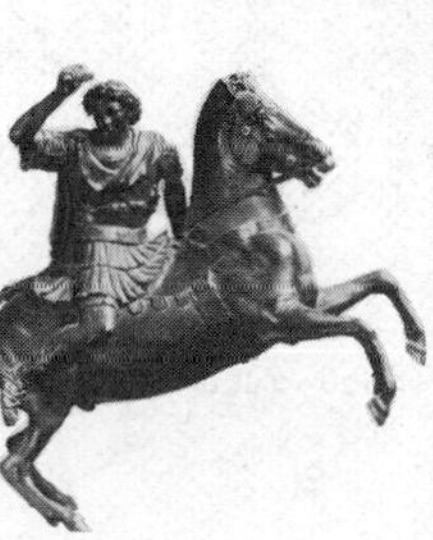

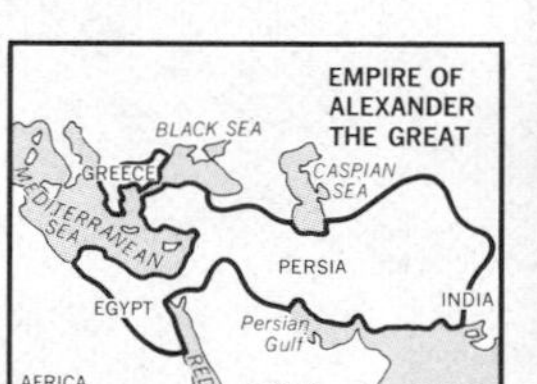

Alexander the Great
Above: Roman bronze statue
Below: Extent of conquests

a·lex·in (ə-lĕk′sĭn) *n.* Also **a·lex·ine** (ə-lĕk′sēn). A blood component, **complement** *(see).* [German *Alexin,* "protection (from bacteria)," from Greek *alexein,* to protect, ward off. See **alek-** in Appendix.*]

a·lex·i·phar·mic (ə-lĕk′sĭ-fär′mĭk) *adj.* Preventing or resisting effects of poison or infection; antidotal; prophylactic. —*n.* An antidote. [Earlier *alexipharmac,* from Greek *alexipharmakos* : *alexein,* to ward off (see **alexin**) + *pharmakon,* poison (see **pharmaco-**).]

A·lex·is (ə-lĕk′sĭs). A masculine given name. [Greek, "defender," from *alexein,* to protect. See **alek-** in Appendix.*]

A·lex·is I Mi·khai·lo·vich (ə-lĕk′sĭs mĭ-KHī′lə-vĭch). 1629–1676. Czar of Russia (1645–76); reformer of laws and religion; father of Peter the Great.

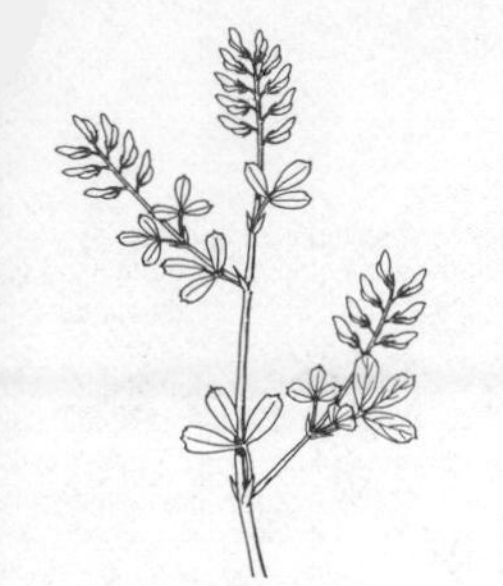

alfalfa

Al·fa code (ăl′fə). *Military.* A code consisting of authorized words standing for each letter of the alphabet. Used to transmit messages without misunderstanding. Typical words are: Alfa, Bravo, Charlie, and Delta.

al·fal·fa (ăl-făl′fə) *n.* A plant, *Medicago sativa,* native to Eurasia, having compound leaves with three leaflets, and clusters of small purple flowers. It is widely cultivated for forage and is used as a commercial source of chlorophyll. Also called "lucerne." [Spanish, from Arabic *al-fasfaṣah.*]

Al·fie·ri (äl-fyâ′rē), Count **Vittorio.** 1749–1803. Italian poet, dramatist, and nationalist leader.

al·fil·a·ri·a, al·fil·e·ri·a (ăl-fĭl′ə-rē′ə) *n.* A plant, *Erodium cicutarium,* native to Europe but widely naturalized in North America, having finely divided leaves and small pink or purplish flowers. Also called "filaree," "pin clover." [American Spanish *alfilerillo,* from Spanish, diminutive of *alfiler,* a pin, from Arabic *al-khilāl,* a brooch.]

Al·fon·so I (ăl-fŏn′sō, -zō). Portuguese name, Afonso Henriques. 1112–1185. First King of Portugal (1139–85).

Al·fon·so XIII (ăl-fŏn′sō, -zō). 1886–1941. Last king of Spain (1886–1931); forced to abdicate; lived in exile.

Al·fred¹ (ăl′frĭd). A masculine given name. [Middle English *Alvredus,* Old English *Ælfrǣd,* "elf counsel" : *ælf,* elf (see **albho-** in Appendix*) + *rǣd,* advice, counsel (see **ar-** in Appendix*).]

Al·fred² (ăl′frĭd). Called "the Great." A.D. 849–899. King of the West Saxons (A.D. 871–899).

al·fres·co (ăl-frĕs′kō) *adv.* Also **al fresco.** In the fresh air; outdoors: *lunch alfresco.* —*adj.* Taking place outdoors; outdoor: *an alfresco party.* [Italian, "in the fresh (air)" : *a il,* in the + *fresco,* fresh, FRESCO.]

Alg. Algeria.

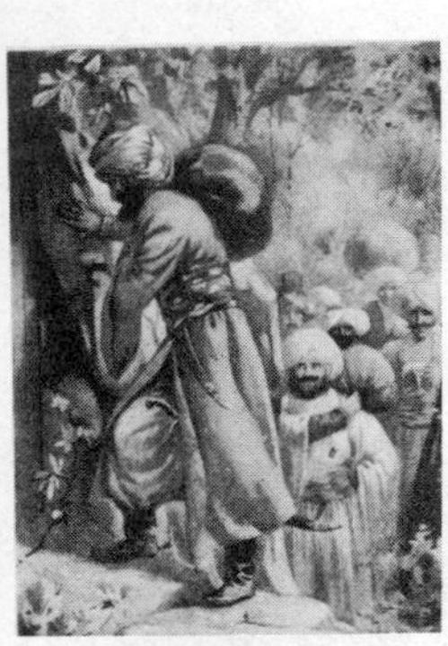

Ali Baba
Shown at the cave entrance

al·gae (ăl′jē) *pl.n. Singular* **-ga** (-gə). Any of various primitive, chiefly aquatic, one-celled or multicellular plants that lack true stems, roots, and leaves but usually contain cholorophyll. Included among the algae are kelps and other seaweeds, and the diatoms. [Latin *algae,* plural of *alga*†, seaweed.] —**al′gal** (ăl′gəl) *adj.*

al·gar·ro·ba, al·ga·ro·ba (ăl′gə-rō′bə) *n.* **1.** A tree, the **mesquite** *(see).* **2.** A tree, the **carob** *(see).* **3.** The edible pod of either of these trees. [Spanish, from Arabic *al-kharrūbah* : *al,* the + *kharrūbah,* CAROB.]

al·ge·bra (ăl′jə-brə) *n.* **1.** A generalization of arithmetic in which symbols, usually letters of the alphabet, represent numbers or members of a specified set of numbers and are related by operations that hold for all numbers in the set. **2.** A set together with operations defined in the set that obey specified laws. Also called "algebraic system." [Medieval Latin, from Arabic *al-jebr, al-jabr,* "the (science of) reuniting" (referring to the solving of algebraic equations) : *al,* the + *jabr,* reunification, bone-setting.] —**al·ge·bra·ist** (ăl′jə-brā′ĭst) *n.*

al·ge·bra·ic (ăl′jə-brā′ĭk) *adj.* **1.** Of, pertaining to, or designating algebra. **2.** Designating an expression, equation, or function in which only numbers, letters, and arithmetic operations are contained or used. **3.** Indicating or restricted to a finite number of algebraic operations. —**al′ge·bra′i·cal·ly** *adv.*

algebraic number. **1.** Any positive or negative number. **2.** A number that is a root of a polynomial equation with rational coefficients.

algebraic operation. Addition, subtraction, multiplication, division, exponentiation, root extraction, or any finite combination of these operations.

algebraic sum. The sum of algebraic quantities produced by arithmetic addition, in which negative quantities are added by the subtraction of corresponding positive quantities.

Al·ge·ci·ras (ăl′jə-sĭr′əs). A Spanish seaport on the Strait of Gibraltar. Population, 66,000.

Al·ger (ăl′jər), **Horatio.** 1834–1899. American clergyman and author of inspirational adventure books for boys.

Al·ge·ri·a (ăl-jĭr′ē-ə). *French* **Al·gé·rie** (ȧl′zhā-rē′). *Abbr.* **Alg.** A republic occupying 847,552 square miles in northwestern Africa; became independent from France in 1962. Population, 10,454,000. Capital, Algiers. —**Al·ge′ri·an** *adj.* & *n.*

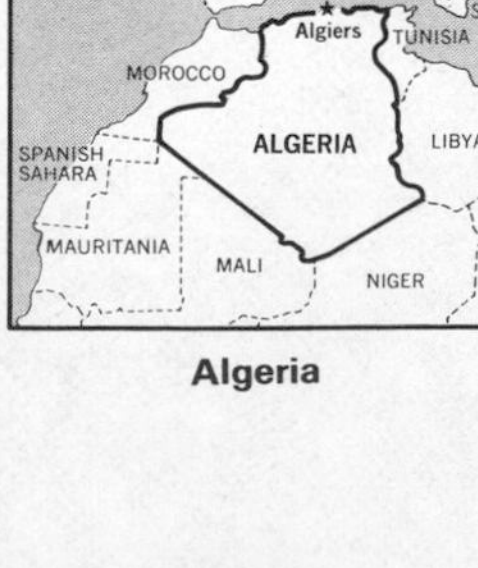

Algeria

-algia. Indicates pain or disease of; for example, **neuralgia.** [Greek, from *algos,* pain. See **algo-**.]

al·gid (ăl′jĭd) *adj.* Cold; chilly. [Latin *algidus,* from *algēre*†, to be cold.] —**al·gid′i·ty** *n.*

Al·giers (ăl-jĭrz′). *French* **Al·ger** (ȧl′zhā′). The capital of Algeria, on the Mediterranean. Population, 884,000.

al·gin (ăl′jĭn) *n.* A gelatinous substance obtained from certain algae, especially the giant kelp, and used as a thickener and emulsifier. [ALG(AE) + -IN.]

algo-. Indicates pain; for example, **algometer.** [Greek, from *algos*†, pain.]

al·goid (ăl′goid′) *adj.* Of or resembling algae.

Al·gol (ăl′gŏl′, -gôl′) *n.* A double, eclipsing, variable star in the constellation Perseus, almost as bright as Polaris. [Arabic *al ghūl,* "the ghoul" : *al,* the + *ghūl,* GHOUL.]

ALGOL (ăl′gŏl) An arithmetic language by which numerical procedures may be precisely presented to a computer in a standard form. [ALG(ORITHMIC) O(RIENTED) L(ANGUAGE).]

al·go·lag·ni·a (ăl′gō-lăg′nē-ə) *n.* Sexual gratification derived from inflicting or experiencing pain. See **masochism, sadism.** [New Latin : ALGO- + Greek *lagneia,* lust, from *lagnos,* lustful (see **slēg-** in Appendix*).]

al·gol·o·gy (ăl-gŏl′ə-jē) *n.* The study of algae. [ALG(AE) + -LOGY.] —**al′go·log′i·cal** (ăl′gə-lŏj′ĭ-kəl) *adj.* —**al·gol′o·gist** *n.*

al·gom·e·ter (ăl-gŏm′ə-tər) *n.* An apparatus for determining sensitivity to pain caused by pressure. [ALGO- + -METER.] —**al′go·met′ric** (ăl′gə-mĕt′rĭk), **al′go·met′ri·cal** (-mĕt′rĭ-kəl) *adj.* —**al·gom′e·try** *n.*

Al·gon·ki·an (ăl-gŏng′kē-ən) *n., pl.* **Algonkian** or **-ans.** **1.** *Geology.* Formerly, late **Proterozoic** *(see).* **2.** Variant of **Algonquian.** [After the rock formations in the Great Lake District, homeland of the Algonquin Indians.]

Al·gon·qui·an (ăl-gŏng′kwē-ən, -kē-ən) *n., pl.* **Algonquian** or **-ans.** Also **Al·gon·ki·an** (-kē-ən). **1.** A principal family of about 50 North American Indian languages spoken in an area from the Atlantic seaboard west to the Rocky Mountains, and from Labrador south to North Carolina and Tennessee, and used by such tribes as the Ojibwa, Delaware, Cree, Fox, Blackfoot, Chippewa, Shawnee, and Arapaho. **2.** A member of a tribe using a language of this family. —*adj.* Also **Al·gon·ki·an.** Of or constituting this language family. [From ALGONQUIN.]

Al·gon·quin (ăl-gŏng′kwĭn, -kĭn) *n., pl.* **Algonquin** or **-quins.** Also **Al·gon·kin** (-kĭn). **1.** Any of several Algonquian-speaking North American Indian tribes formerly inhabiting the region along the Ottawa River and near the northern tributaries of the St. Lawrence River. Now called "Ottawa." **2.** The Algonquian language of these tribes. **3.** Any Indian of these tribes. [Canadian French, from earlier *Algoumequins*† (plural).]

al·go·pho·bi·a (ăl′gō-fō′bē-ə) *n.* Abnormal fear of pain. [New Latin : ALGO- + -PHOBIA.]

al·go·rism (ăl′gə-rĭz′əm) *n. Mathematics.* The Arabic system of numeration; the decimal system. [Middle English *algorisme,* from Old French, from Medieval Latin *algorismus,* after Muhammad ibn-Musa AL-KHWARIZMI.]

al·go·rithm (ăl′gə-rĭth′əm) *n. Mathematics.* Any mechanical or recursive computational procedure. [Variant (influenced by ARITHMETIC) of ALGORISM.] —**al′go·rith′mic** *adj.*

Al·ham·bra (ăl-hăm′brə). A residential city in southwestern California, near Los Angeles, of which it is a suburb. Population, 55,000.

A·li, Muhammad. See Cassius Marcellus **Clay.**

a·li·as (ā′lē-əs, āl′yəs) *n., pl.* **aliases.** An assumed name. —*adv.* Otherwise named: *Johnson, alias Rogers.* [Latin *aliās,* otherwise, from *alius,* other. See **al-¹** in Appendix.*]

A·li Ba·ba (ä′lē bä′bə). In the *Arabian Nights,* a poor woodcutter who gains entrance to the treasure cave of the forty thieves by saying the magic words "Open, Sesame!"

al·i·bi (ăl′ə-bī′) *n., pl.* **-bis.** **1.** *Law.* A form of defense whereby a defendant attempts to prove that he was elsewhere when the crime in question was committed. **2.** *Informal.* An excuse. See Usage note below. —*intr.v.* **alibied, -biing, -bis.** *Informal.* To make an excuse or excuses for oneself. See Usage note below. [Latin *alibī,* elsewhere : *alius,* other (see **al-¹** in Appendix*) + *ubī,* where (see **kwo-** in Appendix*).]

Usage: *Alibi* (noun), in its nonlegal sense of *excuse* (that is, *any excuse*), is acceptable in writing to 41 per cent of the Usage Panel. As an intransitive verb *(they never alibi),* it is acceptable in writing to only 21 per cent of the Panel.

al·i·ble (ăl′ə-bəl) *adj.* Having nutrients; nourishing. [Latin *alibilis,* from *alere,* to nourish. See **al-³** in Appendix.*]

A·li·can·te (ä′lē-kän′tā). A city of Spain, a seaport in the southeast on the Mediterranean. Population, 133,000.

Al·ice (ăl′ĭs). A feminine given name. [Middle English *Alice,* from Old French *Aliz,* contraction of *Adaliz,* from Old High German *Adalhaid,* "nobility," ADELAIDE.]

alice blue. Pale blue. See **color.** [After *Alice* Roosevelt Longworth (born 1884), daughter of Theodore Roosevelt.]

al·i·cy·clic (ăl′ĭ-sī′klĭk, -sĭk′lĭk) *adj.* Of, pertaining to, or designating chemical compounds having both aliphatic and cyclic characteristics or structures. [ALI(PHATIC) + CYCLIC.]

al·i·dade (ăl′ə-dād′) *n.* Also **al·i·dad** (-dăd). **1.** An indicator or sighting apparatus on a plane table, used in angular measurement. **2.** A topographic surveying and mapping instrument with a telescope and graduated vertical circle. [French, from Medieval Latin *allidada,* from Arabic *al-'iḍāda,* "the revolving radius of a circle," from *'aḍud,* humerus.]

a·li·en (ā′lē-ən, āl′yən) *adj.* **1.** Owing political allegiance to another country or government; foreign: *a large alien population.* **2.** Belonging to, characteristic of, or derived from another country, place, society, or person; not one's own; unfamiliar; strange: *"the Negro was compelled to adjust to an utterly alien culture"* (Gordon K. Lewis). **3.** Being inconsistent or opposed; repugnant; adverse. Used with *to: Lying is alien to his nature.* —See Synonyms at **extrinsic.** —*n.* **1.** An unnaturalized foreign resident of a country. **2.** A member of another family, people, region, or the like. **3.** A person who is excluded from some group; an outsider. **4.** *Ecology.* A plant native to one region but naturalized in another. —*tr.v.* **aliened, -ening, -ens.** To transfer (property) to another. [Middle English, from Old French, from Latin *aliēnus,* from *alius,* other. See **al-¹** in Appendix.*]

al·ien·a·ble (āl′yən-ə-bəl, ā′lē-ən-) *adj. Law.* Capable of being transferred to the ownership of another. —**al′ien·a·bil′i·ty** *n.*

al·ien·age (āl′yən-ĭj, ā′lē-ən-) *n.* The state or condition of being alien or an alien.
al·ien·ate (āl′yən-āt′, ā′lē-ən-) *tr.v.* **-ated, -ating, -ates. 1.** To cause (someone previously friendly or affectionate) to become unfriendly or indifferent; estrange: *alienate a friend.* **2.** To remove or dissociate (oneself, for example): *"man cannot alienate himself from his own consciousness"* (Wylie Sypher). **3.** To cause to be transferred; turn away: *"he succeeded . . . in alienating the affections of my only ward"* (Oscar Wilde). **4.** *Law.* To transfer (property) to the ownership of another. —See Synonyms at **estrange.** [Latin *aliēnāre,* from *aliēnus,* ALIEN.] —**al′ien·a′tor** (-ā′tər) *n.*
al·ien·a·tion (āl′yən-ā′shən, ā′lē-ən-) *n.* **1.** The condition of being an outsider; a state of isolation: *"His alienation is far more acute than Holmes's . . . not an eccentric but rather an outcast."* (F.R. Shaw). **2.** *Psychology.* A state of estrangement between the self and the objective world, or between different parts of the personality. **3.** The act of alienating; estrangement; disaffection: *"In the decades after 1795 there was a profound alienation between classes in Britain."* (E.P. Thompson). **4.** *Law.* The act of transferring property, or title to it, to another. **5.** *Psychiatry. Obsolete.* Mental derangement.
al·ien·ee (āl′yən-ē′, ā′lē-ən-ē′) *n. Law.* A person to whom ownership of property is transferred.
al·ien·ism (āl′yən-ĭz′əm, ā′lē-ən-) *n.* **1.** The state or condition of being alien or an alien. **2.** *Obsolete.* Psychiatry.
al·ien·ist (āl′yən-ĭst, ā′lē-ən-) *n.* **1.** *Law.* A physician who has been accepted by a court as an expert on the mental competence of principals or witnesses appearing before it. **2.** *Obsolete.* A psychiatrist. [French *aliéniste,* from *aliéné,* insane, from Latin *aliēnātus,* "estranged," past participle of *aliēnāre,* to ALIENATE.]
al·ien·or (āl′yən-ôr′, ā′lē-ən-) *n. Law.* A person who transfers ownership of property to another.
a·lif (ä′lĭf) *n.* The first letter of the Arabic alphabet. [Arabic.]
a·li·form (ā′lə-fôrm′, ăl′ə-) *adj.* Shaped like a wing; alar. [Latin *āla,* wing (see **aks-** in Appendix*) + -FORM.]
Al·i·garh (ăl′ĭ-gûr′). A city in western Uttar Pradesh, Republic of India, 70 miles southeast of Delhi. Population, 185,000.
a·light[1] (ə-līt′) *intr.v.* **alighted** or **alit** (ə-lĭt′), **alighting, alights. 1.** To come down and settle, as after flight. Used with *on* or *upon: a bird alighting on a branch.* **2.** To dismount. Used with *from.* **3.** *Archaic.* To come upon by chance. Used with *on* or *upon: alight on an answer.* [Middle English *ali(g)hten,* Old English *ālīhtan* : *ā-* (intensive) + *līhtan,* to dismount, lighten, from *līht,* LIGHT (adjective).]
a·light[2] (ə-līt′) *adj.* Burning; lighted; lit up. [Middle English *alight,* Old English *ālīht,* past participle of *ālīhtan,* to light up : A- + *līhtan,* to light, from *līht,* LIGHT.] —**a·light′** *adv.*
a·lign (ə-līn′) *v.* **aligned, aligning, aligns.** Also **aline, alined, alining, alines.** —*tr.* **1.** To arrange in a line. **2.** To ally (oneself, for example) with one side of an argument, cause, or the like. —*intr.* To fall into line. [French *aligner,* from Old French : *a-,* from Latin *ad-,* to + *ligne,* LINE.] —**a·lign′er** *n.*
a·lign·ment (ə-līn′mənt) *n.* Also **a·line·ment. 1.** Arrangement or position in a straight line. **2.** A ground plan. **3.** The act of aligning or the condition of being aligned.
alignment chart. *Mathematics.* A **nomograph** *(see).*
a·like (ə-līk′) *adj.* Having close resemblance; similar. Usually used as a predicate adjective: *"All good books are alike"* (Hemingway). —*adv.* In the same way, manner, or to the same degree: *They dress and walk alike.* See Usage note at **both.** [Middle English *ilik,* Old English *gelīc* : *ge-* (collective prefix) + *līc,* form (see **līk-** in Appendix*).] —**a·like′ness** *n.*
al·i·ment (ăl′ə-mənt) *n.* **1.** Food; nourishment. **2.** Something that supports or sustains: *"Liberty is to faction what air is to fire, an aliment without which it instantly expires."* (James Madison). —*tr.v.* (ăl′ə-mĕnt′) **alimented, -menting, -ments.** To supply with food or other sustenance. [Middle English, from Latin *alimentum,* from *alere,* to nourish. See **al-**[3] in Appendix.*] —**al′i·men′tal** *adj.* —**al′i·men′tal·ly** *adv.*
al·i·men·ta·ry (ăl′ə-mĕn′trē, -tər-ē) *adj.* **1.** Of or pertaining to food or nutrition. **2.** Providing nourishment.
alimentary canal. The mucous-membrane-lined tube of the digestive system, extending from the mouth to the anus and including the pharynx, esophagus, stomach, and intestines.
al·i·men·ta·tion (ăl′ə-mĕn-tā′shən) *n.* **1.** The act or process of giving or receiving nourishment. **2.** Support; sustenance.
A·li Mo·ham·med of Shi·raz. See the **Bab.**
al·i·mo·ny (ăl′ə-mō′nē) *n., pl.* **-nies. 1.** *Law.* An allowance for support made under court order to a divorced person, usually the former wife, by the former spouse, out of the former spouse's income or estate. It is also granted without a divorce, as between legally separated persons, or those whose marriage has been annulled. **2.** Maintenance; sustenance; support. [Latin *alimōnia,* nutriment, support, from *alere,* to nourish. See **al-**[3] in Appendix.*]
al·i·phat·ic (ăl′ə-făt′ĭk) *adj.* Of, pertaining to, or designating organic chemical compounds in which the carbon atoms are linked in open chains rather than rings. [From Greek *aleiphar* (stem *aleiphat-*), oil, from *aleiphein,* to anoint. See **leip-** in Appendix.*]
al·i·quot (ăl′ə-kwŏt′, -kwət) *adj.* **1.** *Mathematics.* Of, pertaining to, or designating an exact divisor or factor of a quantity, especially of an integer. **2.** Contained exactly or an exact number of times. [French *(partie) aliquote,* aliquot (part), from Medieval Latin *(pars) aliquotae,* from Latin *aliquot,* some, several : *alius,* some, other (see **al-**[1] in Appendix*) + *quot,* how many (see **kwo-** in Appendix*).]
Al-Is·kan·da·ri·yah The Arabic name for **Alexandria.**
a·li·un·de (ā′lē-ŭn′dē, ăl′ē-) *adv. Law.* From a source extrinsic to the matter at hand; from elsewhere: *evidence aliunde.* [Latin, from elsewhere : *alius,* other (see **al-**[1] in Appendix*) + *unde,* whence (see **kwo-** in Appendix*).]
a·live (ə-līv′) *adj.* **1.** Having life; in a living state. **2.** In existence or operation; not extinct or inactive: *keep love alive.* **3.** In a state of animation; full of life; lively: *Her face was alive with laughter.* **4.** Now living. Used as an intensive: *the strongest man alive.* —See Synonyms at **aware, living.** —**alive to.** Aware of; sensitive to: *alive to the moods of others.* —**alive with.** Swarming with: *"This pool was alive with grilse"* (Douglas McCraith). [Middle English *alive, on live,* Old English *on līfe* : ON + *līfe,* dative of *līf,* LIFE.] —**a·live′ness** *n.*
a·liz·a·rin (ə-lĭz′ə-rĭn) *n.* Also **a·liz·a·rine** (-rĭn, -rēn′). An orange-red compound, $C_{14}H_8O_4$, used in dyes. [French *alizarine,* from *alizari,* madder, from Spanish, from Arabic *al-'aṣārah,* the juice pressed out : *al,* the + *'aṣara,* he pressed.]
al·ka·hest (ăl′kə-hĕst′) *n.* The hypothetical universal solvent once sought by alchemists. [Medieval Latin *alchahest,* said to have been coined as a pseudo-Arabic word by Paracelsus.]
al·ka·les·cent (ăl′kə-lĕs′ənt) *adj.* Becoming alkaline; slightly alkaline. [ALKAL(I) + -ESCENT.] —**al′ka·les′cence, al′ka·les′cen·cy** *n.*
al·ka·li (ăl′kə-lī′) *n., pl.* **-lis** or **-lies. 1.** *Chemistry.* A hydroxide or carbonate of an **alkali metal** *(see),* the aqueous solution of which is bitter, slippery, caustic, and characteristically basic in reactions. **2.** Any of various soluble mineral salts found in natural water and arid soils. **3.** An alkali metal. [Middle English *alcaly,* from Medieval Latin *alcali,* from Arabic *al-qalīy,* the ashes (of saltwort), from *qalay,* to fry.]
al·ka·li·fy (ăl′kə-lə-fī′, ăl-kăl′ə-fī′) *v.* **-fied, -fying, -fies.** —*tr.* To make alkaline; alkalize. —*intr.* To become alkaline.
alkali metal. Any of a group of soft, white, low-density, low-melting, highly reactive metallic elements, including lithium, sodium, potassium, rubidium, cesium, and francium.
al·ka·lim·e·ter (ăl′kə-lĭm′ə-tər) *n.* **1.** An apparatus for measuring alkalinity. **2.** An apparatus for measuring the amount of carbon dioxide evolved from a solid. —**al′ka·lim′e·try** *n.*
al·ka·line (ăl′kə-lĭn, -līn′) *adj.* **1.** Of, relating to, or containing an alkali. **2.** Having a pH greater than 7.
alkaline earth. 1. An oxide of an alkaline-earth metal. **2.** An alkaline-earth metal. —**al′ka·line-earth′** *adj.*
alkaline-earth metal. Any of a group of metallic elements, especially calcium, strontium, and barium, but generally including beryllium, magnesium, and radium.
al·ka·lin·i·ty (ăl′kə-lĭn′ə-tē) *n.* The alkali concentration or alkaline quality of an alkali-containing substance.
al·ka·lize (ăl′kə-līz′) *v.* **-lized, -lizing, -lizes.** Also **al·ka·lin·ize** (-lĭn-īz′). —*tr.* To make alkaline. —*intr.* To become an alkali. —**al′ka·li·za′tion** *n.*
al·ka·loid (ăl′kə-loid′) *n.* Any of various physiologically active nitrogen-containing organic bases derived from plants, including nicotine, quinine, cocaine, atropine, and morphine. [German : ALKAL(I) + -OID.] —**al′ka·loi′dal** (-loid′l) *adj.*
al·ka·lo·sis (ăl′kə-lō′sĭs) *n.* Pathologically high alkali content in the blood and tissues. [New Latin : ALKAL(I) + -OSIS.]
al·kane series (ăl′kān′). *Chemistry.* The **paraffin series** *(see).* [ALK(YL) + -ANE.]
al·ka·net (ăl′kə-nĕt′) *n.* **1. a.** A European plant, *Alkanna tinctoria,* the roots of which yield a red dye. **b.** The root of this plant, or a dye prepared from it. **2.** Any of several hairy plants of the genus *Anchusa,* native to the Old World, having clusters of blue flowers. Also called "bugloss." **3.** A plant, the **puccoon** *(see).* [Middle English, from Spanish *alcaneta,* diminutive of *alcana,* henna, from Medieval Latin *alchanna,* from Arabic *al-hinnā',* the HENNA.]
al·kene (ăl′kēn′) *n. Chemistry.* An open-chain hydrocarbon, **olefin** *(see).* [ALK(YL) + -ENE.]
al-Khwa·riz·mi (ăl′KHwä-rēz′mē), **Muhammad ibn-Musa.** Also **al-Khowa·riz·mi.** A.D. 780–850? Arab mathematician and author; regarded as the father of algebra.
Al·ko·ran. Variant of **Alcoran.**
Al Ku·wait. See **Kuwait.**
al·kyd resin (ăl′kĭd). *Chemistry.* A widely used durable synthetic resin derived from glycerol and phthalic anhydride. Also called "alkyd." [Blend of ALKYL and ACID.]
al·kyl (ăl′kĭl) *n. Chemistry.* A monovalent radical, such as ethyl or propyl, having the general formula C_nH_{2n+1}. [German : ALC(OHOL) + -YL.]
al·kyl·a·tion (ăl′kə-lā′shən) *n. Chemistry.* Any process in which an alkyl group is added to or substituted in a compound, as in the reaction of olefins with paraffin hydrocarbons to make high-octane fuels.
al·kyne (ăl′kīn′) *n.* Also **al·kine.** Any of a group of open-chain hydrocarbons with a triple bond and the general formula C_nH_{2n-2}. [ALKY(L) + -(I)NE.]
all (ôl) *adj.* **1.** The total entity or extent of: *all Christendom.* **2.** The entire or total number, amount, or quantity of: *all the saints.* **3.** The utmost possible of: *in all truth.* **4.** Every. Used only in phrases such as *all manner, all kinds.* **5.** Any whatsoever: *beyond all doubt.* **6.** Nothing but; only: *He was all skin and bones.* —*pron.* **1.** Each and every one: *All were drowned.* **2.** Each and every thing: *Ten ships sailed and all returned.* See Usage note below. —*n.* **1.** Everything one has: *He gave his all.* **2.** The whole number; totality. —**above all.** Most of all; before everything else. —**after all.** Nevertheless. —**all in all.** Everything being taken into account. —**at all. 1.** In any and every way: *He can't walk at all.* **2.** To any extent; whatever: *no money at all.* —**for all. 1.** To the extent that: *for all I care.* **2.** In spite

of; despite: *For all his knowledge he's a stupid man.* —**in all.** Including everyone or everything: *five desks in all.* —*adv.* **1.** Wholly; entirely; completely: *She is all wrong.* **2.** Each; apiece: *a score of five all.* **3.** Exclusively: *The cake is all for him.* —**all but.** Nearly; almost; on the brink of: *She all but fainted.* —**all in.** *Informal.* Tired; exhausted. —**all of.** Not less than: *It's all of ten miles.* —**all out.** With every effort possible: *He went all out with the new plan.* —**all over. 1.** Finished; completed. **2.** Everywhere: *Books are scattered all over.* **3.** *Informal.* Typically: *That's me all over.* —**all the better (more, worse,** and the like**).** So much the better (more, worse, and the like). [Middle English *al(le),* Old English *all, eall.* See **al-**[5] in Appendix.*]

Usage: *All* is invariably followed by *of* when *all* precedes a pronoun: *All of us rose.* The construction *all of* may also precede nouns: *All of the children came.* But especially in written usage, *of* is often omitted in such an example: *All the children came.* As a pronoun, *all* may take either a singular or plural verb. When the sense is that of *everything* or *the whole,* a singular verb is indicated: *All is not lost.* When *all* refers to a group of persons or things considered individually, in the sense of *each one* or *everyone,* a plural verb is used: *All are now recovered.* Adverbially, *all* is sometimes coupled with *that* in constructions implying comparison: *Is the problem all that difficult?* In writing, however, such an example is acceptable to only 39 per cent of the Usage Panel.

al·la bre·ve (ä′lə brĕv′ā). *Music.* In duple or quadruple meter with the half note being the unit of time. Also called "cut time." [Italian, "according to the breve."]

Al·lah (ăl′ə, ä′lə) *n.* The supreme being in the Moslem religion. [Arabic *Allāh* : *al,* the + *Ilāh,* god.]

Al·la·ha·bad (ăl′ə-hə-băd′, -bäd′). A city and pilgrimage center of the Republic of India, in southern Uttar Pradesh, on the Jumna near its junction with the Ganges. Population, 412,000.

al·la·man·da (ăl′ə-măn′də) *n.* Also **al·la·man·de.** Any of several woody vines of the genus *Allamanda,* native to tropical America, having showy, funnel-shaped yellow flowers. [After Jean N.S. *Allamand* (died 1787), Swiss scientist.]

all-A·mer·i·can (ôl′ə-mĕr′ĭ-kən) *adj.* **1.** Representing the whole of the United States; especially, chosen as the best in the United States. **2.** Composed of Americans or American materials exclusively. **3.** Entirely within the territorial limits of the United States. **4.** Of all the Americas.

All-A·mer·i·can (ôl′ə-mĕr′ĭ-kən) *n. Sports.* A member of a team of players voted best in the United States.

Al·lan. Variant of **Alan.**

al·lan·toid (ə-lăn′toid) *adj.* Also **al·lan·toi·dal** (ăl′ən-toid′l). **1.** Of or having an allantois. **2.** Shaped like a sausage. —*n.* The allantois. [French *allantoïde,* from Old French, from Greek *allantoeidēs (humēn),* "the sausage-shaped (membrane)" : *allantos*†, sausage + -OID.]

al·lan·to·is (ə-lăn′tō-ĭs) *n., pl.* **allantoides** (ăl′ən-tō′ə-dēz). A membranous sac that develops from the hindgut in the embryos of mammals, birds, and reptiles. In mammals it takes part in the formation of the umbilical cord and the placenta. [New Latin, from Greek *allantoeidēs,* ALLANTOID.] —**al′lan·to′ic** (ăl′ən-tō′ĭk) *adj.*

all-a·round. Variant of **all-round.**

al·lay (ə-lā′) *tr.v.* **-layed, -laying, -lays. 1.** To lessen or relieve (pain or grief, for example); reduce the intensity of. **2.** To calm or pacify; set to rest. —See Synonyms at **relieve.** [Middle English *alaien,* Old English *ālecgan* : *ā-,* perfective prefix + *lecgan,* to lay (see **legh-** in Appendix*).] —**al·lay′er** *n.*

all clear. 1. A signal, usually by siren, that an air raid is over. **2.** A term signifying the absence of immediate obstacles or impending danger.

al·le·ga·tion (ăl′ĭ-gā′shən) *n.* **1.** Something alleged. **2.** The act of alleging. **3.** A statement offered without proof, as an excuse or plea; mere assertion. **4.** *Law.* An assertion made by a party which must be proved or supported with evidence.

al·lege (ə-lĕj′) *tr.v.* **-leged, -leging, -leges. 1.** To assert to be true; affirm; declare. **2.** To assert without proof. **3.** To state (a plea or excuse, for example) in support or denial of a claim or accusation. **4.** *Archaic.* To cite or quote, as in confirmation. —See Synonyms at **assert.** [Middle English *alleg(g)en,* perhaps from Old French *alleguer,* from Latin *allēgāre,* to send on a mission, dispatch, cite : *ad-,* toward + *lēgāre,* to charge (see **leg-** in Appendix*).] —**al·lege′a·ble** *adj.* —**al·leg′er** *n.*

al·leged (ə-lĕjd′, ə-lĕj′ĭd) *adj.* Represented as existing or as being such as described but not so proved: *an alleged infringement of regulations.* —**al·leg′ed·ly** (ə-lĕj′ĭd-lē) *adv.*

Al·le·ghe·ny Mountains (ăl′ə-gā′nē). A section of the Appalachian mountain system in Virginia, West Virginia, Maryland, and central Pennsylvania, ranging from 2,000 to 4,800 feet in altitude. Also called the "Alleghenies."

Al·le·ghe·ny River (ăl′ə-gā′nē). A river rising in Pennsylvania and flowing 325 miles, first north into New York, then generally south through Pennsylvania to Pittsburgh, where it joins the Monongahela to form the Ohio.

Allegheny spurge. A low-growing, shrubby plant, *Pachysandra procumbens,* of the southeastern United States, having evergreen leaves and spikes of white or purplish flowers.

Allegheny vine. A plant, the **climbing fumitory** *(see).*

al·le·giance (ə-lē′jəns) *n.* **1.** Loyalty, or the obligation of loyalty, as to a nation, sovereign, or cause: *"the army recognized no real allegiance to the republican régime"* (Gordon A. Craig). **2.** The obligations of a vassal to his overlord. —See Synonyms at **fidelity.** [Middle English *allegeaunce,* from Old French *ligeance,* from *li(e)ge,* LIEGE.] —**al·le′giant** *adj.*

al·le·gor·ic (ăl′ə-gôr′ĭk, -gŏr′ĭk) *adj.* Also **al·le·gor·i·cal** (-ĭ-kəl). Pertaining to, characteristic of, or containing allegory. —**al′le·gor′i·cal·ly** *adv.*

al·le·go·rize (ăl′ə-gô-rīz′, -gə-rīz′) *v.* **-rized, -rizing, -rizes.** —*tr.* **1.** To express as, or in the form of, an allegory. **2.** To interpret allegorically. —*intr.* To use or make allegory. —**al′le·go′ri·za′tion** *n.* —**al′le·go·riz′er** *n.*

al·le·go·ry (ăl′ə-gôr′ē, -gōr′ē) *n., pl.* **-ries. 1.** A literary, dramatic, or pictorial representation the apparent or superficial sense of which both parallels and illustrates a deeper sense just as, for example, the story of the search for the actual Holy Grail may illustrate an inner spiritual search. **2.** An instance of such representation. **3.** Any symbolic representation. [Middle English *allegorie,* from Old French, from Latin *allēgoria,* from Greek, from *allēgorein,* to speak figuratively, "speak in other terms" : *allos,* other (see **al-**[1] in Appendix*) + *agoreuein,* to speak (in public), from *agora,* an assembly (see **ger-**[1] in Appendix*).] —**al′le·go′rist** *n.*

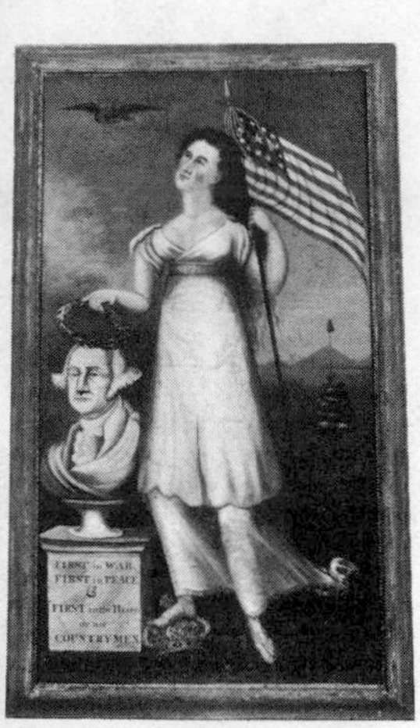

allegory
Early 19th-century painting, "George Washington and Liberty," by unknown artist

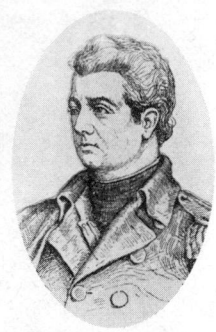

al·le·gret·to (ăl′ə-grĕt′ō, ä′lə-) *adv. Music.* In quick tempo; slower than allegro but faster than andante. Used as a direction. —*n., pl.* **allegrettos.** *Music.* A movement or passage in this tempo. [Italian, diminutive of ALLEGRO.] —**al′le·gret′to** *adj.*

al·le·gro (ə-lĕg′rō, ə-lā′grō) *adv. Music.* In rapid tempo; faster than allegretto but slower than presto. Used as a direction. —*n., pl.* **allegros.** *Music.* A movement or passage in this tempo. [Italian, "lively," from Latin *alacer.* See **al-**[2] in Appendix.*] —**al·le′gro** *adj.*

al·lele (ə-lēl′) *n.* Any of a group of possible mutational forms of a gene. [German *Allel,* short for ALLELOMORPH.] —**al·le′lic** (ə-lē′lĭk, ə-lĕl′ĭk) *adj.*

al·le·lo·morph (ə-lē′lə-môrf′, ə-lĕl′ə-) *n.* An allele. [Greek *allēlōn,* reciprocally, from *allos,* another (see **al-**[1] in Appendix*) + -MORPH.] —**al·le′lo·mor′phic** (ə-lē′lə-môr′-fĭk) *adj.* —**al·le′lo·mor′phism′** *n.*

al·le·lu·ia (ăl′ə-lōō′yə) *interj.* Used as a Christian expression of praise to God or of thanksgiving. [Middle English, from Medieval Latin *allēlūja,* from Late Greek *allēlouia,* from Hebrew *hallelūyāh,* HALLELUJAH.]

al·le·mande (ăl′ə-mănd′, ăl′ə-mănd′) *n.* **1. a.** A stately 16th-century dance in 2/2 time. **b.** A lively, late 18th-century dance in 3/4 time. **2.** *Music.* The first movement of a 17th- or 18th-century suite. [French, feminine of *allemand,* German, from Latin *Alemannus,* singular of ALEMANNI.]

Al·len. Variant of **Alan.**

Al·len (ăl′ən), **Ethan.** 1738–1789. American Revolutionary commander of the Green Mountain Boys of Vermont.

Ethan Allen

Al·len (ăl′ən), **William.** 1532–1594. English Roman Catholic cardinal; sponsor of the Douay Bible.

Al·len·by (ăl′ən-bē), **Edmund Henry Hynman.** First Viscount Allenby. 1861–1936. British commander of Egyptian Expeditionary Force; high commissioner for Egypt (1919–25).

Al·len·ti·ac (ăl′ĕn-tē′ăk) *n., pl.* **Allentiac** or **-acs. 1.** A tribe of South American Indians inhabiting west-central Argentina. **2.** A member of this tribe. **3.** The language of this tribe. —**Al′len·ti′ac** *adj.*

Al·len·town (ăl′ən-toun′). A city of Pennsylvania, in the east on the Lehigh River. Population, 108,000.

Al·lep·pey (ə-lĕp′ē). A seaport in Kerala on the Arabian Sea in the Republic of India. Population, 146,000.

al·ler·gen (ăl′ər-jən) *n.* A substance that causes an allergy. [German *Allergen* : *Allergie,* ALLER(GY) + -GEN.] —**al′ler·gen′ic** (-jĕn′ĭk) *adj.*

al·ler·gic (ə-lûr′jĭk) *adj.* **1.** Characteristic of or concerning allergy. **2.** Having an allergy. **3.** *Informal.* Having a dislike; averse. Used with *to: allergic to work.*

al·ler·gist (ăl′ər-jĭst) *n.* A physician specializing in allergies.

al·ler·gy (ăl′ər-jē) *n., pl.* **-gies. 1.** Hypersensitive or pathological reaction to environmental factors or substances, such as pollens, foods, dust, or microorganisms, in amounts that do not affect most people. **2. Anaphylaxis** *(see).* **3.** *Informal.* An adverse sentiment; dislike; antipathy. [German *Allergie,* "altered reaction" : ALL(O)- + Greek *ergon,* work, effect (see **werg-**[1] in Appendix*).]

al·le·vi·ate (ə-lē′vē-āt′) *tr.v.* **-ated, -ating, -ates.** To make more bearable; reduce (pain, grief, or suffering). See Synonyms at **relieve.** [Late Latin *alleviāre,* to lighten : Latin *ad-,* toward + *levis,* light (see **legwh-** in Appendix*).] —**al·le′vi·a′tor** (-ā′tər) *n.*

al·le·vi·a·tion (ə-lē′vē-ā′shən) *n.* **1.** The act of alleviating. **2.** The state of being alleviated. **3.** A thing that alleviates.

al·le·vi·a·tive (ə-lē′vē-ā′tĭv) *adj.* Also **al·le·vi·a·to·ry** (-ə-tôr′ē, -tōr′ē). Promoting alleviation. —*n.* A thing that relieves.

al·ley[1] (ăl′ē) *n., pl.* **-leys. 1.** A narrow street or passageway between or behind city buildings. **2.** A path between flowerbeds or trees in a garden or park. **3.** A **bowling alley** *(see).* **4.** *Tennis.* The parallel lanes on either side of the court reserved for use in doubles matches. —**up one's alley.** *Slang.* Compatible with one's interests or qualifications. [Middle English *aley,* from Old French *alee,* from the feminine past participle of *aler,* to go, from Latin *ambulāre,* to walk. See **al-**[2] in Appendix.*]

al·ley[2] (ăl′ē) *n., pl.* **-leys.** A large playing marble, often used as the shooter. [Short for ALABASTER.]

alley cat. 1. A homeless cat that roams the alleys and back streets of cities. **2.** *Slang.* A sexually promiscuous person.

al·ley·way (ăl′ē-wā′) *n.* A narrow passage between buildings.

all-fired (ôl′fīrd′) *adj. Slang.* Extreme; excessive. —*adv. Slang.* Extremely; excessively. [Euphemism for *hell-fired.*]

All Fools' Day. April 1, **April Fools' Day** *(see).*

all fours. 1. All four limbs of an animal or person: *A baby crawls on all fours.* **2.** A card game, **seven-up** *(see).*

all hail. *Archaic.* All health. Used as a greeting.

All·hal·low·mas (ôl′hăl′ō-məs) *n.* Also **All·hal·lows** (ôl′hăl′ōz). **All Saints' Day** *(see).*
all-heal (ôl′hēl′) *n.* Any of several plants reputed to have healing powers, as the **self-heal** *(see).*
al·li·a·ceous (ăl′ē-ā′shəs) *adj.* Characteristic of onions or garlic, especially in odor or taste. [Latin *allium,* garlic (see **allium**) + -ACEOUS.]
al·li·ance (ə-lī′əns) *n.* **1. a.** A formal pact of union or confederation between nations in a common cause. **b.** The nations so conjoined. **2.** Any union, relationship, or connection by kinship, marriage, common interest, or the like. **3.** Any affinity, congruence, or conjunction of quality or kind. **4.** The act of becoming or the state of being allied. [Middle English *alliaunce,* from Old French *aliance,* from *alier,* to ALLY.]
al·lied (ə-līd′, ăl′īd′) *adj.* **1.** Joined; united; confederated. **2.** Of a similar nature; related: *allied studies.* **3.** *Capital* **A.** Of or pertaining to the Allies.
Al·lier (à′lyā′). A river rising in south-central France and flowing 255 miles north to the Loire.
Al·lies (ăl′īz′, ə-līz′) *pl.n.* **1.** *World War I.* The nations allied against the Central Powers of Europe. They were Russia, France, Great Britain, and later many others, including the United States. **2.** *World War II.* The nations, primarily Great Britain, Russia, and the United States, allied against the Axis.
al·li·ga·tor (ăl′ə-gā′tər) *n.* **1.** Either of two large, amphibious reptiles, *Alligator mississipiensis,* of the southeastern United States, or *A. sinensis,* of China, having sharp teeth and powerful jaws, and differing from crocodiles in having a broader, shorter snout. **2.** Loosely, any crocodilian reptile. **3.** Leather made from the hide of an alligator. **4.** A tool having strong, adjustable jaws, often toothed. [Earlier *alagarto,* from Spanish *el lagarto* : *el,* the, from Latin *ille,* that (see **al-**[1] in Appendix*) + *lagarto,* lizard, from Latin *lacertus,* LIZARD.]
alligator pear. A tree, the **avocado** *(see),* or its fruit. [Folk etymology, variant of AVOCADO (the trees are said to grow in places infested by alligators).]
alligator snapping turtle. A large freshwater turtle, *Macroclemys temmincki,* of the south-central United States, having a rough carapace and a hooked beak. Also called "alligator snapper."
al·lit·er·ate (ə-lĭt′ə-rāt′) *v.* **-ated, -ating, -ates.** —*intr.* **1.** To use alliteration in speech or writing. **2.** To have or contain alliteration. —*tr.* To form or arrange with alliteration. —**al·lit′er·a′tor** (-ə-rā′tər) *n.*
al·lit·er·a·tion (ə-lĭt′ə-rā′shən) *n.* The occurrence in a phrase or line of speech or writing of two or more words having the same initial sound, for example, *wailing in the winter wind.* [From AD- (to) + Latin *littera,* LETTER.]
al·lit·er·a·tive (ə-lĭt′ə-rā′tĭv, -ər-ə-tĭv) *adj.* Of, manifesting, or characterized by alliteration. —**al·lit′er·a′tive·ly** *adv.* —**al·lit′er·a′tive·ness** *n.*
al·li·um (ăl′ē-əm) *n.* Any of various plants of the genus *Allium,* characterized by their pungent odor, and including the onion, leek, chive, garlic, and shallot. [New Latin *Allium,* from Latin *allium, ālium*†, garlic.]
allo–, all–. Indicates divergence, opposition, or difference; for example, **allopatric.** [Greek, other, altered, from *allos,* other. See **al-**[1] in Appendix.*]
al·lo·cate (ăl′ō-kāt′, ăl′ə-) *tr.v.* **-cated, -cating, -cates. 1.** To designate for a special purpose; set apart. **2.** To distribute according to plan; allot. **3.** To determine the location of; locate. —See Synonyms at **assign.** [Medieval Latin *allocāre,* to place to : Latin *ad-,* toward + *locāre,* to place, from *locus,* place, LOCUS.] —**al′lo·ca·ble** (ăl′ə-kə-bəl) *adj.* —**al′lo·ca′tion** *n.*
al·lo·cu·tion (ăl′ə-kyōō′shən) *n.* A formal and authoritative speech or address, especially one that advises or informs. [Latin *allocūtiō,* from *alloquī* (past participle *allocūtus*), to speak to : *ad-,* to + *loquī,* to speak (see **tolkw-** in Appendix*).]
al·lo·di·um (ə-lō′dē-əm) *n., pl.* **-dia** (-dē-ə). Also **a·lo·di·um.** Land held in absolute ownership, and without obligation or service to any feudal overlord. [Medieval Latin *allodium,* from Frankish *al-ōd-* (unattested). See **al-**[5] in Appendix.*] —**al·lo′di·al** *adj.* —**al·lo′di·al·ly** *adv.*
al·log·a·my (ə-lŏg′ə-mē) *n. Botany.* **Cross-fertilization** *(see).* [ALLO- + -GAMY.] —**al·log′a·mous** *adj.*
al·lo·graph (ăl′ə-grăf′, -gräf′) *n.* Writing, especially a signature, made by one person for another. [ALLO- + -GRAPH.]
al·lom·er·ism (ə-lŏm′ə-rĭz′əm) *n.* Consistency in crystalline form with variation in chemical composition. [ALLO- + Greek *meros,* part (see **smer-**[2] in Appendix*).] —**al·lom′er·ous** *adj.*
al·lom·e·try (ə-lŏm′ə-trē) *n. Biology.* The study of the change in proportion of various parts of an organism as a consequence of growth. [ALLO- + -METRY.] —**al′lo·met′ric** (ăl′ə-mĕt′rĭk) *adj.*
al·lo·morph[1] (ăl′ə-môrf′) *n. Mineralogy.* Obsolete synonym of **paramorph** *(see).* [ALLO- + -MORPH.] —**al′lo·mor′phic** (-môr′fĭk) *adj.* —**al′lo·mor′phism′** *n.*
al·lo·morph[2] (ăl′ə-môrf′) *n. Linguistics.* Any of the variant forms of a morpheme, for example, the phonetic *s* of *cats, z* of *dogs,* and *iz* of *horses* are allomorphs of the English morpheme *s.* [ALLO- + -MORPH.] —**al′lo·mor′phic** (-môr′fĭk) *adj.* —**al′lo·mor′phism′** *n.*
al·lo·nym (ăl′ə-nĭm′) *n.* **1.** The name of one person assumed by another, especially by a writer. **2.** A book by such a writer. [French *allonyme* : ALL(O)- + -ONYM.] —**al·lon′y·mous** (ə-lŏn′ə-məs) *adj.* —**al·lon′y·mous·ly** *adv.*
al·lo·path (ăl′ə-păth′). Also **al·lop·a·thist** (ə-lŏp′ə-thĭst) *n.* A person who practices or advocates allopathy.
al·lop·a·thy (ə-lŏp′ə-thē) *n.* Therapy with remedies that produce effects differing from those of the disease treated. Compare **homeopathy.** [German *Allopathie* : ALLO- + -PATHY.] —**al′lo·path′ic** (ăl′ə-păth′ĭk) *adj.* —**al′lo·path′i·cal·ly** *adv.*
al·lo·pat·ric (ăl′ə-păt′rĭk) *adj. Ecology.* Occurring in separate, widely differing geographic areas. Compare **sympatric.** [From ALLO- + Greek *patra,* fatherland, from *patēr,* father (see **peter** in Appendix*).] —**al′lo·pat′ri·cal·ly** *adv.*
al·lo·phane (ăl′ə-făn′) *n.* An amorphous, translucent, variously colored mineral, essentially hydrous aluminum silicate. [Greek *allophanēs,* "appearing otherwise" : ALLO- + -PHANE.]
al·lo·phone (ăl′ə-fōn′) *n. Linguistics.* Any of the variant forms of a phoneme; for example, the aspirated *p* of *pit* and the unaspirated *p* of *spit* are allophones of the English phoneme *p.* [ALLO- + -PHONE.] —**al′lo·phon′ic** (-fŏn′ĭk) *adj.*
all-or-none (ôl′ər-nŭn′) *adj.* Characterized by either complete response or total lack of response or effect, as in neurological action above a threshold.
al·lot (ə-lŏt′) *tr.v.* **-lotted, -lotting, -lots. 1.** To distribute by lot; apportion. **2.** To give or assign; allocate: *allot three weeks to a project.* —See Synonyms at **assign.** [Middle English *alotten,* from Old French *aloter* : *a-,* from Latin *ad-,* to + *lot,* a portion, lot, from Frankish *lot* (unattested) (see **klêu-** in Appendix*).] —**al·lot′ter** *n.*
al·lot·ment (ə-lŏt′mənt) *n.* **1.** The act of allotting. **2.** That which is allotted. **3.** *Military.* A portion of a serviceman's pay set aside for a member of his family or for insurance.
al·lo·trope (ăl′ə-trōp′) *n.* A structurally differentiated form of an allotropic element. [Back-formation from ALLOTROPY.]
al·lot·ro·py (ə-lŏt′rə-pē) *n.* The existence, especially in the solid state, of two or more crystalline or molecular structural forms of an element. [ALLO- + -TROPY.] —**al′lo·trop′ic** (ăl′ə-trŏp′ĭk), **al′lo·trop′i·cal** *adj.* —**al′lo·trop′i·cal·ly** *adv.*
all′ ot·ta·va (äl ō-tä′və). *Music. Symbol* **8va 1.** A direction placed above or below notes to be performed an octave higher or lower than written. Also called "all' ottava alta," "all' ottava sopra." **2.** A direction placed below notes to be performed an octave lower than written. In this sense, also called "all' ottava bassa," "all' ottava sotta." [Italian, "at the octave."]
al·lot·tee (ə-lŏt′ē′) *n.* One to whom something is allotted.
all-out (ôl′out′) *adj.* Complete; without reservation; out-and-out: *an all-out effort.*
all-o·ver (ôl′ō′vər) *adj.* Covering an entire surface.
al·low (ə-lou′) *tr.v.* **-lowed, -lowing, -lows. 1.** To let do or happen; permit. **2.** To acknowledge or admit; concede: *allow the legality of a claim.* **3.** To permit to have. **4.** To make provision for: *allow time for a coffee break.* **5.** To permit the presence of: *No pets allowed.* **6.** To provide (the needed amount): *allow funds in case of emergency.* **7.** To admit; grant: *I allow that to be true.* —**allow for.** To make an allowance or provision for: *allow for bad weather.* —**allow of.** To permit: *a treatise allowing of several interpretations.* [Middle English *allowen,* from Old French *al(l)ouer,* to permit, approve, a blend of: **(a)** Medieval Latin *allocāre,* to assign, ALLOCATE, and **(b)** Latin *allaudāre,* to give praise to : *ad-,* to + *laudāre,* to praise, LAUD.] —**al·low′a·ble** *adj.* —**al·low′a·bly** *adv.*
Synonyms: *allow, permit, let.* These verbs are compared as they mean to grant or to consent to something. *Allow* implies refraining from any hindrance, whereas *permit* suggests authoritative consent. Inherent in both is capacity to prevent an act. *Let* is less strong in implying authority; often it suggests weak consent or failure to prevent something because one is inattentive or not inclined to act.
al·low·ance (ə-lou′əns) *n.* **1.** The act of allowing. **2.** That which is allowed. **3.** A regular provision of money, food, or the like, as to a dependent. **4.** A price reduction granted as in exchange for used merchandise; discount. **5.** A consideration for possibilities or modifying circumstances: *an allowance for breakage.* —*tr.v.* **allowanced, -ancing, -ances. 1.** To restrict to an allowance. **2.** To put on an allowance.
al·low·ed·ly (ə-lou′ĭd-lē) *adv.* By general admission; admittedly.
al·loy (ăl′oi′, ə-loi′) *n.* **1.** *Metallurgy.* A macroscopically homogeneous mixture or solid solution, usually of two or more metals, the atoms of one replacing or occupying interstitial positions between atoms of the other. **2.** Anything added that lowers value or purity. —*tr.v.* (ə-loi′, ăl′oi′) **alloyed, -loying, -loys. 1.** *Metallurgy.* To combine (metals) to form an alloy. **2.** To lower purity or value of (a metal) by mixing with a cheaper metal. **3.** To debase by the addition of an inferior element. [Old French *aloi,* from *aloier, aleier,* to alloy, to bind, from Latin *alligāre,* to bind to, ALLY.]
all right. 1. Satisfactory; average. **2.** Correct. **3.** Uninjured. **4.** Very well; yes. **5.** Without a doubt: *He's a fool, all right!*
all-right (ôl′rīt′) *adj. Slang.* **1.** Dependable; honorable: *an all-right fellow.* **2.** Good; excellent: *an all-right movie.*
all-round (ôl′round′) *adj.* Also **all-a·round** (ôl′ə-round′). **1.** Comprehensive in extent or depth: *all-round vocational training.* **2.** Able to do many or all things well; generally excellent; versatile: *an all-round student.*
Usage: *All-round* is preferable to the variant form *all-around.* Both are hyphenated and applicable only as adjectives standing before nouns. They should not be confused with *all round* and *all around* used adverbially or prepositionally.
All Saints' Day. November 1, a church festival in honor of all saints. Also called "Allhallowmas," "Allhallows."
all·seed (ôl′sēd′) *n. Botany.* Any of several plants having many seeds, such as **knotgrass** *(see).*
All Souls' Day. November 2, observed by the Roman Catholic Church as a day of prayer for souls in purgatory.
all·spice (ôl′spīs′) *n.* **1.** A tropical American tree, *Pimenta officinalis,* having small white flowers and aromatic berries.

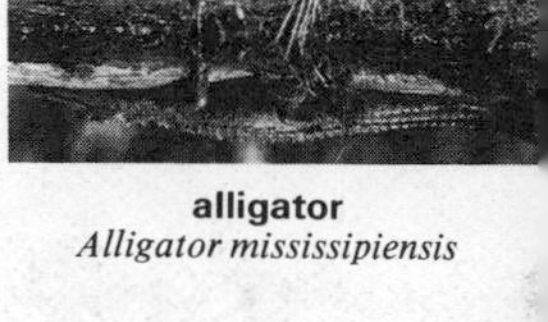

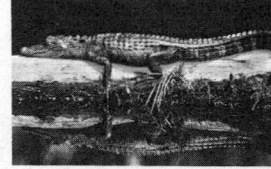

alligator
Alligator mississipiensis

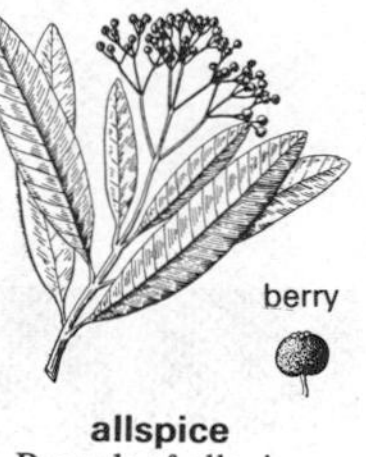

allspice
Branch of allspice
with leaves and berries

2 The dried berries of this tree, used whole or ground as a spice. Also called "pimento." [It seems to combine the flavors of several spices.]
all-star (ôl′stär′) *adj.* Made up wholly of star performers: *a play with an all-star cast.*
all-time (ôl′tīm′) *adj. Informal.* Of all time: *one of the all-time greats of baseball.*
all told. In all; altogether; with everything considered.
al·lude (ə-lo͞od′) *intr.v.* **-luded, -luding, -ludes.** To make an indirect reference to. See Usage note at **allusion.** [Latin *allūdere*, to play with, jest at : *ad-*, to + *lūdere*, to play, from *lūdus*, game (see **leid-** in Appendix*).]
al·lure (ə-lo͝or′) *v.* **-lured, -luring, -lures.** —*tr.* To entice with something desirable; tempt. —*intr.* **1.** To tempt or fascinate. **2.** To be tempting or fascinating. —*n.* The power to entice or tempt; fascination; strong attraction. [Middle English *aluren*, from Old French *aleurrer* : *a-*, from Latin *ad-*, to + *leurrer*, to lure, from *loirre, leurre*, LURE.] —**al·lure′ment** *n.* —**al·lur′er** *n.* —**al·lur′ing·ly** *adv.*
al·lu·sion (ə-lo͞o′zhən) *n.* **1.** The act of alluding; indirect mention. **2.** An indirect, but pointed or meaningful, reference. [Late Latin *allūsiō*, a playing with, from Latin *allūdere* (past participle *allūsus*), to play with, ALLUDE.]
Usage: Allusion and *allude* are often used where the more general terms *reference* and *refer* would be preferable. *Allusion* and *allude* apply to indirect reference that does not identify specifically. *Reference* and *refer*, unless qualified, usually imply direct, specific mention.
al·lu·sive (ə-lo͞o′sĭv) *adj.* Containing or making allusions; suggestive. —**al·lu′sive·ly** *adv.* —**al·lu′sive·ness** *n.*
al·lu·vi·al (ə-lo͞o′vē-əl) *adj.* Of, pertaining to, or composed of **alluvium** *(see).*
alluvial fan. A fan-shaped accumulation of alluvium deposited at the mouth of a ravine. Also called "alluvial cone."
alluvial plain. A plain resulting from the deposit of alluvium.
al·lu·vi·on (ə-lo͞o′vē-ən) *n.* **1. Alluvium** *(see).* **2.** The flow of water against a shore or bank. **3.** Inundation by water; flood. **4.** *Law.* The increasing of land, especially along a river bed, by deposited alluvium. Compare **avulsion.** [Latin *alluviō*, from *alluere*, to wash against : *ad-*, to + *lavere*, to wash (see **lou-** in Appendix*).]
al·lu·vi·um (ə-lo͞o′vē-əm) *n., pl.* **-viums** or **-via** (-vē-ə). Any sediment deposited by flowing water, as in a river bed, flood plain, or delta. Also called "alluvion." [Latin, from the neuter of *alluvius*, alluvial, from *alluere*, to wash against. See **alluvion.**]
al·ly (ə-lī′, ăl′ī′) *v.* **-lied, -lying, -lies.** —*tr.* **1.** To unite or connect in a formal relationship or bond, such as by treaty or other agreement. Used with *to* or *with: The United States allies itself with Great Britain.* **2.** To unite or connect in a personal relationship, such as friendship or marriage. —*intr.* To enter into an alliance. —*n.* (ăl′ī′, ə-lī′), *pl.* **allies.** **1.** One that is united with another in some formal or personal relationship. See **Allies.** **2.** A friend or close associate. —See Synonyms at **partner.** [Middle English *al(l)ien*, from Old French *alier*, from Latin *alligāre*, to bind to : *ad-*, to + *ligāre*, to bind (see **leig-**[1] in Appendix*).]
al·lyl (ăl′ĭl) *n.* The univalent organic radical CH_2:$CHCH_2$. [Latin *allium*, garlic (see **allium**) + -YL (so called because it was first obtained from garlic).] —**al·lyl′ic** *adj.*
allyl alcohol. A colorless, poisonous flammable liquid, CH_2-$CHCH_2OH$, used in poison gas, resins, plastics, and herbicides.
allyl resin. Any of a class of synthetic resins derived from allyl alcohol esters and dibasic acids, and used as laminating adhesives and in varnishes and molding compounds.
Al·ma (ăl′mə). A feminine given name. [Latin, from *almus*, nourishing. See **al-**[3] in Appendix.*]
Al·ma-A·ta (äl′mä-ä-tä′). Formerly **Ver·nyi** (vyěr′nĭ). The capital of the Kazakh S.S.R., in the southeastern part of the republic. Population, 623,000.
Al-Ma·di·na. The Arabic name for **Medina.**
Al·ma·gest (ăl′mə-jĕst′) *n.* **1.** An exhaustive chronicle on astronomy and geography compiled by Ptolemy about A.D. 150. **2.** *Sometimes small* **a.** In medieval science, any similar work concerned with astronomy or alchemy. [Middle English *almageste*, from Old French, from Arabic *al-majisti* : *al*, the + Greek *megistē (suntaxis)*, greatest (collection), feminine of *megistos*, superlative of *megas*, great (see **meg-** in Appendix*).]
Al·ma·gro (äl-mä′grō), **Diego de.** 1475?–1538. Spanish conquistador in Peru and Chile.
al·ma ma·ter, Al·ma Ma·ter (ăl′mə mä′tər, äl′mə). **1.** The school, college, or university that one has attended. **2.** The anthem or school song of an institution of higher learning. [Latin, "cherishing or fostering mother."]
al·ma·nac (ôl′mə-năk′, ăl′-) *n.* **1.** An annual publication including calendars with weather forecasts, astronomical information, tide tables, and other related tabular information. **2.** An annual publication composed of various lists, charts, and tables of useful information in many unrelated fields. [Middle English *almenak*, from Medieval Latin *almanachus*†.]
al·man·dine (ăl′mən-dēn′) *n.* Also **al·man·dite** (-dīt′). A deep violet-red garnet, essentially $FeAl_2Si_3O_{12}$, found in metamorphic rocks and used as a gemstone. [Variant of earlier *alabandine*, from Middle English *alabandina*, from Late Latin *(gemma) alabandīna*, "(gem) of *Alabanda*," town in Caria, ancient district of Asia Minor, famous for jewelry.]
Al·ma-Tad·e·ma (ăl′mə-tăd′ə-mə), Sir **Lawrence.** 1836–1912. Dutch-born English painter of classical scenes.
Al·mei·da (äl-mā′də), **Francisco de.** 1450?–1510. First viceroy of Portuguese India (1505–09).

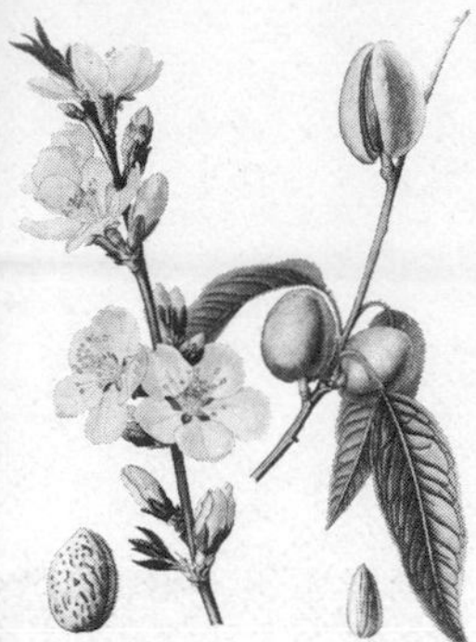
flowers
nuts
inner shell
nutmeat
almond

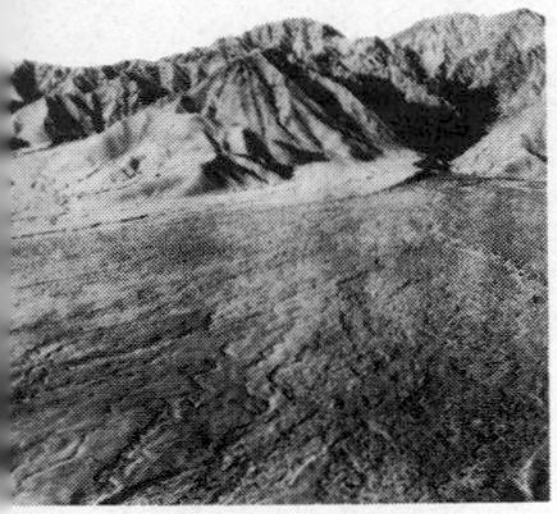
alluvial fan
River emerging from a canyon in mountains of northeastern Mongolia

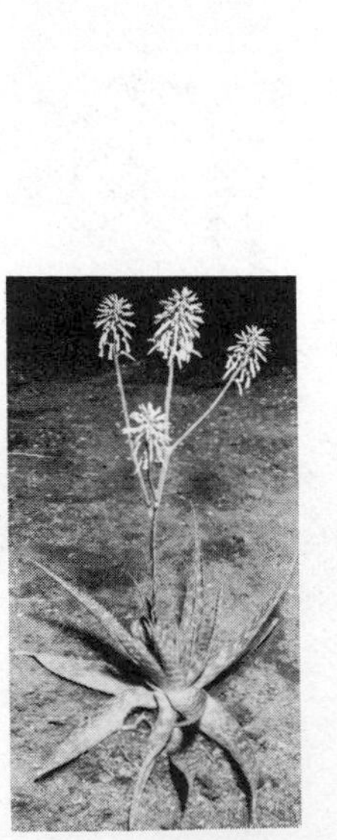
aloe
Aloe grandidentata

al·me·mar (ăl-mē′mär) *n. Judaism.* A **bema** *(see).* [Hebrew *almēmār*, from Arabic *al-minbar*, the pulpit.]
Al·me·rí·a (äl′mā-rē′ä). A seaport of Spain, in the southeast on the Mediterranean. Population, 87,000.
al·mighty (ôl-mī′tē) *adj.* **1.** All-powerful; omnipotent: *almighty God.* **2.** *Informal.* Great: *an almighty din.* —*adv. Slang.* Extremely: *almighty scared.* —**the Almighty.** God. [Middle English *almighty*, Old English *ealmihtig* : *eall*, ALL + *mihtig*, from *miht*, MIGHT.] —**al·might′i·ly** *adv.*
al·mond (ä′mənd, ăm′ənd) *n.* **1.** A small tree, *Prunus amygdalus*, native to the Mediterranean region, having pink flowers and fruit containing an edible nut. **2.** The nut itself, ellipsoid in shape, and having a soft, yellowish-tan shell. **3.** Something having the oval, pointed form of an almond. **4.** Pale tan. See **color.** [Middle English *almande*, from Old French, from Late Latin *amandula*, corruption of Latin *amygdala*, from Greek *amugdalē*†.] —**al′mond** *adj.*
al·mon·er (ăl′mən-ər, ä′mən-) *n.* **1.** One who distributes alms, as for a church or royal family. **2.** *British.* A social worker in a hospital. [Middle English *a(u)moner*, from Old French *aumosnier*, from *amosne*, alms, from Vulgar Latin *alemosina* (unattested), from Late Latin *eleēmosyna*, ALMS.]
al·mon·ry (ăl′mən-rē, ä′mən-) *n., pl.* **-ries.** The house of an almoner; a place at which alms are distributed.
Al·mo·ra·vides (ăl-môr′ə-vīdz′, ăl-mōr′ə-). A Berber dynasty that ruled over North Africa and much of Spain (1056–1145). [Arabic *al-murābitūn*, "the holy ones," from *murābit*, holy man, hermit.]
al·most (ôl′mōst′, ôl-mōst′) *adv.* Slightly short of; not quite; all but; very nearly. See Usage note at **most.** [Middle English *almost*, Old English *(e)almǣst*, completely, for the most part : *eall*, ALL + *mǣst*, MOST.]
alms (ämz) *pl.n.* Money or goods given to the poor in charity. [Middle English *almes, almesse*, Old English *ælmesse*, from Common Germanic *alemosina* (unattested), from Late Latin *eleēmosyna*, from Greek *eleēmosunē*, pity, from *eleēmōn*, pitiful, from *eleos*†, pity.]
alms·house (ämz′hous′) *n.* A poorhouse.
alms·man (ämz′mən) *n., pl.* **-men** (-mĭn). One dependent on alms for his support.
al·ni·co (ăl′nĭ-kō′) *n.* Any of several hard, strong alloys of aluminum, cobalt, copper, iron, nickel, and sometimes niobium or tantalum, used to make strong permanent magnets. [AL(UMINUM) + NI(CKEL) + CO(BALT).]
a·lo·di·um. Variant of **allodium.**
al·oe (ăl′ō) *n.* **1.** Any of various plants of the genus *Aloe*, mostly native to southern Africa, having fleshy, spiny-toothed leaves and red or yellow flowers. **2.** *Plural.* A cathartic drug, **bitter aloes** *(see).* Used with a singular verb. **3.** *Plural.* The fragrant wood of a tree, *Aquilaria agallocha*, of tropical Asia. Used with a singular verb. In this sense, also called "aloes wood" and sometimes "agalloch." [Middle English *aloe*, Old English *aluwe*, from Latin *aloē*, from Greek, probably of Oriental origin.] —**al′o·et′ic** (ăl′ō-ĕt′ĭk) *adj.*
a·loft (ə-lôft′, ə-lŏft′) *adv.* **1.** In or into a high place; high or higher up. **2.** *Nautical.* At or toward the upper rigging. [Middle English, from Old Norse *ā lopt* : *ā*, on, in (see **an**[1] in Appendix*) + *lopt*, air, sky (see **leup-** in Appendix*).]
a·lo·ha (ä-lō′hä′) *n. Hawaiian.* Love. Used as an interjection to express greeting or farewell.
al·o·in (ăl′ō-ĭn) *n.* A bitter crystalline compound obtained from the aloe and used as a laxative.. [ALO(E) + -IN.]
a·lone (ə-lōn′) *adj.* **1.** Apart from other people; single; solitary. **2.** Excluding anything or anyone else; with nothing further; sole; only. —**leave alone. 1.** To allow (someone) to remain by himself. **2.** *Informal.* To refrain from interrupting or interfering with (someone). —**let alone. 1.** To refrain from interrupting or interfering with (someone). **2.** Not to speak of or think of: *I haven't a minute to spare, let alone an hour.* —**let well enough alone.** To be satisfied with things as they are and not try to change them. [Middle English, from *al one* : ALL + ONE.] —**a·lone′** *adv.* —**a·lone′ness** *n.*
Synonyms: alone, lonely, lonesome, solitary. These adjectives are compared as they describe lack of companionship. *Alone* emphasizes isolation from others and does not imply unhappiness. *Lonely* adds to isolation the painful consciousness of it. In *lonesome*, the desire for companionship is more plaintive, but less profound: *lonely for a lover; lonesome for a friend. Solitary* stresses physical isolation, sometimes self-imposed.
a·long (ə-lông′, ə-lŏng′) *adv.* **1.** In a line with; following the length or path of; parallel to. Often used with *by: trees growing along by the river.* **2.** With a progressive onward motion; forward. **3.** In association; together. Usually used with *with.* **4.** As company; as a companion: *Bring your son along.* **5.** *Informal.* Advanced to some degree: *The evening was well along.* **6.** *Informal.* Approaching something, such as a time or an age. Used with *about: along about midnight.* —**all along.** From the very beginning; throughout; always: *I knew all along that this would happen.* —**be along.** *Informal.* To come to; arrive at a place: *Our guests should be along soon.* —**get along. 1.** To go onward. **2.** To manage successfully; survive: *I'll get along somehow.* **3.** To be compatible; agree: *He can't get along with anyone.* **4.** *Slang.* To go away; get out. —*prep.* Over, through, or by the length of. [Middle English *along*, Old English *andlang*, "extending opposite" : *and-*, against, facing (see **anti** in Appendix*) + *lang*, extending, LONG.]
a·long·shore (ə-lông′shôr′, -shōr′, ə-lŏng′-) *adv.* Along, near, or by the shore, either on land or in the water.
a·long·side (ə-lông′sīd′, ə-lŏng′-) *adv.* Along, near, at, or to the

side of anything. —*prep.* By the side of; side by side with.
Usage: *Alongside of* is a variant prepositional form, but *alongside* is capable of standing alone.

a·loof (ə-lo͞of′) *adj.* Distant, especially in one's relations with other people; indifferent: *"I stood at a distance aloof from the uproar of life"* (De Quincey). —*adv.* At a distance, but within view; apart; withdrawn. [From *aloufe!* (obsolete nautical expression), "(steer the ship) up into the wind!" : A- (to) + *loufe,* LUFF.] —**a·loof′ly** *adv.* —**a·loof′ness** *n.*

al·o·pe·ci·a (ăl′ə-pē′shē-ə) *n.* Loss of hair; baldness. [Latin *alopēcia,* mange of fox, baldness, from Greek *alōpekia,* from *alōpēx,* fox. See **wlp-** in Appendix.*] —**al′o·pe′cic** (-pē′sĭk) *adj.*

A·lor (ăl′ôr, ä′lôr). An island (906 square miles) of Indonesia, lying in the south Flores Sea, north of Timor.

a·loud (ə-loud′) *adv.* **1.** In a loud tone. **2.** Louder than a whisper; audibly: *She is afraid to say it aloud.* **3.** With the voice; orally: *Read this passage aloud.*

alp (ălp) *n.* A high mountain, especially one of the **Alps** *(see).*

al·pac·a (ăl-păk′ə) *n.* **1.** A domesticated South American mammal, *Lama pacos,* related to the llama, and having fine, long wool. **2. a.** The silky wool of this animal. **b.** Cloth made from this wool. **3.** A glossy cotton or rayon and wool fabric, usually black. [Spanish, from Aymara *allpaca.*]

al·pen·glow (ăl′pən-glō′) *n.* A rosy glow with which snow-covered mountain peaks are suffused at sunrise or dusk on a clear day. [Partial translation of German *Alpenglühen* : *Alpen,* ALPS + *glühen,* to glow.]

al·pen·horn (ăl′pən-hôrn′) *n.* A curved wooden horn, sometimes as long as 20 feet, used by herdsmen in the Alps to call cows to pasture. [German *Alpenhorn* : *Alpen,* ALPS + *Horn,* horn, from Old High German *horn* (see **ker-**[1] in Appendix*).]

al·pen·stock (ăl′pən-stŏk′) *n.* A long staff with an iron point, used by mountain climbers. [German *Alpenstock* : *Alpen,* ALPS + *Stock,* a staff, from Old High German *stoc* (see **steu-** in Appendix*).]

al·pes·trine (ăl-pĕs′trĭn) *adj. Botany.* Growing at high altitudes; alpine or subalpine. [From Medieval Latin *alpestris,* from *Alpes,* the ALPS.]

al·pha (ăl′fə) *n.* **1.** The first letter in the Greek alphabet, written Α, α. Transliterated in English as *A, a.* See **alphabet. 2.** The first of anything; beginning. **3.** *Astronomy.* The brightest or main star in a constellation. **4.** *Physics.* An **alpha particle** *(see).* —*adj.* **1.** First in order of importance. **2.** *Chemistry.* Closest to the functional group of atoms in a molecule. [Greek, from a Phoenician word akin to Hebrew *āleph,* ALEPH.]

alpha and omega. 1. The first and the last: *"I am Alpha and Omega, the beginning and the ending, saith the Lord"* (Revelation 1:8). **2.** The most important part of something.

al·pha·bet (ăl′fə-bĕt′, -bĭt) *n.* **1.** The letters of a given language, arranged in the order fixed by custom. See table overleaf. **2.** Any system of characters or symbols representing sounds or things. **3.** The basic or elementary principles of anything; rudiments. [Latin *alphabētum,* from Greek *alphabētos* : ALPHA + BETA.]

al·pha·bet·i·cal (ăl′fə-bĕt′ĭ-kəl) *adj.* Also **al·pha·bet·ic** (-bĕt′ĭk). **1.** Arranged in the customary order of the letters of a language. **2.** Of, pertaining to, or expressed by an alphabet. —**al′pha·bet′i·cal·ly** *adv.*

al·pha·bet·ize (ăl′fə-bə-tīz′) *tr.v.* **-ized, -izing, -izes. 1.** To arrange in or put into alphabetical order. **2.** To express by or supply with an alphabet. —**al′pha·bet′i·za′tion** (ăl′fə-bĕt′ə-zā′shən) *n.* —**al′pha·bet·iz′er** *n.*

Alpha Cen·tau·ri (sĕn-tôr′ē) *n.* A double star in Centaurus, the brightest in the constellation, 4.4 light-years from Earth.

Alpha Cru·cis (kro͞o′sĭs) *n.* A double star in the constellation Crux, approximately 230 light-years from Earth.

Alpha Le·o·nis (lē-ō′nĭs). *Astronomy.* A star, **Regulus** *(see).*

al·pha·nu·mer·ic (ăl′fə-no͞o-mĕr′ĭk, -nyo͞o-mĕr′ĭk) *adj.* Also **al·pha·mer·ic** (-fə-mĕr′ĭk). **1.** Consisting of alphabetic and numerical symbols. **2.** Consisting of such symbols and of punctuation marks, mathematical symbols, and other conventional symbols used in computer work.

alpha particle. *Symbol* α *Physics.* A positively charged composite particle, indistinguishable from a helium atom nucleus and consisting of two protons and two neutrons.

alpha privative. The Greek negative prefix *a-* (*an-* before vowels). See **a-** (negative prefix).

alpha ray. A stream of alpha particles.

alpha rhythm. The most common electroencephalographic waveform found in recordings of the electrical activity of the adult cerebral cortex, characteristically 8 to 12 smooth, regular oscillations per second in subjects at rest. Also called "alpha wave." Compare **beta rhythm.**

al·pho·sis (ăl-fō′sĭs) *n. Pathology.* Lack of skin pigment, as in albinism. [New Latin : Greek *alphos,* dull-white leprosy (see **albho-** in Appendix*) + -OSIS.]

al·pine (ăl′pīn′) *adj.* **1.** Of or pertaining to high mountains. **2.** *Biology.* Living or growing on mountains above the timberline. **3.** Intended for or concerned with mountaineering. [Latin *Alpīnus,* of the Alps, from *Alpēs,* the ALPS.]

Al·pine (ăl′pīn′) *adj.* **1.** Of, pertaining to, or characteristic of the Alps or their inhabitants. **2.** Of or pertaining to a subdivision of the Caucasian race predominant around the Alps.

alpine azalea. A low-growing, shrubby plant, *Loiseleuria procumbens,* of northern regions, having small evergreen leaves and clusters of small pink or white flowers.

al·pin·ist (ăl′pə-nĭst) *n.* Also **Al·pin·ist.** A mountain climber. —**al′pin·ism′** *n.*

Alps (ălps). The major mountain system of south-central Europe, forming a 680-mile arc from southern France to Albania. Highest elevation, Mont Blanc (15,781 feet).

Al Qa·hi·rah. The Arabic name for **Cairo.**

al·read·y (ôl-rĕd′ē) *adv.* By this (or a specified) time; before; previously. [Middle English *al redy* : ALL + READY.]
Usage: *Already,* an adverb expressing time, should not be confused with *all ready,* used adjectively to express complete readiness: *At last they were all ready. But the train had already left.*

al·right (ôl-rīt′) *adv.* All right. A common misspelling.

a.l.s., A.L.S. autograph letter signed.

Al·sace (ăl-săs′, -săs′). A former province of eastern France between the Rhine and the Vosges Mountains.

Al·sace-Lor·raine (ăl-săs′lô-rān′, ăl-săs′-). *German* **El·sass-Lo·thring·en** (ĕl′zäs′lō′trĭng-ən). A region of northeastern France, annexed in 1871 by Germany, and recovered by France in 1919.

Al·sa·tian (ăl-sā′shən) *adj.* Of or pertaining to Alsace, its inhabitants, or their culture. —*n.* **1.** A native or inhabitant of Alsace. **2.** *British.* A dog, the **German shepherd** *(see).*

al·sike clover (ăl′sīk′, -sĭk′). A plant, *Trifolium hybridum,* native to Eurasia and widely cultivated for forage, having compound leaves and pink or whitish flowers. [After *Alsike,* town in Sweden, where it was first found.]

al·so (ôl′sō) *adv.* Besides; in addition; likewise; too. [Middle English *also,* Old English *(e)alswā,* even so, altogether thus : *(e)al-,* all (see **al-**[5] in Appendix*) + *swā,* so.]
Synonyms: *also, too, likewise, besides, moreover, furthermore.* These adverbs indicate the presence of, or introduce, something additional. The first three generally imply that the additional element or consideration is equal in weight to what precedes it. *Also* is more formal in sound than *too. Likewise* is very formal in tone, and may imply similarity between elements as well as equality. *Besides* often introduces an additional element that reinforces what has gone before. *Moreover* and *furthermore* frequently stress the importance of the additional element.
Usage: Especially in writing, *also* should not be made to do the work of connectives such as *and* or *and also: He studied French and mathematics, also music and drawing* (preferably substitute *and also* for *also,* or use a simple series). Some grammarians disapprove of *also* used as the first word of a sentence to link it with a preceding sentence: *The package was very bulky. Also, it broke* (preferably *was very bulky and also it broke*).

al·so-ran (ôl′sō-răn′) *n. Informal.* One that is defeated in a race, election, or other competition; a loser.

alt (ălt) *adj. Music.* High; pitched in the first octave above the treble staff. —*n. Music.* **1.** The first octave above the treble staff. **2.** A note or tone in this octave. [Latin *altus,* high, deep. See **al-**[3] in Appendix.*]

alt. 1. alteration. **2.** alternate. **3.** altitude.

Alta. Alberta.

Al·tai Mountains (ăl′tī′). A major mountain system of central Asia, in the Soviet Union, Mongolia, and China. Highest elevation, Belukha (15,157 feet), in the Soviet Union.

Al·ta·ic (ăl-tā′ĭk) *n.* A language family of Europe and Asia, including Turkic, Tungus, Mongolian, and possibly Korean. —*adj.* **1.** Of or pertaining to the Altai Mountains. **2.** Of or pertaining to the Altaic languages.

Al·ta·ir (ăl-tä′ĭr, ăl-târ′) *n.* A very bright, double, variable star in the constellation Aquila, approximately 15.7 light-years from Earth. [Arabic *al-ta'ir,* "the star."]

al·tar (ôl′tər) *n.* **1.** Any elevated place or structure upon which sacrifices may be offered or incense burned, or before which religious ceremonies may be enacted. **2.** In Christian churches, a table or similar structure before which the divine offices are recited and upon which the Eucharist is celebrated. —**lead to the altar.** To marry. [Middle English *alter,* Old English *altar,* from Latin *altāre*†, originally "material for burning sacrificial offerings," hence the altar.]

altar boy. An attendant to an officiating clergyman in the performance of a liturgical service; acolyte.

al·tar·piece (ôl′tər-pēs′) *n.* A painting, carving, or the like placed above and behind an altar.

alt·az·i·muth (ălt-ăz′ə-məth) *n.* A mounting for astronomical telescopes that permits both horizontal and vertical rotation. [ALT(ITUDE) + AZIMUTH.]

al·ter (ôl′tər) *v.* **-tered, -tering, -ters.** —*tr.* **1.** To change or make different; modify. **2.** To adjust (a garment) for a better fit. **3.** *Informal.* To castrate or spay. —*intr.* To change or become different. —See Synonyms at **change.** [Middle English *alteren,* from Old French *alterer,* from Medieval Latin *alterāre,* from Latin *alter,* other. See **al-**[1] in Appendix.*]

al·ter·a·ble (ôl′tər-ə-bəl) *adj.* Capable of being altered. —**al′ter·a·bil′i·ty, al′ter·a·ble·ness** *n.* —**al′ter·a·bly** *adv.*

al·ter·a·tion (ôl′tə-rā′shən) *n. Abbr.* **alt. 1.** The act or procedure of altering. **2.** The condition resulting from altering; a modification; change.

al·ter·a·tive (ôl′tə-rā′tĭv) *adj.* **1.** Tending to alter or produce alteration. **2.** *Medicine.* Tending to restore normal health. —*n.* Also **al·ter·ant** (ôl′tər-ənt). *Medicine.* An alterative treatment or medication.

al·ter·cate (ôl′tər-kāt′) *intr.v.* **-cated, -cating, -cates.** To argue or dispute vehemently. [Latin *altercārī,* to have differences with another, from *alter,* another. See **al-**[1] in Appendix.*]

al·ter·ca·tion (ôl′tər-kā′shən) *n.* A heated and noisy quarrel.

al·ter e·go (ôl′tər ē′gō). **1.** Another side of oneself; a second self. **2.** An intimate or inseparable friend; constant companion. [Latin, "other I."]

al·ter·nate (ôl′tər-nāt′, ăl′-) *v.* **-nated, -nating, -nates.** —*intr.* **1.** To occur in successive turns. Usually used with *with: The rainy season alternates with the dry season.* **2.** To pass from one

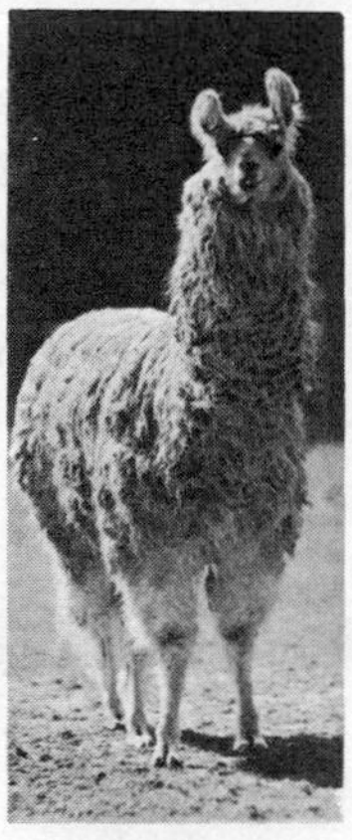

alpaca

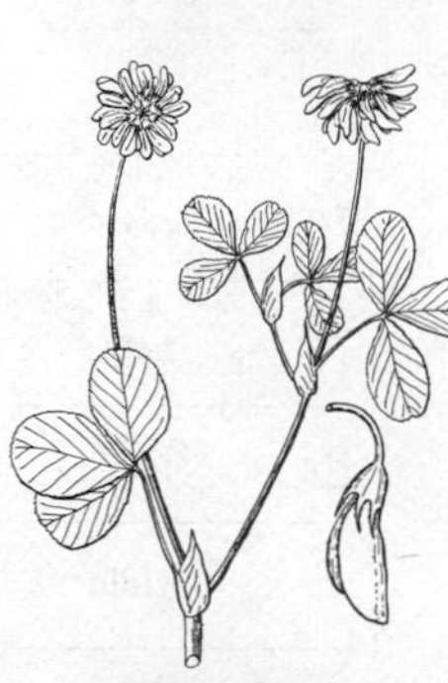

alsike clover

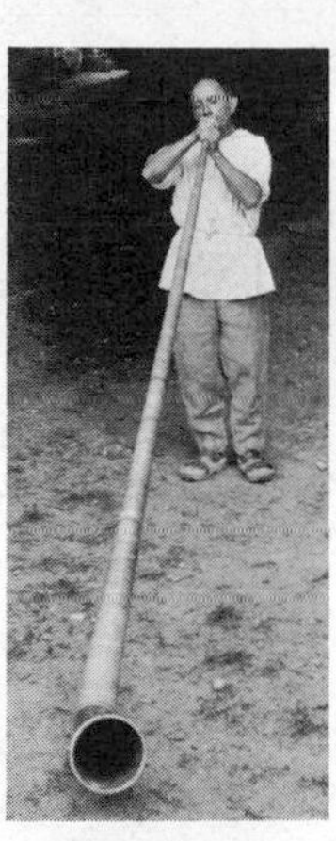

alpenhorn

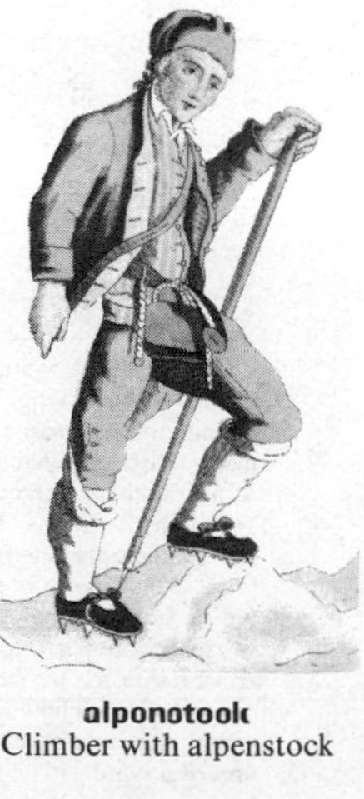

alpenstock
Climber with alpenstock

TABLE OF ALPHABETS

The transliterations shown are those used in the etymologies of this Dictionary. The names of the Hebrew and Greek letters are also entered and defined as English nouns. In some cases the English spelling is different from the transliterated spelling shown here, chiefly in the absence of diacritical marks. Thus the English word "omega" differs from the transliterated form ōmega. For individual histories of the English letters, see the opening page of each letter throughout the Dictionary.

HEBREW

Forms	Name	Sound
א	'aleph	'
ב	bēth	b (bh)
ג	gimel	g (gh)
ד	dāleth	d (dh)
ה	hē	h
ו	waw	w
ז	zayin	z
ח	ḥeth	ḥ
ט	ṭeth	ṭ
י	yodh	y
כ ך	kāph	k (kh)
ל	lāmedh	l
מ ם	mēm	m
נ ן	nūn	n
ס	samekh	s
ע	'ayin	'
פ ף	pē	p (ph)
צ ץ	ṣadhe	ṣ
ק	qōph	q
ר	rēsh	r
ש	sin	s
ש	shin	sh
ת	tāw	t (th)

Vowels are not represented in normal Hebrew writing, but for educational purposes they are indicated by a system of subscript and superscript dots. The transliterations shown in parentheses are used when the letter falls at the end of a word. The transliterations with subscript dots are pharyngeal consonants as in Arabic. The second forms shown are used when the letter falls at the end of a word.

ARABIC

Forms 1	2	3	4	Name	Sound
ا	ا			'alif	'
ب	ب	ـبـ	ـب	bā	b
ت	ت	ـتـ	ـت	tā	t
ث	ث	ـثـ	ـث	thā	th
ج	ج	ـجـ	ـج	jīm	j
ح	ح	ـحـ	ـح	ḥā	ḥ
خ	خ	ـخـ	ـخ	khā	kh
د	ـد			dāl	d
ذ	ـذ			dhāl	dh
ر	ـر			rā	r
ز	ـز			zāy	z
س	س	ـسـ	ـس	sīn	s
ش	ش	ـشـ	ـش	shīn	sh
ص	ص	ـصـ	ـص	ṣād	ṣ
ض	ض	ـضـ	ـض	ḍād	ḍ
ط	ط	ـطـ	ـط	ṭā	ṭ
ظ	ظ	ـظـ	ـظ	ẓā	ẓ
ع	ع	ـعـ	ـع	'ayn	'
غ	غ	ـغـ	ـغ	ghayn	gh
ف	ف	ـفـ	ـف	fā	f
ق	ق	ـقـ	ـق	qāf	q
ك	ك	ـكـ	ـك	kāf	k
ل	ل	ـلـ	ـل	lām	l
م	م	ـمـ	ـم	mīm	m
ن	ن	ـنـ	ـن	nūn	n
ه	ه	ـهـ	ـه	hā	h
و	ـو			wāw	w
ي	ي	ـيـ	ـي	yā	y

The different forms in the four numbered columns are used when the letters are in: (1) isolation; (2) juncture with a previous letter; (3) juncture with the letters on both sides; (4) juncture with a following letter.

Long vowels are represented by the consonants 'alif (for ā), wāw (for ū), and yā (for ī). Short vowels are not usually written; they can, however, be indicated by the following signs: ˊ fatḥa (for a), ˌ kesra (for i), and ˌ ḍamma (for u).

Transliterations with subscript dots represent "emphatic" or pharyngeal consonants, which are pronounced in the usual way except that the pharynx is tightly narrowed during articulation. When two dots are placed over the hā, the new letter thus formed is called tā marbūta, and is pronounced (t).

There are several other diacritical marks indicating such situations as the doubling of a consonant or the elision of a vowel.

GREEK

Forms	Name	Sound
Α α	alpha	a
Β β	beta	b
Γ γ	gamma	g (n)
Δ δ	delta	d
Ε ε	epsilon	e
Ζ ζ	zēta	z
Η η	ēta	ē
Θ θ	thēta	th
Ι ι	iota	i
Κ κ	kappa	k
Λ λ	lambda	l
Μ μ	mu	m
Ν ν	nu	n
Ξ ξ	xi	x
Ο ο	omicron	o
Π π	pi	p
Ρ ρ	rhō	r (rh)
Σ σ ς	sigma	s
Τ τ	tau	t
Υ υ	upsilon	u
Φ φ	phi	ph
Χ χ	khi	kh
Ψ ψ	psi	ps
Ω ω	ōmega	ō

The superscript ' on an initial vowel or rhō, called the rough breathing, represents an aspirate. Lack of aspiration on an initial vowel is indicated by the superscript ', called the smooth breathing. When gamma precedes kappa, xi, khi, or another gamma, it has the value n and is so transliterated. The second lower-case form of sigma is used only in final position.

RUSSIAN

Forms	Sound
А а	a
Б б	b
В в	v
Г г	g
Д д	d
Е е	e
Ж ж	zh
З з	z
И и Й й	i, ĭ
К к	k
Л л	l
М м	m
Н н	n
О о	o
П п	p
Р р	r
С с	s
Т т	t
У у	u
Ф ф	f
Х х	kh
Ц ц	ts
Ч ч	ch
Ш ш	sh
Щ щ	shch
Ъ ъ	''[1]
Ы ы	y
Ь ь	'[2]
Э э	e
Ю ю	yu
Я я	ya

[1] This letter, called tvordiĭ znak, "hard sign," is very rare in modern Russian. It indicates that the previous consonant remains hard even when followed by a front vowel.

[2] This letter, called myakiĭ znak, "soft sign," indicates that the previous consonant is palatalized even when a front vowel does not follow.

state, action, or place to a second, back to the first, and so on indefinitely. Usually used with *between: alternate between optimism and pessimism.* —*tr.* **1.** To do or execute by turns. **2.** To cause to follow in turns; interchange regularly. —*adj.* (ôl′tər-nĭt, ăl′-). *Abbr.* **alt.** **1.** Happening or following in turns; succeeding each other continuously. See Usage note at **alternative.** **2.** Designating or pertaining to every other one of a series: *alternate lines.* **3.** In place of another; substitute: *an alternate plan.* **4.** *Botany.* **a.** Growing at alternating intervals on either side of a stem. Said especially of leaves. Compare **opposite.** **b.** Arranged alternately between other parts, as stamens between petals. —*n.* (ôl′tər-nĭt, ăl′-) *Abbr.* **alt.** A person acting in the place of another; a substitute. [Latin *alternāre,* from *alternus,* by turns, interchangeable, from *alter,* other. See **al-**[1] in Appendix.*] —**al′ter·nate·ness** *n.*

alternate angle. *Geometry.* An angle on one side of a **transversal** *(see)* that cuts two lines, having one of the intersected lines as a side.

al·ter·nate·ly (ôl′tər-nĭt-lē, ăl′-) *adv.* In alternate order or place; by turns. See Usage note at **alternative.**

alternating current. *Abbr.* **ac, A.C.** An electric current that reverses direction in a circuit at regular intervals.

al·ter·na·tion (ôl′tər-nā′shən, ăl′-) *n.* Successive change from one thing to another and back again.

alternation of generations. *Biology.* **Metagenesis** *(see).*

al·ter·na·tive (ôl-tûr′nə-tĭv, ăl-) *n.* **1. a.** The choice between two mutually exclusive possibilities. **b.** A situation presenting such a choice. **c.** Either of these possibilities. **2. a.** One of a number of things from which one must be chosen: *a third alternative.* **b.** A choice or the opportunity to choose among several possibilities. —See Synonyms at **choice.** —*adj.* **1.** Allowing or necessitating a choice between two (or more than two) things. **2.** *Grammar.* Indicating that the words or phrases connected are alternatives: *an alternative conjunction.* **3.** *Logic.* Making two or more assertions, one of which must be true. Said of a proposition. —**al·ter′na·tive·ly** *adv.*

Usage: *Alternative* (noun, adjective) is not necessarily restricted to a choice involving only two, according to 58 per cent of the Usage Panel. (The remainder, who would so restrict it, propose *choice* or *possibility* as substitutes for *alternative,* used as a noun, when more than two things are involved.) In any case, *alternative* and *alternatively* always pertain to choice. *Alternate* and *alternately,* with which they are often confused, have the entirely different basic sense of following by turns, rotating. But *alternate* overlaps the first pair by also pertaining to choice in the sense of substitution (second choice).

al·ter·na·tor (ôl′tər-nā′tər, ăl′-) *n.* An electric generator that produces alternating current.

al·the·a (ăl-thē′ə) *n.* Also **al·thae·a.** **1.** A shrub, the **rose of Sharon** *(see).* **2.** Any plant of the genus *Althaea,* which includes the hollyhock. [Latin, marsh mallows, from Greek *althaia,* "healer," from *althein,* to heal. See **al-**[3] in Appendix.*]

alt·horn (ălt′hôrn′) *n.* A brass wind instrument that sometimes replaces the French horn. Also called "alto horn." [German *Althorn* : *alt,* alto, from Italian *alto,* ALTO + *Horn,* horn, from Old High German (see **ker-**[1] in Appendix*).]

al·though (ôl-*thō*′) *conj.* Also **al·tho.** Regardless of the fact that; even though. [Middle English : *al,* ALL + THOUGH.]

Usage: *Although* and *though* may be used interchangeably in the following typical examples: *Although I was ill, I reported. I reported, though I was ill. Although* is used most often as the first word of concessive clauses. *Though* does not always come first: *ill though I was.* In addition, *though* is the more common term in linking single words or phrases: *wiser though poorer.*

al·tim·e·ter (ăl-tĭm′ə-tər) *n.* An instrument for determining elevation, used especially in aircraft, and commonly based on barometric sensing of pressure changes with altitude or on determination of the frequency delay in a radio signal reflected from ground. [Latin *altus,* high (see **al-**[3] in Appendix*) + -METER.] —**al·tim′e·try** *n.*

Al·ti·pla·no (äl′tē-plä′nō). A high South American plateau in the Andean regions of Bolivia, Peru, and Argentina.

al·ti·tude (ăl′tə-to͞od′, -tyo͞od′) *n. Abbr.* **alt.** **1.** The height of a thing above a reference level, especially above sea level or above the earth's surface. Also called "elevation." **2.** A high location or area. **3.** *Astronomy.* The angular distance of a celestial object above the horizon. **4.** *Geometry.* The perpendicular distance from the base of a geometric figure to the opposite vertex, parallel side, or parallel surface. **5.** A high position or rank. [Middle English, from Latin *altitūdō,* from *altus,* high. See **al-**[3] in Appendix.*] —**al′ti·tu′di·nal** *adj.*

altitude sickness. Illness with symptoms such as nausea, breathlessness, and nosebleed, caused by an oxygen deficiency, as encountered at high altitudes.

al·to (ăl′tō) *n., pl.* **-tos.** *Abbr.* **A.** *Music.* **1.** A low, female singing voice; a contralto. **2.** Originally, a high male singing voice; countertenor. **3.** The range between soprano and tenor. **4.** A singer whose voice lies within this range. **5.** An instrument that sounds within this range, such as an alto saxophone. **6.** A vocal or instrumental part written for such a voice or instrument. —*adj.* Pertaining to this range. [Italian, "high," from Latin *altus,* high. See **al-**[3] in Appendix.*]

al·to·cu·mu·lus (ăl′tō-kyo͞o′myə-ləs) *n.* A cloud formation of rounded, fleecy, white or gray masses. [Latin *altus,* high (see **al-**[3] in Appendix*) + CUMULUS.]

al·to·geth·er (ôl′tə-gĕ*th*′ər, ôl′tə-gĕ*th*′ər) *adv.* **1.** Entirely; completely; utterly. **2.** With all included or counted; in all; all told: *Altogether 100 people were there.* See Usage note below. **3.** On the whole; with everything considered: *Altogether, I'm sorry it happened.* —*n.* A whole. —**in the altogether.** *Informal.* In the nude. [Middle English *al togeder* : *al,* ALL + TOGETHER.]

Usage: *Altogether* and *all together* have different senses. *All together* always applies collectively in the sense of unity, physical or figurative: *prisoners herded all together, nations standing all together. Altogether* may mean *completely (altogether satisfactory);* it may also have the specialized collective sense of *in all, all told,* without reference to proximity: *six men altogether.*

Al·too·na (ăl-to͞o′nə). An industrial city of central Pennsylvania about 80 miles east of Pittsburgh. Population, 69,000.

al·to·re·lie·vo (ăl′tō-rĭ-lē′vō) *n., pl.* **-vos.** Also *Italian* **al·to-ri·lie·vo** (äl′tō-rē-lyā′vō) *pl.* **-vi** (-vē). *Sculpture.* **High relief** *(see).* [Italian *alto rilievo,* "high relief."]

al·to·stra·tus (ăl′tō-strā′təs, -străt′əs) *n.* An extended cloud formation of bluish or gray sheets or layers. [Latin *altus,* high (see **al-**[3] in Appendix*) + STRATUS.]

al·tri·cial (ăl-trĭsh′əl) *adj.* Helpless and naked when hatched, as young pigeons are. [From Latin *altricēs,* plural of *altrix,* feminine of *altōr,* nourisher, from *alere,* to nourish. See **al-**[3] in Appendix.*]

al·tru·ism (ăl′tro͞o-ĭz′əm) *n.* Concern for the welfare of others, as opposed to egoism; selflessness. [French *altruisme,* from *altrui-,* variant of *autrui,* other, from Old French, oblique case of *autre,* other, from Latin *alter,* other. See **al-**[1] in Appendix.*] —**al′tru·ist** *n.* —**al′tru·is′tic** *adj.* —**al′tru·is′ti·cal·ly** *adv.*

al·u·la (ăl′yə-lə) *n., pl.* **-lae** (-lē′). **1.** The feathers attached to the part of a bird's wing corresponding to the thumb. Also called "bastard wing." **2.** A small lobe near the base of the wing in certain insects. [New Latin, diminutive of Latin *āla,* wing. See **aks-** in Appendix.*] —**al′u·lar** (-lər) *adj.*

al·um (ăl′əm) *n.* Any of various double sulfates of a trivalent metal such as aluminum, chromium, or iron, and a univalent metal such as potassium or sodium, especially aluminum potassium sulfate, $AlK(SO_4)_2 \cdot 12H_2O$, widely used in industry as clarifiers, hardeners, and purifiers, and medicinally as topical astringents and styptics. [Middle English, from Old French, from Latin *alūmen*†.]

a·lu·mi·na (ə-lo͞o′mə-nə) *n.* Any of several forms of aluminum oxide, Al_2O_3, occurring naturally as corundum, in a hydrated form in bauxite, and with various impurities as ruby, sapphire, and emery. It is used in aluminum production and in abrasives, refractories, ceramics, and electrical insulation. [New Latin, from Latin *alūmen* (stem *alūmin-*), ALUM.]

a·lu·min·ate (ə-lo͞o′mə-nāt′, -nĭt) *n.* A chemical compound containing aluminum as part of a negative ion.

a·lu·mi·nif·er·ous (ə-lo͞o′mə-nĭf′ər-əs) *adj.* Containing or yielding aluminum, alumina, or alum. [Latin *alūmen* (stem *alūmin-*), ALUM + -FEROUS.]

a·lu·min·ize (ə-lo͞o′mə-nīz′) *tr.v.* **-ized, -izing, -izes.** To coat or cover with aluminum or aluminum paint.

a·lu·mi·nous (ə-lo͞o′mə-nəs) *adj.* Of, pertaining to, or containing aluminum or alum.

a·lu·mi·num (ə-lo͞o′mə-nəm) *n.* Also *chiefly British* **al·u·min·i·um** (ăl′yə-mĭn′ē-əm). *Symbol* **Al** A silvery-white, ductile metallic element, the most abundant in the earth's crust, but found only in combination, chiefly in bauxite. It is used to form many hard, light, corrosion-resistant alloys. Atomic number 13, atomic weight 26.98, melting point 660.2°C, boiling point 2,467°C, specific gravity 2.69, valence 3. See **element.** [New Latin, earlier *alumium* : ALUMINA + -IUM.]

aluminum oxide. *Chemistry.* **Alumina** *(see).*

aluminum sulfate. A white crystalline compound, $Al_2(SO_4)_3$, used chiefly in papermaking, water purification, sanitation, and tanning. Also called "alum."

a·lum·na (ə-lŭm′nə) *n., pl.* **-nae** (-nē′). A female graduate or former student of a school, college, or university. See Usage note at **alumnus.** [Latin, feminine of ALUMNUS.]

a·lum·nus (ə-lŭm′nəs) *n., pl.* **-ni** (-nī′). A male graduate or former student of a school, college, or university. [Latin *alumnus,* a pupil, foster son, from *alere,* to nourish. See **al-**[3] in Appendix.*]

Usage: The plural *alumni* is often used in referring to the graduates or former students of a coeducational institution.

al·um·root (ăl′əm-ro͞ot′, -ro͝ot′) *n.* **1.** Any of various North American plants of the genus *Heuchera,* having clusters of small white, reddish, or green flowers and astringent roots. **2.** The **wild geranium** *(see).*

A·lun·dum (ə-lŭn′dəm) *n.* A trademark for a hard, artificial abrasive of fused alumina, used in making oilstones and grinding wheels. [Probably AL(UMINA) + (CARBOR)UNDUM.]

al·u·nite (ăl′yə-nīt′) *n.* A gray mineral, chiefly $K_2Al_3(OH)_6(SO_4)_3$, used in making alum and fertilizer. Also called "alumstone." [French, from *alun,* alum, from Latin *alūmen,* ALUM.]

Al·va (äl′vä), **Duke of.** Also **Al·ba** (äl′bä). Title of Fernando Álvarez de Toledo. 1508–1582. Spanish statesman; conqueror of Portugal.

Al·va·ra·do (äl′vä-rä′*th*ō), **Pedro de.** 1495?–1541. Spanish conquistador.

al·ve·o·lar (ăl-vē′ə-lər) *adj.* **1.** Of or pertaining to an alveolus. **2.** *Anatomy.* **a.** Pertaining to the jaw section containing the tooth sockets. **b.** Pertaining to the alveoli of the lungs. **3.** *Phonetics.* Formed with the tip of the tongue touching or near the upper alveoli, as the English *t, d,* and *s.* —*n. Phonetics.* A sound produced in this manner. [French *avéolaire,* from *alvéole,* alveolus, from Latin ALVEOLUS.]

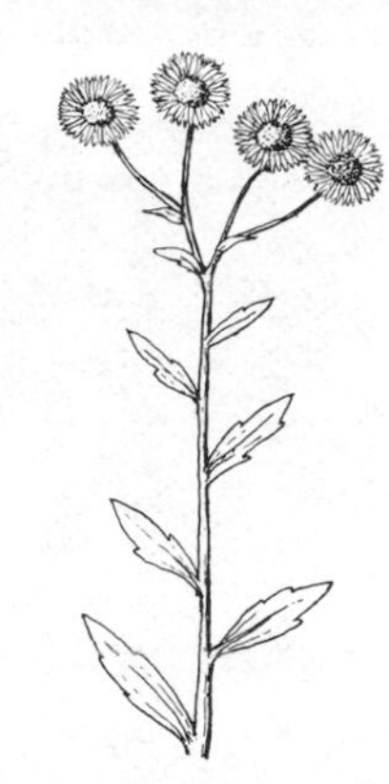

alternate
Alternate leaves of daisy fleabane

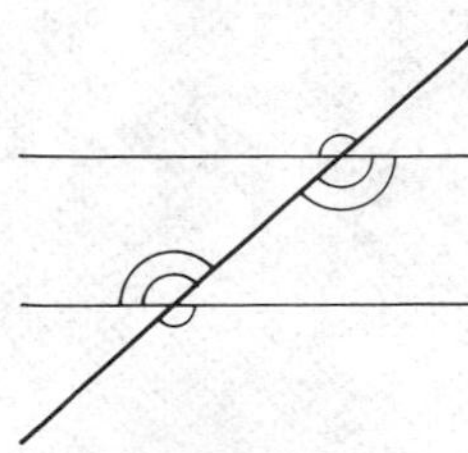

alternate angle
Alternate exterior angles shown by single arc; alternate interior angles shown by double arc

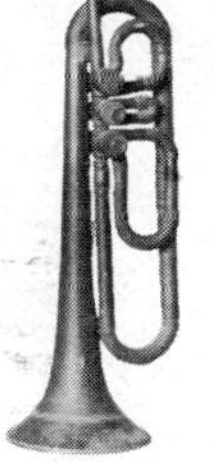

althorn

ă pat/ā pay/âr care/ä father/b bib/ch church/d deed/ĕ pet/ē be/f fife/g gag/h hat/hw which/ĭ pit/ī pie/îr pier/j judge/k kick/l lid, needle/m mum/n no, sudden/ng thing/ŏ pot/ō toe/ô paw, for/oi noise/ou out/o͝o took/o͞o boot/p pop/r roar/s sauce/sh ship, dish/t tight/th thin, path/*th* this, bathe/ŭ cut/ûr urge/v valve/w with/y yes/z zebra, size/zh vision/ə about, item, edible, gallop, circus/ à *Fr.* ami/œ *Fr.* feu, *Ger.* schön/ü *Fr.* tu, *Ger.* über/KH *Ger.* ich, *Scot.* loch/N *Fr.* bon. ***Follows main vocabulary. †Of obscure origin.**

al·ve·o·late (ăl-vē′ə-lĭt) *adj.* Having alveoli; deeply pitted; honeycombed. [Latin *alveolātus*, hollowed, from ALVEOLUS.] —**al′ve′o·la′tion** *n.*

al·ve·o·lus (ăl-vē′ə-ləs) *n., pl.* -li (-lī′). 1. A small cavity or pit, such as a honeycomb cell. 2. A tooth socket in the jawbone. 3. An air sac of the lungs, at the termination of a bronchiole. [Latin, small cavity, diminutive of *alveus*, a cavity, hollow, from *alvus*, a hollow, belly. See aulo- in Appendix.*]

al·ways (ôl′wāz, -wĭz) *adv.* 1. On every occasion; at every time: *He always leaves at six o'clock.* 2. Ceaselessly; continuously; forever: *They will be friends always.* [Middle English *always*, adverbial genitive of *alwei*, Old English *ealne weg*, "(along) all the way" : *ealne*, accusative of *eall*, ALL + *weg*, WAY.]

a·lys·sum (ə-lĭs′əm) *n.* 1. Any of various plants of the genus *Alyssum*, having dense clusters of yellow or white flowers. Sometimes called "madwort." 2. See sweet alyssum. [New Latin, from Greek *alusson*, madwort (believed to cure rabies), from neuter of *alussos*, curing rabies : *a-*, not + *lussa*, rabies, madness (see leuk- in Appendix*).]

am (ăm; *unstressed* əm). The first person singular, present indicative of be.

am amplitude modulation.

Am The symbol for the element americium.

AM amplitude modulation.

Am. America; American.

a.m. ante meridiem (usually small capitals A.M.).

A.M. 1. ante meridiem (usually small capitals A.M.). 2. in the year of the world (Latin *anno mundi*). 3. Master of Arts.

AMA, A.M.A. American Medical Association.

A·ma·ga·sa·ki (ä-mä′gə-sä′kē). An industrial city on Osaka Bay, southern Honshu, Japan. Population, 478,000.

a·mah (ä′mə, ä′mä) *n.* Also **a·ma.** In the Orient, a maidservant who attends children; especially, a wet nurse. [Portuguese *ama*, wet nurse, from Medieval Latin *amma*, from Latin *amma* (unattested), mother. See amma in Appendix.*]

a·main (ə-mān′) *adv. Archaic & Poetic.* 1. With strength and intensity. 2. With speed or haste. 3. Greatly; exceedingly. [A- (on, by) + MAIN (strength).]

Am·a·lek·ite (ăm′ə-lĕk-īt′, ə-măl′ə-kīt′) *n.* A member of an ancient nomadic tribe reputedly descended from Esau's grandson Amalek. Genesis 36:12–16. Exodus 17:8–13. [Hebrew *'Amālēqī*, after *'Amāleq*, Amalek.]

a·mal·gam (ə-măl′gəm) *n.* 1. Any of various alloys of mercury with other metals, as with tin or silver. 2. Any combination or mixture of diverse elements. —See Synonyms at mixture. [Middle English *amalgame*, from Old French, from Medieval Latin *amalgama†*.]

a·mal·ga·mate (ə-măl′gə-māt′) *v.* -mated, -mating, -mates. —*tr.* 1. To mix so as to make a unified whole; blend; unite; combine. 2. To mix or alloy (a metal) with mercury. —*intr.* 1. To combine, unite, or consolidate. 2. To unite or blend with another metal. —See Synonyms at mix. —**a·mal′ga·ma′tive** (-mā′tĭv) *adj.* —**a·mal′ga·ma′tor** (-mā′tər) *n.*

a·mal·ga·ma·tion (ə-măl′gə-mā′shən) *n.* 1. The act of or condition resulting from amalgamating. 2. A consolidation, as of several corporations. 3. *Chemistry.* The dissolving of a metal in mercury to form an alloy.

a·man·dine (ä′män-dēn′) *adj.* Prepared or garnished with almonds: *swordfish amandine.* [French, from *amande*, almond, from Old French *almande*, ALMOND.]

am·a·ni·ta (ăm′ə-nī′tə, -nē′tə) *n.* Any of various mushrooms of the genus *Amanita*, most of which are extremely poisonous. See death cup. [From Greek *amanitai*, mushrooms†.]

a·man·u·en·sis (ə-măn′yōō-ĕn′sĭs) *n., pl.* -ses (-sēz). One employed to take dictation or to copy manuscript. [Latin *āmanuensis*, from *(servus) ā manū*, "(slave) at hand(writing)" : *ab-*, by + *manus*, hand (see man-² in Appendix*).]

A·ma·pá (ä′mä-pä′). A federal territory of northernmost Brazil, occupying about 53,000 square miles between French Guiana and the Amazon delta. Population, 92,000. Capital, Macapá.

am·a·ranth (ăm′ə-rănth′) *n.* 1. Any of various, often weedy, plants of the genus *Amaranthus*, having clusters of small greenish or purplish flowers. See pigweed, tumbleweed, love-lies-bleeding. 2. *Poetic.* An imaginary flower that never fades. 3. Deep reddish purple to dark or grayish, purplish red. —*adj.* color. [New Latin *amaranthus*, variant (influenced by -*anthus*, flower) of Latin *amarantus*, from Greek *amarantos*, unfading : *a-*, not + *marainein*, to waste, wither (see mer-² in Appendix*).]

am·a·ran·thine (ăm′ə-răn′thĭn, -thīn′) *adj.* 1. Of, pertaining to, or resembling the amaranth. 2. Eternally beautiful; unfading; everlasting. 3. Deep purple in color.

am·a·relle (ăm′ə-rĕl′) *n.* A type of sour cherry having pale-red fruit. [German *Amarelle*, from Medieval Latin *amarellum*, from Latin *amārus*, bitter. See om- in Appendix.*]

Am·a·ril·lo (ăm′ə-rĭl′ō). A city and leading commercial center of northern Texas. Population, 138,000.

am·a·ryl·lis (ăm′ə-rĭl′ĭs) *n.* 1. A bulbous plant, *Amaryllis belladonna*, native to southern Africa, having large, lilylike reddish or white flowers. Also called "belladonna lily." 2. Any of several related or similar plants. [After AMARYLLIS.]

Am·a·ryl·lis (ăm′ə-rĭl′ĭs). In classical pastoral poetry, a shepherdess. [Latin girl's name, from Greek *Amarullis*.]

a·mass (ə-măs′) *tr.v.* amassed, amassing, amasses. To pile up or gather up; collect for oneself; accumulate, especially for one's own pleasure or profit. See Synonyms at gather. [Old French *amasser* : *a-*, to, from Latin *ad-* + *masser*, to gather together, from *masse*, a MASS.] —**a·mass′a·ble** *adj.* —**a·mass′ment** *n.*

Amazon¹
Greek wine pitcher from
about 450 B.C.

amaryllis
"Imperator" variety

am·a·teur (ăm′ə-chōōr′, -ə-tər, -ə-tyōōr′) *n.* 1. *Abbr.* a., A. A person who engages in any art, science, study, or athletic activity as a pastime rather than as a profession. 2. *Abbr.* a., A. An athlete who has never participated in competition for money or a livelihood. 3. One lacking professional skill or ease in a certain area, as in art. —*adj.* 1. *Abbr.* a., A. Pertaining to or performed by an amateur. 2. *Abbr.* a., A. Made up of amateurs: *an amateur orchestra.* 3. Not professional; unskillful. [French, from Latin *amātor*, a lover, from *amāre*, to love. See amma in Appendix.*] —**am′a·teur·ism′** *n.*

am·a·teur·ish (ăm′ə-chōōr′ĭsh, -tûr′ĭsh, -tyōōr′ĭsh) *adj.* Characteristic of an amateur; not professional; unskillful. —**am′a·teur′ish·ly** *adv.* —**am′a·teur′ish·ness** *n.*

A·ma·ti (ä-mä′tē) *n.* A violin made by Nicolò Amati or the members of his family.

A·ma·ti (ä-mä′tē), **Nicolò** or **Nicola.** 1596–1684. Italian violin maker of Cremona; master of Stradivari and Guarnieri.

am·a·tive (ăm′ə-tĭv) *adj.* Amorous. [Medieval Latin *amātīvus*, from Latin *amāre*, to love. See amma in Appendix.*] —**am′a·tive·ly** *adv.* —**am′a·tive′ness** *n.*

am·a·tol (ăm′ə-tôl′, -tŏl′) *n.* A highly explosive mixture of ammonium nitrate and trinitrotoluene. [From AM(MONIUM) + (TRINITRO)TOL(UENE).]

am·a·to·ry (ăm′ə-tôr′ē, -tōr′ē) *adj.* Also **am·a·to·ri·al** (ăm′ə-tôr′ē-əl, -tōr′ē-əl). Of, pertaining to, or expressive of love, especially sexual love. [Latin *amātōrius*, from *amātor*, a lover, from *amāre*, to love. See amma in Appendix.*]

am·au·ro·sis (ăm′ô-rō′sĭs) *n.* Total loss of vision; blindness. [Greek *amaurōsis*, from *amauroun*, to darken, from *(a)mauros†*, dark.] —**am′au·rot′ic** (-rŏt′ĭk) *adj.*

a·maze (ə-māz′) *tr.v.* amazed, amazing, amazes. 1. To affect with surprise or great wonder; astonish. 2. *Obsolete.* To bewilder. —See Synonyms at surprise. —*n. Archaic.* Amazement; wonder: *"It fills me with amaze/To see thee, Porphyro!"* (Keats). [Middle English *amasen*, Old English *āmasian†*, to bewilder. See also maze.] —**a·maz′ed·ly** (ə-mā′zĭd-lē) *adv.* —**a·maz′ed·ness** (ə-mā′zĭd-nĭs) *n.*

a·maze·ment (ə-māz′mənt) *n.* 1. A state of extreme surprise or wonder; astonishment. 2. *Obsolete.* Bewilderment; perplexity.

a·maz·ing (ə-mā′zĭng) *adj.* Causing amazement; greatly surprising; wonderful. —**a·maz′ing·ly** *adv.*

Am·a·zon¹ (ăm′ə-zŏn′, -zən) *n.* 1. *Greek Mythology.* A member of a nation of female warriors reputed to have lived in Scythia, near the Black Sea. 2. *Often small a.* Any tall, vigorous, aggressive woman. [Middle English, from Latin *Amāzon*, from Greek. See magh-² in Appendix.*]

Am·a·zon² (ăm′ə-zŏn′, -zən). A river of South America rising in the Peruvian Andes and flowing about 4,000 miles north and then east through northern Brazil to the Atlantic Ocean; navigable by ocean vessels to Iquitos, Peru, 2,400 miles inland.

Amazon ant. Any of several small red ants of the genus *Polyergus*, that take over and enslave the young of other species. [After the legend that the Amazons raised captured children.]

A·ma·zo·nas (ä′mä-zō′näs). A state of Brazil, occupying 614,913 square miles in the northwest. Population, 721,000. Capital, Manaus.

A·ma·zo·nas Territory (ä′mä-sō′näs). A territory of Venezuela, occupying 67,857 square miles in the southern part of the country. Population, 32,000. Capital, Puerto Ayacucho.

Am·a·zo·ni·an¹ (ăm′ə-zō′nē-ən) *adj.* 1. Characteristic of or resembling an Amazon. 2. *Often small a.* Aggressive in a masculine way. Said of women. [From the AMAZON(s).]

Am·a·zo·ni·an² (ăm′ə-zō′nē-ən) *adj.* Of or pertaining to the Amazon River and the regions adjacent to it.

am·a·zon·ite (ăm′ə-zən-īt′) *n.* A green variety of microcline, often used as a semiprecious stone. Also called "amazon stone." [Found near the AMAZON River.]

amb., Amb. ambassador.

am·bage (ăm′bĭj) *n.* 1. *Archaic.* A winding or indirect pathway. 2. *Usually plural. Archaic.* Roundabout ways. [Back-formation from Middle English *ambages*, circumlocutions, from Old French, from Latin *ambāges*, "a going around" : *ambi-*, around + *agere*, to drive, lead (see ag- in Appendix*).] —**am·ba′gious** (ăm-bā′jəs) *adj.*

Am·ba·la (ŭm-bä′lə). A city in eastern Hariana, Republic of India, near the site of recently discovered remains of the oldest prehistoric civilization of India. Population, 106,000.

am·bas·sa·dor (ăm-băs′ə-dər, -dôr′) *n. Abbr.* amb., Amb. 1. A diplomatic official of the highest rank appointed and accredited as representative in residence by one government to another. Also called in full "ambassador extraordinary and plenipotentiary." 2. Any of various diplomatic officials of the highest rank: a. *ambassador-at-large.* An ambassador not assigned to a particular country. b. *ambassador extraordinary.* An ambassador assigned to a specific mission. c. *ambassador plenipotentiary.* An ambassador empowered to negotiate treaties. 3. A diplomatic official heading his country's permanent mission to certain international organizations, such as the United Nations. 4. Any authorized messenger or representative. [Middle English *ambassadour*, from Old French *ambassadeur*, from Old Italian *ambasciator*, from Vulgar Latin *ambactiātor* (unattested), from Medieval Latin *ambactia*, mission, from Germanic *ambakhtaz* (unattested), from Latin *ambactus*, vassal, probably from Celtic. See ag- in Appendix.*] —**am·bas′sa·do′ri·al** (ăm-băs′ə-dôr′ē-əl, -dôr′ē-əl) *adj.* —**am·bas′sa·dor·ship′** *n.*

am·bas·sa·dress (ăm-băs′ə-drĭs) *n. Rare.* 1. The wife of an ambassador. 2. A female ambassador.

am·ber (ăm′bər) *n.* 1. A hard, translucent, yellow, orange, or brownish-yellow fossil resin, found chiefly along the shores of the Baltic Sea, and used for making jewelry and other ornamental objects. **2.** Medium to dark or deep orange yellow. See **color.** **3.** An amber-toned stage light used to simulate sunlight. *—adj.* **1.** Of or relating to amber. **2.** Having an amber color. [Middle English *ambre,* from Old French, from Medieval Latin *ambra, ambar,* from Arabic *'anbar,* ambergris, amber.]

am·ber·gris (ăm′bər-grĭs′, -grēs′) *n.* A waxy, grayish substance formed in the intestines of sperm whales and found floating at sea or washed ashore. It is used as a fixative in perfumes. [Middle English *ambregris,* from Old French *ambre gris* : AMBER + *gris,* gray, from (unattested) Frankish *gris* (see **gher-**[4] in Appendix*).]

am·ber·jack (ăm′bər-jăk′) *n., pl.* **amberjack** or **-jacks.** Any of several food and game fishes of the genus *Seriola,* of temperate and tropical marine waters. [AMBER + JACK (fish).]

ambi–. Indicates both; for example, **ambiversion.** [Latin, round, on both sides. See **ambhi** in Appendix.*]

am·bi·ance (ăm′bē-əns; *French* äN-byäNs′) *n.* Also **am·bi·ence** (ăm′bē-əns). The atmosphere surrounding one; environment. [French, from *ambiant,* surrounding, from Latin *ambiēns,* AMBIENT.]

am·bi·dex·ter (ăm′bĭ-dĕk′stər) *n.* **1.** An ambidextrous person. **2.** A deceitful or hypocritical person. *—adj.* Ambidextrous. [Middle English, from Late Latin : Latin *ambi-,* on both sides + *dexter,* right-handed (see **deks-** in Appendix*).]

am·bi·dex·ter·i·ty (ăm′bĭ-dĕk-stĕr′ə-tē) *n.* **1.** The state or quality of being ambidextrous. **2.** Deceit; hypocrisy.

am·bi·dex·trous (ăm′bĭ-dĕk′strəs) *adj.* **1.** Able to use both hands with equal facility. **2.** Unusually dexterous; adroit. **3.** Deceptive; hypocritical. **—am′bi·dex′trous·ly** *adv.*

am·bi·ent (ăm′bē-ənt) *adj.* Surrounding; encircling. [Latin *ambiēns,* present participle of *ambire,* to go around : *ambi-,* around + *īre,* to go (see **ei-**[1] in Appendix*).]

am·bi·gu·i·ty (ăm′bĭ-gyōō′ə-tē) *n., pl.* **-ties.** **1.** The state of being ambiguous. **2.** Something ambiguous.

am·big·u·ous (ăm-bĭg′yōō-əs) *adj.* **1.** Susceptible of multiple interpretation. **2.** Doubtful or uncertain. [Latin *ambiguus,* uncertain, "going about," from *ambigere,* to wander about : *ambi-,* around + *agere,* to drive, lead (see **ag-** in Appendix*).] **—am·big′u·ous·ly** *adv.* **—am·big′u·ous·ness** *n.*

Synonyms: *ambiguous, equivocal, obscure, recondite, abstruse, vague, cryptic, enigmatic.* These adjectives mean lacking clarity of meaning. *Ambiguous* indicates the presence of two or more possible meanings, usually because of faulty expression. An *equivocal* statement is deliberately unclear or misleading, suggesting a hedging to avoid exposure of one's position. *Obscure* suggests meaning hidden in difficult form, sometimes not worth digging out. *Recondite* and *abstruse,* less pejorative, connote the erudite obscurity of the scholar: *a recondite allusion missed by most readers; abstruse works of philosophy. Vague* primarily indicates a lack of definite form. *Cryptic* suggests a puzzling terseness intended to discourage understanding, and *enigmatic,* great significance hidden in mysterious and challenging form.

am·bit (ăm′bĭt) *n.* **1.** The external boundary of something; a circuit. **2.** The sphere or scope of something. [Middle English, from Latin *ambitus,* a going around, from *ambire* (past participle *ambitus*), to go around. See **ambient.**]

am·bi·tion (ăm-bĭsh′ən) *n.* **1.** An eager or strong desire to achieve something, such as fame or fortune; will to succeed. **2.** The object or goal desired. *—tr.v.* **ambitioned, -tioning, -tions.** To seek with eagerness. [Middle English *ambicioun,* from Old French *ambition,* from Latin *ambitiō,* a going around (for votes), from *ambīre,* to go around. See **ambient.**]

am·bi·tious (ăm-bĭsh′əs) *adj.* **1.** Full of, characterized by, or motivated by ambition. **2.** Greatly desirous; eager. Used with *of* or an infinitive: *"I am not ambitious of ridicule"* (Burke). **3.** Showing or requiring much effort; challenging: *an ambitious plan.* **—am·bi′tious·ly** *adv.* **—am·bi′tious·ness** *n.*

Synonyms: *ambitious, enterprising.* These relate to striving for power, wealth, or success. *Ambitious* is associated with desire for gain or higher station in life, and can suggest ruthlessness of means. *Enterprising* stresses bold, imaginative planning in an effort to succeed, especially in business.

am·biv·a·lence (ăm-bĭv′ə-ləns) *n.* The existence of mutually conflicting feelings or thoughts, such as love and hate together, about some person, object, or idea. [German *Ambivalenz* (coined by Freud) : AMBI- + VALENCE.]

am·biv·a·lent (ăm-bĭv′ə-lənt) *adj.* Exhibiting ambivalence.

am·bi·ver·sion (ăm′bĭ-vûr′zhən, -shən) *n.* A personality trait showing both introversion and extroversion. [AMBI- + (INTRO)VERSION or (EXTRO)VERSION.] **—am′bi·vert′** *n.*

am·ble (ăm′bəl) *intr.v.* **-bled, -bling, -bles.** **1.** To move along smoothly by lifting first both legs on one side and then both on the other. Used of horses and other animals. **2.** To walk slowly; move with a leisurely gait: *"I ambled along, looking in store windows"* (John Howard Griffin). *—n.* **1.** An ambling gait, especially that of a horse. **2.** An unhurried or easy walk; a leisurely pace. [Middle English *amblen,* from Old French *ambler,* from Latin *ambulāre,* to AMBULATE.] **—am′bler** *n.*

am·blyg·o·nite (ăm-blĭg′ə-nīt′) *n.* A white or greenish mineral with composition $(Li,Na)Al(PO_4)(F,OH)$. It is an important source of lithium. [German *Amblygonit,* "the stone with obtuse angles (in its crystals)" : Greek *amblugōnios,* having obtuse angles : *amblus,* blunt (see **mele-** in Appendix*) + *gōnia,* angle (see **genu-**[1] in Appendix*) + -ITE.]

am·bly·o·pi·a (ăm′blē-ō′pē-ə) *n.* Dimness of vision without apparent physical defect or disease of the eye. [New Latin, from Greek *ambluōpia* : *amblus,* blunt, dim (see **mele-** in Appendix*) + -OPIA.] **—am′bly·o′pic** (-ō′pĭk, -ŏp′ĭk) *adj.*

am·bo (ăm′bō) *n., pl.* **-bos** or **ambones** (ăm-bō′nēz). One of the two pulpits or raised stands in early Christian churches from which parts of the service were chanted or read. [Medieval Latin, from Greek *ambōn*†, pulpit, a raised edge or rim.]

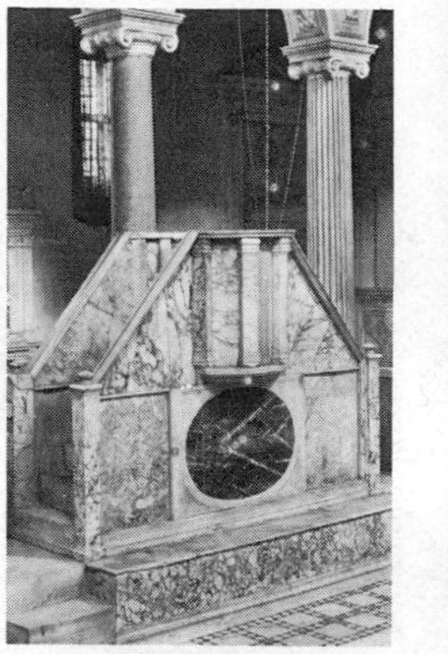
ambo
In the Church of St. Clement, Rome

Am·boi·na (ăm-boi′nə). Also **Am·bon** (äm′bôn). **1.** An island, 314 square miles in area, in the Moluccas, Indonesia. Population, 66,000. **2.** A seaport on the southern coast of this island, capital of the Moluccas. Population, 56,000.

Am·boi·nese (ăm′boi-nēz′, -nēs′) *n.* The language of Amboina.

Am·boise (äN-bwȧz′). A town on the Loire in west-central France; royal residence in the 16th century.

am·boy·na (ăm-boi′nə) *n.* Also **am·boi·na.** The reddish-brown, curly-grained wood of a tree, *Pterocarpus indicus,* of southeastern Asia, used for decorative cabinetwork. [From AMBOINA.]

Am·brose (ăm′brōz′), **Saint.** A.D. 340?–397. Bishop of Milan; author and composer of hymns.

am·bro·sia (ăm-brō′zhə, -zhē-ə) *n.* **1.** *Greek & Roman Mythology.* The food of the gods, thought to impart immortality. Compare **nectar.** **2.** Anything with an especially delicious flavor or fragrance. [Latin, from Greek, "immortality," from *ambrotos,* immortal : *a-,* not + *mbrotos,* archaic form of *brotos,* mortal (see **mer-**[2] in Appendix*).]

am·bro·sial (ăm-brō′zhəl, -zhē-əl) *adj.* Also **am·bro·sian** (-zhən, -zhē-ən). **1.** Suggestive of ambrosia; fragrant or delicious. **2.** Of or worthy of the gods; divine. **—am·bro′sial·ly** *adv.*

Am·bro·sian (ăm-brō′zhən, -zhē-ən) *adj.* Of, by, attributed to, or in the style of Saint Ambrose.

Ambrosian chant. A type of liturgical chant, supposedly introduced by Saint Ambrose and used to the present day in the Cathedral of Milan.

am·bry (ăm′brē) *n., pl.* **-bries.** **1.** A storeroom or cupboard; pantry; closet. **2.** In churches, a niche near the altar for keeping sacred vessels and vestments. [Middle English *aumry,* from Old French *almarie, aumaire,* from Medieval Latin *almārium,* store, from Latin *armārium,* from *arma,* tools, ARMS.]

ambs·ace (āmz′ās′) *n.* Also **ames·ace.** **1.** Double aces, the lowest throw at dice. **2.** Misfortune; bad luck. **3.** The smallest amount or most worthless thing possible. [Middle English *ambes as,* from Old French, from Latin *ambās ās,* "both aces" : *ambās,* feminine accusative of *ambō,* both (see **ambhō** in Appendix*) + *ās,* a unit (see **ace**).]

am·bu·la·crum (ăm′byə-lā′krəm) *n., pl.* **-cra** (-krə). *Zoology.* One of the five radial areas on the undersurface of the starfish and similar echinoderms, on which the tube feet are borne. [New Latin, from Latin *ambulācrum,* walk planted with trees, from *ambulāre,* to AMBULATE.] **—am′bu·la′cral** *adj.*

am·bu·lance (ăm′byə-ləns) *n.* An automobile or other vehicle specially equipped to transport the sick or wounded. [French, from *(hôpital) ambulant,* itinerant (hospital), from Latin *ambulāns,* present participle of *ambulāre,* to AMBULATE.]

ambulance chaser. *Slang.* **1.** A lawyer or a lawyer's agent who obtains clients by persuading victims of accidents to sue for damages. **2.** A lawyer avid for clients.

am·bu·lant (ăm′byə-lənt) *adj.* Moving or walking about; shifting from place to place. [French. See **ambulance.**]

am·bu·late (ăm′byə-lāt′) *intr.v.* **-lated, -lating, -lates.** To walk from place to place; move about. [Latin *ambulāre,* to go about, to walk. See **al-**[2] in Appendix.*] **—am′bu·la′tion** *n.*

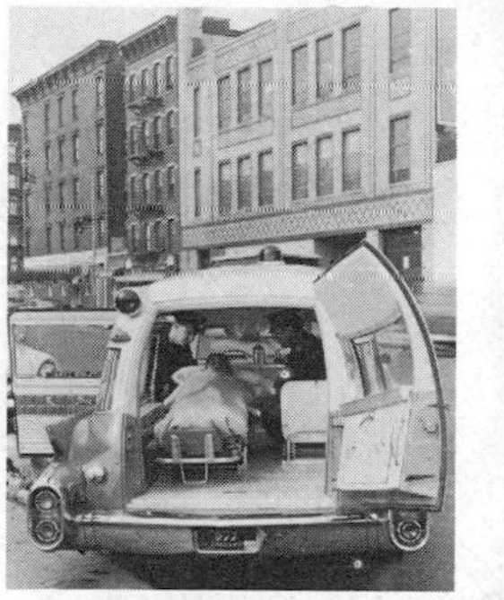
ambulance

am·bu·la·to·ry (ăm′byə-lə-tôr′ē, -tōr′ē) *adj.* **1.** Of, pertaining to, or for walking. **2.** Capable of walking; not bedridden. **3.** Moving about; not stationary. **4.** *Law.* Capable of being changed or revoked, as a will during the life of the testator. *—n., pl.* **ambulatories.** A covered place for walking, as in a cloister.

am·bus·cade (ăm′bə-skād′) *n.* An ambush. *—tr.v.* **ambuscaded, -cading, -cades.** To ambush. [Old French *embuscade,* from Old Italian *imboscata,* feminine past participle of *imboscare,* to ambush, from Vulgar Latin *imboscāre* (unattested), to AMBUSH.] **—am′bus·cad′er** *n.*

am·bush (ăm′bo͝osh′) *n.* **1.** A lying in wait to attack by surprise. **2.** A surprise attack made from a concealed position. **3. a.** Those in hiding to make such an attack. **b.** Their hiding place. **4.** Any hidden peril or trap. *—tr.v.* **ambushed, -bushing, -bushes.** To attack from a concealed position. [From Middle English *embushen,* to ambush, from Old French *embuschier,* from Vulgar Latin *imboscāre* (unattested), "to hide in the bushes" : *in,* in + *boscus* (unattested), bush, from Germanic (see **busk-** in Appendix*).] **—am′bush·er** *n.*

a·me·ba. Variant of **amoeba.**

am·e·be·an. Variant of **amoebaean.**

am·e·bi·a·sis. Variant of **amoebiasis.**

a·me·bo·cyte. Variant of **amoebocyte.**

a·meer. Variant of **emir.**

a·me·lio·rate (ə-mēl′yə-rāt′) *v.* **-rated, -rating, -rates.** *—tr.* To make better; improve. *—intr.* To become better. —See Synonyms at **improve.** [From French *améliorer,* to improve, from Old French *ameillorer* : *a-,* to, from Latin *ad-* + *meillor,* better, from Latin *melior* (see **mel-**[4] in Appendix*).] **—a·me′lio·ra·ble** (-rə-bəl) *adj.* **—a·me′lio·rant** (-rənt) *n.* **—a·me′lio·ra′tive** *adj.* **—a·me′lio·ra′tor** (-rā′tər) *n.*

a·me·lio·ra·tion (ə-mēl′yə-rā′shən) *n.* **1.** The act of ameliorating. **2.** The state of being ameliorated; improvement.

a·men (ā-mĕn′, ä-) *interj.* Used at the end of a prayer or a statement to express approval. *—adv.* Verily; truly. *—n.* **1.** An utterance of this interjection. **2.** Any expression of conviction or assent. [Middle English *amen,* Old English *amen,* from Late Latin *āmēn,* from Greek *amēn,* from Hebrew *āmēn,* certainly, verily.]

A·men (ä′mən). Also **A·mon.** *Egyptian Mythology.* The god of life and reproduction, represented as a man with a ram's head.

a·me·na·ble (ə-mē′nə-bəl, ə-mĕn′ə-) *adj.* **1.** Willing to follow advice or suggestion; tractable; submissive. **2.** Responsible to authority; accountable. **3.** Open or liable to testing, criticism, or judgment. —See Synonyms at **obedient, responsible.** [From French *amener,* to lead, bring, from Old French : *a-,* to, from Latin *ad-* + *mener,* to lead, from Latin *mināre,* to drive (cattle), from *minārī,* "to shout at," threaten, from *minae,* threats (see **men-**[2] in Appendix*).] —**a·me′na·bil′i·ty, a·me′na·ble·ness** *n.* —**a·me′na·bly** *adv.*

Usage: *Amenable* is followed by *to* when it takes a preposition: *amenable to reason.*

amen corner. A church seat reserved for persons leading responsive amens.

a·mend (ə-mĕnd′) *v.* **amended, amending, amends.** —*tr.* **1.** To improve; better. **2.** To remove the faults or errors of; correct; rectify. **3.** To alter (a legislative measure, for example) formally by adding, deleting, or rephrasing. —*intr.* To better one's conduct; reform. —See Synonyms at **correct.** [Middle English *amenden,* from Old French *amender,* alteration of Latin *ēmendāre,* to free from faults : *ex-,* removal, out of + *menda, mendum,* defect, fault (see **mend-** in Appendix*).] —**a·mend′a·ble** *adj.* —**a·mend′a·ble·ness** *n.* —**a·mend′er** *n.*

a·mend·a·to·ry (ə-mĕn′də-tôr′ē, -tōr′ē) *adj.* Serving or tending to amend; corrective.

a·mend·ment (ə-mĕnd′mənt) *n.* **1.** A change for the better; improvement: *"Society may sometimes show signs of repentance and amendment"* (G.G. Coulton). **2.** A correction. **3.** A revision or change. **4.** A formal statement of such a change.

a·mends (ə-mĕndz′) *pl.n.* Reparation or payment made as satisfaction for insult or injury. See Synonyms at **reparation.** [Middle English *amendes,* from Old French, plural of *amende,* reparation, from *amender,* to AMEND.]

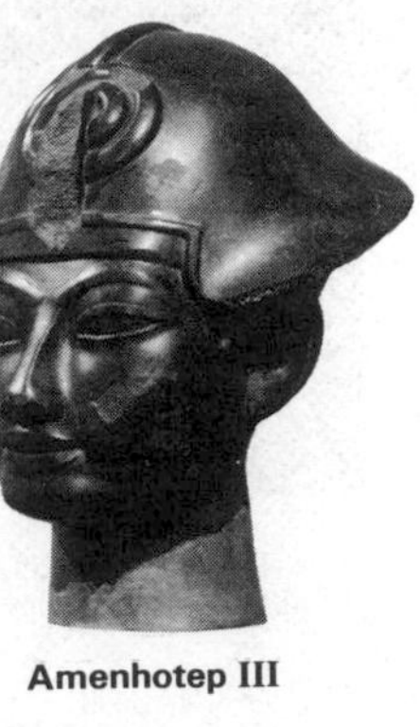

Amenhotep III

A·men·ho·tep III (ä′mən-hō′tĕp). Also **Am·e·no·phis III** (ăm′ə-nō′fĭs). King of Egypt (1411?–1375? B.C.).

A·men·ho·tep IV. See **Akhenaton.**

a·men·i·ty (ə-mĕn′ə-tē, ə-mē′nə-) *n., pl.* **-ties. 1.** Pleasantness; agreeableness. **2.** Anything that increases physical or material comfort: *"It had the same recreational amenities as the others, with the library and gym for the whole place as well"* (Brendan Behan). **3.** *Plural.* Social courtesies; pleasantries; civilities. [Middle English *amenite,* from Old French, from Latin *amoenitās,* from *amoenus*†, pleasant, delightful.]

a·men·or·rhe·a, a·men·or·rhoe·a (ā-mĕn′ə-rē′ə) *n.* Abnormal suppression or absence of menstruation. [New Latin : A- (not) + Greek *mēn,* month (see **mē-**[2] in Appendix*) + -RRHEA, -RRHOEA.]

am·ent[1] (ăm′ənt, ā′mənt) *n. Botany.* A **catkin** *(see).* [New Latin *amentum,* from Latin *ammentum,* a thong, strap. See **ap-**[1] in Appendix.*]

a·ment[2] (ā′mənt, ā′mĕnt′) *n.* A mentally deficient or feeble-minded person. [Latin *āmēns* (stem *āment-*) : *ā-,* out of, away from + *mēns,* mind (see **men-**[1] in Appendix*).]

am·en·ta·ceous (ăm′ən-tā′shəs, ā′mən-) *adj. Botany.* **1.** Resembling or characteristic of an ament; catkinlike. **2.** Having aments, or catkins. [AMENT + -ACEOUS.]

a·men·tia (ā-mĕn′shə) *n.* Subnormal mental development; feeble-mindedness. [Latin *āmentia,* from *āmēns,* AMENT.]

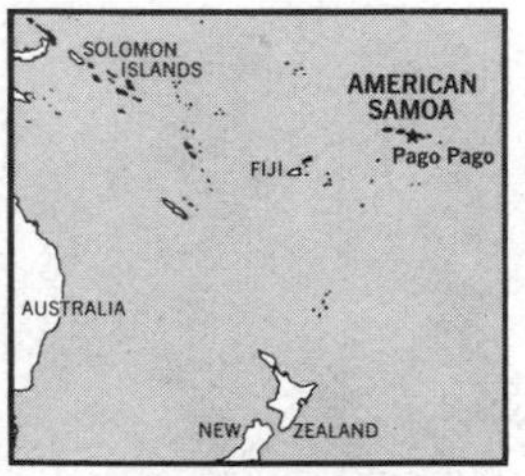

American Samoa

am·en·tif·er·ous (ăm′ən-tĭf′ər-əs, ā′mən-) *adj. Botany.* Bearing aments, or catkins. [AMENT + -FEROUS.]

Amer. America; American.

a·merce (ə-mûrs′) *tr.v.* **amerced, amercing, amerces. 1.** To punish by a fine imposed arbitrarily at the discretion of the court. **2.** To punish by imposing any arbitrary penalty. [Middle English *amercien,* from Norman French *amercier,* from *a merci,* at the mercy of : *a-,* to, from Latin *ad-* + *merci,* mercy, from Latin *mercēs,* wages (see **merc-** in Appendix*).]

A·mer·i·ca (ə-mĕr′ə-kə). *Abbr.* **A., Am., Amer. 1.** The United States of America. **2.** North America. **3.** South America. **4.** North America, Central America, and South America together. In this sense, often called "the Americas." [After *Americus* Vespucius (Latinized form of Amerigo VESPUCCI).]

A·mer·i·can (ə-mĕr′ə-kən) *adj. Abbr.* **A., Am., Amer. 1.** Of, relating to, or characteristic of the United States of America, its people, culture, government, or history. **2.** Of, in, or pertaining to North or South America, or the Western Hemisphere. **3.** Of or pertaining to the Indians inhabiting America. **4.** Indigenous to North or South America. Often used with plant and animal names: *American elm; American elk.* ***Note:*** In this Dictionary, some plants and animals having a common name beginning with *American* are entered under the second element of their name; for example, (American) **beech,** (American) **widgeon,** (American) **alligator.** —*n. Abbr.* **A., Am., Amer. 1.** A native or inhabitant of America. **2.** A citizen of the United States. **3. American English** *(see).*

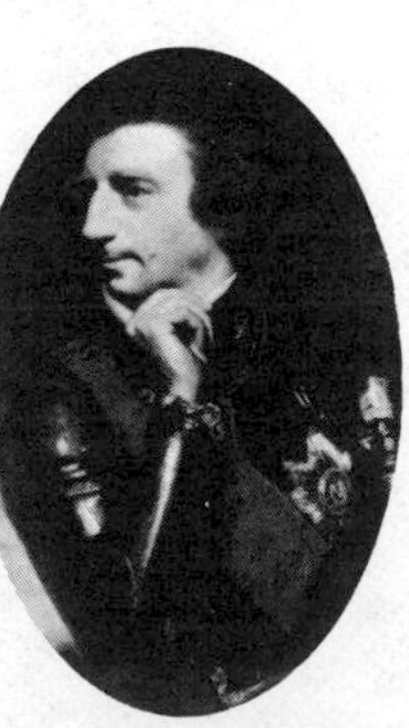

Jeffery Amherst
Contemporary portrait by Sir Joshua Reynolds

A·mer·i·ca·na (ə-mĕr′ə-kä′nə, -kăn′ə, -kā′nə) *pl.n.* A collection of things relating to American history, folklore, or geography. [AMERIC(A) + -ANA.]

American Beauty. 1. A type of rose bearing large, long-stemmed purplish-red flowers. **2.** Medium to dark purplish red. See **color.**

American cheese. A smooth, mild cheddar cheese, white to yellow in color.

American cowslip. A plant, the **shooting star** *(see).*

American eagle. The **bald eagle** *(see),* especially as it appears on the Great Seal of the United States.

American elk. The **wapiti** *(see).*

American English. The English language as used in the United States. Also called "American."

American Expeditionary Forces. *Abbr.* **AEF, A.E.F.** American troops sent to Europe during World War I.

American Falls. That part of Niagara Falls that is within the United States.

American Federation of Labor. *Abbr.* **AFL, A.F.L., A.F.** of **L.** A federation of labor unions organized in 1886, and merged with the Congress of Industrial Organizations in 1955.

American Indian. A member of any of the aboriginal peoples of North America (except the Eskimos), South America, and the West Indies, considered to belong to the Mongoloid ethnic division of the human species.

A·mer·i·can·ism (ə-mĕr′ə-kən-ĭz′əm) *n.* **1.** A custom, trait, or tradition originating in the United States. **2.** A usage of language characteristic of American English. **3.** Allegiance to the United States and its customs and institutions.

A·mer·i·can·ist (ə-mĕr′ə-kən-ĭst) *n.* **1.** One who studies a facet of America, such as its history or geology. **2.** An anthropologist specializing in the study of American aboriginal culture. **3.** A person, other than a U.S. citizen, who is sympathetic to the United States and its policies.

American ivy. A vine, the **Virginia creeper** *(see).*

A·mer·i·can·ize (ə-mĕr′ə-kən-īz′) *v.* **-ized, -izing, -izes.** —*tr.* To assimilate into American culture. —*intr.* To become American in spirit or methods. —**A·mer′i·can·i·za′tion** *n.*

American League. One of the major associations of professional teams in baseball and football.

American Legion. *Abbr.* **A.L.** An organization of U.S. armed forces veterans of World War I, World War II, and the Korean War, founded in 1919.

American Library Association. *Abbr.* **ALA, A.L.A.** An organization of libraries and librarians, founded in 1876.

American plan. A system of hotel management in which a guest pays a fixed daily rate for room, meals, and service.

American Revolution. The war fought between Great Britain and her colonies in North America (1775–83) by which the colonies won independence. Also called "Revolutionary War," "War of Independence," and in Great Britain "War of American Independence." See Treaty of **Paris.**

American sable. The soft, dense, brown fur of a marten, *Martes americana,* of northern North America.

American saddle horse. A three-gaited or five-gaited high-stepping saddle horse of a breed originating in Kentucky.

American Samoa (sə-mō′ə). Seven islands of the Samoan group in the South Pacific, with a combined area of 76 square miles, a U.S. possession administered by the Department of the Interior since 1951. Population, 20,000. Capital, Pago Pago.

American Spanish. The Spanish of the Western Hemisphere.

American Standard Version. *Abbr.* **ASV, ARV** A revised version of the King James Bible published in the United States in 1901. Also called "American Revised Version."

America's Cup. Originally, a trophy won by the yacht *America* in 1851, off the Isle of Wight in England. Now, the prize awarded to the winner of a yacht race between a selected challenger and a selected American yacht.

am·er·ic·i·um (ăm′ə-rĭsh′ē-əm) *n. Symbol* **Am** A white metallic transuranic element of the actinide series, having isotopes with mass numbers from 237 to 246 and half-lives from 25 minutes to 7,950 years. Its longest-lived isotopes, Am 241 and Am 243, are alpha-ray emitters used as radiation sources in research. Atomic number 95, specific gravity 11.7, valences 3, 4, 5, 6. See **element.** [New Latin, from AMERICA.]

A·me·ri·go Ves·puc·ci. See **Vespucci.**

Am·er·ind (ăm′ə-rĭnd′) *n.* An American Indian or an Eskimo. [AMER(ICAN) + IND(IAN).] —**Am′er·in′di·an** *adj. & n.* —**Am′er·in′dic** *adj.*

A·mers·foort (ä′mərz-fōrt′). A commune in the central Netherlands, 12 miles northeast of Utrecht. Population, 74,000.

ames·ace. Variant of **ambsace.**

am·e·thyst (ăm′ə-thĭst) *n.* **1.** A purple or violet form of transparent quartz used as a gemstone. **2.** A purple variety of corundum, used as a gemstone. Also called "Oriental amethyst." **3.** Moderate purple to graying reddish purple. See **color.** [Middle English *ametist,* from Old French *ametiste,* from Latin *amethystus,* from Greek *amethustos,* amethyst, "anti-intoxicant" (amethyst was thought to be a remedy for intoxication) : *a-,* not + *methuskein,* to intoxicate, from *methuein,* to be drunk, from *methu,* wine (see **medhu-** in Appendix*).]

am·e·thys·tine (ăm′ə-thĭs′tĭn, -tīn′) *adj.* **1.** Of or containing amethyst. **2.** Of the color of amethyst.

am·e·tro·pi·a (ăm′ə-trō′pē-ə) *n.* Any eye abnormality, such as nearsightedness, farsightedness, or astigmatism, resulting from faulty refraction. [New Latin : Greek *ametros,* beyond measure, disproportionate : *a-,* without + *metron,* measure (see **mē-**[2] in Appendix*) + -OPIA.]

Am·ga (ŭm-gä′). A river of the Soviet Union, rising in the southern Yakut A.S.S.R. and flowing 1,025 miles generally northeast to join the Aldan, northeast of Yakutsk.

Am·har·a (ăm-hăr′ə). A former province of northern Ethiopia, the rulers of which dominated most of the country from the 12th to 19th century.

Am·har·ic (ăm-hăr′ĭk, äm-hä′rĭk) *n.* A southern Semitic language, the official language in Ethiopia. —*adj.* Of or concerning Amhara.

Am·herst (ăm′ərst), **Jeffery.** Also **Jeffrey.** First Baron Amherst. 1717–1797. British major general sent by Pitt the Elder to command British and American colonial forces in final French and Indian War; victor at Louisburg.

a·mi·a·ble (ā′mē-ə-bəl) *adj.* **1.** Pleasantly disposed; good-natured; agreeable. **2.** Cordial; friendly; sociable; congenial: *an*

ă pat/ā pay/âr care/ä father/b bib/ch church/d deed/ĕ pet/ē be/f fife/g gag/h hat/hw which/ĭ pit/ī pie/îr pier/j judge/k kick/l lid, needle/m mum/n no, sudden/ng thing/ŏ pot/ō toe/ô paw, for/oi noise/ou out/ŏŏ took/ōō boot/p pop/r roar/s sauce/sh ship, dish/

amiable gathering. [Middle English, from Old French, from Late Latin *amīcābilis,* AMICABLE.] —**a'mi·a·bil'i·ty, a'mi·a·ble·ness** *n.* —**a'mi·a·bly** *adv.*

Synonyms: *amiable, affable, good-natured, obliging, agreeable, pleasant.* These adjectives all refer to a tendency to please in social relations. *Amiable* implies friendliness and sweetness of disposition. *Affable* especially fits a person who is easy to approach and difficult to anger. *Good-natured* suggests a tolerant, easygoing disposition; sometimes it also implies a docile nature. *Obliging* specifies disposition to comply with the will of others; *agreeable* adds to this a sense of eagerness to please. *Pleasant* applies broadly to favorable manner or appearance.

am·i·an·thus (ăm'ē-ăn'thəs) *n.* Also **am·i·an·tus** (-təs). An asbestos with fine, silky fibers. [Latin *amiantus,* from Greek *amiantos (lithos),* "unpolluted (stone)" : *a-,* not + *miainein,* to pollute, defile (see **mai-²** in Appendix*).]

am·i·ca·ble (ăm'ĭ-kə-bəl) *adj.* Characterized by or showing friendliness; friendly; peaceable. [Middle English, from Late Latin *amīcābilis,* from Latin *amīcus.* See **amma** in Appendix.*] —**am'i·ca·bil'i·ty, am'i·ca·ble·ness** *n.* —**am'i·ca·bly** *adv.*

am·ice (ăm'ĭs) *n. Ecclesiastical.* A liturgical vestment, consisting of an oblong piece of white linen worn around the neck and shoulders and partly under the alb. [Middle English *amyse,* probably from Old French *amis,* plural of *amit,* amice, from Latin *amictus,* mantle, "(a garment) thrown around one," from *amicīre,* to throw around : *ambi-,* around + *jacere,* to throw (see **yē-** in Appendix*).]

a·mi·cus cu·ri·ae (ə-mē'kəs kyo͝or'ē-ī') *pl.* **amici curiae** (ə-mē'kē kyo͝or'ē-ī'). *Law.* A person invited to advise a court on a matter of law in a case to which he is not a party. [Latin, "friend of the court."]

a·mid (ə-mĭd') *prep.* Also **a·midst** (ə-mĭdst'). Surrounded by; in the middle of. See Synonyms at **among.** [Middle English *amidde,* Old English *onmiddan* : ON + *middan,* dative singular of *midd(e),* middle (see **medhyo-** in Appendix*).]

am·ide (ăm'īd', -ĭd) *n.* **1.** An organic compound, such as acetamide, containing the $CONH_2$ group. **2.** A compound with a metal replacing hydrogen in ammonia, such as sodium amide, $NaNH_2$. [AM(MONIA) + -IDE.] —**a·mid'ic** (ə-mĭd'ĭk) *adj.*

am·i·dol (ăm'ə-dôl', -dōl') *n.* A colorless crystalline compound $(NH_2)_2C_6H_3OH \cdot 2HCl$, used as a photographic developer. [German *Amidol* (trademark) : AMID(E) + (PHEN)OL.]

a·mid·ships (ə-mĭd'shĭps') *adv.* Also **a·mid·ship** (-shĭp'). *Nautical.* Midway between the bow and the stern; toward the middle of the ship; midships.

A·miens (à-myăN'). A manufacturing center of France, in the north on the Somme River; the site of a cathedral of Notre Dame. Population, 106,000.

a·mi·go (ə-mē'gō) *n., pl.* **-gos.** A friend. [Spanish, from Latin *amīcus,* friend. See **amma** in Appendix.*]

a·mine (ə-mēn', ăm'ĭn) *n.* Any of a group of organic compounds of nitrogen, such as ethylamine, $C_2H_5NH_2$, that may be considered ammonia derivatives in which one or more hydrogen atoms has been replaced by a hydrocarbon radical. [AM(MONIUM) + -INE.]

-amine. Indicates an amine; for example, **methylamine.**

a·mi·no (ə-mē'nō, ăm'ə-nō') *adj.* Pertaining to an amine or other chemical compound containing NH_2 combined with a nonacid organic radical. [From AMINO-.]

amino-. *Chemistry.* Indicates replacement of one hydrogen in ammonia by a nonacid organic radical; for example, **aminophenol.** [From AMINE.]

amino acid. 1. Any organic compound containing both an amino group (NH_2) and a carboxylic acid group (COOH). **2.** A compound of the form $NH_2CHRCOOH$, found as essential components of the protein molecule.

a·mi·no·ben·zo·ic acid (ə-mē'nō-bĕn-zō'ĭk, ăm'ə-nō-). Any of three benzoic acid derivatives, $C_7H_7NO_2$, especially the yellowish para form, which is part of the vitamin B complex.

a·mi·no·phe·nol (ə-mē'nō-fē'nōl', ăm'ə-nō-) *n.* One of three organic compounds with composition $C_6H_4NH_2OH$, used as photographic developers and dye intermediates.

a·mi·no·py·rine (ə-mē'nō-pī'rēn', ăm'ə-nō-) *n.* A colorless crystalline compound, $C_{13}H_{17}N_3O$, used to reduce fever and relieve pain. [AMINO- + (ANTI)PYRINE.]

a·mir. Variant of **emir.**

A·mish (ä'mĭsh, ăm'ĭsh) *adj.* Of, concerning, or designating the Mennonite, or Plain People, sect that settled in the United States. —*pl.n.* A Mennonite sect founded in the 17th century by Jacob Ammann, Swiss religious reformer.

a·miss (ə-mĭs') *adj.* Out of proper order. Usually used predicatively: *What is amiss?* —*adv.* In an improper or defective way. —**take amiss.** To misunderstand; feel offended by. [Middle English *a mis* : A- (on, at) + *mis,* a mistake, from *missen,* to miss, Old English *missan* (see **mei-¹** in Appendix*).]

a·mi·to·sis (ā'mī-tō'sĭs, ăm'ə-) *n. Biology.* Cell division characterized by simple nuclear cleavage without the formation of chromosomes. [New Latin : A- (not) + MITOSIS.] —**a'mi·tot'ic** (ā'mī-tŏt'ĭk, ăm'ə-) *adj.* —**a'mi·tot'i·cal·ly** *adv.*

am·i·ty (ăm'ə-tē) *n., pl.* **-ties.** Peaceful relations, as between nations; friendship. [Middle English *amite,* from Old French *amitie,* from Medieval Latin *amīcitās,* from Latin *amīcus,* friend. See **amma** in Appendix.*]

Am·man (ă-măn'). Ancient name **Phil·a·del·phi·a** (fĭl'ə-dĕl'fē-ə). Biblical names **Rab·bah Am·mon** (răb'ä ăm'ŏn), **Rab·bath Am·mon** (răb'ăth). The capital of Jordan, in the northern part of the country. Population, 296,000.

am·me·ter (ăm'mē'tər) *n. Abbr.* **A** An instrument that measures electric current. [AM(PERE) + -METER.]

am·mine (ăm'ēn') *n.* Any of a class of chemical compounds, such as aniline, derived from replacement of hydrogen atoms in ammonia by univalent hydrocarbon radicals. [AMM(ONIA) + -INE.] —**am'mi·no'** (ăm'ə-nō', ə-mē'nō) *adj.*

am·mo (ăm'ō) *n. Military.* Ammunition.

am·mo·cete (ăm'ə-sēt') *n.* The blind, wormlike larva of the lamprey. [New Latin *Ammocoetes* (former genus name), "ones who lie in sand" : Greek *ammos,* sand (see **bhes-¹** in Appendix*) + *koitē,* bed, from *keisthei,* to lie (see **kei-¹** in Appendix*).]

am·mo·nia (ə-mōn'yə) *n.* **1.** A colorless, pungent gas, NH_3, extensively used to manufacture fertilizers and a wide variety of nitrogen-containing organic and inorganic chemicals. **2.** A solution of ammonia in water, **ammonium hydroxide** *(see).* [New Latin, from Latin *(sal) ammōniăcus,* "(salt) of Amen," from Greek *ammōniakos,* from *Ammōn,* AMEN (it was originally obtained from a region near the temple of Amen, in Libya).]

am·mo·ni·ac¹ (ə-mō'nē-ăk') *adj.* Also **am·mo·ni·a·cal** (ăm'ə-nī'ə-kəl). Of, containing, or similar to ammonia.

am·mo·ni·ac² (ə-mō'nē-ăk') *n.* A strong-smelling gum resin from the stems of a plant, *Dorema ammoniacum,* of northern Asia, formerly used in medicine as an expectorant and stimulant. Also called "gum ammoniac." [Middle English *ammonyak,* from Latin *ammōniacum,* from Greek *ammōniakon,* neuter of *ammōniakos,* of Amen. See **ammonia.**]

am·mo·ni·ate (ə-mō'nē-āt') *tr.v.* **-ated, -ating, -ates.** To treat or combine with ammonia. —*n.* A compound that contains ammonia. —**am·mo'ni·a'tion** *n.*

ammonia water. *Chemistry.* **Ammonium hydroxide** *(see).*

am·mon·i·fi·ca·tion (ə-mŏn'ə-fĭ-kā'shən, ə-mō'nə-) *n.* **1.** Impregnation with ammonia or an ammonium compound. **2.** The generation of ammonia or ammonium compounds by the action of bacteria on nitrogenous organic matter in soil.

am·mon·i·fy (ə-mŏn'ə-fī', ə-mō'nə-) *v.* **-fied, -fying, -fies.** —*tr.* To subject to ammonification. —*intr.* To be subjected to ammonification. [AMMONI(A) + -FY.] —**am·mon'i·fi'er** *n.*

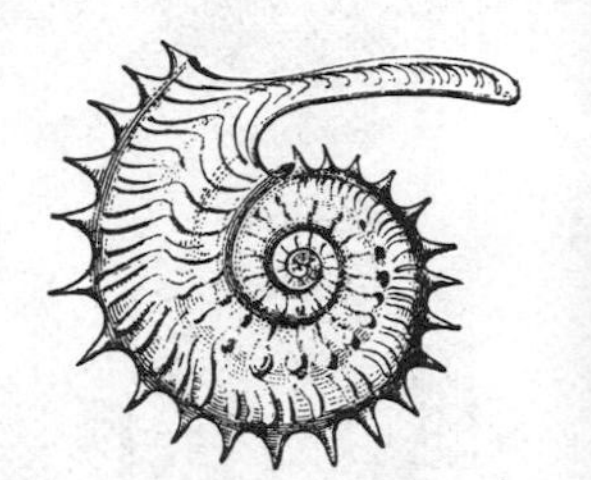

ammonite

am·mon·ite (ăm'ə-nīt') *n.* Also **am·mon·oid** (ăm'ə-noid'). The coiled, flat, chambered shell of any of various extinct mollusks of the class *Cephalopoda,* found as fossils in Mesozoic formations. [New Latin *Ammonītēs,* from Latin *(cornus) Ammōnis,* "(horn) of Amen" (because it resembles the horns of Amen), from *Ammōnis,* genitive of *Ammōn,* AMEN.]

Am·mon·ite (ăm'ə-nīt') *n.* A member of a Semitic people living east of the Jordan River, mentioned frequently in the Old Testament. [Late Latin *Ammonītēs,* the Ammonites, from Hebrew *'Ammōn,* city or people of Amman, from Canaanite *'am-,* "folk."]

am·mo·ni·um (ə-mō'nē-əm) *n.* The chemical ion NH_4^+. [New Latin : AMMON(IA) + -IUM.]

Am·mo·ni·um. The ancient name for **Siwa.**

ammonium carbonate. A white powder with composition $(NH_4)HCO_3 \cdot (NH_4)CO_2NH_2$ used in baking powders, smelling salts, and fire-extinguishing compounds.

ammonium chloride. A slightly hygroscopic white crystalline compound, NH_4Cl, used in dry cells, as a soldering flux, as an expectorant, and in various industrial applications. Also called "sal ammoniac."

ammonium hydroxide. A colorless basic aqueous solution of ammonia, NH_4OH, used as a household cleanser and to manufacture a wide variety of products including textiles, rayon, rubber, fertilizer, and plastic. Also called "ammonia solution."

ammonium nitrate. A colorless crystalline salt, NH_4NO_3, used in fertilizers, explosives, and solid rocket propellants.

ammonium sulfate. A brownish-gray to white crystalline salt, $(NH_4)_2SO_4$, used in fertilizers and water purification.

am·mu·ni·tion (ăm'yə-nĭsh'ən) *n.* **1. a.** The projectiles, along with their fuzes and primers, that can be fired from guns or otherwise propelled. **b.** Any nuclear, biological, chemical, or explosive material used for defense or offense, as rockets, grenades, mines, or the like. **2.** Any means of offense or defense. [Old French *a(m)munition,* from phrase *l'amunition,* originally *la munition,* the MUNITION.]

am·ne·sia (ăm-nē'zhə) *n.* Partial or total loss of memory, especially through shock, psychological disturbance, brain injury, or illness. [New Latin, from Greek *amnēsia* : *a-,* not + *mnasthai,* to remember (see **men-¹** in Appendix*).] —**am·ne'si·ac'** (ăm-nē'zē-ăk', -zhē-ăk'), **am·ne'sic** (ăm-nē'zĭk, -sĭk) *n.* & *adj.* —**am·nes'tic** (ăm-nĕs'tĭk) *adj.*

am·nes·ty (ăm'nəs-tē) *n., pl.* **-ties.** A general pardon for offenders by a government, especially for political offenses. —*tr.v.* **amnestied, -tying, -ties.** To grant amnesty to. [Greek *amnēstia,* "forgetfulness," from *amnēstos,* forgotten : *a-,* not + *mnasthai,* to remember (see **men-¹** in Appendix*).]

am·ni·on (ăm'nē-ən, -ŏn') *n., pl.* **-ons** or **-nia** (-nē-ə). A thin, tough, membranous sac that contains a watery fluid in which the embryo of a mammal, bird, or reptile is suspended. [New Latin, from Greek *amnion*†, sacrificial plate to hold a victim's blood, sac.] —**am'ni·ot'ic** (ăm'nē-ŏt'ĭk), **am'ni·on'ic** (ăm'nē-ŏn'ĭk) *adj.*

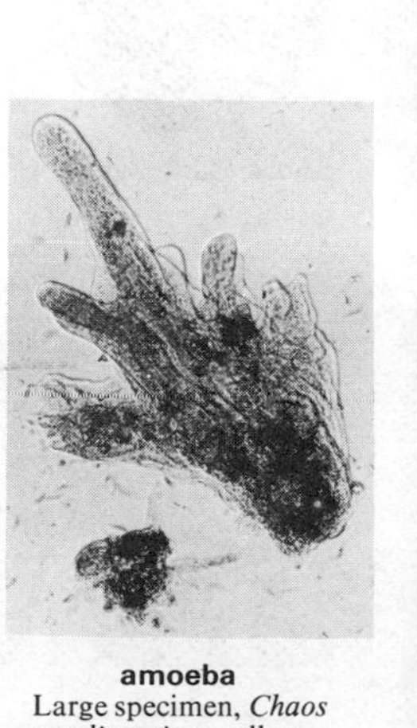

amoeba
Large specimen, *Chaos carolinensis;* small one, *Amoeba proteus* (enlarged 200 diameters)

a·moe·ba, a·me·ba (ə-mē'bə) *n., pl.* **-bas** or **-bae** (-bē). Any of various protozoans of the genus *Amoeba* and related genera, occurring in water, soil, and as internal animal parasites, characteristically having an indefinite, changeable form and moving by means of pseudopodia. [New Latin, from Greek *amoibē,* change, from *ameibein,* to change. See **mei-¹** in Appendix.*] —**a·moe'bic** (-bĭk) *adj.*

am·oe·bae·an, am·oe·be·an, am·e·be·an (ăm'ĭ-bē'ən) *adj.* Alternately answering, as dialogue. [Late Latin *amoebaeus,* from Greek *amoibaios,* from *amoibē,* change. See **amoeba.**]

am·oe·bi·a·sis, am·e·bi·a·sis (ăm'ĭ-bī'ə-sĭs) *n., pl.* **-ses** (-sēz'). An infection caused by amoebas, especially by *Entamoeba histolytica*. [New Latin *amoebiasis* : AMOEB(A) + -IASIS.]

amoebic dysentery. An infectious, inflammatory disease of the colon, caused by *Entamoeba histolytica* and resulting in severe pain and diarrhea.

a·moe·bo·cyte, a·me·bo·cyte (ə-mē'bə-sīt') *n.* Any cell, such as a leucocyte, having amoebic form. [AMOEB(A) + -CYTE.]

a·moe·boid (ə-mē'boid') *adj.* Of or resembling an amoeba, especially in changeable form and means of locomotion.

a·mok. Variant of **amuck.**

a·mo·le (ə-mō'lē) *n.* **1.** Any of several plants, chiefly of southwestern North America, having roots, bulbs, or other parts used as soap, such as the **soap plant** *(see)*. **2.** The parts of these plants used as soap. [Spanish, from Nahuatl *amol(li).*]

A·mon. Variant of **Amen.**

a·mong (ə-mŭng') *prep.* Also **a·mongst** (ə-mŭngst'). **1.** In the midst of; in the company of; surrounded by. **2.** In the group, number, or class of: *He is among the wealthy.* **3.** In the company of; in association with: *traveling among a group of tourists.* **4.** With many; by many or the entire number of: *a custom popular among the Greeks.* **5.** By the joint action of: *Among us, we will get the job done.* **6.** With portions to each of: *Distribute this among you.* **7.** Each with the other; between one another: *Don't fight among yourselves.* —See Usage note at **between.** [Middle English *among*, Old English *on gemang* : *on*, in, ON + *gemang*, a crowd (see **mag-** in Appendix*).]

Synonyms: *among, amid, between.* These prepositions are compared as they pertain to positions in space or to their figurative equivalents. *Among* refers to being surrounded, or approximately so, by objects that are individual and separable: *living among the Indians. Amid* stresses being surrounded but not necessarily by separable things: *a house amid the trees; remain cool amid confusion. Between* refers to a location in space that separates two objects: *standing between two skyscrapers; caught between opposing viewpoints.*

a·mon·til·la·do (ə-mŏn'tə-lä'dō; *Spanish* ä-mōn'tē-lyä'thō) *n., pl.* **-dos.** A pale dry sherry. [Spanish *(vino) amontillado*, "(wine) made in Montilla" : *a-*, to, from Latin *ad-* + *Montilla*, Spanish town.]

a·mor·al (ā-môr'əl, ā-mŏr'əl) *adj.* **1.** Not admitting of moral distinctions or judgments; neither moral nor immoral. **2.** Lacking moral judgment or sensibility; not caring about right and wrong. [A- (not) + MORAL.] —**a'mo·ral'i·ty** (ā'mô-răl'ə-tē), **a·mor'al·ism'** *n.* —**a·mor'al·ly** *adv.*

am·o·ret·to (ăm'ə-rĕt'ō, ä'mə-) *n., pl.* **-retti** (-rĕt'ē) or **-tos.** A cupid. [Italian, diminutive of *Amore*, Cupid, from Latin *Amor*, from *amor*, love, from *amāre*, to love. See **amma** in Appendix.*]

am·o·rist (ăm'ə-rĭst) *n.* One dedicated to love. [From Latin *amor*, love. See **amoretto.**]

Am·o·rite (ăm'ə-rīt') *n.* A member of a people inhabiting Canaan before the Israelites, mentioned frequently in the Old Testament. [From Hebrew *Emōrī.*]

am·o·rous (ăm'ər-əs) *adj.* **1.** Strongly attracted to love, especially sexual love. **2.** Indicative of love: *an amorous glance.* **3.** Of or associated with love: *an amorous poem.* **4.** In love; enamored. Usually used with *of.* [Middle English, from Old French, from Medieval Latin *amōrōsus*, from Latin *amor*, love. See **amoretto.**] —**am'or·ous·ly** *adv.* —**am'or·ous·ness** *n.*

a·mor·phism (ə-môr'fĭz'əm) *n.* The state or quality of being amorphous.

a·mor·phous (ə-môr'fəs) *adj.* **1.** Without definite form; lacking a specific shape. **2.** Of no particular type or character; unorganized; formless: *"a curious linguistic phenomenon: a language amorphous, halting, groping"* (William Barrett). **3.** Lacking distinct crystalline structure. [Greek *amorphos* : *a-*, without + -MORPHOUS.] —**a·mor'phous·ly** *adv.* —**a·mor'phous·ness** *n.*

am·or·ti·za·tion (ăm'ər-tə-zā'shən, ə-môr'tə-) *n.* Also **a·mor·tize·ment** (ə-môr'tĭz-mənt). **1.** The act or process of amortizing. **2.** The money set aside for this purpose. **3.** *Finance.* In reckoning the yield of a bond bought at a premium, the periodic subtraction from its current yield of a proportionate share of the premium between the purchase date and the maturity date. Compare **accumulation.**

am·or·tize (ăm'ər-tīz', ə-môr'tīz') *tr.v.* **-tized, -tizing, -tizes.** **1.** To liquidate (a debt) by installment payments or payment into a sinking fund. **2.** *Accounting.* To write off (expenditures) by prorating over a certain period. **3.** *Law.* To sell or transfer (property) in mortmain. [Middle English *amortisen*, from Old French *amortir* (present stem *amortiss-*), from Vulgar Latin *admortīre* (unattested), to deaden : *ad-*, to + *mortus* (unattested), dead, from Latin *mors*, death (see **mer-²** in Appendix*).] —**am'or·tiz'a·ble** *adj.*

A·mos¹ (ā'məs). A Hebrew prophet of the eighth century B.C.

A·mos² (ā'məs) *n.* A book of the Old Testament containing the prophecies of Amos.

a·mount (ə-mount') *n. Abbr.* **amt.** **1.** The total of two or more quantities; aggregate. **2.** A number; sum. **3.** A principal plus its interest, as in a loan. **4.** The aggregate effect or meaning; import. **5.** Quantity: *a great amount of intelligence.* —*intr.v.* **amounted, amounting, amounts.** **1.** To add up in number or quantity: *The total purchase amounts to ten dollars.* **2.** To be equivalent or tantamount: *accusations amounting to an indictment.* [From Middle English *amounten*, to rise, from Old French *amonter*, from *amont*, upward, "to the mountain" : *a-*, to, from Latin *ad-* + *mont*, mountain, from Latin *mōns* (see **men-²** in Appendix*).]

a·mour (ə-mŏŏr') *n.* A love affair, especially an illicit one: *"the amours of an empress . . . are seldom susceptible of much sentimental delicacy."* (Gibbon). [Middle English, from Old French, from Old Provençal *amor*, from Latin *amor*, love, from *amāre*, to love. See **amma** in Appendix.*]

a·mour-pro·pre (ə-mŏŏr'prôp'r') *n.* Self-respect. [French, "self-love."]

A·moy (ä-moi', ə-moi'). **1.** An island of southern Fukien Province, southeast China, in the Formosa Strait, about 300 miles northeast of Hong Kong. **2.** A major industrial city and port on this island. Population, 308,000.

am·pe·lop·sis (ăm'pə-lŏp'sĭs) *n.* Any of several woody vines of the genus *Ampelopsis*, having small greenish or yellowish flowers. [New Latin *Ampelopsis* : Greek *ampelos*, grapevine, perhaps from Mediterranean + -OPSIS.]

am·per·age (ăm'pər-ĭj, ăm'pîr'ĭj) *n.* The strength of an electric current expressed in amperes.

am·pere (ăm'pîr') *n. Abbr.* **A** **1.** A unit of electric current in the meter-kilogram-second system. It is the steady current that when flowing in straight parallel wires of infinite length and negligible cross section, separated by a distance of one meter in free space, produces a force between the wires of 2×10^{-7} newtons per meter of length. **2.** A unit in the International System specified as one International coulomb per second and equal to 0.999835 ampere. Also shortened to "amp." See **measurement.** [After André Marie AMPÈRE.]

Am·père (äN-pâr'), **André Marie.** 1775–1836. French mathematician and physicist; regarded as father of electrodynamics.

am·pere-hour (ăm'pîr-our') *n. Abbr.* **A·h** The electric charge transferred past a specified circuit point by a current of one ampere in one hour.

am·pere-turn (ăm'pîr-tûrn') *n. Abbr.* **A·turn** A unit of magnetomotive force in the meter-kilogram-second system equal to the magnetomotive force around a path linking one turn of a conducting loop carrying a current of one ampere.

am·per·sand (ăm'pər-sănd') *n.* The character or sign (&) representing *and.* [Contraction of *"and per se and," "& (the sign) by itself (equals) and."*]

am·phet·a·mine (ăm-fĕt'ə-mēn', -mĭn) *n.* **1.** A colorless volatile liquid, $C_9H_{13}N$, used primarily as a central nervous system stimulant. **2.** A phosphate or sulfate of amphetamine, similarly used. [A(LPHA) M(ETHYL) PH(ENYL) ET(HYL) AMINE.]

amphi-. Indicates: **1.** On both sides or ends, or on all sides; for example, **amphipod. 2.** Around; for example, **amphitheceum.** [Latin, from Greek, from *amphi*, around, on both sides, on all sides. See **ambhi** in Appendix.*]

am·phi·ar·thro·sis (ăm'fē-är-thrō'sĭs) *n., pl.* **-ses** (-sēz'). A relatively immobile joint between bony surfaces connected by ligaments or elastic cartilage. [New Latin : AMPHI- + ARTHROSIS.]

am·phib·i·an (ăm-fĭb'ē-ən) *n.* **1.** Any of various cold-blooded, smooth-skinned vertebrate organisms of the class Amphibia, such as a frog, toad, or salamander, characteristically hatching as aquatic larvae that breathe by means of gills and metamorphosing to an adult form having air-breathing lungs. **2.** Any amphibious organism. **3.** An aircraft that can take off and land either on land or on water. **4.** A vehicle that can move over land and on water. —*adj.* Of or pertaining to an amphibian, especially one of the Amphibia. [From New Latin *Amphibia*, plural of *amphibium*, an amphibian, from Greek *amphibion*, neuter of *amphibios*, AMPHIBIOUS.]

am·phi·bi·ot·ic (ăm'fĭ-bī-ŏt'ĭk) *adj.* Living in water during an early stage of development and on land during the adult stage.

am·phib·i·ous (ăm-fĭb'ē-əs) *adj.* **1.** Living or able to live both on land and in water. **2.** Able to operate on both land and water: *amphibious military vehicles.* **3.** Of a mixed or twofold nature. [Greek *amphibios*, "living a double life" : AMPHI- + *bios*, life (see **gwei-** in Appendix*).] —**am·phib'i·ous·ly** *adv.* —**am·phib'i·ous·ness** *n.*

am·phi·bole (ăm'fĭ-bōl') *n.* Any of a large group of structurally similar hydrated double silicate minerals including hornblende and a type of asbestos, containing various combinations of sodium, calcium, magnesium, iron, and aluminum. [French, from Late Latin *amphibolus*, ambiguous (from its many varieties), from Greek *amphibolos*, doubtful, from *amphiballein*, to throw around, doubt : *amphi-* + *ballein*, to throw (see **gwel-¹** in Appendix*).] —**am'phi·bol'ic** (-bŏl'ĭk) *adj.*

am·phib·o·lite (ăm-fĭb'ə-līt') *n.* A chiefly amphibole rock with minor plagioclase and little quartz. [AMPHIBOL(E) + -ITE.]

am·phi·bol·o·gy (ăm'fĭ-bŏl'ə-jē) *n., pl.* **-gies.** Also **am·phib·o·ly** (ăm-fĭb'ə-lē) *pl.* **-lies.** **1.** Ambiguity arising from a grammatical construction that can be understood in more than one way. **2.** A statement containing such ambiguity. [Middle English *amphibologie*, from Late Latin *amphibologia*, from *amphibolia*, from Greek *amphibolia*, from *amphibolos*, ambiguous. See **amphibole.**] —**am·phib'o·log'i·cal** (ăm-fĭb'ə-lŏj'ĭ-kəl) *adj.* —**am·phib'o·log'i·cal·ly** *adv.*

am·phib·o·lous (ăm-fĭb'ə-ləs) *adj.* Characterized by amphibology; having two meanings; ambiguous; equivocal. [From Greek *amphibolos.* See **amphibole.**]

am·phi·brach (ăm'fĭ-brăk') *n. Prosody.* A trisyllabic metrical foot having one accented or long syllable between two unaccented or short syllables (˘¯˘), as in *re·mem'ber.* [Latin *amphibrachys*, from Greek *amphibrakhus*, "short at both ends" : AMPHI- + *brakhus*, short (see **mreghu-** in Appendix*).]

am·phi·coe·lous (ăm'fĭ-sē'ləs) *adj.* Also **am·phi·ce·lous.** Concave on both ends or sides, as the vertebrae of most fishes are. [Late Greek *amphikoilos* : Greek *amphi-*, on both sides + *koilos*, hollow (see **keu-³** in Appendix*).]

am·phic·ty·o·ny (ăm-fĭk'tē-ə-nē) *n., pl.* **-nies.** In ancient Greece, a group of states sharing a common religious center or

amphora

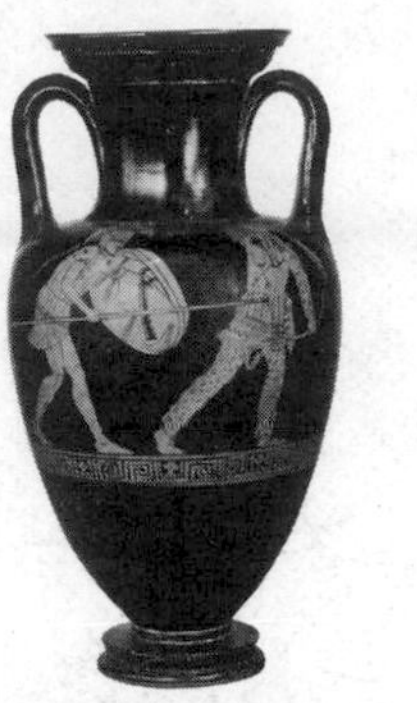

amphora with stand

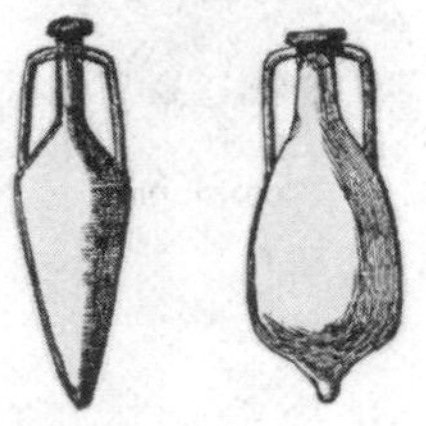

amphorae without stands

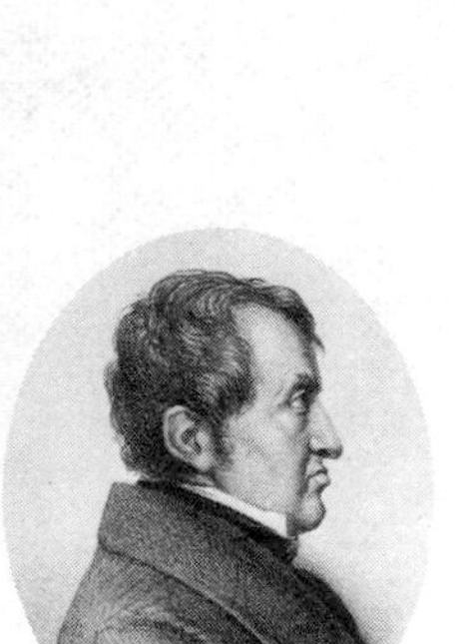

André Marie Ampère

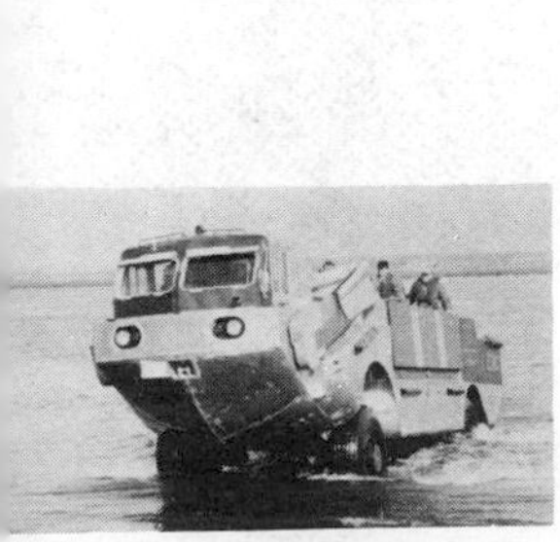

amphibian
U.S. Marine Corps
amphibian coming ashore

ă pat/ā pay/âr care/ä father/b bib/ch church/d deed/ĕ pet/ē be/f fife/g gag/h hat/hw which/ĭ pit/ī pie/îr pier/j judge/k kick/l lid, needle/m mum/n no, sudden/ng thing/ŏ pot/ō toe/ô paw, for/oi noise/ou out/ŏŏ took/ōō boot/p pop/r roar/s sauce/sh ship, dish/

shrine, such as the one at Delphi. [Greek *amphiktuonia,* from *Amphiktuones,* neighbors : AMPHI- + *ktizein,* to found (see **ksei-** in Appendix*).] —**am·phic'ty·on'ic** (-ŏn'ĭk) *adj.*

am·phim·a·cer (ăm-fĭm'ə-sər) *n. Prosody.* A trisyllabic foot having an unaccented or short syllable between two accented or long syllables (¯˘¯), as in *prō domō.* Also called "cretic." [Latin *amphimacrus,* from Greek *amphimakros,* "long at both ends" : AMPHI- + *makros,* long (see **māk-** in Appendix*).]

am·phi·mix·is (ăm'fĭ-mĭk'sĭs) *n.* True sexual reproduction, with fusion of sperm and egg nuclei. [New Latin : AMPHI- + Greek *mixis,* a mingling, from *mignunai,* to mingle (see **meik-** in Appendix*).] —**am'phi·mic'tic** (-mĭk'tĭk) *adj.*

Am·phi·on (ăm-fī'ən). *Greek Mythology.* The son of Zeus and the twin brother of Zethus, with whom he conquered and fortified Thebes, building a wall around the city by charming the stones into place with the music of his magic lyre.

am·phi·ox·us (ăm'fē-ŏk'səs) *n.* A primitive chordate organism, the **lancelet** *(see).* [New Latin, "sharp at both ends" : AMPHI- + Greek *oxus,* sharp (see **ak-** in Appendix*).]

am·phi·pod (ăm'fĭ-pŏd') *n.* Any of numerous small crustaceans of the order Amphipoda, which includes the beach fleas. [From New Latin *Amphipoda,* "having feet on both sides" : AMPHI- + -POD.]

am·phip·ro·style (ăm-fĭp'rō-stīl', ăm'fĭ-prō'stīl') *adj.* Also **am·phip·ro·sty·lar** (ăm-fĭp'rō-stī'lər, ăm'fĭ-prō-stī'lər). *Architecture.* Having a prostyle or set of columns at each end, but none along the sides. [Latin *amphiprostylos,* from Greek *amphiprostulos,* "with pillars in front and behind" : *amphi-,* on both sides + *prostulos,* with pillars in front (see **prostyle**).] —**am·phip'ro·style'** *n.*

am·phis·bae·na (ăm'fĭs-bē'nə) *n.* A mythological serpent having a head at each end of its body. [Latin, from Greek *amphisbaina,* "one that goes in both directions" : *amphis,* both ways, from *amphi-,* on both sides + *bainein,* to go (see **gwā-** in Appendix*).] —**am'phis·bae'nic** *adj.*

am·phi·sty·lar (ăm'fĭ-stī'lər) *adj. Architecture.* Having columns at both front and back or on each side. [From AMPHI- + Greek *stulos;* a pillar (see **stā-** in Appendix*).]

am·phi·the·a·ter (ăm'fə-thē'ə-tər) *n.* Also *chiefly British* **am·phi·the·a·tre. 1.** An oval or round structure having tiers of seats rising gradually outward from an open space or arena at the center. **2.** Any arena where contests are held. **3.** A level area surrounded by upward sloping ground. **4.** An upper, sloping gallery in a theater. [Latin *amphitheatrum,* from Greek *amphitheatron* : AMPHI- + THEATER.] —**am'phi·the·at'ric** (-thē-ăt'rĭk), **am'phi·the·at'ri·cal** *adj.* —**am'phi·the·at'ri·cal·ly** *adv.*

am·phi·the·ci·um (ăm'fĭ-thē'shē-əm, -sē-əm) *n., pl.* **-cia** (-shē-ə, -sē-ə). *Botany.* The outer layer of cells of the spore-containing capsule of a moss. [New Latin : AMPHI- + Greek *thēkion,* diminutive of *thēkē,* a case (see **dhē-¹** in Appendix*).]

am·phit·ri·chous (ăm-fĭt'rĭ-kəs) *adj.* Also **am·phit·ri·chate** (-rĭ-kət). Having a flagellum or flagella at both ends, as certain microorganisms do. [AMPHI- + -TRICHOUS.]

Am·phi·tri·te (ăm'fə-trī'tē). *Greek Mythology.* The wife of Poseidon, goddess of the sea, and one of the Nereids.

am·phit·ro·pous (ăm-fĭt'rə-pəs) *adj. Botany.* Partly inverted, so that the point of attachment is near the middle. Said of an ovule or seed. [AMPHI- + -TROPOUS.]

Am·phit·ry·on (ăm-fĭt'rē-ən). *Greek Mythology.* A king of Thebes and the husband of Alcmene.

am·pho·ra (ăm'fə-rə) *n., pl.* **-rae** (-rē') or **-ras.** A two-handled jar with a narrow neck, used by the ancient Greeks and Romans to carry wine or oil. [Latin *amphora,* from Greek *amphoreus, amphiphoreus* : AMPHI- + *phoreus,* a bearer, from *pherein,* to bear (see **bher-¹** in Appendix*).] —**am'pho·ral** (-rəl) *adj.*

am·pho·ter·ic (ăm'fə-tĕr'ĭk) *adj. Chemistry.* Capable of reacting either as an acid or a base. [From Greek *amphoteros,* either of two, from *amphō,* both. See **amphō-** in Appendix.*]

am·ple (ăm'pəl) *adj.* **-pler, -plest. 1.** Of large or great size, amount, extent, capacity: *an ample living room.* **2.** Large in degree or kind; in abundant measure: *an ample reward.* **3.** Sufficient for a particular need; abundant: *ample provisions for a week.* [Middle English, from Old French, from Latin *amplus*†, wide, ample.] —**am'ple·ness** *n.*

am·plex·i·caul (ăm-plĕk'sĭ-kôl') *adj. Botany.* Having a base that clasps or encircles the stem, as some leaves do. [New Latin *amplexicaulis,* embracing stem : Latin *amplexus,* past participle of *amplectī,* to wind around : AM(BI)- + *plectere,* to plait (see **plek-** in Appendix*) + *caulis,* stem (see **kaul-** in Appendix*).]

am·pli·fi·ca·tion (ăm'plə-fĭ-kā'shən) *n.* **1.** The act or result of amplifying. **2.** An addition to or expansion of any statement or idea. **3.** A statement with such an addition. **4.** *Physics.* **a.** The process of increasing the magnitude of a variable quantity, especially of a voltage or current, without altering any other quality. **b.** The result of such a process.

am·pli·fi·er (ăm'plə-fī'ər) *n.* **1.** One that amplifies, enlarges, or extends. **2.** *Physics.* Any of various devices or electronic circuits that produce amplification.

am·pli·fy (ăm'plə-fī') *v.* **-fied, -fying, -fies.** —*tr.* **1.** To make larger or more powerful; extend; increase. **2.** To add to, as by illustrations; make complete. **3.** To exaggerate. **4.** *Physics.* To produce amplification of. —*intr.* To write or discourse at length; expatiate. [Middle English *amplifien,* from Old French *amplifier,* from Latin *amplificāre* : *amplus,* AMPLE + *facere,* to make (see **dhē-¹** in Appendix*).] —**am'pli·fi·ca'tive** (-fĭ-kā'tĭv), **am·plif'i·ca·to·ry** (ăm-plĭf'ĭ-kə-tôr'ē, -tōr'ē) *adj.*

am·pli·tude (ăm'plə-to͞od', -tyo͞od') *n.* **1.** Greatness of size; magnitude. **2.** Fullness; copiousness. **3.** Breadth or range, as of mind. **4.** *Astronomy.* The angular distance along the horizon from true east or west to the intersection of the vertical circle of a celestial body with the horizon. **5.** *Physics.* The maximum value of a periodically varying quantity. **6.** *Mathematics.* **a.** The maximum ordinate value of a periodic curve. **b.** The angle made with the positive horizontal axis by the vector representation of a complex number. In this sense, also called "argument." [Latin *amplitūdō,* from *amplus,* AMPLE.]

amplitude modulation. *Abbr.* **AM, am** The encoding of a carrier wave by variation of its amplitude in accordance with an input signal. Compare **frequency modulation.**

am·ply (ăm'plē) *adv.* In an ample manner; largely; liberally; sufficiently.

am·poule, am·pule (ăm'po͞ol, -pyo͞ol) *n.* Also **am·pul.** A small glass vial, sealed after filling and used chiefly as a container for a hypodermic injection solution. [French, from Old French, from Latin *ampulla,* AMPULLA.]

am·pul·la (ăm-po͝ol'ə, -pŭl'ə) *n., pl.* **-pullae** (-po͝ol'ē, -pŭl'ē). **1.** A nearly round bottle with two handles used by the ancient Romans for wine, oil, or perfume. **2.** *Ecclesiastical.* **a.** A container used in the church for wine or water at the Eucharist. **b.** A vessel for consecrated wine or holy oil. **3.** *Anatomy.* A small dilation in a canal or duct, especially in the semicircular canal of the ear. [Latin, diminutive of *amp(h)ora,* AMPHORA.] —**am·pul'lar** (-ər) *adj.*

am·pul·la·ceous (ăm'po͝o-lā'shəs) *adj.* **1.** Of or concerning an ampulla. **2.** Resembling an ampulla; bladder-shaped. [Latin *ampullāceus* : AMPULL(A) + -ACEOUS.]

am·pu·tate (ăm'pyo͞o-tāt') *tr.v.* **-tated, -tating, -tates.** To cut off (a part of the body), especially by surgery. [Latin *amputāre,* to cut around : AM(BI)- + *putāre,* to cut (see **peuə-²** in Appendix*).] —**am'pu·ta'tion** *n.* —**am'pu·ta'tor** (-tā'tər) *n.*

am·pu·tee (ăm'pyo͞o-tē') *n.* A person who has had one or more limbs removed by amputation.

am·ri·ta (ŭm-rē'tə) *n.* Also **am·ree·ta.** *Hindu Mythology.* **1.** The ambrosia, prepared by the gods, that bestows immortality. **2.** The immortality achieved by drinking this ambrosia. [Sanskrit *amṛta,* "deathless" : *a-,* without (see **ne** in Appendix*) + *mṛta,* death (see **mer-²** in Appendix*).]

Am·rit·sar (ŭm-rĭt'sər). A city of India, in western Punjab; the center of the Sikh religion. Population, 376,000.

Am·ster·dam (ăm'stər-dăm'). **1.** *Abbr.* **Amst.** The constitutional capital of the Netherlands, a commercial and port city on the IJsselmeer. Population, 868,000. **2.** A city and industrial center of eastern New York State. Population, 29,000.

amt. amount.

am·trac (ăm'trăk') *n.* Also **am·track.** A small, armed, amphibious vehicle first used in World War II to carry troops from ship to shore. [AM(PHIBIOUS) + TRAC(TOR).]

amu *Physics.* atomic mass unit.

a·muck (ə-mŭk') *adv.* Also **a·mok** (ə-mŭk', ə-mŏk'). **1.** In a frenzy to do violence or kill. **2.** In a blind, heedless manner. Used in the phrase *run amuck.* —*adj.* Crazed with murderous frenzy. [Malay *amok,* furious attack.]

A·mu Dar·ya (ä'mo͞o där'yə). Ancient name **Ox·us** (ŏk'səs). A river of central Asia, rising in the Pamirs and flowing about 1,500 miles generally north to the Aral Sea, forming part of the Soviet-Afghanistan border on its course.

am·u·let (ăm'yə lĭt) *n.* An object worn, especially around the neck, as a charm against evil or injury. [Latin *amulētum*†.]

A·mund·sen (ä'mən-sən), **Roald.** 1872–1928. Norwegian explorer; first to reach the South Pole (1911).

A·mund·sen Gulf (ä'mən-sən). An inlet of the Arctic Ocean bounded by the mainland Northwest Territories on the south, Banks Island on the north, and Victoria Island on the west.

A·mund·sen Sea (ä'mən-sən). A part of the South Pacific Ocean, off the Antarctic coast, west of Ross Sea.

A·mur (ä-mo͝or'). A river of eastern Asia, rising in northern Mongolia and flowing about 2,700 miles southeast along the Soviet-Chinese border and northeast to the Sea of Okhotsk.

a·muse (ə-myo͞oz') *tr.v.* **amused, amusing, amuses. 1.** To occupy in an agreeable, pleasing, or entertaining fashion. **2.** To cause to laugh or smile by giving pleasure. **3.** *Archaic.* To delude; deceive; bemuse. [Old French *amuser,* "to cause to idle away time" : *a,* to, from Latin *ad-* + *muser,* to idle, MUSE.] —**a·mus'a·ble** *adj.* —**a·mus'er** *n.*

Synonyms: *amuse, entertain, divert, regale.* These verbs refer to actions that provide pleasure, especially as a means of passing time. *Amuse* is the least specific. *Entertain* suggests more formal, deliberate acts of bringing about pleasure. *Divert* implies distraction from worrisome thought or care. *Regale* means to entertain lavishly.

a·muse·ment (ə-myo͞oz'mənt) *n.* **1.** The state of being amused, entertained, or pleased. **2.** That which amuses.

amusement park. A commercially operated enterprise that supplies refreshments and various forms of entertainment.

a·mus·ing (ə-myo͞o'zĭng) *adj.* **1.** Entertaining or pleasing. **2.** Arousing laughter. —**a·mus'ing·ly** *adv.* —**a·mus'ing·ness** *n.*

a·mu·sive (ə-myo͞o'zĭv, -sĭv) *adj.* Providing amusement.

a·myg·dale (ə-mĭg'dāl) *n.* An amygdule. [Greek *amugdalē,* ALMOND.]

a·myg·da·line (ə-mĭg'də-lĭn, -līn') *adj.* Of, pertaining to, or resembling an almond. [Latin *amygdalīnus,* from Greek *amugdalinos,* from *amugdalē,* ALMOND.]

a·myg·da·loid (ə-mĭg'də-loid') *n.* A volcanic rock containing many amygdules. —*adj.* Also **a·myg·da·loi·dal** (ə-mĭg'də-loid'l). **1.** Almond-shaped. **2.** *Geology.* Resembling amygdaloid. [Latin *amygdala,* ALMOND + -OID.]

a·myg·dule (ə-mĭg'dyo͞ol) *n.* A small gas bubble in lava or other igneous rock filled with secondary minerals such as zeolite, cal-

amulet

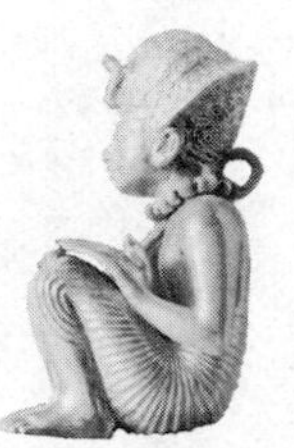

Egyptian

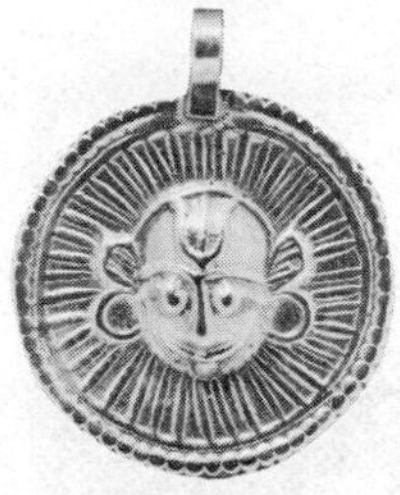

Indian

Moroccan

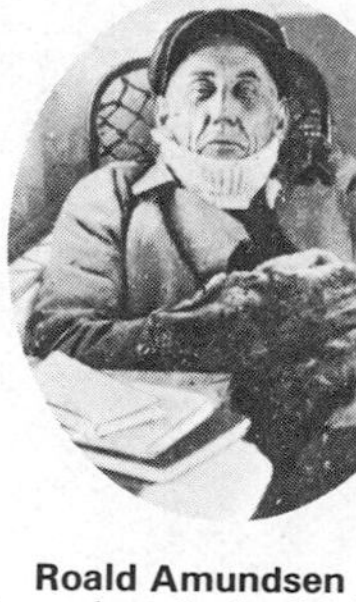

Roald Amundsen
The explorer in the dirigible *Norge* on his 1926 flight over the North Pole

cite, or quartz. [Latin *amygdala*, ALMOND (from its almondlike shape) + (NOD)ULE.]

am·yl (ăm′əl) *n.* The univalent organic radical C_5H_{11}, occurring in several isomeric forms in many organic compounds. Also called "pentyl." [Latin *amylum*, AMYLUM.]

am·y·la·ceous (ăm′ə-lā′shəs) *adj.* Of, pertaining to, or resembling starch; starchy. [AMYL(O)- + -ACEOUS.]

amyl acetate. An organic compound, $CH_3COOC_5H_{11}$, used commercially in isomeric mixtures as a flavoring agent, as a paint and lacquer solvent, and in the preparation of penicillin. Also called "banana oil," "pear oil."

amyl alcohol. Any of eight isomers of the composition $C_5H_{11}OH$, one of which, $CH_3CH_2CH(CH_3)CH_2OH$, is the principal constituent of fusel oil.

am·y·lase (ăm′ə-lās′, -lāz′) *n.* Any of various enzymes that convert starch to sugar. [AMYL(O)- + -ASE.]

amylo–, amyl–. Indicates starch; for example, **amylolysis, amylase.** [From Latin *amylum*, starch, AMYLUM.]

am·y·loid (ăm′ə-loid′) *n.* **1.** A starchlike substance. **2.** *Pathology.* A hard protein deposit resulting from degeneration of tissue. —*adj.* Starchlike. [AMYL(O)- + -OID.]

am·y·lol·y·sis (ăm′ə-lŏl′ə-sĭs) *n.* The enzymatic conversion of starch to sugars. [AMYLO- + -LYSIS.] **—am′y·lo·lyt′ic** (-lō-lĭt′ĭk) *adj.*

am·y·lop·sin (ăm′ə-lŏp′sĭn) *n.* The starch-digesting amylase produced by the pancreas. [AMYLO- + (TRY)PSIN.]

am·y·lose (ăm′ə-lōs′, -lōz′) *n.* The relatively soluble portion of starch. [AMYL(O)- + -OSE.]

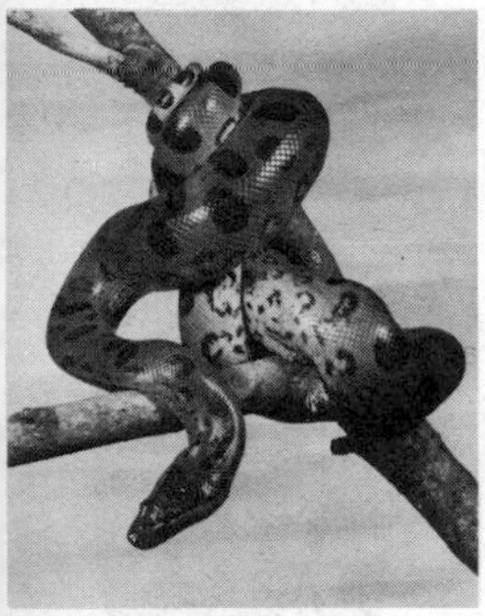

anaconda

am·y·lum (ăm′ə-ləm) *n.* Starch. [Latin, from Greek *amulon*, starch, the finest flour, from neuter of *amulos*, "not ground in a mill," *a-*, not + *mulē*, mill (see **mele-** in Appendix*).]

a·my·o·to·ni·a (ā′mī-ə-tō′nē-ə) *n.* Lack of muscle tone. [New Latin : A- (without) + MYO- + -TONIA.]

an[1] (ăn, ən). The indefinite article, a form of *a* used before words beginning with a vowel or with an unpronounced *h: an elephant; an hour.* See Usage note at **a.** [Middle English *an*, Old English *ān*, one. See **oino-** in Appendix.*]

an[2] (ăn, ən) *conj.* Also **an′.** *Archaic.* And if; if: *"An I may hide my face, let me play Thisby too."* (Shakespeare). [Middle English *an*, Old English *an*, short for AND.]

an–. Indicates not or without; for example, **anaerobe, anosmia.** [Greek *an-*, not, without, lacking. See **ne** in Appendix.*]

–an, –n. Indicates: **1.** Pertaining to, belonging to; or resembling; for example, **cetacean, Mexican. 2.** Believing in or adhering to; for example, **Mohammedan. 3.** *Chemistry.* **a.** A heterocyclic compound; for example, **furan. b.** An anhydride of a carbohydrate; for example, **dextran.** See **-ean, -ian.** [Latin *-ānus*, adjectival suffix.]

An *Physics.* actinon.

AN Anglo-Norman.

an. 1. before (Latin *ante*). **2.** in the year (Latin *annō*).

A.N. Anglo-Norman.

an·a[1] (ăn′ə, ä′nə) *n., pl.* **ana** or **anas. 1.** A collection of various materials that reflect the character of a person or place. **2.** An item in such a collection. [From -ANA.]

an·a[2] (ăn′ə) *adv. Abbr.* **aa** *Pharmacology.* Both in the same quantity; of each. Used to refer to ingredients in prescriptions. [Middle English, from Medieval Latin, from Greek, at the rate of, according to, originally "up." See **an**[1] in Appendix.*]

ana–. Indicates: **1.** Upward progression; for example, **anabolism, anaphase. 2.** Reversion; for example, **anaplasia. 3.** Renewal or intensification; for example, **anaphylaxis.** [In borrowed Greek compounds, *ana-* indicates: 1. Upward, as in **anabasis.** 2. According to, as in **analogy.** 3. Back, as in **anabiosis.** 4. Backward, reversed, as in **anachronism.** 5. Again, anew, as in **anaphora.** Greek, from *ana*, up, throughout, according to. See **an**[1] in Appendix.*]

–ana, –iana. Indicates a collection of assorted material, as facts, anecdotes, and pictures, suggestive of the character of a notable place or person; for example, **Americana.** [New Latin, from Latin *-āna*, "the things pertaining to," neuter plural of *-ānus*, -AN.]

an·a·bae·na (ăn′ə-bē′nə) *n.* Any of various freshwater algae of the genus *Anabaena*, sometimes occurring in drinking water and causing a bad taste and odor. [New Latin *Anabaena*, from Greek *anabainein*, to go up (from their periodic rise to the surface) : *ana-*, up + *bainein*, to go (see **gwā-** in Appendix*).]

an·a·ban·tid (ăn′ə-băn′tĭd) *n.* Any of various tropical freshwater fishes of the family Anabantidae, which includes the **Siamese fighting fish** and the **climbing perch** *(both of which see).* [New Latin *Anabantidae* : *Anabas* (stem *anabant-*), type genus, from Greek *anabas*, aorist participle of *anabainein*, to go up (see **anabaena**) + -IDAE.]

An·a·bap·tist (ăn′ə-băp′tĭst) *n.* A member of one of the radical movements of the Reformation of the 16th century that insisted that only adult baptism was valid and held that true Christians should not bear arms, use force, or hold government office. [New Latin *anabaptista*, "one who is rebaptized," from Late Greek *anabaptizein*, to baptize again : Greek *ana-*, again + *baptizein*, to baptize, from *baptein*, to dip (see **gwebh-**[1] in Appendix*).] **—An′a·bap′tism′** *n.* **—An′a·bap′tist** *adj.*

an·a·bas (ăn′ə-băs) *n.* Any member of the genus *Anabas*, freshwater fishes of Africa and Asia, resembling perch. [New Latin *Anabas.* See **anabantid.**]

a·nab·a·sis (ə-năb′ə-sĭs) *n., pl.* **-ses** (-sēz′). A large-scale military advance; specifically, the Greek expedition across Asia Minor (401 B.C.) led by Cyrus the Younger of Persia, as described by Xenophon. [Greek, a going up or forward, from *anabainein*, to go up. See **anabaena.**]

an·a·bat·ic (ăn′ə-băt′ĭk) *adj.* Of or pertaining to rising wind currents. [Late Greek, *anabatikos*, from Greek, ability to rise, from *anabainein*, to go up. See **anabaena.**]

an·a·bi·o·sis (ăn′ə-bī-ō′sĭs) *n.* A restoring to life from a deathlike condition; resuscitation. [New Latin, from Greek *anabiōsis*, from *anabioun*, to come back to life : *ana-*, back + *bioun*, to live, from *bios*, life (see **gwei-** in Appendix*).]

an·a·bi·ot·ic (ăn′ə-bī-ŏt′ĭk) *adj.* In a state resembling death, but capable of resuscitation. —*n. Medicine.* A resuscitating agent.

a·nab·o·lism (ə-năb′ə-lĭz′əm) *n.* The metabolic process by which simple substances are synthesized into the complex materials of living tissue; constructive metabolism. Compare **catabolism.** [ANA- ("constructive") + (META)BOLISM.] **—an′a·bol′ic** (ăn′ə-bŏl′ĭk) *adj.*

a·nab·o·lite (ə-năb′ə-līt′) *n.* A product of anabolism. **—a·nab′o·lit′ic** (-lĭt′ĭk) *adj.*

a·nach·o·rism (ə-năk′ə-rĭz′əm) *n.* Something out of place or unsuited to its location; a geographical incongruity. Compare **anachronism.** [Greek *ana-*, back + *khōrion*, place, diminutive of *khōros*, place, space, spot (see **ghē-** in Appendix*) + -ISM.]

a·nach·ro·nism (ə-năk′rə-nĭz′əm) *n.* **1.** The representation of something as existing or happening at other than its proper or historical time. **2.** Anything out of its proper time. [French *anachronisme*, from Greek *anakhronismos*, from *anakhronizein*, to be an anachronism : *ana-*, backward, reversed + *khronizein*, to belong to a particular time, from *khronos*, time (see **chronic**).] **—a·nach′ro·nis′tic, a·nach′ro·nis′ti·cal, a·nach′ro·nous** *adj.* **—a·nach′ro·nis′ti·cal·ly, a·nach′ro·nous·ly** *adv.*

an·a·cli·sis (ăn′ə-klī′sĭs, ə-năk′lə-sĭs) *n.* Psychological dependence on others. [New Latin, from Greek *anaklisis*, a leaning back, from *anaklinein*, to lean on : *ana-*, upon + *klinein*, to lean (see **klei-** in Appendix*).] **—an′a·clit′ic** (-klĭt′ĭk) *adj.*

an·a·co·lu·thon (ăn′ə-kə-lōō′thŏn′) *n., pl.* **-thons** or **-tha** (-thə). An abrupt change within a sentence to a second grammatical construction inconsistent with the first, sometimes used for rhetorical effect; for example, *I warned him that if he continues to drink, what will become of him?* [Late Latin, from Greek *anakolouthon*, inconsistent, from *anakolouthos*, inconsistent : *an-*, not + *akolouthos*, following : *a-*, together + *keleuthos*†, path.] **—an′a·co·lu′thic** *adj.*

an·a·con·da (ăn′ə-kŏn′də) *n.* **1.** A large, nonvenomous, arboreal snake, *Eunectes murinus*, of tropical South America, that constricts its prey in its coils. **2.** Any of several similar or related snakes. [Unexplained variant of Singhalese *henakandayā*, perhaps from Dravidian.]

An·a·con·da (ăn′ə-kŏn′də). A city and copper-mining center of southwestern Montana. Population, 12,000.

A·nac·re·on (ə-năk′rē-ən, -ŏn′). 572?–488? B.C. Greek poet; noted for his songs praising love and wine.

A·nac·re·on·tic (ə-năk′rē-ŏn′tĭk) *adj.* In the manner of the poems of Anacreon; specifically, convivial or amatory. —*n.* An Anacreontic poem.

an·a·cru·sis (ăn′ə-krōō′sĭs) *n. Prosody.* One or more unstressed syllables at the beginning of a line of verse, before the reckoning of the normal meter begins. [New Latin, from Greek *anakrousis*, the beginning of a tune, from *anakrouein*, to thrust off : *ana-*, back + *krouein*, to push (see **kreu-**[2] in Appendix*).]

an·a·dem (ăn′ə-dĕm′) *n. Poetic.* A head wreath or garland. [Latin *anadēma*, from Greek, from *anadein*, to bind up : *ana-*, back, up + *dein*, to bind (see **dē-** in Appendix*).]

an·a·di·plo·sis (ăn′ə-dĭ-plō′sĭs) *n.* Rhetorical repetition of the word or phrase that ends one phrase at the beginning of the next phrase. [Latin *anadiplōsis*, from Greek, from *anadiploun*, to reduplicate : *ana-*, again + *diploun*, to double, from *diplous*, double (see **dwō** in Appendix*).]

a·nad·ro·mous (ə-năd′rə-məs) *adj.* Migrating up rivers from the sea to breed in fresh water: *Salmon are anadromous.* Compare **catadromous.** [Greek *anadromos*, a running up : *ana-*, up + *dromos*, a running (see **der-**[1] in Appendix*).]

A·na·dyr (ŭ-nŭ-dĭr′). Also **A·na·dir.** A river of the Soviet Union, rising in northeastern Siberia and flowing 450 miles south, east, and northeast to the Gulf of Anadyr, an inlet of the Bering Sea.

a·nae·mi·a. Variant of **anemia.**

an·aer·obe (ăn′ə-rōb′, ăn-âr′ōb′) *n.* Also **an·aer·o·bi·um** (ăn′ə-rō′bē-əm, ăn′âr-ō′-) *pl.* **-bia** (-bē-ə). A microorganism, as a bacterium, able to live in the absence of free oxygen. [AN- (not) + AEROBE.] **—an′aer·o′bic** (ăn′ə-rō′bĭk, -âr-ō′bĭk) *adj.* **—an′aer·o′bic·al·ly** *adv.*

an·aes·the·sia. Variant of **anesthesia.**

an·a·glyph (ăn′ə-glĭf′) *n.* An ornament carved in low relief. [Greek *anagluphos*, wrought in low relief, from *anagluphein*, to carve in relief : *ana-*, up + *gluphein*, to carve (see **gleubh-** in Appendix*).] **—an′a·glyph′ic, an′a·glyp′tic** (-glĭp′tĭk) *adj.*

an·a·go·ge (ăn′ə-gō′jē) *n.* Also **an·a·go·gy.** A mystical interpretation of a word, passage, or text; specifically, scriptural exegesis that detects allusions to heaven or the afterlife. [Late Latin *anagōgē*, from Late Greek, spiritual uplift, from *anagein*, to uplift, lead up : *ana-*, up + *agein*, to lead (see **ag-** in Appendix*).] **—an′a·gog′ic** (-gŏj′ĭk), **an′a·gog′i·cal** *adj.* **—an′a·gog′i·cal·ly** *adv.*

an·a·gram (ăn′ə-grăm′) *n.* A word or phrase formed by reordering the letters of another word or phrase. [French *anagramme*, from New Latin *anagramma* : ANA- + -GRAM.] **—an′a·gram·mat′ic** (-grə-măt′ĭk) *adj.* **—an′a·gram·mat′i·cal·ly** *adv.*

an·a·gram·ma·tize (ăn′ə-grăm′ə-tīz′) *tr.v.* **-tized, -tizing, -tizes.** To make an anagram of.

An·a·heim (ăn′ə-hīm′). A city in southwestern California, near Los Angeles, site of Disneyland. Population, 104,000.

A·ná·huac (ə-nä′wäk). **1.** The heavily populated and industrially developed central plateau area of Mexico, including the states of Mexico and Puebla and the Federal District. **2.** A former Aztec empire in the valley of Mexico.

a·nal (ā′nəl) *adj.* **1.** Of, pertaining to, or near the anus. **2.** *Psychoanalysis.* Of, pertaining to, or denoting: **a.** The stage of psychosexual development of the infant in which gratification is derived from sensations associated with the anus. **b.** Personality traits originating during toilet training and distinguished as **anal-expulsive** or **anal-retentive** *(both of which see).* [New Latin *analis,* from Latin *ānus,* ANUS.]

anal. 1. analogous; analogy. **2.** analysis; analytic.

a·nal·cime (ə-năl′sēm′) *n.* Also **a·nal·cite** (-sīt′). *Mineralogy.* A white or light-colored zeolite, found in diabase and certain basalts. [French, from Greek *analkimos,* weak (from its weak electric power) : AN- (not) + *alkimos,* stout, brave, from *alkē,* strength (see **alek-** in Appendix*).]

an·a·lects (ăn′ə-lĕkts′) *pl.n.* Also **an·a·lec·ta** (ăn′ə-lĕk′tə). Selections or parts of a literary work or group of works. [Latin *analecta,* from Greek *analekta,* neuter plural of *analektos,* select, choice, from *analegein,* to pick up, gather : *ana-,* up + *legein,* to gather (see **leg-** in Appendix*).] —**an′a·lec′tic** *adj.*

an·a·lem·ma (ăn′ə-lĕm′ə) *n.* A graduated scale, in the shape of a figure eight, indicating the sun's declination and the equation of time for every day of the year, usually found on sundials and globes. [Latin, a sundial, from Greek *analēmma,* a support, from *analambanein,* to take up, restore. See **analeptic.**]

an·a·lep·tic (ăn′ə-lĕp′tĭk) *adj.* Restorative or stimulating. —*n.* An analeptic medication. [Greek *analēptikos,* from *analambanein,* to take up, restore : *ana-,* up + *lambanein,* to take (see **slagw-** in Appendix*).]

a·nal-ex·pul·sive (ā′nəl-ĭk-spŭl′sĭv) *adj. Psychoanalysis.* Designating personality traits such as conceit, suspicion, ambition, and generosity, originating in habits, attitudes, or values associated with infantile pleasure in the expulsion of feces.

anal fin. An unpaired fin in fishes, located on the ventral median line between the tail and the anus.

an·al·ge·si·a (ăn′əl-jē′zē-ə, -zhə) *n. Pathology.* Inability to feel pain while conscious. [New Latin, from Greek *analgēsia,* want of feeling : AN- (not) + Greek *algēsia,* sense of pain, from *algein,* to feel pain, from *algos,* pain (see **algo-**).]

an·al·ge·sic (ăn′əl-jē′zĭk, -sĭk) *n.* A medication that reduces or eliminates pain. —*adj.* Of or causing analgesia.

analog computer. Also **analogue computer.** A computer in which numerical data are represented by analogous physical magnitudes or electrical signals. Compare **digital computer.**

an·a·log·i·cal (ăn′ə-lŏj′ĭ-kəl) *adj.* Of, pertaining to, composed of, or based upon an analogy. —**an′a·log′i·cal·ly** *adv.*

a·nal·o·gize (ə-năl′ə-jīz′) *v.* **-gized, -gizing, -gizes.** —*tr.* To make an analogy to. —*intr.* To think or reason by analogy.

a·nal·o·gous (ə-năl′ə-gəs) *adj. Abbr.* **anal. 1.** Similar or alike in a way that permits the drawing of an analogy. **2.** *Biology.* Similar in function but not in evolutionary origin, as the gills of a fish and the lungs of a mammal. Compare **homologous.** [Latin *analogus,* from Greek *analogos,* proportionate, resembling : *ana-,* according to + *logos,* proportion, word, from *legein,* to speak (see **leg-** in Appendix*).] —**a·nal′o·gous·ly** *adv.* —**a·nal′o·gous·ness** *n.*

Usage: The following deals with appropriate prepositions after *analogous* and *analogy.* Two or more things may be said to be *analogous in* specified qualities or respects, in which case one is *analogous to* or *with* the others. We speak of the *analogy of* or *between* things or of the *analogy of* one *to* or *with* another.

an·a·logue (ăn′ə-lôg′, -lŏg′) *n.* Also **an·a·log. 1.** Something that bears an analogy to something else. **2.** *Biology.* An organ or structure that is similar in function to one in another kind of organism, but is of dissimilar evolutionary origin. **3.** *Chemistry.* A structural derivative of a parent compound. [French, from Greek *analogos,* ANALOGOUS.]

a·nal·o·gy (ə-năl′ə-jē) *n., pl.* **-gies.** *Abbr.* **anal. 1.** Correspondence in some respects, especially in function or position, between things otherwise dissimilar. **2.** A form of logical inference, or an instance of it, based on the assumption that if two things are known to be alike in some respects, then they must be alike in other respects. **3.** *Linguistics.* The creation of forms on the basis of a proportion $a : b = c : x$. For example, in the set *sing* : *sung* = *bring* : *x, x* = *brung* on the analogy of *sung.* —See Synonyms at **likeness.** —See Usage note at **analogous.** [Latin *analogia,* from Greek, from *analogos,* ANALOGOUS.]

an·al·pha·bet·ic (ăn-ăl′fə-bĕt′ĭk) *adj.* **1.** Not alphabetical. **2.** Unable to read; illiterate. —*n.* An illiterate. [Greek *analphabētos* : AN- (not) + *alphabētos,* ALPHABET.]

a·nal-re·ten·tive (ā′nəl-rĭ-tĕn′tĭv) *adj. Psychoanalysis.* Designating personality traits such as meticulousness, avarice, and obstinacy, originating in habits, attitudes, or values associated with infantile pleasure in retention of feces.

a·nal·y·sand (ə-năl′ə-sănd′) *n.* A person who is being psychoanalyzed. [From ANALYZE (by analogy with MULTIPLICAND).]

a·nal·y·sis (ə-năl′ə-sĭs) *n., pl.* **-ses** (-sēz′). *Abbr.* **anal. 1.** The separation of an intellectual or substantial whole into constituents for individual study. Compare **synthesis. 2.** A statement of the results of such a study. **3.** *Chemistry.* **a.** Separation of a substance into constituents or the determination of its composition. **b.** The stated findings of such separation or determination. **4.** *Mathematics.* **a.** Methodology principally involving algebra and calculus as opposed to synthetic geometry, group theory, and number theory. **b.** The method of proof in which a known truth is sought as a consequence of reasoning from the thing to be proved. **5.** Psychoanalysis. [New Latin, from Greek *analusis,* a releasing, from *analuein,* to undo : *ana-,* back + *luein,* to loosen (see **leu-**[1] in Appendix*).]

analysis si·tus (sī′təs). A term formerly used for the mathematical discipline **topology** *(see).* [New Latin, "analysis of region."]

an·a·lyst (ăn′ə-lĭst) *n.* **1.** One who analyzes. **2.** A licensed practitioner of **psychoanalysis** *(see).*

an·a·lyt·ic (ăn′ə-lĭt′ĭk) *adj.* Also **an·a·lyt·i·cal** (-ĭ-kəl). *Abbr.* **anal. 1.** Of or pertaining to analysis. **2.** Dividing into elemental parts or basic principles. **3.** Reasoning from a perception of the parts and interrelations of a subject; using analysis. **4.** *Linguistics.* Expressing a grammatical category by using two or more words instead of an inflected form: *English is analytic in its use of the comparative "more beautiful" insteau of "beautifuler."* [Late Latin *analyticus,* from Greek *analutikos,* from *analuein,* to resolve. See **analysis.**] —**an′a·lyt′i·cal·ly** *adv.*

analytical balance. A balance for chemical analysis.

analytic geometry. The analysis of geometric structures and properties principally by algebraic operations on variables defined in terms of position coordinates.

an·a·lyt·ics (ăn′ə-lĭt′ĭks) *n.* Plural in form, used with a singular verb. The branch of logic dealing with analysis.

an·a·lyze (ăn′ə-līz′) *tr.v.* **-lyzed, -lyzing, -lyzes. 1.** To separate into parts or basic principles so as to determine the nature of the whole; examine methodically. **2.** To make a chemical analysis of. **3.** To make a mathematical analysis of. **4.** To psychoanalyze. [French *analyser,* from *analyse,* analysis, from New Latin ANALYSIS.] —**an′a·lyz′a·ble** *adj.* —**an′a·ly·za′tion** *n.* —**an′a·lyz′er** *n.*

A·nam. See **Annam.**

an·am·ne·sis (ăn′ăm-nē′sĭs) *n., pl.* **-ses** (-sēz′). **1.** *Psychology.* Recalling to memory; recollection. **2.** *Medicine.* The complete case history of a patient. [New Latin, from Greek *anamnēsis,* from *anamimnēskein,* to recall to memory : *ana-,* back + *mimnēskein,* to call to mind (see **men-**[1] in Appendix*).] —**an′am·nes′tic** (-nĕs′tĭk) *adj.* —**an′am·nes′ti·cal·ly** *adv.*

an·a·mor·phic (ăn′ə-môr′fĭk) *adj.* Having, producing, or designating different optical magnification along mutually perpendicular radii: *an anamorphic lens.* [ANA- + -MORPHIC.]

an·a·mor·pho·sis (ăn′ə-môr′fə-sĭs, -môr-fō′sĭs) *n., pl.* **-ses** (-sēz′). *Optics.* An image distorted so that it can be viewed without distortion only from a special angle or with a special instrument. [Medieval Greek *anamorphōsis,* "a forming anew," from Late Greek *anamorphoun,* to transform : *ana-,* again + *morphoun,* to form, from *morphē,* form (see **mer-bh-** in Appendix*).]

an·an·drous (ăn-ăn′drəs) *adj. Botany.* Having no stamens. [Greek *anandros,* "without a man" : AN- (without) + *anēr* (stem *andr-*), man (see **ner-**[2] in Appendix*).]

An·a·ni·as (ăn′ə-nī′əs). A liar who dropped dead when Peter rebuked him. Acts 5:1–6.

an·an·thous (ăn-ăn′thəs) *adj. Botany.* Lacking flowers. [AN- (without) + -ANTHOUS.]

an·a·pest (ăn′ə-pĕst′) *n.* Also **an·a·paest. 1.** A metrical foot composed of two short syllables followed by one long one, written (˘˘¯). **2.** A line of verse in this meter: *"'Twas the night before Christmas and all through the house"* (Clement Moore). [Latin *anapaestus,* from Greek *anapaistos,* "struck back" (an anapest being a dactyl reversed) : *ana-,* back + *paiein,* to strike (see **pēu-** in Appendix*).] —**an′a·pes′tic** *adj.*

an·a·phase (ăn′ə-fāz′) *n. Biology.* The stage of mitosis in which the daughter chromosomes move toward the poles of the nuclear spindle. Also formerly called "diaster." [ANA- ("progressive") + PHASE.]

a·naph·o·ra (ə-năf′ər-ə) *n. Rhetoric.* The deliberate repetition of a word or phrase at the beginning of several successive verses, clauses, or paragraphs. [Late Latin, from Greek *anaphora,* repetition, from *anapherein,* to repeat : *ana-,* again + *pherein,* to carry (see **bher-**[1] in Appendix*).]

an·aph·ro·dis·i·a (ăn-ăf′rə-dĭz′ē-ə, -dĭzh′ə) *n.* Absence or decline of sexual desire. [Greek : AN- (without) + *aphrodisia,* sexual desire (see **aphrodisiac**).] —**an·aph′ro·dis′i·ac** (ăn-ăf′rə-dĭz′ē-ăk′) *adj. & n.*

an·a·phy·lac·toid (ăn′ə-fə-lăk′toid) *adj. Pathology.* **1.** Of or pertaining to an anaphylactic reaction that occurs without causing antibodies. **2.** Of or pertaining to a toxic reaction caused in an unsensitized person by an excessive dose of a substance that causes anaphylaxis in a sensitized person.

an·a·phy·lax·is (ăn′ə-fə-lăk′sĭs) *n.* Hypersensitivity to a foreign substance, especially in animals, induced by a small preliminary or sensitizing injection of the substance. Also called "allergy." [New Latin : ANA- ("intensification") + (PRO)PHYLAXIS.] —**an′a·phy·lac′tic** (-lăk′tĭk) *adj.* —**an′a·phy·lac′ti·cal·ly** *adv.*

an·a·pla·sia (ăn′ə-plā′zhə) *n. Biology.* Reversion of cells to a more primitive or less differentiated form. [ANA- + -PLASIA.]

an·a·plas·tic (ăn′ə-plăs′tĭk) *adj.* **1.** *Surgery.* Pertaining to the restoration of a lost or absent part. **2.** Of or pertaining to anaplasia of cells.

an·a·plas·ty (ăn′ə-plăs′tē) *n.* Plastic surgery. [French *anaplastie,* from Greek *anaplasis,* remodeling, from *anaplassein,* to form anew : *ana-,* anew + *plassein,* to mold (see **pele-**[1] in Appendix*).]

An·a·pur·na. See **Annapurna.**

an·arch (ăn′ärk′) *n.* A leader or adherent of anarchy.

an·ar·chic (ăn-är′kĭk) *adj.* Also **an·ar·chi·cal** (-kĭ-kəl). **1.** Of, like, or promoting anarchy. **2.** Lacking order or control; lawless. —**an·ar′chi·cal·ly** *adv.*

an·ar·chism (ăn′ər-kĭz′əm) *n.* **1.** The theory that all forms of government are oppressive and undesirable, and should be

anchor

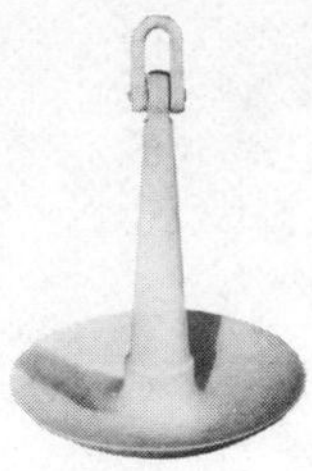

mushroom

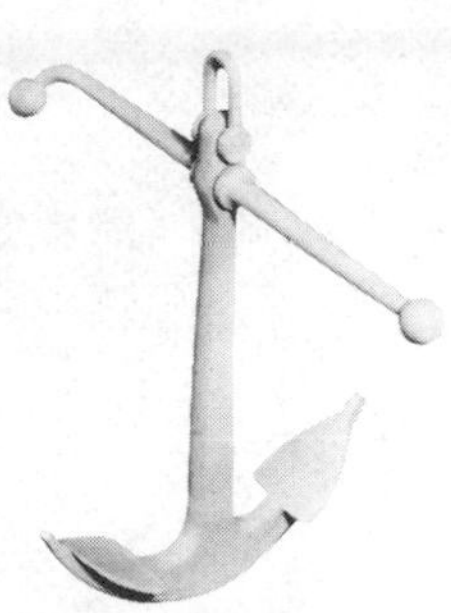

admiralty

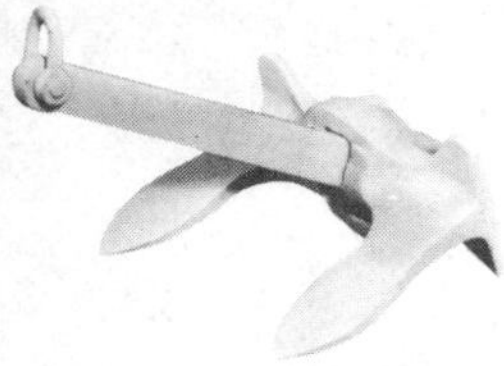

stockless

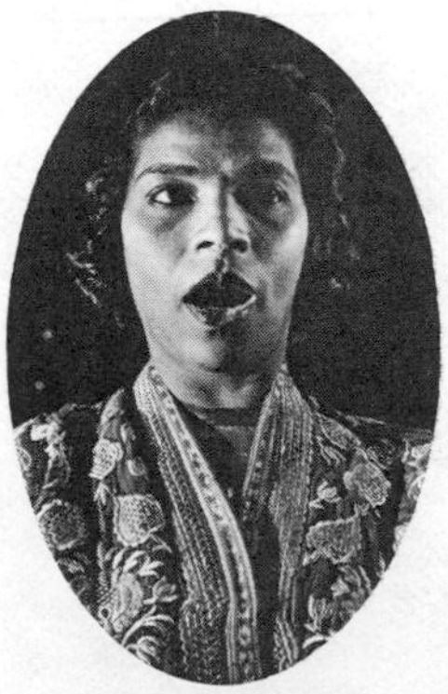

Marian Anderson

abolished. **2.** Active resistance and terrorism against the state, as used by some anarchists. **3.** Rejection of all forms of coercive control and authority: *"he was inclined to anarchism; he hated system and organization and uniformity"* (Bertrand Russell). **—an'ar·chis'tic** (ăn'ər-kĭs'tĭk) *adj.*

an·ar·chist (ăn'ər-kĭst) *n.* A person who advocates or engages in anarchism.

an·ar·cho·syn·di·cal·ism (ăn-är'kō-sĭn'dĭ-kəl-ĭz'əm) *n.* A revolutionary doctrine, **syndicalism** *(see).* [ANARCH(Y) + SYNDICALISM.]

an·ar·chy (ăn'ər-kē) *n., pl.* **-chies. 1.** Absence of any form of political authority. **2.** Political disorder and confusion. **3.** Absence of any cohering principle, as a common standard or purpose. [Greek *anarkhia,* from *anarkhos,* without a ruler : AN- (without) + *arkhos,* ruler, -ARCH.]

an·ar·thri·a (ăn-är'thrē-ə) *n.* Loss of the ability to speak. [New Latin, from Greek *anarthros,* not articulated. See **anarthrous.**] **—an·ar'thric** (-thrĭk) *adj.*

an·ar·throus (ăn-är'thrəs) *adj.* **1.** *Grammar.* Used without an article. **2.** *Zoology.* Lacking joints; unjointed. [Greek *anarthros,* not articulated, without an article : AN- (without) + *arthron,* joint, article (see **ar-** in Appendix*).]

an·a·sar·ca (ăn'ə-sär'kə) *n.* A general accumulation of serum in various tissues and body cavities. [New Latin, from Greek *ana sarka,* "throughout the body" : *ana,* throughout + *sarka,* accusative of *sarx,* flesh (see **twerk-** in Appendix*).] **—an'a·sar'cous** (-sär'kəs) *adj.*

An·a·sta·sia (ăn'ə-stā'zhə), **Grand Duchess.** In full, Anastasia Nicolaievna Romanovna. 1901–1918? Youngest daughter of Nicholas II.

an·as·tig·mat (ăn-ăs'tĭg-măt') *n.* A compound lens corrected for astigmatism and for at least one off-axis zone in the image plane.

an·as·tig·mat·ic (ăn-ăs'tĭg-măt'ĭk) *adj.* **1.** Not astigmatic. Said of a lens that forms an accurate point image of a point object. Also "stigmatic." **2.** Pertaining to a compound lens in which the separate components compensate for the astigmatism of each. [AN- (not) + ASTIGMATIC.]

a·nas·to·mose (ə-năs'tə-mōz', -mōs') *v.* **-mosed, -mosing, -moses.** *—tr.* To join by anastomosis. *—intr.* To connect by anastomosis, as blood vessels.

a·nas·to·mo·sis (ə-năs'tə-mō'sĭs) *n., pl.* **-ses** (-sēz'). **1.** The union or connection of branches, as of rivers, veins of leaves, or blood vessels. **2.** A surgical connection of separate or severed hollow organs to form a continuous channel. [New Latin, from Greek *anastomōsis,* an outlet, opening, from *anastomoun,* to furnish with a mouth : *ana-,* up + *stoma,* a mouth, opening (see **stomen-** in Appendix*).] **—a·nas'to·mot'ic** (-mŏt'ĭk) *adj.*

a·nas·tro·phe (ə-năs'trə-fē) *n. Rhetoric.* Inversion of the normal syntactic order of words: *To market went she.* [Greek *anastrophē,* a turning upside down, from *anastrephein,* to turn upside down : *ana-,* back + *strephein,* to turn (see **strebh-** in Appendix*).]

anat. anatomical; anatomist; anatomy.

an·a·tase (ăn'ə-tās', -tāz') *n.* A rare blue or light-yellow to brown mineral of titanium dioxide. Formerly called "octahedrite." [French, from Greek *anatasis,* extension (from its long crystals), from *anateinein,* to extend, stretch up : *ana-,* up + *teinein,* to stretch (see **ten-** in Appendix*).]

a·nath·e·ma (ə-năth'ə-mə) *n., pl.* **-mas. 1.** A formal ecclesiastical ban, curse, or excommunication. **2.** A vehement denunciation; imprecation; curse: *"the sound of a witch's anathemas in some unknown tongue."* (Hawthorne). **3.** Someone or something cursed, reviled, or shunned. [Late Latin, a curse, a person cursed, an offering, from Greek *anathēma,* votive offering, from *anatithenai,* to dedicate : *ana-,* up + *tithenai,* to put (see **dhē-**[1] in Appendix*).]

a·nath·e·ma·tize (ə-năth'ə-mə-tīz') *tr.v.* **-tized, -tizing, -tizes.** To proclaim an anathema on; denounce or curse. **—a·nath'e·ma·ti·za'tion** *n.*

An·a·to·li·a (ăn'ə-tō'lē-ə). **Asia Minor** *(see).*

An·a·to·li·an (ăn'ə-tō'lē-ən) *adj.* Also **An·a·tol·ic** (-tŏl'ĭk). **1.** Of or pertaining to Anatolia or its inhabitants. **2.** Of or pertaining to a family of extinct languages of ancient Anatolia. *—n.* The Anatolian languages.

an·a·tom·i·cal (ăn'ə-tŏm'ĭ-kəl) *adj.* Also **an·a·tom·ic** (-tŏm'ĭk). *Abbr.* **anat. 1.** Of or pertaining to anatomy. **2.** Of or pertaining to dissection. **3.** Structural as opposed to functional. **—an'a·tom'i·cal·ly** *adv.*

a·nat·o·mist (ə-năt'ə-mĭst) *n. Abbr.* **anat.** An expert in or student of anatomy.

a·nat·o·mize (ə-năt'ə-mīz') *tr.v.* **-mized, -mizing, -mizes. 1.** To dissect. **2.** To analyze in minute detail. **—a·nat'o·mi·za'tion** *n.*

a·nat·o·my (ə-năt'ə-mē) *n., pl.* **-mies.** *Abbr.* **anat. 1.** The structure of a plant or animal, or of any of its parts. **2.** The science of the shape and structure of organisms and their parts. **3.** A treatise on this science. **4.** The dissection of a plant or animal to disclose the various parts, their positions, structure, and interrelation. **5.** A skeleton. **6.** Any detailed examination or analysis. **7.** The human body. [Middle English *anatomie,* from Old French, from Late Latin *anatomia,* from Greek *anatomē,* dissection, from *anatemnein,* to dissect : *ana-,* up + *temnein,* to cut (see **tem-** in Appendix*).]

a·nat·ro·pous (ə-năt'rə-pəs) *adj. Botany.* Inverted, so that the micropyle is next to the hilum, and the embryonic root is at the other end. Said of an ovule. [ANA- (inverted) + -TROPOUS.]

a·nat·to. Variant of **annatto.**

An·ax·ag·o·ras (ăn'ăk-săg'ə-rəs). 500?–428 B.C. Greek philosopher; introduced dualistic explanation of universe.

A·nax·i·man·der (ə-năk'sə-măn'dər). 611–547 B.C. Greek astronomer and philosopher.

ANC Airport code for Anchorage, Alaska.

anc. ancient.

-ance, -ancy. Indicates an action, quality, or condition; for example, **riddance, compliancy.** [Middle English *-ance, -aunce,* from Old French *-ance,* from Latin *-antia,* abstract noun suffix of *-ant-,* stem of *-āns,* present participle ending, -ANT.]

an·ces·tor (ăn'sĕs'tər) *n.* **1.** Any person from whom one is descended, especially if more remote than a grandfather; a forefather. **2.** *Law.* The person from whom an estate has been inherited. **3.** *Biology.* The actual or hypothetical organism or stock from which later kinds have evolved. [Middle English *ancestre, ancessour,* from Old French *ancestre, ancessor,* from Latin *antecessor,* "one that goes before," from *antecessus,* past participle of *antecēdere,* to go before : ANTE- + *cēdere,* to go (see **ked-**[1] in Appendix*).]

an·ces·tral (ăn-sĕs'trəl) *adj.* Pertaining to or evolved from an ancestor or ancestors. **—an·ces'tral·ly** *adv.*

an·ces·tress (ăn'sĕs'trĭs) *n.* A female ancestor.

an·ces·try (ăn'sĕs'trē) *n.; pl.* **-tries. 1.** Ancestral descent or lineage. **2.** Ancestors collectively. [Middle English *ancestrie,* from Old French *ancesserie,* from *ancessour,* ANCESTOR.]

An·chi·ses (ăn-kī'sēz). *Greek & Roman Mythology.* The father of Aeneas, rescued by his son from fallen Troy.

an·chor (ăng'kər) *n.* **1.** A heavy object of iron or steel attached to a vessel by a cable and cast overboard to keep the vessel in place, either by its weight or by its flukes gripping the bottom. **2.** Anything likened to an anchor in giving stability. **—at anchor.** Anchored. *—v.* **anchored, -choring, -chors.** *—tr.* To hold fast by, or as if by, an anchor. *—intr.* To drop anchor; lie at anchor, as a ship. [Middle English *anker,* Old English *ancer, ancor,* from Latin *anc(h)ora,* from Greek *ankura.* See **ank-** in Appendix.*]

an·chor·age (ăng'kər-ĭj) *n.* **1.** A place for anchoring. **2.** A fee charged for the privilege of anchoring. **3. a.** The act of anchoring. **b.** The condition of being at anchor.

An·chor·age (ăng'kər-ĭj). The largest city of Alaska, in the south at the head of Cook Inlet. Population, 44,000.

an·cho·ress (ăng'kə-rĭs) *n.* A female anchorite.

an·cho·rite (ăng'kə-rīt') *n.* Also **an·cho·ret** (-rĕt'). A person who has retired into seclusion for religious reasons; hermit; recluse. [Middle English, from Medieval Latin *anchorita,* variant of Late Latin *anchorēta,* from Late Greek *anakhōrētēs,* "one who withdraws (from the world)," from *anakhōrein,* to withdraw : Greek *ana-,* back + *khōrein,* to make room (see **ghē-** in Appendix*).] **—an'cho·rit'ic** (-rĭt'ĭk) *adj.*

anchor man. 1. One heavily depended upon; mainstay. **2.** *Sports.* The man, usually the strongest of his team, who performs the last stage of a relay race. **3.** *Radio & Television.* The narrator or coordinator of a news broadcast in which several correspondents give reports.

anchor ring. *Geometry.* A **torus** *(see).*

an·cho·vy (ăn'chō'vē, ăn-chō'vē) *n., pl.* **-vies** or **anchovy.** Any of various small, herringlike marine fishes of the family Engraulidae. Several species are widely used as food fish. [Spanish *anchova, anchoa,* perhaps from Basque *anchu.*]

anchovy pear. 1. A tropical American tree, *Grias cauliflora,* that bears edible fruit resembling the mango in taste. **2.** The fruit of this tree. [Perhaps from its use as an hors d'oeuvre.]

an·chu·sa (ăng-kyo͞o'sə) *n.* Any plant of the genus *Anchusa.* See **bugloss.** [New Latin *Anchusa,* from Latin *anchūsa,* a plant used as a cosmetic, from Greek *ankhousa*†, alkanet.]

an·chy·lose. Variant of **ankylose.**

an·chy·lo·sis. Variant of **ankylosis.**

an·cien ré·gime (äɴ-syăɴ' rā-zhēm'). **1.** The political and social system existing in France before the Revolution of 1789. **2.** Any former system. [French, "old regime."]

an·cient[1] (ān'shənt) *adj. Abbr.* **anc. 1.** Very old; aged. **2.** Of, existing, or occurring in times long past; especially, belonging to the historical period prior to the fall of the Western Roman Empire (A.D. 476). —See Synonyms at **old.** *—n.* **1.** A very old person. **2.** A person who lived in ancient times. **3.** *Plural.* The peoples of the classical nations of antiquity. **4.** *Plural.* The ancient Greek and Roman authors. [Middle English *ancien,* from Old French, from Vulgar Latin *anteānus* (unattested), "going before," from Latin *ante,* before. See **anti** in Appendix.*] **—an'cient·ly** *adv.* **—an'cient·ness** *n.*

an·cient[2] (ān'shənt) *n. Obsolete.* **1.** An ensign; a flag. **2.** A flag-bearer or lieutenant. [Variant of ENSIGN.]

Ancient Chinese. The language of ancient China and ancestor of almost all the modern Chinese dialects and of the Chinese loan words in Japanese, Korean, and Vietnamese. The Ancient Chinese pronunciation is reconstructed on the basis of the *Ch'ieh Yün* dictionary published in A.D. 601 and is preserved better in the southern dialects, such as Cantonese and Amoy, than in Mandarin Chinese.

Ancient Greek. The Greek language of historical antiquity, from its first documentation in the 14th century B.C. until the time of the late Roman Empire, divided into two principal dialect areas, **East Greek** and **West Greek** *(both of which see).*

an·cil·lar·y (ăn'sə-lĕr'ē) *adj.* **1.** Subordinate: *"For Degas, sculpture was never more than ancillary to his painting"* (Herbert Read). **2.** Helping; auxiliary. *—n., pl.* **ancillaries.** A servant. [Latin *ancillāris,* servile, from *ancilla,* maidservant, feminine diminutive of *anculus,* servant. See **kwel-**[1] in Appendix.*]

an·cip·i·tal (ăn-sĭp'ə-təl) *adj.* Flattened and two-edged as certain plant stems are. [From Latin *anceps* (stem *ancipit-*), two-headed : AMBI- + *caput,* head (see **kaput-** in Appendix*).]

an·con (ăng′kŏn′) *n., pl.* **ancones** (ăng-kō′nēz). **1.** A projecting bracket used in classical architecture to carry the upper elements of a cornice; a console. **2.** *Anatomy. Obsolete.* The elbow. [Latin *ancōn*, from Greek *ankōn*, elbow, bend of the arm. See ank- in Appendix.*] —**an′co·nal** (-kə-nəl), **an·co′ne·al** (-kō′nē-əl) *adj.*

An·co·na (ăng-kō′nə). A city on the Adriatic coast of central Italy. Population, 105,000.

-ancy. Variant of **-ance.**

an·cy·lo·sto·mi·a·sis (ăn′sĭ-lō-stō-mī′ə-sĭs, ăng′kĭ-lō-) *n.* A disease caused by hookworm infestation and marked by progressive anemia. Also called "hookworm disease." [New Latin : *Ancylostoma*, hookworm (genus), "hook-mouth" : Greek *ankulos*, crooked (see ank- in Appendix*) + *stoma*, mouth (see stomen- in Appendix*) + -IASIS.]

An·cy·ra. The ancient name for Ankara.

and (ənd, ən; *stressed* ănd) *conj.* **1.** Together with or along with; also; in addition; as well as. Used to connect words, phrases, or clauses that have the same grammatical function in a construction: *trials and tribulations; a long and happy life.* **2.** Added to; plus: *Two and two makes four.* **3.** As a result; in consequence: *Seek, and ye shall find.* **4.** *Informal.* To. Used between finite verbs, such as *go, come, try, write,* or *see: try and find it; come and see.* **5.** *Archaic.* Then. Used to begin a sentence: *And he said unto her . . .* **6.** *Archaic.* If: *and it pleases you.* [Middle English *and,* Old English *and, ond.* See en in Appendix.*]

and. *Music.* andante.

And. Andorra.

An·da·lu·sia (ăn′də-lōō′zhə). *Spanish* **An·da·lu·cí·a** (ăn′dä-lōō-thē′ä). A region of Spain, occupying 33,675 square miles in the southwest, and bordering on the Atlantic and the Mediterranean Sea. Population, 99,000. —**An′da·lu′sian** *adj. & n.*

an·da·lu·site (ăn′də-lōō′sīt′) *n.* A mineral aluminum silicate, Al$_2$SiO$_5$, usually found in prisms of various colors. [French *andalousite,* discovered in ANDALUSIA.]

An·da·man and Nic·o·bar Islands (ăn′də-mən; nĭk′ə-bär′). A territory of the Republic of India, with a combined area of 3,143 square miles, comprising two island groups in the Bay of Bengal, the Andaman Islands (2,508 square miles) to the north and the Nicobar Islands (635 square miles) to the south. Population, 64,000. Capital, Port Blair.

An·da·man·ese (ăn′də-mə-nēz′, -nēs′) *n., pl.* **Andamanese.** Also **An·da·man** (ăn′də-mən) (for sense 1). **1.** A member of a Negrito people native to the Andaman Islands. **2.** The agglutinative language of this people, not known to be connected with any other language family. —**An′da·man·ese′** *adj.*

An·da·man Sea (ăn′də-mən). An arm of the Bay of Bengal bounded by the Andaman and Nicobar Islands, Burma, the Malay Peninsula, and Sumatra.

an·dan·te (än-dän′tā, ăn-dăn′tē) *adv. Abbr.* **and.** *Music.* Moderate in tempo; faster than adagio, but slower than allegretto. Used as a direction: *performed andante.* —*adj. Abbr.* **and.** *Music.* Moderately slow: *an andante movement.* —*n. Abbr.* **and.** *Music.* An andante movement or passage. [Italian, "walking," present participle of *andare,* to walk, from Vulgar Latin *ambitāre* (unattested), from Latin *ambulāre,* to AMBULATE.]

an·dan·ti·no (än′dän-tē′nō, ăn′dän-tē′nō) *adv. Music.* Slightly faster than andante in tempo. Used as a direction. —*adj. Music.* Slightly faster than andante: *an andantino section.* —*n., pl.* **andantinos.** *Music.* An andantino movement or passage. [Italian, diminutive of ANDANTE.]

An·de·an (ăn′dē-ən, ăn-dē′ən) *adj.* Of, pertaining to, or like the Andes or their inhabitants.

An·der·sen (ăn′dər-sən), **Hans Christian.** 1805–1875. Danish author of fairy tales.

An·der·son (ăn′dər-sən), **Carl David.** Born 1905. American physicist; detected the positron in cosmic rays.

An·der·son (ăn′dər-sən), **Marian.** Born 1902. American concert and opera contralto.

An·der·son (ăn′dər-sən), **Maxwell.** 1888–1959. American author of modern verse drama.

An·der·son (ăn′dər-sən), **Sherwood.** 1876–1941. American author of short stories and novels.

An·der·son·ville (ăn′dər-sən-vĭl′). A village in southwest Georgia; site of a Confederate prison for Union soldiers during the Civil War.

An·des (ăn′dēz). A 4,000-mile-long mountain system stretching the length of western South America from Venezuela to Tierra del Fuego. Highest elevation, Aconcagua (22,835 feet).

an·de·site (ăn′dē-zīt′) *n.* A gray, fine-grained volcanic rock, chiefly plagioclase and feldspar. [German *Andesit,* from the ANDES.]

An·dhra Pra·desh (ăn′drə prə-dāsh′). A state of the Republic of India, occupying about 105,900 square miles in the southeast. Population, 35,983,000. Capital, Hyderabad.

and·i·ron (ănd′ī′ərn) *n.* One of a pair of metal supports for holding up logs in a fireplace. Also called "firedog." [Middle English *aundiren,* variant of Old French *andier,* firedog, from Gaulish *andero-* (unattested), young bull (andirons were often decorated with heads of animals at the top).]

An·di·zhan (än′dĭ-zhän′). A cotton-trading center of the Soviet Union, in Uzbek. Population, 150,000.

and/or. Used to indicate that either *and* or *or* may be used to connect words, phrases, or clauses depending upon what meaning is intended.

Usage: *And/or* is principally appropriate to legal or commercial usage. It is most useful in setting forth three distinct and exclusive possibilities: either of two things considered separately or the two in combination (that is, one or the other or both)

Thus, *an offense punishable by a fine and/or imprisonment* (fine or imprisonment or both). Where three exclusive possibilities are not stressed (as in *those engaged in television and/or radio*), *and/or* can usually be replaced by either *or* or *and* without loss of meaning. In every case, *and/or* hould be employed with care to avoid the possibility of misinterpretation.

An·dor·ra (ăn-dôr′ə, -dôr′ə). *Abbr.* **And.** A republic occupying 191 square miles in the eastern Pyrenees between France and Spain. Population, 13,000. Capital, Andorra la Vella.

an·dra·dite (ăn-drä′dīt′) *n.* A green to brown or black calcium-iron garnet, Ca$_3$Fe$_2$(SiO$_4$)$_3$. [After José B. de *Andrada* e Silva (died 1838), Brazilian geologist.]

An·dré (än′drā, ăn′drē), **John.** 1751–1780. British army officer; hanged as a spy in the American Revolution for conspiring with Benedict Arnold.

An·dre·a del Sar·to (än-drā′ä děl sär′tō). Original name, Andrea Domenico d'Agnolo di Francesco. 1486–1531. Italian painter.

An·dre·a·nof Islands (ăn′drē-ăn′ôf). An island group extending about 275 miles in the Aleutians.

An·dre·ev (än-drā′yəf), **Leonid Nikolaevich.** Also **An·dre·yev.** 1871–1919. Russian author of plays, novels, and short stories.

An·drew[1] (ăn′drōō). A masculine given name. [Middle English, from Latin *Andreas,* from Greek, probably from *andreios,* manly, from *anēr* (stem *andr-*), man. See ner-² in Appendix.*]

An·drew[2] (ăn′drōō). One of the Apostles, the brother of Simon called Peter.

An·drews (ăn′drōōz), **Thomas.** 1813–1885. Irish physical chemist; experimented on liquefaction of gases.

andro-, andr-. Indicates: **1.** The male sex or masculine; for example, **androgenous.** **2.** *Botany.* Stamen or anther; for example, **androecium.** [Greek, from *anēr* (stem *andr-*), man. See ner-² in Appendix.*]

An·dro·cles (ăn′drə-klēz′). Also **An·dro·clus** (-kləs). A Roman slave held to have been spared in the arena by a lion that remembered him as the man who had once removed a thorn from its paw.

an·droe·ci·um (ăn-drē′shē-əm, -shəm) *n., pl.* **-cia** (-shē-ə, -shə). The stamens of a flower considered collectively. [New Latin : ANDR(O)- + Greek *oikion,* residence, diminutive of *oikos,* house (see weik-¹ in Appendix*).] —**an·droe′cial** (-shəl) *adj.*

an·dro·gen (ăn′drə-jən) *n.* Any of the steroid hormones that develop and maintain masculine characteristics. Compare **estrogen.** [ANDRO- + -GEN.] —**an′dro·gen′ic** (-jěn′ĭk) *adj.*

an·drog·e·nous (ăn-drŏj′ə-nəs) *adj.* Of or pertaining to production of male offspring. [ANDRO- + -GENOUS.]

an·drog·y·nous (ăn-drŏj′ə-nəs) *adj.* **1.** Having female and male characteristics in one; hermaphroditic. **2.** *Botany.* Composed of staminate and pistillate flowers. Said of the flower·spikes of certain sedges. [Latin *androgynus,* from Greek *androgunos* : ANDRO- + -GYNOUS.] —**an·drog′y·ny** *n.*

an·droid (ăn′droid′) *adj.* Possessing human features. —*n.* A synthetic man created from biological materials. A term used in science fiction. Also called "humanoid." [Late Greek *androeidēs,* manlike : ANDR(O)- + -OID.]

An·drom·a·che (ăn-drŏm′ə-kē). *Greek Mythology.* The faithful wife of Hector, captured by the Greeks at the fall of Troy.

an·drom·e·da (ăn-drŏm′ə-də) *n.* Any of several shrubs of the genus *Andromeda,* or of closely related genera. See **Japanese andromeda.** [After ANDROMEDA.]

An·drom·e·da[1] (ăn-drŏm′ə-də). *Greek Mythology.* The daughter of Cepheus and Cassiopeia and wife of Perseus, who had rescued her from a sea monster.

An·drom·e·da[2] (ăn-drŏm′ə-də) *n.* A constellation in the Northern Hemisphere near Lacerta and Perseus.

An·dros (ăn′drəs, -drŏs). An island of Greece, the northernmost of the Cyclades in the Aegean Sea.

An·dros (ăn′drəs, -drŏs), **Sir Edmund.** 1637–1714. English colonial governor of Dominion of New England; imprisoned by colonists and returned to England.

An·dros·cog·gin River (ăn′drə-skŏg′ĭn). A river rising on the northern Maine-New Hampshire border and flowing 175 miles, first south through New Hampshire, and then southeast through Maine to the Kennebec River and the Atlantic Ocean.

An·dros Island (ăn′drəs). The largest island (1,600 square miles) of the Bahamas, lying in the western group. Also shortened to "Andros."

an·dros·ter·one (ăn-drŏs′tə-rōn′) *n.* A male sex hormone, excreted in male urine and synthetically produced from cholesterol. [ANDRO- + STER(OL) + -ONE.]

-androus. *Botany.* Indicates number or type of stamens; for example, **monandrous.** [New Latin *-androus,* from Greek *-andros,* "having men," from *anēr* (stem *andr-*), man. See ner-² in Appendix.*]

-andry. Indicates number of husbands; for example, **monandry.** [From Greek *anēr* (stem *andr-*), man. See **-androus.**]

-ane. *Chemistry.* Indicates a saturated hydrocarbon; for example, **hexane, propane.** [Variant of -ENE, -INE, or -ONE.]

a·near (ə-nîr′) *prep. Archaic & Regional.* Near: "*Now seems it far, and now anear.*" (Scott). —*adv. Archaic.* Nearly: "*The lady shrieks, and well anear does fall in travail*" (Shakespeare). —*tr.v.* **aneared, anearing, anears.** *Archaic.* To approach: "*The castle tonight . . . anears its fall.*" (Elizabeth Barrett Browning).

an·ec·dot·age (ăn′ĭk-dō′tĭj) *n.* **1.** Anecdotes collectively. **2.** Garrulous old age or senility. Used humorously. [Sense 2 is a blend of ANECDOTE and DOTAGE.]

an·ec·do·tal (ăn′ĭk-dōt′l) *adj.* Pertaining to, characterized by, or full of anecdotes.

an·ec·dote (ăn′ĭk-dōt′) *n., pl.* **-dotes** (for both senses) or **-dota**

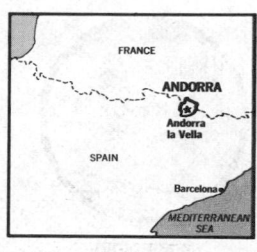

Andorra

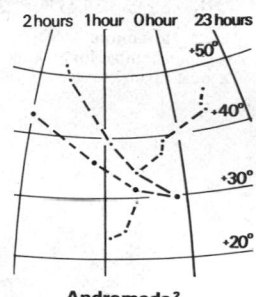

Andromeda²

andiron
Book illustration
by Winslow Homer

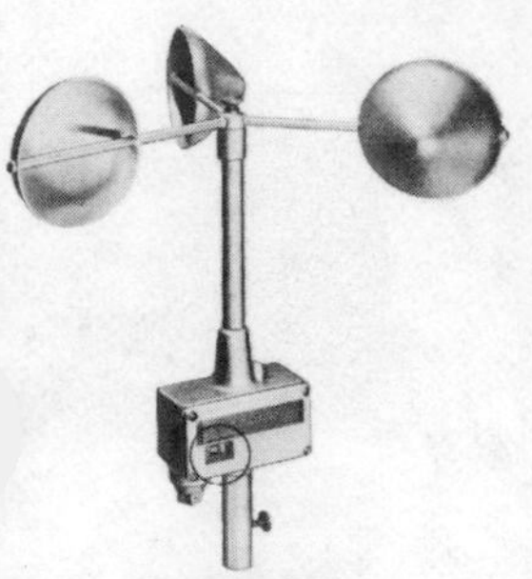

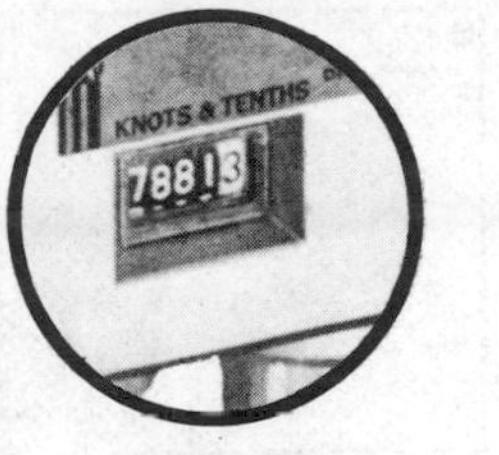

anemometer
Above: Totalizing anemometer
Below: Detail showing totalizing recorder

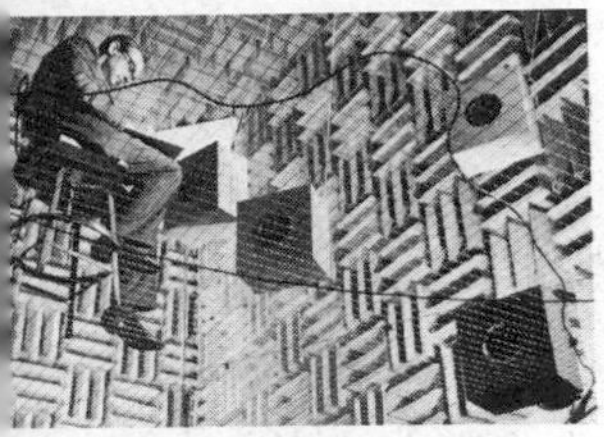

anechoic
Anechoic chamber for making acoustical measurements

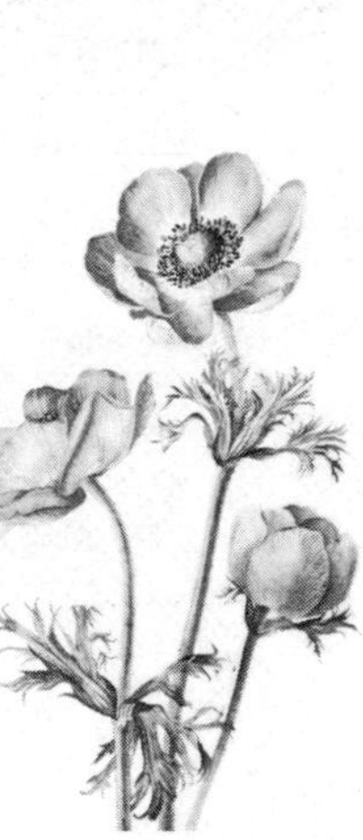

anemone
Anemone coronaria
Poppy anemone

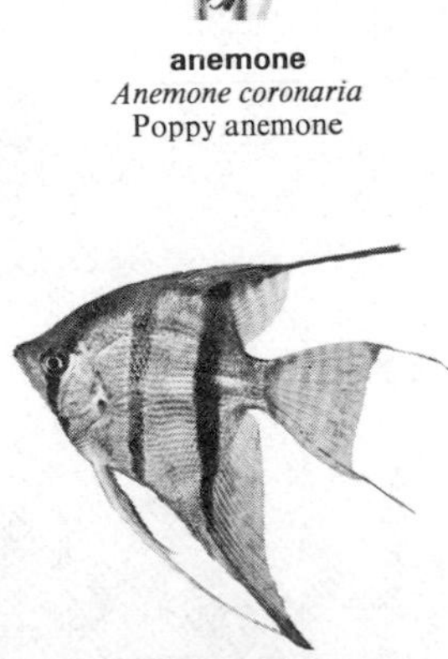

angelfish
Pterophyllum scalare
Freshwater angelfish

(-dō′tə) (for sense 2 only). **1.** A short account of some interesting or humorous incident. **2.** Secret or hitherto undivulged particulars of history or biography. [French, from Greek *anekdota,* "things unpublished," from *anekdotos,* unpublished : AN- (not) + *ekdotos,* given out, from *ekdidonai,* to give out : *ek-,* out + *didonai,* to give (see **dō-** in Appendix*).]

an·ec·dot·ic (ăn′ĭk-dŏt′ĭk) *adj.* Also **an·ec·dot·i·cal** (-ĭ-kəl). **1.** Anecdotal. **2.** Fond of or given to telling anecdotes.

an·ec·dot·ist (ăn′ĭk-dō′tĭst) *n.* A person who tells, collects, or publishes anecdotes.

an·e·cho·ic (ăn′ĕ-kō′ĭk) *adj.* Neither having nor producing echoes: *an anechoic chamber.* [AN- (not) + ECHOIC.]

a·nele (ə-nēl′) *tr.v.* **aneled, aneling, aneles.** *Archaic.* To anoint, especially in administering extreme unction. [Middle English *anelen* : *an,* Old English *an, on,* ON + *elen,* from *ele,* oil, Old English *oele,* from Latin *oleum,* from Greek *elaion,* from *elaia,* olive (see **elaia-** in Appendix*).]

a·ne·mi·a (ə-nē′mē-ə) *n.* Also **a·nae·mi·a.** A pathological deficiency in the oxygen-carrying material of the blood, measured in unit volume concentrations of hemoglobin, red blood cell volume, and red blood cell number. [New Latin, from Greek *anaimia* : *an-,* without + *haima,* blood (see **hemoglobin**).]

a·ne·mic (ə-nē′mĭk) *adj.* Also **a·nae·mic.** **1.** Of or relating to anemia. **2.** Listless and weak; pallid.

anemo–. Indicates wind; for example, **anemology.** [From Greek *anemos,* wind. See **anə-** in Appendix.*]

a·nem·o·chore (ə-nĕm′ə-kôr) *n.* A plant, such as the dandelion, having seeds, spores, or similar reproductive parts that are dispersed by the wind. [ANEMO- + -CHORE.]

a·nem·o·graph (ə-nĕm′ə-grăf′) *n.* A recording anemometer. [ANEMO- + -GRAPH.] —**a·nem′o·graph′ic** *adj.*

an·e·mog·ra·phy (ăn′ə-mŏg′rə-fē) *n.* The science of recording anemometrical measurements. [ANEMO- + -GRAPHY.]

an·e·mol·o·gy (ăn′ə-mŏl′ə-jē) *n.* The scientific study of winds. [ANEMO- + -LOGY.]

an·e·mom·e·ter (ăn′ə-mŏm′ə-tər) *n.* An instrument for measuring wind force and speed. [ANEMO- + -METER.] —**an′e·mo·met′ric** (-mō-mĕt′rĭk), **an′e·mo·met′ri·cal** *adj.*

an·e·mom·e·try (ăn′ə-mŏm′ə-trē) *n. Meteorology.* The determination of wind force and velocity. [ANEMO- + -METRY.]

a·nem·o·ne (ə-nĕm′ə-nē) *n.* **1.** Any of various plants of the genus *Anemone,* of the North Temperate Zone, having white, purple, or red cup-shaped flowers. Some species are also called "windflower." See **pasqueflower.** **2.** A marine invertebrate, the **sea anemone** *(see).* [Latin *anemōnē,* from Greek, perhaps from Semitic.]

anemone fish. Any of various small, brightly colored marine fishes of the genus *Amphiprion,* found near sea anemones.

an·e·moph·i·lous (ăn′ə-mŏf′ə-ləs) *adj.* Pollinated by wind-dispersed pollen. [ANEMO- + -PHILOUS.] —**an′e·moph′i·ly** *n.*

a·nent (ə-nĕnt′) *prep.* Also *rare* **a·nenst** (ə-nĕnst′). **1.** *Archaic & Scottish.* Regarding; concerning. **2.** *Chiefly Regional.* Opposite; close to. **3.** *Obsolete & British Regional.* On a level with; in a line with. [Middle English *anent, onevent,* Old English *onemn, on efen,* alongside, together : ON + *efen,* EVEN.]

an·er·oid (ăn′ə-roid′) *adj.* Not using fluid. [French *anéroïde* : A- (not) + Greek *nēron,* water (see **newo-** in Appendix*).]

aneroid barometer. A barometer in which variations of atmospheric pressure are indicated by the relative bulges of a thin elastic metal disk covering a partially evacuated chamber.

an·es·the·sia (ăn′ĭs-thē′zhə) *n.* Also **an·aes·the·sia.** **1.** Total or partial loss of sensation, especially tactile sensibility, induced by disease or an anesthetic. **2.** Artificially induced unconsciousness or local or general insensibility to pain. [New Latin, from Greek *anaisthēsia,* lack of sensation : *an-,* without + *aisthēsis,* feeling, from *aisthanesthai,* to feel (see **aw-**[2] in Appendix*).]

an·es·the·si·ol·o·gy (ăn′ĭs-thē′zē-ŏl′ə-jē) *n.* Also **an·aes·the·si·ol·o·gy.** The medical study and application of anesthetics. [ANESTHESI(A) + -LOGY.] —**an′es·the′si·ol′o·gist** *n.*

an·es·thet·ic (ăn′ĭs-thĕt′ĭk) *adj.* Also **an·aes·thet·ic.** **1.** Relating to or resembling anesthesia. **2.** Causing anesthesia. **3.** Insensitive. —*n.* Any agent that causes unconsciousness or insensitivity to pain. See **general anesthetic, local anesthetic.** [From Greek *anaisthētos,* without feeling : *an-,* without + *aisthētos,* perceptible, from *aisthanesthai,* perceive (see **anesthesia**).]

an·es·the·tist (ə-nĕs′thə-tĭst) *n.* Also **an·aes·the·tist.** A person, usually a physician, trained to administer anesthetics.

an·es·the·tize (ə-nĕs′thə-tīz′) *tr.v.* **-tized, -tizing, -tizes.** Also **an·aes·the·tize.** To induce anesthesia in. —**an·es′the·ti·za′tion** *n.*

an·es·trus (ăn-ĕs′trəs) *n. Zoology.* An interval of sexual dormancy between two periods of estrus. [New Latin : AN- + ESTRUS.] —**an·es′trous** *adj.*

A·ne·to, Pi·co de. See **Pico de Aneto.**

an·eu·rysm (ăn′yə-rĭz′əm) *n.* Also **an·eu·rism.** A pathological blood-filled dilatation of a blood vessel. [Greek *aneurusma,* from *aneurunein,* to dilate : *ana-,* "throughout" + *eurunein,* to dilate, widen, from *eurus,* wide (see **wer-**[8] in Appendix*).] —**an′eu·rys′mal** (-rĭz′məl) *adj.*

a·new (ə-nōō′, ə-nyōō′) *adv.* **1.** Again. **2.** In a new and different way, form, or manner. [Middle English *anewe, of newe,* Old English *of nīwe* : OF + *nīwe,* NEW.]

an·frac·tu·os·i·ty (ăn-frăk′chōō-ŏs′ə-tē) *n., pl.* **-ties.** **1.** The condition or quality of being anfractuous. **2.** A winding channel, passage, or crevice. **3.** A complicated or involved process.

an·frac·tu·ous (ăn-frăk′chōō-əs) *adj.* Full of twists and turns; winding; tortuous. [French *anfractueux,* from Late Latin *anfractuōsus,* from Latin *anfractus,* a winding : *an-,* from AMBI- + *fractus,* past participle of *frangere,* to break (see **bhreg-** in Appendix*).]

An·ga·ra (ən-gə-rä′). A river of Siberia, flowing 1,300 miles north and west from Lake Baikal to the Yenisei River.

an·ga·ry (ăng′gə-rē) *n.* Also **an·gar·i·a** (ăng-gâr′ē-ə). *International Law.* The right of a belligerent state to seize, use, or destroy the property of a neutral, provided that full compensation is made. [Late Latin *angaria,* service to a lord, from Greek *angareia,* impressment for public service, from *angaros,* mounted courier. See **angelos** in Appendix.*]

an·gel (ān′jəl) *n.* **1.** *Theology.* An immortal, spiritual being attendant upon God. In medieval angelology, one of nine orders of spiritual beings (listed from the highest to lowest in rank): seraphim, cherubim, thrones, dominations or dominions, virtues, powers, principalities, archangels, and angels. **2. a.** A guardian spirit or guiding influence. **b.** *Informal.* A kind and lovable person. **3.** *Christian Science.* God's thoughts passing to man. **4.** *Informal.* A financial backer of an enterprise, especially a dramatic production. **5.** *Military.* Enemy aircraft. [Middle English, from Old French *angele,* from Late Latin *angelus,* from Greek *angelos* (translation of Hebrew *mal'ākh*), messenger. See **angelos** in Appendix.*]

An·ge·la (ăn′jə-lə). A feminine given name. [Late Latin, feminine of *angelus,* ANGEL.]

An·ge·la Me·ri·ci (än′jä-lä mā-rē′chē), **Saint.** 1474?–1540. Italian Roman Catholic nun; founded Ursuline Order.

An·ge·le·no (ăn′jə-lē′nō) *n.* A native or resident of Los Angeles. [American Spanish *Angeleño,* from LOS ANGELES.]

Angel Fall. A waterfall in southeastern Venezuela, dropping over 3,000 feet and considered the highest uninterrupted fall in the world.

an·gel·fish (ān′jəl-fĭsh′) *n., pl.* **angelfish** or **-fishes.** **1.** Any of several brightly colored fishes of the family Chaetodontidae, of warm seas, having laterally compressed bodies. **2.** A freshwater fish, *Pterophyllum scalare,* native to rivers of tropical South America, having a laterally compressed, usually striped body. It is a popular aquarium fish. In this sense, also called "scalare."

angel food cake. A white, almond-flavored sponge cake made of egg whites, sugar, and flour. Also called "angel cake."

an·gel·ic (ăn-jĕl′ĭk) *adj.* Also **an·gel·i·cal** (-ĭ-kəl). **1.** Of, pertaining to, consisting of, or belonging to angels: *angelic hosts.* **2. a.** Suggestive of or fit for an angel; pure and lovely. **b.** *Informal.* Kind and lovable. —**an·gel′i·cal·ly** *adv.*

an·gel·i·ca (ăn-jĕl′ĭ-kə) *n.* **1.** Any of various plants of the genus *Angelica,* having compound leaves and clusters of small white or greenish flowers; especially, *A. Archangelica,* of which the aromatic seeds, leaves, stems, and roots are used in medicine and as flavoring. **2.** The candied stem of this plant. **3.** *Often capital* **A.** A sweet white wine or liqueur. [New Latin, from Medieval Latin *(herba) angelica,* "angelic (herb)," from Late Latin, feminine of *angelicus,* from Greek *angelikos,* from *angelos,* messenger. See **angel.**]

angelica tree. Any of several spiny trees or shrubs, such as the **Hercules'-club** *(see).*

An·gel·i·co (än-jĕl′ĭ-kō), **Fra.** Original name, Guido di Pietro. Also known as Fra Giovanni da Fiesole. 1387–1455. Italian Dominican friar and painter of the Florentine school.

An·gel Island (ān′jəl). The largest island (about one square mile) in San Francisco Bay, California.

an·gel·ol·o·gy (ān′jəl-ŏl′ə-jē) *n.* The branch of theology having to do with angels. [ANGEL + -LOGY.] —**an′gel·o·log′ic** (-ə-lŏj′ĭk), **an′gel·o·log′i·cal** *adj.*

angel shark. Any of several raylike sharks of the genus *Squatina,* having a broad, flat head and body.

An·ge·lus (ăn′jə-ləs) *n.* Also **an·ge·lus.** *Roman Catholic Church.* **1.** A devotional prayer at morning, noon, and night to commemorate the Annunciation. **2.** A bell rung as a call to recite this prayer. [Medieval Latin, *"Angelus (Domini . . .),"* "The Angel (of the Lord)" (the beginning of the liturgy commemorating the Incarnation), from Late Latin *angelus,* ANGEL.]

an·ger (ăng′gər) *n.* **1.** A feeling of extreme displeasure, hostility, indignation, or exasperation toward someone or something; rage; wrath; ire. **2.** *Obsolete.* Trouble; pain; affliction. **3.** *British Regional.* An inflammation or sore. —*v.* **angered, -gering, -gers.** —*tr.* **1.** To make angry; enrage or provoke. **2.** *British Regional.* To make painful or inflamed. —*intr.* To become angry: *She angers too quickly.* [Middle English, from Old Norse *angr,* grief. See **angh-** in Appendix.*]

Synonyms: *anger, rage, fury, ire, wrath, resentment, indignation.* These nouns denote varying degrees of marked displeasure. *Anger,* the most general, denotes strong, usually temporary displeasure without specifying manner of expression. *Rage* and *fury* are closely related in the sense of intense, uncontained, explosive emotion. *Fury* can be more destructive, *rage* more justified by circumstances. *Ire* is a poetic term for anger. *Wrath* applies especially to fervid anger that seeks vengeance or punishment on an epic scale. *Resentment* refers to ill will and suppressed anger generated by a sense of grievance. One feels *indignation* at seeing the mistreatment of someone or something dear and worthy.

an·ger·ly (ăng′gər-lē) *adv. Archaic.* Angrily: *"Again thou blushest angerly."* (Tennyson).

An·gers (äN-zhā′). A city and industrial center of the Loire Valley in western France. Population, 115,000.

An·ge·vin (ăn′jə-vĭn) *adj.* **1.** Of or pertaining to Anjou. **2.** Of or pertaining to the House of Anjou, especially as represented by the Plantagenet kings of England descended from Geoffrey, Count of Anjou. [French, from Old French, from Medieval Latin *Andegavīnus,* from *Andegavia,* ANJOU.] —**An′ge·vin** *n.*

an·gi·na (ăn-jī′nə) *n.* **1.** Any disease, such as croup or diphtheria, in which spasmodic and painful suffocation or spasms occur. **2. Angina pectoris** *(see).* [Latin, quinsy, from Greek *ankhonē,* a strangling. See **angh-** in Appendix.*]

angina pec·to·ris (pĕk′tə-rĭs). Severe paroxysmal pain in the chest, associated with emotional stress and characterized by feelings of suffocation and apprehension. [New Latin, "angina of the chest."]

an·gi·ol·o·gy (ăn′jē-ŏl′ə-jē) *n.* The study of blood and lymph vessels. [Greek *angeion,* vessel, diminutive of *angos*†, vessel + -LOGY.]

an·gi·o·ma (ăn′jē-ō′mə) *n., pl.* **-mas** or **-mata** (-mə-tə). A tumor composed of lymph and blood vessels. [New Latin : Greek *angeion,* vessel (see **angiology**) + **-OMA.**] **—an′gi·om′a·tous** (-ŏm′ə-təs) *adj.*

an·gi·o·sperm (ăn′jē-ə-spûrm′) *n. Botany.* Any plant of the class Angiospermae, characterized by having seeds enclosed in an ovary; a flowering plant. [Greek *angeion,* vessel (see **angiology**) + SPERM.] **—an′gi·o·sper′mous** (-spûr′məs) *adj.*

Ang·kor (ăng′kôr′). A vast group of ruins in northwestern Cambodia, including Angkor Thom, the ancient Khmer capital, and the temple Angkor Wat (or Angkor Vat).

Angl. Anglican.

an·gle[1] (ăng′gəl) *intr.v.* **-gled, -gling, -gles. 1.** To fish with a hook and line. **2.** To try to get something by using schemes, tricks, or other artful means. Used with *for: angle for recognition.* *—n. Obsolete.* A fishhook or fishing tackle. [Middle English *anglen,* from *angel,* a fishhook, Old English *angul, ongul.* See **ank-** in Appendix.*]

an·gle[2] (ăng′gəl) *n.* **1.** *Geometry.* **a.** The figure formed by two lines diverging from a common point. **b.** The figure formed by two planes diverging from a common line. **c.** The rotation required to superimpose either of two such lines or angles on the other. **d.** The space between such lines or surfaces. **e.** A **solid angle** *(see).* **2.** An angular or projecting corner, as of a building. **3. a.** The place, position, or direction from which an object is presented to view. **b.** An aspect, as of a problem, seen from a specific point of view. **4.** *Slang.* A scheme; devious method. —See Synonyms at **phase.** *—v.* **angled, -gling, -gles.** *—tr.* **1.** To move or turn at an angle. **2.** To hit (a ball, for example) at an angle. **3.** *Informal.* To impart a biased aspect or point of view to (a story or anecdote). *—intr.* To continue along or turn itself at angles or by angles: *The path angled through the woods.* [Middle English, from Old French, from Latin *angulus,* angle, corner. See **ank-** in Appendix.*]

An·gle (ăng′gəl) *n.* A member of a Germanic people that migrated to England from southern Denmark in the fifth century A.D., founded the kingdoms of Northumbria, East Anglia, and Mercia, and together with the Jutes and Saxons formed the Anglo-Saxon peoples. [Latin *Anglī, Anglii* (plural), from Germanic. See **ank-** in Appendix.*]

An·gle·doz·er (ăng′gəl-dō′zər) *n.* A trademark for a machine resembling a tractor, used to level or scrape ground, and constructed so that the dirt is pushed off to one side.

angle iron. A length of steel or iron bent at a right angle along its long dimension, used as a lintel to support masonry or as part of a structural framework.

angle of attack. 1. The acute angle between the chord of an airfoil and a line representing the undisturbed relative airflow. **2.** Any other acute angle between two reference lines designating the cant of an airfoil relative to the oncoming air.

angle of incidence. 1. *Physics.* The angle formed by the path of a body or of radiation incident on a surface and a perpendicular to the surface at the point of impact. **2.** *Aviation.* The angle of attack.

angle of reflection. The acute angle formed by the path of a reflected body or reflected radiation with a perpendicular to the surface at the point of reflection.

angle of refraction. The acute angle formed by the path of refracted radiation with a perpendicular to the refracting surface at the point of refraction.

angle of view. The angle included by two lines drawn from opposite extreme corners of an image to the center of a lens.

angle of yaw. The angle between an aircraft's longitudinal axis and its line of travel, as seen from above.

angle plate. A right-angled metal bracket, used on the face plate of a lathe to hold pieces being worked.

an·gle·pod (ăng′gəl-pŏd′) *n.* Any of several plants of the genus *Gonolobus,* of the southern and central United States, having greenish or purple flowers and angular pods.

an·gler (ăng′glər) *n.* **1.** A fisherman who uses a hook. **2.** A scheming person. **3.** An anglerfish.

an·gler·fish (ăng′glər-fĭsh′) *n., pl.* **anglerfish** or **-fishes.** Any of various marine fishes of the order Lophiiformes (or Pediculati), having a long dorsal fin ray that is suspended over the mouth and that serves as a lure to attract prey.

An·gle·sey (ăng′gəl-sē). An island, 275 square miles in area, off the northwestern coast of Wales, of which it is a county. Population, 58,000. County seat, Holyhead.

an·gle·site (ăng′glə-sīt′) *n.* A lead sulfate mineral, occurring in colorless or tinted crysals. [First found at ANGLESEY.]

an·gle·worm (ăng′gəl-wûrm′) *n.* A worm, such as an earthworm, used as bait in fishing.

An·gli·a (ăng′glē-ə). The medieval Latin name for England. [Latin, from *Anglī,* the ANGLE(S).]

An·gli·an (ăng′glē-ən) *adj.* Of or pertaining to the Angles. *—n.* **1.** An Angle. **2.** The Old English dialects of Northumbrian and Mercian.

An·gli·can (ăng′glĭ-kən) *adj.* **1.** *Abbr.* **Angl.** Of, pertaining to, or characteristic of the Church of England or any of the churches related to it in origin and communion, such as the Protestant Episcopal Church. **2.** Of or pertaining to England or the English. *—n.* A member of the Church of England or of any of the churches related to it. [Medieval Latin *Anglicānus,* from *Anglicus,* English, from Latin *Anglī,* ANGLE(S).]

Anglican Church. The Church of England and the churches in other nations that are in complete agreement with it as to doctrine and discipline and are in communion with the Archbishop of Canterbury. Also called "Anglican Communion."

An·gli·can·ism (ăng′glĭ-kən-ĭz′əm) *n.* The doctrine, system, and practice of the Anglican Church.

An·gli·ce (ăng′glə-sē′) *adv.* In the English form: *Firenze,* Anglice *"Florence."* [Medieval Latin *Anglicē,* adverb of *Anglicus,* English, from Latin *Anglī,* the ANGLE(S).]

An·gli·cism (ăng′glə-sĭz′əm) *n.* Also **an·gli·cism. 1.** A word, phrase, or idiom peculiar to the English language, especially as spoken in England; Briticism. **2.** A typically English quality.

An·gli·cize (ăng′glə-sīz′) *v.* **-cized, -cizing, -cizes.** Also **an·gli·cize.** *—tr.* To make English or similar to English in form, idiom, style, or character. *—intr.* To become English in form or character. **—An′gli·ci·za′tion** *n.*

an·gling (ăng′glĭng) *n.* The act, process, or art of fishing with a hook and line and usually a rod.

Anglo–. Indicates English or England; for example, **Anglophile.** [New Latin, from Medieval Latin *Anglī,* the English people, from Latin, the ANGLE(S).]

An·glo-A·mer·i·can (ăng′glō-ə-mĕr′ə-kən) *adj.* Of, relating to, or between England and America, especially the United States; English and American: *Anglo-American cooperation.*

An·glo-Cath·o·lic (ăng′glō-kăth′lĭk, -kăth′ə-lĭk) *n.* A member of the Anglican Communion whose religious convictions emphasize sacramental worship. **—An′glo-Cath′o·lic** *adj.*

An·glo-French (ăng′glō-frĕnch′) *adj.* Of, relating to, or between England and France or their peoples; English and French. *—n. Abbr.* **AF, A.F. Norman French** *(see).*

An·glo-In·di·an (ăng′glō-ĭn′dē-ən) *n.* **1.** A person of English and Indian descent. **2.** The dialect of English used in India. **—An′glo-In′di·an** *adj.*

An·glo-I·rish (ăng′glō-ī′rĭsh) *n.* **1.** A native of England living in Ireland. **2.** A native of Ireland living in England. **3.** A person of mixed Irish and English ancestry. **4.** The dialect of English used in Ireland. **—An′glo-I′rish** *adj.*

An·glo·ma·ni·a (ăng′glō-mā′nē-ə) *n.* An infatuation for English things. **—An′glo·ma′ni·ac′** (-nē-ăk′) *n.*

An·glo-Nor·man (ăng′glō-nôr′mən) *adj.* Of or pertaining to the Normans who settled in England after 1066, their descendants, or their language. *—n.* **1.** One of the Norman settlers in England after 1066, or a descendant of these settlers. **2.** *Abbr.* **AN, A.N. Norman French** *(see).*

An·glo·phile (ăng′glə-fīl′) *n.* Also **an·glo·phile, An·glo·phil** (-fĭl), **an·glo·phil.** An admirer of England and English things. *—adj.* Of or resembling Anglophiles. **—An′glo·phil′i·a** *n.*

An·glo·phobe (ăng′glə-fōb′) *n.* Also **an·glo·phobe.** One who has an aversion to England or English things. *—adj.* Of or similar to Anglophobes. **—An′glo·pho′bi·a** *n.*

An·glo-Sax·on (ăng′glō-săk′sən) *n. Abbr.* **AS, A.S., AS. 1.** A member of one of the Germanic peoples (Angles, Saxons, and Jutes) who settled in Britain in the fifth and sixth centuries. **2.** Any of the descendants of these peoples who were dominant in England until the Norman Conquest of 1066. **3. Old English** *(see).* **4.** Any person of English ancestry. *—adj.* Of, pertaining to, or characteristic of Anglo-Saxons or their descendants, or their language or culture; English.

An·go·la (ăng-gō′lə). Also **Portuguese West Af·ri·ca** (ăf′rĭ-kə). A Portuguese colony occupying 481,351 square miles in southwestern Africa. Population, 4,830,000. Capital, Luanda.

An·go·ra[1] (ăng-gôr′ə, -gōr′ə) *n.* **1.** *Often small* **a. a.** The long, silky hair of the Angora goat. **b.** The fine, light hair of the Angora rabbit, sometimes blended with wool in fabrics. **2.** *Often small* **a.** A yarn or fabric made from either of these fibers. **3.** An Angora cat. **4.** An Angora goat. **5.** An Angora rabbit. [From ANGORA.]

An·go·ra[2]. The former name for **Ankara.**

Angora cat. A long-haired domestic cat.

Angora goat. Any of a breed of domestic goats having long, silky hair.

Angora rabbit. One of a breed of domestic rabbits having long, soft, usually white hair.

an·gos·tu·ra bark (ăng′gəs-tŏŏr′ə, -tyŏŏr′ə). The bitter, aromatic bark of either of two Brazilian trees, *Galipea officinalis* or *Cusparia trifoliata,* formerly used as a tonic. Also called "angostura." [From *Angostura,* former name of Ciudad Bolívar.]

Angostura bitters. A trademark for a bitter aromatic tonic made from water, alcohol, gentian, angostura bark, and vegetable extracts.

an·gry (ăng′grē) *adj.* **-grier, -griest. 1.** Feeling or showing anger; incensed or enraged. Used with *at, with,* or *about.* **2.** Indicative of or resulting from anger: *an angry silence.* **3.** Having a menacing aspect; seeming to threaten: *angry clouds.* **4.** Inflamed: *an angry sore.* [Middle English, from ANGER.] **—an′gri·ly** (-grə-lē) *adv.* **—an′gri·ness** *n.*

angry young man. Also **Angry Young Man.** One of a group of English writers of the 1950's whose works are characterized by vigorous social protest.

angst (ängkst) *n.* A feeling of anxiety. [German *Angst,* from Middle High German *angest,* from Old High German *angust.* See **angh-** in Appendix.*]

ang·strom, Ång·ström (ăng′strəm) *n. Symbol* **Å** A unit of length equal to one hundred-millionth (10^{-8}) of a centimeter, used especially to specify radiation wavelengths. Also called

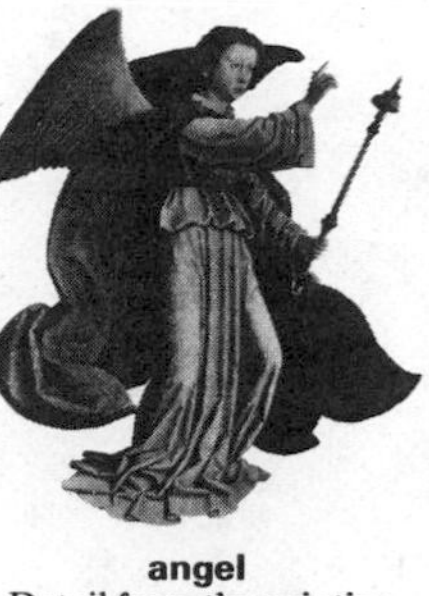

angel
Detail from the painting "Angel of the Annunciation," by Gerard David

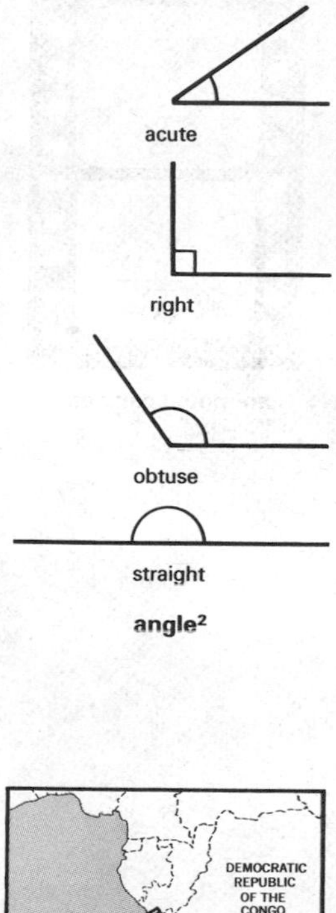

angle[2]

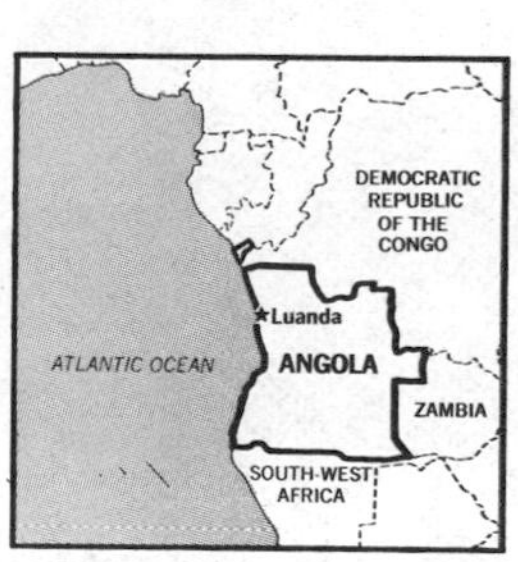

Angola

"angstrom unit." See **measurement**. [After Anders Jonas Ångström.]

Ång·ström (ăng′strəm, ông′-), **Anders Jonas**. 1814–1874. Swedish physicist; pioneer in spectroscopy.

An·guil·la. See **St. Kitts-Nevis-Anguilla**.

an·guil·li·form (ăng-gwĭl′ə-fôrm′) adj. Having the elongated shape of an eel. [New Latin anguilla, from Latin, eel, diminutive of anguis, snake (see angwhi- in Appendix*) + -FORM.]

an·guine (ăng′gwĭn) adj. Of, pertaining to, or resembling a snake; snakelike. [Latin anguinus, from anguis, snake. See angwhi- in Appendix*.]

an·guish (ăng′gwĭsh) n. An agonizing physical or mental pain; torment; torture. See Synonyms at **regret**. —v. **anguished**, **-guishing**, **-guishes**. —tr. To cause to suffer or feel anguish. —intr. To suffer or feel anguish. [Middle English anguisshe, from Old French anguisse, from Latin angustia, straitness, narrowness, from angustus, narrow. See angh- in Appendix*.]

an·guished (ăng′gwĭsht) adj. 1. Filled with anguish. 2. Caused by or expressing anguish: "On thy cold forehead starts the anguished dew." (Coleridge).

an·gu·lar (ăng′gyə-lər) adj. 1. Having, forming, or consisting of an angle or angles. 2. Measured by an angle or degrees of an arc. 3. Bony and lean; gaunt. 4. Lacking grace or smoothness; awkward: an angular gait. 5. Crotchety in manner or disposition; unyielding. —an′gu·lar·ly adv. —an′gu·lar·ness n.

angular acceleration. Physics. The rate of change of angular velocity with respect to time.

an·gu·lar·i·ty (ăng′gyə-lăr′ə-tē) n., pl. **-ties**. 1. The state, condition, or quality of being angular. 2. Plural. Angular forms, outlines, or corners.

angular momentum. Physics. 1. The vector product of the position vector and linear velocity of a particle in motion relative to an axis. 2. The sum of such products, one for each component particle of an extended body, expressible as the product of the angular velocity and the moment of inertia of the body. Also called "moment of momentum."

angular velocity. Physics. A vector quantity describing rotational motion, the magnitude of which is the time rate of change of angle and the direction of which is along the axis of rotation.

an·gu·late (ăng′gyə-lĭt, -lāt′) adj. Also **an·gu·lat·ed** (-lā′tĭd). Having angles or an angular shape. —v. (ăng′gyə-lāt′) **angulated**, **-lating**, **-lates**. —tr. To cause to become angular. —intr. To become angular. —an′gu·late·ly adv.

an·gu·la·tion (ăng′gyə-lā′shən) n. 1. The formation of angles. 2. An angular part, position, or formation.

An·gus (ăng′gəs). Formerly **For·far** (fôr′fär). A county occupying 843 square miles in eastern Scotland. Population, 280,000. County seat, Forfar.

An·halt (än′hält′). A former state of central Germany, a part of East Germany since 1945.

an·hin·ga (ăn-hĭng′gə) n. A bird, the **water turkey** (see). [Portuguese, from Tupi.]

An·hwei (än′hwā′). A province of China, occupying 54,000 square miles in the east-central part of the country. Population, 33,560,000. Capital, Hofei.

anhydr. anhydrous.

an·hy·dride (ăn-hī′drīd′) n. A chemical compound formed from another by the removal of water. [ANHYDR(OUS) + -IDE.]

an·hy·drite (ăn-hī′drīt′) n. A white to grayish or reddish mineral of anhydrous calcium sulfate, CaSO₄, occurring as layers in gypsum deposits. [ANHYDR(OUS) + -ITE.]

an·hy·drous (ăn-hī′drəs) adj. Abbr. **anhyd.** Without water, especially water of crystallization. [Greek anudros, waterless : an-, without + hudōr, water (see wed-¹ in Appendix*.)]

a·ni (ä-nē′) n. Any of several chiefly tropical American birds of the genus Crotophaga, having black plumage and a long tail. [Spanish aní, from Tupi ani.]

An·i·ak·chak Crater (ăn′ē-ăk′chăk′). A large active volcanic crater (six miles wide) in Alaska on the Alaska Peninsula.

an·il (ăn′ĭl) n. Rare. The indigo plant or the blue dye obtained from it. [French, from Portuguese, from Arabic an-nīl, the indigo plant, from Persian nīl, indigo. See nei-¹ in Appendix*.]

an·ile (ăn′īl′, ā′nīl′) adj. Of or like an old woman. [Latin anīlis, from anus, old woman. See an- in Appendix*.]

an·i·line (ăn′ə-lĭn) n. Also **an·i·lin**. A colorless, oily, poisonous benzene derivative, C₆H₅NH₂, used in the manufacture of rubber, dyes, resins, pharmaceuticals, and varnishes. —adj. Also **an·i·lin**. Derived from aniline. [German Anilin : ANIL + -INE.]

aniline dye. Any of numerous synthetic dyes.

anim. Music. animato.

an·i·ma (ăn′ə-mə) n. 1. The soul. 2. In the psychology of Carl Jung: **a**. The soul, or true inner self. **b**. The feminine inner personality, as present in man. Compare **animus**. [Latin, feminine of animus, mind, ANIMUS.]

an·i·mad·ver·sion (ăn′ə-măd-vûr′zhən, -shən) n. 1. Hostile criticism. 2. A critical or censorious remark. Used with on or upon. [Latin animadversiō, from animadvertere, to ANIMADVERT.] —an′i·mad·ver′sive (-vûr′sĭv) adj.

an·i·mad·vert (ăn′ə-măd-vûrt′) intr.v. **-verted**, **-verting**, **-verts**. To remark or comment critically, usually with strong disapproval or censure. Used with on or upon: He felt impelled to animadvert on the wickedness of governments. [Latin animadvertere, to direct the mind to, censure : animus, mind (see ane- in Appendix*) + advertere, to turn toward : ad-, to + vertere, to turn (see wer-³ in Appendix*.)]

an·i·mal (ăn′ə-məl) n. 1. Any organism of the kingdom Animalia, distinguished from plants by certain typical characteristics, such as the power of locomotion, fixed structure and limited growth, and nonphotosynthetic metabolism. 2. Any such organism other than a human being; especially, a mammal. 3. A person of inhuman character or bearing; someone who is bestial or brutish. 4. Animality. Preceded by the: Drinking releases the animal in him. —adj. 1. Of, relating to, or characteristic of animals. 2. Relating to the sensual or physical as distinct from the spiritual nature of man. —See Synonyms at **brute**. [Latin, an animal, from animālis, living, from anima, feminine of animus, breath, soul. See ane- in Appendix*.]

animal crackers. Small cookies baked in various animal shapes.

an·i·mal·cule (ăn′ə-măl′kyōōl) n. Also **an·i·mal·cu·lum** (-kyə-ləm) pl. **-la** (-lə). 1. A microscopic or minute organism usually thought of as an animal, as an amoeba or paramecium. 2. Archaic. A tiny animal, as a mosquito. [New Latin animalculum, diminutive of ANIMAL.] —an′i·mal′cu·lar (-kyə-lər) adj.

animal heat. The heat generated in an animal's body.

animal husbandry. The care and breeding of domestic animals such as cattle, hogs, sheep, and horses.

an·i·mal·ism (ăn′ə-məl-ĭz′əm) n. 1. A state of enjoying sound health and the wholesome satisfaction of physical drives. 2. A state of brutish indifference to all but the physical appetites. 3. The doctrine that man is purely animal with no spiritual nature. —an′i·mal·ist n. —an′i·mal·is′tic (-ĭs′tĭk) adj.

an·i·mal·i·ty (ăn′ə-măl′ə-tē) n. 1. The characteristics or nature of an animal. 2. Animals collectively; the animal kingdom. 3. The animal as distinct from the spiritual nature of man.

an·i·mal·ize (ăn′ə-məl-īz′) tr.v. **-ized**, **-izing**, **-izes**. 1. To make coarse and brutal; sensualize. 2. To endow (a deity) with the attributes of an animal. —an′i·mal·i·za′tion n.

animal kingdom. The category of living organisms that includes all animals. Compare **mineral kingdom, vegetable kingdom**.

animal magnetism. 1. Hypnotism or mesmerism. 2. Magnetic personal presence. 3. Sensualism. 4. Christian Science. "The voluntary or involuntary action of error in all its forms" (Mary Baker Eddy).

animal spirits. Vigorous buoyancy of good health.

animal starch. Glycogen (see).

an·i·mate (ăn′ə-māt′) tr.v. **-mated**, **-mating**, **-mates**. 1. To give life to; fill with life. 2. To impart interest or zest to; enliven: "The party was animated by all kinds of men and women" (René Dubos). 3. To fill with spirit, courage, or resolution; encourage. 4. To inspire to action; prompt. 5. To impart motion or activity to. 6. To make, design, or produce (a cartoon, for example) so as to create the illusion of motion. —adj. (ăn′ə-mĭt). 1. Possessing life; living. 2. Of or relating to animal life as distinct from plant life. 3. Lively; vivacious. [Latin animāre, to fill with breath, from anima, breath, soul. See **animal**.]

an·i·mat·ed (ăn′ə-mā′tĭd) adj. 1. Filled with life, activity, vigor, or spirit; lively; spirited; vigorous: an animated discussion. 2. Made or designed so as to seem alive and moving: an animated doll. 3. Containing or consisting of figures or objects that seem to move in a lifelike manner. —an′i·mat′ed·ly adv.

animated cartoon. A motion picture consisting of a photographed series of drawings.

animated oat. A grass, Avena sterilis, of the Mediterranean region, having spikelets that move or twist in response to changes in moisture.

an·i·ma·tion (ăn′ə-mā′shən) n. 1. The act, process, or result of animating. 2. The condition or quality of being animate; liveliness; spirit; vitality. 3. **a**. The art and process of preparing animated cartoons. **b**. An animated cartoon.

a·ni·ma·to (ä′nē-mä′tō) adv. Abbr. **anim.** Music. In an animated or lively manner. Used as a direction. —a′ni·ma′to adj. [Italian, from Latin animātus, past participle of animāre, to ANIMATE.]

an·i·ma·tor (ăn′ə-mā′tər) n. Also **an·i·mat·er**. 1. One that animates. 2. An artist or technician who prepares or produces an animated cartoon.

an·i·mism (ăn′ə-mĭz′əm) n. 1. Any of various primitive beliefs whereby natural phenomena and things animate and inanimate are held to possess an innate soul. 2. Any theory of psychic concepts or of spiritual beings generally. 3. The hypothesis, first advanced by Pythagoras and Plato, of an immaterial force animating the universe. 4. An 18th-century doctrine that viewed the soul as the vital principle and source of both the normal and the abnormal phenomena of life. [German Animismus, from Latin anima, breath, soul. See **animal**.] —an′i·mist n. —an′i·mis′tic adj.

an·i·mos·i·ty (ăn′ə-mŏs′ə-tē) n., pl. **-ties**. Bitter hostility or open enmity; active hatred. See Synonyms at **enmity**. [Middle English animosite, from Old French, from Late Latin animōsitās, vehemence, spirit, from Latin animōsus, bold, spirited, from animus, soul, mind. See ane- in Appendix*.]

an·i·mus (ăn′ə-məs) n. 1. An animating motive; intention or purpose. 2. A feeling of animosity; bitter hostility or hatred. 3. In the psychology of Carl Jung, the masculine inner personality, as present in women. Compare **anima**. See Synonyms at **enmity**. [Latin, mind, soul. See ane- in Appendix*.]

an·i·on (ăn′ī′ən) n. A negatively charged ion that migrates to an anode, as in electrolysis. Compare **cation**. [Greek, "that which goes up" (i.e., toward the anode), neuter present participle of anienai, to go up : an(a)-, up + ienai, to go (see ei-¹ in Appendix*.)] —an′i·on′ic (-ŏn′ĭk) adj.

an·ise (ăn′ĭs) n. 1. A plant, Pimpinella anisum, native to the Mediterranean region, having clusters of small yellowish-white flowers and licorice-flavored seeds. 2. Aniseed. [Middle English anis, from Old French, from Latin anīsum, from Greek anison†.]

animated cartoon

anise

ă pat/ā pay/âr care/ä father/b bib/ch church/d deed/ĕ pet/ē be/f fife/g gag/h hat/hw which/ĭ pit/ī pie/îr pier/j judge/k kick/l lid, needle/m mum/n no, sudden/ng thing/ŏ pot/ō toe/ô paw, for/oi noise/ou out/ōō took/ōō boot/p pop/r roar/s sauce/sh ship, dish/

an·i·seed (ăn′ĭ-sēd′) *n.* The licorice-flavored seed of the anise plant, used in medicine and as flavoring. [Middle English *anis seed* : ANISE + SEED.]
an·i·sei·ko·ni·a (ăn-ī′sī-kō′nē-ə) *n.* An ocular defect in which image, shape, and size differ in each eye. [New Latin : ANIS(O)- + Greek *eikōn,* image (see **weik-**[3] in Appendix*).] —**an′i′sei·kon′ic** (-kŏn′ĭk) *adj.*
an·i·sette (ăn′ə-sĕt′, -zĕt′) *n.* An anise-flavored liqueur. [French, diminutive of *anis,* ANISE.]
aniso–. Indicates not equal or alike; for example, **anisomerous.** [New Latin, from Greek *anisos,* unequal : AN-, not + *isos,* equal (see **iso-**).]
an·i·sog·a·my (ăn′ī-sŏg′ə-mē) *n. Biology.* A union between markedly different gametes. [ANISO- + -GAMY.] —**an′i·sog′a·mous** (-məs) *adj.*
an·i·som·er·ous (ăn′ī-sŏm′ər-əs) *adj. Botany.* Having or designating floral whorls that have unequal numbers of parts. [ANISO- + -MEROUS.]
an·i·so·met·ric (ăn-ī′sə-mĕt′rĭk) *adj.* Not isometric. [French *anisométrique* : AN- (not) + ISOMETRIC.]
an·i·so·me·tro·pi·a (ăn-ī′sə-mə-trō′pē-ə) *n. Pathology.* Difference in the refractive power of the eyes. [New Latin : Greek *anisometros* : AN- (not) + *isometros,* ISOMETR(IC) + -OPIA.]
an·i·so·trop·ic (ăn-ī′sə-trŏp′ĭk) *adj.* **1.** Not isotropic. **2.** *Physics.* Having properties that differ according to the direction of measurement. [AN- (not) + ISOTROPIC.] —**an′i·sot′ro·pism′** (-sŏt′rə-pĭz′əm), **an′i·sot′ro·py** *n.*
An·jou (ăn′jo͞o′; *French* äN-zho͞o′). A former province of western France. See **Angevin.**
An·ka·ra (ăng′kə-rə, äng′-). Ancient name **An·cy·ra** (ăn-sī′rə). Formerly **An·go·ra** (ăng-gôr′ə). The capital and second-largest city of Turkey, in the center of the Asian part of the country. Population, 650,000.
an·ker·ite (ăng′kə-rīt′) *n.* A dolomitelike mineral in which iron partially replaces magnesium. [German *Ankerit,* after M.J. *Anker* (died 1843), Austrian mineralogist.]
ankh (ăngk) *n.* An ansate cross. [Egyptian.]
An·king (än′kĭng′). Formerly **Hwai·ning** (hwī′nĭng). A city on the Yangtze, the historical capital of Anhwei province, China. Population, 129,000.
an·kle (ăng′kəl) *n.* **1.** The joint, consisting of the bones and related structure, that connects the foot with the leg. **2.** The slender section of the leg immediately above the foot. [Middle English *ankel* and *anclowe,* respectively from Old Norse *ankula* (unattested) and Old English *anclēow.* See **ank-** in Appendix.*]
an·kle·bone (ăng′kəl-bōn′) *n. Anatomy.* The **talus** *(see).*
an·klet (ăng′klĭt) *n.* **1.** An ornament worn around the ankle. **2.** A sock that reaches just above the ankle.
an·ky·lose (ăng′kĭ-lōs′, -lōz′) *v.* **-losed, -losing, -loses.** Also **an·chy·lose** —*tr.* To join or consolidate by ankylosis. —*intr.* To become joined or consolidated by ankylosis. [From New Latin ANKYLOSIS.]
an·ky·lo·sis (ăng′kĭ-lō′sĭs) *n.* Also **an·chy·lo·sis** (ăng′kĭ-). **1.** *Anatomy.* The consolidation of bones or their parts forming a single unit. **2.** *Pathology.* The stiffening of a joint as the result of abnormal bone fusion. [New Latin, from Greek *ankulōsis,* stiffening of the joints, from *ankuloun,* to bend, from *ankulos,* bent, curved, crooked. See **ank-** in Appendix.*] —**an′ky·lot′ic** (-lŏt′ĭk) *adj.*
an·lace (ăn′lĭs) *n.* A two-edged medieval dagger. [Middle English *anlas, anelas*†.]
an·la·ge (än′lä′gə) *n., pl.* **-gen** (-gən) or **-ges.** Also **An·la·ge. 1.** *Embryology.* The initial cell structure from which an embryonic part or organ develops; primordium. **2.** A fundamental principle; foundation. [German *Anlage,* from Middle High German *anlāge,* a request, a laying on : *ane-,* on, from Old High German *ana* (see **an**[1] in Appendix*) + *lāge,* act of laying, from Old High German *āga* (see **legh-** in Appendix*).]
Ann, Anne (ăn). Also **An·na** (ăn′ə). A feminine given name. [Middle English *Anne, Anna,* from Old French, from Late Latin and Late Greek *Anna,* from Hebrew *Ḥannāh,* HANNAH.]
ann. 1. annals. **2.** annual. **3.** annuity.
Ann, Cape (ăn). A peninsula in northern Massachusetts projecting into the Atlantic Ocean northeast of Gloucester.
an·na (ä′nə) *n.* A former copper coin of India and Pakistan, equal to 1/16th of a rupee. [Hindi *ānā,* from Sanskrit *áṇu-*†, small.]
An·na·ba (ä-nä-bä′). *French* **Bône** (bōn). A city of Algeria, in the northeast on the Mediterranean. Population, 139,000.
An·na·bel, An·na·belle (ăn′ə-bĕl′). A feminine given name. [Middle English *Anabel,* probably a misreading for *Amabel,* from Latin *amabilis,* loving, from *amāre,* to love. See **amour.**]
an·nal·ist (ăn′əl-ĭst) *n.* A chronicler. [French *annaliste,* from Old French, from *annales,* annals, from Latin *annālēs,* ANNALS.] —**an′nal·is′tic** *adj.*
an·nals (ăn′əlz) *pl.n. Abbr.* **ann. 1.** A chronological record of the events of successive years. **2.** Any descriptive account or record; history: *"The short and simple annals of the poor"* (Gray). **3.** A periodical journal compiling the records and reports of a particular learned field. [Latin *(librī) annālēs,* "yearly (books)," from *annālis,* yearly, from *annus,* year. See **at-** in Appendix.*]
An·nam (ă-năm′, ăn′ăm′). Also **A·nam.** An administrative region of French Indochina in east-central Vietnam.
An·na·mese (ăn′ə-mēz′, -mēs′) *adj.* Also **An·na·mite** (ăn′ə-mīt′). Of or pertaining to Annam, its inhabitants, their language, or their culture. —*n., pl.* Annamese (for sense 1). Also **An·na·mite. 1.** A native or inhabitant of Annam. **2.** The former name for the language **Vietnamese** *(see).*
An·nap·o·lis (ə-năp′ə-lĭs). The capital of Maryland, on Chesapeake Bay, the seat of the U.S. Naval Academy since 1850. Population, 22,000.
An·nap·o·lis Royal (ə-năp′ə-lĭs). A town in southwestern Nova Scotia, Canada, first settled in 1605, and formerly the capital of the province.
An·na·pur·na (ăn′ə-po͝or′nə, -pûr′nə). Also **An·a·pur·na.** A massif of the Himalayas extending 35 miles in central Nepal. Highest elevation, Annapurna I (26,502 feet).
Ann Ar·bor (ăn är′bər). A city in southeastern Michigan. Population, 67,000.
an·nat·to (ə-nä′tō) *n., pl.* **-tos.** Also **a·nat·to, ar·nat·to** (är-nä′tō). **1.** A small tropical American tree, *Bixa orellana,* having red or pinkish flowers and seeds used in cooking. See **achiote. 2.** A yellowish-red dyestuff obtained from the pulp of annatto seeds. [From Cariban.]
Anne[1]. Variant of **Ann.**
Anne[2] (ăn). 1665–1714. Queen of Great Britain and Ireland (1702–14); daughter of James II.
an·neal (ə-nēl′) *tr.v.* **-nealed, -nealing, -neals. 1.** To subject (glass or metal) to a process of heating and slow cooling in order to toughen and reduce brittleness. **2.** To temper. [Middle English *anelen,* Old English *onǣlan* : ON + *ǣlan,* to set fire to, from *āl,* fire (see **aidh-** in Appendix*).]
Anne·cy (ăn-sē′). A lakeside resort of southeastern France, about 25 miles south of Geneva, Switzerland. Population, 42,000.
an·ne·lid (ăn′ə-lĭd) *adj.* Also **an·nel·i·dan** (ə-nĕl′ə-dən). Of or belonging to the phylum Annelida, which includes the earthworms, leeches, and other worms having cylindrical segmented bodies. —*n.* Also **an·nel·i·dan.** An annelid worm. [New Latin *Annelida,* from French *annélide* : *annelés,* ringed, from *anneler,* to encircle, from Old French *annel,* ring, from Latin *annellus,* diminutive of *ānulus,* small ring (see **annulet**) + -IDE.]
Anne of Cleves (ăn; klēvz). 1515–1557. Queen of England; married (1540) Henry VIII as his fourth wife.
an·nex (ə-nĕks′, ăn′ĕks′) *tr.v.* **-nexed, -nexing, -nexes. 1.** To add or join to; append or attach, especially to a larger or more significant thing. **2.** To incorporate (territory) into an existing country or state. **3.** To add or attach, as an attribute, condition, or consequence. —*n.* (ăn′ĕks′, ăn′ĭks). Also *British* **an·nexe** (ăn′ĭks′). **1.** A building added on to a larger one, or an auxiliary building situated near the main one. **2.** An addition to a record or document; an appendix or addendum. [Middle English *annexen,* from Old French *annexer,* from Latin *annectere* (past participle *annexus*), to bind to : *ad-,* to + *nectere,* to tie (see **ned-** in Appendix*).] —**an·nex′a·ble** *adj.*
an·nex·a·tion (ăn′ĕk-sā′shən) *n.* **1.** The act or process of annexing. **2.** Something that has been annexed. —**an′nex·a′tion·al** *adj.* —**an′nex·a′tion·ism′** *n.* —**an′nex·a′tion·ist** *n.*
An·nie Oak·ley (ăn′ē ōk′lē). *Slang.* A complimentary ticket of admittance; a free ticket or pass. [After Annie OAKLEY, from the association of the punched ticket with one of her bullet-riddled targets.]
an·ni·hi·late (ə-nī′ə-lāt′) *v.* **-lated, -lating, -lates.** —*tr.* **1.** To destroy completely; wipe out; reduce to nonexistence. **2.** To nullify or render void; abolish. **3.** *Informal.* To overwhelm completely; render helpless or ineffective. —*intr.* To participate in annihilation, as do an electron and a positron. [Late Latin *annihilāre,* to reduce to nothing : Latin *ad-,* to + *nihil,* nothing (see **ne** in Appendix*).] —**an·ni′hi·la·bil′i·ty** (ə-nī′ə-lə-bĭl′ə-tē) *n.* —**an·ni′hi·la·ble** (ə-nī′ə-lə-bəl) *adj.* —**an·ni′hi·la′tor** (-lā′tər) *n.*
an·ni·hi·la·tion (ə-nī′ə-lā′shən) *n.* **1.** The act or process of annihilating. **2.** The condition or result of having been annihilated; utter destruction. **3.** *Physics.* The phenomenon in which a particle and an antiparticle, such as an electron and a positron, disappear with a resultant release of energy approximately equivalent to the sum of their masses.
an·ni·ver·sa·ry (ăn′ə-vûr′sər-ē) *n., pl.* **-ries. 1.** The annual recurrence of an event that took place in some preceding year: *a wedding anniversary.* **2.** A commemorative celebration on this date. —*adj.* **1.** Recurring each year, especially on the same date of each year. **2.** Of or for an anniversary. [Middle English *anniversarie,* from Medieval Latin *(diēs) anniversāria,* "anniversary (day)," from Latin *anniversārius,* "returning yearly" : *annus,* year (see **at-** in Appendix*) + *versus,* past participle of *vertere,* to turn (see **wer-**[3] in Appendix*).]
an·no Dom·i·ni (ăn′ō dŏm′ə-nī′, dŏm′ə-nē). *Abbr. Usually small capitals* A.D. *Latin.* In a specified year of the Christian era. Literally, "in the year of the Lord."
Usage: In formal usage, A.D. precedes the date, which is always a specific year rather than a century: *He died* A.D. *961* (not *in the tenth century* A.D.). Informally, it is often used like B.C., which always follows the date and may be applied to any specified period (year, century, or era). When neither abbreviation appears, the time is assumed to be after Christ.
an·no·tate (ăn′ō-tāt′) *v.* **-tated, -tating, -tates.** —*tr.* To furnish (a literary work) with critical commentary or explanatory notes; to gloss. —*intr.* To gloss a text. [Latin *annotāre,* to note down : *ad-,* to + *notāre,* to mark, from *nota,* a mark, note (see **gnō-** in Appendix*).] —**an′no·ta′tive** *adj.* —**an′no·ta′tor** (ăn′ō-tā′tər) *n.*
an·no·ta·tion (ăn′ō-tā′shən) *n.* **1.** The act or process of annotating. **2.** A critical or explanatory note; commentary.
an·nounce (ə-nouns′) *tr.v.* **-nounced, -nouncing, -nounces. 1.** To bring to public notice; to declare or proclaim officially or formally. **2.** To proclaim the presence or arrival of: *announce a caller.* **3.** To make aware or conscious of through the senses. **4.** To serve as an announcer. [Middle English *announcen*

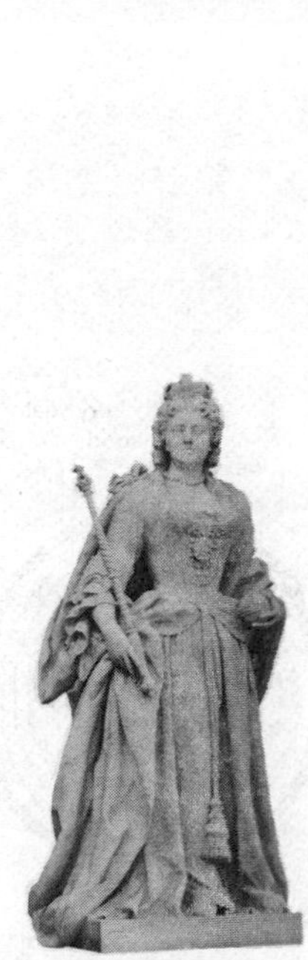

Anne[2]
Statue in the library of Blenheim Palace, England

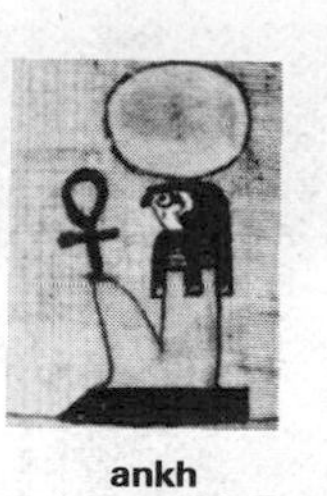

ankh
Illustration on 19th-Dynasty Egyptian papyrus

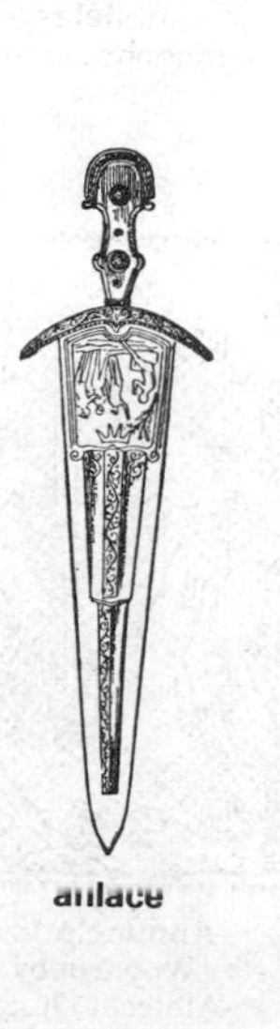

anlace

t tight/th thin, path/*th* this, bathe/ŭ cut/ûr urge/v valve/w with/y yes/z zebra, size/zh vision/ə about, item, edible, gallop, circus/ à *Fr.* ami/œ *Fr.* feu, *Ger.* schön/ü *Fr.* tu, *Ger.* über/KH *Ger.* ich, *Scot.* loch/N *Fr.* bon. ***Follows main vocabulary.** †**Of obscure origin.**

from Old French *annoncer*, from Latin *annuntiāre* : *ad-*, to + *nuntiāre*, to announce, from *nuntius*, messenger (see **neu-**[1] in Appendix*).]

an·nounce·ment (ə-nouns′mənt) *n.* **1.** The act of announcing. **2.** Something that has been announced. **3.** A printed or published statement or notice.

an·nounc·er (ə-noun′sər) *n.* **1.** Someone who announces. **2.** A radio or television performer who provides program continuity and delivers commercial and other announcements.

an·noy (ə-noi′) *v.* **-noyed, -noying, -noys.** —*tr.* **1.** To bother or irritate; disturb slightly. **2.** To injure or harm; molest. —*intr.* To behave in an annoying manner. —*n. Archaic.* Something that annoys. [Middle English *anoien*, from Old French *anoier*, *enuier*, from Late Latin *inodiāre*, to make odious, from Latin *in odiō*, "in hatred," odious : *in*, in + *odiō*, ablative of *odium*, hatred (see **od-**[2] in Appendix*).] —**an·noy′er** *n.*

Synonyms: *annoy, irritate, bother, irk, vex, provoke, aggravate, peeve, rile.* These verbs mean to disturb or disquiet a person and, usually, to stir anger. *Annoy* refers to mild disturbance caused by an act that tries one's patience. *Irritate* is closely related but somewhat stronger. *Bother* implies imposition that affects physical or mental composure. *Irk* stresses the wearisome quality of repeated disturbance. *Vex* applies to an act capable of bringing on anger or perplexity. *Provoke* implies strong and usually deliberate imposition and angry response, and *aggravate* is an approximate but informal equivalent. *Peeve*, also informal, suggests rather minor disturbance that produces a querulous, resentful response. *Rile* implies strong anger, openly displayed.

an·noy·ance (ə-noi′əns) *n.* **1.** Something that annoys; a nuisance. **2.** The act of annoying. **3.** Vexation; irritation.

an·noy·ing (ə-noi′ĭng) *adj.* Causing vexation or irritation; troublesome: *an annoying cough.* —**an·noy′ing·ly** *adv.*

an·nu·al (ăn′yōō-əl) *adj. Abbr.* **ann. 1.** Recurring, done, or performed every year; yearly. **2.** Of or pertaining to the year; determined by a year's time: *an annual income.* **3.** *Botany.* Living and growing for only one year or season. Compare **perennial, biennial.** —*n.* **1.** A periodical published yearly; yearbook. **2.** A plant that lives and grows for only one year or season, during which the life cycle is completed. [Middle English *annuel*, from Old French, from Late Latin *annuālis*, from Latin *annus*, year. See **at-** in Appendix.*] —**an′nu·al·ly** *adv.*

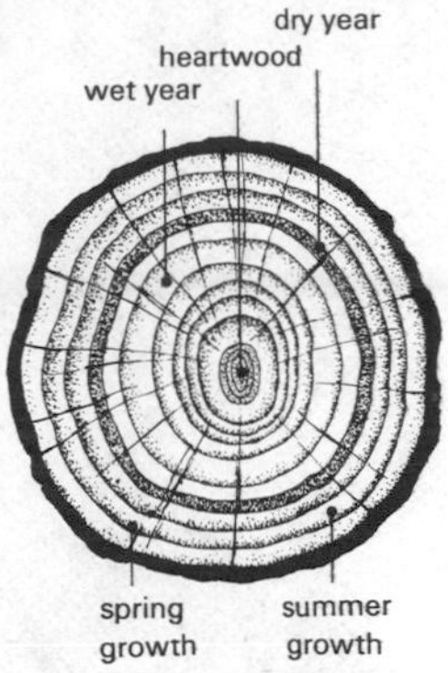
dry year
heartwood
wet year
spring growth
summer growth

annual ring
Cross section showing annual rings

annual ring. One of the concentric layers of wood, especially in a tree trunk, indicating a year's growth in temperate climates and seasonal growth in regions of wet and dry seasons.

an·nu·i·tant (ə-nōō′ə-tənt, ə-nyōō′-) *n.* A person who receives or is qualified to receive an annuity.

an·nu·it coep·tis (ăn′yōō-ĭt sĕp′tĭs). *Latin.* He (God) has favored our undertakings. It is the motto, adapted from the *Aeneid* (IX.625), that appears on the reverse of the Great Seal of the United States.

an·nu·i·ty (ə-nōō′ə-tē, ə-nyōō′-) *n., pl.* **-ties.** *Abbr.* **ann. 1.** The annual payment of an allowance or income. **2.** The right to receive this payment or the obligation to make this payment. **3. a.** The interest or dividends paid annually on an investment of money. **b.** The investment made. [Middle English *annuite*, from Old French, from Medieval Latin *annuitās*, yearly payment, from Latin *annuus*, yearly, from *annus*, year. See **at-** in Appendix.*]

an·nul (ə-nŭl′) *tr.v.* **-nulled, -nulling, -nuls. 1.** To make or declare void or invalid; nullify or cancel, as a marriage or a law. **2.** To obliterate the existence or effect of; annihilate. —See Synonyms at **nullify.** [Middle English *annullen*, from Old French *annuller*, from Late Latin *annullāre*, to make into nothing : Latin *ad-*, to + *nullus*, none, null (see **ne-** in Appendix*).] —**an·nul′la·ble** *adj.*

an·nu·lar (ăn′yə-lər) *adj.* Forming or shaped like a ring. [Old French *annulaire*, from Latin *annulāris*, *ānulāris*, from *annulus*, *ānulus*, ring. See **āno-** in Appendix.*] —**an′nu·lar·ly** *adv.*

annular eclipse. A solar eclipse in which the moon covers all but a bright ring around the circumference of the sun.

annular ligament. A ligament or fibrous band that rings the ankle joint or the wrist joint.

an·nu·late (ăn′yə-lĭt, -lāt′) *adj.* Also **an·nu·lat·ed** (-lā′tĭd). Having or consisting of rings or ringlike segments. [Latin *annulātus*, *ānulātus*, from *annulus*, *ānulus*, ring. See **annulet.**]

an·nu·la·tion (ăn′yə-lā′shən) *n.* **1.** The act or process of forming rings. **2.** A ringlike structure or segment.

an·nu·let (ăn′yə-lĭt) *n. Architecture.* A ringlike molding around the capital of a pillar. [Diminutive formation from Latin *annulus*, *ānulus*, ring. See **āno-** in Appendix.*]

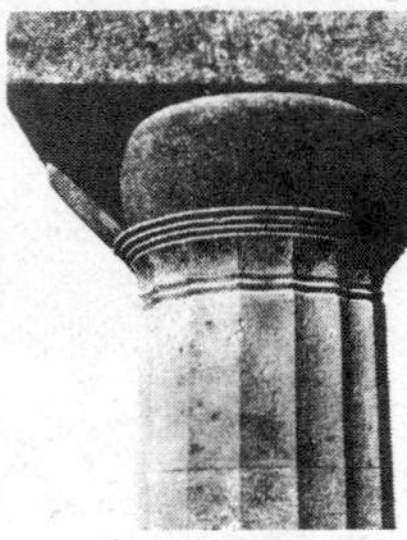

annulet
Doric pillar encircled by four annulets

an·nul·ment (ə-nŭl′mənt) *n.* **1.** The act of annulling. **2.** The retrospective as well as prospective invalidation of a marriage, as for nonconsummation, effected by means of a declaration stating that the marriage was never valid.

an·nu·lus (ăn′yə-ləs) *n., pl.* **-luses** or **-li** (-lī′). **1.** A ringlike figure, part, structure, or marking. **2.** *Geometry.* The figure bounded by and containing the area between two concentric circles. [Latin *annulus*, *ānulus*, ring. See **āno-** in Appendix.*]

an·nun·ci·ate (ə-nŭn′sē-āt′) *tr.v.* **-ated, -ating, -ates.** To announce; proclaim: *"They do not so properly affirm, as annunciate it"* (Lamb). [Latin *annuntiāre*, to ANNOUNCE.] —**an·nun′ci·a′tive, an·nun′ci·a·to′ry** (-ə-tôr′ē, -tōr′ē) *adj.*

an·nun·ci·a·tion (ə-nŭn′sē-ā′shən) *n.* **1.** The act of announcing. **2.** An announcement; proclamation.

An·nun·ci·a·tion (ə-nŭn′sē-ā′shən) *n.* **1.** The angel Gabriel's announcement of the Incarnation. Luke 1:26–38. **2.** The festival, on March 25, in celebration of this event.

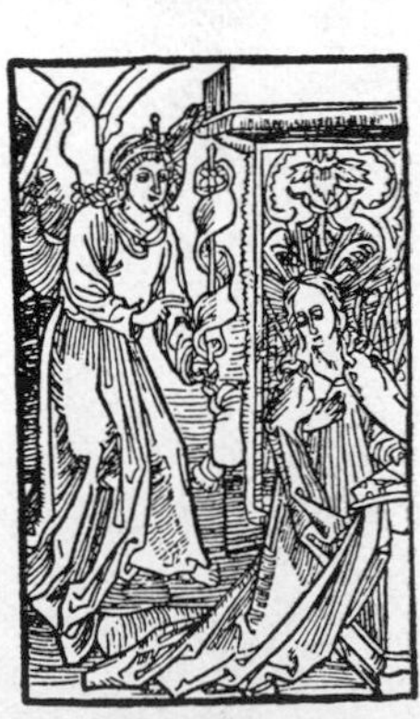

Annunciation
Woodcut by Albrecht Dürer

Annunciation lily. The **Madonna lily** *(see).*

an·nun·ci·a·tor (ə-nŭn′sē-ā′tər) *n.* An electrical signaling device used in hotels or offices to indicate the source of calls on a switchboard.

an·nus mi·rab·i·lis (ăn′əs mĭ-răb′ə-lĭs). **1.** A year of wonders or disasters; fateful year: *"Hungary's blood bath was the saddest event in that annus mirabilis"* (C.L. Sulzberger). **2.** The year 1666, memorable for the great fire of London and the English victory over the Dutch. [New Latin, "wondrous year," originally designating the year 1588 in a forecast of its disasters by Regiomontanus.]

a·no·a (ə-nō′ə) *n.* A small buffalo, *Anoa depressicornis*, of Celebes and the Philippines, having short, pointed horns. [Native name in Celebes.]

an·ode (ăn′ōd′) *n.* **1.** Any positively charged electrode, as of an electrolytic cell, storage battery, or electron tube. **2.** The negatively charged terminal of a primary cell or of a storage battery that is supplying current. [Greek *anodos*, a way up (i.e., from the positive pole into the electrolyte) : *ana-*, up + *hodos*, road, way (see **sed-**[2] in Appendix*).] —**an·o′dal** (ăn-ō′dəl), **an·od′ic** (ăn-ŏd′ĭk) *adj.*

an·o·dize (ăn′ə-dīz′) *tr.v.* **-dized, -dizing, -dizes.** To coat (a metallic surface) electrolytically with a protective oxide. [ANOD(E) + -IZE.]

an·o·dyne (ăn′ə-dīn′) *adj.* **1.** Able to soothe or relieve pain. **2.** Relaxing: *anodyne novels about country life.* **3.** Watered-down; insipid: *anodyne references to progress and freedom.* —*n.* **1.** A medicine that relieves pain. **2.** Anything that soothes or comforts. [Latin *anōdynus*, from Greek *anōdunos*, free from pain : AN- (without) + *odunē*, pain (see **ed-** in Appendix*).]

a·noint (ə-noint′) *tr.v.* **anointed, anointing, anoints. 1.** To apply oil, ointment, or a similar substance to. **2.** To put oil on as a sign of sanctification or consecration in a religious ceremony. [Middle English *anointen*, from Old French *enoindre* (past participle *enoint*), from Latin *inunguere* : *in-*, upon + *unguere*, to smear, anoint (see **ongw-** in Appendix*).] —**a·noint′er** *n.* —**a·noint′ment** *n.*

a·no·le (ə-nō′lē) *n.* Any of various chiefly tropical New World lizards of the genus *Anolis*, characterized by a distensible throat flap and the ability to change color. Also called "chameleon." [New Latin *Anolis*, from French *anolis*, anole, from Cariban.]

a·nom·a·lous (ə-nŏm′ə-ləs) *adj.* Deviating from the normal or common order, form, or rule; abnormal; deviant. [Late Latin *anōmalos*, from Greek, uneven : AN- (not) + *homalos*, even, from *homos*, same (see **sem-**[1] in Appendix*).] —**a·nom′a·lous·ly** *adv.* —**a·nom′a·lous·ness** *n.*

a·nom·a·ly (ə-nŏm′ə-lē) *n., pl.* **-lies. 1.** Deviation from the normal or common order, form, or rule; abnormality. **2.** Anything anomalous, irregular, or abnormal. **3.** *Astronomy.* The angular deviation, as observed from the sun, of a planet from its perihelion. —**a·nom′a·lis′tic** (-lĭs′tĭk′), **a·nom′a·lis′ti·cal** *adj.* —**a·nom′a·lis′ti·cal·ly** *adv.*

an·o·mie, an·o·my (ăn′ə-mē) *n.* **1.** A collapse of the social structures governing a given society. **2.** The state of alienation experienced by an individual or class in such a situation. **3.** Personal disorganization resulting in unsocial behavior. [Greek *anomia*, lawlessness, from *anomos*, without law : *a-*, without + *nomos*, law (see **nem-**[2] in Appendix*).]

a·non (ə-nŏn′) *adv.* **1.** At another time; again. **2.** *Archaic.* In a short time; soon: *"Such good men as he which is anon to be interred"* (Cotton Mather). **3.** *Archaic.* At once; immediately: *"The same is he that heareth the word, and anon with joy receiveth it"* (Matthew 13:20). —**ever and anon.** Time after time; now and then. [Middle English *anon*, *onon*, from Old English *on ān*, "into one," at once : *on*, in, ON + *ān*, one (see **oino-** in Appendix*).]

anon. anonymous.

an·o·nym (ăn′ə-nĭm′) *n.* **1.** An anonymous person. **2.** A pseudonym. [French *anonyme*, from adjective, "anonymous," Late Latin *anōnymus*, ANONYMOUS.]

a·non·y·mous (ə-nŏn′ə-məs) *adj. Abbr.* **a., anon. 1.** Having an unknown or unacknowledged name. **2.** Having an unknown or withheld authorship or agency. [Late Latin *anōnymus*, from Greek *anōnumos*, nameless : AN- (without) + *onoma*, name (see **nomen-** in Appendix*).] —**an′o·nym′i·ty** (ăn′ə-nĭm′ə-tē), **a·non′y·mous·ness** *n.* —**a·non′y·mous·ly** *adv.*

a·noph·e·les (ə-nŏf′ə-lēz′) *n.* Any of various mosquitoes of the genus *Anopheles*, many of which carry the malaria parasite and transmit the disease to man. [New Latin *Anopheles*, "the hurtful ones," from Greek *anōphelēs*, useless, hurtful : AN- (without) + *ophelos*, advantage (see **obhel-** in Appendix*).] —**a·noph′e·line′** (-līn′) *adj.* & *n.*

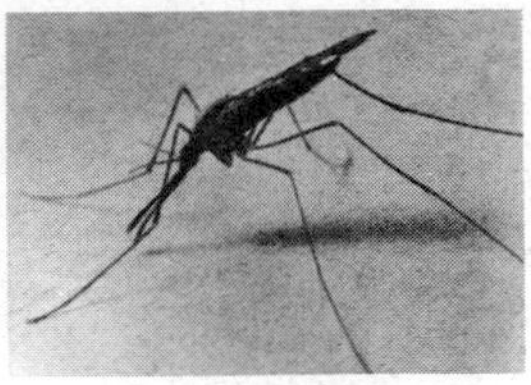

anopheles
Female anopheles mosquito

an·o·rak (ăn′ə-răk′) *n.* A heavy jacket with a hood, worn in polar regions; parka. [Eskimo (Greenland) *ánorâq.*]

an·o·rex·i·a (ăn′ə-rĕk′sē-ə) *n.* Loss of appetite. [Greek *anorexia* : AN- (without) + *orexis*, a longing, from *oregein*, to reach out for (see **reg-**[1] in Appendix*).]

an·or·thite (ăn-ôr′thīt′) *n.* A rare plagioclase feldspar with high calcium oxide content, occurring in igneous rocks. [French : AN- (not) + Greek *orthos*, straight (from its oblique crystals) (see **werdh-** in Appendix*) + -ITE.] —**an′or·thit′ic** (-thĭt′ĭk) *adj.*

an·or·tho·site (ăn-ôr′thə-sīt′) *n.* A plutonic rock, chiefly plagioclase. [French *anorthose* : AN- (not) + Greek *orthos*, straight (see **anorthite**) + -ITE.]

an·os·mi·a (ăn-ŏz′mē-ə) *n.* Loss of the sense of smell. [New Latin : AN- (without) + Greek *osmē*, smell (see **od-**[1] in Appendix*) + -IA.] —**an·os′mic** *adj.*

an·oth·er (ə-nu*th*′ər) *adj.* **1.** An additional; one more. **2.** Distinctly different; some other. **3.** Different, but of the same char-

acter. —*pron.* **1.** An additional one. **2.** A different one. **3.** One of the same kind. [Middle English *an other.*]
Usage: *Another than* is the preferred construction in examples such as *another car than mine was used,* where *another* (adjective) means *different.* An alternative possibility is *another from.* The possessive of *one another* is *one another's* (not *one anothers'*): *They shared one another's interests.*

A·nou·ilh (ȧ-nōō-ē′), **Jean.** Born 1910. French dramatist.

an·ox·e·mi·a (ăn′ŏk-sē′mē-ə) *n.* An abnormal decline in the oxygen content of the blood. [New Latin : AN- (without) + OX(Y)- + -EMIA.] —**an′ox·e′mic** *adj.*

an·ox·i·a (ăn-ŏk′sē-ə) *n.* **1.** Absence of oxygen. **2.** A pathological deficiency of oxygen, especially **hypoxia** *(see).* [AN- (without) + OX(Y)- + -IA.] —**an·ox′ic** *adj.*

ans. answer.

an·sate (ăn′sāt′) *adj.* Also **an·sat·ed** (-tĭd). Having a handle or a part resembling a handle. [Latin *ānsātus,* from *ānsa,* handle. See **ans-** in Appendix.*]

ansate cross. A cross shaped like a T with a loop at the top; an ankh. Also called "crux ansata."

An·schluss (än′shlŏŏs′) *n. German.* A union; specifically, the political union of Nazi Germany and Austria in 1938.

An·selm (ăn′sĕlm′), **Saint.** 1033–1109. Archbishop of Canterbury (1093–1109).

an·ser·ine (ăn′sə-rīn′) *adj.* Also **an·ser·ous** (-rəs) (for sense 3). **1.** Of or belonging to the subfamily Anserinae, which includes the geese. **2.** Of or resembling a goose; gooselike. **3.** Stupid; silly; foolish. [New Latin *Anserinae,* from Latin *ānserīnus,* gooselike, from *ānser,* goose. See **ghans-** in Appendix.*]

An·shan (ăn′shăn). A city of northeastern China, in southern Liaoning Province. Population, 833,000.

an·swer (ăn′sər, än′-) *n. Abbr.* **ans., a., A. 1.** Spoken or written reply, as to a question, statement, request, or letter. **2. a.** A solution or result, as to a problem. **b.** The correct response or solution. **3.** An act in response or retaliation. **4.** *Law.* A defendant's defense against charges filed against him. —*v.* **answered, -swering, -swers.** —*intr.* **1.** Respond in words or action. Used with *to.* **2.** To be liable or accountable. Used with *for.* **3.** To serve the purpose; suffice; do: *"often I do use three words where one would answer"* (Mark Twain). **4.** To correspond; match. Used with *to: answering to the description.* —*tr.* **1.** To reply to. **2.** To respond correctly to. **3.** To fulfill the demands of; serve: *"my fortune has answered my desires"* (Walton). **4.** To conform or correspond to. **5.** To be responsible for; meet; discharge (a claim or debt, for example). [Middle English *answer(e),* Old English *andswaru.* See **swer-**[1] in Appendix.*] —**an′swer·er** *n.*
Synonyms: *answer, respond, reply, retort.* These verbs relate to action taken as the immediate result of a question or other stimulus. *Answer,* the most general, refers to any act that completes a process initiated by another. *Respond* suggests a physical act or change that follows a specific stimulus, but is now also used as a loose equivalent of *reply,* which means to answer in speech or writing to a direct question. *Retort* refers to a sharp, spoken remark of the same style or kind as that used by one's accuser or debating opponent.

an·swer·a·ble (ăn′sər-ə-bəl) *adj.* **1.** Responsible; accountable; liable. **2.** Able to be answered. **3.** Corresponding; suitable. Used with *to.* —See Synonyms at **responsible.** —**an′swer·a·bil′i·ty, an′swer·a·ble·ness** *n.* —**an′swer·a·bly** *adv.*

ant (ănt) *n.* Any of various social insects of the family Formicidae, characteristically having wings only in the males and fertile females, and living in colonies that have a complex social organization. [Middle English *ante, amete,* Old English *ǣmette.* See **mai-**[1] in Appendix.*]

-ant. Indicates performing, promoting, or causing an action; for example, **deodorant, benignant.** [Middle English, from Old French, from Latin *-āns* (stem *ant-*), present participial ending of first conjugation verbs.]

ant. 1. antenna. **2.** antiquarian; antiquity. **3.** antonym.

an·ta (ăn′tə) *n., pl.* **-tae** (-tē′). *Architecture.* **1.** A thickening of the projecting end of the lateral wall of a Greek temple. **2.** A pier that constitutes one boundary of the porch. [Latin *antae* (plural). See **anetā** in Appendix.*]

ANTA (ăn′tə). American National Theatre and Academy.

ant·ac·id (ănt-ăs′ĭd) *adj.* Correcting acidity; neutralizing acids. —*n.* A substance that neutralizes acid, especially a medicinal remedy. [ANT(I)- + ACID.]

An·tae·us (ăn-tē′əs). *Greek Mythology.* A giant, invincible while touching the ground, who was lifted into the air by Heracles and crushed to death.

an·tag·o·nism (ăn-tăg′ə-nĭz′əm) *n.* **1.** Mutual resistance; opposition; hostility. **2.** The condition of being an opposing principle, force, or factor. —See Synonyms at **enmity.**

an·tag·o·nist (ăn-tăg′ə-nĭst) *n.* **1.** One who opposes and actively competes with another; adversary. **2.** *Anatomy.* A muscle that opposes another muscle. **3.** *Pharmacology.* A drug that counteracts or neutralizes another drug. —See Synonyms at **opponent.** —**an·tag′o·nis′tic** *adj.* —**an·tag′o·nis′ti·cal·ly** *adv.*

an·tag·o·nize (ăn-tăg′ə-nīz′) *tr.v.* **-nized, -nizing, -nizes. 1.** To incur the dislike of. **2.** To counteract. [Greek *antagōnizesthai,* to struggle against : *anti-,* against + *agōnizesthai,* to struggle, from *agōn,* contest (see **agony**).]

An·tal·ya (än′täl-yä′). Formerly **A·da·li·a** (ä′dä-lē-yä′). A seaport of southwestern Turkey on the Gulf of Antalya, an inlet of the Mediterranean. Population, 46,000.

Ant·arc·tic (ănt-ärk′tĭk, -är′tĭk) *adj.* Of or pertaining to the regions surrounding the South Pole. —*n.* Antarctica and its surrounding waters. Preceded by *the.* [Middle English *Antartik,* from Medieval Latin *Antarticus,* from Latin *antarcticus,* southern, from Greek *antarktikos* : *anti-,* opposite + ARCTIC.]

Ant·arc·ti·ca (ănt-ärk′tĭ-kə, -är′tĭ-kə). A continent over five million square miles in area, largely contained within the Antarctic Circle, and almost entirely covered by a sheet of ice. Also called "Antarctic Continent."

Antarctic Archipelago. The former name for the **Palmer Archipelago.**

Antarctic Circle. A parallel of latitude, 66 degrees, 33 minutes south, marking the limit of the South Frigid Zone.

Antarctic Ocean. The waters surrounding Antarctica; the southern extensions of the Atlantic, Pacific, and Indian oceans, which appear to constitute a distinct body of water on most world map projections.

Antarctic Peninsula. Formerly **Pal·mer Peninsula** (pä′mər). A peninsula of Antarctica, extending some 700 miles into the Atlantic Ocean. Also called "Graham Land."

An·tar·es (ăn-târ′ēz) *n.* A double and variable star, the brightest in the southern sky, about 424 light-years from earth in the constellation Scorpius. [Greek *antarēs,* "opposite Mars" : *anti-,* opposite + ARES.]

ant cow. An aphid that yields a honeylike substance on which ants feed.

an·te (ăn′tē) *n.* **1.** *Poker.* The stake that each player must put into the pool before receiving his hand, or before receiving new cards. **2.** *Slang.* The amount to be paid as one's share. —*tr.v.* **anted** or **-teed, -teing, -tes. 1.** *Poker.* To put (one's stake) into the pool. Often used with *up.* **2.** *Slang.* To pay (one's share). [From Latin *ante,* before. See **anti** in Appendix.*]

ante-. Indicates: **1.** In front of; for example, **anteroom. 2.** Previous to; for example, **antenatal.** [Latin, from *ante,* before, in front of, previous to. See **anti** in Appendix.*]

ant·eat·er (ănt′ē′tər) *n.* **1.** Any of several tropical American mammals of the family Myrmecophagidae, that lack teeth and feed on ants and termites; especially, *Myrmecophaga tridactyla,* having a long, narrow snout, a long, sticky tongue, and a long, shaggy-haired tail. This species is also called "giant anteater" and sometimes "ant bear." **2.** Any of several other animals that feed on ants, such as the echidna and the pangolin.

an·te·bel·lum (ăn′tē-bĕl′əm) *adj.* Belonging to the period prior to the Civil War. [Latin *ante bellum,* before the war : ANTE- + *bellum,* war (see **duellum** in Appendix*).]

an·te·cede (ăn′tə-sēd′) *tr.v.* **-ceded, -ceding, -cedes.** To go before in rank, place, or time; precede. [Latin *antecēdere* : ANTE- + *cēdere,* to go (see **ked-**[1] in Appendix*).]

an·te·ce·dence (ăn′tə-sēd′əns) *n.* Precedence.

an·te·ce·dent (ăn′tə-sēd′ənt) *adj.* Going before; preceding; prior. —*n.* **1.** One that precedes. **2.** Any occurrence or event prior to another. **3.** *Plural.* One's ancestors, ancestry, or past life. **4.** The word, phrase, or clause to which a relative pronoun refers. **5.** *Mathematics.* The first term of a ratio. **6.** *Logic.* The conditional member of a hypothetical proposition. —See Synonyms at **cause.** —**an′te·ce′dent·ly** *adv.*

an·te·cham·ber (ăn′tĭ-chām′bər) *n.* A smaller room serving as an entryway into a larger room. [French *antichambre* : *anti-,* before, from Latin *ante-* + *chambre,* room, CHAMBER.]

an·te·date (ăn′tĭ-dāt′) *tr.v.* **-dated, -dating, -dates. 1.** To be of an earlier date than; precede in time. **2.** To give a date earlier than the actual date; date back.

an·te·di·lu·vi·an (ăn′tĭ-də-lōō′vē-ən) *adj.* **1.** Occurring or belonging to the era before the Flood. Genesis 7, 8. **2.** Very old; antiquated; primitive. —*n.* **1.** One that lived or existed before the Flood. **2.** A very old person. [From ANTE- + Latin *dīluvium,* flood (see **diluvial**).]

an·te·fix (ăn′tĭ-fĭks′) *n., pl.* **-fixes** or **-fixa** (-fĭk′sə). *Architecture.* An upright ornament along the eaves of a tiled roof to conceal the joints between the rows of tiles. [Latin *antefīxus,* "fastened before" : *ante-,* before + *fīxus,* past participle of *fīgere,* to fasten (see **dhīgw-** in Appendix*).] —**an′te·fix′al** *adj.*

an·te·lope (ăn′tə-lōp′) *n., pl.* **antelope** or **-lopes. 1.** Any of various slender, swift-running, long-horned ruminants of the family Bovidae, of Africa and Asia. **2.** An animal that resembles a true antelope, such as the **pronghorn** *(see).* **3.** Leather made from the hide of an antelope. [Middle English, from Old French *antelop,* a fabulous oriental beast, from Medieval Latin *anthalopus,* from Late Greek *antholops*†.]

an·te·me·rid·i·an (ăn′tē-mə-rĭd′ē-ən) *adj.* Of, pertaining to, or taking place in the morning. [Latin *antemerīdiānus* : *ante-,* before + *merīdiānus,* MERIDIAN.]

an·te me·rid·i·em (ăn′tē mə-rĭd′ē-əm). *Abbr. Usually small capitals* A.M. Also **a.m., A.M.** Before noon. Used chiefly in the abbreviated form to specify the hour: *10:30* A.M. [Latin : *ante-,* before + *merīdiēs,* midday, noon (see **meridian**).]

an·te mor·tem (ăn′tē môr′təm). *Latin.* Before death.

an·te·na·tal (ăn′tē-nāt′l) *adj.* Before birth; prenatal.

an·ten·na (ăn-tĕn′ə) *n., pl.* **-tennae** (-tĕn′ē) (for sense 1) or **-nas** (for sense 2). **1.** One of the paired, flexible, jointed sensory appendages on the head of an insect, myriapod, or crustacean. **2.** *Abbr.* **ant.** A metallic apparatus for sending and receiving electromagnetic waves. In this sense, also called "aerial." [Medieval Latin, from Latin *antemna, antenna*†, sail yard.] —**an·ten′nal** *adj.*

an·ten·nule (ăn-tĕn′yōōl) *n. Zoology.* A small antenna, especially one of the first pair in crustaceans. [French, diminutive of *antenne,* antenna, from Medieval Latin ANTENNA.]

an·te·pen·di·um (ăn′tĭ-pĕn′dē-əm) *n., pl.* **-dia** (-dē-ə). **1.** A hanging for the front of an altar. **2.** A pulpit cloth. [Medieval Latin : Latin *ante-,* in front of + *pendēre,* to hang (see **spen-** in Appendix*).]

antenna

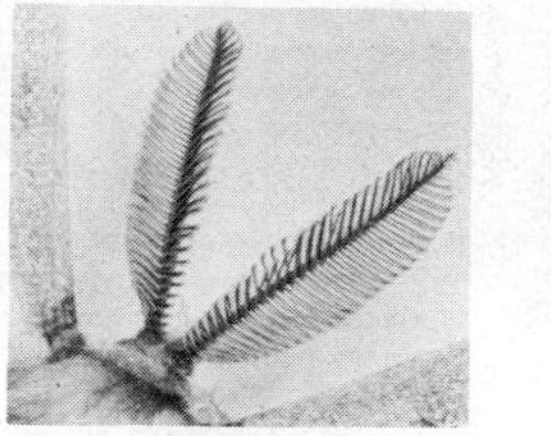

antennae of cecropia moth

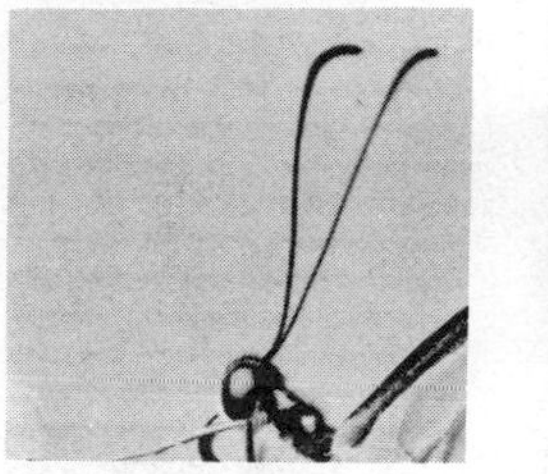

antennae of giant swallowtail

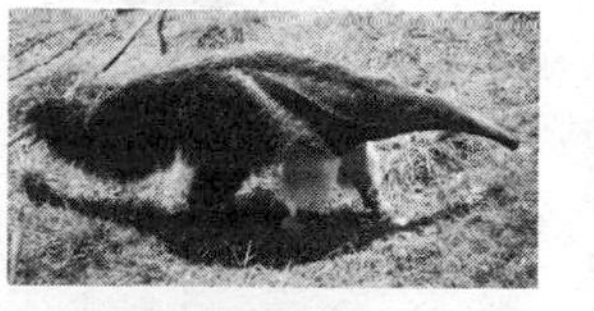

anteater
Myrmecophaga tridactyla
Giant anteater

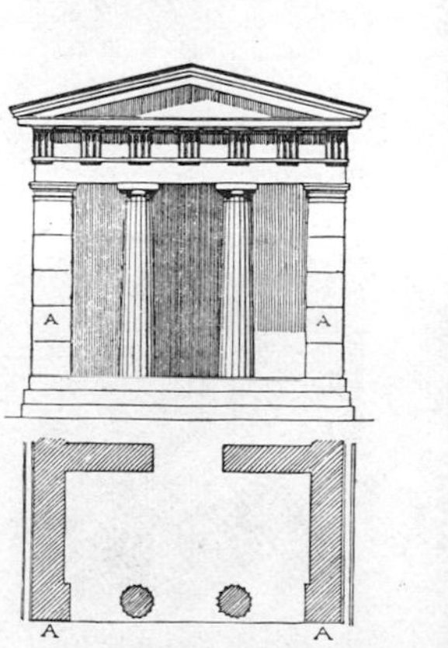

anta
Engraving and diagram of a temple, with antae indicated by A

t tight/th thin, path/*th* this, bathe/ŭ cut/ûr urge/v valve/w with/y yes/z zebra, size/zh vision/ə about, item, edible, gallop, circus/ à *Fr.* ami/œ *Fr.* feu, *Ger.* schön/ü *Fr.* tu, *Ger.* über/KH *Ger.* ich, *Scot.* loch/N *Fr.* bon. ***Follows main vocabulary.** †**Of obscure origin.**

an·te·pe·nult (ăn′tĭ-pē′nŭlt′, -pĭ-nŭlt′) *n.* The third syllable from the end in a word; for example, *te* is the antepenult of the word *antepenult.* [Late Latin *antepaenultima,* feminine of *antepaenultimus,* ANTEPENULTIMATE.]

an·te·pe·nul·ti·mate (ăn′tĭ-pĭ-nŭl′tə-mĭt) *adj.* Second from the last; third from the end in a series. —*n.* An antepenult. [Late Latin *antepaenultimus* : Latin ANTE- + *paenultimus,* PENULT.]

an·te·ri·or (ăn-tîr′ē-ər) *adj.* **1.** Placed in front; located forward. **2.** Prior in time; earlier. **3.** *Abbr.* **a.** Located near the head in lower animals. **b.** Located on or near the front of the body in higher animals. **c.** Located on or near the front of an organ or on the ventral surface of the body in man. **4.** *Botany.* In front of and facing away from the axis or stem. [Latin, comparative of *ante,* before. See **anti** in Appendix.*] —**an·te′ri·or·ly** *adv.*

an·te·room (ăn′tĭ-ro͞om′, -ro͝om′) *n.* A waiting room.

ant·he·li·on (ănt-hē′lē-ən, ăn-thē′-) *n., pl.* **-lia** (-lē-ə) or **-ons.** A luminous, white, halolike area occasionally seen in the sky opposite the sun on the **parhelic circle** *(see).* [Greek *anthēlion,* from *anthēlios,* opposite the sun : *ant(i)-,* opposite + *hēlios,* sun (see **sāwel-** in Appendix*).]

ant·hel·min·tic (ănt′hĕl-mĭn′tĭk, ăn′thĕl-) *adj.* Also **ant·hel·min·thic** (-thĭk). Acting to expel or destroy intestinal worms. —*n.* An anthelmintic remedy; a vermifuge. [ANT(I)- + Greek *helmins* (stem *helminth-*), worm (see **wel-**[3] in Appendix*).]

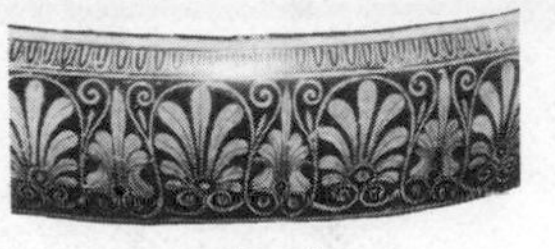

anthemion

an·them (ăn′thəm) *n.* **1.** A hymn of praise or loyalty. **2.** A sacred composition set to words from the Bible. [Middle English *antem, antefn,* Old English *antefn,* antiphonal song, from Medieval Latin *antiphōna,* from Late Greek, "sung responses," neuter plural of *antiphōnos,* singing in response : *anti-,* opposite + *phōnē,* voice (see **bhā-**[2] in Appendix*).]

an·the·mi·on (ăn-thē′mē-ən) *n., pl.* **-mia** (-mē-ə). A pattern of honeysuckle or palm leaves in a radiating cluster, used as a motif in Greek art. [Greek, diminutive of *anthemon,* name of a plant, from *anthos,* flower. See **andh-** in Appendix.*]

an·ther (ăn′thər) *n. Botany.* The organ that is borne at the upper end of a stamen, and that secretes and discharges pollen. [New Latin *anthera,* from Medieval Latin *anthēra,* pollen, from Latin, medicine composed of flowers, from Greek *antherōs,* flowery, from *anthos,* flower. See **andh-** in Appendix.*]

an·ther·id·i·um (ăn′thə-rĭd′ē-əm) *n., pl.* **-ia** (-ē-ə). *Botany.* An organ that produces male sex cells in the algae, fungi, mosses, and ferns. [New Latin : *anthera,* ANTHER + -IDIUM.]

an·ther·o·zo·id (ăn′thər-ə-zō′ĭd) *n. Botany.* A male sex cell produced by an antheridium. [ANTHER + ZO(O)ID.]

an·the·sis (ăn-thē′sĭs) *n. Botany.* The blooming or time of full bloom of a flower. [New Latin, from Greek *anthēsis,* from *anthein,* to bloom, from *anthos,* flower. See **andh-** in Appendix.*]

ant·hill (ănt′hĭl′) *n.* A mound formed by ants or termites in digging or building a nest.

antho–. *Botany.* Indicates a flower; for example, **anthocyanin.** [Greek *anthos,* blossom, flower. See **andh-** in Appendix.*]

an·tho·cy·a·nin (ăn′thō-sī′ə-nĭn) *n.* Any of a class of water-soluble pigments that impart to flowers and other plant parts any of the colors ranging from blue to most shades of red. [ANTHO- + CYANIN(E).]

an·tho·di·um (ăn-thō′dē-əm) *n., pl.* **-dia** (-dē-ə). *Botany.* The flower head of composite plants, such as the aster, thistle, and goldenrod. [New Latin, from Greek *anthōdēs,* flowerlike : ANTHO- + -OID.]

an·thol·o·gize (ăn-thŏl′ə-jīz′) *tr.v.* **-gized, -gizing, -gizes.** To compile or include in an anthology.

an·thol·o·gy (ăn-thŏl′ə-jē) *n., pl.* **-gies.** A collection of literary pieces, such as poems, short stories, or plays, usually suggesting a theme. [New Latin *anthologia,* from Medieval Greek, from Greek, "flower gathering," a collection : ANTHO- + -LOGY.] —**an′tho·log′i·cal** (ăn′thə-lŏj′ĭ-kəl) *adj.* —**an·thol′o·gist** *n.*

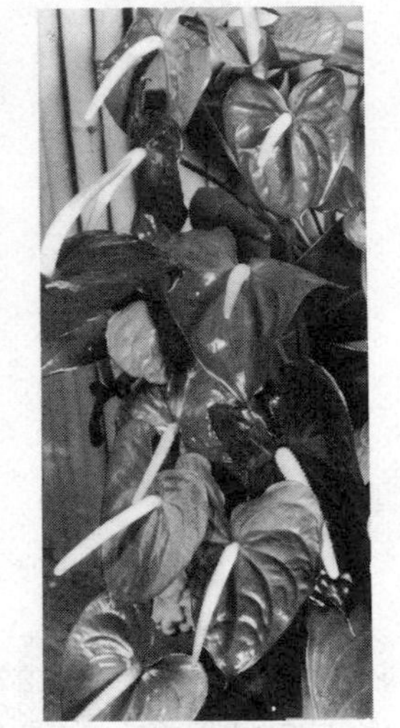

anthurium
An arrangement of anthuriums

An·tho·ny (ăn′thə-nē, ăn′tə-nē). A masculine given name. [Latin *Antōnius*†, name of a Roman gens.]

An·tho·ny (ăn′thə-nē, ăn′tə-nē), **Saint.** A.D. 250?–350? Egyptian anchorite.

An·tho·ny (ăn′thə-nē), **Susan B(rownell).** 1820–1906. American feminist; leader in woman suffrage movement.

An·tho·ny of Padua (ăn′thə-nē, ăn′tə-nē′), **Saint.** 1195–1231. Portuguese Franciscan monk; active in France and Italy.

an·tho·phore (ăn′thə-fôr′, -fōr′) *n. Botany.* A stalklike part in certain flowers, supporting the pistils and corolla. [From Greek *anthophorous,* "flower-bearing" : ANTHO- + -PHOROUS.]

an·tho·tax·y (ăn′thə-tăk′sē) *n.* Also **an·tho·tax·is** (ăn′thə-tăk′sĭs). *Botany.* The arrangement of the parts of a flower. [ANTHO- + -TAXY.]

–anthous. Indicates a flower; for example, **ananthous.** [New Latin *-anthus,* from Greek *anthos,* flower. See **andh-** in Appendix.*]

an·tho·zo·an (ăn′thə-zō′ən) *n.* Any of various marine organisms of the class Anthozoa, growing singly or in colonies, and including the corals and sea anemones. Also called "actinozoan." [New Latin *Anthozoa,* "flowerlike organisms" : ANTHO- + -ZOA.] —**an′tho·zo′an, an′tho·zo′ic** *adj.*

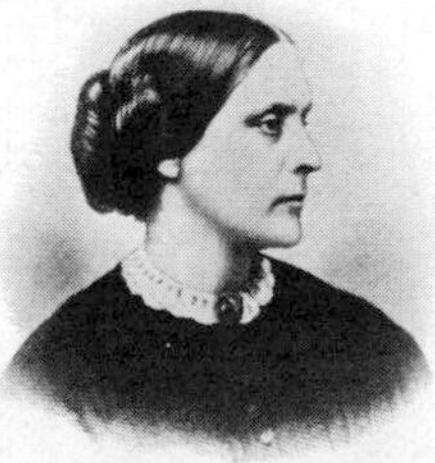

Susan B. Anthony

an·thra·cene (ăn′thrə-sēn′) *n.* A crystalline hydrocarbon, $C_6H_4(CH_2)C_6H_4$, extracted from coal tar and used in the manufacture of dyes and organic chemicals. [Greek *anthrax,* charcoal, coal, ANTHRAX + -ENE.]

an·thra·cite (ăn′thrə-sīt′) *n.* A hard coal having a high carbon content and little volatile matter that burns with a clean flame. Also called "hard coal." [Greek *anthrakitēs,* a kind of coal, from *anthrax,* ANTHRAX.] —**an′thra·cit′ic** (-sĭt′ĭk) *adj.*

an·thrac·nose (ăn-thrăk′nōs′) *n.* Any of several diseases of plants caused by fungi, and characterized by dead spots on the leaves, twigs, or fruit. [French : Greek *anthrax,* charcoal, carbuncle, ANTHRAX + Greek *nosos,* disease (see **noso-**).]

an·thrax (ăn′thrăks′) *n., pl.* **-thraces** (-thrə-sēz′) (for sense 2 only). **1.** *Pathology.* An infectious, usually fatal disease of warm-blooded animals, especially of cattle and sheep, caused by *Bacillus anthracis.* It is transmissible to man, capable of affecting various organs, and especially characterized by malignant ulcers. **2.** A lesion caused by this disease. [Latin, virulent ulcer, from Greek *anthrax*†, charcoal, carbuncle, pustule.]

anthrop. anthropological; anthropology.

an·throp·ic (ăn-thrŏp′ĭk) *adj.* Of or pertaining to man or the era of human life. [Greek *anthrōpikos,* from *anthrōpos,* man. See **anthropo–.**]

anthropo–. Indicates man or human; for example, **anthroposophy.** [From Greek *anthrōpos,* man. See **ner-**[2] in Appendix.*]

an·thro·po·cen·tric (ăn′thrə-pō-sĕn′trĭk) *adj.* **1.** Regarding man as the central fact or final aim of the universe. **2.** Interpreting reality exclusively in terms of human values and experience.

an·thro·po·gen·e·sis (ăn′thrə-pō-jĕn′ə-sĭs) *n.* The scientific study of the origin of man. [New Latin : ANTHROPO- + -GENESIS.] —**an′thro·po·gen′ic** *adj.*

an·thro·poid (ăn′thrə-poid′) *adj.* **1.** Resembling man. Said of the apes of the family Pongidae, which includes gorillas, chimpanzees, orang-utans, and gibbons. **2.** Resembling or characteristic of an ape; apelike. —*n.* **1.** Any member of the family Pongidae. Also called "anthropoid ape." **2.** A person resembling an ape in appearance, behavior, or intelligence. [Greek *anthrōpoeidēs* : ANTHROP(O)- + -OID.] —**an′thro·poi′dal** *adj.*

an·thro·pol·o·gy (ăn′thrə-pŏl′ə-jē) *n. Abbr.* **anthrop., anthropol.** The scientific study of the origin and of the physical, social, and cultural development and behavior of man. [New Latin *anthropologia* : ANTHROPO- + -LOGY.] —**an′thro·po·log′ic, an′thro·po·log′i·cal** (-pə-lŏj′ĭ-kəl) *adj.* —**an′thro·po·log′i·cal·ly** *adv.* —**an′thro·pol′o·gist** *n.*

an·thro·pom·e·try (ăn′thrə-pŏm′ə-trē) *n.* The study and technique of human body measurement for use in anthropological classification and comparison. [ANTHROPO- + -METRY.] —**an′thro·po·met′ric** (-pō-mĕt′rĭk), **an′thro·po·met′ri·cal** *adj.* —**an′thro·po·met′ri·cal·ly** *adv.* —**an′thro·pom′e·trist** *n.*

an·thro·po·mor·phism (ăn′thrə-pō-môr′fĭz′əm) *n.* The attribution of human motivation, characteristics, or behavior to inanimate objects, animals, or natural phenomena. —**an′thro·po·mor′phic** *adj.*

an·thro·po·mor·phize (ăn′thrə-pō-môr′fīz′) *tr.v.* **-phized, -phizing, -phizes.** To ascribe human characteristics to.

an·thro·po·mor·phous (ăn′thrə-pō-môr′fəs) *adj.* **1.** Having or suggesting human form and appearance. **2.** Anthropomorphic. [Greek *anthrōpomorphos* : ANTHROPO- + -MORPHOUS.] —**an′thro·po·mor′phous·ly** *adv.*

an·thro·pop·a·thism (ăn′thrə-pŏp′ə-thĭz′əm) *n.* The attribution of human feelings to nonhuman beings, objects, or natural phenomena. [From Greek *anthrōpopathēs,* with human feelings : ANTHROPO- + *pathos,* feeling (see **-pathy**).] —**an′thro·po·path′ic** (-pō-păth′ĭk) *adj.*

an·thro·poph·a·gi (ăn′thrə-pŏf′ə-jī′) *pl.n. Singular* **-gus** (-gəs). Eaters of human flesh; cannibals. [Latin *anthrōpophagī,* plural of *anthrōpophagus,* from Greek *anthrōpophagos,* man-eating : ANTHROPO- + -PHAGOUS.] —**an′thro·po·phag′ic** (-pō-făj′ĭk), **an′thro·poph′a·gous** *adj.* —**an′thro·poph′a·gy** *n.*

an·thro·pos·o·phy (ăn′thrə-pŏs′ə-fē) *n.* A system of mystical beliefs derived from theosophy. [ANTHROPO- + -SOPHY.] —**an′thro·po·soph′ic** (-pō-sŏf′ĭk), **an′thro·po·soph′i·cal** *adj.*

–anthropus. Indicates man; for example, **Meganthropus.** [New Latin, from Greek *anthrōpos,* man. See **anthropo-.**]

an·thur·i·um (ăn-tho͝or′ē-əm) *n.* Any of various tropical American plants of the genus *Anthurium,* many of which are cultivated as potted plants for their showy flowers or foliage. [New Latin *Anthurium,* "flower-tail" : ANTH(O)- + Greek *oura,* tail (see **ors-** in Appendix*).]

an·ti (ăn′tī′, ăn′tē) *n., pl.* **-tis.** *Informal.* A person who is opposed to a group, policy, proposal, or practice. [From ANTI-.]

anti–, ant–. Indicates: **1.** Opposition to, effectiveness against, or counteraction; for example, **antacid, antibody. 2.** Situation opposite to; for example, **antimere. 3.** Reciprocal correspondence to; for example, **antilogarithm. 4.** Converse operation to; for example, **anticyclone, antinode.** ***Note:*** Many compounds other than those entered here may be formed with *anti-.* In forming compounds, *anti-* is normally joined with the following element without space or a hyphen: *antibody.* However, if the second element begins with a capital letter, it is separated with a hyphen: *anti-American.* It is also preferable to use the hyphen if the second element begins with *i: anti-intellectual.* The hyphen may always be used to aid clarity, as in nonce coinages: *anti-antivivisection,* or when the compound brings together three or more vowels: *anti-aesthetic.* [In borrowed Greek compounds *anti-* indicates : 1. Over against, opposite, as in **antichrist.** 2. Against; opposite, as in **antipathy.** 3. Responding to, as in **antiphon.** 4. Instead of, as in **antonomasia.** 5. Opposite, counterfeiting, as in **antirrhinum.** Greek, from *anti,* opposite, against. See **anti** in Appendix.*]

an·ti·air·craft (ăn′tē-âr′krăft′, -kräft′) *adj. Abbr.* **A.A., AA** Defensive, especially from a surface position, against aircraft or missile attack. —*n.* An antiaircraft weapon.

an·ti·bar·y·on (ăn′tĭ-băr′ē-ŏn, ăn′tī-) *n.* The antiparticle of the **baryon** *(see).*

An·tibes (äɴ-tēb′). A port and resort center on the Riviera in southeastern France. Population, 25,000.

an·ti·bi·o·sis (ăn'tĭ-bī-ō'sĭs, ăn'tī-) n. An association between two or more organisms that is injurious to one of them. Compare **symbiosis**. [New Latin : ANTI- + -BIOSIS.]

an·ti·bi·ot·ic (ăn'tĭ-bī-ŏt'ĭk, ăn'tī-) n. Any of various substances, such as penicillin and streptomycin, produced by certain fungi, bacteria, and other organisms, that are effective in inhibiting the growth of or destroying microorganisms, and are widely used in the prevention and treatment of diseases. —adj. 1. Of or pertaining to antibiotics. 2. Of or pertaining to antibiosis. [New Latin *antibioticus* : ANTI- + BIOTIC.]

an·ti·bod·y (ăn'tĭ-bŏd'ē) n., pl. -ies. 1. Any of various proteins in the blood that are generated in reaction to foreign proteins or polysaccharides, neutralize them, and thus produce immunity against certain microorganisms or their toxins. 2. An object composed of antimatter. [ANTI- + BODY.]

an·tic (ăn'tĭk) n. 1. Often plural. A ludicrous or extravagant act or gesture; caper; prank. 2. Archaic. A clown; merry-andrew. —adj. Ludicrous; odd; fantastic. [Italian *antico*, "ancient," "grotesque," from Latin *antiquus*. See anti in Appendix.*]

an·ti·cat·a·lyst (ăn'tĭ-kăt'l-ĭst, ăn'tī-) n. 1. A substance that retards or arrests a chemical reaction. 2. A substance that reduces or destroys the effectiveness of a catalyst.

an·ti·cath·ode (ăn'tĭ-kăth'ōd', ăn'tī-) n. An electrode that is the target in a cathode ray tube, especially in an x-ray tube.

an·ti·chlor (ăn'tĭ-klôr', -klōr') n. A substance, such as sodium thiosulfate, used to neutralize the excess chlorine or hypochlorite left after bleaching textiles, fiber, or paper pulp. [ANTI- + CHLOR(INE).] —an'ti·chlo·ris'tic adj.

an·ti·cho·lin·er·gic (ăn'tĭ-kō'lə-nûr'jĭk, -kōl'ə-nûr'jĭk, ăn'tī-) adj. Opposing or antagonistic to the physiological action of parasympathetic or other cholinergic nerve fibers.

an·ti·cho·lin·es·ter·ase (ăn'tĭ-kō'lə-nĕs'tə-rās', -rāz', ăn'tī-) n. Any substance that inhibits the activity of **cholinesterase** (see).

an·ti·christ (ăn'tĭ-krīst') n. 1. An enemy of Christ. 2. Capital A. The epithet of the great antagonist who was expected by the early Church to set himself up against Christ in the last days before the Second Coming. [Middle English *Antecrist*, from Old French, from Late Latin *Antichristus*, from Greek *Antikhristos* (I John 2:18) : ANTI- + *Khristos*, CHRIST.]

an·tic·i·pant (ăn-tĭs'ə-pənt) adj. 1. Coming or acting in advance. 2. Expectant. —n. One who anticipates.

an·tic·i·pate (ăn-tĭs'ə-pāt') tr.v. -pated, -pating, -pates. 1. To feel or realize beforehand; foresee. 2. To look forward to; expect. 3. To act in advance so as to prevent; preclude; forestall. 4. To foresee and fulfill in advance. 5. To cause to happen in advance; accelerate. 6. To use in advance, as income not yet available. 7. To pay (a debt) before it is due. —See Synonyms at expect. [Latin *anticipāre*, to take before : *ante-*, before + *capere*, to take (see kap- in Appendix*).] —an·tic'i·pa'tor (-pā'tər) n. —an·tic'i·pa·to'ry (-pə-tôr'ē, -tōr'ē) adj.

Usage: The senses *to feel or realize beforehand, to look forward to* (often with the implication of foretasting pleasure) are approved by 62 per cent of the Usage Panel in the example *He is anticipating a visit with his son.* The minority would restrict *anticipate,* in such a context, to some more overt action (such as preparation for the visit). In the passive, *anticipate,* unlike *expect,* is not followed by an infinitive: *Trouble is expected* (or *expected to occur*). *Trouble is anticipated* (but not *anticipated to occur*). *A large sale is anticipated* (but not *The sale is anticipated to be large*).

an·tic·i·pa·tion (ăn-tĭs'ə-pā'shən) n. 1. The act of anticipating. 2. Something anticipated; expectation. 3. Foreknowledge; intuition; presentiment. 4. Law. The use or assignment of funds from a trust fund before legitimately available for use. 5. Music. The introduction of one note of a new chord before the previous chord is resolved.

an·tic·i·pa·tive (ăn-tĭs'ə-pā'tĭv, -pə-tĭv) adj. Anticipating; expectant. —an·tic'i·pa'tive·ly adv.

an·ti·cler·i·cal (ăn'tĭ-klĕr'ĭ-kəl) adj. Opposed to the Church's influence in political affairs. —an'ti·cler'i·cal·ism' n.

an·ti·cli·max (ăn'tĭ-klī'măks') n. 1. A decline viewed in disappointing contrast with a previous rise: *the anticlimax of a brilliant career.* 2. Something trivial or commonplace coming to conclude a series of significant events. 3. Rhetoric. **a.** A sudden descent from the impressive or significant to the ludicrous or inconsequential. **b.** An instance of this; for example, *For God, for country, and for Yale.* —an'ti·cli·mac'tic (-klī-măk'tĭk) adj. —an'ti·cli·mac'ti·cal·ly adv.

an·ti·cli·nal (ăn'tĭ-klī'nəl) adj. Sloping downward in opposite directions, as an anticline. [ANTI- + -CLINAL.]

an·ti·cline (ăn'tĭ-klīn') n. Geology. A fold with strata sloping downward on both sides from a common crest. [ANTI- + -CLINE.]

an·ti·co·ag·u·lant (ăn'tĭ-kō-ăg'yə-lənt, ăn'tī-) n. Any substance that suppresses or counteracts coagulation, especially of the blood. —adj. Acting as an anticoagulant.

An·ti·cos·ti (ăn'tə-kôs'tē, -kŏs'tē) An island, 130 miles long and 30 miles wide, off Quebec Province, Canada, in the Gulf of St. Lawrence.

an·ti·cy·clone (ăn'tĭ-sī'klōn') n. An extensive system of winds spiraling outward from a high-pressure center, circling clockwise in the Northern Hemisphere and counterclockwise in the Southern Hemisphere. —an'ti·cy·clon'ic (-sī-klŏn'ĭk) adj.

an·ti·dote (ăn'tĭ-dōt') n. 1. A remedy or other agent to counteract the effects of a poison. 2. Anything that relieves or counteracts an injurious effect. [Latin *antidotum*, from Greek *antidoton*, from *antididonai*, to give as a remedy against : ANTI- + *didonai*, to give (see dō- in Appendix*).] —an'ti·dot'al (ăn'tĭ-dōt'l) adj. —an'ti·dot'al·ly adv.

Usage: A thing is said to be an antidote *to, for,* or (less often) *against* something else.

an·ti·en·zyme (ăn'tē-ĕn'zīm', ăn'tī-) n. A substance that neutralizes or counteracts an enzyme. —an'ti·en'zy·mat'ic (-zĭ-măt'ĭk, -zī-măt'ĭk) adj. —an'ti·en·zy'mic (-zī'mĭk) adv.

An·tie·tam (ăn-tē'təm). A creek, tributary of the Potomac River, in western Maryland, near the town of Sharpsburg, the site of a Civil War battle (1862).

an·ti·feb·rile (ăn'tĭ-fĕb'rəl, -fē'brəl, -rīl', ăn'tī-) adj. Able to reduce fever; antipyretic. —n. An antifebrile drug or agent.

an·ti·fed·er·al·ist (ăn'tĭ-fĕd'ər-əl-ĭst, -fĕd'rəl-ĭst, ăn'tī-) n. Also **An·ti·fed·er·al·ist.** One opposed to the ratification of the U.S. Constitution. —an'ti·fed'er·al·ism' n.

an·ti·freeze (ăn'tĭ-frēz') n. A substance, often a liquid such as ethylene glycol or alcohol, mixed with another liquid to lower the freezing point of the latter.

an·ti·gen (ăn'tĭ-jən) n. Also **an·ti·gene** (-jēn). Any substance that, when introduced into the body, stimulates the production of an antibody. [ANTI- + -GEN.] —an'ti·gen'ic (-jĕn'ĭk) adj. —an'ti·gen'i·cal·ly adv. —an'ti·ge·nic'i·ty (-jə-nĭs'ə-tē) n.

An·tig·o·ne (ăn-tĭg'ə-nē'). Greek Mythology. The daughter of Oedipus and Jocasta, who performed funeral rites over her brother's body in defiance of her uncle Creon.

An·ti·gua (ăn-tē'gwə, -gə). An island, 108 square miles in area, in the West Indies; a former British colony, it received internal self-government in 1967 as a state of the West Indies Associated States. Population; 62,000. Capital, Saint Johns. —An·ti'guan adj. & n.

an·ti·he·ro (ăn'tĭ-hîr'ō, ăn'tī-) n. The protagonist in certain forms of modern fiction and drama characterized by a lack of traditional heroic qualities.

an·ti·his·ta·mine (ăn'tĭ-hĭs'tə-mēn', -mĭn) n. Any of various drugs used to reduce physiological effects associated with histamine production in allergies and colds. —an'ti·his'ta·min'ic (-tə-mĭn'ĭk) adj.

an·ti·knock (ăn'tĭ-nŏk') n. A substance, such as tetraethyl lead, added to gasoline to reduce engine knock.

An·ti·Leb·a·non (ăn'tĭ-lĕb'ə-nən). Arabic **Je·bel esh Shar·qi** (jă'băl ăsh shûr'kē). A mountain range running north and south on the border between Syria and Lebanon. Highest elevation, Mount Hermon (9,232 feet).

An·til·les (ăn-tĭl'ēz). The main island group of the West Indies, with the exception of the Bahamas, forming a chain that separates the Caribbean Sea from the Atlantic Ocean. See **Greater Antilles, Lesser Antilles, Netherlands Antilles.** —An·til'le·an (ăn-tĭl'ē-ən, ăn'tĭ-lē'ən) adj. & n.

an·ti·log·a·rithm (ăn'tĭ-lôg'ə-rĭth'əm, ăn'tĭ-lŏg'-, ăn'tī-) n. The number for which a given logarithm stands; for example, where log *x* equals *y,* the *x* is the antilogarithm of *y.* Also called "antilog." See logarithm. —an'ti·log'a·rith'mic adj.

an·ti·ma·cas·sar (ăn'tĭ-mə-kăs'ər) n. A protective covering for the backs of chairs and sofas. [ANTI- + MACASSAR (OIL).]

an·ti·mag·net·ic (ăn'tĭ-măg-nĕt'ĭk) adj. Impervious to the effect of a magnetic field; magnetization resistant. Said especially of watch movements.

an·ti·ma·lar·i·al (ăn'tĭ-mə-lâr'ē-əl, ăn'tī-) adj. Effective against malaria. —n. An antimalarial drug.

an·ti·mat·ter (ăn'tĭ-măt'ər) n. A hypothetical form of matter consisting of antiparticles and having positron-surrounded nuclei composed of antiprotons and antineutrons. See **antiparticle.**

an·ti·mere (ăn'tĭ-mîr') n. Biology. A part or division corresponding to an opposite or similar part in an organism characterized by bilateral or radial symmetry. [ANTI- + -MERE.] —an'ti·mer'ic (-mĕr'ĭk) adj.

an·ti·mi·cro·bi·al (ăn'tĭ-mī-krō'bē-əl) adj. Also **an·ti·mi·cro·bic** (-bĭk). Capable of destroying or suppressing the growth of microorganisms. —n. An antimicrobial agent.

an·ti·mis·sile missile (ăn'tĭ-mĭs'əl). A missile designed to intercept and destroy another missile in flight.

an·ti·mo·ni·al (ăn'tĭ-mō'nē-əl) adj. Of or containing antimony. —n. A medicine with antimony as an ingredient.

an·ti·mo·ny (ăn'tə-mō'nē) n. Symbol **Sb** A metallic element having four allotropic forms the most common of which is a hard, extremely brittle, lustrous, silver-white, crystalline material. It is used in a wide variety of alloys, especially with lead in battery plates, and in the manufacture of flame-proofing compounds, paints, semiconductor devices, and ceramic products. Atomic number 51, atomic weight 121.75, melting point 630.5°C, boiling point 1,380°C, specific gravity 6.691, valences 3, 5. See element. [Middle English, from Medieval Latin *antimonium,* perhaps from Arabic *al-íthmid,* perhaps from Greek *stimmi.* See stibine.]

antimony glance. An antimony ore, **stibnite** (see).

an·ti·neu·tri·no (ăn'tĭ-nōō-trē'nō, ăn'tĭ-nyōō-, ăn'tī-) n., pl. -nos. Physics. The **antiparticle** (see) of the neutrino.

an·ti·neu·tron (ăn'tĭ-nōō'trŏn', ăn'tĭ-nyōō'-, ăn'tī-) n. Symbol **n̄** Physics. The **antiparticle** (see) of the neutron.

an·ti·node (ăn'tĭ-nōd') n. Physics. The region or point of maximum amplitude between adjacent **nodes** (see).

an·ti·no·mi·an (ăn'tĭ-nō'mē-ən) n. Theology. A member of a Christian sect holding that faith alone is necessary to salvation. —adj. Of or pertaining to such a sect or doctrine. [From Medieval Latin *antinomus* : Greek ANTI- + *nomos,* law (see nem-² in Appendix*).] —an'ti·no'mi·an·ism' n.

an·tin·o·my (ăn-tĭn'ə-mē) n., pl. -mies. 1. Opposition; contradiction. 2. Contradiction between inferences or principles that seem equally necessary and reasonable. [Latin *antinomia,* from Greek : ANTI- + *nomos,* law (see nem-² in Appendix*).]

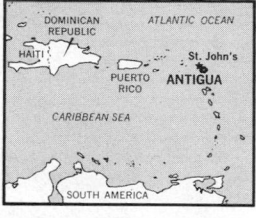

Antigua

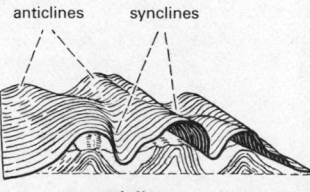

anticline
Sketch of a bed
of limestone

anticlines   synclines

an·ti·nu·cle·on (ăn′tĭ-no͞o′klē-ŏn′, ăn′tĭ-nyo͞o′-, ăn′tī-) *n. Physics.* The **antiparticle** *(see)* of a nucleon.

An·ti·och (ăn′tē-ŏk′). A city on the Orontes River in southern Turkey; capital of ancient Syria. —**An′ti·o′chi·an** (ăn′tē-ō′kē-ən) *adj.* & *n.*

an·ti·ox·i·dant (ăn′tĭ-ŏk′sə-dənt, ăn′tī-) *n.* A chemical compound or substance that inhibits oxidation.

an·ti·par·ti·cle (ăn′tĭ-pär′tĭ-kəl, ăn′tī-) *n.* A subatomic particle, such as a positron, antiproton, or antineutron, having the same mass, average lifetime, spin, magnitude of magnetic moment, and magnitude of electric charge as the particle to which it corresponds, but having the opposite sign of electric charge, opposite intrinsic parity, and opposite direction of magnetic moment. See **annihilation.**

an·ti·pas·to (än′tē-päs′tō) *n., pl.* **-tos** or **-ti** (-tē). An Italian appetizer consisting of an assortment of smoked meats, fish, olives, tomatoes, hot peppers, cheese, and other ingredients, served with oil and vinegar. [Italian : ANTI- (before) + *pasto,* food, from Latin *pastus,* past participle of *pascere,* to feed (see **pā-** in Appendix*).]

an·tip·a·thet·ic (ăn-tĭp′ə-thĕt′ĭk) *adj.* Also **an·tip·a·thet·i·cal** (-ĭ-kəl). **1.** Having an inherent feeling of aversion, repugnance, or opposition. Often used with *to: antipathetic to new ideas.* **2.** Causing a feeling of antipathy. —**an·tip′a·thet′i·cal·ly** *adv.*

an·tip·a·thy (ăn-tĭp′ə-thē) *n., pl.* **-thies. 1.** A strong feeling of aversion or opposition. **2.** The object of aversion. —See Synonyms at **enmity.** [Latin *antipathia,* from Greek *antipatheia,* from *antipathēs,* of opposite feelings : ANTI- (opposite) + *pathos,* feeling (see **-pathy**).]

an·ti·pe·ri·od·ic (ăn′tĭ-pîr′ē-ŏd′ĭk, ăn′tī-) *adj.* Preventing regular recurrence of disease or fever. —*n.* An antiperiodic drug.

an·ti·per·son·nel (ăn′tĭ-pûr′sə-nĕl′, ăn′tī-) *adj. Abbr.* **AP** *Military.* Designed to inflict casualties on the military personnel or civilian population of an enemy country.

an·ti·per·spi·rant (ăn′tĭ-pûr′spə-rənt) *n.* A preparation applied to the skin to decrease or prevent excessive perspiration.

an·ti·phlo·gis·tic (ăn′tĭ-flō-jĭs′tĭk) *adj.* Reducing inflammation or fever. [ANTI- + PHLOGISTIC.] —**an′ti·phlo·gis′tic** *n.*

an·ti·phon (ăn′tə-fŏn′, -fən) *n.* **1.** A devotional composition sung responsively as part of a liturgy. **2.** A short liturgical text chanted responsively before a psalm or canticle. **3.** A response; answer: *a resounding antiphon of dissent.* [Late Latin *antiphona,* from Greek *antiphōna,* sung responses, ANTHEM.]

an·tiph·o·nal (ăn-tĭf′ə-nəl) *adj.* **1.** Pertaining to or resembling an antiphon. **2.** Answering responsively (as in antiphony). —*n.* Variant of **antiphonary.** —**an·tiph′o·nal·ly** *adv.*

an·tiph·o·nar·y (ăn-tĭf′ə-nĕr′ē) *n., pl.* **-ies.** Also **an·tiph·o·nal** (-nəl). A bound collection of antiphons, especially of the responsive choral parts of the divine office. —*adj.* Of or pertaining to such a book.

an·tiph·o·ny (ăn-tĭf′ə-nē) *n., pl.* **-nies. 1.** Responsive or antiphonal singing or chanting. **2.** A composition that is sung responsively; an antiphon. **3.** A sound or other effect that answers or echoes another.

an·tip·o·dal (ăn-tĭp′ə-dəl) *adj.* **1.** Of, pertaining to, or situated on the opposite side or opposite sides of the earth. **2.** Diametrically opposed; exactly opposite.

an·ti·pode (ăn′tĭ-pōd′) *n.* A direct or diametrical opposite. [Back-formation from ANTIPODES.]

an·tip·o·des (ăn-tĭp′ə-dēz′) *pl.n.* **1.** Any two places or regions that are on opposite sides of the earth. **2.** *Often capital* **A.** Australia and New Zealand. **3.** Something that is the exact opposite or contrary of another. Sometimes used with a singular verb. [Middle English, from Latin, from Greek, from *antipous* (stem *antipod-*), with the feet opposite : ANTI- + *pous,* foot (see **ped-**[1] in Appendix*).]

An·tip·o·des (ăn-tĭp′ə-dēz′). A group of rocky, uninhabited islands, 24 square miles in area, off the southeastern coast of New Zealand.

an·ti·pope (ăn′tĭ-pōp′) *n.* A person claiming to be pope in opposition to the one chosen by church law. [Middle English *antipope,* from Old French *antipape,* from Medieval Latin *antipāpa* : ANTI- + *pāpa,* POPE.]

an·ti·pro·ton (ăn′tĭ-prō′tŏn′, ăn′tī-) *n. Physics.* The **antiparticle** *(see)* of the proton.

an·ti·py·ret·ic (ăn′tĭ-pī-rĕt′ĭk) *adj.* Reducing or tending to reduce fever. —*n.* Medication that reduces fever. [ANTI- + PYRETIC.] —**an′ti·py·re′sis** (-rē′sĭs) *n.*

an·ti·py·rine (ăn′tĭ-pī′rēn′) *n.* A white powder, $C_{11}H_{12}N_2O$, used to reduce fever and relieve pain. [German *Antipyrin* (trademark) : ANTI- + PYR(O)- + -INE.]

antiq. 1. antiquarian; antiquary. **2.** antiquities; antiquity.

an·ti·quar·i·an (ăn′tĭ-kwâr′ē-ən) *adj. Abbr.* **ant., antiq. 1.** Of or pertaining to antiquaries or the study of antiquities. **2.** Dealing in or having to do with old rare books. —*n.* An **antiquary** *(see).* —**an′ti·quar′i·an·ism′** *n.*

an·ti·quar·y (ăn′tə-kwĕr′ē) *n., pl.* **-ies.** *Abbr.* **antiq.** A student or dealer of antiquities. Also called "antiquarian." [Latin *antiquārius,* from adjective, of antiquity, from *antiquus,* ANTIQUE.]

an·ti·quate (ăn′tə-kwāt′) *tr.v.* **-quated, -quating, -quates. 1.** To make obsolete or old-fashioned. **2.** To give an antique appearance to. [Latin *antiquāre,* to leave in its ancient state, from *antiquus,* ANTIQUE.] —**an′ti·qua′tion** *n.*

an·ti·quat·ed (ăn′tə-kwā′tĭd) *adj.* **1.** So old as to be no longer useful or suitable; outmoded; obsolete: *antiquated laws.* **2.** Very old; aged. —See Synonyms at **old.** —**an′ti·quat′ed·ness** *n.*

an·tique (ăn-tēk′) *adj.* **1.** Of or belonging to ancient times; especially, of, from, or characteristic of ancient Greece or Rome. **2.** Belonging to, made in, or typical of an earlier period. **3.** Outmoded; old-fashioned. —See Synonyms at **old.** —*n.* **1.** An object having special value because of its age; especially, a work of art or handicraft that is over 100 years old, or, according to a U.S. customs regulation adopted in 1930, made before 1830. **2.** The style or manner of ancient times, especially that of ancient Greek or Roman art. Preceded by *the: an admirer of the antique.* —*tr.v.* **antiqued, -tiquing, -tiques.** To give the appearance of an antique to. [French, from Latin *antīquus,* ancient, former. See **anti** in Appendix.*] —**an·tique′ly** *adv.* —**an·tique′ness** *n.*

an·ti·quer (ăn-tē′kər) *n.* **1.** A collector of antiques. **2.** One who treats or finishes new furniture so as to make it appear old or antique.

an·tiq·ui·ty (ăn-tĭk′wə-tē) *n., pl.* **-ties.** *Abbr.* **ant., antiq. 1.** *Sometimes capital* **A.** Ancient times, especially the times preceding the Middle Ages. **2.** The people, especially the writers, of ancient times. **3.** The quality of being old or ancient; considerable age: *a carving of great antiquity.* **4.** *Usually plural.* Something belonging to or dating from a time long past.

an·ti·ra·chit·ic (ăn′tĭ-rə-kĭt′ĭk, ăn′tī-) *adj.* Curing or preventing rickets. —*n.* An antirachitic drug or food.

An·ti·re·mon·strant (ăn′tĭ-rĭ-mŏn′strənt, ăn′tī-) *n.* One of the Dutch Calvinists who opposed **Arminianism** *(see).*

an·tir·rhi·num (ăn′tə-rī′nəm) *n.* Any plant of the genus *Antirrhinum,* a **snapdragon** *(see).* [New Latin, from Greek *antirrhinon,* "plant having snoutlike flowers" : *anti-,* counterfeiting + *rhis* (stem *rhin-*), nose (see **rhino-**).]

An·ti·sa·na (än′tē-sä′nä). An active volcano, 18,885 feet high, in the Andes in north-central Ecuador.

an·ti·scor·bu·tic (ăn′tĭ-skôr-byo͞o′tĭk, ăn′tī-) *adj.* Curing or preventing scurvy. —*n.* A food or drug that cures or prevents scurvy. [ANTI- + SCORBUTIC.]

an·ti-Sem·ite (ăn′tĭ-sĕm′īt′, ăn′tī-) *n.* A person who is hostile toward or prejudiced against Jews. —**an′ti-Se·mit′ic** (-sə-mĭt′ĭk) *adj.* —**an′ti-Sem′i·tism′** *n.*

an·ti·sep·sis (ăn′tə-sĕp′sĭs) *n.* The destruction of microorganisms that cause disease, fermentation, or putrefaction. Compare **asepsis.** [ANTI- + SEPSIS.]

an·ti·sep·tic (ăn′tə-sĕp′tĭk) *adj.* **1.** Of, pertaining to, or designating antisepsis. **2.** Capable of producing antisepsis. **3.** Thoroughly clean. **4.** Devoid of enlivening or enriching qualities; austere; drab. —*n.* An antiseptic drug or agent. [ANTI- + SEPTIC.] —**an′ti·sep′ti·cal·ly** *adv.*

an·ti·se·rum (ăn′tĭ-sîr′əm) *n., pl.* **-rums** or **-ra** (-rə). Human or animal serum containing antibodies for at least one antigen.

an·ti·slav·er·y (ăn′tĭ-slā′vər-ē, -slāv′rē, ăn′tī-) *adj.* Opposed to or against slavery.

an·ti·so·cial (ăn′tĭ-sō′shəl, ăn′tī-) *adj.* **1.** Shunning the society of others; unsociable. **2.** Opposed to or interfering with the social order. —**an′ti·so′cial·ly** *adv.*

an·ti·spas·mod·ic (ăn′tĭ-spăz-mŏd′ĭk, ăn′tī-) *adj.* Easing or preventing spasms. —*n.* An antispasmodic drug.

An·tis·the·nes (ăn-tĭs′thə-nēz′). 444?–371? B.C. Greek philosopher; founder of the Cynic school.

an·tis·tro·phe (ăn-tĭs′trə-fē) *n.* **1.** In ancient Greek choral poetry or drama, the movement following and in the same meter as the strophe, sung while the chorus moves in the opposite direction from that of the strophe. **2.** The second stanza, and those like it, in a poem consisting of alternating stanzas in contrasting metric form. [Late Latin, from Greek *antistrophē* : ANTI- + STROPHE.] —**an′ti·stroph′ic** (ăn′tĭ-strŏf′ĭk) *adj.* —**an′ti·stroph′i·cal·ly** *adv.*

an·ti·sub·ma·rine (ăn′tĭ-sŭb′mə-rēn′, -sŭb′mə-rēn′, ăn′tī-) *adj. Abbr.* **AS** Directed against enemy submarines.

an·ti·tank (ăn′tĭ-tăngk′) *adj. Abbr.* **AT** Designed or used for combat against tanks or other armored vehicles.

an·tith·e·sis (ăn-tĭth′ə-sĭs) *n., pl.* **-ses** (-sēz′). **1.** Direct contrast; opposition. **2.** The direct or exact opposite. **3.** *Rhetoric.* **a.** The juxtaposition of sharply contrasting ideas in balanced or parallel words, phrases, or grammatical structures; for example, "*He for God only, she for God in him*" (Milton). **b.** The second and contrasting part of such a juxtaposition. **4.** The second stage of the dialectic process. [Late Latin, from Greek, opposition, from *antitithenai,* to oppose : ANTI- + *tithenai,* to set, place (see **dhē-**[1] in Appendix*).]

an·ti·thet·i·cal (ăn′tə-thĕt′ĭ-kəl) *adj.* Also **an·ti·thet·ic** (-ĭk). **1.** Pertaining to, of the nature of, or including antithesis. **2.** Directly opposed in every respect. —See Synonyms at **opposite.** [Late Latin *antitheticus,* from Greek *antithetikos,* from *antitithenai,* to oppose. See **antithesis.**] —**an′ti·thet′i·cal·ly** *adv.*

an·ti·tox·ic (ăn′tĭ-tŏk′sĭk) *adj.* **1.** Counteracting a toxin or poison. **2.** Of or pertaining to an antitoxin.

an·ti·tox·in (ăn′tĭ-tŏk′sĭn) *n.* **1.** An antibody formed in response to, and capable of neutralizing, a poison of biological origin. **2.** An animal serum containing such antibodies.

an·ti·trades (ăn′tĭ-trādz′) *pl.n.* The westerly winds above the trade winds of the tropics, which become the westerly winds of the middle latitudes.

an·ti·trust (ăn′tĭ-trŭst′, ăn′tī-) *adj.* Opposing or concerned with the regulation of trusts, cartels, or similar business monopolies.

an·ti·tus·sive (ăn′tĭ-tŭs′ĭv, ăn′tī-) *adj.* Capable of relieving coughing. —*n.* An antitussive drug.

an·ti·type (ăn′tĭ-tīp′) *n.* **1.** That which is foreshadowed by or identified with an earlier symbol or type, such as a figure in the New Testament who has a counterpart in the Old Testament. **2.** An opposite type. [Medieval Latin *antitypus,* from Greek *antitupos,* "opposite to the die" : *anti-,* opposite + *tupos,* die (see **steu-** in Appendix*).] —**an′ti·typ′i·cal** (-tĭp′ĭ-kəl) *adj.*

an·ti·ven·in (ăn′tĭ-vĕn′ĭn, ăn′tī-) *n.* **1.** An antitoxin active against venom. **2.** An antiserum containing such an antitoxin. [ANTI- + VEN(OM) + -IN.]

ant·ler (ănt′lər) *n.* One of a pair of hard, bony, deciduous growths, usually elongated and branched, that characteristically grow on the heads of male deer and related animals. [Middle English *aunteler,* from Old French *antoillier,* from Vulgar Latin *anteoculāris* (unattested), "before the eyes" : ANTE- + Latin *oculus,* eye (see **okw-** in Appendix*).] —**ant′lered** (ănt′lərd) *adj.*

Ant·li·a (ănt′lē-ə) *n.* A constellation in the Southern Hemisphere near Hydra and Vela. [Latin *antlia,* pump, from Greek *antlia, antlos,* bucket. See **sem-²** in Appendix.*]

ant lion. Any insect of the family Myrmeleontidae, of which the adults resemble dragon flies; especially, the larva of such an insect, which digs holes to trap ants and other insects for food. Also called "doodlebug."

An·to·fa·gas·ta (än′tō-fä-gäs′tä). A city and mineral-exporting seaport of northwestern Chile. Population, 105,000.

An·toi·nette (ăn′twə-nĕt′, ăn′tə-). A feminine given name. [French, from *Antoine,* from Latin *Antōnius,* ANTHONY.]

An·to·ni·a (ăn-tō′nē-ə). A feminine given name. [Italian, feminine of *Antonio,* from Latin *Antōnius,* ANTHONY.]

An·to·ni·nus, Marcus Aurelius. See **Marcus Aurelius Antoninus.**

An·to·ni·nus Pi·us (ăn′tə-nī′nəs pī′əs). A.D. 86–161. Roman emperor (138–161); adopted son and successor to Hadrian.

An·to·ni·us (ăn-tō′nē-əs), **Marcus.** English name, Mark or Marc Antony. 83?–30 B.C. Roman triumvir.

an·to·no·ma·sia (ăn′tə-nō-mā′zhə) *n.* **1.** The substitution of a title or epithet for a proper name, as in calling a king "His Majesty." **2.** The substitution of a personal name for a common noun to designate a member of a group or class, as in calling a libertine "a Don Juan." [Latin, from Greek, from *antonomazein,* to name instead : *ant(i)-,* instead of + *onomazein,* to name, from *onoma,* name (see **nomen-** in Appendix*).]

an·to·nym (ăn′tə-nĭm′) *n. Abbr.* **ant.** A word having a sense opposite to a sense of another word; for example, *light* is an antonym of *dark.* Compare **synonym.** [ANT(I)- + -ONYM.] —**an·ton′y·mous** (ăn-tŏn′ə-məs) *adj.* —**an·ton′y·my** *n.*

an·tre (ăn′tər) *n. Chiefly Poetic.* A cavern or cave. [French, from Latin *antrum,* cave. See **antrum.**]

An·trim (ăn′trĭm). A county occupying 1,098 square miles in Northern Ireland. Population, 290,000. County seat, Belfast.

an·trorse (ăn′trôrs′) *adj. Biology.* Directed forward and upward. [New Latin *antrorsus* : perhaps blend of ANTERIOR and DEXTRORSE.] —**an′trorse′ly** *adv.*

an·trum (ăn′trəm) *n., pl.* **-tra** (-trə). A cavity, usually in bone; especially, either of the sinuses in the upper jaw opening into the nose. [Late Latin, cavity in the body, from Latin, cave, from Greek *antron,* akin to Armenian *ayr,* hole.]

An·tung (än′dŏŏng′, -tŏŏng′). A city and river port of eastern China, at the mouth of the Yalu in Liaoning Province. Population, 370,000.

Ant·werp (ănt′wûrp). *Flemish* **Ant·wer·pen** (änt′vĕr′pən); *French* **An·vers** (äN′vâr′). **1.** A province of Belgium, occupying 1,104 square miles in the north-central part of the country. Population, 1,443,000. **2.** The capital of this province, a port city in the northwest on the Scheldt. Population, 253,000.

A·nu·bis (ə-nōō′bĭs, ə-nyōō′-). *Egyptian Mythology.* A jackal-headed god who conducted the dead to judgment.

A·nu·ra·dha·pu·ra (ŭ-nōō-rä′də-pōō′rä). A town in north-central Ceylon, an ancient capital. Population, 18,000.

a·nu·ran (ə-nŏŏr′ən, ə-nyŏŏr′-) *adj.* Of or pertaining to frogs and toads. —*n.* A frog or toad. [New Latin *Anura,* order of frogs and toads : AN- (without) + Greek *oura,* tail (see **ors-** in Appendix*).]

an·u·re·sis (ăn′yōō-rē′sĭs) *n.* **1.** Inability to urinate. **2.** Anuria. [AN- (without) + Greek *ouresis,* urination, from *ourein,* to urinate, from *ouran,* urine (see **wer-¹²** in Appendix*).] —**an′u·ret′ic** (ăn′yōō-rĕt′ĭk) *adj.*

a·nu·ri·a (ə-nŏŏr′ē-ə, ə-nyŏŏr′-) *n.* **1.** The pathological condition characterized by failure to urinate. **2.** Anuresis. [New Latin : AN- (not) + -URIA.] —**a·nu′ric** *adj.*

a·nu·rous (ə-nŏŏr′əs, ə-nyŏŏr′-) *adj.* Having no tail; tailless. [AN- + -UROUS.]

a·nus (ā′nəs) *n., pl.* **anuses.** The excretory opening of the alimentary canal. [Latin *ānus.* See **āno-** in Appendix.*]

an·vil (ăn′vĭl) *n.* **1.** A heavy block of iron or steel, with a smooth, flat top on which metals are shaped by hammering. **2.** The fixed jaw in a set of calipers, against which the object to be measured is placed. **3.** *Anatomy.* A bone, the **incus** *(see).* [Middle English *anvil(t), anvelt,* Old English *anfealt, anfilt* : *an,* ON + *-fealt,* "beaten" (see **pel-⁶** in Appendix*).]

anx·i·e·ty (ăng-zī′ə-tē) *n., pl.* **-ties. 1.** A state of uneasiness and distress about future uncertainties; apprehension; worry. **2.** A cause of such uneasiness; a worry. **3.** *Psychiatry.* Intense fear or dread lacking an unambiguous cause or a specific threat. **4.** Eagerness. [Latin *anxietās,* from *anxius,* ANXIOUS.]

Synonyms: *anxiety, worry, care, concern, solicitude.* These nouns express troubled states of mind. *Anxiety* suggests feelings of fear and concern detached from objective sources, feeding themselves, as it were. *Worry* implies persistent doubt or fear that produces strong mental agitation. *Care,* often in the plural, implies mental oppression of varying degree arising from heavy responsibilities. *Concern* has more to do with serious thought than with emotion, and stresses personal involvement in the source of mental unrest. *Solicitude* is active concern for the well-being of another person or persons.

anx·ious (ăngk′shəs, ăng′shəs) *adj.* **1.** Worried and strained about some uncertain event or matter; uneasy. **2.** Attended with, showing, or causing such worry; full of anxieties. **3.** Eagerly or earnestly desirous. —See Synonyms at **eager.** [Latin *anxius,* from *angere,* to torment, choke. See **angh-** in Appendix.*] —**anx′ious·ly** *adv.* —**anx′ious·ness** *n.*

Usage: *Anxious* is often followed by *for, about,* or an infinitive: *anxious for* (or *about*) *your safety; anxious to avoid danger.* The adjectives *anxious* and *eager* overlap to some extent, where *anxious* denotes "eagerly or earnestly desirous," but *anxious* is more appropriate in such contexts when there is some implication of apprehension or concern: *"Charlie had never fallen in love, but was anxious to do so on the first opportunity"* (Kipling). Where such implication is absent, *eager* is preferable: *eager to see your new car.* The example *anxious to see your new car* is unacceptable in writing to 72 per cent of the Usage Panel, but acceptable in speech to 63 per cent.

an·y (ĕn′ē) *adj.* **1.** One, no matter which, from three or more; a, an, or some. **2.** Some, regardless of quantity or number. **3.** The smallest quantity or number of; even one. **4.** Every. —*pron.* **1.** Any one or ones among three or more. **2.** Any quantity or part. —*adv.* To any degree or extent; at all. [Middle English *any, eny,* Old English *ænig.* See **oino-** in Appendix.*]

Usage: *Any* (pronoun) can take either a singular or plural verb, depending on how it is construed: *Any of these books is suitable* (that is, *any one*). *But are any* (that is, *some*) *of them available?* In written usage, *any other,* rather than *any,* is appropriate in constructions, such as the following, involving the comparison of like things: *The day seemed longer than any other he had known.* Similarly, *any* (adjective), with a singular noun, is used loosely in the following: *He is the best-known of any living playwright* (preferably *of all living playwrights,* or omit *all*). The preceding example, with *of any,* is unacceptable in writing to 67 per cent of the Usage Panel. *Any* (adverb), as defined above, is appropriate to all levels of usage. It is also used in the same sense, but informally, in interrogative and negative constructions such as *Does it hurt any? The medicine didn't help any.*

An·yang (än′yäng′). A city of China, in central Honan Province; an important archeological site and capital of the ancient Shang dynasty. Population, 153,000.

an·y·bod·y (ĕn′ē-bŏd′ē, -bəd-ē) *pron.* Anyone. See Usage note at **anyone.** —*n., pl.* **anybodies.** A person of some consequence: *everybody who is anybody.*

an·y·how (ĕn′ē-hou′) *adv.* **1.** In any way or by any means whatever; at all. **2.** In any case. **3.** Carelessly; neglectfully.

an·y·more (ĕn′ē-môr′, -mōr′) *adv.* At the present; from now on. Used in negative and interrogative constructions.

an·y·one (ĕn′ē-wŭn′, -wən) *pron.* Anybody; any person.

Usage: *Anyone* and *anybody* (always written as one word in this sense) are singular terms, and take singular verbs. In written usage especially, accompanying personal pronouns and pronominal adjectives should agree in number (singular) with the verb: *Anyone is entitled to change his* (not *their*) *mind occasionally.* The pronoun *anyone* is equivalent to *anybody;* it refers only to persons (indefinitely to any person whatsoever), and stresses *any.* In contrast, *any one* refers to any person or thing of a specified group, and stresses *one.* Thus, *Anyone can succeed if he tries. There are many candidates, any one of whom could do a good job.* The singular *anyone* is used informally (for *all*) in the following typical construction: *She is the most thrifty person of anyone I know* (preferably eliminate *of anyone* or use *all*). The preceding example is unacceptable in writing to 64 per cent of the Usage Panel.

an·y·place (ĕn′ē-plās′) *adv.* To, in, or at any place; anywhere.

an·y·thing (ĕn′ē-thĭng′) *pron.* Any object, occurrence, or matter whatever. —*adv.* To any degree or extent; at all. —**anything but.** By no means; not at all.

an·y·way (ĕn′ē-wā′) *adv.* **1.** In any manner whatever. **2.** Nevertheless; at any rate; anyhow.

Usage: *Anyway* and *any way* are interchangeable only in the sense of anywise or in any way or manner: *Do it anyway* (or *any way*) *you want.* When the sense is in any case, at any rate, or nevertheless, only *anyway* is possible: *He objected, but she went anyway.* When the sense is any course or direction, only *any way* is possible: *Any way we choose will involve danger.*

an·y·ways (ĕn′ē-wāz′) *adv. Nonstandard.* Anyway.

an·y·where (ĕn′ē-hwâr′) *adv.* **1.** To, in, or at any place. **2.** To any extent or degree; at all. —**anywhere from.** Any quantity, degree, time, or the like between given bounds.

an·y·wise (ĕn′ē-wīz′) *adv.* In any way or manner.

An·za (än′thä), **Juan Bautista de.** 1735–1788. Spanish explorer and governor in North America; founded Monterey and San Francisco.

An·zac (ăn′zăk′) *n.* **1.** A soldier in the Australian and New Zealand Army Corps formed in World War I. **2.** Any soldier from New Zealand or Australia. —*adj.* Of or pertaining to this army corps.

An·zi·o (ăn′zē-ō′; *Italian* än′tsyō). A town and port on the western coast of Italy, 33 miles south of Rome, the site of an Allied beachhead in World War II (January 1944).

A.O.H. Ancient Order of Hibernians.

A·o·mor·i (ä′ō-mō′rē). A city of Japan, a seaport on northern Honshu. Population, 232,000.

A-one (ā′wŭn′) *adj.* **1.** *Informal.* First-class; excellent; splendid. **2.** Having a hull and equipment in the best condition. Said of a ship. Also written *A-1.*

aor. aorist.

Ao·ran·gi. See Mount **Cook.**

a·o·rist (ā′ə-rĭst) *n. Abbr.* **aor.** A verb tense originally used in classical Greek. It usually denotes past action without indicating completion, continuation, or repetition of this action.

antler

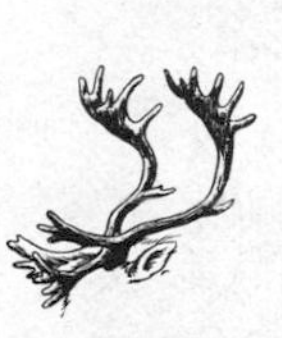

reindeer

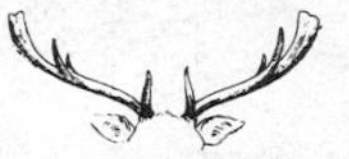

fallow deer

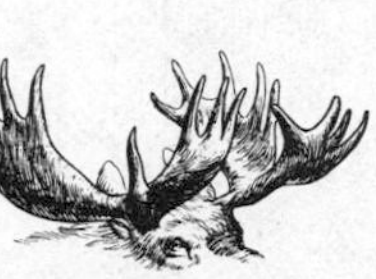

moose

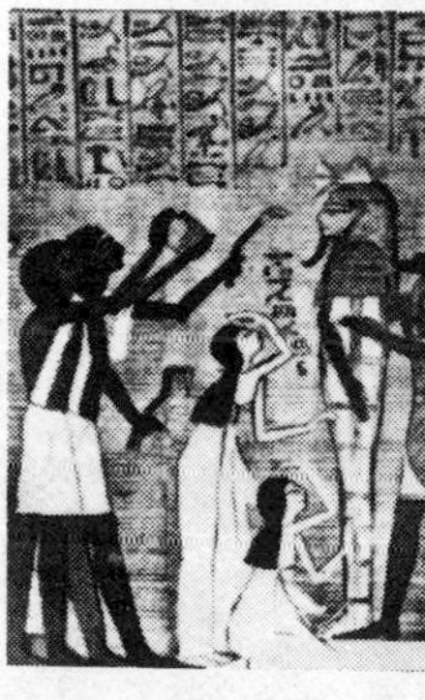

Anubis
The god *(right)* holding a mummy

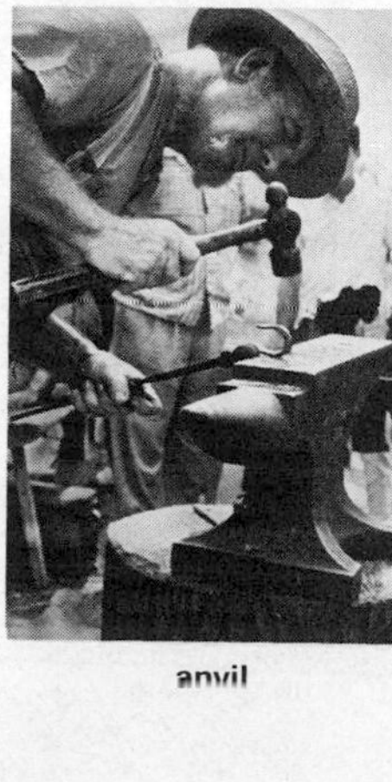

anvil

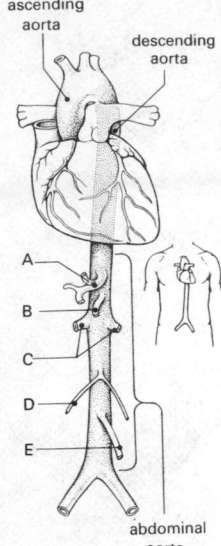

aorta
A. Celiac artery
B. Superior mesenteric artery
C. Renal arteries
D. Spermatic artery
E. Inferior mesenteric artery

ascending aorta

descending aorta

abdominal aorta

—*adj.* Of or in this verb tense. [Greek (*khronos*) *aoristos*, "the indefinite (tense)" : A- (not) + *horistos*, definable, from *horizein*, to delimit, from *horos*, boundary, limit (see **horizon**).] —**a'o·ris'tic** *adj.* —**a'o·ris'ti·cal·ly** *adv.*

a·or·ta (ā-ôr'tə) *n., pl.* **-tas** or **-tae** (-tē') *Anatomy.* The main trunk of the systemic arteries, carrying blood from the left side of the heart to the arteries of all limbs and organs except the lungs. [New Latin, from Greek *aortē*, aorta, "appendices (of the heart)," from *aeirein*, to raise up. See **wer-²** in Appendix.*] —**a·or'tal, a·or'tic** *adj.*

a·ou·dad (ä'ŏŏ-dăd') *n.* A wild sheep, *Ammotragus lervia*, of northern Africa, having long, curved horns and a beardlike growth of hair on the neck and chest. Also called "Barbary sheep." [French, from Berber *audad*.]

AP **1.** airplane. **2.** antipersonnel. **3.** Associated Press.

ap. apothecary.

a.p. **1.** additional premium. **2.** author's proof.

A.P. Associated Press.

A.P.A. **1.** American Philological Association. **2.** American Psychiatric Association.

a·pace (ə-pās') *adv.* At a rapid pace; rapidly; swiftly. [Middle English *apas, apace*, step by step, from Old French *a pas* : *a*, to, from Latin *ad* + *pas*, step, **PACE**.]

a·pache (ə-päsh', ə-păsh'; *French* ä-päsh') *n., pl.* **apaches** (ə-päsh', ə-păsh'; *French* ä-päsh'). A member of the Parisian underworld. [From **APACHE**.]

A·pach·e (ə-păch'ē) *n., pl.* **Apache** or **-es.** **1.** A formerly nomadic Athapascan-speaking tribe of North American Indians inhabiting the southwestern United States and northern Mexico. **2.** A member of this tribe. **3.** Any of the languages of this tribe. [Spanish, probably from Zuñi *Apachu*, enemy.]

a·pach·e dance (ə-păch'ē). A semiacrobatic, violent duet dance, originated in the Parisian underworld and popular in vaudeville and burlesque shows.

Apache plume. A low shrub, *Fallugia paradoxa*, of southwestern United States and Mexico, having white flowers and plumelike fruiting clusters.

Ap·a·lach·ee Bay (ăp'ə-lăch'ē). An inlet of the Gulf of Mexico in northwestern Florida.

Ap·a·lach·i·co·la River (ăp'ə-lăch'ĭ-kō'lə). A river of Florida, formed at the border with Georgia by the confluence of the Chattahoochee and Flint rivers, and flowing 112 miles south to the Gulf of Mexico.

ap·a·nage. Variant of **appanage.**

A·pa·po·ris (ä'pä-pō'rəs). A river of Colombia, rising in the south-central part of the country, and flowing 500 miles south to join the Japurá on the border with Brazil.

a·pa·re·jo (ä'pə-rā'hō, ăp'ə-) *n., pl.* **-jos.** *Southwestern U.S.* A packsaddle made from a stuffed leather pad. [American Spanish, from Spanish, equipment, from *aparejar*, to prepare, from Vulgar Latin *appariculāre* (unattested), to **APPAREL**.]

a·part (ə-pärt') *adv.* **1. a.** In pieces. **b.** To pieces. **2. a.** Separately or at a distance in time, place, or position. **b.** To one side; aside. **3.** One from another. **4.** Separately or aside for a particular function or purpose. **5.** Independently or separately in consideration or thought. **6.** Out of consideration or set aside; aside. —**apart from.** With the exception of; besides. —*adj.* Having individualizing features or characteristics. Used predicatively: *a race apart.* [Middle English, from Old French *a part*, to the side : *a*, to, from Latin *ad-* + **PART**.]

a·part·heid (ə-pärt'hīt', -hāt') *n.* An official policy of racial segregation promulgated in the Republic of South Africa with a view to promoting and maintaining white ascendancy. [Afrikaans, "apartness" : *apart*, separate, from French *à part*, from Old French *a part*, **APART** + *-heid*, -hood.]

a·part·ment (ə-pärt'mənt) *n. Abbr.* **apt. 1.** A room or suite of rooms designed for housekeeping and generally located in a building which includes other such rooms or suites; a flat. **2.** A room. [French *appartement*, from Italian *appartemento*, from *appartare*, to separate, from *a parte*, apart : *a*, to, from Latin *ad* + *parte*, part, from Latin *pars*, **PART**.]

apartment house. A building divided into apartments. Also called "apartment building."

ap·a·tet·ic (ăp'ə-tĕt'ĭk) *adj. Zoology.* Pertaining to or characteristic of coloration serving as natural camouflage. [Greek *apatētikos*, deceptive, from *apateuein*, to cheat, from *apatē†*, deceit, fraud.]

ap·a·thet·ic (ăp'ə-thĕt'ĭk) *adj.* Also **ap·a·thet·i·cal** (-ĭ-kəl). **1.** Feeling or showing little or no emotion. **2.** Uninterested; listless. —See Synonyms at **indifferent.** [Blend of **APATHY** and **PATHETIC.**] —**ap'a·thet'i·cal·ly** *adv.*

ap·a·thy (ăp'ə-thē) *n.* **1.** Lack of emotion or feeling. **2.** Lack of interest in things generally found exciting, interesting, or moving; indifference. [Greek *apatheia*, from *apathēs*, without feeling : A- (without) + *pathos*, feeling (see **-pathy**).]

ap·a·tite (ăp'ə-tīt') *n.* A natural, variously colored calcium fluoride phosphate, Ca₅F(PO₄)₃, with chlorine, hydroxyl, or carbonate sometimes replacing the fluoride. It is a source of phosphorus compounds and is used in the manufacture of fertilizers. [German *Apatit*, "the deceptive stone" (often mistaken for other minerals), from Greek *apatē†*, deceit. See **apatetic.**]

APB all points bulletin (in police communications).

ape (āp) *n.* **1.** Any of various large, tailless Old World primates of the family Pongidae, including the chimpanzee, gorilla, gibbon, and orang-utan. **2.** Broadly, any monkey. **3.** A mimic or imitator. **4.** *Informal.* A clumsy, ill-bred, coarse person. —*tr.v.* **aped, aping, apes.** To mimic. See Synonyms at **imitate.** [Middle English *ape*, Old English *apa*, from Common Germanic *apan-* (unattested).]

aoudad

Aphrodite
Third-century B.C. Greek terra cotta, "The Birth of Aphrodite"

a·peak (ə-pēk') *adv. Nautical.* In a vertical or almost vertical position or direction. [Earlier *apike* : A- + **PIKE** (peak).]

A·pel·doorn (ä'pəl-dōrn). A manufacturing city in the east-central Netherlands. Population, 112,000.

A·pel·les (ə-pĕl'ēz). Greek painter of the fourth century B.C.

ape-man (āp'măn') *n., pl.* **-men** (-mĭn'). Loosely, any of several extinct primates considered intermediate between apes and modern man.

Ap·en·nines (ăp'ə-nīnz'). A mountain range of Italy, extending about 800 miles along the entire length of the peninsula. Highest elevation, Mount Corno (9,560 feet).

a·per·çu (ă-pĕr-sü') *n., pl.* **-çus** (-sü'). *French.* An outline; synopsis; summary.

a·pe·ri·ent (ə-pîr'ē-ənt) *adj.* Gently purgative; laxative. —*n.* A mild laxative. [Latin *aperiēns*, present participle of *aperīre*, to uncover, open. See **wer-⁵** in Appendix.*]

a·pe·ri·od·ic (ā'pîr-ē-ŏd'ĭk) *adj.* Occurring without periodicity; irregular. —**a'pe·ri·od'i·cal·ly** *adv.* —**a·pe'ri·o·dic'i·ty** *n.*

a·pé·ri·tif (ä-pĕr'ə-tēf'; *French* ä-pā-rē-tēf') *n.* A drink of alcoholic liquor or wine taken to stimulate the appetite before a meal. [French, from Old French *aperitif*, from Medieval Latin *aperitīvus*, from Latin *aperīre*, to open. See **wer-⁵** in Appendix.*]

ap·er·ture (ăp'ər-chŏŏr', -chər) *n.* **1.** A hole, gap, slit, or other opening; an orifice. **2.** *Optics.* A usually adjustable opening in an optical instrument that limits the amount of light passing through a lens. [Latin *apertūra*, from *apertus*, open, from the past participle of *aperīre*, to open. See **wer-⁵** in Appendix.*] —**ap'er·tur'al** *adj.*

a·pet·al·ous (ā-pĕt'l-əs) *adj. Botany.* Having no petals. [A- (not) + **PETALOUS**.] —**a·pet'al·y** (ā-pĕt'l-ē) *n.*

a·pex (ā'pĕks') *n., pl.* **apexes** or **apices** (ā'pə-sēz', ăp'ə-). **1.** The highest point of something; vertex. **2.** The culmination. **3.** The pointed end of something; tip. —See Synonyms at **summit.** [Latin *apex*, point, summit, top. See **ap-¹** in Appendix.*]

a·phaer·e·sis, a·pher·e·sis (ə-fĕr'ə-sĭs) *n.* The loss of one or more letters or sounds from the beginning of a word, as in *round* for *around* or *most* for *almost.* [Late Latin, from Greek *aphairesis*, a taking away, from *aphairein*, to take away from : *ap(o)-*, away from + *hairein*, to take (see **heresy**).] —**aph'ae·ret'ic** (ăf'ə-rĕt'ĭk) *adj.*

a·pha·gi·a (ə-fā'jē-ə) *n.* Inability to swallow. [New Latin : A- (not) + -PHAGIA.]

aph·a·nite (ăf'ə-nīt') *n.* Any dense, homogeneous rock with constituents so fine that they cannot be seen by the naked eye. [French : Greek *aphanēs*, unseen : A- (not) + *phainesthai*, to be seen, from *phainein*, to see (see **bhā-¹** in Appendix*) + -ITE.] —**aph'a·nit'ic** (-nĭt'ĭk) *adj.* —**aph'a·nit·ism'** *n.*

a·pha·sia (ə-fā'zhə) *n.* Partial or total loss of the ability to articulate ideas in any form, resulting from brain damage. [New Latin, from Greek : A- (without) + -PHASIA.] —**a·pha'si·ac'** (-zē-ăk') *n.* —**a·pha'sic** *adj. & n.*

a·phe·li·on (ə-fē'lē-ən, ə-fēl'yən) *n., pl.* **-lia** (-lē-ə). The orbital point on a planetary orbit farthest from the sun. Compare **perihelion.** [New Latin, variant of *aphelium* : Greek *ap(o)-*, away from + *hēlios*, sun (see **sāwel-** in Appendix*).]

a·phe·li·o·trop·ic (ə-fē'lē-ō-trŏp'ĭk) *adj. Biology.* Turning away from the sun or source of light, as roots do. [AP(O)- (away from) + HELIOTROPIC.] —**a·phe'li·o·trop'i·cal·ly** *adv.* —**a·phe'li·ot'ro·pism'** (-ŏt'rə-pĭz'əm) *n.*

aph·e·sis (ăf'ə-sĭs) *n.* The loss of a short unstressed vowel from the beginning of a word; for example, *squire* for *esquire.* [New Latin, from Greek *aphesis*, a letting go, from *aphienai*, to let go : *ap(o)-*, away + *hienai*, to send (see **yē-** in Appendix*).] —**a·phet'ic** (ə-fĕt'ĭk) *adj.* —**a·phet'i·cal·ly** *adv.*

a·phid (ā'fĭd, ăf'ĭd) *n.* Any of various small, soft-bodied insects of the family Aphidae, that feed by sucking sap from plants. Also called "plant louse." [From New Latin *aphis* (stem *aphid-*), APHIS.] —**a·phid'i·an** (ə-fĭd'ē-ən) *adj. & n.*

aphid lion. The larva of any of several insects of the family Chrysopidae, such as the lacewing, that feed on aphids.

a·phis (ā'fĭs, ăf'ĭs) *n., pl.* **aphides** (ā'fə-dēz', ăf'ə-). An aphid, especially one of the genus *Aphis.* [New Latin *Aphis†*.]

a·pho·ni·a (ā-fō'nē-ə) *n.* Loss of speech, or voicelessness, as a result of disease or injury to the organs of speech. [New Latin, from Greek *aphōnia*, voicelessness, from *aphōnos*, voiceless : A- (without) + *phōnē*, voice (see **bha-²** in Appendix*).]

a·phon·ic (ā-fŏn'ĭk) *adj.* **1.** *Pathology.* Affected with or having aphonia. **2.** *Phonetics.* Unvoiced.

aph·o·rism (ăf'ə-rĭz'əm) *n.* **1.** A brief statement of a principle. **2.** A tersely phrased statement of a truth or opinion; maxim; an adage. —See Synonyms at **saying.** [Old French *aphorisme*, from Greek *aphorismos*, a delimitation, from *aphorizein*, to mark off by boundaries : *ap(o)-*, off, away from + *horizein*, to limit, from *horos*, boundary, limit (see **horizon**).] —**aph'o·ris'tic** (-rĭs'tĭk) *adj.* —**aph'o·ris'ti·cal·ly** *adv.*

a·pho·tic (ā-fō'tĭk) *adj.* Without light. [A- (not) + PHOTIC.]

aph·ro·dis·i·ac (ăf'rə-dĭz'ē-ăk') *adj.* Stimulating or intensifying sexual desire. —*n.* An aphrodisiac drug or food. [Greek *aphrodisiakos*, from *aphrodisia*, aphrodisiac pleasures, from *aphrodisios*, of Aphrodite, from *Aphroditē*, APHRODITE.]

aph·ro·di·te (ăf'rə-dī'tē) *n.* A brightly colored butterfly, *Argynnis aphrodite*, of North America. [After APHRODITE.]

Aph·ro·di·te (ăf'rə-dī'tē) *n. Greek Mythology.* The goddess of love and beauty, identified with the Roman Venus. Also called "Cytherea." [Greek *Aphroditē*.]

a·phyl·lous (ā-fĭl'əs) *adj. Botany.* Having or bearing no leaves. [Greek *aphyllos* : A- (not) + -PHYLLOUS.] —**a·phyl'ly** (ā-fĭl'ē) *n.*

A·pi·a (ä-pē'ə). The capital of Western Samoa, a seaport on Upolu Island. Population, 22,000.

a·pi·an (ā′pē-ən) *adj.* Of or pertaining to bees. [Latin *apiānus,* from *apis*†, bee.]
a·pi·ar·i·an (ā′pē-âr′ē-ən) *adj.* Pertaining to bees or to the keeping and care of bees. —*n.* An apiarist.
a·pi·a·rist (ā′pē-ə-rĭst, ā′pē-ĕr′ĭst) *n.* A beekeeper.
a·pi·ar·y (ā′pē-ĕr′ē) *n., pl.* **-ies.** A shed or stand containing a number of beehives, in which bees are raised for their honey. [Latin *apiārium,* beehive, from *apis,* bee. See **apian.**]
ap·i·cal (ăp′ĭ-kəl, ā′pĭ-) *adj.* **1.** Of, pertaining to, located at, or constituting the apex. **2.** *Phonetics.* Pertaining to consonants articulated with the tip of the tongue, as *t, d,* and *s.* [New Latin *apicalis,* from Latin *apex* (stem *apic-*), APEX.]
a·pi·ces. Alternate plural of **apex.**
a·pic·u·late (ə-pĭk′yə-lĭt) *adj. Botany.* Ending with a sharp, abrupt tip: *an apiculate leaf.* [From New Latin *apiculus,* a sharp point, diminutive of Latin *apex* (stem *apic-*), APEX.]
a·pi·cul·ture (ā′pĭ-kŭl′chər) *n.* The raising and care of bees. [Latin *apis,* bee (see **apian**) + CULTURE.] —**a′pi·cul′tur·al** *adj.* —**a′pi·cul′tur·ist** *n.*
a·piece (ə-pēs′) *adv.* To or for each one; each: *Give them an apple apiece.* [Middle English *a pece* : A + PIECE.]
A·pis (ā′pĭs) *n.* A sacred bull of the ancient Egyptians.
ap·ish (ā′pĭsh) *adj.* **1.** Slavishly or foolishly imitative. **2.** Silly; tricky; mischievous. —**ap′ish·ly** *adv.* —**ap′ish·ness** *n.*
a·piv·o·rous (ā-pĭv′ər-əs) *adj.* Feeding on bees. [Latin *apis,* bee (see **apian**) + -VOROUS.]
a·pla·cen·tal (ā′plə-sĕn′təl) *adj.* Having no placenta. Said of marsupials and monotremes. [A- (not) + PLACENT(A) + -AL.]
ap·la·nat·ic (ăp′lə-năt′ĭk) *adj.* Of or pertaining to optical systems that correct for spherical aberration and coma. [From Greek *aplanētos,* unable to go astray : A- (not) + *planētos, planēs,* wandering, from *planasthai,* to wander (see **pelə-**[1] in Appendix*).]
a·pla·sia (ə-plā′zhə) *n.* Defective development or congenital absence of tissue, of an organ, or of an organic part. [New Latin : A- (not) + -PLASIA.]
a·plas·tic (ā-plăs′tĭk) *adj.* **1.** Lacking form. **2.** *Pathology.* Unable to form or regenerate tissue. **3.** *Pathology.* Of or relating to aplasia. [A- (not) + -PLASTIC.]
ap·lite (ăp′līt′) *n.* Also **hap·lite.** A fine-grained, light-colored granitic rock consisting primarily of orthoclase and quartz. [German *Aplit* : Greek *haplous,* single, simple (see **haploid**) + -ITE.] —**ap·lit′ic** (ăp-lĭt′ĭk) *adj.*
a·plomb (ə-plŏm′, ə-plŭm′) *n.* Self-confidence; poise; assurance. See Synonyms at **confidence.** [French, uprightness, from Old French *a plomb,* perpendicularly, according to the plummet : *a,* to, from Latin *ad* + *plomb,* plummet, lead weight, from Latin *plumbum,* lead (see **plumbum** in Appendix*).]
apmt. appointment.
ap·ne·a (ăp-nē′ə, ăp′nē-ə) *n.* Also **ap·noe·a.** Transient suspension of respiration. [New Latin, from Greek *apnoia,* absence of respiration : A- (without) + *pnoē,* breathing, from *pnein,* to breathe (see **pneu-** in Appendix*).] —**ap·ne′ic** *adj.*
A·po, Mount (ä′pō). The highest mountain (9,690 feet) in the Philippines, an active volcano on southeastern Mindanao.
apo-, ap-. Indicates: **1.** Being away from; for example, **aphelion. 2.** Lack of; for example, **apogamy. 3.** Separation of; for example, **apocarpous. 4.** *Geology.* Metasomatism; for example, **apophyllite.** [In borrowed Greek compounds, *apo-* indicates: 1. Away from, as in **apogee.** 2. Away, off, as in **apothecary.** 3. Return, as in **apodosis.** 4. Intensive action, as in **aposiopesis.** 5. Keeping off, defense, as in **apology.** 6. Change from an existing state, as in **apotheosis.** 7. Reversal, as in **Apocalypse.** Greek *apo-,* from *apo,* away from, off. See **apo-** in Appendix.*]
APO, A.P.O. Army Post Office.
Apoc. **1.** Apocalypse. **2.** Apocrypha; Apocryphal.
A·poc·a·lypse (ə-pŏk′ə-lĭps′) *n.* **1.** *Abbr.* **Apoc.** The last book of the New Testament, **Revelation** *(see).* **2.** *Small* **a.** A prophetic disclosure or revelation. [Middle English *Apocalipse,* from Late Latin *Apocalypsis,* from Greek *apokalupsis,* revelation, from *apokaluptein,* to uncover : *apo-,* reversal + *kaluptein,* to cover (see **kel-**[4] in Appendix*).]
a·poc·a·lyp·tic (ə-pŏk′ə-lĭp′tĭk) *adj.* Also **a·poc·a·lyp·ti·cal** (-tĭ-kəl). Of or pertaining to a prophetic disclosure or revelation. —**a·poc′a·lyp′ti·cal·ly** *adv.*
ap·o·carp (ăp′ə-kärp′) *n. Botany.* An apocarpous fruit. [Back-formation from APOCARPOUS.]
ap·o·car·pous (ăp′ə-kär′pəs) *adj.* Having distinctly separated carpels. [APO- + -CARPOUS.] —**ap′o·car′py** (ăp′ə-kär′pē) *n.*
ap·o·chro·mat·ic (ăp′ə-krō-măt′ĭk) *adj. Optics.* Corrected for both chromatic and spherical aberration.
a·poc·o·pe (ə-pŏk′ə-pē) *n.* A cutting off or omitting of the last sound or syllable of a word; for example, *goin′* for *going.* [Latin *apocopē,* from Greek *apokopē,* from *apokoptein,* to cut off : *apo-,* off + *koptein,* to cut (see **skep-** in Appendix*).]
ap·o·crine (ăp′ə-krĭn, -krīn′, -krēn′) *adj.* Of or pertaining to a gland that loses part of its cytoplasm in secretion. [APO- + Greek *krinein,* to separate (see **skeri-** in Appendix*).]
A·poc·ry·pha (ə-pŏk′rə-fə) *n.* Plural in form, used with a singular verb. *Abbr.* **Apoc. 1.** The 14 books of the Septuagint included in the Vulgate but considered uncanonical by Protestants because they are not part of the Hebrew Scriptures. Eleven of these books are accepted in the Roman Catholic canon, and appear in the Douay Bible. **2.** Various early Christian writings proposed as additions to the New Testament, but rejected by the major canons. **3.** *Small* **a.** Any writings of questionable authorship or authenticity. [Middle English *Apocripha,* from Medieval Latin *(scripta) apocrypha,* hidden (writings), from Late Latin *apocryphus,* hidden, from Greek *apokruphos,* from *apokruptein,* to hide away : *apo-,* away + *kruptein,* to hide (see **krau-** in Appendix*).]
a·poc·ry·phal (ə-pŏk′rə-fəl) *adj.* **1.** Of questionable authorship or authenticity. **2.** False; counterfeit. **3.** *Capital* **A.** *Abbr.* **Apoc.** Of or having to do with the Apocrypha. —**a·poc′ry·phal·ly** *adv.*
ap·o·dal (ăp′ə-dəl) *adj. Zoology.* Having no limbs, feet, or footlike appendages. [From Greek *apous* (stem *apod-*) : A- (without) + *pous,* foot (see **ped-**[1] in Appendix*).]
ap·o·dic·tic (ăp′ə-dĭk′tĭk) *adj.* Clearly proven or demonstrated; incontestable. [Latin *apodicticus,* from Greek *apodeiktikos,* from *apodeiknunai,* to point out or away from : *apo-,* away from + *deiknunai,* to show (see **deik-** in Appendix*).]
a·pod·o·sis (ə-pŏd′ə-sĭs) *n., pl.* **-ses** (-sēz′). The clause stating the conclusion or consequence of a conditional sentence. Compare **protasis.** [New Latin, from Greek, response (to the protasis), "a giving back," from *apodidonai,* give up or back : *apo-,* return + *didonai,* to give (see **dō-** in Appendix*).]
ap·o·en·zyme (ăp′ō-ĕn′zīm′) *n.* A protein requiring a **coenzyme** *(see)* to function as an enzyme.
a·pog·a·my (ə-pŏg′ə-mē) *n. Botany.* The production of a new plant from a prothallus by budding, without sexual reproduction, as in ferns. [APO- (lack of) + -GAMY.] —**ap′o·gam′ic** (ăp′ə-găm′ĭk), **a·pog′a·mous** (ə-pŏg′ə-məs) *adj.*
ap·o·gee (ăp′ə-jē) *n.* **1.** The point in the orbit of the moon or of an artificial satellite most distant from the earth. Compare **perigee. 2.** The farthest or highest point; apex. [French *apogée,* from New Latin *apogaeum,* from Greek *apogaion,* neuter of *apogaios,* "away from the earth" : *apo-,* away from + *gaia, gē,* earth (see **gē** in Appendix*).] —**ap′o·ge′an** (-jē′ən) *adj.*
a·po·lit·i·cal (ā′pə-lĭt′ĭ-kəl) *adj.* **1.** Having no association with or interest in politics. **2.** Having no political importance. —**a′po·lit′i·cal·ly** *adv.*
A·pol·li·naire (à′pô-lē-nâr′), **Guillaume.** Original name, Wilhelm Appollinaris de Kostrowitzky. 1880–1918. Polish-born French poet.
a·pol·lo (ə-pŏl′ō) *n.* Any young man of great physical beauty. [After Apollo.]
A·pol·lo (ə-pŏl′ō). *Greek Mythology.* The god of the sun, prophecy, music, medicine, and poetry.
ap·ol·lo·ni·an (ăp′ə-lō′nē-ən) *adj.* **1.** *Capital* **A.** Of or pertaining to Apollo or his cult. **2.** Of a theoretical or rational nature; clearly defined and well-ordered; harmonious. Compare **dionysian. 3.** Noble; dignified; serene.
a·pol·o·get·ic (ə-pŏl′ə-jĕt′ĭk) *adj.* **1.** Making an apology. **2.** Explaining or defending in speech or writing. —*n.* A formal defense or apology. —**a·pol′o·get′i·cal·ly** *adv.*
a·pol·o·get·ics (ə-pŏl′ə-jĕt′ĭks) *n.* Plural in form, used with a singular verb. The branch of theology that deals with the defense and proof of Christianity.
ap·o·lo·gi·a (ăp′ə-lō′jē-ə, -jə) *n.* A formal defense or justification. [Latin, APOLOGY.]
a·pol·o·gist (ə-pŏl′ə-jĭst) *n.* A person who argues in defense or justification of another person or cause.
a·pol·o·gize (ə-pŏl′ə-jīz′) *intr.v.* **-gized, -gizing, -gizes. 1.** To make excuse for or regretful acknowledgment of a fault or offense. **2.** To make a formal defense or justification in speech or writing. —**a·pol′o·giz′er** *n.*
ap·o·logue (ăp′ə-lôg′, -lŏg′) *n.* A moral fable. [French *apologue,* from Latin *apologus,* from Greek *apologos,* fable : *apo-,* away, off + *logos,* discourse (see **leg-** in Appendix*).]
a·pol·o·gy (ə-pŏl′ə-jē) *n., pl.* **-gies. 1.** A statement of acknowledgment expressing regret or asking pardon for a fault or offense. **2.** A formal justification or defense. **3.** An inferior substitute. [Old French *apologie,* from Late Latin *apologia,* from Greek *apologiā,* speech in defense : *apo-,* defense + *logos,* discourse, speech (see **leg-** in Appendix*).]
ap·o·mict (ăp′ə-mĭkt′) *n. Biology.* An organism that is the result of apomixis. [APO- + Greek *miktos,* mixed, from *mignunai,* to mix (see **meik-** in Appendix*).]
ap·o·mix·is (ăp′ə-mĭk′sĭs) *n.* A rare reproductive process in which a new individual is produced from a female cell or cells other than the egg cell, often in a manner that mimics sexual reproduction. [New Latin : APO- + Greek *mixis,* a mingling, from *mignunai,* to mix (see **meik-** in Appendix*).]
ap·o·mor·phine (ăp′ə-môr′fēn′) *n.* A poisonous white crystalline alkaloid, $C_{17}H_{17}NO_2$, derived from morphine and used medicinally as an expectorant, emetic, and hypnotic.
ap·o·neu·ro·sis (ăp′ə-nŏŏ-rō′sĭs, ăp′ə-nyŏŏ-) *n., pl.* **-ses** (-sēz′). A sheetlike membrane, resembling a flattened tendon, that invests a muscle or connects it to its insertion. [New Latin, from Greek *aponeurōsis,* from *aponeurousthai,* to become a nerve : *apo-* (change) + *neuron,* nerve (see **snēu-** in Appendix*).] —**ap′o·neu·rot′ic** (-rŏt′ĭk) *adj.*
ap·o·phthegm. Variant of **apothegm.**
a·poph·y·ge (ə-pŏf′ə-jē) *n.* The curvature at the top and bottom of the shaft of a column. [Greek *apophugē,* "escape" : *apo-,* away + *phugē,* flight (see **bheug-**[1] in Appendix*).]
a·poph·yl·lite (ə-pŏf′ə-līt′, ăp′ə-fĭl′īt′) *n.* A white, pale-pink, or pale-green crystalline mineral, essentially $KCa_4FSi_4O_{10} \cdot 8H_2O$. [APO- + PHYLLITE.]
a·poph·y·sis (ə-pŏf′ə-sĭs) *n., pl.* **-ses** (-sēz′). **1.** *Biology.* A swelling, projection, or outgrowth of an organ or part. **2.** *Geology.* A branch from a dike or vein. [New Latin, from Greek *apophusis,* side-shoot : *apo-,* off, away + *phusis,* growth, from *phuein,* to grow (see **bheu-** in Appendix*).] —**a·poph′y·sate, a·poph′y·se′al** (ə-pŏf′ə-sē′əl) *adj.*
ap·o·plec·tic (ăp′ə-plĕk′tĭk) *adj.* **1.** Of, resembling, or causing apoplexy. **2.** Having or exhibiting symptoms of apoplexy. —**ap′o·plec′ti·cal·ly** *adv.*

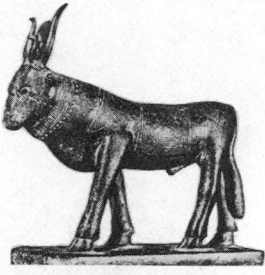

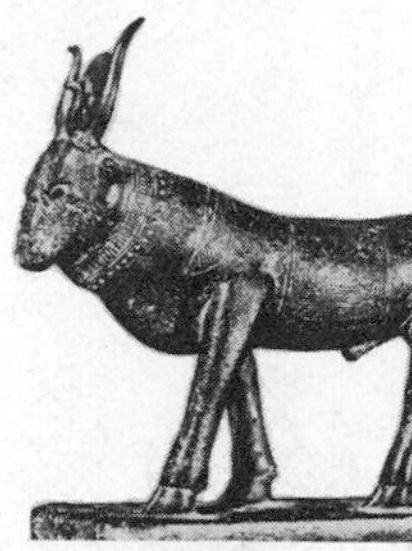
Apis
Bronze statue

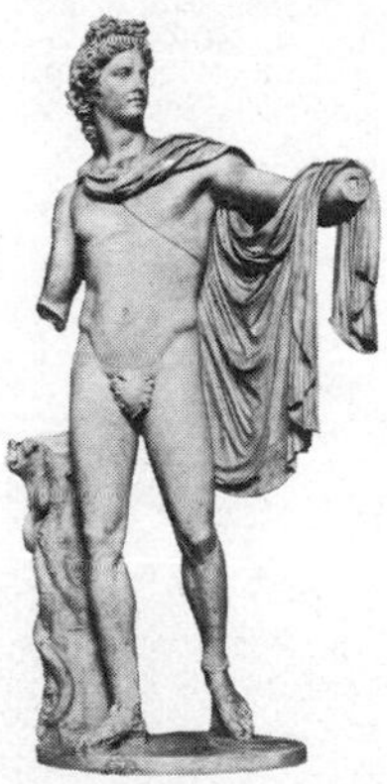
Apollo
Roman copy of 300 B.C. Greek statue

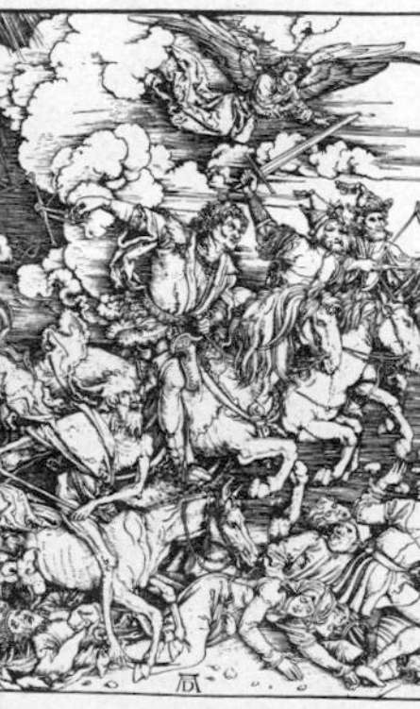
Apocalypse
The Four Horsemen of the Apocalypse, woodcut by Albrecht Dürer

ap·o·plex·y (ăp′ə-plĕk′sē) n. Sudden loss of muscular control, with diminution or loss of sensation and consciousness, resulting from rupture or blocking of a blood vessel in the brain. [Middle English apoplexie, from Old French, from Late Latin apoplēxia, from Greek, from apoplēssein, to cripple by a stroke : apo- (intensive) + plēssein, to strike (see **plāk-²** in Appendix*).]

a·port (ə-pôrt′, ə-pōrt′) adj. Nautical. On or toward the port, or left, side.

ap·o·si·o·pe·sis (ăp′ə-sī′ə-pē′sĭs) n., pl. **-ses** (-sēz). Rhetoric. A sudden and dramatic breaking off of a thought in the middle of a sentence, as though the speaker were unwilling or unable to continue. [Late Latin aposiōpēsis, from Greek, a becoming silent, from aposiōpān, maintain silence : apo- (intensifier) + siōpān, to be silent, from siōpē, silence (see **swi-** in Appendix*).]
—**ap′o·si′o·pet′ic** adj.

a·pos·ta·sy (ə-pŏs′tə-sē) n., pl. **-sies**. An abandonment of one's religious faith, political party, or cause. [Middle English apostasie, from Late Latin apostasia, from Greek, desertion, revolt, from apostanai, "to stand away from," rebel : apo-, away from + stanai, to stand (see **stā-** in Appendix*).]

a·pos·tate (ə-pŏs′tāt′, -tĭt) n. One who forsakes his faith or principles. —adj. Guilty of apostasy. [Middle English, from Late Latin apostata, from Greek apostatēs, deserter, rebel, from apostanai, to rebel. See **apostasy**.]

a·pos·ta·tize (ə-pŏs′tə-tīz′) intr.v. **-tized, -tizing, -tizes**. To give up or abandon one's faith or political party.

a pos·te·ri·o·ri (ä pŏs-tîr′ē-ôr′ē, -ōr′ē, ä pŏs-tîr′ē-ôr′ī′, -ōr′ī′) Logic. Denoting reasoning from facts or particulars to general principles, or from effects to causes; inductive; empirical. Compare **a priori**. [Latin, "from the subsequent."]

a·pos·tle (ə-pŏs′əl) n. **1.** Usually capital **A**. One of a group made up especially of the twelve witnesses chosen by Christ to preach his gospel. Luke 6:13–16. **2.** A missionary of the early Christian Church. **3.** A leader of the first Christian mission to a country or region. **4.** One of the twelve members of the Mormon administrative council. **5.** One who leads or advocates a new cause. [Middle English apostel, apostle, Old English apostol, from Late Latin apostolus, from Greek apostolos, messenger, envoy, from apostellein, to send away from : apo-, away from + stellein, to place (see **stel-¹** in Appendix*).]

Apostles' Creed. A Christian creed traditionally ascribed to the Twelve Apostles that begins, "I believe in God the Father Almighty."

ap·os·tol·ic (ăp′ə-stŏl′ĭk) adj. **1.** Of, pertaining to, or contemporary with the Apostles. **2.** Of or pertaining to the faith, teaching, or practice of the Apostles. **3.** Of or pertaining to the pope as successor of Saint Peter.

Apostolic Fathers. Church fathers, including Clement of Rome, Ignatius of Antioch, and Polycarp of Smyrna, who had received personal instruction from the Apostles themselves or from their disciples.

apostolic see. 1. A bishopric founded, traditionally, by one of the Apostles. **2.** Capital **A**, capital **S**. The See of Rome founded, according to tradition, by the Apostle Peter.

a·pos·tro·phe¹ (ə-pŏs′trə-fē) n. The superscript sign (') used to indicate the omission of a letter or letters from a word, the possessive case, and certain plurals, especially those of numbers and letters. See Usage note at **possessive**. [French, from Old French, from Late Latin apostrophus, from Greek (prosōidia) apostrophos, "(accent of) turning away," from apostrephein, to turn away : apo-, away + strephein, to turn (see **strebh-** in Appendix*).] —**ap′os·troph′ic** (ăp′ə-strŏf′ĭk) adj.

a·pos·tro·phe² (ə-pŏs′trə-fē) n. A digression in discourse; especially, a turning away from an audience to address an absent or imaginary person. [Latin apostrophē, from Greek, from apostrephein, to turn away. See **apostrophe** (sign).] —**ap′os·troph′ic** (ăp′ə-strŏf′ĭk) adj.

a·pos·tro·phize¹ (ə-pŏs′trə-fīz′) v. **-phized, -phizing, -phizes**. —tr. To omit a letter or letters in (a word) by use of an apostrophe. —intr. To connect a word with an apostrophe.

a·pos·tro·phize² (ə-pŏs′trə-fīz′) v. **-phized, -phizing, -phizes**. —tr. To address by apostrophe. —intr. To speak or write in apostrophe.

apothecaries' measure. A system of liquid volume measure used in pharmacy.

apothecaries' weight. A system of weights used in pharmacy and based on an ounce equal to 480 grains and a pound equal to 12 ounces.

a·poth·e·car·y (ə-pŏth′ə-kĕr′ē) n., pl. **-ries**. Abbr. **ap.** One who prepares and sells drugs and medicines; druggist; pharmacist. [Middle English apotecarie, from Medieval Latin apothecārius, from Late Latin, warehouse man, from Latin apothēca, storehouse, from Greek apothēkē, from apotithenai, to put away : apo-, away + tithenai, to put (see **dhē-¹** in Appendix*).]

ap·o·the·ci·um (ăp′ə-thē′shē-əm, -sē-əm) n., pl. **-cia** (-shē-ə, -sē-ə). An open disk-shaped or cup-shaped fruiting body in certain fungi, lined with a spore-bearing layer. [New Latin, from Greek apothēca, storehouse (see **apothecary**).] —**ap′o·the′cial** (ăp′ə-thē′shəl) adj.

ap·o·thegm (ăp′ə-thĕm′) n. Also **ap·o·phthegm**. A terse and witty instructive saying; maxim; proverb. [Greek apophthegma, a pointed saying, from apophthengesthai, to speak out plainly : apo-, away + phthengesthai, to speak, akin to phthongos, sound (see **diphthong**).] —**ap′o·theg·mat′ic** (-thĕg-măt′ĭk), **ap′o·theg·mat′i·cal** adj. —**ap′o·theg·mat′i·cal·ly** adv.

ap·o·them (ăp′ə-thĕm′) n. Geometry. In a regular polygon, the

perpendicular distance from the center to any of the sides. [APO-, away from + Greek thema, position, THEME.]

a·poth·e·o·sis (ə-pŏth′ē-ō′sĭs, ăp′ə-thē′ə-sĭs) n., pl. **-ses** (-sēz′). **1.** Exaltation to divine rank or stature; deification. **2.** An exalted or glorified ideal. [Late Latin apotheōsis, from Greek apotheōsis, from apotheoun, to deify : apo- (change) + theos, god (see **dhēs-** in Appendix*).]

a·poth·e·o·size (ə-pŏth′ē-ə-sīz′, ə-pŏth′ē-ə-sīz′) tr.v. **-sized, -sizing, -sizes**. To glorify; exalt.

app. 1. apparatus. **2.** Library Service. appendix. **3.** applied. **4.** appoint; appointed. **5.** apprentice.

Ap·pa·la·chi·a (ăp′ə-lā′chē-ə, -lăch′ē-ə). The region of the Appalachian Mountains.

Ap·pa·la·chi·an (ăp′ə-lā′chē-ən, -lā′chən, -lăch′ən) adj. Of, from, or pertaining to the Appalachian Mountains or the Appalachian mountain region.

Appalachian Mountains. The major mountain system of eastern North America, extending parallel to the coast for over 1,600 miles from southern Quebec to central Alabama. Highest elevation, Mount Mitchell (6,684 feet), in North Carolina. Also called "the Appalachians."

Appalachian tea. A shrub, the **withe rod** (see).

Appalachian Trail. A system of mountain trails extending for over 2,000 miles along the Appalachian range between Georgia and Maine.

ap·pall (ə-pôl′) tr.v. **-palled, -palling, -palls**. To fill with consternation or dismay. See Synonyms at **dismay**. [Middle English ap(p)allen, from Old French apalir, to grow pale : a-, to, from Latin ad-, to + palir, to grow pale, from Latin pallescere, from pallēre, to be pale (see **pel-²** in Appendix*).]

ap·pall·ing (ə-pô′lĭng) adj. Causing dismay; frightful; horrifying. —**ap·pall′ing·ly** adv.

ap·pa·loo·sa (ăp′ə-lōō′sə) n. A horse of a breed developed in northwestern North America, having a characteristically spotted rump.

ap·pa·nage (ăp′ə-nĭj) n. Also **ap·a·nage**. **1.** Land or some other source of revenue given by a king for the maintenance of a member of the ruling family. **2.** A perquisite. **3.** A natural accompaniment or adjunct. [French apanage, from Old French, from apaner, to make provisions for, from Medieval Latin appānāre : ad-, to + pānis, bread (see **pā-** in Appendix*).]

ap·pa·ra·tus (ăp′ə-rā′təs, -răt′əs) n., pl. **apparatus** or **-tuses**. Abbr. **app. 1.** The totality of means by which a designated function is performed or a specific task executed. **2. a.** A machine. **b.** A group of machines used together or in succession to accomplish a task. **3.** Physiology. A group of organs having a collective function: the respiratory apparatus. **4.** A political organization. **5.** A set of principles or standards, as for judging or testing. [Latin apparātus, equipment, preparation, from past participle of apparāre, to prepare : ad-, to + parāre, to make ready (see **per-⁴** in Appendix*).]

ap·pa·ra·tus cri·ti·cus (ăp′ə-rā′təs krĭt′ĭ-kəs). **1.** Reference materials used in literary research. **2.** Special appendixes, notes, or glossaries in an edition of a text. [New Latin, "critical apparatus."]

ap·par·el (ə-păr′əl) n. **1.** Clothing, especially outer garments; attire. **2.** Anything that covers or adorns. —tr.v. **appareled, -eling, -els**. Also chiefly British. **-elled, -elling. 1.** To clothe; dress. **2.** To adorn; embellish. [Middle English appareil, from Old French apareil, preparation, apparatus, furnishings, from apareillier, to prepare, from Vulgar Latin appariculāre (unattested), from Latin apparāre : ad-, toward + parāre, to make ready (see **per-⁴** in Appendix*).]

ap·par·ent (ə-păr′ənt, ə-pâr′-) adj. **1.** Readily seen; open to view; visible. **2.** Readily understood or perceived; plain or obvious. —See Synonyms at **evident**. [Middle English, from Old French aparent, present participle of aparoir, APPEAR.] —**ap·par′ent·ly** adv. —**ap·par′ent·ness** n.

apparent magnitude. Astronomy. Magnitude (see).

ap·pa·ri·tion (ăp′ə-rĭsh′ən) n. **1.** A ghostly figure; specter. **2.** A sudden or unusual sight. **3.** An appearance. [Middle English apparicioun, from Old French apparicion, from Late Latin apparitiō, appearance, epiphany (translation of Greek epiphaneia), from Latin appārēre, APPEAR.] —**ap′pa·ri′tion·al** adj.

ap·par·i·tor (ə-păr′ə-tər) n. Formerly, an official who was sent to carry out the orders of a civil or ecclesiastical court. [Latin, from appārēre, to serve, APPEAR (as a servant).]

ap·peal (ə-pēl′) n. **1.** An earnest or urgent request, entreaty, or supplication. **2.** A resort or application to some higher authority, as for sanction, corroboration, or a decision: an appeal to reason. **3.** The power of attracting or of arousing interest. **4.** Law. **a.** The transfer of a case from a lower to a higher court for a new hearing. **b.** A request for a new hearing. **c.** A case so transferred. —v. **appealed, -pealing, -peals**. —intr. **1.** To make an earnest or urgent request, as for help or sympathy. **2.** To resort; have recourse, as for sanction or corroboration. **3.** To be attractive or interesting. **4.** Law. To make or apply for an appeal. —tr. Law. To transfer or apply to transfer (a case) to a higher court for rehearing. [Middle English appelen, apelen, from Old French apeler, from Latin appellāre, to apply to, entreat, address. See **pel-⁶** in Appendix*.] —**ap·peal′a·ble** adj. —**ap·peal′er** n. —**ap·peal′ing·ly** adv.

ap·pear (ə-pîr′) intr.v. **-peared, -pearing, -pears**. **1.** To come into view; become visible. **2.** To come into existence. **3.** To seem or look. **4.** To seem likely. **5.** To come before the public; be presented or published. **6.** Law. To present oneself formally before a court as defendant, plaintiff, or counsel. [Middle English apperen, aperen, from Old French aparoir, from Latin appārēre : ad-, toward + pārēre†, to show.]

apostle
Medieval illumination
of the Twelve Apostles

ap·pear·ance (ə-pîr′əns) *n.* **1.** The act or an instance of appearing; a coming into sight. **2.** The act or instance of coming into public view. **3.** The outward aspect of something. **4.** Something that appears; phenomenon. **5.** An apparition. **6.** A pretense or semblance; false show. **7.** *Plural.* Circumstances; outward indications.

ap·pease (ə-pēz′) *tr.v.* **-peased, -peasing, -peases. 1.** To bring peace to; placate; soothe. **2.** To satisfy or relieve: *appease thirst.* —See Synonyms at **pacify.** [Middle English *appesen, apesen,* from Old French *apaisier* : *ap-,* from Latin *ad-,* to + *pais,* peace, from Latin *pāx* (see **pag-** in Appendix*).] —**ap·peas′a·ble** *adj.* —**ap·peas′a·bly** *adv.* —**ap·peas′er** *n.*

ap·pease·ment (ə-pēz′mənt) *n.* **1. a.** The act of appeasing. **b.** The condition of being appeased. **2.** The policy of granting concessions to potential enemies to maintain peace.

ap·pel (ə-pĕl′) *n. Fencing.* A quick stamp of the foot used as a feint to produce an opening. [French, a call, challenge, from *appeler,* to call, from Old French *apeler,* to APPEAL.]

ap·pel·lant (ə-pĕl′ənt) *adj.* Appellate. —*n.* One who appeals a court decision.

ap·pel·late (ə-pĕl′ĭt) *adj.* Having the power to hear appeals and to reverse court decisions. [Latin *appellātus,* past participle of *appellāre,* to APPEAL.]

ap·pel·la·tion (ăp′ə-lā′shən) *n.* **1.** A name or title. **2.** The act of naming. —See Synonyms at **name.** [Middle English *appellacioun,* from Latin *appellātiō,* from *appellāre,* to APPEAL.]

ap·pel·la·tive (ə-pĕl′ə-tĭv) *adj.* **1.** Of or relating to the assignment of names. **2.** *Grammar.* Designating a class; common: *appellative nouns.* —*n.* A name or descriptive epithet. [Middle English, from Late Latin *appellātīvus,* from *appellāre,* to call by name, APPEAL.] —**ap·pel′la·tive·ly** *adv.*

ap·pel·lee (ăp′ə-lē′) *n.* One against whom an appeal is taken. [Old French *apele,* from *apeler,* to APPEAL.]

ap·pend (ə-pĕnd′) *tr.v.* **-pended, -pending, -pends. 1.** To add as a supplement. **2.** To attach; fix to. [Latin *appendere* : *ad-,* to + *pendere,* to hang (see **spen-** in Appendix*).]

ap·pend·age (ə-pĕn′dĭj) *n.* **1.** Something appended. **2.** *Biology.* Any part or organ that is joined to an axis or trunk.

Synonyms: *appendage, appurtenance, adjunct, accessory, addition, attachment.* These nouns denote something added to a principal object. *Appendage* applies to what is likened to a limb in close but subordinate relation to the principal. An *appurtenance* is something that belongs to or goes with the principal without being essential to it, such as a president's limousine. An *adjunct* is added to the principal but has its own function and is self-sustaining, like a tea room in the basement of a bookstore. *Accessory* denotes that which adds to the usefulness or appearance of something already complete in itself. *Addition* refers broadly to anything of the same nature or function added to the principal. An *attachment* usually contributes another function to the principal, to which it is physically linked.

ap·pen·dant (ə-pĕn′dənt) *adj.* **1.** Hanging attached; suspended. **2.** Accompanying; attendant: *faith and its appendant hope.* **3.** *Law.* Belonging to a land grant as a subsidiary right. —*n.* **1.** Something attached or added. **2.** *Law.* A subsidiary right.

ap·pen·dec·to·my (ăp′ən-dĕk′tə-mē) *n., pl.* **-mies.** *Surgery.* The removal of the vermiform appendix. [APPEND(IX) + -ECTOMY.]

ap·pen·di·ci·tis (ə-pĕn′də-sī′tĭs) *n.* Inflammation of the vermiform appendix. [New Latin : APPENDIX + -ITIS.]

ap·pen·dic·u·lar (ăp′ən-dĭk′yə lər) *adj.* Of, pertaining to, or consisting of an appendage or appendages. [From Latin *appendicula,* diminutive of *appendix,* APPENDIX.]

ap·pen·dix (ə-pĕn′dĭks) *n., pl.* **-dixes** or **-dices** (-də-sēz′). *Abbr.* **app. 1. a.** An appendage. **b.** A collection of supplementary material at the end of a book. **2.** The **vermiform appendix** *(see).* [Latin *appendix,* appendage, from *appendere,* APPEND.]

ap·per·ceive (ăp′ər-sēv′) *tr.v.* **-ceived, -ceiving, -ceives.** *Psychology.* To perceive in terms of past perceptions. [Middle English *apperceiven, aperceiven,* from Old French *aperceivre* : *a-,* from Latin *ad-,* toward + *perceivre,* PERCEIVE.]

ap·per·cep·tion (ăp′ər-sĕp′shən) *n. Psychology.* **1.** Conscious perception with full awareness. **2.** The process of understanding by which newly observed qualities of an object are related to past experience. —**ap′per·cep′tive** (-sĕp′tĭv) *adj.*

ap·per·tain (ăp′ər-tān′) *intr.v.* **-tained, -taining, -tains.** To belong as a function or part; pertain properly. Used with *to.* [Middle English *apperteinen,* from Old French *apartenir,* from Vulgar Latin *appartenere* (unattested), variant of Late Latin *appertinēre,* to belong to, PERTAIN.]

ap·pe·tence (ăp′ə-təns) *n.* Also **ap·pe·ten·cy** (-tən-sē) *pl.* **-cies. 1.** A strong craving or desire. **2.** A tendency or proclivity; propensity. [Latin *appetentia,* from *appetens,* present participle of *appetere,* to strive after, desire eagerly. See **appetite.**] —**ap′pe·tent** (-tənt) *adj.*

ap·pe·tite (ăp′ə-tīt′) *n.* **1.** A desire for food or drink. **2.** Any physical craving or desire. **3.** A strong wish or urge to partake of something. [Middle English *appetit, apetit,* from Old French *apetit,* from Latin *appetītus,* from *appetere,* to strive after, desire eagerly : *ad-,* toward + *petere,* to seek (see **pet-**[1] in Appendix*).] —**ap′pe·ti′tive** (ăp′ə-tī′tĭv, ə-pĕt′ə-tĭv) *adj.*

ap·pe·tiz·er (ăp′ə-tī′zər) *n.* A food or drink served before a meal to stimulate the appetite.

ap·pe·tiz·ing (ăp′ə-tī′zĭng) *adj.* Stimulating or appealing to the appetite. —**ap′pe·tiz′ing·ly** *adv.*

Ap·pi·an Way (ăp′ē-ən). An ancient paved road in Italy, extending about 350 miles between Rome and Brindisi by way of Capua. [After *Appius* Claudius Caecus, Roman censor, who inaugurated its construction in 312 B.C.]

appl. applied.

ap·plaud (ə-plôd′) *v.* **-plauded, -plauding, -plauds.** —*intr.* To express approval by clapping the hands. —*tr.* **1.** To express approval of by clapping the hands. **2.** To praise; approve. [Latin *applaudere,* to clap at : *ad-,* to + *plaudere,* to clap (see **explode**).] —**ap·plaud′er** *n.*

ap·plause (ə-plôz′) *n.* Publicly expressed approval, especially when shown by the clapping of hands. [Medieval Latin *applausus,* from Latin, past participle of *applaudere,* APPLAUD.]

ap·ple (ăp′əl) *n.* **1.** A tree, *Pyrus malus,* of temperate regions, having fragrant pink or white flowers and edible fruit. **2.** The firm, rounded fruit of this tree or any of its varieties, having skin that is usually red but may be yellow or green. **3. a.** Any of several trees or plants having fruit resembling the apple, such as the **custard apple** or the **May apple** *(both of which see).* **b.** The fruit of any of these trees or plants. **4.** The hard wood of an apple tree. [Middle English *appel,* Old English *æppel.* See **abel-** in Appendix.*]

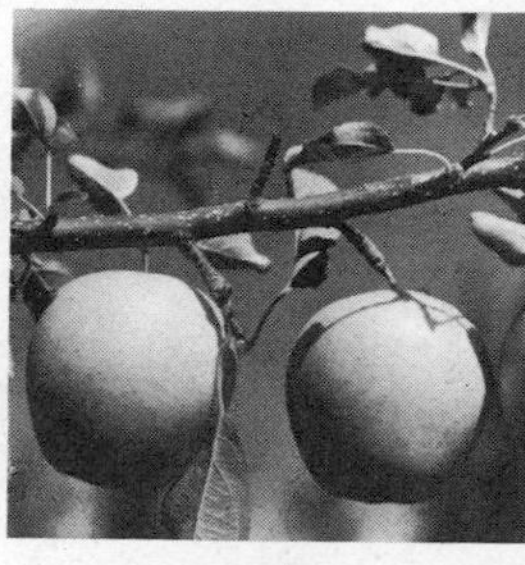
apple
"Golden Delicious" variety

apple green. Moderate or vivid yellow green to light or strong yellowish green. See **color.** —**ap′ple-green′** *adj.*

ap·ple·jack (ăp′əl-jăk′) *n.* Brandy distilled from hard cider.

apple of Peru. A plant, *Nicandra physalodes,* native to tropical America, having tubular blue or whitish flowers.

apple pandowdy. A kind of apple pie, **pandowdy** *(see).*

ap·ple-pie order (ăp′əl-pī′). *Informal.* Very good condition.

ap·ple-pol·ish (ăp′əl-pŏl′ĭsh) *intr.v.* **-ished, -ishing, -ishes.** *Informal.* To seek favor by toadying. —**apple polisher.**

ap·ple·sauce (ăp′əl-sôs′) *n.* **1.** Apples stewed to a pulp, sweetened, and sometimes spiced. **2.** *Slang.* Foolishness; nonsense.

Ap·ple·seed, Johnny. See John **Chapman.**

Ap·ple·ton layer (ăp′əl-tən). The **F layer** *(see)* of the upper atmosphere. [After Sir Edward *Appleton* (1892–1965), British physicist.]

ap·pli·ance (ə-plī′əns) *n.* A device or instrument, especially one operated by electricity and designed for household use. See Synonyms at **tool.** [From APPLY.]

ap·pli·ca·ble (ăp′lĭ-kə-bəl, ə-plĭk′ə-) *adj.* Capable of being applied; appropriate. —**ap′pli·ca·bil′i·ty** *n.* —**ap′pli·ca·bly** *adv.*

ap·pli·cant (ăp′lĭ-kənt) *n.* One who applies, as for a job. [Latin *applicāns,* present participle of *applicāre,* APPLY.]

ap·pli·ca·tion (ăp′lĭ-kā′shən) *n.* **1.** The act of applying or putting something on. **2.** Anything that is applied, such as a cosmetic or curative agent. **3.** The act of putting something to a special use or purpose. **4. a.** A method of applying or using; specific use. **b.** The capacity of being usable; relevance: *"the idea . . . has bearing and application upon the point made"* (Dewey). **5.** Close attention; diligence or effort. **6.** A request, as for a job. **7. a.** A written statement of one's qualifications for employment or admission. **b.** The printed form upon which such a statement is often made: *fill out an application.* —See Synonyms at **effort.** [Middle English *applicacioun,* from Latin *applicātiō,* from *applicāre,* APPLY.]

ap·pli·ca·tive (ăp′lĭ-kā′tĭv, ə-plĭk′ə-) *adj.* **1.** Characterized by actual application to something. **2.** Practical; applicatory. —**ap′pli·ca′tive·ly** *adv.*

ap·pli·ca·tor (ăp′lĭ-kā′tər) *n.* An instrument for applying something, such as medicine or glue.

ap·pli·ca·to·ry (ăp′lĭ-kə-tôr′ē, -tōr′ē, ə-plĭk′ə-) *adj.* Practical.

ap·plied (ə-plīd′) *adj. Abbr.* **app., appl.** Put in practice; used: *applied physics.* Compare **theoretical.**

ap·pli·qué (ăp′lĭ-kā′) *n.* A decoration or ornament, as in needlework or cabinetwork, made by cutting pieces of one material and applying them to the surface of another. —*adj.* Of or like this kind of decoration. —*tr.v.* **appliquéd, -quéing, -qués.** To decorate with appliqué work. [French, past participle of *appliquer,* to put on, apply, from Latin *applicāre,* APPLY.]

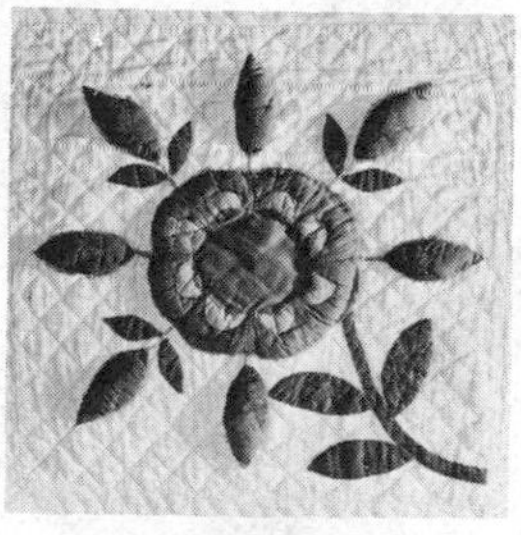
appliqué
Floral design appliquéd to a quilted coverlet

ap·ply (ə-plī′) *v.* **-plied, -plying, -plies.** —*tr.* **1.** To bring into nearness or contact with something; put on, upon, or to. **2.** To put to or adapt for a special use. **3.** To use (an epithet, for example) with reference to a particular person or thing. **4.** To devote (oneself or one's efforts) to something. —*intr.* **1.** To be pertinent or relevant. **2.** To request or seek employment, acceptance, or admission. Used with *for* or *to.* [Middle English *applien, aplien,* from Old French *aplier,* from Latin *applicāre,* to join to, apply to : *ad-,* to + *plicāre,* to fold together (see **plek-** in Appendix*).]

ap·pog·gia·tu·ra (ə-pŏj′ə-tŏŏr′ə; *Italian* äp-pôd′jä-tōō′rä) *n. Music.* An embellishing note, usually one step above or below the note it precedes and indicated by a small note or special sign. [Italian, "a supporting," from *appoggiare,* to lean on, from Vulgar Latin *appodiāre* (unattested) : Latin *ad-,* to + *podium,* balcony, from Greek *podion,* small foot, base, diminutive of *pous* (stem *pod-*), foot (see **ped-**[1] in Appendix*).]

ap·point (ə-point′) *tr.v.* **-pointed, -pointing, -points. 1.** To select or designate to fill an office or position. **2.** To fix or set by authority or by mutual agreement. **3.** To order, require, or enjoin with authority; prescribe. **4.** To furnish; equip. Used chiefly in the past participle as an adjective and in combination: *"Mr. Jackson's mansion was more . . . comfortably appointed"* (J.P. Marquand). **5.** *Law.* To direct the disposition of (property) to a person or persons in exercise of a power granted for this purpose by a preceding deed. [Middle English *appointen, apointen,* from Old French *apointier,* to arrange, from *(rendre) à point,* "(to bring) to a point" : *a-,* from Latin *ad-,* to + *point,* POINT.]

ap·point·ee (ə-poin′tē′) *n.* **1.** A person who is appointed to an office or position. **2.** *Law.* One to whom a power of appointment of property is granted.

ap·point·ive (ə-poin′tĭv) *adj.* Pertaining to or filled by appointment: *an appointive office.*

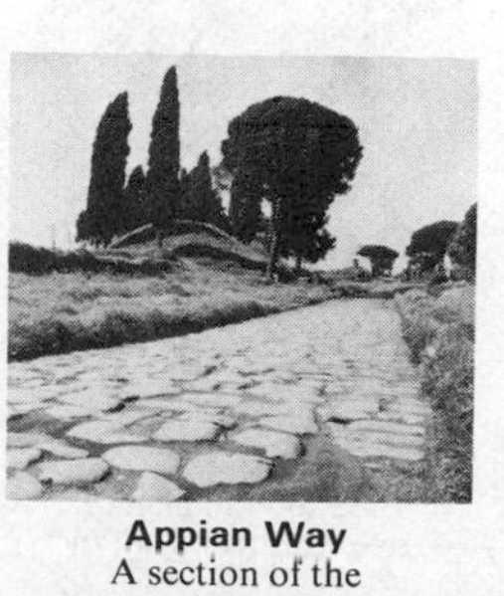
Appian Way
A section of the ancient road

ap·point·ment (ə-point′mənt) *n.* *Abbr.* **apmt.** **1.** The act of appointing or designating for an office or position. **2.** The office or position to which a person has been appointed. **3.** An arrangement to do something or meet someone at a particular time and place. **4.** *Usually plural.* Fittings or equipment. **5.** *Law.* The act of directing the disposition of property by virtue of a power granted for this purpose.

ap·poin·tor (ə-poin′tər, ə-poin′tôr′) *n.* *Law.* One who executes a power of appointment of property.

Ap·po·mat·tox (ăp′ə-măt′əks). The town in central Virginia where General Robert E. Lee surrendered to General Ulysses S. Grant on April 9, 1865, bringing the Civil War to a close. Population, 9,148.

Ap·po·mat·tox River (ăp′ə-măt′əks). A river in eastern Virginia, flowing east for about 150 miles from near the town of Appomattox to the James River.

ap·por·tion (ə-pôr′shən, ə-pōr′-) *tr.v.* **-tioned, -tioning, -tions.** To divide and assign according to some plan or proportion; allot; partition. See Synonyms at **assign.** [Old French *apportionner* : *a-*, from Latin *ad-*, to + *portionner,* to divide into portions, from *portion,* PORTION.]

ap·por·tion·ment (ə-pôr′shən-mənt, ə-pōr′-) *n.* **1.** The act of apportioning or the condition of being apportioned. **2. a.** The proportional distribution of the number of members of the U.S. House of Representatives on the basis of the population of each state. **b.** A similar distribution in other U.S. legislative bodies, such as a state legislature. **c.** The allotment of direct taxes on the basis of state population.

ap·pose (ă-pōz′) *tr.v.* **-posed, -posing, -poses. 1.** To put or apply (one thing) to another. **2.** To arrange (things) near to each other or side by side. [Back-formation from APPOSITION (by analogy with COMPOSE, COMPOSITION).]

ap·po·site (ăp′ə-zĭt) *adj.* Fitting; suitable; appropriate. See Synonyms at **relevant.** [Latin *appositus,* "situated near," past participle of *appōnere,* to place near to, apply to. See **apposition.**] —**ap′po·site·ly** *adv.* —**ap′po·site·ness** *n.*

ap·po·si·tion (ăp′ə-zĭsh′ən) *n.* **1.** *Grammar.* **a.** A construction in which a noun or noun phrase is placed with another as an explanatory equivalent, both having the same syntactic relation to the other elements in the sentence. In the sentence *Copley, the famous painter, was born in Boston, Copley* and *the famous painter* are in apposition. **b.** The relationship between such nouns or noun phrases. **2.** A placing side by side or next to each other. **3.** *Biology.* The growth of successive layers of a cell wall. [Middle English *apposicioun,* from Medieval Latin *appositiō,* from Latin *appōnere* (past participle *appositus*), to place near to, apply to : *ad-*, near, to + *pōnere,* to put (see **apo-** in Appendix*).] —**ap′po·si′tion·al** *adj.* —**ap′po·si′tion·al·ly** *adv.*

ap·pos·i·tive (ə-pŏz′ə-tĭv) *adj.* In or concerning apposition. —*n.* A word or phrase that is in apposition. [From APPOSITION.] —**ap·pos′i·tive·ly** *adv.*

ap·prais·al (ə-prā′zəl) *n.* **1.** The act of appraising. **2.** An expert or official valuation of something, as for taxation.

ap·praise (ə-prāz′) *tr.v.* **-praised, -praising, -praises. 1.** To evaluate, especially in an official capacity. **2.** To estimate the quality, amount, size, and other features of; to judge. —See Synonyms at **estimate.** [Middle English *appreisen,* partly from *preise,* value, PRAISE, partly from Old French *aprisier,* from Late Latin *appretiāre,* to set a value on : *ad-*, to + *pretiāre,* to value, from Latin *pretium,* price (see **per**[1] in Appendix*).] —**ap·prais′a·ble** *adj.* —**ap·praise′ment** *n.* —**ap·prais′er** *n.*

ap·pre·cia·ble (ə-prē′shə-bəl) *adj.* Capable of being noticed, estimated, or measured; noticeable. See Synonyms at **perceptible.** —**ap·pre′cia·bly** *adv.*

ap·pre·ci·ate (ə-prē′shē-āt′) *v.* **-ated, -ating, -ates.** —*tr.* **1.** To estimate the quality, value, significance, or magnitude of. **2.** To be fully aware of or sensitive to; realize. See Usage note below. **3.** To be thankful or show gratitude for. **4.** To admire greatly; enjoy. **5.** To raise in value or price. —*intr.* To go up in value or price. [Late Latin *appretiāre,* to set a value on : *ad-*, to + *pretiāre,* to value, from *pretium,* price (see **per**[1] in Appendix*).] —**ap·pre′ci·a′tor** (-ā′tər) *n.*

Synonyms: *appreciate, value, prize, esteem, treasure, cherish.* These verbs express having a favorable opinion of someone or something. *Appreciate* applies especially to favor based on judgment and assessment. *Value* implies high regard for the importance of the object, while *prize* emphasizes its specialness. *Esteem* suggests respect of a formal sort; *treasure* and *cherish* suggest affectionate regard mixed with pride of possession.

Usage: *Appreciate,* as a synonym for *be fully aware of* or *realize,* is especially appropriate to situations calling for sensitivity and understanding: *I appreciate your problems.* In lesser contexts, *appreciate* is often regarded as an example of genteelism: *I appreciate the lateness of the hour.* Only 47 per cent of the Usage Panel approve the second example, although it is defensible by the definition of *appreciate.*

ap·pre·ci·a·tion (ə-prē′shē-ā′shən) *n.* **1. a.** The act of estimating the qualities of people and things. **b.** A judgment or opinion. **2.** Gratefulness; gratitude. **3.** Awareness or delicate perception, especially of aesthetic qualities or values: *"It is not appreciation of the artist that is necessary so much as appreciation of the art."* (Bertrand Russell). **4.** An expression of criticism; critique. **5.** A rise in value or price.

ap·pre·cia·tive (ə-prē′shə-tĭv, -shē-ā′tĭv) *adj.* Capable of or showing appreciation. —**ap·pre′cia·tive·ly** *adv.*

ap·pre·hend (ăp′rĭ-hĕnd′) *v.* **-hended, -hending, -hends.** —*tr.* **1.** To take into custody; arrest. **2.** To grasp mentally; understand. **3.** To anticipate with anxiety. —*intr.* To understand. [Middle English *apprehenden,* from Latin *apprehendere,* to lay hold on, seize : *ad-*, to + *prehendere,* to seize (see **ghend-** in Appendix*).]

Synonyms: *apprehend, comprehend, grasp, understand.* These verbs refer to varying degrees of mental perception. *Apprehend* is often limited to perception, and does not imply full understanding. *Comprehend* stresses attainment of full understanding. *Grasp* suggests seizing an idea firmly. *Understand,* nearer in meaning to *comprehend,* can also suggest sympathy, compassion, or insight: *My parents don't understand me.*

ap·pre·hen·si·ble (ăp′rĭ-hĕn′sə-bəl) *adj.* Capable of being apprehended or understood. —**ap′pre·hen′si·bly** *adv.*

ap·pre·hen·sion (ăp′rĭ-hĕn′shən) *n.* **1.** A fearful or uneasy anticipation of the future; dread. **2.** A seizing or capturing; arrest. **3.** The ability to apprehend or understand; understanding. **4.** An opinion or estimate. [Middle English *apprehensioun,* from Late Latin *apprehensiō,* from *apprehendere* (past participle *apprehensus*), APPREHEND.]

Synonyms: *apprehension, foreboding, presentiment, misgiving.* These nouns denote concern for something that impends. *Apprehension* refers broadly to anxiety about the future. *Foreboding* is a vague fear of the future, inferred irrationally from clues in the present. *Presentiment* denotes a less certain prophetic sense that something, not necessarily unpleasant, is imminent. *Misgiving,* usually used in the plural, applies to a specific instance of apprehension and stresses mistrust.

ap·pre·hen·sive (ăp′rĭ-hĕn′sĭv) *adj.* **1.** Anxious or fearful about the future; uneasy. **2.** Capable of understanding; quick to apprehend. **3.** Sensitive; perceptive. —**ap′pre·hen′sive·ly** *adv.* —**ap′pre·hen′sive·ness** *n.*

ap·pren·tice (ə-prĕn′tĭs) *n.* *Abbr.* **app. 1.** One bound by legal agreement to work for another for a specific amount of time in return for instruction in a trade, art, or business. **2.** Any beginner; learner. —*tr.v.* **apprenticed, -ticing, -tices.** To place or take on as an apprentice; bind by indenture. [Middle English *aprentis,* from Old French, from *aprendre,* to learn, from Latin *appre(he)ndere,* APPREHEND.] —**ap·pren′tice·ship′** *n.*

ap·pressed (ă-prĕst′) *adj.* Lying flat or pressed closely against something, as leaves on a stem. [From Latin *appressus,* past participle of *apprimere,* to press to : *ad-*, to + *premere,* to press (see **per-**[6] in Appendix*).]

ap·prise (ə-prīz′) *tr.v.* **-prised, -prising, -prises.** Also **ap·prize.** To cause to know; give notice to; inform. Used with *of.* [From French *apprendre* (past participle *appris*), to cause to learn, inform, from Old French *aprendre,* to learn, from Latin *appre(he)ndere,* APPREHEND.]

ap·proach (ə-prōch′) *v.* **-proached, -proaching, -proaches.** —*intr.* To come near or nearer in space, time, or magnitude. —*tr.* **1.** To come near or nearer to. **2.** To cause to come closer. **3.** To come close to in appearance, quality, condition, or other characteristics; to approximate. **4.** To make a proposal to; make overtures to. **5.** To begin to deal with or work on. —*n.* **1.** The act of coming or drawing near. **2.** A fairly close resemblance; an approximation. **3.** A way or means of reaching someone or a destination; an access. **4.** The method used in dealing with or accomplishing something. **5.** *Often plural.* An advance or overture made by one person to another. **6.** *Golf.* The stroke following the drive from the tee with which the player tries to get the ball onto the putting green. **7.** *Plural. Military.* Works such as trenches or bulwarks for the protection of troops besieging a fortified position. [Middle English *aprochen,* from Old French *aprochier,* from Late Latin *appropiāre,* to go nearer to : *ad-*, to + *propius,* nearer, from *prope,* near (see **per**[1] in Appendix*).]

ap·proach·a·ble (ə-prō′chə-bəl) *adj.* **1.** Capable of being approached or reached; accessible. **2.** Easily approached; receptive to overtures; friendly. —**ap·proach′a·bil′i·ty** *n.*

ap·pro·bate (ăp′rə-bāt′) *tr.v.* **-bated, -bating, -bates.** To sanction; authorize. [Middle English *approbaten,* from Latin *approbāre,* APPROVE.] —**ap′pro·ba′tive, ap·pro′ba·to′ry** (ə-prō′bə-tôr′ē, -tōr′ē) *adj.*

ap·pro·ba·tion (ăp′rə-bā′shən) *n.* **1.** Praise; commendation. **2.** Official approval. —See Synonyms at **regard.**

ap·pro·pri·a·ble (ə-prō′prē-ə-bəl) *adj.* Capable of being appropriated.

ap·pro·pri·ate (ə-prō′prē-ĭt) *adj.* Suitable for a particular person, condition, occasion, or place; proper; fitting. See Synonyms at **fit.** —*tr.v.* (ə-prō′prē-āt′) **appropriated, -ating, -ates. 1.** To set apart for a specific use. **2.** To take possession of or make use of exclusively for oneself, often without permission. [Middle English *appropriaten,* from Late Latin *appropriāre* (past participle *appropriātus*), to make one's own : Latin *ad-* to + *propius,* own (see **per**[1] in Appendix*).] —**ap·pro′pri·ate·ly** *adv.* —**ap·pro′pri·ate·ness** *n.* —**ap·pro′pri·a′tive** (-ā′tĭv) *adj.* —**ap·pro′pri·a′tor** (-ā′tər) *n.*

ap·pro·pri·a·tion (ə-prō′prē-ā′shən) *n.* **1.** The act of appropriating to oneself or to a specific use or purpose. **2.** Public funds set aside for a specific purpose. **3.** A legislative act authorizing the expenditure of a designated amount of public funds for a specific purpose.

ap·prov·al (ə-prōō′vəl) *n.* **1.** The act of approving. **2.** An official approbation; a sanction. **3.** Commendation; favorable regard. —**on approval.** For examination or trial by a potential customer without the obligation to buy.

ap·prove (ə-prōōv′) *v.* **-proved, -proving, -proves.** —*tr.* **1.** To regard favorably; commend by word or action; consider right or good. **2.** To confirm or consent to officially; to sanction; ratify. **3.** *Obsolete.* To prove or demonstrate. Used reflexively: *"the letter he spoke of which approves him an intelligent party"* (Shakespeare). —*intr.* To voice or demonstrate approval.

apse

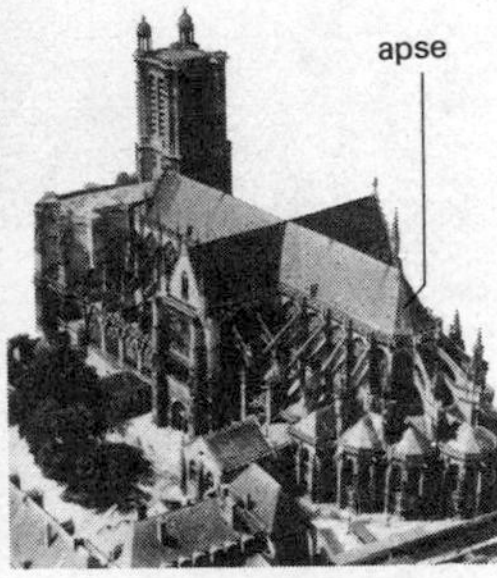

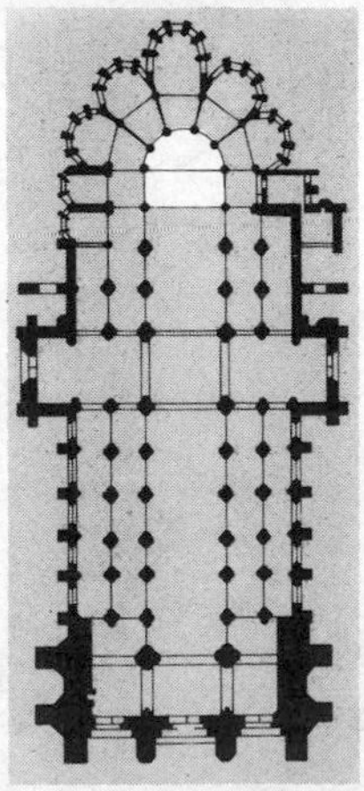

apse
Exterior and plan of Troyes Cathedral, France

ă pat/ā pay/âr care/ä father/b bib/ch church/d deed/ĕ pet/ē be/f fife/g gag/h hat/hw which/ĭ pit/ī pie/îr pier/j judge/k kick/l lid, needle/m mum/n no, sudden/ng thing/ŏ pot/ō toe/ô paw, for/oi noise/ou out/ŏŏ took/ōō boot/p pop/r roar/s sauce/sh ship, dish/

Often used with *of.* [Middle English *approven,* from Old French *aprover,* from Latin *approbāre,* to make good, admit as good : *ad-,* to + *probus,* good (see **per**[1] in Appendix*).] —**ap·prov′a·ble** *adj.* —**ap·prov′ing·ly** *adv.*

Synonyms: *approve, endorse, sanction, certify, accredit, ratify.* These verbs mean to express a favorable opinion of a person, thing, or action, or to signify satisfaction or acceptance. *Approve,* the most widely applicable, may indicate varying degrees of admiration. *Endorse* (or *indorse*), stronger than *approve,* implies expression of support, often by public statement. *Sanction* adds authorization, usually official, to approval. *Certify* and *accredit* imply official endorsement gained upon conforming to set standards. *Ratify* refers to making legal by formal official approval: *a treaty ratified by the legislatures of each of the countries involved.*

approved school. *British.* A reform school.

approx. approximate; approximately.

ap·prox·i·mate (ə-prŏk′sə-mĭt) *adj. Abbr.* **approx. 1.** Almost exact, correct, complete, or perfect. **2.** Very similar; closely resembling. **3.** Close together; near. —*v.* (ə-prŏk′sə-māt′) **approximated, -mating, -mates.** —*tr.* **1.** To come close to; be nearly the same as. **2.** To cause to approach; bring near. —*intr.* To come near or close in degree, nature, quality, or other characteristics. [Late Latin *approximātus,* past participle of *approximāre,* to come near to : Latin *ad-,* to + *proximāre,* to come near, from *proximus,* nearest (see **per**[1] in Appendix*).] —**ap·prox′i·mate·ly** *adv.*

ap·prox·i·ma·tion (ə-prŏk′sə-mā′shən) *n.* **1.** The act, process, or result of approximating. **2.** *Mathematics.* An inexact result adequate for a given purpose. —**ap·prox′i·ma′tive** (-mā′tĭv) *adj.* —**ap·prox′i·ma′tive·ly** *adv.*

appt. appoint; appointed.

ap·pur·te·nance (ə-pûrt′n-əns) *n.* **1.** Something added to another, more important thing; an appendage; accessory. **2.** *Plural.* Any equipment, such as clothing, tools, or instruments, used for a specific purpose or task; gear. **3.** *Law.* A right, privilege, or minor property that is considered incident to the principal property for purposes such as passage of title, conveyance, or inheritance. —See Synonyms at **appendage.** [Middle English *appurtenaunce, apurtenaunce,* from Norman French *apurtenance,* variant of Old French *apertenance,* from Vulgar Latin *appertinentia* (unattested), from Late Latin *appertinēre,* APPERTAIN.]

ap·pur·te·nant (ə-pûrt′n-ənt) *adj.* **1.** *Law.* Constituting an appurtenance. **2.** Belonging, accessory, or incident to.

Apr. April.

a·prax·i·a (ā-prăk′sē-ə) *n.* The inability to perform coordinated movements as a result of lesions in the cerebral cortex. [New Latin, from Greek, inaction : *a-,* without + Greek *praxis,* action, from *prassein,* to do (see **prāk-** in Appendix*).] —**a·prac′tic** (ā-prăk′tĭk) *adj.*

a·pri·cot (ā′prĭ-kŏt′, ăp′rĭ-) *n.* **1.** A tree, *Prunus armeniaca,* native to western Asia and Africa, widely cultivated for its edible fruit. **2.** The juicy, yellow-orange peachlike fruit of this tree. **3.** Moderate, light, or strong orange to strong orange yellow. See **color.** [Earlier *abrecock,* possibly from obsolete Catalan *abercoc,* from Arabic *al-birquq,* "the apricot," from Late Greek *praikokion,* from Latin *(prūnum) praecoquum,* "early-ripening (plum)," from *praecoquere,* to ripen early : *prae-,* before + *coquere,* to ripen, cook (see **pekw-** in Appendix*).]

A·pril (ā′prəl) *n. Abbr.* **Apr.** The fourth month of the year according to the Gregorian calendar. April has 30 days. See **calendar.** [Middle English, from Latin *aprīlis,* perhaps "month of Venus," from Etruscan *apru,* from Greek *Aphrō,* short form of *Aphroditē,* APHRODITE.]

April fool. The victim of a trick played on April Fools' Day.

April Fools' Day. April 1, marked as a day for playing practical jokes. Also called "All Fools' Day."

a pri·o·ri (ä prē-ôr′ē, ā prī-ôr′ī′). **1.** Proceeding from a known or assumed cause to a necessarily related effect; deductive. Compare **a posteriori. 2.** Based on a hypothesis or theory rather than on experiment or experience. **3.** Made before or without examination; not supported by factual study. [Latin, "from the previous (causes or hypotheses)."] —**a pri·or′i·ty** (-ôr′ə-tē) *n.*

a·pron (ā′prən, ā′pərn) *n.* **1.** A garment worn over all or part of the front of the body to protect one's clothes or as a decorative part of a costume. **2.** Anything resembling an apron in appearance or function. **3.** The paved or hand-packed strip in front of and around airport hangars and terminal buildings. **4.** The part of a stage in a theater extending in front of the curtain. **5. a.** A platform of planking or other material at the entrance to a dock. **b.** A covering or structure along the shoreline of a body of water for protection against erosion. **c.** A platform serving a similar purpose below a dam or in a sluiceway. **6.** A continuous conveyor belt. **7.** An area covered by sand and gravel deposited at the front of a glacial moraine. —*tr.v.* **aproned, aproning, aprons.** To cover, protect, or provide with an apron; put an apron or aprons on. [Middle English *(an) apron,* originally *(a) napron,* from Old French *naperon,* diminutive of *nape,* tablecloth, from Latin *mappa,* napkin. See **mappa** in Appendix.*]

ap·ro·pos (ăp′rə-pō′) *adj.* Appropriate; pertinent; opportune. See Synonyms at **relevant.** —*adv.* **1.** Pertinently; relevantly; opportunely. **2.** By the way; incidentally. Used to introduce a remark. —**apropos of.** Speaking of; with reference to. [French *à propos,* "to the purpose."]

apse (ăps) *n.* **1.** *Architecture.* A semicircular or polygonal, usually domed, projection of a building, especially the altar or east end of a church. Also called "apsis." **2.** *Astronomy.* An orbital position, **apsis** *(see).* [Medieval Latin *apsis, absis.* See **apsis.**] —**ap′si·dal** (ăp′sə-dəl) *adj.*

Ap·she·ron (ŭp-shə-rôn′). A peninsula of eastern Azerbaijan S.S.R., extending into the Caspian Sea; site of major Soviet oil fields.

ap·sis (ăp′sĭs) *n., pl.* **-sides** (-sə-dēz′). **1.** *Architecture.* An **apse** *(see).* **2.** *Astronomy.* The point of greatest or least distance of a celestial body from a center of attraction. Also called "apse." [Medieval Latin *apsis, absis,* architectural apse, from Latin, arch, vault, orbit, from Greek *apsis, hapsis,* "a fastening together," from *haptein,* to fasten. See **synapse.**]

apt (ăpt) *adj.* **1.** Exactly suitable; appropriate. **2.** Likely. See Usage note below. **3.** Inclined; given. See Usage note below. **4.** Quick to learn or understand. —See Synonyms at **fit, relevant.** [Middle English, from Latin *aptus,* fit, suited, from the past participle of *apere,* to fasten. See **ap-**[1] in Appendix.*] —**apt′ly** *adv.* —**apt′ness** *n.*

Usage: *Apt* and *likely,* when followed by an infinitive, are often interchangeable. *Likely* is always appropriate when mere probability is involved: *It is likely to snow. He is likely to leave soon.* When probability based on a natural or known tendency is implied, *apt* is the choice: *He is apt to stammer when he is excited.* In similar constructions, in careful usage, *liable* implies the possibility or probability of risk or disadvantage to the subject: *An angry man is liable to say more than he means.* Employment of *liable* in expressing only probability is loose usage: *We are liable* (preferably *likely*) *to go tomorrow.*

apt. apartment.

ap·ter·al (ăp′tər-əl) *adj. Architecture.* Having no columns along the sides. [From Greek *apteros,* wingless, APTEROUS.]

ap·ter·ous (ăp′tər-əs) *adj.* **1.** *Zoology.* Having no wings: *an apterous insect.* **2.** *Botany.* Having no winglike parts or extensions. [Greek *apteros,* wingless : *a-,* without + -PTEROUS.]

ap·ter·yx (ăp′tə-rĭks) *n.* A bird, the **kiwi** *(see).* [New Latin : A- (without) + Greek *pterux,* wing, from *pteron,* feather, wing (see **pet-**[1] in Appendix*).]

ap·ti·tude (ăp′tə-to͞od′, -tyo͞od′) *n.* **1.** A natural or acquired talent or ability; inclination. **2.** Quickness in learning and understanding; intelligence. **3.** The state or quality of being fitting; appropriateness. —See Synonyms at **ability.** [Middle English, from Late Latin *aptitūdō,* fitness, from *aptus,* APT.]

aptitude test. A standardized test designed to measure the ability of an individual to develop skills or acquire knowledge.

Ap·u·lei·us (ăp′yə-lē′əs), **Lucius.** Roman philosopher and satirist of the second century A.D.

A·pu·lia (ə-pyo͞ol′yə). *Italian* **Pu·glia** (po͞o′lyä). A region occupying over 7,000 square miles in southeastern Italy; formerly a Roman province. Population, 3,410,000. Chief city, Bari.

A·pu·re (ä-po͞o′rā). A river of Venezuela, rising on the eastern slopes of the Andes and flowing over 450 miles to the Orinoco.

A·pu·rí·mac (ä′po͞o-rē′mäk). A river rising in south-central Peru and flowing about 500 miles northwest to join the Urubamba and form the Ucayali.

A·pus (ā′pəs) *n.* A constellation in the Southern Hemisphere near Musca and Pavo. [New Latin, from Latin *apus,* the swallow, from Greek *apous,* the swift, "footless" (probably because the swift is seldom seen perching) : *a-,* without + *pous,* foot (see **ped-**[1] in Appendix*).]

A·qa·ba (ä′kä-bä′). A seaport of Jordan at the northern end of the Gulf of Aqaba, an arm of the Red Sea extending about 100 miles between the Sinai Peninsula and northwestern Saudi Arabia. Population, 9,000.

aq·ua (ăk′wə, ä′kwə) *n., pl.* **aquae** (ăk′wē, ä′kwī′) or **-uas. 1.** Water. **2.** *Pharmacy.* Liquid; solution, especially in water. **3.** Light bluish green to light greenish blue. See **color.** [Latin, water. See **akwā-** in Appendix.*] —**aq′ua** *adj.*

aq·ua·cade (ăk′wə-kād′, ä′kwə-) *n.* An entertainment spectacle of swimmers and divers, often performing in unison to the accompaniment of music. [AQUA + (CAVAL)CADE.]

aq·ua for·tis (ăk′wə fôr′tĭs, ä′kwə). Also **aq·ua·for·tis.** *Chemistry.* **Nitric acid** *(see).* [New Latin, "strong water."]

Aq·ua-Lung (ăk′wə-lŭng′, ä′kwə-) *n.* A trademark for a **scuba** *(see),* an underwater breathing apparatus.

aq·ua·ma·rine (ăk′wə-mə-rēn′, ä′kwə-) *n.* **1.** A transparent blue-green variety of beryl, used as a gemstone. **2.** Pale blue to light greenish blue. See **color.** [New Latin *aqua marīna,* from Latin, sea water : *aqua,* AQUA + *marīnus,* of the sea, MARINE.]

aq·ua·naut (ăk′wə-nôt′, ä′kwə-) *n.* A person trained to live in underwater installations and conduct, assist in, or be a subject of scientific research. [AQUA + Greek *nautēs,* sailor, from *naus,* ship (see **nau-**[2] in Appendix*).]

aq·ua·plane (ăk′wə-plān′, ä′kwə-) *n.* A board on which one rides in a standing position while it is pulled over the water by a motorboat. —*intr.v.* **aquaplaned, -planing, -planes.** To ride on an aquaplane. [AQUA + PLANE (surface).]

aqua re·gi·a (rē′jē-ə). A corrosive, fuming, volatile mixture of hydrochloric and nitric acids, used for testing metals and dissolving platinum and gold. Also called "nitrohydrochloric acid." [New Latin, "royal water" (because it dissolves gold, the "royal metal").]

aq·ua·relle (ăk′wə-rĕl′, ä′kwə-) *n.* A drawing done in transparent water colors. [French, from obsolete Italian *acquarella,* water color, from *acqua,* water, from Latin *aqua.* See **akwā-** in Appendix.*] —**aq′ua·rel′list** *n.*

a·quar·ist (ə-kwâr′ĭst) *n.* One who maintains an aquarium.

a·quar·i·um (ə-kwâr′ē-əm) *n., pl.* **-ums** or **-ia** (-ē-ə). **1.** A tank, bowl, or other water-filled enclosure in which living aquatic animals and, often, plants are kept. **2.** A place for the public

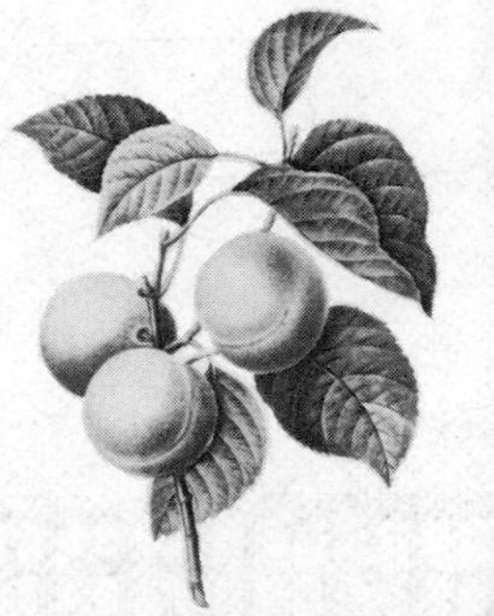

apricot

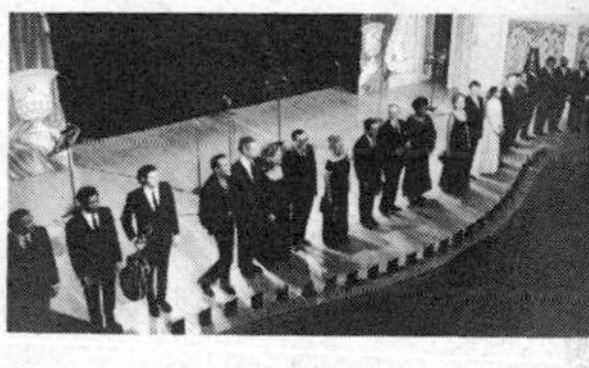

apron
Actors on the apron of the restored Ford's Theater at its dedication in 1968

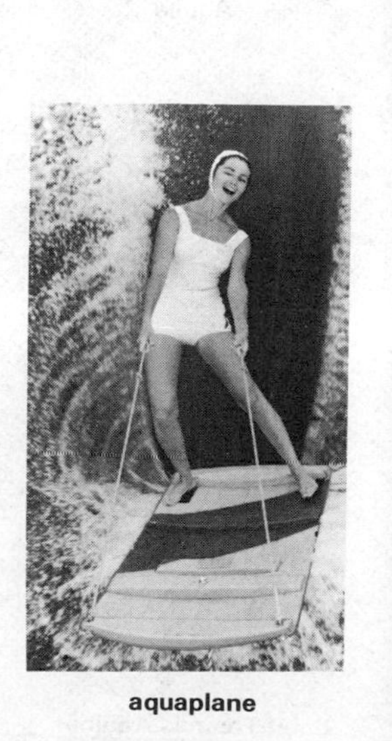

aquaplane

exhibition of such animals and plants. [From Latin *aquārius*, of water, from *aqua*, water. See **akwā-** in Appendix.*]

A·quar·i·us (ə-kwâr′ē-əs) *n.* **1.** A constellation in the equatorial region of the Southern Hemisphere near Pisces and Aquila. **2.** The 11th sign of the **zodiac** *(see)*. Also called the "Water Bearer." [Middle English, from Latin : AQUA + -ARY.]

a·quat·ic (ə-kwŏt′ĭk, ə-kwăt′-) *adj.* **1.** Living or growing in or on the water. **2.** Taking place in or on the water. *—n.* **1.** An aquatic organism. **2.** *Plural.* Sports performed in or on the water. [Old French *aquatique*, from Latin *aquāticus*, from *aqua*, water. See **akwā-** in Appendix.*]

aq·ua·tint (ăk′wə-tĭnt′, ä′kwə-) *n.* **1.** A process of etching capable of producing several tones by varying the etching time of different areas of a copper plate so that the resulting print resembles the flat tints of an ink or wash drawing. **2.** An etching made in this way. *—tr.v.* **aquatinted, -tinting, -tints.** To etch in aquatint. [French *aquatinte*, from Italian *acqua tinta*, "tinted water," watercolor, hence aquatint etching (which imitates watercolor) : *acqua*, water (see **aquarelle**) + *tinta*, tinted, from Latin *tincta*, feminine of *tinctus*, dyed (see **tint**).]

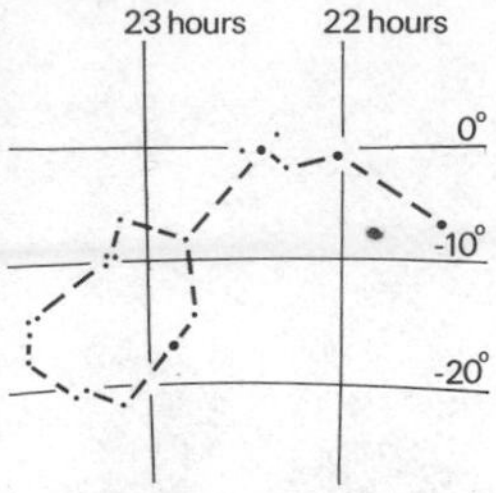

Aquarius

a·qua·vit (ä′kwə-vēt′) *n.* A strong, clear Scandinavian liquor, distilled from potato or grain mash and flavored with caraway seed. [Swedish, Danish, and Norwegian *akvavit*, from Medieval Latin *aqua vītae*, "water of life."]

aqua vi·tae (vī′tē). **1.** Alcohol. **2.** Whiskey, brandy, or other strong liquor. [Middle English *aquavite*, from Medieval Latin *aqua vītae*, "water of life."]

aq·ue·duct (ăk′wə-dŭkt′) *n.* **1.** A conduit designed to transport water from a remote source, usually by gravity. **2.** An elevated structure supporting a conduit or canal passing over a river or low ground. **3.** *Anatomy.* A fluid channel or passage. [Latin *aquae ductus* : *aquae*, genitive of *aqua*, AQUA + DUCT.]

a·que·ous (ā′kwē-əs, ăk′wē-) *adj.* **1.** Pertaining to, similar to, containing, or dissolved in water; watery. **2.** Formed from matter deposited by water, as certain sedimentary rocks. [Medieval Latin *aqueus*, from Latin *aqua*, water, AQUA.]

aqueous humor. A clear, lymphlike fluid in the chamber of the eye between the cornea and the lens.

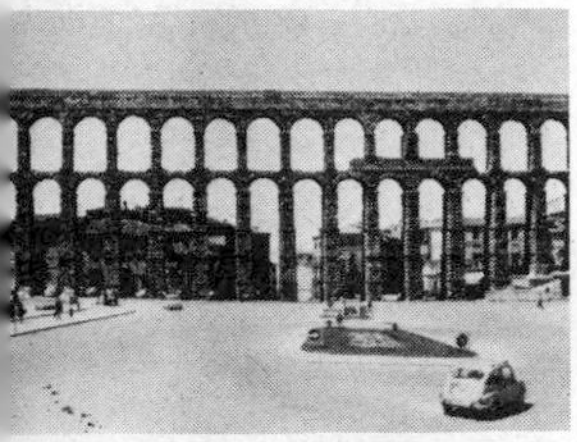
aqueduct
Roman aqueduct in Segovia, Spain

aqui-. Indicates water; for example, **aquiculture.** [Latin, from *aqua*, water. See **akwā-** in Appendix.*]

aq·ui·cul·ture (ăk′wĭ-kŭl′chər, ä′kwĭ-) *n.* A method of plant cultivation, **hydroponics** *(see)*. *—aq′ui·cul′tur·al adj.*

A·quid·neck. The former name for the island of **Rhode Island.**

aq·ui·fer (ăk′wə-fər, ä′kwə-) *n.* A water-bearing rock, rock formation, or group of formations. [AQUI- + -FER.] **—a·quif′er·ous** (ă-kwĭf′ər-əs) *adj.*

Aq·ui·la (ăk′wə-lə) *n.* A constellation in the Northern Hemisphere and the Milky Way near Aquarius and Serpens Cauda. [Latin *aquila*, EAGLE.]

aq·ui·le·gi·a (ăk′wə-lē′jē-ə, -lē′jə) *n.* Any plant of the genus *Aquilegia*; a columbine. [New Latin, from Medieval Latin *aquilēgia*, *aquilējā*†, columbine.]

aq·ui·line (ăk′wə-līn′, -lĭn) *adj.* **1.** Of or similar to an eagle. **2.** Curved or hooked like an eagle's beak: *an aquiline nose.* [Latin *aquilīnus*, from *aquila*, eagle. See **eagle.**]

A·qui·nas (ə-kwī′nəs), **Saint Thomas.** 1225–1274. Italian Dominican monk, philosopher, and theologian.

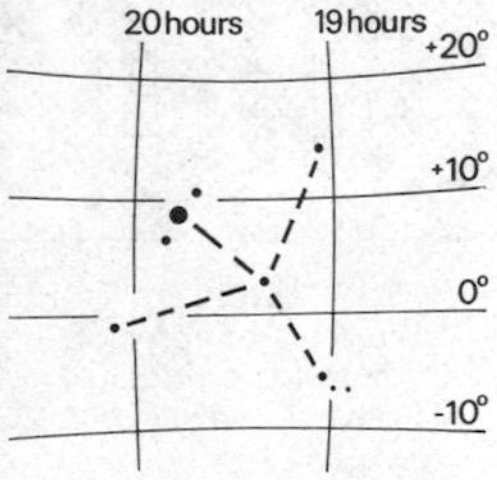

Aquila

Aq·ui·taine (ăk′wə-tān′). A historical region of southwestern France, lying between the Pyrenees and the Garonne River.

ar. Variant of **are** (surface measure).

-ar. Used to form adjectives meaning like, pertaining to, or of the nature of; for example, **titular, polar, astylar.** [Middle English *-ar*, *-er*, from Old French *-er*, from Latin *-āris*, dissimulated alteration (after bases ending in **l**) of *-ālis*, -AL.]

Ar The symbol for the element argon.

AR 1. account receivable. **2.** Arkansas (with Zip Code).

ar. arrival; arrive.

Ar. 1. Arabia; Arabian. **2.** Arabic. **3.** Aramaic.

A.R. 1. Airman Recruit. **2.** army regulation.

A/R account receivable.

A·ra (ā′rə) *n.* A constellation in the Southern Hemisphere near the constellations Norma and Telescopium. [Latin *āra*, altar. See **as-** in Appendix.*]

Ar·ab (ăr′əb) *n.* **1.** A native or inhabitant of Arabia. **2.** Any of a Semitic people originally from Arabia, but later widely scattered throughout the Near East, North Africa, and the Arabian Peninsula. **3.** Loosely, any of a nomadic people living in North African and Near Eastern desert regions. **4.** Any of a breed of swift, intelligent, graceful horses native to Arabia. **5.** A street Arab; waif. *—adj.* Arabian. [Middle English, from Latin *Arabs*, from Greek *Arabs*, *Araps*, from Arabic *'arab*.]

Arab. 1. Arabia; Arabian. **2.** Arabic.

ar·a·besque (ăr′ə-bĕsk′) *n.* **1.** A complex and ornate design of intertwined floral, foliate, and geometrical figures. **2.** *Ballet.* A position in which the dancer stands on one leg, the other leg extended backward with straight knee, and with the arms disposed in any of the various conventional positions. *—adj.* Relating to, in the fashion of, or formed as an arabesque. [French, from Italian *arabesco*, "made or done in the Arabic fashion," from *Arabo*, Arab, from Latin *Arabus*, *Arabs*, ARAB.]

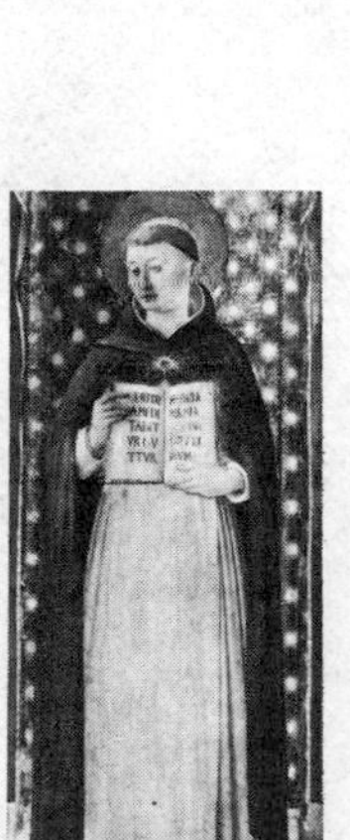
Saint Thomas Aquinas
Painting by
Fra Angelico

A·ra·bi·a (ə-rā′bē-ə). *Abbr.* **Ar., Arab.** A peninsula of southwestern Asia, about one million square miles in area, lying between the Red Sea and the Persian Gulf and including Saudi Arabia, Yemen, and Southern Yemen, as well as a number of sheikdoms. Also called "Arabian Peninsula."

A·ra·bi·an (ə-rā′bē-ən) *adj. Abbr.* **Ar., Arab.** Of or concerning Arabia or the Arabs; Arab. *—n.* **1.** A native or inhabitant of Arabia. **2.** A horse of a breed native to Arabia; Arab.

Arabian camel. The **dromedary** *(see)*.

Arabian Desert. The desert in Egypt between the Nile Valley and the Red Sea.

Arabian primrose. A plant, *Arnebia cornuta*, native to the Orient, having orange flowers spotted with black.

Arabian Sea. That part of the Indian Ocean bounded by eastern Africa, Arabia, and western India.

Ar·a·bic (ăr′ə-bĭk) *adj.* Of or pertaining to Arabia, the Arabs, their language, or their culture. *—n. Abbr.* **Ar., Arab. 1.** The Southwest Semitic language of the Arabs, now spoken in a variety of dialects chiefly in Arabia, Jordan, Syria, Iraq, Palestine, Egypt, and parts of northern Africa. **2.** The literary language of the Koran, as employed in most formal usage in Arabic-speaking countries; classical Arabic.

Arabic numerals. The numerical symbols 1, 2, 3, 4, 5, 6, 7, 8, 9, and 0.

Ar·ab·ist (ăr′ə-bĭst) *n.* A specialist in the Arabic language or culture.

ar·a·ble (ăr′ə-bəl) *adj.* Fit for cultivation. *—n.* Arable land. [Middle English, from Old French, from Latin *arābilis*, from *arāre*, to plow. See **arə-** in Appendix.*]

Arab League. A confederation formed in 1945 by Iraq, Jordan, Lebanon, Saudi Arabia, Egypt, Syria, and Yemen. They were joined in 1959 by Libya, Morocco, Sudan, and Tunisia, and in 1961 by Kuwait.

Ar·a·by (ăr′ə-bē). *Poetic.* Arabia.

A·ra·ca·jú (ä′rä-kä-zhōō′). The capital of Sergipe State, northeastern Brazil, a seaport on the Atlantic. Population, 113,000.

A·rach·ne (ə-răk′nē). *Greek Mythology.* A maiden who was transformed into a spider by Athena for challenging her to a weaving contest. [Latin *Arachnē*, from Greek *Arakhnē*, from *arakhnē*†, spider.]

a·rach·nid (ə-răk′nĭd) *n.* Any of various arthropods of the class Arachnida, such as a spider, scorpion, mite, or tick, characteristically having four pairs of legs. [New Latin *Arachnida*, from Greek *arakhnē*, spider, ARACHNE.] **—a·rach′ni·dan** (ə-răk′nə-dən) *adj. & n.*

a·rach·noid (ə-răk′noid′) *adj.* **1.** Resembling a spider's web. **2.** Of or relating to the arachnids. **3.** Covered with or consisting of thin, soft, entangled hairs like those of a cobweb. *—n.* **1.** An arachnid. **2.** A delicate membrane of the spinal cord and brain, lying between the pia mater and dura mater. [New Latin *arachnoides*, from Greek *arakhnoeidēs*, cobweblike : *arakhnē*, spider, ARACHNE + -OID.]

A·rad (ä-räd′). A city in western Rumania, on the Mureș River. Population, 115,000.

A·ra·fu·ra Sea (ä′rə-fōō′rə). A part of the western Pacific Ocean between New Guinea and Australia.

A·ra·gats, Mount. See Mount **Alagez.**

Ar·a·gon (ăr′ə-gŏn′). *Spanish* **Ar·a·gón** (ä′rä-gōn′). A region of northeastern Spain, formerly an independent kingdom.

Ar·a·go·nese (ăr′ə-gə-nēz′, -nēs′) *adj.* Of or pertaining to Aragon, its inhabitants, language, or culture. *—n., pl.* **Aragonese. 1.** A native or inhabitant of Aragon. **2.** The Spanish dialect spoken in Aragon.

a·rag·o·nite (ə-răg′ə-nīt′, ăr′ə-gə-) *n.* An orthorhombic mineral form of crystalline calcium carbonate, dimorphous with calcite. [First found in ARAGON.]

A·ra·guai·a (ăr′ä-gwī′ä). Also **A·ra·guay·a.** A river of Brazil, rising in south-central Mato Grosso state and flowing 1,100 miles generally north to the Tocantins River.

A·ra·kan Yo·ma (ä-rä-kän′ yō′mä). A range of mountains in Burma, extending about 800 miles and separating Burma from the Republic of India and East Pakistan. Highest elevation, Mount Victoria (10,018 feet).

Ar·al Sea (ăr′əl). *Russian* **A·ral·sko·ye Mo·re** (ŭ-räl′y'-skə-yə mô′ryə). An inland sea of the Soviet Union, occupying 24,500 square miles 175 miles east of the Caspian Sea, with which it was once connected. Also called "Lake Aral."

Ar·am. A Biblical name for ancient Syria.

Ar·a·ma·ic (ăr′ə-mā′ĭk) *n. Abbr.* **Ar., Aram.** A Northwest Semitic language used as the commercial lingua franca for nearly all of southwestern Asia after about 300 B.C. Compare **Biblical Aramaic.** **—Ar′a·ma′ic** *adj.*

Ar·a·me·an, Ar·a·mae·an (ăr′ə-mē′ən) *adj.* Of or pertaining to Aram, its inhabitants, language, or culture. *—n.* **1.** A native or inhabitant of Aram. **2.** The Aramaic language.

Ar·an Islands (ăr′ən). Three islands at the entrance to Galway Bay, off the southwest coast of County Galway, Ireland.

A·ran·sas Pass (ə-răn′səs). A channel in southern Texas leading from the Gulf of Mexico to the Gulf Intracoastal Waterway near Corpus Christi.

A·rap·a·ho (ə-răp′ə-hō′) *n., pl.* **Arapaho** or **-hos.** Also **A·rap·a·hoe. 1.** A tribe of Algonquian-speaking North American Indians formerly centered in the area of the Platte and Arkansas rivers, now settled in Oklahoma and Wyoming. **2.** A member of this tribe. **3.** The language of this tribe. [Crow *aa-raxpé-ahu*, "tatto" : *aa-*, with + *raxpé*, skin + *-ahu*, many.]

ar·a·pai·ma (ăr′ə-pī′mə) *n.* A large South American freshwater food fish, *Arapaima gigas*, sometimes attaining a length of 15 feet. Also called "pirarucu." [Spanish, probably from Tupi.]

Ar·a·rat, Mount (ăr′ə-răt′). *Turkish* **A·ğri Da·ği** (ä′rē dä-ē′). The highest mountain in Turkey (16,945 feet), in the extreme eastern part of the country.

ar·a·ro·ba (ăr′ə-rō′bə) *n.* **1.** A Brazilian tree, *Andira araroba*, having yellowish wood from which a medicinal powder is obtained. **2.** The powder itself, found in cavities in the wood. In this sense, also called "Goa powder." See **chrysarobin.** [Portuguese, probably from Tupi : *arara*, parrot + *yba*, tree.]

A·ras (ä-räs′). *Russian* **A·raks** (ŭ-räks′). Ancient name **A·rax·es**

ă pat/ā pay/âr care/ä father/b bib/ch church/d deed/ĕ pet/ē be/f fife/g gag/h hat/hw which/ĭ pit/ī pie/îr pier/j judge/k kick/l lid, needle/m mum/n no, sudden/ng thing/ŏ pot/ō toe/ô paw, for/oi noise/ou out/ōō took/ōō boot/p pop/r roar/s sauce/sh ship, dish/

(ə-răk′sēz). A river rising in Turkey and flowing 666 miles generally east, forming part of the border between Turkey and the Soviet Union and between Iran and the Soviet Union.
Ar·au·ca·ni·a (ăr′ô-kā′nē-ə). The territory of the Araucanian Indians, a region in central Chile.
Ar·au·ca·ni·an (ăr′ô-kān′yən) *n.* Also **A·rau·can** (ə-rô′kən). **1.** A South American Indian language family spoken in Chile and the western pampas of Argentina. **2.** An Indian of this linguistic stock. **—Ar′au·ca′ni·an** *adj.*
ar·au·car·i·a (ăr′ô-kăr′ē-ə) *n.* Any of several evergreen trees of the genus *Araucaria.* See **bunya, monkey puzzle, Norfolk Island pine.** [New Latin *Araucaria,* from Spanish *Araucano,* (tree) of ARAUCANIA.]
Ar·a·wak (ăr′ə-wäk′) *n., pl.* **Arawak** or **-waks. 1.** An Arawakan-speaking Indian people now living chiefly in certain regions of the Guianas. **2.** A member of this people. **3.** The Arawakan language of this people.
Ar·a·wa·kan (ăr′ə-wä′kən) *n., pl.* **Arawakan** or **-kans. 1.** A South American Indian language family spoken in a wide area comprising the Amazon basin in Brazil, Venezuela, Colombia, the Guianas, Peru, Bolivia, and Paraguay. **2.** An Indian or an Indian people of this linguistic stock. **—Ar′a·wa′kan** *adj.*
ar·ba·lest (är′bə-lĭst) *n.* Also **ar·be·list.** A medieval missile launcher designed on the crossbow principle. [Middle English *arbelast, arblast,* Old English *arblast,* from Old French *arbaleste,* from Late Latin *arcuballista* : Latin *arcus,* bow (see **arkw-** in Appendix*) + BALLISTA.] **—ar′ba·lest′er** (-lĕs′tər) *n.*
Ar·be·la (är-bē′lə). Modern name **Er·bil** (ĭr′bĭl). An ancient Assyrian city in northern Iraq; site of a battle in which Alexander the Great defeated the Persians (331 B.C.).
ar·bi·ter (är′bə-tər) *n.* **1.** One chosen or appointed to judge or decide a disputed issue. **2.** One who has the power to judge or ordain at will. —See Synonyms at **judge.** [Middle English *arbitre,* from Old French, from Latin *arbiter*†, judge.]
ar·bi·tra·ble (är′bə-trə-bəl) *adj.* Subject to arbitration.
ar·bi·trage (är′bə-träzh′) *n.* The purchase of securities on one market for immediate resale on another in order to profit from a price discrepancy. [Old French, arbitration, from *arbitrer,* to arbitrate, from Latin *arbitrārī,* ARBITRATE.]
ar·bit·ra·ment (är-bĭt′rə-mənt) *n.* **1.** The act of arbitrating. **2.** The judgment or award of an arbiter. [Middle English, from Old French *arbitrement,* from *arbitrer,* to judge, arbitrate, from Latin *arbitrārī,* ARBITRATE.]
ar·bi·trar·y (är′bə-trĕr′ē) *adj.* **1.** Determined by whim or caprice. **2.** Based on or subject to individual judgment or discretion. **3.** Established by a court or judge, rather than by a specific law or statute. **4.** Not limited by law; absolute; despotic. —See Synonyms at **dictatorial.** [Middle English, from Latin *arbitrārius,* from *arbiter,* ARBITER.] **—ar′bi·trar′i·ly** (-ə-lē) *adv.* **—ar′bi·trar′i·ness** *n.*
ar·bi·trate (är′bə-trāt′) *v.* **-trated, -trating, -trates.** *—tr.* **1.** To judge or decide as or in the manner of an arbitrator. **2.** To submit to settlement or judgment by arbitration. *—intr.* **1.** To serve as an arbitrator or arbiter. **2.** To refer or submit a dispute to arbitration. [Latin *arbitrārī,* from *arbiter,* ARBITER.]
ar·bi·tra·tion (är′bə-trā′shən) *n.* The process by which the parties to a dispute submit their differences to the judgment of an impartial party appointed by mutual consent or statutory provision. See Synonyms at **mediation.**
ar·bi·tra·tor (är′bə-trā′tər) *n.* **1.** A person chosen to settle the issue between parties engaged in a dispute or controversy. **2.** One having the ability or power to make authoritative decisions; an arbiter. —See Synonyms at **judge.**
Ar·blay, Madame d′. See Fanny **Burney.**
ar·bor[1] (är′bər) *n.* Also *chiefly British* **ar·bour. 1.** A shady garden shelter or bower, often made of rustic work or latticework on which vines, roses, or the like are grown. **2.** *Obsolete.* An orchard or garden. [Middle English *erber, herber,* garden, shady bower, trelliswork, from Old French *erbier, herbier,* herbage, plot of grass, from *herbe,* HERB.]
ar·bor[2] (är′bər) *n.* **1.** An axis or shaft supporting a rotating part on a lathe. **2.** A bar for supporting cutting tools. **3.** A spindle of a wheel, as in watches and clocks. **4.** *Archaic.* A tree. [Latin *arbor*†, tree.]
Arbor Day. A day, usually in the spring, observed by many states of the United States for the community planting of trees.
ar·bo·re·al (är-bôr′ē-əl, är-bōr′-) *adj.* **1.** Pertaining to or resembling a tree. **2.** Living in trees. **—ar·bo′re·al·ly** *adv.*
ar·bo·re·ous (är-bôr′ē-əs, är-bōr′-) *adj.* **1.** Having many trees; wooded. **2.** Resembling or characteristic of a tree; treelike.
ar·bo·res·cent (är′bə-rĕs′ənt) *adj.* Having the form or characteristics of a tree; treelike. [Latin *arborēscēns,* present participle of *arborēscere,* to grow to be a tree, from *arbor,* tree. See **arbor** (shaft).] **—ar′bo·res′cence** *n.*
ar·bo·re·tum (är′bə-rē′təm) *n., pl.* **-tums** or **-ta** (-tə). A place for the scientific study and public exhibition of rare trees. [New Latin, from Latin *arborētum,* a place grown with trees, from *arbor,* tree. See **arbor** (shaft).]
ar·bo·ri·cul·ture (är′bə-rĭ-kŭl′chər, är-bôr′ĭ-, är-bōr′-) *n.* The cultivation of trees for study or for the production of timber.
ar·bor·i·za·tion (är′bər-ə-zā′shən) *n.* **1.** A treelike shape or arrangement, as that of certain minerals or fossils. **2.** The formation of such a shape or arrangement.
ar·bor·ize (är′bə-rīz′) *intr.v.* **-ized, -izing, -izes.** To have or form many branches. [French *arboriser,* to make or become like a tree, from Latin *arbor,* tree. See **arbor** (shaft).]
ar·bor vi·tae (är′bər-vī′tē) *n.* Also **ar·bor vi·tae. 1. a.** Any of several evergreen shrubs and trees of the genus *Thuja,* having tiny, scalelike leaves and egg-shaped cones. **b.** A similar tree of the genus *Thujopsis.* Also called "tree of life." **2.** *Anatomy.* The white matter of the cerebellum, in cross section having the appearance of a tree. [New Latin *arbor vitae,* "tree of life."]
ar·bu·tus (är-byōō′təs) *n.* **1.** Any of several broad-leaved evergreen trees of the genus *Arbutus,* having clusters of white or pinkish flowers. **2.** A plant, **trailing arbutus** *(see).* [New Latin *Arbutus,* from Latin *arbŭtus*†, strawberry tree.]
arc (ärk) *n.* **1.** Anything shaped like a bow, curve, or arch. **2.** *Geometry.* A segment of a curve. **3.** *Electricity.* A luminous discharge of electric current crossing a gap between two electrodes. *—adj. Mathematics.* Designating an inverse trigonometric function: *the arc sine of a quantity.* *—intr.v.* **arced** (ärkt) or **arcked, arcing** (är′kĭng) or **arcking, arcs.** To form an arc. [Middle English *ark,* Old English *arc,* from Latin *arcus,* bow, arc. See **arkw-** in Appendix.*]
ARC, A.R.C. American Red Cross.
Arc, Jeanne d′. See **Joan of Arc.**
ar·cade (är-kād′) *n.* **1.** *Architecture.* **a.** A series of arches supported by columns, piers, or pillars. **b.** An arched, roofed building or part of a building. **2.** A roofed passageway or lane, especially one with shops on either side. *—tr.v.* **arcaded, -cading, -cades.** To provide with or form into an arcade or arcades. Usually used in the past participle: *an arcaded walk.* [French, from Italian *arcata,* from *arco,* arch, from Latin *arcus.* See **arkw-** in Appendix.*]
Ar·ca·di·a (är-kā′dē-ə). **1.** A mountainous region in central Peloponnesus, Greece, often used as a setting by the bucolic poets. **2.** Any place or region thought to epitomize rustic contentment and simplicity.
Ar·ca·di·an (är-kā′dē-ən) *adj.* **1.** Of, pertaining to, or characteristic of Arcadia. **2.** *Sometimes small* **a.** Rustic, peaceful, and simple; pastoral. —See Synonyms at **rural.** *—n.* **1.** A native of Arcadia. **2.** A person who leads or prefers a simple, rural life. **3.** The Ancient Greek dialect of Arcadia, belonging to Arcado-Cyprian.
Ar·ca·do-Cyp·ri·an (är-kā′dō-sĭp′rē-ən) *n.* A branch of East Greek, comprising Arcadian, Pamphylian, and Cypriot.
Ar·ca·dy (är′kə-dē). *Poetic.* Arcadia.
ar·cane (är-kān′) *adj.* Known or understood only by those having special, secret knowledge; esoteric. [Latin *arcānus,* closed, secret, from *arca,* chest. See **arek-** in Appendix.*]
ar·ca·num (är-kā′nəm) *n., pl.* **-na** (-nə). **1.** A profound secret; mystery. **2.** The reputed great secret of nature that alchemists sought to find. **3.** An elixir. [Latin *arcānum,* a mystery, secret, from the neuter of *arcānus,* closed, secret, ARCANE.]
arc-bou·tant (àr-bōō-täN′) *n., pl.* **arcs-boutants** (àr-bōō-täN′). *French.* A **flying buttress** *(see).*
arch[1] (ärch) *n.* **1.** A structural device, especially of masonry, forming the curved, pointed, or flat upper edge of an opening or a support, as in a bridge or doorway. **2.** Any similar structure, as a monument. **3.** Anything curved like an arch. **4.** *Anatomy.* Any of various arch-shaped structures, especially either of two such bony structures of the foot. *—v.* **arched, arching, arches.** *—tr.* **1.** To supply with an arch. **2.** To cause to form an arch or similar curve: *arch one's eyebrows.* **3.** To span: *"the rude bridge that arched the flood"* (Emerson). *—intr.* To form an arch or archlike curve. [Middle English *arche,* from Old French, from Vulgar Latin *arca* (unattested), from Latin *arcus.* See **arkw-** in Appendix.*]
arch[2] (ärch) *adj.* **1.** Chief; principal. **2.** Mischievous; roguish: *an arch glance.* [From ARCH-.] **—arch′ly** *adv.* **—arch′ness** *n.*
arch–. Indicates: **1.** Highest rank or chief status; for example, **archduke, archbishop. 2.** Ultimate of a kind; for example, **archfiend.** [Middle English *arche-, arch-,* from Old English *ærce-, arce-, erce-,* and Old French *arch(e)-,* both from Latin *arch(i)-,* from Greek *arkh(i)-,* from *arkhos,* chief, ruler, from *arkhein,* to begin, rule. See **arkhein** in Appendix.*]
–arch. Indicates a ruler or leader; for example, **matriarch.** [Middle English *-arche,* from Old French, from Late Latin *-archa,* from Latin *-archēs,* from Greek *-arkhēs,* from *arkhos,* ruler, from *arkhein,* to rule. See **arkhein** in Appendix.*]
arch. 1. archaic; archaism. **2.** archery. **3.** archipelago. **4.** architect; architectural; architecture.
Arch. archbishop.
Ar·chae·an. Variant of **Archean.**
archaeo–, archeo–. Indicates ancient times or an early condition; for example, **archaeopteryx.** [New Latin, from Greek *arkhaio-,* from *arkhaios,* ancient, from *arkhē,* beginning, from *arkhein,* to begin. See **arkhein** in Appendix.*]
ar·chae·ol·o·gy, ar·che·ol·o·gy (är′kē-ŏl′ə-jē) *n. Abbr.* **archaeol.** The systematic recovery by scientific methods of material evidence remaining from man's life and culture in past ages, and the detailed study of this evidence. [French *archéologie,* from Late Latin *archaeologia,* "the study of antiquity," from Greek *arkhaiologia* : ARCHAEO- + -LOGY.] **—ar′chae·o·log′i·cal** (-ə-lŏj′ĭ-kəl) *adj.* **—ar′chae·ol′o·gist** *n.*
ar·chae·op·ter·yx (är′kē-ŏp′tər-ĭks) *n.* An extinct primitive bird of the genus *Archaeopteryx,* of the Jurassic period, having lizardlike characteristics and representing a transitional form between reptiles and birds. [New Latin, "ancient-bird" : ARCHAEO- + Greek *pterux,* bird, wing, from *pteron,* feather, wing (see **pet-**[1] in Appendix*).]
Ar·chae·o·zo·ic. Variant of **Archeozoic.**
ar·cha·ic (är-kā′ĭk) *adj.* Also **ar·cha·i·cal** (-ĭ-kəl). *Abbr.* **arch. 1.** Belonging to a much earlier time; ancient: *archaic sculpture.* **2.** No longer current or applicable; antiquated: *archaic laws.* **3.** Designating or characteristic of words and language that were once common, but are now used chiefly to suggest an earlier style or period. —See Synonyms at **old.** [French *ar-*

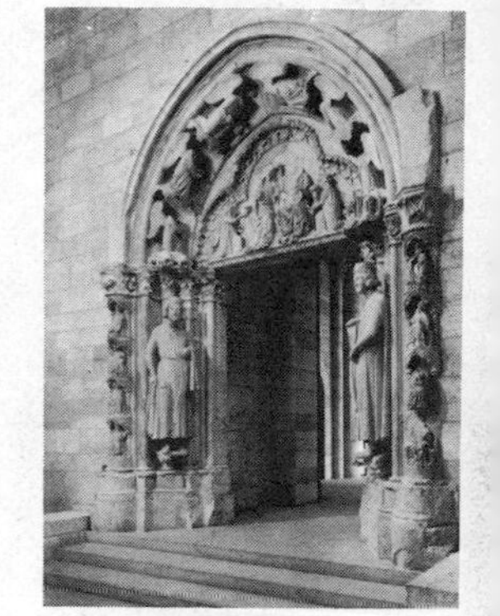

arch[1]
Arched doorway from the Abbey of Moutiers-St.-Jean, Burgundy, now at the Cloisters, Metropolitan Museum of Art, New York City

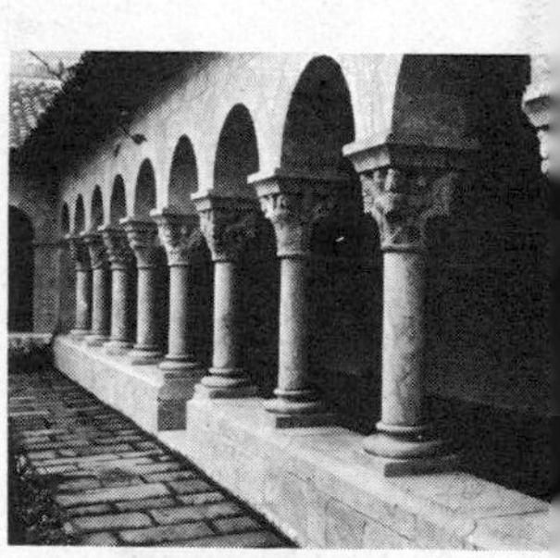

arcade
Detail of an arcade in the Abbey of Saint-Michel-de-Cuxa, southeastern France

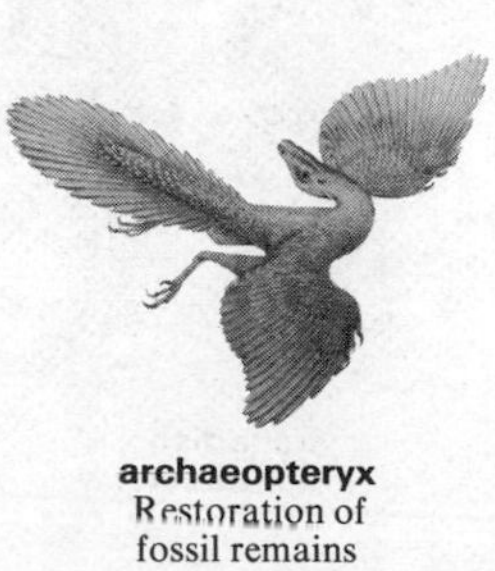

archaeopteryx
Restoration of fossil remains

t tight/th thin, path/*th* this, bathe/ŭ cut/ûr urge/v valve/w with/y yes/z zebra, size/zh vision/ə about, item, edible, gallop, circus/ à *Fr.* ami/œ *Fr.* feu, *Ger.* schön/ü *Fr.* tu, *Ger.* über/KH *Ger.* ich, *Scot.* loch/N *Fr.* bon. ***Follows main vocabulary.** †**Of obscure origin.**

chaïque, from Greek *arkhaikos*, from *arkhaios*, ancient, from *arkhē*, beginning, from *arkhein*, to begin. See **arkhein** in Appendix.*] —**ar·cha'i·cal·ly** *adv.*
Archaic Latin. **Old Latin** *(see)*.
archaic smile. *Fine Arts.* A representation of the human mouth with slightly upturned corners, characteristic of early Greek sculpture produced before the fifth century B.C.
ar·cha·ism (är'kē-ĭz'əm, är'kā-) *n. Abbr.* **arch.** **1.** An archaic word, phrase, idiom, or expression. **2.** An archaic style, quality, or usage. [New Latin *archaeismus*, from Greek *arkhaïsmos*, from *archaios*, ancient, ARCHAIC.] —**ar'cha·ist** *n.* —**ar'cha·is'tic** (-ĭs'tĭk) *adj.*
ar·cha·ize (är'kē-īz', är'kā-) *v.* **-ized, -izing, -izes.** —*tr.* To impart an archaic quality or character to; make archaic. —*intr.* To use archaisms. [Greek *arkhaïzein*, from *arkhaios*, ancient, ARCHAIC.] —**ar'cha·iz'er** *n.*
arch·an·gel (ärk'ān'jəl) *n. Theology.* **1.** A celestial being next in rank above an angel. **2.** *Plural.* The eighth of the nine orders of angels. See **angel.** [Middle English, from Norman French *archangele*, from Late Latin *archangelus*, from Greek *arkhangelos* : ARCH- + ANGEL.] —**arch'an·gel'ic** (-ăn-jĕl'ĭk) *adj.*
Arch·an·gel (ärk'ān'jəl). *Russian* **Ar·khan·gelsk** (ŭr-kän'gəlysk). A city and seaport of the Soviet Union, on the White Sea in the northwestern Russian S.F.S.R. Population, 303,000.
arch·bish·op (ärch-bĭsh'əp) *n. Abbr.* **abp., Abp., Arch., Archbp.** A bishop of the highest rank, heading an archdiocese or province. [Middle English *erchebishop*, *archebishop*, Old English *ærcebiscop*, *arcebiscop*, from Late Latin *archiepiscopus*, from Late Greek *arkhiepiskopos* : ARCH- + *episkopos*, BISHOP.]
arch·bish·op·ric (ärch'bĭsh'əp-rĭk) *n.* **1.** The rank, office, or term of an archbishop. **2.** The area over which an archbishop has jurisdiction.
Archbp. archbishop.
arch·dea·con (ärch-dē'kən) *n.* A church official, chiefly in the Anglican Church, in charge of temporal and other affairs in a diocese, with powers delegated from the bishop. [Middle English *archedeken*, Old English *ærcediakon*, from Late Latin *archidiāconus*, from Late Greek *arkhidiakonos* : ARCH- + DEACON.]
arch·dea·con·ry (ärch-dē'kən-rē) *n., pl.* **-ries.** **1.** The rank, office or jurisdiction of an archdeacon. Also called "archdeaconate," "archdeaconship." **2.** The residence or district of an archdeacon.
arch·di·o·cese (ärch-dī'ə-sĭs, -sēs', -sēz') *n.* A diocese under an archbishop's jurisdiction. —**arch'di·oc'e·san** (-ŏs'ə-sən) *adj.*
arch·du·cal (ärch-do͞o'kəl, -dyo͞o'-kəl) *adj.* Of or pertaining to an archduke or an archduchy.
arch·duch·ess (ärch-dŭch'ĭs) *n.* **1.** The wife or widow of an archduke. **2.** A woman having a rank equivalent to that of an archduke; especially, an Austrian princess.
arch·duch·y (ärch-dŭch'ē) *n., pl.* **-ies.** The territory over which an archduke or an archduchess has authority.
arch·duke (ärch-do͞ok', -dyo͞ok') *n.* In certain royal families, especially that of imperial Austria, a nobleman having a rank equivalent to that of a sovereign prince.
Ar·che·an (är-kē'ən) *adj.* Also **Ar·chae·an.** Of or pertaining to the oldest rocks of the Precambrian era, predominantly igneous in composition. [From Greek *arkhaios*, ARCHAIC.]
arched (ärcht) *adj.* **1.** Forming an arch or a curve like that of an arch. **2.** Provided, made, or covered with an arch or arches.
ar·che·go·ni·um (är'kə-gō'nē-əm) *n., pl.* **-nia** (-nē-ə). *Botany.* The multicellular female sex organ of mosses and related plants, producing a single egg. [New Latin, from Greek *arkhegonos*, "of ancient descent," original, primal : ARCH- + *-gonos*, "-born" (see **genə-** in Appendix*).] —**ar'che·go'ni·al** *adj.* —**ar'che·go'ni·ate** (-nē-ĭt) *adj.*
arch·en·e·my (ärch-ĕn'ə-mē) *n., pl.* **-mies.** **1.** A chief or principal enemy. **2.** *Often capital* **A.** The devil; Satan.
ar·chen·ter·on (är-kĕn'tə-rŏn', -rən) *n.* The embryonic digestive tract, essentially a cavity in the gastrula. [New Latin : ARCH- + ENTERON.] —**ar'chen·ter'ic** *adj.*
archeo–. Variant of **archaeo-.**
ar·che·ol·o·gy. Variant of **archaeology.**
Ar·che·o·zo·ic (är'kē-ə-zō'ĭk) *adj.* Also **Ar·chae·o·zo·ic.** *Geology.* Of, belonging to, or designating the earlier of two generally arbitrary divisions of the Precambrian era. See **geology.** —*n.* Also **Ar·chae·o·zo·ic.** *Geology.* The Archeozoic era. Preceded by *the.* [ARCHEO- + -ZOIC.]
arch·er (är'chər) *n.* **1.** One who shoots with a bow and arrow. **2.** *Capital* **A.** The constellation and sign of the zodiac, **Sagittarius** *(see)*. [Middle English, from Old French *archier*, *archer*, from Late Latin *arcārius*, alteration of *arcuārius*, "of a bow," from Latin *arcus*, arch, bow. See **arkw-** in Appendix.*]
arch·er·fish (är'chər-fĭsh') *n., pl.* **archerfish** or **-fishes.** Any of several small Indo-Australian fishes of the family Toxotidae, capable of capturing insects by squirting water at them.
arch·er·y (är'chər-ē) *n.* **1.** *Abbr.* **arch.** The art, sport, or skill of shooting with a bow and arrows. **2.** The equipment of an archer. **3.** A troop or body of archers.
ar·che·spore (är'kə-spôr', -spōr') *n.* Also **ar·che·spo·ri·um** (-spôr'ē-əm, -spōr'ē-əm) *pl.* **-sporia** (-spôr'ē-ə, -spōr'ē-ə). *Botany.* A spore-bearing cell or mass of cells. [New Latin *archesporium* : ARCH- + *spora*, SPORE.] —**ar'che·spo'ri·al** *adj.*
ar·che·type (är'kə-tīp') *n.* An original model or type after which other similar things are patterned; a prototype. See Synonyms at **ideal.** [Latin *archetypum*, from Greek *arkhetupon*, neuter of *arkhetupos*, first molded as a pattern, exemplary : ARCH- + *tupos*, mold, model (see **sτeu-** in Appendix*).] —**ar'che·typ'al** (-tī'pəl), **ar'che·typ'ic** (-tĭp'ĭk), **ar'che·typ'i·cal** *adj.* —**ar'che·typ'i·cal·ly** *adv.*

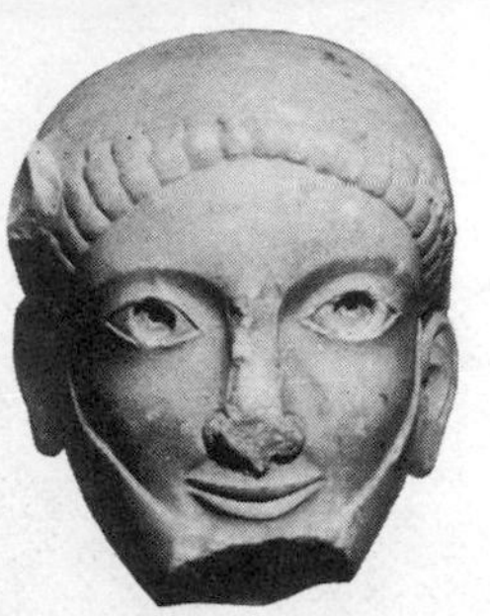

archaic smile
Head of statue found on the Acropolis in Athens

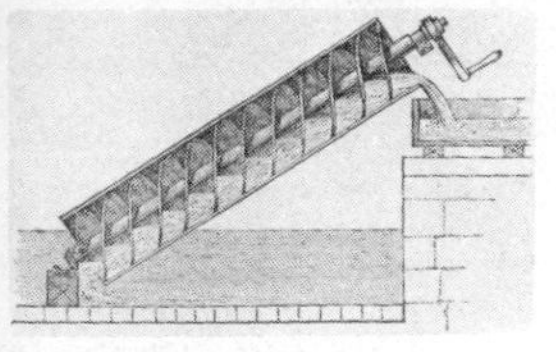

Archimedean screw

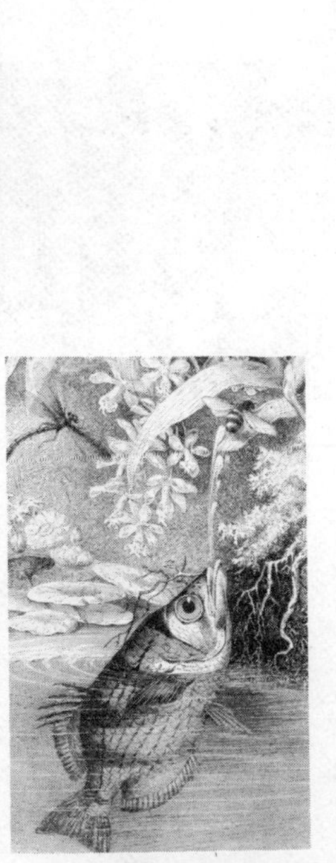

archerfish
Toxotes jaculatrix

arch·fiend (ärch-fēnd') *n.* **1.** A chief or foremost fiend. **2.** Satan; the devil. In this sense, usually preceded by *the.*
Ar·chi·bald (är'chə-bôld'). A masculine given name. [Middle English *Arcebaldus*, from Old French *Archembaldt*, ultimately from Old High German *Erchanbald* : *erchan*, genuine, proper (see **arg-** in Appendix*) + *bald*, bold (see **bhel-²** in Appendix*).]
ar·chi·di·ac·o·nal (är'kĭ-dī-ăk'ə-nəl) *adj.* Of or pertaining to an archdeacon, his duties, or his office. [From Late Latin *archidiāconus*, ARCHDEACON.]
ar·chi·di·ac·o·nate (är'kĭ-dī-ăk'ə-nĭt) *n.* The office or status of an archdeacon. [Medieval Latin *archidiāconātus*, from Late Latin *archidiāconus*, ARCHDEACON.]
ar·chi·e·pis·co·pa·cy (är'kē-ĭ-pĭs'kə-pə-sē) *n., pl.* **-cies.** **1.** Church government by archbishops. **2.** Archiepiscopate. [From Late Latin *archiepiscopus*, ARCHBISHOP.]
ar·chi·e·pis·co·pal (är'kē-ĭ-pĭs'kə-pəl) *adj.* Of or pertaining to an archbishop or an archbishopric. [Medieval Latin *archiepiscopālis*, from Late Latin *archiepiscopus*, ARCHBISHOP.] —**ar'chi·e·pis'co·pal'i·ty** *n.* —**ar'chi·e·pis'co·pal·ly** *adv.*
archiepiscopal cross. A processional crucifix mounted on a tall shaft and borne before an archbishop.
ar·chi·e·pis·co·pate (är'kē-ĭ-pĭs'kə-pĭt, -pāt') *n.* **1.** The rank, office, or term of an archbishop. **2.** Archiepiscopacy. [Medieval Latin *archiepiscopātus*, from Late Latin *archiepiscopus*, ARCHBISHOP.]
ar·chil. Variant of **orchil.**
Ar·chi·lo·chi·an (är'kĭ-lō'kē-ən) *adj.* **1.** Of, pertaining to, or characteristic of Archilochus, Greek satiric poet of the early seventh century B.C., or of the verse form invented by him. **2.** Biting; caustic; trenchant: *His spates of invective have a fine Archilochian verve.* —*n. Greek & Latin Prosody.* Various combinations of iambic trimeters or trochaic tetrameter, as used by Archilochus.
ar·chi·mage (är'kə-māj') *n.* A great magician or chief wizard. [Late Greek *arkhimagos* : ARCH- + *magos*, magician, from Old Persian *maguš* (see **magh-¹** in Appendix*).]
ar·chi·man·drite (är'kə-măn'drīt') *n. Greek Orthodox Church.* **1.** A cleric ranking below a bishop. **2.** The head of a monastery or group of monasteries and the equivalent of a Western abbot. [Late Latin *archimandrītēs*, *archimandrīta*, from Late Greek *arkhimandritēs* : ARCH- + *mandra*†, monastery, from Greek, enclosure, cattle pen.]
Ar·chi·me·de·an (är'kə-mē'dē-ən, -mĭ-dē'ən) *adj.* Of or pertaining to Archimedes or his inventions.
Archimedean screw. An ancient apparatus for raising water, consisting of either a spiral tube around an inclined axis or an inclined tube containing a tight-fitting, broad-threaded screw. Also called "Archimedes' screw."
Ar·chi·me·des (är'kə-mē'dēz). 287?–212 B.C. Greek mathematician; made discoveries in mechanics and hydrostatics.
ar·chine (är-shēn') *n.* Also **ar·shin.** A Russian unit of linear measure equivalent to 28 inches. [Russian *arshin*, of Turkic origin, akin to Turkish and Kazan Tatar *aršyn*, an ell.]
ar·chi·pel·a·go (är'kə-pĕl'ə-gō') *n., pl.* **-goes** or **-gos.** **1.** *Abbr.* **arch.** A large group of islands. **2.** A sea containing a large group of islands, as the Aegean. [From *Archipelago*, the Aegean Sea, from Italian *Arcipelago*, "the Chief Sea" (perhaps a misrendering of Greek *Aigaion pelagos*, the Aegean Sea) : ARCH- + Greek *pelagos*, sea (see **plāk-¹** in Appendix*).] —**ar'chi·pe·lag'ic** (-pə-lăj'ĭk) *adj.*
Ar·chi·pen·ko (är'kĭ-pĕng'kō), **Alexander (Porfirievich).** 1887–1964. Russian-born American abstract sculptor.
archit. architecture.
ar·chi·tect (är'kə-tĕkt') *n. Abbr.* **arch., archt.** **1.** One who designs and supervises the construction of buildings or other large structures. **2.** Any planner or deviser: *"Chief architect and plotter of these woes."* (Shakespeare). [Old French *architecte*, from Latin *architectus*, *architectōn*, from Greek *arkhitektōn*, master builder : ARCH- + *tektōn*, carpenter, craftsman (see **teks-** in Appendix*).]
ar·chi·tec·ton·ic (är'kə-tĕk-tŏn'ĭk) *adj.* Also **ar·chi·tec·ton·i·cal** (-ĭ-kəl). **1.** Of or pertaining to architecture or design. **2.** Having qualities characteristic of architecture; designed and structured. **3.** *Philosophy.* Relating to the scientific systematization of knowledge. [Latin *architectōnicus*, architectural, from Greek *arkhitektōnikos*, from *arkhitektōn*, ARCHITECT.] —**ar'chi·tec·ton'i·cal·ly** *adv.*
ar·chi·tec·ton·ics (är'kə-tĕk-tŏn'ĭks) *n.* Plural in form, used with a singular verb. **1.** The science of architecture. **2.** Structural design, as in a musical work. **3.** *Philosophy.* The scientific systematization of knowledge.
ar·chi·tec·ture (är'kə-tĕk'chər) *n. Abbr.* **arch., archit.** **1.** The art and science of designing and erecting buildings. **2.** A structure or structures collectively. **3.** A style and method of design and construction: *Byzantine architecture.* **4.** Any design or orderly arrangement perceived by man: *the architecture of nature.* [Old French, from Latin *architectūra*, from *architectus*, ARCHITECT.] —**ar'chi·tec'tur·al** *adj.* —**ar'chi·tec'tur·al·ly** *adv.*
ar·chi·trave (är'kə-trāv') *n. Architecture.* **1.** The lowermost part of an entablature, resting directly on top of a column in classical architecture. Also called "epistyle." **2.** The molding around a door or window. [Old French, from Old Italian, "chief beam" : ARCH- + *trave*, beam, from Latin *trabs* (see **treb-** in Appendix*).]
ar·chi·val (är-kī'vəl) *adj.* Of, pertaining to, or kept in archives.
ar·chives (är'kīvz') *pl.n.* **1.** An organized body of records pertaining to an organization or institution. **2.** A place in which such records are preserved. **3.** Any repository of evidence or information: *the archives of the mind.* [French, originally sin-

gular *archive,* from Late Latin *archīum, archīvum,* from Greek *arkheion,* public office (plural *arkheia,* public records, archives), from *arkhē,* beginning, hence first place, government, from *arkhein,* to begin. See **arkhein** in Appendix.*]

ar·chi·vist (är′kə-vĭst, är′kī′-) *n.* One who is in charge of archives; a custodian of archives.

ar·chi·volt (är′kə-vōlt′) *n.* Also **ar·chi·vault** (-vôlt′). *Architecture.* Decorative molding carried around an arched wall opening. [Italian *archivolto, archivolta* : *arco,* arch, from Latin *arcus* (see **arkw-** in Appendix*) + *volta,* vault, from (unattested) Vulgar Latin *volta, volvita* (see **vault**).]

ar·chon (är′kŏn′, -kən) *n.* **1.** One of the nine principal magistrates of ancient Athens. **2.** Any of various officials of the Byzantine Empire. **3.** In certain Gnostic systems, one of several powers believed to be superior to the angels. [Latin *archōn,* from Greek *arkhōn,* "ruler," from the present participle of *arkhein,* to rule. See **arkhein** in Appendix.*] —**ar′chon·ship′** *n.*

arch·priest (ärch′prēst′) *n.* **1.** Formerly, a priest holding first rank among the members of a cathedral chapter, acting as chief assistant to a bishop. **2.** A rural dean. Now used only as a title of honor. [Middle English *archeprest,* from Old French *archeprestre,* from Late Latin *archipresbyter* : ARCHI- + *presbyter,* PRIEST.] —**arch′priest′hood′, arch′priest′ship′** *n.*

archt. architect.

arch·way (ärch′wā′) *n.* **1.** A passageway under an arch. **2.** An arch covering or enclosing an entrance or passageway.

-archy. Indicates rule or government; for example, **oligarchy**. [Middle English *-archie,* from Old French, from Latin *-archia,* from Greek *-arkhia,* from *-arkhēs,* -ARCH.]

ar·ci·form (är′sə-fôrm′) *adj.* Formed like an arc. [Latin *arci-,* from *arcus,* bow (see **arkw-** in Appendix*) + -FORM.]

arcked. Alternate past tense and past participle of **arc**.

arcking. Alternate present participle of **arc**.

arc lamp. An electric lamp in which a current traverses a gas between two incandescent electrodes. Also called "arc light."

arc·tic (ärk′tĭk, är′tĭk) *adj.* **1.** Of, near, or characteristic of the North Pole or polar regions; frigid. **2.** *Usually capital* **A.** Of or relating to a geographic area extending from the North Pole to the northern timberline. —*n.* A warm, waterproof overshoe. [Middle English *artik,* from Medieval Latin *articus,* alteration of Latin *arcticus,* from Greek *arktikos,* from *arktos,* bear, hence the northern constellation Ursa Major, the Great Bear, hence "north." See **r̥kso-** in Appendix.*] —**arc′ti·cal·ly** *adv.*

Arctic Archipelago. An extensive group of islands in the Arctic Ocean between North America and Greenland, part of the Northwest Territories, Canada.

Arctic Circle. A parallel of latitude at 66 degrees, 33 minutes north, marking the limit of the North Frigid Zone.

arctic fox. A fox, *Alopex lagopus,* of arctic regions, having fur that is white or light-gray in winter and brown or blue-gray in summer.

Arctic Ocean. The polar ocean occupying about 5,440,000 square miles between North America and Eurasia.

Arc·tu·rus (ärk-to͝or′əs, -tyo͝or′-) *n.* The brightest star in the constellation Boötes, approximately 36 light-years from earth. [Middle English *Artur, Arcturus,* from Latin *Arcturus,* from Greek *Arktouros,* "guardian of the Bear" (from its position behind the tail of the Ursa Major) : *arktos,* bear (see **r̥ktho-** in Appendix*) + *ouros,* a guard (see **wer-**[4] in Appendix*).] —**Arc·tu′ri·an** *adj.*

ar·cu·ate (är′kyo͞o-ĭt, -āt′) *adj.* Also **ar·cu·at·ed** (-ā′tĭd). Having the form of a bow; curved; arched. [Latin *arcuātus,* past participle of *arcuāre,* to bend like a bow, from *arcus,* bow. See **arkw-** in Appendix.*] —**ar′cu·ate·ly** *adv.*

ar·cu·a·tion (är′kyo͞o-ā′shən) *n.* **1.** The process of bending or curving, or the state of being curved. **2.** *Architecture.* The use of arches or vaults in building.

-ard, -art. Indicates a person who does something to excess; for example, **drunkard, braggart**. [Middle English, from Old French *-ard, -art,* from Common Germanic *-hart, -hard,* "bold, hardy," often found in proper names such as *Reginhart, Raynard, Gerhart, Gerard.* See **kar-**[1] in Appendix.*]

ar·deb (är′dĕb′) *n.* A unit of dry measure of several countries of the Near East, usually equal to 5.6 U.S. bushels, but with variations in different localities. [Colloquial Arabic *ardabb,* from Greek *artabē,* probably from Egyptian.]

Ar·de·bil (är′də-bēl′). Also **Ar·da·bil.** A city in northwestern Iran, the early capital of the Safavid dynasty. Population, 77,000.

ar·den·cy (är′dən-sē) *n.* Strength or intensity of feeling; ardor.

Ar·dennes (är-dĕn′). A forested plateau, east of the Meuse, in northern France, southeastern Belgium, and Luxembourg. It was the scene of bitter fighting in World War I and of the Battle of the Bulge in World War II. Also called "Forest of Ardennes."

ar·dent (är′dənt) *adj.* **1. a.** Expressing or characterized by warmth of passion or desire. **b.** Displaying or characterized by strong enthusiasm or devotion; fervent; zealous: *"an impassioned age, so ardent and serious in its pursuit of art"* (Walter Pater). **2.** Glowing; flashing; fierce: *ardent eyes.* **3.** Hot as fire; burning: *"The temperate yet ardent climate"* (Winston Churchill). [Middle English *ardaunt,* from Old French *ardant,* from Latin *ardēns,* present participle of *ardēre,* to burn. See **as-** in Appendix.*] —**ar′dent·ly** *adv.* —**ar′dent·ness** *n.*

ardent spirits. Strong alcoholic liquors, such as whiskey or gin.

ar·dor (är′dər) *n.* Also *British* **ar·dour.** **1. a.** Great warmth or intensity, as of emotion, passion, or desire. **b.** Strong enthusiasm or devotion; zeal: *"the dazzling conquest of Mexico gave a new impulse to the ardor of discovery"* (William H. Prescott). **2.** Intense heat, as of fire. —See Synonyms at **passion**. [Middle English *ardour,* from Old French, from Latin *ardor,* from *ardēre,* to burn. See **as-** in Appendix.*]

ar·du·ous (är′jo͞o-əs) *adj.* **1.** Demanding great care, effort, or labor; strenuous: *"the arduous work of preparing a Dictionary of the English Language"* (Macaulay). **2.** Testing severely the powers of endurance; full of hardships: *"the effects of a long, arduous, and exhausting war"* (Alexander Hamilton). **3.** Hard to climb or surmount; steep: *an arduous path.* —See Synonyms at **burdensome, hard.** [Latin *arduus,* high, steep, difficult. See **erəd-** in Appendix.*] —**ar′du·ous·ly** *adv.* —**ar′du·ous·ness** *n.*

are[1]. Present tense, indicative plural, and second person singular of **be**.

are[2] (âr, är) *n.* Also **ar** (är). *Abbr.* **a, a.** A metric unit of area equal to 100 square meters. [French, from Latin *ārea,* AREA.]

ar·e·a (âr′ē-ə) *n.* **1.** A flat, open, or unoccupied piece of ground. **2.** A part of the earth's surface; region. **3.** A distinct part or section, as of a building, set aside for a specific function: *"there is an area for business, and an area for friends"* (Richard Condon). **4.** The range or scope of anything: *the whole area of finance.* **5.** The yard of a building; an areaway. **6.** *Abbr.* **A** The measure of a planar region or of the surface of a solid. [Latin *ārea*†, open field.] —**ar′e·al** *adj.*

Synonyms: *area, region, belt, zone, district, locality.* These nouns all mean a division of the space on a surface, but differ in what is implied about the size and boundaries of the division. *Area,* the most inclusive term, means any particular portion of a surface, and suggests a portion that spreads out in all directions from a center, with a vague periphery. If the area is a large, geographical one, it is likely to be called a *region.* If the area is long and narrow, with fairly specific upper and lower limits, it may be called a *belt.* If the area has strictly defined boundaries, especially boundaries fixed arbitrarily so as to set the area apart from adjacent areas, it may be called a *zone: the temperate zone; a demilitarized zone.* If the area is one of human habitation, and is regarded as a subdivision for administrative or jurisdictional purposes, it is a *district.* And if the area is simply a place where a thing in question is to be found, it is a *locality.*

area bombing. The bombing of a particular region with no attempt to hit specific targets within that region.

ar·e·a·way (âr′ē-ə-wā′) *n.* **1.** A small sunken area allowing access or light and air to basement doors or windows. **2.** A passageway, often in close quarters between buildings.

ar·e·ca (ə-rē′kə, ăr′ĭ-kə) *n.* Any of various tall palms of the genus *Areca,* of Southeast Asia, having white flowers and red or orange egg-shaped nuts. See **betel palm**. [New Latin *Areca,* from Portuguese *areca,* from Malayalam *aṭekka, aṭakka.*]

A·re·ci·bo (ä′rā-sē′bō). A city and seaport in northern Puerto Rico. Population, 70,000.

a·re·na (ə-rē′nə) *n.* **1.** The area in the center of an ancient Roman amphitheater where contests and other spectacles were held. **2.** Any similar place: *a boxing arena.* **3.** A sphere or field of conflict, interest, or activity. [Latin *(h)arēna,* sand, arena covered with sand, perhaps from Etruscan.]

ar·e·na·ceous (ăr′ə-nā′shəs) *adj.* **1.** Sandlike in appearance or qualities: *arenaceous limestone.* **2.** Growing in sandy areas. [Latin *(h)arēnaceus* : *(h)arēna,* sand, ARENA + -ACEOUS.]

arena theater. A theater in which the stage is at the center of the auditorium, surrounded by seats, and without a proscenium. Also called "theater-in-the-round."

ar·e·nic·o·lous (ăr′ə-nĭk′ə-ləs) *adj.* Growing or living in sand. [Latin *(h)arēna,* sand, ARENA + -COLOUS.]

aren't (ärnt, är′ənt). Contraction of *are not.* See Usage note at **ain't**.

a·re·o·la (ə-rē′ə-lə) *n., pl.* **-lae** (-lē′) or **-las.** Also **ar·e·ole** (âr′ē-ōl′). **1.** *Biology.* A small space or interstice, such as an area bounded by small veins in a leaf or an insect's wing. **2.** *Anatomy.* A small, dark-colored area around a center portion, as about a nipple or part of the iris of the eye. [New Latin, from Latin *āreola,* diminutive of *ārea,* open place, AREA.] —**a·re′o·lar, a·re′o·late** *adj.* —**a·re′o·la′tion** (ə-rē′ə-lā′shən, âr′ē-ə-) *n.*

Ar·e·op·a·gite (ăr′ē-ŏp′ə-jīt′, -gīt′) *n.* A member of the council of the Areopagus in ancient Athens. —**Ar′e·op·a·git′ic** *adj.*

Ar·e·op·a·gus (ăr′ē-ŏp′ə-gəs) *n.* The highest council of ancient Athens.

A·re·qui·pa (ä′rā-kē′pä). A former Inca city and major modern commercial center in southern Peru. Population, 407,000.

Ar·es (âr′ēz). *Greek Mythology.* The god of war. [Greek *Arēs*†, god of war, the planet Mars.]

a·rête (ə-rāt′) *n.* A sharp, narrow mountain ridge or spur. [French *arête,* fishbone, spiny ridge, from Old French *areste,* from Latin *arista*†, fishbone, spine, beard of grain.]

ar·e·thu·sa (ăr′ə-tho͞o′zə, -sə) *n.* Any of several orchids; especially, *A. bulbosa,* of eastern North America, of the genus *Arethusa,* having a solitary rose-purple flower fringed with yellow. [New Latin *Arethusa,* from Latin, name of a nymph, from Greek *Arethousa*†.]

A·re·ti·no (ä′rā-tē′nō), **Pietro.** 1492–1556. Italian satirist, playwright, and Renaissance political figure.

A·rez·zo (ä-rĕt′tsō). A city on the Arno in central Italy; the birthplace of Petrarch and Vasari. Population, 44,000.

arg. **1.** argent. **2.** silver.

Arg. Argentina; Argentine.

ar·gal[1]. Variant of **argol**.

ar·gal[2] (är′gəl) *adv.* Therefore. Used humorously to indicate a clumsy or absurd reasoning: *"He drowns not himself: argal, he . . . shortens not his own life."* (Shakespeare). [Alteration of Latin *ergo,* therefore. See **reg-**[1] in Appendix.*]

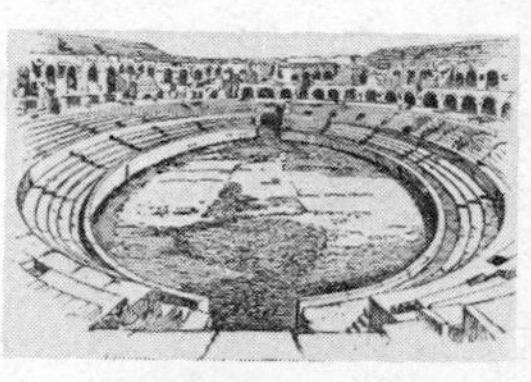

arena
Amphitheater at Nîmes, France

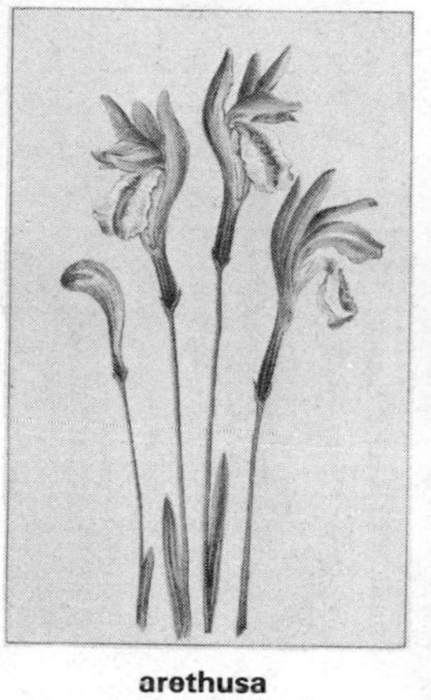

arethusa
Arethusa bulbosa

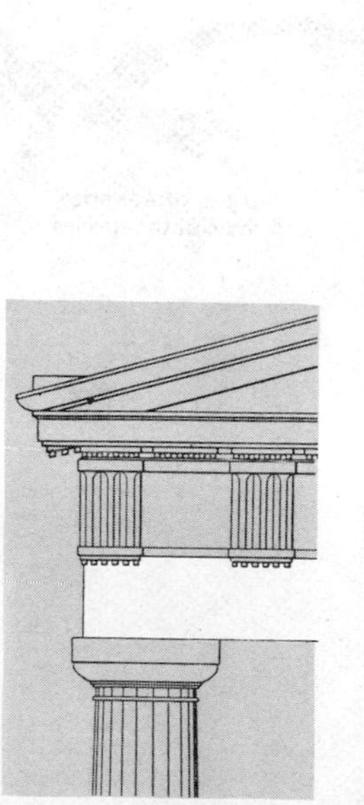

architrave
On a Greek Doric building

ar·ga·li (är′gə-lē) *n., pl.* **argali** or **-lis.** Also **ar·gal** (är′gəl). A wild sheep, *Ovis ammon,* of the mountains of central and northern Asia, having large, spirally curved horns. [Mongolian *argali,* mountain goat.]

Ar·gall (är′gôl′, -gəl), Sir **Samuel.** 1572?–1626. English mariner and colonist in America.

ar·gent (är′jənt) *n.* **1.** *Rare & Poetic.* Silver or anything resembling it. **2.** *Abbr.* **arg.** *Heraldry.* The metal silver, represented by the color white. [Middle English, from Old French, from Latin *argentum.* See **arg-** in Appendix.*] —**ar′gent** *adj.*

Ar·gen·tia (är-jĕn′shə). A U.S. military base on the coast of Newfoundland where Roosevelt and Churchill signed the Atlantic Charter in 1941.

ar·gen·tif·er·ous (är′jən-tĭf′ər-əs) *adj.* Bearing or producing silver. [ARGENT + -FEROUS.]

Ar·gen·ti·na (är′jən-tē′nə; *Spanish* är′hān-tē′nä). *Abbr.* **Arg.** Officially, the Argentine Republic. A republic of southeastern South America, occupying 1,554,326 square miles in the southeastern part of the continent between Chile and the Atlantic. Also called "the Argentine." Population, 22,252,000. Capital, Buenos Aires. [Spanish *(Tierra) Argentina,* "silvery (land)" (with reference to the rivers and lakes), from Latin, feminine of *argentīnus,* silvery, ARGENTINE.]

Ar·gen·ti·na (är′jən-tē′nə; *Spanish* är′hān-tē′nä), **La.** Original name, Antonia Merce. 1890?–1936. Argentine dancer and choreographer; introduced Spanish dance to the concert stage.

ar·gen·tine (är′jən-tīn′, -tēn′) *adj.* Silvery. —*n.* **1.** Silver. **2.** Any of various silvery metals. **3.** Any of several small, silvery marine fishes of the family Argentinidae. [French *argentin,* from Latin *argentīnus,* from *argentum,* silver, ARGENT.]

Ar·gen·tine (är′jən-tēn′, -tīn′) *adj. Abbr.* **Arg.** Of or pertaining to Argentina. —*n.* Also **Ar·gen·tin·e·an** (-tĭn′ē-ən). A native or inhabitant of Argentina.

Ar·gen·ti·no, Lake (är′hān-tē′nō). A lake, 546 square miles in area, in the extreme south of Argentina.

ar·gen·tite (är′jən-tīt′) *n.* A valuable silver ore, Ag_2S, with a lustrous, lead-gray color. [Latin *argentum,* silver, ARGENT + -ITE.]

Ar·geş (är′jĕsh). A river of southern Rumania rising in the Fagaras Mountains and flowing south 180 miles to the Danube.

ar·gil (är′jĭl) *n.* Clay, especially a white clay used by potters. [Middle English *argil, argilla,* from Latin *argilla,* from Greek *argillos.* See **arg-** in Appendix.*]

ar·gil·la·ceous (är′jə-lā′shəs) *adj.* Containing, made of, or resembling clay; clayey. [Latin *argillāceus* : *argilla,* ARGIL + -ACEOUS.]

ar·gil·lite (är′jə-līt′) *n.* A metamorphic rock, intermediate between shale and slate, that does not possess true slaty cleavage. [Latin *argilla,* ARGIL + -ITE.] —**ar′gil·lit′ic** (-lĭt′ĭk) *adj.*

ar·gi·nine (är′jə-nēn′) *n.* An amino acid, $C_6H_{14}N_4O_2$, obtained from plant and animal protein or the digestive action of bacteria, and necessary for nutrition. [German *Arginin* : possibly Greek *arginoeis,* bright, white (see **arg-** in Appendix*) + -INE.]

Ar·give (är′jīv′, -gīv′) *adj.* **1.** Of or designating Argos or Argolis. **2.** Greek. —*n.* A Greek, especially an inhabitant of Argos or Argolis.

Ar·go[1] (är′gō). *Greek Mythology.* The ship in which Jason sailed in search of the Golden Fleece.

Ar·go[2] (är′gō) *n.* A constellation in the Southern Hemisphere, now known by the names of its four smaller parts, **Carina, Puppis, Pyxis,** and **Vela** *(all of which see).* [After the ship ARGO.]

ar·gol (är′gəl) *n.* Also **ar·gal.** Crude **potassium bitartrate** *(see),* a by-product of winemaking. [Middle English *argoile,* from Norman French *argoil*†.]

Ar·go·lis (är′gə-lĭs). A region of ancient Greece, in northeastern Peloponnesus, dominated by the city of Argos. —**Ar·gol′ic** (-gŏl′ĭk), **Ar·go′li·an** (-gō′lē-ən), **Ar′go·lid** *adj.*

ar·gon (är′gŏn′) *n. Symbol* **Ar** A colorless, odorless, inert gaseous element constituting approximately one per cent of the earth's atmosphere, from which it is commercially obtained by fractionation for use in electric lamps, fluorescent tubes, radio vacuum tubes, and as an inert gas shield in arc welding. Atomic number 18, atomic weight 39.94, melting point −189.4°C, boiling point −185.9°C. See **element.** [Greek, neuter of *argos,* inert, idle, "not working" : *a-,* without + *ergon,* work (see **werg-**[1] in Appendix*).]

ar·go·naut (är′gə-nôt′) *n.* A mollusk, the **paper nautilus** *(see).* [New Latin *Argonauta* (genus name), from Latin, ARGONAUT.]

Ar·go·naut (är′gə-nôt′) *n.* **1.** *Greek Mythology.* One who sailed with Jason on the *Argo* in search of the Golden Fleece. **2.** One who went to California in 1849 in search of gold. [Latin *Argonauta, Argonautēs,* from Greek *Argonautēs* : *Argō,* name of Jason's ship + *nautēs,* sailor, from *naus,* ship (see **nāu-**[2] in Appendix*).] —**Ar′go·nau′tic** (-nô′tĭk) *adj.*

Ar·gonne (är-gŏn′, är′gŏn′). A wooded ridge in northeastern France, the scene of heavy fighting in World Wars I and II. Also called "Argonne Forest."

Ar·gos (är′gŏs′, -gəs). A city of Greece 23 miles southwest of Corinth. Possibly the country's oldest city, it figured prominently in myth and legend. Population, 17,000.

ar·go·sy (är′gə-sē) *n., pl.* **-sies.** **1.** A large merchant ship. **2.** A fleet of such ships. [Earlier *argose, ragusye,* from Italian *ragusea,* vessel of *Ragusa,* former name of the port of Dubrovnik, Yugoslavia.]

ar·got (är′gō, -gət) *n.* A specialized vocabulary or set of idioms used by a particular class or group; especially, the jargon of the underworld. See Synonyms at **dialect.** [French *argot*†.] —**ar·got′ic** (är-gŏt′ĭk) *adj.*

ar·gu·a·ble (är′gyōō-ə-bəl) *adj.* That can be argued about.

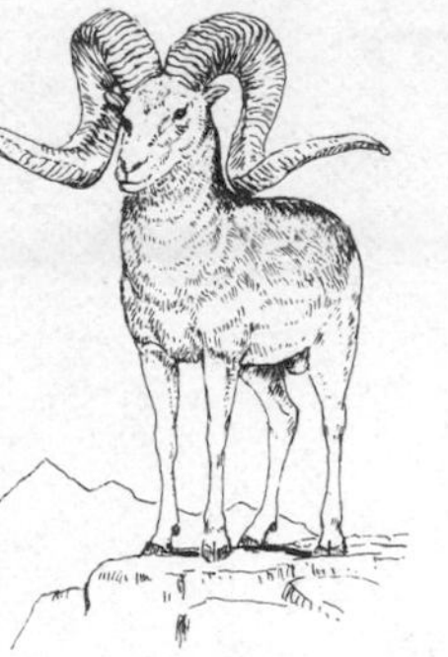

argali

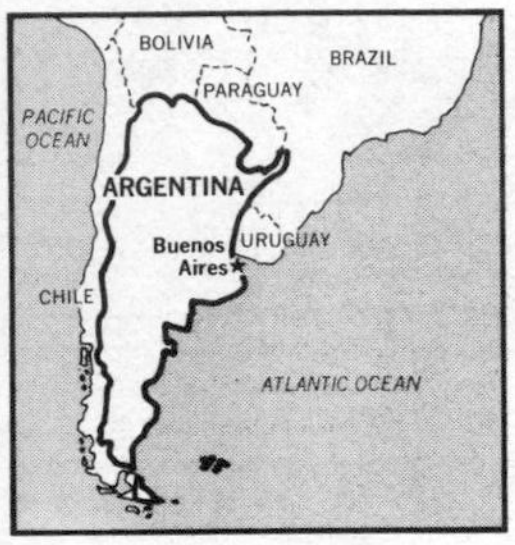

Argentina

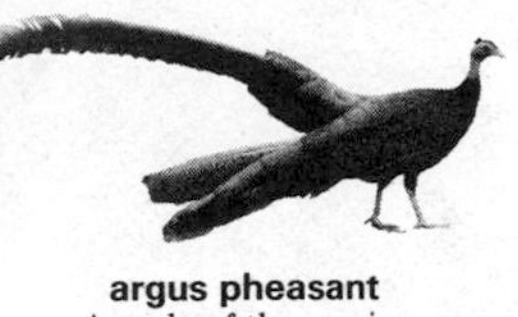

argus pheasant
A male of the species

ar·gue (är′gyōō) *v.* **-gued, -guing, -gues.** —*tr.* **1.** To put forth reasons for or against; debate: *The lawyer argued his case.* **2.** To prove or attempt to prove by reasoning; maintain in argument; contend. **3.** To give evidence of; indicate: *"similarities cannot always be used to argue descent"* (Isaac Asimov). **4.** To persuade or influence, as by presenting reasons: *He argued me into going.* —*intr.* **1.** To put forth reasons for or against an opinion, procedure, proposal, or the like. **2.** To engage in a quarrel; dispute. —See Synonyms at **discuss.** [Middle English *arguen,* from Old French *arguer,* to blame, argue against, from Latin *arguere,* to make clear, assert, prove. See **arg-** in Appendix.*] —**ar′gu·er** *n.*

Synonyms: *argue, quarrel, wrangle, squabble, haggle, bicker.* These verbs are compared as they mean to dispute. *Argue* implies intent to persuade an adversary in debate. *Quarrel* stresses animosity and estrangement. *Wrangle* refers to loud, contentious argument, and *squabble* to minor argument over a petty or trivial matter. *Haggle* specifies verbal bargaining, usually over a price, in a petty way. *Bicker* suggests sharp, recurrent exchange of remarks on a mean or petty level.

ar·gu·fy (är′gyə-fī′) *v.* **-fied, -fying, -fies.** *Regional.* —*tr.* To argue over. —*intr.* To argue stubbornly; wrangle. [ARGUE + -FY.] —**ar′gu·fi′er** *n.*

ar·gu·ment (är′gyə-mənt) *n.* **1. a.** A discussion in which disagreement is expressed about some point; debate. **b.** A quarrel; contention. **c.** *Archaic.* A reason or matter for dispute or contention: *"Sheathed their swords for lack of argument."* (Shakespeare). **2. a.** A course of reasoning aimed at demonstrating the truth or falsehood of something. **b.** A fact or statement offered as proof or evidence. **3. a.** A summary or short statement of the plot or subject of a literary work. **b.** A topic; subject; theme: *"You and love are still my argument."* (Shakespeare). **4.** *Logic.* The minor premise in a syllogism. **5.** *Mathematics.* **a.** The independent variable of a function. **b.** The **amplitude** *(see)* of a complex number. [Middle English, from Old French, from Latin *argūmentum,* from *arguere,* ARGUE.]

Synonyms: *argument, dispute, controversy, wrangling.* These nouns denote discussions involving conflicting points of view. *Argument* is generally the least forceful. *Dispute* stresses division of opinion by its implication of contradictory points of view. Usually it also strongly implies animosity. *Controversy* is especially applicable to major differences over subjects involving many persons rather than two contending individuals. *Wrangling* is noisy, angry discussion notable for lack of dignity.

ar·gu·men·ta·tion (är′gyə-mĕn-tā′shən) *n.* **1.** The presentation and elaboration of an argument. **2.** Deductive reasoning in debate. **3.** A debate.

ar·gu·men·ta·tive (är′gyə-mĕn′tə-tĭv) *adj.* **1.** Given to arguing; disputatious. **2.** Indicative; demonstrative. Used with *of.* **3.** Of or characterized by argument: *an argumentative discourse.* —**ar′gu·men′ta·tive·ly** *adv.* —**ar′gu·men′ta·tive·ness** *n.*

ar·gu·men·tum (är′gyə-mĕn′təm) *n., pl.* **-ta** (-tə). *Logic.* An argument, demonstration, or appeal to reason.

ar·gu·men·tum ad ho·mi·nem (är′gyə-mĕn′təm ăd hŏm′ə-nĕm′). An argument appealing to personal prejudices and emotions rather than to logic or reason. [Latin, "an argument to the man."]

Ar·gun (är-gōōn′). A river of east-central Asia, rising from Lake Hulun Nor in northwestern Manchuria, and forming about 500 miles of the Soviet-Manchurian border on its northerly course to the Shilka with which it forms the Amur.

Ar·gus[1] (är′gəs). *Greek Mythology.* A giant with a hundred eyes who was made guardian of Io and later slain by Hermes.

Ar·gus[2] (är′gəs) *n.* Any alert or watchful person; a guardian. [After the giant ARGUS.]

Ar·gus-eyed (är′gəs-īd′) *adj.* Extremely observant; vigilant.

argus pheasant. A large bird, *Argusianus argus,* of southern Asia and the East Indies, having long tail feathers marked with brilliantly colored eyelike spots. [New Latin, from ARGUS (whose hundred eyes were in Greek myth given after his death to the tail of the peacock).]

ar·gyle (är′gīl′) *n.* Also **ar·gyll, Ar·gyle, Ar·gyll.** **1.** A knitting pattern of varicolored, diamond-shaped areas on a solid color background. **2.** A sock knit in such a pattern. [Originally the pattern on the tartan of the Scottish clan Campbell of Argyle or Argyll.]

Ar·gyll (är-gīl′, är′gīl′). Also **Ar·gyll·shire** (-shĭr, -shər). A county occupying 3,110 square miles in western Scotland. Population, 60,000. County seat, Inverary.

Ar·gy·rol (är′jə-rōl′, -rôl′) *n.* A trademark for a dark-brown silver-protein compound used as a local antiseptic. [Greek *arguros,* silver (see **arg-** in Appendix*) + -OL.]

a·ri·a (ä′rē-ə) *n. Music.* **1.** An air; melody. **2.** A solo vocal piece with instrumental accompaniment, as in an opera or oratorio. [Italian *aria,* melody, "(atmospheric) air," from Latin *āera,* accusative of *āer,* air, from Greek *aēr.* See **wē-** in Appendix.*]

Ar·i·ad·ne (ăr′ē-ăd′nē). *Greek Mythology.* The daughter of Minos and Pasiphae who gave Theseus the thread with which to find his way out of the Minotaur's labyrinth.

Ar·i·an[1] (ăr′ē-ən, âr′-) *adj.* Pertaining to Arius or Arianism. —*n.* A believer in Arianism.

Ar·i·an[2]. Variant of **Aryan.**

-arian. Indicates: **1.** Sect; for example, **Unitarian.** **2.** A belief; for example, **vegetarian.** [Latin *-ārius,* -ARY + -AN.]

Ar·i·an·ism (ăr′ē-ən-ĭz′əm, âr′-) *n. Theology.* The doctrines of Arius, denying that Jesus was of the same substance as God and holding instead that he was only the highest of created beings.

A·ri·ca (ä-rē′kä). A city and seaport in northern Chile, near the border with Peru. Population, 50,000.

ă pat/ā pay/âr care/ä father/b bib/ch church/d deed/ĕ pet/ē be/f fife/g gag/h hat/hw which/ĭ pit/ī pie/îr pier/j judge/k kick/l lid, needle/m mum/n no, sudden/ng thing/ŏ pot/ō toe/ô paw, for/oi noise/ou out/ŏŏ took/ōō boot/p pop/r roar/s sauce/sh ship, dish/

ar·id (ăr′ĭd) *adj.* **1.** Lacking moisture; parched by heat; dry. **2.** Lacking interest or feeling; lifeless; dull. [French *aride,* from Latin *āridus,* from *ārēre,* to be dry or parched. See **as-** in Appendix.*] —**a·rid′i·ty** (ə-rĭd′ə-tē), **ar′id·ness** *n.* —**ar′id·ly** *adv.*

Ar·i·el (âr′ē-əl). The airy spirit who was Prospero's servant in Shakespeare's *The Tempest.*

Ar·ies (âr′ēz, âr′ē-ēz′) *n.* **1.** A constellation in the Northern Hemisphere near Taurus and Pisces. **2.** The first sign of the **zodiac** *(see).* Also called the "Ram." [Latin *ariēs,* ram. See **er-**[4] in Appendix.*]

a·ri·et·ta (är′rē-ĕt′ə) *n.* Also **a·ri·ette** (-ĕt′). A short aria. [Italian, diminutive of ARIA.]

a·right (ə-rīt′) *adv.* Properly; correctly. [Middle English *aright,* Old English *ariht, on riht* : A- (on) + *riht,* RIGHT (noun).]

A·ri·ka·ra (ə-rē′kə-rə) *n., pl.* **Arikara** or **-ras.** Also **A·ri·ca·ra. 1.** A Caddoan-speaking North American Indian tribe, formerly inhabiting the Dakotas. **2.** Any member of this tribe.

ar·il (ăr′əl) *n. Botany.* An outer covering or appendage of some seeds, arising at or near the hilum. It is often fleshy or brightly colored, as in the bittersweet or nutmeg. [New Latin *arillus,* from Medieval Latin *arillus*†, raisin, grape seed.] —**ar′il·late′** (ăr′ə-lāt′) *adj.*

ar·il·lode (ăr′ə-lōd′) *n. Botany.* An appendage or covering that resembles an aril but arises from the micropyle rather than the hilum. [New Latin *arillus,* ARIL + -ODE (like).]

ar·i·ose (ăr′ē-ōs′, ăr′ē-ōs′) *adj. Music.* Songlike; melodic. [Italian *arioso,* from ARIA.]

a·rio·so (ä-ryō′sō) *adv. Music.* In the style of an aria. Used as a direction to the performer. —*adj. Music.* Resembling an aria. —*n., pl.* **ariosos.** A passage or composition in this style. [Italian, from ARIA.]

A·ri·o·sto (ä′rē-ô′stō), **Lodovico.** 1474–1533. Italian poet; author of *Orlando Furioso.*

a·rise (ə-rīz′) *intr.v.* **arose** (ə-rōz′), **arisen** (ə-rĭz′ən), **arising, arises. 1.** To get up, as from a sitting or prone position. **2.** To move upward; ascend. **3.** To come into being; originate. **4.** To result, issue, or proceed. Used with *from.* [Middle English *arisen,* Old English *ārīsan.* See **rīsan** in Appendix.*]

a·ris·ta (ə-rĭs′tə) *n., pl.* **-tae** (-tē). A bristlelike part or process, as the awn of grasses or an antennal appendage of certain insects. [New Latin, from Latin, beard of grain, spine. See **arête.**]

Ar·is·tar·chus (ăr′ĭs-tär′kəs). 220?–150 B.C. Greek critic and grammarian.

Ar·is·tar·chus of Sa·mos (ăr′ĭs-tär′kəs; sā′mŏs′). Greek astronomer of the third century B.C.

a·ris·tate (ə-rĭs′tāt′) *adj.* Having a bristlelike appendage or awn. [Latin *aristātus,* from *arista,* ARISTA.]

Ar·is·ti·des, Ar·is·tei·des (ăr′ĭs-tī′dēz). Called "the Just." Athenian military and political leader of the fifth century B.C.

Ar·is·tip·pus (ăr′ĭs-tĭp′əs). Greek philosopher of the fourth century B.C.; founder of Cyrenaic or Hedonistic school.

ar·is·toc·ra·cy (ăr′ĭs-tŏk′rə-sē) *n., pl.* **-cies. 1.** A hereditary privileged ruling class or nobility. **2.** Government by the nobility or by a privileged minority or upper class. **3.** A state or country having this form of government. **4. a.** Government by the best citizens. **b.** A state having such government. **5.** Any group or class considered to be superior. [Old French *aristocratie,* from Late Latin *aristocratia,* from Greek *aristokratia,* "rule by the best (citizens)" : *aristos,* best (see **ar-** in Appendix*) + -CRACY.]

a·ris·to·crat (ə-rĭs′tə-krăt′, ăr′ĭs-tə-) *n.* **1.** A member of the nobility or aristocracy. **2.** A person having the tastes, opinions, manners, and other characteristics of an upper class. **3.** A person who advocates government by an aristocracy. [French *aristocrate,* from *aristocratie,* ARISTOCRACY.] —**a·ris′to·crat′ic, a·ris′to·crat′i·cal** *adj.* —**a·ris′to·crat′i·cal·ly** *adv.*

Ar·is·toph·a·nes (ăr′ĭs-tŏf′ə-nēz′). 448?–380? B.C. Athenian dramatist; author of many satirical comedies, 11 of them extant.

Ar·is·to·te·li·an (ăr′ĭs-tə-tē′lē-ən, -tēl′yən) *adj.* Also **Ar·is·to·te·le·an.** Of or pertaining to Aristotle or his philosophy. —*n.* **1.** A follower of Aristotle or his teachings. **2.** A person who tends to be empirical or scientific in his methods or thought. —**Ar′is·to·te′li·an·ism′** *n.*

Aristotelian logic. 1. Aristotle's deductive method of logic, especially the theory of the syllogism. **2.** The formal logic based on Aristotle's and dealing with the relations between propositions in terms of their form instead of their content.

Ar·is·tot·le (ăr′ĭs-tŏt′l). 384–322 B.C. Greek philosopher; pupil of Plato; tutor of Alexander the Great; author of works on logic, philosophy, natural science, ethics, politics, and poetics.

a·rith·me·tic (ə-rĭth′mə-tĭk) *n.* **1.** The mathematics of integers under addition, subtraction, multiplication, division, involution, and evolution. **2.** Computation or problem solving involving real numbers and the arithmetic operations. **3.** A book on arithmetic. —*adj.* **ar·ith·met·ic** (ăr′ĭth-mĕt′ĭk). Also **ar·ith·met·i·cal** (-ĭ-kəl). Of or pertaining to arithmetic. [Middle English *ar(i)smet(r)yk, arithmet(r)ik,* from Old French *ar(i)smetique,* from Latin *arithmētica,* from Greek *arithmētikē (tekhnē),* "(the art) of counting," from the feminine of *arithmētikos,* of counting, from *arithmein,* to count, from *arithmos,* number. See **ar-** in Appendix.*] —**ar′ith·met′i·cal·ly** *adv.*

a·rith·me·ti·cian (ə-rĭth′mə-tĭsh′ən) *n.* An arithmetic expert.

arithmetic mean. The number obtained by dividing the sum of a set of quantities by the number of quantities in the set. Also called "average," "mean."

arithmetic progression. A sequence, such as the odd integers 1, 3, 5, 7, . . . , in which each term after the first is formed by adding a constant to each preceding term.

-arium. Indicates a place or housing for; for example, **planetarium, terrarium.** [Latin, from the neuter of *-ārius,* -ARY.]

A·ri·us[1] (ə-rī′əs, âr′ē-əs). Died A.D. 336. Greek Christian theologian condemned as a heretic.

Ari·us[2]. The ancient name for the **Hari Rud.**

Ar·i·zo·na (ăr′ə-zō′nə). *Abbr.* **Ariz.** A southwestern state of the United States, 113,909 square miles in area, bordered on the south by Mexico. It was admitted to the Union in 1912 as the 48th state. Population, 1,302,000. Capital, Phoenix. See map at **United States of America.** —**Ar′i·zo′nan, Ar′i·zo′ni·an** *adj. & n.*

ark (ärk) *n.* **1.** The chest containing the Ten Commandments written on stone tablets, carried by the Hebrews during their desert wanderings. Numbers 10:35. Also called "ark of the covenant." **2.** The **Holy ark** *(see).* **3.** The boat built by Noah for survival during the Flood. Genesis 6–9. **4.** Any large, commodious boat. **5.** A place of shelter or refuge. [Middle English *ark,* Old English *arc, aerc, earc,* from Common Germanic *ark-* (unattested), from Latin *arca,* chest, box, coffer. See **arek-** in Appendix.*]

Ar·kan·sas (är′kən-sô′). *Abbr.* **Ark.** A southern state of the United States, 53,102 square miles in area, with most of its eastern border formed by the Mississippi. It was admitted to the Union in 1836 as the 25th state. Population, 1,786,000. Capital, Little Rock. See map at **United States of America.** —**Ar·kan′san** (-kăn′zən) *adj. & n.*

Ar·kan·sas River (är′kən-sô′, är-kăn′zəs). A river of the south-central United States, rising in the Rocky Mountains of central Colorado and flowing 1,460 miles generally southeast to the Mississippi River, north of Greenville, Mississippi.

Ar·kan·saw·yer (är-kən-sô′yər) *n.* A native of Arkansas.

Ar·khan·gelsk. The Russian name for **Archangel.**

Ark·wright (ärk′rīt′), Sir **Richard.** 1732–1792. British inventor and manufacturer; patented machines for spinning thread.

Arl·berg (ärl′bûrg′; *German* ärl′bĕrk′). An Alpine pass, 5,910 feet high, in western Austria, with a rail tunnel beneath it.

Ar·len (är′lən), **Harold.** Original name, Hyman Arluck. Born 1905. American composer of scores of musical comedies.

Ar·len (är′lən), **Michael.** Original name, Dikran Kouyoumdjian. 1895–1956. Armenian-born English author of popular novels of the 1920's and 1930's.

Arles (ärlz; *French* àrl). **1.** A city of France, on the Rhône in the southeast; a site of Roman ruins. Population, 29,000. **2.** A kingdom formed A.D. 933 by the union of Provence and Burgundy and lasting until 1378.

Ar·ling·ton (är′lĭng-tən). **1.** A county of northern Virginia, an urban area across the Potomac from Washington, D.C.; site of the Arlington National Cemetery. Population, 163,000. **2.** A residential suburb of Boston, Massachusetts. Population, 50,000.

arm[1] (ärm) *n.* **1.** An upper limb of the human body connecting the hand and wrist to the shoulder. **2.** A part similar to an arm, such as the forelimb of an animal, a branch of a tree, or a long part projecting from a central support in a machine. **3.** Anything designed to cover or support the human arm, such as a sleeve on an article of clothing or a projecting support on a chair or sofa. **4.** Anything branching out from a large mass: *an arm of the sea.* **5.** An administrative or functional branch, as of an organization. **6.** Power; authority: *the arm of the law.* —**at arm's length.** At a distance; not on friendly or intimate terms. —**with open arms.** Cordially; hospitably. [Middle English *arm,* Old English *arm, earm.* See **ar-** in Appendix.*]

arm[2] (ärm) *n.* **1.** A weapon, especially a firearm. **2.** A branch of a military force, such as the infantry, cavalry, or air corps. —*v.* **armed, arming, arms.** —*intr.* **1.** To supply or equip oneself with arms. **2.** To prepare oneself for or as if for warfare. —*tr.* **1.** To equip with weapons. **2.** To prepare for war; fortify. **3.** To provide with anything that strengthens, increases efficiency, or the like. **4.** *Military.* To prepare (a bomb, for example) for detonation, as by releasing a safety device. [Back-formation from ARMS (plural).] —**arm′er** *n.*

Arm. Armenia; Armenian.

ar·ma·da (är-mä′də, -mā′də) *n.* **1.** A fleet of warships. **2.** *Capital* **A.** The **Spanish Armada** *(see).* [Spanish, from Medieval Latin *armāta,* army, fleet, from Latin *armātus,* past participle of *armāre,* to arm, from *arma,* arms. See **ar-** in Appendix.*]

ar·ma·dil·lo (är′mə-dĭl′ō) *n., pl.* **-los.** Any of several omnivorous, burrowing mammals of the family Dasypodidae, of southern North America and South America, having a covering of armorlike, jointed, bony plates. [Spanish, diminutive of *armado,* armored, plated, past participle of *armar,* to arm, from Latin *armāre,* from *arma,* arms. See **ar-** in Appendix.*]

Ar·ma·ged·don (är′mə-gĕd′n) *n.* **1.** The scene of a final battle between the forces of good and evil, prophesied in the Bible to occur at the end of the world. Revelation 16:16. **2.** Any decisive conflict. [Late Latin *Armagedōn,* from Greek, from Hebrew *har megiddōn,* the mountain region of *Megiddo,* site of several great battles in the Old Testament.]

Ar·magh (är-mä′). **1.** A county occupying 489 square miles in southern Northern Ireland. Population, 121,000. **2.** Its county seat. Population, 10,000.

ar·ma·ment (är′mə-mənt) *n.* **1.** The weapons and supplies of war with which a military unit is equipped. **2.** *Often plural.* All the military forces and war equipment of a country. **3.** A military force equipped for war. **4.** The process of arming for war. [Late Latin *armāmentum* (singular), from Latin *armāmenta* (plural), implements, equipment, from *arma,* tools, ARMS.]

ar·ma·men·tar·i·um (är′mə-mĕn-târ′ē-əm) *n., pl.* **-ums** or **-ia** (-ē-ə). The complete equipment of a physician or medical institution, including books, supplies, and instruments

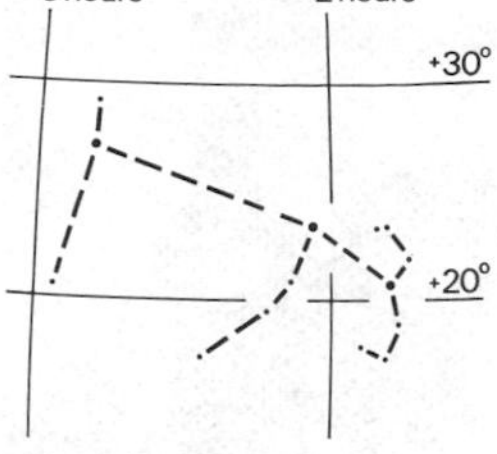

Aries

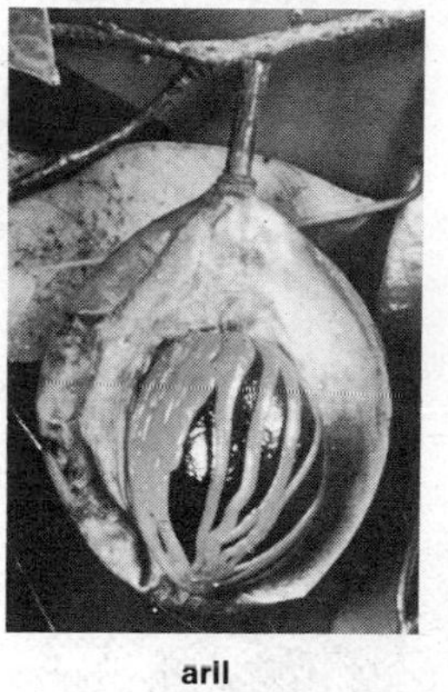
aril
Nutmeg fruit split open to show aril enclosing seed

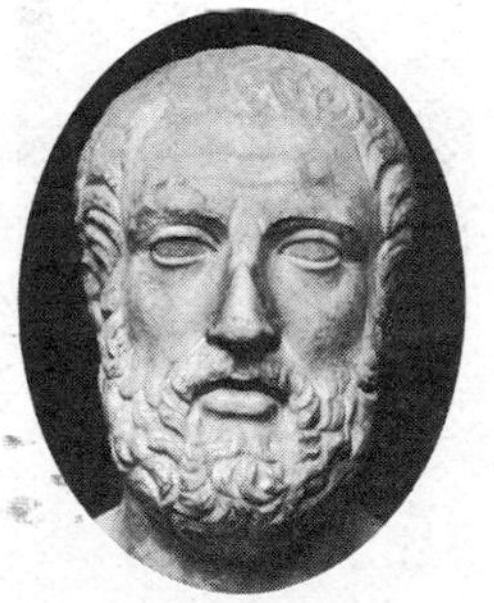
Aristophanes

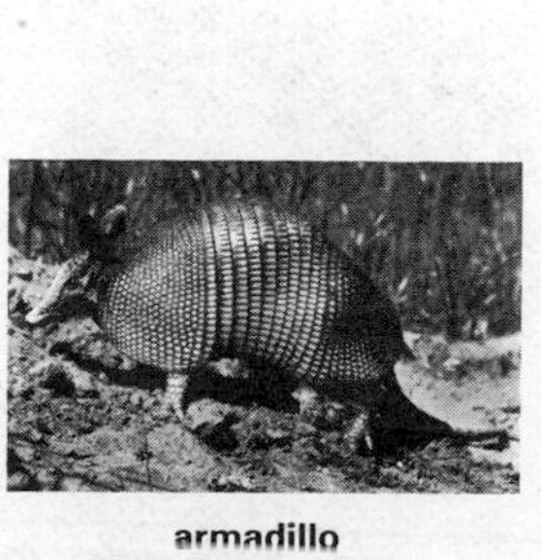
armadillo
Dasypus novemcinctus
Nine-banded armadillo

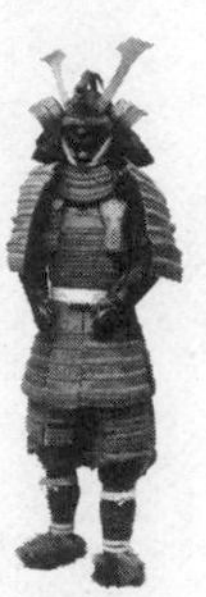

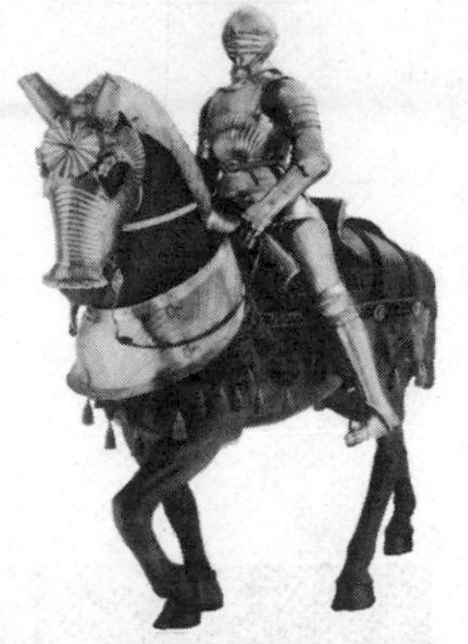

armor
Above: Sixteenth-century Japanese armor of iron and leather
Below: Sixteenth-century German steel armor for man and horse

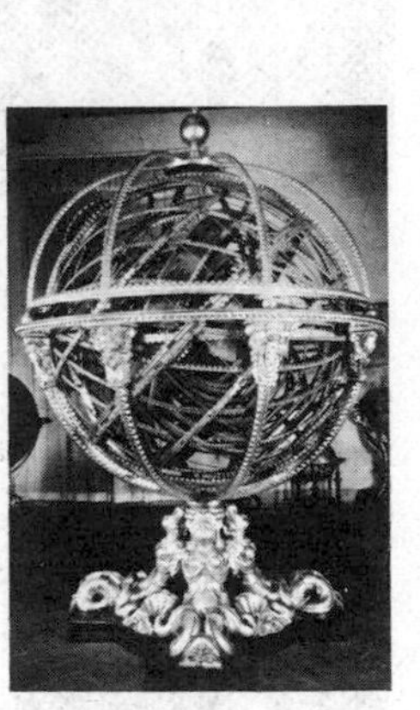

armillary sphere
Late 16th-century model of the universe

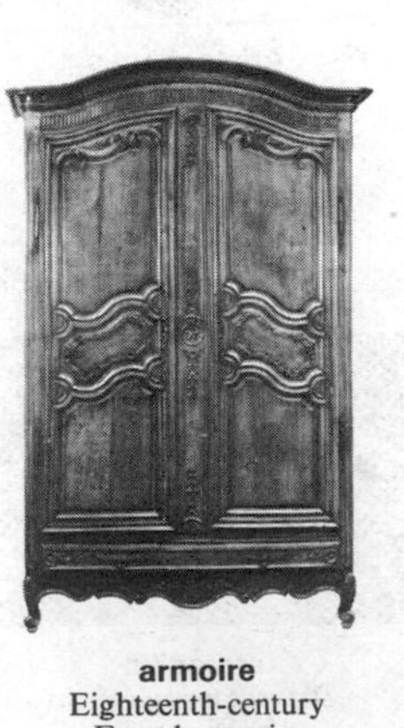

armoire
Eighteenth-century French armoire

ar·ma·ture (är′mə-cho͝or′) *n.* **1.** *Electricity.* **a.** The rotating part of a dynamo consisting essentially of copper wire wound around an iron core. **b.** The moving part of an electromagnetic device such as a relay, buzzer, or loud-speaker. **c.** A piece of soft iron connecting the poles of a magnet. **2.** *Biology.* The protective covering or structure of an animal or plant. **3.** A framework serving as a supporting core for clay sculpture. **4.** Armor. [Latin *armātūra,* equipment, from *armāre,* to arm, from *arma,* weapons, tools. See **ar-** in Appendix.*]

arm·band (ärm′bănd′) *n.* A brassard.

arm·chair (ärm′châr′) *n.* A chair with side structures to support the arms or elbows. *—adj.* Remote from active involvement: *an armchair warrior.*

armed (ärmd) *adj.* **1.** Equipped with weapons. **2.** Having or characterized by an arm or arms of a stated kind or number. Usually used in combination: *strong-armed.*

armed forces. The military forces of a country or countries. Also called "armed services."

Armen. Armenian.

Ar·me·ni·a (är-mē′nē-ə, -mēn′yə). *Armenian* **Ha·ya·stan** (hä′yäs-tän′). *Abbr.* **Arm. 1.** An ancient country of western Asia, now constituting a region divided among the Soviet Union, Turkey, and Iran. **2.** The Armenian S.S.R.

Ar·me·ni·an (är-mē′nē-ən, -mēn′yən) *n. Abbr.* **Arm., Armen. 1.** A native or inhabitant of Armenia. **2.** The Indo-European language of the Armenians. **—Ar·me′ni·an** *adj.*

Ar·me·ni·an Soviet Socialist Republic (är-mē′nē-ən, -mēn′-yən). A constituent republic of the Soviet Union, occupying 11,600 square miles in southern Transcaucasia. Population, 2,134,000. Capital, Yerevan.

ar·met (är′mĕt) *n.* A medieval light helmet with a neck guard and movable visor. [Old French *armet,* partly from *arme,* singular of *armes,* ARMS, and partly from Old Spanish *almete,* from Old French *helmet,* HELMET.]

arm·ful (ärm′fo͝ol′) *n., pl.* **-fuls.** As much as one or both arms can hold.

arm·hole (ärm′hōl′) *n.* An opening for the arm in a garment.

ar·mi·ger (är′mĭ-jər) *n.* **1.** An armorbearer for a knight; a squire. **2.** A person entitled to heraldic arms. [Latin *armiger* : *arma,* ARMS + *gerere,* to carry (see **gerere** in Appendix*).]

ar·mil·lar·y sphere (är′mə-lĕr′ē, är-mĭl′ə-rē). An astronomical model with solid rings, all circles of a single sphere, used to display relationships among the principal celestial circles. [Old French *armillaire,* from Medieval Latin *armilla,* ring, from Latin, arm ring, from *armus,* arm. See **ar-** in Appendix.*]

Ar·min·i·an·ism (är-mĭn′ē-ə-nĭz′əm) *n.* The doctrines of Jacobus Arminius and his followers, opposing the Calvinist doctrine of absolute predestination. **—Ar·min′i·an** *adj. & n.*

Ar·min·i·us (är-mĭn′ē-əs), **Jacobus.** Original name, Jacob Harmensen. 1560–1609. Dutch Protestant theologian.

ar·mip·o·tent (är-mĭp′ə-tənt) *adj. Archaic.* Mighty in arms or battle. [Middle English, from Latin *armipotēns* : *arma,* ARMS + *potēns,* POTENT.] **—ar·mip′o·tence** *n.*

ar·mi·stice (är′mə-stĭs) *n.* A temporary cessation or suspension of hostilities by mutual consent; a truce. [French, from New Latin *armistitium* : Latin *arma,* ARMS + *-stitium,* "stoppage" (see **stā-** in Appendix*).]

Armistice Day. November 11, celebrated as the anniversary of the armistice of World War I in 1918. It has been called **Veterans' Day** *(see)* since 1954.

arm·let (ärm′lĭt) *n.* **1.** A band worn on the arm for ornament or identification. **2.** A small arm, as of the sea.

ar·moire (ärm-wär′, är′mər) *n.* A large ornate cabinet or wardrobe. [Old French, variant of *armaire,* from Latin *armārium,* closet, from *arma,* weapons, tools. See **ar-** in Appendix.*]

ar·mor (är′mər) *n.* Also *British* **ar·mour. 1.** A defensive covering, such as chain mail, worn to protect the body against weapons. **2.** Any tough protective covering, such as the bony scales or plates covering certain animals, or metallic plates on tanks or warships, or wire sheathing. **3.** Anything serving as a safeguard or protection. **4.** The armored vehicles of an army. *—tr.v.* **armored, -moring, -mors.** To cover with armor. [Middle English *armure,* from Old French, from Latin *armātūra,* equipment, from *armāre,* to arm, from *arma,* ARMS.]

ar·mor·bear·er (är′mər-bâr′ər) *n.* One who carries the armor of a warrior.

ar·mor-clad (är′mər-klăd′) *adj.* Wearing or covered with armor.

ar·mored (är′mərd) *adj.* **1.** Clad or covered with armor. **2.** Equipped with armored vehicles, as a military unit.

armored car. 1. A light, armored military vehicle usually having a mounted machine gun and used especially for reconnaissance. **2.** A light armored truck used for transporting money or valuables.

ar·mor·er (är′mər-ər) *n.* **1.** One who makes or repairs armor. **2.** A manufacturer of weapons. **3.** *Military.* An enlisted man in charge of maintenance and repair of the small arms of his unit.

ar·mo·ri·al (är-môr′ē-əl, är-mōr′-) *adj.* Of or pertaining to heraldry or heraldic arms. *—n.* A book or treatise on heraldry.

Ar·mor·ic (är-môr′ĭk, är-mŏr′-) *adj.* Also **Ar·mor·i·can** (är-môr′ə-kən, är-mŏr′-). Of or pertaining to Armorica or the people or language of Armorica. *—n.* **1.** An inhabitant or native of Armorica. **2.** The language of Armorica; Breton.

Ar·mor·i·ca (är-môr′ə-kə, är-mŏr′-). The ancient name for the northwestern part of France, especially Brittany.

armor plate. Specially formulated hard steel plate used to cover warships, vehicles, and fortifications. **—ar′mor-plat′ed** *adj.*

ar·mor·y (är′mər-ē) *n., pl.* **-ies. 1.** A storehouse for arms; an arsenal. **2.** A building for storing arms and military equipment, especially one serving as headquarters for military reserve personnel. **3.** An arms factory. [Middle English *armourie,* from *armure,* ARMOR.]

ar·mour. *British.* Variant of **armor.**

arm·pit (ärm′pĭt′) *n.* The hollow under the arm at the shoulder.

arm·rest (ärm′rĕst′) *n.* A support for the arm, as on a piece of furniture or the inner surface of the door of a vehicle.

arms (ärmz) *pl.n.* **1.** Weapons. **2.** Warfare. **3.** Heraldic bearings. **4.** Insignia, as of a state, official, family, or organization. [Middle English *armes,* from Old French, from Latin *arma,* weapons, tools. See **ar-** in Appendix.*]

Arm·strong (ärm′strông′), **(Daniel) Louis ("Satchmo").** Born 1900. American jazz trumpeter, singer, and conductor.

Arm·strong (ärm′strông′), **Edwin Howard.** 1890–1954. American electrical engineer; invented FM radio.

ar·my (är′mē) *n., pl.* **-mies. 1.** A large body of men organized and trained for warfare on land. **2.** The entire military land forces of a country. **3.** A tactical and administrative military unit consisting of a headquarters, two or more army corps, and auxiliary forces. **4.** Any large group of people organized for a specific cause. **5.** A large multitude, as of people or animals. —See Synonyms at **multitude.** [Middle English *armee,* from Old French, from Medieval Latin *armāta,* army, fleet, from Latin *armātus,* past participle of *armāre,* to arm, from *arma,* arms. See **ar-** in Appendix.*]

Army Air Forces. *Abbr.* **AAF, A.A.F.** The aviation branch of the U.S. Army prior to the establishment of the U.S. Air Force in 1947.

army ant. Any of various chiefly tropical New World ants of the subfamily Dorylinae, forming large colonies that move from place to place. Also called "legionary ant."

Army of the United States. *Abbr.* **AUS** A temporary organization of all military forces during time of war, including the Army Reserves in the National Guard, and Selective Service personnel, as well as the regular U.S. Army.

ar·my·worm (är′mē-wûrm′) *n.* Any of various insect larvae that travel in large groups, destroying crops and other vegetation; especially, the caterpillar of a New World moth, *Leucania* (or *Pseudaletia*) *unipuncta.*

ar·nat·to. Variant of **annatto.**

Arn·hem (ärn′hĕm′, är′nəm). *German* **Arn·heim** (ärn′hīm). A city of the Netherlands, on the Rhine. Population, 130,000.

Arn·hem Land (är′nəm). A region in extreme northern Australia, set aside as a reserve for the Australian aborigines.

ar·ni·ca (är′nĭ-kə) *n.* **1.** Any of various plants of the genus *Arnica,* having bright-yellow, rayed flowers. **2.** A tincture of the dried flower heads of *A. montana,* used for sprains and bruises. [New Latin *Arnica*†.]

Ar·no (är′nō). A river in Tuscany, Italy, rising in the Apennines and flowing about 150 miles first southeast, then northwest, and finally west to the Ligurian Sea near Pisa.

Ar·nold (är′nəld). A masculine given name. [Middle English *Arnald,* from Medieval Latin *Arnoldus* and Old French *Arnaud,* both from Old High German *Arenwald* : *aro, arn,* eagle (see **er-**[2] in Appendix*) + *vald,* power (see **wal-** in Appendix*).]

Ar·nold (är′nəld), **Benedict.** 1741–1801. American army officer in the Revolutionary War; attempted to surrender West Point to British.

Ar·nold (är′nəld), **Henry Harley ("Hap").** 1886–1950. American general of the army; chief of air forces in World War II.

Ar·nold (är′nəld), **Matthew.** 1822–1888. English poet, critic, and educator.

Ar·nold of Vil·la·no·va (är′nəld; vĭl′ə-nō′və). French name, Arnaud de Villeneuve. 1235?–1312? Spanish alchemist.

a·roint (ə-roint′) *tr.v.* **arointed, arointing, aroints.** *Archaic.* Begone; avaunt. Used reflexively in the imperative with *thee:* "*Aroint thee, witch!*" (Shakespeare). [Origin unknown.]

a·ro·ma (ə-rō′mə) *n.* **1.** A pleasant, characteristic odor, as of a plant, spice, or food. **2.** A distinctive, intangible quality; aura. —See Synonyms at **smell.** [Latin *arōma,* from Greek *arōma*†, aromatic herb or spice.]

ar·o·mat·ic (ăr′ə-măt′ĭk) *adj.* **1.** Having an aroma; fragrant, sweet-smelling, or spicy. **2.** *Chemistry.* Of, pertaining to, or containing the six-carbon ring characteristic of the benzene series and related organic groups. *—n.* An aromatic plant or substance. **—ar′o·mat′i·cal·ly** *adv.*

ar·o·ma·tic·i·ty (ăr′ə-mə-tĭs′ə-tē, ə-rō′mə-) *n.* Aromatic quality or character; especially, the distinctive structure or properties of the aromatic chemical compounds.

a·ro·ma·tize (ə-rō′mə-tīz′) *tr.v.* **-tized, -tizing, -tizes. 1.** To make aromatic or fragrant. **2.** *Chemistry.* To subject to a reaction that results in an aromatic compound. **—a·ro′ma·ti·za′tion** *n.*

A·roos·took (ə-ro͞os′to͝ok, ə-ro͞os′-). A river rising in northern Maine and flowing eastward about 140 miles to join the St. John in New Brunswick, Canada.

a·rose. Past tense of **arise.**

a·round (ə-round′) *adv.* **1.** On or to all sides or in all directions. **2.** In a circle or circular motion. **3.** To each member of a group: *enough to go around.* **4.** In or toward the opposite direction, position, or attitude. **5.** From one place to another; here and there: *wander around.* **6.** *Informal.* Close at hand; nearby: *He waited around all day.* **7.** *Informal.* To a specific place or area: *when you come around again.* **8.** *Informal.* To a normal or desired state. **9.** *Informal.* Approximately; about. **—get around.** *Informal.* **1.** To deal or cope with successfully. **2.** To have wide knowledge of worldly matters. **—get around to.** *Informal.* To find time or occasion to give one's attention to. *—prep.* **1.** On all sides of. **2.** So as to enclose, surround, or envelop. **3.** About the circumference or periphery of; encircling. **4.** About the

ă pat/ā pay/âr care/ä father/b bib/ch church/d deed/ĕ pet/ē be/f fife/g gag/h hat/hw which/ĭ pit/ī pie/îr pier/j judge/k kick/l lid, needle/m mum/n no, sudden/ng thing/ŏ pot/ō toe/ô paw, for/oi noise/ou out/o͝o took/o͞o boot/p pop/r roar/s sauce/sh ship, dish/

central point of: *the earth's motion around the sun.* **5.** In or to various places within or near: *driving around the countryside.* **6.** On or to the farther side of: *the house around the corner.* **7.** *Informal.* Approximately at; near. —See Synonyms at **about.** [Middle English : A- (on) + ROUND (noun).]

a·round-the-clock. Variant of **round-the-clock.**

a·rous·al (ə-rou′zəl) *n.* The act of arousing or of being aroused.

a·rouse (ə-rouz′) *v.* **aroused, arousing, arouses.** —*tr.* **1.** To awaken from or as if from sleep. **2.** To stir up; excite; stimulate. —*intr.* To be or become aroused. —See Synonyms at **provoke.** [A- (intensive) + ROUSE.] —**a·rous′er** *n.*

Arp (ärp), **Jean.** Original name, Hans Arp. 1887–1966. French abstract sculptor and painter; a founder of Dada.

Ar·pád (är′päd′). Magyar chieftain of ninth century A.D.; conqueror and national hero of Hungary.

ar·peg·gi·o (är-pĕj′ē-ō′, -pĕj′ō) *n., pl.* **-os.** *Music.* **1.** The playing of the tones of a chord in rapid succession rather than simultaneously. **2.** A chord played or sung in this manner. [Italian *arpeggio,* "chord played as on a harp," from *arpeggiare,* to play the harp, from *arpa,* harp, from Germanic *harpon-* (unattested), HARP.] —**ar·peg′gi·oed′** *adj.*

ar·pent (är-päN′) *n.* Also **ar·pen.** An old French unit of land measurement approximately equivalent to an acre. [French, from Old French, from Vulgar Latin *arependis* (unattested), variant of Latin *arepennis,* half acre, from Gaulish. See **per**[1] in Appendix.*]

ar·que·bus. Variant of **harquebus.**

arr. arrival; arrive; arrived.

ar·rack (ăr′ək, ə-răk′) *n.* A strong alcoholic drink of the Middle East and nearby regions of the Orient, usually distilled from rice or molasses. [Arabic *'araq,* sweet juice, liquor, as in *'araq at-tamr,* fermented juice of the date.]

ar·raign (ə-rān′) *tr.v.* **-raigned, -raigning, -raigns.** **1.** *Law.* To call before a court to answer to an indictment. **2.** To call to account; charge; accuse: *"Johnson arraigned the modern politics of this country as entirely devoid of all principle"* (Boswell). [Middle English *arreinen,* from Old French *araisnier,* from Vulgar Latin *adrationāre* (unattested), "to call to account" : *ad-,* to + Latin *ratiō,* reason, from *rērī* (past participle *ratus*), to think, reckon (see **ar-** in Appendix*).] —**ar·raign′er** *n.*

ar·raign·ment (ə-rān′mənt) *n.* The act or procedure of arraigning or being arraigned; especially, the formal summoning of a prisoner in a law court to answer to an indictment.

Ar·ran (ăr′ən). An island of Scotland, 165 square miles in area, lying in the Firth of Clyde.

ar·range (ə-rānj′) *v.* **-ranged, -ranging, -ranges.** —*tr.* **1.** To put into a deliberate order or relation; dispose. **2.** To plan or prepare for: *arrange a picnic.* **3.** To agree about; settle: *"it has been arranged for him by his family to marry a girl of his own class"* (Edmund Wilson). **4.** *Music.* To reset (music) for other instruments or voices, or for another style of performance. —*intr.* **1.** To come to an agreement. Often used with *with.* **2.** To make preparations; to plan. Often used with *for.* [Middle English *arangen, arengen,* from Old French *arangier, arengier* : *a-,* from *ad,* to + *rengier,* to put in a line, from *renc, reng,* line, row, from Frankish *hring* (unattested), circle, ring (see **sker-**[3] in Appendix*).] —**ar·rang′er** *n.*

ar·range·ment (ə-rānj′mənt) *n.* **1.** The act or process of arranging. **2.** The condition, manner, or result of being arranged; disposal; order. **3.** A collection or set of things that have been arranged. **4.** *Often plural.* A provision or plan made in preparation for some undertaking. **5.** An agreement; settlement; disposition. **6.** *Music.* **a.** An adaptation of a composition for other voices or instruments, or to another style or level of difficulty. **b.** A composition so arranged.

ar·rant (ăr′ənt) *adj.* Egregious; unmitigated; thoroughgoing: *an arrant knave.* [Variant of ERRANT.] —**ar′rant·ly** *adv.*

ar·ras (ăr′əs) *n.* **1.** A tapestry. **2.** A wall hanging, especially of tapestry. [Middle English, from Norman French *(drap de) Arras,* (cloth of) ARRAS.]

Ar·ras (ăr′əs; *French* ȧ-räs′). A city in northern France, noted for its 15th-century tapestries. Population, 41,000.

ar·ray (ə-rā′) *tr.v.* **-rayed, -raying, -rays.** **1.** To arrange or draw up (troops, for example) in battle order. **2.** To deck in finery; adorn: *"even Solomon in all his glory was not arrayed like one of these."* (Matthew 6:29). —*n.* **1.** An orderly arrangement, especially of troops. **2.** An impressive display of numerous persons or objects: *"a heathenish array of monstrous clubs and spears"* (Melville). **3.** Splendid attire; finery. **4.** *Mathematics.* **a.** A rectangular arrangement of quantities in rows and columns, as in a matrix. **b.** Numerical data linearly ordered by magnitude. —See Synonyms at **multitude.** [Middle English *arayen, arrayen,* from Old French *areer, arayer,* from Vulgar Latin *arrēdāre* (unattested), to arrange : *ad,* toward + *rēdāre* (unattested), to provide, from Germanic (see **reidh-** in Appendix*).]

ar·ray·al (ə-rā′əl) *n.* **1.** The act or process of arraying. **2.** Something arrayed; an array.

ar·rear (ə-rîr′) *n.* **1.** *Usually plural.* An unpaid and overdue debt, or an unfulfilled obligation. **2.** *Usually plural.* The state of being behind in fulfilling contracted obligations or payments: *in arrears.* [Middle English *ar(r)ere,* behind, from Old French *arriere, arrere,* from Late Latin *ad retrō,* backward : *ad-,* toward + *retrō,* backward, behind (see **re-** in Appendix*).]

ar·rear·age (ə-rîr′ĭj) *n.* **1.** The state of being in arrears. **2.** An amount owed in payment. **3.** *Rare.* Something held in reserve.

ar·rest (ə-rĕst′) *tr.v.* **-rested, -resting, -rests.** **1.** To prevent the motion, progress, growth, or spread of; stop or check. **2.** To seize and hold under authority of the law. **3.** To capture and hold briefly (the attention, for example); engage: *"In its most gracious architectural forms, it arrests the spectator"* (Kenneth Cragg). —*n.* **1. a.** The act of arresting. **b.** The state of being arrested. **2.** A device for arresting motion, especially of a moving part. —**under arrest.** Detained in legal custody. [Middle English *aresten,* from Old French *arester,* from Vulgar Latin *arrestāre* (unattested), to cause to stop : Latin *ad-,* to + *restāre,* to stop, stay behind : *re-,* back + *stāre,* to stand (see **stā-** in Appendix*).] —**ar·rest′er** *n.* —**ar·rest′ment** *n.*

ar·rest·ing (ə-rĕs′tĭng) *adj.* Attracting and holding the attention; striking. —**ar·rest′ing·ly** *adv.*

Ar·rhe·ni·us (ə-rē′nē-əs, ə-rā′-), **Svante August.** 1859–1927. Swedish chemist; worked on electrolysis.

ar·rhyth·mi·a (ə-rĭth′mē-ə) *n.* Any irregularity in the force or rhythm of the heartbeat. [New Latin, from Greek, from *arrhuthmos,* unrhythmical : *a-,* not + *rhuthmos,* RHYTHM.]

ar·rhyth·mic (ə-rĭth′mĭk) *adj.* Also **ar·rhyth·mi·cal** (-mĭ-kəl). **1.** Lacking rhythm or regularity of rhythm. **2.** *Pathology.* Characterized by arrhythmia. —**ar·rhyth′mi·cal·ly** *adv.*

ar·ri·ère-ban (ăr′ē-âr-bän′, -băn′) *n.* **1.** In medieval France, a royal proclamation by which vassals were summoned to military service. **2.** The vassals so summoned. [French, from Old French *arriereban,* alteration of *arban, herban,* from Old High German *heriban* : *heri,* army (see **koro-** in Appendix*) + *ban,* proclamation (see **bhā-**[2] in Appendix*).]

Ar Ri·mal. See **Rub al Khali.**

ar·ris (ăr′ĭs) *n., pl.* **arris** or **-rises.** *Architecture.* The sharp edge or ridge formed by two surfaces meeting at an angle, as in a molding. [Modification of Old French *areste,* ridge, ARÊTE.]

ar·ri·val (ə-rī′vəl) *n. Abbr.* **ar., arr.** **1.** The act of arriving. **2.** A person or thing that arrives or has arrived. **3.** The reaching of a goal or objective as a result of some process or effort.

ar·rive (ə-rīv′) *intr.v.* **-rived, -riving, -rives.** **1.** To reach a destination; come to a particular place. **2.** To reach a goal or object through some process or effort. Usually used with *at: arrive at a decision.* **3.** To come at length; take place: *The day of crisis has arrived.* **4.** To achieve success or recognition. [Middle English *ariven,* from Old French *ariver,* from Vulgar Latin, *arripāre*† (unattested), to land, come to shore.] —**ar·riv′er** *n.*

ar·ri·viste (ȧ-rē-vēst′) *n., pl.* **-vistes** (-vēst′). A social climber or opportunist; an upstart. [French, from *arriver,* to arrive, from Old French *ariver,* to ARRIVE.]

ar·ro·ba (ə-rō′bə) *n. Archaic.* **1.** A unit of weight in Spanish-speaking countries equal to about 25 pounds. **2.** A unit of weight in Portuguese-speaking countries equal to about 32 pounds. **3.** A liquid measure used in Spanish-speaking countries, having varying value, but approximately equal to 17 quarts when used to measure wine. [Spanish and Portuguese, from Arabic *ar-rub',* the quarter (of a quintal).]

ar·ro·gance (ăr′ə-gəns) *n.* The state or quality of being arrogant; haughtiness; insolent pride.

ar·ro·gant (ăr′ə-gənt) *adj.* **1.** Overly convinced of one's own importance; overbearingly proud; haughty. **2.** Characterized by or arising from haughty self-importance. —See Synonyms at **proud.** [Middle English, from Latin *arrogāns,* present participle of *arrogāre,* ARROGATE.] —**ar′ro·gant·ly** *adv.*

ar·ro·gate (ăr′ə-gāt′) *tr.v.* **-gated, -gating, -gates.** **1.** To appropriate for oneself presumptuously; claim, take, or assume without right. **2.** To attribute to another unwarrantably. [Latin *arrogāre,* to claim for oneself : *ad-,* to + *rogāre,* to ask (see **reg-**[1] in Appendix*).] —**ar′ro·ga′tion** *n.* —**ar′ro·ga′tive** (-gā′tĭv) *adj.* —**ar′ro·ga′tor** (-gā′tər) *n.*

ar·ron·disse·ment (ȧ-rôN-dēs-mäN′) *n. French.* **1.** The chief administrative subdivision of a department in France. **2.** A municipal subdivision of some large French cities.

ar·row (ăr′ō) *n.* **1.** A straight, thin shaft, shot from a bow and usually made of light wood with a pointed head at one end and flight-stabilizing feathers at the other. **2.** Anything similar in form, function, or speed. **3.** A sign or symbol shaped like an arrow and used to indicate direction. [Middle English *arewe, arwe,* Old English *arwe, earh.* See **arkw-** in Appendix.*]

arrow arum. An aquatic or marsh plant, *Peltandra virginica,* of eastern North America, having arrow-shaped leaves and small, densely clustered flowers enclosed in a narrow green spathe.

ar·row·head (ăr′ō-hĕd′) *n.* **1.** The pointed, removable striking tip of an arrow. **2.** Something shaped like an arrowhead, such as a mark indicating a limit on a drawing. **3.** Any aquatic or marsh plant of the genus *Sagittaria,* having arrowhead-shaped leaves and white flowers.

ar·row·root (ăr′ō-ro͞ot′, -ro͝ot′) *n.* **1.** A tropical American plant, *Maranta arundinacea,* having roots that yield an edible starch. **2.** The starch from this plant and from certain plants of the genera *Manihot, Curcuma,* and *Tacca.* [The root was used by the American Indians to absorb poison from arrow wounds.]

ar·row·wood (ăr′ō-wo͝od′) *n.* Any of several small shrubs of the genus *Viburnum,* such as the **dockmackie** *(see),* having straight tough stems formerly used by the Indians to make arrows.

arrow worm. Any of various small, slender marine worms of the phylum Chaetognatha, having prehensile bristles on each side of the mouth.

ar·roy·o (ə-roi′ō) *n., pl.* **-os.** *Southwestern U.S.* **1.** A deep gully cut by an intermittent stream; a dry gulch. **2.** A brook or creek. [Spanish, from Vulgar Latin *arrugium* (unattested), variant of Latin *arrugia*†, mineshaft.]

ar·roz con pol·lo (är-rōth′ kōn pō′lyō, är-rōs′ kōn pō′yō). *Spanish.* A casserole of rice with chicken seasoned with saffron, garlic, and other herbs. Literally, "rice with chicken."

Ar·sa·ni·as. The ancient name for the **Murat.**

arse (ärs) *n. Chiefly British.* Variant of **ass** (buttocks).

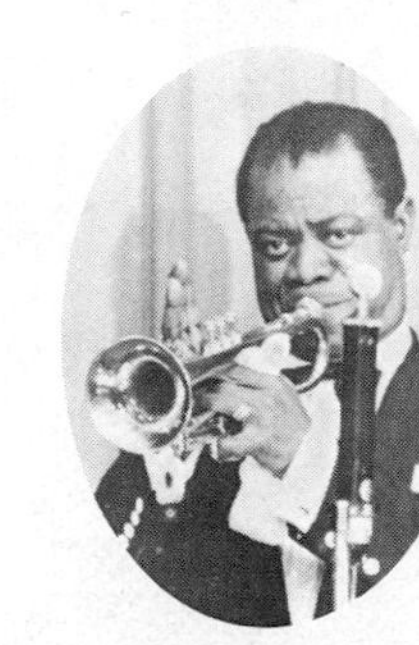

Louis Armstrong

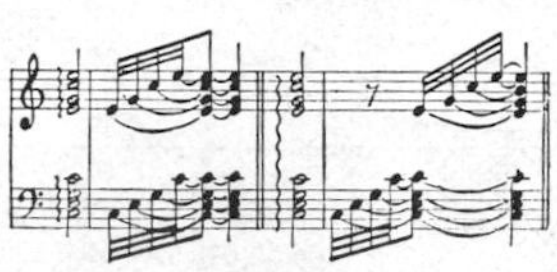

arpeggio
Notation for a keyboard instrument

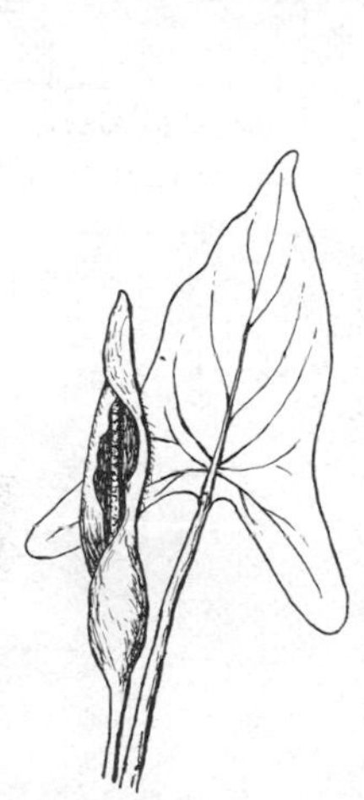

arrow arum

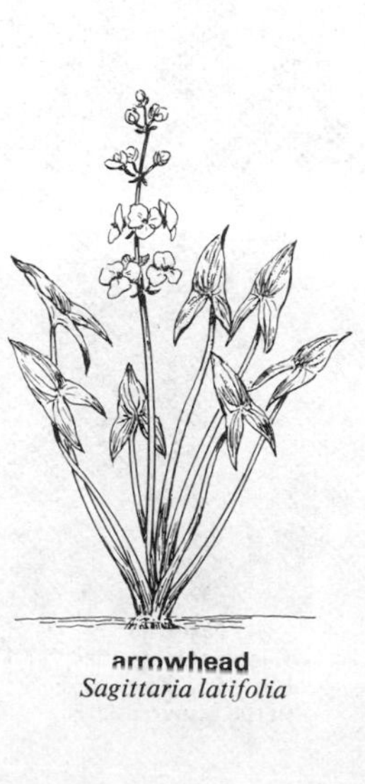

arrowhead
Sagittaria latifolia

ar·se·nal (är′sə-nəl) *n.* **1.** A governmental establishment for the storing, manufacturing, or repairing of arms, ammunition, and other war materiel. **2.** A source of supply for arms and other munitions: *"We must be the great arsenal of democracy."* (F.D. Roosevelt). **3.** A stock of weapons. [Italian *arsenale, arzanale,* originally, naval dockyard, from Arabic *dār-aṣ-ṣinā'ah* : *dār,* house + *aṣ-,* variant of *al-,* the + *ṣinā'ah,* manufacture, from *ṣana'a,* he made.]

ar·se·nate (är′sə-nĭt, -nāt′) *n.* A salt or ester of arsenic acid.

ar·se·nic (är′sə-nĭk) *n.* **1.** *Symbol* **As** A highly poisonous metallic element having three allotropic forms, yellow, black, or gray, of which the brittle, crystalline gray is the most common. Arsenic and its compounds are used in insecticides, weed killers, solid-state doping agents, and various alloys. Atomic number 33, atomic weight 74.922, valence 3 or 5. Gray arsenic melts at 817°C (at 28 atm pressure), sublimes at 613°C, and has a specific gravity of 5.73. See **element. 2. Arsenic trioxide** *(see).* —*adj.* **ar·sen·ic** (är-sĕn′ĭk). Of or containing arsenic, especially with valence 5. [Middle English, from Old French, from Latin *arsenicum, arrenicum,* from Greek *arsenikon, arrhenikon,* yellow orpiment, alteration (influenced by *arsenikos, arrhenikos,* male, virile) of Syriac *zarnīkā,* probably from Iranian. See **ghel-**[2] in Appendix.*]

ar·sen·ic acid (är-sĕn′ĭk). A poisonous white translucent crystalline compound, H_3AsO_4, used to manufacture arsenates.

ar·sen·i·cal (är-sĕn′ĭ-kəl) *adj.* Of or containing arsenic. —*n.* A drug or preparation containing arsenic.

ar·se·nic trioxide (är′sə-nĭk). A poisonous white amorphous powder, As_2O_3, used in insecticides, rat poison, and weed killers. Also loosely called "arsenic."

ar·se·nide (är′sə-nīd′) *n.* A compound of arsenic with a more electropositive element. [ARSEN(IC) + -IDE.]

ar·se·ni·ous (är-sē′nē-əs) *adj.* Of or containing arsenic, especially with valence 3.

ar·se·no·py·rite (är′sə-nō-pī′rīt′) *n.* A silver-white to gray arsenic ore, essentially $FeS_2 \cdot FeAs_2$. Also called "mispickel." [ARSEN(IC) + PYRITE.]

ar·shin. Variant of **archine.**

ar·sine (är-sēn′, är′sēn′) *n.* A colorless, flammable, very poisonous gas, AsH_3, used as a military poison gas, as a solid-state doping agent, and in organic synthesis. [ARS(ENIC) + -INE.]

ar·sis (är′sĭs) *n., pl.* **-ses** (-sēz′). **1.** Originally, the unaccented or shorter part of a foot of verse. **2.** In modern usage, the accented or longer part of a foot of verse. **3.** *Music.* The upbeat, or unaccented part, of a measure. Compare **thesis.** [Late Latin, accented syllable, "raising of the voice," from Greek, unaccented syllable, "raising of the foot in beating time," from *aeirein,* to lift. See **wer-**[2] in Appendix.*]

ar·son (är′sən) *n.* The crime of maliciously burning the building or property of another, or of burning one's own for some improper purpose, as to collect insurance. [Norman French, from Old French, from Medieval Latin *arsiō,* act of burning, from Latin *ardēre* (past participle *arsus*), to burn. See **as-** in Appendix.*] —**ar′son·ist** *n.*

ars·phen·a·mine (ärs-fĕn′ə-mēn′) *n.* A yellow hygroscopic powder, $C_{12}H_{12}N_2O_2As \cdot 2HCl \cdot 2H_2O$, formerly used to treat syphilis. A trademark is "Salvarsan." [ARS(ENIC) + PHEN(YL) + AMINE.]

art[1] (ärt) *n.* **1.** Human effort to imitate, supplement, alter, or counteract the work of nature. **2.** The conscious production or arrangement of sounds, colors, forms, movements, or other elements in a manner that affects the sense of beauty; specifically, the production of the beautiful in a graphic or plastic medium. **3.** The product of these activities; human works of beauty, collectively. **4.** High quality of conception or execution, as found in works of beauty; aesthetic value. **5.** Any field or category of art, such as music, ballet, or literature. **6.** A nonscientific branch of learning; one of the **liberal arts** *(see).* **7. a.** A system of principles and methods employed in the performance of a set of activities: *the art of building.* **b.** A trade or craft that applies such a system of principles and methods: *pursuing the baker's art.* **8.** A specific skill in adept performance, conceived as requiring the exercise of intuitive faculties that cannot be learned solely by study: *the art of writing letters.* **9. a.** *Usually plural.* Artful devices; stratagems; tricks. **b.** Artfulness; contrivance; cunning. **10.** *Printing.* Illustrative material as distinguished from text. [Middle English, from Old French, from Latin *ars* (stem *art-*). See **ar-** in Appendix.*]

art[2] (ärt, ərt). *Archaic.* Second person singular, present indicative of **be.** Used with *thou.*

-art. Variant of **-ard.**

art. 1. article. **2.** artificial. **3.** artillery. **4.** artist.

Ar·taud (är-tō′), **Antonin.** 1896–1948. French surrealist poet, actor, and drama critic; a founder of the theater of cruelty.

ar·te·fact. Variant of **artifact.**

ar·tel (är-tĕl′) *n.* A cooperative enterprise of industrial or agricultural workers in the Soviet Union. [Russian *artel',* from Italian *artieri,* plural of *artiere,* artisan, from *arte,* art, work, from Latin *ars* (stem *art-*). See **ar-** in Appendix.*]

Ar·te·mis (är′tə-mĭs). *Greek Mythology.* The virgin goddess of the hunt and the moon, and twin sister of Apollo. Identified with the Roman goddess Diana.

ar·te·mis·i·a (är′tə-mĭzh′ē-ə, -mĭzh′ə, -mĭz′ē-ə) *n.* Any of various plants of the genus *Artemisia,* which includes sagebrush and wormwood. [Middle English, from Latin, from Greek, "plant sacred to Artemis," from ARTEMIS.]

Ar·te·mus Ward. Pen name of C.F. **Browne** *(see).*

ar·te·ri·al (är-tîr′ē-əl) *adj.* **1.** Of, like, or in an artery or arteries. **2.** Of or designating the blood in the arteries that has absorbed oxygen in the lungs and is bright red. **3.** Of or designating a route of transportation carrying a main flow with many branches. —*n.* A through road or street. —**ar·te′ri·al·ly** *adv.*

ar·te·ri·al·ize (är-tîr′ē-əl-īz′) *tr.v.* **-ized, -izing, -izes.** To convert (venous blood) into arterial blood by absorption of oxygen in the lungs. —**ar·te′ri·al·i·za′tion** *n.*

arterio–, arter–. Indicates an artery or the arteries; for example, **arteriosclerosis.** [Greek *artērio-,* from *artēria,* ARTERY.]

ar·te·ri·ole (är-tîr′ē-ōl′) *n. Anatomy.* One of the small terminal branches of an artery, especially one that connects with a capillary. [New Latin *arteriola,* diminutive of Latin *artēria,* ARTERY.] —**ar·te′ri·o′lar** (-ō′lər, -ə-lər) *adj.*

ar·te·ri·o·scle·ro·sis (är-tîr′ē-ō-sklə-rō′sĭs) *n.* A chronic disease in which thickening and hardening of arterial walls interferes with blood circulation. [New Latin : ARTERIO- + SCLEROSIS.] —**ar·te′ri·o·scle·rot′ic** (-rŏt′ĭk) *adj.*

ar·te·ri·o·ve·nous (är-tîr′ē-ō-vē′nəs) *adj.* Of, pertaining to, or connecting both arteries and veins.

ar·te·ri·tis (är′tə-rī′tĭs) *n.* Inflammation of an artery. [New Latin : ARTER(IO)- + -ITIS.]

ar·ter·y (är′tər-ē) *n., pl.* **-ies. 1.** *Anatomy.* Any of a branching system of muscular tubes that carry blood away from the heart. **2.** A major route of transportation, into which local routes flow. —See Synonyms at **way.** [Middle English *arterie,* from Latin *artēria,* from Greek. See **wer-**[2] in Appendix.*]

ar·te·sian well (är-tē′zhən). A well drilled through impermeable strata to reach water capable of rising to the surface by internal hydrostatic pressure. [French *(puit) artésien,* (well) of ARTOIS, where such wells were first drilled.]

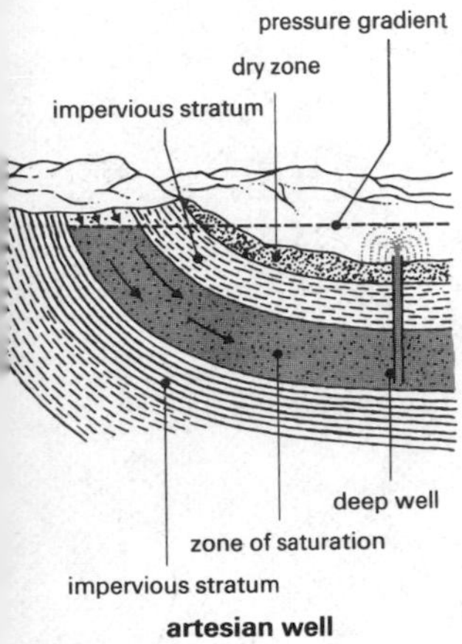
pressure gradient
dry zone
impervious stratum
deep well
zone of saturation
impervious stratum
artesian well

art·ful (ärt′fəl) *adj.* **1.** Exhibiting art or skill. **2.** Skillful, especially in finding the means to an end; clever; ingenious. **3.** Deceitful or tricky; cunning; crafty. **4.** Artificial; not genuine. —See Synonyms at **sly.** —**art′ful·ly** *adv.* —**art′ful·ness** *n.*

ar·thral·gia (är-thrăl′jə, -jē-ə) *n.* Neuralgic pain in a joint. [New Latin : ARTHR(O)- + -ALGIA.] —**ar·thral′gic** (-jĭk) *adj.*

ar·thri·tis (är-thrī′tĭs) *n.* Inflammation of a joint or joints. [Latin, from Greek : ARTHR(O)- + -ITIS.] —**ar·thrit′ic** (är-thrĭt′ĭk) *adj.* & *n.*

arthro–, arthr–. Indicates joint; for example, **arthralgia, arthromere.** [From Greek *arthron.* See **ar-** in Appendix.*]

ar·thro·mere (är′thrə-mîr′) *n.* One of the typical body segments of an arthropod. [ARTHRO- + -MERE.] —**ar′thro·mer′ic** (är-thrə-mĕr′ĭk, -mîr′ĭk) *adj.*

ar·throp·a·thy (är-thrŏp′ə-thē) *n.* Any disease of a joint. [ARTHRO- + -PATHY.]

ar·thro·pod (är′thrə-pŏd′) *n.* Any of numerous invertebrate organisms of the phylum Arthropoda, which includes the insects, crustaceans, arachnids, and myriapods, having a horny, segmented external covering and jointed limbs. [New Latin *Arthropoda* : ARTHRO- + -POD.] —**ar·throp′o·dous** (är-thrŏp′ə-dəs), **ar·throp′o·dal** (-dəl) *adj.*

ar·thro·sis (är-thrō′sĭs) *n., pl.* **-ses** (-sēz′). **1.** A connection or joint between bones. **2.** A degenerative process in a joint. [New Latin, from Greek *arthrōsis* : ARTHR(O)- + -OSIS.]

ar·thro·spore (är′thrə-spôr′, -spōr′) *n. Botany.* A sporelike cell characteristic of segmented filamentous fungi or certain algae. [ARTHRO- + SPORE.] —**ar′thro·spor′ic, ar′thro·spor′ous** *adj.*

Ar·thur[1] (är′thər). A masculine given name. [Middle English *Artur, Artor,* from Medieval Latin *Artorius,* probably from Celtic *arto-* (unattested). See **ṛkso-** in Appendix.*]

Ar·thur[2] (är′thər). Legendary British hero, said to have been king of the Britons in the sixth century A.D.

Ar·thur (är′thər), **Chester Alan.** 1830–1886. Twenty-first President of the United States (1881–85).

Ar·thu·ri·an (är-thŏŏr′ē-ən) *adj.* Of or pertaining to King Arthur and his Knights of the Round Table: *Arthurian legends.*

ar·ti·choke (är′tə-chōk′) *n.* **1.** A thistlelike plant, *Cynara scolymus,* having a large flower head with numerous fleshy, scalelike bracts. **2.** The unopened flower head of this plant, cooked and eaten as a vegetable. Also called "globe artichoke." **3.** The **Jerusalem artichoke** *(see).* [Italian (northern dialect) *articiocco, arciciocco,* alteration of *arcicioffo,* from Old Spanish *alcarchofa,* from Arabic *al-kharshūf,* the artichoke.]

ar·ti·cle (är′tĭ-kəl) *n. Abbr.* **art. 1.** An individual thing in a class; an item: *an article of clothing.* **2.** A small thing. **3.** A particular section or item of a series in a written document, such as a contract, constitution, or treaty. **4.** A nonfictional literary composition that forms an independent part of a publication; a report or essay. **5.** *Grammar.* Any of a class of words used to signal nouns and to specify their application. In English, the articles are *a* and *an* (indefinite articles) and *the* (definite article). **6.** A particular part or subject; a point or specific matter. —*tr.v.* **articled, -cling, -cles. 1.** To set forth or state in articles. **2.** To make specific or formal charges against; accuse. **3.** To bind by articles set forth in a contract. [Middle English, from Old French, from Latin *articulus,* small joint, division, part, diminutive of *artus,* joint. See **ar-** in Appendix.*]

Articles of Confederation. The first constitution of the United States, adopted by the original 13 states in 1781 and lasting until 1788 when the present Constitution was ratified.

ar·tic·u·lar (är-tĭk′yə-lər) *adj.* Of or pertaining to a joint or joints. [Middle English *articuler,* from Latin *articulāris,* from *articulus,* small joint, ARTICLE.] —**ar·tic′u·lar·ly** *adv.*

ar·tic·u·late (är-tĭk′yə-lĭt) *adj.* **1.** Endowed with the power of speech. **2.** Spoken in or divided into clear and distinct words or syllables. **3.** Capable of, speaking in, or characterized by clear, expressive language. **4.** *Biology.* Having joints or segments. —*v.* (är-tĭk′yə-lāt′) **articulated, -lating, -lates.** —*tr.* **1.** To utter (a speech sound or sounds) by moving the necessary organs of

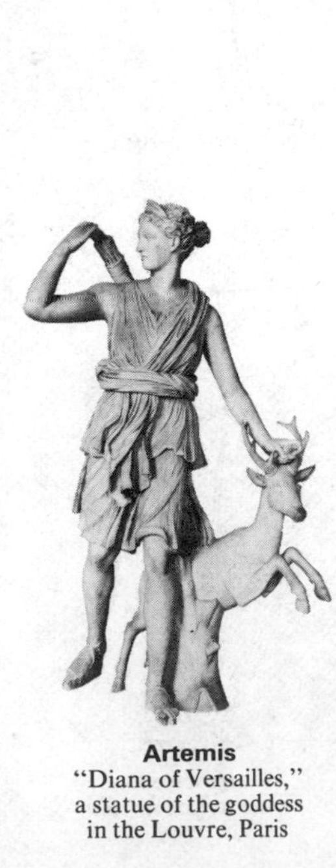
Artemis
"Diana of Versailles,"
a statue of the goddess
in the Louvre, Paris

ă pat/ā pay/âr care/ä father/b bib/ch church/d deed/ĕ pet/ē be/f fife/g gag/h hat/hw which/ĭ pit/ī pie/îr pier/j judge/k kick/l lid, needle/m mum/n no, sudden/ng thing/ŏ pot/ō toe/ô paw, for/oi noise/ou out/ŏŏ took/ōō boot/p pop/r roar/s sauce/sh ship, dish/

speech. **2.** To pronounce distinctly and carefully; enunciate. **3.** To express in coherent verbal form; give words to (an emotion, for example). **4.** To unite by forming a joint or joints. —*intr.* **1.** To utter a speech sound or sounds. **2.** To speak clearly and distinctly. **3.** To form a joint; be jointed. [Latin *articulātus,* jointed, distinct, past participle of *articulāre,* to divide into joints, utter distinctly, from *articulus,* small joint, ARTICLE.] —**ar·tic′u·late·ly** *adv.* —**ar·tic′u·late·ness** *n.*

ar·tic·u·la·tion (är-tĭk′yə-lā′shən) *n.* **1.** The act or process of speaking. **2.** *Phonetics.* **a.** The movements of speech organs employed in producing a particular speech sound. **b.** Any speech sound, especially a consonant. **3. a.** A jointing together or being jointed together. **b.** The method or manner of jointing. **4.** *Zoology.* A joint between bones, or between movable parts of an outside shell. **5.** *Botany.* **a.** A joint between two separable parts, as a leaf and a stem. **b.** A node, or a space on a stem between two nodes. —See Synonyms at **diction.** —**ar·tic′u·la·tive** (är-tĭk′yə-lə-tĭv, -lā′tĭv), **ar·tic′u·la·to′ry** (är-tĭk′yə-lə-tôr′ē, -tōr′ē) *adj.*

ar·tic·u·la·tor (är-tĭk′yə-lā′tər) *n.* **1.** A person who or thing that articulates. **2.** *Phonetics.* A movable organ used in producing speech sounds, such as the tongue, lips, or glottis.

ar·ti·fact (är′tə-făkt′) *n.* Also **ar·te·fact. 1.** An object produced or shaped by human workmanship; especially, a simple tool, weapon, or ornament of archaeological or historical interest. **2.** *Biology.* A structure or substance not normally present, but produced by some external agency or action. [Latin *arte,* by skill, ablative of *ars,* ART + *factum,* something made, neuter past participle of *facere,* to do, make (see **dhē-**[1] in Appendix*).]

ar·ti·fice (är′tə-fĭs) *n.* **1.** A crafty expedient; an artful device or stratagem. **2.** Subtle but base deception; trickery. **3.** Ingenuity; cleverness; skill. [French, from Old French, craftsmanship, from Latin *artificium,* from *artifex,* craftsman : *ars* (stem *art-*), ART + *-fex,* -maker (see **dhē-**[1] in Appendix*).]

Synonyms: *artifice, trick, ruse, wile, feint, stratagem, maneuver, dodge, guile, finesse, subterfuge.* These nouns denote means for achieving an end by indirection. *Artifice* refers to something especially contrived to create a desired effect but not necessarily with intent to deceive. *Trick* often implies willful deception, but can also mean a playful, harmless act. *Ruse* stresses creation of a false impression with the intention of distracting. *Wile* suggests deceiving and trapping a victim by playing on his weak points. *Feint* denotes a deceptive act calculated to distract attention from a person's real end. *Stratagem* implies carefully planned deception. *Maneuver* usually applies more narrowly to a specific strategic move. *Dodge* stresses slyness and quickness in achieving deception. *Guile* refers to treachery, deceit, and cunning in general rather than to a specific application of them. *Finesse* is highly developed skill, often but not invariably associated with craftiness. *Subterfuge* applies to deception practiced especially to evade difficulty or unpleasantness.

ar·tif·i·cer (är-tĭf′ə-sər) *n.* **1.** A skilled worker; craftsman. **2.** A person adept at designing and constructing; an inventor: *"The labyrinth . . . was built by Daedalus, a most skilful artificer."* (Thomas Bulfinch).

ar·ti·fi·cial (är′tə-fĭsh′əl) *adj. Abbr.* **art. 1.** Made by man, rather than occurring in nature. **2.** Made in imitation of something natural. **3.** Feigned; pretended. **4.** Stilted; forced. [Middle English, from Old French, from Latin *artificiālis,* from *artificium,* ARTIFICE.] —**ar′ti·fi′ci·al′i·ty** (är′tə-fĭsh′ē-ăl′ə-tē) *n.* —**ar′ti·fi′cial·ly** *adv.*

Synonyms: *artificial, synthetic, ersatz, simulated, spurious, specious, counterfeit, supposititious.* These adjectives mean not genuine. *Artificial,* broad in meaning and connotation, refers to things resulting from human effort, as distinguished from preexisting nature or character. *Synthetic* applies to a substance designed to appear or function like the original, often with certain advantages. An *ersatz* product is a transparently inferior, often pretentious, imitation. The remaining terms invariably imply fraud. *Simulated* refers to what is not real or true but is intentionally made to appear so. *Spurious* roughly means fraudulent, while *specious* adds the sense of attractiveness or seductiveness: *a spurious document; specious arguments of the Devil. Counterfeit* strongly implies imitation with intent to defraud; *supposititious* suggests the insertion of that which is fraudulent.

artificial horizon. An instrument displaying a line on a flight indicator that lies within the horizontal plane, and about which the pitching and banking movements of an airplane are shown.

artificial insemination. The introduction of semen into the female reproductive organs without sexual contact.

artificial pacemaker. An implanted or external battery-powered device that electrically stimulates and regulates the contraction of the heart in the absence of normal heart function.

artificial respiration. Any of various methods restoring normal breathing in an asphyxiated but living person, usually by rhythmic forcing of air into and out of the lungs.

ar·til·ler·ist (är-tĭl′ər-ĭst) *n.* An artilleryman; gunner.

ar·til·ler·y (är-tĭl′ər-ē) *n. Abbr.* **art., arty. 1.** Large-caliber firing weapons, such as howitzers, cannons, and missile launchers on suitable mounts, which are too heavy to carry and are served by crews. **2.** Troops armed with such guns. **3.** The branch of an armed force that specializes in the use of large, mounted guns. **4.** The science of the use of guns; gunnery. **5.** Catapults, crossbows, slings, and similar devices for discharging missiles. [Middle English *artil(le)rie,* from Old French *artillerie,* from *artillier,* alteration (influenced by *art,* ART) of *atillier,* to fortify, arm, from Latin *apticulāre* (unattested), from *aptāre,* to fit, adapt, from *aptus,* fitting, APT.]

ar·til·ler·y·man (är-tĭl′ər-ē-mən) *n., pl.* **-men** (-mĭn). A soldier in the artillery; an artillerist.

artillery plant. A tropical American plant, *Pilea muscosa,* that releases its pollen with an explosive discharge.

ar·ti·o·dac·tyl (är′tē-ō-dăk′təl) *n.* Any of various hoofed mammals of the order Artiodactyla, which includes cattle, deer, camels, hippopotamuses, and others, having an even number of toes, either two or four, on each foot. —*adj.* Of or belonging to the Artiodactyla. [From New Latin *Artiodactyla,* "the even-toed ones" : Greek *artios,* even, matching (see **ar-** in Appendix*) + DACTYL.] —**ar′ti·o·dac′ty·lous** *adj.*

ar·ti·san (är′tə-zən, -sən) *n.* A person manually skilled in making a particular product; craftsman. [Old French, from Italian *artigiano,* from Vulgar Latin *artitiānus* (unattested), a skilled laborer, from Latin *artītus,* skilled in arts, from *artīre,* to instruct in the arts, from *ars* (stem *art-*), art.]

art·ist (är′tĭst) *n. Abbr.* **art. 1.** One who creates works of art; especially, a painter or sculptor. **2.** Any person who performs his work as if it were an art. **3.** An artiste. [Old French *artiste,* from Medieval Latin *artista,* a student of the liberal arts, Master of Arts, from *ars* (stem *art-*), ART.]

ar·tiste (är-tēst′) *n.* A public performer or entertainer, especially a singer or dancer. [French, from Old French, ARTIST.]

ar·tis·tic (är-tĭs′tĭk) *adj.* **1.** Of, relating to, or befitting art or artists. **2.** Appreciative of or sensitive to art or beauty. —**ar·tis′ti·cal·ly** *adv.*

art·ist·ry (är′tĭs-trē) *n.* **1.** Artistic ability, quality, or workmanship. **2.** The practice or occupation of an artist.

art·less (ärt′lĭs) *adj.* **1.** Without guile, cunning, or deceit; ingenuous; naive. **2.** Free of artificiality; natural; simple. **3.** Lacking art or skill; crude. **4.** Uncultured; ignorant. —See Synonyms at **naive.** —**art′less·ly** *adv.* —**art′less·ness** *n.*

art nou·veau (ärt nōō-vō′). A style of decoration and architecture first current in the 1890's, characterized by linear depiction of sinuous, floral forms. [French, "new art."]

Ar·tois (är-twä′). A region and former province of northern France.

art song. A lyric song intended to be sung in recital, and usually accompanied by a piano.

art·work (ärt′wûrk′) *n.* **1.** Work in the graphic or plastic arts; especially, the hand-making of small decorative or artistic objects. **2.** *Printing.* **a.** Illustrative and decorative matter, as distinguished from text. **b.** Both illustrative matter and type proofs, arranged on a mechanical to be sent to the printer.

art·y (är′tē) *adj.* **-ier, -iest.** *Informal.* Ostentatious or affected in trying to appear artistic. —**art′i·ly** *adv.* —**art′i·ness** *n.*

arty. artillery.

A·ru·ba (ə-rōō′bə). An island, about 70 square miles in area, of the Netherlands Antilles, 20 miles north of the coast of Venezuela. Population, 59,000.

ar·um (âr′əm) *n.* **1.** Any of various plants of the genus *Arum,* having arrow-shaped leaves and small flowers on a spadix surrounded by or enclosed within a spathe. **2.** Any of several similar or related plants, such as the **calla** *(see).* In this sense, usually called "arum lily." [New Latin *Arum,* from Latin *arum,* cuckoopint, from Greek *aron*†.]

a·run·di·na·ceous (ə-rŭn′də-nā′shəs) *adj. Rare.* Of, pertaining to, or resembling a reed; reedlike. [Latin *arundināceus,* from *(h)arundō*†, reed.]

a·rus·pex. Variant of **haruspex.**

A·ru·wi·mi (ä′rə-wē′mē). A river of the Congo (Kinshasa), rising in the northeast near Lake Albert as the Ituri and flowing about 800 miles generally west to the Congo River.

ARV American (Standard) Revised Version.

-ary. Indicates of, engaged in, or connected with; for example, **functionary, parliamentary, reactionary.** [Middle English *-arie,* from Old French *-arie, -aire,* from Latin *-ārius, -āria, -ārium,* noun suffixes, from *-ārius,* adjective suffix.]

Ar·y·an (âr′ē-ən) *n.* Also **Ar·i·an. 1.** A member of the prehistoric people that spoke Proto-Indo-European. **2.** A member of any of the peoples descended from this people, especially: **a.** One of the prehistoric speakers of Indo-Iranian, Common Indic, or Common Iranian. **b.** Any speaker of an Indic or of an Iranian language in historical times. **3.** Proto-Indo-European, or a language or language group descended from it, especially Indo-Aryan. **4.** In Nazi ideology, a Caucasian gentile, especially of Nordic type. —*adj.* Of or pertaining to Aryans or their culture or language. [Sanskrit *ārya* (adjective and noun), noble, Aryan. See **aryo-** in Appendix.*]

Usage: *Aryan* is not a technical linguistic or anthropological term, in any of its senses.

ar·y·te·noid (ăr′ə-tē′noid′, ə-rĭt′n-oid′) *adj. Anatomy.* **1.** Of or pertaining to either of two small cartilages attached to the back of the larynx and to the vocal cords. **2.** Of or pertaining to any of three small muscles of the larynx. —*n.* An arytenoid cartilage or muscle. [From New Latin *arytaenoides,* from Greek *(khondros) arutainoeidēs,* "the ladle-shaped (cartilage)" : *arutaina,* ladle, from *aruein*†, to draw water + -OID.] —**ar′y·te·noi′dal** *adj.*

as[1] (ăz, əz) *adv.* **1.** To the same extent or degree; equally. **2.** For instance: *large carnivores, as the bear or lion.* —*conj.* **1.** To the same degree or quantity that. Often used as the consequent in correlative constructions: *as sweet as sugar; not so bad as you suggest.* See Usage note below. **2.** In the same manner or way that: *Think as I think.* **3.** At the same time that; while. **4.** Since; because. See Usage note below. **5.** With the result or for the reason that: *He studied so as to learn.* **6.** Though: *Great as Milton was, he proved a bad model.* **7.** *Informal.* That: *I don't know as I can.* See Usage note below. —**as for** (or **to**). With

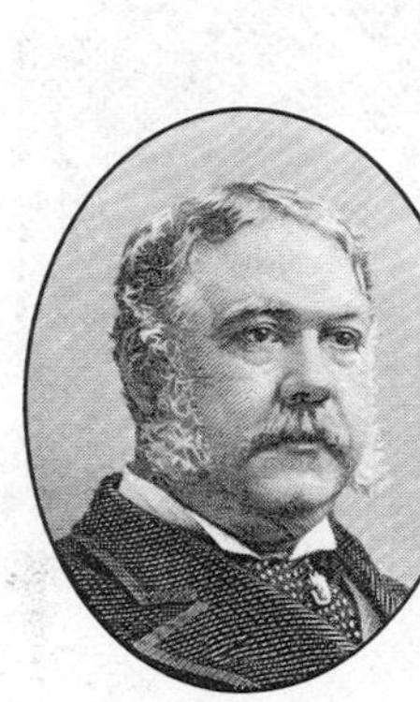

Chester A. Arthur

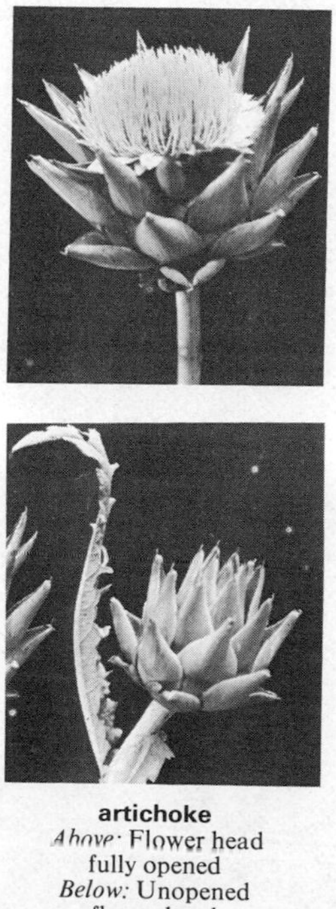

artichoke
Above: Flower head fully opened
Below: Unopened flower head

regard to; concerning. **—as if** (or **though**). In the same way that it would be if. **—as is.** *Informal.* Just the way it is; without making changes. *—pron.* **1.** That; which; who: *I received the same grade as you.* See Usage note below. **2.** A fact that: *The sun is hot, as everyone knows.* **3.** *Regional.* Who or which: *Those as want to can come with me.* *—prep.* In the role, capacity, or function of: *acting as a mediator.* See Usage note below. [Middle English *as, alse, alswa* (adverb and conjunction), Old English *alswā, ealswā, aelswā,* just as, likewise, ALSO.]

Usage: Either *as . . . as* or *so . . . as* may be used in negative comparisons: *She is not as tall* (or *not so tall*) *as her sister.* Though some grammarians prescribe only *so . . . as* in such constructions, either form is acceptable to 57 per cent of the Usage Panel. In positive comparisons, *as . . . as* is the usual construction. Especially in written usage, *as* should be expressed twice in the following typical constructions, to indicate comparison: *This winter is as bad as last, or worse* (not *as bad or worse than last*). *He is as bright as, or brighter than, his brother* (not *as bright or brighter than*). When *as* is used in the sense of *since* or *because,* care must be taken to avoid ambiguity; the following could be taken as a mere reference to time: *I did not hear him enter as I was studying* (preferably *because I was studying*). In all but deliberately informal contexts, *as* is improper for *that, if,* or *whether: We are not sure as we will* (properly *that, if,* or *whether we will*). As a relative pronoun, *as* is properly employed when preceded by *same* or *such,* or in the sense of *a fact that.* In the following example, therefore, it is used loosely: *The treasurer has no veto power, as is held by the president* (properly *such as is held*). When *as* is a preposition (sense of being in the role of) it is invariably followed by a noun or pronoun in the objective case. Otherwise the case of pronouns following *as,* or *as to,* may be nominative or objective, depending on the function of the pronouns: *You like her as much as I* (that is, *as much as I like her*). *You like her as much as me* (that is, *as much as you like me*). See Usage notes at **because, like, well.**

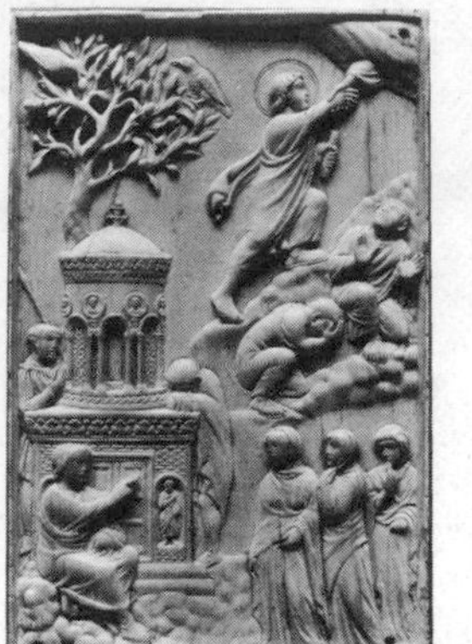

the Ascension
Fifth-century A.D.
ivory panel

as² (ăs) *n., pl.* **asses** (ăs′ēz′, ăs′ĭz). **1.** An ancient Roman coin of copper or copper alloy. **2.** A unit of weight in ancient Rome equal to about one troy pound. [Latin *ās,* a whole, unit, copper coin, possibly from Etruscan.]

As The symbol for the element arsenic.

AS 1. Anglo-Saxon. **2.** antisubmarine.

As. Asia; Asian.

AS., A.S. Anglo-Saxon.

ASA, A.S.A. American Standards Association.

as·a·fet·i·da (ăs′ə-fĕt′ə-də) *n.* Also **as·a·foet·i·da.** A yellow-brown, bitter, offensive-smelling resinous material obtained from the roots of several plants of the genus *Ferula,* formerly used in medicine. [Middle English *asa-fetida,* from Medieval Latin *asafoetida* : *asa,* gum, from Persian *azā*† + Latin *foetida,* feminine of *foetidus,* smelly, FETID.]

A·sa·hi·ga·wa (ä-sä′hē-gä′wä). Also **A·sa·hi·ka·wa** (-kä′wä). A city in central Hokkaido, Japan. Population, 247,000.

A·sa·ma, Mount (ä-sä′mä). An active volcano, 8,340 feet high, in central Honshu, Japan, about 90 miles northwest of Tokyo.

as·a·rum (ăs′ə-rəm) *n.* The dried, strong-scented roots of the wild ginger, *Asarum canadense,* formerly used in medicine and as a flavoring agent. [New Latin, from Latin, wild spikenard, from Greek *asaron*†.]

as·bes·tos (ăs-bĕs′təs, ăz-) *n.* Also **as·bes·tus** (-təs). *Abbr.* **asb.** Either of two incombustible chemical-resistant fibrous mineral forms of impure magnesium silicate, used for fireproofing, electrical insulation, building materials, brake linings, and chemical filters. *—adj.* Of, made of, or containing asbestos. [Latin, an incombustible fiber, probably amianthus, erroneous use of Greek, unslaked lime, from *asbestos,* inextinguishable : *a-,* not + *sbennunai,* to extinguish (see **gwes-** in Appendix*).] **—as·bes′tine** (-tĭn), **as·bes′tic** *adj.*

as·bes·to·sis (ăs′bĕs-tō′sĭs, ăz′-) *n.* Chronic lung inflammation caused by prolonged inhalation of asbestos particles. [New Latin : ASBEST(OS) + -OSIS.]

As·bur·y (ăz′bĕr′ē, -bər-ē), **Francis.** 1745–1816. English Protestant missionary; first bishop of the American Methodists.

ASCAP, A.S.C.A.P. American Society of Composers, Authors, and Publishers.

as·ca·ri·a·sis (ăs′kə-rī′ə-sĭs) *n.* Infestation with nematode worms of the species *Ascaris lumbricoides,* usually in the intestines, but also in the liver, lungs, or stomach. [New Latin : Late Latin *ascaris,* ASCARID + -IASIS.]

as·ca·rid (ăs′kə-rĭd) *n.* Any of various nematode worms of the family Ascaridae, such as the common intestinal parasite *Ascaris lumbricoides.* [Late Latin *ascaris* (stem *ascarid-*), intestinal worm, from Greek *askaris*†.]

as·cend (ə-sĕnd′) *v.* **-cended, -cending, -cends.** *—intr.* **1.** To go or move upward; rise. **2.** To rise gradually. **3.** To slope upward. *—tr.* To move upward upon or along; climb. —See Synonyms at **rise.** [Middle English *ascenden,* from Latin *ascendere* : *ad-,* toward + *scandere,* to climb (see **skand-** in Appendix*).] **—as·cend′a·ble, as·cend′i·ble** *adj.*

as·cen·dan·cy (ə-sĕn′dən-sē) *n.* Also **as·cen·den·cy, as·cen·dance** (-dəns), **as·cen·dence.** The state of being in the ascendant; domination: *"Germany only awaits trade revival to gain an immense mercantile ascendancy."* (Winston Churchill).

as·cen·dant (ə-sĕn′dənt) *adj.* Also **as·cen·dent.** **1.** Inclining or moving upward; ascending; rising. **2.** Dominant in position or influence; superior. *—n.* **1.** The position or state of being dominant or in power: *in the ascendant.* **2.** *Astrology.* The section of the zodiac that rises in the east at the time of a particular event, as a person's birth. **3.** *Rare.* An ancestor.

as·cend·er (ə-sĕn′dər) *n.* **1.** One that ascends. **2.** *Printing.* **a.** The part of certain lower-case letters that extends above most other lower-case letters. **b.** Any letter containing such a part, as *d, f,* or *k.*

as·cend·ing (ə-sĕn′dĭng) *adj.* Going, growing, or moving upward: *a tree with ascending branches.* **—as·cend′ing·ly** *adv.*

as·cen·sion (ə-sĕn′shən) *n.* **1.** The act or process of ascending; ascent. **2.** *Astronomy.* The rising of a star above the horizon. **—the Ascension.** *Theology.* The ascent of Christ into heaven, celebrated on Ascension Day, the 40th day after Easter. Acts 1:9. [Middle English *ascencion,* from Latin *ascensiō,* from *ascendere,* ASCEND.] **—as·cen′sion·al** *adj.*

Ascension Island. A British island, 34 square miles in area, in the South Atlantic about 700 miles northwest of St. Helena with which it is administered. Population, 500.

as·cent (ə-sĕnt′) *n.* **1.** The act or process of ascending. **2.** An advancement, especially in social status. **3.** An upward slope or incline. **4.** A going back in time or genealogical succession. [From ASCEND (by analogy with DESCEND, DESCENT).]

as·cer·tain (ăs′ər-tān′) *tr.v.* **-tained, -taining, -tains.** **1.** To discover through examination or experimentation; find out. **2.** *Archaic.* To make certain and definite. [Middle English *ascertainen,* from Old French *acertainer, acertener* : *a-,* from Latin *ad-,* to + *certain,* CERTAIN.] **—as′cer·tain′a·ble** *adj.* **—as′cer·tain′a·ble·ness** *n.* **—as′cer·tain′a·bly** *adv.* **—as′cer·tain′ment** *n.*

as·cet·ic (ə-sĕt′ĭk) *n.* A person who renounces the comforts of society and leads a life of austere self-discipline, especially as an act of religious devotion. *—adj.* Also **as·cet·i·cal** (-ĭ-kəl). Pertaining to or characteristic of an ascetic; self-denying; austere. See Synonyms at **severe.** [Greek *askētikos,* from *askētēs,* hermit, "one who practices an art," from *askein*†, to work.] **—as·cet′i·cal·ly** *adv.*

as·cet·i·cism (ə-sĕt′ə-sĭz′əm) *n.* **1.** Ascetic practice or discipline. **2.** A doctrine or theory supporting this practice, such as the belief that the ascetic life releases the soul from bondage to the body and permits union with the divine.

Asch (ăsh), **Sholem.** 1880–1957. Polish-born American novelist and dramatist; wrote in Yiddish and English.

As·cham (ăs′kəm), **Roger.** 1515–1568. English humanist writer and scholar; tutor to Queen Elizabeth I.

as·cid·i·an (ə-sĭd′ē-ən) *n.* Any of various saclike marine animals of the class Ascidiacea, which includes the sea squirts. *—adj.* Of or belonging to the Ascidiacea. [From New Latin *Ascidia* (genus name), from Greek *askidion,* little wineskin, from *askos,* wine-skin. See **ascus.**]

as·cid·i·um (ə-sĭd′ē-əm) *n., pl.* **-ia** (-ē-ə). *Botany.* A sac-shaped or bottle-shaped part or organ, such as a leaf of a pitcher plant. [New Latin, from Greek *askidion,* little wineskin, from *askos,* wineskin. See **ascus.**]

as·ci·tes (ə-sī′tēz) *n.* An abnormal accumulation of serous fluid in the abdominal cavity. [Middle English *aschytes,* from Late Latin *ascītēs,* from Greek *askitēs,* from *askos,* bag, belly. See **ascus.**] **—as·cit′ic, as·cit′i·cal** *adj.*

As·cle·pi·us (ăs-klē′pē-əs). *Greek Mythology.* Apollo's son, the god of medicine, identified with the Roman Aesculapius.

asco–. Indicates a saclike or bladderlike part; for example, **ascospore.** [New Latin, from Greek *askos,* bag, bladder. See **ascus.**]

as·co·carp (ăs′kə-kärp′) *n.* *Botany.* A globular structure containing the spore sacs of ascomycetous fungi. [ASCO- + -CARP.] **—as′co·carp′ous** *adj.*

as·co·go·ni·um (ăs′kə-gō′nē-əm) *n., pl.* **-nia** (-nē-ə). *Botany.* A female reproductive structure of certain fungi. [New Latin : ASCO- + -GONIUM.] **—as′co·go′ni·al** *adj.*

as·co·my·cete (ăs′kō-mī′sēt′, -mī′sēt′) *n.* *Botany.* Any of numerous fungi that produce spores in a saclike structure, or ascus. [New Latin *Ascomycetes* : ASCO- + -MYCETE.] **—as′co·my·ce′tous** *adj.*

a·scor·bic acid (ə-skôr′bĭk). A white, crystalline vitamin, $C_6H_8O_6$, found in citrus fruits, tomatoes, potatoes, and leafy green vegetables. It is used to prevent scurvy. Also called "vitamin C." [A- (not) + SCORB(UT)IC.]

as·co·spore (ăs′kə-spôr′, -spōr′) *n.* *Botany.* A sexual spore formed in an ascus. **—as′co·spo′rous** (ăs′kə-spôr′əs, -spōr′əs, ăs-kŏs′pər-əs), **as′co·spor′ic** (-spôr′ĭk, -spŏr′ĭk) *adj.*

as·cot (ăs′kət, -kŏt′) *n.* A kind of scarf or necktie, knotted so that its broad ends are laid flat upon each other. [Said to have been popularized at ASCOT.]

As·cot (ăs′kət). A village of Berkshire, England, near which a famous horse race is held annually.

as·cribe (ə-skrīb′) *tr.v.* **-cribed, -cribing, -cribes.** **1.** To attribute to a specified cause, source, or origin: *"the process which ascribes the Homeric poems to another poet of the same name."* (Charles H. Haskins). **2.** To assign as an attribute. —See Synonyms at **attribute.** [Middle English *ascriben,* from Latin *ascrībere,* to add to in writing : *ad-,* in addition + *scrībere,* to write (see **skeri-** in Appendix*).] **—as·crib′a·ble** *adj.*

as·crip·tion (ə-skrĭp′shən) *n.* **1.** The act of ascribing. **2.** A statement that ascribes. [Latin *ascrīptiō,* from *ascrībere,* ASCRIBE.]

as·cus (ăs′kəs) *n., pl.* **asci** (ăs′ī′, -kī′). *Botany.* A membranous sac in certain fungi, containing ascospores. [New Latin, from Greek *askos*†, wineskin, bag, bladder, belly.]

as·dic (ăz′dĭk) *n.* A sonar device used in antisubmarine warfare. [A(NTI-)S(UBMARINE) D(ETECTION) I(NVESTIGATION) C(OMMITTEE).]

–ase. *Chemistry.* Indicates an enzyme; for example, **amylase.** [From (DIAST)ASE.]

a·sea (ə-sē′) *adv.* Toward or on the sea; at sea.

a·sep·sis (ā-sĕp′sĭs) *n.* The state of being free of pathogenic organisms. Compare **antisepsis**. [A- (without) + SEPSIS.]

a·sep·tic (ā-sĕp′tĭk) *adj.* **1.** Of or pertaining to asepsis. **2.** Lacking animation or emotion: *aseptic smile.* [A- (not) + SEPTIC.]

a·sex·u·al (ā-sĕk′sho͞o-əl) *adj.* **1.** Having no evident sex or sex organs; sexless. **2.** Pertaining to or characterizing reproduction involving a single individual, and without male or female gametes, as in binary fission or budding. [A- (not) + SEXUAL.] —**a·sex′u·al′i·ty** *n.* —**a·sex′u·al·ly** *adv.*

As·gard (ăs′gärd′, äz′-). Also **As·garth** (-gärth′), **As·gar·dhr** (ăs′gär′thr′). *Norse Mythology.* The heavenly residence of the gods and slain heroes of war.

asgd. assigned.

asgmt. assignment.

ash[1] (ăsh) *n.* **1.** The grayish-white to black, soft solid residue of combustion. **2.** *Geology.* Pulverized particulate matter ejected by volcanic eruption. **3.** *Plural.* Ruins. **4.** *Plural.* Human remains, especially after cremation. [Middle English *asshe,* Old English *asce, æsce.* See **as-** in Appendix.*]

ash[2] (ăsh) *n.* **1.** Any of various trees of the genus *Fraxinus,* having compound leaves, clusters of small greenish flowers, and winged seeds. **2.** The durable, close-grained, elastic wood of any of these trees. [Middle English *asshe,* Old English *æsc.* See **os-** in Appendix.*]

a·shamed (ə-shāmd′) *adj.* **1.** Feeling shame or guilt. **2.** Reluctant through fear of shame. [Middle English *ashamed,* Old English *āscamod,* past participle of *āscamian,* to feel shame : *ā-,* intensively + *scamian,* to be ashamed (see **kem-**[1] in Appendix*).] —**a·sham′ed·ly** (ə-shā′mĭd-lē) *adv.* —**a·sham′ed·ness** *n.*

A·shan·ti[1] (ə-shăn′tē, ə-shän′-). A former kingdom and British protectorate of western Africa, now a region of central Ghana. Population, 1,109,000.

A·shan·ti[2] (ə-shăn′tē, ə-shän′-) *n., pl.* **Ashanti** or **-tis.** **1.** An inhabitant of Ashanti. **2.** A language, **Twi** *(see).*

Ash·bur·ton (ăsh′bûr′tən). A river of Western Australia, flowing about 220 miles northwest to the Indian Ocean.

ash can. **1.** A large receptacle, usually of metal, for ashes or trash. **2.** *Slang.* A depth charge.

ash·en[1] (ăsh′ən) *adj.* **1.** Consisting of ashes. **2.** Resembling ashes in color or texture.

ash·en[2] (ăsh′ən) *adj.* Of, pertaining to, or made from the wood of the ash tree.

Ash·er[1] (ăsh′ər). A son of Jacob. Genesis 49:20.

Ash·er[2] (ăsh′ər) *n.* The tribe of Israel descended from Asher.

Ashe·ville (ăsh′vĭl′, -vəl). A commercial city and tourist resort in western North Carolina. Population, 60,000.

A·shi·ka·ga (ä′shē-kä′gä). A city and weaving-industry center of Japan, on Honshu north of Tokyo. Population, 150,000.

Ash·ke·naz·i (äsh′kə-nä′zē, -năz′ē) *n., pl.* **-nazim** (-năz′ĭm, -nä′zĭm). A central or eastern European Jew, generally Yiddish-speaking. Compare **Sephardi.** —**Ash′ke·naz′ic** *adj.*

Ash·kha·bad (ăsh′kə-băd, -bäd′). Formerly **Pol·to·ratsk** (pəl-tŭ-rätsk′). The capital of the Turkmen S.S.R., situated in a fertile oasis near the Iranian border. Population, 226,000.

ash·lar (ăsh′lər) *n.* Also **ash·ler.** **1.** A squared block of building stone. **2.** Masonry of such stones. **3.** A thin, dressed rectangle of stone for facing walls. In this sense, also called "ashlar veneer." [Middle English *asheler,* from Old French *aisselier,* beam, from Latin *axilla,* diminutive of *axis,* board, plank, probably variant of *assis,* akin to *asser*†, beam.]

ash-leaved maple (ăsh′lēvd′). A tree, the **box-elder** *(see).*

a·shore (ə-shôr′, ə-shōr′) *adv.* **1.** Toward or on the shore. **2.** On land; aground.

ash·plant (ăsh′plănt′) *n.* A staff or walking stick made from an ash sapling.

Ash·to·reth (ăsh′tə-rĕth′). The ancient Syrian and Phoenician goddess of sexual love and fertility. Identified with Astarte.

ash·tray (ăsh′trā′) *n.* A receptacle for tobacco ashes.

A·shur (ä′sho͝or′). Also **As·shur, As·sur, A·sur.** *Assyrian Mythology.* The principal deity and god of war and empire.

A·shur·ba·ni·pal (ä′sho͝or-bä′nə-päl′). Also **As·sur·ba·ni·pal** (ä′so͝or-, ä′sho͝or-). King of Assyria (669–26 B.C.).

Ash Wednesday. The seventh Wednesday before Easter and the first day of Lent, on which Roman Catholics customarily place ashes on the forehead in token of penitence.

ash·y (ăsh′ē) *adj.* **-ier, -iest.** **1.** Pertaining to, resembling, or covered with ashes. **2.** Having the color of ashes; pallid; pale.

A·sia (ā′zhə, ā′shə). *Abbr.* **As.** The largest of the earth's continents (16,900,000 square miles), occupying the eastern part of the Eurasian land mass and adjacent islands, and separated from Europe by the Ural Mountains. Population, 1,852,946,000. [Latin, from Greek, "region of the rising sun," from Akkadian *āṣū,* to go out, (of the sun) to set, akin to Hebrew *yātzā′,* went out.]

A·sia Minor (ā′zhə, ā′shə). Formerly **An·a·to·li·a** (ăn′ə-tō′lĭ-ə, -tōl′yə). The western peninsula of Asia, lying between the Black Sea and the Mediterranean and including Asian Turkey.

A·sian (ā′zhən, ā′shən) *adj. Abbr.* **As.** Of or pertaining to Asia or its people. —*n.* A native or inhabitant of Asia.

A·si·at·ic (ā′zhē-ăt′ĭk) *adj.* Asian. —*n.* An Asian.

Asiatic cholera. A disease, a form of **cholera** *(see).*

a·side (ə-sīd′) *adv.* **1.** On or to one side. **2.** Out of one's thoughts or mind; away from consideration: *Put doubts aside.* **3.** On reserve. **4.** Apart; dispensed with: *all joking aside.* —**aside from.** Excluding; excepting. —*n.* **1.** A piece of dialogue that other actors on stage are supposed by dramatic convention not to hear. **2.** A parenthetical departure; digression.

As·i·mov (ăz′ə môf′), **Isaac.** Born 1920. Russian-born American biochemist, educator, and writer.

as·i·nine (ăs′ə-nīn′) *adj.* Like an ass; obstinately stupid or silly; doltish. [Latin *asininus,* from *asinus,* ass. See **asinus** in Appendix.*] —**as′i·nine′ly** *adv.* —**as′i·nin′i·ty** (-nĭn′ə-tē) *n.*

A·sir (ä-sēr′). A mountainous area of southwestern Saudi Arabia on the Red Sea.

ask (ăsk, äsk) *v.* **asked, asking, asks.** —*tr.* **1.** To put a question to. **2.** To seek information about; inquire about. **3.** To request of or for; solicit. **4. a.** To require or call for. **b.** To expect or demand: *ask too much of a child.* **5.** To invite. **6.** *Archaic.* To publish, as marriage banns. —*intr.* **1.** To inquire. Used with *about, after,* or *for.* **2.** To make a request. Often used with *for.* [Middle English *asken, axen,* Old English *āscian, ācsian.* See **ais-** in Appendix.*] —**ask′er** *n.*

Synonyms: *ask, question, inquire, query, interrogate, examine, quiz.* These verbs mean to seek information. *Ask* is the most widely applicable. *Question* implies continuous and careful asking during a given period. *Inquire* may refer to a simple act of asking, but often implies a comprehensive search for information. *Query* usually suggests questioning to settle a doubt. *Interrogate,* a more formal word, applies especially to official questioning. *Examine* refers to close and detailed questioning, and *quiz* to oral or written examination of students.

a·skance (ə-skăns′) *adv.* Also **a·skant** (ə-skănt′). **1.** With a side or oblique glance; sidewise. **2.** With disapproval, suspicion, or distrust. [Earlier *a scanche, a sca(u)nce, a sconce,* obliquely, from Middle English *ascaunce, ascaunces,* "as if to say," "so to speak" : AS + *quances,* as if, from Old French *quanses,* from Medieval Latin *quam si,* alteration of Latin *quasi,* as if, QUASI.]

a·skew (ə-skyo͞o′) *adj.* Crooked; oblique. —*adv.* **1.** To one side; obliquely; awry. **2.** With a sidelong look of contempt; disdainfully. [A- (on) + SKEW.]

a·slant (ə-slănt′, ə-slänt′) *adj.* Oblique; slanting. —*adv.* At a slant; obliquely. —*prep.* Obliquely over or across; athwart.

a·sleep (ə-slēp′) *adj.* **1.** Sleeping. **2.** Inactive; dormant. **3.** Numb: *My leg is asleep.* **4.** Dead: *"concerning them which are asleep . . . sorrow not"* (I Thessalonians 4:13). —*adv.* Into a condition of sleep.

a·slope (ə-slōp′) *adv.* At a slope or slant. —*adj.* Sloping.

As·ma·ra (äz-mä′rə). The capital of Eritrea, Ethiopia, in the southeastern part of the province. Population, 120,000.

As·mo·de·us (ăz′mə-dē′əs). In Jewish demonology, an evil spirit and king of the demons. [Latin *Asmodaeus,* from Greek *Asmodaios,* from Middle Hebrew *Ashmədhay,* from Avestan *Aēsma-daēva,* "spirit of anger" : *aēsma-,* anger (see **eis-**[1] in Appendix*) + *daēva-,* demon (see **deiw-** in Appendix*).]

As·nières (à′nyâr′). An industrial suburb northwest of Paris. Population, 82,000.

a·so·cial (ā-sō′shəl) *adj.* **1.** Avoiding the society of others; not gregarious. **2.** Inconsiderate of others; self-centered.

A·so·ka (ə-sō′kə, ə-shō′kə). Called "the Great." Died 232 B.C. King of Magadha (273–232 B.C.); expanded Indian empire; convert to and promulgator of Buddhism.

A·so·san (ä′sō-sän′). A group of five volcanic cones in central Kyushu, Japan, with the largest crater floor in the world (15 miles long and 10 miles wide).

asp[1] (ăsp) *n.* Any of several venomous Old World snakes, such as the small cobra *Naja haje,* or the horned viper *Cerastes cornutus,* both of Africa and Asia Minor. [Middle English *aspis,* from Latin, from Greek *aspis*†.]

asp[2] (ăsp) *n. Rare.* A tree, the aspen. [See **aspen.**]

as·par·a·gus (ə-spăr′ə-gəs) *n.* **1.** Any of several plants of the genus *Asparagus,* native to Eurasia, having small scales or needlelike branchlets rather than true leaves; especially, the widely cultivated species *A. officinalis.* **2.** The succulent young shoots of this plant, cooked and eaten as a vegetable. [Latin, from Greek *asparagos, aspharagos*†.]

asparagus beetle. A small, spotted beetle, *Crioceris asparagi,* that infests and damages asparagus plants.

asparagus fern. A vine, *Asparagus plumosus,* native to southern Africa, having stems with a fernlike appearance.

as·par·tic acid (ə-spär′tĭk). Also **as·pa·rag·ic acid** (ăs′pə-răj′ĭk). A nonessential amino acid, $C_4H_7NO_4$, found especially in young sugar cane and sugar-beet molasses. [Aspartic, irregularly from ASPARAGUS (because it is obtained by hydrolysis of a crystalline amino acid found in asparagus).]

As·pa·sia (ăs-pā′zhə). 470?–410 B.C. Greek courtesan; mistress of Pericles and conductor of a literary and philosophical salon.

A.S.P.C.A. American Society for the Prevention of Cruelty to Animals.

as·pect (ăs′pĕkt′) *n.* **1.** A particular facial expression; mien; air: *a matron of grim aspect.* **2.** Appearance to the eye, especially when seen from a specific view. **3.** The appearance of an idea, problem, or other object of thought as viewed by the mind: *all aspects of the case.* **4.** A position facing or commanding a given direction; exposure. **5.** A side or surface facing in a particular direction: *the ventral aspect of the body.* **6.** *Astrology.* The configuration of the stars or planets in relation to one another or to the subject. **7.** *Grammar.* A category of the verb denoting primarily the relation of the action to the passage of time, especially in reference to completion, duration, or repetition. Compare **mood.** **8.** *Archaic.* A gaze; look: *"Some other mistress hath thy sweet aspects."* (Shakespeare). —See Synonyms at **phase.** [Middle English, from Latin *aspectus,* a view, past participle of *aspicere,* look at : *ad-,* to + *specere,* to look (see **spek-** in Appendix*).]

aspect ratio. The width to height ratio of a television image.

as·pen (ăs′pən) *n.* Any of several trees of the genus *Populus,* having leaves attached by flattened leafstalks, so that they flutter readily in the wind. *P. tremuloides,* of North America, is

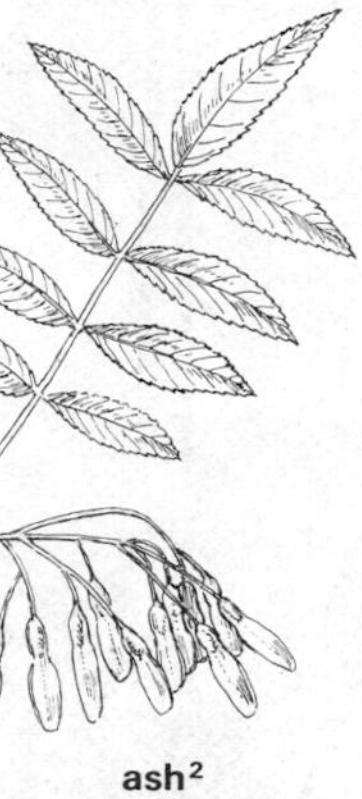

ash[2]
Fraxinus excelsior

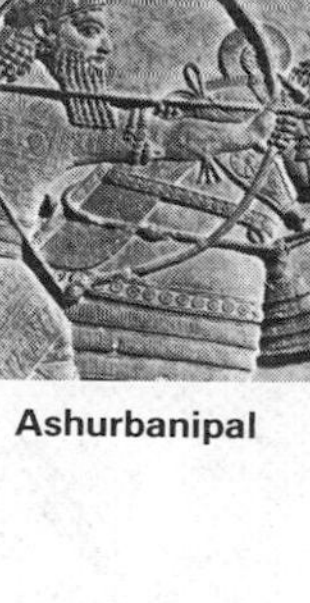

Ashurbanipal

t tight/th thin, path/*th* this, bathe/ŭ cut/ûr urge/v valve/w with/y yes/z zebra, size/zh vision/ə about, item, edible, gallop, circus/ à *Fr.* ami/œ *Fr.* feu, *Ger.* schön/ü *Fr.* tu, *Ger.* über/KH *Ger.* ich, *Scot.* loch/N *Fr.* bon. ***Follows main vocabulary.** †**Of obscure origin.**

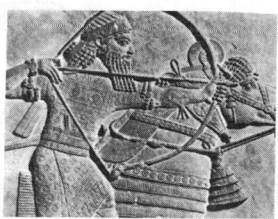

often called "quaking aspen." —*adj.* **1.** Of or relating to an aspen. **2.** Shivering or trembling like the leaves of an aspen. [Middle English *aspen*, of an aspen, from *aspe*, an aspen, Old English *æspe*. See **apsā** in Appendix.*]

As·pen (ăs′pən). A resort town in west-central Colorado, site of an annual music festival. Population, 1,000.

as·per (ăs′pər) *n.* A Turkish money of account reckoned equal to 1/20 of a piaster. [Middle English, from Italian *aspro*, from Medieval Greek *aspron*, from the neuter of *aspros*, shining, newly minted, from Latin *asper*†, rough.]

as·per·ate (ăs′pə-rāt′) *tr.v.* **-ated, -ating, -ates.** To make uneven; roughen. [Latin *asperāre*, from *asper*, rough. See **asper.**]

as·per·ges (ə-spûr′jēz) *n. Roman Catholic Church.* A short rite, preceding the High Mass on Sundays, that consists of sprinkling the altar, clergy, and congregation with holy water. [Latin *asperges (me)*, "thou shalt sprinkle (me)," first word of the rite, from *aspergere*, to sprinkle, ASPERSE.]

aspergill

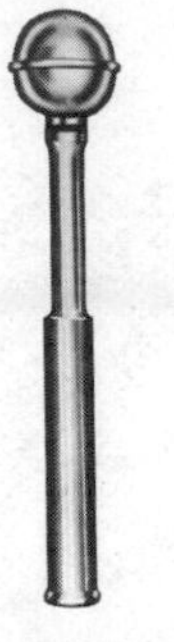

as·per·gill (ăs′pər-jĭl) *n.* Also **as·per·gil·lum** (ăs′pər-jĭl′əm) *pl.* **-la** (-lə) or **-lums.** *Roman Catholic Church.* A brush, perforated container, or other instrument used for sprinkling holy water. Also called "aspersorium." [New Latin *aspergillum*, sprinkler, from Latin *aspergere*, to sprinkle on, ASPERSE.]

as·per·gil·lo·sis (ăs-pûr′jĭ-lō′sĭs) *n.* An infectious disease of the skin, lungs, and other parts of the body, caused by certain fungi of the genus *Aspergillus*. [New Latin : ASPERGILL(US) + -OSIS.]

as·per·gil·lus (ăs′pər-jĭl′əs) *n., pl.* **-gilli** (-jĭl′ī′). Any of various fungi of the genus *Aspergillus*, which includes many common molds. [New Latin, from *aspergillum*, ASPERGILL, from its resemblance to an aspergill brush.]

as·per·i·ty (ăs-pĕr′ə-tē) *n.* **1.** Roughness or harshness, as of surface, weather, or sound. **2.** Ill temper; irritability. [Latin *asperitās*, from *asper*, rough. See **asper.**]

As·pern (äs′pərn). A suburb of Vienna, Austria, near which Napoleon was defeated by an Austrian army (1809).

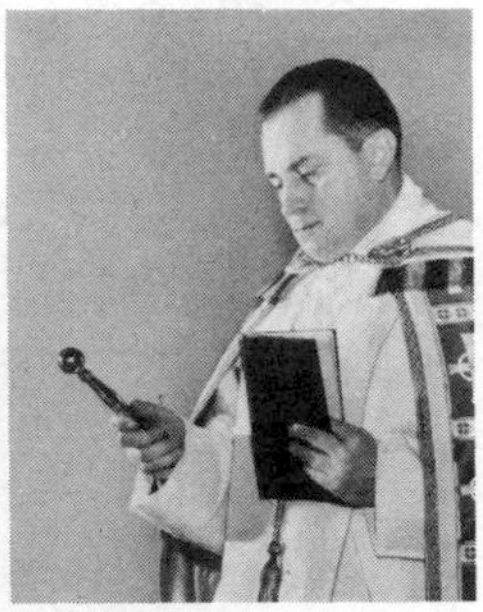

as·perse (ə-spûrs′, ă-) *tr.v.* **-persed, -persing, -perses.** **1.** To spread false charges or insinuations against; defame; slander. **2.** *Rare.* To besprinkle with water or dust. —See Synonyms at **malign.** [Latin *aspergere* (past participle *aspersus*), to sprinkle on, spatter : *ad-*, to + *spargere*, to strew, scatter (see **sphereg-** in Appendix*).] —**as·pers′er, as·per′sor** (-sər) *n.* —**as·per′sive** (-sĭv) *adj.* —**as·per′sive·ly** *adv.*

as·per·sion (ə-spûr′zhən, -shən) *n.* **1.** A calumnious report or remark; slander. **2.** The act of defaming or slandering. **3.** *Rare.* A sprinkling; especially, a baptism by sprinkling.

as·per·so·ri·um (ăs′pər-sôr′ē-əm, -sōr′ē-əm) *n., pl.* **-soria** (-sôr′ē-ə, -sōr′ē-ə) or **-ums.** *Roman Catholic Church.* **1.** A baptismal font. **2.** An **aspergill** *(see)*. [Medieval Latin, from *aspergere*, to sprinkle, ASPERSE.]

as·phalt (ăs′fôlt′) *n.* Also **as·phal·tum** (ăs-fôl′təm), **as·phal·tus** (-təs). **1.** A brownish-black solid or semisolid mixture of bitumens obtained from native deposits or as a petroleum byproduct, used in paving, roofing, and waterproofing. Also called "mineral pitch." **2.** Mixed asphalt and crushed stone gravel or sand, used for paving or roofing. —*tr.v.* **asphalted, -phalting, -phalts.** To pave or coat with asphalt. [Middle English, *asp(h)alt, aspaltoun*, from Late Latin *asphaltus*, from Greek *asphaltos, asphalton*, bitumen, pitch, asphalt, probably "binding agent (used by stone masons)" : *a-*, not + *sphallein*, to cause to fall (see **sphalerite**).] —**as·phal′tic** (ăs-fôl′tĭk) *adj.*

as·phal·tite (ăs′fôl-tīt′) *n.* A solid, dark-colored complex of hydrocarbons, found in natural veins and deposits.

a·spher·ic (ā-sfîr′ĭk, ā-sfĕr′-) *adj.* Also **a·spher·i·cal** (-ĭ-kəl). Varying slightly from sphericity and having only slight aberration. Said of lenses and other optical elements.

as·pho·del (ăs′fə-dəl′) *n.* **1.** An unidentified flower of classical legend, said to resemble the narcissus and to cover the Elysian fields. **2.** Any of several plants of the genus *Asphodeline* or the genus *Asphodelus*, of the Mediterranean region, having clusters of white or yellow flowers. [Latin *asphodelus*, from Greek *asphodelos*†.]

as·phyx·i·a (ăs-fĭk′sē-ə) *n.* Unconsciousness or death caused by lack of oxygen. [New Latin, from Greek *asphuxia*, stopping of the pulse : *a-*, not + *sphuxis*, heartbeat, pulsation, from *sphuzein*, to throb (see **sphygmic**).] —**as·phyx′i·al** *adj.*

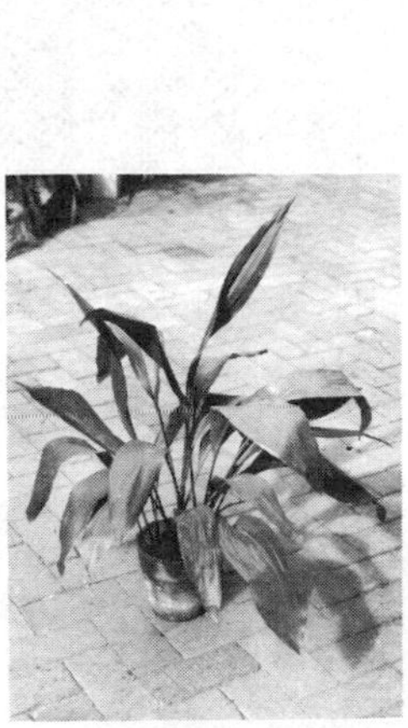

aspidistra
Aspidistra lurida

as·phyx·i·ant (ăs-fĭk′sē-ənt) *adj.* Inducing or tending to induce asphyxia. —*n.* A substance or condition that causes asphyxia.

as·phyx·i·ate (ăs-fĭk′sē-āt′) *v.* **-ated, -ating, -ates.** —*tr.* To cause asphyxia in; smother. —*intr.* To undergo asphyxia; suffocate. —**as·phyx′i·a′tion** *n.* —**as·phyx′i·a′tor** (-ā′tər) *n.*

as·pic¹ (ăs′pĭk) *n.* **1.** A cold dish of meat, fish, vegetables, or fruit combined and set in a gelatin mold. **2.** A jellied garnish of meat or fish stock and gelatin. [French *(sauce)* or *(ragoût) à l'aspic*, from *aspic*, ASPIC (snake), from the different colors of the jelly, as compared with those of the snake.]

as·pic² (ăs′pĭk) *n. Poetic & Archaic.* The asp, a poisonous snake. [Old French, from *aspe*, from Latin *aspis*, ASP (snake).]

as·pic³ (ăs′pĭk) *n. Rare.* A species of lavender, *Lavendula spica*. [French, from Old French, from Old Provençal *espic*, spike (of a grain such as barley), from Latin *spica*, spike. See **spei-** in Appendix.*]

as·pi·dis·tra (ăs′pə-dĭs′trə) *n.* Any of several Asian plants of the genus *Aspidistra;* especially, *A. lurida*, having long, tough, evergreen leaves and small brownish flowers. This species is widely cultivated as a house plant. Also called "cast-iron plant." [New Latin *Aspidistra* : Greek *aspis*† (stem *aspid-*), shield + an obscure ending.]

as·pi·rant (ăs′pər-ənt, ə-spīr′ənt) *n.* One who aspires, especially after advancement, honors, or a high position. —*adj.* **1.** Aspiring for recognition or distinction: *"I receive plenty of letters from poets aspirant."* (Southey). **2.** *Poetic.* Rising; ascending.

as·pi·rate (ăs′pə-rāt′) *tr.v.* **-rated, -rating, -rates.** **1.** *Phonetics.* **a.** To pronounce (a vowel or word) with the initial release of breath associated with English *h*, as in *Hartford*. **b.** To follow (a consonant, especially a stop consonant) with a puff of breath that is clearly audible before the next sound begins, as in English *p, t,* and *k* before vowels. **2.** *Medicine.* To remove (liquids or gases) by means of an aspirator. —*n.* (ăs′pər-ĭt). *Phonetics.* **1.** The speech sound represented by the English *h*. **2.** The puff of air accompanying the release of a stop consonant. **3.** Any speech sound followed by a puff of breath. —*adj.* (ăs′pər-ĭt). *Phonetics.* Aspirated. Said of a speech sound. [Latin *aspīrāre*, to breathe upon, aspirate : *ad-*, to + *spīrāre*, to breathe (see **spirāre** in Appendix*).]

as·pi·ra·tion (ăs′pə-rā′shən) *n.* **1.** Expulsion of breath in speech. **2.** *Phonetics.* **a.** The pronunciation of a consonant with an aspirate. **b.** An aspirate. **3.** *Medicine.* Removal of liquids or gases with an aspirator. **4. a.** A strong desire for high achievement. **b.** An object of such desire; ambitious goal.

as·pi·ra·tor (ăs′pə-rā′tər) *n.* **1.** Any device that removes liquids or gases from a space by suction, especially one used medicinally to evacuate a bodily cavity. **2.** A suction pump used to create a partial vacuum.

as·pir·a·to·ry (ə-spīr′ə-tôr′ē, -tōr′ē) *adj.* Of, concerning, or suited for breathing or suction.

as·pire (ə-spīr′) *intr.v.* **-pired, -piring, -pires.** **1.** To have a great ambition or ultimate desire. **2.** To strive toward an end; aim at: *"All art constantly aspires towards the condition of music."* (Walter Pater). **3.** *Archaic.* To rise upward; soar: *"On what wings dare he aspire?"* (Blake). [Middle English *aspiren*, from Old French *aspirer*, from Latin *aspīrāre*, to breathe upon, favor, desire, ASPIRATE.] —**as·pir′er** *n.* —**as·pir′ing·ly** *adv.*

as·pi·rin (ăs′pər-ĭn, -prĭn) *n.* **1.** A white crystalline compound of acetylsalicylic acid, $CH_3COOC_6H_4COOH$, commonly used in tablet form as an antipyretic and analgesic. **2.** A tablet of aspirin. [AC(ETYL) + *spir(aeic acid)*, old name for salicylic acid, from SPIRAEA + -IN.]

a·squint (ə-skwĭnt′) *adv.* With a sidelong glance. [Middle English : perhaps *a-* + Dutch *schuinte*†, a slope, slant, from *schuin*, sideway, slanting.] —**a·squint′** *adj.*

As·quith (ăs′kwĭth), **Herbert Henry.** First Earl of Oxford and Asquith. 1852–1928. British prime minister (1908–16).

ass¹ (ăs) *n., pl.* **asses** (ăs′ĭz). **1.** Any of several hoofed mammals of the genus *Equus*, resembling and closely related to the horses and zebras, including wild species such as the **onager** *(see)*, and the domesticated donkey. **2.** A vain, self-important, silly, or aggressively stupid person. [Middle English *asse*, Old English *assa*, from Old Irish *asan*, from Latin *asinus*. See **asinus** in Appendix.*]

ass² (ăs) *n., pl.* **asses** (ăs′ĭz). Also *chiefly British* **arse** (ärs). **1.** *Vulgar.* The buttocks. **2.** *Vulgar.* The anus. **3.** *Vulgar.* Coitus. [Earlier *arse*, Middle English *ars, ers*, Old English *aers, ears*. See **ers-** in Appendix.*]

as·sa·gai, as·se·gai (ăs′ə-gī′) *n.* **1.** A light spear or javelin, often with an iron tip, used by southern African tribesmen. **2.** A tree, *Curtisia faginea*, of southern Africa, having wood used for making such spears. [Old French *azagaie*, probably from Old Spanish *azagaya*, from Arabic *az-zaghāyah* : *al*, the + Berber *zaghāyah*, spear.]

as·sai¹ (ä-sī′) *n.* **1.** Any of several palm trees of the genus *Euterpe*, of tropical South America, having edible, fleshy purple fruit. **2.** A beverage made from this fruit. [Brazilian Portuguese *assaí*, from Tupi *assahi*.]

as·sai² (ä-sī′) *adv. Music.* Very. Used in directions: *allegro assai.* [Italian "enough," from Vulgar Latin *ad satis* (unattested), "to the point of sufficiency." See **assets.**]

as·sail (ə-sāl′) *tr.v.* **-sailed, -sailing, -sails.** **1.** To attack with or as if with violent blows; assault. **2.** To attack verbally, as with ridicule or censure. —See Synonyms at **attack.** [Middle English *asailen*, from Old French *asaillir*, from Vulgar Latin *assalīre* (unattested), variant of Latin *assilīre*, to jump on : *ad-*, to + *salīre*, to leap (see **sel-⁴** in Appendix*).] —**as·sail′a·ble** *adj.* —**as·sail′a·ble·ness** *n.* —**as·sail′er** *n.* —**as·sail′ment** *n.*

as·sail·ant (ə-sā′lənt) *n.* A person who assails another.

As·sam (ə-săm′, ă-săm′, ăs′ăm). A state of India occupying 82,276 square miles in the northeast. Population, 11,873,000. Capital, Shillong.

As·sa·mese (ăs′ə-mēz′, -mēs′) *adj.* Of or pertaining to Assam, its people, or their language. —*n., pl.* **Assamese.** **1.** A native or inhabitant of Assam. **2.** The Indo-European Indic language of the Assamese.

as·sas·sin (ə-săs′ĭn) *n.* **1.** *Capital* **A.** A member of a secret order of Moslem fanatics who terrorized and killed Christian Crusaders. **2.** A murderer, especially one who carries out a plot to kill a public official or other prominent person. [French, from Medieval Latin *assassinus*, from Arabic *ḥashshāshīn*, plural of *ḥashshāsh*, "hashish addict," from *ḥashīsh*, HASHISH.]

as·sas·si·nate (ə-săs′ə-nāt′) *tr.v.* **-nated, -nating, -nates.** **1.** To murder (a prominent person). **2.** To destroy or injure treacherously: *assassinate a rival's character.* —**as·sas′si·na′tion** *n.* —**as·sas′si·na′tive** *adj.* —**as·sas′si·na′tor** (-nā′tər) *n.*

assassin bug. Any of various predatory insects of the large family Reduviidae, having short, curved, powerful beaks adapted for sucking blood and capable of inflicting a painful bite. See **conenose, kissing bug.**

As·sa·teague Island (ăs′ə-tēg′). An island extending 33 miles along the Maryland and Virginia coasts, between Chincoteague Bay and the Atlantic Ocean.

as·sault (ə-sôlt′) *n.* **1.** A violent attack, either physical or verbal. **2.** *Military.* **a.** An attack upon a fortified area or place. **b.** The concluding stage of an attack in which there is close combat with the enemy. **3.** *Law.* An unlawful attempt or threat to injure another physically. **4.** Rape. —*v.* **assaulted, -saulting, -saults.** —*tr.* To attack or assail violently. —*intr.* To make an assault. —See Synonyms at **attack.** [Middle English *assaut,* from Old French *asaut, assaut,* from Vulgar Latin *assaltus* (unattested), variant of Latin *assultus,* past participle of *assilīre,* ASSAIL.] —**as·sault′er** *n.*

assault and battery. *Law.* The threat to use force upon another and the carrying out of the threat.

as·say (ăs′ā′, ă-sā′) *n.* **1. a.** The qualitative or quantitative analysis of a substance, especially of an ore or drug. **b.** A substance to be so analyzed. **c.** The result of such an analysis. **2.** Any analysis or examination. **3.** *Obsolete.* An attempt; essay. —*v.* (ă-sā′, ăs′ā′) **assayed, -saying, -says.** —*tr.* **1.** To subject to chemical analysis; make an assay of. **2.** To examine by trial or experiment; put to a test: *assay one's ability.* **3.** To evaluate; assess. **4.** To attempt; try. —*intr.* To be shown by analysis as having a certain proportion, usually of a precious metal. —See Synonyms at **estimate.** [Middle English, from Old French *assai, essai,* trial, ESSAY.] —**as·say′a·ble** *adj.* —**as·say′er** *n.*

as·sem·blage (ə-sĕm′blĭj) *n.* **1. a.** The act of assembling. **b.** The state of being assembled. **2.** A collection of people or things. **3.** A fitting together of parts, as of a machine. **4.** *Fine Arts.* A sculpture consisting of an arrangement of miscellaneous objects, such as scraps of metal, cloth, and string.

as·sem·ble (ə-sĕm′bəl) *v.* **-bled, -bling, -bles.** —*tr.* **1.** To bring or gather together into a group or whole. **2.** To fit or join together the parts of. —*intr.* To gather together; congregate. —See Synonyms at **gather.** [Middle English *assemblen,* from Old French *assembler,* from Vulgar Latin *assimulāre* (unattested), to bring together : Latin *ad-,* to + *simul,* together, at the same time (see **sem-¹** in Appendix*).] —**as·sem′bler** *n.*

as·sem·bly (ə-sĕm′blē) *n., pl.* **-blies.** *Abbr.* **assy. 1. a.** The act of assembling. **b.** The state of being assembled. **2.** A group of persons gathered together for a common purpose. **3.** *Capital* **A.** In certain U.S. states, the lower house of the legislature. **4. a.** The putting together of manufactured parts to make a completed product, especially a machine. **b.** A set of parts so assembled. **6.** *Military.* The signal calling troops to form ranks.

assembly line. A line of factory workers and equipment on which the product being assembled passes consecutively from operation to operation until completed.

as·sem·bly·man (ə-sĕm′blē-mən) *n., pl.* **-men** (-mĭn). A member of a legislative assembly.

as·sent (ə-sĕnt′) *intr.v.* **-sented, -senting, -sents.** To express agreement; concur. Used with *to: assent to his plan.* —*n.* **1.** Agreement, as to a proposal; compliance. **2.** Acquiescence; consent. [Middle English *assenten,* from Old French *assenter,* from Latin *assentārī,* frequentative of *assentīre,* "to join in feeling," agree with : *ad-,* toward + *sentīre,* to feel, think (see **sent-** in Appendix*).] —**as·sent′er, as·sen′tor** (ə-sĕn′tər) *n.* —**as·sent′ing·ly** *adv.* —**as·sen′tive** *adj.* —**as·sen′tive·ness** *n.*

Synonyms: *assent, agree, accede, acquiesce, accept, consent, concur, subscribe.* These verbs mean to go along with another's views, proposals, or actions. *Assent* implies saying "yes" in a formal, somewhat impersonal manner. *Agree* and *accede* are loosely related in the sense of assenting after discussion or persuasion. But *agree* suggests mutual accommodation in a meeting of minds, whereas *accede* implies yielding on the part of one person or group. *Acquiesce* suggests agreeing, despite reservations, because of unwillingness to oppose. *Accept* may indicate agreement with some reluctance. *Consent* indicates complete and voluntary personal commitment to a proposal or desire. *Concur* refers to agreement with another's position, and may suggest that one has reached the same conclusion independently. *Subscribe* indicates hearty consent or approval.

as·sen·ta·tion (ăs′ĕn-tā′shən) *n.* Ill-considered or servile agreement with another's opinions.

as·sert (ə-sûrt′) *tr.v.* **-serted, -serting, -serts. 1.** To state or express positively; affirm. **2.** To defend or maintain (one's rights, for example). —**assert oneself.** To express oneself forcefully or boldly. [Latin *asserere,* "to join to oneself," maintain, claim : *ad-,* to + *serere,* to join (see **ser-³** in Appendix*).] —**as·sert′a·ble, as·sert′i·ble** *adj.* —**as·sert′er, as·ser′tor** (ə-sûr′tər) *n.*

Synonyms: *assert, asseverate, declare, affirm, aver, avow, allege.* These verbs all mean to state; they differ principally in emphasis. To *assert* is to state one's position boldly, and to *asseverate* is to add even greater emphasis to the position taken. *Declare* has the approximate force of *assert,* but may suggest formality of statement and authority in the speaker. *Affirm* and *aver* imply less forcefulness, but stress the speaker's confidence in the validity of his statement. *Avow* emphasizes moral commitment to the statement. *Allege* refers to making a controversial charge or statement without presentation of proof.

as·ser·tion (ə-sûr′shən) *n.* **1.** The act of asserting or declaring. **2.** A declaration stated positively but with no support or attempt at proof. —**as·ser′tion·al** *adj.*

as·ser·tive (ə-sûr′tĭv) *adj.* Inclined to bold assertion; positive. —**as·ser′tive·ly** *adv.* —**as·ser′tive·ness** *n.*

as·ser·to·ry (ə-sûr′tər-ē) *adj.* Asserting or affirming; affirmative. —**as·ser′to·ri·ly** *adv.*

as·ses¹. Plural of **as** (Roman coin).

ass·es². Plural of **ass.**

as·sess (ə-sĕs′) *tr.v.* **-sessed, -sessing, -sesses. 1.** To estimate the value of (property) for taxation. **2.** To set or determine the amount of (a tax, fine, or other payment). **3.** To charge (a person or property) with a tax, fine, or other special payment. **4.** To evaluate; appraise. —See Synonyms at **estimate.** [Middle English *assessen,* from Old French *assesser,* from Latin *assidere* (past participle of *assessus*), "to sit beside," be an assistant judge : *ad-,* near to + *sedēre,* to sit (see **sed-¹** in Appendix*).] —**as·sess′a·ble** *adj.*

as·sess·ment (ə-sĕs′mənt) *n.* **1.** The act of assessing. **2.** An amount assessed.

as·ses·sor (ə-sĕs′ər) *n.* **1.** An official who makes assessments, as for taxation. **2.** An assistant to a judge, selected for his special knowledge of a particular area. **3.** Any adviser or assistant. —**as′ses·so′ri·al** (ăs′ə-sôr′ē-əl, -sōr′ē-əl) *adj.*

as·set (ăs′ĕt′) *n.* **1.** A useful or valuable quality or thing. **2.** A valuable item that is owned. [Back-formation from ASSETS.]

Synonyms: *asset, possession, belongings, effects, property, resource.* These nouns refer to things a person owns, considered as components of wealth. *Asset* technically is used in the plural and refers to an item that can be turned into cash to cover liabilities. Less narrowly the term means any valuable thing or any personal quality or trait of practical value. *Possession* usually applies to any tangible item of value ranging from small to great. *Belongings* denotes the more personal items one owns, such as clothing and jewelry. *Effects* includes belongings and, sometimes, all other movable possessions. *Property* refers broadly to any real or tangible possession. *Resource* denotes any possession on hand or in reserve and available for use; the term thus includes actual and potential wealth.

as·sets (ăs′ĕts′) *pl.n. Accounting.* The entries on a balance sheet showing all of a person's or business' properties and claims against others that may be applied, directly or indirectly, to cover liabilities. Assets include the value of tangible things, such as cash and inventory, and that of intangibles, such as a trademark or good will. [Norman French *asetz,* from Old French *asez,* "enough (to satisfy creditors)," from Vulgar Latin *ad satis* (unattested), "to the point of sufficiency," enough : Latin *ad-,* to + *satis,* sufficient (see **sā-** in Appendix*).]

as·sev·er·ate (ə-sĕv′ə-rāt′) *tr.v.* **-ated, -ating, -ates.** To declare seriously or positively; affirm. See Synonyms at **assert.** [Latin *assevērāre,* to assert earnestly : *ad-,* to + *sevērus,* earnest, serious (see **wero-** in Appendix*).] —**as·sev′er·a′tion** *n.*

As·shur. Variant of **Ashur.**

as·sib·i·late (ə-sĭb′ə-lāt′) *tr.v.* **-lated, -lating, -lates.** *Phonetics.* To make sibilant; pronounce with a hissing sound. [AD- (in addition to) + SIBILATE.] —**as·sib′i·la′tion** *n.*

as·si·du·i·ty (ăs′ə-do͞o′ə-tē, -dyo͞o′ə-tē) *n., pl.* **-ties. 1.** Close and constant application; unflagging effort; diligence. **2.** *Plural.* Constant personal attentions; solicitude.

as·sid·u·ous (ə-sĭj′o͞o-əs) *adj.* **1.** Constant in application or attention; diligent; devoted: *"He was very pious, an assiduous attendant at the sermons"* (Franklin). **2.** Unceasing; persistent. —See Synonyms at **busy.** [Latin *assiduus,* from *assidēre,* to sit beside, attend to : *ad-,* near to + *sedēre,* to sit (see **sed-¹** in Appendix*).] —**as·sid′u·ous·ly** *adv.* —**as·sid′u·ous·ness** *n.*

as·sign (ə-sīn′) *tr.v.* **-signed, -signing, -signs. 1.** To set apart for a particular purpose; designate. **2.** To select for a duty or office; appoint. **3.** To give out as a task; allot. **4.** To ascribe; attribute. **5.** *Law.* To transfer (property, rights, or interests). **6.** *Military.* To place (a unit or personnel) integrally into a particular organization. Compare **attach.** —See Synonyms at **attribute, commit.** —*n. Law.* An assignee. [Middle English *assignen,* from Old French *assigner,* from Latin *assignāre,* to mark out : *ad-,* to + *signāre,* to mark, from *signum,* sign (see **sekw-¹** in Appendix*).] —**as·sign′a·bil′i·ty** *n.* —**as·sign′a·ble** *adj.* —**as·sign′a·bly** *adv.* —**as·sign′er** *n.*

Synonyms: *assign, allot, apportion, allocate.* These verbs refer to distributing something. *Assign* applies to an authoritative act and makes no implication about equality of distribution: *assign a task. Allot* also refers to arbitrary distribution, as of money or time, usually for a specified purpose. *Apportion* refers to division according to prescribed rules, and implies fair distribution. *Allocate* usually means to set something aside from a larger quantity, particularly funds, for a specific purpose.

as·sig·nat (ăs′ĭg-năt′; *French* à-sē-nyà′) *n.* One of the notes of the paper currency issued in France (1789–96) by the revolutionary government backed by the security of confiscated lands. [French, from Latin *assignātum,* "something assigned," *assignāre,* ASSIGN.]

as·sig·na·tion (ăs′ĭg-nā′shən) *n.* **1.** The act of assigning. **2.** Something assigned; assignment. **3.** An appointment for a meeting between lovers; rendezvous; tryst.

as·sign·ee (ə-sī′nē′, ăs′ĭ-nē′) *n. Law.* **1.** A person to whom a transfer of property, rights, or interest is made. **2.** One appointed to act for another; a deputy; an agent.

as·sign·ment (ə-sīn′mənt) *n. Abbr.* **asgmt. 1.** The act of assigning. **2.** Something assigned, such as a task. **3.** A position or post of duty to which one is assigned. **4.** *Law.* **a.** The transfer of a claim, right, interest, or property. **b.** The document or deed by which this transfer is made. —See Synonyms at **task.**

as·sign·or (ə-sī′nôr′, ə-sī′nər, ăs′ə-nôr′) *n. Law.* A person who makes an assignment.

as·sim·i·la·ble (ə-sĭm′ə-lə-bəl) *adj.* Capable of being assimilated. —**as·sim′i·la·bil′i·ty** *n.*

as·sim·i·late (ə-sĭm′ə-lāt′) *v.* **-lated, -lating, -lates.** —*tr.* **1.** *Physiology.* **a.** To consume and incorporate into the body; to digest. **b.** To transform (food) into living tissue; metabolize constructively. **2.** To absorb and incorporate (knowledge, for example). **3.** To make similar; cause to assume a resemblance. **4.** *Linguistics.* To alter (a sound) by assimilation. —*intr.* To become assimilated. [Middle English *assimilaten,* from Latin *assimilāre, assimulāre,* to make similar to : *ad-,* to + *simulāre,*

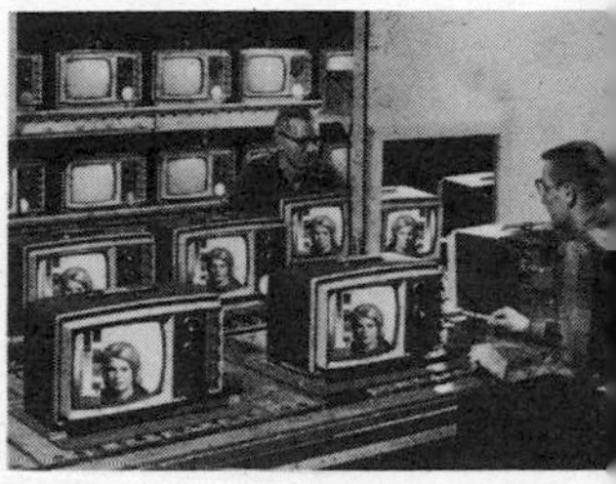

assembly line
Final assembly and testing of television sets

similāre, to simulate, from *similis,* similar (see **sem-**[1] in Appendix*).] —**as·sim′i·la′tor** (-lā′tər) *n.*

as·sim·i·la·tion (ə-sĭm′ə-lā′shən) *n.* **1. a.** The act or process of assimilating. **b.** The condition or process of being assimilated. **2.** *Biology.* The process by which nourishment is changed into living tissue; constructive metabolism. **3.** *Linguistics.* The process by which a sound is modified to make it resemble an adjacent sound. For example, the prefix *in-* in *intolerable* becomes *im-* in *impossible* by assimilation. **4.** *Sociology.* The process whereby a group, as a minority or immigrant group, gradually adopts the characteristics of another culture.

as·sim·i·la·tive (ə-sĭm′ə-lā′tĭv) *adj.* Also **as·sim·i·la·to·ry** (-lə-tôr′ē, -tōr′ē). Marked by or causing assimilation.

As·sin·i·boin (ə-sĭn′ə-boin′) *n., pl.* **Assiniboin** or **-boins. 1.** A tribe of Siouan-speaking North American Indians of northeastern Montana and adjacent regions of Canada. **2.** A member of this tribe. **3.** The language of this tribe. [French *Assiniboine,* from Ojibwa (Western dialect) *assinī-pwān,* "stone-Sioux" : Proto-Algonquian *a′seny-i* (unattested), stone + *pwātha* (unattested), enemy, Sioux.] —**As·sin′i·boin′** *adj.*

As·sin·i·boine (ə-sĭn′ə-boin′). **1.** A river in eastern Saskatchewan, Canada, flowing about 600 miles eastward to join the Red River at Winnipeg. **2.** A mountain, 11,870 feet high, in the Canadian Rocky Mountains.

As·si·si (ə-sē′zē, ə-sē′sē). A town in Umbria, central Italy; a religious center and the birthplace of St. Francis of Assissi.

as·sist (ə-sĭst′) *v.* **-sisted, -sisting, -sists.** *—tr.* To aid; help. *—intr.* **1.** To give aid or support. **2.** To be present; attend. Usually used with *at.* —See Synonyms at **help.** *—n.* **1.** An act of giving aid; help. **2. a.** *Baseball.* A handling of the ball that enables a runner to be put out. **b.** A pass of the ball or puck to the teammate scoring a goal, as in soccer or ice hockey. [Middle English *assisten,* from Old French *assister,* from Latin *assistere,* to stand beside, help : *ad-,* near to + *sistere,* to stand (see **stā-** in Appendix*).] —**as·sist′er** *n.*

as·sis·tance (ə-sĭs′təns) *n.* **1.** The act of assisting. **2.** Aid.

as·sis·tant (ə-sĭs′tənt) *n. Abbr.* **asst.** One that assists; a helper; an aide. *—adj. Abbr.* **asst. 1.** Holding an auxiliary position; subordinate. **2.** Giving aid; auxiliary.

assistant professor. A college teacher who ranks above an instructor and below an associate professor.

As·siut. See **Asyut.**

as·size (ə-sīz′) *n.* **1.** *English History.* **a.** A session of a legislative body or court. **b.** A decree or edict rendered at such a session. **2.** *English History.* **a.** An ordinance regulating weights and measures and the weights and prices of articles of consumption. **b.** The standards so set up. **3.** *English History.* A judicial inquest, the writ by which it is instituted, or the verdict of the jurors. **4.** *Plural.* One of the periodic court sessions held in each of the counties of England and Wales for the trial of civil or criminal cases. **5.** *Plural.* The time or place of such sessions. [Middle English *assise,* from Old French, feminine of *assis,* past participle of *asseior,* to seat, from Vulgar Latin *assedēre* (unattested), from Latin *assidēre,* to sit beside, be an assistant judge. See **assiduous.**]

assn. association.

assoc. associate; association.

as·so·ci·a·ble (ə-sō′shē-ə-bəl, -shə-bəl) *adj.* Capable of being associated. —**as·so′ci·a·bil′i·ty, as·so′ci·a·ble·ness** *n.*

as·so·ci·ate (ə-sō′shē-āt′, -sē-āt′) *v.* **-ated, -ating, -ates.** *—tr.* **1.** To bring into company with another; join in a relationship. **2.** To connect or join together; combine; link. **3.** To connect in the mind or imagination: *"I always somehow associate Chatterton with autumn."* (Keats). *—intr.* **1.** To join in or form a league, union, or association. **2.** To keep company. —See Synonyms at **join.** *—n.* (ə-sō′shē-ĭt, -sē-ĭt, -shē-āt′, -sē-āt′). *Abbr.* **assoc. 1.** A person united with another or others in some action, enterprise, or business; partner; colleague. **2.** A companion; comrade. **3.** Anything that habitually accompanies or is associated with another; an attendant circumstance; a concomitant. **4.** A member of an institution or society who is granted only partial status or privileges. —See Synonyms at **partner.** *—adj.* (ə-sō′shē-ĭt, -sē-ĭt, -shē-āt′, -sē-āt′). *Abbr.* **assoc. 1.** Joined with another or others and having equal or nearly equal status: *an associate editor.* **2.** Having partial status or privileges: *an associate member of the club.* **3.** Following or accompanying; concomitant. [Middle English *associaten,* from Latin *associāre,* to join to : *ad-,* to + *sociāre,* to join, from *socius,* companion (see **sekw-**[1] in Appendix*).]

associate professor. A college or university teacher who ranks below a full professor and above an assistant professor.

as·so·ci·a·tion (ə-sō′sē-ā′shən, -shē-ā′shən) *n.* **1.** The act of associating. **2.** The state of being associated. **3.** *Abbr.* **assn., assoc.** An organized body of people who have some interest, activity, or purpose in common; a society; league. **4.** A mental connection or relation between thoughts, feelings, ideas, or sensations. **5.** *Chemistry.* Any of various processes of chemical combination, such as hydration, solvation, or complex-ion formation, depending on relatively weak chemical bonding. **6.** *Ecology.* A large number of organisms in a specific area with one or two dominant species. —**as·so′ci·a′tion·al** *adj.*

association football. *Chiefly British.* **Soccer** *(see).*

as·so·ci·a·tive (ə-sō′shē-ā′tĭv, -sē-ā′tĭv, -shə-tĭv) *adj.* **1.** Of, characterized by, resulting from, or causing association. **2.** *Mathematics.* Independent of the grouping of elements. Said of mathematical operations: *If* $a + (b + c) = (a + b) + c$, *the operation indicated by* + *is associative.* —**as·so′ci·a·tive·ly** *adv.*

as·soil (ə-soil′) *tr.v.* **-soiled, -soiling, -soils.** *Rare.* **1.** To absolve or pardon. **2.** To atone for. [Middle English *assoilen,* from Old French *assoldre* (stem *assoil-*), from Latin *absolvere,* to set free from : *ab-,* away from + *solvere,* to loosen, set free (see **leu-**[1] in Appendix*).]

as·so·nance (ăs′ə-nəns) *n.* **1.** Resemblance in sound, especially in the vowel sounds of words. **2.** *Prosody.* A partial rhyme in which the accented vowel sounds correspond but the consonants differ, as in *brave* and *vain.* **3.** Rough similarity; approximate agreement. [French, from Latin *assonāns,* present participle of *assonāre,* to sound in response to : *ad-,* to + *sonāre,* to sound (see **swen-** in Appendix*).] —**as′so·nant** *adj.* & *n.*

as·sort (ə-sôrt′) *v.* **-sorted, -sorting, -sorts.** *—tr.* **1.** To separate into groups according to kinds; classify. **2.** To supply with a variety of goods. *—intr.* **1.** To fall into a class; match. **2.** To associate; consort. [Old French *assorter* : *a-,* from Latin *ad-,* to + *sorte,* kind, from Vulgar Latin *sorta* (unattested), kind, from Latin *sors* (stem *sort-*), chance, fortune, lot (see **ser-**[3] in Appendix*).] —**as·sort′a·tive** (ə-sôr′tə-tĭv) *adj.* —**as·sort′er** *n.*

as·sort·ed (ə-sôr′tĭd) *adj.* **1.** Consisting of a number of different kinds; various. **2.** Placed in classes; classified. **3.** Suited or matched. —See Synonyms at **miscellaneous.**

as·sort·ment (ə-sôrt′mənt) *n.* **1.** The act of assorting; separation into classes. **2.** A collection of various things; a variety.

As·souan, As·suan. See **Aswan.**

A.S.S.R. Autonomous Soviet Socialist Republic.

asst. assistant.

as·suage (ə-swāj′) *tr.v.* **-suaged, -suaging, -suages. 1.** To make less severe or burdensome; ease: *"assuage the anguish of your bereavement"* (Lincoln). **2.** To satisfy; appease, as thirst. **3.** To pacify or calm. —See Synonyms at **relieve.** [Middle English *aswagen,* from Old French *assouagier,* from Vulgar Latin *assuāviāre* (unattested), to add sweetness to, sweeten : *ad-,* to + *suāvis,* sweet (see **swād-** in Appendix*).] —**as·suage′ment** *n.*

as·sua·sive (ə-swā′sĭv, -zĭv) *adj.* Soothing. [AD- + *suasive,* persuasive (influenced by ASSUAGE), from Latin *suāsus,* past participle of *suādēre,* to urge (see **swād-** in Appendix*).]

as·sume (ə-so͞om′) *tr.v.* **-sumed, -suming, -sumes. 1.** To put on; don (a garment, for example). **2.** To undertake: *assuming the responsibility.* **3.** To invest oneself formally with: *assume the presidency.* **4.** To take on; adopt: *"the god assumes a human form"* (Ruskin). **5.** To feign; affect. **6.** To take for granted; suppose. **7.** *Theology.* To take up; receive, as into heaven. —See Synonyms at **presume.** [Middle English *assumen,* from Latin *assūmere,* to take to oneself, adopt : *ad-,* to + *sūmere,* to take (see **em-** in Appendix*).] —**as·sum′a·ble** *adj.* —**as·sum′a·bly** *adv.* —**as·sum′er** *n.*

as·sumed (ə-so͞omd′) *adj.* **1.** Pretended; adopted; fictitious: *an assumed name.* **2.** Taken for granted. —**as·sum′ed·ly** *adv.*

as·sum·ing (ə-so͞o′mĭng) *adj.* Presumptuous; pretentious; arrogant. —**as·sum′ing·ly** *adv.*

as·sump·sit (ə-sŭmp′sĭt) *n. Law. Rare.* **1.** An agreement or promise not under seal; a contract. **2.** A legal action to enforce or recover damages for a breach of such an agreement. [New Latin, "he undertook," from *assūmere,* to undertake, ASSUME.]

as·sump·tion (ə-sŭmp′shən) *n.* **1.** The act of assuming. **2.** A statement accepted or supposed true without proof or demonstration. **3.** Presumption or arrogance. **4.** *Logic.* A minor premise. **5.** *Capital* **A. a.** *Theology.* The bodily taking up of the Virgin Mary into heaven after her death. **b.** A church feast on August 15 celebrating this event. [Middle English, from Latin *assumptiō,* a taking up, adoption, from *assūmere,* ASSUME.]

as·sump·tive (ə-sŭmp′tĭv) *adj.* **1.** Of or characterized by assumption: *assumptive facts.* **2.** Taken for granted. **3.** Presumptuous; assuming. —**as·sump′tive·ly** *adv.*

As·sur. Variant of **Ashur.**

as·sur·ance (ə-sho͝or′əns) *n.* **1. a.** The act of assuring. **b.** The state of being assured. **2.** A statement or indication that inspires confidence. **3. a.** Freedom from doubt; certainty. **b.** Self-confidence. **4.** Boldness; audacity. **5.** *Chiefly British.* Insurance. —See Synonyms at **certainty, confidence.**

As·sur·ba·ni·pal. See **Ashurbanipal.**

as·sure (ə-sho͝or′) *tr.v.* **-sured, -suring, -sures. 1.** To inform confidently, with a view to removing doubt. **2.** To cause to feel sure; convince. **3.** To give confidence to; reassure. **4.** To make certain; ensure: *"Nothing in history assures the success of our civilization"* (Herbert J. Muller). **5.** To make safe or secure. **6.** To insure, as against loss. [Middle English *assuren,* from Old French *assurer,* from Medieval Latin *assēcūrāre,* to make sure : Latin *ad-,* to + *sēcūrus,* SECURE.] —**as·sur′a·ble** *adj.* —**as·sur′er** *n.*

Usage: *Assure, ensure,* and *insure* all mean to make secure or certain. *Assure* refers to persons, and it alone has the sense of setting a person's mind at rest: *to assure a leader of one's loyalty.* All three verbs may be applied to the act of making something certain: *Success is assured* (or *ensured* or *insured*). *Ensure* and *insure* also mean to make secure from harm: *to ensure* (or *insure*) *a nation against famine.* Only *insure* is now widely used in the sense of guaranteeing life or property against risk.

as·sured (ə-sho͝ord′) *adj.* **1.** Undoubted; guaranteed; made certain. **2.** Confident; bold. **3.** Insured. —See Synonyms at **sure.** —**as·sur′ed·ly** (-ĭd-lē) *adv.* —**as·sur′ed·ness** *n.*

as·sur·gent (ə-sûr′jənt) *adj.* **1.** Rising or tending to rise. **2.** *Botany.* Slanting or curving upward; ascending. [Latin *assurgēns,* present participle of *assurgere,* to rise up to : *ad-,* to + *surgere,* to SURGE.] —**as·sur′gen·cy** *n.*

assy. assembly.

Assyr. Assyrian.

As·syr·i·a (ə-sîr′ē-ə). An ancient empire of western Asia centered in the upper valley of the Tigris. Capital, Nineveh.

As·syr·i·an (ə-sîr′ē-ən) *adj.* Of or pertaining to Assyria, its people, language, or culture. —*n.* **1.** A native or inhabitant of Assyria. **2.** *Abbr.* **Assyr.** The Semitic language of Assyria.

As·syr·i·ol·o·gy (ə-sîr'ē-ŏl'ə-jē) *n.* The study of the ancient civilization of Assyria. —**As·syr'i·ol'o·gist** *n.*

As·tar·te (ə-stär'tē). *Phoenician Mythology.* The goddess of love and fertility. [Latin *Astartē*, from Greek, from Phoenician *'strt*, akin to Hebrew *'Ashtoreth*.]

a·sta·sia (ə-stā'zhə) *n.* Inability to stand because of muscular incoordination. [New Latin, from Greek instability, from *astatos*, unstable : *a-*, not + *statos*, standing (see **stā-** in Appendix*).]

a·stat·ic (ā-stăt'ĭk) *adj.* Unsteady; unstable. [A- (not) + STATIC.] —**a·stat'i·cal·ly** *adv.* —**a·stat'i·cism'** *n.*

as·ta·tine (ăs'tə-tēn') *n.* *Symbol* **At** A highly unstable radioactive element that resembles iodine in solution and accumulates in the thyroid gland. Its longest lived isotope is At 210, having a half-life of 8.3 hours, and is used in medicine as a radioactive tracer. Atomic number 85, valences probably 1, 3, 5, or 7. See **element.** [From Greek *astatos*, unstable : *a-*, not + *statos*, standing (see **stā-** in Appendix*).]

as·ter (ăs'tər) *n.* **1.** Any of various plants of the genus *Aster*, having rayed, daisylike flowers ranging in color from white to bluish, purple, or pink. **2.** The **China aster** *(see)*. **3.** *Biology.* A star-shaped structure appearing in the cytoplasm of the cell and associated with the centrosome during mitosis. [New Latin, from Latin *astēr*, star, from Greek. See **ster-[3]** in Appendix.*]

-aster. Indicates inferiority or fraudulence; for example, **poetaster.** [Middle English, from Latin, suffix denoting either smallness or partial resemblance (often mildly pejorative).]

as·te·ri·at·ed (ă-stîr'ē-ā'tĭd) *adj.* *Mineralogy.* Exhibiting asterism. [From Greek *asterios*, starry, from *astēr*, star. See **ster-[3]** in Appendix.*]

as·ter·isk (ăs'tə-rĭsk') *n.* **1.** A star-shaped figure (*) used in printing to indicate an omission or a reference to a footnote. **2.** *Linguistics.* This sign used to indicate an unattested form or entity. —*tr.v.* **asterisked, -isking, -isks.** To indicate by means of an asterisk; mark with an asterisk. [Late Latin *asteriscus*, from Greek *asteriskos*, little star, asterisk, from *astēr*, star. See **ster-[3]** in Appendix.*]

as·ter·ism (ăs'tə-rĭz'əm) *n.* **1.** *Printing.* Three asterisks in triangular form used to call attention to a following passage. **2.** *Astronomy.* **a.** A cluster of stars. **b.** A constellation. **3.** *Mineralogy.* A six-rayed starlike figure optically produced in some crystal structures by reflected or transmitted light. [Greek *asterismos*, from *asterizein*, to arrange in constellations, from *astēr*, star. See **ster-[3]** in Appendix.*] —**as'ter·is'mal** *adj.*

a·stern (ə-stûrn') *adv.* *Nautical.* **1.** Behind a vessel. **2.** Toward the rear of a vessel. **3.** To the rear; backward. —**a·stern'** *adj.*

a·ster·nal (ā-stûr'nəl) *adj.* *Anatomy.* **1.** Not connected to the sternum. **2.** Lacking a sternum. [A- (not) + STERNAL.]

as·ter·oid (ăs'tə-roid') *n.* **1.** *Astronomy.* Any of numerous celestial bodies with characteristic diameters between one and several hundred miles and orbits lying chiefly between Mars and Jupiter. Also called "planetoid." **2.** *Zoology.* A starfish. —*adj.* Also **as·ter·oi·dal** (ăs'tə-roid'l). Star-shaped. [Greek *asteroeidēs*, like a star : *astēr*, star (see **ster-[3]** in Appendix*) + -OID.]

As·ter·o·pe. Variant of **Sterope.**

as·the·ni·a (ăs'thə-nē-ə) *n.* Also **as·the·ny** (ăs'thə-nē). *Pathology.* Loss or lack of bodily strength; weakness. [New Latin, from Greek *astheneia*, from *asthenēs*, weak : *a-*, without + *sthenos*†, strength.]

as·then·ic (ăs-thĕn'ĭk) *n.* A slender, lightly muscled human physique. —**as·then'ic, as·then'i·cal** *adj.*

as·the·no·pi·a (ăs'thə-nō'pē-ə) *n.* Eyestrain, especially with headache and dimming of the vision. [New Latin : ASTHEN(IA) + -OPIA.] —**as'the·nop'ic** (-nŏp'ĭk) *adj.*

asth·ma (ăz'mə) *n.* A chronic respiratory disease, often arising from allergies, and accompanied by labored breathing, chest constriction, and coughing. [Middle English *asma*, from Medieval Latin, from Greek *asthma*†.] —**asth·mat'ic** (-măt'ĭk) *adj.* —**asth·mat'i·cal·ly** *adv.*

as·tig·mat·ic (ăs'tĭg-măt'ĭk) *adj.* **1.** Of or having astigmatism. **2.** Correcting astigmatism. —**as'tig·mat'i·cal·ly** *adv.*

a·stig·ma·tism (ə-stĭg'mə-tĭz'əm) *n.* **1.** A refractive defect of a lens that prevents focusing of sharp, distinct images. **2.** Faulty vision caused by such defects in the lens of the eye. [A- (without) + Greek *stigma* (stem *stigmat-*), spot, (tattoo) mark, "focus," from *stizein*, to tattoo (see **steig-** in Appendix*).]

a·stir (ə-stûr') *adj.* **1.** Moving about. **2.** Out of bed; awake. [Scottish *asteer* : A- (on) + *steer*, variant of STIR (noun).]

As·to·lat (ăs'tə-lŏt', -lăt'). An English town in legends of King Arthur, possibly in modern Surrey.

a·stom·a·tous (ā-stŏm'ə-təs, ā-stō'mə-) *adj.* Also **as·tom·ous** (ăs'tə-məs), **a·stom·a·tal** (ā-stŏm'ə-təl, -stō'mə-təl). Having no mouth or stomata. [A- (not) + STOMATOUS.]

As·ton (ăs'tən), **Francis William.** 1877–1945. British scientist; developed the mass spectograph.

a·ston·ied (ə-stŏn'ēd) *adj.* *Archaic.* Bewildered; dazed. [Middle English *aston(y)ed*, past participle of *astonen*, ASTONISH.]

a·ston·ish (ə-stŏn'ĭsh) *tr.v.* **-ished, -ishing, -ishes.** To fill with sudden wonder or amazement; confound. —See Synonyms at **surprise.** [Probably extension (with verbal suffix *-ish*, as in ABOLISH, FINISH) of obsolete *astony*, Middle English *astonen*, *astonien*, from Old French *estoner*, from Vulgar Latin *extonāre* (unattested), to strike with thunder, stun : Latin *ex-*, out of, "by means of" + *tonāre*, to thunder (see **stene-** in Appendix*).] —**a·ston'ish·er** *n.* —**a·ston'ish·ing·ly** *adv.*

a·ston·ish·ment (ə-stŏn'ĭsh-mənt) *n.* **1.** Great surprise or amazement. **2.** A cause of amazement; a marvel.

As·tor (ăs'tər), **John Jacob.** 1763–1848. German-born American fur trader, capitalist, and philanthropist.

As·tor (ăs'tər), **Nancy Witcher Langhorne,** Viscountess. 1879–1964. American-born British political leader, first woman member of House of Commons (1919–1945).

As·to·ri·a (ə-stôr'ē-ə, ə-stōr'-). A seaport of northwestern Oregon, near the mouth of the Columbia River. It was the site of a fur-trading post that was established in 1811 and later bolstered U.S. claims to the Oregon Territory. Population, 11,000.

a·stound (ə-stound') *tr.v.* **astounded, astounding, astounds.** To strike with sudden wonder. See Synonyms at **surprise.** [Originally the past participle of obsolete *astone*, to amaze, from Middle English *astonen*, ASTONISH.] —**a·stound'ing·ly** *adv.*

As·tra·chan (ăs'trə-kăn', -kən) *n.* A tart red or yellow apple of Russian origin. [From ASTRAKHAN.]

a·strad·dle (ə-străd'l) *adv.* In a straddling position; astride. —*prep.* So as to straddle; astride.

As·trae·a (ă-strē'ə). *Greek Mythology.* The goddess of justice. [New Latin, from Greek *astraios*, starry, from *astēr*, star. See **ster-[3]** in Appendix.*]

as·tra·gal (ăs'trə-gəl) *n.* *Architecture.* A narrow, convex molding, often having the form of beading. [Latin *astragalus*, from Greek *astragalos*, "the ball of the ankle joint" (from the shape of the molding). See **osth-** in Appendix.*]

as·trag·a·lus (ə-străg'ə-ləs) *n.*, *pl.* **-li** (-lī'). A bone, the **talus** *(see)*. [New Latin, from Greek *astragalos*, vertebra, the ball of the ankle joint. See **osth-** in Appendix.*] —**as·trag'a·lar** *adj.*

as·tra·khan (ăs'trə-kăn', -kən) *n.* Also **as·tra·chan.** **1.** The curly or wavy fur made from the skins of young lambs from the region of Astrakhan. **2.** A fabric with a curly, looped pile, made to resemble this fur.

As·tra·khan (ăs'trə-kăn', -kən). A city of the Soviet Union, on the Volga delta in the Russian S.F.S.R. Population, 342,000.

as·tral (ăs'trəl) *adj.* **1.** Of, pertaining to, consisting of, emanating from, or resembling the stars. **2.** *Biology.* Pertaining to or shaped like an aster; star-shaped. [Late Latin *astrālis*, from Latin *astrum*, star, from Greek *astron*. See **ster-[3]** in Appendix.*] —**as'tral·ly** *adv.*

as·tra·pho·bi·a (ăs'trə-fō'bē-ə) *n.* Fear of lightning and thunder. [New Latin : Greek *astrapē*, lightning (see **ster-[3]** in Appendix*) + -PHOBIA.]

a·stray (ə-strā') *adv.* **1.** Away from the correct path or direction. **2.** Away from the right or good; toward evil or wrong ways. [Middle English *astray*, *astraie*, from Old French *estraie*, past participle of *estraier*, STRAY.] —**a·stray'** *adj.*

as·trict (ə-strĭkt') *tr.v.* **-tricted, -tricting, -tricts.** To bind, especially by moral or legal obligations. [Latin *astrictus*, past participle of *astringere*, to bind fast, ASTRINGE.] —**as·tric'tion** *n.*

as·tric·tive (ə-strĭk'tĭv) *adj.* Astringent. —*n.* An astringent. —**as·tric'tive·ly** *adv.* —**as·tric'tive·ness** *n.*

a·stride (ə-strīd') *adv.* **1.** With the legs separated so that one is on each side of something. **2.** With the legs wide apart. —*prep.* **1.** Upon or over and with a leg on each side of. **2.** With a part on each side of; spanning or bridging.

as·tringe (ə-strĭnj') *tr.v.* **-tringed, -tringing, -tringes.** To draw together; constrict. [Latin *astringere*, to bind together : *ad-*, to + *stringere*, to bind (see **streig-** in Appendix*).]

as·trin·gent (ə-strĭn'jənt) *adj.* **1.** *Medicine.* Tending to draw together or constrict tissue; contracting; styptic. **2.** Harsh; severe. —*n.* An astringent substance or drug, such as alum. —**as·trin'gen·cy** *n.* —**as·trin'gent·ly** *adv.*

astro-, astr-. Indicates: **1.** Star or star-shaped; for example, **astrocyte.** **2.** That which pertains to outer space; for example, **astronautics.** [Middle English, from Old French, from Latin, from Greek, from *astron*, star. See **ster-[3]** in Appendix.*]

as·tro·bi·ol·o·gy (ăs'trō-bī-ŏl'ə-jē) *n.* **Exobiology** *(see)*.

as·tro·cyte (ăs'trə-sīt') *n.* *Biology.* A star-shaped cell, especially a neuroglial cell. [ASTRO- + -CYTE.]

as·tro·cy·to·ma (ăs'trō-sī-tō'mə) *n.*, *pl.* **-mas** or **-mata** (-mə-tə). A malignant tumor of astrocytes. [ASTROCYT(E) + -OMA.]

as·tro·dome (ăs'trə-dōm') *n.* **1.** A transparent dome on the top of an aircraft, through which celestial observations are made for navigation. **2.** *Capital* **A.** An enclosed stadium, used mainly for sports events, with a translucent dome.

as·tro·dy·nam·ics (ăs'trō-dī-năm'ĭks) *n.* Plural in form, used with a singular verb. The dynamics of celestial bodies.

as·tro·gate (ăs'trə-gāt') *intr.v.* **-gated, -gating, -gates.** To navigate a spacecraft in space. [ASTRO- + (NAVI)GATION.] —**as'tro·ga'tion** (ăs'trə-gā'shən) *n.* —**as'tro·ga'tor** (-gā'tər) *n.*

astrol. astrologer; astrological; astrology.

as·tro·labe (ăs'trə-lāb') *n.* A medieval instrument used to determine the altitude of the sun or other celestial bodies. [Middle English, from Old French, from Medieval Latin *astrolabium*, from Greek *(organon) astrolabon*, "(instrument) for taking the stars" : ASTRO- + *lambanein*, to take (see **slagw-** in Appendix*).]

as·trol·o·gy (ə-strŏl'ə-jē) *n.* *Abbr.* **astrol.** The study of the positions and aspects of heavenly bodies with a view to predicting their influence on the course of human affairs. [Middle English *astrologie*, from Old French, from Latin *astrologia*, from Greek, from *astrologos*, astronomer, (later) astrologer : ASTRO- + *logos*, speech (see **-logy**).] —**as·trol'o·ger** *n.* —**as'tro·log'ic** (ăs'trə-lŏj'ĭk), **as'tro·log'i·cal** *adj.* —**as'tro·log'i·cal·ly** *adv.*

as·trom·e·try (ə-strŏm'ə-trē) *n.* The scientific measurement of the positions and motions of celestial bodies. [ASTRO- + -METRY.] —**as'tro·met'ric** (ăs'trō-mĕt'rĭk), **as'tro·met'ri·cal** *adj.*

astron. astronomer; astronomical; astronomy.

as·tro·naut (ăs'trə-nôt') *n.* A person trained to pilot, navigate, or otherwise participate in the flight of a spacecraft. Also called

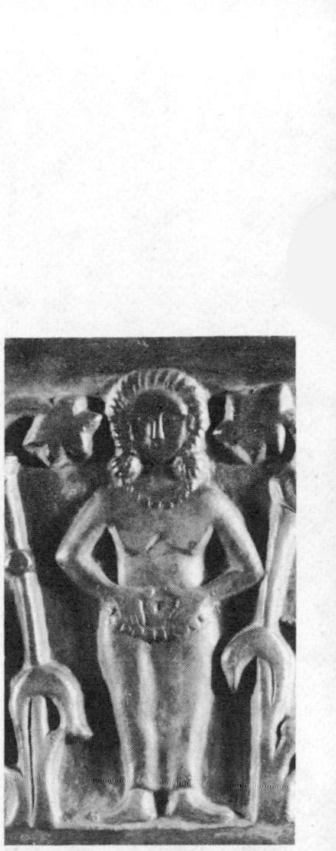

Astarte
Modern metal cast of ancient Phoenician relief found in Ashkelon, Palestine

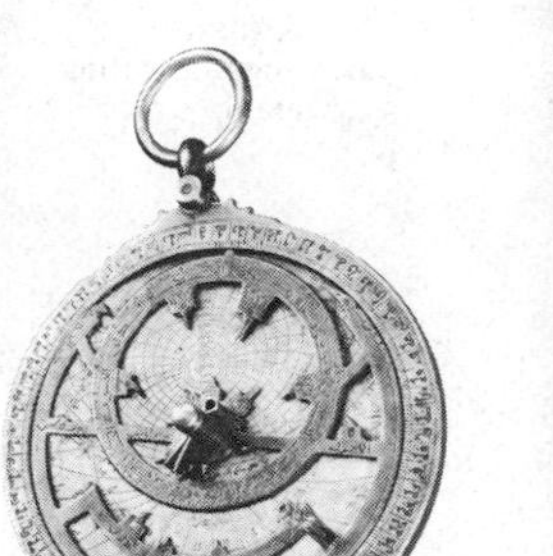

astrolabe
Moorish astrolabe, about 1026

"cosmonaut." [ASTRO- + Greek *nautēs*, sailor, from *naus*, ship (see **nāu-**[2] in Appendix*).]

as·tro·nau·tics (ăs′trə-nô′tĭks) *n.* Plural in form, used with singular verb. The science and technology of space flight. [ASTRO- + Latin *nautica*, neuter plural of *nauticus*, NAUTICAL.] —**as′tro·nau′tic, as′tro·nau′ti·cal** *adj.* —**as′tro·nau′ti·cal·ly** *adv.*

as·tro·nav·i·ga·tion (ăs′trō-năv′ə-gā′shən) *n.* **1.** Navigation of spacecraft. **2. Celestial navigation** *(see).* —**as′tro·nav′i·ga′tor** *n.*

as·tron·o·mer (ə-strŏn′ə-mər) *n. Abbr.* **astron.** A scientist specializing in astronomy. [Middle English, from Late Latin *astronomus*, from Greek *astronomos*, "star-arranger" : ASTRO- + *-nomos*, from *nemein*, to arrange (see **nem-**[2] in Appendix*).]

as·tro·nom·i·cal (ăs′trə-nŏm′ĭ-kəl) *adj.* Also **as·tro·nom·ic** (-nŏm′ĭk). **1.** *Abbr.* **astron.** Of or pertaining to astronomy. **2.** Inconceivably large; immense. —**as′tro·nom′i·cal·ly** *adv.*

astronomical unit. *Abbr.* **A.U.** A unit of length used in measuring astronomical distances, equal to the mean distance of the earth from the sun, approximately 93 million miles.

as·tron·o·my (ə-strŏn′ə-mē) *n. Abbr.* **astron.** The scientific study of the universe beyond the earth, especially the observation, calculation, and theoretical interpretation of the positions, dimensions, distribution, motion, composition, and evolution of celestial bodies and phenomena. [Middle English *astronomie*, from Old French, from Latin *astronomia*, from Greek, from *astronomos*, ASTRONOMER.]

as·tro·pho·tog·ra·phy (ăs′trō-fə-tŏg′rə-fē) *n.* Astronomical photography. —**as′tro·pho′to·graph′ic** (-fō′tə-grăf′ĭk) *adj.*

as·tro·phys·ics (ăs′trō-fĭz′ĭks) *n.* Plural in form, used with a singular verb. The physics of stellar phenomena. —**as′tro·phys′i·cal** *adj.* —**as′tro·phys′i·cist** (-fĭz′ə-sĭst) *n.*

as·tro·sphere (ăs′trō-sfîr′) *n. Biology.* **1.** The central portion of a cell aster; the centrosphere. **2.** The entire cell aster with the exception of the centrosome. [ASTRO- + -SPHERE.]

As·tu·ri·as (ə-stŏŏr′ē-əs, ə-styŏŏr′-; *Spanish* äs-tōō′ryäs). A region and former kingdom and province of northwestern Spain. —**As·tu′ri·an** *adj.* & *n.*

as·tute (ə-stōōt′, ə-styōōt′) *adj.* Keen in judgment: crafty. —See Synonyms at **shrewd.** [Latin *astūtus*, from *astus*, craft. See **wes-**[3] in Appendix.*] —**as·tute′ly** *adv.* —**as·tute′ness** *n.*

As·ty·a·nax (ə-stī′ə-năks′). *Greek Mythology.* The young son of Hector and Andromache, killed by the conquering Greeks.

a·sty·lar (ā-stī′lər) *adj.* Not having columns or pilasters. [A- (without) + Greek *stulos*, pillar (see **stā-** in Appendix*).]

ASU Airport code for Asunción, Paraguay.

A·sun·ción (ä′sōōn-syôn′). The capital of Paraguay, a port on the Paraguay River. Population, 305,000.

a·sun·der (ə-sŭn′dər) *adv.* **1.** Into separate parts or pieces. **2.** Apart from each other either in position or direction. [Middle English *asonder*, Old English *onsundran*, *onsundrum* : *on*, on + *sundran*, *sundrum*, singly, separately, from *sunder*, apart, separate (see **sen-**[2] in Appendix.*)] —**a·sun′der** *adj.*

A·sur. Variant of **Ashur.**

ASV American Standard Version.

As·wan (äs-wăn′, -wŏn′). Also **As·souan, As·suan.** Ancient name, **Sy·e·ne** (sī-ē′nə). A city on the east bank of the Nile in southern Egypt. Population, 48,000.

As·wan Dam (äs-wăn′, -wŏn′). A large dam, 1¼ miles long, across the Nile near the city of Aswan, Egypt. Construction of the new Aswan High Dam, five miles to the south, was begun in 1960.

a·syl·lab·ic (ā′sĭ-lăb′ĭk) *adj.* Not syllabic.

a·sy·lum (ə-sī′ləm) *n., pl.* **-lums** or **-la** (-lə). **1.** An institution for the care of the mentally ill or aged. **2.** A place offering protection or safety. **3.** Formerly, a temple or church affording sanctuary for criminals or debtors. **4.** The protection afforded by a sanctuary: *political asylum.* —See Synonyms at **shelter.** [Middle English *asilum*, from Latin *asylum*, from Greek *asulon*, sanctuary, from *asulos*, inviolable : *a-*, without + *sulon*†, right of seizure.]

a·sym·met·ric (ā′sĭ-mĕt′rĭk) *adj.* Also **a·sym·met·ri·cal** (-rĭ-kəl). *Abbr.* **asym.** Not symmetrical. —**a′sym·met′ri·cal·ly** *adv.*

a·sym·me·try (ā-sĭm′ə-trē) *n.* Lack of symmetry or balance. [Greek *asummetria* : *a-*, without + *summetria*, SYMMETRY.]

a·symp·to·mat·ic (ā′sĭmp-tə-măt′ĭk) *adj.* Neither causing nor exhibiting symptoms. —**a′symp·to·mat′i·cal·ly** *adv.*

as·ymp·tote (ăs′ĭm-tōt′, -ĭmp-tōt′) *n. Mathematics.* A line considered a limit to a curve in the sense that the perpendicular distance from a moving point on the curve to the line approaches zero as the point moves an infinite distance from the origin. [New Latin *asymptōta*, from Greek *(grammē) asumptōtos*, "(a line) not falling together" : *a-*, not + *sumptōtos*, from *sumpiptein*, to fall together : *sun-*, together + *piptein*, to fall (see **pet-**[1] in Appendix*).] —**as′ymp·tot′ic** (-tŏt′ĭk), **as′ymp·tot′i·cal** (-ĭ-kəl) *adj.* —**as′ymp·tot′i·cal·ly** *adv.*

a·syn·chro·nism (ā-sĭng′krə-nĭz′əm) *n.* Lack of synchronism. —**a·syn′chro·nous** (-nəs) *adj.* —**a·syn′chro·nous·ly** *adv.*

a·syn·de·ton (ə-sĭn′də-tŏn′) *n. Rhetoric.* The omission of conjunctions from constructions in which they would normally be used. Compare **parataxis.** [Late Latin, from Greek *asundeton*, from *asundetos*, "without conjunctions," unconnected : *ă-*, not + *sundetos*, bound together, from *sundein*, to bind together : *sun-*, together + *dein*, to bind (see **dē-** in Appendix*).] —**as′yn·det′ic** (ăs′ĭn-dĕt′ĭk) *adj.* —**as′yn·det′i·cal·ly** *adv.*

a·syn·tac·tic (ā′sĭn-tăk′tĭk) *adj.* Not syntactic.

As·yut, As·yût (äs-yōōt′). Also **As·siut.** An industrial city of central Egypt. Population, 122,000.

at[1] (ăt, ət) *prep.* **1. a.** In the location of: *at the market.* **b.** In the position of: *at the center of the page.* **2.** To or toward the direction of: *Look at him.* **3.** Present in; attending: *at the dance.* **4.** In the duration of; during: *at night.* **5.** In the state or condition of: *at peace with one's conscience.* **6.** In the manner of: *at a run.* **7.** To the extent or amount of: *at thirty cents a pound.* **8.** On the exact moment of: *at three o'clock.* **9.** Because of; due to: *rejoice at a victory.* **10.** Through; by way of. **11.** According to: *at one's discretion.* **12.** Dependent upon: *at the mercy of the court.* **13.** Occupied with: *at work.* —**at sea. 1.** On the sea; sailing. **2.** *Informal.* Bewildered; confused. [Middle English *at*, *atte*, Old English *æt*. See **ad-** in Appendix.*]

at[2] (ät) *n., pl.* **at.** A monetary unit equal to 1/100 of the kip of Laos. See table of exchange rates at **currency.** [Siamese.]

aT *Physics.* attotesla.

At The symbol for the element astatine.

AT antitank.

at. attorney.

At·a·brine (ăt′ə-brĭn, -brēn′) *n.* A trademark for an antimalarial preparation, **quinacrine hydrochloride** *(see).*

A·ta·ca·ma Desert (ä′tə-kä′mə). An arid area of northern Chile, possessing major nitrate deposits.

at·a·ghan. Variant of **yataghan.**

At·a·hual·pa (ăt′ə-wäl′pə). Also **A·ta·ba·li·pa** (ä′tä-bä′lē-pä). 1500?–1533. Last Inca emperor; put to death by Pizarro.

At·a·lan·ta (ăt′ə-lăn′tə). *Greek Mythology.* A maiden who agreed to marry any man who could outrun her, and who was defeated by Hippomenes when he dropped three golden apples that she paused to pick up.

at·a·man (ăt′ə-măn′) *n., pl.* **-mans.** A Cossack chief. [Russian, from Polish *hetman*, from German *Hauptmann*, captain, from Middle High German *houbetman*, from Old High German *houbitman* : *houbit*, head (see **kaput** in Appendix*) + *man*, man (see **man-**[1] in Appendix*).]

at·a·mas·co lily (ăt′ə-măs′kō). A plant, *Zephyranthes atamasco*, of eastern North America, having funnel-shaped white or pinkish flowers. Also called "fairy lily." [Algonquian (Virginia) *Attamusco*.]

at·a·rac·tic (ăt′ə-răk′tĭk) *adj.* Also **at·a·rax·ic** (-răk′sĭk). Pertaining to or conducive of calmness and peace of mind. —*n.* Also **at·a·rax·ic.** A drug that reduces nervous tension; a tranquilizer. [Greek *ataraktos*, undisturbed : *a-*, not + *taraktos*, disturbed, from *tarattein*, to disturb (see **dher-**[1] in Appendix*).]

at·a·rax·i·a (ăt′ə-răk′sē-ə) *n.* Peace of mind; emotional tranquillity. [Greek *ataraxia*, from *ataraktos*, ATARACTIC.]

At·a·türk. See **Kemal Atatürk.**

a·tav·ic (ə-tăv′ĭk) *adj.* Of or concerning a remote ancestor.

at·a·vism (ăt′ə-vĭz′əm) *n.* **1.** The reappearance of a characteristic in an organism after several generations of absence, caused by a recessive gene or complementary genes. **2.** An individual or part displaying atavism. Also loosely called "reversion," "throwback." [French *atavisme*, from Latin *atavus*, ancestor, great-great-great-grandfather : *atta*, father (see **atto-** in Appendix*) + *avus*, grandfather (see **awo-** in Appendix*).] —**at′a·vist** *n.* —**at′a·vis′tic** *adj.* —**at′a·vis′ti·cal·ly** *adv.*

a·tax·i·a (ə-tăk′sē-ə) *n.* Also **a·tax·y** (ə-tăk′sē). Loss or lack of muscular coordination. [Greek *ataxia*, from *ataktos*, disorderly : *a-*, not + *taktos*, ordered, from *tattein*, to arrange (see **tāg-** in Appendix*).]

a·tax·ic (ə-tăk′sĭk) *adj.* Of or pertaining to ataxia. —*n.* An individual exhibiting symptoms of ataxia.

At·ba·ra (ăt′bä-rä). A river flowing northwest about 500 miles from northwestern Ethiopia to the Nile in eastern Sudan.

ate. Past tense of **eat.**

-ate[1]. **1.** Indicates: **a.** Possessing; for example, **nervate, affectionate. b.** Shaped like; for example, **lyrate. c.** Having the general characteristics of; for example, **Latinate. 2.** Indicates: **a.** A substance derived from; for example, **stearate. b.** *Chemistry.* The salt or ester of an acid; for example, **nitrate, sulfate. 3.** Used to form verbs with an unrestricted spread of meanings, such as "to make in a specified way," "to apply," "to operate upon"; for example, **aerate, pollinate.** [Middle English *-at*, from Old French, from Latin *-ātus*, ending of the past participle of verbs in *-āre* (first conjugation). It thus appears in: **1.** Participial adjectives; for example, **ornate. 2.** Nouns substantivized from adjectives, either in Latin or in English; for example, **associate. 3.** Verbs originally formed from the corresponding nouns and adjectives in *-ate;* for example, **aggregate, conjugate;** and subsequently, by analogy with these, adopted directly from Latin, taking participial form but infinitive sense; for example, **desiccate, eradicate.**]

-ate[2]. Indicates rank or office; for example, **rabbinate.** In practice restricted to titles for which there is no more usual noun of condition, as those formed with **-ship.** [Latin *-ātus*, an abstract suffix made up of the *-āt-* of *-ātus*, participial ending (-ATE) and the feminine *-us* of fourth declension nouns. It originally designated the collective status of a group, as in **senate,** later the power of a specific type of ruler, as in **triumvirate.**]

at ease. *Military.* **1.** A position of silent rest with the right foot stationary, assumed by soldiers in ranks. **2.** The command to assume this position.

at·el·ier (ăt′l-yā′) *n.* A workshop or studio, especially an artist's studio. [French, from Old French *astelier*, woodpile, hence carpenter's shop, from *astele*, splinter, shaving, chip, from Late Latin *astella*, variant of Latin *astula*, *assula*, diminutive of *assis*, board, plank, probably variant of *axis*. See **ashlar.**]

a tem·po (ä tĕm′pō). *Music.* In normal time; resuming the original tempo. [Italian, "in time."]

a·tem·po·ral (ā-tĕm′pər-əl) *adj.* Independent of time; timeless. [A- (not) + TEMPORAL.]

ATH Airport code for Athens, Greece.

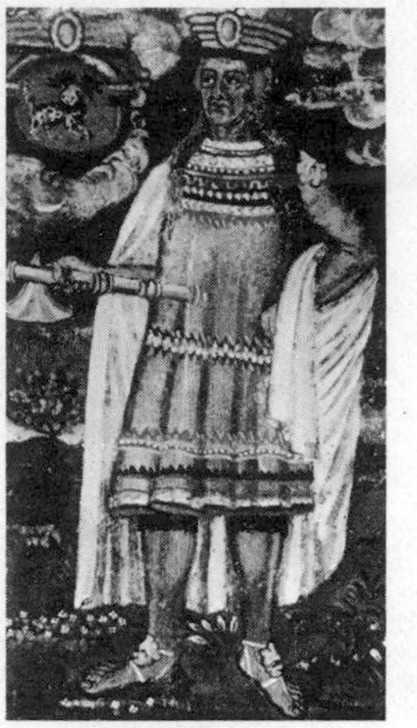

Atahualpa
Miniature painting
by an unknown artist

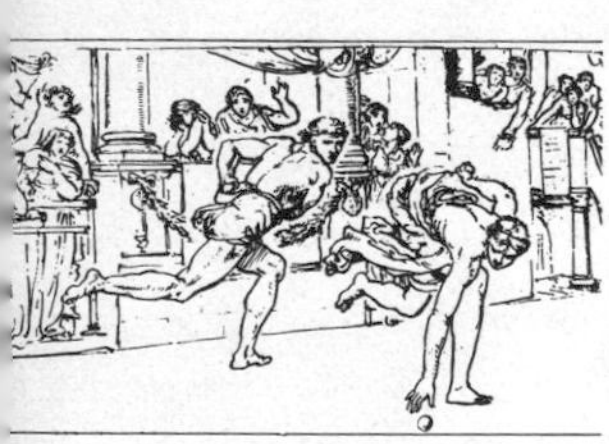

Atalanta
Drawing illustrating
Atalanta's race

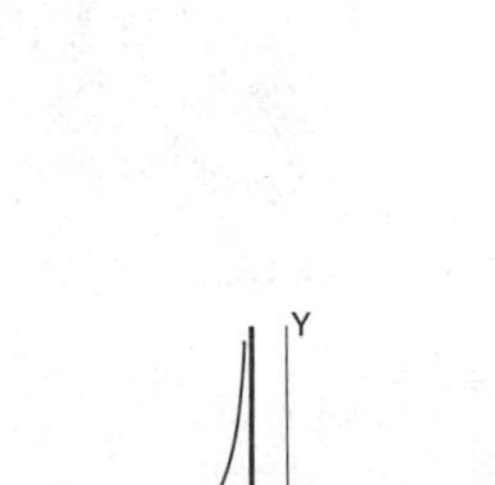

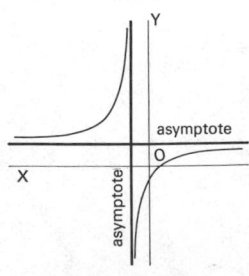

asymptote
Asymptotes of a hyperbola

Ath·a·bas·ca, Ath·a·bas·ka (ăth′ə-băs′kə). **1.** A lake, 3,058 square miles in area, in northern Alberta and Saskatchewan, Canada. **2.** A river of Alberta, Canada, rising in the Rocky Mountains and flowing 765 miles north into this lake.

Ath·a·na·sian (ăth′ə-nā′zhən) *adj.* Of or pertaining to Athanasius. *—n.* A follower of Athanasius and his teachings.

Ath·a·na·sius (ăth′ə-nā′zhəs, -zhē-əs, -shəs, -shē-əs), **Saint.** A.D. 293?–373. Patriarch of Alexandria; opponent of Arianism.

Ath·a·pas·can (ăth′ə-păs′kən) *n.* Also **Ath·a·bas·can** (-băs′kən). **1.** A linguistic stock of North American Indians, including languages of Alaska and northwestern Canada, of the coast of Oregon and California, and the Navaho and Apache languages of the southwestern United States. **2.** A member of an Athapascan-speaking tribe. *—adj.* Of or designating this linguistic stock. [From the name of Lake ATHABASKA, Northern Cree *athapaskaaw,* "there is scattered grass."]

a·the·ism (ā′thē-ĭz′əm) *n.* **1.** Disbelief in or denial of the existence of God. Compare **agnosticism. 2.** Godlessness. [Old French *atheisme,* from *athee,* atheist, from Greek *atheos,* godless : *a-,* without + *theos,* god (see **dhēs-** in Appendix*).]

a·the·ist (ā′thē-ĭst) *n.* One who denies the existence of God.

a·the·is·tic (ā′thē-ĭs′tĭk) *adj.* Also **a·the·is·ti·cal** (-tĭ-kəl). **1.** Pertaining to or characteristic of atheism or of atheists. **2.** Inclined to atheism. **—a′the·is′ti·cal·ly** *adv.* **—a′the·is′tic·ness** *n.*

ath·e·ling (ăth′ə-lĭng, ăth′ə-) *n.* Also **aeth·e·ling.** An Anglo-Saxon nobleman or prince. [Middle English *atheling,* Old English *ætheling,* prince. See **athal-** in Appendix.*]

A·the·na (ə-thē′nə). Also **A·the·ne** (-nē). The Greek goddess of wisdom and the arts. Identified with the Roman goddess Minerva. Also called "Pallas Athena," "Pallas Athene."

Ath·e·nag·o·ras I (ăth′ə-năg′ər-əs). Title of Aristocles Spyrou. Born 1886. Patriarch of Greek Orthodox Church since 1948.

ath·e·ne·um (ăth′ə-nē′əm) *n.* Also **ath·e·nae·um. 1.** An institution, such as a literary club or scientific academy, for the promotion of learning. **2.** A library, reading room, or similar place. [Late Latin *Athēnaeum,* a Roman school of art, after Greek *Athēnaion,* the temple of Athena at Athens, where philosophy was taught, from *Athēnē,* ATHENA.]

Ath·ens (ăth′ənz). *Greek* **A·the·nai** (ə-thē′nī′). The capital of Greece, in the southeast. Population, 1,853,000. [Latin *Athēnae,* from Greek *Athēnai* (plural), "city of Athena," from *Athēnē,* ATHENA.] **—A·the′ni·an** (ə-thē′nē-ən) *n.* & *adj.*

ath·er·o·ma (ăth′ə-rō′mə) *n., pl.* **-mas** or **-mata** (-mə-tə). *Pathology.* **1.** A deposit or degenerative accumulation of pulpy, acellular, lipid-containing materials, especially in arterial walls. **2.** A form of arteriosclerosis induced and characterized by such deposits. [New Latin, from Latin, from Greek *athērōma,* a cyst full of gruellike pus, from *athēra,* gruel, from *athēr*†, beard of grain.] **—ath′er·o·ma·to′sis** (-rō-mə-tō′sĭs) *n.* **—ath′er·om′a·tous** (-rŏm′ə-təs, -rō′mə-təs) *adj.*

ath·er·o·scle·ro·sis (ăth′ə-rō-sklə-rō′sĭs) *n. Pathology.* Atheromatous arteriosclerosis; atheroma. [ATHERO(MA) + SCLEROSIS.] **—ath′er·o·scle·rot′ic** (-rŏt′ĭk) *adj.*

a·thirst (ə-thûrst′) *adj.* **1.** Strongly desirous; eager. Usually used with *for: athirst for freedom* **2.** *Archaic.* Thirsty.

athl. athlete; athletic; athletics.

ath·lete (ăth′lēt′) *n.* **1.** *Abbr.* **athl.** One who takes part in competitive sports. **2.** A person possessing the natural prerequisites for sports competition, as strength, agility, and endurance. [Middle English, from Latin *athlēta,* from Greek *athlētēs,* contestant, from *athlein,* to contend for an award, from *athlon*†, award, prize.]

athlete's foot. A contagious skin infection caused by parasitic fungi usually affecting the feet and sometimes the hands and causing itching, blisters, cracking, and scaling. Also called "dermatophytosis."

ath·let·ic (ăth-lĕt′ĭk) *adj.* **1.** *Abbr.* **athl.** Of, pertaining to, or befitting athletics or athletes. **2.** Physically strong; muscular. **—ath·let′i·cal·ly** *adv.* **—ath·let′i·cism′** (-lĕt′ə-sĭz′əm) *n.*

ath·let·ics (ăth-lĕt′ĭks) *n. Abbr.* **athl. 1.** Athletic activities, as competitive sports. Used with a plural verb. **2.** The principles or system of athletic exercises and training. Used with a singular verb.

athletic supporter. An elastic support for the male genitals, sometimes employing a rigid metallic cup, worn especially in athletic or other strenuous activity. Also called "jockstrap."

ath·o·dyd (ăth′ə-dĭd′) *n.* A simple, essentially tubular, jet engine, as a ramjet. [A(ERO) TH(ERM)ODY(NAMIC) D(UCT).]

at-home (ət-hōm′) *n.* An informal reception at one's home.

Ath·os (ăth′ŏs, ā′thŏs), **Mount.** A peak, 6,670 feet high, in northeastern Greece, in the district of **Mount Athos** *(see).*

a·thwart (ə-thwôrt′) *adv.* **1.** From side to side; crosswise; transversely. **2.** So as to thwart or obstruct; perversely. *—prep.* **1.** From one side to the other of; across. **2.** Contrary to; against. **3.** *Nautical.* Across the course, line, or length of. [Middle English : A- (on) + THWART (side).]

a·tilt (ə-tĭlt′) *adj.* **1.** In a tilted position; inclined upward. **2.** Similar to someone tilting with a lance. **—a·tilt′** *adv.*

-ation. Indicates: **1.** Action or process of; for example, **strangulation, negotiation. 2.** State, condition, or quality of; for example, **isolation, moderation. 3.** Result or product of; for example, **dramatization, civilization.** [Middle English *-acioun,* from Old French *-ation,* from Latin *-ātiō* (stem *-ātiōn-*), abstract noun suffix, from *-ātus,* -ATE.]

A·ti·tlan (ä′tē-tlän′). **1.** A lake of southwestern Guatemala. **2.** An inactive volcano rising to 11,565 feet near this lake.

-ative. Indicates relation, nature, or tendency; for example, **authoritative, illustrative, formative.** [Middle English, from Old French *-atif,* from Latin *-ātīvus,* from *-ātus,* -ATE.]

At·ka Island (ăt′kə, ät′-). The largest, about 1,300 square miles in area, of the Andreanof Islands of southwestern Alaska.

Atka mackerel. A food fish, *Pleurogrammus monopterygius,* of northern Pacific waters.

At·kins, Tommy. See **Tommy Atkins.**

Atl. Atlantic.

At·lan·ta (ăt-lăn′tə). The capital and main city of Georgia, in the northern part of the state. Population, 487,000.

At·lan·te·an (ăt′lăn-tē′ən, ăt-lăn′tē-ən) *adj.* **1.** Of, pertaining to, or like Atlas. **2.** Of or pertaining to Atlantis.

at·lan·tes. *Architecture.* Plural of **atlas.**

At·lan·tic (ăt-lăn′tĭk) *adj.* **1.** *Abbr.* **Atl.** Of, in, near, upon, or pertaining to the Atlantic Ocean. **2.** Of or pertaining to Atlas or to the Atlas Mountains. *—n.* The Atlantic Ocean. [Latin *(mare) Atlanticum,* from Greek *(pelagos) Atlantikos* "(the sea) of Atlas" (the sea lying beyond the Atlas Mountains), from *Atlas* (stem *Atlant-*), ATLAS.]

Atlantic Charter. A declaration of the aims of the Allied Nations in World War II, made jointly by Churchill and Roosevelt as a result of a meeting at sea in August 1941.

Atlantic City. A resort and convention city in southeastern New Jersey. Population, 60,000.

Atlantic Ocean. The second-largest of the earth's oceans (31,830,000 square miles), extending from the Arctic in the north to the Antarctic in the south and from the Americas in the west to Europe and Africa in the east.

Atlantic salmon. A food fish, *Salmo salar,* of northern Atlantic waters.

At·lan·tis (ăt-lăn′tĭs). A legendary island in the Atlantic west of Gibraltar, said by Plato to have sunk beneath the sea.

at·las (ăt′ləs) *n., pl.* **-lases** or **atlantes** (ăt-lăn′tēz) (for sense 4). **1.** A bound collection of maps. **2.** Any volume of tables, charts, or plates that systematically illustrate a subject: *anatomical atlas.* **3.** A large size of drawing paper, measuring 26 by 33 or 34 inches. **4.** *Usually plural. Architecture.* A figure of a man used as a masonry column on a building. **5.** *Anatomy.* The top or first cervical vertebra of the neck, which supports the head. [From representations of the Titan ATLAS upholding the heavens, common in 16th-century books of maps.]

At·las[1] (ăt′ləs). *Greek Mythology.* A Titan condemned to support the heavens upon his shoulders. [Latin, from Greek. See **tel-**[1] in Appendix.*]

At·las[2] (ăt′ləs) *n.* **1.** Any person supporting a great burden. **2.** A kind of intercontinental ballistic missile developed by the U.S. Air Force. [After ATLAS.]

At·las Mountains (ăt′ləs). A mountain system in northwestern Africa, between the Sahara and the Mediterranean. Highest elevation, Djebel Toubkal (13,665 feet).

atm *Physics.* atmosphere.

atm. atmosphere; atmospheric.

at·man (ät′mən) *n. Hinduism.* **1.** The individual soul; the principle of life. **2.** *Capital* **A.** The supreme and universal soul, from which all individual souls arise. [Sanskrit *ātman,* breath, spirit, soul. See **ētmen-** in Appendix.*]

atmo-. Indicates the presence of or relation to vapor; for example, **atmosphere.** [New Latin, from Greek *atmos,* vapor, breath. See **wē-** in Appendix.*]

at·mol·y·sis (ăt-mŏl′ə-sĭs) *n., pl.* **-ses** (-sēz). The separation of a mixture of gases, each with different diffusibility, by diffusion through a porous material. [New Latin : ATMO- + -LYSIS.]

at·mom·e·ter (ăt-mŏm′ə-tər) *n.* An instrument that measures the rate of water evaporation. [ATMO- + -METER.] **—at′mo·met′ric** (ăt′mō-mĕt′rĭk) *adj.* **—at·mom′e·try** *n.*

atmos. atmosphere; atmospheric.

at·mos·phere (ăt′mə-sfîr′) *n.* **1.** *Abbr.* **atm., atmos.** The gaseous mass or envelope surrounding a celestial body, especially that surrounding the earth, and retained by the body's gravitational field. **2.** The atmosphere or climate in a specific place. **3.** *Abbr.* **atm** *Physics.* A unit of pressure equal to 1.01325×10^5 newtons per square meter. **4.** A psychological environment: *He grew up in an atmosphere of austerity.* **5.** The predominant tone or mood of a work of art. **6.** *Informal.* A quality or effect considered to be exotic or romantic in some way. [New Latin *atmosphaera,* "sphere of vapor" : ATMO- + -SPHERE.]

at·mos·pher·ic (ăt′mə-sfîr′ĭk, -sfĕr′ĭk) *adj.* Also **at·mos·pher·i·cal** (-ĭ-kəl). *Abbr.* **atm., atmos. 1.** Of, pertaining to, or existing in the atmosphere. **2.** Produced by, dependent on, or coming from the atmosphere. **—at′mos·pher′i·cal·ly** *adv.*

atmospheric pressure. An exerted pressure of 1 atmosphere.

at·mos·pher·ics (ăt′mə-sfîr′ĭks, -sfĕr′ĭks) *n.* Plural in form, used with a singular verb. **1.** Electromagnetic radiation produced by natural phenomena such as lightning. **2.** Radio interference produced by such radiation. Also called "sferics."

a·toll (ă′tôl′, ă′tŏl′, ā′-) *n.* A ringlike coral island and reef that nearly or entirely encloses a lagoon. [Malayalam *atoḷu,* "reef," native name for the Maldive Islands.]

at·om (ăt′əm) *n.* **1.** Anything considered an irreducible constituent of a specified system. **2.** The irreducible, indestructible material unit of ancient **atomism** *(see).* **3.** *Physics & Chemistry.* A unit of matter, the smallest unit of an element, consisting of a dense, central, positively charged **nucleus** *(see)* surrounded by a system of electrons, equal in number to the number of nuclear protons, the entire structure having an approximate diameter of 10^{-8} centimeter and characteristically remaining undivided in chemical reactions except for limited removal, transfer, or exchange of certain electrons. **4.** This unit regarded as a source of nuclear energy. [Middle English *attome, attomus,* from Latin *atomus,* from Greek *atomos,* indivisible : *a-,* not + *temnein,* to cut (see **tem-** in Appendix*).]

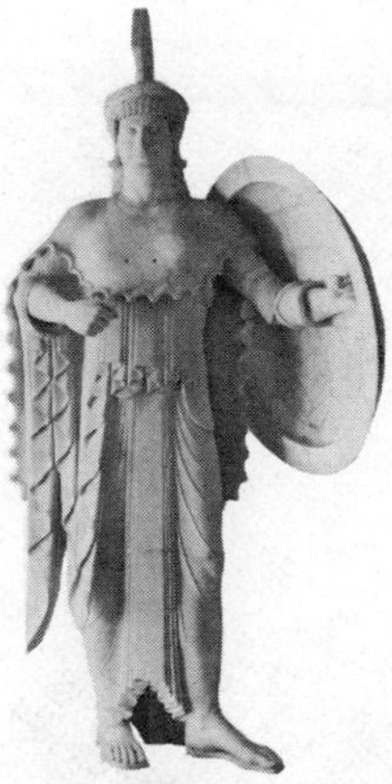

Athena
Marble from Aegina, fifth century B.C.

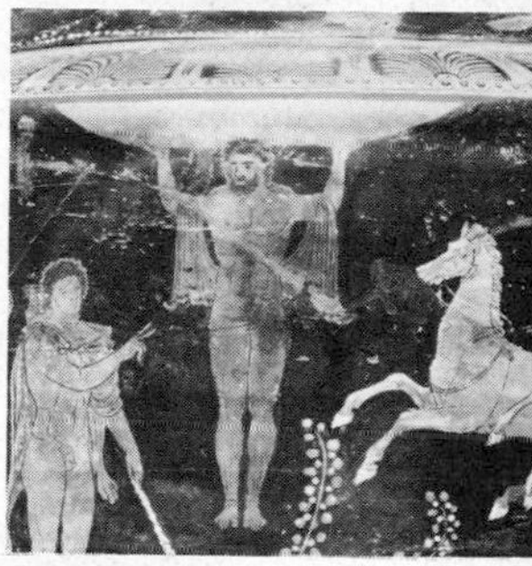

Atlas[1]
Detail of a fourth-century B.C. Greek vase painting

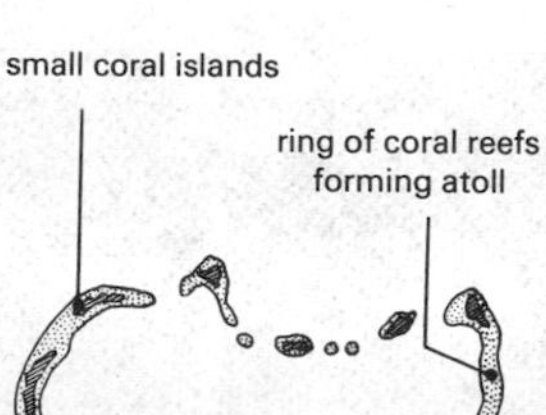

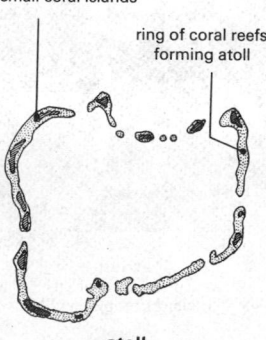

atoll

a·tom·ic (ə-tŏm′ĭk) *adj.* **1.** Of or relating to an atom or atoms. **2.** Of or employing atomic energy: *an atomic submarine.* **3.** Very small; infinitesimal. —**a·tom′i·cal·ly** *adv.*

atomic age. Also **Atomic Age.** The current era as characterized by the discovery, technological applications, and sociopolitical consequences of atomic energy.

atomic bomb. **1.** An explosive weapon of great destructive power derived from the rapid release of energy in the fission of heavy atomic nuclei, as of uranium 235. **2.** Any bomb deriving its destructive power from the release of nuclear energy. Also called "atom bomb," "A-bomb." See **hydrogen bomb.**

atomic clock. An extremely precise timekeeping device regulated in correspondence with a characteristic invariant frequency of an atomic or molecular system.

atomic energy. **1.** The energy released from an atomic nucleus in fission or fusion. **2.** This energy regarded as a source of practical power.

Atomic Energy Commission. *Abbr.* **AEC, A.E.C.** A five-member advisory board formed in the United States in 1946 for the domestic control of atomic energy.

at·o·mic·i·ty (ăt′ə-mĭs′ə-tē) *n.* **1.** The state of being composed of atoms. **2.** *Chemistry.* **a.** The number of atoms in a molecule. **b.** Valence.

atomic mass. The mass of an atomic system or constituent, usually expressed in atomic mass units.

atomic mass unit. *Abbr.* **amu** A unit of mass equal to $\frac{1}{12}$ the mass of the carbon isotope with mass number 12, approximately 1.6604×10^{-24} gram.

atomic number. *Symbol* **Z** The number of protons in an atomic nucleus.

atomic pile. A **nuclear reactor** *(see).*

atomic reactor. A **nuclear reactor** *(see).*

atomic theory. **1.** The physical theory of the structure, properties, and behavior of the atom. **2.** Atomism.

atomic weight. *Abbr.* **at wt** The average weight of an atom of an element, usually expressed relative to one atom of the carbon isotope taken to have a standard weight of 12.

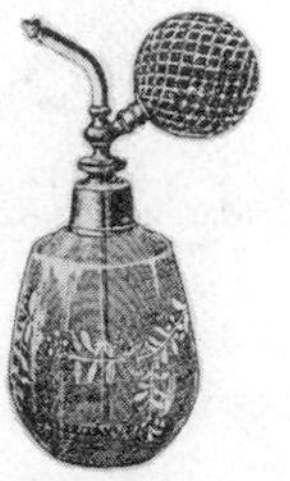

atomizer
French perfume atomizer

at·om·ism (ăt′əm-ĭz′əm) *n.* **1.** The ancient theory of Democritus, Epicurus, and Lucretius, according to which simple, indivisible, and indestructible atoms are the basic components of the entire universe. **2.** *Sociology.* Any theory according to which social institutions and processes arise solely from the acts of individual men. **3.** *Political Science.* **a.** The division or tendency to divide into subclasses, groups, or units of a given society. **b.** The foregoing tendency accompanied by or arising from a strong subjective individualism. —**at′om·ist** *n.* —**at′-om·is′tic** (-ĭs′tĭk), **at′om·is′ti·cal** *adj.* —**at′om·is′ti·cal·ly** *adv.*

at·om·ize (ăt′əm-īz′) *tr.v.* **-ized, -izing, -izes. 1.** To reduce or separate into atoms. **2. a.** To reduce (a liquid) to a spray. **b.** To spray (a liquid) in this form. **3.** To subject to bombardment with atomic weapons. —**at′om·i·za′tion** *n.*

at·om·iz·er (ăt′əm-ī′zər) *n.* A device for producing a fine spray, especially of perfume or medicine.

atom smasher. An atomic particle **accelerator** *(see).*

at·o·my¹ (ăt′ə-mē) *n., pl.* **-mies.** *Archaic.* **1.** A tiny particle. **2.** A tiny being: *"Drawn with a team of little atomies"* (Shakespeare). [From Latin *atomī,* plural of *atomus,* ATOM.]

at·o·my² (ăt′ə-mē) *n., pl.* **-mies.** *Archaic.* A skeleton or a gaunt person. [From *an atomy,* improper spelling of ANATOMY.]

a·to·nal (ā-tō′nəl) *adj. Music.* Lacking a tonal center. —**a·to′-nal·ly** *adv.*

a·to·nal·ism (ā-tō′nəl-ĭz′əm) *n. Music.* **1.** The lack of a tonal center or key, as a principle of musical composition. **2.** The theory of atonal composition.

a·to·nal·i·ty (ā′tō-năl′ə-tē) *n. Music.* A style of composition in which tonal center or key is disregarded.

a·tone (ə-tōn′) *v.* **atoned, atoning, atones.** —*intr.* **1.** To make amends, as for a sin or fault. Used with *for.* **2.** *Archaic.* To agree. —*tr. Archaic.* **1.** To expiate. **2.** To reconcile or harmonize. **3.** To conciliate; appease. [Middle English *atonen,* to be reconciled, from *at one,* of one mind, in accord : AT + ONE.] —**a·ton′a·ble, a·tone′a·ble** *adj.* —**a·ton′er** *n.*

a·tone·ment (ə-tōn′mənt) *n.* **1.** Amends or reparation made for an injury or wrong; expiation; recompense. **2.** In the Hebrew Scriptures, man's reconciliation with God after having transgressed the covenant. **3.** *Capital* **A.** *Theology.* **a.** The redemptive life and death of Christ. **b.** The reconciliation of God and man thus brought about by Christ. **4.** *Christian Science.* The radical obedience and purification, exemplified in the life of Jesus, by which humanity finds man's oneness with God. **5.** *Archaic.* Reconciliation; concord.

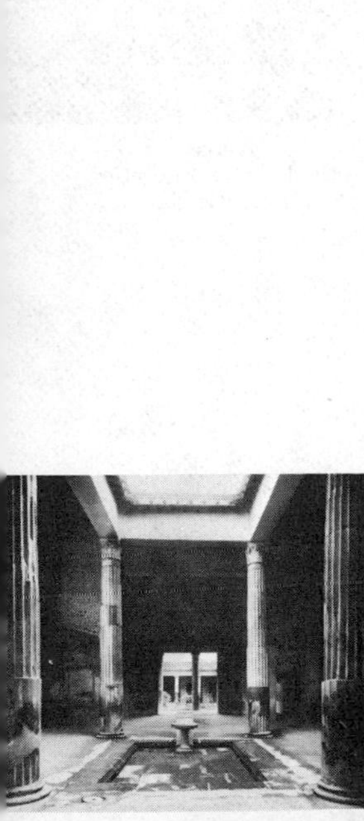

atrium
Inner court of an ancient Pompeian villa

a·ton·ic (ā-tŏn′ĭk) *adj.* **1.** Not accented: *atonic words and syllables.* **2.** *Pathology.* Pertaining to, caused, or characterized by atony. —*n.* A word, syllable, or sound that is unaccented. [French *atonique,* from Greek *atonos.* See **atony.**] —**at′o·nic′i·ty** (ăt′ə-nĭs′ə-tē) *n.*

at·o·ny (ăt′ə-nē) *n. Pathology.* **1.** Insufficient muscular tone. **2.** *Phonetics.* Lack of accent or stress. [Late Latin *atonia,* from Greek, from *atonos,* not stretched : *a-,* without + *tonos,* a stretching, TONE.]

a·top (ə-tŏp′) *adv. Archaic.* On or at the top. —*prep.* On top of. —**a·top′** *adj.*

-ator. Indicates one who or that which acts or does; for example, **aviator, radiator.** [Middle English *-atour,* from Old French, from Latin *-ātor* : *-ātus,* -ATE + -OR.]

-atory. Indicates pertinence to, characteristic of, result of, or effect of; for example, **perspiratory, amendatory.** [Middle English, from Latin *-ātōrius* : *-ātus,* -ATE + *-ōrius,* -ORY.]

ATP *Biochemistry.* adenosine triphosphate.

at·ra·bil·ious (ăt′rə-bĭl′yəs) *adj.* Also **at·ra·bil·i·ar** (-bĭl′ē-ər). **1.** Inclined to melancholy. **2.** Having a peevish disposition; surly. [From Latin *ātra bīlis,* black bile (translation of Greek *melankholia,* MELANCHOLY) : *ātra,* feminine of *āter,* black (see **āter-** in Appendix*) + *bīlis,* BILE.] —**at′ra·bil′ious·ness** *n.*

A·trek (ä-trĕk′). A river rising in northeastern Iran and forming part of the border between Iran and the Soviet Union on its 300-mile course to the Caspian Sea.

A·treus (ā′trōōs′, ā′trē-əs). *Greek Mythology.* A king of Mycenae, father of Agamemnon and Menelaus.

a·tri·o·ven·tric·u·lar (ā′trē-ō-vĕn-trĭk′yə-lər) *adj. Anatomy.* Pertaining to the atria and the ventricles of the heart.

a·trip (ə-trĭp′) *adj.* Just clear of the bottom. Said of an anchor. [A- (on) + TRIP (to raise an anchor).] —**a·trip′** *adv.*

a·tri·um (ā′trē-əm) *n., pl.* **atria** (ā′trē-ə) or **-ums. 1.** An open central court, especially in an ancient Roman house. **2.** A bodily cavity or chamber, as in the heart. Also called "auricle." [Latin *ātrium.* See **āter-** in Appendix.*] —**a′tri·al** *adj.*

a·tro·cious (ə-trō′shəs) *adj.* **1.** Extremely evil or cruel; monstrous: *an atrocious crime.* **2.** Exceptionally bad; abominable: *atrocious decor; atrocious behavior.* [From Latin *ātrōx* (stem *ātrōc-*), "dark-looking," horrible, cruel. See **āter-** in Appendix.*] —**a·tro′cious·ly** *adv.* —**a·tro′cious·ness** *n.*

a·troc·i·ty (ə-trŏs′ə-tē) *n., pl.* **-ties. 1.** Atrocious condition, quality, or behavior; monstrousness; vileness. **2.** An atrocious action, situation, or object; outrage.

at·ro·phy (ăt′rə-fē) *n.; pl.* **-phies. 1.** *Pathology.* The emaciation or wasting of tissues, organs, or the entire body. **2.** Any wasting away or diminution: *moral atrophy.* —*v.* **atrophied, -phying, -phies.** —*tr.* To cause to wither; affect with atrophy. —*intr.* To waste away; wither. [Late Latin *atrophia,* from Greek, from *atrophos,* ill-nourished : *a-,* without + *trophē,* nourishment (see **threph-** in Appendix*).] —**a·troph′ic** (ā-trŏf′-ĭk), **at′ro·phous** (-fəs) *adj.*

at·ro·pine (ăt′rə-pēn′, -pĭn) *n.* Also **at·ro·pin** (-pĭn). An extremely poisonous, bitter, crystalline alkaloid, $C_{17}H_{23}NO_3$, obtained from belladonna and related plants. It is used to dilate the pupil of the eye and as an anesthetic and antispasmodic. [German *Atropin,* from New Latin *Atropa,* genus of belladonna, deadly nightshade, from Greek *atropos,* unchangeable, inflexible. See **Atropos.**]

At·ro·pos (ăt′rə-pŏs′, -pəs). *Greek Mythology.* One of the three Fates. [Greek, from *atropos,* inexorable, inflexible : *a-,* not + *trop-,* stem of *trepein,* to turn (see **trep-²** in Appendix*).]

A.T.S. 1. American Temperance Society. **2.** Army Transport Service.

att. 1. attached. **2.** attention. **3.** attorney.

at·tach (ə-tăch′) *v.* **-tached, -taching, -taches.** —*tr.* **1.** To fasten on or affix to; connect or join. **2.** To connect as an adjunct or associated part. **3.** To affix or append; add, as a signature. **4.** To ascribe or assign: *I attach no significance to the threat.* **5.** To bind by personal ties, as of affection or loyalty: *He's very attached to his mother.* **6.** To appoint officially. **7.** *Military.* To assign (personnel) to a unit on a temporary basis. Compare **assign. 8.** *Law.* To seize (persons or property) by legal writ. —*intr.* To adhere. [Middle English *attachen,* from Old French *attacher, estachier,* to fasten (with a stake), from *estache,* stake, from Frankish *stakka* (unattested). See **steg-²** in Appendix.*] —**at·tach′a·ble** *adj.* —**at·tach′er** *n.*

at·ta·ché (ăt′ə-shā′, ă-tă′shā′) *n.* A person officially assigned to the staff of a diplomatic mission to serve in some particular capacity: *a cultural attaché.* [French, "one attached (to a diplomatic mission)," past participle of *attacher,* ATTACH.]

attaché case. A briefcase resembling a small suitcase, with hinges and flat sides.

at·tach·ment (ə-tăch′mənt) *n.* **1.** The act of attaching or the condition of being attached. **2.** Something that serves to attach one thing to another; a tie, band, or fastening. **3.** Fond regard; affection. **4.** A supplementary part; an accessory. **5.** *Law.* **a.** The legal seizure of a person or property. **b.** The writ ordering such a seizure. —See Synonyms at **appendage.**

at·tack (ə-tăk′) *v.* **-tacked, -tacking, -tacks.** —*tr.* **1.** To set upon with violent force; begin hostilities against or conflict with. **2.** To bombard with hostile criticism. **3.** To start work on with purpose and vigor: *attack a problem.* **4.** To begin to affect harmfully. —*intr.* To make an attack; launch an assault. —*n.* **1.** The act of attacking; an assault. **2.** Occurrence of or seizure by a disease. **3.** The initial movement in any task or undertaking. **4.** *Music.* The manner in which a passage or phrase is begun. [French *attaquer,* from Old French, from Old Italian *attaccare,* variant of *estaccare* (unattested), to attach, join (battle), from *stacca* (unattested), stake, from Gothic *stakka* (unattested). See **steg-²** in Appendix.*] —**at·tack′er** *n.*

Synonyms: *attack, bombard, assail, storm, assault, beset.* These verbs mean to set upon physically or, in some cases, figuratively. *Attack* applies to any offensive action, physical or verbal, and especially to the beginning of planned aggression. *Bombard* suggests showering with bombs or shells or, figuratively, with words: *bombarded with questions. Assail,* literally and figuratively, implies repeated and violent attacks. *Storm* refers to a sudden, sweeping attempt for quick, total victory. *Assault* almost always implies physical contact and sudden, intense violence. *Beset* suggests encirclement by an enemy force or by adversity and attack from all sides.

at·tain (ə-tān′) *v.* **-tained, -taining, -tains.** —*tr.* **1.** To gain, reach, or accomplish by mental or physical effort. **2.** To arrive at, as in time. —*intr.* To succeed in gaining or reaching; arrive at. Usually used with *to: He attained to the highest office in the land.* —See Synonyms at **reach.** [Middle English *atteignen,* from Old French *ataindre* (stem *ataign-*), to reach to, from Vulgar Latin *attangere* (unattested), from Latin *attingere* : *ad-*, to + *tangere*, to touch (see **tag-** in Appendix*).]

at·tain·a·ble (ə-tā′nə-bəl) *adj.* Capable of being attained. —**at·tain′a·bil′i·ty, at·tain′a·ble·ness** *n.*

at·tain·der (ə-tān′dər) *n.* **1.** The loss of all civil rights legally consequent to a death sentence or to outlawry for a capital offense. See **bill of attainder. 2.** *Archaic.* Dishonor. [Middle English *attendre,* conviction, from Norman French, "corruption of blood (of a criminal)," from Old French *ataindre,* to affect, infect, ATTAIN.]

at·tain·ment (ə-tān′mənt) *n.* **1.** The act of attaining. **2.** Something that is attained; an acquirement or acquisition.

at·taint (ə-tānt′) *tr.v.* **-tainted, -tainting, -taints. 1.** *Law.* To condemn by a sentence of attainder. **2.** *Archaic.* To impart stigma to; to disgrace. **3.** *Obsolete.* To accuse or prove guilty. Used with *of.* —*n.* **1.** Attainder. **2.** *Archaic.* A disgrace; stigma. [Middle English *attaynten,* from Old French *ataint,* past participle of *ataindre,* to convict, originally, to affect, infect, ATTAIN.]

At·ta·lid (ăt′ə-lĭd) *n.* A member of a Hellenistic dynasty that ruled Pergamum from 282 to 133 B.C. —**At′ta·lid** *adj.*

at·tar (ăt′ər) *n.* Also **ot·tar** (ŏt′ər), **ot·to** (ŏt′ō). A fragrant essential oil or perfume obtained from the petals of flowers, especially certain species of roses. [Persian *'aṭir,* perfumed, from *'iṭr,* perfume, from Arabic.]

At·ta·wa·pis·kat (ăt′ə-wə-pĭs′kət). A river of Canada, rising in north-central Ontario and flowing 465 miles generally north to James Bay.

at·tempt (ə-tĕmpt′) *tr.v.* **-tempted, -tempting, -tempts. 1.** To endeavor to do or make; to try. **2.** *Archaic.* To tempt. **3.** *Archaic.* To attack with the intention of subduing. —*n.* **1.** An effort or try. **2.** An attack; an assault: *an attempt on one's life.* [Middle English *attempten,* from Old French *attempter,* from Latin *attemptāre* : *ad-*, to + *temptāre,* to try, TEMPT.] —**at·tempt′a·ble** *adj.* —**at·tempt′er** *n.*

at·tend (ə-tĕnd′) *v.* **-tended, -tending, -tends.** —*tr.* **1.** To be present at: *attend class.* **2.** To accompany as a circumstance or follow as a result: *The speech was attended by wild applause.* **3.** To accompany as an attendant or servant; wait upon. **4.** To take care of or charge of (a sick person, for example). **5.** To listen to; heed. **6.** *Archaic.* To wait for; expect. —*intr.* **1.** To be present. **2.** To pay attention; heed. **3.** To remain ready to serve; wait. Used with *on* or *upon: We attend upon your wishes.* **4.** *Obsolete.* To delay or wait. —**attend to.** To apply or direct oneself: *Please attend to the matter at once.* [Middle English *attenden,* from Old French *atendre,* from Latin *attendere,* to stretch toward, direct attention to : *ad-*, toward + *tendere,* to stretch (see **ten-** in Appendix*).] —**at·tend′er** *n.*

at·ten·dance (ə-tĕn′dəns) *n.* **1.** The act of attending. **2.** The persons or number of persons who are present, as at a class.

at·ten·dant (ə-tĕn′dənt) *n.* **1.** One who attends; especially, one who waits on another. **2.** One who is present, as at a class. **3.** An accompanying thing or circumstance; a consequence or concomitant. —*adj.* Accompanying or consequent: *attendant circumstances.* —**at·tend′ant·ly** *adv.*

at·ten·tion (ə-tĕn′shən) *n. Abbr.* **att., attn. 1.** Concentration of the mental powers upon an object; a close or careful observing or listening. **2.** The ability or power to concentrate mentally. **3.** Observant consideration; notice: *Your suggestion has come to our attention.* **4.** Consideration or courtesy: *attention to others' feelings.* **5.** *Usually plural.* An act of courtesy, consideration, or gallantry indicating romantic interest. **6.** *Military.* **a.** The posture assumed by a soldier, with the body erect, eyes to the front, arms at the sides, and heels together. **b.** A command to assume this position. [Middle English *attencioun,* from Latin *attentiō,* from *attendere,* ATTEND.] —**at·ten′tion·al** *adj.*

at·ten·tive (ə-tĕn′tĭv) *adj.* **1.** Paying attention; observant; listening. **2.** Courteous or devoted; considerate; thoughtful. —**at·ten′tive·ly** *adv.* —**at·ten′tive·ness** *n.*

at·ten·u·ate (ə-tĕn′yo͞o-āt′) *v.* **-ated, -ating, -ates.** —*tr.* **1.** To make slender, fine, or small. **2.** To reduce in strength, force, value, or amount; weaken. **3.** To lessen in density; to dilute or rarefy (a liquid or gas). **4.** *Bacteriology.* To make (a pathogenic microorganism) less virulent. —*intr.* To become thin, weak, or fine. —*adj.* (ə-tĕn′yo͞o-ĭt). **1.** Thinned; diluted; weakened. **2.** *Botany.* Gradually tapering to a point; slender and pointed. [Latin *attenuāre,* to make thin : *ad-*, to + *tenuāre,* to make thin, from *tenuis,* thin (see **ten-** in Appendix*).] —**at·ten′u·a·ble** *adj.* —**at·ten′u·a′tion** *n.*

at·test (ə-tĕst′) *v.* **-tested, -testing, -tests.** —*tr.* **1.** To affirm to be correct, true, or genuine; corroborate. **2.** To certify by signature or oath; affirm in an official capacity. **3.** To supply evidence of: *"the vast palaces attest its wealth"* (H.D.F. Kitto). **4.** To constitute documentary or other material proof of the former existence of. Used especially in archaeology and historical linguistics. **5.** To put under oath. —*intr.* To bear witness; give testimony. Used with *to: I attest to his good faith.* —*n. Archaic.* Attestation. [French *attester,* from Old French, from Latin *attestārī* : *ad-*, to + *testārī,* to be witness, from *testis,* witness (see **trei-** in Appendix*).] —**at·test′ant** *n.* —**at′tes·ta′tion** (ăt′ĕs-tā′shən, ăt′ə-stā′-) *n.* —**at·test′er, at·tes′tor** (-tər) *n.*

Att. Gen. attorney general.

at·tic (ăt′ĭk) *n.* **1.** A story or room directly below the roof of a house. **2.** *Architecture.* A low wall or story above the cornice of a classical façade. [From *Attic story,* originally a small top story having square columns in the ATTIC style.]

At·tic (ăt′ĭk) *adj.* **1.** Of, pertaining to, or characteristic of ancient Attica, Athens, or the Athenians. **2.** *Sometimes small* **a.** Characterized by classical purity and simplicity. —*n.* The Ancient Greek dialect of Athens, in which the bulk of Classical Greek literature is written, belonging to Attic-Ionic.

At·ti·ca (ăt′ĭ-kə). **1.** The hinterland of Athens in ancient Greece. **2.** An administrative division of modern Greece. Population, 2,058,000. Capital, Athens.

At·tic-I·on·ic (ăt′ĭk-ī-ŏn′ĭk) *n.* A branch of East Greek comprising Attic and Ionic.

At·ti·cism (ăt′ə-sĭz′əm) *n.* **1.** Something characteristic of the Attic Greek language. **2.** An expression characterized by conciseness and elegance. **3.** A simple, elegant style of rhetoric.

At·ti·cize (ăt′ə-sīz′) *v.* **-cized, -cizing, -cizes.** —*intr.* To affect or conform to Attic custom, style, or usage. —*tr.* To render Attic in custom, style, or usage.

Attic salt. Dry, delicate, pointed wit. Also called "Attic wit."

At·ti·la (ăt′ə-lə, ə-tĭl′ə). Called "the Scourge of God." A.D. 406?–453. King of the Huns (434–53), invader of Europe.

at·tire (ə-tīr′) *tr.v.* **-tired, -tiring, -tires.** To dress, especially in elaborate or splendid garments; clothe. —*n.* **1.** Clothing; array. **2.** *Heraldry.* The antlers of a deer. [Middle English *attiren,* from Old French *atirier,* to arrange into ranks, put in order : *a-*, from Latin *ad-*, to + *tire,* order, rank (see **tier**).]

At·tis (ăt′ĭs). *Phrygian Mythology.* A god of fertility, the consort of Cybele.

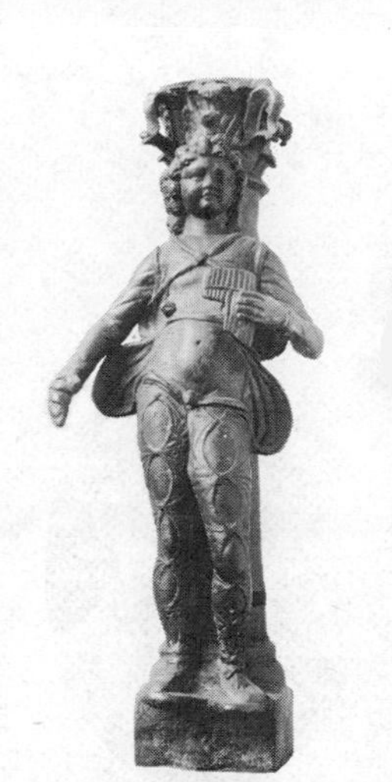

Attis
Roman sculpture of the god against a column found at Edirne (Adrianapolis), Turkey

at·ti·tude (ăt′ə-to͞od′, -tyo͞od′) *n.* **1.** A position of the body or manner of carrying oneself, indicative of a mood or condition: *"men . . . sprawled alone or in heaps, in the careless attitudes of death"* (John Reed). **2.** A state of mind or feeling with regard to some matter; disposition: *"My attitude towards historicism is one of frank hostility"* (Karl Popper). **3.** *Aviation.* The orientation of an aircraft's axes relative to some reference line or plane, such as the horizon. **4.** *Aerospace.* The orientation of a spacecraft relative to its direction of motion. **5.** *Ballet.* A position in which a dancer stands on one leg with the other bent backward. [French, from Italian *attitudine,* disposition, from Late Latin *aptitūdō,* faculty, fitness, from Latin *aptus,* fit, APT.] —**at′ti·tu′di·nal** (ăt′ə-to͞od′n-əl, -tyo͞od′n-əl) *adj.*

at·ti·tu·di·nize (ăt′ə-to͞od′n-īz′, -tyo͞od′n-īz′) *intr.v.* **-nized, -nizing, -nizes.** To assume an affected attitude; to posture.

Att·lee (ăt′lē), **Clement Richard.** 1883–1967. Prime Minister of the United Kingdom (1945–51).

attn. attention.

atto–. *Abbr.* **a** Indicates one-quintillionth (10^{-18}); for example, **attotesla.** [Danish or Norwegian *atten,* eighteen, from Old Norse *āttjān.* See **oktō** in Appendix.*]

at·torn (ə-tûrn′) *intr.v.* **-torned, -torning, -torns.** *Law.* To acknowledge a new owner as one's landlord. [Middle English *attournen,* from Old French *atorner,* to turn to, assign to : *a-*, from Latin *ad-*, to + *torner,* to turn, from Latin *tornāre,* to turn on a lathe, from *tornus,* lathe, from Greek *tornos* (see **ter-²** in Appendix*).] —**at·torn′ment** *n.*

at·tor·ney (ə-tûr′nē) *n., pl.* **-neys.** *Abbr.* **at., att., atty.** A person legally appointed or empowered to act for another; especially, an attorney at law. See Synonyms at **lawyer.** —**by attorney.** By proxy. [Middle English *attourney,* from Old French *atorne,* "one appointed," past participle of *atorner,* to appoint, ATTORN.] —**at·tor′ney·ship′** *n.*

attorney at law. One who is qualified to represent a party in a court of law and to prepare and manage his case; a lawyer.

attorney general *pl.* **attorneys general.** *Abbr.* **A.G., Att. Gen., Atty. Gen. 1.** The chief law officer and legal counsel of the government of a state or the United States. The U.S. Attorney General is a Cabinet member, heading the Department of Justice. **2.** In some states, a public prosecutor.

at·to·tes·la (ăt′ō-tĕs′lə) *n. Physics. Abbr.* **aT** One-quintillionth (10^{-18}) of a tesla.

at·tract (ə-trăkt′) *v.* **-tracted, -tracting, -tracts.** —*tr.* **1.** To cause to draw near or adhere. **2.** To draw or direct to oneself by some quality or action: *sugar attracts insects.* **3.** To evoke interest or admiration in; to allure. —*intr.* To possess or use the power of attraction; be magnetic or alluring. [Middle English *attracten,* from Latin *attrahere* (past participle *attractus*) : *ad-*, toward + *trahere,* to draw (see **tragh-** in Appendix*).] —**at·tract′a·ble** *adj.* —**at·trac′tor** (ə-trăk′tər), **at·tract′er** *n.*

at·trac·tion (ə-trăk′shən) *n.* **1.** The act or capability of attracting. **2.** The quality of attracting; allure; charm. **3.** A feature, characteristic, or factor that attracts: *Money was not the least of her attractions.* **4.** A public spectacle or entertainment.

at·trac·tive (ə-trăk′tĭv) *adj.* **1.** Having the power to attract. **2.** Pleasing to the eye or mind; appealing. **3.** Personally engaging; charming. —**at·trac′tive·ly** *adv.* —**at·trac′tive·ness** *n.*

attrib. attribute; attributive.

at·trib·ute (ə-trĭb′yo͞ot) *tr.v.* **-uted, -uting, -utes.** To regard or assign as belonging to or resulting from someone or something; ascribe. —*n.* (ăt′rə-byo͞ot′). *Abbr.* **attrib. 1.** A quality or characteristic belonging to a person or thing; a distinctive feature: *"Travel has lost the attributes of privilege and fashion."* (John Cheever). **2.** An object associated with and serving to identify a character, personage, or office: *Lightning bolts are the attribute of Zeus.* **3.** *Grammar.* An adjective or a phrase used as an adjective. —See Synonyms at **quality.** [Latin *attribuere* : *ad-*, to + *tribuere,* to allot, grant (see **tribute**).] —**at·trib′ut·a·ble** *adj.* —**at·trib′ut·er, at·trib′u·tor** (-yo͞o-tər) *n.*

Synonyms: *attribute, ascribe, impute, credit, assign, refer.* These verbs mean to declare as belonging to an owner, time, class, or cause. Though the two are now virtually interchangeable, one most precisely *attributes* abstract qualities and possessions and *ascribes* concrete things and effects. *Impute* suggests a fault or guilt, and *credit,* an accomplishment or success.

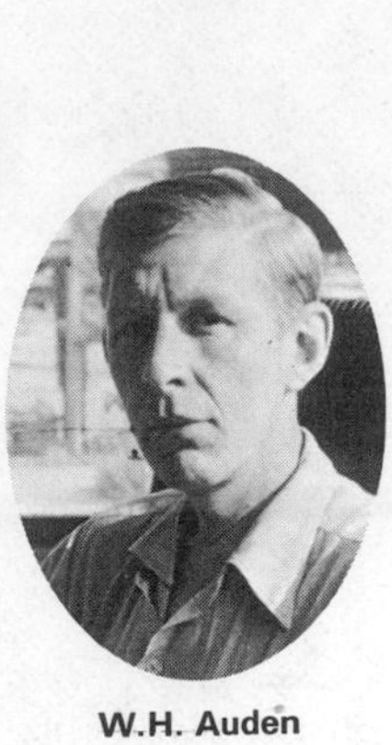

W.H. Auden

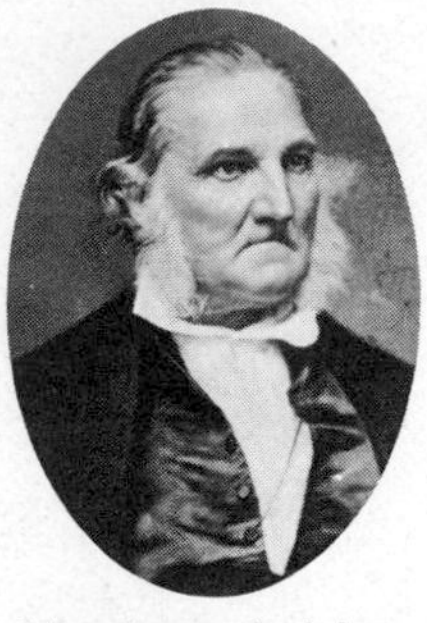

John James Audubon
Photograph by Mathew Brady

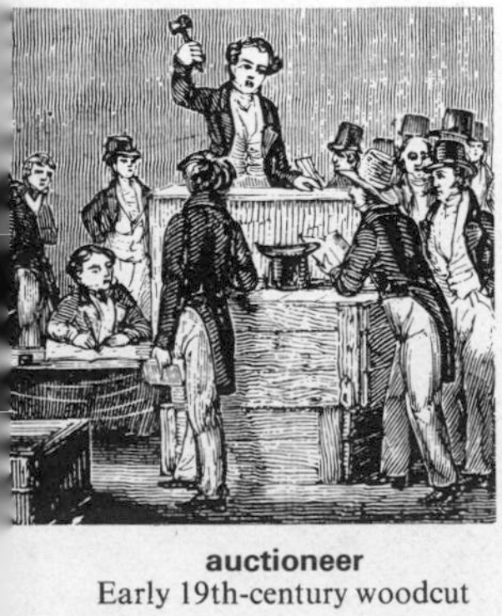

auctioneer
Early 19th-century woodcut

To *assign* is to place within a class, type, or period. To *refer* is to put more approximately in a category. Thus, a psychologist *attributes* Darwin's genius to childhood trauma; a scholar *ascribes* unsigned letters to Darwin; a historian *imputes* the decline of humanism to Darwin; a biologist *credits* modern experimental methods to Darwin or *credits* him with founding modern biology; a fundamentalist *assigns* him to the body of heretics; and a librarian *refers* his minor works to the stacks.

at·tri·bu·tion (ăt′rə-byōō′shən) *n.* **1.** The act of attributing. **2.** Something that is ascribed; an attribute.

at·trib·u·tive (ə-trĭb′yə-tĭv) *n. Abbr.* **attrib.** *Grammar.* A word or word group, such as an adjective or the equivalent of an adjective, that is placed adjacent to the noun it modifies without a linking verb. In the phrases *the pale girl* and *John's hands, pale* and *John's* are attributives. Compare **predicate.** —*adj.* **1.** *Abbr.* **attrib.** *Grammar.* Of or functioning as an attributive, as an adjective. **2.** Of or having the nature of an attribution or attribute. **3.** Of an attributed origin: *an attributive Rubens.* —**at·trib′u·tive·ly** *adv.* —**at·trib′u·tive·ness** *n.*

at·trit·ed (ə-trī′tĭd) *adj.* Also *rare* **at·trite** (ə-trīt′). Worn down by attrition. [Latin *attrītus,* past participle of *atterere,* to rub away. See **attrition.**]

at·tri·tion (ə-trĭsh′ən) *n.* **1.** A rubbing away or wearing down by friction. **2.** A gradual diminution in number or strength due to constant stress. **3.** *Theology.* Repentance for sin motivated by fear of punishment rather than by love of God. [Middle English *attricioun,* from Medieval Latin *attrītiō,* "chastisement," from Latin, a rubbing against, from *atterere,* to rub against : *ad-,* toward, against + *terere,* to rub (see **ter-**[2] in Appendix*).] —**at·tri′tion·al, at·tri′tive** (ə-trī′tĭv) *adj.*

At·tu (ăt′tōō). The westernmost of the Aleutian Islands, occupied by Japan in 1942 and recaptured by U.S. forces in 1943.

At·tucks (ăt′əks), **Crispus.** 1723?–1770. American patriot; one of the men killed by British forces at Boston Massacre; believed to have been a runaway slave.

at·tune (ə-tōōn′, ə-tyōōn′) *tr.v.* **-tuned, -tuning, -tunes. 1.** To tune. **2.** To bring into harmony. **3.** To accustom to a special perception: *an ear attuned to dissonance.* [AD- (to) + TUNE.]

atty. attorney.

Atty. Gen. attorney general.

A·tu·o·na (ä′tōō-ô′nä). The capital of the Marquesas Islands in the South Pacific; the burial place of Gauguin. Population, 670.

a·twain (ə-twān′) *adv. Archaic.* In two: *broken atwain.*

a·twit·ter (ə-twĭt′ər) *adj.* In a state of nervous excitement.

at wt atomic weight.

a·typ·i·cal (ā-tĭp′ĭ-kəl) *adj.* Also **a·typ·ic** (-ĭk). Not typical; varying from the type. —**a·typ′i·cal·ly** *adv.*

Au The symbol for the element gold (Latin *aurum*).

A.U. astronomical unit.

au·bade (ō-bäd′) *n.* A musical composition intended to be played or sung at dawn or early in the morning. [French, from Old French, from Old Provençal *auba, alba,* dawn, from Vulgar Latin *alba* (unattested), feminine of Latin *albus,* white. See **albho-** in Appendix.*]

Aube (ōb). A navigable river in northeastern France, flowing 140 miles northwest to the Seine.

au·berge (ō-bĕrzh′) *n.* An inn or tavern. [French, from Old French, from Old Provençal *alberga,* inn, shelter, camp, from Vulgar Latin *arberga* (unattested), army camp, from Germanic. See **koro-** in Appendix.*]

au·ber·gine (ō′bĕr-zhēn′, ō′bər-jīn) *n.* A vegetable, the **eggplant** *(see).* [French, from Catalan *alberginia,* from Arabic *al-bādindjān,* from Persian *bādin-gān,* from Sanskrit *vatin-ganaḥ*†.]

Au·brey (ô′brē). A masculine given name. [French *Auberi,* from German *Alberich,* "ruler of elfs" : *alb,* elf, from Middle High German (see **albho-** in Appendix*) + *-rich,* ruler, from Old High German (see **reg-**[1] in Appendix*).]

au·burn (ô′bərn) *n.* Moderate reddish brown to brown. See **color.** [Middle English *aborne,* blond, from Old French *auborne, alborne,* from Medieval Latin *alburnus,* whitish, from Latin *albus,* white. See **albho-** in Appendix.*] —**au′burn** *adj.*

Au·bus·son (ō-bü-sôɴ′). A town in central France, long famous for its carpets and tapestries.

Auck·land (ôk′lənd). A city and seaport of New Zealand, on northern North Island. Population, 149,000.

Auck·land Islands (ôk′lənd). An uninhabited island group of New Zealand, 300 miles south of South Island.

au cou·rant (ō kōō-räɴ′). *French.* Informed on current affairs; up-to-date. Literally, "in the current."

auc·tion (ôk′shən) *n.* **1.** A public sale in which property or items of merchandise are sold to the highest bidder. **2.** The bidding in the game of bridge. **3. Auction bridge** *(see).* —*tr.v.* **auctioned, -tioning, -tions.** To sell at or by an auction. Usually used with *off.* [Latin *auctiō,* (a sale by) increase (of bids), from *augēre,* to increase. See **aug-**[1] in Appendix.*]

auction bridge. A variety of the game of bridge in which tricks made in excess of the contract are scored toward game. Also called "auction."

auc·tion·eer (ôk′shə-nîr′) *n.* A person who conducts an auction. —*tr.v.* **auctioneered, -eering, -eers.** To auction.

auc·to·ri·al (ôk-tôr′ē-əl, ôk-tōr′-) *adj.* Of or pertaining to an author. [From Latin *auctor,* AUTHOR.]

aud. audit; auditor.

au·da·cious (ô-dā′shəs) *adj.* **1.** Fearlessly daring; bold. **2.** Lacking restraint or circumspection; arrogantly insolent. —See Synonyms at **brave, reckless.** [Old French *audacieux,* from *audace,* boldness, from Latin *audācia,* from *audāx* (stem *audāc-*), bold, from *audēre,* to dare, "be eager," from *avidus,* AVID.] —**au·da′cious·ly** *adv.* —**au·da′cious·ness** *n.*

au·dac·i·ty (ô-dăs′ə-tē) *n., pl.* **-ties. 1.** Boldness; daring; intrepidity. **2.** Unrestrained impudence; insolence; presumption. **3.** An instance of boldness or presumption. —See Synonyms at **temerity**

Au·den (ôd′n), **W(ystan) H(ugh).** Born 1907. English-born American poet, critic, and playwright.

au·di·bil·i·ty (ô′də-bĭl′ə-tē) *n.* The capacity to be heard.

au·di·ble (ô′də-bəl) *adj.* Capable of being heard. [Late Latin *audībilis,* from Latin *audīre,* to hear. See **aw-**[2] in Appendix.*] —**au′di·ble·ness** *n.* —**au′di·bly** *adv.*

au·di·ence (ô′dē-əns) *n.* **1.** A gathering of spectators or listeners, as at a concert. **2.** The readers, hearers, or viewers reached by a book, radio broadcast, or television program. **3.** A formal hearing or conference with a king, pope, or other personage. **4.** An opportunity to be heard or to express one's views. **5.** The act of hearing or attending. [Middle English, from Old French, from Latin *audientia,* from *audiēns,* present participle of *audīre,* to hear. See **aw-**[2] in Appendix.*]

au·di·ent (ô′dē-ənt) *adj.* Hearing; listening. [Latin *audiēns,* present participle of *audīre,* to hear. See **aw-**[2] in Appendix.*]

au·dile (ô′dĭl′) *adj.* Capable of learning chiefly from auditory, rather than tactile or visual, stimuli. —*n.* An audile person. [From Latin *audīre,* to hear. See **aw-**[2] in Appendix.*]

au·di·o (ô′dē-ō′) *adj.* **1.** Of or pertaining to audible sound. **2. a.** Of or pertaining to the broadcasting of sound. **b.** Of or pertaining to the high-fidelity reproduction of sound. —*n.* **1.** The audio part of television equipment. **2.** Audio broadcasting or reception. **3.** Audible sound. [From AUDIO-.]

audio–. Indicates sound or hearing; for example, **audiometer.** [From Latin *audīre,* to hear. See **aw-**[2] in Appendix.*]

audio frequency. *Abbr.* **a.f., A.F., AF** A range of frequencies, usually from 15 cycles per second to 20,000 cycles per second, characteristic of signals audible to the normal human ear.

au·di·om·e·ter (ô′dē-ŏm′ə-tər) *n. Medicine.* An instrument for measuring hearing thresholds for pure tones of normally audible frequencies. [AUDIO- + -METER.] —**au′di·o·met′ric** (-ō-mĕt′rĭk) *adj.* —**au′di·om′e·try** *n.*

au·di·o·phile (ô′dē-ō-fīl′) *n.* A high-fidelity audio hobbyist. [AUDIO- + -PHILE.]

au·di·o·vis·u·al (ô′dē-ō-vĭzh′ōō-əl) *adj. Abbr.* **A.V. 1.** Both audible and visible. **2.** Of or pertaining to educational materials, such as filmed or televised lectures, that present information in both audible and visible form.

au·dit (ô′dĭt) *n. Abbr.* **aud. 1.** An examination of records or accounts to check their accuracy. **2.** An adjustment or correction of accounts. **3.** An examined and verified account. **4.** *Rare.* An audience or hearing. —*v.* **audited, -diting, -dits.** —*tr.* **1.** To examine, verify, or correct (accounts, records, or claims). **2.** To register for and attend (a college course) without receiving academic credit. —*intr.* To examine accounts. [Middle English, from Latin *audītus,* a hearing, from the past participle of *audīre,* to hear. See **aw-**[2] in Appendix.*]

au·di·tion (ô-dĭsh′ən) *n.* **1.** The act or sense of hearing. **2.** A presentation of something heard; a hearing: *"many a dizzy venture at the Opera House had owed its audition to her"* (Ronald Firbank). **3.** A trial hearing, as of an actor, musician, or other performer. —*v.* **auditioned, -tioning, -tions.** —*tr.* To give (someone) an audition. —*intr.* To perform or be tested in an audition. [Latin *audītiō,* from *audīre,* to hear. See **audit.**]

au·di·tive (ô′də-tĭv) *adj.* Auditory.

au·di·tor (ô′də-tər) *n. Abbr.* **aud. 1.** One who hears; listener. **2.** One who audits accounts. **3.** One who audits courses. [Middle English *auditour,* from Old French *auditeur,* from Latin *audītor,* hearer (in Medieval Latin, also one who audits accounts), from *audīre,* to hear. See **aw-**[2] in Appendix.*]

au·di·to·ri·um (ô′də-tôr′ē-əm, -tōr′ē-əm) *n., pl.* **-ums** or **-toria** (-tôr′ē-ə, -tōr′ē-ə). **1.** A room to accommodate the audience in a school, theater, or other building. **2.** A large building for public meetings or artistic performances. [Latin *audītōrium,* from *audīre,* to hear. See **aw-**[2] in Appendix.*]

au·di·to·ry (ô′də-tôr′ē, -tōr′ē) *adj.* Of or pertaining to the sense, the organs, or the experience of hearing. [Late Latin *audītōrius,* from Latin *audīre,* to hear. See **aw-**[2] in Appendix.*]

auditory nerve. *Anatomy.* The **acoustic nerve** *(see).*

Au·du·bon (ô′də-bŏn′, -bən), **John James.** 1785–1851. French-born American naturalist and painter.

au fait (ō fĕ′). *French.* Skilled or knowledgeable; expert. Literally, "to the point."

Auf·klä·rung (ouf′klā′rōōng) *n. German.* The Enlightenment.

au fond (ō fôɴ′). *French.* Basically; fundamentally. Literally, "at the bottom."

auf Wie·der·seh·en (ouf vē′dər-zā′ən). *German.* Until we see one another again; farewell.

aug. augmentative.

Aug. August.

Au·ge·an (ô-jē′ən) *adj.* Exceedingly filthy from long neglect. [From *Augeas,* legendary king of Elis, who left his stable uncleaned for thirty years.]

au·gend (ô′jĕnd′) *n. Mathematics.* A quantity to which another quantity, the addend, is added. [Latin *augendum,* "the thing to be increased," from *augendus,* gerundive of *augēre,* to increase. See **aug-**[1] in Appendix.*]

au·ger (ô′gər) *n.* **1.** A tool, larger than a gimlet, for boring wood. **2.** A large tool for boring into the earth. [Middle English *an auger,* originally *a nauger,* Old English *nafogār,* "tool for piercing wheel hubs." See **nobh-** in Appendix.*]

Au·ghra·bies Falls (ō-grä′bēs). Formerly **King Geor·ge's Falls** (jôr′jəz). A drop of 480 feet on the Orange River in northwestern Cape of Good Hope Province, South Africa.

ă pat/ā pay/âr care/ä father/b bib/ch church/d deed/ĕ pet/ē be/f fife/g gag/h hat/hw which/ĭ pit/ī pie/îr pier/j judge/k kick/l lid, needle/m mum/n no, sudden/ng thing/ŏ pot/ō toe/ô paw, for/oi noise/ou out/ŏŏ took/ōō boot/p pop/r roar/s sauce/sh ship, dish/

aught[1] (ôt) *pron.* Also **ought. 1.** All: *For aught we know he may have changed his name.* **2.** *Archaic.* Anything whatever; any least part. —*adv.* Also **ought.** *Archaic.* At all; in any respect. [Middle English *aught,* ought, Old English *āuht, āwiht,* "eve a thing," anything. See **aiw-** in Appendix.*]

aught[2] (ôt) *n.* Also **ought. 1.** A cipher; the symbol 0; zero. **2.** *Archaic.* Nothing. [From *an aught,* originally *a* NAUGHT.]

au·gite (ô′jīt′) *n.* A dark-green to black pyroxene mineral that contains large amounts of aluminum, iron, and magnesium. [Latin *augītēs,* a precious stone, from Greek *augitēs,* from *augē,* ray, brightness. See **aug-**[2] in Appendix.*]

aug·ment (ôg-mĕnt′) *v.* **-mented, -menting, -ments.** —*tr.* To make greater, as in size, extent, or quantity; enlarge; increase. —*intr.* To become greater; enlarge. —See Synonyms at **increase.** —*n.* (ôg′mĕnt′). **1.** An enlargement or increase. **2.** A morphological indication of past tense in Greek and Sanskrit verbs, consisting of the prefixing of a vowel or the lengthening of the initial vowel. [Middle English *augmenten,* from Old French *augmenter,* from Late Latin *augmentāre,* from *augmentum,* increase, from Latin *augēre,* to increase. See **aug-**[1] in Appendix.*] —**aug·ment′a·ble** *adj.*

aug·men·ta·tion (ôg′mĕn-tā′shən) *n.* **1. a.** The act or process of augmenting. **b.** The condition of being augmented. **2.** Something that enlarges or increases; an addition. **3.** *Music.* The repetition of a theme in notes of usually double time value.

aug·men·ta·tive (ôg-mĕn′tə-tĭv) *adj.* Also **aug·men·tive** (ôg-mĕn′tĭv). **1.** Having the tendency or ability to augment. **2.** *Grammar.* Producing an increase in the size or intensity of the meaning of the original word, as the word *up* in the phrase *eat up.* —*n.* Also **aug·men·tive.** *Abbr.* **aug., augm.** An augmentative word or affix.

aug·men·ted (ôg-mĕn′tĭd) *adj. Music.* Larger by a semitone than the corresponding major or perfect interval.

au gra·tin (ō grät′n, grăt′n, ô; *French* ō grȧ-tăN′). Covered with bread crumbs or bread crumbs and grated cheese and browned in an oven. [French, "with the crust (of bread crumbs)."]

Augs·burg (ouks′bŏŏrk′). A city and commercial center of West Germany in south-central Bavaria. Population, 210,000.

au·gur (ô′gər) *n.* **1.** One of a group of religious officials of ancient Rome who foretold events by observing and interpreting signs and omens. **2.** A seer or prophet; soothsayer. —*v.* **augured, -guring, -gurs.** —*tr.* **1.** To predict or prognosticate, as from signs or omens. **2.** To serve as an omen of; betoken. —*intr.* **1.** To conjecture or foretell from signs or omens. **2.** To be a sign or omen: *"an immoderate display of emotion that scarcely augured well for married happiness"* (Philip Horton). —See Synonyms at **foretell.** [Latin, a senior priest of divination. See **aug-**[1] in Appendix.*] —**au′gu·ral** (ô′gyə-rəl) *adj.*

au·gu·ry (ô′gyə-rē) *n., pl.* **-ries. 1.** The art, ability, or practice of auguring; divination. **2.** The rite performed by an augur. **3.** A sign or omen; an indication. [Middle English *augurie,* from Old French, from Latin *augurium,* from *augur,* AUGUR.]

au·gust (ô-gŭst′) *adj.* **1.** Inspiring awe or admiration; majestic. **2.** Venerable for reasons of age or high rank. —See Synonyms at **grand.** [Latin *augustus,* venerable, magnificent. See **aug-**[1] in Appendix.*] —**au·gust′ly** *adv.* —**au·gust′ness** *n.*

Au·gust (ô′gəst) *n. Abbr.* **Aug.** The eighth month of the year according to the Gregorian calendar. August has 31 days. See **calendar.** [Middle English *August,* Old English *August,* from Latin *(mensis) Augustus,* (month) of Augustus, after AUGUSTUS Caesar.]

Au·gus·ta (ô-gŭs′tə). **1.** A city of Georgia, in the east on the Savannah; formerly, the capital of the state (1785–95). Population, 71,000. **2.** The capital of Maine, in the south on the Kennebec River. Population, 22,000.

Au·gus·tan (ô-gŭs′tən) *adj.* **1.** Pertaining to or characteristic of Augustus Caesar or his reign or times. **2.** Pertaining to or characteristic of any era resembling Augustus Caesar's in tastes and principles. —*n.* An artist of an Augustan age.

Augustan age. 1. The reign of Augustus Caesar, the golden age of Latin literature. **2.** A similar period of great literary achievement, as during the reign of the English Queen Anne.

Au·gus·tine (ô′gə-stēn′, ô-gŭs′tĭn), **Saint** A.D. 354–430. Early Christian church father and author.

Au·gus·tin·i·an (ô′gə-stĭn′ē-ən) *adj.* **1.** Pertaining to Saint Augustine or his doctrines. **2.** Designating or belonging to any of several orders following or influenced by his rule. —*n.* **1.** A follower of the principles and doctrines of Saint Augustine. **2.** A monk or friar belonging to any of the Augustinian orders. —**Au′gus·tin′i·an·ism′, Au·gus′tin·ism′** *n.*

Au·gus·tus[1] (ô-gŭs′təs) *n.* A title of the Roman emperors that after Hadrian became specifically the title of the senior emperor as distinct from his junior colleague, the **Caesar** *(see).* [Latin *Augustus,* AUGUST, "Imperial Majesty," was adopted by Octavian as a personal title when he acquired supreme power.]

Au·gus·tus[2] (ô-gŭs′təs). Original name, Gaius Octavius. After 44 B.C. (as the adopted son of Julius Caesar), Gaius Julius Caesar Octavianus. Known as Octavian. 63 B.C.–A.D. 14. Founder of the imperial Roman government.

au jus (ō zhü′). Served with the natural juices or gravy: *roast beef au jus.* [French, "with juice."]

auk (ôk) *n.* Any of several sea birds of the family Alcidae, of northern regions, having a chunky body and short wings, such as the **razor-billed auk** *(see).* [Norwegian *alk, alka,* from Old Norse *ālka.* See **el-**[2] in Appendix.*]

auk·let (ôk′lĭt) *n.* Any of various small auks of the genus *Aethia* and related genera, of northern Pacific coasts and waters.

au lait (ō lĕ′). With milk. [French, "with milk."]

auld (ôld) *adj. Scottish.* Old.

auld lang syne (ôld lăng zīn′, sīn′). The good old days long past. [Scottish, "old long since" : AULD + LANGSYNE.]

au·lic (ô′lĭk) *adj.* Pertaining to a royal court; courtly. [French *aulique,* from Latin *aulicus,* from Greek *aulikos,* from *aulē,* court. See **au-**[1] in Appendix.*]

Aulic Council. The emperor's privy council in the Holy Roman Empire, established in 1501 and dissolved in 1806.

Au·lis (ô′lĭs). An ancient town in Boeotia, east-central Greece, on the Gulf of Euboea, traditionally the place from which the Greek fleet embarked for Troy at the start of the Trojan War.

au na·tu·rel (ō nȧ-tü-rĕl′). **1.** In a natural state; nude. **2.** Cooked simply. Said of food. [French, "in the natural."]

aunt (ănt, änt) *n.* **1.** The sister of one's father or mother. **2.** The wife of one's uncle. [Middle English *aunte,* from Norman French, from Old French *ante,* from Latin *amita,* paternal aunt. See **amma** in Appendix.*]

aunt·ie (ăn′tē, än′-) *n.* Also **aunt·y.** A familiar form of **aunt.**

au·ra (ôr′ə) *n., pl.* **-ras** or **aurae** (ôr′ē). **1.** An invisible breath or emanation. **2.** A distinctive air or quality that characterizes a person or thing: *an aura of nobility.* **3.** A soft breeze. **4.** *Pathology.* A sensation, as of a cold breeze, preceding the onset of certain nervous disorders. [Middle English, from Latin, breeze, from Greek. See **wē-** in Appendix.*]

au·ral[1] (ôr′əl) *adj.* Of, pertaining to, or perceived by the ear. [From Latin *auris,* ear. See **ous-** in Appendix.*]

au·ral[2] (ôr′əl) *adj.* Characterized by or pertaining to an aura.

au·rar. Plural of **eyrir.**

au·re·ate (ôr′ē-ĭt) *adj.* **1.** Of a golden color; gilded. **2.** Speaking in or characterized by a florid and pompous style. [Middle English *aureat,* from Medieval Latin *aureātus,* from Latin *aureus,* golden, from *aurum,* gold. See **aurum** in Appendix.*] —**au′re·ate·ly** *adv.* —**au′re·ate·ness** *n.*

Au·re·lian (ô-rēl′yən). Latin name, Lucius Domitius Aurelianus. A.D. 212?–275. Roman emperor (A.D. 270–275).

Au·re·lius. See **Marcus Aurelius Antoninus.**

au·re·ole (ôr′ē-ōl′) *n.* Also **au·re·o·la** (ô-rē′ə-lə). **1.** A circle of light or radiance surrounding the head or body of a representation of a deity or holy person; a halo. **2.** A bright circumferential region around a luminous celestial body, as around the sun or moon, especially when observed through a haze or fog. [Middle English *aureole, auriole,* from Old French *auriole,* from Medieval Latin *(corōna) aureola,* golden (crown), from Latin *aureolus,* golden, from *aurum,* gold. See **aurum** in Appendix.*]

Au·re·o·my·cin (ôr′ē-ō-mī′sĭn) *n.* A trademark for **chlortetracycline** *(see).* [Latin *aureus,* golden (see **aureate**) + -MYCIN.]

au re·voir (ō rə-vwȧr′). *French.* Until we meet again; good-by.

au·ric (ôr′ĭk) *adj.* Of, pertaining to, derived from, or containing gold, especially with valence 3. [From Latin *aurum,* gold. See **aurum** in Appendix.*]

Au·ric (ôr′ĭk), **Georges.** Born 1899. French composer.

au·ri·cle (ôr′ĭ-kəl) *n.* Also **au·ric·u·la** (ô-rĭk′yə-lə) *pl.* **-lae** (-lē′) or **-las. 1. a.** *Anatomy.* The external part of the ear; pinna. **b.** An **atrium** *(see)* of the heart. **2.** *Biology.* Any earlike part, process, or appendage, especially at the base of an organ. [Latin *auricula,* diminutive of *auris,* ear. See **ous-** in Appendix.*] —**au′ri·cled** (-kəld) *adj.*

au·ric·u·la (ô-rĭk′yə-lə) *n., pl.* **-las** or **-lae** (-lē′). **1.** A species of primrose, *Primula auricula,* native to the Alps, having clusters of variously colored flowers. Also called "bear's-ear." **2.** Variant of **auricle.** [New Latin, "little ear" (from the shape of the leaves), from Latin, AURICLE.]

au·ric·u·lar (ô-rĭk′yə-lər) *adj.* **1.** Of or pertaining to the sense or organs of hearing. **2.** Perceived by or spoken into the ear: *an auricular confession.* **3.** Having the shape of an ear. **4.** Of or pertaining to an auricle of the heart. —*n. Plural.* The feathers covering the opening of a bird's ear. [Late Latin *auriculāris,* from *auricula,* AURICLE.] —**au·ric′u·lar·ly** *adv.*

au·ric·u·late (ô-rĭk′yə-lĭt, -lāt′) *adj.* Also **au·ric·u·lat·ed** (-lāt′ĭd). **1.** Having ears or earlike parts or extensions: *an auriculate leaf.* **2.** Having the shape of an ear. [From Latin *auricula,* AURICLE.] —**au·ric′u·late·ly** *adv.*

au·rif·er·ous (ô-rĭf′ər-əs) *adj.* Containing gold; gold-bearing. Said of rocks or gravels. [Latin *aurifer* : *aurum,* gold (see **aurum** in Appendix*) + -FER.]

au·ri·flamme. Variant of **oriflamme.**

au·ri·form (ôr′ə-fôrm′) *adj.* Ear-shaped. [Latin *auris,* ear (see **ous-** in Appendix*) + -FORM.]

Au·ri·ga (ô-rī′gə) *n.* A constellation in the Northern Hemisphere near Lynx and Perseus. Also called the "Charioteer." [Latin *aurīga,* charioteer. See **ōs-** in Appendix.*]

Au·rig·na·cian (ôr′ĭg-nā′shən, ôr′ēn-yā′shən) *adj.* Also **au·rig·na·cian.** *Archaeology.* Of or relating to the Old World Upper Paleolithic culture between Mousterian and Solutrean, associated with Cro-Magnon man, and characterized by artifacts such as figures of stone and bone, graphic art work, and the use of dress and adornment. [After *Aurignac,* commune in France, near which such artifacts were found.]

Au·riol (ô-ryôl′), **Vincent.** 1884–1966. French statesman and first president of the Fourth Republic (1947–54).

au·rochs (ou′rŏks′, ô′-) *n.* **1.** An extinct bovine mammal, *Bos taurus primigenius,* of northern Africa, Europe, and western Asia, believed to be the forerunner of domestic cattle. Also called "urus." **2.** Loosely, the European bison, or wisent. [German, from Old High German *ūrohso* : *ūro,* bison, from Germanic *ūrus* (unattested) + *ohso,* ox (see **wegw-** in Appendix*).]

au·ro·ra (ô-rôr′ə, ô-rōr′ə, ə-) *n.* **1.** High-altitude, many-colored, flashing luminosity, visible in night skies of polar and sometimes temperate zones, and thought to be caused by injection of

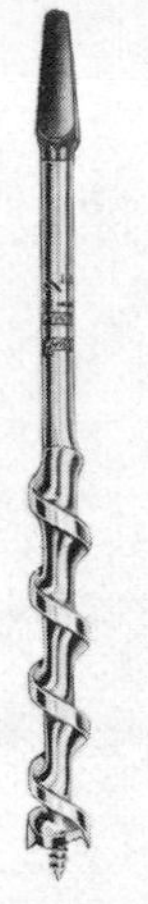

auger
Auger bit, to be used with a hand or power brace

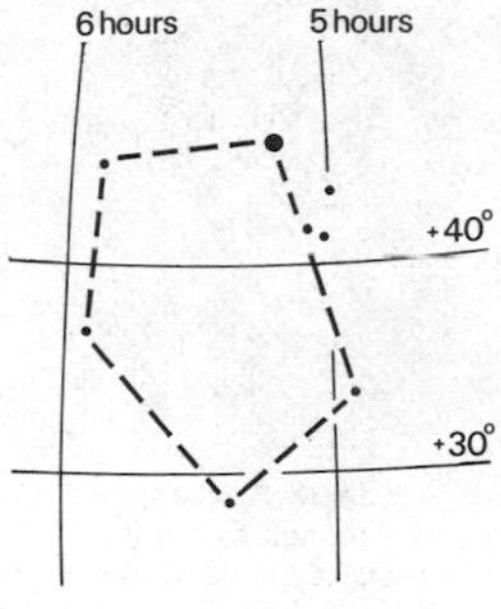

Auriga

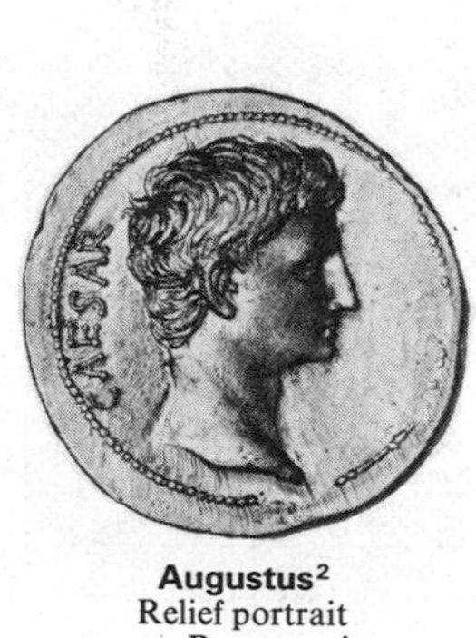

Augustus[2]
Relief portrait on a Roman coin

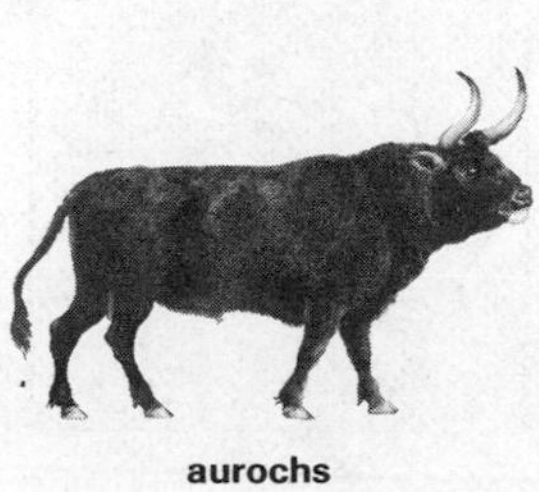

aurochs

charged particles, especially of solar origin, into the earth's magnetic field. Compare **airglow**. **2.** *Poetic.* The dawn. **3.** *Rare.* An early part or stage; a beginning. [Latin *aurōra*, dawn. See **awes-** in Appendix.*]

Au·ro·ra¹ (ô-rôr′ə, ô-rōr′ə, ə-). *Roman Mythology.* The goddess of the dawn, identified with the Greek goddess Eos.

Au·ro·ra² (ô-rôr′ə, ô-rōr′ə, ə-). **1.** A residential city of Colorado, in the northeast near Denver, of which it is a suburb. Population, 49,000. **2.** A city and industrial center in northeastern Illinois. Population, 64,000.

aurora aus·tra·lis (ô-strā′lĭs). Aurora occurring in southern regions. Also called "southern lights." [New Latin : AURORA + AUSTRAL.]

aurora bo·re·al·is (bôr′ē-ăl′ĭs, bōr′-). Aurora occurring in northern regions. Also called "northern lights." [New Latin : AURORA + BOREAL.]

au·ro·ral (ô-rôr′əl, ô-rōr′-, ə-) *adj.* Also *poetic* **au·ro·re·an** (-ē-ən) (for sense 1). **1.** Pertaining to or resembling the dawn. **2.** *Meteorology.* Pertaining to, caused by, or like an aurora. —**au·ro′ral·ly** *adv.*

au·rous (ôr′əs) *adj.* Of or pertaining to gold, especially with valence 1. [Late Latin *aurōsus*, from Latin *aurum*, AURUM.]

au·rum (ôr′əm) *n.* The element gold. [Latin, gold. See **aurum** in Appendix.*]

AUS Airport code for Austin, Texas.

Aus. **1.** Australia. **2.** Austria.

Au·sa·ble River (ô-sā′bəl). A river 20 miles long in northeastern New York State, flowing into Lake Champlain through Ausable Chasm, a deep, two-mile gorge.

Ausch·witz. The German name for **Oświęcim.**

aus·cul·tate (ô′skəl-tāt′) *v.* **-tated, -tating, -tates.** *Medicine.* —*tr.* To examine (a person) by auscultation. —*intr.* To examine by auscultation. [From AUSCULTATION.] —**aus′cul·ta′tive** *adj.* —**aus·cul′ta·to′ry** (ô-skŭl′tə-tôr′ē, -tōr′ē) *adj.*

aus·cul·ta·tion (ô′skəl-tā′shən) *n.* **1.** The act of listening. **2.** *Medicine.* Diagnostic monitoring of the sounds made by internal organs or any internal bodily part. [Latin *auscultātiō*, from *auscultāre*, to listen to. See **ous-** in Appendix.*]

Aus·gleich (ous′glĭKH′) *n., pl.* **-gleiche** (-glī′KHə). *German.* Compromise; agreement; specifically, the treaty between Hungary and Austria in 1867 organizing their dual monarchy.

aus·pex (ô′spĕks′) *n., pl.* **auspices** (ô′spə-sēz′). An augur of ancient Rome, especially one who interpreted omens taken from the actions of birds. [Latin. See **auspice.**]

aus·pi·cate (ô′spĭ-kāt′) *tr.v.* **-cated, -cating, -cates.** *Rare.* To begin or inaugurate with a ceremony designed to bring good luck. [Latin *auspicārī*, from *auspex*, bird augur. See **auspice.**]

aus·pice (ô′spĭs) *n., pl.* **auspices** (ô′spə-sēz′). **1.** *Usually plural.* Protection or support; patronage. **2.** A portent, omen, or augury, especially when observed in the actions of birds. **3.** Observation of and divination from the actions of birds. [Latin *auspicium*, bird divination, from *auspex* (stem *auspic-*), a bird augur : *au-*, from *avis*, bird (see **awi-** in Appendix*) + *-spex*, from *specere*, to look (see **spek-** in Appendix*).]

aus·pi·cious (ô-spĭsh′əs) *adj.* **1.** Attended by favorable circumstances; propitious. **2.** Marked by success; fortunate; prosperous. —See Synonyms at **favorable.** —**aus·pi′cious·ly** *adv.* —**aus·pi′cious·ness** *n.*

Aust. Austria; Austrian.

Aus·ten (ôs′tən), **Jane.** 1775–1817. English novelist.

aus·ten·ite (ôs′tən-īt′) *n.* A nonmagnetic solid solution of ferric or carbon carbide in iron, used in making corrosive-resistant steel. [French, after Sir William Roberts-*Austen* (1843–1902), British metallurgist.] —**aus′ten·it′ic** (-ĭt′ĭk) *adj.*

Aus·ter (ôs′tər) *n. Poetic.* The personification of the south wind. [Latin *auster*†, south wind, the south.]

aus·tere (ô-stîr′) *adj.* **1.** Severe or stern in disposition or appearance; somber; grave: *"an austere man that never laughed or smiled"* (Alan Paton). **2.** Strict or severe in moral discipline; ascetic. **3.** Without adornment or ornamentation; simple; bare. **4.** *Archaic.* Bitter or sour to the taste; astringent. —See Synonyms at **severe.** [Middle English, from Old French, from Latin *austērus*, from Greek *austēros*, harsh, rough, severe. See **saus-** in Appendix.*] —**aus·tere′ly** *adv.* —**aus·tere′ness** *n.*

aus·ter·i·ty (ô-stĕr′ə-tē) *n., pl.* **-ties.** **1.** The quality of being austere. **2.** Severely simple living conditions, especially as an economic policy: *wartime austerity.* **3.** *Usually plural.* An ascetic habit or practice: *Hermits were renowned for their austerities.*

Aus·ter·litz (ôs′tər-lĭts′, ous′-). *Czech* **Slav·kov** (släf′kôf). A town in Moravia, Czechoslovakia, near the site of Napoleon I's victory over the Russian and Austrian armies (1805).

Aus·tin (ôs′tən). The capital of Texas, in the south-central part of the state, on the Colorado River. Population, 187,000.

Aus·tin (ôs′tən), **Alfred.** 1835–1913. English poet laureate (1896–1913).

Aus·tin (ôs′tən), **Stephen Fuller.** 1793–1836. American colonizer and political leader in Republic of Texas.

Austl. Australia; Australian.

aus·tral (ôs′trəl) *adj.* Of, pertaining to, or coming from the south: *austral winds.* [Middle English, from Latin *austrālis*, from *auster*, south, AUSTER.]

Aus·tral·a·sia (ôs′trəl-ā′zhə, -ā′shə). The islands of Oceania in the South Pacific, together with Australia, New Zealand, New Guinea, and associated islands; sometimes, all of Oceania. —**Aus′tral·a′sian** *adj* & *n.*

Aus·tra·lia (ô-strāl′yə). *Abbr.* **Aus., Austl.** **1.** A continent, 2,948,366 square miles in area, lying southeast of Asia between the Pacific and Indian oceans. **2.** Officially, the Commonwealth of Australia. A country and member of the Commonwealth of Nations, comprising this continent, the island of Tasmania, two external territories and a number of dependencies. Population, 11,360,000. Capital, Canberra. [Latin *(Terra) Austrālis*, "Southern (Land)," from *austrālis*, southern, from *auster*, AUSTER.]

Aus·tra·lian (ô-strāl′yən) *n. Abbr.* **Austl.** **1.** A native or citizen of the Commonwealth of Australia. **2.** An aborigine of Australia. **3.** *Abbr.* **Austl.** Any of the languages of the Australian aborigines. —*adj.* **1.** *Abbr.* **Austl.** Of or pertaining to Australia or its inhabitants and their languages or cultures. **2.** *Ecology.* Of or designating the zoogeographic region that includes Australia and the islands adjacent to it, including New Guinea.

Australian Alps. A mountain chain in southeastern Australia. Highest elevation, Mt. Kosciusko (7,316 feet).

Australian Antarctic Territory. A sector of Antarctica including most of the land between 45 degrees and 160 degrees east longitude, claimed by Australia.

Australian ballot. A printed ballot on which the names of all candidates and the texts of propositions appear, distributed to the voter at the polls and marked in secret.

Australian Capital Territory. *Abbr.* **A.C.T.** Formerly **Federal Capital Territory.** A territory, 911 square miles in area, in New South Wales, Australia, containing Canberra, the federal capital. Population, 89,000.

Australian crawl. A swimming stroke, a variation of the **crawl** *(see)* executed with an eight-beat flutter kick to each stroke.

Australian terrier. A small dog of a breed developed in Australia, having a coarse blackish coat with tan markings.

Aus·tral Islands. See **Tubuai Islands.**

Aus·tra·loid (ôs′trə-loid′) *adj.* Of or relating to an ethnic group including the Australian aborigines. [AUSTRAL(IAN) + -OID.]

aus·tra·lo·pith·e·cine (ô-strā′lō-pĭth′ə-sīn′) *n.* Any of several extinct manlike primates of the genera *Australopithecus* and *Paranthropus* or *Zinjanthropus*, known chiefly from Pleistocene fossil remains found in southern and eastern Africa. —*adj.* Of, pertaining to, or characteristic of the australopithecines. [From New Latin *Australopithecus*, "southern ape" : AUSTRAL + New Latin *pithēcus*, ape, from Greek *pithēkos* (see **pithecanthropus**).]

Aus·tra·sia (ô-strā′zhə, -shə). The eastern portion of the Frankish kingdom from the sixth to the eighth century, consisting of parts of eastern France, western Germany, and the Netherlands. [Medieval Latin *Austrāsia*, *Ostrāsia*, "the Eastern country," from Frankish *ōstra-* (unattested), eastern. See **awes-** in Appendix.*] —**Aus·tra′sian** *adj.*

Aus·tri·a (ôs′trē-ə). *Abbr.* **Aus., Aust.** *German* **Ös·ter·reich** (œs′tə-rīKH). A landlocked federal republic, formerly an empire, occupying 32,375 square miles in central Europe. Population, 7,074,000. Capital, Vienna. [New Latin, from German *Österreich*, "the eastern kingdom" : *öster*, eastern, from Old High German *ōstar* (see **awes-** in Appendix*) + *Reich*, kingdom, rule, from Old High German *rikki* (see **reg-¹** in Appendix*).] —**Aus′tri·an** *adj.* & *n.*

Aus·tri·a-Hun·ga·ry (ôs′trē-ə-hŭng′gə-rē). A former dual monarchy of central Europe, formed by the union of Austria, Bohemia, and Hungary and of areas of Poland, Rumania, Yugoslavia, and Italy, and dismembered in 1919.

Austro–¹. Indicates southern; for example, **Austro-Asiatic.** [From Latin *auster*, the south, AUSTER.]

Austro–². Indicates Austrian; for example, **Austro-Hungarian.**

Aus·tro-A·si·at·ic (ôs′trō-ā′zhē-ăt′ĭk) *n.* A family of languages of southeastern Asia, believed to have been once dominant in northeastern India and Indochina. —*adj.* Of or pertaining to this family of languages.

Aus·tro-Hun·gar·i·an (ôs′trō-hŭng-gâr′ē-ən) *adj.* Of or pertaining to Austria-Hungary.

Aus·tro·ne·sia (ôs′trō-nē′zhə, -shə). The islands in the Pacific including Indonesia, Melanesia, Micronesia, and Polynesia. [New Latin, "southern islands" : AUSTRO- + *-nēsia*, from Greek *nēsos*, island (see **snā-** in Appendix*).]

Aus·tro·ne·sian (ôs′trō-nē′zhən, -shən) *adj.* Of or pertaining to Austronesia, its peoples, or their languages. —*n.* A family of languages spoken in Austronesia, including the Indonesian, Melanesian, Micronesian, and Polynesian subfamilies. Also called "Malayo-Polynesian."

au·ta·coid (ô′tə-koid′) *n.* Also **au·to·coid.** *Biochemistry.* Any organic substance, such as a hormone, formed in an organ and secreted into the blood, lymph, or sap, from which it acts on other parts of the organism. [AUT(O)- + Greek *akos*, cure (see **yēk-** in Appendix*).]

au·tar·chy (ô′tär′kē) *n., pl.* **-chies.** **1.** Absolute rule or power; autocracy. **2.** A country under such rule. **3. Autarky** *(see).* [Greek *autarkhia*, from *autarkhos*, self-governing : AUT(O)- + -ARCH.] —**au·tar′chic, au·tar′chi·cal** *adj.*

au·tar·ky (ô′tär′kē) *n., pl.* **-kies.** **1.** A policy of national self-sufficiency and nonreliance on imports or economic aid. **2.** A self-sufficient region or country. Also called "autarchy." [Greek *autarkeia*, self-sufficiency, from *autarkēs*, self-sufficient : AUT(O)- + *arkein*, to suffice (see **arek-** in Appendix*).] —**au·tar′kic, au·tar′ki·cal** *adj.*

au·te·col·o·gy (ô′tĭ-kŏl′ə-jē) *n.* The ecology of a species or individual organisms in relation to the environment. [AUT(O)- + ECOLOGY.]

auth. **1.** authentic. **2.** author. **3.** authority. **4.** authorized.

au·then·tic (ô-thĕn′tĭk) *adj. Abbr.* **auth.** **1. a.** Worthy of trust, reliance, or belief: *authentic records.* **b.** Having an undisputed origin; genuine. **2.** *Law.* Executed with due process of law: *an authentic deed.* **3.** *Music.* **a.** Designating a medieval mode having a range from its final tone to the octave above it.

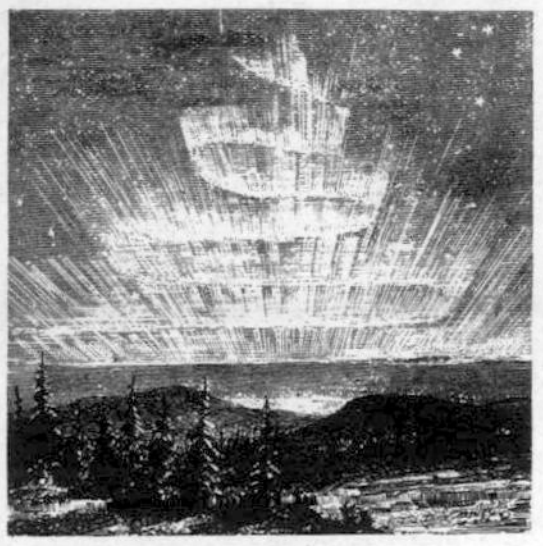

aurora borealis
Observed in Alaska, December 27, 1865

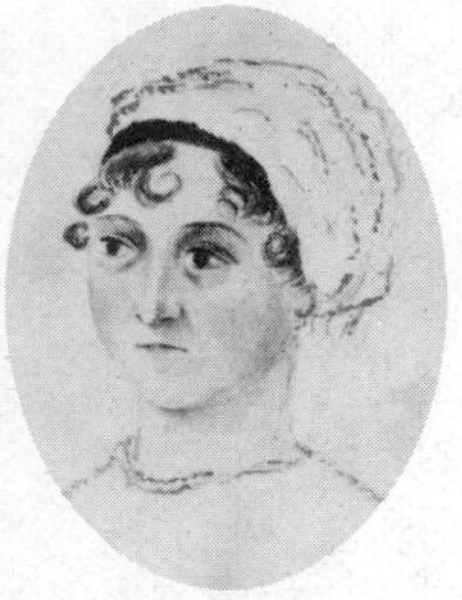

Jane Austen
Sketch by her sister Cassandra

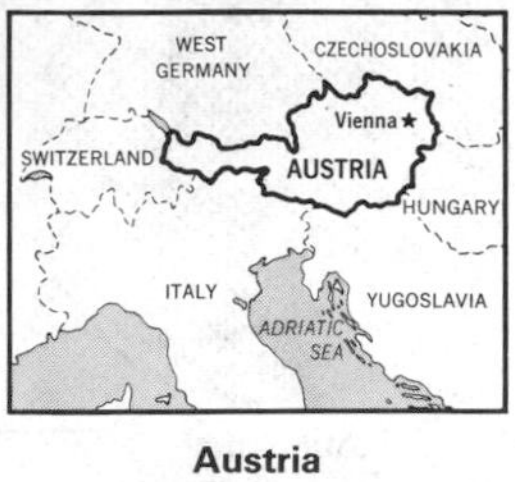

Austria

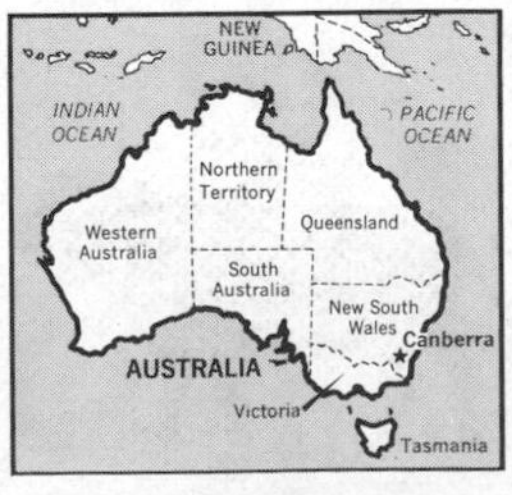

Australia

ă pat/ā pay/âr care/ä father/b bib/ch church/d deed/ĕ pet/ē be/f fife/g gag/h hat/hw which/ĭ pit/ī pie/îr pier/j judge/k kick/l lid, needle/m mum/n no, sudden/ng thing/ŏ pot/ō toe/ô paw, for/oi noise/ou out/o͝o took/o͞o boot/p pop/r roar/s sauce/sh ship, dish/

b. Designating a cadence with the dominant chord immediately preceding the tonic chord. Compare **plagal.** —See Synonyms at **real.** [Middle English *autentik,* from Old French *autentique,* from Late Latin *authenticus,* from Greek *authentikos,* genuine, authoritative, from *authentēs*†, perpetrator, author.] —**au·then′ti·cal·ly** *adj.*

au·then·ti·cate (ô-thĕn′tĭ-kāt′) *tr.v.* **-cated, -cating, -cates.** **1.** To establish as worthy of belief: *authenticate a story.* **2.** To confirm as authentic; prove or verify as genuine, as a painting. **3.** To invest with legal validity, as a deed. —See Synonyms at **confirm.** —**au·then′ti·ca′tion** *n.* —**au·then′ti·ca′tor** (-tər) *n.*

au·then·tic·i·ty (ô′thĕn-tĭs′ə-tē) *n.* The condition or quality of being authentic, trustworthy, or genuine.

au·thor (ô′thər) *n.* **1.** *Abbr.* **auth. a.** The original writer of a literary work. **b.** One who practices writing as his profession. **c.** An author's works collectively. **2.** The beginner, originator, or creator of anything. —*tr.v.* **authored, -thoring, -thors. 1.** To be the author of; write. See Usage note below. **2.** To originate; create: *author a new fashion in hairstyling.* See Usage note below. [Middle English *autour,* from Old French *autor,* from Latin *auctor,* creator, from *augēre* (past participle *auctus*), to create, increase. See **aug-**¹ in Appendix.*]

Usage: *Author,* as a transitive verb *(to author a book),* is unacceptable in writing to 81 per cent of the Usage Panel. After being rare for a long time, the verb has had a revival, though many consider it unnecessary and graceless.

au·thor·ess (ô′thər-ĭs) *n.* A female author. Sometimes considered disparaging.

au·thor·i·tar·i·an (ə-thôr′ə-târ′ē-ən, ə-thŏr′-, ô-) *adj.* Characterized by or favoring absolute obedience to authority, as against individual freedom. —*n.* One who believes in or practices authoritarian policies. —**au·thor′i·tar′i·an·ism′** *n.*

au·thor·i·ta·tive (ə-thôr′ə-tā′tĭv, ə-thŏr′-, ô-) *adj.* **1.** Having or arising from proper authority; official: *authoritative sources.* **2.** Wielding authority; commanding. —See Synonyms at **dictatorial.** —**au·thor′i·ta′tive·ly** *adv.* —**au·thor′i·ta′tive·ness** *n.*

au·thor·i·ty (ə-thôr′ə-tē, ə-thŏr′-, ô-) *n., pl.* **-ties.** *Abbr.* **auth. 1.** The right and power to command, enforce laws, exact obedience, determine, or judge. **2. a.** A person or group invested with this right and power: *"In authoritarian ethics an authority states what is good for man"* (Erich Fromm). **b.** *Plural.* Government officials having this right and power. **3.** Power delegated to others; authorization: *You have my authority to decide.* **4.** *Often capital* **A.** A public agency or corporation with administrative powers limited to a specified field: *the Transit Authority.* **5. a.** An accepted source of expert information or advice, as a book or person. **b.** A quotation or citation from such a source used in defense or support of one's actions, opinions, or the like. **6.** An expert in a given field: *an authority on plants.* **7.** Power to influence or persuade resulting from knowledge or experience: *write with authority.* **8.** A claim to be accepted or believed: *on the authority of the press.* **9.** An authoritative statement or decision that provides adequate grounds for a course of action or that may be taken as a precedent. [Middle English *autorite, auctorite,* from Old French *auctorite,* from Latin *auctōritās,* from *auctor,* AUTHOR.]

au·thor·i·za·tion (ô′thər-ə-zā′shən) *n.* **1.** The act of conferring authority; permission. **2.** Legal power, right, or sanction.

au·thor·ize (ô′thə-rīz′) *tr.v.* **-ized, -izing, -izes. 1.** To grant authority or power to. **2.** To approve or give permission for; to sanction: *authorize a highway project.* **3.** To be sufficient grounds for; justify. [Middle English *autorisen,* from Old French *autoriser,* from Medieval Latin *auctorizāre,* from Latin *auctor,* AUTHOR.] —**au′thor·iz′er** *n.*

au·thor·ized (ô′thə-rīzd′) *adj. Abbr.* **auth. 1.** Invested with authority; authoritative. **2.** Sanctioned by law or command.

Authorized Version. *Abbr.* **A.V.** The **King James Bible** *(see).*

au·thor·ship (ô′thər-shĭp′) *n.* **1.** The profession or occupation of writing. **2.** A source or origin, as of a book or idea.

au·tism (ô′tĭz′əm) *n.* **1.** Abnormal subjectivity; acceptance of fantasy rather than reality. **2.** A form of childhood schizophrenia characterized by acting out and withdrawal. In this sense, also called "infantile autism." [New Latin *autismus* : AUT(O)- + -ISM.] —**au·tis′tic** (-tĭk) *adj.*

au·to (ô′tō) *n., pl.* **-tos.** *Informal.* An automobile. —*intr.v.* **autoed, -toing, -tos.** *Informal.* To go by or ride in an automobile. [Short for AUTOMOBILE.]

auto-¹, **aut-.** Indicates: **1.** Acting or directed from within; for example, **autogenesis, autism. 2.** Self; same; for example, **autobiography.** [Greek, from *autos*†, self.]

auto-². Indicates self-propelled; for example, **autobus.** [From AUTOMOBILE.]

auto. 1. automatic. **2.** automotive.

au·to·an·ti·bod·y (ô′tō-ăn′tĭ-bŏd′ē) *n., pl.* **-ies.** An antibody thought to act against cells of the organism in which it is formed.

au·to·bahn (ou′tō-bän′) *n., pl.* **-bahns** or **-bahnen** (-bä′nən). A superhighway in Germany. [German *Autobahn* : AUTO- (automobile) + *Bahn,* road, from Middle High German *ban, bane* (see **bhen-** in Appendix*).]

au·to·bi·og·ra·phy (ô′tō-bī-ŏg′rə-fē, -bē-ŏg′rə-fē) *n., pl.* **-phies.** The story of a person's life written by himself; memoirs. [AUTO- + BIOGRAPHY.] —**au′to·bi·og′ra·pher** *n.* —**au′to·bi′o·graph′ic** (ô′tō-bī′ə-grăf′ĭk), **au′to·bi′o·graph′i·cal** *adj.* —**au′to·bi′o·graph′i·cal·ly** *adv.*

au·to·bus (ô′tō-bŭs′) *n., pl.* **-buses** or **-busses.** *Rare.* A bus. [AUTO- (automobile) + BUS.]

au·to·ca·tal·y·sis (ô′tō-kə-tăl′ə-sĭs) *n., pl.* **-ses** (-sēz′). Catalysis of a chemical reaction by one of the products of the reaction.

au·to·chrome (ô′tə-krōm′) *n.* A photographic plate once used in three-color photography. [French : AUTO- + -CHROME.]

au·toch·thon (ô-tŏk′thən) *n., pl.* **-thons** or **-thones** (-thə-nēz′). **1.** *Plural.* The earliest known or aboriginal inhabitants of a particular place. **2.** *Ecology.* Any indigenous plant or animal. [Greek *autokhthōn,* "one sprung from the land itself," indigenous : AUTO- + *khthōn,* earth (see **dhghem-** in Appendix*).]

au·toch·tho·nous (ô-tŏk′thə-nəs) *adj.* Also **au·toch·tho·nal** (-thə-nəl), **au·toch·thon·ic** (-thŏn′ĭk). Native to a particular place; aboriginal; indigenous. —**au·toch′thon·ism′** (-thə-nĭz′-əm), **au·toch′tho·ny** (-thə-nē) *n.* —**au·toch′tho·nous·ly** *adv.*

au·to·clave (ô′tō-klāv′) *n.* A strong, pressurized, steam-heated vessel, used to establish special conditions for chemical reactions, for sterilization, and for cooking. [French, "self-locking" : AUTO- + Latin *clāvis,* key (see **klēu-** in Appendix*).]

au·to·coid. Variant of **autacoid.**

au·toc·ra·cy (ô-tŏk′rə-sē) *n., pl.* **-cies. 1.** Government by a single person having unlimited power; despotism. **2.** A country or state having this form of government. [From AUTOCRAT.]

au·to·crat (ô′tə-krăt′) *n.* **1.** A ruler having absolute or unrestricted power; despot. **2.** Any arrogant and domineering person. [French *autocrate,* from Greek *autokratēs,* ruling by oneself : AUTO- + -CRAT.] —**au′to·crat′ic, au′to·crat′i·cal** *adj.* —**au′to·crat′i·cal·ly** *adv.*

au·to-da-fé (ou′tō-də-fā′, ô′tō-) *n., pl.* **au·tos-da-fé** (ou′tōz-, ô′tōz-). **1.** The public announcement of the sentences imposed on persons tried by the Inquisition. **2.** The public execution of these sentences by the secular authorities, especially the burning of heretics at the stake. [Portuguese *auto da fé,* "act of the faith" : *auto,* act, from Latin *āctus,* ACT + *da,* of the + *fé,* faith, from Latin *fidēs* (see **bheidh-** in Appendix*).]

au·to·di·dact (ô′tō-dī′dăkt′) *n.* A person who is self-taught. [Greek *autodidaktos,* self-taught : AUTO- + *didaktos,* taught (see **didactic**).] —**au′to·di·dac′tic** *adj.*

au·toe·cious (ô-tē′shəs) *adj. Biology.* Having all stages of a life cycle occur on the same host. Said especially of certain parasitic fungi. [AUT(O)- + *-oecious,* from Greek *oikos,* house (see **weik-**¹ in Appendix*).] —**au·toe′cism′** *n.*

au·to·er·o·tism (ô′tō-ĕr′ə-tĭz′əm) *n.* Also **au·to·e·rot·i·cism** (ô′tō-ĭ-rŏt′ə-sĭz′əm). Self-arousal and self-satisfaction of sexual desire, as by masturbation. —**au′to·e·rot′ic** (-ĭ-rŏt′ĭk) *adj.*

au·tog·a·my (ô-tŏg′ə-mē) *n.* **1.** *Botany.* Fertilization of a flower by its own pollen; self-fertilization. **2.** *Biology.* The union of nuclei within and arising from a single cell, as in certain protozoans. [AUTO- + -GAMY.] —**au·tog′a·mous** (-məs) *adj.*

au·to·gen·e·sis (ô′tō-jĕn′ə-sĭs) *n. Biology.* **Abiogenesis** *(see).* —**au′to·ge·ne′tic** (-jə-nĕt′ĭk) *adj.* —**au′to·ge·net′i·cal·ly** *adv.*

au·tog·e·nous (ô-tŏj′ə-nəs) *adj.* Also **au·to·gen·ic** (ô′tə-jĕn′ĭk). Self-generated; self-produced. [Greek *autogenēs,* self-producing : AUTO- + -GENOUS.] —**au·tog′e·nous·ly** *adv.*

au·to·gi·ro (ô′tō-jī′rō) *n., pl.* **-ros.** Also **au·to·gy·ro.** An aircraft powered by a conventional propeller and supported in flight by a freewheeling, horizontal rotor mounted above the fuselage, that provides lift by rotating as it is pulled through the air. [AUTO- + Greek *guros,* circle (see **gēu-** in Appendix*).]

au·to·graph (ô′tə-grăf′, -gräf′) *n.* **1.** A person's own signature or handwriting. **2.** A manuscript in the author's handwriting. —*tr.v.* **autographed, -graphing, -graphs. 1.** To write one's name or signature on or in; to sign. **2.** To write in one's own handwriting. —*adj.* **1.** Written in a person's own handwriting. **2.** Containing signatures or autographs. [Latin *autographum,* from Greek *autographon,* autograph manuscript, from *autographos,* written by oneself : AUTO- + -GRAPH.] —**au′to·graph′ic, au′to·graph′i·cal** *adj.* —**au′to·graph′i·cal·ly** *adv.*

au·tog·ra·phy (ô-tŏg′rə-fē) *n.* **1.** The writing of something in one's own handwriting. **2.** Autographs collectively.

au·to·harp (ô′tō-härp′) *n.* A musical instrument, similar to a zither, on which a desired chord can be selected by depressing a particular damper. [Originally a trademark : AUTO- (self) + HARP.]

au·to·hyp·no·sis (ô′tō-hĭp-nō′sĭs) *n.* **1.** The act or process of hypnotizing oneself. **2.** A self-induced hypnotic state. —**au′to·hyp·not′ic** (-nŏt′ĭk) *adj.*

au·to·in·fec·tion (ô′tō-ĭn-fĕk′shən) *n.* Infection, as with recurrent boils, caused by germs or viruses persisting on or in the body.

au·to·in·oc·u·la·tion (ô′tō-ĭn-ŏk′yə-lā′shən) *n.* **1.** Inoculation with a vaccine made from substances in the recipient's own body. **2.** A secondary infection caused by a disease already in the body.

au·to·in·tox·i·ca·tion (ô′tō-ĭn-tŏk′sə-kā′shən) *n.* Self-poisoning caused by endogenous microorganisms, metabolic wastes, or other toxins in the body. Also called "autotoxemia."

au·to·load·ing (ô′tō-lō′dĭng) *adj.* **Semiautomatic** *(see).*

au·tol·y·sate (ô-tŏl′ə-sāt′, -zāt′) *n. Biochemistry.* An end product of autolysis.

au·tol·y·sin (ô-tŏl′ə-sĭn, ô′tə-lī′sĭn) *n. Biochemistry.* A substance that causes autolysis. [AUTOLYS(IS) + -IN.]

au·tol·y·sis (ô-tŏl′ə-sĭs) *n. Biochemistry.* The destruction of tissues or cells of an organism by autogenous substances, such as enzymes. [AUTO- + -LYSIS.] —**au′to·lyt′ic** (ô′tə-lĭt′ĭk) *adj.*

au·to·mat (ô′tə-măt′) *n.* A restaurant in which the customers obtain food from closed compartments by depositing coins therein. [From trademark *Automat,* from AUTOMATIC.]

au·to·mate (ô′tə-māt′) *v.* **-mated, -mating, -mates.** —*tr.* **1.** To convert (a process, factory, or machine) to automation. **2.** To control or operate by automation. —*intr.* To convert to or make use of automation. [Back-formation from AUTOMATIC.]

au·to·mat·ic (ô′tə-măt′ĭk) *adj. Abbr.* **auto. 1. a.** Acting or oper-

autograph

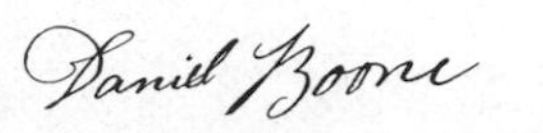

Daniel Boone

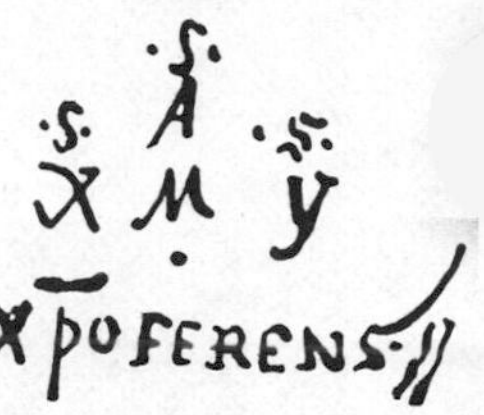

Christopher Columbus

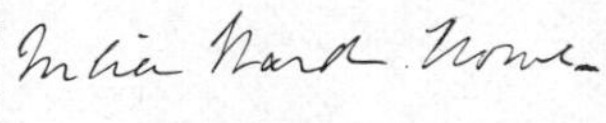

Julia Ward Howe

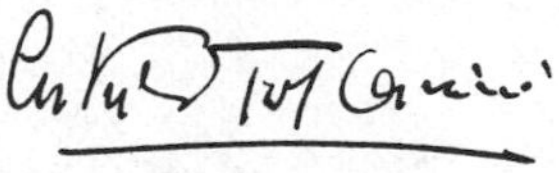

Arturo Toscanini

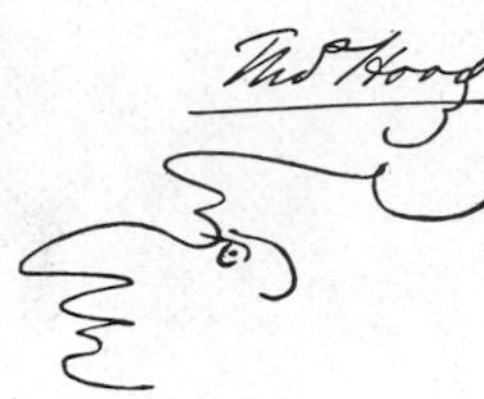

Thomas Hood

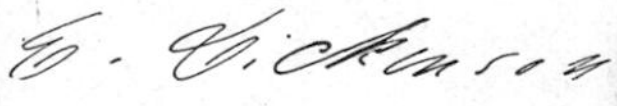

Emily Dickinson

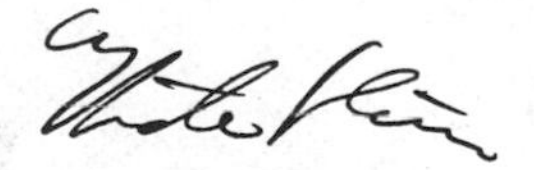

Gertrude Stein

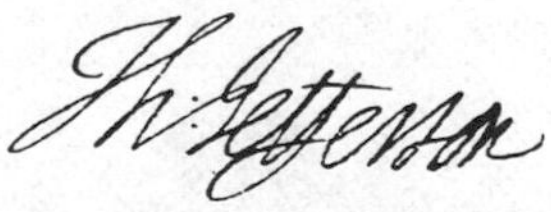

Thomas Jefferson

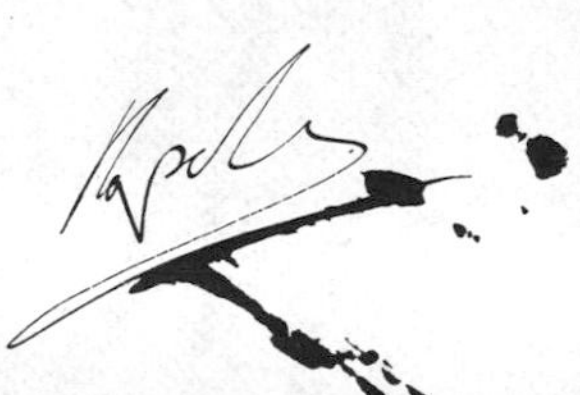

Napoleon

ating in a manner essentially independent of external influence or control; self-moving. **b.** Self-regulating. **2.** Lacking volition, intention, or conscious planning; involuntary; reflex. **3.** Capable of firing continuously until ammunition is exhausted. Said of firearms. In this sense, also "full-automatic." Compare **semi-automatic.** —See Synonyms at **spontaneous.** —*n.* **1.** An automatic firearm, especially an automatic pistol. **2.** An automatic machine or device. [Greek *automatos,* acting by itself, spontaneous, acting of one's own will : AUTO- + *-matos,* willing (see **men-**[1] in Appendix*).] —**au'to·mat'i·cal·ly** *adv.*

au·tom·a·tic·i·ty (ô-tŏm'ə-tĭs'ə-tē) *n.* **1.** The state of being automatic. **2.** Automatic action.

automatic pilot. An aircraft control mechanism that automatically maintains altitude, preset course, and steadiness. Also called "autopilot," "robot pilot."

automatic pistol. A pistol that can be fired automatically or semiautomatically.

automatic rifle. A light machine gun that can be fired automatically or semiautomatically, normally the latter.

au·to·ma·tion (ô'tə-mā'shən) *n.* **1.** The automatic operation or control of a process, equipment, or a system. **2.** The totality of mechanical and electronic techniques and equipment used to achieve such operation or control. **3.** The condition of being automatically controlled or operated. [From AUTOMATIC.] —**au'to·ma'tive** *adj.*

au·tom·a·tism (ô-tŏm'ə-tĭz'əm) *n.* **1. a.** The state or quality of being automatic. **b.** Automatic mechanical action. **2.** *Philosophy.* The theory that all living organisms are automatons. **3.** *Physiology.* **a.** The automatic operation of organs and cells, such as the beating of the heart. **b.** Performance of an act without conscious control, as in the operation of the reflexes. **4.** The effort at suspension of consciousness made by certain surrealist writers and artists in order to express subconscious ideas and feelings. [AUTOMAT(ON) + -ISM.] —**au·tom'a·tist** *n.*

au·tom·a·ton (ô-tŏm'ə-tən, -tŏn') *n., pl.* **-tons** or **-ta** (-tə). **1.** A **robot** *(see).* **2.** One that behaves in an automatic or mechanical fashion. [Latin, self-operating machine, from Greek *automaton,* neuter of *automatos,* AUTOMATIC.] —**au·tom'a·tous** *adj.*

au·to·mo·bile (ô'tə-mō-bēl', -mō'bēl', ô'tə-mō-bēl') *n.* A self-propelled land vehicle, as a four-wheeled passenger vehicle propelled by an internal-combustion engine. —*adj.* Automotive. [French : AUTO- + MOBILE.] —**au'to·mo·bil'ist** *n.*

au·to·mo·tive (ô'tə-mō'tĭv) *adj. Abbr.* **auto. 1.** Self-moving; self-propelling. **2.** Of or pertaining to self-propelled vehicles.

au·to·nom·ic (ô'tə-nŏm'ĭk) *adj.* Also **au·to·nom·i·cal** (-ĭ-kəl). **1.** Independent; autonomous. **2.** *Physiology.* Of or pertaining to the autonomic nervous system. **3.** Resulting from internal causes; self-generated; spontaneous. —**au'to·nom'i·cal·ly** *adv.*

autonomic nervous system. The division of the vertebrate nervous system that regulates involuntary action, as of the intestines, heart, and glands, and comprises the sympathetic nervous system and the parasympathetic nervous system.

au·ton·o·mous (ô-tŏn'ə-məs) *adj.* **1. a.** Independent. **b.** Self-contained. **2. a.** Independent of the laws of another state or government; self-governing. **b.** Of or pertaining to an autonomy. **3.** Autonomic. [Greek *autonomos,* self-ruling : AUTO- + *nomos,* law (see **nem-**[2] in Appendix*).] —**au·ton'o·mous·ly** *adv.*

au·ton·o·my (ô-tŏn'ə-mē) *n., pl.* **-mies. 1.** The condition or quality of being self-governing. **2.** Self-government or the right of self-government; self-determination; independence. **3.** A self-governing state, community, or group. [Greek *autonomia,* from *autonomos,* AUTONOMOUS.] —**au·ton'o·mist** *n.*

au·to·phyte (ô'tə-fīt') *n. Botany.* An autotrophic plant. [AUTO- + -PHYTE.] —**au'to·phyt'ic** (-fĭt'ĭk) *adj.*

au·to·pi·lot (ô'tō-pī'lət) *n.* An **automatic pilot** *(see).*

au·to·plas·ty (ô'tō-plăs'tē) *n.* Surgical repair or replacement with tissue taken from the same body as that on which the surgery is performed. [AUTO- + -PLASTY.] —**au'to·plas'tic** *adj.* —**au'to·plas'ti·cal·ly** *adv.*

au·top·sy (ô'tŏp'sē, ô'təp-) *n., pl.* **-sies.** The examination of a dead body to determine the cause of death. Also called "necropsy," "post-mortem." [New Latin *autopsia,* from Greek, a seeing for oneself : AUT(O)- + Greek *opsis,* sight (see **okw-** in Appendix*).] —**au·top'sic, au·top'si·cal** *adj.* —**au·top'sist** *n.*

au·to·some (ô'tə-sōm') *n.* Any chromosome that is not a sex chromosome. [AUTO- + (CHROMO)SOME.] —**au'to·so'mal** (-sō'məl) *adj.*

au·to·sug·ges·tion (ô'tō-səg-jĕs'chən) *n. Psychology.* The process by which a person induces self-acceptance of an opinion, belief, or plan of action. —**au'to·sug·gest'i·bil'i·ty** *n.* —**au'to·sug·gest'i·ble** *adj.* —**au'to·sug·ges'tive** *adj.*

au·tot·o·mize (ô-tŏt'ə-mīz') *v.* **-mized, -mizing, -mizes.** —*tr.* To cause the autotomy of (a body part). —*intr.* To undergo autotomy.

au·tot·o·my (ô-tŏt'ə-mē) *n. Zoology.* The spontaneous casting off of a body part, as the tail of certain lizards, for self-protection. [AUTO- + -TOMY.] —**au'to·tom'ic** (ô'tə-tŏm'ĭk) *adj.*

au·to·tox·e·mi·a (ô'tō-tŏk-sē'mē-ə) *n.* Also **au·to·tox·ae·mi·a, au·to·tox·i·co·sis** (-tŏk'sĭ-kō'sĭs). *Pathology.* **Autointoxication** *(see).* [AUTO- + TOXEMIA.]

au·to·tox·in (ô'tō-tŏk'sĭn) *n.* A poison that acts on the organism in which it is generated. —**au'to·tox'ic** *adj.*

au·to·trans·form·er (ô'tō-trăns-fôr'mər) *n.* An electrical transformer in which the primary and secondary coils have some or all windings in common.

au·to·troph (ô'tə-trŏf') *n. Biology.* An autotrophic organism, such as a green plant. [Back-formation from AUTOTROPHIC.]

au·to·troph·ic (ô'tə-trŏf'ĭk, -trō'fĭk) *adj. Biology.* Designating or characterizing plants or plantlike organisms capable of manufacturing their own food by synthesis of inorganic materials, as in photosynthesis. [AUTO- + TROPHIC.] —**au'to·troph'i·cal·ly** *adv.* —**au·tot'ro·phy** (ô-tŏt'rə-fē) *n.*

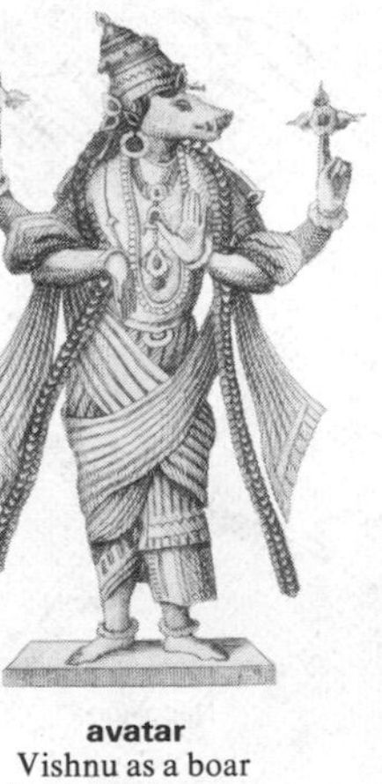

avatar
Vishnu as a boar in his third avatar

au·to·truck (ô'tō-trŭk') *n.* A truck operated by a motor.

au·tumn (ô'təm) *n.* **1.** The season of the year between summer and winter, lasting from the autumnal equinox to the winter solstice and from September to November in the Northern Hemisphere; fall. **2.** A time or period of maturity verging on decline. [Middle English *autumpne,* from Old French *autompne,* from Latin *autumnus,* possibly from Etruscan.] —**au·tum'nal** (-tŭm'nəl) *adj.* —**au·tum'nal·ly** *adv.*

autumnal equinox. The **equinox** *(see)* of September 22 or 23 when the sun crosses the celestial equator going north to south, marking the start of autumn. Compare **vernal equinox.**

autumn crocus. A plant, *Colchicum autumnale,* native to Europe and northern Africa, having pink or purplish flowers that bloom in the fall. Also called "meadow saffron."

au·tun·ite (ō-tŭn'īt', ô'tən-īt') *n.* A yellowish fluorescent, minor ore of uranium with composition $Ca(UO_2)_2(PO_4)_2 \cdot 10H_2O$. [First found at *Autun,* town in France.]

Au·vergne (ō-vârn'). A region of central France.

aux. auxiliary.

aux·e·sis (ôg-zē'sĭs, ôk-sē'-) *n. Biology.* An increase in the size of a cell without cell division. [Greek *auxēsis,* growth, from *auxanein,* to grow, increase. See **aug-**[1] in Appendix.*]

aux·il·ia·ry (ôg-zĭl'yər-ē, -zĭl'ər-ē) *adj. Abbr.* **aux. 1.** Giving assistance or support; aiding; helping. **2.** Subsidiary; supplementary; additional. **3.** Held in or used as a reserve: *auxiliary troops.* **4.** *Nautical.* Equipped with a motor to supplement the sails. —*n., pl.* **auxiliaries. 1.** One that assists or helps; an assistant. **2.** A group or organization that assists or is supplementary to a larger one: *a women's auxiliary.* **3.** *Plural.* Foreign troops serving a country in war. **4.** An auxiliary verb. **5.** *Nautical.* A sailing vessel equipped with a motor. **6.** *Naval.* A vessel designed for and used in other than combat services, such as a tug or a supply ship. [Latin *auxiliārius,* from *auxilium,* help. See **aug-**[1] in Appendix.*]

auxiliary verb. *Grammar.* A verb that accompanies particular forms of the main verb of a clause to form a phrasal unit expressing the tense, mood, voice, or aspect of the main verb. *Have, may, can, must,* and *will* are some auxiliary verbs: *He will come. You must go.*

aux·in (ôk'sĭn) *n.* Any of several plant hormones, or similar substances produced synthetically, that affect growth by causing larger, elongated cells to develop. [Greek *auxein,* to grow (see **aug-**[1] in Appendix*) + -IN] —**aux·in'ic** *adj.*

Av (ôv, äb) *n.* Also **Ab** (äb, ôv). The 11th month of the year on the Hebrew calendar, usually coinciding with August. See **calendar.** [Hebrew *ābh,* from Akkadian *abu.*]

av. 1. avenue. **2.** average. **3.** avoirdupois.

Av. avenue.

a.v. ad valorem.

A.V. 1. audio-visual. **2.** Authorized Version.

a·vail (ə-vāl') *v.* **availed, availing, avails.** —*tr.* To be of use or advantage to; to assist; to help: *Nothing can avail him now.* —*intr.* To be of use, value, or advantage; serve. —**avail (oneself) of.** To make use of. —*n.* Use, benefit, or advantage. Now used chiefly in the phrase *to* (or *of*) *no avail.* [Middle English *availen* : A- (intensive) + *vailen,* to avail, from Old French *valoir* (stem *vail-*), to be worth, from Latin *valēre,* to be strong, be worth (see **wal-** in Appendix*).] —**a·vail'ing·ly** *adv.*

a·vail·a·ble (ə-vā'lə-bəl) *adj.* Accessible for use; at hand; usable. —**a·vail'a·bil'i·ty, a·vail'a·ble·ness** *n.* —**a·vail'a·bly** *adv.*

av·a·lanche (ăv'ə-lănch', -länch') *n.* **1.** A fall or slide of a large mass of snow, rock, or other material down a mountainside. **2.** Something resembling such an overwhelming fall or slide. —*v.* **avalanched, -lanching, -lanches.** —*intr.* To fall, as an avalanche. —*tr.* To overwhelm. [French, from Swiss French *avalantse,* from Savoyard *lavantse,* from Vulgar Latin (unattested) *labanca*†.]

avalanche lily. A plant, *Erythronium montanum,* of western North America, having nodding white flowers. [So called because it grows near the snow line and blooms when the snow begins to melt.]

Av·a·lon (ăv'ə-lŏn'). Also **Av·al·lon.** *Celtic Mythology.* An island paradise in the western seas where King Arthur and other heroes went at death.

Av·a·lon Peninsula (ăv'ə-lŏn'). A peninsula, about 4,000 square miles in area, of southeastern Newfoundland, Canada; the site of its capital, St. John's.

a·vant-garde (ä'vänt-gärd'; *French* à-väN-gàrd') *n.* **1.** A group, as of writers and artists, regarded as pre-eminent in the invention and application of new techniques in a given field. **2.** The admirers of such a group and critics acting as its spokesmen. —*adj.* **1.** Of or belonging to the vanguard, as in the arts. **2.** Ahead of the times. [French, VANGUARD.]

av·a·rice (ăv'ə-rĭs) *n.* An extreme desire to amass wealth; cupidity. [Middle English, from Old French, from Latin *avāritia,* from *avārus,* greedy, from *avēre*†, to desire.]

av·a·ri·cious (ăv'ə-rĭsh'əs) *adj.* Immoderately fond of accumulating wealth. —**av'a·ri'cious·ly** *adv.* —**av'a·ri'cious·ness** *n.*

a·vast (ə-văst', ə-väst') *interj.* A nautical command to desist: *Avast heaving there.* [Shortened from Dutch *houd vast,* "hold fast" : *houd,* imperative of *houden,* to hold, from Middle Dutch (see **kel-**[5] in Appendix*) + *vast,* fast, from Middle Dutch (see **past-** in Appendix*).]

av·a·tar (ăv'ə-tär') *n.* **1. a.** One regarded as the incarnation or embodiment of some known model or category. **b.** An entity regarded as an extreme or notably complete manifestation of its

ă pat/ā pay/âr care/ä father/b bib/ch church/d deed/ĕ pet/ē be/f fife/g gag/h hat/hw which/ĭ pit/ī pie/îr pier/j judge/k kick/l lid, needle/m mum/n no, sudden/ng thing/ŏ pot/ō toe/ô paw, for/oi noise/ou out/ŏŏ took/ōō boot/p pop/r roar/s sauce/sh ship, dish/

kind; exemplar; archetype: *an avatar of stupidity.* **2.** *Hindu Mythology.* The descent to earth of a deity in human or animal form. Used as a generic term for the incarnations of Vishnu. [Sanskrit *avatāra,* descent, from *avatarati,* he descends : *ava,* down (see **au-**[3] in Appendix*) + *tarati,* he crosses (see **ter-**[1] in Appendix*).]

a·vaunt (ə-vônt′, ə-vänt′) *interj. Archaic.* A command to be gone. [Middle English, from Old French *avant,* "forward," "go away!" See **vanguard.**]

AVC, A.V.C. **1.** American Veteran's Committee. **2.** automatic volume control.

avdp. avoirdupois.

A·ve (ä′vā) *n.* The Ave Maria. [Middle English, from Latin *ave, have,* "hail," perhaps from Carthaginian.]

ave., Ave. avenue

A·ve·lla·ne·da (ä′vā-yä-nā′*th*ä). A city and industrial suburb of Buenos Aires, Argentina. Population, 330,000.

A·ve Ma·ri·a (ä′vā mə-rē′ə). Also **A·ve Mar·y** (ā′vē mâr′ē). **1.** A Roman Catholic prayer, based on the greetings of Gabriel and Elizabeth to the Virgin Mary. Luke 1:28, 42. Also called "Hail Mary." **2. a.** A recitation of this prayer. **b.** The hour (as at dawn and sunset) when it is customarily said. **3.** One of the small beads on a rosary used to count recitations of this prayer. [Middle English, from Medieval Latin, "Hail Mary!"]

a·venge (ə-vĕnj′) *v.* **avenged, avenging, avenges.** —*tr.* **1.** To take revenge or exact satisfaction for (a wrong, injury, or the like): *avenge a murder.* **2.** To take vengeance on behalf of: *avenge one's sister.* —*intr.* To take vengeance. [Middle English *avengen* : *a-,* from Latin *ad-,* to + *vengen,* to revenge, from Old French *vengier,* from Latin *vindicāre,* from *vindex* (stem *vindic-*), protector, avenger (see **deik-** in Appendix*).] —**a·veng′er** *n.* —**a·veng′ing·ly** *adv.*

Usage: *Avenge* is generally used in the sense of achieving justice, whereas *revenge* (verb) stresses retaliation. *Avenge* usually has for its subject someone other than the person wronged; the latter, or the wrong itself, often serves as the object in such constructions: *He avenged his father* (or *his father's murder*). *Revenge* usually has for its subject the person wronged, and is often used reflexively: *He revenged himself* (or *the wrong done him*). Both verbs are often used with *on* or *upon.*

av·ens (ăv′ĭnz) *n., pl.* **avens** or **-enses. 1.** Any of various plants of the genus *Geum,* having irregularly shaped leaves, white, yellow, or reddish flowers, and plumed seed clusters. **2.** Any of several related plants of the genus *Dryas,* of mountainous and arctic regions. [Middle English *avence,* from Old French, from Medieval Latin *avencia*†.]

Av·en·tine Hill (ăv′ən-tīn′, -tēn′). One of the seven hills of Rome.

a·ven·tu·rine (ə-vĕn′chə-rēn′, -rĭn) *n.* Also **a·ven·tu·rin** (ə-vĕn′chə-rĭn). **1.** An opaque or semitranslucent brown glass flecked with small metallic particles, often of copper or chromic oxide. **2.** Any of several varieties of quartz or feldspar flecked with particles of mica, hematite, or other materials. Also called "sunstone." [French, from *aventure,* accident, ADVENTURE; so called because of its accidental discovery.] —**a·ven′tu·rine′** *adj.*

av·e·nue (ăv′ə-no͞o′, -nyo͞o′) *n. Abbr.* **av., Av., ave., Ave. 1. a.** A wide street or thoroughfare. **b.** Any path resembling such a thoroughfare: *"the avenue of foam that the ship had plowed through the ocean"* (Ludwig Bemelmans). **2. a.** A path or lane lined with trees. **b.** *Chiefly British.* The drive leading to a country house. **3.** An opening or means of approach to a given place, activity, or goal: *new avenues of trade.* [French, from Old French, approach, avenue, feminine past participle of *avenir,* to approach, arrive, from Latin *advenīre,* to come to : *ad-,* to + *venīre,* to come (see **gwā-** in Appendix*).]

a·ver (ə-vûr′) *tr.v.* **averred, averring, avers. 1.** To declare in a positive or dogmatic manner; affirm. **2.** *Law.* To assert formally as a fact; justify or prove (a plea). —See Synonyms at **assert.** [Middle English *averren,* from Old French *averer,* from Medieval Latin *adverāre,* to assert as true : *ad-,* to + *vērus,* true (see **wēros** in Appendix*).] —**a·ver′ment** *n.* —**a·ver′ra·ble** *adj.*

av·er·age (ăv′rĭj, ăv′ər-ĭj) *n. Abbr.* **av., avg. 1.** *Mathematics.* **a.** A number that typifies a set of numbers of which it is a function. **b.** The **arithmetic mean** *(see).* **2. a.** A relative proportion or degree indicating position or achievement: *a class average.* **b.** A representative type. **3.** *Marine Law.* **a.** The incurrence of and loss due to damage at sea to a ship or cargo. **b.** The equitable distribution of such a loss among concerned parties. **c.** Any charges incurred through such a loss. —*adj.* **1.** Of, pertaining to, or constituting a mathematical average. **2.** Typical; usual. **3.** *Marine Law.* Assessed in compliance with the laws of average. —*v.* **averaged, -aging, -ages.** —*tr.* **1.** To calculate the average of. **2.** To accomplish or obtain an average of: *average three hours work a day.* **3.** To distribute proportionately. —*intr.* **1.** To be or amount to an average. **2.** To buy or sell more goods or shares to obtain more than an average price. —**average out.** *Informal.* To attain an average eventually. —**on the average.** As a mean rate, amount, or the like. [Earlier *averie,* financial loss on damaged shipping, hence such loss shared equitably among investors, hence numerical average, from Old French *avarie,* damage to shipping, from Old Italian *avaria,* from Arabic *'awārīyah,* damaged goods, from *'awar,* fault, blemish.]

Synonyms: *average, medium, mediocre, fair, middling, indifferent, run-of-the-mill, so-so, tolerable.* These adjectives indicate rank or position on a scale of evaluation. *Average* and *medium* apply to what is midway between extremes on such a scale; usually they imply both sufficiency and lack of distinction. *Mediocre* stresses the undistinguished aspect of what is average. *Fair* suggests rank above the average but substantially below the highest. *Middling* refers to middle position, less favorably than *average* but less unfavorably than *mediocre. Indifferent* is close to *mediocre,* and suggests inadequacy. *Run-of-the-mill* suggests uniform mediocrity. *So-so* suggests what is just passable. *Tolerable* suggests more favorably what is acceptable.

A·ver·no (ä-vĕr′nō). Ancient name **A·ver·nus** (ə-vûr′nəs). A small crater lake, ten miles west of Naples, Italy; regarded by the ancient Romans as the entrance to the underworld.

A·ver·ro·ës (ə-vĕr′ō-ēz′, ăv′ə-rō′ēz). Also **A·ver·rho·ës.** *Arabic* **ibn-Rushd** (ĭb′n-rōsht). 1126–1198. Spanish-born Arab philosopher and physician.

a·verse (ə-vûrs′) *adj.* **1. a.** Opposed; reluctant. Used postpositively or predicatively and used with *to.* **b.** Actuated by aversion: *"Men are ever in extremes; either doating or averse."* (Congreve). **2.** *Botany.* Turned away from the central stem or axis. [Latin *āversus,* past participle of *āvertere,* AVERT.] —**a·verse′ly** *adv.* —**a·verse′ness** *n.*

Usage: A person is said to be *averse to* or, less often, *averse from* something. *Aversion* is principally used with *to* or, less often, with *for, toward,* or *from.* Both *averse* and *adverse* (apart from botanical senses) express opposition, but from different points of view. To be *averse* to something indicates opposition on the subject's part. That which is *adverse* to a person or thing reflects opposition contrary to the subject's will.

a·ver·sion (ə-vûr′zhən, -shən) *n.* **1.** Intense dislike. Used with *to.* **2.** A feeling of extreme repugnance. —See Usage note at **averse.**

a·vert (ə-vûrt′) *tr.v.* **averted, averting, averts. 1.** To turn away: *avert one's eyes.* **2.** To ward off or prevent: *avert disaster.* [Middle English *averten,* from Old French *āvertir,* from Vulgar Latin *āvertīre* (unattested), variant of Latin *āvertere* : *ab-,* away from + *vertere,* to turn (see **wer-**[3] in Appendix*).] —**a·vert′ed·ly** (ə-vûr′tĭd-lē) *adv.* —**a·vert′i·ble, a·vert′a·ble** *adj.*

A·ves·ta (ə-vĕs′tə) *n.* The sacred writings of the ancient Persians. [Middle Persian *apastāk*†, text.]

A·ves·tan (ə-vĕs′tən) *n.* The eastern dialect of Old Iranian, in which the Avesta was written, which is the oldest attested group in the Indo-Iranian branch of Indo-European. Also formerly called "Zend." —*adj.* Of or pertaining to the Avesta or to the language in which it was written. [From AVESTA.]

avg. average.

a·vi·an (ā′vē-ən) *adj. Zoology.* Of, pertaining to, or characteristic of birds. [From Latin *avis,* bird. See **awi-** in Appendix.*]

a·vi·ar·y (ā′vē-ĕr′ē) *n., pl.* **-ies.** Any large enclosure specially built to hold a great number of live birds in confinement. [Latin *aviārium,* from *avis,* bird. See **awi-** in Appendix.*] —**a′vi·a·rist** (ā′vē-ə-rĭst, -ĕr′ĭst) *n.*

a·vi·a·tion (ā′vē-ā′shən, ăv′ē-) *n. Abbr.* **avn. 1.** The operation of aircraft. **2.** The production of aircraft. **3.** Military aircraft. [French, from Latin *avis,* bird. See **awi-** in Appendix.*]

aviation medicine. The branch of medicine comprising **aeromedicine** and **space medicine** *(both of which see).*

a·vi·a·tor (ā′vē-ā′tər, ăv′ē-) *n.* One who operates aircraft; a pilot. [French *aviateur,* from *aviation,* AVIATION.]

a·vi·a·trix (ā′vē-ā′trĭks, ăv′ē-) *n., pl.* **-trixes.** A female aviator.

Av·i·cen·na (ăv′ə-sĕn′ə). *Arabic* **ibn-Si·na** (ĭb′ən-sē′nä). A.D. 980–1037. Arab philosopher and physician.

a·vi·cul·ture (ā′vĭ-kŭl′chər, ăv′ĭ-) *n.* The raising or keeping of birds. [Latin *avis,* bird (see **awi-** in Appendix*) + CULTURE.] —**a′vi·cul′tur·ist** *n.*

av·id (ăv′ĭd) *adj.* **1. a.** Eager. Often used with *of* or *for: avid for adventure.* **b.** Greedy. **2.** Enthusiastic; ardent: *an avid sportsman.* —See Synonyms at **eager.** [French *avide,* from Latin *avidus,* from *avēre,* to long for. See **avarice.**] —**av′id·ly** *adv.*

av·i·din (ăv′ə-dĭn) *n.* A protein in egg albumin, capable of inactivating biotin, consequently inhibiting the growth of certain bacteria. [AVID + -IN, from its affinity for biotin.]

a·vid·i·ty (ə-vĭd′ə-tē) *n.* **1. a.** Eagerness. **b.** Greed. **2.** *Chemistry.* **a.** The dissociation-dependent strength of an acid or base. **b.** Degree of **affinity** *(see).*

a·vi·fau·na (ā′və-fô′nə, ăv′ə-) *n.* All the birds of a specific region or time division. [New Latin : Latin *avis,* bird (see **awi-** in Appendix*) + FAUNA.] —**a′vi·fau′nal** *adj.*

av·i·ga·tion (ăv′ə-gā′shən) *n.* Airborne operation and navigation of aircraft. [AVI(ATION) + (NAVI)GATION.] —**av′i·ga′tor** (-gā′tər) *n.*

A·vi·gnon (à-vē-nyôN′). A city on the Rhône in southeastern France; a seat of the papacy (1309–77). Population, 73,000.

a·vi·on·ics (ā′vē-ŏn′ĭks, ăv′ē-) *n.* Plural in form, used with a singular verb. The science and technology of electronics applied to aeronautics and astronautics. [AVI(ATION) + (ELECTR)ONICS.] —**a′vi·on′ic** *adj.*

a·vir·u·lent (ā-vĭr′yə-lənt, ā-vĭr′ə-lənt) *adj. Medicine.* Not infective or virulent.

a·vi·ta·min·o·sis (ā-vī′tə-mĭn-ō′sĭs) *n.* A disease caused by deficiency of vitamins. [A- (without) + VITAMIN + -OSIS.]

avn. aviation.

av·o·ca·do (ăv′ə-kä′dō) *n., pl.* **-dos. 1.** A tropical American tree, *Persea americana,* cultivated for its edible fruit. **2.** The oval or pear-shaped fruit of this tree, having leathery green or blackish skin, a large seed, and bland, greenish-yellow pulp. Also called "alligator pear." [Spanish *aguacate,* from Nahuatl *ahuacatl,* "testicle" (from the shape of the fruit).]

avocado

av·o·ca·tion (ăv′ō-kā′shən) *n.* **1.** An activity engaged in, usually for enjoyment, in addition to one's regular work or profession; hobby. **2.** *Archaic.* One's regular work or profession. [Latin *āvocātiō,* a calling away, diversion, from *āvocāre,* to call away : *ab-,* away + *vocāre,* to call (see **wekw-** in Appendix*).]

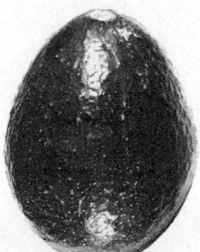

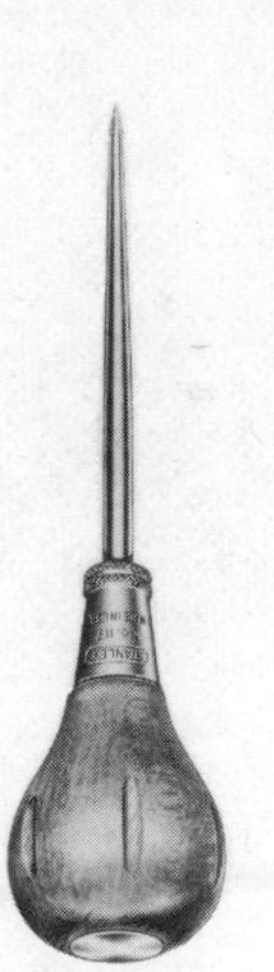
awl

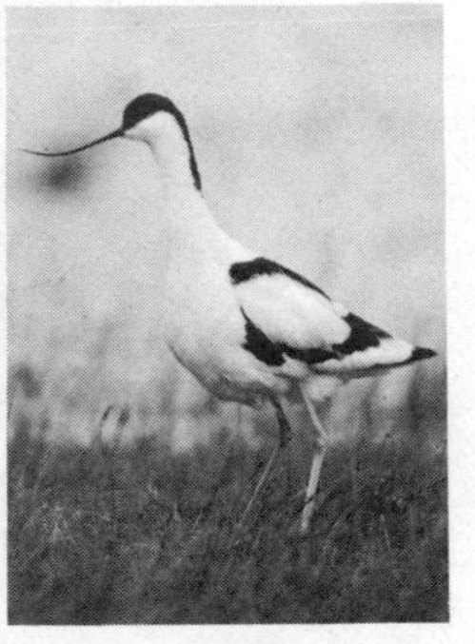
avocet
Recurvirostra avosetta

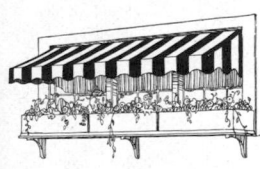

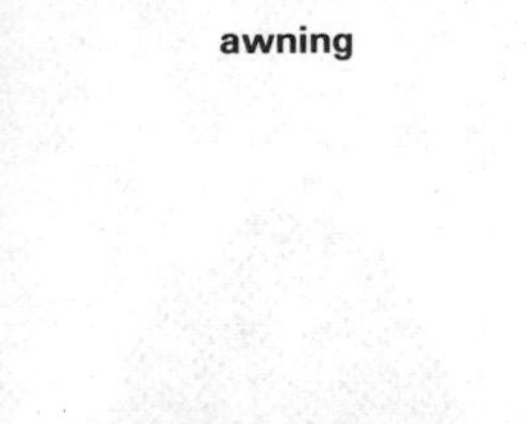
awning

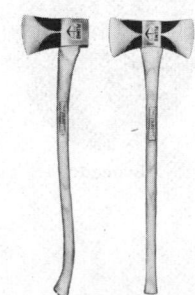

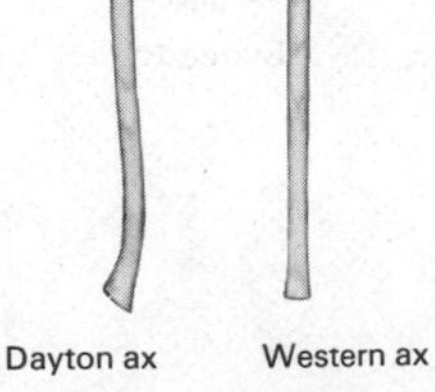
Dayton ax Western ax
ax

av·o·cet (ăv′ə-sĕt′) *n.* Any of several long-legged shore birds of the genus *Recurvirostra,* having a long, slender, upturned beak. [French *avocette,* from Italian *avocetta*†.]

a·vo·di·re (ăv′ə-də-rā′, -dĭ-rā′) *n.* **1.** A tree, *Turreanthus africana,* of western Africa, having light-colored wood with a clearly marked grain. **2.** The wood of this tree, used in decorative cabinetwork. [French *avodiré*†.]

A·vo·ga·dro (ä′və-gä′drō, ăv′ə-), **Amedeo.** 1776–1856. Italian physicist.

Avogadro number. Also **Avogadro's number.** *Abbr.* **N** The number of molecules in a mole of a substance, approximately 6.0225×10^{23}. Also called "Avogadro constant."

Avogadro's law. The principle that equal volumes of different gases under identical conditions of pressure and temperature contain the same number of molecules. Also called "Avogadro's hypothesis," "Avogadro's principle," "Avogadro's rule."

a·void (ə-void′) *tr.v.* **avoided, avoiding, avoids. 1.** To keep away from; stay clear of; shun. **2.** *Law.* To annul or make void; invalidate. **3.** *Obsolete.* To empty or void. —See Synonyms at **escape.** [Middle English *avoiden,* from Norman French *avoider,* from Old French *esvuidier,* "to empty out," hence to leave : *es-,* from Latin *ex-,* out + *vuidier,* to empty, from Vulgar Latin *vocitus* (unattested), empty, from Latin *vocāre,* to be empty (see **eu-**[2] in Appendix*).] —**a·void′a·ble** *adj.* —**a·void′a·bly** *adv.* —**a·void′er** *n.*

a·void·ance (ə-void′əns) *n.* **1.** The act of avoiding or shunning something. **2.** *Law.* A making void; an annulment.

av·oir·du·pois (ăv′ər-də-poiz′) *n. Abbr.* **av., avdp., avoir. 1.** Avoirdupois weight. **2.** *Informal.* Weight; heaviness. Said of a person. [Middle English *avoir de pois,* "commodities sold by weight," from Old French *aver de peis* : *aver,* property, from *aver, aveir,* to possess, have, from Latin *habēre* (see **ghabh-** in Appendix*) + *de,* of, from Latin *dē* + *pois, peis,* weight, from *peser,* to weigh, POISE.]

avoirdupois weight. A system of weights and measures, used in most English-speaking countries, based on a pound containing 16 ounces or 7,000 grains and equal to 453.59 grams. See **measurement.**

A·von (ā′vŏn, ā′vən). A river rising in Warwickshire, England, and flowing 96 miles southwest past Stratford to the Severn.

A·von, Earl of. See Anthony **Eden.**

a·vouch (ə-vouch′) *tr.v.* **avouched, avouching, avouches. 1.** To take responsibility for; to guarantee. **2.** To assert positively; affirm. **3.** To acknowledge one's responsibility for; confess; avow. [Middle English *avouchen,* from Old French *avochier,* from Latin *advocāre,* to call on (as adviser) : *ad-,* to + *vocāre,* to call (see **wekw-** in Appendix*).]

a·vow (ə-vou′) *tr.v.* **avowed, avowing, avows.** To acknowledge openly; confess: *avow guilt.* See Synonyms at **acknowledge, assert.** [Middle English *avowen,* from Old French *avouer,* from Latin *advocāre,* to call on (as adviser), appeal to. See **avouch.**] —**a·vow′a·ble** *adj.* —**a·vow′a·bly** *adv.* —**a·vow′er** *n.*

a·vow·al (ə-vou′əl) *n.* An admission or acknowledgment.

a·vowed (ə-voud′) *adj.* Frankly acknowledged; confessed: *an avowed rebel.* —**a·vow′ed·ly** (ə-vou′ĭd-lē) *adv.*

a·vulse (ə-vŭls′) *tr.v.* **avulsed, avulsing, avulses.** To tear off forcibly; rip away. [Latin *avellere* (past participle *avulsus*), to tear off : *ab-,* away + *vellere,* to pull (see **wel-**[4] in Appendix*).]

a·vul·sion (ə-vŭl′shən) *n.* **1.** A ripping off; forcible separation. **2.** A part removed in this way. **3.** *Law.* **a.** The removal by erosion of soil from one property onto another. **b.** A shift in the course of a boundary stream. In this sense, compare **alluvion.**

a·vun·cu·lar (ə-vŭng′kyə-lər) *adj.* Of, pertaining to, or resembling an uncle, especially a benevolent uncle. [From Latin *avunculus,* maternal uncle. See **awo-** in Appendix.*]

a.w. all water (transportation).

A/W actual weight.

a·wait (ə-wāt′) *v.* **awaited, awaiting, awaits.** —*tr.* **1.** To wait for. **2.** To be in store for. **3.** *Obsolete.* To lie in ambush for. —*intr.* To wait. —See Synonyms at **expect.** [Middle English *awaiten,* from Old North French *awaitier,* watch for, wait on : *a-,* from Latin *ad-,* to + *waitier,* to watch, WAIT.]

A·wa·ji (ä′wä-jē). An island of Japan, about 230 square miles in area, lying between Shikoku and Honshu.

a·wake (ə-wāk′) *v.* **awoke** (ə-wōk′) or *rare* **awaked, awaked** or *rare* **awoke, awaking, awakes.** —*tr.* **1.** To rouse from sleep; waken. **2.** To stir the interest of; excite. **3.** To stir up (memories or fears, for example). —*intr.* **1.** To wake up. **2.** To become alert. **3.** To become aware or cognizant. Often used with *to: They awoke to reality.* —See Usage note at **wake.** —*adj.* **1.** Not asleep. **2.** Alert; vigilant; watchful. —See Synonyms at **aware.** [Middle English *awaken, awakien,* Old English *awacan, awacian* : *a-* (intensive) + *wacan, wacian,* to be awake, WAKE.]

a·wak·en (ə-wā′kən) *v.* **-ened, -ening, -ens.** —*tr.* To cause to wake up. —*intr.* To wake up; awake. —See Usage note at **wake.** [Middle English *awak(e)nen,* Old English *āwæcnan, āwæcnian* : A- (on) + *wæcnan, wæcnian,* to waken (see **weg-**[2] in Appendix*).]

a·wak·en·ing (ə-wā′kən-ĭng) *adj.* **1.** Waking up. **2.** Rousing; exciting. —*n.* **1.** The act of waking; an emergence from sleep. **2.** A stirring up; a rousing of attention or interest.

a·ward (ə-wôrd′) *tr.v.* **awarded, awarding, awards. 1.** To grant as merited or due. **2.** To declare as legally due: *awarded damages to the plaintiff.* **3.** To bestow for performance or quality: *award a prize.* —*n.* **1.** A decision, as one made by a judge or arbitrator. **2.** Something awarded, as a medal or a sum of money. [Middle English *awarden,* from Norman French *awarder,* variant of Old North French *eswarder,* to judge after careful observation : *es-,* from Latin *ex-,* out + *warder,* to observe, keep, judge, from Germanic (see **wer-**[4] in Appendix*).] —**a·ward′a·ble** *adj.* —**a·ward′er** *n.*

a·ware (ə-wâr′) *adj.* Conscious; cognizant. Often used with *of: aware of their limitations.* [Middle English *awar, iwar,* Old English *gewær.* See **wer-**[4] in Appendix.*] —**a·ware′ness** *n.*

Synonyms: *aware, cognizant, conscious, sensible, alive, awake, alert, watchful, vigilant.* These adjectives mean to be mindful or heedful of something. *Aware* implies knowing something either by perception or by means of information. *Cognizant* is a rather formal equivalent of *aware* stressing sure knowledge and the recognition of it. *Conscious* emphasizes recognition of something sensed or felt. *Sensible* implies knowledge gained by sensing or perceiving, and suggests appreciation of it. *Alive* stresses keenness of perception, and *awake* suggests being aroused to the presence of something. *Alert* stresses both knowledge and capability of swift, apt response. *Watchful* and *vigilant* imply acute perception of what is dangerous or potentially so.

a·wash (ə-wŏsh′, ə-wôsh′) *adj.* **1.** Level with or washed by waves. **2.** Flooded. **3.** Floating on waves. —**a·wash′** *adv.*

a·way (ə-wā′) *adv.* **1.** From a particular place: *run away from home.* **2.** At a distance. **3.** In a different direction; aside: *He glanced away.* **4.** Out of existence: *The music faded away.* **5.** From one's possession or notice: *He gave the plot away.* **6.** Continuously: *He worked away at his job.* **7.** Immediately: *Fire away!* **8.** *Slang.* In a penal or mental institution: *put away for robbery.* —**away with. 1.** Take away. **2.** Go away. Often used imperatively: *Away with you!* —**do** (or **make**) **away with. 1.** To get rid of. **2.** To murder. —*adj.* **1.** Absent: *He is away from home.* **2.** At a distance: *He is miles away.* [Middle English *away, on way,* from Old English *aweg, oweg, onweg,* "on the way (from)" : *a-, on,* ON + *weg,* WAY.]

aWb *Physics.* attoweber.

awe (ô) *n.* **1. a.** An emotion of mingled reverence, dread, and wonder inspired by something majestic or sublime. **b.** Respect, tinged with fear, for authority. **2.** *Archaic.* The power to inspire reverence or fear. **3.** *Obsolete.* Dread. —*tr.v.* **awed, awing** or **aweing, awes.** To inspire with awe. [Middle English *awe, age, aghe,* from Old Norse *agi.* See **agh-**[1] in Appendix.*]

a·wea·ry (ə-wîr′ē) *adj.* Tired; weary.

a·weath·er (ə-wĕth′ər) *adv. Nautical.* To windward.

a·weigh (ə-wā′) *adj. Nautical.* Hanging just clear of the bottom. Said of an anchor. [A- (on) + WEIGH.]

awe·some (ô′səm) *adj.* **1.** Inspiring awe. **2.** Expressing or characterized by awe. —**awe′some·ly** *adv.* —**awe′some·ness** *n.*

awe-strick·en (ô′strĭk′ən) *adj.* Also **awe-struck** (-strŭk′). Full of awe.

aw·ful (ô′fəl) *adj.* **1.** Extremely bad or unpleasant; terrible; horrible. **2.** Dreadful; appalling; fearsome. **3.** Great: *an awful fool.* [Middle English *awful, aweful* : AWE + -FUL.] —**aw′ful·ly** *adv.* —**aw′ful·ness** *n.*

a·while (ə-hwīl′) *adv.* For a short time.

Usage: *Awhile* is not preceded by *for,* though the noun *while* can be. Each of the following is possible: *stay awhile; stay for a while; stay a while* (but not *stay for awhile*).

awk·ward (ôk′wərd) *adj.* **1.** Not graceful; ungainly. **2.** Not dexterous; clumsy; unskillful. **3.** Hard to handle; unwieldy: *an awkward bundle.* **4.** Difficult or dangerous: *an awkward climb.* **5.** Inconvenient; uncomfortable: *an awkward pose.* **6.** Causing embarrassment; trying: *an awkward predicament.* [Middle English *awkeward,* "in the wrong direction," awry : *awke,* backhanded, perverse, wrong, from Old Norse *öfugr,* turned backward (see **apo-** in Appendix*) + -WARD.] —**awk′ward·ly** *adv.* —**awk′ward·ness** *n.*

Synonyms: *awkward, clumsy, maladroit, inept, gauche, bungling, ungainly, unwieldy.* These adjectives refer to lack of grace or skill in movement, manner, or performance. *Awkward* and *clumsy,* the least specific, are often interchangeable. *Clumsy* emphasizes lack of dexterity in physical movement. *Awkward* applies both to physical movement and to embarrassing conditions and situations. *Maladroit* implies lack of tact or skill in relationships with other persons. *Inept* applies to inappropriate actions and speech. *Gauche* (French for "left") usually suggests boorishness. *Bungling* implies gross incompetence in performance. *Ungainly* suggests a visible lack of grace in form or movement. *Unwieldy* describes objects whose size or shape make them difficult to handle.

awl (ôl) *n.* A pointed tool for making holes, as in wood or leather. [Middle English *aule, al,* Old English *eal, al, ael,* from Germanic *āl-* (unattested), perhaps of Anatolian origin.]

awl·wort (ôl′wûrt′, -wôrt′) *n.* A small aquatic plant, *Subularia aquatica,* of the Northern Hemisphere, having a tuft of narrow, pointed leaves and minute white flowers. [From the shape of its leaves.]

awn (ôn) *n. Botany.* A slender, bristlelike terminal process, such as those found at the tips of the spikelets in many grasses. [Middle English *awne, agene,* from Old Norse *ǫgn.* See **ak-** in Appendix.*]

awn·ing (ô′nĭng) *n.* A rooflike structure, as of canvas, stretched over a frame as a shelter from weather. [Origin uncertain.]

a·woke. Past tense and rare past participle of **awake.**

A.W.O.L., a.w.o.l., AWOL, awol (ā′wôl′) *Military.* Absent (or absence) without leave.

a·wry (ə-rī′) *adv.* **1.** Turned or twisted toward one side; askew. **2.** Away from the correct course; amiss; wrong. [Middle English *awrie, on wry* : ON + *wry,* twisted, WRY.] —**a·wry′** *adj.*

ax, axe (ăks) *n., pl.* **axes. 1.** A tool with a bladed head mounted on a handle, used for felling or splitting lumber. **2.** Any similar tool or weapon, as a battle-ax. —**get the ax.** *Informal.* To be

fired from one's job. **—have an ax to grind.** To pursue a selfish or subjective aim. *—tr.v.* **axed, axing, axes.** To work on with an ax. [Middle English *ax, axe,* Old English *æx, aces.* See **agwesi-** in Appendix.*]

ax. axiom.

Ax·el Hei·burg (ăk′səl hī′bûrg). An island of the Northwest Territories, Canada; the largest (13,200 square miles) of the Sverdrup group in the Arctic Ocean.

a·xen·ic (ā-zĕn′ĭk, ā-zē′nĭk) *adj. Biology.* Free of symbionts or parasites; uncontaminated. [A- (without) + XEN(O)- + -IC.]

ax·es. 1. Plural of **axis.** 2. Plural of **ax.**

ax·i·al (ăk′sē-əl) *adj.* 1. Pertaining to or forming an axis. 2. Located on, around or in the direction of an axis. [AXI(S) + -AL.] **—ax′i·al·ly** *adv.*

ax·il (ăk′sĭl) *n.* The angle between the upper surface of a leafstalk, flower stalk, branch, or similar part, and the stem or axis from which it arises. [Latin *axilla,* armpit, **axilla.**]

ax·il·la (ăk-sĭl′ə) *n., pl.* **axillae** (ăk-sĭl′ē). The armpit, or an analogous part. [Latin *axilla,* armpit. See **aks-** in Appendix.*]

ax·il·lar (ăk-sĭl′ər, ăk′sə-lər) *adj.* Axillary. *—n.* One of the feathers in the axilla of a bird's wing.

ax·il·lar·y (ăk′sə-lĕr′ē) *adj.* 1. *Anatomy.* Of, relating to, or near the axilla. 2. *Botany.* Of, pertaining to, or located in an axil: *axillary buds.* *—n., pl.* **axillaries.** An axillar.

ax·i·ol·o·gist (ăk′sē-ŏl′ə-jĭst) *n.* An expert in or student of axiology.

ax·i·ol·o·gy (ăk′sē-ŏl′ə-jē) *n. Philosophy.* The study of the nature of values and value judgments. [Greek *axios,* worth, worthy (see **ag-** in Appendix*) + -LOGY.] **—ax′i·o·log′i·cal** (-ə-lŏj′ĭ-kəl) *adj.* **—ax′i·o·log′i·cal·ly** *adv.*

ax·i·om (ăk′sē-əm) *n.* 1. A self-evident or universally recognized truth; maxim. 2. An established rule, principle, or law. 3. *Abbr.* **ax.** *Mathematics & Logic.* **a.** An undemonstrated proposition concerning an undefined set of elements, properties, functions, and relationships; postulate. **b.** A self-evident or accepted principle. [Latin *axiōma,* from Greek, "that which is thought fitting or worthy," from *axioun,* to think worthy, from *axios,* worthy. See **ag-** in Appendix.*]

ax·i·o·mat·ic (ăk′sē-ə-măt′ĭk) *adj.* Also **ax·i·o·mat·i·cal** (-ĭ-kəl). 1. Of, pertaining to, or resembling an axiom; self-evident: *"It is axiomatic that the Negro is religious, which is to say that he stands in fear of the God our ancestors gave us"* (James Baldwin). 2. Aphoristic. **—ax′i·o·mat′i·cal·ly** *adv.*

ax·is (ăk′sĭs) *n., pl.* **axes** (ăk′sēz′). 1. A straight line about which a body or geometrical object rotates or may be conceived to rotate. 2. *Mathematics.* **a.** An unlimited line, half-line, or line segment serving to orient a space or a geometrical object, especially a line about which the object is symmetrical. **b.** A reference line from which distances or angles are measured in a coordinate system. 3. A center line to which parts of a structure or body may be referred. 4. *Fine Arts.* An imaginary line to which elements of the work are referred for measurement or symmetry. 5. *Anatomy.* The second cervical vertebra on which the head turns. **b.** Any of various central structures, as the spinal column, or standard abstract lines used as a positional referent. 6. *Botany.* The main stem or central part about which organs or plant parts such as branches are arranged. 7. *Capital* **A.** The alliance of Germany and Italy (1936), later including Japan and other nations, that opposed the Allies in World War II. Preceded by *the.* [Latin *axis,* hub, axis, axle. See **aks-** in Appendix.*]

ax·is deer (ăk′sĭs). A deer, *Axis axis,* of central Asia, having a brown coat with white spots. Also called "chital." [New Latin *Axis,* from Latin *axis†,* an unidentified Indian animal.]

ax·ite (ăk′sīt′) *n. Anatomy.* One of the terminal fibers of an **axon** *(see).* [AX(ON) + -ITE.]

ax·le (ăk′səl) *n.* 1. A supporting shaft or member upon which a wheel or wheels revolve. 2. The spindle of an axletree. 3. Either end of an axletree. [Middle English *axil, axel,* from Old Norse *öxull.* See **aks-** in Appendix.*]

ax·le·tree (ăk′səl-trē′) *n.* A crossbar or rod supporting a vehicle, as a drawn cart, and having terminal spindles on which the wheels revolve.

ax·man (ăks′mən) *n., pl.* **-men** (-mĭn). A man who wields an ax; especially, a worker who fells trees or chops logs.

Ax·min·ster (ăks′mĭn′stər) *n.* A kind of carpet with stiff jute backing and long, soft cut-wool pile, formerly handmade in Axminster, England.

ax·o·lotl (ăk′sə-lŏt′l) *n.* Any of several western North American and Mexican salamanders of the genus *Ambystoma,* that, unlike most amphibians, often retain their external gills and become sexually mature without undergoing metamorphosis. [Nahuatl : *atl,* water + *xolotl,* servant, spirit.]

ax·on (ăk′sŏn′) *n.* Also **ax·one** (ăk′sōn′). The core of a nerve fiber that generally conducts impulses away from the nerve cell. Also called "neuraxon." [New Latin, from Greek *axōn,* axis. See **aks-** in Appendix.*]

ax·seed (ăks′sēd′) *n.* A plant, the **crown vetch** *(see).* [From its ax-shaped pods.]

ay¹ (ī) *interj. Archaic.* Used to express surprise or distress. [Middle English *ai, ey, ei.*]

ay². 1. Variant of **aye** (affirmative). 2. Variant of **aye** (always).

A·ya·cu·cho (ä′yä-kōō′chō). A city in south-central Peru, near the site of the battle (1824) that secured Peru's independence from Spain. Population, 21,000.

a·yah (ä′yə) *n.* A native maid or nurse in India. [Hindi *āyā, āya,* from Portuguese *aia,* nursemaid, from Latin *avia,* grandmother. See **awo-** in Appendix.*]

aye¹ (ī) *n.* Also **ay.** An affirmative vote or voter. *—adv.* Also **ay.**

Yes; yea. [Earlier *ay, ei,* originally *I,* probably the same word as the pronoun *I,* used as an affirmative answer.]

aye² (ā) *adv.* Also **ay.** *Poetic.* Always; ever. [Middle English *ay, ei,* from Old Norse *ei.* See **aiw-** in Appendix.*]

aye-aye (ī′ī′) *n.* A lemur, *Daubentonia madagascariensis,* of Madagascar, having large ears, a long, bushy tail, and rodentlike teeth. [French, from Malagasay *aiay,* probably imitative of its cry.]

A·ye·sha. See **Aisha.**

a·yin (ä′yĭn) *n.* Also **a·in.** The 16th letter of the Hebrew alphabet. See **alphabet.** [Hebrew *'ayin.*]

Ayles·bur·y (ālz′bər-ē). The county seat of Buckinghamshire, England.

Ay·ma·ra (ī′mä-rä′) *n.* 1. An Indian people inhabiting Bolivia and Peru. 2. **a.** A member of this people. **b.** The language of this people. 3. A language family consisting of the Aymara language. **—Ay′ma·ran′** *adj. & n.*

Ay·mé (ĕ-mā′), **Marcel.** Born 1902. French novelist, short-story writer, and dramatist.

Ayr (âr). 1. Also **Ayr·shire** (âr′shĭr, -shər). A county of Scotland, occupying 1,132 square miles in the southwest. Population, 348,000. 2. The county seat of this county, a port on the Firth of Clyde. Population, 46,000.

Ayr·shire (âr′shĭr, -shər) *n.* 1. One of a breed of brown and white dairy cattle originating in Ayr. 2. Variant of **Ayr** (county).

Ayr·ton (âr′tən), **William Edward.** 1847–1908. English electrical engineer and inventor.

A·yub Khan (ä′yōōb kän′), **Mohammad.** Born 1907. Indian-born Pakistani statesman and military leader; president of Pakistan (1958–69).

A·yut·tha·ya (ä-yōō′tä-yä). Also **A·yu·thi·a** (ä-yōō′thē-ä), **A·yu·dhy·a** (ä-yōōt′ə-yə). 1. The ancient capital of Siam until its destruction by the Burmese in 1767, plans for the reconstruction of which were announced in 1966. 2. A town of Thailand, about 80 miles north of Bangkok, on the site of this ancient capital. Population, 25,000.

AZ Arizona (with Zip Code).

az. 1. azimuth. 2. azure.

a·zal·ea (ə-zāl′yə) *n.* Any of a group of deciduous or evergreen shrubs, part of the genus *Rhododendron,* of the North Temperate Zone, many of which are cultivated for their showy, variously colored flowers. [New Latin, "the dry plant" (growing in dry soil), from Greek, feminine of *azaleos,* dry. See **as-** in Appendix.*]

a·zan (ä-zän′) *n.* The Moslem summons to prayer, called by the muezzin from a minaret of a mosque five times a day. [Arabic *adhān,* from *adhina,* to proclaim. See **muezzin.**]

A·za·ña (ä-thä′nyä), **Manuel.** 1880–1940. Spanish statesman; president of the Spanish Republic (1936–39).

A·za·zel (ə-zā′zəl, ăz′ə-zĕl′). 1. In ancient Hebrew tradition, the rebel leader of the angels who seduced mankind. 2. In Milton's *Paradise Lost,* one of the fallen angels in league with Satan. [Hebrew *'azāzēl,* "removal," hence scapegoat (ritually "sent" into the wilderness) : *'ez,* goat + *'azl,* to go.]

a·zed·a·rach (ə-zĕd′ə-răk′) *n.* 1. A tree, the **chinaberry** *(see).* 2. The astringent bark of this tree, formerly used in medicine as an emetic. [French *azedarac,* from Persian *āzād-dirakht : āzād,* free (see **gene-** in Appendix*) + *dirakht,* tree (see **deru-** in Appendix*).]

A·ze·glio (ä-zĕ′lyô), **Marchese d'.** Title of Massimo Taparelli. 1798–1866. Italian statesman and author.

A·zer·bai·jan (ä′zər-bī-jän′, äz′ər-). Also **A·zer·bai·dzhan, Azar·bai·jan.** 1. The Azerbaijan S.S.R. 2. A former province of northwestern Iran, now divided into Eastern Azerbaijan (28,448 square miles; population, 2,012,000), with its capital at Tabriz, and Western Azerbaijan (13,664 square miles; population, 719,000) with its capital at Rezaiyeh.

A·zer·bai·ja·ni (ä′zər-bī-jä′nē, äz′ər-) *n., pl.* **Azerbaijani** or **-nis.** 1. A native or inhabitant of Azerbaijan. 2. The Turkic language of Azerbaijan.

A·zer·bai·jan Soviet Socialist Republic (ä′zər-bī-jän′, äz′ər-). A constituent republic of the Soviet Union, 33,100 square miles in area, on the Caspian Sea in eastern Transcaucasia. Population, 4,518,000. Capital, Baku.

A·zil·ian (ə-zĭl′yən) *adj. Archaeology.* Of or denoting a western European culture following the Magdalenian era and preceding the Neolithic. [After le Mas d'*Azil,* village in the French Pyrenees, where such artifacts were found.]

az·i·muth (ăz′ə-məth) *n. Abbr.* **az.** 1. The horizontal angular distance from a fixed reference direction to a position, object, or object referent, as to a great circle intersecting a celestial body, usually measured clockwise in degrees along the horizon from a point due south. 2. *Military.* The lateral deviation of a projectile or bomb. [Middle English, from Old French *azimut,* from Arabic *as-sumūt,* plural of *as-samt,* "the way," compass bearing, from Latin *semita†, path.]

az·i·muth·al (ăz′ə-mŭth′əl) *adj.* Of or relating to azimuth. **—az′i·muth′al·ly** *adv.*

azimuthal equidistant projection. A map projection of the earth designed so that a straight line from a given point on the map to any other point gives the shortest distance between the two points.

az·ine (ăz′ēn′, ā′zēn′) *n.* A six-membered heterocyclic compound containing one or more atoms of nitrogen, as pyridine. [AZ(O)- + -INE.]

azine dye. Any of various dyes derived from **phenazine** *(see).*

az·o (ăz′ō) *adj. Chemistry.* Containing a nitrogen group. [From AZO-.]

aye-aye

azalea
Rhododendron canescens
Mountain azalea

axolotl
Ambystoma mexicanum
Mexican axolotl

azo-, az-. *Chemistry.* Indicates the presence of a nitrogen group, especially one attached at both ends in a covalent bond to other groups; for example, **azobenzene, azole.** [From French *azote,* nitrogen, "lifeless" (unlike the life-sustaining oxygen) : A- (not) + Greek *zōē,* life (see **gwei-** in Appendix*).]

Azo. Azores.

az·o·ben·zene (ăz′ō-běn′zēn′, -běn-zēn′) *n.* A yellow or orange crystalline compound, $C_6H_5N_2C_6H_5$, used in the manufacture of dyes and as a fumigant.

azo dye. Any of various red, brown, or yellow acidic or basic dyes derived from azobenzene.

a·zo·ic (ā-zō′ĭk, ə-) *adj.* Of or pertaining to geological periods that precede the appearance of life. [A- (not) + -ZOIC.]

az·ole (ăz′ōl′, ā′zōl′) *n.* Any organic compound having a five-membered heterocyclic ring with two double bonds. [AZ(O)- (because it contains atoms of nitrogen) + -OLE.]

a·zon·ic (ā-zŏn′ĭk) *adj.* Not restricted to any particular zone or region; not local.

A·zores (ā′zōrz, ə-zôrz′). *Portuguese* **A·ço·res** (ä-sō′rĭs). *Abbr.* **Azo.** Three island groups in the North Atlantic 900 miles west of Portugal, of which they are administrative districts. Population, 328,000. Main city, Ponta Delgada, on the island of São Miguel.

az·o·te·mi·a (ăz′ə-tē′mē-ə) *n. Pathology.* **Uremia** *(see).* [New Latin : French *azote,* nitrogen (see **azo-**) + -EMIA.] —**az′o·te′mic** (-mĭk) *adj.*

az·oth (ăz′ŏth′, -ōth′) *n. Alchemy.* **1.** Mercury. **2.** Paracelsus' universal remedy. [Arabic *az-zā′ūq,* the mercury.]

a·zo·to·bac·ter (ā-zō′tō-băk′tər, ə-) *n.* Any of various nitrogen-fixing bacteria of the family Azotobacteraceae. [New Latin : French *azote,* nitrogen (see **azo-**) + BACTER(IA).]

az·o·tu·ri·a (ăz′ə-tŏor′ē-ə, -tyŏor′ē-ə) *n.* Increase of nitrogenous substances in the urine. [New Latin : French *azote,* nitrogen (see **azo-**) + -URIA.]

Az·ov (ăz′ôf′, -ŏf′, ā′zôf′; *Russian* ə-zôf′), **Sea of.** The northern arm of the Black Sea, occupying 14,000 square miles in the southern Soviet Union.

Az·ra·el (ăz′rā-ĕl′). The angel who separates the soul from the body at death in Moslem and Jewish legend. [Arabic *Azrā′īl,* from Hebrew *'Āzar'ēl,* "God has helped."]

Az·tec (ăz′tĕk′) *n.* **1.** A member of an Indian people of Central Mexico noted for their advanced civilization before Cortés invaded Mexico in 1519. **2.** Their language, Nahuatl. —*adj.* Also **Az·tec·an** (ăz′tĕk′ən). Of the Aztecs, their language, culture, or empire. [Spanish *Azteca,* from Nahuatl *Aztecatl* (plural *Azteca*) : *Azt(a)lan,* the supposed place of origin of the people, "near the crane" : *aztatl* (plural *azta*), crane + *tlan,* near + -*tecatl,* suffix denoting origin.]

Aztec Ruins National Monument. An area of 27 acres in northwestern New Mexico, reserved to protect the ruins of a pre-Columbian Indian town.

az·ure (ăzh′ər) *adj. Abbr.* **az.** Of the color azure. —*n.* **1.** Light purplish blue. See **color. 2.** *Abbr.* **az.** An azure pigment. **3.** *Poetic.* The blue sky. [Middle English, from Old French *azur,* from Old Spanish *azul, azur,* from Arabic *allāzaward,* lapis lazuli, from Persian *lāzhuward,* LAPIS LAZULI.]

az·u·rite (ăzh′ə-rīt′) *n.* An azure-blue vitreous mineral of basic copper carbonate, $2CuCO_3 \cdot Cu(OH)_2$, used as a copper ore and as a gemstone. [French : Old French *azur,* AZURE + -ITE.]

az·y·gous (ăz′ĭ-gəs) *adj. Biology.* Occurring singly; unpaired. [New Latin *azygos,* from Greek *azugos,* unwedded, unpaired : *a-,* without + *zugon,* yoke (see **yeug-** in Appendix*).]

ă pat/ā pay/âr care/ä father/b bib/ch church/d deed/ĕ pet/ē be/f fife/g gag/h hat/hw which/ĭ pit/ī pie/îr pier/j judge/k kick/l lid, needle/m mum/n no, sudden/ng thing/ŏ pot/ō toe/ô paw, for/oi noise/ou out/ŏŏ took/ōō boot/p pop/r roar/s sauce/sh ship, dish/

Aztec Ruins National Monument
A section of the ruins showing
the circular top *(right)* of an
underground ceremonial chamber

Bb

| | | | | | | | | | | | | |
|1|2|3|4|5|6|7|8|9|10|11|12|13|14|

Phoenician   Greek   Roman   Medieval   Modern

Around 1000 B.C. the Phoenicians and other Semites of Syria and Palestine began to use a graphic sign in the forms (1,2,3). They gave it the name bēth, meaning "house," and used it for the consonant b. After 900 B.C. the Greeks borrowed the sign from the Phoenicians, altering it to put the triangle in the lower rather than the upper part (4). They also changed its name to bēta. Gradually the Greeks created a more symmetrical form by filling up two triangles and reversing the orientation (5). In its ultimate Greek development the sign appears in a rounded form (6). It passed unchanged via Etruscan to the Roman alphabet (7). The Roman Monumental Capital (8) is the prototype of our modern capital, printed (11) and written (12). The written Roman form (7) developed into the late Roman and medieval Uncial (9) and Cursive (10), in which the upper loop is reduced or omitted. These are the bases of our modern small letter, printed (13) and written (14).

b, B (bē) *n., pl.* **b's** or *rare* **bs, B's** or **Bs. 1.** The second letter of the modern English alphabet. See **alphabet. 2.** Any of the speech sounds represented by this letter.

b, B, b., B. *Note:* As an abbreviation or symbol, *b* may be a small or a capital letter, with or without a period. Established forms or those generally preferred precede the definition. When no form is given, all four forms are in general use in that sense. **1. B.** bachelor. **2. B.** bacillus. **3. b** *Physics.* barn. **4. B** baryon number. **5. b., B.** base. **6. b., B.** *Music.* basso. **7. B.** Baumé scale. **8. b., B.** bay. **9. B.** Bible. **10. B** *Chess.* bishop. **11. b., B.** bolivar. **12. B.** book. **13. b., B.** born. **14. B** The symbol for the element boron. **15. b., B.** breadth. **16. B.** British. **17. b., B.** brother. **18. B.** brotherhood. **19. B** A human blood type of the ABO group. See **ABO. 20.** The second in a series. **21. B** The second best or highest in quality or rank: *grade B meat; a mark of B on an English theme.* **22. B** *Music.* **a.** The seventh tone in the scale of C major, or the second tone in the relative minor scale. **b.** The key or a scale in which B is the tonic. **c.** A written or printed note representing this tone. **d.** A string, key, or pipe tuned to the pitch of this tone.

Ba The symbol for the element barium.

B.A. 1. Bachelor of Arts. **2.** British Academy. **3.** British Association (for the Advancement of Science).

baa (bă, bä) *intr.v.* **baaed, baaing, baas.** To make a bleating sound, as a sheep does. —*n.* The bleat of a sheep. [Imitative.]

Baa·de (bä'də), **Walter.** 1893–1960. German-born American astronomer; measured interstellar distances.

Ba·al (bā'əl) *n., pl.* **-alim** (-ə-lĭm). **1.** Any of various local fertility and nature gods of the ancient Semitic peoples, considered to be false idols by the Hebrews. **2.** *Sometimes small* **b.** Any false god or idol: "*Baalim / Forsake their temples dim.*" (Milton). [Hebrew *bá'al,* owner, master, lord.]

Baal·bek (bäl'bĕk', bā'əl-). Ancient name **He·li·op·o·lis** (hē'lē-ŏp'ə-lĭs). A town in Lebanon, about 35 miles northeast of Beirut. It is the site of ruins of a Roman religious center.

Baal Shem Tov (bäl' shĕm' tōv'). Also **Baal Shem Tob** (tōb'). Original name, Israel ben Eliezer. 1700?–1760. Jewish religious leader, healer, and educator; founded modern Chassidism in Poland.

Bab (băb), **the.** Title of Ali Mohammed of Shiraz. 1819–1850. Persian founder of Babism. [Persian *bāb,* gate, from Arabic.]

Bab. Babylonia; Babylonian.

ba·ba (bä'bə) *n.* A leavened rum cake, usually made with raisins. Also called "baba au rhum." [French, from Polish, "old woman." See **baba-** in Appendix.*]

Ba·bar. See **Baber.**

ba·bas·su (bä'bə-sōō') *n.* A Brazilian palm tree, *Orbignya*

martiana (or *O. speciosa*), bearing hard nuts that yield an oil similar to coconut oil. [Brazilian Portuguese *babaçú,* probably a native name.]

bab·bitt (băb'ĭt) *tr.v.* **-bitted, -bitting, -bitts.** To line or face with Babbitt metal. —*n. Capital* **B. Babbitt metal** (*see*).

Bab·bitt (băb'ĭt) *n.* A member of the American middle class whose attachment to its ideals is such as to make of him a model of narrow-mindedness and self-satisfaction. Used disparagingly. [After George F. *Babbitt,* main character in Sinclair Lewis' novel *Babbitt* (1922).] —**Bab'bitt·ry** *n.*

Babbitt metal. 1. A soft, silvery, antifriction alloy composed of tin with small amounts of copper and antimony. **2.** Loosely, any antifriction alloy. Also called "Babbitt." [After Isaac *Babbitt* (1799–1862), American inventor.]

bab·ble (băb'əl) *v.* **-bled, -bling, -bles.** —*intr.* **1.** To utter a meaningless confusion of words or sounds: "*the telescreen was still babbling away about pig iron and the overfulfillment of the Ninth Three-Year Plan*" (George Orwell). **2.** To talk foolishly or idly; to chatter. **3.** To make a continuous low, murmuring sound, as flowing water. —*tr.* **1.** To utter in a rapid, indistinct voice. **2.** To blurt out impulsively; disclose without careful consideration. —*n.* **1.** Inarticulate or meaningless talk or sounds. **2.** Idle or foolish talk; chatter; prattle. **3.** A continuous murmuring sound. [Middle English *babelen.* See **baba-** in Appendix.*] —**bab'bler** *n.*

babe (bāb) *n.* **1.** *Archaic.* A baby; an infant. **2.** *Slang.* An innocent or naive person. **3.** *Slang.* A girl or young woman. —**babe in the woods.** *Slang.* A naive or easily victimized person in an unfamiliar or dangerous situation. [Middle English *babe.* See **baba-** in Appendix.*]

ba·bel (bā'bəl, băb'əl) *n.* Also **Ba·bel. 1.** A confusion of sounds, voices, or languages: "*in the babel of two hundred voices he would forget himself*" (Conrad). **2.** A scene of noise and confusion. —See Synonyms at **noise.** [From **BABEL.**]

Ba·bel (bā'bəl, băb'əl). A city (now thought to be Babylon) in Shinar where, according to the Book of Genesis, the construction of a heaven-reaching tower was interrupted by the confusion of tongues. [Hebrew *Bābhél,* from Akkadian *Bāb-ilu,* "gate of God."]

Bab el Man·deb (băb' ĕl män'dĕb). A strait, 17 miles wide, between eastern Africa and the southern tip of Arabia, linking the Red Sea with the Gulf of Aden.

Ba·bel·thu·ap (bä'bəl-tōō'äp). Also **Pa·lau** (pä-lou'). The largest island (120 square miles) of the Palau group in the southwestern Pacific Ocean.

Ba·ber, Ba·bar, Ba·bur (bä'bər). Original name, Zahir ud-Din Mohammed. 1483–1530. Mongol conqueror of India.

Ba·bi (bä'bē) *n.* **1.** Babism (*see*). **2.** A follower of the Bab.

Ba·bia Gó·ra (bä'byä gōō'rä). The highest (5,659 feet) of the Beskids Mountains, in the West Beskids on the border between Poland and Czechoslovakia.

ba·bies'-breath. Variant of **baby's-breath.**

Ba·bin·ski reflex (bə-bĭn'skē). A normal reflex in infants that is abnormal in adults, consisting of the upward extension rather than flexion of the toes, or of the great toe alone, when the sole of the foot is stroked. Also called "Babinski sign." [After J.F.F. *Babinski* (1857–1932), French neurologist.]

bab·i·ru·sa (băb'ə-rōō'sə, bä'bə-) *n.* Also **bab·i·rus·sa, bab·i·rous·sa.** A wild pig, *Babyrousa babyrussa,* of the East Indies, having long, upward-curving tusks in the male. [Malay *bābīrūsa* : *bābi,* hog + *rūsa,* deer.]

Bab·ism (bä'bĭz'əm) *n.* The beliefs and practices of a 19th-century Persian religious sect, founded about 1844 by the Bab,

babirusa
A male of the species

Ali Mohammed of Shiraz, in which polygamy, concubinage, begging, trading in slaves, and the use of alcohol or drugs were forbidden. Also called "Babi."

Ba·bi Yar (bä′bē yär′). A ravine outside Kiev, Ukrainian S.S.R., where the Jews of the city were killed by German troops in 1941. The notoriety of the site was established through the poem *Babi Yar* (1961) by Yevgeny Yevtushenko.

bab·ka (bäb′kə) *n.* A Polish coffee cake flavored with orange rind, rum, almonds, and raisins. [Polish, "little old woman," diminutive of *baba*, old woman. See **baba-** in Appendix.*]

ba·boon (bă-bo͞on′) *n.* **1.** Any of several chiefly African monkeys of the genus *Chaeropithecus* (or *Papio*) and related genera, having an elongated, doglike muzzle. **2.** *Slang.* A brutish person. [Middle English *baboyne*, from Old French *babuin*, gaping figure, baboon, probably a blend of *babine*, pendulous lip, and *baboue*, grimace. See **baba-** in Appendix.*]

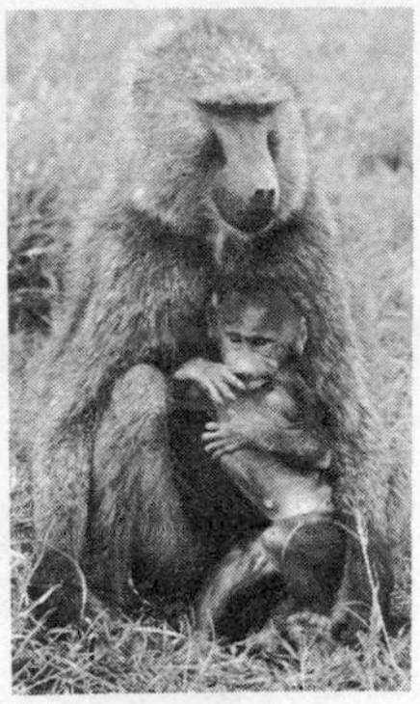

baboon
Papio anubis
Olive baboons

ba·boon·er·y (bă-bo͞o′nə-rē) *n.* Behavior characteristic of baboons or boors.

ba·bu (bä′bo͞o) *n.* Also **ba·boo.** **1.** A form of address in Hindi equivalent to *Esquire* or *Mister.* **2. a.** A Hindu clerk possessing a prerequisite degree of literacy in English. **b.** A native of India who has acquired some superficial education in English. Sometimes used disparagingly. [Hindi *bābū*, "father." See **baba-** in Appendix.*]

ba·bul (bə-bo͞ol′) *n.* A tree, *Acacia arabica*, of northern Africa and India. It is a source of gum arabic, of a hardwood, and of tannin. [Persian *babūl*†.]

Ba·bur. See **Baber.**

ba·bush·ka (bə-bo͝osh′kə) *n.* A woman's head scarf, folded triangularly and tied under the chin. [Russian, "grandmother," diminutive of *baba*, old woman. See **baba-** in Appendix.*]

Ba·bu·yan Islands (bä′bo͞o-yän′). A group of 24 islands in the Philippines, separated from the northern coast of Luzon by the Babuyan Channel.

ba·by (bā′bē) *n.*, *pl.* **-bies.** **1.** A very young boy or girl; an infant. **2.** The youngest member of a family or group. **3.** A very young animal. **4.** An adult or young person who acts like an infant. **5.** *Slang.* A girl or young woman. Used as a term of familiarity. **6.** *Slang.* An object of personal concern or interest: *The project was his baby.* —*adj.* **1.** Of or pertaining to a baby or babies. **2.** Infantile; childish. **3.** Small in comparison with others of the same kind. —*tr.v.* **babied, -bying, -bies.** To treat oversolicitously; coddle. See Synonyms at **pamper.** [Middle English *babie*. See **baba-** in Appendix.*] —**ba′by·hood** *n.*

baby blue. Very light to very pale greenish or purplish blue. See **color.** —**ba′by-blue′** *adj.*

ba·by-blue-eyes (bā′bē-blo͞o′īz′) *n.* Used with a singular or plural verb. A low-growing plant, *Nemophila menziesii*, of California, having bell-shaped blue flowers.

baby book. An album of photographs and other items serving as a record of a child's development from infancy.

baby carriage. A small four-wheeled carriage for an infant. Also called "baby buggy."

baby face. *Slang.* An adult having the plump, smooth face associated with babyhood. —**ba′by-faced′** *adj.*

baby farm. An establishment where small children may be boarded. Often used disparagingly. —**baby farming.**

ba·by·ish (bā′bē-ĭsh) *adj.* **1.** Like a baby; childlike. **2.** Childish; immature. —**ba′by·ish·ly** *adj.* —**ba′by·ish·ness** *n.*

Bab·y·lon[1] (băb′ə-lən, -lŏn′). The capital of ancient Babylonia, situated in Mesopotamia on the Euphrates River. [Latin *Babylōn*, from Greek *Babulōn*, from Akkadian *Bāb-ilāni*, "gate of the gods" : *bāb*, gate + *ilāni*, plural of *ilu*, god.]

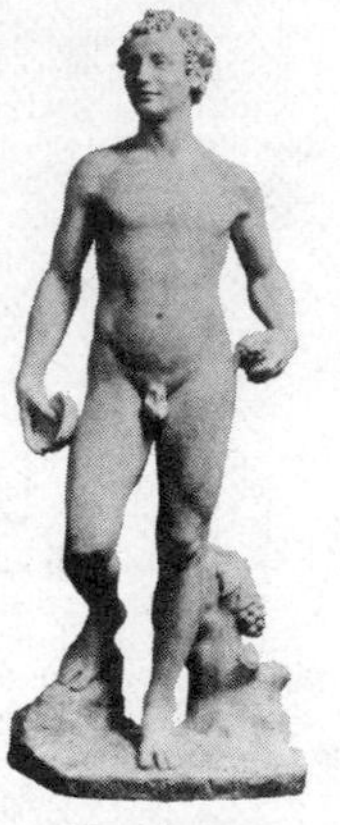

Bacchus
Sixteenth-century marble statue by Domenico Poggini

Bab·y·lon[2] (băb′ə-lən, -lŏn′) *n.* **1.** Any city or place of great luxury and corruption. **2.** Any place of captivity or exile. [From BABYLON.]

Bab·y·lo·ni·a (băb′ə-lō′nē-ə). *Abbr.* **Bab.** An ancient empire in the lower Euphrates Valley of southwestern Asia, prominent from about 2000 to 1000 B.C. Capital, Babylon.

Bab·y·lo·ni·an (băb′ə-lō′nē-ən) *adj. Abbr.* **Bab.** **1.** Of or pertaining to ancient Babylonia or Babylon, their people, culture, or language. **2.** Characterized by a luxurious, pleasure-seeking, and immoral way of life. —*n. Abbr.* **Bab.** **1.** A native or inhabitant of ancient Babylon or Babylonia. **2.** The Semitic language of the Babylonians, a form of Akkadian.

Babylonian captivity. **1.** The deportation of the Jews to Babylonia and their period of exile there, initiated by Nebuchadnezzar II in 597 B.C. and formally terminated by Cyrus in 538 B.C. Also called "Babylonian exile." **2.** The period (1309–77) when the Clementine claimants to the papacy resided at Avignon.

ba·by's-breath, ba·bies'-breath (bā′bēz-brĕth′) *n.* **1.** Any plant of the genus *Gypsophila;* especially, *G. paniculatum*, having numerous small white flowers in branching clusters. **2.** Any of several other plants with small, pleasantly scented flowers.

ba·by-sit (bā′bē-sĭt′) *intr.v.* **-sat** (-săt′), **-sitting, -sits.** To act as a baby sitter.

baby sitter. Someone engaged to care for one or more children when the parents are not at home. Also called "sitter."

baby talk. **1.** The early speech of a very young child. **2.** Halting or infantile speech. **3.** An intentionally shallow explanation.

ba·by-tears (bā′bē-tîrz′) *n.* Also **ba·by's-tears** (bā′bēz-tîrz′). Plural in form, used with a singular or plural verb. A creeping plant, *Helxine soleirolii*, native to Corsica, having numerous very small leaves and minute green flowers.

baby tooth. A **milk tooth** *(see).*

Ba·car·di (bə-kär′dē) *n.* **1.** A trademark for a brand of rum originally distilled in Cuba. **2.** A cocktail made with this rum, containing lime or lemon juice and sugar or grenadine.

bac·ca·lau·re·ate (băk′ə-lôr′ē-ĭt) *n.* **1.** The degree of **Bachelor** *(see)*, conferred upon graduates of most U.S. colleges and universities. **2.** A farewell address in the form of a sermon delivered to the graduating class in most U.S. colleges and universities and in some high schools. [Medieval Latin *baccalaureātus*, from *baccalaureus*, variant (influenced by *bacca lauri*, "laurel berry") of *baccalārius*, BACHELOR.]

bac·ca·rat (bä′kə-rä′, băk′ə-) *n.* Also **bac·ca·ra.** A card game in which the winner is the player holding two or three cards totaling closest to nine. [French *baccara*†.]

bac·cate (băk′āt′) *adj.* **1.** Bearing berries. **2.** Resembling a berry in texture or form. [From Latin *bāca, bacca*, berry, possibly akin to *Bacchus*, BACCHUS.]

Bac·chae (băk′ē) *pl.n.* The priestesses and female followers of Bacchus. [Latin, from Greek *Bakkhai*, plural of *Bakkhē*, priest of Bacchus, from *Bakkhos*, BACCHUS.]

bac·cha·nal (băk′ə-năl′, -näl′, băk′ə-nəl) *n.* **1.** A participant in the Bacchanalia. **2.** *Sometimes plural.* The Bacchanalia. **3.** Any drunken or riotous celebration. **4.** A reveler. —*adj.* Of, pertaining to, or typical of the worship of Bacchus; bacchanalian. [Latin *bacchānālis*, of Bacchus, from BACCHUS.]

Bac·cha·na·lia (băk′ə-năl′yə, -nā′lē-ə) *n.*, *pl.* **Bacchanalia.** **1.** *Plural.* The ancient Roman festival in honor of Bacchus. **2.** *Small* **b.** A riotous or drunken festivity; an orgy. [Latin *bacchānālia*, neuter plural of *bacchānālis*, BACCHANAL.]

bac·cha·na·lian (băk′ə-năl′yən, -nā′lē-ən) *adj.* **1.** Of or pertaining to the Bacchanalia. **2.** Characterized by riotous, drunken revelry; orgiastic. —*n.* A drunken reveler; a bacchanal.

bac·chant (bə-kănt′, -känt′, băk′ənt) *n.*, *pl.* **-chants** or **bacchantes** (bə-kăn′tēz, -kän′tēz, -kănts′, -känts′). **1.** A priest or votary of Bacchus. **2.** A boisterous reveler. —*adj.* **1.** Wine-loving. **2.** Riotous; carousing. [Latin *bacchāns*, present participle of *bacchārī*, to celebrate the festival of Bacchus, from Greek *bakkhān*, from *Bakkhos*, BACCHUS.]

bac·chan·te (bə-kăn′tē, -kän′tē, -kănt′, -känt′) *n.* **1.** A priestess or female votary of Bacchus. **2.** A female participant in a drunken or orgiastic revel. [French, from Latin *bacchāns*, BACCHANT.]

Bac·chic (băk′ĭk) *adj.* **1.** Of or pertaining to Bacchus. **2.** *Small* **b.** Drunken and carousing; bacchanalian.

Bac·chus (băk′əs). The god of grape-growing and of wine, often identified with Dionysus. [Latin, from Greek *Bakkhos*, from a non-Indo-European language in Anatolia.]

bac·cif·er·ous (băk-sĭf′ər-əs) *adj. Botany.* Bearing berries. [Latin *baccifer*, bearing berries : *bacca*, berry (see **baccate**) + -FEROUS.]

bac·ci·form (băk′sə-fôrm′) *adj.* Having the shape of a berry. [Latin *bacca*, berry (see **baccate**) + -FORM.]

bach (băch) *intr.v.* **bached, baching, baches.** Also **batch.** *Slang.* To live alone and keep house for oneself. Used especially in the expression *bach it.* [Short for BACHELOR.]

Bach (bäKH), **Johann Sebastian.** 1685–1750. German composer and organist; father of four sons who were also composers: **Wilhelm Friedemann** (1710–1784); **Karl Philipp Emanuel** (1714–1788); **Johann Christoph Friedrich** (1732–1795); **Johann Christian** (1735–1782).

bach. bachelor.

Ba·chan. See **Batjan.**

bach·e·lor (băch′ə-lər, băch′lər) *n.* **1.** *Abbr.* **bach.** An unmarried man. **2. a.** In feudal times, a young knight in the service of another knight. Also called "bachelor-at-arms." **b.** A **knight bachelor** *(see).* **3.** *Capital* **B.** *Abbr.* **B. a.** A college or university degree signifying completion of the undergraduate curriculum and graduation. **b.** A person holding such a degree. **4.** A young male fur seal who is kept from the breeding territory by older males. [Middle English *bacheler*, from Old French, squire, from Medieval Latin *baccalārius*†.] —**bach′e·lor·dom** *n.* —**bach′e·lor·hood′** *n.* —**bach′e·lor·ship′** *n.*

Bachelor of Arts. *Abbr.* **B.A., A.B.** **1.** An academic degree conferred by a college or university upon a person who has completed the first four years of required study in the liberal arts or humanities. Compare **Master of Arts, Doctor of Philosophy.** **2.** A person who has received this degree.

Bachelor of Science. *Abbr.* **B.S., B.Sc., S.B.** **1.** An academic degree conferred by a college or university upon a person who has completed the first four years of required study in the sciences. Compare **Master of Science, Doctor of Philosophy.** **2.** A person who has received this degree.

bach·e·lor's-but·ton (băch′ə-lərz-bŭt′n, băch′lərz-) *n.* **1.** A plant, the **cornflower** *(see).* **2.** The common European daisy. See **daisy.** **3.** Any of several other plants having buttonlike flowers or flower heads.

bac·il·lar·y (băs′ə-lĕr′ē, bə-sĭl′ə-rē) *adj.* Also **ba·cil·lar** (bə-sĭl′ər, băs′ə-lər). **1.** Rod-shaped. **2.** Of, pertaining to, or caused by bacilli. [From BACILLUS.]

ba·cil·lus (bə-sĭl′əs) *n.*, *pl.* **-cilli** (-sĭl′ī′). **1.** *Abbr.* **B.** Any of various rod-shaped, aerobic bacteria of the genus *Bacillus*, often occurring in chainlike formations. **2.** Any of various bacteria; especially, a rod-shaped bacterium. —See Synonyms at **germ.** [New Latin, from Late Latin, diminutive of Latin *baculum*, rod, stick. See **bak-** in Appendix.*]

bac·i·tra·cin (băs′ə-trā′sĭn) *n.* An antibiotic obtained from the bacterium *Bacillus subtilis* and used externally as a salve. [BACI(LLUS) + Margaret *Tracy*, an American child in whose blood it was first isolated in 1945 + -IN.]

back[1] (băk) *n.* **1. a.** The region of the vertebrate body located nearest the spine, in man consisting of the rear area from the neck to the pelvis. **b.** The analogous dorsal region in other animals, such as insects. **2.** The backbone or spine. **3.** The part or area farthest from the front. **4.** The part opposite to or behind that adapted for use or view. **5.** The reverse side, as of a coin or sheet of paper. **6.** A part that supports or strengthens from the rear. **7. a.** The part of a book where the pages are stitched together into the binding. **b.** The binding itself. **8.** A football player taking a position behind the line of scrimmage. **—at one's back.** Following closely behind. **—behind someone's back.** Without someone's knowledge or approval. **—(flat) on one's back.** Incapacitated or helpless; bedridden. **—get off someone's back.** To cease pestering or scolding someone. **—get one's** (or **put someone's**) **back up.** To become or cause to become angry or stubbornly opposed. **—in back of.** At the rear of; behind. See Usage note below. **—turn one's back on. 1.** To turn away from in contempt or anger. **2.** To ignore the plight of. **3.** To renounce; forsake. **—with one's back to the wall.** In a desperate position from which one cannot retreat. *—v.* **backed, backing, backs.** *—tr.* **1.** To cause to move backward or in a reverse direction. Sometimes used with *up.* **2.** To furnish or strengthen with a back or backing. **3.** To provide support, assistance, or encouragement for (a contending force). **4.** To adduce evidence in support of; substantiate. Often used with *up: backing up an argument with facts.* **5.** To bet on. **6.** To form the back or background of. **7.** To endorse by signing on the back of. *—intr.* **1.** To move backward. Often used with *up.* **2.** To shift to a counterclockwise direction. Used of the wind. Compare **veer.** —See Synonyms at **support. —back and fill. 1.** To maneuver a vessel in a narrow channel by alternately filling and spilling the sails. **2.** To vacillate in one's actions or decisions. **—back down.** To withdraw from a position, opinion, or commitment; abandon a former stand. **—back off.** To retreat or draw away. **—back out of.** To withdraw from (an enterprise or plan) before completion. *—adj.* **1.** Located or placed in the rear. **2.** Distant from a center of activity; remote. **3.** Of a past date; not current. **4.** Owing or due from an earlier time; in arrears. **5.** In a backward direction. **6.** *Phonetics.* Articulated with the tongue pulled to the rear of the mouth. *—adv.* **1.** At, to, or toward the rear or back; backward. **2.** In, to, or toward a former location. **3.** In, to, or toward a former condition. **4.** In, to, or toward a past time. **5.** In reserve or concealment. **6.** In check. **7.** In withdrawal. **8.** In return. **9.** In retort. **—go back on. 1.** To fail to keep (a promise or commitment). **2.** To betray or desert (a person). [Middle English *bak,* Old English *bæc,* from Common Germanic *bakam* (unattested).]

Usage: Fifty-three per cent of the Usage Panel condemn *back of* (for *behind*) in writing: *a mile back of the front lines.* Fifty per cent reject *in back of* (for *behind*) in writing: *the location in back of a warehouse.*

back[2] (băk) *n.* A shallow vat or tub used chiefly by brewers. [Dutch *bak,* from French *bac,* from Old French, from Vulgar Latin *bacca*†, a water vessel, perhaps from Celtic.]

back·bench·er (băk′bĕn′chər) *n. British.* One of the junior Members of Parliament, who sit in the rear benches in the House of Commons, where the front benches are reserved for government officeholders and their counterparts in the opposition party.

back·bite (băk′bīt′) *v.* **-bit** (-bĭt′), **-bitten** (-bĭt′n) or *informal* **-bit, -biting, -bites.** *—tr.* To slander the character or reputation of (an absent person). *—intr.* To speak spitefully or slanderously of a person behind his back. **—back′bit′er** *n.*

back·board (băk′bôrd′, -bōrd′) *n.* **1.** A board placed under the mattress of a bed to make it firmer. **2.** *Basketball.* The elevated, vertical board from which the basket projects.

back·bone (băk′bōn′) *n.* **1.** The vertebrate spine or spinal column. **2.** Anything that resembles a backbone in appearance or position, such as the keel of a ship. **3.** A main support or major sustaining factor: *"Doubt and the Land League were the backbone of the conflict with England"* (Sean O'Faolain). **4.** Strength of character; fortitude; determination. —See Synonyms at **courage. —back′boned′** *adj.*

back·break·ing (băk′brā′kĭng) *adj.* Demanding great physical exertion; exhausting; arduous. **—back′break′er** *n.*

back·court (băk′kôrt′, -kōrt′) *n.* **1.** In tennis and other net games, the part of a court between the service line and the base line. **2.** In other games, such as handball or basketball, the part of the playing area farthest from the goal or target wall. **—back′court′** *adj.*

back·cross (băk′krôs′, -krŏs′) *v.* **-crossed, -crossing, -crosses.** *Genetics. —tr.* To mate (a first-generation hybrid) with a parent or member of the parental stock. *—intr.* To breed or cross in this way. *—n. Genetics.* The act or process of producing offspring by backcrossing.

back·door (băk′dôr′, -dōr′) *adj.* Done or formed secretly or surreptitiously; clandestine.

back·drop (băk′drŏp′) *n.* **1.** A painted curtain hung at the back of a stage set. **2.** The setting, as of a historical event.

backed (băkt) *adj.* Having or furnished with a back or backing. Usually used in combination: *a low-backed chair.*

back·er (băk′ər) *n.* **1.** One who supports or gives aid to a person, group, or enterprise. **2.** One who bets on a contestant. **3.** A worker who provides or works with backs or backing.

back·field (băk′fēld′) *n. Football.* **1.** The players stationed behind the line of scrimmage. **2.** The area occupied by these players.

back·fire (băk′fīr′) *n.* **1.** A fire started purposely in the path of an oncoming fire so that the latter will be extinguished on reaching an area that has already been burned out. **2.** An explosion of prematurely ignited fuel or of unburned exhaust gases in an internal-combustion engine. **3.** An explosion of ammunition in the breech of a gun. *—intr.v.* **backfired, -firing, -fires. 1.** To start or employ a backfire. **2.** To explode in or make the sound of a backfire. **3.** To produce an unexpected and undesired result.

back-for·ma·tion (băk′fôr-mā′shən) *n.* Also **back formation.** *Linguistics.* **1.** The creation of a new word by the deletion of what is mistakenly construed to be an affix from an existing word. *Laze* is a back-formation from *lazy,* on the analogy of pairs such as *haze* and *hazy.* **2.** The process of forming words in this way.

back·gam·mon (băk′găm′ən) *n.* A game for two persons, played on a specially marked board with pieces whose moves are determined by throws of dice. [BACK + GAMMON.]

back·ground (băk′ground′) *n.* **1.** The ground located behind closer areas. **2. a.** The space in pictorial representation, usually appearing as if in the distance, arranged to provide relief for the principal objects. **b.** The general scene or surface against or upon which designs, patterns, figures, or the like are seen or represented. **3.** An area or position of relative obscurity or unimportance. **4.** Underlying or supporting causes, events, or settings. **5.** A person's experience, training, and education, often in a specified area. **6.** Subdued music or sounds heard as accompaniment to dialogue or action, especially in a dramatic performance. **7.** Sound or radiation present at a relatively constant low level at any specific location. **—back′ground′** *adj.*

back·hand (băk′hănd′) *n.* **1.** *Sports.* A stroke or motion, as of a racket, made with the back of the hand facing outward and the arm moving forward. Compare **forehand. 2.** Handwriting characterized by letters that slant to the left. *—adj.* Backhanded. *—adv.* With a backhanded stroke or motion. *—tr.v.* **backhanded, -handing, -hands.** To perform or catch backhand.

back·hand·ed (băk′hăn′dĭd) *adj.* **1.** Made with the back of the hand or with the back of the hand facing outward and moving away from the body. **2.** Slanting toward the left. **3.** Containing a disguised insult or rebuke. **4.** Twisted or formed in a direction opposite to the normal one: *backhanded rope.* **—back′hand′ed·ly** *adv.* **—back′hand′ed·ness** *n.*

back·hoe (băk′hō′) *n.* A machine used in excavating, having a digging device attached to a hinged extension that draws it toward the operator with a motion like that used in hoeing.

back·house (băk′hous′) *n.* A back yard toilet.

back·ing (băk′ĭng) *n.* **1.** Material that provides support or strength from the back. **2.** Support or aid; endorsement. **3.** Those who provide aid or support.

back·lash (băk′lăsh′) *n.* **1.** A sudden or violent backward whipping motion. **2.** An antagonistic reaction to some prior action construed as a threat, as in the context of social or race relations. **3.** A snarl in the part of a fishing line wound around the reel. **4.** The play resulting from loose connections between gears or other mechanical elements, which is most evident on reversal of movement.

back·less (băk′lĭs) *adj.* Having no back; especially, of a dress, cut to the waist in back.

back·list (băk′lĭst′) *n.* A publisher's list of older titles kept in print.

back·log (băk′lŏg′, -lôg′) *n.* **1.** A large log placed at the back of a fire to support other logs and maintain heat. **2.** A reserve supply or source. **3.** An accumulation, especially of unfinished work or unfilled orders. *—v.* **backlogged, -logging, -logs.** *—tr.* To acquire as a backlog. *—intr.* To become a backlog.

back matter. *Printing.* **End matter** *(see).*

back number. 1. An out-of-date periodical or newspaper. **2.** *Informal.* An out-of-date or old-fashioned person or thing.

back·rest (băk′rĕst′) *n.* A rest for the back.

Back River (băk). A river in Canada, rising in the central Northwest Territories and flowing 600 miles northeast into the Arctic Ocean.

back·saw (băk′sô′) *n.* A saw that is reinforced by a metal band along its back edge.

back·scat·ter (băk′skăt′ər) *n.* The deflection of waves or particles through angles greater than 90 degrees by electromagnetic or nuclear forces. Also called "backscattering."

back seat. 1. A seat in the back, especially of a vehicle or an auditorium. **2.** *Informal.* A subordinate position.

back-seat driver (băk′sēt′). *Informal.* **1.** An automobile passenger who constantly advises, corrects, or nags the driver. **2.** Any person who persists in giving unsolicited advice.

back·set (băk′sĕt′) *n.* **1.** A setback; reversal. **2.** An eddy or countercurrent in water.

back·sheesh, back·shish. Variants of **baksheesh.**

back·side (băk′sīd′) *n.* **1.** The back or rear part of something. **2.** *Informal.* The buttocks; rump.

back·slap·per (băk′slăp′ər) *n.* An excessively hearty, extroverted person. **—back′slap′ping** *n. & adj.*

back·slide (băk′slīd′) *intr.v.* **-slid** (-slĭd′), **-slid** or **-slidden** (-slĭd′n), **-sliding, -slides.** To revert to sin, wrongdoing, or the like, especially in religious practice. **—back′slid′er** *n.*

back·space (băk′spās′) *intr.v.* **-spaced, -spacing, -spaces.** To move the carriage of a typewriter back one or more spaces by striking the key used for this purpose. *—n.* The key on a typewriter used for backspacing. Also called "backspacer," "backspace key."

back·spin (băk′spĭn′) *n.* A spin that tends to retard, arrest, or reverse the linear motion of an object, especially of a ball.

back·stage (băk′stāj′) *adv.* **1.** In or toward the dressing rooms behind the performing area in a theater. **2.** In or toward a place closed to public view; privately. *—adj.* (băk′stāj′). **1.** Occurring or situated behind the performing area of a theater. **2.** Not open or known to the public; private or concealed.

back·stairs (băk′stârz′) *n.* A secondary or service staircase at

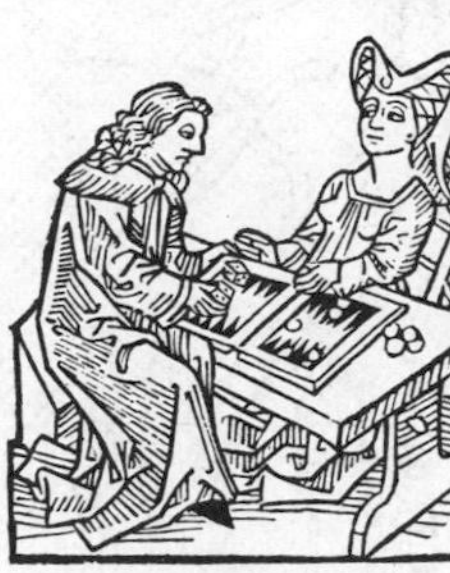

backgammon
Wood engraving by
Erhard Ratdolt
of Augsburg

the back of a house. —*adj.* Also **back·stair** (-stâr′). Furtively carried on; concealed; clandestine: *backstairs gossip.*

back·stay (băk′stā′) *n.* **1.** A rope or shroud extending from the top of the mast aft to the ship's side or stern to help support the mast. **2.** A support at or for the back of something.

back·stitch (băk′stĭch′) *n.* A stitch made by inserting the needle at the midpoint of the preceding stitch, so that each stitch overlaps another by half its length. —*v.* **backstitched, -stitching, -stitches.** —*intr.* To sew with such stitches. —*tr.* To make such stitches.

back·stop (băk′stŏp′) *n.* A screen or fence used to prevent a ball from being thrown or hit far out of a playing area, as in baseball or tennis. —*tr.v.* **backstopped, -stopping, -stops. 1.** To serve as a backstop for. **2. a.** To support. **b.** To substitute for (another) in an emergency.

back·stretch (băk′strĕch′) *n.* The part of an oval racecourse farthest from the spectators and opposite the homestretch, usually a straightaway.

back·stroke (băk′strōk′) *n.* **1.** A backhanded stroke. **2.** A stroke or motion made in return or as a recoil. **3.** A swimming stroke that resembles an inverted crawl. It is executed with the swimmer on his back, using a flutter kick, and moving his arms in upward and backward motions.

back·swept (băk′swĕpt′) *adj.* Swept or angled backward.

back·swim·mer (băk′swĭm′ər) *n.* Any of various insects of the family Notonectidae, that swim or float on their backs.

back·sword (băk′sôrd′, -sōrd′) *n.* **1.** A sword with only one cutting edge. **2.** A stick used in fencing practice, a **singlestick** *(see).* **3.** One who fights with a backsword.

back talk. Impudent contradiction; an insolent retort.

back·track (băk′trăk′) *intr.v.* **-tracked, -tracking, -tracks. 1.** To go back over the course by which one has come. **2.** To reverse one's position or policy; to retreat.

back-up (băk′ŭp′) *n.* **1.** A reserve, as of provisions. **2.** Support or backing. **3.** An overflow caused by clogged plumbing. —*adj.* Extra; standby: *a back-up pilot.*

back·ward (băk′wərd) *adv.* Also **back·wards** (-wərdz). **1.** To or toward the back or rear. **2.** With the back leading. **3.** In a manner or order that reverses the customary. **4.** To, toward, or into the past. **5.** Toward a worse condition. —*adj.* **1.** Directed or facing toward the back or rear. **2.** Done or arranged in reverse or in a manner contrary to the usual. **3.** Unwilling to act; reluctant; shy. **4.** Behind others in progress or development. —**back′ward·ly** *adv.* —**back′ward·ness** *n.*

back·wash (băk′wŏsh′, -wôsh′) *n.* **1.** Water moved backward, as by the action of oars or a motor. **2.** A backward flow of air, as from the propeller of an airplane. **3.** A condition resulting from some disturbing or irregular event; aftermath.

back water. To cause a boat to slow, stop, or reverse its motion, by placing the blade of an oar or paddle in the water and pushing it toward the bow.

back·wa·ter (băk′wô′tər, -wŏt′ər) *n.* **1.** Water held or pushed back by or as if by a dam or current; especially, a body of stagnant or still water thus formed. **2.** A place or situation regarded as stagnant or backward: *a cultural backwater.*

back·woods (băk′wŏŏdz′, -wŏŏdz′) *pl.n.* Heavily wooded, uncultivated, thinly settled areas. —**back′woods′** *adj.*

back·woods·man (băk′wŏŏdz′mən, -wŏŏdz′mən) *n., pl.* **-men** (-mĭn). **1.** One who lives or was brought up in the backwoods. **2.** One unfamiliar with the customs of urban life; a rustic.

back yard. Also **back·yard** (băk′yärd′). A yard at the rear of a house.

ba·con (bā′kən) *n.* The salted and smoked meat from the back and sides of a pig. —**bring home the bacon.** *Informal.* **1.** To provide food and other necessities. **2.** To make good; succeed. [Middle English *bacon, bakoun,* from Old French *bacon, bacun,* from Frankish *bako* (unattested), ham, from Common Germanic *bakkon* (unattested), perhaps akin to *bakam* (unattested), BACK.]

Ba·con (bā′kən), **Francis.** Baron Verulam and Viscount St. Albans. 1561–1626. English philosopher and essayist.

Ba·con (bā′kən), **Nathaniel.** 1647–1676. English colonist in America; reformer and leader of a rebellion in Virginia (1676).

Ba·con (bā′kən), **Roger.** Called "the Admirable Doctor." 1214?–1294. English scientist, encyclopedist, alchemist, philosopher, and Franciscan monk.

Ba·co·ni·an (bā-kō′nē-ən) *adj.* Of, pertaining to, or characteristic of the works or thought of Francis Bacon. —*n.* **1.** A follower of the doctrines of Francis Bacon. **2.** One who believes in the Baconian theory.

Baconian theory. The theory that Francis Bacon was the author of the plays attributed to Shakespeare.

bact. bacteria; bacterial.

bac·te·re·mi·a (băk′tə-rē′mē-ə) *n.* The presence of viable bacteria in the blood. [New Latin : BACTER(IO)- + -EMIA.] —**bac′te·re′mic** *adj.* —**bac′te·re′mi·cal·ly** *adv.*

bac·te·ri·a (băk-tîr′ē-ə) *pl.n. Singular* **-terium** (-tîr′ē-əm). *Abbr.* **bact.** Any of numerous unicellular microorganisms of the class Schizomycetes, occurring in a wide variety of forms, existing either as free-living organisms or as parasites, and having a wide range of biochemical, often pathogenic, properties. See Synonyms at **germ.** [New Latin, plural of *bacterium,* from Greek *baktērion,* diminutive of *baktron,* rod. See **bak-** in Appendix.*] —**bac·te′ri·al** *adj.* —**bac·te′ri·al·ly** *adv.*

bac·te·ri·cide (băk-tîr′ə-sīd′) *n.* A substance that destroys bacteria. [BACTERI(O)- + -CIDE.] —**bac·te′ri·ci′dal** *adj.*

bac·te·rin (băk′tə-rĭn) *n.* A vaccine prepared from dead bacteria. [BACTER(IO)- + -IN.]

bacterio–, bacteri–, bacter–. Indicates bacteria, bacterial activity, or relationship to bacteria; for example, **bacteriophage, bactericide, bacteroid.** [From BACTERIA.]

bacteriol. bacteriologist; bacteriology.

bac·te·ri·ol·o·gist (băk-tîr′ē-ŏl′ə-jĭst) *n. Abbr.* **bacteriol.** One who specializes in bacteriology.

bac·te·ri·ol·o·gy (băk-tîr′ē-ŏl′ə-jē) *n. Abbr.* **bacteriol.** The study of bacteria, especially in relation to medicine and agriculture. [BACTERIO- + -LOGY.] —**bac·te′ri·o·log′ic** (-ə-lŏj′ĭk), **bac·te′ri·o·log′i·cal** *adj.* —**bac·te′ri·o·log′i·cal·ly** *adv.*

bac·te·ri·ol·y·sis (băk-tîr′ē-ŏl′ə-sĭs) *n.* The dissolution of bacteria. [New Latin : BACTERIO- + -LYSIS.] —**bac·te′ri·o·lyt′ic** (-ə-lĭt′ĭk) *adj.*

bac·te·ri·o·phage (băk-tîr′ē-ə-fāj′) *n.* A submicroscopic, usually viral, organism that destroys bacteria. Also called "phage." [BACTERIO- + -PHAGE.] —**bac·te′ri·o·phag′ic** (-făj′ĭk), **bac·te′ri·oph′a·gous** (-ŏf′ə-gəs) *adj.* —**bac·te′ri·o·phag′i·cal·ly** *adv.*

bac·te·ri·os·co·py (băk-tîr′ē-ŏs′kə-pē) *n.* The study of bacteria with microscopes. [BACTERIO- + -SCOPY.] —**bac·te′ri·o·scop′ic** (-ē-ə-skŏp′ĭk), **bac·te′ri·o·scop′i·cal** *adj.* —**bac·te′ri·o·scop′i·cal·ly** *adv.* —**bac·te′ri·os′co·pist** *n.*

bac·te·ri·o·sta·sis (băk-tîr′ē-ō-stā′sĭs) *n.* The arrestment or inhibition of bacterial growth and reproduction. [New Latin : BACTERIO- + -STASIS.] —**bac·te′ri·o·stat′ic** (-stăt′ĭk) *adj.* —**bac·te′ri·o·stat′i·cal·ly** *adv.*

bac·te·ri·um. Singular of **bacteria.**

bac·te·rize (băk′tə-rīz′) *tr.v.* **-rized, -rizing, -rizes.** To change or cause a change in by means of bacteria. —**bac′te·ri·za′tion** *n.*

bac·te·roid (băk′tə-roid′) *adj.* Also **bac·te·roi·dal** (băk′tə-roid′l). Resembling bacteria in appearance or action. —*n.* Any of various structurally modified bacteria, such as those occurring on the roots of leguminous plants. [BACTER(IO)- + -OID.]

Bac·tri·a (băk′trē-ə). An ancient country of southwestern Asia, now a district of northern Afghanistan known as Balkh. —**Bac′tri·an** *adj.* & *n.*

Bactrian camel. A two-humped camel, *Camelus bactrianus,* native to central and southwestern Asia. Compare **dromedary.**

bac·u·li·form (băk′yə-lə-fôrm′, bə-kyōō′lə-) *adj.* Rod-shaped. [Latin *baculum,* stick, staff (see **bak-** in Appendix*) + -FORM.]

bad[1] (băd) *adj.* **worse** (wûrs), **worst** (wûrst). **1.** Inferior; poor. **2.** Evil; wicked; sinful. **3.** Misbehaving; disobedient; naughty. **4.** Disagreeable; unpleasant; disturbing: *bad news.* **5.** Unfavorable: *bad reviews.* **6.** Rotten; spoiled; decomposed. **7.** Injurious in effect; detrimental: *bad habits.* **8.** Defective; poor; inadequate: *a bad telephone connection.* **9.** Faulty or incorrect: *bad grammar.* **10.** Not valid or genuine: *a bad check.* **11.** Severe; violent; intense: *a bad cold.* **12.** In poor health; in pain; ill. See Usage note below. **13.** Sorry; regretful; unhappy. See Usage note below. —**in bad.** *Informal.* In trouble or disfavor. —**not half** (or **so**) **bad.** *Informal.* Reasonably good. —*n.* **1.** That which is bad: *weighing the good against the bad.* **2.** Wickedness. —*adv. Informal.* Badly. See Usage note. [Middle English *badde,* perhaps ultimately from Old English *bǣdan,* to compel, afflict. See **bheidh-** in Appendix.*] —**bad′ness** *n.*

Synonyms: *bad, evil, wicked.* These terms are compared as they pertain to departure from moral or ethical standards. *Bad* is most inclusive and generally weakest, although it can be applied with great stress. *Evil* emphasizes inherent capacity for harm or corruptive influence, and thereby more directly implies moral transgression. *Wicked* pertains not only to potential for wrong but to premeditated practice of it.

Usage: *Bad* (adjective), not *badly,* is the proper form following linking verbs such as *feel* and *look: He felt bad* (ill). *He looked bad* (ill). According to 75 per cent of the Usage Panel, *bad* is the only acceptable form in the foregoing examples, in writing; 69 per cent accept only *bad* in speech. In the example *I felt bad* (regretful), 61 per cent specify only *bad,* in writing, but 55 per cent accept *badly* in speech. *Bad,* used as an adverb, as in *His tooth ached so bad* (properly, *severely*) *he could not sleep,* is unacceptable in writing to 92 per cent of the Panel, and in speech to 75 per cent.

bad[2]. *Archaic.* A past tense of **bid.**

Ba·da·joz (bä′*th*ä-hôth′). A city of southwestern Spain, on the Guadiana River. Population, 103,000.

bad blood. Bitterness between two or more persons.

bad·der·locks (băd′ər-lŏks′) *n.* Plural in form, used with a singular or plural verb. An edible seaweed, *Alaria esculenta,* having long, yellowish-green fronds. [Origin obscure.]

bade. A past tense of **bid.**

Ba·den (bäd′n). A region of southwestern Germany that was a grand duchy (1809–1918) and then a state or administrative division of the Weimar Republic, the Third Reich, and West Germany successively, being merged with adjacent territories in 1951 to form the present state of Baden-Württemberg.

Ba·den-Ba·den (bäd′n-bäd′n). A spa, famous for its mineral baths, in Baden-Württemberg, West Germany.

Ba·den-Pow·ell (bäd′n-pō′əl), **Robert Stephenson Smyth.** First Baron Baden-Powell. 1857–1941. British soldier and colonialist; founder of the Boy Scouts (1908).

Ba·den-Würt·tem·berg (bäd′n-vürt′əm-bĕrκ′). A state of West Germany, formed in 1951, and including the former state of Baden. Population, 8,257,000. Capital, Stuttgart.

badge (băj) *n.* **1.** A device or emblem worn as an insignia of rank, office, or membership in an organization, or as an award or honor. **2.** Any characteristic mark: *"the five-cent straw hat which in the Negro's race had been the badge of his enslavement"* (Faulkner). —See Synonyms at **sign.** —*tr.v.* **badged, badging, badges.** To award or mark with a badge. [Middle English *bag(g)e,* from Norman French *bage*†.]

badg·er (băj′ər) *n.* **1.** Any of several carnivorous, burrowing

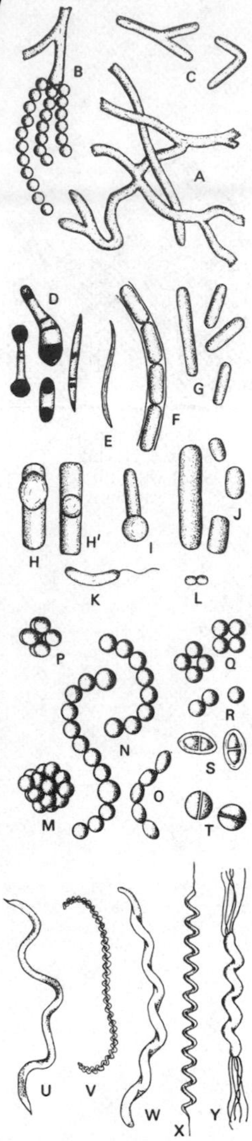

bacteria
A. *Actinomyces bovis*
B. *Streptomyces* species
C. *Mycobacterium tuberculosis*
D. *Corynebacterium diphtheriae*
E. *Fusobacterium fusiforme*
F. *Sphaerotilus natans*
G. *Salmonella typhosa*
H, H′. *Bacillus* species
I. *Clostridium tetani*
J. *Bacillus megaterium*
K. *Vibrio comma*
L. *Brucella abortus*
M. *Staphylococcus aureus*
N. *Streptococcus pyogenes*
O. *Streptococcus lactis*
P. *Sarcina homarus*
Q. *Gaffkya tetragena*
R. Single cocci in fission
S. *Diplococcus pneumoniae*
T. *Neisseria gonorrhoeae*
U. *Borrelia recurrentis*
V. *Leptospira icterohaemorrhagae*
W. *Spirochaeta plicatilis*
X. *Treponema pallidum*
Y. *Spirillum minus*

animals of the family Mustelidae, such as *Meles meles*, of Eurasia, or *Taxidea taxus*, of North America, having short legs, long claws on the front feet, and a heavy, grizzled coat. **2.** The fur or hair of a badger. **3.** Any of several mammals related to or resembling the badger, such as the **honey badger** *(see)*, or, in Australia, the wombat or the bandicoot. **4.** *Capital* **B.** *Slang.* A native or inhabitant of Wisconsin. —*tr.v.* **badgered, -ering, -ers.** To harry persistently with chidings or entreaties; pester. See Synonyms at **harass.** [Possibly from BADGE (from the white mark on its forehead).]

Badger State. The nickname for Wisconsin.

Bad Go·des·berg. See **Godesberg.**

bad·i·nage (băd′ə-näzh′) *n.* Light, playful banter; flippant repartee. —*tr.v.* **badinaged, -naging, -nages.** To tease or amuse with badinage. [French, from *badin,* fool, joker, from Provençal, from *badar,* to gape, from Vulgar Latin *batāre* (unattested). See **bat-** in Appendix.*]

bad·lands (băd′lăndz′) *pl.n.* An extensive area of barren land characterized by roughly eroded ridges, peaks, and mesas.

Bad Lands. An extensive, barren, and deeply eroded region of southwestern South Dakota and northwestern Nebraska.

Badlands National Monument. A 122,972-acre tract of the Bad Lands in South Dakota, reserved to protect the rock formations and fossils.

bad·ly (băd′lē) *adv.* **1.** In a bad manner. See Usage note at **bad.** **2.** Very much; greatly.

Usage: *Badly,* denoting "very much" in constructions signifying need or want, is approved in writing by 88 per cent of the Usage Panel: *The building is badly in need of renovation.*

bad·man (băd′măn′) *n., pl.* **-men** (-mĕn′). *Informal.* A criminal, outlaw, or hoodlum.

bad·min·ton (băd′mĭn′tən) *n.* A game played by volleying a shuttlecock back and forth over a high, narrow net by means of a light, long-handled racket. [After *Badminton,* the country seat of the Duke of Beaufort in Gloucestershire, England.]

B.A.E. Bureau of Agricultural Economics.

Bae·da. See **Bede.**

Bae·de·ker (bā′dĭ-kər) *n.* **1.** Any of a series of guidebooks to Europe published by Karl Baedeker (1801–1859), a German publisher, or his company. **2.** *Informal.* Any guidebook.

Baeke·land (bāk′lănd′), **Leo Hendrik.** 1863–1944. Belgian-born American chemist; inventor of Bakelite.

Baer (bâr), **Karl Ernst von.** 1792–1876. Estonian naturalist; pioneer embryologist; worked in Germany and Russia.

Baf·fin (băf′ĭn), **William.** 1584–1622. English navigator and explorer; searched for Northwest Passage.

Baf·fin Bay (băf′ĭn). An arm of the Atlantic Ocean off northeastern Canada, separating Greenland and Baffin Island.

Baf·fin Island (băf′ĭn). Formerly **Baf·fin Land.** A Canadian island, about 185,000 square miles in area, lying between Greenland and mainland Canada.

baf·fle (băf′əl) *tr.v.* **-fled, -fling, -fles. 1.** To foil; thwart; frustrate: *"secret writing which shall baffle investigation"* (Poe). **2.** To check (someone) in his efforts at solution by confusing; perplex to the point of helplessness; stymie. **3.** To impede the force or movement of; interfere with. —See Synonyms at **puzzle.** —*n.* Any structure used to impede, regulate, or alter flow direction, as of a gas, of sound, or of a liquid. [Perhaps obscurely related to French *bafouer*†, to hoodwink, deceive.] —**baf′fle·ment** *n.* —**baf′fler** *n.*

baf·fling (băf′lĭng) *adj.* **1.** Of a nature that defies solution or understanding; bewildering. **2.** *Nautical.* Shifting in direction and tending to impede or interfere with progress. Said of winds. —**baf′fling·ly** *adv.* —**baf′fling·ness** *n.*

Ba·fing (bə-făng′). A river rising in western Guinea and flowing 350 miles northward to the Senegal River in western Mali.

bag (băg) *n.* **1.** *Abbr.* **bg.** A container in the form of a sack or pouch, made from a flexible material, such as paper, cloth, plastic, or leather. **2.** A woman's handbag; purse. **3.** A suitcase, satchel, or other piece of hand luggage. **4.** An organic sac or pouch, such as the udder of a cow. **5.** Something resembling a bag or pouch. **6.** *Nautical.* The bulging part of a sail. **7. a.** The amount held in a bag; bagful. **b.** *British.* A unit of dry measure equal to three bushels. **8.** The amount of game killed or permitted to be killed in a single day or hunting expedition. **9.** *Baseball.* A base. **10.** *Informal.* A collection of persons or things: *His friends were a mixed bag.* **11.** *Slang.* An area of classification, interest, or skill: *Cooking is not my bag.* **12.** *Slang.* An unattractive woman: *a disagreeable old bag.* —**holding the bag.** *Informal.* Having full responsibility or blame thrust upon one. —**in the bag.** *Slang.* Assured of successful outcome; virtually accomplished or won. —*v.* **bagged, bagging, bags.** —*tr.* **1.** To put into a bag. **2.** To cause to bulge like a bag. **3.** To capture or kill, as game. **4.** *Informal.* To gain possession of; capture. —*intr.* **1.** To hang or bulge loosely. **2.** To swell out. [Middle English *bagge,* from Old Norse *baggi*†.]

bag and baggage. *Informal.* With all one's belongings: *He moved out bag and baggage.*

ba·gasse (bə-găs′) *n.* The dry pulp remaining from sugar cane after the juice has been extracted. [French, from Spanish *bagazo,* dregs, from *baga,* pod, husk, from Latin *bāca, bacca,* berry. See **baccate.**]

bag·a·telle (băg′ə-tĕl′) *n.* **1.** An unimportant or insignificant thing; a trifle. **2.** A short piece of light verse or music. **3.** A game played on an oblong table with a cue and balls. [French, from Italian *bagatella,* diminutive formation from Latin *bāca, bacca,* berry. See **baccate.**]

ba·gel (bā′gəl) *n.* A ring-shaped roll with a tough, chewy texture, made from plain yeast dough that is dropped briefly into nearly boiling water and then baked. [Yiddish *beygel,* ultimately from Middle High German *bouc,* ring, bracelet, from Old High German *boug.* See **bheug-**³ in Appendix.*]

bag·ful (băg′fo͝ol′) *n., pl.* **-fuls** or **bagsful.** The amount held by or contained in a bag.

bag·gage (băg′ĭj) *n.* **1.** The trunks, bags, parcels, and suitcases in which one carries one's belongings while traveling; luggage. **2.** The movable equipment and supplies of an army; impedimenta. **3. a.** A wanton or immoral woman. **b.** An impudent or saucy girl or woman. [Middle English *bagage,* from Old French, from *bague*†, bundle, pack.]

bag·gage·mas·ter (băg′ĭj-măs′tər, -mäs′tər) *n.* One who is in charge of receiving or dispatching baggage at a railway station, bus terminal, or similar place.

bag·ging (băg′ĭng) *n.* Material used for making bags.

bag·gy (băg′ē) *adj.* **-gier, -giest.** Bulging or hanging loosely: *"Watt's trousers, which he wore very baggy, in order to conceal the shape of his legs"* (Samuel Beckett). —**bag′gi·ly** *adv.* —**bag′gi·ness** *n.*

Bagh·dad (băg′dăd′). Also **Bag·dad.** The capital of Iraq, located in the middle of the country on the Tigris River. Population, 2,124,000.

bag·man (băg′mən) *n., pl.* **-men** (-mĭn). **1.** *Slang.* A person who collects money for racketeers. **2.** *British.* A traveling salesman.

bagn·io (băn′yō) *n., pl.* **-ios. 1.** A brothel. **2.** *Obsolete.* A prison for slaves in the Orient. **3.** *Obsolete.* A public bathhouse in Italy or Turkey. [Italian *bagno,* "bath," from Latin *balneum,* from Greek *balaneion.* See **balneal.**]

bag·pipe (băg′pīp′) *n.* A musical instrument having a flexible bag inflated either by a tube with valves or by bellows, a double-reed melody pipe, and from one to four drone pipes. Often used in the plural. —**bag′pip′er** *n.*

ba·guette (bă-gĕt′) *n.* Also **ba·guet. 1.** A gem cut into the form of a narrow rectangle. **2.** The form of such a gem. **3.** *Architecture.* A narrow, convex molding. [French, "small rod," from Italian *bacchetta,* diminutive of *bacchio,* rod, from Latin *baculum,* stick, staff. See **bak-** in Appendix.*]

Ba·gui·o (bä′gē-ō′). The summer capital of the Republic of the Philippines, situated at an elevation of about 5,000 feet on northern Luzon Island. Population, 29,000.

bag·worm (băg′wûrm′) *n.* The larva of any of several moths of the family Psychidae, that encloses itself in a characteristic fibrous case, and that feeds upon and destroys tree foliage.

bah (bä, bă) *interj.* Used to express impatient rejection or contempt. [French (imitative).]

ba·ha·dur (bə-hô′do͝or, -hä′do͝or) *n.* A Hindu title of respect. [Hindi *bahādur,* hero, from Persian *bahādur*†, brave.]

Ba·ha·i (bä-hä′ē, -hī′) *adj.* Of, pertaining to, or designating a religion founded in 1863 by Bahaullah, and emphasizing the spiritual unity of all mankind. —*n.* A teacher of or believer in the Bahai faith. [Persian *bahā′ī,* "of Glory," from *Bahā′ u′llāh,* Bahaullah, "Glory of God."] —**Ba·ha′ism′** (bə-hä′ĭz′əm, -hī′ĭz′əm) *n.* —**Ba·ha′ist** *adj.* & *n.*

Ba·ha·ma Islands (bə-hä′mə). Also **Ba·ha·mas** (-məz). A self-governing British colony comprising an archipelago of over 700 islands in the Atlantic Ocean between Florida and Hispaniola. Population, 139,000. Capital, Nassau. —**Ba·ha′mi·an** (bə-hā′mē-ən, -hä′mē-ən) *adj.* & *n.*

Ba·ha·sa Indonesia (bä-hä′sə). The Malay language that is the official language of the Republic of Indonesia.

Ba·ha·ul·lah (bä-hä′o͞o-lä′). Original name, Hussein Ali. 1817–1892. Persian religious leader; follower of the Bab and founder of Bahaism; exiled.

Ba·ha·wal·pur (bə-hä′wəl-po͝or′). A former state, 17,494 square miles in area, of Punjab in northwestern India, and now a province of West Pakistan.

Ba·hi·a (bä-ē′ə). Also **Ba·í·a. 1.** An Atlantic coast state of eastern Brazil, 217,460 square miles in area. Population, 5,991,000. Capital, Salvador. **2.** The former name for **Salvador.**

Ba·hí·a Blan·ca (bä-ē′ä blăng′kä). A seaport of Argentina, 350 miles southwest of Buenos Aires. Population, 113,000.

Bah·rein (bä-rān′). Also **Bah·rain, Bah·rayn. 1.** A British-protected sheikdom comprising an archipelago in the Persian Gulf between Qatar and Saudi Arabia. Population, 182,000. Capital, Manama. **2.** The largest island of this archipelago.

Bahr el Az·raq. The Arabic name for the **Blue Nile.**

Bahr el Gha·zal (bär′ ĕl gə-zäl′). A province in southwestern Sudan, 82,530 square miles in area. Capital, Wau.

Bahr el Jeb·el (bär′ ĕl jĕb′əl). The portion of the Nile that flows through Sudan to Lake No.

Bah·ret Lut. The Arabic name for the **Dead Sea.**

baht (bät) *n., pl.* **bahts** or **baht. 1.** The basic monetary unit of Thailand, equal to 100 satangs. See table of exchange rates at **currency. 2.** A note worth one baht. [Thai *bāt.*]

Bai·da. See **Beida.**

Bai·kal (bī-kôl′, -käl′). A freshwater lake, the largest (about 13,000 square miles) in Eurasia and said to be the deepest in the world, located in Soviet Central Asia, in the Buryat A.S.S.R.

bail¹ (bāl) *n.* **1.** Security, usually a sum of money, exchanged for the release of an arrested person, as a guarantee of his appearance for trial. **2.** Release from imprisonment provided by the payment of such security. **3.** The person who provides such security. —**go bail for.** To supply bail for; act as security for. —*tr.v.* **bailed, bailing, bails. 1.** To secure the release of (a person) by providing bail. Often used with *out.* **2.** To release (a person) for whom bail has been paid. **3.** *Informal.* To extricate (another) from a difficult situation. Used with *out.* **4.** To deliver or transfer (property) to another for a special purpose, but without permanent transference of ownership. [Middle Eng-

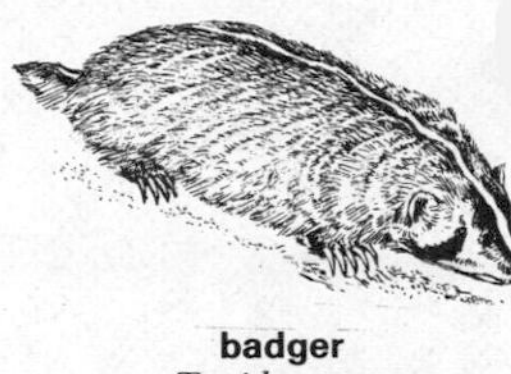

badger
Taxidea taxus

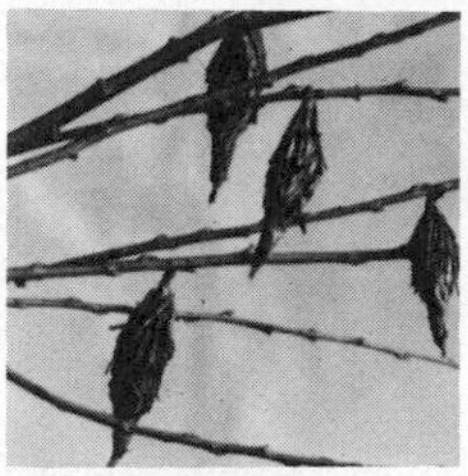

bagworm
Branches with cases of bagworm larvae attached

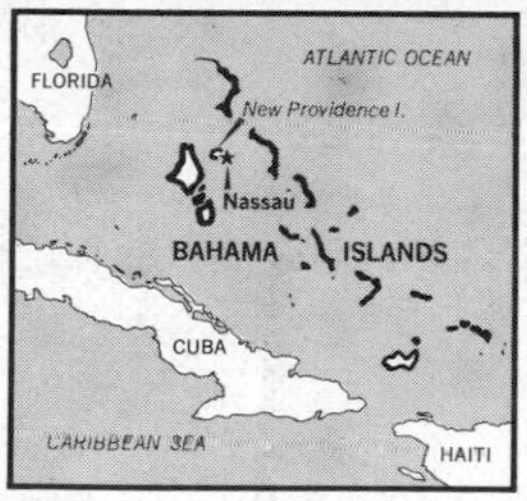

Bahama Islands

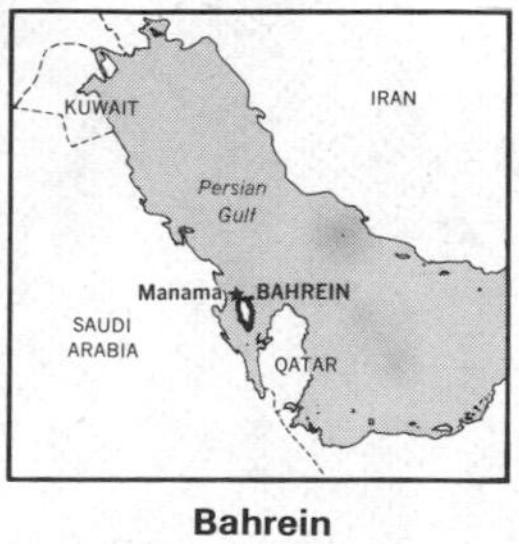

Bahrein

lish *baile*, "custody," from Old French *bail*, from *baillier*, to take charge of, carry, from Latin *bājulāre*, from *bājulus*†, carrier.] —**bail′er** *n.*

bail[2] (bāl) *v.* **bailed, bailing, bails.** —*tr.* **1.** To remove (water) from a boat by repeatedly filling a container and emptying it over the side. **2.** To empty (a boat) of water by this means. Usually used with *out.* —*intr.* To empty a boat of water by scooping or dipping. —**bail out. 1.** To parachute from an aircraft. **2.** *Slang.* To abandon a project or enterprise. —*n.* A container used for bailing. [Middle English *baille*, bucket, from Old French, probably from Vulgar Latin *bājula* (unattested), "carrier (of water)," from Latin *bājulus*, carrier. See **bail** (security).] —**bail′er** *n.*

bail[3] (bāl) *n.* **1.** The arched, hooplike handle of a pail, kettle, or similar container. **2.** An arch or hoop, such as those used to support the top of a covered wagon. [Middle English *baile*, handle, probably from Scandinavian, akin to Old Norse *beyla*, a swelling. See **bheug-**[3] in Appendix.*]

bail[4] (bāl) *n.* **1.** *Cricket.* One of the two crossbars that form the top of a wicket. **2.** A pole or bar used to separate horses in an open stable. [Possibly from Old French *bail*†, crossbeam, possibly from Latin *bājulus*, carrier. See **bail** (security).]

bail·a·ble (bā′lə-bəl) *adj.* **1.** Eligible for bail. **2.** Allowing or admitting of bail: *a bailable offense.*

Bai·le A·tha Cli·ath. The Gaelic name for **Dublin.**

bail·ee (bā-lē′) *n.* A person to whom property is bailed.

bai·ley (bā′lē) *n., pl.* **-leys.** The outer wall of a castle or the space enclosed by it. [Middle English *bailly*, *baile*, from Old French *baille*, enclosed court, from *bailler*, to enclose, from Latin *bājulāre*, to carry. See **bail** (security).]

Bai·ley (bā′lē), **Liberty Hyde.** 1858–1954. American horticulturist, botanist, and educator.

Bai·ley (bā′lē), **Nathan** or **Nathaniel.** Died 1742. English lexicographer; compiler of *Dictionarium Britannicum* (1730).

Bailey bridge. A steel bridge designed to be shipped in parts and assembled rapidly. [Designed by Sir Donald *Bailey* (born 1901), British engineer.]

bail·ie (bā′lē) *n.* **1.** A Scottish municipal officer corresponding to an English alderman. **2.** *Obsolete.* A bailiff. [Middle English *bailli*, from Old French, variant of *baillif*, BAILIFF.]

bail·iff (bā′lĭf) *n.* **1.** A court attendant entrusted with a variety of duties, such as the custody of prisoners under arraignment, the protection of jurors, and the maintenance of order in a courtroom during a trial. **2.** An official who assists a British sheriff and who has the power to execute writs, processes, and arrests. **3.** *Chiefly British.* An overseer of an estate; steward. [Middle English *baillif*, from Old French, from Medieval Latin *bājulīvus*, from Latin *bājulus*, carrier, "person in charge." See **bail** (security).]

bail·i·wick (bā′lĭ-wĭk′) *n.* **1.** The office or district of a bailiff. **2.** A person's specific area of interest, skill, or authority. [Middle English *bailliwik* : BAILIE + *wik*, dwelling, WICK.]

bail·ment (bāl′mənt) *n. Law.* **1.** The process of providing bail for an accused person. **2.** The act of delivering goods or personal property to another in trust.

bail·or (bā′lər, bā-lôr′) *n. Law.* A person who bails property to another.

bails·man (bālz′mən) *n., pl.* **-men.** (-mĭn). *Law.* One who provides bail or security for another.

Bai·ly's beads (bā′lēz). Bright spots of sunlight that appear briefly around the edge of the moon's disk immediately before and after the central phase in a solar eclipse. [After Francis *Baily* (1774–1844), British astronomer.]

bain-ma·rie (băn′mə-rē′) *n., pl.* **bains-ma·rie** (băn′mə-rē′). A device consisting of a large pan containing hot water in which smaller pans may be set to cook slowly or keep warm. [French, from Medieval Latin *balneum Mariae*, "bath of Maria" (mistranslation of Medieval Greek *kaminos Marias*, "furnace of Maria"), after *Maria*, sister of Moses and an alleged alchemist.]

Bai·ram (bī-räm′, bī′räm′) *n.* Either of two Moslem festivals occurring after Ramadan. [Turkish *bayrām*.]

Baird (bârd), **John Logie.** 1888–1946. British inventor; pioneer in development of television.

Baird Mountains (bârd). The mountains at the western end of the Brooks Range in northern Alaska.

bairn (bârn) *n. Scottish.* A child. [Middle English *barn*, Old English *bearn*. See **bher-**[1] in Appendix.*]

bait[1] (bāt) *n.* **1. a.** Food or other lure placed on a hook or in a trap and used in the taking of fish, birds, or other animals. **b.** Worms, fish, and the like used for this purpose. **2.** Any enticement; a temptation. **3.** *Chiefly British.* A stop for food or rest during a trip. —*v.* **baited, baiting, baits.** —*tr.* **1.** To place food or other lure in or on (a trap or fishing hook). **2.** To lure or entice, especially by trickery or strategy. **3.** To set dogs upon (a chained animal, for example) for sport. **4.** To attack or torment, especially with persistent insult, criticism, or ridicule. **5.** To tease. **6.** *Rare.* To feed (an animal) on a journey. —*intr. Rare.* To stop for food or rest during a trip. —See Synonyms at **harass.** [Middle English, partly from Old Norse *beita*, to hunt with dogs, harass, and partly from Old Norse *beita* (a separate word), pasture, food, fish bait. See **bheid-** in Appendix.*] —**bait′er** *n.*

bait[2]. *Falconry.* Variant of **bate.**

baize (bāz) *n.* A cotton or woolen material napped to imitate felt, often bright green in color, and used chiefly as a cover for gaming tables. [French *baie* (plural *baies*), from *bai*, BAY (probably its original color).]

Ba·ja Ca·li·for·nia (bä′hä kä′lē-fôr′nyä). A state of Mexico, 27,655 square miles in area, occupying the northern half of the Lower California Peninsula. Population, 670,000. Capital, Mexicali.

Ba·ja Ca·li·for·nia Sur (bä′hä kä′lē-fôr′nyä so͝or). A territory of Mexico, 27,979 square miles in area, occupying the southern half of the Lower California Peninsula. Population, 89,000. Capital, La Paz.

bake (bāk) *v.* **baked, baking, bakes.** —*tr.* **1.** To cook (bread, pastry, or other food) with continuous, even, dry heat, especially in an oven. **2.** To harden, dry, or otherwise affect by subjecting to heat in or as if in an oven. —*intr.* **1.** To cook food, primarily bread or pastry, by baking. **2.** To become cooked by baking. **3.** To become hard, dry, or otherwise affected by exposure to steady, dry heat. —*n.* **1. a.** The act or process of baking. **b.** The amount baked. **2.** A social gathering at which food is baked and served. Sometimes used in combination: *a clambake.* [Middle English *baken*, Old English *bacan*. See **bhē-** in Appendix.*]

baked-ap·ple berry (bākt′ăp′əl). A plant, the **cloudberry** *(see).*

bake·house (bāk′hous′) *n.* A bakery.

Ba·ke·lite (bā′kə-līt′) *n.* A trademark for any of a group of thermosetting plastics having high chemical and electrical resistance and used in a variety of manufactured articles. [Invented by Leo H. BAEKELAND.]

bak·er (bā′kər) *n.* **1.** One who bakes. **2.** A portable oven.

Ba·ker (bā′kər), **George Pierce.** 1866–1935. American professor of drama, author, editor, and lexicographer.

Ba·ker, Mount (bā′kər). **1.** A peak, 12,406 feet high, in northern Colorado. **2.** A peak, 10,750 feet high, of the Cascade Range in Washington.

Ba·ker Lake (bā′kər). A lake occupying 1,029 square miles in north-central Northwest Territories, Canada.

baker's dozen. A group of 13; one dozen plus one. [From the former custom among bakers of adding an extra roll to every dozen purchased as a safeguard against the possibility that 12 rolls might weigh light.]

Ba·kers·field (bā′kərz-fēld′). A city in California, at the southern end of the San Joaquin Valley. Population, 57,000.

bak·er·y (bā′kə-rē) *n., pl.* **-ies. 1.** A place where products such as bread, cake, and pastries are baked. **2.** A store where baked goods are sold. In this sense, also called "bakeshop."

bak·ing (bā′kĭng) *n.* **1.** The act or process of baking. **2.** The amount baked. —**bak′ing** *adj.*

baking powder. Any of various powdered mixtures of baking soda, starch, and at least one slightly acidic compound such as cream of tartar, used as a leavening agent in baking.

baking soda. A chemical compound, **sodium bicarbonate** *(see).*

ba·kla·va (bä′klə-vä′) *n.* A dessert made of paper-thin layers of pastry, chopped nuts, and honey. [Turkish.]

Ba·koy (bä-koi′). A river rising in northern Guinea and flowing about 250 miles north to the Bafing, with which it forms the Senegal River in western Mali.

bak·sheesh (băk′shēsh′, băk-shēsh′) *n.* Also **bak·shish, back·sheesh, back·shish.** In Turkey, Egypt, India, and other Eastern countries, a gratuity or gift of alms. [Persian *bakhshish*, from *bakhshīdan*, to give. See **bhag-**[1] in Appendix.*]

Bakst (bäkst), **Leon (Nikolaievich).** Original surname, Rosenberg. 1866?–1924. Russian painter; set-designer for ballets.

Ba·ku (bä-ko͞o′). The capital of the Azerbaijan S.S.R., a seaport on the Caspian Sea. Population, 1,147,000.

Ba·ku·nin (bä-ko͞o′nĭn), **Mikhail.** 1814–1876. Russian pamphleteer; active as anarchist in several European countries.

BAL (băl) A colorless, oily, viscous liquid, $C_3H_5(SH)_2(OH)$, used as an antidote for poisoning caused by lewisite, organic arsenic compounds, and heavy metals including mercury and gold. [B(RITISH) A(NTI-)L(EWISITE).]

BAL Airport code for Baltimore, Maryland.

bal. balance.

Ba·la·ki·rev (bä′lə-kē′rĕf), **Mili Alexeievich.** 1837–1910. Russian pianist and composer.

bal·a·lai·ka (băl′ə-lī′kə) *n.* A Russian musical instrument with a triangular body and three strings. [Russian. See **baba-** in Appendix.*]

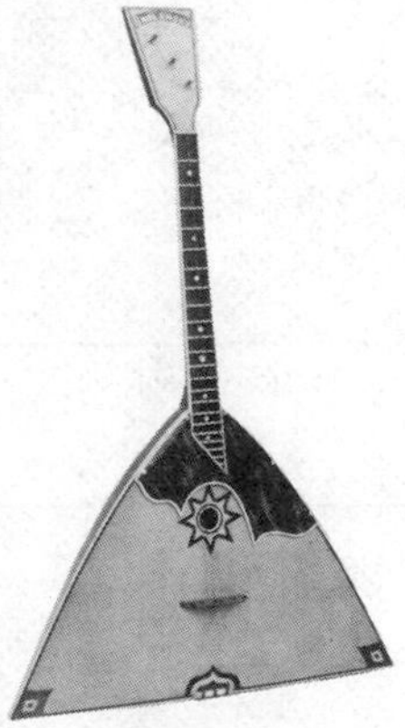

balalaika

bal·ance (băl′əns) *n. Abbr.* **bal. 1.** A weighing device consisting essentially of a rigid, uniformly dense beam, horizontally suspended by a low-friction support at its center, with identical weighing pans hung at either end, one of which holds an unknown weight while the effective weight in the other is increased by known amounts until the beam is level and motionless. **2.** A figurative weighing device capable of determining the outcome of events: *lives hanging in the balance.* **3.** A stable state characterized by cancellation of all forces by equal opposing forces. **4.** A state of bodily equilibrium. **5.** A stable mental or psychological state; emotional equilibrium. **6.** A harmonious or satisfying arrangement or proportion of parts or elements, as in a design or composition. **7.** An influence or force tending to produce equilibrium; a counterpoise. **8.** The difference in magnitude between opposing forces or influences. **9.** *Bookkeeping.* **a.** Equality of totals in the debit and credit sides of an account. **b.** The difference between such totals, either on the credit or the debit side of an account. **10.** *Informal.* Anything that remains or is left over. See Usage note below. **11.** *Chemistry.* Equality of the number, kinds, and net electric charge of reacting species on each side of a chemical equation. **12.** *Mathematics.* Equality with respect to the net number of reduced symbolic quantities on each side of an equation. **13.** A **balance wheel** *(see).* **14.** A dance movement first toward and then away from one's partner. **15.** *Capital* **B.** *Astronomy.* A constellation and sign of the zodiac, **Libra** *(see).* —See Synonyms at **proportion, remainder.**

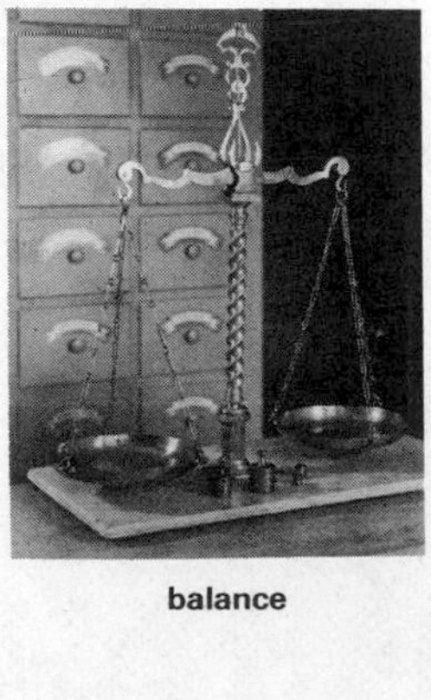

balance

—strike a balance. To reach or achieve a state or position between extremes. —v. **balanced, -ancing, -ances.** —tr. **1.** To weigh or poise in or as if in a balance. **2.** To compare as if weighing in the mind. **3.** To bring into or maintain in a state of equilibrium. **4.** To act as an equalizing weight or force to; to offset; to counterbalance. **5.** *Bookkeeping.* **a.** To compute the difference between the debits and credits of (an account). **b.** To reconcile or equalize the sums of the debits and credits of (an account). **c.** To settle by paying what is owed. **6.** To bring into or keep in equal or satisfying proportion or harmony. **7.** *Mathematics.* To bring (an equation) into mathematical balance. **8.** *Chemistry.* To bring (a chemical equation) into chemical balance. **9.** To move toward and then away from (one's dance partner). —intr. **1.** To be in or come into equilibrium. **2.** To be equal or equivalent. **3.** To sway or waver as if losing or regaining equilibrium. **4.** To move toward and then away from one's dance partner. [Middle English, from Old French, from Vulgar Latin *bilancia* (unattested), scales, from Late Latin *(libra) bilanx,* (a balance) having two scales : Latin *bi-,* double + *lanx†,* scale, plate, pan.]
Usage: Balance (noun), in its extended sense of *remainder* or *rest,* is often condemned, especially when the usage departs far from the literal bookkeeping sense. Only 53 per cent of the Usage Panel accepts the following example in writing: *The balance of the time is your own.*
balanced fund. A mutual fund with a portfolio that includes bonds or preferred stocks as well as common stocks.
balance of payments. A systematic recording of a nation's total payments to foreign countries, including the price of imports and the outflow of capital and gold, and its total receipts from abroad, including the price of exports and the inflow of capital and gold.
balance of power. A distribution of power between nations, often by means of alliance and counteralliance, whereby no one nation is able to dominate or conquer the others.
balance of trade. The difference in value between the total exports and imports of a nation.
bal·anc·er (băl′ən-sər) n. **1.** One that balances. **2.** A rudimentary insect wing, a **halter** *(see).*
balance sheet. *Abbr.* **B.S.** A statement of the assets and liabilities of a business or individual at a specified date.
balance wheel. A wheel that regulates rate of movement in machine parts, as in a watch.
Bal·an·chine (băl′ən-chēn′, băl′ən-chēn′), **George.** Original name, Georgi Balanchinvadze. Born 1904. Russian-born American choreographer.
Ba·la·ra·ma (bŭl′ə-rä′mä). *Hinduism.* The eighth incarnation of Vishnu and elder brother of Krishna. Also called "Rama."
bal·as (băl′əs) n. A rose-red to orange spinel, a semiprecious gem. [Middle English, from Old French *balais,* from Arabic *bálakhsh,* from Persian *Badhakhshān,* a region in northeastern Iran, where the gem is found.]
ba·la·ta (bə-lä′tə) n. **1.** A tropical American tree, *Manilkara bidentata* (or *Mimusops balata*), that yields a latexlike sap. Also called "bully tree." **2.** A tough, nonelastic, rubberlike gum obtained from this sap and used for golf-ball covers, industrial belting, and gaskets. [American Spanish, from Cariban.]
Bal·a·ton, Lake (băl′ə-tŏn′). *German* **Plat·ten·see** (plät′n-zā′). A lake in Hungary, 266 square miles in area, about 55 miles southwest of Budapest.
bal·bo·a (băl-bō′ə; *Spanish* bäl-bō′ä) n. **1.** The basic monetary unit of Panama, equal to 100 centesimos. See table of exchange rates at **currency. 2.** A coin worth one balboa. [After Vasco Núñez de BALBOA.]
Bal·bo·a (băl-bō′ə; *Spanish* bäl-bō′ä). A seaport in the Panama Canal Zone, on the Pacific coast, adjacent to Panama City. Its suburb, Balboa Heights, is the administrative center of the Panama Canal Zone.
Bal·bo·a (băl-bō′ə; *Spanish* bäl-bō′ä), **Vasco Núñez de.** 1475–1517. Spanish explorer and colonial governor; discovered the Pacific Ocean (1513).
bal·brig·gan (băl-brĭg′ən) n. **1.** A knitted unbleached-cotton underwear fabric. **2.** *Usually plural.* Underclothing made of this fabric. [From *Balbriggan,* Irish seaport where it was first manufactured.]
bal·co·ny (băl′kə-nē) n., pl. **-nies. 1.** A platform that projects from the wall of a building and is surrounded by a railing, balustrade, or parapet. **2.** A gallery that projects over the main floor in a theater or auditorium. [Italian *balcone,* from Old Italian, scaffold, from Germanic. See **bhelg-** in Appendix.*]
bald (bôld) adj. **balder, baldest. 1.** Lacking hair on the top of the head. **2.** Lacking natural or usual covering: *a bald spot on the lawn.* **3.** Having white feathers or markings on the head: *a bald eagle.* **4.** Lacking ornament; bare; unadorned. **5.** Undisguised; blunt: *a bald statement.* —See Usage note at **balding.** [Middle English *ballede,* perhaps Old English *bællede* (unattested). See **bhel-¹** in Appendix.*] —**bald′ly** adv. —**bald′ness** n.
bal·da·chin (bôl′də-kĭn, băl′-) n. Also **bal·da·quin, bal·da·chi·no** (băl′də-kē′nō). **1.** A rich fabric of silk and gold brocade. **2.** A canopy of fabric carried in church processions or placed over an altar, throne, or dais. **3.** *Architecture.* A stone or marble structure built in the form of a canopy, especially over the altar of a church. [Italian *baldacchino,* from Old Italian, from *Baldacco,* BAGHDAD, famous in the Middle Ages for its brocades.]
bald cypress. A cone-bearing but deciduous tree, *Taxodium distichum,* of the southeastern United States, growing in swamps and damp ground.
bald eagle. A North American eagle, *Haliaeetus leucocephalus,* having a dark body and a white head and tail. It appears on the

national emblem of the United States. Also called "American eagle."
bal·der·dash (bôl′dər-dăsh′) n. Nonsense. [Origin unknown.]
bald-faced (bôld′făst′) adj. **1.** Having a white face or face markings. **2.** Brash; undisguised.
bald-head (bôld′hĕd′) n. **1.** A person whose head is bald. **2.** Any of several birds having white markings on the head.
bald-head·ed (bôld′hĕd′ĭd) adj. Having a bald head. —adv. Recklessly; precipitately.
balding (bôld′ĭng) adj. *Informal.* Becoming bald.
Usage: The form balding (becoming bald), used as an adjective, is accepted by 55 per cent of the Usage Panel. Representative responses are those of Isaac Asimov, "distasteful but necessary," and Katherine Anne Porter, "entirely vulgar."
bald·pate (bôld′pāt′) n. **1.** A baldheaded person. **2.** An American duck, the **widgeon** *(see).*
bal·dric (bôl′drĭk) n. A belt, usually of ornamented leather, worn across the chest to support a sword or bugle. [Middle English *baud(e)rik,* from Old French *baldrei, baudrei†.*]
Bald·win (bôld′wĭn) n. A red-skinned American variety of apple. [Developed by Colonel Loammi *Baldwin* (1740–1807), American engineer and soldier.]
Bald·win (bôld′wĭn), **James (Arthur).** Born 1924. American author of novels, plays, short stories, and essays.
Bald·win (bôld′wĭn), **Stanley.** First Earl Baldwin of Bewdley. 1867–1947. British statesman; prime minister (1923–24, 1924–29, and 1935–37).
bale¹ (bāl) n. A large bound package of raw or finished material. —tr.v. **baled, baling, bales.** To wrap in bales. [Middle English, probably from Old French, from Germanic. See **bhel-²** in Appendix.*] —**bal′er** n.
bale² (bāl) n. *Poetic.* **1.** Evil influence. **2.** Mental suffering; anguish. [Middle English *bale,* Old English *balu, bealu.* See **bheleu-** in Appendix.*]
Bâle. The French name for **Basel.**
Bal·e·ar·ic Islands (băl′ē-ăr′ĭk; bə-lîr′ĭk). *Spanish* **Is·las Ba·le·a·res** (ēz′läz bä′lä-ä′räs). An island group in the Mediterranean, east of Spain; a province of Spain including Majorca and Minorca. Population, 443,000. Capital, Palma.
ba·leen (bə-lēn′) n. **Whalebone** *(see).* [Middle English *balene,* whale, baleen, from Old French *baleine,* from Latin *ballaena,* whale. See **bhel-²** in Appendix.*]
bale·ful (bāl′fəl) adj. **1.** Harmful or malignant in intent or effect. **2.** Portending evil; dire. —See Synonyms at **sinister.** —**bale′ful·ly** adv. —**bale′ful·ness** n.
Usage: Baleful usually applies to that which menaces, exerts evil influence, or foreshadows evil: *a baleful look.* Baneful is said most often of that which is literally poisonous or destructive: *the baneful hemlock.*
Bal·four (băl′fŏŏr′), **Arthur James.** First Earl of Balfour. 1848–1930. British statesman; prime minister (1902–05).
Ba·li (bä′lē). An island province of Indonesia, 2,146 square miles in area, lying off the eastern end of Java. Population, 1,101,000. Capital, Singaradja.
Ba·li·nese (bä′lə-nēz′, -nēs′) adj. Of or pertaining to Bali, its people, culture, or language. —n. **1.** A native or inhabitant of Bali. **2.** The Indonesian language spoken in Bali.
balk (bôk) v. **balked, balking, balks.** Also **baulk.** —intr. **1.** To stop short and refuse to go on. **2.** To refuse obstinately or abruptly; shrink. Used with *at: He balked at the very idea of compromise.* **3.** *Sports.* To make an incomplete or misleading move, especially an illegal one. —tr. **1.** To put obstacles in the way of; check or thwart. **2.** *Rare.* To let go by; miss: *balk an opportunity.* **3.** *Obsolete.* To heap in, or form into ridges. —See Synonyms at **frustrate, hinder.** —n. Also **baulk. 1.** A hindrance, check, or defeat. **2.** A blunder or failure. **3. a.** *Baseball.* An illegal motion; especially, a false move to throw the ball, made by the pitcher when there are runners on base. **b.** In various other sports, an incomplete or misleading motion. **4. a.** An unplowed strip of land. **b.** A ridge between furrows. **5.** A wooden beam or rafter. **6.** One of the spaces between the cushion and the **balk line** *(see).* [Middle English *balken,* to plow up in ridges, from *balk,* ridge, bar, Old English *balc, balca,* bank, ridge in plowing, from Old Norse *balkr,* partition. See **bhelg-** in Appendix.*] —**balk′er** n.
Bal·kan (bôl′kən) adj. **1.** Of or pertaining to the Balkan Peninsula or the Balkan Mountains. **2.** Of or pertaining to the Balkan States or their inhabitants.
Bal·kan·ize (bôl′kə-nīz′) tr.v. **-ized, -izing, -izes.** Also **bal·kan·ize.** To divide (a region or territory) into small, often hostile, units. [From the division of the Balkan countries by the Great Powers in the early 20th century.] —**Bal′kan·i·za′tion** n.
Balkan Mountains. *Bulgarian* **Sta·ra Pla·ni·na** (stä′rä plä′nĭ-nä′). A range of mountains extending across northern Bulgaria, from the Black Sea to the border of Yugoslavia. Highest elevation, 7,800 feet.
Balkan Peninsula. A peninsula in southeastern Europe, bounded by the Mediterranean and Aegean seas to the south, the Adriatic and Ionian seas to the west, and the Black Sea to the east.
Balkan States. The countries that occupy the Balkan Peninsula: Albania, Bulgaria, Greece, Rumania, and Yugoslavia. Also called "the Balkans."
Balkan War. Either of two wars fought between Turkey and the Balkan States (1911–13), in both of which Turkey was defeated.
Balkh. The modern name for **Bactria.**
Bal·khash (bäl-käsh′). A salt lake, about 7,000 square miles in area, of Kazakhstan in Soviet central Asia.

bald cypress

bald eagle

Bal·kis (băl′kĭs). The name given in the Koran to the Queen of Sheba.

balk line. On a billiard table, a line drawn parallel to one end, from behind which opening shots with the cue ball are made.

balk·y (bô′kē) *adj.* **-ier, -iest.** Given to stopping at, or as if at, an obstacle: *a balky horse.* See Synonyms at **contrary.**

ball[1] (bôl) *n.* **1. a.** A spherical or almost spherical body. **b.** Any spherical entity: *a ball of flame.* **2. a.** Any of various rounded movable objects used in sports and games. **b.** A game, especially baseball, played with such an object. **3.** *Sports.* A ball moving, thrown, hit, or kicked in a particular manner: *a low ball.* **4.** *Baseball.* A pitched ball not swung at by the batter that does not pass through the strike zone. **5. a.** A solid projectile of spherical or pointed shape, as that shot from a cannon. **b.** Projectiles of this kind collectively. **6.** A rounded part or protuberance, especially of the body: *the ball of the foot.* **7.** *Plural. Vulgar.* The testicles. **8.** *Plural. Vulgar.* Nonsense. —*interj. Plural. Vulgar.* Used to express annoyance, disapproval, or disagreement. —**be on the ball.** *Slang.* To be alert, competent, or efficient. —**carry the ball. 1.** *Football.* To hold the ball and attempt to advance it. **2.** *Informal.* To carry the burden of, or take the initiative in (a project). —**have something on the ball.** *Slang.* To have ability or acumen. —**play ball. 1.** To begin or resume a ball game or other activity. **2.** *Informal.* To cooperate. —*v.* **balled, balling, balls.** —*tr.* To form into a ball. —*intr.* To become formed into a ball. —**ball up.** *Slang.* To confuse or bungle; muddle. [Middle English *bal,* from Old Norse *böllr.* See **bhel-**[2] in Appendix.*]

ball[2] (bôl) *n.* A formal gathering for social dancing. —**have a ball.** *Slang.* To have a very enjoyable time. [French *bal,* from Old French, from *baller,* to dance, from Late Latin *ballāre,* from Greek *ballizein.* See **gwel-**[1] in Appendix.*]

bal·lad (băl′əd) *n.* **1.** A narrative poem, often of folk origin and intended to be sung, consisting of simple stanzas and usually having a recurrent refrain. **2.** The music for such a poem. **3.** A popular song of a romantic or sentimental nature. [Middle English *balade,* from Old French *ballade,* from Provençal *balada,* piece to be accompanied by dancing, from *balar,* to dance, from Late Latin *ballāre.* See **ball** (dance).]

bal·lade (bə-läd′, bă-) *n.* **1.** *Prosody.* A verse form usually consisting of three stanzas of eight or ten lines each, with the same concluding line in each stanza, and an envoy, or brief final stanza, ending with the same last line as that of the preceding stanzas. **2.** A musical composition, usually for the piano, having the romantic or dramatic quality of a ballad. [Early form of BALLAD.]

bal·lad·eer (băl′ə-dîr′) *n.* One who sings ballads.

bal·lad·mon·ger (băl′əd-mŭng′gər, -mŏng′gər) *n.* **1.** A seller or peddler of popular ballads. **2.** An inferior poet.

bal·lad·ry (băl′ə-drē) *n.* **1.** Ballads collectively. **2.** The art of making or singing ballads.

ballad stanza. A four-line stanza often used in ballads, rhyming in the second and fourth lines, and having four metrical feet in the first and third lines, and three in the second and fourth.

ball-and-sock·et joint (bôl′ən-sŏk′ĭt). A joint consisting of a spherical knob or knoblike part fitted into a socket so that some degree of motion is possible in nearly any direction.

bal·last (băl′əst) *n.* **1.** Any heavy material placed in the hold of a ship or the gondola of a balloon to enhance stability. **2.** Coarse gravel or crushed rock laid to form a bed for roads or railroads. **3.** That which gives stability, especially to character. —*tr.v.* **ballasted, -lasting, -lasts. 1.** To stabilize or provide with ballast. **2.** To fill (a railroad bed) with ballast. [Perhaps from Old Swedish or Old Danish *barlast,* "bare load" (cargo carried only for its weight) : *bar,* bare (see **bhoso-** in Appendix*) + *last,* load (see **klā-** in Appendix*).]

ball bearing. *Abbr.* **bb, b.b. 1.** A friction-reducing bearing, consisting essentially of a ring-shaped track containing freely revolving hard metal balls against which a rotating shaft or other part turns, either in direct contact with the balls or with a second matched ring. **2.** A hard ball used in such a bearing.

ball cock. A self-regulating device controlling the supply of water in a tank, cistern, or toilet by means of a float connected to a valve that opens or closes with a change in water level.

bal·le·ri·na (băl′ə-rē′nə) *n.* **1.** A principal female dancer in a corps de ballet. **2.** *Informal.* Any female ballet dancer. Compare **prima ballerina.** [Italian, from *ballare,* to dance, from Late Latin *ballāre.* See **ball** (dance).]

bal·let (bă-lā′, băl′ā′) *n.* **1.** An artistic dance form characterized by grace and precision of movement and an elaborate formal technique. **2.** A theatrical presentation of group or solo dancing to a musical accompaniment, usually in costume and with scenic effects, and conveying a story, theme, or atmosphere. **3.** A musical composition written or used for ballet. **4.** A company or group that performs ballet. [French, from Italian *balletto,* diminutive of *ballo,* a dance, from *ballare,* to dance, from Late Latin *ballāre.* See **ball** (dance).]

bal·let·o·mane (bă-lĕt′ə-mān′) *n.* An ardent admirer of the ballet. [Blend of BALLET and MANIA.] —**bal·let′o·ma′ni·a** (bă-lĕt′ə-mā′nē-ə, -mān′yə) *n.*

ball·flow·er (bôl′flou′ər) *n. Architecture.* An ornament in the form of a ball cupped in the petals of a circular flower.

ball game. 1. A game played with a ball; especially, a baseball game. **2.** *Informal.* Any competition, such as a political race: *This makes the Presidential contest a whole new ball game.*

bal·lis·ta (bə-lĭs′tə) *n., pl.* **-tae** (-tē′). A military engine used in ancient and medieval warfare to hurl heavy projectiles. [Latin, from Greek *ballein,* to throw. See **gwel-**[1] in Appendix.*]

bal·lis·tic (bə-lĭs′tĭk) *adj.* **1.** Of or pertaining to ballistics. **2.** Of or pertaining to projectiles, their motion, or their effects. [From BALLISTA.] —**bal·lis′ti·cal·ly** *adv.*

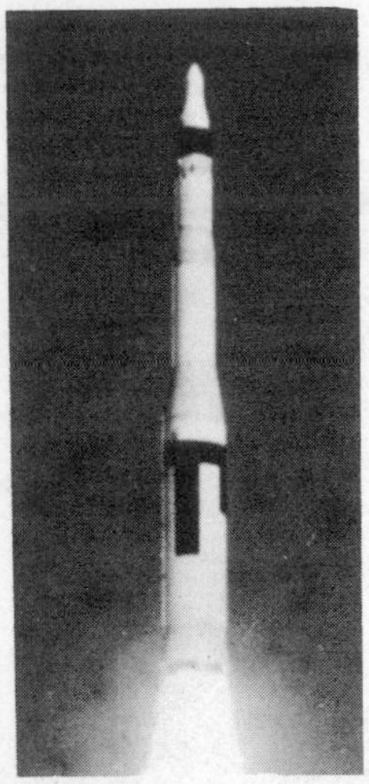
ballistic missile

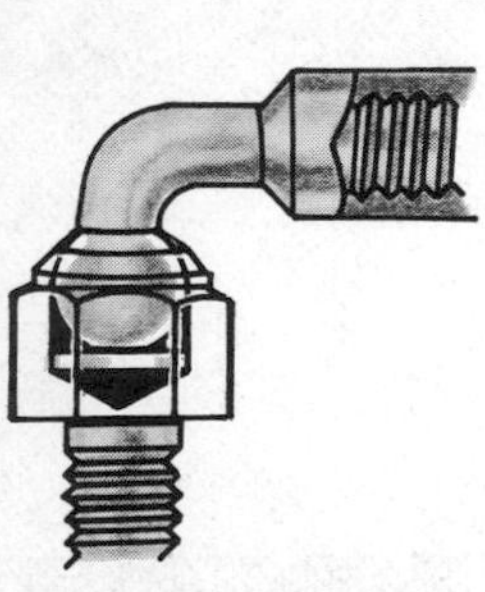
ball-and-socket joint

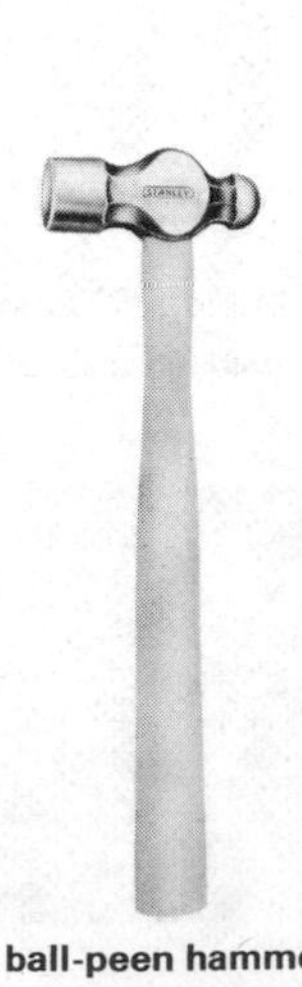
ball-peen hammer

ballistic missile. A projectile that assumes a free-falling trajectory after an internally guided, self-powered ascent. Compare **guided missile.**

bal·lis·tics (bə-lĭs′tĭks) *n.* Plural in form, used with a singular verb. **1. a.** The study of the dynamics of projectiles. **b.** The study of the flight characteristics of projectiles. **2. a.** The study of the functioning of firearms. **b.** The study of the firing, flight, and effect of ammunition. —**bal′lis·ti′cian** (băl′ĭ-stĭsh′ən) *n.*

bal·lo·net (băl′ə-nā′) *n.* One of several small auxiliary gasbags placed inside a balloon or a nonrigid airship that can be inflated or deflated during flight to control and maintain shape and buoyancy. [French *ballonnet,* diminutive of *ballon,* BALLOON.]

bal·loon (bə-lo͞on′) *n.* **1.** A spherical, flexible, nonporous bag inflated with a gas lighter than air, such as helium, that causes it to rise and float in the atmosphere; especially, such a bag with sufficient capacity to lift a suspended gondola. **2.** Any of variously shaped, brightly colored, inflatable rubber bags used as toys. **3.** A rounded or irregularly shaped outline containing the words a character in a cartoon is represented as saying. —*v.* **ballooned, -looning, -loons.** —*intr.* **1.** To ascend or ride in a balloon. **2.** To expand or swell out like a balloon. —*tr.* To cause to expand by or as if by inflating. [French *ballon,* from Italian *pallone,* augmentative of *palla,* ball, from Middle High German *balle.* See **bhel-**[2] in Appendix.*] —**bal·loon′ist** *n.*

balloon flower. A plant, *Platycodon grandiflorum,* native to Asia, cultivated for its showy, blue, bell-shaped flowers.

balloon sail. A comparatively large foresail, used when going before the wind in races to supplement or replace a jib.

balloon tire. A pneumatic tire with a wide tread, inflated to low pressure, and now used chiefly on trucks.

balloon vine. A vine, *Cardiospermum halicacabum,* native to tropical America, having inflated, ornamental, three-valved pods.

bal·lot (băl′ət) *n.* **1.** A written or printed paper or ticket used to cast or register a vote, especially a secret vote. **2.** The act, process, or method of voting, especially by the use of secret ballots or voting machines. **3.** A list of candidates running for office; a ticket. **4.** The total of all votes cast in an election. **5.** The right to vote; franchise. **6.** Formerly, a small ball used to register a vote. —*v.* **balloted, -loting, -lots.** —*intr.* **1.** To cast a ballot; to vote. **2.** To draw lots. —*tr.* To vote or decide on by casting a ballot. [Italian *ballotta,* small ball or pebble used for voting, diminutive of (dialectal) *balla,* ball, from Middle High German *balle.* See **bhel-**[2] in Appendix.*] —**bal′lot·ter** *n.*

bal·lotte·ment (bə-lŏt′mənt) *n.* A technique for detecting or examining a floating object in the body, as: **a.** The use of a finger to push sharply against the uterus and detect the presence or position of a fetus by its return impact. **b.** A test for a floating kidney in which the kidney is moved by alternating external digital pressures. [French, a tossing, from *ballotter,* to toss, from *ballotte,* diminutive of *balle,* ball, from Frankish *balla* (unattested). See **bhel-**[2] in Appendix.*]

ball-peen hammer (bôl′pēn′). A hammer having one hemispherical end of the head.

ball·play·er (bôl′plā′ər) *n.* One who plays baseball.

ball-point pen (bôl′point′). A pen having as its writing point a small ball bearing that transfers ink stored in a cartridge onto a writing surface. Also called "ball pen," "ball point."

ball·room (bôl′ro͞om′, -ro͝om′) *n.* A large room for dancing.

ball valve. A valve regulated by the position of a free-floating ball that moves in response to fluid or mechanical pressure.

bal·ly·hoo (băl′ē-ho͞o′) *n., pl.* **-hoos.** *Informal.* **1.** Sensational or clamorous advertising. **2.** Noisy shouting or uproar. —*tr.v.* **ballyhooed, -hooing, -hoos.** *Informal.* To advertise by sensational methods; publicize exaggeratedly. [Origin unknown.] —**bal′ly·hoo′er** *n.*

bal·ly·rag. Variant of **bullyrag.**

balm (bäm) *n.* **1.** An aromatic, oily resin exuded by various chiefly tropical trees and shrubs, and used in medicine. **2.** Any tree or shrub yielding such a substance. **3.** Any aromatic ointment, oil, unguent, or similar substance. **4.** An aromatic herb, *Melissa officinalis,* native to Eurasia, having clusters of small, fragrant white flowers. Also called "lemon balm." **5.** Any of several similar aromatic plants. **6.** A pleasing, aromatic fragrance. **7.** Something that soothes, heals, or comforts. [Middle English *baume, basme,* from Old French *basme,* from Latin *balsamum,* BALSAM.]

bal·ma·caan (băl′mə-kăn′) *n.* A loose, full overcoat with raglan sleeves, originally made of rough, woolen cloth. [After *Balmacaan,* an estate near Inverness, Scotland.]

balm of Gilead. 1. An aromatic evergreen tree of the genus *Commiphora;* especially, *C. opobalsamum,* of Africa and Asia Minor. **2.** A fragrant resin obtained from this tree. **3.** A North American deciduous tree, *Populus candicans,* having broad, heart-shaped leaves. **4.** A fragrant resin obtained from the **balsam fir** *(see).*

Bal·mor·al (băl-môr′əl, -mŏr′əl) *n.* **1.** A brimless Scottish cap with a flat, round top. **2.** *Sometimes small* **b.** A heavy, laced walking shoe. [After *Balmoral Castle,* Scotland.]

balm·y (bä′mē) *adj.* **-ier, -iest. 1.** Having the quality or fragrance of balm. **2.** Mild and pleasant: *a balmy breeze.* **3.** *Slang.* Eccentric in behavior. [Sense 3, variant of BARMY.] —**balm′i·ly** *adv.* —**balm′i·ness** *n.*

bal·ne·al (băl′nē-əl) *adj.* Of or pertaining to baths or bathing. [From Latin *balneum,* bath, from Greek *balaneion*†.]

bal·ne·ol·o·gy (băl′nē-ŏl′ə-jē) *n.* Medical therapy with mineral baths. [Latin *balneum,* bath (see **balneal**) + -LOGY.]

ă pat/ā pay/âr care/ä father/b bib/ch church/d deed/ĕ pet/ē be/f fife/g gag/h hat/hw which/ĭ pit/ī pie/îr pier/j judge/k kick/l lid, needle/m mum/n no, sudden/ng thing/ŏ pot/ō toe/ô paw, for/oi noise/ou out/o͝o took/o͞o boot/p pop/r roar/s sauce/sh ship, dish/

ba·lo·ney (bə-lō′nē) *n.* Also **bo·lo·ney**. **1.** *Informal.* Variant of **bologna**. **2.** *Slang.* Nonsense.

bal·sa (bôl′sə) *n.* **1.** A tree, *Ochroma lagopus,* of tropical America, having wood that is unusually light in weight. **2.** The wood of this tree. **3.** A raft consisting of a frame fastened to buoyant cylinders of wood or metal. [Spanish *balsa*†.]

bal·sam (bôl′səm) *n.* **1.** An oily or gummy oleoresin, usually containing benzoic or cinnamic acids, obtained from the exudations of any of various trees and shrubs, and used as a base for cough syrups, other medications, and perfumes. See **balsam of Peru, balsam of Tolu, Canada balsam. 2.** Any similar substance, especially a fragrant ointment used as medication. **3.** Any of various trees yielding an aromatic, resinous substance; especially, the **balsam fir** *(see).* **4.** Any of several plants of the genus *Impatiens;* especially, *I. balsamina,* cultivated for its double flowers of various colors. [Latin *balsamum,* from Greek *balsamon,* from Hebrew *bāsām,* "spice."]

balsam apple. A tropical vine, *Momordica balsamina,* native to the Old World, having yellow flowers and warty, orange fruit.

balsam fir. An evergreen tree, *Abies balsamea,* of northeastern North America, having small needles and cones about 2½ inches long. Also called "balsam," "Canada balsam."

bal·sam·ic (bôl-săm′ĭk) *adj.* **1.** Of, pertaining to, or resembling balsam. **2.** Containing or yielding balsam.

bal·sam·if·er·ous (bôl′sə-mĭf′ər-əs) *adj.* Yielding balsam.

balsam of Peru. The aromatic resin of a tropical American tree, *Myroxylon pereirae,* used in the manufacture of perfumes and other products.

balsam of To·lu (tə-lo͞o′). The aromatic resin of a tropical American tree, *Myroxylon toluiferum,* used in cough remedies and in the manufacture of perfumes. Also called "tolu."

balsam pear. A tropical vine, *Momordica charantia,* native to the Old World, having yellow-orange fruit.

balsam poplar. A North American tree, *Populis balsamifera,* having large buds coated with a gummy, fragrant resin. Also called "tacamahac."

bal·sam·root (bôl′səm-ro͞ot′, -ro͝ot′) *n.* Any of several plants of the genus *Balsamorhiza,* of the western United States; especially, *B. sagittata,* having rayed yellow flowers and an aromatic root.

Bal·sas, Rí·o de las (rē′ō dā läz bäl′säs). A river rising in south-central Mexico and flowing 426 miles south and then west to the Pacific Ocean.

Balt (bôlt) *n.* A member of the Baltic-speaking people inhabiting the southeastern shores of the Baltic Sea and formerly occupying a wide area bounded by Danzig, Riga, Moscow, and Kiev.

Bal·tha·sar (băl-thā′zər, -thăz′ər, bôl′thə-zär′, băl′-). Also **Bal·tha·zar**. One of the Magi who came to the infant Jesus.

Bal·ti (bŭl′tē) *n.* A Tibeto-Burman language of the people of northern Kashmir.

Bal·tic (bôl′tĭk) *adj.* **1.** Of or pertaining to the Baltic Sea, or to the Baltic States and their inhabitants or cultures. **2.** Of or designating a group of languages of the Indo-European family, consisting of Lithuanian, Lettish, and Old Prussian. See **Balto-Slavic.** —*n.* The Baltic language group.

Baltic Sea. A long arm of the Atlantic Ocean in northern Europe, about 163,000 square miles in area, and bordered by Sweden, Finland, the Soviet Union, Poland, East and West Germany, and Denmark.

Baltic States. The formerly sovereign states of Estonia, Latvia, and Lithuania, on the eastern coast of the Baltic Sea, incorporated as republics of the Soviet Union in 1940.

Bal·ti·more (bôl′tə-môr′, -mōr′). The largest city of Maryland and a leading seaport of the United States, on upper Chesapeake Bay. Population, 939,000. —**Bal′ti·mo′re·an** *adj.* & *n.*

Bal·ti·more, Lord. See George **Calvert.**

Baltimore oriole. An American songbird, *Icterus galbula,* of which the male has bright-orange, black, and white plumage. [After Lord BALTIMORE (the colors of the male are the same as those in Lord Baltimore's coat of arms).]

Bal·to-Sla·vic (bôl′tō-slä′vĭk, -slăv′ĭk) *n.* A subfamily of the Indo-European language family, composed of the Baltic group and the Slavic group.

Ba·lu·chi (bə-lo͞o′chē) *n., pl.* **Baluchi** or **-chis. 1.** A native or inhabitant of Baluchistan. **2.** The Iranian language of the Baluchi people.

Ba·lu·chi·stan (bə-lo͞o′chĭ-stăn′, -stän′). A region in western West Pakistan, about 134,000 square miles in area, with a coastline on the Arabian Sea. Principal city, Quetta.

ba·lu·chi·there (bə-lo͞o′chĭ-thîr′) *n.* A very large, extinct, rhinoceroslike mammal of the genus *Baluchitherium,* of the Oligocene and Miocene epochs. [New Latin *Baluchitherium* : BALUCHI(STAN) + -THERE.]

bal·us·ter (băl′ə-stər) *n.* One of the posts or supports of a handrail. [French *balustre,* from Italian *balaustro,* from *balaustra,* flower of the pomegranate (from the shape of the post), from Latin *balaustium,* from Greek *balaustion*†.]

bal·us·trade (băl′ə-strād′) *n.* A rail and the row of posts that support it, as along the edge of a staircase. [French, from Italian *balaustrata,* from *balaustro,* BALUSTER.]

Bal·zac (bôl′zăk′, băl′-; *French* bȧl-zȧk′), **Honoré de.** 1799–1850. French author of short stories and novels.

Ba·ma·ko (băm′ə-kō′). The capital and largest city of the Republic of Mali, in the south on the Niger River. Population, 120,000.

Bam·ba·ra (băm-bä′rä) *n., pl.* **Bambara** or **-ras. 1.** A Negroid people of the upper Niger River valley. **2.** The Mande language of this people.

bam·bi·no (băm-bē′nō, bäm-) *n., pl.* **-nos** or **-ni** (-nē). **1.** A child; baby. **2.** A representation of the infant Jesus. [Italian, diminutive of *bambo,* child, fool. See **baba-** in Appendix.*]

bam·boo (băm-bo͞o′) *n., pl.* **-boos. 1.** Any of various mostly tropical grasses of the genus *Bambusa,* having hard-walled stems with ringed joints. **2.** The hollow woody stems of these plants, used in a variety of constructions, crafts, and manufactures. **3.** Any of various tall, bamboolike grasses of the genera *Arundinaria, Phyllostachys,* and *Dendrocalamus.* [Probably from Malay *bambū.*] —**bam·boo′** *adj.*

bam·boo·zle (băm-bo͞o′zəl) *tr.v.* **-zled, -zling, -zles.** *Informal.* To trick or deceive by elaborate misinformation; hoodwink. See Synonyms at **deceive.** [Probably a cant variant of *bumbazzle,* from *bombace,* padding, BOMBAST.] —**bam·boo′zle·ment** *n.* —**bam·boo′zler** *n.*

ban[1] (băn) *tr.v.* **banned, banning, bans. 1.** To prohibit (something), especially by official decree. **2.** *Rare.* To heap curses upon; execrate. —*n.* **1.** In feudal times, a summons to arms. **2.** An excommunication or condemnation by church officials. **3.** A prohibition imposed by law or official decree. **4.** Censure through public opinion. **5.** A curse or imprecation. [Middle English *bannen,* to summon, banish, curse, partly from Old English *bannan,* to summon, proclaim, and partly from Old Norse *banna,* to prohibit, curse. See **bhā-**[2] in Appendix.*]

ban[2] (băn) *n.* Formerly, a provincial governor and warlord in Hungary, Croatia, or Slavonia. [Serbo-Croatian *bān,* lord, from Turkish, akin to *bayan,* rich.]

ban[3] (bän) *n., pl.* **bani** (bä′nē). A coin equal to 1/100 of the leu of Rumania. See table of exchange rates at **currency.** [Rumanian, from Serbo-Croatian *bān,* BAN (warlord).]

ba·nal (bə-näl′, -năl′, bā′nəl) *adj.* Repeating a worn-out convention or type; unaffecting and drearily predictable: *"a classical oedipal fantasy if you like, but if it were only this the story would be banal."* (Selma Fraiberg). See Synonyms at **trite.** [French, commonplace, from Old French, shared (as by tenants in a feudal jurisdiction), from *ban,* summons to military service, from Frankish *ban* (unattested). See **bhā-**[2] in Appendix.*] —**ba·nal′i·ty** (bə-năl′ə-tē, bā-) *n.* —**ba·nal′ly** *adv.*

ba·nan·a (bə-năn′ə) *n.* **1.** Any of several treelike tropical or subtropical plants of the genus *Musa;* especially, *M. sapientum,* a widely cultivated species having long, broad leaves and hanging clusters of edible fruit. **2.** The crescent-shaped fruit of any of these plants, having white, pulpy flesh and thick, easily removed yellow or reddish skin. [Portuguese and Spanish, from a native West African name.]

banana oil. 1. A liquid mixture of nitrocellulose and amyl acetate, or a similar solvent, having a bananalike odor. **2.** An organic compound, **amyl acetate** *(see).* **3.** *Slang.* Insincere flattery; nonsensical exaggeration.

Ba·na·ras. A former name for **Varanasi.**

ban·co (băng′kō, bäng′-) *n., pl.* **-cos.** A bet in certain gambling games for the entire amount the banker offers to accept. —*interj.* Used to announce this bet. [Italian *banco, banca,* BANK (financial establishment).]

Ban·croft (băn′krôft′), **George.** 1800–1891. American historian and diplomat; founder of U.S. Naval Academy (1845).

band[1] (bănd) *n.* **1.** A thin strip of flexible material used to encircle and bind one object or to hold a number of objects together. **2.** A narrow strip of fabric used to trim, finish, or reinforce articles of clothing. Often used in combination: *a waistband.* **3.** Any strip or stripe that contrasts with its surroundings in color, texture, or material. **4. a.** A neckband or collar. **b.** *Plural.* The two strips hanging from the front of a collar as part of the dress of certain clergymen, scholars, and lawyers. **c.** A high collar popular in the 16th and 17th centuries. **5.** *Biology.* Any chromatically or functionally differentiated strip or stripe in or on an organism. **6.** *Physics.* **a.** A range of some physical variable, as of radiation wavelength or frequency. **b.** A range of very closely spaced electron energy levels in solids, the distribution and nature of which determine the electrical properties of a material. **7.** *Bookbinding.* The cords across the back of a book, to which the quires or sheets are attached. —*tr.v.* **banded, banding, bands. 1.** To tie, bind, or encircle with a band. **2.** To mark or identify with a band. [Middle English, from Old French *bande,* bond, tie, link, from Germanic. See **bhendh-** in Appendix.*]

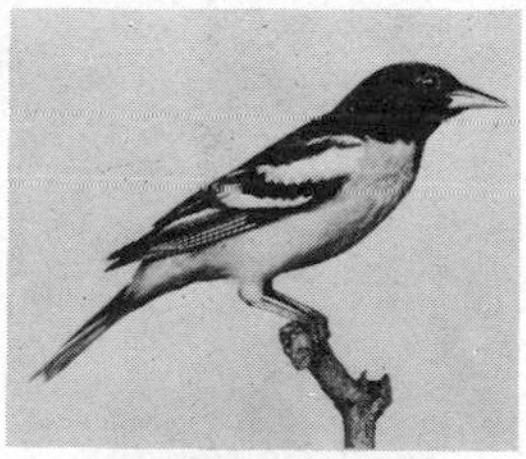

Baltimore oriole
A male of the species

band[2] (bănd) *n.* **1. a.** A group of people joined in a common purpose. **b.** A group of animals. **2.** A group of musicians who play together. —*v.* **banded, banding, bands.** —*tr.* To assemble or unite in a group. —*intr.* To form a group; unite. Often used with *together: to band together for warmth.* [Old French *bande,* a troop, from Italian *banda,* from Latin-Langobardic *bandum* (unattested), standard. See **bhā-**[1] in Appendix.*]

band[3] (bănd) *n.* **1.** *Usually plural.* A physical restraint; a manacle or fetter. **2.** A moral or legal restraint; a bond. [Middle English, from Old Norse. See **bhendh-** in Appendix.*]

band·age (băn′dĭj) *n.* A strip of fabric or other material used as a protective covering for a wound or other injury. —*tr.v.* **bandaged, -aging, -ages.** To apply such a covering to. [French, from *bande,* BAND (strip).] —**band′ag·er** *n.*

Band-Aid (bănd′ād′) *n.* A trademark for an adhesive bandage with a gauze pad in the center, used for protecting cuts.

ban·dan·na, ban·dan·a (băn-dăn′ə) *n.* A large handkerchief or scarf, usually brightly colored, and traditionally figured in white on red or blue. [Probably from Portuguese *bandana,* from Hindi *bāndhnū,* a dyeing process in which the cloth is tied at various points, from *bāndhnā,* to tie, from Sanskrit *bandhnāti.* See **bhendh-** in Appendix.*]

Ban·da O·ri·en·tal. The former name for **Uruguay.**

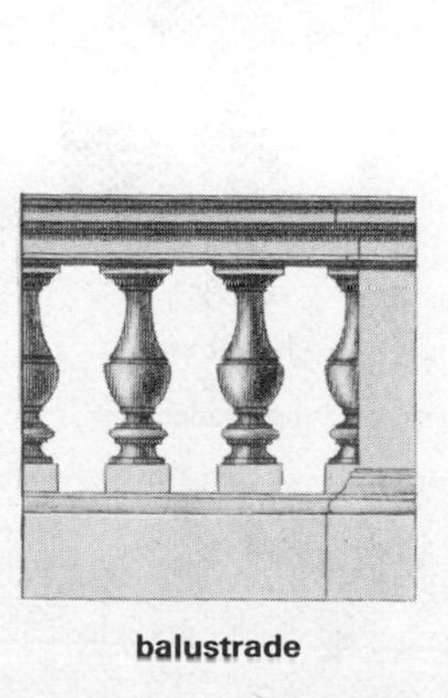

balustrade

banjo clock

Ban·da Sea (băn′də, bän′-). An arm of the Pacific Ocean, 625 miles long and 275 miles wide, in the Indonesian Archipelago, southeast of Sulawesi and north of Timor.

band·box (bănd′bŏks′) n. A lightweight, rounded box originally designed to hold collars but now used for any small articles of apparel.

ban·deau (băn-dō′) n., pl. **-deaux** (-dōz′) or **-deaus.** 1. A narrow band for the hair; a fillet. 2. A brassiere. [French, from Old French bandel, diminutive of bande, BAND (strip).]

ban·de·ril·la (băn′də-rē′ə, -rēl′yə; Spanish bän′dā-rē′lyä) n. In bullfighting, a decorated barbed dart that is thrust into the bull's neck or shoulder muscles by a banderillero. [Spanish, diminutive of bandera, banner, from Vulgar Latin bandāria (unattested), BANNER.]

ban·de·ril·le·ro (băn′də-rē-âr′ō, -rēl-yâr′ō; Spanish bän′dā-rē-lyä′rō) n., pl. **-ros.** In bullfighting, one whose role is to implant the banderillas. [Spanish, from BANDERILLA.]

ban·de·role, ban·de·rol (băn′də-rōl′) n. Also **ban·ne·rol** (băn′ə-rōl′). 1. A narrow forked flag or streamer attached to a staff or lance or flown from a masthead. 2. Art & Architecture. A representation of a ribbon or scroll bearing an inscription. 3. A square flag, sometimes carried at a funeral and placed over a tomb. [French, from Italian banderuola, diminutive of bandiera, banner, from Vulgar Latin bandāria (unattested), BANNER.]

ban·di·coot (băn′dĭ-kōōt′) n. 1. Any of several ratlike marsupials of the family Peramelidae, of Australia and adjacent islands, having a long, tapering snout and long hind legs. 2. Any of several large rats of the genera Bandicota and Nesokia, of southeastern Asia. In this sense, now usually called "bandicoot rat" and sometimes "mole-rat." [Telegu pandikokku : pandi, pig + kokku, bandicoot.]

ban·dit (băn′dĭt) n., pl. **-dits** or **banditti** (băn-dĭt′ē) (for sense 1). 1. A robber. 2. An outlaw; gangster. [Italian bandito, from the past participle of bandire, to band together, from Germanic. See bhā-¹ in Appendix.*] —**ban′dit·ry** n.

Ban·djer·ma·sin. The Dutch name for Banjarmasin.

band·mas·ter (bănd′măs′tər, -mäs′tər) n. One who conducts a musical band.

ban·dog (băn′dôg′, -dŏg′) n. A dog formerly kept chained as a watchdog or because of its ferocious nature. [Middle English band-dogge : BAND (fetter) + DOG.]

ban·do·leer, ban·do·lier (băn′də-lîr′) n. A belt fitted with small pockets or loops for carrying cartridges and worn across the chest by soldiers. [French bandoulière, from Spanish bandolera, from banda, sash, probably from Germanic. See bhā-¹ in Appendix.*]

ban·dore (băn′dôr′, -dōr′) n. Also **ban·do·ra** (băn-dôr′ə, -dōr′ə). An ancient musical instrument resembling a guitar. Also called "pandore." [Portuguese bandurra, from Late Latin pandūra, a three-stringed lute, from Greek pandoura. See pandoura in Appendix.*]

band-pass filter (bănd′păs′). An electric filter that blocks all signals but those within a selected frequency range.

band saw. A power saw consisting essentially of a toothed metal band coupled to and continuously driven around the circumferences of two wheels.

band shell. A bandstand equipped at the rear with a concave, almost hemispheric wall that serves as a sounding board.

bands·man (băndz′mən) n., pl. **-men** (-mĭn). A musician who plays an instrument in a band.

band·stand (bănd′stănd′) n. A platform for a band or orchestra, often roofed when outdoors.

Ban·dung (bän′dŏŏng). Dutch **Ban·doeng.** The third-largest city of Indonesia, situated in western Java, about 80 miles southeast of Djakarta. Population, 973,000.

band·wag·on (bănd′wăg′ən) n. 1. An elaborately decorated wagon used to transport musicians in a parade. 2. Informal. A cause or party that attracts increasing numbers of adherents. —**climb** (or **get**) **on the bandwagon.** Informal. To support or shift support to a party or cause whose fortunes appear to be rising.

ban·dy (băn′dē) tr.v. **bandied, bandying, bandies.** 1. To toss, throw, or strike back and forth: "A sunrise breeze bandied the curtains." (Truman Capote). 2. To give and take (words or blows); to exchange. 3. To discuss in a casual or frivolous manner. 4. To pass around or along indiscriminately. —adj. Bowed or bent in an outward curve: bandy legs. —n., pl. **bandies.** 1. A kind of field hockey; shinny. 2. A stick, bent at one end, used in playing this game. [Perhaps from Old French bander†, to bandy at tennis, oppose oneself against.]

ban·dy-leg·ged (băn′dē-lĕg′ĭd) adj. Having legs that bend outward; bowlegged. [From BANDY.]

bane (bān) n. 1. Poetic. Fatal injury or ruin. 2. A cause of death, destruction, or ruin. 3. A deadly poison. Used in combination: henbane; wolf's-bane. [Middle English bane, Old English bana, slayer, cause of death or destruction, ruin. See bhen- in Appendix.*]

flowers

bane·ber·ry (bān′bĕr′ē) n., pl. **-ries.** 1. Any plant of the genus Actaea, having clusters of white flowers and red or white poisonous berries. Sometimes called "cohosh." 2. A berry of any of these plants.

bane·ful (bān′fəl) adj. Full of venom or harm; destructive; pernicious: "Criticism is really, in itself, a baneful and injurious employment." (Matthew Arnold). See Usage note at baleful.

Banff (bămf). 1. Also **Banff·shire** (bămf′shîr, -shər). A county, 630 square miles in area, of northeastern Scotland. Population, 46,000. 2. The county seat of this county. 3. A resort town of Alberta, Canada, near Lake Louise in Banff National Park. Population, 3,500.

baneberry
Actaea alba
White baneberry

bang¹ (băng) n. 1. The sudden loud noise of an explosion. 2. A sudden loud impact or thump. 3. Informal. A sudden burst of action. 4. Slang. A sense of excitement; thrill. —v. **banged, banging, bangs.** —tr. 1. To hit noisily; strike heavily and repeatedly: "banging the table with his fist till the beer glasses danced" (Frank Norris). 2. To close suddenly and loudly; to slam. 3. To handle noisily or violently: bang the dishes in the sink. 4. Vulgar Slang. To have sexual intercourse with (a woman). —intr. 1. To make a sudden loud noise, as in an explosion. 2. To crash noisily against or into something. —adv. 1. With a bang. 2. Exactly; precisely: The arrow hit bang on the target. [Probably from Scandinavian, akin to Old Norse bang, a hammering. See bheg- in Appendix.*]

bang² (băng) n. Hair cut straight across the forehead, near eyebrow level. Often used in the plural. —tr.v. **banged, banging, bangs.** To cut (hair) straight across. [Perhaps ultimately from Old Norse banga, to cut off (perhaps imitative).]

bang³. Variant of bhang.

Ban·ga·lore (băng′gə-lôr′). The capital of Mysore, Republic of India, 190 miles west of Madras. Population, 947,000.

ban·ga·lore torpedo (băng′gə-lôr′). A piece of metal pipe filled with an explosive, used primarily to clear a path through barbed wire or to detonate land mines. [From BANGALORE.]

Bang·ka (băng′kə). Also **Ban·ka.** An island of Indonesia, 4,610 square miles in area, off the southeastern coast of Sumatra. Population, 205,000.

bang·kok (băng′kŏk′, băng-kŏk′) n. 1. A fine straw used to make hats. 2. A hat made of this straw. [The hat is manufactured in BANGKOK.]

Bang·kok (băng′kŏk′, băng-kŏk′). Thai **Krung Thep** (krŏŏng′ tāp′). The capital of Thailand, 23 miles up the Chao Phraya River from the Gulf of Siam. Population, 1,669,000.

ban·gle (băng′gəl) n. 1. A rigid bracelet or anklet, especially one with no clasp. 2. An ornament hung from a bracelet, necklace, or the like. [Hindi bangri†, glass bracelet.]

Ban·gor (băng′gôr, -gər). A river port and city of southern Maine, on the Penobscot River. Population, 39,000.

bang·tail (băng′tāl′) n. Slang. A racehorse. [Probably BANG (cut) + TAIL.]

Ban·gui (bäng′gə). The capital and largest city of the Central African Republic, on the Ubangi River, about 640 miles northeast of Brazzaville. Population, 111,000.

Bang·we·u·lu (băng′wə-ōō′lōō). A shallow, swampy lake, about 50 miles long, in northeastern Zambia, central Africa.

ba·ni. Plural of ban (coin).

ban·ian¹ (băn′yən) n. 1. A Hindu merchant or trader belonging to a caste whose members eat no meat. 2. A loose shirt, jacket, or gown worn in India. [Portuguese, from Gujarati vāṇiyo, from Sanskrit vāṇija, merchant. See wen- in Appendix.*]

ban·ian². Variant of banyan.

ban·ish (băn′ĭsh) tr.v. **-ished, -ishing, -ishes.** 1. To force to leave a country or place by official decree; exile. 2. To drive away; expel: "The radiance of the first plum blossoms could banish winter from her bones." (Oliver Statler). [Middle English banishen, from Old French banir (present stem baniss-), from Vulgar Latin bannire (unattested), from Germanic. See bhā-² in Appendix.*] —**ban′ish·er** n. —**ban′ish·ment** n.

Synonyms: banish, exile, expatriate, deport, transport, extradite. These verbs mean to send away from a place of residence. Banish applies broadly to forced departure from a country by official decree. Exile specifies departure from one's country, either through compulsion or voluntary action. Expatriate pertains to departure from one's native country, forced or voluntary, and usually implies formal change of citizenship. Deport denotes the act of sending an alien abroad by governmental order. Transport pertains to the sending abroad (usually to a penal colony) of one convicted of a crime. Extradite applies to the delivery of an accused or convicted person to the state or country having jurisdiction over him.

ban·is·ter (băn′ĭ-stər) n. Also **ban·nis·ter.** 1. A baluster. 2. Often plural. The handrail or balustrade of a staircase. [Variant of BALUSTER.]

Ban·jer·ma·sin (băn′jər-mä′sĭn). Dutch **Ban·djer·ma·sin.** A city of Indonesia, on Borneo, in southeastern Kalimantan. Population, 214,000.

ban·jo (băn′jō) n., pl. **-jos** or **-joes.** A fretted stringed instrument, probably invented in the United States, having a hollow circular body with a stretched diaphragm of vellum upon which the bridge rests, and a narrow neck. [Southern Negro pronunciation of BANDORE.] —**ban′jo·ist** n.

banjo clock. A large, pendulum clock having a shape suggestive of a banjo.

bank¹ (băngk) n. 1. Any piled-up mass, as of snow or clouds; a mound; ridge. 2. A steep natural incline. 3. An artificial embankment. 4. Often plural. The slope of land adjoining a body of water, especially adjoining a lake, river, or sea. 5. Often plural. A large elevated area of a sea floor. 6. Billiards. The cushion of a billiard or pool table. 7. Aviation. The lateral tilting of an aircraft executed in a turn. —See Synonyms at shoal. —v. **banked, banking, banks.** —tr. 1. To border or protect with a ridge or embankment. 2. To pile up; amass: bank earth along a wall. 3. To cover (a fire) with ashes, fresh fuel, or the like to insure continued low burning. 4. To construct with a slope rising to the outside edge. 5. Aviation. To tilt (an aircraft) laterally in flight. 6. Billiards. To strike (a ball) so that it rebounds from the table's cushion. —intr. 1. To take the form of or rise in a bank or banks. 2. Aviation. To tilt an aircraft laterally when turning. [Middle English banke, probably from Old Danish banke, sandbank. See bheg- in Appendix.*]

bank[2] (băngk) *n. Abbr.* **bk. 1.** A business establishment authorized to perform one or more of the following services: receive and safeguard money and other valuables; lend money at interest; execute bills of exchange, such as checks and drafts; purchase and exchange foreign currency; and issue notes of circulation or currency. **2.** The offices or building in which such an establishment is located. **3. a.** The funds owned by a gambling establishment. **b.** The funds held by a dealer or banker in some gambling games. **4.** The reserve pieces, cards, chips, or play money in some games from which the players may draw, as in poker or dominoes. **5.** A supply or stock for use in emergencies: *a blood bank.* **6.** Any place of safekeeping or storage. **7.** *Obsolete.* A moneychanger's table or place of business. *—v.* **banked, banking, banks.** *—tr.* To deposit (money) in a bank. *—intr.* **1.** To transact business with a bank; maintain a bank account. **2.** To operate a bank. **3.** To hold the bank in some gambling games. **4.** *Informal.* To have confidence in. Used with *on.* —See Synonyms at **rely.** [French *banque,* from Italian *banca,* bench, moneychanger's table, from Old High German *banc.* See **bheg-** in Appendix.*]

bank[3] (băngk) *n.* **1.** A set of similar or matched things arranged in a row: *a bank of elevators.* **2.** A row of keys on a keyboard. **3.** *Nautical.* **a.** A bench for rowers in a galley. **b.** A row of oars in a galley. **4.** *Journalism.* The lines of type under a headline. **5.** *Printing.* A slanting table on which type matter in galleys or sheets is stored or corrected before being made up in pages. *—tr.v.* **banked, banking, banks.** To arrange or set up in a row: *"Every street was banked with purple-blooming trees"* (Doris Lessing). [Middle English *bank,* from Old French *banc,* from Germanic. See **bheg-** in Appendix.*]

Ban·ka. See **Bangka.**

bank·a·ble (băng'kə-bəl) *adj.* Acceptable to or at a bank.

bank acceptance. A draft or bill of exchange drawn upon and accepted by a bank. Also called "banker's acceptance."

bank account. Funds deposited in a bank that are credited to and subject to withdrawal by the depositor.

bank annuities. *British.* **Consols** *(see).*

bank barn. A barn built into a hillside as protection against wind and cold, with a back entrance at the second-floor level.

bank·book (băngk'bŏŏk') *n.* A book held by a depositor in which his deposits and withdrawals are recorded by his bank. Also called "passbook."

bank discount. The interest on a loan, computed in advance, and deducted at the time the loan is made.

bank·er[1] (băng'kər) *n.* **1.** A person who owns or serves as an officer of a bank. **2.** The player in charge of the bank in some gambling games.

bank·er[2] (băng'kər) *n.* A person or boat engaged in cod fishing on the Newfoundland banks.

bank·er[3] (băng'kər) *n.* A workbench used by masons and sculptors.

bank holiday. 1. A weekday on which the banks are legally closed. **2.** *British.* One of five days regarded as legal holidays, when banks are ordered to remain closed.

bank·ing (băng'kĭng) *n. Abbr.* **bkg.** The business of a bank or the occupation of a banker.

bank note. A note issued by an authorized bank representing its promise to pay a specific sum to the bearer on demand and acceptable as money. Also called "bank bill."

bank paper. 1. Bank notes. **2.** Securities, drafts, bills of exchange, and other commercial paper acceptable by a bank.

bank rate. The rate of discount established by a country's central bank or banks.

bank·roll (băngk'rōl') *n.* **1.** A roll of paper money. **2.** *Informal.* A person's ready cash. *—tr.v.* **bankrolled, -rolling, -rolls.** *Slang.* To underwrite the expense of (a show, for example).

bank·rupt (băngk'rŭpt', -rəpt) *n. Abbr.* **bkpt. 1.** *Law.* An individual or corporate debtor, who, upon voluntary petition or one invoked by his creditors, is judged legally insolvent and whose remaining property is thereafter administered for his creditors or distributed among them in accordance with law. **2.** Any person unable to pay his creditors in full. **3.** One depleted of some resource or quality: *an intellectual bankrupt.* *—adj.* **1.** Subject to legal procedure because of insolvency; legally declared a bankrupt. **2.** Financially ruined; impoverished. **3.** Depleted; destitute: *bankrupt in manners.* *—tr.v.* **bankrupted, -rupting, -rupts.** To cause to become bankrupt. [French *banqueroute,* from Italian *banca rotta,* "broken counter," symbol of an insolvent moneychanger : *banca,* moneychanger's table (see **bank,** financial) + *rotta,* past participle of *rompere,* to break, from Latin *rumpere* (see **reup-** in Appendix*).] **—bank'rupt·cy** *n.*

bankrupt worm. A roundworm of the genus *Trichostrongylus* that causes gastroenteritis in sheep and cattle. [So called because it can bring bankruptcy to cattle raisers.]

Banks (băngks), Sir **Joseph.** 1743–1820. British botanist; circumnavigated the world with James Cook.

Banks Island (băngks). The westernmost island of the Arctic Archipelago, occupying 26,400 square miles.

ban·ner (băn'ər) *n.* **1.** A piece of cloth attached to a staff and used as a standard by a monarch, knight, or military commander. **2. a.** The flag of a nation, state, army, or sovereign. **b.** An ensign bearing a motto or legend, as of a club. **3.** *Journalism.* A headline spanning the width of a newspaper page. **4.** *Botany.* A type of petal, a **standard** *(see).* *—adj.* Outstanding; superior. [Middle English *banere,* from Old French *baniere,* from Vulgar Latin *bandāria* (unattested), from Late Latin *bandum,* standard, from Germanic. See **bhā-**[1] in Appendix.*]

ban·ner·et[1] (băn'ər-ĭt, -ə-rĕt') *n.* Also **ban·ner·ette** (băn'ə-rĕt'). A small banner. [Middle English *baneret,* from Old French *banerete,* diminutive of *baniere,* BANNER.]

ban·ner·et[2] (băn'ər-ĭt, -ə-rĕt') *n.* **1.** A feudal knight entitled to lead men into battle under his own standard. **2.** The rank of such a knight, between knight bachelor and baron. Also called "knight banneret." [Middle English *baneret,* from Old French, "bannered," from *baniere,* BANNER.]

ban·ner·ol. Variant of **banderole.**

ban·nis·ter. Variant of **banister.**

ban·nock (băn'ək) *n.* Also **bon·nock** (bŏn'ək). *Scottish & British Regional.* A griddlecake, usually unleavened, made of oatmeal, barley, or wheat flour. [Middle English *bannok,* Old English *bannuc*†.]

Ban·nock·burn (băn'ək-bûrn', băn'ək-bûrn'). A town in Stirlingshire, Scotland, near which Robert the Bruce defeated the English under Edward II (June 1314).

banns (bănz) *pl.n.* Also **bans.** A spoken or published announcement in a church of an intended marriage. [Middle English *banes,* plural of *bane, ban,* proclamation, partly from Old English *gebann* and partly from Old French *ban,* from Frankish *ban* (unattested). See **bhā-**[2] in Appendix.*]

ban·quet (băng'kwĭt) *n.* **1.** An elaborate and sumptuous repast. **2.** A ceremonial dinner honoring a particular guest or occasion. *—v.* **banqueted, -queting, -quets.** *—tr.* To entertain at a banquet. *—intr.* To partake of a banquet; to feast. [Old French, diminutive of *banc,* bench, from Germanic. See **bheg-** in Appendix.*] **—ban'quet·er** *n.*

ban·quette (băng-kĕt') *n.* **1.** *Military.* A platform lining a trench or parapet wall where soldiers may stand when firing. **2.** *Southern U.S.* A sidewalk. **3.** A long upholstered bench, either placed against or built into a wall. **4.** Any ledge or shelf, as on a buffet. [French, from Provençal *banqueta,* diminutive of *banca,* bench, from Germanic. See **bheg-** in Appendix.*]

ban·shee (băn'shē) *n.* Also **ban·shie.** A female spirit in Gaelic folklore believed to presage a death in the family by wailing outside the house. [Irish Gaelic *bean sídhe,* "woman of the fairies," from Old Irish *ben síde* : *ben,* woman (see **gwen-** in Appendix*) + *síde*†, fairy folk.]

ban·tam (băn'təm) *n.* **1.** Any of various breeds of diminutive domestic fowl. **2.** A small but aggressive person. *—adj.* **1.** Diminutive; miniature. **2.** Spirited or aggressive. [From the belief that the fowl were native to BANTAM.]

Ban·tam (băn'təm). A town in northwestern Java that was the site of the first Dutch settlement in the East Indies.

ban·tam·weight (băn'təm-wāt') *n.* A boxer in the weight class of 112 to 118 pounds.

ban·ter (băn'tər) *n.* Good-humored teasing; playful repartee. *—v.* **bantered, -tering, -ters.** *—tr.* To tease or mock gently. *—intr.* To exchange mildly teasing remarks. [Origin obscure.] **—ban'ter·er** *n.* **—ban'ter·ing·ly** *adv.*

Ban·ting (băn'tĭng), Sir **Frederick Grant.** 1891–1941. Canadian physiologist; discovered insulin with C.H. **Best** *(see).*

bant·ling (bănt'lĭng) *n.* A young child. [Possibly a variant of German *Bänkling,* bastard, from *Bank,* bench (i.e., "a child begotten on a bench"), from Old High German *banc.* See **bheg-** in Appendix.*]

Ban·tu (băn'tōō) *n., pl.* **Bantu** or **-tus. 1.** A member of any of several Negro tribes of central and southern Africa. **2.** A family of languages spoken by the Bantu, including Kongo, Luba, Kikuyu, Luganda, Nyanja, Swahili, and Zulu. [Bantu *Ba-ntu,* "people" : *ba-,* plural prefix + *ntu,* "man."] **—Ban'tu** *adj.*

ban·yan (băn'yən) *n.* Also **ban·ian.** A tree, *Ficus benghalensis,* of tropical India and the East Indies, having large, oval leaves, reddish fruit, and many aerial roots that develop into additional trunks. [From BANIAN, after one such tree near Bandar Abbas, Iran, beneath which Banians had built a pagoda.]

ban·zai (bän'zī') *n.* A Japanese battle cry, patriotic cheer, or greeting. [Japanese, "(may you live) ten thousand years," from Chinese *wan⁴ sui⁴* : *wan⁴,* ten thousand + *sui⁴,* year.]

banzai attack. A desperate, suicidal attack used by Japanese troops in World War II. Also called "banzai charge."

ba·o·bab (bā'ō-băb', bä'-) *n.* A tree, *Adansonia digitata,* of tropical Africa, having a trunk up to 30 feet in diameter, large, pendulous white flowers, and hard-shelled, fleshy fruit called "monkey bread." [Probably a native Central African name.]

Bao Dai (bou' dī'). Title of Nguyen Vinh Thuy. Born 1913. Emperor of Annam (1925–45) and of Viet Nam (1949–55).

Bap., Bapt. Baptist.

bap·tism (băp'tĭz'əm) *n.* **1.** A Christian sacrament, symbolic of spiritual regeneration, in which, as a result of the use of water and the recital of a form of words, the recipient is cleansed of original sin and admitted into Christianity or a specific Christian church. **2.** Any ceremony, trial, or experience by which one is initiated, purified, or given a name. **3.** *Christian Science.* A submergence in Spirit or purification by Spirit. [Middle English *bapteme,* from Old French *bapteme, baptesme,* from Late Latin *baptisma,* from Greek, from *baptizein,* to BAPTIZE.] **—bap·tis'mal** (-məl) *adj.* **—bap·tis'mal·ly** *adv.*

baptism of fire. 1. A soldier's first experience of actual combat conditions. **2.** Any severe ordeal experienced for the first time.

Bap·tist (băp'tĭst) *n. Abbr.* **Bap., Bapt. 1.** A member of any of various Protestant denominations believing that the sacrament of baptism should be given only to adult members upon a profession of faith and usually by immersion. **2.** *Small* **b.** One who baptizes. **—the Baptist.** John the Baptist. **—Bap'tist** *adj.*

bap·tis·ter·y (băp'tĭs-trē) *n., pl.* **-ies.** Also **bap·tis·try. 1.** A part of a church, or a separate building, used for baptizing. **2.** A font used for baptism. **3.** A tank for baptizing by total immersion used in Baptist churches.

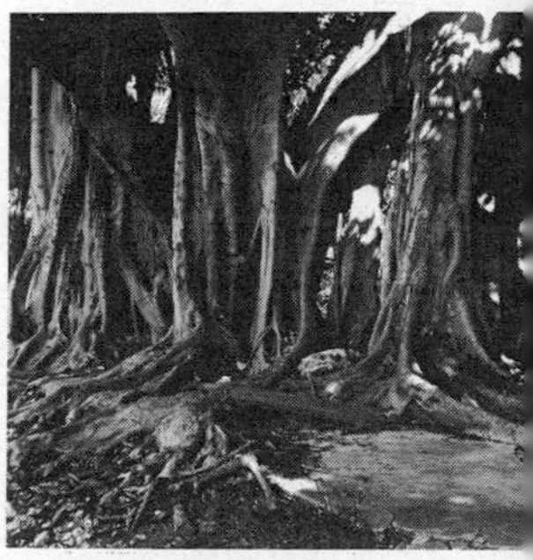

banyan

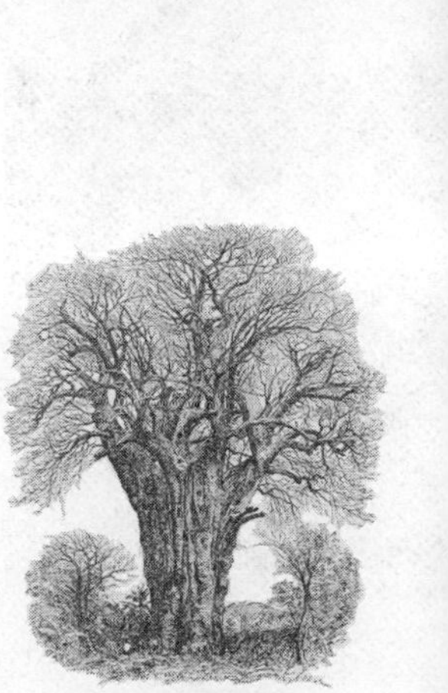

baobab

t tight/th thin, path/*th* this, bathe/ŭ cut/ûr urge/v valve/w with/y yes/z zebra, size/zh vision/ə about, item, edible, gallop, circus/ à *Fr.* ami/œ *Fr.* feu, *Ger.* schön/ü *Fr.* tu, *Ger.* über/KH *Ger.* ich, *Scot.* loch/N *Fr.* bon. ***Follows main vocabulary.** †**Of obscure origin.**

bap·tize (băp-tīz′, băp′tīz′) *v.* **-tized, -tizing, -tizes.** —*tr.* **1.** To dip or immerse in water or to sprinkle water on (a person) during a baptismal ceremony. **2. a.** To cleanse or purify. **b.** To initiate. **3.** To give a first or Christian name to. —*intr.* To administer baptism. [Middle English *baptizen,* from Old French *baptiser,* from Late Latin *baptizāre,* from Greek *baptizein,* from *baptein,* to dip. See **gwebh-**[1] in Appendix.*] —**bap·tiz′er** *n.*

bar[1] (bär) *n.* **1.** A relatively long, straight, rigid piece of any solid material used, for example, as a fastener, support, barrier, or structural or mechanical member. **2. a.** A solid oblong block of a substance, such as soap or candy. **b.** A rectangular block of a precious metal. **c.** A unit of quantity based on such a block. **3.** Anything that impedes or prevents; an obstacle. **4.** A sandbar. **5.** A stripe or band, such as one formed by light or color. **6.** *Heraldry.* A pair of horizontal parallel lines drawn across a shield. **7.** *Law.* **a.** The nullifying, defeating, or preventing of a claim or action. **b.** The process by which this is done. **8.** The railing in a courtroom enclosing the part of the room where the judges and lawyers sit, witnesses are heard, and prisoners are tried. **9.** A particular system of law courts. **10.** Any tribunal or place of judgment. **11. a.** Lawyers collectively. **b.** The profession of law. **12.** *Music.* **a.** A vertical line dividing a staff into equal measures. **b.** A measure. **c.** A **double bar** *(see).* **13. a.** A counter at which drinks, usually alcoholic, and sometimes meals are served. **b.** An establishment or room containing such a counter. —See Synonyms at **obstacle, shoal.** —*tr.v.* **barred, barring, bars. 1.** To fasten securely with a bar. **2.** To shut in or out with or as if with bars. **3.** To obstruct or impede; to block. **4.** To exclude. **5.** To mark with bars or stripes. **6.** *Music.* To indicate measures by using bars. **7.** *Law.* To stop (an action or claim) by legal objection. —See Synonyms at **hinder.** —*prep.* Excluding; except for; barring: *That was his best performance, bar none.* [Middle English *barre,* from Old French, from Vulgar Latin (unattested) *barra*†.]

bar[2] (bär) *n.* A unit of pressure equal to 10^5 newtons per square meter or 0.98697 standard atmosphere. See **measurement.** [German, from Greek *baros,* weight. See **gwer-**[2] in Appendix.*]

BAR Browning automatic rifle.

bar. 1. barometer; barometric. **2.** barrel.

Ba·rab·bas (bə-răb′əs). A condemned thief whose release was demanded of Pilate by the multitude instead of that of Jesus. Mark 15:6–11, John 18:40.

Bar·a·nof Island (băr′ə-nôf′). An island, 1,607 square miles in area, of the Alexander Archipelago of Alaska.

Ba·ra·nov (bŭ-rä′nəf, băr′ə-nŏf′), **Aleksandr Andreevich.** 1746–1819. Russian fur trader in Alaska; first governor of Russian America.

Bá·rá·ny (bä′rän′yə), **Robert.** 1876–1936. Austrian otologist.

Bar·a·tar·i·a Bay (băr′ə-târ′ē-ə). An inlet of the Gulf of Mexico in the Mississippi delta in Louisiana, used as headquarters by Jean Laffite (about 1809–14).

bar·a·the·a (băr′ə-thē′ə) *n.* A soft fabric of silk and cotton or silk and wool. [From *Barathea,* a former trademark.]

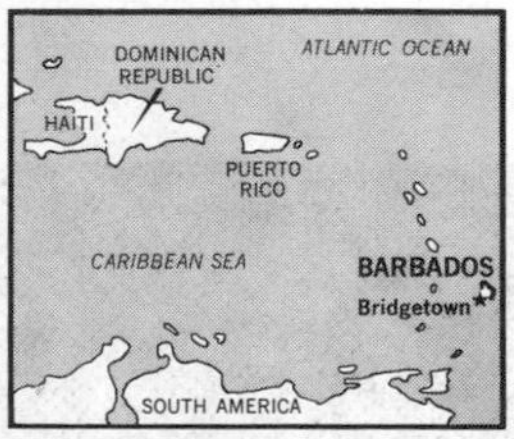

Barbados

barb[1] (bärb) *n.* **1.** A sharp point projecting in reverse direction to the main point of a weapon or tool, as on an arrow, fishhook, or spear. **2.** A cutting or biting remark. **3.** *Botany.* A hooked bristle or hairlike projection. **4.** *Ornithology.* One of the many parallel filaments projecting from the main shaft of a feather. **5.** Any of various Old World freshwater fishes of the genus *Barbus* (or *Puntius*) and related genera, many of which are popular in home aquariums. **6.** *Obsolete.* A beard. **7.** A white linen covering for a woman's head, throat, and chin, worn in medieval times. —*tr.v.* **barbed, barbing, barbs.** To provide or furnish with a barb or barbs. [Middle English *barbe,* beard, beardlike appendage, from Old French, from Latin *barba,* beard. See **bhardhā** in Appendix.*]

barb[2] (bärb) *n.* **1.** A horse of a breed introduced into Spain from northern Africa by the Moors. **2.** One of a breed of domestic pigeons having dark plumage. [French *barbe,* Barbary horse, from Italian *barbero,* from *Barberia,* BARBARY.]

Bar·ba·dos (bär-bā′dōs, -dəs). *Abbr.* **Barb.** The easternmost island of the West Indies, 166 square miles in area, a former British colony independent since 1966, lying about 100 miles east of St. Vincent. Population, 245,000. Capital, Bridgetown.

Barbados cherry. A tropical and semitropical American shrub, *Malpighia glabra,* bearing edible, acid red fruit.

Barbados gooseberry. A cactus, the **blade-apple** *(see).*

Bar·ba·ra (bär′brə, -bər-ə). A feminine given name. [Latin, feminine of *barbarus,* foreign, BARBAROUS.]

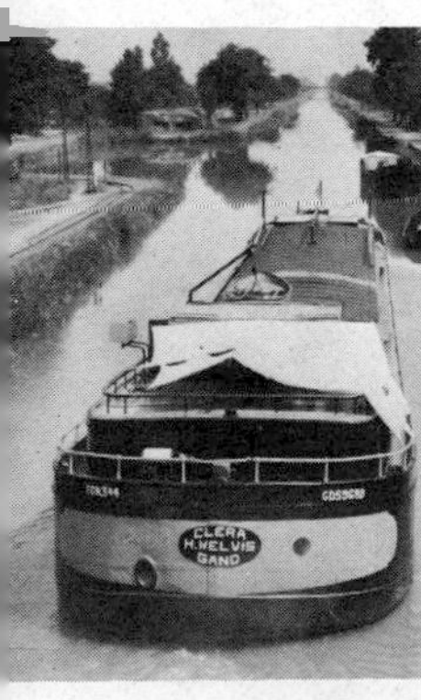
barge
On the Rhône-Rhine Canal in eastern France

bar·bar·i·an (bär-bâr′ē-ən) *n.* **1.** Originally, a foreigner; especially, one not Greek or Roman and therefore regarded as uncivilized. **2.** One belonging to a people or tribe considered to have a primitive civilization. **3.** A fierce, brutal, or cruel person. **4.** An insensitive, uncultured person; boor: *"he is merely a barbarian on the loose in a museum"* (Yvor Winters). —*adj.* Characteristic of or resembling a barbarian; rough and uncivilized. [French *barbarien,* from Latin *barbaria,* foreign country, from *barbarus,* BARBAROUS.] —**bar·bar′i·an·ism′** *n.*

bar·bar·ic (bär-băr′ĭk) *adj.* **1.** Of, pertaining to, or characteristic of a barbarian or barbarians. **2.** Marked by crudeness or wildness of taste, style, or manner.

bar·ba·rism (bär′bə-rĭz′əm) *n.* **1.** An instance, act, trait, or custom characterized by brutality or coarseness. **2. a.** The use of words or forms considered incorrect or nonstandard in a language. **b.** A specific word or form so used. [Old French *barbarisme,* from Latin *barbarismus,* from Greek *barbarismos,* foreign or incorrect speech, from *barbaros,* foreign, BARBAROUS.]

Usage: Barbarism applies to an uncivilized condition generally, with emphasis on crudity of taste, and to crudity of expression in particular. *Barbarity* primarily denotes grossly cruel behavior.

bar·bar·i·ty (bär-băr′ə-tē) *n., pl.* **-ties. 1.** Harsh or cruel conduct. **2.** An inhuman, brutal act. **3.** Crudity; coarseness. —See Usage note at **barbarism.**

bar·ba·rize (bär′bə-rīz′) *v.* **-ized, -izing, -izes.** —*tr.* To make crude or barbarous; to corrupt. —*intr.* To become barbarous.

Bar·ba·ros·sa. See **Frederick I.**

Bar·ba·ros·sa (bär′bə-rŏs′ə), **Khair ed-Din.** 1466?–1546. Greek-born Turkish corsair; with his brother, **Koruk** (1474?–1518), raided Spanish ports and shipping; captured Algiers, Tunis, and Nice; virtually ruled the Mediterranean (1541–44).

bar·ba·rous (bär′bər-əs) *adj.* **1.** Primitive in culture and customs; uncivilized. **2.** Characterized by savagery; cruel; brutal. **3.** Lacking refinement or culture; coarse; boorish. **4.** Characteristic of language that violates classical or accepted usage standards. —See Synonyms at **cruel.** [Latin *barbarus,* from Greek *barbaros,* non-Greek, foreign, rude. See **baba-** in Appendix.*] —**bar′ba·rous·ly** *adv.* —**bar′ba·rous·ness** *n.*

Bar·ba·ry (bär′bə-rē). A region of northern Africa stretching from Egypt's western border to the Atlantic Ocean.

Barbary ape. A tailless monkey, *Macaca sylvana,* of Gibraltar and northern Africa. Also called "magot."

Bar·ba·ry Coast (bär′bə-rē). **1.** The Mediterranean coastal area of Barbary and the Barbary States. **2.** A district of San Francisco before the 1906 earthquake notorious for its brothels and gambling houses.

Barbary sheep. The **aoudad** *(see).*

Bar·ba·ry States (bär′bə-rē). Formerly, the collective name for Algeria, Tunisia, Tripoli, and, sometimes, Morocco, where piracy flourished until the early 19th century.

bar·bas·co (bär-bäs′kō) *n., pl.* **-cos.** Any of several tropical American trees of the genus *Lonchocarpus,* used locally as the source of a poison for killing fish. [American Spanish, from Spanish, perhaps from Latin *verbascum*†, a plant, mullein.]

bar·bate (bär′bāt′) *adj.* Having a beard, or tufted hairs resembling a beard. [Latin *barbātus,* from *barba,* beard. See **barb.**]

bar·be·cue (bär′bĭ-kyōō′) *n.* **1.** A grill, pit, or outdoor fireplace for roasting meat. **2. a.** A whole animal carcass or section thereof roasted over an open fire or on a spit. **b.** Any meat roasted or broiled in this fashion. **3.** A social gathering, usually held outdoors, at which food is prepared in this way. —*tr.v.* **barbecued, -cuing, -cues.** To roast, broil, or grill (meat) over live coals or an open fire, often basting it with a seasoned sauce. [American Spanish *barbacoa,* from Haitian Creole, framework of sticks set on posts, from Taino.]

barbed (bärbd) *adj.* **1.** Having a barb or barbs. **2.** Piercing or stinging: *a barbed statement.*

barbed wire. Twisted strands of fence wire with barbs at regular intervals. Also called "barbwire."

bar·bel (bär′bəl) *n.* **1.** One of the slender, whiskerlike sensory organs on the head of certain fishes, such as catfish. **2.** Any of several Old World freshwater fish of the genus *Barbus.* [Middle English, from Old French, from Late Latin *barbellus,* diminutive of *barbus,* barbel (the fish), from Latin *barba,* beard (from its beardlike fleshy filaments). See **bhardhā** in Appendix.*]

bar·bell (bär′bĕl′) *n.* A bar with adjustable weights at each end, lifted for sport or exercise. [BAR + BELL.]

bar·bel·late (bär′bə-lāt′, bär-bĕl′ĭt, -āt′) *adj.* Having minute, hooked bristles or hairs. [From New Latin *barbella,* short stiff hair, diminutive of Latin *barbula,* little beard, diminutive of *barba,* beard. See **bhardhā** in Appendix.*]

bar·ber (bär′bər) *n.* One whose business is to cut hair, and to shave or trim beards. —*tr.v.* **barbered, -bering, -bers. 1.** To cut the hair of. **2.** To shave or trim the beard of. [Middle English *barbour,* from Old French *barbeor,* from Medieval Latin *barbātor,* from *barba,* beard, from Latin. See **barbel.**]

Bar·ber (bär′bər), **Samuel.** Born 1910. American composer.

bar·ber·ry (bär′bĕr′ē) *n., pl.* **-ries.** Any of various shrubs of the genus *Berberis,* having small leaves, clusters of yellow flowers, and small orange or red berries. [Variant (influenced by BERRY) of Middle English *barbere,* from Old French *berberis, berbere,* from Arabic *barbāris.*]

bar·ber·shop (bär′bər-shŏp′) *n.* The place of business of a barber. —*adj. Informal.* Designating male voices singing sentimental songs in close harmony: *a barbershop quartet.*

barber's itch. Any of various skin eruptions on the neck, especially ringworm. Not in technical use.

bar·bet (bär′bĭt) *n.* Any of various tropical birds of the family Capitonidae, having a broad bill bristled at the base and brightly colored plumage, related to the toucans. [French, from Latin *barbātus,* BARBATE.]

bar·bette (bär-bĕt′) *n.* **1.** A platform or mound within a fort high enough to permit firing of guns over the parapet. **2.** An armored protective cylinder around a revolving turret on a warship. [French, diminutive of *barbe,* beard, from Old French, from Latin *barba.* See **bhardhā** in Appendix.*]

bar·bi·can (bär′bĭ-kən) *n.* A tower or other fortification on the approach to a castle or town, especially one at a gate or drawbridge. [Middle English, from Old French *barbacane,* from Medieval Latin *barbacana,* perhaps from Arabic *bâb-al-baqara,* "gate with holes."]

bar·bi·cel (bär′bə-sĕl′) *n. Ornithology.* One of many minute projections that fringe the edges of the barbules of feathers and interlock with those on adjacent barbules. [New Latin *barbicella,* diminutive of Latin *barba,* beard. See **bhardhā** in Appendix.*]

bar·bi·tal (bär′bə-tôl′) *n.* A white crystalline compound, $C_8H_{12}N_2O_3$, used as a sedative. [BARBIT(URIC ACID) + (VERON)AL.]

bar·bi·tu·rate (bär-bĭch′ər-ĭt, -ə-rāt′, bär′bə-to͝or′ĭt, -to͝or′āt′, -tyo͝or′ĭt, -tyo͝or′āt′) *n.* **1.** A salt or ester of barbituric acid. **2.** Any of a group of barbituric acid derivatives used as sedatives or hypnotics. [BARBITUR(IC ACID) + -ATE.]

bar·bi·tu·ric acid (bär′bə-to͝or′ĭk, -tyo͝or′ĭk). An organic acid, $C_4H_4N_2O_3$, used in the manufacture of barbiturates and some plastics. [Partial translation of German *Barbitursaure* : perhaps from the name BARBARA + UR(IC) + ACID.]

Bar·bi·zon school (bär′bə-zŏn′). A 19th-century group of landscape painters in France, among them Corot, Daubigny, Millet, and Rousseau. [From *Barbizon,* a small village near Paris, where they worked.]

Bar·bu·da (bär-bo͞o′də). An island, 62 square miles in area, in the Leeward Islands, 30 miles north of Antigua, from which it is administered as part of the West Indies Associated States.

bar·bule (bär′byo͞ol) *n. Biology.* A small barb or pointed projection; especially, one of the small projections fringing the edges of the barbs of feathers. [Latin *barbula,* diminutive of *barba,* beard. See **bhardhā** in Appendix.*]

barb·wire (bärb′wīr′) *n.* **Barbed wire** *(see).*

Bar·ca (bär′kə). The family name of many notables of ancient Carthage, including Hannibal and other Carthaginian generals.

bar·ca·role (bär′kə-rōl′) *n.* Also **bar·ca·rolle. 1.** A Venetian gondolier's song, with a rhythm suggestive of rowing. **2.** A musical composition imitating this. [French, from Italian *barcaruola,* from *barcaruolo,* gondolier, from *barca,* barge, from Late Latin *barca,* BARK (ship).]

Bar·ce·lo·na (bär′sə-lō′nə; *Spanish* bär′thā-lō′nä). **1.** A province of Spain, 2,968 square miles in area, in the northeast on the Mediterranean Sea. Population, 2,872,000. **2.** The capital of this province, Spain's principal seaport and industrial center. Population, 1,696,000.

B.Arch. Bachelor of Architecture.

bar chart. A **bar graph** *(see).*

bard[1] (bärd) *n.* **1.** One of an ancient Celtic order of singing poets who composed and recited verses on the legends and history of their tribes. **2.** Any poet, especially an exalted national poet. —See Synonyms at **poet.** [Middle English, from Gaelic and Irish *bárd* and Welsh *bardd.* See **gwerə-**[1] in Appendix.*] —**bard′ic** *adj.*

bard[2] (bärd) *n.* Also **barde.** Any piece of armor used to protect or ornament a horse. —*tr.v.* **barded, barding, bards.** To equip (a horse) with bards. [Old French *barde,* probably from Old Italian *barda,* from Arabic *barda'ah,* stuffed packsaddle.]

Bar·deen (bär-dēn′), **John.** Born 1908. American physicist; discovered the transistor effect with W.H. **Brattain** and W.B. **Shockley** *(see).*

Bard of Avon. William Shakespeare, so called because he was born and buried at Stratford-on-Avon.

bare[1] (bâr) *adj.* **barer, barest. 1.** Without the usual or appropriate covering or clothing; naked: *a bare head.* **2.** Exposed to view; undisguised: *He laid bare the secret agreements between the unions.* **3.** Lacking the usual furnishings, equipment, or decoration: *walls bare of pictures.* **4.** Without addition, adornment, or qualification; simple; plain: *the bare facts.* **5.** Just sufficient; mere: *the bare necessities of life.* **6.** *Obsolete.* Bareheaded. —See Synonyms at **empty.** —*tr.v.* **bared, baring, bares.** To make bare; strip of covering; reveal. —See Synonyms at **strip.** [Middle English *bare,* Old English *bær.* See **bhoso-** in Appendix.*] —**bare′ness** *n.*

bare[2]. *Archaic.* Past tense of **bear.**

bare·back (bâr′băk′) *adj.* Also **bare·backed** (bâr′băkt′). On a horse, pony, or other animal with no saddle: *a bareback rider.* —**bare′back′** *adv.*

bare·faced (bâr′fāst′) *adj.* **1. a.** Having no covering over the face. **b.** Having no beard. **2.** Unconcealed; without disguise. **3.** Presumptuous and shameless; brazen: *a barefaced lie.* —See Synonyms at **shameless.** —**bare′fac′ed·ly** (-fā′sĭd-lē, -fāst′lē) *adv.* —**bare′fac′ed·ness** *n.*

bare·foot (bâr′fo͝ot′) *adj.* Also **bare·foot·ed** (-fo͝ot′ĭd). Wearing nothing on the feet. —**bare′foot′** *adv.*

ba·rege (bə-rĕzh′) *n.* Also **ba·rège.** A sheer fabric woven of silk or cotton and wool, used for women's apparel. [French *barège,* first made in *Barèges,* France.]

bare·hand·ed (bâr′hăn′dĭd) *adj.* **1.** Having no covering on the hands. **2.** With the hands alone; unaided by tools or weapons. —**bare′hand′ed** *adv.*

bare·head·ed (bâr′hĕd′ĭd) *adj.* Having no head covering. —**bare′head′ed** *adv.*

Ba·reil·ly (bə-rā′lē). Also **Ba·re·li.** A commercial city of Uttar Pradesh, Republic of India. Population, 274,000.

bare·leg·ged (bâr′lĕg′ĭd, -lĕgd′) *adj.* Having the legs uncovered. —**bare′leg′ged** *adv.*

bare·ly (bâr′lē) *adv.* **1.** By a very little; hardly. **2.** Without disguise; openly. —See Synonyms at **hardly.**

Ba·rents (băr′ənts, bä′rənts), **Willem.** 1550?–1597. Dutch explorer of Arctic waters; sought Northeast Passage.

Ba·rents Sea (băr′ənts, bä′rənts). The part of the Arctic Ocean lying north of Norway and the Soviet Union, and south of Spitsbergen and Franz Josef Land.

bar·fly (bär′flī′) *n., pl.* **-flies.** *Slang.* One who frequents bars.

bar·gain (bär′gĭn) *n.* **1.** An agreement or contract, especially one involving the sale and purchase of goods or services. **2.** The terms or conditions of such an agreement: *"he met his part of the bargain by giving us what we had asked for"* (E.C. Dunn). **3.** The property acquired or services rendered as a result of such an agreement. **4.** Something offered or acquired at a price advantageous to the buyer. —**into the bargain.** Over and above what is expected. —**strike a bargain.** To agree on the terms of a purchase or joint undertaking. —*v.* **bargained, -gaining, -gains.** —*intr.* **1.** To negotiate the terms of a sale, exchange, or other agreement. **2.** To arrive at an agreement. —*tr.* To exchange; to trade: *He bargained his watch for a meal.* —**bargain for.** To expect; count on. [Middle English *bargaynen,* from Old French *bargaignier,* haggle in the market, probably from Germanic. See **bhergh-**[1] in Appendix.*] —**bar′gain·er** *n.*

barge (bärj) *n.* **1.** A long, large boat, usually flat-bottomed, unpowered, and towed by other craft, used for transporting freight. **2.** A large pleasure boat used for parties, pageants, or formal ceremonies. **3.** *Slang.* Any old or unwieldy boat or ship. **4.** *Naval.* A power boat reserved for the use of a flag officer. —*v.* **barged, barging, barges.** —*tr.* To carry by barge. —*intr. Informal.* **1.** To move about clumsily. **2.** To collide. Used with *into.* **3.** To enter rudely and abruptly; intrude. Used with *in* or *into.* [Middle English, from Old French *barge,* perhaps from Medieval Latin *barica* (unattested), from Greek *baris,* BARK (ship).]

barge·board (bärj′bôrd′, -bōrd′) *n. Architecture.* A board, often ornately carved, attached along the projecting edge of a gable roof. [Origin unknown.]

bar·gee (bär-jē′) *n. British.* A bargeman.

barge·man (bärj′mən) *n., pl.* **-men** (-mĭn). The master or a crew member of a barge.

bar·ghest (bär′gĕst) *n.* Also **bar·guest.** A goblin, often in the shape of a dog, believed to portend misfortune. [Perhaps dialectal *bargh,* ridge, from Middle English *bergh,* hill, Old English *beorg* (see **bhergh-**[2] in Appendix*) + dialectal *ghest,* variant of GHOST.]

bar graph. A graph consisting of parallel, usually vertical, bars or rectangles with lengths proportional to specified quantities in a set of data. Also called "bar chart."

Ba·ri (bä′rə). *Italian* **Ba·ri del·le Pu·glie** (bä′rə dĕl′lā po͞o′lyä). A city and Adriatic seaport of southeastern Italy. Population, 330,000.

ba·ril·la (bə-rēl′yə, -rē′yə) *n.* **1.** Either of two Old World plants, *Salsola kali* or *S. soda,* or a similar plant, *Halogeton soda,* burned to obtain a form of sodium carbonate. **2.** The sodium carbonate thus obtained. [Spanish *barrilla*†.]

bar·ite (bâr′īt′) *n.* A colorless crystalline mineral of barium sulfate that is the chief source of barium chemicals. Also called "barytes," "heavy spar." [Greek *barutēs,* weight, from *barus,* heavy. See **gwer-**[2] in Appendix.*]

bar·i·tone (băr′ə-tōn′) *n.* Also **bar·y·tone. 1.** A male singer or voice having a range higher than a bass and lower than a tenor. **2.** A part written for a voice having such a range. **3.** A brass wind instrument with a similar range. —*adj.* **1.** Of or pertaining to a baritone. **2.** Having the range of a baritone. [Italian *baritono,* from Greek *barutonos,* deep sounding : *barus,* heavy (see **gwer-**[2] in Appendix*) + *tonos,* pitch, TONE.]

bar·i·um (bâr′ē-əm, băr′-) *n. Symbol* **Ba** A soft, silvery-white, alkaline-earth metal, used to deoxidize copper, in various alloys, and in rat poison. Atomic number 56, atomic weight 137.34, melting point 725°C, boiling point 1,140°C, specific gravity 3.50, valence 2. See **element.** [From earlier *baryta,* variant of barytes, earlier form of BARITE.] —**bar′ic** *adj.*

barium sulfate. A fine white powder, $BaSO_4$, used as a pigment, as a filler for textiles, rubbers, and plastics, and as an indicator in x-ray photography of the digestive tract.

barium yellow. 1. A pigment made of barium chromate, $BaCrO_4$. **2.** Light or moderate greenish yellow to brilliant yellow. See **color.**

bark[1] (bärk) *n.* **1.** The harsh, abrupt sound uttered by a dog. **2.** Any sound similar to this, such as a gunshot or cough. —*v.* **barked, barking, barks.** —*intr.* **1.** To utter the harsh, abrupt cry of a dog. **2.** To make a sound similar to a bark. **3.** *Informal.* To cough. **4.** To speak sharply; to snap: *He barked at his assistant.* **5.** *Informal.* To work as a barker. —*tr.* To utter in a loud, harsh voice. —**bark up the wrong tree.** *Informal.* To wastefully misdirect one's energies. [From Middle English *berken,* to bark, Old English *beorcan.* See **bherg-** in Appendix.*]

bark[2] (bärk) *n.* **1.** The outer covering of the woody stems, branches, roots, and main trunks of trees and other woody plants, as distinguished from the cambium and inner wood. **2.** A specific kind of bark used for a special purpose, as in tanning or medicine. **3.** Dark olive brown. See **color.** —*tr.v.* **barked, barking, barks. 1.** To remove bark from (a tree or log). **2.** To rub off the skin of; to bruise. **3.** To cover or enclose with bark. **4.** To treat medically, tan, or dye using bark. [Middle English *barke,* from Old Norse *börkr,* from North Germanic *barkuz* (unattested).]

bark[3] (bärk) *n.* Also **barque. 1.** A sailing ship with from three to five masts, all of them square-rigged except the after mast, which is fore-and-aft rigged. Compare **barkentine. 2.** *Poetic.* Any boat, especially a small sailing vessel. [Middle English *barke,* boat, from Old French *barque,* probably from Italian *barca,* from Late Latin, small boat, bark, barge, from Greek *baris,* Egyptian barge, from Egyptian, akin to Coptic *barī,* barge.]

bark beetle. Any of various small insects of the family Scolytidae that damage trees by boring along the surface of the wood.

bar·keep·er (bär′kē′pər) *n.* Also **bar·keep** (bär′kēp′). **1.** A person who owns or runs a bar for the sale of alcoholic beverages. **2.** A bartender.

bar·ken·tine (bär′kən-tēn′) *n.* Also **bar·quen·tine.** A sailing ship

bark[2]

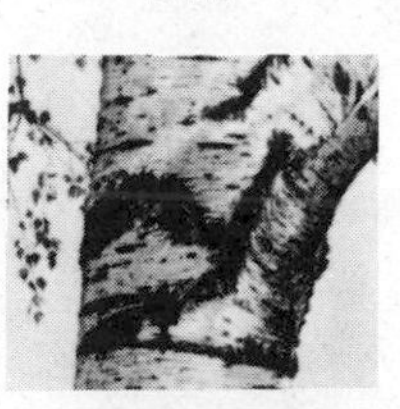
weeping birch

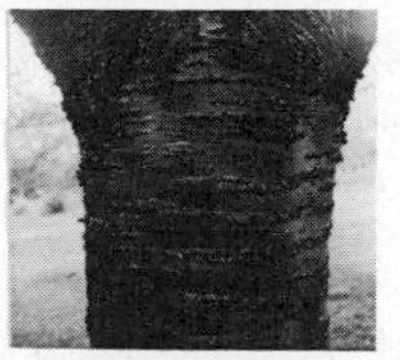
cherry

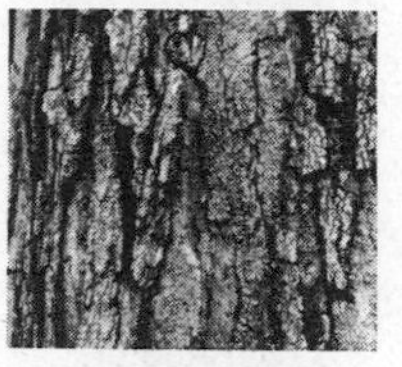
sugar maple

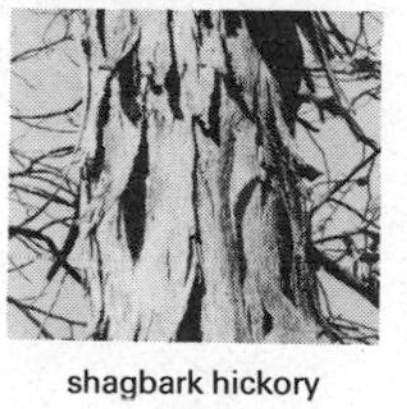
shagbark hickory

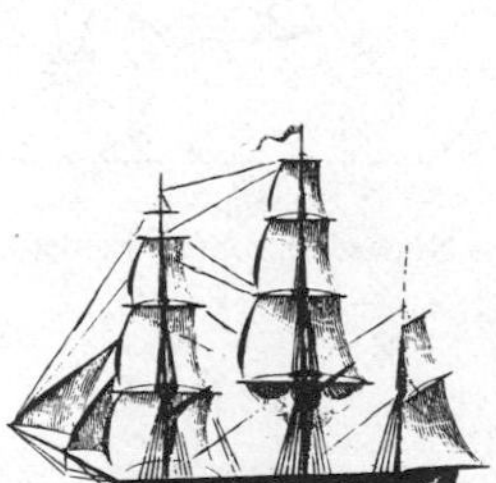
bark[3]

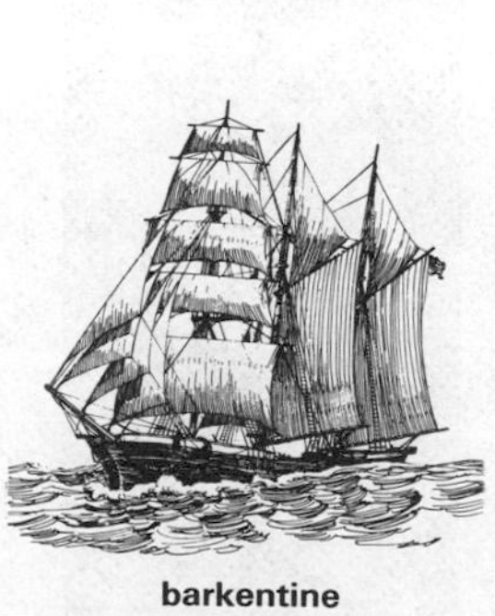
barkentine

with from three to five masts of which only the foremast is square-rigged, the other masts being fore-and-aft rigged. Compare **bark**. [Probably blend of BARK (boat) and BRIGANTINE.]

bark·er¹ (bär′kər) n. 1. One making a barking sound. 2. *Informal.* An employee who stands before the entrance to a show and solicits customers with loud, colorful sales talk.

bark·er² (bär′kər) n. 1. A workman who removes bark from trees or prepares it for tanning. 2. A machine that removes the bark from logs.

Bark·ing (bär′kĭng). A borough of London, England, comprising the former administrative divisions of Barking and Dagenham. Population, 179,000.

barking deer. The muntjac (*see*).

Bark·ley (bär′klē), **Alben William.** 1877–1956. Vice President of the United States under Harry S Truman (1949–53).

bark·y (bär′kē) adj. -ier, -iest. Covered with, containing, or resembling bark.

bar-le-duc (bär′lə-dook′) n. Also **Bar-le-Duc.** A savory preserve made of white currants or gooseberries and served with roast meat. [From *Bar-le-Duc,* town in northeastern France.]

bar·ley (bär′lē) n. 1. A cereal grass, *Hordeum vulgare,* bearing bearded flower spikes with edible seeds. 2. The grain of this plant, used as food and in making beer, ale, and whiskey. [Middle English *barrlig,* originally "of barley," Old English *bærlic,* from *bære, bere,* barley. See bhares- in Appendix.*]

bar·ley·corn (bär′lē-kôrn′) n. 1. The seed or grain of barley. 2. Formerly, a unit of measure equal to the width of a grain of barley, or approximately ⅓ inch.

Bar·ley·corn, John. See John Barleycorn.

barley sugar. A clear, hard candy made by boiling down sugar, formerly with an extract of barley added.

barm (bärm) n. The yeasty foam that rises to the surface of fermenting malt liquors. [Middle English *berme,* Old English *beorma.* See bhreu-² in Appendix.*]

bar·maid (bär′mād′) n. A woman who serves drinks in a bar.

bar·man (bär′mən) n., pl. -men (-mĭn). A bartender.

Bar·me·ci·dal (bär′mə-sīd′l) adj. Also **Bar·me·cide** (bär′mə-sīd′). Plentiful or abundant in appearance only; illusory: *a Barmecide feast.* [From *Barmecide,* name of an eighth-century noble Persian family, one of whom served a beggar an imaginary feast in the *Arabian Nights.*]

bar mitz·vah (bär mĭts′və). Also **bar miz·vah.** *Judaism.* 1. A thirteen-year-old Jewish male, considered an adult and thenceforth responsible for his moral and religious duties. 2. The ceremony conferring and celebrating this status. [Hebrew *bar mitzvāh,* "son of command."]

barm·y (bär′mē) adj. -ier, -iest. 1. Full of barm; frothy; foamy. 2. *British Slang.* Out of one's mind; crazy.

barn (bärn) n. 1. A large farm building used for storing grain, hay, and other farm products, and for sheltering livestock. 2. A large shed for the housing of railroad cars, trucks, or other vehicles. 3. *Physics. Symbol* **b** A unit of area equal to 10⁻²⁴ square centimeter, used to express nuclear cross sections. [Middle English *bern,* from Old English *bern, berern* : *bere,* BARLEY + *ern, ærn,* place, house, from (unattested) Common Germanic *razn-* (see ransack).]

Bar·na·bas (bär′nə-bəs), **Joses** or **Joseph.** Christian leader of the first century A.D.; missionary with Paul to Cyprus and Asia Minor.

Bar·na·by (bär′nə-bē). A masculine given name. [Middle English *Barnabe,* from Late Latin *Barnabas,* from Late Greek, from Hebrew, "son of exhortation" : Aramaic *bar,* son + *nābhā,* prophecy.]

bar·na·cle (bär′nə-kəl) n. 1. Any of various marine crustaceans of the order Cirripedia, that in the adult stage form a hard shell and remain attached to a submerged surface, thus fouling ship bottoms. 2. Formerly, the barnacle goose. [Middle English *bernak, bernacle,* barnacle goose, from Medieval Latin *bernaca, bernaca†,* barnacle, barnacle goose (from the belief that the geese were produced from the shellfish which supposedly clung to trees).] —**bar′na·cled** adj.

barnacle goose. A waterfowl, *Branta leucopsis,* of northern Europe and Greenland, having black, white, and gray plumage.

Bar·nard (bär′nərd), **Christiaan Neethling.** Born 1923. South African surgeon; performed first human heart transplant (1967).

Bar·nard (bär′nərd), **Edward Emerson.** 1857–1923. American astronomer; studied Jupiter and the Milky Way.

Bar·nard (bär′nərd), **Henry.** 1811–1900. American educator.

Bar·na·ul (bər-nŭ-ool′). A city of the Soviet Union, a port on the Ob River in southwestern Siberia. Population, 357,000.

barn dance. A social gathering, usually held in a barn, with music and square dancing.

Bar·ne·gat Bay (bär′nĭ-gät, -gĭt). A narrow inlet of the Atlantic Ocean, extending for 30 miles between the eastern coast of New Jersey and a line of offshore islands.

Barnes (bärnz), **Albert Coombs.** 1873–1951. American physician, discoverer of Argyrol, and art collector.

Bar·net (bär′nĭt). A borough of London, England, comprising the former administrative divisions of Barnet, East Barnet, Finchley, Friern Barnet, and Rendon. Population, 318,000.

barn owl. A predatory nocturnal bird, *Tyto alba,* having light-brown and white plumage, and often frequenting barns and other buildings.

barn·storm (bärn′stôrm′) intr.v. -stormed, -storming, -storms. 1. To travel about the countryside presenting plays, lecturing, or making political speeches. 2. To appear at county fairs and carnivals in exhibitions of stunt flying and parachute jumping. —**barn′storm′er** n.

barn swallow. A widely distributed bird, *Hirundo rustica,* having a deeply forked tail, a dark-blue back, and tan underparts. [The bird often builds its nest in the eaves of barns.]

Bar·num (bär′nəm), **P(hineas) T(aylor).** 1810–1891. American showman; circus producer.

barn·yard (bärn′yärd′) n. The yard or area of ground surrounding a barn, often enclosed by a fence. —adj. 1. Of or pertaining to a barnyard: *a barnyard fence.* 2. Rustic; earthy: *barnyard humor.*

baro-. Indicates weight or pressure; for example, **barometer.** [From Greek *baros,* weight. See gwer-² in Appendix.*]

Ba·ro·da (bə-rō′də). A city and cotton textile center of southeastern Gujarat State, Republic of India. Population, 323,000.

bar·o·gram (bär′ə-grăm′) n. A graphic record produced by a barograph. [BARO- + -GRAM.]

bar·o·graph (bär′ə-grăf′, -gräf′) n. A recording barometer. [BARO- + -GRAPH.] —**bar′o·graph′ic** adj.

ba·rom·e·ter (bə-rŏm′ə-tər) n. 1. *Abbr.* **bar.** An instrument for measuring atmospheric pressure, used in weather forecasting and in determining elevation. 2. Anything that gives notice of fluctuations; an indicator: *"The school has always served as a social barometer, a reflection of national historical trends."* (Paul P. Mok). [BARO- + -METER.] —**bar′o·met′ric** (bär′ə-mĕt′rĭk), **bar′o·met′ri·cal** adj. —**bar′o·met′ri·cal·ly** adv. —**ba·rom′e·try** n.

bar·on (bär′ən) n. 1. *History.* **a.** A feudal tenant holding his rights and title directly from the king or another feudal superior. **b.** A lord or nobleman; peer. 2. A member of the lowest rank of nobility in Great Britain, certain European countries, and Japan. 3. *Abbr.* **Bn., bn.** The rank or title of such a nobleman. 4. A man with great and coercive power in a specified sphere of commercial activity; magnate. 5. A cut of beef consisting of a double sirloin. [Middle English, from Old French, accusative of *ber,* from Medieval Latin *barō†* (stem *barōn-),* man, warrior.]

bar·on·age (bär′ə-nĭj) n. 1. The rank, title, or dignity of a baron. 2. A list of barons. 3. All of the peers of a kingdom.

bar·on·ess (bär′ə-nĭs) n. 1. The wife or widow of a baron. 2. A woman holding a barony in her own right.

bar·on·et (bär′ə-nĭt, bär′ə-nĕt′) n. 1. A British hereditary title of honor, ranking next below a baron, held by commoners. 2. *Abbr.* **Bart., Bt.** The bearer of such a title. [Middle English, diminutive of BARON.]

bar·on·et·age (bär′ə-nĭt-ĭj, -nĕt′ĭj) n. 1. The rank or dignity of a baronet. 2. A list of baronets. 3. Baronets collectively.

bar·on·et·cy (bär′ə-nĭt-sē, -nĕt′sē) n., pl. -cies. The dignity or rank of a baronet.

ba·rong (bä-rông′, -rŏng′) n. A large, broad-bladed knife used by the Moros of the Philippines. [Native Philippine name, probably akin to Malay PARANG.]

ba·ro·ni·al (bə-rō′nē-əl) adj. 1. Of or pertaining to a baron or barony. 2. Suited for or befitting a baron; stately; grand.

bar·o·ny (bär′ə-nē) n., pl. -nies. 1. The domain of a baron. 2. The rank or dignity of a baron.

ba·roque (bə-rōk′) adj. 1. Of, pertaining to, or characteristic of a style in art and architecture developed in Europe from about 1550 to 1700 and typified by elaborate and ornate scrolls, curves, and other symmetrical ornamentation. 2. Of, pertaining to, or characteristic of a style of musical composition that flourished in Europe from about 1600 to 1750, marked by chromaticism, strict forms, and elaborate ornamentation. 3. Ornate or flamboyant in style; richly ornamented: *"his addiction to a baroque luxuriance of language"* (Orville Prescott). 4. Irregular in shape: *baroque pearls.* —n. 1. The baroque style in art, architecture, and music. 2. The period during which baroque styles flourished, roughly from 1550 to 1750. 3. Any work, such as a building or sculpture, in the baroque style. [French, from Italian *barocco,* after the founder of the style, Frederigo Barocci (1528–1612).]

Ba·rot·se·land (bə-rŏt′sē-lănd′). A province in western Zambia, Africa, a former British protectorate (1891–1911).

ba·rouche (bə-roosh′) n. A four-wheeled carriage with a collapsible top, two double seats inside opposite each other, and a box seat outside in front for the driver. [German *Barutsche,* from Italian *baroccio,* earlier *biroccio,* from Late Latin *birotium* (unattested), two-wheeled, from Latin *birotus* : BI- + *rota,* wheel (see ret- in Appendix*).]

barque. Variant of bark (ship).

bar·quen·tine. Variant of barkentine.

Bar·qui·si·me·to (bär′kə-sə-mä′tō). The third-largest city of Venezuela, situated in the northwest, 165 miles west of Caracas. Population, 200,000.

bar·rack¹ (bär′ĭk) tr.v. -racked, -racking, -racks. To house in barracks.

bar·rack² (bär′ĭk) v. -racked, -racking, -racks. *Australian & British.* —intr. To shout against a player or team participating in a game. —tr. To shout against (a player); jeer at. [From native Australian *borak,* banter, chaff.] —**bar′rack·er** n.

bar·racks (bär′ĭks) n. Plural in form, used with a singular or plural verb. 1. *Abbr.* **bks.** A building or group of buildings used to house soldiers. 2. Any large unadorned building used for temporary occupancy. [From French *baraque,* from Italian *baracca,* soldier's tent, from Spanish *barraca,* mud hut, perhaps from Catalan *barraca†.*]

barracks bag. A soldier's cloth bag, usually with a drawstring, for the storage of clothing or laundry in the barracks.

bar·ra·coon (bär′ə-koon′) n. A barracks in which slaves and convicts were temporarily confined. [Spanish *barracón,* augmentative of *barraca,* hut. See barracks.]

bar·ra·cu·da (bär′ə-koo′də) n., pl. barracuda or -das. Any of

barometer
Mercury barometer

adjustable barometer scale

mercury column

glass thermometer

metal housing

reservoir

barouche
Nineteenth-century model

barn owl

various voracious, mostly tropical, marine fishes of the genus *Sphyraena*, having a long, narrow body and projecting jaws with fanglike teeth. [Spanish *barracuda*†.]

bar·rage[1] (bär′ĭj) *n.* **1.** The formation of an artificial obstruction in a watercourse, especially to promote irrigation: *the barrage of the Nile.* **2.** The artificial barrier thus formed; a dam. [French, from *barrer*, to bar, from *barre*, BAR.]

bar·rage[2] (bə-räzh′) *n.* **1.** A heavy curtain of artillery fire placed in front of friendly troops to screen and protect them. **2.** Any rapid, concentrated discharge of missiles, as from small arms. **3.** An overwhelming, concentrated outpouring, as of words or blows: *a barrage of questions.* —*tr.v.* **barraged, -raging, -rages.** To direct a barrage at. [French, from *(tir de) barrage*, barrier (fire), from BARRAGE (barrier).]

barrage balloon. A balloon anchored singly or in a series over a military objective to hinder the passage of enemy aircraft.

bar·ra·mun·da (băr′ə-mŭn′də) *n., pl.* **barramunda** or **-das.** Also **bar·ra·mun·di** (băr′ə-mŭn′dē) *pl.* **barramundi** or **-dis.** Any of several Australian food fishes, such as the river fish *Scleropages leichhardtdii*, or the lungfish *Neoceratodus forsteri.* [Native Australian name.]

bar·ran·ca (bə-răng′kə) *n. Southwestern U.S.* A deep ravine or gorge. [Spanish, probably from Iberian.]

Bar·ran·quil·la (bär′räng-kē′yä). The second-largest city of Colombia, on the Magdalena, eight miles upstream from the Caribbean Sea. Population, 521,070.

bar·ra·tor (băr′ə-tər) *n.* Also **bar·ra·ter.** *Law.* One who commits barratry. [Middle English *baratour*, from Old French *barateor*, swindler, from *barater*, to cheat, to BARTER.]

bar·ra·try (băr′ə-trē) *n., pl.* **-tries. 1.** *Law.* The offense of exciting or stirring up quarrels or groundless lawsuits. **2.** *Maritime Law.* An unlawful breach of duty on the part of a ship's master or crew, resulting in injury to the ship's owner. **3.** The sale or purchase of positions in the church or state. [Middle English *barratrie*, the purchase of church offices, from Old French *baraterie*, deception, from *barater*, to cheat, to BARTER.] —**bar′ra·trous** *adj.* —**bar′ra·trous·ly** *adv.*

Bar·rault (bà-rō′), **Jean-Louis.** Born 1910. French actor, director, and theatrical manager.

barred owl. A North American owl, *Strix varia*, having barred, brownish plumage, a streaked belly, and a strident, hooting cry.

bar·rel (băr′əl) *n.* **1.** A large, cylindrical container, usually made of wooden staves bound together with hoops, and having a flat top and bottom of equal diameter. **2.** The quantity that a barrel with a given or standard capacity will hold. **3.** *Abbr.* **bar., bbl, bbl., bl.** Any of various units of volume or capacity. In the U.S. Customary System it varies, as a liquid measure, from 31 to 42 gallons as established by law or usage. See **measurement. 4.** The metal, cylindrical part of a firearm through which the bullet travels. **5.** A cylinder that contains a movable piston. **6.** The drum of a capstan. **7.** The cylinder within the mechanism of a timepiece that contains the mainspring. **8.** The cylindrical part or hollow shaft of any of various other instruments and mechanisms. **9.** *Informal.* A large quantity: *a barrel of fun.* —*v.* **barreled** or **-relled, -reling** or **-relling, -rels.** —*tr.* To put or pack in a barrel or barrels. —*intr. Slang.* To move at a high speed. [Middle English *barel*, from Old French *baril*, probably from *barre*, BAR (rod).]

barrel chair. A large, upholstered chair having a high, rounded back resembling a half barrel.

bar·rel·house (băr′əl-hous′) *n.* **1.** A disreputable, old-time saloon or bawdyhouse. **2.** An early style of jazz characterized by free group improvisation and an accented two-beat rhythm.

barrel organ. A portable musical instrument operated by the action of a revolving barrel with pegs or pins which open air valves leading from a bellows to a series of pipes.

barrel roll. A flight maneuver in which an aircraft makes a complete rotation on its longitudinal axis while approximately maintaining its original direction.

bar·ren (băr′ən) *adj.* **1. a.** Not producing offspring; childless or fruitless. **b.** Incapable of producing offspring; infertile; sterile. **2.** Lacking vegetation, especially useful vegetation; unproductive. **3.** Unproductive of results or gains; unprofitable. **4.** Devoid; lacking: *writing barren of insight.* **5.** Lacking in liveliness or interest; meager. —See Synonyms at **empty, sterile.** —*n.* A tract of unproductive land, often with a scrubby growth of trees. Usually used in the plural: *the pine barrens of New Jersey.* [Middle English *barein(e)*, from Old French *baraigne, barhaine*†.] —**bar′ren·ly** *adv.* —**bar′ren·ness** *n.*

Barren Grounds. Also **Barren Lands.** A treeless, sparsely inhabited plain in northern Canada, extending westward from Hudson Bay to Great Slave and Great Bear lakes.

barren strawberry. A low-growing plant, *Waldsteinia fragarioides*, of eastern North America, having yellow flowers and small, dry, inedible fruit.

bar·ret (băr′ĭt) *n.* A flat cap; especially, a **biretta** *(see).* [French *barrette*, from Italian *barretta, berretta*, BIRETTA.]

Bar·rett, Elizabeth. See Elizabeth Barrett **Browning.**

bar·rette (bə-rĕt′, bä-) *n.* A small clasp used by women for holding the hair in place. [French, diminutive of *barre*, BAR.]

bar·ri·cade (băr′ə-kād′, băr′ə-kād′) *n.* **1.** A structure set up across a route of access, for defense or the obstruction of passage. **2.** Anything acting to obstruct passage; a barrier. —See Synonyms at **bulwark.** —*tr.v.* **barricaded, -cading, -cades. 1.** To close off or block with a barricade. **2.** To keep in or out by means of a barricade. [French, from Old French, from *barrique*, barrel (the earliest barricades were made of earth-filled barrels), from Spanish *barrica*, from *barril*, barrel, akin to Old French *baril*, BARREL.] —**bar′ri·cad′er** *n.*

Bar·rie (băr′ē), Sir **James M(atthew).** 1860–1937. British novelist and playwright; author of *Peter Pan.*

bar·ri·er (băr′ē-ər) *n.* **1.** A fence, wall, or other structure built to bar passage. **2.** Anything, material or immaterial, that acts to obstruct or prevent passage. **3.** A boundary or limit: *the sound barrier.* **4.** Anything that separates or holds apart: *"Jay's father was the one barrier between them."* (James Agee). **5.** A movable gate that keeps racehorses in line before the start of a race. **6.** *Plural.* The palisades or fences enclosing the lists of a medieval tournament. **7.** *Geology.* A section of the Antarctic ice shelf that extends beyond the coastline, resting partly on the ocean floor. —See Synonyms at **obstacle.** [Middle English *barrere*, from Old French *barriere*, probably from *barre*, BAR.]

barrier reef. A long, narrow ridge of coral or rock parallel to and relatively near a coastline, separated from the coastline by a lagoon too deep for coral growth.

bar·ring (bär′ĭng) *prep.* Unless (something) occurs; excepting: *Barring strong headwinds, the plane will arrive on schedule.*

bar·ri·o (bä′ryō) *n., pl.* **-os. 1.** An enclave, ward, or district in a Latin-American country or in the Philippines. **2.** A chiefly Spanish-speaking community or neighborhood in a U.S. city. [Spanish, from Arabic *barrī*, of an open area, from *barr*, open area, open country, outside.]

bar·ris·ter (băr′ĭ-stər) *n. Chiefly British.* A lawyer admitted to plead at the bar in the superior courts. Compare **solicitor.** See Synonyms at **lawyer.** [Obscurely from BAR (railing).]

bar·room (bär′rōōm′, -rŏŏm′) *n.* A room or building in which alcoholic beverages are sold at a counter or bar.

bar·row[1] (băr′ō) *n.* **1. a.** A flat, rectangular tray or cart having handles at each end. **b.** The load carried on such a tray. **2.** A **wheelbarrow** *(see).* [Middle English *bar(o)we*, Old English *bearwe*, basket, wheelbarrow. See **bher-**[1] in Appendix.*]

bar·row[2] (băr′ō) *n. Archaeology.* A large mound of earth or stones placed over a burial site. [Middle English *borewe, burgh*, Old English *beorg*. See **bhergh-**[2] in Appendix.*]

bar·row[3] (băr′ō) *n.* A pig that has been castrated before reaching sexual maturity. [Middle English *barow*, Old English *bearg, barg*. See **bher-**[2] in Appendix.*]

Bar·row, Point (băr′ō). The northernmost point of Alaska, 71 degrees 20 minutes north latitude, on the Arctic Ocean.

Bar·ry (băr′ē). A masculine given name. [Irish *Bearrach*, from Old Irish *Berrach, Bearrach*†.]

Bar·ry, Comtesse du. See **Du Barry.**

Bar·ry (băr′ē), **Philip.** 1896–1949. American playwright.

Bar·ry·more (băr′ĭ-môr′, -mōr′), **Lionel.** 1878–1954. American actor; brother of actress **Ethel** (1879–1959) and actor **John** (1882–1942).

bar sinister. 1. *Heraldry.* A bend or baton sinister held to signify bastardy. **2.** A hint or proof of illegitimate birth.

Bart. baronet.

bar·tend·er (bär′tĕn′dər) *n.* One who mixes and serves alcoholic drinks at a bar.

bar·ter (bär′tər) *v.* **-tered, -tering, -ters.** —*intr.* To trade goods or services without the exchange of money. —*tr.* To exchange (goods or services) without using money: *He bartered his watch for food.* —*n.* **1.** The act or practice of bartering. **2.** An exchange of agreements or concessions by two or more sides; a bargaining. **3.** Something that is bartered. [Middle English *barteren*, probably from Old French *barater*, to barter, cheat, perhaps from Vulgar Latin *prattāre* (unattested), cheat, do, from Greek *prattein*, to do, manage. See **prāk-** in Appendix.*] —**bar′ter·er** *n.*

Barth (bärt), **Karl.** 1886–1968. Swiss Protestant theologian.

Bar·thol·di (bär-thŏl′dē; *French* bàr-tôl-dē′), **Frédéric Auguste.** 1834–1904. French sculptor of the Statue of Liberty.

Bar·thol·o·mew (bär-thŏl′ə-myōō′), **Saint.** Sometimes called Nathanael. One of the Twelve Apostles. Mark 3:18.

bar·ti·zan (bär′tə-zən, bär′tə-zăn′) *n.* Also **bar·ti·san.** *Architecture.* A small, overhanging turret on a wall or tower. [Scottish *bartisane*, variant of *bratticing*, timberwork, from BRATTICE.] —**bar′ti·zaned** (bär′tə-zənd, bär′tə-zănd′) *adj.*

Bart·lett (bärt′lĭt) *n.* A widely grown English variety of pear having large, juicy, yellow fruit. [Named by Enoch *Bartlett* (1779–1860), American merchant.]

Bart·lett (bärt′lĭt), **John.** 1820–1905. American editor and publisher; compiler of *Familiar Quotations.*

Bart·lett (bärt′lĭt), **Robert Abram.** 1875–1946. American explorer of the Arctic.

Bar·tók (bär′tôk), **Béla.** 1881–1945. Hungarian pianist-composer; resident in America (1940–45).

Bar·to·lom·me·o (bär′tō-lōm-mâ′ō), **Fra.** Original name, Bartolommeo di Pagolo del Fattorino. 1475–1517. Italian painter of the Florentine school.

Bar·ton (bärt′n), **Clara.** In full, Clarissa Harlowe Barton. 1821–1912. Founder of the American Red Cross (1881).

Bar·tram (bär′trəm), **John.** 1699–1777. American botanist.

Bar·uch (bâr′ək) *n.* A book of the Old Testament Apocrypha.

Ba·ruch (bə-rōōk′), **Bernard Mannes.** 1870–1965. American financier and adviser to Presidents.

bar·y·cen·ter (băr′ə-sĕn′tər) *n. Physics.* **Center of mass** *(see).* [Greek *barus*, heavy (see **gwer-**[2] in Appendix*) + CENTER.]

bar·y·on (băr′ē-ŏn′) *n.* Any of a family of subatomic particles, including the nucleon and hyperon multiplets, that participate in strong interactions, have half-integral spins, and are generally more massive than mesons. See **particle.** [Greek *barus*, heavy (see **gwer-**[2] in Appendix*) + -ON.] —**bar′y·on′ic** *adj.*

baryon number. *Symbol* **B** A quantum number equal to the difference between the number of baryons and the number of antibaryons in a system of subatomic particles.

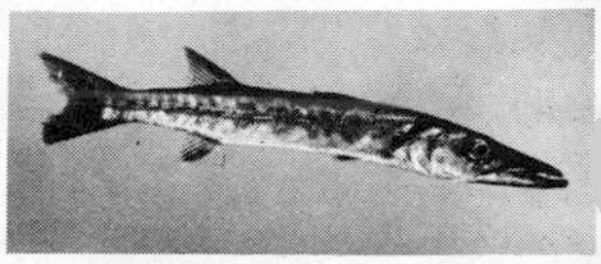

barracuda
Sphyraena borealis
Northern barracuda

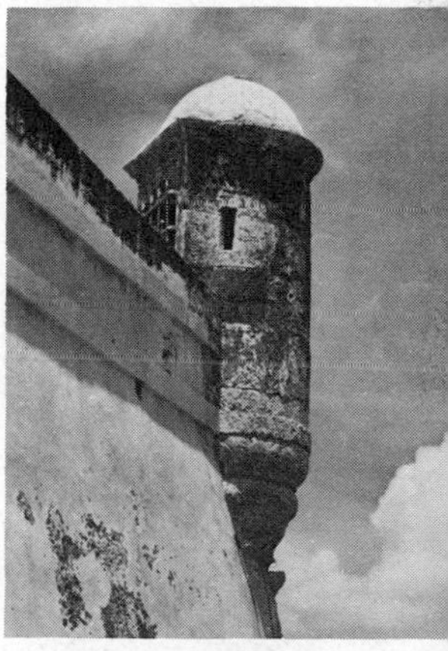

bartizan
On the corner of a 16th-century fortress in Cartagena, Colombia

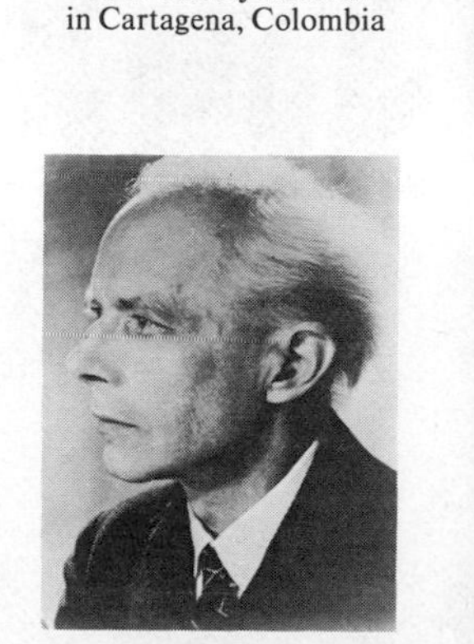

Béla Bartók

t tight/th thin, path/*th* this, bathe/ŭ cut/ûr urge/v valve/w with/y yes/z zebra, size/zh vision/ə about, item, edible, gallop, circus/ à *Fr.* ami/œ *Fr.* feu, *Ger.* schön/ü *Fr.* tu, *Ger.* über/KH *Ger.* ich, *Scot.* loch/N *Fr.* bon. ***Follows main vocabulary.** †**Of obscure origin.**

bar·y·sphere (băr′ə-sfîr′) *n.* The earth's central core, the **centrosphere** *(see).* [Greek *barus,* heavy (see **gwer-**[2] in Appendix*) + -SPHERE.]

ba·ry·tes (bə-rī′tēz) *n.* A mineral, **barite** *(see).*

bar·y·tone. Variant of **baritone.**

B.A.S. **1.** Bachelor of Agricultural Science. **2.** Bachelor of Applied Science.

bas·al (bā′səl, -zəl) *adj.* **1.** Pertaining to, located at, or forming a base. **2.** Of primary importance; basic. **—bas′al·ly** *adv.*

basal metabolic rate. The rate at which energy is used by an organism at complete rest, measured in humans by the heat given off per unit time.

basal metabolism. The least amount of energy required to maintain vital functions in an organism at complete rest.

ba·salt (bə-sôlt′, bā′sôlt′) *n.* **1.** A hard, dense, dark volcanic rock composed chiefly of plagioclase, augite, and magnetite, and often having a glassy appearance. **2.** A kind of black, unglazed pottery. In this sense, also called "basaltware." [Earlier *basaltes,* from Latin *basaltēs,* manuscript error for *basanītēs (lapis),* touchstone, from Greek *basanitēs,* from *basanos,* from Egyptian *bakhan.*] **—ba·sal′tic** (bə-sôl′tĭk) *adj.*

B.A.Sc. **1.** Bachelor of Agricultural Science. **2.** Bachelor of Applied Science.

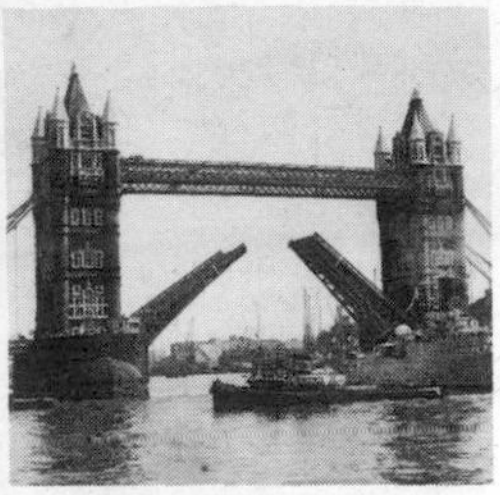

bascule
Tower Bridge, London, with roadway halves raised by bascules to permit the passage of ships

bas·cule (băs′kyōōl) *n.* A device counterbalanced so that when one end is lowered, the other is raised. [French, seesaw, from earlier *basse cule,* variant (influenced by *basse,* low) of earlier *bacule* : *bat(t)re,* to beat, BATTER + *cul,* buttocks, from Latin *cūlus* (see **skeu-** in Appendix*).]

base[1] (bās) *n. Abbr.* **b., B.** **1.** The lowest or supporting part or layer; foundation; bottom. **2.** The fundamental principle or underlying concept of a system or theory. **3.** The fundamental ingredient from which a mixture is prepared; chief constituent: *a paint with an oil base.* **4.** The fact, observation, or premise from which a measurement or reasoning process is begun. **5.** *Sports.* A goal, starting point, or safety area; specifically, one of the four corners of a baseball infield marked by a bag or plate. **6.** A center of organization, supply, or activity; headquarters. **7.** *Military.* **a.** A fortified center of operations. **b.** A supply center for a large force. **8.** *Architecture.* The lowest part of a structure, considered as a separate architectural unit: *the base of a column.* **9.** *Heraldry.* The lower part of a shield. **10.** *Linguistics.* A morpheme or morphemes regarded as a form to which affixes or other bases may be added. For example, in the words *filled* and *refill, fill* is the base. **11.** *Mathematics.* **a.** The side or face of a geometric figure to which an altitude is or is thought to be drawn. **b.** The number that is raised to various powers to generate the principal counting units of a number system. **c.** The number raised to the logarithm of a designated number in order to produce that designated number. **12.** A line used as a reference for measurement or computations. **13.** *Chemistry.* **a.** Any of a large class of compounds, including the hydroxides and oxides of metals, having a bitter taste, a slippery solution, the ability to turn litmus blue, and the ability to react with acids to form salts. **b.** A molecular or ionic substance capable of combining with a proton to form a new substance. **c.** A substance that provides a pair of electrons for a covalent bond with an acid. **—off base.** **1.** *Baseball.* Not touching the base occupied. **2. a.** Badly mistaken or inaccurate. **b.** In a state of unpreparedness. **—***adj.* **1.** Forming or serving as a base. **2.** Situated at or near the base or bottom. **—***tr.v.* **based, basing, bases.** **1.** To form or make a base for. **2.** To find a basis for; establish. [Middle English, from Old French, from Latin *basis,* pedestal, base, from Greek. See **gwā-** in Appendix.*]

Synonyms: *base, basis, foundation, ground, groundwork.* These nouns all pertain to what underlies and supports. *Base* is applied chiefly to material things: *the base of a fountain. Basis* is used in a nonphysical sense: *the basis of a rumor. Foundation* applies physically and figuratively, and more comprehensively than either of the foregoing. It stresses firmness of support for something of relative magnitude: *a philosophy with a foundation in truth. Ground* may denote an actual working surface in arts and crafts; more often, in the plural, it is used figuratively in the sense of a justifiable reason: *grounds for complaint. Groundwork* is most often applied figuratively, with the sense of foundation or a necessary preliminary.

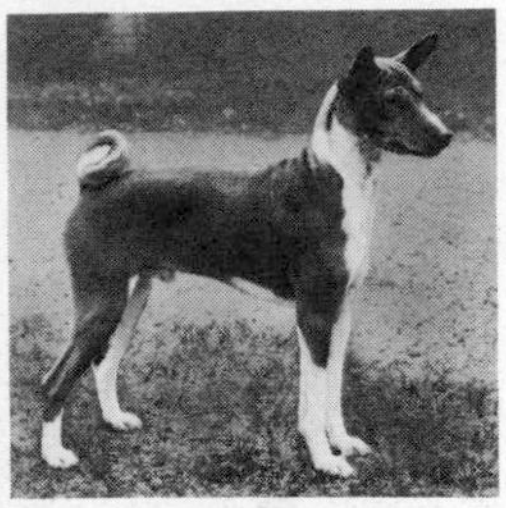

basenji

base[2] (bās) *adj.* **baser, basest.** **1.** *Archaic.* Of low birth, rank, or position. **2.** Characteristic of a person of low station; servile; menial. **3.** Having or proceeding from low moral standards; treacherous; contemptible. **4.** Inferior in quality or value; unrefined; shabby. **5.** Containing inferior substances: *a base metal.* **6.** Valueless, or greatly depreciated in value; debased: *base currency.* **7.** Corrupted by extraneous elements: *base Latin.* **8.** *Obsolete.* Short in stature. —See Synonyms at **mean** (ignoble). **—***n. Obsolete.* Bass. [Middle English *bas,* low, inferior, from Old French, from Late Latin *bassus,* fat, low. See **bassus** in Appendix.*] **—base′ly** *adv.* **—base′ness** *n.*

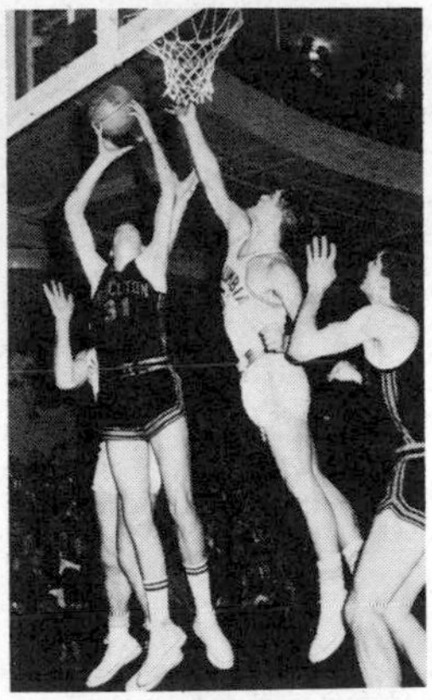

basketball
Intercollegiate competition between the Columbia and Princeton teams

base·ball (bās′bôl′) *n.* **1.** A game played with a wooden bat and hard ball by two opposing teams of nine players, each team playing alternately in the field and at bat, the players at bat having to run a course of four bases laid out in a diamond pattern in order to score. **2.** The ball used in this game.

base·board (bās′bôrd′, -bōrd′) *n.* **1.** A molding that conceals the joint between an interior wall and a floor. **2.** Any board or plate that serves as a base of something.

base·born (bās′bôrn′) *adj.* **1.** Of humble birth. **2.** Born of unwed parents; illegitimate. **3.** Ignoble; contemptible.

base·burn·er (bās′bûr′nər) *n.* A stove or furnace that automatically replenishes consumed coal or other fuel from above.

base hit. *Baseball.* A hit by which the batter reaches base safely, without an error or force play being made.

Ba·sel (bä′zəl). Also **Basle** (bäl). *French* **Bâle** (bäl). The principal commercial city of Switzerland, in the northwest on the Rhine River. Population, 213,000.

base·less (bās′lĭs) *adj.* Having no basis or foundation.

base level. The lowest level to which a land surface can be reduced by the action of running water.

base line. **1.** A line serving as a base for measurement or comparison. **2.** *Baseball.* A path between successive bases, bounded by imaginary lines within which a base runner must stay. **3.** *Tennis.* A line bounding each back end of a court.

base·man (bās′mən) *n., pl.* **-men** (-mĭn). *Baseball.* A player assigned to first, second, or third base.

base·ment (bās′mənt) *n.* **1.** The substructure or foundation of a building. **2.** The lowest habitable story of a building, usually below ground level. [Probably BASE (bottom) + -MENT.]

ba·sen·ji (bə-sĕn′jē) *n., pl.* **-jis.** A small dog of a breed originally from Africa, having a short, smooth coat, and not uttering the barking sound characteristic of most dogs. [From Bantu.]

base runner. A member of a baseball team at bat who has safely reached or is trying to reach a base.

ba·ses[1]. Plural of **basis.**

bas·es[2]. Plural of **base.**

bash (băsh) *tr.v.* **bashed, bashing, bashes.** *Informal.* To strike with a heavy and crushing blow. Often used with *in.* **—***n.* **1.** *Informal.* A heavy, crushing blow. **2.** *Slang.* A celebration; party. [Probably akin to English dialectal *bask,* to beat severely, and Swedish *baska,* to beat, from Germanic.]

Ba·shan (bā′shən). A fertile agricultural region of ancient Palestine, northeast of the Sea of Galilee.

ba·shaw (bə-shô′) *n. Obsolete.* A **pasha** *(see).*

bash·ful (băsh′fəl) *adj.* **1.** Inclined to shrink from notice through shyness; diffident; self-conscious. **2.** Characterized by, showing, or resulting from social shyness or self-consciousness. —See Synonyms at **shy.** [Middle English *baschen,* to abash, short for *abashen,* to ABASH + -FUL.] **—bash′ful·ly** *adv.* **—bash′ful·ness** *n.*

bash·i·ba·zouk (băsh′ē-bə-zōōk′) *n.* A member of the Turkish irregulars, a 19th-century cavalry troop noted for its brutality. [Turkish *başibozuk,* irregular soldier : *bas.* head + *bozuk,* depraved, out of order.]

Ba·shi Channel (bä′shē). A channel about 90 miles wide between southern Taiwan and the northernmost islands of the Philippines.

Bash·kir Autonomous Soviet Socialist Republic (bäsh-kîr′). An administrative division, 55,430 square miles in area, of the western Russian S.F.S.R. Population, 3,696,000. Capital, Ufa.

bash·lyk (băsh′lĭk) *n.* A fitted cloth hood that covers the head and ears and is worn primarily in the Soviet Union. [Russian, from Turkish *başlik,* hood : *baş,* head + *-lik,* purposive suffix.]

basi-, baso-. Indicates: **1.** The base or lower part; for example, **basipetal.** **2.** A chemical base; for example, **basophil.** [From Latin *basis,* BASIS.]

ba·sic (bā′sĭk) *adj.* **1.** Of, pertaining to, or constituting a basis; underlying; fundamental. **2.** *Chemistry.* **a.** Producing, resulting from, or pertaining to a base. **b.** Containing a base, especially in excess of acid. **3.** *Geology.* Containing little silica. Said of igneous rocks. **—***n.* Something that is basic.

ba·si·cal·ly (bā′sĭk-lē) *adv.* Fundamentally; essentially.

Basic English. A simplified, copyrighted form of English with a vocabulary of 850 English words and a short list of non-English words, intended to provide a basis for an auxiliary language and for the introductory teaching of English. [Coined by Charles Ogden, B(RITISH) A(MERICAN) S(CIENTIFIC) I(NTERNATIONAL) C(OMMERCIAL).]

ba·sic·i·ty (bā-sĭs′ə-tē) *n. Chemistry.* The quality or degree of being a base.

basic process. A method of steel production that uses a furnace lined with a basic refractory material.

ba·sid·i·o·my·cete (bə-sĭd′ē-ō-mī′sēt′, -mī-sēt′) *n.* Any fungus of the class Basidiomycetes, which includes the mushrooms, puffballs, and other fungi that bear spores on a basidium. [New Latin *Basidiomycetes* : BASIDI(UM) + -MYCETE.] **—ba·sid′i·o·my·ce′tous** (-sē′təs) *adj.*

ba·sid·i·o·spore (bə-sĭd′ē-ō-spôr′, -spōr′) *n. Mycology.* A spore formed on a basidium. [BASIDI(UM) + SPORE.]

ba·sid·i·um (bə-sĭd′ē-əm) *n., pl.* **-ia** (-ē-ə). A club-shaped cell characteristic of basidiomycetous fungi, on which sexual spores, usually four, are borne at the tip. [New Latin : BASI- + *-idium,* diminutive suffix.] **—ba·sid′i·al** *adj.*

Ba·sie (bā′sē), **William ("Count").** Born 1904. American jazz pianist, composer, and conductor.

ba·si·fy (bā′sə-fī′) *tr.v.* **-fied, -fying, -fies.** *Chemistry.* To make basic. [BAS(E) + -FY.] **—ba′si·fi·ca′tion** *n.* **—ba′si·fi′er** *n.*

bas·il (băz′əl, bāz′əl) *n.* **1.** An herb, *Ocimum basilicum,* native to the Old World, having spikes of small white flowers and aromatic leaves used as seasoning. Also called "sweet basil." **2.** A related plant, *Satureja vulgaris,* native to Europe and widely naturalized in North America, having dense clusters of small pink or purplish flowers. This species is also called "wild basil." [Middle English *basile,* from Old French, from Medieval Latin *basilicum,* from Greek *basilikon,* "royal," from *basileus,* king. See **basilica.**]

Bas·il (băz′əl, bāz′əl), **Saint.** Called "the Great." A.D. 330?–379? Greek Christian leader; bishop of Caesarea; opposed Arianism and founded monastic institutions.

Ba·si·lan (bə-sē′län′). **1.** A group of Philippine islands off the southeastern coast of Mindanao. **2.** The principal island of this

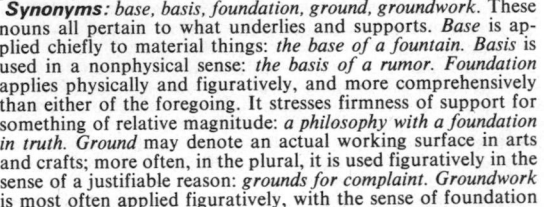

ă pat/ā pay/âr care/ä father/b bib/ch church/d deed/ĕ pet/ē be/f fife/g gag/h hat/hw which/ĭ pit/ī pie/îr pier/j judge/k kick/l lid, needle/m mum/n no, sudden/ng thing/ŏ pot/ō toe/ô paw, for/oi noise/ou out/ŏŏ took/ōō boot/p pop/r roar/s sauce/sh ship, dish/

group, 495 square miles in area, separated from Mindanao by the Basilan Strait.

bas·i·lar (băs′ə-lər) *adj.* Also **bas·i·lar·y** (-lĕr′ē). Pertaining to or located at or near the base, especially the base of the skull. [New Latin *basilaris,* from Latin *basis,* BASE (bottom).]

ba·sil·ic (bə-sĭl′ĭk) *adj.* Also **ba·sil·i·cal** (-ĭ-kəl), **ba·sil·i·can** (-kən) (for sense 1). **1.** Of or pertaining to a basilica. **2.** Important or prominent; royal; kingly. [From French *basilique,* basilica, from Latin *basilica,* BASILICA.]

ba·sil·i·ca (bə-sĭl′ĭ-kə) *n.* **1.** Any of various oblong buildings of ancient Rome having two rows of columns dividing the interior into a nave and two side aisles, used as a court or place of assembly. **2.** A building of this kind or design used as a Christian church. **3.** *Roman Catholic Church.* **a.** Any of several ancient churches in Rome. **b.** A church or cathedral accorded certain ceremonial rights by the pope. [Latin, from Greek *basilikē (stoa),* "royal (portico, court)," from *basileus*†, king.]

Ba·si·li·ca·ta (bä-zē′lə-kä′tä). Ancient name **Lu·ca·nia** (lo͞o-kān′yə, -kā′nē-ə). A region of southern Italy occupying 3,856 square miles in the area northwest of the Gulf of Taranto.

bas·i·lisk (băs′ə-lĭsk′, băz′-) *n.* **1.** A legendary serpent or dragon with lethal breath and glance. Compare **cockatrice. 2.** Any of various tropical American lizards of the genus *Basiliscus,* having an erectile crest at the back of the head. [Middle English, from Latin *basiliscus,* from Greek *basiliskos,* "princelet," diminutive of *basileus,* king. See **basilica.**]

ba·sin (bā′sən) *n.* **1.** An open, rounded vessel used especially for holding liquids. **2.** The amount contained in such a vessel. **3.** A washbowl; a sink. **4. a.** An artificially enclosed area of a river or harbor, so designed that the water level remains unaffected by tidal changes. **b.** A small enclosed or partly enclosed body of water. **5.** A region drained by a single river system. **6.** *Geology.* **a.** A tract of land in which the rock strata are tilted toward a common center. **b.** Any bowl-shaped depression in the surface of the land or ocean floor. [Middle English *ba(s)cin,* from Old French *bacin,* from Late Latin *bacchinus* (unattested), from Vulgar Latin *bacca* (unattested), water vessel, BACK (vat).]

bas·i·net (băs′ə-nĕt′, băs′ə-nĭt) *n.* A light, round, close-fitting medieval helmet, often with a visor. [Middle English *bacinet,* from Old French, diminutive of *bacin,* BASIN.]

ba·sip·e·tal (bā-sĭp′ə-təl) *adj. Botany.* Developing or growing from the top toward the base, as certain forms of inflorescence do. [BASI- + -PETAL.] —**ba·sip′e·tal·ly** *adv.*

ba·sis (bā′sĭs) *n., pl.* **-ses** (-sēz′). **1.** A foundation upon which something rests. **2.** The chief or most stable component of anything; fundamental ingredient. **3.** Principle; criterion. —See Synonyms at **base.** [Latin, pedestal, foot, base, from Greek. See **gwā-** in Appendix.*]

bask (băsk, bäsk) *intr.v.* **basked, basking, basks. 1.** To expose oneself pleasantly to warmth. **2.** To thrive in the presence of a pleasant or advantageous influence. [Middle English *basken,* akin to Norwegian dialectal *baska,* to splash in the water, and to BASH.]

Bas·ker·ville (băs′kər-vĭl), **John.** 1706–1775. British typographer and publisher.

bas·ket (băs′kĭt) *n.* **1.** *Abbr.* **bsk. a.** A container made of interwoven material, such as rushes, twigs, or strips of wood. **b.** The amount a basket will hold. **2.** Something resembling such a container in shape or function. **3.** *Basketball.* **a.** Either of the two goals, each consisting of a metal hoop from which an open-bottomed circular net is suspended. **b.** The score, normally worth two points, made by throwing the ball through the basket. [Middle English, from Norman French *basket*†.]

bas·ket·ball (băs′kĭt-bôl′) *n.* **1.** A game played between two teams of five players each, the object being to throw the ball through an elevated basket on the opponent's side of the rectangular court. **2.** The round, inflated ball used in this game.

basket hilt. A sword hilt with a basket-shaped guard serving to cover and protect the hand.

bas·ket·ry (băs′kĭt-rē) *n.* **1.** The craft or process of making baskets. **2.** Baskets collectively.

basket star. Any of various marine organisms of the class Ophiuroidea, related to the starfishes, and having slender, many-branched arms. Also called "basket fish."

basket weave. A textile weave consisting of double threads interlaced to produce a checkered pattern similar to that of a woven basket.

basking shark. A very large shark, *Cetorhinus maximus,* that feeds on plankton and often floats near the surface of the water.

Basle. See **Basel.**

bas mitz·vah, bas miz·vah. Variants of **bat mitzvah.**

baso-. Variant of **basi-.**

ba·so·phil (bā′sə-fĭl) *n.* A cell, especially a white blood cell, having granules that exhibit an affinity for basic dyes. [BASO- + -PHIL(E).] —**ba′so·phil′ic, ba·soph′i·lous** (bə-sŏf′ə-ləs) *adj.*

Ba·sov (bä′səf), **Nikolai Gennediyevich.** Born 1922. Soviet physicist; worked in quantum electronics.

basque (băsk) *n.* A woman's close-fitting bodice. [French, variant (influenced by *basquine,* petticoat) of earlier *baste,* from Provençal *basta,* perhaps from Germanic. See **bhendh-** in Appendix.*]

Basque (băsk) *n.* **1.** One of a people of unknown origin inhabiting the western Pyrenees in France and Spain. **2.** The language of the Basques, of no known relationship to any other language. [French, from Latin *Vascō*†.] —**Basque** *adj.*

Basque Provinces (băsk). A region comprising three provinces of northern Spain, 2,739 square miles in area, bordering on the Bay of Biscay, with a largely Basque population.

Bas·ra (bŭs′rə, bäs′-). Also **Bas·rah, Bus·ra** (bŭs′rə), **Bus·rah.** A major port and the third-largest city of Iraq, 75 miles from the Persian Gulf on the Shatt al-Arab. Population, 159,000.

bas-re·lief (bä′rĭ-lēf′) *n. Sculpture.* **Low relief** *(see).* [French, from Italian *bassorilievo,* low relief : *basso,* low, from Late Latin *bassus,* BASE (low) + *rilievo,* relief (see **mezzo-relievo**).]

bass[1] (băs) *n., pl.* **bass** or **basses. 1.** Any of several North American freshwater fishes of the family Centrarchidae, related to but larger than the sunfishes. **2.** Any of various marine fishes of the family Serranidae, such as the **sea bass** and the **striped bass** *(both of which see).* [Middle English, variant of dialectal *barse,* Old English *bærs.* See **bhar-** in Appendix.*]

bass[2] (bās) *n.* **1.** A low-pitched tone. **2.** The tones in the lowest register of a musical instrument. **3.** The lowest part in vocal or instrumental part music. **4.** A male singing voice of the lowest range. **5.** A man who has such a singing voice. **6.** A musical instrument that produces tones in a low register; especially, a **double bass** *(see).* —*adj.* Having a deep tone; low in pitch. [Middle English *bas,* low, BASE.]

bass[3] (băs) *n.* A fibrous plant product, **bast** *(see).* [Variant of BAST.]

Bass (băs), **Sam.** 1851–1878. American bandit leader in Nebraska and Texas; shot by Texas Rangers.

Bas·sa·no (bäs-sä′nō), **Jacopo.** Original name, Giacomo da Ponte. 1510–1592. Venetian painter; founder of European genre painting.

bass clef (bās). A musical clef that designates F below middle C as being on the fourth line above the bottom of the staff.

bass drum (bās). A large drum having a cylindrical body and two heads, both of which are struck to produce a low, resonant sound.

bas·set[1] (băs′ĭt) *n.* A dog, the **basset hound** *(see).* [French, Old French, from *basset,* short and low, from *bas,* low, BASE.]

bas·set[2] (băs′ĭt) *n. Geology.* An outcropping of rock at the edge of a stratum. —*intr.v.* **bassetted, -setting, -sets.** *Geology.* To emerge as an outcrop. [Probably from French *basset,* a type of stool used as a low table, from *bas,* low, BASE.]

Basse-Terre (bäs′târ′). **1.** A mountainous island forming the western part of Guadeloupe (French West Indies). **2.** The administrative seat of the Overseas Department of Guadeloupe, at the southern end of this island. Population, 19,000.

Basse·terre (bäs′târ′). The capital and principal seaport of St. Kitts and the Territory of St. Kitts-Nevis-Anguilla, Leeward Islands, one of the West Indies Associated States. Population, 16,000.

basset horn. A tenor clarinet in F, having a range of $3\frac{1}{2}$ octaves pitched between the range of an alto clarinet and that of a bass clarinet. [German *Bassetthorn* : Italian *bassetto,* diminutive of BASSO + *Horn,* horn, from Old High German *horn* (see **ker-**[1] in Appendix*).]

basset hound. A short-haired dog of a breed originating in France, having a long body, short, crooked forelegs, and long, drooping ears.

bass horn. A **tuba** *(see).*

bas·si·net (băs′ə-nĕt′) *n.* An oblong basket resting on legs, used as a crib for an infant. [French, small basin, from Old French *bacinet,* diminutive of *bacin,* BASIN.]

bas·so (băs′ō, bä′sō) *n., pl.* **-sos** or **-si** (-sē). *Abbr.* **b., B.** A bass singer, especially an operatic bass. [Italian, from Late Latin *bassus,* fat, short, low. See **bassus** in Appendix.*]

bas·soon (bə-so͞on′, bă-) *n.* A low-pitched woodwind instrument with a double reed, having a long wooden body attached to a lateral tube that leads to the mouthpiece. [French *basson,* from Italian *bassone,* augmentative of BASSO.] —**bas·soon′ist** *n.*

bas·so pro·fun·do (băs′ō prə-fŭn′dō, bä′sō prō-fo͞on′dō) *pl.* **basso profundos** or **bassi profundi** (bä′sē prō-fo͞on′dē). **1.** A bass voice of the lowest range. **2.** A singer having such a voice. [Italian, "deep bass."]

bas·so-re·lie·vo (băs′ō-rĭ-lē′vō) *n., pl.* **-vos.** Also *Italian* **bas·so-ri·lie·vo** (bä′sō-rē-lyâ′vō) *pl.* **-vi** (-vē). *Sculpture.* **Low relief** *(see).* [Italian *bassorilievo,* BAS-RELIEF.]

Bass Strait (băs). A channel, 185 miles long and from 80 to 150 miles wide, between mainland Australia and Tasmania.

bass viol (bās). *Music.* **1.** A **double bass** *(see).* **2.** A **viola da gamba** *(see).*

bass·wood (băs′wo͝od′) *n.* **1.** Any of several linden trees of eastern North America; especially, *Tilia americana,* having clusters of fragrant yellowish flowers. **2.** The soft, light-colored wood of any of these trees.

bast (băst) *n.* **1.** *Botany.* The fibrous or somewhat woody outer layer of the stems of certain plants, such as flax, hemp, and ramie. **2.** Fibrous material obtained from such plants or from certain trees, and used to make cordage and textiles. Sometimes called "bass." [Middle English *baste,* Old English *bæst,* from Common Germanic *bastaz* (unattested).]

bas·tard (băs′tərd) *n.* **1.** An illegitimate child. **2.** Any product of irregular, inferior, or dubious origin. **3.** *Slang.* An obnoxious or nasty person. Used as an epithet of abuse. **4.** *Slang.* A fellow. Often used with mild contempt: *poor bastard.* —*adj.* **1.** Born of unwed parents; illegitimate. **2.** Not genuine; spurious. **3.** Of inferior breed or kind. **4.** Resembling a known kind or species, but not truly such: *bastard toadflax.* [Middle English, from Old French, perhaps *(fils de) bast,* "packsaddle (son)," from Medieval Latin *bastum,* packsaddle, perhaps from Vulgar Latin *bastāre* (unattested), to carry, from Greek *bastazein*†, to lift, bear.] —**bas′tard·ly** *adj.*

bas·tard·ize (băs′tər-dīz′) *tr.v.* **-ized, -izing, -izes.** To debase; corrupt. —**bas′tard·i·za′tion** *n.*

bastard toadflax. Any plant of the genus *Comandra;* especially,

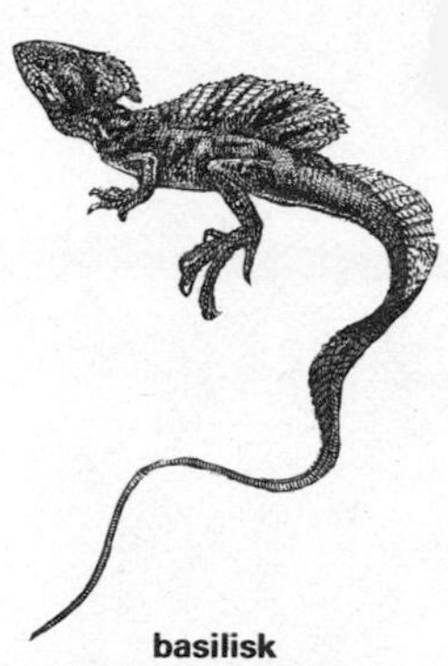

basilisk
Basiliscus plumbifrons
Double-crested basilisk

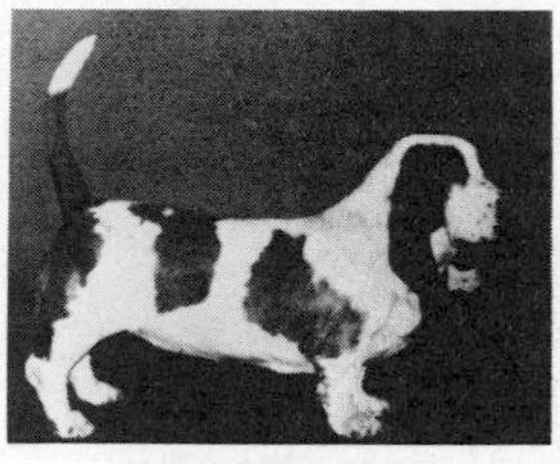

basset hound

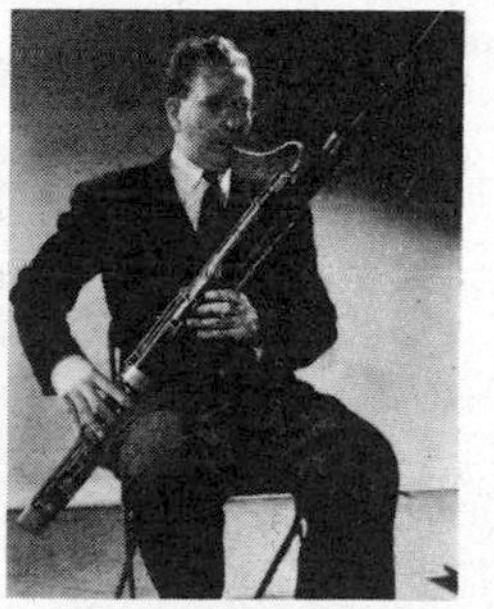

bassoon

t tight/th thin, path/*th* this, bathe/ŭ cut/ûr urge/v valve/w with/y yes/z zebra, size/zh vision/ə about, item, edible, gallop, circus/ à *Fr.* ami/œ *Fr.* feu, *Ger.* schön/ü *Fr.* tu, *Ger.* über/KH *Ger.* ich, *Scot.* loch/N *Fr.* bon. ***Follows main vocabulary. †Of obscure origin.**

C. umbellata, of eastern North America, having rounded clusters of small greenish flowers.

bastard wing. *Ornithology.* An **alula** *(see)*.

bas·tard·y (băs′tər-dē) *n.* **1.** The condition of being of illegitimate birth; illegitimacy. **2.** The begetting of a bastard.

baste[1] (bāst) *tr.v.* **basted, basting, bastes.** To sew loosely with large running stitches so as to hold together temporarily. [Middle English *basten*, from Old French *bastir*, to build, prepare, baste, from Common Germanic *bastjan* (unattested), to sew with bast, from *bastaz* (unattested), BAST.]

baste[2] (bāst) *tr.v.* **basted, basting, bastes.** To pour pan drippings or sauce over (meat) while cooking. [Origin obscure.]

baste[3] (bāst) *tr.v.* **basted, basting, bastes. 1.** To beat vigorously; thrash: *"I took a broom and basted her till she cried out extremely"* (Pepys). **2.** To berate. [Perhaps ultimately from Old Norse *beysta*, to thrash, strike. See **bhau-** in Appendix.*]

bas·tille (băs-tēl′) *n.* Also **bas·tile.** A prison; jail. [Middle English, from Old French, probably a variant of *bastide*, from Provençal *bastida*, from the past participle of *bastir*, to build. See **baste** (to sew).]

Bas·tille (băs-tēl′; *French* bȧs-tē′y'). A fortress in Paris used as a prison until captured on July 14, 1789, at the outset of the French Revolution. [French, from Old French, BASTILLE.]

bas·ti·na·do (băs′tə-nā′dō, -nä′dō) *n., pl.* **-does.** Also **bas·ti·nade** (băs′tə-nād′, -näd′). **1.** A beating with a stick or cudgel, especially on the soles of the feet. **2.** A stick or cudgel. *—tr.v.* **bastinadoed, -doing, -does.** Also **bas·ti·nade, -naded, -nading, -nades.** To subject to a beating; thrash. [Spanish *bastonada*, from *baston*, stick, from Late Latin *bastum*. See **baton.**]

bast·ing (bā′sting) *n.* **1.** The act of sewing together loosely. **2.** The thread used to baste. **3.** *Plural.* The loose stitches used to baste material.

bas·tion (băs′chən, băs′tē-ən) *n.* **1.** A projecting part of a rampart or other fortification: *"Albany is a small long stockaded fort with four bastions in it."* (Sir Edmund Andros). **2.** Any well-fortified or defended position. **3.** Something regarded as a defensive stronghold. —See Synonyms at **bulwark.** [French, from earlier *bastillon*, from Old French *bastille*, BASTILLE.]

bast·naes·ite (băst′nə-sīt′) *n.* A yellowish to reddish-brown mineral fluorocarbonate, used as a rare-earth ore.

Bas·togne (băs-tōn′; *French* bȧs-tôn′y'). A town in southeastern Belgium, near the Luxembourg border, that was a key point of the U.S. defensive line during the Battle of the Bulge (winter, 1944–45). Population, 6,000.

Ba·su·to·land. The former name for **Lesotho.**

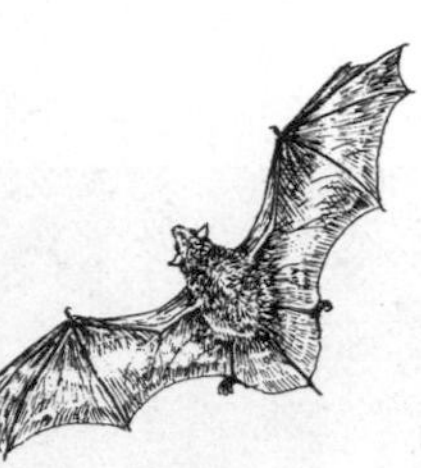

bat[2]
Eptesicus fuscus
Big brown bat

bat[1] (băt) *n.* **1.** A stout wooden stick or club; cudgel. **2.** A blow, as with a stick. **3. a.** *Baseball.* A rounded wooden club, wider and heavier at the hitting end and tapering at the handle, used to strike the ball. **b.** *Cricket.* A wooden club of similar function, having a broad, flat-surfaced hitting end and a distinct, narrow handle. **c.** The club or racket used in other games, such as a squash racket. **4.** *Slang.* A binge; spree. **—at bat.** *Baseball & Cricket.* Taking one's turn to bat. **—go to bat for.** *Informal.* To support or defend. **—(right) off the bat.** *Informal.* Without hesitation; immediately. *—v.* **batted, batting, bats.** *—tr.* **1.** To hit with, or as if with, a club or bat. **2.** *Baseball.* To have (some specified score) as a batting average. **3.** *Informal.* To produce in a hurried manner. Usually used with *out.* **4.** *Informal.* To discuss or consider at length. Usually used with *around.* *—intr.* **1.** *Baseball.* **a.** To use a bat. **b.** To have a turn at bat. **2.** *Slang.* To go from place to place aimlessly; wander. [Middle English *bat*, Old English *batt*, cudgel, club, possibly a Romance borrowing, ultimately from Latin *battuere*, to beat (see **battuere** in Appendix*), or possibly an independent imitative formation.]

bat[2] (băt) *n.* **1.** Any of various nocturnal flying mammals of the order Chiroptera, having membranous wings that extend from the forelimbs to the hind limbs or tail. **2.** *Slang.* An ugly, nagging woman; shrew. **—have bats in the belfry.** *Slang.* To be eccentric; have foolish or crazy ideas. [Variant of Middle English *bakke*, from Scandinavian, Middle Swedish *-bakka*, deformation of Old Norse *-blaka* in *ledhrblaka*, "leather-flapper," bat. See **bhlag-** in Appendix.*]

bat[3] (băt) *tr.v.* **batted, batting, bats.** To wink or flutter: *to bat one's eyelashes.* **—bat an eye.** To evince some sign of surprise or emotion. [Probably a variant of BATE (flap).]

bat. battalion.

Ba·taan (bə-tăn′, -tän′). A peninsula of western Luzon, Republic of the Philippines, surrendered in World War II to the Japanese by U.S. and Philippine forces (1942) and retaken by American forces (February, 1945).

Ba·tan Islands (bə-tän′). A group of islands occupying 76 square miles, north of Luzon, Republic of the Philippines. Population, 10,000.

Ba·ta·vi·a. The former name for **Djakarta.**

batch[1] (băch) *n.* **1.** An amount produced at one baking: *a batch of cookies.* **2.** The quantity produced as the result of one operation: *a batch of cement.* **3.** The quantity of material needed for one operation: *a batch of dough.* **4.** A group of persons or things: *"Bryan was working on a second batch of peace treaties."* (John Dos Passos). [Middle English *bacche*, Old English *bæcce* (unattested), from *bacan*, to BAKE.]

batch[2]. Variant of **bach.**

bate[1] (bāt) *tr.v.* **bated, bating, bates. 1.** To lessen the force of; moderate: *bate one's breath.* **2.** To take away; subtract. [Middle English *baten*, short for *abaten*, to ABATE.]

bate[2] (bāt) *intr.v.* **bated, bating, bates.** Also **bait.** *Falconry.* To flap the wings wildly, as if in impatience. [Middle English *baten*, from Old French *bat(t)re*, to beat, BATTER.]

ba·teau (bă-tō′) *n., pl.* **-teaux** (-tōz′). A light, flat-bottomed boat, used especially in Louisiana and Canada. [Canadian French, from French, from Old French *batel*, from Old English *bāt*. See **bheid-** in Appendix.*]

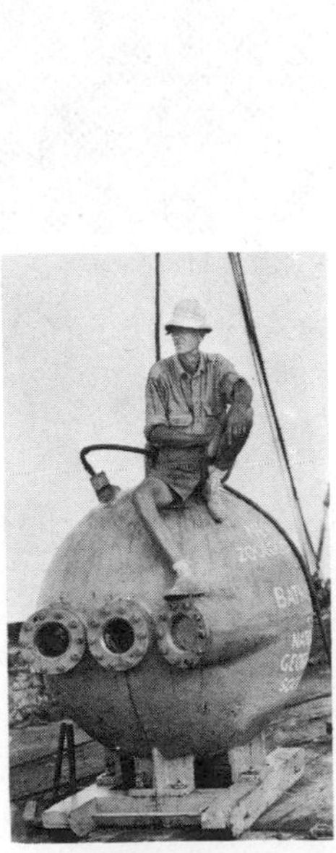

bathysphere
William Beebe seated on the bathysphere in which he made many deep-sea diving expeditions

bateau bridge. A **pontoon bridge** *(see)*.

bat·fish (băt′fĭsh′) *n., pl.* **batfish** or **-fishes.** Any of various marine anglerfishes of the family Ogcocephalidae, having a retractable appendage above the mouth.

bat·fowl (băt′foul′) *intr.v.* **-fowled, -fowling, -fowls.** To catch roosting birds at night by blinding them with a light.

bath[1] (băth, bäth) *n., pl.* **baths** (bă*th*z, băths, bä*th*z, bäths). **1.** The act of washing, dipping, or immersing the body in water. **2.** The water used for bathing. **3.** A bathtub. **4.** A liquid, or a liquid and its container, used to regulate the temperature of, soak, or otherwise act upon an immersed object. **5.** A bathroom. **6.** *Often plural.* A group of rooms or building equipped for bathing. **7.** *Often plural.* A resort providing therapeutic baths; spa. [Middle English *bath*, Old English *bæth*. See **bhē-** in Appendix.*]

bath[2] (băth) *n.* An ancient Hebrew unit of liquid measure, equal to approximately ten U.S. gallons. [Hebrew.]

Bath (băth, bäth). A city of Somersetshire in southwestern England, situated on the Avon, and famous for its mineral baths that are still fed by a reservoir built by the Romans in the first century A.D. Population, 83,000.

Bath brick. Fine calcareous and siliceous silt pressed into blocks and used for scouring and polishing metal. [From BATH.]

Bath chair. A hooded wheelchair used for transporting invalids, as at a spa. [First used at BATH.]

bathe (bā*th*) *v.* **bathed, bathing, bathes.** *—intr.* **1.** To take a bath; wash oneself. **2.** To go swimming. **3.** To become immersed in or as if in liquid. *—tr.* **1.** To immerse in liquid. **2.** To wash or wet. **3.** To apply a liquid to for soothing or healing purposes. **4.** To suffuse. [Middle English *bathen*, Old English *bathian*. See **bhē-** in Appendix.*] **—bath′er** *n.*

ba·thet·ic (bə-thĕt′ĭk) *adj.* Characterized by bathos. [Probably a blend of BATHOS and PATHETIC.]

bath·house (băth′hous′, bäth′-) *n.* **1.** A building equipped for bathing. **2.** A building with dressing rooms for swimmers.

batho–. Variant of **bathy-.**

bath·o·lith (băth′ə-lĭth′) *n.* Also **bath·o·lite** (-līt′). Igneous rock that has melted and intruded surrounding strata at great depths. [German : BATHO- + -LITH.] **—bath′o·lith′ic** *adj.*

ba·thom·e·ter (bə-thŏm′ə-tər) *n.* An instrument used to measure the depth of water. [BATHO- + -METER.]

ba·thos (bā′thŏs′) *n.* **1. a.** A ludicrously abrupt transition from an elevated to a commonplace style. **b.** An anticlimax. **c.** The lowest point; a nadir. **2. a.** Insincere or grossly sentimental pathos; maudlinism. **b.** Extreme triteness or dullness. [Greek, depth, from *bathus*, deep. See **gwadh-** in Appendix.*]

bath·robe (băth′rōb′, bäth′-) *n.* A loose-fitting robe worn before and after bathing and for lounging.

bath·room (băth′ro͞om′, -ro͝om′, bäth′-) *n.* A room equipped for taking a bath or shower and usually also containing a sink and toilet.

Bath·she·ba (băth-shē′bə, băth′shĭ-bə). The wife of Uriah and later of David and, by David, the mother of Solomon. II Samuel 11–12.

bath·tub (băth′tŭb′, bäth′-) *n.* An oblong tub for bathing.

Bath·urst (băth′ərst). The capital of Gambia, on an island at the mouth of the Gambia River. Population, 40,000.

bathy–, batho–. Indicates deepness or some relationship to depth; for example, **bathyscaph, bathometer.** [From Greek *bathus*, deep, and *bathos*, depth, from *bathus*. See **gwadh-** in Appendix.*]

ba·thym·e·try (bə-thĭm′ə-trē) *n.* The measurement of the depth of large bodies of water. [French *bathymétrie* : BATHY- + -METRY.] **—bath′y·met′ric** (băth′ə-mĕt′rĭk), **bath′y·met′ri·cal** *adj.* **—bath′y·met′ri·cal·ly** *adv.*

bath·y·scaph (băth′ĭ-skăf′) *n.* Also **bath·y·scaphe** (-skăf′, -skāf′). A free-diving, self-contained deep-sea research vessel, consisting essentially of a large flotation hull with a manned observation capsule fixed to its underside. [BATHY- + Greek *skaphē*, basin, light boat (see **skep-** in Appendix*).]

bath·y·sphere (băth′ĭ-sfîr′) *n.* A reinforced, spherical deep-diving chamber, manned, and lowered by cable. [BATHY- + -SPHERE.]

ba·tik (bə-tēk′, băt′ĭk) *n.* Also **bat·tik. 1.** A method of dyeing print into a fabric in which parts of the cloth, not intended to be dyed, are covered with removable wax. **2.** The print that is dyed into cloth by this method. **3.** The cloth so dyed. [Malay, from Javanese, "painted."] **—ba·tik′** *adj.*

Ba·tis·ta (bä-tēs′tä), **Fulgencio.** Born 1901. Cuban political leader; dictator (1933–40); president (1940–44 and 1952–59).

ba·tiste (bə-tēst′, bă-) *n.* A fine, plain-woven fabric made from various fibers and used especially for clothing. [Earlier *baptist cloth* (translation of French *toile de Batiste*), first made by *Baptiste* of Cambrai (13th century).]

Ba·tjan (bä′chän). Also **Ba·chan.** A large island (914 square miles) in the Moluccas, Indonesia, lying southwest of Halmahera Island.

bat·man (băt′mən) *n., pl.* **-men** (-mĭn). The soldier servant of a British army officer. [Obsolete *bat*, packsaddle, from Middle English *batt*, from Old French *bat*, *bast*, from Vulgar Latin *bastum* (unattested), a carrying, perhaps from Vulgar Latin *bastāre* (unattested), to carry (see **bastard**) + MAN.]

bat mitz·vah (bät mĭts′və). Also **bat miz·vah, bas mitz·vah** (bäs), **bas miz·vah.** *Judaism.* **1.** A girl who reaches the age of Jewish duty and responsibility, usually between twelve and fourteen

ă pat/ā pay/âr care/ä father/b bib/ch church/d deed/ĕ pet/ē be/f fife/g gag/h hat/hw which/ĭ pit/ī pie/îr pier/j judge/k kick/l lid, needle/m mum/n no, sudden/ng thing/ŏ pot/ō toe/ô paw, for/oi noise/ou out/o͝o took/o͞o boot/p pop/r roar/s sauce/sh ship, dish/

years. **2.** In some congregations, the ceremony marking the arrival of a girl's religious commitment. See **bar mitzvah.** [Hebrew *bat mitzvāh,* "daughter of commandment" : *bat,* daughter + *mitzvāh,* command, commandment.]

ba·ton (bə-tŏn′, băt′n) *n.* **1.** A short staff carried by some public officials as a symbol of office. **2.** A slender wooden stick or rod used by a conductor to direct an orchestra or band. **3.** The hollow metal rod with heavy rubber tips twirled by a drum major or majorette. [French *bâton,* from Old French *baton,* from Late Latin *bastum,* stick, perhaps from Vulgar Latin *bastāre* (unattested), to carry. See **bastard.**]

Bat·on Rouge (băt′n ro͞ozh′). The capital of Louisiana and an important river port on the eastern bank of the Mississippi River, 70 miles northwest of New Orleans. Population, 152,000.

ba·tra·chi·an (bə-trā′kē-ən) *adj.* Of or pertaining to frogs and toads. —*n.* A frog or toad. [New Latin *Batrachia* (former order name, now Salienta), from Greek *batrakhos*†, frog.]

bats (băts) *adj. Slang.* Eccentric; insane.

bats·man (băts′mən) *n., pl.* **-men** (-mĭn). *Baseball & Cricket.* A batter.

batt (băt) *n.* A mass of cotton fibers, **batting** *(see).*

bat·tal·ion (bə-tăl′yən) *n. Abbr.* **bat., batt., bn., Bn. 1.** A tactical military unit, typically consisting of a headquarters company and four infantry companies, or a headquarters battery and four artillery batteries. **2.** An indefinite number of military troops. [Old French *battaillon,* from Old Italian *battaglione,* augmentative of *battaglia,* troop, from Vulgar Latin *battālia* (unattested), BATTLE.]

Bat·ta·ni, al- (ăl′bə-tä′nē). In full, abu-ʿAbdullāh Muhammad ibn-Jābir al-Battāni. Latin name, Albategnius. A.D. 850?–929. Arab astronomer; introduced table of sines.

bat·ten[1] (băt′n) *intr.v.* **-tened, -tening, -tens. 1.** To become fat. **2.** To thrive and prosper, especially at another's expense: *slum lords who batten on the poor.* [Ultimately from Old Norse *batna,* to improve. See **bhad-** in Appendix.*]

bat·ten[2] (băt′n) *n.* **1.** A narrow strip of wood, used for flooring. **2.** One of several flexible strips of wood placed in pockets at the outer edge of a sail to keep it flat. —*tr.v.* **battened, -tening, -tens. 1.** To furnish with battens: *batten a sail.* **2.** To fasten or make secure with battens. Usually used with *up* or *down: batten down the hatches.* [From French *bâton,* BATON.]

bat·ter[1] (băt′ər) *v.* **-tered, -tering, -ters.** —*tr.* **1.** To hit heavily and repeatedly with violent blows. **2.** To damage by heavy wear. —*intr.* To pound repeatedly with heavy blows. —*n. Printing.* **1.** A damaged area on the face of type or on a plate. **2.** The defect in print resulting from such damaged type. [Middle English *bateren,* from Old French *bat(t)re,* to beat, from Latin *battuere.* See **battuere** in Appendix.*]

bat·ter[2] (băt′ər) *n. Baseball & Cricket.* The player at bat.

bat·ter[3] (băt′ər) *n.* A thick, beaten liquid mixture, as of flour, milk, and eggs, used in cooking. [Middle English *bater,* probably from *bateren,* to BATTER.]

bat·ter[4] (băt′ər) *n.* A slope, as of the outer side of a wall, that recedes from bottom to top. —*tr.v.* **battered, -tering, -ters.** To construct so as to slope thus. [Possibly from BATTER (verb).]

bat·ter·ing-ram (băt′ər-ĭng-răm′) *n.* **1.** A heavy beam used in ancient warfare to batter down walls and gates. **2.** Any device resembling this or used for similar purposes.

Bat·ter·sea (băt′ər-sē). A former administrative division of London, England, now part of **Wandsworth** *(see).*

bat·ter·y (băt′ə-rē) *n., pl.* **-ies. 1. a.** A beating or pounding. **b.** *Law.* The unlawful beating of another person. Compare **assault and battery. 2. a.** An emplacement for one or more pieces of artillery. **b.** A set of guns or other heavy artillery, as on a warship. **c.** *Abbr.* **btry.** The basic tactical artillery unit, corresponding to the company in the infantry. **3.** An array or grouping of like things to be used together. **4.** The pitcher and catcher on a baseball team. **5.** The percussion section of an orchestra. **6.** A device for generating an electric current by chemical reaction. [French *batterie,* from *battre,* to beat, from Old French *bat(t)re,* to BATTER.]

Bat·ter·y, the (băt′ə-rē). A park at the southern tip of Manhattan Island on the upper end of New York Bay in New York City, where coastal artillery was mounted during colonial and Revolutionary times.

bat·tik. Variant of **batik.**

bat·ting (băt′ĭng) *n.* **1.** The action of one who bats. **2.** Cotton or wool fiber wadded together and used for stuffing furniture and mattresses. Also called "batt," "cotton batting." [Sense 2, from the beating of raw cotton or wool to clean it.]

bat·tle (băt′l) *n.* **1.** A large-scale combat between two armed forces. **2.** Armed fighting; combat: *wounded in battle.* **3.** Any intense competition; struggle. —*v.* **battled, -tling, -tles.** —*intr.* To engage in or as if in battle. —*tr.* To fight against. [Middle English *bataille,* from Old French, from Vulgar Latin *battālia* (unattested), from Late Latin *battuālia,* fighting and fencing exercises, from Latin *battuere,* to BATTER.]

bat·tle-ax, bat·tle-axe (băt′l-ăks′) *n., pl.* **-axes. 1.** A heavy broad-headed ax, formerly used as a weapon. **2.** *Slang.* An overbearing woman; virago.

battle cruiser. A warship with less heavy armor than a battleship, and with the speed of a cruiser.

battle cry. 1. A shout uttered by troops in battle. **2.** A slogan used by the proponents of a cause.

bat·tle·dore (băt′l-dôr′, -dōr′) *n.* **1.** An early form of badminton played with a flat wooden paddle and a shuttlecock. Also called "battledore and shuttlecock." **2.** The paddle used in this game. [Middle English *batildore,* perhaps from Old Provençal *batedor,* a beater, from Old French *bat(t)re,* to beat, BATTER.]

bat·tle·field (băt′l-fēld′) *n.* A field or area where a battle is fought. Also called "battleground."

bat·tle·ment (băt′l-mənt) *n.* A parapet built on top of a wall, with indentations for defense or decoration. [Middle English *batelment,* from Old French *bataillier,* to provide with battlements, from *batailles,* battlements, plural of *bataille,* BATTLE.] —**bat′tle·ment′ed** (-mĕn′tĭd) *adj.*

battle royal *pl.* **battles royal. 1.** A battle in which numerous combatants participate. **2.** A fight to the finish. **3.** An intense altercation.

bat·tle·ship (băt′l-shĭp′) *n.* Any of a class of modern warships of the largest size, carrying the greatest number of guns and batteries and clad with the heaviest armor.

battleship gray. Medium gray. See **color.**

bat·tle·wag·on (băt′l-wăg′ən) *n. Slang.* A battleship.

bat·tue (bă-to͞o′, -tyo͞o′; *French* bȧ-tü′) *n.* **1.** The driving of wild game from cover by beaters toward waiting hunters. **2.** A hunt employing this procedure. [French, from the feminine past participle of *bat(t)re,* to beat, BATTER.]

bat·ty (băt′ē) *adj.* **-tier, -tiest.** *Slang.* Eccentric; insane.

Ba·tum (bə-to͞om′). Also **Ba·tu·mi** (bə-to͞o′mē). The capital of the Adzhar A.S.S.R., a port city on the Black Sea coast of the Georgian S.S.R. Population, 82,000.

bau·ble (bô′bəl) *n.* **1.** A small, showy ornament or trinket. **2.** A baton surmounted with a grotesquely carved head, carried by a court jester as a mock scepter of his office. [Middle English *babel, babulle,* from Old French *babel, baubel*†, plaything.]

Bau·de·laire (bōd-lâr′), **Charles.** 1821–1867. French poet.

Bau·douin I (bō-dwăN′). Born 1930. King of Belgium since 1951.

Bau·haus (bou′hous′). An institute founded in 1919 in Weimar, Germany, for the study of art, design, and architecture and noted for its development of a style of functional architecture and its experimental use of building materials. [German, "architecture house."]

baulk. Variant of **balk.**

Baum (bäm, bôm), **L(yman) Frank.** 1856–1919. American author of the *Oz* series of books for children.

Bau·mé scale (bō-mā′). *Abbr.* **Bé, B.** A hydrometer scale that separately covers liquids with specific gravities greater and less than 1. [After Antoine *Baumé* (1728–1804), French pharmacist; inventor of a hydrometer.]

baum marten (boum). The fur of any of several Eurasian martens. [Partial translation of German *Baummarder* : *Baum,* tree, from Old High German *boum* (see **bheu-** in Appendix*) + MARTEN.]

baux·ite (bôk′sīt′) *n.* The principal ore of aluminum, 30 to 75 per cent $Al_2O_3 \cdot nH_2O$, with ferric oxide and silica as impurities. [French, first found at Les *Baux,* southern France.]

Bav. Bavaria; Bavarian.

Ba·var·i·a (bə-vâr′ē-ə). *German* **Bay·ern** (bī′ərn). *Abbr.* **Bav.** The largest state (27,119 square miles) of West Germany, in the southern part of the country. Population, 9,976,000. Capital, Munich.

Ba·var·i·an (bə-vâr′ē-ən) *adj. Abbr.* **Bav.** Of or pertaining to Bavaria, its inhabitants, or their dialect. —*n. Abbr.* **Bav. 1.** A native or inhabitant of Bavaria. **2.** The High German dialect spoken in Bavaria and Austria.

bawd (bôd) *n.* **1.** A woman who keeps a brothel; a madam. **2.** A prostitute. [Middle English *bawde,* probably from Old French *baude, baud,* lively, bold, from Old High German *bald,* bold. See **bhel-**[2] in Appendix.*]

bawd·ry (bô′drē) *n.* Obscene or coarse language dealing with sex. [Middle English *bawdery,* from *bawde,* BAWD.]

bawd·y (bô′dē) *adj.* **-ier, -iest.** Humorously coarse; vulgar; lewd. —**bawd′i·ly** *adv.* —**bawd′i·ness** *n.*

bawd·y·house (bô′dē-hous′) *n.* A house of prostitution.

bawl (bôl) *v.* **bawled, bawling, bawls.** —*intr.* **1.** To cry loudly, as from pain or annoyance; to howl. **2.** To cry out loudly and vehemently; to shout. —*tr.* To utter in a loud, vehement voice. —**bawl out.** *Informal.* To reprimand or scold in a loud voice. —*n.* A loud, extended outcry; a wail. [Middle English *baulen,* probably from Scandinavian, akin to Icelandic *baula,* to low. See **bhel-**[4] in Appendix.*] —**bawl′er** *n.*

bay[1] (bā) *n.* **1.** *Abbr.* **b., B.** A body of water partly enclosed by land, but having a wide outlet to the sea. **2.** A broad stretch of low land between hills. **3.** An arm of prairie partly enclosed by woodland. [Middle English *baye,* from Old French *baie,* from Old Spanish *bahia,* perhaps from Iberian.]

bay[2] (bā) *n.* **1.** *Architecture.* A part of a building or other structure marked off by vertical elements. **2. a.** A **bay window** *(see).* **b.** Any opening or recess in a wall. **3.** An extension of a building; wing. **4.** A compartment in a barn, used for storing hay or grain. **5.** A ship's sickbay. **6.** A compartment in an aircraft: *the bomb bay.* [Middle English, from Old French *baee,* an opening, from *baer,* to gape, from Vulgar Latin *batāre* (unattested), to yawn, gape. See **bat-** in Appendix.*]

bay[3] (bā) *adj.* Reddish-brown: *a bay colt.* —*n.* **1.** A reddish brown. See **color. 2.** An animal, especially a horse, of this color. [Middle English, from Old French *bai,* from Latin *badius.* See **badyo-** in Appendix.*]

bay[4] (bā) *n.* **1.** A deep, prolonged barking, especially of hounds closing in on prey. **2.** The position of one cornered by pursuers and forced to turn and fight at close quarters. **3.** The position of one checked or kept at a safe distance. —*v.* **bayed, baying, bays.** —*intr.* To utter a deep, prolonged bark or howl. —*tr.* **1.** To pursue or challenge with barking: *"I had rather be a dog, and bay the moon"* (Shakespeare). **2.** To express by barking. **3.** To bring to bay: *"too big for the dogs which tried to bay it"*

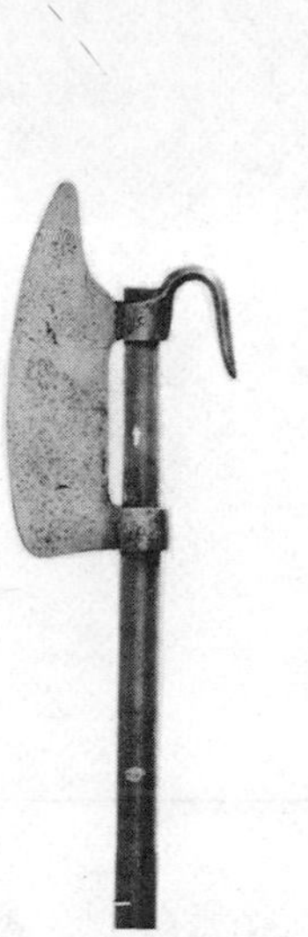

battle-ax
Scottish battle-ax of the 15th and 16th centuries

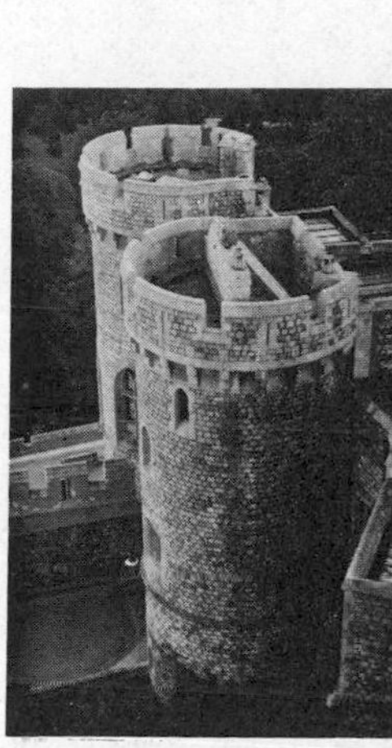

battlement
Battlements on a tower entrance to Windsor Castle, England

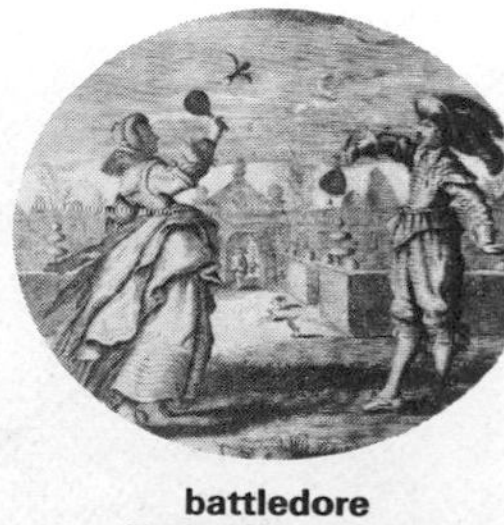

battledore
Early 18th-century engraving of a couple playing battledore

t tight/th thin, path/*th* this, bathe/ŭ cut/ûr urge/v valve/w with/y yes/z zebra, size/zh vision/ə about, item, edible, gallop, circus/ à *Fr.* ami/œ *Fr.* feu, *Ger.* schön/ü *Fr.* tu, *Ger.* über/KH *Ger.* ich, *Scot.* loch/N *Fr.* bon. *Follows main vocabulary. †Of obscure origin.

(Faulkner). [Middle English *baien,* short for *abaien,* from Old French *abaiier, abayer,* from Vulgar Latin *abbaiāre* (unattested). See **bat-** in Appendix.*]

bay[5] (bā) *n.* **1.** A laurel, *Laurus nobilis,* native to the Mediterranean area, having stiff, glossy, aromatic leaves. Also called "bay laurel," "bay tree." **2.** Any of several similar trees or shrubs. **3.** *Usually plural.* A crown or wreath made of the leaves and branches of the bay or similar plants, given in classical times as a sign of honor. **4.** *Plural.* Renown; honor. [Middle English *baye,* laurel berry, from Old French *baie,* from Latin *bāca,* berry. See **Bacchus.**]

ba·ya·dere (bī′ə-dīr′, -dâr′) *n.* A fabric with contrasting horizontal stripes. [French *bayadère,* Hindu dancing girl, from Portuguese *bailadeira,* from *bailar,* to dance, from Late Latin *ballāre,* from Greek *ballizein.* See **gwel-**[1] in Appendix.*]

bay·ber·ry (bā′běr′ē) *n., pl.* **-ries. 1.** Any of several aromatic shrubs or small trees of the genus *Myrica;* especially, *M. pensylvanica,* of eastern North America, bearing gray, waxy berries. **2.** A tropical American tree, *Pimenta acris,* yielding an oil used in making bay rum. Also called "bay rum tree." **3.** The fruit of any of these trees or shrubs.

Bay City. A city of Michigan, in the east near the southern end of Saginaw Bay. Population, 54,000.

Bay·ern. The German name for **Bavaria.**

Ba·yeux tapestry (bä-yōō′, bä-; *French* bȧ-yœ′). An 11th- or 12th-century tapestry, 20 inches wide by 231 feet long, embroidered with scenes depicting the Norman Conquest of England, and preserved in the town of Bayeux in northwestern France.

Bayle (bāl), **Pierre.** 1647–1706. French philosopher and critic.

bay leaf. The dried, aromatic leaf of the bay, *Laurus nobilis,* or of the bayberry, *Pimenta acris,* used as seasoning in cooking.

bay lynx. The bobcat *(see).*

Bay of. For names of actual bays, see the specific element of the name; for example, **Biscay, Bay of; Fundy, Bay of.**

bay·o·net (bā′ə-nĭt, -nĕt′, bā′ə-nĕt′) *n.* A knife adapted to fit the muzzle end of a rifle and used in close combat. —*tr.v.* **bayoneted** *or* **-netted, -neting** *or* **-netting, -nets.** To stab or prod with a bayonet. [French *baïonnette,* first manufactured at BAYONNE (France).]

bayonet

Ba·yonne (bā-yōn′ *for sense 1;* bȧ-yôn′ *for sense 2*). **1.** A seaport of northeastern New Jersey, on Upper New York Bay. Population, 74,000. **2.** A seaport of southwestern France, 13 miles north of the Spanish border. Population, 31,000.

bay·ou (bī′ōō, bī′ō) *n., pl.* **-ous.** *Southern U.S.* A marshy, sluggish body of water tributary to a lake or river. [Louisiana French, from Choctaw *bayuk.*]

Bay·reuth (bī-roit′). A city in Bavaria, West Germany, situated 40 miles northeast of Nuremberg and noted for its annual Wagnerian festival. Population, 62,000.

bay rum. An aromatic liquid obtained by distilling the leaves of the bayberry tree, *Pimenta acris,* with rum, and now also synthesized from alcohol, water, and various oils.

bay rum tree. A tree, the **bayberry** *(see).*

Bay State. The nickname for Massachusetts.

bay tree. 1. A tree, the bay *(see).* **2.** The **California laurel** *(see).*

bay window. 1. A large window or series of windows projecting from the wall of a building and forming a recess within. Also called "bay." **2.** *Slang.* A protruding belly; paunch.

bay window

bay·wood (bā′wŏŏd′) *n. Rare.* The wood of a tropical American mahogany, *Swietenia macrophylla.* [After the *Bay* of Campeche, Mexico.]

ba·zaar (bə-zär′) *n.* Also **ba·zar. 1.** An Oriental market, usually consisting of a street lined with shops and stalls. **2.** A shop or part of a store for the sale of miscellaneous articles. **3.** A fair at which miscellaneous articles are sold, usually for charitable purposes. [Earlier *bazarro, bazar,* probably from Italian *bazarro,* from Turkish, from Persian *bāzār,* from Middle Persian *bāchār,* from Old Persian *abécharish†.*]

ba·zoo·ka (bə-zōō′kə) *n.* A portable military weapon consisting of a long, metal, smoothbore tube for firing small, armor-piercing, explosive rockets at short range. [After the *bazooka,* a crude wind instrument made of pipes, invented and named by American comedian Bob Burns (1896–1956).]

bb, b.b. ball bearing.

BB (bē′bē′) *n.* A standard size of lead shot that measures 0.18 inch in diameter. [Perhaps from the letter *b.*]

B.B.A. Bachelor of Business Administration.

BBB, B.B.B. Better Business Bureau.

BBC, B.B.C. British Broadcasting Corporation.

BB gun. A small air rifle for firing BB shot.

bbl, bbl. barrel.

B.C. 1. Bachelor of Chemistry. **2.** Bachelor of Commerce. **3.** before Christ (usually small capitals B.C.). See Usage note at **anno Domini. 4.** British Columbia.

B.C.E. 1. Bachelor of Chemical Engineering. **2.** Bachelor of Civil Engineering.

BCG bacillus Calmette-Guérin (tuberculosis vaccine).

B.Ch.E. Bachelor of Chemical Engineering.

B.C.L. 1. Bachelor of Canon Law. **2.** Bachelor of Civil Law.

BCN Airport code for Barcelona, Spain.

B.C.S. 1. Bachelor of Chemical Science. **2.** Bachelor of Commercial Science.

bd. 1. board. **2.** bond. **3.** *Bookbinding.* bound.

B.D. 1. Bachelor of Divinity. **2.** bank draft. **3.** bills discounted.

BDA Airport code for Bermuda.

bdel·li·um (děl′ē-əm) *n.* **1.** An aromatic gum resin similar to myrrh, produced by various trees of the genus *Commiphora,* of western Asia and Africa. **2.** A substance mentioned in the

Bible, variously interpreted to be carbuncle, rock crystal, pearl, or gum resin. Numbers 11:7. [Latin, from Greek *bdellion,* probably from Hebrew *bədōlaḥ.*]

bd. ft. board foot.

bdl. bundle.

bds. *Bookbinding.* bound in boards.

B.D.S. Bachelor of Dental Surgery.

BDSA Business and Defense Services Administration.

be (bē) *intr.v.*

	1st person	2nd person	3rd person
Present Tense			
singular	**am** (ăm)	**are** (är)†	**is** (ĭz)
plural	**are**	**are**	**are**
†*Archaic 2nd person singular* **art** (ärt)			
Past Tense			
singular	**was** (wŭz, wŏz)	**were** (wûr)‡	**was**
plural	**were**	**were**	**were**
‡*Archaic 2nd person singular* **wast** (wŏst) *or* **wert** (wûrt)			

Present Participle: being (bē′ĭng) **Present Subjunctive: be**
Past Participle: been (bĭn) **Past Subjunctive: were**

1. To exist in actuality; have reality or life: *I think, therefore I am.* **2.** To exist in a specified place; stay; reside: *"Oh, to be in England,/ Now that April's there"* (Robert Browning). **3.** To occupy a specified position: *The food is on the table.* **4.** To take place; occur. **5.** To go. Used chiefly in the past and perfect tenses: *Have you ever been to Italy?* **6.** *Archaic.* To belong; befall. Used in the subjunctive: *Peace be unto you.* **7.** Used as a copula linking a subject and a predicate nominative, adjective, or pronoun, in such senses as: **a.** To equal in meaning or identity: *"To be a Christian was to be a Roman."* (James Bryce). **b.** To signify; symbolize: *A is excellent, C is passing.* **c.** To belong to a specified class or group: *Man is a primate.* **d.** To have or show a specified quality or characteristic: *She is lovely. All men are mortal.* **8.** Used as an auxiliary verb in certain constructions, as: **a.** With the past participle of a transitive verb to form the passive voice: *The mayoral election is held annually. Our club may be disbanded for lack of funds.* **b.** With the present participle of a verb to express a continuing action: *We are working to improve housing conditions.* **c.** With the present participle or the infinitive of a verb, to express intention, obligation, or future action: *She is to eat her dinner before she may play. He is leaving next month.* **d.** With the past participle of certain intransitive verbs of motion to form the perfect tense: *"Where be those roses gone which sweetened so our eyes?"* (Philip Sidney). [The paradigm of the verb "to be" in English is composed of elements derived from three different Indo-European roots, as follows: 1. Be; been: Middle English *be(e)n; be(o)n,* Old English *bēon; bēon,* to come to be. See **bheu-** in Appendix.* 2. Am; art; is; are (singular and plural): Middle English *am; art, eart; is; are* (singular), *aren* (plural); Old English *eam, eom; eart; is; (e)aron* (plural only). See **es-** and **er-**[1] in Appendix.* 3. Was; were: Middle English *wes, was; ware, were* (singular), *weren, were* (plural); Old English *wæs; wære* (singular) *wæron* (plural). See **wes-**[3] in Appendix.*]

be-. Indicates: **1.** A complete or profuse covering or affecting; for example, **becloud, besmear. 2.** A thorough or excessive degree; for example, **bewilder. 3.** An action that causes a condition to exist; for example, **besot, befriend.** [In Middle English be- indicates: 1. Thoroughly, as in **beloved, betray.** 2. On all sides, as in **besiege.** 3. About, over, in relation to, as in **betroth, bequest.** Old English *be-, bi-* indicates: 1. About, over, as in **bethink.** 2. On all sides, as in **beset.** 3. Away, away from, as in **benumb.** See **ambhi** in Appendix.*]

Be The symbol for the element beryllium.

Bé Baumé scale.

B.E. 1. Bachelor of Education. **2.** Bachelor of Engineering. **3.** Bank of England. **4.** Board of Education.

B/E 1. bill of entry. **2.** bill of exchange.

beach (bēch) *n.* **1.** The shore of a body of water, especially when sandy or pebbly. **2.** The sand or pebbles on a shore. —*tr.v.* **beached, beaching, beaches.** To haul or drive (a boat) ashore. [Earlier *bayche, baich†.*]

beach·comb·er (bēch′kō′mər) *n.* **1.** One who lives on what he can find or beg on beaches or wharf areas. **2.** A long wave rolling in toward a beach. [Sense 2, from COMB, in the sense "to break with foam."]

beach flea. Any of various small, jumping crustaceans of the family Talitridae, living on sandy beaches at or near the tide line. Also called "sand hopper."

beach grass. Any grass of the genus *Ammophila,* growing mostly on sandy shores and dunes and having spikelets in long, crowded clusters.

beach·head (bēch′hĕd′) *n.* **1.** A position on an enemy shoreline captured by advance troops of an invading force. **2.** A first achievement that opens the way for further development.

beach·la·mar (bēch′lə-mär′) *n.* A dialect, **bêche-de-mer** *(see).*

beach pea. Either of two similar North American plants, *Lathyrus maritimus,* of the Atlantic coast, or *L. littoralis,* of the Pacific coast, having purplish flowers and sprawling stems.

beach plum. A seacoast shrub, *Prunus maritima,* of northeastern North America, having white flowers and edible plumlike fruit.

beach wormwood. A seacoast plant, *Artemisia stelleriana,* native to Asia, covered with dense, white down and having small yellow flowers. Also called "dusty miller."

bea·con (bē′kən) *n.* **1.** A signal fire; especially, one used to warn of an enemy's approach. **2.** A lighthouse or other signaling or guiding device on a coast. **3.** A radio transmitter that emits a characteristic signal as a warning or guide. **4.** Anything that warns or guides. —*v.* **beaconed, -coning, -cons.** —*tr.* To provide a beacon for. —*intr.* To serve as a beacon. [Middle English *beken,* sign, standard, Old English *bēacen.* See **bhā-**[1] in Appendix.*]

Bea·cons·field, Earl of. See **Disraeli.**

bead (bēd) *n.* **1.** A small, ball-shaped piece of glass, metal, wood, or other material pierced for stringing or threading. **2.** *Plural.* **a.** A necklace made of such pieces. **b.** A rosary. **3.** Any small, round object, especially: **a.** A small drop of moisture. **b.** A bubble of gas in a liquid. **c.** A small knob of metal on the muzzle of a rifle or gun, used for sighting. **4.** *Architecture.* A strip of material, usually wood, with one molded edge placed flush against the inner part of a door or window frame, used as a sash guide or as the stop against which a door closes. Also called "bead butt." —**count** (or **say** or **tell**) **one's beads.** To pray with a rosary. —**draw a bead on.** To take careful aim at. —*v.* **beaded, beading, beads.** —*tr.* To ornament or cover with beads. —*intr.* To collect into beads. [Middle English *bede, bead,* prayer, prayer bead, bead, Old English *gebed,* prayer. See **bhedh-**[2] in Appendix.*]

bead·ing (bē′dĭng) *n.* **1.** Beads or material used for beads. **2.** Ornamentation with beads. **3.** A narrow, half-rounded molding. **4.** Any narrow strip of trimming. **5.** A narrow piece of openwork lace through which ribbon may be run. **6.** Bubbles or froth, as on the rim of a glass.

bea·dle (bēd′l) *n.* **1.** A minor parish official in an English church, whose duties include keeping order and ushering during services. **2.** An official at an English university who supervises and walks before processions. **3.** *Judaism.* A **shammes** *(see).* [Middle English *bedele, bidel,* herald, messenger, beadle, Old English *bydel.* See **bheudh-** in Appendix.*]

Bea·dle (bēd′l), **George Wells.** Born 1903. American geneticist; worked on enzymes.

bea·dle·dom (bēd′l-dəm) *n.* Petty bureaucratic officiousness.

bead·work (bēd′wûrk′) *n.* **1.** Decorative work in beads. **2.** *Architecture.* Beaded molding.

bead·y (bē′dē) *adj.* **-ier, -iest.** **1.** Small, round, and shiny: *beady eyes.* **2.** Decorated or covered with beads.

bea·gle (bē′gəl) *n.* One of a breed of small hounds having short legs, drooping ears, and a smooth coat with white, black, and tan markings. [Middle English *begle,* perhaps from Old French *beegueule,* noisy person : probably *beer,* to gape, from (unattested) Vulgar Latin *batāre* (see **bay,** opening) + *gueule,* throat, from Latin *gula* (see **gwel-**[5] in Appendix*).]

beak (bēk) *n.* **1.** The horny, projecting structure forming the mandibles of a bird; a bill. **2.** A part or organ resembling this, as in some turtles, insects, or fish. **3.** Any hard, cone-shaped, or pointed structure or part. **4.** *Informal.* A person's nose. [Middle English *bec, bek,* from Old French *bec,* from Latin *beccus,* from Gaulish.]

beak·er (bē′kər) *n.* **1. a.** A large drinking cup with a wide mouth. **b.** The contents of such a cup. **2.** An open glass cylinder with a pouring lip, used as a standard laboratory container, and mixing and heating vessel. [Middle English *biker, beker,* from Old Norse *bikarr,* probably from Vulgar Latin *bicārium* (unattested), possibly from Greek *bikos,* drinking-jar, possibly from Egyptian *bik,* oil vessel. See also **pitcher.**]

beam (bēm) *n.* **1.** A squared-off log or large, oblong piece of timber, metal, or stone, used especially in construction. **2.** *Nautical.* **a.** The breadth of a ship at the widest point. **b.** A transverse structural member of the framing of a vessel, used to support a deck and to brace the sides against stress. **c.** The shank of an anchor. **3.** *Informal.* The width across the hips. **4.** A steel tube or wooden roller with flanged ends on which the warp is wound in a loom. **5.** An oscillating lever connected to an engine piston rod and used to transmit power to the crankshaft. **6.** The bar of a balance, from which weighing pans are suspended. **7.** One of the main stems of a deer's antlers. **8.** The main horizontal bar on a plow to which the share, colter, and handles, if any, are attached. **9. a.** A ray of light. **b.** A group of particles traveling together in close parallel trajectories. **10.** A **radio beam** *(see).* —**on the beam. 1.** Following the radio beam. Said of an aircraft. **2.** *Informal.* On the right track; operating correctly. —*v.* **beamed, beaming, beams.** —*tr.* To emit or transmit: *beaming the message.* —*intr.* **1.** To radiate light; to shine. **2.** To smile expansively. [Middle English *beme, beem,* Old English *bēam,* tree, beam. See **bheu-** in Appendix.*]

beam-ends (bēm′ĕndz′) *pl.n.* The ends of a ship's beams. —**on her beam-ends.** Listing so far over that the beams are nearly vertical and there is danger of capsizing.

beam·ish (bē′mĭsh) *adj.* Beaming; smiling; cheerful.

beam·y (bē′mē) *adj.* **-ier, -iest.** **1.** Broad in the beam. **2.** Emitting beams, as of light; radiant.

bean (bēn) *n.* **1.** Any of several plants of the genus *Phaseolus,* having compound leaves, white or yellow flowers, and seed-bearing pods. See **lima bean, string bean. 2.** The edible seed or pod of any of these plants. **3.** Any of several related plants bearing similar pods and seeds. See **broad bean. 4.** Any of various other seeds or pods resembling beans, such as the coffee bean or the vanilla bean. **5.** *Slang.* The head. **6.** *Plural. Slang.* A small amount: *I don't know beans about the stock market.* **7.** *British Slang.* A fellow; chap. —**spill the beans.** To disclose that which was not meant to be disclosed. —*tr.v.* **beaned, beaning, beans.** *Slang.* To hit on the head with a thrown object, especially a pitched baseball. [Middle English *ben(e),* Old English *bēan.* See **bha-bhā** in Appendix.*]

Bean (bēn), **Roy.** Called himself "the Law West of the Pecos." 1825?–1903. American frontiersman; unorthodox justice of the peace at Langtry, Texas.

bean·bag (bēn′băg′) *n.* A small bag filled with dried beans and used for throwing in games.

bean ball. A baseball pitch aimed at the batter's head.

bean beetle. The **Mexican bean beetle** *(see).*

bean caper. A plant of the genus *Zygophyllum;* especially, *Z. fabago,* a shrub of the Middle East, bearing edible buds used as capers.

bean curd. A soft soybean cheese of the Orient. [Translation of Chinese (Mandarin) *tou*[4] *fu*[4] : *tou*[4], bean + *fu*[4], curdled.]

bean·ie (bē′nē) *n.* A small brimless cap.

bean·o (bē′nō) *n.* A form of bingo, especially one using beans as markers. [Perhaps blend of BINGO and BEAN.]

bean·pole (bēn′pōl′) *n.* **1.** A thin pole used to support bean vines. **2.** *Slang.* A very tall, thin person.

bean sprout. A young, tender shoot of certain beans, such as the soybean or the mung bean, used in Chinese cooking.

bean·stalk (bēn′stôk′) *n.* The stem of a bean plant.

bean tree. Any of various trees, such as the catalpa, that bear beanlike fruit.

bear[1] (bâr) *v.* **bore** (bôr, bōr) or *archaic* **bare** (bâr), **borne** (bôrn, bōrn) (for all senses) or **born** (for sense 11 only; see Usage note below), **bearing, bears.** —*tr.* **1.** To support; hold up: *"They hardly seem to tread the earth, but are borne in some more genial element"* (William Hazlitt). **2.** To carry on one's person; convey. **3.** To carry as if in the mind; maintain: *bearing love for others.* **4.** To transmit at large; relate: *bearing glad tidings.* **5.** To have as a visible characteristic: *bearing a scar on his right arm.* **6.** To have as a visible quality or form; exhibit: *"A thousand different shapes it bears"* (Cowley). **7.** To carry (oneself) in a specified way; to conduct. **8.** To be accountable for; assume. **9.** To have a tolerance for; endure: *"better fitted than others to bear the diseases of the country"* (Darwin). **10.** To have a susceptibility to; admit to: *The case will bear investigation.* **11.** To give birth to. See Usage note below. **12.** To produce; yield: *"Tall trunks bore unexpected pale flowers"* (William Golding). **13.** To offer; render: *bearing witness.* **14.** To move by steady pressure; to push: *"boats against the current, borne back ceaselessly into the past."* (F. Scott Fitzgerald). —*intr.* **1.** To yield a product; to produce. **2.** To withstand stress, difficulty, or attrition. Often used with *up.* **3.** To have relevance; apply. **4.** To exert pressure. **5.** To exert oneself determinedly; to forge. **6.** To proceed in a specified direction: *"I bore right, to avoid the Beduin"* (T.E. Lawrence). —See Synonyms at **convey.** —**bear arms against.** To attack with arms; wage war on. —**bear out.** To prove right or justified; confirm: *The results bear out his claims.* —**bear with.** To be patient or tolerant with. [Bear, bore, borne; Middle English *beren, bare, boren,* Old English *beran, bær, boren.* See **bher-**[1] in Appendix.*]

Synonyms: *bear, endure, stand, suffer, abide, tolerate.* These verbs are compared in the sense of withstanding, sustaining, or putting up with. *Bear* pertains broadly to capacity for such an act. *Endure* specifies a continuing capacity to face pain or hardship. The remaining terms are more descriptive of the manner of withstanding or accepting. *Stand* implies resoluteness of spirit. *Suffer* and the less emphatic *abide* suggest resignation and forbearance. *Tolerate,* in its principal application (to something other than pain), connotes reluctant acceptance despite mental reservations.

Usage: In the sense of "give birth to" the past participle *borne* is the usual form for all active constructions and for passive constructions when followed by *by.* The past participle *born* is the correct form for all other passive constructions indicating the fact of birth: *Three children were borne by her, one of whom was born deaf.*

bear[2] (bâr) *n.* **1.** Any of various usually omnivorous mammals of the family Ursidae, having a shaggy coat and a short tail, and walking with the entire lower surface of the foot touching the ground. See **grizzly bear, polar bear. 2.** Any of various animals resembling a bear in some respect, such as the **koala** *(see).* **3. a.** A person who is awkward, clumsy, or ill-mannered. **b.** One who shows endurance or a special aptitude: *a bear for hard work.* **4.** *Capital* **B.** *Astronomy.* Either of two constellations, the **Great Bear** or the **Little Bear** *(both of which see).* **5.** *Stock Market.* An investor or concern that sells shares in the expectation that prices will fall. Compare **bull.** [Middle English *bere,* Old English *bera.* See **bher-**[3] in Appendix.*]

bear·a·ble (bâr′ə-bəl) *adj.* Capable of being borne; endurable; tolerable. —**bear′a·bly** *adv.*

bear·bait·ing (bâr′bā′tĭng) *n.* The former sport of setting dogs to attack or torment a chained bear.

bear·ber·ry (bâr′bĕr′ē) *n., pl.* **-ries.** A trailing shrub, *Arctostaphylos uva-ursi,* of northern regions, having small evergreen leaves, white or pink flowers, and red berries. Also called "kinnikinnick" and sometimes "crowberry."

bear·cat (bâr′kăt′) *n. Slang.* A person, animal, or machine regarded as especially vigorous or fierce.

beard (bîrd) *n.* **1. a.** The hair on the chin, cheeks, and throat of a man. **b.** This hair allowed to grow and cover the skin. **2.** Any similar hairy or hairlike growth such as that on or near the face of certain mammals. **3.** A tuft or group of bristles on certain plants; an awn. **4.** The barb or hook of a fishhook, arrow, or the like. **5.** *Printing.* The part of a piece of type between the face and the shoulder; neck. —*tr.v.* **bearded, bearding, beards. 1.** To furnish with a beard. **2.** To grasp by the beard. **3.** To confront boldly. [Middle English *berd,* Old English *beard.* See **bhardhā** in Appendix.*]

Beard (bîrd), **Charles Austin.** 1874–1948. American educator

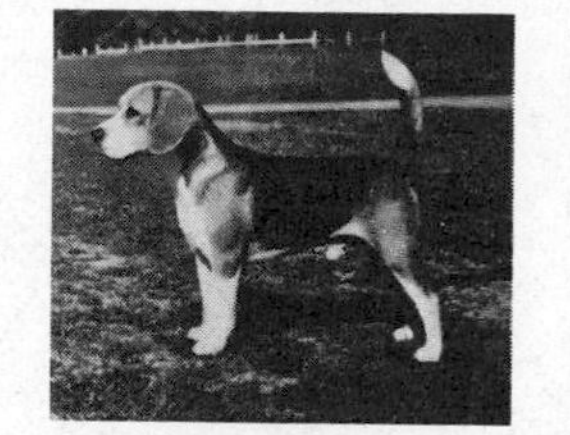

beagle

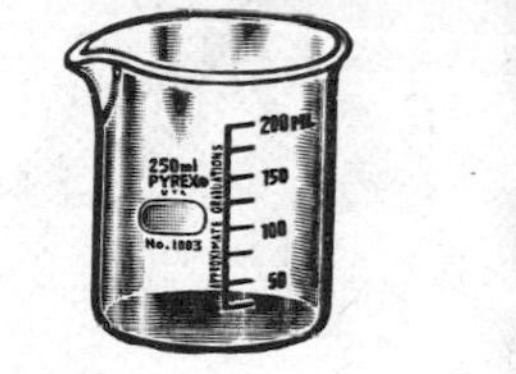

beaker

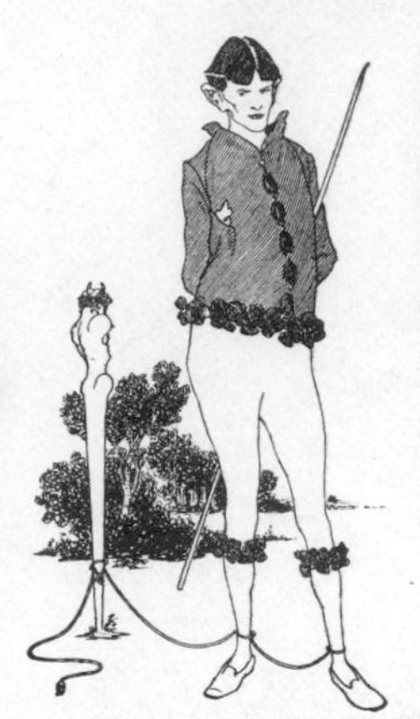

Aubrey Beardsley
Self-portrait drawn in 1896

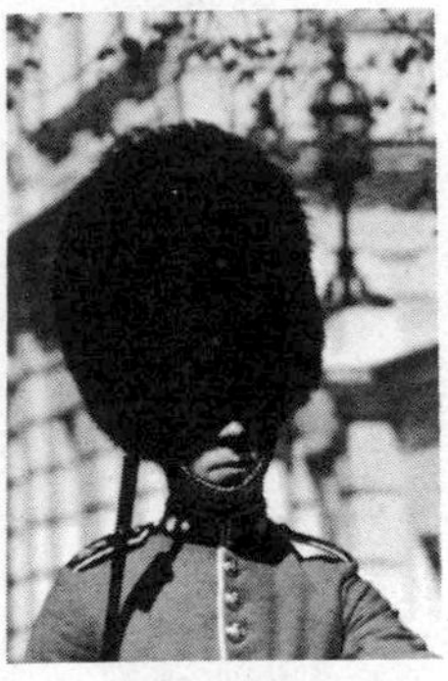

bearskin
British Grenadier Guard

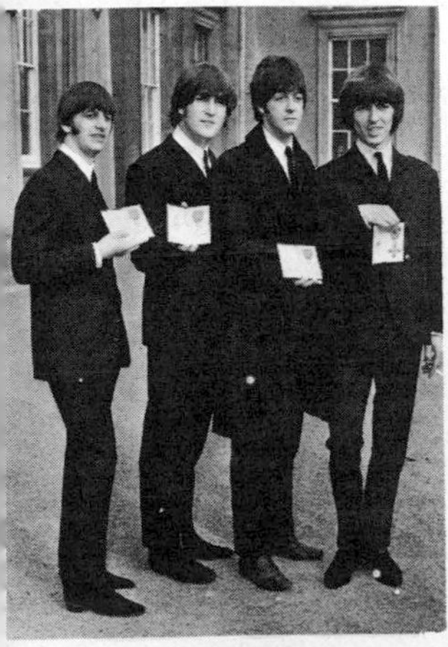

the Beatles
Left to right: Ringo, John, Paul, and George, with medals awarded by the British Crown in 1965

and, with his wife, **Mary R(itter)** (1876–1958), author of works on American history.

Beard (bîrd), **Daniel Carter.** 1850–1941. American writer and illustrator; founder of the first Boy Scout troop in America.

bearded iris. Any of many varieties of iris having beardlike growths at the bases of the three lower, recurved petals.

bearded vulture. A bird, the **lammergeier** *(see).*

beard·less (bîrd′lĭs) *adj.* **1. a.** Having no beard. **b.** Having the beard shaved off; clean-shaven. **2. a.** Not old enough to have a beard. **b.** Immature; inexperienced. **—beard′less·ness** *n.*

Beards·ley (bîrdz′lē), **Aubrey Vincent.** 1872–1898. British illustrator; worked in black and white style of art nouveau.

beard-tongue (bîrd′tŭng′) *n.* Any of various plants of the genus *Penstemon,* mostly of North America, having variously colored, tubular, two-lipped flowers.

bear·er (bâr′ər) *n.* **1.** One that carries or supports. **2.** A porter. **3.** A person who presents for payment a check or other redeemable note. **4.** Any fruit-bearing plant.

bear garden. 1. A place where bears are confined and exhibited, as for bearbaiting. **2.** A place or scene of tumult.

bear grass. 1. A tall plant, *Xerophyllum tenax,* of northwestern North America, having narrow, grasslike leaves and white flowers in a large terminal cluster. **2.** Any of several similar or related plants, especially any of several species of yucca.

bear·ing (bâr′ĭng) *n.* **1.** The manner in which a person carries or conducts himself; deportment; mien. **2.** *Machinery.* **a.** Any part that supports another part or structure. **b.** A device that supports, guides, and reduces the friction of motion between fixed and moving machine parts. **3.** Anything that bears weight or acts as a support. **4.** The part of an architectural arch or beam that rests on a support. **5. a.** The act or period of producing fruit or offspring. **b.** The quantity produced; the yield. **6.** Direction, especially angular direction measured from one position to another using geographical or celestial reference lines. **7.** *Usually plural.* The position or situation of a person or object relative to the surroundings. **8.** Relevancy, relationship, or connection between persons, objects, or concepts: *"he expressly denies its bearing upon social life altogether"* (John Henry Newman). **9.** *Heraldry.* A charge or device on a field.

Synonyms: *bearing, carriage, manner, demeanor, air, mien, presence.* These nouns pertain to distinctive personal qualities. *Bearing,* the most inclusive, applies to both physical posture and conduct in general. *Carriage* denotes physical bearing. *Manner* denotes one's characteristic way of acting; the plural *manners* applies especially to the social proprieties. *Demeanor* is behavior considered as a mirror of personality. *Air* pertains broadly to distinctive appearance, and *mien* to bearing in general and to facial expression in particular. *Presence* denotes the quality of commanding respectful attention.

bearing rein. A rein for a horse, a **checkrein** *(see).*

bear·ish (bâr′ĭsh) *adj.* **1.** Like a bear; clumsy; boorish. **2.** *Stock Market.* Causing, characterized by, or expecting a depression in the price of stocks. **—bear′ish·ly** *adv.* **—bear′ish·ness** *n.*

béarnaise sauce. **Sauce béarnaise** *(see).*

Bear River (bâr). A river rising in northeastern Utah and flowing about 350 miles, first north to Wyoming, then northwest to Idaho, and finally south into Great Salt Lake in Utah.

bear's-ear (bârz′îr′) *n.* A plant, the **auricula** *(see).*

bear·skin (bâr′skĭn′) *n.* **1.** Something, as a rug, made from the skin of a bear. **2.** A tall military headdress made of black fur.

beast (bēst) *n.* **1.** Any animal except man; especially, any large, four-footed animal. **2.** The qualities of an animal; animal nature. **3.** A brutal person. [Middle English *beste,* from Old French, from Latin *bēstia*†.]

beast epic. A long satirical verse narrative in which the characters are animals with human feelings and motives.

beast·ly (bēst′lē) *adj.* **-lier, -liest. 1.** Resembling or characteristic of a beast; bestial. **2.** Disagreeable; nasty; abominable. —See Synonyms at **brute.** —*adv. Chiefly British Informal.* Very. **—beast′li·ness** *n.*

beast of burden. An animal used for transporting loads.

beat (bēt) *v.* **beat, beaten** (bēt′n) or **beat, beating, beats.** —*tr.* **1.** To strike or hit repeatedly. **2.** To punish by hitting or whipping; flog. **3.** To pound or strike against repeatedly: *waves beating the shore.* **4.** To shape or break by repeated blows; to forge. **5.** To make flat by pounding or trampling. **6.** To mix rapidly with an instrument to a frothy consistency: *beat two eggs in a bowl.* **7.** To flap (wings, for example). **8.** To sound (a signal), as on a drum. **9.** To mark or count (time or rhythm) with the hands or with a baton. **10.** To defeat or subdue. **11.** *Informal.* To excel or surpass; be superior to. **12.** *Slang.* To perplex or baffle. —*intr.* **1.** To inflict repeated blows. **2.** To throb or pulsate rhythmically. **3.** *Physics.* To cause beating by superposing waves of different frequencies. **4.** To emit sound when struck: *The gong beat thunderously.* **5.** To sound a signal, as on a drum. **6.** To admit of rapid whipping to a froth. **7.** To hunt through woods or underbrush in search of game. **8.** *Nautical.* To progress against the wind by tacking. —See Synonyms at **defeat, pulsate. —beat about** (or **around**) **the bush.** To approach a subject in a roundabout manner. **—beat a retreat.** To flee or withdraw. **—beat back.** To force to retreat or withdraw. **—beat down.** To force or persuade (a seller) to accept a lower price. **—beat it.** *Slang.* To get going; go away. **—beat off.** To drive away. **—beat up.** *Informal.* To give a thorough beating to; thrash. —*n.* **1.** A stroke or blow, especially one that produces a sound or acts as a signal. **2.** A periodic pulsation or throb. **3.** *Physics.* An amplitude pulse produced by beating. **4.** *Music.* **a.** A regular and rhythmical unit of time. **b.** The gesture given by a conductor or the symbol representing this unit of time. **5.** The measured and rhythmical sound of verse; meter. **6.** The area regularly covered by a policeman, sentry, or newspaper reporter. **7.** *Journalism Slang.* The reporting of a news item obtained ahead of one's competitors. **8.** A member of the **beat generation** *(see).* —See Synonyms at **rhythm.** —*adj. Informal.* Worn-out; fatigued. [Beat, beat, beaten; Middle English *beten, bette, beten,* Old English *bēatan, bēot, bēaten.* See **bhau-** in Appendix.*]

beat·en (bēt′n) *adj.* **1.** Made thin or formed by hammering. **2. a.** Worn by many footsteps; much traveled: *a beaten path.* **b.** Worn by continuous use; tattered. **3.** Tired and worn-out. **—off the beaten track** (or **path**). Not well-known; unusual.

beat·er (bē′tər) *n.* **1.** One that beats, especially an instrument for beating: *a carpet beater.* **2.** A person who drives wild game from under cover for a hunter.

beat generation. A group belonging to the generation coming to maturity after World War II that asserted a loss of faith in Western cultural traditions and rejected conventional norms of dress and behavior.

be·a·tif·ic (bē′ə-tĭf′ĭk) *adj.* Showing or producing exalted joy or blessedness: *a beatific smile.* [Late Latin *beātificus* : Latin *beātus,* blessed, from the past participle of *beāre,* to make happy (see **deu-²** in Appendix*) + *facere,* to do (see **dhē-¹** in Appendix*).] **—be′a·tif′i·cal·ly** *adv.*

be·at·i·fi·ca·tion (bē-ăt′ə-fĭ-kā′shən) *n.* **1.** The act of beatifying. **2.** The state of being beatified. **3.** *Roman Catholic Church.* An act of the pope declaring that a deceased person is beatified, usually as the step prior to canonization.

be·at·i·fy (bē-ăt′ə-fī′) *tr.v.* **-fied, -fying, -fies. 1.** To make blessedly happy. **2.** *Roman Catholic Church.* To proclaim (a deceased person) to be one of the blessed and thus worthy of public religious honor. Compare **canonize. 3.** To exalt above all others. [Late Latin *beātificāre,* from *beātificus,* BEATIFIC.]

beat·ing (bē′tĭng) *n.* **1.** Punishment by whipping, flogging, or thrashing. **2.** A defeat. **3.** A throbbing or pulsation, as of the heart. **4.** *Physics.* The periodic alternation of amplitude maxima and minima produced by interference between two waves of different frequency.

be·at·i·tude (bē-ăt′ə-tōōd′, -tyōōd′) *n.* **1.** Supreme blessedness or happiness. **2.** *Capital* **B.** Any of nine declarations of blessedness made by Jesus in the Sermon on the Mount. Matthew 5:3–11. [Latin *beātitūdo,* from *beātus,* blessed. See **beatific.**]

Beat·les (bēt′əlz), **the.** English quartet of composers and musicians; members are John Lennon (born 1940), Ringo Starr (original name, Richard Starkey; born 1940), (James) Paul McCartney (born 1942), and George Harrison (born 1943).

beat·nik (bēt′nĭk) *n.* **1.** A member of the **beat generation** *(see).* **2.** A person who acts and dresses with pointed, often exaggerated, disregard for what is thought proper and who is given to radical and extravagant social criticism or self-expression. [BEAT + (NUD)NIK.]

Bea·ton (bēt′n), **Cecil Walter Hardy.** Born 1904. English photographer, painter, and theatrical designer.

Be·a·trice (bē′ə-trĭs). A feminine given name. [Italian *Beatrice,* from Late Latin *Beātrix,* from *beātus,* blessed. See **beatific.**]

beau (bō) *n., pl.* **beaus** or **beaux** (bōz). **1.** The sweetheart of a woman or girl. **2.** A man excessively interested in fine clothes and social etiquette; a dandy. [French, fine, handsome, from Latin *bellus,* pretty, handsome, fine. See **deu-²** in Appendix.*]

Beau Brum·mell (bō brŭm′əl). A dandy; fop. [After George Bryan *("Beau") Brummell* (1778–1840), British dandy.]

Beau·fort scale (bō′fərt). A scale on which successive ranges of wind velocities are assigned code numbers from 0 to 12 or from 0 to 17, corresponding to names from *calm* to *hurricane.* [After Sir Francis *Beaufort* (1774–1857), British admiral.]

Beau·fort Sea (bō′fərt). A part of the Arctic Ocean lying off the coasts of northwestern Canada and northeastern Alaska.

beau geste (bō zhĕst′) *pl.* **beaux gestes** (bō zhĕst′) or **beau gestes** (bō zhĕst′). **1.** A gracious gesture. **2.** A gesture noble in form but meaningless in substance. [French, "beautiful gesture."]

beau i·de·al (bō ī-dē′əl) *pl.* **beau ideals. 1.** The concept of perfect beauty. **2.** An idealized type or model. [French *beau idéal,* "ideal beauty."]

Beau·mar·chais (bō-mȧr-shā′), **Pierre Augustin Caron de.** 1732–1799. French dramatist and pamphleteer.

beau monde (bō mŏnd′; *French* bō môNd′) *pl.* **beaux mondes** (bō môNd′) or **beau mondes** (bō mŏndz′). Fashionable society. [French, "beautiful world."]

Beau·mont (bō′mŏnt). An industrial city and port of eastern Texas, on the Gulf of Mexico. Population, 119,000.

Beau·mont (bō′mŏnt), **Francis.** 1584–1616. English dramatist; collaborated with John **Fletcher** *(see).*

Beau·mont (bō′mŏnt), **William.** 1785–1853. American military surgeon; pioneer in study of digestive processes.

Beau·re·gard (bō′rə-gärd), **Pierre Gustave Toutant de.** 1818–1893. American Confederate general.

beaut (byōōt) *n. Slang.* Something outstanding of its kind: *"When I make a mistake, it's a beaut."* (Fiorello H. La Guardia). [Short for BEAUTY.]

beau·te·ous (byōō′tē-əs, -tyəs) *adj.* Beautiful, especially to the sight. **—beau′te·ous·ly** *adv.* **—beau′te·ous·ness** *n.*

beau·ti·cian (byōō-tĭsh′ən) *n.* One skilled in cosmetic treatments, as in a beauty parlor. [BEAUT(Y) + -ICIAN.]

beau·ti·ful (byōō′tə-fəl) *adj.* Having beauty in any of its forms. —*n.* Beauty, as an aesthetic or philosophical principle. Preceded by *the.* **—beau′ti·ful·ly** *adv.* **—beau′ti·ful·ness** *n.*

Synonyms: *beautiful, lovely, pretty, handsome, comely, fair.* All these adjectives apply to that which appeals to the senses or mind. *Beautiful,* the most comprehensive, applies to what stirs a heightened response of the senses and of the mind on its highest level. *Lovely* pertains to that which inspires ardent emotion rather than intellectual appreciation. *Pretty* suggests only sensory appeal of a limited and superficial nature. *Handsome* stresses visual appeal by reason of conformity to ideals of form and proportion. *Comely* is usually restricted to wholesome physical attractiveness. *Fair,* in this context, emphasizes visual appeal deriving from freshness and purity.

beau·ti·fy (byōō′tə-fī′) *v.* **-fied, -fying, -fies.** *—tr.* To make beautiful: *"Grace and tenderness of feeling beautify Surrey's work"* (Tucker Brooke). *—intr.* To become beautiful. [BEAUT(Y) + -FY.] **—beau′ti·fi·ca′tion** *n.* **—beau′ti·fi′er** *n.*

beau·ty (byōō′tē) *n., pl.* **-ties. 1.** A pleasing quality associated with harmony of form or color, excellence of craftsmanship, truthfulness, originality, or other, often unspecifiable property. **2.** Appearance or sound that arouses a strong, contemplative delight; loveliness: *a woman who has preserved her youthful beauty.* **3.** A person or thing that arouses such delight; especially, a woman widely regarded as beautiful. **4.** A part, characteristic, or attribute that arouses such delight; a specific excellence or grace: *"discern the beauties . . . with pleasure, and the imperfections with dislike"* (Addison). **5.** The feature that is most effective, gratifying, or telling: *The beauty of the venture is that we stand to lose nothing.* **6.** *Informal.* An outstanding or conspicuous example. [Middle English *beau(l)te,* from Old French *bealte, beaute,* from Vulgar Latin *bellitās* (unattested), from Latin *bellus,* pretty, handsome, fine. See **deu-²** in Appendix.*]

beau·ty·ber·ry (byōō′tē-bĕr′ē) *n., pl.* **-ries.** Any shrub of the genus *Callicarpa,* having glistening, purplish, berrylike fruit. *C. americana,* of southeastern North America, is also called "Bermuda mulberry," "French mulberry."

beau·ty·bush (byōō′tē-bŏŏsh′) *n.* A shrub, *Kolkwitzia amabilis,* native to China, widely cultivated for its profusely blooming pink flowers.

beauty parlor. An establishment providing women with services that include hair treatment, manicures, facials, and the like. Also called "beauty salon," "beauty shop."

beauty spot. 1. A small black mark penciled or glued on a woman's face or shoulders to accentuate the fairness of her skin. Also called "patch." **2.** A mole or freckle.

Beau·voir (bō-vwär′), **Simone de.** Born 1908. French writer; a founder of existentialism.

beaux. Alternate plural of **beau.**

beaux-arts (bō-zär′) *pl.n. French.* The fine arts.

bea·ver¹ (bē′vər) *n.* **1.** A large, aquatic rodent of the genus *Castor,* having thick brown fur, webbed hind feet, a paddlelike, hairless tail, and chisellike front teeth adapted for gnawing bark and felling trees used to build dams. **2.** The fur of a beaver. **3.** A full beard. **4.** A top hat, originally made of the beaver's underfur. **5.** A napped wool fabric, similar to felt, used for outer garments. **6.** Grayish brown to light or dark grayish yellowish brown. See **color.** [Middle English *bever,* Old English *be(o)for.* See **bher-³** in Appendix.*]

bea·ver² (bē′vər) *n.* **1.** A movable piece of medieval armor attached to a helmet or breastplate to protect the mouth and chin. **2.** The visor on a helmet. [Middle English *baviere,* from Old French, from *baver,* to slaver, from (unattested) Vulgar Latin *baba* (imitative).]

bea·ver·board (bē′vər-bôrd′, -bōrd′) *n.* A light, semirigid building material of compressed wood pulp, used for walls and partitions. [From the former trademark *Beaverboard.*]

Bea·ver·brook (bē′vər-brŏŏk′), **First Baron.** Title of William Maxwell Aitken. 1879–1964. Canadian-born British newspaper publisher and public official.

be·bop (bē′bŏp′) *n.* A type of music, **bop** *(see).* [Imitative of a two-beat phrase in this music.]

BEC Bureau of Employees' Compensation.

be·calm (bĭ-käm′) *tr.v.* **-calmed, -calming, -calms. 1.** To render (a ship) motionless for lack of wind. **2.** To make calm or still; soothe.

be·came. Past tense of **become.**

be·cause (bĭ-kôz′, -kŭz′) *conj.* For the reason that; since. See Usage note below. **—because of.** By reason of; on account of. [Middle English *bi cause* : *bi,* BY + CAUSE.]

Usage: *Because* is the most specific of the conjunctions used to express cause or reason and always indicates an unequivocal causal relationship: *He stayed behind because he was ill. Inasmuch as* is direct but less forceful; the clause it introduces justifies or more fully explains what has preceded. *For* (after a comma) is less direct in indicating cause; the elements it links are more independent: *He stayed behind, for he was ill. Since* is often a weak form of *because,* but its connotation of time implies that what it introduces makes the preceding matter follow by logical sequence or inference: *He stayed behind, since he had become ill. As* (after a comma except when it begins the sentence) is the weakest in indicating cause, and must be used with great care to avoid confusion with mere reference to time. When *because* follows a negative, ambiguity must also be guarded against: *We did not go because we were unprepared* (more clearly, *We were unprepared, so we did not go,* or, in another sense, *Our failure to go was not due to lack of preparation).* Avoid also the redundant construction *the reason is because* (properly *the reason is,* followed by a noun or a clause).

bec·ca·fi·co (bĕk′ə-fē′kō) *n., pl.* **-cos.** Any small songbird or warbler of various genera, eaten as a delicacy in Italy. [Italian, "figpecker" : *beccare,* to peck, from *becco,* beak, from Latin *beccus,* BEAK + *fico,* fig, from Latin *ficus,* FIG.]

bé·cha·mel sauce (bā′shə-mĕl′). A white sauce of butter, flour, milk or cream, and seasonings. [French *sauce béchamelle,* invented by Louis de *Béchamel,* steward of Louis XIV.]

be·chance (bĭ-chăns′, -chäns′) *v.* **-chanced, -chancing, -chances.** *Rare. —intr.* To happen; chance. *—tr.* To befall; happen to. [BE- + CHANCE (verb).]

bêche-de-mer (bĕsh′də-mâr′) *n., pl.* **bêches-de-mer** (bĕsh′də-mâr′). **1.** A marine animal, the **trepang** *(see),* or a food prepared from it. **2.** A lingua franca that combines Malay and English, spoken in the southwest Pacific. In this sense, also called "beach-la-mar." [Pseudo-French, from earlier English *biche de mer,* from Portuguese *bicho do mar,* "sea worm" : *bicho,* worm, from Late Latin *bēstulus,* diminutive of Latin *bēstia,* BEAST + *mar,* sea, from Latin *mare* (see **mori-** in Appendix*). The designation of the language is probably from the use of trepang as an important trade item in this area.]

Bech·u·a·na (bĕch′ōō-ä′nə) *n., pl.* **Bechuana** or **-nas. 1.** A member of a Bantu people inhabiting Botswana in south-central Africa. **2.** The Bantu language of this people.

Bech·u·a·na·land. See **Botswana.**

beck¹ (bĕk) *n.* A gesture of beckoning or summons. **—at one's beck and call.** Very willingly obedient. [Middle English, from *becken,* to beckon, short for *beknen,* to BECKON.]

beck² (bĕk) *n. British.* A small brook. [Middle English, from Old Norse *bekkr.* See **bhegw-** in Appendix.*]

Beck·en·ham (bĕk′ə-nəm). A former administrative division of London, England, now part of **Bromley** *(see).*

beck·et (bĕk′ĭt) *n. Nautical.* A device, such as a looped rope, hook and eye, strap, or grommet, for holding or fastening loose ropes, spars, or oars in position. [Origin unknown.]

Beck·et (bĕk′ĭt), **Thomas à.** Known as Saint Thomas Becket. 1118?–1170. English Roman Catholic martyr; appointed archbishop of Canterbury (1162) by Henry II; assassinated.

Beck·ett (bĕk′ĭt), **Samuel.** Born 1906. Irish playwright, novelist, and poet; resident in France.

beck·on (bĕk′ən) *v.* **-oned, -oning, -ons.** *—tr.* **1.** To signal or summon (another), as by nodding or waving. **2.** To attract as if with gestures: *"a lovely, sunny country that seemed to beckon them on to the Emerald City"* (L. Frank Baum). *—intr.* **1.** To make a summoning or signaling gesture. **2.** To have a strong attraction; be enticing. *—n.* A gesture or motion of summons. [Middle English *beknen,* Old English *bēcnan, bīecnan.* See **bhā-¹** in Appendix.*] **—beck′on·er** *n.* **—beck′on·ing·ly** *adv.*

be·cloud (bĭ-kloud′) *tr.v.* **-clouded, -clouding, -clouds. 1.** To darken with clouds. **2.** To confuse; to obscure.

be·come (bĭ-kŭm′) *v.* **-came** (-kām′), **-come, -coming, -comes.** *—intr.* To grow or come to be: *"All women become like their mothers."* (Oscar Wilde). *—tr.* **1.** To be appropriate or suitable to: *"it would not become me . . . to interfere with parties"* (Swift). **2.** To show to advantage; look good with. **—become of.** To be the fate or subsequent condition of. [Middle English *becomen,* Old English *becuman.* See **gwā-** in Appendix.*]

be·com·ing (bĭ-kŭm′ĭng) *adj.* **1.** Appropriate; suitable; proper. **2.** Pleasing or attractive to the eye. **—be·com′ing·ly** *adv.* **—be·com′ing·ness** *n.*

Bec·que·rel (bĕ-krĕl′, bĕk′ə-rĕl′), **Antoine Henri.** 1852–1908. French physicist; discovered natural radioactivity.

Becquerel ray. *Obsolete.* Radiation associated with radioactivity. [After Antoine Henri BECQUEREL.]

bed (bĕd) *n.* **1. a.** A piece of furniture for reclining and sleeping, typically consisting of a flat, rectangular frame, a mattress resting on springs, and bedclothes. **b.** A bedstead. **c.** A mattress or a mattress with bedclothes. **2.** Any place or surface upon which one may rest or sleep. **3.** A place where one may sleep for a night; lodging. **4.** A place for lovemaking. **5.** A marital relationship, with its rights and intimacies. **6.** A small plot of cultivated or planted land: *flower bed.* **7.** The bottom of a watercourse or other body of water. **8.** A supporting, underlying, or securing part, especially: **a.** A layer of food surmounted by another kind of food: *lobster on a bed of rice.* **b.** A foundation of crushed rock or a similar substance for a road or railroad; roadbed. **c.** A layer of mortar upon which stones or bricks are laid. **d.** The heavy table of a printing press in which the type form is placed. **9.** *Geology.* **a.** A rock mass of large horizontal extent bounded, especially above, by physically different material. **b.** A deposit, as of ore, parallel to the local stratification. **—put** (or **go**) **to bed.** *Journalism.* To go to press; be printed. *—v.* **bedded, bedding, beds.** *—tr.* **1.** To furnish with a bed or sleeping place. **2.** To put to bed. **3.** To make a bed for; spread litter for. Usually used with *down: He bedded down the sheep under a lean-to.* **4. a.** To prepare (soil) for planting. **b.** To plant in a prepared bed of soil. **5.** To lay flat or arrange in layers. **6.** To embed. **7.** To have sexual intercourse with: *"Within two weeks Cyrus had wooed, wedded, bedded, and impregnated her."* (Steinbeck). *—intr.* **1.** To go to bed. **2.** To form layers or strata. **—go to bed (with).** *Slang.* To have sexual intercourse. [Middle English *bed(e),* Old English *bed(d).* See **bhedh-¹** in Appendix.*]

bed and board. 1. Sleeping accommodations and meals. **2.** One's home; especially, the home of a married couple: *She has left his bed and board.*

be·daub (bĭ-dôb′) *tr.v.* **-daubed, -daubing, -daubs. 1.** To smear; soil. **2.** To ornament in a vulgar and showy fashion.

be·daz·zle (bĭ-dăz′əl) *tr.v.* **-zled, -zling, -zles.** To dazzle so completely as to confuse or blind. **—be·daz′zle·ment** *n.*

bed·bug (bĕd′bŭg′) *n.* Also **bed bug.** A wingless, bloodsucking insect, *Cimex lectularius,* that has a flat, reddish body and a disagreeable odor and that often infests human dwellings.

bed·cham·ber (bĕd′chām′bər) *n.* A bedroom

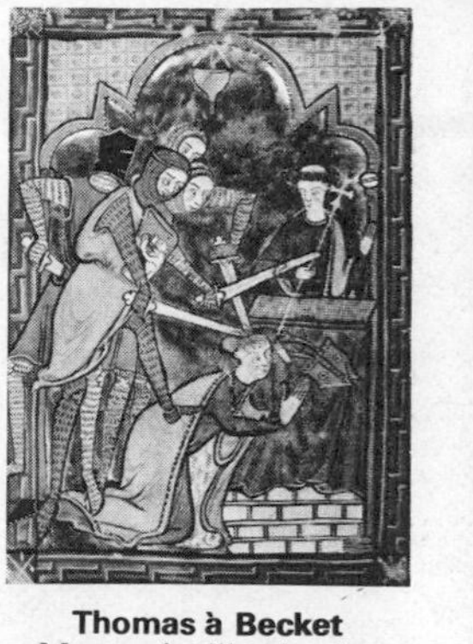

Thomas à Becket
Manuscript illumination showing the saint's assassination

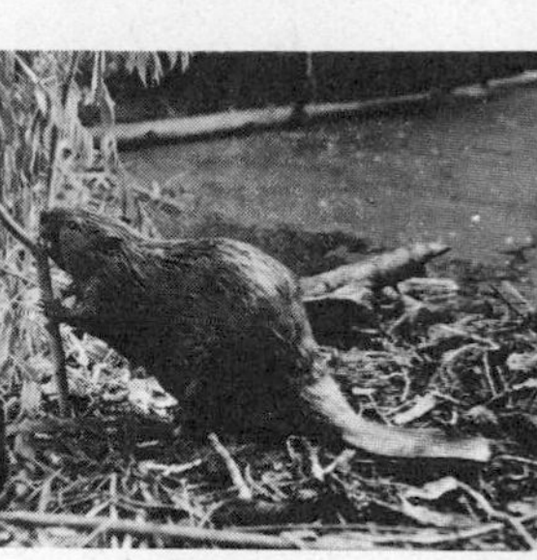

beaver¹
Castor canadensis
American beaver

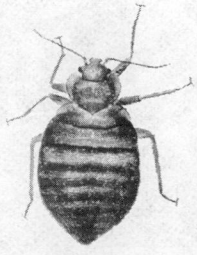

bedbug

bed·clothes (bĕd′klōz′, -klō*thz*′) *pl.n.* Coverings, such as sheets and blankets, ordinarily used on a bed.
bed·ding (bĕd′ĭng) *n.* **1.** Bedclothes. **2.** Straw or similar material for animals to sleep on. **3.** Something that forms a foundation or bottom layer. **4.** A placing of growing plants in a massed group. **5.** *Geology.* Stratification of rocks into beds.
Bed·ding·ton and Wal·ling·ton (bĕd′ĭng-tən; wŏl′ĭng-tən). A former administrative division of London, England, now part of **Sutton** *(see).*
Bede (bēd), **Saint.** Also **Bae·da** (bē′də). Known as the Venerable Bede. A.D. 673–735. English historian, teacher, and theologian.
be·deck (bĭ-dĕk′) *tr.v.* **-decked, -decking, -decks.** To deck out or adorn in a showy fashion; cover with decorations.
bedes·man (bēdz′mən) *n., pl.* **-men** (-mĭn). An almsman.
be·dev·il (bĭ-dĕv′əl) *tr.v.* **-iled, -iling, -ils.** Also *chiefly British* **-illed, -illing.** **1.** To torment devilishly; plague; harass. **2.** To worry, annoy, or frustrate. **3.** To possess as with a devil; bewitch. **4.** To spoil; to ruin. —**be·dev′il·ment** *n.*
be·dew (bĭ-dōō′, -dyōō′) *tr.v.* **-dewed, -dewing, -dews.** To wet with or as if with dew.

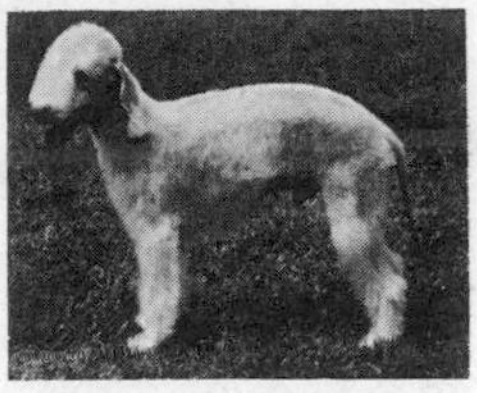
Bedlington terrier

bed·fast (bĕd′făst′, -fäst′) *adj.* Confined to bed; bedridden.
bed·fel·low (bĕd′fĕl′ō) *n.* **1.** A person with whom one shares a bed; bedmate. **2.** A temporary associate, collaborator, or ally.
Bed·ford (bĕd′fərd). **1.** *Abbr.* **Beds, Beds.** Also **Bed·ford·shire** (-shîr, -shər). A county occupying 473 square miles in central England. Population, 312,000. **2.** The capital of this county, on the Ouse. Population, 53,000.
Bedford cord. A heavy cotton or woolen fabric in a ribbed weave with wide or narrow raised cords, much like corduroy. [From BEDFORD.]
be·dight (bĭ-dīt′) *tr.v.* **-dight, -dight** or **-dighted, -dighting, -dights.** *Rare.* To dress or adorn. [Middle English *bedighten* : *be-*, thoroughly + DIGHT.]
be·dim (bĭ-dĭm′) *tr.v.* **-dimmed, -dimming, -dims.** To make dim.
be·di·zen (bĭ-dī′zən, -dĭz′ən) *tr.v.* **-zened, -zening, -zens.** To dress or ornament vulgarly or tastelessly. [BE- + DIZEN.] —**be·di′zen·ment** *n.*

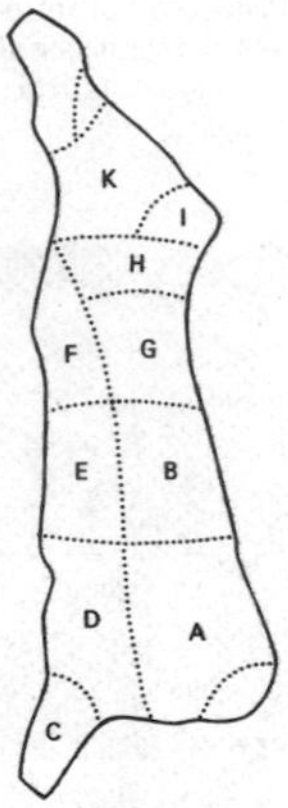

beef
A. Chuck
B. Ribs
C. Shank
D. Brisket
E. Plate
F. Flank
G. Loin (tenderloin and porterhouse)
H. Sirloin
I. Rump
K. Round

bed·lam (bĕd′ləm) *n.* **1.** Any place or situation of noisy uproar and confusion. **2.** A lunatic asylum; madhouse. [Middle English *Bedlem, Bethlem,* Hospital of St. Mary of *Bethlehem,* in southeastern London, which was an asylum at one time.]
bed·lam·ite (bĕd′lə-mīt′) *n.* A madman; lunatic.
Bed·ling·ton terrier (bĕd′lĭng-tən). A dog of a breed developed in England, having a woolly grayish or brownish coat. [From *Bedlington,* England.]
Bed·loe's Island, Bed·loe Island. Former names for **Liberty Island.**
bed·mate (bĕd′māt′) *n.* One with whom a bed is shared.
bed molding. 1. The molding between the corona and frieze of an entablature. **2.** Any molding below a projecting part.
bed of roses. A state of idyllic comfort or luxury.
Bed·ou·in (bĕd′ōō-ĭn) *n.* Also **Bed·u·in.** An Arab of any of the nomadic tribes of the deserts of North Africa, Arabia, and Syria. [Middle English *Bedoin,* from Old French *beduin,* from Arabic *badāwīn,* plural of *badāwī,* from *badw,* desert.]
bed·pan (bĕd′păn′) *n.* **1.** A metal, glass, or plastic receptacle for the excreta of bedridden persons. **2.** A **warming pan** *(see).*
bed·plate (bĕd′plāt′) *n.* A metal plate, frame, or platform serving as a base or support for a machine.
bed·post (bĕd′pōst′) *n.* Any of the four vertical posts at the corners of some beds.
be·drag·gle (bĭ-drăg′əl) *tr.v.* **-gled, -gling, -gles.** To make wet and limp. [BE- + DRAGGLE.]
bed·rid·den (bĕd′rĭd′n) *adj.* Also **bed·rid** (-rĭd′). Confined to one's bed because of illness or infirmity. [Middle English *bedreden, bedrede,* Old English *bedrida,* from noun, "one who is bedridden" : BED + *rīda,* a rider, from *rīdan,* to RIDE.]
bed·rock (bĕd′rŏk′) *n.* **1.** The solid rock that underlies all soil, sand, clay, gravel, and loose material on the earth's surface. **2.** The lowest or bottom level. **3.** Fundamental principles.
bed·roll (bĕd′rōl′) *n.* A portable roll of bedding used especially by campers and others who sleep outdoors.
bed·room (bĕd′rōōm′, -rŏŏm′) *n.* A room for sleeping in.
Beds, Beds. Bedford.
bed·side (bĕd′sīd′) *n.* The space alongside a bed, especially the bed of a sick person. —*adj.* Near a bed: *a bedside table.*
bedside manner. The attitude and conduct of a doctor in the presence of a patient, intended to inspire confidence.

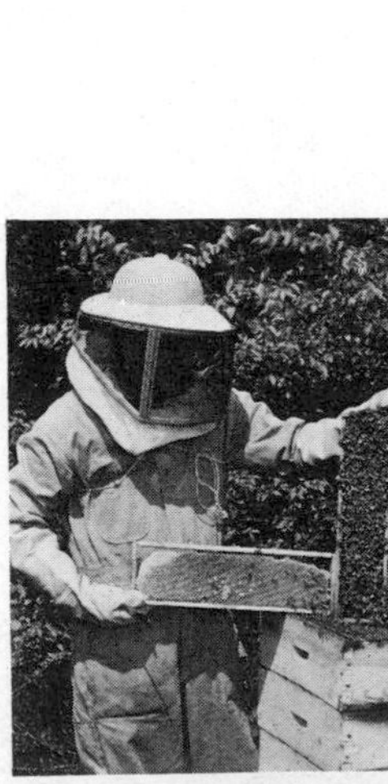
beekeeper
In protective clothing while removing a bee-covered honey frame from a hive

bed·sore (bĕd′sôr′, -sōr′) *n.* A pressure-induced ulceration of the skin with necrosis and sometimes deep muscular infection, occurring during long confinement to bed.
bed·spread (bĕd′sprĕd′) *n.* A usually decorative bed covering.
bed·spring (bĕd′sprĭng′) *n.* **1.** The network of springs supporting the mattress of a bed. **2.** Any of these springs.
bed·stead (bĕd′stĕd′) *n.* The frame supporting a bed.
bed·straw (bĕd′strô′) *n.* Any of various plants of the genus *Galium,* having whorled leaves, small white or yellow flowers, and prickly burrs. [From its former use as a mattress stuffing.]
bed·time (bĕd′tīm′) *n.* The time when one goes to bed.
bee[1] (bē) *n.* **1.** Any of various winged, hairy-bodied, usually stinging insects of the order Hymenoptera, including many solitary species as well as the social members of the family Apidae, and characterized by specialized structures for sucking nectar and gathering pollen from flowers. See **honeybee. 2.** A social gathering where people combine work, competition, and amusement: *"There was a 'bee' to-day for making a road up to the church."* (Anne Langton). [Middle English *bee,* Old English *bēo.* See **bhei-**[1] in Appendix.*]
bee[2] (bē) *n.* A **bee block** *(see).* [Middle English *bege,* a ring of metal, Old English *bēag.* See **bheug-**[3] in Appendix.*]
bee[3] (bē) *n.* The letter *b.*
bee balm. A plant, **Oswego tea** *(see).*
Bee·be (bē′bē), **(Charles) William.** 1877–1962. American naturalist and author; explored ocean in bathysphere.
bee block. *Nautical.* A piece of hardwood on either side of a bowsprit through which forestays are reeved. Also called "bee."
bee·bread (bē′brĕd′) *n.* A brownish substance consisting of a mixture of pollen and nectar, fed by bees to their larvae.
beech (bēch) *n.* **1.** Any tree of the genus *Fagus,* characterized by smooth, light-colored bark and edible nuts partly enclosed in a prickly husk; especially, *F. grandifolia,* of eastern North America, and *F. sylvatica,* of Europe. **2.** The wood of any of these trees. [Middle English *beche,* Old English *bēce.* See **bhāgo-** in Appendix.*] —**beech** *adj.*
Bee·cham (bē′chəm), Sir **Thomas.** 1879–1961. British conductor of opera and symphony orchestras.
beech·drops (bēch′drŏps′) *n.* Plural in form, used with a singular or plural verb. A leafless plant, *Epifagus virginiana,* of eastern North America, that has brownish or purplish flowers and is parasitic on the roots of the beech tree.
Bee·cher (bē′chər), **Henry Ward.** 1813–1887. American Protestant clergyman, editor, and abolitionist leader.
Bee·cher (bē′chər), **Lyman.** 1775–1863. American Protestant theologian; father of Henry Ward Beecher and Harriet Beecher Stowe.
beech mast. The nuts of the beech tree; beechnuts.
beech·nut (bēch′nŭt′) *n.* The small, edible nut of the beech tree.
bee-eat·er (bē′ē′tər) *n.* Any of various chiefly tropical Old World birds of the family Meropidae, having brightly colored plumage and feeding chiefly on bees.
beef (bēf) *n., pl.* **beeves** (bēvz) or **beefs** (only form for sense 4). **1.** A full-grown steer, bull, ox, or cow, especially one intended for use as meat. **2.** The flesh of a slaughtered full-grown steer, bull, ox, or cow. **3.** *Informal.* Human muscle; brawn. **4.** *Slang.* A complaint. —*intr.v.* **beefed, beefing, beefs.** *Slang.* To complain. —**beef up.** *Slang.* To reinforce; build up. [Middle English *boef, beef,* beef, ox, from Old French *boef,* from Latin *bōs* (stem *bov-*), ox. See **gwou-** in Appendix.*] —**beef** *adj.*
beef bour·gui·gnon (bŏŏr′gē-nyōn′). Also *French* **boeuf bour·gui·gnon** (bœf′ bōōr-gē-nyôN′). Braised beef cubes simmered in a seasoned red-wine sauce with mushrooms, carrots, and onions. [Partial translation of French *boeuf bourguignon,* from *bourguignon,* Burgundy style, from *Bourgogne,* BURGUNDY.]
beef·burg·er (bēf′bûr′gər) *n.* A hamburger.
beef·eat·er (bēf′ē′tər) *n.* **1.** A yeoman of the royal guard in England or a warder of the Tower of London. **2.** One who eats beef.
bee fly. Any of various flies of the family Bombyliidae, resembling bees and having larvae that are parasitic on the young of bees, wasps, and other insects.
beef·steak (bēf′stāk′) *n.* A slice of beef, as from the loin or the hindquarters, suitable for broiling or frying.
beefsteak fungus. An edible fungus, *Fistularia hepatica,* growing on decaying wood and having a large, irregularly shaped reddish cap. [Perhaps because the cap resembles a piece of raw beef.]
beef stro·ga·noff (strō′gə-nôf′, -nŏf′, strō-gän′ôf). Thinly sliced beef fillet sautéed and served with mushrooms and sour cream. [After Count Paul *Stroganoff,* 19th-century Russian diplomat.]
beef tea. Broth made from beef extract or by boiling pieces of lean beef, often used as a restorative.
beef·wood (bēf′wŏŏd′) *n.* Any of various trees of the genus *Casuarina,* mostly native to Australia, having small, scalelike leaves and flowers. Sometimes called "she-oak." [Perhaps from its reddish color.]
beef·y (bē′fē) *adj.* **-ier, -iest. 1.** Resembling beef. **2.** Muscular in build; heavy; brawny: *a beefy wrestler.* —**beef′i·ness** *n.*
bee gum. 1. A hollow gum tree in which bees hive. **2.** A beehive, especially one in a hollow gum tree.
bee·hive (bē′hīv′) *n.* **1.** A hive, either natural or man-made, for bees. **2.** Any place teeming with activity.
bee·keep·er (bē′kē′pər) *n.* One who keeps bees; an apiarist.
bee·line (bē′līn′) *n.* A fast, straight course. [From the belief that a pollen-laden bee flies straight back to its hive.]
Be·el·ze·bub (bē-ĕl′zĭ-bŭb′). **1.** The Devil. **2.** In Milton's *Paradise Lost,* the chief of the fallen angels, next to Satan in power. [Late Latin, from Greek *Beelzeboub,* from Hebrew *bá'al zəbūb,* "lord of flies," god of the Ekronites (II Kings 1:2) : *bá'al,* lord + *zəbūb,* fly.]
bee moth. Either of two moths, *Galleria mellonella* or *Achroia grisella,* that lay their eggs in beehives, where the larvae feed on the honeycombs and the young bees. Also called "wax moth."
been. Past participle of **be.**
bee plant. Any of various fragrant, nectar-bearing plants that attract bees.
beer (bîr) *n.* **1.** A fermented alcoholic beverage brewed from malt and flavored with hops. **2.** Any of various drinks made from extracts of roots and plants. [Middle English *ber(e),* Old English *bēor,* from a West Germanic word, from Late Latin *biber,* a drink, from Latin *bibere,* to drink. See **pōi-**[1] in Appendix.*]
Beer (bär), **Wilhelm.** 1797–1850. German banker and astronomer; published maps of the moon and Mars.
beer and skittles. *Slang.* Easygoing existence.
Beer·bohm (bîr′bōm′), Sir **Max.** 1872–1956. English critic and caricaturist.

ă pat/ā pay/âr care/ä father/b bib/ch church/d deed/ĕ pet/ē be/f fife/g gag/h hat/hw which/ĭ pit/ī pie/îr pier/j judge/k kick/l lid, needle/m mum/n no, sudden/ng thing/ŏ pot/ō toe/ô paw, for/oi noise/ou out/ŏŏ took/ōō boot/p pop/r roar/s sauce/sh ship, dish/

Beers (bîrz), **Clifford Whittingham.** 1876–1943. American humanitarian; founder of the mental-hygiene movement.
Beer·she·ba (bîr-shē′bə). The capital city of the Negev, Israel, 45 miles southwest of Jerusalem. Population, 52,000.
beer·y (bîr′ē) *adj.* **-ier, -iest. 1.** Smelling or tasting of beer. **2.** Affected or produced by beer.
beest·ings (bē′stĭngz) *n.* Plural in form, used with a singular or plural verb. The first milk given by a cow or other mammal after parturition. [Middle English *bestynge* (singular), Old English *bēsting* (unattested), from *bēost,* beestings, akin to Middle Dutch *biest,* Old High German *biost*†.]
bee-stung (bē′stŭng′) *adj.* Compressed in a pout: *bee-stung lips.*
bees·wax (bēz′wăks′) *n.* **1.** The yellowish to dark-brown wax secreted by the honeybee for making honeycombs. **2.** Commercial wax obtained by processing and purifying the crude wax of the honeybee and used in making candles, crayons, and polishes. [From *bee's wax.*]
bees·wing (bēz′wĭng′) *n.* **1.** A thin crust of tartar scales that sometimes forms on old port or other old wines. **2.** Wine affected by this crust. [From *bee's wing.*]
beet (bēt) *n.* **1.** Any of several widely cultivated plants of the genus *Beta;* especially, *B. vulgaris,* having leaves sometimes eaten as greens and a thickened, fleshy root. See **sugar beet. 2.** The bulbous root of this plant, characteristically dark red in color, eaten as a vegetable. [Middle English *bete,* Old English *bēte,* from Latin *bēta*†.]
Bee·tho·ven (bā′tō-vən), **Ludwig van.** 1770–1827. German composer.
bee·tle¹ (bēt′l) *n.* **1.** Any of numerous insects of the order Coleoptera, having biting mouth parts and front wings modified to form horny wing covers that overlie the membranous rear wings when at rest. **2.** Loosely, any insect resembling a beetle. [Middle English *bityl,* Old English *bitela,* probably from *bītan,* to BITE.]
bee·tle² (bēt′l) *adj.* Jutting; overhanging: *beetle brows.* —*intr.v.* **beetled, -tling, -tles.** To overhang. [Middle English *bitel-(brouwed),* having shaggy or protruding (eyebrows), possibly after the BEETLE, from the bushy antennae of some varieties.]
bee·tle³ (bēt′l) *n.* **1.** A heavy mallet with a large wooden head. **2.** A small wooden household mallet. **3.** A heavy wooden club used in stamping and finishing handmade linen. **4.** A cloth-finishing machine that stamps cloth with revolving wooden hammers. —*tr.v.* **beetled, -tling, -tles. 1.** To pound with a beetle. **2.** To stamp and finish (cloth) with a beetle. [Middle English *betel,* Old English *bīetel.* See **bhau-** in Appendix.*]
bee·tle·bung (bēt′l-bŭng′) *n.* A tree, the **sour gum** *(see).* [Origin obscure.]
bee·tle·weed (bēt′l-wēd′) *n.* A plant, the **galax** *(see).*
bee tree. 1. A hollow tree in which bees live. **2.** A tree, such as the basswood, having flowers rich in nectar.
beet·root (bēt′ro͞ot′, -ro͝ot′) *n. British.* The beet.
beetroot purple. Deep to very deep purplish red. See **color.**
beeves. A plural of **beef.**
Bee·wee (bē′wē′) *adj. Informal.* British West Indian: *Beewee dollars.* [From *B.W.I.,* abbreviation of British West Indies.]
bef. before.
B.E.F. British Expeditionary Force.
be·fall (bĭ-fôl′) *v.* **-fell** (-fĕl′), **-fallen** (-fôl′ən), **-falling, -falls.** —*intr.* To come to pass; happen. —*tr.* To happen to: *"There shall no evil befall thee."* (Psalms 91:10). —See Synonyms at **happen.** [Middle English *befallen,* Old English *befeallen,* to fall, belong. See **phol-** in Appendix.*]
be·fit (bĭ-fĭt′) *tr.v.* **-fitted, -fitting, -fits.** To be suitable to or appropriate for: *His fate befits his actions.*
be·fit·ting (bĭ-fĭt′ĭng) *adj.* Appropriate; suitable; proper. —**be·fit′ting·ly** *adv.*
be·fog (bĭ-fôg′, -fŏg′) *tr.v.* **-fogged, -fogging, -fogs. 1.** To cover or obscure with or as if with fog; make foggy. **2.** To cause confusion in; muddle.
be·fool (bĭ-fo͞ol′) *tr.v.* **-fooled, -fooling, -fools. 1.** To make a fool of; to hoodwink; trick; deceive. **2.** To treat as a fool.
be·fore (bĭ-fôr′, -fōr′) *adv.* **1.** In front; ahead; in advance. **2.** In the past; previously. —*prep. Abbr.* **bef. 1.** In front of; ahead of. **2.** Prior to. **3.** Awaiting: *Your happiness lies before you.* **4.** In the presence of: *He ordered the man to be brought before him.* **5.** Under the consideration or jurisdiction of: *the case before the court.* **6.** In preference to; sooner than. **7.** In advance of, or in precedence of, as in rank, condition, or development: *The prince is before his brother in the line of succession.* —*conj.* **1.** In advance of the time when: *before he went.* **2.** Rather than; sooner than: *He would die before he would betray his country.* [Middle English *before(n),* Old English *beforan.* See **per¹** in Appendix.*]
be·fore·hand (bĭ-fôr′hănd′, bĭ-fōr′-) *adv.* In anticipation; in advance; early: *He arrived beforehand.* —**be·fore′hand′** *adj.*
be·fore·time (bĭ-fôr′tīm′, bĭ-fōr′-) *adv. Rare.* Formerly.
be·foul (bĭ-foul′) *tr.v.* **-fouled, -fouling, -fouls. 1.** To make dirty; to soil. **2.** To speak badly of; cast aspersions upon.
be·friend (bĭ-frĕnd′) *tr.v.* **-friended, -friending, -friends.** To act as a friend to; aid; assist.
be·fud·dle (bĭ-fŭd′l) *tr.v.* **-dled, -dling, -dles. 1.** To confuse; perplex. **2.** To stupefy with or as if with alcoholic drink.
beg¹ (bĕg) *v.* **begged, begging, begs.** —*tr.* **1.** To ask for as charity. **2.** To ask earnestly for, or of; entreat. —*intr.* **1.** To solicit alms. **2.** To make a humble or urgent plea. —**beg off.** To seek release from (a penalty or obligation). —**beg the question. 1.** To presuppose the conclusion in one's argument. **2.** To equivocate. [Middle English *beggen*†.]
Synonyms: *beg, crave, beseech, implore, entreat, importune. Beg* and *crave* apply to the act of asking for something one cannot claim as a right, in a way that is earnest, humble, and designed to stir pity. *Beseech* emphasizes earnestness and implies great anxiety. *Implore* intensifies the senses of earnestness, humility, and anxiety. *Entreat* pertains to persuasive pleading calculated to overcome opposition. *Importune* adds the sense of persistent and sometimes harassing pleading.
beg² (bĕg, bāg) *n.* A governor or other official of the Ottoman Empire or Mogul Empire; bey. [Ottoman Turkish, BEY.]
be·gan. Past tense of **begin.**
be·get (bĭ-gĕt′) *tr.v.* **-got** (-gŏt′) or *rare* **-gat** (-găt′), **-gotten** (-gŏt′n) or **-got, -getting, -gets. 1.** To father; sire. **2.** To cause to exist. [Middle English *begeten,* to acquire, procreate, Old English *begietan.* See **ghend-** in Appendix.*] —**be·get′ter** *n.*
beg·gar (bĕg′ər) *n.* **1.** One who solicits alms for a living. **2.** One who has no money; an impoverished person; a pauper. **3.** A rascal; rogue. —*tr.v.* **beggared, -garing, -gars. 1.** To impoverish; make a beggar of. **2.** To exhaust the resources of: *Her beauty beggars all description.* [Middle English *begger(e), beggar(e),* from *beggen,* to BEG.]
beg·gar·ly (bĕg′ər-lē) *adj.* Of or pertaining to a beggar; very poor: *a beggarly pension.* —**beg′gar·li·ness** *n.*
beg·gar's-lice (bĕg′ərz-līs′) *pl.n.* **1.** Any of several plants bearing small, prickly fruit that cling readily to clothing or the fur of animals, such as the **stickseed** *(see).* Used with a singular or plural verb. **2.** The seeds of such a plant.
beg·gar-ticks (bĕg′ər-tĭks′) *pl.n.* **1.** Any of several plants having seeds that cling to clothing, often by means of barbed bristles; especially, the **bur marigold** and the **tick trefoil** *(both of which see).* Used with a singular or plural verb. **2.** The seeds of any of these plants.
beg·gar·weed (bĕg′ər-wēd′) *n.* A West Indian plant, *Desmodium purpureum,* grown as forage in the southern United States.
beg·gar·y (bĕg′ə-rē) *n.* **1.** Extreme poverty; penury. **2.** The state or condition of being a beggar. **3.** Beggars collectively.
be·gin (bĭ-gĭn′) *v.* **-gan** (-găn′), **-gun** (-gŭn′), **-ginning, -gins.** —*intr.* **1.** To start to do something; commence. **2.** To come into being: *when life began.* —*tr.* **1.** To start to do; commence. **2.** To cause to come into being; originate; start. [Begin, began, begun; Middle English *beginnen, bigan, begun,* Old English *beginnan, began, begunnen,* from West Germanic *bi-ginnan* (unattested).]
Synonyms: *begin, commence, start, initiate, inaugurate. Begin* and *commence* are equivalent in meaning, though *commence* is sometimes felt to be stronger in suggesting initiative. *Start* is often interchangeable with *begin* and *commence* but can specify a setting out from a specific point, following inaction, or (transitively) a setting in motion. *Initiate* applies to the act of taking the first steps in a process, without reference to what follows. *Inaugurate* pertains to a formal beginning.
be·gin·ner (bĭ-gĭn′ər) *n.* **1.** One who begins something. **2.** One who is just starting to learn or do something; a novice.
be·gin·ning (bĭ-gĭn′ĭng) *n.* **1.** The act or process of bringing or being brought into being; a start; commencement. **2.** The time when something begins or is begun: *"In the beginning God created the heaven and the earth."* (Genesis 1:1). **3.** The place where something begins or is begun: *at the beginning of the road.* **4.** The source or origin of something: *"The fear of the Lord is the beginning of wisdom."* (Psalms 111:10). **5.** The first part: *the beginning of the play.* **6.** *Often plural.* The early or rudimentary phase: *the beginnings of history.*
be·gird (bĭ-gûrd′) *tr.v.* **-girt** (-gûrt′) or **-girded, -girt, -girding, -girds.** To gird or encircle; surround.
be·gone (bĭ-gôn′, -gŏn′) *interj.* Used as an order of dismissal. [Middle English: BE (imperative) + GONE.]
be·go·nia (bĭ-gōn′yə) *n.* Any of various plants of the genus *Begonia,* mostly native to the tropics but widely cultivated, having leaves that are often brightly colored or veined and irregular, waxy flowers of various colors. [New Latin, after Michel *Bégon* (1638–1710), governor of Santo Domingo.]
be·got. Past tense and alternate past participle of **beget.**
be·got·ten. Past participle of **beget.**
be·grime (bĭ-grīm′) *tr.v.* **-grimed, -griming, -grimes.** To smear or soil with dirt or grime.
be·grudge (bĭ-grŭj′) *tr.v.* **-grudged, -grudging, -grudges. 1. a.** To envy the possession or enjoyment of: *She begrudged his youth.* **b.** To envy for a possession: *She begrudged him his youth.* **2.** To give with reluctance. —See Synonyms at **envy.**
be·guile (bĭ-gīl′) *tr.v.* **-guiled, -guiling, -guiles. 1.** To deceive by guile; delude: *"The serpent beguiled me and I did eat."* (Genesis 3:13). **2. a.** To take away from by guile; cheat. Used with *of* or *out of.* **b.** To divert: *"to beguile you from the grief of a loss so overwhelming"* (Lincoln). **3.** To cause to vanish unnoticed or without pain: *"The history of a soldier's wound beguiles the pain of it."* (Sterne). —See Synonyms at **deceive, lure.** [BE- + GUILE (verb).] —**be·guile′ment** *n.* —**be·guil′er** *n.*
be·guine (bĭ-gēn′) *n.* **1.** A ballroom dance based on a native dance of Martinique and St. Lucia. **2.** The music for this dance. [American French *béguine,* from French *béguin,* hood, flirtation (as in *avoir un béguin pour quelqu'un,* "to be sweet on someone"), probably from Old French *Beguine,* BEGUINE.]
Beg·uine (bĕg′ēn′) *n.* A member of any of several Roman Catholic lay sisterhoods existing in the Netherlands since the 12th century. [Old French *Beguine,* possibly feminine of *beguin, begard,* mendicant, from Middle Dutch *beggaert,* beggar, related to Middle English *beggen,* BEG.]
be·gum (bē′gəm) *n.* A Moslem lady of rank. [Urdu *begam,* from Ottoman Turkish *begim,* possessive of *beg,* BEY.]
be·gun. Past participle of **begin.**
be·half (bĭ-hăf′, -häf′) *n.* Interest, support, or benefit. Used

chiefly in the phrases *in behalf of* and *on behalf of.* See Usage note. [Middle English *(on min) behalfe,* "on my side" : *be,* BY + *half,* side, HALF.]

Usage: *In behalf of* and *on behalf of* have distinct senses, and therefore cannot be used interchangeably in most cases, according to 58 per cent of the Usage Panel. They restrict *in behalf of* to the senses of *in the interest of, for the benefit of;* and *on behalf of* to *as the agent of, on the part of.* The other Panel members accept either construction in any of these senses.

Be·han (bē′ən), **Brendan (Francis).** 1923–1964. Irish playwright and novelist.

Be·har. See **Bihar.**

be·have (bĭ-hāv′) *v.* **-haved, -having, -haves.** —*intr.* **1.** To act, react, function, or perform in a particular way. **2. a.** To conduct oneself in a specified way. **b.** To conduct oneself in a proper way. —*tr.* **1.** To conduct (oneself) properly. **2.** To conduct (oneself) in some specified way. [Middle English *behaven,* to hold oneself in a certain way : *be-,* thoroughly + *haven,* to HAVE.]

be·hav·ior (bĭ-hāv′yər) *n.* Also *chiefly British* **be·hav·iour.** **1.** The manner in which one behaves; deportment; demeanor. **2.** The actions or reactions of persons or things under specified circumstances. —**be·hav′ior·al** *adj.* —**be·hav′ior·al·ly** *adv.*

Synonyms: *behavior, conduct, deportment.* These all pertain to one's actions considered as a means of evaluation by others. *Behavior* applies to actions on specific occasions involving essentially external and sometimes superficial relationships. *Conduct* applies to actions in more significant relationships, considered from the standpoint of morals and ethics. *Deportment* more narrowly pertains to actions measured by a prevailing social code of behavior.

be·hav·ior·ism (bĭ-hāv′yə-rĭz′əm) *n.* The psychological school holding that objectively observable organismic behavior constitutes the essential or exclusive scientific basis of psychological data and investigation and stressing the role of environment as a determinant of human and animal behavior. —**be·hav′ior·ist** *n.* —**be·hav′ior·is′tic** *adj.*

be·head (bĭ-hĕd′) *tr.v.* **-headed, -heading, -heads.** To separate the head from; decapitate. [Middle English *beheveden,* Old English *behēafdian* : *be-,* away from + *hēafdian,* to behead, from *hēafod,* HEAD.]

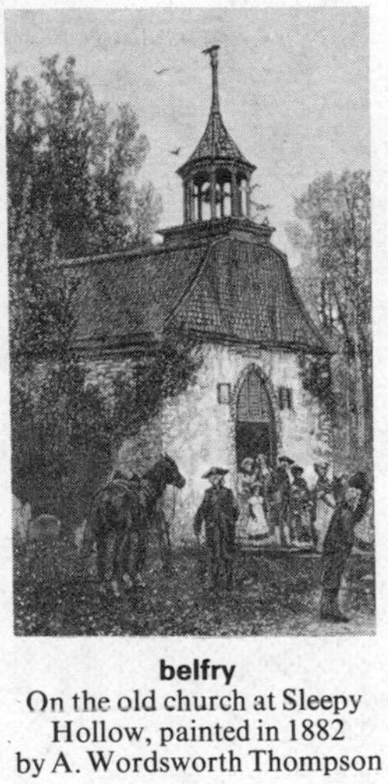

belfry
On the old church at Sleepy Hollow, painted in 1882 by A. Wordsworth Thompson

be·he·moth (bĭ-hē′məth, bē′ə-môth′) *n.* **1.** A huge animal, possibly the hippopotamus. Job 40:15–24. **2.** Something enormous in size. [Hebrew *bəhēmōth,* intensive plural ("great beast") of *bəhēmāh,* beast.]

be·hest (bĭ-hĕst′) *n.* An order or authoritative command; a request or bidding. [Middle English *behest,* promise, command, Old English *behǣs.* See **kei-**[3] in Appendix.*]

be·hind (bĭ-hīnd′) *adv.* **1.** In, to, or toward the rear: *He walked behind.* **2.** In a place or condition that has been passed or left: *He left his gloves behind.* **3.** In arrears; late: *behind in her payments.* **4.** Below the standard level; in an inferior position: *fall behind in class.* **5.** Slow: *His watch is running behind.* **6.** *Rare.* In reserve; yet to come: *There is no more behind.* —*prep.* **1.** At the back of or in the rear of: *She sat behind him.* See Usage note at **back.** **2.** On the farther side of; beyond: *behind the door.* **3.** In a place or time that has been passed or left by: *Their worries are behind them.* **4.** After (a set time); later than: *The plane was behind schedule.* **5.** Inferior to; less advanced than: *behind us in technology.* **6.** Hidden or concealed by: *behind the scenes.* **7.** Serving to support: *He had the army behind him.* —*n.* *Informal.* The buttocks. [Middle English *bihinden,* Old English *behindan, bihindan.* See **ko-** in Appendix.*]

be·hind·hand (bĭ-hīnd′hănd′) *adv.* **1.** In arrears. **2.** Behind time; slow. **3.** In a backward state. —**be·hind′hand′** *adj.*

Be·his·tun (bā′hĭs-tōōn′). Also **Bi·si·tun** (bē′sə-tōōn′), **Bi·su·tun.** A village in western Iran; site of a monument with Babylonian, Old Persian, and Elamite cuneiform inscriptions that provided a clue to the decipherment of cuneiform.

be·hold (bĭ-hōld′) *tr.v.* **-held** (-hĕld′), **-holding, -holds.** To gaze at; look upon. See Synonyms at **see.** —*interj.* Used to express amazement. [Middle English *beholden,* Old English *behealdan,* to possess, hold, observe. See **kel-**[5] in Appendix.*]

be·hold·en (bĭ-hōl′dən) *adj.* Obliged; indebted. [Middle English *beholden,* bound by obligation, Old English *behealden,* past participle of *behealdan,* to hold, BEHOLD.]

be·hoof (bĭ-hōōf′) *n.* *Rare.* Benefit; advantage; use. [Middle English *behove,* Old English *behōf.* See **kap-** in Appendix.*]

be·hoove (bĭ-hōōv′) *v.* **-hooved, -hooving, -hooves.** —*tr.* To be necessary or proper for. Used impersonally: *"It behooved him now to be a man and learn to live without her."* (Louis Auchincloss). —*intr.* *Rare.* To be appropriate or fit. Used impersonally. [Middle English *behoven,* Old English *behōfian,* to require, be needful or fitting. See **kap-** in Appendix.*]

Beh·ring, Vitus. See **Bering.**

Bei·da (bā′də). Also **Bai·da.** *Arabic* **Al Bay·da** (ăl bā′də). A town in Cyrenaica, Libya; site of the king's palace and a proposed capital of the country. Population, 13,000.

Bei·der·becke (bī′dər-bĕk′), **Leon Bismarck ("Bix").** 1903–1931. American jazz composer, cornetist, and pianist.

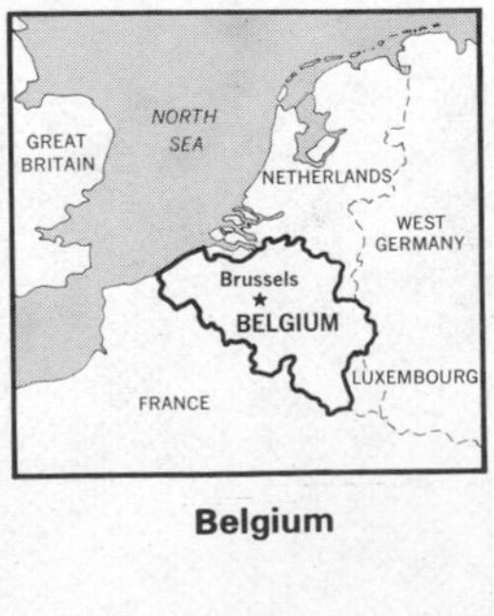

Belgium

beige (bāzh) *n.* **1.** A soft fabric of undyed and unbleached wool. **2.** Light grayish brown, or yellowish brown to grayish yellow. See **color.** [French, from Old French *bege*†.] —**beige** *adj.*

be·ing (bē′ĭng) *n.* **1.** Existence; a state of existence; a condition of particular existence. **2. a.** An object, idea, or symbol that exists, is thought to exist, or is represented as existing. **b.** A person: *"The artist after all is a solitary being."* (Virginia Woolf). **3.** *Capital* **B.** God: *the Supreme Being.* **4.** One's basic or essential nature. **5.** *Philosophy.* **a.** That which can be conceived as existing. **b.** Absolute existence in its perfect and unqualified state; the essence of existence.

Bei·ra (bā′ə-rə). A port city of eastern Mozambique, situated on Mozambique Channel. Population, 59,000.

Bei·rut (bā-rōōt′). *French* **Bey·routh** (bā-rōōt′). The capital and principal seaport of Lebanon, on the eastern Mediterranean. Population, 500,000.

Be·ja (bā′jə) *n., pl.* **Beja.** **1.** A pastoral tribe of people living as nomads in the area between the Nile River and the Red Sea. **2.** One of this people. **3.** The Cushitic language of this people.

Bé·ké·sy (bā′kā-shē), **Georg von.** Born 1899. Hungarian-born American physicist; worked in acoustics.

bel (bĕl) *n.* The logarithm to the base 10 of the ratio of two levels of power, voltage, current, or sound intensity. [After Alexander Graham BELL.]

Bel (bĕl). *Babylonian Mythology.* The god of heaven and earth.

be·la·bor (bĭ-lā′bər) *tr.v.* **-bored, -boring, -bors.** **1.** To beat, hit, or whip; to attack with blows. **2.** To thrash or assail verbally. **3.** To go over repeatedly or for an absurd amount of time; harp upon: *"This is a point that passes by too easily, so I propose to belabor it."* (William Dean Howells).

Be·las·co (bə-lăs′kō), **David.** 1854–1931. American theatrical producer, director, and playwright.

be·lat·ed (bĭ-lā′tĭd) *adj.* Tardy; too late: *a belated birthday card.* [BE- + obsolete *lated,* from LATE.] —**be·lat′ed·ly** *adv.* —**be·lat′ed·ness** *n.*

be·lay (bĭ-lā′) *v.* **-layed, -laying, -lays.** —*tr.* **1.** *Nautical.* To secure or make fast (a rope) by winding on a cleat or pin. **2.** To secure (a mountain climber) at the end of a length of rope. —*intr.* **1.** To be made secure. **2.** *Rare.* To stop. Used chiefly in the imperative: *Belay there!* —*n.* In mountain climbing, the securing of a rope on a rock or other projection. [Middle English *beleggen,* to beset, surround, Old English *belecgan,* to cover, surround. See **legh-** in Appendix.*]

Be·la·ya. See **Byelaya.**

belaying pin. *Nautical.* A short, removable wooden or metal pin, fitted in a hole in the rail of a boat, and used for securing running gear.

bel can·to (bĕl kän′tō). A style of operatic singing characterized by rich tonal lyricism and brilliant display of vocal technique. [Italian, "beautiful singing."]

belch (bĕlch) *v.* **belched, belching, belches.** —*intr.* **1.** To expel gas noisily from the stomach through the mouth; to eruct. **2.** To expel the contents violently; erupt: *The volcano belched with a roar.* **3.** To issue spasmodically; gush forth. —*tr.* **1.** To expel (gas) noisily from the stomach through the mouth; to eruct. **2.** To eject violently from within: *The volcano belched hot lava.* —*n.* A belching; an eructation. [Middle English *belchen,* perhaps Old English *bealcan* or *b(i)elcan* (unattested). See **bhel-**[4] in Appendix.*] —**belch′er** *n.*

bel·dam (bĕl′dəm) *n.* Also **bel·dame** (bĕl′dəm). An old woman, especially one who is loathsome or ugly. [Middle English, grandmother : Old French *bel-,* prefix indicating respect, from *belle,* beautiful, BELLE + DAME.]

be·lea·guer (bĭ-lē′gər) *tr.v.* **-guered, -guering, -guers.** **1.** To besiege by surrounding with troops: *"around the beleaguered Four Courts the heavy guns roared"* (Liam O'Flaherty). **2.** To harass; plague; beset. [Dutch *belegeren* : *be-,* around (see **ambhi** in Appendix*) + *leger,* camp, from Middle Dutch (see **legh-** in Appendix*).] —**be·lea′guer·er** *n.*

Be·lém (bə-lĕm′). The capital of Pará State in northern Brazil, on the Rio Pará. Population, 402,000.

bel·em·nite (bĕl′əm-nīt′) *n.* A pointed, cigar-shaped fossil, the internal shell of any of various extinct cephalopods related to the cuttlefish. Also called "thunderstone." [New Latin *belemnites,* from Greek *belemnon,* dart. See **gwel-**[1] in Appendix.*]

Bel·fast (bĕl′făst′, -fäst′, bĕl-făst′, -fäst′). The capital of Northern Ireland and county seat of County Antrim, situated at the head of Belfast Lough, an inlet of the North Channel, on the eastern coast. Population, 410,000.

bel·fry (bĕl′frē) *n., pl.* **-fries.** **1.** A tower or steeple in which one or more bells are hung. **2.** The part of a tower or steeple in which the bells are hung. [Middle English *berfrey,* portable siege tower, bell tower, from Old French *berfrei,* from Germanic. See **bhergh-**[2] in Appendix.*] —**bel′fried** *adj.*

Belg. Belgian; Belgium.

Bel·gae (bĕl′gī′, -jē′) *pl.n.* An ancient Gallic people who formerly inhabited what is now Belgium and northern France. [Latin, from Gaulish *Belgae*†.]

Bel·gian (bĕl′jən) *n.* *Abbr.* **Belg.** A native or inhabitant of Belgium. See **Fleming** and **Walloon.** —**Bel′gian** *adj.*

Bel·gian Congo (bĕl′jən). A former Belgian colony in western central Africa. See **Congo, Democratic Republic of the.**

Bel·gian East Africa (bĕl′jən). The former Belgian trust territory of Ruanda-Urundi, now comprising the independent countries of Burundi and Rwanda.

Belgian hare. A large, reddish-brown rabbit of a domestic breed developed in England from Belgian stock.

Bel·gic (bĕl′jĭk) *adj.* Of or pertaining to Belgium or the Belgians, to the Netherlands, or to the Belgae.

Bel·gium (bĕl′jəm). *French* **Bel·gique** (bĕl-zhēk′). Officially, Kingdom of Belgium. *Abbr.* **Belg.** A kingdom of northwestern Europe, 11,750 square miles in area. Population, 9,428,000. Capital, Brussels. [Latin, after the BELGAE.]

Bel·grade (bĕl′grād′, bĕl-grād′). The capital of Yugoslavia and of the Republic of Serbia, situated in the east at the confluence of the Danube and Sava rivers. Population, 598,000.

Bel·gra·vi·a (bĕl-grā′vē-ə). A fashionable residential district in the southwestern part of London, England.

ă pat/ā pay/âr care/ä father/b bib/ch church/d deed/ĕ pet/ē be/f fife/g gag/h hat/hw which/ĭ pit/ī pie/îr pier/j judge/k kick/l lid, needle/m mum/n no, sudden/ng thing/ŏ pot/ō toe/ô paw, for/oi noise/ou out/ŏŏ took/ōō boot/p pop/r roar/s sauce/sh ship, dish/

Be·li·al (bē′lē-əl, bēl′yəl). **1.** A satanic personification of wickedness and ungodliness alluded to in the New Testament. II Corinthians 6:15. **2.** In Milton's *Paradise Lost,* one of the fallen angels who rebelled against God. [Hebrew *bəlīyya'al,* "uselessness" : *bəlīy,* without + *ya'al,* use.]

be·lie (bĭ-lī′) *tr.v.* **-lied, -lying, -lies. 1.** *Archaic.* To tell lies about; slander; defame. **2.** To misrepresent or picture falsely; disguise: *"He spoke roughly in order to belie his air of gentility"* (Joyce). **3.** To show to be false: *Their laughter belied their grief.* **4.** To disappoint or leave unfulfilled. [Middle English *belien,* Old English *belēogan.* See **leugh-** in Appendix.*] **—be·li′er** *n.*

be·lief (bĭ-lēf′) *n.* **1.** The mental act, condition, or habit of placing trust or confidence in a person or thing; faith. **2.** Mental acceptance or conviction in the truth or actuality of something. **3.** Something believed or accepted as true; especially, a particular tenet, or a body of tenets, accepted by a group of persons. —See Synonyms at **opinion.** [Middle English *beleve,* Old English *bileafe, gelēafa.* See **leubh-** in Appendix.*]

be·lieve (bĭ-lēv′) *v.* **-lieved, -lieving, -lieves.** *—tr.* **1.** To accept as true or real. **2.** To credit with veracity; have confidence in; trust. **3.** To expect or suppose; think: *I believe that he will come shortly.* *—intr.* **1.** To have faith, especially religious faith. **2.** To have faith or confidence; to trust. Used with *in: I believe in his ability.* **3.** To have confidence in the truth, value, or existence of something. Used with *in: "Edison did not believe in the cinema"* (Ivor Montagu). **4.** To think or judge: *How could you believe so badly of him?* [Middle English *bileven, beleven,* Old English *belēfan, gelēfan.* See **leubh-** in Appendix.*] **—be·liev′a·ble** *adj.* **—be·liev′er** *n.*

be·like (bĭ-līk′) *adv. Archaic.* Perhaps; probably. [Middle English : *be-, bi,* BY + LIKE.]

Be·lin·da (bə-lĭn′də). A feminine given name. [Perhaps from Old High German *Bettindis*†.]

Bel·i·sar·i·us (bĕl′ĭ-sâr′ē-əs). A.D. 505?–565. General of the Eastern Roman Empire; served Emperor Justinian.

Be·li·toeng. A Dutch name for **Billiton.**

be·lit·tle (bĭ-lĭt′l) *tr.v.* **-tled, -tling, -tles. 1.** To represent or speak of as small or unimportant; depreciate; disparage. **2.** To cause to seem less or little. —See Synonyms at **decry. —be·lit′tle·ment** *n.* **—be·lit′tler** *n.*

Be·li·tung. See **Billiton.**

Be·lize (bə-lēz′). The capital and a seaport of British Honduras, Central America, situated on the Caribbean at the mouth of the Belize River. Population, 33,000.

bell[1] (bĕl) *n.* **1.** A hollow metal instrument, usually cup-shaped with a flared opening. It emits a metallic tone when struck. **2.** Something shaped like a bell, as: **a.** The round, flared mouth of some musical wind instruments. **b.** The corolla of a flower. **c.** A hollow, usually inverted vessel, such as a diving bell. **3.** *Nautical.* **a.** A stroke on a bell to mark the hour. **b.** The time indicated by the striking of a bell, divided into half hours. *—v.* **belled, belling, bells.** *—tr.* **1.** To put a bell on. **2.** To shape or cause to flare like a bell. *—intr.* To assume the form of a bell. **—bell the cat.** To perform a daring action. [Middle English *belle,* Old English *belle.* See **bhel-**[4] in Appendix.*]

bell[2] (bĕl) *n.* The bellowing or baying cry of certain animals, such as a deer in rut or a beagle on the hunt. *—intr.v.* **belled, belling, bells.** To bellow; bay. [Middle English *bellen,* to bay, Old English *bellan.* See **bhel-**[4] in Appendix.*]

Bell (bĕl), **Alexander Graham.** 1847–1922. Scottish-born American inventor; patented the first telephone (1876).

bel·la·don·na (bĕl′ə-dŏn′ə) *n.* **1.** A poisonous Eurasian plant, *Atropa belladonna,* having purplish-red, bell-shaped flowers and small black poisonous berries. Also called "deadly nightshade." **2.** An atropine powder or tincture derived from the leaves and roots of the belladonna and used to treat asthma, colic, and hyperacidity. [Italian, "fair lady" (supposedly from its use in cosmetics) : *bella,* feminine of *bello,* fine, beautiful, from Latin *bellus* (see **deu-**[2] in Appendix*) + DONNA.]

belladonna lily. A plant, the **amaryllis** *(see).*

Bel·la·my (bĕl′ə-mē), **Edward.** 1850–1898. American socialist novelist; author of *Looking Backward.*

Bel·lay (bĕ-lā′), **Joachim du.** 1522?–1560. French poet.

bell·bird (bĕl′bûrd′) *n.* Any of various tropical American birds of the family Cotingidae, having a characteristic bell-like call.

bell·boy (bĕl′boi′) *n.* A boy or man employed by a hotel to carry luggage, run errands, and the like. Also called "bellhop."

bell buoy. A buoy fitted with a warning bell that is activated by the movement of the waves.

belle (bĕl) *n.* **1.** An attractive and much-admired girl or woman. **2.** The most attractive girl or woman at a given place: *the belle of the ball.* [French, "beautiful," from Latin *bella,* feminine of *bellus,* handsome, pretty. See **deu-**[2] in Appendix.*]

Belle (bĕl). A feminine given name. [French, BELLE.]

Bel·leau Wood (bĕl′ō; *French* bĕ-lō′). A small forest near Château-Thierry, France, where U.S. Marines in World War I halted the German drive on Paris (1918).

Belle Isle (bĕl īl′). An island, about 15 square miles in area, at the northern entrance to the Strait of Belle Isle, between southeastern Labrador and northwestern Newfoundland.

Bel·ler·o·phon (bə-lĕr′ə-fŏn′). *Greek Mythology.* The Corinthian hero who, with the aid of the winged horse Pegasus, slew the Chimera.

belles-let·tres (bĕl-lĕt′rə) *n.* Plural in form, used with a singular verb. Literature regarded for its aesthetic value rather than for its didactic or informative content. [French, "fine letters" (literature).] **—bel·let′rism′** *n.* **—bel·let′rist** *n.* **—bel′le·tris′tic** (bĕl′ə-trĭs′tĭk) *adj.*

bell·flow·er (bĕl′flou′ər) *n.* Any of various plants of the genus *Campanula,* characteristically having blue, bell-shaped flowers. See **harebell, bluebell.**

bel·li·cose (bĕl′ĭ-kōs′) *adj.* Warlike in manner or temperament; pugnacious. See Synonyms at **belligerent.** [Middle English, from Latin *bellicōsus,* from *bellicus,* of war, from *bellum,* earlier *duellum,* war. See **duellum** in Appendix.*] **—bel′li·cose′ly** *adv.* **—bel′li·cos′i·ty** (-kŏs′ə-tē), **bel′li·cose′ness** *n.*

bel·lig·er·ence (bə-lĭj′ər-əns) *n.* A warlike or hostile attitude, nature, or inclination.

bel·lig·er·en·cy (bə-lĭj′ər-ən-sē) *n.* The state of being at war or engaged in a warlike conflict.

bel·lig·er·ent (bə-lĭj′ər-ənt) *adj.* **1.** Given to or marked by hostile or aggressive behavior: *"Raymie bared his teeth like a belligerent mouse."* (Sinclair Lewis). **2.** Of, pertaining to, or engaged in warfare: *the belligerent powers.* *—n.* One that is belligerent. [Latin *belligerāns,* present participle of *belligerāre,* to wage war, from *belliger,* waging war : *bellum,* war (see **bellicose**) + *gerere,* to bear, carry (see **gerere** in Appendix*).] **—bel·lig′er·ent·ly** *adv.*

Synonyms: *belligerent, bellicose, pugnacious, contentious, quarrelsome. Belligerent* may specify actual combat, or conduct or temper conducive to hostilities. In the latter sense it is closely related to *bellicose* and *pugnacious,* although *pugnacious* more often applies to a natural inclination to aggressiveness than to a specific instance of hostility. *Contentious,* which implies chronic argumentativeness, and *quarrelsome,* which suggests perversity and bad temper, are weaker terms.

Bel·lings·hau·sen (bĕl′ĭngz-hou′zən), **Fabian Gottlieb von.** 1778–1852. Russian naval officer; circumnavigated the world (1803); explored Antarctica (1819–21).

Bel·lings·hau·sen Sea (bĕl′ĭngz-hou′zən). An arm of the South Pacific Ocean off the coast of Antarctica, extending from Alexander I Island to Thurston Island.

Bel·li·ni (bə-lē′nē; *Italian* bāl-lē′nē). Italian family of painters of the Venetian school, including **Jacopo** (1400?–1470?) and his sons **Gentile** (1429?–1507) and **Giovanni** (1430?–1516).

Bel·li·ni (bə-lē′nē; *Italian* bāl-lē′nē), **Vincenzo.** 1801–1835. Italian composer of operas.

bell jar. A cylindrical glass vessel with a rounded top and an open base used to protect and display fragile objects or to establish a controlled atmosphere or environment in scientific experiments. Also called "bell glass."

bell·man (bĕl′mən) *n., pl.* **-men** (-mĭn). A **town crier** *(see).*

bell metal. An alloy of tin and copper used to make bells.

bell-mouthed (bĕl′mouthd′, -moutht′) *adj.* Having a flaring, bell-shaped mouth, as a flask.

Bel·loc (bĕl′ŏk′, -ək), **Hilaire.** Pen name of Joseph Hilary Pierre Belloc. 1870–1953. French-born English writer.

Bel·lo·na (bə-lō′nə). The Roman goddess of war. [Latin *Bellōna,* from *bellum,* war. See **duellum** in Appendix.*]

bel·low (bĕl′ō) *v.* **-lowed, -lowing, -lows.** *—intr.* **1.** To roar, as a bull. **2.** To shout in a deep voice. *—tr.* To utter in a loud and powerful voice: *"bellowing something between a cheer and a shout"* (Alan Sillitoe). *—n.* **1.** The roar of a bull, elephant, or other large animal. **2.** A very loud utterance; a shout: *"the hoarse bellow of voices all crying together"* (Katherine Anne Porter). **3.** The sound of artillery, thunder, or the like. [Middle English *belwen,* Old English *belgan* (unattested). See **bhel-**[4] in Appendix.*] **—bel′low·er** *n.*

Bel·low (bĕl′ō), **Saul.** Born 1915. American novelist.

bel·lows (bĕl′ōz, -əz) *n.* Plural in form, sometimes used with a singular verb. **1.** An apparatus for producing a strong current of air, as for sounding a pipe organ or increasing the draft to a fire. It consists of a flexible, valved air chamber that is contracted and expanded by pumping to force the air through a nozzle. **2.** Something resembling a bellows, such as the pleated windbag of an accordion. **3.** The lungs. [Middle English *belwes, belows,* plural of *belu, below,* probably from Old English *belga,* plural of *bel(i)g, bælig,* bag, bellows. See **belly.**]

Bel·lows (bĕl′ōz), **George Wesley.** 1882–1925. American painter and graphic artist.

bell pepper. 1. A pepper plant, *Capsicum frutescens grossum,* cultivated for its edible fruit. **2.** The mild-flavored, bell-shaped fruit of this plant, usually red when ripe but often eaten when green. Also called "sweet pepper."

bells of Ireland. Plural in form, used with a singular or plural verb. A plant, the **shellflower** *(see).*

bell·weth·er (bĕl′wĕth′ər) *n.* **1.** A male sheep, usually castrated, with a bell hung from its neck, that is followed by a flock of sheep. **2.** One that is followed, as a leader.

bell·wort (bĕl′wûrt′, -wôrt′) *n.* Any plant of the genus *Uvularia,* of eastern North America, having yellow, bell-shaped flowers. Also called "merry-bells."

bel·ly (bĕl′ē) *n., pl.* **-lies. 1.** The part of the body of mammals between the rib cage and the pelvis that contains the intestines; the abdomen. **2.** The underside of the body of certain vertebrates, such as snakes and fish. **3. a.** The stomach. **b.** The appetite for food; gluttony. **4.** Any part that bulges or protrudes: *the belly of a sail.* **5.** The womb; uterus. **6.** The deep, hollow interior of something: *a ship's belly.* **7.** The bulging part of a muscle. **8.** The front part of the body of a stringed musical instrument. In this sense, also called "table." *—v.* **bellied, -lying, -lies.** *—intr.* To swell out; to bulge: *"mud-colored clouds bellied downwards from the sky"* (Hardy). *—tr.* To cause to bulge. [Middle English *bely, baly,* Old English *bel(i)g, bæl(i)g,* bag, purse, bellows. See **bhelgh-** in Appendix.*]

bel·ly·ache (bĕl′ē-āk′) *n.* An ache or pain in the stomach or abdomen. *—intr.v.* **bellyached, -aching, -aches.** *Slang.* To grumble or complain, especially in a whining manner.

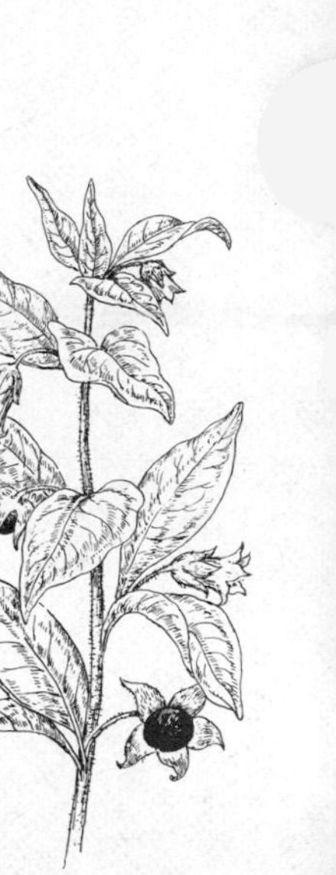

belladonna

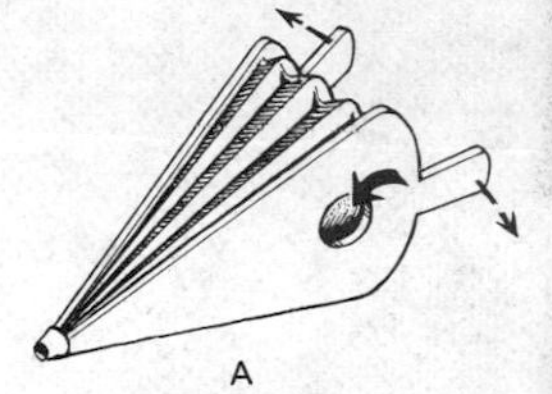

A

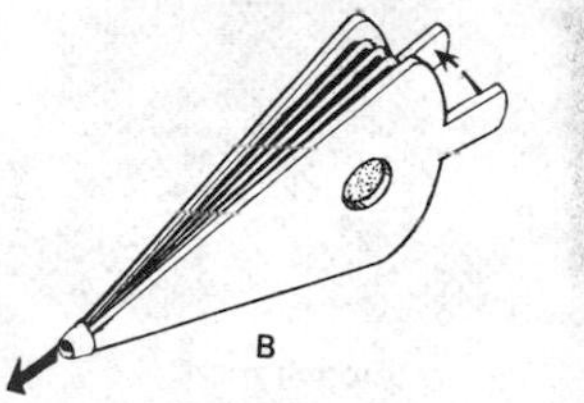

B

bellows
A. Air is admitted through open valve *(large arrow)* as bellows is expanded
B. Valve closes and air is expelled through nozzle *(large arrow)* as bellows is compressed

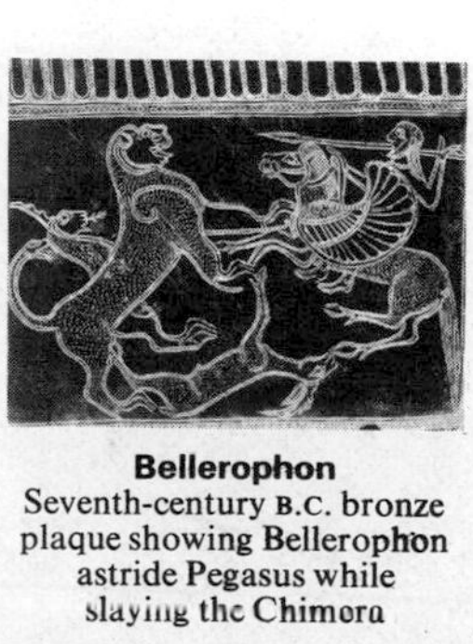

Bellerophon
Seventh-century B.C. bronze plaque showing Bellerophon astride Pegasus while slaying the Chimera

bel·ly·band (bĕl′ē-bănd′) *n.* **1.** A band passed around the belly of an animal to secure something, as a saddle. **2.** An encircling cloth band for holding in the protruding navel of a baby.
bel·ly·but·ton (bĕl′ē-bŭt′n) *n. Informal.* The navel.
bel·ly·ful (bĕl′ē-fo͝ol′) *n. Informal.* An amount that satisfies or exceeds what one desires or can endure.
belly laugh. A deep, jovial laugh.
bel·ly·whop (bĕl′ē-hwŏp′) *intr.v.* **-whopped, -whopping, -whops.** *Slang.* **1. a.** To coast while lying belly down on a sled. **b.** To cast oneself on a sled belly down, after making a short run to gain speed. **2.** To dive striking the chest or chest and belly flat against the water. *—n.* Also **bel·ly·whop·per** (-hwŏp′ər). *Slang.* A dive performed in this manner.
Bel·mon·te (bĕl-môn′tā), **Juan.** 1893–1962. Spanish bullfighter; considered the father of modern bullfighting.
Be·lo Ho·ri·zon·te (bā′lō ô′rē-zŏn′tē). The capital city of Minas Gerais State, in eastern Brazil. Population, 693,000.
be·long (bĭ-lông′, -lŏng′) *intr.v.* **-longed, -longing, -longs. 1.** To be the property or concern of. Used with *to: "the earth belongs to the living"* (Jefferson). **2.** To be part of or in natural association with something. **3.** To be a member of an organization. Used with *to: belong to a fraternity.* **4.** To have a proper or suitable place: *Those clothes belong in the closet.* [Middle English *belongen* : *be-,* thoroughly + *longen,* to suit (see **long,** to yearn).]
be·long·ing (bĭ-lông′ĭng, bĭ-lŏng′-) *n.* **1.** *Plural.* Personal possessions; effects. **2.** Close and secure relationship: *a sense of belonging.* —See Synonyms at **asset.**
Be·lo·rus·sia. See **Byelorussian Soviet Socialist Republic.**
Be·lo·rus·sian. Variant of **Byelorussian.**
Be·lo·stok. A Russian name for **Białystok.**
be·lov·ed (bĭ-lŭv′ĭd, -lŭvd′) *adj.* Held in great affection. *—n.* One that is beloved. [Middle English, past participle of *beloven,* to love thoroughly : *be-,* thoroughly + *loven,* to love, Old English *lufian* (see **leubh-** in Appendix*).]
be·low (bĭ-lō′) *adv.* **1.** In or to a lower place; beneath. **2. a.** On or to a lower floor; downstairs. **b.** *Nautical.* On or to a lower deck. **3.** Farther down or on, as on a page. **4.** In or to hell or Hades. **5.** On earth. **6.** In a lower rank or class. *—prep.* **1.** Lower than; beneath. **2.** Unworthy of or unsuitable to the rank or dignity of. [Middle English *bilooghe* : *bi,* BY + *loogh, lowe,* LOW.]
***Synonyms:** below, under, beneath, underneath. Below,* in its principal physical sense, denotes only position lower than a given point of reference. *Under* specifies position directly below, lower than the point of reference and in approximately vertical line with it. *Below* is also used to indicate direction and distance in a horizontal plane: *a town on the Hudson below Albany. Beneath* may have the basic sense of *below* or, more often, of *under. Underneath* combines the basic sense of *under* with that of at least partial concealment. Figuratively, *below* indicates deficiency or lesser status in a general way: *below normal; below one's rank. Under* indicates specific deficiency or explicitly subordinate relationship: *under legal age; serve under a captain. Beneath* applies to deficiency in moral or social senses: *beneath ordinary decency; beneath one's level.*
Bel·sen (bĕl′zən). A village in West Germany, about 30 miles north of Hanover, the site of a Nazi concentration camp.
Bel·shaz·zar (bĕl-shăz′ər). The son of Nebuchadnezzar II and the last king of Babylon, who was warned of his downfall and death by the handwriting on the wall. Daniel 5:25.
belt (bĕlt) *n.* **1.** A band of leather, cloth, or other flexible material, worn around the waist to support clothing, secure tools or weapons, or serve as decoration. **2.** A **seat belt** *(see).* **3.** *Naval.* A strip of armor surrounding a warship at the water line. **4. a.** An encircling route or highway. **b.** A **belt line** *(see).* **5.** A continuous band or chain for transferring motion or power or conveying materials from one wheel or shaft to another. See **fan belt. 6.** A geographical region that is distinctive in some specific way. **7.** *Slang.* A powerful blow; a punch. **8.** *Slang.* A strong emotional reaction. **9.** *Slang.* A drink of hard liquor. —See Synonyms at **area.** —**below the belt. 1.** *Boxing.* In the area below the waistline, where a blow is foul. **2.** Not according to rule; unfair. —**tighten one's belt.** To become thrifty and frugal. *—tr.v.* **belted, belting, belts. 1.** To encircle; gird: *"your insular city of the Manhattoes, belted around by wharves"* (Melville). **2.** To attach with or as if with a belt. **3.** To mark with or as if with a belt. **4.** To strike with a belt. **5.** *Slang.* To strike forcefully; to punch. **6.** *Slang.* To sing in a loud and forceful manner. Often used with *out: belt a song; belt out a note.* [Middle English *belt,* Old English *belt,* from Common Germanic *baltjaz* (unattested), from Latin *balteus,* probably from Etruscan.]
Bel·tane (bĕl′tān′, -tĭn) *n.* **1.** May Day in the old Scottish calendar. **2.** The ancient Celtic May Day celebration. [Middle English *beltane,* from Scottish Gaelic *bealltainn,* probably from Old Celtic *belote(p)nia* (unattested). See **bhel-**[1] in Appendix.*]
belt highway. A highway circumventing an urban area.
belt·ing (bĕl′tĭng) *n.* **1.** Belts collectively. **2.** The material used to make belts.
belt line. A transportation line, as of trains, trolleys, or buses, that makes a complete circuit of an urban area.
be·lu·ga (bə-lo͞o′gə) *n.* **1.** The **white whale** *(see).* **2.** A sturgeon, *Huso huso,* of the Black and Caspian seas, whose roe is used for caviar. Also called "beluga sturgeon." [Russian *byeluga,* sturgeon, and *byelukha,* white whale : *byelii,* white (see **bhel-**[1] in Appendix*) + *-uga, -ukha,* augmentative suffix.]
Be·lu·kha (bə-lo͞o′kə). The highest elevation, 15,157 feet, of the Altai Mountains in the Soviet Union, near Mongolia.

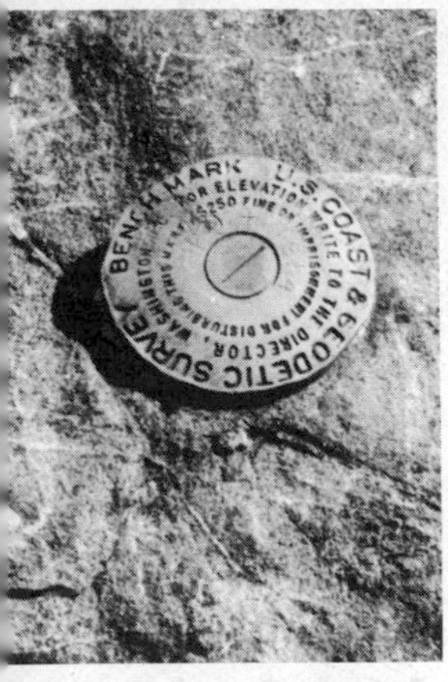

bench mark
U.S. Coast & Geodetic Survey bench mark on a stone outcropping of Monhegan Island, Maine

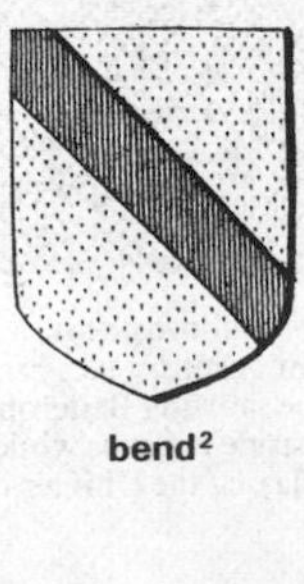
bend[2]

bel·ve·dere (bĕl′və-dîr′) *n.* A structure, such as a summerhouse or an open, roofed gallery, situated so as to command a fine view. [Italian *bel, bello,* beautiful, from Latin *bellus* (see **deu-**[2] in Appendix*) + *vedere,* view, "to see," from Latin *vidēre* (see **weid-** in Appendix*).]
Bel·zo·ni (bāl-tsō′nē), **Giovanni Battista.** 1778–1823. Italian inventor, showman, explorer, and Egyptologist.
B.E.M. British Empire Medal.
be·ma (bē′mə) *n., pl.* **-mata** (-mə-tə). **1.** Also **bi·mah** (bē′mə) *pl.* **-mahs.** *Judaism.* The platform from which services are conducted in a synagogue. Also called "almemar." **2.** *Eastern Orthodox Church.* The enclosed area about the altar; the sanctuary. [Late Latin *bēma,* from Greek, platform. See **gwā-** in Appendix.*]
be·mean (bĭ-mēn′) *tr.v.* **-meaned, -meaning, -means.** To lower in dignity or estimation; debase: *"Galloway fell to bemeaning Sam for cowardice"* (T.S. Stribling). [BE- + MEAN (base).]
Be·mel·mans (bē′məl-mənz, bĕm′əl-), **Ludwig.** 1898–1962. Austrian-born American artist, illustrator, and author.
be·mire (bĭ-mīr′) *tr.v.* **-mired, -miring, -mires. 1.** To soil with mud. **2.** To bog down in mud. Usually used in the passive.
be·moan (bĭ-mōn′) *v.* **-moaned, -moaning, -moans.** *—tr.* **1.** To lament; mourn over. **2.** To express pity or grief for. *—intr.* To mourn; lament. [Middle English *bemenen,* Old English *bemǣnan* : *be-,* about, over + *mǣnan,* to moan (see **mei-no-** in Appendix*).]
be·muse (bĭ-myo͞oz′) *tr.v.* **-mused, -musing, -muses.** To confuse or stupefy.
be·mused (bĭ-myo͞ozd′) *adj.* In deep thought; engrossed.
ben[1] (bĕn) *n. Scottish.* The inner room or parlor of a house. *—adv. Scottish.* Inside; within. *—prep. Scottish.* Within. [Middle English *ben, binne(n),* within, Old English *binnan* : *be,* BY + *innan,* within (see **en** in Appendix*).]
ben[2] (bĕn) *n. Scottish.* A mountain peak. Used in names of mountains: *Ben Nevis.* [Scottish Gaelic *beann,* peak, height. See **bend-** in Appendix.*]
ben[3] (bĕn) *n.* Any of several Asiatic trees of the genus *Moringa,* bearing winged seeds that yield an oil used in perfumes and cosmetics. [Dialectal Arabic *bēn,* from Arabic *bān.*]
Be·na·res. A former name for **Varanasi.**
Ben Bel·la (bĕn bĕl′ə), **Ahmed.** Born 1919. Algerian statesman; premier (1962–65); president (1963–65).
bench (bĕnch) *n.* **1.** A long seat, usually made of wood or stone and without a back, for two or more persons. **2.** A thwart in a boat. **3. a.** The seat for judges in a courtroom. **b.** The office or position of a judge. **4.** The judge or judges composing a court. **5. a.** A seat occupied by persons in some official capacity: *the bench of bishops.* **b.** The office of the persons occupying such a seat. **6.** A strong worktable, as one used in carpentry. **7.** A platform on which animals, especially dogs, are exhibited. **8.** *Sports.* **a.** The place where the players on an athletic team sit while they are not participating in the game. **b.** The reserve players on an athletic team. **9. a.** A level, narrow stretch of land interrupting a declivity. **b.** A level elevation of land along a shore or coast, especially one marking a former shoreline. *—tr.v.* **benched, benching, benches. 1.** To furnish with a bench or benches. **2.** To seat on a bench, especially in judicial capacity. **3.** To show (dogs) in a bench show. **4.** *Sports.* To keep out or remove (a player) from a game. [Middle English *bench,* Old English *benc.* See **bheg-** in Appendix.*]
bench·er (bĕn′chər) *n.* **1.** *British.* A member of the inner or higher bar who acts as a governor of one of the Inns of Court. **2.** *Rare.* One who occupies an official bench, as a magistrate.
Bench·ley (bĕnch′lē), **Robert Charles.** 1889–1945. American humorist, critic, and actor.
bench mark. A surveyor's mark made on some stationary object of previously determined position and elevation, and used as a reference point in tidal observations and surveys.
bench show. An indoor exhibition of small animals; especially, a competitive dog show.
bench warrant. *Law.* A warrant issued by a judge or court, ordering the apprehension of an offender.
bend[1] (bĕnd) *v.* **bent** (bĕnt) or *rare* **bended, bending, bends.** *—tr.* **1.** To bring (a bow) into tension by drawing it with a string. **2. a.** To cause to assume a curved or angular shape. **b.** To force to assume a different shape or direction. **3.** To cause to swerve from a straight line; turn; deflect. **4.** To turn or direct (one's eyes or attention, for example): *"And to my cries . . . Thine ear with favor bend."* (Milton). **5.** To influence coercively; subdue. **6.** To decide; to resolve. Used in the passive, with *on: He was bent on leaving.* **7.** To apply (the mind) closely; concentrate. **8.** *Nautical.* To fasten: *bend a mainsail onto the boom.* *—intr.* **1. a.** To turn or be altered from straightness or from an initial shape or position: *Wire bends easily.* **b.** To assume a curved, crooked, or angular form or direction: *The saplings bent in the wind.* **2.** To take a new direction; to swerve. **3.** To incline the body; to stoop. **4.** To bow in submission; yield. **5.** To apply oneself closely; concentrate. Used with *to.* *—n.* **1.** The act or fact of bending. **2.** The state of being bent. **3.** Something bent; a curve; crook. **4.** *Nautical.* **a.** *Plural.* The thick planks in a ship's side; the wales. **b.** A knot that joins a rope to a rope or another object. —**the bends. Caisson disease** *(see).* [Bend, bent, bent; Middle English *benden, bente* and *bende, bente* and *bende,* Old English *bendan, bende, bended.* See **bhendh-** in Appendix.*]
bend[2] (bĕnd) *n. Heraldry.* A band passing from the upper dexter corner of the escutcheon to the lower sinister corner. [Middle English *bend,* Old English *bend,* ribbon, band. See **bhendh-** in Appendix.*]

Ben Da·vis (bĕn dā′vĭs). A variety of large red winter apple, grown in western North America, and used for cooking.

Ben Day. Also **ben·day** (bĕn-dā′), **Ben·day, ben day. 1.** A method of adding a tone to a printed image by imposing a transparent sheet of dots or other patterns on the image at some stage of a photographic reproduction process. **2.** A screen or pattern used in this process. [Invented by *Benjamin Day* (1838–1916), New York printer.]

bend·er (bĕn′dər) *n.* **1.** One that bends. **2.** *Slang.* A drinking spree. **3.** *British Slang.* A sixpence.

bend sinister. *Heraldry.* A band passing from the upper sinister corner of the escutcheon to the lower dexter corner.

ben·e. Variant of **benne.**

be·neath (bĭ-nēth′) *adv.* **1.** In a lower place; below. **2.** Underneath. *—prep.* **1.** Below; under. **2.** Covered by: *The earth lay beneath a blanket of snow.* **3.** Under the power or influence of. **4.** Lower than in rank or station; inferior to: *An earl is beneath a duke.* **5.** Unworthy of; unbefitting: *It is beneath him to beg.* —See Synonyms at **below.** [Middle English *benethe(n),* Old English *binithan* : *bi,* BY + *nithan, neothan,* from below, below (see **ni** in Appendix*).]

Ben·e·dic·i·te (bĕn′ə-dĭs′ə-tē) *n.* **1.** A canticle, used in various Christian churches, beginning *"Benedicite, omnia opera Domini Domino"* ("All ye works of the Lord, bless the Lord"). **2.** *Small* **b.** Any invocation of a blessing. [Middle English, from Latin, imperative of *benedīcere,* to bless. See **benediction.**]

ben·e·dict (bĕn′ə-dĭkt′) *n.* Also **ben·e·dick** (-dĭk′). A confirmed bachelor, newly wed. [After *Benedick,* a character in Shakespeare's *Much Ado About Nothing.*]

Ben·e·dict (bĕn′ə-dĭkt′). A masculine given name. [Middle English, from Latin *benedictus,* blessed. See **benediction.**]

Ben·e·dict XIV (bĕn′ə-dĭkt′). Original name, Prospero Lambertini. 1675–1758. Pope (1740–58); educator and author.

Ben·e·dict XV (bĕn′ə-dĭkt′). Original name, Giacomo della Chiesa. 1854–1922. Pope (1914–22); active in war relief.

Ben·e·dic·tine (bĕn′ə-dĭk′tĭn, -tēn′) *adj.* Of or pertaining to Saint Benedict of Nursia or his order. *—n.* (bĕn′ə-dĭk′tĭn, -tēn′ *for sense 1;* bĕn′ə-dĭk′tēn′ *for sense 2*). **1.** A monk or nun belonging to the order founded by Saint Benedict. **2.** A trademark for a liqueur made originally by Benedictine monks.

ben·e·dic·tion (bĕn′ə-dĭk′shən) *n.* **1.** A blessing or the act of blessing. **2.** An invocation of divine blessing, usually at the end of a service. **3.** *Usually capital* **B.** *Roman Catholic Church.* A short service consisting of prayers, the singing of a Eucharistic hymn, and the blessing of the congregation with the Host. Also called "Benediction of the Blessed Sacrament." **4.** The state of blessedness. [Middle English *benediccioun,* from Old French *benediction,* from Latin *benedictiō,* from *benedictus,* blessed, from *benedīcere,* to bless, speak well of : *bene,* well (see **deu-²** in Appendix*) + *dīcere,* to say (see **deik-** in Appendix*).] *—***ben′e·dic′tive, ben′e·dic′to·ry** (-dĭk′tə-rē) *adj.*

Ben·e·dict of Nur·si·a (bĕn′ə-dĭkt′; nûr′shē-ə, -shə), **Saint.** Italian monk of the early sixth century A.D.; founder of the Benedictine order (about A.D. 529).

Ben·e·dic·tus (bĕn′ə-dĭk′təs) *n.* **1.** A canticle that begins, *"Benedictus qui venit in nomine Domini"* ("Blessed is he that cometh in the name of the Lord"). Matthew 21:9. **2.** A canticle starting *"Benedictus Dominus Deus Israel"* ("Blessed be the Lord God of Israel"). Luke 1:68. **3.** A musical setting of either of these canticles. [Latin, "blessed." See **benediction.**]

ben·e·fac·tion (bĕn′ə-făk′shən) *n.* **1.** The act of conferring help or a benefit. **2.** A charitable gift or deed. [Late Latin *benefactiō,* from *benefactus,* past participle of *benefacere,* to do well : Latin *bene,* well (see **deu-²** in Appendix*) + *facere,* to do (see **dhē-¹** in Appendix*).]

ben·e·fac·tor (bĕn′ə-făk′tər) *n.* One who gives financial or other aid. [Late Latin, from *benefactiō,* BENEFACTION.]

ben·e·fac·tress (bĕn′ə-făk′trĭs) *n.* A female benefactor.

be·nef·ic (bə-nĕf′ĭk) *adj.* Exerting a beneficent influence; beneficent. [Latin *beneficus.* See **beneficence.**]

ben·e·fice (bĕn′ə-fĭs) *n.* **1.** *Ecclesiastical.* **a.** A church office, as a rectory, endowed with fixed capital assets. **b.** The revenue from such assets. **2.** A landed estate granted in feudal tenure. *—tr.v.* **beneficed, -ficing, -fices.** To endow or provide with a benefice. [Middle English, from Old French, from Medieval Latin *beneficium,* from Latin, favor, benefit, from *beneficus,* beneficent. See **beneficence.**]

be·nef·i·cence (bə-nĕf′ə-səns) *n.* **1.** The quality of charity or kindness: *"the transience of nature's beneficence stimulated thrift"* (Homer W. Smith). **2.** A charitable act or gift. [Old French, from Latin *beneficentia,* from *beneficus,* beneficent, generous : *bene,* well (see **deu-²** in Appendix*) + *facere,* to do (see **dhē-¹** in Appendix*).]

be·nef·i·cent (bə-nĕf′ə-sənt) *adj.* **1.** Characterized by or performing acts of kindness or charity: *"even cruel savage brutes . . . have at times . . . beneficent impulses"* (W.H. Hudson). **2.** Conferring benefit; beneficial. *—***be·nef′i·cent·ly** *adv.*

ben·e·fi·cial (bĕn′ə-fĭsh′əl) *adj.* **1.** Promoting a favorable result; enhancing well-being; advantageous. **2.** *Law.* Receiving or having the right to receive proceeds or other advantages: *a beneficial interest in sales.* [From BENEFICE, in the obsolete sense "benefit."] *—***ben′e·fi′cial·ly** *adv.* *—***ben′e·fi′cial·ness** *n.*

Synonyms: *beneficial, profitable, advantageous.* These adjectives apply to that which promotes gain. *Beneficial* is said of whatever enhances well-being; *profitable,* of what yields usually material gain; and *advantageous,* of that which affords improvement in relative position or in chances of success.

ben·e·fi·ci·ar·y (bĕn′ə-fĭsh′ē-ĕr-ē, -fĭsh′ə-rē) *n., pl.* **-ies. 1.** One who receives a benefit. **2.** *Law.* The recipient of funds, property, or other benefits from an insurance policy, will, or other settlement. **3.** *Ecclesiastical.* The holder of a benefice. *—adj.* Pertaining to or holding a feudal benefice. [Medieval Latin *beneficiārius,* from Latin, of a favor, from *beneficium,* favor, BENEFICE.]

ben·e·fit (bĕn′ə-fĭt) *n.* **1.** Anything that promotes or enhances well-being; advantage. **2.** *Archaic.* An act of charity; a kindly deed. **3.** A payment or series of payments to one in need. **4.** A public entertainment, performance, or social event held to raise funds for a person or cause. *—v.* **benefited, -fiting, -fits.** *—tr.* To be helpful or advantageous to. *—intr.* To improve or gain advantage; to profit. Used with *from.* [Middle English *benfet,* from Norman French, from Latin *benefactum,* benefit, good deed, from *bene facere,* to do well : *bene,* well (see **deu-²** in Appendix*) + *facere,* to do (see **dhē-¹** in Appendix*).]

benefit of clergy. 1. The exemption from trial or punishment except by church court given to the clergy in the Middle Ages. **2.** Marriage: *cohabiting without benefit of clergy.*

benefit of the doubt. A favorable judgment granted in the absence of full evidence.

benefit society. An association that guarantees its members financial aid in times of need, as by hospitalization insurance, by the collection of dues. Also called "benefit association."

Ben·e·lux (bĕn′ə-lŭks′) *n.* The tripartite customs union formed by Belgium, the Netherlands, and Luxembourg in 1947. [BE(LGIUM) + NE(THERLANDS) + LUX(EMBOURG).]

Be·neš (bĕ′nĕsh), **Eduard.** 1884–1948. President of Czechoslovakia (1935–38, in exile 1939–45; 1946–48).

Be·nét (bĭ-nā′), **Stephen Vincent.** 1898–1943. American poet and short-story writer; brother of W.R. Benét.

Be·nét (bĭ-nā′), **William Rose.** 1886–1950. American writer and editor; brother of S.V. Benét.

Be·ne·ven·to (bĕn-ĭ-vĕn′tō; *Italian* bā-nā-vĕn′tō). Ancient name **Ben·e·ven·tum** (bĕn-ə-vĕn′təm). A city of southern Italy, 35 miles northeast of Naples. It is the site of a Roman victory over Pyrrhus in 275 B.C. Population, 55,000.

be·nev·o·lence (bə-nĕv′ə-ləns) *n.* **1.** An inclination or tendency to perform charitable acts; good will. **2.** A kindly act. **3.** *English History.* A compulsory tax or payment exacted by some sovereigns without the consent of Parliament.

be·nev·o·lent (bə-nĕv′ə-lənt) *adj.* **1.** Characterized by benevolence; kindly. **2.** Of or concerned with charity: *a benevolent fund.* —See Synonyms at **kind.** [Middle English, from Latin *benevolēns,* "wishing well" : *bene,* well (see **deu-²** in Appendix*) + *volēns,* present participle of *velle,* to wish (see **wel-²** in Appendix*).] *—***be·nev′o·lent·ly** *adv.*

Ben·gal (bĕn-gôl′, bĕng-gôl′). A region of northeastern India and a former province of British India, divided in 1947 into East Bengal, now in East Pakistan, and West Bengal, Republic of India. *—***Ben′ga·lese′** (bĕn′gə-lēz′, bĕng′gə-, -lēs′) *adj. & n.*

Ben·gal, Bay of (bĕn-gôl′, bĕng-gôl′). That part of the Indian Ocean between India on the west and Burma on the east.

Ben·ga·li (bĕn-gô′lē, bĕng-gô′-) *n.* **1.** An inhabitant of Bengal. **2.** The modern Indic language spoken in Bengal. *—adj.* Of or characteristic of Bengal, its inhabitants, or its language.

ben·ga·line (bĕng′gə-lēn′, bĕng′gə-lēn′) *n.* A fabric having a crosswise ribbed effect made of silk, wool, or synthetic fibers. [French, from its similarity to a fabric made in BENGAL.]

Bengal light. A type of firework that burns with a brilliant, sustained blue light, formerly used for signaling.

Ben·ga·si (bĕn-gä′zē). Also **Ben·ga·zi, Ben·gha·zi.** One of the two capitals of Libya and the country's second-largest city, situated on the Mediterranean coast in the northeast, 610 miles east of Tripoli. Population, 71,000.

Ben·guel·a (bĕn-gĕl′ə, bĕng-). A seaport and provincial capital of Angola. Population, 23,000.

Ben-Gur·i·on (bĕn-go͝or′ē-ən), **David.** Original surname, Green. Born 1886. Polish-born Israeli statesman; first prime minister of Israel (1948–53); again prime minister (1955–63).

Be·ni (bā′nē). A river rising in western Bolivia and flowing 1,000 miles north to join the Mamoré at the Brazilian border.

be·night·ed (bĭ-nī′tĭd) *adj.* **1.** Overtaken by darkness or night. **2.** In moral or intellectual darkness; unenlightened; ignorant. [BE- + NIGHT.] *—***be·night′ed·ly** *adv.* *—***be·night′ed·ness** *n.*

be·nign (bĭ-nīn′) *adj.* **1.** Of a kind disposition. **2.** Manifesting gentleness and mildness. **3.** Tending to promote well-being; beneficial: *"spread the benign influence of the gospel"* (Horatio Greenough). **4.** *Pathology.* Not malignant: *a benign tumor.* Compare **malignant.** —See Synonyms at **favorable, kind.** [Middle English *benigne,* from Old French, from Latin *benignus,* "well-born" : *bene,* well (see **deu-²** in Appendix*) + -GENOUS.] *—***be·nign′ly** *adv.*

be·nig·nant (bĭ-nĭg′nənt) *adj.* **1.** Favorable; beneficial. **2.** Kind and gracious. *—***be·nig′nant·ly** *adv.*

be·nig·ni·ty (bĭ-nĭg′nə-tē) *n., pl.* **-ties.** Also **be·nig·nan·cy** (-nən-sē). **1.** The quality or condition of being benign. **2.** A kindly or gracious act.

Be·ni Ha·san (bĕ-nē hä′săn). A village of Egypt, on the Nile, 75 miles north of Asyut; site of tombs dating from 2000 B.C.

Be·nin (bĕ-nēn′). **1.** A former native kingdom of western Africa, now a province of Nigeria. **2.** The former name for the French possessions on the Guinea coast, including Dahomey.

Be·nin, Bight of (bĕ-nēn′). An indentation of the Gulf of Guinea along the coasts of Togo, Dahomey, and Nigeria.

ben·i·son (bĕn′ə-zən, -sən) *n.* A blessing or benediction. [Middle English *benes(u)n,* from Old French *beneisson,* from Latin *benedictiō,* BENEDICTION.]

ben·ja·min (bĕn′jə-mən) *n.* A resin, **benzoin** *(see).* [Variant (influenced by the name) of earlier *benjoin,* BENZOIN.]

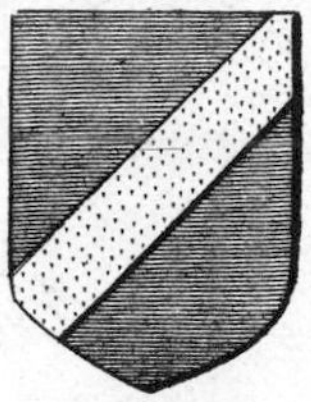

bend sinister

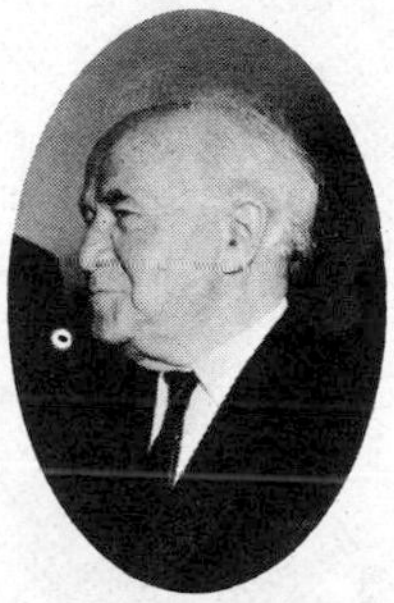

David Ben-Gurion
During a 1961 visit to U.N. headquarters

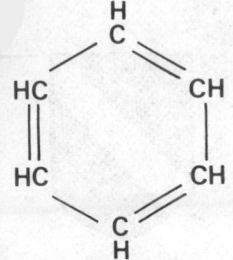

benzene ring
Each C represents a
carbon atom, each H
a hydrogen atom, and
the straight lines
are chemical bonds

Ben·ja·min[1] (bĕn′jə-mən). A masculine given name. [Hebrew, "son of the right hand" : bēn, son + yāmīn, "right hand."]

Ben·ja·min[2] (bĕn′jə-mən). The youngest son of Jacob and Rachel, favorite son of Jacob. Genesis 35:18.

Ben·ja·min[3] (bĕn′jə-mən) n. The tribe of Israel descended from Benjamin. —**Ben′ja·mite′** (-mīt′) adj. & n.

Ben·ja·min (bĕn′jə-mən), **Judah Philip.** 1811–1884. British-born American lawyer and political figure; secretary of state of Confederate States of America (1862–65); later, queen's counsel in England.

benjamin bush. The spicebush (see).

Ben Lo·mond (bĕn lō′mənd). A mountain, 3,192 feet high, on the eastern shore of Loch Lomond in Scotland.

ben·ne, ben·ni, ben·e (bĕn′ē) n. A plant, the sesame (see), or its seeds or oil. [Of African origin, akin to Mandingo bēne.]

ben·net (bĕn′ĭt) n. See herb bennet.

Ben·nett (bĕn′ĭt), **(Enoch) Arnold.** 1867–1931. English writer.

Ben·nett (bĕn′ĭt), **James Gordon**[1]. 1795–1872. Scottish-born American newspaper publisher; founded the New York Herald (1835); father of J.G. Bennett.

Ben·nett (bĕn′ĭt), **James Gordon**[2]. 1841–1918. American newspaper publisher; editor of New York Herald; founder of New York Evening Telegram; son of J.G. Bennett.

Ben Ne·vis (bĕn nĕ′vĭs, nĕv′ĭs). The highest elevation, 4,406 feet, in Great Britain, in the Grampians, Scotland.

Ben·ning·ton (bĕn′ĭng-tən). A town in Vermont near which, in 1777, the Americans under General John Stark defeated the British. Population, 13,000.

ben·ny (bĕn′ē) n., pl. -nies. Slang. An amphetamine tablet. [From BENZEDRINE.]

Be·noît de Sainte-Maure (bə-nwä′ də sănt-môr′). French trouvère of the 12th century; author of the Roman de Troie.

Be·no·ni (bə-nō′nī′). A city in the gold-mining area of southern Transvaal, Republic of South Africa, about 20 miles east of Johannesburg. Population, 141,000.

bent[1] (bĕnt). Past tense and past participle of bend. —adj. 1. Deviating from a straight line; crooked. 2. On a fixed course of action; determined: "I perceived he was bent on refusing my mediation" (Emily Brontë). 3. Headed toward; on the way to. —n. 1. The state of being crooked. 2. An individual tendency, disposition, or inclination: "The natural bent of my mind was to science." (Thomas Paine). 3. The limit of endurance. Used chiefly in the phrase to the top of one's bent. 4. A structural member or framework used for strengthening a bridge or trestle transversely.

bent[2] (bĕnt) n. 1. Any of several grasses of the genus Agrostis, some species of which are used in lawn mixtures and for hay. Also called "bent grass." 2. The stiff stalk of various grasses. 3. Rare. A moor; heath. [Middle English bent, grassy plain, Old English beonet- (attested in place names), from West Germanic binut- (unattested).]

Bent (bĕnt), **Charles.** 1799–1847. American fur trader and pioneer; with his brother, **William** (1809–1869), established Bent's Fort, principal trading post of early Southwest.

Ben·tham (bĕn′thəm), **Jeremy.** 1748–1832. English philosopher and jurist; a proponent of utilitarianism.

Ben·tham·ism (bĕn′thə-mĭz′əm) n. The utilitarian philosophy of Jeremy Bentham, holding that pleasure is the chief end of life and that the greatest happiness for the greatest number should be the ultimate goal of man. —**Ben′tham·ite′** (-mīt′) n.

ben·thos (bĕn′thŏs′) n. 1. The bottom of the sea or of a lake, especially at considerable depths. 2. The organisms living on sea or lake bottoms. [Greek, depth of the sea. See gwadh- in Appendix.*] —**ben′thic** (bĕn′thĭk), **ben′thal** (-thəl) adj.

Ben·ton (bĕnt′n), **Thomas Hart**[1]. 1782–1858. American political figure; granduncle of the painter T.H. Benton.

Ben·ton (bĕnt′n), **Thomas Hart**[2]. Born 1889. American easel painter and muralist; grandnephew of T.H. Benton.

ben·ton·ite (bĕn′tə-nīt′) n. Either of two principally aluminum silicate clays, containing some magnesium and iron, distinguished by sodium or calcium content with corresponding high or low swelling capacity, and used in various adhesives, cements, and ceramic fillers. [After Fort Benton, Montana.] —**ben′ton·it′ic** (-nĭt′ĭk) adj.

bent·wood (bĕnt′wood′) n. Wood that has been steamed until pliable and then bent into shape. —adj. Of or designating a style of furniture made of wood so treated.

Be·nue (bā′nwä). Also **Bin·ue** (bĭn′wä). A river rising in north-central Cameroun and flowing 870 miles west to join the Niger in south-central Nigeria.

be·numb (bĭ-nŭm′) tr.v. -numbed, -numbing, -numbs. 1. To make numb, especially by cold. 2. To make inactive; stupefy: "the anesthetic afternoon benumbs, sickens our senses" (Karl Shapiro). [Middle English benomen, past participle of benimen, to take away, Old English beniman : be-, away + niman, to take (see nem-² in Appendix*).] —**be·numb′ment** n.

Benz (bĕnts), **Karl Friedrich.** 1844–1929. German engineer; built first gasoline-powered automobile (1885).

benz·al·de·hyde (bĕn-zăl′də-hīd′) n. A colorless or yellowish, strongly reactive, volatile oil, C_6H_5CHO, used as a solvent, flavoring, and in perfumery. [German Benzaldehyd : BENZ(OIN) + ALDEHYDE.]

Ben·ze·drine (bĕn′zə-drēn′) n. A trademark for a brand of amphetamine (see).

ben·zene (bĕn′zēn′, bĕn-zēn′) n. A clear, colorless, highly refractive, flammable liquid, C_6H_6, derived from petroleum and used in or to manufacture a wide variety of chemical products including DDT, detergents, insecticides, and motor fuels. In nontechnical use, also called "benzol." [BENZ(OIN) + -ENE.]

benzene ring. The hexagonal ring structure in the benzene molecule and its substitutional derivatives, each vertex of which is occupied and distinguished by a carbon atom. Also called "benzene nucleus."

benzene series. A series of chemically related aromatic hydrocarbons containing the benzene ring, the simplest member of which is benzene.

ben·zi·dine (bĕn′zə-dēn′) n. A yellowish, white, or reddish-gray crystalline powder, $C_{12}H_{12}N_2$, used in dyes and to detect blood stains. [Probably BENZ(ENE) + -ID(E) + -INE.]

ben·zine (bĕn′zēn, bĕn-zēn′) n. Also **ben·zin** (bĕn′zĭn). A mixture of hydrocarbons, ligroin (see). [German Benzin : BENZ(OIN) + -INE.]

ben·zo·ate (bĕn′zō-āt′) n. A salt or ester of benzoic acid. [BENZ(OIN) + -ATE.]

benzoate of soda. Chemistry. Sodium benzoate (see).

ben·zo·ic acid (bĕn-zō′ĭk). A white crystalline acid, C_6H_5CO-OH, used to season tobacco and in perfumes, dentifrices, and germicides. [BENZO(IN) + -IC + ACID.]

ben·zo·in (bĕn′zō-ĭn, -zoin′) n. 1. Any of several resins containing benzoic acid, obtained as a gum from various trees of the genus Styrax, used in ointments, perfumes, and medicine. Also called "benjamin," "gum benjamin," "gum benzoin." 2. Any of various aromatic shrubs and trees of the genus Lindera, which includes the spicebush. 3. A white or yellowish crystalline compound, $C_{14}H_{12}O_2$, derived from benzaldehyde and used as an antiseptic. [Earlier benjoin, from French, from New Latin benzoe, from Arabic lubān jāwī, "frankincense of Java."]

ben·zol (bĕn′zôl′, -zōl′) n. Benzene (see). Not in technical use. [German Benzol : BENZ(OIN) + -OL.]

ben·zo·phe·none (bĕn′zō-fĭ-nōn′, -fē′nōn′) n. A white crystalline compound, $(C_6H_5)_2CO$, used in perfumery and in medicine. Also called "diphenylketone." [BENZO(IN) + PHEN(OL) + -ONE.]

ben·zo·yl (bĕn′zō-ĭl′) n. The univalent radical C_6H_5CO derived from benzoic acid. [German : BENZO(IN) + -YL.]

benzoyl peroxide. A flammable white granular solid, $(C_6H_5CO)_2O_2$, used as a bleaching agent for flour, fats, waxes, and oils, as a polymerization catalyst, and in pharmaceuticals.

ben·zyl (bĕn′zĭl, -zēl′) n. The univalent radical $C_6H_5CH_2$ derived from toluene. [BENZ(OIN) + -YL.]

Be·o·wulf (bā′ə-wo͞olf′). The hero of an anonymous Old English epic poem believed to have been composed in northern England between A.D. 650 and 750.

Bep·pu (bĕp′o͞o). A city on Beppu Bay, in northeastern Kyushu Island, Japan, with numerous hot springs, geysers, and mud volcanoes. Population, 129,000.

be·queath (bĭ-kwēth′, -kwēth′) tr.v. -queathed, -queathing, -queaths. 1. Law. To give (property) to a person by will. 2. To pass on or hand down. [Middle English bequethen, Old English becwethan, to say, bequeath : be-, about, over + cwethan, to say, speak (see gwet-² in Appendix*).] —**be·queath′al** (bĭ-kwē′thəl, -thəl) n. —**be·queath′er** n. —**be·queath′ment** n.

be·quest (bĭ-kwĕst′) n. 1. The act of bequeathing. 2. That which is bequeathed. [Middle English : be-, about + -quiste, a decree, Old English -cwiss (see gwet-² in Appendix*).]

BER Airport code for Berlin, Germany.

Be·rar (bā-rär′). A region of west-central India, and a part of Maharashtra State (since 1960).

be·rate (bĭ-rāt′) tr.v. -rated, -rating, -rates. To rebuke or scold harshly. See Synonyms at scold. [BE- + RATE (verb).]

Ber·ber (bûr′bər) n. 1. A member of one of several Moslem tribes of North Africa. 2. The Afro-Asiatic languages of these tribes. —**Ber′ber** adj.

Ber·be·ra (bûr′bĕr-ə). A seaport in Somalia, on the Gulf of Aden. Capital of former British Somaliland. Population, 20,000.

ber·ber·ine (bûr′bə-rēn′) n. A bitter-tasting yellow alkaloid, $C_{20}H_{19}NO_5$, obtained from the root of a North American plant, Hydrastis canadensis, from the barberry, and from other plants, and used in medicine. [German Berberin : New Latin Berberis (genus), from Old French berberis, BARBERRY + -IN.]

ber·ceuse (bĕr-sœz′) n., pl. -ceuses (-sœz′). 1. A cradlesong or lullaby. 2. A musical composition with a soothing accompaniment, usually in moderate ⁶/₈ time. [French, from bercer, to rock, from Gallo-Roman bertiare (unattested), from Gaulish bertā- (unattested), "to shake." See bher-¹ in Appendix.*]

Berch·tes·ga·den (bĕrKH′təs-gäd′n). A resort town in southeastern West Germany, ten miles south of Salzburg, Austria, where Adolf Hitler maintained a retreat. Population, 6,000.

Ber·dya·ev (bĕr-dyä′əf), **Nikolai Aleksandrovich.** 1874–1948. Russian existentialist philosopher.

be·reave (bĭ-rēv′) tr.v. -reaved or -reft (-rĕft′), -reaving, -reaves. 1. To deprive (of life or hope, for example): "To a man bereft of the sense of purpose" (G. Wilson Knight). 2. To leave desolate, especially by death: "cry aloud for the man who is dead, for the woman and children bereaved" (Alan Paton). [Bereave, bereft, bereft; Middle English bireven, birefte, bireft, Old English berēafian, berēafode, berēafod. See reup- in Appendix.*] —**be·reave′ment** n. —**be·reav′er** n.

Ber·en·gar·i·a (bĕr′ən-gâr′ē-ə). Princess of Navarre and queen of England in the 13th century; wife of Richard the Lion-Hearted.

Ber·e·ni·ce (bĕr′ə-nī′sē). A ruined city of ancient Egypt, founded by Ptolemy II in 300 B.C., and situated on the Red Sea.

Ber·en·son (bĕr′ən-sən), **Bernard** or **Bernhard.** 1865–1959. Lithuanian-born American art historian, critic, and collector.

be·ret (bə-rā′) n. A round, visorless cloth cap, worn originally

bentwood
Nineteenth-century
bentwood rocking chair

beret

by male Basques. [French *béret,* from Old Gascon *barret,* cap, from Late Latin *birrus*†, hooded cape.]

be·ret·ta. Variant of **biretta.**

Be·re·zi·na (byə-ryā′zyĭ-nə). A navigable river rising in northeastern Byelorussia and flowing generally southeast 365 miles to join the Dnieper west of Gomel. Napoleon's forces suffered great losses crossing this river, on their retreat from Moscow (1812).

berg (bûrg) *n.* An **iceberg** *(see).*

Berg (bĕrĸʜ), **Alban.** 1885–1935. Austrian composer.

Ber·ga·ma (bĕr′gä-mä′). A town in western Turkey, about 60 miles north of Izmir, the site of ancient Pergamum.

Ber·ga·mo (bĕr′gä-mō). An industrial center in Lombardy, Italy, 30 miles northeast of Milan. Population, 120,000.

ber·ga·mot (bûr′gə-mŏt′) *n.* **1.** A small, spiny tree, *Citrus aurantium bergamia,* bearing sour, pear-shaped fruit, the rind of which yields an aromatic oil. Also called "bergamot orange." **2.** The oil itself, used in perfumery. Also called "bergamot oil." **3.** Any of several plants of the genus *Monarda;* especially, the **wild bergamot** *(see).* [French *bergamote,* from Italian *bergamotta,* probably from Turkish *beg-armūdī,* "bey's pear."]

Ber·gen (bûr′gən, bär′-). A seaport and the second-largest city of Norway, situated in the southwest. Population, 117,000.

Ber·ger (bĕr′gər), **Hans.** 1873–1941. German psychiatrist; pioneer in electroencephalography.

Ber·ge·rac, Cyrano de. See **Cyrano de Bergerac.**

Berg·man (bûrg′mən; *Swedish* bär′y′-män′), **Ingmar.** Born 1918. Swedish screenwriter and director of motion pictures.

Berg·mann (bûrg′mən), **Peter Gabriel.** Born 1915. German-born American theoretical physicist.

berg·schrund (bĕrk′shrŏŏnt′) *n. Geology.* A crevasse at the head of a glacier which separates the moving ice from stationary ice adhering to the valley walls. [German *Bergschrund* : *Berg,* mountain, from Old High German *bĕrg* (see **bhergh-²** in Appendix*) + *Schrunde,* crack, from Old High German *scrunta* (see **sker-¹** in Appendix*).]

Berg·son (bĕrg′sən; *French* bĕrg-sôɴ′), **Henri (Louis).** 1859–1941. French philosopher.

Berg·so·ni·an (bĕrg-sō′nē-ən) *adj.* Of or pertaining to Henri Bergson or to his philosophy. —**Berg·so′ni·an** *n.*

Berg·son·ism (bĕrg′sə-nĭz′əm) *n.* Bergson's philosophy, which contends that all living forms arise from a persisting natural force, the **élan vital** *(see).*

be·rhyme (bĭ-rīm′) *tr.v.* **-rhymed, -rhyming, -rhymes. 1.** To celebrate in verse. **2.** To lampoon in verse.

Be·ri·a (bə-rē′ə, bĕr′ē-ə), **Lavrenti Pavlovich.** 1899–1953. Soviet chief of security under Stalin; executed for treason.

ber·i·ber·i (bĕr′ē-bĕr′ē) *n.* A thiamine deficiency disease of the peripheral nervous system, endemic in eastern and southern Asia, and characterized by partial paralysis of the extremities, emaciation, and anemia. [Singhalese, reduplication of *beri,* weakness.]

Be·ring (bîr′ĭng, bâr′-), **Vitus.** Also **Beh·ring.** 1680–1741. Danish navigator; explored Arctic seas for Russia.

Be·ring Sea (bîr′ĭng, bâr′-). The part of the North Pacific bounded by Alaska on the east, the Aleutian Islands to the southeast, Kamchatka Peninsula on the west, and Siberia to the northwest. It is joined to the Arctic Ocean by the Bering Strait.

Bering time. The time in northern Alaska and the Aleutian Islands, which lie in the 11th time zone west of Greenwich.

Berke·le·ian (bär′klē-ən, bûr′-) *adj.* Of or pertaining to George Berkeley or his philosophy. —**Berke′le·ian** *n.*

Berke·le·ian·ism (bär′klē-ə-nĭz′əm, bûr′-) *n.* The philosophy of George Berkeley, holding that material objects have no independent being but exist only as concepts of a human or divine mind.

Berke·ley (bûrk′lē *for sense 1;* bärk′lē *for sense 2).* **1.** A city and educational center of western California, situated on San Francisco Bay. Population, 111,000. **2.** A town in Gloucester, England, where Edward II was murdered (1327).

Berke·ley (bärk′lē), **George.** 1685–1753. Irish educator, philosopher, and Anglican bishop; active in America (1728–31).

Berke·ley (bärk′lē), **Sir William.** 1606–1677. English colonial administrator; governor of Virginia (1642–76).

berke·li·um (bûrk′lē-əm) *n. Symbol* **Bk** A synthetic transuranic element having 9 isotopes with mass numbers from 243 to 250 and half-lives from 3 hours to 1,380 years. Atomic number 97, valences 3, 4. See **element.** [New Latin, after BERKELEY (California).]

Berk·shire¹ (bärk′shîr, -shər). *Abbr.* **Berks, Berks.** A county, 725 square miles in area, in the Thames River valley in southern England. Population, 504,000. County seat, Reading.

Berk·shire² (bûrk′shîr, -shər) *n.* One of a domestic breed of black swine that originated in Berkshire, England, having white feet and faces.

Berk·shire Hills (bûrk′shîr, -shər). A range of hills in western Massachusetts. Highest elevation, Mount Greylock (3,491 feet). Also called "the Berkshires."

Ber·lich·ing·en (bĕr′lĭĸʜ-ĭng′ən), **Götz** or **Gottfried von.** 1480–1562. German revolutionary; leader of the Peasants' Revolt (1524–26).

ber·lin (bər-lĭn′) *n.* **1.** A light wool used in making clothing, especially gloves. Also called "Berlin wool." **2.** A four-wheeled covered carriage. **3.** Variant of **berline.** [After BERLIN.]

Ber·lin (bĕr-lĭn′; *German* bĕr-lēn′). The former capital of Germany and of Prussia, now a divided city entirely surrounded by East Germany. East Berlin, under Soviet control after 1945, became the capital of East Germany in 1949 (population, 1,071,000). The sectors under American, British, and French

control became West Berlin, associated politically and economically with West Germany (population, 2,200,000). —**Ber·lin′er** *n.*

Ber·lin (bĕr-lĭn′), **Irving.** Original name, Israel Baline. Born 1888. American-composer and lyricist of musical comedies.

ber·line (bər-lĭn′) *n.* Also **ber·lin.** A limousine with a glass window between the front and rear seats. [French, after BERLIN, where it originated.]

Ber·li·ner (bûr′lĭ-nər), **Emile.** 1851–1929. German-born American inventor; developed the flat phonograph record (1904).

Ber·li·oz (bĕr′lē-ōz′; *French* bĕr-lyôz′), **(Louis) Hector.** 1803–1869. French composer of operas and program music.

berm (bûrm) *n.* Also **berme. 1. a.** A narrow ledge or shelf, as along a slope. **b.** A shoulder of a road. **2.** A ledge between the parapet and the moat in a fortification. [French *berme,* from Dutch *berm,* slope, edge of a dike or dam, from Middle Dutch *berme.* See **bhrem-²** in Appendix.*]

Ber·me·jo (bĕr-mā′hō). A river rising in northern Argentina and flowing 1,000 miles southeast to join the Paraguay River. Along its middle course, also called "Teuco."

Ber·mond·sey (bûr′mənd-zē). A former administrative division of London, England, now part of **Southwark** *(see).*

Ber·mu·da (bər-myōō′də). **1.** Formerly **Som·ers Islands** (sŭm′ərz). A British colony in the Atlantic Ocean about 570 miles southeast of Cape Hatteras, North Carolina. It is an archipelago of over 350 small islands with a total area of about 21 square miles. Population, 48,000. Capital, Hamilton. **2.** The largest island of the group. In this sense, also called "Main Island." —**Ber·mu′di·an** (-dē-ən) *adj.* & *n.*

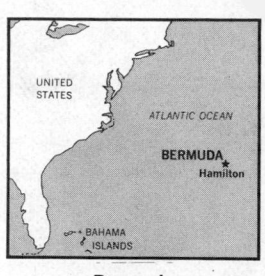

Bermuda

Bermuda buttercup. A plant, *Oxalis cernua,* native to southern Africa and naturalized in Bermuda, having yellow flowers.

Bermuda grass. A grass, *Cynodon dactylon,* that has wiry, creeping rootstocks and is used for lawns and pasturage in warm regions. Also called "scutch grass," "wiregrass."

Bermuda lily. A lily, *Lilium longiflorum,* cultivated extensively in Bermuda, having large, white, trumpet-shaped flowers. Also called "Easter lily."

Bermuda mulberry. A species of **beautyberry** *(see).*

Bermuda onion. A large, mild-flavored, yellow-skinned variety of onion. [First brought from Europe to Bermuda.]

Bermuda rig. A fore-and-aft rig, distinguished by a tall triangular mainsail, widely used on cruising and racing vessels. Also called "Marconi rig."

Bermuda shorts. Shorts that end slightly above the knees.

Bern (bûrn, bĕrn). Also **Berne.** The capital of Switzerland, on the Aar River in the northwestern part of the country. Population, 167,000. —**Ber·nese′** (bûr-nēz′, -nēs′) *n.* & *adj.*

Ber·na·dette (bûr′nə-dĕt′), **Saint.** Original name, Marie Bernarde Soubirous. 1844–1879. French peasant girl; canonized 1933; her visions were responsible for establishment of the shrine at Lourdes, France.

Ber·na·dotte (bûr′nə-dŏt′), **Count Folke.** 1895–1948. Swedish humanitarian; assassinated while United Nations mediator in Palestine.

Ber·nard (bûr′nərd, bər-närd′). A masculine given name. [Norman French *Bernard,* from German *Bernhard* : Old High German *bero,* a bear (see **bher-³** in Appendix*) + *harti,* stern, bold (see **kar-¹** in Appendix*).]

Ber·nard (bĕr-när′), **Claude.** 1813–1878. French physiologist; studied nervous and digestive systems.

Ber·nard·ine (bûr′nər-dĭn, -dēn′) *adj.* **1.** Of or pertaining to Saint Bernard of Clairvaux. **2.** Of or pertaining to the Cistercians, the order of monks reformed by Saint Bernard in 1115. —*n.* A member of a Cistercian order.

Ber·nard of Clair·vaux (bər-närd′ əv klâr-vō′), **Saint.** 1090–1153. French monastic reformer and political figure.

Bernese Alps. Also **Ber·nese O·ber·land** (ō′bər-lănd′, -länt′). A range of the Alps in south-central Switzerland. Highest elevation, Finsteraarhorn (14,032 feet).

Bern·hardt (bûrn′härt′, bĕrn′-), **Sarah.** Original name, Rosine Bernard. 1844–1923. French actress.

Ber·ni·ni (bĕr-nē′nē), **Giovanni Lorenzo.** 1598–1680. Italian sculptor, architect, and painter of early baroque period.

Ber·noul·li (bər-nōō′lē). Swiss family of mathematicians, including **Jakob** or **Jacques** (1654–1705), his brother **Johann** or **Jean** (1667–1748), and Johann's son **Daniel** (1700–1782).

Bernoulli distribution. *Statistics.* The **binomial distribution** *(see).* [After Jakob BERNOULLI.]

Bernoulli effect. The phenomenon of internal pressure reduction with increased stream velocity in a fluid. [After Daniel BERNOULLI.]

Bernoulli's law. 1. *Statistics.* The probability theorem stating that for a very large number of independent repeated Bernoulli trials the observed relative frequency of successes will approximate the probability of success on each trial. Also called "law of large numbers." **2.** *Physics.* The relationship between internal fluid pressure and fluid velocity, essentially a statement of the conservation of energy, that has as a consequence the Bernoulli effect. Also called "Bernoulli's theorem." [Statistics law, after Jakob BERNOULLI; physics law, after Daniel BERNOULLI.]

Bernoulli trial. *Statistics.* An experiment having just two possible results, usually denoted *success* and *failure,* with the property that the occurrence of one excludes the occurrence of the other in any given trial. [After Jakob BERNOULLI.]

Bern·stein (bûrn′stīn′), **Leonard.** Born 1918. American conductor, pianist, and composer of musical comedies, ballets, and symphonies.

ber·ret·ta. Variant of **biretta.**

Giovanni Bernini
A self-portrait

berlin

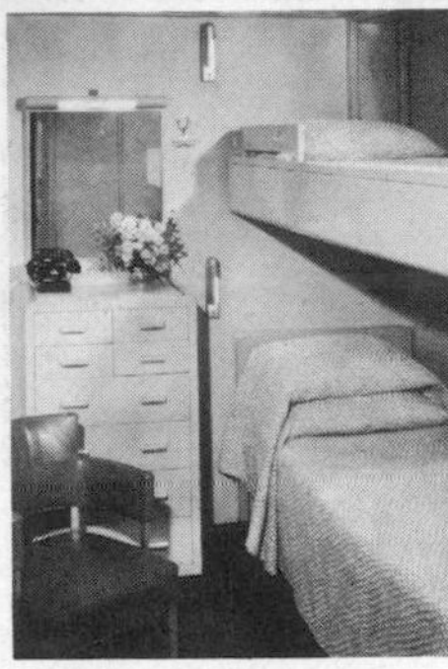

berth
Berths in a cabin on the liner S.S. *United States*

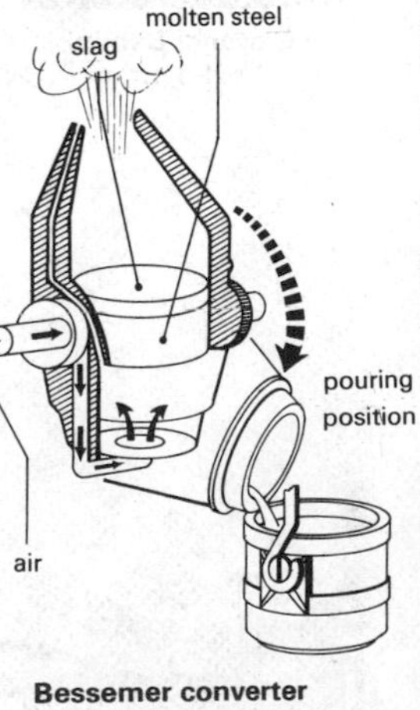

Bessemer converter

ber·ry (bĕr′ē) *n., pl.* **-ries. 1.** Any of various usually fleshy, edible fruits, such as the strawberry, blackberry, or raspberry. **2.** *Botany.* A fleshy fruit, such as the grape, blueberry, or tomato, developed from a single ovary and having few or many seeds, but not a single stone. See **hesperidium, pepo. 3.** Any of various seeds or dried kernels, such as that of the coffee plant. **4.** The small, dark egg of certain crustaceans or fishes. —*intr.v.* **berried, -rying, -ries. 1.** To hunt for or gather berries. **2.** To produce or bear berries. [Middle English *berye,* Old English *beri(g)e.* See **bhā-¹** in Appendix.*]

Ber·ry (bĕ-rē′). Also **Ber·ri.** A region, former province, and former duchy of central France.

ber·seem (bər-sēm′) *n.* A clover, *Trifolium alexandrinum,* native to northern Africa and southwestern Asia, grown for soil improvement in dry regions of southwestern North America. Also called "Egyptian clover." [Arabic *barsīm, birsīm,* from Coptic *bersīm.*]

ber·serk (bər-sûrk′, -zûrk′) *adj.* **1.** Destructively or frenetically violent. **2.** Deranged. —*n.* A berserker. —**ber·serk′** *adv.*

ber·serk·er (bər-sûr′kər, -zûr′kər) *n. Norse Mythology.* A fierce warrior who fought in battle with frenzied violence and fury. [Old Norse *berserkr,* "bear's skin" : *björn* (stem *ber-*), a bear (see **bher-³** in Appendix*) + *serkr,* shirt, from Germanic *sarkiz* (unattested).]

berth (bûrth) *n.* **1.** A built-in bed or bunk in a ship or railroad sleeping car. **2.** *Nautical.* A space at a wharf for a ship to dock or anchor. **3.** *Nautical.* Enough space for a ship to maneuver; sea room. **4.** A position of employment, especially on a ship. —**give a wide berth to.** To stay at a substantial distance from; avoid. —*v.* **berthed, berthing, berths.** —*tr.* **1.** To bring (a ship) to a berth. **2.** To provide (a ship) with a berth. **3.** To provide a bunk for, as on a ship or a railroad sleeping car. —*intr.* To come to a berth; dock. [Earlier *birth, byrth,* probably from BEAR (to proceed in a certain direction).]

ber·tha (bûr′thə) *n.* A wide, deep collar, often of lace, that covers the shoulders of a low-necked dress. [French *berthe,* after Queen *Bertha,* mother of Charlemagne.]

Ber·tha (bûr′thə). A feminine given name. [German, from Old High German *Beratha,* "the bright one," from *beraht,* bright, shining. See **bherəg-** in Appendix.*]

Ber·the·lot (bĕr-tə-lō′), **Pierre Eugène Marcelin.** 1827–1907. French organic chemist and political figure.

Ber·til·lon system (bûr′tə-lŏn′; *French* bĕr-tē-yôN′). A former system for identifying persons by means of a record of various body measurements, coloring, and markings. [Developed by Alphonse *Bertillon* (1853–1914), French criminologist.]

Ber·wick (bĕr′ĭk). Also **Ber·wick·shire** (-shĭr, -shər). A county of southeastern Scotland, 457 square miles in area. Population, 22,000. County seat, Duns.

Ber·wyn (bûr′wĭn). A city in Illinois, west of Chicago. Population, 54,000.

ber·yl (bĕr′əl) *n.* A mineral, essentially aluminum beryllium silicate, $Be_3Al_2Si_6O_{18}$, occurring in hexagonal prisms. It is the chief source of beryllium and is used as a gem. [Middle English, from Old French, from Latin *bēryllus,* from Greek *bērullos,* of Dravidian origin, probably from *Vēlūr* (modern *Bēlūr*), city in southern India.] —**ber′yl·line** (-ə-lĭn, -līn′) *adj.*

beryl blue. Light to very light greenish blue. See **color.**

beryl green. Light to brilliant bluish green. See **color.**

be·ryl·li·um (bə-rĭl′ē-əm) *n. Symbol* **Be** A high-melting, lightweight, corrosion-resistant, rigid, steel-gray metallic element used as an aerospace structural material, as a moderator and reflector in nuclear reactors, and in a copper alloy used for springs, electrical contacts, and nonsparking tools. Atomic number 4, atomic weight 9.0122, melting point 1,278°C, boiling point 2,970°C, specific gravity 1.848, valence 2. See **element.** [New Latin, from BERYL.]

Ber·ze·li·us (bər-zā′lē-əs, bər-zē′-), Baron **Jöns Jakob.** 1779–1848. Swedish chemist; discovered several elements; introduced system of writing chemical symbols; improved methods of analysis and electrolysis.

Bes (bĕs). *Egyptian Mythology.* A god of music and revelry.

Be·san·çon (bə-zäN-sôN′). A city of eastern France, between the Vosges and Jura mountains. Population, 96,000.

be·seech (bĭ-sēch′) *tr.v.* **-sought** (-sôt′) or **-seeched, -seeching, -seeches. 1.** To address an earnest or urgent request to; implore. **2.** To request earnestly; beg for. —See Synonyms at **beg.** [Middle English *besechen,* to seek : *be-,* thoroughly + *sechen, seken,* to SEEK.] —**be·seech′er** *n.*

be·seem (bĭ-sēm′) *tr.v.* **-seemed, -seeming, -seems.** *Archaic.* To be appropriate for; befit. [Middle English *besemen,* to seem, appear to do well : *be-,* thoroughly + *semen,* to SEEM.]

be·set (bĭ-sĕt′) *tr.v.* **-set, -setting, -sets. 1.** To attack from all sides. **2.** To trouble persistently; harass: *"forever frightened and beset by a ghostly band of doubts"* (Sherwood Anderson). **3.** To surround; hem in. **4.** To stud, as with jewels. —See Synonyms at **attack.** [Middle English *besetten,* Old English *besettan* : *be-,* on all sides + SET (place).] —**be·set′ment** *n.*

be·set·ting (bĭ-sĕt′ĭng) *adj.* Constantly troubling or attacking.

be·shrew (bĭ-shrōō′) *tr.v.* **-shrewed, -shrewing, -shrews.** *Archaic.* To invoke evil upon; to curse. [Middle English *beshrewen,* to corrupt, curse : *be-,* thoroughly + *shrewen,* to curse, from *shrewe,* a SHREW.]

be·side (bĭ-sīd′) *prep.* **1.** Next to. **2.** In comparison with. **3.** Except for. See Usage note at **besides. 4.** Apart from. —**beside oneself.** Out of one's senses with excitement; extremely agitated. —*adv.* In addition to. [Middle English *biside,* Old English *be sīdan* : *be,* BY + *sīdan,* dative of *sīde,* SIDE.]

be·sides (bĭ-sīdz′) *adv.* **1.** In addition; also. **2.** Moreover; furthermore. **3.** Otherwise; else. —See Synonyms at **also.** —*prep.* **1.** In addition to. **2.** Except for. [Middle English *bisides,* adverbial genitive of *biside,* BESIDE.]

Usage: In modern usage, the senses *in addition to* and *except for* are conveyed more often by *besides* than *beside.* Thus: *He had few friends besides us.*

be·siege (bĭ-sēj′) *tr.v.* **-sieged, -sieging, -sieges. 1.** To surround with aggressive intent; lay siege to. **2.** To crowd around; hem in. **3.** To harass or importune, as with requests. [Middle English *besegen* : *be-,* on all sides + *sege,* SIEGE.] —**be·siege′ment** *n.* —**be·sieg′er** *n.*

Bes·kids (bĕs′kĭdz, bĕ-skēdz′). Either of two mountain ranges, the East Beskids and the West Beskids, in the western Carpathians along the eastern border of Czechoslovakia. Highest elevation, Babia Góra (5,659 feet) in the West Beskids.

be·smear (bĭ-smĭr′) *tr.v.* **-smeared, -smearing, -smears. 1.** To smear over. **2.** To tarnish.

be·smirch (bĭ-smûrch′) *tr.v.* **-smirched, -smirching, -smirches. 1.** To soil; sully. **2.** To dim the purity or luster of; to tarnish; dishonor. —**be·smirch′er** *n.* —**be·smirch′ment** *n.*

be·som (bē′zəm) *n.* **1.** A bundle of twigs attached to a handle, and used as a broom. **2.** A broom of any kind. **3.** *Rare.* The broom plant. [Middle English *besem,* Old English *bes(e)ma,* from West Germanic *besmo-* (unattested).]

be·sot (bĭ-sŏt′) *tr.v.* **-sotted, -sotting, -sots.** To muddle or stupefy, especially with liquor. [BE- + SOT.]

be·sought. Past tense and past participle of **beseech.**

be·span·gle (bĭ-spăng′gəl) *tr.v.* **-spangled, -spangling, -spangles.** To ornament or cover with spangles.

be·spat·ter (bĭ-spăt′ər) *tr.v.* **-tered, -tering, -ters. 1.** To spatter or soil thoroughly, as with mud. **2.** To asperse; defame.

be·speak (bĭ-spēk′) *tr.v.* **-spoke** (-spōk′) or *archaic* **-spake** (-spāk′), **-spoken** (-spō′kən) or **-spoke, -speaking, -speaks. 1.** To be or give a sign of; indicate; signify. **2.** *Archaic.* To speak to; address. **3.** To engage or claim in advance; to reserve. **4.** To foretell; portend. [Middle English *bespeken,* to speak, order, Old English *bisprecan.* See **spreg-** in Appendix.*]

be·spec·ta·cled (bĭ-spĕk′tə-kəld) *adj.* Wearing eyeglasses.

be·spoke (bĭ-spōk′) *adj.* Also **be·spo·ken** (bĭ-spō′kən). *Chiefly British.* **1.** Made-to-order. **2.** Dealing in custom-made articles.

be·spread (bĭ-sprĕd′) *tr.v.* **-spread, -spreading, -spreads.** To cover or spread over, usually thickly.

be·sprent (bĭ-sprĕnt′) *adj. Poetic.* Besprinkled. [Middle English *bespreynt,* past participle of *besprengen,* to besprinkle, Old English *besprengan* : *be-,* around, over + *sprengan,* to scatter, burst (see **spergh-** in Appendix*).]

be·sprin·kle (bĭ-sprĭng′kəl) *tr.v.* **-kled, -kling, -kles.** To sprinkle over, as with water. [Middle English *besprengeln,* frequentative of *besprengen,* to besprinkle. See **besprent.**]

Bes·sa·ra·bi·a (bĕs′ə-rā′bē-ə). A former Rumanian region, about 18,000 square miles in area, now part of the Moldavian S.S.R., situated between the Prut and Dniester rivers. —**Bes′sa·ra′bi·an** *adj.* & *n.*

Bes·sel (bĕs′əl), **Friedrich Wilhelm.** 1784–1846. Prussian astronomer and mathematician.

Bes·se·mer (bĕs′ə-mər), Sir **Henry.** 1813–1898. British metallurgist and inventor.

Bessemer converter. A large pear-shaped container in which molten iron is converted to steel by the Bessemer process. [After Sir Henry BESSEMER.]

Bessemer process. A method for making steel by blasting compressed air through molten iron, burning out excess carbon and other impurities. [After Sir Henry BESSEMER.]

best (bĕst) *adj.* Superlative of **good. 1.** Surpassing all others in quality; most excellent. **2.** Most satisfactory, suitable, or useful; most desirable: *the best solution.* **3.** Greatest; largest: *the best part of a journey.* —*adv.* Superlative of **well. 1.** In the best way; most creditably or advantageously. **2.** To the greatest degree or extent; most: *"He was certainly the best hated man in the ship."* (Maugham). —**had best.** Should; ought to. —*n.* **1.** That which is best among several. **2.** The best person or persons. **3.** The best condition or quality: *look your best.* **4.** One's best clothing. **5.** The best effort one can make: *doing his best.* **6.** One's warmest wishes or regards: *Give them my best.* —**at best. 1.** Interpreted most favorably; at most. **2.** Under the most favorable conditions. —**for the best.** For the ultimate good. —**get** (or **have**) **the best of.** To defeat, surpass, or outwit. —**make the best of.** To do as well as possible under unfavorable conditions. —*tr.v.* **bested, besting, bests.** To prevail over; surpass; defeat: *"I'm a rough customer, I expect, but I know when I'm bested."* (Nathanael West). [Middle English *best,* Old English *bet(e)st.* See **bhad-** in Appendix.*]

Best (bĕst), **Charles Herbert.** Born 1899. American-born Canadian physiologist; discovered insulin with Frederick **Banting** *(see).*

be·stead (bĭ-stĕd′) *tr.v.* **-steaded** or **-stead, -steading, -steads.** *Archaic.* To be of service to; avail; aid. —*adj. Archaic.* Placed; located. [BE- + STEAD (to help).]

bes·tial (bĕs′chəl, bĕst′yəl) *adj.* **1.** Of or pertaining to an animal. **2.** Having the qualities of, or behaving in the manner of, a brute; savage. **3.** Subhuman in intelligence. —See Synonyms at **brute.** [Middle English, from Old French, from Late Latin *bēstiālis,* from Latin *bēstia,* BEAST.] —**bes′tial·ly** *adv.*

bes·ti·al·i·ty (bĕs′chē-ăl′ə-tē, bĕs′tē-ăl′-) *n., pl.* **-ties. 1.** The quality of being bestial; animal nature. **2.** An action or conduct marked by repugnant carnality or brutality: *"the bestialities of the sailors were intensified by the gloom of the rabbit-warren quarters"* (L.M. Kable). **3.** Sexual relations between a human being and a lower animal; sodomy.

bes·tial·ize (bĕs′chə-līz′, bĕst′yə-) *tr.v.* **-ized, -izing, -izes.** To make bestial; brutalize.

bes·ti·ar·y (bĕs′chē-ĕr′ē, bĕs′tē-) *n., pl.* **-ies.** A medieval collection of allegorical fables about the habits and traits of animals, each fable followed by an interpretation of its moral significance. [Medieval Latin *bēstiārium,* from Latin *bēstia,* BEAST.]

be·stir (bĭ-stûr′) *tr.v.* **-stirred, -stirring, -stirs.** To cause to become active; rouse. [Middle English *bestiren* : *be-,* thoroughly + STIR (arouse).]

best man. The bridegroom's chief attendant at a wedding.

be·stow (bĭ-stō′) *tr.v.* **-stowed, -stowing, -stows.** **1.** To present as a gift or honor; confer. Used with *on* or *upon.* **2.** To give in marriage. **3.** To apply; use: *"On Hester Prynne's story . . . I bestowed much thought."* (Hawthorne). **4.** *Archaic.* To store; to house. [Middle English *bestowen,* : *be-* (intensive) + STOW.] **—be·stow′able** *adj.* **—be·stow′al, be·stow′ment** *n.*

be·strad·dle (bĭ-străd′l) *tr.v.* **-dled, -dling, -dles.** To straddle.

be·strew (bĭ-stroo͞′) *tr.v.* **-strewed, -strewed** or **-strewn** (-stroo͞n′), **-strewing, -strews.** **1.** To strew (a surface) with things so as to cover it. **2.** To scatter or cast things profusely on a surface. **3.** To lie scattered over or about.

be·stride (bĭ-strīd′) *tr.v* **-strode** (-strōd′), **-stridden** (-strĭd′n), **-striding, -strides.** **1.** To sit or stand on with the legs widely spread; straddle. **2.** To step over. [Middle English *bestriden,* Old English *bestrīdan* : *be-,* over + *strīdan,* to STRIDE.]

best seller. A book or other product that is among those sold in the largest numbers. **—best′-sell′ing** *adj.*

bet (bĕt) *n.* **1.** An agreement between two parties that the one proved wrong about an uncertain outcome will forfeit a stipulated thing or sum to the other; a wager. **2.** The fact, event, or outcome on which a wager is made. **3.** The object or amount risked in a wager; the stake. **4.** The person or thing upon which a stake is placed. **—***v.* **bet** or *rare* **betted, betting, bets.** **—***tr.* **1.** To stake (an object or amount, for example) in a bet. **2.** To make a bet with. **3.** To make a bet on (a contestant or an outcome). **4.** To maintain confidently, as if making a bet. **—***intr.* To make or place a bet. **—you bet.** *Informal.* Surely. [Perhaps short for ABET in the sense of "instigation."]

bet. between.

be·ta (bā′tə, bē′-). **1.** The second letter in the Greek alphabet, written Β, β. Transliterated in English as *B, b.* See **alphabet.** **2.** The second item in a series or system of classification. **3.** *Physics.* **a.** A beta particle. **b.** A beta ray. [Greek *bēta,* from Hebrew *bēth,* BETH.]

be·ta·ine (bē′tə-ēn′) *n.* A sweet, crystalline alkaloid, $C_5H_{11}NO_2$, occurring in sugar beets and other plants and used in treatment of muscular degeneration. [Latin *bēta,* BEET + -INE.]

be·take (bĭ-tāk′) *tr.v.* **-took** (-to͝ok′), **-taken, -taking, -takes.** **1.** To cause (oneself) to go or move. **2.** *Archaic.* To commit or apply (oneself) to something: *He betook himself to fasting.*

beta particle. A high-speed electron or positron, especially one emitted in radioactive decay.

beta ray. A stream of beta particles, especially of electrons.

beta rhythm. The second most common waveform occurring in electroencephalograms of the adult brain, characteristically having a frequency from 18 to 30 cycles per second and associated with an alert waking state. Also called "beta wave." Compare **alpha rhythm.**

be·ta·tron (bā′tə-trŏn′, bē′-) *n.* A fixed-radius magnetic induction electron **accelerator** *(see)* capable of accelerating electrons to energies of a few million to a few hundred million electron volts. [BETA + -TRON.]

be·tel (bēt′l) *n.* A climbing Asiatic plant, *Piper betle,* the leaves of which are chewed with the betel nut by people of southeastern Asia to induce both stimulating and narcotic effects. [Portuguese *betel, betle,* from Malayalam *veṭṭila.*]

Be·tel·geuse (bēt′l-jo͞oz′, bĕt′l-jœz′) *n.* Also **Be·tel·geux.** A bright-red intrinsic variable star, 527 light years from Earth, in the constellation Orion. [French *Bételgeuse,* from Arabic *bīt al-jauzā′,* "shoulder of the Giant (Orion)."]

betel nut. Also **be·tel·nut** (bēt′l-nŭt′). The seed of the fruit of the betel palm, chewed, together with betel leaves and lime, by many people of southeastern Asia.

betel palm. A palm tree, *Areca catechu,* of tropical Asia, having featherlike leaves and orange or scarlet fruit.

bête noire (bĕt nwär′). Someone or something that one especially dislikes or avoids. [French, "black beast."]

beth (bĕt) *n.* The second letter of the Hebrew alphabet. See **alphabet.** [Hebrew *bēth,* "house."]

Beth·a·ny (bĕth′ə-nē). A village of Biblical Palestine, two miles east of Jerusalem, where Jesus raised Lazarus from the dead. John 11:1, 43–44.

Be·the (bā′tə), **Hans Albrecht.** Born 1906. German-born American theoretical physicist.

beth·el (bĕth′əl, bĕ′thĕl′) *n.* **1.** A hallowed or holy place. **2.** A chapel for seamen. [Hebrew *bēth 'Ēl,* "house of God."]

Beth·el (bĕth′əl). A town of Biblical Palestine, 11 miles north of Jerusalem. Genesis 28:19.

Be·thes·da[1] (bĭ-thĕz′də). A pool in Jerusalem believed to have healing properties. John 5:2–4.

Be·thes·da[2] (bĭ-thĕz′də). An urban center in Maryland; a suburb of Washington, D.C. Population, 57,000.

be·think (bĭ-thĭngk′) *v.* **-thought** (-thôt′), **-thinking, -thinks.** **—***tr.* **1.** *Archaic.* To reflect upon; think about; consider. **2.** To remind (oneself); remember. Often used reflexively: *"I bethought me of the Lord's Prayer."* (Ralph Flanders). **—***intr.* *Archaic.* To meditate; ponder. [Middle English *bethinken,* Old English *bethencan* : *be-,* about + *thencan,* to THINK.]

Beth·le·hem (bĕth′lĭ-hĕm, bĕth′lē-əm). **1.** A town in Israeli-occupied Jordan, five miles south of Jerusalem, and the Palestinian village of Biblical times where David lived and Jesus was born. **2.** A city in east-central Pennsylvania, on the Lehigh River, near the New Jersey border. Population, 75,000.

Beth·nal Green (bĕth′nəl). A former administrative division of London, England, now part of **Tower Hamlets** *(see).*

Beth·sa·i·da (bĕth-sā′ĭ-də). A town of Biblical Palestine on the northeastern shore of the Sea of Galilee. John 1:44.

Be·thune (bĭ-tho͞on′), **Mary McLeod.** 1875–1955. American educator and government official.

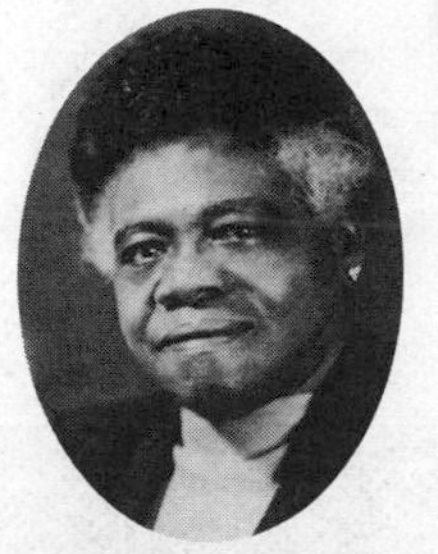

Mary McLeod Bethune

be·tide (bĭ-tīd′) *v.* **-tided, -tiding, -tides.** **—***tr.* To happen to: *Woe betide you if you harm his son.* **—***intr.* To take place; befall: *Whatever betides, he'll make every effort to help.* —See Synonyms at **happen.** [Middle English *betiden* : *be-,* thoroughly + *tiden,* to happen, Old English *tīdan* (see **dā-** in Appendix*).]

be·times (bĭ-tīmz′) *adv.* **1.** Early; in good time: *He awoke betimes.* **2.** *Archaic.* Quickly; soon. [Middle English, adverbial genitive of *betime* : *be,* BY + TIME.]

Bet·je·man (bĕch′ə-mən), **John.** Born 1906. English poet.

be·to·ken (bĭ-tō′kən) *tr.v.* **-kened, -kening, -kens.** To give a sign or portent of: *Those clouds betoken snow.* See Synonyms at **foretell.** [Middle English *betokenen,* Old English *bitācnian* (unattested). See **deik-** in Appendix.*] **—be·to′ken·er** *n.*

bet·o·ny (bĕt′ə-nē) *n., pl.* **-nies.** **1.** Any of several plants of the genus *Stachys;* especially, *S. officinalis,* native to Eurasia, having a spike of reddish-purple flowers. **2.** A plant, the **lousewort** *(see).* [Middle English *betone,* from Old French *betoine,* from Latin *bētonica, vettonica,* probably after the *Vettones,* an ancient Iberian tribe.]

be·took. Past tense of **betake.**

be·tray (bĭ-trā′) *tr.v.* **-trayed, -traying, -trays.** **1.** To give aid or information to an enemy of; commit treason against or be a traitor to: *betray one's nation.* **2.** To be disloyal or faithless to: *betray a promise.* **3.** To divulge in a breach of confidence: *"A servant . . . betrayed their presence . . . to the Germans."* (William Styron). **4.** To make known unintentionally: *"Only the young have the right to betray their ignorance"* (Henry Adams). **5.** To show; reveal; indicate: *"If their works betray imperfections"* (James Madison). **6.** To deceive; lead astray: *"I betrayed thy budding youth into a false and unnatural relation with my decay."* (Hawthorne). **7.** To seduce and forsake (a woman). —See Synonyms at **reveal, deceive.** [Middle English *betrayen* : *be-,* thoroughly + *trayen,* to betray, from Old French *trair,* from Latin *trādere* : *trāns-,* over + *dare,* to give (see **dō-** in Appendix*).] **—be·tray′al, be·tray′ment** *n.* **—be·tray′er** *n.*

be·troth (bĭ-trōth′, bĭ-trôth′) *tr.v.* **-trothed, -trothing, -troths.** **1.** To promise to give in marriage. **2.** To promise to marry. [Middle English *betrouthen* : *be-,* in relation to + *trouthe,* TROTH.]

be·troth·al (bĭ-trō′thəl, -trô′thəl) *n.* Also **be·troth·ment** (bĭ-trōth′mənt, -trôth′mənt). **1.** The act of becoming betrothed or of betrothing. **2.** A mutual promise to marry; an engagement.

be·trothed (bĭ-trōthd′, bĭ-trôtht′) *n.* A person who is engaged to be married.

bet·ter[1] (bĕt′ər) *adj.* Comparative of **good.** **1.** Greater in excellence or higher in quality. **2.** More useful, suitable, or desirable. **3.** Larger; greater: *the better part of a summer.* **4.** Healthier than before. **—better off.** In a better or wealthier condition. **—***adv.* Comparative of **well.** **1.** In a more useful or desirable way. **2.** To a greater or higher extent or degree. **3.** More: *better than a year.* See Usage note below. **—go (someone) one better.** To outdo or outwit. **—had better.** Have to; ought to; must. **—think better of.** To change one's mind about (a course of action) after reconsideration. **—***n.* **1.** Something more useful, excellent, desirable, or suitable. **2.** *Usually plural.* One's superiors, especially in social standing, competence, or intelligence. **—for the better.** Resulting in an improvement. **—get** (or **have**) **the better of.** To gain an advantage over. **—***v.* **bettered, -tering, -ters.** **—***tr.* **1.** To improve. Often used reflexively. **2.** To surpass or exceed. **—***intr.* To become better. —See Synonyms at **improve.** [Middle English *bettre,* Old English *betera.* See **bhad-** in Appendix.*]

Usage: The adverbial use of *better* in the sense of *more* is unacceptable in writing to 69 per cent of the Usage Panel, on the basis of this typical example: *The distance is better than a mile.* "Rustic and illogical," notes Dwight Macdonald. "Is anything *better,* or *worse,* than a mile?"

bet·ter[2]. Variant of **bettor.**

bet·ter·ment (bĕt′ər-mənt) *n.* **1.** An improvement. **2.** *Usually plural.* Any improvement, excluding mere repairs, that adds to the value of real property.

Bet·ter·ton (bĕt′ər-tən), **Thomas.** 1635?–1710. English actor.

bet·tor (bĕt′ər) *n.* Also **bet·ter.** One who bets.

be·tween (bĭ-twēn′) *prep. Abbr.* **bet., betw.** **1.** Intermediate in the space separating two places or things: *between the trees.* **2.** Intermediate to two times, quantities, or degrees: *between 11 o'clock and 12 o'clock.* **3.** Connecting spatially: *a path between the house and the road.* **4.** Connecting in reciprocal action or effort. See Usage note below. **5.** By the combined efforts of: *Between them, they succeeded.* **6.** In the combined ownership of: *They had three dollars between them.* **7.** Either one or the other of: *choose between riding and walking.* —See Synonyms at **among.** **—between you and me.** In strictest confidence. **—***adv.* In an intermediate space, position, or time; in the interim. **—in between.** In an intermediate situation. [Middle English *betwene,* Old English *betwēonum.* See **dwō** in Appendix.*]

Usage: *Between* (rather than *among*) is the correct preposition

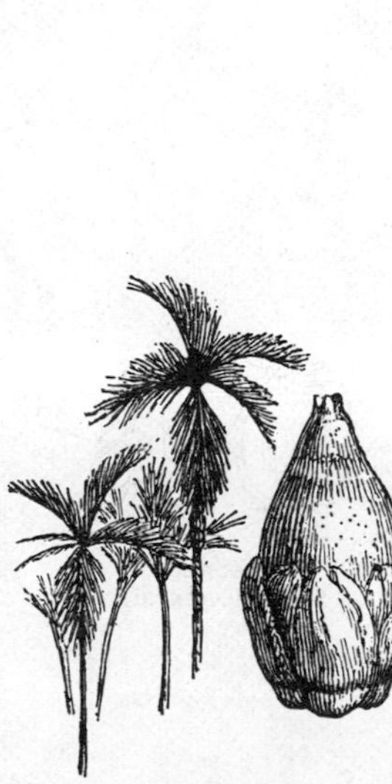

betel palm
The palm with its fruit, the betel nut

t tight/th thin, path/*th* this, bathe/ŭ cut/ûr urge/v valve/w with/y yes/z zebra, size/zh vision/ə about, item, edible, gallop, circus/ à *Fr.* ami/œ *Fr.* feu, *Ger.* schön/ü *Fr.* tu, *Ger.* über/KH *Ger.* ich, *Scot.* loch/N *Fr.* bon. ***Follows main vocabulary.** †**Of obscure origin.**

when only two persons or things serve as objects: *choose between good and evil. Between* is also the proper choice, according to 70 per cent of the Usage Panel, when more than two are involved, provided they are considered individually and in a close working relationship: *a treaty between five nations. Among* is applied to three or more when they are considered collectively and no close relationship is indicated: *spoils divided among the machine's backers.* The remaining 30 per cent of the Panel invariably restricts *between* to two and *among* to more than two. *Between* is always followed by pronouns in the objective case—specifically, by *me: between you and me.* The form *between you and I,* in writing, is condemned by 99 per cent of the Panel and in speech by 96 per cent. John Kieran notes: "If the position of the pronouns is reversed, the crime is glaringly exposed: *between I and you.* Who could say that in cold blood?" *Between* should never be followed by *each* or *every* and a singular noun, as in *an intermission between each act* (properly, *after each* or *between each act and the next*). When *between* is used with two objects to denote choice, *and* is the only proper connective of the objects: *choose between luxury and integrity* (not *luxury or integrity*).

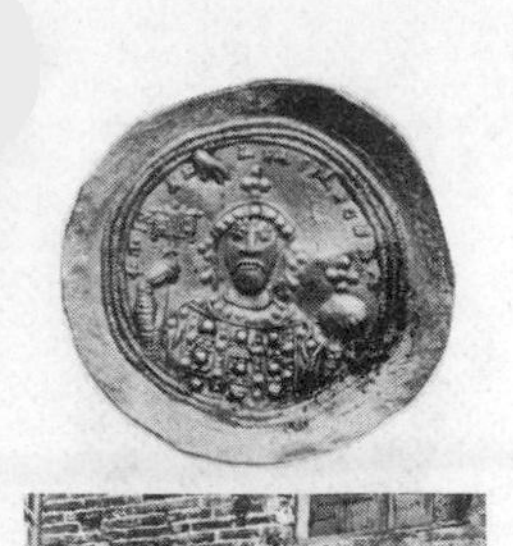

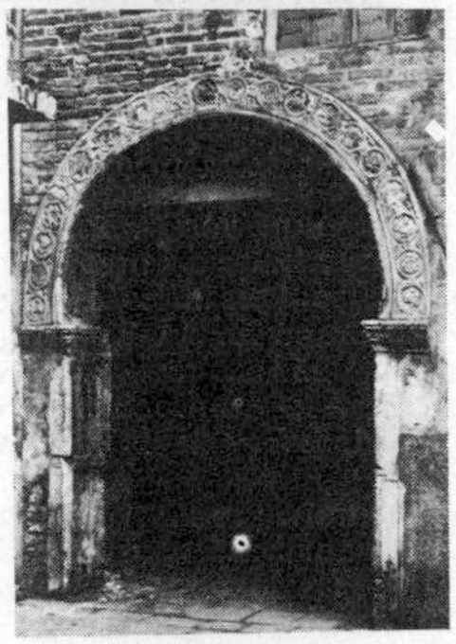

bezant
Above: Gold Byzantine coin
Below: Sculptured bezants above an arched 13th-century Venetian doorway

be·twixt (bĭ-twĭkst′) *adv. Archaic.* Between. —*prep. Archaic.* Between. —**betwixt and between.** In an intermediate or indecisive state; in a middle position; neither wholly one nor the other. [Middle English *betwix(te),* Old English *betwēohs, betwihs.* See **dwō** in Appendix.*]

Beu·lah (byo͞o′lə). **1.** The land of Israel. Isaiah 62:4. **2.** The land of peace described in Bunyan's *Pilgrim's Progress.*

Beu·then. The German name for **Bytom.**

BeV *Physics.* Billion (10^9) electron volts. The abbreviation GeV is preferred in standard international usage.

Bev·an (bĕv′ən), **Aneurin.** 1897–1960. British socialist leader.

Bev·a·tron (bĕv′ə-trŏn) *n. Physics.* A **proton synchrotron** *(see)* at the University of California. [BEV + -TRON.]

bev·el (bĕv′əl) *n.* **1.** The angle or inclination of a line or surface that meets another at any angle but 90 degrees. **2.** A rule with an adjustable arm, used to measure or draw angles or to fix a surface at an angle. In this sense, also called "bevel square." —*adj.* Inclined at an angle; slanted. —*v.* **beveled, -eling, -els.** Also *chiefly British* **-elled, -elling.** —*tr.* To cut at an inclination that forms an angle other than a right angle. —*intr.* To be inclined; to slope. [Old French *bevel* (unattested), from *baif,* open-mouthed, from *bayer,* to gape. See **bay** (space).]

bevel gear. Either of a pair of gears with teeth surfaces cut so that the gear shafts are not parallel.

bev·er·age (bĕv′rĭj, bĕv′ə-rĭj) *n.* Any of various liquid refreshments, usually excluding water. [Middle English *beverege,* from Old French *bevrage,* from Vulgar Latin *biberāticum* (unattested), from Latin *bibere,* to drink. See **pōi-**[1] in Appendix.*]

Bev·er·idge (bĕv′ər-ĭj), Sir **William Henry.** First Baron Tuggal. 1879–1963. British economist and sociologist.

Bev·er·ly (bĕv′ər-lē). Also **Bev·er·ley.** A feminine or masculine given name. [Middle English : *bever,* BEAVER + *ley,* LEA.]

Bev·in (bĕv′ĭn), **Ernest.** 1884–1951. British labor leader and foreign secretary (1945–51).

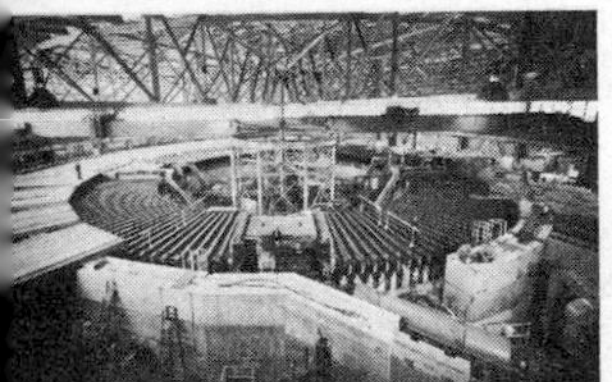

Bevatron

bev·y (bĕv′ē) *n., pl.* **-ies. 1.** A group of animals or birds, especially larks or quail. **2.** A group or assemblage. —See Synonyms at **flock.** [Middle English *bevy*†.]

be·wail (bĭ-wāl′) *v.* **-wailed, -wailing, -wails.** —*tr.* To express sorrow or regret over; cry or complain about. —*intr.* To wail or lament. —**be·wail′er** *n.* —**be·wail′ment** *n.*

be·ware (bĭ-wâr′) *v.* **-wared, -waring, -wares.** —*tr.* To be on guard against; be cautious of. Used chiefly in the imperative or infinitive. —*intr.* To be wary or careful. Used chiefly in the imperative or infinitive. [Middle English *be war* : BE (imperative) + *war(e),* WARY.]

be·wil·der (bĭ-wĭl′dər) *tr.v.* **-dered, -dering, -ders. 1.** To confuse or befuddle, especially with numerous conflicting situations, objects, or statements. **2.** *Rare.* To cause to become lost. —See Synonyms at **puzzle.** [BE- + archaic *wilder,* to stray, probably from WILDERNESS.]

be·wil·dered (bĭ-wĭl′dərd) *adj.* In a state of perplexity; thoroughly confused. —**be·wil′dered·ly** *adv.*

be·wil·der·ing (bĭ-wĭl′dər-ĭng) *adj.* Clouding the mind with a multiplicity of impressions or choices; confusing; perplexing. —**be·wil′der·ing·ly** *adv.*

be·wil·der·ment (bĭ-wĭl′dər-mənt) *n.* **1.** The condition of being bewildered. **2.** A situation of perplexity or confusion; a tangle.

be·witch (bĭ-wĭch′) *tr.v.* **-witched, -witching, -witches. 1.** To place under one's power by magic; cast a spell over. **2.** To captivate completely; fascinate; charm. [Middle English *bewicchen* : *be-,* thoroughly + *wicchen,* to bewitch, Old English *wiccian* (see **weik-**[2] in Appendix*).] —**be·witch′er** *n.* —**be·witch′er·y, be·witch′ment** *n.*

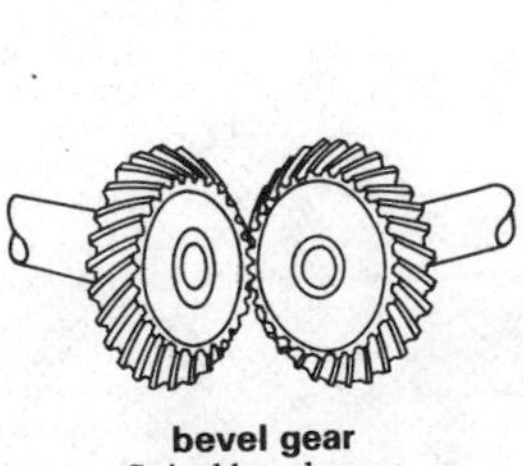

bevel gear
Spiral bevel gears

be·witch·ing (bĭ-wĭch′ĭng) *adj.* Enchanting as if with a magical spell; fascinating. —**be·witch′ing·ly** *adv.*

be·wray (bĭ-rā′) *tr.v.* **-wrayed, -wraying, -wrays.** *Rare.* To disclose, especially inadvertently; betray. [Middle English *bewreien* : *be-,* thoroughly + *wreien,* to accuse, Old English *wrēgan,* from Germanic *wrōgian* (unattested).]

Bex·ley (bĕk′slē). A borough of London, England, comprising the former administrative divisions of Bexley, Crayford, Erith, and part of Chislehurst and Sidcup. Population, 210,000.

bey (bā) *n.* **1.** A provincial governor in the Ottoman Empire. **2.** A native ruler of the former kingdom of Tunis. **3.** A Turkish title of honor and respect. [Turkish, prince, lord, gentleman, from Ottoman Turkish *beg.*]

be·yond (bē-ŏnd′) *prep.* **1.** Farther away than; on the far side of. **2.** After (a specified time); later than. **3.** Past or outside the limits, reach, or scope of: *"He was simple beyond analysis"* (Henry Adams). —*adv.* Farther along. [Middle English *beyonde,* Old English *begeondan* : *be,* BY + *geondan,* farther, from *geond,* yonder (see **i-** in Appendix*).]

bez·ant (bĕz′ənt, bə-zănt′) *n.* Also **bez·zant, byz·ant** (bĭz′ənt, bĭ-zănt′). **1.** A gold coin issued in Byzantium; solidus. **2.** *Architecture.* A flat disk, used as an ornament. [Middle English *besant,* from Old French, from Latin *Byzantius,* of BYZANTIUM.]

bez·el (bĕz′əl) *n.* Also **bez·il. 1.** A slanting surface or bevel on the edge of various cutting tools. **2.** The upper, faceted portion of a cut gem, above the girdle. **3.** A groove or flange designed to hold the beveled edge of a watch crystal or a gem. [Probably from Old French *besel*† (unattested).]

be·zique (bə-zēk′) *n.* A card game similar to pinochle, played with a deck of 64 cards. [French *bésigue*†.]

be·zoar (bē′zôr′, -zōr′) *n.* A hard gastric or intestinal mass, found chiefly in ruminants and once considered an antidote to poison. [Middle English *bezear,* from Old French *bezar,* from Arabic *bāzahr,* from Persian *pād-zahr* : *pād,* protecting against, (see **pā-** in Appendix*) + *zahr,* poison, from (unattested) Old Persian *jathra-* (see **gwhen-**[1] in Appendix*).]

Bez·wa·da. The former name for **Vijayavada.**

bf, bf. boldface.

b.f. 1. boldface. **2.** *Accounting.* brought forward.

B/F *Accounting.* brought forward.

B.F.A. Bachelor of Fine Arts.

bg. bag.

B.G. Brigadier General.

Bha·gal·pur (bä′gəl-po͝or′). A city of the Republic of India, in the east on the Ganges. Population, 154,000.

Bha·ga·vad-Gi·ta (bŭg′ə-vəd-gē′tə) *n.* A sacred Hindu text in the form of a philosophical dialogue that is incorporated into the *Mahabharata,* an ancient Sanskrit epic. [Sanskrit *Bhagavad-gītā,* "Song of the Blessed One" : *Bhágaḥ,* god of wealth, "the allotter," from *bhájati,* apportion, enjoy (see **bhag-**[1] in Appendix*) + *gītā,* a song (see **gēi-**[2] in Appendix*).]

bhang (băng) *n.* Also **bang. 1.** A plant, **hemp** *(see).* **2.** Any of several narcotics made from hemp. [Hindi *bhāng,* from Sanskrit *bhaṅgā*†, hemp.]

Bha·rat. The Hindi name for **India.**

Bhat·pa·ra (bät-pä′rə). A city in West Bengal, Republic of India, 22 miles north of Calcutta. Population, 135,000.

Bhau·na·gar (bou-nŭg′ər). Also **Bhav·na·gar** (bou-nŭg′ər). A seaport of the Republic of India, in the west on the Gulf of Cambay. Population, 171,000.

Bhn. *Metallurgy.* Brinell number.

Bho·pal (bō-päl′). The capital of the state of Madhya Pradesh, Republic of India, in the west-central part of the state. Population, 213,000.

bhp, b.hp. brake horsepower.

Bhu·ba·nes·war (bo͝ov′ə-nāsh′wər). The capital of Orissa State, Republic of India, situated in the southeast, near the Bay of Bengal. Population, 38,000.

Bhu·tan (bo͞o-tăn′, -tän′). Also **Bho·tan** (bō-). A kingdom occupying 18,000 square miles in the Himalaya Mountains between the northern border of the Republic of India and Tibet. Population, 800,000. Capital, Thimphu.

Bhu·tan·ese (bo͞o′tə-nēz′, -nēs′) *n., pl.* **Bhutanese.** Also **Bhu·ta·ni** (bo͞o-tä′nē) *pl.* **Bhutani** or **-nis** (-nēz); **Bho·ta·ni** (bō-tä′nē). **1.** A native or inhabitant of Bhutan. **2.** The Sino-Tibetan language spoken in Bhutan. —*adj.* Of or characteristic of Bhutan, its people, or their language and culture.

BHX Airport code for Birmingham, England.

bi-, bin-. Indicates: **1.** Two; for example, **binocular. 2. a.** Appearance or occurrence in intervals of two; for example, **bicentennial. b.** Appearance or occurrence twice during; for example, **biweekly.** See Usage note at **bimonthly. 3.** Occurrence on both sides or directions; for example, **biconcave, bilateral. 4.** *Chemistry.* **a.** An element or group in twice the proportion necessary for stability; for example, **sodium bicarbonate. b.** Of organic compounds, a double radical; for example, **bitartrate.** [Latin *bi-, bin-,* from *bis,* twice. See **dwō** in Appendix.*]

Bi The symbol for the element bismuth.

Bi·a·fra (bē-ä′frə, bē-ăf′rə). A region of eastern Nigeria; embarked on a secessionist movement in May, 1967.

Bi·a·fra, Bight of (bīt əv bē-ä′frə, bē-ăf′rə). A wide inlet of the Gulf of Guinea, off the coasts of Nigeria and Cameroun.

Bi·ak (bē-yăk′). The largest (948 square miles) of the Schouten Islands of Indonesia, off the northern coast of West Irian.

bi·a·ly (bē-ä′lē) *n., pl.* **-lys.** A flat, round baked roll topped with onion flakes. [From BIALYSTOK.]

Bia·ly·stok (bē-ä′lĭ-stôk′). *Russian* **Be·lo·stok** (byĕ′lə-stôk′), **Bye·lo·stok.** An industrial city of northeastern Poland, near the border of Byelorussia. Population, 134,000.

bi·an·nu·al (bī-ăn′yo͞o-əl) *adj.* Happening twice each year; semiannual. See Usage note at **bimonthly.** —**bi·an′nu·al·ly** *adv.*

Bi·ar·ritz (bē′ə-rĭts′). A resort city of southwestern France, on the Bay of Biscay. Population, 21,000.

bi·as (bī′əs) *n.* **1.** A line cutting diagonally across the grain of fabric: *cut cloth on the bias.* **2. a.** Preference or inclination that inhibits impartial judgment; prejudice. **b.** A specified instance of this. **3. a.** A weight or irregularity in a ball that causes it to swerve, as in lawn bowling. **b.** The tendency of such a ball to swerve. **4.** The fixed voltage applied to an electrode. —*adj.* Slanting or diagonal; oblique: *a bias fold.* —*adv.* Obliquely; aslant. —*tr.v.* **biased** or **biassed, biasing** or **biassing, biases** or **biasses. 1.** To cause to have a prejudiced view; to prejudice or influence. **2.** To apply a small voltage to (a grid). [From Old French *biais,* oblique, from Old Provencal, perhaps from Greek *epikarsios*†, oblique.]

bi·au·ric·u·lar (bī'ô-rĭk'yə-lər) *adj.* Also **bi·au·ric·u·late** (-lĭt, -lāt'). Possessing two auricles.

bi·ax·i·al (bī-ăk'sē-əl) *adj.* Having two axes. —**bi·ax'i·al'i·ty** (-ăl'ə-tē) *n.* —**bi·ax'i·al·ly** *adv.*

bib (bĭb) *n.* **1.** A piece of cloth worn under the chin by small children, to protect the clothing during meals. **2.** The part of an apron or pair of overalls worn over the chest. —*v.* **bibbed, bibbing, bibs.** —*tr.* To drink; imbibe. —*intr.* To indulge in drinking; tipple. [From Middle English *bibben,* to tipple, drink, perhaps from Latin *bibere.* See **pōi-**[1] in Appendix.*]

Bib. Bible; Biblical.

bib and tucker. *Informal.* Clothing; outfit. Usually used in the phrase *one's best bib and tucker.*

bibb (bĭb) *n.* **1.** A bracket on the mast of a ship to support the trestletrees. **2.** A **bibcock** *(see).* [Variant of BIB (napkin).]

bib·ber (bĭb'ər) *n.* A tippler; drinker. [From BIB (to drink).]

Bibb lettuce (bĭb). A kind of lettuce forming a small head and having tender, dark-green leaves. [Developed in Kentucky about 1850 by a Jack *Bibb.*]

bib·cock (bĭb'kŏk') *n.* A faucet with a nozzle that is bent downward. Also called "bibb." [BIB (napkin) + COCK.]

bi·be·lot (bĭb'lō; *French* bē-blō') *n.* A trinket. [French, from Old French *beubelet,* from a reduplication of *bel,* beautiful, from Latin *bellus,* handsome, fine. See **deu-**[2] in Appendix.*]

bibl., Bibl. Biblical.

Bi·ble (bī'bəl) *n. Abbr.* **B., Bib. 1.** The sacred book of Christianity, a collection of ancient writings including the books of both the Old Testament and the New Testament, and, in the Roman Catholic (Douay) Bible, the deuterocanonical books. See **Old Testament, New Testament, Apocrypha, King James Bible, Revised Version, Revised Standard Version, Douay Bible, Vulgate. 2.** The Old Testament, the sacred book of Judaism. See **Hebrew Scriptures. 3.** Any book or collection of writings constituting the sacred text of a religion. **4.** *Small* **b.** Any book considered authoritative in its field. [Middle English, from Old French, from Medieval Latin *biblia,* from Greek *(ta) biblia,* "(the) books," plural of *biblion,* book, originally a diminutive of *biblos, bublos,* papyrus, scroll, book, after *Bublos,* Phoenician port from which the Egyptian papyrus was exported to Greece.]

Bible Belt. Those sections of the United States, especially in the South and Middle West, where Protestant fundamentalism prevailed. [Coined by H.L. Mencken, about 1925.]

Bible paper. A thin, strong, opaque printing paper used for Bibles and reference books. Also called "India paper."

Bib·li·cal (bĭb'lĭ-kəl) *adj.* Also **bib·li·cal.** *Abbr.* **Bib., Bibl., bibl. 1.** Of, pertaining to, or contained in the Bible. **2.** In keeping with the nature of the Bible, especially: **a.** Suggestive of the personages or times depicted in the Bible. **b.** Suggestive of the prose or narrative style of the King James Bible. [Obsolete *biblic,* probably from Medieval Latin *biblicus,* from *biblia,* BIBLE.] —**Bib'li·cal·ly** *adv.*

Biblical Aramaic. A form of Aramaic that was the original language of the non-Hebrew portions of the Old Testament, such as certain passages in Ezra, Daniel, and Jeremiah. Also called "Chaldee." Compare **Aramaic.**

Bib·li·cist (bĭb'lə-sĭst) *n.* Also **Bib·list** (bĭb'lĭst). **1.** An expert on the Bible. **2.** A person who interprets the Bible literally. [From obsolete *biblic,* BIBLICAL.]

biblio–. Indicates books; for example, **bibliomania.** [From Greek *biblion,* book. See **Bible.**]

bib·li·o·film (bĭb'lē-ō-fĭlm') *n.* A type of microfilm used especially to photograph the pages of books.

bibliog. bibliographer; bibliography.

bib·li·og·ra·pher (bĭb'lē-ŏg'rə-fər) *n.* Also **bib·li·o·graph** (bĭb'lē-ə-grăf', -gräf'). *Abbr.* **bibliog. 1.** One versed in the description and cataloguing of printed matter. **2.** One who compiles a bibliography.

bib·li·og·ra·phy (bĭb'lē-ŏg'rə-fē) *n., pl.* **-phies.** *Abbr.* **bibliog. 1.** A list of the works of a specific author or publisher, or of sources of information in print on a specific subject. **2. a.** The description and identification of the editions, dates of issue, authorship, and typography of books, or other written material. **b.** A compilation of such information. [French *bibliographie,* from New Latin *bibliographia* : BIBLIO- + -GRAPHY.] —**bib'li·o·graph'i·cal** (bĭb'lē-ə-grăf'ĭ-kəl), **bib'li·o·graph'ic** *adj.* —**bib'li·o·graph'i·cal·ly** *adv.*

bib·li·ol·a·try (bĭb'lē-ŏl'ə-trē) *n.* **1.** Excessive adherence to a literal interpretation of the Bible. **2.** Extreme devotion to or concern with books. [BIBLIO- + -LATRY.] —**bib'li·ol'a·ter** *n.* —**bib'li·ol'a·trous** *adj.*

bib·li·o·man·cy (bĭb'lē-ō-măn'sē) *n., pl.* **-cies.** Divination by interpretation of a passage chosen at random from a book, especially the Bible. [BIBLIO- + -MANCY.]

bib·li·o·ma·ni·a (bĭb'lē-ō-mā'nē-ə, -mān'yə) *n.* An exaggerated liking for acquiring and owning books. [BIBLIO- + -MANIA.] —**bib'li·o·ma'ni·ac'** (-ăk') *n.* & *adj.* —**bib'li·o·ma·ni'a·cal** (-mə-nī'ə-kəl) *adj.*

bib·li·o·phile (bĭb'lē-ə-fīl') *n.* Also **bib·li·o·phil** (-fĭl'), **bib·li·oph·i·list** (bĭb'lē-ŏf'ə-lĭst). **1.** One who loves books. **2.** A book collector. [French : BIBLIO- + -PHILE.] —**bib'li·oph'i·lism'** *n.* —**bib'li·oph'i·lis'tic** *adj.*

bib·li·o·pole (bĭb'lē-ə-pōl') *n.* Also **bib·li·op·o·list** (bĭb'lē-ŏp'ə-lĭst). A person who deals in rare books. [Latin *bibliopōla,* from Greek *bibliopōlēs* : BIBLIO- + *pōlēs,* seller, from *pōlein,* to sell (see **pel-**[5] in Appendix*).] —**bib'li·o·pol'ic** (-pŏl'ĭk), **bib'li·o·pol'i·cal** *adj.* —**bib'li·op'o·ly** (-ŏp'ə-lē), **bib'li·op'o·lism'** (-ŏp'ə-lĭz'əm) *n.* —**bib'li·op'o·lis'tic** *adj.*

bib·li·o·the·ca (bĭb'lē-ə-thē'kə) *n.* **1.** A book collection; library. **2.** A catalogue of books. [Latin *bibliothēca,* from Greek *bibliothēkē,* "case for books" : BIBLIO- + *thēkē,* receptacle, case (see **dhē-**[1] in Appendix*).] —**bib'li·o·the'cal** *adj.*

bib·li·ot·ics (bĭb'lē-ŏt'ĭks) *n.* Plural in form, usually used with a singular verb. The examination of written documents to determine authorship or authenticity. [From BIBLIO-.]

Bib·list. Variant of **Biblicist.**

bib·u·lous (bĭb'yə-ləs) *adj.* Given to or marked by convivial drinking. [Latin *bibulus,* from *bibere,* to drink. See **pōi-**[1] in Appendix.*] —**bib'u·lous·ly** *adv.* —**bib'u·lous·ness** *n.*

bi·cam·er·al (bī-kăm'ər-əl) *adj.* Composed of two houses, chambers, or branches: *a bicameral legislature.* [BI- + Late Latin *camera,* room, CHAMBER.]

bi·cap·su·lar (bī-kăp'sə-lər, -syo͞o-lər) *adj. Botany.* **1.** Having two capsules. **2.** Having a capsule with two cells.

bi·car·bon·ate (bī-kär'bə-nāt', -nĭt) *n.* The radical group HCO_3 or a compound, such as sodium bicarbonate, containing it.

bicarbonate of soda. *Chemistry.* **Sodium bicarbonate** *(see).*

bice blue (bīs). Moderate blue, the color of azurite. See **color.** [Partial translation of French *azur bis,* "dark blue" : AZURE + *bis,* brown, tawny, from Old French *bis*†.]

bice green. Moderate yellow green, the color of malachite. See **color.** [See **bice blue.**]

bi·cen·ten·a·ry (bī'sĕn-tĕn'ə-rē, bī-sĕn'tə-nĕr'ē) *n., pl.* **-ries.** A bicentennial. —**bi'cen·ten'a·ry** *adj.*

bi·cen·ten·ni·al (bī'sĕn-tĕn'ē-əl) *adj.* **1.** Happening once every 200 years. **2.** Lasting for 200 years. **3.** Pertaining to a 200th anniversary. —*n.* A 200th anniversary or its celebration.

bi·cen·tric (bī-sĕn'trĭk) *adj.* Having two centers. —**bi'cen·tric'i·ty** (-trĭs'ə-tē) *n.*

bi·ceps (bī'sĕps') *n., pl.* **biceps** or **-cepses** (-sĕp'sĭz). Any muscle having two heads or points of origin, especially: **a.** The large muscle at the front of the upper arm that flexes the elbow joint. **b.** The large muscle at the back of the thigh that flexes the knee joint. [New Latin, from Latin, "two-headed" : BI- + *-ceps,* from *caput,* head (see **kaput** in Appendix*).]

Bi·chat (bē-shä'), **Marie François Xavier.** 1771–1802. French anatomist; regarded as founder of histology.

bi·chlo·ride (bī-klôr'īd', -klōr'īd') *n. Chemistry.* **Dichloride** *(see).*

bi·chro·mate (bī-krō'māt', -mĭt) *n. Chemistry.* **Dichromate** *(see).*

bi·cip·i·tal (bī-sĭp'ə-təl) *adj.* Of or pertaining to the biceps. [From New Latin *biceps* (stem *bicipit-*), BICEPS.]

bick·er (bĭk'ər) *intr.v.* **-ered, -ering, -ers. 1.** To engage in a petty quarrel; to squabble. **2.** *Poetic.* To flicker; glisten; quiver. —See Synonyms at **argue.** —*n.* A petty quarrel; a tiff. [Middle English *bikeren*†, to attack.] —**bick'er·er** *n.*

Bi·col. Variant of **Bikol.**

bi·col·or (bī'kŭl'ər) *adj.* Also **bi·col·ored** (bī'kŭl'ərd). Having two colors.

bi·con·cave (bī'kŏn-kāv', bī-kŏn'kāv') *adj.* Concave on both sides or surfaces. —**bi'con·cav'i·ty** (-kăv'ə-tē) *n.*

bi·con·vex (bī'kŏn-vĕks', bī-kŏn'vĕks') *adj.* Convex on both sides or surfaces. —**bi'con·vex'i·ty** *n.*

bi·corn (bī'kôrn') *adj.* Also **bi·cor·nu·ate** (bī-kôr'nyo͞o-ĭt, -āt'). **1.** Having two horns or two horn-shaped parts. **2.** Shaped like a crescent. [Latin *bicornis* : BI- + *cornū,* horn (see **ker-**[1] in Appendix*).]

bi·cor·po·ral (bī-kôr'pər-əl) *adj.* Also **bi·cor·po·re·al** (bī'kôr-pôr'ē-əl, -pōr'ē-əl). Having two distinct bodies or main parts.

bi·cus·pid (bī-kŭs'pĭd) *adj.* Also **bi·cus·pi·date** (-pə-dāt'). Having two points or cusps, as the crescent moon. —*n.* A bicuspid tooth, especially a **premolar** *(see).* [New Latin *bicuspis* (stem *bicuspid-*) : BI- + Latin *cuspis,* point, CUSP.]

bi·cy·cle (bī'sĭk'əl, -sĭ-kəl) *n.* A vehicle, usually designed for one person, consisting of a metal frame mounted upon two wire-spoked wheels with narrow rubber tires in tandem. It has a seat, handlebars for steering, and two pedals or a small motor by which it is driven. —*intr.v.* **bicycled, -cling, -cles.** To ride or travel on a bicycle. [French : BI- + Greek *kuklos,* circle, wheel (see **kwel-**[1] in Appendix*).] —**bi'cy·clist** *n.*

bi·cy·clic (bī-sī'klĭk, -sĭk'lĭk) *adj.* Also **bi·cy·cli·cal** (bī-sī'klĭ-kəl, -sĭk'lĭ-kəl). **1.** Consisting of or having two cycles. **2.** *Botany.* Composed of or arranged in two distinct whorls, as the petals of a flower. **3.** *Chemistry.* Consisting of or containing molecules consisting of two fused rings.

bid (bĭd) *v.* For transitive senses 1, 2, 3: **bade** (băd, bād) or *archaic* **bad** (băd), **bidden** (bĭd'ən) or **bid, bidding, bids.** For remaining senses: **bid, bid, bidding, bids.** —*tr.* **1.** To direct; command; enjoin. **2.** To utter (a greeting or salutation). **3.** To invite to attend; to summon. **4.** *Card Games.* To state one's intention to take (tricks of a certain number or suit): *bid four hearts.* **5.** To offer or propose (an amount) as a price. —*intr.* **1.** To make an offer to pay or accept a specified price. **2.** To seek to win or attain something; strive. —See Synonyms at **command.** ***Note:*** In the following phrases the past tense and past participle is **bid.** —**bid defiance.** To refuse to submit; offer resistance. —**bid fair.** To appear likely; seem. —**bid in.** To outbid on one's own property at an auction in order to raise the final selling price. —**bid up.** In an auction or card game, to increase the amount bid. —*n.* **1. a.** An offer or proposal of a price, as for an item at an auction or for a contract. **b.** The amount offered or proposed. **2.** An invitation, especially one offering membership in a group or club. **3.** *Card Games.* **a.** The act of bidding. **b.** The number of tricks or points declared. **c.** The trump or no-trump declared. **d.** The turn of a player to bid. **4.** An earnest effort; a striving: *a bid for first place.* See Usage note below. [Bid, bade, bidden; from two verbs: 1. Middle English *bidden,* ask, beseech, demand, command, *bad, beden,* Old English *biddan, bæd* (plural *bǣdon*), *(ge)beden.* See **bhedh-**[2] in Appendix.* 2. Middle English *beden,* to offer, pre-

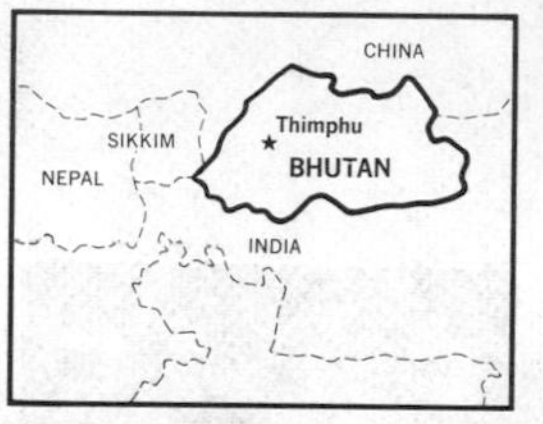

Bhutan

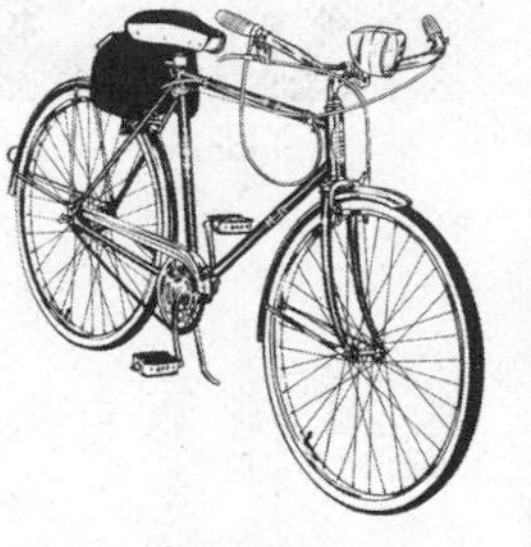
bicycle
Lightweight bicycle with hand-operated brakes

sent, proclaim, command (last sense adopted from *bidden*), *bead, boden,* Old English *bēodan, bēad* (plural *budon*), *(ge)boden.* See **bheudh-** in Appendix.*] —**bid′der** *n.*

Usage: *Bid* (noun), in the noncommercial sense of effort or striving, is acceptable in writing to 82 per cent of the Usage Panel: *a bid to restore harmony in the party.*

b.i.d. *Medicine.* twice a day (Latin *bis in die*).

bi·dar·ka (bī-där′kə) *n.* A hide-covered canoe used by Eskimos of Alaska. [Russian *baidarka,* diminutive of *baidara*†.]

bid·da·ble (bĭd′ə-bəl) *adj.* **1.** Worth bidding on. **2.** Docile; tractable: *"make him as biddable as a house-dog"* (Yeats).

bid·den. A past participle of **bid.**

bid·ding (bĭd′ĭng) *n.* **1.** A demand that something be done; a command. **2.** A request to appear; a summons. **3.** The bids collectively, as at an auction or in playing cards. —**at the bidding of.** At the service of. —**do the bidding of.** To follow the orders of.

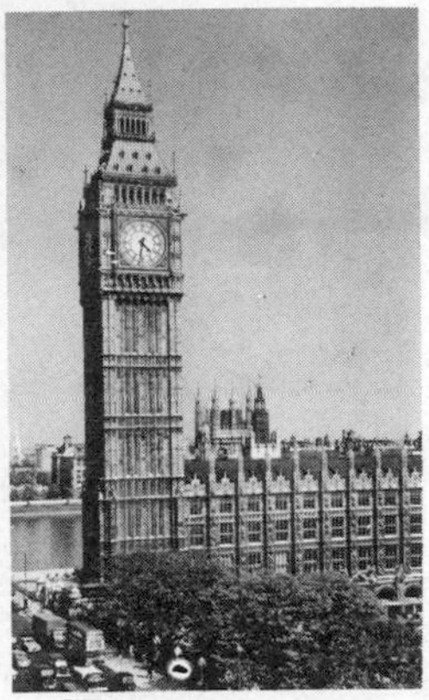

Big Ben

Bid·dle (bĭd′l), **George.** Born 1885. American painter and sculptor.

Bid·dle (bĭd′l), **John.** 1615–1662. English Unitarian theologian; banished and imprisoned for blasphemy.

Bid·dle (bĭd′l), **Nicholas.** 1786–1844. American financier; opponent of President Jackson in national bank controversy.

bid·dy[1] (bĭd′ē) *n., pl.* **-dies.** A hen; fowl. [Possibly imitative of a call used for chickens.]

bid·dy[2] (bĭd′ē) *n., pl.* **-dies.** *Slang.* A garrulous old woman. [Pet form of BRIDGET.]

bide (bīd) *v.* **bided** or **bode** (bōd), **bided, biding, bides.** —*intr.* **1.** To stay in some condition or state; remain the same: *"England shall bide till Judgement Tide."* (Kipling). **2. a.** To wait; tarry: *bide for a while.* **b.** To stay: *to bide at home.* **c.** To be left; remain: *"Waters stink soon, if in one place they bide."* (Donne). —*tr.* To await. Used only in the phrase *bide one's time.* [Bide, bode; Middle English *biden, bod* (past singular), Old English *bīdan, bād.* See **bheidh-** in Appendix.*]

bi·den·tate (bī-dĕn′tāt′) *adj.* Having two teeth or two toothlike processes.

bi·det (bē-dā′) *n.* A basinlike fixture designed to be straddled for bathing the genitals and the posterior parts. [French, "small horse," possibly from Old French *bider*†, to trot.]

Bie·der·mei·er (bē′dər-mī′ər) *adj.* **1.** Of or pertaining to a type of German furniture of the first half of the 19th century, modeled after Empire styles. **2.** Staid and conventional; philistine. [After Gottlieb *Biedermeier,* the imaginary author of poems written by L. Eichroth (1827–1892), German poet.]

Biel (bēl). *French* **Bienne** (byĕn). A manufacturing city and railroad junction in northwestern Switzerland. Population, 67,000.

Bie·le·feld (bē′lə-fĕlt′). An industrial city of North Rhine-Westphalia, West Germany, about 40 miles east of Münster. Population, 170,000.

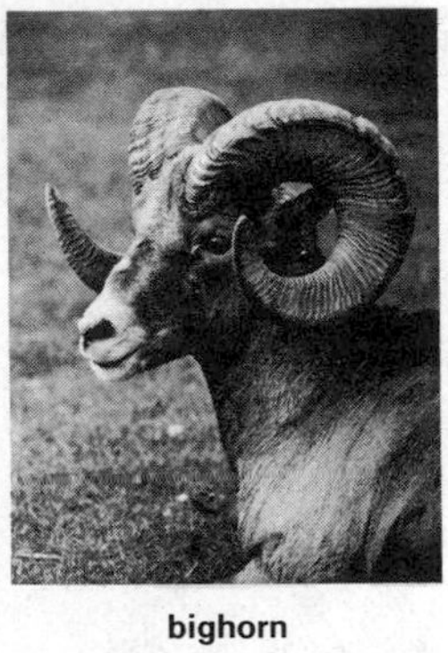

bighorn

bi·en·ni·al (bī-ĕn′ē-əl) *adj.* **1.** Lasting or living for two years. **2.** Happening every second year. **3.** Having a normal life cycle of two years. Compare **annual, perennial.** —*n.* **1.** An event that occurs once every two years. **2.** A plant that normally requires two years to reach maturity, producing leaves in the first year, blooming and producing fruit in its second year, and then dying. —See Usage note at **bimonthly.** [From BIENNIUM.] —**bi·en′ni·al·ly** *adv.*

bi·en·ni·um (bī-ĕn′ē-əm) *n., pl.* **-ums** or **-ennia** (-ĕn′ē-ə). A two-year period. [Latin : BI- + *annus,* year (see **at-** in Appendix*).]

bier (bîr) *n.* A stand on which a corpse, or a coffin containing a corpse, is placed to lie in state or to be carried to the grave. [Middle English *bere,* Old English *ber, bær.* See **bher-**[1] in Appendix.*]

Bierce (bîrs), **Ambrose (Gwinett).** 1842–1914? American short-story writer; disappeared in Mexico (1913).

bi·fa·cial (bī-fā′shəl) *adj.* **1.** Having two faces, fronts, or façades. **2.** *Botany.* Having upper and lower surfaces that are distinct and dissimilar. **3.** Having two opposing surfaces that are alike.

biff (bĭf) *tr.v.* **biffed, biffing, biffs.** *Slang.* To strike or punch. —*n. Slang.* A blow or cuff. [Imitative.]

bi·fid (bī′fĭd) *adj.* Divided or cleft into two parts or lobes. [Latin *bifidus* : BI- + -FID.] —**bi·fid′i·ty** *n.* —**bi′fid·ly** *adv.*

bi·fi·lar (bī-fī′lər) *adj.* Fitted with or involving the use of two threads or wires. [BI- + FILAR.] —**bi·fi′lar·ly** *adv.*

bi·flag·el·late (bī-flăj′ə-lĭt, -lāt′) *adj. Biology.* Having two flagella: *a biflagellate protozoan.*

bi·fo·cal (bī-fō′kəl) *adj.* **1.** Having two different focal lengths. **2.** Correcting for both near and distant vision.

bi·fo·cals (bī-fō′kəlz) *pl.n.* Eyeglasses with bifocal lenses, used for both near and distant vision.

bi·fo·li·ate (bī-fō′lē-ĭt, -āt′) *adj.* Having two leaves.

bi·fo·li·o·late (bī-fō′lē-ə-lāt′, -lĭt) *adj.* Having two leaflets.

bi·fo·rate (bī-fôr′āt′, -fōr′āt′, bĭ′fə-rāt′) *adj. Biology.* Having two openings or perforations. [BI- + Latin *forātus,* past participle of *forāre,* to pierce, bore (see **bher-**[2] in Appendix*).]

bi·forked (bī′fôrkt′) *adj.* Divided into two branches; bifurcate.

bi·form (bī′fôrm′) *adj.* Also **bi·formed** (-fôrmd′). Having a combination of features or qualities of two distinct forms.

bi·fur·cate (bī′fər-kāt′, bī-fûr′kāt′) *v.* **-cated, -cating, -cates.** —*tr.* To divide or separate into two parts or branches. —*intr.* To separate into two parts; fork. —*adj.* (bī′fər-kāt′, -kĭt, bī-fûr′kāt′, -kĭt). Also **bi·fur·cat·ed** (-kā′tĭd). Forked or divided into two parts. [Medieval Latin *bifurcātus* (adjective), from Latin *bifurcus,* two-forked : BI- + *furca,* forked stake (see **fork**).] —**bi′fur·cate′ly** *adv.* —**bi′fur·ca′tion** *n.*

big (bĭg) *adj.* **bigger, biggest. 1.** Of considerable size, number, quantity, magnitude, or extent; large. **2. a.** *Obsolete.* Of great force or violence: *"Farewell the plumed troop and the big wars"* (Shakespeare). **b.** Having great intensity; great; strong. **3.** Grown-up. **4.** Pregnant. Used with *with: big with child.* **5.** Filled up; brimming over. **6.** Having or exercising considerable authority, control, or influence. **7.** Conspicuous in position, wealth, or importance; prominent; influential. **8.** Of great significance; important; momentous. **9.** Loud and firm; resounding. **10.** Bountiful; generous; kindly. **11.** *Informal.* Self-important; boastful; pompous. —See Synonyms at **large.** —**big on.** *Informal.* Enthusiastic about; partial to: *big on meat and potatoes.* —*adv.* **1.** Pompously; pretentiously; boastfully: *"Toad talked big about all he was going to do in the days to come."* (Kenneth Grahame). **2.** With considerable success; in an outstanding manner. [Middle English *big, byg,* strong, stout, full-grown, probably from Scandinavian, akin to Norwegian dialectal *bugge,* strong man. See **beu-**[1] in Appendix.*] —**big′gish** *adj.* —**big′ly** *adv.* —**big′ness** *n.*

big·a·mist (bĭg′ə-mĭst) *n.* One who commits bigamy.

big·a·mous (bĭg′ə-məs) *adj.* **1.** Involving bigamy. **2.** Guilty of bigamy. —**big′a·mous·ly** *adv.*

big·a·my (bĭg′ə-mē) *n., pl.* **-mies.** *Law.* The criminal offense of marrying one person while still legally married to another. [Middle English *bigamie,* from Old French, from *bigame,* bigamous, from Late Latin *bigamus* : BI- + -GAMOUS.]

big·ar·reau (bĭg′ə-rō′) *n.* Any of several varieties of sweet cherry with firm, often light-colored flesh. [French, from *bigarrer,* to variegate : BI- + Old French *garre*†, variegated.]

big bang theory. A cosmological theory, the **expanding universe theory** *(see).*

Big Ben. 1. The bell in the clock tower of the Houses of Parliament in London, England. **2.** The clock itself.

Big Bend National Park. A national park, 1,080 square miles in area, in western Texas on the Mexican border.

Big Bertha. A large cannon used by the Germans in World War I. [Translation of German *dicke Bertha,* "fat Bertha," after *Bertha* Krupp von Bohlen und Halbach (1886–1957), proprietress of the Krupp Works, where the cannon was made.]

big brother. 1. An older brother, or someone having a similar protective relationship. **2.** *Capital* **B,** *capital* **B.** A vague, threatening figure representing the all-seeing, omnipresent power of an authoritarian government. [Sense 2, from *Big Brother,* a character in George Orwell's novel *1984.*]

Big Dipper. An asterism in the constellation Ursa Major, consisting of seven stars, four forming the bowl and three the handle of a dipper-shaped configuration. Also called the "Plow," the "Wain," the "Wagon."

bi·gem·i·nal (bī-jĕm′ə-nəl) *adj.* Occurring in pairs; twinned. [From Late Latin *bigeminus,* doubled : BI- + Latin *geminus,* paired, double, twin (see **yem-** in Appendix*).]

big·eye (bĭg′ī′) *n.* Any of several marine fishes of the family Priacanthidae, having large eyes and reddish scales.

big game. 1. Large animals or fish hunted or caught for sport. **2.** *Slang.* An important objective. —**big′-game′** *adj.*

big·gi·ty (bĭg′ə-tē) *adj.* Also **big·ge·ty.** *Informal.* Self-important; conceited; stuck-up. [From BIG.]

big·head (bĭg′hĕd′) *n.* **1.** *Informal.* Conceit; egotism. **2.** Any of various diseases of animals characterized by swelling of the head. —**big′head′ed** *adj.* —**big′head′ed·ness** *n.*

big-heart·ed (bĭg′här′tĭd) *adj.* Generous; charitable. —**big′-heart′ed·ly** *adv.* —**big′-heart′ed·ness** *n.*

big·horn (bĭg′hôrn′) *n.* A wild sheep, *Ovis canadensis,* of the mountains of western North America, having massive, curved horns in the male. Also called "mountain sheep," "Rocky Mountain sheep."

Big·horn Mountains (bĭg′hôrn′). A range in north-central Wyoming, part of the Rocky Mountains. Highest elevation, Cloud Peak (13,165 feet).

Big·horn River (bĭg′hôrn′). A river rising in west-central Wyoming and flowing 336 miles north to join the Yellowstone River in Montana.

big house. Also **Big House.** *Slang.* A penitentiary.

bight (bīt) *n.* **1. a.** A loop in a rope. **b.** The middle or slack part of an extended rope. **2.** A bend or curve, especially in a shoreline. **3.** A wide bay formed by such a bend or curve. —*tr.v.* **bighted, bighting, bights.** To tie in or secure with a bight of a rope. [Middle English *byght,* bend, bay, armpit, Old English *byht,* bend, angle. See **bheug-**[3] in Appendix.*]

big-league (bĭg′lēg′) *adj.* **Major-league** *(see).*

big·mouth (bĭg′mouth′) *n.* **1.** Broadly, any of various fishes having unusually large mouths. **2.** *Slang.* A loud-mouthed or gossipy person. —**big′mouthed′** (-mouthd′, -moutht′) *adj.*

big·no·ni·a (bĭg-nō′nē-ə) *n.* A plant of the genus *Bignonia;* especially, the **cross-vine** *(see).* [New Latin, after the Abbé Jean-Paul *Bignon* (1662–1743), librarian to Louis XV.]

big·ot (bĭg′ət) *n.* A person of strong conviction or prejudice, especially in matters of religion, race, or politics, who is intolerant of those who differ with him. [French, from Old French *bigot*†, a pejorative term for the Normans.]

big·ot·ed (bĭg′ə-tĭd) *adj.* Being or characteristic of a bigot. —**big′ot·ed·ly** *adv.* —**big′ot·ed·ness** *n.*

big·ot·ry (bĭg′ə-trē) *n.* The attitude, state of mind, or behavior characteristic of a bigot; intolerance.

big shot. *Slang.* An important or influential person.

big time. *Slang.* The most prestigious level of attainment in a competitive field. —**big′-time′** *adj.* —**big′-tim′er** *n.*

big top. *Informal.* **1.** The main tent of a circus. **2.** The circus.

big tree. The **giant sequoia** *(see).*

big wheel. *Slang.* A person of importance or authority.

big·wig (bĭg′wĭg′) n. Informal. An important person; dignitary.

Bi·har (bĭ-här′). Also **Be·har** (bĭ-här′). A state of the Republic of India, 67,198 square miles in area, bordering on Nepal in the north, and East Pakistan in the east. Population, 46,457,000. Capital, Patna.

Bi·ha·ri (bē-hä′rē) n. 1. A native or inhabitant of Bihar. 2. The Indic language spoken in northeastern India. —**Bi·ha′ri** adj.

bi·hour·ly (bī-our′lē) adj. Happening or done once every two hours. —adv. Every two hours.

bi·jou (bē′zhōō′) n., pl. **-joux** (-zhōō′). 1. A small, exquisitely wrought trinket. 2. Any charming, delicately made thing. [French, from Breton bizou, ring with a stone, from biz†, finger.]

bi·jou·te·rie (bē-zhōō′tə-rē′) n. A collection of jewelry or trinkets. [French, from BIJOU.]

Bi·ka·ner (bĭk′ə-nĕr′, bē′kŭn-âr′). A city of the Republic of India, in the Thar Desert in the northwest, and celebrated for its woolen goods. Population, 162,000.

bike (bīk) n. Informal. A bicycle. —intr.v. **biked, biking, bikes.** Informal. To ride a bicycle. [Short for BICYCLE.]

bi·ki·ni (bĭ-kē′nē) n. A very brief two-piece bathing suit worn by women. [French, after BIKINI atoll (referring to the "atomic" impact of the first bikinis).]

Bi·ki·ni (bĭ-kē′nē). An atoll in the Marshall Islands, in the western Pacific Ocean, the site of atomic bomb tests by the United States in 1946.

Bi·kol (bē-kōl′) n., pl. **Bikol** or **-kols** (for sense 2). Also **Bi·col.** 1. A language of the Indonesian subfamily, spoken on the island of Luzon in the Philippines. 2. One of the Malayan peoples of Luzon who speak this language.

bi·la·bi·al (bī-lā′bē-əl) adj. 1. Phonetics. Pronounced or articulated with both lips. Said of certain consonants, such as b, p, m, and w. 2. Pertaining to or having a pair of lips. —n. Phonetics. A bilabial sound or consonant. —**bi·la′bi·al·ly** adv.

bi·la·bi·ate (bī-lā′bē-ĭt, -āt′) adj. Botany. Having two lips. Said of a flower or corolla.

bil·an·der (bĭl′ən-dər, bī-lăn′-) n. A small two-masted sailing vessel, used especially on canals in the Low Countries. [Dutch bijlander, "ship that sails by the land" : bij, by, from Middle Dutch bie (see ambhi in Appendix*) + land, land, from Middle Dutch (see lendh-² in Appendix*).]

bi·lat·er·al (bī-lăt′ər-əl) adj. 1. Of, pertaining to, or having two sides; two-sided. 2. Having two symmetrical sides. 3. Affecting or undertaken by two sides equally; binding on both parties. —**bi·lat′er·al·ism′, bi·lat′er·al·ness** n. —**bi·lat′er·al·ly** adv.

Bil·ba·o (bĭl-bä′ō). A port city of northern Spain, on an inlet of the Bay of Biscay. Population, 351,000.

bil·ber·ry (bĭl′bĕr′ē) n., pl. **-ries.** 1. Any of several shrubby or woody plants of the genus Vaccinium, having edible blue or blackish berries. The European species, V. myrtillus, is also called "whortleberry." 2. The fruit of any of these plants. [Probably from Scandinavian, akin to Danish böllebaer : bolle, ball, round roll (see bhel-² in Appendix*) + baer, berry.]

bil·bo (bĭl′bō) n., pl. **-boes.** An iron bar with sliding fetters, formerly used to shackle the feet of prisoners. [Possibly after BILBAO, famous for its ironworks.]

bile (bīl) n. 1. Physiology. A bitter, alkaline, brownish-yellow or greenish-yellow liquid that is secreted by the liver, stored in the gallbladder, and discharged into the duodenum, and that aids in digestion, chiefly by saponifying fats. 2. Bitterness of temper; irascibility; ill humor; spleen. [French, from Latin bīlis, from Old Latin bis(t)lis (unattested), probably from Celtic, akin to Old Cornish bistel†.]

bilge (bĭlj) n. 1. The lowest inner part of a ship's hull. 2. Water that collects in this part. Also called "bilge water." 3. The bulge of a barrel or cask. 4. Slang. Stupid talk; nonsense. —v. **bilged, bilging, bilges.** —intr. 1. To spring a leak in the bilge. 2. To bulge or swell. —tr. To break open the bilge of. [Probably variant of BULGE.] —**bilg′y** adj.

bilge keel. Either of two beams or fins fastened lengthwise along the outside of a ship's bilge to inhibit heavy rolling.

bil·har·zi·a·sis (bĭl′här-zī′ə-sĭs) n. A disease, schistosomiasis (see). [New Latin : Bilharzia, schistosomes discovered by T. Bilharz (1825–1862), German parasitologist + -IASIS.]

bil·i·ar·y (bĭl′ē-ĕr′ē) adj. Of or pertaining to bile.

bi·lin·e·ar (bī-lĭn′ē-ər) adj. Mathematics. Linear with respect to each of two variables or positions.

bi·lin·gual (bī-lĭng′gwəl) adj. 1. Able to speak two languages with equal skill. 2. Written or expressed in two languages. —n. A bilingual person. [Latin bilinguis : bi- + lingua, tongue (see dnghu in Appendix*).] —**bi·lin′gual·ly** adv.

bi·lin·gual·ism (bī-lĭng′gwə-lĭz′əm) n. Habitual use of two languages, especially in speaking.

bil·ious (bĭl′yəs) adj. 1. Of, pertaining to, or containing bile; biliary. 2. Pertaining to, characterized by, or experiencing gastric distress caused by sluggishness of the liver or gall bladder. 3. Reminiscent of bile or bilious distress, especially in color. 4. Of a peevish disposition; sour-tempered; irascible. —**bil′ious·ly** adv. —**bil′ious·ness** n.

bil·i·ru·bin (bĭl′ə-rōō′bĭn, bĭl′ə-) n. A reddish-yellow organic compound, $C_{33}H_{36}O_6N_4$, derived from hemoglobin during normal and pathological destruction of erythrocytes. [Latin bīlis, BILE + ruber, red (see reudh- in Appendix*) + -IN.]

-bility. Indicates quality or state of being; for example, **capability.** [Middle English -bilite, from Old French, from Latin -bilitās, from -bilis, adjective suffix. See -able.]

bil·i·ver·din (bĭl′ə-vûr′dĭn) n. A green compound, $C_{33}H_{34}O_6N_4$, occurring in bile, sometimes formed by oxidation of bilirubin. [Swedish : bili-, from Latin bīlis, BILE + obsolete French verd,

green, from Latin viridis, from virēre, to be green (see virēre in Appendix*) + -IN.]

bilk (bĭlk) tr.v. **bilked, bilking, bilks.** 1. To defraud, cheat, or swindle. 2. To evade payment of. 3. To balk or frustrate. 4. To elude. —n. 1. One who cheats. 2. A hoax or swindle. [Perhaps an alteration of BALK (to refuse to go farther).] —**bilk′er** n.

bill¹ (bĭl) n. 1. An itemized list or statement of fees or charges. 2. A statement or list of particulars, such as a playbill or menu. 3. The entertainment offered by a theater. 4. An advertising poster or similar public notice. 5. A piece of legal paper money. 6. A bill of exchange (see) or a similar commercial note. 7. A draft of a proposed law presented for approval to a legislative body. 8. Law. A document presented to a court and containing a formal statement of a case, complaint, or petition. —**fill the bill.** Informal. To be quite satisfactory; meet all necessary requirements. —**foot the bill.** Informal. To pay the complete cost of. —tr.v. **billed, billing, bills.** 1. To present a statement of costs or charges to. 2. To enter on a statement of costs or a particularized list. 3. To advertise, announce, or schedule, either by public notice or as part of a program. [Middle English bille, from Norman French, from Medieval Latin billa, variant of bulla, seal affixed to a document, document, from Latin, bubble, ball, amulet. See beu-¹ in Appendix*.]

bill² (bĭl) n. 1. The beak of a bird. 2. A beaklike mouth part, as of a turtle. 3. The visor of a cap. 4. The tip of the fluke of an anchor. —intr.v. **billed, billing, bills.** To touch beaks together. —**bill and coo.** To kiss and murmur amorously. [Middle English bile, Old English bile. See bhei-² in Appendix*.]

bill³ (bĭl) n. 1. A pruning implement, a **billhook** (see). 2. A halberd or similar weapon with a hooked blade and a long handle. [Middle English bil, Old English bil. See bhei-² in Appendix*.]

bil·la·bong (bĭl′ə-bông′, -bŏng′) n. Australian. 1. A dead-end channel extending from the main stream of a river. 2. A stream bed filled with water only in the rainy season. 3. A stagnant pool or backwater. [Native Australian name : billa, river, water + bong, dead.]

bill·board (bĭl′bôrd′, -bōrd′) n. 1. A structure for the display of advertisements in public places or alongside highways. 2. Broadcasting. The opening listing of title, sponsors, products, talent, and the like, designed to stimulate audience interest in the program to follow.

bil·let¹ (bĭl′ĭt) n. 1. A lodging for troops in a nonmilitary building. 2. A written order directing that such quarters be provided. 3. Any assigned quarters. 4. Informal. A position of employment; job. —v. **billeted, -leting, -lets.** —tr. 1. To quarter (soldiers), especially in nonmilitary buildings. 2. To serve (a person) with an order to provide such quarters. 3. To assign lodging to. —intr. To be quartered; to lodge. [Middle English bylett, from Old French billette, bullette, diminutives of bulle, document, from Medieval Latin bulla, document, BILL.]

bil·let² (bĭl′ĭt) n. 1. A short, thick piece of firewood. 2. One of a series of square or log-shaped decorations forming part of a molding. 3. A bar of iron or steel in an intermediate stage of manufacture. 4. a. The part of a harness strap that passes through a buckle. b. A loop or pocket for securing the tongue of a harness strap. [Middle English, from Old French billette, billot, diminutive of bille, log, block, tree trunk, from Medieval Latin billus, billa, branch, trunk, probably from Celtic, akin to Irish bile†, sacred tree, large tree.]

bil·let-doux (bĭl′ā-dōō′, bĭl′ē-) n., pl. **billets-doux** (bĭl′ā-dōōz′, bĭl′ē-). A love letter. [French : billet, short note, from Old French billette, bullette, short note, BILLET + doux, sweet, from Latin dulcis (see dĮku- in Appendix*).]

bill·fish (bĭl′fĭsh′) n., pl. **billfish** or **-fishes.** 1. Any of various fishes of the family Istiophoridae, such as a marlin or sailfish, having an elongated, swordlike or spearlike snout and upper jaw. 2. Any of various other fishes having long, pointed jaws.

bill·fold (bĭl′fōld′) n. A folding pocket-sized case for carrying money and personal documents.

bill·head (bĭl′hĕd′) n. A sheet of paper with a business name and address printed at the top, used for making out bills.

bill·hook (bĭl′hŏŏk′) n. An implement with a curved blade attached to a handle, used especially for clearing brush and for rough pruning. Also called "bill."

bil·liard (bĭl′yərd) n. A shot in billiards; a carom. —adj. Of, pertaining to, or used in billiards. [From BILLIARDS.]

bil·liards (bĭl′yərdz) n. Plural in form, used with a singular verb. 1. A game played on a rectangular, cloth-covered table with raised, cushioned edges, in which a long, tapering cue is used to hit three small, hard balls against one another or the side cushions of the table. 2. Any of several similar games, such as one played on a table with pockets. Compare pool. [From French billard, bent stick, billiard cue, from Old French, from bille, log. See billet (stick).]

bill·ing (bĭl′ĭng) n. The relative importance of performers as indicated by the position and type size in which their names are listed on programs, theater marquees, or advertisements.

Bil·lings (bĭl′ĭngz). A city of Montana, in the south on the Yellowstone River. Population, 53,000.

Bil·lings (bĭl′ĭngz), **Josh.** Pen name of Henry Wheeler Shaw. 1818–1885. American humorist.

bil·lings·gate (bĭl′ĭngz-gāt′; British bĭl′ĭngz-gĭt) n. Foulmouthed abuse. [With allusion to scurrilous fishmongers at Billingsgate, London.]

bil·lion (bĭl′yən) n. 1. The cardinal number represented by 1 followed by 9 zeros, usually written 10^9. Called in British usage "milliard." See **number.** 2. In British usage, the cardinal number represented by 1 followed by 12 zeros, usually written 10^{12}. See **number**. **3.** An indefinitely large number. [French : BI- + (M)ILLION.] **—bil′lion** *adj.*

bil·lion·aire (bĭl′yə-nâr′) *n.* A person whose wealth amounts to at least a billion dollars, pounds, or comparable monetary units. [BILLION + (MILLION)AIRE.]

bil·lionth (bĭl′yənth) *n.* **1.** The ordinal number one billion in a series. See **number**. **2.** One of a billion equal parts. **—bil′lionth** *adj.* & *adv.*

Bil·li·ton (bə-lē′tŏn′). Also **Be·li·tung** (bə-lē′to͝ong). *Dutch* **Be·li·toeng**. An island, 1,866 square miles in area, of the Republic of Indonesia, in the Java Sea, off the southeastern coast of Sumatra. Population, 102,000.

bill of attainder. A former legislative act pronouncing a person guilty of a crime, usually treason, without trial and subjecting him to capital punishment and **attainder** *(see).*

bill of exchange. *Abbr.* **B/E** A written order directing that a specified sum of money be paid to a specified person. Also called "bill."

bill of fare. A menu.

bill of health. A certificate stating whether or not there is infectious disease aboard a ship or in her port of departure, and given to the ship's master for presentation at the next port of arrival. **—clean bill of health.** *Informal.* A satisfactory attestation as to condition.

bill of lading. *Abbr.* **B/L** A document listing and acknowledging receipt of goods for shipment.

bill of rights. **1.** A formal summary of those rights and liberties considered essential to a people or group of people. **2.** *Capital* **B**, *capital* **R**. The first ten amendments to the Constitution of the United States. **3.** *Capital* **B**, *capital* **R**. A declaration of rights restricting the power of the crown, enacted by the English Parliament in 1689.

bill of sale. *Abbr.* **B.S.** A document that attests a transference of the ownership of personal property.

bil·lon (bĭl′ən) *n.* **1.** An alloy of gold or silver with a greater proportion of another metal such as tin or copper, used in making coins. **2.** An alloy of silver with a high percentage of copper, used in making medals and tokens. [French, from Old French, ingot, from *bille,* log. See **billet** (stick).]

bil·low (bĭl′ō) *n.* **1.** A large wave or ocean swell. **2.** A great swell or surge, as of smoke or sound. **—*v.*** **billowed, -lowing, -lows.** **—*intr.*** To surge or roll in or as if in billows. **—*tr.*** To cause to swell or rise in billows. [From Old Norse *bylgja.* See **bhelgh-** in Appendix.*] **—bil′low·i·ness** *n.* **—bil′low·y** *adj.*

bill·post·er (bĭl′pō′stər) *n.* One who posts notices, posters, or advertisements. Also called "billsticker." **—bill′post′ing** *n.*

bil·ly¹ (bĭl′ē) *n., pl.* **-lies.** *Informal.* A short wooden club. [Probably from the name *Billy,* pet form of WILLIAM.]

bil·ly² (bĭl′ē) *n., pl.* **-lies.** *Australian.* A metal pot or kettle used in camp cooking. [Short for *billycan* : *billa,* a native Australian word for water + CAN (container).]

bil·ly·cock (bĭl′ē-kŏk′) *n. British.* A man's felt hat with a low crown, similar to a derby. [Possibly after *Billy* or William *Coke,* nephew of Thomas William Coke, Earl of Leicester (1752–1842), for whom the first billycock was made.]

billy goat. *Informal.* A male goat.

Billy the Kid. Original name, William H. Bonney. 1859–1881. American bandit of the Southwest; killed in ambush.

bi·lo·bate (bī-lō′bāt′) *adj.* Also **bi·lo·bat·ed** (-bā′tĭd), **bi·lobed** (bī′lōbd′). Divided into or having two lobes.

bi·loc·u·lar (bī-lŏk′yə-lər) *adj.* Also **bi·loc·u·late** (-lĭt, -lāt′). *Biology.* Divided into or containing two chambers, cavities, or cells. [BI- + LOCULUS.]

Bi·lox·i¹ (bə-lŭk′sē, -lŏk′sē) *n., pl.* **Biloxi** or **-is.** One of a tribe of Siouan-speaking North American Indians originally inhabiting the area of the lower Mississippi River.

Bi·lox·i² (bə-lŭk′sē, -lŏk′sē). An industrial and resort city in southern Mississippi, on the Gulf of Mexico. Population, 44,000.

bil·sted (bĭl′stĕd′) *n.* A tree, the **sweet gum** *(see).* [Origin unknown.]

bil·tong (bĭl′tŏng′, -tông′) *n. South African.* Narrow strips of meat, dried in the sun. [Afrikaans : *bil,* buttock, from Middle Dutch *bille* (see **bhel-²** in Appendix*) + *tong,* tongue, from Middle Dutch *tonghe* (see **dn̥ghū** in Appendix*).]

bi·mah. Variant of **bema**.

bi·man·u·al (bī-măn′yo͞o-əl) *adj.* Using or requiring the use of both hands. **—bi·man′u·al·ly** *adv.*

bi·mes·tri·al (bī-mĕs′trē-əl) *adj.* Bimonthly. [From Latin *bimē(n)stris* : BI- + *mēnsis,* month (see **mē-²** in Appendix*).]

bi·me·tal·lic (bī′mə-tăl′ĭk) *adj.* **1.** Consisting of two metals. **2.** Of, based on, or employing the principles of bimetallism.

bi·met·al·lism (bī-mĕt′l-ĭz′əm) *n.* **1.** The use of gold and silver as the monetary standard of currency and value. **2.** The doctrine advocating such a standard. **—bi·met′al·list** *n.*

Bim·i·ni (bĭm′ə-nē). Also **Bim·i·nis** (-nĭz). A group of small islands, nine square miles in total area, in the Bahamas.

bi·mod·al (bī-mōd′l) *adj.* Having two distinct statistical modes. **—bi′mo·dal′i·ty** (bī′mō-dăl′ə-tē) *n.*

bi·mo·lec·u·lar (bī′mə-lĕk′yə-lər) *adj.* Pertaining to, consisting of, or affecting two molecules.

bi·month·ly (bī-mŭnth′lē) *adj.* **1.** Happening every two months. **2.** *Nonstandard.* Happening twice a month; semimonthly. See Usage note below. **—*adv.*** **1.** Once every two months. **2.** *Nonstandard.* Twice a month; semimonthly. See Usage note below. **—*n., pl.*** **bimonthlies.** A publication issued bimonthly.

Usage: *Bimonthly* is rigidly restricted to the sense of *once in two months,* and *biweekly* to that of *once in two weeks,* according to 84 per cent of the Usage Panel. The remainder also accept the corresponding secondary senses of *twice a month* and *twice a week,* which are more properly expressed by *semimonthly* and *semiweekly.* An even stricter distinction exists between *biannual* (twice a year) and *biennial* (once in two years, lasting for two years). *Biyearly,* in strict usage, means *once in two years,* and *semiyearly* means *twice a year.*

bi·mo·tored (bī-mō′tərd) *adj.* Possessing, especially powered by, two motors.

bin (bĭn) *n.* **1.** A storage receptacle or container. **2.** *Slang.* An insane asylum. **—*tr.v.*** **binned, binning, bins.** To place or store in a bin. [Middle English *binne,* Old English *binn, binne,* basket, crib. See **bhendh-** in Appendix.*]

bin–. Variant of **bi–**.

bi·nal (bī′nəl) *adj.* Twofold; double. [From Latin *bīnī,* two by two. See **dwō** in Appendix.*]

bi·na·ry (bī′nə-rē) *adj.* **1.** Characterized by or composed of two different parts; twofold; double. **2.** *Chemistry.* Consisting of, or containing only molecules consisting of, just two kinds of atoms. **3.** Of, designating, or belonging to a number system that has 2 as its base. **—*n., pl.*** **binaries.** An entity consisting of two distinct parts, especially a **binary star** *(see).* [Late Latin *bīnārius,* from *bīnī,* two by two. See **dwō** in Appendix.*]

binary fission. **Fission** *(see),* especially of a cell or of an atomic nucleus, that results in just two approximately equal products.

binary star. A stellar system consisting of two stars orbiting about a common center of mass and often appearing as a single visual or telescopic object. Also called "visual binary," "binary," "double star."

bi·nate (bī′nāt′) *adj. Botany.* Consisting of two parts or divisions; growing in pairs: *a binate leaf.* [From Latin *bīnī,* two by two. See **dwō** in Appendix.*] **—bi′nate′ly** *adv.*

bin·au·ral (bī-nôr′əl, bĭn-ôr′əl) *adj.* **1.** Having or related to two ears; hearing with both ears. **2.** Of or pertaining to sound transmission from two sources, which may vary acoustically, as in tone or pitch, relative to a listener. Compare **stereophonic**. [BIN- + AURAL.]

bind (bīnd) *v.* **bound** (bound), **binding, binds.** **—*tr.*** **1.** To tie or secure, as with a rope or cord. **2.** To fasten or wrap by encircling with a belt, girdle, or the like. **3.** To bandage. Often used with *up: bind up a wound.* **4.** To hold or restrain with or as if with bonds. **5.** To compel, obligate, or unite, as with a sense of moral duty. **6.** *Law.* To place under legal obligation by contract or oath. **7.** To make certain or irrevocable: *bind a bargain.* **8.** To hold or employ as an apprentice; to indenture. Often used with *out* or *over.* **9.** To cause to cohere or stick together in a mass. **10.** To enclose and fasten (a book) between covers. **11.** To furnish with an edge or border for reinforcement or ornamentation. **12.** To constipate. **—*intr.*** **1.** To tie up or fasten anything. **2.** To be tight and uncomfortable. **3.** To become stiff, compact, or solid; cohere; jam. **4.** To be obligatory or compulsory. **—bind over.** *Law.* To hold on bail or place under bond. **—*n.*** **1. a.** Something that binds. **b.** The act of binding. **c.** The state of being bound. **2.** *Informal.* A difficult situation or dilemma. [Bind, bound, bound; Middle English *binden, bond, b(o)unden,* Old English *bindan, band* (plural *bundon*), *bunden.* See **bhendh-** in Appendix.*]

bind·er (bīn′dər) *n.* **1.** One who binds books by trade; a bookbinder. **2.** Something used to tie or fasten, such as a cord, rope, or band. **3.** A notebook cover with rings or clamps for holding sheets of paper. **4.** A material used to ensure uniform consistency, solidification, or adhesion to a surface, as the eggs in batter or the gum in paint. **5. a.** An attachment on a reaping machine that ties grain in bundles. **b.** A machine that reaps and ties grain. **6.** *Law.* A payment or written statement making an agreement legally binding until the completion of a formal contract, especially an insurance contract.

bind·er·y (bīn′də-rē) *n., pl.* **-ies.** A shop where books are bound.

bind·ing (bīn′dĭng) *n.* **1.** The action or process of one that binds. **2.** Something that binds or is used as a binder. **3.** The cover that holds together the pages of a book. **4.** A strip sewn or attached over or along the edge of something for protection, reinforcement, or ornamentation. **—*adj.*** **1.** Serving to bind. **2.** Uncomfortably tight and confining. **3.** Having the power to hold to an agreement or commitment; obligatory. **—bind′ing·ly** *adv.* **—bind′ing·ness** *n.*

binding energy. **1.** The energy released in binding a group of particles into a single system, especially a group of nucleons into an atomic nucleus. **2.** The work required to remove an atomic electron to an infinitely remote position from its orbit.

bin·dle stiff (bĭnd′l). *Slang.* A migrant worker or hobo who carries his own bedroll. [*Bindle,* alteration of BUNDLE.]

bind·weed (bīnd′wēd′) *n.* **1.** Any of several trailing or twining plants of the genus *Convolvulus,* having pink or white trumpet-shaped flowers. **2.** Any of various similar trailing or twining plants.

bine (bīn) *n.* **1.** The flexible stem of any of various climbing and twining plants, such as the hop, woodbine, or bindweed. **2.** Any of these plants. [Variant of dialectal *bind,* clinging vine, Middle English *bynde,* from *binden,* to BIND.]

Bi·net-Si·mon scale (bĭ-nā′sī′mən). Any of a series of early psychological tests of childhood intelligence. Also called "Binet Scale," "Binet-Simon test." See **Stanford-Binet scale**. [After Alfred *Binet* (1857–1911) and Théodore *Simon* (1873–1961), French psychologists.]

binge (bĭnj) *n. Slang.* **1.** A drunken spree or revel. **2.** A period of uncontrolled self-indulgence: *a crying binge.* [British dialectal *binge*†, to fill a boat with water, to drink heavily.]

Bing·ham·ton (bĭng′əm-tən). An industrial city of southern

New York State, on the Susquehanna near the Pennsylvania border. Population, 76,000.

bin·go (bĭng′gō) *n.* A game of chance in which players place markers on a pattern of numbered squares, according to numbers drawn and announced by a caller. Compare **lotto, keno.** —*interj.* Used to express pleasurable surprise or unexpected satisfaction. [Originally the winner's exclamation, from *bing,* ringing sound, sound expressing surprise (imitative).]

Binh·dinh (bĭn′dĭn′). Also **Binh Dinh.** A city of southeastern South Vietnam, near the South China Sea. Population, 147,000.

bin·na·cle (bĭn′ə-kəl) *n.* The nonmagnetic stand on which a ship's compass case is supported. [Earlier *bittacle,* from Middle English *bitakle,* from Spanish *bitácula* or Portuguese *bitácola,* from Latin *habitāculum,* little house, from *habitāre,* to dwell, abide, from *habēre* (past participle of *habitus*), to have. See **ghabh-** in Appendix.*]

bin·oc·u·lar (bə-nŏk′yə-lər, bī-) *adj.* 1. Pertaining to, used by, or involving both eyes at the same time. 2. Having two eyes arranged to produce stereoscopic vision. —*n.* Also *rare* **bin·o·cle** (bĭn′ə-kəl) (for sense 2). 1. *Usually plural.* An optical device, such as a pair of field glasses, designed for use by both eyes at once. 2. Any binocular optical device. [BIN- + OCULAR.] —**bin·oc′u·lar′i·ty** *n.* —**bin·oc′u·lar·ly** *adv.*

bi·no·mi·al (bī-nō′mē-əl) *adj.* Consisting of or pertaining to two names or terms. —*n.* 1. *Mathematics.* An expression consisting of two terms connected by a plus or minus sign; a polynomial in two terms. 2. A taxonomic name in **binomial nomenclature** *(see).* [New Latin *binōmium* : BI- + Greek *nomos,* portion, part (see **nem-**[2] in Appendix*).] —**bi·no′mi·al·ly** *adv.*

binomial distribution. *Statistics.* The frequency distribution of the probability of a specified number of successes in an arbitrary number of repeated independent Bernoulli trials. Also called "Bernoulli distribution."

binomial nomenclature. A system of classifying plants and animals by a double name, the first of which is the name of the genus and the second that of the species within the genus; for example, *Odobenus rosmarus,* the walrus.

binomial theorem. A mathematical theorem that specifies the expansion of a binomial to any power without requiring the explicit multiplication of the binomial terms.

bi·nu·cle·ate (bī-nōō′klē-ĭt, -āt′, bī-nyōō′-) *adj.* Also **bi·nu·cle·ar** (-ər), **bi·nu·cle·at·ed** (-ā′tĭd). Having two nuclei.

Bin·ue. See **Benue.**

bio-, bi-. Indicates life or living organisms; for example, *biocide, bionics.* [Greek, from *bios,* life, mode of life. See **gwei-** in Appendix.*]

bi·o·as·say (bī′ō-ăs′ā′, -ă-sā′) *n.* Evaluation of a drug by comparison of its effect with that of a standard on a test organism.

bi·o·as·tro·nau·tics (bī′ō-ăs′trə-nô′tĭks) *n.* Plural in form, used with a singular verb. The study of the biological and medical effects of space flight.

bi·o·cat·a·lyst (bī′ō-kăt′l-ĭst) *n.* A substance that initiates or modifies the rate of a biological process. —**bi′o·cat′a·lyt′ic** (-ĭt′ĭk) *adj.*

bi·o·chem·ist (bī′ō-kěm′ĭst) *n.* A scientist whose specialty is biochemistry.

bi·o·chem·is·try (bī′ō-kěm′ĭs-trē) *n.* The chemistry of biological substances and processes. —**bi′o·chem′i·cal, bi′o·chem′ic** *adj.* —**bi′o·chem′i·cal·ly** *adv.*

bi·o·cide (bī′ə-sīd′) *n.* A substance, such as a pesticide or an antibiotic, that is capable of destroying living organisms. [BIO- + -CIDE.] —**bi′o·ci′dal** (-sīd′l) *adj.*

bi·o·cli·ma·tol·o·gy (bī′ō-klī′mə-tŏl′ə-jē) *n.* The study of the effects of climatic conditions on organic life. —**bi′o·cli′ma·to·log′i·cal** (-tə-lŏj′ĭ-kəl) *adj.*

bi·o·e·lec·tric·i·ty (bī′ō-ĭ-lěk-trĭs′ə-tē, bī′ō-ē′lěk-) *n.* The electricity produced in organisms and living cells. —**bi′o·e·lec′tric, bi′o·e·lec′tri·cal** *adj.*

bi·o·fla·vo·noid (bī′ō-flā′və-noid′) *n.* Any of a group of biologically active substances found widely in plants and functioning in the maintenance of the walls of small blood vessels. [BIO- + FLAVON(E) + -OID.]

biog. biographer; biographical; biography.

bi·o·gen·e·sis (bī′ō-jěn′ə-sĭs) *n.* Also **bi·og·e·ny** (bī-ŏj′ə-nē). 1. The doctrine that living organisms develop only from other living organisms and not from nonliving matter. 2. The generation of living organisms from other living organisms. —**bi′o·ge·net′ic** (-jə-nět′ĭk), **bi′o·ge·net′i·cal, bi·og′e·nous** (bī-ŏj′ə-nəs) *adj.* —**bi′o·ge·net′i·cal·ly** *adv.*

bi·o·ge·og·ra·phy (bī′ō-jē-ŏg′rə-fē) *n.* The biological study of the geographical distribution of plants and animals. —**bi′o·ge′o·graph′ic** (-jē′ə-grăf′ĭk), **bi′o·ge′o·graph′i·cal** *adj.* —**bi′o·ge′o·graph′i·cal·ly** *adv.*

bi·og·ra·pher (bī-ŏg′rə-fər, bē-) *n. Abbr.* **biog.** One who writes a biography.

bi·o·graph·i·cal (bī′ə-grăf′ĭ-kəl) *adj.* Also **bi·o·graph·ic** (-grăf′-ĭk). *Abbr.* **biog.** 1. Containing, consisting of, or pertaining to the facts or events in a person's life. 2. Of or pertaining to biography as a literary form. —**bi′o·graph′i·cal·ly** *adv.*

bi·og·ra·phy (bī-ŏg′rə-fē, bē-) *n., pl.* **-phies.** *Abbr.* **biog.** A written account of a person's life; a life history. [New Latin *biographia,* from Medieval Greek : BIO- + -GRAPHY.]

biol. biological; biologist; biology.

bi·o·log·i·cal (bī′ə-lŏj′ĭ-kəl) *adj.* Also **bi·o·log·ic** (-lŏj′ĭk). *Abbr.* **biol.** 1. Of or pertaining to biology. 2. Of, pertaining to, caused by, or affecting life or living organisms. —*n. Pharmacology.* A drug derived from a biological source. Often used in the plural. —**bi′o·log′i·cal·ly** *adv.*

biological clock. An intrinsic biological mechanism responsible for the periodicity or other time-dependent aspects of certain classes of behavior in living organisms.

biological warfare. Warfare in which disease-producing microorganisms or organic biocides are used to destroy livestock, crops, or human life.

bi·ol·o·gist (bī-ŏl′ə-jĭst) *n. Abbr.* **biol.** One who is trained in or specializes in biology.

bi·ol·o·gy (bī-ŏl′ə-jē) *n. Abbr.* **biol.** 1. The science of life and life processes, including the study of structure, functioning, growth, origin, evolution, and distribution of living organisms. 2. The life processes or characteristic phenomena of any group or category of living organisms. 3. The plant and animal life of a specific region or place. [German *Biologie* : BIO- + -LOGY.]

bi·o·lu·mi·nes·cence (bī′ō-lōō′mə-něs′əns) *n.* The emission of visible light by living organisms such as the firefly, various fish, fungi, bacteria, and other organisms. —**bi′o·lu′mi·nes′cent** *adj.*

bi·ol·y·sis (bī-ŏl′ə-sĭs) *n.* Death caused or accompanied by lysis. [New Latin : BIO- + -LYSIS.] —**bi′o·lyt′ic** (bī′ə-lĭt′ĭk) *adj.*

bi·ome (bī′ōm′) *n. Ecology.* A community of living organisms of a single major ecological region. [BI(O)- + -OME.]

bi·o·met·rics (bī′ō-mět′rĭks) *n.* Plural in form, used with a singular verb. Also **bi·om·e·try** (bī-ŏm′ĭ-trē). The statistical study of biological data. —**bi′o·met′ric, bi′o·met′ri·cal** *adj.* —**bi′o·met′ri·cal·ly** *adv.*

bi·on·ics (bī-ŏn′ĭks) *n.* Plural in form, used with a singular verb. The application of biological principles to the study and design of engineering, especially electronic, systems. [BI(O)- + (ELECTR)ONICS.]

bi·o·nom·ics (bī′ə-nŏm′ĭks) *n.* Plural in form, used with a singular verb. Ecology *(see).* [From French *bionomique,* pertaining to ecology, from *bionomie,* ecology : BIO- + -NOMY.] —**bi′o·nom′ic, bi′o·nom′i·cal** *adj.* —**bi′o·nom′i·cal·ly** *adv.*

bi·ont (bī′ŏnt′) *n.* A living organism. —**bi·on′tic** (bī-ŏn′tĭk) *adj.* [BI(O)- + Greek *ōn* (stem *ont-*), existing, from *einai,* to be, exist (see **es-** in Appendix*).]

bi·o·phys·i·cist (bī′ō-fĭz′ə-sĭst) *n.* A scientist whose specialty is biophysics.

bi·o·phys·ics (bī′ō-fĭz′ĭks) *n.* Plural in form, used with a singular verb. The physics of biological processes. —**bi′o·phys′i·cal** *adj.* —**bi′o·phys′i·cal·ly** *adv.*

bi·o·plasm (bī′ō-plăz′əm) *n.* Living protoplasm, especially as distinguished from its nonliving content. [BIO- + -PLASM.]

bi·op·sy (bī′ŏp′sē) *n., pl.* **-sies.** The gross and microscopic examination of tissues removed from the body as an aid to medical diagnosis. [French *biopsie* : BI(O)- + -OPSY.] —**bi·op′sic** (bī-ŏp′sĭk) *adj.*

bi·o·scope (bī′ə-skōp′) *n.* An early motion-picture projector, used about 1900. [BIO- + -SCOPE.]

bi·os·co·py (bī-ŏs′kə-pē) *n., pl.* **-pies.** Medical examination of a body to determine whether it is dead. [BIO- + -SCOPY.]

-biosis. Indicates a specific way of living; for example, **symbiosis.** [New Latin, from Greek *biōsis,* way of life, from *bioun,* to live, from *bios,* mode of life. See **gwei-** in Appendix.*]

bi·o·sphere (bī′ə-sfîr′) *n.* The totality of regions of the earth that support self-sustaining and self-regulating ecological systems. [BIO- + -SPHERE.]

bi·o·syn·the·sis (bī′ō-sĭn′thə-sĭs) *n.* The production of complex substances from simple ones by or with living organisms. —**bi′o·syn·thet′ic** (-thět′ĭk) *adj.* —**bi′o·syn·thet′i·cal·ly** *adv.*

Biot (byō), **Jean Baptiste.** 1774–1862. French physicist; studied polarization of light.

bi·o·ta (bī-ō′tə) *n.* The animal and plant life of a particular region considered as a total ecological entity. [New Latin, from Greek *biotē,* way of life, from *bios,* life. See **bio-**.]

bi·o·tech·nol·o·gy (bī′ō-těk-nŏl′ə-jē) *n.* The engineering and biological study of relationships between man and machines.

bi·ot·ic (bī-ŏt′ĭk) *adj.* Pertaining to life or specific life conditions. [Greek *biōtikos,* from *bios,* mode of life. See **bio-**.]

biotic potential. 1. The likelihood of survival of a specific organism in a specific environment, especially in an unfavorable environment. 2. The growth rate of a population that maintains a stable age distribution.

bi·o·tin (bī′ə-tĭn) *n.* A colorless crystalline vitamin, $C_{10}H_{16}N_2$-O_3S, often considered in the vitamin B complex and found in large quantities in liver, egg yolk, milk, and yeast. Also called "vitamin H." [Greek *biotos,* life, from *bios,* life, mode of life (see **gwei-** in Appendix*) + -IN.]

bi·o·tite (bī′ə-tīt′) *n.* A dark-brown to black mica, K(Mg, Fe)$_3$AlSi$_3$O$_{10}$(OH)$_2$, found in igneous and metamorphic rocks. [German *Biotit,* after J.B. BIOT.] —**bi′o·tit′ic** (-tĭt′ĭk) *adj.*

bi·o·tope (bī′ə-tōp′) *n.* A limited ecological region or niche in which the environment is suitable for certain forms of life. [BIO- + Greek *topos,* place (see **topic**.)]

bi·o·type (bī′ə-tīp′) *n.* A group of organisms having identical genetic but varying physical characteristics. —**bi′o·typ′ic** (-tĭp′ĭk) *adj.*

bip·a·rous (bĭp′ər-əs) *adj.* 1. *Biology.* Producing two offspring in a single birth. 2. *Botany.* Having two axes or branches, as certain flower clusters. [BI- + -PAROUS.]

bi·par·ti·san (bī-pär′tĭ-zən) *adj.* Consisting of or supported by members of two parties, especially two major political parties. —**bi·par′ti·san·ism′** *n.* —**bi·par′ti·san·ship′** *n.*

bi·par·tite (bī-pär′tīt′) *adj.* Also **bi·part·ed** (bī-pär′tĭd). 1. Having or consisting of two parts. 2. Having two corresponding parts, one for each party: *a bipartite treaty.* 3. *Botany.* Divided into two, almost to the base. —*Said of certain leaves.* [Latin *bipartitus,* past participle of *bipartire,* to divide into two parts : BI- + *partire,* to part, from *pars,* a share, part (see **perə-** in Appendix.*] —**bi·par′tite·ly** *adv.* —**bi·par·ti′tion** (-tĭsh′ən) *n.*

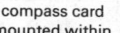
compass card
mounted within

lamp

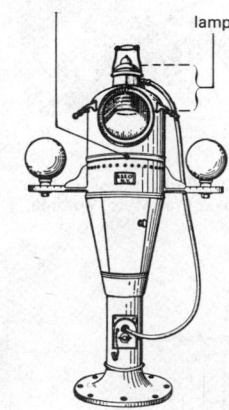

binnacle

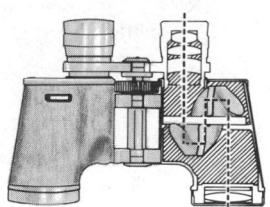

binoculars

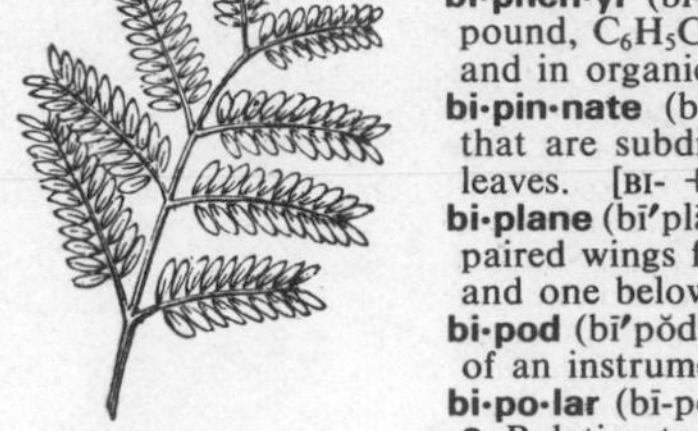

bipinnate
Bipinnate leaves

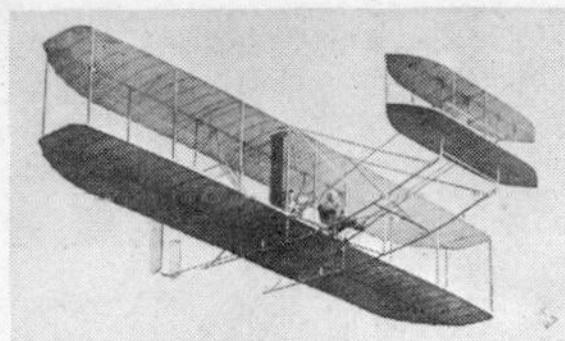

biplane
Wright Brothers' airplane over Fort Myer, Virginia, in 1908

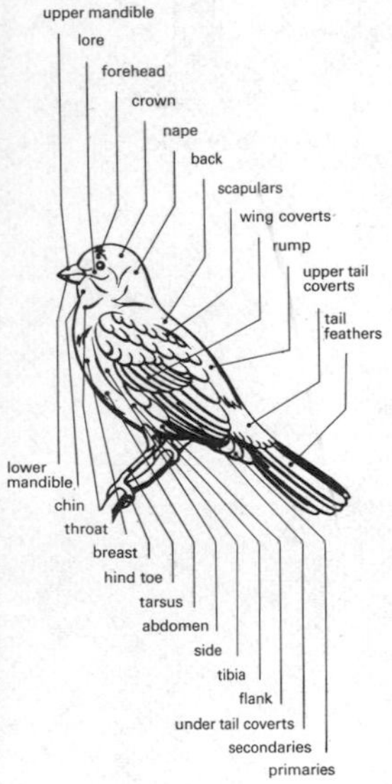

bird

bi·ped (bī′pĕd′) *n.* An animal with two feet. *—adj.* Also **bi·ped·al** (bī-pĕd′l). Having two feet; two-footed. [Latin *bipēs,* "two-footed" : BI- + -PED.]

bi·pet·al·ous (bī-pĕt′l-əs) *adj. Botany.* Having two petals; dipetalous.

bi·phen·yl (bī-fĕn′əl, -fē′nəl) *n.* A colorless crystalline compound, $C_6H_5C_6H_5$, used as a heat-transfer agent, in fungicides, and in organic synthesis. Also called "diphenyl."

bi·pin·nate (bī-pĭn′āt′) *adj. Botany.* Having opposite leaflets that are subdivided into opposite leaflets. Said of compound leaves. [BI- + PINNATE.] **—bi·pin′nate′ly** *adv.*

bi·plane (bī′plān′) *n.* An early aircraft distinguished by single or paired wings fixed at two different levels, especially one above and one below the fuselage. Compare **monoplane.**

bi·pod (bī′pŏd′) *n.* A stand having two legs, as for the support of an instrument or a weapon. [BI- + -POD.]

bi·po·lar (bī-pō′lər) *adj.* **1.** Pertaining to or having two poles. **2.** Relating to or involving both of the earth's poles. **3.** Having or expressing two opposite or contradictory ideas or qualities. **—bi′po·lar′i·ty** (-lăr′ə-tē) *n.*

bi·pro·pel·lant (bī′prə-pĕl′ənt) *n.* A two-component rocket propellant, such as liquid hydrogen and liquid oxygen, combined as fuel and oxidizer. Also called "dipropellant."

bi·quad·rat·ic (bī′kwŏ-drăt′ĭk) *adj. Mathematics.* Of or pertaining to the fourth degree. *—n. Mathematics.* An algebraic equation of the fourth degree.

bi·quar·ter·ly (bī-kwôr′tər-lē) *adj.* Happening or appearing two times during each three-month period of the year.

bi·ra·cial (bī-rā′shəl) *adj.* Of, for, or consisting of members of two races. **—bi·ra′cial·ism′** *n.*

bi·ra·di·al (bī-rā′dē-əl) *adj.* Both bilaterally and radially symmetrical.

birch (bûrch) *n.* **1.** Any of several deciduous trees of the genus *Betula,* common in the Northern Hemisphere, and having white, yellowish, or gray bark that can be separated from the wood in sheets. **2.** The hard, close-grained wood of any of these trees. **3.** A rod from a birch tree, used to administer a whipping. *—tr.v.* **birched, birching, birches.** To whip (someone) with or as if with a birch rod. [Middle English *birche,* Old English *birce, beorc(e).* See **bhereg-** in Appendix.*]

Birch·er (bûr′chər) *n.* Also **Birch·ite** (bûr′chīt′), **Birch·ist** (bûr′chĭst). **1.** A member of the **John Birch Society** *(see).* **2.** A supporter of its doctrines and activities. **—Birch′ism′** *n.*

bird (bûrd) *n.* **1.** Any member of the class Aves, which includes warm-blooded, egg-laying feathered vertebrates with forelimbs modified to form wings. **2.** A bird hunted as game. **3.** *Aerospace Slang.* A rocket or guided missile. **4.** A target, a **clay pigeon** *(see).* **5.** The feather-tipped object used in playing badminton, a **shuttlecock** *(see).* **6.** *Slang.* One who is odd or remarkable. **7.** *British Slang.* A young woman. **8.** *Slang.* A derisive sound of disapproval or derision. Used chiefly in the expression *give (someone) the bird.* **—for the birds.** *Slang.* Objectionable or worthless. *—intr.v.* **birded, birding, birds. 1.** To observe and identify birds in their natural surroundings. **2.** To trap, shoot, or catch birds. [Middle English *byrd, bryd,* young bird, Old English *brid*†.]

bird·brain (bûrd′brān′) *n. Slang.* A silly, light-minded person.

bird·cage (bûrd′kāj′) *n.* A cage for birds.

bird·call (bûrd′kôl′) *n.* **1.** The song of a bird. **2. a.** An imitation of the song of a bird. **b.** A small device for producing this.

bird cherry. A cherry tree, *Prunus padus,* native to Eurasia, having clusters of white flowers and small black fruit.

bird colonel. *Military Slang.* A full colonel. [From the eagle insignia worn by a full colonel.]

bird dog. 1. A dog used to hunt game birds; gun dog. **2.** *Slang.* One who seeks out something for another.

bird·farm (bûrd′färm′) *n. Naval Slang.* An aircraft carrier.

bird-foot violet (bûrd′fo͝ot′). Also **bird's-foot violet** (bûrdz′-). A North American violet, *Viola pedata,* having blue flowers and leaves divided into narrow lobes.

bird·house (bûrd′hous′) *n.* **1.** An aviary. **2.** A small box made as a nesting place for birds.

bird·ie (bûr′dē) *n.* **1.** *Informal.* A small bird. **2.** *Golf.* One stroke under par for any hole. **3.** A **shuttlecock** *(see).*

bird·lime (bûrd′līm′) *n.* **1.** A sticky substance smeared on branches or twigs to capture small birds. **2.** Something that captures and ensnares. *—tr.v.* **birdlimed, -liming, -limes. 1.** To smear with birdlime. **2.** To catch with birdlime.

bird·man (bûrd′mən) *n., pl.* **-men** (-mĭn). **1.** A fowler or ornithologist. **2.** *Slang.* An aviator.

bird of paradise. Any of various birds of the family Paradisaeidae, native to New Guinea and adjacent areas, usually having brilliant plumage and long tail feathers in the male.

bird-of-par·a·dise flower (bûrd′əv-pâr′ə-dīs′). A perennial plant, *Strelitzia reginae,* having purple bracts and large orange or yellow flowers with blue tongues. [From its stalks of colorful flowers resembling birds of paradise.]

bird of passage. A migratory bird or a transient person.

bird of prey. Any of various predatory carnivorous birds such as the eagle or hawk.

bird pepper. 1. A plant, *Capsicum frutescens,* that is the probable ancestor of the mild peppers and many of the pungent peppers. **2.** The narrow, extremely pungent fruit of this plant.

bird·seed (bûrd′sēd′) *n.* A mixture of various kinds of seeds used for feeding birds, especially caged birds.

bird's-eye (bûrdz′ī′) *n.* **1.** Any of various plants having small, brightly colored flowers, such as the bird's-eye primrose or the bird's-eye speedwell. **2. a.** A fabric woven with a pattern of small diamonds, each having a dot in the center. **b.** The pattern of such a fabric. *—adj.* **1.** Dappled or patterned with spots thought to resemble birds' eyes: *bird's-eye maple.* **2.** Seen from high above or from a remote distance: *a bird's-eye view.*

Birds·eye (bûrdz′ī′), **Clarence C.** 1886–1956. American inventor; developed the first practical method of quick-freezing foods.

bird's-eye primrose. A plant, *Primula farinosa,* native to Eurasia, having clusters of small, purplish, yellow-throated flowers.

bird's-eye speedwell. A weak-stemmed plant, *Veronica chamaedrys,* native to Eurasia, having small, bright-blue flowers.

bird's-foot (bûrdz′fo͝ot′) *n., pl.* **bird's-foots.** Any of various plants that have flowers, leaves, or pods resembling a bird's foot or claw, such as the bird's-foot trefoil.

bird's-foot fern. A fern, *Pellaea mucronata,* native to California, having fronds with wiry leaves grouped to resemble a bird's foot.

bird's-foot trefoil. A sprawling plant, *Lotus corniculatus,* having yellow flowers and clusters of seed pods resembling the claws of a bird.

bird's-nest fungus (bûrdz′nĕst′). Any of various fungi of the family Nidulariaceae, having a cuplike fruiting body containing several round, egglike structures that enclose the spores.

bird's-nest soup. A Chinese soup made from a gelatinous coating on the nests of certain swifts native to the Orient. [Translation of Chinese (Mandarin) *yen*^{4} *wo*^{1} *t'ang*^{1} : *yen*^{4}, the swallow or swift + *wo*^{1}, nest + *t'ang*^{1}, soup.]

birds of a feather. People who are alike in some way. Used chiefly in the saying *Birds of a feather flock together.*

bird watcher. A person who observes and identifies birds in their natural surroundings. **—bird watching.**

bi·re·frin·gence (bī′rĭ-frĭn′jəns) *n.* The resolution or splitting of a light wave into two waves with mutually perpendicular vibration directions by an optically anisotropic medium such as calcite, topaz, or quartz. Also called "double refraction." [BI- + Latin *refringens,* REFRINGENT.] **—bi′re·frin′gent** *adj.*

bi·reme (bī′rēm′) *n.* An ancient galley equipped with two tiers of oars on each side. [Latin *birēmis* : BI- + *rēmus,* oar (see **ere-**^{1} in Appendix*).]

bi·ret·ta (bə-rĕt′ə) *n.* Also **be·ret·ta, ber·ret·ta, bir·ret·ta.** A stiff square cap that is worn by Roman Catholic clergy and is black for a priest, purple for a bishop, and red for a cardinal. Also called "barret." [Italian *berretta* or Spanish *birreta,* from Medieval Latin *birretum,* cap, from Late Latin *birrus,* hooded cloak. See **beret.**]

Bir·ken·head (bûr′kən-hĕd′). A seaport and industrial city of northwestern England, situated on the south bank of the Mersey River, opposite Liverpool. Population, 149,000.

birl (bûrl) *v.* **birled, birling, birls.** *—tr.* To cause (a floating log) to spin rapidly by rotating with the feet. *—intr.* To whirr; hum. *—n.* A whirring noise; a hum. [Blend of BIRR and WHIRL.]

birl·ing (bûr′lĭng) *n.* A game of skill among lumberjacks in which two competitors try to balance on a floating log while spinning it with their feet. Also called "logrolling."

Bir·ming·ham (bûr′mĭng-hăm′ *for senses 1, 2;* bûr′mĭng-əm *for sense 3*). **1.** The principal commercial and industrial city of Alabama, in the north-central part of the state. Population, 341,000. **2.** A suburb of Detroit, Michigan, in the southeastern part of the state. Population, 26,000. **3.** The second-largest city in England, an industrial center about 100 miles northwest of London. Population, 1,103,000.

Bi·ro·bi·dzhan (bĭr′ō-bĭ-jän′, -jăn′). A region occupying 14,000 square miles in the southeastern Soviet Union, on the Manchurian border. Also called "Jewish Autonomous Oblast." Population, 172,000.

birr (bûr) *n.* A whirring sound. [Middle English *bir(re), byrr,* strong wind, onrush, from Old Norse *byrr,* favorable wind. See **bher-**^{1} in Appendix.*]

birth (bûrth) *n.* **1.** The beginning of existence; fact of being born. **2.** Any beginning or origin. **3. a.** The act of bearing young; parturition. **b.** The passage of a child from the uterus. **4.** Ancestry; parentage: *a man of noble birth.* **5.** Origin; lineage: *a Southerner by birth.* **—give birth to.** To bring forth. *—tr.v.* **birthed, birthing, births.** *Chiefly Regional.* **1.** To deliver (a baby). **2.** To bear (a child). [Middle English *birth,* from Old Norse *burdhr.* See **bher-**^{1} in Appendix.*]

birth canal. The cavity of the uterus and the vagina traversed by the fetus in parturition.

birth certificate. An official record of a person's parentage, and the date, place, and time of birth.

birth control. Voluntary limitation or control of the number of children conceived, especially by planned use of contraceptive techniques.

birth·day (bûrth′dā′) *n.* **1.** The day of one's birth. **2.** The anniversary of one's birth.

birth·mark (bûrth′märk′) *n.* A mole, mark, or blemish present on the body from birth; nevus.

birth·place (bûrth′plās′) *n.* The place where someone is born or where something originates.

birth·rate (bûrth′rāt′) *n.* The number of births in a specified population per unit time, especially per year. Also called "natality."

birth·right (bûrth′rīt′) *n.* **1.** Any privilege granted a person by virtue of his birth. **2.** Any special privilege accorded the first-born. —See Synonyms at **right.**

birth·root (bûrth′ro͞ot′, -ro͝ot′) *n.* Any of several North American plants of the genus *Trillium;* especially, *T. erectum,* having purplish flowers with an unpleasant odor and tuberlike roots, formerly used as an aid in childbirth.

ă pat/ā pay/âr care/ä father/b bib/ch church/d deed/ĕ pet/ē be/f fife/g gag/h hat/hw which/ĭ pit/ī pie/îr pier/j judge/k kick/l lid, needle/m mum/n no, sudden/ng thing/ŏ pot/ō toe/ô paw, for/oi noise/ou out/o͝o took/o͞o boot/p pop/r roar/s sauce/sh ship, dish/

birth·stone (bûrth′stōn′) *n.* A jewel associated with a specific month and thought to bring good luck to a person born in that month.
birth trauma. **1.** An injury sustained by an infant during birth. **2.** An emotional shock sustained by an infant during birth.
birth·wort (bûrth′wûrt′, -wôrt′) *n.* Any of several tropical woody vines of the genus *Aristolochia,* having reddish or brownish, usually unpleasantly scented flowers. [Formerly believed to aid in parturition.]
bis (bĭs) *adv.* Twice; again; encore. Used especially as a direction in music. [French, from Latin, twice. See **dwō** in Appendix.*]
BIS, B.I.S. **1.** Bank for International Settlements. **2.** British Information Service.
Bi·sa·yan. Variant of **Visayan.**
Bi·sa·yan Islands. See **Visayan Islands.**
Bis·cay, Bay of (bĭs′kā). An inlet of the Atlantic Ocean bordered on the south by Spain and on the east and northeast by France.
biscay green. Moderate yellow green. See **color.**
Bis·cayne Bay (bĭs-kān′, bĭs′kān′). An inlet of the Atlantic Ocean, 40 miles long and from 2 to 10 miles wide, along the southeastern coast of Florida.
bis·cuit (bĭs′kĭt) *n., pl.* **-cuits** or **biscuit. 1.** A small cake of shortened bread leavened with baking powder or soda. **2.** *British.* A thin, crisp cracker of unleavened bread. **3.** Pale brown; beige. See **color. 4.** *Ceramics.* Pottery that has been fired once but not glazed. Also called "bisque." [Middle English *besquite,* from Old French *bescoit, bescuit,* from (unattested) Medieval Latin *biscoctus (panis),* "twice-cooked (bread)" : Latin *bis-,* BI- + *coctus,* past participle of *coquere,* to cook (see **pekw-** in Appendix*).]
biscuit tor·to·ni (tôr-tō′nē). A rich ice-cream dessert usually flavored with almonds, often garnished with whipped cream, and served in a paper cup. [Probably invented by *Tortoni,* 19th-century restaurateur in Paris.]
bi·sect (bī′sĕkt′, bī-sĕkt′) *v.* **-sected, -secting, -sects.** —*tr.* To cut or divide into two equal parts. —*intr.* To split; fork: *The road bisects at the intersection.* [BI- + -SECT.] —**bi′sec′tion** *n.* —**bi′sec′tion·al** *adj.* —**bi′sec′tion·al·ly** *adv.*
bi·sec·tor (bī′sĕk′tər, bī-sĕk′-) *n.* Anything that bisects, especially a straight line that bisects an angle.
bi·ser·rate (bī-sĕr′āt′) *adj. Biology.* **1.** Having serrations that are themselves serrated; doubly serrate. **2.** Serrated on both sides: *biserrate antennae.*
bi·sex·u·al (bī-sĕk′shōō-əl) *adj.* **1.** Of or pertaining to both sexes. **2.** Having both male and female organs; hermaphroditic. **3.** Sexually attracted to members of both sexes. —*n.* **1.** A bisexual organism; a hermaphrodite. **2.** A person who is sexually attracted to members of both sexes. —**bi·sex′u·al·ism′, bi′sex·u·al′i·ty** (-ăl′ə-tē) *n.* —**bi·sex′u·al·ly** *adv.*
bish·op (bĭsh′əp) *n.* **1.** *Abbr.* **bp.** A high-ranking Christian clergyman, in modern churches usually in charge of a diocese and in some churches regarded as having received the highest ordination in unbroken succession from the apostles. **2.** *Abbr.* **B** A miter-shaped chessman that can move diagonally across any number of unoccupied spaces of the same color. **3.** Mulled port spiced with oranges, sugar, and cloves. [Middle English *bisshop,* Old English *biscop, bisceop,* from Vulgar Latin *biscopus* (unattested), variant of Late Latin *episcopus,* from Greek *episkopos,* guardian, overseer : *epi-,* on, over + *skopos,* one who watches (see **spek-** in Appendix*).]
bish·op·ric (bĭsh′əp-rĭk) *n.* **1.** The office or rank of a bishop. **2.** The diocese of a bishop. [Middle English *bisshopriche, bisshoprike,* Old English *bisceoprice* : BISHOP + *rice,* realm (see **reg-**[1] in Appendix*).]
bish·op's-cap (bĭsh′əps-kăp′) *n.* A plant, the **miterwort** *(see).*
bishop's purple. Moderate reddish purple. See **color.**
bishop's violet. Moderate reddish purple to vivid purple. See **color.**
Bi·si·tun. See **Behistun.**
Bis·marck (bĭz′märk). The capital of North Dakota, on the Missouri River in the south-central part of the state. Population, 27,000.
Bis·marck (bĭz′märk), Prince **Otto Eduard Leopold von.** Called the "Iron Chancellor." 1815–1898. First chancellor of the German Empire.
Bis·marck Archipelago (bĭz′märk). A group of over 100 islands, with a combined area of 19,815 square miles, in the southwestern Pacific Ocean, northeast of New Guinea. Population, 183,000.
Bis·marck Mountains (bĭz′märk). A range of mountains in northeastern New Guinea. Highest elevation, Mount Wilhelm (over 15,000 feet).
bis·muth (bĭz′məth) *n. Symbol* **Bi** A white, crystalline, brittle, highly diamagnetic metallic element used in alloys to form sharp castings for objects sensitive to high temperatures and in various low-melting alloys for fire-safety devices. Atomic number 83, atomic weight 208.980, melting point 271.3°C, boiling point 1,560°C, specific gravity 9.747, valences 3, 5. See **element.** [New Latin *bisemutum,* Latinization of German *Wismut*†.] —**bis′muth·al** *adj.*
bis·na·ga, biz·na·ga (bĭs-nä′gə) *n.* Any of several spiny, globe-shaped or barrel-shaped cacti of the southwestern United States and Mexico. [Spanish *biznaga,* alteration of earlier *vitznauac* (by confusion with *biznaga,* parsnip), from Nahuatl *huitznahuac,* "having spines around" : *huitztli,* spine, thorn + *nahuac,* around.]
bi·son (bī′sən, -zən) *n.* **1.** A hoofed mammal, *Bison bison,* of western North America, having a dark-brown coat, a shaggy mane, and short, curved horns. Also called "buffalo." **2.** A similar, somewhat smaller animal, *B. bonasus,* of Europe. In this sense, also called "wisent." [Latin *bisōn,* from Germanic. See **weis-**[1] in Appendix.*]
bisque[1] (bĭsk) *n.* **1.** A thick, rich soup made from meat, fish, or shellfish. **2.** Any thick cream soup. **3.** Ice cream mixed with crushed macaroons or nuts. [French *bisque*†.]
bisque[2] (bĭsk) *n.* **1.** *Ceramics.* **Biscuit** *(see).* **2. a.** Pale orange yellow to yellowish gray. **b.** A color ranging in various industries from moderate yellowish pink to grayish yellow. See **color.** [From BISCUIT.]
bisque[3] (bĭsk) *n.* An advantage allowed an inferior player in certain games; especially, a free point taken when desired in a tennis set. [French *bisque*†.]
Bis·sau (bĭ-sou′). The capital of Portuguese Guinea, on an inlet of the North Atlantic Ocean. Population, 56,000.
bis·sex·tile (bī-sĕks′tĭl, -tīl′, bĭ-) *adj.* **1.** Of or pertaining to a leap year. **2.** Of or pertaining to the extra day falling in a leap year. —*n.* A leap year. [Late Latin *bissextilis,* from Latin *bissextus,* intercalary day in the Julian calendar, which followed February 24, the sixth day before the calends of March : *bis,* twice, BI- + *sextus,* sixth (see **sweks** in Appendix*).]
bis·ter (bĭs′tər) *n.* Also **bis·tre. 1.** A water-soluble, yellowish-brown pigment made from soot obtained from beech or other wood. **2.** Grayish to yellowish brown. See **color.** [French *bistre*†.] —**bis′ter, bis′tered** *adj.*
bis·tort (bĭs′tôrt′) *n.* Any of several plants of the genus *Polygonum,* especially: **1.** A Eurasian plant, *P. bistorta,* having pointed clusters of small, pinkish flowers. **2.** A similar plant, *P. bistortoides,* of the mountains of western North America, having oval clusters of pink or white flowers. [Old French *bistorte,* "twice-twisted" : Latin *bis,* twice, BI- + *tortus,* past participle of Latin *torquēre,* to twist (see **terkw-** in Appendix*).]
bis·tou·ry (bĭs′tə-rē) *n., pl.* **-ries.** A surgical knife for minor incisions. [French *bistouri,* from Old French *bistorie, bistorit,* dagger, from Italian (northern dialect) *bistorino* (unattested), variant of *pistorino,* "of Pistoia," from *Pistoja,* Pistoia, Italy (where sharp knives were made).]
bis·tro (bē′strō, bĭs′trō) *n., pl.* **-tros.** A small bar, tavern, or nightclub. [French *bistro*†.]
bi·sul·cate (bī-sŭl′kāt′) *adj.* Cleft or cloven, as a hoof. [BI- + SULCATE.]
bi·sul·fate (bī-sŭl′fāt′) *n. Chemistry.* The inorganic acid group HSO_4 or any compound containing it.
bi·sul·fide (bī-sŭl′fīd′) *n. Chemistry.* A **disulfide** *(see).*
bi·sul·fite (bī-sŭl′fīt′) *n. Chemistry.* The inorganic acid group HSO_3 or any compound containing it.
Bi·su·tun. See **Behistun.**
bit[1] (bĭt) *n.* **1.** A small piece, portion, or amount. **2.** A brief amount of time; moment. **3. a.** An entertainment routine given regularly by a performer; an act. **b.** A short scene or episode in a play, movie, or the like. **4.** A small and insignificant role, as in a play or movie, usually containing a few spoken lines. **5.** *Informal.* A particular kind of behavior or activity. See Usage note below. **6.** *Informal.* An amount equal to $\frac{1}{8}$ of a dollar. Used only in even multiples: *two bits a head.* **7.** *British.* A small coin: *a threepenny bit.* —**a bit (of).** Somewhat; to some extent: *a bit of a bore.* —**bit by bit.** Little by little; gradually. —**do one's bit.** To make one's contribution; carry one's share. —*adj.* Small and insignificant. See Usage note. [Middle English *bit,* Old English *bita,* piece bitten off, morsel. See **bheid-** in Appendix.*]
Usage: The theatrical term *bit part* (or *bit role*) is acceptable in writing to 92 per cent of the Usage Panel. But *bit* (noun), in the sense of *distinctive activity or behavior (to do the intellectual bit),* is unacceptable to 87 per cent of the Usage Panel.
bit[2] (bĭt) *n.* **1.** The sharp part of a tool, as the blade of a knife. **2.** A pointed and threaded tool for drilling and boring that is secured in a brace, bitstock, or drill press. **3.** The part of a key that enters the lock and engages the bolt or tumblers. **4.** The metal mouthpiece of a bridle, serving to control, curb, and direct an animal. See **harness. 5.** Anything that controls, guides, or curbs. —*tr.v.* **bitted, bitting, bits. 1.** To place a bit in the mouth of (a horse). **2.** To check or control, as if with a bit. **3.** To make or grind a bit on (a key). [Middle English *bitt,* cutting edge, mouthpiece of a bridle, Old English *bite,* a sting, bite. See **bheid-** in Appendix.*]
bit[3] (bĭt) *n. Computers.* **1.** A single character of a language having just two characters, such as either of the binary digits 0 or 1. **2.** A unit of information equivalent to the choice of either of two equally likely states of an information-containing system. **3.** A unit of information storage capacity, as of a computer memory. [BI(NARY) (DIGI)T.]
bit[4]. Past tense and alternate past participle of **bite.** See Usage note at **bite.**
bi·tar·trate (bī-tär′trāt′) *n. Chemistry.* The tartrate of an acid.
bitch (bĭch) *n.* **1.** A female dog or other canine animal. **2.** *Slang.* A spiteful or lewd woman. **3.** *Slang.* A complaint. **4.** *Slang.* A difficult or confounding problem. —*intr.v.* **bitched, bitching, bitches.** *Slang.* **1.** To complain; grumble. **2.** To botch; bungle. Used with *up.* [Middle English *bicche,* Old English *bicce,* female dog, from Germanic *bekjōn-* (unattested).]
bitch·y (bĭch′ē) *adj.* **-ier, -iest.** *Slang.* Malicious, spiteful, or ill-tempered. —**bitch′i·ness** *n.*
bite (bīt) *v.* **bit** (bĭt), **bitten** (bĭt′n) or **bit** (see Usage note below), **biting, bites.** —*tr.* **1.** To cut, grip, or tear with or as if with the teeth. **2.** To pierce the skin of with the teeth, fangs, or stinger. **3.** To cut into with a sharp instrument. **4.** To grip, grab, or seize. **5.** To eat into; corrode. **6.** To cause to sting or smart.

bit[2]
Bits with a brace

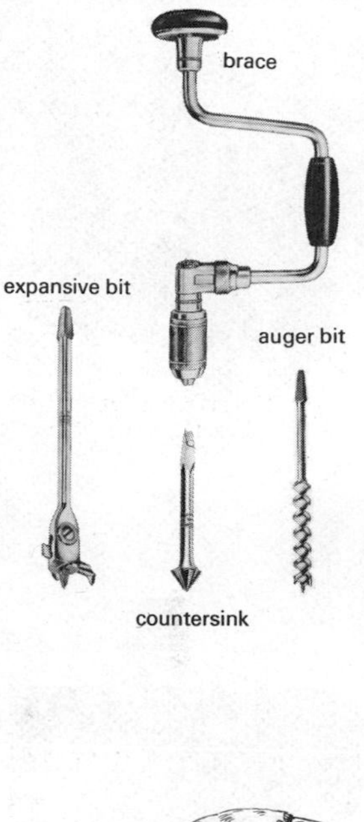
brace
expansive bit
auger bit
countersink

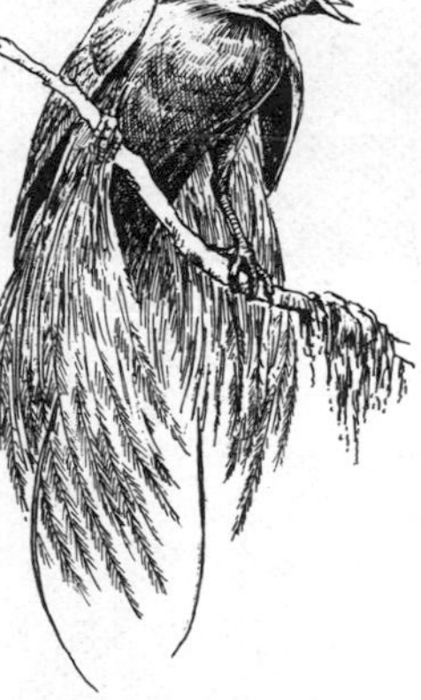

bird of paradise
Paradisaea apoda
A male of the species

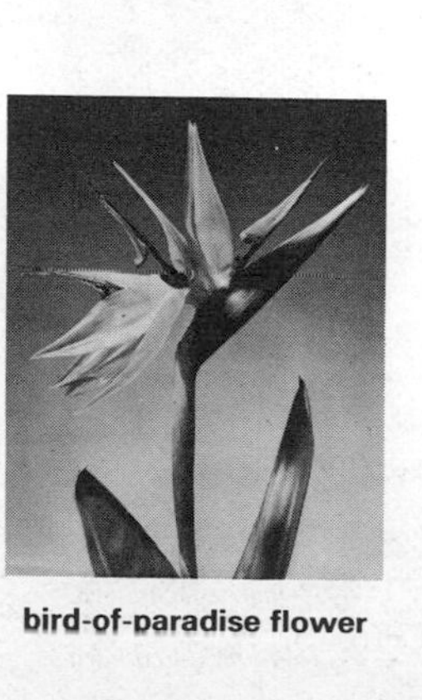

bird-of-paradise flower

—*intr.* **1.** To grip, cut into, or injure something with or as if with the teeth. **2.** To have a stinging effect or a sharp taste. **3.** To take or swallow bait. **4.** To be taken in by a ploy or deception. —**bite the dust.** To fall dead, especially in combat. —*n.* **1.** The act of biting. **2.** A wound or injury resulting from biting. **3. a.** A stinging or smarting sensation. **b.** An incisive, penetrating quality. **4.** An amount of food taken into the mouth at one time; mouthful. **5.** *Informal.* A light meal or snack. **6.** A secure grip or hold applied by a tool or machine upon a working surface. **7.** *Dentistry.* The angle at which the upper and lower teeth meet. **8.** The corrosive action of acid upon an etcher's metal plate. —**put the bite on.** *Slang.* To borrow money from. [Bite, bit, bitten; Middle English *biten, bot* (past plural *biten*), *biten,* Old English *bītan, bāt* (past plural *biton*), *biten.* See **bheid-** in Appendix.*] —**bit'a·ble, bite'a·ble** *adj.* —**bit'er** *n.*

Usage: Of the two participles *bitten* and *bit,* only *bitten* is now standard in the passive. *The boy was bitten* (not *bit*) *by the dog.*

Bi·thyn·i·a (bĭ-thĭn'ē-ə). An ancient country of northwestern Asia Minor, on the Black Sea.

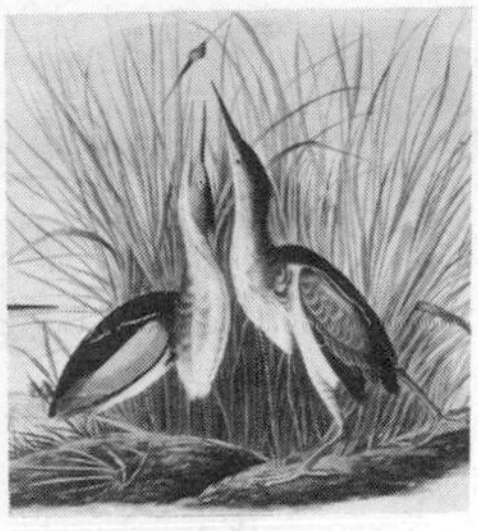

bittern[1]
Ixobrychus exilis
Least bittern

bit·ing (bī'tĭng) *adj.* **1.** Causing a stinging sensation. **2.** Incisive; caustic: *"biting remarks revealed her attitude of contempt"* (D.H. Lawrence). —See Synonyms at **incisive.** —**bit'ing·ly** *adv.* —**bit'ing·ness** *n.*

bit·stock (bĭt'stŏk') *n.* A brace or handle in which a drilling or boring bit is secured.

bitt (bĭt) *n.* A vertical post set on the deck of a ship and used to secure cables. —*tr.v.* **bitted, bitting, bitts.** To wind (a cable) around a bitt. [Probably of Low German origin, akin to Low German and Dutch *beting.* See **bheid-** in Appendix.*]

bit·ten. Alternate past participle of **bite.** See Usage note at **bite.**

bit·ter (bĭt'ər) *adj.* **-terer, -terest. 1.** Having or being a taste that is sharp, acrid, and unpleasant. **2.** Causing sharp pain to the body or discomfort to the mind; harsh. **3.** Difficult or distasteful to accept or admit: *the bitter truth.* **4.** Exhibiting or proceeding from strong animosity: *bitter foes.* **5.** Marked by anguished resentfulness or rancor: *"He was already a bitter elderly man with a gray face"* (John Dos Passos). —*v.* **bittered, -tering, -ters.** —*tr.* To make bitter. —*intr.* To become bitter. [Middle English *bitter,* Old English *biter.* See **bheid-** in Appendix.*] —**bit'ter·ly** *adv.* —**bit'ter·ness** *n.*

bitter almond. A variety of the common almond, *Prunus amygdalus amara,* having bitter kernels that yield a very poisonous oil.

bitter aloes. Plural in form, used with a singular verb. A cathartic drug derived from the juice of the fleshy leaves of a tropical plant, *Aloe barbadensis.*

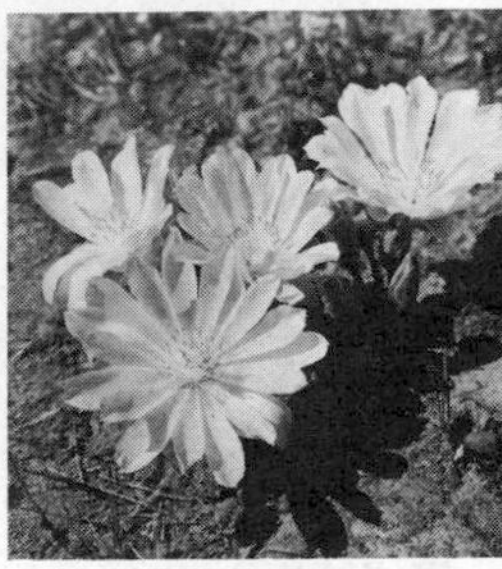

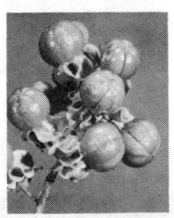

bitterroot

bitter apple. A plant, the **colocynth** *(see),* or its fruit.

bitter cress. Any of various plants of the genus *Cardamine,* having white or purplish flowers and often edible leaves.

bitter end. 1. *Nautical.* The end of a rope or cable that is wound around a bitt. **2.** A final, painful, or disastrous extremity; the absolute end.

Bitter Lakes. Two lakes, Great Bitter Lake and Little Bitter Lake, in Egypt, crossed and connected by the Suez Canal.

bit·tern[1] (bĭt'ərn) *n.* Any of several wading birds of the genera *Botaurus* and *Ixobrychus,* having mottled, brownish plumage, and notable for its deep, resonant cry. [Middle English *botor, bitter,* from Old French *butor,* from Vulgar Latin *būtitaurus* (unattested), "bird that bellows like an ox" : Latin *būtiō,* bittern (see **beu-[2]** in Appendix*) + *taurus,* ox, bull (see **tauro-** in Appendix*).]

bit·tern[2] (bĭt'ərn) *n.* The solution of bromides, magnesium, and calcium salts remaining after sodium chloride is crystallized out of sea water. [From BITTER.]

bit·ter·nut (bĭt'ər-nŭt') *n.* A hickory tree, *Carya cordiformis,* of eastern North America, having nuts with bitter kernels.

bitter principle. *Pharmacology.* Any of a large number of bitter substances, frequently of vegetable origin.

bit·ter·root (bĭt'ər-ro͞ot', -ro͝ot') *n.* A plant, *Lewisia rediviva,* of western North America, having showy pink or white flowers and a starchy, edible root.

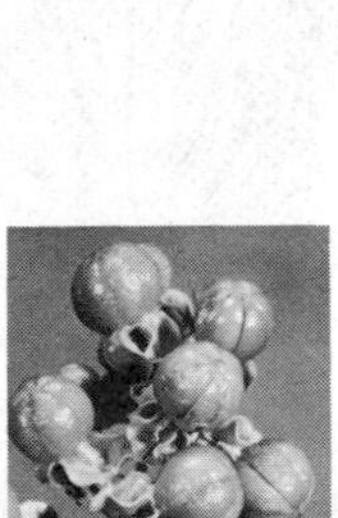

Bitterroot Range. Also **Bitter Root Range.** A range of the Rocky Mountains along the Idaho-Montana border. Highest elevation, Garfield Mountain (10,961 feet).

bit·ters (bĭt'ərz) *pl.n.* A bitter, usually alcoholic liquid made with herbs or roots and used in cocktails or as a tonic.

bit·ter·sweet (bĭt'ər-swēt') *n.* **1.** A North American woody vine, *Celastrus scandens,* having orange or yellowish fruits that split open to expose seeds enclosed in fleshy scarlet arils. **2.** A sprawling vine, *Solanum dulcamara,* native to Eurasia, having purple flowers and poisonous scarlet berries. Also called "nightshade." **3.** Dark to deep reddish orange. See **color.** —*adj.* **1.** Bitter and sweet at the same time. **2.** Producing a mixture of pain and pleasure. **3.** Having the color bittersweet.

bit·ter·weed (bĭt'ər-wēd') *n.* Any of various plants that yield or contain a bitter principle, such as the **ragweed** *(see),* or plants of the genus *Picris.*

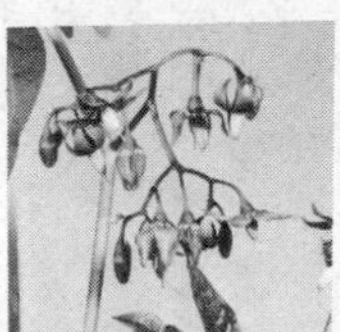

bittersweet
Above: Fruit of *Celastrus scandens*
Below: Flowers of *Solanum dulcamara*

Bitt·ner (bĭt'nər), **John Joseph.** 1904–1961. American biologist; engaged in cancer research.

bi·tu·men (bĭ-to͞o'mən, bĭ-tyo͞o'-) *n.* Any of various mixtures of hydrocarbons and other substances, occurring naturally or obtained by distillation from coal or petroleum, found in asphalt and tar, and used for surfacing roads and for waterproofing. [Middle English *bithumen,* from Latin *bitūmen,* probably from Gaulish *bet* (unattested). See **gwet-[1]** in Appendix.*] —**bi·tu'mi·noid'** (-mə-noid') *adj.*

bi·tu·mi·nize (bĭ-to͞o'mə-nīz', bĭ-tyo͞o'-) *tr.v.* **-nized, -nizing, -nizes.** To treat with bitumen. —**bi·tu'mi·ni·za'tion** *n.*

bi·tu·mi·nous (bĭ-to͞o'mə-nəs, bĭ-tyo͞o'-, bī-) *adj.* **1.** Like or containing bitumen. **2.** Of or pertaining to bituminous coal.

bituminous coal. A mineral coal that burns with a smoky, yellow flame, yielding volatile bituminous constituents. Also called "soft coal."

bi·va·lent (bī-vā'lənt) *adj.* **1.** *Chemistry.* Having valence 2. **2.** *Genetics.* Composed of two homologous chromosomes, or two sets of such chromosomes. —**bi·va'lence, bi·va'len·cy** *n.*

bi·valve (bī'vălv') *n.* A mollusk, such as an oyster or clam, having a shell consisting of two hinged parts. —*adj.* Also **bi·val·vate** (-văl'vāt'), **bi·val·vu·lar** (-văl'vyə-lər) (for sense 2). **1.** Having such a shell. **2.** Consisting of two similar separable parts.

bi·var·i·ate (bī-vâr'ē-ĭt, -āt') *adj.* Having two variables.

biv·ou·ac (bĭv'o͞o-ăk, bĭv'wăk) *n.* A temporary encampment made by soldiers in the field. —*intr.v.* **bivouacked, -acking, -acks** or **-acs.** To encamp in a bivouac. [French, earlier *biwacht,* probably from Swiss German *beiwacht,* "supplementary night watch," from German *Beiwache, Beiwacht* : *bei,* by, at, from Old High German *bī* (see **ambhi** in Appendix*) + *Wache,* watch, from Old High German *wahha* (see **weg-[2]** in Appendix*).]

Bi·wa, Lake (bē'wä). The largest lake (260 square miles) in Japan, situated in south-central Honshu, northeast of Kyoto.

bi·week·ly (bī-wēk'lē) *adj.* **1.** Happening every two weeks. **2.** *Nonstandard.* Happening twice a week; semiweekly. See Usage note at **bimonthly.** —*n., pl.* **biweeklies.** A publication issued every two weeks. —*adv.* **1.** Every two weeks. **2.** *Nonstandard.* Twice a week; semiweekly. See Usage note at **bimonthly.**

bi·year·ly (bī-yîr'lē) *adj.* **1.** Happening every two years. **2.** *Nonstandard.* Happening twice a year; semiyearly. See Usage note at **bimonthly.** —*adv.* **1.** Every two years. **2.** *Nonstandard.* Twice a year; semiyearly. See Usage note at **bimonthly.**

bi·zarre (bĭ-zär') *adj.* Strikingly unconventional and far-fetched in style or appearance; odd; grotesque. See Synonyms at **fantastic.** [French, originally "handsome," "brave," from Spanish *bizarro,* from Basque *bizar,* beard ("bearded," hence "spirited").] —**bi·zarre'ly** *adv.* —**bi·zarre'ness** *n.*

Bi·zet (bē-zā'), **Georges.** Original name, Alexandre César Léopold Bizet. 1838–1875. French composer.

biz·na·ga. Variant of **bisnaga.**

B.J. Bachelor of Journalism.

Bjerk·nes (byûrk'nəs), **Jakob Aall Bonnevie.** Born 1897. Norwegian-born American meteorologist; studied air masses.

Bk The symbol for the element berkelium.

bk. 1. bank. **2.** book.

bkg. banking.

bklr. *Printing.* black letter.

bkpg. bookkeeping.

bkpt. bankrupt.

bks. barracks.

bl. 1. barrel. **2.** black. **3.** blue.

B.L. 1. Bachelor of Laws. **2.** Bachelor of Letters; Bachelor of Literature.

B/L bill of lading.

B.L.A. Bachelor of Liberal Arts.

blab (blăb) *v.* **blabbed, blabbing, blabs.** —*tr.* To reveal (a secret), especially through unreserved talk. —*intr.* **1.** To talk of secret matters. **2.** To chatter indiscreetly. —*n.* **1.** A person who blabs. **2.** Lengthy chatter. [Middle English *blabben,* akin to *blabberen,* to BLABBER.] —**blab'by** *adj.*

blab·ber (blăb'ər) *intr.v.* **-bered, -bering, -bers.** To chatter. —*n* **1.** Idle chatter. **2.** One who blabs. [Middle English *blabberen,* from an imitative Germanic root *blab-* (unattested).]

blab·ber·mouth (blăb'ər-mouth') *n., pl.* **-mouths** (-mouthz). *Slang.* One who chatters indiscreetly and at length.

black (blăk) *adj.* **blacker, blackest.** *Abbr.* **bl., blk. 1.** Being of the darkest achromatic visual value; producing or reflecting comparatively little light and having no predominant hue. **2.** Having no light whatsoever: *a black cave.* **3.** Belonging to an ethnic group having dark skin; especially, Negroid. **4.** Dark in color or having parts that are dark in color. Used with animal and plant names: *black bass; black birch.* **5.** Soiled, as from soot. **6.** Evil; sinister: *black deeds.* **7.** Cheerless and depressing; gloomy. **8.** Angered; sullen. **9.** *Sometimes capital* **B.** Attended with disaster; calamitous: *the stock-market crash on Black Friday.* **10.** Of or designating a form of humor dealing with the abnormal and grotesque aspects of life and society and evoking a sense of the comedy of human despair and failure. **11.** Indicating or incurring censure or dishonor: *"man . . . has written one of his blackest records as a destroyer on the oceanic islands"* (Rachel Carson). **12.** *Informal.* Absolute; confirmed: *a black villain.* **13.** Wearing black clothing: *the black knight.* **14.** Served without milk or cream. Said of coffee. —*n. Abbr.* **bl., blk. 1.** An achromatic color value of minimum lightness or maximum darkness; one extreme of the neutral gray series, the opposite being white. Although strictly a response to zero stimulation of the retina, the perception of black appears to depend on contrast with surrounding color stimuli. See **color. 2.** Clothing of this color, especially for mourning. **3.** Any member of a Negroid people; a Negro. **4.** A black-colored chess or checker piece. —**in the black.** On the credit side of a ledger; prosperous. —*tr.v.* **blacked, blacking, blacks. 1.** To make black or dirty; to soil. **2.** To put black dye, paint, or polish on. —See Usage note at **blacken.** [Middle English *blak,* Old English *blæc.* See **bhel-[1]** in Appendix.*] —**black'ly** *adv.* —**black'ness** *n.*

Black (blăk), **Joseph.** 1728–1799. Scottish chemist; discovered carbon dioxide; a pioneer in quantitative analysis.

ă pat/ā pay/âr care/ä father/b bib/ch church/d deed/ĕ pet/ē be/f fife/g gag/h hat/hw which/ĭ pit/ī pie/îr pier/j judge/k kick/l lid, needle/m mum/n no, sudden/ng thing/ŏ pot/ō toe/ô paw, for/oi noise/ou out/o͝o took/o͞o boot/p pop/r roar/s sauce/sh ship, dish/

black alder. **1.** A deciduous holly, *Ilex verticillata,* of eastern North America, bearing bright-scarlet berries. **2.** A tree, *Alnus glutinosa,* native to Eurasia, having dark bark.
black·a·moor (blăk′ə-mŏŏr′) *n.* Any dark-skinned person; especially, an African Negro. [Earlier *black More* : BLACK + *More,* earlier form of MOOR.]
black-and-blue (blăk′ən-blōō′) *adj.* Discolored from coagulation of blood below the surface of the skin.
Black and Tans. **1.** The Royal Irish Constabulary, a force of about 6,000 British soldiers sent to Ireland to suppress the Sinn Fein rebellion of 1919–21. **2.** *Singular.* A member of this force. [So called from the color of the uniform.]
black-and-tan terrier (blăk′ən-tăn′). See **Manchester terrier.**
black and white. **1.** Print or writing. **2.** A picture or photograph in tones of black and white.
black art. **Black magic** *(see).*
black·ball (blăk′bôl′) *n.* **1.** A small, black ball used as a negative ballot. **2.** A negative vote that blocks the admission of an applicant to an organization. *—tr.v.* **blackballed, -balling, -balls.** **1.** To vote against; especially, to veto the admission of. **2.** To exclude from a social group; ostracize. **—black′ball′er** *n.*
black bass. Any of several North American freshwater game fishes of the genus *Micropterus.*
black bear. Either of two black or dark-brown bears, *Euarctos* (or *Ursus*) *americanus,* of North America, or *Selenarctos thibetanus,* of Asia.
Black·beard. See Edward **Teach.**
black belt. **1.** Any part of a state or city having a predominantly Negro population. **2.** A region of rich, black soil extending from Georgia across central Alabama and Mississippi.
black·ber·ry (blăk′bĕr′ē, -bər-ē) *n., pl.* **-ries.** **1.** Any of several woody plants of the genus *Rubus,* having canelike, usually thorny stems and black, glossy, edible berries. See **black raspberry, dewberry, loganberry.** **2.** The fruit of any of these plants.
blackberry lily. A plant, *Belamcanda chinensis,* having spotted orange flowers and a seed cluster that resembles a blackberry.
black bile. One of the four **humors** *(see)* of medieval physiology, supposed to cause melancholia.
black bindweed. A vine, *Polygonum convolvulus,* native to Europe and naturalized as a weed in North America.
black birch. A North American tree, *Betula lenta,* having dark, brownish bark and twigs and leaves that yield an aromatic oil. Also called "cherry birch," "sweet birch."
black·bird (blăk′bûrd′) *n.* **1.** Any of various New World birds of the family Icteridae, having black or predominantly black plumage in the male. See **cowbird, grackle, redwing.** **2.** An Old World songbird, *Turdus merula,* of which the male is black with a yellow bill. This species is also called "merle."
black·board (blăk′bôrd′, -bōrd′) *n.* A panel, once black, now often colored, for writing on with chalk; chalkboard.
black·bod·y (blăk′bŏd′ē) *n., pl.* **-ies.** *Physics.* A theoretically perfect absorber of all incident radiation.
blackbody radiation. *Physics.* The characteristic thermal radiation emitted by a blackbody at a specific temperature.
black book. A record of people liable to punishment.
black box. A device or theoretical construct, especially an electric circuit, with known or specified performance characteristics but unknown or unspecified constituents and means of operation.
black bryony. A climbing European plant, *Tamus communis,* having small, greenish flowers and poisonous red berries.
black·buck (blăk′bŭk′) *n.* An antelope, *Antilope cervicapra,* of India, of which the male has a dark back and spiral horns.
Black·burn (blăk′bərn). A city and textile center in northwestern England. Population, 103,000.
Black·burn, Mount (blăk′bərn). An elevation, 16,140 feet high, of the Wrangell Mountains in southeastern Alaska.
black calla. A plant, *Arum palaestinum,* native to the southeastern Mediterranean region, having green and blackish-purple flowers resembling those of the calla lily.
Black Canyon. **1.** A canyon of the Colorado River between Arizona and Nevada. **2.** A canyon of the Gunnison River in southwestern Colorado.
black·cap (blăk′kăp′) *n.* **1.** The **black raspberry** *(see).* **2.** A small European bird, *Sylvia atricapilla,* of which the male is gray with a black crown. **3.** Any of various black-crowned birds.
black·cock (blăk′kŏk′) *n.* The male of the **black grouse** *(see).*
black cohosh. A tall plant, *Cimicifuga racemosa,* of eastern North America, having long clusters of small, whitish flowers. Also called "black snakeroot."
black crappie. An edible North American fish, *Pomoxis nigromaculatus,* having dark, mottled coloring. Also called "calico bass," "strawberry bass."
black·damp (blăk′dămp′) *n.* A gas composed of a mixture of carbon dioxide and nitrogen, found in mines after fires and explosions of combustible gases. Also called "chokedamp."
Black Death. A form of plague that was pandemic throughout Europe and much of Asia for several years following 1353. [From the dark splotches it causes on the skin.]
black diamond. **1.** A variety of dark diamond, **carbonado** *(see).* **2.** *Plural.* Coal.
black·en (blăk′ən) *v.* **-ened, -ening, -ens.** *—tr.* **1.** To make black. **2.** To sully; defame. *—intr.* To become black or dark. **—black′en·er** *n.*
Usage: Transitively, *blacken* is used principally to express the figurative sense of sullying or defaming, while the verb *black* expresses the literal sense of making black. One *blackens* a name or reputation; one *blacks* (applies blacking to) boots, a stove, or the face, and *blacks* (by punching or bumping) an eye.
Black·ett (blăk′ĭt), **Patrick Maynard Stuart.** Born 1897. British physicist; worked on cloud chamber detection of nuclear reactions.
black eye. **1.** A bruised discoloration of the flesh surrounding the eye, resulting from a blow. **2.** A heavy defeat; bad setback.
black-eyed pea (blăk′īd′). The edible seed of the **cowpea** *(see).*
black-eyed Susan. **1.** Any of several North American plants of the genus *Rudbeckia;* especially, *R. hirta,* having hairy stems and leaves, and flowers with orange-yellow rays and dark-brown centers. **2.** A vine, *Thunbergia alata,* native to tropical Africa, having white or orange-yellow flowers with purple throats.
black·face (blăk′fās′) *n.* **1.** Makeup for a conventionalized comic travesty of the Negro in a minstrel show or the like. **2.** An actor in a minstrel show. **3.** *Printing.* Boldface type. *—adj.* **1.** Performing in blackface. **2.** *Printing.* Boldface.
black·fish (blăk′fĭsh′) *n., pl.* **blackfish** or **-fishes.** **1.** Any of various dark-colored fishes, such as: **a.** A freshwater fish, *Dallia pectoralis,* of far northern regions. **b.** The **tautog** *(see).* **2.** The **pilot whale** *(see).*
black fly. Any of various small, dark-colored, biting flies of the family Simuliidae. Also called "buffalo gnat."
Black·foot (blăk′fŏŏt′) *n., pl.* **Blackfoot** or **-feet.** **1.** Any of three tribes of Algonquian-speaking Indians formerly inhabiting the regions of Montana, Alberta, and Saskatchewan. **2.** A member of one of these tribes. **3.** The Algonquian language spoken by these tribes. [Translation of Blackfoot *Siksika;* said to be so named because the soles of their moccasins were black from walking across burned prairie.] **—Black′foot′** *adj.*
Black Forest. *German* **Schwarz·wald** (shvärts′vält′). A wooded mountain region in southwestern West Germany.
Black Friar. A Dominican friar. [From the black mantles worn by the Dominican friars.]
black grouse. A Eurasian game bird, *Lyrurus tetrix,* of which the black male is called "blackcock," the mottled female is called "greyhen," and for which the collective plural is "black game."
black·guard (blăg′ərd, -ärd) *n.* **1.** A scoundrel. **2.** A scurrilous person. *—adj.* Of or like a blackguard; foulmouthed; ruffianly. *—v.* **blackguarded, -guarding, -guards.** *—tr.* To abuse or revile. *—intr.* To behave in a ruffianly manner. [Originally, the kitchen workers and menials of a noble household or of an army.] **—black′guard·ism′** *n.* **—black′guard·ly** *adj. & adv.*
black gum. A tree, the **sour gum** *(see).*
Black Hand. A secret society, organized for acts of terrorism and blackmail, composed mainly of Sicilians, active in the United States in the early 20th century. Compare **Mafia.**
black haw. A shrub, *Viburnum prunifolium,* with white flower clusters and purple-black fruit.
Black Hawk (blăk′ hôk′). Indian name, Ma-ka-tae-mish-kia-kiak. 1767–1838. American Indian; leader of the Fox and Sauk Indians in the Black Hawk War (1832).
black·head (blăk′hĕd′) *n.* **1.** A plug of dried fatty matter capped with blackened dust and epithelial debris that clogs a pore of the skin. Also called "comedo." **2.** *Veterinary Medicine.* An infectious, often fatal, liver and intestinal disease of turkeys and some wildfowl. Also called "infectious enterohepatitis." **3.** Any of various birds with dark head markings.
black·heart (blăk′härt′) *n.* A disease of potatoes and other plants, in which the inner tissues darken.
black-heart·ed (blăk′här′tĭd) *adj.* Evil by nature; wicked.
Black Hills. A mountainous region, rich in mineral deposits, in southwestern South Dakota and northeastern Wyoming. Highest elevation, Harney Peak (7,242 feet).
Black Hole of Calcutta. **1.** A small dungeon at Calcutta, India, in which 123 of the 146 British prisoners confined there on June 20, 1756, died of suffocation. **2.** *Small* **b,** *small* **h.** A military lockup. In this sense, also called "black hole."
black horehound. A strong-smelling plant, *Ballota nigra,* native to Europe, having clusters of purple flowers.
black humor. The humor of the morbid and the absurd, especially in its development as a literary genre.
black·ing (blăk′ĭng) *n.* **1.** **Lamp black** *(see).* **2.** A black paste or liquid used as shoe polish.
black·ish (blăk′ĭsh) *adj.* Somewhat black. **—black′ish·ly** *adv.*
black·jack[1] (blăk′jăk′) *n.* A small leather-covered bludgeon with a short flexible shaft or strap, used as a hand weapon. *—tr.v.* **blackjacked, -jacking, -jacks.** **1.** To hit with a blackjack. **2.** To coerce by threats. [BLACK + JACK (tool).]
black·jack[2] (blăk′jăk′) *n.* An oak tree, *Quercus marilandica,* of the southeastern United States, having blackish bark. Also called "blackjack oak." [BLACK + JACK (tool).]
black·jack[3] (blăk′jăk′) *n.* A card game in which the object is to accumulate cards with a total count nearer to 21 than that of the dealer. Also called "twenty-one." [BLACK + JACK (knave in cards).]
black·jack[4] (blăk′jăk′) *n.* A tankard made of tarred or waxed leather. [BLACK + Middle English *jakke,* leather coat, container, from Old French *jacque* (see **jacket**).]
black·jack[5] (blăk′jăk′) *n.* Sphalerite or zinc sulfide ore. [BLACK + JACK (impertinent, worthless person); miners' term for this worthless mixture in lead ore.]
black knot. A disease of plum and cherry trees caused by a fungus, *Dibotryon morbosa,* and resulting in black, knotlike swellings on the branches.
black·leg (blăk′lĕg′) *n.* **1.** *Veterinary Medicine.* An infectious, usually fatal, gas gangrene affecting the heavily muscled upper parts of the legs of sheep and cattle. **2.** A bacterial or fungous

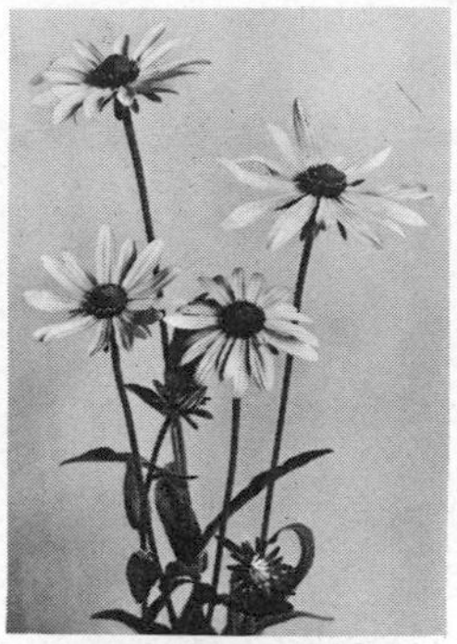

black-eyed Susan
Rudbeckia hirta

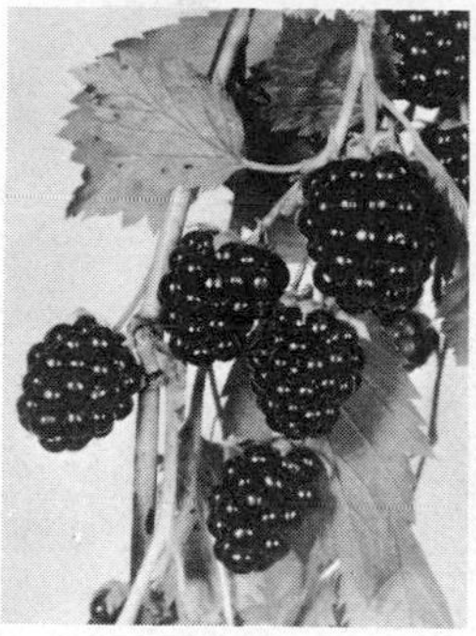

blackberry

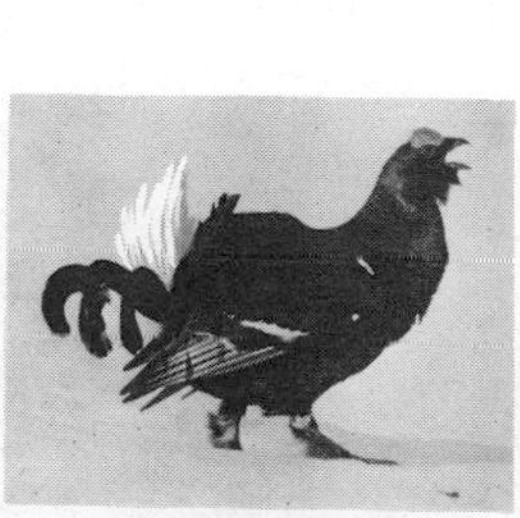

black grouse
A blackcock performing the mating dance

t tight/th thin, path/*th* this, bathe/ŭ cut/ûr urge/v valve/w with/y yes/z zebra, size/zh vision/ə about, item, edible, gallop, circus/ à *Fr.* ami/œ *Fr.* feu, *Ger.* schön/ü *Fr.* tu, *Ger.* über/KH *Ger.* ich, *Scot.* loch/N *Fr.* bon. ***Follows main vocabulary. †Of obscure origin.**

plant disease that causes the stems of plants to turn black. **3.** One who cheats at cards, especially a professional gambler; cardsharp. **4.** *British.* A strikebreaker; scab.

black letter. *Abbr.* **bklr.** *Printing.* A heavy type face having very broad counters and thick, ornamental serifs. Also called "Gothic," "church text," "Old English." —**black′-let′ter** *adj.*

black light. Invisible ultraviolet or infrared radiation.

black·list (blăk′lĭst′) *n.* A list of persons or organizations to be disapproved, boycotted, or suspected of disloyalty. —*tr.v.* **blacklisted, -listing, -lists.** To place (a name) on a blacklist.

black magic. Magic as practiced in league with the Devil; witchcraft. Also called "black art." See Synonyms at **magic.**

black·mail (blăk′māl′) *n.* **1.** Extortion by the threat of exposure or criminal prosecution. **2.** Money extorted in this manner. **3.** Tribute formerly paid to freebooters along the Scottish border for protection from pillage. —*tr.v.* **blackmailed, -mailing, -mails. 1.** To extort money or something of value from (a person) by means of blackmail. **2.** To coerce by means of blackmail. [BLACK + *mail,* tribute, Middle English *maill, male,* Old English *māl,* agreement, from Old Norse *māl,* speech, agreement (see **mōd-** in Appendix*).] —**black′mail′er** *n.*

Black Maria. A patrol wagon.

black market. An illicit market in which goods are sold in violation of price controls, rationing, or other restrictions.

black-mar·ket (blăk′mär′kĭt) *tr.v.* **-keted, -keting, -kets.** To trade on a black market. —**black marketer, black marketeer.**

black mass. A travesty of the Roman Catholic Mass belonging to the reputed observances of Satanism.

black measles. A severe form of measles, characterized by a dark rash.

black medic, black medick. A cloverlike plant, *Medicago lupulina,* native to Europe, having compound leaves, small yellow flower heads, and black pods. Also called "nonesuch."

Black·more (blăk′môr, -mōr), **Richard Doddridge.** 1825–1900. British novelist; author of *Lorna Doone.*

Black Mountains. A range of the Blue Ridge Mountains in western North Carolina. Highest elevation, Mount Mitchell (6,684 feet).

Black Muslim. A member of the **Nation of Islam** *(see).* Used by nonmembers.

black mustard. A plant, *Brassica nigra,* native to Eurasia, having clusters of yellow flowers. Its pungent seeds, ground to a powder, are a source of the condiment mustard.

black nightshade. A plant, the **deadly nightshade** *(see).*

black oak. A deciduous tree, *Quercus velutina,* of eastern North America, having hard, durable wood. Also called "quercitron."

black out. 1. To produce or undergo a blackout. **2.** To suppress or delete by censorship.

black·out (blăk′out′) *n.* **1.** The extinguishing or concealing of lights that might be visible to enemy aircraft during an air raid at night. Compare **dim-out. 2.** In the theater, the sudden extinguishing of all stage lights to indicate passage of time, or to mark the end of an act or a scene. **3.** A temporary loss of consciousness. **4.** A suppression or stoppage, as of news.

black pepper. See **pepper.**

black·poll (blăk′pōl′) *n.* A North American warbler, *Dendroica striata,* of which the male has a black cap.

Black·pool (blăk′pōōl′). A seaside resort in Lancashire, England, on the Irish Sea. Population, 150,000.

black poplar. A shade tree, *Populus nigra,* native to Eurasia, having spreading branches and pointed, triangular leaves. See **Lombardy poplar.**

Black Power. A movement among American Negroes to achieve social equality through political power gained by uniting the Negro community in specifically Negro political and cultural institutions, as distinguished from seeking integration into the white community: *"Black Power therefore calls for black people to consolidate behind their own, so that they can bargain from a position of strength."* (Stokely Carmichael and Charles V. Hamilton).

Black Prince. See **Edward, Prince of Wales.**

black raspberry. 1. A prickly shrub, *Rubus occidentalis,* of eastern North America, bearing black fruit. **2.** The fruit of this plant. Also called "blackcap."

Black River. *Annamese* **Song Bo** (sông′ bō′). A river rising in Yunnan Province, southern China, and flowing 500 miles southeast through northern North Vietnam to join the Red River.

Black Rod. A British official, the chief usher of various institutions, including the House of Lords.

black rot. Any of various plant diseases caused by fungi or bacteria and resulting in darkening of the leaves and decay.

Black Sea. A large inland sea, 178,000 square miles in area, between Europe and Asia Minor, connected with the Aegean Sea by the Bosporus, the Sea of Marmara, and the Dardanelles.

black sheep. 1. A sheep with black fleece. **2.** A person considered undesirable or disgraceful by his family or group.

Black Shirt. A member of a fascist party organization having a black shirt as part of its uniform.

black·smith (blăk′smĭth′) *n.* **1.** One who forges and shapes iron with an anvil and hammer. **2.** One who makes, repairs, and fits horseshoes. [Middle English *blaksmith,* "a worker in black metal" (iron).] —**black′smith′ing** *n.*

black·snake (blăk′snāk′) *n.* **1.** Broadly, any of various dark-colored, chiefly nonvenomous snakes, such as the black racer, *Coluber constrictor,* or the black rat snake, *Elaphe obsoleta,* of North America. **2.** *Western U.S.* A long, tapering, braided rawhide or leather whip with a snapper on the end.

black snakeroot. A plant, the **black cohosh** *(see).*

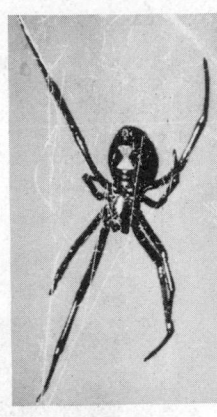

Black
black letter

black widow

black spot. Any of various plant diseases caused by fungi or bacteria and resulting in small black spots on the leaves.

black spruce. An evergreen tree, *Picea mariana,* of northern North America, growing mostly in bogs. Sometimes called "spruce pine."

Black·stone (blăk′stən, -stōn′), Sir **William.** 1723–1780. British jurist; author of the *Commentaries.*

black·strap (blăk′străp′) *n.* A dark, very thick molasses used in the manufacture of industrial alcohol, and as an ingredient in cattle feed. Also called "blackstrap molasses."

black-tailed deer (blăk′tāld′). Also **black-tail deer** (blăk′tāl′). The **mule deer** *(see).*

black tea. A dark tea, the leaf of which is fully fermented or oxidized before drying. Compare **green tea, oolong.**

black thorn. A shrub, the **pear haw** *(see).*

black·thorn (blăk′thôrn′) *n.* A thorny Eurasian shrub, *Prunus spinosa,* having clusters of white flowers and bluish-black, plumlike fruit. Also called "sloe."

black tie. 1. A black bow tie worn with a dinner jacket. **2.** Semiformal evening wear for men, typically requiring a dinner jacket. —**black′-tie′** *adj.*

black·top (blăk′tŏp′) *n.* A bituminous material, such as asphalt, used to pave roads. —*tr.v.* **blacktopped, -topping, -tops.** To pave with blacktop.

Black Vol·ta (vŏl′tə). A river of western Africa rising in Upper Volta and flowing 500 miles south and then east through Ghana to join the White Volta and form the Volta.

black vomit. 1. A vomit consisting of bloody matter. **2.** Severe yellow fever with symptomatic regurgitation of such vomit.

black vulture. A carrion-eating bird, *Coragyps atratus,* of central North America and South America, having black plumage and a bald, black head.

black walnut. 1. A deciduous tree, *Juglans nigra,* of eastern North America, having dark, hard wood and edible nuts. **2.** The grained wood of this tree, used for cabinetwork.

Black Watch. 1. A Highland regiment of the British Army, the men of which wear uniforms of a dark-blue and dark-green tartan. **2.** *Often small* **b,** *small* **w.** The tartan of the Black Watch.

black·wa·ter fever (blăk′wô′tər, -wŏt′ər). A severe, frequently fatal malaria with symptomatic excretion of blood in the urine.

Black·well (blăk′wĕl, -wəl), **Elizabeth.** 1821–1910. British physician; resident of America (1832–69); first woman awarded M.D. degree.

Black·wells Island. The former name for **Welfare Island.**

black widow. A New World spider, *Latrodectus mactans,* of which the extremely venomous female is black with red markings. [From the fact that the female eats its mate.]

blad·der (blăd′ər) *n.* **1.** *Anatomy.* Any of various distensible membranous sacs found in most animals, especially the **urinary bladder** *(see).* **2.** Anything resembling such a sac: *the bladder of a football.* **3.** *Botany.* An inflated, hollow structure, such as the air sac in certain seaweeds. **4.** *Pathology.* A blister, pustule, or cyst filled with fluid or air. [Middle English *bladdre,* Old English *blǽdre.* See **bhlē-²** in Appendix.*]

bladder campion. A plant, *Silene cucubalus,* native to Europe, having white flowers and an inflated calyx.

blad·der·nose (blăd′ər-nōz′) *n.* An aquatic mammal, the **hooded seal** *(see).*

blad·der·nut (blăd′ər-nŭt′) *n.* Any of several shrubs or small trees of the genus *Staphylea,* of the North Temperate Zone, having small, whitish flowers and inflated seed pods.

bladder worm. The bladderlike, encysted larva of the tapeworm.

blad·der·wort (blăd′ər-wûrt′, -wôrt′) *n.* Any of various aquatic plants of the genus *Utricularia,* having violet or yellow flowers, and, in most species, small bladders that trap minute aquatic animals.

bladder wrack. A rockweed, *Fucus vesiculosus,* having forked, brownish-green fronds with air-filled bladders.

blad·der·y (blăd′ər-ē) *adj.* **1.** Resembling a bladder; bladderlike. **2.** Possessing a bladder or bladders.

blade (blād) *n.* **1.** The flat-edged cutting part of a sharpened tool or weapon. **2. a.** A sword. **b.** A swordsman. **3.** A gay, reckless young man. **4.** Any flat, thin structural member or section: *the blade of an oar.* **5.** *Anatomy.* The **scapula** *(see).* **6.** *Botany.* **a.** The leaf of a grass or similar plant. **b.** The expanded, usually green part of a leaf, as distinguished from the leafstalk. **7.** *Phonetics.* The upper surface of the tongue, just behind the tip. [Middle English *blade,* Old English *blæd,* leaf, blade. See **bhel-³** in Appendix.*] —**blad′ed** *adj.*

blade-ap·ple (blād′ăp′əl) *n.* A spiny, vinelike, tropical American cactus, *Pereskia aculeata,* having true leaves, white flowers, and pulpy yellow fruit. Also called "Barbados gooseberry."

Bla·go·vesh·chensk (blä′gə-vyĕsh′chĕnsk). A city and river port of the Soviet Union in Asia, situated in the east on the northern bank of the Amur River. Population, 114,000.

blah (blä) *n. Slang.* Worthless nonsense; drivel. [Imitative.]

blain (blān) *n.* A skin sore; blister; blotch. [Middle English *blein, blain,* an inflammatory swelling, Old English *blegen.* See **bhlei-** in Appendix.*]

Blaine (blān), **James Gillespie.** 1830–1893. American political figure; twice Secretary of State (1881; 1889–92).

Blake (blāk), **William.** 1757–1827. English poet and engraver.

blam·a·ble (blā′mə-bəl) *adj.* Also **blame·a·ble.** Deserving of blame; culpable. —**blam′a·ble·ness** *n.* —**blam′a·bly** *adv.*

blame (blām) *tr.v.* **blamed, blaming, blames. 1.** To hold responsible; accuse. **2.** To find fault with; to censure. **3.** To place responsibility for (something) on a person. See Usage note below. —See Synonyms at **criticize.** —*n.* **1.** The responsibility for a fault or error. **2.** Censure; condemnation. [Middle English *blamen,* from Old French *blamer,* earlier *blasmer,* from Vulgar Latin *blastēmāre* (unattested), alteration of Late Latin *blasphēmāre,* to reproach, BLASPHEME.] —**blam′er** *n.*

Synonyms: *blame, fault, guilt.* These nouns are compared in the sense of responsibility for an offense. *Blame* stresses censure arising from something for which one is held liable. *Fault* usually applies to a cause of failure ascribed specifically to a person or persons. *Guilt* applies to serious, willful breaches of a standard of conduct and stresses the moral culpability, rather than practical shortcoming, of the offender.

Usage: The construction *blame . . . on (blame the present crisis on your predecessor)* is acceptable in writing to 82 per cent of the Usage Panel. The remainder specify *blame your predecessor for* or *place the blame on your predecessor.*

blamed (blāmd). Euphemism for **damned.**

blame·ful (blām′fəl) *adj.* Deserving of blame; blameworthy. —**blame′ful·ly** *adv.* —**blame′ful·ness** *n.*

blame·less (blām′lĭs) *adj.* Free from blame or guilt; innocent. —**blame′less·ly** *adv.* —**blame′less·ness** *n.*

blame·wor·thy (blām′wûr′thē) *adj.* Deserving of blame; reprehensible. —**blame′wor′thi·ness** *n.*

Blanc, Cape (blăɴ). A cape on the coast of Tunisia, the northernmost point of the African continent.

Blanc, Mont. See **Mont Blanc.**

Blan·ca Peak (blăng′kə). The highest elevation (14,363 feet) of the Sangre de Cristo Mountains of southern Colorado.

blanc fixe (blăngk′ fĭks′). Powdered barium sulfate used as a base for water-color pigments. [French, "fixed white."]

blanch (blănch, blänch) *v.* **blanched, blanching, blanches.** Also **blench** (blĕnch). —*tr.* **1.** To take color from; to bleach. **2.** To whiten (a growing food plant, such as celery) by covering to cut off direct light. **3.** To whiten (a metal) by soaking in acid or by coating with tin. **4.** To loosen the skin of (almonds, for example) by scalding. **5.** To cause to turn pale. —*intr.* To turn white or become pale. [Middle English *blaunchen,* from Old French *blanchir,* from *blanche,* feminine of *blanc,* white, from Vulgar Latin *blancus* (unattested), from Germanic. See **bhel-**[1] in Appendix.*] —**blanch′er** *n.*

Blan·chard (blăɴ-shär′), **(Jean Pierre) François.** 1753–1809. French balloonist; inventor of a parachute.

blanc·mange (blə-mänj′; *French* bläɴ-mäɴzh′) *n.* A flavored and sweetened milk pudding, thickened with cornstarch. [Middle English *blancmanger,* dish of chopped chicken or fish with rice, from Old French, "white food" : *blanc,* white (see **blanch**) + *manger,* food, from *mangier,* to eat (see **mange**).]

bland (blănd) *adj.* **blander, blandest. 1.** Characterized by a moderate, undisturbing, or tranquil quality: **a.** Pleasant in manner; ingratiating. **b.** Free of irritation; soothing: *a bland diet.* **c.** Mild; balmy. **2.** Lacking a distinctive character; mediocre; dull. [Latin *blandus,* caressing, flattering, "soft-spoken." See **mel-**[1] in Appendix.*] —**bland′ly** *adv.* —**bland′ness** *n.*

blan·dish (blăn′dĭsh) *tr.v.* **-dished, -dishing, -dishes.** To coax by flattery or wheedling; cajole. [Middle English *blandishen,* from Old French *blandir* (present stem *blandiss-*), from Latin *blandīrī,* from *blandus,* flattering, BLAND.] —**blan′dish·er** *n.* —**blan′dish·ment** *n.*

blank (blăngk) *adj.* **blanker, blankest. 1.** Bearing no writing, print, or marking of any kind. **2.** Not finished or filled in: *a blank questionnaire.* **3.** Having no finishing grooves or cuts: *a blank key.* **4.** Expressing nothing; vacuous; vacant: *"Although his gestures were elaborate, his face was blank."* (Nathanael West). **5.** Devoid of activity or character; empty. **6.** Barren; fruitless: *blank efforts.* **7.** Utter; complete: *a blank refusal.* —See Synonyms at **empty.** —*n.* **1.** An empty space; a void. **2. a.** An empty space on a document to be filled in. **b.** A document having one or more such spaces. **3.** An unfinished material, part, or article, such as a key form, that is prepared and stored for eventual finishing. **4.** A gun cartridge with a charge of powder but no bullet. Also called "blank cartridge." **5.** A lottery ticket that wins no prize. **6.** A mark, usually a dash (—), indicating the omission of a word or letter. **7.** The center white circle of a target; bull's eye. **8.** Any goal or target. —**draw a blank.** *Informal.* To fail utterly; achieve nothing. —*tr.v.* **blanked, blanking, blanks. 1.** To remove from view; obliterate: *"at times the strong glare of the sun blanked it from sight"* (Richard Wright). **2.** To omit; delete; invalidate. Often used with *out.* **3.** To prevent (an opponent in a game or sport) from scoring. **4.** *Machinery.* To punch or stamp from flat stock, especially with a die. Often used with *out.* [Middle English *bla(u)nk,* white, not written on, from Old French *blanc.* See **blanch.**] —**blank′ly** *adv.* —**blank′ness** *n.*

blank endorsement. An endorsement on a check or negotiable note that names no payee, making it payable to the bearer. Also called "endorsement in blank."

blan·ket (blăng′kĭt) *n.* **1.** A large piece of wool or other thick cloth used as a covering for warmth, especially on a bed. **2.** A thick layer that covers or encloses: *a blanket of snow.* —*adj.* Covering a wide range of conditions or requirements: *a blanket insurance policy.* —*tr.v.* **blanketed, -keting, -kets. 1.** To cover with or as if with a blanket. **2.** To conceal or suppress as if with a blanket. **3.** To apply to generally and uniformly without exception: *The fare increase blankets the airlines.* **4.** *Nautical.* To cut off (a sailboat) from the wind by passing close on the windward side. [Middle English, originally, a white woolen material, from Old French *blanquet, blanchet,* diminutive of *blanc,* white. See **blanch.**]

blan·ket flow·er (blăng′kĭt-flou′ər) *n.* The **gaillardia** *(see).*

blanket stitch. The buttonhole stitch, as used for edging around a blanket.

blan·ket-stitch (blăng′kĭt-stĭch′) *tr.v.* **-stitched, -stitching, -stitches.** To sew (something) with a blanket stitch.

blank verse. Verse consisting of unrhymed lines, usually of iambic pentameter.

Blan·tyre-Lim·be (blăn-tīr′lĭm′bā). The largest city of Malawi, in the southern part of the country. Population, 130,000.

blare (blâr) *v.* **blared, blaring, blares.** —*intr.* To sound loudly and insistently. —*tr.* To utter or exclaim loudly. —*n.* **1.** A loud, strident noise. **2.** Flamboyance. [Middle English *bleren,* to bellow, from Middle Dutch. See **bhlē-**[1] in Appendix.*]

blar·ney (blär′nē) *n.* Smooth, flattering talk. —*v.* **blarneyed, -neying, -neys.** —*tr.* To beguile with blarney. —*intr.* To flatter. [After the BLARNEY STONE.]

Blar·ney Stone (blär′nē). A stone in Blarney Castle, Blarney, County Cork, Ireland, said to impart skills of eloquence and flattery to those who kiss it.

bla·sé (blä-zā′, blä′zā) *adj.* **1.** Having no more capacity or appetite for enjoyment, especially from habitual and excessive indulgence; sophisticated. **2.** Filled with ennui; weary. [French, past participle of *blaser,* to blunt, cloy, surfeit, "to cause to be bloated with strong liquor," from Middle Dutch *blasen,* to blow up, cause to swell. See **bhlē-**[2] in Appendix.*]

blas·pheme (blăs-fēm′) *v.* **-phemed, -pheming, -phemes.** —*tr.* **1.** To speak of (God or something sacred) in an irreverent or impious manner. **2.** To revile; execrate: *"and every tongue/ Cursed and blasphemed him as he passed"* (Shelley). —*intr.* To speak blasphemy. [Middle English *blasfemen, blasphemen,* from Old French *blasfemer,* from Late Latin *blasphēmāre,* to reproach, blaspheme, from Greek *blasphēmein,* from *blasphēmos,* evil-speaking, BLASPHEMOUS.] —**blas·phem′er** *n.*

blas·phe·mous (blăs′fə-məs) *adj.* Impiously irreverent. See Synonyms at **profane.** [Late Latin *blasphēmus,* from Greek *blasphēmos,* evil-speaking, impious. See **bha-**[2] in Appendix.*] —**blas′phe·mous·ly** *adv.* —**blas′phe·mous·ness** *n.*

blas·phe·my (blăs′fə-mē) *n., pl.* **-mies. 1. a.** Any contemptuous or profane act, utterance, or writing concerning God. **b.** Any irreverent or impious act or utterance. **2.** *Theology.* The act of claiming for oneself the attributes and rights of God. **3.** *Judaism.* **a.** Any word or deed meant to dishonor or revile the being or the work of God, as a curse or profanity. **b.** The mention of the sacred, ineffable name of God.

blast (blăst, bläst) *n.* **1. a.** A strong gust of wind. **b.** The battering effect of such a gust. **2.** A forcible stream of air, gas, or steam from an opening, especially one in a blast furnace to aid combustion. **3. a.** The blowing of a whistle or wind instrument. **b.** The sound or noise produced by this. **4. a.** An explosion, as of dynamite. **b.** The effect of such an explosion. **c.** The charge of dynamite or other explosive so used. **5.** Any disease of plants that results in failure of flowers to open, or failure of fruit or seeds to mature. **6.** Any destructive or damaging influence. **7.** A violent verbal assault or outburst. **8.** *Slang.* A big or wild party. —See Synonyms at **wind.** —**(at) full blast.** At full speed, volume, or capacity. —*v.* **blasted, blasting, blasts.** —*tr.* **1.** To tear to pieces by or as by explosion; blow up. **2.** To cause to deteriorate; ruin; frustrate: *"Our hopes were all blasted at one blow."* (Frederick Douglass). **3.** To cause to shrivel, wither, or mature imperfectly by or as if by blast or blight. **4.** To make, dislodge, or open (something) by or as by explosion: *blast a channel through the reefs.* **5.** *Slang.* To attack or criticize vigorously. **6.** *Slang.* To damn. Used euphemistically. **7.** *Slang.* To shoot. Used with *down.* —*intr.* **1.** To detonate explosives. **2.** To emit a sudden loud noise. **3.** To wither, shrivel, or mature imperfectly. **4.** *Slang.* To attack or criticize with vigor. Used with *away.* **5.** *Slang.* To shoot. **6.** *Electronics.* To distort sound recording or transmission by overloading a microphone or loud-speaker. [Middle English *blast,* Old English *blǣst.* See **bhlē-**[2] in Appendix.*] —**blast′er** *n.*

-blast. Indicates a germ, sprout, or growth; for example, **erythroblast.** [From Greek *blastos,* shoot, bud. See **melōdh-** in Appendix.*]

blast·ed (blăs′tĭd, bläs′-) *adj.* **1.** Blighted; withered; shriveled. **2.** *Slang.* Damned.

blas·te·ma (blă-stē′mə) *n., pl.* **-mas** or **-mata** (-mə-tə). A segregated region of embryonic cells from which a specific organ develops. [New Latin, from Greek *blastēma,* offspring, offshoot, from *blastos,* sprout, bud. See **melōdh-** in Appendix.*] —**blas·te′mal** (blă-stē′məl), **blas′te·mat′ic** (blăs′tə-măt′ĭk), **blas·te′mic** (blă-stē′mĭk) *adj.*

blast furnace. Any furnace in which combustion is intensified by a blast of air.

-blastic. Indicates buds, sprouts, or growth; for example, **diploblastic.**

blasting gelatin. A **dynamite** *(see)* containing nitrocellulose in addition to nitroglycerin.

blasto-. Indicates growth, budding, or germination; for example, **blastoderm.** [From Greek *blastos.* See **-blast.**]

blas·to·coel, blas·to·coele (blăs′tə-sēl′) *n. Embryology.* The cavity of a **blastula** *(see).* Also called "segmentation cavity." [BLASTO- + *-coel,* variant of -CELE.] —**blas′to·coel′ic** *adj.*

blas·to·cyst (blăs′tə-sĭst) *n. Embryology.* The **germinal vesicle** *(see).* —**blas·to·cys′tic** *adj.*

blas·to·derm (blăs′tə-dûrm′) *n.* The layer of cells surrounding the blastocoel. It gives rise to the **germinal disc** *(see)* from which the embryo develops in most placental vertebrates. [BLASTO- + -DERM.] —**blas′to·der·mat′ic, blas′to·der′mic** *adj.*

blas·to·disc (blăs′tə-dĭsk′) *n.* Also **blas·to·disk.** *Embryology.* The **germinal disc** *(see).*

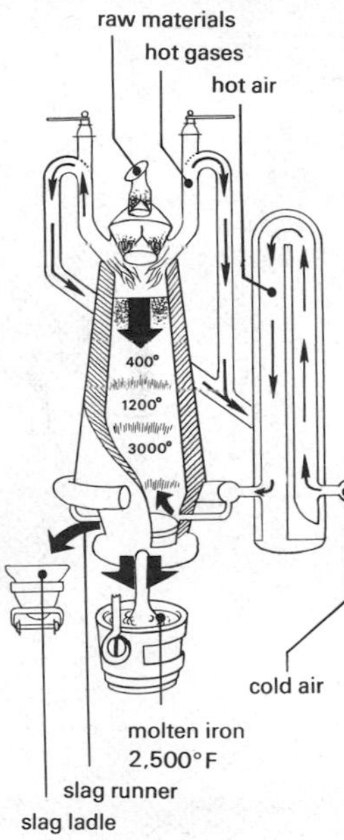
raw materials
hot gases
hot air
400°
1200°
3000°
cold air
molten iron
2,500°F
slag runner
slag ladle

blast furnace

blast off. To commence flight; take off. Used of rockets or space vehicles.
blast·off (blăst′ôf′, bläst′-) *n.* Also **blast-off.** *Aerospace.* The launching of a rocket or space vehicle.
blas·to·gen·e·sis (blăs′tə-jĕn′ĭ-sĭs) *n. Biology.* **1.** The theory that inherited characteristics are transmitted from parent to offspring by germ plasm. **2.** Reproduction by budding. —**blas′to·ge·net′ic, blas′to·gen′ic** *adj.*
blas·to·mere (blăs′tə-mîr′) *n.* A cell formed during the cleavage of a fertilized ovum. [BLASTO- + -MERE.] —**blas′to·mer′ic** *adj.*
blas·to·pore (blăs′tə-pôr′, -pōr′) *n.* The mouthlike opening into the primitive intestinal cavity of the gastrula. [BLASTO- + PORE (orifice).] —**blas′to·po′ral** (-pôr′əl, -pōr′əl) *adj.*
blas·tu·la (blăs′chōō-lə) *n., pl.* **-las** or **-lae** (-lē′). An early embryonic form, consisting essentially of a hollow cellular sphere. Also called "blastosphere." [New Latin, from Greek *blastos,* bud, germ. See **melədh-** in Appendix.*] —**blas′tu·lar** (-lər) *adj.* —**blas′tu·la′tion** (-lā′shən) *n.*
blat (blăt) *v.* **blatted, blatting, blats.** —*tr. Informal.* To blurt out or blab. —*intr.* To bleat or baa, as a sheep. [Imitative.]
bla·tant (blā′tənt) *adj.* **1.** Unpleasantly loud and noisy. **2.** Offensively conspicuous; obtrusive; obvious: *blatant lie.* **3.** *Rare.* Bellowing. Said of animals. —See Synonyms at **vociferous.** [First used by Spenser ("*the blattant beast,*" a symbol of calumny), probably from Latin *blatīre,* to blab, gossip. See **blat-** in Appendix.*] —**bla′tan·cy** *n.* —**bla′tant·ly** *adv.*
Usage: *Blatant* and *flagrant* are often confused. *Blatant* stresses offensiveness and obtrusiveness, primarily from the standpoint of noise and bluster. *Flagrant* emphasizes wrong or evil that is glaring or notorious. Therefore, one who blunders is guilty of a *blatant* (not *flagrant*) error; one who willfully violates a pledge commits a *flagrant* act.
blath·er (blă*th*′ər) *v.* **-ered, -ering, -ers.** Also **bleth·er** (blĕ*th*′ər). —*intr.* To talk nonsense; babble. —*tr.* To speak foolishly or nonsensically. —*n.* Also **bleth·er.** Absurd or foolish talk; nonsense. [Middle English *blether,* from Old Norse *bladhra,* to prattle, akin to *bladhra,* bladder. See **bhlē-[2]** in Appendix.*] —**blath′er·er** *n.*
blath·er·skite (blă*th*′ər-skīt′) *n.* **1.** A babbling, foolish person. **2.** Absurd and foolish talk. [Earlier *bletherskate* : BLATHER + SKATE (fish).]
blaze[1] (blāz) *n.* **1.** A brilliant burst of fire; a flame. **2.** Any bright, hot, steady light or glare. **3.** A destructive fire, especially one that spreads rapidly. **4.** A sudden outburst, as of emotion or activity. **5.** *Plural. Slang.* Hell. Used as a euphemism. —*v.* **blazed, blazing, blazes.** —*intr.* **1.** To burn with a bright flame. **2.** To shine brightly. **3.** To be deeply excited, as by emotion. **4.** To shoot rapidly and continuously. Usually used with *away.* —*tr.* **1.** *Rare.* To cause to burn. **2.** To shine or be resplendent with: *Her eyes blazed fire.* [Middle English *blase,* Old English *blæse,* torch, bright fire. See **bhel-[1]** in Appendix.*] —**blaz′ing·ly** *adv.*
Synonyms: *blaze, flame, flare, flash, glare, incandescence, glow.* These nouns relate to the visible signs of combustion, especially to a brightly burning light. *Blaze* primarily stresses intensity and magnitude of combustion and especially implies vivid illumination. *Flame* more narrowly pertains to a jet or tongue of fire. *Flare* applies to a sudden, brief, intensely brilliant but unsteady burst of light, and *flash* to an even shorter burst. *Glare* emphasizes continuing intensity of blinding light. *Incandescence* suggests the intense brilliance of something white-hot. *Glow* primarily stresses light, often in the absence of visible flame; it particularly suggests steadiness of radiation and absence of intense brilliance.
blaze[2] (blāz) *n.* **1.** A white or light-colored spot on the face of a horse or other animal. **2.** A mark cut on a tree to indicate a trail. —*tr.v.* **blazed, blazing, blazes.** **1.** To mark (a tree) by cutting the bark. **2.** To indicate (a trail) by marking trees in this manner. [Probably from Middle Low German *bles.* See **bhel-[1]** in Appendix.*]
blaz·er (blā′zər) *n.* **1.** One that blazes. **2.** A lightweight, informal sports jacket, often striped or brightly colored.
blazing star. **1.** A North American plant, *Chamaelirium luteum,* having a long cluster of small white flowers. Also called "devil's bit." **2.** Any of various North American plants of the genus *Liatris,* having clusters of tuftlike purple or pinkish flowers. Also called "button snakeroot." **3.** A plant, *Mentzelia laevicaulis,* of western North America, having large, pale-yellow flowers.
bla·zon (blā′zən) *tr.v.* **-zoned, -zoning, -zons.** **1.** To describe (a coat of arms) in proper heraldic terms. **2.** To paint or depict (a coat of arms) with accurate heraldic detail. **3.** To adorn or embellish with or as if with blazons: *"the stars and moons and suns blazoned on that sacred wall"* (G.K. Chesterton). **4.** To announce; proclaim. Often used with *abroad.* —*n.* **1.** A coat of arms. **2.** The heraldic description or representation of a coat of arms. **3.** An ostentatious or showy display. [From Middle English *blasoun,* shield, coat of arms, from Old French *blason*†.] —**bla′zon·er** *n.* —**bla′zon·ment** *n.*
bla·zon·ry (blā′zən-rē) *n., pl.* **-ries.** **1.** The art of properly and accurately describing or representing armorial bearings. **2.** A coat of arms. **3.** Any showy or brilliant display.
bld. boldface.
bldg. building.
bleach (blēch) *v.* **bleached, bleaching, bleaches.** —*tr.* **1.** To remove the color from by means of sunlight, chemical agents, or the like. **2.** To make white or colorless. —*intr.* To become white or colorless. —*n.* **1.** Any chemical agent used for bleaching, by either oxidation or reduction. **2.** The degree of bleaching obtained. **3.** The act of bleaching. [Middle English *blechen,* Old English *blǣcan.* See **bhel-[1]** in Appendix.*]
bleach·er (blē′chər) *n.* **1.** One that bleaches. **2.** *Usually plural.* An unroofed outdoor grandstand for seating spectators. [Sense 2, from the bleaching effect of exposure to sun.]
bleaching powder. Any powder, such as chlorinated lime or calcium hypochlorite, used in solution as a bleach.
bleak[1] (blēk) *adj.* **bleaker, bleakest.** **1.** Exposed to the elements; unsheltered; barren. **2.** Cold and cutting; harsh. **3.** *Chiefly Regional.* Pale and wan; sickly; ashen. **4.** Gloomy and somber; depressing; dreary: *"Life in the Aràn Islands has always been bleak and difficult."* (John M. Synge). [Middle English *bleike,* pale, from Old Norse *bleikr,* shining, white. See **bhel-[1]** in Appendix.*] —**bleak′ly** *adv.* —**bleak′ness** *n.*
bleak[2] (blēk) *n.* A European freshwater fish of the genus *Alburnus,* having silvery scales used in the manufacture of artificial pearls. [Middle English *bleke,* probably from Old Norse *bleikja,* "white color." See **bhel-[1]** in Appendix.*]
blear (blîr) *tr.v.* **bleared, blearing, blears.** **1.** To blur (the eyes) with or as with tears. **2.** To blur; dim. —*adj.* Bleary. [Middle English *bleren,* probably of Low German origin, akin to Low German *blerr-*† (in *blerr-oged,* bleary-eyed).]
blear·y (blîr′ē) *adj.* **-ier, -iest.** **1.** Blurred or dimmed by or as by tears. **2.** Vague or indistinct; blurred. **3.** Exhausted; worn-out. —**blear′i·ly** *adv.* —**blear′i·ness** *n.*
blear·y-eyed (blîr′ē-īd′) *adj.* Also **blear-eyed** (blîr′īd′). **1.** With eyes blurred by or as by tears. **2.** Dull of mind or perception.
bleat (blēt) *v.* **bleated, bleating, bleats.** —*intr.* **1.** To utter the cry of a calf, goat, or sheep. **2.** To utter any similar sound, especially a whine. —*tr.* To utter in a whining voice. —*n.* **1.** The characteristic cry of a goat, sheep, or calf. **2.** Any similar sound, as a whining cry. [Middle English *bleten,* Old English *blǣtan.* See **bhlē-[1]** in Appendix.*] —**bleat′er** *n.*
bleb (blĕb) *n.* **1.** A small blister or pustule. Compare **bulla.** **2.** An air bubble. [Perhaps variant of BLOB.] —**bleb′by** *adj.*
bleed (blēd) *v.* **bled** (blĕd), **bleeding, bleeds.** —*intr.* **1.** To lose or emit blood. **2.** To suffer loss of blood, as a casualty in battle. **3.** To feel sympathetic grief or anguish: *My heart bleeds for you.* **4.** To exude sap or similar fluid, as a bruised plant does. **5.** *Slang.* To pay out money, especially an exorbitant amount. **6.** To become mixed or run, as dyes in wet cloth or paper. **7.** To show through a layer of paint, as a stain or resin in wood. **8.** *Printing.* To be printed so as to go over the edge or edges of a page, either purposely or by trimming the margins too closely. Often used with *off.* —*tr.* **1. a.** To take blood from, either surgically or with leeches. **b.** To extract sap or juice from. **2.** To exude (blood or sap, for example). **3. a.** To draw liquid or gaseous contents from; to drain. **b.** To draw off (liquid or gaseous matter) from a container. **4.** *Slang.* To obtain money from, especially by improper means. **5.** *Printing.* **a.** To print (an illustration, for example) so that it will go over the edge or edges of a page. **b.** To trim (a page or sheet, for example) too closely so as to mutilate the printed or illustrative matter. —*n.* *Printing.* **1.** Illustrative matter that purposely bleeds. **2.** A page trimmed so as to bleed. Also called "bleed page." **3.** The part thus trimmed off. [Bleed, bled, bled; Middle English *bleden, bledde, bledde,* Old English *blēdan, blēdde, blēdd,* from Common Germanic *blōthjan* (unattested), from *blōtham* (unattested), BLOOD.]
bleed·er (blē′dər) *n.* **1.** A **hemophiliac** (*see*). **2.** One who draws blood for medical purposes; bloodletter.
bleed·ing-heart (blē′dĭng-härt′) *n.* Any of several plants of the genus *Dicentra,* having finely divided leaves and nodding, pink flowers with two short, curved spurs; especially, the widely cultivated species *D. spectabilis,* native to Japan.
blem·ish (blĕm′ĭsh) *tr.v.* **-ished, -ishing, -ishes.** To impair or spoil by a flaw; mar. —*n.* A flaw or defect; a stain; disfigurement. [Middle English *blemisshen,* from Old French *blemir, blesmir* (present stem *blemiss-*), to make pale, from Germanic. See **bhel-[1]** in Appendix.*] —**blem′ish·er** *n.*
Synonyms: *blemish, imperfection, fault, defect, flaw.* All of these denote loss or absence of perfection. *Blemish* applies to some manifest characteristic that is held to mar the appearance or character of a thing, whereas *imperfection* and *fault* apply more comprehensively to any deficiency or shortcoming in make-up. *Defect* denotes serious functional or structural shortcoming; *flaw* refers to a small but fundamental weakness or dislocation, such as a fissure in a gem.
blench[1] (blĕnch) *intr.v.* **blenched, blenching, blenches.** To draw back or shy away, as from fear; to quail; flinch. See Synonyms at **recoil.** [Middle English *blenchen,* to deceive, start aside, evade, Old English *blencan,* to deceive. See **bhel-[1]** in Appendix.*] —**blench′er** *n.*
blench[2]. Variant of **blanch.**
blend (blĕnd) *v.* **blended** or **blent** (blĕnt), **blending, blends.** —*tr.* **1.** To combine or mix so as to render the constituent parts indistinguishable from one another. **2.** To mix (different varieties or grades) so as to obtain a new mixture of some particular quality or consistency. —*intr.* **1.** To form a uniform mixture; intermingle: *"The smoke blended easily into the odor of the other fumes."* (Norman Mailer). **2.** To become merged into one; unite: *"Evil dreams and evil waking were blended into a long tunnel of misery"* (J.R.R. Tolkien). **3.** To pass imperceptibly into one another; harmonize: *"standing motionless beside that door, as though trying to make myself blend with the dark wood."* (Faulkner). —See Synonyms at **mix.** —*n.* **1.** That which is blended; a mixture. **2.** The act of blending. **3.** *Linguistics.* A word produced by combining parts of other words, such as *smog,* from *smoke* and *fog;* portmanteau word. —See Syno-

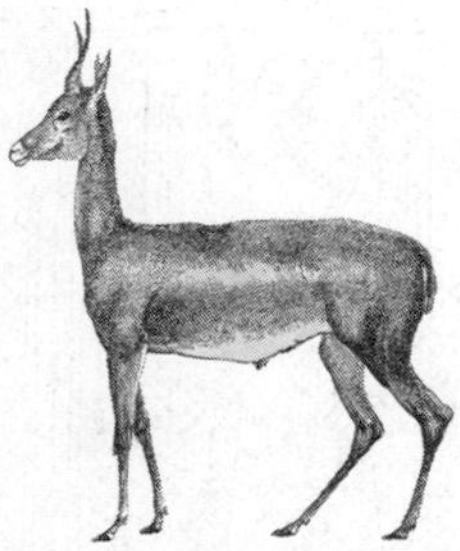

blesbok

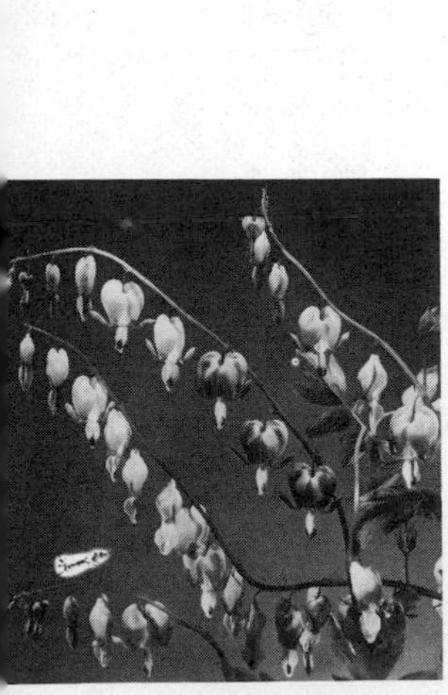

bleeding-heart
Dicentra spectabilis

ă pat/ā pay/âr care/ä father/b bib/ch church/d deed/ĕ pet/ē be/f fife/g gag/h hat/hw which/ĭ pit/ī pie/îr pier/j judge/k kick/l lid, needle/m mum/n no, sudden/ng thing/ŏ pot/ō toe/ô paw, for/oi noise/ou out/ŏŏ took/ōō boot/p pop/r roar/s sauce/sh ship, dish/

nyms at **mixture**. [Middle English *blenden*, from Old Norse *blanda* (stem *blend-*). See **bhel-¹** in Appendix.*]

blende (blĕnd) *n.* **1.** Any of various shiny minerals composed chiefly of metallic sulfides. **2.** A mineral, **sphalerite** *(see).* [German *Blende*, short for *blendendes Erz*, "deceptive ore" (often mistaken, on account of its metallic gleam, for a lead ore), from *blenden*, to blind, deceive, from Old High German *blenten*. See **bhel-¹** in Appendix.*]

blended whiskey. Whiskey that is a blend of two or more straight whiskeys, or a blend of whiskey and neutral spirits.

blend·er (blĕn′dər) *n.* **1.** One that combines or blends. **2.** A mechanical device for combining ingredients, as in cooking.

blending inheritance. *Genetics.* Inheritance of characters intermediate between those of parents widely divergent in those characters.

blen·ny (blĕn′ē) *n., pl.* **-nies.** Any of numerous small, elongated marine fishes, chiefly of the families Blenniidae and Clinidae. [Latin *blennius*, *blendius*, from Greek *blennos*, "slime" (from the slimy coating on its scales). See **mel-¹** in Appendix.*]

blent. Alternate past tense and past participle of **blend**.

bleph·a·ri·tis (blĕf′ə-rī′tĭs) *n.* Inflammation of the eyelid. [New Latin : Greek *blepharon*†, eyelid + -ITIS.]

bleph·a·ro·spasm (blĕf′ə-rō-spăz′əm) *n.* Uncontrollable winking, caused by involuntary contraction of an eyelid muscle. [New Latin *blepharospasmus* : BLEPHAR(ITIS) + SPASM.]

Blé·riot (blā-ryō′), **Louis.** 1872–1936. French engineer and aviator; first to fly the English Channel (1909).

bles·bok (blĕs′bŏk′) *n., pl.* **blesbok** or **-boks.** Also **bles·buck** (-bŭk′). An African antelope, *Damaliscus albifrons*, having curved horns and a face marked with white. [Afrikaans : *bles*, white mark on animal's face, from Middle Dutch (see **bhel-¹** in Appendix*) + *bok*, buck, from Middle Dutch *boc* (see **bhugo-** in Appendix*).]

bless (blĕs) *tr.v.* **blessed** or **blest** (blĕst), **blessing, blesses. 1.** To make holy by religious rite; sanctify. **2.** To make the sign of the cross over, so as to sanctify. **3.** To invoke divine favor upon. **4.** To preserve from evil. Used as an exclamation: *Bless my soul!* **5.** To honor as holy; glorify: *Bless the Lord.* **6.** To confer well-being or prosperity upon. **7.** To endow or favor, as with talent. [Middle English *blessen*, Old English *blētsian*, *blædsian*, from Common Germanic *blōthisōjan* (unattested), "to hallow with blood," from *blōtham* (unattested), BLOOD.] **—bless′er** *n.*

bless·ed (blĕs′ĭd) *adj.* Also **blest** (blĕst). **1.** Made sacred by a religious rite; consecrated. **2.** Worthy of profound respect or worship. **3.** *Roman Catholic Church.* Enjoying the eternal happiness of heaven. Used as a title for those who have been beatified. **4.** Enjoying happiness; fortunate. **5.** Bringing happiness or bliss. **6.** Damned. Used euphemistically or as an intensive. **—bless′ed·ly** *adv.* **—bless′ed·ness** *n.*

Blessed Sacrament. *Roman Catholic Church.* The consecrated Host.

Blessed Virgin. *Abbr.* **B.V.** The Virgin Mary.

bless·ing (blĕs′ĭng) *n.* **1. a.** The act of one who blesses. **b.** The prescribed words or ceremony for such an act. **2.** An expression or utterance of good wishes. **3.** A special favor granted by God. **4.** Anything promoting or contributing to happiness, well-being, or prosperity; a boon. **5.** Approbation: *This plan has my blessing.* **6.** A short prayer before or after a meal.

blest. 1. Alternate past tense and past participle of **bless**. **2.** Variant of **blessed**.

bleth·er. Variant of **blather**.

bleu cheese. Blue cheese *(see).*

blew. Past tense of **blow**.

Bligh (blī), **William.** 1754–1817. British naval officer, explorer, and colonial administrator; captain of mutinied ship *Bounty*.

blight (blīt) *n.* **1.** Any of several plant diseases that result in sudden dying of leaves, growing tips, or an entire plant. **2.** An environmental condition that injures or kills plants or animals, as air pollution. **3.** One that withers hopes or ambitions, impairs growth, or halts prosperity. **4.** The state or result of being blighted. **—***v.* **blighted, blighting, blights.** **—***tr.* **1.** To cause to decline or decay. **2.** To ruin; destroy. **3.** To frustrate: *a mishap that blighted his hopes.* **—***intr.* To suffer blight. [Origin unknown.]

blight·y (blī′tē) *n.* Also **Blight·y.** *British Slang.* England; home. [Hindi *bilāyatī*, *wilāyatī*, "foreign," "English," from Arabic *wilāyat*, district, realm, from *waliya*, he rules.]

blimp¹ (blĭmp) *n.* A nonrigid, buoyant aircraft. [Probably (type) B + LIMP.]

blimp² (blĭmp) *n. Chiefly British.* One whose views exhibit a blend of ultraconservative jingoism and misinformation. [From Colonel *Blimp*, a cartoon character invented by David Low.]

blind (blīnd) *adj.* **blinder, blindest. 1.** Without the sense of sight. **2.** Of or for sightless persons. **3.** Performed without the use of sight: *blind flying.* **4.** Performed without preparation, forethought, or knowledge: *a blind attempt.* **5.** Unable or unwilling to perceive or understand. **6.** Not based on reason or evidence: *blind faith.* **7.** *Informal.* Drunk. **8.** Acting without human control: *blind fate.* **9. a.** Difficult to comprehend or see; illegible: *blind writings.* **b.** Illegibly or incompletely addressed: *blind mail.* **10. a.** Hidden from sight: *a blind seam.* **b.** Screened from the view of an oncoming driver: *a blind intersection.* **11.** Closed at one end: *a blind socket.* **12.** Having no opening: *a blind wall.* **13.** *Botany.* Failing to flower. **—***n.* **1.** Something that hinders vision or shuts out light: *a Venetian blind.* **2.** A shelter for concealing hunters, especially duck hunters. **3.** Any subterfuge; a decoy. **—***adv.* **1.** Without being able to see; blindly: *fly blind.* **2.** *Informal.* Into a stupor: *They drank themselves blind.* **—***tr.v.* **blinded, blinding, blinds. 1.** To deprive of sight. **2.** To dazzle. **3.** To deprive (a person) of his powers of perception or judgment. **4.** To eclipse. **5.** To deprive of light; darken. [Middle English *blind*, Old English *blind*, blind, obscure. See **bhel-¹** in Appendix.*] **—blind′ly** *adv.* **—blind′ness** *n.*

blind alley. 1. A passageway open only at one end; dead end. **2.** *Informal.* Any project that fails to produce results.

blind date. *Informal.* **1.** A social engagement between a man and a woman who have not previously met. **2.** Either of the persons keeping such an engagement.

blind·er (blīn′dər) *n.* **1.** One that causes blinding. **2.** *Plural.* A pair of leather flaps attached to a horse's bridle to curtail side vision. Also called "blinkers." **3.** *Western U.S.* A cloth used to cover a horse's eyes during saddling or shoeing.

blind·fish (blīnd′fĭsh′) *n., pl.* **blindfish** or **-fishes.** Any of various fishes having rudimentary, nonfunctioning eyes; especially, the **cavefish** *(see).*

blind·fold (blīnd′fōld′) *tr.v.* **-folded, -folding, -folds. 1.** To cover the eyes with or as if with a bandage. **2.** To hamper the sight or comprehension of; mislead; delude. **—***n.* A bandage over the eyes. **—***adj.* **1.** With eyes covered. **2.** Reckless. [From Middle English *blindfolde*, *blindfelde*, past participle of *blindfellen*, to strike blind, from Old English *geblindfellian*, "to strike blind" : *ge-*, Y- + BLIND + *fellan*, to strike down, FELL.]

blind gut. *Anatomy.* The **cecum** *(see).*

blind hinge. A hinge so constructed that it allows the hinged piece to swing shut by its own weight unless held open.

blind·ing (blīn′dĭng) *adj.* **1.** Tending to make sightless. **2.** Dazzling; overpowering. **—blind′ing·ly** *adv.*

blind·man's buff (blīnd′mănz′). A game in which one person, blindfolded, tries to catch and identify one of the other players. [*Buff*, short for BUFFET (a blow).]

blind pig. *Slang.* An illegal saloon, a **blind tiger** *(see).*

blind spot. 1. *Anatomy.* The small, optically insensitive region where the optic nerve enters the retina of the eye. **2.** Any part of an area that cannot be directly observed. **3.** An area where radio reception is weak. **4.** A subject about which one is markedly ignorant or prejudiced.

blind staggers. Plural in form, used with a singular verb. A disease of horses, the **staggers** *(see).*

blind·sto·ry (blīnd′stôr′ē, -stōr′ē) *n., pl.* **-ries.** *Architecture.* A story having no windows.

blind tiger. *Slang.* An establishment where alcoholic beverages are sold illegally. Also called "blind pig."

blind·worm (blīnd′wûrm′) *n.* A lizard, the **slowworm** *(see).* [Perhaps so called because its eyes close after death.]

bli·ni (blē′nē) *pl.n.* Small buckwheat pancakes served with caviar or sour cream. [Russian, plural of *blin*, pancake, from Old Russian *blinŭ*, *mlinŭ*. See **mele-** in Appendix.*]

blink (blĭngk) *v.* **blinked, blinking, blinks.** **—***intr.* **1.** To close and open one or both eyes rapidly. **2.** To look through half-closed eyes, as in a bright glare; to squint. **3.** To shine with intermittent gleams; flash on and off. **4.** To look with pretended ignorance. Used with *at*. See Usage note below. **5.** To become startled or dismayed. Usually used with *at*. **—***tr.* **1.** To close and open (the eyes or an eye) rapidly. **2.** To close the eyes to; ignore or overlook. See Usage note below. **3.** To signal (a message) with a flashing light. **—***n.* **1.** The act or an instance of blinking; a brief closing of the eyes. **2.** A quick look or glimpse; a glance. **3.** The time it takes to blink. **4.** A flash of light; a gleam; a twinkle; a glimmer. **5.** An **iceblink** *(see).* **—on the blink.** *Slang.* Not in proper working condition; out of order. [Middle English *blinken*, partly a variant of *blenchen*, BLENCH (flinch), and perhaps partly from Middle Dutch *blinken*, to glitter. See **bhel-¹** in Appendix.*]

Usage: The verb *blink* used transitively and without a preposition expresses evasion in the sense of deliberate refusal to face or recognize: *blink* (not *blink at*) *ugly facts.* In an intransitive sense, *blink at* (or, more frequently, *wink at*) expresses evasion by condoning or tolerating: *blink at dishonest practices.* The first construction pertains basically to shirking and the second to complicity.

blink·ard (blĭng′kərd) *n.* **1.** A person who blinks habitually or chronically. **2.** An obtuse person.

blink·er (blĭng′kər) *n.* **1.** A light that blinks in order to convey a message or warning. Also called "blinker light." **2.** *Slang.* An eye. **3.** *Plural.* Goggles. **4.** *Plural.* **Blinders** *(see).*

blintz (blĭnts) *n.* Also **blin·tze** (blĭn′tsə). A thin, rolled pancake filled with cream cheese or cottage cheese, fruit, or seasoned mashed potatoes, and often served with sour cream. [Yiddish *blintse*, from Russian *blinyets*, diminutive of *blin*, BLINI.]

blip (blĭp) *n.* A spot of light on a radar screen. [Imitative.]

bliss (blĭs) *n.* **1.** Serene happiness. **2.** The ecstasy of salvation; spiritual joy. **3.** A cause of great delight or happiness. —See Synonyms at **ecstasy**. [Middle English *blis(se)*, Old English *bliss*, *blīths*, from Common Germanic *blīthsjo* (unattested), from *blīthiz* (unattested), BLITHE.] **—bliss′ful** *adj.* **—bliss′ful·ly** *adv.* **—bliss′ful·ness** *n.*

blis·ter (blĭs′tər) *n.* **1.** A thin, rounded swelling of the skin, containing watery matter, caused by burning or irritation. **2.** A similar swelling on a plant. **3.** An air bubble on a painted surface or in a casting. **4.** A rounded, often transparent protuberance on certain aircraft, used for observation or as a gun position. **—***v.* **blistered, -tering, -ters.** **—***tr.* **1.** To cause a blister or blisters to form upon. **2.** To reprove harshly. **—***intr.* To break out in blisters. [Middle English *blester*, *blister*, possibly from Old French *blestre*, from Middle Dutch *bluyster*, "swelling." See **bhlei-** in Appendix.*] **—blis′ter·y** *adj.*

blister beetle. Any of various beetles of the family Meloidae,

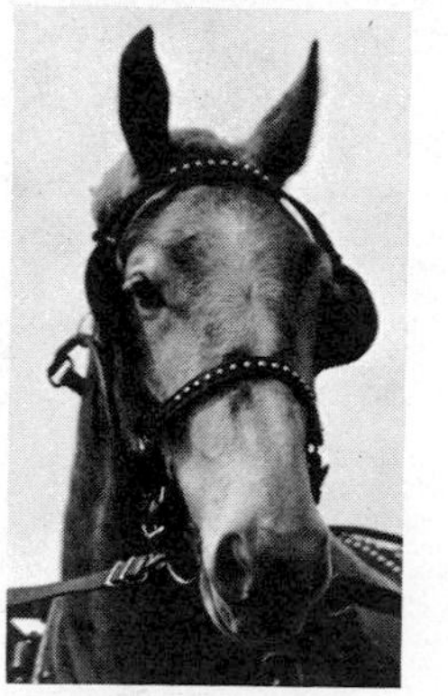

blinders
Farm horse with blinders

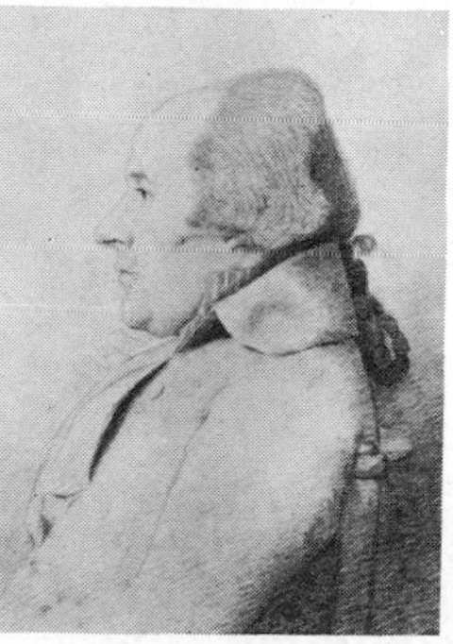

Captain Bligh
Contemporary portrait in pencil

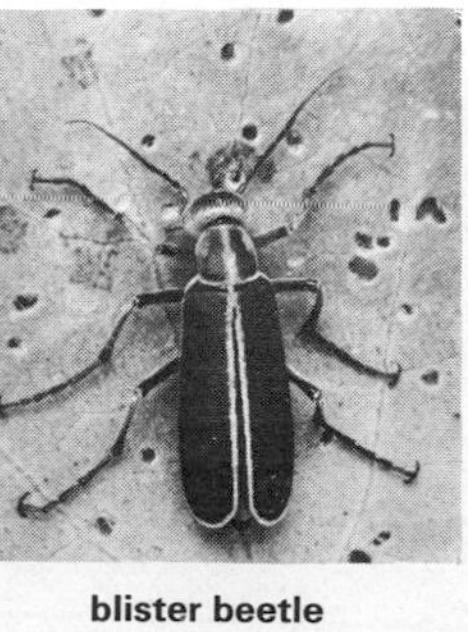

blister beetle

that secrete a substance capable of blistering the skin. Some species cause damage to crops. See **Spanish fly.**

blister copper. An almost pure copper produced in an intermediate stage of copper refining. [From its blistered surface.]

blister rust. Any of several diseases of pine trees, caused by various fungi of the genus *Cronartium* and resulting in cankers and blisters on the bark.

B.Lit. Bachelor of Literature (Latin *Baccalaureus Litterarum*).

blite (blīt) *n.* See **strawberry blite.** [Middle English, from Latin *blitum*, orach, from Greek *bliton.* See **mele-** in Appendix.*]

blithe (blīth, blīth) *adj.* **1.** Filled with gaiety; cheerful. **2.** Frivolous; casual; carefree: *blithe optimism.* —See Synonyms at **jolly.** [Middle English *blithe*, Old English *blīthe*, from Common Germanic *blīthiz*† (unattested), gentle, mild.] —**blithe'ly** *adv.* —**blithe'ness** *n.*

blith·er·ing (blĭth'ər-ĭng) *adj.* Talking senselessly; jabbering. [From *blither*, variant of BLATHER.]

blithe·some (blīth'səm, blīth'-) *adj.* Cheerful; merry. —**blithe'some·ly** *adv.* —**blith'some·ness** *n.*

blitz (blĭts) *n.* **1.** A blitzkrieg. **2.** An intensive air raid or series of air raids. **3.** Any intense campaign. —*tr.v.* **blitzed, blitzing, blitzes.** To subject to a blitz. [From BLITZKRIEG.]

blitz·krieg (blĭts'krēg') *n.* **1.** A swift, sudden military offensive, usually by combined air and land forces. **2.** Any swift, concerted effort. [German *Blitzkrieg*, "lightning war" : *Blitz*, lightning, from Middle High German *blicz*, from *bliczen*, to flash, from Old High German *blĕcchazen* (see **bhel-**[1] in Appendix*) + *Krieg*, war, from Middle High German *kriec*, from Old High German *chrēg*, stubbornness (see **gwer-**[2] in Appendix*).]

Blitz·stein (blĭts'stīn), **Marc.** 1903–1964. American composer.

bliz·zard (blĭz'ərd) *n.* **1.** A violent windstorm accompanied by intense cold and driving snow. **2.** A very heavy snowstorm with high winds. [Origin unknown.]

blk. **1.** black. **2.** block. **3.** bulk.

B.LL. Bachelor of Laws (Latin *Baccalaureus Legum*).

bloat (blōt) *v.* **bloated, bloating, bloats.** —*tr.* **1.** To cause to swell up or inflate, as with liquid or gas. **2.** To puff up, as with vanity. **3.** To cure (herring or other fish) by soaking in brine and half-drying in smoke. —*intr.* To become swollen or inflated. —*n.* *Veterinary Medicine.* A swelling of the rumen or intestinal tract of a domestic animal, caused by the gases of fermentation of green forage. [From *bloat*, swollen, earlier *blowt*, soft, flabby, from Middle English *blout*, probably from Old Norse *blautr*, soft, wet, soaked. See **bhleu-** in Appendix.*]

bloat·er (blō'tər) *n.* A herring lightly smoked and salted.

blob (blŏb) *n.* **1.** A soft, amorphous mass. **2.** A shapeless splotch or daub of color. —*tr.v.* **blobbed, blobbing, blobs.** To splash or mark with blobs; to splotch. [Middle English, bubble (imitative).]

bloc (blŏk) *n.* **1.** A group of persons, parties, or nations united for common action. **2.** A coalition, often bipartisan, of U.S. legislators acting together for some common interest: *the farm bloc.* [French, from Old French, BLOCK.]

Bloch (blŏk), **Ernest.** 1880–1959. Swiss-born American composer of orchestral and chamber music.

Bloch (blŏk), **Felix.** Born 1905. Swiss-born American physicist; engaged in research on nuclear magnetic moments.

Bloch (blŏk), **Konrad Emil.** Born 1909. German-born American biochemist; worked on fatty-acid metabolism.

block (blŏk) *n. Abbr.* **blk. 1.** A solid piece of wood or other hard substance having one or more flat sides. **2.** Such a piece used as a construction member or as a supporting or strengthening piece. **3.** Such a piece upon which chopping or cutting is done: *a butcher's block.* **4.** Such a piece upon which persons are beheaded: *"the men of Tudor England could outface the block and the stake"* (Christopher Morris). **5.** A stand from which articles are displayed at an auction. **6.** A mold or form upon which something is shaped or displayed: *a hat block.* **7.** A piece of wood, stone, or other substance prepared for engraving. **8. a.** A pulley or a system of pulleys set in a casing. **b.** The casting containing the cylinders of an internal-combustion engine. **9.** A group acting or regarded as a unit; a bloc. **10.** A set of like items sold or handled as a unit, as shares of stock. **11.** *Philately.* A group of four or more unseparated stamps forming a rectangle. **12.** *Canadian.* A group of townships in an unsurveyed area. **13. a.** A rectangular section of a city or town bounded on each side by consecutive streets. **b.** A segment of a street bounded by successive cross streets, including its buildings and inhabitants. **14.** A large building divided into separate units, such as apartments. **15.** A length of railroad track controlled by signals. See **block system. 16.** An act of obstructing or hindering. **17.** An obstacle or hindrance. **18.** *Sports.* An act of bodily obstruction; specifically, in football, legal interference with an opposing player to clear the path of the ballcarrier. **19.** *Medicine.* Interruption, especially obstruction, of a neural, digestive, or other physiological process. **20.** *Psychology.* Sudden cessation of a thought process without an immediate observable cause, sometimes considered a consequence of repression. **21.** *Slang.* A person's head. Used especially in the phrase *knock one's block off.* **22.** A blockhead. —See Synonyms at **obstacle.** —**on the block.** Up for sale at an auction. —*v.* **blocked, blocking, blocks.** —*tr.* **1.** To shape into a block or blocks. **2.** To support, strengthen, or retain in place by means of a block or blocks. **3.** To shape, mold, or form with or on a block: *block a hat.* **4.** To stop or impede the passage of or movement through; hinder or obstruct: *block traffic.* **5.** *Sports.* To impede the movement of (one's opponent or the ball) by means of physical interference. **6.** *Medicine.* To interrupt the proper functioning of (a physiological process). **7.** *Psychology.* To fail to remember. **8.** To run (trains) on the **block system** *(see).* —*intr.* *Sports.* To obstruct the movement of an opponent. —See Synonyms at **hinder.** —**block out. 1.** To plan or project broadly without details; sketch out. **2.** To obscure from view. —**block up. 1.** To raise on a block or blocks, as a house or boat. **2.** To fill with solid material: *block up the windows of an old house.* [Middle English *blok(ke)*, from Old French *bloc*, from Middle Dutch *blok*, trunk of a tree, from Germanic.] —**block** *adj.* —**block'er** *n.*

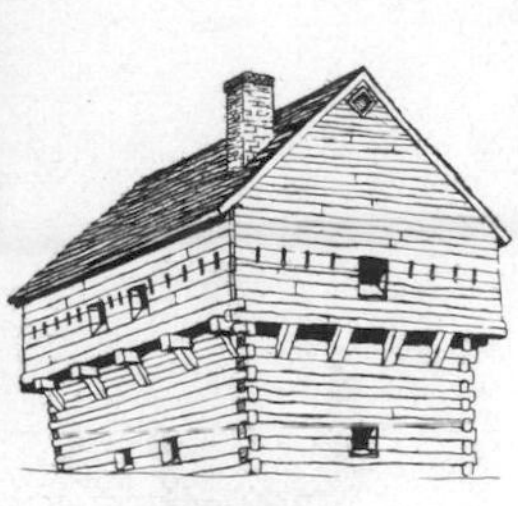

blockhouse
Blockhouse at the site of the Battle of Saratoga, showing slits for rifles and openings for downward fire

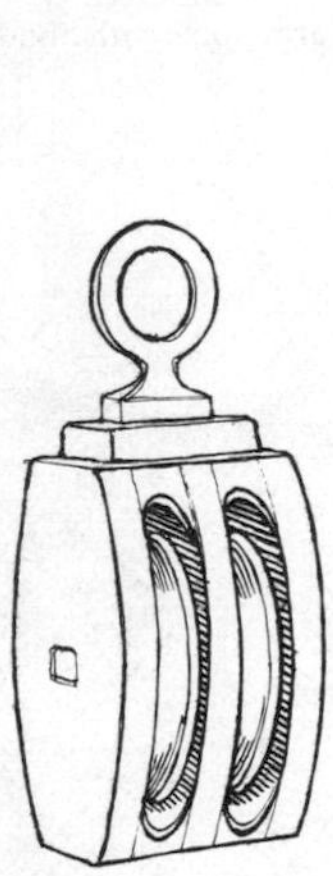

block

Block (blŏk), **Herbert Lawrence.** Pen name, Herblock. Born 1909. American editorial cartoonist.

block·ade (blŏ-kād') *n.* **1.** The closing off of a city, coast, harbor, or other area to traffic and communication by hostile ships or forces. **2.** The forces employed to close such an area. —*tr.v.* **blockaded, -ading, -ades.** To set up a blockade against. [From BLOCK (after AMBUSCADE).] —**block·ad'er** *n.*

block·ade-run·ner (blŏ-kād'rŭn'ər) *n.* A ship or person that goes through or past a blockade. —**block·ade'-run'ning** *n.*

block·age (blŏk'ĭj) *n.* **1.** The act of blocking or obstructing. **2.** An obstruction.

block and tackle. An apparatus of pulley blocks and ropes or cables used for hauling and hoisting heavy objects.

block·bust·er (blŏk'bŭs'tər) *n. Informal.* **1.** A bomb capable of destroying a city block. **2.** Anything of devastating effect.

block·head (blŏk'hĕd') *n.* A stupid person; dolt.

block·house (blŏk'hous') *n.* **1.** A military fortification constructed of concrete or other sturdy material, with loopholes for defensive firing or for observation. **2.** *Aerospace.* A heavily reinforced building used for launch operations of missiles and space launch vehicles. **3.** A house made of squared timbers.

block·ish (blŏk'ĭsh) *adj.* **1.** Like or resembling a block. **2.** Dull; stupid. —**block'ish·ly** *adv.* —**block'ish·ness** *n.*

Block Island. An island and summer resort of Rhode Island, in the Atlantic Ocean, about ten miles off the south coast.

block lava. Lava formed into sharp, angular blocks.

block letter. 1. A letter printed or written sans serif. **2.** *Printing.* A sans-serif style of type. —**block'-let'ter** *adj.*

block plane. A small plane used by carpenters for cutting across the grain of wood.

block printing. Printing from engraved or carved wooden or linoleum blocks.

block signal. A fixed signal at the beginning of a railroad block, indicating whether or not trains may enter.

block system. A system for controlling and safeguarding the flow of railway trains in which track is divided into sections or blocks, each controlled by automatic signals.

block tin. An impure commercial tin cast in blocks.

block·y (blŏk'ē) *adj.* **-ier, -iest.** Resembling a block; stocky.

Bloem·fon·tein (blo͞om'fŏn-tān'). The capital and largest city of the Orange Free State, Republic of South Africa, situated about 100 miles southeast of Kimberley. Population, 145,000.

bloke (blōk) *n. British Slang.* A fellow; man. [Origin unknown.]

blond (blŏnd) *adj.* **blonder, blondest.** Also *feminine* **blonde** (for sense 1). See Usage note below. **1.** Having fair hair and skin and usually light eyes. Said of persons. **2.** Of a flaxen or golden color or of any light shade of auburn or pale yellowish brown. Said of human hair. **3.** Light-colored: *blond furniture.* —*n.* Also *feminine* **blonde** (for sense 1). See Usage note below. **1.** A blond person. **2.** Light yellowish brown to dark grayish yellow. See **color.** [Old French, probably from Germanic. See **bhel-**[1] in Appendix.*] —**blond'ish** *adj.* —**blond'ness** *n.*

Usage: *Blond* and *brunet*, as adjectives, may be used of both sexes. As nouns, they are usually restricted to males. *Blonde* and *brunette*, as nouns and adjectives, are used only of females.

blood (blŭd) *n.* **1.** The fluid circulated by the heart through the vertebrate vascular system, carrying oxygen and nutrients throughout the body and waste materials to excretory channels. **2.** A functionally similar fluid in an invertebrate. **3.** A fluid resembling blood, such as the juice of certain plants. **4.** Loosely, life; lifeblood. **5.** Bloodshed; murder. **6.** Temperament; temper; disposition. **7.** Descent from a common ancestor; parental lineage. **8.** Family relationship; kinship. **9.** Descent from noble or royal lineage. Preceded by *the: a princess of the blood.* **10.** Recorded descent from purebred stock. Said of animals. **11.** Racial or national ancestry. **12.** Personnel: *new blood in the organization.* **13.** A dashing young man; a rake; a dandy. —**in cold blood.** Dispassionately; deliberately; coldly. —**make one's blood boil.** To make extremely angry. —**make one's blood run cold.** To terrify. —*tr.v.* **blooded, blooding, bloods. 1. a.** To give (a hound or hunting dog) its first taste of blood. **b.** To initiate a novice who has successfully followed hounds from find to death by marking his face with the blood of the fox. **2.** To subject (recruits) to the baptism of fire. —*adj.* Purebred: *a blood mare.* [Middle English *blood*, Old English *blōd*, from Common Germanic *blōtham* (unattested).]

blood bank. 1. A place where whole blood or plasma is typed, processed, and stored for future use in transfusion. **2.** A reserve of such blood or plasma.

blood bath. A savage and indiscriminate killing; a massacre.

blood count. 1. The number of red and white corpuscles in a specific volume of blood. **2.** The determination of this number.

blood·cur·dling (blŭd'kûrd'lĭng) *adj.* Causing great horror; terrifying. —**blood'cur'dling·ly** *adv.*

blood·ed (blŭd'ĭd) *adj.* **1.** Having blood or a temperament of a specified kind. Used in combination: *a cold-blooded reptile; a hot-blooded person.* **2.** Thoroughbred.

blood fluke. A trematode worm, a **schistosome** *(see).*

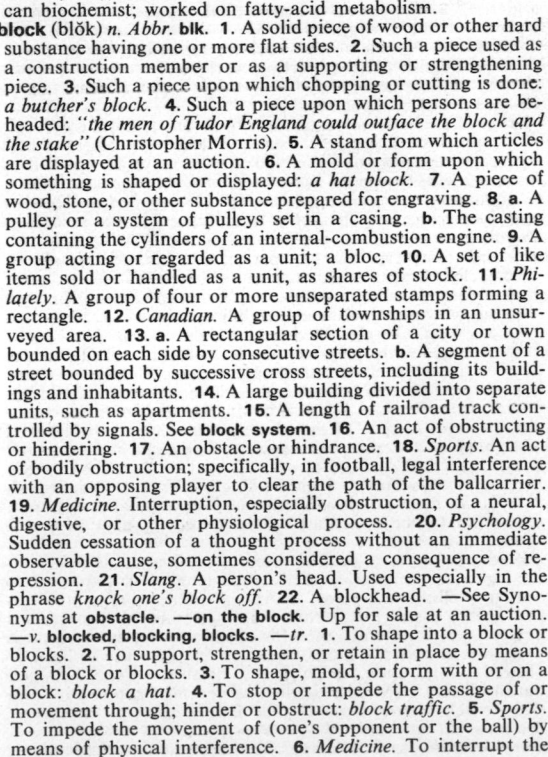

blood group. Any of several immunologically distinct, genetically determined classes of human blood, clinically identified by characteristic agglutination reactions. Also called "blood type."
blood·guilt (blŭd′gĭlt′) *n.* Guilt owing to murder or bloodshed. —**blood′guilt′i·ness** *n.* —**blood′guilt′y** *adj.*
blood heat. The usual temperature (98.6°F) of human blood.
blood·hound (blŭd′hound′) *n.* **1.** One of a breed of hounds with a smooth coat, drooping ears, sagging jowls, and a keen sense of smell. **2.** *Informal.* Any relentless pursuer.
blood·less (blŭd′lĭs) *adj.* **1.** Having no blood. **2.** Pale and anemic in color. **3.** Achieved without bloodshed. **4.** Lacking spirit. **5.** Cruel. —**blood′less·ly** *adv.* —**blood′less·ness** *n.*
blood·let·ting (blŭd′lĕt′ĭng) *n.* **1.** The bleeding of a vein as a therapeutic measure; bleeding; venesection. **2.** A draining away, as of lifeblood. **3.** **Bloodshed** *(see).* —**blood′let′ter** *n.*
blood·line (blŭd′līn′) *n.* Direct line of descent; strain; pedigree.
blood·mo·bile (blŭd′mə-bēl) *n.* A motor vehicle equipped for collecting blood from donors.
blood money. **1.** Money paid as compensation to the next of kin of a murder victim. **2.** Money paid to a hired killer. **3.** Money gained at the cost of another's life or livelihood.
blood plasma. The pale-yellow or gray-yellow, protein-containing fluid portion of the blood in which the corpuscles are normally suspended. Also called "plasma."
blood platelet. A constituent of blood, a **platelet** *(see).*
blood poisoning. **1.** Any condition in which the blood contains poisons, **toxemia** *(see).* **2.** A pathological condition resulting from the presence of poisons in the blood, **septicemia** *(see).*
blood pressure. The pressure of the blood within the arteries, primarily maintained by contraction of the left ventricle.
blood pudding. A sausage prepared from cooked swine's blood and suet. Also called "blood sausage."
blood red. Moderate to vivid red. See **color.** —**blood′-red′** *adj.*
blood relation. A person who is related by birth rather than by marriage. Also called "blood relative." —**blood relationship.**
blood·root (blŭd′ro͞ot′, -ro͝ot′) *n.* A woodland plant, *Sanguinaria canadensis,* of eastern North America having a fleshy rootstock, red juice, and a single pale flower. Also called "red puccoon."
blood·shed (blŭd′shĕd′) *n.* **1.** The shedding of blood. **2.** Carnage. Also called "bloodletting." —**blood′shed′der** *n.*
blood·shot (blŭd′shŏt′) *adj.* Red and irritated: *bloodshot eyes.*
blood·stain (blŭd′stān′) *n.* A stain caused by blood. —*tr.v.* **bloodstained, -staining, -stains.** To spot or stain with blood.
blood·stone (blŭd′stōn′) *n.* A variety of deep-green chalcedony flecked with red jasper. Also called "heliotrope."
blood stream. The stream of blood flowing through the circulatory system of a living body.
blood·suck·er (blŭd′sŭk′ər) *n.* **1.** Any animal that sucks blood, as a leech. **2.** One who clings to or preys upon another; parasite. —**blood′suck′ing** *adj.* & *n.*
blood test. A usually diagnostic examination of a blood sample, especially to detect syphilis.
blood·thirst·y (blŭd′thûr′stē) *adj.* **1.** Thirsting for bloodshed; murderous; cruel. **2.** Thirsting for violence. —**blood′thirst′i·ly** *adv.* —**blood′thirst′i·ness** *n.*
blood type. **Blood group** *(see).*
blood vessel. Any elastic, tubular canal, such as an artery, vein, or capillary, through which blood circulates.
blood·worm (blŭd′wûrm′) *n.* Any of various segmented worms of the genera *Polycirrus* and *Enoplobranchus,* having bright-red bodies and often used for bait.
blood·wort (blŭd′wûrt′, -wôrt′) *n.* Any of various chiefly South American plants of the family Haemodoraceae, having roots that contain a red juice.
blood·y (blŭd′ē) *adj.* **-ier, -iest.** **1.** Stained with blood. **2.** Of, characteristic of, or containing blood. **3.** Accompanied by or giving rise to bloodshed: *a bloody fight.* **4.** Bloodthirsty; cruel. **5.** Suggesting the color of blood; blood-red. **6.** *British Vulgar.* Used as an intensive: *bloody fool.* —*adv. British Vulgar.* Used as an intensive: *bloody well right.* —*tr.v.* **bloodied, -ying, -ies.** To stain, spot, or color with or as if with blood. —**blood′i·ly** *adv.* —**blood′i·ness** *n.*
bloody mary. Also **Bloody Mary.** A drink usually made with vodka, tomato juice, and seasonings.
Bloody Mary. See **Mary I.**
bloom¹ (blo͞om) *n.* **1.** The flower or blossoms of a plant. **2. a.** The condition or time of being in flower: *a rose in bloom.* **b.** A condition or time of vigor, freshness, and beauty; prime: *"the radiant bloom of Greek genius"* (Edith Hamilton). **3.** A fresh, rosy complexion. *"She was short, plump, and fair, with a fine bloom"* (Jane Austen). **4.** *Botany.* A delicate, powdery coating, such as that on some fruits, as the plum, or on some leaves and stems. **5.** A similar coating, as on newly minted coins. —*v.* **bloomed, blooming, blooms.** —*intr.* **1.** To bear flowers. **2.** To shine with health and vigor; to glow. **3.** To grow or flourish. —*tr.* **1.** To cause to flower. **2.** To cause to flourish. [Middle English *blom, blome,* from Old Norse *blōm, blōmi.* See **bhel-³** in Appendix.*] —**bloom′y** *adj.*
bloom² (blo͞om) *n.* **1.** A bar of steel, usually over 36 square inches in cross section, prepared for rolling. **2.** A mass of wrought iron ready for further working. [Middle English *blome,* lump of metal, Old English *blōma.* See **bhel-³** in Appendix.*]
bloom·er¹ (blo͞o′mər) *n.* **1. a.** A plant that blooms. **b.** One who attains full development of his abilities. **2.** *Slang.* A blunder.
bloom·er² (blo͞o′mər) *n.* **1.** A costume formerly worn by women and girls that was composed of loose trousers gathered about the ankles and worn under a short skirt. **2.** *Plural.* **a.** Wide, loose trousers gathered at the knee and formerly worn by women and girls as an athletic costume. **b.** Women's underpants of similar design. [Advocated by Amelia BLOOMER.]
Bloom·er (blo͞o′mər), **Amelia (Jenks).** 1818–1894. American social reformer; agitated for woman's suffrage.
Bloom·field (blo͞om′fēld′). A city in northeastern New Jersey near Newark. Population, 52,000.
Bloom·field (blo͞om′fēld′), **Leonard.** 1887–1949. American linguist and educator.
bloom·ing (blo͞o′mĭng) *adj.* **1.** Flowering; blossoming. **2.** Flourishing; growing. **3.** *Slang.* Utter; thorough. Used as an intensive: *a blooming idiot.* [Sense 3, probably a euphemism for BLOODY.] —**bloom′ing·ly** *adv.* —**bloom′ing·ness** *n.*
bloop·er (blo͞o′pər) *n.* **1.** *Baseball.* A short, weakly hit fly ball that carries just beyond the infield. **2.** *Informal.* A faux pas. [From *bloop,* sound of such a hit (imitative).]
blos·som (blŏs′əm) *n.* **1.** A flower or mass of flowers. Said especially of plants that yield edible fruit. **2.** The condition or time of flowering: *peach trees in blossom.* —*intr.v.* **blossomed, -soming, -soms.** **1.** To come into flower; to bloom. **2.** To develop; flourish: *She blossomed into a beauty.* [Middle English *blosme,* Old English *blōstm, blōstma.* See **bhel-³** in Appendix.*] —**blos′som·y** *adj.*

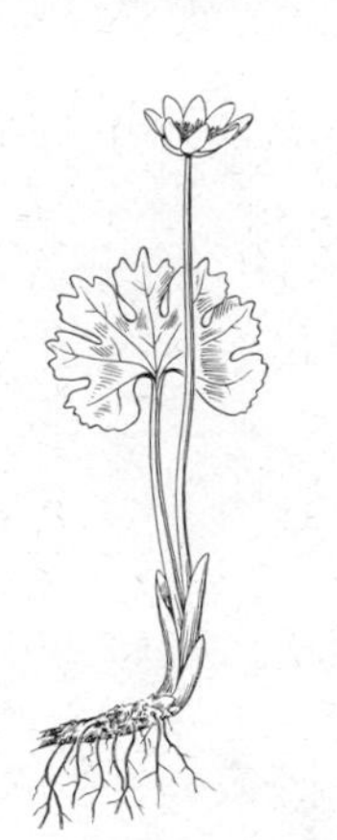
bloodroot

blot¹ (blŏt) *n.* **1.** A spot; a stain: *a blot of ink.* **2.** A stain on one's reputation or character; a disgrace: *"O indignity, O blot/To honour and Religion"* (Milton). **3.** Something that detracts from beauty or excellence: *"Let not the name of George the Third be a blot on the page of history."* (Jefferson). —*v.* **blotted, blotting, blots.** —*tr.* **1.** To spot or stain. **2.** To bring moral disgrace to. **3.** To obliterate; cancel. Used with *out:* *"Whosoever hath sinned against me, him will I blot out of my book."* (Exodus 32:33). **4.** To make obscure; darken; hide. Usually used with *out: clouds blotting out the moon.* **5.** To destroy utterly; annihilate. Used with *out.* **6.** To dry or soak up with absorbent material. —*intr.* **1.** To spill or spread in a blot or blots. **2.** To become blotted; absorb or soak up: *a paper that blots easily.* —See Synonyms at **erase.** [Middle English *blot, blotte,* perhaps from Old French *blotte, blostre,* clod of earth, probably from Germanic. See **bhlei-** in Appendix.*]
blot² (blŏt) *n.* **1.** An exposed piece in backgammon. **2.** *Archaic.* A weak point. [Probably from Dutch *bloot,* "naked," from Middle Dutch, naked, poor. See **bhleu-** in Appendix.*]
blotch (blŏch) *n.* **1.** A spot or blot; a splotch. **2.** A discoloration on the skin; blemish. **3.** Any of various plant diseases caused by fungi and resulting in brown or black dead areas on leaves or fruit. —*v.* **blotched, blotching, blotches.** —*tr.* To mark with blotches. Used chiefly in the past participle as an adjective: *"They were all blotched with insect bites."* (Richard Hughes). —*intr.* To become blotched. [Probably a blend of BLOT and BOTCH.] —**blotch′i·ness** *n.* —**blotch′y** *adj.*

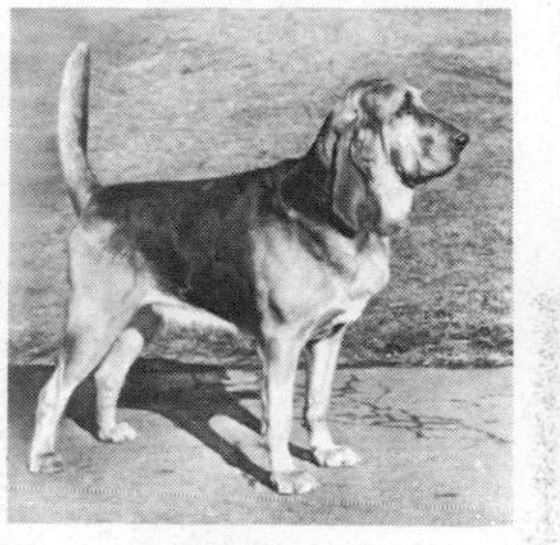
bloodhound

blot·ter (blŏt′ər) *n.* **1.** A piece or pad of blotting paper. **2.** A book containing daily records of occurrences or transactions: *a police blotter.*
blotting paper. Absorbent paper used to blot a surface by soaking up excess ink.
blouse (blous, blouz) *n.* **1.** A woman's or child's loosely fitting shirtwaist extending from the neck to the waist or slightly below the waist. **2.** A loosely fitting garment resembling a long shirt, sometimes belted at the waist, and worn especially by European workmen. **3.** The service coat or tunic worn by members of the U.S. Army. —*v.* **bloused, blousing, blouses.** —*intr.* To hang loose and full. —*tr.* To drape loosely. [French *blouse*†.]
blow¹ (blō) *v.* **blew** (blo͞o), **blown** (blōn), **blowing, blows.** —*intr.* **1.** To be in a state of motion, as the wind. **2.** To move along or be carried by or as if by the wind: *Her hat blew away.* **3.** To expel a current of air, as from the mouth or from a bellows. **4.** To produce a sound by expelling a current of air, as in sounding a musical wind instrument. **5.** To breathe hard; pant. **6.** To storm: *It blew all night.* **7.** To spout water and air, as a whale. **8.** *Slang.* To boast. **9.** *Slang.* To go away; depart. —*tr.* **1.** To cause to move by means of a current of air. **2.** To expel (air) from the mouth. **3.** To cause air to be expelled from. **4.** To drive a current of air upon, in, or through. **5.** To clear out or make free of obstruction by forcing air through. **6.** To shape or form (glass, for example) by forcing air or gas through at the end of a pipe. **7. a.** To cause (a wind instrument) to sound. **b.** To sound: *"a bugle blew the cease-fire"* (Frank Richards). **8.** To cause (a horse) to be out of breath. **9.** To cause to explode. Usually used with an adverb. **10.** To lay or deposit eggs in. Used of a fly. **11.** To melt or disable (a fuse). **12.** *Slang.* To spend (money) freely. **13.** *Vulgar Slang.* To perform fellatio upon. **14.** *Slang.* To handle ineptly. —**blow hot and cold.** To vacillate between favor and opposition. —**blow in.** *Slang.* To arrive. —**blow over.** **1.** To subside; to wane: *The storm blew over quickly.* **2.** To be forgotten: *The scandal will soon blow over.* —*n.* **1. a.** A blast of air or wind. **b.** A storm. **2.** The act of blowing. **3.** *Slang.* An act of bragging. [Blow, blew, blown; Middle English *blowen, blew, blowen,* Old English *blāwan, blēow, blāwen.* See **bhlē-²** in Appendix.*]
blow² (blō) *n.* **1.** A sudden hard stroke or hit, as with the fist or an instrument. **2.** A sudden unexpected shock or calamity. **3.** A sudden unexpected attack. —**come to blows.** To begin to fight. [Middle English (northern dialect) *blaw,* perhaps from Germanic *bleuwan* (unattested), to strike.]
blow³ (blō) *n.* A mass of blossoms: *peach blow.* —*v.* **blew** (blo͞o), **blown** (blōn), **blowing, blows.** —*intr.* To bloom. —*tr.* **1.** To cause to bloom. **2.** To produce (blossoms). [From Middle English *blowen,* to blossom, Old English *blōwan.* See **bhel-³** in Appendix.*]

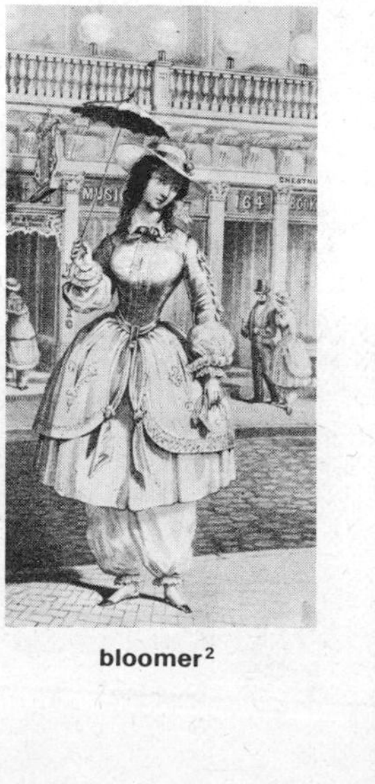
bloomer²

blow·er (blō′ər) *n.* **1.** One that blows; especially, a mechanical device, such as a fan. **2.** *Slang.* A braggart.
blow·fish (blō′fĭsh′) *n., pl.* **blowfish** or **-fishes.** The **puffer** *(see).*
blow·fly (blō′flī′) *n., pl.* **-flies.** Any of several flies of the family Calliphoridae, that deposit their eggs in carcasses or carrion or in open sores and wounds.
blow·gun (blō′gŭn′) *n.* A long narrow pipe through which darts or pellets may be blown. Also called "blowpipe."
blow·hard (blō′härd′) *n. Slang.* A boaster; braggart.
blow·hole (blō′hōl′) *n.* **1.** A nostril at the highest point on the head of whales and other cetaceans. **2.** A hole in ice through which whales, dolphins, and other aquatic mammals come up for air. **3.** A vent to permit the escape of air or other gas.
blow·job (blō′jŏb′) *n. Vulgar Slang.* An act or instance of fellatio.
blown[1] (blōn) *adj.* **1.** Inflated; distended. **2.** Out-of-breath; panting. **3.** Flyblown. **4.** Formed by blowing: *blown glass.*
blown[2] (blōn) *adj.* Completely expanded or opened. Often used in combination: *a full-blown flower.*
blow off. 1. To release or let off, as steam from a boiler. **2.** *Slang.* To give vent to one's thoughts, problems, or emotions.
blow·off (blō′ôf′, -ŏf′) *n.* **1.** Something blown off, as a gas. **2.** A device or channel for blowing off something.
blow out. 1. To extinguish or be extinguished by blowing, as a candle. **2.** To burst suddenly, as a tire. **3.** To burn out or melt, as a fuse. **4.** To fail, as an electrical apparatus.
blow·out (blō′out′) *n.* **1. a.** A sudden rupture or bursting, as of an automobile tire. **b.** The hole made so. **c.** The ruptured object. **2.** A sudden escape of a confined gas. **3.** The burning out of a fuse. **4.** *Slang.* A large party or social affair.
blow·pipe (blō′pīp′) *n.* **1.** A metal tube in which a flow of gas is mixed with a controlled flow of air to concentrate the heat of a flame. **2.** A **blowgun** *(see).* **3.** A long narrow iron pipe used to gather, work, and blow molten glass.
blow·torch (blō′tôrch′) *n.* A usually portable gas burner that produces a flame typically hot enough to melt soft metals.
blow up. 1. To come into being: *A storm blew up off the coast.* **2.** To explode. **3.** To lose one's temper. **4.** To enlarge the size of (a photographic print). **5.** To fill with air.
blow·up (blō′ŭp′) *n.* **1.** An explosion. **2.** A violent outburst of temper. **3.** A photographic enlargement.
blow·y (blō′ē) *adj.* **-ier, -iest.** Windy; breezy.
blow·zy (blou′zē) *adj.* **-zier, -ziest.** Also **blow·sy. 1.** Having a coarsely ruddy and bloated appearance. **2.** Disheveled; frowzy; unkempt: *blowzy hair.* —See Synonyms at **sloppy.** [From dialectal *blowse,* beggar wench, slattern, probably from blowzy, windy, from BLOW.]
BLS Bureau of Labor Statistics.
B.L.S. Bachelor of Library Science.
blub·ber[1] (blŭb′ər) *v.* **-bered, -bering, -bers.** —*intr.* To weep and sob in a noisy manner. —*tr.* **1.** To utter while crying and sobbing: *The child blubbered his name.* **2.** To make wet and swollen by weeping. —See Synonyms at **cry.** —*n.* A loud weeping and sobbing. [Middle English *bloberen, blubren,* to bubble, foam, from *blober, bluber,* foam, bubble (imitative).] —**blub′ber·er** *n.* —**blub′ber·ing·ly** *adv.*
blub·ber[2] (blŭb′ər) *n.* **1.** The thick layer of fat between the skin and the muscle layers of whales and other marine mammals. **2.** Excessive body fat. —*adj.* Swollen and protruding. [Middle English *blober, bluber,* foam, bubble, entrails, fish or whale oil. See **blubber** (verb).] —**blub′ber·y** *adj.*
blu·cher (blo͞o′chər, -kər) *n.* **1.** A high shoe or half boot. **2.** A shoe having the vamp and tongue made of one piece and the top lapping over the vamp. [After G.L. von BLÜCHER.]
Blü·cher (blo͞o′kər; *German* blü′ᴋʜər), **Gebhard Leberecht von.** 1742–1819. Prussian field marshal.
bludg·eon (blŭj′ən) *n.* A short, heavy club, usually of wood, that has one end loaded or thicker than the other. —*tr.v.* **bludgeoned, -eoning, -eons. 1.** To hit with or as if with a bludgeon. **2.** To threaten or bully. [Origin unknown.] —**bludg′eon·er, bludg′eon·eer′** (-ə-nîr′) *n.*

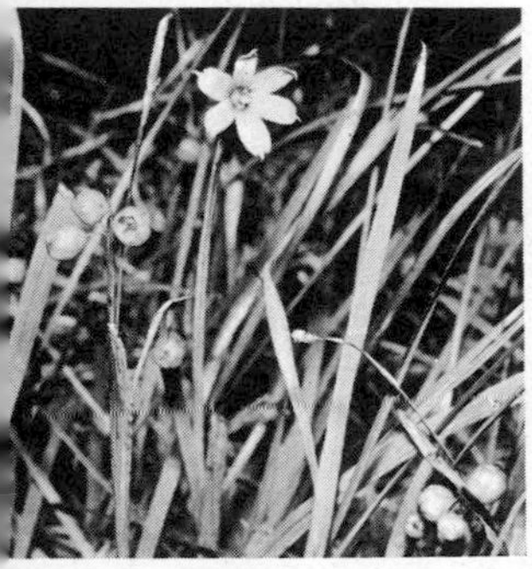
blue-eyed grass

blue (blo͞o) *n.* **1.** *Abbr.* **bl.** Any of a group of colors that may vary in lightness and saturation, whose hue is that of a clear sky; the hue of that portion of the spectrum lying between green and violet; one of the additive or light primaries; one of the psychological primary hues, evoked in the normal observer by radiant energy of wavelength approximately 475 nanometers. See **color, primary color. 2. a.** Any pigment or dye imparting this color. **b.** Bluing. **3. a.** Any object of this color. **b.** Blue dress or clothing: *the girls in blue.* **4.** A person who wears a blue uniform. **5.** *Sometimes capital* **B. a.** A member of the Union Army in the Civil War. **b.** The Union Army itself. Compare **gray. 6.** *Plural.* The blue uniform of the U.S. Navy. **7.** A small blue butterfly of the family Lycaenidae. **8.** A **bluestocking** *(see).* —**into the blue.** At a far distance or into the unknown. —**out of the blue. 1.** From an unexpected, unforeseen, or unknown source. **2.** At a completely unexpected time. —**the blue. 1.** The sea. **2.** The sky. **3.** *Theater.* Risqué humor. —*adj.* **bluer, bluest. 1.** *Abbr.* **bl.** Of the color blue. **2.** Bluish, or having parts that are blue or bluish. Used with plant and animal names: *blue spruce, blue whale.* **3.** Having a gray or purplish color, as from cold or contusion. **4.** Wearing blue. **5. a.** Gloomy; depressed. **b.** Dismal; dreary: *a blue day.* **6.** Puritanical; strict. **7.** Fiercely intellectual. Usually said of a woman. **8.** Aristocratic; patrician. **9.** Indecent; risqué: *a blue joke.* —See Synonyms at **sad.** —**once in a blue moon.** Very seldom; rarely. —*v.* **blued, bluing, blues.** —*tr.* **1.** To make blue. **2.** To use bluing on. —*intr.* To become blue. [Middle English *bleu, blewe,* from Old French *bleu,* from Common Romance *blāvus* (unattested), from Germanic. See **bhel-**[1] in Appendix.*] —**blue′ly** *adv.* —**blue′ness** *n.*

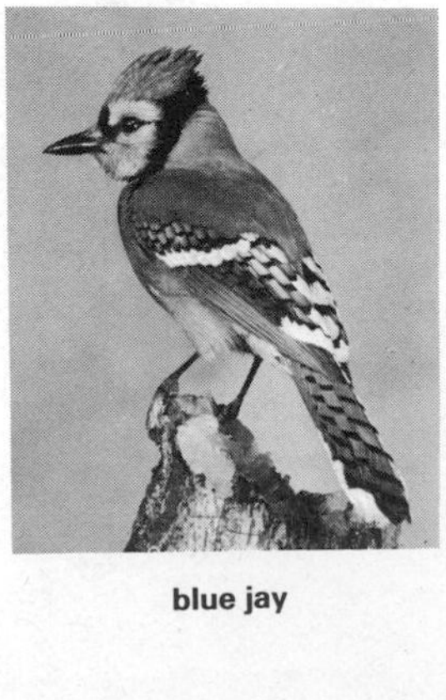
blue jay

blue baby. An infant born with bluish skin caused by inadequate oxygenation of the blood, a symptom of a congenital cardiac or pulmonary defect.
blue·back salmon (blo͞o′băk′). The **sockeye salmon** *(see).*
blue·beard (blo͞o′bîrd′) *n.* Also **Blue·beard.** Any man thought to be a wife-slayer or a killer of women.
Blue·beard (blo͞o′bîrd′). The central character of a folk tale who married and murdered one wife after another.
blue·bell (blo͞o′bĕl′) *n.* Any of various plants having blue, bell-shaped flowers, especially: **a.** A European plant, *Scilla non-scripta,* having grasslike leaves and a one-sided cluster of fragrant, blue-violet flowers. This species is the bluebell of England. **b.** The **harebell** *(see),* which is the bluebell of Scotland. **c.** Any of various plants of the genus *Mertensia.*
blue·ber·ry (blo͞o′bĕr′ē, -bər-ē) *n., pl.* **-ries. 1.** Any of several North American shrubs of the genus *Vaccinium,* having small, urn-shaped flowers and edible berries. **2.** The juicy blue, purplish, or blackish berry of any of these shrubs.
blue·bill (blo͞o′bĭl′) *n.* A duck, the **scaup** *(see).*
blue·bird (blo͞o′bûrd′) *n.* Any of several North American birds of the genus *Sialia,* having blue plumage and, in the male of most species, a rust-colored breast.
blue blood. 1. Noble or aristocratic descent. **2.** A member of the aristocracy or other high social group. [Translation of Spanish *sangre azul;* probably from the blue color of the veins of fair-complexioned aristocrats.] —**blue′-blood′ed** *adj.*
blue·blos·som (blo͞o′blŏs′əm) *n.* A shrub, *Ceanothus thyrsiflorus,* of the west coast of the United States, having profuse clusters of small blue flowers. Also called "California lilac."
blue·bon·net (blo͞o′bŏn′ĭt) *n.* **1.** A plant, *Lupinus subcarnosus,* of Texas and adjacent regions, having compound leaves and clusters of blue flowers. **2.** Any of several other plants having blue flowers. **3.** A broad, blue woolen cap worn in Scotland. **4.** A Scotsman wearing such a cap.
blue book. Also **blue·book** (blo͞o′bo͝ok′), **Blue Book. 1.** An official publication of the British government, so named for its blue covers. **2.** An official list of persons in the employ of the U.S. government. **3.** *Informal.* A book listing the names of socially prominent people. **4.** A blank notebook with blue covers in which to write college examinations.
blue·bot·tle (blo͞o′bŏt′l) *n.* **1.** Any of several flies of the genus *Calliphora,* having a bright metallic-blue body and breeding in decaying organic matter. **2.** A plant, the **cornflower** *(see).*
blue cheese. A semisoft cheese made of cow's milk, having a greenish-blue mold and flavor similar to Roquefort cheese. Also called "bleu cheese."
blue chip. 1. *Finance.* A stock that sells at a high price because of public confidence in its long record of steady earnings. Also called "blue-chip stock." **2.** A valuable asset held in reserve. **3.** A blue-colored poker chip of high value. —**blue′-chip′** *adj.*
blue·coat (blo͞o′kōt′) *n.* A person who wears a blue uniform, especially a policeman. —**blue′coat′ed** *adj.*
blue cohosh. A plant, *Caulophyllum thalictroides,* of eastern North America, having compound leaves and a cluster of greenish or purplish flowers. Also called "papoose-root."
blue-col·lar (blo͞o′kŏl′ər) *adj.* Of or pertaining to wage earners in jobs performed in rough clothing and often involving manual labor, especially when such workers are regarded as a social class. Compare **white-collar.**
blue·curls (blo͞o′kûrlz′) *n.* Also **blue curls.** Plural in form, used with a singular or plural verb. Any of several North American plants of the genus *Trichostema,* having blue, two-lipped flowers with long, curved stamens.
blue devils. 1. *Slang.* Delirium tremens. **2.** *Informal.* A feeling of depression or despondency.
blue dicks. Plural in form, used with a singular or plural verb. A plant, *Brodiaea capitata,* of the western United States, having a rounded cluster of blue flowers.
blue-eyed grass (blo͞o′īd′). Any of various plants of the genus *Sisyrinchium,* mostly of North America, having grasslike leaves and small, starlike blue flowers.
blue-eyed Mary. A plant, *Collinsia verna,* of eastern North America, having two-lipped blue and white flowers.
blue·fish (blo͞o′fĭsh′) *n., pl.* **bluefish** or **-fishes. 1.** A voracious food and game fish, *Pomatomus saltatrix,* of temperate and tropical waters of the Atlantic and Indian oceans. **2.** Broadly, any of various other fishes that are predominantly blue in color.
blue flag. Any of several wild irises having blue flowers, especially *Iris versicolor,* of eastern North America.
blue fox. 1. The **arctic fox** *(see)* during its summer color phase, when its pelt is bluish gray. **2.** The fur of such a fox.
blue·gill (blo͞o′gĭl′) *n.* A common, edible sunfish, *Lepomis macrochirus,* of North American lakes and streams.
blue·grass (blo͞o′grăs′, -gräs′) *n.* Any of several grasses of the genus *Poa;* especially, *P. pratensis,* native to Eurasia but naturalized throughout North America. This species is also called "Kentucky bluegrass."
Bluegrass Country. A region in central Kentucky noted for its abundant bluegrass and also for the breeding of racehorses. Also called "Bluegrass Region," "the Bluegrass."
Bluegrass State. The nickname for Kentucky.
blue-green algae (blo͞o′grēn′). Any of the algae of the division Cyanophyta (or Myxophyceae), considered to be among the simplest forms of plants.
blue grouse. A wildfowl, *Dendragapus obscurus,* of western North America, having predominantly gray plumage. Also called "dusky grouse," "sooty grouse."
blue gum. A tall timber tree, *Eucalyptus globulus,* native to

Australia, having aromatic leaves and outer bark that peels off in shreds.

blue·head (blōō'hĕd') *n.* A marine fish, *Thalassoma bifasciatum,* of tropical Atlantic waters, the male of which has a blue head and a green body.

blue·hearts (blōō'härts') *n.* Plural in form, used with a singular or plural verb. A hairy plant, *Buchnera americana,* of central North America, having a spike of deep-purple flowers.

blue·ing. Variant of **bluing.**

blue·ish. Variant of **bluish.**

blue·jack (blōō'jăk') *n.* An oak tree, *Quercus cinerea,* of the southern United States, having narrow, unlobed leaves. [BLUE + (BLACK)JACK (oak).]

blue·jack·et (blōō'jăk'ĭt) *n.* An enlisted man in the U.S. or British Navy; a sailor. [From the blue jacket of the Navy.]

blue jay. A North American bird, *Cyanocitta cristata,* having a crested head and predominantly blue plumage.

blue jeans. Heavy blue denim trousers, **jeans** *(see).*

blue law. **1.** In colonial New England, one of a body of laws designed to enforce certain moral standards, and particularly prohibiting specified forms of entertainment or recreation on Sundays. **2.** Any law designed to regulate Sunday activities. [From BLUE (puritanical).]

Blue Lodge. *Freemasonry.* A lodge in which the first three degrees, bearing blue decorations, are conferred.

blue mold. Any of several fungi of the genus *Penicillium,* forming a bluish growth on food and other surfaces.

Blue Mountains. **1.** A range in northeastern Oregon, extending into southeastern Washington. Highest elevation, Rock Creek Butte (9,097 feet). **2.** A range in the Eastern Highlands of New South Wales, Australia. Highest elevation, about 4,460.

Blue Nile. *Arabic* **Bahr el Az·raq** (bä'hər ăl äz'rŏk). A river rising in the highlands of central Ethiopia and flowing about 1,000 miles southeast and then northwest to Khartoum, Sudan, where it joins the White Nile, with which it forms the Nile.

blue·nose (blōō'nōz') *n.* **1.** A puritanical person. **2.** *Usually capital* **B.** A person or ship from Nova Scotia.

blue-pen·cil (blōō'pĕn'səl) *tr.v.* **-ciled, -ciling, -cils.** To edit, revise, or correct with or as with a blue pencil.

blue peter. *Nautical.* A blue flag with a white square in the center, flown to signal that a ship is ready to sail. [Probably from the name PETER.]

blue point. A type of edible oyster found chiefly off Blue Point, Great South Bay, Long Island, New York.

blue·print (blōō'prĭnt') *n.* **1.** A photographic reproduction, as of architectural plans or technical drawings, rendered as white lines on a blue background. Also called "cyanotype." **2.** Any carefully designed plan. —*tr.v.* **blueprinted, -printing, -prints. 1.** To make a blueprint of. **2.** To lay a plan for.

blue ribbon. **1.** The first prize; highest award or honor. **2.** The badge of various temperance societies. **—blue'-rib'bon** *adj.*

blue-rib·bon jury (blōō'rĭb'ən). A jury whose members have been specially selected. Also called "blue-ribbon panel."

Blue Ridge. A range of the Appalachians in the eastern United States, extending 600 miles from southern Pennsylvania to northern Georgia. Also called "Blue Ridge Mountains."

blues (blōōz) *n.* Plural in form, sometimes used with a singular verb. **1.** A state of depression or melancholy. **2.** A style of jazz evolved from southern American Negro secular songs and usually distinguished by slow tempo and flatted thirds and sevenths.

blue-sky law (blōō'skī'). A law designed to protect the public from buying fraudulent securities.

blue spruce. An evergreen tree, *Picea pungens,* of the Rocky Mountain region, having bluish-green needles.

blue·stock·ing (blōō'stŏk'ĭng) *n.* A pedantic or scholarly woman. [After the *Blue Stocking Society,* name given derisively to a predominantly female club of 18th-century London, in allusion to unconventional blue worsted stockings worn by Benjamin Stillingfleet, a member.] **—blue'stock'ing** *adj.*

blue·stone (blōō'stōn') *n.* **1.** A bluish-gray sandstone used for paving and building. **2.** Any similar stone.

blue streak. *Informal.* **1.** Anything moving very fast. **2.** A rapid and seemingly interminable stream of words.

blu·ets (blōō'ĭts) *n.* Plural in form, used with a singular or plural verb. A slender, low-growing plant, *Houstonia caerulea,* of eastern North America, having small, light-blue flowers with yellow centers. Also called "innocence," "Quaker-ladies." [French *bleuet, bluet,* diminutives of *bleu,* BLUE.]

blue vitriol. *Chemistry.* **Copper sulfate** *(see).*

blue·weed (blōō'wēd') *n.* A plant, **viper's bugloss** *(see).*

blue whale. A very large whale, *Sibbaldus musculus,* having a bluish-gray back and longitudinal grooves along the throat and belly. Also called "sulphur-bottom."

bluff[1] (blŭf) *v.* **bluffed, bluffing, bluffs.** —*tr.* **1.** To mislead, deceive, or hoodwink. **2.** To impress, deter, or intimidate by a display of confidence greater than the facts support. **3.** To try to mislead (opponents) in poker by heavy betting on a poor hand or by little or no betting on a good one. —*intr.* To feign strength when in a state of weakness, or the reverse. —*n.* **1.** The act or practice of bluffing. **2.** One who bluffs. **—call someone's bluff.** To challenge or expose someone's bluff. [Dutch *bluffen,* to boast, from Middle Dutch, to swell up (probably imitative).] **—bluff'a·ble** *adj.* **—bluff'er** *n.*

bluff[2] (blŭf) *n.* A steep headland, promontory, river bank, or cliff. —*adj.* **bluffer, bluffest. 1.** Presenting a broad, steep front. **2.** Having a rough, blunt but not unkind manner. —See Synonyms at **gruff.** [Possibly from obsolete Dutch *blaf*†, flat, broad.] **—bluff'ly** *adv.* **—bluff'ness** *n.*

blu·ing (blōō'ĭng) *n.* Also **blue·ing. 1.** Any of various coloring agents used to counteract the yellowing of laundered fabrics. **2.** A rinsing agent used to give a silver tint to graying hair.

blu·ish (blōō'ĭsh) *adj.* Also **blue·ish.** Somewhat or slightly blue. **—blu'ish·ness** *n.*

bluish green. Any of a group of colors that may vary in lightness and saturation, whose hue is more bluish than green, but not so blue as a greenish blue. **—blu'ish-green'** *adj.*

Blum (blōōm), **Léon.** 1872–1950. Premier of France (1936–37 and 1946–47).

Blu·men·bach (blōō'mən-bäkн'), **Johann Friedrich.** 1752–1840. German anthropologist; first to classify man into five races.

blun·der (blŭn'dər) *n.* A stupid and grave mistake; a clumsy, foolish act or remark. —*v.* **blundered, -dering, -ders.** —*intr.* **1.** To move awkwardly or clumsily; stumble about. **2.** To make a stupid mistake because of ignorance or confusion. —*tr.* **1.** To botch or bungle. **2.** To say stupidly or thoughtlessly. [Middle English *blund(e)ren, blond(e)ren,* to proceed blindly, bungle, probably from Old Norse *blunda,* to shut the eyes. See **bhel-**[1] in Appendix.*] **—blun'der·er** *n.* **—blun'der·ing·ly** *adv.*

blun·der·buss (blŭn'dər-bŭs') *n.* **1.** A short musket of wide bore and flaring muzzle, formerly used to scatter shot at close range. **2.** A stupid, clumsy person. [Alteration (influenced by BLUNDER) of Dutch *donderbus* : *donder,* thunder, from Middle Dutch *doner* (see **stene-** in Appendix*) + *bus,* gun, from Middle Dutch *busse,* box, tube, from Late Latin *buxis,* BOX.]

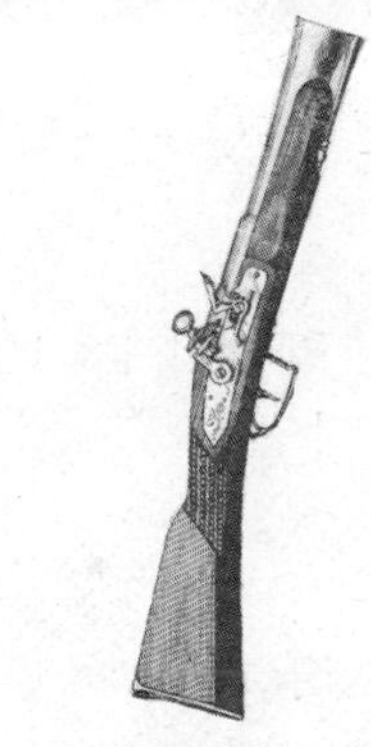

blunderbuss
Flintlock blunderbuss with walnut stock and silver mountings

blunt (blŭnt) *adj.* **blunter, bluntest. 1.** Having a thick, dull edge or end; not sharp or pointed. **2.** Having an abrupt and frank manner; brusque. **3.** Slow to understand or perceive; dull. —See Synonyms at **dull, gruff.** —*v.* **blunted, blunting, blunts.** —*tr.* **1.** To make blunt. **2.** To make less sensitive or emotional: *"Division of purpose blunted our offensive spirit"* (T.E. Lawrence). —*intr.* To become blunt. [Middle English *blont, blunt*†, dull, blunt, stupid.] **—blunt'ly** *adv.* **—blunt'ness** *n.*

blur (blûr) *v.* **blurred, blurring, blurs.** —*tr.* **1.** To make indistinct and hazy in outline or appearance; to obscure. **2.** To smear or stain; to smudge. **3.** To lessen the perception of; to dim. —*intr.* **1.** To become indistinct. **2.** To make blurs by smearing. —*n.* **1.** A smear or blot; a smudge. **2.** A hazy and indistinct image to the sight or mind. [Possibly related to BLEAR.] **—blur'ry** *adj.*

blurb (blûrb) *n.* A brief commendatory publicity notice, as on a book jacket. [Coined in 1907 by Gelett Burgess (1866–1951), American humorist and illustrator.]

blurt (blûrt) *tr.v.* **blurted, blurting, blurts.** To utter suddenly and impulsively. Often used with *out.* —*n.* A sudden utterance or statement. [Probably imitative.]

blush (blŭsh) *v.* **blushed, blushing, blushes.** —*intr.* **1.** To become suddenly red in the face from modesty, embarrassment, or shame; to flush. **2.** To become red or rosy. **3.** To feel ashamed or regretful about something. Usually used with *at* or *for.* —*tr.* **1.** To give a reddish hue to. **2.** To reveal by blushing. —*n.* **1.** A sudden reddening of the face from modesty, embarrassment, or shame: *"There's a blush for won't, and a blush for shan't,/ And a blush for having done it"* (Keats). **2.** A red or rosy color. —*adj.* Having the rosy color of a blush. **—at** (or **on**) **first blush.** At first sight or glance. [Middle English *blusshen, blisshen,* Old English *blyscan.* See **bhel-**[1] in Appendix.*] **—blush'er** *n.* **—blush'ful** *adj.* **—blush'ing·ly** *adv.*

blus·ter (blŭs'tər) *v.* **-tered, -tering, -ters.** —*intr.* **1.** To blow in loud, violent gusts, as wind in a storm. **2.** To speak noisily and boastfully. **3.** To threaten ineffectually. —*tr.* To force or bully with swaggering threats. —*n.* **1.** A violent, gusty wind. **2.** Turbulence or noisy confusion. **3.** Swaggering talk. [Middle English *blusteren,* probably akin to Low German *blüstern.*] **—blus'ter·er** *n.* **—blus'ter·y, blus'ter·ous** *adj.*

blvd. boulevard.

Bly, Nellie. See Elizabeth **Seaman.**

b.m. **1.** board measure. **2.** bowel movement.

B.M. **1.** Bachelor of Medicine. **2.** Bachelor of Music. **3.** British Museum.

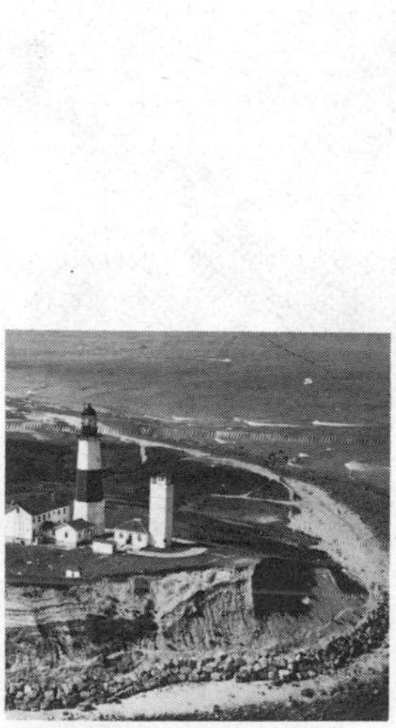

bluff[2]
Lighthouse on a bluff of Montauk Point, eastern Long Island, New York

B.M.E. **1.** Bachelor of Mechanical Engineering. **2.** Bachelor of Mining Engineering.

B.Mus. Bachelor of Music.

bn., Bn. **1.** baron. **2.** battalion.

B.N.A. British North America.

B'nai B'rith (bnā' brĭth'). A Jewish international fraternal society. [Hebrew *bənē bərith,* "sons of the covenant."]

bo (bō) *n., pl.* **bos.** *Slang.* A fellow; pal. Often used as a form of address. [Probably short for HOBO or BOZO.]

b.o. **1.** box office. **2.** branch office. **3.** buyer's option.

bo·a (bō'ə) *n.* **1.** Any of various large, nonvenomous, chiefly tropical snakes of the family Boidae, which includes the pythons, anaconda, boa constrictor, and other snakes that coil around and crush their prey. **2.** A long, fluffy scarf made of fur, feathers, or other soft material. [New Latin *Boa* (genus), from Latin *boa*†, a large water snake.]

Bo·ab·dil (bō'əb-dēl'). Original name, Abu Abdullah. Last Moorish king of Granada (1482–83 and 1486–92).

boa constrictor. A large, nonvenomous snake, *Constrictor constrictor,* of tropical America, having brown markings.

Bo·ad·i·ce·a (bō-ăd'ə-sē'ə). Also **Bou·dic·ca** (bōō-dĭk'ə). Died A.D. 62. British queen; led an unsuccessful revolt against the Romans.

Bo·a·ner·ges[1] (bō'ə-nûr'jēz). The name given by Jesus to the Apostles John and James. Mark 3:17.

Bo·a·ner·ges[2] (bō'ə-nûr'jēz) *n.* Plural in form, used with a singular verb. A vociferous, loud-voiced preacher or orator. [Hebrew *bənē reghesh,* "sons of thunder."]

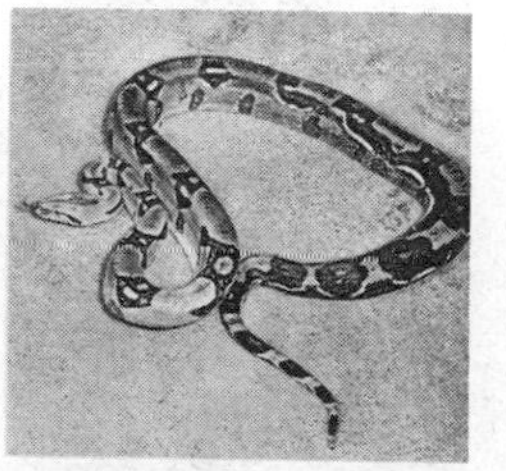

boa constrictor

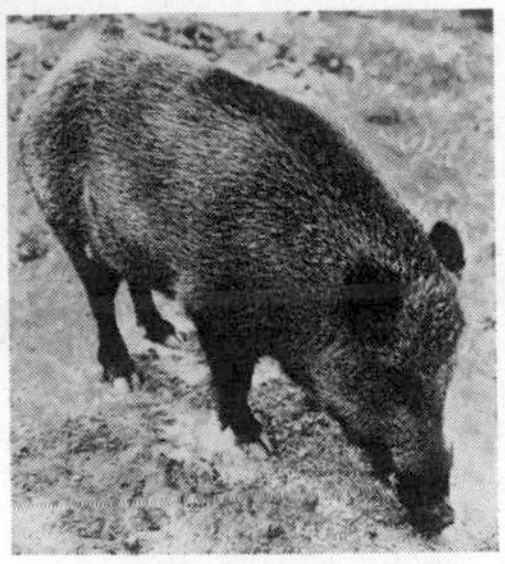

boar
A wild boar

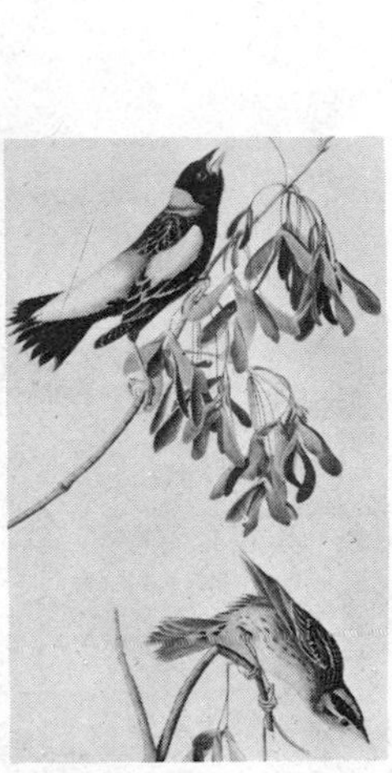

male female
bobolink

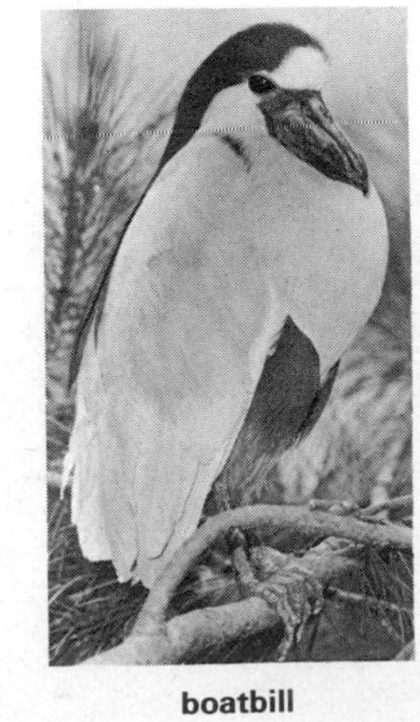

boatbill

boar (bôr, bōr) *n.* **1.** Any uncastrated male pig. **2.** A wild pig, *Sus scrofa,* of Eurasia and northern Africa, having dense, dark bristles. It is the ancestor of the domestic hog. Also called "wild boar." [Middle English *bor,* Old English *bār,* from West Germanic *bairoz* (unattested).]

board (bôrd, bōrd) *n. Abbr.* **bd. 1.** A long, flat slab of sawed lumber; plank. **2.** A flat piece of wood or similarly rigid material, adapted for a special use. **3.** A flat surface on which a game is played. **4.** The hard pasteboard cover of a book. **5.** *Plural.* A theater stage. Used with *the.* **6. a.** A table, especially one set for serving food. **b.** Food or meals collectively: *board and lodging.* **7.** A table at which official meetings are held; council table. **8.** An organized body of administrators: *a board of trustees.* **9.** An electrical-equipment panel. **10.** A border or edge. **11.** *Plural.* The wooden structure enclosing an ice-hockey rink. **12.** *Nautical.* **a.** The side of a ship. **b.** A leeboard. **c.** A centerboard. —**across the board.** *Informal.* **1.** Designating a bet that a horse or dog will win, place, or show. **2.** Affecting all members or divisions equally. —**go by the board. 1.** To be swept overboard. **2.** To be ruined, unnoticed, or ignored. —**on board.** Aboard. —**tread the boards.** To perform on or as if on a theater stage. —*v.* **boarded, boarding, boards.** —*tr.* **1.** To cover or close with boards. Used with *up: board up a door.* **2.** To furnish with meals in return for pay. **3.** To house where board is furnished. **4.** To enter or go aboard (a vehicle or ship). **5.** To come alongside (a ship). **6.** *Obsolete.* To approach. —*intr.* To receive meals in return for pay. [Middle English *bord,* Old English *bord,* plank, table, border, ship's side. See **bherdh-** in Appendix.*]

board·er (bôr′dər, bōr′-) *n.* **1.** One who pays a homeowner a stipulated sum for regular meals or meals and lodging. **2.** A person who is detailed to go aboard an enemy ship.

board foot *pl.* **board feet.** *Abbr.* **bd. ft.** A unit of lumber measurement equal to one foot square by one inch thick.

boarding house. Also **board·ing·house** (bôr′dĭng-hous′, bōr′-). A private home that takes in paying guests and provides meals and lodging.

boarding school. A school where pupils are provided with meals and lodging. Compare **day school.**

board measure. *Abbr.* **b.m.** Measurement in board feet.

board of trade. 1. An association of bankers and businessmen to promote common commercial interests. **2.** *Capital* **B,** *capital* **T.** A British governmental committee dealing with problems of trade and commerce.

board rule. A measuring stick for determining board feet.

board·walk (bôrd′wôk′, bōrd′-) *n.* **1.** A walk made of wooden planks. **2.** A promenade, especially of planks, along a beach or waterfront.

boar·fish (bôr′fĭsh′, bōr′-) *n., pl.* **boarfish** or **-fishes.** Any of several marine fishes of the genus *Antigonia,* having a deep, flattened body and bright-red coloring.

boar·hound (bôr′hound′, bōr′-) *n.* A large dog, such as the Great Dane, used for hunting wild boars.

boar·ish (bôr′ĭsh, bōr′-) *adj.* Like a boar; coarse; lecherous; brutish. —**boar′ish·ly** *adv.* —**boar′ish·ness** *n.*

Bo·as (bō′ăz′), **Franz.** 1858–1942. German-born American anthropologist; studied North American Indian tribes.

boast[1] (bōst) *v.* **boasted, boasting, boasts.** —*intr.* **1.** To brag about one's own accomplishments, talents, or possessions. **2.** To speak with pride. Often used with *of.* —*tr.* **1.** To brag about with excessive pride. **2.** To take pride in, or be enhanced by, the possession of. See Usage note below. —*n.* **1.** An instance of bragging. **2.** That which one brags about. [Middle English *bosten,* from *bost,* bragging, threat, perhaps from Germanic, akin to German dialectal *bauste(r)n,* to swell. See **beu-**[1] in Appendix.*] —**boast′er** *n.* —**boast′ing·ly** *adv.*

Synonyms: *boast, brag, crow, vaunt. Boast* is the most general of the verbs for the expression of vanity, primarily by vocal means. *Brag,* used in more informal contexts, implies exaggerated claims, blatancy, and often an air of insolence. *Crow,* also informal in tone, stresses exultation and noisy rejoicing over a victory or achievement. *Vaunt* is distinctive in emphasizing ostentatious display as strongly as vocal extravagance; it is appropriate to formal usage and often appears as the participle *vaunted,* used as an attributive adjective.

Usage: *Boast* (verb), in its transitive sense *to take pride in possessing,* is well established but distasteful to some because of the association with the primary sense of boasting. As an example in writing, *The college boasts one of the finest auditoriums in New York* is acceptable to 55 per cent of the Usage Panel.

boast[2] (bōst) *tr.v.* **boasted, boasting, boasts.** To shape or form (stone) roughly with a broad chisel. [Origin unknown.]

boast·ful (bōst′fəl) *adj.* Tending to boast or brag. —**boast′ful·ly** *adv.* —**boast′ful·ness** *n.*

boat (bōt) *n.* **1. a.** A relatively small, usually open craft of a size that might be carried on a ship. **b.** An inland vessel of any size. **2.** A ship. Not in nautical usage. **3.** A dish shaped like a boat: *a gravy boat.* —**in the same boat.** In the same situation. —*v.* **boated, boating, boats.** —*intr.* To travel by boat. —*tr.* **1.** To transport by boat. **2.** To place in a boat. [Middle English *bo(o)t,* from Old English *bāt* and Old Norse *bātr.* See **bheid-** in Appendix.*]

boat·bill (bōt′bĭl′) *n.* A tropical American wading bird, *Cochlearius cochlearius,* having a large bill shaped like an inverted boat. Also called "boat-billed heron."

boat·er (bō′tər) *n.* **1.** One who boats. **2.** A stiff straw hat with a flat crown.

boat hook. A pole with a metal point and hook at one end, used to maneuver boats and other floating objects.

boat·house (bōt′hous′) *n.* A house in which boats are kept.

boat·load (bōt′lōd′) *n.* The number of passengers or quantity of cargo that a boat can safely carry.

boat·man (bōt′mən) *n., pl.* **-men** (-mĭn). One who works on, deals with, or operates boats. —**boat′man·ship′** *n.*

boat·swain (bō′sən) *n.* Also **bo's'n, bo·sun.** A warrant officer or petty officer in charge of a ship's deck crew, rigging, anchors, and cables, who has a whistle as his badge of office. [Middle English *botswein,* Old English *bātswān* : BOAT + SWAIN.]

boatswain's chair. A short board secured by ropes and used as a seat by sailors when working aloft or over a ship's side.

boat-tailed grackle (bōt′tāld′). A bird, *Cassidix mexicanus,* of the southern United States and Mexico, having a long tail, and glossy black plumage in the male.

boat train. A train scheduled to meet a boat.

Bo·az (bō′ăz). The husband of Ruth. Ruth 2:4.

bob[1] (bŏb) *n.* **1.** A quick jerking movement of the head or body. **2.** A tap or a light blow. **3.** Any small knoblike pendent object: *a plumb bob.* **4.** A fishing float or cork. **5.** A small lock or curl of hair. **6.** A short haircut on a woman or child. **7.** The docked tail of a horse. **8.** A bobsled or a bob skate. —*v.* **bobbed, bobbing, bobs.** —*intr.* **1.** To move up and down: *The cork bobbed on the water.* **2.** To curtsy or bow. **3.** To grab at floating or hanging objects with the teeth. Usually used with *for: He bobbed for apples.* **4.** To fish with a bob. —*tr.* **1.** To move (especially the head) up and down. **2.** To hit lightly and quickly; to tap. **3.** To cut short: *She bobbed her hair.* —**bob up.** To appear suddenly, as a cork emerging from under water. [As "a pendent object," Middle English *bobbe(,* cluster of flowers or fruit. As verb "to move up and down," Middle English *bobben* (probably expressive).] —**bob′ber** *n.*

bob[2] (bŏb) *n., pl.* **bob.** *British Slang.* A shilling. [Origin unknown.]

Bo·ba·dill·a (bō′vä-*thē*′lyä), **Francisco de.** Spanish colonial administrator; viceroy of the Indies (1499–1502).

bob·bin (bŏb′ĭn) *n.* **1.** A spool or reel that holds thread or yarn for spinning, weaving, knitting, sewing, or making lace. **2.** Narrow braid used as trimming. [French *bobine* (expressive).]

bob·bi·net (bŏb′ə-nĕt′) *n.* A machine-woven net fabric with hexagonal meshes. [BOBBI(N) + NET.]

bobbin lace. An intricate handmade lace made by interlacing thread around small notched pins or bobbins stuck into a pillow according to a certain pattern. Also called "pillow lace."

bob·ble (bŏb′əl) *v.* **-bled, -bling, -bles.** —*intr.* To bob up and down. —*tr.* To fumble (a ball, for example). —*n.* A fumble or a miss; a blunder. [Frequentative of BOB (verb).]

bob·by (bŏb′ē) *n., pl.* **-bies.** *British Slang.* A policeman. [After Sir Robert PEEL, who was Home Secretary of England when the Metropolitan Police Force was created (1828).]

bobby pin. A small metal hair clip with the ends pressed tightly together. [From BOB (lock of hair).]

bobby socks. Also **bobby sox.** *Informal.* Ankle socks worn by girls or women. [From the name *Bobby,* pet form for ROBERT (influenced by BOBBY PIN).]

bob·by·sox·er (bŏb′ē-sŏk′sər) *n.* Also **bobby soxer.** *Informal.* A teen-age girl of the 1940's who followed current fads. [From the BOBBY SOCKS worn by the teen-age girls.]

bob·cat (bŏb′kăt′) *n.* A wild cat, *Lynx rufus,* of North America, having spotted reddish-brown fur, tufted ears, and a short tail. Also called "bay lynx." [From its bobbed tail.]

bob·o·link (bŏb′ə-lĭngk′) *n.* An American migratory songbird, *Dolichonyx oryzivorus,* of which the male has black, white, and yellowish plumage. Also called "reedbird," "ricebird." [Originally *bobolincon;* imitative of its call.]

Bo·bruisk (bŭ-brōō′ĭsk). A city of Byelorussia, on the Berezina River, 90 miles southeast of Minsk. Population, 115,000.

bob skate. A skate having two parallel bearing edges. [BOB(SLED) + SKATE.]

bob·sled (bŏb′slĕd′) *n.* **1.** A long racing sled with a steering mechanism controlling the front runners. **2. a.** A long sled made of two shorter sleds joined in tandem. **b.** Either of these two smaller sleds. —*intr.v.* **bobsledded, -sledding, -sleds.** To ride or race in a bobsled. [From BOB (short).]

bob·stay (bŏb′stā′) *n. Nautical.* A rope or chain used to steady the bowsprit. [From BOB (up-and-down motion).]

bob·tail (bŏb′tāl′) *n.* **1.** A short or shortened tail. **2.** A horse or other animal having such a tail. —*adj.* **1.** Having the tail short or cut short; abbreviated; curtailed. —*tr.v.* **bobtailed, -tailing, -tails. 1.** To cut the tail of (a horse or other animal); to dock. **2.** To cut short; abbreviate.

bob·white (bŏb-hwīt′) *n.* A small North American quail, *Colinus virginianus,* having brown plumage with white markings. Sometimes called "partridge." [Imitative of its call.]

bo·cac·cio (bə-kä′chō, -chē-ō′) *n., pl.* **-cios.** A rockfish, *Sebastodes paucispinis,* of American Pacific waters. [American Spanish (influenced by Giovanni BOCCACCIO), from Spanish *bocacha,* big mouth, augmentative of *boca,* mouth, from Latin *bucca.* See **beu-**[1] in Appendix.*]

Boc·cac·cio (bō-kä′chē-ō′; *Italian* bōk-kät′chō), **Giovanni.** 1313–1375. Italian poet, diplomat, and author.

Boc·che·ri·ni (bōk′kā-rē′nē), **Luigi.** 1743–1805. Italian composer and violoncellist.

Boche (bŏsh, bôsh) *n. Slang.* Also **boche.** A German. Used disparagingly. [French, short for *alboche* : probably *al-,* from *allemand,* German (see **allemande**) + *caboche,* pate, hard skull, from Old French *caboce,* head (see **cabbage**).]

Bo·chum (bō′KHōōm). A city of West Germany situated in the Ruhr, nine miles east of Essen. Population, 362,000.

bock beer (bŏk). A strong dark beer, the first that is drawn

ă pat/ā pay/âr care/ä father/b bib/ch church/d deed/ĕ pet/ē be/f fife/g gag/h hat/hw which/ĭ pit/ī pie/îr pier/j judge/k kick/l lid, needle/m mum/n no, sudden/ng thing/ŏ pot/ō toe/ô paw, for/oi noise/ou out/ōō took/ōō boot/p pop/r roar/s sauce/sh ship, dish/

from the vats in springtime. Also called "bock." [German *Bockbier,* from (Munich dialect) *Oambock, Ambock,* variants of *Eimbecker Bier;* first made at *Eimbeck,* city in Hanover.]

bo·da·cious (bō-dā′shəs) *adj. Slang.* Intrepidly bold or daring; audacious. [Blend of BOLD and AUDACIOUS.]

bode[1] (bōd) *tr.v.* **boded, boding, bodes. 1.** To be an omen of: *His ill will bodes no good.* **2.** *Obsolete.* To predict; foretell. —See Synonyms at **foretell.** [Middle English *boden,* Old English *bodian,* to announce, proclaim, from *boda,* messenger. See **bheudh-** in Appendix.*]

bode[2]. Alternate past tense of **bide.**

bo·de·ga (bō-dā′gə) *n.* **1.** A wineshop, sometimes combined with a grocery. **2.** A warehouse for wine storage. [Spanish, from Latin *apothēca,* from Greek *apothēkē,* storehouse, from *apotithenai,* to put away : *apo-,* away + *tithenai,* to put, place (see **dhē-**[1] in Appendix*).]

Bo·den·see. The German name for Lake of **Constance.**

bo·dhi·satt·va (bō′dĭ-sŭt′və) *n. Buddhism.* One who, out of compassion, forgoes nirvana in order to save others. [Sanskrit, "one whose essence is enlightenment" : *bodhi,* enlightenment, from *bodhati,* he awakes (see **bheudh-** in Appendix*) + *sattva,* essence, from *sat, sant,* existing (see **es-** in Appendix*).]

bod·ice (bŏd′ĭs) *n.* **1.** The fitted part of a dress that extends from the waist to the shoulder. **2.** A woman's laced outer garment, worn like a vest over a blouse. **3.** *Obsolete.* A corset. [Originally *bodies,* plural of BODY.]

bod·ied (bŏd′ēd) *adj.* **1.** Having a body. **2.** Having a specified kind of body. Used in combination: *strong-bodied.*

bod·i·less (bŏd′ē-lĭs, bŏd′ə-) *adj.* Having no body, form, or substance; incorporeal. —**bod′i·less·ness** *n.*

bod·i·ly (bŏd′ə-lē) *adj.* **1.** Of, pertaining to, within, or exhibited by the body: *bodily organs.* **2.** Physical as opposed to mental or spiritual: *bodily welfare.* —*adv.* **1.** In the flesh; in person: *He was bodily but not mentally present.* **2.** As a complete physical entity: *He carried her bodily from the room.*

bod·ing (bō′dĭng) *n.* An omen or foreboding, especially of evil.

bod·kin (bŏd′kĭn) *n.* **1.** A small, sharply pointed instrument for making holes in fabric or leather. **2.** A blunt needle for pulling tape or ribbon through a series of loops or a hem. **3.** A long hairpin, usually with an ornamental head. **4.** *Printing.* An awl or pick for extracting letters from set type. **5.** *Obsolete.* A dagger or stiletto. [Middle English *boidekyn*†.]

Bo·do·ni (bō-dō′nē) *n. Printing.* A style of typeface. [Designed by Giambattista *Bodoni* (1740–1813), Italian printer.]

bod·y (bŏd′ē) *n., pl.* **-ies. 1. a.** The entire material structure and substance of an organism, especially of a human being or an animal. **b.** A corpse or carcass. **2. a.** The trunk or torso of a human being or animal. **b.** The part of a garment covering the torso. **3.** *Law.* **a.** A person. **b.** A group of individuals regarded as an entity; corporation. **4.** A number of persons, concepts, or things regarded collectively; a group: *We walked out in a body.* **5.** The main or central part of something, as: **a.** The nave of a church. **b.** The content of a book or document exclusive of prefatory matter, codicils, indexes, and the like. **c.** The passenger- and cargo-carrying part of an aircraft, ship, or vehicle. **d.** The sound box of a musical instrument. **6.** Any bounded aggregate of matter: *a body of water.* **7.** Consistency of substance, as in paint, textiles, wine, and the like: *a sauce with body.* **8.** *Printing.* The part of a block of type underlying the impression surface. —*tr.v.* **bodied, -ying, -ies. 1.** To furnish with a body. **2.** To give shape to. Usually followed by *forth: "Imagination bodies forth the form of things unknown."* (Shakespeare). [Middle English *body,* Old English *bodig,* from Germanic *bot-* (unattested), container.]

Synonyms: *body, corpse, remains, carcass, cadaver. Body* denotes the physical organism of a person or animal, alive or dead. *Corpse* and *remains* apply to the body of a dead person. *Carcass* primarily denotes the body of a dead animal; it is applied to a person, alive or dead, only derogatorily or humorously. *Cadaver* is a corpse used for dissection and study. *Remains* is considered genteel by some; others find its literal connotations clinical and rather grisly.

body corporate. *Law.* A **corporation** *(see).*

bod·y·guard (bŏd′ē-gärd′) *n.* **1.** A person or group of persons, usually armed, responsible for the physical safety of one or more specific persons. **2.** An escort or retinue.

body politic. The people collectively of a politically organized nation or state: *"a body politique never dieth"* (Milton).

body snatcher. A person who steals corpses from graves.

Boe·o·tia (bē-ō′shə). An ancient province of southeastern Greece, on the long peninsula between the Gulf of Corinth and the Straits of Euboea. Principal city, Thebes.

Boe·o·tian (bē-ō′shən) *adj.* **1.** Of or pertaining to Boeotia or its inhabitants. **2.** Stupid; boorish. —*n.* **1.** An inhabitant of Boeotia. **2.** A stupid, boorish person.

Boer (bōr, bôr, bo͝or) *n.* A Dutch colonist or a descendant of a Dutch colonist in South Africa. —*adj.* Of or pertaining to the Boers. [Dutch, "peasant," "farmer," from Middle Dutch *gheboer.* See **bheu-** in Appendix.*]

Boer War. A war (1899–1902) in which Great Britain defeated the Boers of the Orange Free State and the Transvaal Republic in South Africa. Also called "South African War."

Bo·e·thi·us (bō-ē′thē-əs), **Anicius Manlius Severinus.** Roman Christian philosopher of the late fifth and early sixth centuries A.D; translated Aristotle.

boeuf bourguignon. *French.* **Beef bourguignon** *(see).*

Bo·fors gun (bō′fôrz′). A double-barreled, automatic antiaircraft gun. [First made at the munitions works in *Bofors,* Sweden.]

bog (bôg, bŏg) *n.* Soft, waterlogged ground; a marsh; swamp. —*v.* **bogged, bogging, bogs.** —*tr.* To hinder; slow; impede. Often used with *down.* —*intr.* To be hindered and slowed. Usually used with *down.* [Scottish and Irish Gaelic *bogach,* from *bog,* soft. See **bheug-**[3] in Appendix.*] —**bog′gish** *adj.* —**bog′gish·ness** *n.*

bog asphodel. Either of two related bog plants, *Narthecium americanum,* of the southeastern United States, or *N. ossifragum,* of Europe, having a cluster of yellow flowers.

bog·bean (bôg′bēn′, bŏg′-) *n.* A plant, the **buckbean** *(see).*

bo·gey (bō′gē) *n., pl.* **-geys. 1.** Variant of **bogy** (hobgoblin). **2.** *Golf.* **a.** An estimated standard score. **b.** One stroke over par on a hole. **3.** *Military Slang.* Any unidentified flying aircraft.

bo·gey·man. Variant of **boogieman.**

bog·gle (bŏg′əl) *v.* **-gled, -gling, -gles.** —*intr.* **1.** To hesitate or evade as if in fear or doubt. **2.** To shy away from; start with fright. —*tr.* To make a botch of; bungle. —See Synonyms at **object.** —*n.* The act of boggling. [Probably from *boggle,* Northern dialectal variant of BOGLE.] —**bog′gler** *n.*

bog·gy (bô′gē, bŏg′ē) *adj.* **-gier, -giest. 1.** Like a bog; swampy. **2.** Full of bogs. —**bog′gi·ness** *n.*

bog hole. A hole containing soft mud or quicksand.

bo·gie[1] (bō′gē) *n.* Also **bo·gy. 1.** A railroad car or locomotive undercarriage with two, four, or six wheels that swivels so that curves may be negotiated. Also called "bogie truck." **2.** One of several wheels or supporting and aligning rollers inside the tread of a tractor or tank. In this sense, also called "bogie wheel." [Origin unknown.]

bo·gie[2]. Variant of **bogy** (hobgoblin).

bo·gle (bō′gəl) *n.* A hobgoblin, a **bogy** *(see).* [Scottish *bogill,* from Welsh *bygel,* ghost, or *bwgwl,* menace, akin to Cornish *buccaboo,* the devil, BUGABOO.]

Bo·gor (bō′gôr). An industrial city of Java, Indonesia, about 35 miles south of Djakarta. Population, 124,000.

Bo·go·tá (bō′gə-tä′; *Spanish* bô-gô-tä′). The capital and largest city of Colombia, situated in the Cordillera Central at an elevation of 8,660 feet. Population, 1,697,000.

bog rosemary. A low-growing evergreen shrub, *Andromeda glaucophylla,* of northern regions, growing in wet ground, and having small pink flowers. Also called "moorwort."

bog·trot·ter (bôg′trŏt′ər, bŏg′-) *n.* **1.** A person who lives in or frequents bogs. **2.** An Irishman. Used disparagingly.

bo·gus (bō′gəs) *adj.* Counterfeit; fake. [From *bogus,* a device for making counterfeit money, perhaps alteration of BOGLE.]

bog·wood (bôg′wo͝od′, bŏg′-) *n.* Wood that has been preserved in a peat bog.

bo·gy[1] (bō′gē) *n., pl.* **-gies.** Also **bo·gey, bo·gie. 1.** An evil or mischievous spirit; hobgoblin. Also called "bogle." **2.** Something that causes annoyance or harassment. [Perhaps related to BOGLE.] —**bo′gy·ism′** *n.*

bo·gy[2]. Variant of **bogie** (railroad car undercarriage).

bo·gy·man. Variant of **boogieman.**

Boh. Bohemia; Bohemian.

bo·hea (bō-hē′) *n.* A black Chinese tea. The name originally referred to the choicest grade but later was applied to an inferior variety. [Chinese (Fukien dialect) *bu-i,* corresponding to Mandarin Chinese *wu*[3]*i*[2], after *Wu-i Shan,* a range of hills in northern Fukien Province, where the black tea was grown.]

Bo·he·mi·a[1] (bō-hē′mē-ə). *Czechoslovakian* **Če·chy** (chĕKH′ē). *Abbr.* **Boh.** A region and former province of western Czechoslovakia, 20,100 miles in area. [From Latin *Boihaemum,* "home of the Boii" : Celtic *Boii,* "fighters," name of the Celtic people who originally inhabited this region (see **bhei-**[2] in Appendix*) + Latin *-haemum,* "home," from Germanic (see **kei-**[1] in Appendix*).]

Bo·he·mia[2] (bō-hē′mē-ə) *n.* Also **bo·he·mia. 1.** A community of persons with artistic or literary tastes who adopt manners and mores conspicuously different from those expected or approved of by the majority of society. **2.** The district in which they live.

Bo·he·mi·an[1] (bō-hē′mē-ən) *n. Abbr.* **Boh. 1.** A native or inhabitant of Bohemia. **2.** A Gypsy. **3.** *Archaic.* The language of the Czechs. [Sense 2 from the belief that Gypsies came from Bohemia.] —**Bo·he′mi·an** *adj.*

Bo·he·mi·an[2] (bō-hē′mē-ən) *n.* Also **bo·he·mi·an.** A person with artistic or literary interests who disregards conventional standards of behavior. [From BOHEMIAN (Gypsy).] —**Bo·he′mi·an** *adj.* —**Bo·he′mi·an·ism′** *n.*

Bohemian Brethren. A religious society organized in the 15th century by the Hussites.

Bohemian Forest. *German* **Böh·mer·wald** (bœ′mər-vält). A heavily forested mountain region of central Europe, on the border of West Germany and Czechoslovakia.

Bo·hol (bō′hôl). An island, 1,492 square miles in area, of the central Philippines, at the northern end of the Mindanao Sea.

Bohr (bōr), **Niels Henrik David.** 1885–1962. Danish theoretical physicist; major contributor to quantum theory and to the theory of nuclear reactions and nuclear fission.

Bohr theory. A model of atomic structure, in which electrons travel around the nucleus in orbits determined by quantum conditions on angular momentum. [After Niels BOHR.]

bo·hunk (bō′hŭngk) *n. Slang.* A person from east-central Europe, especially a laborer. Used disparagingly. Also shortened to "hunky." [BO(HEMIAN) + HUNG(ARIAN).]

boil[1] (boil) *v.* **boiled, boiling, boils.** —*intr.* **1.** To vaporize a liquid by the application of heat. **2.** To reach the **boiling point** *(see).* **3.** To undergo the action of boiling; especially, to cook by boiling. **4.** To be in a state of agitation, as boiling water; seethe. **5.** To be greatly excited, as with rage or passion. —*tr.* **1.** To heat to the boiling point. **2.** To cook or clean by boiling.

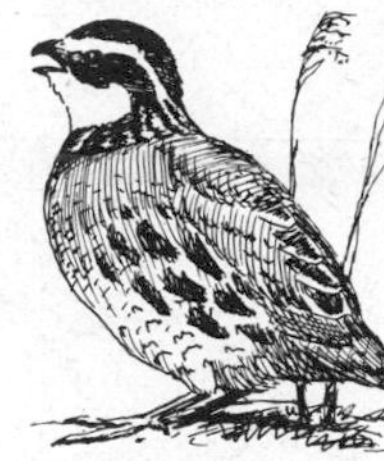

bobwhite

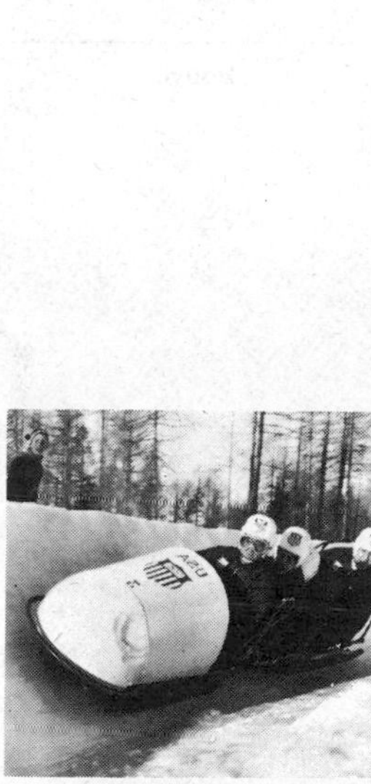

bobsled
U.S. team competing in the 1956 Olympics in the Dolomites of northeastern Italy

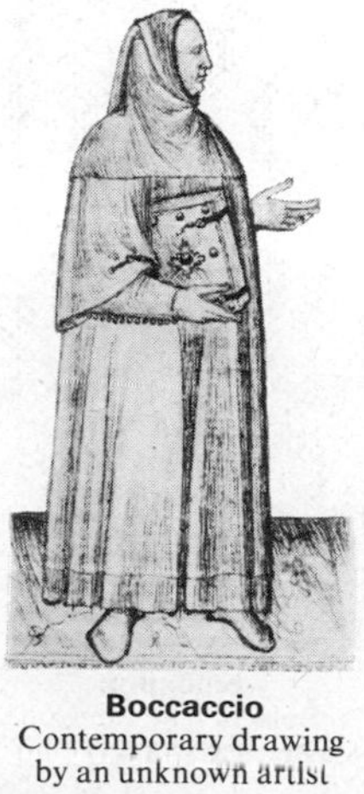

Boccaccio
Contemporary drawing by an unknown artist

3. To separate by evaporation as a result of boiling. **—boil away.** To evaporate by boiling. **—boil down. 1.** To reduce in bulk or size by boiling. **2.** To condense or summarize. **—boil over. 1.** To overflow while boiling. **2.** To explode in rage or passion. *—n.* The state, condition, or act of boiling. [Middle English *boillen,* from Old French *bo(u)illir,* from Latin *bullire,* to bubble, boil. See **beu-¹** in Appendix.*]

Synonyms: *boil, simmer, seethe, stew.* All of these verbs have physical senses and related figurative ones. *Boil* refers to heating up to the vaporizing (boiling) point, with consequent bubbling up of gases; figuratively, it pertains to the act of being stirred by intense emotion, especially anger. *Simmer* refers to the less agitated state of heating to or near the boiling point, and figuratively to being stirred by pent-up anger. *Seethe,* a strong term, emphasizes in both senses the turbulence of steady boiling at high temperature. *Stew* refers to slow, gentle boiling and to emotional upset that is persistent but not violent in expression.

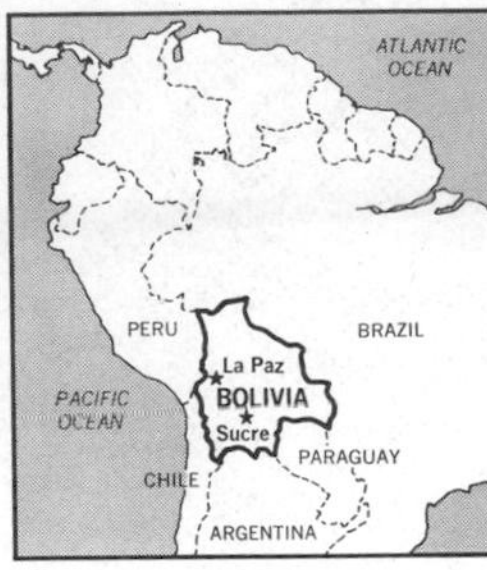

Bolivia

boil² (boil) *n.* A painful, pus-filled swelling of the skin and subcutaneous tissue caused by bacterial infection. Also called "furuncle." Compare **carbuncle.** [Middle English *bile, bule, boyl,* Old English *býl, býle.* See **beu-¹** in Appendix.*]

Boi·leau-Des·pré·aux (bwȧ-lō′dā-prā-ō′), **Nicolas.** 1636–1711. French poet and critic; arbiter of classicism.

boil·er (boi′lər) *n.* **1.** An enclosed vessel in which water is heated and circulated, either as hot water or as steam, for heating or power. **2.** A container for boiling liquids, such as a kettle or double boiler. **3.** A storage tank for hot water.

boil·er·mak·er (boi′lər-mā′kər) *n.* **1.** One who makes or repairs boilers. **2.** *Slang.* A drink of whiskey with beer as a chaser.

boil·er·plate (boi′lər-plāt′) *n.* **1.** A steel plate used in making the shells of steam boilers. **2.** *Journalism.* Material, such as syndicated features and sometimes repeated items like the masthead, available in plate or mat form.

boiling point. 1. *Abbr.* **bp, b.p.** The temperature at which a liquid boils, especially under standard atmospheric conditions. **2.** *Informal.* The point at which a person loses his temper.

Bois de Bou·logne (bwä′ də bo͞o-lōn′; *French* bwäd-bo͞o-lôn′y′). A park in Paris, France, 2,155 acres in area.

bois de rose (bwä′ də rōz′). Grayish red. See **color.** [French, "rosewood."]

Boi·se (boi′zē, -sē). The capital and largest city of Idaho, situated in the Boise River valley, in the southwestern part of the state. Population, 52,000.

Bois-le-Duc. The French name for **'s Hertogenbosch.**

bois·ter·ous (boi′stər-əs, -strəs) *adj.* **1.** Rough and stormy; violent and turbulent. **2.** Loud, noisy, and unrestrained. —See Synonyms at **vociferous.** [Middle English *boistres,* variant of *boist(e)ous*†, rude, fierce, stout.] **—bois′ter·ous·ly** *adv.* **—bois′ter·ous·ness** *n.*

Bo·i·to (bō′ē-tō′), **Arrigo.** 1842–1918. Italian operatic composer, librettist, and novelist.

Boj·a·dor, Cape (bŏj′ə-dôr). A cape on the west-central coast of Spanish Sahara, northwestern Africa.

Bo·kha·ra. See **Bukhara.**

Bol. Bolivia.

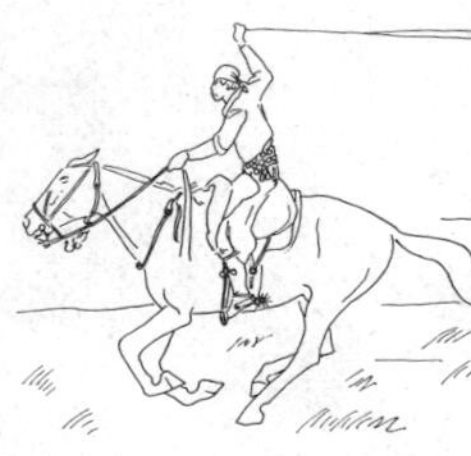
bola
Argentine Gaucho preparing to release bola

bo·la (bō′lə) *n.* Also **bo·las** (-ləs). A rope with weights attached, used in South America to catch cattle or game by entangling the legs. [American Spanish *bolas,* plural of Spanish *bola,* ball, from Latin *bulla,* bubble, round object. See **beu-¹** in Appendix.*]

bold (bōld) *adj.* **bolder, boldest. 1.** Fearless and daring; courageous. **2.** Requiring or exhibiting courage and bravery. **3.** Unduly forward and brazen in manner. **4.** Clear and distinct to the eye; standing out prominently: *a bold handwriting.* **5.** Abrupt; steep, as a cliff. **6.** Designating boldface type. —See Synonyms at **brave, shameless. —make bold.** To take the liberty; dare. [Middle English *bold,* Old English *bald, beald.* See **bhel-²** in Appendix.*] **—bold′ly** *adv.* **—bold′ness** *n.*

bold·face (bōld′fās′) *n. Abbr.* **bf, bf., b.f., bld.** *Printing.* Type cut with thick, heavy lines so as to give a conspicuous black impression. *—adj. Abbr.* **bf, bf., b.f., bld.** Printed in boldface. *—tr.v.* **boldfaced, -facing, -faces. 1.** To mark (copy) for printing in boldface. **2.** To print or set in boldface.

bold-faced (bōld′fāst′) *adj.* **1.** Impudent; brazen. **2. a.** Printed or set in boldface. **b.** Marked for printing in boldface.

bole¹ (bōl) *n.* The trunk of a tree. [Middle English, from Old Norse *bolr.* See **bhel-²** in Appendix.*]

bole² (bōl) *n.* Moderate reddish brown. See **color.** [Middle English, a red clay, from Medieval Latin *bōlus,* clod of earth, BOLUS.] **—bole** *adj.*

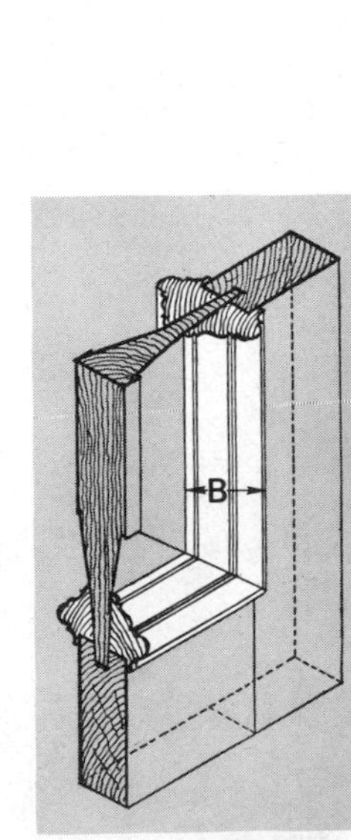

bolection
Bolection molding on a paneled wooden door

bo·lec·tion (bō-lĕk′shən) *n.* A molding that projects outward from the surface of a panel. [Origin unknown.]

bo·le·ro (bō-lâr′ō) *n., pl.* **-ros. 1.** A short jacket, usually with no front fastening, worn by both men and women. **2.** A Spanish dance in triple meter. **3.** The music for this dance. [Spanish, apparently from *bola,* ball. See **bola.**]

bo·le·tus (bō-lē′təs) *n., pl.* **-tuses** or **-ti** (-tī′). Also **bo·lete** (bō′lēt). Any fungus of the genus *Boletus,* having an umbrella-shaped cap with spore-bearing tubules on the underside. Some species are poisonous and others edible. [New Latin *Boletus,* from Latin *bōlētus*†, fungus.]

Bol·eyn (bo͝ol′ĭn, bō-lĭn′), **Anne.** 1507–1536. Queen of England; married (1533) to Henry VIII as his second wife; mother of Elizabeth I; beheaded.

bo·lide (bō′līd) *n.* A meteoric fireball. [French, from Latin *bolis,* from Greek *bolis*†, missile.]

Bol·ing·broke. See **Henry IV** of England.

bol·i·var (bŏl′ə-vər; *Spanish* bō-lē′vär) *n., pl.* **-vars** or *Spanish* **bolivares** (bō-lē-vä′rĕs). *Abbr.* **b., B. 1.** The basic monetary unit of Venezuela, equal to 100 centimos. See table of exchange rates at **currency. 2.** A coin worth one bolivar. [After Simón BOLÍVAR.]

Bo·lí·var, Pi·co. See **Pico Bolívar.**

Bo·lí·var (bō-lē′vär), **Simón.** Called "the Liberator." 1783–1830. Venezuelan leader in South American struggles for national independence.

bo·liv·i·a (bə-lĭv′ē-ə) *n.* A woolen cloth with a soft pile resembling plush. [Probably because Bolivian alpaca is used in its manufacture.]

Bo·liv·i·a (bə-lĭv′ē-ə). *Abbr.* **Bol.** A republic of South America, 424,163 square miles in area, separated from the Pacific Ocean by Peru and Chile. Population, 3,520,000. Capitals, La Paz and Sucre. **—Bo·liv′i·an** *adj.* & *n.*

boll (bōl) *n.* The rounded seed pod or capsule of certain plants, such as flax or cotton. [Middle English *bolle,* from Middle Dutch. See **bhel-²** in Appendix.*]

bol·lard (bŏl′ərd) *n.* A thick post on a ship or wharf, used for securing ropes and hawsers. [Middle English : probably BOLE (tree trunk) + -ARD.]

bol·lix (bŏl′ĭks) *tr.v.* **-lixed, -lixing, -lixes.** Also **bol·lox** (-əks), **-loxed, -loxing, -loxes.** *Slang.* To throw into confusion; botch or bungle. Usually used with *up.* [From earlier *bollocks, ballocks,* testicles, Middle English *ballocks,* Old English *beallucas.* See **bhel-²** in Appendix.*]

boll weevil. A small, grayish, long-snouted beetle, *Anthonomus grandis,* of Mexico and the southern United States, having destructive larvae that hatch in and damage cotton bolls.

boll·worm (bōl′wûrm′) *n.* **1.** The larva of a moth, *Pectinophora gossypiella,* that is very destructive to growing cotton. **2.** The **corn earworm** *(see).*

bo·lo (bō′lō) *n., pl.* **-los.** A long, heavy, single-edged machete used in the Philippines. [Spanish, name in the Philippines.]

bo·lo·gna (bə-lō′nə, -nē, -nyə) *n.* Also *informal* **ba·lo·ney** (-nē), **bo·lo·ney.** A seasoned smoked sausage made of mixed meats. [After BOLOGNA, Italy.]

Bo·lo·gna (bō-lō′nyä). An industrial city and railroad center of northern Italy. Population, 482,000. It is the seat of the oldest European university (1088).

bo·lom·e·ter (bō-lŏm′ə-tər) *n.* An instrument that measures radiant heat by correlating the radiation-induced change in electrical resistance of a blackened metal foil with the amount of radiation absorbed. [Greek *bolē,* beam, ray (see **gwel-¹** in Appendix*) + -METER.] **—bo′lo·met′ric** (bō′lō-mĕt′rĭk) *adj.* **—bo′lo·met′ri·cal·ly** *adv.*

Bol·she·vik (bōl′shə-vĭk′, bŏl′-) *n., pl.* **-viks** or **-viki** (bōl′shə-vē′kē). **1. a.** A participant in the Russian Revolution belonging to the Communist Party of the Soviet Union. **b.** A member of the left-wing majority group of the Russian Social Democratic Party adopting Lenin's theses on party organization (1903). Compare **Menshevik. 2.** *Often small* **b.** Any extreme radical: *a literary bolshevik.* [Russian *Bol'shevik,* "one of the majority" : *bol'shii,* greater, from *bol'shoi,* large (see **bel-** in Appendix*) + noun suffix *-vik.*] **—Bol′she·vik′** *adj.*

Bol·she·vism (bōl′shə-vĭz′əm, bŏl′-) *n.* Also **bol·she·vism. 1.** The strategy developed by the Bolsheviks between 1903 and 1917 with a view to seizing state power and establishing the dictatorship of the proletariat. **2.** Soviet Communism.

Bol·she·vist (bōl′shə-vĭst, bŏl′-) *n.* Also **bol·she·vist.** A Bolshevik. **—Bol′she·vist, Bol′she·vis′tic** *adj.*

bol·son (bōl′sən) *n. Southwestern U.S.* A flat arid valley surrounded by mountains and draining into a shallow central lake. [Spanish, "big pouch," augmentative of *bolsa,* purse, from Late Latin *bursa.* See **bursa.**]

bol·ster (bōl′stər) *n.* A long, narrow pillow or cushion. *—tr.v.* **bolstered, -stering, -sters. 1.** To support with a pillow. **2.** To support or prop up. Often used with *up.* **3.** To apply padding to. [Middle English *bolster,* Old English *bolster,* cushion. See **bhelgh-** in Appendix.*] **—bol′ster·er** *n.*

bolt¹ (bōlt) *n.* **1.** A bar made of wood or metal that slides into a socket and is used to fasten doors and gates. **2.** A metal bar or rod in the mechanism of a lock thrown or withdrawn by turning the key. **3.** A metal pin with a head on one end and screw thread on the other, used with a nut to fasten two or more bored or threaded parts. **4. a.** A sliding metal bar that positions the cartridge in breech-loading rifles, closes the breech, and ejects the spent cartridge. **b.** A similar device in any breech mechanism. **5.** A short, heavy arrow with a thick head, especially used with a crossbow. **6.** A flash of lightning or a thunderbolt. **7.** Any sudden or unexpected event. **8.** A sudden movement toward or away from something. **9.** A large roll of cloth of a definite length, especially as it comes from the loom. **—bolt from the blue.** A sudden, usually shocking, surprise. **—shoot one's bolt.** To do all that one can. *—v.* **bolted, bolting, bolts.** *—tr.* **1.** To secure or lock with or as if with a bolt or bolts. **2.** *Archaic.* To shoot or discharge (an arrow or other missile). **3.** To arrange or roll (lengths of cloth, for example) on a bolt. **4.** To eat hurriedly and with little chewing; gulp. **5.** To desert or withdraw support from (a political party). **6.** To utter impulsively; blurt out. *—intr.* **1.** To move or spring suddenly toward or from something. **2.** To break from the rider's control and run away. Used of a horse. **3.** To make off suddenly; run away. **4.** To break away from a political party or its policies. **5.** *Horticulture.* To flower or produce seeds prematurely. [Middle English *bolt,* Old English *bolt,* heavy arrow. See **bheld-** in Appendix.*]

bolt² (bōlt) *tr.v.* **bolted, bolting, bolts.** To pass through a sieve; sift. [Middle English *bulten, bolten,* from Old French *buleter,* from Middle Dutch *biutelen.* See **beu-¹** in Appendix.*]

bolt·er[1] (bōl′tər) *n.* **1.** A horse given to bolting. **2.** *Informal.* One who gives up membership in his political party or withdraws support from that party's candidates or policies.

bolt·er[2] (bōl′tər) *n.* **1.** A machine used for sifting, especially for sifting flour. **2.** One who operates this machine.

Bol·ton (bōl′tən). In full, **Bol·ton-le-Moors** (-lə-mŏŏrz′). A city and textile-manufacturing center in northwestern England, 11 miles northwest of Manchester. Population, 158,000.

bol·to·ni·a (bōl-tō′nē-ə) *n.* Any of several North American plants of the genus *Boltonia,* having daisylike flowers with white, violet, or pinkish rays. [New Latin, after James *Bolton,* 18th-century English botanist.]

bolt·rope (bōlt′rōp′) *n.* A rope sewn into the outer edge of a sail to prevent the sail from tearing.

Boltz·mann (bôlts′män), **Ludwig.** 1844–1906. Austrian physicist; developed statistical mechanics and applied it to the kinetic theory of gases.

bo·lus (bō′ləs) *n., pl.* **-luses. 1.** A small round mass. **2.** *Pharmacology.* A large pill or tablet. [Medieval Latin *bōlus,* from Greek *bōlos*†, lump, clod.]

Bo·lyai (bō′yô-ē), **János.** 1802–1860. Hungarian mathematician; developed non-Euclidian geometry.

BOM Airport code for Bombay, India.

bomb (bŏm) *n.* **1.** An explosive weapon detonated by impact, proximity to an object, a timing mechanism, or other predetermined means. **2.** Any of various weapons detonated to release smoke, gas, pellets, poisons, or other destructive materials. **3.** *Football Slang.* A very long forward pass designed to achieve great yardage in a single play. **4. a.** A container capable of withstanding high internal pressure. **b.** A vessel for storing compressed gas. **c.** A portable, manually operated container that ejects a spray, foam, or gas under pressure. **5.** *Slang.* A dismal failure or complete fiasco. **—the bomb.** Nuclear weapons collectively. *—v.* **bombed, bombing, bombs.** *—tr.* To attack, damage, or destroy with a bomb or bombs. *—intr.* **1.** To drop a bomb or bombs. **2.** *Slang.* To fail miserably. Usually used with *out.* [French *bombe,* from Italian *bomba,* probably from Latin *bombus,* booming, humming, from Greek *bombos.* See **bamb-** in Appendix.*]

bom·bard (bŏm′bärd′) *n.* An early form of cannon that fired stone balls. *—tr.v.* (bŏm-bärd′) **bombarded, -barding, -bards. 1.** To attack with bombs, explosive shells, or missiles. **2.** To attack persistently. **3.** To irradiate (an atom). **4.** To attack with a bombard. —See Synonyms at **attack.** [Middle English *bombarde,* cannon, from Old French, from Medieval Latin *bombarda,* probably from Latin *bombus,* booming. See **bomb.**] **—bom·bard′er** *n.* **—bom·bard′ment** *n.*

bom·bar·dier (bŏm′bər-dîr′) *n.* **1.** *Military.* The member of an aircraft crew who operates the bombing equipment. **2.** *British.* A noncommissioned artillery officer. **3.** A soldier who operated a bombard. [French, from Old French *bombarde,* BOMBARD.]

bombardier beetle. Any of various beetles of the genus *Brachinus* and related genera, that expel an acrid secretion from the posterior end of the abdomen.

bom·bar·don (bŏm-bärd′n, bŏm′bər-dən) *n.* **1.** A brass musical instrument resembling a tuba but with a lower pitch; a bass or contrabass tuba. **2.** A 16-foot reed stop on the organ. [French, from Italian *bombardone,* augmentative of *bombardo,* from *bombarda,* bombard, from Medieval Latin. See **bombard.**]

bom·bast (bŏm′băst′) *n.* **1.** Grandiloquent and pompous speech or writing. **2.** Formerly, a soft material used for padding. [Earlier *bombace,* cotton padding, from Old French, from Late Latin *bombax,* cotton, silk, alteration of Latin *bombyx,* silkworm, silk, from Greek *bombux,* of Oriental origin, akin to Turkish *pambuk,* cotton.] **—bom·bast′er** *n.*

Synonyms: *bombast, declamation, rant, fustian, claptrap, rodomontade.* All these terms designate speech or writing that emphasizes extravagance of style or delivery, usually at the expense of content. *Bombast,* applicable to speech and writing, stresses inflation of style without ruling out the possibility of substantial content. *Declamation* applies principally to formal oratory and the speaking of verse drama but may imply clamorous, empty display. *Rant,* said chiefly of speech, emphasizes turgidity and violence of style. *Fustian* stresses contrast between pretentious style of writing or speech and absurd or commonplace content. *Claptrap* is insincere, worthless speech or writing, calculated to win applause. *Rodomontade* is boastful speech and bluster.

bom·bas·tic (bŏm-băs′tĭk) *adj.* Characterized by bombast; pompous; grandiloquent. **—bom·bas′ti·cal·ly** *adv.*

Bom·bay (bŏm-bā′). **1.** The second-largest city of the Republic of India, the capital of Maharashtra State, and the country's most important west-coast port. Population, 2,772,000; urban area, 4,152,000. **2.** A state of India until its division in 1960 into Gujarat and Maharashtra states.

Bombay duck. 1. A food fish, *Harpodon nehereus,* of India. **2.** The dried flesh of this fish or a dish prepared from it.

Bombay hemp. A plant, **sunn** *(see),* or the tough fiber obtained from its stems.

bom·ba·zine (bŏm′bə-zēn′) *n.* Also **bom·ba·sine.** A fine twilled fabric of silk and worsted or cotton, often dyed black and used for mourning clothes. [French *bombasin,* from Late Latin *bombacīnum,* variant of *bombȳcīnum,* from Latin, neuter of *bombȳcīnus,* silken, from *bombyx,* silk. See **bombast.**]

bomb bay. The compartment in the fuselage of a military aircraft from which bombs are dropped.

bombe (bŏm; *French* bôɴb) *n.* A frozen dessert, a mold or melon containing two or more layers of ice cream of different flavors. [French, "bomb" (from its shape).]

bombed (bŏmd) *adj. Slang.* Drunk.

bomb·er (bŏm′ər) *n.* **1.** A military aircraft designed to carry and drop bombs. **2.** One who bombs.

bomb·proof (bŏm′prōōf′) *adj.* Designed and constructed to resist destruction by bombs. *—n.* A bomb shelter.

bomb rack. A framework or mechanical holder for bombs on a military aircraft.

bomb·shell (bŏm′shĕl′) *n.* **1.** A bomb. **2.** A shocking surprise.

bomb shelter. A shelter, often below ground, built to resist bombardment.

bomb·sight (bŏm′sīt′) *n.* A device in aircraft for aiming bombs.

bom·by·cid (bŏm′bĭ-sĭd) *n.* A moth of the family Bombycidae, which includes the silkworms. [New Latin *Bombycidae,* from Latin *bombyx,* silkworm. See **bombast.**]

Bo·mu (bō′mōō). Also **Mbo·mu** (əm-bō′mōō). A river rising in the southeastern Central African Republic and flowing 500 miles west to join the Uele River to form the Ubangi River.

Bon (bōn) *n.* A Japanese Buddhist festival held in July to honor ancestral spirits. Also called "Feast of Lanterns." [Japanese *bon,* basin, sacrificial vessel (later used as a festive lantern), from Chinese (Mandarin) *p'ên*[2].]

Bon, Cape (bŏn; *French* bôɴ). A peninsula of extreme northeastern Tunisia, extending 50 miles northeastward into the Mediterranean Sea.

bo·na fide (bō′nə fīd′, fī′dē, bŏn′ə). **1.** Done or made in good faith; sincere: *a bona fide offer.* **2.** Authentic; genuine: *a bona fide Rembrandt.* [Latin, "in good faith."]

Bon·aire (bôn′âr′). An island, 95 square miles in area, of the Netherlands Antilles, lying off the northern coast of Venezuela. Population, 6,000.

bo·nan·za (bə-năn′zə) *n.* **1.** A rich mine, vein, or pocket of ore. **2.** Any source of great wealth or prosperity. [Spanish, fair weather, prosperity, from Vulgar Latin *bonacia* (unattested), from Latin *bonus,* good (after Latin *malacia,* calm at sea, taken as if from *malus,* bad). See **deu-**[2] in Appendix.*]

Bo·na·parte (bō′nə-pärt′; *French* bô-nà-pàrt′). *Italian* **Buo·na·par·te** (bwô′nä-pär′tā). A Corsican family, including the brothers **Napoleon I** *(see);* **Joseph** (1768–1844), king of Naples (1806–08) and of Spain (1808–13); **Lucien** (1775–1840), prince of Canino; **Louis** (1778–1846), king of Holland (1806–10); **Jérôme** (1784–1860), king of Westphalia (1807–13).

Bo·na·part·ist (bō′nə-pär′tĭst) *n.* A follower or supporter of Napoleon Bonaparte, his policies and dynastic claims, or of the Bonaparte family. **—Bo′na·part′ism′** *n.*

Bon·a·ven·ture (bŏn′ə-vĕn′chər), **Saint.** *Italian* **Bo·na·ven·tu·ra** (bō′nä-vän-tōō′rä). Original name, Giovanni di Fidanza. 1221–1274. Italian Franciscan monk, philosopher, and educator; canonized in 1482.

bon·bon (bŏn′bŏn′) *n.* A candy having a center of fondant, fruit, or nuts, and coated with chocolate or fondant. [French, baby-talk reduplication of *bon,* good, from Latin *bonus.* See **deu-**[2] in Appendix.*]

bon·bon·nière (bŏn′bŏn-yâr′; *French* bôɴ-bô-nyâr′) *n.* **1.** A small ornate box or dish for candy. **2.** A confectioner's store. [French, from *bonbon,* BONBON.]

bond (bŏnd) *n. Abbr.* **bd. 1.** Anything that binds, ties, or fastens together: **a.** *Usually plural.* A shackle; a fetter. **b.** A cord, rope, or band. **2.** *Usually plural. Archaic.* Captivity; confinement. **3.** *Often plural.* A uniting force or tie; a link: *"A mystic bond of brotherhood makes all men one."* (Carlyle). **4.** A binding agreement; covenant. **5.** The duty, promise, or obligation by which one is bound: *"To trust a man on his oath or bond"* (Shakespeare). **6. a.** A substance or an agent that causes two or more objects or parts to cohere. **b.** Such a union or cohesion. **7.** *Chemistry.* A **chemical bond** *(see).* **8.** *Law.* **a.** Any written and sealed obligation, especially one requiring payment of a stipulated amount of money on or before a given day. **b.** A sum of money paid as bail or surety. **c.** One who acts as bail; bondsman. **9.** *Finance.* A certificate of debt issued by a government or corporation, guaranteeing payment of the original investment plus interest by a specified future date. **10.** *Commerce.* The state or condition of storing taxable goods in a warehouse until the taxes or duties due on them are paid. **11.** An insurance contract in which an agency guarantees payment to an employer in the event of unforeseen financial loss through the actions of an employee. **12.** Any overlapping arrangement of bricks or other masonry components in a wall. **13.** A type of paper, **bond paper** *(see).* **—bottled in bond.** Said of whiskies bottled under government supervision prior to paying duties and stored in a bonded warehouse for a stipulated period. *—v.* **bonded, bonding, bonds.** *—tr.* **1.** To mortgage or place a guaranteed bond on. **2.** To furnish bond or surety for. **3.** To place (an employee or merchandise, for example) under bond or guarantee. **4.** To join securely, as with glue or cement. **5.** To lay (bricks or other building materials) in an overlapping pattern for solidity. *—intr.* To secure or hold something together with or as with a bond or bonds. [Middle English *bond, band,* from Old Norse *band.* See **bhendh-** in Appendix.*] **—bond′a·ble** *adj.* **—bond′er** *n.*

bond·age (bŏn′dĭj) *n.* **1.** The condition of a slave or serf; serfdom; servitude. **2.** A state of subjection to any force, power, or influence. **3.** In early English law, **villeinage** *(see).* —See Synonyms at **servitude.** [Middle English, from Medieval Latin *bondāgium,* from Middle English *bonde,* serf, peasant, Old English *bōnda,* householder, from Old Norse *bōndi, būandi,* "tiller of the soil," husbandman, from the present participle of *būa,* to live, dwell. See **bheu-** in Appendix.*]

bonded warehouse. A warehouse certified by the U.S. Department of Internal Revenue in which goods may be stored pending payment of duties or taxes.

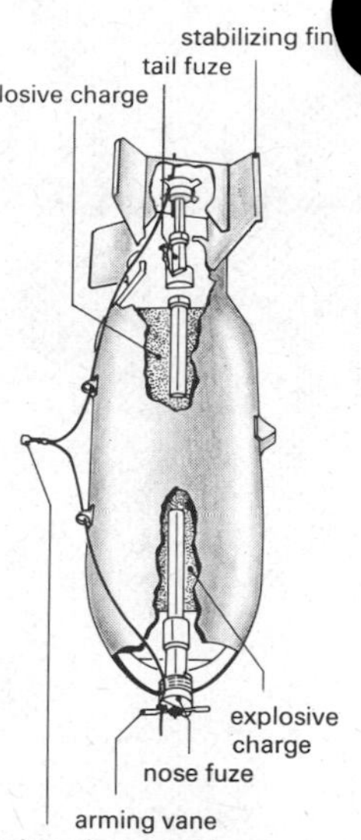
stabilizing fin
tail fuze
explosive charge
explosive charge
nose fuze
arming vane
arming-wire assembly

bomb

bolt[1]

carriage bolt
hex bolt
A325
heavy hex structural bolt

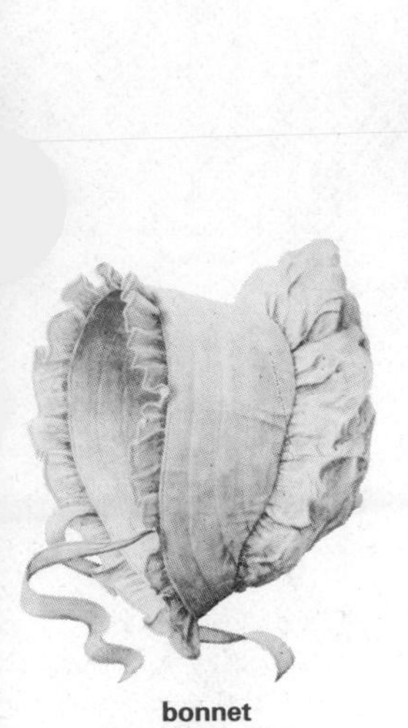

bonnet
Late 19th-century sunbonnet

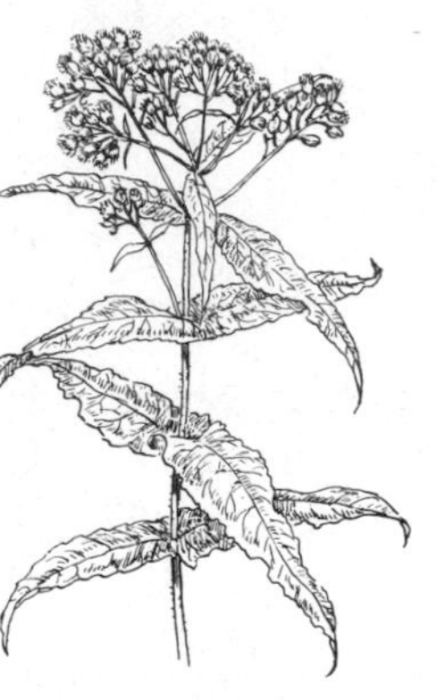

boneset
Eupatorium perfoliatum

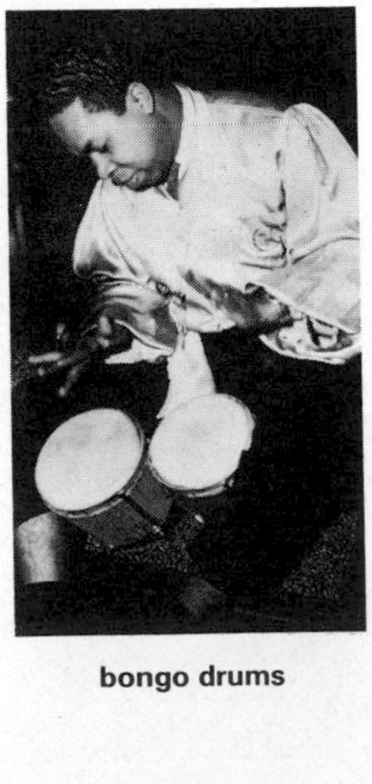

bongo drums

bond·hold·er (bŏnd′hōl′dər) *n.* The owner of a bond or bonds.
bond·maid (bŏnd′mād′) *n.* A female bondservant.
bond paper. A superior grade of strong white paper made wholly or in part from rag pulp. Also called "bond."
bond·ser·vant (bŏnd′sûr′vənt) *n.* **1.** A person obligated to service without wages. **2.** A slave or serf. Also called "bondman," "bondslave," "bondsman." [*Bond-*, from Middle English *bonde,* serf. See **bondage.**]
bonds·man (bŏndz′mən) *n., pl.* **-men** (-mĭn). **1.** A male **bondservant** *(see).* **2.** A person who provides bond or surety for another.
bone (bōn) *n.* **1. a.** The dense, semirigid, porous, calcified connective tissue of the skeleton of most vertebrates. **b.** Any of numerous anatomically distinct skeletal structures made of this material. **c.** A piece of this material. **2.** *Plural.* **a.** The skeleton. **b.** The body. **3.** An animal structure or material, such as ivory, resembling bone. **4.** Something made of bone or of material resembling bone, especially: **a.** A piece of whalebone or similar material used as a corset stay. **b.** *Plural. Informal.* Dice. **5. a.** *Plural.* Flat clappers made of bone or wood used by the end man in a minstrel show. **b.** *Capital* **B.** *Plural.* The end man in a minstrel show. Used with a singular verb. Also called "Mr. Bones." **—feel in one's bones.** To have an intuition of. **—have a bone to pick with.** To have grounds for a dispute with. **—make no bones about.** To be frank and candid about. *—v.* **boned, boning, bones.** *—tr.* **1.** To remove the bones from. **2.** To stiffen (a corset or piece of clothing) with whalebone or similar material. **3.** To fertilize with bone meal. *—intr. Slang.* To study intensely, usually at the last minute. Often used with *up on.* [Middle English *bon, ban,* from Old English *bān,* from Common Germanic *baina-* (unattested).]
Bône. The French name for **Annaba.**
bone ash. The white, powdery calcium phosphate ash of burned bones, used as a fertilizer, in making ceramics, and in cleaning and polishing compounds. Also called "bone earth."
bone·black (bōn′blăk′) *n.* Also **bone black.** A black pigment containing about 10 per cent charcoal, made by roasting bones in an airtight container and used in polishes, as a filtering medium, and in decolorizing sugar. Also called "bone charcoal."
bone china. Porcelain made of clay mixed with bone ash.
bone conduction. The transmission of sound by bone, especially to the inner ear by the bones of the skull.
bone-dry (bōn′drī′) *adj.* Without a trace of moisture; very dry.
bone·fish (bōn′fĭsh′) *n., pl.* **bonefish** or **-fishes.** A marine game fish, *Albula vulpes,* of warm waters, having silvery scales. [From its many small bones.]
bone·head (bōn′hĕd′) *n. Slang.* A stupid or dense person. **—bone′head′ed** *adj.* **—bone′head′ed·ness** *n.*
bone meal. Bones crushed and ground to a coarse powder, used as plant fertilizer and animal feed.
bone of contention. Grounds or cause for dispute or disagreement; the subject of a dispute.
bone oil. A dark-brown, foul-smelling oil obtained by destructive distillation of bones and used primarily as a denaturant for alcohol.
bon·er (bō′nər) *n. Slang.* A blunder. [Origin uncertain.]
bone·set (bōn′sĕt′) *n.* Any of various plants of the genus *Eupatorium;* especially, *E. perfoliatum,* of eastern North America, having broad clusters of small white flowers. Also called "thoroughwort" and sometimes "agueweed" or "feverwort." [So called because it supposedly helps set broken bones.]
bon·fire (bŏn′fīr′) *n.* A large outdoor fire. [Middle English *banefyre,* a fire in which bones were burned : BONE + FIRE.]
bong (bŏng, bông) *n.* A deep ringing sound, as of a bell. *—v.* **bonged, bonging, bongs.** *—tr.* To announce or proclaim with or as with such a ringing sound: *bong the hour.* *—intr.* To ring. [Imitative.]
bon·go (bŏng′gō) *n., pl.* **-gos.** An antelope, *Boocercus eurycerus,* of central Africa, having a reddish-brown coat with white stripes and spirally twisted horns in both sexes. [Native African name.]
bongo drums. A pair of connected drums having parchment heads that can be tuned, played by beating with the hands. Also called "bongos," "bongoes." [American Spanish *bongó* (probably imitative).]
Bon·heur (bŏ-nûr′; *French* bô-nœr′), **Rosa.** 1822–1899. Full name, Marie Rosalie Bonheur. French painter of animals.
bon·ho·mie (bŏn′ə-mē′) *n.* Also **bon·hom·mie.** A pleasant and affable disposition; good nature; geniality. [French, from *bonhomme,* good-natured man : *bon,* good, from Latin *bonus* (see **deu-**[2] in Appendix*) + *homme,* man, from Latin *homo* (see **dhghem-** in Appendix*).]
bon·i·face (bŏn′ə-fĭs, -fās′) *n.* An innkeeper. [After *Boniface,* an innkeeper in the *Beaux Stratagem,* by George FARQUHAR.]
Bon·i·face (bŏn′ə-fās′), **Saint.** Original name, Winfred or Wynfrith. A.D. 680?–755. English Benedictine missionary in Germany; archbishop of Mainz; martyred.
Bo·nin Islands (bō′nĭn). *Japanese* **O·ga·sa·wa·ra Ji·ma** (ō-gä′sä-wä′rä jē′mä). An archipelago of 15 islands, about 500 miles south of Japan, under U.S. administration after World War II until restored to Japan in 1968.
bo·ni·to (bə-nē′tō) *n., pl.* **bonito** or **-tos.** Also **bo·ni·ta** (-tə). **1.** Any of several marine food and game fishes of the genus *Sarda,* related to and resembling the tuna. **2.** Any of several similar fishes. [Spanish, "beautiful" (from its appearance), from Latin *bonus,* good. See **deu-**[2] in Appendix.*]
bon mot (bôN′ mō′) *pl.* **bons mots** (bôN′ mōz′). A clever saying, usually a terse and apt witticism. [French, "good word."]
Bonn (bŏn). The capital of the German Federal Republic, situated on the west bank of the Rhine, 16 miles southeast of Cologne. Population, 142,000.
Bon·nard (bô′nàr′), **Pierre.** 1867–1947. French impressionist painter and lithographer.
bonne (bôn) *n.* A female servant; maid. [French, feminine of *bon,* good, from Latin *bonus.* See **deu-**[2] in Appendix.*]
bonne femme (bôn′ fĕm′). Designating simple, home-style cooking. [French *(à la) bonne femme,* "(in the manner of) a good housewife."]
bon·net (bŏn′ĭt) *n.* **1.** A hat that is held in place by ribbons tied under the chin. **2.** *Scottish.* A brimless cap worn by men. **3.** A feather headdress worn by some American Indians. **4.** A removable metal plate over a valve or other machinery part. **5.** *British.* The hood of an automobile. **6.** A wind screen for a chimney. **7.** *Nautical.* A strip of canvas laced to a fore-and-aft sail to increase sail area. *—tr.v.* **bonneted, -neting, -nets.** To put a bonnet on. [Middle English *bonet,* from Old French, from Medieval Latin *abonnis*†, cap.]
Bon·net (bô-nĕ′), **Charles.** 1720–1793. Swiss naturalist; discovered parthenogenesis.
Bon·ne·ville Dam (bŏn′ə-vĭl′). A dam, 170 feet high, across the Columbia River about 35 miles east of Portland, Oregon.
Bon·ne·ville Salt Flats (bŏn′ə-vĭl′). A barren plain, part of the bed of prehistoric Lake Bonneville in northwestern Utah, situated west of Great Salt Lake in Great Salt Lake Desert, site of land-speed tests in measured-mile racing.
Bon·ney, William H. See **Billy the Kid.**
bon·nock. Variant of **bannock.**
bon·ny (bŏn′ē) *adj.* **-nier, -niest.** Also **bon·nie.** *Chiefly Scottish.* **1.** Pleasing or attractive to the eye; pretty; fair. **2.** Healthy; robust. **3.** Cheerful; pleasant. [Perhaps from Old French *bon,* good, from Latin *bonus.* See **deu-**[2] in Appendix.*] **—bon′ni·ly** *adv.* **—bon′ni·ness** *n.*
bon·ny·clab·ber (bŏn′ē-klăb′ər) *n. British Regional.* Sour clotted milk. [Probably from Irish *bainne clabair,* "milk of the churn-dasher" : *bainne,* milk, from Middle Irish *banne,* milk, drop + *clabair,* genitive of *clabaire*†, dasher (part of a churn).]
Bo·non·ci·ni (bō′nōn-chē′nē). Also **Buo·non·ci·ni** (bwô′-). Italian family of composers, including **Giovanni Maria** (1640–1678) and his sons **Giovanni Battista** (1670–1755) and **Marcantonio** (1675–1726).
bon·sai (bōn-sī′) *n., pl.* **bonsai. 1.** The art of growing dwarfed, ornamentally shaped trees or shrubs in small, shallow pots. **2.** A tree or shrub grown by this method. [Japanese, "potted plant" : *bon,* basin, pot, from Chinese (Mandarin) *p'ên*[2] + *sai,* to plant, from Chinese (Mandarin) *tsai*[1].]
bon·spiel (bŏn′spēl′) *n.* Also **bon·spell** (-spəl). *Scottish.* A curling match. [Probably from Dutch *bon(d)spel* (unattested), "league game" : *bond,* league, from Middle Dutch *bont* (see **bhendh-** in Appendix*) + *spel,* game, from Middle Dutch, from Germanic *spillōn* (unattested), to play (see **spiel**).]
bon·te·bok (bŏn′tə-bŏk′) *n.* A nearly extinct South African antelope, *Damaliscus pygargus,* having a reddish coat, a white rump, and a white mark on the face. [Afrikaans : *bont,* spotted, from Middle Dutch, probably from Latin *punctus,* spotted, pierced (see **point**) + *bok,* buck, from Middle Dutch *boc* (see **bhugo-** in Appendix*).]
bon ton (bŏn′ tŏn′). **1.** Sophisticated manners; style. **2.** Stylish or fashionable society. [French, "good tone."]
bo·nus (bō′nəs) *n., pl.* **-nuses. 1.** Something given or paid in addition to the usual or expected. **2.** Money paid to a state by a company in return for a corporate charter. **3.** A grant from a government to veterans of the armed forces. **4.** An extra dividend paid from profits. **5.** A premium paid for a loan. [From Latin *bonus,* good. See **deu-**[2] in Appendix.*]
Synonyms: *bonus, bounty, subsidy, dividend, premium, prize, reward, gratuity.* Each of these nouns designates some form of extra payment. *Bonus* usually applies to money in excess of what is normally received or strictly due, given in consideration of superior achievement or as a share in profits. *Bounty* generally pertains to a grant from a government, designed to encourage a specific desirable activity, such as the destruction of vermin. *Subsidy* refers to a large grant, usually by a government, in support of an enterprise regarded as in the public interest but not self-sustaining. *Dividend* usually refers to distribution of profits to shareholders or policyholders. *Premium* is generally something given as an incentive to business or commercial activity, as a discount or special wage rate. *Prize,* in this context, usually implies competitive achievement. *Reward* refers broadly to payment for a specific effort and emphasizes the merit of the accomplishment (or, less often, its evil). *Gratuity* pertains to voluntary payment in appreciation of services rendered, such as a tip, and emphasizes generosity.
bon vi·vant (bôN vē-väN′) *pl.* **bons vivants** (bôN vē-väN′). *French.* A person who enjoys good food and drink and lives luxuriously.
bon voy·age (bôN vwä-yàzh′). A phrase used to wish a departing traveler a pleasant journey. [French, "good trip."]
bon·y (bō′nē) *adj.* **-ier, -iest. 1.** Of, pertaining to, resembling, or made of bone. **2.** Having an internal skeleton of bones. **3.** Having many bones. **4.** Having protruding or prominent bones; lean; gaunt. **—bon′i·ness** *n.*
bonze (bŏnz) *n.* A Mahayana Buddhist monk, especially of China, Japan, and adjacent countries. [French *bonze* or Portuguese *bonzo,* from Japanese *bonsō,* from Chinese *fan*[2] *sêng*[1] : *fan*[2] (earlier also pronounced *bon*[2]), Buddhist, from Sanskrit *brāhmaṇas,* BRAHMAN + *sêng*[1], monk.]
bon·zer (bŏn′zər) *adj. Australian Slang.* Excellent; very good. [Perhaps an alteration of BONANZA.]

ă pat/ā pay/âr care/ä father/b bib/ch church/d deed/ĕ pet/ē be/f fife/g gag/h hat/hw which/ĭ pit/ī pie/îr pier/j judge/k kick/l lid, needle/m mum/n no, sudden/ng thing/ŏ pot/ō toe/ô paw, for/oi noise/ou out/ŏŏ took/ōō boot/p pop/r roar/s sauce/sh ship, dish/

boo (bo͞o) *n., pl.* **boos.** A vocal sound uttered to show contempt, scorn, or disapproval. —*interj.* Used to frighten or surprise or to express disapproval or derision. —*v.* **booed, booing, boos.** —*intr.* To utter "boo." —*tr.* To say "boo" to. [Imitative.]
boob (bo͞ob) *n.* **1.** *Slang.* A stupid or foolish person; simpleton; dolt. **2.** *Vulgar.* A woman's breast. [Short for BOOBY.]
boob·oi·sie (bo͞ob′wä-zē′) *n.* The class of the population composed of the stupid and gullible. [BOOB + (BOURGE)OISIE (coined by H.L. Mencken).]
boo-boo (bo͞o′bo͞o) *n., pl.* **-boos.** *Slang.* A stupid or thoughtless mistake; a blunder. [Perhaps altered from BOOHOO.]
boo·by (bo͞o′bē) *n., pl.* **-bies.** **1.** A stupid person; dolt; dunce. **2.** *Vulgar.* A woman's breast. **3.** Any of several tropical sea birds of the genus *Sula,* resembling and related to the gannets. [Spanish *bobo,* from Latin *balbus,* stammering. See **baba-** in Appendix.* Sense 2, imitative of the sound of sucking.]
booby hatch. **1.** *Nautical.* A raised covering over a small hatchway. **2.** *Slang.* An asylum or hospital for the insane. [Sense 1, from BOOBY (bird), since these birds commonly light there at sea. Sense 2, from BOOBY (dunce).]
booby prize. An insignificant or comical award given to the person who receives the lowest score in a game or contest.
booby trap. **1.** A concealed or camouflaged device designed to be triggered by some unsuspecting action of the intended victim. **2.** Any device or situation that catches a person off guard.
boo·dle (bo͞od′l) *n. Slang.* **1.** Money, especially counterfeit money. **2.** Money accepted as a bribe. **3.** Stolen goods; swag. **4.** A crowd or mob; caboodle. —*v.* **boodled, -dling, -dles.** *Slang.* —*intr.* To accept a bribe. —*tr.* To bribe or swindle. [From Dutch *boedel,* estate, effects, from Middle Dutch *bōdel,* riches, property. See **bheu-** in Appendix.*] —**boo′dler** *n.*
boog·ie·man (bo͝og′ē-măn′, bo͞o′gē-) *n., pl.* **-men** (-mĕn′). Also **boog·y·man, boog·ey·man, bo·gy·man** (bō′gē-), **bo·gey·man.** A hobgoblin; a terrifying specter. [*Boogie,* alteration of *booger,* from dialectal *boggart,* specter, hobgoblin, akin to BOGLE.]
boog·ie-woog·ie (bo͝og′ē-wo͝og′ē) *n.* A style of jazz piano playing characterized by a repeated rhythmic and melodic pattern in the bass. [Imitative.] —**boog′ie-woog′ie** *adj.*
boo·hoo (bo͞o′ho͞o′) *intr.v.* **-hooed, -hooing, -hoos.** To weep noisily. —*n., pl.* **boohoos.** Noisy weeping. [Imitative.]
book (bo͝ok) *n. Abbr.* **b., B., bk.** **1.** A volume made up of written or printed pages fastened along one side and encased between protective covers. **2.** Any written or printed literary work. **3.** A bound volume of blank or ruled pages. **4. a.** Any of the volumes in which financial transactions are recorded. **b.** *Plural.* Such records collectively. **5.** A main division of a larger written or printed work: *a book of the Old Testament.* **6.** A **libretto** *(see).* **7.** The script of a play. **8.** *Capital* **B.** The Bible. Often used with *The.* **9.** A set of standards, rules, conventions, or policies. Used with *the: He runs the company by the book.* **10.** *Plural. Informal.* Studies; lessons. Used with *the.* **11.** Something regarded as a source of knowledge: *the book of life.* **12.** A small packet of similar items bound together: *a book of matches.* **13.** A record of bets placed on a race. **14.** *Card Games.* The number of tricks needed before any tricks can have scoring value, as the first six tricks taken by the declaring side in bridge. **15.** A bundle of tobacco leaves sliced lengthwise. —**bring to book.** **1.** To compel to explain or account for. **2.** To reprimand. —**by the book.** According to established rules. —**close the books.** **1.** *Bookkeeping.* To make no further entries in and to draw up statements from the records as they stand. **2.** To bring to an end. —**in one's book.** In one's opinion. —**keep books.** To keep financial records of. —**like a book.** Thoroughly; completely: *She knows him like a book.* —**make book.** *Slang.* To accept bets as a bookmaker, especially on a sporting event. —**one for the books.** *Informal.* Something noteworthy. —**on the books.** **1.** Recorded or registered. **2.** Enlisted or enrolled. —**throw the book at.** *Slang.* **1.** To make all possible charges against (an offender or lawbreaker, for example). **2.** To reprimand or punish severely. —*tr.v.* **booked, booking, books.** **1.** To list or register in or as if in a book. **2.** To record charges against (a person) on a police blotter. **3.** To arrange for in advance; reserve (tickets, for example). **4.** To hire (entertainers, for example). [Middle English *bok,* Old English *bōc,* written document, composition. See **bhāgo-** in Appendix.*]
book·bind·er·y (bo͝ok′bīn′də-rē) *n., pl.* **-ies.** A business establishment where books are bound.
book·bind·ing (bo͝ok′bīn′dĭng) *n.* The art, trade, or profession of binding books. —**book′bind′er** *n.*
book·case (bo͝ok′kās′) *n.* A piece of furniture with shelves for holding books.
book club. **1.** An organization that sells books, usually at a discount, to members who have agreed to buy a minimum number. **2.** A club for the reading and discussion of books.
book end. A prop placed at the end of a row of books to keep them upright.
book·ie (bo͝ok′ē) *n. Slang.* A **bookmaker** *(see).*
book·ing (bo͝ok′ĭng) *n.* An engagement, as for a performance by an entertainer.
book·ish (bo͝ok′ĭsh) *adj.* **1.** Of, relating to, or resembling a book. **2.** Fond of books; studious. **3.** Relying on book learning. **4.** Pedantic; dull. —**book′ish·ly** *adv.* —**book′ish·ness** *n.*
book jacket. A **dust jacket** *(see).*
book·keep·ing (bo͝ok′kē′pĭng) *n. Abbr.* **bkpg.** The art or practice of recording the accounts and transactions of a business. —**book′keep′er** *n.*
book learning. Knowledge gained from books rather than from practical experience. Also called "booklore." —**book′-learn′ed** (bo͝ok′lûr′nĭd) *adj.*
book·let (bo͝ok′lĭt) *n.* A small bound book or pamphlet, usually with paper covers.
book·lore (bo͝ok′lôr′, -lōr′) *n.* **Book learning** *(see).* [Middle English *boklore,* Old English *bōclār* : BOOK + LORE.]
book·louse (bo͝ok′lous′) *n., pl.* **-lice** (-līs′). Any of various small, often wingless insects of the order Psocoptera (or Corrodentia), some species of which damage books.
book·mak·er (bo͝ok′mā′kər) *n.* **1.** One who edits, prints, publishes, or binds books. **2.** Someone who accepts and pays off bets, as on a horse race. In this sense, also *slang* "bookie."
book·man (bo͝ok′mən) *n., pl.* **-men** (-mĭn). **1.** Someone who spends much time studying or reading; student; scholar. **2.** Someone whose occupation is selling books.
book·mark (bo͝ok′märk′) *n.* A marker, such as a ribbon or a strip of leather, placed between the pages of a book.
book·mo·bile (bo͝ok′mō-bēl′) *n.* A small truck or trailer equipped to serve as a mobile lending library.
Book of Common Prayer. The book of services and prayers used in the Church of England and, with certain modifications, in the other churches of the Anglican Communion.
Book of Mormon. The sacred text of the Mormon Church. See **Mormon.**
book·plate (bo͝ok′plāt′) *n.* A label pasted on the inside cover of a book and bearing the owner's name or other identification.
book·rack (bo͝ok′răk′) *n.* **1.** A small rack or shelf for books. **2.** A frame or rack for supporting an open book. In this sense, also called "bookstand," "bookrest."
book review. A critical analysis of a book.
book·sel·ler (bo͝ok′sĕl′ər) *n.* A person who sells books.
book·stall (bo͝ok′stôl′) *n.* A stall or stand where books are sold.
book·stand (bo͝ok′stănd′) *n.* **1.** A small counter where books are sold. **2.** A **bookrack** *(see).*
book·store (bo͝ok′stôr′, -stōr′) *n.* A store where books are sold. Also called "bookshop."
book·worm (bo͝ok′wûrm′) *n.* **1.** The larva of any of various insects that infest books and feed on the paste in the bindings. **2.** One who spends much time reading or studying.
Boole (bo͞ol), **George.** 1815–1864. British mathematician, logician, and author.
Bool·e·an algebra (bo͞o′lē-ən). Any of various algebraic systems based on mathematical forms and relationships borrowed from the symbolic logic of George Boole.
boom[1] (bo͞om) *v.* **boomed, booming, booms.** —*intr.* **1.** To make a deep, resonant, usually sustained sound: *"A row of guns were booming at a distant enemy"* (Stephen Crane). **2.** To flourish or progress swiftly or vigorously: *Business boomed.* —*tr.* **1.** To give forth or utter with a deep, resonant sound. Often used with *out.* **2.** To cause to grow or flourish; boost. —*n.* **1.** A booming sound, as of an explosion. **2.** A time of prosperity. Compare **bust.** **3.** A sudden increase, as in growth, wealth, or popularity. —*adj.* Of or resulting from a boom: *boom prices.* [Middle English *bomben, bummen* (imitative).]
boom[2] (bo͞om) *n.* **1.** *Nautical.* A long spar extending from a mast to hold or extend the foot of a sail. **2.** A long pole extending upward at an angle from the mast of a derrick to support or guide objects lifted or suspended. **3.** *Lumbering.* **a.** A barrier composed of a chain of floating logs enclosing other free-floating logs. **b.** The area enclosed by such a barrier. **4.** A floating barrier serving to obstruct navigation. **5.** A long, movable arm used to maneuver a microphone. —*tr.v.* **boomed, booming, booms.** **1.** *Nautical.* To extend (a sail) on a boom. Used with *out.* **2.** To obstruct (a river or the mouth of a harbor, for example) with a floating barrier. [Dutch, tree, pole, from Middle Dutch. See **bheu-** in Appendix.*]
boo·mer·ang (bo͞o′mə-răng′) *n.* **1.** A flat, curved wooden missile, some types of which can be hurled so that they return to the thrower. It is used as a weapon by Australian aborigines. **2.** A statement or course of action that rebounds detrimentally against its originator. —*intr.v.* **boomeranged, -anging, -angs.** To result in adverse effect upon the originator; to backfire. [Native Australian word, variously recorded as *wo-mur-rāng, būmarin.*]
boom town. A town showing very sudden growth and prosperity, as through the discovery of local mineral resources.
boon[1] (bo͞on) *n.* **1.** Something beneficial or pleasant that is bestowed; a blessing: *"Despotism was a boon to Italian art."* (Will Durant). **2.** A favor or request: *"If you mean to please any people, you must give them the boon which they ask"* (Burke). [Middle English *bone,* prayer, thing prayed for, hence favor, from Old Norse *bōn,* prayer, request. See **bhā-**[2] in Appendix.*]
boon[2] (bo͞on) *adj.* **1.** Jolly; convivial: *a boon companion.* **2.** *Archaic.* Kind; generous. [Middle English *bone,* "good," from Old French *bon,* from Latin *bonus.* See **deu-**[2] in Appendix.*]
boon·docks (bo͞on′dŏks′) *pl.n. Slang.* **1.** Wild and dense brush; jungle. Preceded by *the.* **2.** Back country; hinterland. Preceded by *the.* [Tagalog *bundok,* mountain.]
boon·dog·gle (bo͞on′dôg′əl, -dŏg′əl) *intr.v.* **-gled, -gling, -gles.** *Informal.* To waste time on pointless and unnecessary work. —*n.* Pointless, unnecessary, and time-wasting work. [Originally, the plaited leather cord worn around the neck by Boy Scouts (coined in 1925 by R.H. Link, American scoutmaster), hence, any insignificant handicraft.] —**boon′dog′gler** *n.*
Boone (bo͞on), **Daniel.** 1734–1820. American pioneer; explored and settled Kentucky.
boor (bo͝or) *n.* **1.** A peasant. **2.** A person with rude, clumsy manners and little refinement; bumpkin. [Dutch *boer,* farmer, peasant, from Middle Dutch *gheboer.* See **bheu-** in Appendix.*]
boor·ish (bo͝or′ĭsh) *adj.* Like a boor; rude; ill-mannered. —**boor′ish·ly** *adv.* —**boor′ish·ness** *n.*

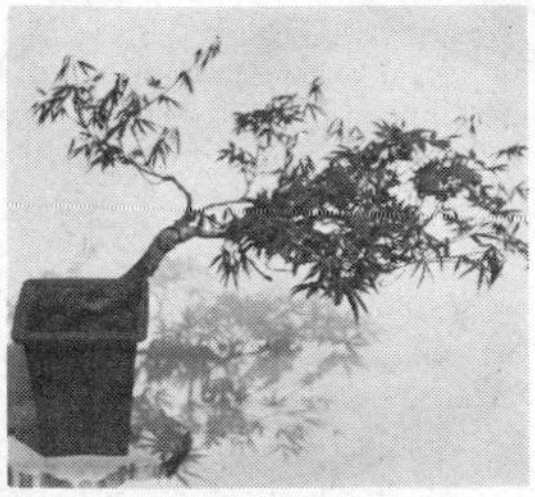

bonsai
Dwarfed maple tree

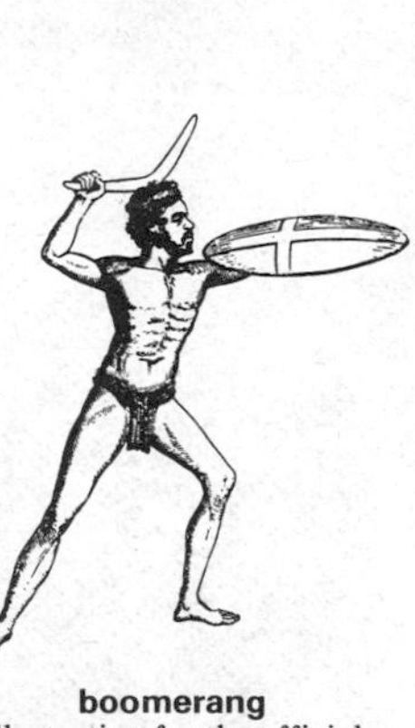

boomerang
Illustration for the official narrative of Charles Wilkes' mid-19th-century expedition, showing an Australian aborigine with a boomerang and shield

boost (bo͞ost) *tr.v.* **boosted, boosting, boosts. 1.** To raise or lift by or as if by pushing up from behind or below. **2.** To increase; to raise. **3.** To promote vigorously; advocate actively. —See Synonyms at **lift.** —*n.* **1.** A lift or help. **2.** An increase: *a boost in salary.* [Perhaps from BOUSE.]
boost·er (bo͞o′stər) *n.* **1.** Any device for increasing power or effectiveness. **2.** One that actively promotes something, such as a cause. **3.** *Electronics.* A radio-frequency amplifier. **4. a.** A rocket that assists the main propulsive system of an aircraft or spacecraft. **b.** A rocket used to launch a missile or space vehicle. In this sense, also called "booster rocket," "launch vehicle." **5.** A supplementary dose of a vaccine injected to maintain immunity. In this sense, also called "booster shot."
booster cable. An electric cable used to connect a discharged automobile battery to a power source for charging. Also called "jumper cable."
boot[1] (bo͞ot) *n.* **1.** A protective piece of footgear, usually leather, covering the foot and part or all of the leg. **2.** A protective sheath for a horse's leg. **3.** An instrument of torture formerly used to crush the foot and leg. **4.** Any protective covering or sheath, especially: **a.** A protective flap for the driver of an open automobile or other vehicle. **b.** A patch for the inner casing of an automobile tire to protect a weak spot or break. **5.** *British.* An automobile trunk. **6.** A scabbard on a saddle or vehicle to hold a gun. **7.** *Music.* A box to hold the reed in a reed pipe of an organ. **8.** A light or white patch on the leg of an animal. **9.** A kick. **10.** *U.S. Military.* A new recruit. —**bet your boots.** To be certain. —**lick the boots of.** To be obsequious toward. —**the boot.** *Slang.* Dismissal, as from work. —*tr.v.* **booted, booting, boots. 1.** To put boots on. **2.** To torture with the boot. **3.** To kick. **4.** *Slang.* To discharge; dismiss. [Middle English *bote,* from Old French *bote*†.]

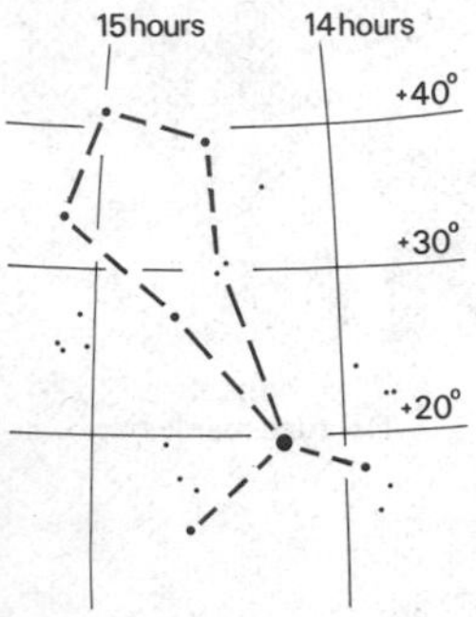

Boötes

boot[2] (bo͞ot) *intr.v.* **booted, booting, boots.** *Archaic.* To be of help or advantage; to avail. —*n.* **1.** *Regional.* Something given in addition. **2.** *Archaic.* Advantage; avail. —**to boot.** In addition; besides. [Middle English *bote,* Old English *bōt,* advantage, addition, recompense. See **bhad-** in Appendix.*]
boot·black (bo͞ot′blăk′) *n.* A person who cleans and polishes shoes for a living.
boot camp. *U.S. Military.* A training camp for recruits. [So called because the recruits wear boots.]
boot·ed (bo͞o′tĭd) *adj.* **1.** Wearing boots. **2.** Having the legs covered with feathers, as some birds do.
boo·tee (bo͞o′tē) *n.* Also **boo·tie.** A soft, usually knitted, shoe for a baby. [Diminutive of BOOT (shoe).]
Bo·ö·tes (bō-ō′tēz) *n.* A constellation in the Northern Hemisphere near Virgo and Canes Venatici. [Latin *Boōtēs,* from Greek, "plowman," from *boōtein,* to plow, from *bous,* ox. See **gwou-** in Appendix.*]
booth (bo͞oth) *n., pl.* **booths** (bo͞othz, bo͞oths). **1.** A small enclosed compartment, usually accommodating only one person and providing privacy: *a telephone booth.* **2.** A seating area in a restaurant that has a table and seats whose backs serve as partitions. **3.** A small stall or stand for the display and sale of goods. [Middle English *both, b(o)uth,* from Old Danish *bōth,* dwelling, stall. See **bheu-** in Appendix.*]
Booth (bo͞oth). Family of evangelists, including **William** (1829–1912), British founder of Salvation Army; his daughter, **Evangeline Cory** (1865–1950), British-born American commander of Salvation Army; and his son, **Ballington** (1859–1940), British-born American founder of Volunteers of America.

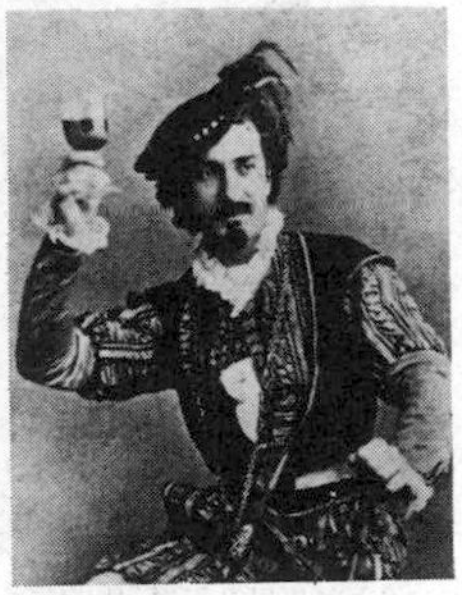
Edwin Thomas Booth

Booth (bo͞oth), **Edwin Thomas.** 1833–1893. American actor and theatrical manager; brother of J.W. Booth.
Booth (bo͞oth), **John Wilkes.** 1838–1865. American actor; assassin of Abraham Lincoln; brother of E.T. Booth.
Boo·thi·a, Gulf of (bo͞o′thē-ə). An inlet, about 250 miles long, of the Arctic Ocean in northeastern Canada between the Boothia and Melville peninsulas.
Boo·thi·a Peninsula (bo͞o′thē-ə). A peninsula of northeastern Canada, west of Baffin Island, whose tip is the northernmost point of the North American mainland.
boot·jack (bo͞ot′jăk′) *n.* A forked device for holding a boot secure while the foot is being withdrawn.
boot·leg (bo͞ot′lĕg′) *v.* **-legged, -legging, -legs.** —*tr.* To make, sell, or transport (alcoholic liquor, for example) for sale illegally. —*intr.* To engage in bootlegging. —*n.* **1.** Goods smuggled or illicitly produced or sold. **2.** The part of a tall boot above the instep. —*adj.* Produced, sold, or transported for sale illegally. *bootleg gin.* [From smugglers' practice of carrying liquor in the legs of tall boots.] —**boot′leg′ger** *n.*
boot·less (bo͞ot′lĭs) *adj.* Having no advantage or benefit; useless; unavailing; fruitless: *a bootless effort.* —**boot′less·ly** *adv.* —**boot′less·ness** *n.*

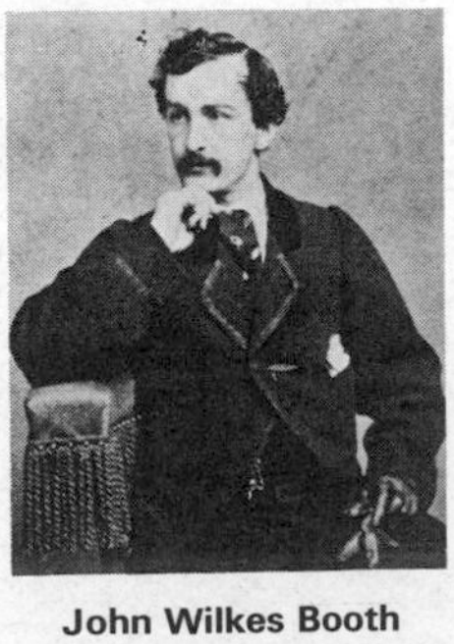
John Wilkes Booth

boot·lick (bo͞ot′lĭk′) *v.* **-licked, -licking, -licks.** —*tr.* To be servile toward. —*intr.* To behave in a servile manner; to fawn. —**boot′lick′er** *n.*
boots (bo͞ots) *n., pl.* **boots.** *British.* A servant; especially, one in a hotel who cleans and shines shoes.
boot·strap (bo͞ot′străp′) *n.* A leather or cloth loop sewn at each side or the top rear of a boot to help in pulling the boot on. —**by one's (own) bootstraps.** By one's own efforts. Usually used in the phrase *pull oneself up by one's bootstraps.*
boot tree. A **shoetree** *(see).*
boo·ty (bo͞o′tē) *n., pl.* **-ties. 1.** Plunder taken from an enemy in time of war. **2.** Any seized or stolen goods. **3.** Any valuable prize, award, or gain. [Middle English *bottyne,* from Old French *butin,* from Middle Low German *būte,* exchange, from Common Germanic *būti-ōn* (unattested).]
booze (bo͞oz) *n. Informal.* **1.** Alcoholic drink; especially, hard liquor. **2.** A drinking spree. —*intr.v.* **boozed, boozing, boozes.** *Informal.* To drink alcoholic beverages excessively or chronically. [Middle English *bousen,* to carouse, from Middle Dutch *būsen*†] —**booz′er** *n.* —**booz′y** *adj.*
bop[1] (bŏp) *tr.v.* **bopped, bopping, bops.** *Informal.* To hit or strike. —*n.* A blow; a punch. [Imitative.]
bop[2] (bŏp) *n.* A style of jazz characterized by rhythmic and harmonic complexity and a brilliant style of execution. Also called "bebop." [Short for BEBOP.]
bor. borough.
bo·ra (bôr′ə, bōr′ə) *n.* A violent cold wind from the northeast blowing on the Dalmatian coast of Yugoslavia in winter. [Italian (Venetian dialect), from Latin *Boreās,* BOREAS.]
bor·age (bôr′ĭj, bŏr′-) *n.* A plant, *Borago officinalis,* native to southern Europe and northern Africa, having hairy leaves and star-shaped blue flowers. The young, cucumber-flavored leaves are sometimes used as seasoning. [Middle English, from Old French *bourrache,* from Medieval Latin *borrāgō,* probably from Arabic *abū 'āraq,* "father of sweat" (from its use medicinally as a sudorific).]
Bo·rah (bôr′ə, bōr′ə), **William Edgar.** 1865–1940. American political leader; chairman U.S. Senate Foreign Relations Committee (1924–33); a noted isolationist.
bo·rane (bôr′ān′, bōr′-) *n.* Any of a series of boron-hydrogen compounds. [BOR(ON) + -ANE.]
bo·rate (bôr′āt′, bōr′-) *n.* A salt of boric acid.
bo·rax (bôr′ăks′, -əks, bōr′-) *n.* **1.** A hydrated **sodium borate** *(see).* **2.** An anhydrous sodium borate used in the manufacture of glass and various ceramics. [Middle English *boras, borax,* from Old French *boras,* from Medieval Latin *borax,* from Arabic *būraq,* from Persian *būrah*†.]
bo·ra·zon (bôr′ə-zŏn′, bōr′-) *n.* An extremely hard boron nitride formed at very high pressures and temperatures. [BOR(ON) + AZ(O)- + -ON.]
Bor·deaux[1] (bôr-dō′). A seaport of southwestern France, on the Garonne estuary. Population, 250,000; urban area, 462,000.
Bor·deaux[2] (bôr-dō′) *n., pl.* **Bordeaux** (bôr-dōz′). Any of the red or white wines produced in the regions around Bordeaux.
Bordeaux mixture. A mixture of copper sulfate, lime, and water, used as a fungicide. [Translation of French *bouillie bordelaise.*]
bordelaise sauce. Sauce bordelaise *(see).*
bor·del·lo (bôr-dĕl′ō) *n., pl.* **-los.** Also **bor·del** (bôrd′l). A house of prostitution; brothel. [Italian, from Old French *bordel,* "small house," "hut," brothel, from *borde,* wooden hut, from Frankish *borda* (unattested), from *bord* (unattested), board, plank. See **bherdh-** in Appendix.*]
Bor·den (bôrd′n), **Gail.** 1801–1874. American inventor, surveyor, newspaper publisher, and western pioneer; first produced condensed milk, coffee, tea, cocoa, and beef extracts.
Bor·den (bôrd′n), **Lizzie Andrew.** 1860–1927. American woman accused and acquitted of ax murder of parents (1892) in Massachusetts.
bor·der (bôr′dər) *n.* **1.** A margin, rim, or edge around or along something. **2.** A design or a decorative strip on the edge or rim of something. **3.** A strip of ground in which ornamental plants or shrubbery is planted. **4.** The line or frontier area separating political divisions or geographical regions; a boundary. **5.** *Capital* **B.** The boundary and adjacent areas between England and Scotland. Often used in the plural. —See Synonyms at **boundary.** —*adj.* Of, pertaining to, forming, or located on a border. —*tr.v.* **bordered, -dering, -ders. 1.** To put a border, rim, or edging on. **2.** To lie along or adjacent to the border of. —**border on** (or **upon**). **1.** To adjoin. **2.** To be almost like; approach in character: *an act that borders on heroism.* [Middle English *bordure,* from Old French, from *border,* to border, from *bord,* side of a vessel, border, from Frankish *bord* (unattested), board, plank. See **bherdh-** in Appendix.*] —**bor′der·er** *n.*
Synonyms: *border, margin, edge, verge, brink, brow, rim, brim.* All these words refer to the line or narrow area that marks the outmost bound of a surface. *Border* refers either to the boundary (limiting line) of a surface or, more often, to the area that immediately adjoins the boundary. *Margin* is an area, adjacent to the boundary, that is more or less precisely definable as to width and often distinguishable in other respects from the rest of the surface. *Edge* may refer specifically to the precise bounding line formed by the continuous convergence of two surfaces of a solid. *Verge* is an extreme terminating line or edge; figuratively it indicates extreme closeness to, or the imminence of, a thing or condition. *Brink* denotes the edge of a steep incline or slope; figuratively it indicates the imminence of an extreme condition, such as disaster or war. *Brow* is the upper edge of a steep incline. *Rim* denotes the edge of a surface that is circular or curved, such as a wheel or cymbal. *Brim* applies to the upper edge or inner side of the rim of a vessel or container, such as a cup.
bor·der·land (bôr′dər-lănd′) *n.* **1.** Land located on or near a border or frontier. **2.** An uncertain or indeterminate area, situation, or condition.
bor·der·line (bôr′dər-līn′) *n.* Also **border line. 1.** A line that establishes or marks a border. **2.** An indefinite line between two qualities or conditions: *"The border line between slavery and freedom"* (Frederick Douglass). —*adj.* Verging on a given quality or condition; indeterminate; dubious: *a borderline case of paranoia.*
Border States. The former slave states of Delaware, Maryland, Kentucky, and Missouri, adjacent to northern free states and caught between opposing forces in the Civil War. None of them seceded.

ă pat/ā pay/âr care/ä father/b bib/ch church/d deed/ĕ pet/ē be/f fife/g gag/h hat/hw which/ĭ pit/ī pie/îr pier/j judge/k kick/l lid, needle/m mum/n no, sudden/ng thing/ŏ pot/ō toe/ô paw, for/oi noise/ou out/o͝o took/o͞o boot/p pop/r roar/s sauce/sh ship, dish/

Bor·det (bôr'dĕ'), **Jules Jean Baptiste Vincent.** 1870–1961. Belgian bacteriologist.

bor·dure (bôr'jər) *n. Heraldry.* A border around a shield. [Middle English, BORDER.]

bore[1] (bôr, bōr) *v.* **bored, boring, bores.** —*tr.* **1.** To make a hole in or through (something), as with a drill or auger. **2.** To make (a tunnel, for example) by drilling, digging, or burrowing. —*intr.* **1.** To make a hole in or through something by or as if by drilling. **2.** To be capable of being pierced or drilled. **3.** To proceed or advance steadily or laboriously: *"All night they bored through the hot darkness."* (Steinbeck). —*n.* **1.** A hole or passage made by or as if by drilling. **2.** The interior diameter of a hole, tube, cylinder, or the like. **3.** The caliber of a firearm. **4.** A drilling tool. [Middle English *boren,* Old English *borian.* See **bher-**[2] in Appendix.*]

bore[2] (bôr, bōr) *tr.v.* **bored, boring, bores.** To tire with dullness, repetition, or tediousness. —*n.* One arousing boredom. [Origin unknown.]

bore[3] (bôr, bōr) *n.* A high and often dangerous wave caused by the surge of a flood tide upstream in a narrowing estuary or by colliding tidal currents. Also called "eagre." [Middle English *bare,* from Old Norse *bāra,* wave, billow. See **bher-**[1] in Appendix.*]

bore[4]. Past tense of **bear.**

bo·re·al (bôr'ē-əl, bōr'-) *adj.* **1.** Pertaining to the north; northern. **2.** Of or concerning the north wind. **3.** *Capital* **B.** Of or pertaining to the forest areas and tundras of the North Temperate Zone and Arctic region. [Middle English *boriall,* from Late Latin *boreālis,* from Latin *Boreās,* BOREAS.]

Bo·re·as (bôr'ē-əs, bōr'-). **1.** The north wind. **2.** The god personifying the north wind in Greek mythology. [Middle English, from Latin *Boreās,* from Greek *Boreas.* See **gwer-**[1] in Appendix.*]

bore·cole (bôr'kōl', bōr'-) *n.* A vegetable, **kale** *(see).* [Dutch *boerenkool,* "peasants' cabbage" : *boer,* BOOR (peasant) + *kool,* cabbage, from Latin *caulis,* stalk (see **cole**).]

bore·dom (bôr'dəm, bōr'-) *n.* The condition of being bored.

Bo·rel·li (bō-rĕl'lē), **Giovanni Alfonso.** 1608–1679. Italian mathematician and physiologist.

bor·er (bôr'ər, bōr'-) *n.* **1.** A tool used for boring or drilling. **2.** One who works with such a tool. **3.** An insect or insect larva, such as the **corn borer** *(see),* that bores into plants. **4.** Any of various mollusks that bore into soft rock or wood.

Bor·ghe·se (bōr-gā'zā). An Italian noble family; originated in Siena; influential in Roman art and politics from the 16th to the early 19th century.

Bor·gia (bôr'jä, -jə). *Spanish* **Bor·ja** (bôr'hä). An Italian family influential in church and government from the 14th to the 16th century; originated in Spain.

Bor·gia, Alfonso. See **Calixtus III.**

Bor·gia (bôr'jä, -jə), **Cesare.** 1475?–1507. Italian cardinal and political and military leader; son of Rodrigo Borgia.

Bor·gia (bôr'jä, -jə), **Lucrezia.** Duchess of Ferrara. 1480–1519. Italian noblewoman; patron of the arts; daughter of Rodrigo Borgia.

Bor·gia, Rodrigo. See **Alexander VI.**

Bor·glum (bôr'gləm), **Gutzon.** Full name, John Gutzon de la Mothe Borglum. 1867–1941. American sculptor of monuments at Mount Rushmore.

bo·ric (bôr'ĭk, bōr'-) *adj.* Of, pertaining to, derived from, or containing boron.

boric acid. A white or colorless crystalline compound, H_3BO_3, used as an antiseptic, preservative, and in fireproofing compounds, cosmetics, cements, and enamels.

boric oxide. A hard, colorless, transparent glass, B_2O_3, used in heat-resistant glassware, as a fire-resistant paint additive, and in the production of boron.

bo·ride (bôr'īd', bōr'-) *n.* A binary compound of boron with a more electropositive element or radical. [BOR(ON) + -IDE.]

bor·ing[1] (bôr'ĭng, bōr'-) *n.* **1.** The making of a hole by or as if by drilling. **2.** A hole made in this way. **3.** *Plural.* The material, chips, or dust produced by such drilling.

bor·ing[2] (bôr'ĭng, bōr'-) *adj.* Uninteresting and tiresome; dull.
Synonyms: *boring, monotonous, tedious, irksome, tiresome, humdrum, dismal, dreary.* These adjectives all mean to be burdensome in the sense of inducing discontent and mental weariness. *Boring* implies dullness that causes listlessness and lack of interest. *Monotonous* stresses unchanging lack of variety. *Tedious* suggests slowness, long-windedness, and dullness. *Irksome* describes what is demanding of time and effort and yet is dull, distasteful, or otherwise unrewarding. *Tiresome* intensifies the sense of *irksome,* and *humdrum* refers to what is commonplace, trivial, or characterized by unexciting routine. In this comparison *dismal* and *dreary* apply to what is depressingly dull.

Bor·mann (bôr'män'), **Martin Ludwig.** Born 1900. German political leader; third deputy of Nazi party; disappeared (1945).

born (bôrn). A past participle of **bear.** See Usage note at **bear.** —*adj.* **1.** *Abbr.* **b., B.** Brought into life or being. **2.** Having an innate quality or talent: *a born artist.*

Born (bôrn), **Max.** Born 1882. German-born British physicist; worked on quantum theory.

borne (bôrn, bōrn). A past participle of **bear.** See Usage note at **bear.**

Bor·ne·o (bôr'nē-ō'). An island of the Indonesian Archipelago, 296,696 square miles in area, lying between the Sulu and Java seas of the western Pacific Ocean. It is divided into Kalimantan (Indonesian Borneo), the Malaysian states of Sarawak and Sabah, and the British-protected sultanate of Brunei.

Born·holm (bôrn'hōm', -hōlm') A Danish island, 227 square

miles in area, in the Baltic Sea, 25 miles off the southern coast of Sweden. Population, 48,000.

born·ite (bôr'nīt') *n.* A brownish-bronze copper ore with composition Cu_5FeS_4. [After Ignaz von *Born* (1742–1791), Austrian mineralogist.]

Bor·nu (bôr'nōō). A former Moslem native kingdom in western Africa and now a province, about 50,000 square miles in area, of northeastern Nigeria.

Bo·ro·din (bôr'ə-dēn'), **Aleksandr Porfirevich.** 1834–1887. Russian nationalist composer and chemist.

Bo·ro·di·no (bôr'ə-dē'nō; *Russian* bə-rə-dyĭ-nô'). A village of the Soviet Union, 70 miles west of Moscow, near which Napoleon defeated the Russians on September 7, 1812.

bo·ron (bôr'ŏn', bōr'-) *n. Symbol* **B** A soft, brown, amorphous or crystalline, nonmetallic element, extracted chiefly from kernite and borax, and used in flares, propellant mixtures, nuclear reactor control elements, abrasives, and hard metallic alloys. Atomic number 5, atomic weight 10.811, melting point 2,300°C, sublimation 2,550°C, specific gravity (crystal) 2.34, valence 3. See **element.** [BOR(AX) + (CARB)ON.]

boron carbide. An extremely hard, black, crystalline compound or solid solution, B_4C, used as an abrasive, in control rods for nuclear reactors, and as a reinforcing filament in composite structural materials.

bo·ro·sil·i·cate glass (bôr'ō-sĭl'ĭ-kĭt, bōr'ō-, -kāt'). A strong heat-resistant glass that contains a minimum of five per cent boric oxide.

bor·ough (bûr'ō, bûr'ə) *n. Abbr.* **bor. 1.** A self-governing incorporated town in certain U.S. states. **2.** One of the five administrative units of New York City. **3.** *British.* **a.** A town having a municipal corporation and certain rights, such as self-government. **b.** A town that sends one or more representatives to Parliament. [Middle English *burgh, borough,* Old English *burg, burh,* fortress, fortified town. See **bhergh-**[2] in Appendix.*]

bor·ough-Eng·lish (bûr'ō-ĭng'glĭsh) *n.* An old custom in certain boroughs of England whereby the right to inherit an estate went to the youngest son or, in default of issue, to the youngest brother.

bor·row (bôr'ō, bōr'ō) *v.* **-rowed, -rowing, -rows.** —*tr.* **1.** To obtain or receive (something) on loan with the promise or understanding of returning it or its equivalent. **2.** To adopt or use as one's own: *They borrowed his ideas.* **3.** In subtraction, to increase a figure in the minuend by ten and make up for it by decreasing the next larger denomination by one. —*intr.* To take or receive a loan; obtain or receive something. [Middle English *borwen,* Old English *borgian.* See **bhergh-**[1] in Appendix.*] —**bor'row·er** *n.*

Bor·row (bôr'ō, bōr'ō), **George.** 1803–1881. English linguist, author, and authority on gypsies.

borscht (bôrsht) *n.* Also **borsht, borsch** (bôrsh). A Russian beet soup served hot or cold, often with sour cream. [Russian *borshch,* "cow parsnip" (the original base of the soup). See **bhar-** in Appendix.*]

borscht circuit. *Slang.* The predominantly Jewish resort hotels of the Catskill Mountains that employ entertainers. [So called with reference to borscht as an item of the cuisine.]

bort (bôrt) *n.* **1.** Poorly crystallized diamonds used for industrial cutting and abrasion. **2.** An impure diamond, a **carbonado** *(see).* [Probably from Dutch *boort,* possibly from Old French *bourt,* bastard, from Latin *burdus,* hinny. See **bher-**[1] in Appendix.*] —**bort'y** *adj.*

bor·zoi (bôr'zoi') *n.* A rather large, slenderly built dog of a breed originating in Russia, having a narrow, pointed head and a silky, predominantly white coat. Also called "Russian wolfhound." [Russian *borzoi†,* "swift."]

BOS Airport code for Boston, Massachusetts.

bos·cage (bŏs'kĭj) *n.* Also **bos·kage.** A mass of trees or shrubs; thicket; underwood; grove. [Middle English *boskage,* from Old French *boscage,* from *bosc,* forest, from Germanic. See **busk-** in Appendix.*]

Bosch (bŏs, bôs), **Hieronymus.** Original name, van Aken or van Aeken. 1450?–1516. Dutch painter.

bosh (bŏsh) *n. Informal.* Meaningless talk or opinions; nonsense. [Turkish *boş,* empty, useless.]

bosk (bŏsk) *n.* A small wooded area or thicket. [Back-formation from BOSKY.]

bos·ky (bŏs'kē) *adj.* **1.** Covered with bushes, shrubs, or trees; wooded. **2.** Shaded by trees or bushes. [From Middle English *bosk,* wooded, from *bosk, bush,* bush, from Old Norse *buskr.* See **busk-** in Appendix.*] —**bos'ki·ness** *n.*

bo's'n. Variant of **boatswain.**

Bos·ni·a and Her·ze·go·vi·na (bŏz'nē-ə; hĕrt'sə-gō-vē'nə). Two Balkan regions, about 20,000 square miles in area, now constituting an autonomous republic of Yugoslavia. Population, 3,278,000. Capital, Sarajevo.

Bos·ni·an (bŏz'nē-ən) *adj.* Also **Bos·ni·ac** (-nē-ăk'). Of or pertaining to Bosnia. —*n.* Also **Bos·ni·ac. 1.** A native of Bosnia. **2.** Their Serbo-Croatian language.

bos·om (bŏŏz'əm, bōō'zəm) *n.* **1.** The chest of a human being; especially, the female breasts. **2.** The part of a garment covering the chest. **3.** The center or heart: *in the bosom of one's family.* **4.** The chest considered as the source of emotion. —*adj.* Beloved; intimate: *a bosom friend.* [Middle English *bosom,* Old English *bōsm.* See **beu-**[1] in Appendix.*]

bos·on (bō'sŏn) *n.* A particle, such as a photon, pion, or alpha particle, having zero or integral spin and obeying statistical rules that permit any number of identical particles to occupy the same quantum state. Compare **fermion.** [After Jagadis Chandra *Bose* (1858–1937), Indian physicist and biologist.]

borzoi

---

 t tight/th thin, path/*th* this, bathe/ŭ cut/ûr urge/v valve/w with/y yes/z zebra, size/zh vision/ə about, item, edible, gallop, circus/ à *Fr.* ami/œ *Fr.* feu, *Ger.* schön/ü *Fr.* tu, *Ger.* über/KH *Ger.* ich, *Scot.* loch/N *Fr.* bon. *Follows main vocabulary. †Of obscure origin.

Bos·po·rus (bŏs′pər-əs). Also **Bos·pho·rus** (bŏs′fər-əs). *Turkish* **Ka·ra·de·niz Bo·ğa·zı** (kä′rä-dĕng-ēz′ bō′ä-zĭ′). A narrow strait between European and Asian Turkey, linking the Black Sea with the Sea of Marmara.

boss¹ (bôs, bŏs) *n.* **1. a.** An employer or supervisor of workers; manager; foreman. **b.** Someone who makes decisions or exercises authority. **2.** A professional politician who controls a party or political machine. —*v.* **bossed, bossing, bosses.** —*tr.* **1.** To supervise or control. **2.** To command in an arrogant or domineering manner. Often used with *around.* —*intr.* To be or act as a boss. —*adj.* **1.** Foremost; chief; head. **2.** *Slang.* First-rate; topnotch. [Dutch *baas,* master, from Middle Dutch *baes,* from Germanic *basa-* (unattested).]

boss² (bôs, bŏs) *n.* **1.** A circular protuberance or knoblike swelling. **2.** A raised area used as ornamentation. **3.** *Architecture.* A raised ornament, as at the intersection of the ribs in vaulted roofs. **4.** *Machinery.* **a.** An enlarged part of a shaft to which another shaft is coupled or to which a wheel or gear is keyed. **b.** A hub, especially of a propeller. **5.** *Bookbinding.* A metal ornament used for protecting the corners or centers of books. —*tr.v.* **bossed, bossing, bosses. 1.** To decorate with bosses. **2.** To emboss. [Middle English *boce,* from Old French, from Vulgar Latin *bottia* (unattested). See **cabbage.**]

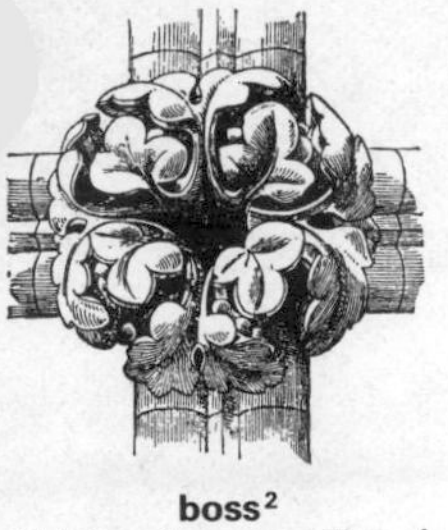

boss²
Thirteenth-century French architectural boss

boss³ (bôs, bŏs) *n.* A cow or calf. [Origin unknown.]

bos·sism (bô′sĭz′əm, bŏs′ĭz′əm) *n.* The domination of a political organization by a political boss.

boss·y¹ (bô′sē, bŏs′ē) *adj.* **-ier, -iest.** Commanding, domineering, or overbearing. —**boss′i·ly** *adv.* —**boss′i·ness** *n.*

boss·y² (bô′sē, bŏs′ē) *adj.* Decorated with studs or similar raised ornaments.

bos·sy³ (bô′sē, bŏs′ē) *n., pl.* **-sies.** *Informal.* A cow or calf. [From BOSS (cow).]

Bos·ton (bô′stən, bŏs′tən). The capital and chief port of Massachusetts. Population, 697,000. —**Bos·to′ni·an** (bô-stō′nē-ən, bŏs-) *adj.* & *n.*

Boston bag. A handbag or satchel for books and papers, with handles on both sides of the top opening.

Boston bull. A dog, the **Boston terrier** *(see).*

Boston cream pie. A cake with a custard filling.

Boston fern. A fern, *Nephrolepis exaltata bostoniensis,* having arching or drooping fronds with opposite leaflets.

Boston ivy. A widely cultivated climbing woody vine, *Parthenocissus tricuspidata,* native to Asia, that has three-lobed leaves and that frequently covers the outer walls of buildings. Also called "Japanese ivy."

Boston lettuce. A type of cultivated lettuce forming a rounded head and having soft-textured, yellow-green leaves.

Boston Massacre. A riot in Boston (March 5, 1770) between a local mob and British troops who in self-defense killed five men.

Bos·ton Mountains (bŏs′tən). A ridge 1,000 to 2,000 feet high in the Ozark Mountains of northwestern Arkansas.

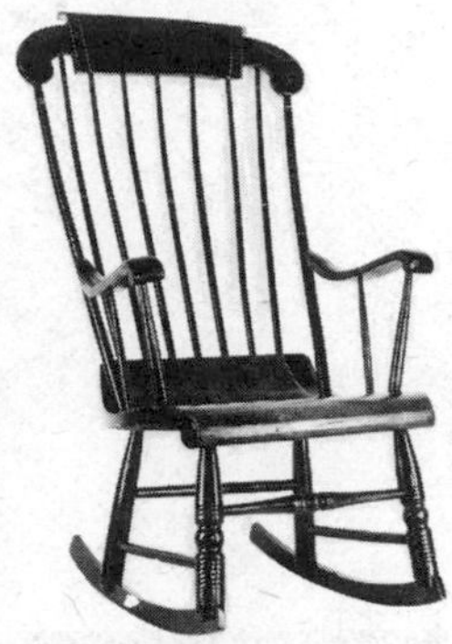

Boston rocker

Boston rocker. A 19th-century American wooden rocking chair with a curved seat, a high spindled back, and usually a headpiece with stenciled decorations.

Boston Tea Party. A protest staged by American colonists in Boston (December 16, 1773) against the British tax on imported tea. The colonists disguised as Indians boarded British ships in Boston Harbor and threw chests of tea overboard.

Boston terrier. A small dog of a breed that originated in New England as a cross between a bull terrier and a bulldog. Also called "Boston bull."

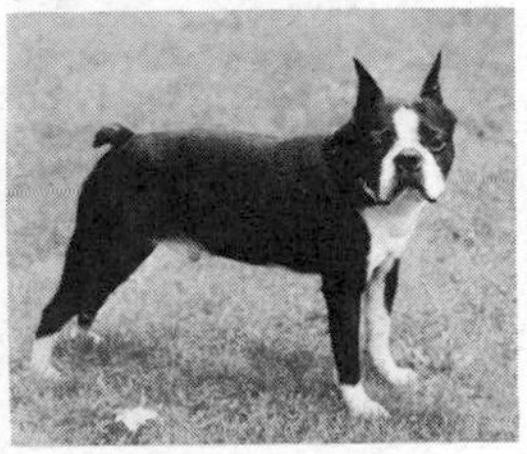

Boston terrier

bo·sun. Variant of **boatswain.**

Bos·well (bŏz′wĕl′, -wəl) *n.* An assiduous and devoted admirer, student, and recorder of another's words and deeds. [After James BOSWELL.]

Bos·well (bŏz′wĕl′, -wəl), **James.** 1740–1795. Scottish lawyer and writer; biographer of Samuel Johnson.

Bos·worth Field (bŏz′wûrth). Site of the final battle in the Wars of the Roses, near Leicester in central England, where Richard III, the last Plantagenet king, was defeated on August 22, 1485, by Henry Tudor.

bot (bŏt) *n.* Also **bott.** The parasitic larva of a botfly. [Middle English, probably of Low German origin, akin to Dutch *bot*†.]

bot. 1. botanical; botanist; botany. **2.** bottle.

bo·tan·i·cal (bə-tăn′ĭ-kəl) *adj.* Also **bo·tan·ic** (bə-tăn′ĭk). *Abbr.* **bot. 1.** Of or pertaining to plants or plant life: *a collection of botanical specimens.* **2.** Of or pertaining to the science of botany. —*n.* A drug, medicinal preparation, or similar substance obtained from a plant or plants. [French *botanique,* from Late Latin *botanicus,* from Greek *botanikos,* from *botanē*†, pasture, herb, plant.] —**bo·tan′i·cal·ly** *adv.*

bot·a·nist (bŏt′n-ĭst) *n. Abbr.* **bot.** One who specializes in the study of plants.

bot·a·nize (bŏt′n-īz′) *v.* **-nized, -nizing, -nizes.** —*intr.* **1.** To secure plants for botanical study. **2.** To examine plants scientifically. —*tr.* To investigate (an area) for botanical study. —**bot′a·niz′er** *n.*

bot·a·ny (bŏt′n-ē) *n., pl.* **-nies.** *Abbr.* **bot. 1.** The biological science of plants. **2.** The plant life of a particular area or district. **3.** The characteristics and phenomena of a plant group or category: *the botany of grasses.* **4. a.** A book or scholarly work on botany. **b.** A particular system of botany: *the botany of Linnaeus.* [From BOTANICAL.]

Bot·a·ny Bay (bŏt′n-ē). An inlet of the Tasman Sea on the eastern coast of New South Wales, Australia. Nearby is the site of a former penal colony.

botch (bŏch) *tr.v.* **botched, botching, botches. 1.** To ruin through clumsiness. **2.** To make or perform clumsily; bungle. **3.** To repair or mend clumsily. —*n.* **1.** A ruined or defective piece of work: *"I have made a miserable botch of this description."* (Hawthorne). **2.** A badly repaired part or flaw: *"Let it stick as a notorious botch of deformity."* (Milton). [Middle English *bocchen*†, to patch up, mend.] —**botch′er** *n.*

botch·y (bŏch′ē) *adj.* **-ier, -iest.** Carelessly or clumsily done or made; imperfect. —**botch′i·ly** *adv.*

bot·fly (bŏt′flī′) *n., pl.* **-flies.** Also **bot fly.** Any of various winged insects, chiefly of the genera *Gasterophilus* and *Oestrus,* having larvae that are parasitic on man and on sheep, horses, and other animals.

both (bōth) *adj.* The two; the two in conjunction: *Both boys arrived.* —*pron.* The one and the other: *Both are patriots.* —*conj.* As well; together; equally. Used correlatively with *and* to show that each of two coordinated words or things in coordinated phrases or clauses is included: *both Keats and Shelley.* See Usage note below. [Middle English *bothe, bathe,* from Old Norse *bāthir.* See **ambhō** in Appendix.*]

Usage: *Both* refers to two, in careful usage. Thus, in *deficient in both content, organization, and style,* eliminate *both. Both* is usually redundant in combination with *as well as, equal, equally, alike,* and *together.* In all of the following, omit *both: deficient in both content as well as style; they are both equal; they are both equally bad; they are both alike; they both appeared together in the film. Both* is loosely used for *each* in the following: *Both* (properly *each*) *accused the other. There is a toll booth on both sides of the road* (preferably *on each side* or *booths on both sides*). In formal usage, constructions such as *both girls* and *both the girls* are generally preferred to *both of the girls.* The construction *the both* is avoided in careful usage: *gave it to the both of us* (omit *the*). Possessive constructions with *both* are now most formally, and usually most clearly, expressed by *of both: the mothers of both* (rather than *both their mothers*); *the fault of both* (preferable to *both their fault* or *both's fault*). In written usage, *both* and *and,* in combination, are usually construed as parallel; generally each is followed by a word or phrase that corresponds grammatically to what follows the other: *in both India and China; both in India and in China* (rather than *both in India and China*); *considered both as assets and as liabilities* (or *as both assets and liabilities*).

Bo·tha (bō′tə), **Louis.** 1862–1919. South African statesman and military leader; first prime minister of Union of South Africa.

Bo·the (bō′tə), **Walther Wilhelm Georg Franz.** 1891–1957. German theoretical physicist; worked on quantum theory.

both·er (bŏth′ər) *v.* **-ered, -ering, -ers.** —*tr.* **1.** To irritate, particularly by small annoyances; pester; harass. **2. a.** To make agitated or nervous; fluster. **b.** To make confused or perplexed; bewilder; puzzle. **3.** To thrust oneself in without invitation or warrant; disturb. **4.** To give trouble to: *a back condition that bothers him constantly.* —*intr.* **1.** To trouble or concern oneself. **2.** To cause trouble. —See Synonyms at **annoy.** —*n.* A cause or state of disturbance. —*interj. Chiefly British.* Used to express mild irritation. [Perhaps from Irish *buaidhrim,* I vex, from Old Irish *buadrim.* See **gwōu-** in Appendix.*]

both·er·a·tion (bŏth′ə-rā′shən) *n.* Irritation; vexation; bother.

both·er·some (bŏth′ər-səm) *adj.* Causing vexation or irritation; troublesome.

Both·ni·a, Gulf of (bŏth′nē-ə). A northern arm of the Baltic Sea between Sweden and Finland.

Both·well (bŏth′wəl), **Earl of.** Title of James Hepburn. 1536?–1578. Scottish Protestant nobleman; third husband of Mary, Queen of Scots; died in exile in Denmark.

bo tree (bō). An Asiatic tree, the **peepul** *(see).* According to Buddhist tradition, this is the tree under which the Buddha attained enlightenment. [Singhalese *bo,* from Pali *bodhi(taru),* "(tree of) wisdom," from Sanskrit *bodhi,* wisdom, enlightenment, from *bodhati,* he awakes. See **bheudh-** in Appendix.*]

bot·ry·oi·dal (bŏt′rē-oid′l) *adj.* Also **bot·ry·oid** (bŏt′rē-oid′). Formed like a bunch of grapes. [From Greek *botruoeidēs* : *botrus*†, bunch of grapes + -OID.] —**bot′ry·oi′dal·ly** *adv.*

Bot·swa·na (bŏt-swä′nə). A republic occupying 222,000 square miles in southern Africa. Formerly, a British protectorate called Bechuanaland, it became independent in 1966. Population, 559,000. Capital, Gaberones.

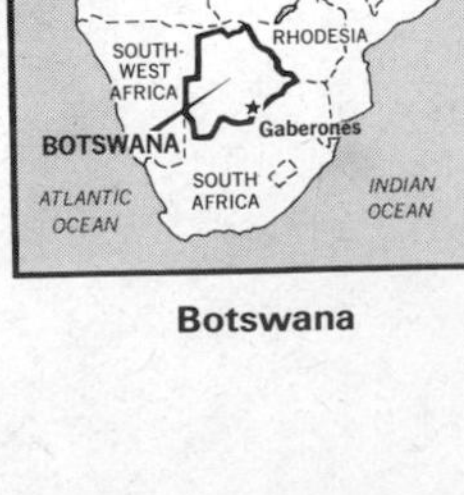

Botswana

bott. Variant of **bot.**

Bot·ti·cel·li (bŏt′ĭ-chĕl′ē; *Italian* bōt′tē-chĕl′lē), **Sandro.** Original name, Alessandro di Mariano dei Filipepi. 1444?–1510. Italian painter of Florentine school.

bot·tle (bŏt′l) *n. Abbr.* **bot. 1.** A receptacle, usually glass, having a narrow neck and mouth that can be plugged, corked, or capped. **2.** The quantity a bottle contains. —**hit the bottle.** *Slang.* To drink intoxicating liquor to excess. —**the bottle. 1.** Intoxicating drink: *addicted to the bottle.* **2.** Milk or formula fed to a baby from a bottle: *brought up on the bottle.* —*tr.v.* **bottled, -tling, -tles. 1.** To place in a bottle or bottles. **2.** To confine as if in a bottle. Used with *up: bottle up one's emotions.* [Middle English *botel,* from Old French *botele, botaille,* from Medieval Latin *butticula,* diminutive of Late Latin *buttis,* cask, akin to Greek *putine, butinē*†.] —**bot′tler** *n.*

bot·tle·brush (bŏt′l-brŭsh′) *n.* Any of various shrubs or trees of the genera *Callistemon* and *Melaleuca,* native to Australia. They have dense spikes of flowers with protruding stamens that suggest a brush used to clean bottles.

bottle club. A private establishment where patrons may purchase bottles of liquor and keep them for consumption after legal closing hours.

bottled gas. Gas, such as butane or propane, stored under pressure in portable tanks.

bottled in bond. See **bond.**

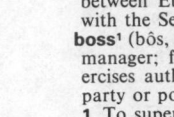

ă pat/ā pay/âr care/ä father/b bib/ch church/d deed/ĕ pet/ē be/f fife/g gag/h hat/hw which/ĭ pit/ī pie/îr pier/j judge/k kick/l lid, needle/m mum/n no, sudden/ng thing/ŏ pot/ō toe/ô paw, for/oi noise/ou out/ŏŏ took/ōō boot/p pop/r roar/s sauce/sh ship, dish/

bottle gentian. A plant, *Gentiana andrewsii,* of eastern and central North America, having deep-blue flowers that remain closed. Also called "closed gentian."
bottle gourd. A vine, the **calabash** *(see),* or its fruit.
bottle green. Dark to moderate or grayish green. See **color.** —**bot′tle-green′** *adj.*
bot·tle·neck (bŏt′l-nĕk′) *n.* **1.** The narrow part of a bottle near the top. **2.** A narrow or obstructed section of a highway, pipeline, or the like. **3.** Any hindrance to production or progress. —*tr.v.* **bottlenecked, -necking, -necks.** To impede or slow down by creating a bottleneck.
bot·tle-nosed dolphin (bŏt′l-nōzd′). Any of several marine mammals of the genus *Tursiops,* having a short, protruding beak. Also called "bottlenose."
bottle tree. Any of several trees of the genus *Stercula* (or *Brachychiton*), native to Australia, characterized by a bottlelike swelling of the trunk.
bot·tom (bŏt′əm) *n.* **1.** The lowest or deepest part of anything. **2.** The underside. **3.** The supporting part of something; a foundation; base. **4.** The basic underlying quality; essence. **5.** The land below a body of water: *a river bottom.* **6.** *Often plural.* Low-lying alluvial land adjacent to a river; bottom land. **7.** *Nautical.* The part of a ship's hull below the water line. **8.** A ship: *"English merchants did much of their overseas trade in foreign bottoms."* (G.M. Trevelyan). **9.** *Plural.* The trousers of pajamas. **10.** *Informal.* The buttocks. **11.** The seat of a chair. **12.** Staying power; stamina: *A horse with good bottom.* —**at bottom.** Basically; actually. —**bottoms up.** *Informal.* Drain your glass. —*adj.* Lowest; undermost; fundamental. —*v.* **bottomed, -toming, -toms.** —*tr.* **1.** To provide with an underside or foundation. **2.** To establish on a foundation or basis; ground; found. Used with *on* or *upon: The theory is bottomed on questionable assumptions.* **3.** To grasp the meaning of; fathom: *bottom a mystery.* —*intr.* **1.** To be based or grounded. Used with *on* or *upon.* **2.** To rest on or touch the bottom: *The submarine bottomed on the ocean floor.* —**bottom out.** To descend to the lowest point possible, after which only a rise may occur: *Steel stocks bottomed out in the market.* [Middle English *botme,* Old English *botm.* See **bhudh-** in Appendix.*]
bottom dollar. *Slang.* The last of one's money: *bet one's bottom dollar.*
bottom land. Low land along a river; bottom.
bot·tom·less (bŏt′əm-lĭs) *adj.* **1.** Having no bottom. **2.** Unfathomable; limitless.
bot·tom·ry (bŏt′əm-rē) *n.* A contract by which a shipowner borrows money to finance a voyage, pledging the vessel as security. [Earlier *bottomary,* from Dutch *bodemerij,* from *bodem,* (ship's) bottom, hull. See **bhudh-** in Appendix.*]
Bot·trop (bôt′rôp). A city of West Germany, situated in the Ruhr industrial region. It was formed in 1919 by merging several villages built over coal mines. Population, 113,000.
bot·u·lin (bŏch′ŏŏ-lĭn) *n.* Any of several nerve toxins produced by the bacterium *Clostridium botulinum* and found in improperly canned or improperly smoked foods. [New Latin *botulinus,* from Latin *botulus,* sausage. See **gwet-³** in Appendix.*]
bot·u·lism (bŏch′ŏŏ-lĭz′əm) *n.* An often fatal food poisoning caused by botulin and characterized by vomiting, abdominal pain, coughing, muscular weakness, and visual disturbance. [German *Botulismus,* "sausage-poisoning," from Latin *botulus,* sausage. See **gwet-³** in Appendix.*]
Bou·cher (bōō-shā′), **François.** 1703–1770. French rococo artist; court painter to Louis XV.
Bou·ci·cault (bōō′sĭ-kō′), **Dion.** Original name, Dionysius Lardner Boursiquot. 1820?–1890. Irish actor and author of farces and melodramas.
bou·cle (bōō-klā′) *n.* **1.** A type of yarn, usually three-ply and having one thread looser than the others, which produces a rough-textured cloth. **2.** Fabric woven or knitted from this yarn. [French, curled, past participle of *boucler,* to curl, from Old French *boucle,* curl of hair, BUCKLE.]
Bou·dic·ca. See **Boadicea.**
bou·doir (bōō′dwär′, -dwôr′) *n.* A woman's private sitting room, dressing room, or bedroom. [French, "place for pouting," from Old French *bouder,* to pout, sulk (imitative).]
bouf·fant (bōō-fänt′) *adj.* Puffed-out; full: *a bouffant hair style.* [French, puffed, full, present participle of *bouffer,* to swell, puff up (the cheeks), from Old French (imitative).]
bouffe (bōōf) *n.* Comic opera. See **opera buffa.**
Bou·gain·ville (bōō′gən-vĭl′). The largest (3,880 square miles) of the Solomon Islands in the southwestern Pacific, administered by Australia as part of the Trust Territory of New Guinea. Population, 64,000.
Bou·gain·ville (bōō-găN-vēl′), **Louis Antoine de.** 1729–1811. French explorer, military leader, and scientist.
bou·gain·vil·le·a (bōō′gən-vĭl′ē-ə, -vĭl′yə) *n.* Also **bou·gain·vil·lae·a.** Any of several woody tropical American vines of the genus *Bougainvillea,* having inconspicuous flowers surrounded by showy red, purple, or orange bracts. [After Louis Antoine de BOUGAINVILLE.]
bough (bou) *n.* A large branch of a tree. [Middle English *bow, bough,* Old English *bōg, bōh.* See **bhāghu-** in Appendix.*]
bought. Past tense and past participle of **buy.**
bought·en. *Regional.* Alternate past participle of **buy.**
bou·gie (bōō′zhē, -jē) *n.* **1.** A wax candle. **2.** *Medicine.* **a.** A slender, pliable implement inserted into a bodily canal, as the urethra or rectum. **b.** A suppository. [French, from Old French, a fine wax imported from *Bougie,* town in Algeria.]
Bou·guer·eau (bōō-grō′), **Adolphe William.** 1825–1905. French academic painter.
bouil·la·baisse (bōō′yə-bās′) *n.* A highly seasoned fish stew made with several kinds of fish and shellfish. [French, earlier *bouille-abaisse,* from Provençal *bouiabaisso,* "boil (and) settle" (jocular command to the pot, because the fish is rapidly cooked) : *boui,* imperative of *bouie,* to boil, from Latin *bullīre* (see **beu-¹** in Appendix*) + *abaisso,* imperative of *abeissa,* to lower, from Vulgar Latin *abbassiāre* (unattested), ABASE.]
bouil·lon (bōōl′yŏn′, bōōl′yŏn′, -yən) *n.* A clear thin broth made typically by simmering beef or chicken in water with seasonings. [French, from Old French, from *boulir,* to boil, from Latin *bullīre.* See **beu-¹** in Appendix.*]
boul. boulevard.
Bou·lan·ger (bōō-läN-zhā′), **Georges Ernest Jean Marie.** 1837–1891. French military and political leader.
boul·der (bōl′dər) *n.* Also **bowl·der.** A large rounded stone block lying on the surface of the ground, or sometimes imbedded in the soil, and generally different in composition from other rocks in the immediate vicinity. [Middle English *bulder (ston),* from Scandinavian, akin to dialectal Swedish *bullersten,* stone in a stream : *buller-,* "rounded object" (see **bhel-²** in Appendix*) + *sten,* stone.]
Boul·der (bōl′dər). A city in northern Colorado, 25 miles northwest of Denver. Population, 38,000.
Boulder Canyon. A former canyon of the Colorado River, between Arizona and Nevada, now inundated by Lake Mead.
Boulder Dam. The former name for **Hoover Dam.**
bou·le¹ (bōō′lē, bōō-lā′) *n.* **1. a.** *Capital* **B.** The senate of 400 founded in ancient Athens by Solon. **b.** A legislative assembly in any of the states of ancient Greece. **2.** *Capital* **B.** The lower house of the modern Greek legislature. [Greek *boulē,* "will," "council." See **gwel-¹** in Appendix.*]
boule² (bōōl) *n.* A pear-shaped synthetic sapphire, ruby, or other alumina-based gem, produced by fusing and tinting alumina. [French, "ball," from Latin *bulla,* bubble, ball. See **beu-¹** in Appendix.*]
boule³. Variant of **buhl.**
boul·e·vard (bōōl′ə-värd′, bōō′lə-) *n. Abbr.* **blvd., boul.** A broad city street, often tree-lined and landscaped. [French, from Old French *boloart, belouart,* rampart, promenade converted from an old rampart, from Middle Dutch *bolwerc,* from Middle High German, BULWARK.]
bou·le·var·dier (bōō′lə-vär-dyā′, bōōl′ə-vär-dîr′) *n.* A man about town. [French, a man who frequents boulevards, from BOULEVARD.]
boulle. Variant of **buhl.**
Bou·logne (bōō-lōn′, -loin′; *French* bōō-lôn′y′). In full **Bou·logne-sur-Mer** (-sür-mâr′). A seaport on the English Channel on the coast of northern France. Napoleon collected a fleet here in 1808 for his proposed invasion of England. Population, 49,000.
Bou·logne-Bil·lan·court (bōō-lôn′y′-bē-yäN-kōōr′). An industrial city and suburb of Paris, France, situated to the southwest on the Seine. Population, 107,000.
bounce (bouns) *v.* **bounced, bouncing, bounces.** —*intr.* **1. a.** To rebound elastically from a collision. **b.** To collide and rebound elastically several times in succession. **2.** To bound thumpingly: *The child bounced into the room.* **3.** *Informal.* To be sent back by a bank as valueless: *The check bounced.* —*tr.* **1.** To cause (a body) to collide and rebound. **2.** *Slang.* **a.** To expel by force. **b.** To dismiss from employment. —*n.* **1.** A bound or rebound. **2.** A sudden spring or leap. **3. a.** A loud or heavy blow or thump. **b.** *Archaic.* The sound of an explosion: *"He speaks plain cannon fire, and smoke and bounce."* (Shakespeare). **4.** Capacity to bounce; spring: *A ball with bounce.* **5.** Spirit; liveliness; vigor. **6.** *Slang.* Expulsion; dismissal. **7.** *British.* Impudent bluster; vaunt: *"The whole story is a bounce of his own."* (De Quincey). [Middle English *bunsen, bonchen,* to beat, thrust, stamp (probably imitative).]
bounc·er (boun′sər) *n.* **1.** One that bounces. **2.** *Slang.* A person employed to expel disorderly persons from a public place.
bounc·ing (boun′sĭng) *adj.* **1.** Vigorous; healthy: *a bouncing baby.* **2.** Big; strapping; exaggerated. —**bounc′ing·ly** *adv.*
bouncing Bet. A plant, *Saponaria officinalis,* native to the Old World, having rounded clusters of fragrant pink or white flowers. Also called "soapwort." [*Bet,* pet form of ELIZABETH (from its flower clusters, suggesting bouncing girls).]
bounc·y (boun′sē) *adj.* **-ier, -iest. 1.** Characterized by a capacity to bound or spring. **2.** Having vigor and buoyancy; lively. —**bounc′i·ly** *adv.*
bound¹ (bound) *intr.v.* **bounded, bounding, bounds. 1.** To leap forward or upward; to spring. **2.** To progress by bounds. —*n.* **1.** A leap; jump. **2.** A bounce. [French *bondir,* to bounce, originally "to rebound," from Old French, to resound, from Vulgar Latin *bombitīre* (unattested), to hum, buzz, from Latin *bombīre,* to buzz, from *bombus,* a deep hollow sound, buzz, from Greek *bombos.* See **bamb-** in Appendix.*]
bound² (bound) *n.* **1.** *Usually plural.* A boundary; limit: *His joy knew no bounds.* **2.** *Plural.* The territory on, within, or near limiting lines: *the bounds of the kingdom.* —See Synonyms at **boundary.** —**out of bounds. 1.** Beyond boundaries, as of a playing field. **2.** Transgressing moral or conventional limits. —*v.* **bounded, bounding, bounds.** —*tr.* **1.** To provide a limit to. **2.** To constitute the boundary or limit of. **3.** To identify and set the boundaries of; demarcate. —*intr.* To border on another country, state, or place; adjoin. —See Synonyms at **limit.** [Middle English *bounde,* from Old French *bunde, bodne,* from Medieval Latin *bodina,* from Gaulish *bodina*† (unattested).]
bound³ (bound). Past tense and past participle of **bind.** —*adj.* **1.** Confined by bonds; tied. Often used in combination: *muscle-*

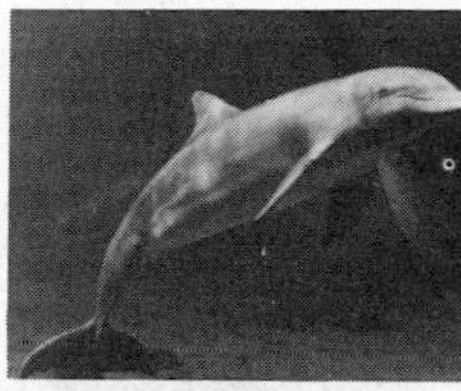

bottle-nosed dolphin
Tursiops truncatus

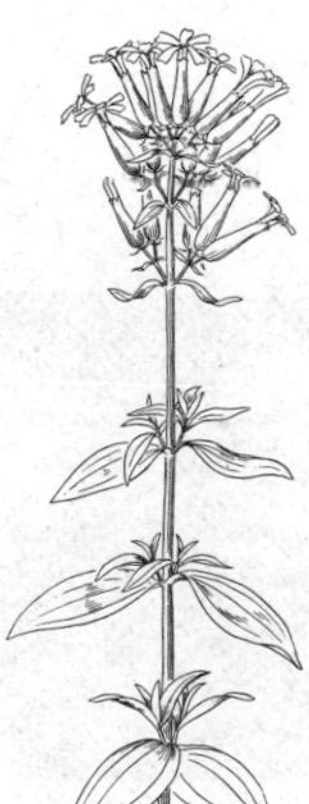

bouncing Bet

bound; snowbound. **2.** Under legal or moral obligation; under contract: *bound by his promise.* **3.** Indentured: *a bound apprentice.* **4.** *Abbr.* **bd.** Equipped with a cover or binding: *bound volumes.* **5.** Predetermined; certain: *We are bound to be late.* **6.** Determined; resolved: *He's bound to be mayor.* **7.** Constipated. —**bound up in** (or **with**). **1.** Inseparably connected with. **2.** Wholly dedicated to: *She is bound up in her career.*

bound⁴ (bound) *adj.* Headed for; going toward: *bound for home.* [Middle English *boun,* prepared, ready to go, from Old Norse *būinn,* past participle of *būa,* to dwell, prepare. See **bheu-** in Appendix.*]

bound·a·ry (boun′drē, -də-rē) *n., pl.* **-ries. 1.** Something that indicates a border or limit. **2.** The border or limit so indicated. [Earlier *bounder,* from BOUND (limit).]

Synonyms: *boundary, border, frontier, limit, bound, end, confine. Boundary* is usually applied geographically to a precisely defined terminating line of a country, city, or the like. *Border* may be used in this exact sense or more broadly to denote the territory immediately adjoining a boundary. *Frontier* denotes either the part of a country that faces toward or fronts an adjoining country or (within a country) the remote, imprecisely defined area that marks the farthest settlement. Figuratively the term applies to any newly explored branch of knowledge. *Limit* (often in the plural) is interchangeable with *boundary* in a physical sense; figuratively it indicates an extent beyond which an activity or function cannot or should not take place. *Bound* (usually plural) is interchangeable with *boundary,* physically: *The ball went out of bounds;* figuratively it has the sense of limit: *the bounds of good taste. End* (often plural) in this comparison emphasizes remoteness or extreme limit in all senses: *the ends of the earth; the end of his rope. Confine* (usually plural) is used physically and figuratively to denote enclosure or limitation.

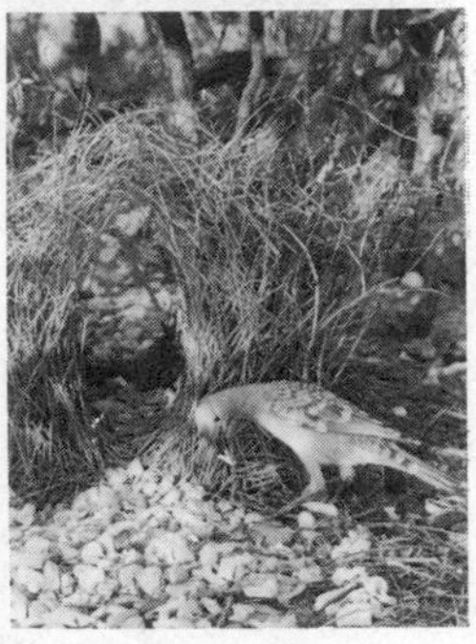

bowerbird
Chlamydera nuchalis

boundary layer. *Physics.* The nearly motionless fluid layer found immediately adjacent to a boundary, such as the surface of a solid, past which the fluid flows.

Boundary Peak. The highest elevation (13,145 feet) in Nevada, in the southwest on the California-Nevada border.

bound·en (boun′dən) *adj.* **1.** Under obligation; obliged. **2.** Obligatory: *his bounden duty.* [From *bounden,* obsolete past participle of BIND.]

bound·er (boun′dər) *n.* **1.** One that bounds. **2.** *Chiefly British.* A vulgar, cocksure fellow.

bound form. A linguistic element that always occurs as part of another word, as *-ly* in *lovely.* Compare **free form.**

bound·less (bound′lĭs) *adj.* Without limit; infinite. See Synonyms at **infinite.** —**bound′less·ly** *adv.* —**bound′less·ness** *n.*

boun·te·ous (boun′tē-əs) *adj.* **1.** Giving generously and kindly **2.** Copious; plentiful. [Middle English *bountevous, bounteuous* from Old French *bontif, bontive,* benevolent, from *bonte,* BOUNTY.] —**boun′te·ous·ly** *adv.* —**boun′te·ous·ness** *n.*

boun·ti·ful (boun′tĭ-fəl) *adj.* **1.** Generous. **2.** Abundant; plentiful. —**boun′ti·ful·ly** *adv.* —**boun′ti·ful·ness** *n.*

boun·ty (boun′tē) *n., pl.* **-ties. 1.** Liberality in giving. **2.** Something that is given liberally. **3.** A reward, inducement, or payment, especially one given by a government for acts beneficial to the state, such as killing predatory animals, growing certain crops, starting certain industries, or enlisting for military service. —See Synonyms at **bonus.** [Middle English *bounte,* from Old French *bonte,* from Latin *bonitās,* goodness, from *bonus,* good. See **deu-²** in Appendix.*]

bounty hunter. One who hunts predatory animals or criminals and outlaws for a bounty.

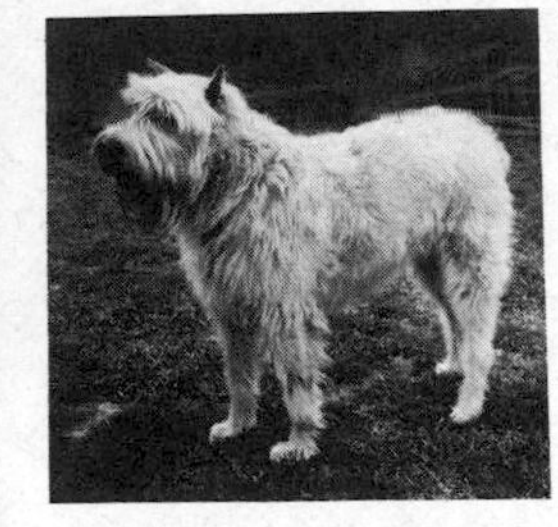

Bouvier des Flandres

bounty jumper. One who deserts the army, having enlisted only for the sake of the bounty, as during the Civil War.

bou·quet (bō-kā′, bo͞o- *for sense 1;* bo͞o-kā′ *for sense 2*) *n.* **1.** A cluster of flowers; nosegay. **2.** The fragrance typical of a wine or a liqueur. —See Synonyms at **smell.** [French, from Old North French *bosquet,* clump, diminutive of Old French *bosc,* forest, from Germanic. See **busk-** in Appendix.*]

bou·quet gar·ni (bō-kā′ gär-nē′, bo͞o-) *pl.* **bouquets garnis** (bō-kāz′ gär-nē′, bo͞o-). A bunch of herbs tied together or wrapped in cheesecloth, immersed in a soup or stew as seasoning. [French, "garnished bouquet."]

bour·bon (bûr′bən) *n.* A whiskey distilled from a fermented mash containing not less than 51 per cent corn. [Originally made in *Bourbon* County, Kentucky.]

Bour·bon (bo͝or′bən; *French* bo͞or-bôN′). A French royal family including rulers of France (1589–1793 and 1814–30); of Spain (1700–1808, 1814–68, and 1874–1931); and of Naples (1735–1805 and 1815–60).

bour·don (bo͝or′dən) *n.* **1.** The monotonic drone bass of a bagpipe. **2.** An organ stop, commonly of the 16-foot pipes. [Middle English *burdoun,* from Old French *bourdon,* drone, from Medieval Latin *burdō* (imitative).]

bourg (bo͝org; *French* bo͞or) *n.* **1.** A medieval village, especially one situated near a castle. **2.** A French market town. [Middle English, fortified town, from Old French, from Late Latin *burgus.* See **bhergh-²** in Appendix.*]

bour·geois¹ (bo͝or-zhwä′, bo͝or′zhwä′) *n., pl.* **bourgeois. 1.** One belonging to the bourgeoisie. **2.** *Plural.* The middle class; the bourgeoisie. **3.** One whose attitudes and behavior are marked by conformity to the standards and conventions of the middle class. **4.** In Marxist theory, a member of the property-owning class; a capitalist, as opposed to a member of the proletariat. —*adj.* Of or typical of the middle class. Often used disparagingly to suggest such qualities as mediocrity or a preoccupation with respectability and material values. [French, from Old French *burgeis,* from *bourg,* fortified town, BOURG.]

bour·geois² (bər-jois′) *n. Printing.* A size of type, approximately 9-point. [Possibly from its middling size between long primer and brevier.]

Bour·geois (bo͝or-zhwä′), **Léon Victor Auguste.** 1851–1925. French statesman; an organizer and first chairman of League of Nations.

bour·geoise (bo͝or-zhwäz′, bo͝or′zhwäz′) *n., pl.* **-geoises** (-zhwä′-zĭz). A female member of the bourgeoisie. —**bour·geoise′** *adj.*

bour·geoi·sie (bo͝or′zhwä-zē′) *n.* **1.** The class of tradesmen; the middle class. **2.** In Marxist theory, the social group opposed to the proletariat in the class struggle; the capitalist class. [French, from BOURGEOIS.]

bour·geon. Variant of **burgeon.**

Bour·gogne. The French name for **Burgundy.**

Bour·gui·ba (bo͝or-gē′bə), **Habib ben Ali.** Born 1903. Tunisian nationalist leader and statesman; first premier (1956) and first president (since 1957).

Bourke-White (bûrk′hwīt′), **Margaret.** Born 1906. American photographer and author.

bourn¹ (bôrn, bōrn, bo͝orn) *n.* Also **bourne.** A stream or small brook. [Middle English *burne,* variant of *burn,* BURN (brook).]

bourn² (bôrn, bōrn, bo͝orn) *n.* Also **bourne.** *Archaic.* **1.** The terminal point of a trip or course of action; a goal. **2.** A boundary, as between properties. [French *bourne,* from Old French *bonne, bodne,* BOUND (limit).]

Bourne·mouth (bôrn′məth, bōrn′-, bo͝orn′-). A seaside resort in south-central England, on the English Channel. Population, 151,000.

bour·rée (bo͞o-rā′, bo͞o-) *n.* **1.** An old French dance resembling the gavotte, and usually in quick duple time beginning with an upbeat. **2.** The music for this dance. [French, "fagot" (probably from its rude movements), from *bourrer,* to stuff, from Old French *bourre,* stuffing, fluff, from Late Latin *burra,* shaggy garment. See **burl.**]

bourse (bo͝ors) *n.* Also **Bourse.** The stock exchange of a city of continental Europe, especially Paris. [French, "purse," from Late Latin *bursa,* from Greek. See **bursa** in Appendix.*]

bouse (bouz) *v.* **boused, bousing, bouses.** Also **bowse.** *Nautical.* —*tr.* To hoist or pull up with a tackle. —*intr.* To hoist. [Origin unknown.]

bou·stro·phe·don (bo͞o′strə-fēd′n, -fē′dŏn′) *n.* An ancient method of writing in which the lines are inscribed alternately from right to left and from left to right. [Greek *boustrophēdon,* turning like an ox (while plowing) : *bous,* ox (see **gwou-** in Appendix*) + *strephein,* to turn (see **strebh-** in Appendix*).] —**bou·stroph′e·don′ic** (-strŏf′ə-dŏn′ĭk) *adj.*

bout (bout) *n.* **1.** A contest between antagonists; a match: *a wrestling bout.* **2.** A period of time spent in a particular way; a spell: *"His tremendous bouts of drinking had wrecked his health"* (Thomas Wolfe). [Earlier *bought,* a turn (as in plowing), Middle English *bought,* bend, turn, from Middle Low German *bucht.* See **bheug-³** in Appendix.*]

bou·tique (bo͞o-tēk′) *n.* A small retail shop that specializes in gifts, fashionable clothes, and accessories. [French, from Old Provençal *botica,* from Greek *apothēkē,* storeroom, from *apotithenai,* to put away : *apo-,* away + *tithenai,* to put, place (see **dhē-¹** in Appendix*).]

bou·ton·niere (bo͞o′tə-nîr′, -tən-yâr′) *n.* Also **bou·ton·nière.** A flower or small bunch of flowers worn in a buttonhole, usually on a lapel. [Old French, from *bouton,* BUTTON.]

bou·var·di·a (bo͞o-vär′dē-ə) *n.* Any of several tropical American shrubs of the genus *Bouvardia,* having clusters of white or red, often fragrant flowers. [New Latin *Bouvardia;* after Charles *Bouvard* (died 1658), French physician.]

Bou·vier des Flan·dres (bo͞o-vyā′ də flăn′dərz; *French* bo͞o-vyā′ dā flăN′dr′) *pl.* **Bouviers des Flandres.** A rough-coated dog of a breed originally used in Belgium for herding and guarding cattle. [French, "cowherd of Flanders."]

bo·vid (bō′vĭd) *adj.* Of or belonging to the family Bovidae, which includes hoofed, hollow-horned ruminants such as cattle, sheep, goats, and buffaloes. —*n.* A member of the Bovidae. [New Latin *Bovidae,* from Latin *bōs,* ox, cow. See **bovine.**]

bo·vine (bō′vīn′, -vēn′) *adj.* **1.** Of, pertaining to, or resembling an ox, cow, or other animal of the genus *Bos.* **2.** Sluggish; dull; stolid. —*n.* A bovine animal. [Late Latin *bovīnus,* from Latin *bōs* (stem *bov-*), ox, cow. See **gwou-** in Appendix.*]

bow¹ (bou) *n.* **1.** The front section of a ship or boat. **2.** The oar or oarsman closest to the bow of a boat. —*adj.* Of or close to the bow. [Middle English, from Middle Low German *boog.* See **bhāghu-** in Appendix.*]

bow² (bou) *v.* **bowed, bowing, bows.** —*intr.* **1.** To bend or curve downward; stoop. **2.** To incline the body or head or bend the knee in greeting, consent, courtesy, acknowledgment, submission, or veneration. **3.** To yield or comply; submit. —*tr.* **1.** To bend (the head, knee, or body) in order to express greeting, consent, courtesy, submission, or veneration. **2.** To convey (greeting or consent, for example) by bowing. **3.** To escort deferentially and with bows: *He bowed us into the restaurant.* **4.** To cause to acquiesce; submit. **5.** To cause to bend downward; overburden. Often used with *down: Grief bowed him down.* —See Synonyms at **yield.** —**bow and scrape.** To behave in an obsequious manner. —**bow out.** To remove oneself from a situation or agreement. —*n.* An inclination of the head or body, as in greeting, consent, courtesy, acknowledgment, submission, or veneration. —**make one's bow.** To enter or retire formally. —**take a bow.** To recognize and accept applause or an introduction. [Middle English *bowen,* Old English *būgan.* See **bheug-³** in Appendix.*]

bow³ (bō) *n.* **1.** Something that is bent, curved, or arched: *a bow in a road.* **2.** A weapon consisting of a curved, sometimes recurved, stave of a resilient material, especially wood, strung taut from end to end and used to launch arrows. **3.** An archer, or archers collectively. **4.** A rod having horsehair drawn tightly between its two raised ends, used in playing instruments of the violin and viol families. **5.** A knot usually having two loops and two ends; bowknot. **6. a.** A frame for the lenses of a pair of eyeglasses. **b.** The part of such a frame passing over the ear. **7.** A rainbow. **8.** An oxbow. —*v.* **bowed, bowing, bows.** —*tr.* **1.** To bend (something) into the shape of a bow. **2.** To play (a stringed instrument) with a bow. —*intr.* **1.** To bend into a curve or bow. **2.** To play a stringed instrument with a bow. [Middle English *bowe,* Old English *boga,* bow, arch. See **bheug-**[3] in Appendix.*]

bow compass (bō). A drawing compass with legs that are connected by an adjustable metal spring band.

Bow·ditch (bou′dĭch), **Nathaniel.** 1773–1838. American mathematician and astronomer.

bowd·ler·ize (bōd′lə-rīz′, boud′-) *tr.v.* **-ized, -izing, -izes.** To expurgate prudishly. [After Thomas *Bowdler* (1754–1825), English editor who published an expurgated edition of Shakespeare's works.] —**bowd′ler·ism′** *n.* —**bowd′ler·i·za′tion** *n.*

bow·el (bou′əl, boul) *n.* **1.** An intestine, especially in man. **2.** *Usually plural.* The digestive tract below the stomach. **3.** *Plural.* The interior of anything: *in the bowels of the ship.* **4.** *Plural. Archaic.* The seat of pity or the gentler emotions. —*tr.v.* **boweled, -eling, -els.** Also *chiefly British* **-elled, -elling.** To remove the bowels or entrails from; disembowel. [Middle English *b(o)uel,* from Old French *bo(u)el, boiel,* from Latin *botellus,* diminutive of *botulus,* sausage. See **gwet-**[3] in Appendix.*]

bow·er[1] (bou′ər) *n.* **1.** A shaded, leafy recess; an arbor. **2.** *Rare.* A private chamber; boudoir. **3.** *Poetic.* A rustic cottage; a country retreat. —*tr.v.* **bowered, -ering, -ers.** To enclose in or as in a bower; embower. [Middle English *bour,* dwelling, inner apartment, Old English *būr.* See **bheu-** in Appendix.*] —**bow′er·y** *adj.*

bow·er[2] (bou′ər) *n.* In certain card games, such as euchre, either of the two highest cards, the jack of trumps (right bower) or the jack of the same color as the trump (left bower), except when the joker (best bower) is used. [German *Bauer,* "farmer," "peasant," jack (in cards), from Middle High German *būre, gebūre,* from Old High German *gibūro.* See **bheu-** in Appendix.*]

bow·er[3] (bou′ər) *n.* The heaviest of a ship's anchors, carried at the bow. Also called "bower anchor."

bow·er·bird (bou′ər-bûrd′) *n.* Any of various birds of the family Ptilonorhynchidae, of Australia and New Guinea. The males of many species build bowers of grasses, twigs, and colored materials to attract females.

bow·er·y (bou′ər-ē, bou′rē) *n., pl.* **-ies.** A farm or plantation owned by one of the early Dutch settlers of New York. [Dutch *bouwerij,* farm, estate, from *bouwen,* to cultivate, from Middle Dutch. See **bheu-** in Appendix.*]

Bow·er·y, the (bou′ər-ē, bou′rē). A street and section of lower Manhattan, New York City, frequented by derelicts. [From BOWERY (originally Peter Stuyvesant's estate).]

bow·fin (bō′fĭn′) *n.* A freshwater fish, *Amia calva,* of central and eastern North America. Also called "dogfish," "mudfish."

bow·front (bō′frŭnt′) *adj.* Having an outward-curving front: *a bowfront bureau.*

bow·head (bō′hĕd′) *n.* A whale, *Balaena mysticetus,* of Arctic seas, having a large head. [From the curved top of its head.]

Bow·ie (bō′ē, bōō′ē), **James.** 1790?–1836. American-born Mexican colonist; colonel in Texas army; killed at the Alamo.

bow·ie knife (bō′ē, bōō′ē). A single-edged steel hunting knife, about 15 inches in length, having a hilt and a crosspiece. [Popularized by Colonel James BOWIE (probably designed by his brother, Rezin P. Bowie).]

bow·knot (bō′nŏt′) *n.* A knot with large, decorative loops.

bowl[1] (bōl) *n.* **1. a.** A hemispherical vessel, wider than deep, for food or fluids. **b.** The contents of such a vessel. **2.** A drinking goblet. **3.** A bowl-shaped part, as of a spoon. **4. a.** A bowl-shaped edifice such as an amphitheater or a football stadium. **b.** Any of various football games played after the usual season between selected teams. **5.** A bowl-shaped topographical depression. [Middle English *bolle,* Old English *bolla.* See **bhel-**[2] in Appendix.*]

bowl[2] (bōl) *n.* **1.** A large, wooden ball weighted or slightly flattened so as to roll with a bias. **2.** A roll or throw of the ball, as in bowling. **3.** *Machinery.* A revolving cylinder or drum. —*v.* **bowled, bowling, bowls.** —*intr.* **1.** To participate in a game of bowling. **2.** To throw or roll a ball in bowling. **3.** To move smoothly and rapidly. Usually used with *along.* **4.** *Cricket.* To hurl the ball from one end of the pitch toward the batsman at the other, in a manner distinguished from throwing. —*tr.* **1.** To throw or roll (a ball) in bowling. **2.** To make or achieve by bowling. **3.** *Cricket.* To retire (a batsman) with a bowled ball that knocks the bails off the wicket. Used with *out.* —**bowl over. 1.** To knock over with something rolled. **2.** To take by surprise; astound. [Middle English *boule, bowle,* originally "ball," from Old French *boule,* from Latin *bulla.* See **beu-**[1] in Appendix.*]

bowl·der. Variant of **boulder.**

bow·leg (bō′lĕg′) *n.* A leg having an outward curvature in the region of the knee.

bow·leg·ged (bō′lĕg′ĭd, -lĕgd′) *adj.* Having bowlegs.

bowl·er[1] (bō′lər) *n.* One that bowls.

bowl·er[2] (bō′lər) *n. Chiefly British.* A man's hat, a **derby** *(see).* [After John *Bowler,* 19th-century London hatmaker.]

bow·line (bō′lĭn, -līn′) *n.* **1.** *Nautical.* A rope leading forward from the leech of a square sail to hold the leech forward when sailing close-hauled. **2.** A knot forming a loop that does not slip. In this sense, also called "bowline knot." —**on a bowline.** *Nautical.* Close-hauled. [Middle English *bouline,* probably from Middle Low German *bōlīne* : *boog,* BOW (of a ship) + *līne,* line, from Latin *līnea* (see **line**).]

bowl·ing (bō′lĭng) *n.* **1.** A game played by rolling a ball down a wooden alley in order to knock down a triangular group of ten pins. Also called "tenpins." **2.** Any of various similar games, such as skittles or ninepins. **3. Lawn bowling** *(see).*

bowling alley. 1. A smooth, level, wooden alley used in bowling. **2.** A building or room containing such alleys.

bowling green. A level grassy area for lawn bowling.

bow·man[1] (bō′mən) *n., pl.* **-men** (-mĭn). An archer.

bow·man[2] (bou′mən) *n., pl.* **-men** (-mĭn). An oarsman stationed at the bow of a boat.

bow·man's root (bō′mənz). A plant, *Gillenia trifoliata,* of eastern North America, having compound leaves and small white or pinkish flowers. Also called "Indian physic."

bow pen (bō). A bow compass with a pen at the end of one leg.

Bow River (bō). A river of Canada rising on the eastern slopes of the Canadian Rockies and flowing 315 miles southeast through Alberta to the South Saskatchewan River.

bowse. *Nautical.* Variant of **bouse.**

bow·shot (bō′shŏt′) *n.* The distance an arrow can be shot.

bow·sprit (bou′sprĭt′, bō′-) *n.* A spar extending forward from the stem of a ship. [Middle English *bouspret,* from Middle Low German *bōchsprēt, bugsprēt.* See **sper-**[4] in Appendix.*]

bow·string (bō′strĭng′) *n.* The string of a bow.

bowstring hemp. 1. Any of various plants of the genus *Sansevieria,* having thick, erect leaves. **2.** The fiber from the leaves of these plants, used for cordage and in packing.

bow tie (bō). A man's small necktie tied in the shape of a bow.

bow window (bō). A bay window built in a curve.

bow-wow (bou′wou′) *n.* The bark of a dog. [Imitative.]

bow·yer (bō′yər) *n.* **1.** An archer. **2.** One who makes bows.

box[1] (bŏks) *n.* **1.** *Abbr.* **bx.** A rectangular container, typically having a lid or cover. **2.** *Abbr.* **bx.** The amount or quantity such a container can hold. **3.** A separated compartment in a public place, as a theater, for the accommodation of a small group. **4.** A small structure serving as a shelter: *a sentry box.* **5.** *British.* A small country house in hunting country: *a shooting box.* **6.** A **box stall** *(see).* **7.** The raised seat for the driver of a coach or carriage. **8.** *Baseball.* **a.** An area marked out by chalk lines where the batter stands. **b.** Any of various designated areas for other team members, such as the pitcher, catcher, and coaches. **9.** Featured printed matter enclosed by hairlines, a border, or white space and placed within or between text columns. **10.** A cut in the side of a tree through which sap is collected. **11.** An insulating, enclosing, or protective casing or part in a machine. **12.** An awkward or perplexing situation. **13.** *Vulgar Slang.* The female pudendum. —*tr.v.* **boxed, boxing, boxes. 1.** To pack in a box. **2.** To confine as if in a box. Often used with *in* or *up.* **3.** *Nautical.* To boxhaul. —**box the compass. 1.** To name the points of the compass in proper order. **2.** To make a complete revolution or reversal. [Middle English *box,* Old English *box,* from Late Latin *buxis,* variant of Latin *pyxis,* box (made of boxwood), from Greek *puxis,* from *puxos,* box tree. See **puxos** in Appendix.*]

box[2] (bŏks) *n.* A blow or slap with the hand: *a box on the ear.* —*v.* **boxed, boxing, boxes.** —*tr.* **1.** To hit with the hand or fist. **2.** To take part in a boxing match with. —*intr.* To fight with the fists; to spar. [Middle English *box*†.]

box[3] (bŏks) *n., pl.* **box** or **boxes. 1.** Any evergreen tree or shrub of the genus *Buxus;* especially, *B. sempervirens,* used for hedges, borders, and garden mazes. Also called "boxwood." **2.** The wood of this tree, **boxwood** *(see).* **3.** Any of several trees whose timber or foliage resembles that of box. [Middle English *box,* Old English *box,* from Latin *buxus,* from Greek *puxos.* See **puxos** in Appendix.*]

box calf. Calfskin treated with chromium salts and having square markings on the grain. [Named in the United States after Joseph *Box,* 19th-century London bootmaker.]

box·car (bŏks′kär′) *n.* **1.** An enclosed and covered railway car for the transportation of freight. **2.** *Plural.* In the game of craps, a pair of sixes on the first throw.

box coat. 1. A heavy overcoat formerly worn by coachmen. **2.** A coat designed to hang loose from the shoulders. [From BOX (seat for coach driver).]

box·el·der (bŏks′ĕl′dər) *n.* A maple tree, *Acer negundo,* of North America, having compound leaves with lobed leaflets. Also called "ash-leaved maple."

box·er[1] (bŏk′sər) *n.* One who boxes; specifically, a pugilist.

box·er[2] (bŏk′sər) *n.* One that packs boxes.

box·er[3] (bŏk′sər) *n.* A short-haired dog of a breed developed in Germany, having a brownish coat and a short, square-jawed muzzle. [German *Boxer,* from English BOXER, from its pugnacious nature.]

Box·er (bŏk′sər) *n.* A member of a secret society in China that attempted in 1900 to drive foreigners from the country by violence and to force Chinese Christians to renounce their religion. [Rough translation of Mandarin Chinese *i*[4] *hê*[2] *ch'üan*[2], "righteous harmonious fists," altered from *i*[4] *hê*[2] *t'uan*[2], "Righteous Harmonious Brigade" (name of the society) : *i*[4], righteousness + *hê*[2], harmony + *t'uan*[2], brigade.]

box·fish (bŏks′fĭsh′) *n., pl.* **boxfish** or **-fishes.** A tropical marine fish, the **trunkfish** *(see).*

box·haul (bŏks′hôl′) *tr.v.* **-hauled, hauling, -hauls.** To turn (a

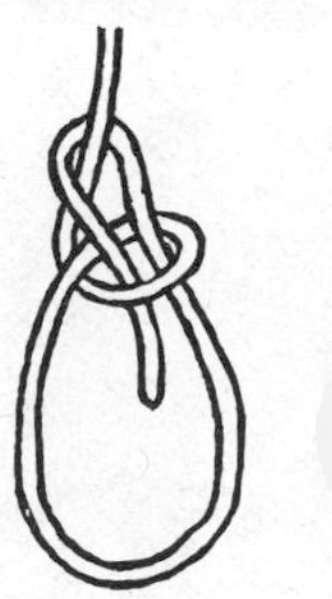
bowline
A bowline knot

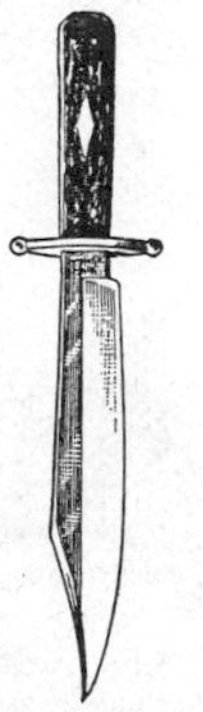
bowie knife

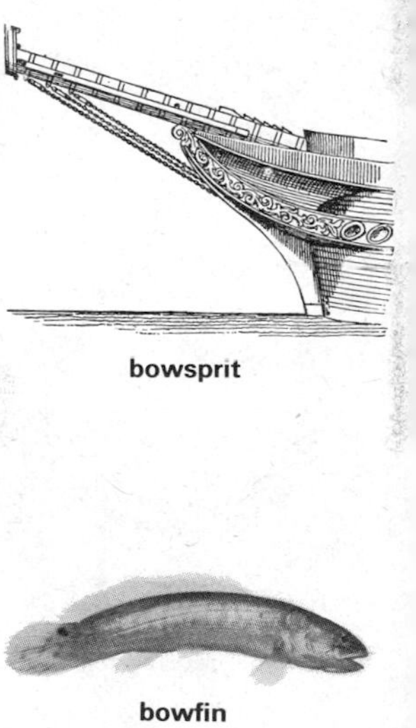
bowsprit

bowfin

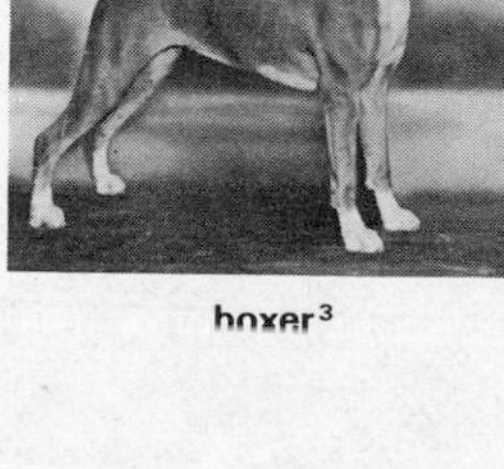
boxer[3]

t tight/th thin, path/*th* this, bathe/ŭ cut/ûr urge/v valve/w with/y yes/z zebra, size/zh vision/ə about, item, edible, gallop, circus/ à *Fr.* ami/œ *Fr.* feu, *Ger.* schön/ü *Fr.* tu, *Ger.* über/KH *Ger.* ich, *Scot.* loch/N *Fr.* bon. ***Follows main vocabulary.** †**Of obscure origin.**

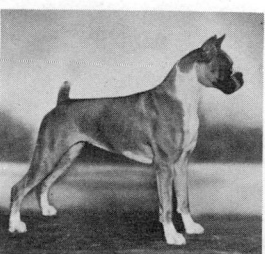

square-rigged ship) about on her heel by bracing her sails aback.

box·ing[1] (bŏk′sĭng) *n.* Material used for a box or boxes.

box·ing[2] (bŏk′sĭng) *n.* The sport of fighting with the fists.

Boxing Day. *British.* The first weekday after Christmas, observed as a holiday, when Christmas gifts or boxes were traditionally given to household employees and other service workers.

boxing glove. A heavily padded leather glove worn in boxing.

box kite. A tailless kite consisting of a rectangular, box-shaped frame, encircled with cloth or paper bands.

box office. **1.** *Abbr.* **b.o.** A ticket office, as of a theater or stadium. **2.** The drawing power of a theatrical entertainment or of a performer; popular appeal. —**box′-of′fice** *adj.*

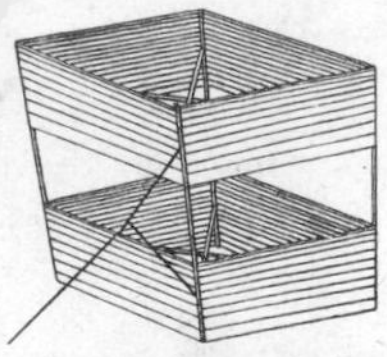

box kite

box pleat. A double pleat formed by two facing folds.

box score. A printed summary of a baseball or basketball game, in the form of a table listing each player and the statistics for his performance.

box seat. A seat in a box at a theater, concert hall, or stadium.

box set. A stage set with a ceiling and three walls.

box spring. A bedspring consisting of a frame enclosed with cloth and containing rows of coil springs.

box stall. An enclosed stall for a single animal.

box·thorn (bŏks′thôrn′) *n.* A shrub, the **matrimony vine** *(see).*

box turtle. Any of several North American turtles of the genus *Terrapene,* having a high-domed shell.

box·wood (bŏks′wo͝od′) *n.* **1.** A shrub or tree, **box** *(see).* **2.** The hard, light-yellow wood of this tree, used to make musical instruments, rulers, inlays, and engraving blocks.

box·y (bŏk′sē) *adj.* **-ier, -iest.** Like a box.

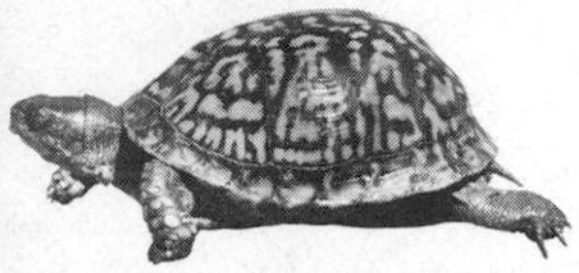

box turtle
Terrapene carolina

boy (boi) *n.* **1.** A male child or youth. **2.** *Informal.* Any grown man; a fellow. **3.** A manservant. —*interj.* Used as a mild exclamation. [Middle English *boye, bay, bye,* originally "male servant," "knave," possibly from Norman French *abuié, embuié* (unattested), "fettered," from Old French *embuier,* to fetter, from Vulgar Latin *imboiāre* (unattested) : *in-,* in + *boiae,* collar for the neck, fetters, from Greek *boeiai (dorai),* ox(hides), hence thongs made from oxhide, from *bous,* ox. See **gwou-** in Appendix.*] —**boy′hood′** *n.*

bo·yar (bō-yär′) *n.* Also **bo·yard.** **1.** A member of a former Russian aristocratic order abolished by Peter I. **2.** A member of a former aristocratic class of Rumania. [Earlier *boiaren,* from Russian *boyarin,* from Old Russian, "of the highest rank," from Old Slavic *boljarinŭ,* from Old Turkic *boila,* a title.]

boy·cott (boi′kŏt′) *tr.v.* **-cotted, -cotting, -cotts.** To abstain from using, buying, or dealing with, as a protest or means of coercion. —*n.* The act or an instance of boycotting. [After Charles C. *Boycott* (1832–1897), land agent for the Earl of Erne, County Mayo, Ireland, who was ostracized by the tenants for refusing to lower the rents.] —**boy′cott′er** *n.*

Boy·den (boid′n), **Seth.** 1788–1870. American inventor.

boy friend. **1.** A male friend. **2.** *Informal.* A favored male companion or sweetheart of a girl or woman.

boy·ish (boi′ish) *adj.* Characteristic of or befitting a boy: *a boyish prank.* —**boy′ish·ly** *adv.* —**boy′ish·ness** *n.*

Boyle (boil), **Robert.** 1627–1691. English chemist, physicist, and theologian; formulated Boyle's law.

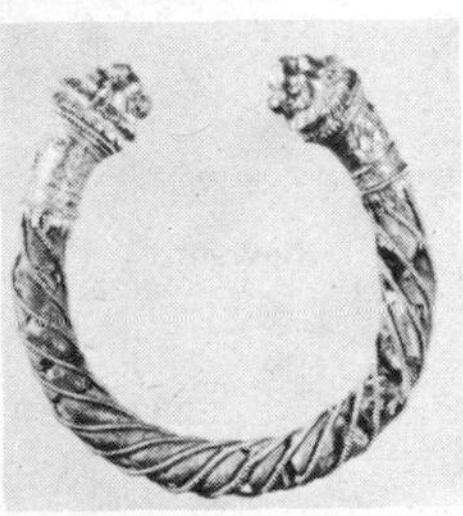

bracelet
Third-century B.C.
Greek bracelet of
blue glass and gold

Boyle's law. The principle that at a fixed temperature the pressure of a confined ideal gas varies inversely with its volume.

Boyne (boin). A river rising in northeastern Ireland and flowing 70 miles northeast to the Irish Sea. The battle in which the deposed James II was defeated by William III of England was fought along its banks (1690).

Boy Scout. A member of a worldwide organization of young men and boys, founded in England in 1908, for character development and citizenship training.

boy·sen·ber·ry (boi′zən-bĕr′ē) *n., pl.* **-ries.** **1.** A prickly bramble hybridized from the loganberry and various blackberries and raspberries. **2.** The large, wine-red, edible berry borne by this plant. [Developed by Rudolph *Boysen,* 20th-century American horticulturist.]

Boz. Pen name of Charles **Dickens** *(see).*

bo·zo (bō′zō) *n., pl.* **-zos.** *Slang.* A fellow; guy. [Possibly from Spanish *bozo*†, "down growing on the cheeks of youths."]

bp boiling point.

bp. bishop.

B.P. **1.** Bachelor of Pharmacy. **2.** Bachelor of Philosophy. **3.** bills payable. **4.** British Pharmacopoeia.

B/P bills payable.

bpd, b.p.d. barrels per day.

B.Pd., B.Pe. Bachelor of Pedagogy.

B.P.E. Bachelor of Physical Education.

B.Ph., B.Phil. Bachelor of Philosophy.

B.P.O.E. Benevolent and Protective Order of Elks.

Br The symbol for the element bromine.

br. **1.** branch. **2.** brief. **3.** bronze. **4.** brother. **5.** brown.

Br. **1.** Breton. **2.** Britain; British. **3.** Brother (religious).

B/R bills receivable.

bra (brä) *n.* A brassiere.

Bra·bant (brə-bănt′, -bänt′). **1.** A former duchy of the Netherlands, now divided between the Netherlands and Belgium. **2.** A province, 1,268 square miles in area, of central Belgium. Population, 2,085,000. Capital, Brussels. —**Bra·bant′ine** (brə-băn′tīn, -tĭn′) *adj.*

brab·ble (brăb′əl) *intr.v.* **-bled, -bling, -bles.** To quarrel noisily; to wrangle. —*n.* A petty dispute; a squabble. [Possibly from Middle Dutch *brabbelen,* to jabber (imitative).] —**brab′bler** *n.*

brace (brās) *n., pl.* **braces** or **brace** (for sense 13 only). **1.** A device that holds or fastens two or more parts together or in place; a clamp. **2.** Any device that steadies or holds something erect, as a supporting beam in a building. **3.** *Plural. Chiefly British.* A pair of suspenders. **4.** *Medicine.* An appliance used to support a bodily part. **5.** *Often plural. Dentistry.* An arrangement of bands and wires fixed to the teeth to correct irregular alignment. **6.** *Nautical.* A rope by which a yard is swung and secured on a square-rigged ship. **7.** *Archery.* A protective pad strapped to the bow arm. **8.** *Music.* A leather loop that slides to change the tension on the cords of a drum. **9.** *Music.* A set of connected staves. **10.** A cranklike handle with an adjustable aperture at one end for securing and turning a bit. **11.** *Printing.* One of two symbols { }, used to connect written or printed lines. **12.** *Mathematics.* Either of a pair of symbols, { }, used to indicate aggregation or to clarify the grouping of quantities when parentheses and square brackets have already been used. Also loosely called "bracket." **13.** A pair of like things: *a brace of partridges.* **14.** *Military.* An extremely stiff and straight position of attention. —See Synonyms at **couple.** —*v.* **braced, bracing, braces.** —*tr.* **1.** To furnish with a brace or braces. **2.** To support or hold steady with or as if with a brace or braces. **3.** To prepare or position so as to be ready for an impact or danger. **4.** To invigorate; stimulate: *"The freshness of the September morning inspired and braced him"* (Hardy). **5.** *Nautical.* To turn (the yards of a ship) by the braces. —*intr.* **1.** To get ready; make preparations. **2.** *Military.* To assume a position of rigid attention. —**brace up.** To summon one's strength or endurance. [Middle English, arm guard, support, from Old French *brace,* the two arms, from Latin *bracchia,* plural of *bracchium,* arm, from Greek *brakhiōn.* See **mreghu-** in Appendix.*]

brace·let (brās′lĭt) *n.* **1.** An ornamental band or chain encircling the wrist. **2.** *Plural. Slang.* Handcuffs. [Middle English, from Old French *bracelet,* diminutive of *bracel,* "little arm," armlet, from Latin *bracchiāle,* from *bracchium,* arm. See **brace.**]

brac·er[1] (brā′sər) *n.* **1.** Something or someone that braces. **2.** *Informal.* A stimulating drink; tonic.

brac·er[2] (brā′sər) *n.* An arm or wrist guard worn by archers and fencers. [Middle English, arm guard, from Old French *brasseure,* from *bras,* arm, from Latin *bracchium.* See **brace.**]

bra·ce·ro (brə-sâr′ō) *n., pl.* **-ros.** A Mexican agricultural or industrial laborer permitted to enter the United States and work for a limited period of time. Compare **wetback.** [Spanish, manual laborer, from *brazo,* arm, from Latin *bracchium,* from Greek *brakhiōn.* See **mreghu-** in Appendix.*]

brach (brăch) *n. Obsolete.* A bitch hound. [Back-formation from Middle English *braches* (plural), from Old French *braches,* plural of *brachet, brac,* from Common Romance *bracco* (unattested), from Old High German *braccho,* dog that tracks game by scent. See **bhreg-** in Appendix.*]

bra·chi·al (brā′kē-əl, brăk′ē-) *adj.* Of, pertaining to, or resembling the arm or a similar or homologous part. [Latin *bracchialis,* from *bracchium,* arm, BRACHIUM.]

bra·chi·ate (brā′kē-ĭt, brăk′ē-, -āt′) *adj. Botany.* Having widely spreading branches arranged in pairs. —*intr.v.* (brā′kē-āt′, brăk′ē-) **brachiated, -ating, -ates.** To swing by the arms from branch to branch, as certain apes do. [Latin *bracchiātus,* from *bracchium,* arm, BRACHIUM.] —**bra′chi·a′tion** *n.*

brach·i·o·pod (brăk′ē-ə-pŏd′, brā′kē-) *n.* Any of various marine invertebrates of the phylum Brachiopoda, having bivalve dorsal and ventral shells and a pair of tentacled, armlike structures on either side of the mouth. Also called "lamp shell." [BRACHI(UM) + -POD.] —**brach′i·o·pod′** *adj.*

bra·chi·um (brā′kē-əm, brăk′ē-) *n., pl.* **brachia** (brā′kē-ə, brăk′ē-ə). An arm or a homologous anatomical structure, such as a flipper or wing. [Latin *bracchium,* arm, forearm, from Greek *brakhiōn.* See **mreghu-** in Appendix.*]

brachy–. Indicates shortness; for example, **brachyuran.** [From Greek *brakhus,* short. See **mreghu-** in Appendix.*]

brach·y·ce·phal·ic (brăk′ē-sə-făl′ĭk) *adj.* Also **brach·y·ceph·a·lous** (-sĕf′ə-ləs). Having a short, almost round head, the width of which is at least 80 per cent as great as the length. Also "brachycranic." See **cephalic index.** [BRACHY- + -CEPHALIC.] —**brach′y·ceph′a·ly** (brăk′ē-sĕf′ə-lē), **brach′y·ceph′a·lism′** (brăk′ē-sĕf′ə-lĭz′əm) *n.*

brach·y·dac·tyl·ic (brăk′ē-dăk-tĭl′ĭk) *adj.* Also **brach·y·dac·ty·lous** (-dăk′tə-ləs). Having abnormally short fingers or toes. —**brach′y·dac·tyl′i·a** (-dăk-tĭl′ē-ə), **brach′y·dac′tyl·ism′** (-dăk′tə-lĭz′əm), **brach′y·dac′ty·ly** (-dăk′tə-lē) *n.*

bra·chyl·o·gy (brə-kĭl′ə-jē) *n., pl.* **-gies.** **1.** Brief, concise speech. **2.** A shortened or condensed phrase or expression. [Late Latin *brachylogia,* from Greek *brakhulogia* : BRACHY- + -LOGY.]

bra·chyp·ter·ous (brə-kĭp′tər-əs) *adj.* Having short wings. Said of certain insects. [Greek *brakhupteros* : BRACHY- + -PTEROUS.] —**bra·chyp′ter·ism′** (-tə-rĭz′əm) *n.*

brach·y·u·ran (brăk′ē-yo͝or′ən) *adj.* Also **brach·y·u·ral** (-əl), **brach·y·u·rous** (-əs). Of or belonging to the Brachyura, a group of crustaceans characterized by a short abdomen concealed under the cephalothorax, and including the true crabs. —*n.* A member of the Brachyura. [New Latin *Brachyura,* "short-tailed ones" : BRACHY- + *-ura,* plural of *-urus,* -UROUS.]

brac·ing (brā′sĭng) *adj.* Invigorating. —*n.* **1.** A brace. **2.** Braces collectively. —**brac′ing·ly** *adv.* —**brac′ing·ness** *n.*

brack·en (brăk′ən) *n.* **1.** A fern, *Pteridium aquilinum,* having tough stems and branching, finely divided fronds. Also called "brake." **2.** An area overgrown with this fern. **3.** Any large, coarse fern. [Middle English (northern dialect) *braken,* from Old Norse *brakni* (unattested). See **bhreg-** in Appendix.*]

brack·et (brăk′ĭt) *n.* **1.** A simple rigid structure in the shape of an L, one arm of which is fixed to a vertical surface, with the other projecting horizontally to support a shelf or other weight. **2.** Any of various functionally similar wall-anchored fixtures adapted to support loads. **3.** A small shelf or shelves supported by brackets. **4. a.** Either of a pair of symbols, [ ], used to enclose written or printed material or to indicate a mathematical expression considered in some sense a single quantity. Also called "square bracket." See Usage note below. **b.** Either of a pair of symbols, < >, similarly used and in mathematics used especially together to indicate the average of a contained quantity. Also called "angle bracket." **c.** *Mathematics.* Loosely, a **brace** *(see).* **5.** A classification or grouping; especially, one of taxpayers according to income. **6.** *Military.* The space between two rounds of artillery, the first aimed beyond a target and the second aimed short of it, used to determine range. —*tr.v.* **bracketed, -eting, -ets. 1.** To support with a bracket or brackets. **2.** To place within brackets. **3.** To classify or group together. **4.** *Military.* To fire beyond and short of (a target) in order to determine range. [Earlier *bragget,* from Old French *braguette,* codpiece, diminutive of *brague,* mortise, breeches (in plural), from Old Provençal *braga,* from Latin *brāca.* See **brāc-** in Appendix.*]

Usage: Brackets, the signs used to set off or enclose words or passages in writing, are employed most often to indicate the insertion of something other than the writer's own words: a portrait of [Theodore] Roosevelt. Such explanatory additions occur frequently in material being quoted. Brackets are also used to set off an editor's comments from a printed text. Parentheses should not be used for these purposes. A secondary use of brackets is to enclose material that is inserted within something already in parentheses: (Newton [Mass.], April 1970).

bracket fungus. Any of various fungi that form shelflike growths on tree trunks and wood structures.

brack·ish (brăk′ĭsh) *adj.* **1.** Containing some salt; briny: *"You could cut the brackish winds with a knife/Here in Nantucket"* (Robert Lowell). **2.** Distasteful; unpalatable. [From British dialectal *brack,* briny, brine, from Dutch *brak,* salty, from Middle Dutch *brac*†.] —**brack′ish·ness** *n.*

bract (brăkt) *n.* A leaflike plant part, usually small but sometimes showy and sometimes brightly colored, located either below a flower or on the stalk of a flower cluster. [From New Latin *bractea,* from Latin *bractea,* properly *brattea*†, metal plate or leaf.] —**brac′te·al** (brăk′tē-əl) *adj.*

brac·te·ate (brăk′tē-ĭt, -āt′) *adj. Botany.* Bearing bracts. [New Latin *bracteatus,* from *bractea,* BRACT.]

brac·te·o·late (brăk′tē-ə-lĭt, -lāt′) *adj. Botany.* Bearing small bracts, or bracteoles.

brac·te·ole (brăk′tē-ōl) *n.* Also **bract·let** (-lĭt). *Botany.* A small or secondary bract. [New Latin *bracteola,* from Latin, diminutive of *bractea,* metal plate or leaf. See **bract.**]

brad (brăd) *n.* A tapered nail with a small head or a slight side projection instead of a head. [Middle English *brad, brod,* from Old Norse *broddr,* spike. See **bhar-** in Appendix.*]

brad·awl (brăd′ôl′) *n.* A small awl with a chisel edge, used to make holes in wood for brads or screws.

Brad·bur·y (brăd′bĕr′ē), **Ray (Douglas).** Born 1920. American author of science fiction.

Brad·dock (brăd′ək), **Edward.** 1695–1755. British military leader; commander in chief during French and Indian War (1754–55).

Brad·ford (brăd′fərd). An industrial city in Yorkshire, northern England. Population, 298,000.

Brad·ford (brăd′fərd), **William**¹. 1590–1657. English Puritan colonist in America; five times governor of Plymouth colony.

Brad·ford (brăd′fərd), **William**². 1663–1752. English Quaker colonist in America; printer and publisher.

Brad·ley (brăd′lē), **Henry.** 1845–1923. English lexicographer; editor of *Oxford English Dictionary.*

Brad·ley (brăd′lē), **James.** 1693–1762. British astronomer; discovered stellar aberration; estimated the speed of light.

Brad·ley (brăd′lē), **Omar Nelson.** Born 1893. American General of the Army.

Brad·street (brăd′strēt′), **Anne (Dudley).** 1612–1672. English Puritan poet and colonist in America; daughter of Thomas Dudley; wife of Simon Bradstreet.

Brad·street (brăd′strēt′), **Simon.** 1603–1697. English colonial administrator; governor of Massachusetts Bay Colony (1679–86 and 1689–92); husband of Anne Bradstreet.

brady-. Indicates slowness; for example, **bradylogia.** [New Latin, from Greek *bradus*†, slow.]

Bra·dy (brā′dē), **James Buchanan ("Diamond Jim").** 1856–1917. American financier and philanthropist.

Bra·dy (brā′dē), **Mathew B.** 1823?–1896. American photographic pioneer; made photographic record of Civil War.

brad·y·car·di·a (brăd′ĭ-kär′dē-ə) *n.* Abnormally slow heartbeat, as less than 60 beats per minute. [New Latin : BRADY- + Greek *kardia,* heart (see **cardia**).] —**brad′y·car′dic** *adj.*

brad·y·lo·gi·a (brăd′ĭ-lō′jē-ə) *n.* Abnormally slow speech. [New Latin : BRADY- + -LOGY.]

brae (brā) *n. Scottish.* A hillside; slope. [Middle English (Scottish and northern dialects) *bra,* from Old Norse *brā,* eyelash. See **bherək-** in Appendix.*]

brag (brăg) *v.* **bragged, bragging, brags.** —*intr.* To talk boastfully about oneself. —*tr.* To assert boastfully. —See Synonyms at **boast.** —*n.* **1.** Arrogant or boastful speech or manner. **2.** Something boasted of. **3.** A braggart; boaster. **4.** A card game similar to poker. —*adj.* **bragger, braggest.** Exceptionally fine. [Middle English *braggen,* probably from *brag*†, "spirited," "mettlesome," hence boastful.] —**brag′ger** *n.*

Bragg (brăg), **Braxton.** 1817–1876. American military leader; commander of Confederate forces at battle of Chickamauga.

Bragg (brăg), Sir **William Henry.** 1862–1942. British physicist; worked on x-ray spectrometry.

Bragg (brăg), Sir **William Lawrence.** Born 1890. British physicist; worked on crystal structure and x rays with Sir William Henry Bragg, his father.

brag·ga·do·ci·o (brăg′ə-dō′shē-ō) *n., pl.* **-os. 1.** A braggart. **2. a.** Empty or pretentious bragging. **b.** Swaggering manner; cockiness. [After *Braggadocchio,* name coined by Spenser for his personification of boasting : *braggad-,* alteration of BRAGGART + *-occio,* Italian augmentative suffix.]

Bragg angle. The angle between an incident x-ray beam and a set of crystal planes for which the secondary radiation displays maximum intensity as a result of constructive interference. [After William Henry BRAGG and William Lawrence BRAGG.]

brag·gart (brăg′ərt) *n.* One given to loud, empty boasting; a bragger. —*adj.* Boastful. [French *bragard,* from *braguer,* to brag, obscurely related to Middle English *braggen,* BRAG.]

Bragg's law. The fundamental law of x-ray crystallography, $n\lambda = 2d\sin\Theta$, where n is an integer, λ is the wavelength of a beam of x rays incident on a crystal with lattice planes separated by distance d, and Θ is the Bragg angle.

Bra·gi (brä′gē). Also **Bra·ge** (brä′gə). *Norse Mythology.* The son of Odin, husband of Ithunn, and god of poetry.

Bra·he (brä′ə), **Tycho.** 1546–1601. Danish astronomer and author; observed stellar and planetary positions precisely.

Brah·ma¹ (brä′mə) *n. Hinduism.* **1.** The personification of divine reality in its creative aspect as a member of the Hindu triad. See **Vishnu, Shiva. 2.** Variant of **Brahman.** [Sanskrit *bráhman,* prayer, the universal soul, the Absolute, akin to *brahmán-,* priest. See **Brahman.**]

Brah·ma² (brä′mə, brā′-) *n.* Also **brah·ma.** A large domestic fowl of a breed originating in Asia, and having feathered legs. [Short for *Brahmaputra;* first brought from Lakhimpur, on the BRAHMAPUTRA River.]

Brah·ma³. Variant of **Brahman** (cattle).

Brah·man (brä′mən) *n., pl.* **-mans** (for senses 2, 3). Also **Brah·ma** (-mə) (for senses 1, 3), **Brah·min** (-mĭn) (for senses 2, 3). **1.** *Hinduism.* The essential divine reality of the universe; the eternal spirit from which all being originates and to which all returns. **2.** *Hinduism.* A member of the highest caste, originally composed of priests but now occupationally diversified. **3.** One of a breed of domestic cattle developed in the southern United States from stock originating in India, and having a hump between the shoulders and a pendulous dewlap. [Sanskrit *brāhmaṇas,* member of the Brahman caste, from *brahmán-,* priest. See **bhlagmen-** in Appendix.*] —**Brah·man′ic** (-măn′ĭk), **Brah·man′i·cal** *adj.*

Brah·man·ism (brä′mən-ĭz′əm) *n.* Also **Brah·min·ism** (brä′mĭn-). **1.** The religious practices and beliefs of ancient India as reflected in the Vedas, the earliest religious texts. **2.** The social caste system of the Brahmans of India. —**Brah′man·ist** *n.*

Brah·ma·pu·tra (brä′mə-po͞o′trə). A river of Asia, rising in southwestern Tibet and flowing 1,800 miles, first east, then west through Assam, India, and south in East Pakistan to form with the Ganges a delta on the Bay of Bengal.

Brah·min (brä′mĭn) *n.* **1.** A highly cultured and socially exclusive person; especially, a member of one of the old New England families. **2.** Variant of **Brahman** (except for sense 1). —**Brah·min′ic, Brah·min′i·cal** *adj.*

Brah·min·ism (brä′mĭn-ĭz′əm) *n.* **1.** The attitude or conduct typical of a social or cultural elite. **2.** Variant of **Brahmanism.**

Brahms (brämz), **Johannes.** 1833–1897. German composer.

braid (brād) *tr.v.* **braided, braiding, braids. 1.** To interweave three or more strands of; to plait. **2.** To decorate or edge with an ornamental trim. **3.** To produce by interweaving: *braid a rug.* **4.** To fasten or decorate (hair) with a band or ribbon. —*n.* **1.** A narrow length of fabric, hair, or other material that has been braided or plaited. **2.** A thin, flat, woven strip of cloth used for binding or decorating fabrics; an ornamental trim. **3.** A ribbon or band used to fasten the hair. [Middle English *breyden,* to move quickly, pull, twist, braid, Old English *bregdan.* See **bherək-** in Appendix.*] —**braid′er** *n.*

braid·ing (brā′dĭng) *n.* Braided embroidery.

brail (brāl) *n.* A line used to furl loose-footed sails. —*tr.v.* **brailed, brailing, brails.** To gather in (a sail) with brails. Usually used with *up.* [Middle English *brayle,* from Old French *brail, braiel,* belt, girdle, from Medieval Latin *brācāle,* from Latin *brāca,* breeches. See **brāc-** in Appendix.*]

Bră·i·la (brə-ē′lə). A city of east-central Rumania on the Danube River. Population, 109,000.

Braille (brāl) *n.* Also **braille.** A system of writing and printing for the blind, in which varied arrangements of raised dots representing letters and numerals can be identified by touch. [Invented by Louis BRAILLE.]

Braille (brāl; *French* brī), **Louis.** 1809–1852. French musician, educator, and inventor; blind from childhood.

brain (brān) *n.* **1.** The portion of the central nervous system in the vertebrate cranium that is responsible for the interpretation of sensory impulses, the coordination and control of bodily activities, and the exercise of emotion and thought. **2.** A functionally similar portion of the invertebrate nervous system. **3.** *Often plural.* Intellectual capacity. **4.** *Slang.* A highly intelligent person. **5.** *Often plural.* The supreme planner, as of a movement. —See Synonyms at **mind.** —**on the brain.** Obsessively in mind. —*tr.v.* **brained, braining, brains. 1.** To smash in the skull of. **2.** *Slang.* To hit on the head. [Middle English *brain,* Old English *brægen.* See **mregh-mo** in Appendix.*]

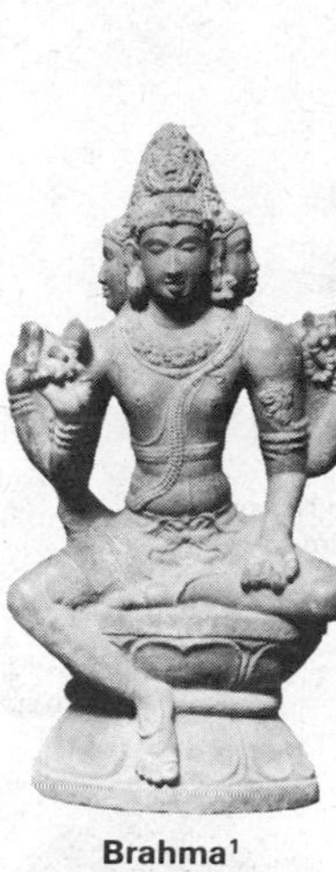

Brahma¹
Seated statue
from the Chola Dynasty
(10th to 11th century)

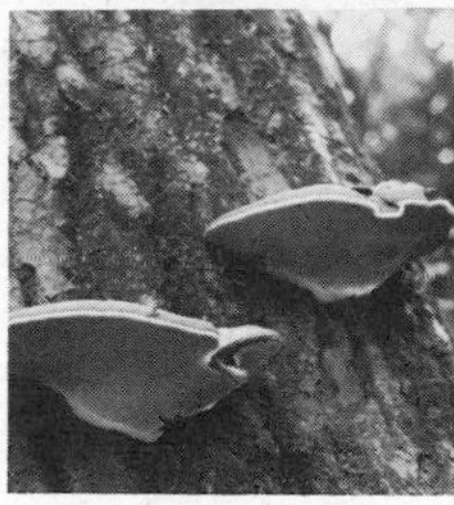

bracket fungus
Polyporus applanatus

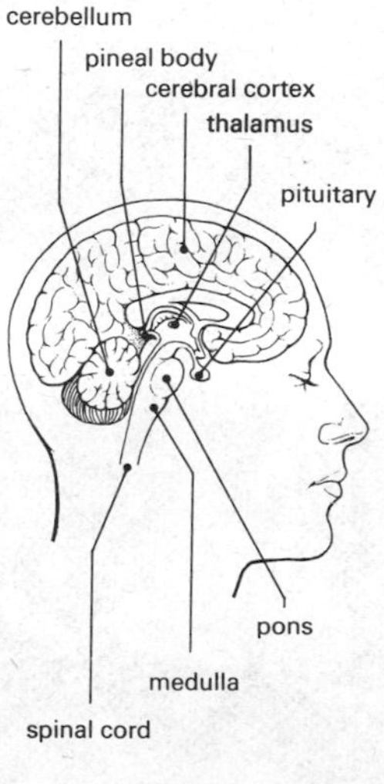
cerebellum
pineal body
cerebral cortex
thalamus
pituitary
pons
medulla
spinal cord

brain

brain child. *Informal.* An original idea, plan, or the like, attributed to a specific person or group.
brain coral. Any of several corals of the genus *Meandrina,* forming rounded colonies that resemble the human brain.
brain fever. *Pathology.* **Encephalitis** *(see).*
brain·less (brān′lĭs) *adj.* **1.** Devoid of intelligence; stupid. **2.** Lacking a brain. **—brain′less·ly** *adv.* **—brain′less·ness** *n.*
brain·pan (brān′păn′) *n.* The part of the skull that contains the brain; cranium.
brain·sick (brān′sĭk′) *adj.* Of, pertaining to, or induced by insanity; mad. **—brain′sick′ly** *adv.* **—brain′sick′ness** *n.*
brain·stem (brān′stĕm′) *n.* The part of the brain consisting of the medulla oblongata, pons, and mesencephalon and connecting the spinal cord to the forebrain and cerebrum.
brain·storm (brān′stôrm′) *n.* **1.** A sudden and violent disturbance in the brain. **2.** A sudden clever, whimsical, or foolish idea.
brain trust. Also *chiefly British* **brains trust.** A group of experts who serve as unofficial advisers and policy planners, especially in a government. **—brain truster.**
brain·wash (brān′wŏsh′, -wôsh′) *tr.v.* **-washed, -washing, -washes.** To subject to brainwashing. [Back-formation from BRAINWASHING.]
brain·wash·ing (brān′wŏsh′ĭng, -wôsh′ĭng) *n.* Intensive indoctrination, usually political, aimed at changing a person's basic convictions and attitudes and replacing them with a fixed and unquestioned set of beliefs. [Translation of Mandarin Chinese *hsi*[3] *nao*[3] : *hsi*[3], to wash + nao[3], brain.]
brain wave. **1.** A rhythmic fluctuation of electric potential between parts of the brain. **2.** A sudden inspiration.
brain·y (brā′nē) *adj.* **-ier, -iest.** *Informal.* Intelligent; learned; smart. **—brain′i·ly** *adv.* **—brain′i·ness** *n.*
braise (brāz) *tr.v.* **braised, braising, braises.** To cook (meat or vegetables) by browning in fat, then simmering in a small quantity of liquid in a covered container. [French *braiser,* from *braise,* hot charcoal, from Old French *brese,* from Germanic. See **bhreu-**[2] in Appendix.*]

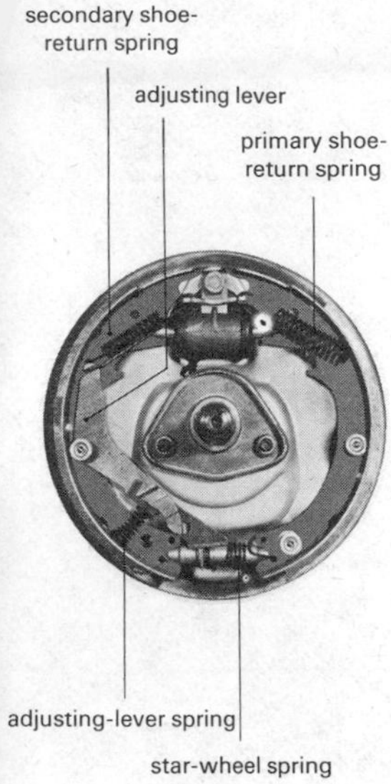
secondary shoe-return spring
adjusting lever
primary shoe-return spring
adjusting-lever spring
star-wheel spring
brake[1]
Self-adjusting passenger-car brake

brake[1] (brāk) *n.* **1.** A device for slowing or stopping motion, as of a vehicle or machine, especially by contact friction. **2.** *Often plural.* Any check that slows or stops action. **3.** A device for separating the fibers of flax or hemp by crushing or beating. **4.** A heavy harrow for breaking clods of earth. **5.** A handle on a pump or other machine. **6.** *Obsolete.* An instrument of torture; the rack. **—*v.*** **braked, braking, brakes.** **—*tr.*** **1.** To reduce the speed of with or as if with a brake. **2.** To crush (flax or hemp) in a brake. **3.** To break up (clods of earth) with a harrow. **—*intr.*** To operate or apply a brake or brakes. [Middle English *brake,* crushing instrument, pestle, flax brake, from Middle Dutch *braeke.* See **bhreg-** in Appendix.*]
brake[2] (brāk) *n.* Any of several ferns, especially **bracken** *(see).* [Middle English, variant of BRACKEN.]
brake[3] (brāk) *n.* An area overgrown with dense brushwood, briers, and undergrowth; a thicket. [Middle English *(ferne)-brake,* Old English *(fearn)braca,* bed of fern : FERN + *bracu* (unattested), dense growth, thicket (see **bhreg-** in Appendix*).]
brake[4]. Variant of **break** (carriage).
brake[5]. *Archaic.* Past tense of **break.**
brake·age (brā′kĭj) *n.* The action or capacity of a brake.
brake band. A flexible belt that is tightened around a brake drum to arrest the motion of a wheel or shaft.
brake drum. A metal cylinder to which pressure is applied by a braking mechanism in order to arrest rotation of the wheel or shaft to which the cylinder is attached.
brake fluid. The liquid used in a hydraulic brake cylinder.
brake horsepower. *Abbr.* **bhp., b.hp.** The actual or useful horsepower of an engine, usually determined from the force exerted on a dynamometer connected to the drive shaft.
brake·man (brāk′mən) *n., pl.* **-men** (-mĭn). Also *British* **brakes·man** (brāks′mən). A railroad employee who assists the conductor and checks on the operation of the train's brakes.
brake shoe. A curved metal block that presses against and thereby arrests the rotation of a wheel or brake drum.
braking rocket. *Aerospace.* A **retrorocket** *(see).*
Bra·man·te (brä-män′tā). Original name, Donato d'Agnolo. 1444–1514. Italian architect of the High Renaissance.
bram·ble (brăm′bəl) *n.* **1.** Any prickly plant or shrub of the genus *Rubus,* especially the blackberry or the raspberry. **2.** Any prickly shrub or bush. [Middle English *brembel,* Old English *brǣmbel, brēmel.* See **bhrem-**[2] in Appendix.*] **—bram′bly** *adj.*
bram·bling (brăm′blĭng) *n.* A finch, *Fringilla montifringilla,* of northern Eurasia, having black, white, and rust-brown plumage. [BRAMB(LE) + -LING.]
bran (brăn) *n.* **1.** The seed husk or outer coating of cereals such as wheat, rye, and oats, separated from the flour by sifting or bolting. **2.** Cereal by-products used as a food. [Middle English *bran, bren,* from Old French *bran,* probably from Gaulish *brenno-*† (unattested).]

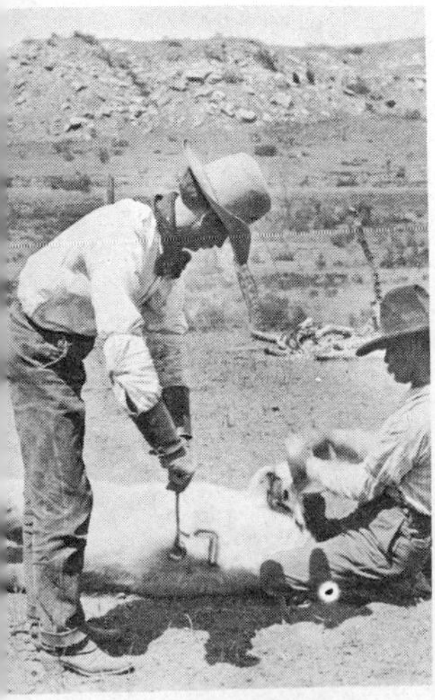
branding iron
Texas cowboys branding a calf

branch (brănch, bränch) *n. Abbr.* **br.** **1.** A secondary woody stem or limb growing from the trunk or main stem of a tree, bush, or shrub, or from another secondary limb. **2.** Any part resembling or structurally analogous to a branch. **3.** A limited part of a larger or more complex body, as: **a.** An academic or vocational field of specialization. **b.** A local unit of a business. **c.** A division of a family, tribe, or other group believed to stem from a common ancestor. **4.** *Linguistics.* A subdivision of a family of languages. **5. a.** A tributary of a river. **b.** Any small stream, creek, or brook. **6.** *Geometry.* A part of a curve that is separated, as by discontinuities or extreme points. **—*v.*** **branched, branching, branches.** **—*intr.*** **1.** To put forth or spread out in branches. **2.** To separate into subdivisions; diverge. **—*tr.*** **1.** To separate (something) into or as if into branches. **2.** To embroider with a design of flowers or foliage. **—branch off.** **1.** To divide into branches; to fork. **2.** To separate from the main part or course; diverge. **—branch out.** To enlarge the scope of one's interest, business, or activities. [Middle English *braunche,* from Old French *branche,* from Late Latin *branca,* foot, paw, perhaps from Gaulish, akin to Irish *bracc*†, arm.]
-branch. *Zoology.* Indicates gills; for example, **elasmobranch.** [New Latin *-branchia,* from Latin *branchia,* BRANCHIA.]
bran·chi·a (brăng′kē-ə) *n., pl.* **-chiae** (-kē-ē). *Zoology.* A gill or similar breathing organ. [Latin, from Greek *brankhia*†, gills.] **—bran′chi·al** *adj.*
bran·chi·ate (brăng′kē-ĭt, -āt′) *adj.* Having branchiae or gills.
bran·chi·o·pod (brăng′kē-ə-pŏd′) *n.* Any of various crustaceans of the subclass Branchiopoda, characteristically having a segmented body and flattened, limblike appendages. [New Latin *Branchiopoda* : Latin *branchia,* gill, BRANCHIA + -POD.]
Bran·cusi (brŏng′kōōsh, brăn-kōō′sē), **Constantin.** 1876–1957. Rumanian-born French abstract sculptor.
brand (brănd) *n.* **1.** A trademark or distinctive name identifying a product or a manufacturer. **2.** The make of a product thus marked: *a popular brand of soap.* **3.** A mark indicating identity or ownership, burned on the hide of an animal with a hot iron. **4.** A mark formerly burned into the flesh of criminals. **5.** Any mark of disgrace or notoriety; a stigma. **6.** An iron that is heated and used for branding. **7.** A piece of burning or charred wood. **8.** *Archaic.* A sword: *"So flash'd and fell the brand Excalibur"* (Tennyson). **—*tr.v.*** **branded, branding, brands.** **1.** To mark with or as if with a brand. **2.** To mark with disgrace or infamy; stigmatize. [Middle English *brand,* fire, torch, sword, Old English *brand,* piece of burning wood. See **bhreu-**[2] in Appendix.*]
Bran·deis (brăn′dīs), **Louis Dembitz.** 1856–1941. American jurist; Associate Justice U.S. Supreme Court (1916–39).
Bran·den·burg (brăn′dən-bûrg; *German* brän′dən-bōōrkh). **1.** A former German duchy around which, as the seat of the Hohenzollern dynasty, the kingdom of Prussia grew during the 16th and 17th centuries. **2.** A state of East Germany, established in 1949. Capital, Potsdam. **3.** A city of this state, on the Havel River, about 35 miles southwest of Berlin. Population, 88,000.
branding iron. A metal rod heated and used for branding.
bran·dish (brăn′dĭsh) *tr.v.* **-dished, -dishing, -dishes.** **1.** To wave or flourish menacingly, as a weapon. **2.** To display ostentatiously. **—*n.*** A menacing or defiant wave or flourish. [Middle English *braundisshen,* from Old French *brandir* (present stem *brandiss-*), from *brand,* sword, blade, from Germanic. See **bhreu-**[2] in Appendix.*] **—bran′dish·er** *n.*
brand·ling (brănd′lĭng) *n.* A common reddish-brown earthworm, *Eisenia foetida,* often used as bait. [BRAND (because of its red markings) + -LING.]
brand-new (brănd′nōō′, -nyōō′) *adj.* Also **bran-new** (brăn′nōō′, -nyōō′). In fresh and unused condition; completely new.
bran·dy (brăn′dē) *n., pl.* **-dies.** An alcoholic liquor distilled from wine or from fermented fruit juice. **—*tr.v.*** **brandied, -dying, -dies.** To mix, flavor, or preserve with brandy. [Earlier *brandy wine,* from Dutch *brandewijn, brantwijn* : *brant,* past participle of *branden,* to burn, distill (see **bhreu-**[2] in Appendix*) + WINE.]
Bran·dy·wine (brăn′dē-wīn′). A creek in southeastern Pennsylvania and northern Delaware; site of Washington's defeat by the British under General Howe in 1777.
branks (brăngks) *n.* Plural in form, sometimes used with a singular verb. A metal bridle with a bit to restrain the tongue, formerly used to punish scolds. [Possibly an alteration of earlier *bernaks,* plural of Middle English *bernak,* bridle, from Norman French *bernac.* See **barnacle** (horse's bit).]
bran·ni·gan (brăn′ĭ-gən) *n. Slang.* **1.** A noisy or confused quarrel. **2.** A spree; binge. [Probably from the proper name *Brannigan.*]
bran·ny (brăn′ē) *adj.* **-nier, -niest.** Of or containing bran.
brant (brănt) *n., pl.* **brant** or **brants.** Also *British* **brent** (brĕnt). Any of several wild geese of the genus *Branta,* that breed in arctic regions; especially, *B. bernicla,* having a black neck and head. [Probably from Scandinavian, akin to Swedish *brandgas,* "burnt goose" (from its black color) : *brand,* firebrand, from Old Norse *brandr* (see **bhreu-**[2] in Appendix*) + *gas,* goose.]
Brant (brănt), **Joseph.** Original name, Thayendanegea. 1742–1807. American Indian leader; chief of the Mohawk; fought for the British during the Revolutionary War.
Brant·ford (brănt′fərd). A city and industrial center in southeastern Ontario, Canada. Population, 55,000.
Braque (bräk), **Georges.** 1882–1963. French cubist painter.
brash[1] (brăsh) *adj.* **brasher, brashest.** **1.** Hasty and unthinking; rash. **2.** Impudent; saucy. **3.** Brittle. Said of wood or timber. —See Synonyms at **shameless.** [Perhaps imitative, influenced by BREAK and RASH.] **—brash′ly** *adv.* **—brash′ness** *n.*
brash[2] (brăsh) *n.* A mass or pile of rubble or fragments. [Probably from French *brèche,* breach, from Old French, from Old High German *brehha,* fracture, from *brehhan,* to break. See **bhreg-** in Appendix.*]
Brash·er (brăsh′ər), **Rex.** 1869–1960. American ornithologist and artist.
bra·sier. Variant of **brazier.**
Bra·sil. The Portuguese name for **Brazil.**
Bra·sí·lia (brə-zē′lyə). The capital of Brazil since 1960, in a

Federal District within Goiás State, 600 miles northwest of Rio de Janeiro. Population of Federal District, 141,000.

bras·i·lin. Variant of **brazilin.**

Bra·şov (brä-shôv′). *German* **Kron·stadt** (krōn′shtät′). Formerly **Sta·lin** (stä′lĭn). An industrial city of central Rumania. Population, 137,000.

brass (brăs, bräs) *n.* **1.** An alloy of copper and zinc with other metals in varying lesser amounts. **2.** Ornaments, objects, or utensils made of brass. **3.** *Plural. Music.* Wind instruments, such as the French horn and trombone, made of brass. **4.** A memorial plaque or tablet made of brass. **5.** *Machinery.* A bushing sleeve or similar lining for a bearing, made from a copper alloy. **6.** *Informal.* Blatant self-assurance; effrontery; nerve. **7.** *Slang.* High-ranking military officers or other high officials. **8.** *British Slang.* Money. [Middle English *bras,* Old English *bræs.* See **ferrum** in Appendix.*] —**brass** *adj.*

bras·sard (brə-särd′, brăs′ärd′) *n.* Also **bras·sart** (brə-särt′, brăs′ärt′). **1.** A cloth badge worn around the upper arm. **2.** A piece of armor for the arm. [French, alteration of earlier *brassal,* from Provencal, from *bras,* arm, from Latin *brachium,* from Greek *brakhiōn.* See **mreghu-** in Appendix.*]

brass·bound (brăs′bound′, bräs′-) *adj.* Firmly and inflexibly established; rigid: *a brassbound tradition.*

brass hat. *Slang.* **1.** A high-ranking military officer. **2.** Any high-ranking official. [Because of the gold braid on his cap.]

brass·ie (brăs′ē, brä′sē) *n.* Also **brass·y** *pl.* **-ies.** A wooden golf club with a brass-plated face, used for long low shots.

bras·siere, bras·sière (brə-zîr′) *n.* A woman's undergarment worn to support and give contour to the breasts. [French *brassière,* from Old French *braciere,* armor for the arm, arm guard, from *bras,* arm, from Latin *brachium,* from Greek *brakhiōn.* See **mreghu-** in Appendix.*]

brass knuckles. A weapon consisting of a metal strip or chain with holes or links into which the fingers fit.

brass tacks. *Informal.* Essential facts. Used chiefly in the phrase *get* (or *come*) *down to brass tacks.*

brass·y¹ (brăs′ē, brä′sē) *adj.* **-ier, -iest. 1.** Of or decorated with brass. **2.** Resembling brass in color. **3.** Like or characterized by the sound of brass instruments: *"the band was now playing some brassy march"* (Robert Penn Warren). **4.** Cheap and showy; flashy. **5.** *Informal.* Brazen; insolent; impudent. —**brass′i·ly** *adv.* —**brass′i·ness** *n.*

brass·y². Variant of **brassie.**

brat (brăt) *n.* A child, especially a nasty one. [Probably from dialectal *brat,* coarse garment, Middle English *brat,* Old English *bratt,* cloak, from Old Irish *bratt*†.] —**brat′ty** *adj.*

Bra·ti·sla·va (brä′tĭ-slä′və, brăt′ĭ-). *German* **Press·burg** (prĕs′-bŏŏrk′); *Hungarian* **Po·zsony** (pō′zhōn-y′). A river port and industrial city of south-central Czechoslovakia, on the Danube near the borders of Austria and Hungary. Population, 266,000.

Brat·tain (brăt′n), **Walter Houser.** Born 1902. American physicist; discovered the transistor effect with John **Bardeen** and William **Shockley** *(see).*

brat·tice (brăt′ĭs) *n.* **1.** A partition, especially one erected in a mine for ventilation. **2.** Formerly, a temporary breastwork erected during a siege. —*tr.v.* **bratticed, -ticing, -tices.** To equip with a brattice. [Middle English *bretais,* defensive structure, from Norman French *breteske,* variants of Old French *bretesque,* from Medieval Latin *(turris) brittisca,* perhaps "British (tower)," parapet (this type of fortification originated in Great Britain), probably from Latin *Britto,* BRITON.]

brat·tle (brăt′l) *n.* A rattling or clattering sound. —*intr.v.* **brattled, -tling, -tles.** To rush with such a sound. [Imitative.]

brat·wurst (brăt′wûrst′; *German* brät′vŏŏrsht′) *n.* A sausage made with finely chopped, seasoned fresh pork. [German *Bratwurst,* from Old High German *brātwurst* : *brāt(o),* meat (see **bhreu-²** in Appendix*) + *wurst,* sausage, WURST.]

Braun (broun), **Eva.** 1910–1945. German mistress of Adolf Hitler; allegedly married to him before committing suicide.

Braun (broun), **Karl Ferdinand.** 1850–1918. German physicist; pioneer of wireless telegraphy.

Braun (broun), **Wernher Magnus Maximilian von.** Born 1912. German-born American rocket engineer.

Braun·schweig. The German name for **Brunswick.**

Braun·schwei·ger (broun′shwī′gər; *German* broun′shvī′gər) *n.* A smoked liver sausage. [German, "Brunswick sausage," from *Braunschweig,* BRUNSWICK.]

bra·va·do (brə-vä′dō) *n., pl.* **-does** or **-dos. 1.** Defiant or swaggering show of courage; false bravery. **2.** An instance of such behavior. [Spanish *bravada, bravata,* from *bravo,* BRAVE.]

brave (brāv) *adj.* **braver, bravest. 1.** Possessing or displaying courage; valiant. **2.** Making a fine display; splendid. **3.** *Archaic.* Excellent. —*n.* **1.** A North American Indian warrior. **2.** A courageous person. **3.** *Obsolete.* A bully. **4.** *Obsolete.* A boast or challenge. —*v.* **braved, braving, braves.** —*tr.* **1.** To undergo or face courageously. **2.** To defy; to challenge: *"Together they would brave Satan and all his legions"* (Emily Brontë). **3.** *Obsolete.* To make splendid. —*intr. Obsolete.* To boast. [Old French *brave,* courageous, noble, from Italian and Spanish *bravo,* from Vulgar Latin *brabus* (unattested), wild, savage, altered from Latin *barbarus,* foreign, barbarous, from Greek *barbaros.* See **baba-** in Appendix.*] —**brave′ly** *adv.* —**brave′ness** *n.*

Synonyms: *brave, courageous, fearless, intrepid, bold, daring, audacious, gallant, valiant, valorous, doughty, game, gritty, mettlesome, plucky, dauntless, undaunted.* These adjectives all apply to admirable human action in difficult conditions. *Brave,* the least specific, is frequently associated with an innate quality, and *courageous* with the act of consciously rising to a specific test by drawing on a reserve of moral strength and righteousness. *Fearless* emphasizes, besides absence of fear, resolute self-possession; *intrepid* adds to this the sense of invulnerability to fear in any situation. *Bold* and *daring* stress not only readiness to meet danger but a desire to seize initiative; *audacious* intensifies those qualities, often to the point of recklessness. *Gallant* also implies indifference to danger, together with a noble display of courage, often in a losing cause. *Valiant,* said principally of persons, pertains to the bravery or courage of heroes, and *valorous* to their deeds. On a lower and perhaps more contemporary plane, *doughty* suggests formidableness (now usually humorously), and *game* and *gritty* imply dogged persistence and capacity for resisting pain. *Mettlesome* stresses spirit and love of challenge; *plucky* stresses spirit and heart in the face of unfavorable odds. *Dauntless* refers to courage that resists subjection or intimidation; *undaunted* more strongly suggests such courage that has been put to actual test.

brav·er·y (brā′və-rē, brāv′rē) *n., pl.* **-ies. 1.** The state or quality of being brave; courage. **2.** Splendor, as of attire; show.

bra·vis·si·mo (brä-vĭs′ĭ-mō′) *interj.* Used to express great approval. [Italian, superlative of *bravo,* BRAVO.]

bra·vo¹ (brä′vō, brä-vō′) *interj.* Used to express approval. —*n., pl.* **bravos.** A shout or cry of "bravo." [Italian, fine, BRAVE.]

bra·vo² (brä′vō) *n., pl.* **-voes** or **-vos.** A hired assassin; killer. [Italian, "wild," "brave." See **brave.**]

bra·vu·ra (brə-vyŏŏr′ə) *n.* **1.** *Music.* Brilliant technique or style in performance. **2.** A showy manner or display. [Italian, "bravery," spirit, from *bravo,* BRAVE.] —**bra·vu′ra** *adj.*

braw (brô) *adj.* **brawer, brawest.** *Scottish.* Fine or splendid. [Earlier *brawf,* Scottish variant of BRAVE.]

brawl (brôl) *n.* **1.** A noisy quarrel or fight. **2.** *Slang.* A loud party. —*intr.v.* **brawled, brawling, brawls. 1.** To quarrel noisily. **2.** To flow noisily, as water. [Middle English *brawlen, brallen,* probably related to Dutch and Low German *brallen* (imitative).] —**brawl′er** *n.* —**brawl′ing·ly** *adv.*

brawn (brôn) *n.* **1.** Solid and well-developed muscles. **2.** Muscular strength and power. **3.** *British.* **a.** A pig. **b.** A pickled or preserved preparation, made from meat of the head or feet of a pig. [Middle English, from Norman French *braun,* variant of Old French *braon,* flesh, muscle, from Germanic. See **bhreu-²** in Appendix.*]

brawn·y (brô′nē) *adj.* **-ier, -iest.** Strong and muscular. —**brawn′i·ly** *adv.* —**brawn′i·ness** *n.*

bray¹ (brā) *v.* **brayed, braying, brays.** —*intr.* **1.** To utter a loud, harsh cry, as a donkey. **2.** To sound loudly and harshly. —*tr.* To utter loudly and harshly. —*n.* **1.** A loud, harsh cry, as of a donkey. **2.** Any sound resembling this. [Middle English *brayen,* to make noise, roar, from Old French *braire,* probably from Celtic.] —**bray′er** *n.*

bray² (brā) *tr.v.* **brayed, braying, brays. 1.** To crush and pound in or as if in a mortar. **2.** To spread (ink) thinly over a surface. [Middle English *brayen,* from Old French *breier,* to break, from Germanic. See **bhreg-** in Appendix.*]

bray·er (brā′ər) *n. Printing.* A small hand roller used to spread ink thinly and evenly over type.

Braz. Brazil; Brazilian.

braze¹ (brāz) *tr.v.* **brazed, brazing, brazes. 1.** To make of or decorate with brass. **2.** To make hard like brass. [Middle English *brasen,* Old English *brasian,* from *bræs,* BRASS.]

braze² (brāz) *tr.v.* **brazed, brazing, brazes.** To solder (two pieces of metal) together using a hard solder with a high melting point. [Probably from French *braser,* from Old French, to burn, from *brese,* burning coals, from Germanic. See **bhreu-²** in Appendix.*] —**braz′er** *n.*

bra·zen (brā′zən) *adj.* **1.** Made of brass. **2.** Resembling brass in color, quality, or hardness. **3.** Having a loud, resonant sound like that of a brass trumpet. **4.** Impudent; bold. —See Synonyms at **shameless.** —*tr.v.* **brazened, -zening, -zens.** To face or undergo with bold or brash self-assurance. Usually used with *out.* [Middle English *brasen,* Old English *bræsen,* from *bræs,* BRASS.] —**bra′zen·ly** *adv.* —**bra′zen·ness** *n.*

bra·zen-faced (brā′zən-fāst′) *adj.* Impudent and shameless.

bra·zier¹ (brā′zhər) *n.* Also **bra·sier.** One who works in brass. [Middle English *brasier,* from *bras,* BRASS.]

bra·zier² (brā′zhər) *n.* Also **bra·sier.** A metal pan for holding burning coals or charcoal. [French *brasier,* from *braise,* burning coals, from Old French *brese,* from Germanic. See **bhreu-²** in Appendix.*]

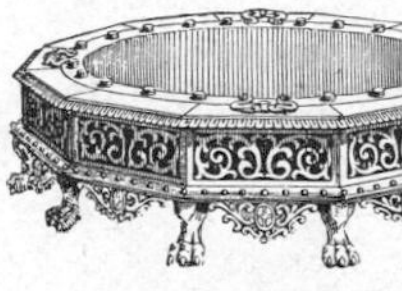

brazier²

Bra·zil (brə-zĭl′). *Abbr.* **Braz.** *Portuguese* **Bra·sil** (brä-zĭl′). Officially, United States of Brazil. A republic of South America, the fifth-largest country in the world, occupying 3,287,203 square miles. Population, 70,967,000. Capital, Brasília. [Portuguese, from Spanish *Brasil,* short for *(tierra de) brasil,* "(land of) brazilwood," from Old French *bresil,* BRAZILWOOD.] —**Bra·zil′ian** *adj.* & *n.*

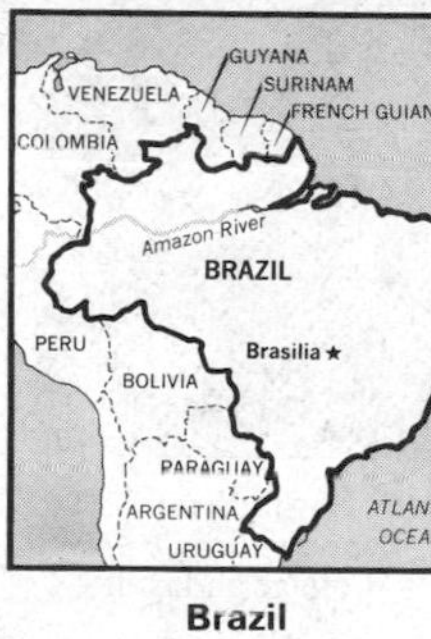

Brazil

braz·i·lin (brăz′ə-lĭn, brə-zĭl′ən) *n.* Also **bras·i·lin.** A crystalline compound, $C_{16}H_{14}O_5$, obtained from brazilwood and used as a dye. [French *brésiline,* from *brésil,* brazilwood, from Old French *bresil.* See **brazilwood.**]

Brazil nut. 1. A tree, *Bertholletia excelsa,* of tropical South America, bearing hard, round, woody pods that contain about 20 to 30 nuts. **2.** The edible nut of this tree. [After BRAZIL.]

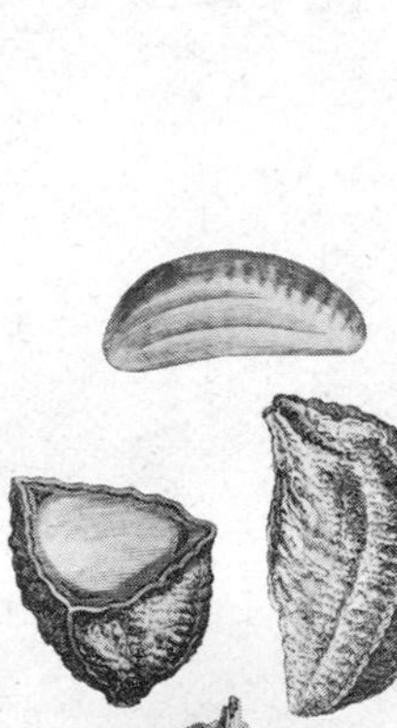

Brazil nut
Nuts and open pod

bra·zil·wood (brə-zĭl′wŏŏd′) *n.* The red wood of any of several tropical trees of the genus *Caesalpinia,* used for cabinetwork and as the source of a red or purple dye. [Middle English *brasil,* from Old French *bresil,* "red-dye wood," probably from *brese,* burning coals, from Germanic. See **bhreu-²** in Appendix.*]

Braz·os River (brăz′əs). A river rising in northwestern Texas

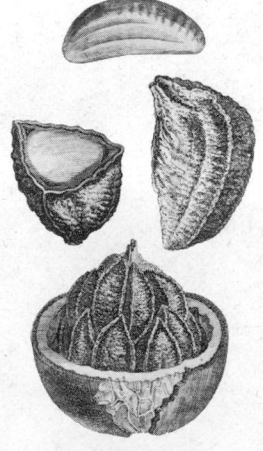

and flowing 870 miles, generally southeast, to the Gulf of Mexico west of Galveston.

Braz·za (brá-zä'), **Pierre Paul François Camille Savorgnan de.** 1852–1905. French explorer of central Africa.

Braz·za·ville (brăz'ə-vĭl'). The capital of the Republic of Congo, a river port on the northern bank of the Congo, 225 miles from the Atlantic Ocean. Population, 136,000.

breach (brēch) *n.* **1.** A violation or infraction, as of a law, legal obligation, or promise. **2.** A gap or rift, especially in a solid structure such as a dike or fortification: *"The first breach in . . . the monolith of international communism opened new horizons"* (John C. Bennett). **3.** A breaking up or disruption of friendly relations; an estrangement. **4.** The leaping of a whale from the water. **5.** The breaking of waves or surf. **6.** *Obsolete.* A wound; an injury. —*v.* **breached, breaching, breaches.** —*tr.* To make a hole or gap in; break through. —*intr.* To leap from the water. Used of a whale. [Middle English *breche, brek,* partly from Old French *breche,* from Old High German *brehha,* from *brehhan,* to break, and partly from Old English *brǣc, brēc,* from *brecan,* to break. See **bhreg-** in Appendix.*]

Synonyms: *breach, infraction, violation, transgression, trespass, encroachment, infringement.* These nouns apply to the act of one who commits a legal or moral offense. *Breach* and *infraction* are applied to any failure to keep the law or to fulfill one's duties, obligations, word, or the like, whether intentional or otherwise. *Violation* is broadly applicable to such an act committed willfully, and more strongly suggests injury. *Transgression* refers to violation, generally of divine or moral law, in which sense it denotes sin. *Trespass* refers either to violation of moral or statutory law; in the latter sense it denotes forceful violation of another's rights, possessions, or person. In all senses it implies willful intrusion. *Encroachment* is the act of gradual intrusion on another's rights, territory, or other possessions, generally by stealth. *Infringement* is used broadly in the sense of infraction or violation and specifically to denote encroachment on another's rights, such as the rights granted by a copyright.

breach of promise. The failure to fulfill a promise, especially a promise to marry someone.

bread (brĕd) *n.* **1.** A staple food made from flour or meal mixed with a liquid, usually combined with a leavening agent, and kneaded, shaped into loaves, and baked. **2.** Food in general, regarded as necessary for sustaining life. **3. a.** The necessities of life; livelihood: *earn one's bread.* **b.** Something that nourishes; sustenance: *"My bread shall be the anguish of my mind"* (Spenser). —*tr.v.* **breaded, breading, breads.** To coat with bread crumbs, especially before cooking. [Middle English *bread, bred,* Old English *brēad.* See **bhreu-**[2] in Appendix.*]

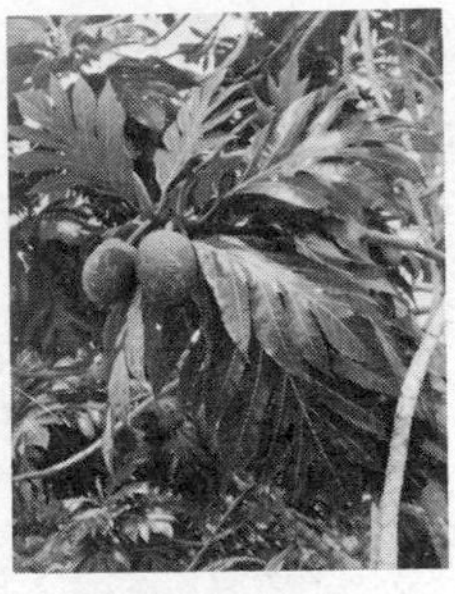

breadfruit
Artocarpus communis
Foliage and fruit

bread and butter. *Informal.* A means of support; livelihood.

bread-and-butter (brĕd'n-bŭt'ər) *adj.* **1.** Influenced by or undertaken out of necessity: *a bread-and-butter job.* **2.** Expressive of gratitude for hospitality: *a bread-and-butter note.*

bread·bas·ket (brĕd'băs'kĭt, -bäs'kĭt) *n.* **1.** A basket for serving bread. **2.** A geographical region serving as a principal source of grain supply. **3.** *Slang.* The stomach.

bread·board (brĕd'bôrd', -bōrd') *n.* **1.** A board on which bread is sliced. **2.** *Slang.* An experimental model, especially of an electric circuit; a prototype.

bread·fruit (brĕd'fro͞ot') *n.* **1.** A tree, *Artocarpus communis* (or *A. incisa*), of Polynesia, having deeply lobed leaves and round, usually seedless fruit. **2.** The edible fruit of this tree, having a texture like that of bread, when baked or roasted.

bread line. A line of persons waiting to be given free food, either from a relief agency or as charity.

bread mold. A fungus, *Rhizopus nigricans,* that forms a dense, cottony growth on bread and other foods.

bread·nut (brĕd'nŭt') *n.* **1.** A tree, *Brosimum alicastrum,* of Central America and the West Indies, bearing round, nutlike fruit. **2.** The fruit of this tree, ground to produce a substitute for wheat flour.

bread·root (brĕd'ro͞ot', -ro͝ot') *n.* A plant, *Psoralea esculenta,* of the central North American plains, having an edible, starchy root. Also called "prairie turnip."

bread·stuff (brĕd'stŭf') *n.* **1.** Bread. **2.** Flour, meal, or grain used in the baking of bread.

breadth (brĕdth) *n.* **1.** *Abbr.* **b., B.** The measure or dimension from side to side of something, as distinguished from length or thickness; width. **2.** A piece of something, usually produced in a standard width: *a breadth of canvas.* **3.** Wide extent or scope. **4.** Freedom from narrowness, as of views or interests. [Middle English *brede,* Old English *brǣdu,* from Common Germanic *braidjōn* (unattested), from *braithaz* (unattested), BROAD.]

Usage: *Breadth* and *broadness* are seldom interchangeable. *Breadth* expresses measure or scope, physical or otherwise, and lack of narrowness (figurative). *Broadness* often implies grossness or coarseness (lack of desirable restraint).

breadth·wise (brĕdth'wīz') *adv.* Also **breadth·ways** (-wāz'). In the direction of the breadth. —**breadth'wise'** *adj.*

bread·win·ner (brĕd'wĭn'ər) *n.* One who supports a family or household by his or her earnings.

break (brāk) *v.* **broke** (brōk) or *archaic* **brake** (brāk), **broken** (brō'kən), **breaking, breaks.** See Usage note at **broken.** —*tr.* **1.** To disjoin or reduce to pieces with sudden or violent force; to smash. **2.** To crack without actually separating into pieces. **3.** To render unusable or inoperative. **4.** To part or pierce the surface of. **5.** To cause to burst. **6.** To fracture a bone of. **7.** To force or make a way through; penetrate. **8.** To force one's way out of; escape from. **9.** To put an end to by force or strong opposition: *break a strike.* **10.** To fail to conform to; act contrary to; violate. **11.** To discontinue abruptly; interrupt; suspend. **12.** To cause to give up a habit. **13.** To train to obey; to tame. **14.** To disrupt or destroy the order or regularity of: *break ranks.* **15.** To destroy the completeness of: *break a set of books.* **16.** To lessen in force or effect: *break a fall.* **17.** To weaken or destroy, as in spirit or health: *"For a hero loves the world till it breaks him"* (Yeats). **18.** To overwhelm with grief or sorrow: *break one's heart.* **19.** To cause to be without money or to go into bankruptcy. **20.** To reduce in rank; demote. **21.** To reduce to or exchange for smaller monetary units: *break a dollar.* **22.** To surpass or outdo: *break a record.* **23.** To make known, as news. **24.** To find the solution or key to. **25.** *Law.* To invalidate (a will) by judicial action. **26.** *Electricity.* To open: *break a circuit.* —*intr.* **1.** To become separated into pieces or fragments; come apart. **2.** To become unusable or inoperative. **3.** To give way; to collapse. **4.** To diminish or discontinue abruptly: *His fever broke.* **5.** To scatter or disperse. **6.** To move away or escape suddenly. **7.** To change direction suddenly. **8.** To come into being or notice, especially suddenly. **9.** To emerge above the surface of water. **10.** To be overwhelmed with sorrow. Used of the heart. **11.** To begin abruptly to utter or produce something. Used with *into, out into,* or *out in:* *"like the flower of the prairie sugar cane when it breaks into bloom"* (Ronald Firbank). **12.** To come to an end; dismiss. Often used with *up: The game will break up in ten minutes.* **13.** To drop rapidly and considerably. Used of stock prices. **14.** To collapse or crash into surf or spray, as waves. **15.** To change from one tone quality or musical register to another. **16.** *Baseball.* To curve near or over the plate. Used of a pitch. **17.** *Informal.* To occur in a particular way: *Things are breaking well for him.* —**break bread.** To eat or share a meal. —**break camp.** To pack up equipment and leave a campsite. —**break in. 1.** To train or adapt for some purpose. **2.** To enter forcibly or suddenly. **3.** To interrupt. —**break in on** (or **upon**). To interrupt or intrude on. —**break into. 1.** To enter forcibly, suddenly, or illegally. **2.** To interrupt: *"No one would have dared to break into his abstraction"* (Alan Paton). —**break off. 1.** To stop suddenly, as in speaking. **2.** To discontinue (a relationship). **3.** To detach or become detached. —**break out. 1.** To begin or arise suddenly. **2.** To escape, as from prison. **3.** To become affected with eruptions or with a rash. Used of the skin. —**break with.** To discontinue a relationship with. —*n.* **1.** The act of breaking; a separating into parts. **2.** The result of breaking; a fracture or crack. **3.** A beginning or opening: *the break of day.* **4.** A dash, especially to escape. **5.** An interruption or disruption of continuity or regularity. **6.** A pause or interval, as from work. **7.** A sudden or marked change. **8.** *Informal.* A chance occurrence; especially, an unexpected opportunity. **9.** A severing of ties. **10.** A sudden decline in prices, especially in the stock market. **11.** *Prosody.* A caesura. **12.** *Printing.* **a.** The space between two paragraphs. **b.** A series of three dots (. . .) used to indicate an omission in a text. **13.** *Electricity.* Interruption of a flow of current. **14.** *Music.* **a.** The point at which a register or a tonal quality changes to another register or tonal quality. **b.** The change itself. **c.** In jazz, a solo cadenza played during the pause between the regular phrases or choruses of a melody. **15.** *Baseball & Cricket.* The swerving of a ball from a straight path of flight when thrown. **16.** *Billiards.* The opening shot. **17.** *Billiards & Croquet.* A run, or unbroken series of successful shots. **18.** *Bowling.* Failure to score a strike or a spare in a given frame. **19.** Also **brake.** A high, open, horse-drawn carriage with four wheels. —See Synonyms at **opportunity.** [Break, broke, broken; Middle English *breken, brok* (or *brak*), *broken,* Old English *brecan, bræc* (plural *brǣcon*), *brocen.* See **bhreg-** in Appendix.*]

Synonyms: *break, crack, fracture, rupture, burst, split, splinter, shatter, shiver, smash, crush.* These verbs describe the effect of sudden application of force. *Break,* the least specific, usually involves separation of a rigid object into parts; sometimes, however, it is used in the sense of *crack,* which specifies adherence of parts. *Fracture* applies to breaking or cracking of a rigid body. *Rupture* refers to breaking apart or tearing of a soft or pliable substance; sometimes rupturing (as in the case of a blood vessel) results from internal force and thus has the basic sense of *burst. Split* refers to the breaking of a rigid substance lengthwise or in the direction of the grain. *Splinter* involves splitting into thin and sharp separate pieces. *Shatter* pertains to the breaking of a rigid object into many small, scattered pieces. *Shiver* likewise indicates fragmentation by sudden force but especially suggests fine splinters. *Smash* stresses force of impact and complete change of form of a rigid body but is otherwise not specific. *Crush* refers to the effect of great external force, to change of form, or to reduction into fine particles.

break·a·ble (brā'kə-bəl) *adj.* Capable of being broken. See Synonyms at **fragile.** —*n.* Articles capable of being broken easily. Usually used in the plural. —**break'a·ble·ness** *n.*

break·age (brā'kĭj) *n.* **1.** The act or process of breaking. **2.** A quantity broken. **3. a.** Loss or damage as a result of breaking. **b.** An allowance for such a loss or damage.

break·a·way (brāk'ə-wā') *adj.* **1.** Designating a theatrical prop designed to fall apart easily. **2.** Capable of independent action: *a breakaway political group.* —*n.* A breakaway object.

break·bone fever (brāk'bōn'). A viral disease, **dengue** *(see).*

break down. 1. To fail to function; cease to be useful or operable. **2.** To have a physical or mental collapse. **3.** To become or cause to become distressed or upset. **4.** To overcome (opposition, for example). **5.** To consider in parts; analyze. **6.** To effect or undergo chemical decomposition.

break·down (brāk'doun') *n.* **1.** The act or process of breaking down and failing to function or the condition resulting from this. **2.** *Electricity.* The failure of an insulator or insulating medium to prevent discharge or current flow. **3.** A collapse in physical or mental health. **4.** An analysis, outline, or summary consisting of itemized data or essentials. **5.** Disintegration or decomposition into parts or elements.

breakdown voltage. The potential difference in volts at which a normally insulating medium becomes conducting because an electric discharge occurs in it.

break·er[1] (brā′kər) *n.* **1.** One that breaks. **2.** A machine or plant for breaking up some hard substance, such as rock or coal. **3.** *Electricity.* A **circuit breaker** *(see).* **4.** A wave that crests or breaks into foam, especially against a shoreline.

break·er[2] (brā′kər) *n.* A small water cask for use on a ship's lifeboat. [Spanish *bareca, barrica, barril,* barrel, akin to Old French *baril,* BARREL.]

break·fast (brĕk′fəst) *n.* The first meal of the day. —*intr.v.* **breakfasted, -fasting, -fasts.** To eat breakfast. [Middle English *brekfast, brekefast,* from *breken faste,* to break (one's) fasting : BREAK + *faste,* a fast, from Old Norse *fasta* (see **past-** in Appendix*).] —**break′fast·er** *n.*

break·front (brāk′frŭnt′) *n.* A high, wide cabinet or bookcase having a central section projecting beyond the end sections.

break·ing (brā′kĭng) *n.* *Linguistics.* The change of a simple vowel to a diphthong, often caused by the influence of neighboring consonants. In Old English, for example, simple *e* often became diphthongal *eo* under the influence of a following *r* plus another consonant, as *berg,* a hill, became *beorg.* Also called "vowel fracture." [Translation of German *Brechung.*]

breaking and entering. *Law.* The gaining of unauthorized access, as by forcing a lock, to another's premises for the purpose of committing a crime.

break·neck (brāk′nĕk′) *adj.* Heedless of safety; dangerous; headlong: *breakneck speed.*

Break·spear, Nicholas. See **Adrian IV.**

break·through (brāk′thro͞o′) *n.* **1.** An act of breaking through an obstacle or restriction. **2.** A military offensive that penetrates an enemy's lines of defense. **3.** A major achievement or success that permits further progress, as in technology.

break up. 1. To disperse; scatter. **2.** To take apart; separate. **3.** To put a stop to; discontinue. **4.** To sever or become severed. Used of a relationship. **5.** *Informal.* To lose or cause to lose control or composure. **6.** *Slang.* To convulse with laughter.

break·up (brāk′ŭp′) *n.* **1.** The act of breaking up; a separation or dispersal. **2.** *Informal.* A loss of control or composure.

break·wa·ter (brāk′wô′tər, -wŏt′ər) *n.* A barrier that protects a harbor or shore from the full impact of waves.

bream[1] (brēm) *n., pl.* **bream** or **breams. 1.** Any of several European freshwater fishes of the genus *Abramis,* having a flattened body and silvery scales. **2.** Any of several similar or related fishes. [Middle English *breme,* from Old French *breme, bresme,* from Germanic. See **bherək-** in Appendix.*]

bream[2] (brēm) *tr.v.* **breamed, breaming, breams.** To clean (a wooden ship's hull) by applying heat to soften the pitch, and then by scraping. [Probably from Dutch *brem,* broom, furze, from Middle Dutch *bremme.* See **bhrem-**[2] in Appendix.*]

breast (brĕst) *n.* **1. a.** The human mammary gland. **b.** A homologous organ in other mammals. **2.** A source of nourishment. **3.** The superior ventral surface of the body, extending from the neck to the abdomen. **4.** This part of the human body regarded as the seat of affection or emotion. **5.** The section of a garment that covers this part of the body. **6.** Anything likened to this part of the body: *the breast of a hill.* —**make a clean breast of.** To make a full confession of. —*tr.v.* **breasted, breasting, breasts.** To encounter or advance against manfully; confront boldly: "*Waves of tiny soldiers breasted the small hills.*" (Ross Lockridge, Jr.). [Middle English *brest,* Old English *brēost.* See **bhreus-**[1] in Appendix.*]

breast·bone (brĕst′bōn′) *n.* *Anatomy.* The **sternum** *(see).*

breast-feed (brĕst′fēd′) *tr.v.* **-fed** (-fĕd′), **-feeding, -feeds.** To feed (a baby) mother's milk from the breast; suckle.

breast·plate (brĕst′plāt′) *n.* **1.** A piece of armor plate that covers the breast. **2.** A square cloth set with 12 precious stones representing the 12 tribes of Israel, worn by a Jewish high priest. **3.** The plastron of a turtle's or tortoise's shell.

breast stroke. A swimming stroke in which one lies face down in the water and extends the arms in front of the head, then sweeps them both back laterally under the surface of the water while performing a frog kick.

breast·work (brĕst′wûrk′) *n.* A temporary, quickly constructed fortification, usually breast-high. See Synonyms at **bulwark.**

breath (brĕth) *n.* **1.** The air inhaled and exhaled in respiration. **2.** The act or process of breathing; respiration. **3.** The capacity to breathe. **4.** A single respiration. **5.** Exhaled air, as evidenced by vapor, odor, or heat. **6.** A momentary pause or rest. **7. a.** A momentary stirring of air. **b.** A slight gust of fragrant air. **8.** A trace or suggestion. **9.** A soft-spoken sound; a whisper. **10.** *Phonetics.* Exhalation of air without vibrating the vocal cords, as in the articulation of *p* and *s.* Compare **voice.** —**catch one's breath.** To pause until one's normal breathing is regained. —**in the same breath.** At the same time. —**out of breath.** Breathless, as from exertion. —**save one's breath.** To refrain from futile entreaties. —**take one's breath away.** To leave one as if breathless from awe or surprise. —**under** (or **below**) **one's breath.** In a whisper or muted voice. [Middle English *breth,* vapor, air from the lungs, Old English *brǣth,* odor, exhalation. See **bhreu-**[2] in Appendix.*]

breathe (brēth) *v.* **breathed, breathing, breathes.** —*intr.* **1.** To inhale and exhale air. **2.** To be alive; to live. **3.** To move or blow gently, as air. **4.** To be exhaled or emanated, as a fragrance. **5.** To pause to rest or regain breath: *Give me a moment to breathe.* —*tr.* **1.** To inhale and exhale during respiration. **2.** To impart (a quality) as if by breathing; instill: *breathe life into a portrait.* **3.** To exhale; emit. **4.** To utter, especially quietly; to whisper: *Don't breathe a word of this.* **5.** To make apparent; to manifest. **6.** To allow (a person or animal) to rest or regain breath. **7.** *Obsolete.* To tire or exhaust. **8.** *Phonetics.* To utter with a voiceless exhalation of air. [Middle English *brethen,* from *breth,* BREATH.] —**breath′a·ble** *adj.*

breath·er (brē′thər) *n.* **1.** One who breathes in a specified manner. **2.** *Informal.* A strenuous or exhausting task. **3.** *Informal.* A short rest period.

breath·ing (brē′thĭng) *n.* **1. a.** The act or process of respiration. **b.** A single breath. **2.** The time required to take one's breath. **3.** Either of two marks used in Greek to indicate aspiration of an initial sound (‘) or the absence of such aspiration (’).

breathing space. 1. Sufficient space to permit ease of breathing or movement. **2.** An opportunity to rest or give thought to a situation. In this sense, also called "breathing spell."

breath·less (brĕth′lĭs) *adj.* **1.** Without breath; not breathing; dead. **2.** Having no air or breeze; still. **3.** Out-of-breath. **4.** Holding the breath from excitement or suspense. **5.** Inspiring or marked by sudden excitement that takes the breath away: *a breathless flight.* —**breath′less·ly** *adv.* —**breath′less·ness** *n.*

breath·tak·ing (brĕth′tā′kĭng) *adj.* Inspiring awe; exciting.

breath·y (brĕth′ē) *adj.* **-ier, -iest.** Marked by audible or noisy breathing: *a breathy voice.*

brec·ci·a (brĕch′ē-ə, brĕsh′-) *n.* Rock composed of sharp-angled fragments cemented in a fine matrix. [Italian, from Old High German *brehha,* breaking, fragment, from *brehhan,* to break. See **bhreg-** in Appendix.*] —**brec′ci·at′ed** (-ā′tĭd) *adj.*

Brecht (brĕKHt), **Bertolt.** 1898–1956. German playwright and poet; exiled in America and Scandinavia (1933–47).

Breck·in·ridge (brĕk′ĭn-rĭj), **John Cabell.** 1821–1875. Vice President of the United States under James Buchanan (1857–61); served Confederacy as general and Secretary of War.

Brec·on·shire (brĕk′ən-shîr, -shər). Formerly **Breck·nock·shire** (brĕk′näk-). A county occupying 733 square miles in southeastern Wales. Population, 55,000. County seat, Brecknock.

bred. Past tense and past participle of **breed.**

Bre·da (brā′də). An industrial city in the southwestern Netherlands. Population, 114,000.

brede (brēd) *n.* *Archaic.* An ornamental braided or embroidered edging; a braid.

breech (brēch) *n.* **1.** The lower rear portion of the human trunk; the buttocks. **2.** The lower part of a pulley. **3.** The part of a firearm to the rear of the barrel or, in a cannon, to the rear of the bore. —*tr.v.* **breeched, breeching, breeches.** *Archaic & Regional.* To clothe with breeches. [Middle English *breech,* Old English *brēc,* breeches, plural of *brōc,* leg covering. See **bhāg-** in Appendix.*]

breech·block (brēch′blŏk′) *n.* The metal part that closes the breech end of the barrel of a breechloading gun and that is removed to insert a cartridge and replaced before firing.

breech·cloth (brēch′klôth′) *n.* Also **breech·clout** (-klout′). A cloth worn to cover the loins; loincloth.

breech delivery. Delivery of a fetus with the buttocks or feet appearing first.

breech·es (brĭch′ĭz) *pl.n.* **1.** Trousers extending to or just below the knee. **2.** *Informal.* Any trousers. [Plural of BREECH.]

breeches buoy. An apparatus used for rescues at sea, consisting of sturdy canvas breeches attached at the waist to a ring buoy that is suspended from a pulley running along a rope from ship to shore or from ship to ship.

breech·ing (brĭch′ĭng, brē′chĭng) *n.* **1.** The strap of a harness that passes behind a draft animal's haunches. **2.** The parts of a gun that make up the breech. **3.** Formerly, a rope securing the breech of a cannon to the side of a ship to control the recoil.

breech·load·er (brēch′lō′dər) *n.* Any gun or firearm loaded at the breech. —**breech′load′ing** *adj.*

breech presentation. The position of a fetus during labor in which the buttocks or feet first appear in the cervix.

breed (brēd) *v.* **bred** (brĕd), **breeding, breeds.** —*tr.* **1.** To produce (offspring); give birth to or hatch. **2.** To bring about; engender. **3. a.** To cause to reproduce; raise. **b.** To develop new or improved strains in (animals or plants). **4.** To rear or train; bring up. —*intr.* **1.** To produce offspring. **2.** To gain origin and sustenance; be nurtured. —*n.* **1.** A genetic strain or type of organism, usually a domestic animal, having consistent and recognizable inherited characteristics; especially, such a strain developed and maintained by man. **2.** A kind; sort. **3.** *Western U.S.* A half-breed. An offensive term used derogatorily. [Breed, bred (past tense and past participle); Middle English *breden, bred,* Old English *brēdan, bredd* (unattested). See **bhreu-**[2] in Appendix.*]

breed·er (brē′dər) *n.* **1.** A person who breeds animals or plants. **2.** An animal kept to produce offspring. **3.** One that breeds; a cause; source. **4.** *Physics.* A breeder reactor.

breeder reactor. A nuclear reactor that produces, as well as consumes, fissionable material; especially, one that produces more fissionable material than it consumes.

breeder tulip. A type of garden tulip having tall stems and flowers with muted colors.

breed·ing (brē′dĭng) *n.* **1.** One's line of descent: *a man of noble breeding.* **2.** Training in the proper forms of social and personal conduct. —See Synonyms at **culture.**

Breed's Hill (brēdz). A hill near **Bunker Hill** *(see);* site of a monument commemorating the Battle of Bunker Hill.

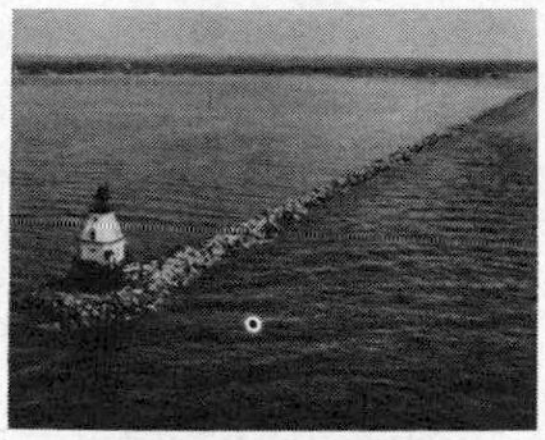

breakwater
U.S. Coast Guard light station at the tip of a breakwater

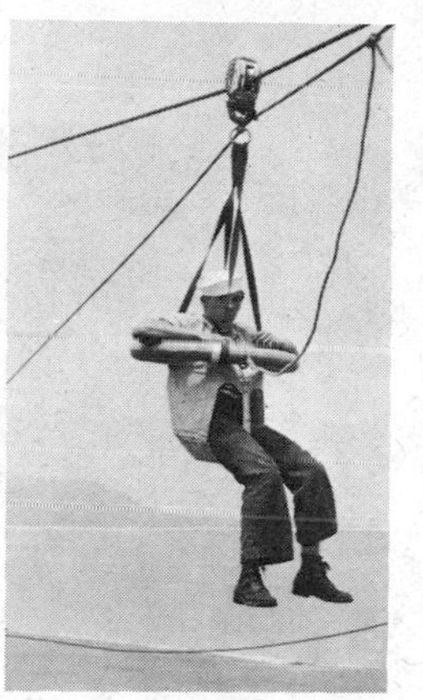

breeches buoy

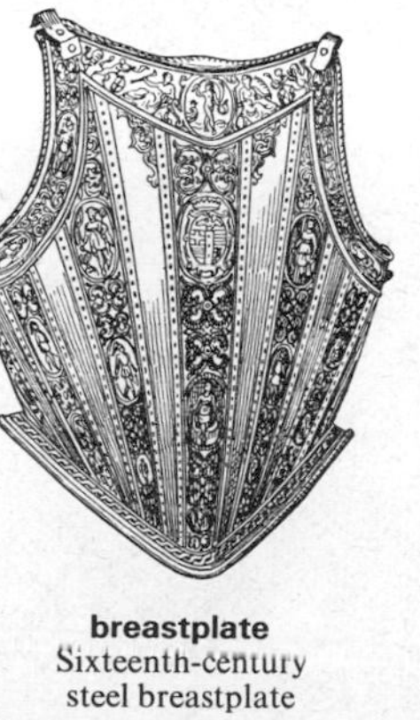

breastplate
Sixteenth-century steel breastplate

breeks (brēks) *pl.n. Scottish.* Breeches. [From Middle English (northern dialect) *breke,* variant of *brech,* BREECH.]

breeze[1] (brēz) *n.* **1.** A light air current; gentle wind. **2.** *Meteorology.* A wind of from 4 to 31 miles per hour. **3.** *Chiefly British Informal.* A commotion or disturbance; an argument. **4.** *Informal.* An easily accomplished task. —See Synonyms at **wind.** —*intr.v.* **breezed, breezing, breezes. 1.** To blow lightly. **2.** *Informal.* To move swiftly and effortlessly. —**breeze up.** *Nautical.* To blow more strongly. Used of wind. [Perhaps from Old Spanish *briza*†, northeast wind.]

breeze[2] (brēz) *n. Rare.* A gadfly or similar insect. [Middle English *brese,* Old English *brēosa*†.]

breeze[3] (brēz) *n. British.* The refuse left when coal, coke, or charcoal is burned, used in brickmaking and as a concrete filler. [Probably from French *braise,* burning coals, from Old French *brese,* from Germanic. See **bhreu-[2]** in Appendix.*]

breeze·way (brēz′wā′) *n.* A roofed, open-sided passageway connecting two structures, such as a house and a garage.

breez·y (brē′zē) *adj.* **-ier, -iest. 1.** Exposed to breezes; windy. **2.** Fresh and animated; lively; sprightly. —**breez′i·ly** *adv.* —**breez′i·ness** *n.*

breg·ma (brĕg′mə) *n., pl.* **-mata** (-mə-tə). *Anatomy.* The junction of the sagittal and coronal sutures at the top of the skull. [New Latin, from Late Latin, the front part of the head, from Greek. See **mregh-mo-** in Appendix.*] —**breg·mat′ic** *adj.*

Breit (brīt), **Gregory.** Born 1899. Russian-born American nuclear physicist.

Bre·men (brĕm′ən; *German* brā′mən). **1.** A state, 156 square miles in area, in northern West Germany. Population, 733,000. **2.** The capital of this state and a port of entry, on the Weser River, 46 miles from the North Sea. Population, 588,000.

Brem·er·ha·ven (brĕm′ər-hä′vən; *German* brā′mər-hä′fən). A seaport of northern West Germany, on the Weser estuary about ten miles from the North Sea. Population, 145,000.

brems·strah·lung (brĕms′shträ′ləng) *n.* The electromagnetic radiation produced by an electrically charged subatomic particle, such as an electron, subjected to a change in velocity, as by deceleration in the electric field of an atomic nucleus. [German *Bremsstrahlung,* braking radiation : *Bremse,* brake, from Middle High German, clamp, from Middle Low German *premese,* from *pramen,* to press, akin to Middle High German *pfrengen*†, to press + *Strahlung,* radiation, from *strahlen,* to radiate, from *Strahl,* ray, beam, from Old High German *strāla,* arrow, lightning bolt (see **ster-[2]** in Appendix*).]

Bren·da (brĕn′də). A feminine given name. [Shetland dialect, perhaps from Old Norse *Brand*†.]

Bren gun (brĕn). *Military.* A .303 caliber gas-operated, air-cooled submachine gun, adopted by the British Army in World War II. [BR(NO), Czechoslovakia, where it was first made + EN(FIELD), England, where it was manufactured.]

Bren·ner Pass (brĕn′ər). A pass through the eastern Alps between southern Austria and northeastern Italy. It is the lowest (4,500 feet) of the Alpine passes.

brent. *British.* Variant of **brant.**

Brent (brĕnt). A borough of London, England, comprising the former administrative divisions of Wembley and Willesden. Population, 296,000.

Brent·ford and Chis·wick (brĕnt′fərd; chĭz′ĭk). A former administrative division of London, now part of **Hounslow** *(see).*

br'er (brûr, brĕr) *n. Southern U.S.* Brother.

Bre·scia (brā′shä). An industrial city of north-central Italy, 50 miles east of Milan. Population, 191,000.

Bres·lau. The German name for **Wroclaw.**

Brest (brĕst). **1.** A city and Atlantic seaport in extreme western France. Population, 136,000. **2.** Formerly **Brest Li·tovsk** (brĕst lə-tôfsk′, -tôvsk′). *Polish* **Brześć nad Bu·giem** (bzhĕsts′y′ näd bo͞o′gyĕm). A city of southwestern Byelorussia, where the Treaty of Brest-Litovsk was signed in 1918 between the Soviet Union and the Central Powers. Population, 73,000.

Bre·tagne. The French name for **Brittany.**

breth·ren. *Archaic.* Plural of **brother.**

Bret·on (brĕt′n) *n.* **1.** A native or inhabitant of Brittany. **2.** *Abbr.* **Br.** The Celtic language of Brittany. [French, from Old French, BRITON.] —**Bret′on** *adj.*

Bre·ton·neau (brə-tô-nō′), **Pierre.** 1778–1862. French surgeon; gave name to diphtheria; described typhoid fever.

Bret·ton Woods (brĕt′n). A resort in north-central New Hampshire in the White Mountains. It was the site in 1944 of an international monetary conference that established the International Monetary Fund and the World Bank.

Breu·er (broi′ər), **Marcel Lajos.** Born 1902. Hungarian-born American architect and designer of furniture and interiors.

Breu·ghel. See **Brueghel.**

brev. brevet.

breve (brĕv, brēv) *n.* **1.** A symbol (˘) placed over a vowel to show that it has a short sound. Compare **macron. 2.** *Prosody.* A similar symbol used to indicate that a syllable is short or unstressed. **3.** *Music.* A single note equivalent to two whole notes. **4.** *Archaic.* A letter of authority, especially one from a pope. [Middle English, variant of *bref,* BRIEF.]

bre·vet (brə-vĕt′; *British* brĕv′ĭt) *n. Abbr.* **brev., bvt.** A commission, often granted as an honor, promoting a military officer in rank without an increase in pay or authority. —*tr.v.* **brevetted** or **-veted, -vetting** or **-veting, -vets.** To promote by brevet. —*adj.* Held or awarded by brevet. [Middle English, from Old French *brevet,* diminutive of *bref,* letter, BRIEF.]

bre·vet·cy (brə-vĕt′sē) *n., pl.* **-cies.** A rank awarded by brevet.

bre·vi·ar·y (brē′vē-ĕr-ē, brĕv′-ē-) *n., pl.* **-ies.** *Ecclesiastical.* A book containing the hymns, offices, and prayers for the canonical hours. [Latin *breviārium,* summary, abridgment, from *breviāre,* to abridge, from *brevis,* short, BRIEF.]

bre·vier (brə-vîr′) *n. Printing.* A size of type, 8-point. [Dutch, "type size for breviaries," from Latin *breviārium,* BREVIARY.]

brev·i·ty (brĕv′ə-tē) *n.* **1.** Briefness of duration. **2.** Concise expression; terseness. [Latin *brevitās,* from *brevis,* BRIEF.]

brew (bro͞o) *v.* **brewed, brewing, brews.** —*tr.* **1.** To make (ale or beer) from malt and hops by infusion, boiling, and fermentation. **2.** To make (a beverage) by boiling, steeping, or mixing various ingredients. **3.** To concoct; devise. —*intr.* **1.** To make ale or beer as an occupation. **2.** To be imminent; impend: *"In spite of storms brewing on every frontier"* (John Dos Passos). —*n.* **1.** A beverage made by brewing. **2.** The quantity of beverage brewed at one time. [Middle English *brewen,* Old English *brēowan.* See **bhreu-[2]** in Appendix.*] —**brew′er** *n.*

brew·age (bro͞o′ĭj) *n.* **1.** Something prepared by brewing. **2.** The process of brewing.

brewer's yeast. A yeast, *Saccharomyces cerevisiae,* used in brewing and as a source of B complex vitamins.

brew·er·y (bro͞o′ər-ē) *n., pl.* **-ies.** An establishment for the manufacture of malt liquors.

brew·house (bro͞o′hous′) *n.* A brewery.

brew·ing (bro͞o′ĭng) *n.* **1.** The act or process of producing malt liquors. **2.** The quantity brewed at one time; a brew. **3.** The act of concocting or devising.

brew·is (bro͞o′ĭs, bro͞oz) *n. Regional.* **1.** A broth. **2.** Bread soaked in broth, gravy, milk, or the like. [Middle English *browis, brewes,* from Old French *broez, bro(u)ez,* from *breu,* broth, from Germanic. See **bhreu-[2]** in Appendix.*]

Brew·ster (bro͞o′stər), **William.** 1567–1644. English Puritan colonist; a leader of the Pilgrims at Plymouth, Massachusetts.

Brezh·nev (brĕzh′nĕf; *Russian* brĕzh-nyôf′), **Leonid Ilyich.** Born 1906. Soviet statesman; first secretary of the Communist Party (since 1964).

Br. Gu. British Guiana.

Br. Hond. British Honduras.

Br. I. British India.

Bri·an (brī′ən). Also **Bry·an.** A masculine given name. [Middle English, probably from Celtic.]

Bri·an Bo·ru (brī′ən bô-ro͞o′). Irish Gaelic, Boramhe or Boroimhe. A.D. 926–1014. High King of unified Ireland (1002–14).

Bri·and (brē-äN′), **Aristide.** 1862–1932. French statesman; 11 times premier.

Bri·ansk. See **Bryansk.**

bri·ar[1] (brī′ər) *n.* Also **bri·er. 1.** A shrub or small tree, *Erica arborea,* of southern Europe, having a hard, woody root used to make tobacco pipes. Also called "tree heath." **2.** A pipe made from briarroot or from a similar wood. [French *bruyère,* heath, from Gallo-Roman *brūcaria* (unattested), from *brūcus,* from Gaulish *brūko* (unattested). See **wer-[3]** in Appendix.*]

bri·ar[2]. Variant of **brier** (bush).

bri·ard (brē-är′, -ärd′) *n.* A sturdily built, rough-coated dog of an ancient French breed. [French, from *Brie,* France.]

Bri·ar·e·us (brī-âr′ē-əs). *Greek Mythology.* A giant who aided Zeus and the Olympians against the Titans.

bri·ar·root (brī′ər-ro͞ot′, -ro͝ot′) *n.* The hard, woody root of the briar.

bri·ar·wood (brī′ər-wo͝od′) *n.* Wood from the root of the briar.

bribe (brīb) *n.* **1.** Anything, such as money, property, or a favor, offered or given to someone in a position of trust to induce him to act dishonestly. **2.** Something offered or serving to influence or persuade. —*v.* **bribed, bribing, bribes.** —*tr.* **1.** To give, offer, or promise a bribe to. **2.** To gain influence over or corrupt by bribery. —*intr.* To give, offer, or promise bribes. [Middle English *briben,* to purloin, steal, from Old French *briber, brimber*†, to beg.] —**brib′a·ble** *adj.* —**brib′er** *n.*

brib·er·y (brī′bə-rē) *n., pl.* **-ies.** The act of giving, offering, or taking a bribe.

bric-a-brac (brĭk′ə-brăk′) *n.* Objects collectively, usually small, displayed in a room as ornaments and valued for their antiquity, rarity, or curiosity value. [French *bric-à-brac* (expressive formation).]

brick (brĭk) *n.* **1.** A molded, rectangular block of clay, baked by the sun or in a kiln until hard, and used as a building and paving material. **2.** These blocks collectively. **3.** Any object shaped like such a block. **4.** *Informal.* A splendid fellow. —**make bricks without straw.** To try to do something while lacking a needed component. —*tr.v.* **bricked, bricking, bricks. 1.** To construct, line, or pave with brick. **2.** To close or wall with brick. Usually used with *up* or *in: He bricked up the windows of the old house.* [Middle English *brike, breke,* probably from Middle Dutch *bricke,* akin to Middle Low German *brike*†.] —**brick** *adj.* —**brick′y** *adj.*

brick·bat (brĭk′băt′) *n.* **1.** A piece of brick, especially one used as a weapon or missile. **2.** A blunt remark or criticism.

brick cheese. A brick-shaped semisoft cheese that is sweet in taste and smooth of texture.

brick·kiln (brĭk′kĭln′, -kĭl′) *n.* A kiln in which bricks are baked.

brick·lay·er (brĭk′lā′ər) *n.* A person skilled in building with bricks. —**brick′lay′ing** *n.*

brick red. 1. Moderate reddish brown. **2.** Moderate to strong brown. See **color.** —**brick′-red′** *adj.*

brick·work (brĭk′wûrk′) *n.* **1.** A structure made of bricks. **2.** Construction with bricks.

brick·yard (brĭk′yärd′) *n.* A place where bricks are made.

bri·dal (brīd′l) *n.* A marriage ceremony; a wedding. —*adj.* Of or pertaining to a bride or a marriage ceremony; nuptial. [Middle English *bridale,* wedding feast, Old English *brȳdealu,* "bride ale" : BRIDE + ALE.]

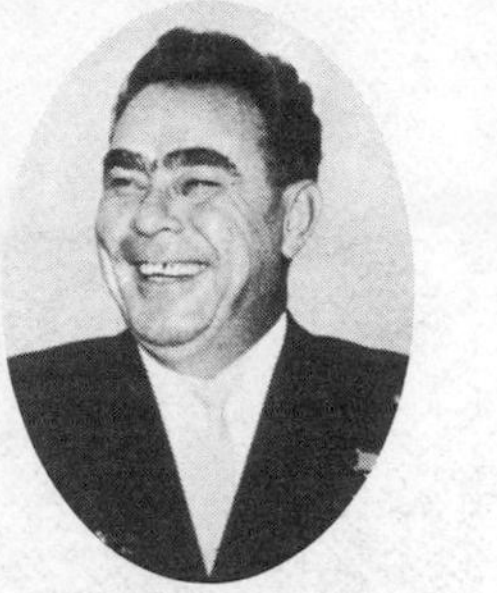

Leonid Brezhnev
Photographed in Belgrade, Yugoslavia, in 1962

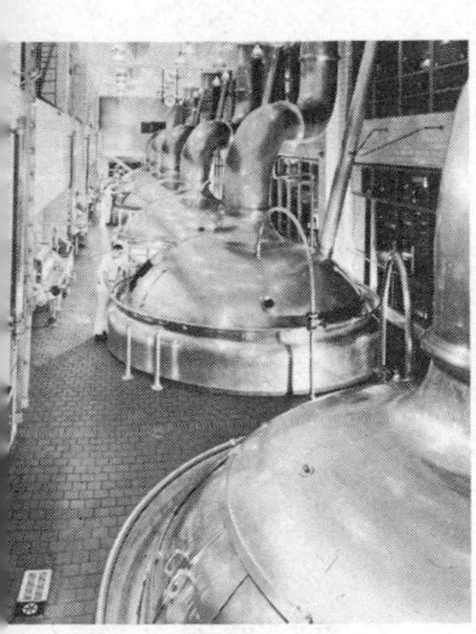

brewery
Copper brewing kettles in a commercial brewery

Bri·dal·veil (brīd′l-vāl′). Also **Bridal Veil.** A waterfall, 620 feet high, in Yosemite National Park, east-central California.
bridal wreath. Either of two related shrubs, *Spiraea prunifolia* or *S. vanhouttei,* cultivated for their profuse white flowers.
bride[1] (brīd) *n.* A woman who has recently been married or is about to be married. [Middle English *bride,* Old English *brȳd,* from Common Germanic *brūdhiz* (unattested).]
bride[2] (brīd) *n.* A loop, bar, or tie connecting pattern segments in lacework or needlework. [French, "bridle," from Middle High German *brīdel,* rein. See **bherek-** in Appendix.*]
Bride, Saint. See Saint **Bridget** (Irish).
bride·groom (brīd′grōōm′, -grŏŏm′) *n.* A man who has recently been married or is about to be married. [Alteration (influenced by GROOM) of Middle English *bridegome,* Old English *brȳdguma* : *brȳd,* BRIDE + *guma,* man (see **dhghem-** in Appendix*).]
brides·maid (brīdz′mād′) *n.* A woman, usually young and unmarried, who attends the bride at a wedding. Compare **maid of honor, matron of honor.**
bridge[1] (brĭj) *n.* **1.** A structure spanning and providing passage over a waterway, railroad, or other obstacle. **2.** Anything resembling or analogous to such a structure in form or function. **3.** The upper bony ridge of the human nose. **4.** The part of a pair of eyeglasses that rests against this ridge. **5.** *Music.* **a.** A thin, upright piece of wood in some stringed instruments that supports the strings above the soundboard. **b.** A transitional passage connecting two subjects or movements. **6.** *Dentistry.* A fixed or removable replacement for one or several, but not all, of the natural teeth, usually anchored at each end to a natural tooth. **7.** *Nautical.* A crosswise platform above the main deck of a ship from which the ship is controlled. **8.** *Billiards.* A notched piece of wood or a rest made with the hand on which to steady the cue. Also called "rest." **9.** *Electricity.* Any of various circuits containing a branch that connects two points of equal potential and consequently carries no current when the circuit is suitably adjusted. **—burn one's bridges (behind one).** To eliminate the possibility of retreat. *—tr.v.* **bridged, bridging, bridges. 1.** To build a bridge over. **2.** To cross by or as if by a bridge. [Middle English *brigge,* Old English *brycg.* See **bhrū-** in Appendix.*] **—bridge′a·ble** *adj.*
bridge[2] (brĭj) *n.* Any of several card games derived from whist, played with one deck of cards divided equally among four people. [Earlier *biritch,* probably from Russian *birich,* caller, announcer of official proclamations, probably from *bir,* taxes, from Turkic *ber-* (unattested), "to give."]
bridge·board (brĭj′bôrd′, -bōrd′) *n.* A notched board at either side of a staircase, that supports the treads and risers.
bridge·head (brĭj′hĕd′) *n.* A military position established by advance troops on the enemy's side of a river or pass to afford protection for the main attacking force. [Translation of French *tête de pont.*]
Bridge of Sighs. 1. An elevated passageway over a canal in Venice, Italy, connecting the Doge's Palace and the prison. **2.** A passageway in New York City that formerly connected the Tombs prison with the criminal court building.
Bridge·port (brĭj′pôrt′, -pōrt′). An industrial city in southwestern Connecticut, on Long Island Sound. Population, 155,000.
Bridg·er (brĭj′ər), **James ("Jim").** 1804–1881. American mountain man and explorer; discovered Great Salt Lake.
Bridg·es (brĭj′ĭz), **Harry.** In full, Alfred Bryant Renton Bridges. Born 1900. Australian-born American labor leader.
Bridg·es (brĭj′ĭz), **Robert (Seymour).** 1844–1930. English poet and essayist; poet laureate (1913–30).
Bridg·es Creek. See **Wakefield.**
Bridg·et (brĭj′ĭt). A feminine given name. [Irish *Brighid,* from Old Irish *Brigit,* name of a Celtic fire goddess. See **bhregh-**[2] in Appendix.*]
Bridg·et[1] (brĭj′ĭt), **Saint.** Also **Brig·id** (brĭj′ĭd, brē′ĭd). In England **Bride** (brīd). A.D. 453–523. Irish Roman Catholic religious leader and a patron saint of Ireland.
Bridg·et[2] (brĭj′ĭt), **Saint.** 1303–1373. Swedish Roman Catholic religious leader; founded Brigittine or St. Saviour order.
Bridge·town (brĭj′toun′). The capital of Barbados, on the southwestern coast of the island. Population, 94,000.
bridge·work (brĭj′wûrk′) *n. Dentistry.* **a.** A bridge. **b.** Prosthetics involving a bridge or bridges.
bridg·ing (brĭj′ĭng) *n.* Wooden braces between beams, as of a floor or roof, that provide reinforcement and distribution of stress.
Bridg·man (brĭj′mən), **Percy Williams.** 1882–1961. American physicist; performed research on high-pressure phenomena.
bri·dle (brīd′l) *n.* **1.** The harness fitted about a horse's head, consisting of a headstall, bit, and reins, used to restrain or guide the animal. **2.** Any device or condition that controls or restrains free movement; a curb or check. **3.** *Nautical.* A span of chain, wire, or rope that can be secured at both ends to an object and slung from its center point. **4.** A bridling gesture. *—v.* **bridled, -dling, -dles.** *—tr.* **1.** To put a bridle on. **2.** To control or restrain with or as if with a bridle. *—intr.* **1.** To lift the head and draw in the chin as an expression of scorn or resentment. **2.** To become scornful, angry, or take offense. —See Synonyms at **restrain.** [Middle English *bridel,* Old English *brīdel.* See **bherek-** in Appendix.*] **—bri′dler** *n.*
bridle hand. The left hand, in which the reins are usually held, as by a cavalryman.
bridle path. A trail for saddle horses or pack horses.
bri·dle-wise (brīd′l-wīz′) *adj.* Trained to respond to pressure of the rein on the neck rather than a pull on the bit.
bri·doon (brĭ-dōōn′) *n.* A cavalry bit resembling a snaffle that may be reined independently of the curb bit. [French *bridon,* from *bride,* a bridle. See **bride** (loop).]
Brie (brē) *n.* A mold-ripened, whole-milk cheese, the center of which is soft. [French, first made in *Brie,* France.]
brief (brēf) *adj.* **briefer, briefest. 1.** Short in time or duration. **2.** Short in length or extent. **3.** Condensed in expression; succinct. **4.** Curt; abrupt. *—n.* **1.** A short or condensed statement. **2.** *Abbr.* **br.** A condensation or abstract of a large document or series of documents. **3.** *Abbr.* **br.** *Law.* **a.** An abstract of all of the documents affecting the title of real property. **b.** A document containing all facts and points of law pertinent to a specific case, filed by an attorney before arguing the case in court. **4.** *Roman Catholic Church.* A papal letter pertaining to matters of discipline. **5.** A briefing. **6.** *Plural.* Short, tight-fitting underpants. **—in brief.** In short; in a few words. *—tr.v.* **briefed, briefing, briefs. 1.** To summarize. **2.** To give concise preparatory instructions or advice to. **3.** *British.* To send a legal brief to. **4.** *British.* To hire (an attorney) as counsel. [As an adjective, Middle English *bref,* from Old French *bref,* from Latin *brevis;* as a noun, Middle English *bref,* letter of authority, from Old French *brief,* from Late Latin *breve,* summary, from Latin, neuter of *brevis,* short. See **mreghu-** in Appendix.*] **—brief′ly** *adv.* **—brief′ness** *n.*
Usage: *Brief* (adjective) is largely restricted to time (duration). *Short* is used for both time and extent (physical measurement). Thus, *short* (or *brief*) *visit; short* (not *brief*) *hair; short trunks* (here *brief* would emphasize lack of extent, and be used only facetiously). Applied to time, *brief* sometimes implies conscious effort to be concise, and *short* may imply curtailment.
brief·case (brēf′kās′) *n.* A portable rectangular case of leather or similar material. [From BRIEF (document).]
brief·ing (brē′fĭng) *n.* **1.** The act or procedure of giving or receiving concise preparatory instructions, information, or advice. **2.** The information conveyed during this procedure.
brief·less (brēf′lĭs) *adj.* Having no brief, thus no clients. Said of a lawyer.
bri·er[1] (brī′ər) *n.* Also **bri·ar.** Any of various thorny plants or bushes, especially a prickly-stemmed rosebush. [Middle English *brere,* Old English *brǣr, brērt.*] **—bri′er·y** *adj.*
bri·er[2]. Variant of **briar** (shrub).
Bri·eux (brē-œ′), **Eugène.** 1858–1932. French dramatist.
brig[1] (brĭg) *n.* A two-masted sailing ship, square-rigged on both masts, carrying two or more headsails and a quadrilateral gaff sail or spanker aft of the mizzenmast. [Short for BRIGANTINE.]
brig[2] (brĭg) *n.* **1.** A ship's prison. **2.** *Military Slang.* A guardhouse. [Probably from BRIG (ship).]
bri·gade (brĭ-gād′) *n.* **1.** *Abbr.* **brig. a.** A military unit consisting of a variable number of combat battalions, with supporting services. Three such units frequently form a division. **b.** Formerly, a unit of the U.S. Army composed of two or more regiments commanded by a brigadier general. **2.** Any group of persons organized for a specific purpose. *—tr.v.* **brigaded, -gading, -gades.** To form into a brigade. [French, from Old French, from Old Italian *brigata,* troop, company, from *brigare,* to form a troop, fight, from *briga,* strife, perhaps from Celtic. See **gwer-**[2] in Appendix.*]
brig·a·dier general (brĭg′ə-dîr′) *pl.* **brigadier generals.** *Abbr.* **B.G., Brig. Gen.** An officer ranking between a colonel and a major general in the U.S. Army, Air Force, and Marine Corps. Also called "brigadier." [French, from BRIGADE.]
brig·and (brĭg′ənd) *n.* A robber or freebooter, especially one of a band of bandits. [Middle English *brigaunt,* foot soldier, bandit, from Old French *brigand,* from Old Italian *brigante,* from the past participle of *brigare,* to fight. See **brigade.**] **—brig′and·age** (-ən-dĭj), **brig′and·ism′** *n.*
brig·an·tine (brĭg′ən-tēn′) *n.* A two-masted sailing ship, square-rigged on the foremast and having a fore-and-aft mainsail with square maintopsails. [French, from Old French *brigandin,* from Italian *brigantino,* "pirate ship," from *brigante,* BRIGAND.]
Brig. Gen. brigadier general.
Briggs (brĭgz), **Henry.** 1561–1631. English mathematician; published logarithm tables; invented modern long division.
bright (brīt) *adj.* **brighter, brightest. 1. a.** Emitting or reflecting light; shining. **b.** Comparatively high on the scale of **brightness** *(see).* See **color. 2.** Characterizing a dyestuff that produces a highly saturated color; brilliant in color; vivid. **3.** Glorious; splendid. **4.** Full of promise and hope; auspicious. **5.** Happy; cheerful. **6.** Smart; intelligent. —See Synonyms at **intelligent.** *—n.* **1.** Flue-cured tobacco. **2.** A thin, flat paintbrush used for highlighting. **3.** *Plural.* High-beam headlights. *—adv.* In a bright manner. [Middle English *bright,* Old English *beorht.* See **bherəg-** in Appendix.*] **—bright′ly** *adv.*
Synonyms: *bright, brilliant, radiant, lustrous, lambent, luminous, incandescent, effulgent. Bright* can be applied to anything that emits or reflects light. The terms that follow are more specific. A *brilliant* object is intensely bright and striking by reason of the sparkle, glitter, or gleam that it emits or reflects; figuratively the term applies to outstanding personal qualities. A *radiant* object radiates light; figuratively the term applies to that which, like a smile, reveals inner light and warmth. A *lustrous* object originates no light but reflects an agreeable sheen. *Lambent* is said of that which, like a flame, casts soft, flickering light; figuratively it suggests a subtle playfulness, as of style or wit. Physically, *luminous* is broadly applicable to anything bright, but is said especially of that which shines in the dark or figuratively of that which is remarkably clear or enlightened. *Incandescent* stresses burning brilliance, as of something white-

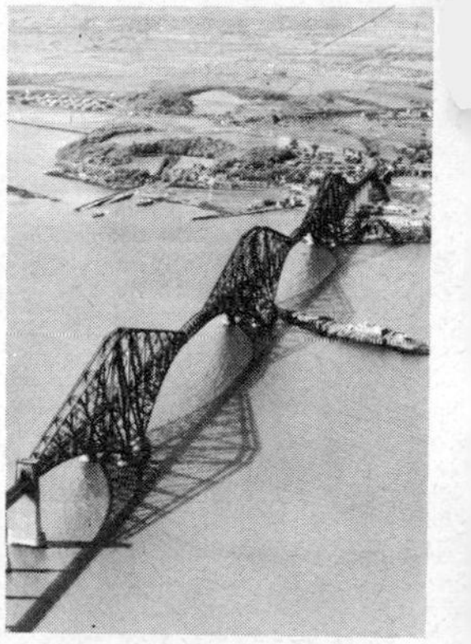

bridge[1]
The 3,770-foot Forth Bridge near Edinburgh, Scotland

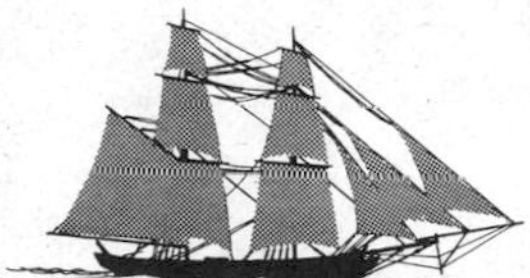

brig[1]

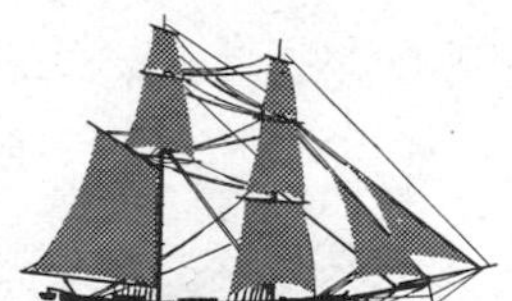

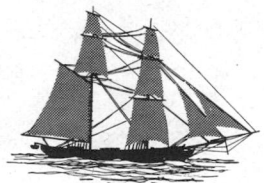

brigantine

hot. *Effulgent,* physically and figuratively, means intensely radiant.

bright·en (brīt′n) *v.* **-ened, -ening, -ens.** —*tr.* **1.** To make bright or brighter. **2.** To make more cheerful. —*intr.* **1.** To become bright or brighter. **2.** To become more cheerful.

bright·ness (brīt′nĭs) *n.* **1.** The state or quality of being bright. **2.** The effect or sensation by means of which an observer is able to distinguish differences in **luminance** *(see).* **3.** The dimension of a color that represents its similarity to one of a series of achromatic colors ranging from very dim (dark) to very bright (dazzling). See **color.**

Brigh·ton (brīt′n). A popular seaside resort on the English Channel, 50 miles south of London. Population, 163,000.

Bright's disease (brīts). Chronic **nephritis** *(see).* [First described by Richard *Bright* (1789–1858), British physician.]

bright·work (brīt′wûrk′) *n.* Metal parts or fixtures, especially on a ship, made bright by polishing.

Brig·id, Saint. See Saint **Bridget** (Irish).

Brill (brĭl), **Abraham Arden.** 1874–1948. Austrian-born American psychiatrist; translator of Jung and Freud.

brill (brĭl) *n., pl.* **brill** or **brills.** An edible flatfish, *Scophthalmus rhombus,* of European waters. [Perhaps from Cornish *brȳthel,* mackerel, from Old Cornish *brȳth*†, spotted, speckled.]

Bril·lat-Sa·va·rin (brē′yȧ′sȧ′vȧ′răN′), **Anthelme.** 1755–1826. French politician and gourmet; author of *Physiology of Taste.*

bril·liance (brĭl′yəns) *n.* Also **bril·lian·cy** (-yən-sē). **1.** Extreme brightness. **2.** Sharpness and clarity of musical tone. **3.** Splendor; magnificence. **4.** Exceptional clarity and agility of intellect or invention.

bril·liant (brĭl′yənt) *adj.* **1.** Full of light; shining. **2. a.** Brightly vivid in color. **b.** Designating a color that has a combination of high lightness and strong saturation. See **color.** **3.** *Music.* Sharp and clear in tone. **4.** Glorious; splendid; magnificent. **5.** Superb; excellent; wonderful. **6.** Marked by extraordinary powers of intellect or invention. —See Synonyms at **bright, intelligent.** —*n.* **1.** A precious gem, especially a diamond, finely cut in any of various forms, with numerous facets. **2.** *Printing.* A small size of type, about 3½-point. [French *brillant,* present participle of *briller,* to shine, from Italian *brillare,* perhaps from *brillo,* beryl, from Latin *bēryllus,* BERYL.] —**bril′liant·ly** *adv.* —**bril′liant·ness** *n.*

bril·lian·tine (brĭl′yən-tēn′) *n.* **1.** An oily, perfumed hairdressing. **2.** A glossy fabric made from cotton and worsted or cotton and mohair. [French *brillantine,* from *brillant,* BRILLIANT.]

brim (brĭm) *n.* **1.** The rim or uppermost edge of a cup or other vessel. **2.** A projecting rim or edge: *the brim of a hat.* **3.** A border or edge, especially one surrounding a body of water. —See Synonyms at **border.** —*v.* **brimmed, brimming, brims.** —*tr.* To fill to the brim. —*intr.* To be full to the brim. —**brim over.** To overflow. [Middle English *brimme,* from Germanic, akin to Middle High German *brem.* See **bhrem-²** in Appendix.*]

brim·ful (brĭm′fo͝ol′) *adj.* Also **brim·full.** Completely full.

brim·stone (brĭm′stōn′) *n. Obsolete.* **Sulfur** *(see).* [Middle English *brimston,* Late Old English *brynstān.* See **bhreu-²** in Appendix.*] —**brim′ston′y** *adj.*

brin (brĭn) *n.* One of the ribs of a fan. [French *brin*†.]

Brin·di·si (brēn′dē-zē). Ancient name **Brun·di·si·um** (brŭn-dĭz′ē-əm, -dĭzh′ē-əm). A seaport of southeastern Italy, on the Adriatic Sea. Population, 63,000.

brin·dle (brĭnd′l) *adj.* Brindled. —*n.* **1.** A brindled color. **2.** A brindled animal.

brin·dled (brĭnd′əld) *adj.* Tawny or grayish with streaks or spots of a darker color. Said of an animal. [Variant of earlier *brinded, brended,* from Middle English *brende,* perhaps from Scandinavian, akin to Old Norse *brandr,* piece of burning wood. See **bhreu-²** in Appendix.*]

brine (brīn) *n.* **1.** Water saturated with or containing large amounts of a salt, especially of sodium chloride. **2. a.** The water of a sea or ocean. **b.** A large body of salt water. **3.** Salt water used for preserving and pickling foods. —*tr.v.* **brined, brining, brines.** To immerse or pickle in brine. [Middle English *brine,* Old English *brȳne*†, from Germanic.]

Bri·nell hardness (brĭ-nĕl′). The relative hardness of metals and alloys, determined by forcing a steel ball into a test piece under standard conditions and measuring the surface area of the resulting indentation. [After Johann A. *Brinell* (1849–1925), Swedish engineer.]

Brinell number. *Abbr.* **Bhn.** The numerical value assigned to the Brinell hardness of metals and alloys.

brine shrimp. Any of various small crustaceans of the genus *Artemia.* [So called because they have been observed living in highly saline water.]

bring (brĭng) *tr.v.* **brought** (brôt), **bringing, brings.** **1.** To take with oneself to a place; convey or carry along: *brought enough money with him.* See Usage note below. **2.** To carry as an attribute or contribution: *brought years of experience to his new post.* **3.** To lead or force into a specified state, situation, or location: *brought to grief.* **4.** To succeed in persuading; induce: *His confession brought others to confess.* **5.** To cause to occur as a consequence or concomitant: *Floods brought death to the valley.* **6.** To cause to become apparent to the mind; recall: *bring back memories.* **7.** *Law.* To advance or set forth (charges or evidence, for example) in a court. **8.** To sell for; fetch. —**bring about.** **1.** To cause to happen. **2.** To turn (a ship). —**bring around** (or **round**). **1.** To cause to adopt an opinion or course of action. **2.** To cause to recover consciousness. —**bring down.** **1.** To cause to fall or collapse. **2.** To fell. —**bring down the house.** *Informal.* To cause wild or general applause. —**bring forth.** **1.** To give rise to; to effect; produce. **2.** To disclose; reveal. —**bring forward.** **1.** To present; adduce: *bring forward an opinion.* **2.** *Accounting.* To carry (a sum) from one page or column to another. —**bring in.** **1.** To give or submit (a verdict). **2.** To produce or yield (profits or income). —**bring off.** To accomplish successfully. —**bring on.** **1.** To result in; to cause. **2.** To cause to appear: *bring on the dessert.* —**bring out.** **1.** To reveal or expose. **2.** To produce or publish. —**bring over.** To win over. —**bring to.** **1.** To cause to recover consciousness. **2.** To cause (a ship) to turn into the wind and lose way. —**bring up.** **1.** To take care of and educate (a child); to rear. **2.** To introduce into discussion; to mention. **3.** To vomit or cough up. [Bring, brought, brought; Middle English *bringen, broughte, brought,* Old English *bringan, brōhte, brōht.* See **bher-¹** in Appendix.*] —**bring′er** *n.*

Usage: In the sense of conveying or escorting, *bring* properly indicates movement toward a place identified with the speaker; it implies *come* (here) *with. Take* indicates movement away from such a place and implies *go* (there) *with.* Thus one *takes* checks to the bank and *brings* home cash. One may be asked to *bring* proof of identity. *Fetch* involves going to a specified place, getting something, then returning with it. *Brung,* as the past tense and past participle of *bring,* is an illiteracy.

bring·ing-up (brĭng′ĭng-ŭp′) *n.* The care, training, and education of a child; upbringing.

brink (brĭngk) *n.* **1. a.** The upper edge of a steep or vertical declivity: *the brink of a cliff.* **b.** The margin of land bordering a body of water. **2.** The verge of something: *on the brink of discovery.* —See Synonyms at **border.** [Middle English *brinke, brenk,* akin to Middle Dutch *brink*†, slope.]

brink·man·ship (brĭngk′mən-shĭp′) *n.* The practice, especially in international politics, of seeking advantage by creating the impression that one is willing and able to pass the brink of nuclear war rather than concede. [BRINK + (GAMES)MANSHIP.]

brin·y (brī′nē) *adj.* **-ier, -iest.** Of, pertaining to, or resembling brine; salty. —*n. Slang.* The sea. —**brin′i·ness** *n.*

bri·o (brē′ō) *n.* Vigor; vivacity. [Italian, "vivacity," from Gaulish *brigo-* (unattested), might, strength. See **gwer-²** in Appendix.*]

bri·oche (brē-ôsh′, -ōsh′) *n.* A soft, light-textured roll or bun made from eggs, butter, flour, and yeast. [French, from Old French, from *brier,* dialectal form of *broyer,* to knead, from Germanic. See **bhreg-** in Appendix.*]

bri·o·lette (brē′ə-lĕt′) *n.* A pear-shaped gem, especially a diamond, cut with long triangular facets. [French, *bri(ll)olette,* probably an irregular diminutive of *brillant,* BRILLIANT.]

bri·quette, bri·quet (brĭ-kĕt′) *n.* A block of compressed coal dust or charcoal, used for fuel and kindling. [French *briquette,* from *brique,* brick, from Middle Dutch *bricke,* BRICK.]

bri·sance (brĭ-zäns′) *n.* The shattering effect of a sudden release of energy, as in an explosion. [French, from *brisant,* present participle of *briser,* to break, from Vulgar Latin *brisāre,* from Gaulish. See **bhrēi-** in Appendix.*] —**bri·sant′** *adj.*

Bris·bane (brĭz′bən, -bān) *n.* The capital, principal seaport, and largest city of Queensland, Australia, situated in the southeast near the Pacific Ocean. Population, 664,000.

brisk (brĭsk) *adj.* **brisker, briskest.** **1.** Moving or acting quickly; lively; energetic: *a brisk walk.* **2.** Keen or sharp in speech or manner: *a brisk greeting.* **3.** Stimulating and invigorating: *a brisk wind.* **4.** Effervescent: *"A cup of wine that's brisk and fine"* (Shakespeare). —See Synonyms at **nimble.** [Probably a variant of BRUSQUE.] —**brisk′ly** *adv.* —**brisk′ness** *n.*

bris·ket (brĭs′kĭt) *n.* **1.** The chest of an animal. **2.** The ribs and meat from this part. [Middle English *brusket,* probably from a Scandinavian compound akin to Old Norse *brjōst,* breast (see **bhreus-¹** in Appendix*) + *ket*†, meat.]

bris·ling (brĭz′lĭng, brĭs′-) *n.* A fish, the **sprat** *(see).* [Norwegian, alteration (influenced by *brisa,* to flash) of Low German *bretling,* from *bret,* broad, from Common Germanic *braithaz* (unattested), BROAD.]

bris·tle (brĭs′əl) *n.* A short, coarse, stiff hair or hairlike part. —*v.* **bristled, -tling, -tles.** —*intr.* **1.** To erect the bristles, as an angry, excited, or frightened animal: *The hog bristled with fear.* **2.** To react with agitation to anger, excitement, or fear. Often used with *up: He bristled up in anger.* **3.** To stand erectly on end like bristles: *His hair bristled.* **4.** To be covered or thick with or as if with bristles: *The path bristled with thorns.* —*tr.* **1.** To cause to stand erect like bristles; stiffen. Often used with *up: "Boy, bristle thy courage up."* (Shakespeare). **2.** To furnish or supply with bristles; put bristles on. **3.** To ruffle; disturb. [Middle English *bristil, brustel,* from *brust,* bristle, Old English *byrst.* See **bhar-** in Appendix.*] —**bris′tly** *adj.*

bris·tle·tail (brĭs′əl-tāl′) *n.* Any of various wingless insects of the order Thysanura, such as the silverfish, having bristlelike posterior appendages.

Bris·tol (brĭs′təl). **1.** A city and port in southwestern England, six miles inland from the Severn River estuary. Population, 431,000. **2.** A city in east-central Connecticut, 15 miles southwest of Hartford, once noted for clockmaking. Population, 51,000. **3.** An urban and industrial area in southeastern Pennsylvania, on the Delaware River. Population, 59,000.

Bristol board. A smooth, heavy pasteboard of fine quality. Also called "Bristol paper."

Bris·tol Channel (brĭs′təl). An inlet of the Atlantic Ocean extending 85 miles between Wales and southwestern England.

brit (brĭt) *n.* Also **britt.** **1.** The young of herring and similar fish. **2.** Minute marine organisms, such as crustaceans of the genus *Calanus,* that are a major source of food for many fish and whales. [Perhaps from Cornish *brȳthel,* mackerel. See **brill.**]

Brit. Britain; British.

ă pat/ā pay/âr care/ä father/b bib/ch church/d deed/ĕ pet/ē be/f fife/g gag/h hat/hw which/ĭ pit/ī pie/îr pier/j judge/k kick/l lid, needle/m mum/n no, sudden/ng thing/ŏ pot/ō toe/ô paw, for/oi noise/ou out/o͝o took/o͞o boot/p pop/r roar/s sauce/sh ship, dish/

Brit·ain (brĭt′n). *Abbr.* **Br., Brit.** See **Great Britain.** [Middle English *Bretayne,* from Old French *Bretaigne,* from Latin *Brittānia,* BRITANNIA.]
Usage: *Britain* is a geographical and political term. The nouns *Briton* and *British* apply to the people of Great Britain.
Bri·tan·nia (brĭ-tăn′yə, -tăn′ē-ə). **1.** The Latin name for Britain. **2.** The ancient Roman province in Great Britain. **3.** *Poetic.* Great Britain. **4.** A female personification of Great Britain or the British Empire. [Latin *Brittānia, Britannia,* from *Britannī,* Britons, from *Britto,* BRITON.]
bri·tan·nia (brĭ-tăn′yə, -tăn′ē-ə) *n.* Also **Bri·tan·nia.** A white alloy of tin with copper, antimony, and sometimes bismuth and zinc. It is used in the manufacture of tableware. Also called "britannia metal." [From BRITANNIA.]
Bri·tan·nic (brĭ-tăn′ĭk) *adj.* British. Used chiefly in the phrase *His* (or *Her*) *Britannic Majesty.*
britch·es (brĭch′ĭz) *pl.n. Informal.* Breeches. **—too big for one's britches.** *Informal.* Overconfident; cocky; arrogant. [Variant of BREECHES.]
Brit·i·cism (brĭt′ə-sĭz′əm) *n.* Also **Brit·ish·ism** (brĭt′ĭsh-ĭz′əm). A word, phrase, or idiom characteristic of or peculiar to English as it is spoken in Great Britain.
Brit·ish (brĭt′ĭsh) *adj. Abbr.* **B., Br. 1.** Of, pertaining to, or characteristic of Great Britain, the United Kingdom, or the British Empire. **2.** Of, pertaining to, or characteristic of the ancient Britons. *—n.* **1.** The people of Great Britain. Usually preceded by *the.* **2.** *Abbr.* **B., Brit., Br.** The language spoken in Great Britain, **British English** *(see).* **3. a.** The language spoken by the ancient Britons. **b.** The languages that developed from it: Welsh, Cornish, and Breton. [Middle English *Bruttische, Brytysshe,* Old English *Brettisc, Bryttisc,* pertaining to the ancient Britons, from *Bret,* Briton, from Latin *Britto,* BRITON.]
British A·mer·i·ca (ə-mĕr′ə-kə). **1.** Also **British North A·mer·i·ca.** Formerly, the British possessions in North America north of the United States; specifically, Canada. **2.** Sometimes, all British possessions in or near the Americas.
British Ant·arc·tic Territory (ănt-ärk′tĭk, -är′tĭk). Formerly **Falk·land Island Dependencies** (fôk′lənd). A group of islands and territory administered by the British from the Falkland Islands, and including the South Georgia, South Sandwich, South Orkney, and South Shetland groups, and sections of Antarctica. Capital, Stanley, in the Falklands.
British Bor·ne·o. The former name for British possessions on the island of Borneo.
British Cam·e·roons. See **Cameroons.**
British Co·lum·bi·a (kə-lŭm′bē-ə). *Abbr.* **B.C.** The westernmost province of Canada, 366,255 square miles in area, with its western border on the Pacific Ocean and Alaska. Population, 1,789,000. Capital, Victoria, on Vancouver Island. See map at **Canada. —British Columbian.**
British Commonwealth of Nations. The former name for the **Commonwealth of Nations.**
British East Af·ri·ca (ăf′rĭ-kə). Collectively, the former British territories in eastern Africa, including Kenya, Uganda, Tanganyika, and Zanzibar.
British Empire. The former British Commonwealth of Nations and all geographical and political units formerly under British control, including colonies, dependencies, trust territories, and protectorates.
British English. The English language as spoken, pronounced, and written in England, as compared with the English spoken elsewhere. Also called "British."
Brit·ish·er (brĭt′ĭsh-ər) *n. Informal.* **1.** A native of Great Britain. **2.** Sometimes, any British subject.
British Gui·a·na. *Abbr.* **Br. Gu.** The former name for **Guyana.**
British Hon·du·ras (hŏn-do͝or′əs, -dyo͝or′əs). *Abbr.* **Br. Hond.** A British crown colony, 8,867 square miles in area, on the Caribbean coast of Central America, bordered by Guatemala and Mexico. Population, 90,000. Capital, Belize.
British In·di·a (ĭn′dē-ə). *Abbr.* **Br. I.** That part of India exclusive of the Indian states, under direct British administration until 1947. See **India.**
British Isles. A group of islands off the northwestern coast of Europe, about 120,000 square miles in area, comprising Great Britain, Ireland, and adjacent smaller islands.
British Ma·lay·a (mə-lā′ə). The former British possessions on the Malay Peninsula and Malay Archipelago.
British New Guin·ea. The former name for the Territory of **Papua.**
British North A·mer·i·ca. *Abbr.* **B.N.A.** See **British America.**
British North Bor·ne·o. The former name for **Sabah.**
British Sol·o·mon Islands. See **Solomon Islands.**
British So·ma·li·land. See **Somalia.**
British thermal unit. *Abbr.* **Btu** The quantity of heat required to raise the temperature of one pound of water by one degree Fahrenheit. See **measurement.**
British To·go·land (tō′gō-lănd′). That part of the former German colony of Togo, later attached to the British Gold Coast crown colony, and now part of Ghana. See **Togoland.**
British Virgin Islands. A British colony in the West Indies, east of Puerto Rico, comprising about 30 islands. Population, 9,000. Capital, Road Town, on Tortola Island.
British West Af·ri·ca (ăf′rĭ-kə). *Abbr.* **B.W.A.** The former British possessions in western Africa, including Nigeria, Gambia, Sierra Leone, and the Gold Coast, and the trust territories of Togoland and Cameroons.
British West In·dies (ĭn′dēz). *Abbr.* **B.W.I.** The former name for the islands of the West Indies that were colonies or self-governing colonies of the United Kingdom.
Brit·on (brĭt′n) *n.* **1.** A native of Britain. **2.** One of a Celtic people who inhabited ancient Britain before the Roman invasion. [Middle English *Breton, Bryton,* from Old French *Breton,* from Latin *Britto* (stem *Brittōn-*), from Common Celtic *Britto(s)* (unattested).]
britt. Variant of **brit.**
Brit·ta·ny (brĭt′n-ē). *French* **Bre·tagne** (brə-tàn′y′). A region and former province of France on a peninsula extending into the Atlantic between the English Channel and Bay of Biscay.
brittany blue. Moderate greenish blue. See **color.**
Brit·ten (brĭt′n), **(Edward) Benjamin.** Born 1913. British composer, conductor, and pianist.
brit·tle (brĭt′l) *adj.* **1.** Likely to break; fragile: *brittle porcelain.* **2.** Difficult to deal with; snappish: *a brittle disposition.* —See Synonyms at **fragile.** *—n.* A confection of caramelized sugar to which nuts are added: *peanut brittle.* [Middle English *brotel, britel,* Old English *brytel* (unattested). See **bhreu-**[1] in Appendix.*] **—brit′tle·ness** *n.*
brittle star. Any of various marine organisms of the class Ophiuroidea, related to and resembling the starfish but having long, slender, whiplike arms. Also called "serpent star."
Br·no (bûr′nō). *German* **Brünn** (brün). The second-largest city of Czechoslovakia, in southern Moravia. Population, 327,000.
bro. brother.
broach[1] (brōch) *n.* **1.** A tapered and serrated tool used to shape or enlarge a hole. **2.** The hole made by such a tool. **3.** A spit for roasting meat. **4.** A narrow mason's chisel. **5.** A gimlet for tapping or broaching casks. **6.** Variant of **brooch.** *—tr.v.* **broached, broaching, broaches. 1. a.** To begin to talk about: *broach a subject.* **b.** To announce: *"Ernest broached his plans for spending the next year or two."* (Samuel Butler). **2.** To pierce in order to draw off liquid: *broach a keg.* **3.** To draw off (a liquid) by piercing a hole in a cask, keg, or other container. **4.** To shape or enlarge (a hole) with a broach. —See Synonyms at **vent.** [Middle English *broche,* pointed rod or pin, from Old French, a spit, from Vulgar Latin *brocca* (unattested), a spike. See **brocade.**] **—broach′er** *n.*
broach[2] (brōch) *v.* **broached, broaching, broaches.** *Nautical. —tr.* To cause to veer broadside to the wind and waves. *—intr.* To veer broadside to the wind and waves. Used with *to.* [Perhaps from BROACH (in the obsolete sense of "to turn on a spit").]
broad (brôd) *adj.* **broader, broadest. 1.** Wide from side to side. See Usage note below. **2.** Large in expanse; spacious: *a broad lawn.* See Usage note below. **3.** Widely diffused; open; clear: *broad daylight.* **4.** Covering a wide scope; general: *a broad rule.* **5.** Liberal; tolerant. **6.** Main; essential: *the broad facts of the matter.* **7.** Plain and clear; obvious: *a broad hint.* **8.** Outspoken; unrestrained. **9.** Vulgar; ribald: *a broad joke.* **10.** Heavily dialectal: *a broad accent.* **11.** *Phonetics.* Indicating a vowel that is pronounced with the tongue placed low and flat and with the oral cavity wide open, especially as when the *a* in *bath* is pronounced like the *a* in *bard.* *—n.* **1.** The broad part of something. **2.** *Slang.* A woman or girl. *—adv.* Fully; completely. [Middle English *brood,* Old English *brād,* from Common Germanic *braithaz* (unattested). See also **breadth, brisling.**] **—broad′ly** *adv.*
Usage: The adjectives *broad* and *wide* are both used as indications of horizontal extent. *Broad* is generally the choice when the word it modifies is a surface or expanse considered as such *(broad shoulders, broad river). Wide* is employed when the sense stresses space (distance across a surface), considered specifically *(the frame is five feet wide)* or indefinitely but emphatically *(the river is wide here).* Often the terms are interchangeable, but, especially in more figurative senses, the choice is governed solely by established idiom *(broad smile, wide mouth).*
broad arrow. 1. An arrow with a wide, barbed head. **2.** A wide arrowhead mark identifying British government property.
broad·ax, broad·axe (brôd′ăks′) *n., pl.* **-axes.** An ax with a wide, flat head and a short handle; battle-ax.
broad bean. 1. A plant, *Vicia faba,* native to the Old World, cultivated for its edible pods and seeds. **2.** The somewhat flattened seed of this plant. Also called "fava bean," "horse bean."
broad·bill (brôd′bĭl′) *n.* **1.** Any of various birds of the family Eurylaimidae, of Africa and tropical Asia, having a short, wide bill and brightly colored plumage. **2.** Any of several other broad-billed birds, as the shoveler. **3.** The **swordfish** *(see).*
broad·brim (brôd′brĭm′) *n.* **1.** A hat with a broad, flat brim, as those worn by Quakers. **2.** *Capital* **B.** *Informal.* A member of the Society of Friends; a Quaker.
broad·cast (brôd′kăst′, -käst′) *v.* **-cast** or **-casted, -casting, -casts.** *—tr.* **1.** To transmit (a program) by radio or television. **2.** To make known over a wide area: *broadcast rumors.* **3.** To sow (seed) over a wide area, especially by hand. *—intr.* **1.** To transmit a radio or television program. **2.** To participate in a radio or television program. *—n.* **1.** Transmission of a radio or television program or signal. **2.** A radio or television program, or the duration of such a program. **3.** The act of scattering seed. *—adj.* **1.** Of or pertaining to transmission by radio or television. **2.** Scattered over a wide area. *—adv.* In a scattered manner; far and wide. **—broad′cast′er** *n.*
Broad-Church (brôd′chûrch′) *adj.* Of or pertaining to members of the Anglican Communion favoring liberalism of doctrine and ritual. Compare **High-Church, Low-Church. —Broad′-Church′man** *n.*
broad·cloth (brôd′klôth′, -klŏth′) *n.* **1.** A densely textured woolen cloth with a plain or twill weave and a lustrous finish. **2.** A closely woven silk, cotton, or synthetic fabric with a narrow crosswise rib.

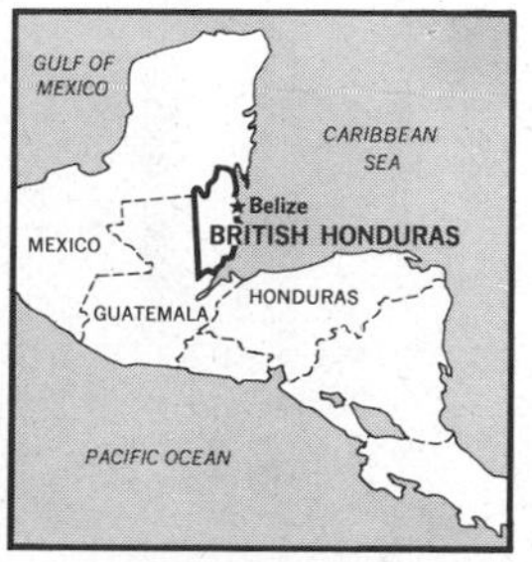

British Honduras

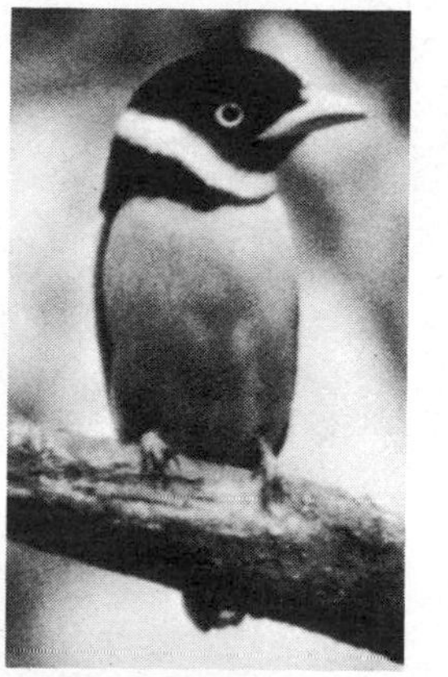
broadbill
Eurylaimus ochromalus

t tight/th thin, path/*th* this, bathe/ŭ cut/ûr urge/v valve/w with/y yes/z zebra, size/zh vision/ə about, item, edible, gallop, circus/ à *Fr.* ami/œ *Fr.* feu, *Ger.* schön/ü *Fr.* tu, *Ger.* über/KH *Ger.* ich, *Scot.* loch/N *Fr.* bon. *Follows main vocabulary. †Of obscure origin.

broad·en (brôd′n) v. **-ened, -ening, -ens.** —tr. To make broad or broader. —intr. To become broad or broader.

broad gauge. A railroad track with a width between the rails greater than the standard gauge of 56½ inches.

broad-gauge (brôd′gāj′) adj. Also **broad-gage, broad-gauged** (-gājd′), **broad-gaged.** 1. Having a broad gauge. 2. Informal. Having a wide scope; not narrow; liberal.

broad hatchet. A hatchet with a wide, flat blade.

broad-head (brôd′hĕd′) n. 1. A flat steel arrowhead with two sharp edges. 2. An arrow with such a head.

broad jump. In track and field events, a jump made for distance rather than height, either from a stationary position, *standing broad jump,* or a moving start, *running broad jump.*

broad-leaf (brôd′lēf′) n. Any of various tobacco plants having broad leaves.

broad-leaved (brôd′lēvd′) adj. Also **broad-leaf** (-lēf′), **broad-leafed** (-lēft′). Having relatively broad leaves. Said of evergreens such as the rhododendron and holly to distinguish them from needle-bearing evergreens such as the pines and spruces.

broad-loom (brôd′lōōm′) adj. Designating carpet woven on a wide loom and from 4½ feet to 18 feet in width. —n. A broadloom carpet.

broad-mind-ed (brôd′mīn′dĭd) adj. Having liberal or tolerant views. —**broad′-mind′ed-ly** adv. —**broad′-mind′ed-ness** n.

broad-ness (brôd′nĭs) n. The state, quality, or aspect of being broad. See Usage note at **breadth.**

Broads, The (brôdz). A low-lying region of marsh land and waterways in Norfolk and Suffolk, on the eastern coast of England.

broad seal. The official public seal of a state or nation.

broad-side (brôd′sīd′) n. 1. The side of a ship above the water line. 2. a. All the guns on one side of a warship. b. Their simultaneous discharge. 3. An explosive verbal attack or denunciation. 4. A large sheet of paper printed on one side. Also called "broadsheet." 5. Any broad, unbroken surface. —adv. With the side turned to a given object.

broad-spec-trum (brôd′spĕk′trəm) adj. Broad; widely applicable or effective: *a broad-spectrum drug.*

broad-sword (brôd′sôrd′, -sōrd′) n. A cutting sword with a wide blade.

broad-tail (brôd′tāl′) n. 1. A breed of sheep, the **karakul** (see). 2. The black pelt of a prematurely born karakul sheep, having a flat surface with wavy markings. Compare **Persian lamb.**

Broad-way¹ (brôd′wā′). A thoroughfare of New York extending the entire length of Manhattan Island, through the Bronx, and as far as Albany.

Broad-way² (brôd′wā′). 1. The principal theater district of New York City, located on or near Broadway. 2. This district thought of as representing the American theater industry; the American legitimate stage: *a career in motion pictures and on Broadway.* Compare **off-Broadway.** —**Broad′way′** adj.

Bro-ca (brō′kə; French brô-kä′), **Paul.** 1824–1880. French surgeon and anthropologist; pioneer in brain surgery.

bro-cade (brō-kād′) n. A heavy fabric interwoven with a rich, raised design. —tr.v. **brocaded, -cading, -cades.** To weave (cloth) with a raised design. [Earlier *brocado,* from Spanish or Portuguese, from Italian *broccato,* embossed fabric, from *brocco,* twisted thread, shoot, from Vulgar Latin *brocca* (unattested), a spike, from Latin *brocchus,* from Celtic *brokko-* (unattested), badger. See also **brock.**]

broc-a-tel, broc-a-telle (brŏk′ə-tĕl′) n. A very heavy fabric resembling brocade, but with a more highly raised design. [French *brocatelle,* from Italian *broccatello,* diminutive of *broccato,* BROCADE.]

broc-co-li (brŏk′ə-lē) n. 1. A plant, *Brassica oleracea italica,* closely related to the cabbage and cauliflower, having a branched, greenish flower head. 2. The flower head of this plant, eaten as a vegetable before the green, tightly clustered buds have opened. [Italian, plural of *broccolo,* cabbage sprout, diminutive of *brocco,* shoot. See **brocade.**]

bro-ché (brō-shā′) adj. Woven with a raised pattern or design; brocaded. [French, past participle of *brocher,* to stitch, from *broche,* knitting needle, spit, from Old French, a spit, from Vulgar Latin *brocca* (unattested), a spike. See **brocade.**]

bro-chette (brō-shĕt′) n. A small spit or skewer upon which meat, fish, or vegetables are roasted or broiled. [French, from Old French, diminutive of *broche,* spit. See **broché.**]

bro-chure (brō-shŏor′) n. A small pamphlet or booklet. [French, "a stitching" (from the loose stitching of the pages), from *brocher,* to stitch. See **broché.**]

brock (brŏk) n. British. 1. A badger. 2. Regional. An unsavory character; skunk. [Middle English *brock,* Old English *broc,* from Celtic *brokko-* (unattested), badger. See also **brocade.**]

Brock-en (brŏk′ən). The highest elevation (3,747 feet) of the Harz Mountains in western East Germany, near the border with West Germany.

brock-et (brŏk′ĭt) n. 1. A two-year-old stag with its first horns. 2. Any of several small deer of the genus *Mazama,* of South America, having short, unbranched horns. [Middle English *broket,* from Old North French *brocard,* from *broque,* the horn of an animal, any pointed implement, variant of Old French *broche,* a spit. See **broché.**]

Brock-ton (brŏk′tən). A manufacturing city in southeastern Massachusetts, 19 miles south of Boston. Population, 73,000.

bro-gan (brō′gən) n. A heavy, ankle-high work shoe. [Irish-Gaelic *brógan,* diminutive of *bróg.* BROGUE (shoe).]

Bro-glie (brō-glē′; French brô′y′), **Louis Victor de.** Born 1892. French physicist; predicted wave properties of the electron; awarded Nobel Prize in physics (1929).

brogue¹ (brōg) n. A strong dialectal accent, especially a strong Irish accent. [From BROGUE (shoe), with reference to the shoes of Irish and Scottish peasants.]

brogue² (brōg) n. 1. A heavy shoe of untanned leather, formerly worn in Scotland and Ireland. 2. A strong oxford shoe, usually with ornamental perforations. [Irish and Scottish Gaelic *bròg,* from Old Irish *bróc,* shoe, apparently from Old Norse *brók,* trousers. See **brāc-** in Appendix.*]

broi-der (broi′dər) tr.v. **-dered, -dering, -ders.** Obsolete. To ornament with needlework; embroider.

broil¹ (broil) v. **broiled, broiling, broils.** —tr. 1. To cook by direct radiant heat, as over a grill or under an electric coil. 2. To expose to great heat. —intr. To be exposed to great heat. —n. 1. The act or condition of broiling. 2. Something broiled. [Middle English *broillen, brulen,* from Old French *brul(l)er,* earlier *brusler,* to burn, perhaps from Vulgar Latin *brustulāre* (unattested), perhaps from Germanic. See **eus-** in Appendix.*]

broil² (broil) n. A rowdy argument; a brawl. —intr.v. **broiled, broiling, broils.** To engage in a brawl. [From obsolete *broil,* to confound, disturb, from Middle English *broilen,* from Old French *brouiller,* perhaps from *breu,* broth. See **brewis.**]

broil-er (broi′lər) n. 1. One who broils. 2. a. A small electric oven used for broiling. b. The part of a stove used for broiling. 3. A tender young chicken suitable for broiling.

broke (brōk). Past tense and *nonstandard* past participle of **break.** See Usage note at **broken.** —adj. Informal. 1. Lacking funds. 2. Bankrupt.

bro-ken (brō′kən). Past participle of **break.** See Usage note below. —adj. 1. Forcibly fractured into two or more pieces; shattered. 2. Violated; transgressed, as promises. 3. Fragmentary; incomplete: *a broken set of books.* 4. Disorganized; routed: *broken troops.* 5. Intermittently stopping and starting; discontinuous. 6. Varying abruptly, as in pitch: *broken sobs.* 7. Spoken imperfectly: *broken English.* 8. Topographically rough; uneven. 9. Subdued; humbled: *a broken spirit.* 10. Tamed and trained: *a broken stallion.* 11. Weakened; exhausted: *broken health.* 12. Crushed by grief: *a broken heart.* 13. Financially ruined; bankrupt. 14. Not functioning.

Usage: Broken, not broke, is the proper past participle of *break.* Thus, *He has broken* (not *broke*) *his arm. The bone is broken* (not *broke*).

bro-ken-down (brō′kən-doun′) adj. 1. Out of working order. 2. Decayed; infirm.

bro-ken-heart-ed (brō′kən-här′tĭd) adj. Grievously sad.

broken wind. A disease of horses, the **heaves** (see).

bro-ker (brō′kər) n. 1. One who acts as an agent for others in negotiating contracts, purchases, or sales in return for a fee or commission. 2. A stockbroker. [Middle English, peddler, pawnbroker, go-between, from Norman French *brocour†.*]

bro-ker-age (brō′kər-ĭj) n. 1. The business of a broker. 2. A fee or commission paid to a broker.

bro-mate (brō′māt′) n. A salt of bromic acid. —tr.v. **bromated, -mating, -mates.** 1. To treat (a substance) chemically with a bromate. 2. Loosely, to combine (a substance) chemically with bromine. [Probably German *Bromat* : BROM(O)- + -ATE.]

Brom-berg. The German name for **Bydgoszcz.**

brome (brōm) n. Any grass of the genus *Bromus,* having spikelets in loose, often drooping clusters. Also called "brome grass." [New Latin *Bromus,* from Latin *bromos,* oats, from Greek *bromos†.*]

bro-me-li-ad (brō-mē′lē-ăd′) n. Any of various mostly epiphytic plants of the family Bromeliaceae, which includes the pineapple, Spanish moss, and many species grown as house plants. [From New Latin *Bromelia* (type genus), after Olaf *Bromelius* (died 1705), Swedish botanist.]

bro-mic acid (brō′mĭk). A corrosive, colorless liquid, HBrO₃, used in making dyes and pharmaceuticals. [From French *bromique* : BROM(O)- + -IC.]

bro-mide (brō′mīd′) n. 1. A binary compound of bromine. 2. A sedative, **potassium bromide** (see). 3. a. A commonplace remark or notion; platitude. b. A tiresome person; bore. 4. A photographic print on paper that has been treated with bromine and silver. — See Synonyms at **cliché.** [BROM(INE) + -IDE.] —**bro-mid′ic** (-mĭd′ĭk) adj.

bro-mi-nate (brō′mə-nāt′) tr.v. **-nated, -nating, -nates.** To combine (a substance) with bromine or a bromine compound. [BROMIN(E) + -ATE.] —**bro′mi-na′tion** n.

bro-mine (brō′mēn′) n. Symbol Br A heavy, volatile, corrosive, reddish-brown, nonmetallic liquid element, having a highly irritating vapor. It is used in producing gasoline antiknock mixtures, fumigants, dyes, and photographic chemicals. Atomic weight 79.909, atomic number 35, melting point −7.2°C, boiling point 58.78°C, valences 1, 3, 5, 7. See **element.** [French *brome,* from Greek *brōmos†,* stench + -INE.]

bro-mism (brō′mĭz′əm) n. Also **bro-min-ism** (brō′mə-nĭz′əm). Poisoning from overuse of bromides. Symptoms include skin eruptions, headache, sleepiness, apathy, and loss of strength. [Probably French *bromisme* : BROM(O)- + -ISM.]

Brom-ley (brŏm′lē). A borough of southeastern London, England, comprising the former administrative divisions of Beckenham, Bromley, Penge, Orpington, and part of Chislehurst and Sidcup. Population, 294,000.

bromo-. Indicates bromine as the principal element in a chemical compound; for example, **bromoacetone.** [Probably from French *brome,* BROMINE.]

bro-mo-ac-e-tone (brō′mō-ăs′ə-tōn′) n. Also **brom-ac-e-tone** (brō-măs′ə-tōn′). A colorless liquid, CH₂BrCOCH₃, used as a constituent of tear gas. [BROMO- + -ACETONE.]

bron-chi. Plural of **bronchus.**

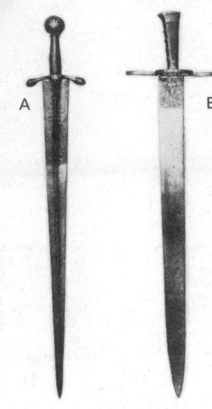

broadsword
A. Italian four-faced broadsword made about 1520
B. German two-edged broadsword made about 1552

brocade
Detail of an 18th-century French brocaded silk

bron·chi·a (brŏng′kē-ə) *pl.n. Singular* **-chium** (-kē-əm). *Anatomy.* Bronchial tubes smaller than the bronchi and larger than bronchioles. [Late Latin, from Greek *bronkhia,* plural of *bronkhion,* diminutive of *bronkhos,* windpipe, BRONCHUS.]

bron·chi·al (brŏng′kē-əl) *adj. Anatomy.* Of or pertaining to the bronchi, the bronchia, or the bronchioles.

bronchial asthma. A usually allergic asthma of the bronchi.

bronchial tube. *Anatomy.* A bronchus or any of its branches.

bron·chi·ec·ta·sis (brŏng′kē-ĕk′tə-sĭs) *n. Pathology.* Chronic dilation of the bronchial tubes, with cough and formation of mucopurulent matter. [New Latin : BRONCH(O)- + *ectasis,* dilation, from Greek *ektasis,* stretching, from *ekteinein,* to stretch out : *ek-,* out + *teinein,* to stretch (see **ten-** in Appendix*).]

bron·chi·ole (brŏng′kē-ōl′) *n. Anatomy.* Any of the fine, thin-walled, tubular extensions of a bronchus.

bron·chi·tis (brŏng-kī′tĭs) *n.* Chronic or acute inflammation of the mucous membrane of the bronchial tubes. [New Latin : BRONCH(O)- + -ITIS.] —**bron·chit′ic** (-kĭt′ĭk) *adj.*

broncho-, bronch-. Indicates the bronchi or windpipe; for example, **bronchoscope, bronchitis.** [Late Latin, from Greek *bronkh(o)-,* from *bronkhos,* windpipe, BRONCHUS.]

bron·cho·pneu·mon·ia (brŏng′kō-nōō-mōn′yə, -nyōō-mōn′yə) *n.* Inflammation of the lungs spreading from and following infection of the bronchi.

bron·cho·scope (brŏng′kə-skōp′) *n.* A slender tubular instrument with a small light on the end for inspection of the interior of the bronchi. [BRONCHO- + -SCOPE.]

bron·chus (brŏng′kəs) *n., pl.* **-chi** (-kī′, -kē′). *Anatomy.* Either of two main branches of the trachea, leading directly to the lungs. [New Latin, from Greek *bronkhos,* trachea, windpipe, throat. See **gwerə-²** in Appendix.*]

bron·co (brŏng′kō) *n., pl.* **-cos.** Also **bron·cho.** A wild or semi-wild horse or pony of western North America. [Mexican Spanish, from Spanish, rough, wild, possibly from Latin *broncus,* variant of *brocchus,* projecting (used of an animal's teeth). See **brocade.**]

bron·co·bust·er (brŏng′kō-bŭs′tər) *n.* A cowboy who breaks wild horses to the saddle.

Bron·të (brŏn′tē). English family of novelists, including **Anne** (pen name, Acton Bell), 1820–1849; **Charlotte** (pen name, Currer Bell), 1816–1855; **Emily Jane** (pen name, Ellis Bell), 1818–1848.

bron·to·saur (brŏn′tə-sôr′) *n.* Also **bron·to·sau·rus** (brŏn′tə-sôr′əs). A very large, herbivorous dinosaur of the genus *Apatosaurus* (or *Brontosaurus*), of the Jurassic period. [New Latin *Brontosaurus* : Greek *brontē,* thunder (see **bhrem-¹** in Appendix*) + -SAUR.]

Bronx, the (brŏngks). The northernmost and only mainland borough of New York City, separated from Manhattan by the Harlem River. Population, 1,425,000. —**Bronx′ite** *n.*

Bronx cheer. *Slang.* An expression of derision or contempt, a **raspberry** *(see).*

Bronx cocktail. A cocktail of gin and orange juice, and sometimes vermouth or bitters.

bronze (brŏnz) *n.* **1.** *Abbr.* **br. a.** Any of various alloys of copper and tin, sometimes with traces of other metals. **b.** Any of various alloys of copper, with or without tin, and antimony, phosphorus, or other components. **2.** A work of art made of bronze. **3.** Moderate yellowish to olive brown. See **color. 4.** A pigment of this color. —*adj.* Of or like bronze. —*tr.v.* **bronzed, bronzing, bronzes.** To give the appearance of bronze to. [French, from Italian *bronzo*†.] —**bronz′y** *adj.*

Bronze Age. A period of human culture between the Stone Age and the Iron Age, characterized by weapons and implements made of bronze.

Bronze Star. A U.S. Army decoration awarded for heroism or meritorious achievement in ground combat.

brooch (brōch, brōōch) *n.* Also **broach.** A large decorative pin or clasp. [Middle English *broche,* brooch, BROACH (tool).]

brood (brōōd) *n.* **1.** The young of certain animals, as birds or fish; especially, a group of young birds or fowl hatched at one time and cared for by the same mother. **2.** The children in one family. —See Synonyms at **flock.** —*v.* **brooded, brooding, broods.** —*tr.* **1.** To sit on or hatch (eggs). **2.** To protect (young) by or as if by covering with the wings. —*intr.* **1.** To sit on or hatch eggs. **2.** To hover envelopingly: *"that gentle heat that brooded on the waters"* (Thomas Browne). **3.** To ponder moodily; sulk. —*adj.* Kept for breeding: *a brood mare.* [Middle English *brood,* Old English *brōd.* See **bhreu-²** in Appendix.*] —**brood′ing·ly** *adv.*

brood·er (brōō′dər) *n.* **1.** One that broods. **2.** A heated enclosure in which young chickens or other fowl are raised.

brood·y (brōō′dē) *adj.* **-ier, -iest. 1.** Moody; meditative. **2.** Inclined to sit on eggs to hatch them. Said of chickens and other poultry.

brook¹ (brŏŏk) *n.* A small, natural freshwater stream. [Middle English *brook, broke,* Old English *brōc,* from West Germanic *brōka* (unattested).]

brook² (brŏŏk) *tr.v.* **brooked, brooking, brooks.** To put up with; bear; tolerate. Usually used in the negative. [Middle English *brouken, broken,* enjoy, to use (as food), to stomach, Old English *brūcan.* See **bhrūg-** in Appendix.*]

Brooke (brŏŏk), **Edward William.** Born 1919. American lawyer and political leader; U.S. senator from Massachusetts (since 1967); first Negro senator since Reconstruction.

Brooke (brŏŏk), **Rupert.** 1887–1915. English poet.

Brook Farm. A utopian socialist community with Fourierist connections (1841–47), founded near West Roxbury (now in Boston), Massachusetts, under the leadership of George Ripley.

brook·ite (brŏŏk′īt′) *n.* A red-brown to black titanium dioxide mineral with characteristic orthorhombic crystals. [After Henry J. *Brooke* (died 1857), English mineralogist.]

brook·let (brŏŏk′lĭt) *n.* A small brook.

brook·lime (brŏŏk′līm′) *n.* Either of two closely related trailing plants, *Veronica americana,* of North America, and *V. beccabunga,* native to Eurasia, growing in moist places and having small blue flowers. [Variant (influenced by LIME) of Middle English *brokelemke* : *broke,* BROOK + *lemke,* a kind of brooklime, Old English *hleomoce,* akin to Middle Low German *lōmeke*†.]

Brook·line (brŏŏk′līn′). A residential town in eastern Massachusetts, near Boston. Population, 54,000.

Brook·lyn (brŏŏk′lĭn). An industrial and residential borough of New York City, at the southwestern end of Long Island. Population, 2,627,000. —**Brook′lyn·ite** *n.*

Brooks (brŏŏks), **Van Wyck.** 1886–1963. American literary historian, critic, and translator.

Brooks Range (brŏŏks). A mountain range in Alaska, north of the Arctic Circle. Highest elevation, Mt. Michelson (9,239 feet).

brook trout. A freshwater game fish, *Salvelinus fontinalis,* of eastern North America. Also called "speckled trout."

brook·weed (brŏŏk′wēd′) *n.* Either of two related plants, *Samolus valerandi* of Europe and *S. floribundus* of North America, both having small white flowers and growing in moist areas. Also called "water pimpernel."

broom (brōōm, brŏŏm) *n.* **1.** A brush of twigs, broomcorn straw, or synthetic bristles, bound together, attached to a stick or handle, and used for sweeping. **2.** Any shrub of the genus *Cytisus,* native to Eurasia, having compound leaves and yellow or white flowers. **3.** Any of several similar or related shrubs, especially of the genus *Genista.* —*tr.v.* **broomed, brooming, brooms.** To sweep with a broom. [Middle English *broom,* broom made of broom twigs, broom plant, Old English *brōm,* broom plant. See **bhrem-²** in Appendix.*] —**broom′y** *adj.*

broom·corn (brōōm′kôrn′, brŏŏm′-) *n.* A grass, *Sorghum vulgare technicum,* having flower clusters with stiff, branching stalks that are used to make brooms and brushes.

broom moss. Any moss of the genus *Dicranum,* especially *D. scoparium,* having leaves turned to one side along the stem.

broom·rape (brōōm′rāp′, brŏŏm′-) *n.* Any of several leafless, parasitic plants of the genus *Orobanche,* having yellow, purple, or reddish-brown flowers and living on the roots of other plants. [Translation of New Latin *rapum genistae,* "tuber of Genista (a genus of broom)" (from the resemblance of one of the parasitic growths to a tuber on the roots of broom).]

broom·stick (brōōm′stĭk′, brŏŏm′-) *n.* The long handle of a broom.

bros. brothers.

broth (brôth, brŏth) *n., pl.* **broths** (brôths, brô*th*z, brŏths, brŏ*th*z). **1.** The water in which meat, fish, or vegetables have been boiled; stock. **2.** A thin, clear soup based on stock, to which rice, barley, meat, or vegetables may be added. [Middle English *broth,* Old English *broth.* See **bhreu-²** in Appendix.*]

broth·el (brŏth′əl, brŏ*th*′-, brô′thəl, -*th*əl) *n.* A house of prostitution. [Short for earlier *brothel-house,* from Middle English *brothel,* prostitute, worthless fellow, from *brothen,* gone to ruin, Old English *brothen,* past participle of *brēothan,* to deteriorate. See **bhreu-¹** in Appendix.*]

broth·er (brŭ*th*′ər) *n., pl.* **brothers** or *archaic* **brethren** (brĕ*th*′rən). *Abbr.* **br., bro., b., B. 1.** A male having the same mother and father as another, *full brother,* or having one parent in common with another, *half brother.* **2.** One who shares a common ancestry, allegiance, character, or purpose with another or others, specifically: **a.** A kinsman. **b.** A fellow man. **c.** A fellow member, as of a fraternity or union. **d.** A close male friend; comrade: *"Such a gallant set of fellows! Such a band of brothers!"* (Lord Nelson). **e.** *Informal.* Friend; fellow. Used in direct address. **3.** *Ecclesiastical. Abbr.* **Br. a.** A member of a men's religious order who is not in holy orders, but engages in the work of the order. **b.** A lay member of a religious order of men. **c.** *Capital* **B.** A form of address for such a person: *Brother Luke.* [Middle English *brother,* Old English *brōthor.* See **bhrāter-** in Appendix.*]

broth·er·hood (brŭ*th*′ər-hŏŏd′) *n.* **1.** The state or relationship of being a brother or brothers. **2.** The quality of being brotherly; fellowship. **3.** *Abbr.* **B.** An association of men united for common purposes; a fraternity, union, society, or similar organization. **4.** All the members of a specific profession or trade.

broth·er-in-law (brŭ*th*′ər-ĭn-lô′) *n., pl.* **brothers-in-law. 1.** The brother of one's husband or wife. **2.** The husband of one's sister. **3.** The husband of the sister of one's husband or wife.

Brother Jon·a·than (jŏn′ə-thən). *British Archaic.* **1.** The people or government of the United States. **2.** An American. Also called "Jonathan." [Originally applied by British soldiers to American patriots during the Revolutionary War (probably from the frequent use of Biblical given names in the American colonies).]

broth·er·ly (brŭ*th*′ər-lē) *adj.* Characteristic of or befitting brothers; fraternal. —**broth′er·li·ness** *n.* —**broth′er·ly** *adv.*

Brothers of the Christian Schools. The official name for the **Christian Brothers** *(see).*

brougham (brōōm, brōō′əm, brō′əm) *n.* **1.** A closed four-wheeled carriage with an open driver's seat in front. **2.** An automobile with an open driver's seat. **3.** An electrically powered automobile resembling a coupé. [After Henry Peter *Brougham,* Baron Brougham and Vaux (1778–1868), Scottish jurist.]

brought. Past tense and past participle of **bring.**

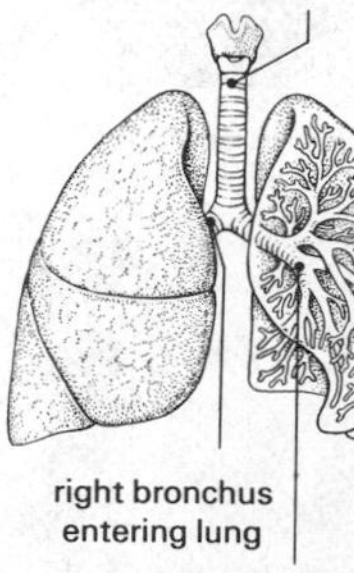

bronchia

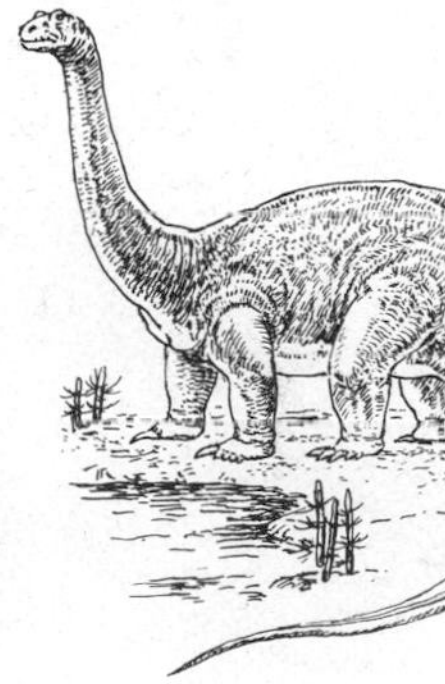

brontosaur

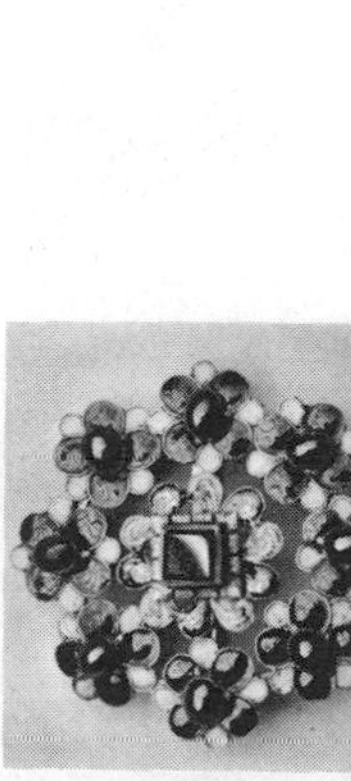

brooch
Nineteenth-century Austrian rosette of enamel, silver, and garnets

brou·ha·ha (brōō′hä-hä′) *n.* An uproar; a hubbub. [French (probably imitative).]
Broun (brōōn), **(Matthew) Heywood (Campbell).** 1888–1939. American journalist; first president of the American Newspaper Guild.
brow (brou) *n.* **1.** *Anatomy.* **a.** The superciliary ridge over the eyes. **b.** The hair growing on this ridge; an eyebrow. **c.** The forehead. **2.** A facial expression; countenance: *"Speak you this with a sad brow?"* (Shakespeare). **3.** The edge of a steep place. —See Synonyms at **border.** [Middle English *brow,* Old English *brū,* eyelash, eyelid, eyebrow. See **bhrū-** in Appendix.*]
brow·beat (brou′bēt′) *tr.v.* **-beat, -beaten** (-bēt′n), **-beating, -beats.** To intimidate or subject with an overbearing or imperative manner; domineer.
Brow·der (brou′dər), **Earl Russell.** Born 1891. American Communist leader; twice Presidential candidate (1936, 1940).
brown (broun) *n. Abbr.* **br.** Any of a group of colors between red and yellow in hue that are medium to low in lightness, and low to moderate in saturation. See **color.** —*adj.* **browner, brownest. 1.** *Abbr.* **br.** Of the color brown. **2.** Deeply suntanned. —*v.* **browned, browning, browns.** —*tr.* To make brown; specifically, to cook until brown. —*intr.* To become brown: *"foam/That browns and dwindles as the wave goes home"* (Rupert Brooke). [Middle English *broun, brown,* Old English *brūn.* See **bher-³** in Appendix.*] —**brown′ness** *n.*
Brown (broun), **Charles Brockden.** 1771–1810. American novelist, editor, and pamphleteer.
Brown (broun), **John.** 1800–1859. American abolitionist leader; seized Harpers Ferry (1859); executed.

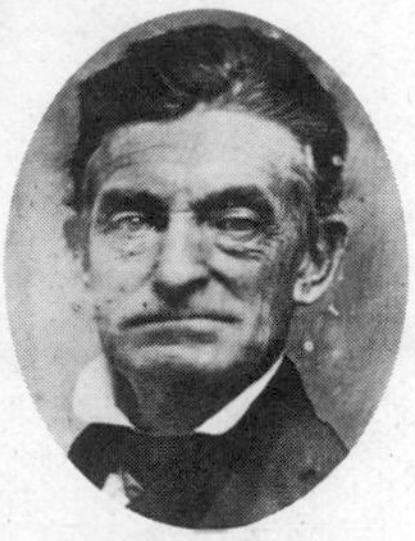
John Brown

Brown (broun), **Robert.** 1773–1858. Scottish botanist; classified Australian plant life and collected new plant species; described Brownian motion in liquids.
brown algae. Brownish, chiefly marine algae of the division Phaeophyta, which includes the rockweeds and the kelps.
brown bear. A very large bear, *Ursus arctos,* of Alaska and northern Eurasia, having brown to yellowish fur.
brown Bet·ty (bĕt′ē). Also **brown bet·ty.** A baked pudding of chopped or sliced apples, bread crumbs, raisins, sugar, butter, and spices. [*Betty,* pet form of ELIZABETH.]
brown bread. Any bread made of a dark flour, as graham or whole-wheat bread.
brown coal. A type of coal, **lignite** *(see).*
Browne (broun), **Charles Farrar.** Pen name, Artemus Ward. 1834–1867. American humorist and lecturer.
Browne (broun), Sir **Thomas.** 1605–1682. English physician, author, and rhetorician.
Brown·i·an motion (brou′nē-ən). The random motion of microscopic particles suspended in a liquid or gas, caused by collision with molecules of the surrounding medium. Also called "Brownian movement." [Described by Robert BROWN.]
brown·ie (brou′nē) *n.* **1.** *Folklore.* A small sprite supposed to do helpful work at night, especially domestic chores. **2.** A flat, moist, cakelike chocolate cooky with nuts. [Diminutive of BROWN. The sprite was thought of as a "wee brown man."]

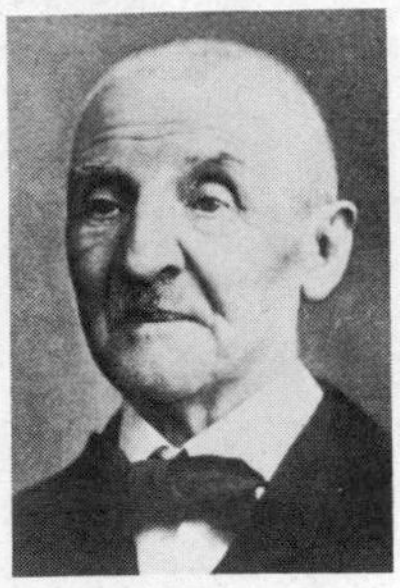
Anton Bruckner

Brown·ie¹ (brou′nē) *n.* A junior Girl Scout, at the ages of seven and eight. [From BROWNIE (sprite).]
Brown·ie² (brou′nē) *n.* A trademark for a box camera.
Brown·ing (brou′nĭng), **Elizabeth Barrett.** 1806–1861. English poet; wife of Robert Browning.
Brown·ing (brou′nĭng), **Robert.** 1812–1889. English poet; author of 300 works, including dramatic monologues.
Brown·ing automatic rifle (brou′nĭng). *Abbr.* **BAR** A .30 caliber air-cooled, automatic or semiautomatic, gas-operated, magazine-fed rifle used in World Wars I and II. [Invented by John Moses *Browning* (1855–1926), American firearms designer.]
Browning machine gun. A .30 or .50 caliber automatic machine gun capable of firing ammunition at a rate of more than 500 rounds per minute. [See **Browning automatic rifle.**]
brown-nose (broun′nōz′) *n. Vulgar Slang.* One who obsequiously curries favor with his superiors; sycophant; toady. —*v.* **brown-nosed, -nosing, -noses.** *Vulgar Slang.* —*intr.* To behave like a brown-nose; ingratiate oneself obsequiously. —*tr.* To seek the favor of obsequiously. [From the contemptuous metaphor seen also in the vulgar slang expression *Kiss my arse!*]
brown·out (broun′out′) *n.* A partial extinguishing or dimming of lights in a city, especially as a defensive measure against enemy bombardment. [After BLACKOUT.]
brown patch. A disease of grasses caused by a fungus, *Pellicularia filamentosa,* and resulting in circular dying areas.
brown rat. The **Norway rat** *(see).*
brown rice. Unpolished rice grains, retaining the germ and the yellowish outer layer containing the bran.
brown rot. 1. A disease of peaches and similar fruits, caused by fungi of the genus *Monolinia.* **2.** A disease of citrus trees, caused by fungi of the genus *Phytophthora.*
Brown Shirts. A Nazi militia, **Sturmabteilung** *(see).* [Translation of German *Braunhemd.*]

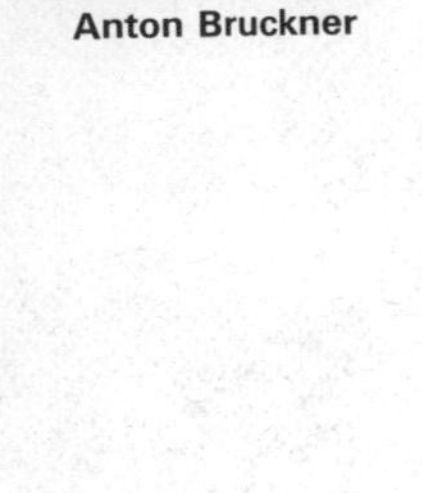

Brunei

brown·stone (broun′stōn′) *n.* **1.** A brownish-red sandstone once widely used as a building material, especially for façades of houses. **2.** A house built or faced with such stone. **3.** Grayish brown. See **color.** —**brown′stone′** *adj.*
brown study. A state of deep thought, melancholy, or reverie.
brown sugar. Unrefined or partially refined sugar.
Browns·ville (brounz′vĭl). A city and port of entry in southern Texas, on the Rio Grande, opposite Matamoros, Mexico. Population, 48,000.
Brown Swiss. One of a hardy breed of dairy cattle that originated in Switzerland.
brown-tail moth (broun′tāl′). A small white and brown moth, *Euproctis phaeorrhoea,* hairy caterpillars of which damage shade-tree foliage and cause an irritating skin rash.
brown thrasher. A North American bird, *Toxostoma rufum,* having a reddish-brown back and a dark-streaked breast.
brown trout. A freshwater fish, *Salmo trutta,* native to Europe but naturalized in North America, having yellow-brown sides with reddish spots.
browse (brouz) *v.* **browsed, browsing, browses.** —*intr.* **1.** To inspect in a leisurely and casual way. **2.** To feed on leaves, young shoots, and other vegetation. —*tr.* **1.** To look through or over casually. **2. a.** To nibble; to crop. **b.** To graze on. —*n.* Young twigs, leaves, and tender shoots of plants or shrubs that animals eat. [From Old French *broust, brost,* shoot, twig, from Germanic. See **bhreus-¹** in Appendix.*] —**brows′er** *n.*
BRU Airport code for Brussels, Belgium.
Bru·beck (brōō′bĕk), **David Warren ("Dave").** Born 1920. American jazz pianist, composer, and conductor.
Bruce (brōōs). A masculine given name. [From the surname of Robert the BRUCE.]
Bruce, Robert the. See **Robert I.**
bru·cel·lo·sis (brōō′sə-lō′sĭs) *n.* **1.** A disease of man, **undulant fever** *(see).* **2.** A disease of cattle caused by the bacillus *Brucella abortus* and resulting in abortions in newly infected animals. In this sense, also called "contagious abortion." [New Latin : *Brucella,* after Sir David *Bruce* (1855–1931), British bacteriologist + -OSIS.]
bruc·ine (brōō′sēn′, -sĭn) *n.* A poisonous white crystalline alkaloid, $C_{23}H_{26}O_4N_2 \cdot 2H_2O$, derived from nux vomica seeds. [After James *Bruce* (1730–1794), Scottish explorer in Africa.]
Bruck·ner (brŏŏk′nər), **Anton.** 1824–1896. Austrian composer.
Brue·ghel (brœ′gəl), **Pieter.** Also **Brue·gel, Breu·ghel.** 1525?–1569. Flemish painter; father of two sons who were also painters: **Pieter** (1564?–1637) and **Jan** (1568–1625).
Bruges (brōōzh). *Flemish* **Brug·ge** (brüg′ə). The capital of West Flanders, northwestern Belgium. Population, 52,000.
brugh (brōōKH) *n. Scottish.* A borough.
bru·in (brōō′ĭn) *n.* A bear. [Dutch *bruin,* "brown," from Middle Dutch *bruun.* See **bher-³** in Appendix.*]
bruise (brōōz) *v.* **bruised, bruising, bruises.** —*tr.* **1.** *Medicine.* To injure the surface of (the skin) without rupture. **2.** To dent or mar. **3.** To pound into fragments; crush. **4.** To hurt psychologically; offend. —*intr.* To become discolored, as the skin does after a hard, dull blow. —*n.* **1.** *Medicine.* An injury in which the skin is not broken; a contusion. **2.** An injury to one's feelings or expectations. [Middle English *brusen, brisen,* to crush, mangle, from Old English *brȳsan* (see **bhreus-²** in Appendix*) and Old French *bruisier*†, to break, crush.]
bruis·er (brōō′zər) *n. Slang.* A large, powerfully built man.
bruit (brōōt) *tr.v.* **bruited, bruiting, bruits.** To spread news of; repeat. —*n.* **1.** *Archaic.* A rumor. **2.** *Archaic.* A din; a clamor. **3.** *Medicine.* An abnormal sound heard in auscultation. [Middle English, noise, from Old French, from the past participle of *bruire,* to roar, from Vulgar Latin *brūgere* (unattested), variant of Latin *rugīre,* to roar. See **reu-** in Appendix.*]
bru·mal (brōō′məl) *adj.* Of, pertaining to, or characteristic of winter; wintry. [Latin *brūmālis,* from *brūma,* winter solstice, "the shortest day," from *brevima* (unattested), the shortest, from *brevis,* short. See **mreghu-** in Appendix.*]
brume (brōōm) *n.* Heavy fog or mist; dense vapor. [French, mist, winter, from Old French, from Old Provençal *bruma,* from Latin *brūma.* See **brumal.**] —**bru′mous** *adj.*
brum·ma·gem (brŭm′ə-jəm) *adj.* Cheap and showy; meretricious. —*n.* Any cheap and gaudy imitation, especially of jewelry. [Variant of BIRMINGHAM, England (with reference to counterfeit coins made there in the 17th century).]
Brum·mell, Beau. See **Beau Brummell.**
brunch (brŭnch) *n.* A meal eaten late in the morning as a combination of breakfast and lunch. [BR(EAKFAST) + (L)UNCH.]
Brun·di·si·um. The ancient name for **Brindisi.**
Bru·nei (brōō-nī′). A British-protected sultanate, 2,226 square miles in area, on the northern coast of the island of Borneo. Population, 105,876. Capital, Brunei.
Bru·nel·le·schi (brōō′nə-lĕs′kē; *Italian* brōō′näl-lās′kē), **Filippo.** 1377?–1446. Florentine architect and engineer.
bru·net (brōō-nĕt′) *adj.* Also *feminine* **bru·nette.** Dark or brown in color. Said of the hair, eyes, and skin. —*n.* Also *feminine* **bru·nette.** A person with brown hair. See Usage note at **blond.** [French, from Old French, from *brun,* brown, from Germanic. See **bher-³** in Appendix.*]
Brun·hild (brōōn′hilt). In the *Nibelungenlied,* a legendary queen of Iceland who is won as a bride by Gunther.
Brünn. The German name for **Brno.**
Brünn·hil·de (brōōn-hĭl′də). The heroine of Wagner's *Ring of the Nibelung,* a Valkyrie who is placed in a circle of fire by Wotan and is eventually released by Siegfried.
Bru·no (brōō′nō), **Giordano.** 1548?–1600. Italian philosopher.
Bru·no of Co·logne (brōō′nō; kə-lōn′), **Saint.** 1030?–1101. German educator; founder of Carthusian order of monks.
Bruns·wick (brŭnz′wĭk). *German* **Braun·schweig** (broun′shvīk′). **1.** A former state in central Germany. **2.** An industrial city of West Germany, about 90 miles southeast of Hamburg. Population, 289,000.
Bruns·wick stew (brŭnz′wĭk). A stew of rabbit or squirrel meat and onions. [Originated in *Brunswick* County, Virginia.]
brunt (brŭnt) *n.* **1.** The main impact, force, or burden, as of a blow. **2.** *Obsolete.* A violent attack. [Middle English *brunt*†.]
Bru·sa. See **Bursa.**
brush¹ (brŭsh) *n.* **1.** Any of various devices consisting of bristles, fibers, or other flexible material fastened into a handle, for

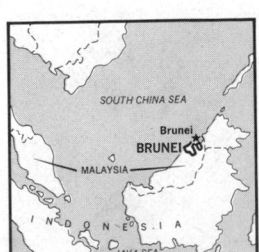

such uses as scrubbing, polishing, applying paint, or grooming the hair. **2.** The act of using such a device. **3.** A light touch in passing; a graze. **4.** A brief contact or encounter. **5.** The bushy tail of a fox or other animal. **6.** The style in which a painter applies paint. **7.** *Electricity.* A yielding or sliding connection completing a circuit between a fixed and a moving, especially rotating, conductor. —*v.* **brushed, brushing, brushes.** —*tr.* **1.** To use a brush on, so as to clean, polish, or groom. **2.** To apply with or as if with motions of a brush. **3.** To remove with or as if with motions of a brush. **4.** To dismiss abruptly or curtly. Used with *aside* or *off: brushed the matter aside.* **5.** To touch lightly in passing; graze against. —*intr.* **1.** To use or apply a brush. **2.** To move past something so as to touch it lightly. —**brush up.** To refresh one's memory. [Middle English *brusshe,* from Old French *broisse, brosse,* perhaps from *broce,* BRUSH (brushwood).] —**brush'er** *n.* —**brush'y** *adj.*

brush[2] (brŭsh) *n.* **1. a.** A dense growth of bushes or shrubs. **b.** Land covered by such a growth. **2.** Sparsely populated woodland. **3.** Cut or broken branches. [Middle English *brusch(e),* from Old French *broce,* from Vulgar Latin *bruscia* (unattested). See **bhreus-**[2] in Appendix.*] —**brush'y** *adj.*

brush discharge. A faintly visible, relatively slow, crackling discharge of electricity without sparking.

brushed (brŭsht) *adj.* Of or designating knitted or woven fabrics that have a nap produced by brushing.

brush fire. A fire in low-growing, scrubby trees and brush.

brush-off (brŭsh'ôf', -ŏf') *n. Slang.* An abrupt dismissal.

brush·wood (brŭsh'wo͝od') *n.* **1.** Cut or broken-off branches. **2. a.** Dense undergrowth. **b.** An area covered by such growth.

brush·work (brŭsh'wûrk') *n.* **1.** Work done with a brush. **2.** The manner in which a painter applies paint with his brush.

brusque (brŭsk) *adj.* Also **brusk.** Abrupt and curt in manner or speech; discourteously blunt. See Synonyms at **gruff.** [French *brusque,* lively, fierce, harsh, from Italian *brusco,* sour, sharp, perhaps a blend of Latin *rūscum*†, butcher's broom, and Late Latin *brūcus,* heather, from (unattested) Gaulish *brūko* (see **wer-**[3] in Appendix*).] —**brusque'ly** *adv.* —**brusque'ness** *n.*

brus·que·rie (brüs'kə-rē') *n. French.* Brusqueness; curtness.

Brus·sels (brŭs'əlz). *French* **Bru·xelles** (brü-sĕl', brük-sĕl'); *Flemish* **Brus·sel** (brüs'əl). The capital of Belgium, in the north-central part of the country. Population, 1,066,000.

Brussels carpet. A machine-made carpet consisting of small, colored woolen loops that form a heavy, patterned pile.

Brussels lace. Net lace with an appliqué design, formerly made by hand but now usually made by machine.

Brussels sprouts. **1.** A variety of cabbage, *Brassica oleracea gemmifera,* having a stout stem studded with budlike heads. **2.** The small edible heads of this plant.

brut (bro͞ot) *adj.* Very dry. Said of wines, especially champagne. Compare **sec.** [French, raw, rough, from Old French, from Latin *brūtus,* heavy. See **gwer-**[2] in Appendix.*]

Brut (bro͞ot). Any of several medieval chronicles devoted to the lore and early history of Britain, beginning with the story of its traditional founder, Brutus, a mythical descendant of Aeneas. [Middle English *Brout,* from Middle Welsh *Brut,* from Medieval Latin *Brutus,* name of the legendary founder of Britain.]

bru·tal (bro͞ot'l) *adj.* **1.** Characteristic of a brute; cruel. **2.** Crude or unfeeling in manner or speech. **3.** Harsh; unrelenting. —See Synonyms at **brute.** —**bru'tal·ly** *adv.*

bru·tal·i·ty (bro͞o-tăl'ə-tē) *n., pl.* **-ties.** **1.** The state or quality of being brutal. **2.** A brutal act.

bru·tal·ize (bro͞ot'l-īz') *tr.v.* **-ized, -izing, -izes.** **1.** To render brutal. **2.** To treat brutally. —**bru'tal·i·za'tion** *n.*

brute (bro͞ot) *n.* **1.** Any animal other than man; a beast. **2.** A brutal person. —*adj.* **1.** Of or relating to beasts; animal: *"None of the brute creation requires more than food and shelter."* (Thoreau). **2.** Characteristic of a brute: **a.** Entirely physical or instinctive: *brute force.* **b.** Lacking reason or intelligence. **3.** Savage; cruel. **4.** Gross; coarse. [Middle English, from Old French *brut,* rough. See **brut.**] —**brut'ism'** *n.*

Synonyms: *brute, animal, brutish, brutal, beastly, bestial.* These adjectives apply to behavior characteristic of lower animals. *Brute,* the least derogatory, stresses the fundamental powers possessed by all creatures: *brute instinct. Animal* emphasizes physical nature distinguished from intellect or spirit: *animal vitality. Brutish,* said principally of manners, stresses marked lack of human refinement and sensibility. *Brutal,* said of physical acts, stresses unfeeling cruelty. *Beastly* is applied to what is considered beneath man and is often used as a counter word meaning merely very disagreeable. *Bestial* usually implies the vileness of moral degradation.

bru·ti·fy (bro͞o'tə-fī') *v.* **-fied, -fying, -fies.** —*tr.* To brutalize. —*intr.* To become brutalized. [BRUT(E) + -FY.]

brut·ish (bro͞o'tĭsh) *adj.* **1.** Of or characteristic of a brute. **2.** Crude in feeling or manner. **3.** Sensual; carnal. —See Synonyms at **brute.** —**brut'ish·ly** *adv.* —**brut'ish·ness** *n.*

Brut·ti·um. The ancient name for **Calabria.**

Bru·tus (bro͞o'təs), **Marcus Junius.** 85?–42 B.C. Roman political and military leader; participated in assassination of Julius Caesar.

Bru·xelles. The French name for **Brussels.**

Bry·an. Variant of **Brian.**

Bry·an (brī'ən), **William Jennings.** 1860–1925. American statesman and lawyer; three times Presidential candidate (1896, 1900, and 1908).

Bry·ansk (brē-änsk'). Also **Bri·ansk.** A city of the western Soviet Union, on the Desna River. Population, 267,000.

Bry·ant (brī'ənt), **William Cullen.** 1794–1878. American poet and newspaper editor.

Bryce Canyon National Park (brīs). A national park in southern Utah, 56 square miles in area, notable for its rock formations and canyons.

Bryn·hild (brĭn'hĭld'). A Valkyrie in the *Volsunga Saga* who is revived from an enchanted sleep by Sigurd.

bryo-. Indicates moss; for example, **bryophyte.** [New Latin, from Greek *bruon,* moss, akin to Greek *bruein,* to swell. See **embryo.**]

bry·ol·o·gy (brī-ŏl'ə-jē) *n.* The botany of bryophytes. [BRYO- + -LOGY.] —**bry'o·log'i·cal** (brī'ə-lŏj'ĭ-kəl) *adj.*

bry·o·ny (brī'ə-nē) *n., pl.* **-nies.** Either of two European plants, the **black bryony** or the **white bryony** *(both of which see).* [Latin *bryōnia,* from Greek *bruōnia,* akin to Greek *bruein,* to swell. See **embryo.**]

bry·o·phyte (brī'ə-fīt') *n.* Any plant of the major botanical division Bryophyta, which includes the true mosses, peat mosses, and liverworts. [New Latin *Bryophyta* : BRYO- + -PHYTE.] —**bry'o·phyt'ic** (-fĭt'ĭk) *adj.*

bry·o·zo·an (brī'ə-zō'ən) *n.* Any of various small aquatic animals of the phylum Bryozoa, that reproduce by budding and form mosslike or branching colonies. Also called "polyzoan." —*adj.* Of or belonging to the Bryozoa. Also "polyzoan." [New Latin *Bryozoa,* plural of *bryozoon* : BRYO- + -ZOON.]

Bryth·on (brĭth'ən, -ŏn') *n.* **1.** An ancient Celtic Briton of Cornwall, Wales, or Cumbria. **2.** One who speaks a Brythonic language. [Welsh, from Common Celtic *Brittones* (unattested), plural of *Brittos* (unattested), a BRITON.]

Bry·thon·ic (brĭ-thŏn'ĭk) *adj.* Of, pertaining to, or characteristic of the Brythons or their language. —*n.* The branch of the Celtic languages that includes Welsh, Breton, and Cornish.

Brześć nad Bu·giem. The Polish name for **Brest,** Byelorussia.

B.S. **1.** Bachelor of Science. **2.** balance sheet. **3.** bill of sale.

B.S.A. **1.** Bachelor of Science in Agriculture. **2.** Boy Scouts of America.

BSB Airport code for Brasília, Brazil.

B.Sc. Bachelor of Science.

B.S.Ed. Bachelor of Science in Education.

bsh. bushel.

bsk. basket.

Bt. baronet.

B.T., B.Th. Bachelor of Theology.

btry. battery.

Btu British thermal unit.

bu bushel.

bu. **1.** bureau. **2.** bushel.

bub (bŭb) *n. Informal.* Fellow. Used as a term of affection or familiarity in direct address. [From *bubby,* possibly a baby-talk variant of BROTHER.]

bub·ble (bŭb'əl) *n.* **1.** A rounded, generally spherical, thin-walled and hollow, or sometimes solid, object, often occurring naturally in an otherwise homogeneous medium as a result of the local accumulation of gas: *soap bubble.* **2.** A small globule of gas trapped in a liquid or solid, as in a carbonated beverage or in hardened glass. **3.** A sound made by or as if by the forming and bursting of bubbles. **4.** Anything insubstantial, groundless, or ephemeral, such as a scheme that comes to nothing. **5.** A glass or plastic dome, usually transparent. —*v.* **bubbled, -bling, -bles.** —*intr.* **1.** To form or give off bubbles, as a boiling liquid. **2.** To move or flow with a gurgling sound. **3.** To display irrepressible activity or emotion. —*tr.* To cause to form bubbles. [Middle English *bobelen* (imitative).] —**bub'bly** *adj.*

bubble and squeak. *Chiefly British.* Cabbage and potatoes fried together. [From the sounds made in cooking it.]

bubble chamber. *Physics.* An apparatus for detecting the paths of charged particles, or inferring the paths of electrically neutral particles, by examination of trails of bubbles that form on ions produced in a superheated liquid. Compare **cloud chamber.**

bubble gum. Chewing gum that can be blown into bubbles.

bub·bler (bŭb'lər) *n.* A drinking fountain in which the water flows through a small vertical nozzle.

bub·by (bŭb'ē) *n., pl.* **-bies.** *Slang.* A breast of a woman. Formerly in standard use: *"And rudely with your pretty bubbies play"* (Dryden). [Origin obscure.]

Bu·ber (bo͞o'bər), **Martin.** 1878–1965. Austrian existentialist philosopher and Judaic scholar.

bu·bing·a (bo͞o-bĭng'ə) *n.* A tree, the **kevazingo** *(see),* or its wood. [Bantu.]

bu·bo (bo͞o'bō, byo͞o'-) *n., pl.* **-boes.** An inflamed swelling of a lymphatic gland, especially in the area of the armpit or groin. [Middle English, from Medieval Latin *bubo,* from Greek *boubōn,* groin, swollen gland. See **beu-**[1] in Appendix.*] —**bu·bon'ic** (-bŏn'ĭk) *adj.*

bubonic plague. A contagious, usually fatal epidemic disease caused by bacteria of the genus *Pasteurella,* transmitted by fleas from infected rats and characterized by chills, fever, vomiting, diarrhea, and buboes.

Bu·ca·ra·man·ga (bo͞o'kä-rä-mäng'gä). A city and transportation center of north-central Colombia. Population, 229,000.

buc·cal (bŭk'əl) *adj.* Of or pertaining to the cheeks or mouth cavity. [From Latin *bucca,* cheek. See **beu-**[1] in Appendix.*]

buc·ca·neer (bŭk'ə-nîr') *n.* A pirate, especially one of the freebooters who preyed upon Spanish shipping in the West Indies during the 17th century. [French *boucanier,* pirate, "one who cures meat on a barbecue frame" (as done by 17th-century French pirates), from *boucaner,* to cure meat, from *boucan,* barbecue frame, from Tupi *mocaen.*]

Bu·ceph·a·lus (byo͞o-sĕf'ə-ləs). The war horse of Alexander the Great. [Latin *Būcephalus,* from Greek *Boukephalos,* "bull-headed" : *bous,* bull (see **gwou-** in Appendix*) + -CEPHALOUS.]

Brussels sprouts

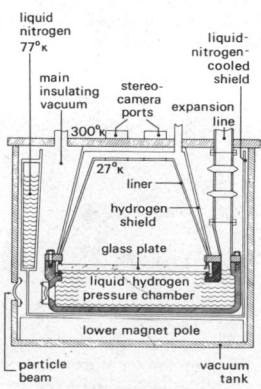

bubble chamber

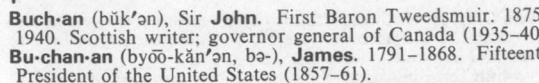

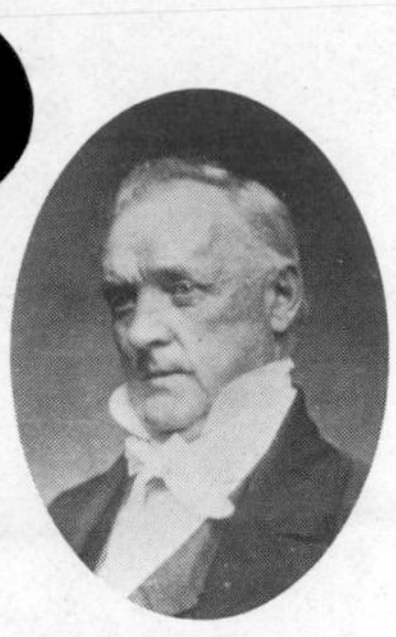
James Buchanan

Buch·an (bŭk′ən), Sir **John.** First Baron Tweedsmuir. 1875–1940. Scottish writer; governor general of Canada (1935–40).
Bu·chan·an (byōō-kăn′ən, bə-), **James.** 1791–1868. Fifteenth President of the United States (1857–61).
Bu·cha·rest (bōō′kə-rĕst′, byōō′-). *Rumanian* **Bu·cu·reş·ti** (bōō′kōō-rĕsht′, -rĕsh′tē). The capital of Rumania, in the southeastern part of the country. Population, 1,372,000.
Bu·chen·wald (bōō′kən-wôld′, bŏŏk′ən-; *German* bŏŏKH′ən-vält′). A village northeast of Weimar, East Germany; also the name of a nearby Nazi concentration camp.
Büch·ner (büKH′nər), **Georg.** 1813–1837. German poet.
buck[1] (bŭk) *n.* **1.** The adult male of some animals, such as the deer or rabbit. **2.** *Informal.* **a.** A robust or high-spirited young man. **b.** A fop. [Middle English *bukke,* Old English *buc,* stag, and *bucca,* he-goat. See **bhugo-** in Appendix.*]
buck[2] (bŭk) *v.* **bucked, bucking, bucks.** *—intr.* **1.** To leap forward and upward suddenly; rear up. Used of a horse or mule. **2.** To move rapidly forward with the head lowered; to butt. **3.** To move with sudden forward jerks; to jolt. **4.** To resist stubbornly and obstinately; to balk. **5.** *Informal.* To strive determinedly. Used with *for.* *—tr.* **1.** To throw (a rider or burden) by bucking. **2.** To butt against with the head. **3.** *Football.* To charge into (an opponent's line) carrying the ball. **4.** To oppose directly and stubbornly; turn against. **—buck up.** *Informal.* To summon one's courage or spirits. *—n.* An act of bucking. [From BUCK (deer).] **—buck′er** *n.*
buck[3] (bŭk) *adj. Military Slang.* Of the lowest rank in a specified category: *a buck private.* [Perhaps from BUCK (young man).]
buck[4] (bŭk) *n.* **1.** A sawhorse. **2.** A leather-covered frame used for gymnastic vaulting. [Short for SAWBUCK.]
buck[5] (bŭk) *n. Slang.* A dollar. [Short for BUCKSKIN (a unit of trade with the American Indians).]
buck[6] (bŭk) *n.* A counter or marker formerly placed before a poker player to mark him as the next dealer. **—pass the buck.** To shift responsibility or blame to someone else. [Short for earlier *buckhorn knife,* from its use for this purpose.]
Buck (bŭk), **Pearl (Sydenstricker).** Born 1892. American novelist; awarded Nobel Prize in literature (1938).
buck and wing. A fast solo tap dance with much springing of the legs and heel-clicking.
buck·a·roo, (bŭk′ə-rōō′) *n., pl.* **-roos.** Also **buck·e·roo.** A cowboy. [Variant of Spanish *vaquero,* from *vaca,* a cow, from Latin *vacca.* See **wak-** in Appendix.*]

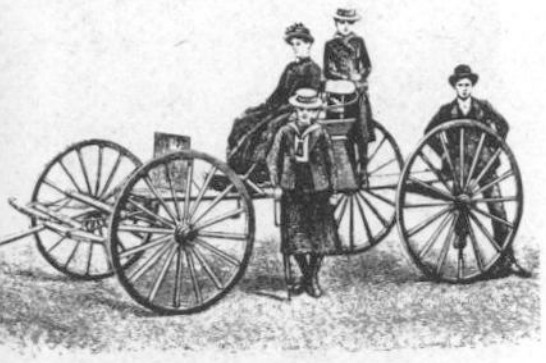
buckboard

buck·bean (bŭk′bēn′) *n.* A marsh plant, *Menyanthes trifoliata,* having a creeping rootstock and white or reddish flowers. Also called "bogbean." [Translation of Dutch *boksboon.*]
buck·board (bŭk′bôrd′, -bōrd′) *n.* A four-wheeled open carriage with the seat attached to a flexible board extending from the front to the rear axle. [From obsolete *buck,* body of a wagon, "trunk of a body," from Middle English *buke,* belly, Old English *būc.* See **beu-**[1] in Appendix.*]
buck·et (bŭk′ĭt) *n.* **1.** A cylindrical vessel used for holding or carrying liquids or solids; pail. **2.** Any of various machine compartments that receive and convey material, such as the scoop of a steam shovel. **3.** The amount that a bucket will hold. **—kick the bucket.** *Slang.* To die. *—v.* **bucketed, -eting, -ets.** *—tr.* **1.** To hold, carry, or put in a bucket. **2.** To ride (a horse) long and hard. *—intr.* **1.** To move or proceed rapidly and jerkily. **2.** To make haste; hustle. [Middle English *buket, boket,* from Norman French *buket,* bucket, tub, perhaps from Old English *būc,* belly, pitcher. See **beu-**[1] in Appendix.*]
bucket seat. A seat with a rounded or molded back, as in sports cars and airplanes.

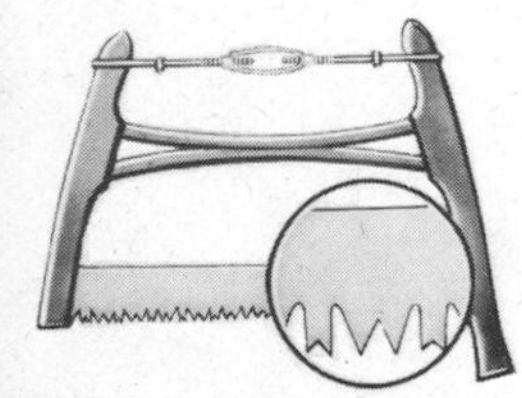
bucksaw

bucket shop. A fraudulent brokerage operation that accepts orders to buy or sell securities or commodities but delays executing the orders on the gamble that prices will change adversely to the interests of the customer, so that it can pocket what the customer thinks he has lost. [Originally a place where small amounts of commodity gambling transactions took place and where the customer could buy liquor in buckets.]
buck·eye (bŭk′ī′) *n.* **1.** Any of several North American trees of the genus *Aesculus,* having compound leaves and erect clusters of white or reddish flowers. See **horse chestnut. 2.** The glossy brown nut of any of these trees. [From the seed's appearance.]
Buckeye State. The nickname for Ohio.
buck fever. *Informal.* Nervous excitement felt by a novice hunter at the first sight of game.
buck·hound (bŭk′hound′) *n.* A hound used for hunting deer.
Buck·ing·ham (bŭk′ĭng-əm), **First Duke of.** Title of George Villiers. 1592–1628. English courtier.
Buck·ing·ham Palace (bŭk′ĭng-əm). The official London residence of the British sovereign.
Buck·ing·ham·shire (bŭk′ĭng-əm-shîr, -shər). Also **Buck·ing·ham** (bŭk′ĭng-əm). *Abbr.* **Bucks., Bucks** A county, 749 square miles in area, of south-central England. Population, 488,000. County seat, Aylesbury.

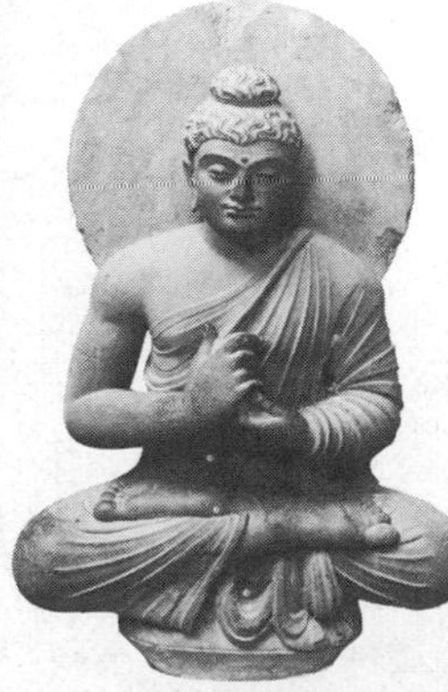
Buddha[2]
Indian sculpture of Buddha meditating in the full lotus position

buck·ish (bŭk′ĭsh) *adj.* Foppish; dandified. **—buck′ish·ly** *adv.*
buck·le[1] (bŭk′əl) *n.* **1.** A clasp, especially a metal frame with one or more movable tongues for fastening two strap or belt ends. **2.** An ornament that resembles such a clasp. *—v.* **buckled, -ling, -les.** *—tr.* To fasten or secure with a buckle. *—intr.* To become fastened or attached with a buckle. **—buckle down.** To apply oneself with determination. [Middle English *bocle,* from Old French *boucle,* metal ring, buckle, from Latin *buccula,* cheek strap of a helmet, diminutive of *bucca,* cheek. See **beu-**[1] in Appendix.*]
buck·le[2] (bŭk′əl) *v.* **-led, -ling, -les.** *—intr.* **1.** To bend, warp, or crumple under pressure or heat. **2.** To collapse. *—tr.* To cause to bend, warp, or crumple. **—buckle under.** To surrender to (another's authority); yield. *—n.* A bend, bulge, or other distortion. [Middle English *boclen,* from Old French *boucler,* "to fasten with a buckle," from *boucle,* BUCKLE.]
buck·ler (bŭk′lər) *n.* **1.** A small round shield either carried or worn on the arm. **2.** A means of protection; a defense. *—tr.v.* **bucklered, -lering, -lers.** To shield with or as if with a buckler; protect. [Middle English *boc(e)ler,* from Old French *bocler, boucler,* from *boucle,* boss on a shield, BUCKLE.]
buck·o (bŭk′ō) *n., pl.* **-oes. 1.** A bully. **2.** *Anglo-Irish.* A young man; lad. [From BUCK (young man).]
buck·ra (bŭk′rə) *n. Chiefly Southeastern Slang.* A white man. Often used disparagingly by Negroes. [Perhaps from Efik *m′ba′-ka²-ra²,* "master."]
buck·ram (bŭk′rəm) *n.* **1.** A coarse cotton fabric heavily sized with glue, used for stiffening garments and in bookbinding. **2.** *Obsolete.* Stiffness; formality. *—adj.* Made of buckram or resembling it in stiffness. *—tr.v.* **buckramed, -raming, -rams.** To stiffen with buckram. [Middle English *bokram,* a fine linen, from Old French *boquerant,* obscurely from BUKHARA, from where the fine linen was once imported.]
Bucks., Bucks Buckinghamshire.
buck·saw (bŭk′sô′) *n.* A wood-cutting saw, usually set in an H-shaped frame. [From BUCK (sawhorse).]
buck·shee (bŭk′shē) *n. British Military Slang.* **1.** A windfall or gratuity. **2.** An extra ration. *—adj.* Free of charge; gratis. [Variant of BAKSHEESH.]
buck·shot (bŭk′shŏt′) *n.* A large lead shot for shotgun shells. [Originally the distance at which a buck could be shot.]
buck·skin (bŭk′skĭn′) *n.* **1.** The skin of a male deer. **2.** A strong, grayish-yellow leather once made from deerskins but now usually made from sheepskins. **3.** *Plural.* A pair of breeches or shoes made from this leather. **4.** *Capital* **B.** A person wearing clothes of this leather; especially, an American soldier of the Revolutionary War. **5.** A horse of the grayish-yellow color of this leather. *—adj.* Made of buckskin.
buck·thorn (bŭk′thôrn′) *n.* Any shrub or tree of the genus *Rhamnus;* especially, *R. cathartica,* native to Eurasia, having spine-tipped branches and small greenish flowers. [Translation of New Latin *cervi spina.*]
buck·tooth (bŭk′tōōth′) *n., pl.* **-teeth** (-tēth′). A prominent, projecting upper front tooth. [From BUCK (deer).] **—buck′-toothed′** (bŭk′tōōtht′) *adj.*
buck·wheat (bŭk′hwēt′) *n.* **1.** Any plant of the genus *Fagopyrum;* especially, *F. esculentum,* native to Asia, having fragrant white flowers and small triangular seeds. **2.** The edible seeds of this plant, often ground into flour. **3.** The flour itself. [Partial translation of Middle Dutch *boecweite,* "beech wheat" (because its seeds resemble beech nuts) : *boek,* beech (see **bhago-** in Appendix*) + *weite,* wheat.]
bu·col·ic (byōō-kŏl′ĭk) *adj.* **1.** Of or characteristic of shepherds and flocks; pastoral. **2.** Of or characteristic of the countryside or its people; rustic. —See Synonyms at **rural.** *—n.* **1.** A pastoral poem. **2.** A farmer or shepherd; a rustic. [Latin *būcolicus,* from Greek *boukolikos,* from *boukolos,* cowherd : *bous,* cow (see **gwou-** in Appendix*) + *-kolos,* herd (see **kwel-**[1] in Appendix*).] **—bu·col′i·cal·ly** *adv.*
Bu·co·vi·na (bōō′kə-vē′nə). Also **Bu·ko·vi·na.** A region in east-central Europe, and a former province of Rumania, divided in 1945 between the Ukrainian S.S.R. and Rumania.
Bu·cu·reş·ti. The Rumanian name for **Bucharest.**
bud[1] (bŭd) *n.* **1.** *Botany.* **a.** A small protuberance on a stem or branch, often enclosed in protective scales, and containing an undeveloped shoot, leaves, or flowers. **b.** The stage or condition of having buds. **2.** *Biology.* **a.** An asexually produced protuberance, as on a polyp, that develops into a mature, complete organism. **b.** Any small, rounded organic part resembling a plant bud. **3.** An undeveloped person or thing. **—in bud.** Budding. **—in the bud.** In an incipient or undeveloped state. **—nip in the bud.** To stop (something) in its initial stage. *—v.* **budded, budding, buds.** *—intr.* **1.** To put forth or produce a bud or buds. **2.** To begin to develop or grow from or as if from a bud. **3.** To be in an undeveloped stage or condition. *—tr.* **1.** To cause to put forth buds. **2.** *Horticulture.* To graft a bud onto (a plant). [Middle English *budde,* bud, perhaps from Low German *but,* perhaps from Old French *boter,* to push forth, from Germanic. See **beu-**[1] in Appendix.*] **—bud′der** *n.*
bud[2] (bŭd) *n.* Fellow; mister. Used in informal address. [Short for BUDDY.]
Bu·da·pest (bōō′də-pĕst′; *Hungarian* bōō′dô-pĕsht′). The capital of Hungary, situated in the north-central part of the country. Population, 1,900,000.
Bud·dha[1] (bōō′də, bŏŏd′ə). Title of Gautama Siddhartha. 563?–483? B.C. Indian philosopher; founder of Buddhism.
Bud·dha[2] (bōō′də, bŏŏd′ə) *n.* **1.** A Buddhist sage who has achieved a state of perfect illumination in accordance with the teachings of Gautama Buddha. **2.** A representation of Gautama Buddha. [Sanskrit, "awakened," past participle of *bōdhati,* he awakes, becomes aware. See **bheudh-** in Appendix.*]
Buddh Ga·ya (bŏŏd′ gə-yä′). A town and holy Buddhist pilgrimage center in central Bihar State, Republic of India.
Bud·dhism (bōō′dĭz′əm, bŏŏd′ĭz′-) *n.* **1.** The doctrine, attributed to Gautama Buddha, that suffering is inseparable from existence but that inward extinction of the self and of the senses culminates in a state of illumination beyond both suffering and existence. **2.** The religion of eastern and central Asia represented by the many differing sects that profess this doctrine and venerate Gautama Buddha. **—Bud′dhist** *n. & adj.* **—Bud·dhis′tic, Bud·dhis′ti·cal** *adj.*
bud·dle (bŭd′l) *n.* An inclined trough on which ore is separated

from waste by washing with running water. [Origin unknown.]

bud·dle·ia (bŭd′lē-ə, bŭd-lē′ə) *n.* A shrub of the genus *Buddleia,* the **butterfly bush** *(see).* [After Adam *Buddle* (died 1715), British botanist.]

bud·dy (bŭd′ē) *n., pl.* **-dies.** *Informal.* **1.** A good friend; comrade; pal. **2.** Brother; friend. Used in direct address as a term of familiarity or condescension. [Probably from a baby-talk variant of BROTHER.]

budge[1] (bŭj) *v.* **budged, budging, budges.** —*intr.* **1.** To move or stir slightly. **2.** To alter a position or attitude. —*tr.* **1.** To cause to move slightly. **2.** To cause to alter a position or attitude. [Earlier *bouge,* from Old French *bouger, bougier,* from Vulgar Latin *bullicāre* (unattested), from Latin *bullīre,* to boil. See **beu-**[1] in Appendix.*]

budge[2] (bŭj) *n.* Fur, usually lambskin, formerly used to trim academic robes. —*adj.* **1.** Trimmed with or wearing budge. **2.** Extremely formal; solemn. [Middle English *bugee, bogey*†.]

budg·er·i·gar (bŭj′ə-rē-gär′) *n.* A parakeet, *Melopsittacus undulatus,* native to Australia, having green, yellow, or blue plumage. It is a popular cage bird. Also *informal* "budgie." [Native Australian name : *budgeri,* good + *gar,* cockatoo.]

budg·et (bŭj′ĭt) *n.* **1.** An itemized summary of probable expenditures and income for a given period, usually embodying a systematic plan for meeting expenses. **2.** The total sum of money allocated for a particular purpose or time period. **3.** A stock or collection with definite limits. —*tr.v.* **budgeted, -eting, -ets.** **1.** To plan in advance the expenditure of (money or time, for example). **2.** To enter or plan for in a budget. [Middle English *bouget,* wallet, from Old French *bougette,* diminutive of *bouge,* leather bag, from Latin *bulga,* from Gaulish. See **bhelgh-** in Appendix.*] —**budg′et·ar′y** (bŭj′ə-tĕr′ē) *adj.*

budg·ie (bŭj′ē) *n. Informal.* A bird, the **budgerigar** *(see).*

BUE Airport code for Buenos Aires, Argentina.

Bue·na·ven·tu·ra (bwā′nä-vĕn-to͞o′rä). A port city in western Colombia. Population, 97,000.

Bue·na Vis·ta (bwā′nə vĭs′tə). A historic battlefield south of Saltillo, Mexico, where U.S. forces under Zachary Taylor defeated the Mexicans under Santa Anna (1847).

Bue·nos Ai·res (bwā′nəs âr′ēz, ī′rēz, bō′nəs; *Spanish* bwā′nōs ī′rās). **1.** A province of Argentina, 118,722 square miles in area, with borders on the Atlantic Ocean and Río de la Plata. Population, 5,458,000. Capital, La Plata. **2.** The capital of Argentina and largest city of the Southern Hemisphere, situated on the southwestern shore of the Río de la Plata estuary. Population, 3,876,000.

Bue·nos Ai·res, Lake (bwā′nəs âr′ēz, ī′rēz, bō′nəs; *Spanish* bwā′nōs ī′rās). A lake extending over 75 miles from southeastern Chile into southwestern Argentina.

buff[1] (bŭf) *n.* **1.** A soft, thick, undyed leather made chiefly from the skins of buffalo, elk, or oxen. **2.** The color of this leather; pale, light, or moderate yellowish pink to yellow, including moderate orange yellow to light yellowish brown. See **color.** **3.** A military coat made of this leather. **4.** *Informal.* The bare skin. Used chiefly in the phrase *in the buff.* **5.** A polishing implement covered with a soft material, such as velvet or leather. —*adj.* **1.** Made of buff. **2.** Of the color of buff. —*tr.v.* **buffed, buffing, buffs.** **1.** To polish or shine with a buff. **2.** To make the color of buff. [Originally "buffalo," from Old French *buffle,* from Vulgar Latin *būfalus* (unattested), BUFFALO.]

buff[2] (bŭf) *tr.v.* **buffed, buffing, buffs.** To deaden the shock of. —*n.* A buffet; a blow. [As verb, from obsolete *buff,* "to sound as a soft body when struck" (perhaps imitative); as noun, from Middle English *buffe,* from Old French, BUFFET.]

buff[3] (bŭf) *n. Informal.* One who is enthusiastic and knowledgeable about a given subject: *a Civil War buff.* [Originally a New York volunteer fireman, hence an enthusiast, from the firemen's buff uniforms.]

buf·fa·lo (bŭf′ə-lō′) *n., pl.* **-loes** or **-los** or **buffalo.** **1. a.** Any of several oxlike Old World mammals of the family Bovidae, such as *Syncerus caffer,* of Africa, having massive, downward-curving horns, or the **water buffalo** *(see).* **b.** A related North American animal, the **bison** *(see).* **2.** The **buffalo fish** *(see).* —*tr.v.* **buffaloed, -loing, -loes.** *Slang.* To intimidate. [Portuguese *bufalo,* from Vulgar Latin *būfalus* (unattested), from Latin *būbalus,* from Greek *boubalos,* African antelope, buffalo, probably from *bous,* cow, ox. See **gwou-** in Appendix.*]

Buf·fa·lo (bŭf′ə-lō′). The second-largest city of New York State, situated at the northeastern end of Lake Erie on the Niagara River. Population, 533,000.

buffalo berry. **1.** Either of two North American shrubs, *Shepherdia argentea* or *S. canadensis,* having small yellowish flowers and red or yellowish berries. **2.** The berry of either of these shrubs.

Buffalo Bill. See William Frederick **Cody.**

buffalo bug. The **carpet beetle** *(see).* Also "buffalo beetle."

buffalo fish. Any of several North American freshwater fishes of the genus *Ictiobus,* having a humped back.

buffalo gnat. The **black fly** *(see).*

buffalo grass. A short grass, *Buchloe dactyloides,* of the plains east of the Rocky Mountains.

buffalo robe. The dressed skin of the North American bison, used as a lap robe, cape, or blanket.

buff·er[1] (bŭf′ər) *n.* An implement used to shine or polish, as a soft cloth or a buffing wheel.

buff·er[2] (bŭf′ər) *n.* **1.** Something that lessens or absorbs the shock of an impact. **2.** One that protects by intercepting or moderating adverse pressures or influences. **3.** Something that interposes between two rival powers, lessening the danger of conflict. Often used attributively: *a buffer zone.* **4.** *Chemistry.* A substance capable of maintaining the relative concentrations of hydrogen and hydroxyl ions in a solution by neutralizing, within limits, added acids or bases. —*tr.v.* **buffered, -ering, -ers.** *Chemistry.* To treat (a solution) with a buffer. [Probably from BUFF (deaden the shock of).]

buf·fet[1] (bə-fā′, bo͞o-) *n.* **1.** A large sideboard with drawers and cupboards. **2. a.** A counter or table from which meals or refreshments are served. **b.** A restaurant having such a counter. **3.** A meal at which guests serve themselves from various dishes displayed on a table or sideboard. [French *buffet*†.]

buf·fet[2] (bŭf′ĭt) *n.* A blow or cuff with or as if with the hand. —*v.* **buffeted, -feting, -fets.** —*tr.* **1.** To hit or club, especially repeatedly. **2.** To strike against forcefully; to batter. **3.** To force (one's way) with or as if with crude blows. —*intr.* **1.** To struggle; contend. **2.** To force one's way by struggling. [Middle English, from Old French, diminutive of *buffe,* blow (imitative).] —**buf′fet·er** *n.*

Buf·fet (bü-fĕ′), **Bernard.** Born 1928. French painter.

buffing wheel. A wheel covered with a soft material, such as velvet or leather, for shining and polishing metal.

buf·fle·head (bŭf′əl-hĕd′) *n.* A small North American duck, *Bucephala albeola,* having black and white plumage and a densely feathered, rounded head. Also called "butterball." [From obsolete *buffle,* a buffalo (from the duck's large head), from Old French. See **buff** (leather).]

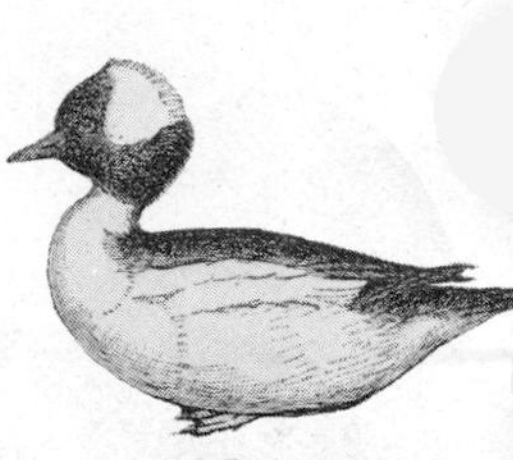
bufflehead
A male of the species

buf·fo (bo͞o′fō) *n., pl.* **-fi** (-fē). A male opera singer. [Italian, "puff of wind," from *buffare,* to puff. See **buffoon.**]

Buf·fon (bü-fôN′), Comte **Georges Louis Leclerc de.** 1707–1788. French naturalist and theoretical biologist.

buf·foon (bə-fo͞on′) *n.* **1.** A clown; jester. **2.** A witless person given to making coarse jokes. [French *bouffon,* from Italian *buffone,* from *buffare,* to puff (imitative).] —**buf·foon′er·y** *n.*

bug (bŭg) *n.* **1.** Any of various wingless or four-winged insects of the order Hemiptera, and especially the suborder Heteroptera, having mouth parts adapted for piercing and sucking. **2.** Broadly, any insect or similar organism. **3.** *Informal.* A disease-producing microorganism. **4.** A mechanical, electrical, or other systemic defect or difficulty. **5.** *Slang.* An enthusiast or devotee; a buff: *a hi-fi bug.* **6.** A small hidden microphone or other device used for eavesdropping. See Usage note below. —*v.* **bugged, bugging, bugs.** —*intr.* To protrude. Used of eyes. —*tr.* **1.** *Slang.* To annoy; pester. **2.** To eavesdrop on, especially with electronic devices. See Usage note below. [Origin obscure.]

Usage: *Bug* and *bugging,* as nouns or verbs in the sense of electronic eavesdropping, are acceptable in writing to 69 per cent of the Usage Panel and in speech to 86 per cent.

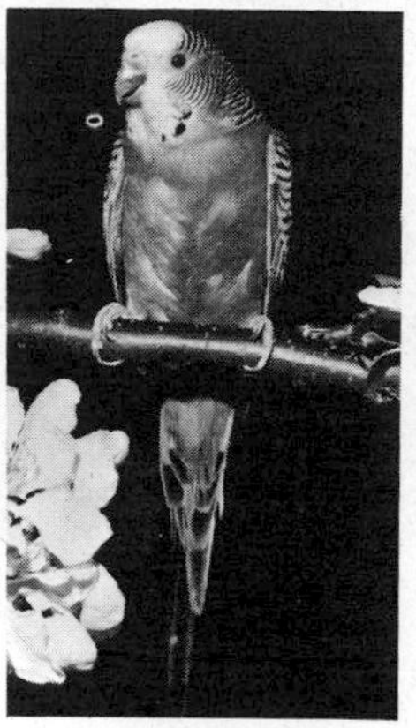
budgerigar

Bug (bo͞og). **1.** A river rising in the southwestern Ukraine and flowing 500 miles southeast to the Dnieper estuary. Also called "Southern Bug." **2.** A river rising in the southwestern Ukraine and flowing 450 miles generally northwest, forming part of the Polish-Soviet border before joining the Narew River in Poland.

bug·a·boo (bŭg′ə-bo͞o′) *n., pl.* **-boos.** **1.** A bugbear. **2.** A steady source of concern. [Perhaps from Celtic, akin to Cornish *buccaboo,* the devil. Compare **bugbear** and **bogle.**]

Bu·gan·da (bo͞o-găn′də, byo͞o-). A federated state of Uganda occupying 25,631 square miles in the southern part of the country. Capital, Kampala.

bug·bane (bŭg′bān′) *n.* Any of several plants of the genus *Cimicifuga;* especially, *C. americana,* of eastern North America, having clusters of small white flowers supposed to repel insects.

bug·bear (bŭg′bâr′) *n.* **1.** An object of obsessive dread. **2.** *Archaic.* A hobgoblin or bogie. [Obsolete *bug,* from Middle English *bugge,* possibly from Middle Welsh *bwg(a),* ghost, akin to Cornish *buccaboo,* the devil, BUGABOO + BEAR.]

bug-eyed (bŭg′īd′) *adj. Slang.* Agog.

bug·ger (bŭg′ər, bo͝og′-) *n.* **1.** *Vulgar.* A sodomite. **2.** A contemptible or disreputable person. **3.** *Slang.* A fellow; a chap. —*v.* **buggered, -gering, -gers.** *Vulgar.* —*intr.* To practice buggery. —*tr.* To practice buggery with. [Middle English *bougre,* a heretic, from Middle Dutch *bugger,* from Old French *bougre,* from Medieval Latin *Bulgarus,* a Bulgarian (the Eastern Orthodox Bulgarians were regarded as heretics).]

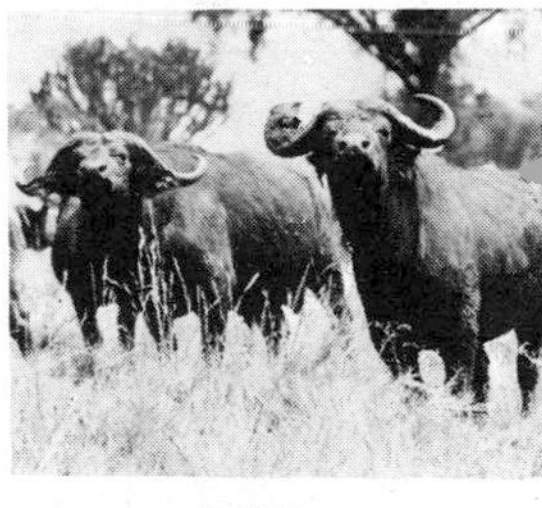
buffalo
Syncerus caffer

bug·ger·y (bŭg′ə-rē, bo͝og′-) *n. Vulgar.* Sodomy.

bug·gy[1] (bŭg′ē) *n., pl.* **-gies.** **1.** A small, light, four-wheeled horse-drawn carriage. **2.** A baby carriage. [Origin unknown.]

bug·gy[2] (bŭg′ē) *adj.* **-gier, -giest.** **1.** Infested with bugs. **2.** *Slang.* Crazy. —**bug′gi·ness** *n.*

bug·house (bŭg′hous′) *n. Slang.* An insane asylum. [From BUGGY (crazy).]

bu·gle[1] (byo͞o′gəl) *n.* **1.** A brass wind instrument somewhat shorter than a trumpet, and without keys or valves. **2.** A hunting horn. —*v.* **bugled, -gling, -gles.** —*intr.* To play a bugle. —*tr.* To call, signal, or summon by sounding a bugle. [Middle English *bugle,* buffalo, horn, bugle, from Old French, from Latin *būculus,* diminutive of *bōs,* ox. See **gwou-** in Appendix.*] —**bu′gler** *n.*

bu·gle[2] (byo͞o′gəl) *n.* A tubular glass or plastic bead used to ornament women's clothing. Also called "bugle bead." —*adj.* Also **bu·gled** (-gəld). Decorated with such beads. [Origin unknown.]

bu·gle[3] (byo͞o′gəl) *n.* Any of several plants of the genus *Ajuga,* native to Eurasia, having spikes or dense clusters of small blue or white flowers. Also called "bugleweed." [Middle English, from Old French, from Late Latin *bugula,* perhaps from Latin *bugillō,* from Gaulish.]

bu·gle·weed (byo͞o′gəl-wēd′) *n.* **1.** Any plant of the genus *Lycopus;* especially, *L. virginicus,* having small, whitish flowers

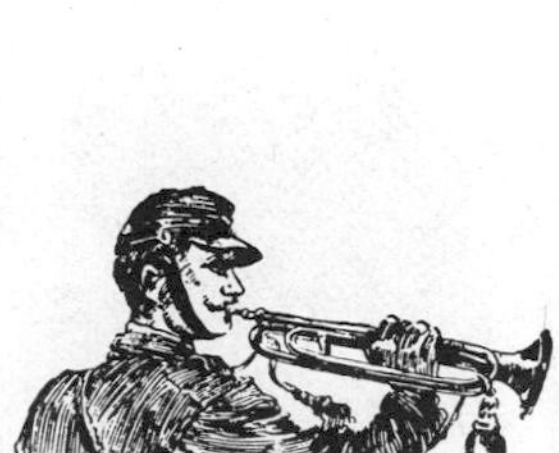
bugle[1]
Bugler in the Civil War

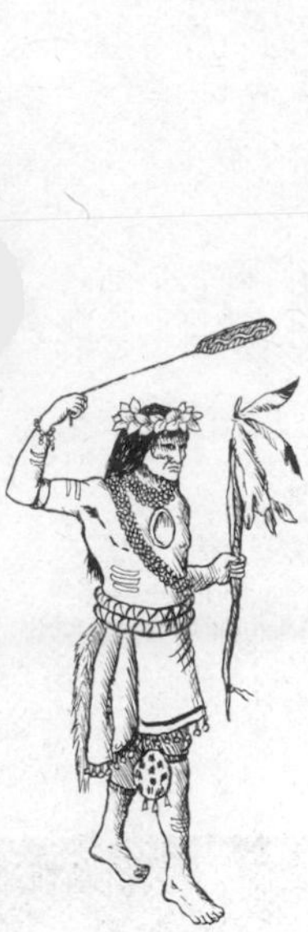

bullroarer
Hopi medicine man using a bullroarer in a ceremonial dance

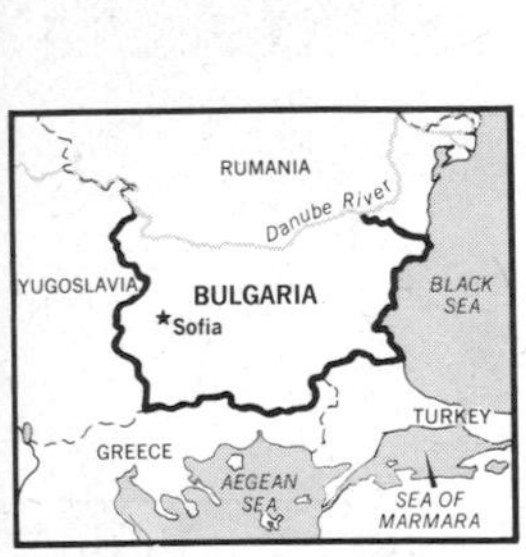

Bulgaria

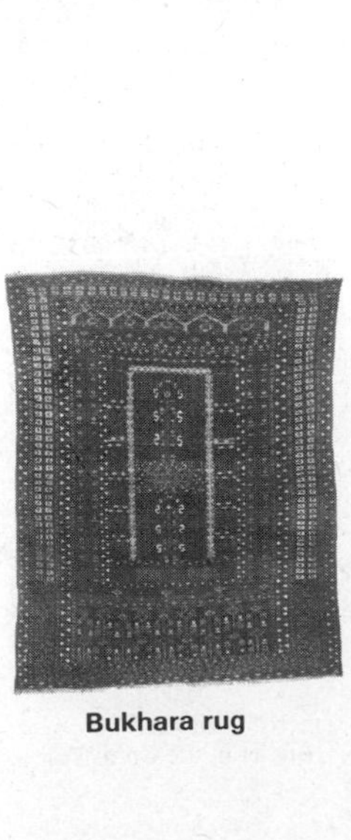

Bukhara rug

and an aromatic odor. Also called "water horehound." **2.** A plant, the **bugle** *(see)*. [Perhaps from its tubular flowers.]

bu·gloss (byōō′glŏs′, -glôs′) *n.* Any of several plants of the genera *Lycopsis, Echium,* and *Anchusa,* having hairy stems and leaves, and clusters of blue flowers. See **alkanet.** [Middle English *buglosse,* from Old French, from Latin *būglōssa,* from Greek *bouglōssos,* "ox-tongued" (from the broad, rough leaves) : *bous,* ox (see **gwou-** in Appendix*) + *glōssa,* tongue (see **glōgh-** in Appendix*).]

bug moss. Any moss of the genus *Buxbaumia,* characterized by a flattened, asymmetric capsule borne on a rough stalk.

bug·seed (bŭg′sēd′) *n.* Any of several low-growing plants of the genus *Corispermum,* having narrow leaves and flat seeds.

bug·sha (bōōg′shä) *n.* A monetary unit equal to 1/40 of the riyal of Yemen. See table of exchange rates at **currency.** [Arabic.]

buhl (bōōl) *n.* Also **boule, boulle. 1.** A style of furniture decoration in which elaborate designs are inlaid with tortoiseshell, ivory, and metals of various colors. **2.** A piece of furniture so decorated. Also called "buhlwork." [After André C. *Boule* (1642–1732), French woodcarver.]

buhr·stone (bûr′stōn′) *n.* Also **burr·stone.** A tough limestone impregnated with silica, from which millstones were formerly made. [Variant of *bur(r)stone* : perhaps BUR + STONE.]

build (bĭld) *v.* **built** (bĭlt) or *archaic* **builded, building, builds.** —*tr.* **1.** To form by combining materials or parts; to erect; construct. **2.** To give form to according to a definite plan or process; to fashion; mold; create. **3.** To establish and strengthen; create and add to: *build a savings account.* **4.** To establish a basis for; found or ground: *build an argument on fact.* **5.** *Card Games.* To accumulate combinations or sequences of (cards) according to suit or number. —*intr.* **1.** To construct something or have something constructed: *"Each of the three architects built in a different style"* (Dwight Macdonald). **2.** To be a builder. **3.** To develop an idea, argument, theory, or the like. Used with *on* or *upon.* **4.** *Card Games.* To accumulate combinations or sequences of cards. **5.** To progress toward a maximum, as of intensity, excitement, or the like. —**build in.** To construct as an integral or permanent part of. —*n.* The physical make-up of a person or thing: *an athletic build.* [Middle English *bilden,* Old English *byldan,* from *bold,* a dwelling. See **bheu-** in Appendix.*]

build·er (bĭl′dər) *n.* **1.** One that builds; especially, a person who contracts for and supervises the construction of a building. **2.** An abrasive or filler used in a soap or a detergent.

build·ing (bĭl′dĭng) *n.* **1.** *Abbr.* **bldg.** Something that is built; a structure; an edifice. **2.** The act, process, art, or occupation of constructing.

Synonyms: *building, structure, edifice, pile.* All these nouns apply to something built. *Building* is the basic, broadly applicable term of this group. *Structure* usually implies considerable size and emphasizes physical make-up with respect to material and design. *Edifice* invariably implies something large or otherwise imposing; it may be applied figuratively to a receptacle of knowledge or ideals. *Pile* suggests the massiveness of stone and frequently indicates a cluster of buildings.

build up. 1. To construct in stages or by degrees. **2.** To renew the strength or health of. **3.** To establish and strengthen; create and add to: *build up a business.* **4.** To increase, as in value, quality, beauty, reputation, or the like: *build up a small role.* **5.** To magnify (a person or thing) by extravagant praise or publicity. **6.** To fill up (an area) with buildings.

build-up (bĭld′ŭp′) *n.* Also **build·up. 1.** The act of amassing or increasing; a reinforcing. **2.** *Informal.* Extravagant praise; widely favorable publicity, especially by a systematic campaign.

built. Past tense and past participle of **build.**

built-in (bĭlt′ĭn′) *adj.* **1.** Constructed as part of a larger unit; not detachable: *a built-in cabinet.* **2.** Forming a permanent or essential element or quality: *a built-in escape clause.*

built-up (bĭlt′ŭp′) *adj.* **1.** Made by fastening several layers or sections one on top of the other: *a built-up roof.* **2.** Occupied by several buildings.

Bu·jum·bu·ra (bōō′jəm-bōōr′ə, bōō-jōōm′bōōr′ə). Formerly **U·sum·bu·ra** (ōō-sōōm-bōōr′ə). The capital of Burundi, in the western part of the country at the northern end of Lake Tanganyika. Population, 47,000.

Bu·kha·ra (bōō-kä′rə, -hä′rə). Also **Bo·kha·ra** (bō-). A city of Uzbek S.S.R. situated east of the Amu Darya River, about 125 miles west of Samarkand. Population, 69,000.

Bukhara rug. Also **Bokhara rug.** A kind of Turkoman rug, usually having a black-and-white pattern of large and small octagons on a red, brownish-red, or sometimes tan ground.

Bu·kha·rin (bōō-KHä′rĭn), **Nikolai Ivanovich.** 1888–1938. Bolshevik theoretician and revolutionary; executed for treason.

Bu·ko·vi·na. See **Bucovina.**

bul. bulletin.

Bu·la·wa·yo (bōō′lə-wä′yō, -wā′ō). A city and trade center of Rhodesia, situated in the southwest. Population, 214,000.

bulb (bŭlb) *n.* **1.** *Botany.* A modified underground stem, such as that of the onion or tulip, usually surrounded by scalelike modified leaves, and containing stored food for the undeveloped shoots of the new plant enclosed within it. **2.** Loosely, an underground stem or root resembling this, such as a corm, rhizome, or tuber. **3.** Any plant that grows from a bulb. **4.** A rounded projection or part of something: *the bulb of a syringe.* **5.** An incandescent lamp or its glass housing. **6.** *Anatomy.* Any of various rounded, enlarged, or bulb-shaped structures, especially the **medulla oblongata** *(see)*. [Latin *bulbus,* bulb, onion, from Greek *bolbos*†, name of various bulbous plants.]

bul·bar (bŭl′bər, -bär′) *adj.* Of, pertaining to, or characteristic of a bulb, especially of the medulla oblongata: *bulbar poliomyelitis.*

bul·bil (bŭl′bĭl′) *n. Botany.* A small bulblike part growing above ground on a flower stalk or in a leaf axil. [French *bulbille,* diminutive of *bulbe,* bulb, from Latin *bulbus,* BULB.]

bul·bous (bŭl′bəs) *adj.* **1.** Resembling a bulb in shape. **2.** *Botany.* Bearing bulbs or growing from a bulb.

bul·bul (bōōl′bōōl′) *n.* **1.** Any of various chiefly tropical Old World songbirds of the family Pycnonotidae, having grayish or brownish plumage. **2.** A songbird thought to be a nightingale, often mentioned in Persian poetry. [Persian, from Arabic.]

Bul·finch (bōōl′fĭnch′), **Thomas.** 1796–1867. American mythologist; author of *The Age of Fable.*

Bulg. Bulgaria; Bulgarian.

Bul·ga·nin (bōōl-gä′nĭn, -găn′ĭn), **Nikolai Aleksandrovich.** Born 1895. Soviet statesman; premier (1955–58).

Bul·gar·i·a (bŭl-gâr′ē-ə, bōōl-). *Bulgarian* **Bul·ga·ri·ya** (bŭl-gä′rē-yä). *Abbr.* **Bulg.** Officially, People's Republic of Bulgaria. A republic, 42,796 square miles, on the Balkan Peninsula, on the Black Sea. Population, 8,211,000. Capital, Sofia.

Bul·gar·i·an (bŭl-gâr′ē-ən, bōōl-) *adj. Abbr.* **Bulg.** Of, pertaining to, or characteristic of Bulgaria, its inhabitants, or their language. —*n.* Also **Bul·gar** (bŭl′gər, bōōl′gär′) (for sense 1). *Abbr.* **Bulg. 1.** A native or inhabitant of Bulgaria. **2.** The Slavic language spoken by Bulgarians.

bulge (bŭlj) *n.* **1.** A protruding part; an outward curve or a swelling. **2.** The rounded lower section of a ship's hull. **3.** *Slang.* An advantage. —*v.* **bulged, bulging, bulges.** —*tr.* To cause to curve outward. —*intr.* To swell up; grow larger or rounder. [Middle English, wallet, pouch, from Old French *bouge,* from Latin *bulga,* leather bag, probably from Gaulish. See **bhelgh-** in Appendix.*] —**bulg′i·ness** *n.* —**bulg′y** *adj.*

Bulge, Battle of the. The last major German counteroffensive of World War II, launched December 16, 1944, and repulsed by January 25, 1945. [So called because the line of combat formed a large bulge deep into Belgium.]

bu·lim·i·a (byōō-lĭm′ē-ə) *n.* Insatiable appetite. [New Latin, from Greek *boulimia* : *bous,* ox, cow (see **gwou-** in Appendix*) + *limos,* hunger, famine (see **leud-** in Appendix*).]

bulk[1] (bŭlk) *n.* **1.** Great size, mass, or volume. **2. a.** A distinct mass or portion of matter, especially a large one. **b.** The body of a human being, especially a large and corpulent body. **3.** The major portion or greater part of something: *"the great bulk of necessary work can never be anything but painful"* (Bertrand Russell). **4.** Thickness of paper or cardboard in relation to weight. **5.** *Abbr.* **blk.** A ship's hold or the cargo stowed there. **6. Bulkage** *(see)*. —**in bulk. 1.** Unpackaged; loose. **2.** In large numbers, amounts, or volume. —*v.* **bulked, bulking, bulks.** —*intr.* **1.** To be or appear to be massive in size, volume, importance, or consequence; loom: *"shopkeeping naturally bulks large among London occupations"* (G.D.H. Cole and Raymond Postgate). **2.** To grow or increase in size or importance. Usually used with *up.* **3.** To cohere or form a mass: *Certain paper pulps bulk well.* —*tr.* **1.** To cause to swell or expand. Usually used with *out.* **2.** To cause to cohere or form a mass. [Middle English *bulke, bolke,* heap, mass, body, from Old Norse *bulki,* cargo. See **bhel-**[2] in Appendix.*]

bulk[2] (bŭlk) *n.* A frame structure, such as a stall or booth, projecting from the front of a building. [Perhaps ultimately from Old Norse *balkr,* partition, low wall. See **bhelg-** in Appendix.*]

bulk·age (bŭl′kĭj) *n.* Any substance that stimulates peristalsis by increasing the bulk of material in the intestine.

bulk·head (bŭlk′hĕd′) *n.* **1.** One of the upright partitions dividing a ship into compartments and serving to prevent the spread of leakage or fire. **2.** A wall or embankment constructed in a mine or tunnel to protect against earth slides, fire, water, or gas. **3.** A horizontal or sloping structure providing access to a cellar stairway or to an elevator shaft. [From BULK (frame structure).]

bulk·y (bŭl′kē) *adj.* **-ier, -iest. 1.** Extremely large; massive. **2.** Clumsy; unwieldy. —**bulk′i·ly** *adv.* —**bulk′i·ness** *n.*

bull[1] (bōōl) *n.* **1. a.** An adult male bovine mammal. **b.** The uncastrated adult male of domestic cattle. **2.** The male of certain other mammals, such as the elephant and moose. **3.** An exceptionally large, strong, and aggressive man. **4.** *Stock Market.* A person who buys commodities or securities in anticipation of a rise in prices or who tries by speculative purchases to effect such a rise, in order to sell later at a profit. Compare **bear. 5.** Anyone who is optimistic about business conditions. **6.** *Capital* **B.** The constellation and sign of the zodiac, **Taurus** *(see)*. **7.** *Slang.* A policeman or detective. **8.** *Slang.* Empty, foolish talk; nonsense. —**shoot the bull.** *Slang.* To spend time talking; talk foolishly. —*v.* **bulled, bulling, bulls.** —*tr.* **1.** *Stock Market.* To engage in speculative buying so as to raise the price of (stocks) or prices in (a market). **2.** To push; to force. Usually used with *through: bull one's way through a crowded bus.* —*intr.* **1.** *Stock Market.* To rise in price. **2.** To push ahead or through forcefully. —*adj.* **1.** Male. **2.** Resembling a bull; large and strong. **3.** *Stock Market.* Characterized by rising prices: *a bull market.* [Middle English *bule, bole,* from Old English *bula,* from Old Norse *boli.* See **bhel-**[2] in Appendix.*]

bull[2] (bōōl) *n.* **1.** An official document issued by the pope and sealed with a bulla. **2.** The bulla itself. [Middle English *bulle,* from Old French *bulle,* from Medieval Latin *bulla,* seal, BULLA.]

bull[3] (bōōl) *n. Informal.* A blunder. [Origin obscure.]

Bull, John. See **John Bull.**

bull. bulletin.

bul·la (bōōl′ə) *n., pl.* **bullae** (bōōl′ē). **1.** A round seal affixed to a papal bull. **2.** *Pathology.* A large blister or vesicle. Compare **bleb.** [Sense 1, Medieval Latin, from Latin, bubble, seal; sense 2, Latin, bubble, seal. See **beu-**[1] in Appendix.*]

bul·lace (bo͝ol′ĭs) *n.* A plum, the **damson** *(see).* [Middle English *bolas,* from Old French *buloce, beloce,* sloe, probably from Medieval Latin *bollucat*†.]

bullace grape. The **muscadine** *(see).*

bul·late (bo͝ol′āt′, bŭl′-) *adj.* Having a puckered or blistered appearance: *bullate leaves.* [From New Latin *bulla,* bubble, from Latin. See **beu-**[1] in Appendix.*]

bull·bat (bo͝ol′băt′) *n.* A bird, the **nighthawk** *(see).* [From its roaring sound in flight.]

bull dike. *Vulgar Slang.* A female homosexual who affects mannish clothes and mannerisms.

bull·dog (bo͝ol′dôg′, -dŏg′) *n.* **1.** A short-haired dog of a breed characterized by a large head, strong, square jaws with dewlaps, and a stocky body. **2.** A short-barreled revolver or pistol of a large caliber. **3.** A **tapadera** *(see).* **4.** A heat-resistant material used to line puddling furnaces. **5.** *British.* A proctor's assistant at Oxford or Cambridge. —*adj.* Resembling or having the qualities of a bulldog; stubborn. —*tr.v.* **bulldogged, -dogging, -dogs.** *Western U.S.* To throw (a steer) by seizing its horns and twisting its neck until the animal falls.

bulldog edition. The early morning edition of a daily newspaper.

bull·doze (bo͝ol′dōz′) *tr.v.* **-dozed, -dozing, -dozes. 1.** To clear, dig up, or move with a bulldozer. **2.** *Slang.* To coerce by intimidation; to bully. [Perhaps BULL + DOSE.]

bull·doz·er (bo͝ol′dō′zər) *n.* **1.** A tractor, usually with endless-link treads and having a vertical metal scoop in front for moving earth and rocks, used especially to clear or grade land. **2.** *Slang.* An overbearing or bullying person.

bul·let (bo͝ol′ĭt) *n.* **1.** A spherical or pointed cylindrical metallic projectile that is fired from a pistol, rifle, or other relatively small firearm. **2.** Such a projectile in a metal casing; a cartridge. **3.** Any object of similar shape, action, or effect. **4.** *Printing.* A heavy dot (•) used to call attention to a particular passage. [French *boulette,* diminutive of *boule,* ball, from Old French, from Latin *bulla,* bubble, ball. See **beu-**[1] in Appendix.*]

bul·le·tin (bo͝ol′ə-tən, -tĭn) *n. Abbr.* **bul., bull. 1.** A printed or broadcast statement on a matter of public interest. **2.** A periodical published by an organization or society. —*tr.v.* **bulletined, -tining, -tins.** To inform by bulletin. [French, probably from Old French *bullette,* from *bulle,* BULL (document).]

bulletin board. A board mounted on a wall, on which notices are posted.

bul·let·proof (bo͝ol′ĭt-pro͞of′) *adj.* Impenetrable by bullets. —*tr.v.* **bulletproofed, -proofing, -proofs.** To make impenetrable by bullets.

bull fiddle. A **double bass** *(see).*

bull·fight (bo͝ol′fīt′) *n.* A public spectacle, especially in Spain and Mexico, in which a fighting bull is engaged in a series of traditional maneuvers culminating usually with the matador's ceremonial execution of the bull by sword. —**bull′fight′er** *n.* —**bull′fight′ing** *n.*

bull·finch (bo͝ol′fĭnch′) *n.* **1.** A European bird, *Pyrrhula pyrrhula,* having a short, thick bill and, in the male, a red breast. **2.** Any of several other similar finches. [From its thick neck.]

bull·frog (bo͝ol′frôg′, -frŏg′) *n.* Any of several large frogs, chiefly of the genus *Rana;* especially, *R. catesbeiana,* of North America, having a characteristic deep, resonant croak.

bull·head (bo͝ol′hĕd′) *n.* **1.** Any of several North American freshwater catfishes of the genus *Ictalurus.* **2.** Any of several fishes of the family Cottidae, such as the **sculpin** and the **miller's thumb** *(both of which see).*

bull·head·ed (bo͝ol′hĕd′ĭd) *adj.* Very stubborn; obstinate; headstrong. See Synonyms at **obstinate.** —**bull′head′ed·ly** *adv.* —**bull′head′ed·ness** *n.*

bull·horn (bo͝ol′hôrn′) *n.* An electric megaphone that amplifies the volume of a voice or other sounds. Compare **megaphone.**

bul·lion (bo͝ol′yən) *n.* **1.** Gold or silver considered with respect to quantity rather than value. **2.** Gold or silver in the form of bars, ingots, or plates. **3.** A heavy lace trimming made of twisted gold or silver threads. [Middle English, from Norman French, "mint," perhaps variant of Old French *bouillon,* "a boiling," from *bouillir,* to BOIL.]

bull·ish (bo͝ol′ĭsh) *adj.* **1.** Like a bull. **2.** Stubborn; bullheaded. **3.** Causing, expecting, or characterized by rising stock-market prices. —**bull′ish·ly** *adv.* —**bull′ish·ness** *n.*

Bul·litt (bŭl′ĭt), **William Christian.** 1891–1967. American diplomat and ambassador to the Soviet Union (1933–36).

bull·mas·tiff (bo͝ol′măs′tĭf, -mäs′tĭf) *n.* A heavy-set dog of a breed developed from the bulldog and the mastiff, having a smooth, brownish coat.

Bull Moose. Also **Bull Mooser.** A member or supporter of Theodore Roosevelt's **Progressive Party** *(see).* [From the emblem of the party.]

bull·necked (bo͝ol′nĕkt′) *adj.* Having a short, thick neck.

bull·nose (bo͝ol′nōz′) *n.* A contagious disease of swine caused by the bacillus *Actinomyces necrophorus* and characterized by an infection and swelling of the snout.

bul·lock (bo͝ol′ək) *n.* **1.** A castrated bull; a steer. **2.** A young bull. [Middle English *bullok,* Old English *bulluc,* diminutive of *bula,* BULL.]

bull·pen (bo͝ol′pĕn′) *n.* **1.** A pen for confining bulls. **2.** *Informal.* A place for the temporary detention of prisoners. **3.** *Baseball.* An area where relief pitchers warm up during a game.

bull·ring (bo͝ol′rĭng′) *n.* A circular arena for bullfights.

bull·roar·er (bo͝ol′rôr′ər, -rōr′ər) *n.* A small wooden slat attached to a string, that makes a roaring noise when whirled.

Bull Run (bo͝ol′ rŭn′). A creek in northeastern Virginia near Manassas, the scene of two Civil War battles (July 1861 and August 1862) in which the Confederates defeated the Union forces.

bull session. *Informal.* A random, informal group discussion.

bull's eye. Also **bull's-eye** (bo͝olz′ī′). **1. a.** The small central circle on a target. **b.** A shot that hits this circle. **2.** Anything that precisely achieves a desired goal. **3.** A thick, circular piece of glass set in a roof, pavement, ship's deck, or the like, to admit light. **4.** Any circular opening or window. **5. a.** A plano-convex lens used to concentrate light. **b.** A lantern or lamp having such a lens. **6.** *Nautical.* A small round or oval wooden pulley. **7.** A piece of round, hard candy.

bull·shit (bo͝ol′shĭt′) *n. Vulgar Slang.* Foolish, uninformed, or exaggerated talk. —*intr.v.* **bullshit** or **-shitted, -shitting, -shits.** *Vulgar Slang.* To utter such talk. —**bull′shit′ter** *n.*

bull snake. Any of several nonvenomous North American snakes of the genus *Pituophis,* having yellow and brown or black markings. Some species are also called "gopher snake."

bull terrier. A dog of a breed developed by crossing a bulldog and a terrier, having a short, usually white coat.

bull thistle. A coarse weed, *Cirsium vulgare,* native to Eurasia, having spiny stems and leaves and purple flowers. [From its large head.]

bull tongue. A heavy plow with a single shovel.

bull·whip (bo͝ol′hwĭp′) *n.* A long, plaited rawhide whip with a knotted end. —*tr.v.* **bullwhipped, -whipping, -whips.** To whip with a bullwhip.

bul·ly[1] (bo͝ol′ē) *n., pl.* **-lies. 1.** A person who is habitually cruel to smaller or weaker people. **2.** *Archaic.* A hired ruffian. **3.** *Obsolete.* A pimp. **4.** *Obsolete.* A fine fellow. **5.** *Obsolete.* A sweetheart. —*v.* **bullied, -lying, -lies.** —*tr.* To intimidate with superior size or strength. —*intr.* To behave like a bully. —*adj. Informal.* **1.** Excellent; splendid. **2.** Dashing; gallant. —*interj.* Used to express approval. [Originally "sweetheart," probably from Middle Dutch *boele,* lover, from Middle High German *buole,* perhaps of baby-talk origin.]

bul·ly[2] (bo͝ol′ē) *n.* Canned or pickled beef. [French *bouilli,* boiled (beef), from the past participle of *bouillir,* to BOIL.]

bul·ly·rag (bo͝ol′ē-răg′) *tr.v.* **-ragged, -ragging, -rags.** Also **bal·ly·rag** (băl′ē-răg′). To mistreat or intimidate by bullying or hazing.

bully tree. A tropical American tree, the **balata** *(see).* [By folk etymology, variant of BALATA.]

bul·rush (bo͝ol′rŭsh′) *n.* **1.** Any of various grasslike sedges of the genus *Scirpus,* growing in wet places. **2.** Broadly, any of various marsh plants, such as the cattail. [Middle English *bulrish* : perhaps *bule,* BULL (in the sense "large") + *rish,* RUSH.]

bul·wark (bo͝ol′wərk, bŭl′-, -wôrk′) *n.* **1.** A wall or wall-like structure raised as a defensive fortification; rampart. **2.** Anything serving as a principal defense against attack or encroachment: *"We have seen the necessity of the Union, as our bulwark against foreign danger"* (James Madison). **3.** A breakwater. **4.** *Usually plural.* The part of a ship's side that is above the upper deck. —*tr.v.* **bulwarked, -warking, -warks. 1.** To fortify with a bulwark. **2.** To provide defense or protection for. [Middle English *bulwerke,* from Middle High German *bolwerc* : *bole,* plank (see **bhel-**[2] in Appendix*) + *werc,* work, from Old High German (see **werg-**[1] in Appendix*).]

Synonyms: *bulwark, barricade, breastwork, earthwork, rampart, bastion, parapet.* All of these nouns refer to structures used or regarded as a defense against attack. *Bulwark* applies to any wall-like fortification, and figuratively to anything relied upon heavily for protection. *Barricade* pertains broadly to any barrier but implies hasty construction to meet an imminent threat. *Breastwork* denotes a low defensive wall, especially a temporary one built in haste. *Earthwork* specifies a defensive embankment of earth, usually in the field. A *rampart,* the main defensive structure around a guarded place, is permanent, high, and broad. The projecting sections of a *rampart* are called *bastions,* from which defenders have a wide range of view and fire. Both terms are used figuratively, *bastion* implying great defensive strength. *Parapet* applies to any low fortification, typically a wall atop a *rampart.*

bum[1] (bŭm) *n.* **1.** A tramp; hobo. **2.** A person who avoids work and seeks to live off others. —**on the bum.** *Slang.* **1.** Living as a hobo or tramp. **2.** Out of order; broken. —*v.* **bummed, bumming, bums.** *Informal.* —*intr.* **1.** To live by begging and scavenging from place to place. Often used with *around.* **2.** To loaf. —*tr.* To acquire by begging or sponging. —*adj. Slang.* **1.** Of poor quality; worthless. **2.** Disabled; malfunctioning: *a bum shoulder.* [From earlier *bummer,* a loafer, probably from German *bummler,* from *bummeln*†, to loaf.]

bum[2] (bŭm) *intr.v.* **bummed, bumming, bums.** *Chiefly British.* To make a humming sound; to drone. [Middle English *bumben* (imitative).]

bum[3] (bŭm) *n. Chiefly British Slang.* The buttocks. [Middle English *bom*†.]

bum·bail·iff (bŭm′bā′lĭf) *n. British.* A sheriff's deputy or county court bailiff. Used disparagingly. [From BUM (buttocks), since he pursues and catches from behind.]

bum·ble[1] (bŭm′bəl) *v.* **-bled, -bling, -bles.** —*intr.* To speak or behave in a clumsy or faltering manner. —*tr.* To bungle; botch. [Variant of BUNGLE.]

bum·ble[2] (bŭm′bəl) *intr.v.* **-bled, -bling, -bles.** To make a humming or droning sound; to buzz. —*n.* A droning sound; a buzz. [Middle English *bomblen* (imitative).]

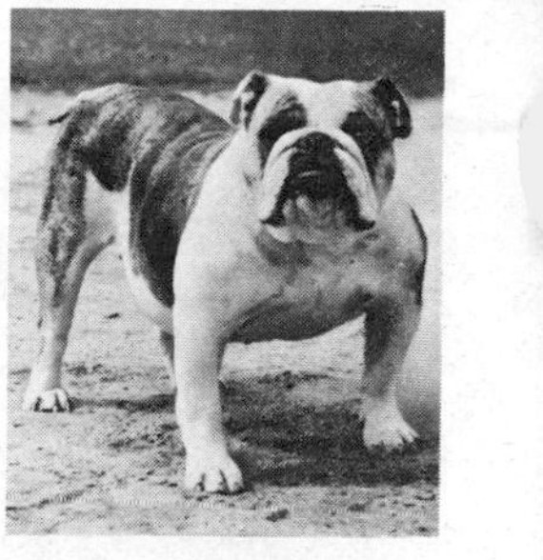

bulldog

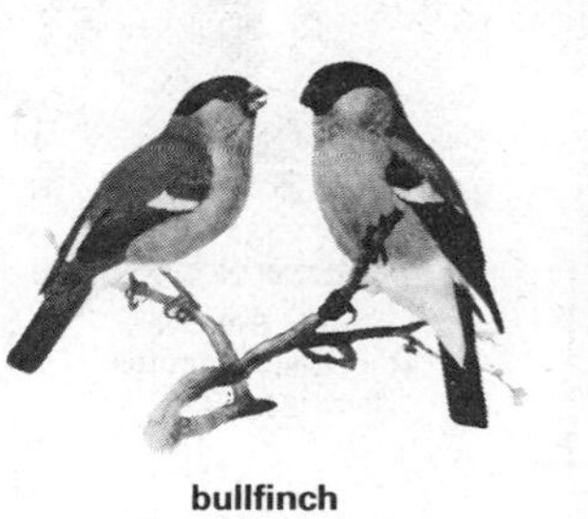

bullfinch
Pyrrhula pyrrhula

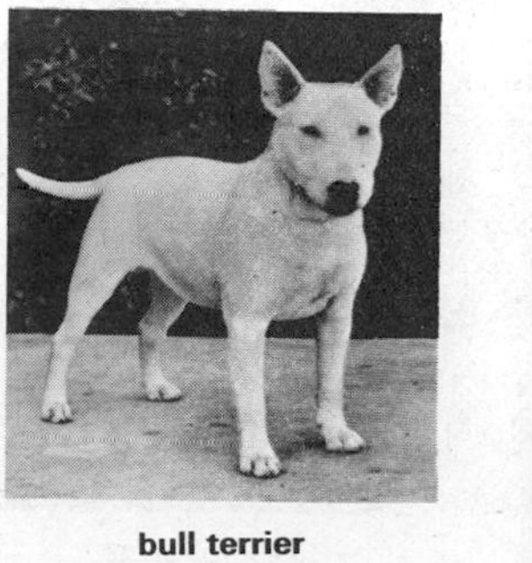

bull terrier

bum·ble·bee (bŭm′bəl-bē′) *n.* Any of various large, hairy bees of the genus *Bombus.* [BUMBLE + BEE.]

bum·boat (bŭm′bōt′) *n.* A small boat used to peddle provisions and small wares to ships anchored offshore. [Probably Dutch *bom*†, a kind of fishing boat + BOAT.]

bump (bŭmp) *v.* **bumped, bumping, bumps.** —*tr.* **1.** To strike or collide with. **2.** To cause to knock against an obstacle. **3.** To knock to a new position; displace. **4.** *Informal.* To displace from a position or job; oust. —*intr.* **1.** To hit or knock with force. Often used with *against* or *into.* **2.** To proceed with jerks and jolts. **3.** To thrust the pelvis forward, in or as if in a burlesque striptease. —**bump off.** *Slang.* To murder. —*n.* **1.** A light blow, collision, or jolt. **2.** A slight swelling or lump. **3.** One of the natural protuberances on the human skull. **4.** A sudden violent upward air current striking an airplane in flight. **5.** A forward thrust of the pelvis, as performed by or as if by a burlesque stripteaser. [Imitative.]

bump·er[1] (bŭm′pər) *n.* **1.** One that bumps. **2.** Either of two metal structures, typically horizontal bars, attached to the front and rear of an automobile to absorb the impact of a collision. **3.** A similar protective device on other objects.

bump·er[2] (bŭm′pər) *n.* **1.** A drinking vessel filled to the brim. **2.** Something unusually or extraordinarily large. —*tr.v.* **bumpered, -ering, -ers. 1.** To fill to the brim. **2.** To propose a toast to. —*adj.* Unusually full or abundant: *a bumper crop.* [Perhaps from BUMP (lump, hence something large).]

bump·kin (bŭmp′kĭn, bŭm′-) *n.* Also **bum·kin** (bŭm′-) (for sense 2). **1.** An awkward, untutored rustic. **2.** A short spar projecting from the deck of a ship, used to extend a sail or secure a block or stay. [Perhaps originally "Dutchman," probably from Dutch *boomken,* "little tree," squat person, diminutive of *boom,* tree, from Middle Dutch. See **bheu-** in Appendix.*]

bump·tious (bŭmp′shəs) *adj.* Crudely forward and self-assertive in behavior; pushy. [Perhaps a blend of BUMP and FRACTIOUS.] —**bump′tious·ly** *adv.* —**bump′tious·ness** *n.*

bump·y (bŭm′pē) *adj.* **-ier, -iest. 1.** Covered with lumps or protuberances: *a bumpy head.* **2.** Causing jerks and jolts: *a bumpy road.* —**bump′i·ly** *adv.* —**bump′i·ness** *n.*

bum's rush. *Slang.* Forcible ejection from a place.

bun (bŭn) *n.* **1.** A small bread roll, often sweetened or spiced. **2.** A tight roll of hair worn at the back of a woman's head. [Middle English *bunne*†.]

Bu·na (bōō′nə, byōō′-) *n.* A trademark for synthetic rubber made by polymerization of butadiene and sodium. [BU(TADIENE) + NA (the symbol for sodium).]

bunch (bŭnch) *n.* **1.** A group of like items growing, fastened, or placed together; a cluster or tuft. **2.** *Informal.* A small group of people. **3.** A lump or swelling. —*v.* **bunched, bunching, bunches.** —*tr.* To gather or form into a cluster or tuft. —*intr.* **1.** To form a cluster or tuft. **2.** To swell; protrude. [Middle English *bunche*†.] —**bunch′y** *adj.*

bunch·ber·ry (bŭnch′bĕr′ē) *n., pl.* **-ries.** A plant, the **dwarf cornel** *(see).*

Bunche (bŭnch), **Ralph Johnson.** Born 1904. American diplomat and United Nations undersecretary (since 1954).

bunch·flow·er (bŭnch′flou′ər) *n.* A bog plant, *Melanthium virginicum,* of the eastern United States, having narrow leaves and a branching cluster of greenish flowers.

bunch grass. Any of various grasses growing in clumps.

bun·co (bŭng′kō) *n., pl.* **-cos.** Also **bun·ko.** *Informal.* A swindle in which an unsuspecting person is cheated; confidence game. —*tr.v.* **buncoed, -coing, -cos.** Also **bun·ko.** To swindle, as by a confidence game. [Spanish *banca,* name of a card game, "bank" (in gambling), from Italian *banca,* BANK (financial establishment).]

bun·combe. Variant of **bunkum.**

bund[1] (bŭnd) *n.* **1.** An embankment or dike. **2.** A street running along a harbor or waterway. [Hindi *band,* from Persian. See **bhendh-** in Appendix.*]

bund[2] (bŏŏnd, bŭnd) *n.* **1.** A confederation or league. **2.** *Often capital* **B.** A pro-Nazi German-American organization of the 1930's. [German *Bund,* "league," from Middle High German *bunt.* See **bhendh-** in Appendix.*] —**bund′ist** *n.*

Bun·del·khand (bŏŏn′dəl-kŭnd′). A region of east-central India, 10,000 square miles in area, now incorporated mainly in Madhya Pradesh.

Bun·des·rat (bŏŏn′dəs-rät′) *n.* Also **Bun·des·rath** (-rät′). **1.** Formerly, a federal legislative council composed of representatives from the 26 states of the German Empire. **2.** The upper house of the federal legislature of West Germany. **3.** The federal council of certain countries, as of Switzerland and Austria. [German *Bundesrat* : *Bundes,* genitive of BUND + *Rat,* counsel, council, from Old High German *rāt* (see **ar-** in Appendix*).]

Bun·des·tag (bŏŏn′dəs-täg′) *n.* The lower house of the federal legislature of West Germany. [German : *Bundes,* genitive of BUND + *-tag,* meeting, from Middle High German *tagen,* to meet, from *tag,* day, from Old High German *tac* (see **dhegwh-** in Appendix*).]

bun·dle (bŭnd′l) *n. Abbr.* **bdl. 1.** A number of objects bound, wrapped, or otherwise held together. **2.** Anything wrapped or tied up for carrying; a package. **3.** *Biology.* A cluster or strand of specialized cells. **4.** *Botany.* A **vascular bundle** *(see).* **5.** *Slang.* A large sum of money. —*v.* **bundled, -dling, -dles.** —*tr.* **1.** To tie, wrap, fold, or otherwise secure together. **2.** To dispatch quickly and with little fuss; to hustle. Usually used with *off.* **3.** To dress warmly. Used with *up.* —*intr.* **1.** To leave hastily and unceremoniously. Used with *away* or *off.* **2.** To sleep in the same bed while fully clothed, a custom practiced by engaged couples in early New England. [Middle English *bundel,* probably from Middle Dutch, sheaf of papers, bundle. See **bhendh-** in Appendix.*] —**bun′dler** *n.*

bung (bŭng) *n.* **1.** A stopper for the hole through which a cask is filled or emptied. **2.** The hole itself; a bunghole. —*tr.v.* **bunged, bunging, bungs. 1.** To close (a bunghole) with a cork or stopper. **2.** *Slang.* To beat up; bruise; maul. Often used with *up.* [Middle English *bunge,* from Middle Dutch *bonghe,* perhaps variant of *bonne,* perhaps from Late Latin *puncta,* hole, from the feminine past participle of Latin *pungere,* to prick. See **peuk-** in Appendix.*]

bun·ga·low (bŭng′gə-lō′) *n.* **1.** A small cottage, usually of one story. **2.** In India, a thatched or tiled house having one story and surrounded by a wide verandah. [Earlier *bungale,* perhaps from Gujarati *bangalo,* from Hindi *baṅglā,* "of Bengal."]

bung·hole (bŭng′hōl′) *n.* The hole in a cask, keg, or barrel through which liquid is poured in or drained out.

bun·gle (bŭng′gəl) *v.* **-gled, -gling, -gles.** —*intr.* To work or act ineptly or inefficiently. —*tr.* To manage (a task) badly; mishandle; botch. —*n.* A clumsy or inept job or performance. [Perhaps from Scandinavian, akin to Swedish (dialectal) *bangla,* to work ineffectually. See **bheg-** in Appendix.*] —**bun′gler** *n.*

bun·gling (bŭng′glĭng) *adj.* Performing clumsily or ineptly; incompetent. See Synonyms at **awkward.** —**bun′gling·ly** *adv.*

bun·ion (bŭn′yən) *n.* A painful, inflamed swelling at the bursa of the big toe. [Probably from earlier dialectal *bunny, bony,* swelling, from Old French *buigne*†, bump on the head.]

bunk[1] (bŭngk) *n.* **1.** A narrow bed attached like a shelf against a wall. **2.** A narrow bed, usually a double-decker. **3.** *Informal.* Any place for sleeping. —*intr.v.* **bunked, bunking, bunks. 1.** To sleep in a bunk. **2.** To go to bed. [Possibly short for BUNKER.]

bunk[2] (bŭngk) *n. Slang.* Twaddle. [Short for BUNKUM.]

bun·ker (bŭng′kər) *n.* **1.** A bin or tank for fuel storage, as on a ship. **2.** A sand trap serving as an obstacle on a golf course. **3.** A fortified earthwork, as for the protection of a gun emplacement. —*tr.v.* **bunkered, -kering, -kers. 1.** To store (fuel) in a bunker. **2.** To drive (a golf ball) into a sand trap or obstacle. [Earlier Scottish *bonker*†.]

Bun·ker Hill (bŭng′kər). A hill in Charlestown, Massachusetts, near which the first major battle of the American Revolution was fought (June 17, 1775). In this battle the British won the field but suffered far heavier losses.

bunk·house (bŭngk′hous′) *n.* Sleeping quarters on a ranch or in a camp.

bunk·mate (bŭngk′māt′) *n.* A person with whom one shares rough sleeping quarters.

bun·ko. Variant of **bunco.**

bun·kum (bŭng′kəm) *n.* Also **bun·combe.** Empty or meaningless talk, especially by a politician; claptrap. [From *Buncombe* County, North Carolina, from a remark made around 1820 by Felix Walker, U.S. congressman, who made a fatuous speech, calling it "a speech for Buncombe."]

bun·ny (bŭn′ē) *n., pl.* **-nies.** A rabbit. Used chiefly as a child's term. [From dialectal *bun*†, squirrel.]

bunny hug. A dance in ragtime rhythm popular in the United States during the early part of the 20th century.

Bun·sen (bŭn′sən; *German* bōōn′zən), **Robert Wilhelm.** 1811–1899. German chemist and inventor.

Bun·sen burner (bŭn′sən). A small laboratory burner consisting of a vertical metal tube connected to a gas source, and producing a very hot flame from a mixture of gas and air let in through adjustable holes at the base. [Invented by Robert Wilhelm BUNSEN.]

bunt[1] (bŭnt) *v.* **bunted, bunting, bunts.** —*tr.* **1.** To butt (something) with or as if with the horns or head. **2.** *Baseball.* To bat (a pitched ball) with a half swing, and with the upper hand supporting the middle of the bat, so that the ball rolls slowly in front of the infielders. —*intr. Baseball.* To bunt a pitch. —*n.* **1.** A butt with or as if with the horns or head. **2.** *Baseball.* **a.** The act of bunting. **b.** A bunted ball. [Probably from Celtic, akin to Breton *bounta,* to butt.]

bunt[2] (bŭnt) *n.* **1.** *Nautical.* The middle section of a square sail. **2.** The sagging middle part of a fishnet. [Possibly from Middle Low German *bunt,* bundle. See **bhendh-** in Appendix.*]

bunt[3] (bŭnt) *n.* A disease of wheat, rye, and other cereal grasses, caused by fungi of the genus *Tilletia* and resulting in sooty black spores in place of normal seeds. [Origin unknown.]

bunt·ing[1] (bŭn′tĭng) *n.* **1.** A light cotton or woolen cloth used for making flags. **2.** Flags collectively. **3.** Long, colored strips of cloth used for festive decoration. [Origin unknown.]

bunt·ing[2] (bŭn′tĭng) *n.* Any of various birds of the family Fringillidae, having short, cone-shaped bills. [Middle English *buntynge*†.]

bunt·ing[3] (bŭn′tĭng) *n.* A snug-fitting, hooded sleeping bag for infants. [From "Bye, Baby Bunting," a nursery rhyme, origin and meaning unknown.]

bunt·line (bŭnt′lĭn, -līn′) *n. Nautical.* A rope that keeps a square sail from bellying when it is being hauled up for furling.

Bunt·line, Ned. Pen name of Edward Z.C. **Judson** *(see).*

bun·ya (bŭn′yə) *n.* Also **bun·ya-bun·ya** (bŭn′yə-bŭn′yə). An evergreen tree, *Araucaria bidwilli,* native to Australia, having sharp-pointed, close-set leaves and large cones. [Native Australian name.]

Bun·yan (bŭn′yən), **John.** 1628–1688. English preacher; author of *Pilgrim's Progress.*

Buo·na·par·te. See **Bonaparte.**

Buo·nar·ro·ti, Michelangelo. See **Michelangelo.**

Buo·non·ci·ni. See **Bononcini.**

buoy (bōō′ē, boi) *n.* **1.** *Nautical.* A float moored in water as a warning of danger under the surface or as a marker for a chan-

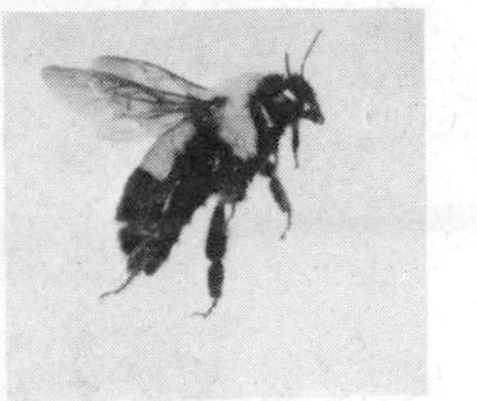

bumblebee

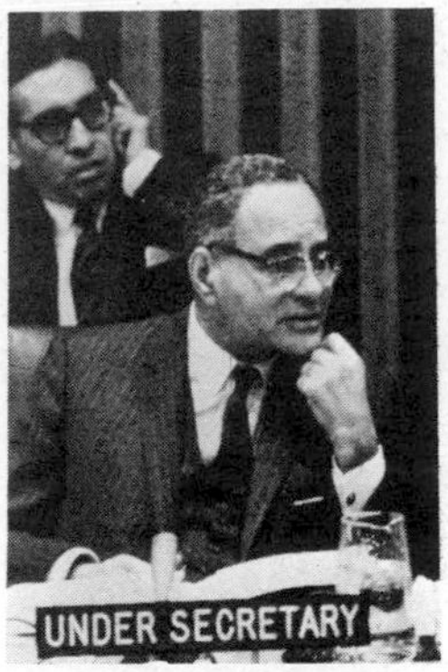

Ralph Bunche
At a U.N. committee meeting in 1962

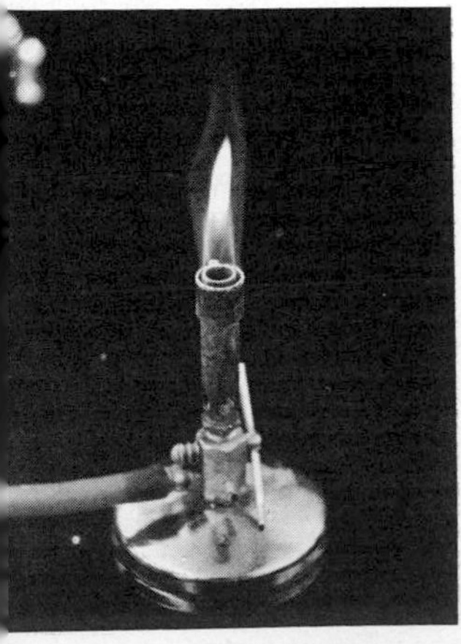

Bunsen burner

ă pat/ā pay/âr care/ä father/b bib/ch church/d deed/ĕ pet/ē be/f fife/g gag/h hat/hw which/ĭ pit/ī pie/îr pier/j judge/k kick/l lid, needle/m mum/n no, sudden/ng thing/ŏ pot/ō toe/ô paw, for/oi noise/ou out/ŏŏ took/ōō boot/p pop/r roar/s sauce/sh ship, dish/

nel. See **bell buoy**. **2**. A device made of cork or other buoyant material for keeping a person afloat. In this sense, also called "life buoy." —*tr.v.* **buoyed, buoying, buoys**. **1**. *Nautical*. To mark (a water hazard or a channel) with a buoy. **2**. To keep afloat. **3**. To uplift the spirits of; to cheer; hearten. [Middle English *boye*, probably from Old French *boie*, perhaps from Old High German *bouhhan*. See **bhā-**[1] in Appendix.*]

buoy·an·cy (boi′ən-sē, bo͞o′yən-) *n.* Also **buoy·ance** (-əns, -yəns). **1**. The tendency or capacity to remain afloat in a liquid or to rise in air or gas. **2**. The upward force of a fluid upon a floating or immersed object. **3**. The ability to recover quickly from setbacks. **4**. Lightness of spirit; cheerfulness.

buoy·ant (boi′ənt, bo͞o′yənt) *adj.* Having buoyancy. [Spanish *buoyante*, present participle of *boyar*, to float, from *boya*, buoy, from Old French *boie*, BUOY.] —**buoy′ant·ly** *adv.*

bu·pres·tid (byo͞o-prĕs′tĭd) *n.* Any of various often brightly colored beetles of the family Buprestidae, many of which are destructive wood borers as larvae. [New Latin *Buprestidae* : *Buprestis* (genus name), from Latin *būprestis*, a venomous beetle whose sting caused cattle to swell up, from Greek *bouprēstis* : *bous*, ox, cow (see **gwou-** in Appendix*) + *prēthein*†, to blow up + -ID.]

bur[1] (bûr) *n.* Also **burr**. **1**. **a**. The rough, prickly, or spiny fruit husk, seed pod, or flower of various plants, such as the chestnut or the burdock. **b**. A plant producing burs. **2**. A persistently clinging or nettlesome person or thing. **3**. Any of various rotary cutting tools designed to be attached to a drill. [Middle English *burre*, probably from Scandinavian, akin to Old Swedish *borre*. See **bhar-** in Appendix.*]

bur[2]. **1**. Variant of **burr** (rough edge). **2**. Variant of **burr** (guttural trill). **3**. Variant of **burr** (washer).

Bur. **1**. bureau. **2**. Burma.

bu·ran (bo͞o-rän′) *n.* Also **bu·ra** (-rä′). A violent windstorm of the steppes of Russia, accompanied in summer by dust and in winter by snow. [Russian, from Turkic, akin to Turkish and Kazan Tatar *buran*.]

Bur·bage (bûr′bĭj), **Richard**. 1567?–1619. English actor and theatrical manager; associated with Shakespeare.

Bur·bank (bûr′bangk′). A city in southern California, ten miles northwest of Los Angeles. Population, 90,000.

Bur·bank (bûr′băngk′), **Luther**. 1849–1926. American horticulturist; developed many new plant varieties.

bur·ble (bûr′bəl) *n.* **1**. A rushing or bubbling sound. **2**. A rapid, excited flow of speech. **3**. *Aviation*. A separation in the boundary layer of air about a moving streamlined body, causing a breakdown in the smooth airflow and resulting in turbulence. —*intr.v.* **burbled, -bling, -bles**. **1**. To bubble; to gurgle. **2**. To speak quickly and excitedly. [Middle English *burblen*, to flow with a bubbling sound (imitative).]

bur·bot (bûr′bət) *n., pl.* **burbot** or **-bots**. A freshwater fish, *Lota lota*, of the Northern Hemisphere, related to and resembling the cod. [Middle English *borbot*, from Old French *bourbotte*, *bourbete*, from *bourbeter*, to burrow in the mud, from *bourbe*†, mud.]

bur cucumber. **1**. A climbing vine, *Sicyos angulatus*, of eastern North America, having lobed leaves, small greenish flowers, and bristly, egg-shaped fruit. **2**. The fruit of this plant.

bur·den[1] (bûrd′n) *n.* Also *archaic* **bur·then** (bûr′*th*ən). **1**. **a**. Something that is carried. **b**. Something that is difficult to bear physically or emotionally. **2**. A responsibility or duty. **3**. **a**. The amount of cargo that a vessel can carry. **b**. The weight of the cargo carried by a vessel at one time. **4**. The carrying of heavy loads: *a beast of burden*. —*tr.v.* **burdened, -dening, -dens**. Also *archaic* **bur·then**. **1**. To load or overload. **2**. To weigh down; oppress. [Middle English *burden*, *burthen*, Old English *byrthen*. See **bher-**[1] in Appendix.*]

bur·den[2] (bûrd′n) *n.* **1**. The bass accompaniment to a song. **2**. The chorus or refrain of a musical composition. **3**. The drone of a bagpipe. **4**. A recurring idea or theme. [Variant (influenced by BURDEN, load) of BOURDON, from the idea of the burden being carried along by the melody.]

burden of proof. The responsibility of giving proof for a disputed charge or allegation. [Translation of Latin *onus probandi*.]

bur·den·some (bûrd′n-səm) *adj.* Heavy; hard to bear; onerous. —**bur′den·some·ly** *adv.* —**bur′den·some·ness** *n.*

Synonyms: *burdensome, onerous, oppressive, harsh, arduous, demanding, rigorous, exacting*. These adjectives all apply to what taxes the body or mind. *Burdensome* is generally associated with actual hardship of body, and *onerous* with the figuratively heavy load imposed by something irksome, annoying, or otherwise unwelcome. *Oppressive* and *harsh* pertain to severe trial of body or spirit. The remaining adjectives imply active efforts to overcome hardship. *Arduous* emphasizes the expenditure of sustained, exhausting labor. *Demanding* and *rigorous* apply to that which imposes severe conditions, and *exacting* further intensifies the sense of uncompromising demands, as for high standards of performance or for strict observance of rules.

bur·dock (bûr′dŏk′) *n.* Any of several coarse, weedy plants of the genus *Arctium*, native to Eurasia, having large, heart-shaped leaves and purplish flowers surrounded by hooked bristles. [BUR + DOCK (plant).]

bu·reau (byo͝or′ō) *n., pl.* **-reaus** or **bureaux** (byo͝or′ōz). **1**. A chest of drawers. **2**. *Chiefly British*. A writing desk or writing table with drawers. **3**. *Abbr.* **Bur., bu.** **a**. A government department or subdivision of a department. **b**. An office, usually of a large organization, that performs a specific duty: *a news bureau*. **c**. A business that offers information of a specified kind: *a travel bureau*. [French, bureau, woolen material used to cover writing desks, from Old French, from *bure*, coarse woolen stuff, possibly from Vulgar Latin *būra* (unattested), from Late Latin *burra*, shaggy garment. See **burl**.]

bu·reauc·ra·cy (byo͞o-rŏk′rə-sē) *n., pl.* **-cies**. **1**. **a**. Administration of a government chiefly through bureaus staffed with nonelective officials. **b**. The officials staffing such bureaus. **2**. Government marked by diffusion of authority among numerous offices and adherence to inflexible rules of operation. **3**. Any administration in which the need to follow complex procedures impedes effective action. [French *bureaucratie* : BUREAU + -CRACY.]

bu·reau·crat (byo͝or′ə-krăt′) *n.* **1**. An official of a bureaucracy. **2**. Any official who insists on rigid adherence to rules, forms, and routines. —**bu′reau·crat′ic** *adj.* —**bu′reau·crat′i·cal·ly** *adv.*

Usage: In American usage, *bureaucrat* is almost invariably derogatory unless the context establishes otherwise.

bu·rette (byo͞o-rĕt′) *n.* Also **bu·ret**. A uniform-bore glass tube with fine gradations and a stopcock at the bottom, used especially in laboratory procedures for accurate fluid dispensing and measurement. [French, originally "cruet," from Old French, cruet for sacramental wine, from *buire*, pitcher, variant of *buie*, from Frankish *būk* (unattested). See **beu-**[1] in Appendix.*]

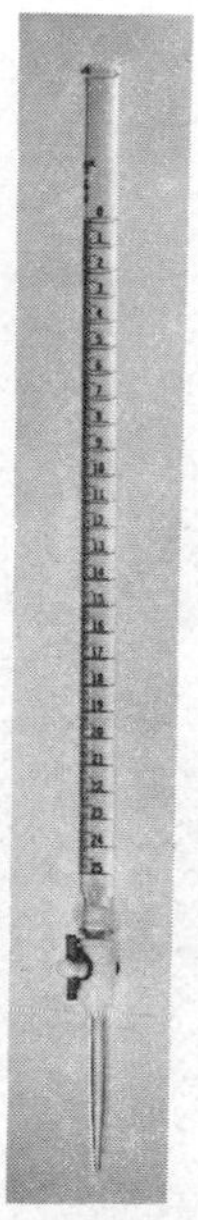
burette

burg (bûrg) *n.* **1**. A fortified town. **2**. *Informal*. A city or town. [Old English *burg*, *burh*. See **bhergh-**[2] in Appendix.*]

bur·gage (bûr′gĭj) *n.* A tenure in England and Scotland under which property of the king or a lord in a town was held for a yearly rent. [Middle English, from Medieval Latin *burgāgium*, from *burgus*, fortified town, from Old English *burg*, BURG.]

bur·gee (bûr′jē, bər-jē′) *n.* A small distinguishing flag displayed by a yacht. [Perhaps from Channel Islands French *bourgeais*, shipowner, from Old French *burgeis*, owner, BURGESS.]

Bur·gen·land (bo͝or′gən-länt′). A province in southeastern Austria, 1,530 square miles in area. Population, 271,000. Capital, Eisenstadt.

bur·geon (bûr′jən) *v.* **-geoned, -geoning, -geons**. Also **bour·geon**. —*intr.* **1**. To put forth new buds, leaves, or greenery; begin to sprout, grow, or blossom. **2**. To develop rapidly; flourish. See Usage note below. —*tr.* To put forth (buds, for example); to sprout. —*n.* Also **bour·geon**. A bud, sprout, or newly developing growth. [Middle English *burgenen*, from *burjon*, a bud, from Old French, from Vulgar Latin *burriō* (stem *burriōn-*) (unattested), from Late Latin *burra*, shaggy garment (probably from the down on some buds). See **burl**.]

Usage: The verb *burgeon* and its participle *burgeoning*, used as an adjective, are properly restricted to actual or figurative budding and sprouting, that is, to what is newly emerging: *the burgeoning talent of the boy Mozart*. They are not mere substitutes for the more general *expand*, *grow*, and *thrive*, as 51 per cent of the Usage Panel noted in rejecting the following example: *the burgeoning population of Queens*.

burg·er (bûr′gər) *n.* *Informal*. A hamburger.

bur·gess (bûr′jĭs) *n.* **1**. A freeman or citizen of an English borough. **2**. Formerly, a member of the English Parliament, representing a town, borough, or university. **3**. A member of the lower house of the colonial legislature of either Virginia or Maryland. [Middle English *burgeis*, from Old French, from Vulgar Latin *burgensis* (unattested), from Late Latin *burgus*, fortified place, from Germanic. See **bhergh-**[2] in Appendix.*]

Bur·gess (bûr′jĭs), **Thornton Waldo**. 1874–1965. American author of nature books for children.

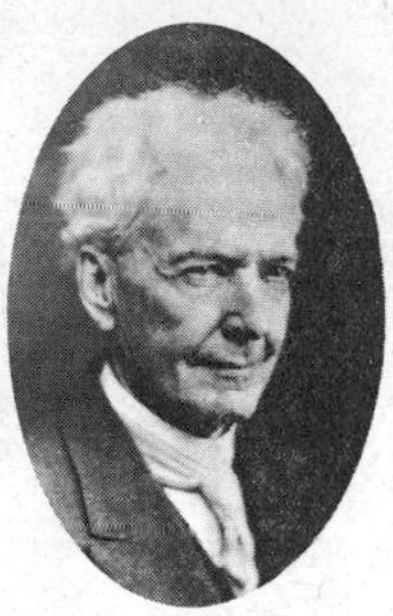
Luther Burbank

burgh (bûrg) *n.* A chartered town or borough in Scotland. [Scottish, variant of BOROUGH.] —**burgh′al** *adj.*

burgh·er (bûr′gər) *n.* **1**. A member of the mercantile class of a medieval city. **2**. A solid citizen; bourgeois. [Either German *Bürger*, from Middle High German *burgære*, from Old High German *burgāri*, town-dweller, from *burg*, fortified place (see **bhergh-**[2] in Appendix*) or Dutch *burger*, from Middle Dutch *burgher*, from Middle High German *burgære*.]

Burgh·ley, Baron. See William **Cecil**.

bur·glar (bûr′glər) *n.* One who commits burglary; housebreaker. [Norman French *burgler*, from Medieval Latin *burgulator*, probably variant of *burgātor*, town thief, from Late Latin *burgus*, fortress, from Germanic. See **bhergh-**[2] in Appendix.*]

bur·glar·i·ous (bər-glâr′ē-əs) *adj.* Pertaining to burglary.

bur·glar·ize (bûr′glə-rīz′) *tr.v.* **-ized, -izing, -izes**. To commit burglary in. See Synonyms at **rob**.

bur·glar·proof (bûr′glər-pro͞of′) *adj.* Secure against burglary.

bur·gla·ry (bûr′glə-rē) *n., pl.* **-ries**. The crime of breaking into and entering a house with intent to commit a felony.

bur·gle (bûr′gəl) *v.* **-gled, -gling, -gles**. *Informal*. —*tr.* To burglarize. —*intr.* To commit burglary. [Back-formation from BURGLAR.]

bur·go·mas·ter (bûr′gə-măs′tər, -mäs′tər) *n.* In the Netherlands, Flanders, Austria, and Germany, the principal magistrate of a city or town, comparable to a mayor. [Partial translation of Dutch *burgemeester* : *burg*, town, from Middle Dutch *burch* (see **bhergh-**[2] in Appendix*) + MASTER.]

bur·goo (bûr′go͞o, bər-go͞o′) *n., pl.* **-goos**. **1**. Thick oatmeal gruel, originally served to sailors. **2**. *Southern U.S.* **a**. A thick, spicy soup or stew of meat and vegetables. **b**. A picnic or gathering where this dish is served. [Perhaps from Arabic *burghul*, from Persian *burghul*†, "bruised grain."]

Bur·gos (bo͝or′gōs). A city in north-central Spain, site of a famous Gothic cathedral. Population, 89,000.

Bur·goyne (bər-goin′), **John**. Called "Gentleman Johnny." 1722–1792. British general; defeated at Battle of Saratoga (1777).

bur·grave (bûr′grāv′) *n.* *German History*. **1**. The appointed

t tight/th thin, path/*th* this, bathe/ŭ cut/ûr urge/v valve/w with/y yes/z zebra, size/zh vision/ə about, item, edible, gallop, circus/ à *Fr.* ami/œ *Fr.* feu, *Ger.* schön/ü *Fr.* tu, *Ger.* über/KH *Ger.* ich, *Scot.* loch/N *Fr.* bon. ***Follows main vocabulary. †Of obscure origin.**

governor of a town or military fortress. **2.** The hereditary lord of a town and its surroundings. [German *Burggraf*, from Middle High German *burcgrāve* : *burc*, fortress, from Old High German *burg* (see **bhergh-**[2] in Appendix*) + *grāve*, count, from Old High German *grāvo* (see **gravo-** in Appendix*).]

Bur·gun·dy[1] (bûr′gən-dē). *French* **Bour·gogne** (bo͞or-gôn′y′). A region, formerly a duchy and province, of southeastern France. —**Bur·gun′di·an** (bər-gŭn′dē-ən) *adj.* & *n.*

Bur·gun·dy[2] (bûr′gən-dē) *n., pl.* **-dies. 1. a.** Any of various red or white wines produced in Burgundy. **b.** Any of various similar wines produced elsewhere. **2.** *Small* **b.** Dark grayish or blackish purple to dark purplish red or reddish brown. See **color.**

bur·i·al (bĕr′ē-əl) *n.* The interment of a dead body. [Middle English *biriel, buryel*, grave, singular of *buriels*, Old English *byrgels*. See **bhergh-**[1] in Appendix.*] —**bur′i·al** *adj.*

bu·rin (byo͝or′ĭn, bûr′-) *n.* **1.** A pointed steel cutting tool used in engraving or in carving stone. **2.** The style or technique of an engraver's work. [French, perhaps from Italian *burino*, from Germanic. See **bher-**[2] in Appendix.*]

burke (bûrk) *tr.v.* **burked, burking, burkes. 1.** To murder (someone) by suffocation so as to leave the body intact and suitable for dissection. **2.** To suppress quietly and unceremoniously. [After William *Burke* (1792–1829), Irish murderer executed in Edinburgh, Scotland, for this crime.]

Burke (bûrk), **Edmund.** 1729–1797. British statesman and philosopher.

burl (bûrl) *n.* **1.** A knot, lump, or slub in yarn or cloth. **2.** A large, rounded excrescence on the trunk or branch of a tree. **3.** The strongly marked wood from such an excrescence, usually cut into thin pieces and used as veneer. —*tr.v.* **burled, burling, burls.** To dress or finish (cloth) by removing burls or loose threads. [Middle English *burle*, from Old French *bourle*, diminutive of *bourre*, coarse wool, from Late Latin *burra*†, shaggy garment.] —**burl′er** *n.*

bur·lap (bûr′lăp′) *n.* A coarsely woven cloth made of fibers of jute, flax, or hemp, used to make bags, to reinforce linoleum, and in interior decoration. [Origin obscure.]

Bur·leigh, Baron. See William **Cecil.**

bur·lesque (bər-lĕsk′) *n.* **1.** A literary or dramatic work that makes a subject appear ridiculous by treating it in an incongruous style, as by presenting a lofty subject with vulgarity, or the inconsequential with mock dignity. **2.** Any ludicrous or mocking imitation; a travesty. **3.** Vaudeville entertainment characterized by broad, ribald comedy, dancing, and display of nudity. —See Synonyms at **caricature.** —*v.* **burlesqued, -lesquing, -lesques.** —*tr.* To imitate mockingly: *"always bringing junk . . . home, as if he were burlesquing his role as provider"* (John Updike). —*intr.* To use the methods or techniques of burlesque. —*adj.* **1.** Mockingly and ludicrously imitative. **2.** Of, pertaining to, or characteristic of theatrical burlesque, especially in its ribald aspects. [French, from Italian *burlesco*, from *burla*, joke, ridicule, from Vulgar Latin *burrula* (unattested), diminutive of Late Latin *burra*, trifle, bit of nonsense, perhaps from *burra*, shaggy garment. See **burl.**] —**bur·lesque′ly** *adv.* —**bur·les′quer** *n.*

bur·ley (bûr′lē) *n., pl.* **-leys.** Also **Bur·ley.** A light-colored tobacco grown chiefly in Kentucky. [Probably from *Burley*, a proper name.]

Bur·ling·ton (bûr′lĭng-tən). **1.** A city and shipping center in southeastern Iowa, on the Mississippi. Population, 32,000. **2.** A city in northern North Carolina, about 20 miles east of Greensboro. Population, 33,000. **3.** The largest city of Vermont, and an important shipping center, on the eastern shore of Lake Champlain. Population, 36,000.

bur·ly (bûr′lē) *adj.* **-lier, -liest.** Heavy, strong, and muscular; husky. [Middle English *burli, borlich*, stately, big, probably from Old English *būrlic* (unattested), exalted. See **bher-**[1] in Appendix.*] —**bur′li·ly** *adv.* —**bur′li·ness** *n.*

Bur·ma (bûr′mə). *Abbr.* **Bur.** Officially, Union of Burma. A republic of southeastern Asia, 263,590 square miles in area, on the eastern shore of the Bay of Bengal and the Andaman Sea. Population, 24,229,000. Capital, Rangoon.

bur marigold. Any of various plants of the genus *Bidens*, having yellow flowers and pointed seeds that cling to fur and clothing. Also called "beggar-ticks," "sticktight."

Bur·ma Road (bûr′mə). A highway extending about 700 miles between Kunming, China, and Lashio, Burma, and used as an Allied supply route in World War II.

Bur·mese (bər-mēz′, -mēs′) *adj.* Also **Bur·man** (bûr′mən). Of, pertaining to, or characteristic of Burma, its natives and inhabitants, their language, or their culture. —*n., pl.* **Burmese.** Also **Bur·man** (for sense 1) *pl.* **-mans. 1.** A native or inhabitant of Burma. **2.** The Sino-Tibetan language spoken in Burma.

burn[1] (bûrn) *v.* **burned** or **burnt** (bûrnt), **burning, burns.** —*tr.* **1. a.** To cause to undergo combustion. **b.** To destroy with fire. **2.** To damage or injure by fire, heat, or a heat-producing agent. **3.** *Slang.* To kill or execute. **4.** *Slang.* To electrocute. **5.** To produce by fire or heat: *burn a clearing in the brush.* **6.** To use as a fuel. **7.** To impart a sensation of intense heat to: *The chili burned his mouth.* **8.** To brand (an animal). **9.** To harden or impart a finish to by subjecting to intense heat; to fire. **10.** To sunburn. **11.** *Card Games.* To remove (the top card) and place it at the bottom of the deck before dealing. —*intr.* **1.** To be on fire; undergo combustion; to flame. **2.** To emit heat or light by or as if by means of fire: *"Arleon's inspiration burned in his mind like a star."* (Lord Dunsany). **3.** To be destroyed, injured, damaged, or changed by or as if by fire. **4.** To feel or look hot. **5.** To be consumed with strong emotion. **6.** *Slang.* To be electrocuted. —**burn up.** *Informal.* To make or become very annoyed; enrage. —*n.* **1.** An injury produced by fire, heat, or a heat-producing agent. Burns are classified in order of increasing seriousness: a *first-degree burn* produces redness of the skin, a *second-degree burn* produces blistering, and a *third-degree burn* destroys and chars the skin tissue. **2.** A burned place or area. **3.** The process or result of firing or burning, as in the manufacture of bricks. **4.** A sunburn. **5.** *Aerospace.* One firing of a rocket. [Middle English *bernen, burnen*, from Old English *beornan, byrnan* (intransitive) and *bærnan* (transitive). See **bhreu-**[2] in Appendix.*]

Synonyms: *burn, scorch, singe, sear, char, parch.* These verbs mean to injure or alter by heat. *Burn* can apply to the effect of exposure to any source of heat. *Scorch* usually refers to contact with flame or heated metal, and involves superficial (surface) burning that discolors, damages texture, or makes brittle. *Singe* specifies superficial and momentary burning of edges through nearness to the heat source. *Sear* applies to surface burning of organic tissue, as by branding, cauterizing, or application of intense flame, as to meat. *Char* pertains to the reduction of a burning substance to carbon, or to any blackening or disintegration due to fire. *Parch* emphasizes surface drying and, often, fissuring by long exposure to flame or sun.

burn[2] (bûrn) *n. Chiefly Scottish.* A small stream; brook. Often used in compound Scottish place names: *Bannockburn.* [Middle English *burn, burne*, Old English *burn, burna*, spring, fountain. See **bhreu-**[2] in Appendix.*]

Burne-Jones (bûrn′jōnz′), Sir **Edward Coley.** 1833–1898. British Pre-Raphaelite painter and decorative artist.

burn·er (bûr′nər) *n.* **1.** One that burns something. **2.** The part of a stove, furnace, or lamp that is lighted to produce a flame. **3.** A device in which something is burned: *an oil burner.*

bur·net (bər-nĕt′, bûr′nĭt) *n.* Any of several plants of the genus *Sanguisorba*, having cucumber-flavored leaves and clusters of small white, red, or greenish flowers. [Middle English, dark brown (from the brownish-red flowers), from Old French *burnete, brunette*, BRUNETTE.]

Bur·net (bər-nĕt′, bûr′nĭt), Sir **(Frank) Macfarlane.** Born 1899. Australian physician; studied immunology.

Bur·nett (bər-nĕt′), **Frances Hodgson.** 1849–1924. British-born American author of children's books; creator of "Little Lord Fauntleroy."

burn·ing (bûr′nĭng) *adj.* **1.** Characterized by intense emotion; passionate. **2.** Urgent; pressing: *"the issues that seem so burning in Washington"* (John F. Kennedy). —**burn′ing·ly** *adv.*

burning bush. 1. Any of several plants or shrubs having foliage that turns bright red, such as the **wahoo** and the **summer cypress** *(both of which see).* **2.** The **gas plant** *(see).* [So called from the burning bush in Exodus 3:2.]

burning glass. A convex lens used to focus the sun's rays and produce heat, especially for ignition. Also called "sunglass."

bur·nish (bûr′nĭsh) *v.* **-nished, -nishing, -nishes.** —*tr.* To polish, smooth, or make glossy by or as if by rubbing. —*intr.* To become smooth and glossy. —*n.* A smooth, glossy finish or appearance; luster. [Middle English *burnischen*, from Old French *burnir* (present stem *burniss-*), variant of *brunir*, "to make brown," burnish, from *brun*, brown, shining, from Germanic. See **bher-**[3] in Appendix.*] —**bur′nish·er** *n.*

bur·noose (bər-no͞os′) *n.* Also **bur·nous.** A hooded cloak worn by Arabs. [French *burnous*, from Arabic *bournous*, from Greek *birros*, cloak with a hood, from Latin *birrus* (attested only in Late Latin). See **beret.**]

burn out. 1. To stop burning from lack of fuel. **2.** To wear out or become inoperative as a result of heat or friction. **3.** To become exhausted, especially as a result of overwork or dissipation.

burn·out (bûrn′out′) *n.* **1.** A failure in a device attributable to burning, excessive heat, or friction. **2.** *Aerospace.* The termination of rocket or jet-engine operation because of fuel exhaustion or shutoff.

Burns (bûrnz), **Robert.** 1759–1796. Scottish poet.

Burn·side (bûrn′sīd′), **Ambrose E(verett).** 1824–1881. American military and political leader; twice relieved of command of Union forces in Civil War.

burn·sides (bûrn′sīdz′) *pl.n.* Heavy side whiskers and a moustache, worn with the chin clean-shaven. [After Ambrose E. BURNSIDE, who wore them.]

burnt (bûrnt). Alternate past tense and past participle of **burn.** —*adj.* Affected by or as if by burning; scorched.

burnt offering. An offering, such as a slaughtered animal, burned on an altar as a religious sacrifice.

burnt sienna. 1. A reddish-brown pigment prepared by calcining raw sienna. **2.** Dark reddish orange. Also called "sienna." See **color.**

bur oak. A timber tree, *Quercus macrocarpa*, of eastern North America, having acorns enclosed within a deep, fringed cup.

burp (bûrp) *n. Informal.* A belch. —*v.* **burped, burping, burps.** *Informal.* —*intr.* To belch. —*tr.* To cause (a baby) to belch, especially after feeding. [Imitative.]

burp gun. A portable, lightweight machine gun.

burr[1] (bûr) *n.* Also **bur. 1.** A rough edge or area remaining on metal or other material after it has been cast, cut, or drilled. **2.** Any rough protuberance; especially a burl on a tree. —*tr.v.* **burred, burring, burrs.** Also **bur. 1.** To form a rough edge on. **2.** To remove a rough edge or edges from. [Middle English *burre*, rough edge, BUR.]

burr[2] (bûr) *n.* Also **bur. 1.** A rough, guttural trilling of the letter *r*, produced by the uvula vibrating against the back of the tongue, as in Scottish pronunciation. **2.** Any similar guttural

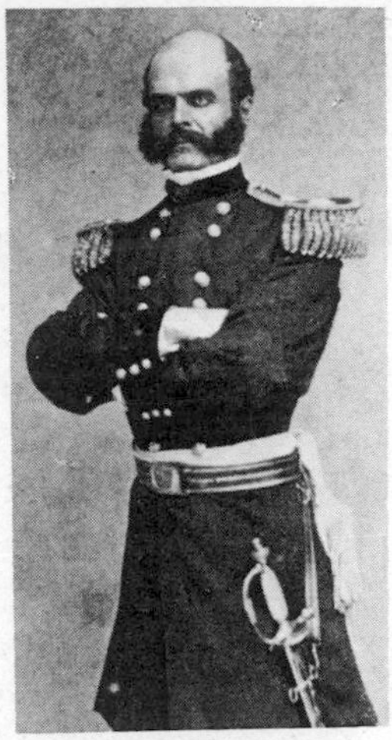

Ambrose Burnside

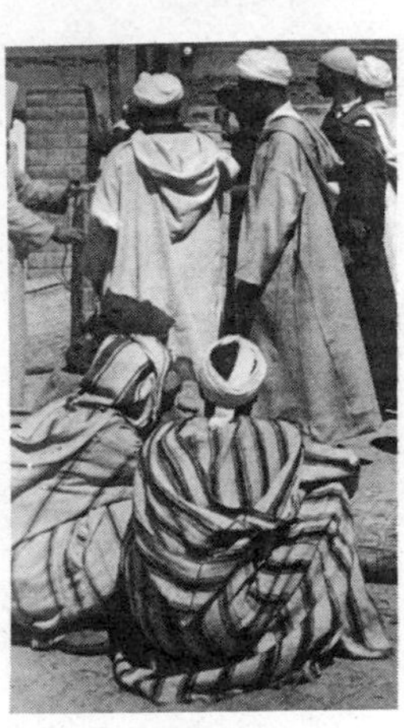

burnoose
Moroccans wearing burnooses

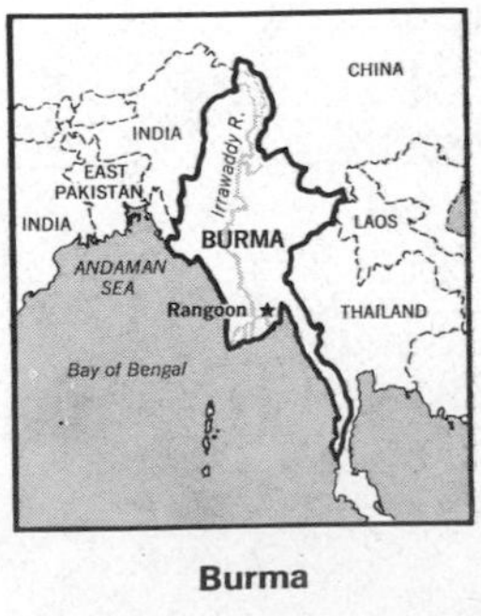

Burma

ă pat/ā pay/âr care/ä father/b bib/ch church/d deed/ĕ pet/ē be/f fife/g gag/h hat/hw which/ĭ pit/ī pie/îr pier/j judge/k kick/l lid, needle/m mum/n no, sudden/ng thing/ŏ pot/ō toe/ô paw, for/oi noise/ou out/o͝o took/o͞o boot/p pop/r roar/s sauce/sh ship, dish/

pronunciation or speech sound. **3.** A buzzing or whirring sound. —*v.* **burred, burring, burrs.** Also **bur.** —*tr.* To pronounce with a burr. —*intr.* **1.** To speak with a burr. **2.** To make a buzzing or whirring sound. [Imitative, probably associated with BUR, from its roughness.] —**bur'ry** *adj.*

burr[3] (bûr) *n.* Also **bur.** **1.** A washer that fits around the smaller end of a rivet. **2.** A blank punched from a sheet of metal. [Variant of obsolete *burrow*†.]

burr[4]**.** Variant of **bur.**

Burr (bûr), **Aaron.** 1756–1836. Vice President of the United States under Thomas Jefferson (1801–05); fatally wounded Alexander Hamilton in a duel.

bur reed. Any of various marsh plants of the genus *Sparganium,* having narrow leaves and round, prickly fruit.

bur·ro (bûr'ō, bo͝or'ō) *n., pl.* **-ros.** A small donkey, especially one used as a pack animal. [Spanish, from *borrico,* donkey, from Late Latin *burricus*†, small horse.]

Bur·roughs (bûr'ōz), **Edgar Rice.** 1875–1950. American writer; creator of Tarzan.

Bur·roughs (bûr'ōz), **John.** 1837–1921. American naturalist and author.

bur·row (bûr'ō) *n.* **1.** A hole or tunnel dug in the ground by a small animal, such as a rabbit or a mole, for habitation or refuge. **2.** Any similar narrow or snug place. —*v.* **burrowed, -rowing, -rows.** —*intr.* **1.** To dig a burrow. **2.** To live or hide in a burrow. **3.** To move or progress through something as if by digging or tunneling: *"Suddenly the train is burrowing through the pinewoods"* (William Styron). —*tr.* **1.** To make by or as if by tunneling. **2.** To dig a burrow in or through. **3.** To hide or seclude (oneself) in a burrow. [Middle English *borow,* probably a variant of *borugh,* fortified place, "lair." See **borough.**] —**bur'row·er** *n.*

burrowing owl. A small, long-legged owl, *Speotyto cunicularia,* of American prairies, that nests in burrows dug by animals such as prairie dogs or rabbits.

burr·stone. Variant of **buhrstone.**

bur·ry (bûr'ē) *adj.* **-rier, -riest.** **1.** Like a bur; prickly. **2.** Full of or covered with burs.

bur·sa (bûr'sə) *n., pl.* **-sae** (-sē) or **-sas.** A saclike bodily cavity, especially one located between joints or at points of friction between moving structures. [New Latin, from Medieval Latin, bag, purse, from Greek. See **bursa** in Appendix.*]

Bur·sa (bo͝or-sä', bûr'sə). Also **Bru·sa** (bro͞o-sä', bro͞o'sə). A city of Turkey, the first capital of the Ottoman Empire, in the northwest near the Sea of Marmara. Population, 154,000.

bur·sal (bûr'səl) *adj.* **1.** *Anatomy.* Of or functioning as a bursa. **2.** Pertaining to the public revenue; fiscal.

bur·sar (bûr'sər, -sär') *n.* **1.** A treasurer or similar official in charge of funds, as at a college or university. **2.** A scholarship student at a Scottish university. [Sense 1, Medieval Latin *bursārius,* from *bursa,* purse (see **bursa**); sense 2, French *boursier,* from *bourse,* purse, from Medieval Latin *bursa.*]

bur·sa·ry (bûr'sə-rē) *n., pl.* **-ries.** **1.** A treasury, especially of a public institution or religious order. **2.** A scholarship granted to a student at a Scottish university. [Medieval Latin *bursāria,* from *bursa,* purse. See **bursa.**] —**bur·sar'i·al** (bər-sâr'ē-əl) *adj.*

burse (bûrs) *n.* **1.** *Rare.* A purse. **2.** *Ecclesiastical.* A flat cloth case for carrying the piece of linen, or corporal, that is used in celebrating the Eucharist. [Medieval Latin *bursa.* See **bursa.**]

bur·seed (bûr'sēd') *n.* A plant, the **stickseed** *(see).*

bur·si·form (bûr'sə-fôrm') *adj. Anatomy.* Shaped like a pouch or sac. [Medieval Latin *bursa,* bag, purse (see **bursa**) + -FORM.]

bur·si·tis (bər-sī'tĭs) *n.* Inflammation of a bursa, especially of one of the shoulder, elbow, or knee joints. [New Latin BURS(A) + -ITIS.]

burst (bûrst) *v.* **burst, bursting, bursts.** —*intr.* **1.** To come open or fly apart suddenly or violently, especially from internal pressure. **2.** To be full to the point of breaking open; swell. **3.** To come forth, emerge, or arrive suddenly and in full force. **4.** To become audible or visible suddenly. **5.** To give sudden utterance or expression. Used with *into: burst into song.* —*tr.* **1.** To cause to come open or fly apart with sudden violence. **2.** To cause to swell or become full to the point of breaking open. —See Synonyms at **break.** —*n.* **1.** A sudden breaking open or flying apart; an explosion. **2.** The result of bursting; a breach or rupture. **3.** A sudden, vehement outbreak or occurrence: *"blow with the strength of a hurricane in fitful bursts"* (Conrad). **4.** An abrupt, intense increase or display: *a burst of speed.* **5.** *Military.* **a.** The explosion of a projectile or bomb on impact or in the air. **b.** The number of bullets fired from an automatic weapon by one pull of the trigger. [Middle English *bersten,* Old English *berstan.* See **bhres-** in Appendix.*]

bur·then. *Archaic.* Variant of **burden.**

bur·ton (bûrt'n) *n. Nautical.* A light tackle having double or single blocks, used to hoist or tighten rigging. [Earlier *Breton (takles), Brytton (takles),* probably from BRETON.]

Bur·ton (bûrt'n), Sir **Richard Francis.** 1821–1890. British Orientalist and adventurer.

Bur·ton (bûrt'n), **Robert.** 1577–1640. English clergyman, scholar, and writer; author of *The Anatomy of Melancholy.*

Bu·run·di (bo͝o-ro͞on'dē). An independent country (since 1962) of central Africa, 10,750 square miles in area, northwest of Tanzania. Population, 3,274,000. Capital, Bujumbura.

bur·weed (bûr'wēd') *n.* Any of various plants that bear burs, such as the burdock.

bur·y (bĕr'ē) *tr.v.* **-ied, -ying, -ies.** **1.** To place in the ground; conceal by covering over with earth. **2.** To place (a dead body) in a grave, a tomb, or in the sea; inter. **3.** To cover from view; hide. **4.** To embed; immerse or sink. **5.** To occupy (oneself) with deep concentration. **6.** To put an end to; forget; abandon. —See Synonyms at **hide.** —**bury the hatchet.** To make peace; cease hostility. [Middle English *berien, burien,* Old English *byrgan.* See **bhergh-**[1] in Appendix.*] —**bur'i·er** *n.*

Bur·yat Autonomous Soviet Socialist Republic (bo͝or-yät'). An administrative division, 135,650 square miles in area, of the southeastern Russian S.F.S.R. Population, 762,000. Capital, Ulan-Ude.

burying beetle. Any of various black or black and orange beetles of the genus *Necrophorus,* that bury dead mice and other small animals, on which they feed and lay their eggs. Also called "sexton beetle."

bus (bŭs) *n., pl.* **buses** or **busses.** **1.** A long motor vehicle, sometimes with two decks, for carrying passengers. Also called "omnibus." **2.** *Informal.* A large or clumsy automobile. **3.** A four-wheeled cart for carrying dishes in a restaurant. **4.** *Electricity.* A **bus bar** *(see).* —*v.* **bused** or **bussed, busing** or **bussing, buses** or **busses.** *Informal.* —*tr.* To transport in a bus. —*intr.* To travel in a bus. [Short for OMNIBUS.]

Usage: *Bus,* as a transitive verb *(to bus children),* is acceptable in writing to only 48 per cent of the Usage Panel, but in speech to 60 per cent. The Panel is about evenly divided in preference between *busing* and *bussing* for the present participle.

bus. business.

bus bar. *Electricity.* A conducting bar that carries heavy currents to supply several electric circuits. Also called "bus."

bus boy. A restaurant employee who clears away dirty dishes and serves as a waiter's assistant.

bus·by (bŭz'bē) *n., pl.* **-bies.** A tall, full-dress, fur hat worn in certain regiments of the British Army. [Origin unknown.]

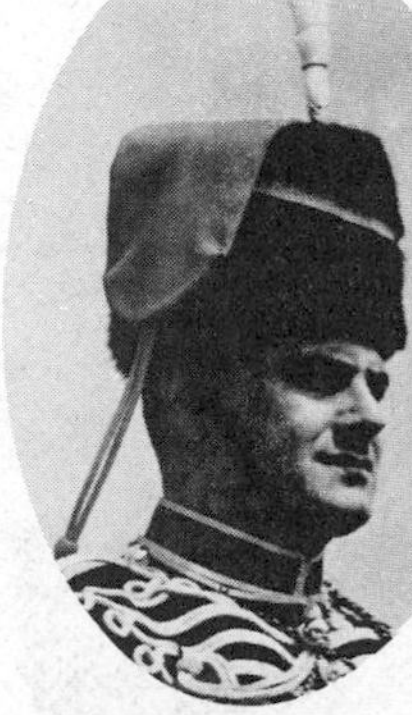

busby

bush[1] (bo͝osh) *n.* **1.** Any low, branching, woody plant, usually smaller than a tree; shrub. **2.** A thick growth of shrubs; thicket. **3. a.** Land covered with a dense growth of shrubs. **b.** Land remote from settlement; backland. Preceded by *the.* **4.** A fox's tail. **5. a.** A clump of ivy formerly used as the sign of a tavern. **b.** *Obsolete.* A tavern. —**beat around** (or **about**) **the bush.** To delay in getting to the point. —*v.* **bushed, bushing, bushes.** —*intr.* **1.** To grow or branch out like a shrub or bush. **2.** To extend in a bushy growth. —*tr.* To decorate, protect, or support with shrubs or bushes. [Middle English *busshe,* perhaps from Middle Low German *busch.* See **busk-** in Appendix.*]

bush[2] (bo͝osh) *tr.v.* **bushed, bushing, bushes.** To furnish or line with a bushing. [From earlier *bush,* BUSHING.]

Bush (bo͝osh), **Vannevar.** Born 1890. American electrical engineer and educator.

bush baby. A small primate, the **galago** *(see).*

bush bean. A shrubby plant, *Phaseolus vulgaris humilis,* a variety of the string bean.

bush·buck (bo͝osh'bŭk') *n.* An African antelope, *Tragelaphus scriptus,* having white markings and twisted horns. Also called "harnessed antelope." [Translation of Afrikaans *bosbok.*]

bush clover. Any of various plants or shrubs of the genus *Lespedeza,* having compound leaves with three leaflets, and clusters of purple or yellowish flowers.

bushed (bo͝osht) *adj. Informal.* Extremely tired; exhausted. See Synonyms at **tired.** [Probably from BUSH (wilderness).]

bush·el[1] (bo͝osh'əl) *n. Abbr.* **bu, bu., bsh.** **1. a.** A unit of volume or capacity in the U.S. Customary System, used in dry measure and equal to 4 pecks or 2,150.42 cubic inches. **b.** A unit of volume or capacity in the British Imperial System, used in dry and liquid measure, and equal to 2,219.36 cubic inches. See **measurement.** **2.** A container with the capacity of this unit. **3.** *Informal.* A large amount; a great deal. [Middle English *busshel, boyschel,* from Old French *boissiel,* from *boisse,* one sixth of a bushel, from Gaulish *bostia*† (unattested), handful.]

bush·el[2] (bo͝osh'əl) *tr.v.* **-eled** or **-elled, -eling** or **-elling, -els.** To alter or mend (clothing). [German *bosseln,* to mend, do small jobs, probably from Middle High German *bōzeln,* to knock, tap repeatedly, from *bōzen,* to knock, shove, from Old High German *bōzan.* See **bhau-** in Appendix.*] —**bush'el·er, bush'el·man** (-mən) *n.*

bush honeysuckle. Any of several North American shrubs of the genus *Diervilla,* having yellow flowers that turn reddish.

Bu·shi·do (bo͞o'shē-dō') *n.* Also **bu·shi·do.** The traditional code of the Japanese samurai, stressing self-discipline, bravery, and simple living. [Japanese *bushidō,* "the way of the warrior" : *bushi,* warrior, knight, from Chinese *wu*[3]*shih*[4], "man of arms" : *wu*[3], military + *shih*[4], man + *dō,* way, path, from Chinese *tao*[4].]

bush·ing (bo͝osh'ĭng) *n.* **1.** A fixed or removable metal lining used to constrain, guide, or reduce friction. **2.** An insulating lining for an aperture through which a conductor passes. **3.** An adapter threaded to permit joining of pipes with different diameters. [From earlier *bush,* from Middle Dutch *busse,* bushing of a wheel, wheel box, from Late Latin *buxis,* BOX.]

bush league. *Baseball Slang.* A minor league.

bush-league (bo͝osh'lēg') *adj. Slang.* **1.** *Baseball.* Of or belonging to a minor league. **2.** Second-rate. —**bush'-lea'guer** *n.*

Bush·man (bo͝osh'mən) *n., pl.* **-men** (-mĭn). **1.** A member of a nomadic Negroid people of southwestern Africa, characteristically of short stature. **2.** Any of several Khoisan languages spoken by this people. **3.** *Small* **b.** *Chiefly Australian.* A backwoodsman. [Translation of Afrikaans *boschjesman.*]

Burundi

bush·mas·ter (bo͝osh'măs'tər, -mäs'tər) *n.* A large, venomous snake, *Lachesis muta,* of tropical America, having brown and grayish markings.

Bush·nell (bo͝osh'nəl), **David.** 1742?–1824. American inventor of primitive submarine, "Bushnell's Turtle," used in Revolutionary War.

bush pig. A hog, *Potamochoerus porcus,* of southern Africa,

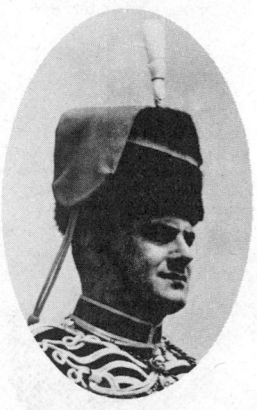

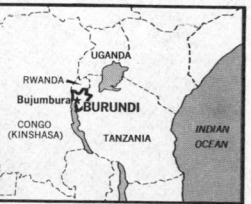

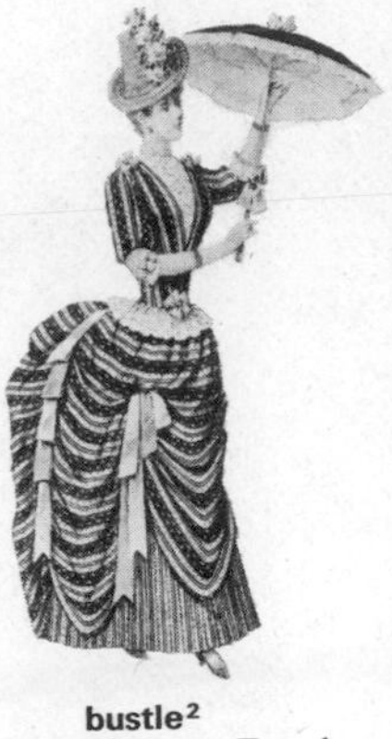

bustle[2]
Nineteenth-century French fashion plate showing a dress with a bustle

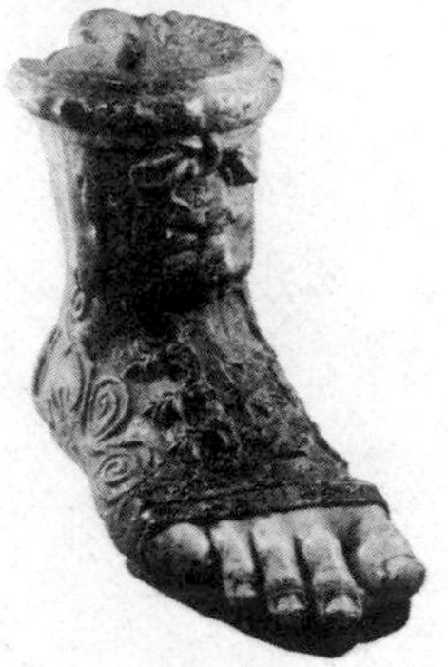

buskin
Fragment of an ancient Roman statue

bustard
Otis tarda

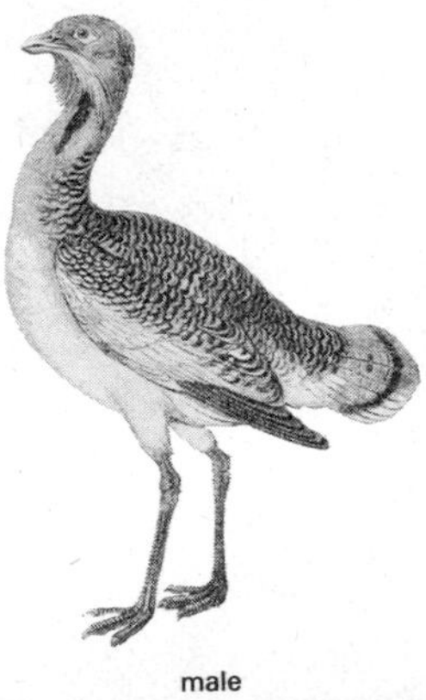

male

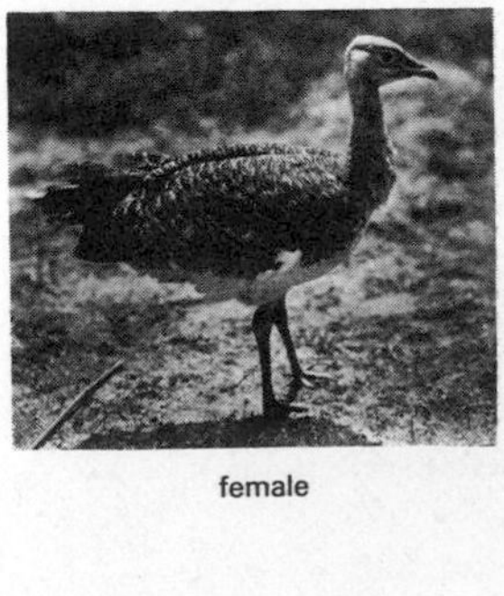

female

having long tufts of hair on the face and ears. [Translation of Afrikaans *bosvark.*]

bush poppy. The **tree poppy** *(see).*

bush·rang·er (bŏŏsh′rān′jər) *n.* **1.** One who lives in the back country or bush. **2.** *Australian.* An outlaw who lives in the bush.

bush·tit (bŏŏsh′tĭt′) *n.* Either of two small, long-tailed birds, *Psaltriparus minimus* or *P. melanotis,* of western North America, having predominantly gray plumage.

bush·whack (bŏŏsh′hwăk′) *v.* **-whacked, -whacking, -whacks.** —*intr.* **1.** To make one's way through thick woods by cutting away bushes and branches. **2.** To travel through the woods, as in scouting. **3.** To fight as a guerrilla in the back country or bush. —*tr.* To attack suddenly from a place of concealment; to ambush. [Back-formation from BUSHWHACKER.]

bush·whack·er (bŏŏsh′hwăk′ər) *n.* **1.** One that bushwhacks. **2.** A woodsman. **3.** A guerrilla, especially a Confederate guerrilla during the Civil War. [BUSH + whacker, one who whacks, from WHACK.]

bush·y (bŏŏsh′ē) *adj.* **-ier, -iest. 1.** Overgrown with bushes. **2.** Shaggy. —**bush′i·ly** *adv.* —**bush′i·ness** *n.*

bus·i·ly (bĭz′ə-lē) *adv.* In a busy manner.

busi·ness (bĭz′nĭs) *n. Abbr.* **bus. 1.** The occupation, work, or trade in which a person is engaged. **2.** Commercial, industrial, or professional dealings; the buying and selling of commodities or services. **3.** Any commercial establishment, such as a store or factory. **4.** Volume or amount of commercial trade. **5.** Commercial policy or practice. **6.** One's rightful or proper concern or interest; responsibility: *"The business of America is business."* (Calvin Coolidge). **7.** Serious work or endeavor that pertains to one's job: *went to Tokyo on business.* **8.** An affair or matter: *a peculiar business.* **9.** *Theater.* An incidental action performed by an actor on the stage to fill a pause between lines or to provide interesting detail. **10.** *Obsolete.* The condition of being busy. —**mean business.** To be in dead earnest. [Middle English *bissinesse,* diligence, state of being busy, Old English *bisignis,* care, solicitude, from *bisig,* BUSY.]

Synonyms: *business, industry, commerce, trade, traffic.* These nouns apply to forms of activity that have the objective of supplying commodities. *Business* pertains broadly to all gainful activity, though it usually excludes the professions and farming. *Industry* is the production and manufacture of goods and commodities, especially on a large scale, and *commerce* and *trade,* the exchange and distribution of commodities. Often *commerce* is applied to exchange of commodities for money, as within a country, while *trade* refers to exchange of commodities for commodities, as between countries. *Traffic* may suggest illegal trade, as in narcotics.

busi·ness·like (bĭz′nĭs-līk′) *adj.* **1.** Methodical; systematic; efficient. **2.** Purposeful; earnest. —**busi′ness·like′ness** *n.*

busi·ness·man (bĭz′nĭs-măn′) *n., pl.* **-men** (-mĕn′). A man engaged in business.

busi·ness·wom·an (bĭz′nĭs-wŏŏm′ən) *n., pl.* **-women** (-wĭm′ĭn). A woman engaged in business.

busk[1] (bŭsk) *n.* **1.** A thin, flexible strip of wood, whalebone, plastic, or metal sewn in a woman's undergarment as stiffening. **2.** *Regional.* A corset. [French *busc,* from Italian *busco,* splinter, from Germanic. See **busk-** in Appendix.*]

busk[2] (bŭsk) *intr.v.* **busked, busking, busks.** *British.* To entertain by singing and dancing, especially in streets and public places. [Origin unknown.] —**busk′er** *n.*

bus·kin (bŭs′kĭn) *n.* **1.** A foot and leg covering reaching halfway to the knee, resembling a laced half boot. **2.** A thick-soled laced half boot, worn by actors of Greek and Roman tragedies. Compare **sock. 3.** Tragedy. [Old French *bouzequin, brousequin,* akin to Spanish *borzeguí,* Italian *borzacchino*†.]

bus·man (bŭs′mən) *n., pl.* **-men** (-mĭn). One who runs a bus.

busman's holiday. *Informal.* A vacation on which a person engages in recreation similar to his usual work. [A bus driver might go for a drive on a holiday.]

Bus·ra, Bus·rah. See **Basra.**

buss (bŭs) *v.* **bussed, bussing, busses.** *Regional.* —*tr.* To kiss with a loud smacking sound. —*intr.* To kiss loudly. —*n. Regional.* A smacking kiss. [Perhaps imitative.]

bus·ses. 1. Alternate plural of **bus. 2.** Alternate third person singular of **bus.**

bust[1] (bŭst) *n.* **1. a.** A woman's bosom. **b.** *Archaic.* The human chest. See Usage note at **breast. 2.** A piece of sculpture representing a person's head, shoulders, and upper chest. [French *buste,* from Italian *busto,* piece of sculpture, probably from Latin *būstum,* place where the bodies of the dead were burned and buried, tomb, past participle of *būrere* (unattested), to burn, short for *ambūrere,* to burn around, scorch : AMBI- + *ūrere,* to burn (see **eus-** in Appendix*).]

bust[2] (bŭst) *v.* **busted, busting, busts.** *Slang.* —*tr.* **1.** To burst or break. **2.** To break up (a trust or monopoly). **3.** To break or tame (a horse). **4.** To cause to become bankrupt or short of money. **5.** To reduce the rank of; demote. **6.** To hit or punch. **7.** To place under arrest. —*intr.* **1.** To burst or break. **2.** To become bankrupt or short of money. —*n. Slang.* **1.** A failure; a flop. **2.** A state of bankruptcy. **3.** A time or period of widespread financial depression. Compare **boom. 4.** A punch or blow. **5.** A spree. **6.** An arrest. [Variant of BURST.]

bus·tard (bŭs′tərd) *n.* Any of various large Old World birds of the family Otididae, frequenting open, grassy regions. [Middle English *bustarde,* possibly from Norman French *bustarde* (unattested), blend of Old French *bistarde* and *oustarde,* both perhaps from Latin *avis tarda,* "slow bird" : *avis,* bird (see **awi-** in Appendix*) + *tarda,* feminine of *tardus,* slow (see **tardy**).]

bust·er (bŭs′tər) *n. Slang.* **1.** One who bursts or breaks up: *a crime buster.* **2.** One who breaks horses; a broncobuster. **3.** Something especially large or remarkable. **4.** A spree. **5.** *Often capital* **B.** A man or boy. Used in direct address.

bus·tle[1] (bŭs′əl) *v.* **-tled, -tling, -tles.** —*intr.* To hurry energetically and busily. —*tr.* To cause to hurry. —*n.* Excited activity; commotion; stir. [Probably a variant of obsolete *buskle,* frequentative of dialectal *busk,* to prepare, from Middle English *busken,* from Old Norse *buāsk* : *būa,* to prepare (see **bheu-** in Appendix*) + *-sk,* reflexive ending (see **seu-**[2] in Appendix*).]

bus·tle[2] (bŭs′əl) *n.* **1.** A frame or pad to support and distend the fullness of the back of a woman's skirt. **2.** A bow, peplum, or gathering of material at the back of a skirt below the waist. [Perhaps from German *Buschel*†, a bunch, pad.]

bust·y (bŭs′tē) *adj.* **-ier, -iest.** *Informal.* Full-bosomed.

bus·y (bĭz′ē) *adj.* **-ier, -iest. 1.** Actively engaged in some form of work; occupied. **2.** Crowded with activity: *a busy morning.* **3.** Meddlesome; prying. **4.** Temporarily in use. Said of a telephone line. **5.** Cluttered with minute detail to the point of distracting attention from the focal point: *a busy design.* —*tr.v.* **busied, -ying, -ies.** To make busy; occupy. Often used reflexively. [Middle English *bisy, busy,* Old English *bysig, bisig,* akin to Middle Low German *besich*†.] —**bus′y·ness** *n.*

Synonyms: *busy, industrious, diligent, assiduous, sedulous.* All these words suggest active or sustained effort to accomplish something. *Busy* primarily applies to one engaged in present activity, without definite implication of kind, continuity, or duration of activity. *Industrious* implies continuing activity and a natural inclination to be so engaged. *Diligent* suggests intense activity in the accomplishment of a specific goal; often it implies keen interest in work of one's choosing. *Assiduous* emphasizes sustained devotion to work. *Sedulous* adds to assiduity the sense of earnest, persistent, painstaking labor.

bus·y·bod·y (bĭz′ē-bŏd′ē) *n., pl.* **-ies.** A person who meddles or pries into the affairs of others.

busy signal. A series of sharp buzzing tones heard over a telephone when the number dialed is in use.

bus·y·work (bĭz′ē-wûrk′) *n.* Activity meant to take up time but not necessarily to yield productive results.

but (bŭt; *unstressed* bət) *conj.* **1.** On the contrary. **2.** Contrary to expectation; however; yet. **3.** Except; save. See Usage note below. **4.** With the exception that; except that. Used to introduce a dependent clause with *that* expressed: *They should have resisted but that they lacked courage.* **5.** Without the result that: *It never rains but it pours.* **6.** Other than: *I have no goal but to end war.* **7.** That. Often used after a negative. See Usage note below. **8.** That . . . not. Used after a negative or question: *There never is a tax law presented but someone will oppose it.* **9.** Who . . . not; which . . . not: *None came to him but were treated well.* **10.** *Archaic.* Unless; if not: *"Beshrew me but I love her heartily"* (Shakespeare). **11.** *Archaic & Nonstandard.* Than: *"No sooner acquainted my brother, but he immediately wanted to propose it."* (Fielding). —*prep.* With the exception of; barring; save. See Usage note below. —**but for.** Were it not for: *But for luck, he would still be poor.* —*adv.* No more than; only; just. See Usage note below. —**all but.** Nearly; almost: *His poem is all but finished.* —*n.* An objection, restriction, or exception: *no ifs, ands, or buts.* [Middle English *bute, but* (conjunction and adverb), Old English *būtan, būte* (conjunction and preposition). See **ud-** in Appendix.*]

Synonyms: *but, however, still, yet, nevertheless.* Each of these words introduces a statement in opposition to what precedes it. *But,* which notes but does not stress the opposition, is the most widely applicable: *He was ill, but he kept the appointment.* In the same example, *however* would soften the contrast between the two elements: *Still, yet,* and *nevertheless,* in the same example, emphasize contrast.

Usage: *But* in the sense of *except* is often followed by a pronoun in constructions such as *No one heard it but me* (less often, *I*). The choice of the proper pronoun depends on whether one construes *but* as a preposition or as a conjunction. When *but* and the word that follows it occur at the end of the sentence, *but* is usually considered a preposition, and the word that follows it is in the objective case. In the preceding example, 60 per cent of the Usage Panel term *but me* the only acceptable form; 29 per cent accept either pronoun, and 11 per cent specify *I.* In the following typical example, *but* is construed as a conjunction, and the pronoun agrees in case with the word that precedes *but.* Thus, *No one* (subject) *but I* (nominative) *heard it.* In the construction *but that* (for *that*), *but* is usually redundant: *There is no doubt but that he will try* (omit *but*). This example, with *but that,* is unacceptable in writing to 66 per cent of the Usage Panel. *But what* is even more objectionable: *There is no doubt but what he will try* (substitute *that* for *but what*). The preceding example, with *but what,* is unacceptable in written usage to 95 per cent of the Panel, who also reject *There is no one but what would find it distracting* (properly *no one who would not find*). *But,* as a conjunction synonymous with *however, still, yet,* or *nevertheless,* should not be used in combination with any of those terms in a single sentence, as in *He was tired, but he went nevertheless* (eliminate *nevertheless*). When *but* is an adverb meaning *only,* it is similarly redundant in combination with *only: They have but only a short time* (eliminate *but* or *only*). In the same example, *but just* and *but merely* would be equally objectionable. Beware also of the form of double negation common to constructions involving *but* in the sense of *only,* as in *It won't take but an hour* (correctly *It will take but an hour*). See Usage notes at **cannot, help.**

but-. Indicates a chemical compound containing four carbon atoms; for example, **butane.** [From BUTYRIC.]

bu·ta·di·ene (byo͞o′tə-dī′ēn′, -dī-ēn′) *n.* A colorless, highly flammable hydrocarbon, C_4H_6, obtained from petroleum and used in the manufacture of synthetic rubber. [BUTA(NE) + DI- + -ENE.]

bu·tane (byo͞o′tān′) *n.* Either of two isomers of a gaseous hydrocarbon, C_4H_{10}, produced synthetically from petroleum and used as a household fuel, refrigerant, aerosol propellant, and in the manufacture of synthetic rubber. [BUT- + -ANE.]

bu·ta·no·ic acid (byo͞o′tə-nō′ĭk). *Chemistry.* **Butyric acid** *(see).* [From BUTAN(E) + -IC.]

bu·ta·nol (byo͞o′tə-nôl′, -nōl′) *n.* **1.** A butyl alcohol derived naturally from the bacterial fermentation of grain and used as a solvent for resins, in plasticizers, hydraulic fluids, and as a dehydrating agent. **2.** An isomeric alcohol derived from the cracking of petroleum or natural gas and used as a solvent in varnishes, lacquers, and paint removers. [BUTAN(E) + -OL.]

bu·ta·none (byo͞o′tə-nōn′) *n.* A colorless, flammable ketone, C_4H_8O, used in lacquers, paint removers, cements and adhesives, celluloid, and cleaning fluids. Also called "methyl ethyl ketone." [BUTAN(E) + -ONE.]

butch (bo͝och) *n. Slang.* A female homosexual with mannish or aggressive traits. [From *butch,* a haircut usually associated with young ruffians, from *Butch,* a pet name for a young boy.] **—butch** *adj.*

butch·er (bo͝och′ər) *n.* **1.** One who slaughters and dresses animals for food or market. **2.** One who sells meats. **3.** One guilty of cruel or pointless killing. **4.** A vender of candy, magazines, and the like on a train. **5.** One who bungles; botcher. *—tr.v.* **butchered, -ering, -ers. 1.** To slaughter or dress (animals) for market. **2.** To kill cruelly or pointlessly. **3.** To spoil by botching; to bungle. [Middle English *bo(u)cher,* from Norman French, from Old French *bouchier,* from *boc,* he-goat. See **bhugo-** in Appendix.*] **—butch′er·er** *n.*

butch·er·bird (bo͝och′ər-bûrd′) *n.* Any of various birds that impale their prey on thorns; especially, a **shrike** *(see).*

butcher's broom. A shrub, *Ruscus aculeatus,* native to Europe, having stiff, prickle-tipped, flattened stems resembling true leaves. [Formerly used as a broom by butchers.]

butch·er·y (bo͝och′ə-rē) *n., pl.* **-ies. 1.** The trade of a butcher. **2.** A slaughterhouse. **3.** Wanton or cruel killing; carnage.

Bute (byo͞ot). **1.** An island of Scotland, 46 square miles in area, lying in the Firth of Clyde. **2.** Also **Bute·shire** (byo͞ot′shîr, -shər). A county of Scotland comprising this island, Arran, and others. Population, 22,000. County seat, Rothesay.

Bu·te·nandt (bo͞o′tə-nänt′), **Adolf Friedrich.** Born 1903. German chemist; shared the Nobel Prize in chemistry (1939) for work on sex hormones with Leopold **Ružička** *(see);* declined by order of Nazi government.

bu·te·o (byo͞o′tē-ō′) *n., pl.* **-os.** Any of various hawks of the genus *Buteo,* characterized by broad wings and broad, rounded tails. [New Latin, from Latin *būteō,* a kind of falcon or hawk. See **beu-**[2] in Appendix.*]

but·ler (bŭt′lər) *n.* A male head servant in a household, in charge of the plate, table, and liquors. [Middle English *buteler,* servant in charge of the wine cellar, from Old French *bouteillier,* a bottle bearer, from *bouteille, botele,* BOTTLE.]

But·ler (bŭt′lər), **Benjamin Franklin.** 1818–1893. American political and military leader; a Union general in the Civil War.

But·ler (bŭt′lər), **Samuel**[1]. 1612–1680. English poet and epigrammatist; author of *Hudibras.*

But·ler (bŭt′lər), **Samuel**[2]. 1835–1902. English novelist; author of *The Way of All Flesh.*

But·le·rov (bo͞ot′lə-rôf′), **Alexander Mikhailovich.** 1828–1886. Russian chemist; first noted chemical structure of compounds.

butler's pantry. A serving and storage room between the kitchen and the dining room.

butt[1] (bŭt) *v.* **butted, butting, butts.** *—tr.* To hit or push against with the head or horns; ram. *—intr.* **1.** To hit or push something with the head or horns. **2.** To project forward or out. **—butt in** (or **into**). *Informal.* To interfere or meddle; intrude. *—n.* A push or blow with the head or horns. [Middle English *butten,* from Norman French *buter, boter,* from Common Romance *bottare* (unattested), from Germanic. See **bhau-** in Appendix.*]

butt[2] (bŭt) *v.* **butted, butting, butts.** *—tr.* To attach the ends of; abut. *—intr.* To be joined at the ends. *—n.* **1. a.** The act of joining two objects end to end. **b.** A **butt joint** *(see).* **2.** A **butt hinge** *(see).* [From BUTT (end).]

butt[3] (bŭt) *n.* **1.** A person or thing serving as an object of ridicule or contempt. **2.** A target. **3.** *Plural.* A target range. **4.** A mound of earth, a wall, or another obstacle behind a target for stopping the shot. **5.** *Obsolete.* A limit; goal. [Middle English *butte,* target, from Old French *but*†.]

butt[4] (bŭt) *n.* **1.** The larger or thicker end of something: *the butt of a rifle.* **2.** An unburned end, as of a cigarette. **3.** A short or broken remnant; a stub. **4.** *Slang.* A cigarette. **5.** *Informal.* The buttocks; the rear end. [Middle English *but, butte,* thicker end, from Germanic, possibly akin to Old Norse *būtr,* block of wood. See **bhau-** in Appendix.*]

butt[5] (bŭt) *n.* **1.** A large cask. **2.** A unit of volume equal to 126 U.S. gallons. [Middle English, from Norman French *but,* variant of Old French *bot, bout,* from Late Latin *buttis.* See **bottle.**]

butte (byo͞ot) *n.* A hill rising abruptly above the surrounding area and having sloping sides and a flat top. [French, from Old French *but,* BUTT (mound behind targets).]

Butte (byo͞ot). A city and important mining center in southwestern Montana. Population, 28,000.

but·ter[1] (bŭt′ər) *n.* **1.** A soft, yellowish or whitish emulsion of butterfat, water, air, and sometimes salt, churned from milk or cream and processed for use in cooking and as a food. **2.** Any of various similar substances, especially: **a.** A spread made from fruit, nuts, or other foods, as *apple butter.* **b.** A vegetable fat having a nearly solid consistency at ordinary temperatures, as *cocoa butter.* **3.** *Informal.* Flattery. *—tr.v.* **buttered, -tering, -ters. 1.** To put butter on or in. **2.** *Informal.* To flatter. Usually used with *up.* [Middle English *buter(e),* Old English *butere,* from West Germanic, from Latin *būtӯrum,* from Greek *bouturon,* "cow cheese" : *bous,* cow (see **gwou-** in Appendix*) + *turos,* cheese (see **teuə-** in Appendix*).]

butt·er[2] (bŭt′ər) *n.* One that butts with the head or horns.

but·ter-and-eggs (bŭt′ər-ən-ĕgz′) *n.* Plural in form, used with a singular or plural verb. A North American plant, *Linaria vulgaris,* having numerous narrow leaves and a spike of spurred pale-yellow and orange flowers. Also called "toadflax."

but·ter·ball (bŭt′ər-bôl′) *n.* **1.** A ball of butter. **2.** *Informal.* A fat or chubby person. **3.** A duck, the **bufflehead** *(see).*

butter bean. 1. The **wax bean** *(see).* **2.** *Regional.* The **lima bean** *(see).* [From the yellow pods of the wax bean.]

but·ter·bur (bŭt′ər-bûr′) *n.* Any of several plants of the genus *Petasites,* having woolly leaves and stems and fragrant whitish or purple flowers. [Its leaves are said to have been used to wrap butter.]

but·ter·cup (bŭt′ər-kŭp′) *n.* Any of various plants of the genus *Ranunculus,* characteristically having glossy yellow flowers. *R. acris,* native to Europe, is common throughout North America. Some species are also called "crowfoot."

but·ter·fat (bŭt′ər-făt′) *n.* The oily content of milk from which butter is made, consisting largely of the glycerides of oleic, stearic, and palmitic acids.

but·ter·fin·gers (bŭt′ər-fĭng′gərz) *n.* Plural in form, used with a singular verb. A clumsy or awkward person who drops things. **—but′ter·fin′gered** *adj.*

but·ter·fish (bŭt′ər-fĭsh′) *n., pl.* **butterfish** or **-fishes. 1.** A marine food fish, *Poronotus triacanthus,* of the North American Atlantic coast, having a flattened body. **2.** Any of various similar or related fishes. [From its slippery mucous coating.]

but·ter·fly (bŭt′ər-flī′) *n., pl.* **-flies. 1.** Any of various insects of the order Lepidoptera, characteristically having slender bodies, knobbed antennae, and four broad, usually colorful wings. **2.** A frivolous pleasure-seeker: *a social butterfly.* **3.** The **butterfly stroke** *(see).* [Middle English *butterflie,* from Old English *buttorflēoge* : *buter(e),* BUTTER + FLY, perhaps from the belief that butterflies steal milk and butter.]

butterfly bush. Any of several shrubs of the genus *Buddleia,* cultivated for their clusters of purplish or white flowers.

butterfly fish. Any of various tropical marine fishes of the family Chaetodontidae, most of which are brightly colored.

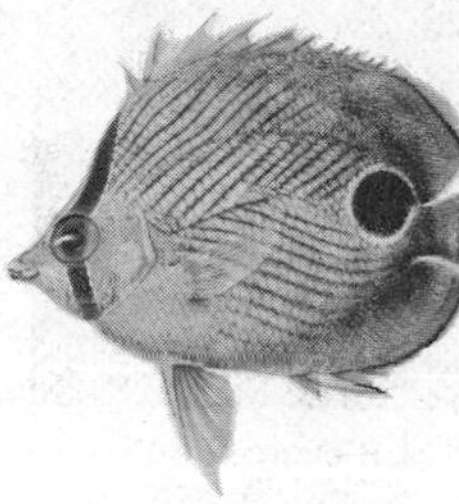

butterfly fish
Chaetodon capistratus

butterfly pea. A twining vine, *Clitoria mariana,* of the eastern United States, having compound leaves and pale-blue flowers.

butterfly stroke. A swimming stroke, a variation of the breast stroke, in which both arms are drawn upward out of the water and forward with a simultaneous up-and-down kick of the feet.

butterfly table. A small drop-leaf table, the leaves of which have brackets shaped like a butterfly's wings.

butterfly valve. 1. A disk turning on a diametrical axis inside a pipe, used as a throttle valve or damper. **2.** A valve composed of two semicircular plates hinged on a common spindle, used to permit flow in one direction only. [Its action somewhat resembles that of a butterfly's wings.]

butterfly weed. A North American plant, *Asclepias tuberosa,* having flat-topped clusters of bright-orange flowers. Also called "orange milkweed," "pleurisy root."

but·ter·milk (bŭt′ər-mĭlk′) *n.* **1.** The sour liquid that remains after the butterfat has been removed from whole milk or cream by churning. **2.** Milk soured with certain microorganisms.

but·ter·nut (bŭt′ər-nŭt′) *n.* **1.** A tree, *Juglans cinerea,* of eastern North America, having compound leaves and egg-shaped nuts. Also called "white walnut." **2.** The edible, oily nut of this tree. **3.** The hard, grayish-brown wood of this tree. **4.** The bark of this tree, or an extract obtained from it, formerly used as a laxative. **5.** A brownish color or dye obtained from butternut bark. **6.** *Plural.* Clothing dyed with butternut extract. **7.** *Informal.* A Confederate soldier or partisan in the Civil War. **8.** The **souari nut** *(see).* [From the oiliness of the nut. Sense 7, from homemade uniforms dyed with butternut extract.]

but·ter·scotch (bŭt′ər-skŏch′) *n.* **1.** A syrup, sauce, or flavoring made by melting butter, brown sugar, and sometimes artificial flavorings. **2.** A hard, sticky candy made from these ingredients. [Perhaps originally made in Scotland.]

but·ter·weed (bŭt′ər-wēd′) *n.* **1.** A plant, *Senecio glabellus,* of the southern and central United States, having yellow flowers. **2.** The **horseweed** *(see).* [From its yellow flowers.]

but·ter·wort (bŭt′ər-wûrt′, -wôrt′) *n.* Any plant of the genus *Pinguicula;* especially, *P. vulgaris,* of wet places, having violet-blue, spurred flowers and fleshy, greasy leaves. Sometimes called "sheepweed." [From the oiliness of the leaves.]

but·ter·y[1] (bŭt′ə-rē) *adj.* **1.** Resembling, containing, or spread with butter. **2.** *Informal.* Effusively and insincerely flattering. **—but′ter·i·ness** *n.*

but·ter·y[2] (bŭt′ə-rē) *n., pl.* **-ies.** *Chiefly British.* **1.** A pantry or wine cellar. **2.** A place in colleges and universities where students may buy provisions. [Middle English *boteri, buttrie,* from Old French *boterie,* from *bot,* BUTT (cask).]

butt hinge. A hinge composed of two plates attached to abutting surfaces of a door and door jamb and joined by a pin. Also called "butt." [From BUTT (abut).]

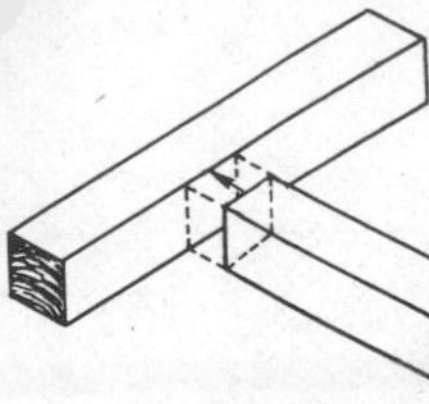

butt joint

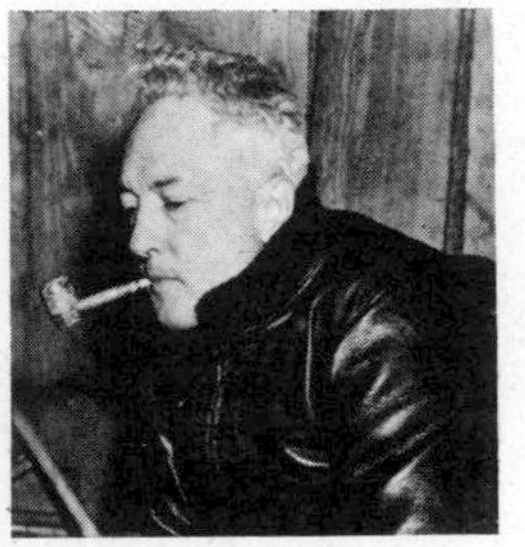

Richard Byrd
At Little America, Antarctica, in 1947

butt joint. A joint formed by two abutting surfaces placed squarely together. Also called "butt." [From BUTT (abut).]
but·tock (bŭt′ək) *n.* **1.** Either of the two rounded parts of the rump. **2.** *Plural.* The rump. Also called "nates." [Middle English, possibly from Old English *buttuc,* end, strip of land, ridge. See **bhau-** in Appendix.*]
but·ton (bŭt′n) *n.* **1.** A generally disk-shaped fastener used to join two parts of a garment by fitting through a buttonhole or loop. **2.** Such an object used for decoration. **3.** Any of various objects of similar appearance, especially: **a.** A push-button switch. **b.** *Fencing.* The tip of a foil. **c.** A fused metal or glass globule. **4.** Any of various knoblike organic structures, especially: **a.** The head of a small mushroom. **b.** The tip of a rattlesnake's tail. **5.** A round flat emblem bearing a design or printed information and pinned to the front of a garment. **6.** *Slang.* The end of the chin. **—on the button.** *Informal.* Exactly; precisely. **—***v.* **buttoned, -toning, -tons.** **—***tr.* **1.** To furnish with a button or buttons. **2.** To fasten with a button or buttons. **—***intr.* To admit of being fastened with a button or buttons. [Middle English *boton,* from Old French *bouton,* bud, button, from *bouter,* to strike against, thrust, pierce, from Common Romance *bottare* (unattested), from Germanic. See **bhau-** in Appendix.*] **—but′ton·er** *n.* **—but′ton·y** *adj.*
but·ton·ball (bŭt′n-bôl′) *n.* A North American tree, the **sycamore** *(see).* [From its buttonlike fruit.]
but·ton·bush (bŭt′n-bo͝osh′) *n.* A North American shrub, *Cephalanthus occidentalis,* having spherical clusters of small white flowers.
but·ton·hole (bŭt′n-hōl′) *n.* **1.** A slit in a garment or piece of fabric for fastening a button. **2.** *Chiefly British.* A boutonniere. **—***tr.v.* **buttonholed, -holing, -holes.** **1.** To make a buttonhole in. **2.** To sew with a buttonhole stitch. **3.** To accost and detain in conversation. **—but′ton·hol′er** *n.*
buttonhole stitch. A loop stitch that forms a reinforced edge, as around a buttonhole. Also called "close stitch."
but·ton·hook (bŭt′n-ho͝ok′) *n.* A small hook for buttoning shoes or gloves.
but·ton·mold (bŭt′n-mōld′) *n.* The core of a covered button.
but·ton·quail (bŭt′n-kwāl′) *n.* Any of various small, quaillike Old World birds of the family Turnicidae.
button snakeroot. **1.** A plant, the **blazing star** *(see).* **2.** A plant, the **rattlesnake master** *(see).* [Probably from its buttonlike umbels.]
but·ton·wood (bŭt′n-wo͝od′) *n.* A North American tree, the **sycamore** *(see).* [From the buttonlike fruit.]
butt plate. A metal plate on the butt end of a gunstock.
but·tress (bŭt′rĭs) *n.* **1.** A structure, usually brick or stone, built against a wall for support or reinforcement. See **flying buttress.** **2.** Anything resembling a buttress. **3.** A horny growth on the heel of a horse's hoof. **4.** Anything that serves to support, prop, or reinforce. **—***tr.v.* **buttressed, -tressing, -tresses.** **1.** To support or reinforce with a buttress. **2.** To sustain, prop, or bolster: *buttress an argument with evidence.* [Middle English *butres, boteras,* from Old French *bouterez,* shortened from *(ars) bouterez,* thrusting (arch), from *bouter,* to strike against, butt, from Common Romance *bottare* (unattested), from Germanic. See **bhau-** in Appendix.*]
butt shaft. A blunt, unbarbed arrow.
butt weld. A welded butt joint.
butt-weld (bŭt′wĕld′) *tr.v.* **-welded, -welding, -welds.** To join by a butt weld.
Bu·tung (bo͞o′to͝ong). An island of Indonesia, about 2,000 square miles in area, off the southeastern coast of Sulawesi. Population, 253,000.
bu·tyl (byo͞ot′l, byo͞o′tĭl) *n.* A hydrocarbon radical, C_4H_9, with the structure of butane and valence 1. [BUT- + -YL.]
butyl alcohol. One of four isomeric alcohols widely used as solvents and in organic synthesis, each having the formula C_4H_9OH.
bu·ty·lene (byo͞ot′l-ēn′) *n.* Any of three gaseous isomeric ethylene hydrocarbons, C_4H_8, used principally in making synthetic rubbers. [BUTYL + -ENE.]
butyl rubber. A synthetic rubber produced by copolymerization of a butylene (98 per cent) with isoprene or butadiene (2 per cent), outstanding in gaseous impermeability and used in tires, inner tubes, insulation, and as a binder fuel in solid propellants for rockets.
bu·ty·ra·ceous (byo͞o′tə-rā′shəs) *adj.* Resembling butter in appearance, consistency, or chemical properties; buttery. [Latin *būtȳrum,* BUTTER + -ACEOUS.]
bu·tyr·al·de·hyde (byo͞o′tə-răl′də-hīd′) *n.* A transparent, extremely flammable liquid, $CH_3(CH_2)_2CHO$, used in synthesizing resins. [BUTYR(IC) + ALDEHYDE.]
bu·ty·rate (byo͞o′tə-rāt′) *n.* A salt or ester of butyric acid. [BUTYR(IC) + -ATE.]
bu·tyr·ic (byo͞o-tĭr′ĭk) *adj.* **1.** Of, pertaining to, containing, or derived from butter. **2.** Of, pertaining to, or derived from butyric acid. [From Latin *būtȳrum,* BUTTER.]
butyric acid. Either of two colorless isomeric acids, C_3H_7COOH, occurring in animal milk fats and used in disinfectants, emulsifying agents, and pharmaceuticals. Also called "butanoic acid."
bu·ty·rin (byo͞o′tə-rĭn) *n.* Any one of three isomeric glyceryl esters of butyric acid, naturally present in butter. [Earlier *butirine,* from French : Latin *būtȳrum,* BUTTER + -INE.]
bux·om (bŭk′səm) *adj.* **1.** Healthily plump and ample of figure. Said of a woman. **2.** *Archaic.* Lively; blithe; vivacious. **3.** *Obsolete.* Obedient; yielding. [Earlier, flexible, gay, comely, Middle English *buhsum, buxum,* obedient, humble, bending, from Old English *gebūhsum* (unattested), easy to bend, pliable, from *būgan,* to bend. See **bheug-**[3] in Appendix.*] **—bux′om·ly** *adv.* **—bux′om·ness** *n.*
Bux·te·hu·de (bo͝oks′tə-ho͞o′də), **Dietrich.** 1637–1707. Swedish composer and organist; resident in Germany.
buy (bī) *v.* **bought** (bôt), **bought** or *regional* **boughten** (bôt′n), **buying, buys.** **—***tr.* **1.** To acquire in exchange for money or its equivalent; to purchase. **2.** To be capable of purchasing: *"nor was it for . . . money or what money buys that I burned"* (Virgilia Peterson). **3.** To acquire by sacrifice, exchange, or trade. **4.** To bribe. **5.** *Slang.* To accept the truth or feasibility of. **—***intr.* To purchase goods; act as a purchaser: *"since the system buys in bulk it is able to obtain larger discounts"* (John Tebbel). **—buy in** (or **into**). **1.** To purchase stock or interest, as in a company. **2.** To purchase back for the original owner, as at an auction when the bidding is low. **3.** *Slang.* To pay money in exchange for joining (a social or business group). **—buy off.** To bribe in order to proceed without interference, or to be exempted from an obligation or from prosecution. **—buy out.** To purchase the controlling stock, business rights, or interests of. **—buy up.** To purchase all that is available of. **—***n.* **1.** Anything bought or capable of being bought; a purchase. See Usage note below. **2.** *Informal.* Something that is underpriced; a bargain. See Usage note below. [Buy, bought (past tense), bought (past participle); Middle English *byen* (earlier *byggen*), *bo(g)hte, (i)bo(g)ht,* Old English *bycgan, bohte, geboht,* from Germanic *bugjan* (unattested).] **—buy′a·ble** *adj.*
Usage: *Buy,* as a noun denoting a purchase or bargain, is appropriate only to commercial usage. Its use in a more general context, as in the following example, is unacceptable in writing to 61 per cent of the Usage Panel: *Luxury gained at the expense of liberty is never a good buy.*
buy·er (bī′ər) *n.* **1.** One who buys goods; a customer. **2.** A purchasing agent, especially one who buys for a retail store.
buyers' market. *Economics.* A market condition characterized by prices at or near cost, occurring when the supply of commodities exceeds market demand.
buzz[1] (bŭz) *v.* **buzzed, buzzing, buzzes.** **—***intr.* **1.** To make a low droning or vibrating sound like that of a bee. **2.** To talk excitedly in low tones. **3.** To move quickly and busily; bustle. **—***tr.* **1.** To cause to buzz: *hornets buzzing their wings.* **2.** To utter (gossip) in a rapid, low voice. **3.** *Informal.* To fly low over: *The plane buzzed the control tower.* **4.** To signal (a person) with a buzzer. **5.** *Informal.* To telephone (a person). **—***n.* **1.** A rapidly vibrating, humming, or droning sound. **2.** A low murmur, as of many hushed voices speaking at once: *a buzz of talk.* **3.** *Informal.* A telephone call. **4.** *Slang.* A pleasant intoxication, as from alcohol. [Middle English *bussen* (attested only in the verbal noun *bussyng*), to drone (imitative).]
buzz[2] (bŭz) *tr.v.* **buzzed, buzzing, buzzes.** *British.* To drink (a bottle or cup) to the last drop. [From BUZZ (sound).]
buz·zard (bŭz′ərd) *n.* **1.** Any of various North American vultures, such as the **turkey buzzard** *(see).* **2.** *Chiefly British.* Any hawk of the genus *Buteo.* **3.** An avaricious or unpleasant person. [Middle English *busard,* from Old French, alteration of *buson,* from Latin *būteō.* See **beu-**[2] in Appendix.*]
Buz·zards Bay (bŭz′ərdz). An inlet of the Atlantic Ocean, 30 miles long, in southeastern Massachusetts.
buzz bomb. A **robot bomb** *(see)* of World War II. [From the buzzing noise made by its pulsejet engine.]
buzz·er (bŭz′ər) *n.* Any of various electric signaling devices that make a buzzing sound, such as a doorbell.
buzz saw. A **circular saw** *(see).* [From the sound it makes.]
B.V. Blessed Virgin.
B.V.M. Blessed Virgin Mary.
bvt. brevet; brevetted.
B.W.A. British West Africa.
B.W.I. British West Indies.
bx. box.
by[1] (bī) *prep.* **1.** Next to; close to: *the window by the door.* **2.** With the use of; through: *He came by the back road.* **3.** Up to and beyond; past: *He drove by the house.* **4.** In the period of; during: *sleeping by day.* **5.** Not later than: *by 5:00 P.M.* **6.** In the amount of: *letters by the thousands.* **7.** To the extent of: *shorter by two inches.* **8.** According to: *by his own account.* **9.** In the presence or name of. Used in oaths: *I swear by the book.* **10.** Through the agency or action of: *killed by a bullet.* **11.** In succession to; after: *day by day.* **12.** In behalf of; for: *He does well by his employees.* **13.** Used to link certain expressions to be taken together and indicating: **a.** Multiplication of quantities. **b.** Coordination of measurements: *a room 12 by 18 feet.* **c.** Alteration of a compass direction: *north by northeast.* **—by the way.** Incidentally. **—***adv.* **1.** On hand; nearby: *stand by.* **2.** Aside; away: *He put it by for later.* **3.** Up to, alongside, and past: *The car raced by.* **4.** Into the past: *as years go by.* **—by and large.** On the whole; for the most part. [Middle English *by,* Old English *bī, bi, be.* See **ambhi** in Appendix.*]
Synonyms: *by, through, with.* These prepositions indicate the agency or means by which something is accomplished. *By* usually introduces directly the agent (person) or agency (power): *named by him; struck by lightning. Through,* the least direct, is often followed by a person, in the sense of intermediary *(apply through a friend),* or by a word naming a condition as cause or means *(fail through indecision). With* is usually followed by an inanimate object denoting physical instrument *(fight with a sword)* or instrumentality *(soothe with kind words).*
by[2]**.** Variant of **bye.**
by–, bye–. Indicates: **1.** Close at hand or near; for example, **bystander.** **2.** Out of the way or aside; for example, **byroad,**

bye-election. 3. Secondary or incidental; for example, **by-product.** [Middle English *by-, bi-,* from BY.]

by and by. At a later time; before long. [Middle English, side by side, again and again, one by one, from BY.]

by-and-by (bī′ən-bī′) *n.* **1.** Some future time or occasion. **2.** The hereafter.

by-bid-der (bī′bĭd′ər) *n.* A person who bids at an auction to raise prices for the owner.

by-blow (bī′blō′) *n.* **1.** An indirect or chance blow. **2.** An illegitimate child; a bastard. [Sense 2 from the idea of a child begotten incidentally or by chance.]

Byd-goszcz (bĭd′gôshch). *German* **Brom-berg** (brôm′běrk′). A major industrial city in northern Poland, near the Vistula, 140 miles northwest of Warsaw. Population, 250,000.

bye (bī) *n.* Also **by. 1.** A secondary matter; side issue. **2.** *Sports.* The position of one who draws no opponent for a round in a tournament and so advances to the next round. **3.** *Golf.* One or more holes remaining unplayed at the end of a match. **4.** *Cricket.* A run made on a ball not touched by the batsman. —**by the bye.** Incidentally; by the way. —*adj.* Also **by.** Secondary; incidental. [From BY (aside, hence, "secondary").]

bye-. Variant of **by-.**

bye-bye (bī′bī′) *interj. Informal.* Good-by. [Baby-talk form for (GOOD-)BY.]

Bye-la-ya (byĕ′lə-yə). Also **Be-la-ya.** A navigable river of the Soviet Union, rising in the southern Urals in the Bashkir A.S.S.R. and flowing 880 miles to join the Kama.

by-e-lec-tion (bī′ĭ-lĕk′shən) *n.* Also **bye-e-lec-tion.** A special election, especially in the United Kingdom, held between general elections to fill a vacancy in a legislature.

Bye-lo-rus-sian (byĕl′ō-rŭsh′ən) *adj.* Also **Be-lo-rus-sian** (bĕl′ō-). Of or pertaining to the Byelorussian S.S.R., its people, or their language. —*n.* Also **Be-lo-rus-sian. 1.** A native or inhabitant of the Byelorussian S.S.R. **2.** The language of the Byelorussians. Also called "White Russian."

Byelorussian Soviet Socialist Republic. Also **Bye-lo-rus-sia** (byĕl′ō-rŭsh′ə), **Be-lo-rus-sia** (bĕl′ō-). One of the 15 republics of the Soviet Union, 80,134 square miles in area, situated in the southwest, in Europe. Population, 8,500,000. Capital, Minsk. Also called "White Russia."

Bye-lo-stok. A Russian name for **Bia-ly-stok.**

by-gone (bī′gôn′, -gŏn′) *adj.* Past; gone by; former: *bygone days.* —*n.* A past occurrence. —**let bygones be bygones.** To let past differences be reconciled.

by-lane (bī′lān′) *n.* A side road; byway.

by-law (bī′lô′) *n.* **1.** A secondary law. **2.** A law or rule governing the internal affairs of an organization. [Middle English *bilawe, bylawe,* "village law," probably from Old Norse *bȳlög* (unattested) : *bȳr,* village (see **bheu-** in Appendix*) + *lög* (see **legh-** in Appendix*).]

by-line (bī′līn′) *n.* Also **by-line.** A line at the head of a newspaper or magazine article with the author's name. —*tr.v.* **by-lined, -lining, -lines.** Also **by-line.** To write under a by-line. —**by′-lin′er** *n.*

by-name (bī′nām′) *n.* **1.** A surname. **2.** A nickname.

by-pass (bī′păs′, -päs′) *n.* Also **by-pass. 1.** A road or highway that passes around or to one side of an obstructed or congested area, a detour. **2.** A pipe or channel to conduct gas or liquid around another pipe or a fixture. **3.** Any means of circumvention. **4.** *Electricity.* A **shunt** (*see*). —*tr.v.* **by-passed, -passing, -passes.** Also **by-pass. 1.** To go around instead of through; avoid (an obstacle). **2.** To proceed heedless of; ignore: *by-passing office procedures.* **3.** To cause (piped liquid, for example) to follow a by-pass.

by-past (bī′păst′, -päst′) *adj.* Past; former; bygone.

by-path (bī′păth′, -päth′) *n., pl.* **-paths** (-păthz, -päthz). An indirect or little-used path.

by-play (bī′plā′) *n.* Secondary action or speech taking place while the main action proceeds, especially on a theater stage.

by-prod-uct (bī′prŏd′əkt) *n.* **1.** Something produced in the making of something else. **2.** A secondary result; side effect.

Byrd (bûrd), **Richard Evelyn.** 1888–1957. American polar explorer.

Byrd Land (bûrd). Formerly **Ma-rie Byrd Land** (mə-rē′ bûrd′). A large section of Antarctica extending eastward about 800 miles from the Ross Shelf Ice, claimed by Richard E. Byrd for the United States in 1929.

byre (bīr) *n.* A cowshed or barn. [Middle English *byre,* Old English *bȳre,* stall, hut. See **bheu-** in Appendix.*]

byr-nie (bûr′nē) *n. Archaic.* A breastplate or a coat or shirt of mail. [Middle English *brinie,* from Old Norse *brynja.* See **bhreug-**[1] in Appendix.*]

by-road (bī′rōd′) *n.* A side road; back road.

By-ron (bī′rən), **George Gordon.** Sixth Baron Byron of Rochdale. 1788–1824. English poet.

By-ron-ic (bī-rŏn′ĭk) *adj.* Of or characteristic of Byron or his works. —**By-ron′i-cal-ly** *adv.*

bys-sus (bĭs′əs) *n., pl.* **-suses** or **byssi** (bĭs′ī′). **1.** *Zoology.* A mass of filaments by means of which certain bivalve mollusks, such as mussels, attach themselves to fixed surfaces. **2.** A fine-textured linen of ancient times, used by the Egyptians as wrapping for mummies. [Latin, from Greek *bussos,* flax, linen, through a Semitic intermediary (such as Hebrew *būṣ,* linen cloth), from Egyptian *w′ḏ,* linen.]

by-stand-er (bī′stăn′dər) *n.* A person who is present at some event without participating in it.

by-street (bī′strēt′) *n.* A side street or road.

by-talk (bī′tôk′) *n.* Unimportant talk; small talk.

By-tom (bē′tôm′, bī′-). *German* **Beu-then** (boi′tən). A city in south-central Poland, northwest of Katowice. Population, 192,000.

by-way (bī′wā′) *n.* **1.** A side road; byroad. **2.** A secondary or overlooked field of study.

by-word (bī′wûrd′) *n.* **1.** A well-known saying; proverb. **2.** One that proverbially represents a type, class, or quality. **3.** An object of notoriety. **4.** A nickname or epithet. [Middle English *biword,* Old English *bīword* (translation of Latin *prōverbium,* PROVERB) : BY + WORD.]

by-work (bī′wûrk′) *n.* Work done during one's spare time.

byz-ant. Variant of **bezant.**

Byz-an-tine (bĭz′ən-tēn′, -tīn′, bĭ-zăn′tĭn) *adj.* **1.** Of, pertaining to, or characteristic of Byzantium, its inhabitants, or their culture. **2.** Of or designating the style of architecture developed from the fifth century A.D. in Byzantium, characterized by round arches, massive domes, intricate spires and minarets, and extensive use of mosaic. **3.** Of or designating the style of painting and design developed in Byzantium, characterized by formality of design, frontal, stylized presentation of figures, rich use of color, especially gold, and generally religious subject matter. **4.** Of the Eastern Orthodox Church or the rites performed in it. —*n.* A native or inhabitant of Byzantium.

Byzantine Empire. *Arabic* **Rum** (rōōm). The eastern part of the later Roman Empire, founded by Constantine in A.D. 330 and continuing after the fall of Rome as its successor until 1453; its capital was Constantinople. Also called "Eastern Roman Empire."

By-zan-ti-um (bĭ-zăn′shē-əm, -tē-əm). **1.** A Greek city on the site of which Constantine built the city of Constantinople (now Istanbul) in A.D. 330. **2.** The Byzantine Empire and its culture.

BZV Airport code for Brazzaville, Congo.

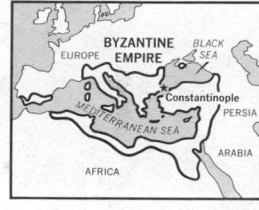

Byzantine Empire
At its greatest extent
under Justinian I

---

t tight/th thin, path/*th* this, bathe/ŭ cut/ûr urge/v valve/w with/y yes/z zebra, size/zh vision/ə about, item, edible, gallop, circus/
à *Fr.* ami/œ *Fr.* feu, *Ger.* schön/ü *Fr.* tu, *Ger.* über/KH *Ger.* ich, *Scot.* loch/N *Fr.* bon. *Follows main vocabulary. †Of obscure origin.

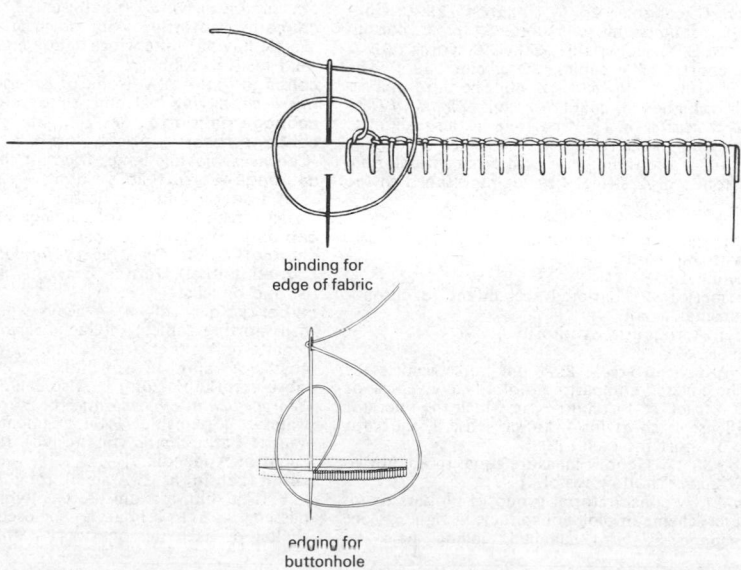

binding for
edge of fabric

edging for
buttonhole

buttonhole stitch

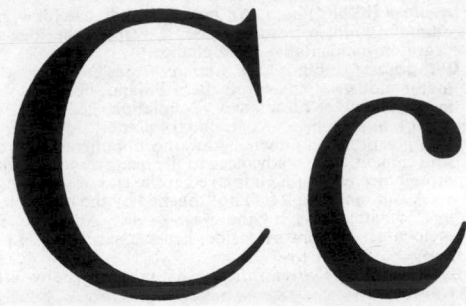

Cc

| 1 | 2 | 3 | 4 | 5 | 6 | 7 | 8 | 9 | 10 | 11 | 12 | 13 | 14 | 15 | 16 |

Phoenician   Greek   Roman   Medieval   Modern

Around 1000 B.C. *the Phoenicians and other Semites of Syria and Palestine began to use a graphic sign in the forms (1,2). They gave it the name* gīmel, *meaning "camel," and used it for the consonant g. After 900* B.C. *the Greeks borrowed the sign from the Phoenicians in the forms (3,4) and later developed other forms reversing the orientation (5,6,7). They also changed its name to* gamma, *but used it with the same consonantal value. The Greek form (5) passed via Etruscan to the Roman alphabet (8,9). The Romans used the sign originally for both the sound g (writing* Caius *for* Gaius*) and for the sound k. In the course of time they developed a graphic differentiation for the two sounds. They used the original form (9) for the sound k, and later also for other palatalized sounds such as s and c, and developed a new modification for the sound g (see* G*). The Roman Monumental Capital (10) is the prototype of our modern capital, printed (13) and written (14). The written Roman form (9) developed into the late Roman and medieval Uncial (11) and Cursive (12), which are the bases of our modern small letter, printed (15) and written (16).*

c, C (sē) *n., pl.* **c's** *or rare* **cs, C's** *or* **Cs. 1.** The third letter of the modern English alphabet. See **alphabet. 2.** Any of the speech sounds represented by this letter.

c, C, c., C. *Note:* As an abbreviation or symbol, *c* may be a small· or a capital letter, with or without a period. Established forms or those generally preferred precede the definition. When no form is given, all four forms are in general use in that sense. **1. c** *Physics.* candle. **2. C** *Electricity.* capacitance. **3. c.,** C. capacity. **4. c., C.** cape. **5. c** carat. **6. C** The symbol for the element carbon. **7. c., C.** carton. **8. c., C.** case. **9. c., C.** *Baseball.* catcher. **10. C.** Catholic. **11. C** Celsius. **12. C.** Celtic. **13. c., C.** cent. **14. c** centi-. **15. C** centigrade. **16. c., C.** centime. **17. c., C.** century. **18. C.** chancellor. **19. c., C.** chapter. **20. C** *Physics.* charge conjugation. **21. C.** chief. **22. c., C.** church. **23. C.** circa. **24. C.** city. **25. C.** cloudy. **26. C.** companion. **27. c., C.** congius. **28. C.** Congress. **29. C.** Conservative. **30. c, C** *Mathematics.* constant. **31. c., C.** consul. **32. c., C.** copy. **33. c., C.** copyright. **34. c., C.** corps. **35. C** coulomb. **36. C.** court. **37. c** cubic. **38. c.** cup. **39. C** The Roman numeral for 100 (Latin *centum*). **40.** The third in a series. **41. C** The third highest in quality or rank: *a mark of C on a term paper.* **42. C** *Music.* **a.** The first tone in the scale of C major, or the third tone in the relative minor scale. **b.** The key or a scale in which C is the tonic. **c.** A written or printed note representing this tone. **d.** A string, key, or pipe tuned to the pitch of this tone.

ca circa.

Ca The symbol for the element calcium.

CA California (with Zip Code).

c.a. chartered accountant.

C.A. 1. Central America. **2.** chartered accountant. **3.** chronological age. **4.** consular agent.

CAA, C.A.A. Civil Aeronautics Authority.

Ca·a·ba. See Kaaba.

cab[1] (kăb) *n.* **1.** A **taxicab** *(see).* **2.** A one-horse vehicle for public hire. **3.** The covered compartment of a heavy vehicle or machine, such as a truck or locomotive, in which the operator or driver sits. [Sense 1, short for TAXICAB; sense 2, short for CABRIOLET; sense 3, short for CABIN.]

cab[2] (kăb) *n.* Also **kab.** A Hebrew measure equal to about two quarts. [Hebrew *qabh,* "hollow vessel."]

ca·bal (kə-băl') *n.* **1.** A conspiratorial group of plotters or intriguers. **2.** A secret scheme or plot; conspiracy; intrigue. —See Synonyms at **conspiracy.** —*intr.v.* **caballed, -balling, -bals.** To

form a cabal; to plot; conspire; scheme. [French *cabale,* from Medieval Latin *cabala,* CABALA. The term was popularized during the reign of Charles II, when it was applied to the ministry of C(lifford), A(rlington), B(uckingham), A(shley), and L(auderdale).]

cab·a·la (kăb'ə-lə, kə-bä'lə) *n.* Also **cab·ba·la, kab·a·la, kab·ba·la. 1.** *Often capital* **C.** An occult theosophy of rabbinical origin, widely transmitted in medieval Europe, based on an esoteric interpretation of the Hebrew Scriptures. **2.** A secret doctrine resembling the Cabala. [Medieval Latin, from Hebrew *qabbālāh,* received doctrine, tradition, from *qābal,* to receive.] —**cab'a·lism'** *n.* —**cab'a·list** *n.* —**cab'a·lis'tic** (kăb'ə-lĭs'tĭk) *adj.* —**cab'a·lis'ti·cal·ly** *adv.*

cab·al·le·ro (kăb'ə-lâr'ō; *Spanish* käb'əl-yâr'ō) *n., pl.* **-ros. 1.** A Spanish gentleman; cavalier. **2.** *Southwestern U.S.* A horseman. [Spanish, from Late Latin *caballārius,* a horse groom, from Latin *caballus,* a horse. See **cavalier.**]

ca·ban·a (kə-băn'ə, -băn'yə) *n.* Also **ca·ba·ña** (kə-bä'nyə). A shelter on a beach used as a bathhouse. [Spanish *cabaña,* from Late Latin *capanna,* hut, CABIN.]

cab·a·ret (kăb'ə-rā') *n.* **1.** A restaurant providing short programs of live entertainment. **2.** The floor show billed by such a place. [French, from Old French, from Middle Dutch *cabret, cambret,* from Old Picard *camberet,* small room, from *cambre,* room, from Late Latin *camera,* CHAMBER.]

cab·bage (kăb'ĭj) *n.* **1.** An edible plant, *Brassica oleracea capitata,* grown in temperate climates throughout the world and having a short, thick stalk, and a large head formed by tightly overlapping green or reddish leaves. **2.** An edible leaf bud of the **cabbage palm** *(see).* **3.** *Slang.* Money, especially in the form of bills. —*intr.v.* **cabbaged, -baging, -bages.** To form or grow in a head, as cabbage does. [Middle English *caboche,* from Old North French, variant of Old French *caboce,* "head" : perhaps *ca-,* pejorative prefix + *boce,* a bump, swelling, from Vulgar Latin *bottia†* (unattested).]

cabbage butterfly. Any of several butterflies of the genus *Pieris,* having white wings lightly marked with black, and larvae that feed on cabbage.

cabbage palm. A tropical American palm tree, *Roystonea oleracea,* having leaf buds that are edible when young.

cabbage palmetto. See **palmetto.**

cabbage rose. A prickly shrub, *Rosa centifolia,* native to the Caucasus, having large, fragrant, many-petaled pink flowers.

cab·bage·worm (kăb'ĭj-wûrm') *n.* Any of several caterpillars that feed on and are destructive to cabbage; especially, the bright-green larva of the **cabbage butterfly** *(see).*

cab·ba·la. Variant of **cabala.**

cab·by (kăb'ē) *n., pl.* **-bies.** *Informal.* A cab driver.

Cab·ell (kăb'əl), **James Branch.** 1879–1958. American essayist and novelist.

ca·ber (kā'bər, kä'-) *n.* A heavy wooden pole heaved in a Scottish sporting contest. [Gaelic *cabar,* from Vulgar Latin *caprio* (unattested), rafter, from Latin *capra,* she-goat, from *caper,* hegoat. See **kapro-** in Appendix.*]

cab·e·zon (kăb'ə-zŏn') *n.* Also **cab·e·zone.** A large, edible fish, *Scorpaenichthys marmoratus,* of North American Pacific coastal waters. [Spanish *cabezón,* augmentative of *cabeza,* head, from Vulgar Latin *capitia* (unattested), from Latin *caput,* head. See **kaput** in Appendix.*]

cab·in (kăb'ĭn) *n.* **1.** A small, roughly built house; cottage; hut. **2. a.** In a ship, a room used as living quarters by an officer or passenger. **b.** In a boat, an enclosed compartment serving as a shelter or as living quarters. **c.** In an airplane, the enclosed

cabbage

ă pat/ā pay/âr care/ä father/b bib/ch church/d deed/ĕ pet/ē be/f fife/g gag/h hat/hw which/ĭ pit/ī pie/îr pier/j judge/k kick/l lid/
needle/m mum/n no, sudden/ng thing/ŏ pot/ō toe/ô paw, for/oi noise/ou out/ŏŏ took/ōō boot/p pop/r roar/s sauce/sh ship, dish/

space for the crew, passengers, or cargo. —*v.* **cabined, -ining, -ins.** —*tr.* **1.** To lodge in a cabin. **2.** To confine, as in a cabin. —*intr.* To live in a cabin or a small area. [Middle English *cabane,* from Old French, from Old Provençal, from Late Latin *capanna*†, hut, cabin.]
cabin boy. A boy servant aboard a ship.
cabin class. A class of accommodations on some passenger ships, lower than first class and higher than tourist class. —**cab′in-class′** *adj.* & *adv.*
cabin cruiser. A powerboat with a cabin. Also called "cruiser."
Ca·bin·da (kə-bĭn′də). **1.** A territory of Angola, 3,000 square miles in area, forming an exclave lying between the two Congo republics on the Atlantic coast of Africa. Population, 59,000. **2.** The capital of this territory, a seaport just north of the mouth of the Congo. Population, 4,000.
cab·i·net (kăb′ə-nĭt) *n.* **1.** An upright, cupboardlike repository with shelves, drawers, or compartments for the safekeeping or display of a collection of objects or materials. **2.** A small or private room set aside for some specific activity. **3.** *Often capital* **C.** The body of persons appointed by a chief of state or a prime minister to head the executive departments of the government and to act as his official advisers. —*adj.* **1.** Of suitable value, beauty, or size to be kept or displayed in a cabinet: *a cabinet edition.* **2.** Belonging or relating to a political cabinet: *a cabinet minister.* **3.** Used for cabinetwork: *teak and other heavy cabinet woods.* [Old French, diminutive of Old North French *cabine*†, a gambling house.]
cab·i·net·mak·er (kăb′ə-nĭt-mā′kər) *n.* A craftsman specializing in making fine articles of wooden furniture.
cab·i·net·work (kăb′ə-nĭt-wûrk′) *n.* Finished woodwork made by a cabinetmaker.
ca·ble (kā′bəl) *n.* **1.** A strong, large-diameter, heavy steel or fiber rope. **2.** *Electricity.* A bound or sheathed group of mutually insulated conductors. **3. a.** *Nautical.* A heavy rope or chain for mooring or anchoring a ship. **b.** A unit of nautical length equal to 720 feet in the United States and 608 feet in England. Also called "cable's length." **4.** A cablegram. **5.** A **cable stitch** *(see).* —*v.* **cabled, -bling, -bles.** —*tr.* **1. a.** To send a cablegram to. **b.** To transmit (a message) by telegraph. **2.** To supply or fasten with a cable or cables. —*intr.* To send a cablegram. [Middle English, from Norman French, from Medieval Latin *capulum,* rope for fastening cattle, from Latin *capere,* to take. See **kap-** in Appendix.*]
cable car. A car used on a cableway or cable railway.
ca·ble·gram (kā′bəl-grăm′) *n.* A telegram sent by submarine cable.
ca·ble-laid (kā′bəl-lād′) *adj.* Made of three ropes of three strands each, twisted together counterclockwise.
cable railway. A railroad on which the cars are moved by an endless cable driven by a stationary engine.
cable stitch. A stitch in knitting that produces a twisted rope design. Also called "cable."
ca·blet (kā′blĭt) *n.* A cable-laid rope with a circumference of less than ten inches; a small cable. [Diminutive of CABLE.]
ca·ble·way (kā′bəl-wā′) *n.* A conveyor system in which cars, buckets, or other carrier units are suspended from and run on wire cables strung between elevated supports.
cab·man (kăb′mən) *n., pl.* **-men** (-mĭn). The driver of a cab, especially a horse-drawn cab.
cab·o·chon (kăb′ə-shŏn′) *n.* **1.** A highly polished, convex-cut, unfaceted gem. **2.** This style of cutting. —*adv.* In cabochon: *a sapphire cut cabochon.* [Old French, augmentative of Old North French *caboche, caboce,* head, CABBAGE.]
ca·boo·dle (kə-bo͞od′l) *n. Informal.* The lot, group, or bunch. Used chiefly in the phrase *the whole kit and caboodle.* [Perhaps *ca-,* probably short for KITH or KIT + BOODLE.]
ca·boose (kə-bo͞os′) *n.* **1.** The last car on a freight train, having kitchen and sleeping facilities for the train crew. **2.** *Obsolete.* **a.** A ship's galley. **b.** Any of various cast-iron cooking ranges used in such galleys during the early 19th century. **c.** An outdoor oven or fireplace. [Probably from Dutch *kabuis,* from Middle Low German *kabūse*†.]
Cab·ot (kăb′ət), **John.** Italian name, Giovanni Caboto. 1450–1498. Italian explorer in English service; discovered mainland of North America (1497); father of Sebastian Cabot.
Cab·ot (kăb′ət), **Sebastian.** 1476?–1557. English explorer and cartographer; in service of Spain (1509–47); son of John Cabot.
cab·o·tage (kăb′ə-täzh′) *n.* Trade or navigation in coastal waters. [French, from *caboter,* to coast, probably from Spanish *cabo,* cape, headland, from Latin *caput,* head. See **kaput** in Appendix.*]
Cab·ot Strait (kăb′ət). A 60-mile-wide channel between southwestern Newfoundland and Cape Breton Island, Canada, connecting the Gulf of St. Lawrence with the Atlantic Ocean.
Ca·bral (kə-bräl′), **Pedro Álvares.** 1460?–1526? Portuguese navigator; discovered and claimed Brazil for Portugal (1500).
ca·bret·ta (kə-brĕt′ə) *n.* A soft, kidlike leather made from sheepskin having coarse, hairlike wool, and used for making gloves and shoe uppers. [Spanish and Portuguese *cabra,* goat (see **cabrilla**) + Spanish *-etta,* diminutive suffix.]
ca·bril·la (kə-brē′yə, -brĭl′ə) *n.* Any of various sea basses, especially *Epinephelus guttatus,* of tropical waters. [Spanish, diminutive of *cabra,* goat, from Latin *capra,* she-goat, from *caper,* he-goat. See **kapro-** in Appendix.*]
Ca·bri·ni (kə-brē′nē), Saint **Frances Xavier.** 1850–1917. Founder of the Missionary Sisters of the Sacred Heart; first American canonized (1946).
cab·ri·ole (kăb′rē-ōl′) *n.* A form of furniture leg, characteristic of Queen Anne and Chippendale furniture, that curves outward and then narrows downward into an ornamental foot. [French, "caper" (from its resemblance to the foreleg of a capering animal). See **cabriolet.**]
cab·ri·o·let (kăb′rē-ə-lā′) *n.* **1.** A two-wheeled, one-horse carriage with two seats and a folding top. **2.** A coupelike automobile with a collapsible top; a convertible coupe. [French, diminutive of *cabriole,* caper (in allusion to its bounding motion), from Old French, from Old Italian *capriola,* from *capriolo,* roebuck, from Latin *capreolus,* wild goat, chamois, from *caper,* he-goat. See **kapro-** in Appendix.*]
cab·stand (kăb′stănd′) *n.* A place where taxicabs are stationed.
ca·ca·o (kə-kä′ō, -kā′ō) *n., pl.* **-os.** **1.** An evergreen tropical American tree, *Theobroma cacao,* having yellowish flowers and reddish-brown seed pods. Also called "chocolate tree." **2.** The seed of this tree, used in making chocolate, cocoa, and cocoa butter. In this sense, also called "cacao bean." [Spanish, from Nahuatl *cacahuatl,* cacao beans.]
cacao butter. **Cocoa butter** *(see).*
Cac·ci·ni (kät-chē′nĭ), **Giulio.** 1550?–1618. Italian singer and composer of early music dramas.
cach·a·lot (kăsh′ə-lŏt′, kăsh′ə-lō′) *n.* The **sperm whale** *(see).* [French, from Spanish, from Portuguese *cacholotte,* "fish with a big head," from *cachola*†, head.]
cache (kăsh) *n.* **1.** A hole or similar hiding place used by pioneers or explorers for storing provisions and other necessaries in the wilderness. **2.** A place for concealment and safekeeping, as of valuables. **3.** A store of goods hidden in a cache. —*tr.v.* **cached, caching, caches.** To store in a hiding place for future use. See Synonyms at **hide.** [French, from *cacher,* to hide, from Vulgar Latin *coācticāre* (unattested), to compress, from Latin *coāctāre,* to constrain, from *cōgere* (past participle *coāctus*), to drive together : *com-,* together + *agere,* to drive (see **ag-** in Appendix*).]
ca·chec·tic (kă-kĕk′tĭk) *adj.* Pertaining to or characterized by cachexia. [French *cachectique,* from Latin *cachecticus,* from Greek *kakhektikos,* from *kakhexia,* CACHEXIA.]
cache·pot (kăsh-pō′, kăsh′pŏt′) *n.* An ornamental container for a flowerpot. [French : CACHE + *pot,* pot, from Old French, perhaps from Low German (see **pott-** in Appendix*).]
ca·chet (kă-shā′) *n.* **1.** A seal on a letter or document. **2.** A mark of distinction, individuality, or authenticity. **3. a.** A commemorative design stamped on an envelope to mark some postal or philatelic event. **b.** A motto forming part of a postal cancellation. **4.** A kind of wafer capsule formerly used by pharmacists for presenting an unpleasant-tasting drug. [Old French, from *cacher,* to hide, press together. See **cache.**]
ca·chex·i·a (kă-kĕk′sē-ə) *n.* A general wasting of the body during a chronic disease. [Late Latin, from Greek *kakhexia,* bad condition of the body : CAC(O)- + *hexis,* condition, from *ekhein,* to hold, be in a condition (see **segh-** in Appendix*).]
cach·in·nate (kăk′ə-nāt′) *intr.v.* **-nated, -nating, -nates.** To laugh loud, hard, or convulsively; guffaw. [Latin *cachinnāre*†.] —**cach′in·na′tion** *n.*
ca·chou (kă-sho͞o′, kăsh′o͞o) *n.* **1.** An astringent, **catechu** *(see).* **2.** A pastille used to sweeten the breath. [French, from Portuguese *cachu,* from Malayalam *kāccu.*]
ca·chu·cha (kä-cho͞o′chä) *n.* An Andalusian solo dance in 3/4 time. [Spanish, "small boat," probably from *cacho,* shard, saucepan, probably from Vulgar Latin *cacculus* (unattested), alteration of Latin *caccabus,* pot, from Greek *kakkabos,* probably from Semitic, akin to Akkadian *kukubu,* vessel.]
ca·cique (kə-sēk′) *n.* Also **ca·zique** (-zēk′). **1.** An Indian chief, especially in the Spanish West Indies and other parts of Latin America during colonial and postcolonial times. **2.** A local political boss in Spain or Latin America. **3.** Any of various tropical orioles. [Spanish, of Arawakan origin, akin to Arawak *kassequa,* chief, Taino *cacique.*]
cack·le (kăk′əl) *v.* **-led, -ling, -les.** —*intr.* **1.** To make the shrill cry characteristic of a hen after laying an egg. **2.** To laugh or talk in a similar manner. —*tr.* To utter in cackles. —*n.* **1.** The act or sound of cackling. **2.** Shrill, brittle laughter. **3.** Foolish chatter. [Middle English *cakelen,* probably from Middle Low German *kakeln* (imitative).] —**cack′ler** *n.*
caco–. Indicates bad, incorrect, or unpleasant; for example, **cacography.** [Greek *kako-,* from *kakos,* bad. See **kakka-** in Appendix.*]
cac·o·dyl (kăk′ə-dĭl′) *n.* **1.** The arsenic group $As(CH_3)_2$. **2.** A poisonous oil, $As_2(CH_3)_4$, with an obnoxious garlicky odor. [Greek *kakōdēs,* bad-smelling : CACO- + *-ōdēs,* from *ozein,* to smell (see **od-**[1] in Appendix*) + -YL.] —**cac′o·dyl′ic** *adj.*
cac·o·e·thes (kăk′ō-ē′thēz) *n.* A mania or irresistible compulsion; a pernicious habit. [Latin, from Greek *kakoēthes,* from the neuter of *kakoēthēs,* ill-disposed, abominable, malignant : CACO- + *ēthos,* custom, disposition (see **seu-**[2] in Appendix*).]
cac·o·gen·ics (kăk′ə-jĕn′ĭks) *n.* Plural in form, usually used with a singular verb The study of racial degeneration, **dysgenics** *(see).* [CACO- + -GENIC(S).] —**cac′o·gen′ic** *adj.*
ca·cog·ra·phy (kă-kŏg′rə-fē) *n.* **1.** Bad handwriting, as opposed to calligraphy **2.** Incorrect spelling, as opposed to orthography. [CACO- + -GRAPHY.]
cac·o·mis·tle (kăk′ə-mĭs′əl) *n.* Also **cac·o·mix·le** (-mĭk′səl). Either of two small, carnivorous mammals, *Bassariscus astutus,* of the southwestern United States, or *Jentinkia sumichrasti,* of Central America, having grayish or brownish fur and a black-banded tail. Also called "ringtail," "ring-tailed cat." [Mexican Spanish, from Nahuatl *tlacomiztli* : *tlaco,* half + *miztli,* a mountain lion.]
ca·coph·o·nous (kă-kŏf′ə-nəs) *adj.* Also **cac·o·phon·ic** (kăk′ə-fŏn′ĭk), **cac·o·phon·i·cal** (-ĭ-kəl). Having a harsh, unpleasant

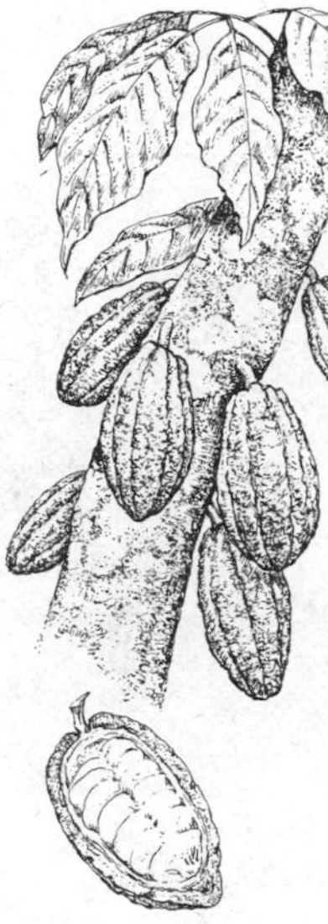

cacao
Above: Branch with seed pods
Below: Opened pod with seeds

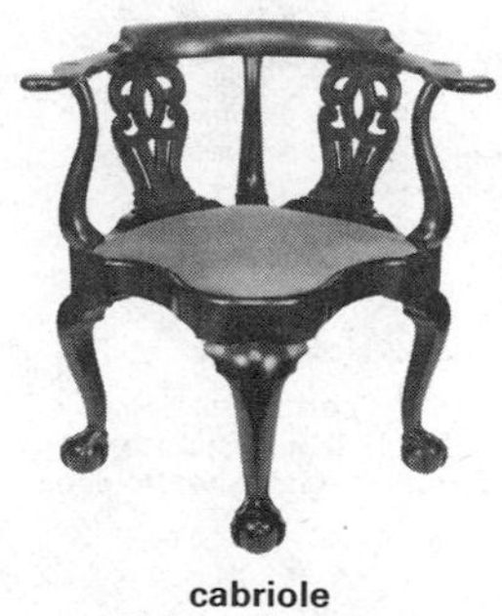

cabriole
Eighteenth-century mahogany corner chair with cabriole legs

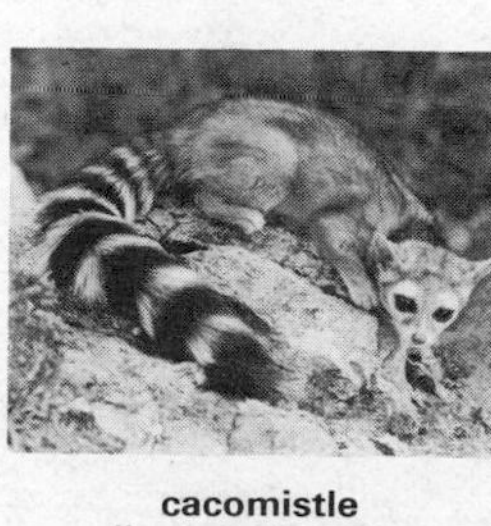

cacomistle
Bassariscus astutus

sound; discordant. [Greek *kakophōnos* : CACO- + *phōnē*, sound (see **bhā-**[2] in Appendix*).] —**ca·coph'o·nous·ly** *adv.*

ca·coph·o·ny (kă-kŏf'ə-nē) *n., pl.* **-nies.** **1.** Jarring, discordant sound; dissonance. **2.** Harsh or unharmonious use of language, as opposed to euphony. [French *cacophonie*, from Greek *kakophōnia*, from *kakophōnos*, CACOPHONOUS.]

cac·tus (kăk'təs) *n., pl.* **-ti** (-tī') or **-tuses.** Any of a large group of plants of the family Cactaceae, mostly native to arid regions of the New World. They are characterized by thick, fleshy, often prickly stems that function as leaves and in some species have showy flowers and edible fruit. [New Latin, from Latin, the cardoon, from Greek *kaktos*†.]

ca·cu·mi·nal (kă-kyōō'mə-nəl) *adj.* *Phonetics.* Pronounced with the tip of the tongue turned back and up toward the roof of the mouth; retroflex; cerebral. —*n.* *Phonetics.* A cacuminal consonant. [From Latin *cacūmen*, summit, treetop, point. See **keu-**[2] in Appendix.*]

cad (kăd) *n.* An ungentlemanly man. [Short for CADDIE.] —**cad'dish** *adj.* —**cad'dish·ly** *adv.* —**cad'dish·ness** *n.*

ca·das·ter (kə-dăs'tər) *n.* Also **ca·das·tre.** A public record, survey, or map of the value, extent, and ownership of land as a basis of taxation. [French *cadastre*, from Italian *cadastro*, variant of Old Italian *catastico*, from Late Greek *katastikhon*, notebook, "line by line" : *kata-*, down from + *stikhos*, line, verse (see **steigh-** in Appendix*).] —**ca·das'tral** *adj.*

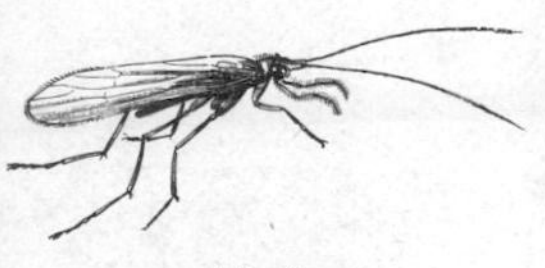

caddis fly
Phryganea striata

ca·dav·er (kə-dăv'ər) *n.* A dead body, especially one intended for dissection. See Synonyms at **body.** [Latin, from *cadere*, to fall, "die." See **kad-** in Appendix.*] —**ca·dav'er·ic** *adj.*

ca·dav·er·ine (kə-dăv'ə-rēn') *n.* A syrupy, colorless fuming ptomaine, $NH_2(CH_2)_5NH_2$, formed from decaying animal flesh. [CADAVER + -INE.]

ca·dav·er·ous (kə-dăv'ər-əs) *adj.* **1.** Corpselike: *"his waistcoat is pea-green, imparting a most cadaverous hue to his melancholy countenance"* (R.S. Surtees). **2.** Of corpselike pallor: *"I saw a cadaverous face appear at a small window"* (Dickens). —**ca·dav'er·ous·ly** *adv.* —**ca·dav'er·ous·ness** *n.*

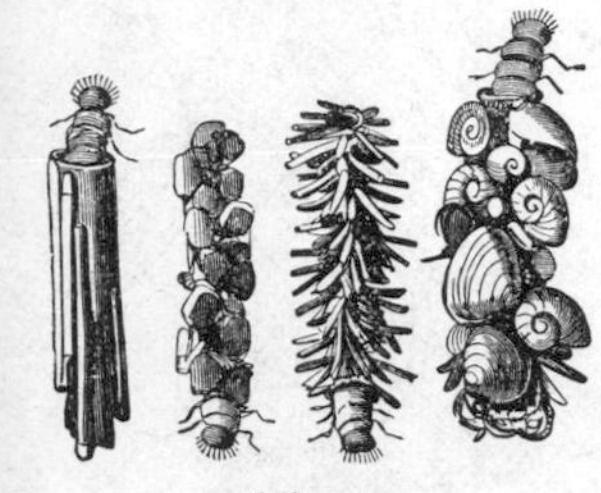

caddis worm
Larva cases of caddis worms

cad·die (kăd'ē) *n.* Also **cad·dy** *pl.* **-dies.** **1.** One hired to serve as attendant to a golfer, especially by carrying his clubs. **2.** *Scottish.* A boy who does odd jobs. —*intr.v.* **caddied, -dying, -dies.** Also **caddy.** To serve as a caddie. [French *cadet*, CADET.]

cad·dis (kăd'ĭs) *n.* Also **cad·dice.** A coarse woolen fabric, yarn, or ribbon binding. [Middle English *cadas*, from Old French *cadaz*, from Old Provençal *cadarz*†.]

caddis fly. Also **caddice fly.** Any of various four-winged insects of the order Trichoptera, found near lakes and streams. [*Caddis*, from obsolete *cad*, variant of COD (pod), from the tube in which the larva lives.]

caddis worm. Also **caddice worm.** The aquatic, wormlike larva of the caddis fly, enclosed in a cylindrical case covered with grains of sand, fragments of shell, or the like.

Cad·do (kăd'ō) *n., pl.* **Caddo** or **-dos.** A member of a North American Indian confederacy of Caddoan linguistic stock, formerly living in Arkansas, Louisiana, and eastern Texas. [Probably from Caddoan *Kädohädächo*, "real chiefs."]

Cad·do·an (kăd'ō-ən) *n.* A family of North American Indian languages formerly spoken in three separate areas west of the Mississippi. These areas were the Dakotas, Nebraska and Kansas, and Oklahoma, Arkansas, Texas, and Louisiana.

cad·dy[1] (kăd'ē) *n., pl.* **-dies.** A small box or other container, especially for holding tea. [Originally "a container of one catty of tea," from Malay *kati*, CATTY.]

cad·dy[2]. Variant of **caddie.**

cade[1] (kād) *adj.* Left by its mother and raised by hand: *a cade calf.* [Middle English *cad*†.]

cade[2] (kād) *n.* A shrub, *Juniperus oxycedrus*, of the Mediterranean region, the wood of which yields an oily brown liquid used to treat skin ailments. [French, from Old Provençal, from Medieval Latin *catanus*, probably from Gaulish *catănos* (unattested).]

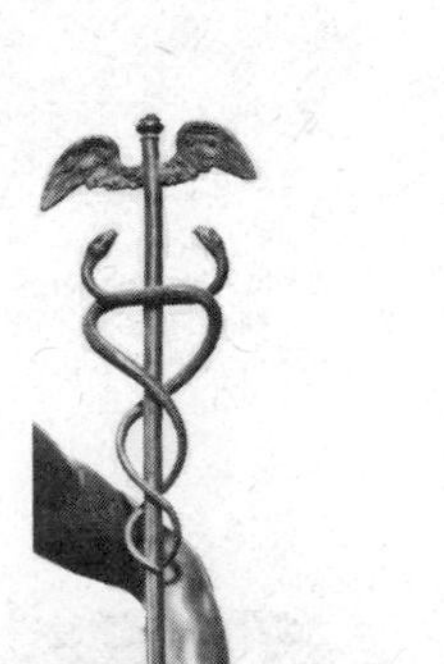

caduceus
Detail from a statue of Hermes by Giovanni Bologna

Cade (kād), **Jack.** English rebel; led march on London (1450); killed resisting arrest.

-cade. Indicates procession or parade; for example, **motorcade.** [From CAVALCADE.]

ca·delle (kə-dĕl') *n.* A small blackish beetle, *Tenebroides mauritanicus*, both the larval and adult forms of which damage stored grain and packaged foods. [French, from Provençal *cadello*, from Latin *catella*, feminine of *catellus*, *catulus*, offspring. See **kat-**[1] in Appendix.*]

ca·dence (kād'əns) *n.* Also **ca·den·cy** (kād'ən-sē) *pl.* **-cies.** **1.** Balanced, rhythmic flow, as of poetry or oratory. **2.** The measure or beat of movement, as in dancing or marching. **3. a.** A falling inflection of the voice, as at the end of a sentence. **b.** The general inflection or modulation of the voice. **4.** *Music.* A progression of chords moving to a harmonic close or point of rest. —See Synonyms at **rhythm.** [Middle English, from Old French, from Old Italian *cadenza*, from *cadere*, to fall, from Latin. See **kad-** in Appendix.*] —**ca'denced** *adj.*

ca·dent (kād'ənt) *adj.* **1.** Having cadence or rhythm. **2.** *Archaic.* Falling. [Latin *cadēns*, present participle of *cadere*, to fall. See **kad-** in Appendix.*]

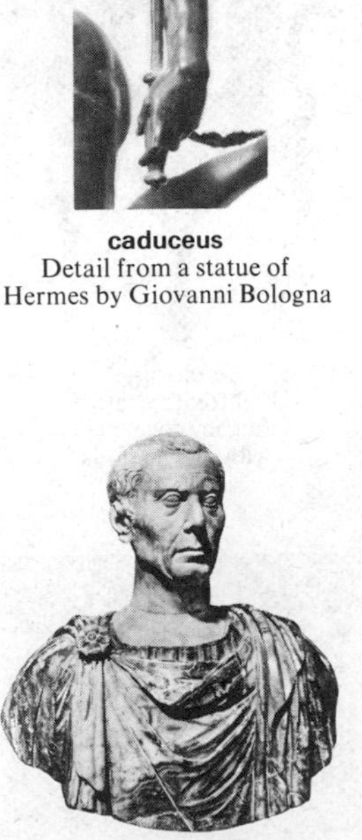

Julius Caesar
Roman bust in the Capitoline Museum, Rome, Italy

ca·den·za (kə-dĕn'zə) *n.* **1.** An elaborate ornamental flourish interpolated into an aria or other vocal piece. **2.** An extended, virtuosic section for the soloist near the end of a movement of a concerto. [Italian, from Old Italian, CADENCE.]

ca·det (kə-dĕt') *n.* **1.** A student training to be an officer at a military school. **2.** A younger son or brother. **3.** *Slang.* A pimp. [French, from Gascon dialect *capdet*, captain, chief, from Late Latin *capitellum*, "small head," from Latin *caput*, head. See **kaput** in Appendix.*] —**ca·det'ship'** *n.*

cadge (kăj) *v.* **cadged, cadging, cadges.** *Informal.* —*tr.* To get by begging. —*intr.* To beg. [Back-formation from *cadger*, carrier, Middle English *cadgear*, from *caggen*†, to carry wares.]

Cad·il·lac (kăd'l-ăk'; *French* kȧ-dē-yȧk'), Sieur **Antoine de la Mothe.** 1658–1730. French fur trader and colonial administrator in America; founded Detroit (1701).

Cá·diz (kə-dĭz', kā'dĭz; *Spanish* kä'thēth'). A city of southeastern Spain, a seaport northwest of Gibraltar on the Gulf of Cádiz; an inlet of the Atlantic Ocean. Population, 128,000.

Cad·me·an (kăd-mē'ən) *adj.* Pertaining to, associated with, or resembling Cadmus.

Cadmean victory. A victory achieved at ruinous cost to the victor. [Translation of Greek *Kadmeia nikē*, from such a victory among the warriors who sprang from the dragon's teeth sown by Cadmus.]

cad·mi·um (kăd'mē-əm) *n.* *Symbol* **Cd** A soft, bluish-white metallic element, occurring primarily in zinc, copper, and lead ores. It is easily cut with a knife and is used in low-friction, fatigue-resistant alloys, solders, dental amalgams, nickel-cadmium storage batteries, and in rustproof electroplating. Atomic number 48, atomic weight 112.40, melting point 320.9°C, boiling point 765°C, specific gravity 8.65, valence 2. See **element.** [New Latin, from Latin *cadmia*, zinc ore, CALAMINE (because cadmium is found together with calamine in the ore).] —**cad'mic** (-mĭk) *adj.*

Cad·mus (kăd'məs) *n.* *Greek Mythology.* A Phoenician prince who killed a dragon and sowed its teeth, from which sprang up an army of men who fought one another until only five survived; with these Cadmus founded the city of Thebes.

cad·re (kăd'rē) *n.* **1.** A framework. **2.** A nucleus of trained personnel around which a larger organization can be built and trained. [French, from Italian *quadro*, from Latin *quādrum*, a square, from *quādrus*. See **kwetwer-** in Appendix.*]

ca·du·ce·us (kə-dōō'sē-əs, kə-dyōō'-) *n., pl.* **-cei** (-sē-ī'). **1. a.** An ancient herald's wand or staff. **b.** *Mythology.* A winged staff with two serpents twined around it, carried by Hermes. **2.** A similar staff used as the symbol of the medical profession. [Latin *cādūceus*, from Greek (Doric) *karukeion*, from *karux*, herald. See **kar-**[2] in Appendix.*] —**ca·du'ce·an** (-sē-ən) *adj.*

ca·du·ci·ty (kə-dōō'sə-tē, kə-dyōō'-) *n.* **1.** The frailty of old age; senility. **2.** Perishability; impermanence. [French *caducité*, from *caduc*, frail, falling, from Latin *cadūcus*, CADUCOUS.]

ca·du·cous (kə-dōō'kəs, kə-dyōō'-) *adj.* **1.** *Biology.* Dropping off or shedding at an early stage of development, as the gills of amphibians or the leaves of certain plants. **2.** Not long-lasting; impermanent; transitory. [Latin *cadūcus*, falling, frail, from *cadere*, to fall. See **kad-** in Appendix.*]

cae·cil·ian (sĭ-sĭl'yən, -sĭl'ē-ən, sĭ-sēl'-) *n.* Any of various legless, burrowing, wormlike amphibians of the order Gymnophiona, of tropical regions. [From New Latin *Caecilia*, type genus, from Latin *caecilia*, lizard, from *caecus*, blind (in allusion to a lizard's small eyes). See **kaiko-** in Appendix.*]

cae·cum. Variant of **cecum.**

Caed·mon (kăd'mən). English poet of the seventh century A.D.; described by Bede.

Cae·li·an (sē'lē-ən). One of the seven hills of Rome.

Cae·lum (sē'ləm) *n.* A constellation in the Southern Hemisphere near Columba and Eridanus. [New Latin, from Latin *caelum*, sculptor's chisel. See **skhai-** in Appendix.*]

Caen (käɴ). A city in Normandy, northwestern France; a main target of the Allied invasion in World War II (1944). Population, 91,000.

Caer·nar·von (kär-när'vən). Also **Car·nar·von.** **1.** Also **Caer·nar·von·shire** (-shĭr, -shər), **Car·nar·von·shire.** A county of Wales, occupying 569 square miles in the northwest. Population, 122,000. **2.** The county seat of this county, in the west near the border with Anglesey. Population, 9,000.

Cae·sar (sē'zər) *n.* **1.** A surname of the early Roman emperors that after Hadrian became the title of the junior imperial colleague of the **Augustus** *(see).* **2.** A dictator or autocrat: *"And she shall be sole victress, Caesar's Caesar."* (Shakespeare). [*Caesar* was first the surname of the Julio-Claudians in imitation of Augustus, whose official name, as the adopted son of Julius Caesar, was Gaius Julius *Caesar* Octavianus; the name, a cognomen within the Julian gens, is of Etruscan origin.]

Cae·sar (sē'zər), **Gaius Julius.** 100–44 B.C. Roman statesman, general, and historian; dictator (49–44 B.C.); assassinated.

Cae·sa·re·a (sē'zə-rē'ə, sĕs'ə-, sĕz'ə-). An ancient seaport and capital of Roman Palestine, built by Herod the Great on the northwestern coast of Israel, about 20 miles south of Haifa.

Cae·sa·re·a Maz·a·ca. The ancient name for **Kayseri.**

Cae·sar·e·an (sĭ-zâr'ē-ən) *adj.* Also **Cae·sar·i·an, Ce·sar·e·an, Ce·sar·i·an.** Pertaining to Julius Caesar or the Caesars. —*n.* *All spellings.* A Caesarean section.

Caesarean section. Also **caesarean section.** A surgical incision through the abdominal wall and uterus, performed to extract a fetus. [From an unhistorical tradition that the eponymous ancestor of the Roman family *Caesar* (or Julius *Caesar* himself) was born by this operation, and named *ā caesō mātris ūterē*, "from the *incised* womb of his mother," from *caesus*, past participle of *caedere*, to cut; see **skhai-** in Appendix.*]

Cae·sar·ism (sē'zə-rĭz'əm) *n.* Military dictatorship. —**Cae'sar·ist** *n.* —**Cae'sar·is'tic** *adj.*

caesar salad. A salad made with greens, crumbled cheese, croutons, and, as its most distinctive ingredient, a raw egg.

cae·si·um. Variant of **cesium.**

caes·pi·tose. Variant of **cespitose.**

caes·tus. Variant of **cestus** (boxing glove).

cae·su·ra (sĭ-zhōōr'ə, -zyōōr'ə, -zōōr'ə) *n., pl.* **-ras** or **-surae**

ă pat/ā pay/âr care/ä father/b bib/ch church/d deed/ĕ pet/ē be/f fife/g gag/h hat/hw which/ĭ pit/ī pie/îr pier/j judge/k kick/l lid, needle/m mum/n no, sudden/ng thing/ŏ pot/ō toe/ô paw, for/oi noise/ou out/ŏŏ took/ōō boot/p pop/r roar/s sauce/sh ship, dish/

(-zhŏŏr′ē, -zyŏŏr′ē, -zŏŏr′ē). Also **ce·su·ra.** **1.** A pause in a line of verse dictated by sense or natural speech rhythm rather than by metrics. It is conventionally indicated by a parallel slash: *"Drink deep, / or taste not the Pierian Spring"* (Pope). **2.** *Latin & Greek Prosody.* A break in a line caused by the ending of a word within a foot, especially when this coincides with a sense division: *"Arma virumque cano / Troiae qui primus ab oris"* (Virgil). **3.** *Music.* A pause or breathing at a point of rhythmic division in a melody. [Latin, "a cutting off," from *caedere,* to cut off. See **skhai-** in Appendix.*] —**cae·su′ral, cae·su′ric** *adj.*
C.A.F. cost and freight.
ca·fé (kă-fā′, kə-) *n.* A coffee house, restaurant, or bar. [French, coffee, from Turkish *kahve.* See **coffee.**]
ca·fé au lait (kă-fā′ ō lā′). **1.** Coffee served with hot milk. **2.** A light coffee color. [French, "coffee with milk."]
café brû·lot (brü-lō′) *pl.* **café brûlots** (brü-lōz′). A drink made by adding coffee to sugar, spices, and orange peel blazed with brandy. [Louisianian French, "burned brandy coffee."]
café noir (nwär′). Coffee served without cream or milk. [French, "black coffee."]
caf·e·te·ri·a (kăf′ə-tîr′ē-ə) *n.* A restaurant in which the customers are served at a counter and carry their meals to tables. [American Spanish, coffee shop, from Spanish *cafetero,* coffee maker or seller, from *café,* coffee, from Turkish *kahve.* See **coffee.**]
caf·feine (kă-fēn′, kăf′ē-ĭn) *n.* Also **caf·fein.** A bitter white alkaloid, $C_8H_{10}N_4O_2 \cdot H_2O$, derived from coffee, tea, and kola nuts, and used as a stimulant and diuretic. [German *Kaffein,* from *Kaffee,* coffee, from French *café.* See **café.**]
caf·tan (kăf′tən, kăf-tăn′) *n.* Also **kaf·tan.** In the Near East, a full-length tunic with long sleeves and a sash at the waist, worn under a coat. [Russian *kaftan,* from Turkish *kaftān.*]
Ca·ga·yan (kä′gä-yän′). A river rising in northeastern Luzon, Republic of the Philippines, and flowing 220 miles north into Babuyan Channel.
cage (kāj) *n.* **1.** A structure for confining birds or animals, enclosed on at least one side by a grating of wires or bars in order to let in air and light. **2. a.** Any enclosure that serves as a means of confining prisoners. **b.** Anything that confines. **3.** Any framework having a cagelike appearance or construction. **4.** An elevator car. **5.** *Baseball.* **a.** A backstop used for batting practices. **b.** A catcher's mask. **6.** *Basketball.* The basket. **7.** *Hockey.* The goal, made of a network frame. —*tr.v.* **caged, caging, cages.** To put in a cage; lock up or confine. [Middle English, from Old French, from Latin *cavea,* a hollow, enclosure, from *cavus,* hollow. See **keu-**[3] in Appendix.*]
Cage (kāj), **John.** Born 1912. American composer.
cage·ling (kāj′lĭng) *n.* A caged bird.
cag·ey (kā′jē) *adj.* **-ier, -iest.** Also **cag·y.** Wary; careful; shrewd. [Origin unknown.] —**cag′i·ly** *adv.* —**cag′i·ness** *n.*
Ca·glia·ri (kä′lyä-rē). The capital of Sardinia, Italy, and a seaport on the southern shore of the island. Population, 755,000.
Ca·glio·stro (kä-lyô′strō), Count **Alessandro di.** Original name, Giuseppe Balsamo. 1743–1795. Italian adventurer and magician.
ca·hier (kä-yā′) *n.* **1.** A number of pages gathered together, as in a loose-leaf binder; notebook. **2.** A report, as of the proceedings at a meeting. [French, from Old French *caier, quaer,* from Latin *quaternī,* a group of four (leaves), from *quater,* four times. See **kwetwer-** in Appendix.*]
Ca·ho·ki·a Mounds (kə-hō′kī-ə). A group of pre-Columbian Indian mounds, one of which is the largest earthwork of this kind in the United States, situated in southeastern Illinois, near East St. Louis.
ca·hoots (kə-hōōts′) *pl.n. Informal.* Collaboration of a questionable nature. Used in the phrase *in cahoots.* [Perhaps from French *cahute,* cabin, hut, from Old French, blend of *cabane,* CABIN, and *hutte,* HUT.]
CAI Airport code for Cairo, Egypt.
Cai·a·phas (kā′ə-fəs, kī′-), **Joseph.** Jewish High Priest (A.D. 18?–36); president of council condemning Jesus. Matthew 26.
Cai·cos (kā′kəs). One of the two groups of islands comprising the British-administered **Turks and Caicos Islands** *(see).*
Cai·jan. Variant of **Cajun.**
cai·man (kā′mən, kā-măn′, kī-măn′) *n., pl.* **-mans.** Also **cay·man.** Any of various tropical American crocodilians of the genus *Caiman* and related genera, resembling and closely related to the alligators. [Spanish *caimán,* from Carib *cayman,* perhaps of African origin.]
cain. Variant of **kain.**
Cain[1] (kān). The eldest son of Adam and Eve, who killed his brother Abel out of jealousy. Genesis 4. [Latin, from Greek *Kain,* from Hebrew *Qayin,* "creature."]
Cain[2] (kān) *n.* A murderer. —**raise Cain.** *Slang.* To create a great disturbance or uproar; make trouble. [From CAIN.]
-caine. Indicates a synthetic alkaloid in anesthetic drugs; for example, **eucaine.** [From (CO)CAINE.]
Cain·ite (kā′nīt′) *n.* **1.** A member of a Gnostic sect of possibly pre-Christian origin, who regarded the God of the Old Testament as the cause of all evil and venerated those who had opposed him, from Cain to Judas Iscariot. **2.** One of the race of Cain who dwelt in the Land of Nod. Genesis 5: 16–24.
ca·ïque (kä-ēk′) *n.* **1.** A long, narrow rowboat used in the Middle East. **2.** A small sailing vessel used in the eastern Mediterranean. [French, from Italian *caicco,* from Turkish *kayık.*]
caird (kârd) *n. Scottish.* An itinerant tinker or handyman. [Scottish Gaelic *ceard,* artist, craftsman, from Old Irish *cerd,* art, artist. See **kerd-**[2] in Appendix.*]
Caird Coast (kârd). A section of Coats Land on the south eastern coast of the Weddell Sea in Antarctica; part of the British Antarctic Territory.
cairn (kârn) *n.* Also **karn.** A mound of stones erected as a landmark or memorial. [Middle English *carne,* from Celtic *kar-n-, kr-ag-* (both unattested).] —**cairned** (kârnd) *adj.*
cairn·gorm (kârn′gôrm′) *n.* A smoky-brown or yellow variety of quartz, used as a semiprecious gem. Also called "smoky quartz." [After *Cairngorm* Mountains, Scotland, its locality.]
Cairn terrier. A small dog of a breed developed in Scotland, having a broad head and a rough, shaggy coat. [So called because it hunts among cairns.]
Cai·ro (kī′rō *for sense 1;* kâr′ō *for sense 2*). **1.** *Arabic* **Al Qa·hi·rah** (äl kä′hĭ-rō). The capital of Egypt and the largest city in Africa, on the Nile in the northeastern part of the country. Population, 3,346,000. **2.** A town in Illinois at the confluence of the Ohio and Mississippi rivers; an important Union military base during the Civil War. Population, 9,000.
cais·son (kā′sŏn′, -sən) *n.* **1.** A watertight structure within which construction work is carried on. **2.** A watertight float, a **camel** *(see).* **3.** A floating structure used to close off the entrance to a dock or canal lock. **4.** A large box open at the top and one side, designed to fit against the side of a ship and used to repair damaged hulls under water. **5.** *Military.* **a.** A large box used to hold ammunition. **b.** A horse-drawn vehicle, usually two-wheeled, once used to carry ammunition. [French, from Old French *casson,* from Italian *cassa,* chest, box, from Latin *capsa.* See **kap-** in Appendix.*]
caisson disease. A disorder in divers and caisson and tunnel workers caused by a too rapid return from high pressure to atmospheric pressure, characterized by pains in the joints, cramps, paralysis, and eventual death unless treated by gradual decompression. Also called "aeroembolism," "the bends," "decompression sickness," "tunnel disease."
Caith·ness (kāth′nĕs′, kāth-nĕs′). A county of Scotland, occupying 686 square miles in the extreme northeast. Population, 28,000. County seat, Wick.
cai·tiff (kā′tĭf) *n.* A base coward; wretch. —*adj.* Base and cowardly. [Middle English *caitif,* prisoner, captive, wretch, from Old North French, from Latin *captīvus,* CAPTIVE.]
Ca·ja·mar·ca (kä′hä-mär′kä). A city of northeastern Peru, in the Andes; the scene of the capture of the last Inca ruler by Pizarro (1532). Population, 23,000.
caj·e·put (kăj′ə-pət, -pŏŏt′) *n.* Also **caj·u·put.** A tree, *Melaleuca leucadendron,* native to Australia, having whitish flowers and leaves that yield an aromatic oil. [Malay *kayu puteh* : *kayu,* tree + *puteh,* white.]
ca·jole (kə-jōl′) *tr.v.* **-joled, -joling, -joles.** To coax; wheedle. [French *cajoler,* "to chatter like a caged jay," alteration (influenced by French *cage,* cage) of earlier *gaioler,* from Picard *gaiole,* bird cage, from Late Latin *caveola,* diminutive of Latin *cavea,* a hollow, enclosure. See **cage.**] —**ca·jol′er** *n.* —**ca·jol′er·y** *n.* —**ca·jol′ing·ly** *adv.*
Ca·jun (kā′jən) *n.* Also **Cai·jan, Ca·jan.** A native of Louisiana believed to be descended from the French exiles from Acadia. [Alteration of ACADIAN.]
cake (kāk) *n.* **1.** A sweet baked mixture of flour, liquid, eggs, and other ingredients in loaf or rounded layer form. **2.** A flat, thin mass of dough or batter, baked or fried, as a pancake. **3.** A patty of fried food, as a fishcake. **4.** A shaped or molded piece, as of soap or ice. —**take the cake.** *Informal.* To win the prize; be outstanding. —*v.* **caked, caking, cakes.** —*tr.* To cause to form into a cake. —*intr.* To become formed into a compact mass. [Middle English *cake, kake,* from Old Norse *kaka.* See **kak-**[2] in Appendix.*]
cakes and ale. The good things in life.
cake·walk (kāk′wôk′) *n.* **1.** Formerly, a promenade or walk in which those performing the most complex and unusual steps won cakes as prizes. **2. a.** A strutting dance based on this promenade. **b.** The music for this dance. —*intr.v.* **cakewalked, -walking, -walks.** To perform a cakewalk. —**cake′walk′er** *n.*
cal calorie (small).
Cal calorie (large).
cal. **1.** calendar. **2.** caliber.
Cal. California (unofficial).
Cal·a·bar (kăl′ə-bär′). A seaport of Nigeria, in the southeast on the Gulf of Guinea. Population, 47,000.
Calabar bean. The dark-brown poisonous seed of a woody vine, *Physostigma venenosum,* of tropical Africa. It is the source of the drug **physostigmine** *(see).* Also called "ordeal bean." [After CALABAR.]
cal·a·bash (kăl′ə-băsh′) *n.* **1.** A vine, *Lagenaria siceraria,* native to the Old World, bearing large, hard-shelled gourds. Also called "bottle gourd." **2.** A tropical American tree, *Crescentia cujete,* bearing large, rounded fruit. Also called "bottle gourd." **3.** The fruit of a calabash. **4.** A utensil, such as a dish, ladle, or tobacco pipe, made from the fruit of a calabash. [Obsolete French *calabasse,* from Spanish *calabaza*†.]
cal·a·boose (kăl′ə-bōōs′) *n. Slang.* A jail. [Louisiana French *calabouse,* from Spanish *calabozo*†, a dungeon.]
Ca·la·bri·a (kə-lā′brē-ə; *Italian* kä-lä′brē-ä). Ancient name **Brut·ti·um** (brŭt′ē-əm). A region of Italy, occupying 5,823 square miles in the extreme southwest. Population, 2,045,000. Capital, Cosenza.
ca·la·di·um (kə-lā′dē-əm) *n.* Any of various tropical plants of the genus *Caladium,* widely cultivated as potted plants for their showy, variegated foliage. [New Latin *Caladium,* from Malay *kĕladi,* an aroid.]
Ca·lah. The Biblical name for **Kalakh.**

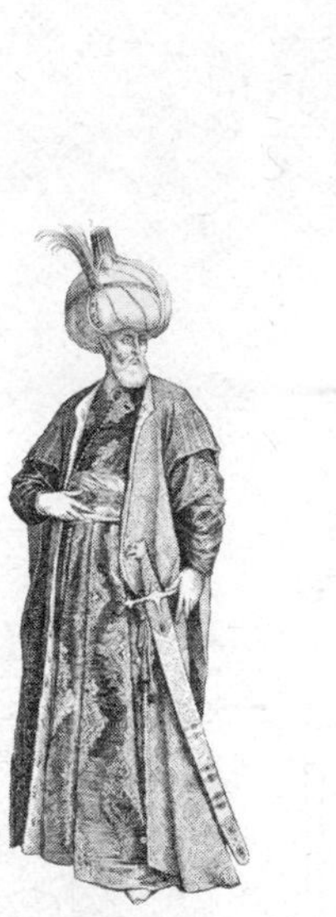

caftan
Turkish caftan worn under a short-sleeved outer garment

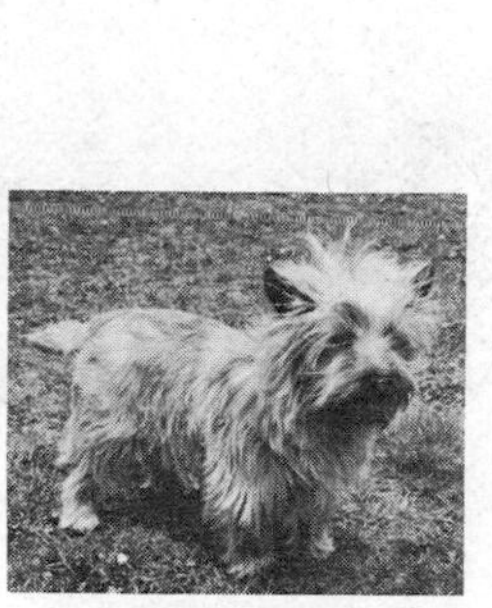

Cairn terrier

caïque

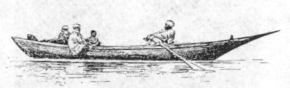

Ca·lais (kă-lā′, kăl′ā). A seaport and industrial city of northwestern France, on the Strait of Dover, opposite Dover, England. Population, 70,000.

cal·a·man·co (kăl′ə-măng′kō) *n., pl.* **-cos** or **-coes.** A glossy woolen fabric with a checked pattern on only one side. [Spanish *calamaco,* perhaps modification of Latin *calamaucus,* felt cap, of Oriental origin.]

cal·a·man·der (kăl′ə-măn′dər) *n.* The hard, black-and-brown-striped wood of certain tropical Asiatic trees of the genus *Diospyros,* used in furniture. [Probably from Dutch *kalamander(hout),* calamander (wood), perhaps after COROMANDEL COAST.]

Ca·la·mian Islands (kä′lä-myän′). An island group of the Republic of the Philippines, consisting of 3 large islands and 95 small ones, occupying 677 square miles, between Mindoro and Palawan islands.

cal·a·mine (kăl′ə-mīn′, -mĭn) *n.* **1.** A white or sometimes iron- or copper-stained mineral, essentially $Zn_4Si_2O_7(OH)_2 \cdot H_2O$. Also called "hemimorphite." **2.** *Pharmacology.* A pink, odorless, tasteless powder of zinc oxide with a small amount of ferric oxide, dissolved in mineral oils and used in skin lotions. [French, from Medieval Latin *calamīna,* alteration of Latin *cadmia,* from Greek *kadmeia,* "Cadmean (earth)" (first found near Thebes, city founded by Cadmus), from *kadmeios,* of Cadmus, from *Kadmos,* CADMUS.]

cal·a·mint (kăl′ə-mĭnt′) *n.* Any of several aromatic plants of the genus *Satureja;* especially, *S. calamintha,* native to Eurasia, having clusters of purplish or pink flowers. [Middle English *calament,* from Old French, from Medieval Latin *calamentum,* variant of Late Latin *calaminthē,* from Greek *kalaminthē*†.]

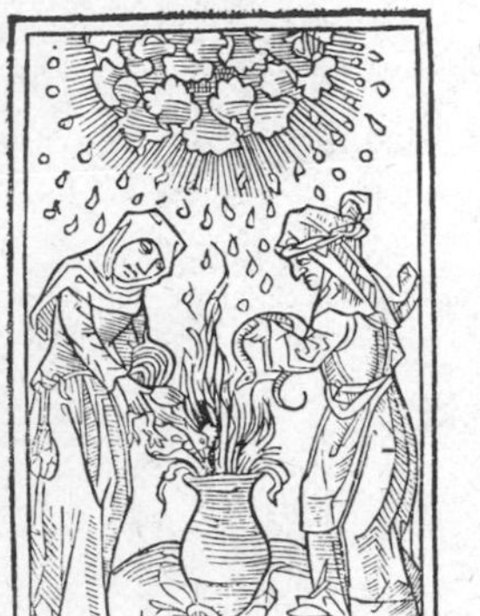

caldron
Fifteenth-century woodcut of witches

cal·a·mite (kăl′ə-mīt) *n.* Any of various extinct treelike plants of the genus *Calamites,* resembling the horsetails, but much larger, and known only as fossils. [New Latin *Calamites,* from Late Greek *kalamitēs,* reedlike, from Greek, of a reed, from *kalamos,* a reed. See **koləm-** in Appendix.*]

ca·lam·i·tous (kə-lăm′ə-təs) *adj.* Causing or involving a disaster. —**ca·lam′i·tous·ly** *adv.* —**ca·lam′i·tous·ness** *n.*

ca·lam·i·ty (kə-lăm′ə-tē) *n., pl.* **-ties.** **1.** A disaster. **2.** Dire distress. —See Synonyms at **disaster.** [Middle English *calamite,* from Old French, from Latin *calamitās.* See **kel-**[2] in Appendix.*]

Calamity Jane. Original name, Martha Jane Canary (Burke). 1852?–1903. American frontierswoman.

cal·a·mon·din (kăl′ə-mŏn′dĭn) *n.* **1.** A citrus tree, *Citrus mitis,* of the Philippine Islands. **2.** The acid, globular fruit of this tree, resembling a small orange. [Tagalog *kalamunding.*]

cal·a·mus (kăl′ə-məs) *n., pl.* **-mi** (-mī′). **1.** A plant, the **sweet flag** *(see),* or its aromatic root. **2.** Any of various tropical Asiatic palms of the genus *Calamus,* from some of which rattan is obtained. **3.** A part of a feather, a **quill** *(see).* [Latin, reed, cane, from Greek *kalamos.* See **koləm-** in Appendix.*]

ca·lan·do (kä-län′dō) *adj. Music.* Gradually diminishing in tempo and volume. —*adv. Music.* In a calando manner. [Italian, from Latin *calandum,* a slackening, from *calāre, chalāre,* to let fall, slacken, from Greek *khalan.* See **ghē-** in Appendix.*]

ca·lash (kə-lăsh′) *n.* Also **ca·lèche** (kə-lĕsh′). **1.** A carriage with low wheels and a collapsible top. **2.** The top of such a carriage. **3.** A woman's folding bonnet, fashionable in the late 18th century. [French *calèche,* from German *Kalesche,* from Czech *kolesa,* plural of *koleso,* wheel, from *kolo* (stem *koles-*), wheel, from Old Church Slavonic. See **kwel-**[1] in Appendix.*]

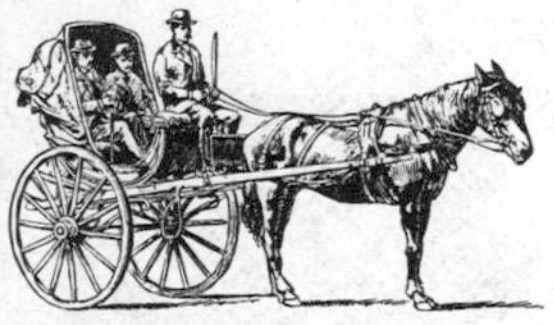

calash

cal·a·thus (kăl′ə-thəs) *n., pl.* **-thi** (-thī′). A vase-shaped basket represented in Greek painting and sculpture. [Latin, from Greek *kalathos*†.]

cal·a·ver·ite (kăl′ə-vâr′īt′) *n.* A rare ore of gold, essentially gold telluride, $AuTe_2$, often containing a small amount of silver. [Discovered in *Calaveras,* county in California.]

cal·ca·ne·us (kăl-kā′nē-əs) *n., pl.* **-nei** (-nē-ī′). Also **cal·ca·ne·um** (-nē-əm) *pl.* **-nea** (-nē-ə). The quadrangular bone at the back of the tarsus. Also called "heel bone." [Latin, "heel," from *calx,* heel. See **calk.**] —**cal·ca′ne·al** *adj.*

cal·car[1] (kăl′kär′) *n., pl.* **calcaria** (kăl-kâr′ē-ə). An anatomical spur or spurlike projection. [Latin, spur, from *calx,* heel. See **calk.**]

cal·car[2] (kăl′kär′) *n.* **1.** An oven for calcining or annealing. **2.** A furnace used in glassmaking for preparing frit. [Italian *calcara,* from Late Latin *calcāria (fornāx),* lime-kiln, from *calcārius,* of lime, from Latin *calx,* chalk, lime, from Greek *khalix,* pebble. See **calcium.**]

cal·car·e·ous (kăl-kâr′ē-əs) *adj.* Composed of, containing, or characteristic of calcium carbonate, calcium, or limestone; chalky. [Latin *calcārius,* from *calx,* lime. See **calcar.**]

cal·ced·o·ny. Variant of **chalcedony.**

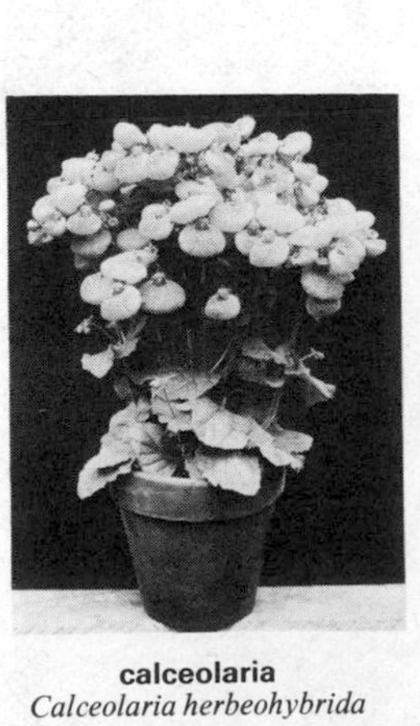

calceolaria
Calceolaria herbeohybrida

cal·ce·i·form (kăl′sē-ə-fôrm′) *adj. Botany.* Slipper-shaped; calceolate. [Latin *calceus,* shoe (see **calceolate**) + -FORM.]

cal·ce·o·lar·i·a (kăl′sē-ə-lâr′ē-ə) *n.* Any of various plants of the genus *Calceolaria,* native to tropical America and widely cultivated for their yellow, speckled, slipper-shaped flowers. Also called "slipperwort." [New Latin, from Latin *calceolārius,* shoemaker, from *calceolus,* small shoe. See **calceolate.**]

cal·ce·o·late (kăl′sē-ə-lāt′) *adj. Botany.* Shaped like a slipper, as the blossoms of some orchids. [From Latin *calceolus,* diminutive of *calceus*†, shoe.]

cal·ces. Alternate plural of **calx.**

Cal·chas (kăl′kəs). *Greek Mythology.* A soothsayer who accompanied the Greeks during the Trojan War.

calci-, calc-. Indicates lime or calcium; for example, **calciferous, calcite.** [From Latin *calx,* lime, limestone. See **calcar.**]

cal·cic (kăl′sĭk) *adj.* Composed of, containing, derived from, or pertaining to calcium or lime. [CALC(I)- + -IC.]

cal·ci·cole (kăl′sĭ-kōl′) *n. Botany.* A plant that thrives in soil rich in lime. [French : CALCI- + *-cole,* dweller, from Latin *-cola* (see **-colous**).] —**cal·cic′o·lous** (-sĭk′ə-ləs) *adj.*

cal·cif·er·ol (kăl-sĭf′ə-rôl′, -rōl′) *n.* **Vitamin D_2** *(see).* [CALCIF(EROUS) + (ERGOST)EROL.]

cal·cif·er·ous (kăl-sĭf′ər-əs) *adj.* Of, forming, or containing calcium or calcium carbonate. [CALCI- + -FEROUS.]

cal·cif·ic (kăl-sĭf′ĭk) *adj.* Producing salts of lime, as in the formation of eggshells in birds and reptiles.

cal·ci·fi·ca·tion (kăl′sə-fĭ-kā′shən) *n.* **1.** Impregnation with calcium or calcium salts, as with calcium carbonate. **2.** Hardening, as of tissue, by such impregnation. **3.** A substance, such as petrified wood, or a part so impregnated.

cal·ci·fuge (kăl′sə-fyōōj′) *n.* A plant that does not thrive in lime-rich soil. —**cal·cif′u·gal** (-sĭf′yə-gəl), **cal·cif′u·gous** *adj.*

cal·ci·fy (kăl′sə-fī′) *v.* **-fied, -fying, -fies.** —*tr.* To make stony or chalky by deposition of calcium salts. —*intr.* To become stony or chalky by deposition of calcium salts. [CALCI- + -FY.]

cal·ci·mine (kăl′sə-mīn′) *n.* Also **kal·so·mine.** A white or tinted liquid containing zinc oxide, water, glue, and coloring matter, used as a wash for walls and ceilings. Also *British* "distemper." —*tr.v.* **calcimined, -mining, -mines.** To cover or wash with calcimine. [Alteration of trademark *Kalsomine.*]

cal·ci·na·tion (kăl′sə-nā′shən) *n.* **1.** The act or process of calcining. **2.** The calcined state.

cal·cine (kăl′sīn′, kăl-sīn′) *v.* **-cined, -cining, -cines.** —*tr.* To heat (a substance) to a high temperature but below the melting or fusing point, causing loss of moisture, reduction, or oxidation. —*intr.* To undergo calcination. [Middle English *calcinen,* from Old French *calciner,* from Medieval Latin *calcīnāre,* from Latin *calx,* lime. See **calcium.**]

cal·cite (kăl′sīt′) *n.* A common crystalline form of natural calcium carbonate, the basic constituent of limestone, marble, and chalk. [CALC(I)- + -ITE.] —**cal·cit′ic** (-sĭt′ĭk) *adj.*

cal·ci·um (kăl′sē-əm) *n. Symbol* **Ca** A silvery, moderately hard metallic element, constituting approximately three per cent of the earth's crust, a basic component of bone, shells, and leaves. It occurs naturally in limestone, gypsum, and fluorite, and its compounds are used to make plaster, quicklime, Portland cement, and metallurgic and electronic materials. Atomic number 20, atomic weight 40.08, melting point 842 to 848°C, boiling point 1,487°C, specific gravity 1.55, valence 2. See **element.** [New Latin, from Latin *calx,* lime, limestone, from Greek *khalix*†, pebble.]

calcium carbide. A grayish-black crystalline compound, CaC_2, obtained by heating pulverized limestone or quicklime with carbon and used to generate acetylene gas, as a dehydrating agent, and in the manufacture of graphite and hydrogen.

calcium carbonate. A colorless or white crystalline compound, $CaCO_3$, occurring naturally as chalk, limestone, marble, and other forms and used in a wide variety of manufactured products including commercial chalk, medicines, and dentifrices.

calcium chloride. A white deliquescent compound, $CaCl_2$, used chiefly as a drying agent, refrigerant, and preservative, and for controlling dust and ice on roads.

calcium cyanamide. A gray-black compound, $Ca(CN)_2$, used as a fertilizer and weed killer.

calcium fluoride. A white powder, CaF_2, used in emery wheels, carbon electrodes, and cements.

calcium hydroxide. A soft white powder, $Ca(OH)_2$, used in making mortar, cements, calcium salts, paints, hard rubber products, and petrochemicals. Also called "slaked lime."

calcium hypochlorite. A white crystalline solid, $Ca(OCl)_2$, used as a bactericide, fungicide, and bleaching agent.

calcium light. An intense white light produced by incandescent lime, **limelight** *(see).*

calcium oxalate. A white crystalline powder, CaC_2O_4, used to make oxalic acid and found in many plant cells.

calcium oxide. A white caustic lumpy powder, CaO, used as a refractory, as a flux, in manufacturing steel, glassmaking, waste treatment, insecticides, and as an industrial alkali. Also called "lime," "quicklime," "unslaked lime," "calx."

calcium phosphate. Any of several phosphate compounds, especially: **a.** A white crystalline powder, $CaHPO_4$ or $CaHPO_4 \cdot 2H_2O$, used as a food, as a plastic stabilizer, and in glass. Also called "dibasic calcium phosphate." **b.** A colorless deliquescent powder, $CaH_4(PO_4)_2 \cdot H_2O$, used in baking powders, as a plant food, plastic stabilizer, and in glass. Also called "monobasic calcium phosphate." **c.** A white amorphous powder, $Ca_3(PO_4)_2$, used in ceramics, rubber, fertilizers, plastic stabilizers, and as a food supplement. Also called "tribasic calcium phosphate."

calc-sin·ter (kălk′sĭn′tər) *n.* Natural calcium carbonate, chiefly in the form of stalagmites or stalactites. See **travertine.** [German *Kalksinter* : *Kalk,* lime, from Old High German, from Latin *calx* (see **calcium**) + *Sinter,* slag, SINTER.]

calc·spar, calc-spar (kălk′spär′) *n.* A natural calcium carbonate, **calcite** *(see).* [Partial translation of Swedish *kalkspat* : *kalk,* lime, from Old Swedish, from Middle Low German, from Latin *calx,* lime (see **calcium**) + SPAR (mineral).]

calc-tu·fa (kălk′tōō′fə, -tyōō′fə) *n.* Also **calc-tuff** (-tŭf′). A porous or spongy deposit of calcium carbonate found in calcareous mineral springs. [CALC(AREOUS) + TUFA.]

cal·cu·la·ble (kăl′kyə-lə-bəl) *adj.* Capable of being calculated or estimated. **2.** That may be counted on; dependable; reliable. —**cal′cu·la·bil′i·ty** *n.*

cal·cu·late (kăl′kyə-lāt′) *v.* **-lated, -lating, -lates.** —*tr.* **1.** To

ă pat/ā pay/âr care/ä father/b bib/ch church/d deed/ĕ pet/ē be/f fife/g gag/h hat/hw which/ĭ pit/ī pie/îr pier/j judge/k kick/l lid, needle/m mum/n no, sudden/ng thing/ŏ pot/ō toe/ô paw, for/oi noise/ou out/ŏŏ took/ōō boot/p pop/r roar/s sauce/sh ship, dish/

ascertain by computation; reckon. **2.** To make an estimate of; evaluate. **3.** To fit for a purpose; make suitable for. Usually used in the passive voice: *calculated to go 100 miles per hour.* **4.** *Regional.* **a.** To purpose; intend. **b.** To think; suppose. —*intr.* **1.** To execute a mathematical process. **2.** *Regional.* To suppose; think; guess. —**calculate on.** To count, depend, or rely on. [Latin *calculāre,* from *calculus,* small stone (used in reckoning), diminutive of *calx,* lime, limestone, from Greek *khalix,* pebble. See **calcium.**]

Synonyms: calculate, compute, reckon, estimate. These verbs describe ways of getting more or less abstract results by mathematics. *Calculate,* the most comprehensive, can apply to all mathematical operations, simple or complex, but usually implies a relatively high level of abstraction or procedural complexity. *Compute* applies, in general, to essentially straightforward, though possibly lengthy, arithmetic operations. *Reckon* suggests simple arithmetic. *Estimate* implies rough approximation of a result without immediate need for exactness.

cal·cu·lat·ed (kăl′kyə-lā′tĭd) *adj.* **1.** Estimated with forethought: *a calculated risk.* **2.** Likely; apt: *a stratagem calculated to succeed.* **3.** Determined by mathematical calculation. —**cal′cu·lat′ed·ly** *adv.*

cal·cu·lat·ing (kăl′kyə-lā′tĭng) *adj.* **1.** Performing calculations: *a calculating machine.* **2. a.** Shrewd; crafty. **b.** Coldly scheming or conniving.

cal·cu·la·tion (kăl′kyə-lā′shən) *n.* **1.** The act, process, or result of calculating. **2.** An estimate based upon probabilities. **3.** Deliberation; foresight. —**cal′cu·la′tive** *adj.*

cal·cu·la·tor (kăl′kyə-lā′tər) *n.* **1.** A person who performs calculations. **2.** A keyboard machine for the automatic performance of arithmetic operations. **3.** A set of mathematical tables used to aid in calculating.

cal·cu·lous (kăl′kyə-ləs) *adj. Medicine.* Pertaining to, caused by, or having a calculus or calculi.

cal·cu·lus (kăl′kyə-ləs) *n., pl.* -**li** (-lī′) *or* -**luses.** **1.** *Pathology.* An abnormal concretion in the body, usually formed of mineral salts; a stone, as in the gall bladder, kidney, or urinary bladder. **2.** *Mathematics.* **a.** A method of analysis or calculation using a special symbolic notation. **b.** The combined mathematics of differential and integral calculus. [Latin, small stone used in reckoning, reckoning. See **calculate.**]

calculus of variations. The mathematical analysis of the maxima and minima of definite integrals, the integrands of which are functions of independent variables, dependent variables, and the derivatives of one or more dependent variables.

Cal·cut·ta (kăl-kŭt′ə). The capital of West Bengal, Republic of India, a port on the Hooghly River about 80 miles inland from the Bay of Bengal. Population, 2,927,000.

Cal·der (kôl′dər), **Alexander.** Born 1898. American sculptor.

cal·de·ra (kăl-dâr′ə, -dîr′ə) *n.* A large crater formed by volcanic explosion or by collapse of a volcanic cone. [Spanish, "kettle," "boiler," from Late Latin *caldāria,* CALDRON.]

Cal·de·rón de la Bar·ca (kăl′dā-rôn′ dā lä bär′kä), **Pedro.** 1600–1681. Spanish poet and playwright.

cal·dron (kôl′drən) *n.* Also **caul·dron.** A large kettle or vat for boiling. [Middle English *caud(e)ron, caldron,* from Old North French *caud(e)ron,* from Late Latin *caldāria,* from Latin, bath, from *caldārius,* suitable for warming, from *cal(i)dus,* warm. See **kel-¹** in Appendix.*]

Cald·well (kôl′dwĕl′, -dwəl), **Erskine.** Born 1903. American author.

Ca·leb¹ (kā′ləb). A masculine given name. [Hebrew *Kālēbh,* "like a dog," "faithful," from *kelebh,* dog.]

Ca·leb² (kā′ləb). A Hebrew leader. He and Joshua were the only two allowed to enter the Promised Land. Numbers 14:24.

ca·lèche. Variant of **calash.**

Cal·e·do·nia (kăl′ə-dōn′yə, -dō′nē-ə). *Poetic.* Scotland. —**Cal′e·do′nian** *adj. & n.*

Caledonian Canal. A ship canal, 60 miles long, across central Scotland, connecting the North Sea with the Atlantic Ocean.

cal·en·dar (kăl′ən-dər) *n. Abbr.* **cal. 1.** Any of various systems of reckoning time in which the beginning, length, and divisions of a year are arbitrarily defined or otherwise established. **2.** A table showing the months, weeks, and days in at least one specific year. **3.** A list or schedule, especially one arranged in chronological order, as of cases on a court docket. **4.** *Library Service.* A chronological list of documents or manuscripts, usually annotated. **5.** *Obsolete.* A guide; example. —*tr.v.* **calendared, -daring, -dars.** To enter on a calendar; to list; schedule. —**Chinese calendar.** The lunar calendar of the Chinese, supposed to have begun in 2397 B.C. Years are reckoned in cycles of 60, each year having a particular name that is a combination of two characters derived schematically from two series of signs, the celestial and the terrestrial. Months are reckoned also in cycles of 60 that are renewed every 5 years, and each month consists of 28 to 30 days. —**ecclesiastical calendar.** A lunisolar calendar used in Roman Catholic and many Protestant countries, reckoning the year from Advent Sunday. —**Gregorian calendar.** The calendar now in use throughout most parts of the world, introduced by Pope Gregory XIII in 1582 and adopted by England and the American colonies in 1752. Also called "New Style." —**Hebrew** or **Jewish calendar.** The lunisolar calendar used by the Hebrews, reckoning time from the year of creation, 3761 B.C., and based on a metonic cycle of 19 years, with the 3rd, 6th, 8th, 11th, 14th, 17th, and 19th years of each cycle designated leap years. —**Hindu calendar.** The lunisolar calendar of the Hindus, believed to date in its modern form from A.D. 400. The solar year is divided into 12 months in accordance with the successive entrances of the sun into the

MONTHS OF THREE PRINCIPAL CALENDARS

GREGORIAN		HEBREW		MOSLEM	
		Months correspond approximately to those in parentheses		Beginning of year retrogresses through the solar year of the Gregorian calendar	
name	number of days	name	number of days	name	number of days
January	31	Tishri (September–October)	30	Muharram	30
February in leap year	28 29	Heshvan in some years (October–November)	29 30	Safar	29
March	31	Kislev in some years (November–December)	29 30	Rabi I	30
April	30	Tevet (December–January)	29	Rabi II	30
May	31	Shevat (January–February)	30	Jumada I	30
June	30	Adar* in leap year (February–March)	29 30	Jumada II	29
July	31	Nisan (March–April)	30	Rajab	30
August	31	Iyar (April–May)	29	Sha`ban	29
September	30	Sivan (May–June)	30	Ramadan	30
October	31	Tammuz (June–July)	29	Shawwal	29
November	30	Av (July–August)	30	Dhu'l-Qa dah	30
December	31	Elul (August–September)	29	Dhu'l-Hijja in leap year	29 30

*Adar is followed in leap year by the intercalary month Veadar, or Adar Sheni, having 29 days.

signs of the zodiac, the months varying in length from 29 to 32 days. —**Julian calendar.** The calendar prescribed by Julius Caesar, introduced in 46 B.C. and replaced in most countries by the Gregorian calendar. Also called "Old Style." —**Moslem calendar.** The calendar used in Moslem countries reckoning time from July 16, A.D. 622, the day after the Hegira, based on a cycle of 30 years, 19 of which have 354 days each and 11 of which are leap years, having 355 days each. —**Revolutionary calendar.** The calendar introduced in France on October 24, 1793, by the National Convention and abolished under Napoleon on December 31, 1805, reckoning time from September 22, 1792, the date of the founding of the First Republic. —**Roman calendar.** An ancient Roman lunar calendar designating the day of the new moon as the **calends** *(see),* the day of the full moon as the **ides** *(see),* and the ninth day before the ides as the **nones** *(see).* [Middle English *calender,* from Norman French, from Medieval Latin *kalendārium,* from Latin, a moneylender's account book (because the monthly interest was due on the calends), from *kalendae,* the CALENDS.]

cal·en·der (kăl′ən-dər) *n.* A machine in which paper or cloth is made smooth and glossy by being pressed through rollers. —*tr.v.* **calendered, -dering, -ders.** To press in a calender. [French *calendre,* from Medieval Latin *calendra, celendra,* from Latin *cylindrus,* cylinder, roller, from Greek *kulindros,* from *kulindein,* to roll. See **skel-³** in Appendix.*] —**cal′en·der·er** *n.*

ca·len·dri·cal (kə-lĕn′drĭ-kəl) *adj.* Of, pertaining to, or used in a calendar.

cal·ends (kăl′əndz) *n., pl.* **calends.** Also **kal·ends.** In the ancient Roman calendar, the day of the new moon and the first day of the month. [Middle English *kalendes,* from Latin *kalendae.* See **kel-³** in Appendix.*] —**ca·len′dal** (kə-lĕn′dəl) *adj.*

ca·len·du·la (kə-lĕn′jŏŏ-lə) *n.* Any plant of the genus *Calendula,* having orange-yellow flowers; especially, the **pot marigold** *(see).* [New Latin *Calendula,* from Medieval Latin *calendula,* marigold, from Latin *kalendae,* CALENDS (perhaps because it was thought to be a cure for menstrual disorders).]

cal·en·ture (kăl′ən-chŏŏr′) *n.* A mild, brief, or sometimes persistent tropical fever. [Spanish *calentura,* from *calentar,* to heat, from Latin *calēns,* present participle of *calēre,* to be warm. See **kel-¹** in Appendix.*]

calf¹ (kăf, käf) *n., pl.* **calves** (kăvz, kävz). **1.** A young cow or bull. **2.** The young of certain other mammals, such as the elephant or whale. **3.** Calfskin leather. **4.** A large, floating chunk of ice split from a glacier, iceberg, or floe. **5.** An awkward, callow youth. —**kill the fatted calf.** To prepare a feast of welcome; celebrate in grand style. [Middle English *calf, kelf,* Old English *cealf,* from West Germanic *kalbam* (unattested).]

calf² (kăf, käf) *n., pl.* **calves** (kăvz, kävz). The fleshy, muscular back part of the human leg, between the knee and ankle. [Middle English, from Old Norse *kalfi,* perhaps from West Germanic *kalbam* (unattested), CALF (animal).]

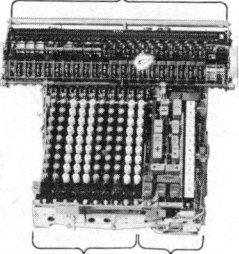

digital display dials

digital input keyboard

arithmetic operations

calculator

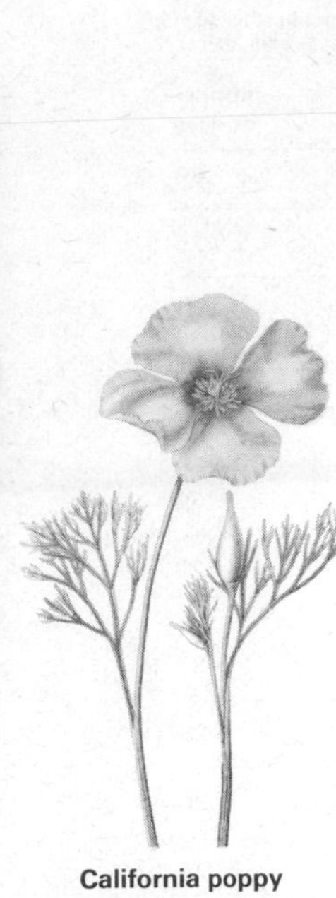

California poppy

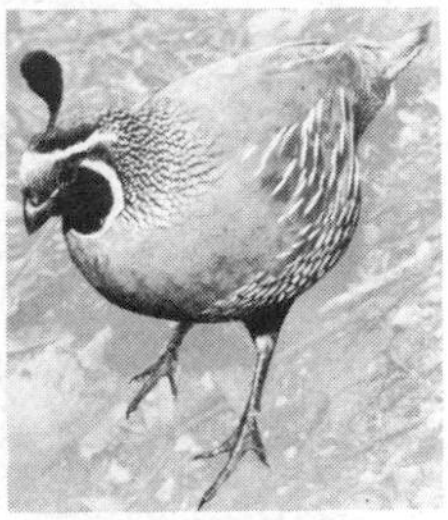

California quail

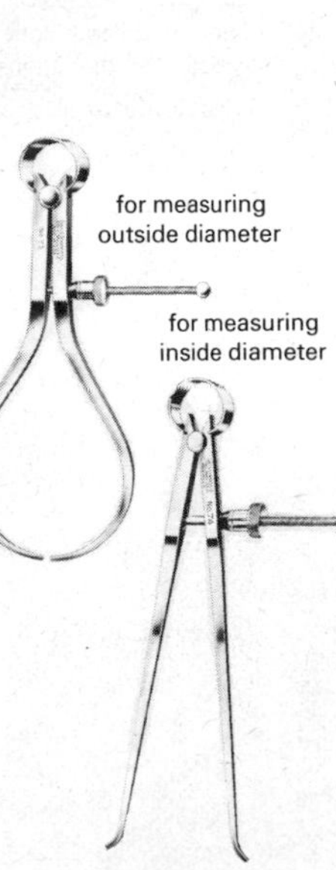

caliper
Glass blower's calipers

calf's-foot jelly (kăvz′fo͝ot′, kăvz′-). Also **calves'-foot jelly.** A gelatinous food made by boiling calves' feet.
calf·skin (kăf′skĭn′, käf′-) *n.* **1.** The hide of a calf. **2.** *Abbr.* **cf.** Fine leather made from the hide of a calf. In this sense, also called "calf."
Cal·ga·ry (kăl′gə-rē). The second-largest city of Alberta, Canada, situated in the southwest in the center of a ranching area. Population, 311,000.
Cal·houn (kăl-ho͞on′), **John Caldwell.** 1782–1850. Vice President of the United States under John Quincy Adams and Andrew Jackson (1825–32).
Ca·li (kä′lē). A city of west-central Colombia, in the valley of the Cauca River. Population, 638,000.
Cal·i·ban (kăl′ə-băn′). In Shakespeare's *Tempest,* the grotesque, brutish slave. [Perhaps alteration of CARIBAN.]
cal·i·ber (kăl′ə-bər) *n.* Also *chiefly British* **cal·i·bre. 1.** *Abbr.* **cal. a.** The diameter of the inside of a tube. **b.** The diameter of the bore of a gun. **c.** The diameter of a bullet or shell. **2.** Degree of worth or distinction. [Old French *calibre,* from Old Italian *calibro,* from Arabic *qālib,* shoemaker's last, probably from Greek *kalapous,* "wooden foot" : *kalon,* wood, firewood, from *kaiein,* to burn (see **kēu-** in Appendix*) + *pous,* foot (see **ped-**[1] in Appendix*).]
cal·i·brate (kăl′ə-brāt′) *tr.v.* **-brated, -brating, -brates. 1.** To check, adjust, or systematically standardize the graduations of a quantitative measuring instrument. **2.** To determine the caliber of (a tube). —**cal′i·bra′tion** *n.* —**cal′i·bra′tor** (-brā′tər) *n.*
ca·li·ces. Plural of **calix.**
ca·li·che (kə-lē′chē; *Spanish* kä-lē′chā) *n.* **1. a.** A crude sodium nitrate occurring naturally in Chile, Peru, and the southwestern United States, used as fertilizer. **b. Sodium nitrate** *(see).* **2.** A hard soil layer cemented by calcium carbonate and found in deserts and other arid or semiarid regions. [American Spanish, from Spanish, pebble in a brick, chip of limestone, from *cal,* lime, limestone, from Latin *calx,* from Greek *khalix,* pebble. See **calcium.**]
cal·i·co (kăl′ĭ-kō) *n., pl.* **-coes** or **-cos. 1.** A coarse cloth, usually printed with bright designs. **2.** *British.* White cotton cloth. —*adj.* **1.** Made of calico. **2.** Resembling printed calico; spotted; mottled: *a calico cat.* [After CALICUT.]
cal·i·co·back (kăl′ĭ-kō-băk′) *n.* The **harlequin bug** *(see).*
calico bass. A fish, the **black crappie** *(see).* [From the colored spots on its body.]
calico bush. A shrub, the **mountain laurel** *(see).*
Cal·i·cut. The former name for **Kozhikode.**
ca·lif. Variant of **caliph.**
Cal·i·for·nia (kăl′ə-fôrn′yə, -fôr′nē-ə). *Abbr.* **Calif.** A Pacific Coast state of the United States, 158,693 square miles in area, bounded by Mexico to the south; the 31st state to be admitted to the Union (1850). Population, 18,084,000. Capital, Sacramento. See map at **United States of America.** —**Cal′i·for′nian** *adj.* & *n.*
Cal·i·for·nia, Gulf of (kăl′ə-fôrn′yə, -fôr′nē-ə). An inlet of the Pacific Ocean, extending 700 miles between the peninsula of Lower California and northwestern Mexico.
California Current. A cold ocean current in the Pacific, flowing southeastward off the west coast of North America.
California fuchsia. A plant, *Zauschneria californica,* of western North America, cultivated for its tubular scarlet flowers.
California laurel. An aromatic evergreen tree, *Umbellularia californica,* of the North American Pacific Coast, having clusters of yellowish-green flowers and yellowish-green fleshy fruit. Its attractively grained wood is used to make bowls and plates and in cabinetwork. Also called "bay tree," "Oregon myrtle."
California lilac. A shrub, the **blueblossom** *(see).*
California nutmeg. An evergreen tree, *Torreya californica,* having spiny, pointed leaves and purple-streaked, greenish fruit.
California poppy. A plant, *Eschscholtzia californica,* of the Pacific Coast of North America, having finely divided bluish-green leaves and orange-yellow flowers.
California quail. A plump, chunky bird, *Lophortyx californicus,* of western North America, having gray and brown plumage and a curving black plume on the crown of the head.
cal·i·for·ni·um (kăl′ə-fôr′nē-əm) *n.* *Symbol* **Cf** A synthetic element produced in trace quantities by helium isotope bombardment of curium. All isotopes are radioactive, chiefly by emission of alpha particles. Atomic number 98, mass numbers 244 to 254, half-lives varying from 25 minutes to 800 years. See **element.** [New Latin; discovered at the University of *California.*]
ca·lig·i·nous (kə-lĭj′ə-nəs) *adj. Rare.* Dark; gloomy; shadowy: *"Her lone little room, full of caliginous corners and nooks"* (Bulwer-Lytton). [Old French *caligineux,* from Latin *cālīginōsus,* dark, from *cālīgō*†, darkness.]
Ca·lig·u·la (kə-lĭg′yə-lə). Original name, Gaius Caesar. A.D. 12–41. Emperor of Rome (37–41).
cal·i·pash (kăl′ə-păsh′, kăl′ə-păsh′) *n.* An edible, gelatinous, greenish substance lying beneath a turtle's upper shell. [Probably alteration of Spanish *carapacho,* CARAPACE.]
cal·i·pee (kăl′ə-pē′, kăl′ə-pē′) *n.* An edible, gelatinous, yellowish substance lying beneath a turtle's lower shell. [Probably alteration of CALIPASH.]
cal·i·per (kăl′ə-pər) *n.* Also **cal·li·per. 1.** *Usually plural.* An instrument consisting essentially of two curved hinged legs and used to measure internal and external dimensions. **2.** *Usually plural.* A large instrument having a fixed and a movable arm on a graduated stock, used for measuring the diameters of logs and similar objects. **3.** A **vernier caliper** *(see).* —*v.* **calipered, -pering, -pers.** —*tr.* To measure (something) with calipers. —*intr.* To determine dimensions by using calipers. [Variant of CALIBER.]
ca·liph (kā′lĭf, kăl′ĭf) *n.* Also **ca·lif, kha·lif.** The secular and religious head of a Moslem state. [Middle English *caliphe, califfe,* from Old French *calife,* from Arabic *khalīfa,* "successor," from *khalafa,* to succeed.]
ca·liph·ate (kā′lĭf-āt′, kăl′ĭf-, -ĭt) *n.* The office, jurisdiction, or reign of a caliph.
cal·i·sa·ya (kăl′ə-sā′ə) *n.* The bark of any tree of the genus *Cinchona,* from which quinine is obtained, especially *C. calisaya.* Also called "calisaya bark," "yellowbark." [Spanish, probably after *Calisaya,* 17th-century Peruvian Indian who taught the Spanish the use of quinine contained in the bark.]
cal·is·then·ics (kăl′əs-thĕn′ĭks) *pl.n.* Also **cal·lis·then·ics. 1.** Simple gymnastic exercises designed to develop muscular tone and to promote physical well-being. **2.** The practice of such exercises. Used with a singular verb. [CAL(L)I- + Greek *sthenos,* strength (see **sthenia**).] —**cal′is·then′ic** *adj.*
ca·lix (kā′lĭks, kăl′ĭks) *n., pl.* **calices** (kā′lə-sēz′, kăl′ə-). *Ecclesiastical.* A chalice. [Latin. See **kal-**[1] in Appendix.*]
Ca·lix·tus III (kə-lĭk′stəs). Original name, Alfonso Borgia. 1378–1458. Pope (1455–58); first Borgia elected to papacy.
calk[1] (kôk) *n.* **1.** A pointed extension on the toe or heels of a horseshoe designed to prevent slipping. **2.** A spiked plate fixed on the bottom of a shoe to prevent slipping and preserve the sole. —*tr.v.* **calked, calking, calks. 1.** To supply with or fasten on calks. **2.** To cut or injure with a calk. [Short for earlier *calkin,* Middle English *kakun,* from Middle Dutch *calcoen,* hoof of a horse, from Old Norman French *calcain,* heel, from Latin *calcāneum, calcāneus,* from *calx*†.]
calk[2]. Variant of **caulk.**
call (kôl) *v.* **called, calling, calls.** —*tr.* **1.** To cry out in a loud tone; announce; proclaim. **2.** To summon. **3.** To convoke or convene (a meeting). **4.** To summon to a particular career or pursuit. **5.** To awaken. **6.** To telephone (someone). **7. a.** To make a characteristic cry, as a bird. **b.** To lure by imitating such a cry. **8.** To name. **9.** To estimate as being; consider: *I call that fair.* **10.** To designate; label: *Nobody calls me a liar.* **11.** To bring to action or under consideration: *call a case to court.* **12.** To demand payment of (a loan or bond issue). **13.** *Baseball.* **a.** To stop (a game) because of bad weather or darkness. **b.** To indicate a decision in regard to (a pitch, ball, strike, or player). **14.** *Billiards.* **a.** To predict (the outcome of a shot) before playing. **b.** To ask (another player) to do so. **15.** To forecast or predict accurately. **16.** *Poker.* To demand to see the hand of (an opponent) by equaling his bet. **17.** *Informal.* To demand that a person make good a boast or support a statement with facts: *call a bluff.* **18.** To shout (directions) in rhythm for square dances. —*intr.* **1.** To telephone. **2.** To pay a short visit. **3.** To attract attention by shouting. —**call back. 1.** To bid to come back; to recall. **2.** To retract or disavow. **3.** To telephone repeatedly or in return. —**call down. 1.** To invoke, as from heaven. **2.** *Informal.* To find fault with or berate. —**call for. 1.** To go and get or stop for. **2.** To be appropriate for; to warrant. —**call forth.** To evoke. —**call in. 1.** To collect or request payment of. **2.** To take out of circulation: *calling in silver dollars.* **3.** To summon for assistance or consultation: *call in a specialist.* —**call into being.** To create or cause to exist. —**call into question.** To raise doubt about. —**call off. 1.** To cancel or postpone. **2.** To restrain or recall. **3.** To read aloud, as from a list of names. —**call on** (or **upon**). **1.** To pay a short visit to. **2.** To request or order (someone) to do something. —**call out. 1.** To shout. **2.** To cause to assemble; summon: *call out the guard.* —**call up. 1.** To telephone (someone). **2.** To summon into military service: *called up for active duty.* **3.** To remember or cause to remember: *calling up old times.* **4.** To bring forth for action or discussion. —*n.* **1.** A shout or loud cry. **2. a.** The characteristic cry of an animal, especially a bird. **b.** An instrument or sound made to imitate such a cry, used as a lure. **3.** Need or occasion: *There was no call for that remark.* **4.** Demand: *There isn't much call for buggy whips today.* **5.** A claim on a person's time or life: *the call of duty.* **6.** A short visit; especially, one made as a formality or for business or professional purposes. **7.** A summons or invitation. **8. a.** A signal, as made by a horn or bell. **b.** The sounding of a horn to encourage hounds during a hunt. **9.** A vocation, as to the ministry. **10.** A roll call. **11.** *Theater.* A posted notice of rehearsal times. **12.** *Baseball.* The decision of an umpire. **13.** An instruction in square dancing to begin a different step or set. **14.** A demand or request for payment of a debt, as by redeeming bonds. **15.** *Finance.* **a.** An agreement in which a trader may, for a fee, buy a certain quantity of a stock or commodity for a specified price within a limited period of time. **b.** A demand for payment due on the stock bought on margin when the value has shrunk. In this sense, compare **put, straddle.** —**on call. 1.** Payable on demand. **2.** Available whenever summoned. —**within call.** Easily summoned; accessible. [Middle English *callen,* Old English *ceallian,* to call, shout, from Old Norse *kalla.* See **gal-**[2] in Appendix.*]
cal·la (kăl′ə) *n.* **1.** Any of several tropical or semitropical plants of the genus *Zantedeschia;* especially, *Z. aethiopica,* widely cultivated for its large, showy white spathe that encloses a yellow spadix. Also called "calla lily," "arum lily." **2.** A marsh plant, *Calla palustris,* of the North Temperate Zone, having small, densely clustered greenish flowers partly enclosed in a spreading white spathe. Also called "water arum." [New Latin *Calla,* from Greek *kallaia,* wattle of a cock, probably from *kallos,* beauty. See **kal-**[2] in Appendix.*]
Cal·la·o (kä-yä′ō). The principal seaport of Peru, situated on

ă pat/ā pay/âr care/ä father/b bib/ch church/d deed/ĕ pet/ē be/f fife/g gag/h hat/hw which/ĭ pit/ī pie/îr pier/j judge/k kick/l lid, needle/m mum/n no, sudden/ng thing/ŏ pot/ō toe/ô paw, for/oi noise/ou out/o͝o took/o͞o boot/p pop/r roar/s sauce/sh ship, dish/

the Pacific Ocean eight miles west of Lima. Population, 161,000.

call·board (kôl′bôrd′, -bōrd′) *n. Theater.* A backstage bulletin board for posting instructions and notices.

call·boy (kôl′boi′) *n.* **1.** One who tells actors when it is time for them to go on stage. **2.** A bellboy.

call·er[1] (kô′lər) *n.* **1.** Someone or something that calls or cries out. **2.** A person paying a short visit. **3.** One who calls out the figures in square dancing.

cal·ler[2] (kăl′ər) *adj. Scottish.* **1.** Fresh. Used of food, especially fish. **2.** Cool and refreshing, as a breeze. [Middle English *calour,* earlier *calvur*†.]

call girl. *Informal.* A prostitute hired by telephone.

call house. *Informal.* A house of prostitution.

calli–. Indicates beauty; for example, **calliopsis.** [Latin, from Greek *kalli-,* from *kallos,* beauty. See **kal-**[2] in Appendix.*]

cal·lig·ra·phy (kə-lĭg′rə-fē) *n.* **1.** The art of fine handwriting. **2.** Penmanship; handwriting. [French *calligraphie,* from Greek *kalligraphia* : CALLI- + -GRAPHY.] —**cal·lig′ra·pher, cal·lig′ra·phist** *n.* —**cal′li·graph′ic** (kăl′ə-grăf′ĭk) *adj.*

call·ing (kô′lĭng) *n.* **1.** An inner urge; a strong impulse. **2.** An occupation, profession, or career.

calling card. A card bearing one's name and often one's address and telephone number, used for social or business purposes.

cal·li·o·pe (kăl′ē-ōp′, kə-lī′ə-pē′) *n.* A musical instrument fitted with steam whistles, played from a keyboard. It is usually heard at carnivals and circuses. [After CALLIOPE (the Muse).]

Cal·li·o·pe (kə-lī′ə-pē′). *Greek Mythology.* The Muse of epic poetry. [Latin, from Greek *Kalliopē,* "beautiful-voiced" : CALLI- + *ops,* voice (see **wekw-** in Appendix*).]

cal·li·op·sis (kăl′ē-ŏp′sĭs) *n.* A plant, the **coreopsis** *(see).* [New Latin, "having beautiful eyes" (with reference to its achenes) : CALLI- + -OPSIS.]

cal·li·per. Variant of **caliper.**

cal·li·pyg·i·an (kăl′ə-pĭj′ē-ən) *adj.* Also **cal·li·pyg·ous** (-pī′gəs). Having beautifully proportioned buttocks. [From Greek *kallipugos* : CALLI- + *pugē,* buttocks (see **pygidium**).]

Cal·lis·the·nes (kə-lĭs′thə-nēz′). Greek philosopher of the fourth century B.C.; chronicler of Alexander the Great.

cal·lis·then·ics. Variant of **calisthenics.**

Cal·lis·to[1] (kə-lĭs′tō). *Greek Mythology.* A nymph, beloved of Zeus and thus hated by Hera, who changed her into a bear. Zeus then placed her in the sky as the constellation Ursa Major. [Latin, from Greek *Kallistō,* perhaps from *kallistos,* the most beautiful, from *kallos,* beautiful. See **kal-**[2] in Appendix.*]

Cal·lis·to[2] (kə-lĭs′tō) *n.* One of the 12 moons of Jupiter, the largest known moon of any planet. [After CALLISTO.]

call letters. The identifying code letters or numbers of a radio or television transmitting station.

call loan. A loan repayable on demand at any time.

call market. The market for call money.

call money. Money lent by banks, usually to stockbrokers, subject to repayment on demand at any time.

call number. A number used in libraries to classify a book and indicate its placement on the shelves.

cal·los·i·ty (kă-lŏs′ə-tē, kə-) *n., pl.* **-ties.** **1.** The condition of being calloused. **2.** Hardheartedness; insensitivity. [Middle English *callosite,* from Old French, from Latin *callōsitās,* from *callōsus,* hardened, CALLOUS.]

Cal·lot (kȧ-lō′), **Jacques.** 1592–1635. French painter and engraver; raised etching to an independent art.

cal·lous (kăl′əs) *adj.* **1.** Having calluses; toughened. **2.** Emotionally hardened; insensitive; unfeeling. —*v.* **calloused, -lousing, -louses.** —*tr.* To make callous. —*intr.* To become callous. —See Usage note at **callus.** [Middle English, from Old French *calleuse,* from Latin *callōsus,* from *callum, callus,* hard skin, CALLUS.] —**cal′lous·ly** *adv.* —**cal′lous·ness** *n.*

cal·low (kăl′ō) *adj.* **1.** Immature; inexperienced. **2.** Not yet having feathers; unfledged, as a bird. [Originally, "bald," hence unfledged, Middle English *calwe,* bald, Old English *calu.* See **gal-**[1] in Appendix.*] —**cal′low·ness** *n.*

call rate. The rate of interest charged on call loans.

cal·lus (kăl′əs) *n., pl.* **-luses.** **1. a.** A localized thickening and enlargement of the horny layer of the skin. **b.** The hard bony tissue that surrounds the ends of a fractured bone. **2.** *Botany.* Hardened tissue that develops over a wound or cut end of a woody stem. —*intr.v.* **callused, -lusing, -luses.** To form or develop a callus. [Latin *callus, callum*†.]

Usage: *Callus* has only the physical sense of thickening of skin in general usage. *Callous* (adjective, verb) has both that physical sense and the figurative one of emotional insensitivity, but it cannot properly be used as a noun.

calm (käm) *adj.* **calmer, calmest.** **1.** Nearly or completely motionless; undisturbed. **2.** Not excited or agitated; composed; quiet. —*n.* **1.** An absence or cessation of motion; stillness. **2.** Serenity; tranquillity; peace. **3.** *Meteorology.* A condition of little or no wind. —*v.* **calmed, calming, calms.** —*tr.* To make calm; to quiet. —*intr.* To become calm or quiet. Often used with *down.* [Middle English *calme,* from Old French, from Old Italian *calma,* from Late Latin *cauma,* heat of the day, hence, a rest or resting place in the heat of the day, from Greek *kauma,* burning heat, from *kaiein,* to burn. See **kēu-** in Appendix.*] —**calm′ly** *adv.* —**calm′ness** *n.*

Synonyms: *calm, tranquil, placid, serene, still, quiet, halcyon, peaceful.* These adjectives describe absence of movement, noise, or emotion. *Calm,* in both its physical and figurative senses, implies freedom from agitation. *Tranquil* adds to *calm* the idea of a more enduring state: *tranquil life.* A *placid* person is not easily shaken by emotion, and *placid* waters are unruffled. *Serene* suggests a lofty, even spiritual calm. *Still* and *quiet* are related in emphasizing absence of all noise. *Still* has the additional sense of absence of motion. *Halcyon* has the meaning of both *calm* and *tranquil* and suggests happiness: *halcyon days of youth. Peaceful* implies aversion to conflict.

calm·a·tive (kä′mə-tĭv, kăl′mə-) *adj.* Having relaxing or pacifying properties; sedative. —*n.* A sedative or tranquilizer. [From CALM (after SEDATIVE).]

cal·o·mel (kăl′ə-mĕl′, -məl) *n.* A white, tasteless compound, Hg_2Cl_2, used as a purgative. [French, from New Latin *calomelas,* "beautiful black" (calomel, though white, was originally developed from a black powder) : Greek *kalos,* beautiful (see **kal-**[2] in Appendix*) + *melas,* black (see **mel-**[2] in Appendix*).]

ca·lor·ic (kə-lôr′ĭk, -lŏr′ĭk) *adj.* Relating or pertaining to heat or calories. —*n.* A hypothetically indestructible, uncreatable, highly elastic, self-repellent, all-pervading fluid, formerly thought responsible for the production, possession, and transfer of heat. [French *calorique,* from Latin *calor,* heat. See **calorie.**]

cal·o·rie (kăl′ər-ē) *n.* **1.** *Abbr.* **cal** Any of several approximately equal units of heat, each measured as the quantity of heat required to raise the temperature of 1 gram of water by 1°C from a standard initial temperature, especially from 3.98°C, 14.5°C, or 19.5°C, at 1 atmosphere pressure. Also called "gram calorie," "small calorie." **2.** *Abbr.* **cal** The unit of heat equal to 1/100 the quantity of heat required to raise the temperature of 1 gram of water from 0 to 100°C at 1 atmosphere pressure. Also called "mean calorie." **3.** *Abbr.* **Cal** The unit of heat equal to the amount of heat required to raise the temperature of 1 kilogram of water by 1°C at 1 atmosphere pressure. Also called "kilogram calorie," "large calorie." **4.** The unit of heat equal to 4.184 joules. Also called "thermochemical calorie." [French, from Latin *calor,* heat. See **kel-**[1] in Appendix.*]

cal·o·rif·ic (kăl′ə-rĭf′ĭk) *adj.* Pertaining to or generating heat. [French *calorifique,* from Latin *calorificus* : *calor,* heat (see **calorie**) + -FIC.]

cal·o·rim·e·ter (kăl′ə-rĭm′ə-tər) *n.* **1.** An apparatus for measuring heat. **2.** The part of such an apparatus, usually a sample container, in which the heat measured causes a change of state. [Latin *calor,* heat (see **calorie**) + -METER.]

ca·lotte (kə-lŏt′) *n.* A skullcap, especially one worn by Roman Catholic clergymen. [French, diminutive of Old French *cale,* cap, from Germanic. See **skel-**[1] in Appendix.*]

ca·loy·er (kə-loi′ər, kăl′ə-yər) *n.* A monk of the Eastern Orthodox Church. [French, from obsolete Italian *caloiero,* from Medieval Greek *kalogēros,* venerable, "handsome old man" : Greek *kalos,* beautiful (see **kal-**[2] in Appendix*) + *gēras,* old age (see **ger-**[2] in Appendix*).]

cal·pac (kăl′păk′, kăl-păk′) *n.* Also **cal·pack, kal·pak.** A large black cap, usually of sheepskin or felt, worn in Turkey, Armenia, and other Near Eastern regions. [Turkish *kalpāk.*]

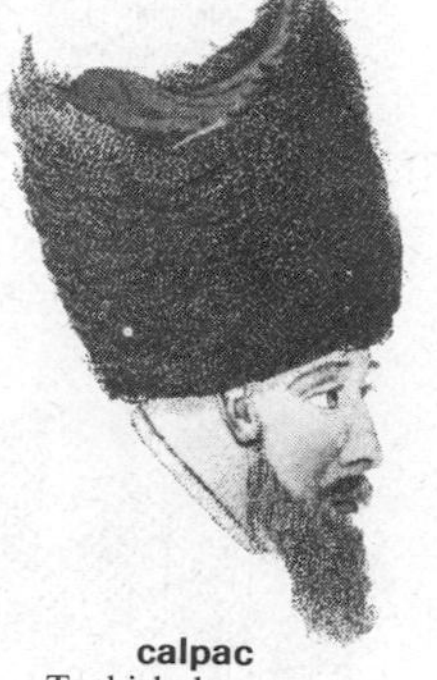

calpac
Turkish dragoman wearing a calpac

Cal·pe. The ancient name for the Rock of **Gibraltar.**

calque (kălk) *n. Linguistics.* **1.** A form of semantic borrowing in which a word is given a special extended meaning by analogy with that of a word having the same basic meaning in another language; for example, Latin *māteriēs,* growing wood, timber, acquired the philosophical sense "matter" by analogy with Greek *hulē,* wood, hence matter. **2. Loan translation** *(see).* —*tr.v.* **calqued, calquing, calques.** To model (the meaning of a word) upon that of an analogous word in another language. [French, tracing, imitation, close copy, from *calquer,* to trace, copy, make an impression of, from Italian *calcar,* to press, from Latin *calcāre,* to trample, stamp, from *calx,* a heel. See **skel-**[3] in Appendix.*]

cal·trop (kăl′trəp) *n.* Also **cal·trap.** **1.** *Military.* An iron ball with four projecting spikes so arranged that when three of the spikes were on the ground, the fourth pointed upward. It was formerly used to delay the advance of mounted and unmounted troops. Also called "crowfoot." **2.** Any of several plants having spiny burs or bracts, as members of the genera *Tribulus* and *Kallstroemia.* [Middle English *cal(ke)trap(pe),* from Old French *chauchetrap,* iron ball with spikes, and Old English *calcatrippe,* spiny plant, brambles, both from Medieval Latin *calcatrappa, calcatrippa,* "foot trap" : Latin *calcāre,* to tread, from *calx,* heel (see **calk**) + Medieval Latin *trappa,* trap, from Germanic (see **der-**[1] in Appendix*).]

cal·u·met (kăl′yə-mĕt′, -mət, kăl′yə-mĕt′) *n.* A long-stemmed, ornamented pipe used by North American Indians for ceremonial purposes. Also called "peace pipe." [Canadian French, from French (Normandy dialect), variant of French *chalumeau,* a straw, from Late Latin *calamellus,* little reed, from *calamus,* a reed. from Greek *kalamos.* See **koləm-** in Appendix.*]

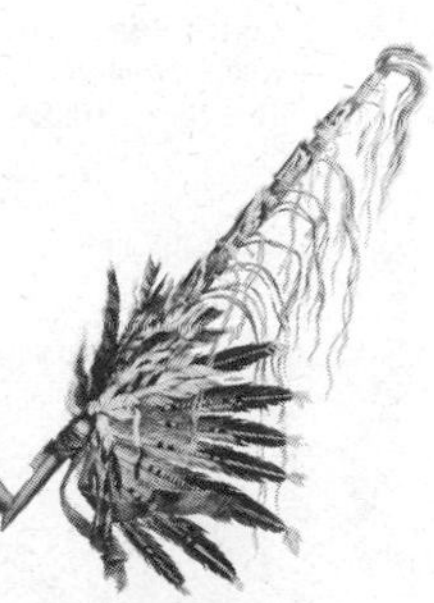

calumet

ca·lum·ni·ate (kə-lŭm′nē-āt′) *tr.v.* **-ated, -ating, -ates.** To make false statements about; to slander. See Synonyms at **malign.** [Latin *calumniārī,* from *calumnia,* CALUMNY.] —**ca·lum′ni·a′tion** *n.* —**ca·lum′ni·a′tor** (-ā′tər) *n.*

ca·lum·ni·ous (kə-lŭm′nē-əs) *adj.* Also **ca·lum·ni·a·to·ry** (-ə-tôr′ē, -tōr′ē). Containing or implying calumny; slanderous; defamatory. —**ca·lum′ni·ous·ly** *adv.*

cal·um·ny (kăl′əm-nē) *n., pl.* **-nies.** **1.** A false statement, maliciously or knowingly made to injure someone. **2.** The utterance of such statements; slander. [Middle English, from Old French *calomnie,* from Latin *calumnia,* "trickery," "deception," from *calvī,* to deceive, trick. See **kēl-** in Appendix.*]

Cal·va·dos (kăl′və-dôs′, -dōs′; *French* kȧl-vȧ-dôs′) *n.* A French brandy made from apples. [French; originally made in *Calvados,* department in Normandy.]

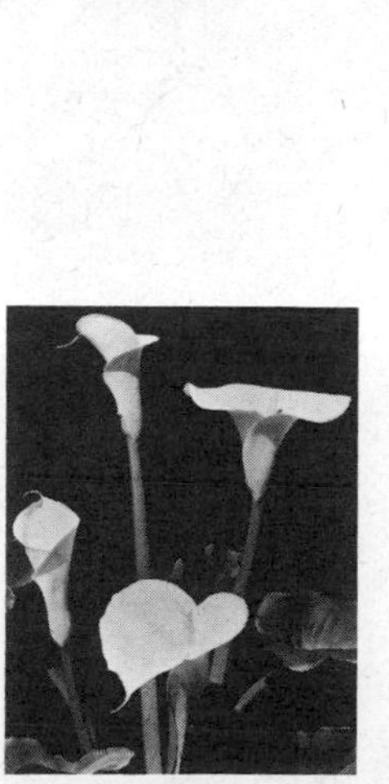

calla
Zantedeschia aethiopica

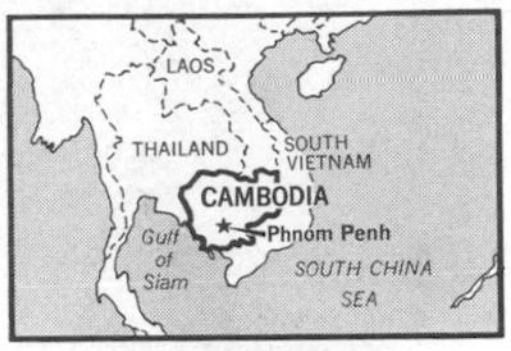

Cambodia

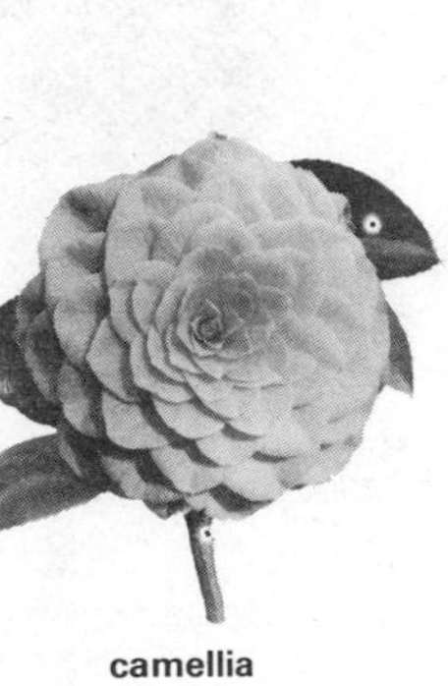
camellia
Camellia japonica
"Pope Pius" variety

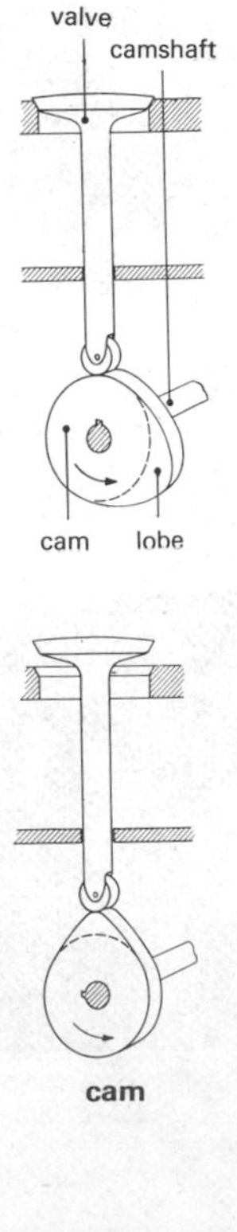

cam

cal·va·ry (kăl′vər-ē) *n., pl.* **-ries.** A sculptured depiction of the Crucifixion. [After CALVARY.]

Cal·va·ry (kăl′vər-ē). The hill outside the ancient city of Jerusalem where Jesus was crucified. [Middle English *Calvarie,* Old English *Calvarie,* from Late Latin *Calvāria,* from Latin *calvāria,* skull (translation of Greek *kranion,* translation of Aramaic *gulgūtha,* GOLGOTHA), from *calva,* scalp, from *calvus,* bald. See **keləwo-** in Appendix.*]

Calvary cross. *Heraldry.* A Latin cross set on three steps.

calve (kăv, käv) *v.* **calved, calving, calves.** —*intr.* **1.** To give birth to a calf. **2.** To break up and lose a portion of itself. Used of a glacier or an iceberg. —*tr.* **1.** To give birth to (a calf). **2.** To set loose (a mass of ice). [Middle English *calven,* Old English *cealfian,* from *cealf,* CALF (young cow).]

Cal·vert (kăl′vərt). English family of colonists in America, including **George,** First Baron Baltimore (1580?–1632); his son **Cecilius** (1605–1675), Second Baron and recipient of Maryland charter; another son, **Leonard** (1606–1647), first governor of Maryland (1634–47); and Cecilius' son **Charles** (1637–1715), Third Baron and governor (1661–75) and proprietor (1675–1715) of Maryland.

calves. Plural of **calf.**

calves'-foot jelly. Variant of **calf's-foot jelly.**

Cal·vin (kăl′vĭn). A masculine given name. [Latin *Calvīnus,* from *calvus,* bald. See **keləwo-** in Appendix.*]

Cal·vin (kăl′vĭn), **John.** Original name, Jean Chauvin or Caulvin. 1509–1564. French theologian and religious reformer; resident in Switzerland.

Cal·vin (kăl′vĭn), **Melvin.** Born 1911. American chemist; worked on photosynthesis.

Cal·vin·ism (kăl′vĭn-ĭz′əm) *n.* **1.** The religious doctrines of John Calvin, which emphasize the supremacy of the Scriptures in the revelation of truth, the omnipotence of God, the sinfulness of man, the salvation of the elect by God's grace alone, and a rigid moral code. **2.** Agreement with or advocacy of such doctrines. —**Cal′vin·ist** *n.* & *adj.* —**Cal′vin·is′tic, Cal′vin·is′ti·cal** *adj.* —**Cal′vin·is′ti·cal·ly** *adv.*

calx (kălks) *n., pl.* **calxes** or **calces** (kăl′sēz′). **1.** The crumbly residue left after a mineral or metal has been calcined or roasted. **2.** Lime; chalk. **3. Calcium oxide** *(see).* [Latin, lime, limestone, from Greek *khalix,* pebble. See **calcium.**]

cal·y·cine (kă′lə-sīn′, kăl′ə-) *adj.* Of, pertaining to, or resembling a calyx.

ca·ly·cle (kă′lĭ-kəl, kăl′ĭ-) *n. Botany.* An **epicalyx** *(see).* [French *calicule,* from Latin *calyculus,* diminutive of *calyx,* bud, CALYX.] —**ca·lyc′u·late′** (kə-lĭk′yə-lāt′, -lĭt) *adj.*

ca·lyc·u·lus (kə-lĭk′yə-ləs) *n., pl.* **-li** (-lī′). *Biology.* A small cup-shaped structure. [Latin, CALYCLE.] —**ca·lyc′u·lar** *adj.*

Cal·y·don (kăl′ə-dŏn′, -dən). An ancient city in west-central Greece, north of the Gulf of Patras.

Cal·y·don, Gulf of. See Gulf of **Patras.**

ca·lyp·so¹ (kə-lĭp′sō) *n.* An orchid, *Calypso bulbosa,* of the North Temperate Zone, having a pinkish flower with a slipper-shaped lip. [After CALYPSO.]

ca·lyp·so² (kə-lĭp′sō) *n.* A type of music originated in the West Indies, notably in Trinidad, characterized by improvised lyrics on topical or broadly humorous subjects. [After CALYPSO.]

Ca·lyp·so (kə-lĭp′sō). *Greek Mythology.* A sea nymph who delayed Odysseus on her island, Ogygia, for seven years. [Latin, from Greek *Kalupsō,* "she who conceals," from *kaluptein,* to cover, conceal. See **kel-⁴** in Appendix.*]

ca·lyp·tra (kə-lĭp′trə) *n. Botany.* **1.** The protective cap covering the spore case of a moss or related plant. **2.** Any similar hoodlike or caplike structure. [New Latin, from Greek *kaluptra,* veil, covering, from *kaluptein,* to cover, conceal. See **kel-⁴** in Appendix.*] —**ca·lyp′trate′** *adj.*

ca·lyp·tro·gen (kə-lĭp′trə-jən) *n. Botany.* A layer of actively dividing cells at the end of a root tip, from which the root cap is formed. [CALYPTR(A) + -GEN.]

ca·lyx (kā′lĭks, kăl′ĭks) *n., pl.* **-lyxes** or **calyces** (kā′lə-sēz′, kăl′ə-). **1.** The outer protective covering of a flower, consisting of a series of leaflike, usually green segments called sepals. Compare **corolla. 2.** A cuplike or funnel-shaped animal structure. [Latin, from Greek *kalux.* See **kal-¹** in Appendix.*]

cam (kăm) *n.* An eccentric or multiply curved wheel mounted on a rotating shaft and used to produce variable or reciprocating motion in another engaged or contacted part. [Perhaps from French *came,* from German *Kamm,* "comb," from Old High German *kamb.* See **gembh-** in Appendix.*]

Ca·ma·güey (kä′mä-gwā′). A city in east-central Cuba. Population, 191,000.

ca·ma·ra·de·rie (kä′mə-rä′də-rē, kăm′ə-) *n.* Good will and lighthearted rapport between or among friends; comradeship. [French, from *camarade,* COMRADE.]

cam·a·ril·la (kăm′ə-rĭl′ə, -rē′yə) *n.* **1.** Any of various secret and unofficial advisers to the Spanish kings. **2.** Any group of confidential·advisers; a cabal. [Spanish, "small room," from *cámara,* room, from Late Latin *camera,* from Latin, arched roof, from Greek *kamara,* vault. See **kamer-** in Appendix.*]

cam·as (kăm′əs) *n.* Also **cam·ass, quam·ash** (kwä′mĭsh). **1.** Any of several North American plants of the genus *Camassia;* especially, *C. quamash,* of western North America, having a showy cluster of blue or white flowers and an edible bulb. **2.** The **death camas** *(see).* [Chinook jargon *kamass.*]

Cam·ba·luc. See **Khanbalik.**

Cam·bay, Gulf of (kăm-bā′). An arm of the Arabian Sea on the northwestern coast of India.

cam·ber (kăm′bər) *n.* **1. a.** A slightly arched surface, as of a road, a ship's deck, or an airfoil. **b.** The condition of being so arched. **2.** A setting of automobile wheels closer together at the bottom than at the top. —*v.* **cambered, -bering, -bers.** —*tr.* To give a slight arch to. —*intr.* To arch slightly. [From Middle English *ca(u)mber,* curved, arched, from Old French *cambre,* from Latin *camur(us)*†, bent or curved inward.]

Cam·ber·well (kăm′bər-wĕl′, -wəl). A former administrative division of London, now part of **Southwark** *(see).*

Camberwell beauty. A butterfly, the **mourning cloak** *(see).* [After CAMBERWELL.]

cam·bist (kăm′bĭst) *n.* **1.** A manual giving exchange rates of different currencies and equivalents of different weights and measures. **2.** A dealer in or expert on international exchange. [French *cambiste,* from Italian *cambista,* from *cambio,* exchange, from *cambiare,* to exchange, from Late Latin *cambiāre.* See **skamb-** in Appendix.*] —**cam′bism′, cam′bis·try** *n.*

cam·bi·um (kăm′bē-əm) *n.* A layer of cells in the stems and roots of vascular plants that gives rise to phloem and xylem. [New Latin, "that which changes into new layers," from Medieval Latin, exchange, from Latin *cambiāre,* to exchange. See **skamb-** in Appendix.*] —**cam′bi·al** *adj.*

Cam·bo·di·a (kăm-bō′dē-ə). An independent constitutional monarchy occupying 66,800 square miles in southeastern Asia, bordering on the Gulf of Siam. Population, 5,749,000. Capital, Phnom Penh. —**Cam·bo′di·an** *n.* & *adj.*

cam·bo·gi·a (kăm-bō′jē-ə) *n.* A resin, **gamboge** *(see).* [New Latin, variant of *gambogium, cambugium,* GAMBOGE.]

Cam·brai (kăm-brā′; *French* käN-brĕ′). A textile-manufacturing city of northern France, on the Scheldt River.

Cam·bri·a (kăm′brē-ə). The Latin name for Wales. [Latin, from Welsh *Cymry,* from Old Welsh *kombrogī* (unattested), Welshmen, "compatriots" : *kom-,* with (see **kom** in Appendix*) + *bro,* border, region (see **merg-** in Appendix*).]

Cam·bri·an¹ (kăm′brē-ən) *adj.* Of or pertaining to Wales; Welsh. —*n.* A Welshman.

Cam·bri·an² (kăm′brē-ən) *adj.* Of, belonging to, or designating the geologic time, system of rocks, and sedimentary deposits of the first period of the Paleozoic era, characterized by warm seas and desert land areas. See **geology.** —*n. Geology.* The Cambrian period. Preceded by *the.* [After CAMBRIA, Wales, where rocks and fossils of this period were found.]

cam·bric (kām′brĭk) *n.* A finely woven white linen or cotton fabric. [Earlier *cameryk,* from obsolete Flemish *kameryk,* after *Kameryk,* CAMBRAI, where it was first made.]

cambric tea. A drink for children, made of hot water, milk, sugar, and usually a small amount of tea. [So called because it is thin and white like CAMBRIC.]

Cam·bridge (kām′brĭj). **1.** A city and county seat of Cambridgeshire and Ely, in eastern England, about 50 miles northeast of London; site of Cambridge University. Population, 167,000. **2.** A city in eastern Massachusetts, on the Charles River opposite Boston; site of Harvard University and the Massachusetts Institute of Technology. Population, 108,000.

Cam·bridge·shire and E·ly (kām′brĭj-shĭr, -shər; ē′lē). A county of southeastern England, covering an area of 830 square miles. Population, 295,000. County seat, Cambridge.

Cam·by·ses (kăm-bī′sēz). King of Persia (529–522 B.C.); son of Cyrus the Great; extended rule through Nile Valley.

Cam·den (kăm′dən). **1.** A borough of London, England, comprising the former administrative divisions of Hampstead, Holborn, and St. Pancras. Population, 246,000. **2.** A city in southwestern New Jersey, on the Delaware. Population, 117,000.

came¹ (kām) *n.* A grooved lead bar used to secure the panes in stained glass or latticework windows. [Origin unknown.]

came². Past tense of **come.**

cam·el (kăm′əl) *n.* **1.** A humped, long-necked ruminant mammal of the genus *Camelus,* domesticated in Old World desert regions as a beast of burden and as a source of wool, milk, and meat. See **Bactrian camel, dromedary. 2.** A device used to raise a sunken vessel. In this sense, also called "caisson." [Middle English *camel, chamel,* from Old English *camel,* Norman French *camel,* and Old French *chamel,* all from Latin *camēlus,* from Greek *kamēlos,* from Semitic, akin to Hebrew and Phoenician *gāmāl,* Arabic *jamal.*]

cam·el·back (kăm′əl-băk′) *adj.* Having a shape characterized by a hump or upward curve.

cam·el·eer (kăm′ə-lîr′) *n.* A person who drives or rides a camel.

ca·mel·lia (kə-mēl′yə) *n.* **1.** Any of several shrubs or trees of the genus *Camellia,* native to Asia; especially, *C. japonica,* having shiny evergreen leaves and showy, variously colored flowers. **2.** The flower of a camellia. Also called "japonica." [New Latin; first described by Georg Josef *Kamel* (1661–1706), Moravian Jesuit missionary.]

ca·mel·o·pard (kə-mĕl′ə-pärd′) *n.* **1.** *Archaic.* A giraffe. **2.** *Heraldry.* A bearing resembling a giraffe, but represented with long curved horns. [Medieval Latin *camēlopardus,* from Latin *camēlopardalis,* from Greek *kamēlopardalis* : *kamēlos,* CAMEL + *pardalis,* variant of *pardos,* PARD (leopard), so called because the giraffe has a head like a camel's and the spots of a leopard.]

Ca·mel·o·par·da·lis (kə-mĕl′ō-pär′də-lĭs) *n.* A constellation in the Northern Hemisphere near Ursa Major and Cassiopeia. [New Latin, from Latin *camēlopardalis,* CAMELOPARD.]

Cam·e·lot (kăm′ə-lŏt′). The legendary town where King Arthur had his court.

camel's hair. Also **camel hair. 1.** The soft, fine hair of a camel or a substitute for it. **2.** A soft, heavy cloth, usually light tan, made chiefly of camel's hair. —**cam′el's-hair′** *adj.*

Cam·em·bert (kăm′əm-bâr′) *n.* A creamy, mold-ripened

ă pat/ā pay/âr care/ä father/b bib/ch church/d deed/ĕ pet/ē be/f fife/g gag/h hat/hw which/ĭ pit/ī pie/îr pier/j judge/k kick/l lid, needle/m mum/n no, sudden/ng thing/ŏ pot/ō toe/ô paw, for/oi noise/ou out/ŏŏ took/ōō boot/p pop/r roar/s sauce/sh ship, dish/

French cheese that softens on the inside as it matures. [French; first made at Camembert, village in Normandy.]
cam·e·o (kăm′ē-ō′) *n., pl.* **-os. 1.** A technique of engraving in relief on a gem or other stone, especially with layers of different hues, cut so the raised design is of one color and the background of another. Compare **intaglio. 2.** A gem so cut. **3.** A medallion with a profile cut in raised relief. **4.** A brief but dramatic appearance of a prominent actor or actress in a single scene on a television show or in a motion picture. Also called "cameo role." *—tr.v.* **cameoed, -oing, -os. 1.** To make into or like cameo. **2.** To portray in sharp, delicate relief, as in a literary composition. [Middle English *cameu,* from Italian *cam(m)eo* and Old French *camaïeu,* possibly from Arabic *qamā'il,* plural of *qum'ūl,* flower bud.]
cam·er·a (kăm′ər-ə, kăm′rə) *n., pl.* **-as** or **-erae** (-ə-rē′) (for sense 4). **1.** Any apparatus for taking photographs, generally consisting of a lightproof enclosure having an aperture with a shuttered lens through which the image of an object is focused and recorded on a photosensitive film or plate. **2.** The part of a television transmitting apparatus that receives the primary image on a light-sensitive cathode tube and transforms it into electrical impulses. **3.** A **camera obscura** *(see).* **4.** A room or chamber; specifically, a judge's private office. **—in camera.** *Law.* Privately. [Late Latin, room, from Latin, arched roof, from Greek *kamara,* vault. See **kamer-** in Appendix.*]
cam·er·al (kăm′ər-əl) *adj.* **1.** Pertaining to a judge's chamber and to the judicial affairs that take place there. **2.** Pertaining to public finance and state business or to a council that manages such matters. [Medieval Latin *camerālis,* from *camera,* office, department of state, from Late Latin, room, CAMERA.]
cam·er·a lu·ci·da (kăm′ər-ə lo͞o′sĭ-də) *n.* An optical device that projects a virtual image of an object onto a plane surface, especially for tracing. [New Latin, "light chamber" : CAMERA + Latin *lūcida,* feminine of *lūcidus,* LUCID.]
cam·er·a·man (kăm′ər-ə-măn′, kăm′rə-) *n., pl.* **-men** (-mĕn′). A person who operates a motion picture or television camera.
cam·er·a ob·scu·ra (kăm′ər-ə ŏb-skyo͝or′ə). A darkened chamber in which the real image of an object is received through a small opening or lens and focused in natural color onto a facing surface. [New Latin, "dark chamber" : CAMERA + Latin *obscūra,* feminine of *obscūrus,* OBSCURE.]
cam·er·lin·go (kăm′ər-lĭng′gō) *n., pl.* **-gos.** Also **cam·er·len·go** (-lĕng′gō). *Roman Catholic Church.* The cardinal who manages the pope's secular affairs. [Italian *camarlingo,* from Germanic *kamarling* (unattested), "chamber servant" : *kamar* (unattested), room, from Late Latin *camera,* CAMERA + -LING.]
Cam·e·roon¹ (kăm′ə-ro͞on′). A volcanic mountain rising to 13,350 feet in western Cameroun.
Cam·e·roon². See **Cameroun.**
Cam·e·roons, British (kăm′ə-ro͞onz′). A former British mandate in western Africa, divided by plebiscite in 1961 between Nigeria and Cameroun.
Cameroons, French. A former French mandate in western Africa, which became the Federal Republic of Cameroun on January 1, 1960.
Cam·e·roun (kăm′ə-ro͞on′). Also **Cam·e·roon.** Officially, Federal Republic of Cameroun. A republic of central Africa, 166,800 square miles in area, with a coastline on the Bight of Biafra. Population, 5,000,000. Capital, Yaoundé.
Ca·mille (kə-mēl′). Also **Ca·mil·la** (kə-mĭl′ə). A feminine given name. [French *Camille,* from Latin *Camilla,* from *camilla,* feminine of *camillus,* noble youth assisting at religious rites, probably from Etruscan.]
cam·i·on (kăm′ē-ən; *French* kȧ-myôN′) *n.* **1.** A low, sturdy wagon. **2.** A truck. [French, from Old French *chamion*†.]
ca·mi·sa (kə-mē′sə) *n. Southwestern U.S.* A shirt or chemise. [Spanish, from Late Latin *camīsia*†, shirt.]
cam·i·sa·do (kăm′ə-sā′dō, -sä′dō) *n., pl.* **-dos.** *Archaic.* A surprise attack by night. [Probably from obsolete Spanish *camisada,* "shirted" (because attackers wore white shirts over armor for identification), from *camisa,* shirt, CAMISA.]
ca·mise (kə-mēz′, -mēs′) *n.* A loose shirt, shift, or tunic. [Arabic *qamīs,* from Late Latin *camīsia,* shirt, CAMISA.]
cam·i·sole (kăm′ə-sōl′) *n.* **1.** A woman's sleeveless underbodice. **2.** A short negligee. [French, from Old Provençal *camisolla,* diminutive of *camisa,* shirt, from Late Latin *camīsia,* CAMISA.]
Cam·lan (kăm′lən). The legendary battlefield where King Arthur was mortally wounded.
cam·let (kăm′lĭt) *n.* **1.** A kind of rich cloth of Oriental origin, supposed to have been made formerly of camel's hair and silk, and later made of goat's hair and silk or other combinations. **2.** A garment made from this cloth. [Middle English *chamelet,* from Old French *c(h)amelot,* from Arabic *ḥamlat.*]
Cam·o·ëns (kăm′ō-ənz′, kə-mō′ənz), **Luiz Vaz de.** Portuguese name, **Ca·mões** (kə-moiNsh′). 1524–1580. Portuguese poet.
cam·o·mile. Variant of **chamomile.**
Ca·mor·ra (kə-môr′ə, -mŏr′ə) *n.* **1.** A Neapolitan secret society organized about 1820, notorious for practicing violence and blackmail. Compare **Mafia. 2.** Any unscrupulous, clandestine group. [Italian, perhaps from *camorra*†, a kind of smock-frock (said to have been worn by members of this society).] **—Ca·mor′rism′** (kə-môr′ĭz′əm, kə-mŏr′-) *n.* **—Ca·mor′rist** *n.*
cam·ou·flage (kăm′ə-fläzh′, -fläj′) *n.* **1.** *Military.* The method or result of concealing people or things from the enemy by making them appear to be part of the natural surroundings. **2.** Any means of concealment; dissimulation. *—v.* **camouflaged, -flaging, -flages.** *—tr.* To conceal by altering the appearance; disguise. *—intr.* To use camouflage. [French, from *camoufler,* to disguise, perhaps from *camouflet,* smoke blown into someone's nose, hence "disguise," alteration of earlier *chault mouflet,* "hot face" : *chault, chaud,* hot, from Old French, from Latin *calĭdus,* from *calēre,* to be hot (see **kel-**¹ in Appendix*) + *mouflet,* diminutive of *moufle,* fat face, from German *Muffel,* snout, mouth (probably imitative).] **—cam′ou·flag′er** *n.*
camp¹ (kămp) *n.* **1. a.** A place where a body of men, such as soldiers, miners, or sportsmen, are temporarily lodged in tents, huts, or other makeshift shelters. **b.** The shelters in such a place or the persons using them. **2.** A place consisting of more or less permanent cabins or other shelters, used for vacationing or other recreational purposes. **3.** Military service; army life. **4.** A group of persons, parties, or states favorable to a common cause, doctrine, or political system: *the socialist camp.* *—v.* **camped, camping, camps.** *—tr.* To shelter or lodge in a camp; encamp. *—intr.* **1.** To make or set up a camp. Often used with *down.* **2.** To live in or as if in a camp: *We camped in the apartment until the furniture arrived.* [Old French, from Old North French, from Latin *campus*†, open field.] **—camp′er** *n.*
camp² (kămp) *n.* **1.** An affectation or appreciation of manners and tastes commonly thought to be outlandish, vulgar, or banal. **2.** Banality or artificiality, when appreciated for its humor. *—adj.* Having the qualities or style of camp. *—intr.v.* **camped, camping, camps.** To act in an outlandish or effeminate manner. [Origin obscure.] **—camp′y** *adj.*
Cam·pa·gna (käm-pä′nyä). Also **Cam·pa·gna di Ro·ma** (dē rō′mä). A region of about 800 square miles surrounding Rome.
cam·paign (kăm-pān′) *n.* **1.** A series of military operations undertaken to achieve a specific objective within a given area. **2.** An operation undertaken, as by means of propaganda, to attain some political, social, or commercial goal. *—intr.v.* **campaigned, -paigning, -paigns.** To engage in a campaign. [French *campagne,* from Old French, battlefield, from Italian *campania,* from Late Latin *campānia,* countryside, from Latin *Campānia,* CAMPANIA.] **—cam·paign′er** *n.*
Cam·pa·nia (kăm-pān′yə, -pā′nē-ə). A region of southern Italy, 5,214 square miles in area, on the Tyrrhenian Sea. Population, 4,756,000. Capital, Naples. [Latin *Campānia,* "the place of fields," from *campānius,* of open fields, from *campus,* field, plain. See **camp.**] **—Cam·pa′ni·an** *adj.* & *n.*
cam·pa·ni·le (kăm′pə-nē′lē) *n., pl.* **-les** (-lēz) or **-li** (-lē). A bell tower, especially one near but not attached to a church. [Italian, from *campana,* bell, from Late Latin *campāna,* bell (made of metal produced in Campania), from Latin *campānus,* of Campania, from *Campānia,* CAMPANIA.]
cam·pa·nol·o·gy (kăm′pə-nŏl′ə-jē) *n.* The art or study of bell casting and ringing. [New Latin *campanologia* : Late Latin *campāna,* bell (see **campanile**) + -LOGY.] **—cam′pa·nol′o·gist** *n.*
cam·pan·u·la (kăm-păn′yə-lə) *n.* Any of various plants of the genus *Campanula,* which includes the bellflowers. [New Latin, diminutive of Late Latin *campāna,* bell. See **campanile.**]
cam·pan·u·late (kăm-păn′yə-lĭt, -lāt′) *adj.* Also **cam·pan·i·form** (-ə-fôrm′). Bell-shaped. [From New Latin *campanula,* small bell. See **campanula.**]
Camp·bell (kăm′bəl), **Alexander.** 1788–1866. Irish-born American clergyman; with his father, **Thomas** (1763–1854), founded the Disciples of Christ.
Camp·bell (kăm′bəl), Sir **Malcolm.** 1885–1948. English racer; established speed records for automobile and speedboat; his son, **Donald Malcolm** (1921–1967), broke these records.
Camp·bell (kăm′bəl), Mrs. **Patrick.** Original name, Beatrice Stella Tanner. 1867–1940. British actress.
Camp·bell (kăm′bəl), **Thomas.** 1777–1844. Scottish poet.
Camp·bell-Ban·ner·man (kăm′bəl-băn′ər-mən), Sir **Henry.** 1836–1908. British statesman; Liberal Party leader during Boer War; prime minister (1905–08).
Camp·bel·lite (kăm′bə-līt′) *n.* A member of the Disciples of Christ, a sect founded by Thomas and Alexander Campbell. The term is not recognized by the membership.
Cam·pe·che (kăm-pē′chē; *Spanish* käm-pā′chā). **1.** A state of southeastern Mexico, 19,670 square miles in area, on the western part of the Yucatán peninsula. Population, 186,000. **2.** Its capital. Population, 44,000.
Cam·pe·che, Gulf of (kăm-pē′chē; *Spanish* käm-pā′chā). Also **Bay of Cam·pe·che.** A wide inlet of the Gulf of Mexico along the southeastern coast of Mexico.
cam·pes·tral (kăm-pĕs′trəl) *adj.* Pertaining to or growing in uncultivated land or open fields. [From Latin *campester,* of the fields, from *campus,* field. See **camp.**]
camp·fire (kămp′fīr′) *n.* **1.** An outdoor fire in a camp, used for warmth or cooking. **2.** A meeting held around such a fire.
campfire girl. A member of the Camp Fire Girls, an organization for girls, from seven through eighteen, that strives to instill good values and character and develop practical skills.
camp follower. 1. A civilian who follows an army from place to place to sell goods or services; especially, a prostitute. **2.** One who follows but does not belong to a main body or group.
camp·ground (kămp′ground′) *n.* An area used for setting up a camp or holding a camp meeting.
cam·phene (kăm′fēn′) *n.* A colorless crystalline compound, $C_{10}H_{16}$, used in the manufacture of synthetic camphor. [CAMPH(OR) + -ENE.]
cam·phire (kăm′fīr′) *n. Archaic.* Henna. [Obsolete variant of CAMPHOR (mistranslation of Hebrew *kōfur,* henna, in Song of Solomon 1:14).]
cam·phor (kăm′fər) *n.* A volatile crystalline compound, $C_{10}H_{16}O$, obtained from camphor tree wood or synthesized and used as an insect repellent, in the manufacture of film, plastics, lacquers, and explosives, and medicinally as a stimulant, ex-

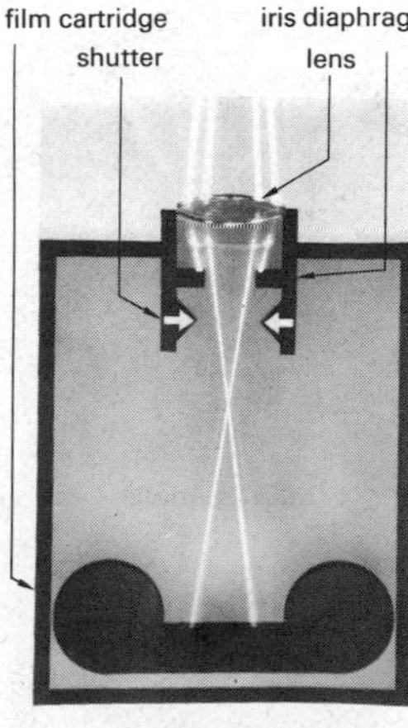

camera
Simple camera body

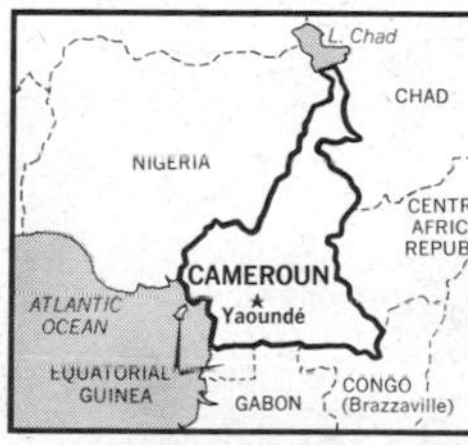

Cameroun

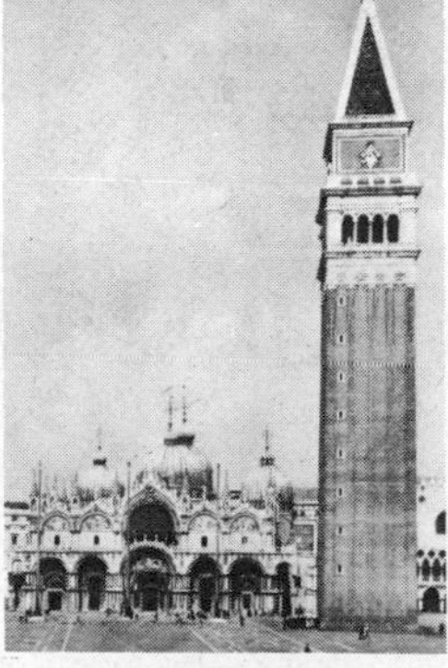
campanile
In the Piazza San Marco, Venice

pectorant, and diaphoretic. [Middle English *ca(u)mfre,* from Old French *camphre,* from Medieval Latin *camphora,* from Arabic *kāfūr,* from Malay *kāpūr,* chalk.] —**cam·phor'ic** *adj.*
cam·phor·ate (kăm'fə-rāt') *tr.v.* **-ated, -ating, -ates.** To treat or impregnate with camphor.
camphor ice. A skin ointment consisting of camphor, white wax, spermaceti, and castor oil.
camphor tree. An evergreen tree, *Cinnamomum camphora,* native to eastern Asia, having aromatic wood that is a source of camphor.
Cam·pi·na Gran·de (kăɴm-pē'nä grän'dĕ). A city of Brazil, in eastern Paraíba State. Population, 116,000.
Cam·pi·nas (kăɴm-pē'näs). A city of São Paulo, Brazil, 45 miles north of the city São Paulo. Population, 180,000.
cam·pi·on (kăm'pē-ən) *n.* Any of various plants of the genus *Lychnis* or related genera, having red, pink, or white flowers. [Probably from *campion,* obsolete variant of CHAMPION; applied first to *lychnis coronaria,* "crowning lychnis" (whose leaves were formerly used to make crowns for athletic champions).]
Cam·pi·on (kăm'pē-ən), **Thomas.** 1567–1620. English poet; composed songs for voice and lute.
camp meeting. An evangelistic gathering held in a tent or outdoors and often lasting a number of days.
cam·po (kăm'pō; *Spanish* käm'pō) *n., pl.* **campos** (kăm'pōz; *Spanish* käm'pōs). In South America, a large, grassy plain with occasional bushes and small trees. [American Spanish, from Spanish, field, from Latin *campus.* See **camp.**]
Cam·po·bel·lo (kăm'pō-bĕl'ō). An island in the Bay of Fundy off the southwestern coast of New Brunswick, Canada, site of a summer home of Franklin D. Roosevelt.
Cam·po·for·mi·do (käm'pō-fôr'mē-dō'). Formerly **Cam·po For·mi·o** (fôr'mē-ō). A village of northeastern Italy, southwest of Udine, where a treaty was signed in 1797 between France and Austria, ending the first phase of the Napoleonic Wars.
camp·o·ree (kăm'pə-rē') *n.* An assembly or gathering of Boy Scouts on the local or district level. Compare **jamboree.** [CAMP + (JAMB)OREE.]
Cam·pos (kăɴm'po͞os). A city of southeastern Brazil, on the Paraíba River, 35 miles from its mouth. Population, 132,000.
camp robber. A bird, the **Canada jay** *(see).*
camp·site (kămp'sīt') *n.* An area suitable for camping.
camp·stool (kămp'sto͞ol') *n.* A light folding stool.
cam·pus (kăm'pəs) *n., pl.* **-puses. 1.** The grounds of a school, college, or university. **2.** In ancient Rome, a field used for various events, such as games, military exercises, and public meetings. [Latin *campus,* field, plain (first used at Princeton University). See **camp.**]
Cam·ranh Bay (kăm'răn'). An inlet of the South China Sea on the southeastern coast of South Vietnam.
cam·shaft (kăm'shăft', -shäft') *n.* An engine shaft fitted with a cam or cams.
Ca·mus (kȧ-mü'), **Albert.** 1913–1960. French novelist.
can[1] (kăn; *unstressed* kən) *v.* Past tense **could,** present tense **can** or *archaic* **canst** (for second person singular). Used as an auxiliary, followed by an infinitive without *to,* or with the infinitive understood, to indicate: **1.** Ability: *I can meet you today.* **2.** Possession of a specified power, right, or means: *The President can veto congressional bills.* **3.** Possession of a specified capacity or skill: *He can tune the harpsichord as well as play it.* **4.** Possible contingency: *I wonder if she can be alive.* **5.** *Informal.* A requesting or granting of permission: *Can I be excused? No, you cannot.* See Usage note below. [Can, could; Middle English *can, coude* (also *couthe*), Old English *can* (also *con*), *cūthe,* first and third person present and past indicative of *cunnan,* to know how. See **gnō-** in Appendix.*]
Usage: *Can,* in formal usage, is employed to indicate ability to do something, and *may* to express permission to do it: *Those who need an additional day to prepare may have it. May I have an additional day?* Using these as examples in writing, 70 per cent of the Usage Panel specify *may* as the only acceptable form in the first, and 77 per cent specify *may* in the second. In formal speech, 60 per cent of the Panel specify *may* as the proper choice in the second example. However, with some interrogative constructions (requests for permission involving a negative) and in outright negative statements (refusals of requests), a form of *can* is permissible, and sometimes preferable, on all levels of speech: *Why can't I have an additional day to prepare* (acceptable to 89 per cent). *You cannot* (or *can't*) *have additional time* (acceptable to 72 per cent). Many Panel members regard *mayn't* (*why mayn't I have*) as awkward and unnatural, though technically proper.
can[2] (kăn) *n.* **1.** A metal container. **2. a.** An airtight container, usually made of tin-coated iron, in which foods or beverages are preserved. **b.** The contents of such a container; a canful. **3.** *Slang.* **a.** A jail or prison. **b.** A toilet or rest room. **c.** The buttocks. —*tr.v.* **canned, canning, cans. 1.** To seal (vegetables, fruit, or jam) in a can or jar for future use; to preserve. **2.** *Slang.* To make a recording of: *can the audience's applause.* **3.** *Slang.* **a.** To dismiss from employment or school. **b.** To quit or dispense with: *can the chatter.* [Middle English *canne,* Old English *canne,* from Common Germanic *kannōn-* (unattested).] —**can'ner** *n.*
can. 1. canceled. **2.** canon. **3.** canto.
Can. Canada; Canadian.
Ca·na (kā'nə). A village in northern Palestine, four miles northeast of Nazareth, where Jesus performed His first miracle by changing water into wine. John 2:1, 11.
Ca·naan[1] (kā'nən). The fourth son of Ham and grandson of Noah. Genesis 9:18, 25–26; 10.

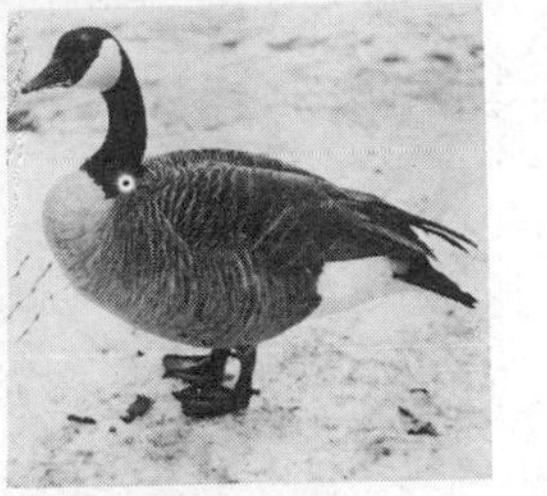
Canada goose

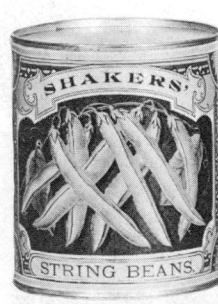

can[2]
Can for string beans made by Shakers around the turn of the century

Ca·naan[2] (kā'nən). In Biblical times, the part of Palestine between the Jordan River and the Mediterranean Sea; the Promised Land. Often used for all of Palestine. [Late Latin *Chanaan,* from Greek *Khanaan, Kanaan,* from Hebrew *kəna'an,* probably from Canaanite.]
Ca·naan·ite (kā'nən-īt') *n.* **1.** One of the Semitic inhabitants of the ancient land of Canaan before its conquest by the Israelites. **2.** The Semitic language of these inhabitants of Canaan. **3.** A member of a Jewish sect of extremely zealous anti-Romans; specifically, one of the Twelve Apostles, Simon Zelotes. Matthew 10:4. —**Ca'naan·it'ic** (-ĭt'ĭk) *adj.*
Can·a·da (kăn'ə-də). *Abbr.* **Can.** The second-largest country (3,851,809 square miles) in the world, and the oldest member of the Commonwealth of Nations, occupying the northern half of North America, with the exception of Alaska, Greenland, and St. Pierre and Miquelon. Population, 19,785,000. Capital, Ottawa. —**Ca·na'di·an** (kə-nā'dē-ən) *adj.* & *n.*
Canada balsam. 1. A tree, the **balsam fir** *(see).* **2.** A viscous, yellowish, transparent resin obtained from the balsam fir and used as a mounting cement for microscopic specimens.
Canada goose. A common wild goose, *Branta canadensis,* of North America, having grayish plumage, a black neck and head, and a white face patch.
Canada jay. A bird, *Perisoreus canadensis,* of North American conifer forests, having gray plumage and a black-capped head. Also called "camp robber," "moosebird," "whiskey jack."
Canada mayflower. A plant, the **wild lily of the valley** *(see).*
Canada thistle. A weedy plant, *Cirsium arvense,* native to Eurasia, having prickly leaves and clusters of purplish flowers.
Canadian bacon. Cured rolled bacon from the loin of a pig.
Canadian Falls. A section of Niagara Falls, 160 feet high and 2,500 feet wide, separated from the American Falls by Goat Island in the Niagara River just above Niagara Falls. Also called "Horseshoe Falls."
Canadian French. The French language as spoken and written in Canada, chiefly in Quebec and the Maritime Provinces.
Canadian River. A river rising in northern New Mexico and flowing 900 miles to the Arkansas River.
Canadian Shield. See **Laurentian Plateau.**
ca·naille (kə-nī', -nāl') *n.* The masses; rabble; riffraff; mob. [French, from Italian *canaglia,* "pack of dogs," from *cane,* dog, from Latin *canis.* See **kwon-** in Appendix.*]
ca·nal (kə-năl') *n.* **1.** A man-made waterway or artificially improved river used for irrigation, shipping, or travel. **2.** *Anatomy.* A tube or duct. **3.** *Astronomy.* One of the faint, hazy markings resembling straight lines on the surface of Mars, now thought to be geological features. —*tr.v.* **canalled** or **-naled, -nalling** or **-naling, -nals. 1.** To dig an artificial waterway through. **2.** To provide with a canal or canals. [Middle English, tube, from Latin *canālis,* channel, from *canna,* reed, from Greek *kanna.* See **kanna** in Appendix.*]
Ca·na·let·to (kä'nä-lāt'tō), **Antonio.** Original name, Canale. 1697–1768. Italian painter and etcher.
can·a·lic·u·lus (kăn'ə-lĭk'yə-ləs) *n., pl.* **-li** (-lī'). *Anatomy.* A small bodily channel, especially a tear duct. [Latin, diminutive of *canālis,* conduit, channel, CANAL.] —**can'a·lic'u·lar** (-lər) *adj.*
ca·nal·i·za·tion (kə-năl'ə-zā'shən, kăn'əl-ə-) *n.* **1.** The act or an instance of canalizing. **2.** A system of canals.
ca·nal·ize (kə-năl'īz', kăn'əl-) *tr.v.* **-ized, -izing, -izes. 1.** To furnish with, build, or convert into a canal or canals. **2.** To channel into a particular direction; provide an outlet for.
canal rays. Positively charged ions formed in a gas by electrical discharge and attracted to the cathode of the discharge tube. Not in current technical use. [Translation of German *Kanalstrahl* (because the ions pass through fissures in the cathode).]
Canal Zone. *Abbr.* **C.Z.** A strip of territory, 10 miles wide and 372 square miles in land area, across the Isthmus of Panama, under lease to the United States for the operation of the Panama Canal. Also called "Panama Canal Zone."
Can·an·dai·gua Lake (kăn'ən-dā'gwə). One of the Finger Lakes of western New York State.
can·a·pé (kăn'ə-pā', -pē) *n.* A cracker or small, thin piece of bread or toast spread with cheese, meat, or relish, and served as an appetizer. [French, "couch" ("seat" for the relish), from Medieval Latin *canapeum.* See **canopy.**]
ca·nard (kə-närd') *n.* A false or unfounded story. [French *canard,* "duck" (from the expression *vendre des canards à moitié,* "to half-sell ducks," swindle, deceive), from Old French *canart,* duck, from *caner,* to cackle (imitative).]
ca·nar·y (kə-nâr'ē) *n., pl.* **-ies. 1.** A songbird, *Serinus canaria,* native to the Canary Islands, that is greenish to yellow and has long been bred as a cage bird. **2.** A sweet white wine, similar to Madeira, from the Canary Islands. **3.** A lively 16th-century French and English court dance. **4.** Light to moderate or vivid yellow. Also called "canary yellow." See **color.** [French *canari* (bird), *canarie* (wine, dance), from Old Spanish *canario,* "of the Canary Islands," from *Islas Canarias,* CANARY ISLANDS.]
canary grass. A grass, *Phalaris canariensis,* native to Europe, having straw-colored seeds used to feed birds.
Canary Islands. *Spanish* **Is·las Ca·nar·i·as** (ēz'läs kä-nä'ryäs). A group of islands, 2,912 square miles in area, in the Atlantic Ocean off the northwestern coast of Africa, comprising two provinces of Spain, Las Palmas and Santa Cruz de Tenerife. Also called "Canaries." Population, 909,000. [Spanish *Islas Canarias,* from Late Latin *Canariae Insulae,* "the Isles of Dogs," from the large dogs once bred there, from Latin *canis,* dog. See **kwon-** in Appendix.*]
ca·nas·ta (kə-năs'tə) *n.* A card game for two to six players, related to rummy and requiring two decks of cards. [Spanish,

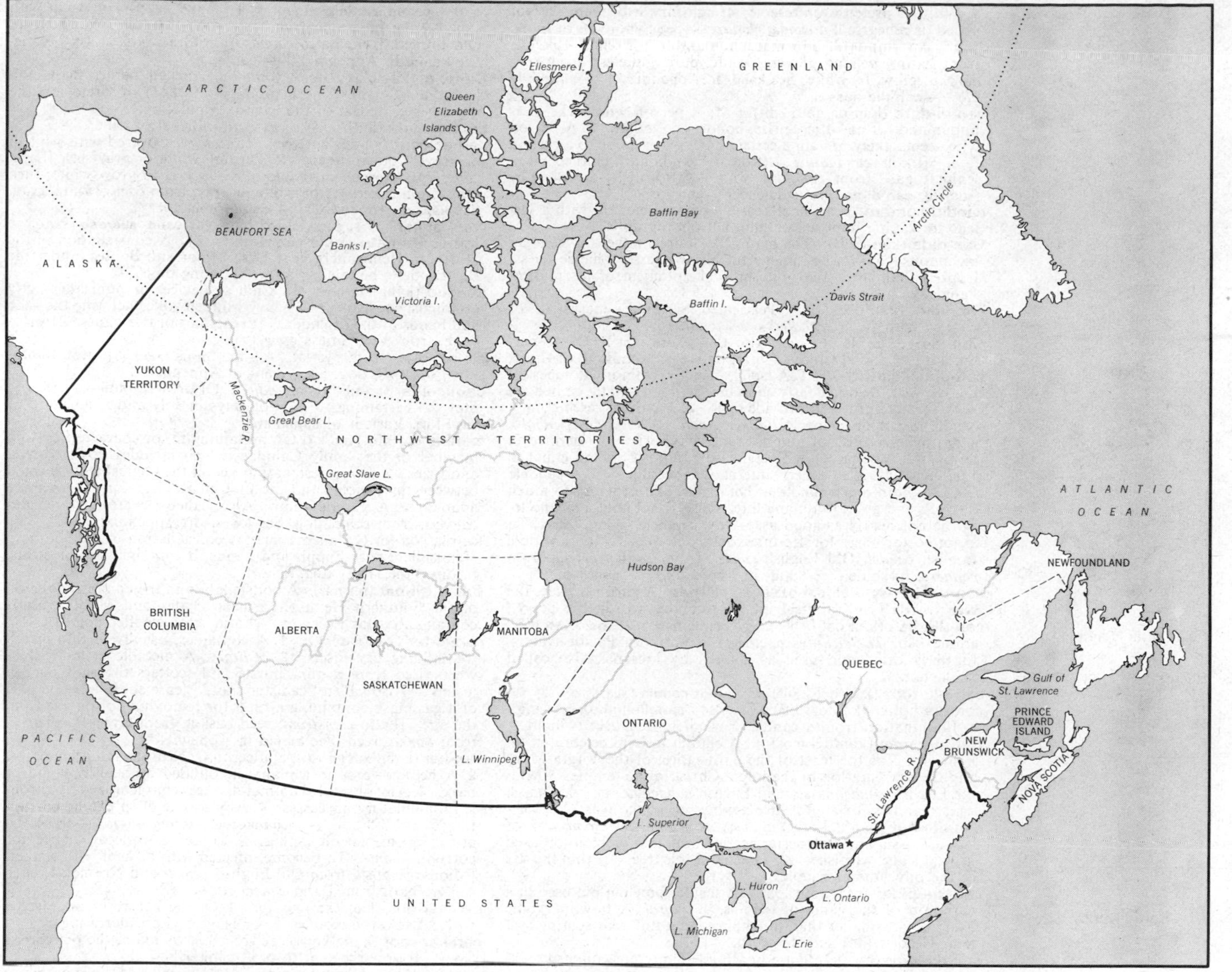

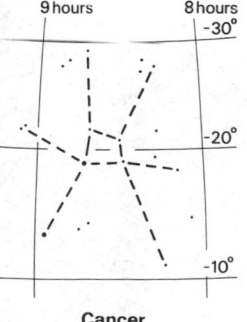

Canada

"basket" (from the use of two decks, or a "basketful," of cards), from *canasto, canastro,* basket, from Latin *canistrum,* CANISTER.]

Ca·nav·er·al, Cape. The former name for Cape **Kennedy**.

Can·ber·ra (kăn′bĕr′ə, -bər-ə). The capital of Australia, in the Australian Capital Territory, on the Murrumbidgee in southeastern New South Wales. Population, 89,000.

can·can (kăn′kăn′) *n.* An exuberant dance performed by women and marked by high kicking. [French, from *cancan,* baby-talk reduplication of *canard,* duck, CANARD (from its waddling movements).]

can·cel (kăn′səl) *v.* **-celed, -celing, -cels.** Also *chiefly British* **-celled, -celling.** —*tr.* **1.** To cross out with lines or other markings. **2.** To annul or invalidate. **3.** To mark or perforate (a postage stamp or check, for example) to indicate that it may not be used again. **4.** To equalize or make up for; neutralize; offset. **5.** *Mathematics.* **a.** To remove a common factor from the numerator and denominator of a fractional expression. **b.** To remove a common factor or term from both members of an equation or inequality. **6.** *Printing.* To omit or delete. —*intr.* To balance or neutralize one another. Used with *out.* —See Synonyms at **erase, nullify.** —*n. Abbr.* **canc. 1. a.** The omission or deletion of typed or printed matter. **b.** The matter omitted or deleted, or its replacement. **2.** *Library Service.* Any part of a book used as a substitute for an original part of the book. [Middle English *cancellen,* from Old French *canceller,* from Latin *cancellāre,* to make like a lattice, cross out, from *cancellī,* lattice, diminutive of *cancer, carcer,* jail. See **carcer** in Appendix.*] —**can′cel·a·ble** *adj.* —**can′cel·er** *n.*

can·cel·late (kăn′sə-lāt′, -lĭt) *adj.* Also **can·cel·lat·ed** (-lā′tĭd) or **can·cel·lous** (kăn′səl-əs, kăn-sĕl′əs). *Anatomy.* Having a coarse netlike or spongy structure. Said of bone. [Latin *cancellātus,* past participle of *cancellāre,* to make like a lattice. See **cancel.**]

can·cel·la·tion (kăn′sə-lā′shən) *n.* Also **can·ce·la·tion. 1.** The act of canceling. **2.** Marks or perforations indicating canceling. **3.** Something that has been canceled.

can·cer (kăn′sər) *n.* **1. a.** Any of various malignant neoplasms that manifest invasiveness and a tendency to metastasize to new sites. **b.** The pathological condition characterized by such growths. **2.** A pernicious, spreading evil. [Latin *cancer,* crab, creeping ulcer (formed after Greek *karkinōma,* CARCINOMA). See **kar-**¹ in Appendix.*] —**can′cer·ous** *adj.*

Can·cer (kăn′sər) *n.* **1.** A constellation in the Northern Hemisphere near Leo and Gemini. **2.** The fourth sign of the **zodiac** *(see).* Also called the "Crab." [Middle English, from Latin *cancer,* crab. See **kar-**¹ in Appendix.*]

can·cer·root (kăn′sər-rōōt′, -rŏŏt′) *n.* Any of several leafless, parasitic plants of the genus *Orobanche* or related genera; especially, *O. uniflora,* having whitish or purplish flowers. [Formerly used to treat cancer.]

can·croid (kăng′kroid′) *adj.* **1.** Similar to a cancer. **2.** Similar to a crab. —*n.* A skin cancer. [Latin *cancer* (stem *cancr-*), crab, CANCER + -OID.]

can·del·a (kăn-dĕl′ə) *n. Abbr.* **cd** A unit of luminous intensity equal to ¹/₆₀ of the luminous intensity per square centimeter of a blackbody radiating at the temperature of solidification of platinum (2,046°K). Also called "candle," "standard candle." See **measurement.** [Latin *candēla,* CANDLE.]

can·de·la·brum (kăn′də-lä′brəm, -lăb′rəm, -lā′brəm) *n., pl.* **-bra** (-brə) or **-brums.** Also **can·de·la·bra** *pl.* **-bras.** A large decorative candlestick having several arms or branches. [Latin *candēlābrum,* from *candēla,* CANDLE.]

can·dent (kăn′dənt) *adj. Rare.* Having a white-hot glow; incandescent. [Latin *candēns,* present participle of *candēre,* to shine, glow. See **kand-** in Appendix.*]

can·des·cence (kăn-dĕs′əns) *n. Rare.* The state of being white hot; incandescence. [Latin *candēscēns,* present participle of *candēscere,* inceptive of *candēre,* to shine, glow. See **candid.**] —**can·des′cent** (-ənt) *adj.* —**can·des′cent·ly** *adv.*

Can·di·a (kăn′dē-ə). **1.** Crete. **2.** *Greek* **He·rak·li·on** (hĭ-răk′lē-ən). A seaport of Greece, the largest city of Crete, situated on the island's northern coast. Population, 63,000.

Can·di·a, Sea of. See Sea of **Crete.**

can·did (kăn′dĭd) *adj.* **1.** Without prejudice; impartial; fair;

9 hours   8 hours

Cancer

candelabrum

2. Without pretense or reserve; straightforward; open. 3. Not posed or rehearsed: *a candid picture.* —See Synonyms at **frank.** —*n.* An unposed informal photograph. [French *candide,* from Latin *candidus,* glowing, white, pure, guileless, from *candēre,* to glow, be white. See **kand-** in Appendix.*] —**can′did·ly** *adv.* —**can′did·ness** *n.*

can·di·date (kăn′də-dāt′, -dĭt) *n.* **1.** A person who seeks or is nominated for an office, prize, honor, or the like. **2.** A person who seems likely to gain a certain position or come to a certain fate. [Latin *candidātus,* "(Roman candidate) clothed in a white toga," from *candidus,* white, CANDID.] —**can′di·da·cy** (-də-sē), **can′di·da·ture′** (-də-cho͝or′, -chər) *n.*

candid camera. Any small, easily operated camera with a fast lens for taking unposed or informal photographs.

Can·dide (kăn-dēd′). The hero of Voltaire's novel *Candide,* an ingenuous youth who, in his travels, witnesses chance catastrophes that mock the philosophical optimism of his master, Pangloss.

can·died (kăn′dēd) *adj.* Permeated, covered, encrusted, or cooked with sugar: *candied sweet potatoes.*

Can·di·ot (kăn′dē-ŏt′) *adj.* Also **Can·di·ote** (-ōt′). Of or pertaining to Candia, Crete. —*n.* A native or inhabitant of Crete.

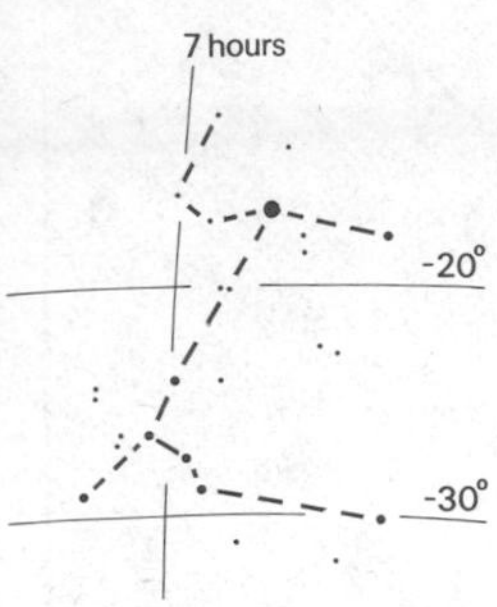

Canis Major

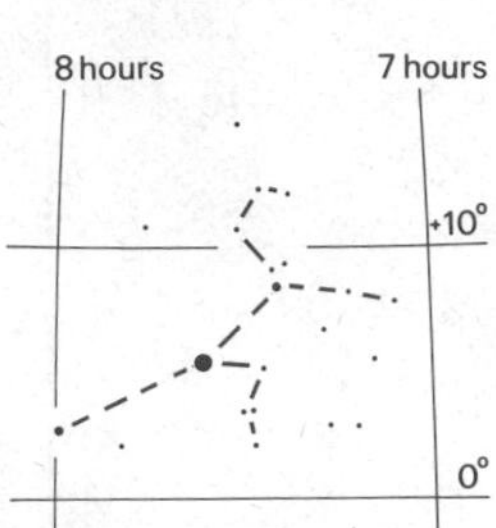

Canis Minor

can·dle (kăn′dəl) *n.* **1.** A solid, usually cylindrical mass of tallow, wax, or other fatty substance with an axially embedded wick that is burned to provide light. **2.** Anything resembling a candle in use or shape: *a Roman candle.* **3.** *Physics. Symbol* **c a.** An obsolete unit of luminous intensity, originally defined in terms of a wax candle with standard composition and equal to 1.02 candelas. Also called "international candle." **b.** A **candela** *(see).* —**burn one's candle at both ends.** To expend too much of one's energy in too many directions. —**not hold a candle to.** To be not nearly as good as. —*tr.v.* **candled, -dling, -dles.** To examine (an egg) for freshness in front of a light. [Middle English *candel,* Old English *candel,* from Latin *candēla,* from *candēre,* to shine. See **kand-** in Appendix.*] —**can′dler** *n.*

can·dle·ber·ry (kăn′dəl-bĕr′ē) *n., pl.* **-ries.** A shrub or tree, the **wax myrtle** *(see),* or its fruit. [From the wax in the berry.]

can·dle·fish (kăn′dəl-fĭsh′) *n., pl.* **candlefish** or **-fishes.** An oily, edible fish, *Thaleichthys pacificus,* of northern Pacific waters, formerly dried and used as a torch by Indians. Also called "eulachon."

can·dle-foot (kăn′dəl-fo͝ot′) *n.* A **foot-candle** *(see).*

can·dle·light (kăn′dəl-līt′) *n.* Also **can·dle·light·ing** (-ĭng). **1.** Illumination from a candle or candles. **2.** Dusk; twilight.

Can·dle·mas (kăn′dəl-məs) *n.* A church festival celebrated on February 2 as the feast of the purification of the Virgin Mary and the presentation of the infant Christ in the temple. [Middle English *candelmasse,* Old English *candelmæsse* : CANDLE + -MAS (candles for church use are blessed at the feast).]

can·dle·nut (kăn′dəl-nŭt′) *n.* **1.** A tree, *Aleurites moluccana,* of tropical Asia and Polynesia, bearing nuts that yield an oil used in paints and varnishes. **2.** The nut of this tree. [From the use of the oily nuts as candles.]

can·dle·pin (kăn′dəl-pĭn′) *n.* **1.** A slender bowling pin used in a variation of the game of tenpins. **2.** *Plural.* A bowling game using a ball smaller than in tenpins and a different scoring system. Used with a singular verb.

can·dle·pow·er (kăn′dəl-pou′ər) *n.* Luminous intensity expressed in standard candles.

can·dle·stick (kăn′dəl-stĭk′) *n.* A holder, often ornamental, with cups or spikes for a candle or candles. Also called "candleholder." [Middle English *candlestikke,* Old English *candelsticca* : CANDLE + STICK (rod).]

can·dle·wick (kăn′dəl-wĭk′) *n.* The wick of a candle.

can·dle·wick·ing (kăn′dəl-wĭk′ĭng) *n.* **1.** Soft, heavy cotton thread similar to that used to make wicks for candles. **2.** Embroidery made of tufts of such thread.

can·dle·wood (kăn′dəl-wo͝od′) *n.* **1.** A tree, the **ocotillo** *(see).* **2.** The resinous wood of this or similar plants.

Can·dolle (kän-dôl′), **Augustin Pyrame de.** 1778–1841. Swiss botanist; perfected system of plant classification.

can·dor (kăn′dər) *n.* Also *chiefly British* **can·dour.** **1.** Frankness of expression; sincerity; straightforwardness. **2.** Freedom from prejudice; impartiality. —See Synonyms at **truth.** [Latin *candor,* whiteness, purity, frankness, from *candēre,* to glow, be white. See **kand-** in Appendix.*]

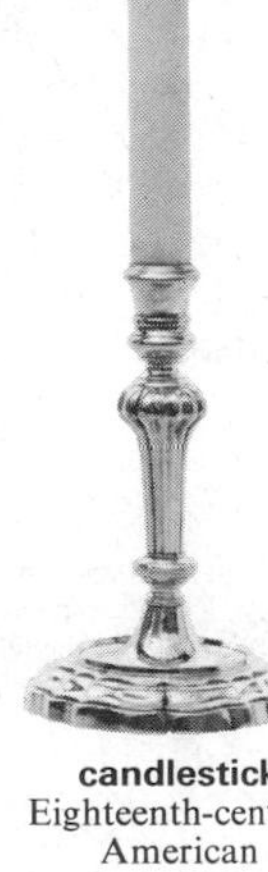

candlestick
Eighteenth-century American

can·dy (kăn′dē) *n., pl.* **-dies.** **1.** Any of numerous kinds of rich, sweet confections made with sugar, corn syrup, or similar substances, often combined with chocolate, dairy products, fruits, or nuts. **2.** A single piece of such a confection. —*v.* **candied, -dying, -dies.** —*tr.* **1.** To reduce to sugar crystals. **2.** To cook, preserve, saturate, or coat with sugar or syrup. **3.** To make pleasant or agreeable; sweeten. —*intr.* **1.** To crystallize, as sugar. **2.** To become coated with sugar or syrup. [Short for *sugar candy,* Middle English *sugre candi,* from Old French *sucre candi,* from Old Italian *zucchero candi* : *zucchero,* SUGAR + *candi,* from Arabic *qandi,* candied, from *qand,* cane sugar, from Dravidian, akin to Tamil *kaṇṭu.*]

can·dy·tuft (kăn′dē-tŭft′) *n.* Any of various plants of the genus *Iberis,* having clusters of white, red, or purplish flowers. [*Candy,* obsolete variant of CANDIA + TUFT.]

cane (kān) *n.* **1. a.** A slender, jointed stem, woody but usually flexible, as of bamboo, rattan, or certain palm trees. **b.** Any plant having such a stem. **c.** Such stems, or strips of such stems, used for wickerwork. **2.** A grass, *Arundinaria gigantea,* of the southeastern United States, having long stiff stems and often forming canebrakes. **3.** The long, woody stem of a raspberry, blackberry, certain roses, or similar plants. **4. Sugar cane** *(see).* **5.** A stick used as an aid in walking. **6.** A rod used for flogging. —*tr.v.* **caned, caning, canes.** **1.** To make, supply, or repair with cane. **2.** To hit or beat with a cane. [Middle English, from Old French, from Latin *canna,* from Greek *kanna,* reed, cane. See **kanna** in Appendix.*] —**can′er** *n.*

Ca·ne·a (kä-nē′ə). *Greek* **Kha·ni·a.** Ancient name, **Cy·do·ni·a** (sĭ-dō′nē-ə, -nyə). The capital (since 1841) of Crete, on the northwestern coast of the island. Population, 38,000.

cane·brake (kān′brāk′) *n.* A dense thicket of cane.

ca·nes·cent (kə-nĕs′ənt) *adj.* **1.** *Biology.* Covered with whitish or grayish down; hoary. **2.** Turning white or grayish. [Latin *cānēscēns,* present participle of *cānēscere,* to grow white, turn gray, from *cānēre,* to be white or gray, from *cānus,* white, gray. See **kas-** in Appendix.*] —**ca·nes′cence** *n.*

cane sugar. A sugar yielded by sugar cane, **sucrose** *(see).*

Ca·nes Ve·nat·i·ci (kā′nēz vĭ-năt′ə-sī′). A constellation in the Northern Hemisphere near Ursa Major and Boötes, under the Big Dipper's handle. [Latin, "hunting dogs."]

cangue (kăng) *n.* An old Chinese device for punishing petty criminals, consisting of a heavy wooden yoke enclosing the neck and hands of the offender. [French, from Portuguese *canga,* a yoke, from Vietnamese *gong.*]

Ca·nic·u·la (kə-nĭk′yə-lə). A star, **Sirius** *(see).* [Latin, diminutive of *canis,* dog. See **kwon-** in Appendix.*]

ca·nic·u·lar (kə-nĭk′yə-lər) *adj.* **1.** Of or pertaining to the Dog Star. **2.** Pertaining to the dog days in July and August.

can·i·kin. Variant of **cannikin.**

ca·nine (kā′nīn′) *adj.* **1.** Of, pertaining to, or characteristic of a member of the family Canidae, which includes dogs, wolves, and foxes. **2.** Of or designating one of the conical teeth located between the incisors and the first bicuspids. —*n.* **1.** A canine animal. **2.** A canine tooth. Also called "eyetooth." [Latin *canīnus,* from *canis,* dog. See **kwon-** in Appendix.*]

Ca·nis Ma·jor (kā′nĭs mā′jər). A constellation in the Southern Hemisphere near Puppis and Lepus. It contains the star Sirius. [Latin, "the larger dog."]

Canis Mi·nor (mī′nər). A constellation in the equatorial region of the Southern Hemisphere near Hydra and Monoceros. It contains the star Procyon. [Latin, "the smaller dog."]

can·is·ter (kăn′ĭs-tər) *n.* **1.** A container, usually of thin metal, for holding dry foods. **2.** *Military.* A metallic cylinder that, when fired from a gun, bursts and scatters the shot packed inside it. Also called "canister shot," "case shot." **3.** The part of a gas mask containing a filter for removing poison gas from the air. [Latin *canistrum,* reed basket, from Greek *kanastron,* from *kanna,* reed. See **kanna** in Appendix.*]

can·ker (kăng′kər) *n.* **1.** An ulcerous sore of the mouth and lips. **2.** A necrotic area in a plant surrounded by healthy wood or bark. **3.** Any of several animal diseases characterized by chronic inflammatory processes. **4.** Any source of spreading corruption or debilitation. —*v.* **cankered, -kering, -kers.** —*tr.* **1.** To attack or infect with canker. **2.** To cause to decay or become corrupt. —*intr.* To become infected with or as if with canker. [Middle English, from Old English *cancer* and Norman French *cancre,* both from Latin *cancer,* CANCER.]

can·ker·ous (kăng′kər-əs) *adj.* **1.** Of the nature of or infected with a canker; ulcerous. **2.** Causing canker; ulcerating.

can·ker·root (kăng′kər-ro͞ot′, -ro͝ot′) *n.* A plant, the **goldthread** *(see).* [Formerly used to treat canker.]

canker sore. A small, painful ulcer usually of the mouth.

can·ker·worm (kăng′kər-wûrm′) *n.* The larva of either of two moths, *Paleacrita vernata* or *Alsophila pometaria,* that are destructive to fruit and shade trees.

can·na (kăn′ə) *n.* Any of various tropical plants of the genus *Canna,* having broad leaves and showy red or yellow flowers. [New Latin *Canna,* from Latin *canna,* reed, CANE.]

can·na·bin (kăn′ə-bĭn) *n.* A resinous material extracted from cannabis. [CANNAB(IS) + -IN.]

can·na·bis (kăn′ə-bĭs) *n.* **1.** A plant of the genus *Cannabis,* **hemp** *(see).* **2.** The dried flowering tops of the hemp plant. See **marijuana, hashish.** [New Latin, from Latin, hemp, from Greek *kannabis.* See **kannabis** in Appendix.*] —**can′na·bic** *adj.*

Can·nae (kăn′ē). An ancient city in southeastern Italy where, during the Second Punic War, the Romans suffered a devastating defeat by Hannibal's forces, 216 B.C.

canned (kănd) *adj.* **1.** Preserved and sealed in a can or jar. **2.** *Informal.* Recorded or taped: *"So if television is to have canned laughter, how about canned tears?"* (Jack Paar).

canned heat. An alcohol or paraffin fuel packed in small cans and used to heat food.

can·nel (kăn′əl) *n.* A bituminous coal that burns brightly with much smoke. Also called "cannel coal." [From *cannel coal,* dialectal form for *candle coal* (from its bright flame).]

can·nel·lo·ni (kăn′nĕl-lō′nē) *pl.n.* An Italian pasta dish of large-sized macaroni stuffed with forcemeat or some cheese mixture, baked, and served with tomato sauce or cream sauce. [Italian, plural of *cannellone,* CANNELON.]

can·ne·lon (kăn-lôN′) *n.* A hollow roll of puff paste stuffed with finely chopped meat or some sweet filling and baked or fried. [From Italian *cannellone,* tubular soup noodle, from *cannello,* small tube, diminutive of *canna,* cane, reed, from Latin, from Greek *kanna.* See **kanna** in Appendix.*]

can·ner·y (kăn′ər-ē) *n., pl.* **-ies.** An establishment where meat, vegetables, or other foods are canned.

Cannes (kăn; *French* kån). A seaport and fashionable resort city of southeastern France, on the Mediterranean. Population, 59,000.

can·ni·bal (kăn′ə-bəl) *n.* **1.** A person who eats the flesh of human beings. **2.** Any animal that feeds on others of its own kind. [From Spanish *Caníbalis, Caríbales,* name (recorded by

Columbus) of the man-eating Caribs of Cuba and Haiti, from Arawakan *caniba, cariba*, Caribbean tribal name, akin to Cariban *caribe*, CARIB.] —**can′ni·bal·ism′** *n.* —**can′ni·bal·is′tic** *adj.*
can·ni·bal·ize (kăn′ə-bə-līz′) *tr.v.* **-ized, -izing, -izes. 1.** To remove serviceable parts from (damaged airplanes, tanks, or other machinery) for use in the repair of other equipment. **2.** To deprive (an organization) of personnel or equipment for use in another organization. [Originally, "to eat human flesh," from CANNIBAL.] —**can′ni·bal·i·za′tion** *n.*
can·ni·kin (kăn′ĭ-kĭn) *n.* Also **can·i·kin. 1.** A little can or cup. **2.** A wooden bucket. [Probably from Dutch *kanneken*, from Middle Dutch *canneken*, diminutive of *canne*, can, vessel, from Common Germanic *kannōn-* (unattested), CAN.]
can·ning (kăn′ĭng) *n.* The act, process, or business of preserving foods in airtight containers.
Can·ning (kăn′ĭng), **George.** 1770–1827. British statesman; foreign secretary (1822–27) and prime minister (1827).
Can·niz·za·ro (kän′nēd-dzä′rō), **Stanislao.** 1826–1910. Italian chemist and political leader.
can·non (kăn′ən) *n., pl.* **cannon** or **-nons. 1.** A weapon for firing projectiles, consisting of a heavy metal tube mounted on a carriage. **2.** Any heavy firearm larger than 0.60 caliber. See **gun, howitzer, mortar. 3.** The loop at the top of a bell by which it is suspended. **4.** A round bit for a horse. Also called "cannon bit." **5.** The bone located between the hock or knee and the fetlock of a horse or ruminant. Also called "cannon bone." **6.** *British.* A carom made in billiards. —*v.* **cannoned, -noning, -nons.** —*tr.* **1.** To bombard or batter with cannon. **2.** *British.* To cause to carom, as in billiards. —*intr.* **1.** To fire cannon. **2.** *British.* To carom; make a carom. [Middle English *canon*, from Old French, from Italian *cannone*, "large tube, barrel," from *canna*, reed, tube, from Latin, reed, CANE.]
Can·non (kăn′ən), **Joseph Gurney.** Called "Uncle Joe." 1836–1926. American political leader; member of U.S. House of Representatives for 46 years; its speaker and virtual dictator (1903–11).
can·non·ade (kăn′ə-nād′) *v.* **-aded, -ading, -ades.** —*tr.* To assault or bombard with cannon fire. —*intr.* To deliver heavy artillery fire. —*n.* An extended, usually heavy, discharge of artillery. [Old French *canonade*, discharge of artillery, from Italian *cannonata*, from *cannone*, CANNON.]
can·non·ball (kăn′ən-bôl′) *n.* Also **cannon ball. 1.** A round projectile fired from a cannon. **2.** A jump into water made with the arms grasping the upraised knees. **3.** Something moving with great speed, such as a fast train. —*intr.v.* **cannonballed, -balling, -balls. 1.** To travel rapidly in the manner of a cannonball. **2.** To make a cannonball dive.
can·non·eer (kăn′ə-nîr′) *n.* A gunner or artilleryman. [Old French *canonier*, from *canon*, CANNON.] —**can′non·eer′ing** *n.*
cannon fodder. Soldiers considered as expendable materials of warfare. [Translation of German *Kanonenfutter*.]
can·non·ry (kăn′ən-rē) *n., pl.* **-ries. 1.** Artillery; cannons collectively. **2.** Artillery fire.
cannon shot. 1. Ammunition for a cannon. **2.** A shot or shots fired by cannon. **3.** The firing distance of a cannon.
can·not (kăn′ŏt, kă-nŏt′) *v.* The negative form of **can.**
Usage: *Cannot but*, sometimes criticized as a form of double negative, is nevertheless acceptable to 68 per cent of the Panel in this typical example: *One cannot but admire his courage*. Alternative ways of expressing this include *can but admire, can only admire, must admire, cannot help admiring*. See Usage notes at **help, seem.**
can·nu·la (kăn′yə-lə) *n., pl.* **-las** or **-lae** (-lē′). Also **can·u·la.** A tube inserted into a bodily cavity to drain fluid or insert medication. [New Latin, from Latin, diminutive of *canna*, a reed, tube, CANE.]
can·nu·late (kăn′yə-lāt′) *tr.v.* **-lated, -lating, -lates.** Also **can·u·late.** To insert a cannula. —*adj.* Also **can·nu·lar** (kăn′yə-lər). Tubular; hollow. —**can′nu·la′tion** *n.*
can·ny (kăn′ē) *adj.* **-nier, -niest. 1.** Having or showing knowledge and skill in applying it; fully competent. **2.** Assiduous in the safekeeping and advancement of one's interests; shrewd. **3.** Attentive to all factors and considerations; prudent. **4.** Susceptible of human understanding; explicable; natural. Used with a negative: *events not canny to strangers*. **5.** *Chiefly Scottish.* **a.** Pleasant; attractive. **b.** Gentle; mild; steady. [From CAN (to know how, be able).] —**can′ni·ly** *adv.* —**can′ni·ness** *n.*
ca·noe (kə-no͞o′) *n.* A light, slender boat with pointed ends, propelled by paddles. —*v.* **canoed, -noeing, -noes.** —*tr.* To carry or send by canoe. —*intr.* To travel in or propel a canoe. [Earlier *canoa*, from Spanish, from Arawakan (recorded by Columbus), from Cariban.] —**ca·noe′ist** *n.*
canoe birch. The **paper birch** *(see)*.
can·on¹ (kăn′ən) *n. Abbr.* **can. 1.** An ecclesiastical law or code of laws established by a church council. **2.** A secular law, rule, or code of law. **3.** A basis for judgment; standard; criterion. **4.** The books of the Bible officially recognized by the Church. **5.** *Often capital* **C.** The part of the Mass beginning after the Sanctus and ending just before the Lord's Prayer. **6.** The calendar of saints accepted by the Roman Catholic Church. **7.** An authoritative list, as of the works of an author. **8.** *Music.* A composition or passage in which the same melody is repeated by one or more voices, overlapping in time in the same or a related key. See **fugue, round. 9.** *Printing.* A size of type, 48-point. [Middle English *cano(u)n*, from Old English and Old French *canon*, both from Late Latin *canōn*, from Latin, measuring line, rule, model, from Greek *kanōn*, rod, rule. See **kanna** in Appendix.*]
can·on² (kăn′ən) *n.* **1.** One of a chapter of priests serving in a cathedral or collegiate church. **2.** A member of a religious community living under common rules and bound by vows. [Middle English *cano(u)n*, from Norman French *canunie*, from Late Latin *canōnicus*, one living under a rule, from *canōn*, CANON (rule).]
ca·ñon. *Spanish.* Variant of **canyon.**
can·on·ess (kăn′ən-ĭs) *n.* A member of a religious community of women, living under a common rule but not bound by vows.
ca·non·i·cal (kə-nŏn′ĭ-kəl) *adj.* Also **ca·non·ic** (-ĭk). **1.** Pertaining to, required by, or abiding by canon law. **2.** Of or appearing in the Biblical canon. **3.** Authoritative; officially approved; orthodox. —**ca·non′i·cal·ly** *adv.* —**can′on·ic′i·ty** (kăn′ə-nĭs′ə-tē) *n.*
canonical hours. 1. *Ecclesiastical.* **a.** A special form of prayer, prescribed by canon law, normally to be recited at specified times of the day, either in common or individually. They are matins (with lauds), prime, tierce, sext, nones, vespers, and complin. **b.** The times of day set aside for these prayers. **2.** *British.* The hours between 8:00 A.M. and 3:00 P.M., during which marriages may legally take place in parish churches.
ca·non·i·cals (kə-nŏn′ĭ-kəlz) *pl.n.* The dress prescribed by canon for officiating clergy.
ca·non·i·cate (kə-nŏn′ĭ-kāt′, -kĭt) *n.* The office or dignity of a canon; canonry. [Medieval Latin *canōnicātus*, from Late Latin *canōnicus*, a canon, from *canōn*, CANON (rule).]
can·on·ist (kăn′ən-ĭst) *n.* A person skilled in canon law. —**can′on·is′tic, can′on·is′ti·cal** *adj.*
can·on·ize (kăn′ə-nīz′) *tr.v.* **-ized, -izing, -izes. 1.** To declare (a deceased person) to be a saint and entitled to be fully honored as such by the Roman Catholic Church. Compare **beatify. 2.** To include in the Biblical canon. **3.** To approve as being within canon law. **4.** To glorify; exalt. —**can′on·i·za′tion** *n.* —**can′on·iz′er** *n.*
canon law. The body of officially established rules governing the faith and practice of the members of a Christian church.
can·on·ry (kăn′ən-rē) *n., pl.* **-ries. 1.** The position or benefice of a canon. **2.** Canons collectively.
Ca·no·pic (kə-nō′pĭk, -nŏp′ĭk) *adj.* **1.** Of, pertaining to, or from the ancient city of Canopus. **2.** Designating an ancient Egyptian vase, urn, or jar used to hold the remains of the dead.
Ca·no·pus¹ (kə-nō′pəs) *n.* A star in the constellation Carina, 650 light-years from Earth, the second-brightest star in the sky. [Latin, from Greek *Kanōpos*†.]
Ca·no·pus² (kə-nō′pəs). An ancient city of Egypt, about 15 miles east of Alexandria, the site of a temple to Serapis.
can·o·py (kăn′ə-pē) *n., pl.* **-pies. 1.** A cloth covering fastened or held horizontally above a person or an object for protection or ornamentation. **2.** *Architecture.* An ornamental, rooflike structure. **3.** Any high covering: *"spreads out into a vast canopy of foliage"* (Thomas Huxley). **4.** *Aviation.* **a.** The transparent, movable enclosure over an aircraft's cockpit. **b.** The hemispherical surface of a parachute. —*tr.v.* **canopied, -pying, -pies.** To overhang with a canopy; form a canopy over: *Mist canopied the landscape*. [Middle English *canape, canope*, from Medieval Latin *canapeum, canopeum*, (couch with a) mosquito net, from Latin *cōnōpeum*, mosquito net, from Greek *kōnōpion*, after the city *Kanōpos*, CANOPUS, where it probably originated (but influenced by *kōnōps*, mosquito).]
ca·no·rous (kə-nôr′əs, -nōr′əs, kăn′ər-əs) *adj.* Tuneful. [Latin *canōrus*, from *canor*, tune, melody, from *canere*, to sing. See **kan-** in Appendix.*] —**ca·no′rous·ly** *adv.* —**ca·no′rous·ness** *n.*
Ca·nos·sa (kə-nŏs′ə; *Italian* kä-nôs′sä). A village in northern Italy where, in 1077, the Holy Roman Emperor Henry IV of Germany submitted to the authority of Pope Gregory VII.
Ca·no·va (kä-nō′vä), **Antonio.** 1757–1822. Italian sculptor.
Can·so, Strait of (kăn′sō). A deep, mile-wide channel between northeastern Nova Scotia, Canada, and southern Cape Breton Island.
canst (kănst). *Archaic.* The second person singular present tense of **can.** Used with *thou*.
cant¹ (kănt) *n.* **1.** Angular deviation from a vertical or horizontal plane or surface; inclination; slant; slope. **2. a.** A thrust or motion that tilts something. **b.** The tilt caused by such a motion. **3.** An outer corner, as of a building. **4.** A slanted edge or surface. —*v.* **canted, canting, cants.** —*tr.* **1.** To set at an oblique angle; cause to slant or tilt. **2.** To give a slanting edge to; bevel. **3.** To change the direction of suddenly. —*intr.* **1.** To tilt to one side; to slant. **2.** To take an oblique direction or course; swing around, as a ship. [Middle English, side, edge, from Norman French, from Latin *cant(h)us*, iron tire, rim of a wheel, from Celtic. See **kantho-** in Appendix.*]
cant² (kănt) *n.* **1.** Whining speech, as used by beggars. **2.** Discourse recited monotonously or mechanically. **3.** Hypocritically pious language. **4.** The special vocabulary peculiar to the members of a group on the fringe of society, as thieves; argot. **5.** The special terminology understood among the members of a profession, discipline, or class, but obscure to the general population; jargon. —See Synonyms at **dialect.** —*intr.v.* **canted, canting, cants. 1.** To speak in a whining, pleading tone. **2.** To speak tediously or sententiously; moralize. **3.** To use special jargon or argot. [Probably from Norman French *cant*, singing, jargon, from *canter*, to sing, tell, from Latin *cantāre*, frequentative of *canere*, to sing. See **kan-** in Appendix.*] —**cant′ing·ly** *adv.* —**cant′ing·ness** *n.*
can't (kănt, känt). Contraction of *cannot*. See Usage notes at **can, cannot.**
Cant. Cantonese.
can·ta·bi·le (kän-tä′bē-lā′) *adj. Music.* In a smooth, lyrical, flowing style. Used as a direction to the performer. —*n. Music.*

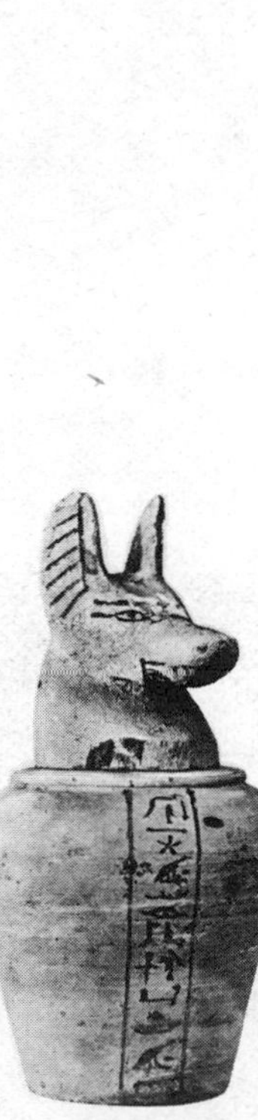
Canopic
Jackal-headed Canopic jar

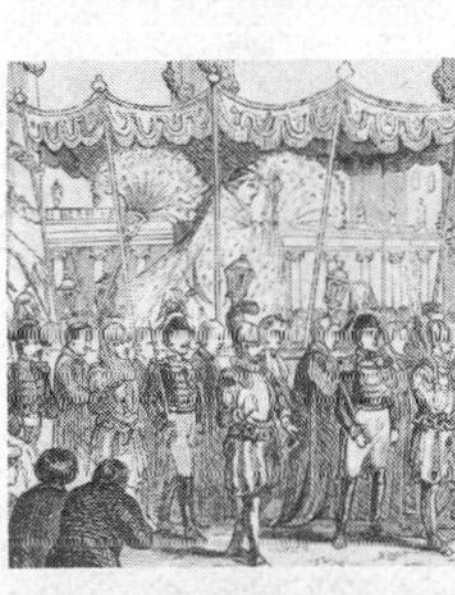
canopy

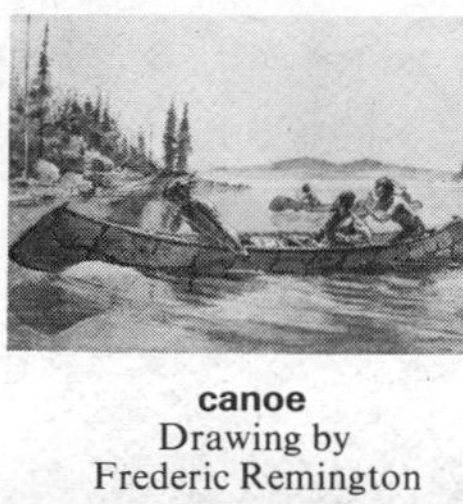
canoe
Drawing by
Frederic Remington

A cantabile passage or movement. [Italian, from Late Latin *cantābilis,* singable, from Latin *cantāre,* frequentative of *canere,* to sing. See **kan-** in Appendix.*] —**can·ta′bi·le** *adv.*

Can·ta·bri·an Mountains (kăn-tā′brē-ən). A range of mountains extending about 300 miles in northern and northwestern Spain. Highest elevation, 8,794 feet.

Can·ta·brig·i·an (kăn′tə-brĭj′ē-ən) *adj.* **1.** Of or pertaining to Cambridge, England, or Cambridge, Massachusetts. **2.** Of or pertaining to Cambridge University. —*n.* **1.** A native or resident of Cambridge. **2.** A student or graduate of Cambridge University or Cambridge High and Latin School. [From *Cantabrigia,* Medieval Latin form of CAMBRIDGE.]

can·ta·la (kăn-tä′lə) *n.* **1.** A century plant, *Agave cantula,* native to tropical America, cultivated for its coarse, tough fiber. **2.** The fiber of this plant. [Origin unknown.]

can·ta·le·ver, can·ta·liv·er. Variants of **cantilever.**

can·ta·loupe (kăn′tə-lōp′) *n.* Also **can·ta·loup. 1.** A variety of melon, *Cucumis melo cantalupensis,* having fruit with a ribbed, rough rind and aromatic orange flesh. **2.** Any of several similar melons. **3.** The fruit of any of these plants. [French *cantaloup,* from Italian *cantalupo,* first grown at *Cantalupo,* a papal villa near Rome.]

can·tank·er·ous (kăn-tăng′kər-əs) *adj.* Ill-tempered and quarrelsome; disagreeable; contrary. [Probably from Middle English *contekour,* rioter, brawler, from *contek,* quarrel, strife, from Norman French *contek*† (influenced by CANKEROUS).] —**can·tank′er·ous·ly** *adv.* —**can·tank′er·ous·ness** *n.*

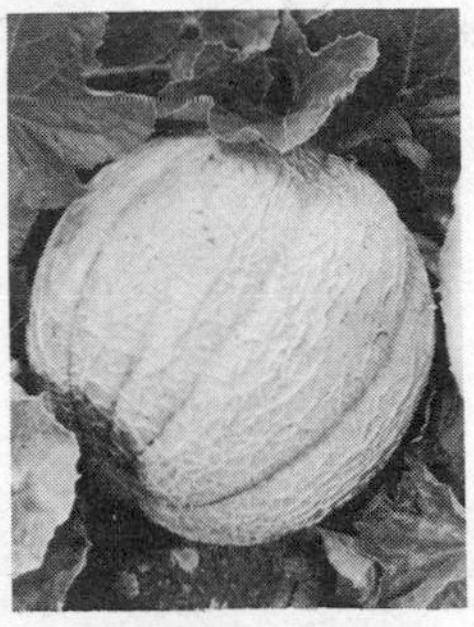

cantaloupe

can·ta·ta (kən-tä′tə) *n.* A vocal and instrumental composition comprising choruses, solos, and recitatives. [Italian *(aria) cantata,* "sung (aria)," from *cantare,* to sing, from Latin *cantāre.* See **cant** (jargon).]

can·teen (kăn-tēn′) *n.* **1. a.** A store for on-base military personnel. See **Post Exchange. b.** *British.* A club for soldiers. **2.** An institutional recreation hall or cafeteria. **3.** A temporary or mobile eating place, especially one set up in an emergency. **4. a.** A mess kit. **b.** A box divided into compartments containing a set of cooking gear. **5.** A flask for drinking water of the kind carried by soldiers. [French *cantine,* from Italian *cantina,* a wine cellar, from *canto,* edge, from Latin *cant(h)us,* iron tire, rim of a wheel, from Celtic. See **kantho-** in Appendix.*]

can·ter (kăn′tər) *n.* A gait slower than the gallop but faster than the trot. —*v.* **cantered, -tering, -ters.** —*intr.* To move or ride at a canter. —*tr.* To make (a horse) go at a canter. [Short for *Canterbury gallop,* the slow pace at which mounted pilgrims rode to Canterbury.]

Can·ter·bur·y (kăn′tər-bĕr′ē). **1.** A cathedral city of Kent, in southeastern England; the ecclesiastical center of England since A.D. 597. Population, 33,000. **2.** A city of Australia, in New South Wales, and a suburb of Sydney. Population, 114,000. [Middle English *Canterbury,* Old English *Cantwarabyrig,* "the town of the Kentish people" : *Cant, Cent,* KENT + *-wara,* genitive plural of *-ware,* inhabitant (see **wer-⁵** in Appendix*) + *burg, byrig,* fortified place, town (see **bhergh-** in Appendix*).]

Canterbury bells. Used with a singular or plural verb. A plant, *Campanula medium,* native to Europe, widely cultivated for its showy, bell-shaped violet-blue flowers. [The flowers resemble the small bells on the horses of Canterbury pilgrims.]

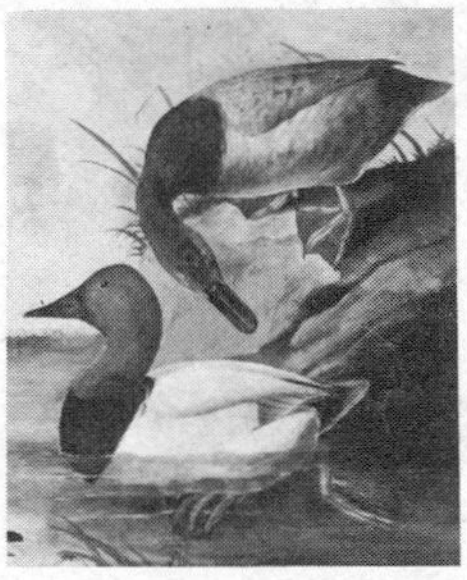

canvasback
Painting by
John James Audubon

can·thar·i·des (kăn-thăr′ə-dēz′) *pl.n. Singular* **cantharis** (kăn′thə-rĭs). Used with a singular or plural verb. A toxic preparation of the crushed, dried bodies of the beetle *Lytta vesicatoria* (or *Cantharis vesicatoria*), formerly used as a counterirritant for skin blisters and as an aphrodisiac. Also called "Spanish fly." [Latin, plural of *cantharis,* from Greek *kantharis,* blister beetle, from *kantharos*†, dung beetle.]

cant hook. A **peavey** *(see).* [From CANT (angle).]

can·thus (kăn′thəs) *n., pl.* **-thi** (-thī′). The corner at either side of the eye, formed by the meeting of the upper and lower eyelids. [Late Latin, from Greek *kanthos*†.]

can·ti·cle (kăn′tĭ-kəl) *n.* A song or chant; specifically, a nonmetrical hymn with words taken directly from a Biblical text. [Middle English, from Latin *canticulum,* diminutive of *cantus,* song, from *canere,* to sing. See **kan-** in Appendix.*]

Canticle of Canticles. In the Douay Bible, the **Song of Solomon** *(see).*

can·ti·le·ver (kăn′tə-lē′vər, -lĕv′ər) *n.* Also **can·ta·le·ver, can·ta·liv·er** (-lĭv′ər). **1.** A projecting beam or other structure supported only at one end. **2.** A beam or other member projecting beyond a fulcrum and supported by a balancing member or a downward force behind the fulcrum. **3.** A bracket or block supporting a balcony or cornice. —*tr.v.* **cantilevered, -vering, -vers.** Also **can·ta·le·ver, can·ta·liv·er.** To extend outward or build as a cantilever. [Possibly CANT (slope, edge) + LEVER (beam, bar).]

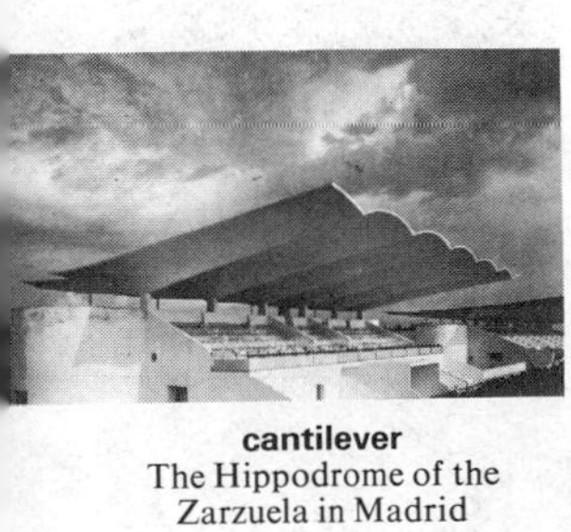

cantilever
The Hippodrome of the
Zarzuela in Madrid

cantilever bridge. A bridge formed by two projecting beams or trusses that are joined in the center by a connecting member and are supported on piers and anchored by counterbalancing members.

can·til·late (kăn′tə-lāt′) *v.* **-lated, -lating, -lates.** —*tr.* To chant or recite in a musical monotone, as in Jewish or other rituals. —*intr.* To recite in a musical monotone. [Latin *cantillāre,* to sing in a low voice, hum, from *cantāre,* frequentative of *canere,* to sing. See **kan-** in Appendix.*] —**can′til·la′tion** *n.*

can·ti·na (kăn-tē′nə) *n. Southwestern U.S.* An establishment that serves liquor; a bar or saloon. [Spanish, canteen, wine cellar, from Italian *cantina,* CANTEEN.]

can·tle (kăn′təl) *n.* **1.** The rear part of a saddle. **2.** A corner or portion, especially when cut off from something, as a piece of land or cheese; a slice. [Middle English *cantel,* from Norman French, diminutive of *cant,* corner, CANT.]

can·to (kăn′tō) *n., pl.* **-tos.** *Abbr.* **can.** One of the principal divisions of a long poem. [Italian, from Latin *cantus,* song, from *canere,* to sing. See **kan-** in Appendix.*]

can·ton (kăn′tən, -tŏn′) *n.* **1. a.** A small territorial division of a country, especially one of the states of Switzerland. **b.** A subdivision of an arrondissement in France. **2.** *Heraldry.* A small, square division of a shield, usually in the upper right corner. **3.** A division of a flag, usually rectangular, occupying the upper corner next to the staff. —*tr.v.* (kăn′tən, -tŏn′ *for sense 1;* kăn-tōn′, -tŏn′ *for sense 2*) **cantoned, -toning, -tons. 1.** To divide into parts, especially cantons or territorial districts. **2.** To assign quarters to (troops); billet. [French, corner, subdivision, from Old French, from Italian *cantone,* augmentative of *canto,* corner, from Latin *cant(h)us,* iron tire, rim of a wheel, from Celtic. See **kantho-** in Appendix.*] —**can′ton·al** (kăn′tən-əl, kăn-tŏn′əl) *adj.*

Can·ton (kăn′tŏn′, kăn-tŏn′ *for sense 1;* kăn′tən *for sense 2*). **1.** *Chinese* **Kwang·chow** (kwäng′jō′). The capital of Kwangtung Province, China, a river port on the Chu Kiang. Population, 1,840,000. **2.** A city in northeastern Ohio; the site of the home of President McKinley. Population, 114,000.

Can·ton crepe (kăn′tŏn′, -tən). A soft fabric of silk or similar material with a finely crinkled texture. It is similar to crêpe de Chine but heavier. [Originally made at CANTON, China.]

Can·ton·ese (kăn′tə-nēz′, -nēs′) *n., pl.* **Cantonese. 1.** *Abbr.* **Cant.** *Chinese* **Yüeh** (yōō-ā′). The Chinese dialect spoken in Kwangtung and Kwangsi provinces in southern China. **2.** A native or inhabitant of Kwangtung Province in southern China. —**Can′ton·ese′** *adj.*

Canton flannel. A heavy, soft cotton cloth with a woolly nap on one side, used mainly for baby clothes. Also called "flannelette," "swan's-down." [Originally made at CANTON, China.]

can·ton·ment (kăn-tōn′mənt, kăn-tŏn′-) *n.* **1.** A group of more or less temporary buildings for housing troops. **2.** The assignment of troops to temporary quarters.

Can·ton River. See **Chu Kiang.**

can·tor (kăn′tər) *n.* **1.** The official soloist or chief singer of the liturgy in a synagogue. **2.** The person who leads a church choir or congregation in singing; precentor. [Latin, singer, from *canere,* to sing. See **kan-** in Appendix.*]

can·trip (kăn′trĭp) *n. Scottish.* **1.** A magic spell; a witch's trick. **2.** A mischievous trick; prank. [Origin obscure.]

can·tus fir·mus (kăn′təs fîr′məs, fûr′məs). A pre-existing melody serving as the basis of a polyphonic composition by the addition of contrapuntal voices, as in 15th-century polyphony. [Medieval Latin "fixed melody."]

Ca·nuck (kə-nŭk′) *n. Slang.* A Canadian; specifically, a French Canadian. Often used disparagingly. [Possibly a mispronunciation (by Indians) of CANADIAN.]

can·u·la. Variant of **cannula.**

can·u·late. Variant of **cannulate.**

Ca·nute (kə-nōōt′, -nyōōt′). Also **Cnut** (knōōt), **Knut.** Called "the Great." A.D. 994?–1035. King of England (1016?–35), of Denmark (1018–35), and of Norway (1028–35).

can·vas (kăn′vəs) *n.* **1.** A heavy, coarse, closely woven fabric of cotton, hemp, or flax, used for making tents and sails. **2. a.** A piece of such material on which a painting is made, especially an oil painting. **b.** A painting of this kind. **3.** Sailcloth. **4.** A sail, or sails collectively. **5.** A tent or tents collectively, especially a circus tent. **6.** A fabric of coarse open weave, used as a foundation for needlework. **7.** The floor of a ring in which boxing or wrestling takes place. —**under canvas. 1.** In a tent or tents. **2.** With sails spread. [Middle English *canevas,* from Norman French, from Vulgar Latin *cannabāceus* (unattested), "made of hemp," from Latin *cannabis,* hemp, from Greek *kannabis.* See **kannabis** in Appendix.*]

can·vas·back (kăn′vəs-băk′) *n.* A North American duck, *Aythya valisneria,* having a reddish-brown head and neck and a whitish back.

can·vass (kăn′vəs) *v.* **-vassed, -vassing, -vasses.** —*tr.* **1.** To examine carefully or discuss thoroughly; scrutinize. **2. a.** To go through (a region) or go to (persons) to solicit votes, orders, subscriptions, or the like. **b.** To conduct a survey (of public opinion) on a given subject; to poll. —*intr.* **1.** To make a thorough examination or conduct a detailed discussion. **2.** To solicit political support, sales orders, or opinions. —*n.* **1.** An examination or discussion. **2. a.** A solicitation of votes, sales orders, or opinions. **b.** A survey of public opinion. [From CANVAS, probably from the idea of "tossing a person in a canvas sheet," hence to criticize, harangue.] —**can′vass·er** *n.*

can·yon (kăn′yən) *n. Spanish* **ca·ñon** (kä-nyōn′). A narrow chasm with steep cliff walls, formed by running water; a gorge. [American Spanish *cañon,* from Spanish, pipe, tube, conduit, augmentative of *caña,* tube, cane, from Latin *canna,* a reed, from Greek *kanna.* See **kanna** in Appendix.*]

Canyon de Chel·ly National Monument (də shā′). An area of 83,840 acres in northeastern Arizona, reserved to protect ruins of cliff dwellings.

Can·yon·lands National Park (kăn′yən-lăndz′). A national park occupying 257,640 acres in southeastern Utah.

can·zo·ne (kăn-zō′nē; *Italian* kän-tsō′nā) *n., pl.* **-nes** (-nēz, -nāz) or **-ni** (-nē). **1.** A poetic form that was the dominant lyric genre of the Italian 13th century, consisting of a sequence of equal stanzas with various standard rhyme schemes developed as a synthesis of pre-existing Provençal forms by Dante and others. **2.** A polyphonic song form evolving from this and resembling the madrigal in style. [Italian, from Latin *cantiō* (accusative *cantiōnem*), song, from *canere,* to sing. See **kan-** in Appendix.*]

ă pat/ā pay/âr care/ä father/b **bib**/ch **church**/d **deed**/ĕ pet/ē be/f **fife**/g **gag**/h **hat**/hw **which**/ĭ pit/ī pie/îr pier/j **judge**/k **kick**/l **lid, needle**/m **mum**/n **no, sudden**/ng **thing**/ŏ pot/ō toe/ô paw, for/oi noise/ou out/ŏŏ took/ōō boot/p **pop**/r **roar**/s **sauce**/sh **ship, dish**/

can·zo·net (kăn′zə-nĕt′) *n.* A short, lighthearted song or air. [Italian *canzonetta,* diminutive of CANZONE.]
caou·tchouc (kou-cho͝ok′, -cho͝ok′) *n.* Natural rubber. See **rubber.** [French, from obsolete Spanish *cauchuc,* from Quechua.]
cap (kăp) *n.* **1.** A covering for the head, usually soft and close-fitting, and either brimless or having a visor or narrow ruffle. **2.** A special head covering worn to indicate rank, occupation, or membership in a particular group: *a cardinal's cap.* **3.** Any of numerous objects similar to a head covering in form, use, or position: *a bottle cap.* **4.** *Architecture.* The capital of a column. **5.** The top part, or pileus, of a mushroom or similar fungus. **6. a.** A percussion cap. **b.** A small explosive charge enclosed in paper for use in a toy gun. **7.** Any of several sizes of writing paper. See **foolscap, legal cap.** —**set one's cap for.** To attempt to attract and win (a man) as a lover or husband. —*tr.v.* **capped, capping, caps. 1.** To put a cap on. **2.** To lie over or on top of; serve as a cap for; cover: *Snow capped the hills.* **3.** To apply the finishing touch to; complete: *cap a meal with dessert.* **4.** To surpass; outdo. [Middle English *cappe,* Old English *cæppe,* from Late Latin *cappa,* hood, probably from Latin *caput,* head. See **kaput** in Appendix.*]
cap. 1. capacity. **2.** capital (city). **3.** capital letter.
C.A.P. Civil Air Patrol.
ca·pa·bil·i·ty (kā′pə-bĭl′ə-tē) *n., pl.* **-ties. 1.** The quality of being capable; physical, mental, or moral capacity; ability. **2.** *Usually plural.* Potential ability: *live up to one's capabilities.* **3.** The capacity to be used, treated, or developed for a specific purpose.
ca·pa·ble (kā′pə-bəl) *adj.* Having capacity or ability; competent; efficient; able: *a capable administrator.* —**capable of. 1.** Having the mental or physical capacity for; qualified for. **2.** Open to; susceptible to: *an error capable of remedy.* [French, from Old French, from Late Latin *capābilis,* "able to hold," from *capere,* to hold. See **kap-** in Appendix.*] —**ca′pa·ble·ness** *n.* —**ca′pa·bly** *adv.*
ca·pa·cious (kə-pā′shəs) *adj.* Able to contain a large quantity; spacious; roomy. [From Latin *capāx* (stem *capāc-*), able to hold, from *capere,* to hold, contain, take. See **kap-** in Appendix.*] —**ca·pa′cious·ly** *adv.* —**ca·pa′cious·ness** *n.*
ca·pac·i·tance (kə-păs′ə-təns) *n. Symbol* **C 1.** The ratio of charge to potential on an electrically charged, isolated conductor. **2.** The ratio of the electric charge transferred from one to the other of a pair of conductors to the resulting potential difference between them. Formerly called "capacity." [CAPACIT(Y) + -ANCE.] —**ca·pac′i·tive** *adj.* —**ca·pac′i·tive·ly** *adv.*
ca·pac·i·tate (kə-păs′ə-tāt′) *tr.v.* **-tated, -tating, -tates. 1.** To render fit; make qualified; enable. **2.** To qualify legally: *capacitated to vote.* [CAPACIT(Y) + -ATE.] —**ca·pac′i·ta′tion** *n.*
ca·pac·i·tor (kə-păs′ə-tər) *n.* An electric circuit element used to store charge temporarily, consisting in general of two metallic plates separated by a dielectric. Formerly called "condenser."
ca·pac·i·ty (kə-păs′ə-tē) *n., pl.* **-ties.** *Abbr.* **c., C., cap. 1.** The ability to receive, hold, or absorb. **2.** A measure of this ability; volume. **3.** The maximum amount that can be contained: *a trunk filled to capacity.* **4.** The maximum or optimum amount of production: *factories operating below capacity.* **5.** The ability to learn or retain knowledge. **6.** The ability to do something; faculty; aptitude. Used with *of, for,* or an infinitive: *a capacity for self-expression.* **7.** The quality of being suitable for or receptive to specified treatment: *the capacity of elastic to be stretched.* **8.** The position in which one functions; role: *his capacity as host.* **9.** Legal qualification or authority: *the capacity to make an arrest.* **10.** *Electricity.* **a.** *Obsolete.* **Capacitance** *(see).* **b.** A measure of the electric output of a generator. —See Synonyms at **ability.** —*adj.* As large or numerous as possible in a given setting: *a capacity crowd on opening night.* [Middle English *capacite,* from Old French, from Latin *capācitās,* from *capāx* (stem *capāc-*), CAPACIOUS.]
cap-a-pie, cap-à-pie (kăp′ə-pē′) *adv.* From head to foot. [Old French *(de) cap a pie,* from Old Provençal *de cap a pe* : *cap,* head, from Latin *caput* (see **kaput** in Appendix*) + *pe,* foot, from Latin *pēs* (see **ped-**[1] in Appendix*).]
ca·par·i·son (kə-păr′ə-sən) *n.* **1.** A cover, usually ornamental, placed over a horse's saddle or harness; trappings. **2.** Richly ornamented clothing; finery. —*tr.v.* **caparisoned, -soning, -sons.** To outfit with a caparison. [Old French *caparaçon,* from Spanish *caparazón,* saddle blanket, "mantle with hood," probably from *capa,* CAPE (garment).]
cape[1] (kāp) *n.* A sleeveless garment fastened at the throat and worn hanging over the shoulders. [French, from Old Provençal *cape* and Spanish *capa,* both from Late Latin *cappa,* hood, cloak, from Latin *caput,* head. See **kaput** in Appendix.*]
cape[2] (kāp) *n. Abbr.* **c., C.** A point or head of land projecting into a sea or other body of water; promontory. Compare **peninsula.** —**the Cape. 1.** See Cape **Cod. 2.** See Cape of **Good Hope.** [Middle English *cap,* from Old French, from Old Provençal, from Latin *caput,* head. See **kaput** in Appendix.*]
Cape, Cape of. For names of actual capes, see the specific element of the name, as **Hatteras, Cape; Good Hope, Cape of.** Other names beginning with *Cape* are entered under **Cape.**
Cape Bret·on Island (brĕt′n, brĭt′n). An island, 3,975 square miles in area, of northeastern Nova Scotia, Canada, separated from the mainland by the Strait of Canso.
Cape Coast. Formerly **Cape Coast Castle.** A port city of south-central Ghana on the Gulf of Guinea, the capital of the former British Gold Coast colony and once a shipping point for slaves. Population, 41,000.
Cape Cod Bay. The southern part of Massachusetts Bay, partially enclosed by the curve of Cape Cod.
Cape Cod Canal. A sea-level canal across the base of Cape Cod, connecting Buzzards Bay with Cape Cod Bay.
Cape Cod cottage. A compact one- or one-and-a-half-story house surfaced with wood shingles and clapboards, with a simple gabled roof and a massive central chimney.
Cape cowslip. Any of various bulbous South African plants of the genus *Lachenalia,* having clusters of drooping red or yellow flowers and widely cultivated as a potted plant.
Cape Dutch. A language of South Africa, **Afrikaans** *(see).*
Cape Fear River. A river rising in central North Carolina and flowing 200 miles southeast to the Atlantic Ocean.
Cape gooseberry. A plant, *Physalis peruviana,* native to tropical America, having yellow flowers and edible yellow berries.
Cape jasmine. A species of **gardenia** *(see).*
cap·e·lin (kăp′ə-lĭn, kăp′lĭn) *n.* Also **cap·lin** (kăp′lĭn). A small, edible marine fish, *Mallotus villosus,* of northern Atlantic and Pacific waters, related to and resembling the smelts. [Canadian French *capelan,* from French, codfish, from Old Provençal *cappellan,* "chaplain," from Medieval Latin *cappellānus,* CHAPLAIN.]
Ca·pel·la (kə-pĕl′ə) *n.* A double star in Auriga, the brightest star in the constellation, approximately 46 light-years from Earth. [New Latin, from Latin, diminutive of *capra,* she-goat, from *caper,* goat. See **kapro-** in Appendix.*]
Cape of Good Hope Province. Also **Cape Province.** Formerly **Cape Colony.** *Afrikaans* **Kaap·land** (käp′länt). The southernmost province of the Republic of South Africa, about 278,000 square miles in area, with coastlines on the Atlantic and Indian oceans. Population, 5,363,000. Capital, Cape Town.
ca·per[1] (kā′pər) *n.* **1.** A playful leap or hop; a skip. **2.** A wild escapade. —*intr.v.* **capered, -pering, -pers.** To leap or frisk about; frolic; gambol. [Short for CAPRIOLE.] —**ca′per·er** *n.*
ca·per[2] (kā′pər) *n.* **1.** A spiny, trailing shrub, *Capparis spinosa,* of the Mediterranean region. **2. a.** A pickled flower bud of this shrub, used as a condiment. **b.** Any similar pickled bud or pod. [From earlier *capres* (mistaken as plural), Middle English *caperis,* from Latin *capparis,* from Greek *kapparis*†.]
cap·er·cail·lie (kăp′ər-kāl′yē, -kā′lē) *n.* Also **cap·er·cail·zie** (-kāl′zē, -kāl′yē). A large grouse, *Tetrao urogallus,* of northern Europe, having dark plumage and a fanlike tail. [Scottish Gaelic *capalcoille,* "horse of the woods" : *capall,* horse, probably from Latin *caballus* (see **cavalier**) + *coille,* forest, probably from Old Irish *caill* (see **kel-**[2] in Appendix*).]
Ca·per·na·um (kə-pûr′nē-əm). A city of Biblical Palestine, on the northwestern shore of the Sea of Galilee.
cape·skin (kāp′skĭn′) *n.* Soft leather made from sheepskin. [Originally made in CAPE OF GOOD HOPE PROVINCE.]
Ca·pet (kā′pĭt, kăp′ĭt; *French* kȧ-pĕ′), **Hugh** or **Hugues.** A.D. 940?–996. King of France (987–996).
Ca·pe·tian (kə-pē′shən) *adj.* Pertaining or belonging to the French dynasty (987–1328) founded by Hugh Capet. —*n.* A member of this dynasty.
Cape Town. Also **Cape·town** (kāp′toun′). The legislative capital of the Republic of South Africa and the capital of Cape of Good Hope Province, situated on the southwestern tip of Africa. Population, 508,000.
Cape Verde Islands (vûrd). *Portuguese* **I·lhas do Ca·bo Ver·de** (ē′lyəzh do͞o kä′bo͞o vĕr′dĭ). A group of islands occupying 1,557 square miles in the Atlantic Ocean about 400 miles west of Senegal, Africa, and constituting an overseas territory of Portugal. Population, 202,000. Capital, Praia.
Cape York Peninsula (yôrk). A 450-mile-long peninsula of northeastern Queensland, Australia, between the South Pacific Ocean and the Gulf of Carpentaria.
cap gun. A **cap pistol** *(see).*
caph. Variant of **kaph.**
ca·pi·as (kā′pē-əs) *n. Law.* A writ authorizing an officer to arrest the person specified therein. [Middle English, from Latin *capias,* "You are to arrest" (first word of the writ), from *capere,* to seize, take. See **kap-** in Appendix.*]
cap·il·lar·i·ty (kăp′ə-lăr′ə-tē) *n., pl.* **-ties.** The interaction between contacting surfaces of a liquid and a solid that distorts the liquid surface from a planar shape.
cap·il·lar·y (kăp′ə-lĕr′ē) *adj.* **1.** Pertaining to or resembling a hair; fine and slender. **2.** Having a very small internal diameter. Said of tubes. **3.** *Anatomy.* In, of, or pertaining to the capillaries. **4.** *Physics.* Of or pertaining to capillarity. —*n., pl.* **capillaries. 1.** *Anatomy.* One of the minute blood vessels that connect the arteries and veins. **2.** Any tube with a small internal diameter. [Latin *capillāris,* from *capillus*†, hair.]
capillary attraction. The force that results from greater adhesion of a liquid to a solid surface than internal cohesion of the liquid itself and that causes the liquid to be raised against a vertical surface, as is water in a clean glass tube.
capillary repulsion. The force that results from greater internal cohesion of a liquid than adhesion of the liquid to a solid surface and that causes the liquid to be depressed against a vertical surface, as is mercury in a glass tube.
cap·il·li·ti·um (kăp′ə-lĭsh′ē-əm) *n., pl.* **-litia** (-lĭsh′ē-ə). A network of sterile, threadlike structures among the spores in slime molds and puffball fungi. [New Latin, from Latin, the hair collectively, from *capillus,* hair. See **capillary.**]
cap·i·tal[1] (kăp′ə-təl) *n.* **1.** *Abbr.* **cap.** A town or city that is the official seat of government in a state, nation, or other political entity. **2.** Wealth in the form of money or property, owned, used, or accumulated in business by an individual, partnership, or corporation. **3.** Any form of material wealth used or available for use in the production of more wealth. **4. a.** *Accounting.* The remaining assets of a business after all liabilities have been

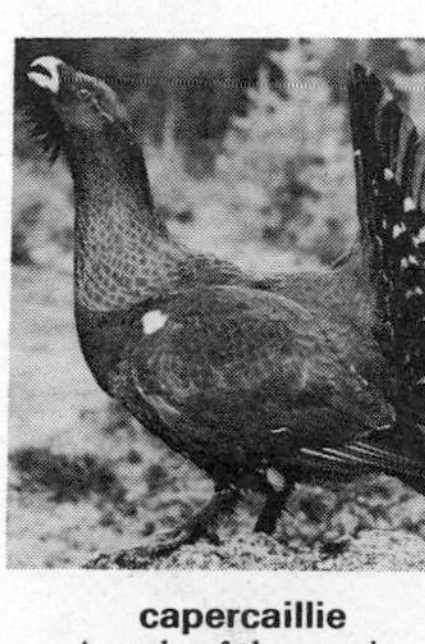
capercaillie
A male of the species

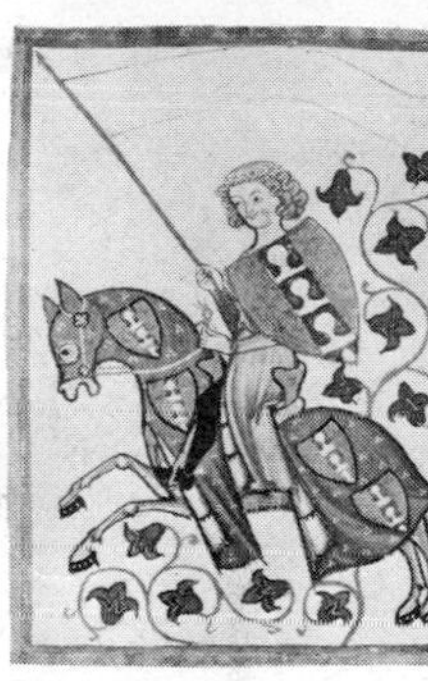
caparison

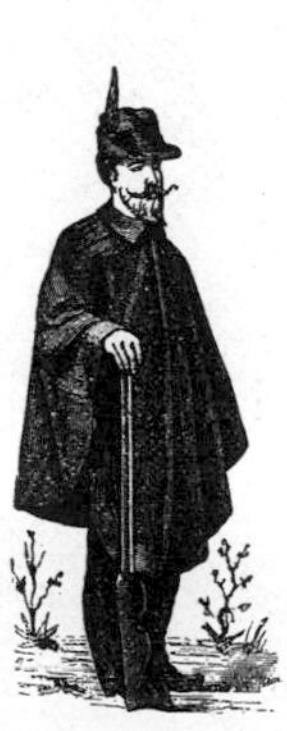
cape[1]

t tight/th thin, path/*th* this, bathe/ŭ cut/û urge/v valve/w with/y yes/z zebra, size/zh vision/ə about, item, edible, gallop, circus/ ȧ *Fr.* ami/œ *Fr.* feu, *Ger.* schön/ü *Fr.* tu, *Ger.* über/KH *Ger.* ich, *Scot.* loch/N *Fr.* bon. ***Follows main vocabulary.** †**Of obscure origin.**

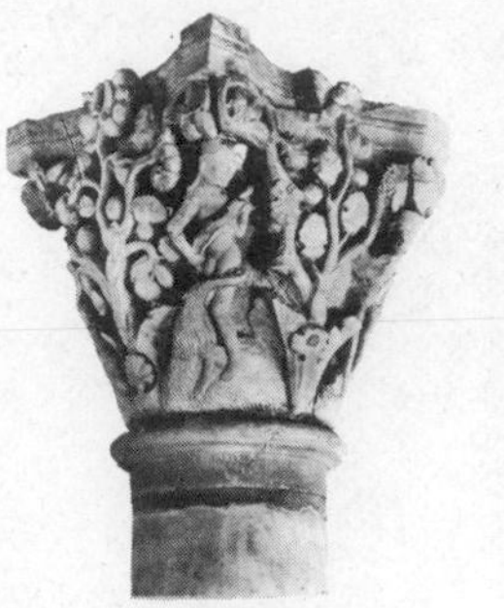

capital²
Twelfth-century capital in the church of the Benedictine Abbey at Cluny, France

capsule

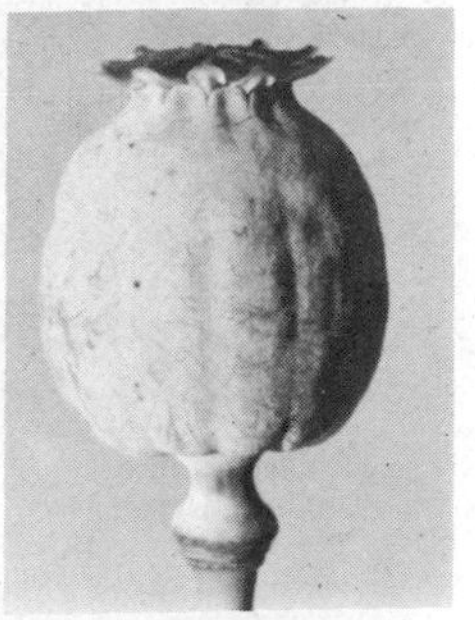

opium poppy

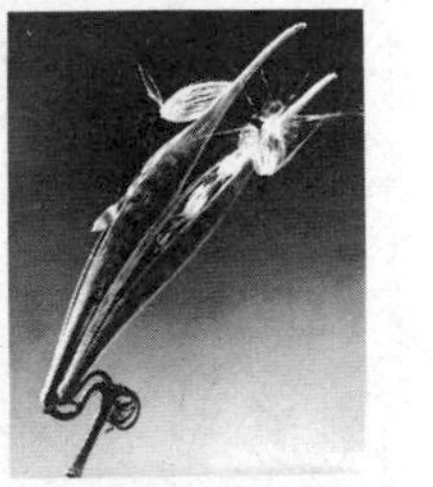

butterfly weed

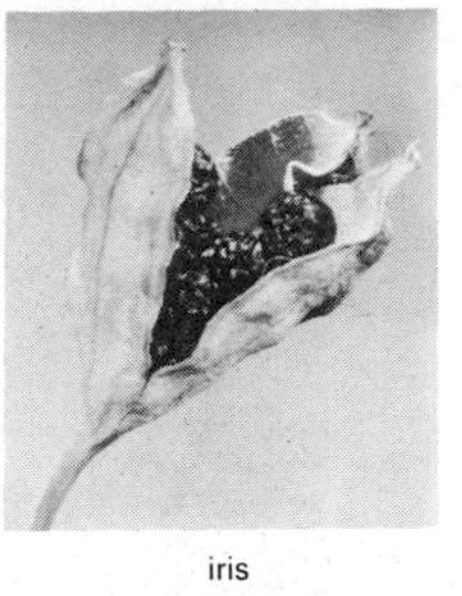

iris

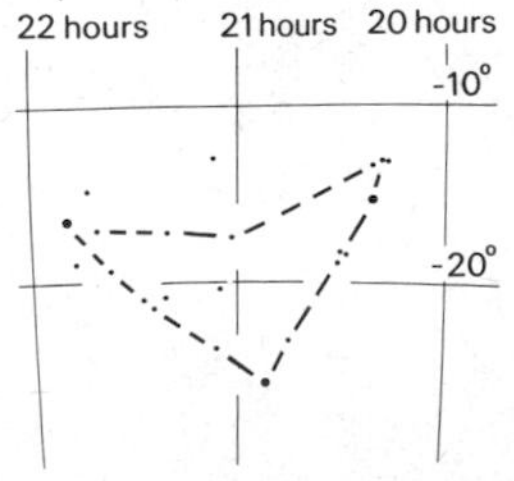

Capricornus

deducted; net worth. **b.** The funds contributed to a business by the owners or stockholders. **5.** Capitalists considered as a group or class. **6.** Any asset or advantage. **7.** A **capital letter** *(see)*. *—adj.* **1.** First and foremost; chief; principal. **2.** Of or pertaining to a political capital; politically important. **3.** First-rate; excellent: *a capital fellow.* **4.** Extremely serious; fatal: *a capital blunder.* **5.** Involving death or calling for the death penalty: *capital punishment.* **6.** Of or pertaining to monetary capital. **7.** Designating an upper-case letter. [Middle English, from Old French, from Latin *capitālis,* "of the head," important, chief, from *caput,* head. See **kaput** in Appendix.*]

cap·i·tal² (kăp′ə-təl) *n. Architecture.* The top part, or head, of a pillar or column. [Middle English *capitale,* from Norman French *capitel,* from Late Latin *capitellum,* "small head," from Latin *caput,* head. See **kaput** in Appendix.*]

capital account. **1.** An account stating the amount of funds and assets invested in a business by the owners or stockholders, including retained earnings; the owner's interest in the firm. **2.** *Accounting.* A statement of the net worth of a business enterprise at a given time.

capital expenditure. Funds spent for additions or improvements to plant or equipment.

capital gain. Profit from the sale of capital assets.

capital goods. Goods used in the production of commodities; producers' goods. Compare **consumer goods.**

cap·i·tal·ism (kăp′ə-təl-ĭz′əm) *n.* **1.** An economic system characterized by freedom of the market with increasing concentration of private and corporate ownership of production and distribution means, proportionate to increasing accumulation and reinvestment of profits. **2.** A political or social system regarded as being based on this. Compare **socialism.**

cap·i·tal·ist (kăp′ə-təl-ĭst) *n.* **1.** An investor of capital in business; especially, one having a major interest in an important enterprise. **2.** Any person of great wealth. *—adj.* Of or pertaining to capitalism or capitalists.

cap·i·tal·is·tic (kăp′ə-təl-ĭs′tĭk) *adj.* Pertaining to capitalism or capitalists. **—cap′i·tal·is′ti·cal·ly** *adv.*

cap·i·tal·i·za·tion (kăp′ə-təl-ə-zā′shən) *n.* **1.** The act, practice, or result of capitalizing. **2. a.** The total value of owners' shares in a business firm; total investment of owners. **b.** The authorized or outstanding stock or bonds in a corporation. **3.** The process of converting anticipated future income into present value.

cap·i·tal·ize (kăp′ə-təl-īz′) *v.* **-ized, -izing, -izes.** *—tr.* **1.** To utilize as capital; convert into capital. **2.** To supply with capital or investment funds. **3.** To authorize a certain amount of capital stock of (a business). **4.** To convert (debt) into capital stock or shares. **5.** To estimate the present value of (a stock, annuity, or real estate, for example). **6.** *Accounting.* To include (expenditures) in business accounts as assets instead of expenses. **7. a.** To write or print in upper-case letters. **b.** To begin a word with an upper-case letter. *—intr.* To turn to advantage; profit by; exploit. Often used with *on: capitalize on an opponent's error.* **—cap′i·tal·iz′a·ble** *adj.* **—cap′i·tal′i·zer** *n.*

capital letter. *Abbr.* **cap.** An upper-case letter; a letter written or printed in a size larger than and often in a form differing from its corresponding lower-case letter.

capital levy. A tax on capital assets or real property.

capital punishment. The infliction of the death penalty for the commission of certain crimes.

capital ship. A warship, such as a battleship or aircraft carrier, of the largest class.

capital stock. **1.** The total amount of stock authorized for issue by a corporation. **2.** The total stated or par value of the permanently invested capital of a corporation.

cap·i·tate (kăp′ə-tāt′) *adj.* **1.** *Zoology.* Enlarged or globular at an end, as some tentacles and bones are. **2.** *Botany.* Forming a headlike mass or dense cluster, as the inflorescence of certain flowers. [Latin *capitātus,* having a head, from *caput* (stem *capit-*), head. See **kaput** in Appendix.*]

cap·i·ta·tion (kăp′ə-tā′shən) *n.* **1.** A counting or assessing of individuals by head. **2.** A tax fixed at an equal sum per person; a per capita or poll tax. [Late Latin *capitātiō,* from *caput* (stem *capit-*), head, person. See **kaput** in Appendix.*] **—cap′i·ta′tive** *adj.*

Cap·i·tol (kăp′ə-təl) *n.* **1.** The ancient temple of Jupiter on the Capitoline Hill in Rome. **2.** *Often small* **c.** The building in which a state legislature assembles. **3.** The building in Washington, D.C., occupied by the Congress of the United States. [Middle English *Capitol(ie),* Jupiter's temple in Rome, from Old French *Capitolie,* from Latin *Capitōlium,* probably "the chief (temple)," from *caput,* head. See **kaput** in Appendix.*]

Capitol Hill. **1.** The hill in Washington, D.C., upon which the Capitol stands. **2.** The U.S. Congress itself.

Cap·i·to·line (kăp′ə-tə-līn′) *adj.* **1.** Of or pertaining to the Roman Capitol or to the Capitoline Hill. **2. a.** Used as a title of Jupiter representing the eternal indestructibility associated with the Capitol. **b.** Pertaining to Jupiter in this capacity. *—n.* One of the seven hills upon which Rome was built.

Capitol Reef National Monument. An area of 33,000 acres in south-central Utah, reserved to protect its cliff dwellings, petrified trees, and geologic formations.

ca·pit·u·lar (kə-pĭch′o͝o-lər) *adj.* Pertaining or belonging to a chapter, especially an ecclesiastical chapter: *capitular clergy.* [Medieval Latin *capitulāris,* from *capitulum,* (ecclesiastical) chapter, from Late Latin, division (of a book), chapter. See **capitulate.**] **—ca·pit′u·lar·ly** *adv.*

ca·pit·u·lar·y (kə-pĭch′o͝o-lĕr′ē) *adj.* Of or pertaining to a chapter; capitular. *—n., pl.* **capitularies.** **1.** A member of a chapter. **2.** *Plural.* Ordinances or a set of them; especially, those promulgated by Charlemagne and his successors.

ca·pit·u·late (kə-pĭch′o͝o-lāt′) *intr.v.* **-lated, -lating, -lates.** **1.** To surrender under specified conditions; come to terms. **2.** To give up all resistance; acquiesce. —See Synonyms at **yield.** [Originally "to propose or make terms (of surrender)," from Medieval Latin *capitulāre,* to draw up under heads or chapters, from Late Latin *capitulum,* chapter, from Latin, heading, from *caput,* head. See **kaput** in Appendix.*] **—ca·pit′u·lant** *n.* **—ca·pit′u·la′tor** (-lā′tər) *n.*

ca·pit·u·la·tion (kə-pĭch′o͝o-lā′shən) *n.* **1.** The act of capitulating. **2.** The instrument containing the terms of surrender. **3.** An enumeration of the main parts of a subject; an outline; summary. —See Synonyms at **surrender.** **—ca·pit′u·la·to′ry** (-lə-tôr′ē, -tōr′ē) *adj.*

ca·pit·u·lum (kə-pĭch′o͝o-ləm) *n., pl.* **-la** (-lə). **1.** *Botany.* A dense, headlike cluster of stalkless flowers. **2.** *Anatomy.* A small knob or head-shaped part, as the end of a bone or the knoblike tip of an insect's antenna. [New Latin, from Latin, diminutive of *caput,* head. See **kaput** in Appendix.*]

cap·lin. Variant of **capelin.**

ca·po (kā′pō′) *n., pl.* **-pos.** A small movable bar placed across the fingerboard of a guitar or other similar instrument for altering the pitch of all the strings simultaneously. [Italian *capo (di tastro),* "cap (of the keys)," from Latin *caput,* head. See **kaput** in Appendix.*]

ca·pon (kā′pŏn′, -pən) *n.* A rooster castrated to improve the quality of its flesh for food. Compare **poulard.** [Middle English *capon,* Old English *capūn* and Norman French *capon,* both from Latin *capō* (stem *cāpōn-*). See **skep-** in Appendix.*]

cap·o·ral (kăp′ə-rəl, kăp′ə-răl′) *n.* A strong, dark cigarette and pipe tobacco. [French *(tabac de) caporal,* "corporal's tobacco" (superior to *tabac de soldat,* soldier's tobacco), from Italian *caporale,* corporal, from *capo,* head, chief, from Latin *caput,* head. See **kaput** in Appendix.*]

ca·pote (kə-pōt′) *n.* **1.** A long cloak or coat, usually hooded. **2.** The movable top of a vehicle such as a buggy. [French, from Old French *cape,* CAPE (cloak).]

Ca·po·te (kə-pō′tē), **Truman.** Born 1924. American novelist and playwright.

ca·pouch. Variant of **capuche.**

Cap·pa·do·ci·a (kăp′ə-dō′shē-ə, -shə). An ancient region of eastern Asia Minor, now forming the central part of Turkey. **—Cap′pa·do′cian** *adj.* & *n.*

cap·per (kăp′ər) *n.* **1.** One that caps or makes caps. **2.** *Slang.* One who acts as a decoy, as for a gambler. **3.** *Slang.* A person employed at an auction to raise bids.

cap pistol. A toy pistol with a hammer action that detonates a mildly explosive cap. Also called "cap gun."

cap·re·o·late (kăp′rē-ə-lāt′, kə-prē′-) *adj. Biology.* Having or like tendrils. [From Latin *capreolus,* wild goat, wooden prop (suggesting horns), supporting tendrils of vines. See **capriole.**]

Ca·pri (kä′prē). A mountainous island of Italy, about five square miles in area, south of the Bay of Naples.

cap·ric acid (kăp′rĭk). A white crystalline compound, $CH_3(CH_2)_8COOH$, obtained by distilling coconut oil and used in the manufacture of perfumes and fruit flavors. Also called "decanoic acid." [From Latin *caper,* goat (from the unpleasant odor of the acid). See **kapro-** in Appendix.*]

ca·pric·cio (kə-prē′chō, -chē-ō′) *n., pl.* **-cios** or **-ci** (-chē). **1.** *Music.* An instrumental work with an improvisatory style and a free form. **2.** A prank or caper. **3.** A fanciful whim. [Italian, CAPRICE.]

ca·pric·ci·o·so (kə-prē′chō′sō) *adj. Music.* Lively and free. Used as a direction. [Italian, from *capriccio,* CAPRICE.]

ca·price (kə-prēs′) *n.* **1.** An impulsive change of mind. **2.** An inclination to make such changes. **3.** *Music.* A capriccio. [French, from Italian *capriccio,* "head with hair standing on end," hence horror, whim (in sense influenced by *capra,* goat, from Latin *caper*) : *capo,* head, from Latin *caput* (see **kaput** in Appendix*) + *riccio,* hedgehog, from Latin *ēricius,* from *ēr,* hedgehog (see **ghers-** in Appendix*).]

Synonyms: *caprice, whim, whimsy, vagary, freak.* These nouns denote an erratic or unexpected notion, act, or quality. *Caprice* strongly suggests lack of apparent motivation, and can imply wanton or willful behavior. *Whim* and *whimsy* can both mean a quaint or fanciful idea, but *whim* reserves the suggestion of sudden inspiration, and *whimsy* more often refers to the literary quality or humor of being playful and fanciful. *Vagary* emphasizes the erratic and unpredictable, even irresponsible, nature of a notion or act. *Freak,* synonymous with *whim* and *vagary* in an old sense, now more commonly means a rare and highly improbable occurrence, or a grotesque variation from a type.

ca·pri·cious (kə-prĭsh′əs, -prē′shəs) *adj.* Characterized by or subject to whim; impulsive and unpredictable; fickle. **—ca·pri′cious·ly** *adv.* **—ca·pri′cious·ness** *n.*

Cap·ri·corn (kăp′rĭ-kôrn′) *n.* **1.** Variant of **Capricornus.** **2. Tropic of Capricorn** *(see).*

Cap·ri·cor·nus (kăp′rĭ-kôr′nəs) *n.* Also **Cap·ri·corn.** **1.** A constellation in the equatorial region of the Southern Hemisphere, near Aquarius and Sagittarius. **2.** The tenth sign of the **zodiac** *(see).* Also called the "Goat." [Latin (translation of Greek *aigokeros,* "goat-horned") : *caper,* goat (see **kapro-** in Appendix*) + *cornū,* horn (see **ker-¹** in Appendix*).]

cap·ri·fi·ca·tion (kăp′rə-fĭ-kā′shən) *n.* A method of assuring pollination of the edible fig by having certain wasps carry pollen from the flowers of the caprifig to those of the edible variety. [Latin *caprificātiō,* from *caprificāre,* to ripen figs by caprification, from *caprificus,* CAPRIFIG.]

cap·ri·fig (kăp′rə-fĭg′) *n.* A wild variety of fig, *Ficus carica sylvestris,* of the eastern Mediterranean region, used in the caprification of the edible fig. [Middle English *caprifige, caprificus,* from Latin *caprificus,* "goat fig" : *caper,* goat (see **kapro-** in Appendix*) + *fīcus,* FIG.]

cap·ri·ole (kăp′rē-ōl′) *n.* **1.** An upward leap made by a trained horse without going forward and with all feet off the ground. **2.** A leap or jump. —*intr.v.* **caprioled, -oling, -oles.** To perform a capriole. [French, from Italian *capriola,* "leap of a goat," from *capriolo,* wild goat, roebuck, from Latin *capreolus,* diminutive of *caper,* goat. See **kapro-** in Appendix.*]

caps. capsule.

Cap·sa. The ancient name for **Gafsa.**

cap screw. A long-threaded bolt, usually with a square head, used in fastening machine parts.

Cap·si·an (kăp′sē-ən) *adj.* Of or designating a Paleolithic culture of northern Africa and southern Europe. [French *capsien,* after *Capsa,* ancient name of GAFSA, near which remains of the culture were found.]

cap·si·cin (kăp′sə-sĭn) *n.* Also **cap·sa·i·cine** (kăp-sā′ə-sĭn). A peppery, reddish-brown liquid, $C_{18}H_{27}O_3N$, obtained from plants of the genus *Capsicum,* and used in flavoring vinegar and pickles and medicinally as an irritant. [CAPSIC(UM) + -IN.]

cap·si·cum (kăp′sĭ-kəm) *n.* **1.** Any of various tropical plants of the genus *Capsicum.* See **pepper. 2.** The dried fruit of pungent varieties of *C. frutescens,* used medicinally as a gastric stimulant and counterirritant. [New Latin, probably from Latin *capsa,* box (from its podlike fruit). See **capsule.**]

cap·size (kăp′sīz′, kăp-sīz′) *v.* **-sized, -sizing, -sizes.** —*intr.* To overturn. —*tr.* To cause to turn over. [Origin unknown.]

cap·stan (kăp′stən) *n.* **1.** *Nautical.* An apparatus consisting of a vertical cylinder rotated manually or by motor, used for hoisting weights by winding in a cable. Compare **windlass. 2.** *Electronics.* A small cylindrical pulley used to regulate the speed of magnetic tape in a tape recorder. [Middle English, from Old Provençal *cabestan, cabestran,* from *cabestre,* rope noose, from Latin *capistrum,* halter, from *capere,* to take, seize. See **kap-** in Appendix.*]

cap·stone (kăp′stōn′) *n.* Also **cope·stone** (kōp′-). **1.** The top stone of a structure or wall. Compare **coping. 2.** The crowning or final stroke; culmination; acme.

cap·su·lar (kăp′sə-lər, -syŏŏ-lər) *adj.* Of, pertaining to, or characteristic of a capsule.

cap·su·late (kăp′sə-lāt′, -syŏŏ-lāt′, -lĭt) *adj.* Also **cap·su·lat·ed** (-lā′tĭd). In or formed into a capsule. —**cap′su·la′tion** *n.*

cap·sule (kăp′səl, -syŏŏl) *n. Abbr.* **caps. 1.** *Pharmacology.* A soluble, gelatinous sheath enclosing a dose of an oral medicine. **2.** A seal or airtight cap, as for the mouth of a bottle. **3.** *Anatomy.* A fibrous, membranous, or fatty envelope enclosing an organ or part, such as the sac surrounding the kidney. **4.** *Microbiology.* A mucopolysaccharide layer enveloping certain bacteria. **5.** *Botany.* **a.** A fruit that contains two or more seeds and that dries and splits open. **b.** The spore case of a moss or other bryophyte. **6.** A pressurized modular compartment of an aircraft or spacecraft, especially one designed to accommodate a crew or to be ejected if required. —*adj.* Condensed into a small or brief unit; concise; compact: *a capsule description.* [French, from Latin *capsula,* diminutive of *capsa,* box, chest. See **kap-** in Appendix.*]

cap·tain (kăp′tən) *n.* **1.** One who commands, leads, or guides others, specifically: **a.** The officer in command of a ship; skipper. **b.** A precinct chief in a police or fire department. **c.** The designated leader of a team or crew in sports. **2.** *Abbr.* **Capt. a.** A commissioned officer in the Army, Air Force, or Marine Corps who ranks below a major and above a first lieutenant. **b.** A commissioned officer in the Navy who ranks below a commodore or rear admiral and above a commander. **3.** A figure in the forefront; leader: *a captain of industry.* —*tr.v.* **captained, -taining, -tains.** To command or direct. [Middle English *capitane, captein,* from Old French *capitain(e),* from Late Latin *capitāneus,* chief, from Latin *caput,* head. See **kaput** in Appendix.*] —**cap′tain·cy** *n.* —**cap′tain·ship′** *n.*

cap·tion (kăp′shən) *n.* **1.** A title, short explanation, or description accompanying an illustration or photograph. **2.** A subtitle in a motion picture. **3.** A title or heading, as of a document or chapter in a book. **4.** *Law.* The part of a legal document that states the time, place, and authority of its execution. —*tr.v.* **captioned, -tioning, -tions.** To furnish a caption for. [Originally "arrest," hence record of execution of a commission, from Middle English *capcioun,* arrest, seizure, from Latin *captiō,* from *capere,* to seize, take. See **kap-** in Appendix.*]

cap·tious (kăp′shəs) *adj.* **1.** Marked by a disposition to find fault and make petty criticisms; carping. **2.** Intended to entrap or confuse; likely to perplex; deceptive, as a question. [Middle English *capcious,* from Old French *captieux,* from Latin *captiōsus,* "ensnaring," from *captiō,* seizure, CAPTION.] —**cap′tious·ly** *adv.* —**cap′tious·ness** *n.*

cap·ti·vate (kăp′tə-vāt′) *tr.v.* **-vated, -vating, -vates. 1.** *Archaic.* To capture. **2.** To fascinate by special charm or beauty; enrapture. [Late Latin *captīvāre,* to capture, from Latin *captīvus,* CAPTIVE.] —**cap′ti·va′tion** *n.* —**cap′ti·va′tor** (-vā′tər) *n.*

cap·tive (kăp′tĭv) *n.* **1.** One who is forcibly confined, restrained, or subjugated, as a prisoner. **2.** One who is enslaved by a strong emotion or passion. —*adj.* **1.** Held as prisoner. **2.** Under restraint or control. **3.** Captivated; enraptured. **4.** Obliged to be present: *a captive audience.* [Middle English *captif,* from Latin *captīvus,* from *capere,* to seize. See **kap-** in Appendix.*]

cap·tiv·i·ty (kăp-tĭv′ə-tē) *n., pl.* **-ties.** The state or a period of being captive.

cap·tor (kăp′tər, -tôr′) *n.* One who takes or keeps a person or thing as a captive. [Late Latin, from Latin *capere,* to seize. See **kap-** in Appendix.*]

cap·ture (kăp′chər) *tr.v.* **-tured, -turing, -tures. 1.** To take captive; seize or catch by force or craft. **2.** To win possession or control of, as in a contest. **3.** To succeed in preserving in a fixed form: *capture a likeness in a painting.* —*n.* **1.** The act of capturing; seizure. **2.** One that is seized, caught, or won; a catch or prize. **3.** *Physics.* The phenomenon in which an atomic nucleus absorbs a subatomic particle, often with the subsequent emission of radiation. [French, from Old French, from Latin *captūra,* from *capere,* to seize. See **kap-** in Appendix.*]

ca·puche (kə-pōōch′, -pōōsh′) *n.* Also **ca·pouch.** A hood on a cloak; especially, the long, pointed cowl worn by a Capuchin monk. [Italian *cappuccio,* from *cappa,* hood, from Late Latin, hood, cloak, from Latin *caput,* head. See **kaput** in Appendix.*]

cap·u·chin (kăp′yŏŏ-chĭn, kə-pyōō′-, -shĭn) *n.* **1.** *Capital* **C.** A monk belonging to the Order of Friars Minor Capuchins, a branch that broke away from the Franciscans in 1525. **2.** A hooded cloak worn by women. **3.** Any of several long-tailed monkeys of the genus *Cebus,* of Central and South America, many of which have hoodlike tufts of hair on the head. In this sense, also called "sapajou." [French, from Old French, from Italian *cappuccino,* "hooded one," from *cappuccio,* CAPUCHE.]

cap·y·ba·ra (kăp′ĭ-bä′rə, -băr′ə) *n.* A large, short-tailed, semiaquatic rodent *Hydrochoerus hydrochaeris,* of tropical South America, often attaining a length of four feet. [Portuguese *capibara,* from Tupi.]

car (kär) *n.* **1.** An automobile. **2.** A conveyance with wheels that runs along tracks, as a streetcar or railroad car. **3.** *Archaic.* A chariot. **4.** A boxlike enclosure for passengers on a conveyance, as an elevator car or cable car. [Middle English *car(re),* cart, wagon, from Norman French, from Vulgar Latin *carra* (unattested), variant of Latin *carrus,* two-wheeled wagon. See **kers-**[2] in Appendix.*]

car. carat.

car·a·bao (kăr′ə-bou′, kä′rə-) *n., pl.* **-baos.** The **water buffalo** *(see).* [Visayan *karabáw,* akin to Malay *karbaw.*]

car·a·bin, car·a·bine. Variants of **carbine.**

car·a·bi·neer, car·a·bi·nier. Variants of **carbineer.**

car·a·cal (kăr′ə-kăl′) *n.* A wild cat, *Lynx caracal,* of Africa and southern Asia, having short, fawn-colored fur and long, tufted ears. [French, from Turkish *kara kūlāk,* "black ear" : *kara,* black + *kulak,* ear.]

Car·a·cal·la (kăr′ə-kăl′ə). Real name, Marcus Aurelius Antoninus. Original name, Bassianus. A.D. 188–217. Emperor of Rome (A.D. 211–217); assassinated.

ca·ra·ca·ra (kä′rə-kä′rə, kə-rä′kə-rä′) *n.* Any of several large, carrion-eating or predatory birds of the subfamily Caracarinae, of South and Central America and the southern United States, related to the hawks and falcons. [Spanish *caracara* and Portuguese *caracará,* from Tupi *caracara* (imitative).]

Ca·ra·cas (kə-rä′kəs, -răk′əs). The capital and largest city of Venezuela, situated about eight miles south of the Caribbean coast at an elevation of over 3,000 feet. Population, 1,639,000.

car·ack. Variant of **carrack.**

car·a·cole (kăr′ə-kōl′) *n.* Also **car·a·col** (-kŏl). A half turn to either side performed by a horseman. —*intr.v.* **caracoled, -coling, -coles.** To perform a caracole or caracoles. [French, from Spanish *caracol*†, snail, winding stair.]

car·a·cul (kăr′ə-kəl) *n.* **1.** The loosely curled fur of a karakul lamb. **2.** Variant of **karakul.**

ca·rafe (kə-răf′) *n.* A glass bottle for serving water or wine at the table; decanter. [French, from Italian *caraffa,* from Spanish *garaffa,* from Arabic *gharrāf,* from *gharafa,* to dip.]

car·a·geen. Variant of **carrageen.**

car·a·mel (kăr′ə-məl, kär′məl) *n.* **1.** A smooth, chewy candy made with sugar, butter, cream or milk, and flavoring. **2.** Burnt sugar, used for coloring and sweetening foods. [French, from Old Spanish, probably from Late Latin *calamellus,* diminutive of Latin *calamus,* reed, cane, from Greek *kalamos.* See **kolem-** in Appendix.*]

car·a·mel·ize (kăr′ə-mə-līz′, kär′mə-līz′) *v.* **-ized, -izing, -izes.** —*tr.* To convert (sugar) into caramel. —*intr.* To change to caramel. —**car′a·mel·i·za′tion** *n.*

ca·ran·gid (kə-răn′jĭd, -răng′gĭd) *n.* Any of various fishes of the family Carangidae, which includes the jacks and pompanos. —*adj.* Of or belonging to the Carangidae. [New Latin *Carangidae* : *Caranx* (genus), from French *carangue,* mackerel, from Spanish *caranga*† + -IDAE.]

car·a·pace (kăr′ə-pās′) *n.* **1.** *Zoology.* A hard bony or chitinous outer covering, such as the fused dorsal plates of a turtle, or the portion of the exoskeleton covering the head and thorax of a crustacean. **2.** Any similar protective covering. [French, from Spanish *carapacho,* from a pre-Roman Iberian root *kar-,* scale.]

car·at (kăr′ət) *n.* **1.** *Abbr.* **c, car.** A unit of weight for precious stones, equal to 200 milligrams. **2.** Variant of **karat.** [French, from Old French, from Medieval Latin *carratus,* from Arabic *qīrāṭ,* small weight, carat, from Greek *keration,* "little horn," carat, diminutive of *keras,* horn. See **ker-**[1] in Appendix.*]

Ca·ra·vag·gio (kä′rä-väd′jō), **Michelangelo Amerighi** or **Merisi da.** 1565?–1609. Italian painter.

car·a·van (kăr′ə-văn′) *n.* **1.** A company of travelers journeying together, especially across a desert. **2.** A single file of vehicles or pack animals. **3.** A large covered vehicle; van. **4.** *Chiefly British.* A trailer or home on wheels. [French *caravane* or Italian *caravana, carovana,* from Persian *kārwān*†.]

car·a·van·sa·ry (kăr′ə-văn′sə-rē) *n., pl.* **-ries.** Also **car·a·van·se·rai** (-rī′). **1.** In the Near or Far East, an inn built around a large

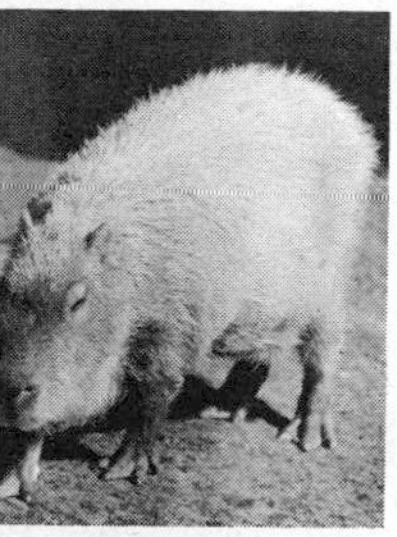

capybara

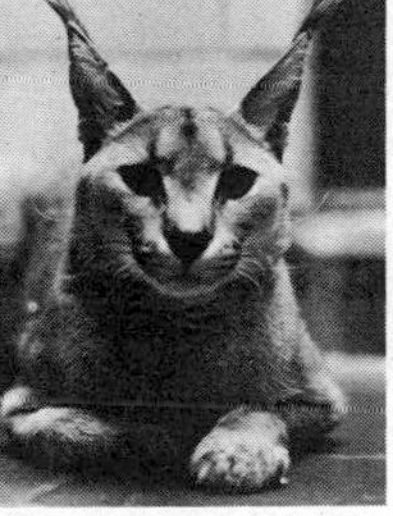

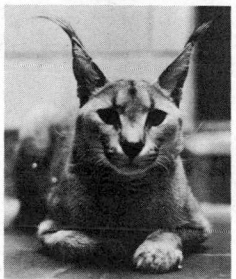

caracal

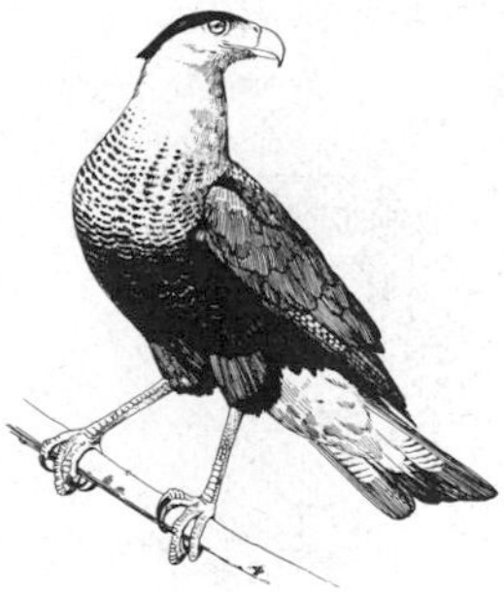

caracara
Polyborus cheriway

court for accommodating caravans. **2.** Any large inn or hostelry. [Persian *kārwānsarāī* : *kārwān*, CARAVAN + *sarāī*, palace, inn (see **ter-**[1] in Appendix*).]

car·a·vel (kăr′ə-vĕl′) *n.* Also **car·a·velle, car·vel** (kär′vəl, -vĕl′). A small, light sailing ship of the kind used by the Spanish and Portuguese in the 15th and 16th centuries. [Old French *caravelle, carvelle,* from Old Portuguese *caravela,* diminutive of *cáravo,* ship, from Late Latin *cārabus,* a small wicker boat, from Greek *karabos*†, light ship.]

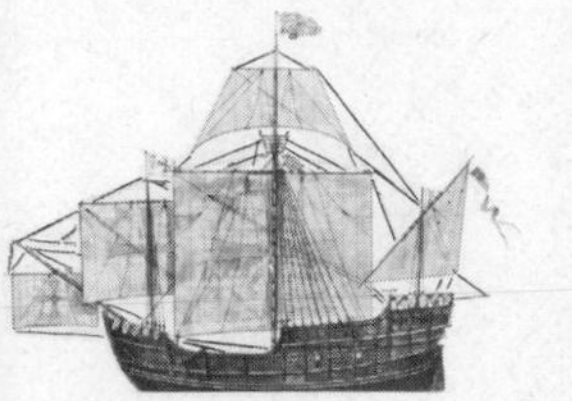
caravel

car·a·way (kăr′ə-wā′) *n.* **1.** A plant, *Carum carvi,* native to Eurasia, having finely divided leaves and clusters of small, whitish flowers. **2.** The pungent, aromatic seeds of this plant, used in baking and cooking. [Middle English *car(a)way,* probably from Old Spanish *alcarahueya* and Medieval Latin *carvi,* both from Arabic *alkarawyā,* probably from Greek *karon*†.]

car barn. Also **car·barn** (kär′bärn′). A shed for housing streetcars or buses.

car·bide (kär′bīd′) *n.* A binary carbon compound, especially calcium carbide, consisting of carbon and a more electropositive element. [CARB(O)- + -IDE.]

car·bine (kär′bīn′, -bēn′) *n.* Also **car·a·bin** (kăr′ə-bĭn), **car·a·bine** (-bīn′, -bēn′). A light shoulder rifle with a short barrel, originally for cavalry use. [French *carabine,* carbine, carbineer, from Old French *carabin,* cavalryman, soldier armed with a musket, probably derisively from *escarrabin,* "one who lays out plague corpses," variant of *escarabilh, scarabée,* dung beetle, from Latin *scarabeus,* a beetle. See **scarab.**]

car·bi·neer (kär′bə-nîr′) *n.* Also **car·a·bi·neer** (kăr′ə-), **car·a·bi·nier.** A soldier armed with a carbine.

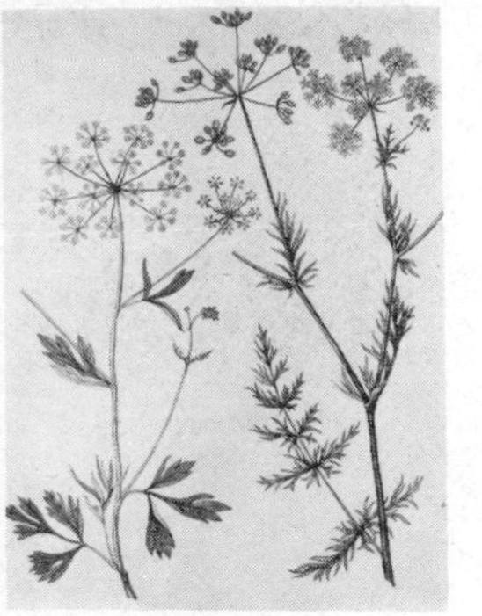
caraway

car·bi·nol (kär′bə-nôl′, -nōl′) *n.* **1.** Wood alcohol, **methanol** *(see).* **2.** An alcohol derived from methanol. [German *Karbinol* : CARB(O)- + -IN + -OL.]

carbo–, carb–. Indicates carbon; for example, **carbohydrate, carbolic acid.** [French, from *carbone,* CARBON.]

car·bo·hy·drate (kär′bō-hī′drāt′) *n.* Any of a group of chemical compounds, including sugars, starches, and cellulose, containing carbon, hydrogen, and oxygen only, with the ratio of hydrogen to oxygen atoms usually 2:1. [CARBO- + HYDRATE (carbohydrates were formerly classified as hydrates).]

car·bo·lat·ed (kär′bə-lā′tĭd) *adj.* Containing or treated with carbolic acid.

car·bol·ic acid (kär-bŏl′ĭk). An organic compound, **phenol** *(see).* [CARB(O)- + Latin *oleum,* OIL + -IC.]

car·bon (kär′bən) *n. Symbol* **C** **1.** A naturally abundant nonmetallic element that occurs in many inorganic and in all organic compounds, exists in amorphous, graphitic, and diamond allotropes, and is capable of chemical self-bonding to form an enormous number of chemically, biologically, and commercially important long-chain molecules. Atomic number 6; atomic weight 12.01115; sublimes above 3,500°C; boiling point 4,827°C; specific gravity of amorphous carbon 1.8 to 2.1, of diamond 3.15 to 3.53, of graphite 1.9 to 2.3; valences 2, 3, 4. See **element.** **2. a.** A sheet of carbon paper. **b.** A copy made by using carbon paper. **3.** *Electricity.* **a.** Either of two rods through which current flows to form an arc in lighting or in welding. **b.** A carbonaceous electrode in an electric cell. *—adj.* **1.** Of, pertaining to, or like carbon. **2.** Treated with carbon. [French *carbone,* from Latin *carbō* (stem *carbōn-*), charcoal. See **ker-**[4] in Appendix.*] **—car′bon·ous** *adj.*

carbon 14. A naturally radioactive carbon isotope with atomic mass 14 and half-life 5,700 years, used in dating ancient carbon-containing objects. Also called "radiocarbon."

car·bo·na·ceous (kär′bə-nā′shəs) *adj.* Consisting of, containing, pertaining to, or yielding carbon. [CARBON + -ACEOUS.]

car·bo·na·do[1] (kär′bə-nā′dō, -nä′dō) *n., pl.* **-does** or **-dos.** A piece of scored and broiled fish, fowl, or meat. *—tr.v.* **carbonadoed, -doing, -dos.** **1.** To score and broil (fish, fowl, or meat). **2.** *Archaic.* To slice; slash; chop. [Spanish *carbonada,* from *carbón,* charcoal, coal, from Latin *carbō,* CARBON.]

car·bo·na·do[2] (kär′bə-nā′dō, -nä′dō) *n., pl.* **-does.** A form of opaque or dark-colored diamond, chiefly Brazilian, used for drills. Also called "black diamond," "bort." [Portuguese, "carbonated," from *carbone,* carbon, from French, CARBON.]

Car·bo·na·ri (kär′bō-nä′rē) *pl.n. Singular* **-ro.** The members of a secret society originally organized in Naples in the early 19th century to establish a republic. [Italian, plural of *Carbonaro,* from *carbonaro,* charcoal burner, from Latin *carbōnārius,* from *carbō* (stem *carbōn-*), charcoal. See **ker-**[4] in Appendix.*] **—Car′bo·na′rism′** *n.* **—Car′bo·na′rist** *n. & adj.*

car·bon·ate (kär′bə-nāt′) *tr.v.* **-ated, -ating, -ates.** **1.** To charge with carbon dioxide gas, as a beverage. **2.** To burn to carbon; carbonize. **3.** To change into a carbonate. *—n.* (kär′bə-nāt′, -nĭt). A salt or ester of carbonic acid. **—car′bon·a′tion** *n.* **—car′bon·a′tor** (-ā′tər) *n.*

carbonated water. Soda water *(see).*

carbon bisulfide. Carbon disulfide *(see).*

carbon black. Any of various finely divided forms of carbon derived from the incomplete combustion of natural gas or petroleum oil and used principally in rubber and ink.

carbon copy. **1.** *Abbr.* **C.C., c.c.** A replica, as of a letter, made by using carbon paper. **2.** *Informal.* Any close copy or reproduction; duplicate.

carbon cycle. **1.** *Astrophysics.* The **carbon-nitrogen cycle** *(see).* **2.** *Biology.* The cycle of natural processes in which atmospheric carbon in the form of carbon dioxide is converted to carbohydrates by photosynthesis, metabolized by animals, and ultimately returned to the atmosphere as a carbon dioxide waste or decomposition product.

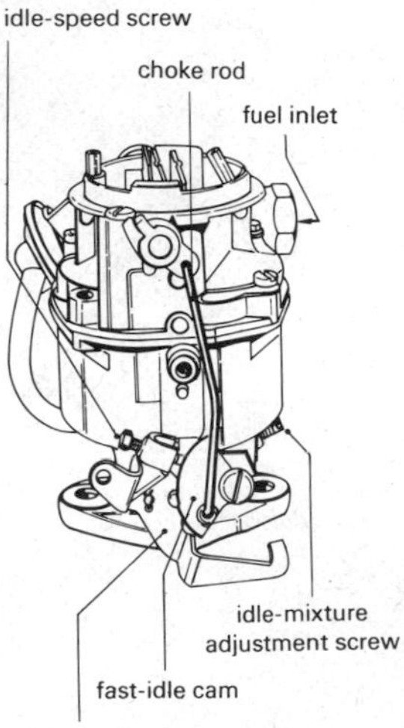

idle-speed screw
choke rod
fuel inlet
idle-mixture adjustment screw
fast-idle cam
throttle lever

carburetor

carbon dioxide. A colorless, odorless, incombustible gas, CO_2, formed during respiration, combustion, and organic decomposition and used in food refrigeration, carbonated beverages, inert atmospheres, fire extinguishers, and aerosols.

carbon disulfide. A clear flammable liquid, CS_2, used to manufacture viscose rayon and cellophane, as a solvent for fats, rubber, resins, waxes, and sulfur, and in matches, fumigants, and pesticides. Also called "carbon bisulfide."

car·bon·ic acid (kär-bŏn′ĭk). A weak, unstable acid, H_2CO_3, present in solutions of carbon dioxide in water.

carbonic acid gas. Carbon dioxide.

car·bon·if·er·ous (kär′bə-nĭf′ər-əs) *adj.* Producing, containing, or pertaining to carbon or coal. [CARBON + -FEROUS.]

Car·bon·if·er·ous (kär′bə-nĭf′ər-əs) *adj. Geology.* Of, belonging to, or designating a division of the Paleozoic era following the Devonian and preceding the Permian, including the Mississippian and Pennsylvanian periods. It was characterized, especially in the Pennsylvanian, by swamp formation and deposition of plant remains later hardened into coal. See **geology.** *—n. Geology.* The Carboniferous period. Preceded by *the.*

car·bo·ni·um (kär-bō′nē-əm) *n.* A positively charged organic ion, such as H_3C, having one less electron than a corresponding free radical and behaving chemically as if the positive charge were localized on the carbon atom.

car·bon·i·za·tion (kär′bən-ə-zā′shən) *n.* **1.** The process of carbonizing. **2.** The destructive distillation of bituminous coal to obtain coke and other fractions.

car·bon·ize (kär′bə-nīz′) *tr.v.* **-ized, -izing, -izes.** **1.** To reduce or convert to carbon, as by partial burning. **2.** To coat or combine with carbon. **—car′bon·iz′er** *n.*

carbon monoxide. A colorless, odorless, highly poisonous gas, CO, formed by the incomplete combustion of carbon or any carbonaceous material, including gasoline.

car·bon-ni·tro·gen cycle (kär′bən-nī′trə-jən). A chain of thermonuclear reactions in which nitrogen isotopes are formed in intermediate stages and carbon acts essentially as a catalyst to convert four protons into one helium nucleus, the entire sequence thought to generate significant amounts of energy in certain classes of stars. Also called "carbon cycle," "nitrogen cycle."

carbon paper. A lightweight paper faced on one side with a dark waxy pigment that is transferred by the impact of typewriter keys or by writing pressure to any copying surface, as paper.

carbon process. A photographic printing process using permanent pigments, such as carbon, contained in a sensitized tissue or film of gelatin.

carbon tetrachloride. A poisonous, nonflammable, colorless liquid, CCl_4, used in fire extinguishers and as a solvent.

car·bon·yl (kär′bə-nĭl′, -nēl′) *n.* **1.** The bivalent radical CO. **2.** A metal compound, such as $Ni(CO)_4$, containing the CO group. [CARBON + -YL.] **—car′bon·yl′ic** *adj.*

carbonyl chloride. A poisonous gas, **phosgene** *(see).*

Car·bo·run·dum (kär′bə-rŭn′dəm) *n.* A trademark for a silicon carbide abrasive.

car·box·yl (kär-bŏk′səl) *n.* A univalent radical, COOH, characteristic of all organic acids. [CARB(O)- + OX(Y)- + -YL.] **—car′box·yl′ic** (-sĭl′ĭk) *adj.*

car·box·yl·ase (kär-bŏk′sə-lās′, -lāz′) *n.* A plant enzyme that produces acetaldehyde and carbon dioxide from pyruvic acid.

car·boy (kär′boi′) *n.* A large glass or plastic bottle, usually encased in a protective basket or crate and often used to hold corrosive liquids. [Persian *qarāba,* from Arabic *qarrābah.*]

car·bun·cle (kär′bŭng′kəl) *n.* **1.** A painful, localized, pus-producing, sometimes fatal infection of the skin and subcutaneous tissue. Compare **boil.** **2.** *Obsolete.* A deep-red garnet, unfaceted and convex. [Middle English, from Old French, from Latin *carbunculus,* small glowing ember, tumor, diminutive of *carbō* (stem *carbōn-*), charcoal, ember. See **ker-**[4] in Appendix.] **—car′bun′cled** *adj.* **—car·bun′cu·lar** (-kyə-lər) *adj.*

car·bu·ret (kär′bə-rāt′, kär′byə-, -rĕt′) *tr.v.* **-reted** or **-retted, -reting** or **-retting, -rets.** To combine or mix with carbon or hydrocarbons, so as to increase available fuel energy. [From obsolete *carbure(t),* carbide, from French *carbure,* from Latin *carbō,* CARBON.]

car·bu·re·tor (kär′bə-rā′tər, kär′byə-) *n.* Also *chiefly British* **car·bu·ret·tor** (-rĕt′ər). A device used in gasoline engines to produce an efficient explosive vapor of fuel and air. [From CARBURET.]

car·bu·rize (kär′byə-rīz′) *tr.v.* **-rized, -rizing, -rizes.** **1.** To treat (iron or steel, for example) with carbon. **2.** To treat with hydrocarbons. [CARBUR(ET) + -IZE.] **—car′bu·ri·za′tion** *n.*

car·ca·jou (kär′kə-jōō′, -zhōō′) *n. Canadian.* An animal, the wolverine. [Canadian French, from Algonquian *karkajou.*]

car·ca·net (kär′kə-nĕt′, -nĭt) *n. Rare.* A jeweled necklace, collar, or headband. [From Old French *carcan,* collar, akin to Medieval Latin *carcannum*†.]

car·cass (kär′kəs) *n.* Also *archaic* **car·case.** **1.** The dead body of an animal, especially one slaughtered and gutted. **2.** The body of a human being. Used humorously or disparagingly. **3.** Something from which the substance or character is gone: *the carcass of a once-glorious empire.* **4.** A framework or basic structure, as of a ruined building. —See Synonyms at **body.** [French *carcasse,* from Old French *c(h)arcois*†.]

Car·cas·sonne (kär′kə-sôn′, -sŏn′; *French* kȧr-kȧ-sôn′). A city of southern France, on the Aude River; the only complete medieval fortified town extant in Europe. Population, 37,000.

Car·che·mish (kär′kə-mĭsh′, kär-kē′mĭsh). An ancient Hittite city on the Euphrates in Turkey, near the Syrian border.

car·cin·o·gen (kär-sĭn′ə-jən, kär′sĭn-ə-jĕn′) *n.* A cancer-causing

ă pat/ā pay/âr care/ä father/b bib/ch church/d deed/ĕ pet/ē be/f fife/g gag/h hat/hw which/ĭ pit/ī pie/îr pier/j judge/k kick/l lid, needle/m mum/n no, sudden/ng thing/ŏ pot/ō toe/ô paw, for/oi noise/ou out/ŏŏ took/ōō boot/p pop/r roar/s sauce/sh ship, dish/

substance. [Greek *karkinos,* cancer, crab (see **kar-**[1] in Appendix*) + -GEN.] —**car'cin·o·gen'ic** *adj.*

car·ci·no·ma (kär'sə-nō'mə) *n., pl.* **-mas** or **-mata** (-mə-tə). A malignant tumor derived from epithelial tissue. [Latin *carcinōma,* cancerous ulcer, from Greek *karkinōma,* from *karkinos,* cancer, crab. See **kar-**[1] in Appendix.*] —**car'ci·nom'a·tous** (-nŏm'ə-təs, -nō'mə-təs) *adj.* —**car'ci·no'ma·toid** *adj.*

car·ci·no·ma·to·sis (kär'sə-nō'mə-tō'sĭs) *n.* The existence of carcinomas at many bodily sites. [New Latin : Latin *carcinōma* (stem *carcinōmat-*), CARCINOMA + -OSIS.]

card[1] (kärd) *n.* **1.** A small, flat piece of stiff paper or thin pasteboard, usually rectangular, with numerous uses: **a.** One of a set bearing significant numbers, symbols, and figures, used in numerous games and in divination. See **cards. b.** One used to send messages; a post card. **c.** One printed with a suitable illustration and greeting and sent in an envelope, as for Christmas. **d.** One bearing a person's name and other information, used for purposes of identification or classification, as a calling card or draft card. **e.** One used for cataloguing information in a file, as a reference card. **2.** A notice or advertisement printed on cardboard. **3.** A program of events, as at horse races. **4.** A circular piece of paper bearing the 32 points of a compass. **5.** *Informal.* An amusing or eccentric person. —**have a card up one's sleeve.** To have a secret resource or plan held in reserve. —**in the cards.** Likely or destined to occur. —**put (or lay) one's cards on the table.** To make a frank and clear revelation, as of one's motives. —*v.* **carded, carding, cards.** —*tr.* **1.** To furnish with or attach to a card. **2.** To list on a card or cards; to catalogue. —*intr. Rare.* To play at cards. [Middle English *carde,* from Old French *carte,* from Latin *charta,* leaf of papyrus, from Greek *khartēs,* probably from Egyptian.]

card[2] (kärd) *n.* **1.** A wire-toothed brush used to disentangle fibers, as of wool, prior to spinning. **2.** A similar device used to raise the nap on a fabric. —*tr.v.* **carded, carding, cards.** To comb out or brush with a card. [Middle English *carde,* from Old French, from *carder,* to card, from Old Provençal *cardar,* from Vulgar Latin *caritāre* (unattested), from Latin *cārere,* to card. See **kars-** in Appendix.*] —**card'er** *n.*

Card. *Roman Catholic Church.* cardinal.

car·da·mom, car·da·mum (kär'də-məm) *n.* Also **car·da·mon** (-mən). **1.** A tropical Asiatic perennial plant, *Elettaria cardamomum,* having large, hairy leaves and capsular fruit, the seeds of which are used as a condiment and in medicine. Also called "grains of paradise." **2.** An East Indian plant, *Amomum cardamomum,* the seeds of which are used as an inferior substitute for true cardamom seed. [Latin *cardamōmum,* from Greek *kardamōmon* : *kardamon*†, cress + *amōmon*†, an Indian spice.]

card·board (kärd'bôrd', -bōrd') *n.* A thin, stiff pasteboard made of paper pulp, used for making cartons and signs.

card catalog. *Library Service.* A listing, especially of books in a library, made with a separate card for each item and arranged in alphabetical order. Also called "catalog."

car·di·a (kär'dē-ə) *n.* The opening of the esophagus into the stomach. [New Latin, from Greek *kardia,* heart, cardiac orifice of the stomach. See **kerd-**[1] in Appendix.*]

car·di·ac (kär'dē-ăk') *adj.* **1.** Of, near, or pertaining to the heart. **2.** Of or pertaining to the cardia. —*n.* A person with a heart disorder. [Latin *cardiacus,* from Greek *kardiakos,* from *kardia,* heart. See **kerd-**[1] in Appendix.*]

cardiac muscle. The striated muscle of the heart.

car·di·al·gi·a (kär'dē-ăl'jē-ə) *n.* **Heartburn** *(see).* [New Latin, from Greek *kardialgia* : CARDI(O)- + -ALGIA.]

Car·diff (kär'dĭf). The major port and industrial city of Wales, situated on Bristol Bay. Population, 260,000.

car·di·gan (kär'dĭ-gən) *n.* A sweater or knitted jacket opening down the front. [After James Thomas Brudenell, Seventh Earl of *Cardigan* (1797–1868), British army officer.]

Car·di·gan·shire (kär'dĭ-gən-shĭr, -shər). Also **Car·di·gan** (-dĭ-gən). A county of Wales, occupying 690 square miles in the west. Population, 54,000. County seat, Aberystwyth.

car·di·nal (kärd'n-əl, kärd'nəl) *adj.* **1.** Of foremost importance; pivotal. **2.** Of a dark to deep or vivid red color. —*n.* **1.** *Abbr.* **Card.** *Roman Catholic Church.* A member of the Sacred College or College of Cardinals. Members are appointed by the pope and elect a new pope when the Holy See is vacated. **2.** Dark to deep or vivid red, as a cardinal's cassock. See **color. 3.** A North American bird, *Richmondena cardinalis,* having a crested head, a short, thick bill, and bright-red plumage in the male. **4.** A short, hooded cloak, originally of scarlet cloth, worn by women in the 18th century. **5.** A **cardinal number.** [Middle English, from Old French, from Late Latin *cardinālis,* from Latin, principal, of a hinge, from *cardō*† (stem *cardin-*), hinge.]

car·di·nal·ate (kärd'n-əl-ĭt, kärd'nəl-, -āt') *n.* Also **car·di·nal·ship** (-shĭp'). *Roman Catholic Church.* **1.** The College of Cardinals. **2.** The position, rank, dignity, or term of a cardinal.

cardinal fish. Any of various small red or reddish tropical marine fishes of the family Apogonidae, many species of which are mouthbreeders.

cardinal flower. A plant, *Lobelia cardinalis,* of eastern North America, having a terminal cluster of brilliant scarlet flowers.

cardinal number. A number, such as 3 or 11 or 412, used to indicate quantity but not order. See **number.** Compare **ordinal number.**

cardinal point. One of the four principal directions on a compass: north, south, east, or west.

cardinal sins. The **seven deadly sins** *(see).*

cardinal tetra. A small, brilliantly colored freshwater fish, *Cheirodon axelrodi,* native to tropical South America and popular in home aquariums.

cardinal virtues. The four qualities of justice, prudence, fortitude, and temperance. Also called "natural virtues."

cardio-, cardi-. Indicates the heart; for example, **cardiogram, cardioid.** [Greek *kardi(o)-,* from *kardia,* heart. See **kerd-**[1] in Appendix.*]

car·di·o·gram (kär'dē-ə-grăm') *n.* The curve traced by a cardiograph, used in the diagnosis of heart defects. [CARDIO- + -GRAM.]

car·di·o·graph (kär'dē-ə-grăf', -gräf') *n.* An instrument used to record the mechanical movements of the heart. [French *cardiographe* : CARDIO- + -GRAPH.]

car·di·oid (kär'dē-oid') *n.* A heart-shaped plane curve, the locus of a fixed point on a circle that rolls on the circumference of another circle with the same radius. [CARDI(O)- + -OID.]

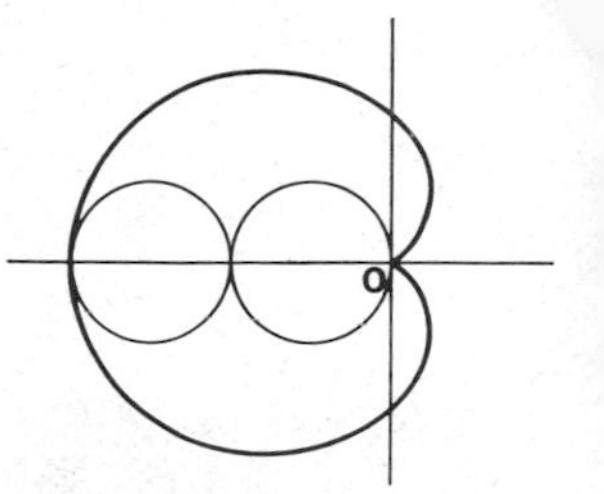

cardioid

car·di·ol·o·gist (kär'dē-ŏl'ə-jĭst) *n.* A physician who specializes in diagnosis and treatment of heart disease.

car·di·ol·o·gy (kär'dē-ŏl'ə-jē) *n.* The medical study of the diseases and functioning of the heart. [CARDIO- + -LOGY.]

car·di·o·meg·a·ly (kär'dē-ō-mĕg'ə-lē) *n. Pathology.* **Megalocardia** *(see).* [CARDIO- + *megaly,* from MEGALO-.]

car·di·o·res·pir·a·to·ry (kär'dē-ō-rĕs'pər-ə-tôr'ē, -rĭ-spī'rə-tôr'ē, -tōr'ē) *adj.* Pertaining to the heart and the lungs.

car·di·o·vas·cu·lar (kär'dē-ō-văs'kyə-lər) *adj.* Pertaining to or involving the heart and the blood vessels.

car·doon (kär-dōōn') *n.* A plant, *Cynara cardunculus,* of southern Europe, closely related to the artichoke, and having spiny leaves, purple flowers, and an edible leafstalk. [French *cardon,* from Provençal, from Late Latin *cardō,* thistle, from Latin *carduus,* thistle, artichoke. See **kars-** in Appendix.*]

cards (kärdz) *pl.n.* Usually used with a singular verb. **1.** Any game played with cards, as bridge, pinochle, or poker, usually in decks of 52 cards divided into four suits: spades, hearts, diamonds, and clubs. **2.** The playing of such games.

card·sharp (kärd'shärp') *n.* Also **card·sharp·er** (-shär'pər). A person expert in cheating at cards. —**card'sharp'ing** *n.*

care (kâr) *n.* **1.** Mental distress and uncertainty; worry. **2.** Mental suffering; grief. **3.** An object or source of worry, attention, or solicitude. **4.** Caution; heedfulness: *handling with care.* **5.** Protection; supervision; charge: *in the care of a nurse.* **6.** Attentiveness to detail; painstaking application; conscientiousness: *a report prepared with great care.* —See Synonyms at **anxiety.** —**(in) care of.** *Abbr.* **c/o, c.o.** At the address of; in custody of. Used in addressing mail. —*v.* **cared, caring, cares.** —*intr.* **1.** To have a strong feeling or opinion; be concerned or interested. **2.** To object; to mind. Usually used with *if* and in negative or interrogative constructions: *I won't care if you borrow my car.* —*tr.* **1.** To wish; be inclined. Used with an infinitive: *We don't care to attend.* **2.** To be concerned to the degree of: *"I care not a curse for the critics."* (Sterne). [Middle English *care,* Old English *caru, cearu.* See **gar-** in Appendix.*]

CARE (kâr) Cooperative for American Remittances Everywhere. A nonprofit organization set up after World War II to send packages of food and clothing to needy people overseas.

ca·reen (kə-rēn') *v.* **-reened, -reening, -reens.** —*intr.* **1.** To move rapidly and in an uncontrolled manner; to lurch or swerve in motion. See Usage note below. **2.** To lean to one side; to heel, as a ship sailing in the wind. **3.** *Nautical.* To turn a ship on its side for cleaning, caulking, or repairing. —*tr. Nautical.* **1.** To cause (a ship) to lean to one side; to tilt. **2.** To lean (a ship) on one side for cleaning, caulking, or repairing. **3.** To clean, caulk, or repair (a ship in this position). —*n.* **1.** The act or process of careening a ship. **2. a.** The position of a careened ship. **b.** The place where a ship is careened. [From French *(en) carène,* "(on) the keel," from Old French *carene,* keel, from Old Italian *carena,* from Latin *carina,* keel of a ship, nutshell. See **kar-**[1] in Appendix.*] —**ca·reen'er** *n.*

Usage: *Careen,* in the sense of moving rapidly and in an uncontrolled manner, is now established in American usage, though still disputed by some. It is acceptable in that sense to 62 per cent of the Usage Panel in the example *The car careened across the icy pavement and into a group of pedestrians.* The minority would restrict *careen* to the senses of leaning and tilting, as in nautical usage, and specify *career* for the sense of rapid forward movement.

ca·reen·age (kə-rē'nĭj) *n.* **1.** A place for careening ships. **2.** The charge for careening.

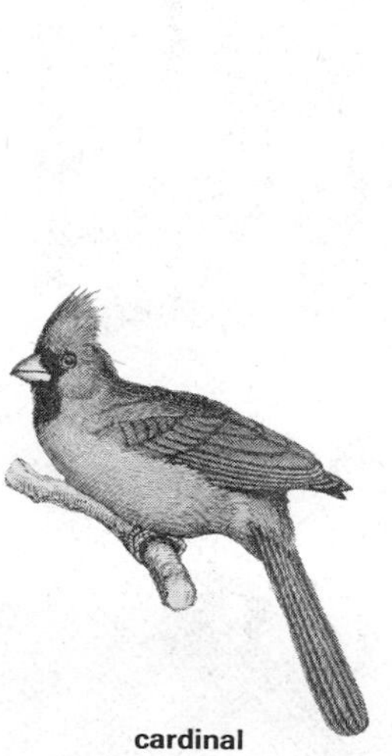

cardinal

ca·reer (kə-rîr') *n.* **1. a.** A chosen pursuit; life work: *a military career.* **b.** Success in one's profession: *He has a career before him.* **2.** *Archaic.* **a.** A path or course. **b.** A rapid course or swift progression, as of the sun through the heavens. **c.** A charge at full tilt. **3. a.** Speed. Often used with *full: "My hasting days fly on with full career."* (Milton). **b.** The moment of highest pitch or peak activity. Often used with *full: The Republic was now in the full career of its triumphs.* —*intr.v.* **careered, -reering, -reers.** To move or run at full speed; go headlong; rush: *"Thus the night fled away . . . and he careering on it."* (Hawthorne). See Usage note at **careen.** [French *carrière,* racecourse, course, career, from Old French, from Old Provençal *carriera,* street, from Medieval Latin *(via) carrāria,* (road) for vehicles, from Latin *carrus,* a kind of vehicle. See **kers-**[2] in Appendix.*]

ca·reer·ism (kə-rîr'ĭz'əm) *n.* The practice of seeking one's professional advancement by all possible means. —**ca·reer'ist** *n.*

care·free (kâr'frē') *adj.* Free of worries and responsibilities.

care·ful (kâr'fəl) *adj.* **1.** Cautious in thought, speech, or action; circumspect; prudent. **2.** Thorough; painstaking; conscientious: *careful investigation.* **3.** Solicitous; protective. Used with *of* or *for: "Herdsman, careful of the herd"* (Joyce). **4.** *Archaic.* Full of cares or anxiety: *"thou art careful and troubled about many things"* (Luke 10:41). —**care'ful·ly** *adv.* —**care'ful·ness** *n.*

t tight/th thin, path/*th* this, bathe/ŭ cut/ûr urge/v valve/w with/y yes/z zebra, size/zh vision/ə about, item, edible, gallop, circus/
à *Fr.* ami/œ *Fr.* feu, *Ger.* schön/ü *Fr.* tu, *Ger.* über/KH *Ger.* ich, *Scot.* loch/N *Fr.* bon. ***Follows main vocabulary.** †**Of obscure origin.**

care·less (kâr′lĭs) *adj.* **1.** Inattentive; negligent. **2.** Marked by or resulting from lack of thought, thoroughness, or planning: *a careless mistake.* **3.** Inconsiderate: *a careless remark.* **4.** Unconcerned; unmindful: *careless about her health.* **5.** Unstudied; effortless: *careless grandeur.* **6.** Free from cares; cheerful: *"Good-humoured, easy, and careless, he presided over his whale boat as if the most deadly encounter were but a dinner"* (Melville). —**care′less·ly** *adv.* —**care′less·ness** *n.*

Synonyms: *careless, heedless, thoughtless, inadvertent, indifferent.* These adjectives apply to actions or attitudes demonstrating little or no concern for what results. *Careless* pertains to lack of care or attentiveness and can imply negligence. *Heedless* implies inattentiveness to the point of recklessness. *Thoughtless* suggests action without consideration for others. *Inadvertent* applies only to actions that are unintentional. *Indifferent* emphasizes not caring one way or the other about consequences.

ca·ress (kə-rĕs′) *n.* A gentle touch or gesture of fondness, tenderness, or love. —*tr.v.* **caressed, -ressing, -resses. 1.** To touch or stroke in an affectionate or loving manner. **2.** To treat fondly, kindly, or favorably. [French *caresse,* from Italian *carezza,* endearment, from *caro,* dear, from Latin *cārus.* See **kā-** in Appendix.*] —**ca·ress′er** *n.* —**ca·ress′ing·ly** *adv.*

car·et (kăr′ĭt) *n.* A proofreading symbol used to indicate where something is to be inserted in a line of printed or written matter. See table at **symbol.** [Latin, "there is lacking," from *carēre,* to cut off, be without. See **kes-²** in Appendix.*]

care·tak·er (kâr′tā′kər) *n.* A person employed to look after or take charge of goods, property, or a person; custodian.

Ca·rew (kə-ro͞o′, kâr′ē), **Thomas.** 1595?–1639? English Cavalier poet.

care·worn (kâr′wôrn′, -wōrn′) *adj.* Showing the effects of care; weary from worry. See Synonyms at **haggard.**

car·fare (kär′fâr′) *n.* Fare charged a passenger.

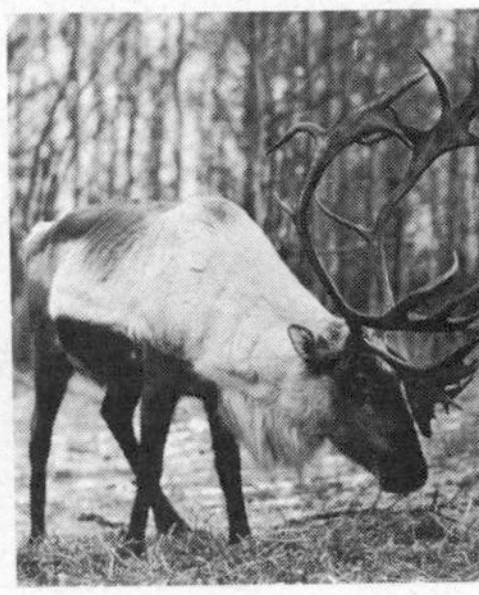

caribou

car·go (kär′gō) *n., pl.* **-goes** or **-gos.** The freight carried by a ship, airplane, or other vehicle. [Spanish *cargo, carga,* load, cargo, from *cargar,* to load, from Late Latin *carricāre,* from Latin *carrus,* a kind of vehicle. See **kers-²** in Appendix.*]

car·hop (kär′hŏp′) *n.* A waiter at a drive-in restaurant.

Car·i·a (kâr′ē-ə). An ancient region of southwestern Asia Minor with a coastline on the Aegean Sea and its capital at Halicarnassus.

Car·ib (kăr′ĭb) *n., pl.* **Carib** or **-ibs.** Also **Car·i·ban** (kăr′ə-bən, kə-rē′bən) (for senses 1a, 1b). **1. a.** A group of peoples of American Indians of northern South America and the Lesser Antilles. **b.** A member of one of these peoples. **2.** Any of the languages of these peoples. [American Spanish *Caribe,* from Spanish, from Cariban *caribe,* "brave."] —**Car′ib** *adj.*

Car·i·ban (kăr′ə-bən, kə-rē′bən) *n., pl.* **Cariban** or **-bans. 1.** Variant of **Carib. 2.** A language family of the Lesser Antilles and South America, comprising the languages spoken by the Caribs. —**Car′i·ban** *adj.*

Car·ib·be·an (kăr′ə-bē′ən, kə-rĭb′ē-ən) *n.* A Carib Indian. —*adj.* **1.** Of or pertaining to the Caribbean Sea and its islands. **2.** Of or pertaining to the Carib or their language.

Caribbean Sea. An extension of the Atlantic Ocean, 750,000 square miles in area, bounded by the coasts of Central and South America and the major islands of the West Indies. Also called the "Caribbean."

ca·ri·be (kə-rē′bē, kăr′ə-bē′) *n.* A fish, the **piranha** *(see).* [American Spanish, CARIB.]

Car·i·boo Mountains (kăr′ə-bo͞o′). A range of the Rocky Mountains in east-central British Columbia, Canada. Highest elevation, 11,750 feet.

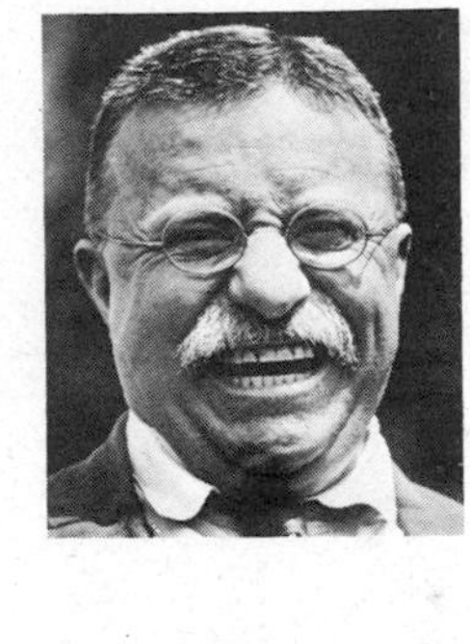

car·i·bou (kăr′ə-bo͞o′) *n., pl.* **caribou** or **-bous.** A deer, *Rangifer tarandus,* of arctic regions of the New World, having antlers in both sexes. See **reindeer.** [Canadian French, from Proto-Algonquian *mekālixpowa* (unattested), "snow shoveler" : *mekāl-* (unattested), to scrape + *-ixpo-* (unattested), snow.]

car·i·ca·ture (kăr′ĭ-kə-cho͝or′) *n.* **1.** A representation, especially pictorial, in which the subject's distinctive features or peculiarities are deliberately exaggerated or distorted to produce a comic or grotesque effect. **2.** The process or art of creating such representations. **3.** An imitation or copy so inferior as to be absurd. —*tr.v.* **caricatured, -turing, -tures.** To represent or imitate in or as in a caricature; satirize. [French, from Italian *caricatura,* caricature, "exaggeration," from *caricare,* to load, from Late Latin *carricāre,* from Latin *carrus,* a kind of vehicle. See **kers-²** in Appendix.*] —**car′i·ca·tur′ist** *n.*

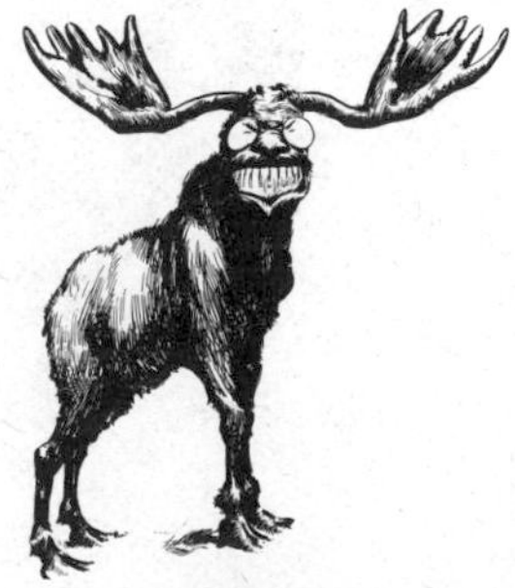

caricature
Above: Theodore Roosevelt
Below: Roosevelt caricatured as a bull moose in a 1912 cartoon

Synonyms: *caricature, burlesque, parody, travesty, satire, lampoon, takeoff, spoof.* These nouns denote artistic forms in which a person or thing is imitated or otherwise depicted in an amusing and generally critical manner. A *caricature,* usually pictorial, grossly exaggerates a peculiar feature of a person, group, or thing with intent to ridicule. *Burlesque,* usually a stage work, suggests outlandish mimicry and broad comedy to provoke laughter. *Parody, travesty, satire,* and *lampoon* generally apply to written works or to their dramatizations. *Parody* implies ludicrous treatment of a generally trivial theme, employing the manner and style of a well-known composition or writer. A *travesty* keeps to the theme or subject of the original but treats it with a heavy hand and an ironic and absurd manner. *Satire* usually involves holding up to ridicule the follies and vices of a people or a time, and is often associated with social reform. *Lampoon* refers to an abusive attack in a broadly humorous vein. *Takeoff,* an informal term, suggests good-humored imitation in written or dramatic form. *Spoof* is often interchangeable with *parody* but stresses lightheartedness.

car·ies (kâr′ēz) *n.* Decay of a bone or tooth. [Latin *cariēs,* caries, decay. See **ker-⁵** in Appendix.*]

car·il·lon (kăr′ə-lŏn′, kə-rĭl′yən) *n.* A set of bells in a tower played from a keyboard or by some other mechanism. —*intr.v.* **carillonned, -lonning, -lons.** To play a carillon. [French, variant of Old French *carignon, quarregnon,* from Vulgar Latin *quadriniō* (unattested), set of four bells, variant of Late Latin *quaterniō,* set of four, from *quaternī,* four each, from *quater,* four times. See **kwetwer-** in Appendix.*]

car·il·lon·neur (kăr′ə-lŏn-ûr′, kə-rĭl′yən-ər) *n.* A person who plays a carillon.

ca·ri·na (kə-rī′nə) *n., pl.* **-nae** (-nē′). *Biology.* A keel-shaped ridge, such as that on the breastbone of a bird or in the petals of certain flowers. [New Latin, from Latin *carīna,* keel. See **kar-¹** in Appendix.*]

Ca·ri·na (kə-rī′nə) *n.* A constellation in the Southern Hemisphere near Volans and Vela and containing the star Canopus. [Latin *Carīna,* "the Keel," from *carīna.* See **carina.**]

car·i·nate (kăr′ə-nāt′, -nĭt) *adj.* Also **car·i·nat·ed** (-nā′tĭd). *Biology.* Having or shaped like a keel; ridged.

Ca·rin·thi·a (kə-rĭn′thē-ə). *German* **Kärn·ten** (kĕrn′tən). A province, formerly a duchy, of Austria, occupying 4,460 square miles in the southern part of the country. Population, 495,000. Capital, Klagenfurt.

car·i·o·ca (kăr′ē-ō′kə) *n.* **1.** A South American ballroom dance that originated in Rio de Janeiro. **2.** The music for this dance. **3.** *Capital* **C.** Variant of **Cariocan.** [Portuguese *Carioca,* CARIOCAN.]

Car·i·o·can (kăr′ē-ō′kən) *n.* Also **Car·i·o·ca** (-kə). A native or resident of Rio de Janeiro, Brazil. [Portuguese *Carioca,* from Tupi, "(dweller in) a white house" : *cari,* white + *oca,* house.]

car·i·ole (kăr′ē-ōl′) *n.* Also **car·ri·ole. 1.** A small, open one-horse carriage with two wheels. **2.** A light, covered cart. [French *carriole,* from Old Provençal *carriola,* diminutive of *carri,* chariot, from Vulgar Latin *carrium* (unattested), from Latin *carrus,* a kind of vehicle. See **kers-²** in Appendix.*]

car·i·ous (kâr′ē-əs) *adj.* Having caries; decayed. —**car′i·os′i·ty** (-ŏs′ə-tē), **car′i·ous·ness** *n.*

carl, carle (kärl) *n.* **1.** *Archaic.* A peasant or farmer. **2.** *Obsolete.* A bondman; serf. **3.** *Regional.* A rude person; churl. [Middle English *carl,* from Old English *carl* (used only in compounds), from Old Norse *karl,* man, freeman. See **karlaz** in Appendix.*]

Carl (kärl). A masculine given name. [German *Karl,* from Middle High German *karl,* man, from Old High German *karal.* See **karlaz** in Appendix.*]

car·ling (kär′lĭng, -lĭn) *n.* Also **car·line** (-lĭn). *Nautical.* One of the short timbers running fore and aft that connect the transverse beams supporting the deck of a ship. [French *carlingue,* from Old French *cal(l)ingue,* probably from Old Norse *kerling,* "old woman," from *karl,* man. See **karlaz** in Appendix.*]

Car·lisle (kär-līl′). The county seat of Cumberland, England, in the northwestern part of the county. Population, 57,000.

Carl·ist (kär′lĭst) *n.* **1.** In Spain, a supporter of Don Carlos, the pretender to the throne, or his heirs. **2.** In France, a supporter of Charles X and his line. —**Carl′ism′** *n.*

car·load (kär′lōd′) *n. Abbr.* **c.l. 1.** The amount a car carries or is able to carry. **2.** The official minimum weight necessary to ship freight at the carload rate.

Car·los (kär′lōs′), **Don.** In full, Carlos Maria Isidro de Borbón. 1788–1855. Spanish pretender; leader of the Carlists.

Car·los de Aus·tri·a (kär′lōs′ *thä* ous′trē-ä), **Don.** 1545–1568. Prince of Asturias and heir to the throne of Spain; son of Philip II; died mysteriously.

Car·lo·ta (kär-lō′tä). Original name, Marie Charlotte Amélie. 1840–1927. Empress of Mexico (1864–67) and wife of Maximilian, Archduke of Austria.

Car·lo·vin·gi·an. Variant of **Carolingian.**

Car·low (kär′lō). **1.** A county of the Republic of Ireland, occupying 346 square miles in the southeast. Population, 33,000. **2.** The county seat of this county. Population, 8,000.

Carls·bad¹ (kärlz′băd′). A city on the Pecos River in southeastern New Mexico. Population, 26,000.

Carls·bad². The German name for **Karlovy Vary.**

Carls·bad Caverns National Park (kärlz′băd′). An area of 71 acres in southeastern New Mexico, containing the Carlsbad Caverns, a series of huge limestone caves.

Carl·son (kärl′sən), **Evans Fordyce.** 1896–1947. U.S. Marine Corps general in World War II.

Carls·ru·he. See **Karlsruhe.**

Car·lyle (kär-līl′), **Thomas.** 1795–1881. English essayist and historian.

car·man (kär′mən) *n., pl.* **-men** (-mĭn). **1.** A motorman or conductor, as of a streetcar. **2.** A man who drives a car or cart.

Car·mar·then (kər-mär′*th*ən, kär-). **1.** Also **Car·mar·then·shire** (-shîr, -shər). A county of Wales, occupying 919 square miles in the southwest. Population, 168,000. **2.** The county seat of this county. Population, 13,000.

Car·mel, Mount (kär′məl). A ridge extending about 15 miles across northwestern Israel to the Mediterranean. Highest elevation, about 1,800 feet.

Car·mel·ite (kär′mə-līt′) *n.* **1.** A monk or mendicant friar belonging to the order of Our Lady of Mount Carmel, founded by St. Berthold at Mount Carmel in 1155. Also called "White Friar." **2.** A member of a community of nuns of this order, founded in 1452. —**Car′mel·ite′** *adj.*

Car·men (kär′mən). A feminine or masculine given name. [Spanish, from Latin, song, poem. See **kan-** in Appendix.*]

car·min·a·tive (kär-mĭn′ə-tĭv, kär′mə-nā′tĭv) *adj.* Inducing expulsion of gas from the stomach and intestines. [Middle English, from Medieval Latin *carminātīvus,* from *carmināre* (past participle *carminātus*), to card wool, to comb out impurities, from Latin *carmen*, a card for wool, from *cārere*, to card. See **kars-** in Appendix.*] —*n.* A carminative drug.

car·mine (kär′mĭn, -mīn′) *n.* **1.** A strong to vivid red color. See **color**. **2.** A crimson pigment derived from **cochineal** (*see*). —*adj.* Vivid-red or purplish-red. [French *carmin*, from Medieval Latin *carminium* : Arabic *qirmiz*, KERMES + Latin *minium*, MINIUM.]

car·nage (kär′nĭj) *n.* **1.** Massive slaughter, as in war; massacre. **2.** *Obsolete.* Corpses, especially of men killed in battle: *a battlefield bloody with carnage.* [Old French, from Medieval Latin *carnāticum*, slaughter of animals, from Latin *carō* (stem *carn-*), flesh, meat. See **sker-**[1] in Appendix.*]

car·nal (kär′nəl) *adj.* **1.** Relating to the desires and appetites of the flesh or body; sensual; animal. **2.** Worldly or earthly; not spiritual; not holy or sanctified. [Middle English, from Medieval Latin *carnālis*, from Latin *carō* (stem *carn-*), flesh. See **sker-**[1] in Appendix.*] —**car′nal·ist** *n.* —**car·nal′i·ty** (kär-năl′ə-tē) *n.* —**car′nal·ly** *adv.*

carnal knowledge. Sexual intercourse.

car·nall·ite (kär′nəl-īt′) *n.* A white, brownish, or reddish mineral, $KCl \cdot MgCl_2 \cdot 6H_2O$, used to manufacture potash salts. [German *Carnallit*, after Rudolf von *Carnall* (1804–1874), German mining engineer.]

Car·nar·von. See **Caernarvon**.

Car·nar·von·shire. See **Caernarvon** (county).

car·nas·si·al (kär-năs′ē-əl) *adj.* Adapted for tearing apart flesh. Said of teeth. —*n.* The last upper premolar and the first lower molar teeth in carnivorous mammals. [From French *carnassier*, carnivorous, from Provençal, from *carnasso*, meat in abundance, from *carn*, flesh, from Latin *carō* (stem *carn-*). See **sker-**[1] in Appendix.*]

car·na·tion (kär-nā′shən) *n.* **1. a.** A plant, *Dianthus caryophyllus*, native to Eurasia, widely cultivated for its fragrant white, pink, or red flowers with fringed petals. **b.** The flower of this plant. **2.** *Plural. Rare.* Flesh-colored tints used in painting. [Old French, flesh-colored, carnation, from Old Italian *carnagione*, complexion, from *carne*, flesh, from Latin *carō* (stem *carn-*), flesh. See **sker-**[1] in Appendix.*]

car·nau·ba (kär-nô′bə, -nou′bə) *n.* **1.** A palm tree, *Copernica cerifera*, of tropical South America. **2.** A hard wax obtained from the leaves of this tree, used as a polish and in candles. In this sense, also called "carnauba wax." [Portuguese, probably of Tupi origin.]

Car·ne·gie (kär′nə-gē, kär-nĕg′ē), **Andrew.** 1835–1919. Scottish-born American industrialist and humanitarian.

car·nel·ian (kär-nēl′yən) *n.* Also **cor·nel·ian** (kôr-). A pale to deep red or reddish-brown variety of clear chalcedony, used in jewelry. [Middle English *corneline*, from Old French, probably "cherry-colored," from *cornelle*, CORNEL (cherry).]

Car·nic Alps (kär′nĭk). *German* **Kar·ni·sche Al·pen** (kär′nĭsh-ə äl′pən). A range of the Alps in southern Austria and northern Italy. Highest elevation, Kellerwand (9,220 feet).

Car·ni·o·la (kär′nē-ō′lə, kär-nyō′lə). *German* **Krain** (krīn); *Slovene* **Kranj** (krä′nyə). A region in northwestern Yugoslavia, formerly belonging to Austria, but since 1947 a part of Yugoslavia. —**Car′ni·o′lan** *adj.* & *n.*

car·ni·val (kär′nə-vəl) *n.* **1.** The season just before Lent, marked by merrymaking and feasting. See **Mardi gras**. **2.** Any time of revelry; a festival. **3.** A traveling amusement show, having a Ferris wheel, side shows, and the like. [Italian *carnevale*, from Old Italian *carnelevare*, "the putting away of flesh," Shrovetide, from Medieval Latin *carnelevāmen* : Latin *carō* (stem *carn-*), flesh (see **sker-**[1] in Appendix*) + *levāre*, to raise, remove (see **legwh-** in Appendix*).]

car·ni·vore (kär′nə-vôr′, -vōr′) *n.* **1.** *Zoology.* Any animal belonging to the order Carnivora, which includes predominantly flesh-eating mammals such as dogs, cats, bears, and weasels. **2.** Any flesh-eating or predatory organism, such as a bird of prey or an insectivorous plant. [French, from Latin *carnivorus*, CARNIVOROUS.]

car·niv·o·rous (kär-nĭv′ər-əs) *adj.* **1.** Belonging or pertaining to the order Carnivora. **2.** Flesh-eating or predatory. **3.** *Botany.* Capable of trapping and absorbing insects or other small organisms; insectivorous. Said of plants such as the pitcher plant and the Venus's-flytrap. [Latin *carnivorus* : *carō* (stem *carn-*), flesh (see **sker-**[1] in Appendix*) + -VOROUS.] —**car·niv′o·rous·ly** *adv.* —**car·niv′o·rous·ness** *n.*

Car·not (kȧr-nō′), **Nicolas Léonard Sadi.** 1796–1832. French physicist; pioneer in thermodynamics.

Carnot cycle. The thermodynamic cycle of an ideal heat engine, consisting of an adiabatic compression, an isothermal expansion, an adiabatic expansion, and an isothermal compression, the sequence restoring the initial conditions of the system. [After N.L.S. CARNOT.]

car·no·tite (kär′nə-tīt′) *n.* A yellow uranium ore with composition $K_2(UO_2)_2(VO_4)_2 \cdot 3H_2O$. [French, after M.A. *Carnot* (died 1920), French inspector general of mines.]

car·ny (kär′nē) *n.*, *pl.* **-nies.** Also **car·ney** *pl.* **-neys.** *Slang.* **1.** A carnival. **2.** A person who works with a carnival.

car·ob (kăr′əb) *n.* An evergreen tree, *Ceratonia siliqua*, of the Mediterranean region, having compound leaves and edible pods. Also called "algarroba." See **St. John's bread**. [Old French *caro(u)be*, from Medieval Latin *carrūbium*, from Arabic *kharrūbah*.]

ca·roche (kə-rōch′, -rōsh′) *n.* Also **ca·roach, ca·roch.** A stately carriage of the 16th and 17th centuries. [Old French *carroche*, from Old Italian *carroccio*, augmentative of *carro*, vehicle, from Latin *carrus*. See **kers-**[2] in Appendix.*]

car·ol (kăr′əl) *v.* **-oled, -oling, -ols.** Also *chiefly British* **-olled, -olling.** —*tr.* **1.** To celebrate in song. **2.** To sing joyously. —*intr.* **1.** To sing in a joyous manner; warble. **2.** To go from house to house singing Christmas songs. —*n.* **1.** A song of praise or joy, especially for Christmas. **2.** An old round dance often accompanied by singing. [Middle English *carolen*, from Old French *caroler*, from *carole*, a carol, perhaps from Late Latin *choraula*, choral song, from Latin *choraula*, *choraulēs*, one who accompanies a chorus, from Greek *khoraulēs*, from *khoraulein*, to accompany a chorus : *khoros*, CHORUS + *aulein*, to play the flute, from *aulos*, pipe, flute (see **aulo-** in Appendix*).] —**car′ol·er** *n.*

Car·ol (kăr′əl). A feminine given name. [Medieval Latin *Carolus*, CHARLES.]

Car·ol II (kăr′əl). 1893–1953. King of Rumania (1930–40); abdicated.

Car·o·le·an (kăr′ə-lē′ən) *adj.* Of or relating to Charles I or Charles II of England, or their times. [From Medieval Latin *Carolus*, CHARLES.]

Car·o·li·na (kăr′ə-lī′nə). An English colony, first settled in 1653, divided into what became the present North and South Carolina in 1729. —**the Carolinas.** North and South Carolina.

Carolina allspice. A shrub, *Calycanthus floridus*, of the southeastern United States, having fragrant brownish flowers and aromatic wood.

Carolina parakeet. A green and yellow parakeet, *Conuropsis carolinensis*, formerly common in the southeastern United States but extinct since the beginning of the 20th century.

Car·o·line[1] (kăr′ə-līn′, -lĭn). A feminine given name. [Italian *Carolina*, diminutive of *Carlo*, from Medieval Latin *Carolus*, CHARLES.]

Car·o·line[2] (kăr′ə-līn′, -lĭn) *adj.* Relating to the life and times of Charles I or Charles II of England; Carolinian. [New Latin *Carolinius*, from Medieval Latin *Carolus*, CHARLES.]

Car·o·line Islands (kăr′ə-līn′). An archipelago of some 680 islands and atolls with a combined area of 460 square miles, in the Pacific Ocean east of the Philippines. In 1947, the islands were awarded to the United States; now part of the United Nations Trust Territory of the Pacific Islands.

Car·o·lin·gi·an (kăr′ə-lĭn′jē-ən) *adj.* Also **Car·lo·vin·gi·an** (kär′-lə-vĭn′jē-ən). Related to or belonging to the Frankish dynasty that was founded by Pepin the Short in A.D. 751 and that lasted until A.D. 987 in France and A.D. 911 in Germany. —*n.* Also **Car·lo·vin·gi·an.** A member of this dynasty. [French *Carolingien*, variant of *Carlovingien*, probably a blend of Medieval Latin *Carolus*, CHARLES and *Mérovingien*, MEROVINGIAN.]

Car·o·lin·i·an (kăr′ə-lĭn′ē-ən) *adj.* **1.** Of or relating to the Carolinas. **2.** Of or relating to Charles I or Charles II of England; Caroline. **3.** Of or relating to Charlemagne and his times. —*n.* A native or resident of North or South Carolina.

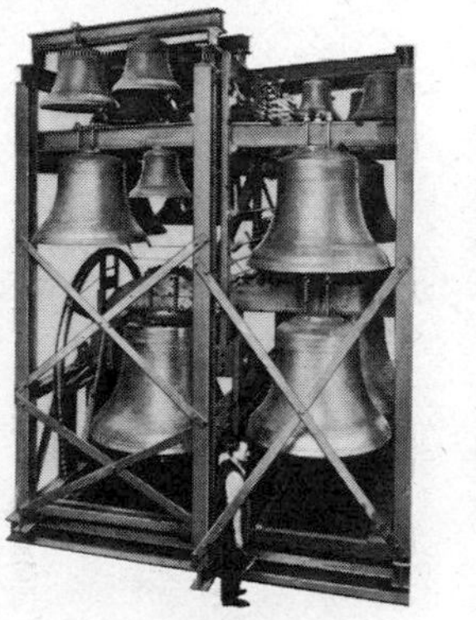

carillon
Part of the bells and framework of a large carillon

car·om (kăr′əm) *n.* Also **car·rom.** **1. a.** *Billiards.* A shot in which the cue ball successively strikes two other balls; a billiard. **b.** A similar shot in related games, such as pool. **2.** A collision followed by a rebound. —*v.* **caromed, -oming, -oms.** Also **car·rom.** —*intr.* **1.** To collide with and rebound. Usually used with *off*: *The boat caromed off the dock.* **2.** To make a carom, as in billiards. —*tr.* To cause to carom. [Earlier *carambole*, from Spanish *carambola*, a kind of fruit, from Portuguese, from Marathi *karambal*†.]

car·o·tene (kăr′ə-tēn′) *n.* Also **car·ro·tene, car·o·tin** (-tĭn), **car·ro·tin.** An orange-yellow to red hydrocarbon, $C_{40}H_{56}$, existing in three isomeric forms, occurring in many plants as a pigment, and converted to vitamin A in the animal liver. [German *Karotin* : Latin *carōta*, CARROT + -ENE.]

ca·rot·e·noid (kə-rŏt′ə-noid′) *n.* Any of a class of yellow- to deep-red pigments, such as the carotenes, occurring in many vegetable oils and some animal fats. [CAROTEN(E) + -OID.]

Ca·roth·ers (kə-rŭth′ərz), **Wallace Hume.** 1896–1937. American chemist; worked on synthetics, such as nylon.

ca·rot·id (kə-rŏt′ĭd) *n.* Either of the two major arteries in the neck that carry blood to the head. —*adj.* Of or pertaining to either of the two major arteries of the neck. [French *carotide*, from Greek *karōtides*, from *karoun*, to stupefy (it was once thought that pressure on the carotids causes a stupor). See **ker-**[1] in Appendix.*]

ca·rous·al (kə-rou′zəl) *n.* A jovial, riotous drinking party; boisterous merrymaking; revelry.

ca·rouse (kə-rouz′) *n.* Boisterous, drunken merrymaking; a carousal. —*intr.v.* **caroused, -rousing, -rouses.** To drink excessively; go on a drinking spree. [Old French *carrousse*, from (*boire*) *carous*, (to drink) all out, from German *garaus* (*trinken*) : *gar*, quite, entirely, from Old High German *garo*, from adjective, complete (see **gwher-** in Appendix*) + *aus*, out, from Old High German *ūz* (see **ud-** in Appendix*).] —**ca·rous′er** *n.*

car·ou·sel, car·rou·sel (kăr′ə-sĕl′, -zĕl′) *n.* **1.** A **merry-go-round** (*see*). **2.** A tournament in which knights or horsemen engaged in various exercises and races. [French *carrousel*, probably from Italian dialectal *carosello*†, a kind of tournament.]

carp[1] (kärp) *intr.v.* **carped, carping, carps.** To find fault and complain constantly; harp on petty grievances; nag or fuss. [Middle English *carpen*, from Old Norse *karpa*, to boast. See **ger-**[3] in Appendix.*] —**carp′er** *n.*

carp[2] (kärp) *n.*, *pl.* **carp** or **carps.** **1.** An edible freshwater fish, *Cyprinus carpio*, frequently bred in ponds and lakes. **2.** Any of various other fishes of the family Cyprinidae. [Middle English *carpe*, from Old French, from Late Latin *carpa*†.]

-carp. *Botany.* Indicates fruit or similar reproductive structure; for example, **mesocarp**. [New Latin *-carpium*, from Greek *-karpion*, from *karpos*, fruit. See **kerp-** in Appendix.*]

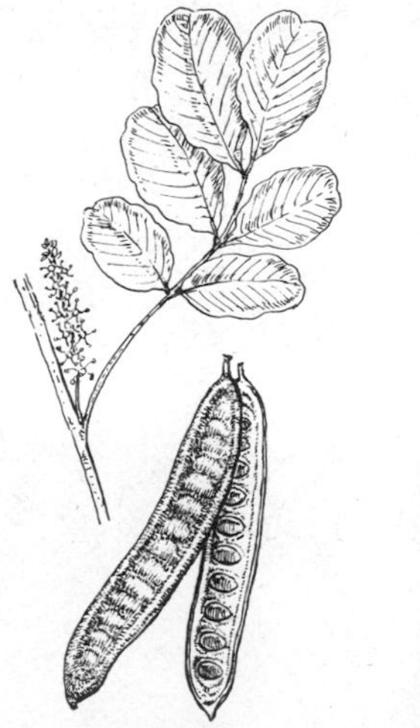

carob
Above: Foliage and flowers
Below: Pod

t tight/th thin, path/*th* this, bathe/ŭ cut/ûr urge/v valve/w with/y yes/z zebra, size/zh vision/ə about, item, edible, gallop, circus/ à *Fr.* ami/œ *Fr.* feu, *Ger.* schön/ü *Fr.* tu, *Ger.* über/KH *Ger.* ich, *Scot.* loch/N *Fr.* bon. ***Follows main vocabulary.** **†Of obscure origin.**

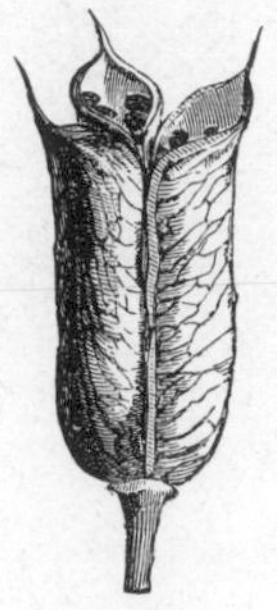

carpel
Fruit of aconite, composed of three carpels

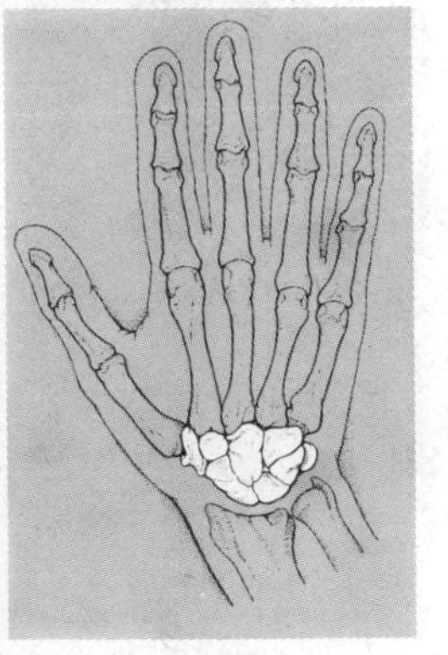

carpus

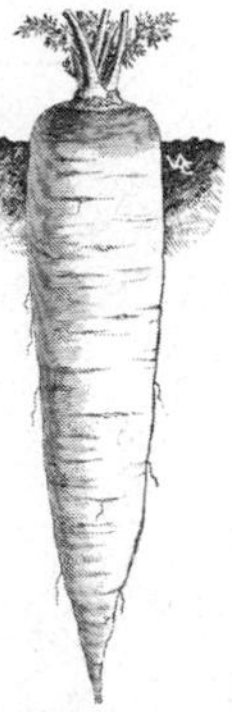

carrot

car·pal (kär′pəl) *adj. Anatomy.* Of, pertaining to, or near the carpus. —*n.* Any bone of the carpus. [New Latin *carpalis,* from Greek *karpos,* wrist. See **kwerp-** in Appendix.*]

Car·pa·thi·an Mountains (kär-pā′thē-ən). Also **Car·pa·thi·ans.** A mountain system of eastern Europe, extending in a 1,000-mile arc through Czechoslovakia, Hungary, the Soviet Union, and Rumania, and forming a continuation of the Alps. Highest elevation, Gerlachovka (8,737 feet).

Car·pa·tho-U·kraine (kär-pā′thō-yo͞o′krān). A name for that part of **Ruthenia** *(see)* that once constituted a province of Czechoslovakia.

car·pel (kär′pəl) *n. Botany.* The central, ovule-bearing female organ of a flower, consisting of a modified leaf forming one or more sections of the pistil. [New Latin *carpellum,* from Greek *karpos,* fruit. See **kerp-** in Appendix.*] —**car′pel·lar·y** *adj.*

car·pel·late (kär′pə-lāt′, -lĭt) *adj. Botany.* Having carpels.

Car·pen·tar·i·a (kär′pən-târ′ē-ə), **Gulf of.** A wide, shallow inlet of the Arafura Sea, over 400 square miles in area, in northern Australia, between Cape York Peninsula and Arnhem Land.

car·pen·ter (kär′pən-tər) *n.* One whose occupation is constructing, finishing, and repairing wooden objects and structures. —*v.* **carpentered, -tering, -ters.** —*tr.* To make, build, or repair (wooden structures). —*intr.* To work as a carpenter. [Middle English, from Norman French, from Latin *carpentārius (artifex),* carriage(-maker), from adjective, of a carriage, from *carpentum,* two-wheeled carriage, wagon, from Celtic. See **kers-**[2] in Appendix.*] —**car′pen·try** *n.*

carpenter ant. Any of various ants of the genus *Camponotus,* that nest in and are destructive to wood.

carpenter bee. Any of various bees of the families Xylocopidae and Ceratinidae, that do not live in colonies and that bore tunnels into wood to lay their eggs.

carpenter moth. Any of various moths of the family Cossidae, the larvae of which are harmful to the wood of various trees.

car·pet (kär′pĭt) *n.* **1. a.** A thick, heavy covering for a floor, usually made of wool or synthetic fibers; rug. **b.** The fabric used for this. **2.** A surface of similar function or appearance: *a carpet of leaves and pine needles.* —**on the carpet. 1.** Under discussion or consideration. **2.** In the position of being reprimanded by one in authority. —*tr.v.* **carpeted, -peting, -pets.** To cover with or as with a carpet: *"the pool was carpeted with green sponge"* (Rachel Carson). [Middle English *carpete,* from Old French *carpite,* from Old Italian *carpita,* from *carpire,* to pluck, tear, from Latin *carpere.* See **kerp-** in Appendix.*]

car·pet·bag (kär′pĭt-băg′) *n.* An old-fashioned kind of traveling bag made of carpet fabric.

car·pet·bag·ger (kär′pĭt-băg′ər) *n.* **1.** A Northerner who went to the South after the Civil War for political or financial advantage. Compare **scalawag. 2.** A nonresident politician who represents or seeks to represent a locality for political self-interest. —**car′pet·bag′ger·y, car′pet·bag′gism′** *n.*

carpet beetle. Any of various small beetles of the genera *Anthrenus* and *Attagenus,* having larvae injurious to fabrics, furs, and other plant and animal products. Also called "buffalo beetle," "buffalo bug."

carpet knight. A soldier, originally a knight, who has spent his life in ease away from battle. Used disparagingly.

car·pet·weed (kär′pĭt-wēd′) *n.* A low-growing, weedy plant, *Mollugo verticillata,* forming dense mats and having whorled leaves and small, greenish-white flowers.

-carpic. Variant of **-carpous.**

carp·ing (kär′pĭng) *adj.* Naggingly critical; faultfinding; complaining. —**carp′ing·ly** *adv.*

carpo-. Indicates fruit or similar reproductive structure; for example, **carpogonium, carpology.** [From Greek *karpos,* fruit. See **kerp-** in Appendix.*]

car·po·go·ni·um (kär′pə-gō′nē-əm) *n., pl.* **-nia** (-nē-ə). *Botany.* The female structure producing sex cells in certain red algae. [New Latin : CARPO- + -GONIUM.] —**car′po·go′ni·al** *adj.*

car·pol·o·gy (kär-pŏl′ə-jē) *n.* The area of botany concerned with fruit and seeds. [CARPO- + -LOGY.]

car·poph·a·gous (kär-pŏf′ə-gəs) *adj.* Feeding on fruit; fruit-eating. [Greek *karpophagos* : CARPO- + -PHAGOUS.]

car·po·phore (kär′pə-fôr′, -fōr′) *n. Botany.* **1.** The elongated part of the axis of certain flowers, to which the carpels are attached. **2.** A fruiting body or the stalk of a fruiting body in a fungus. [CARPO- + -PHORE.]

car·port (kär′pôrt′, -pōrt′) *n.* A roof projecting from the side of a building, used as a shelter for an automobile.

car·po·spor·an·gi·um (kär′pə-spô-răn′jē-əm) *n., pl.* **-gia** (-jē-ə). A specialized sporangium in red algae, in which carpospores are formed. [New Latin : CARPO- + SPORANGIUM.]

car·po·spore (kär′pə-spôr′, -spōr′) *n. Botany.* A nonmotile haploid or diploid spore formed within the carpogonium of red algae. [CARPO- + SPORE.]

-carpous, -carpic. Indicates a specified number or kind of fruit; for example, **polycarpous, monocarpic.** [New Latin *-carpus,* from Greek *karpos,* fruit. See **kerp-** in Appendix.*]

car·pus (kär′pəs) *n., pl.* **-pi** (-pī′). *Anatomy.* **1. a.** The **wrist** *(see).* **b.** The bones of the wrist. **2.** Any joint corresponding to the wrist in quadrupeds. [New Latin, from Greek *karpos,* wrist. See **kwerp-** in Appendix.*]

car·rack (kăr′ək) *n.* Also **car·ack.** A type of merchant ship used in the 14th, 15th, and 16th centuries; galleon. [Middle English *caryk, carrake,* from Old French *caraque,* from Old Spanish *carraca,* from Arabic *qarāqir,* plural of *qurqūr,* carrack.]

car·ra·geen (kăr′ə-gēn′) *n.* Also **car·ra·gheen, car·a·geen.** A seaweed, **Irish moss** *(see).* [It grows abundantly around *Carragheen,* near Waterford, Ireland.]

Car·ran·za (kə-răn′zə; *Spanish* kär-rän′sä), **Venustiano.** 1859–1920. Mexican revolutionist and statesman; president (1915–20); opponent of Huerta, Villa, and Zapata; assassinated.

car·rel (kăr′əl) *n.* Also **car·rell.** A nook near the stacks in a library, used for private study. [Perhaps from Middle English *carole,* round dance, from Old French, CAROL.]

Car·rel (kə-rĕl′, kăr′əl), **Alexis.** 1873–1944. French surgeon and biologist in America (1905–39); discovered a method of suturing blood vessels.

car·riage (kăr′ĭj; kăr′ē-ĭj *for sense 6b*) *n.* **1.** A four-wheeled, horse-drawn passenger vehicle, often of an elegant design. **2.** *British.* A railroad car for passengers. **3.** A perambulator; baby carriage. **4.** A wheeled support or frame for moving a heavy object, such as a cannon. **5.** A moving part of a machine for holding or shifting another part. **6. a.** The act or process of transporting or carrying. **b.** The cost of or charge for transporting. **7.** The manner of holding and moving one's head and body; posture. **8.** *Archaic.* The manner of executing or carrying out; management; administration. —See Synonyms at **bearing.** [Middle English *cariage,* from Old North French, from *carier,* to transport in a vehicle, CARRY.]

carriage dog. The **Dalmatian** *(see).*

carriage trade. Wealthy patrons, as of a restaurant or theater.

car·rick bend (kăr′ĭk). *Nautical.* A type of knot used to fasten two cables or hawsers together. [From obsolete *carrick,* carrack, from Middle English *caryk,* CARRACK.]

carrick bitt. *Nautical.* Either of the two posts that support the windlass on a ship's deck. [Probably from obsolete *carrick.* See **carrick bend.**]

car·ri·er (kăr′ē-ər) *n.* **1.** One that transports or conveys. **2.** One that deals in transporting passengers or goods. **3.** A mechanism or device by which something is conveyed or conducted. **4.** *Medicine.* A person or animal at least temporarily immune to a pathogen that it transmits directly or indirectly to others; vector. **5.** *Electronics.* **a.** A **carrier wave** *(see).* **b.** A charge-carrying entity, especially an electron or a hole in a semiconductor. **6.** An **aircraft carrier** *(see).*

Car·ri·er (kăr′ē-ər), **Willis Haviland.** 1876–1950. American engineer; inventor of air conditioning.

carrier pigeon. A **homing pigeon** *(see),* especially one trained to carry messages.

carrier wave. An electromagnetic wave that can be modulated in frequency, amplitude, phase, or otherwise to transmit speech, music, images, or other signals.

car·ri·ole. Variant of **cariole.**

car·ri·on (kăr′ē-ən) *n.* Dead and decaying flesh. —*adj.* **1.** Of or similar to carrion. **2.** Carrion-eating. [Middle English *carion, caroine,* from Norman French *caroine,* from Vulgar Latin *carōnia* (unattested), from Latin *carō* (stem *carn-*), flesh. See **sker-**[1] in Appendix.*]

carrion crow. A European crow, *Corvus corone.*

carrion flower. 1. A climbing vine, *Smilax herbacea,* of eastern North America, having clusters of small, greenish flowers with an odor of decaying flesh. **2.** Any of several other plants having flowers with an unpleasant odor.

Car·roll (kăr′əl), **Charles.** Known as Carroll of Carrollton. 1737–1832. American Revolutionary leader.

Car·roll (kăr′əl), **Lewis.** Pen name of Charles Lutwidge Dodgson. 1832–1898. English author and mathematician; creator of *Alice in Wonderland.*

car·rom. Variant of **carom.**

car·ro·nade (kăr′ə-nād′) *n.* A short, large-caliber cannon, formerly used for firing at close range. [From the *Carron* iron works, Carron, Scotland.]

car·ron oil (kăr′ən). *Medicine.* A mixture of limewater and oil, used for treating burns. [After the *Carron* iron works, Scotland, from its use in treating the burns of workers there.]

car·rot (kăr′ət) *n.* **1.** A widely cultivated plant, *Daucus carota sativa,* having finely divided leaves, flat clusters of small white flowers, and an edible, yellow-orange root. **2.** The long, tapering root of this plant, eaten as a vegetable. [Old French *carotte,* from Latin *carōta,* from Greek *karōton.* See **ker-**[1] in Appendix.*]

car·ro·tin, car·ro·tene. Variants of **carotene.**

car·rot·y (kăr′ət-ē) *adj.* **1.** Similar to a carrot, especially in color. **2.** Having carrot-colored hair.

car·rou·sel. Variant of **carousel.**

car·ry (kăr′ē) *v.* **-ried, -rying, -ries.** —*tr.* **1.** To bear or convey from one place to another; transport: *carry mail.* **2.** To make known, take, bring, or communicate (a message, for example). **3.** To serve as a means for the conveyance or transmission of; transmit. **4.** To hold or bear while moving. **5.** To hold or be capable of holding. **6.** To support or sustain the responsibility of. **7.** To keep or have on one's person. **8.** To be pregnant with. **9. a.** To hold and move (the body or a part of it) in a particular way. **b.** To behave or conduct (oneself) in a specified manner. **10.** To extend or continue in a certain direction or to a given point or degree. **11.** To cause to move; drive; impel. **12.** To take or seize, especially by force; capture: *"the Turks carried the defences of Jebel Subh"* (T.E. Lawrence). **13.** To gain victory, support, or acceptance for; especially, to secure the adoption of. **14.** To win most of the votes of: *Their candidate carried New England and the Midwest.* **15.** To be successful in; win. **16.** To win over; gain the interest of: *His enthusiasm carried the audience.* **17.** To support or corroborate; give validity to (a claim, for example). **18. a.** To have as a customary or necessary attribute or accompaniment: *an appliance carrying a full-year guarantee.* **b.** To involve necessarily as a condition, consequence, effect, or the like: *The crime carried a five-year* *sentence.* **19.** To transfer from one place (as a column, page, or book) to another. **20.** To keep in stock; offer for sale: *carry a line of dresses.* **21.** To keep in one's accounts: *carry a loss over to the following year.* **22.** To place before the public, as through a mass medium: *The press conference was carried by all networks.* **23.** To produce as a crop. **24.** To support or sustain (livestock). **25.** To sing (a melody, for example) on key: *She can't carry a tune.* **26.** *Golf.* To cover (a distance). **27.** *Hunting.* To keep and follow (a scent). —*intr.* **1.** To act as a bearer: *teach a dog to fetch and carry.* **2. a.** To be transmitted or conveyed; cover a range: *a voice that carries well.* **b.** To have or exert propulsive force: *equipped with guns that carry well.* **3.** To admit of being transported in a certain manner: *Heavy loads do not carry easily.* **4.** To hold the neck and head in a certain way. Used of a horse. **5.** To be accepted or approved: *The proposal carried by a wide margin.* —See Synonyms at **convey.** —**carry away.** To move or excite greatly: *carried away by desire.* —**carry forward. 1.** To progress with: *carry forward the program.* **2.** *Accounting.* To transfer (an entry) to the next column, page, book, or to another account. —**carry off. 1.** To cause the death of: *carried off by a fever.* **2.** To handle (a situation, for example) successfully. **3.** To win, as a prize, award, or honor. **4.** To seize and run away with; abduct. **5.** To face with courage; brave out. —**carry on. 1.** To conduct; administer: *carry on the affairs of state.* **2.** To engage in: *carry on a love affair.* **3.** To continue without halting: *carry on in the face of disaster.* **4.** To behave in an excited, improper, or silly manner; act hysterically or childishly. —**carry out. 1.** To put into practice or effect: *carry out a plan.* **2.** To follow or obey: *carry out instructions.* **3.** To bring to a conclusion; accomplish. —**carry through. 1.** To accomplish; complete. **2.** To enable to endure; sustain: *Fortitude carried him through the ordeal.* —*n., pl.* **carries. 1.** The act or process of carrying. **2.** A portage, as between two navigable rivers or other bodies of water. **3. a.** The range of a gun or projectile. **b.** The distance traveled by a golf ball. [Middle English *carien,* from Old North French *carier,* to transport in a vehicle, from *car(re),* vehicle, from Latin *carrus.* See **kers-²** in Appendix.*]

car·ry·all (kăr'ē-ôl') *n.* **1. a.** A covered one-horse carriage with two seats. **b.** A closed automobile with two lengthwise seats facing each other. **2.** A large bag, basket, or pocketbook.

carrying charge. The interest charged on the balance owed when paying in installments.

carry over. 1. *Accounting.* To transfer (an entry) to another column, page, book, or account. **2.** To continue at another time; put off: *carry over a problem until the next meeting.*

car·ry·o·ver (kăr'ē-ō'vər) *n.* **1.** A part or quantity, as of goods or commodities, left over or held for future use. **2.** *Accounting.* A sum transferred to a new column, page, book, or account.

Car·shal·ton (kər-shôl'tən). A former administrative division of London, England, now part of **Sutton** (*see*).

car·sick (kär'sĭk') *adj.* Nauseated by vehicular motion.

Car·son (kär'sən), **Christopher** ("**Kit**"). 1809–1868. American frontiersman, trapper, Indian agent, and guide.

Car·son City (kär'sən). The capital of Nevada, situated in the southwestern part of the state. Population, 5,200.

Car·stensz, Mount (kär'stənz). A mountain, 16,400 feet high, in the Snow Mountains of West Irian.

cart (kärt) *n.* **1.** A two-wheeled vehicle drawn by a horse or other animal and used for transporting goods. **2.** An open two-wheeled business or pleasure carriage, such as a village cart or dog cart. **3.** Any small, light vehicle moved by hand, such as a grocery cart or golf cart. —*v.* **carted, carting, carts.** —*tr.* **1. a.** To convey in a cart. **b.** To convey laboriously, as in a cart; lug. **2.** To remove or transport (a person or thing) in an unceremonious manner or by force. Used with *away* or *off: He was carted off to jail.* —*intr.* To use carts as a means of removing or transporting goods. [Middle English *carte, cart,* partly from Old English *cræt,* partly from Old Norse *kartr.* See **ger-³** in Appendix.*] —**cart'a·ble** *adj.* —**cart'er** *n.*

cart·age (kär'tĭj) *n. Abbr.* **ctge. 1.** The act or process of transporting by cart. **2.** The cost of transporting by cart.

Car·ta·ge·na (kär'tə-gā'nə; *Spanish* kär'tä-hā'nä). **1.** A seaport of northwestern Colombia, on the Caribbean coast. Population, 198,000. **2.** A seaport of southeastern Spain, on the Mediterranean. Population, 131,000.

Carte (kärt), **Richard D'Oyly**. 1844–1901. British theatrical producer; associated with W.S. Gilbert and Arthur Sullivan.

carte blanche (kärt blänsh') *pl.* **cartes blanches.** Unrestricted power to act at one's own discretion; full permission; unconditional authority. [French, "blank card."]

car·tel (kär-tĕl') *n.* **1.** A combination of independent business organizations formed to regulate production, pricing, and marketing of goods by the members. **2.** An official agreement between governments at war, especially concerning the exchange of prisoners. **3.** In some European countries, a political group united in a common cause; a bloc. —See Synonyms at **monopoly.** [Old French, from Old Italian *cartello,* letter of defiance, placard, from *carta,* card, from Latin *charta,* leaf of papyrus. See **card.**]

Car·ter·et (kär'tə-rĕt'), **John.** First Earl Granville. 1690–1763. British statesman and diplomat; adviser to George II.

Car·te·sian (kär-tē'zhən) *adj.* Of or pertaining to the philosophy or methods of Descartes. —**Car·te'sian·ism'** *n.*

Cartesian coordinate. A coordinate in a Cartesian coordinate system.

Cartesian coordinate system. 1. A two-dimensional coordinate system in which the coordinates of a point are its distances from two intersecting, often perpendicular, straight lines, the distance from each being measured along a straight line parallel to the other. **2.** A three-dimensional coordinate system in which the coordinates of a point are its distances from each of three intersecting, often mutually perpendicular, planes along lines parallel to the intersection of the other two.

Car·thage (kär'thĭj). *Latin* **Car·tha·go** (kär-tä'gō). An ancient city and state on the northern coast of Africa, nine miles northeast of modern Tunis. It was the seat of a sea power dominant in the western Mediterranean until its defeat by Rome in the second century B.C.

Car·tha·gin·i·an (kär'thə-jĭn'ē-ən) *adj.* Of or pertaining to Carthage or its language or culture. —*n.* **1.** A native of Carthage. **2.** Phoenician, as spoken by the Carthaginians.

Carthaginian Wars. The Punic Wars (*see*).

Car·thu·sian (kär-thōō'zhən) *n. Roman Catholic Church.* A member of a contemplative order founded during the 11th century in Chartreuse, France, by St. Bruno. —*adj.* Of or pertaining to the Carthusian order.

Car·tier (kár-tyā'), Sir **George Étienne.** 1814–1873. Canadian statesman and industrialist.

Car·tier (kár-tyā'), **Jacques.** 1491–1557. French explorer; claimed the St. Lawrence River valley for France (1534).

Car·tier-Bres·son (kár-tyā'brĕs-sôN'), **Henri.** Born 1908. French photographer.

car·ti·lage (kär'tə-lĭj) *n.* A tough white fibrous connective tissue attached to the articular surfaces of bones, a major constituent of the fetal and young vertebrate skeleton that is largely converted to bone with maturation. Also called "gristle." [Latin *cartilāgo.*]

cartilage bone. A bone developed from cartilage. Compare **membrane bone.**

car·ti·lag·i·nous (kär'tə-lăj'ə-nəs) *adj.* **1.** Of or pertaining to cartilage. **2.** Having a skeleton consisting mainly of cartilage.

car·to·gram (kär'tə-grăm') *n.* A presentation of statistical data in geographical distribution using lines, dots, and the like on a map. [French *cartogramme* : *carte,* map, *CARD* + -*GRAM.*]

car·tog·ra·phy (kär-tŏg'rə-fē) *n. Abbr.* **cartog.** The art or technique of making maps or charts. [French *cartographie* : *carte,* map, *CARD* + -*GRAPHY.*] —**car·tog'ra·pher** *n.* —**car'to·graph'ic** (kär'tə-grăf'ĭk), **car'to·graph'i·cal** *adj.*

car·ton (kärt'n) *n.* **1.** *Abbr.* **C., c., ctn.** A cardboard box or other container, especially: **a.** A box closed by flaps on the top or on one end, used for transporting goods. **b.** A small container for liquids: *a carton of milk.* **2.** The contents of such a box or container: *a carton of cigarettes.* **3.** In riflery: **a.** A small white disk at the center of a target's bull's eye. **b.** A shot hitting such a disk. [French, from Italian *cartone,* pasteboard, augmentative of *carta,* card, from Latin *charta,* leaf of papyrus. See **card.**]

car·toon (kär-tōōn') *n.* **1.** A drawing, as in a newspaper or magazine, depicting a humorous situation, often accompanied by a caption; a pictorial joke. **2.** A pictorial satire or comment on a subject of current public interest, usually accompanied by words; a caricature. **3.** A preliminary sketch, similar in size to the fresco, mosaic, tapestry, or the like that is to be copied from it. **4.** An animated cartoon. **5.** A comic strip. —*v.* **cartooned, -tooning, -toons.** —*tr.* To sketch a humorous or satirical representation of; caricature. —*intr.* To draw satirical or humorous sketches. [Italian *cartone,* pasteboard, *CARTON.*] —**car·toon'ist** *n.*

car·touche, car·touch (kär-tōōsh') *n.* **1.** *Architecture.* A scroll-like tablet used either to provide space for an inscription or for ornamental purposes. **2.** In ancient Egyptian hieroglyphics, an oval or oblong figure that encloses characters expressing the names or epithets of royal or divine personages. **3.** A case containing the combustible materials in some varieties of fireworks. **4.** *Obsolete.* **a.** A heavy paper cartridge case. **b.** A cartridge. [French, cartridge, from Italian *cartoccio,* from *carta,* paper, card. See **carton.**]

car·tridge (kär'trĭj) *n.* **1. a.** A tubular metal or cardboard and metal case containing the propellant powder and primer of small arms ammunition or shotgun shells. **b.** Such a case loaded with shotgun pellets. **c.** Such a case fitted with a projectile, such as a bullet, for use in rifled small arms, machine guns, or the like. Also called "round." **2.** A small modular unit of equipment, especially: **a.** A removable case containing the stylus and electric conversion circuitry in a phonograph pickup. **b.** A case containing reeled magnetic tape, a pickup reel, guide and feed mechanisms, used instead of separate reels in certain tape recorders and players. **c.** A case with photographic film that can be loaded directly into a camera. **d.** A disposable or refillable ink reservoir for a pen. [From earlier *cartage,* variant of French *CARTOUCHE* (cartridge).]

cartridge belt. A belt for carrying ammunition, with loops or pockets for cartridges or clips of cartridges.

cartridge clip. A metal container or frame for holding cartridges to be loaded into an automatic rifle or pistol.

car·tu·lar·y (kär'chōō-lĕr'ē) *n., pl.* -**ies.** Also **char·tu·lar·y** (kär'-). A collection of deeds or charters, especially a register of titles to all the property of an estate or monastery. [Medieval Latin *c(h)artulārium,* from Latin *chartula,* little paper, diminutive of *charta,* leaf of papyrus. See **card.**]

cart·wheel (kärt'hwēl') *n.* **1.** The wheel of a cart. **2.** A somersault or handspring in which the body turns over sideways with the arms and legs spread like the spokes of a wheel. **3.** *Slang.* A silver dollar or other large coin.

cart·wright (kärt'rīt') *n.* An artisan who makes carts.

Cart·wright (kärt'rīt'), **Edmund.** 1743–1823. British inventor of the power loom.

car·un·cle (kär'ŭng'kəl, kə-rŭng'-) *n.* **1.** *Anatomy.* A fleshy,

cartouche
Sixteenth-century
engraved design

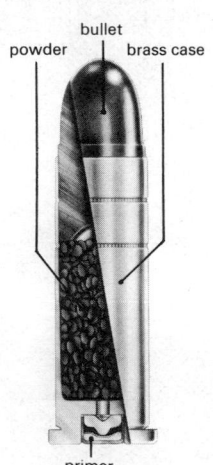

cartridge

ă pat/ā pay/âr care/ä father/b bib/ch church/d deed/ĕ pet/ē be/f fife/g gag/h hat/hw which/ĭ pit/ī pie/îr pier/j judge/k kick/l lid, needle/m mum/n no, sudden/ng thing/ŏ pot/ō toe/ô paw, for/oi noise/ou out/ōō took/ōō boot/p pop/r roar/s sauce/sh ship, dish/t tight/th thin, path/th this, bathe/ŭ cut/ûr urge/v valve/w with/y yes/z zebra, size/zh vision/ə about, item, edible, gallop, circus/ à *Fr.* ami/œ *Fr.* feu, *Ger.* schön/ü *Fr.* tu, *Ger.* über/KH *Ger.* ich, *Scot.* loch/N *Fr.* bon. *Follows main vocabulary. †Of obscure origin.

naked outgrowth, such as a fowl's wattles. **2.** *Botany.* An excrescence on a seed at or near the hilum. [Obsolete French *caruncule,* from Latin *caruncula,* diminutive of *carō* (stem *carn-*), flesh. See **sker-**[1] in Appendix.*] —**ca·run'cu·lar** *adj.* —**ca·run'cu·late', ca·run'cu·lat'ed, ca·run'cu·lous** *adj.*

Ca·ru·so (kə-rōō'sō), **Enrico.** 1873–1921. Italian operatic tenor.

carve (kärv) *v.* **carved** or *archaic* **carven** (kär'vən), **carving, carves.** —*tr.* **1. a.** To divide into pieces by cutting; slice: *carve a fowl.* **b.** To divide by parceling out. Used with *up: carve up an estate.* **2.** To cut with a sharp instrument; cleave. **3.** To cut (something) into a desired shape; fashion by cutting: *carve the wood into a figure.* **4.** To produce or form by cutting: *carve initials in the bark.* **5.** To decorate by carving. **6.** To furrow or mark as with carving: *"A million wrinkles carved his skin."* (Tennyson). —*intr.* **1.** To engrave or cut figures as a hobby or trade. **2.** To disjoint, slice, and serve meat or poultry. —**carve out. 1.** To make or form by carving; cut out: *"The bright share carved out the furrow clean."* (William Morris). **2.** To achieve by exertion or ability: *carve out a career.* —*n.* An act or stroke of slicing or carving. [Middle English *kerven, carven,* Old English *ceorfan.* See **gerebh-** in Appendix.*] —**carv'er** *n.*

car·vel. Variant of **caravel.**

car·vel-built (kär'vəl-bĭlt', kär'vĕl'-) *adj.* Designating a boat or ship built with the hull planks lying flush or edge to edge, rather than overlapping. Compare **clinker-built.**

carvel joint. A joining of a ship's planks so that they lie edge to edge; flush joint.

Car·ver (kär'vər), **George Washington.** 1864?–1943. American agricultural chemist and educator.

Car·ver (kär'vər), **John.** 1576?–1621. English Pilgrim colonist in America; first governor of Plymouth Colony (1620–21).

carv·ing (kär'vĭng) *n.* **1.** Cutting of wood, stone, or other material to form a figure or design. **2.** The figure or design so formed.

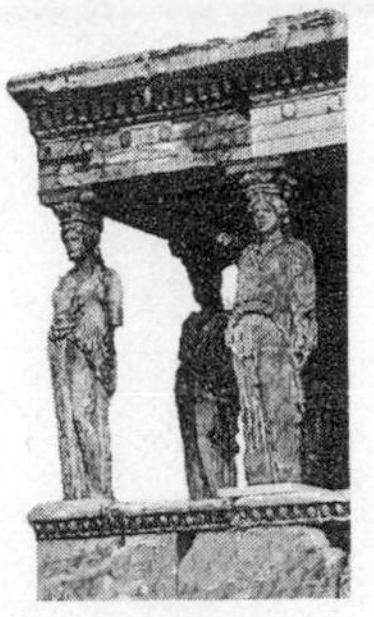

caryatid
Section of the porch of the Erechtheum on the Acropolis at Athens

car·y·at·id (kăr'ē-ăt'ĭd) *n., pl.* **-ids** or **-atides** (-ăt'ə-dēz'). *Architecture.* A supporting column sculptured in the form of a woman. Compare **telamon.** [Latin *Caryātidēs* (plural), from Greek *Karuatidēs,* caryatids, priestesses of Artemis at *Karuai,* village in Laconia.] —**car'y·at'i·dal** (-ăt'ə-dəl), **car'y·at'i·de'an** (-ăt'ə-dē'ən), **car'y·a·tid'ic** (-ə-tĭd'ĭk) *adj.*

caryo-. Variant of **karyo-.**

car·y·op·sis (kăr'ē-ŏp'sĭs) *n., pl.* **-opses** (-ŏp'sēz') or **-opsides** (-ŏp'sə-dēz'). *Botany.* A one-celled, one-seeded dry fruit having its outer coat fused to its surface, as a grain of barley or wheat. [New Latin : CARY(O)- + -OPSIS.]

ca·sa·ba (kə-sä'bə) *n.* Also **cas·sa·ba.** A variety of **winter melon** *(see)* having a yellow rind and sweet, whitish flesh. [From *kassaba,* former name of Turgutlu, Turkey.]

Cas·a·blan·ca (kăs'ə-blăng'kə, kä'sə-bläng'kə). *Arabic* **Dar-el-Bei·da** (där-ăl-bā'də). A city and major seaport of Morocco, in the northwest on the Atlantic; the site of a wartime conference (January 1943) between Prime Minister Winston Churchill and President Franklin D. Roosevelt. Population, 1,085,000.

Ca·sals (kə-sälz'), **Pablo.** Born 1876. Spanish cellist; resident in France (from 1936) and Puerto Rico (from 1956).

Cas·a·no·va (kăs'ə-nō'və, kăz'-) *n.* A romantic or promiscuous man; libertine. [After G.J. CASANOVA DE SEINGALT.]

Ca·sa·no·va de Sein·galt (kăz'ə-nō'və də săN'gál, kăs'-; *Italian* kä'zä-nô'vä də săn'gál), **Giovanni Jacopo.** Known as Casanova. 1725–1798. Italian amorous adventurer.

ca·sa·va. Variant of **cassava.**

Cas·bah (kăz'bä', käz'-). Also **Kas·bah. 1.** In northern Africa, the citadel and palace of a sovereign. **2.** The native quarter in any of several cities in northern Africa, notably the city of Algiers. [French, from Arabic (north African dialect) *qaṣbah,* from Arabic *qaṣabah,* fortress.]

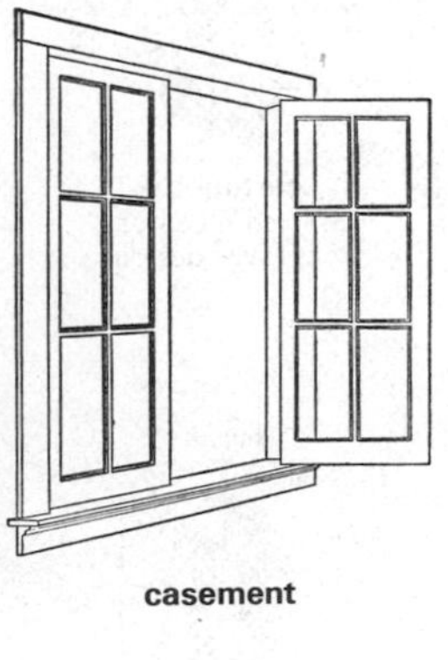

casement

cas·cade (kăs-kād') *n.* **1.** A waterfall or a series of small waterfalls over steep rocks. **2.** *Physics.* An analogous structure or phenomenon, as: **a.** A cosmic-ray shower generated by the successive alternate production of electron pairs by pair production and of photons by bremsstrahlung, continuing until the energy of each single particle is below the threshold for pair production. **b.** A process occurring in an electrical discharge in a gas by which at least one member of an ion pair is accelerated by the field to sufficiently high energy to produce another pair of ions in a collision. **3.** *Electricity.* A series of components or networks, the output of each of which serves as the input for the next. **4.** *Chemistry.* A series of compressed gases of successively lower boiling points, the expansion of which produces successively lower temperatures. —*intr.v.* **cascaded, -cading, -cades.** To fall from one level to another in a continuous series. [French, from Italian *cascata,* from *cascare,* to fall, from Vulgar Latin *casicāre* (unattested), from Latin *cadere* (past participle *cāsus*). See **kad-** in Appendix.*]

Cascade Range. The northern section of the Sierra Nevada Mountains, extending from northeastern California to western Oregon and Washington. Highest elevation, Mount Rainier (14,408 feet).

cas·car·a (kăs-kăr'ə) *n.* **1.** The cascara buckthorn. **2.** Cascara sagrada. [Spanish *cáscara,* bark, from *cascar,* to break, break off, from Vulgar Latin *quassicāre* (unattested), from Latin *quassāre,* from *quatere* (past participle *quassus*), to shake. See **kwēt-** in Appendix.*]

cascara buckthorn. A shrub or tree, *Rhamnus purshiana,* of northwestern North America, of which the bark is the source of cascara sagrada.

cascara sa·gra·da (sə-grä'də). The dried bark of the cascara buckthorn, used as a stimulant, cathartic, and laxative.

cas·ca·ril·la (kăs'kə-rĭl'ə) *n.* **1.** A shrub, *Croton eluteria,* of the West Indies, having bitter, aromatic bark. **2.** The bark of this shrub, used as a tonic. In this sense, also called "cascarilla bark." [Spanish, diminutive of *cáscara,* bark. See **cascara.**]

Cas·co Bay (kăs'kō). An Atlantic Ocean inlet in Maine.

case[1] (kās) *n.* **1.** An instance or exemplification of the existence or occurrence of something. **2. a.** An occurrence of disease or disorder. **b.** A client, as of a physician, psychiatrist, or attorney. **3.** A set of circumstances or state of affairs; the situation. **4.** A set of reasons, arguments, or supporting facts offered in justification of a statement, action, situation, or thing: *the case for socialized medicine.* **5.** A question or problem; a matter: *a case of honor.* **6.** *Law.* **a.** An action or suit, or just grounds for an action. **b.** The facts or evidence offered in support of a claim. **7.** *Informal.* A peculiar or eccentric person. **8.** *Linguistics.* **a.** The syntactic relationship of a noun, pronoun, or adjective to the other words of a sentence, indicated in inflected languages by the assumption of declensional endings, and in noninflected languages by the position of the words within the sentence. **b.** The form or position of a word that indicates this relationship. **c.** Such forms, positions, or relationships collectively. **9. a.** *Linguistics.* A pattern of inflection of nouns, pronouns, and adjectives, to express different syntactic functions in a sentence; for example, *I* and *him* are respectively in the nominative and objective cases in *I like him.* **b.** The form of such an inflected word. —See Synonyms at **example.** —**in any case.** Regardless of what occurred or will occur. —**in case.** If it happens that; if. —*tr.v.* **cased, casing, cases.** *Slang.* To examine carefully, as in planning a crime: *case the bank before robbing it.* [Middle English *cas,* an occurrence, from Old French, from Latin *cāsus,* fall, event, occurrence, from the past participle of *cadere,* to fall. See **kad-** in Appendix.*]

case[2] (kās) *n.* **1.** A container or receptacle. **2.** A decorative or protective covering or cover. **3.** *Abbr.* **C., c., cs.** A box with its contents. **4.** A set or pair, as of pistols. **5.** The frame or framework of a window, door, or stairway. **6.** *Printing.* A shallow, compartmented tray for storing type or type matrices. —*tr.v.* **cased, casing, cases.** To put into, cover, or protect with a case. [Middle English, from Old North French *casse,* from Latin *capsa,* chest, case. See **kap-** in Appendix.*]

ca·se·ate (kā'sē-āt') *intr.v.* **-ated, -ating, -ates.** To undergo caseation. [From Latin *cāseus,* CHEESE.]

ca·se·a·tion (kā'sē-ā'shən) *n.* The necrotic degeneration of bodily tissue into a cheeselike substance. [From CASEATE.]

case·hard·en (kās'härd'n) *tr.v.* **-ened, -ening, -ens. 1.** To harden the surface of (iron or steel) by high-temperature shallow infusion of carbon followed by quenching. **2.** To harden the spirit or emotions; make callous. [From CASE (covering).]

case history. An organized set of facts relevant to the development of an individual or group condition under study or treatment, especially in sociology, psychiatry, or medicine.

ca·se·in (kā'sē-ĭn, kā'sēn') *n.* A white, tasteless, odorless milk and cheese protein, used to make plastics, adhesives, paints, and foods. [Probably French *caséine* : Latin *cāseus,* CHEESE + -IN.]

case knife. 1. A knife kept in a sheath or case. **2.** A table knife.

case law. Law based on judicial decision and precedent rather than statute.

case·mate (kās'māt') *n. Military.* **1.** On a warship, a fortified enclosure for artillery. **2.** On a rampart, an armored compartment for artillery. [Old French, from Italian *casamatta,* perhaps from Greek *khasmata,* plural of *khasma,* gap, CHASM.] —**case'mat'ed** *adj.*

case·ment (kās'mənt) *n.* **1.** A window sash that opens outward by means of hinges. **2.** A window with such sashes. **3.** A case or covering. [Middle English *casement*†.] —**case'ment·ed** *adj.*

Case·ment (kās'mənt), Sir **Roger David.** 1864–1916. British diplomat and Irish nationalist; executed for treason.

ca·se·ous (kā'sē-əs) *adj.* Resembling cheese. [From Latin *cāseus,* CHEESE.]

ca·sern (kə-zûrn') *n.* Also **ca·serne.** A military barracks. [French *caserne,* from Old French, small room for the night watch, from Old Provençal *cazerna,* group of four persons, from Vulgar Latin *quaderna* (unattested), from Latin *quaterni,* four each, from *quater,* four times. See **kwetwer-** in Appendix.*]

Ca·ser·ta (kä-zĕr'tä). A city of Italy, 16 miles northeast of Naples; the Mediterranean headquarters of the Allies during World War II and site of the surrender of the German forces in Italy and Yugoslavia (April 29, 1945). Population, 50,000.

case shot. 1. A **canister** *(see).* **2.** The shot in a canister. **3.** A shrapnel shell.

case study. A detailed analysis of an individual or group, especially as an exemplary model of medical, psychological, or social phenomena.

case·work (kās'wûrk') *n.* The part of a social worker's duties dealing with the problems of a particular case.

case·worm (kās'wûrm') *n.* An insect larva, such as a caddis fly, that constructs a protective case around its body.

cash[1] (kăsh) *n.* **1.** Ready money; currency or coins. **2.** Payment for goods or services in money or by check. —*tr.v.* **cashed, cashing, cashes.** To exchange for or convert into ready money: *cash a check.* —**cash in. 1.** To convert to ready money. **2.** *Slang.* To die. —**cash in on.** To take advantage of. [Old French *casse,* money box, CASE (box).]

cash[2] (kăsh) *n., pl.* **cash.** Any of various Oriental coins of small denomination; especially, a copper and lead coin with a square hole in its center. [Portuguese *caixa,* from Tamil *kācu,* a small copper coin, from Sanskrit *karṣa*†, a certain weight.]

ca·shaw. Variant of **cushaw.**

cash·book (kăsh'bŏŏk') *n.* A book in which a record of cash receipts and expenditures is kept.

cash crop. A crop grown especially for sale, and that usually provides an important source of income.
cash discount. *Abbr.* **c.d.** A reduction in the price of an item for sale allowed if payment is made within a stipulated period.
cash·ew (kăsh′ōō, kə-shōō′) *n.* **1.** A tropical American evergreen tree, *Anacardium occidentale,* bearing kidney-shaped nuts that protrude from a fleshy receptacle. **2.** The nut of this tree, edible only when roasted. In this sense, also called "cashew nut." [Portuguese *cajú, acajú,* from Tupi *acajú.*]
cash·ier¹ (kă-shîr′) *n.* **1.** The officer of a bank or business concern in charge of paying and receiving money. **2.** An employee whose major function is to handle cash transactions for any of various business operations, such as a restaurant or supermarket. [Dutch *cassier,* from French *caissier,* from *caisse,* money box, from Old French *casse,* CASE (box).]
cash·ier² (kă-shîr′) *tr.v.* **-iered, -iering, -iers.** To dismiss from a position of command or responsibility, especially for disciplinary reasons. [Dutch *casseren,* from Old French *casser,* to discharge, annul, from Latin *quassāre,* to shake, break in pieces, from *quassus,* past participle of *quatere,* to shake. See **kwēt-** in Appendix.*]
cashier's check. A check drawn by a bank on its own funds and signed by the bank's cashier.
cash·mere (kăzh′mîr′, kăsh′-) *n.* Also **kash·mir. 1.** Fine, downy wool growing beneath the outer hair of the Cashmere goat. **2.** A soft fabric made of wool from this goat, or from similar fibers. [From KASHMIR.]
Cash·mere. Variant of **Kashmir.**
Cashmere goat. Also **Kashmir goat.** A goat native to the Himalayan regions of India and Tibet, prized for its wool.
cash register. A machine having a series of numbered levers for tabulating the amount of sales transactions, a space for showing their amount, a paper tape for making a permanent and cumulative record of them, and a drawer or drawers in which cash may be kept.
cas·i·mere. Variant of **cassimere.**
cas·ing (kā′sĭng) *n.* **1.** The act of encasing. **2.** A case; an outer cover. **3.** The cleaned intestines of cattle, sheep, or hogs for wrapping sausage meat. **4.** The frame or framework for a window or door. **5.** A metal pipe or tube used as a lining for water, oil, or gas wells.
ca·si·no (kə-sē′nō) *n., pl.* **-nos. 1.** A summer or country house in Italy. **2.** A public room or house for entertainment, especially for gambling. **3.** Variant of **cassino.** [Italian, diminutive of *casa,* house, from Latin *casa*†, hut, cottage.]
cask (kăsk, käsk) *n. Abbr.* **ck., csk. 1.** A barrel of any size. **2.** The quantity contained in a barrel. [Spanish *casco,* helmet, cask, perhaps from *cascar,* to crack, break, from Vulgar Latin *quassicāre* (unattested), to shake, break, from Latin *quassāre.* See **cashier** (to dismiss).]
cas·ket (kăs′kĭt, käs′-) *n.* **1.** A small case or chest for jewels or other valuables. **2.** A coffin. *—tr.v.* **casketed, -keting, -kets.** To enclose in a casket. [Middle English, from Old French *cassette.* See **cassette.**]
Cas·lon (kăz′lən) *n. Printing.* A style of type designed by the English type founder William Caslon (1692–1766).
Cas·par (kăs′pər). Also **Gas·par** (găs-pär′). One of the three Magi who came to the infant Jesus. See **Balthasar, Melchior.**
Cas·par Milque·toast (kăs′pər mĭlk′tōst′). See **milquetoast.**
Cas·pi·an Sea (kăs′pē-ən). The largest inland body of water in the world (153,000 square miles), often classified as a salt lake, extending from the Kazakh S.S.R. into northern Iran.
casque (kăsk) *n.* **1.** A helmet or other armor for the head. **2.** *Zoology.* A helmetlike structure or protuberance. [French, from Spanish *casco,* CASK.] **—casqued** (kăskt) *adj.*
Cass (kăs), **Lewis.** 1782–1866. American diplomat, political leader, and governor of Michigan Territory (1813–31).
cas·sa·ba. Variant of **casaba.**
Cas·san·dra¹ (kə-săn′drə). A daughter of Priam, King of Troy, endowed with the gift of prophecy but fated by Apollo never to be believed.
Cas·san·dra² (kə-săn′drə) *n.* Anyone who utters unheeded prophecies. [From CASSANDRA.]
cas·sa·reep (kăs′ə-rēp′) *n.* The boiled juice of the cassava root, used as a condiment. [Earlier *casserepo,* of Cariban origin.]
cas·sa·tion (kă-sā′shən) *n.* Abrogation; annulment. [Middle English *cassacioun,* from Old French *cassation,* from *casser,* to annul. See **cashier** (dismiss).]
Cas·satt (kə-săt′), **Mary.** 1845–1926. American impressionist painter.
cas·sa·va (kə-sä′və) *n.* Also **ca·sa·va. 1.** Any of various tropical American plants of the genus *Manihot;* especially, *M. esculenta* (or *M. utilissima*), having a large, starchy root. Also called "manioc." **2.** A starch derived from the root of this plant, used to make tapioca and as a staple food in the tropics. [Spanish *cazabe,* cassava bread, from Taino *caçábi.*]
Cas·se·grain·i·an telescope (kăs′ə-grā′nē-ən). A reflecting telescope in which a concave primary mirror reflects incident light to a convex secondary mirror that in turn reflects the light back through a central perforation in the primary and onto the focal plane. [Invented by N. *Cassegrain,* 17th-century French physician and inventor.]
Cas·sel. See **Kassel.**
cas·se·role (kăs′ə-rōl′) *n.* **1.** A dish, usually of earthenware, glass, or cast iron, in which food is both baked and served. **2.** Food prepared and served in such a dish. **3.** *Chemistry.* A small-handled, deep porcelain crucible used for heating and evaporating. [French, saucepan, from Old French, from *casse,* ladle, dripping pan, from Old Provençal *cassa,* from Medieval Latin *cattia,* dipper, from Greek *kuathion,* small ladle, diminutive of *kuathos*†, ladle.]
cas·sette (kă-sĕt′) *n.* **1.** A light proof camera cartridge, usually metal, for daylight loading of photographic film. **2.** A **tape cartridge** *(see).* [French, small box, from Old French, diminutive of *casse,* CASE (box).]
cas·sia (kăsh′ə) *n.* **1.** Any of various chiefly tropical trees, shrubs, and plants of the genus *Cassia,* having compound leaves, usually yellow flowers, and long pods. See **senna. 2.** A tree, *Cinnamomum cassia,* of tropical Asia, having bark similar to cinnamon but of inferior quality. **3.** The bark of this tree, used as a spice. [Middle English *cassia,* Old English *cassia,* from Latin *cas(s)ia,* a kind of plant, from Greek *kas(s)ia,* from Semitic, akin to Akkadian *kasia.*]
cas·si·mere (kăz′ə-mîr′, kăs′-) *n.* Also **cas·i·mere.** A plain or twilled woolen cloth for men's apparel. [From *Cassimere,* variant of KASHMIR.]
Cas·si·ni (*Italian* käs-sē′nē; *French* kȧ-sē-nē′), **Giovanni Domenico** or **Jean Dominique.** 1625–1712. Italian-born French astronomer; studied parallax of sun.
cas·si·no (kə-sē′nō) *n.* Also **ca·si·no.** A card game for two to four players in which cards on the table are matched by cards in the hand. [From CASINO.]
Cas·si·o·do·rus (kăs′ē-ə-dôr′əs, -dōr′əs), **Flavius Magnus Aurelius.** Roman statesman and historian of sixth century A.D.
Cas·si·o·pe·ia (kăs′ē-ə-pē′ə) *n.* A W-shaped constellation in the Northern Hemisphere near Camelopardalis and Cepheus.
Cas·si·rer (kä-sē′rər), **Ernst.** 1874–1945. German philosopher.
cas·sis (kä-sēs′) *n.* **1.** A European bush, *Ribes nigrum,* that bears black currants. **2.** A cordial made from the berries of this bush. [French, from Latin *cassia,* CASSIA.]
cas·sit·e·rite (kə-sĭt′ə-rīt′) *n.* A light-yellow, red-brown, or black mineral, SnO_2, an important tin ore. Also called "tinstone." [French *casiterite,* from Greek *kassiteros,* tin, from Elamite *kassi-ti-ra,* "coming from the land of the Kassi," an Elamite people.]
Cas·sius Lon·gi·nus (kăsh′əs lŏn-jī′nəs), **Gaius.** Died 42 B.C. Roman general and conspirator.
cas·sock (kăs′ək) *n.* A long garment, usually black, reaching to the feet and worn by clergymen and others assisting in church services. [Old French *casaque,* from Persian *kazagand*†, padded jacket.]
cas·so·war·y (kăs′ə-wĕr′ē) *n., pl.* **-ies.** Any of several large, flightless birds of the genus *Casuarius,* of New Guinea and adjacent areas, having a large, bony projection on the top of the head and brightly colored wattles. [Malay *kĕsuari.*]
cast (kăst, käst) *v.* **cast, casting, casts.** *—tr.* **1.** To throw with violence or force; hurl; toss; fling. **2.** To throw off or away; lose. **3.** To shed; to molt. **4.** To throw forth; to drop. **5. a.** To throw down; throw on the ground. **b.** *Archaic.* To overthrow; to defeat, as in wrestling. **6.** To put or place, especially with haste or violence. **7.** To throw aside; dismiss; discard; get rid of. **8.** To deposit or give (a ballot). **9.** To turn or direct. **10.** To cause to fall upon or over something or in a certain direction, as if by throwing. **11.** *Archaic.* To bestow; confer. Used with *upon: "The government I cast upon my brother"* (Shakespeare). **12. a.** To draw (lots). **b.** To throw (dice). **13.** To give birth to or bear prematurely: *The cow cast a calf.* **14.** *Hunting.* To cause (hounds) to scatter and circle in search of a lost scent. **15. a.** To choose actors for (a play or movie). **b.** To assign a certain role to (an actor). **c.** To assign an actor to (a part). **16.** To form (liquid metal or plaster) into a particular shape by pouring into a mold. **17.** To arrange in some system. **18.** To contrive; devise. **19.** To calculate or compute; add up (a column of figures). **20.** To calculate astrologically; to forecast. **21.** To warp; twist. **22.** *Obsolete.* To consider; ponder: *"I'll do it with ease, I have cast it all"* (Jonson). **23.** *Printing.* To stereotype or electroplate. **24.** *Nautical.* To turn (a ship); change to the opposite tack. *—intr.* **1.** To throw; especially, to throw out a lure or bait at the end of a fishing line. **2. a.** To add a column of figures; make calculations. **b.** To calculate horoscopes, tides, or the like. **c.** To conjecture or forecast. **3.** To receive form or shape in a mold. **4.** To search for a lost scent in hunting with hounds. **5.** *Nautical.* **a.** To veer to leeward from a former course; fall off. **b.** To put about; tack. **6.** To choose the actors for a play, movie, or the like. **7.** *Obsolete.* To turn or revolve something in the mind; ponder; scheme. —See Synonyms at **throw. —cast about. 1.** To search or look for. **2.** To devise means; contrive; scheme. **—cast aside.** To discard or reject as useless. **—cast back. 1.** To refer to something past. **2.** To show resemblance to a remote ancestor. **—cast down. 1.** To bend and turn downward; lower the eyes or head. **2.** To make sad; discourage. **—cast in one's lot with.** To share the fate or fortune of someone. **—cast on.** To make the first row of stitches in knitting. **—cast one's ballot.** To vote. **—cast out.** To drive out by force; expel. **—cast up. 1.** To vomit; eject. **2.** To add up; calculate. **3.** To turn upward; raise suddenly the eyes or head. *—n.* **1. a.** The act of casting or throwing. **b.** The distance thrown. **2. a.** The throwing of a fishing line or net into the water. **b.** The line or net thrown. **c.** *British.* The leader with flies or baited hooks attached. **3. a.** A throw of dice. **b.** The number thrown. **c.** A stroke of fortune or fate; lot. **4. a.** *Obsolete.* A turning of the eye in any direction; a glance or look. **b.** A permanent twist or turn, especially to one side. **5.** A quantity or thing thrown off, out, or away, as the mass of waste and earth excreted by an earthworm, the skin shed by an insect, or a mass of feathers, bones, and other matter ejected from the crop of an owl. **6. a.** The addition of a column of figures; a calculation. **b.** A conjecture or forecast. **7. a.** The act of casting or

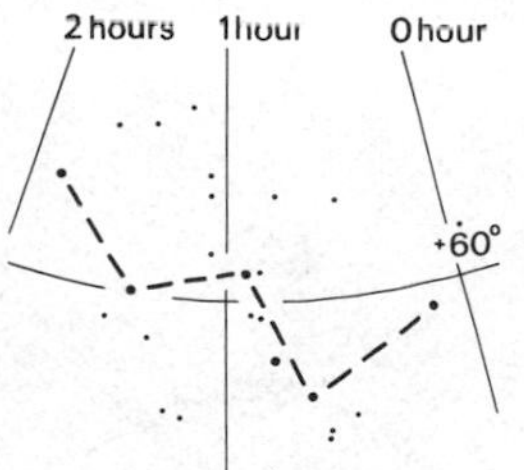

Cassiopeia

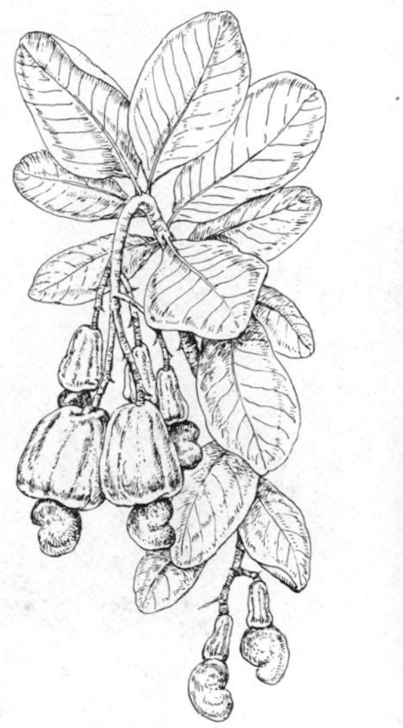
cashew

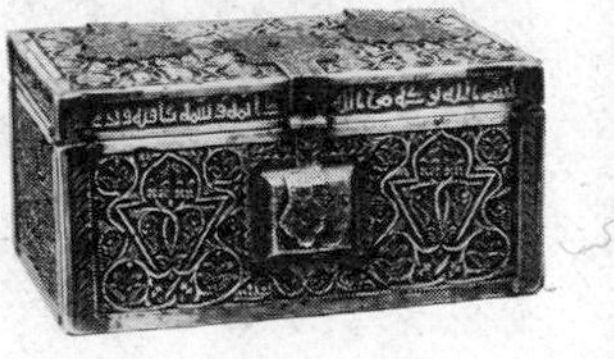
casket
Moorish ivory casket

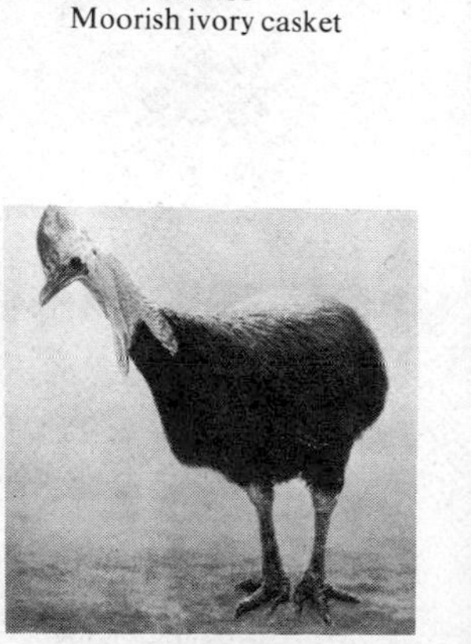
cassowary
Casuarius casuarius

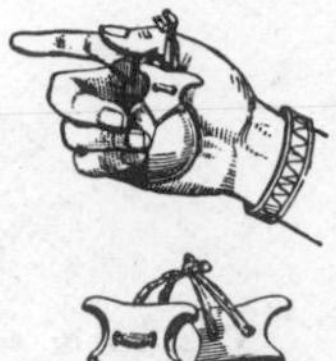

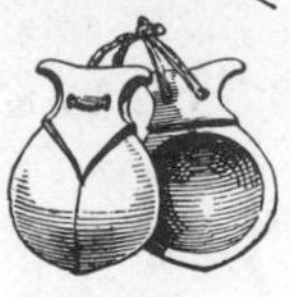

castanets

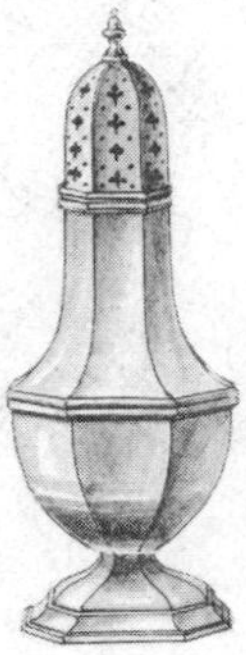

caster

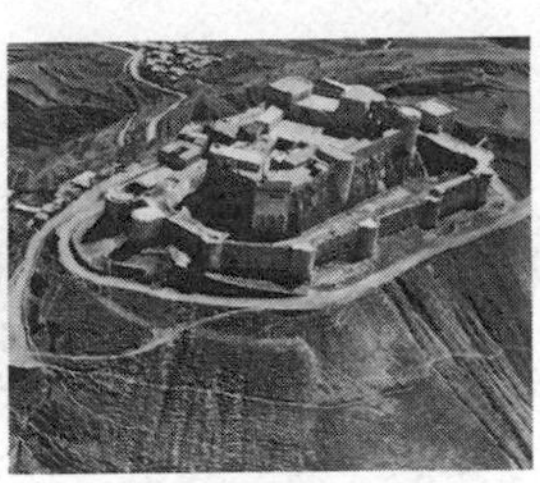

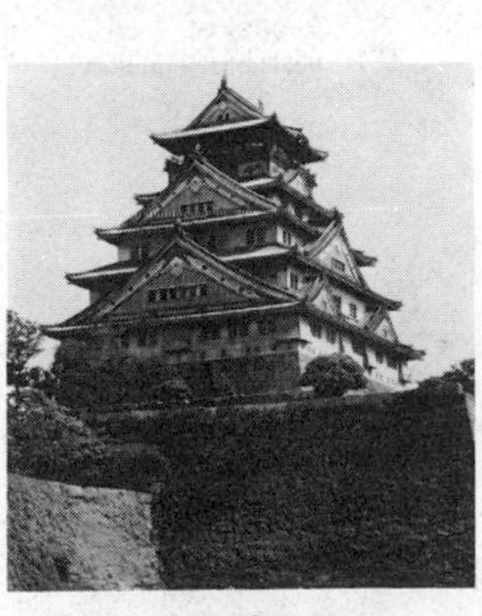

castle
Above: Eleventh-century castle built by the Knights Hospitalers at Kerak, Jordan
Below: Sixteenth-century castle built by warlord Toyotomu Hideyoshi at Osaka, Japan

founding. **b.** The amount of molten material poured into a mold at a single operation. **c.** Something formed by this means. **8. a.** An impression formed in a mold or matrix; a mold: *a cast of his face made in plaster.* **b.** *Geology.* A mineral substance that fills a hole in place of an object, such as a shell, that has been dissolved out of a rock or earth mass. **9.** The form in which something is made or constructed; arrangement; disposition. **10.** The actors in a play, movie, or the like: *a very strong cast.* **11.** *Surgery.* A rigid dressing, usually made of gauze and plaster of Paris, for immobilizing a broken bone, an arthritic joint, or part or all of the spine. Also called "plaster cast." **12.** A slight trace of color. **13.** Outward form or look; appearance. **14.** Sort; type; kind. **15.** Inclination; tendency. **16.** A distortion of shape. **17.** A pair of hawks released by a falconer at one time. **18.** *Hunting.* The circling of hounds to pick up a scent. —See Synonyms at **flock.** [Middle English *casten,* to throw, from Old Norse *kasta†.*]

Cas·ta·gno (käs-tä′nyō), **Andrea del.** 1423–1457. Italian painter of the Florentine school.

cas·ta·nets (kăs′tə-nĕts′) *pl.n.* A pair of slightly concave shells of ivory or hardwood, held in the palm of the hand by a connecting cord over the thumb and clapped together with the fingers as a rhythmical accompaniment to dancing. [Spanish *castañeta,* from *castaña,* chestnut, from Latin *castanea,* CHESTNUT.]

cast away. **1.** To reject; get rid of. **2.** To throw away; squander. **3.** To shipwreck.

cast·a·way (kăst′ə-wā′, käst′-) *adj.* **1.** Shipwrecked; cast adrift or ashore. **2.** Discarded; thrown away. —*n.* **1.** A shipwrecked person. **2.** A discarded or rejected person or thing.

caste (kăst, käst) *n.* **1.** One of the four major hereditary classes into which Hindu society is divided. Each caste is distinctly separated from the others by restrictions placed upon occupation and marriage. See **Brahman, Kshatriya, Vaisya, Sudra.** **2.** Any social class separated from others by distinctions of hereditary rank, profession, or the like. **3.** A social system, or the principle of grading society, based on these distinctions. **4.** The social position or status conferred by such a system: *lose caste.* —*adj.* Of or characterized by caste: *caste distinctions.* [Portuguese *casta,* caste, race, breed, from the feminine of *casto,* pure, chaste, from Latin *castus.* See **kes-²** in Appendix.*]

cas·tel·lan (kăs′tə-lən) *n.* The governor or keeper of a castle. [Middle English *castelleyn,* from Old North French *castelain,* from Latin *castellānus,* occupant of a castle, from adjective, "of a castle," from *castellum,* CASTLE.]

cas·tel·la·ny (kăs′tə-lā′nē) *n., pl.* **-nies.** **1.** The jurisdiction of a castellan. **2.** The lands appertaining to a castle.

cas·tel·lat·ed (kăs′tə-lā′tĭd) *adj.* Furnished with turrets and battlements in the style of a castle. [Medieval Latin *castellātus,* past participle of *castellāre,* to fortify as a castle, from Latin *castellum,* CASTLE.] —**cas′tel·la′tion** *n.*

cast·er (kăs′tər, käs′-) *n.* Also **cas·tor** (except sense 1). **1.** A person or thing that casts. **2.** A small wheel on a swivel, attached under a piece of furniture or other heavy object, to make it easier to move. **3. a.** A small bottle or cruet for condiments. **b.** A stand for holding a set of these bottles.

cas·ti·gate (kăs′tə-gāt′) *tr.v.* **-gated, -gating, -gates.** **1.** To punish or chastise. **2.** To criticize severely. —See Synonyms at **punish.** [Latin *castīgāre,* to correct, punish : *castus,* pure (see **kes-²** in Appendix*) + *agere,* to do, make (see **ag-** in Appendix*).] —**cas′ti·ga′tion** *n.* —**cas′ti·ga′tor** (-gā′tər) *n.*

Cas·ti·glio·ne (käs′tē-lyō′nā), Conte **Baldassare.** 1478–1529. Italian diplomat and author of *The Courtier.*

Cas·tile (kăs-tēl′). *Spanish* **Cas·ti·lla** (kä-stē′lyä). A region and former kingdom of Spain extending from the Bay of Biscay in the north to Andalusia in the south.

Castile soap. Also **castile soap.** A fine, hard, white, odorless soap made with olive oil and sodium hydroxide.

Cas·til·ian (kăs-tĭl′yən) *n.* **1.** Originally, the dialect of Castile, now the standard form of the Spanish language as spoken in Spain. **2.** A native or inhabitant of Castile. —*adj.* Of or pertaining to Castile, its people, or their language and culture.

cast·ing (kăs′tĭng, käs′-) *n.* **1.** The act or process of making casts or molds. **2.** The throwing of a fishing line. **3.** The selection of actors or performers. **4.** That which is cast in a mold, as a metal piece. **5.** That which is cast off or out, as skin, earth excreted by worms, or the like.

casting vote. The vote of a presiding officer in an assembly or council, given to decide a question when the votes of the members are tied.

cast iron. A hard, brittle nonmalleable iron-carbon alloy containing 2.0 to 4.5 per cent carbon, 0.5 to 3 per cent silicon, and lesser amounts of sulfur, manganese, and phosphorus.

cast-i·ron (kăst′ī′ərn, käst′-) *adj.* **1.** Made of cast iron. **2.** Hard; rigid; inflexible: *a cast-iron rule.*

cast-iron plant. The **aspidistra** *(see).*

cas·tle (kăs′əl, käs′-) *n.* **1.** A fort or fortified group of buildings usually dominating the surrounding country and held by a vassal of a ruler in feudal societies, especially in medieval Europe. **2.** A former stronghold of this kind converted to residential use; mansion. **3.** The citadel of a fortified medieval town. **4.** Any building similar to or resembling a castle. **5.** Any place of privacy, security, or refuge. **6. a.** A small defensive tower on the deck of a medieval warship. Compare **forecastle.** **b.** A small tower carried on the back of an elephant in war. **7.** *Chess.* The **rook** *(see).* —*v.* **castled, -tling, -tles.** —*tr.* **1.** To place in or as if in a castle. **2.** *Chess.* To move (the king) from his own square two squares to one side and then, in the same move, bring the rook from that side to the square immediately past the new position of the king. —*intr. Chess.* To move the king and rook in this manner. [Middle English *castel,* from Old English *castel* and Old North French *castel,* both from Late Latin *castellum,* village, from Latin *castellum,* castle, diminutive of *castrum,* fortified place. See **kes-²** in Appendix.*]

cas·tled (kăs′əld, käs′-) *adj.* **1.** Having a castle or castles. **2.** Built like a castle; fortified.

Cas·tle·reagh (kăs′əl-rā, käs′-), **Viscount.** Title of Robert Stewart. Later Marquis of Londonderry. 1769–1822. British foreign secretary (1812–22).

cast off. **1.** To discard or reject. **2.** To let go; set loose. **3.** To make the last row of stitches in knitting. **4.** To estimate the space a manuscript will occupy when set into type.

cast-off (kăst′ôf′, -ŏf′, käst′-) *adj.* Discarded; rejected.

cast·off (kăst′ôf′, -ŏf′, käst′-) *n.* **1.** Someone or something that has been discarded or thrown away. **2.** *Printing.* A calculation of the amount of space a manuscript will occupy when set into type.

cas·tor¹ (kăs′tər, käs′-) *n.* **1.** An oily, brown, odorous substance obtained from glands in the groin of the beaver and used as a perfume fixative. **2.** A beaver hat. **3.** A heavy wool fabric, used especially for overcoats. [Middle English, beaver, from Latin, from Greek *kastōr,* from *Kastōr,* of CASTOR AND POLLUX.]

cas·tor². Variant of **caster.**

Cas·tor (kăs′tər, käs′-) *n.* A double star in the constellation Gemini, the brightest star in the group, approximately 46 light-years from Earth.

Cas·tor and Pol·lux (kăs′tər, käs′-; pŏl′əks). *Greek Mythology.* The twin sons of Leda and brothers of Helen and Clytemnestra, transformed by Zeus into the constellation Gemini. Also called "Dioscuri."

castor bean. **1.** The castor-oil plant. **2.** A seed of this plant. [CASTOR (OIL) + BEAN.]

castor oil. A colorless or yellowish oil extracted from castor-oil plant seeds and used as a cathartic and a fine lubricant. [Probably from a mistaken connection with the substance CASTOR.]

cas·tor-oil plant (kăs′tər-oil′, käs′-). A large plant, *Ricinus communis,* native to tropical Africa and Asia, grown for ornament and for the commercial extraction of castor oil from its poisonous seeds.

cas·trate (kăs′trāt′) *tr.v.* **-trated, -trating, -trates.** **1.** To remove the testicles of; geld. **2.** To remove the ovaries of; spay. **3.** To bowdlerize. [Latin *castrāre.* See **kes-²** in Appendix.*]

Cas·tries (kă-strē′, kăs′trēs′). The capital of the British colony of St. Lucia in the West Indies, a seaport on St. Lucia Island. Population, 4,000.

Cas·tro (kăs′trō; *Spanish* käs′trō), **Fidel.** In full, Fidel Castro Ruz. Born 1927. Cuban revolutionary; premier (since 1959).

cas·u·al (kăzh′o͞o-əl) *adj.* **1.** Occurring by chance. **2.** Unpremeditated; not planned. **3.** Informal; relaxed. **4.** Without specific purpose; aimless; unconcerned. **5.** Careless; negligent. **6.** Pertaining to or associated with accidents. —See Synonyms at **chance.** —*n.* **1.** *British.* A person who receives temporary welfare relief. **2.** A person who works at irregular intervals. **3.** *Military.* A soldier temporarily attached to a unit while awaiting permanent assignment. [Middle English *casuel,* from Old French, from Late Latin *cāsuālis,* from Latin *cāsus,* fall, chance, CASE.] —**cas′u·al·ly** *adv.* —**cas′u·al·ness** *n.*

cas·u·al·ty (kăzh′o͞o-əl-tē) *n., pl.* **-ties.** **1.** An unfortunate accident, especially one involving loss of life. **2.** One who is injured or killed in an accident. **3. a.** One injured, killed, captured, or missing in action against an enemy. **b.** *Usually plural.* Loss in numbers through injury, death, or other cause. [Middle English *casuelte,* from *casuel,* CASUAL.]

cas·u·a·ri·na (kăzh′o͞o-ə-rī′nə) *n.* Any of various trees of the genus *Casuarina,* which includes the beefwoods. [New Latin, from Malay *kĕsuari,* CASSOWARY (from the resemblance of its twigs to the drooping feathers of the cassowary).]

cas·u·ist (kăzh′o͞o-ĭst) *n.* One who determines what is right and wrong in matters of conscience or conduct. Often used disparagingly. [French *casuiste,* from Spanish *casuista,* from Latin *cāsus,* chance, CASE.]

cas·u·is·tic (kăzh′o͞o-ĭs′tĭk) *adj.* Of or pertaining to casuists or casuistry. —**cas′u·is′ti·cal·ly** *adv.*

cas·u·ist·ry (kăzh′o͞o-ĭs-trē) *n.* The determination of right and wrong in questions of conduct or conscience by the application of general principles of ethics. [From CASUIST.]

ca·sus bel·li (kā′səs bĕl′ī′, kä′səs bĕl′ē′). An act or event that justifies a declaration of war. [Latin, "occasion of war."]

cat (kăt) *n.* **1.** A carnivorous mammal, *Felis catus* (or *F. domesticus*), domesticated since early times as a catcher of rats and mice and as a pet, and existing in several distinctive breeds and varieties. **2.** Any of the other animals of the family Felidae, which includes the lion, tiger, leopard, and lynx. **3.** The fur of a domestic cat. **4.** A spiteful or gossiping woman. **5.** A cat-o'-nine-tails. **6.** A catfish. **7.** *Nautical.* **a.** A cathead. **b.** A device for raising an anchor to the cathead. **c.** A catboat. **8.** *Slang.* A man. **9.** *Slang.* A Caterpillar tractor. —**let the cat out of the bag.** To let a secret be known. —*tr.v.* **catted, catting, cats.** **1.** To flog with a cat-o'-nine-tails. **2.** To hoist an anchor to the cathead. [Middle English *cat(te),* Old English *cat(t),* from Common Germanic *kattuz* (unattested), probably from Late Latin *cattus, catta,* perhaps of Hamitic origin.]

cat. catalogue.

cata–. Indicates: **1.** Reversing of a process; for example, **cataplasia.** **2.** Lower in position or down from; for example, **cataphyll, catadromous.** [In borrowed Greek compounds *kata-* indicates: 1. Down, as in **catabolism.** 2. Down from, as in **catalepsy.** 3. Off or away, as in **catalectic.** 4. Against, as in **category.** 5. Completely or thoroughly, as in **catachresis.** 6. According to,

ă pat/ā pay/âr care/ä father/b bib/ch church/d deed/ĕ pet/ē be/f fife/g gag/h hat/hw which/ĭ pit/ī pie/îr pier/j judge/k kick/l lid, needle/m mum/n no, sudden/ng thing/ŏ pot/ō toe/ô paw, for/oi noise/ou out/o͝o took/o͞o boot/p pop/r roar/s sauce/sh ship, dish/

as in **catechize.** Greek *kata-,* from *kata,* down, down from, according to. See **kat-**[1] in Appendix.*]

ca·tab·o·lism (kə-tăb′ə-lĭz′əm) *n.* The metabolic change of complex into simple molecules. Compare **anabolism.** [From Greek *katabolē,* a throwing down, from *kataballein,* to throw down : *kata-,* down + *ballein,* to throw (see **gwel-**[1] in Appendix*).] —**cat′a·bol′ic** (kăt′ə-bŏl′ĭk) *adj.* —**cat′a·bol′i·cal·ly** *adv.*

ca·tab·o·lize (kə-tăb′ə-līz′) *v.* **-lized, -lizing, -lizes.** —*tr.* To break down (complex molecules) by metabolic processes. —*intr.* To undergo catabolism.

cat·a·chre·sis (kăt′ə-krē′sĭs) *n., pl.* **-ses** (-sēz′). **1. a.** Strained use of a word or phrase, as for rhetorical effect. **b.** A deliberately paradoxical figure of speech. **2.** The use of a wrong word in a context. [Latin *catachrēsis,* from Greek *katakhrēsis,* excessive use, misuse, from *katakhrēsthai,* to misuse, make full use of : *kata-,* completely + *khrēsthai,* to use (see **gher-**[7] in Appendix*).] —**cat′a·chres′tic** (-krĕs′tĭk) *adj.*

cat·a·clysm (kăt′ə-klĭz′əm) *n.* **1.** A violent and sudden change in the earth's crust. **2.** Any violent upheaval. **3.** A devastating flood. —See Synonyms at **disaster.** [French *cataclysme,* from Latin *cataclysmos,* deluge, flood, from Greek *kataklusmos,* from *katakluzein,* to deluge, inundate : *kata-,* down + *kluzein,* to wash (see **kleu-**[2] in Appendix*).] —**cat′a·clys′mic** (-klĭz′mĭk), **cat′a·clys′mal** (-klĭz′məl) *adj.*

cat·a·combs (kăt′ə-kōmz′) *pl.n.* A series of underground chambers or tunnels with recesses for graves. [From Old French *catacombe,* a subterranean chamber, probably from Old Italian *catacomba,* from Late Latin *catacumba*†.]

ca·tad·ro·mous (kə-tăd′rə-məs) *adj.* Migrating down river to breed in marine waters. Compare **anadromous.** [CATA- + -DROMOUS.]

cat·a·falque (kăt′ə-fălk′, -fôlk′, -fôk′) *n.* The raised structure upon which a coffin rests during a state funeral. [French, from Italian *catafalco,* from Vulgar Latin *catafalicum* (unattested), scaffold : Latin *cata-,* down from + *fala,* scaffold, siege tower, from Etruscan *falas*.]

Cat·a·lan (kăt′l-ăn′, -ən) *adj.* Of or pertaining to Catalonia, its people, language, or culture. —*n.* **1.** A native or inhabitant of Catalonia. **2.** The Romance language of Catalonia.

cat·a·lase (kăt′l-ās′, -āz′) *n.* An enzyme in the blood and tissues that catalyzes the decomposition of hydrogen peroxide into water and oxygen. [CATAL(YSIS) + -ASE.]

cat·a·lec·tic (kăt′l-ĕk′tĭk) *adj.* Designating a verse that lacks part of the last foot. [Late Latin *catalēcticus,* from Greek *katalēktikos,* incomplete, from *katalēgein,* to leave off : *kata-,* off, away + *lēgein,* to leave off, stop (see **slēg-** in Appendix*).]

cat·a·lep·sy (kăt′l-ĕp′sē) *n.* Muscular rigidity, lack of awareness of environment, and lack of response to external stimuli, often associated with epilepsy, schizophrenia, and hysteria. [Learned respelling of earlier *catalency,* from Middle English *cathalempsia,* from Medieval Latin *catalepsia,* from Late Latin *catalēpsis,* from Greek *katalēpsis,* "a seizing," from *katalambanein,* to seize : *kata-,* down from + *lambanein,* to take, seize (see **slagw-** in Appendix*).] —**cat′a·lep′tic** *adj.*

Cat·a·li·na Island. See **Santa Catalina.**

cat·a·lo (kăt′l-ō′) *n., pl.* **-loes** or **-los.** Also **cat·ta·lo.** A hardy, fertile hybrid resulting from a cross between the American buffalo, or bison, and domestic cattle. [CAT(TLE) + (BUFF)ALO.]

cat·a·logue (kăt′l-ôg′, -ŏg′) *n.* Also **cat·a·log** (only form for senses 2 and 3). *Abbr.* **cat. 1.** A systematized list, usually in alphabetical order, often with descriptions of the listed items. **2.** *Library Service.* A **card catalog** *(see).* **3.** *Library Service.* A publication containing such a list. —*v.* **catalogued, -loguing, -logues.** Also **cat·a·log.** —*tr.* To list in a catalogue; make a catalogue of. —*intr.* To make a catalogue. [Middle English *cateloge,* from Old French *catalogue,* from Late Latin *catalogus,* an enumeration, from Greek *katalogos,* from *katalegein,* to recount, enumerate : *kata-,* thoroughly + *legein,* to gather, speak (see **leg-** in Appendix*).] —**cat′a·logu′er** *n.*

Cat·a·lo·ni·a (kăt′l-ō′nē-ə, -nyə). *Spanish* **Ca·ta·lu·ña** (kä′tä-lo͞o′nyä). A region and former republic of northeastern Spain, bordering on France to the north and the Mediterranean Sea to the east.

ca·tal·pa (kə-tăl′pə, -tôl′pə) *n.* Any of several chiefly North American trees of the genus *Catalpa,* having large leaves, showy clusters of whitish flowers, and long, slender pods. Also called "Indian bean." [Creek *kutuhlpa,* "head with wings" (from the shape of its flowers).]

ca·tal·y·sis (kə-tăl′ə-sĭs) *n.* The action of a catalyst, especially modification of the rate of a chemical reaction by a catalyst. [Greek *katalusis,* dissolution, from *kataluein,* to dissolve : *kata-,* down + *luein,* to loosen, release (see **leu-**[1] in Appendix*).] —**cat′a·lyt′ic** (kăt′l-ĭt′ĭk) *adj.* —**cat′a·lyt′i·cal·ly** *adv.*

cat·a·lyst (kăt′l-ĭst) *n.* **1.** *Chemistry.* A substance, usually present in small amounts relative to the reactants, that modifies, especially increases, the rate of a chemical reaction without being consumed in the process. **2.** One that precipitates a process or event, especially without being involved in or changed by the consequences. [From CATALYSIS (by analogy with ANALYST and ANALYSIS).]

catalytic cracker. An oil refinery unit in which catalytic **cracking** *(see)* of petroleum is performed.

cat·a·lyze (kăt′l-īz′) *tr.v.* **-lyzed, -lyzing, -lyzes.** To modify the rate of (a chemical reaction) as a catalyst. —**cat′a·lyz′er** *n.*

cat·a·ma·ran (kăt′ə-mə-răn′) *n.* **1.** A boat with two parallel hulls. **2.** A raft of logs or floats lashed together. [Tamil *kaṭṭumaram* : *kaṭṭu-,* to tie + *maram,* tree, timber.]

cat·a·me·ni·a (kăt′ə-mē′nē-ə) *n. Physiology.* Menses. [New Latin, from Greek *katamēnia,* neuter plural of *katamēnios,* monthly : *kata-,* according to + *mēn,* month (see **mē-**[2] in Appendix*).] —**cat′a·me′ni·al** *adj.*

cat·a·mite (kăt′ə-mīt′) *n.* A boy kept by a pederast. [Latin *catamītus,* from *Catamītus,* Ganymede, from Etruscan *Catmite,* from Greek *Ganumēdēs,* GANYMEDE (cupbearer of the gods).]

cat·a·mount (kăt′ə-mount′) *n.* Also **cat·a·moun·tain** (kăt′ə-moun′tən). Any of various wild felines, such as a mountain lion or a lynx. [Short for catamountain, variant of earlier *cat of the mountain.*]

Ca·ta·nia (kə-tān′yə; *Italian* kä-tä′nyä). The second-largest city of Sicily, Italy, on the eastern shore. Population, 364,000.

cat·a·pho·re·sis (kăt′ə-fə-rē′sĭs) *n. Chemistry.* **Electrophoresis** *(see).* [New Latin : CATA- + -PHORESIS.] —**cat′a·pho·ret′ic** (-rĕt′ĭk) *adj.* —**cat′a·pho·ret′i·cal·ly** *adv.*

cat·a·phyll (kăt′ə-fĭl′) *n. Botany.* A modified or rudimentary leaf, such as a bud scale. [CATA- + -PHYLL (translation of German *Niederblatt,* "lower leaf").]

cat·a·pla·sia (kăt′ə-plā′zhə, -zhē-ə) *n.* Degenerative reversion of cells or tissue to a less differentiated form. [New Latin : CATA- + -PLASIA.] —**cat′a·plas′tic** (-plăs′tĭk) *adj.*

cat·a·plasm (kăt′ə-plăz′əm) *n. Medicine.* A **poultice** *(see).* [Old French *cataplasme,* from Late Latin *cataplasma,* from Greek *kataplasma,* from *kataplassein,* to plaster over : *kata-,* thoroughly + *plassein,* to mold (see **plasma**).]

cat·a·pult (kăt′ə-pŭlt′) *n.* **1.** An ancient military machine for hurling large stones, arrows, or other missiles. **2.** A mechanism for launching aircraft without a runway, as from the deck of a ship. **3.** A slingshot. —*v.* **catapulted, -pulting, -pults.** —*tr.* To hurl or launch from or as if from a catapult. —*intr.* To become catapulted; spring up abruptly. [Old French *catapulte,* from Latin *catapulta,* from Greek *katapaltēs, katepeltēs* : *kata-,* down + *pallein,* to sway, brandish (see **pōl-** in Appendix*).]

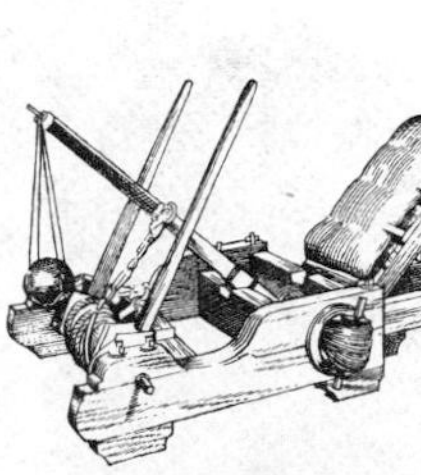

catapult
Roman catapult

cat·a·ract (kăt′ə-răkt′) *n.* **1.** A very large waterfall. **2.** A great downpour. **3.** *Pathology.* Opacity of the lens or capsule of the eye, causing partial or total blindness. [Middle English *cataracte,* floodgate, from Old French, portcullis, cataract (of the eye), from Latin *catarractēs,* waterfall, portcullis, from Greek *katar(rh)aktēs,* "a down-swooping," from *katarassein,* to dash down : *kata-,* down + *rassein,* to strike (see **wrāgh-**[2] in Appendix*).]

ca·tarrh (kə-tär′) *n.* Inflammation of mucous membranes, especially of the nose and throat. [Old French *catarrhe,* from Late Latin *catarrhus,* from Greek *katarrhous,* a flowing down, from *katarrhein,* to flow down : *kata-,* down + *rhein,* to flow (see **sreu-** in Appendix*).] —**ca·tarrh′al, ca·tarrh′ous** *adj.*

cat·arrh·ine (kăt′ə-rīn′) *adj.* Of or designating a group of primates that includes the Old World monkeys, apes, and man, characterized by close-set nostrils directed forward or downward. —*n.* A catarrhine primate. [New Latin *Catarrhina,* from Greek *katarrhin,* hook-nosed : *kata-,* down + *rhis* (stem *rhin-*), nose (see **rhino-**).]

ca·tas·ta·sis (kə-tăs′tə-sĭs) *n., pl.* **-ses** (-sēz′). **1.** In classical tragedy, the intensified part of the action directly preceding the catastrophe. **2.** The climax of a play. [Greek *katastasis,* settlement, establishment, from *kathistanai,* to set in order, bring down : *kata-,* down + *histanai,* to set, place (see **stā-** in Appendix*).]

ca·tas·tro·phe (kə-tăs′trə-fē) *n.* **1.** A great and sudden calamity; disaster. **2.** A sudden violent change in the earth's surface; cataclysm. **3.** The dénouement of a play, especially a classical tragedy. —See Synonyms at **disaster.** [Greek *katastrophē,* from *katastrephein,* to turn down, overturn : *kata-,* down + *strephein,* to turn (see **strebh-** in Appendix*).] —**cat′a·stroph′ic** (kăt′ə-strŏf′ĭk) *adj.* —**cat′a·stroph′i·cal·ly** *adv.*

cat·a·to·ni·a (kăt′ə-tō′nē-ə) *n.* A schizophrenic disorder characterized by plastic immobility of the limbs, stupor, negativism, and mutism. [New Latin, from German *Katatonie* : CATA- + -TONIA.] —**cat′a·ton′ic** (-tŏn′ĭk) *adj.* & *n.*

cat·a·wam·pus (kăt-ə-wŏm′pəs) *adj.* Also **cat·ty·wam·pus** (kăt′ē-). *Slang.* **1.** Cater-cornered; slantwise. **2.** Evil; malicious. [Origin uncertain.]

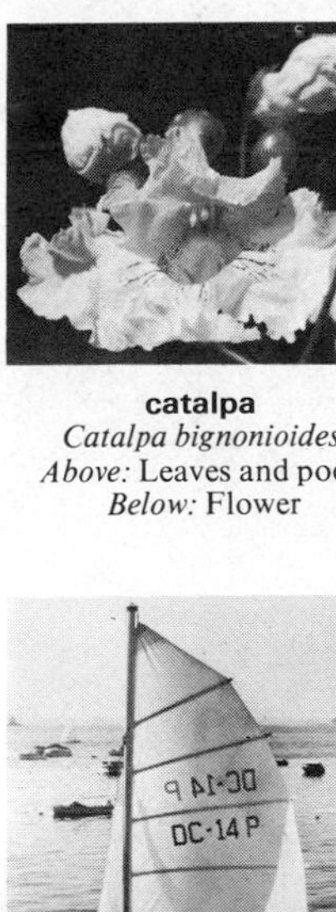

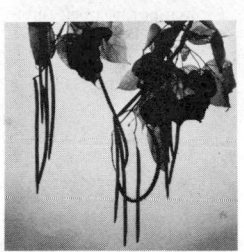

catalpa
Catalpa bignonioides
Above: Leaves and pods
Below: Flower

Ca·taw·ba (kə-tô′bə) *n., pl.* **Catawba** or **-bas** (only form for sense 4). **1.** A Siouan-speaking tribe of North American Indians formerly living along the Catawba River in the Carolinas. **2.** A member of this tribe. **3.** The Siouan language of this tribe. **4.** A light-red North American grape developed from the fox grape, *Vitis labrusca.* **5.** Wine made from these grapes.

Ca·taw·ba River (kə-tô′bə). A river rising in the Blue Ridge Mountains of western North Carolina and flowing 250 miles south into South Carolina.

cat·bird (kăt′bûrd′) *n.* A North American songbird, *Dumetella carolinensis,* having predominantly slate-gray plumage. [From one of its calls, resembling the mewing of a cat.]

cat·boat (kăt′bōt′) *n.* A broad-beamed sailboat carrying a single sail on a mast stepped well forward.

cat·bri·er (kăt′brī′ər) *n.* Any of several thorny vines of the genus *Smilax;* especially, *S. rotundifolia,* having heart-shaped leaves, small green flowers, and blackish berries. Also called "greenbrier." [CAT + BRIER (from its prickles).]

cat·call (kăt′kôl′) *n.* A harsh or shrill call or whistle expressing disapproval or derision. —*v.* **catcalled, -calling, -calls.** —*tr.* To express disapproval of with catcalls. —*intr.* To sound catcalls.

catch (kăch) *v.* **caught** (kôt), **catching, catches.** —*tr.* **1.** To capture or seize, especially after a chase. **2.** To take by trapping or snaring. **3.** To come upon suddenly, unexpectedly, or accidentally. **4. a.** To lay hold of forcibly or suddenly; grasp. **b.** To grab so as to stop the motion of. **5. a.** To overtake. **b.** To reach in time to board, attend, or the like. **6. a.** To entangle; grip. **b.** To cause to become suddenly or accidentally hooked, en-

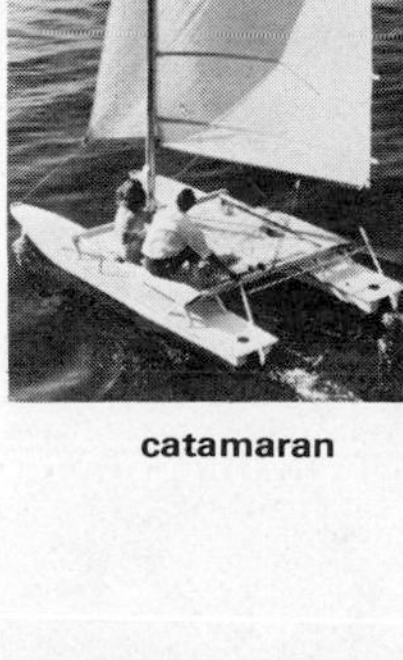

catamaran

tangled, or the like. **7.** To hit; strike. **8.** To check (oneself) in some sort of action. **9.** To become subject to or contract, as by exposure or contagion. **10.** To become affected by or imbued with, as by sympathy or imitation. **11.** To take or get suddenly, momentarily, or quickly. **12.** To seize mentally or by the senses; apprehend. **13.** To apprehend and reproduce accurately by or as if by artistic means. **14.** To attract and fix; to arrest. **15.** *Informal.* To see (a theatrical performance, for example). *—intr.* **1.** To become held, entangled, or fastened. **2.** To act or move so as to hold someone or something. **3.** To be communicable or infectious; to spread. **4.** To take fire; kindle; burn. **5.** *Baseball.* To act as catcher. **—catch at. 1.** To try to catch; snatch or grab at. **2.** To clutch at gratefully or eagerly. **—catch it.** *Informal.* To receive some form of punishment or scolding. **—catch on.** *Informal.* **1.** To understand or perceive. **2.** To become popular. **—catch one's breath. 1.** To rest so as to be able to go on. **2.** To cease breathing briefly. **—catch up. 1.** To lift up suddenly; grab; snatch. **2.** To attach or fasten with loops. **3.** To detect (someone) in a mistake. **4.** To come up from behind; overtake. **5.** To become involved with, often unwillingly. Used in the passive: *caught up in the scandal.* **6.** To bring up to date. Used with *on* or *with: catch up on one's correspondence.* **7.** To absorb completely; engross. Used in the passive: *He is caught up in his work.* **—catch up with** (or **to**). To overtake. *—n.* **1.** The act of catching; a taking and holding. **2.** Something that catches, especially a device for fastening or for checking motion. **3.** Something that is caught. **4.** The amount caught. **5.** A choking or stoppage of the breath or voice. **6.** A stop or break in a mechanism. **7.** *Informal.* A person or thing worth catching. **8.** *Informal.* A tricky or unsuspected condition or drawback. **9.** A snatch or fragment. **10.** *Music.* A canonical, often rhythmically intricate composition for three or more voices, popular especially in the 17th and 18th centuries. **11.** *Sports.* **a.** The grabbing and holding of a thrown, kicked, or batted ball before it hits the ground. **b.** A game of throwing and catching a ball. *—adj.* **1.** Tricky. **2.** Designed to attract attention. [Catch, caught, caught; Middle English *cacchen, cauhte, cauht,* to chase, catch, from Old North French *cachier,* to hunt, from Vulgar Latin *captiāre* (unattested), from Latin *captāre,* to chase, strive to seize, from *capere* (past participle *captus*), to take, seize. See **kap-** in Appendix.*]

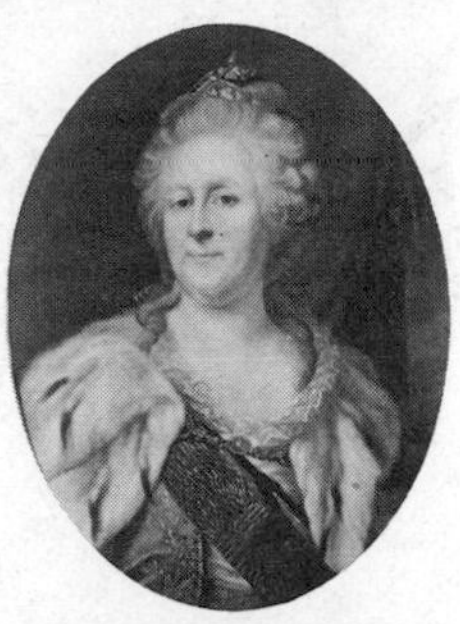

Catherine the Great
Contemporary portrait by
Giovanni Batista Lampi I

catch·all (kăch′ôl′) *n.* **1.** A box, closet, or other receptacle for a variety of odds and ends. **2.** Something, such as a phrase or law, that covers a variety of situations. **—catch′all′** *adj.*

catch-as-catch-can (kăch′əz-kăch′kăn′) *n.* A style of wrestling in which a contestant is permitted to hold his opponent below the waist and to trip and tackle. *—adj.* Seizing any opportunity or using any available means; not planned.

catch·er (kăch′ər) *n.* **1.** One that catches. **2.** *Abbr.* **C., c.** The baseball player whose position is behind home plate and who signals for and receives pitches.

catch·fly (kăch′flī′) *n., pl.* **-flies.** Any of several plants of the genus *Silene* and related genera, having white, pink, or red flowers with characteristically sticky stems and calyxes.

catch·ing (kăch′ĭng) *adj.* **1.** Infectious. **2.** Attractive; alluring.

catch·ment (kăch′mənt) *n.* **1.** A catching or collecting of water. **2.** A structure, such as a basin or reservoir, for collecting or draining water. **3.** The amount of water so collected.

catch·pen·ny (kăch′pĕn′ē) *adj.* Designed and made to sell without concern for quality; cheap. *—n., pl.* **catchpennies.** A catchpenny item.

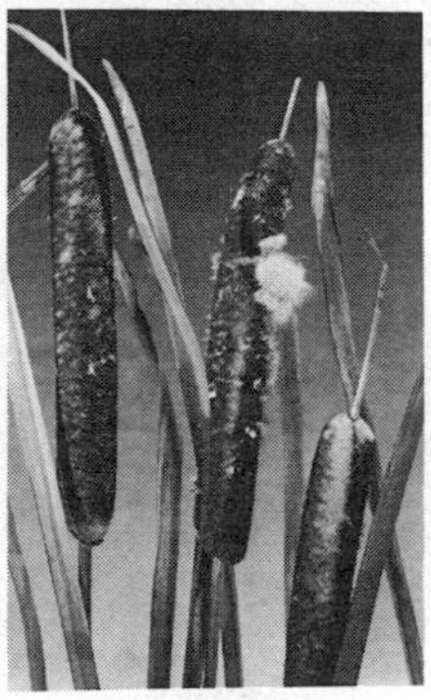

cattail
Typha latifolia

catch·pole (kăch′pōl′) *n.* Also **catch·poll.** Formerly, a sheriff's officer, especially one who arrested debtors. [Middle English *cacchepol,* Old English *cæccepol,* from Old North French *cachepol,* "chicken chaser" : *cachier,* variant of Old French *chacier,* to hunt, CHASE + *poul, pol,* rooster, from Latin *pullus,* young animal, young fowl (see **pōu-** in Appendix*).]

catch·up. Variant of **ketchup.**

catch·word (kăch′wûrd′) *n.* **1.** An often repeated word or slogan. Also called "catch phrase." **2.** *Printing.* A word placed at the head of a column or page, as in a dictionary or encyclopedia, to indicate the first or last entry on the page. **3.** The first word of a page printed at the bottom of the preceding page.

catch·y (kăch′ē) *adj.* **-ier, -iest. 1.** Attractive; alluring. **2.** Easily remembered. **3.** Tricky; deceptive. **4.** Fitful; spasmodic.

cat·e·che·sis (kăt′ə-kē′sĭs) *n., pl.* **-ses** (-sēz′). Instruction of catechumens. [Late Latin *catēchēsis,* from Greek *katēkhēsis,* from *katēkhein,* CATECHIZE.] **—cat′e·chet′i·cal** (-kĕt′ĭ-kəl) *adj.*

cat·e·chism (kăt′ə-kĭz′əm) *n.* **1.** A short book giving, in question-and-answer form, a brief summary of the basic principles of a religion. **2.** A book of similar form giving instruction in other subjects. **3.** A question-and-answer examination, as of a political figure. [Late Latin *catēchismus,* from Late Greek *katēkhismos,* from *katēkhizein,* to CATECHIZE.]

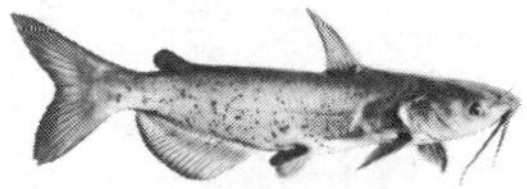

catfish
Ictalurus punctatus
Channel catfish

cat·e·chist (kăt′ə-kĭst) *n.* A person who catechizes, especially one who instructs catechumens in preparation for baptism. [Late Latin *catēchista,* from Late Greek *katēkhistēs,* from *katēkhizein,* to CATECHIZE.] **—cat′e·chis′tic** (-kĭs′tĭk), **cat′e·chis′ti·cal** (-tĭ-kəl) *adj.*

cat·e·chize (kăt′ə-kīz′) *tr.v.* **-chized, -chizing, -chizes. 1.** To teach orally (the principles of a religious creed) by means of questions and answers. **2.** To question searchingly or persistently: *"Boswell was eternally catechizing him on all kinds of subjects"* (Macaulay). [Late Latin *catēchizāre,* from Late Greek *katēkhizein,* from Greek *katēkhein,* to teach by word of mouth : *kata-,* according to + *ēkhein,* to sound, from *ēkhē,* sound (see **swāgh-** in Appendix*).] **—cat′e·chi·za′tion** (-kə-zā′shən) *n.* **—cat′e·chi′zer** *n.*

cat·e·chu (kăt′ə-chōō′) *n.* Any of several water-soluble, resinous, astringent substances used in tanning and dyeing, as that obtained from a tree, *Acacia catechu,* of southern Asia, or from a woody vine, *Uncaria gambier,* of Malaya. Also called "cachou," "cutch." [Probably from Malay *kachu,* probably from Dravidian, akin to Malayalam *kāccu,* CACHOU.]

cat·e·chu·men (kăt′ə-kyōō′mən) *n.* **1.** One who is being taught the principles of Christianity; a neophyte. **2.** One who is being instructed in any subject at an elementary level. [Middle English *cathecumyn,* from Old French *cathecumene,* from Late Latin *catēchūmenus,* from Greek *katēkhoumenos,* present passive participle of *katēkhein,* to CATECHIZE.]

cat·e·gor·i·cal (kăt′ə-gôr′ĭ-kəl, -gŏr′ĭ-kəl) *adj.* **1.** Without exception or qualification; absolute; certain. **2.** Of, concerning, or included in a category. **—cat′e·gor′i·cal·ly** *adv.* **—cat′e·gor′i·cal·ness** *n.*

categorical imperative. In Kant's ethical system, an absolute and universally binding moral law as opposed to **hypothetical imperative** *(see).*

cat·e·go·rize (kăt′ə-gə-rīz′) *tr.v.* **-rized, -rizing, -rizes.** To put into categories; classify. **—cat′e·go·ri·za′tion** *n.*

cat·e·go·ry (kăt′ə-gôr′ē, -gōr′ē) *n., pl.* **-ries. 1.** A specifically defined division in a system of classification; a class. **2.** *Logic.* Any of the basic classifications into which all knowledge can be placed. In this sense, also called "predicament." [Late Latin *catēgoria,* accusation, predicament, category of predicables, from Greek *katēgoria,* from *katēgorein,* to accuse : *kata-,* against + *-agorein,* to speak publicly, from *agora,* assembly (see **ger-**[1] in Appendix*).]

ca·te·na (kə-tē′nə) *n., pl.* **-nae** (-nē′) or **-nas.** A closely linked series. [Latin *catēna*†, chain.]

cat·e·nar·y (kăt′ə-nĕr′ē, kə-tē′nər-ē) *n., pl.* **-ies. 1.** The curve theoretically formed by a perfectly flexible, uniformly dense and thick, inextensible cable suspended from two points. **2.** Anything having the shape of this curve. **3.** The overhead wire system of an electric railroad. *—adj.* Of or resembling a catenary. [New Latin *catenaria,* from Latin *catēnāria,* feminine of *catēnārius,* of a chain, from *catēna,* CATENA.]

cat·e·nate (kăt′ə-nāt′) *tr.v.* **-nated, -nating, -nates.** To connect in a series of ties or links; form into a chain. [Latin *catēnāre,* from *catēna,* CATENA.] **—cat′e·na′tion** *n.*

ca·ten·u·late (kə-tĕn′yə-lĭt) *adj.* Consisting or formed of chain-like links. [From Latin *catēnula,* little chain, diminutive of Latin *catēna,* CATENA.]

ca·ter (kā′tər) *v.* **-tered, -tering, -ters.** *—intr.* **1.** To provide food or entertainment, usually for large dinners, banquets, and the like. **2.** To provide anything wished for or needed. *—tr.* To provide food service for. [From obsolete *cater,* a buyer of provisions, caterer, from Middle English *catour,* short for *acatour,* from Norman French, from *acater,* to buy, from Vulgar Latin *accaptāre* (unattested), to buy, procure, from Latin *acceptāre,* to ACCEPT.] **—ca′ter·er** *n.*

cat·er·cor·nered (kăt′ər-kôr′nərd, kăt′ē-) *adj.* Also **cat·er·cor·ner** (-nər), **cat·ty-cor·nered** (kăt′ē-kôr′nərd). Diagonal. *—adv.* Diagonally. [From obsolete *cater,* four at dice, from Middle English, from Old French *quatre,* four, from Latin *quattuor.* See **kwetwer-** in Appendix.*]

cat·er·pil·lar (kăt′ər-pĭl′ər, kăt′ə-) *n.* **1. a.** The wormlike often brightly colored, hairy, or spiny larva of a butterfly or moth. **b.** Any of various similar insect larvae. **2.** *Capital* **C.** A trademark for a tractor equipped with a pair of endless chain treads. [Middle English *catyrpel,* probably from Old French *catepelose,* "hairy cat" : *cate,* female cat, from Late Latin *catta,* CAT + *pelose, pelouse,* feminine of *pelous,* hairy, from Latin *pilōsus,* from *pilus,* hair (see **pilo-** in Appendix*).]

cat·er·waul (kăt′ər-wôl′) *intr.v.* **-wauled, -wauling, -wauls. 1.** To cry or screech like a cat in heat. **2.** To make any discordant sound or shriek. **3.** To have a noisy argument. *—n.* **1.** The cry of cats in heat. **2.** Any similar cry. [Middle English *caterw(r)awen,* perhaps from Low German *katerwaulen* : *kater,* tomcat, from Common Germanic *kattuz* (unattested), CAT + *waulen,* to screech (perhaps imitative).]

cat·face (kăt′fās′) *n.* Also **cat·fac·ing** (-fā′sĭng). A deformity of fruit resulting from insect stings or disease.

cat·fall (kăt′fôl′) *n.* A cable, rope, or chain used to raise an anchor to the cathead.

cat·fish (kăt′fĭsh′) *n., pl.* **catfish** or **-fishes.** Any of numerous scaleless, chiefly freshwater fishes of the order Siluriformes, characteristically having whiskerlike barbels extending from the upper jaw.

cat·gut (kăt′gŭt′) *n.* A tough, thin cord or thread made from the dried intestines of certain animals, used for stringing musical instruments and tennis rackets and for surgical ligatures. [The reason for the naming is unknown.]

cath. cathedral.

ca·thar·sis (kə-thär′sĭs) *n., pl.* **-ses** (-sēz′). **1.** *Medicine.* Purgation, especially for the digestive system. **2.** A purifying or figurative cleansing of the emotions. **3.** *Psychoanalysis.* **a.** A technique used to relieve tension and anxiety by bringing repressed material to consciousness. **b.** The result of this process; abreaction. [New Latin, from Greek *katharsis,* from *kathairein,* to purge, purify, from *katharos*†, pure.]

ca·thar·tic (kə-thär′tĭk) *adj.* Inducing catharsis; purgative; cleansing. *—n.* A cathartic agent, especially a laxative. [Late Latin *catharticus,* from Greek *kathartikos,* from *kathairein,* to purge, purify. See **catharsis.**]

Ca·thay (kă-thā′). *Archaic & Poetic.* China. [Medieval Latin *Cataya, Kitai,* from Old Turkic *Qitay, Qitan,* name of an Altaic Turkic tribe that ruled China as the Liao Dynasty (A.D. 907–1101).]

ă pat/ā pay/âr care/ä father/b bib/ch church/d deed/ĕ pet/ē be/f fife/g gag/h hat/hw which/ĭ pit/ī pie/îr pier/j judge/k kick/l lid, needle/m mum/n no, sudden/ng thing/ŏ pot/ō toe/ô paw, for/oi noise/ou out/ŏŏ took/ōō boot/p pop/r roar/s sauce/sh ship, dish/

cat·head (kăt′hĕd′) *n.* A beam projecting outward from the bow of a ship, and used as a support to lift the anchor. [CAT (nautical) + HEAD.]

ca·the·dra (kə-thē′drə) *n., pl.* **-drae** (-drē). **1.** The official chair or throne of a bishop. **2.** The office or see of a bishop. **3.** The official chair of an office or position, as of a professor. [Latin, chair, from Greek *kathedra,* seat : *kata-,* down + *hedra,* seat (see **sed-**[1] in Appendix*).]

ca·the·dral (kə-thē′drəl) *n. Abbr.* **cath. 1.** The principal church of a bishop's see and one that contains his official throne. **2.** Any large or important church. *—adj.* **1.** Of, pertaining to, or containing a bishop's official throne. **2.** Relating to or issuing from a chair of office or authority; authoritative. **3.** Of or pertaining to a cathedral. [Originally *cathedral church,* from Middle English *cathedral,* of a cathedra, from Old French, from Late Latin *cathedrālis,* from Latin *cathedra,* CATHEDRA.]

Cath·er (kăth′ər), **Willa Sibert.** 1876–1947. American author.

Cath·e·rine, Kath·e·rine (kăth′rĭn, -ər-ĭn). A feminine given name. [Middle English *Katerine,* from Old French *Caterine,* from Latin *Katerina, Katharina* (influenced by Greek *katharos,* pure), from Greek *Aikaterina*†.]

Cath·e·rine I (kăth′rĭn, -ər-ĭn). 1684?–1727. Empress of Russia (1725–27); second wife of and successor to Peter the Great.

Cath·e·rine II (kăth′rĭn, -ər-ĭn). Called "the Great." 1729–1796. Empress of Russia (1762–96).

Cath·e·rine, Mount. The English name for **Jebel Katherina.**

Cath·e·rine de Mé·di·cis (kăth′rĭn də mĕd′ə-chē, mā′də-sēs′, kăth′ə-rĭn). 1519–1589. Queen of France (1547–59).

Cath·e·rine of Aragon (kăth′rĭn, -ər-ĭn). 1485–1536. Queen of England; first wife of Henry VIII.

Cath·e·rine of Siena (kăth′rĭn, -ər-ĭn), **Saint.** 1347–1380. Italian mystic.

catherine wheel. A firework similar to a pinwheel. [After St. *Catherine* of Alexandria (died A.D. 307), who was condemned to be tortured on a wheel.]

cath·e·ter (kăth′ə-tər) *n. Medicine.* A slender, flexible tube of metal, rubber, or plastic inserted into a body channel, such as a vein, to distend or maintain an opening to an internal cavity. [Late Latin *catheter,* from Greek *kathetēr,* something inserted, from *kathienai,* let fall, send down : *kata-,* down + *hienai,* to send (see **yē-** in Appendix*).]

cath·e·ter·ize (kăth′ə-tə-rīz′) *tr.v.* **-ized, -izing, -izes.** To introduce a catheter into a bodily passage. **—cath′e·ter·i·za′tion** *n.*

ca·thex·is (kə-thĕk′sĭs) *n.* The concentration of emotional energy upon some object or idea. [New Latin, from Greek *kathexis,* a holding, retention, from *katekhein,* to hold fast : *kata-,* down + *ekhein,* to have, hold (see **segh-** in Appendix*).]

Cath·leen, Kath·leen (kăth-lēn′). A feminine given name. [Irish, from Middle English *Catlin,* from Old French *Cateline,* variant of *Caterine,* CATHERINE.]

cath·ode (kăth′ōd′) *n.* **1.** Any negatively charged electrode, as of an electrolytic cell, storage battery, or electron tube. **2.** The positively charged terminal of a primary cell or of a storage battery that is supplying current. [Greek *kathodos,* way down, descent : *kata-,* down + *hodos,* way (see **sed-**[2] in Appendix*).] **—ca·thod′ic** (kă-thŏd′ĭk) *adj.* **—ca·thod′i·cal·ly** *adv.*

cathode follower. A vacuum-tube amplifying circuit with input connections between the control grid and the remote end of the cathode load, output connections between terminals of the cathode load, and usually high input impedance, low output impedance, and gain less than but approaching unity.

cathode ray. 1. A stream of electrons emitted by the cathode in electrical discharge tubes. **2.** An electron in such a stream.

cath·ode-ray tube (kăth′ōd-rā′). A vacuum tube in which a hot cathode emits electrons that are accelerated as a beam through a relatively high voltage anode, further focused or deflected electrostatically or electromagnetically, and allowed to fall on a fluorescent screen.

cath·o·lic (kăth′lĭk, kăth′ə-lĭk) *adj.* **1.** Universal; general; all-inclusive. **2.** Broad and comprehensive in interests, sympathies, or the like; liberal. [Old French *catholique,* from Late Latin *catholicus,* from Greek *katholikos,* from *katholou,* in general : *kata-,* according to + *holou,* neuter genitive of *holos,* whole (see **sol-** in Appendix*).] **—ca·thol′i·cal·ly** (kə-thŏl′ĭk-lē) *adv.*

Cath·o·lic (kăth′lĭk, kăth′ə-lĭk) *adj. Abbr.* **C. 1.** Of or pertaining to the universal Christian church. **2.** Of or pertaining to the ancient undivided Christian church. **3. a.** Of or designating those churches that have claimed to be representatives of the ancient undivided church: *Roman Catholic, Eastern Orthodox, Anglican,* and *Old Catholic.* **b.** Of or concerning the Roman Catholic Church. **4.** Pertaining to the Western Church as opposed to the Eastern Orthodox Church. *—n. Abbr.* **C.** A member of any Catholic church, especially Roman Catholic.

Catholic Church. Roman Catholic Church *(see).*

Ca·thol·i·cism (kə-thŏl′ə-sĭz′əm) *n.* The faith, doctrine, system, and practice of a Catholic church, especially the Roman Catholic Church. See **Roman Catholicism.**

cath·o·lic·i·ty (kăth′ə-lĭs′ə-tē) *n.* **1.** The condition or quality of being catholic; liberality; broad-mindedness. **2.** General acceptance; universality. **3.** *Capital* **C.** Roman Catholicism.

ca·thol·i·cize (kə-thŏl′ə-sīz′) *v.* **-cized, -cizing, -cizes.** *—tr.* **1.** To make catholic. **2.** To convert to Catholicism. *—intr.* **1.** To become catholic. **2.** To be converted to Catholicism.

ca·thol·i·con (kə-thŏl′ə-kŏn′) *n.* A universal remedy; panacea. [French, from Medieval Latin, from Greek *katholikon,* neuter of *katholikos,* CATHOLIC.]

cat·house (kăt′hous′) *n., pl.* **-houses** (-hou′zəz). *Slang.* A house of prostitution; a brothel.

Cat·i·line (kăt′l-īn′). Latin name, Lucius Sergius Catilina. 108?–62 B.C. Roman politician; conspired to assassinate the consuls; attacked and foiled by Cicero; executed.

cat·i·on (kăt′ī′ən) *n.* An ion having a positive charge and, in electrolytes, characteristically moving toward a negative electrode. Compare **anion.** [Greek *kation,* neuter of *katiōn,* present participle of *katienai,* to go down : *kata-,* down + *ienai,* to go (see **ei-**[1] in Appendix*).] **—cat′i·on′ic** (-ŏn′ĭk) *adj.*

cat·kin (kăt′kĭn′) *n. Botany.* A dense, often drooping flower cluster, such as that of a birch, consisting of small, scalelike flowers. Also called "ament." [Translation of obsolete Dutch *katteken,* "little cat" (the cluster resembles a kitten's tail).]

cat·like (kăt′līk′) *adj.* Like a cat; stealthy; silent.

cat·ling (kăt′lĭng) *n.* Also **cat·lin** (kăt′lĭn) (for sense 2). **1.** Catgut for stringing a musical instrument. **2.** *Surgery.* A long amputation knife with a two-edged blade. [CAT + -LING.]

cat nap. A short nap; light sleep.

cat·nip (kăt′nĭp′) *n.* A hairy, aromatic plant, *Nepeta cataria,* native to Eurasia, to which cats are strongly attracted.

Ca·to (kā′tō), **Marcus Porcius**[1]. Called "the Elder" or "the Censor." 234–149 B.C. Roman consul and censor.

Ca·to (kā′tō), **Marcus Porcius**[2]. Surname, Uticensis. Called "the Younger." 95–46 B.C. Roman statesman; opponent of Catiline and Caesar; great-grandson of Cato the Elder.

cat-o′-nine-tails (kăt′ə-nīn′tālz′) *n.* A whip consisting of nine knotted cords fastened to a handle, formerly used for flogging. [So called because it leaves marks like the scratches of a cat.]

ca·top·tric (kə-tŏp′trĭk) *adj.* Also **ca·top·tri·cal** (-trĭ-kəl). Of or pertaining to mirrors and reflected images. [Greek *katoptrikos,* from *katoptron,* mirror : *kata-,* against, cata- + *optos,* visible (see **okw-** in Appendix*) + -TRON.] **—ca·top′trics** *n.*

cat rig. The rig of a **catboat** *(see).*

cat's cradle. A child's game in which an intricately looped string is transferred from the hands of one player to the next, resulting in a succession of different loop patterns.

cat's-eye (kăts′ī′) *n.* **1.** Any of various semiprecious gems displaying a band of reflected light that shifts position as the gem is turned. **2.** A colored reflector attached to the back of a vehicle to indicate its presence on the road at night.

Cats·kill Mountains (kăts′kĭl′). A mountain range in southeastern New York. Highest elevation, Slide Mountain (4,204 feet). Also called the "Catskills."

cat's-paw (kăts′pô′) *n.* Also **cats·paw. 1.** A person used by another as a dupe or tool. **2.** A light breeze that ruffles small areas of a water surface. **3.** *Nautical.* A hitch in the bight of a rope, on which a tackle is hooked. ["These he useth as the monkey did the cat's paw to scrape the nuts out of the fire." M. Hawke, *Killing Is Murder* (1657).]

cat·sup. Variant of **ketchup.**

cat·tail (kăt′tāl′) *n.* Any of several marsh plants of the genus *Typha;* especially, *T. latifolia,* having long, straplike leaves and a dense, cylindrical head of minute brown flowers. Also called "reed mace."

cat·ta·lo. Variant of **catalo.**

Cat·te·gat. See **Kattegat.**

cat·tle (kăt′l) *pl.n.* **1.** Various animals of the genus *Bos,* especially those of the domesticated species *B. taurus,* raised in many breeds for meat and dairy products. **2.** *Obsolete.* Domestic animals. **3.** Human beings. Used contemptuously or humorously: *"Boys and women are for the most part cattle of this color."* (Shakespeare). [Middle English *catel,* personal property, livestock, from Old North French, from Medieval Latin *capitāle,* property, from Latin, neuter of *capitālis,* chief, primary, from *caput,* head. See **kaput** in Appendix.*]

cat·tle·man (kăt′l-mən, -măn′) *n., pl.* **-men** (-mĭn, -mĕn′). A man who tends or raises cattle.

cattle prod. An electrified prod designed for driving cattle.

cat·tle·ya (kăt′lē-ə) *n.* Any orchid of the genus *Cattleya,* having showy rose-purple or white flowers. [New Latin, after William *Cattley* (died 1832), British patron of botany.]

Cat·ton (kăt′n), **Bruce.** Born 1899. American historian.

cat·ty[1] (kăt′ē) *n., pl.* **-ties.** Also **cat·tie.** An Asian unit of weight generally equivalent to $1\frac{1}{3}$ pounds avoirdupois. [Malay *kati.*]

cat·ty[2] (kăt′ē) *adj.* **-tier, -tiest. 1.** Catlike; stealthy. **2.** Subtly cruel or malicious; spiteful: *a catty remark.* **—cat′ti·ly** *adv.* **—cat′ti·ness** *n.*

cat·ty-cor·nered. Variant of **cater-cornered.**

cat·ty·wam·pus. Variant of **catawampus.**

Ca·tul·lus (kə-tŭl′əs), **Gaius Valerius.** Roman poet of the first century B.C.

cat·walk (kăt′wôk′) *n.* A narrow platform or pathway, as on the sides of a bridge.

cat whisker. A fine, pointed wire formerly used to make electrical contact with the surface of a crystal detector.

Cau·ca (kou′kä). A river of Colombia, rising in the northwest and flowing 600 miles northward to join the Magdalena.

Cau·ca·sian (kô-kā′zhən, -kăzh′ən, -kā′shən, -kăsh′ən) *n.* **1.** A native or inhabitant of the Caucasus. **2.** A member of the Caucasoid ethnic division. **3.** The group of languages spoken in the area of the Caucasus that are neither Indo-European nor Altaic, including Circassian and Georgian. *—adj.* Also **Cau·cas·ic** (kô-kăs′ĭk). **1.** Of or pertaining to the Caucasus region, its people, or their languages and culture. **2.** Caucasoid. [After the CAUCASUS (from an old belief that the "Aryan" race originated there).]

Cau·ca·soid (kô′kə-soid′) *adj.* **1.** *Anthropology.* Of, pertaining to, or designating a major ethnic division of the human species having certain distinctive physical characteristics such as skin color varying from very light to brown, and fine hair ranging from straight to wavy or curly. This division is considered to

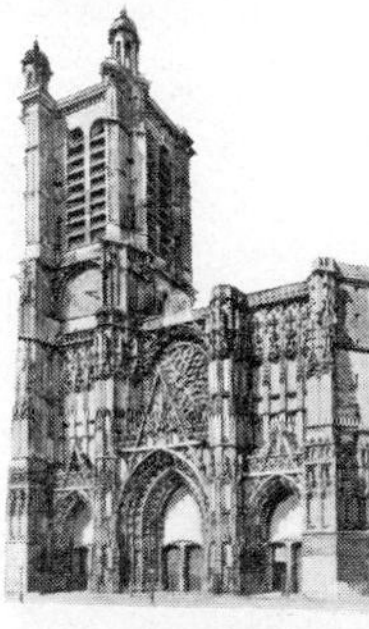

cathedral
Cathedral at Troyes, France, eastern façade

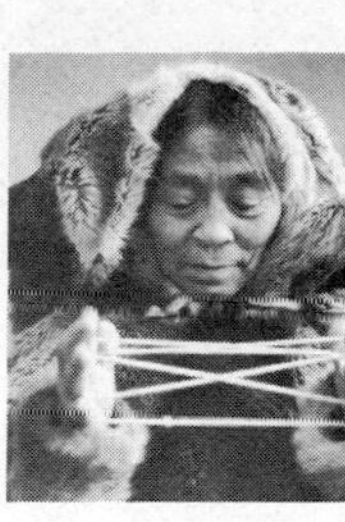

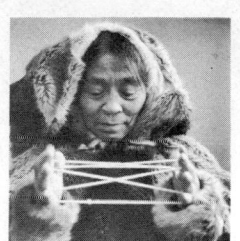

cat's cradle
Eskimo woman displaying the loop position frequently used in cat's cradle

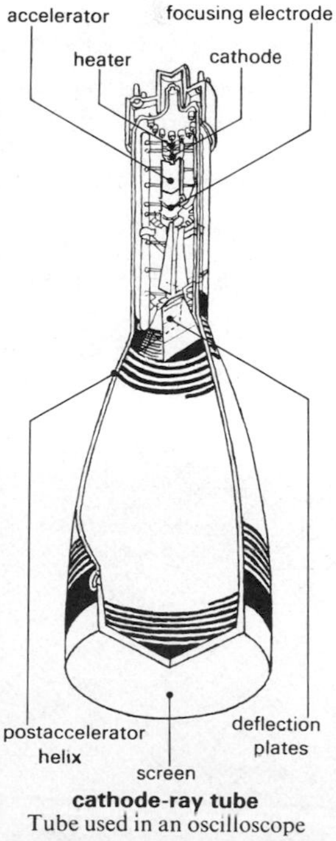
accelerator
focusing electrode
heater
cathode
postaccelerator helix
screen
deflection plates

cathode-ray tube
Tube used in an oscilloscope

include groups of peoples indigenous to or inhabiting Europe, northern Africa, southwestern Asia, and the Indian subcontinent, and persons of this ancestry in other parts of the world. **2.** Of, pertaining to, or characteristic of Caucasoids. —*n.* A member of the Caucasoid ethnic division.

Cau·ca·sus (kô′kə-səs). Also **Cau·ca·sia** (kô-kā′zhə, -shə). **1.** A region in the Soviet Union covering 154,250 square miles between the Black and Caspian seas. **2.** A range of mountains extending 900 miles and dividing the Caucasus region from northwest to southeast. Highest elevation, Mount Elbrus (18,480 feet).

Cau·ca·sus In·di·cus. The ancient name for the **Hindu Kush.**

cau·cus (kô′kəs) *n., pl.* **-cuses** or **-cusses.** **1.** A meeting of the members of a political party to decide upon questions of policy and the selection of candidates for office. **2.** *British.* A committee within a political party charged with determining policy. —*intr.v.* **caucused** or **-cussed, -cusing** or **-cussing, -cuses** or **-cusses.** To assemble in or hold a caucus. [Earlier *corcas,* probably of Algonquian origin, perhaps akin to *caucauasu* (Virginia Algonquian word for "counselor" recorded by Captain John Smith).]

cau·dad (kô′dăd′) *adv. Anatomy.* Toward the tail or posterior part of the body. [Latin *cauda,* tail (see **caudate**) + -AD.]

cau·dal (kôd′l) *adj.* **1.** *Anatomy.* Of, at, or near the tail or hind parts; posterior. **2.** *Zoology.* Taillike. [New Latin *caudalis,* from Latin *cauda,* tail. See **caudate.**] —**cau′dal·ly** *adv.*

caudal fin. The tail fin of a fish.

cau·date (kô′dāt′) *adj.* Also **cau·dat·ed** (-dā′tĭd). Having a tail. [New Latin *caudatus,* from Latin *cauda*†, tail.]

cau·dex (kô′dĕks′) *n., pl.* **-dices** (-də-sēz′) or **-dexes.** *Botany.* **1.** The thickened base of the stem of some perennial plants. **2.** A woody, trunklike stem, such as that of a tree fern. [Latin *caudex, cōdex*†, stem, tree trunk.]

cau·di·llo (kou-*thē*′lyō, -*thē*′yō) *n., pl.* **-llos.** In Spanish-speaking countries, a military leader who sets himself up as a dictator. [Spanish, chieftain, from Late Latin *capitellum,* small head, diminutive of *caput,* head. See **kaput** in Appendix.*]

cau·dle (kôd′l) *n.* A warm beverage given to ailing persons, consisting of wine or ale mixed with sugar, eggs, bread, and various spices. [Middle English *caudel,* from Old North French *caudel, chaudel,* from *chaud,* warm, from Latin *cal(i)dus.* See **kel-**[1] in Appendix.*]

caught. Past tense and past participle of **catch.**

caul (kôl) *n.* **1.** A portion of the membrane that surrounds a fetus and that sometimes covers its head at birth. **2.** The large omentum covering the intestines. [Middle English *calle,* probably from Old French *cale,* cap, from Germanic. See **skel-**[1] in Appendix.*]

caul·dron. Variant of **caldron.**

cau·les·cent (kô-lĕs′ənt) *adj. Botany.* Having a stem showing above the ground. [Latin *caulis,* stem (see **kaul-** in Appendix*) + -ESCENT.]

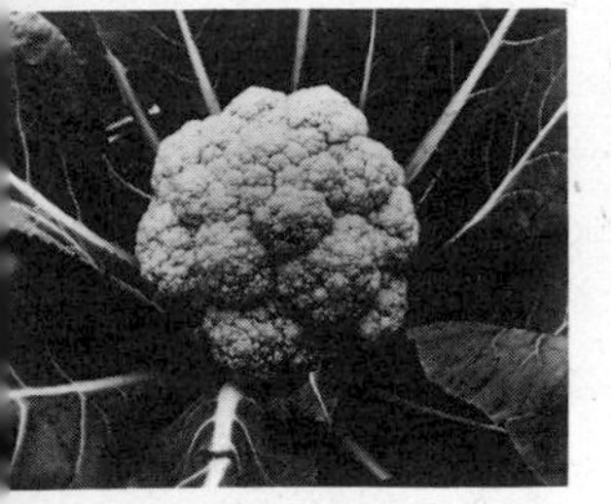

cauliflower

cau·li·cle (kô′lĭ-kəl) *n. Botany.* A small stem. [Latin *cauliculus,* diminutive of *caulis,* stem. See **kaul-** in Appendix.*]

cau·li·flow·er (kô′lĭ-flou′ər, kŏl′ĭ-) *n.* **1.** A plant, *Brassica oleracea botrytis,* related to the cabbage and broccoli and having an enlarged, crowded flower head. **2.** The compact, whitish flower head of this plant, eaten as a vegetable. [Earlier *colie-florie,* probably from Italian *caoli-fiori,* plural of *cavolo-fiore,* "flowered cabbage" : *cavolo,* cabbage, from Late Latin *caulus,* variant of Latin *caulis* (see **kaul-** in Appendix*) + *fiore,* flower, from Latin *flōs* (stem *flōr-*) (see **bhel-**[3] in Appendix*).]

cauliflower ear. An ear deformed by repeated blows.

cau·line (kô′līn′, -lĭn) *adj. Botany.* Of, having, or growing on a stem. [New Latin *caulinus,* from Latin *caulis,* stalk, stem. See **kaul-** in Appendix.*]

caulk (kôk) *tr.v.* **caulked, caulking, caulks.** Also **calk.** **1.** *Nautical.* To make (a boat) watertight by packing seams with oakum or tar. **2.** To make (pipes, for example) watertight or airtight by filling in cracks. [Middle English *ca(u)lken,* from Old North French *cauquer,* to trample, tread, from Latin *calcāre,* from *calx* (stem *calc-*), a heel. See **calk.**] —**caulk′er** *n.*

caus·al (kô′zəl) *adj.* **1.** Pertaining to or involving a cause. **2.** Constituting or expressing a cause. —*n.* A word or grammatical element expressing a cause or reason. —**caus′al·ly** *adv.*

cau·sal·i·ty (kô-zăl′ə-tē) *n., pl.* **-ties.** **1.** The relationship between cause and effect. **2.** A causal agency, force, or quality.

cau·sa·tion (kô-zā′shən) *n.* **1.** The act or process of causing. **2.** A cause. **3.** The relationship between cause and effect.

caus·a·tive (kô′zə-tĭv) *adj.* **1.** Functioning as a cause; effective. **2.** Designating a verb or verbal affix that expresses causation. In the phrase *to fell a tree, fell* is a causative verb. —*n.* A word or form expressing causation. —**caus′a·tive·ly** *adv.*

cause (kôz) *n.* **1.** That which produces an effect, result, or consequence; the person, event, or condition responsible for an action or result. **2.** A basis for an action or decision; ground; reason; motive. **3.** Good or sufficient reason or ground. **4.** A goal or principle served with dedication and zeal. **5.** The interests of a person or group engaged in a struggle: *"The cause of America is in great measure the cause of all mankind."* (Thomas Paine). **6.** *Law.* **a.** The ground for legal action. **b.** A lawsuit. **7.** A subject under debate or discussion. —*tr.v.* **caused, causing, causes.** To be the cause of; effect; make happen; bring about. [Middle English, from Old French, from Latin *causa*†, reason, purpose, motive, lawsuit.] —**caus′a·ble** *adj.* —**cause′less** *adj.* —**caus′er** *n.*

Synonyms: *cause, reason, occasion, antecedent.* These nouns denote things or prior conditions that bring about, or are associated with, certain effects. A *cause,* singly or as one of a series, must exist for an effect logically to occur: *Deficiency in vitamin C is the cause of scurvy. Reason* refers to what explains the occurrence or nature of an effect and suggests an effort of human thought: *There was no reason for the accident.* An *occasion* is the situation or time that permits existing causes to come into play: *The occasion for the robbery was the absence of the regular night watchman. Antecedent* refers to that which has gone before. It implies a relationship, not necessarily causal, with the thing or effect in question.

cause cé·lè·bre (kōz sā-lĕb′r′) *pl.* **causes célèbres** (kōz sā-lĕb′r′). *French.* **1.** A celebrated legal case. **2.** An issue arousing heated public debate and partisanship.

cau·se·rie (kōz-rē′) *n. French.* **1.** A chat. **2.** A short, conversational piece of writing.

cause·way (kôz′wā′) *n.* **1.** A raised roadway, as across water or marshland. **2.** A paved highway. [Middle English *caucewei* : *cauce,* from Old North French *cauciee,* from Vulgar Latin *calciāta* (unattested), paved (as with limestone), from Latin *calx* (stem *calc-*), limestone, small stone, from Greek *khalix,* small stone (see **calcium**) + *wei,* WAY.]

caus·tic (kôs′tĭk) *adj.* **1.** Able to burn, corrode, dissolve, or otherwise eat away by chemical action. **2.** Marked by sharp and bitter wit; cutting: *"Her new clothes were the subject of caustic comment."* (Willa Cather). **3.** *Optics.* Of or pertaining to light emitted from a point source and reflected or refracted from a curved surface. —See Synonyms at **sarcastic.** —*n.* A caustic material or substance. [Latin *causticus,* from Greek *kaustikos,* from *kaiein,* to burn. See **kēu-** in Appendix.*] —**caus′ti·cal·ly** *adv.* —**caus·tic′i·ty** (kôs-tĭs′ə-tē) *n.*

caustic potash. **Potassium hydroxide** *(see).*

caustic soda. **Sodium hydroxide** *(see).*

cau·ter·ize (kô′tə-rīz′) *tr.v.* **-ized, -izing, -izes.** To burn or sear with a cautery. [Old French *cauteriser,* from Late Latin *cautērizāre,* to brand, from Greek *kautēriazein,* from *kautērion,* branding iron. See **cautery.**] —**cau′ter·i·za′tion** *n.*

cau·ter·y (kô′tər-ē) *n., pl.* **-ies.** **1.** A caustic agent or a very hot or very cold instrument used to destroy aberrant tissue. **2.** Cauterization. [Latin *cautērium,* branding iron, from Greek *kautērion,* from *kaiein,* to burn. See **kēu-** in Appendix.*]

cau·tion (kô′shən) *n.* **1.** Forethought to avoid danger or harm. **2.** A warning; admonishment. **3.** *Informal.* Someone or something that is striking or alarming. —*tr.v.* **cautioned, -tioning, -tions.** To warn against danger; put on guard. See Synonyms at **warn.** [Middle English *caucion,* from Old French *caution,* from Latin *cautiō,* a guarding, from *cavēre* (past participle *cautus*), to watch, take heed. See **keu-**[1] in Appendix.*] —**cau′tion·ar′y** (-shə-nĕr′ē) *adj.*

cau·tious (kô′shəs) *adj.* Showing or practicing caution; wary; careful. —**cau′tious·ly** *adv.* —**cau′tious·ness** *n.*

Cau·ve·ry (kô′və-rē). Also **Ka·ve·ri** (kä′və-rē). A river of southern India, sacred to the Hindus, flowing 475 miles southeast to a wide delta in Madras on the Bay of Bengal.

cav. **1.** cavalier. **2.** cavalry.

cav·al·cade (kăv′əl-kād′, kăv′əl-kād′) *n.* **1.** A ceremonial procession, especially of horsemen or horse-drawn carriages. **2.** A colorful procession or display. [French, from Old French, from Old Italian *cavalcata,* from *cavalcare,* to ride on horseback, from Late Latin *caballicāre,* from Latin *caballus,* horse. See **cavalier.**]

cav·a·lier (kăv′ə-lîr′) *n. Abbr.* **cav.** **1.** A gentleman accomplished in arms. **2.** A gallant. **3.** A lady's dancing partner. —*adj.* **1.** Haughty; arrogant. **2.** Carefree and gay; offhand. [Old French, from Old Italian *cavaliere,* from Late Latin *caballārius,* horseman, rider, from Latin *caballus*†, horse.]

Cav·a·lier (kăv′ə-lîr′) *n.* A supporter of Charles I of England in his struggles against Parliament; a Royalist. —**Cav′a·lier′** *adj.*

cav·a·lier·ly (kăv′ə-lîr′lē) *adv.* With an ill-considered sureness verging on arrogance: *"he cavalierly dismisses the theory of both Freud and Jung"* (Walter Sutton). —*adj.* Haughty.

Cavalier poets. A group of English poets, including Lovelace and Suckling, associated with the court of Charles I.

ca·val·la (kə-văl′ə) *n., pl.* **-las** or **cavalla.** Also **ca·val·ly** (kə-văl-ē′) *pl.* **-lies** or **cavally.** **1.** Any of various tropical marine food fishes of the family Carangidae. **2.** The **king mackerel** *(see).* [Spanish *caballa,* horse mackerel, from Late Latin, feminine of Latin *caballus,* horse. See **cavalier.**]

cav·al·ry (kăv′əl-rē) *n., pl.* **-ries.** *Abbr.* **cav.** Troops trained to fight on horseback or, more recently, in armored vehicles. [Old French *cavallerie,* from Old Italian *cavalleria,* cavalry, chivalry, from *cavaliere,* CAVALIER.] —**cav′al·ry·man** *n.*

Cav·an (kăv′ən). **1.** A county of the Republic of Ireland, occupying 730 square miles in the northeast. Population, 57,000. **2.** The county seat of this county. Population, 3,200.

cave (kāv) *n.* A hollow beneath the earth's surface, often having an opening in the side of a hill or cliff. See Synonyms at **hole.** —*v.* **caved, caving, caves.** —*tr.* To hollow out. —*intr. Informal.* To fall in; to collapse. [Middle English, from Old French, from Latin *cava,* from the neuter plural of *cavus,* hollow. See **keu-**[3] in Appendix.*]

ca·ve·at (kā′vē-ăt′, kăv′ē-, kä′vē-) *n.* **1.** *Law.* A formal notice filed by an interested party with a court or officer, requesting the postponement of a proceeding until he is heard. **2.** A warning or caution. [Latin, let him beware, from *cavēre,* to beware, take care. See **keu-**[1] in Appendix.*]

ca·ve·at emp·tor (kā′vē-ăt′ ĕmp′tôr′, kăv′ē-, kä′vē-). *Latin.* Let the buyer beware.

cave·fish (kāv′fĭsh′) *n., pl.* **cavefish** or **-fishes.** Any of various freshwater fishes of the family Amblyopsidae, of subterranean waters, having rudimentary eyes. Also called "blindfish."

ă pat/ā pay/âr care/ä father/b bib/ch church/d deed/ĕ pet/ē be/f fife/g gag/h hat/hw which/ĭ pit/ī pie/îr pier/j judge/k kick/l lid, needle/m mum/n no, sudden/ng thing/ŏ pot/ō toe/ô paw, for/oi noise/ou out/o͝o took/o͞o boot/p pop/r roar/s sauce/sh ship, dish/

cave in. **1.** To fall in; collapse, as from being undermined. **2.** To cause to collapse. **3.** *Informal.* To cease resistance.
cave-in (kāv′ĭn′) *n.* An action of caving in.
Cav·ell (kăv′əl), **Edith Louisa.** 1865–1915. British nurse; executed by the Germans for aiding the escape of Allied soldiers.
cave man. **1.** A prehistoric man who lived in caves. **2.** *Informal.* One who is crude or brutal, especially toward women. **—cave′-man′** *adj.*
Cav·en·dish (kăv′ən-dĭsh), **Henry.** 1731–1810. British chemist and physicist; determined composition of air and water and calculated mean density of earth.
Cav·en·dish (kăv′ən-dĭsh), Sir **Thomas.** 1555?–1592. English navigator; led third expedition to circumnavigate the globe.
cav·ern (kăv′ərn) *n.* A large cave. *—tr.v.* **caverned, -erning, -erns.** **1.** To enclose in or as if in a cavern. **2.** To hollow out. [Middle English *caverne,* from Old French, from Latin *caverna,* from *cavus,* hollow. See **keu-³** in Appendix.*]
cav·ern·ous (kăv′ər-nəs) *adj.* **1.** Filled with caverns. **2.** Like a cavern in depth, vastness, or obscurity. **3.** Filled with cavities; porous. **—cav′ern·ous·ly** *adv.*
ca·vet·to (kə-vĕt′ō) *n., pl.* **-vetti** (-vĕt′ē) or **-tos.** A concave molding for cornices, shaped like a circular quadrant. [Italian, from *cavo,* hollow, from Latin *cavus.* See **keu-³** in Appendix.*]
cav·i·ar (kăv′ē-är′) *n.* Also **cav·i·are.** The roe of a sturgeon or other large fish, salted, seasoned, and eaten as a relish or delicacy. [Earlier *caviari, cavialy,* probably from French *caviar,* from Old Italian *caviaro,* from Turkish *havyār.*]
cav·i·corn (kăv′ə-kôrn′) *adj. Zoology.* Having hollow horns, as distinguished from bony antlers. [From New Latin *Cavicornia* (former designation of bovines) : Latin *cavus,* hollow (see **cave**) + *cornū,* horn (see **ker-¹** in Appendix*).]
cav·il (kăv′əl) *v.* **-iled, -iling, -ils.** Also *chiefly British* **-illed, -illing.** *—intr.* To raise unnecessary or trivial objections; to carp. Used with *at, about,* or *with.* *—tr.* To quibble about; detect petty flaws in. *—n.* A captious or trivial objection. [Old French *caviller,* from Latin *cavillārī,* to satirize, criticize, quibble, from *cavilla,* a jeering. See **kēl-** in Appendix.*] **—cav′il·er** *n.*
cav·i·ta·tion (kăv′ə-tā′shən) *n.* The sudden formation and collapse of low-pressure bubbles in liquids by means of mechanical forces, as those resulting from rotation of a marine propeller. [From CAVITY.]
cav·i·ty (kăv′ə-tē) *n., pl.* **-ties.** **1.** A hollow or hole. **2.** A hollow area within the body: *a sinus cavity.* **3.** A pitted area in a tooth caused by **caries** *(see).* —See Synonyms at **hole.** [French *cavité,* Old French *cavete,* from Late Latin *cavitās,* hollowness, from Latin *cavus,* hollow. See **cave.**]
ca·vort (kə-vôrt′) *intr.v.* **-vorted, -vorting, -vorts.** **1.** To bound or prance about in a sprightly manner; to caper. **2.** To make merry; to sport; to frolic. [Perhaps variant of CURVET.]
Ca·vour (kä-vōōr′), Conte **Camillo Benso di.** 1810–1861. Italian nationalist leader; premier of Sardinia (1852–59).
ca·vy (kā′vē) *n., pl.* **-vies.** Any of various short-tailed or apparently tailless South American rodents of the family Caviidae, which includes the guinea pig and the capybara. [New Latin *Cavia,* probably from Galibi *cabiai.*]
caw (kô) *n.* The hoarse, raucous sound uttered by a crow or similar bird. *—intr.v.* **cawed, cawing, caws.** To utter the characteristic sound of a crow. [Imitative.]
Cawn·pore. See **Kanpur.**
Cax·ton (kăk′stən), **William.** 1422?–1491. English printer; published first book printed in English (1474?).
cay (kē, kā) *n.* A small, low islet composed largely of coral or sand; a key. [Spanish *cayo,* probably from Old French *quai, cay,* QUAY.]
Cay·enne (kī-ĕn′, kā-). The capital of French Guiana, on Cayenne Island. Population, 19,000.
cay·enne pepper (kī-ĕn′, kā-). A condiment made from the very pungent fruit of a variety of the plant *Capsicum frutescens.* Also called "cayenne," "red pepper." [Earlier *kian, chian* (influenced by *Cayenne* Island), from Tupi *kyinha.*]
cay·man. Variant of **caiman.**
Cay·man Islands (kā-măn′, kā′mən). Also **Cay·mans** (kā-mănz′, kā′mənz). A group of three islands administered as a British colony, Grand Cayman, Little Cayman, and Cayman Brac, in the Caribbean Sea northwest of Jamaica. Population, 9,000. Capital, Georgetown, on Grand Cayman.
Ca·yu·ga (kā-yōō′gə, kī-) *n., pl.* **Cayuga** or **-gas.** **1.** A tribe of Iroquoian-speaking Indians formerly living around Cayuga and Seneca lakes in central New York. **2.** A member of this tribe. **3.** The language spoken by this tribe. **—Ca·yu′ga** *adj.*
Ca·yu·ga Lake (kā-yōō′gə, kī-). One of the Finger Lakes of central New York State, about 40 miles long and 2 miles wide.
cay·use (kī-yōōs′) *n. Western U.S.* A horse; especially, an Indian pony. [After the CAYUSE Indians.]
Cay·use (kī-yōōs′) *n., pl.* **Cayuse** or **-uses.** **1.** A tribe of Sahaptin-speaking Indians of Oregon. **2.** A member of this tribe. **3.** The language of this tribe. **—Cay·use′** *adj.*
ca·zique. Variant of **cacique.**
Cb The symbol for the element columbium.
C.B.D. cash before delivery.
cc cubic centimeter.
cc. chapters.
c.c., C.C. carbon copy.
C.C.A. Circuit Court of Appeals.
CCC **1.** Civilian Conservation Corps. **2.** Commodity Credit Corporation.
C.C.F. Cooperative Commonwealth Federation of Canada.
C clef. A clef sign used to form any of three clefs, soprano, alto, or tenor, by locating the tone C (320 cycles per second) on, respectively, the lowest line of the staff, the middle line, or the fourth (next to the highest) line.
CCS **1.** Airport code for Caracas, Venezuela. **2.** combined chiefs of staff.
CCU Airport code for Calcutta, India.
cd *Physics.* candela.
Cd The symbol for the element cadmium.
c.d. cash discount.
C.D. civil defense.
Cdr. commander.
Ce The symbol for the element cerium.
C.E. **1.** chemical engineer. **2.** civil engineer. **3.** common era.
Ce·a·rá (sā′ə-rä′). A state of northeastern Brazil, 57,370 square miles in area, with a coastline on the Atlantic Ocean. Population, 3,682,000. Capital, Fortaleza.
cease (sēs) *v.* **ceased, ceasing, ceases.** *—tr.* To put an end to; discontinue. *—intr.* To come to an end; stop. *—n.* Cessation. Used in the phrase *without cease.* [Middle English *ces(s)en,* from Old French *cesser,* from Latin *cessāre,* to delay, stop, frequentative of *cēdere* (past participle *cessus*), to CEDE.]
cease-fire (sēs′fīr′) *n.* **1.** An order to cease firing. **2.** A suspension of active hostilities; truce.
cease·less (sēs′lĭs) *adj.* Without stop; endless. See Synonyms at **continual.** **—cease′less·ly** *adv.*
Ce·bu (sā-bōō′). **1.** An island, 1,707 square miles in area, in the Visayan Islands, Republic of the Philippines. **2.** The principal city of this island, on the eastern coast. Population, 251,000.
Če·chy. The Czech name for **Bohemia.**
Ce·cil (sē′səl, sĕs′əl). A masculine given name. [Middle English, from Latin *Caecilius,* name of a Roman gens, from *caecus,* blind. See **kaiko-** in Appendix.*]
Cec·il (sĕs′əl, sĭs′əl), Lord **(Edward Christian) David.** Born 1902. British biographer.
Cec·il (sĕs′əl, sĭs′əl), **Robert.** First Earl of Salisbury and First Viscount Cranborne. 1563?–1612. English statesman; adviser to Elizabeth I and James I; son of William Cecil.
Cec·il (sĕs′əl, sĭs′əl), **Robert Arthur Talbot Gascoyne.** Third Marquis of Salisbury. 1830–1903. English statesman; three times prime minister (1885–1902).
Cec·il (sĕs′əl, sĭs′əl), **William.** First Baron Burghley or Burleigh. 1520–1598. English statesman; chief secretary of state to Elizabeth I; father of Robert Cecil.
Ce·cil·ia (sĭ-sēl′yə). Also **Cec·i·ly** (sĕs′ə-lē), **Cic·e·ly.** A feminine given name. [Middle English, from Latin *Caecilia,* feminine of *Caecilius.* See **Cecil.**]
Ce·cil·ia (sĭ-sēl′yə), **Saint.** Roman martyr of the third century A.D.; patron saint of music and of the blind.
ce·cro·pi·a moth (sĭ-krō′pē-ə). A large North American moth, *Hyalophora cecropia,* having wings with red, white, and black markings. [*Cecropia,* from New Latin, after *Cecrops,* Greek mythological king portrayed as half-man, half-dragon.]
ce·cum (sē′kəm) *n., pl.* **-ca** (-kə). Also **cae·cum.** **1.** A cavity with only one opening. **2.** *Anatomy.* The large blind pouch forming the beginning of the large intestine. In this sense also called "blind gut." [New Latin, from Latin *(intestinum) caecum,* blind (intestine), from *caecus,* blind. See **kaiko-** in Appendix.*] **—ce′cal** (sē′kəl) *adj.*
CED Council for Economic Development.
ce·dar (sē′dər) *n.* **1.** Any of several coniferous evergreen trees of the genus *Cedrus,* native to the Old World, such as the **cedar of Lebanon** *(see).* **2.** Any of various similar evergreen trees, mostly of the genera *Thuja, Chamaecyparis,* and *Juniperus.* **3.** The durable, aromatic, often reddish wood of a cedar. [Middle English *cedre,* from Old French, from Latin *cedrus,* cedar, juniper, from Greek *kedros*†.]
Ce·dar (sē′dər). A river flowing from southeastern Minnesota 330 miles southeast through Iowa to the Iowa River.
cedar of Lebanon. A tall evergreen tree, *Cedrus libani,* of Asia Minor, having short dark needles and fragrant hard wood. [Translation of Late Latin *cedrus libani* (translation of Hebrew *arzē Ləbānōn*).]
Cedar Rapids. An industrial city and railroad center in eastern Iowa on the Cedar River. Population, 92,000.
cedar waxwing. A North American bird, *Bombycilla cedrorum,* having a crested head and predominantly brown plumage. Also called "cedarbird." [Probably so called because it eats the berries of the red cedar.]
cede (sēd) *tr.v.* **ceded, ceding, cedes.** **1.** To surrender possession of officially or formally. **2.** To yield; grant. —See Synonyms at **relinquish.** [Old French *ceder,* from Latin *cēdere,* withdraw, yield. See **ked-¹** in Appendix.*]
ce·di (sē′dē) *n.* **1.** The basic monetary unit of Ghana, equal to 100 pesewa. See table of exchange rates at **currency.** **2.** A note worth one cedi.
ce·dil·la (sĭ-dĭl′ə) *n.* A mark (̧) placed beneath the letter *c* in the spelling of French, Portuguese, and Spanish, to indicate that the letter is to be pronounced (s), as in the French word *garçon.* The cedilla is also used for various purposes in Turkish and Rumanian spelling. [Obsolete Spanish *cedilla,* diminutive of *ceda,* the letter zee, from Late Latin *zēta,* ZETA (so called because a small *z* was formerly used to make a hard *c* sibilant).]
Ced·ric (sĕd′rĭk, sē′drĭk). A masculine given name. [Probably a mistake in Sir Walter Scott's *Ivanhoe* for *Cerdic*†, name of the traditional founder of Wessex.]
cee (sē) *n.* The letter *c.*
cei·ba (sā′bə) *n.* Any of various large tropical trees of the genus *Ceiba,* which includes the silk-cotton tree, the source of the silky fiber kapok. [New Latin, from Spanish, probably from Arawakan.]

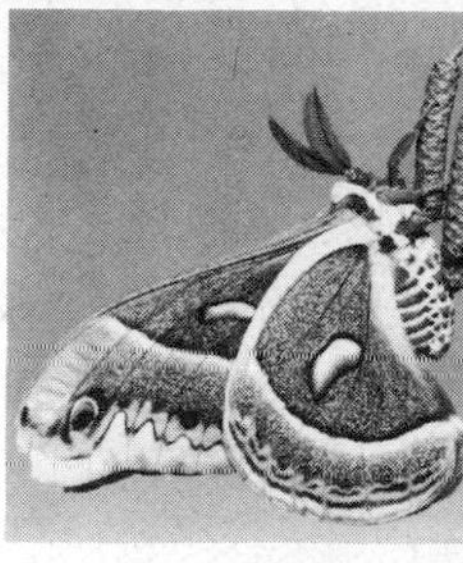
cecropia moth

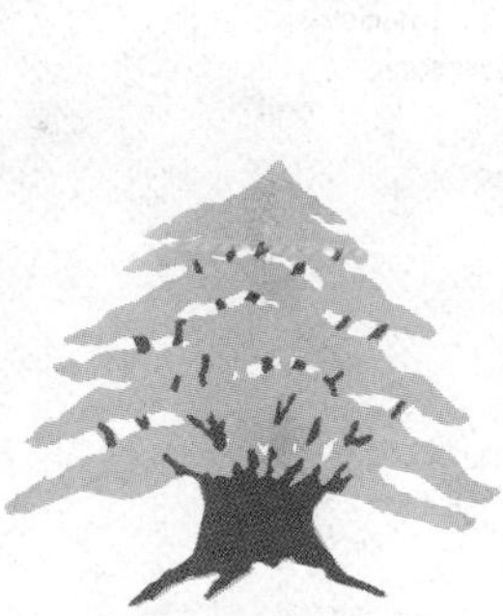
cedar of Lebanon
Stylized cedar as shown on the Lebanese flag

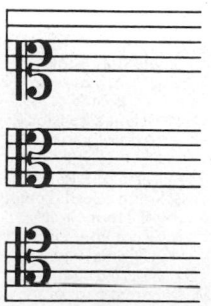

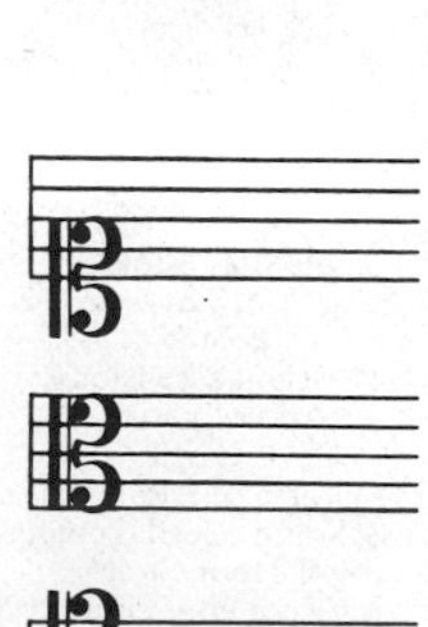
C clef
Above: Soprano clef
Center: Alto clef
Below: Tenor clef

ceil (sēl) *tr.v.* **ceiled, ceiling, ceils. 1.** To make a ceiling for. **2.** To provide (a ship) with interior planking. [Middle English *celen,* perhaps a back-formation from *celing,* CEILING.]

ceil·ing (sē′lĭng) *n.* **1.** The interior upper surface of a room. **2.** The planking applied to the interior framework of a ship. **3.** A maximum limit. **4.** Any of various vertical boundaries, especially of atmospheric visibility, cloud cover altitude, or operable aircraft altitude. [Middle English *celing*†.]

ceil·om·e·ter (sē-lŏm′ə-tər) *n.* A photoelectric instrument for ascertaining cloud heights. [CEIL(ING) + -METER.]

cel·a·don (sĕl′ə-dŏn′) *n.* Also **cé·la·don. 1.** Pale to very pale green. Also called "celadon green." See **color. 2.** Pale to very pale blue. Also called "celadon blue." See **color.** [French *céladon,* from *Céladon,* wan character in d'Urfé's *"Astrée"* (1610).] —**cel′a·don′** *adj.*

Ce·lae·no[1] (sĭ-lē′nō). *Greek Mythology.* One of the Pleiades.

Ce·lae·no[2] (sĭ-lē′nō) *n.* One of the six stars in the Pleiades cluster visible to the naked eye. [After CELAENO.]

cel·an·dine (sĕl′ən-dīn′, -dēn′) *n.* **1.** A plant, *Chelidonium majus,* native to Eurasia, having deeply divided leaves, yellow flowers, and yellow-orange juice. Also called "swallowwort." **2.** The **lesser celandine** *(see).* [Middle English *celidoine,* from Old French, from Medieval Latin *celidonia,* from Latin *chelidonia, chelidonium,* from Greek *khelidonion,* from *khelidōn,* swallow (the ancients associated the plant with the habits of the swallow). See **ghel-**[1] in Appendix.*]

-cele[1]**.** Indicates a tumor or hernia; for example, **cystocele.** [From Greek *kēlē*†, tumor.]

-cele[2]**, -coel, -coele.** Indicates a hollow chamber; for example, **hematocele, blastocoel, blastocoele.** [New Latin *-cela, -coela,* from Greek *koilos,* hollow. See **keu-**[3] in Appendix.*]

Cel·e·bes. The former name for **Sulawesi.**

Cel·e·bes Sea (sĕl′ə-bēz, sə-lē′bēz). The part of the western Pacific Ocean between the islands of Sulawesi and Mindanao.

cel·e·brant (sĕl′ə-brənt) *n.* **1.** The priest officiating at the celebration of the Eucharist. **2.** A person who participates in a religious ceremony or rite. **3.** A participant in any celebration.
Usage: *Celebrant,* in the sense of a participant in any celebration (*New Year's Eve celebrant*), is acceptable to 51 per cent of the Usage Panel. *Celebrator* is an undisputed alternative.

cel·e·brate (sĕl′ə-brāt′) *v.* **-brated, -brating, -brates.** —*tr.* **1.** To observe (a day or event) with ceremonies of respect, festivity, or rejoicing. **2.** To perform (a religious ceremony). **3.** To announce publicly; proclaim. **4.** To extol; praise. —*intr.* **1.** To observe an occasion with appropriate ceremony, festivity, or merrymaking. **2.** To perform a religious ceremony. —See Synonyms at **observe.** [Latin *celebrāre,* to frequent, fill, celebrate, from *celeber,* numerous, much frequented. See **kel-**[5] in Appendix.*] —**cel′e·bra′tion** *n.* —**cel′e·bra′tor** (-brā′tər) *n.* —**ce·leb′ra·to′ry** (-tôr′ē, -tōr′ē) *adj.*

cel·e·brat·ed (sĕl′ə-brā′tĭd) *adj.* Famous.

ce·leb·ri·ty (sə-lĕb′rə-tē) *n., pl.* **-ties. 1.** A famous person. **2.** Notoriety or renown; fame. [Latin *celebritās,* from *celeber,* numerous. See **kel-**[5] in Appendix.*]

ce·le·ri·ac (sə-lîr′ē-ăk′, sĭ-lĕr′-) *n.* A variety of celery, *Apium graveolens rapaceum,* cultivated for its edible, turniplike root. [From CELERY.]

ce·ler·i·ty (sə-lĕr′ə-tē) *n.* Swiftness; quickness; speed. [Middle English *celerite,* from Old French, from Latin *celeritās,* from *celer,* swift. See **kel-**[5] in Appendix.*]

cel·er·y (sĕl′ər-ē) *n.* A plant, *Apium graveolens dulce,* native to Eurasia and widely cultivated for its edible stalks and its small seeds, used as seasoning. [French *céleri,* from Italian (Lombardy dialect) *seleri,* plural of *selero,* from Late Latin *selīnum,* from Greek *selinon*†, celery.]

celery cabbage. Chinese cabbage *(see).*

ce·les·ta (sə-lĕs′tə) *n.* Also **ce·leste** (sə-lĕst′). A musical instrument having a keyboard and metal plates struck by hammers that produce bell-like tones. [French *célesta,* coined from *céleste,* celestial, from Latin *caelestis,* CELESTIAL.]

ce·les·tial (sə-lĕs′chəl) *adj.* **1.** Of or pertaining to the sky or the heavens. **2.** Of, from, or suggestive of heaven; spiritual; divine. **3.** *Usually capital* **C.** Of or pertaining to the Chinese people or to the former Chinese Empire. —*n.* **1.** A heavenly being; a god or an angel. **2.** *Capital* **C.** *Archaic.* A Chinese person. Usually used humorously. [Middle English, from Old French, from Latin *caelestis,* from *caelum*†, sky, heaven.]

Celestial Empire. The Chinese Empire. [Translation of Chinese *t'ien*[1] *ch'ao*[2], "heavenly empire" (from the belief that the emperors were sons of Heaven).]

celestial equator. A great circle on the celestial sphere in the same plane as the earth's equator.

celestial globe. A model of the celestial sphere showing the stars and other celestial bodies.

celestial navigation. Ship or aircraft navigation based on the positions of celestial bodies. Also called "astronavigation."

celestial pole. Either of two diametrically opposite points at which the extensions of the earth's axis intersect the celestial sphere.

celestial sphere. An imaginary sphere of infinite extent with the earth at its center. The stars, planets, and other heavenly bodies appear to be located on its imaginary surface.

cel·es·tite (sĕl′ĭs-tīt′, sə-lĕs′tīt′) *n.* An important white, red-brown, or light-blue strontium ore, essentially strontium sulfate, $SrSO_4$. [German *Zölestin,* from Latin *caelestis,* CELESTIAL (from its blue color).]

Ce·lia (sēl′yə). A feminine given name. [Short for CECILIA.]

ce·li·ac (sē′lē-ăk′) *adj.* Also **coe·li·ac.** Of or relating to the abdomen. [Latin *coeliacus,* from Greek *koiliakos,* from *koilia,* bowels, abdomen, from *koilos,* hollow. See **keu-**[3] in Appendix.*]

celiac disease. A chronic nutritional disturbance of infants and young children, caused by improper absorption of fats and resulting in malnutrition, distended abdomen, and diarrhea.

cel·i·ba·cy (sĕl′ə-bə-sē) *n.* The condition of being unmarried, especially by reason of religious vows. [Latin *caelibātus,* celibacy, from *caelebs*†, unmarried.]

cel·i·bate (sĕl′ə-bĭt) *n.* One who remains unmarried, especially by religious vow. —*adj.* Unmarried. [From Latin *caelebs* (stem *caelib-*), unmarried. See **celibacy.**]

cell (sĕl) *n.* **1.** A narrow, confining room, as in a prison, asylum, or convent. **2.** A small and humble abode, such as a cave or hut. **3.** *Ecclesiastical.* A small religious house dependent on a larger one, as a priory within an abbey. **4.** The primary organizational unit of a political party of Leninist structure, consisting of three or more members living or working in the same place or engaged in the same occupation. **5.** A small group of Christian lay persons working for the propagation of the faith. **6.** *Biology.* The smallest structural unit of an organism that is capable of independent functioning, consisting of one or more nuclei, cytoplasm, various organelles, and inanimate matter, all surrounded by a semipermeable plasma membrane. **7.** *Biology.* A small, enclosed cavity or space, such as a compartment in a honeycomb or within a plant ovary, or an area bordered by veins in an insect's wing. **8.** *Electricity.* **a.** A single unit for electrolysis or for conversion of chemical into electric energy, usually consisting of a container with electrodes and an electrolyte. **b.** A single unit that converts radiant energy into electric energy: *a solar cell.* —*v.* **celled, celling, cells.** —*tr.* To store in a honeycomb. —*intr.* To live in a cell. [Middle English *celle,* from Old French, from Latin *cella,* cella, storeroom, chamber. See **kel-**[4] in Appendix.*]

cel·la (sĕl′ə) *n., pl.* **cellae** (sĕl′ē′). The inner room of an ancient Greek or Roman temple. [Latin *cella,* cella, CELL.]

cel·lar (sĕl′ər) *n.* **1.** A room used for storage, usually beneath the ground or under a building. **2.** A dark, cool room for storing wines. **3.** A stock of wines. —*tr.v.* **cellared, -laring, -lars.** To store in a cellar. [Middle English *celer,* from Norman French, from Late Latin *cellārium,* storehouse, larder, from Latin *cella,* storeroom, CELL.]

cel·lar·age (sĕl′ər-ĭj) *n.* **1.** A fee charged for storage in a cellar. **2.** A cellar, or cellars collectively.

cel·lar·er (sĕl′ər-ər) *n.* The member of a medieval monastic community who was responsible for dealings with outside tradesmen and for the maintenance of adequate supplies of food and drink. [Middle English *celerer,* from Norman French, from Late Latin *cellāriārius,* from *cellārium,* CELLAR.]

cel·lar·et (sĕl′ə-rĕt′) *n.* A cabinet used for storing bottles of wine. [Diminutive of CELLAR.]

cell-block (sĕl′blŏk′) *n.* A unit of cells in a prison.

Cel·li·ni (chə-lē′nē; *Italian* chĕl-lē′nē), **Benvenuto.** 1500–1571. Italian goldsmith and sculptor; author of *Autobiography.*

cel·lo (chĕl′ō) *n., pl.* **-los.** Also **′cel·lo.** A four-stringed instrument of the violin family, pitched lower than the viola but higher than the double bass. Also called "violoncello." [Short for VIOLONCELLO.] —**cel′list** *n.*

cel·loi·din (sĕ-loid′n) *n.* A pure pyroxylin in which specimen sections are embedded for microscopic examination. [CEL-L(ULOSE) + -OID + -IN.]

cel·lo·phane (sĕl′ə-fān′) *n.* A thin, flexible, transparent cellulose material made from wood pulp and used as a moisture-proof wrapping. [CELL(ULOSE) + -PHANE.]

cel·lu·lar (sĕl′yə-lər) *adj.* **1.** Pertaining to or resembling a cell. **2.** Consisting of or containing a cell or cells.

cel·lu·lase (sĕl′yə-lās′, -lāz′) *n.* Any of several enzymes found in fungi, bacteria, and lower animals, that hydrolyze cellulose. [CELLUL(OSE) + -ASE.]

cel·lule (sĕl′yōōl) *n.* A small cell. [French, monk's cell, from Latin *cellula,* small apartment, diminutive of *cella,* CELL.]

cel·lu·li·tis (sĕl′yə-lī′tĭs) *n.* Inflammation of subcutaneous tissue. [New Latin : Latin *cellula,* cell (see **cellule**) + -ITIS.]

Cel·lu·loid (sĕl′yə-loid′) *n.* A trademark for a colorless, flammable material made from nitrocellulose and camphor and used for toys, toilet articles, photographic film, and as a substitute for materials such as ivory and amber. [CELLUL(OSE) + -OID.]

cel·lu·lose (sĕl′yə-lōs′, -lōz′) *n.* An amorphous carbohydrate polymer, $(C_6H_{10}O_5)_x$, the main constituent of all plant tissues and fibers, used in the manufacture of many fibrous products, including paper, textiles, and explosives. [French, from *cellule,* biological cell, CELLULE.] —**cel′lu·los′ic** *adj.*

cellulose acetate. A cellulose resin used in lacquers, photographic film, transparent sheeting, and cigarette filters.

cellulose nitrate. A tough thermoplastic, **nitrocellulose** *(see).*

ce·lom. Variant of **coelom.**

Cel·o·tex (sĕl′ə-tĕks) *n.* A trademark for a building board made of compressed bagasse, used for insulation and soundproofing.

Cel·si·us (sĕl′sē-əs, -shəs) *adj. Abbr.* **C** Of or pertaining to a temperature scale that registers the freezing point of water as 0°C and the boiling point as 100°C under normal atmospheric pressure. Also called "centigrade." The designation *Celsius* has been official since 1948, but *centigrade* remains in common use. [Originally devised by Anders *Celsius* (1701–1744), Swedish astronomer.]

Cel·sus (sĕl′səs), **Aulus Cornelius.** Roman medical author of the first century A.D.

celt (sĕlt) *n.* A prehistoric axlike tool. [Late Latin *celtis, celtes*†, chisel, a possible misreading of *certe,* surely, in a disputed text of the Vulgate (Job 19:24) (influenced in form by CELT).]

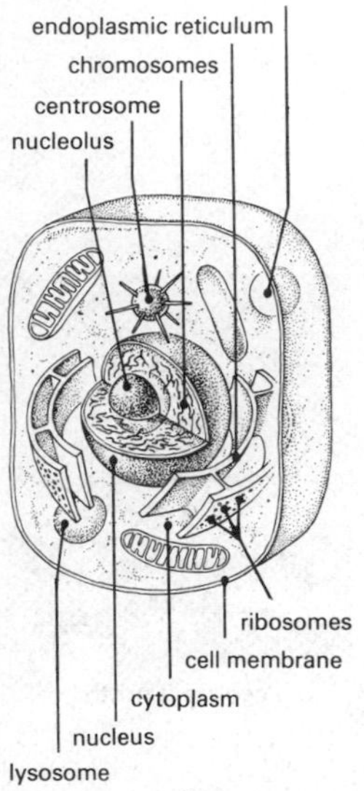
vacuole
endoplasmic reticulum
chromosomes
centrosome
nucleolus
ribosomes
cell membrane
cytoplasm
nucleus
lysosome

cell

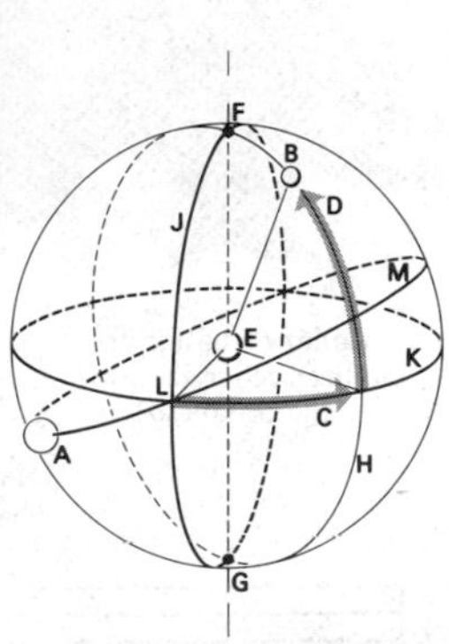
F
B
D
J
M
E
K
L
C
A
H
G

celestial sphere
A. Sun
B. Star
C. Right ascension
D. Declination
E. Earth
F. North celestial pole
G. South celestial pole
H. Hour circle
J. Zero hour circle
K. Celestial equator
L. Vernal equinox
M. Apparent path of the sun

Celt (kĕlt, sĕlt) *n.* Also **Kelt** (kĕlt). **1.** One of an ancient people of western and central Europe, including the Britons and the Gauls. **2.** A speaker or a descendant of speakers of a Celtic language. [French *Celte,* singular of *Celtes,* from Latin *Celtae,* from Greek *Keltoi*†.]

Celt·ic (kĕl′tĭk, sĕl′-) *n.* Also **Kelt·ic** (kĕl′tĭk). *Abbr.* **C., Celt.** A subfamily of the Indo-European family of languages, subdivided into the Brythonic branch, consisting of Cornish, Welsh, and Breton, and the Goidelic branch, consisting of Irish Gaelic, Scottish Gaelic, and Manx. —*adj.* Also **Kelt·ic.** Of or pertaining to the Celtic people and languages.

Celtic Church. The Church as it existed throughout the British Isles until the end of the sixth century A.D. and as it held out, at variance with the Church of Rome, in Wales and Ireland for some time.

Celtic cross. An upright cross superimposed on a circle.

Celt·i·cism (kĕl′tə-sĭz′əm, sĕl′-) *n.* **1.** A Celtic custom. **2.** A fondness for Celtic customs. **3.** A Celtic idiom.

Celt·i·cist (kĕl′tə-sĭst, sĕl′-) *n.* A specialist in Celtic culture.

cem·ba·lo (chĕm′bə-lō′) *n., pl.* **-los.** A harpsichord. [Italian, short for *clavicembalo,* from Medieval Latin *clāvicymbalum* : Latin *clāvis,* key (see **klēu-** in Appendix*) + *cymbalum,* CYMBAL.] —**cem′ba·list** *n.*

ce·ment (sĭ-mĕnt′) *n.* **1.** Any of various construction adhesives, consisting essentially of powdered, calcined rock and clay materials, that form a paste with water and can be molded or poured to set as a solid mass. See **Portland cement, hydraulic cement.** **2.** Any substance that hardens to act as an adhesive; glue. **3.** *Geology.* A chemically precipitated substance that binds particles of clastic rocks. **4.** Variant of **cementum.** —*v.* **cemented, -menting, -ments.** —*tr.* **1.** To bind with or as if with cement. **2.** To cover or coat with cement. —*intr.* To become cemented. [Middle English *siment, cyment,* from Old French *ciment,* from Latin *caementum,* rough quarried stone, and its plural *caementa,* marble chips (used to make lime), from *caedere,* to cut, hew. See **skhai-** in Appendix.*] —**ce·ment′er** *n.*

ce·men·ta·tion (sē′mĕn-tā′shən) *n.* **1.** The process or result of cementing. **2.** A metallurgical coating process in which iron or steel is immersed in a powder of another metal, such as zinc, chromium, or aluminum, and heated to a temperature below the melting point of either.

ce·ment·ite (sĭ-mĕn′tīt′) *n.* A hard brittle iron carbide, Fe_3C, found in steel with more than 0.85 per cent carbon. [From CEMENT.]

cement mixer. A **concrete mixer** *(see).*

ce·ment·um (sĭ-mĕn′təm) *n.* Also **ce·ment** (sĭ-mĕnt′). A bony substance covering the root of a tooth. [New Latin, from Latin *caementum,* rough stone, CEMENT.]

cem·e·ter·y (sĕm′ə-tĕr′ē) *n., pl.* **-ies.** A place for burying the dead; graveyard. [Middle English *cimitery,* from Late Latin *coemētērium,* from Greek *koimētērion,* sleeping room, burial place, from *koiman,* to put to sleep. See **kei-**[1] in Appendix.*]

cen. **1.** central. **2.** century.

cen·a·cle (sĕn′ə-kəl) *n.* A small dining room, usually on an upper floor. [Middle English, from Old French, from Late Latin *cēnāculum,* dining room, the Cenacle of the Last Supper, from Latin *cēna,* dinner. See **sker-**[1] in Appendix.*]

-cene. Indicates a recent geological period; for example, **Neocene.** [From Greek *kainos,* new, fresh. See **ken-**[3] in Appendix.*]

cen·o·bite (sĕn′ə-bīt′, sē′nə-) *n.* Also **coen·o·bite.** A member of a religious convent or community. [Late Latin *coenobita,* from *coenobium,* convent, from Greek *koinobion,* life in community : *koinos,* common (see **kom** in Appendix*) + *bios,* life (see **gwei-** in Appendix*).] —**cen′o·bit′ic** (-bĭt′ĭk), **cen′o·bit′i·cal** *adj.* —**cen′o·bit′ism′** (sĕn′ə-bīt-ĭz′əm, sē′nə-) *n.*

ce·no·gen·e·sis (sē′nō-jĕn′ə-sĭs, sĕn′ō-) *n.* Also **coe·no·gen·e·sis.** The environmentally determined development of characteristics or structures in an organism. [Greek *kainos,* fresh, new (see **ken-**[3] in Appendix*) + GENESIS.] —**ce′no·ge·net′ic** (-jə-nĕt′ĭk) *adj.* —**ce′no·ge·net′i·cal·ly** *adv.*

cen·o·taph (sĕn′ə-tăf′, -täf′) *n.* A monument erected in honor of a dead person whose remains lie elsewhere. [Old French *cenotaphe,* from Latin *cenotaphium,* from Greek *kenotaphion,* empty tomb : *kenos,* empty (see **ken-**[4] in Appendix*) + *taphos,* tomb (see **dhembh-** in Appendix*).] —**cen′o·taph′ic** *adj.*

Ce·no·zo·ic (sē′nə-zō′ĭk, sĕn′ə-) *adj.* Of, belonging to, or designating the latest era of geologic time, which includes the Tertiary and Quaternary periods and is characterized by the evolution of mammals, birds, plants, modern continents, and glaciation. See **geology.** —*n. Geology.* The Cenozoic era. Preceded by *the.* [Greek *kainos,* new, fresh (see **ken-**[3] in Appendix*) + -ZOIC.]

cense (sĕns) *tr.v.* **censed, censing, censes.** **1.** To perfume with incense. **2.** To offer incense to. [Middle English *censen,* short for *encensen,* to burn incense, from Old French *encenser,* from *encens,* INCENSE (noun).]

cen·ser (sĕn′sər) *n.* An incense vessel. Also called "thurible." [Middle English *censer,* from Old French *censier,* short for *encensier,* from *encens,* INCENSE (noun).]

cen·sor (sĕn′sər) *n.* **1.** An authorized examiner of literature, plays, or other material, who may prohibit what he considers morally or otherwise objectionable. **2.** An official, as in the military or a prison, who examines personal mail and official dispatches to remove any information considered secret or improper. **3.** Any person who condemns or censures. **4.** In ancient Rome, one of two officials responsible for supervising the public census and public behavior and morals. **5.** *Psychoanalysis. Rare.* The agent responsible for **censorship** *(see).* —*tr.v.* **censored, -soring, -sors.** To examine and expurgate. [Latin *cēnsor,* from *cēnsēre,* to assess, estimate, judge. See **kens-** in Appendix.*] —**cen·so′ri·al** (sĕn-sôr′ē-əl, sĕn-sōr′-) *adj.*

cen·so·ri·ous (sĕn-sôr′ē-əs, sĕn-sōr′-) *adj.* **1.** Tending to reprimand or censure; faultfinding. **2.** Expressing censure. [Latin *cēnsōrius,* of a censor, from *cēnsor,* CENSOR.] —**cen·so′ri·ous·ly** *adv.* —**cen·so′ri·ous·ness** *n.*

cen·sor·ship (sĕn′sər-shĭp′) *n.* **1.** The act or process of censoring. **2.** The office or authority of a censor. **3.** A program or policy of censoring. **4.** *Psychoanalysis.* The inhibition by either ego or superego of conscious awareness of painful feelings or ideas.

cen·sur·a·ble (sĕn′shər-ə-bəl) *adj.* Deserving censure. —**cen′sur·a·ble·ness, cen′sur·a·bil′i·ty** *n.* —**cen′sur·a·bly** *adv.*

cen·sure (sĕn′shər) *n.* An expression of blame or disapproval. —*v.* **censured, -suring, -sures.** —*tr.* To criticize severely; blame. —*intr.* To express severe criticism or disapproval. —See Synonyms at **criticize.** [Latin *cēnsūra,* censorship, the office of a censor, from *cēnsor,* CENSOR.] —**cen′sur·er** *n.*

cen·sus (sĕn′səs) *n.* An official, usually periodic, enumeration of population. [Latin *cēnsus,* registration of citizens, from *cēnsēre,* to assess, tax. See **kens-** in Appendix.*]

cent (sĕnt) *n. Abbr.* **c., C., ct.** **1. a.** *Symbol* ¢ A monetary unit equal to $1/100$ of the dollar of the United States. **b.** A monetary unit equal to $1/100$ of the dollar of Australia, Canada, Ethiopia, Guyana, Liberia, Malaysia, New Zealand, Trinidad and Tobago, Western Samoa, Hong Kong, and Singapore. **c.** A monetary unit equal to $1/100$ of the guilder of the Netherlands, Surinam, and the Netherlands Antilles, the leone of Sierra Leone, the piaster of South Vietnam, the rand of the Republic of South Africa, the rupee of Ceylon and Mauritius, and the yuan of the Republic of China. **d.** A monetary unit equal to $1/100$ of the shilling of Kenya, Tanzania, Uganda, and the Somali Republic. See table of exchange rates at **currency.** **2. a.** A coin worth one cent. Also called "penny." **b.** A note worth one cent. [Old French, "hundred," from Latin *centum.* See **dekm̥** in Appendix.*]

cent. **1.** centime. **2.** central. **3.** century.

cen·tal (sĕn′təl) *n. Rare.* A hundredweight. [From Latin *centum,* hundred. See **dekm̥** in Appendix.*]

cen·taur (sĕn′tôr′) *n.* **1.** *Greek Mythology.* One of a race of monsters, born of Ixion, having the head, arms, and trunk of a man and the body and legs of a horse. **2.** *Capital* **C.** Variant of **Centaurus.** [Middle English *Centaur,* from Latin *Centaurus,* from Greek *Kentauros*†, originally the name of a primitive Thessalian tribe.]

Cen·tau·rus (sĕn-tôr′əs) *n.* Also **Cen·taur** (sĕn′tôr′). A constellation in the Southern Hemisphere near Vela and Lupus. [Latin, CENTAUR.]

cen·tau·ry (sĕn′tôr′ē) *n., pl.* **-ries.** **1.** Any of several plants of the genus *Centaurium,* native to Eurasia; especially, *C. umbellatum,* having clusters of rose-purple flowers. **2.** A plant of the genus *Centaurea,* which includes the cornflower and knapweed. [Middle English *centaure,* from Old French *centaure,* from Late Latin *centaurea,* variant of Latin *centaureum,* from Greek *kentaureion,* centaury, from *Kentauros,* CENTAUR (its medicinal properties were found by the centaur Chiron, a physician).]

cen·ta·vo (sĕn-tä′vō) *n., pl.* **-vos.** **1.** A monetary unit equal to $1/100$ of the colon of El Salvador, the cordoba of Nicaragua, the escudo of Portugal, the lempira of Honduras, the cruzeiro of Brazil, the peso of Argentina, Bolivia, Colombia, Cuba, the Dominican Republic, Mexico, and the Philippines, the quetzal of Guatemala, the sol of Peru, and the sucre of Ecuador. See table of exchange rates at **currency.** **2.** A coin worth one centavo. [Spanish, "a hundredth," from Latin *centum,* hundred. See **dekm** in Appendix.*]

cen·te·nar·i·an (sĕn′tə-nâr′ē-ən) *n.* A person one hundred years old or older. [From Latin *centēnārius,* CENTENARY.] —**cen′te·nar′i·an** *adj.*

cen·ten·a·ry (sĕn-tĕn′ə-rē, sĕn′tə-nĕr′ē) *adj.* **1.** Of or pertaining to a 100-year period. **2.** Occurring once every 100 years. —*n., pl.* **centenaries.** **1.** A 100-year period. **2.** A 100th anniversary. [Latin *centēnārius,* of a hundred, from *centēnī,* a hundred each, from *centum,* hundred. See **dekm** in Appendix.*]

cen·ten·ni·al (sĕn-tĕn′ē-əl) *adj.* **1.** Of or pertaining to an age or period of 100 years. **2.** Occurring once every 100 years. **3.** Of or pertaining to a 100th anniversary. —*n.* A 100th anniversary or a celebration of this. [Latin *centum,* hundred (see **dekm̥** in Appendix*) + (BI)ENNIAL.] —**cen·ten′ni·al·ly** *adv.*

cen·ter (sĕn′tər) *n.* Also *chiefly British* **cen·tre.** *Abbr.* **ctr.** **1.** A point equidistant or at the average distance from all points on the sides or outer boundaries of anything; middle. **2.** *Geometry.* **a.** A point equidistant from the vertexes of a regular polygon. **b.** A point equidistant from all points on the circumference of a circle or on the surface of a sphere. **3.** A point around which something revolves; axis. **4.** A part of an object that is surrounded by the rest; core. **5.** A place of concentrated activity or influence. **6.** A person or thing that is the chief object of attention, interest, activity, or emotion. **7.** A person, object, or group occupying a middle position. **8.** A political policy or group representing a compromise between the **right** and **left** *(both of which see).* **9. a.** The ring circling the bull's eye of a target. **b.** A shot that hits this ring. **10.** In some team sports, a player who holds a middle position on the field, court, or forward line. —*v.* **centered, -tering, -ters.** Also *chiefly British* **centre, -tred, -tring, -tres.** —*tr.* **1.** To place in or on a center. **2.** To concentrate at a center. **3.** To determine the center of. **4.** *Football.* To pass (the ball) from the line to a back. —*intr.* **1.** To be concentrated; cluster. **2.** To have a central theme or concern.

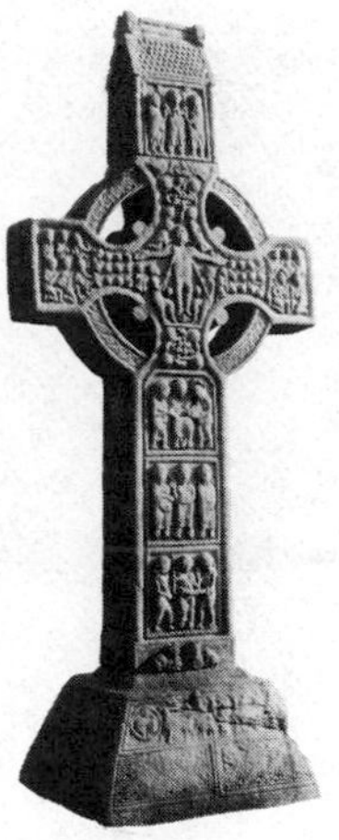

Celtic cross

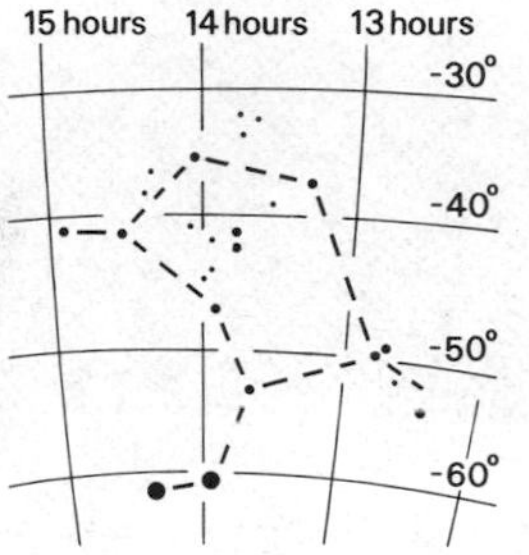

Centaurus

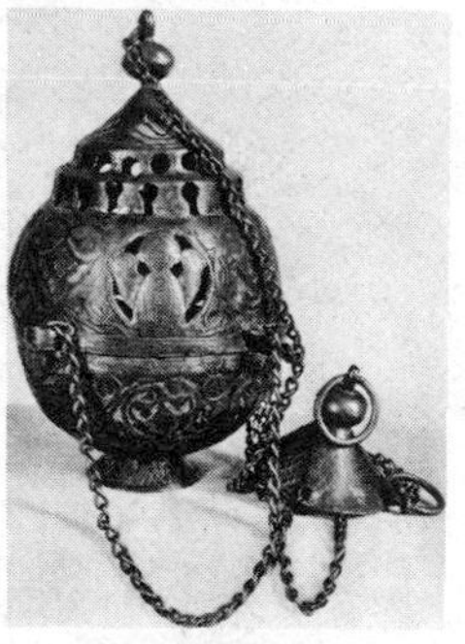

censer
Fourteenth-century French

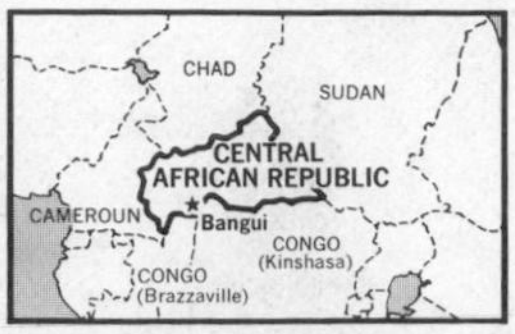

Central African Republic

See Usage note below. —*adj.* Also *chiefly British* **cen·tre.** Central; middle. [Middle English *centre,* from Old French, from Latin *centrum,* center, stationary point of a compass, from Greek *kentron,* sharp point, stationary point of a pair of compasses, from *kentein,* to prick. See **kent-** in Appendix.*]

Usage: *Center,* as an intransitive verb, is properly used with *on, upon, in,* or *at: The dispute centers on the effects of automation.* The familiar construction *center around* (or *about*) is often condemned as a misconception of *center* (point or focus). In the preceding example, *dispute centers around the effects* is unacceptable in writing to 68 per cent of the Usage Panel; but *revolves around* (or *about*) is permissible.

center bit. A bit having a sharp center point, used in carpentry for boring holes.

cen·ter·board (sĕn′tər-bôrd′, -bōrd′) *n. Nautical.* A flat board or metal plate that can be lowered through the bottom of a sailboat to prevent drifting and provide stability.

center of gravity. *Abbr.* **c.g.** The point in or near a body at which the gravitational potential energy of the body is equal to that of a single particle of the same mass located at that point and through which the resultant of the gravitational forces on the component particles of the body acts.

center of mass. *Abbr.* **c.m.** The point about which the sum of all the linear moments of mass of the particles in a body is zero. Also called "barycenter."

cen·ter·piece (sĕn′tər-pēs′) *n.* A decorative object or arrangement placed at the center of a dining table.

center punch. A tool with a sharp point used in metalworking to mark centers or center lines on pieces to be drilled.

cen·tes·i·mal (sĕn-tĕs′ə-məl) *adj.* **1.** Hundredth. **2.** Pertaining to or divided into hundredths. [From Latin *centēsimus,* hundredth, from *centum,* hundred. See **dekm̥** in Appendix.*] —**cen·tes′i·mal·ly** *adv.*

cen·tes·i·mo[1] (sĕn-tĕs′ə-mō′; *Italian* chān-tā′zē-mō′) *n., pl.* **-mos** or **-mi** (-mē). A monetary unit equal to 1/100 of the lira of Italy. See table of exchange rates at **currency.** [Italian, "hundredth," from Latin *centēsimus,* CENTESIMAL.]

cen·tes·i·mo[2] (sĕn-tĕs′ə-mō′; *Spanish* sĕn-tĕ′sē-mō′) *n., pl.* **-mos** (-mōs′). A coin equal to 1/100 of the balboa of Panama, the escudo of Chile, and the peso of Uruguay. See table of exchange rates at **currency.** [Spanish, "hundredth," from Latin *centēsimus,* CENTESIMAL.]

centi-, cent-. *Abbr.* **c** Indicates a hundredth; for example, **centinewton, centile.** [French, from Latin *centum,* hundred. See **dekm̥** in Appendix.*]

cen·ti·grade (sĕn′tĭ-grād′) *adj.* **1.** Consisting of or divided into 100 degrees. **2.** *Abbr.* **C** Designating a temperature scale, **Celsius** *(see).* [French : CENTI- + GRADE.]

cen·ti·gram (sĕn′tĭ-grăm) *n. Abbr.* **cg** One hundredth (10^{-2}) of a gram. See **measurement.**

cen·tile (sĕn′tĭl, -tĭl′) *n.* **Percentile** *(see).* [CENT(I)- + -ILE.]

cen·ti·li·ter (sĕn′tə-lē′tər) *n. Abbr.* **cl** One hundredth (10^{-2}) of a liter. See **measurement.** [French *centilitre* : CENTI- + LITER.]

cen·time (săn′tēm′; *French* säN-tēm′) *n. Abbr.* **c., C., cent.** **1. a.** A monetary unit equal to 1/100 of the franc of France, Belgium, Burundi, Cameroun, Central African Republic, Chad, Congo (Brazzaville), Dahomey, Gabon, Guinea, Ivory Coast, Luxembourg, Malagasy Republic, Mali, Mauritania, Niger, Rwanda, Senegal, Switzerland, Togo, Upper Volta, and of various overseas departments and territories of France. See table of exchange rates at **currency.** **b.** A coin worth one centime. Also called, in Switzerland, "rappen." **2. a.** A coin equal to 1/100 of the dinar of Algeria. **b.** A monetary unit equal to 1/100 of the gourde of Haiti. See table of exchange rates at **currency.** [French, from *cent,* hundred. See **cent.**]

cen·ti·me·ter (sĕn′tə-mē′tər, sän′-) *n.* Also **cen·ti·me·tre.** *Abbr.* **cm** A unit of length equal to 1/100 of a meter or 0.3937 inch. See **measurement.** [French *centimètre* : CENTI- + -METER.]

cen·ti·me·ter-gram-sec·ond system (sĕn′tə-mē′tər-grăm′sĕk′-ənd). *Abbr.* **cgs, CGS** A coherent system of units for mechanics, electricity, and magnetism, in which the basic units of length, mass, and time are the centimeter, gram, and second.

cen·ti·mo (sĕn′tə-mō; *Spanish* sĕn′tē-mō) *n., pl.* **-mos.** **1.** A monetary unit equal to 1/100 of the bolivar of Venezuela, the colon of Costa Rica, the guarani of Paraguay, and the peseta of Spain. See table of exchange rates at **currency.** **2.** Any of several coins worth one centimo. [Spanish *céntimo,* from French *centime,* CENTIME.]

cen·ti·new·ton (sĕn′tə-nōō′tən, -nyōō′tən) *n. Abbr.* **cN** One hundredth (10^{-2}) of a newton. See **measurement.**

cen·ti·pede (sĕn′tə-pēd′) *n.* Any of various wormlike arthropods of the class Chilopoda, having numerous body segments, each with a pair of legs, the front pair modified into venomous biting organs. Compare **millipede.** [Latin *centipeda* : CENTI- + -PEDE.]

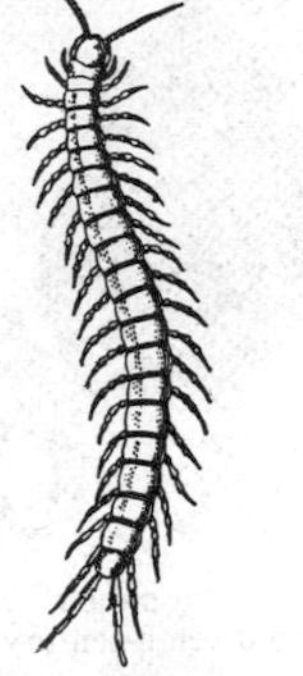

centipede
Genus *Scolopendra*

cen·ti·poise (sĕn′tə-poiz′) *n. Abbr.* **cP** One hundredth (10^{-2}) of a poise. See **measurement.**

cent·ner (sĕnt′nər) *n.* **1.** A unit of weight corresponding to the hundredweight, equal to 110.23 pounds, used in several European countries. **2.** An assaying unit equal to one dram. [German *Zentner,* from Old High German *centenāri,* from Medieval Latin *centēnārius,* weighing a hundred pounds, from Latin, CENTENARY.]

cen·to (sĕn′tō) *n., pl.* **-tos.** A literary work pieced together from the works of several authors: *"the whole is a cento of fragments or short poems worked up by a redactor"* (H.G. Evelyn-White). [Latin *centō,* patchwork, cento. See **kentho-** in Appendix.*]

cen·tral (sĕn′trəl) *adj. Abbr.* **cen., cent.** **1.** At, in, near, or being the center. **2.** Constituting that from which other things proceed, or upon which they depend; controlling: *central offices.* **3.** Dominant; principal; essential. **4.** *Anatomy & Physiology.* **a.** Denoting that part of the nervous system constituted by the brain and spinal cord. **b.** Of or pertaining to a centrum. **5.** *Phonetics.* Pronounced with the tongue in a neutral position, as *e* in *mister.* —*n.* **1.** A telephone exchange. **2.** A telephone-exchange operator. [Latin *centrālis,* from *centrum,* CENTER.] —**cen′tral·ly** *adv.*

Central African Republic. Formerly **U·ban·gi-Sha·ri** (yōō-băng′gē-shä′rē, ōō-băng′gē-). A country of central Africa, 238,220 square miles in area. Population, 1,256,000. Capital, Bangui.

Central A·mer·i·ca (ə-mĕr′ĭ-kə). *Abbr.* **C.A.** The region extending from the southern boundary of Mexico to the northern boundary of Colombia. —**Central American.**

central angle. An angle having radii as sides, and the center of a circle as its vertex.

Central Intelligence Agency. *Abbr.* **CIA** The coordinating agency for U.S. Federal intelligence activities.

cen·tral·ism (sĕn′trəl-ĭz′əm) *n.* The assignment of power and authority to a central leadership in an organization. —**cen′tral·ist** *n.* & *adj.* —**cen′tral·is′tic** (sĕn′trəl-ĭs′tĭk) *adj.*

cen·tral·i·ty (sĕn-trăl′ə-tē) *n.* **1.** The state or quality of being central. **2.** The tendency to be or remain at the center.

cen·tral·ize (sĕn′trəl-īz′) *v.* **-ized, -izing, -izes.** —*tr.* **1.** To draw into or toward the center. **2.** To bring under a single, central authority. —*intr.* To come together at a center; concentrate. —**cen′tral·i·za′tion** *n.* —**cen′tral·iz′er** *n.*

Central Kar·roo. See **Great Karroo.**

central nervous system. The portion of the vertebrate nervous system consisting of the brain and spinal cord.

Central Powers. The alliance comprising Germany, Austria-Hungary, Bulgaria, and Turkey that opposed the Allies in World War I.

Central Provinces and Be·rar. The former name for **Madhya Pradesh.**

Central Standard Time. *Abbr.* **CST, C.S.T.** The local civil time of the 90th meridian west of Greenwich, England, six hours earlier than Greenwich time, observed in the central United States. Also called "Central Time." See **standard time.**

Central Valley. A valley about 450 miles long in central California, between the Sierra Nevada and the Coast Ranges.

cen·tre. *Chiefly British.* Variant of **center.**

cen·tric (sĕn′trĭk) *adj.* Also **cen·tri·cal** (sĕn′trĭ-kəl). **1.** At, of, or having a center. **2.** *Physiology.* Of or originating at a nerve center. [Greek *kentrikos,* from *kentron,* CENTER.] —**cen′tri·cal·ly** *adv.* —**cen·tric′i·ty** (sĕn-trĭs′ə-tē) *n.*

cen·trif·u·gal (sĕn-trĭf′yə-gəl, -trĭf′ə-gəl) *adj.* **1.** Moving or directed away from a center or axis. Compare **centripetal.** **2.** Operated by means of centrifugal force. **3.** *Physiology.* Pertaining to impulses transmitted away from a nerve center; efferent. **4.** *Botany.* Developing outward from a center or axis. [From New Latin *centrifugus* : Latin *centrum,* CENTER + *fugere,* to flee (see **bheug-**[1] in Appendix*).] —**cen·trif′u·gal·ly** *adv.*

centrifugal force. The component of apparent force on a body in curvilinear motion, as observed from that body, that is directed away from the center of curvature or axis of rotation; the equilibrant of centripetal force.

cen·tri·fuge (sĕn′trə-fyōōj′) *n.* Any apparatus consisting essentially of a compartment spun about a central axis to separate contained materials of different density or to simulate gravity with centrifugal force. —*tr.v.* **centrifuged, -fuging, -fuges.** To separate, dehydrate, or test by means of a centrifuge. [French, from New Latin *centrifugus,* CENTRIFUGAL.] —**cen·trif′u·ga′tion** (sĕn-trĭf′yə-gā′shən, sĕn-trĭf′ə-) *n.*

cen·tri·ole (sĕn′trē-ōl′) *n. Genetics.* A tiny cylindrical organelle, considered a pole of the mitotic figure and located at the center of a centrosome. [Latin *centrum,* CENTER + -OLE.]

cen·trip·e·tal (sĕn-trĭp′ə-təl) *adj.* **1.** Directed or moving toward a center or axis. Compare **centrifugal.** **2.** Operated by centripetal force. **3.** *Physiology.* Pertaining to nerve impulses transmitted toward the central nervous system; afferent. **4.** *Botany.* Developing inward, toward the center or axis, as some forms of inflorescence do. [From New Latin *centripetus* : Latin *centrum,* CENTER + -PETAL.] —**cen·trip′e·tal·ly** *adv.*

centripetal force. The component of force acting on a body in curvilinear motion that is directed toward the center of curvature or axis of rotation.

cen·trist (sĕn′trist) *n.* One taking a position in the political center. [CENTR(O)- + -IST.]

centro-, centr-. Indicates center; for example, **centromere, centrist.** [From Greek *kentron,* CENTER.]

cen·tro·bar·ic (sĕn′trə-băr′ĭk) *adj.* Of or relating to the center of gravity. [Late Greek *kentrobarikos,* from Greek *kentrobarikē,* the theory of the center of gravity : *kentron,* CENTER + *bareos,* genitive of *baros,* weight (see **gwer-**[2] in Appendix*).]

cen·troid (sĕn′troid′) *n.* **1.** The center of mass of an object having constant density. **2.** The point in a system of masses each of whose coordinates is a weighted mean of coordinates of the same dimension of points within the system, the weights being determined by the density function of the system. [CENTR(O)- + -OID.]

cen·tro·mere (sĕn′trə-mîr′) *n. Genetics.* The region of a chromosome to which the spindle fiber is attached during mitosis. [CENTRO- + -MERE.]

cen·tro·some (sĕn′trə-sōm′) *n. Genetics.* A small mass of differentiated cytoplasm containing the **centriole** *(see).* [CENTRO- + -SOME (body).] —**cen′tro·so′mic** *adj.*

cen·tro·sphere (sĕn′trə-sfîr′) *n.* **1.** *Genetics.* The mass of cyto-

plasm surrounding the centriole in a centrosome. **2.** The central core of the earth. In this sense, also called "barysphere."
cen·trum (sĕn′trəm) *n., pl.* **-trums** or **-tra** (-trə). The major part of a vertebra, exclusive of the bases of the neural arch. [Latin, CENTER.]
cen·tum (kĕn′təm) *adj.* Of, pertaining to, or comprising the group of Indo-European languages that retained the velar *k*, and the labiovelar *kw* of primitive Indo-European. Compare **satem.** [From Latin *centum*, hundred (an arbitrarily chosen word in which initial *c* represents initial Indo-European *k*). See **dekm̥** in Appendix.*]
cen·tu·ple (sĕn′tə-pəl, sĕn-to͞o′pəl, -tyo͞o′pəl) *adj.* Multiplied by a hundred; hundredfold. —*tr.v.* **centupled, -pling, -ples.** To increase a hundredfold. [French, from Late Latin *centuplus* : Latin *centum*, hundred (see **dekm̥** in Appendix*) + *-plus*, "-fold" (see **pel-**³ in Appendix*).]
cen·tu·pli·cate (sĕn-to͞o′plĭ-kāt′, sĕn-tyo͞o′-) *tr.v.* **-cated, -cating, -cates.** To multiply by one hundred. —*adj.* (sĕn-to͞o′plĭ-kĭt, sĕn-tyo͞o′-). Hundredfold. —*n.* (sĕn-to͞o′plĭ-kĭt, sĕn-tyo͞o′-). A number that has been increased a hundredfold. [Latin *centuplicāre*, from *centuplex*, hundredfold : *centum*, hundred (see **dekm̥** in Appendix*) + *-plex*, "-fold" (see **plek-** in Appendix*).] —**cen·tu′pli·ca′tion** *n.*
cen·tu·ri·al (sĕn-to͝or′ē-əl, sĕn-tyo͝or′-) *adj.* **1.** Of or pertaining to a century in the Roman army. **2.** Of, pertaining to, or marking a period of 100 years.
cen·tu·ried (sĕn′chə-rēd) *adj.* Hundreds of years old: *"This centuried eclipse of woe."* (Byron).
cen·tu·ri·on (sĕn-to͝or′ē-ən, sĕn-tyo͝or′-) *n.* An officer commanding a century in the Roman army. [Middle English *centurioun*, from Old French *centurion*, from Latin *centuriō*, from *centuria*, CENTURY.]
cen·tu·ry (sĕn′chə-rē) *n., pl.* **-ries.** *Abbr.* **C., c., cen., cent. 1.** A period of 100 years. **2.** Each of the successive periods of 100 years before or since the advent of the Christian era. **3.** A unit of the Roman army, originally consisting of 100 men. **4.** One of the 193 electoral divisions of the Roman people. **5.** A group of 100 things. [Latin *centuria*, a group of a hundred, from *centum*, hundred. See **dekm̥** in Appendix.*]
century plant. Any of several fleshy plants of the genus *Agave*, some species of which bloom only once in 10 to 20 years and then die; especially, *A. americana*, having large grayish leaves and greenish flowers.
ceorl (chā′ôrl) *n.* In Anglo-Saxon England, a freeman of the lowest class. Also called "churl." [Old English *ceorl*, CHURL.]
Ce·os. The ancient name for **Keos.**
ceph·a·lad (sĕf′ə-lăd′) *adv. Zoology.* Toward the head or anterior section. [CEPHAL(O)- + -AD (toward).]
ce·phal·ic (sə-făl′ĭk) *adj.* **1.** Of or relating to the head or skull. **2.** Located on, in, or near the head. [Old French *cephalique*, from Latin *cephalicus*, from Greek *kephalikos*, from *kephalē*, head. See **ghebhel-** in Appendix.*]
-cephalic. Indicates head or skull; for example, **orthocephalic.** [From Greek *-kephalos*, -CEPHALOUS.]
cephalic index. The ratio of the maximum width of the head to its maximum length, multiplied by 100. Compare **cranial index.**
ceph·a·lin (sĕf′ə-lĭn) *n.* Also **keph·a·lin** (kĕf′-). *Biochemistry.* A phosphatide derived from the brain and spinal cord, usually of cattle, and used as a hemostatic agent. [CEPHAL(O)- + -IN.]
ceph·a·li·za·tion (sĕf′ə-lə-zā′shən) *n. Zoology.* The gradually increasing concentration of the brain and sensory organs in the head during animal evolution. [CEPHAL(O)- + -IZ(E) + -ATION.]
cephalo-, cephal-. Indicates head; for example, **cephalopod, cephalad.** [Latin, from Greek *kephalo-*, from *kephalē*, head. See **ghebhel-** in Appendix.*]
ceph·a·lo·chor·date (sĕf′ə-lō-kôr′dāt′) *adj.* Of or belonging to the subphylum Cephalochordata, which includes primitive forerunners of the vertebrates such as the lancelet. —*n.* A member of the Cephalochordata. [New Latin *Cephalochordata* : CEPHALO- + CHORDATE.]
Ceph·a·lo·ni·a (sĕf′ə-lō′nē-ə, -lōn′yə). *Greek* **Ke·phal·li·ni·a** (kĕf′ə-lə-nē′ə). The largest of the Ionian Islands (287 square miles), off the western coast of Greece.
ceph·a·lo·pod (sĕf′ə-lə-pŏd′) *n.* Any of various mollusks of the class Cephalopoda, such as an octopus or nautilus, having a beaked head, an internal shell in some species, and prehensile tentacles. —*adj.* Also **ceph·a·lop·o·dous** (-lŏp′ə-dəs). Of, pertaining to, or belonging to the Cephalopoda. [New Latin *Cephalopoda* : CEPHALO- + -POD.] —**ceph′a·lop′o·dan** (sĕf′ə-lŏp′ə-dən) *n.* & *adj.*
ceph·a·lo·tho·rax (sĕf′ə-lō-thôr′ăks′, -thōr′ăks′) *n.* The anterior section of arachnids and many crustaceans, consisting of the fused head and thorax.
-cephalous. Indicates a head; for example, **hydrocephalous.** [New Latin *-cephalus*, from Greek *-kephalos*, from *kephalē*, head. See **ghebhel-** in Appendix.*]
-cephalus. Indicates an abnormality of the head; for example, **hydrocephalus.** [New Latin *-cephalus*, -CEPHALOUS.]
-cephaly. Indicates a head; for example, **megalocephaly.** [From Greek *-kephalos*, -CEPHALOUS.]
Ce·phe·id variable (sē′fē-ĭd, sĕf′ē-). Any of a class of intrinsically variable stars with exceptionally regular periods of light pulsation. Also called "Cepheid." [From CEPHEUS.]
Ce·pheus¹ (kē′fyo͞os). *Greek Mythology.* An Ethiopian king, father of Andromeda.
Ce·pheus² (sē′fyo͞os′, -fē-əs) *n.* A constellation in the Northern Hemisphere near Cassiopeia and Draco. [Latin *Cēpheus*, from Greek *Kēpheus*, a mythical king.]
ce·ra·ceous (sə-rā′shəs) *adj.* Waxy or waxlike. [Latin *cēra*, wax (see **cerate**) + -ACEOUS.]
Ce·ram (sā′räm′). An island of Indonesia, 6,622 square miles in area, west of New Guinea.
ce·ram·al (sə-răm′əl) *n.* An alloy, **cermet** *(see).* [CERAM(IC) + AL(LOY).]
ce·ram·ic (sə-răm′ĭk) *n.* **1.** Any of various hard, brittle, heat-resistant and corrosion-resistant materials made by firing clay or other minerals and consisting of one or more metals in combination with a nonmetal, usually oxygen. **2.** *Plural* **a.** Objects made of such materials. **b.** The art or technique of making objects of such materials, especially from fired clay or porcelain. Used with a singular verb. [Probably French *céramique*, "of pottery," from Greek *keramikos*, from *keramos*, potter's clay, earthenware. See **ker-**⁴ in Appendix.*] —**ce·ram′ic** *adj.* —**ce·ram′ist** *n.*
Ce·ram Sea (sā′räm′). A section of the Pacific Ocean in the central Molucca Islands of Indonesia.
ce·ras·tes (sə-răs′tēz) *n., pl.* **cerastes.** Any of several venomous snakes of the genus *Cerastes*, such as the **horned viper** *(see).* [Middle English, from Latin *cerastēs*, from Greek *kerastēs*, horned (serpent), from *keras*, horn. See **ker-**¹ in Appendix.*]
ce·rate (sîr′āt′) *n.* A hard, unctuous, fat- or wax-based solid, sometimes medicated, formerly applied to the skin directly or on dressings. [Latin *cērātum*, a wax plaster, wax salve, from *cēra*, wax, akin to Greek *kēros*†, wax.]
ce·rat·ed (sîr′ā′tĭd) *adj.* **1.** Coated with wax; waxed. **2.** Possessing a cere. [Latin *cērātus*, from the past participle of *cērāre*, to wax, from *cēra*, wax. See **cerate.**]
ce·rat·o·dus (sə-răt′ə-dəs) *n., pl.* **-duses.** Any of various extinct lungfishes of the genus *Ceratodus*, of the Triassic and Cretaceous periods. [New Latin *Ceratodus*, "horn-tooth" : Greek *keras* (stem *kerat-*), horn (see **ker-**¹ in Appendix*) + *odous*, tooth (see **dent-** in Appendix*).]
cer·a·toid (sĕr′ə-toid′) *adj.* Hornlike. [Greek *keratoeidēs* : *keras* (stem *kerat-*), horn (see **ker-**¹ in Appendix*) + -OID.]
Cer·ber·us (sûr′bər-əs). *Greek & Roman Mythology.* A three-headed dog guarding the entrance of Hades. [Latin, from Greek *Kerberos*†.] —**Cer·be′re·an** (-bîr′ē-ən) *adj.*
cer·car·i·a (sər-kâr′ē-ə) *n., pl.* **-iae** (-ē-ē) or **-as.** The parasitic larva of a trematode worm, having a tail that disappears in the adult stage. [New Latin, "the tailed one" : Greek *kerkos*, tail (see **ker-**² in Appendix*) + *-aria*, from *-arius*, -ARY.] —**cer·car′i·al** *adj.*
cer·co·pi·the·coid (sûr′kō-pĭ-thē′koid′, -pĭth′ə-koid′) *adj.* Of or belonging to the family Cercopithecidae, which includes monkeys such as the baboons, mandrills, macaques, and langurs. —*n.* Also **cer·co·pi·the·cid** (-sĭd′). A member of the Cercopithecidae. [Latin *cercopithēcus*, long-tailed ape, from Greek *kerkopithēkos* : *kerkos*, tail (see **ker-**² in Appendix*) + *pithēkos*, ape (see **Pithecanthropus**) + -OID.]
cere¹ (sîr) *tr.v.* **cered, cering, ceres.** To wrap in or as if in cerecloth, as a corpse. [Middle English *ceren*, to cover with wax, from Old French *cirer*, from Latin *cērāre*, from *çēra*, wax. See **cerate.**]
cere² (sîr) *n.* A fleshy or waxlike swelling at the base of the upper part of the beak in certain birds, such as parrots and some birds of prey. [Middle English *sere*, from Old French *cire*, from Medieval Latin *cēra*, from Latin, wax. See **cerate.**] —**cered** *adj.*
ce·re·al (sîr′ē-əl) *n.* **1.** An edible grain, such as wheat, oats, or corn. **2.** A grass producing such a grain. **3.** A food prepared from such a grain. —*adj.* Of or pertaining to cereals. [Latin *cereālis*, of grain, "of Ceres," from *Cerēs*, CERES.]
cer·e·bel·lum (sĕr′ə-bĕl′əm) *n., pl.* **-lums** or **-bella** (-bĕl′ə). The structure of the brain responsible for regulation and coordination of complex voluntary muscular movement, lying posterior to the pons and medulla oblongata and inferior to the occipital lobes of the cerebral hemispheres. [Medieval Latin, from Latin, diminutive of *cerebrum*, brain. See **ker-**¹ in Appendix.*] —**cer′e·bel′lar** (-bĕl′ər) *adj.*
ce·re·bral (sə-rē′brəl, sĕr′ə-brəl) *adj.* **1.** Of or pertaining to the brain or cerebrum. **2.** Appealing to or marked by the workings of the intellect; intellectually refined. —**ce·re′bral·ly** *adv.*
cerebral cortex. The extensive outer layer of gray tissue of the cerebral hemispheres, largely responsible for higher nervous functions. Also called "pallium."
cerebral hemisphere. Either hemisphere of the cerebrum of the brain, divided by the longitudinal cerebral fissure.
cerebral palsy. Impaired muscular power and coordination from brain damage usually occurring at or before birth.
cer·e·brate (sĕr′ə-brāt′) *intr.v.* **-brated, -brating, -brates.** To think; ponder. [Back-formation from CEREBRATION.]
cer·e·bra·tion (sĕr′ə-brā′shən) *n.* The action of thinking; thought. [From Latin *cerebrum*, CEREBRUM.]
cer·e·bro·side (sĕr′ə-brō-sīd′) *n.* Any of various compounds found in the brain and other nerve tissue, yielding on decomposition a fatty acid, an unsaturated amino-alcohol, and a sugar. [CEREBR(UM) + -OS(E) + -IDE.]
ce·re·bro·spi·nal (sə-rē′brō-spī′nəl, sĕr′ə-brō-) *adj.* Of or pertaining to the brain and spinal cord. [CEREBR(UM) + SPINAL.]
cerebrospinal fluid. The serumlike fluid that bathes the lateral ventricles of the brain and the cavity of the spinal cord.
cerebrospinal meningitis. An acute infectious, epidemic meningitis that is often fatal. Also called "spinal meningitis," "cerebrospinal fever."
ce·re·brum (sə-rē′brəm, sĕr′ə-brəm) *n., pl.* **-brums** or **-bra** (-brə). The large rounded structure of the brain occupying most of the cranial cavity, divided into two cerebral hemispheres by a deep

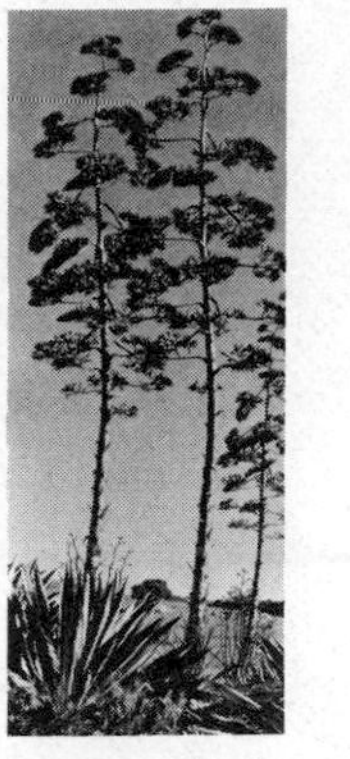

century plant
Agave americana

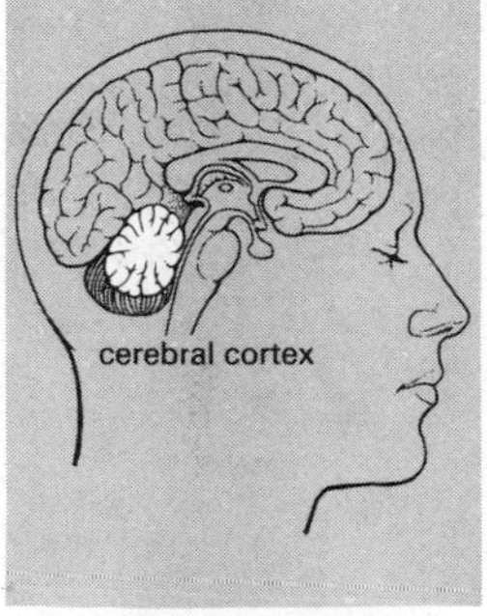

cerebral cortex

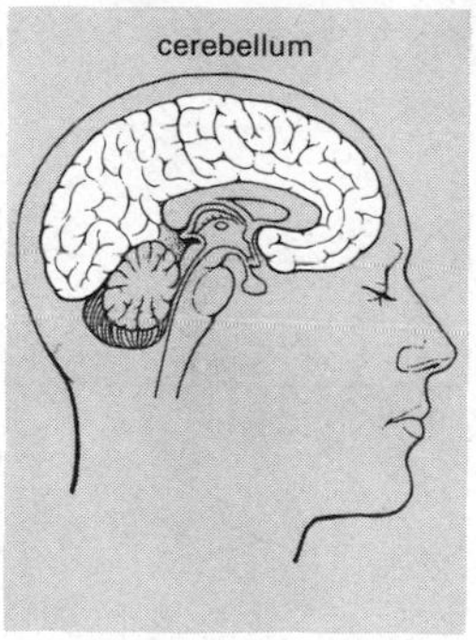

cerebellum

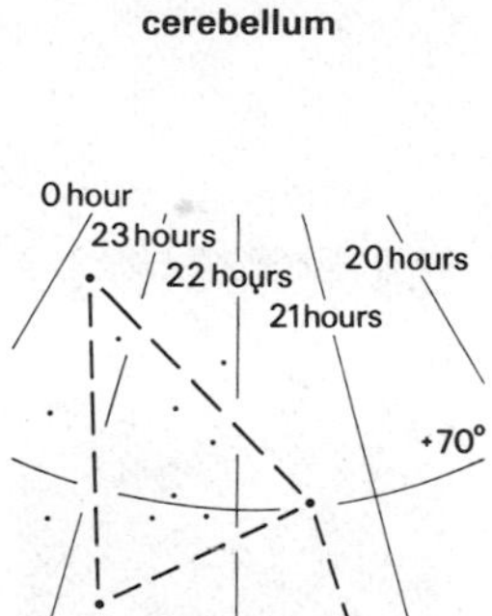

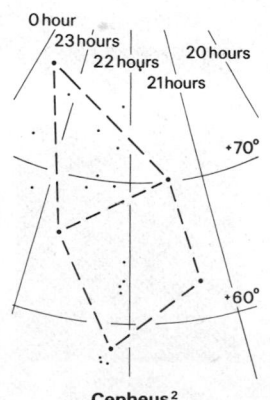

Cepheus²

median sagittal groove and joined at the bottom by the corpus callosum. [Latin, brain. See **ker-**[1] in Appendix.*]
cere·cloth (sîr′klôth′, -klŏth′) *n.* Cloth coated with wax, formerly used for wrapping the dead.
cere·ment (sîr′mənt) *n.* Also **cere·ments** (-məntz). Cerecloth.
cer·e·mo·ni·al (sĕr′ə-mō′nē-əl) *adj.* Of or characterized by ceremony; formal; ritual. See Usage note below. —*n.* A set of ceremonies prescribed for an occasion; a rite. —**cer′e·mo′ni·al·ism′** *n.* —**cer′e·mo′ni·al·ist** *n.* —**cer′e·mo′ni·al·ly** *adv.*
Usage: *Ceremonial* (adjective) is applicable chiefly to things; *ceremonious,* to persons and things. *Ceremonial* is primarily a categorizing term pertaining to ceremony in general *(ceremonial occasions, ceremonial garb). Ceremonious* stresses formality and display, often in the unfavorable sense of pompousness.
cer·e·mo·ni·ous (sĕr′ə-mō′nē-əs) *adj.* **1.** Fond of ceremony; elaborately polite. **2.** Characterized by ceremony; rigidly formal. —See Usage note at **ceremonial.** —**cer′e·mo′ni·ous·ly** *adv.* —**cer′e·mo′ni·ous·ness** *n.*
cer·e·mo·ny (sĕr′ə-mō′nē) *n., pl.* **-nies. 1.** A formal act or set of acts performed as prescribed by ritual, custom, or etiquette. **2.** A conventional social gesture or act without intrinsic purpose. **3.** Strict observance of formalities or etiquette. —**stand on ceremony.** To insist on or behave with excessive formality. [Middle English *ceremonie,* from Old French, from Latin *caerimōnia*†, sacredness, religion, religious rite.]
Če·ren·kov (sə-rĕng′kôf), **Pavel Alekseevic.** Born 1904. Soviet physicist; worked on the velocity of high-energy particles; discovered the Čerenkov effect.
Čerenkov effect. The emission of light by a particle passing through a transparent nonconducting solid at a speed greater than the speed of light in that solid. [Discovered by P.A. ČERENKOV.]
Čerenkov radiation. Light emitted in the Čerenkov effect.
Ce·res[1] (sîr′ēz). *Roman Mythology.* The goddess of agriculture; identified with the Greek goddess Demeter. [Latin *Cerēs.* See **ker-**[3] in Appendix.*]
Ce·res[2] (sîr′ēz) *n.* The first asteroid to be discovered (1801), having an orbit between Mars and Saturn. [After CERES.]
ce·re·us (sîr′ē-əs) *n.* Any of several tall tropical American cacti of the genus *Cereus* or other genera, such as the **night-blooming cereus** *(see).* [New Latin, "candle" (from the shape), from Latin, taper, from *cēra,* wax. See **cerate.**]
ce·ric oxide (sîr′ĭk, sĕr′ĭk). A pale yellow-white powder, CeO_2, used in ceramics, to polish glass, and to sensitize photosensitive glass. [From CERIUM.]
cer·iph. *Chiefly British.* Variant of **serif.**
ce·rise (sə-rēs′, -rēz′) *n.* Deep to vivid purplish red. See **color.** [French, from Old French, CHERRY.] —**ce·rise′** *adj.*
ce·ri·um (sîr′ē-əm) *n. Symbol* **Ce** A lustrous, iron-gray, malleable, metallic rare-earth element that occurs chiefly in the minerals monazite and bastnaesite, exists in four allotropic states, is a constituent of lighter flint alloys, and is used in various metallurgical and nuclear applications. Atomic number 58, atomic weight 140.12, melting point 795°C, boiling point 3,468°C, specific gravity 6.67 to 8.23, valences 3, 4. See **element.** [New Latin, from the asteroid CERES.]
cer·met (sûr′mĕt′) *n.* A material consisting of processed ceramic particles bonded with metal and used in high-strength and high-temperature applications. Also called "ceramal." [CER(AMIC) + MET(AL).]
CERN (sûrn) The research center of the European Council for Nuclear Research in Geneva. [French *C(onseil) E(uropéen Pour) R(echerches) N(ucléaires).*]
Cer·nă·u·ţi. The Rumanian name for **Chernovtsy.**
cer·nu·ous (sûr′nyōō-əs) *adj. Botany.* Hanging downward; drooping; nodding. [Latin *cernuus*†.]
ce·ro (sîr′ō) *n., pl.* **-ros** or **cero. 1.** An edible fish, *Scomberomorus regalis,* of western Atlantic waters, having silvery sides and a dark-blue back. Sometimes called "pintado." **2.** A fish, the **king mackerel** *(see).* [Spanish *sierra,* sawfish, saw, SIERRA.]
ce·ro·tic acid (sə-rō′tĭk, -rŏt′ĭk). An acid, $C_{25}H_{51}COOH$, occurring in waxes, such as beeswax and carnauba wax. [From Latin *cērōtum,* wax plaster, from Greek *kērōton,* from *kēros,* wax. See **cerate.**]
ce·ro·type (sîr′ə-tīp′, sĕr′ə-) *n.* The process of preparing a printing surface for electrotyping by first engraving on a wax-coated metal plate. [Greek *kēros,* wax (see **cerate**) + -TYPE.]
ce·rous (sîr′əs) *adj.* Of, pertaining to, or containing cerium, especially with valence 3. [CER(IUM) + -OUS.]
Cer·ro de Pun·ta (sĕr′rō *th*ā pōōn′tä). The highest elevation (4,400 feet) in Puerto Rico, part of the Cordillera Central.
Cer·ro Gor·do (sĕr′rō gôr′*th*ō). A mountain pass between Veracruz and Jalapa in southern Mexico, the site of an American victory (1847) in the Mexican War.
cert. certificate; certification; certified.
cer·tain (sûrt′n) *adj.* **1.** Definite; fixed; determined. **2.** Sure; inevitable; destined. **3.** Established beyond doubt or question; indisputable. **4.** Unfailing; dependable; unerring. **5.** Confident; assured; positive. **6.** Not specified or identified but usually assumed to be known: *a certain woman.* **7.** Some but not much; limited: *to a certain degree.* —See Synonyms at **sure.** —*pron.* An indefinite but limited number; some. —**for certain.** Surely; without doubt. [Middle English, from Old French, from Vulgar Latin *certānus* (unattested), from Latin *certus,* past participle of *cernere,* to decide, determine. See **skeri-** in Appendix.*]
Usage: *Certain* (adjective) is often preceded by *more* or *most* or terms such as *fairly* and *reasonably,* even though by definition *certain* is seemingly absolute in most of its senses. The following typical example is acceptable on all levels to 83 per cent of the Usage Panel: *Nothing is more certain than an extremist's hatred of compromise.*
cer·tain·ly (sûrt′n-lē) *adv.* Beyond a doubt; by all means.
cer·tain·ty (sûrt′n-tē) *n., pl.* **-ties. 1.** The fact, quality, or state of being certain. **2.** A clearly established fact.
Synonyms: *certainty, certitude, assurance, conviction.* These nouns mean freedom from any doubt. *Certainty,* the strongest, means a sure thing, belief in which is based on thorough examination of all evidence. *Certitude* implies a firm belief based more often on faith than on objective reasoning. *Assurance* relates closely to *certitude* and stresses as its foundation self-confidence, again resulting more from subjective experience than from objective examination. *Conviction* generally implies that a prior doubt existed and now has been removed because one has been convinced or assured of the truth.
cer·tes (sûr′tēz) *adv. Archaic.* Certainly; truly; verily. [Middle English, from Old French, from Vulgar Latin *certās* (unattested), from Latin *certus,* CERTAIN.]
certif. certificate.
cer·tif·i·cate (sər-tĭf′ĭ-kĭt) *n. Abbr.* **cert., certif., ct., ctf. 1.** A document testifying to a fact, qualification, or promise. **2. a.** A document issued to a person completing a course of study not leading to a diploma. **b.** A document certifying that a person may officially practice in certain professions. **3.** A written statement legally authenticated. Compare **guarantee, license, voucher.** —*tr.v.* (sər-tĭf′ə-kāt′) **certificated, -cating, -cates.** To authorize by a certificate. [Middle English *certificat,* from Old French, from Medieval Latin *certificātum,* from the neuter past participle of Late Latin *certificāre,* CERTIFY.]
certificate of deposit. A certificate from a bank stating that the named person has a specified sum on deposit.
cer·ti·fi·ca·tion (sûr′tə-fĭ-kā′shən) *n. Abbr.* **cert. 1.** The act of certifying or certificating. **2.** The state of being certified. **3.** A certified statement.
cer·ti·fied (sûr′tə-fīd′) *adj. Abbr.* **cert. 1.** Guaranteed in writing; vouched for; endorsed. **2.** Holding a certificate. **3.** Committed to a mental institution.
certified check. A check guaranteed by a bank to be covered by sufficient funds on deposit.
certified mail. Uninsured first-class mail whose delivery is recorded by having the addressee sign for it.
certified public accountant. *Abbr.* **C.P.A.** A public accountant who has received a certificate stating that he has met the state's legal requirements.
cer·ti·fy (sûr′tə-fī′) *v.* **-fied, -fying, -fies.** —*tr.* **1. a.** To confirm formally as true, accurate, or genuine; testify to or vouch for in writing. **b.** To guarantee as meeting a standard; attest. **2.** To acknowledge in writing on the face of (a check) that the signature of the drawer is genuine and that the depositor has sufficient funds on deposit for its payment. **3.** To declare legally insane. **4.** To assure or make certain; tell positively. —*intr.* To testify. Usually used with *to.* —See Synonyms at **approve.** [Middle English *certifien,* from Old French *certifier,* from Late Latin *certificāre,* to make certain : Latin *certus,* CERTAIN + *facere,* to make (see **dhē-**[1] in Appendix*).] —**cer′ti·fi′a·ble** *adj.* —**cer′ti·fi′a·bly** *adv.* —**cer′ti·fi′er** *n.*
cer·ti·o·ra·ri (sûr′shē-ə-râr′ē, -rä′rē) *n. Law.* A writ from a higher court to a lower one requesting a transcript of the proceedings of a case for review. [Medieval Latin *certiorārī volumus,* "we wish to be certified" (words used in the writ), from *certiorāre,* to inform, certify, from *certior,* comparative of *certus,* CERTAIN.]
cer·ti·tude (sûr′tə-tōōd′, -tyōōd′) *n.* Complete assurance. See Synonyms at **certainty.** [Middle English, from Late Latin *certitūdō,* from Latin *certus,* CERTAIN.]
ce·ru·le·an (sə-rōō′lē-ən) *adj.* Sky-blue; azure. [From Latin *caeruleus,* dark-blue, azure, dissimilated from Old Latin *caelo-lo* (unattested), from Latin *caelum,* sky. See **celestial.**]
cerulean blue. Light to vivid blue or greenish blue. See **color.**
ce·ru·men (sə-rōō′mən) *n.* A yellowish waxy secretion of the external ear; earwax. [New Latin, from Latin *cēra,* wax. See **cerate.**]
ce·ruse (sə-rōōs′, sîr′ōōs′) *n.* **White lead** *(see).* [Middle English, from Old French, from Latin *cērussa,* perhaps from Greek *kēroessa* (unattested), white wax cosmetic, from *kēroun,* to wax, from *kēros,* wax. See **cerate.**]
ce·rus·site (sə-rŭs′īt′, sîr′ə-sīt′) *n.* Also **ce·ru·site** (sə-rōō′sīt′, sîr′ə-sīt′). Natural lead carbonate, $PbCO_3$, a lead ore. [German *Zerussit* : Latin *cērussa,* CERUSE + -ITE.]
Cer·van·tes Sa·a·ve·dra (sər-văn′tēz sä′ä-vē′drä; *Spanish* thĕr-vän′tās sä′ä-vā′*th*rä), **Miguel de.** 1547–1616. Spanish author of novels, plays, and tales; creator of Don Quixote.
cer·vi·cal (sûr′vĭ-kəl) *adj. Anatomy.* Pertaining to a neck or a cervix. [New Latin *cervicalis,* from Latin *cervīx,* CERVIX.]
cer·vi·ci·tis (sûr′və-sī′tĭs) *n.* Inflammation of the cervix of the uterus. [New Latin : CERVIX + -ITIS.]
cer·vine (sûr′vīn′) *adj.* Pertaining to, resembling, or characteristic of a deer. [Latin *cervīnus,* from *cervus,* deer. See **ker-**[1] in Appendix.*]
cer·vix (sûr′vĭks) *n., pl.* **-vixes** or **-vices** (-və-sēz′, -vī′sēz). *Anatomy.* **1.** The neck. **2.** Any neck-shaped anatomical structure, as the narrow outer end of the uterus. [Latin *cervīx,* neck. See **ker-**[1] in Appendix.*]
Ce·sar·e·an, Ce·sar·i·an. Variants of **Caesarean.**
ce·si·um (sē′zē-əm) *n.* Also **cae·si·um.** *Symbol* **Cs** A soft, silvery-white ductile metal, liquid at room temperature, the most electropositive and alkaline of the elements. It is used in photo-

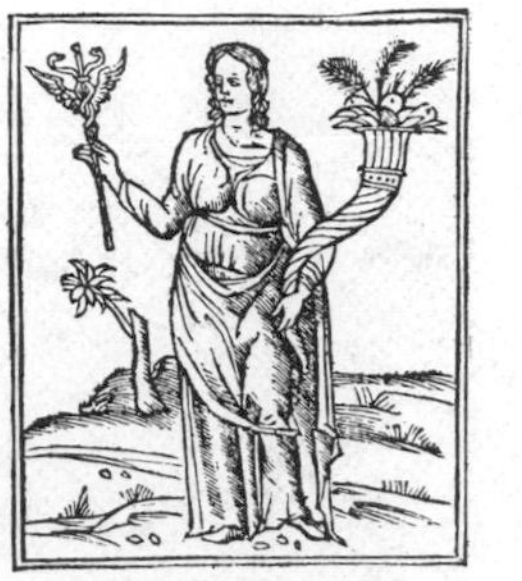

Ceres[1]
Sixteenth-century woodcut

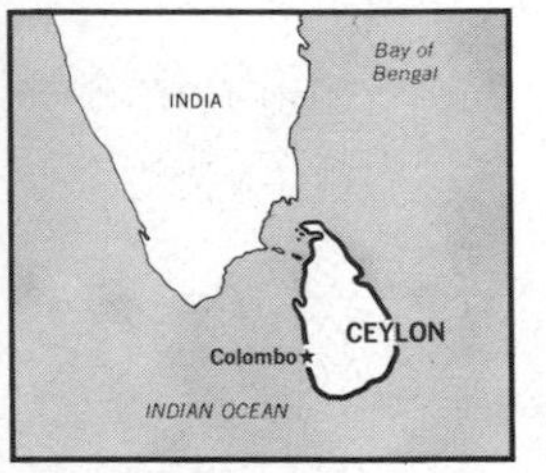

Ceylon

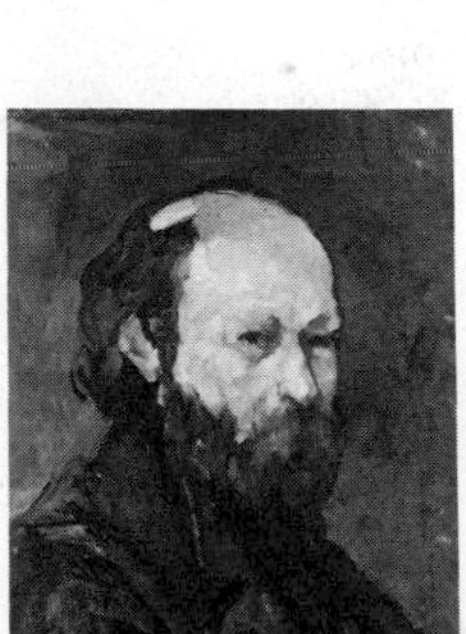

Cézanne
A self-portrait painted in oil about 1877

electric cells and to catalyze hydrogenation of some organic compounds. Atomic number 55, atomic weight 132.905, melting point 28.5°C, boiling point 690°C, specific gravity 1.87, valence 1. See **element**. [New Latin, from Latin *caesius*†, bluish-gray (from its blue spectral lines).]

Čes·ko·slo·ven·sko. The Czech name for **Czechoslovakia**.

ces·pi·tose (sĕs′pĭ-tōs′) *adj.* Also **caes·pi·tose**. *Botany.* Growing in dense tufts or turflike clumps; matted. [New Latin *caespitosus*, from Latin *caespes*† (stem *caespit-*), turf, grassy plain.] —**ces′pi·tose′ly** *adv.*

cess¹ (sĕs) *n.* A tax; levy. [Middle English *cessen*, short for *assessen*, ASSESS.]

cess² (sĕs) *n. Irish.* Luck: *Bad cess to thee!* [Possibly short for SUCCESS.]

ces·sa·tion (sĕ-sā′shən) *n.* A ceasing; discontinuance. [Middle English *cessacioun*, from Latin *cessātiō*, from *cessāre*, CEASE.]

ces·sion (sĕsh′ən) *n.* **1.** An act of ceding; a surrendering, as of territory to another country by treaty. **2.** A ceded territory. [Middle English, from Old French, from Latin *cessiō*, from *cēdere* (past participle *cessus*), to yield. See **ked-¹** in Appendix.*]

ces·sion·ar·y (sĕsh′ən-ĕr′ē) *n., pl.* **-ies.** One to whom a cession is made; transferee; assignee.

cess·pool (sĕs′po͞ol′) *n.* **1.** A covered hole or pit for receiving sediment or drained sewage. **2.** A filthy place. Also called "cesspit." [Variant (influenced by pool) of earlier *cesperalle*, drainpipe, from Middle English *suspiral*, from Old French *souspirail*, breathing hole, from *sou(s)pirer*, to breathe, from Latin *suspīrāre*, to sigh, breathe out : *sub-*, out from under + *spīrāre*, to breathe (see **spīrāre** in Appendix*).]

ces·tode (sĕs′tōd′) *n.* Any flatworm of the class Cestoda, including tapeworms. [New Latin *Cestoda*, variant of *Cestoidea*, "ribbon-shaped ones" : Latin *cestus*, CESTUS (belt) + -OID.]

ces·tus¹ (sĕs′təs) *n., pl.* **-ti** (-tī′). A belt or girdle. [Latin *cestus*, girdle, belt, from Greek *kestos*. See **kent-** in Appendix.*]

ces·tus² (sĕs′təs) *n., pl.* **-tuses.** Also **caes·tus**. A covering for the hand, made of leather straps weighted with iron or lead, worn by ancient Roman boxers. [Latin *caestus*, *cestus*, boxing glove, from *caedere*, to strike. See **skhai-** in Appendix.*]

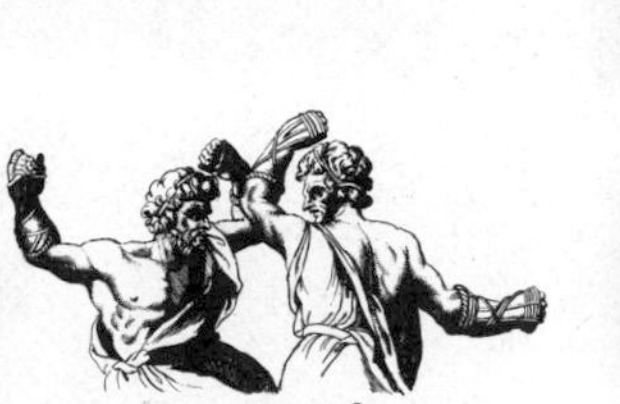

cestus²

ce·su·ra. Variant of **caesura**.

ce·ta·ce·an (sĭ-tā′shən) *adj.* Also **ce·ta·ceous** (-shəs). Of or belonging to the order Cetacea, which includes fishlike aquatic mammals such as the whale and porpoise. —*n.* An aquatic mammal of the order Cetacea. [From New Latin *Cetacea*, from the neuter plural of *cetaceus*, of whales : Latin *cētus*, whale, from Greek *kētos*† + -ACEOUS.]

ce·tane (sē′tān′) *n.* A colorless liquid, $C_{16}H_{34}$, used as a solvent and in standardized hydrocarbons. [Latin *cētus*, whale (so called because it belongs to a series of compounds found in sperm whale oil) (see **cetacean**) + -ANE.]

cetane number. The performance rating of a diesel fuel, expressed as the percentage of cetane that must be mixed with liquid methylnaphthalene to produce the same ignition performance as the diesel fuel being rated. Also called "cetane rating." Compare **octane number**.

cete (sēt) *n.* A company of badgers. See Synonyms at **flock**. [Probably from Latin *coetus*, *coitus*, meeting, reunion, assembly, COITUS.]

ce·te·ris pa·ri·bus (sĕt′ə-rĭs păr′ə-bəs, kā′tə-rĭs). *Abbr.* **cet. par.** *Latin.* Other things being equal.

ce·tol·o·gy (sĭ-tŏl′ə-jē) *n.* The zoology of whales and related aquatic mammals. [Latin *cētus*, whale (see **cetacean**) + -LOGY.] —**ce′to·log′i·cal** (-tə-lŏj′ĭ-kəl) *adj.* —**ce·tol′o·gist** *n.*

cet. par. ceteris paribus.

Ce·tus (sē′təs) *n.* A constellation in the equatorial region of the Southern Hemisphere near Aquarius and Eridanus. [Latin *cētus*, whale. See **cetacean**.]

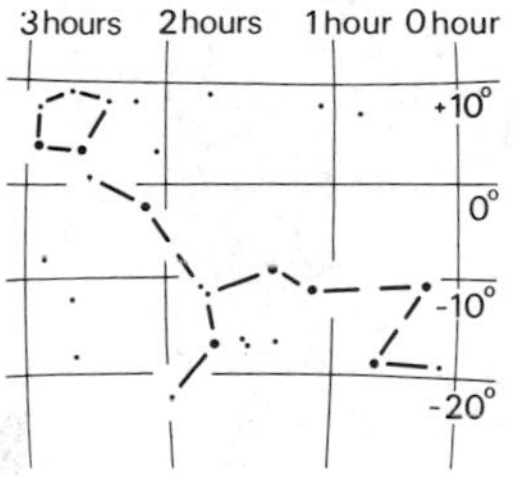

Cetus

Ceu·ta (sā′o͞o-tä). A Spanish port and presidio on the coast of Morocco, opposite Gibraltar. Population, 76,000.

Cé·vennes (sā-vĕn′). A mountain range in southern France, west of the Rhone. Highest elevation, 5,753 feet.

Cey·lon (sĭ-lŏn′). *Abbr.* **Cey.** An independent country and a member of the Commonwealth of Nations, an island 25,332 square miles in area, in the Indian Ocean off the southeastern coast of India. Population, 10,625,000. Capital, Colombo. —**Cey′lo·nese′** *adj.* & *n.*

Ceylon moss. A red seaweed, *Gracilaria lichenoides*, of the East Indies, used for making agar.

Cé·zanne (sā-zăn′), **Paul.** 1839–1906. French painter; a leader of the postimpressionist school.

Cf The symbol for the element californium.

cf. **1.** calfskin. **2.** compare (Latin *confer*).

c.f. **1.** *Baseball.* center field; center fielder. **2.** cost and freight.

C.F. cost and freight.

C/F *Accounting.* carried forward.

c.f.i., C.F.I. cost, freight, and insurance.

cg centigram.

c.g. **1.** center of gravity. **2.** consul general.

C.G. **1.** coast guard. **2.** commanding general. **3.** consul general.

cgs, CGS centimeter-gram-second (system of units).

C.G.T. General Confederation of Labor (French *Confédération Générale du Travail*).

ch chain (measurement).

ch. **1.** chaplain. **2.** chapter. **3.** check. **4.** chief. **5.** child; children. **6.** church.

Ch. **1.** chaplain. **2.** chief. **3.** China; Chinese. **4.** church.

c.h., C.H. **1.** clearing-house. **2.** courthouse. **3.** customhouse.

Cha·blis (shă-blē′) *n.* A very dry, white Burgundy wine produced in the region of Chablis, a town in north-central France.

cha-cha (chä′chä′) *n.* Also **cha-cha-cha** (chä-chä-chä′). A rhythmic ballroom dance that originated in Latin America. —*intr.v.* **cha-chaed, -chaing, -chas.** To dance the cha-cha. [American Spanish *cha-cha-cha* (expressive formation).]

chac·ma (chăk′mə) *n.* A grayish-black baboon, *Chaeropithecus ursinus* (or *Papio ursinus*), of southern and eastern Africa. [Hottentot.]

Cha·co (chä′kō). Also **Gran Cha·co** (grän chä′kō). A region in southern South America, 100,000 square miles in area, lying between the Pilcomayo and Paraguay rivers and divided among Bolivia, Paraguay, and Argentina.

cha·conne (shă-kôn′) *n.* **1.** A slow and stately dance of the 18th century. **2.** The music for this dance. **3.** A musical form consisting of variations based on a reiterated harmonic pattern. Compare **passacaglia**. [French, from Spanish *chacona* (perhaps imitative of the castanets used for the music).]

Chad (chăd). *French* **Tchad** (chȧd). Officially, Republic of Chad. A country occupying 495,368 square miles in north-central Africa. Population, 2,800,000. Capital, Fort-Lamy.

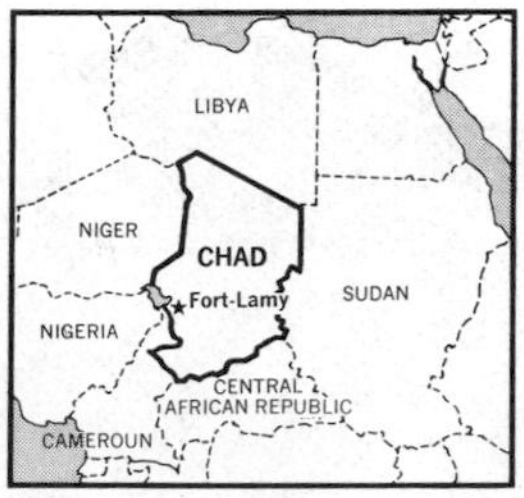

Chad

Chad, Lake (chăd). *French* **Lac Tchad** (lȧk chȧd′). A lake in north-central Africa. Its area ranges from 5,000 to 10,000 square miles.

Chad·wick (chăd′wĭk′), Sir **James.** Born 1891. British physicist; discovered the neutron (1932).

Chaer·o·ne·a (kĕr′ə-nē′ə, kĭr′-). An ancient city, long in ruins, in eastern Greece; the site of the victory of Philip II of Macedonia over the Boeotians and Athenians (338 B.C.) and of Sulla's victory over Mithridates VI (86 B.C.).

chae·ta (kē′tə) *n., pl.* **-tae** (-tē′). *Zoology.* A bristle, or seta, of certain worms. [New Latin, from Greek *khaitē*, long hair. See **ghait-** in Appendix.*]

chae·tog·nath (kē′tŏg-năth′) *n.* Any of various marine worms of the phylum Chaetognatha, which includes the arrow worms. [New Latin *Chaetognatha*, "bristle-jaw" (so named from the spines at the jaws) : CHAETA + *gnathos*, jaw (see **genu-²** in Appendix*).]

chafe (chāf) *v.* **chafed, chafing, chafes.** —*tr.* **1.** To wear away or irritate by rubbing. **2.** To annoy; vex. **3.** To heat or warm by rubbing. —*intr.* **1.** To cause friction; rub. **2.** To become worn or sore from rubbing. **3.** To be or become annoyed. —*n.* **1.** Warmth, wear, or soreness produced by friction. **2.** Annoyance; irritation; vexation. [Middle English *chaufen*, from Old French *chauf(f)er*, to warm (by rubbing), from Vulgar Latin *calefāre* (unattested), variant of Latin *calefacere* : *calēre*, to be warm (see **kel-¹** in Appendix*) + *facere*, to make (see **dhē-¹** in Appendix*).]

chaf·er (chā′fər) *n.* Any of various beetles of the family Scarabaeidae, such as a cockchafer or a member of the genus *Macrodactylus*. [Middle English *cheaffer*, Old English *ceafor*. See **geph-** in Appendix.*]

chaff¹ (chăf) *n.* **1.** The husks of grain after separation from the seed. **2.** Finely cut straw or hay used as fodder. **3.** Trivial or worthless matter. **4.** Strips of metal foil released in the atmosphere to inhibit radar. [Middle English *chaf(f)*, Old English *ceaf*. See **geph-** in Appendix.*]

chaff² (chăf) *v.* **chaffed, chaffing, chaffs.** —*tr.* To make fun of good-naturedly; to tease. —*intr.* To engage in good-natured teasing. —*n.* Good-natured teasing; banter. [Probably a blend of CHAFF (trivia) and CHAFE (to irritate).] —**chaff′er** *n.*

chaf·fer (chăf′ər) *v.* **-fered, -fering, -fers.** —*intr.* **1.** To bargain or haggle. **2.** To bandy words. —*tr.* **1.** To bandy (words). **2.** *Obsolete.* To buy and sell; barter. —*n.* **1.** A bargaining or haggling. **2.** *Obsolete.* A buying and selling; trade. [Middle English *chaffare*, *cheapfare*, trade, merchandise : *chep*, trade (see **cheap**) + FARE.] —**chaf′fer·er** *n.*

chaf·finch (chăf′ĭnch) *n.* A small European songbird, *Fringilla coelebs*, having predominantly reddish-brown plumage. [Middle English *chaffynche*, Old English *ceaffinc* : CHAFF + FINCH.]

chafing dish. A dish set above a heating device, used to cook or maintain the warmth of food at the table.

Cha·gall (shə-gäl′), **Marc.** Born 1887. Russian painter and illustrator; resident in France.

Cha·gas disease (shä′gəs). A South American form of trypanosomiasis caused by the protozoan *Trypanosoma cruzi*. [First described by Carlos *Chagas* (1879–1934), Brazilian physician.]

Chag·a·tai (chăg′ə-tī′) *n.* Also **Jag·a·tai** (jăg′ə-tī′). A Middle Turkic dialect, the literary language of the empire of Tamerlane in Central Asia (1405–1502). [After *Chagatai* (died 1242), second son of Genghis Khan, who inherited the Central Asian portion of the Mongol Empire (1207).]

Cha·gres (chä′grās). A river rising in central Panama and flowing through Gatun Lake to the Caribbean.

cha·grin (shə-grĭn′) *n.* A feeling of embarrassment or humiliation caused by failure or disappointment. —*tr.v.* **chagrined, -grining, -grins.** To cause to feel chagrin; humiliate. Usually used in the passive. [French, sadness, from *chagrin*†, sad.]

chain (chān) *n.* **1.** A connected, flexible series of links, usually of metal, used for binding, connecting, or other purposes. **2.** Anything that restrains or confines. **3.** *Plural.* Bonds, fetters, or shackles. **4.** *Plural.* Captivity or oppression; bondage. **5.** Any series of connected or related things: *a chain of coincidences.* **6.** A number of establishments, such as stores, restaurants, or theaters, under common ownership or management. **7.** A mountain range. **8.** *Chemistry.* A group of atoms bonded in a spatial configuration resembling a chain. **9.** *Abbr.* **ch a.** A measuring instrument for surveying, consisting of 100 linked pieces of iron or steel. **b.** The length of this instrument as a unit of length, equal to 100 links or 66 feet. Also called "Gunter's chain." **10.** *Abbr.* **ch a.** A similar instrument used in engineer-

chain

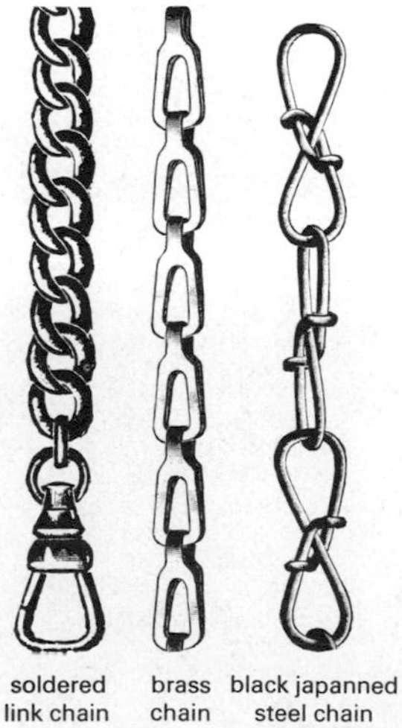

soldered link chain — brass chain — black japanned steel chain

t tight/th thin, path/*th* this, bathe/ŭ cut/ûr urge/v valve/w with/y yes/z zebra, size/zh vision/ə about, item, edible, gallop, circus/ à *Fr.* ami/œ *Fr.* feu, *Ger.* schön/ü *Fr.* tu, *Ger.* über/KH *Ger.* ich, *Scot.* loch/N *Fr.* bon. ***Follows main vocabulary.** †**Of obscure origin.**

ing. **b.** The length of this instrument used as a unit of length, equal to 100 feet. Also called "engineer's chain." —See Synonyms at **series**. —*tr.v.* **chained, chaining, chains. 1.** To bind or make fast with a chain or chains. **2.** To bind or fetter; confine. [Middle English *chayne, cheyne,* from Old French *chaine, chaeine,* from Latin *catēna,* CATENA.]

Chain (chān), **Ernst Boris.** Born 1906. German-born British biochemist; helped to develop penicillin.

chain fern. Any of various ferns of the genus *Woodwardia,* having spore cases borne in chainlike lines along the midribs of the fronds.

chain gang. A group of convicts chained together and set to outdoor labor.

chain letter. A letter instructing the recipient to send out multiple copies, so that its circulation increases in a geometrical progression as long as the instructions are followed.

chain mail. Flexible armor of joined metal links or scales.

chain·man (chān′mən) *n., pl.* **-men** (-mĭn). *Surveying.* Either of the two persons who hold the measuring chain.

chain·o·mat·ic (chā′nə-măt′ĭk) *n.* A balance with an adjustable calibrated chain suspended from the beam, used to weigh small masses accurately. [From *Chainomatic,* a trademark.]

chain pump. A pump that lifts water by means of containers, attached to an endless chain, that pass under water and up over a wheel.

chain-re·act (chān′rē-ăkt′) *intr.v.* **-acted, -acting, -acts.** To undergo a chain reaction.

chain-reacting pile. A **nuclear reactor** *(see).*

chain reaction. 1. A series of events, each of which induces or otherwise influences its successor. **2.** *Physics.* A multistage nuclear reaction so constituted, especially a self-sustaining series of fissions in which the average number of neutrons produced per unit of time exceeds the number absorbed or lost. **3.** *Chemistry.* A series of reactions in which one product of a reacting set is a reactant in the following set.

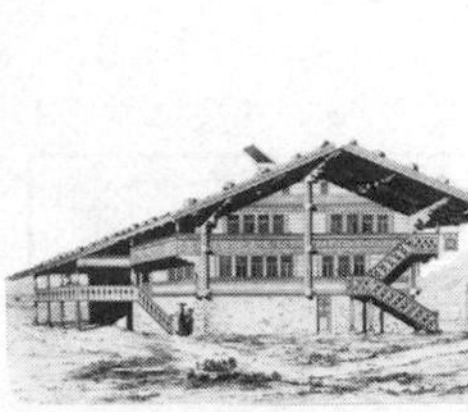

chalet

chain saw. A power saw with teeth linked in an endless chain.

chain-smoke (chān′smōk′) *v.* **-smoked, -smoking, -smokes.** —*intr.* To smoke cigarettes or cigars in continuing succession. —*tr.* To smoke (cigarettes or cigars) in continuing succession. —**chain smoker.**

chain stitch. A decorative stitch in which loops are connected like the links of a chain.

chain store. Any of a number of retail stores under the same ownership.

chair (châr) *n.* **1.** A piece of furniture consisting of a seat, legs, and back, and often arms, designed to accommodate one person. **2.** A seat of office, authority, or dignity, as that of a bishop. **3.** The office or position of a person having authority, as a judgeship. **4.** A person who holds such an office or position; especially, the chairman of a meeting. **5.** *Slang.* The electric chair. **6.** A seat carried about on poles; a sedan chair. **7.** A metal block for supporting and holding railroad track in position. —**take the chair.** To preside at a meeting as chairman. —*tr.v.* **chaired, chairing, chairs. 1.** To put or seat in a chair. **2.** To install in a position of authority, especially as chairman. See Usage note below. **3.** To preside over (a meeting). See Usage note below. **4.** *British.* To carry (a person) aloft in triumph, usually in a chair. [Middle English *chaiere, chare,* from Old French *chaiere,* bishop's chair, from Latin *cathedra,* chair, from Greek *kathedra,* seat : *kata-,* down + *hedra,* seat (see **sed-**[1] in Appendix*).]

Usage: Chair (verb), in the sense to preside over, has rather wide journalistic use, but is less well established in more formal writing. The same is true of *chairman* (verb). But *chair,* in the sense to install in office, has long been established.

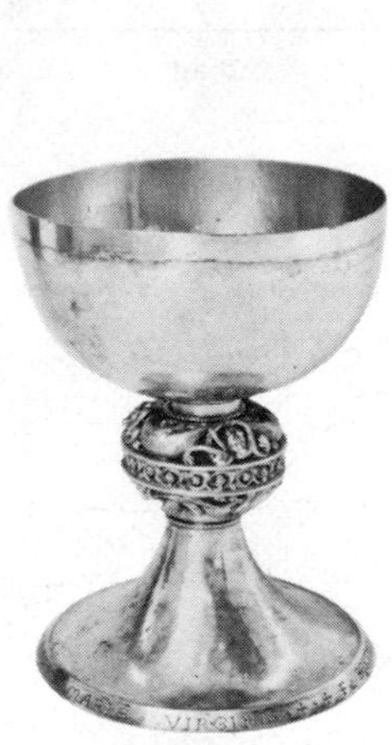

chalice
Thirteenth-century silver chalice

chair car. A **parlor car** *(see).*

chair lift. A cable-suspended, power-driven chair assembly used to transport people up or down mountains. See **ski lift.**

chair·man (châr′mən) *n., pl.* **-men** (-mĭn). *Abbr.* **chm. 1.** One who presides over an assembly, meeting, committee, or board. **2.** One who carries or wheels others in a chair. —*tr.v.* **chairmanned, -manning, -mans.** To act as chairman of. See Usage note at **chair.**

chair·man·ship (châr′mən-shĭp′) *n.* The office or term of a chairman.

chair·wom·an (châr′wo͝om′ən) *n., pl.* **-women** (-wĭm′ən). A woman who serves as a chairman.

chaise (shāz) *n.* **1.** Any of various light, open carriages, often with a collapsible hood; especially, a two-wheeled carriage drawn by one horse. **2.** A **post chaise** *(see).* [French, chair, seat, from Old French, variant of *chaire, chaiere,* CHAIR.]

chaise longue (shāz′ lông′) *pl.* **chaise longues** or **chaises longues** (shāz′ lông′). A reclining chair with a seat long enough to support the outstretched legs of the sitter. Also mistakenly called "chaise lounge." [French, "long chair."]

cha·lah. Variant of **challah.**

cha·la·za (kə-lā′zə) *n., pl.* **-zae** (-zē′) or **-zas. 1.** *Zoology.* One of two spiral bands of tissue in an egg, connecting the yolk to the lining membrane. **2.** *Botany.* The part of an ovule that is opposite the micropyle and that serves as a point of attachment for the integuments and the nucellus. [New Latin, from Greek *khalaza,* hailstone, small cyst. See **gheləd-** in Appendix.*]

chal·ced·o·ny (kăl-sĕd′n-ē) *n., pl.* **-nies.** Also **cal·ced·o·ny.** A translucent to transparent milky or grayish quartz with distinctive microscopic crystals arranged in slender fibers in parallel bands. [Middle English *calcedonie,* from Late Latin *chalcēdonius,* from Greek *khalkēdōn,* a mystical stone (Revelation 21:19), perhaps after *Khalkēdōn,* ancient town in Asia Minor.] —**chal′ce·don′ic** *adj.*

chal·cid (kăl′sĭd) *n.* Any of various minute wasps of the superfamily Chalcidoidea, of which the larvae of many species are parasitic on the larval stages of other insects. Also called "chalcid wasp." [From New Latin *Chalcis* (genus), "copper (fly)" (from its metallic color and sheen), from Greek *khalkos,* copper. See **ghelegh-** in Appendix.*]

Chal·cid·i·ce (kăl-sĭd′ə-sē′). *Greek* **Khal·ki·di·kí** (käl′kə-*th*ĭ-kē′). A peninsula of north-central Greece extending into the Aegean Sea east of the Gulf of Salonika.

Chal·cis (kăl′sĭs). *Modern Greek* **Khal·kis** (kăl′kĭs). An ancient city of southeastern Greece, on the western coast of Euboea, in ancient times the invasion point for Persian campaigns against Greece. Population, 25,000.

chal·co·cite (kăl′kə-sīt′) *n.* An important copper ore, essentially CuS_2. [French *chalcos(ine)* : Greek *khalkos,* copper (see **ghelegh-** in Appendix*) + -ITE.]

chal·co·py·rite (kăl′kə-pī′rīt′) *n.* An important copper ore, essentially $CuFeS_2$. Also called "copper pyrites." [New Latin *chalcopyrites* : Greek *khalkos,* copper (see **ghelegh-** in Appendix*) + PYRITES.]

Chal·de·a (kăl-dē′ə). Also **Chal·dae·a.** An ancient region in southern Babylonia along the Euphrates River and the Persian Gulf in southwestern Asia.

Chal·de·an (kăl-dē′ən) *n.* Also **Chal·dae·an, Chal·dee** (kăl′dē′, kăl-dē′). **1.** A member of an ancient Semitic people who ruled in Babylonia. **2.** The Semitic language of Chaldeans. **3.** A person versed in occult learning; an astrologer, soothsayer, or sorcerer. —**Chal·de′an** *adj.* —**Chal·da′ic** (-dā′ĭk) *n.* & *adj.*

Chal·dee. 1. Biblical Aramaic *(see).* **2.** Variant of **Chaldean.**

chal·dron (chôl′drən) *n.* A unit of dry measure, as for coke, coal, or lime, equal to 32 to 36 bushels, formerly used in England. [Old French *chauderon,* from *chaudiere,* kettle, from Late Latin *caldāria,* CALDRON.]

cha·let (shă-lā′) *n.* **1.** A dwelling with a gently sloping overhanging roof, common in Switzerland and other Alpine regions. **2.** The hut of a herdsman in the Alps. [French, from Swiss French, cabin, possibly a diminutive of *cala* (unattested), stone shelter, from a Mediterranean root *cal-,* "stone."]

Cha·leur Bay (shə-lo͝or′, -lûr′). An inlet of the Gulf of St. Lawrence between the Gaspé Peninsula of southeastern Quebec and New Brunswick, Canada.

Cha·lia·pin (shə-lyä′pĭn), **Feodor Ivanovich.** 1873–1938. Russian-born French operatic basso.

chal·ice (chăl′ĭs) *n.* **1.** A cup or goblet. **2. a.** A cup for the consecrated wine of the Eucharist. **b.** The wine itself. **3.** A cup-shaped blossom. [Middle English, from Norman French, from Latin *calix,* cup, goblet. See **kal-**[1] in Appendix.*]

chal·i·co·there (kăl′ĭ-kō-thîr′) *n.* Any of various extinct ungulate mammals of the Eocene to Pleistocene epochs, having distinctive three-clawed, three-toed feet. [New Latin *Chalicotherium* (genus), "fossil beast" : Greek *khalix,* stone, pebble (see **calcium**) + Greek *thērion,* diminutive of *thēr,* beast (see **ghwer-** in Appendix*).]

chalk (chôk) *n.* **1.** A soft, compact calcium carbonate, $CaCO_3$, with varying amounts of silica, quartz, feldspar, or other mineral impurities, generally gray-white or yellow-white and derived chiefly from fossil seashells. **2.** A piece of chalk or chalklike substance, frequently colored, used for marking on a blackboard or other surface. **3.** A mark or picture made with chalk. **4.** A reckoning, as of credit given; a tally. —*tr.v.* **chalked, chalking, chalks. 1.** To mark, draw, or write with chalk. **2.** To smear or cover with chalk. **3.** To make pale; whiten. **4.** To treat (soil, for example) with chalk. —**chalk up. 1.** To earn or score: *chalk up points.* **2.** To credit: *Chalk that up to experience.* —*adj.* Made with chalk. [Middle English *chalk,* Old English *cealc,* from Latin *calx,* stone, pebble, from Greek *khalix.* See **calcium.**] —**chalk′i·ness** *n.* —**chalk′y** *adj.*

chalk·board (chôk′bôrd′, -bōrd′) *n.* A panel, usually green or black, for writing on with chalk; a blackboard.

chalk·stone (chôk′stōn′) *n. Pathology.* A **tophus** *(see).*

chalk talk. A lecture, often informal, illustrated with diagrams chalked on a blackboard.

chal·lah (KHä′lə) *n.* Also **cha·lah, hal·lah** (KHä′lə, hä′lə). A loaf of yeast-leavened, white egg bread, usually braided, traditionally eaten by Jews on the Sabbath, holidays, and ceremonial occasions. [Hebrew *ḥallāh.*]

chal·lenge (chăl′ənj) *n.* **1.** A call to engage in a contest or fight. **2.** A demand for an explanation; a calling into question. **3.** A sentry's call for identification. **4.** The quality of requiring full use of one's abilities, energy, or resources: *a career that offers a challenge.* **5.** A claim that a vote is invalid or that a voter is unqualified. **6.** *Law.* A formal objection, especially to the qualifications of a juror or jury. —*v.* **challenged, -lenging, -lenges.** —*tr.* **1.** To call to engage in a contest or fight. **2.** To take exception to; dispute. **3.** To order to halt and be identified. **4.** *Law.* To object formally to (a juror or jury, for example). **5.** To claim that (a voter) is unqualified or that (a vote) is invalid. **6.** To have due claim to; call for. **7.** To summon to action, effort, or use; stimulate: *a problem that challenges the imagination.* —*intr.* **1.** To make or give voice to a challenge. **2.** To begin barking upon picking up the scent. Used of hunting dogs. [Middle English *c(h)alenge,* accusation, challenge, from Old French *c(h)alenge,* from Latin *calumnia,* trickery, false accusation, from *calvī,* to deceive. See **kēl-** in Appendix.*] —**chal′lenge·a·ble** *adj.* —**chal′leng·er** *n.*

chal·lis (shăl′ē) *n.* Also **chal·lie.** A light clothing fabric usually printed and made of wool, cotton, or rayon. [Possibly from the English surname *Challis.*]

chal·one (kăl′ōn′) *n.* A hormone that inhibits a metabolic process. [Greek *khalōn*, present participle of *khalan*, to slacken, let down. See **ghē-** in Appendix.*]

cha·lyb·e·ate (kə-lĭb′ē-ĭt, -lē′bē-ĭt) *adj.* **1.** Impregnated with or containing salts of iron. **2.** Tasting like iron, as mineral-spring water. *—n.* Water or medicine containing iron in solution. [New Latin *chalybeatus*, from Latin *chalybs*, steel, from Greek *khalups*, from *Khalups*†, the Chalybes, ancient people in Asia Minor famous for their work in iron and steel.]

cham (kăm) *n. Archaic.* A Tatar or Mogul khan. [French, from Persian *khān*, from Turkish, KHAN.]

Cha·mae·leon (kə-mēl′yən, -mē′lē-ən) *n.* Also **Cha·me·leon.** A constellation in the southern polar region near Apus and Mensa.

cham·ber (chām′bər) *n.* **1. a.** A room in a house, especially a bedroom. **b.** *Plural. Chiefly British.* A suite of rooms; an apartment. **2.** A judge's office. **3.** A room in a palace or official residence where an important personage receives visitors. **4.** A hall for the meeting of an assembly, especially a legislative assembly. **5.** A legislative, judicial, or deliberative assembly. **6.** A board or council: *a chamber of commerce.* **7.** A place where governmental funds are received and held; treasury. **8.** Any enclosed space or compartment; cavity. **9. a.** An enclosed space at the bore of a gun that holds the charge. **b.** The part of a cylinder of a revolver that receives the cartridge. *—tr.v.* **chambered, -bering, -bers. 1.** To put in or as in a chamber; enclose; confine. **2.** To furnish with a chamber. [Middle English *chambre*, from Old French, from Late Latin *camera, camara*, from Latin, vault, arched roof, from Greek *kamara*. See **kamer-** in Appendix.*]

chambered nautilus. A cephalopod mollusk, *Nautilus pompilius*, of the Pacific and Indian oceans, having a coiled and partitioned shell lined with a pearly layer. Also called "pearly nautilus."

cham·ber·lain (chām′bər-lĭn) *n.* **1.** An official who manages the household of a sovereign or nobleman; a chief steward. **2.** A high-ranking officer in various royal courts. **3.** An official who receives the rents and fees of a municipality; a treasurer. [Middle English *chamberleyn*, from Old French *chamberlenc*, from Frankish *kamerling* (unattested), bedchamber servant : Common Germanic *kamer-* (unattested), chamber, from Late Latin *camera*, CHAMBER + -LING.]

Cham·ber·lain (chām′bər-lĭn), **(Arthur) Neville.** 1869–1940. British prime minister (1937–40); son of Joseph Chamberlain.

Cham·ber·lain (chām′bər-lĭn), **Joseph.** 1836–1914. British political leader; father of Neville Chamberlain.

Cham·ber·lain (chām′bər-lĭn), **Owen.** Born 1920. American physicist; discovered the antiproton with E. **Segrè** *(see).*

Cham·ber·lin (chām′bər-lĭn), **Thomas Chrowder.** 1843–1928. American geologist; formulated planetesimal hypothesis of earth's origin.

cham·ber·maid (chām′bər-mād′) *n.* A female servant who cleans and cares for bedrooms, now chiefly in hotels.

chamber music. Music appropriate for performance in a private room or small concert hall and composed for a group of instruments such as a trio or quartet.

chamber of commerce. *Abbr.* **C. of C.** An association of businessmen and merchants for the promotion of business interests in its community.

chamber pot. A portable vessel used in a bedroom as a toilet.

Cham·bers (chām′bərz), **(Jay David) Whittaker.** 1901–1961. American journalist and recanted Communist agent (1924–39); accuser of Alger **Hiss** *(see).*

Cham·be·zi (chăm-bē′zē, -bā′zē). A river rising in northern Zambia and flowing 300 miles southwest to the swamps of Lake Bangweulu; one of the headstreams of the Congo.

Cham·bord (shäN-bôr′). A village near the Loire in north-central France; the site of a famous chateau built by Francis I.

cham·bray (shăm′brā′) *n.* A fine, lightweight type of gingham, woven with white threads across a colored warp. [After *Cambrai*, France.]

Cham·do (chäm′dō′). *Chinese* **Chang·tu** (chäng′dōō′). A region of south-central China, east of Tibet.

cha·me·leon (kə-mēl′yən, -mē′lē-ən) *n.* **1.** Any of various tropical Old World lizards of the family Chamaeleonidae, characterized by their ability to change color. **2.** A similar lizard, the **anole** *(see).* **3.** A changeable or inconstant person. [Middle English *camelion*, from Latin *chamaeleōn*, from Greek *khamaileōn*, "ground lion" : *khamai*, on the ground (see **dhghem-** in Appendix*) + *leōn*, LION.] **—cha·me′le·on′ic** (-lē-ŏn′ĭk) *adj.*

Cha·me·leon. Variant of **Chamaeleon.**

cham·fer (chăm′fər) *tr.v.* **-fered, -fering, -fers. 1.** To cut off the edge or corner of; bevel. **2.** To cut a groove in; to flute. *—n.* **1.** A flat surface made by cutting off the edge or corner of something, such as a block of wood. **2.** A furrow or groove, as in a piece of wood. [Perhaps a back-formation from *chamfering*, from French *chanfrein*, a bevel, from Old French *chanfrein(t)*, past participle of *chanfraindre*, to break the edge off : *chant*, edge, rim, from Latin *canthus*, iron ring of a wheel, from Celtic (see **kantho-** in Appendix*) + *fraindre*, to break, from Latin *frangere* (see **bhreg-** in Appendix*).]

cham·fron (chăm′frən) *n.* Also **cham·frain, chan·fron** (chăn′frən). Medieval armor for the front of a horse's head. [Middle English *shamfron*, from Old French *chanfrein*, from *chafrener*, to harness a horse : *chief*, head, from Latin *caput* (see **kaput** in Appendix*) + *frener*, to bridle, from Latin *frēnare*, from *frēnum*, bridle (see **ghren-** in Appendix*).]

cha·mi·so (chə-mē′sō) *n., pl.* **-sos.** Also **cha·mise** (chə-mēz′). A shrub, *Adenostoma fasciculatum*, of California, having clusters of small white flowers and forming dense thickets. [American Spanish, from Spanish *chamizo*, burnt stick, from Portuguese *chamiço*, from *chamiça*, dried wood, heather, from *chama*, flame, from Latin *flamma*. See **bhel-**[1] in Appendix.*]

Cha·mi·zal (chä-mĭ-säl′). An area of about 600 acres, once in Mexico and later, when the Rio Grande changed its course in the 19th century, in El Paso, Texas; to be restored to Mexico by moving the river northward according to a 1964 treaty.

cham·ois (shăm′ē; *French* shăm-wä′ *for sense 1 only*) *n., pl.* **chamois** (shăm′ēz; *French* shăm-wä′ *for sense 1 only*). Also **cham·my, sham·my** (for sense 2) *pl.* **-mies. 1.** A hoofed mammal, *Rupricapra rupricapra*, of mountainous regions of Europe, having upright horns with backward-hooked tips. **2.** The soft leather made from the hide of this animal or others such as deer or sheep. **3.** Moderate to grayish yellow. See **color.** *—tr.v.* **chamoised, -oising, -oises.** Also **sham·my, -mied, -mying, -mies** (for sense 2). **1.** To dress or prepare like chamois. **2.** To polish or dry with chamois leather. [Old French, probably from Late Latin *camox*†.]

cham·o·mile, cam·o·mile (kăm′ə-mīl′) *n.* **1.** Any of various plants of the genus *Anthemis;* especially, *A. nobilis*, an aromatic plant native to Eurasia, having finely dissected leaves and white flowers. **2.** Any of several similar plants of the genus *Matricaria;* especially, *M. chamomilla*, native to Eurasia. [Middle English *camomille*, from Old French, from Late Latin *chamomilla*, from Latin *chamaemēlon*, from Greek *khamaemēlon*, "earth-apple" : *khamai*, on the ground (see **dhghem-** in Appendix*) + *mēlon*, apple (see **mēlon** in Appendix*).]

Cha·mo·nix (shȧ-mô-nē′). A valley of eastern France, north of Mont Blanc; the site of the resort town of Chamonix-Mont-Blanc.

champ[1] (chămp) *v.* **champed, champing, champs.** Also **chomp** (chŏmp). *—tr.* **1.** To bite upon with restlessness or impatience. **2.** To chew upon noisily. **3.** *Scottish.* To crush or trample. *—intr.* To work the jaws and teeth vigorously: *champ at the bit.* *—n.* Also **chomp.** The act of chewing or biting vigorously. [Possibly imitative.]

champ[2] (chămp) *n. Informal.* A champion.

cham·pagne (shăm-pān′) *n.* **1.** A sparkling white wine produced in Champagne, France, or any similar wine made elsewhere. **2.** Pale orange yellow to grayish yellow or yellowish gray. See **color.** *—adj.* Of, for, or pertaining to this wine or color.

Cham·pagne (shăm-pān′; *French* shäN-pȧn′y′). A region and former province of northeastern France, famous for its wines.

cham·paign (shăm-pān′) *n.* Level and open country; a plain. *—adj.* Pertaining to or like champaign; level and open. [Middle English *champayn*, from Old French *champagne*, from Late Latin *campānia*, from Latin *Campānia*, Campagna (province in Middle Italy), from *campus*, plain, field. See **camp.**]

Cham·paign (shăm-pān′). A city of east-central Illinois. Population, 50,000.

cham·pak (chăm′păk′, chŭm′pŭk) *n.* Also **cham·pac.** A tree, *Michelia champaca*, of India and the East Indies, having yellow flowers and yielding a camphorlike substance and an oil used in perfumes. [Hindi *campak*, from Sanskrit *campaka*, probably of Austro-Asiatic origin.]

cham·per·ty (chăm′pər-tē) *n., pl.* **-ties.** *Law.* An illegal sharing in the proceeds of a lawsuit by an outside party who has promoted it. [Middle English *champartie*, from Norman French, from Old French *champart*, division of farm produce : *champ*, field, from Latin *campus* (see **camp**) + *part*, PART.] **—cham′per·tous** (-təs) *adj.*

cham·pi·gnon (shăm-pĭn′yən; *French* shäN-pē-nyôN′) *n.* An edible mushroom, especially the common species *Agaricus campestris.* [French, from Old French *champigneul*, probably from Vulgar Latin *(fungus) campāniolus* (unattested), "(fungus) growing in the fields," from Late Latin *campānia*, countryside, CHAMPAIGN.]

cham·pi·on (chăm′pē-ən) *n.* **1.** One that holds first place or wins first prize in a contest, especially in sports. **2.** One who fights for, defends, or supports a cause or another person: *"Russia has long played the role of champion of the colored peoples"* (Brewton Berry). **3.** One who fights; a warrior. *—tr.v.* **championed, -oning, -ons. 1.** To fight as champion of; defend; support: *"championed the government and defended the system of taxation"* (Samuel Chew). **2.** *Obsolete.* To defy or challenge. —See Synonyms at **support.** *—adj.* Holding first place or prize; superior to all others. [Middle English *champi(o)un*, from Old French *champion*, probably from West Germanic *kampjo* (unattested), warrior, from *kamp* (unattested), battlefield, from Latin *campus*, field. See **camp.**]

cham·pi·on·ship (chăm′pē-ən-shĭp′) *n.* **1.** The position or title of a champion. **2.** Defense or support; advocacy. **3.** A competition or series of competitions held to determine a winner.

Cham·plain, Lake (shăm-plān′). A lake 125 miles long and 435 square miles in area, between eastern New York State and western Vermont.

Cham·plain (shăm-plān′), **Samuel de.** 1567?–1635. French explorer, cartographer, founder of Quebec (1608); governor of New France (1633–35).

Cham·pol·lion (shäN-pô-lyôN′), **Jean François.** 1790–1832. French archaeologist and Egyptologist; deciphered the Rosetta Stone.

chan. channel.

Chan. chancellor.

Chanc. 1. chancellor. **2.** chancery.

chance (chăns, chäns) *n.* **1. a.** The abstract nature or quality shared by unexpected, random, or unpredictable events; contingency. **b.** This quality regarded as a cause of such events;

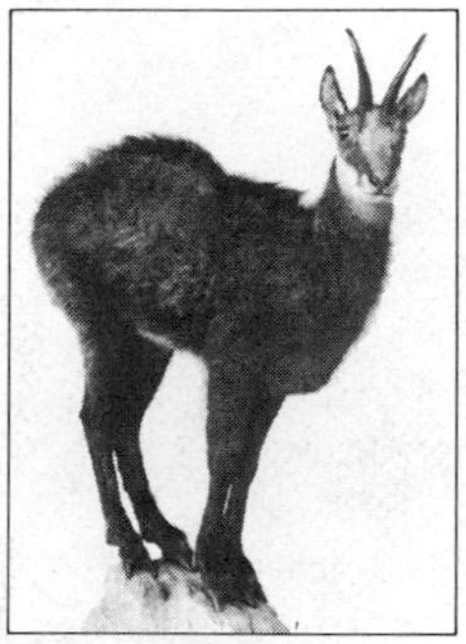

chamois

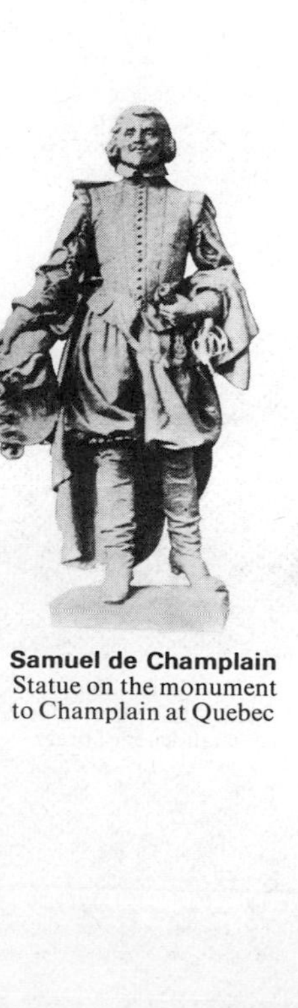

Samuel de Champlain
Statue on the monument to Champlain at Quebec

luck. 2. The likelihood of occurrence of an event; probability. 3. a. An opportunity. b. A risk or hazard; gamble. c. A raffle or lottery ticket. 4. a. An unexpected, random, or unpredicted event. b. A fortuitous event. 5. *Baseball.* An opportunity to make a putout or an assist that counts as an error if unsuccessful. —See Synonyms at **opportunity.** —*v.* **chanced, chancing, chances.** —*intr.* To happen by chance; occur by accident. —*tr.* To take the risk or hazard of. —See Synonyms at **happen.** —**chance on** (or **upon**). To find or meet accidentally; happen upon. —*adj.* Occurring as or in consequence of chance. See Synonyms below. [Middle English, from Old French, from Vulgar Latin *cadentia* (unattested), "a fall," happening, from Latin *cadere,* to fall. See **kad-** in Appendix.*]

Synonyms: *chance, random, casual, haphazard, desultory.* These adjectives apply to what lacks purposefulness or method. *Chance* implies total absence of design or predictability: *my chance meeting with a friend. Random* applies to things that happen to occur or be selected without the aid of a governing mind or design. *Casual* suggests lack of deliberation or formality; *haphazard,* a carelessness or a willful leaving to chance; and *desultory,* an absence of relation among things in a series.

chance·ful (chăns′fəl, chäns′-) *adj.* 1. Eventful. 2. *Rare.* Full of chance; risky. 3. *Obsolete.* Dependent upon chance.

chan·cel (chăn′səl, chän′-) *n.* The space around the altar of a church for the clergy and choir, often enclosed by a lattice or railing. [Middle English *chauncel,* from Old French *chancel,* from Late Latin *cancellus,* altar, from Latin *cancellī,* grating, lattice, plural diminutive of *cancer,* lattice. See **carcer** in Appendix.*]

chan·cel·ler·y (chăn′səl-ər-ē, -slər-ē, chän′-) *n., pl.* **-ies.** 1. The rank, position, or dignity of a chancellor. 2. The office or department of a chancellor or the building in which it is located. 3. The official place of business of an embassy, consulate, or legation. [Middle English *chancelerie,* from Old French, from *chancelier,* CHANCELLOR.]

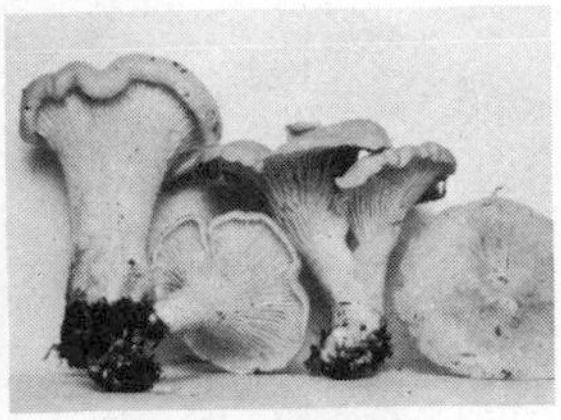

chanterelle

chan·cel·lor (chăn′səl-ər, -slər, chän′-) *n. Abbr.* **Chan., Chanc., C.** 1. Any of various officials of high rank; especially: a. A secretary to a king or nobleman. b. *British.* The chief secretary of an embassy. c. The chief minister of state in some European countries. 2. a. *British.* The honorary or titular head of a university. b. The president of certain American universities. 3. The presiding judge of a court of chancery or equity in some states of the United States. [Middle English *cha(u)nceler,* from Norman French *chanceler,* from Old French *chancelier,* from Late Latin *cancellārius,* secretary, doorkeeper, from *cancellus,* grating, CHANCEL.] —**chan′cel·lor·ship′** *n.*

Chancellor of the Exchequer. In the British Government, the highest minister of finance and a member of the Cabinet.

Chan·cel·lors·ville (chăn′səl-ərz-vĭl′, -slərz-vĭl′, chän′-). Also **Chan·cel·lor** (chăn′səl-ər, -slər, chän′-). A town in northeastern Virginia, the site of a Confederate victory in the Civil War (1863). Population, 29,000.

chance-med·ley (chăns′mĕd′lē, chäns′-) *n.* 1. *Law.* A sudden quarrel resulting in an unpremeditated homicide. 2. A random or haphazard action. [Middle English, from Norman French *chance medlee,* "mixed chance" : Old French *chance,* CHANCE + *medlee,* past participle of *medler,* MEDDLE.]

chan·cer·y (chăn′sər-ē, chän′-) *n., pl.* **-ies.** *Abbr.* **Chanc.** 1. a. A court with jurisdiction in equity, as distinguished from one with jurisdiction in common law. Also called "court of chancery." b. The proceedings and practice of a court of chancery; equity. 2. A court of public record; an office of archives. 3. In Great Britain, one of the five divisions of the High Court of Justice, presided over by the Lord High Chancellor. 4. A chancellery. —**in chancery.** 1. *Law.* In litigation or pending in a court of chancery. 2. *Wrestling.* With the head locked firmly in an opponent's arm and held against his chest. 3. *Informal.* In an embarrassing or hopeless predicament. [Middle English *chancerie,* contraction of *chancelerie,* CHANCELLERY.]

Chan·chiang (chän′chyäng′). A city in southwestern Kwangtung Province, China, known as Fort Bayard under the French (1899–1946). Population, 166,000.

chan·cre (shăng′kər) *n.* A dull-red, hard, insensitive lesion that is the first manifestation of syphilis. [French, from Latin *cancer,* ulcer, CANCER.]

chan·croid (shăng′kroid′) *n.* A soft, nonsyphilitic, usually venereal, lesion of the genital region. [French *chancroïde* : CHANCR(E) + -OID.]

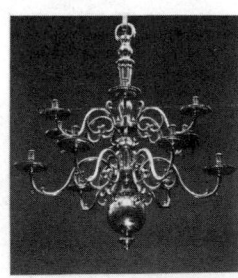

chandelier
Mid-18th-century Dutch chandelier of brass

chanc·y (chăn′sē, chän′-) *adj.* **-ier, -iest.** 1. Uncertain or hazardous. 2. *Scottish.* Lucky; propitious.

chan·de·lier (shăn′də-lîr′) *n.* A branched fixture that holds a number of light bulbs or candles, and is usually suspended from a ceiling. [French, from Old French, from Vulgar Latin *candēlārum* (unattested), from Latin *candēlābrum,* CANDELABRUM.]

chan·delle (shăn-dĕl′) *n.* A sudden, steep climbing turn of an aircraft, executed to alter flight direction and gain altitude simultaneously. [French, "candle," from Old French. See **chandler.**]

Chan·der·na·gore (chŭn′dər-nə-gôr′). A former territory of French India, on the Hooghly River 20 miles north of Calcutta, an integral part of the Republic of India since 1954.

Chan·di·garh (chŭn′dē-gər). The capital (since 1966) of Hariana and Punjab states, Republic of India, in northeastern Hariana. Population, 89,000.

chan·dler (chăn′dlər, chän′-) *n.* 1. A person who makes or sells candles. 2. A dealer in specified goods or equipment: *a ship chandler.* [Middle English *chandeler,* from Old French *chandelier,* from *c(h)andelle,* candle, from Latin *candēla,* CANDLE.]

chan·dler·y (chăn′dlər-ē, chän′-) *n., pl.* **-ies.** 1. The stock or business of a chandler. 2. A place where candles are stored.

Chan·dra·se·khar (chŭn′drə-shā′kər), **Subrahmanyan.** Born 1910. Indian-born American astrophysicist.

Cha·nel (shȧ-nĕl′), **Gabrielle ("Coco").** Born 1883? French dress designer.

Cha·ney (chā′nē), **Lon.** 1883–1930. American actor in silent films.

chan·fron. Variant of **chamfron.**

Chang·an. The former name for **Sian.**

Chang·chow (chäng′jō′). 1. The former name for **Lungshi.** 2. The former name for **Wusih.**

Ch'ang·chun (chäng′chōōn′). Formerly **Hsin·king** (shĭn′jĭng′). The capital of Kirin Province, China, an industrial city in south-central Manchuria. Population, 988,000.

change (chānj) *v.* **changed, changing, changes.** —*tr.* 1. a. To cause to be different; alter. b. To give a completely different form or appearance to; transform. 2. To give and receive reciprocally; interchange. 3. To exchange for or replace by another, usually of the same kind or category: *change one's name.* 4. To lay aside, abandon, or leave for another; switch: *change methods; change planes.* 5. To give or receive the equivalent of (money) in lower denominations or in foreign currency. 6. To put fresh clothes or coverings on: *change a baby.* —*intr.* 1. To become different or altered. 2. To go from one phase to another. Used of the moon. 3. To make an exchange. 4. To transfer from one vehicle to another. 5. To put on other clothing. 6. To become deeper in tone. Used of the voice. —**change hands.** To pass from one owner to another. —**change off.** 1. To alternate with another person in performing a task. 2. To perform two tasks at once by alternating, or a single task by alternate means. —*n.* Also **'change** (for sense 9). 1. a. The process or condition of changing; alteration or modification; transformation. b. The replacing of one thing for another; substitution. 2. A transition from one state, condition, or phase to another: *the change of seasons.* 3. Something different; variety. 4. A different or fresh set of clothing. 5. The money of smaller denomination given or received in exchange for money of higher denomination. 6. The balance of money returned when an amount given is more than what is due. 7. Any small coins. 8. *Music.* a. A pattern or order in which bells are rung. b. A shift in key. 9. A market or exchange where business is transacted. —**ring the changes.** 1. To ring bells with every possible variation. 2. To do or say something in every possible manner. [Middle English *changen,* from Old French *changier,* from Late Latin *cambiāre,* probably from Celtic. See **skamb-** in Appendix.*] —**chang′er** *n.*

Synonyms: *change, alter, vary, modify, transform, convert, transmute.* These verbs mean to make or become different. *Change* implies a fundamental difference or a substitution of one thing for another: *change his mind; change trains. Alter* usually means to make less of a difference or adjustment. *Vary* implies shifting circumstances or conditions that cause differences with some regularity. *Modify* can mean to restrict, limit, or qualify, and sometimes to make less extreme. *Transform* refers to complete change in outer form or appearance and often also in character and function. *Convert* can refer to moderate change designed to adapt something to new use or different conditions; to chemical change; to change in belief or doctrine; or to the exchange of something for equivalent value, either in the same form *(convert dollars into pounds)* or a different form *(convert real estate into cash). Transmute* suggests almost magical basic change that elevates something in value.

change·a·ble (chān′jə-bəl) *adj.* 1. Liable to change; capricious. 2. Capable of being altered. 3. Changing color or appearance when seen from different angles: *changeable taffeta.* —**change′a·bil′i·ty, change′a·ble·ness** *n.* —**change′a·bly** *adv.*

change·ful (chānj′fəl) *adj.* Having the propensity or the ability to change; given to frequent changes; variable. —**change′ful·ly** *adv.* —**change′ful·ness** *n.*

change·less (chānj′lĭs) *adj.* Immutable; unchanging; enduring. —**change′less·ly** *adv.* —**change′less·ness** *n.*

change·ling (chānj′lĭng) *n.* 1. A child secretly exchanged for another by the fairies. 2. *Archaic.* A changeable, fickle person. 3. *Archaic.* A simple-minded person; idiot.

change of life. The **menopause** *(see).*

change ringing. The ringing of a set of chimes or bells with every possible unrepeated variation.

Chang·kiang. The official name for the **Yangtze.**

Chang·sha (chäng′shä′). The capital of Hunan Province, in southeastern China, on the Siang River. Population, 709,000.

Chang·tu. The Chinese name for **Chamdo.**

chan·nel[1] (chăn′əl) *n. Abbr.* **chan.** 1. The bed of a stream or river. 2. The deeper part of a river or harbor; especially, a deep navigable passage. 3. A broad strait: *the English Channel.* 4. A tubular passage for liquids. 5. A course or passage through which something may be moved or directed: *a channel of thought.* 6. *Plural.* Official routes of communication. 7. *Electronics.* A specified frequency band for the transmission and reception of electromagnetic signals, as for television signals. 8. A trench, furrow, or groove. 9. A rolled metal bar with a bracket-shaped section. In this sense, also called "channel bar," "channel iron." —*tr.v.* **channeled, -neling, -nels.** Also *chiefly British* **-nelled, -nelling.** 1. To make or cut channels in: *"No more shall trenching war channel her fields."* (Shakespeare). 2. To form a channel or flute in. 3. To direct or guide along some desired course. [Middle English *chanel,* from Old French, from Latin *canālis,* CANAL.]

chan·nel[2] (chăn′əl) *n. Nautical.* A wood or steel ledge projecting from a sailing vessel's sides to spread the shrouds and keep

them clear of the gunwales. [Earlier *chainwale* : CHAIN (fastening) + WALE (plank).]
channel bass. A fish, the **red drum** *(see).*
channel black. A finely divided carbon black, formed on iron plate by direct exposure to a natural gas flame and used in inks, paints, typewriter ribbons, crayons, and polishes. Also called "gas black." [From CHANNEL (metal bar).]
Channel Islands. A group of nine British islands in the English Channel off Normandy, with an area of about 75 square miles, and including the islands of Jersey, Guernsey, Alderney, and Sark. Population, 112,000. Capital, St. Helier on Jersey.
chan·nel·ize (chăn′əl-īz′) *tr.v.* **-ized, -izing, -izes.** To channel. —**chan′nel·i·za′tion** *n.*
Chan·ning (chăn′ĭng), **William Ellery.** 1780–1842. American Protestant clergyman; a founder of Unitarianism.
chan·son (shăn′sən; *French* shäN-sôN′) *n.* A song. Now archaic except with reference to specifically French genres. [French, from Old French, from Latin *cantiō,* from *cantāre,* to CHANT.]
chan·son de geste (shäN-sôN′ də zhĕst′) *pl.* **chansons de geste** (shäN-sôN′). A genre of Old French epic poem falling into cycles of poems celebrating the deeds of heroic or historical figures. [French, "song of heroic deeds."]
chant (chănt, chänt) *n.* Also *archaic* **chaunt** (chônt, chänt). **1.** A short, simple melody in which a number of syllables or words are sung on each note. **2.** A psalm or canticle sung in this manner. **3.** A song or melody. **4.** A monotonous rhythmic voice. —*v.* **chanted, chanting, chants.** —*tr.* **1.** To sing or intone to a chant. **2.** To celebrate in song. **3.** To say in the manner of a chant. —*intr.* **1.** To sing; especially, to sing chants. **2.** To speak monotonously. [Middle English, probably from *chanten,* to sing, from Old French *chanter,* from Latin *cantāre,* to sing, frequentative of *canere,* to sing. See **kan-** in Appendix.*]
chant·age (chăn′tĭj, chän′-; *French* shäN-tȧzh′) *n.* Blackmail. [French, from *chanter,* to sing, CHANT.]
chant·er (chăn′tər, chän′-) *n.* **1.** A person who chants, as a chorister or precentor. **2.** A priest who sings in the chantry. **3.** In a bagpipe, the pipe on which the melody is played. In this sense, also called "chanter pipe."
chan·te·relle (shăn′tə-rĕl′, shän′-) *n.* An edible yellow mushroom, *Cantharellus cibarius,* having a pleasant fruity odor. [French, from New Latin *cantharella,* "little cup" (from its shape), diminutive of Latin *cantharus,* drinking vessel, from Greek *kantharos*†.]
chan·teuse (shäN-tœz′) *n.* A woman singer; especially, a nightclub singer. [French, feminine of *chanteur,* singer, from *chanter,* to sing, CHANT.]
chant·ey (shăn′tē, chăn′-) *n., pl.* **-eys.** Also **chant·y, shant·y** (shăn′tē) *pl.* **-ies, shant·ey** *pl.* **-eys.** A song sung by sailors to the rhythm of their movements while working. [Probably from French *chantez,* imperative of *chanter,* to sing, CHANT.]
chan·ti·cleer (chăn′tə-klîr′, shăn′-) *n.* A cock or rooster: *"I hear the strain of strutting chanticleer."* (Shakespeare). [Middle English *Chantecler,* from Old French *Chantecler* (the cock in *Reynard the Fox*) : *chanter,* to CHANT + *cler,* CLEAR.]
Chan·til·ly (shăn-tĭl′ē; *French* shäN-tē-yē′). A town of northern France, famous for its delicate lace. Population, 8,000.
chan·try (chăn′trē, chän′-) *n., pl.* **-tries.** *Ecclesiastical.* **1.** An endowment to cover expenses for the saying of masses and prayers, usually for the soul of the founder of the endowment. **2.** An altar or chapel endowed for this purpose. [Middle English *chaunterie,* from Old French *chanterie,* from *chanter,* to CHANT.]
Cha·nu·kah (KHä′nŏŏ-kə) *n.* Also **Ha·nuk·kah, Ha·nu·kah.** A Jewish festival beginning on the 25th day of the month of Kislev and lasting eight days. It commemorates the victory of the Maccabees over the Syrians in 165 B.C. and the rededication of the Temple at Jerusalem. Also called "Feast of Lights," "Feast of Dedication." [Hebrew *ḥanukkāh,* "dedication," from *ḥānakh,* he dedicated.]
Cha·nute (shə-nōōt′), **Octave.** 1832–1910. French-born American civil engineer; pioneer in construction and flight of gliders.
Ch'ao·an (chou′än′). Also **Chao·chow** (chou′jō′). A city in eastern Kwangtung Province, southeastern China, on the Han River 20 miles north of Swatow. Population, 594,700.
Chao Phra·ya (chou prä′yə). Formerly **Mae Nam, Me·nam** (mä′näm′). A river formed by the confluence of the Ping and Nan rivers in central Thailand and flowing 150 miles south into the Gulf of Siam.
cha·os (kā′ŏs′) *n.* **1.** Any condition or place of total disorder or confusion. **2.** *Often capital* **C.** The disordered state of unformed matter and infinite space supposed by some religious cosmological views to have existed prior to the ordered universe. **3.** *Obsolete.* A vast abyss or chasm. [Latin, from Greek *khaos,* empty space, chaos. See **ghēu-** in Appendix.*] —**cha·ot′ic** (kā-ŏt′ĭk) *adj.* —**cha·ot′i·cal·ly** *adv.*
chap¹ (chăp) *v.* **chapped, chapping, chaps.** —*tr.* To cause (the skin) to split or roughen, especially as a result of cold or exposure. —*intr.* To split or become rough and sore. —*n.* A sore roughening of the skin, caused by cold or exposure. [Middle English *chappen,* possibly of Low German origin, akin to Middle Low German *kappen.* See **skep-** in Appendix.*]
chap² (chăp) *n.* **1.** *Informal.* A man or boy; a fellow. **2.** *British Regional.* A customer; purchaser. [Short for CHAPMAN.]
chap. chapter.
Cha·pa·la (chä-pä′lä). The largest lake in Mexico (408 square miles), lying 20 miles southeast of Guadalajara.
cha·pa·re·jos (chä′pä-rä′hōs, shăp′ə-rā′ōs) *pl.n.* Also **cha·pa·ra·jos** *Southwestern U.S.* Heavy leather trousers worn by cowboys, **chaps** *(see).* [Probably from Mexican Spanish *chaparreras* (influenced by Spanish *aparejo,* equipment), from *chaparro,* CHAPARRAL.]
chap·ar·ral (shăp′ə-răl′) *n.* A dense thicket of shrubs and small trees, especially in the southwestern United States and Mexico. [Spanish, from *chaparro,* evergreen oak, probably from Basque *txapar,* diminutive of *saphar,* thicket.]
chaparral cock. A bird, the **roadrunner** *(see).*
chaparral pea. A thorny shrub, *Pickeringia montana,* of California, having showy reddish-purple flowers and forming dense thickets.
chap·book (chăp′bŏŏk′) *n.* A small book or pamphlet containing poems, ballads, stories, or religious tracts. [Originally, "a book sold by chapmen" : CHAP(MAN) + BOOK.]
chape (chāp, chăp) *n.* A metal tip or mounting on a scabbard or sheath. [Middle English, from Old French, cape, covering, from Late Latin *cappa,* hood, "head covering," from Latin *caput,* head. See **kaput** in Appendix.*]
cha·peau (shă-pō′; *French* shȧ-pō′) *n., pl.* **-peaux** (-pōz′; *French* -pō′) or **-peaus** (-pōz′). A hat. [French, from Old French *chapel,* from Vulgar Latin *cappellus* (unattested), diminutive of Late Latin *cappa,* head covering. See **chape.**]
chap·el (chăp′əl) *n.* **1.** A place of Christian worship that is smaller than and subordinate to a church. **2.** A place of worship in a college, hospital, or other institution. **3.** The services held at a chapel. **4.** A recess or room in a church set apart for special or small services. **5.** In England, any place of worship for those not connected with or not members of the established church. **6.** A choir or orchestra connected with a chapel, court, or the like. **7. a.** An association of workers in a print shop. **b.** *Rare.* A printing house or print shop. [Middle English, from Old French *chapele,* from Medieval Latin *capella,* originally a shrine containing the cape of St. Martin of Tours, diminutive of Late Latin *cappa,* cape. See **chape.**]
chap·er·on (shăp′ə-rōn′) *n.* Also **chap·er·one.** A person, especially an older or married woman, who for propriety supervises a group of young unmarried people or accompanies a young unmarried woman in public. —*tr.v.* **chaperoned, -oning, -ons.** To act as chaperon to or for. See Synonyms at **accompany.** [French, "hood," protection, protectress, from Old French, from *chape,* CHAPE.] —**chap′er·on′age** (shăp′ə-rō′nĭj) *n.*
chap·fall·en (chăp′fô′lən, chŏp′-) *adj.* Also **chop·fall·en** (chŏp′-). Dejected; disheartened; crestfallen. [From *chaps,* variant of CHOPS.]
chap·i·ter (chăp′ə-tər) *n. Architecture.* The capital of a column. [Middle English *chapitre,* from Latin *capitulum.* See **chapter.**]
chap·lain (chăp′lĭn) *n. Abbr.* **ch., Ch.** **1.** A clergyman attached to a chapel. **2.** A clergyman or layman who conducts religious services for a legislative assembly or other organization. **3.** A clergyman attached to a military unit. [Middle English *chapeleyn,* from Old French *chapelain,* from Medieval Latin *cappellānus,* from *capella,* CHAPEL.] —**chap′lain·cy, chap′lain·ship′** *n.*
chap·let (chăp′lĭt) *n.* **1.** A wreath or garland for the head. **2.** *Roman Catholic Church.* **a.** A string of prayer beads having one third the number of a rosary's beads. **b.** The prayers counted on such beads. **3.** Any string of beads. **4.** *Architecture.* A small molding carved in a way resembling a string of beads. [Middle English *chapelet,* from Old French, diminutive of *chapel,* CHAPEAU.] —**chap′let·ed** *adj.*
Chap·lin (chăp′lĭn), **Charles Spencer ("Charlie").** Born 1889. British motion-picture actor, producer, director, writer, and composer; worked in America (1913–52).
chap·man (chăp′mən) *n., pl.* **-men** (-mĭn). **1.** *British.* A peddler. **2.** *Archaic.* A dealer or merchant. [Middle English *chapman,* Old English *cēapman* : *cēap,* trade (see **cheap**) + MAN.]
Chap·man (chăp′mən), **Frank Michler.** 1864–1945. American ornithologist and author.
Chap·man (chăp′mən), **George.** 1559?–1634. English poet, dramatist, and translator of Homer.
Chap·man (chăp′mən), **John.** Called "Johnny Appleseed." 1775?–1845. American pioneer; hero of many legends.
chaps (chăps, shăps) *pl.n.* Heavy leather trousers without a seat, worn over ordinary trousers by cowboys to protect their legs. Also called "chaparejos." [Short for Mexican Spanish *chaparreras,* CHAPAREJOS.]
chap·ter (chăp′tər) *n. Abbr.* **chap., ch., c., C.** **1.** Any of the main divisions of a book or other writing, usually numbered or titled. **2.** A period or sequence of events, as in history, that marks a distinct change of pattern. **3.** A local branch of a club, fraternity, or other organization. **4.** *Ecclesiastical.* **a.** An assembly of the canons of a church. **b.** The canons collectively. **5.** *Ecclesiastical.* An assembly of the members or representatives of a religious house, community, or order. **6.** A meeting of any society or order. **7.** A short Scriptural passage read after the psalms in certain church services. —*tr.v.* **chaptered, -tering, -ters.** To divide (a book or other writing) into chapters. [Middle English *chapitre,* from Old French, from Late Latin *capitulum,* from Latin, small head, chapiter, from *caput,* head. See **kaput** in Appendix.*]
chapter house. **1.** A building in which the chapter of a cathedral or monastery assembles. **2.** A house in which a chapter of a fraternity or sorority lives and holds its meetings.
Cha·pul·te·pec (chə-pōōl′tə-pĕk′). A Mexican fortress on a hill three miles southwest of Mexico City; captured by American forces during the Mexican War (1847).
char¹ (chär) *v.* **charred, charring, chars.** —*tr.* **1.** To burn the surface of; scorch. **2.** To reduce to charcoal by incomplete combustion. —*intr.* **1.** To become scorched. **2.** To become reduced to charcoal. —See Synonyms at **burn.** —*n.* A sub-

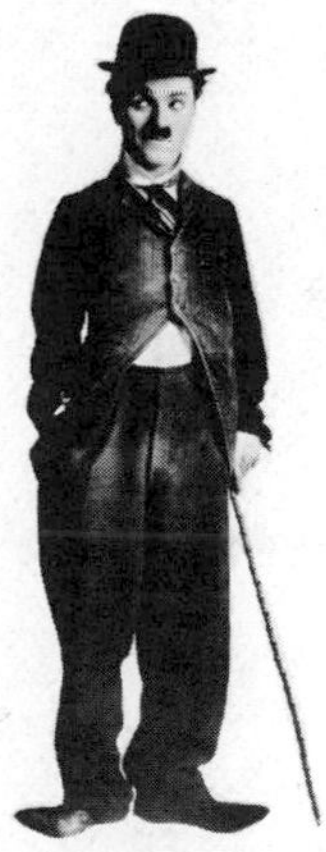

Charlie Chaplin

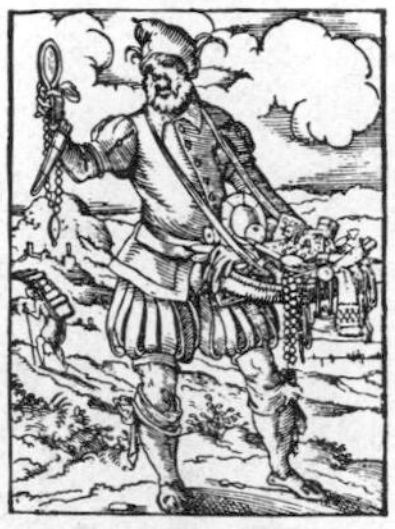

chapman
Sixteenth-century German woodcut

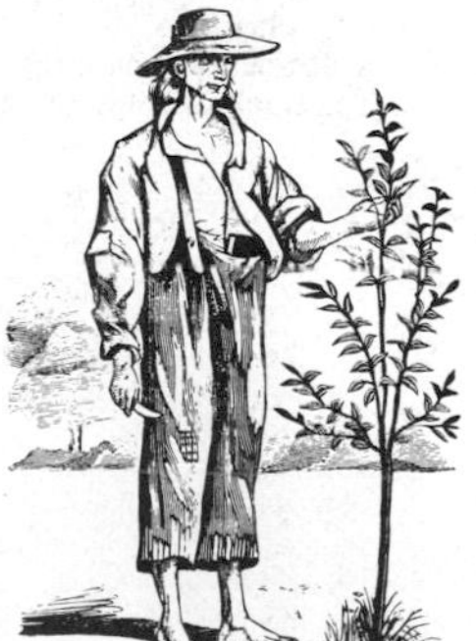

John Chapman
Engraving of "Johnny Appleseed" planting an apple tree

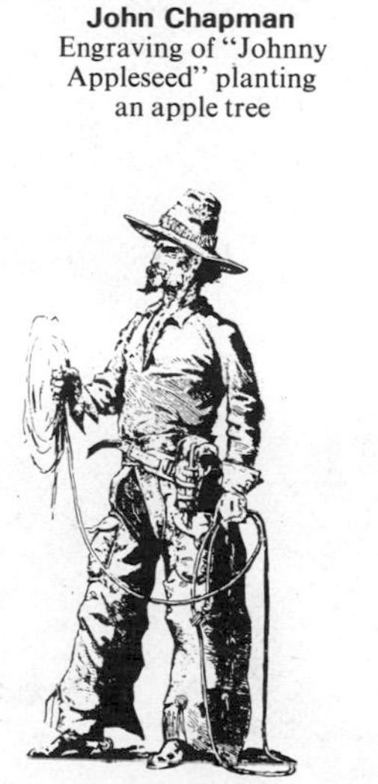

chaps
Frederic Remington drawing of a cowboy wearing chaps

stance that has been charred; charcoal. [Back-formation from CHARCOAL.]

char² (chär) *n., pl.* **char** or **chars.** Also **charr.** Any of several fishes of the genus *Salvelinus,* related to the trout; especially, the widely distributed species *S. alpinus.* [Origin unknown.]

char³ (châr) *n.* Also *British* **chare** (châr). **1.** A chore or odd job, especially a household task. **2.** A charwoman. *—intr.v.* **charred, charring, chars.** Also *British* **chare, chared, charing, chares. 1.** To do small jobs, tasks, or chores. **2.** To work as a charwoman. [Middle English *char(re),* piece of work, Old English *cierr, cyrr,* piece of work, a turning, from West Germanic *karzi* (unattested).]

char. charter.

char·a·banc (shăr′ə-băng′) *n., pl.* **-bancs.** Also **char·a·bank.** *British.* A large bus, often used for sightseeing. [French *char à bancs,* "carriage with benches."]

char·a·cin (kăr′ə-sĭn) *n.* Also **char·a·cid** (-sĭd). Any of numerous chiefly tropical freshwater fishes of the family Characidae, many of which are popular aquarium fishes. [New Latin *Characinidae* (earlier family name) : *Charax* (genus), from Greek *kharax,* a kind of fish, pointed stake (see **gher-⁵** in Appendix*) + -IDAE.]

char·ac·ter (kăr′ĭk-tər) *n.* **1.** The combination of qualities or features that distinguishes one person, group, or thing from another. **2.** One such distinguishing feature or attribute; a characteristic. **3.** The combined moral or ethical structure of a person or group. **4.** Moral or ethical strength; integrity; fortitude. **5.** Reputation: *"I have not the character of being half as prudent as I really am."* (Anne Langton). **6.** Status; capacity; role: *in his character as a father.* **7.** *Informal.* A person who is peculiar or eccentric. **8.** A personage. **9.** A person portrayed in a drama, novel, or other artistic piece. **10.** A description of a person's attributes, traits, or abilities. **11.** A formal written statement as to competency and dependability, given by an employer to a former employee; a recommendation. **12.** A symbol or mark used in a writing system, such as a letter of the alphabet. **13.** A style of printing or writing. **14.** A symbol used in secret writing; a cipher or code. **15.** *Genetics.* Any structure, function, or attribute determined by a gene or group of genes. —See Synonyms at **disposition, quality, type.** —**in** (or **out of**) **character.** Consistent (or not consistent) with the general character or role. *—adj.* **1.** Acting in usually supporting roles that emphasize traits markedly different from those of the actor himself: *a character actor.* **2.** Of or calling for such a style of performance: *a character part.* *—tr.v.* **charactered, -tering, -ters. 1.** To write, print, engrave, or inscribe. **2.** *Rare.* To portray, describe, or represent. [Learned respelling of Middle English *caracter,* from Old French *caractere,* from Latin *charactēr,* character, mark, instrument for branding, from Greek *kharaktēr,* engraved mark, brand, from *kharassein,* to brand, sharpen, from *kharax,* pointed stake. See **gher-⁵** in Appendix.*]

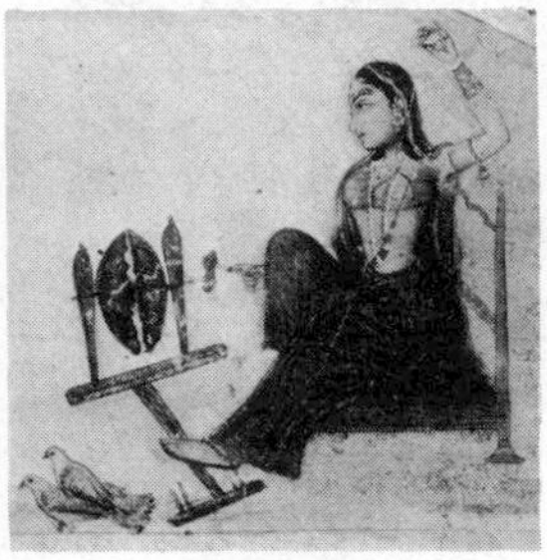

charkha
Late 18th-century painting of the Lucknow school

char·ac·ter·is·tic (kăr′ĭk-tə-rĭs′tĭk) *adj.* Pertaining to, indicating, or constituting a distinctive character, quality, or disposition; typical. *—n.* **1.** A distinguishing feature or attribute. **2.** *Mathematics.* The integral part of a logarithm as distinguished from the mantissa: *6 is the characteristic of the logarithm 6.3214.* —**char′ac·ter·is′ti·cal·ly** *adv.*

Synonyms: *characteristic, individual, distinctive, peculiar, typical.* These adjectives indicate a trait, feature, or quality that identifies or sets apart someone or something. *Characteristic* designates the identifying and especially the intrinsic feature: *the zebra's characteristic stripes. Individual* lends to *characteristic* a personal quality that more definitely sets apart the person or thing: *students judged by individual performance. Distinctive* adds to *individual* the idea of an outstanding, worthwhile quality or feature. *Peculiar* emphasizes a trait belonging solely to one person or one thing. In this sense it does not necessarily relate to oddness: *a mellow sound peculiar to the cello. Typical,* the most common of these terms, describes features, qualities, or behavior broadly applicable to a species, group, or class.

char·ac·ter·i·za·tion (kăr′ĭk-tər-ə-zā′shən) *n.* **1.** The act of characterizing. **2.** A description or representation of a person's qualities or peculiarities. **3.** The creation or delineation of a character or characters on the stage or in writing, especially by imitating or describing actions, gestures, or speeches.

char·ac·ter·ize (kăr′ĭk-tə-rīz′) *tr.v.* **-ized, -izing, -izes. 1.** To describe the qualities or peculiarities of. **2.** To be a distinguishing trait or mark of. **3.** To give character to, as on the stage or in a novel. —**char′ac·ter·iz′er** *n.*

char·ac·ter·y (kăr′ĭk-tər-ē, kə-răk′-) *n., pl.* **-ies.** *Archaic.* **1.** The use of characters or symbols to express or convey thought and meaning. **2.** Such characters or symbols collectively.

cha·rades (shə-rādz′) *n.* Plural in form, sometimes used with a singular verb. **1.** A parlor game in which words or phrases are represented in pantomime, sometimes syllable by syllable, until they are guessed by the other players. **2.** *Singular.* An episode in this game or the word so represented. [French, from Provençal *charrado,* chat, from *charra,* to chat (imitative).]

char·coal (chär′kōl′) *n.* **1.** A black, porous carbonaceous material, produced by the destructive distillation of wood and used as a fuel, filter, and absorbent. **2.** A drawing pencil or crayon made from this substance. **3.** A drawing executed with such a pencil or crayon. **4.** Dark grayish brown to black or dark purplish gray. See **color.** *—tr.v.* **charcoaled, -coaling, -coals.** To draw, write, or blacken with charcoal. [Middle English *charcole* : perhaps Old French *charbon,* charcoal, from Latin *carbō* (see **carbon**) + COAL.]

charcoal rot. A disease of plants caused by a fungus, *Macrophomina phaseoli,* and resulting in black, decayed tissue.

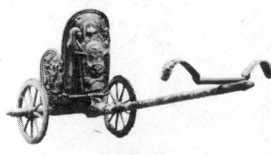

chariot
Sixth-century B.C. Etruscan chariot

Char·cot (shär-kō′), **Jean Baptiste Etienne Auguste.** 1867–1936. French explorer of the Antarctic; son of J.M. Charcot.

Char·cot (shär-kō′), **Jean Martin.** 1825–1893. French neurologist and educator; father of J.B.E.A. Charcot.

Char·cot's disease (shär-kōz′). **Multiple sclerosis** *(see).*

chard (chärd) *n.* A variety of beet, *Beta vulgaris cicla,* having large, succulent leaves used as a vegetable. Also called "Swiss chard," "leaf beet." [French *carde,* edible stalks of the cardoon, from Old French, cardoon, from Late Latin *cardō,* from Latin *carduus,* artichoke. See **kars-** in Appendix.*]

Char·din, Pierre Teilhard de. See **Teilhard de Chardin.**

Char·don·net (shär-dô-nā′), Count **Louis Marie Hilaire Bernigaud.** 1839–1924. French chemist; inventor of rayon.

chare. *British.* Variant of **char** (odd job).

Cha·rente (shä-ränt′). A navigable river rising in west-central France and flowing 225 miles west into the Bay of Biscay.

Char·gaff (chär′gŏf), **Erwin.** Born 1905. Austrian-born American biochemist; worked on nucleic acid molecule.

charge (chärj) *v.* **charged, charging, charges.** *—tr.* **1.** To place a burden on; entrust with a duty, responsibility, task, or obligation. **2.** To place an order or injunction upon; command. **3.** To instruct, warn, or urge authoritatively. **4.** To blame, accuse, or impute something to. Often used with *with.* **5.** To set or ask (a given amount) as a price. **6.** To hold financially liable; demand payment from. **7.** To postpone payment on (a service or purchase) by recording as a debt. **8.** To attack violently: *The soldiers charged the fort.* **9.** To direct or put (a weapon) into position for use. **10.** To load (a gun or other firearm). **11.** To fill (any substance) with another substance. **12.** *Electricity.* **a.** To cause formation of a net electric charge on or in (a conductor, for example). **b.** To energize (a storage battery). **13. a.** To excite or intensify: *The argument was charged with emotion.* **b.** To cause to be saturated; impregnate: *The air was charged with perfume.* **14.** To fill or put in or on (a thing) that which it is adapted or intended to receive: *charge a furnace with coal.* **15.** *Heraldry.* To place a bearing on. *—intr.* **1.** To make an onset; to attack violently. **2.** To demand or ask payment. **3.** To make an entry to one's debit. **4.** To lie down or squat at command. Used of dogs. —See Synonyms at **command.** —**charge off.** To consider as a loss. *—n.* **1.** Care, custody, or supervision: *have charge of; be in the charge of.* **2.** An obligation or responsibility. **3.** A person or thing entrusted to one's care or management. **4.** An order, command, or injunction. **5.** An address, given by a judge to a jury at the end of a trial, of instruction about such matters as legal points and the weight of evidence. **6.** An accusation or indictment. **7.** *Abbr.* **chg.** Expense; cost; price. **8.** *Abbr.* **chg.** Any financial burden, as a tax or lien. **9.** *Abbr.* **chg.** A debt or an entry in an account recording a debt. **10. a.** An attack or onset. **b.** The command for this. **11.** A load or burden. **12.** The maximum quantity of anything that an apparatus or container can hold at one time. **13.** The quantity of explosive to be set off at one time. **14.** *Electricity.* **a.** The intrinsic property of matter responsible for all electric phenomena, in particular for the force of the electromagnetic interaction, occurring in two forms arbitrarily designated *negative* and *positive.* **b.** A measure of this property. **c.** By extension, the net measure of this property possessed by a body or contained in a bounded region of space. **15.** *Heraldry.* A bearing or figure. —See Synonyms at **price.** —**get a charge out of.** *Informal.* To derive pleasure from; enjoy. [Middle English *chargen,* to load, from Old French *chargier,* from Late Latin *carricāre,* from Latin *carrus,* a kind of vehicle. See **kers-²** in Appendix.*]

charge·a·ble (chär′jə-bəl) *adj.* **1.** That may be or is suitable to be charged, as to an account. **2.** Liable to be accused. **3.** Liable to become a public charge or responsibility.

charge account. A business arrangement of credit in which the customer receives purchases or services prior to payment.

charge-a-plate (chärj′ə-plāt′) *n.* A small piece of metal or plastic embossed with a person's name and address, presented by a customer at a store in order to buy on credit. [From former trademark *Chargaplate.*]

charge conjugation. *Symbol* **C** *Physics.* **1.** A mathematical operator that changes the sign of the charge and of the magnetic moment of every particle in the system to which it is applied. **2.** Loosely, the theoretical conversion of matter to antimatter or of antimatter to matter.

char·gé d'af·faires (shär-zhā′ də-fâr′) *pl.* **chargés d'affaires** (shär-zhā′, shär-zhāz′). **1.** A governmental official temporarily placed in charge of diplomatic affairs while the ambassador or minister is absent. Also in full "chargé d'affaires ad interim." **2.** A diplomatic representative of the lowest rank, accredited by his government to the minister of foreign affairs of another. [French, "(one) charged with affairs."]

charge density. The electric charge per unit area or per unit volume of a body or of a region of space.

charg·er¹ (chär′jər) *n.* **1.** One that charges. **2.** A horse trained for battle; cavalry horse. **3.** An instrument that charges or replenishes storage batteries.

charg·er² (chär′jər) *n. Archaic.* A large, shallow dish; platter. [Middle English *chargeour*†.]

Cha·ri. The French name for the **Shari.**

char·i·ly (châr′ə-lē) *adv.* In a chary manner; sparingly; carefully.

char·i·ness (châr′ē-nĭs) *n.* **1.** The quality of being chary; carefulness; frugality. **2.** *Obsolete.* Strict integrity.

Cha·ri-Nile (shä′rē-nīl′) *n.* A branch of the Nilo-Saharan language family. Also formerly called "Nilo-Hamitic."

char·i·ot (chăr′ē-ət) *n.* **1.** An ancient, horse-drawn, two-wheeled vehicle, used in war, races, and processions. **2.** A light, four-

wheeled carriage used for occasions of ceremony or for pleasure. —*v.* **charioted, -oting, -ots.** —*tr.* To convey or drive (someone) in a chariot. —*intr.* To ride in or drive a chariot. [Middle English, from Old French, from *char*, vehicle, from Latin *carrus*. See **kers-**[2] in Appendix.*]
char·i·o·teer (chăr′ē-ə-tîr′) *n.* **1.** A person who drives a chariot. **2.** *Capital* **C.** The constellation **Auriga** *(see)*.
cha·ris·ma (kə-rĭz′mə) *n., pl.* **-mata** (-mə-tə). Also **char·ism** (kăr′ĭz′əm). **1.** A rare quality or power attributed to those persons who have demonstrated an exceptional ability for leadership and for securing the devotion of large numbers of people. **2.** *Theology.* A divinely inspired gift or power, such as the ability to perform miracles. [Greek *kharisma*, favor, divine gift, from *kharizesthai*, to favor, from *kharis*, grace, favor. See **gher-**[6] in Appendix.*] —**char′is·mat′ic** (kăr′ĭz-măt′ĭk) *adj.*
char·i·ta·ble (chăr′ə-tə-bəl) *adj.* **1.** Generous in giving money or other help to the needy. **2.** Mild or tolerant in judging others; lenient. **3.** Of, for, or concerned with charity: *a charitable organization.* —**char′i·ta·ble·ness** *n.* —**char′i·ta·bly** *adv.*
char·i·ty (chăr′ə-tē) *n., pl.* **-ties.** **1.** The provision of help or relief to the poor; almsgiving. **2.** Something that is given to help the needy; alms. **3.** An institution, organization, or fund established to help the needy. **4.** An act or feeling of benevolence, good will, or affection. **5.** Indulgence or forbearance in judging others; leniency. **6.** *Theology.* **a.** The benevolence of God toward man. **b.** The love of man for his fellow men; brotherly love. —See Synonyms at **mercy.** [Middle English *charite*, Christian love, from Old French, from Latin *cāritās*, love, regard, from *cārus*, dear. See **kā-** in Appendix.*]
cha·riv·a·ri (shĭv′ə-rē′, shĭv′ə-rē′) *n., pl.* **-ris.** Also **chiv·a·ree, shiv·a·ree.** A noisy mock serenade to newly-weds. [French, from Late Latin *caribaria*, headache, from Greek *karēbaria*, "heavy head" : *karē*, *kara*, head (see **ker-**[1] in Appendix*) + *barus*, heavy (see **gwer-**[2] in Appendix*).]
char·kha (chûr′kə, chär′-) *n.* Also **char·ka.** In India, a spinning wheel, especially one used for cotton. [Hindi *carkha*, from Persian *charkha*, wheel. See **kwel-**[1] in Appendix.*]
char·la·tan (shär′lə-tən) *n.* A person who claims to possess knowledge or skill that he does not have; a quack. See Synonyms at **impostor.** [French, from Italian *ciarlatano*, variant of *cerretano*, inhabitant of *Cerreto*, village near Spoleto, Italy, famous for its quacks.] —**char′la·tan′ic** (-tăn′ĭk), **char′la·tan′i·cal** *adj.* —**char′la·tan·ism′, char′la·tan·ry** *n.*
Char·le·magne (shär′lə-măn′). Known as "Charles the Great," "Charles I." A.D. 742–814. King of the Franks (768–814); crowned emperor of the Romans (800).
Char·le·roi (shȧr-lə-rwä′). Also **Char·le·roy.** A city of south-central Belgium; the site of the first battle (1914) of World War I. Population, 26,000.
Charles[1] (chärlz). *Abbr.* **Chas.** A masculine given name. [French, from Medieval Latin *Carolus*, from Middle High German *karl*, man, from Old High German *karal*. See **karlaz** in Appendix.*]
Charles[2] (chärlz). Born 1948. Prince of Wales; eldest son of Elizabeth II.
Charles I[1]. See **Charlemagne.**
Charles I[2]. See **Charles II** (Holy Roman Emperor).
Charles I[3]. See **Charles V.**
Charles I[4] (chärlz). Title of Charles Stuart. 1600–1649. King of England (1625–49); beheaded.
Charles II[1] (chärlz). Called "the Bald." A.D. 823–877. Holy Roman Emperor (875–877); king of France as Charles I (840–877).
Charles II[2] (chärlz). 1630–1685. King of England following Restoration (1660–85); son of Charles I of England.
Charles V (chärlz). 1500–1558. Holy Roman Emperor (1519–56); king of Spain as Charles I (1516–56); expanded empire through Europe and America; abdicated.
Charles VII (chärlz). 1403–1461. King of France (1422–61); defeated English at Orléans (1429) with aid of Joan of Arc.
Charles IX (chärlz). 1550–1574. King of France (1560–74); son of Catherine de Médicis.
Charles X (chärlz). 1757–1836. King of France (1824–30); brother of Louis XVI and Louis XVIII; abdicated.
Charles, Cape (chärlz). A cape in Virginia at the northern entrance to Chesapeake Bay opposite Cape Henry.
Charles (shärl), **Jacques Alexandre César.** 1746–1823. French physicist; experimented with thermodynamics.
Charles Edward Stuart. See **Stuart,** Charles Edward.
Charles Mar·tel (chärlz mär-tĕl′). A.D. 689?–741. Frankish ruler of Austrasia; victor over Moslems (732); grandfather of Charlemagne.
Charles River (chärlz). A river about 60 miles long in eastern Massachusetts, flowing into Boston Harbor and separating the city of Boston from Cambridge.
Charles's law. The physical law that the volume of a fixed mass of gas held at a constant pressure varies directly with the absolute temperature. Also called "Gay-Lussac's law." [Formulated by Jacques CHARLES.]
Charles the Great. See **Charlemagne.**
Charles·ton[1] (chärl′stən). **1.** A seaport of southeastern South Carolina, situated on an inlet of the Atlantic Ocean. Population, 81,000. **2.** The capital and largest city of West Virginia, in the western part of the state. Population, 105,000.
Charles·ton[2] (chärl′stən) *n.* A fast dance in 4/4 time, popular during the 1920's. [After CHARLESTON, South Carolina.]
Charles·town (chärlz′toun′). A former city of eastern Massachusetts, now the oldest part of Boston.
char·ley horse (chär′lē). *Informal.* A cramp or stiffness of various muscles in the body, especially in the arm or leg, caused by injury or excessive exertion. [Probably from the use of *Charley* (pet form of CHARLES) as a name for lame horses.]
Char·lie (chär′lē) *n. Slang.* A member of the Vietcong. [Originally *Victor Charlie*, code words for the letters *VC*.]
char·lock (chär′lək, -lŏk′) *n.* A weedy plant, *Brassica kaber*, native to Eurasia, having hairy stems, foliage, and yellow flowers. [Middle English *cherlok*, *carlok*, Old English *cerlic*†.]
char·lotte (shär′lət) *n.* **1.** A cold dessert, **charlotte russe** *(see)*. **2.** A dessert, served either hot or cold, consisting of a mold of sponge cake or bread with a filling of fruits, whipped cream, custard, or the like. [French, from the given name.]
Char·lotte[1] (shär′lət). A feminine given name. [French, from Italian *Carlotta*, feminine diminutive of *Carlo*, Charles, from Latin *Carolus*, CHARLES.]
Char·lotte[2] (shär′lət). The largest city of North Carolina, situated in the southwestern part of the state. Population, 202,000.
Char·lotte A·ma·lie (shär′lət ə-mäl′yə). Formerly **St. Thom·as** (tŏm′əs). The capital of the Virgin Islands of the United States, a seaport on the southern shore of St. Thomas Island. Population, 13,000.
char·lotte russe (shär′lət ro͞os′). A cold dessert of Bavarian cream set in a mold lined with ladyfingers. Also called "charlotte." [French, "Russian charlotte."]
Char·lottes·ville (shär′ləts-vĭl′). A city of central Virginia, 70 miles northwest of Richmond; site of the homes of Thomas Jefferson and James Monroe. Population, 29,000.
Char·lotte·town (shär′lət-toun′). The capital of Prince Edward Island Province, Canada, a seaport on the southern coast. Population, 19,000.
charm[1] (chärm) *n.* **1.** The power or quality of pleasing, attracting, or fascinating. **2.** A particular quality or feature that fascinates or attracts: *"The charm of friendship is liberty."* (Gibbon). **3.** A trinket or small ornament worn on a bracelet or other jewelry. **4.** Anything that is worn for its supposed magical effect, as in warding off evil; an amulet. **5.** Any action or formula thought to have magical power. **6.** The chanting of a magic word or verse; an incantation. —*v.* **charmed, charming, charms.** —*tr.* **1.** To attract or delight greatly or irresistibly; fascinate. **2.** To act upon with or as if with magic; bewitch. —*intr.* **1.** To be alluring or pleasing. **2.** To act as an amulet or charm. **3.** To employ spells. [Middle English *charme*, chant, magic spell, from Old French, from Latin *carmen*, song, incantation. See **kan-** in Appendix.*] —**charm′ing·ly** *adv.*

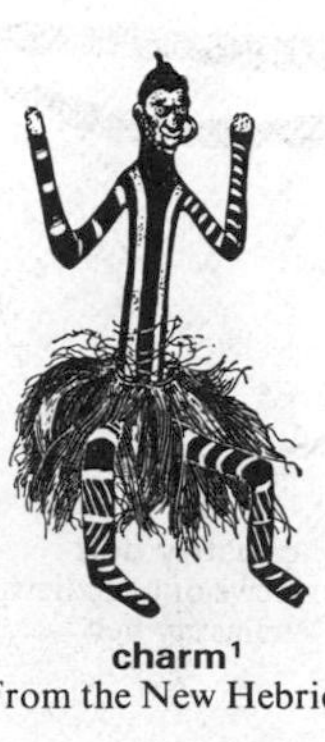

charm[1]
From the New Hebrides

charm[2] (chärm) *n.* **1.** *Archaic.* A confused sound of voices or bird calls. **2.** A company of finches. [Middle English *cherme* (influenced by *charme*, incantation, CHARM), Old English *cirm*, *cierm*, clamor, cry. See **gar-** in Appendix.*]
charm·er (chär′mər) *n.* **1.** One who charms or has the power to charm, especially a girl or woman. **2.** A sorcerer.
char·nel (chär′nəl) *n.* A charnel house. —*adj.* Resembling, suggesting, or suitable for receiving the dead. [Middle English, from Old French, from Medieval Latin *carnāle*, from Late Latin *carnālis*, carnal, from Latin *carō* (stem *carn-*), flesh. See **sker-**[1] in Appendix.*]
charnel house. A building, room, or vault in which the bones or bodies of the dead are placed.
Char·on (kâr′ən). *Greek Mythology.* The ferryman who conveyed the dead to Hades over the river Styx.

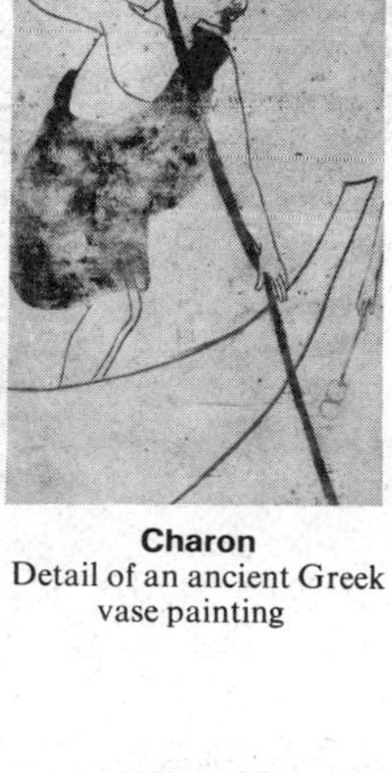

Charon
Detail of an ancient Greek vase painting

char·qui (chär′kē) *n.* Cured or jerked meat, **jerky** *(see)*. [Spanish, from Quechua *ch'arki*.]
charr. Variant of **char** (fish).
chart (chärt) *n.* **1.** A map showing coastlines, water depths, or other information of use to navigators. **2.** An outline map on which special information, as weather data, can be plotted. **3.** A sheet presenting information in the form of graphs or tables. **4.** A **graph** *(see)*. —*tr.v.* **charted, charting, charts.** **1.** To make a chart of. **2.** To plan in detail. [Old French *charte*, from Latin *charta*, papyrus leaf, paper. See **card.**]
char·ta·ceous (kär-tā′shəs) *adj.* Like paper; papery. [Late Latin *chartāceus*, from Latin *charta*, papyrus leaf. See **card.**]
char·ter (chär′tər) *n. Abbr.* **char.** **1.** A document issued by a sovereign, legislature, or other authority, creating a public or private corporation, as a city, college, or bank, and defining its privileges and purposes. **2.** A written grant from the sovereign power of a country conferring certain rights and privileges upon a person, a corporation, or the people. **3.** *Often capital* **C.** A document outlining the principles, functions, and organization of a corporate body; statute; constitution. **4.** An authorization from a central organization to establish a local branch or chapter. **5.** A special privilege or immunity. **6.** A **charter party** *(see)*. **7.** The hiring or leasing of an aircraft, vessel, or other vehicle. **8.** Any written instrument given as evidence of agreement, transfer, or contract; deed. —*tr.v.* **chartered, -tering, -ters.** **1.** To grant a charter to; establish by charter. **2.** To hire or lease by charter. **3.** To hire (a vehicle). [Middle English *chartre*, from Old French, from Latin *chartula*, diminutive of *charta*, papyrus leaf. See **card.**] —**char′ter·er** *n.*
char·ter·age (chär′tər-ĭj) *n.* **1.** The act or business of chartering, especially ships. **2.** The fee charged by a ship broker.
charter colony. *U.S. History.* A colony, such as Massachusetts, Connecticut, or Rhode Island, created by a royal charter exempting it from direct interference by the Crown.
chartered accountant. *Abbr.* **c.a., C.A.** *British.* A member of one of the institutes of accountants granted a royal charter.
char·ter·house (chär′tər-hous′) *n.* A Carthusian monastery. [By folk etymology from Norman French *chartrouse*, the *Chartreuse* monastery. See **chartreuse.**]
Char·ter·house (chär′tər-hous′). **1.** A London hospital found-

ed in 1611 on the site of a Carthusian monastery. **2.** The public school into which this hospital was later converted. In 1872 this school was moved to Surrey.

charter member. An original member or founder of an organization.

Charter of the United Nations. The charter adopted at an international conference in San Francisco in 1945 establishing the United Nations as a permanent organization.

charter party. A contract for the commercial leasing of a vessel or space on a vessel. Also called "charter."

Chart·ism (chär′tĭz′əm) *n.* The principles and practices of a party of social and political reformers, chiefly workingmen, active in England from 1838 to 1848. Their views were stated in the People's Charter, published in 1838. —**Chart′ist** *n.* & *adj.*

chart·ist (chär′tĭst) *n.* A stock-market specialist who interprets market action, predicts trends, or forecasts price movements of individual stocks, using charts and graphic records.

Chartres (shärt, shär′trə; *French* shȧr′tr′). A city in north-central France, 55 miles southwest of Paris, noted for its Gothic cathedral. Population, 29,000.

char·treuse (shär-trōōz′, -trōōs′; *French* shȧr-trœz′) *n.* **1.** A yellow, pale-green, or white liqueur made by the Carthusian monks. **2.** *Capital* **C.** A trademark for this liqueur. **3.** Strong to brilliant greenish yellow to moderate or strong yellow green. See **color.** [French, first made at *la Grande Chartreuse,* Carthusian monastery, near Grenoble.] —**char·treuse′** *adj.*

char·tu·lar·y. Variant of **cartulary.**

char·wom·an (chär′wo͝om′ən) *n., pl.* **-women** (-wĭm′ĭn). *British.* A woman hired to do cleaning or similar work, usually in a large building. [CHAR (chore) + WOMAN.]

char·y (châr′ē) *adj.* **-ier, -iest. 1.** Careful; wary. **2.** Fastidious; finicky. **3.** Shy: *chary of meeting people.* **4.** Sparing: *chary of compliments.* [Middle English *charig, charry,* cherished, dear, Old English *cearig,* sorrowful. See **gar-** in Appendix.*]

Cha·ryb·dis (kə-rĭb′dĭs). *Greek Mythology.* A whirlpool off the Sicilian coast, opposite the cave of **Scylla** *(see).*

Chas. Charles.

chase[1] (chās) *v.* **chased, chasing, chases.** —*tr.* **1.** To pursue in order to catch or overtake. **2.** To follow (game) in order to capture or kill; hunt. **3.** To follow earnestly or regularly; run after. **4.** To put to flight; drive. Often used with *away, out,* or *off.* —*intr.* **1.** To go or follow in pursuit. **2.** *Informal.* To go hurriedly; rush. —*n.* **1.** The act of chasing; pursuit. **2.** The sport of hunting. Preceded by *the.* **3.** That which is hunted or pursued; a quarry. **4.** *British.* **a.** A privately owned, unenclosed game preserve. **b.** The right to hunt or keep game on the land of others. —**give chase.** To pursue; chase. [Middle English *chacen, chasen,* from Old French *chasser, chacier,* from Vulgar Latin *captiāre* (unattested), from Latin *captāre,* to seize, frequentative of *capere,* to take. See **kap-** in Appendix.*]

chase[2] (chās) *n. Printing.* A rectangular steel or iron frame into which pages or columns of type are locked for printing or plate making. [Probably from French *châsse,* a case, frame, from Latin *capsa,* box, case. See **kap-** in Appendix.*]

chase[3] (chās) *n.* **1. a.** A groove cut in any object; slot: *the chase for the quarrel on a crossbow.* **b.** A trench or channel for drainpipes or wiring. **c.** A longitudinal groove for a tenon or tongue. **2.** The part of a gun in front of the trunnions. —*tr.v.* **chased, chasing, chases. 1.** To decorate (metal) by engraving or embossing. **2. a.** To groove; indent. **b.** To cut (the thread of a screw). [Old French *chas,* "enclosure," from Latin *capsus,* from *capsa,* box. See **kap-** in Appendix.*]

Chase (chās), **Salmon P(ortland).** 1808–1873. American political leader and jurist; Secretary of the Treasury (1861–64); Chief Justice of the United States (1864–73).

Chase (chās), **Samuel.** 1741–1811. American Revolutionary leader and jurist; Associate Justice of the U.S. Supreme Court (1796–1811); impeached but acquitted.

Chase (chās), **Stuart.** Born 1888. American economist and writer.

chas·er[1] (chā′sər) *n.* **1.** One that chases or pursues. **2.** A gun on the bow or stern of a ship, used during pursuit or flight. Also called "chase gun." **3.** *Informal.* A drink of water, beer, or the like taken after hard liquor.

chas·er[2] (chā′sər) *n.* **1.** One who decorates metal by engraving or embossing; a worker who chases metal. **2.** A steel tool for cutting or finishing screw threads.

chasm (kăz′əm) *n.* **1.** A deep cleft or crack in the earth's surface; an abyss or narrow gorge. **2.** A sudden interruption of continuity; a gap; hiatus. **3.** Any marked difference of opinion, interests, loyalty, or the like. [Latin *chasma,* from Greek *khasma.* See **ghei-** in Appendix.*] —**chas′mal** (kăz′məl) *adj.*

chas·sé (shă-sā′) *n.* A dance movement consisting of one or more quick, gliding steps with the same foot always leading. —*intr.v.* **chasséd, -séing, -sés.** To make or perform a chassé. [French, from the past participle of *chasser,* to chase, from Old French *chacier,* to CHASE.]

chasse·pot (shăs′pō) *n.* A type of breech-loading rifle introduced into the French army in 1866. [French, invented by Antoine *Chassepot* (1833–1905), French gunsmith.]

chas·seur (shă-sûr′) *n.* **1.** A soldier, especially one of certain light cavalry or infantry troops of the French army, trained for rapid maneuvers. **2.** A huntsman. **3.** A uniformed footman. [French, from Old French *chaceour,* from *chacier,* to CHASE.]

Chas·si·dim (KHä-sē′dĭm) *pl.n. Singular* **Chas·sid** (KHä′sĭd). Also **Has·si·dim, Ha·si·dim.** A sect of Jewish mystics founded in Poland (about 1750) in opposition to the formalistic Judaism of the period and ritual laxity. [Hebrew *ḥasīdhīm,* "pious ones," from *ḥāsīdh,* pious.] —**Chas·si′dic** *adj.* —**Chas·si′dism′** *n.*

chas·sis (shăs′ē, chăs′ē) *n., pl.* **chassis** (shăs′ēz, chăs′ēz). **1.** The rectangular steel frame, supported on springs and attached to the axles, that holds the body and motor of an automotive vehicle. **2.** The landing gear of an aircraft, including the wheels, floats, and other structures, that support the aircraft on land or water. **3.** The frame on which a casement gun carriage moves forward and backward. **4.** The framework to which the functioning parts of a radio, television, phonograph, or other electronic equipment are attached. [French *châssis,* from Old French *chassis,* from Vulgar Latin *capsīcium* (unattested), from Latin *capsa,* box. See **kap-** in Appendix.*]

chaste (chāst) *adj.* **chaster, chastest. 1.** Morally pure; decent; modest. **2. a.** Abstaining from unlawful sexual intercourse; virtuous. **b.** Celibate. **3.** Pure or simple in literary or artistic style; not ornate or extreme. [Middle English, from Old French, from Latin *castus,* morally pure. See **kes-**[2] in Appendix.*] —**chaste′ly** *adv.* —**chaste′ness** *n.*

chas·ten (chā′sən) *tr.v.* **-tened, -tening, -tens. 1.** To punish, either physically or morally; chastise. **2.** To restrain; moderate. **3.** To refine; purify: *chasten one's style.* [Variant of obsolete *chaste,* from Middle English *chasten, chastien,* from Old French *chastier,* from Latin *castigāre,* to CASTIGATE.] —**chas′ten·er** *n.*

chaste tree (chāst). A shrub, *Vitex agnus-castus,* of southern Europe, often cultivated for its spikes of lilac-blue flowers. Also called "hemp tree." [Translation of New Latin *agnus castus,* by folk etymology (influenced by Latin *agnus,* lamb) from Greek *agnos*† (confused with *hagnos,* holy, chaste).]

chas·tise (chăs-tīz′) *tr.v.* **-tised, -tising, -tises. 1.** To punish, usually by beating. **2.** *Rare.* To purify. **3.** To criticize severely. —See Synonyms at **punish.** [Middle English *chastisen,* variant of *chastien,* CHASTEN.] —**chas·tis′a·ble** *adj.* —**chas·tise′ment** (chăs-tīz′mənt, chăs′tĭz-mənt) *n.* —**chas·tis′er** *n.*

chas·ti·ty (chăs′tə-tē) *n.* **1.** The state or quality of being chaste or pure. **2.** Celibacy; virginity. [Middle English *chastete,* from Old French, from Latin *castitās,* from *castus,* CHASTE.]

chastity belt. Any of various devices supposed to have been worn by medieval women to prevent sexual intercourse.

chas·u·ble (chăz′yə-bəl, chăs′-) *n.* A long, sleeveless vestment worn over the alb by the priest at Mass. [French, from Old French, from Late Latin *casubla,* hooded garment, variant of *casula,* cloak, probably from Latin, diminutive of *casa,* house. See **casino.**]

chat (chăt) *intr.v.* **chatted, chatting, chats.** To converse in an easy, informal, or familiar manner. —*n.* **1.** An informal or familiar conversation. **2.** Any of several birds known for their chattering call, such as: **a.** Any of several Old World birds of the genus *Saxicola.* **b.** A North American bird, *Icteria virens,* having a yellow breast and a greenish back. This species is also called "yellow-breasted chat." [Middle English *chatten,* short for *chatteren,* to CHATTER.]

cha·teau (shă-tō′) *n., pl.* **chateaux** (shă-tōz′; *French* shȧ-tō′). Also *French* **châ·teau** (shȧ-tō′). **1.** A French castle or manor house. **2.** A country house, especially one resembling a French castle. [French *château,* from Old French *chastel,* from Latin *castellum,* CASTLE.]

Châ·teau·bri·and (shȧ-tō-brē-äN′) *n.* Also **châ·teau·bri·and. 1.** A double-thick tender center cut of beef tenderloin. **2.** Such a cut of steak in which a pocket is cut and filled with various seasonings before grilling. [Probably invented by the chef of François René, Vicomte de CHÂTEAUBRIAND.]

Châ·teau·bri·and (shȧ-tō-brē-äN′), Vicomte **François René de.** 1768–1848. French author, diplomat, and political leader.

Châ·teau-Thier·ry (shȧ-tō′tyĕ-rē′). A town in northern France on the Marne about 55 miles east of Paris; the site of heavy fighting (1918) in World War I. Population, 9,000.

chat·e·lain (shăt′ə-lān′) *n.* The keeper of a castle; a castellan. [Middle English *chateleyn,* from Old French *chastelain,* from Latin *castellānus,* from *castellum,* CASTLE.]

chat·e·laine (shăt′ə-lān′) *n.* **1.** The lady or mistress of a castle, chateau, or large, fashionable household. **2.** A clasp or chain worn at the waist for holding keys, a purse, or a watch.

Chat·ham, First Earl of. See **Pitt.**

Chat·ham Island (chăt′əm). **1.** The largest (347 square miles) of the Chatham Islands. **2.** See **San Cristóbal.**

Chat·ham Islands (chăt′əm). A group of islands belonging to New Zealand and located in the southwestern Pacific Ocean about 500 miles east of South Island.

cha·toy·ant (shə-toi′ənt; *French* shȧ-twȧ-yäN′) *adj.* Having a changeable luster. —*n.* A chatoyant stone or gemstone, such as the cat's-eye. [French, present participle of *chatoyer,* gleam like a cat's eyes, from *chat,* cat, from Late Latin *cattus,* CAT.]

Chat·ta·hoo·chee (chăt′ə-hōō′chē). A river rising in northeastern Georgia and flowing 436 miles southwest and then south to join the Flint River at the Florida border.

Chat·ta·noo·ga (chăt′ə-nōō′gə). An industrial city and port of southeastern Tennessee, on the Tennessee River; the site of the battles of Chickamauga, Missionary Ridge, and Lookout Mountain during the Civil War. Population, 130,000.

chat·tel (chăt′l) *n.* **1.** An article of personal, movable property. **2.** A slave. [Middle English *chatel,* property, goods, from Old French, from Medieval Latin *capitāle,* from Latin, chief, head, from *capitālis,* CAPITAL.]

chattel mortgage. A mortgage on personal property as security for an obligation or debt.

chat·ter (chăt′ər) *v.* **-tered, -tering, -ters.** —*intr.* **1.** To utter a rapid series of short, inarticulate, speechlike sounds. Used of a bird or animal. **2.** To talk rapidly, incessantly, and on a trivial subject; jabber. **3.** To click together quickly, as the teeth from cold. **4.** To vibrate or rattle while in operation, as a power tool.

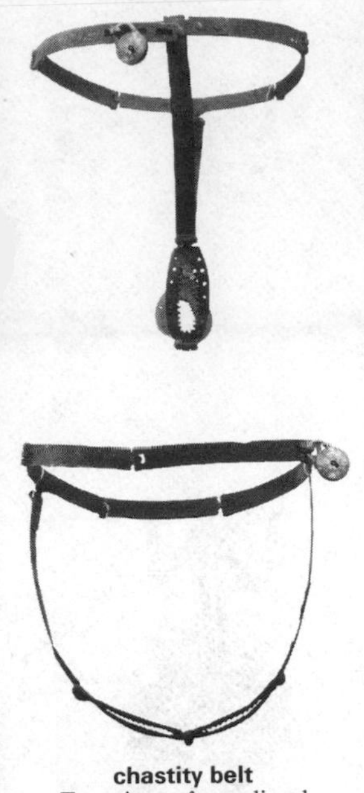

chastity belt
Two views of a medieval chastity belt

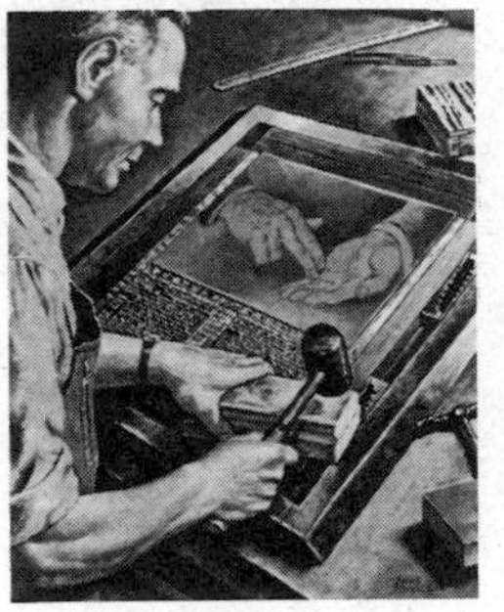

chase[2]
Compositor working with a chase

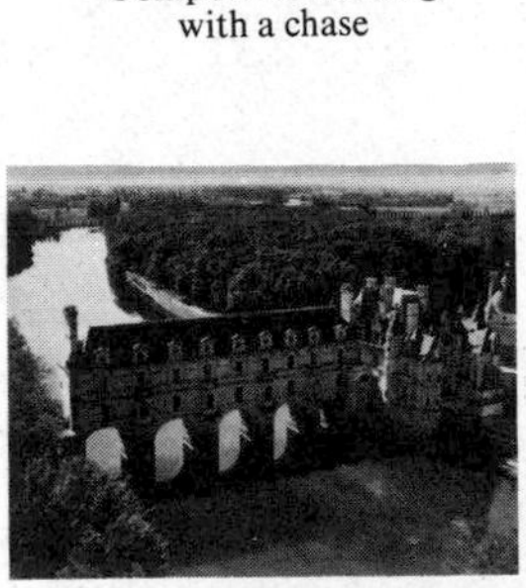

chateau
Château de Chenonceaux, in the Loire Valley of central France

—*tr.* To utter in a rapid and aimless way. —See Synonyms at **speak.** —*n.* **1.** Idle or trivial talk. **2.** The jabbering of an animal or bird. **3.** A rattling or clicking, as of the teeth. **4.** The rattling or vibration, as of a power tool in operation. [Middle English *chat(t)eren* (imitative).] —**chat'ter·er** *n.*

chat·ter·box (chăt'ər-bŏks') *n.* An extremely talkative person.

Chat·ter·ji (chä'tər-jē), **Bankim Chandra.** 1838–1894. Indian author of pioneer Bengali novels.

chatter mark. Also **chat·ter·mark** (chăt'ər-märk'). **1.** A riblike marking on wood or metal, caused by vibration of a cutting tool. **2.** *Geology.* One of a series of short scars on a glaciated rock surface.

Chat·ter·ton (chăt'ər-tən), **Thomas.** 1752–1770. English poet; author of spurious medieval writings; committed suicide.

chat·ty (chăt'ē) *adj.* **-tier, -tiest. 1.** Given to informal conversation. **2.** Informal; familiar. —**chat'ti·ly** *adv.* —**chat'ti·ness** *n.*

Chau·cer (chô'sər), **Geoffrey.** 1340?–1400. English poet; author of *The Canterbury Tales.*

Chau·ce·ri·an (chô-sĭr'ē-ən) *adj.* Of, pertaining to, or characteristic of Chaucer or his writings. —*n.* A scholar specializing in the writings of Chaucer.

chaud·froid (shō-frwä') *n.* **1.** A jellied white or brown sauce used as an aspic for cold meats or fish. **2.** Molded cold meat or fish dishes garnished with a chaudfroid sauce. [French, "hot-cold" : *chaud,* hot, from Old French, from Latin *calidus* (see **kel-¹** in Appendix*) + *froid,* cold, from Old French, from Vulgar Latin *frigidus* (unattested), from Latin *frīgidus,* FRIGID.]

chauf·feur (shō'fər, shō-fûr') *n.* One employed to drive a private automobile. —*v.* **chauffeured, -feuring, -feurs.** —*tr.* To serve as a driver for (someone). —*intr.* To serve as a chauffeur. [French, stoker, from *chauffer,* to warm, from Old French *chaufer.* See **chafe.**]

chaul·moo·gra (chôl-mōō'grə) *n.* Any of several trees of tropical Asia, especially *Taraktogenos kurzii* and those of the genus *Hydnocarpus,* having seeds that yield an oil used in treating leprosy. [Bengali *cāulmugrā* : *cāul,* rice + *mugrā,* hemp.]

chaunt. *Archaic.* Variant of **chant.**

chausses (shōs) *pl.n.* Medieval armor of mail for the legs and feet. [Middle English *chauces,* from Old French, from Medieval Latin *calcia,* clothing for the leg, from Latin *calceus,* shoe. See **calceate.**]

Chau·tau·qua¹ (shə-tô'kwə). A town in southwestern New York, near the northern end of Chautauqua Lake; the site of a summer adult education program started in 1874.

Chau·tau·qua² (shə-tô'kwə) *n.* The annual summer educational and recreational assembly formerly held in the town of Chautauqua. Also called "Chautauqua Assembly."

chau·vin·ism (shō'vən-ĭz'əm) *n.* Militant and boastful devotion to and glorification of one's country; fanatical patriotism. [French, *chauvinisme,* after Nicholas *Chauvin,* legendary French soldier extremely devoted to Napoleon.] —**chau'vin·ist** *n.* —**chau'vin·is'tic** *adj.* —**chau'vin·is'ti·cal·ly** *adv.*

Chá·vez (chä'väs), **Carlos.** Born 1899. Mexican composer, conductor, and educator.

chaw (chô) *v.* **chawed, chawing, chaws.** *Regional.* —*intr.* To chew. —*tr.* To chew (something). —*n. Regional.* A chew.

cha·yo·te (chä-yō'tā) *n.* **1.** A tropical American vine, *Sechium edule,* bearing squashlike fruit. **2.** The fruit itself, cooked and eaten as a vegetable. [Spanish, from Nahuatl *chayotli.*]

cha·zan, chaz·zen (KHä'zən) *n.* Also **haz·zan.** A cantor in a synagogue. [Late Hebrew *ḥazzān,* officer, cantor.]

Ch.E. chemical engineer.

cheap (chēp) *adj.* **cheaper, cheapest. 1.** Relatively low in cost; inexpensive. **2.** Charging low prices: *a cheap restaurant.* **3.** Worth more than the price. **4.** Costing little effort: *a cheap victory.* **5.** Of small value. **6.** Of poor quality. **7.** Not worthy of respect; vulgar. **8.** Stingy; miserly. **9.** *Economics.* **a.** Obtainable at a low rate of interest. **b.** Devalued, as in buying power. —*adv.* Inexpensively. [From Middle English *chep,* sale, bargain, purchase, Old English *cēap,* from West Germanic *kaupaz* (unattested), trader, from Latin *caupō.* See **caupo** in Appendix.*] —**cheap'ly** *adv.* —**cheap'ness** *n.*

cheap·en (chē'pən) *v.* **-ened, -ening, -ens.** —*tr.* **1.** To make cheap or cheaper. **2.** To deprecate; disparage; belittle. —*intr.* To become cheap or cheaper. —**cheap'en·er** *n.*

cheap·skate (chēp'skāt') *n.* Also **cheap skate.** *Slang.* A stingy person; miser. [CHEAP + SKATE (chap).]

cheat (chēt) *v.* **cheated, cheating, cheats.** —*tr.* **1.** To deceive by trickery; swindle. **2.** To mislead; fool. **3.** To elude; escape: *cheat death.* —*intr.* **1.** To act dishonestly; practice fraud. **2.** *Informal.* To be unfaithful to one's spouse. Sometimes used with *on: cheating on his wife.* —*n.* **1.** A fraud or swindle. **2.** A swindler. **3.** *Law.* The fraudulent acquisition of another's property. **4.** A grass, *Bromus secalinus,* having rough blades and wheatlike ears. In this sense, also called "chess." [Middle English *cheten,* to revert, short for *acheten,* variant of *escheten,* from *eschete,* ESCHEAT.] —**cheat'er** *n.* —**cheat'ing·ly** *adv.*

cheat·ers (chē'tərz) *pl.n. Slang.* Eyeglasses; spectacles.

che·bec (chĭ-bĕk') *n.* A small bird, the **least flycatcher** *(see).* [Imitative.]

Che·bok·sa·ry (chĕ'bŏk-sä'rē). The capital of the Chuvash A.S.S.R., on the Volga River. Population, 163,000.

Che·chen-In·gush Autonomous Soviet Socialist Republic (chĭ-chĕn'ĭn-gōōsh'). Also **Che·che·no-In·gush A.S.S.R.** (chĭ-chĕn'ô-ĭn-gōōsh'). An administrative division, 7,350 square miles in area, of the southwestern Russian S.F.S.R. Population, 987,000. Capital, Groznyy.

check (chĕk) *n.* Also *chiefly British* **cheque** (for sense 10). **1.** An abrupt halt or stop; a delay; rebuff. **2.** A restraint or control. **3.** One that restrains or controls. **4.** Supervised control, as of accuracy or efficiency. **5.** A standard of comparison to verify accuracy; test. **6.** A mark to show verification or approval. **7.** A ticket or slip of identification: *a baggage check.* **8.** A bill at a restaurant or bar. **9.** A chip or counter used in gambling games. **10.** *Abbr.* **ch., ck.** A written order to a bank to pay the amount specified from funds on deposit; draft. **11. a.** A pattern of small squares, as on a chessboard. **b.** One of the squares of such a pattern. **c.** A fabric patterned with such squares. **12.** A small crack or chink. **13.** *Chess.* **a.** A move that directly attacks an opponent's king but does not constitute a checkmate. **b.** The position or tactical condition of a king so attacked. **14.** *Ice Hockey.* The act of impeding an opponent in control of the puck, either by blocking his progress with the body or by jabbing at the puck with the stick. —**in check.** Under restraint; in control. —*interj.* **1.** *Chess.* A declaration made to an opponent that his king is in check. **2.** *Informal.* Used to express affirmation. —*v.* **checked, checking, checks.** —*tr.* **1.** To arrest the motion of abruptly; halt. **2.** To hold in restraint; curb. **3.** To slow the growth of; retard. **4.** To rebuke; rebuff. **5.** To test or examine, as for accuracy or efficiency; verify; investigate. **6.** To put a check mark on or next to. Often used with *off.* **7.** To deposit for temporary safekeeping: *check one's hat.* **8.** To make cracks or chinks in. **9.** *Chess.* To move so as to put (an opponent's king) under direct attack. **10.** *Ice Hockey.* To impede an opponent in control of the puck, either by using the body to block the opponent, *body check,* or by jabbing at the puck with the hockey stick, *poke check.* —*intr.* **1.** To come to an abrupt halt; stop; pause. **2.** To have item-for-item correspondence; agree. **3.** To make an examination or investigation to determine accuracy or verification. Usually used with *on* or *upon.* **4.** To write a check on a bank account. **5.** To crack in a pattern of checks, as paint. **6.** To pause to relocate a scent. Used of hunting dogs. **7.** *Chess.* To place an opponent's king in check. **8.** In falconry, to abandon the proper game and follow baser prey. Used with *at.* —See Synonyms at **restrain, delay.** —**check in.** To register, as at a hotel. —*adj.* **1.** Marked in a pattern of checks or squares. **2.** Serving to verify or control. [Middle English *chek,* attack, quarrel, check at chess, from Old French *eschec, eschac,* from Arabic *shāh,* king, check at chess, from Persian, king. See **ksei-²** in Appendix.*] —**check'a·ble** *adj.*

check·book (chĕk'bŏŏk') *n.* A book containing blank checks, issued by a bank.

checked (chĕkt) *adj.* **1.** Having a pattern of checks or squares. **2.** Held in check; restrained. **3.** *Phonetics.* Situated in a stopped or closed syllable. Used of a vowel.

check·er (chĕk'ər) *n.* Also *chiefly British* **cheq·uer. 1.** One of the disks used in the game of checkers. **2. a.** A pattern of checks or squares. **b.** One of the squares in such a pattern. **3.** One who checks, examines, or supervises. **4.** One who receives items for temporary storage or safekeeping: *a baggage checker.* **5.** A cashier. **6.** The fruit of the **service tree** *(see).* —*tr.v.* **checkered, -ering, -ers. 1.** To mark with a checked or squared pattern. **2.** To diversify in color, shading, or character; change; alter. [Middle English, from *cheker,* chessboard, from Old French *eschequier,* from *eschec,* CHECK.]

check·er·ber·ry (chĕk'ər-bĕr'ē) *n., pl.* **-ries. 1.** A plant, the **wintergreen** *(see).* **2.** The red, edible, spicy berry of this plant. [CHECKER (tree) + BERRY.]

check·er·bloom (chĕk'ər-blōōm') *n.* A plant, *Sidalcea malvaeflora,* of California, having long clusters of rose-pink flowers. [CHECKER (tree) + BLOOM.]

check·er·board (chĕk'ər-bôrd', -bōrd') *n.* A game board divided into 64 squares of two alternating colors on which chess and checkers are played.

check·ered (chĕk'ərd) *adj.* **1.** Divided into squares. **2.** Marked by light and dark patches; diversified in color. **3.** Marked by great changes or fluctuating or diverse shifts in fortune: *a checkered career.*

check·ers (chĕk'ərz) *n.* Plural in form, used with a singular verb. A game played on a checkerboard by two persons, each with 12 pieces. Also *chiefly British* "draughts."

checking account. A bank account in which checks may be written against amounts on deposit.

check list. Any list in which items can be compared, scheduled, verified, or identified.

check·mate (chĕk'māt') *tr.v.* **-mated, -mating, -mates. 1.** *Chess.* To attack (an opponent's king) in such manner that no escape or defense is possible, thus ending the game. **2.** To defeat completely. —*n.* **1.** *Abbr.* **chm.** *Chess.* **a.** A move that constitutes an inescapable and indefensible attack on an opponent's king. **b.** The position or strategic condition of a king so attacked. **2.** Utter defeat. —*interj. Chess.* A call declaring the checkmate of an opponent's king. [Middle English *chekmate,* from Old French *eschec mat,* from Arabic *shāh māt,* the king is perplexed or dead : *shāh,* king (see **check**) + *māt,* dead, perplexed, probably from Proto-Semitic *mawit* (unattested).]

check·off (chĕk'ôf', -ŏf') *n.* The collecting of dues from members of a union by authorized deduction from their wages.

check out. 1. To pay one's bill and depart, as from a hotel or motel. **2.** To investigate; confirm. **3.** To test for performance. **4.** To correspond, upon investigation, to what is expected. **5.** To process through a supermarket check-out.

check-out (chĕk'out') *n.* **1.** The time at which a guest must vacate a hotel or motel room or be charged for another day's occupancy. **2.** The enumeration of and charging for goods being purchased, as in a supermarket. **3.** A test, as of a machine, for proper functioning. **4.** An investigation or inspection. —**check'-out'** *adj.*

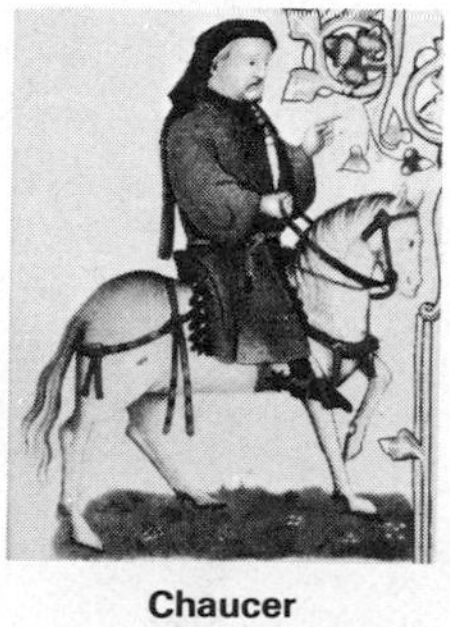

Chaucer
The poet depicted in an illustration for a 15th-century manuscript of *The Canterbury Tales*

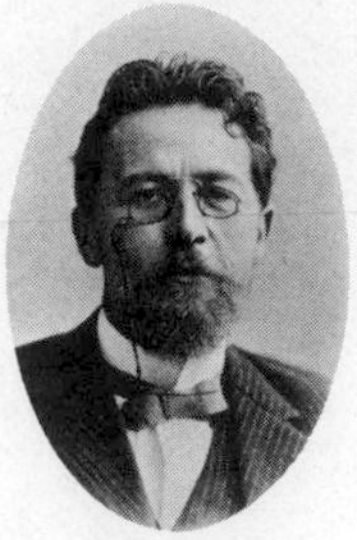
Chekhov

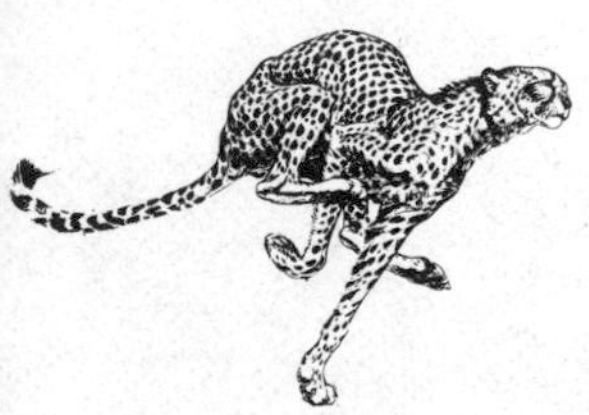
cheetah

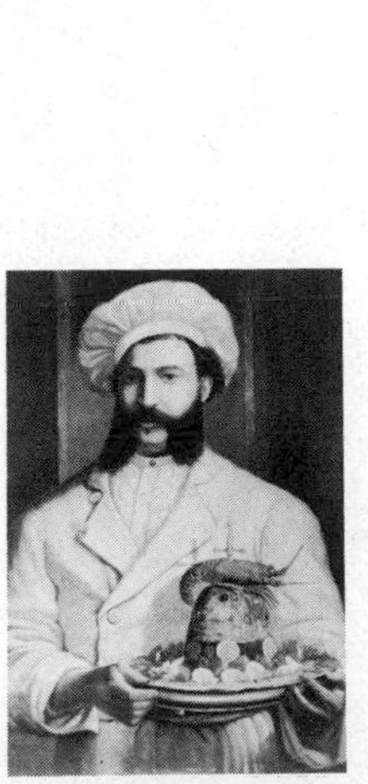
chef
Portrait of Jules Harder, chef at the Palace Hotel, San Francisco, painted in 1874 by Joseph Harrington

check·point (chĕk′point′) *n.* A place where surface traffic is stopped for inspection.

check·rein (chĕk′rān′) *n.* **1.** A short rein connected from a horse's bit to the saddle, to keep a horse from lowering its head. **2.** A rein joining the bit of one of a span of horses to the driving rein of the other horse. Also called "bearing rein."

check·room (chĕk′ro͞om′, -ro͝om′) *n.* A place where hats, coats, packages, or other items may be stored temporarily.

check·row (chĕk′rō′) *n. Agriculture.* A row, as of corn, in which the distance between plants is the same as the distance between adjacent rows to permit cross cultivation. —*tr.v.* **checkrowed, -rowing, -rows.** To plant in checkrows.

checks and balances. The system of maintaining a balance of power between various branches of a government.

check·up (chĕk′ŭp′) *n.* **1.** A thorough examination, as for verification or accuracy. **2.** A physical examination.

Ched·dar (chĕd′ər) *n.* Also **ched·dar.** Any of several types of smooth, hard cheese varying in flavor from mild to extra sharp. Also called "Cheddar cheese." [First made in *Cheddar*, village in Somerset, England.]

cheek (chēk) *n.* **1.** The fleshy part of either side of the face below the eye and between the nose and ear. **2.** Something resembling this in shape or position, such as either of two sides of something. **3.** *Plural.* The buttocks. **4.** Sauciness; impudence. —See Synonyms at **temerity.** —**cheek by jowl.** Side by side; intimate. —*tr.v.* **cheeked, cheeking, cheeks.** *Informal.* To speak impudently to. [Middle English *che(e)ke*, Old English *cēce, cēace*, from Germanic *kēkōn-* (unattested).]

cheek·bone (chēk′bōn′) *n.* A bone in the upper cheek, the **zygomatic bone** *(see).*

Cheek·to·wa·ga (chēk′tə-wä′gə). An urban area in northeastern New York State, just east of Buffalo. Population, 65,000.

cheek·y (chē′kē) *adj.* **-ier, -iest.** Saucy; impudent; brazen. —**cheek′i·ly** *adv.* —**cheek′i·ness** *n.*

cheep (chēp) *n.* A faint, shrill sound like that of a young bird; chirp. —*v.* **cheeped, cheeping, cheeps.** —*tr.* To utter with a chirp. —*intr.* To chirp; peep. [Imitative.] —**cheep′er** *n.*

cheer (chîr) *n.* **1.** Gaiety; animation; happiness. **2.** Anything that gives joy or happiness; comfort. **3.** A shout of approval, encouragement, or congratulation. **4.** Food or drink; refreshment. —*v.* **cheered, cheering, cheers.** —*tr.* **1.** To fill with joy; comfort. Often used with *up.* **2.** To encourage with or as if with cheers; urge. Often used with *on.* **3.** To salute or acclaim with cheers; applaud. —*intr.* **1.** To shout cheers; applaud. **2.** To become cheerful. Often used with *up.* [Middle English *chere*, cheer, disposition, countenance, face, from Old French *ch(i)ere*, face, from Late Latin *cara*, from Greek *karē, kara*, head. See **ker-**[1] in Appendix.*] —**cheer′er** *n.* —**cheer′ing·ly** *adv.*

cheer·ful (chîr′fəl) *adj.* **1.** Being in good spirits; happy. **2.** Promoting cheer; pleasant. **3.** Hearty; willing: *cheerful labor.* —See Synonyms at **glad.** —**cheer′ful·ly** *adv.* —**cheer′ful·ness** *n.*

cheer·i·o (chîr′ē-ō′) *interj. Chiefly British Informal.* Used in greeting or parting. [From CHEER.]

cheer·lead·er (chîr′lē′dər) *n.* One who leads group cheering.

cheers (chîrz) *interj.* Used as a toast.

cheer·y (chîr′ē) *adj.* **-ier, -iest.** In good spirits; cheerful. —**cheer′i·ly** *adv.* —**cheer′i·ness** *n.*

cheese[1] (chēz) *n.* **1. a.** A solid food prepared from the pressed curd of milk. **b.** A molded mass of this substance. **2.** Something like cheese in shape or consistency. **3.** *Plural.* **a.** The common mallow, *Malva rotundifolia*, a creeping plant having pale-lavender or white flowers and flat, round, ridged fruits. **b.** The fruit of this plant. [Middle English *chese*, Old English *cēse*, from Germanic *kasjus* (unattested), from Latin *cāseus*†.]

cheese[2] (chēz) *tr.v.* **cheesed, cheesing, cheeses.** *Slang.* To stop. —**cheese it!** Look out! Get away fast! [Origin unknown.]

cheese[3] (chēz) *n. Slang.* An important person. Usually used sarcastically in the phrase *big cheese.* [Hindi *chīz*, thing, from Persian. See **kwo-** in Appendix.*]

cheese·burg·er (chēz′bûr′gər) *n.* A hamburger topped with melted cheese.

cheese·cake (chēz′kāk′) *n.* Also **cheese cake** (for sense 1). **1.** A cake made of sweetened curds, eggs, milk, sugar, and flavorings. **2.** *Slang.* **a.** A photograph of a pretty girl scantily clothed. **b.** Such photographs collectively.

cheese·cloth (chēz′klôth′, -klŏth′) *n.* A coarse, loosely woven cotton gauze, originally used for wrapping cheese.

cheese·par·ing (chēz′pâr′ĭng) *n.* **1.** A paring of cheese rind. **2.** Something of little or no value. **3.** Stinginess; parsimony. —*adj.* Miserly; stingy.

chees·y (chē′zē) *adj.* **-ier, -iest.** **1.** Like cheese. **2.** *Slang.* Of poor quality; shoddy; inadequate. —**chees′i·ness** *n.*

chee·tah (chē′tə) *n.* Also **che·tah.** A long-legged, swift-running wild cat, *Acinonyx jubatus*, of Africa and southwestern Asia, having black-spotted, tawny fur and nonretractile claws. It is sometimes trained to pursue game. Also called "hunting leopard." [Hindi *cītā*, from Sanskrit *citrakāya*, tiger : *citra*, speckled (see **skai-** in Appendix*) + *kāya*, body (see **kwei-**[2] in Appendix*).]

Chee·ver (chē′vər), **John.** Born 1912. American author of novels and short stories.

chef (shĕf) *n.* A cook; especially, the chief cook of a large kitchen staff. [French, from Old French *chief, chef*, CHIEF.]

chef-d'oeu·vre (shĕ-dœ′vr′) *n., pl.* **chefs-d'oeuvre** (shĕ-). *French.* A masterpiece. [French, "chief work."]

Che·foo (jŭ′fo͞o′). Officially **Yen·tai** (yĕn′tī′). A city of eastern China, a seaport on the northern coast of the Shantung Peninsula. Population, 140,000.

chef's salad. Tossed salad greens, usually garnished with a chef's choice of julienne strips of cheese or meats.

Che·ju (chā′jo͞o′). *Japanese* **Sai·shu** (sī′sho͞o). **1.** Formerly **Quel·part** (kwĕl′pärt). An island, 713 square miles in area, lying 50 miles off the southern coast of South Korea, of which it constitutes a province. **2.** The capital of Cheju, on the northern coast of the island. Population, 57,905.

Che·ka (chā′kä) *n.* The Soviet security service organized in 1918 by Lenin. Reorganized successively as GPU, OGPU, NKVD, and MVD, it acquired in 1954 ministry-level structure and the designation **KGB** *(see).* [Russian, short for *Chrezvychayhaya Komissiy*, "extraordinary commission."]

Che·khov (chĕk′ôf′), **Anton Pavlovich.** Also **Tche·khov, Che·kov.** 1860–1904. Russian author of plays and short stories.

Che·kiang (jŭ′jyäng′). A province of China, 39,300 square miles in area, with a coastline on the East China Sea. Population, 25,280,000. Capital, Hangchow.

Che·kist (chĕk′ĭst) *n.* A Cheka cadre or officer: *"Its* [KGB] *officers still refer to themselves as Chekists, a term both fearful and glamorous"* (New York Times). [CHEK(A) + -IST.]

che·la[1] (chā′lä) *n. Anglo-Indian.* A pupil of a guru. [Hindi *celā*, from Sanskrit *ceṭa, ceṭaka*†, slave.]

che·la[2] (kē′lə) *n., pl.* **-lae** (-lē′). A pincerlike claw, as of a lobster, crab, or similar crustacean. [New Latin, variant of obsolete English *chely*, from Latin *chēlē*, from Greek *khēlē*†, claw.]

che·late (kē′lāt′) *adj.* **1.** *Zoology.* Having or characteristic of a chela. **2.** *Chemistry.* Of or pertaining to a heterocyclic ring containing a metal ion attached by coordinate bonds to at least two nonmetal ions in the same molecule. —*tr.v.* **chelated, -lating, -lates.** To form a ring compound by joining a chelating agent to a metal ion. —**che′late′** *n.* —**che·la′tion** *n.*

che·lic·er·a (kĭ-lĭs′ər-ə) *n., pl.* **-erae** (-ə-rē′). Either of the first pair of appendages near the mouth of a spider or other arachnid, often modified for grasping. [New Latin : CHELA (claw) + Greek *keras*, horn (see **ker-**[1] in Appendix*).]

che·li·form (kē′lə-fôrm′) *adj.* Having the shape of a chela; pincerlike. [New Latin CHELA (claw) + -FORM.]

Chel·li·an, Chel·le·an (shĕl′ē-ən) *adj. Archaeology.* **Abbevillian** *(see).* [From *Chelles*, France, where some archaeological specimens were found.]

che·loid. Variant of **keloid.**

che·lo·ni·an (kĭ-lō′nē-ən) *adj. Zoology.* Of or belonging to the order Chelonia, which includes the turtles and tortoises. —*n.* A member of the Chelonia. [From New Latin *Chelonia*, from Greek *khelōnē*, tortoise. See **ghelū-** in Appendix.*]

Chel·sea (chĕl′sē). A former borough of London, England, now part of **Kensington and Chelsea** *(see).*

Chel·ten·ham (chĕlt′nəm, chĕlt′n-əm). A city and resort of Gloucestershire, southwestern England. Population, 75,000.

Che·lya·binsk (chĭ-lyä′bĭnsk). A city of the Soviet Union in Asia, situated in the eastern foothills of the central Ural Mountains. Population, 805,000.

Che·lyus·kin, Cape (chĭ-lyo͞os′kĭn). The northernmost point of Asia, situated at the tip of the Taimyr Peninsula in Siberia.

chem–, chemi–. Variants of **chemo-.**

chem. chemical; chemist; chemistry.

chem·ic (kĕm′ĭk) *adj. Archaic.* **1.** Chemical. **2.** Alchemic. —*n. Obsolete.* An alchemist.

chem·i·cal (kĕm′ĭ-kəl) *adj. Abbr.* **chem.** **1.** Of or pertaining to chemistry. **2.** Of or pertaining to the properties or actions of chemicals. —*n.* A substance produced by or used in a chemical process. [Earlier *chimical*, from *chimic*, an alchemist, from New Latin *chimicus*, from Medieval Latin *alchimicus*, from *alchimia, alchymia*, ALCHEMY.] —**chem′i·cal·ly** *adv.*

chemical bond. Any of several forces or mechanisms, especially the **ionic bond, covalent bond,** and **metallic bond** *(all of which see),* by which atoms or ions are bound in a molecule or crystal.

chemical engineering. The technology of large-scale chemical and chemical materials production. —**chemical engineer.**

Chemical Mace. A trademark for a mixture of organic chemicals used in aerosol form as a weapon to disable with intense burning eye pain, blepharospasm, acute bronchitis, and respiratory irritation. Also called "Mace."

chemical warfare. Warfare using chemicals other than explosives, especially irritants, asphyxiants, contaminants, poisons, and incendiaries, as direct weapons.

chem·i·lu·mi·nes·cence (kĕm′ĭ-lo͞o′mə-nĕs′əns) *n.* The emission of light as a result of a chemical reaction at environmental temperatures.

che·min de fer (shə-măN′ də fâr′). A gambling game, a variation of baccarat. [French, "railroad."]

che·mise (shə-mēz′) *n.* **1.** A woman's loose, shirtlike undergarment. **2.** A woman's dress hanging straight from the shoulders. In this sense, also called "shift." [Middle English, from Old French, shirt, from Late Latin *camisia*, linen shirt, nightgown. See **camisia.**]

chem·i·sette (shĕm′ĭ-zĕt′) *n.* **1.** A short, sleeveless bodice, formerly worn by women. **2.** A blouse front formerly worn by women; a dickey. [French, diminutive of CHEMISE.]

chem·i·sorb (kĕm′ĭ-sôrb′) *tr.v.* **-sorbed, -sorbing, -sorbs.** Also **chem·o·sorb** (kĕm′ə-sôrb′). To take up and chemically bind a substance on the surface of another substance. [CHEMI- + (AB)SORB.] —**chem′i·sorp′tion** (kĕm′ĭ-sôrp′shən) *n.*

chem·ist (kĕm′ĭst) *n. Abbr.* **chem.** **1.** A scientist specializing in chemistry. **2.** *Chiefly British.* A pharmacist. **3.** *Obsolete.* An alchemist. [Earlier *chimist*, from New Latin *chimista*, short for Medieval Latin *alchymista*, ALCHEMIST.]

chem·is·try (kĕm′ĭs-trē) *n., pl.* **-tries.** *Abbr.* **chem.** **1.** The science of the composition, structure, properties, and reactions of matter, especially of atomic and molecular systems. **2.** The composition, structure, properties, and reactions of a substance. **3.** Behavior or functioning, as of a complex of emotions: *the chemistry of love.* [Earlier *chimistrie,* from *chimist,* CHEMIST.]

Chem·nitz. The former name for **Karl-Marx-Stadt.**

chemo–, chemi–, chem–. Indicates chemicals or chemical reactions; for example, **chemisorb, chemosmosis, chemotaxis.** [New Latin, from Late Greek *khēmeia,* ALCHEMY.]

chem·o·pro·phy·lax·is (kĕm′ō-prō′fə-lăk′sĭs, kē′mō-) *n.* The use of chemicals to prevent infectious disease. **—chem′o·pro′-phy·lac′tic** *adj.*

chem·o·re·cep·tion (kĕm′ō-rĭ-sĕp′shən, kē′mō-) *n.* The reaction of a sense organ to a chemical stimulus. **—chem′o·re·cep′tive** *adj.* **—chem′o·re′cep·tiv′i·ty** (-rē′sĕp-tĭv′ə-tē) *n.*

chem·o·re·cep·tor (kĕm′ō-rĭ-sĕp′tər, kē′mō-) *n.* A nerve ending or sense organ, as of smell or taste, sensitive to chemical stimuli.

chem·os·mo·sis (kĕm′ŏz-mō′sĭs, -ŏs-mō′sĭs) *n.* The phenomenon of ionic or molecular transport across a membrane. [CHEM(O)- + OSMOSIS.] **—chem′os·mot′ic** (-mŏt′ĭk) *adj.*

chem·o·sphere (kĕm′ə-sfîr′, kē′mō-) *n.* The region of the atmosphere between 20 and 120 miles altitude in which photochemical reactions initiated by solar radiation occur.

chem·o·syn·the·sis (kĕm′ō-sĭn′thə-sĭs, kē′mō-) *n.* The synthesis of organic substances such as food nutrients, using the energy of chemical reactions. **—chem′o·syn·thet′ik** (-thĕt′ĭk) *adj.* **—chem′o·syn·thet′i·cal·ly** *adv.*

chem·o·tax·is (kĕm′ō-tăk′sĭs, kē′mō-) *n.* Characteristic orientation or motion of a freely moving living organism relative to a chemical substance. [New Latin : CHEMO- + -TAXIS.] **—chem′o·tac′tic** (-tăk′tĭk) *adj.* **—chem′o·tac′ti·cal·ly** *adv.*

chem·o·ther·a·py (kĕm′ō-thĕr′ə-pē, kē′mō-) *n.* The treatment of disease with chemicals. **—chem′o·ther′a·peu′tic** (-pyōō′tĭk, kē′mō-) *adj.*

chem·ot·ro·pism (kĕm-ŏt′rə-pĭz′əm) *n.* Movement or growth of an organism, especially a plant, in response to chemical stimuli. [German *Chemotropismus* : CHEMO- + -TROPISM.] **—chem′o·trop′ic** (-ō-trŏp′ĭk, kē′mō-) *adj.*

Che·mul·po. The Korean name for **Inchon.**

chem·ur·gy (kĕm′ər-jē, kĕ-mûr′-) *n.* The development of new industrial chemical products from organic raw materials, especially from those of agricultural origin. [CHEM(O)- + -URGY.] **—chem·ur′gic** (kĕ-mûr′jĭk), **chem·ur′gi·cal** *adj.*

Che·nab (chə-näb′). A river rising in Kashmir and flowing 675 miles west along the foot of the Himalayas and then southwest to join the Sutlej River in east-central West Pakistan.

Cheng·chow (jŭng′jō′). Formerly **Cheng·hsien** (jŭng′shyĕn′). A city of China, on the Yellow River in northern Honan Province, of which it is the capital. Population, 785,000.

Cheng·teh (chŭng′dŭ′). Also **Cheng·te.** Formerly **Je·hol** (jə-hōl′). A city in northeastern China, northeast of Peking; the summer residence of Manchu emperors. Population, 120,000.

Cheng·tu (chŭng′dōō′). The capital of Szechwan Province, central China. Population, 1,107,000.

Ché·nier (shā-nyā′), **André Marie de.** 1762–1794. French poet; guillotined.

che·nille (shə-nēl′) *n.* **1.** A soft, tufted cord of silk, cotton, or worsted used in embroidery or for fringing. **2.** Fabric made of this cord, commonly used for bedspreads or rugs. [French, "caterpillar," from Latin *canicula,* diminutive of *canis,* dog (from its hairy pile). See **kwon-** in Appendix.*]

Chen·nault (shə-nôlt′), **Claire Lee.** 1890–1958. American Air Force general in World War II.

che·no·pod (kē′nə-pŏd′, kĕn′ə-) *n.* Any plant of the goosefoot family, Chenopodiaceae, which includes spinach and beets as well as many common weeds. [New Latin *Chenopodiaceae,* from *Chenopodium* (genus) : Greek *khēn,* goose (see **ghans-** in Appendix*) + -PODIUM.]

Chen·sto·khov. The Russian name for **Częstochowa.**

Cheops (kē′ŏps). Original name, Khu-fu. King of Egypt of the fourth dynasty (2900?–2877 B.C.); erected Great Pyramid.

cheque. *Chiefly British.* Variant of **check** (bank).

cheq·uer. *Chiefly British.* Variant of **checker.**

Cher (shâr). A river rising in central France and flowing 220 miles northwest to the Loire near Tours.

Cher·bourg (shâr′bŏŏrg′; *French* shĕr-bōōr′). A seaport and naval base of northwestern France, on the northern coast of the Cotentin Peninsula. Population, 37,000.

Cher·bourg Peninsula. See **Cotentin Peninsula.**

Che·rem·kho·vo (chə-rĕm′kə-vō′). A city of the Soviet Union, in Asia, 80 miles northwest of Irkutsk. Population, 113,000.

Che·ri·bon. See **Tjirebon.**

cher·i·moy·a (chĕr′ĭ-moi′ə) *n.* **1.** A tropical American tree, *Annona cherimola,* having yellow flowers and edible fruit with white, soft, aromatic pulp. **2.** The fruit of this tree. [American Spanish *chirimoya,* from Quechua *chirimuya.*]

cher·ish (chĕr′ĭsh) *tr.v.* **-ished, -ishing, -ishes. 1.** To hold dear; treat with affection and tenderness. **2.** To keep fondly in mind; entertain. —See Synonyms at **appreciate.** [Middle English *cherissen, cherishen,* from Old French *cherir* (present stem *cheriss-*), from *cher,* dear, from Latin *cārus.* See **kā-** in Appendix.*] **—cher′ish·er** *n.* **—cher′ish·ing·ly** *adv.*

Cher·kessk (chĕr-kĕsk′). The capital of the Karachay-Cherkess Autonomous Region of the Soviet Union, on the Kuban River about 110 miles northeast of the Black Sea. Population, 53,000.

Cher·ni·gov (chĕr-nē′gôf). A city of the Soviet Union, on the Desna River in the Ukrainian S.S.R. Population, 126,000.

Cher·nov·tsy (chĕr-nôf′tsē). *Rumanian* **Cer·nă·u·ţi** (chĕr′-nə-ōōts′, -ōōt′sē); *German* **Czer·no·witz** (chĕr′nō-vĭts). A city of the Soviet Union, in the western Ukrainian S.S.R., on the Prut River near the Rumanian border. Population, 172,000.

cher·no·zem (chĕr′nə-zĕm′, chĕr′nə-zhôm′) *n.* A very black topsoil, rich in humus, typical of cool to temperate semiarid regions, such as the grasslands of European Russia. [Russian, contraction of *chĕrnaya zemlya,* "black earth" : *chĕrnyĭ,* black (see **kers-**[1] in Appendix*) + *zemlya,* earth, from Old Russian (see **dhghem-** in Appendix*).]

Cher·o·kee (chĕr′ə-kē′, chĕr′ə-kē′) *n., pl.* **Cherokee** or **-kees. 1.** An Iroquoian-speaking tribe of North American Indians, formerly inhabiting North Carolina and northern Georgia and now settled in Oklahoma. **2.** A member of this tribe. **3.** The language of this tribe. [Cherokee *tsalaki.*] **—Cher′o·kee′** *adj.*

Cherokee rose. A climbing rose, *Rosa laevigata,* of Chinese origin, having large, white, fragrant flowers.

Cherokee Strip. Also **Cherokee Outlet.** A strip of land occupying 12,000 square miles in modern northern Oklahoma, that was guaranteed to the Cherokee Indians (1828 and 1833), purchased by the United States in 1891, and opened to settlers in 1893.

che·root (shə-rōōt′, chə-) *n.* Also **she·root.** A cigar with square-cut ends. [Tamil *curuṭṭu, śurruṭṭu,* from *śuruḷ,* a curl.]

cher·ry (chĕr′ē) *n., pl.* **-ries. 1.** Any of several trees of the genus *Prunus,* having small, fleshy, globe-shaped or heart-shaped fruit with a small, hard stone; especially, *P. avium,* the common sweet cherry, and *P. cerasus,* the sour cherry. **2.** The fruit or wood of any of these trees. **3.** Moderate or strong red to purplish red. See **color. 4.** *Vulgar Slang.* The hymen considered as a symbol of virginity. [Middle English *chery,* from Norman French *cherise,* variant of Old French *cerise,* from Vulgar Latin *ceresia* (unattested), from Latin *cerasus,* cherry tree, from Greek *kerasos*†.] **—cher′ry** *adj.*

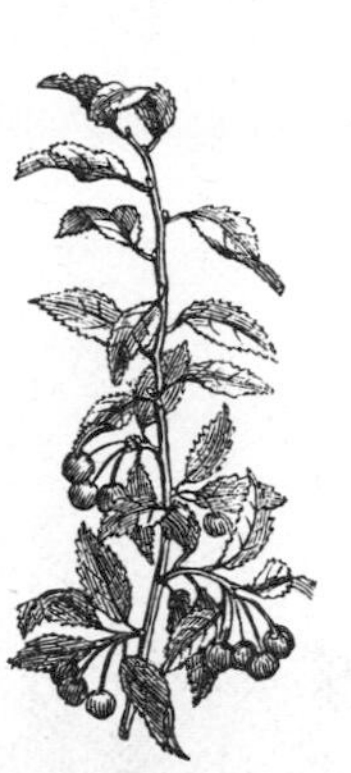

cherry
Prunus cerasus
Sour cherry

cherry birch. The **black birch** *(see).*

cherry laurel. A frequently cultivated European shrub, *Prunus laurocerasus,* having evergreen foliage and white flowers.

cherry pepper. The very pungent red, yellow, or purplish fruit of a tropical plant, *Capsicum frutescens cerasiforme.*

cherry picker. Any of various large, usually mobile cranes having a long, maneuverable, obliquely vertical boom often supporting a work platform.

cherry plum. A tree, the **myrobalan** *(see).*

cher·ry·stone (chĕr′ē-stōn′) *n.* A clam, the quahog, when half-grown and of comparatively small size.

cherry tomato. A variety of the common tomato, *Lycopersicum esculentum cerasiforme,* having small red or yellow fruit.

cher·so·nese (kûr′sə-nēz′, -nēs′) *n.* A peninsula. [Latin *chersonēsus,* from Greek *khersonēsos* : *khersos,* dry land (see **ghers-** in Appendix*) + *nēsos,* island (see **snā-** in Appendix*).]

chert (chûrt) *n.* **1.** Any of various microscopically crystalline mineral varieties of silica. **2.** A siliceous rock of chalcedonic or opaline silica occurring in limestone. [Origin unknown.]

cher·ub (chĕr′əb) *n., pl.* **-ubim** (-ə-bĭm′, -yə-bĭm′) (for senses 1, 2) or **-ubs** (for senses 3, 4). **1.** A winged celestial being. Genesis 3:24. **2.** *Theology.* One of the second order of angels. See **angel. 3.** A representation of an angelic cherub, portrayed as a winged child with a chubby, rosy face. **4.** Any person, especially a child, with an innocent or chubby face. [Hebrew *kərūbh.*] **—che·ru′bic** (chə-rōō′bĭk) *adj.* **—che·ru′bi·cal·ly** *adv.*

Che·ru·bi·ni (kâr-ə-bē′nē; *Italian* kā′rōō-bē′nē), **Maria Luigi Carlo Zenobio Salvatore.** 1760–1842. Italian composer of operas and sacred music.

cher·vil (chûr′vəl) *n.* **1.** An aromatic plant, *Anthriscus cerefolium,* native to Eurasia, having leaves used in soups and salads. **2.** Any of several related plants, especially *Chaerophyllum bulbosum,* having an edible root. [Middle English *cherville,* Old English *cerfille,* from West Germanic *kervila* (unattested), from Latin *chaerephylla,* from Greek *khairephullon* : *khairein,* to delight in (see **gher-**[6] in Appendix*) + *phullon,* leaf (see **bhel-**[3] in Appendix*).]

cher·vo·nets (chĕr-vô′nĕts) *n., pl.* **-vontsi** (-vônt′sē). A former monetary unit and gold coin of the Soviet Union, equal to ten roubles. [Russian, from Old Russian *červonyi*†.]

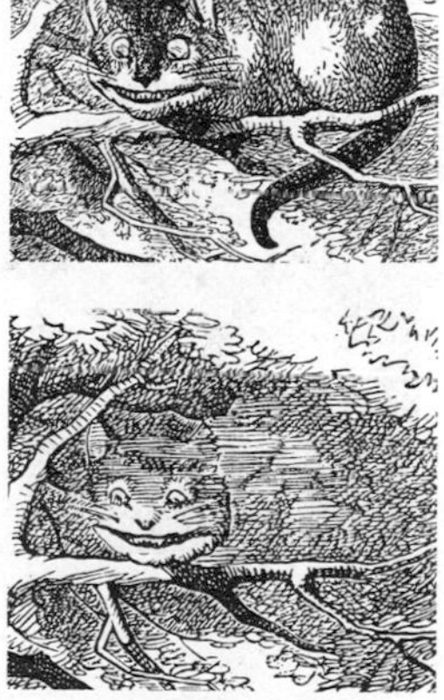

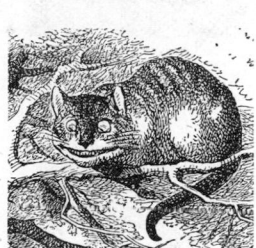

Cheshire cat
Details from illustrations by Sir John Tenniel for Lewis Carroll's *Alice's Adventures in Wonderland*

Cher·well (chär′wĕl, -wəl). A river of England, rising in Northamptonshire, and flowing about 30 miles south to the Thames at Oxford.

Ches. Cheshire.

Ches·a·peake Bay (chĕs′ə-pēk′). An inlet of the Atlantic Ocean, about 200 miles long, in Virginia and Maryland.

Chesapeake Bay retriever. A hunting dog of a breed developed in the United States, having a thick, short, brownish coat.

Chesh·ire (chĕsh′ər, -îr). *Abbr.* **Ches., Chesh.** A county of England, occupying 1,015 square miles in the northwest. Population, 1,430,000. County seat, Chester.

Chesh·ire cat (chĕsh′ər, -îr). In *Alice's Adventures in Wonderland,* by Lewis Carroll, a grinning cat that gradually disappeared until only its grin remained visible.

chesh·ire cheese (chĕsh′ər, -îr). A hard, yellow English cheese made from cow's milk. [From CHESHIRE.]

chess[1] (chĕs) *n.* A board game for two players, each possessing an initial force of a king, a queen, two bishops, two knights, two rooks, and eight pawns, all maneuvered following individual rules of movement with the objective of checkmating the opposing king. [Middle English *ches,* short for Old French *esches,* plural of *eschec,* CHECK (at chess).]

chess[2] (chĕs) *n.* Any of several weedy grasses, especially **cheat** *(see).* [Origin unknown.]

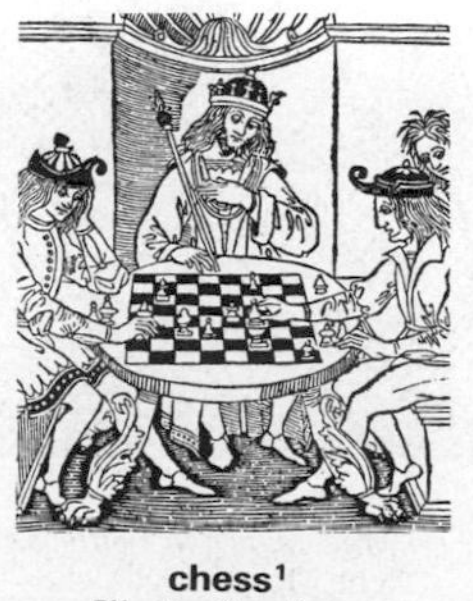

chess[1]
Illustration for a 15th-century treatise on playing chess

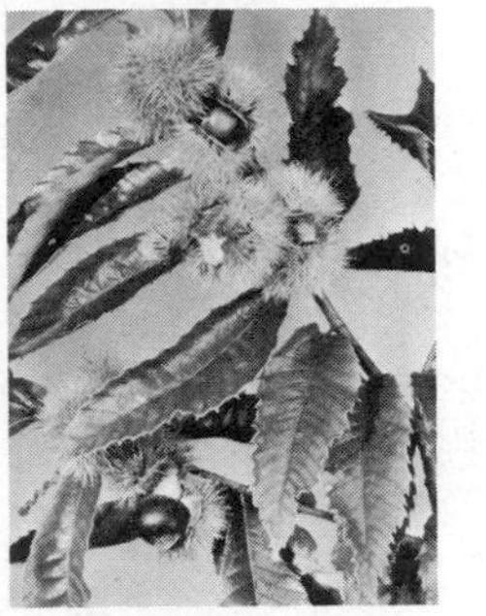

chestnut

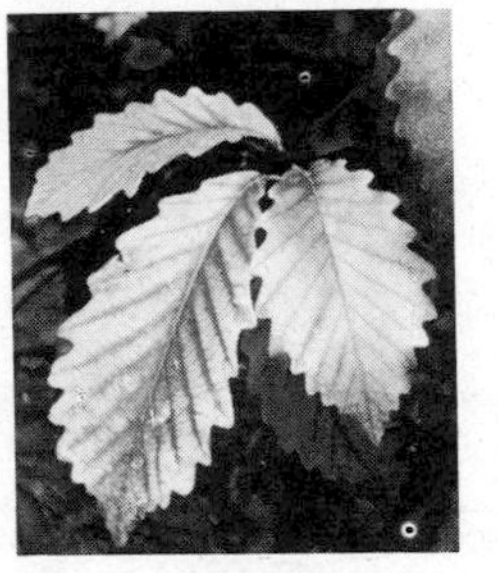

chestnut oak

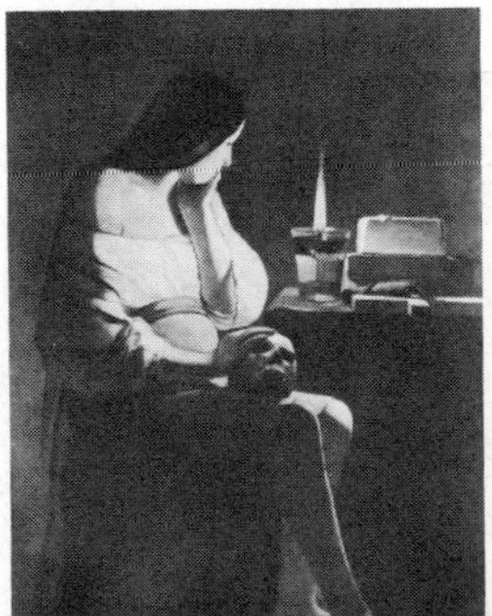

chiaroscuro
La Madeleine à la Veilleuse
("The Mary Magdalene Beside Her Night Lamp"), a painting by Georges de La Tour

chess[3] (chěs) *n., pl.* **chess** or **chesses**. One of the floor boards of a pontoon bridge. [Middle English *ches,* tier, from Old French *chasse,* frame, from Latin *capsa,* box. See **kap-** in Appendix.*]

chess·board (chěs′bôrd′, -bōrd′) *n.* A board used in playing chess, marked with 64 squares.

chess·man (chěs′mǎn′, -mən) *n., pl.* **-men** (-měn′, -mǐn). Any of the pieces used in playing the game of chess.

chest (chěst) *n.* **1.** The part of the body between the neck and the abdomen, enclosed by the ribs and the breastbone. **2. a.** A sturdy box with a lid and often a lock, used for storage and protection of articles. **b.** A small closet or cabinet with shelves for storing supplies. **3. a.** The treasury of a public institution. **b.** The funds kept there. **4. a.** A box for the shipping of certain goods, such as tea. **b.** The quantity packed in such a box. **5.** A sealed receptacle for liquid, gas, or steam. **6.** A bureau or dresser. [Middle English *chest,* Old English *cest, cist,* box, from West Germanic *kistā* (unattested), from Latin *cista,* from Greek *kistē.* See **kistā** in Appendix.*] —**chest′ed** (chěs′tĭd) *adj.*

Ches·ter[1] (chěs′tər). A masculine given name. [Probably from Middle English *chestre,* town, Old English *ceaster,* fortified town, from Latin *castrum,* camp. See **kes-**[2] in Appendix.*]

Ches·ter[2] (chěs′tər). A city of southeastern Pennsylvania, on the Delaware River. Population, 64,000.

ches·ter·field (chěs′tər-fēld′) *n.* **1.** A single-breasted or double-breasted overcoat, usually with concealed buttons and a velvet collar. **2.** A large, overstuffed sofa with upright armrests. [Named after an Earl of *Chesterfield* of the 19th century.]

Ches·ter·field (chěs′tər-fēld′), **Fourth Earl of.** Title of Philip Dormer Stanhope. 1694–1773. English statesman and author.

Ches·ter·field·i·an (chěs′tər-fēl′dē-ən) *adj.* Pertaining to or characteristic of Lord Chesterfield; debonair; urbane; elegant.

Ches·ter·field Inlet (chěs′tər-fēld′). An inlet of Hudson Bay extending about 250 miles into eastern Keewatin District, Northwest Territories, Canada.

Ches·ter·ton (chěs′tər-tən), **G(ilbert) K(eith).** 1874–1936. English journalist, novelist, poet, and critic.

Chester White. A white hog of a breed that originated in Chester County, Pennsylvania.

chest·nut (chěs′nŭt′, -nət) *n.* **1.** Any of several trees of the genus *Castanea,* of the Northern Hemisphere, bearing nuts enclosed in a prickly bur. *C. dentata,* of eastern North America, has been almost completely exterminated by the **chestnut blight** *(see).* **2.** The nut of any of these trees, edible when cooked. **3.** The hard wood of these trees, used in furniture and as a building material. **4.** The **horse chestnut** *(see).* **5.** Grayish brown to moderate reddish brown. See **color.** **6.** A reddish-brown horse. **7.** A small, hard callus on the inner surface of a horse's foreleg. **8. a.** An old and stale joke. **b.** Anything lacking freshness or originality, as a song or story. [Earlier *chesten nut* : Middle English *chesten, chasteine,* chestnut, from Old French *chastaigne,* from Latin *castanea,* from Greek *kasteneat* + NUT.] —**chest′nut′** *adj.*

chestnut blight. A disease of the native American chestnut tree, caused by a fungus, *Endothia parasitica,* and resulting in cankers on the trunk and branches and eventual death.

chestnut oak. A tree, *Quercus prinus,* of eastern and central North America, having leaves with wavy edges like those of the chestnut.

chest register. The lower register of the human voice. Also called "chest voice."

chest·y (chěs′tē) *adj.* **-ier, -iest.** *Informal.* **1.** Having a large or well-developed chest. **2.** Arrogant; proud; conceited.

che·tah. Variant of **cheetah.**

cheth. Variant of **heth.**

Chet·nik (chět′nĭk) *n., pl.* **-niks** or **Chetnici** (chět-nē′tsē). A Serbian guerrilla fighter in World War II. [Serbian *četnik,* from *četa*†, troop.]

che·val-de-frise (shə-văl′də-frēz′) *n., pl.* **chevaux-de-frise** (shə-vō′-). **1.** An obstacle composed of barbed wire or spikes attached to a wooden frame, used to block enemy advancement and, formerly, to hinder enemy cavalry. **2.** An obstacle in the form of jagged glass or spikes set in the masonry on the top of a wall. [French, "Frisian horse." It was first used in Friesland to compensate for a lack of cavalry.]

che·va·let (shə-vă-lā′) *n.* The bridge of a stringed musical instrument. [French, diminutive of *cheval,* horse, from Latin *caballus.* See **cavalier.**]

che·val glass (shə-văl′). A long mirror mounted on swivels in a frame. [From French *cheval,* support, "horse." See **chevalet.**]

chev·a·lier (shěv′ə-lîr′) *n.* **1.** A member of certain orders of knighthood or merit, as the Legion of Honor in France. **2.** *French History.* **a.** A nobleman of the lowest rank. **b.** A cadet of the nobility. **3.** A knight. **4.** A chivalrous, gallant man. [Middle English *chevaler,* from Old French *chevalier,* from Late Latin *caballārius,* horseman, CAVALIER.]

che·ve·lure (shəv-lür′) *n.* A head of hair. [Old French, from Latin *capillātūra,* the hair, from *capillus.* See **capillary.**]

Chev·i·ot (shěv′ē-ət *for sense 1;* chěv′ē-ət, chē′vē- *for sense 2*) *n.* **1.** One of a breed of sheep with short, thick wool, originally raised in the Cheviot Hills. **2.** *Small* **c.** A woolen fabric with a coarse twill weave, used chiefly for suits and overcoats and originally made from the wool of the Cheviot sheep.

Chev·i·ot Hills (chěv′ē-ət, chē′vē-). A range of hills extending about 35 miles along the boundary between England and Scotland. Highest elevation, The Cheviot (2,676 feet).

chev·ron (shěv′rən) *n.* **1.** A badge or insignia consisting of stripes meeting at an angle, worn on the sleeve of a military, naval, or police uniform to indicate rank, merit, or length of service. **2.** *Heraldry.* A device shaped like an inverted V. **3.** Any V-shaped pattern, especially a kind of fret used in architecture. [Middle English, from Old French, beam, rafter, from Vulgar Latin *capriō* (unattested), from Latin *capra,* feminine of *caper,* goat. See **kapro-** in Appendix.*]

chev·ro·tain (shěv′rə-tān′) *n.* Any of several small, hornless ruminants of the genera *Hyemoschus* and *Tragulus* of central Africa and southeastern Asia. Also called "mouse deer." [French *chevrotin,* from Old French, diminutive of *chevrot,* kid, diminutive of *chevre,* goat, from Latin *capra.* See **chevron.**]

chev·y. Variant of **chivvy** (noun).

chew (cho͞o) *v.* **chewed, chewing, chews.** —*tr.* **1.** To bite and grind with the teeth; masticate. **2.** To meditate upon; ruminate; ponder. —*intr.* **1.** To make a crushing and grinding motion with the teeth. **2.** To cogitate; meditate. **3.** *Informal.* To use chewing tobacco. —**chew out.** *Slang.* To scold or reprimand. —**chew the rag.** *Slang.* To argue or discuss. —*n.* **1.** The act of chewing. **2.** That which is chewed or intended for chewing: *a chew of tobacco.* [Middle English *chewen,* Old English *cēowan.* See **gyeu-** in Appendix.*] —**chew′er** *n.*

chewing gum. A sweetened, flavored preparation for chewing, usually made of chicle.

che·wink (chĭ-wĭngk′) *n.* A bird, the **towhee** *(see).* [Imitative of its note.]

Chey·enne[1] (shī-ăn′, -ĕn′) *n., pl.* **Cheyenne** or **-ennes.** **1.** A tribe of Algonquian-speaking North American Indians, formerly inhabiting central Minnesota and North and South Dakota, now settled in Montana and Oklahoma. **2.** A member of this tribe. **3.** The Algonquian language of this tribe. [Canadian French, from Dakota *šahíyena.*] —**Chey·enne′** *adj.*

Chey·enne[2] (shī-ăn′, -ĕn′). The capital of Wyoming, in the southeast near the Colorado border. Population, 44,000.

Chey·enne River (shī-ăn′, -ĕn′). A river rising in eastern Wyoming and flowing 290 miles first southeast and then northeast to the Missouri near Pierre, South Dakota.

chez (shā) *prep. French.* At the home of; at; by.

chg. charge.

chi (kī) *n.* The 22nd letter in the Greek alphabet, written Χ, χ. Transliterated in English as *kh,* often also as *ch.* See **alphabet.** [Greek *khi.* See **X.**]

CHI Airport code for Chicago, Illinois.

Chi·ai (jē′ī′). A city in west-central Taiwan. Population, 191,000.

Chia·mus·su. The Japanese name for **Kiamusze.**

Chi·an (kī′ən) *adj.* Pertaining to or coming from Chios. —*n.* A native or inhabitant of Chios.

Chiang Kai-shek (jyäng′ kī′shěk′, chyäng′, chăng′). Original name, Chiang Chung-cheng. Born 1887. Chinese military leader and first president of Republic of China (1928–31); again president (since 1948); removed government to Taiwan (1949).

Chi·an·ti (kē-än′tē, -ăn′tē) *n.* **1.** A dry red wine produced in the Monti Chianti region of Italy. **2.** Any similar wine.

Chian·ti, Mon·ti (mōn′tē kyän′tē). A range of the Apennines in central Italy. Highest elevation, 2,930 feet.

chiao (tyou) *n., pl.* **chiao.** A monetary unit equal to 1/10 of the yuan of the People's Republic of China. See table of exchange rates at **currency.** [Mandarin Chinese *chiao*[3], "an animal's horn," "liquid measure made from a horn."]

Chi·a·pas (chē-ä′päs). A state of Mexico, occupying 28,730 square miles on the southeastern coast. Population, 1,323,000. Capital, Tuxtla Gutiérrez.

chi·a·ro·scu·ro (kē-är′ə-sko͝or′ō, -skyo͝or′ō) *n., pl.* **-ros.** Also **chi·a·ro·o·scu·ro** (kē-är′ə-ō-sko͝or′ō, -skyo͝or′ō). **1.** The technique of using light and shade in pictorial representation. **2.** The arrangement of light and dark elements in a pictorial work of art. Also called "clair-obscure." [Italian : *chiaro,* light, clear, from Latin *clārus,* clear (see **kel-**[3] in Appendix*) + *oscuro,* dark, from Latin *obscūrus* (see **skeu-** in Appendix*).] —**chi·a′ro·scu′rist** *n.*

chi·as·ma (kī-ăz′mə) *n., pl.* **-mata** (-mə-tə) or **-mas.** Also **chi·asm** (kī′ăz′əm). **1.** *Anatomy.* A crossing or intersection of two tracts, as of nerves or ligaments. **2.** *Genetics.* A point of contact between homologous chromosomes, considered the cytological manifestation of crossing over. [New Latin, from Greek *khiasma,* cross, piece of wood, from *khiazein,* to mark with the letter chi, from *khi,* CHI.] —**chi·as′mal, chi·as′mic, chi′as·mat′ic** (-măt′ĭk) *adj.*

chi·as·ma·ty·py (kī-ăz′mə-tī′pē) *n. Genetics.* The meiotic twisting between pairs of homologous chromosomes that produces chiasmata. [French *chiasmatypie* : CHIASMA + -TYPE.]

chi·as·mus (kī-ăz′məs) *n., pl.* **-mi** (-mī′). A rhetorical inversion of the second of two parallel structures, as *He went to the theater, but home went she.* [New Latin, from Greek *khiasmos,* from *khiazein,* to mark with the letter chi, from *khi,* CHI.]

chi·as·to·lite (kī-ăs′tə-līt′) *n.* A mineral variety of andalusite with carbonaceous impurities regularly arranged along the longer axis of the crystal. Also called "macle." [German *Chiastolith* : Greek *khiastos,* crossed, past participle of *khiazein,* to mark with the letter chi, from *khi,* CHI + -LITE.]

chiaus (chous, choush) *n.* An official Turkish messenger, emissary, or sergeant. [Turkish *çavuş.*]

Chi·ba (chē′bə). A city of eastern Honshu, Japan, on the northeastern shore of Tokyo Bay. Population, 301,000.

Chib·cha (chĭb′chə) *n., pl.* **Chibcha** or **-chas.** **1.** An extinct tribe of Indians, once inhabiting Colombia. **2.** A member of this tribe. **3.** The extinct language of this tribe.

Chib·chan (chĭb′chən) *n.* **1.** A South American or Central American Indian ethnic stock including the Chibcha. **2.** The language spoken by these people. —*adj.* Of or concerning this ethnic or language group.

ă pat/ā pay/âr care/ä father/b bib/ch church/d deed/ĕ pet/ē be/f fife/g gag/h hat/hw which/ĭ pit/ī pie/îr pier/j judge/k kick/l lid, needle/m mum/n no, sudden/ng thing/ŏ pot/ō toe/ô paw, for/oi noise/ou out/o͝o took/o͞o boot/p pop/r roar/s sauce/sh ship, dish/

chi·bouk (chĭ-bo͝ok′, shĭ-) *n.* Also **chi·bouque.** A Turkish tobacco pipe with a long stem and a red clay bowl. [French *chibouque,* from Turkish *çubuk, cibuk.*]

chic (shēk) *adj.* **1.** Sophisticated; stylish. **2.** Dressed smartly and fashionably; modish. —*n.* **1.** Sophistication in dress and manner; elegance. **2.** Stylishness; fashionableness. [French, from German *Schick,* skill, Middle High German *schicken*†, to arrange, prepare.] —**chic′ly** *adv.*

Chi·ca·go (shə-kä′gō, -kô′gō, -kä′gə). The second-largest city in the United States, at the southern end of Lake Michigan in northeastern Illinois. Population, 3,550,000. —**Chi·ca′go·an** *n.*

chi·ca·lo·te (chē′kə-lō′tē) *n.* A prickly poppy, *Argemone platyceras,* of the southwestern United States and tropical America, having grayish foliage and large white flowers. [Spanish, from Nahuatl *chicalotl.*]

chi·cane (shĭ-kān′) *v.* **-caned, -caning, -canes.** —*tr.* **1.** To trick; deceive. **2.** To quibble over; cavil. —*intr.* To use tricks or chicanery. —*n.* **1.** Chicanery. **2.** In bridge or whist, a hand without trumps. [French *chicaner,* from Old French *chicaner*†, to quibble.] —**chi·can′er** *n.*

chi·can·er·y (shĭ-kā′nər-ē) *n., pl.* **-ies. 1.** Deception by trickery or sophistry. **2.** A trick; subterfuge.

chic·co·ry. Variant of **chicory.**

Chich·a·gof Island (chĭch′ə-gôf′). An island of Alaska, 2,100 square miles in area, in the Alexander Archipelago.

Chi·chén-It·zá (chĭ-chĕn′-ĭt-sä′). A village in northeastern Yucatán State, Mexico; the site of extensive Mayan ruins.

chi·chi (shē′shē) *adj.* Ostentatiously stylish; showy. [French *chichi* (expressive formation).]

chick (chĭk) *n.* **1.** A young chicken. **2.** The young of any bird. **3.** A child. **4.** *Slang.* A girl; young woman. [Middle English *chike,* short for *chiken,* CHICKEN.]

chick·a·dee (chĭk′ə-dē′) *n.* Any of several small, plump North American birds of the genus *Parus,* having predominantly gray plumage and a dark-crowned head. [Imitative of its cry.]

Chick·a·mau·ga (chĭk′ə-mô′gə). A town in northwestern Georgia near Chickamauga Creek, the site of a Union defeat in the campaign for Chattanooga, Tennessee (1863).

chick·a·ree (chĭk′ə-rē′). A squirrel, *Tamiascurus douglasi,* of northwestern North America, resembling and closely related to the red squirrel. [Imitative of its cry.]

Chick·a·saw (chĭk′ə-sô′) *n., pl.* **Chickasaw** or **-saws. 1.** A tribe of Muskhogean-speaking North American Indians, originally of Mississippi, later removed to Oklahoma. **2.** A member of this tribe. **3.** The language of this tribe. —**Chick′a·saw′** *adj.*

chick·en (chĭk′ən) *n.* **1.** The common domestic fowl or its young. **2.** Any of various similar or related birds, such as the **prairie chicken** *(see).* **3.** The flesh of the common domestic fowl. **4.** *Slang.* A young woman. —*adj. Slang.* Afraid; timid. —*intr.v.* **chickened, -ening, -ens.** *Slang.* To act in a cowardly manner; lose one's nerve. Usually used with *out.* [Middle English *chiken,* Old English *cīcen.* See **ku-** in Appendix.*]

chicken breast. A chest deformity marked by a projecting sternum, occurring as the result of rickets. Also called "pigeon breast." —**chick′en-breast′ed** *adj.*

chicken colonel. *Military Slang.* A full colonel. [From the eagle insignia worn by a full colonel.]

chicken feed. *Slang.* A trifling amount of money.

chicken hawk. Any of various hawks that prey on or have the reputation of preying on chickens.

chick·en-heart·ed (chĭk′ən-här′tĭd) *adj.* Cowardly; timid.

chick·en-liv·ered (chĭk′ən-lĭv′ərd) *adj.* Cowardly; timid.

chicken pox. An acute contagious viral disease, usually of young children, characterized by skin eruption, slight fever, and mild constitutional symptoms. Also called "varicella." [Supposedly from the mildness of the disease.]

chicken shit. *Vulgar Slang.* **1.** Annoying duties or requirements regarded as unnecessary and demeaning. **2.** Petty, mean behavior or attitudes. **3.** Lying or empty talk worthy of scorn. —**chick′en-shit′** *adj.*

chicken wire. A light-gauge galvanized wire fencing, usually made with hexagonal mesh and used for bounding chicken runs and similar enclosures.

chick·pea (chĭk′pē′) *n.* **1.** A bushy plant, *Cicer arietenum,* grown in the Mediterranean region and central Asia and bearing edible seeds. **2.** One of the pealike seeds of this plant, widely used as food. Also called "garbanzo." [Earlier *chichpease* : Middle English *chiche,* chickpea, from Old French, from Latin *cicer*† + *pease,* PEA.]

chick·weed (chĭk′wēd′) *n.* Any of various plants of the genera *Cerastium* and *Stellaria;* especially, *S. media,* a low, weedy plant having small white flowers. [So called because it is eaten by chickens.]

chic·le (chĭk′əl) *n.* The coagulated milky juice of the sapodilla, used as the principal ingredient of chewing gum. [Spanish, from Nahuatl *chictli.*]

chi·co (chē′kō) *n., pl.* **-cos.** A species of greasewood, *Sarcobatus vermiculatus.* [Shortened from CHICALOTE.]

Chic·o·pee (chĭk′ə-pē). A city of southwestern Massachusetts, on the Connecticut River near Springfield. Population, 62,000.

chic·o·ry (chĭk′ər-ē) *n., pl.* **-ries.** Also **chic·co·ry. 1.** A plant, *Cichorium intybus,* having usually blue flowers and leaves, used in salads. **2.** The root of this plant, dried, roasted, and ground for mixing with coffee or as a coffee substitute. Also called "succory." See **endive.** [Middle English *cicoree,* from Old French, from Latin *cichorium,* from Greek *kikhora*†.]

chide (chīd) *v.* **chided** or **chid** (chĭd), **chided** or **chid** or **chidden** (chĭd′n), **chiding, chides.** —*intr.* To scold; rebuke; reprimand. —*tr.* **1.** To state one's disapproval of. **2.** To goad; impel. [Middle English *chiden,* Old English *cīdan,* from *cīd*†, strife.] —**chid′er** *n.* —**chid′ing·ly** *adv.*

chief (chēf) *n. Abbr.* **C., ch., Ch. 1.** One who is highest in rank or authority; a leader. **2.** *Usually capital* **C.** *Nautical.* A chief petty officer; the chief engineer of a ship. **3.** *Slang.* A boss. **4.** *Heraldry.* The upper section of a shield. **5.** *Rare.* The highest or most important part of something. —**in chief. 1.** Having the highest or most important position: *the commander in chief.* **2.** Chiefly. —*adj.* **1.** Highest in rank, authority, or office. **2.** Principal; most important. —*adv. Archaic.* Chiefly. [Middle English *chief, chef,* from Old French, from Vulgar Latin *capum* (unattested), from Latin *caput,* head. See **kaput** in Appendix.*]

Synonyms: *chief, principal, main, leading, foremost, primary, prime.* These adjectives, often interchangeable, refer to being first, either in rank or in importance. *Chief* most commonly applies to a person who is highest in rank and authority: *chief magistrate.* Used figuratively, *chief* implies maximum importance: *A man's chief concern is supporting his family. Principal* usually stresses importance of persons or things rather than personal authority, but can be applied to persons in the sense of rank or standing. *Main* usually applies to things with reference to importance: *main building on a campus; main event of a boxing program. Leading,* applicable to persons and things, often suggests in the former a record of achievement, personal magnetism, or capacity for influencing others. *Foremost* is closely related to *leading,* but more strongly emphasizes first position and the sense of forging ahead of others in a given field. *Primary,* applicable to things, stresses first in the sense of origin, sequence, or development: *primary school.* It can also mean first in the sense of basic or fundamental. *Prime* emphasizes first in authority, power, or quality: *prime minister; prime ribs of beef.*

chief justice. Also **Chief Justice.** *Abbr.* **C.J.** The presiding judge of a court of several judges, especially of the U.S. Supreme Court.

chief·ly (chēf′lē) *adv.* **1.** Above all; especially. **2.** Mostly; mainly. —*adj.* Of or similar to a chief.

chief of staff. *Abbr.* **C. of S., C.S. 1.** The ranking officer of the U.S. Army, Navy, or Air Force, responsible to the secretary of his branch and to the President. **2.** *Military.* The senior staff officer at the division level or higher.

chief of state. One who serves as the formal head of a nation.

chief·tain (chēf′tən) *n.* **1.** The leader of a clan or tribe. **2.** The leader or head of any group. [Middle English *chieftaine, cheftaine,* from Old French *chevetain,* from Late Latin *capitāneus,* from Latin *caput,* head. See **kaput** in Appendix.*]

chiff·chaff (chĭf′chăf′) *n.* A small European warbler, *Phylloscopus collybita,* with yellowish plumage. [Imitative of its cry.]

chif·fon (shĭ-fŏn′, shĭf′ŏn′) *n.* **1.** A fabric of sheer silk or rayon. **2.** *Usually plural.* Ribbons, laces, or other ornamental accessories for women's clothing. —*adj.* **1.** Of or relating to chiffon. **2.** *Cooking.* Having a light and fluffy consistency. [French, "rag," from *chiffe,* old rag, variant of Old French *chipe,* from Middle English *chip,* CHIP.]

chif·fo·nier (shĭf′ə-nîr′) *n.* Also **chif·fon·nier.** A narrow, high chest of drawers or bureau, often with a mirror attached. [French *chiffonnier,* "bureau for rags," from CHIFFON.]

chig·ger (chĭg′ər) *n.* **1.** Any of various small six-legged larvae of mites of the family Trombidiidae, causing intensely irritating itching when lodged on the skin. Also called "chigoe," "jigger," "harvest bug," "harvest mite." **2.** A flea, the **chigoe** *(see).* [Variant of CHIGOE.]

chi·gnon (shēn-yŏn′, shēn′yŏn′) *n.* A roll or knot of hair worn at the back of the head by women. [French, variant of Old French *chaignon,* chain, from Vulgar Latin *catēniō* (unattested), from Latin *catēna,* CATENA.]

chig·oe (chĭg′ō, chē′gō) *n. Zoology.* **1.** A small tropical flea, *Tunga penetrans,* of which the fertile female burrows under the skin, causing intense irritation and sores that may become severely infected. Also called "chigger," "jigger," "sand flea." **2.** A mite, the **chigger** *(see).* [Cariban *chigo.*]

Chih·li. The former name for **Hopei.**

Chih·li, Gulf of. The former name for the Gulf of **Po Hai.**

Chi·hua·hua[1] (chĭ-wä′wä, -wə). **1.** A state of Mexico, occupying 94,822 square miles in the northeast. Population, 1,374,000. **2.** The capital of this state, an industrial city in the center of the state. Population, 198,000.

Chi·hua·hua[2] (chĭ-wä′wä, -wə) *n.* A very small dog of a breed originating in Mexico, having pointed ears and a smooth coat. [From CHIHUAHUA.]

chil·blain (chĭl′blān′) *n.* An inflammation followed by itchy irritation on the hands, feet, or ears, resulting from exposure to moist cold. [CHIL(L) + BLAIN.] —**chil′blained** *adj.*

child (chīld) *n., pl.* **children** (chĭl′drən). **1.** *Abbr.* **ch.** Any person between birth and puberty. **2. a.** An unborn infant; fetus. **b.** An infant; a baby. **3.** One who is childish or immature. **4.** A son or daughter; an offspring. **5.** *Plural.* In Biblical usage, members of a tribe; descendants. **6.** The figurative offspring of anything: *a child of nature.* —**with child.** Pregnant. [Child, children; Middle English *child(e), childre(ns),* Old English *cild, cildra,* from Common Germanic *kiltham* (unattested).] —**child′less** *adj.* —**child′less·ness** *n.*

child·bear·ing (chīld′bâr′ĭng) *n.* The process of parturition.

child·bed (chīld′bĕd′) *n.* The state of a woman in childbirth.

childbed fever. Puerperal fever *(see).*

child·birth (chīld′bûrth′) *n.* Parturition.

childe (chīld) *n. Archaic.* A child of noble birth. [Middle English *child(e),* childe, CHILD.]

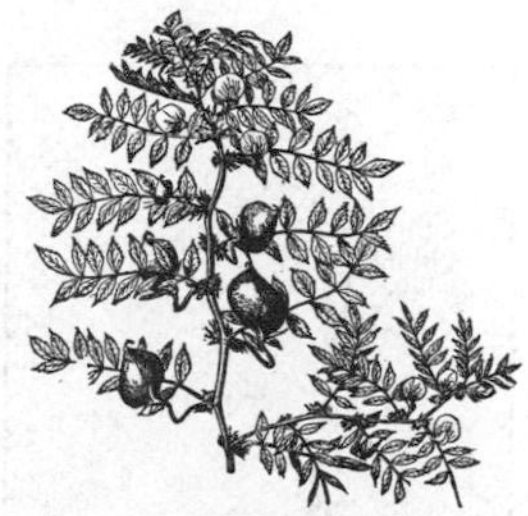

chickpea

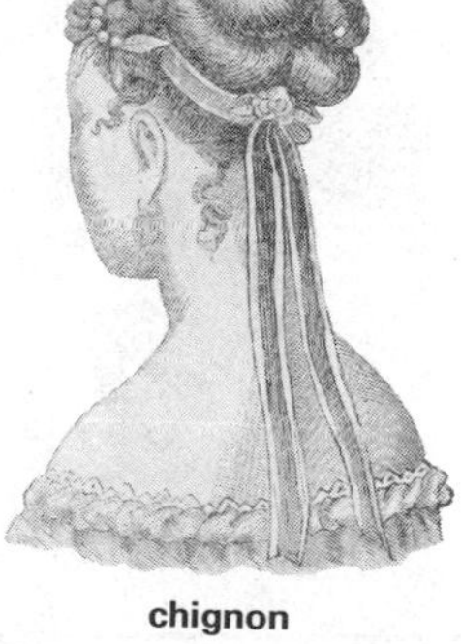

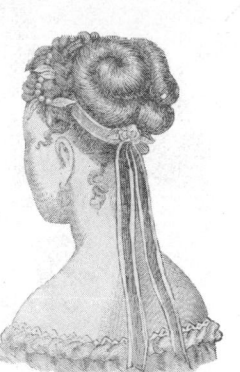

chignon

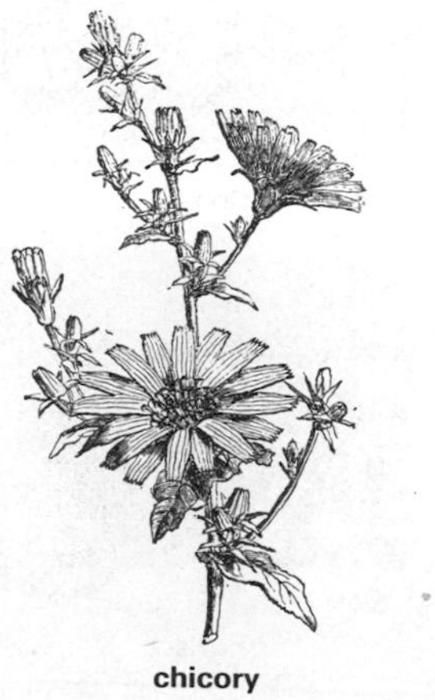

chicory

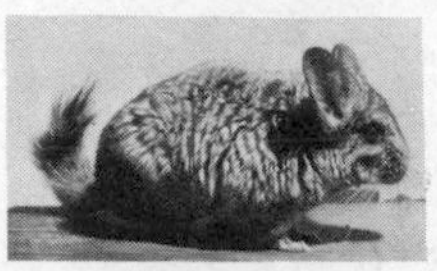
chinchilla

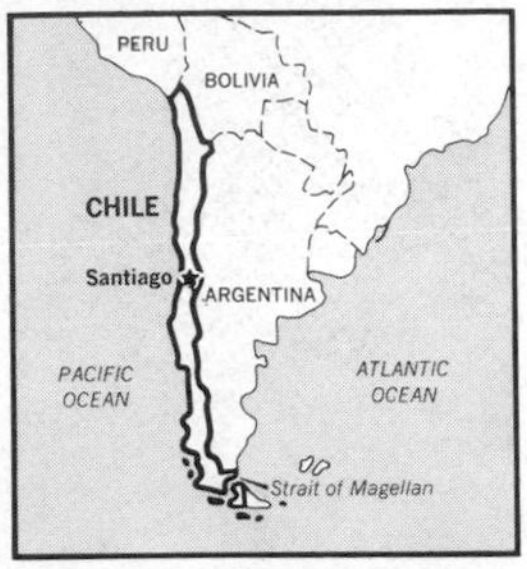

Chile

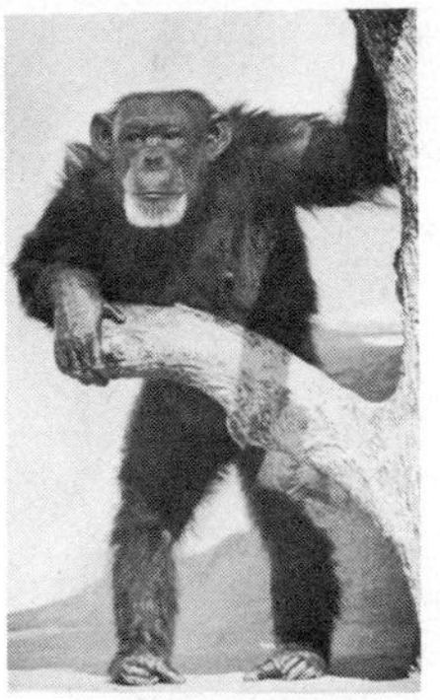
chimpanzee

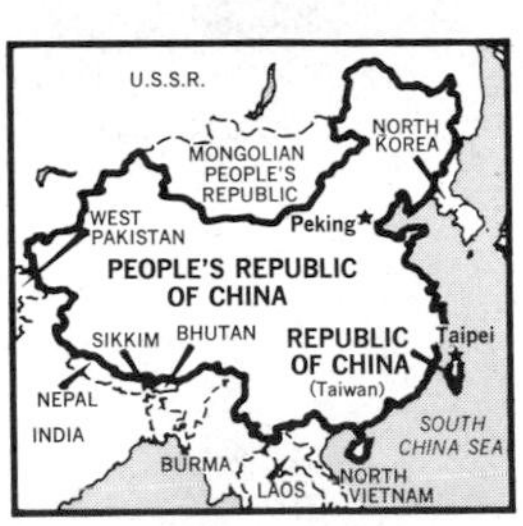

China

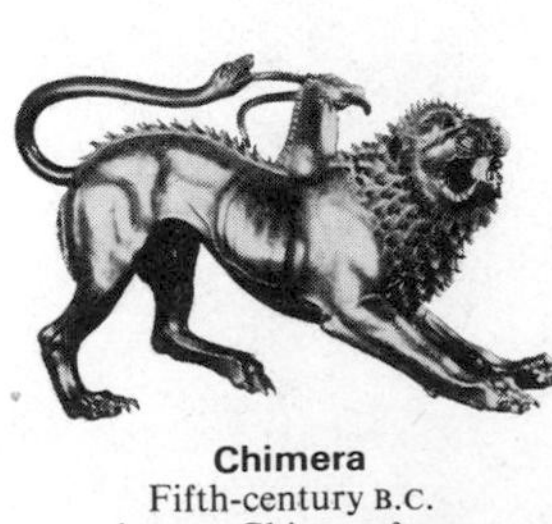
Chimera
Fifth-century B.C.
bronze Chimera from
Arezzo, Italy

child·hood (chīld′ho͝od′) *n.* The time or state of being a child.
child·ish (chīl′dĭsh) *adj.* **1.** Of, similar to, or suitable for a child. **2.** Foolish; puerile. —**child′ish·ly** *adv.* —**child′ish·ness** *n.*
Usage: Childish applied to adults is almost invariably a term of reproach but lacks such connotation when applied to children. *Childlike* is generally favorable on all age levels, suggesting endearing traits characteristic of children.
child labor. The full-time employment of children under a minimum legal age.
child·like (chīld′līk′) *adj.* Also *rare* **child·ly** (chīld′lē). Like or befitting a child, as in innocence. See Usage note at **childish.**
chil·dren. Plural of **child.**
Children of Israel. The Jews; Hebrews.
child's play. Anything that is very easy to do; a trivial matter.
Chil·e (chĭl′ē; *Spanish* chē′lā). Officially, Republic of Chile. A republic of western South America, with an area of 286,297 square miles, stretching from Peru to the southern tip of the continent. Population, 8,515,000. Capital, Santiago de Chile. —**Chil′e·an** (chĭl′ē-ən) *adj.* & *n.*
chil·e con car·ne (chĭl′ē kŏn kär′nē). Also **chil·i con car·ne.** A highly spiced dish made of red peppers, meat, and sometimes beans. Also called "chili." [Spanish, "chili with meat."]
Chile saltpeter. *Chemistry.* **Sodium nitrate** *(see).*
chil·i (chĭl′ē) *n., pl.* **-ies.** Also **chil·e, chil·li. 1. a.** The very pungent fruit of several varieties of a woody plant, *Capsicum frutescens.* **b.** A condiment made from the dried fruits of this plant. **2. Chile con carne** *(see).* [Spanish *chile, chili,* from Nahuatl *chilli.*]
chil·i·ad (kĭl′ē-ăd′) *n.* **1.** A group containing 1,000 elements. **2.** One thousand years. [Late Latin *chīliās* (stem *chīliad-*), from Greek *khilias,* thousand, from *khilioi,* thousand. See **gheslo-** in Appendix.*]
chil·i·asm (kĭl′ē-ăz′əm) *n. Theology.* The doctrine stating that Christ will reign on earth for 1,000 years. [New Latin *chilasmus,* probably from Greek *khiliasmos,* from *khilias,* CHILIAD.] —**chil′i·ast′** (-ăst′) *n.* —**chil′i·as′tic** *adj.*
chili sauce. A spiced sauce made with chilies and tomatoes.
Chil·koot Pass (chĭl′ko͞ot′). A pass in the Rocky Mountains of southeastern Alaska, extending about 30 miles to the southwestern Yukon Territory, Canada.
chill (chĭl) *n.* **1.** A moderate but penetrating coldness. **2.** A sensation of coldness, as with a fever. **3.** A checking or dampening of enthusiasm, spirit, or joy. **4.** A sudden numbing fear or dread. —*adj.* **1.** Chilly. **2.** Dispiriting; discouraging: *"Chill penury repressed their noble rage."* (Gray). —*v.* **chilled, chilling, chills.** —*tr.* **1.** To affect with cold. **2.** To discourage; dispirit. **3.** To lower in temperature. **4.** *Metallurgy.* To harden a metallic surface by rapid cooling. —*intr.* **1.** To be seized with cold. **2.** To become cold: *This jelly chills quickly.* **3.** *Metallurgy.* To become hard by rapid cooling. [Middle English *chile, chele,* frost, Old English *c(i)ele.* See **gel-**[3] in Appendix.*] —**chill′ing·ly** *adv.* —**chill′ness** *n.*
chill·er (chĭl′ər) *n.* One that chills or frightens; a thriller.
chill·y (chĭl′ē) *adj.* **-ier, -iest. 1.** Cool or cold enough to cause shivering. **2.** Seized with cold; shivering. **3.** Distant and cool; unfriendly. —**chill′i·ly** *adv.* —**chill′i·ness** *n.*
Chi·lo·e (chē′lō-ā′). An island of Chile, 4,700 square miles in area, lying in the Pacific off the southwestern coast.
chi·lo·pod (kī′lə-pŏd′) *n.* Any of various arthropods of the class Chilopoda, which includes the centipedes. [New Latin *Chilopoda,* "foot jaws" (the foremost pair of legs are jawlike appendages) : Greek *kheilos,* lip (see **ghelunā** in Appendix*) + -POD.]
Chil·tern Hills (chĭl′tərn). A range of chalk hills in south-central England, extending 45 miles northeast from the Thames River.
Chil·tern Hundreds (chĭl′tərn). *British.* A now merely formal office applied for by Members of Parliament when they wish to resign from the House of Commons. [CHILTERN (HILLS) + HUNDRED(S) (administrative division).]
Chi·lung. See **Keelung.**
Chim·bo·ra·zo (chĭm′bə-rä′zō, shĭm′-; *Spanish* chēm′bō-rä′sō). The highest mountain of Ecuador (20,561 feet), in the western range of the Andes.
chime[1] (chīm) *n.* **1.** An apparatus for striking a bell or bells to produce a musical sound. **2.** *Usually plural.* A set of bells tuned to the musical scale and used as an orchestral instrument. **3.** A single bell. **4.** The musical sound produced by a bell or bells. **5.** Agreement; accord. —*v.* **chimed, chiming, chimes.** —*intr.* **1.** To sound with a harmonious ring when struck. **2.** To make a musical sound by striking a chime. **3.** To agree; harmonize. Usually used with *with.* —*tr.* **1.** To produce (music) by striking, as a bell. **2.** To strike (a bell) to produce music. **3.** To make known (the hour) by ringing bells. **4.** To call, send, or welcome by ringing bells. —**chime in. 1.** To break into, as a conversation; interrupt. **2.** To join in harmoniously. [Middle English *chime, chimbe,* cymbal, chime, perhaps from Old French *chimbe,* from Latin *cymbalum,* CYMBAL.] —**chim′er** *n.*
chime[2] (chīm) *n.* Also **chimb** (chīm), **chine** (chīn). The rim of a cask. [Middle English *chimbe,* Old English *cim(b)-.* See **gembh-** in Appendix.*]
chi·me·ra (kī-mîr′ə, kə-) *n.* Also **chi·mae·ra** (for sense 1). **1.** *Capital* **C.** *Greek Mythology.* A fire-breathing monster represented with the head of a lion, the body of a goat, and the tail of a serpent. **2.** A creation of the imagination; an impossible and foolish fancy. **3.** *Biology.* An organism, especially a plant, containing tissues from at least two genetically distinct parents. [Latin *Chimaera,* from Greek *khimaira,* chimera, "she-goat." See **ghei-**[2] in Appendix.*]
chi·mer·i·cal (kī-mĕr′ĭ-kəl, -mîr′ĭ-kəl, kə-) *adj.* Also **chi·mer·ic** (kī-mĕr′ĭk, -mîr′ĭk). **1.** Like a chimera; imaginary; unreal. **2.** Given to unrealistic fantasies. —**chi·mer′i·cal·ly** *adv.*
chim·ney (chĭm′nē) *n.* **1.** A passage through which smoke and gases escape from a fire or furnace; flue. **2. a.** The usually vertical structure containing a flue. **b.** The part of such a structure that rises above a roof. **3.** *Chiefly British.* A smokestack, as of a ship or locomotive. **4.** A glass tube for enclosing the flame of a lamp. **5.** Anything resembling a chimney, such as a narrow cleft in a cliff. [Middle English *chimenee,* from Old French *cheminee,* from Late Latin *caminata,* from Latin *camīnus,* furnace, from Greek *kaminos*†.]
chim·ney·piece (chĭm′nē-pēs′) *n.* **1.** The mantel of a fireplace. **2.** A decoration over a fireplace.
chimney pot. A pipe placed on the top of a chimney to improve the draft.
chimney sweep. Also **chimney sweeper.** A worker employed at cleaning soot from chimneys.
chimney swift. A small, dark, swallowlike New World bird, *Chaetura pelagica,* that frequently nests in chimneys.
chimp (chĭmp) *n. Informal.* A chimpanzee.
chim·pan·zee (chĭm′păn-zē′, chĭm-păn′zē) *n.* An anthropoid ape, *Pan troglodytes,* of tropical Africa, having dark hair, gregarious, somewhat arboreal habits, and a high degree of intelligence. [Native West African name.]
chin (chĭn) *n.* The central forward portion of the lower jaw. —*v.* **chinned, chinning, chins.** —*tr.* **1.** To pull (oneself) up with the arms while grasping an overhead horizontal bar until one's chin is level with the bar. **2.** To place (a violin) under the chin. —*intr.* **1.** *Informal.* To chatter. **2.** To chin oneself. [Middle English *chin,* Old English *cin(n).* See **genu-**[2] in Appendix.*]
Chin. China; Chinese.
chi·na (chī′nə) *n.* **1.** High quality porcelain or ceramic ware, originally made in China. **2.** Any porcelain ware. Also called "chinaware." —*adj.* Made of china.
Chi·na (chī′nə). *Abbr.* **Ch., Chin.** A country occupying 3,782,612 square miles in east-central Asia, which has in consequence of civil war been divided since 1949 into two political entities: **a.** Officially, People's Republic of China. A republic occupying the 3,768,727 square miles comprising the territory of China proper. Population, 800,000,000. Capital, Peking. **b.** Officially, Republic of China. A republic, 13,885 square miles in area, occupying Taiwan and nearby smaller islands. Population, 12,429,000. Capital, Taipei. [Sixteenth-century English, ultimately from Sanskrit *Chīna,* said to be from Chinese *Ch'in*[2], a dynastic name (255–204 B.C.) of the country. See **Sino-.**]
China aster. A plant, *Callistephus chinensis,* native to China, widely cultivated for its showy, variously colored flowers.
chi·na·ber·ry (chī′nə-bĕr′ē) *n., pl.* **-ries. 1.** A spreading tree, *Melia azedarach,* native to Asia, widely grown for its white or purple flower clusters. Also called "China tree," "azedarach." **2.** A soapberry tree, *Sapindus marginatus* (or *S. saponaria*), of the West Indies, Mexico, and the southwestern United States. **3.** The fruit of either of these trees.
Chi·na·man (chī′nə-mən) *n., pl.* **-men** (-mĭn). A Chinese man. An offensive or patronizing term.
Chi·nan. See **Tsinan.**
China rose. A shrub, *Rosa chinensis,* that has fragrant red or pink flowers and is the original ancestor of many cultivated hybrid roses.
China Sea. A western portion of the Pacific Ocean along the eastern coast of Asia, extending from southern Japan to the Malay Peninsula. See **East China Sea, South China Sea.**
Chi·na·town (chī′nə-toun′) *n.* A neighborhood inhabited by Chinese people.
chin·ca·pin. Variant of **chinquapin.**
chinch (chĭnch) *n. Regional.* A bedbug. [Spanish *chinche,* from Latin *cīmex* (stem *cīmic-*), bug. See **cimex.**]
chinch bug. A small black and white insect, *Blissus leucopterus,* that is very destructive to grains and grasses.
chin·che·rin·chee (chĭng′kə-rĭn-chē′) *n.* Also **chin·ke·rin·chee.** A bulbous plant, *Ornithogalum thyrsoides,* of southern Africa, having long clusters or spikes of white or yellow flowers. [Origin unknown.]
chin·chil·la (chĭn-chĭl′ə) *n.* **1.** A squirrellike rodent, *Chinchilla laniger,* native to the mountains of South America and widely raised in captivity for its soft pale-gray fur. **2.** The fur of this animal. **3.** A thick, twilled cloth of wool and cotton, used for overcoats. [Spanish, probably from Aymara.]
Chin·chow (jĭn′jō′). An industrial city of northeastern China, in southwestern Liaoning Province. Population, 400,000.
Chin·co·teague Bay (shĭng′kə-tēg′, chĭng′-). A long, narrow bay in northeastern Virginia and southeastern Maryland, separating Assateague Island from the mainland.
Chincoteague pony. A type of small, inbred North American horse that runs wild on certain islands off the Virginia coast. [From *Chincoteague* Island, Chincoteague Bay, where the breed developed.]
chin·cough (chĭn′kôf′, -kŏf′) *n.* **Whooping cough** *(see).* [By folk etymology (influenced by CHINE, spine) from CHINK (sound) + COUGH.]
chine[1] (chīn) *n.* **1.** The backbone; spine. **2.** A cut of meat containing part of the backbone. **3.** A ridge or crest. **4.** The line of intersection between the side and bottom of a flatbottom or V-bottom boat. [Middle English *chyne,* from Old French *eschine,* probably from Germanic. See **skei-** in Appendix.*]
chine[2]. Variant of **chime** (barrel rim).
Chi·nese (chī-nēz′, -nēs′) *adj. Abbr.* **Ch., Chin.** Of or pertaining to China, its culture, people, or languages. —*n., pl.* **Chinese.**

ă pat/ā pay/âr care/ä father/b bib/ch church/d deed/ĕ pet/ē be/f fife/g gag/h hat/hw which/ĭ pit/ī pie/îr pier/j judge/k kick/l lid, needle/m mum/n no, sudden/ng thing/ŏ pot/ō toe/ô paw, for/oi noise/ou out/o͝o took/o͞o boot/p pop/r roar/s sauce/sh ship, dish/

1. a. A native or inhabitant of China. b. A person of Chinese ancestry. 2. One of a group of Sino-Tibetan languages and dialects spoken in China, including Mandarin, Cantonese, Fukien, Amoy, and Shanghai. 3. Mandarin, the standard language of China.
Chinese anise. A tree, the **star anise** *(see)*, or its fruit.
Chinese cabbage. A Chinese plant, *Brassica pekinensis*, related to the common cabbage, having a cylindrical head of crisp, edible leaves. Also called "celery cabbage," "pe-tsai."
Chinese calendar. The lunar calendar of the Chinese people. See **calendar.**
Chinese Chippendale. Chippendale furniture characterized by certain Oriental influences.
Chinese date. A tree, the **jujube** *(see)*, or its fruit.
Chinese evergreen. A plant, *Aglaonema simplex*, of tropical Asia, that has glossy, pointed green leaves and is widely grown as a house plant. Also called "Japanese leaf."
Chinese gooseberry. A plant, the **kiwi** *(see)*, or its fruit.
Chinese houses. A plant, *Collinsia bicolor*, of California, having showy white and rose-purple flowers.
Chinese ink. **India ink** *(see)*.
Chinese lantern. 1. A decorative, collapsible lantern of thin, brightly colored paper. 2. One of the papery, inflated seed cases of the **winter cherry** *(see)*.
Chinese lantern plant. The **winter cherry** *(see)*.
Chinese puzzle. 1. A very intricate puzzle. 2. Any very difficult problem.
Chinese red. **Vermilion** *(see)*.
Chinese Revolution. 1. The revolution of 1911–12 in which the Republic of China was founded. 2. The revolution culminating in the proclamation of the People's Republic of China (1949).
Chinese sacred lily. A variety of the polyanthus narcissus, *Narcissus tazetta orientalis*, that has fragrant yellow and white flowers and is frequently grown as a house plant.
Chinese Tur·ke·stan. See **Turkestan.**
Chinese white. A paint pigment, **zinc oxide** *(see)*.
Chinese windlass. *Machinery.* A **differential windlass** *(see)*.
Chinese wood oil. **Tung oil** *(see)*.
Ch'ing. See **Manchu.**
Ching·ford (chĭng′fərd). A former administrative division of London, England, now part of **Waltham Forest** *(see)*.
Ch'ing-hai, Ching·hai. See **Tsinghai.**
Chin Hills (chĭn). A mountainous region of western Burma, along the border with Assam, Republic of India. Highest elevation, Mt. Victoria (10,018 feet).
Chin·ju (jĭn′jo͞o′). A city of South Korea, in a cotton-producing area, about 55 miles west of Pusan. Population, 77,000.
chink[1] (chĭngk) *n.* A crack or fissure; narrow opening. —*tr.v.* **chinked, chinking, chinks.** 1. To make chinks in. 2. To fill cracks or chinks in. [Perhaps variant of earlier *chine*, from Middle English *chine*, crack, Old English *cinu, cine.* See **gēi-**[1] in Appendix.*] —**chink′y** *adj.*
chink[2] (chĭngk) *n.* A short, metallic sound. —*v.* **chinked, chinking, chinks.** —*tr.* To strike (something) and make this sound. —*intr.* To produce this sound. [Imitative.]
Chink (chĭngk) *n. Slang.* A Chinese. An offensive term used derogatorily. [Perhaps from CHINESE (influenced by CHINK, crevice, supposedly a reference to narrow slanting eyes).]
chin·ke·rin·chee. Variant of **chincherinchee.**
Chin·nam·po (chē′näm′pō). Also **Nam·po** (näm′pō). A city of southwestern North Korea, on Korea Bay, 25 miles southwest of Pyongyang.
Chin·ne·reth, Sea of. The Old Testament name for the Sea of **Galilee.**
chi·no (chē′nō, shē′-) *n., pl.* **-nos.** 1. A coarse, twilled cotton fabric used for uniforms and sports clothes. 2. *Plural.* Boys' and men's trousers of this material. [American Spanish *chino*†, "toasted" (from its original tan color).]
chi·noi·se·rie (shē-nwȧz-rē′) *n. French.* 1. A style in art reflecting Chinese influence through use of elaborate decoration and intricate patterns. 2. An object in this style.
Chi·nook (shə-no͝ok′, chə-) *n., pl.* **Chinook** or **-nooks.** 1. A tribe of North American Indians formerly inhabiting the Columbia River basin in Oregon and speaking one of the Chinookan languages. 2. A member of this tribe. 3. The language of this tribe. 4. *Small* **c.** A moist, warm wind blowing from the sea on the Oregon and Washington coasts. 5. *Small* **c.** A warm, dry wind that descends from the eastern slopes of the Rocky Mountains, causing a rapid rise in temperature. [Salish *c'inuk.*]
Chi·nook·an (shə-no͝ok′ən, chə-) *n.* A North American Indian language family of Washington and Oregon. —*adj.* Of or pertaining to the Chinook Indians, their language, or their culture.
Chinook jargon. A language combining simple English, French, Chinookan, and other Indian dialects, formerly used by Indians and fur traders of the Pacific Northwest.
Chinook salmon. A salmon, *Oncorhynchus tshawytscha*, of northern Pacific waters, valued as a food fish. Also called "king salmon," "quinnat salmon."
chin·qua·pin (chĭng′kə-pĭn′) *n.* Also **chin·ca·pin, chin·ka·pin.** 1. A small, shrubby tree, *Castanea pumila*, of the eastern United States. 2. A large evergreen tree, *Castanopsis chrysophella*, of the Pacific Coast of North America. Also called "giant chinquapin." 3. The nut of either of these trees. [Of Algonquian origin, akin to Algonquian (Virginia) *chechinkamin*, chestnut.]
chintz (chĭnts) *n.* Also **chints.** A printed and glazed cotton fabric, usually of bright colors. [Variant of earlier *chints*, plural of *chint*, from Hindi *chīnt*, from Sanskrit *citra*, many-colored, bright. See **skai-** in Appendix.*]
chintz·y (chĭnt′sē) *adj.* **-ier, -iest.** 1. Of or relating to, or decorated with chintz. 2. Gaudy; trashy; cheap.
Chin·wang·tao (chĭn′hwäng′dou′). A seaport of China, in northeastern Hopei, on the Gulf of Po Hai. Population, 210,000.
Chi·os (kē′ŏs′, kī′-). 1. A Greek island, about 350 square miles in area, in the Aegean Sea off the western coast of Turkey. 2. The capital and chief port of this island. Population, 22,000.
chip[1] (chĭp) *n.* 1. A small piece broken or cut off. 2. A crack or other mark caused by chipping. 3. A small disk or counter, used in poker and other games to represent money. 4. *Electronics.* A minute square of a thin semiconducting material, such as silicon or germanium, doped and otherwise processed to have specified electrical characteristics; especially, such a square before attachment of electrical leads and packaging as an electronic component or integrated circuit. 5. A thin slice of edible material: *a potato chip.* 6. *Plural.* French-fried potatoes. *Chiefly British* except in the phrase *fish and chips.* 7. Wood, palm leaves, straw, or similar material, cut and dried for weaving. 8. A fragment of dried animal dung, used as fuel. 9. Anything that is worthless. —*v.* **chipped, chipping, chips.** —*tr.* 1. To break a small piece from; to fragment. 2. To chop or cut with an ax or other implement. 3. To shape or carve by cutting or chopping. —*intr.* To become broken off. —**chip in.** *Informal.* 1. To contribute money, labor, or the like. 2. To interject; interrupt. 3. To put up chips or money as one's bet in poker and other games. [Middle English *chip*, Old English *cipp*†, beam, piece cut off a beam.]
chip[2] (chĭp) *intr.v.* **chipped, chipping, chips.** To cheep, as a bird. —*n.* A chirp, as made by some birds. [Imitative.]
chip[3] (chĭp) *n. Wrestling.* A trick method of throwing one's opponent. [Perhaps ultimately from Old Norse *kippr*, a pull, from *kippa*†, to pull, snatch.]
Chip·e·wy·an (chĭp′ə-wī′ən) *n., pl.* **Chipewyan** or **-ans.** Also **Chip·pe·wai·an, Chip·pe·wy·an.** 1. A tribe of Athapascan-speaking North American Indians living in Canada in the area between Great Slave Lake and Lake Athabasca on the west and Hudson Bay on the east. 2. A member of this tribe. 3. The language spoken by this tribe. [Cree *čīpwayān*, "pointed skin," parka wearer : *cīpw-*, pointed + *-ayān*, skin.]
chip·munk (chĭp′mŭngk′) *n.* A small rodent, *Tamias striatus*, of eastern North America, or any of several similar rodents of the genus *Eutamias*, of western North America and northern Asia, resembling a squirrel but smaller and having a striped back. Compare **ground squirrel.** [Variant of earlier *chitmunk*, from Algonquian.]
chipped beef. Dried beef smoked and sliced very thin.
Chip·pen·dale (chĭp′ən-dāl′) *adj.* Of, pertaining to, or designating a type of furniture characterized by flowing lines and rococo ornamentation. [After Thomas *Chippendale* (1718–1779), English cabinetmaker.]
chip·per[1] (chĭp′ər) *n.* A person or thing that chips or cuts.
chip·per[2] (chĭp′ər) *intr.v.* **-pered, -pering, -pers.** 1. To chirp or twitter, as a bird. 2. To babble. [From CHIP (to chirp).]
chip·per[3] (chĭp′ər) *adj. Informal.* Active; cheerful; brisk; pert. See Synonyms at **nimble.** [Origin obscure.]
Chip·pe·wa (chĭp′ə-wô′, -wä′, -wā′) *n., pl.* **Chippewa** or **-was.** Also **Chip·pe·way** (-wā′). **Ojibwa** *(see)*.
Chip·pe·wa River (chĭp′ə-wô′, -wä′). A river rising in northwestern Wisconsin and flowing about 180 miles south and southwest to the Mississippi at the Minnesota border.
chipping sparrow. A small North American sparrow, *Spizella passerina*, having a reddish-brown crown.
chip·py (chĭp′ē) *n., pl.* **-pies.** 1. The chipping sparrow. 2. *Slang.* A prostitute. [From CHIP (to chirp).]
chip shot. *Golf.* A short, lofted stroke, used in approaching the green. Also called "chip."
Chi·re. The Portuguese name for the **Shire.**
chi-rho (kī′rō, kē′-) *n.* A monogram and symbol for Christ, consisting of the superimposed Greek letters chi (X) and rho (P), often embroidered on altar cloths and clerical vestments. [CHI + RHO, first two letters of Greek *khristos*, CHRIST.]
chiro–. Indicates of or with the hand; for example, **chiropractic.** [Latin, from Greek *kheir*, hand. See **ghesor-** in Appendix.*]
chi·rog·ra·phy (kī-rŏg′rə-fē) *n.* **Penmanship** *(see)*. [French *chirographie*, from Old French *chirographe*, autograph, from Latin *chīrographum*, from Greek *kheirographon*, holograph, manuscript, from *kheirographos*, written with one's own hand : CHIRO- + -GRAPH.] —**chi·rog′ra·pher** *n.* —**chi′ro·graph′ic** (kī′rə-grăf′ĭk), **chi′ro·graph′i·cal** *adj.*
chi·ro·man·cy (kī′rə-măn′sē) *n.* The art or practice of foretelling a person's future by studying the palm of his hand; palmistry. [Middle English *ciromancie*, from Medieval Latin *chiromantia*, from Greek *kheiromantis*, palmist : CHIRO- + *mantis*, seer, diviner (see **-mancy**).] —**chi′ro·man′cer** *n.*
Chi·ron (kī′rŏn′). *Greek Mythology.* The wise centaur who tutored Achilles, Hercules, and Asclepius.
chi·rop·o·dy (kə-rŏp′ə-dē, shə-) *n. Medicine.* **Podiatry** *(see)*. [From New Latin *chiropodologia*, treatment of hand and foot ailments : CHIRO- + -POD + -LOGY.] —**chi·rop′o·dist** *n.*
chi·ro·prac·tic (kī′rə-prăk′tĭk) *n.* A system of therapy in which disease is considered the result of neural malfunction and manipulation of the spinal column and other bodily structures is the preferred method of treatment. [CHIRO- + Greek *praktikos*, effective, PRACTICAL.] —**chi′ro·prac′tor** (-tər) *n.*
chi·rop·ter·an (kī-rŏp′tər-ən) *n.* A flying mammal of the order Chiroptera, which includes the bats. [From New Latin *Chiroptera* : CHIRO- + -PTER.] —**chi·rop′ter·an** *adj.*

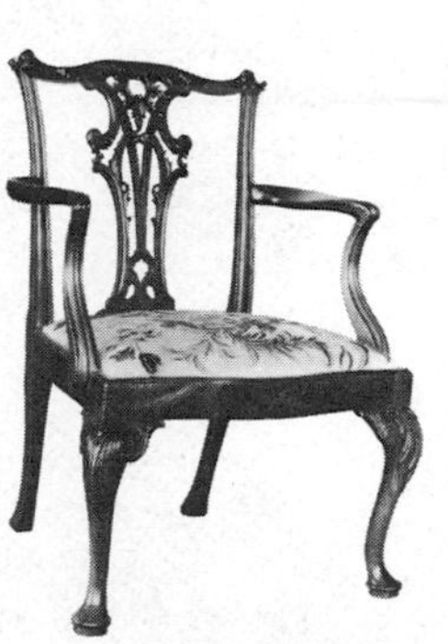

Chippendale
Chippendale armchair made of mahogany

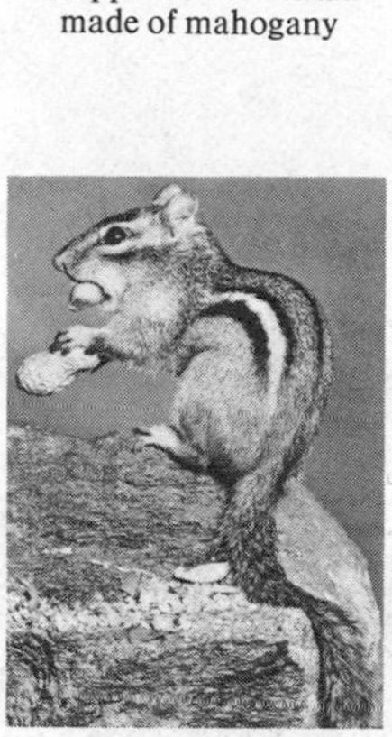

chipmunk
Tamias striatus
Eastern chipmunk

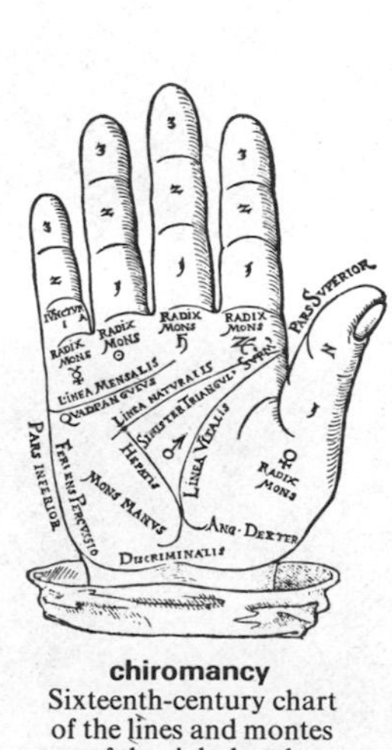

chiromancy
Sixteenth-century chart of the lines and montes of the right hand

chirp (chûrp) *v.* **chirped, chirping, chirps.** —*intr.* **1.** To utter a short, high-pitched sound, as a small bird; tweet; peep. **2.** To speak in a quick, sprightly manner. —*tr.* To utter with a short, high-pitched sound. —*n.* A short, high-pitched sound; a tweet; a peep. [Middle English *chirpen* (attested only in gerund *chirpinge*), to chirp, twitter (imitative).] —**chirp′er** *n.*

chirr (chûr) *intr.v.* **chirred, chirring, chirrs.** To make a harsh, trilled sound, as a cricket does. —*n.* A harsh, trilling sound, such as that made by crickets. [Imitative.]

chir·rup (chûr′əp, chĭr′-) *v.* **-ruped, -ruping, -rups.** —*intr.* **1.** To utter a series of chirps; to twitter. **2.** To make clicking, clucking sounds with the lips, as in urging on a horse. —*tr.* **1.** To sound with chirps. **2.** To make clucking sounds to. —*n.* **1.** A series of chirps; a twitter. **2.** A series of clucks or clicking sounds, such as those made to urge on a horse. [Variant of CHIRP.]

chi·rur·geon (kī-rûr′jən) *n. Archaic.* A surgeon. [Middle English *cirurgien, surgien,* SURGEON.]

chis·el (chĭz′əl) *n.* A metal tool with a sharp, beveled edge, used to cut and shape stone, wood, or metal. —*v.* **chiseled, -eling, -els.** Also *chiefly British* **-elled, -elling.** —*tr.* **1.** To shape or cut with a chisel. **2.** *Slang.* **a.** To cheat or swindle. **b.** To obtain by deception. —*intr.* **1.** To use a chisel. **2.** *Slang.* To use unethical methods; cheat. [Middle English, from Old North French, from Vulgar Latin *cīsellus, caesellus* (both unattested), diminutive formation from *caedere* (past participle *caesus*), to cut. See **skhai-** in Appendix.*] —**chis′el·er** *n.*

Chi·shi·ma Ret·to. The Japanese name for the **Kurile Islands.**

Chis·holm Trail (chĭz′əm). A former cattle trail from San Antonio, Texas, to Abilene, Kansas. [After Jesse *Chisholm* (1806–1868), Indian trader.]

Chi·şi·nău. The Rumanian name for **Kishinev.**

Chis·le·hurst and Sid·cup (chĭz′əl-hûrst′; sĭd′kəp). A former administrative division of London, England, of which one portion is now part of **Bexley** *(see),* and another portion is part of **Bromley** *(see).*

chit[1] (chĭt) *n.* **1.** A statement of an amount owed for food and drink; a check; bill. **2.** *Chiefly British.* A short letter; note. [Short for earlier *chitty,* from Hindi *ciṭṭha,* note, pass, from Sanskrit *citra,* bright, variegated. See **skai-** in Appendix.*]

chit[2] (chĭt) *n.* A child, especially a pert girl. [Middle English *chitte*†, young animal.]

Chi·ta (chĭ-tä′). A city of the Soviet Union, a major industrial center on the Trans-Siberian Railroad east of Ulan-Ude. Population, 198,000.

chi·tal (chē′təl) *n.* The **axis deer** *(see).* [Hindi *cītal,* from Sanskrit *citrala,* spotted, from *citra,* bright, variegated. See **skai-** in Appendix.*]

chit·chat (chĭt′chăt′) *n.* **1.** Casual conversation; small talk. **2.** Gossip. —*intr.v.* **chitchatted, -chatting, -chats.** To indulge in small talk. [Dissimilated reduplication of CHAT.]

chi·tin (kī′tĭn) *n.* A semitransparent horny substance, primarily a mucopolysaccharide, forming the principal component of crustacean shells, insect exoskeletons, and the cell walls of certain fungi. [French *chitine,* from New Latin CHITON (mollusk).] —**chi′tin·ous** *adj.*

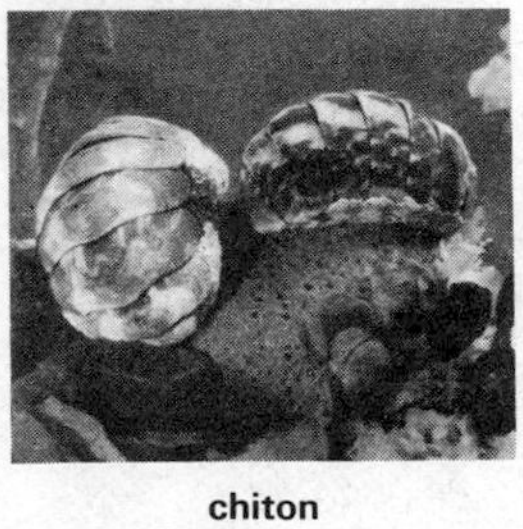

chiton
Genus *Chiton*

chi·ton (kīt′n, kī′tŏn′) *n.* **1.** A tunic worn by men and women in ancient Greece. **2.** Any of various marine mollusks of the class Amphineyra, living on rocks and having shells consisting of eight overlapping transverse plates. Sometimes called "sea cradle." [New Latin, mollusk (with tuniclike shell), from Greek *khitōn,* tunic, from Semitic, akin to Hebrew *kəthōnet.*]

Chi·tral (chĭ-träl′). A river rising in northern West Pakistan and flowing 300 miles generally south to the Kabul in Afghanistan.

Chit·ta·gong (chĭt′ə-gŏng′, -gông′). The principal port of East Pakistan, on the Karnaphuli River, 12 miles from the Bay of Bengal. Population, 364,000.

chit·tam·wood (chĭt′əm-wo͝od′) *n.* Any of various North American trees, especially a **smoke tree** *(see).* [Probably a Muskhogean word, akin to Choctaw *shitimmi,* to puff.]

chit·ter (chĭt′ər) *intr.v.* **-tered, -tering, -ters.** To twitter or chatter, as a bird. [Middle English *chiteren* (imitative).]

chit·ter·lings (chĭt′lĭnz) *pl.n.* Also **chit·lins, chit·lings.** The small intestines of pigs, cooked and eaten as food. [Middle English *chiterling,* probably diminutive of Old English *cieter* (unattested), intestines. See **ku-** in Appendix.*]

chiv. Variant of **shiv.**

chiv·al·ric (shĭ-văl′rĭk, shĭv′əl-) *adj.* Chivalrous.

chiv·al·rous (shĭv′əl-rəs) *adj.* **1.** Having the qualities of gallantry and honor attributed to an ideal knight. **2.** Of or pertaining to chivalry. —**chiv′al·rous·ly** *adv.* —**chiv′al·rous·ness** *n.*

chiv·al·ry (shĭv′əl-rē) *n., pl.* **-ries. 1. a.** The medieval institution of knighthood. **b.** The principles and customs of this institution. **2. a.** The qualities idealized by knighthood, such as bravery, courtesy, and honesty. **b.** The manifestation of any of these qualities. **3.** A group of knights or gallant gentlemen. [Middle English *chivalrie,* from Old French *chevalerie,* knightliness, from *chevalier,* knight, from Late Latin *caballārius,* horseman, CAVALIER.]

chiv·a·ree. Variant of **charivari.**

chive (chīv) *n.* **1.** A plant, *Allium schoenoprasum,* native to Eurasia, having purplish flowers and hollow, grasslike leaves. **2.** *Usually plural.* The leaves of this plant, used as a seasoning. [Middle English *cyve, cheve,* from Old French *cive,* from Latin *cēpa,* onion, perhaps akin to Greek *kapia*†, onions.]

chiv·vy, chiv·y (chĭv′ē) *v.* **-vied, -vying, -vies.** Also **chev·y** (chĕ′vē). *British.* —*tr.* To chase or harass. —*intr.* To scurry. —*n., pl.* **chivvies, chivies.** Also **chev·y** (chĕ′vē). *British.* **1.** A hunt or chase. **2.** A hunting cry. [English dialectal *chevy,* short for *chevy chase,* confusion, pursuit, from *Chevy Chase,* name of a Middle English ballad about the battle of Otterburn (1388), which arose from a hunt *(chase)* near the CHEVIOT HILLS.]

Chka·lov (chə-kä′lôf). Formerly **O·ren·burg** (ōr′ən-bo͝org). A city and trade center of the Soviet Union on the Ural River near the southern end of the Ural Mountains. Population, 293,000.

chl. chloroform.

Chlad·ni (kläd′nē), **Ernst Florens Friedrich.** 1756–1827. German physicist; founded science of acoustics.

chlam·y·date (klăm′ə-dāt′) *adj. Zoology.* Having a mantle. Said of mollusks. [Latin *chlamydātus,* from *chlamys,* CHLAMYS.]

chla·myd·e·ous (klə-mĭd′ē-əs) *adj. Botany.* Having or pertaining to a floral envelope. [From Latin *chlamys* (stem *chlamyd-*), mantle, CHLAMYS.]

chla·myd·o·spore (klə-mĭd′ə-spôr′, -spōr′) *n.* A thick-walled fungus spore derived from a hyphal cell; a resting spore. [Latin *chlamys* (stem *chlamyd-*), mantle, CHLAMYS + SPORE.]

chla·mys (klā′mĭs, klăm′ĭs) *n., pl.* **-myses** or **chlamydes** (klăm′ə-dēz′). A short mantle fastened at the shoulder, worn by men in ancient Greece. [Latin *chlamys,* from Greek *khlamus*†.]

chlo·ral (klôr′əl, klōr′-) *n.* A colorless, mobile oily liquid, CCl_3CHO, a penetrating lung irritant, used to manufacture DDT and chloral hydrate. [French : CHLOR(O)- + AL(COHOL).]

chloral hydrate. A colorless crystalline compound, $CCl_3CH(OH)_2$, used medicinally as a sedative and hypnotic.

chlo·ra·mine (klôr′ə-mēn′, klōr′-) *n.* Any of several compounds containing nitrogen and chlorine, especially an unstable colorless liquid, NH_2Cl, used to make hydrazine. [CHLOR(O)- + AM(MONIA) + -INE.]

chlo·ram·phen·i·col (klôr′ăm-fĕn′ĭ-kôl′, klōr′-, -kōl′) *n.* An antibiotic, $C_{11}H_{12}Cl_2N_2O_5$, derived from the soil bacterium *Streptomyces venezuelae,* or synthesized. [CHLOR(O)- + AM(IDE) + PHE(NO)- + NI(TRO)- + (GLY)COL.]

chlo·rate (klôr′āt′, klōr′-) *n.* The inorganic group ClO_3 or a compound containing it. [CHLOR(O)- + -ATE.]

chlor·dane (klôr′dān′, klōr′-) *n.* Also **chlor·dan** (-dăn′). A colorless, odorless viscous liquid, $C_{10}H_6Cl_8$, used as an insecticide. [CHLOR(O)- + (IN)D(ENE) + -ANE.]

chlo·rel·la (klə-rĕl′ə) *n.* Any of various green algae of the genus *Chlorella,* widely used in studies of photosynthesis. [New Latin *Chlorella* : CHLOR(O)- + *-ella,* diminutive suffix.]

chlo·ren·chy·ma (klə-rĕng′kə-mə) *n.* Plant tissue, especially stem tissue, containing chlorophyll. [CHLOR(OPHYLL) + -ENCHYMA.]

chlo·ric (klôr′ĭk, klōr′-) *adj.* Of, pertaining to, or containing chlorine. [CHLOR(O)- + -IC.]

chloric acid. A strongly oxidizing, unstable acid, $HClO_3 \cdot 7H_2O$.

chlo·ride (klôr′īd′, klōr′-) *n.* Any binary compound of chlorine. [CHLOR(O)- + -IDE.] —**chlo·rid′ic** (klə-rĭd′ĭk) *adj.*

chlo·rin·ate (klôr′ə-nāt′, klōr′-) *tr.v.* **-ated, -ating, -ates.** To treat or combine with chlorine or with a chlorine compound. —**chlo′ri·na′tion** *n.* —**chlo′ri·na′tor** (-nā′tər) *n.*

chlorinated lime. A white powder of varying composition, as $CaCl(ClO) \cdot 4H_2O$, produced by chlorinating slaked lime and used as a bleach. Also called "chloride of lime," "bleaching powder."

chlo·rine (klôr′ēn′, klōr′-, -ĭn) *n. Symbol* **Cl** A highly irritating, greenish-yellow gaseous halogen, capable of combining with nearly all other elements, produced principally by electrolysis of sodium chloride and used widely to purify water, as a disinfectant, a bleaching agent, and in the manufacture of many important compounds including chloroform and carbon tetrachloride. Atomic number 17, atomic weight 35.45, freezing point −100.98°C, boiling point −34.6°C, specific gravity 1.56 (−33.6°C), valences 1, 3, 5, 7. See **element.** [CHLOR(O)- + -INE.]

chlo·rite[1] (klôr′īt′, klōr′-) *n.* A generally green or black secondary mineral, $(Mg, Fe, Al)_6(Si, Al)_4O_{10}(OH)_8$, often formed by metamorphic alteration of primary dark rock minerals. [Latin *chlōritis,* a green precious stone, from Greek *khlōritis,* from *khlōros,* greenish yellow. See **ghel-**[2] in Appendix.*]

chlo·rite[2] (klôr′īt′, klōr′-) *n.* The inorganic group ClO_2 or a compound containing it. [CHLOR(O)- + -ITE.]

chloro-, chlor-. Indicates: **1.** The color green; for example, **chlorosis. 2.** The presence of chlorine; for example, **chloroform, chlorate.** [From Greek *khlōros,* greenish yellow. See **ghel-**[2] in Appendix.*]

chlo·ro·ben·zene (klôr′ō-bĕn′zēn′, -bĕn-zēn′, klōr′-) *n.* A colorless, volatile flammable liquid, C_6H_5Cl, used to prepare phenol, DDT, aniline, and as a general solvent.

chlo·ro·form (klôr′ə-fôrm′, klōr′-) *n. Abbr.* **chl.** A clear, colorless heavy liquid, $CHCl_3$, used in refrigerants, propellants, and resins, and as an anesthetic. —*tr.v.* **chloroformed, -forming, -forms. 1.** To anesthetize or kill with chloroform. **2.** To apply chloroform to. [CHLORO- + FORM(YL).]

chlo·ro·hy·drin (klôr′ō-hī′drĭn, klōr′-) *n.* An aliphatic organic chemical compound that is both an alkyl chloride and an alcohol, frequently containing a single chlorine atom and a single hydroxyl group on adjacent carbon atoms. [CHLORO- + HYDR(O)- + -IN.]

Chlo·ro·my·ce·tin (klôr′ō-mī-sēt′n, klōr′-) *n.* A trademark for **chloramphenicol** *(see).* [CHLORO- + MYCET(O)- + -IN.]

chlo·ro·phyll (klôr′ə-fĭl, klōr′-) *n.* Also **chlo·ro·phyl.** Any of a group of related green pigments found in photosynthetic organisms, especially: **a.** *Chlorophyll a,* a waxy blue-black microcrystalline green-plant pigment, $C_{55}H_{72}MgN_4O_5$, with a characteristic blue-green alcohol solution. **b.** *Chlorophyll b,* a similar green-plant pigment, $C_{55}H_{70}MgN_4O_6$, having a brilliant green alcohol solution. [French *chlorophylle* : CHLORO- + -PHYLL.]

ă pat/ā pay/âr care/ä father/b bib/ch church/d deed/ĕ pet/ē be/f fife/g gag/h hat/hw which/ĭ pit/ī pie/îr pier/j judge/k kick/l lid, needle/m mum/n no, sudden/ng thing/ŏ pot/ō toe/ô paw, for/oi noise/ou out/o͝o took/o͞o boot/p pop/r roar/s sauce/sh ship, dish/

chlo·ro·pic·rin (klôr′ə-pĭk′rĭn, klōr′-) *n.* An oily colorless liquid, CCl_3NO_2, used to make poison gas, in dyestuffs, disinfectants, insecticides, and fumigants. Also called "nitrochloroform," "vomiting gas." [CHLORO- + PICR(O)- + -IN.]
chlo·ro·plast (klôr′ə-plăst′, klōr′-) *n.* Also **chlo·ro·plas·tid** (klôr′ə-plăs′tĭd, klōr′-). *Botany.* A plastid containing chlorophyll in photosynthetic plants. [CHLORO- + -PLAST.]
chlo·ro·prene (klôr′ə-prēn′, klōr′-) *n.* A colorless liquid, C_4H_5Cl, used as the monomer of neoprene rubber. [CHLORO- + (ISO)PRENE.]
chlo·ro·sis (klə-rō′sĭs) *n.* **1.** *Botany.* An abnormal condition of plants, characterized by absence of or deficiency in green pigment and caused by lack of light, mineral deficiency, or genetic disorders. **2.** *Pathology.* An iron-deficiency anemia chiefly affecting girls at puberty and characterized by greenish skin color. Also called "greensickness." [CHLOR(O)- + -OSIS.]
chlor·prom·a·zine (klôr-prŏm′ə-zēn′, -prō′mə-zēn′, klōr-) *n.* An oily liquid, $C_{17}H_{19}ClN_2S$, derived from phenothiazine and used as a sedative, tranquilizer, and antiemetic. [CHLOR(O)- + PRO(PYL) + METH(YL) + AZINE.]
chlor·tet·ra·cy·cline (klôr′tĕt-rə-sī′klēn′, klōr′-) *n.* An antibiotic, $C_{22}H_{23}ClN_2O_8$, obtained from the soil bacterium *Streptomyces aureofaciens.*
chm. **1.** chairman. **2.** *Chess.* checkmate.
cho·an·o·cyte (kō-ăn′ə-sīt′) *n. Biology.* One of the flagellated cells that line the body cavity of a sponge. Also called "collar cell." [Greek *khoanē,* funnel, from *khein,* to pour (see **gheu-** in Appendix*) + -CYTE.]
chock (chŏk) *n.* **1.** A block or wedge placed under something, such as a boat, barrel, or wheel, to keep it from moving. **2.** *Nautical.* A heavy fitting of metal or wood with two jaws curving inward, through which a rope or cable may be run. —*tr.v.* **chocked, chocking, chocks. 1.** To fit with or secure by a chock or chocks. **2.** To place (a boat) on chocks. —*adv.* **1.** As completely as possible. **2.** As close as possible: *chock up against the railing.* [Origin obscure.]
chock-a-block (chŏk′ə-blŏk′) *adj.* **1.** *Archaic.* Drawn so close as to have the blocks touching. Said of a ship's hoisting tackle. **2.** Squeezed together; jammed. —**chock′-a-block′** *adv.*
chock-full (chŏk′fo͝ol′, chŭk′-) *adj.* Also **chuck-full, choke-full.** Completely filled; stuffed: *chock-full of candy.* [Middle English *chokkeful,* possibly from CHOCK (to ram tight with chocks).]
choc·o·late (chôk′lĭt, chô′kə-lĭt, chŏk′-) *n.* **1.** Husked, roasted, and ground cacao seeds, often combined with a sweetener or flavoring agent. **2.** A candy or beverage made from this. **3.** Grayish to deep reddish brown to deep grayish brown. See **color.** [Spanish, from Aztec *xocolatl* : *xococ,* bitter + *atl,* water.] —**choc′o·late** *adj.*
chocolate tree. The **cacao** *(see).*
Choc·taw (chŏk′tô) *n., pl.* **Choctaw** or **-taws. 1.** A tribe of Muskhogean-speaking Indians, formerly living in southern Mississippi and Alabama, now settled in Oklahoma. **2.** A member of this tribe. **3.** The Muskhogean language of this tribe. [Choctaw *Chahta.*]
choice (chois) *n.* **1.** The act of choosing; selection; election. **2.** The power, right, or liberty of choosing; option. **3.** The person or thing chosen. **4. a.** A sufficient number or variety from which to choose. **b.** A supply chosen with care. **5.** That which is best or preferable above others; the best part. **6.** An alternative. —*adj.* **choicer, choicest. 1.** Of fine quality; select; excellent. **2.** Selected with care. **3.** Of the U.S. Government grade of meat higher than *good* and lower than *prime.* [Middle English *chois,* from Old French, from *choisir,* to choose, from Gothic *kausjan* (unattested). See **geus-** in Appendix.*]
Synonyms: *choice, alternative, option, preference, selection, election.* Each of these terms involves the privilege of choosing. *Choice* implies broadly the freedom of choosing from a set of persons or things. *Alternative* emphasizes choice between only two possibilities or courses of action. *Option* stresses the power to choose, and is widely used in the sense of granting exclusive rights to make a choice. *Preference* indicates choice based on one's values, bias, or predilections. *Selection* suggests a wide variety of things or persons to choose from. *Election* emphasizes use of judgment and wisdom in making a choice with an important end in view.
choir (kwīr) *n.* **1. a.** An organized company of singers, especially one performing church music or singing in a church. **b.** The part of a church used by such singers. **2.** *Architecture.* The part of a cruciform church between the nave and the main altar; chancel. **3.** Any musical group or band, or a section of one. —*v.* **choired, choiring, choirs.** —*tr.* To perform (a musical composition) in chorus. —*intr.* To sing in chorus. [Earlier *quier, quire,* Middle English *quere,* from Old French *cuer,* from Medieval Latin *chorus,* from Latin *chorus,* dance, CHORUS.]
Choi·seul (shwä-zœl′). One of the Solomon Islands, 1,500 square miles in area, in the southwestern Pacific, southeast of Bougainville.
choke (chōk) *v.* **choked, choking, chokes.** —*tr.* **1.** To interfere with or terminate normal breathing of (a person, for example), especially by constricting or breaking the windpipe or by polluting the air. **2.** To stop by or as if by strangling; to silence; suppress. Often used with *off, down,* or *back: choke back tears.* **3.** To reduce the air intake of (a carburetor), thereby enriching the fuel mixture. **4.** To check or slow down the movement, growth, or action of. **5.** To block up or obstruct by filling or crowding; to clog; congest. **6.** To fill completely; to jam; pack. **7.** To grip (a bat, racket, or club) at a point nearer the hitting surface; shorten one's grip on. —*intr.* **1.** To become suffocated; have difficulty in breathing, swallowing, or speaking. **2.** To be blocked up or obstructed. —**choke up. 1.** *Informal.* To be unable to speak because of strong emotion. **2.** *Informal.* To fail to perform effectively because of nervous agitation or tension. —*n.* **1.** The act or sound of choking. **2.** That which constricts or chokes; a narrow part, such as the chokebore of a gun. **3.** A device used in an internal-combustion engine to enrich the fuel mixture by reducing the flow of air to the carburetor. [Middle English *choken, cheken,* short for *achoken, acheken,* Old English *ācēocian,* from Germanic *kēkōn-* (unattested), CHEEK.]
choke·ber·ry (chōk′bĕr′ē) *n., pl.* **-ries. 1.** Any of various North American shrubs of the genus *Aronia,* having bitter-tasting red, black, or purple fruit. **2.** The fruit of this shrub. [From its bitter fruit.]
choke·bore (chōk′bôr′, -bōr′) *n.* **1.** A shotgun bore which narrows toward the muzzle to prevent wide scattering of the shot. **2.** A gun with a bore of this kind.
choke·cher·ry (chōk′chĕr′ē) *n., pl.* **-ries. 1.** A North American shrub or tree, *Prunus virginiana,* having long clusters of white flowers and very astringent dark-red or blackish fruit. **2.** The fruit of this shrub. [From the bitter fruit.]
choke·damp (chōk′dămp′) *n.* A gaseous mixture, **black damp** *(see).* [So called because it causes suffocation in mines.]
choke-full. Variant of **chock-full.**
chok·er (chō′kər) *n.* **1.** One that chokes. **2.** *Informal.* **a.** A necklace that fits closely around the throat. Also called "dog collar." **b.** A high, tight collar. **c.** A narrow fur neckpiece.
chole-, chol-. Indicates the presence of or relation to gall or bile; for example, **cholecyst, choline.** [From Greek *kholē,* bile, gall. See **ghel-²** in Appendix.*]
cho·le·cyst (kō′lə-sĭst′, kŏl′ə-) *n. Rare.* The gallbladder. [New Latin *cholecystis* : CHOLE- + CYST.]
chol·er (kŏl′ər, kō′lər) *n.* **1.** *Archaic.* **a.** One of the four humors of the body thought in the Middle Ages to cause anger and bad temper when present in excess; bile. **b.** Biliousness. **2.** Anger; irritability. [Middle English *colre, coler(a),* from Old French *colere,* from Latin *cholera,* bilious diarrhea, from Greek *kholera,* from *kholē,* bile, gall. See **ghel-²** in Appendix.*]
chol·er·a (kŏl′ər-ə) *n.* An acute infectious epidemic disease caused by the microorganism *Vibrio comma,* often fatal, and characterized by watery diarrhea, vomiting, cramps, suppression of urine, and collapse. Also called "Asiatic cholera," "Indian cholera," "epidemic cholera." [Latin *cholera,* bilious diarrhea. See **choler.**] —**chol′e·ra′ic** (-ə-rā′ĭk) *adj.* —**chol′e·roid′** (-ə-roid′) *adj.*
cholera in·fan·tum (ĭn-făn′təm). *Rare.* Infantile diarrhea. [Latin, "cholera of children."]
cholera mor·bus (môr′bəs). *Rare.* Acute gastroenteritis occurring in summer and autumn and marked by severe cramps, diarrhea, and vomiting. Also called "cholera nostras." [Latin, "the disease cholera."]
chol·er·ic (kŏl′ə-rĭk, kə-lĕr′ĭk) *adj.* **1.** *Archaic.* Causing biliousness. **2.** Bad-tempered. —**chol′er·i·cal·ly, chol′er·ic·ly** *adv.*
cho·les·ter·ol (kə-lĕs′tə-rôl′, -rōl′) *n.* A glistening white soapy crystalline substance, $C_{27}H_{45}OH$, the most common animal sterol, a precursor of a form of vitamin D and a universal tissue constituent, occurring notably in bile, gallstones, the brain, blood cells, plasma, egg yolk, and seeds. Also called "cholesterin." [CHOLE- + Greek *stereos,* hard, solid (see **ster-¹** in Appendix*) + -OL. So called because first found in gallstones.]
cho·lic acid (kō′lĭk, kŏl′ĭk). An abundant crystalline bile acid, $C_{24}H_{40}O_5$. [Greek *kholikos,* bilious, from *kholē,* bile. See **ghel-²** in Appendix.*]
cho·line (kō′lēn′, kŏl′ēn′) *n.* A natural amine, $C_5H_{15}NO_2$, often classed in the vitamin B complex and a precursor of acetylcholine. [CHOL(E)- + -INE (from its function in preventing fat accumulation in the liver).]
cho·lin·er·gic (kō′lə-nûr′jĭk, kŏl′ə-) *adj.* **1.** Activated by or capable of liberating the **acetylcholine** *(see).* **2.** Having physiological effects similar to acetylcholine. [(ACETYL)CHOLIN(E) + Greek *ergon,* work (see **werg-¹** in Appendix*) + -IC.]
cho·lin·es·ter·ase (kō′lə-nĕs′tə-rās′, -rāz′, kŏl′ə-) *n.* An enzyme that hydrolyzes acetylcholine to form acetic acid and choline. Also called "acetylcholinesterase." [CHOLIN(E) + ESTERASE.]
chol·la (choi′ə) *n.* Any of several very spiny cacti of the genus *Opuntia,* characterized by cylindrical rather than flattened stem segments. See **prickly pear.** [Mexican Spanish, from Spanish *cholla,* head, possibly from Old French *cholle,* head, from Germanic. See **geulo-** in Appendix.*]
Cho·lon (chō′lôn′). A city in South Vietnam, southwest of Saigon of which it is a suburb. Population, 431,000.
Cho·lu·la (chə-lo͞o′lə). A town in southeastern Mexico, eight miles west of the city of Puebla; site of the remains of the ancient pyramid of Quetzalcoatl. Population, 13,000.
Cho·mo·lung·ma. The Tibetan name for Mount **Everest.**
chomp. Variant of **champ** (bite).
chon (chŏn) *n., pl.* **chon.** A coin equal to $1/100$ of the won, the monetary unit of South Korea. See table of exchange rates at **currency.** [Korean.]
chondri-. Variant of **chondro-.**
chon·dri·fy (kŏn′drə-fī′) *v.* **-fied, -fying, -fies.** —*tr.* To change into cartilage. —*intr.* To become cartilage. [CHONDRI- + -FY.] —**chon′dri·fi·ca′tion** *n.*
chon·dri·o·some (kŏn′drē-ə-sōm′) *n. Biology.* A **mitochondrion** *(see).* [CHONDRI- + -SOME.]
chon·drite (kŏn′drīt′) *n.* A stone of meteoric origin characterized by chondrules. [CHONDR(O)- + -ITE.] —**chon′drit′ic** (-drĭt′ĭk) *adj.*
chondro-, chondr-, chondri-. Indicates: **1.** Relation to car-

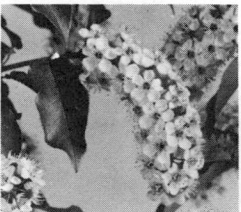

chokecherry

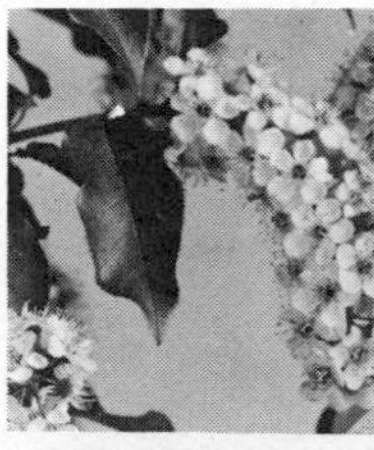

flowers

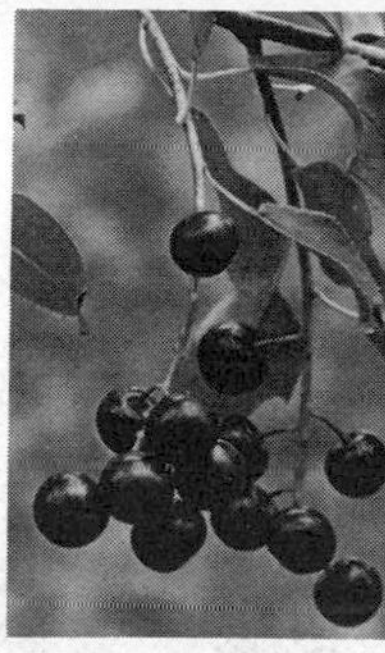

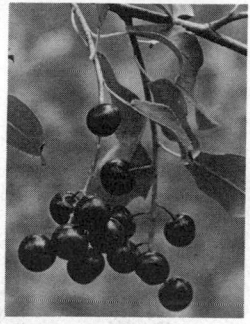

fruit

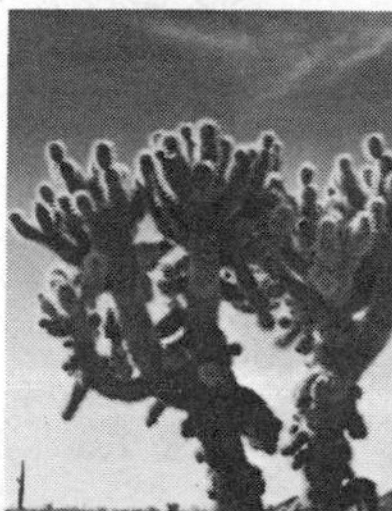

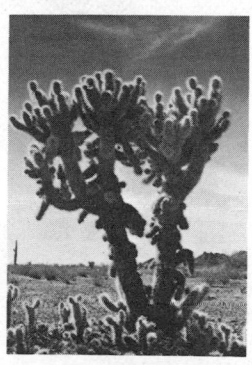

cholla

tilage; for example, **chondroma, chondrify. 2.** Granule or chondrule; for example, **chondrite.** [From Greek *khondros,* granule, cartilage. See **ghren-** in Appendix.*]
chon·dro·cra·ni·um (kŏn′drō-krā′nē-əm) *n., pl.* **-ums** or **-nia** (-nē-ə). The embryonic cranium, especially as distinguished from the **osteocranium** *(see).*
chon·dro·ma (kŏn-drō′mə) *n., pl.* **-mas** or **-mata** (-mə-tə). A cartilaginous growth. [New Latin : CHONDR(O)- + -OMA.]
chon·drule (kŏn′drōōl) *n. Geology.* A small round granule of extraterrestrial origin found embedded in some meteorites. [CHONDR(O)- + -ULE.]
Chong·jin (chŏng′jĭn′). *Japanese* **Sei·shin** (sā′shēn′). A city of North Korea, a seaport in the northeast on the Sea of Japan. Population, 184,000.
choose (chōōz) *v.* **chose** (chōz), **chosen** (chō′zən), **choosing, chooses.** *—tr.* **1.** To select from a number of possible alternatives; decide upon and pick out. **2.** To prefer above others. **3.** To want; desire: *choose to go.* *—intr.* To make a choice; select; decide. [Choose, Middle English *chosen,* Old English *cēosan* (later *ceōsan*). Chose, chosen; Middle English *chosen* (past plural), *chosen,* both from the infinitive *chosen.* See **geus-** in Appendix.*] **—choos′er** *n.*
Synonyms: *choose, select, elect, pick.* These verbs apply to making a choice. *Choose* implies the use of judgment in taking one of several persons, things, or courses. *Select* stresses care and comparison in choosing from a large variety. *Elect* strongly suggests deliberation in making a selection, usually between alternatives: *He elected to stay home. Pick,* like *select,* indicates some care in choosing but implies less deliberation than *elect.*
choos·y (chōō′zē) *adj.* **-ier, -iest.** Also **choos·ey.** Unwilling to settle for less than the best; hard to please. **—choos′i·ness** *n.*
chop[1] (chŏp) *v.* **chopped, chopping, chops.** *—tr.* **1.** To cut by striking with a heavy, sharp tool, such as an axe. **2.** To make by cutting in this way. **3.** To cut into bits; mince. **4.** To cut short (words or phrases). **5.** *Sports.* To hit or hit at with a short, swift, downward stroke. *—intr.* **1.** To make heavy, cutting strokes. **2.** To move roughly or suddenly. *—n.* **1.** The act of chopping. **2.** A swift, short, cutting blow or stroke. **3.** A chopped-off piece; especially, a cut of meat, usually taken from the rib, shoulder, or loin and containing a bone. **4.** A short, irregular motion of waves. [Middle English *choppen,* variant of *chappen,* CHAP (to split).]
chop[2] (chŏp) *intr.v.* **chopped, chopping, chops.** To change direction suddenly; swerve, as a ship in the wind. [Originally, "to exchange," from Middle English *choppen,* variant of *chappen, chepen,* to barter, trade, Old English *cēapian,* from Common Germanic *kaupjan* (unattested), from *kaupaz* (unattested), trader, from Latin *caupō.* See **caupō** in Appendix.*]
chop[3] (chŏp) *n.* **1.** In the Far East, an official stamp or permit. **2.** *Anglo-Indian.* Quality: *first chop.* [Hindi *chhāpↄ,* seal.]
chop·fall·en. Variant of **chapfallen.**
chop·house[1] (chŏp′hous′) *n.* A restaurant that specializes in serving chops and steaks.
chop·house[2] (chŏp′hous′) *n.* A customhouse in China.
Cho·pin (shō′păn′; *French* shō-păN′), **Frédéric François.** 1810–1849. Polish pianist and composer of works for piano and orchestra; resident in France (from 1829).
chop·per (chŏp′ər) *n.* **1.** One that chops. **2.** A device that interrupts an electric current or beam of radiation. **3.** *Slang.* A helicopter. **4.** *Plural. Slang.* The jaws.
chop·py (chŏp′ē) *adj.* **-pier, -piest.** Also **chop·ping.** Abruptly shifting or breaking, as waves or winds: *choppy seas.*
chops (chŏps) *pl.n.* The jaws, cheeks, or jowls of animals or man. [Origin unknown.]
chop·sticks (chŏp′stĭks′) *pl.n.* A pair of slender sticks made of wood or ivory, used as eating utensils in China, Japan, and some other Asian countries. [Pidgin English *chop,* fast, probably from Cantonese *kap,* corresponding to Mandarin Chinese *chi*[2], fast, hurried + STICK(S). A loose translation of Cantonese *fai chi* and Mandarin *kwai*[4] *tse*[0], "fast ones" (originally a boatman's substitute for *chu*[4], chopsticks, which is a homonym of *chu*[4], to stop, stand still, an unlucky word for boatmen).]

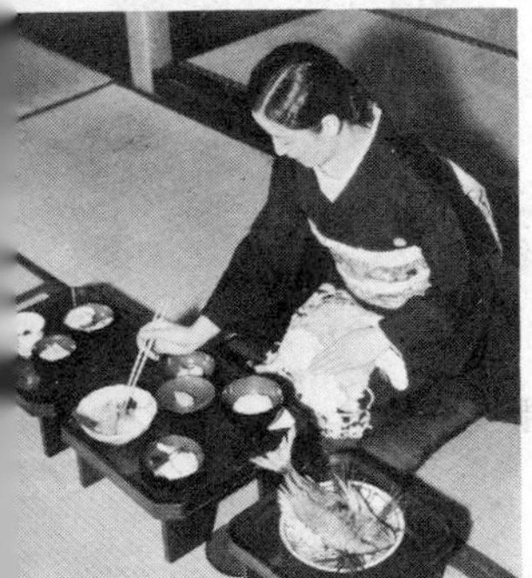

chopsticks
Woman using chopsticks

chop su·ey (chŏp sōō′ē). A Chinese-American dish consisting of small pieces of meat or chicken cooked with bean sprouts and other vegetables and served with rice. [Cantonese *tsap sui,* corresponding to Mandarin Chinese *cha*[2] *sui*[4], "mixed pieces."]
cho·rag·ic (kə-răj′ĭk) *adj.* Of or pertaining to a choragus.
cho·ra·gus (kə-rā′gəs) *n., pl.* **-gi** (-jī′). In Greek drama: **a.** The leader of the chorus. **b.** An elected official supervising the production of dramatic performances in the festival of Dionysus at Athens. [Latin, from Greek *khoragos* : *khoros,* CHORUS + *-agos,* leader, from *agein,* to lead (see **ag-** in Appendix*).]
cho·ral (kôr′əl, kōr′-) *adj.* **1.** Of or pertaining to a chorus or choir. **2.** Written for performance by a chorus. [Medieval Latin *chorālis,* from *chorus,* CHORUS.] **—cho′ral·ly** *adv.*
cho·rale (kə-răl′, -räl′) *n.* Also **cho·ral. 1.** A Protestant hymn tune. **2.** A harmonized hymn, especially one for organ: *a Bach chorale.* **3.** A chorus or choir. [German *Choral(gesang),* "choral (song)," from Medieval Latin *chorālis,* CHORAL.]
chorale prelude. *Music.* A composition for organ, chiefly in baroque style, characterized by an elaborate contrapuntal structure based on the melody of a hymn or chorale.
choral speaking. The recitation of poetry or prose by a chorus.
chord[1] (kôrd, kōrd) *n.* **1.** A combination of three or more usually concordant tones sounded simultaneously. **2.** Any kind of harmony, as of color. **3.** An emotional feeling or response: *Her words struck a sympathetic chord.* *—v.* **chorded, chording, chords.** *—tr.* To furnish with chords. *—intr.* To accord or form a chord; harmonize. [Respelled (influenced by Latin *chorda,* strings, CORD) from Middle English *cord,* agreement, harmony, short for ACCORD.]
chord[2] (kôrd, kōrd) *n.* **1.** *Geometry.* A line segment that joins two points on a curve. **2.** *Aviation.* A straight line connecting the leading and trailing edges of an airfoil. **3.** *Archaic.* The string of a musical instrument. [Respelled (influenced by Latin *chorda,* string) from CORD.]
chord[3]**.** Variant of **cord.**
chord·al (kôrd′l) *adj.* **1.** *Music.* **a.** Of or pertaining to the strings of a musical instrument. **b.** Relating to or consisting of a harmonic chord. **c.** Giving prominence to harmonic rather than contrapuntal structure: *chordal music.* **2.** *Fine Arts.* Of or pertaining to combinations of colors.
chor·date (kôr′dāt′, -dĭt) *n. Zoology.* Any of numerous animals belonging to the phylum Chordata, which includes all vertebrates and certain marine animals having a notochord, such as the lancelets. [New Latin *Chordata,* from *chorda,* notochord, from Latin, CORD.]
chore (chôr, chōr) *n.* **1.** A routine or minor task. **2.** *Plural.* **a.** Any daily or routine domestic tasks. **b.** The routine morning and evening tasks of a farmer, as the feeding of livestock. **3.** An unpleasant or burdensome task. —See Synonyms at **task.** *—intr.v.* **chored, choring, chores.** To work at chores: *His uncle let him chore for his board.* [Variant of CHARE, CHAR.]
-chore. Indicates a plant distributed by a specific agency; for example, **anemochore, zoochore.** [From Greek *khōrein,* to move, spread abroad. See **ghē-** in Appendix.*]
cho·re·a (kô-rē′ə, kō-) *n.* A nervous disorder, especially of children, marked by uncontrollable and irregular movements of the muscles of the arms, legs, and face. Also called "St. Vitus' dance." [Latin *chorea,* dance, from Greek *khoreia,* choral dance, from *khoros,* dance, CHORUS.]
cho·re·o·graph (kôr′ē-ə-grăf′, -gräf′, kōr′-) *v.* **-graphed, -graphing, -graphs.** *—tr.* To create the choreography of (a ballet or other stage work). *—intr.* To serve as a choreographer.
cho·re·og·ra·pher (kôr′ē-ŏg′rə-fər, kōr′-) *n.* One who creates, arranges, or directs dances for stage performance, especially ballet dances.
cho·re·og·ra·phy (kôr′ē-ŏg′rə-fē, kōr′-) *n.* Also **cho·reg·ra·phy** (kə-rĕg′rə-fē). **1.** The art of creating and arranging ballets or dances. **2.** The art and technique of dance notation. **3.** The art of dancing. [French *chorégraphie* : Greek *khoreios,* of a dance, from *khoros,* dance, CHORUS + -GRAPHY.] **—cho′re·o·graph′ic** (kôr′ē-ə-grăf′ĭk, kōr′-) *adj.*
cho·ri·amb (kôr′ē-ămb′, kōr′-) *n., pl.* **-ambs.** Also **cho·ri·am·bus** (kôr′ē-ăm′bəs, kōr′-) *pl.* **-bi** (-bī′) or **-buses. 1.** *Greek & Latin Prosody.* A metrical foot consisting of a trochee followed by an iamb, much employed in Aeolic poetry and in the choric odes of tragedy. **2.** *Prosody.* A foot of verse used in lyric poetry having two unstressed syllables flanked by the two rhythmic stresses marking the first and last syllables of the foot. [Late Latin *choriambus,* from Greek *khoriambos* : *khoreios,* of a chorus, hence trochee, from *khoros,* CHORUS + *iambos,* IAMBUS.]
cho·ri·am·bic (kôr′ē-ăm′bĭk, kōr′-) *adj.* Consisting of or characterized by choriambs. *—n.* **1.** A choriamb. **2.** A verse in which choriambs make the characteristic rhythm: *"Sweet the kisses of death set on thy lips."* (Swinburne).
cho·ric (kôr′ĭk, kōr′-, kŏr′-) *adj.* Of or pertaining to a singing or speaking chorus; in the style of a chorus. Used only with reference to Greek poetry and drama: *choric dance.* [Late Latin *choricus,* from Greek *khorikos,* from *khoros,* CHORUS.]
cho·rine (kôr′ēn′, kōr′-) *n. Slang.* A chorus girl.
cho·ri·on (kôr′ē-ŏn′, kōr′-) *n.* The outer membrane enclosing the embryo in reptiles, birds, and mammals. [Greek *khorion,* afterbirth. See **gher-**[1] in Appendix.*] **—cho′ri·on′ic** *adj.*
chor·is·ter (kôr′ĭs-tər, kōr′-, kŏr′-) *n.* **1.** A choir singer; especially, a choirboy. **2.** A choir leader. [Learned respelling of Middle English *queristre,* from Norman French *cueristre* (unattested), from Medieval Latin *chorista,* from *chorus,* CHORUS.]
cho·rog·ra·phy (kə-rŏg′rə-fē) *n.* **1.** The technique of mapping a region or district. **2.** *Archaic.* A description or map of a region. [Latin *chōrographia,* from Greek *khōrographia* : *khōros,* place, specific area (see **ghē-** in Appendix*) + -GRAPHY.] **—cho·rog′ra·pher** *n.* **—cho′ro·graph′ic** (kôr′ə-grăf′ĭk, kōr′-), **cho′ro·graph′i·cal** *adj.* **—cho′ro·graph′i·cal·ly** *adv.*
cho·roid (kôr′oid′, kōr′-) *n.* Also **cho·roi·de·a** (kô-roi′dē-ə, kō-). The dark-brown vascular coat of the eye between the sclera and the retina. *—adj.* Also **cho·ri·oid** (kôr′ē-oid′, kōr′-). *Anatomy.* **1.** Resembling the chorion. **2.** Resembling the corium. **3.** Of or pertaining to the choroid. [Greek *khoroeidēs,* scribal error for *khorioeidēs,* resembling an afterbirth : *khorion,* afterbirth, CHORION + -OID.]
chor·tle (chôrt′l) *intr.v.* **-tled, -tling, -tles.** To chuckle throatily: *"He chortled in his joy."* (Lewis Carroll). *—n.* A snorting, joyful chuckle. [Blend of CHUCKLE and SNORT, coined by Lewis Carroll.] **—chor′tler** *n.*
cho·rus (kôr′əs, kōr′-) *n., pl.* **-ruses. 1.** *Music.* **a.** A composition in four or more parts written for a large number of singers. **b.** A song refrain in which the audience joins the soloist. **c.** *Jazz.* A repeat of the opening statement played by the whole group. **d.** *Jazz.* A solo section based on the main melody and played by a member of the group. **e.** A body of singers who perform choral compositions. **f.** A body of vocalists and dancers who support the soloists and leading actors in operas, musical comedies, and revues. **2. a.** In drama or poetry recitation, a group of persons who speak or sing a given part or composition in unison. **b.** In Elizabethan drama, an actor who recites the prologue and epilogue to a play and sometimes comments on the action. **3.** In Greek poetry and drama: **a.** A ceremonial

ă pat/ā pay/âr care/ä father/b bib/ch church/d deed/ĕ pet/ē be/f fife/g gag/h hat/hw which/ĭ pit/ī pie/îr pier/j judge/k kick/l lid, needle/m mum/n no, sudden/ng thing/ŏ pot/ō toe/ô paw, for/oi noise/ou out/ŏŏ took/ōō boot/p pop/r roar/s sauce/sh ship, dish/

dance performed to the singing of odes. **b.** The portion of a drama consisting of choric dance and ode. **c.** The body of actors whose choric performance comments upon and accompanies the action of the play. **4. a.** Any speech, song, or other utterance made in concert by many people. **b.** Any simultaneous utterance by a number of persons or animals. —**in chorus.** With simultaneous utterance; all together. —*v.* **chorused** or **chorussed, -rusing** or **-russing, -ruses** or **-russes.** —*tr.* **1.** To sing or utter in chorus. **2.** To furnish with a refrain or chorus. —*intr.* To speak or sing in chorus: *"Then they all chorused upon me."* (Richardson). [Latin *chorus,* from Greek *khoros,* dance, chorus. See **gher-²** in Appendix.*]

chorus girl. A girl who dances in a theatrical chorus.

Cho·rzów (KHô′zhōōf′). An industrial city and mining center of southwestern Poland. Population, 153,000.

chose¹. Past tense of **choose.**

chose² (shōz) *n. Law.* An item of personal property; chattel. [French *chose,* "thing," from Old French, from Latin *causa,* thing, CAUSE.]

cho·sen (chō′zən). Past participle of **choose.** —*adj.* **1.** Selected from or preferred above others. **2.** *Theology.* Elect. —*n., pl.* **chosen. 1.** One of the elect. **2.** The elect collectively.

Cho·sen (chō′sĕn′). **1.** A name traditionally designating Korea since the second millennium B.C. **2.** The official name of Korea as a Japanese province (1910–45). See **Korea.**

chosen people. The Israelites regarded as the people chosen to receive God's revelation. Nehemiah 9:8.

Cho·ta Nag·pur (chō′tə näg′pŏŏr′). A forested plateau region in northern Orissa and southern Bihar states, Republic of India.

chott (shŏt) *n.* Also **shott. 1.** The depression surrounding a salt marsh, especially in North Africa. **2.** The bed of a dried salt marsh. [French, from Arabic *shaṭṭ,* "river bank."]

Chou (jō). A Chinese dynasty that ruled from 1122 to 255 B.C., enlarging the empire and promoting philosophy.

Chou En-lai (jō′ ĕn′lī′). Born 1898. Chinese communist leader; premier (since 1949).

chough (chŭf) *n.* A crowlike Old World bird of the genus *Pyrrhocorax,* having black plumage and red legs. [Middle English *choge, chowe,* from Germanic, akin to Old English *cēo,* jackdaw, jay, Middle Dutch *cauwe,* chough (imitative).]

choush. Variant of **chiaus.**

Chou Shan (jō′ shän′). A group of islands belonging to China, in the East China Sea near the mouth of Hangchow Bay.

Chou·teau (shōō-tō′). American family of Western pioneers and fur traders, including **Jean Pierre** (1758–1859); his sons, **Auguste Pierre** (1786–1838) and **Pierre** (1789–1865); and his half brother, **René Auguste** (1749–1829).

chow¹ (chou) *n.* Also **chow chow.** A heavy-set dog of a breed originating in China, having a long, dense, reddish-brown or black coat and a blackish tongue. [Perhaps Pidgin English, from Cantonese *kao* and Mandarin Chinese *kou³,* dog.]

chow² (chou) *n. Slang.* Food; victuals. —*intr.v.* **chowed, chowing, chows.** *Slang.* To eat. [Pidgin English, probably from Mandarin Chinese *ch'ao³,* to stir, fry, cook.]

chow-chow (chou′chou′) *n.* A relish consisting of chopped vegetables pickled in mustard. [Pidgin English, probably reduplication of Mandarin Chinese *cha²,* mixed.]

chow·der (chou′dər) *n.* A thick soup or stew containing fish or shellfish, especially clams, and vegetables, often in a milk base. [French *chaudière,* stew pot, from Old French, from Late Latin *caldāria,* caldron, from Latin *caldārius,* suitable for heating, from *caldus, calidus,* hot. See **kel-¹** in Appendix.*]

chow mein (chou′ mān′). A Chinese-American dish consisting of any of various combinations of stewed vegetables and meat, served over fried noodles. [Cantonese, variant of Mandarin Chinese *ch'ao³ mien⁴,* "fried noodles."]

Chr. Christ; Christian.

chres·ard (krĕs′ərd) *n.* Water present in the soil and available for plant absorption. [Greek *khrēsis,* use, from *khrēsthai,* to use (see **gher-⁷** in Appendix*) + *ardein*†, to water.]

Chrês·tien de Troyes (krā-tyăN′ də trwä′). Also **Chré·tien de Troyes.** French trouvère of the late 12th century.

chres·tom·a·thy (krĕs-tŏm′ə-thē) *n., pl.* **-thies.** A selection of literary passages, used in studying literature or a language. [Greek *khrēstomatheia,* "useful learning" : *khrēstos,* useful, from *khrēsthai,* to use (see **gher-⁷** in Appendix*) + *-matheia,* learning, from *manthanein,* to learn (see **mendh-** in Appendix*).] —**chres′to·math′ic** *adj.*

chrism (krĭz′əm) *n.* Also **chris·om** (for sense 2). *Ecclesiastical.* **1.** A mixture of oil and balsam consecrated by a bishop and used for anointing in various church sacraments, such as baptism and confirmation. **2.** Any sacramental anointing, especially upon confirmation into the Eastern Orthodox Church. [Middle English *crisme,* Old English *crisma,* from Late Latin *chrisma,* from Greek *khrisma,* ointment, from *khriein,* to anoint. See **ghrēi-** in Appendix.*] —**chris′mal** (krĭz′məl) *adj.* —**chris′ma′tion** *n.*

chris·om (krĭz′əm) *n. Ecclesiastical.* **1.** A white cloth or robe worn by an infant at baptism. **2.** *Archaic.* An infant wearing a baptismal robe; baby. **3.** Variant of **chrism.** [Middle English *crisom,* variant of *crisme,* CHRISM.]

Christ (krīst) *n. Abbr.* **Chr. 1.** The Anointed; the Messiah, as foretold by the prophets of the Old Testament. **2. Jesus** *(see).* **3.** *Christian Science.* "The divine manifestation of God, which comes to the flesh to destroy incarnate error." (Mary Baker Eddy). —*interj.* Used as an oath. [Middle English *Crist,* Old English *Crist,* from Latin *Christus,* from Greek *Khristos,* "the anointed (one)," from *khriein,* to anoint. See **ghrēi-** in Appendix.*] —**Christ′li·ness** *n.* —**Christ′ly** *adj.*

Christ·church (krīst′chûrch′). The largest city of South Island, New Zealand, near the eastern coast. Population, 159,000.

christ·cross (krĭs′krôs′, -krŏs′) *n.* **1.** *Archaic.* A symbol of the cross, formerly placed before the alphabet in a child's hornbook. **2.** The cross marked for a signature by someone who cannot write.

chris·ten (krĭs′ən) *tr.v.* **-tened, -tening, -tens. 1.** To baptize into a Christian church. **2.** To give a name to at baptism. **3.** To name and dedicate ceremonially: *christen a ship.* **4.** *Informal.* To use for the first time. [Middle English *cristen, cristnen,* Old English *cristnian,* from *Cristen,* CHRISTIAN.]

Chris·ten·dom (krĭs′ən-dəm) *n.* **1.** Christians collectively. **2.** The Christian world. **3.** *Obsolete.* Christianity. [Middle English *Cristendom,* Old English *Cristendōm* : *Cristen,* CHRISTIAN + -DOM.]

chris·ten·ing (krĭs′ə-nĭng) *n.* The Christian sacrament of baptism, including the bestowal of a name upon an infant.

Christ·hood (krīst′hŏŏd′) *n.* The state of being the Christ.

Chris·tian¹ (krĭs′chən). A masculine given name. [Latin *Christiānus,* believer in Christ, CHRISTIAN.]

Chris·tian² (krĭs′chən) *adj.* **1.** Professing belief in Jesus as Christ or following the religion based on his teachings. **2.** Pertaining to or derived from Jesus or his teachings. **3.** Manifesting the qualities or spirit of Christ; Christlike. **4.** Pertaining to or characteristic of Christianity or its adherents. **5.** *Informal.* Neighborly; decent. —*n.* **1.** *Abbr.* **Chr.** One who professes belief in Jesus as the Christ or follows the religion based on his teachings. **2.** One who lives according to the teachings of Jesus. **3.** *Informal.* **a.** A human being as distinguished from an animal. **b.** A decent human being. [Middle English *Cristen, Christen,* Old English *Crīsten,* from Latin *Christiānus,* from Greek *Khristianos,* from *Khristos,* CHRIST.] —**Chris′tian·ly** *adv.*

Chris·tian X (krĭs′chən). 1870–1947. King of Denmark (1912–1947).

Christian Brothers. An order of Roman Catholic laymen dedicated to the education of the poor. Also officially called "Brothers of the Christian Schools."

Christian era. The period beginning with the birth of Jesus (conventionally in A.D. 1). Dates in this era are marked A.D., and dates before it, B.C.

chris·ti·a·ni·a (krĭs′tē-ä′nē-ə, krĭs′chē-ăn′ē-ə) *n.* A ski turn in which the body is swung from a crouching position to change direction or to make a stop. Also called "christiania turn," "christy." [Norwegian, from CHRISTIANIA.]

Chris·ti·a·ni·a. The former name for **Oslo,** Norway.

Chris·ti·an·i·ty (krĭs′chē-ăn′ə-tē) *n., pl.* **-ties. 1.** The Christian religion, founded on the teachings of Jesus. **2.** A particular system of the Christian religion. **3.** Christians as a group; Christendom. **4.** The state or fact of being a Christian.

Chris·tian·ize (krĭs′chən-īz′) *v.* **-ized, -izing, -izes.** —*tr.* **1.** To convert to Christianity. **2.** To instill with Christian principles and qualities. —*intr.* To adopt Christianity. —**Chris′tian·i·za′tion** *n.* —**Chris′tian·iz′er** *n.*

Christian Science. *Abbr.* **C.S.** The church and the religious system founded by Mary Baker **Eddy** *(see),* emphasizing healing through spiritual means as an important element of Christianity, and teaching pure divine goodness as underlying the scientific reality of existence. Also officially called "Church of Christ, Scientist." —**Christian Scientist.**

Chris·tie (krĭs′tē), **Agatha (Mary Clarissa).** Born 1891. English author of mystery novels and plays.

Chris·ti·na (krĭs-tē′nə). 1626–1689. Queen of Sweden (1632–54); daughter of Gustavus Adolphus; abdicated and converted to Roman Catholicism.

Christ·like (krīst′līk′) *adj.* Having the spiritual qualities or attributes of Christ. —**Christ′like′ness** *n.*

Christ·mas (krĭs′məs) *n.* **1.** December 25, a holiday celebrated by Christians as the anniversary of the birth of Jesus. **2.** The Christian church festival extending from December 24 (Christmas Eve) through January 6 (Epiphany). In this sense, also called "Christmastide." [Middle English *Cristesmasse,* Old English *Crīstesmæsse* : *Cristes,* genitive of *Crīst,* CHRIST + *mæsse,* -MAS.]

Christmas berry. A shrub, the **toyon** *(see).*

Christmas cactus. A spineless, epiphytic cactus, *Zygocactus truncatus,* of South America, cultivated as a house plant for its showy red flowers. Also called "crab cactus."

Christmas Eve. 1. The evening before Christmas. **2.** Loosely, the day before Christmas.

Christmas fern. The **dagger fern** *(see).*

Christmas Island. 1. An island, 64 square miles in area, in the Indian Ocean about 260 miles south of Java. **2.** The largest (225 square miles) of the Line Islands, in the Pacific about 1,200 miles south of Honolulu; the site of British and American nuclear experiments.

Christmas rose. An evergreen plant, *Helleborus niger,* native to Europe, having a poisonous root and white or pinkish-green flowers that bloom in late fall or winter. Also called "hellebore," "winter rose."

Christmas tree. An evergreen or artificial tree decorated with lights and ornaments during the Christmas season.

Chris·tol·o·gy (krĭs-tŏl′ə-jē) *n., pl.* **-gies. 1.** The study of Christ's person and qualities. **2.** Any doctrine or theory based on Christ or his teachings. [CHRIST + -LOGY.] —**Chris′to·log′i·cal** (-tə-lŏj′ĭ-kəl) *adj.*

Chris·tophe (krē-stôf′), **Henri.** 1767–1820. Haitian revolutionary leader; king of Haiti (1811–20); committed suicide.

Chris·to·pher (krĭs′tə-fər) *n.* A masculine given name. [Middle English *Christophre,* from Late Latin *Christophorus,* from

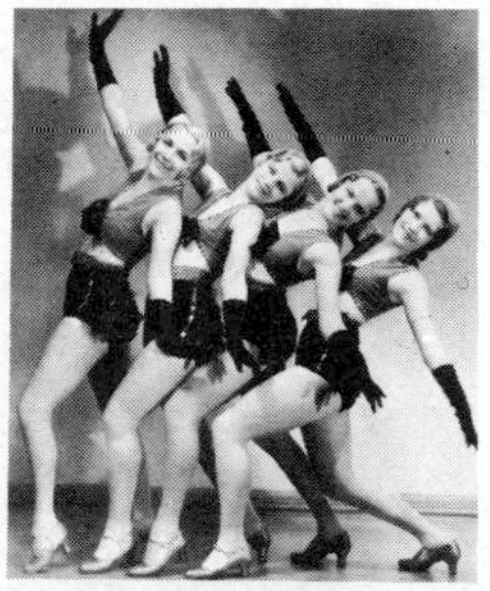

chorus girl
Chorus line at the New Amsterdam Theater, New York City, in 1937

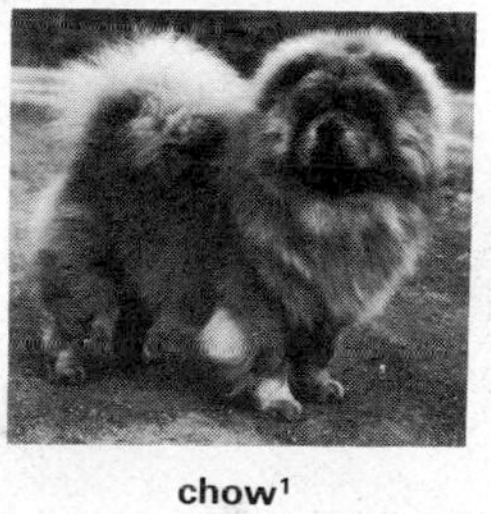

chow¹

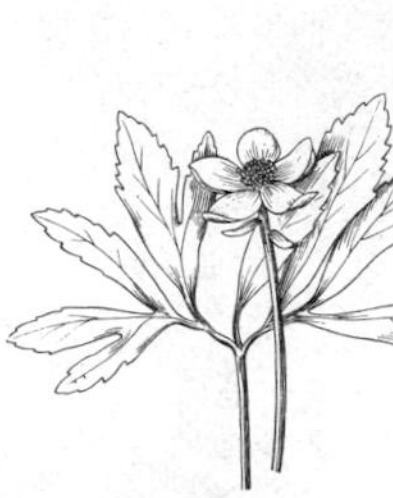

Christmas rose

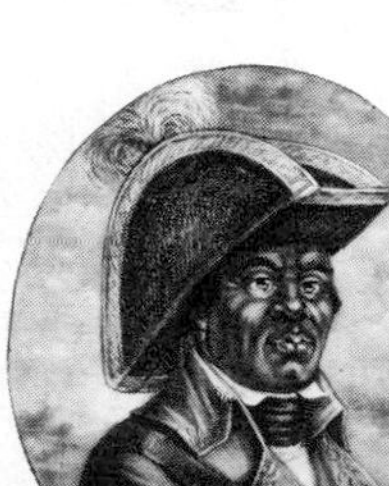

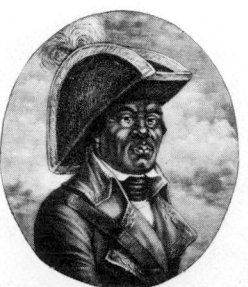

Henri Christophe

Late Greek *Khristophoros*, "Christbearer"; from the legend that St. Christopher carried Jesus across a river.]

Chris·to·pher (krĭs′tə-fər), **Saint.** Legendary Christian martyr of the third century A.D.; patron saint of travelers.

Christ's-thorn (krīsts′thôrn′) *n.* Any of several plants of the Near East having spiny thorns and popularly believed to have been used for Christ's crown of thorns, such as the jujube or *Paliurus spina-christi.*

chris·ty (krĭs′tē) *n., pl.* **-ties.** A ski turn, the **christiania** *(see).*

Chris·ty (krĭs′tē), **Howard Chandler.** 1873–1952. American illustrator, portraitist, and sculptor.

chro·ma (krō′mə) *n.* That aspect of color in the Munsell color system by which a sample appears to differ from a gray of the same lightness or brightness. Chroma corresponds to **saturation** *(see)* of the perceived color. See **color.** [Greek *khrōma,* color. See **ghrēu-** in Appendix.*]

chro·mate (krō′māt′) *n.* A salt or ester of chromic acid. [CHROM(O)- + -ATE.]

chro·mat·ic (krō-măt′ĭk) *adj.* **1. a.** Pertaining to colors or color. **b.** Pertaining to color perceived to have a saturation greater than zero. **2. a.** *Music.* Of, pertaining to, or based on the chromatic scale. **b.** Pertaining to chords or harmonies based on nonharmonic tones. [Greek *khrōmatikos,* from *khrōma,* color, modification of musical tone. See **ghrēu-** in Appendix.*] —**chro·mat′i·cal·ly** *adv.* —**chro·mat′i·cism′** *n.*

chromatic aberration. Color distortion in an image produced by a lens because of the dependence of lens refractivity on the wavelength of light and marked by a variation in the focusing of colors.

chro·ma·tic·i·ty (krō′mə-tĭs′ə-tē) *n.* The aspect of color that includes consideration of its dominant wavelength and purity. See **color.**

chro·mat·ics (krō-măt′ĭks) *n.* Plural in form, used with a singular verb. The scientific study of color. Also called "chromatology." —**chro′ma·tist** (-mə-tĭst) *n.*

chromatic scale. *Music.* A scale consisting of 12 semitones.

chro·ma·tid (krō′mə-tĭd) *n. Genetics.* Either of two daughter strands of a duplicated chromosome while still joined by a single centromere. [CHROMAT(O)- + -ID.]

chro·ma·tin (krō′mə-tən) *n. Genetics.* A complex of nucleic acids and proteins, characterized by intense staining with basic dyes. [CHROMAT(O)- + -IN.]

chromato-, chromat-. Indicates: **1.** Color, staining, or pigmentation; for example, **chromatophore, chromatid. 2.** Chromatin; for example, **chromatolysis.** [From Greek *khrōma* (stem *khrōmat-*), color. See **ghrēu-** in Appendix.*]

chro·mat·o·gram (krō-măt′ə-grăm′) *n.* The absorbent column or strip of material containing the stratographically differentiated constituents separated from a solution or mixture by chromatography. [CHROMATO- + -GRAM.]

chro·ma·tog·ra·phy (krō′mə-tŏg′rə-fē) *n.* Separation of complex mixtures by percolation through a selectively adsorbing medium, as through a column of magnesia, gelatin, or starch, yielding stratified, sometimes chromatically distinct, constituent layers. [CHROMATO- + -GRAPHY.] —**chro′ma·tog′ra·pher** *n.* —**chro·mat′o·graph′ic** (krō-măt′ə-grăf′ĭk, krō′mə-tə-) *adj.*

chro·ma·tol·y·sis (krō′mə-tŏl′ə-sĭs) *n. Biology.* The solution and disintegration of stainable material, as of chromatin, within a cell. [CHROMATO- + -LYSIS.]

chro·mat·o·phore (krō-măt′ə-fôr′, krō′mə-tə-, -fōr′) *n. Biology.* A pigment-containing or pigment-producing cell; especially, a pigment-containing animal cell, as in certain lizards, that by expansion or contraction can change the overall color of the skin. Also called "pigment cell." [CHROMATO- + -PHORE.] —**chro′ma·to·phor′ic** *adj.*

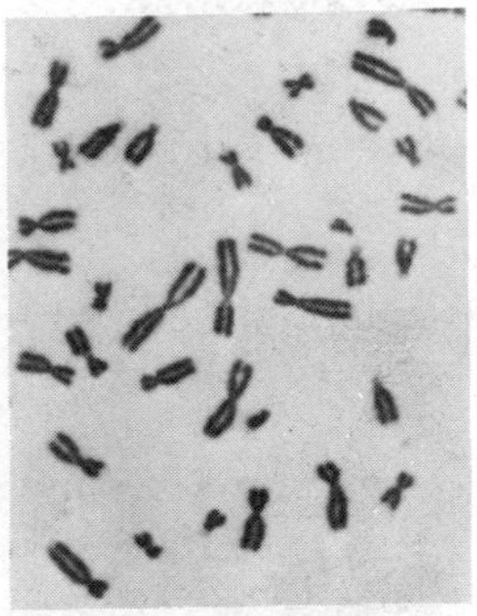

chromosome
Chromosomes from a lymphocyte of a normal human male

chrome (krōm) *n.* **1. a.** Chromium. **b.** Anything plated with a chromium alloy. **2.** A pigment containing chromium. —*tr.v.* **chromed, chroming, chromes. 1.** To plate with chromium. **2.** To tan or dye with a chromium compound. [French, from Greek *khrōma,* color (from the brilliant colors of the chromium compounds). See **ghrēu-** in Appendix.*]

-chrome. Indicates pigment, color, or colored; for example, **autochrome.** [From Greek *khrōma,* color. See **ghrēu-** in Appendix.*]

chrome alum. A violet-red crystalline compound, $CrK(SO_4)_2 \cdot 12H_2O$, used in tanning, as a mordant, and in photography.

chrome green. 1. Any of a class of green pigments consisting of chrome yellow and iron blue in various proportions. **2.** Very dark yellowish green to moderate or strong green. See **color.**

chrome red. A light orange to red pigment consisting of basic lead chromate with varying proportions of $PbCrO_4$ and PbO.

chrome yellow. Lead chromate, $PbCrO_4$, a yellow pigment often combined with lead sulfate, $PbSO_4$, for lighter hues.

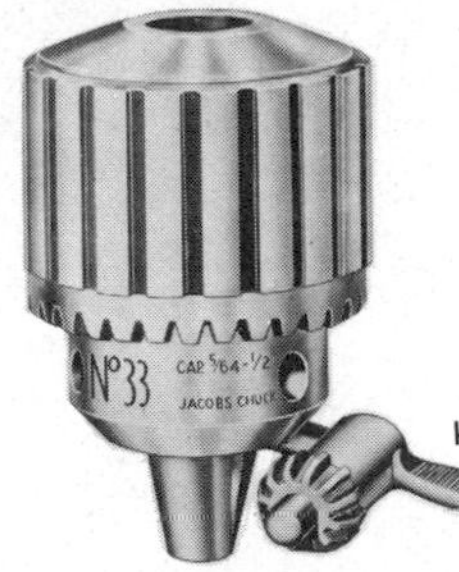

chuck²

chro·mic (krō′mĭk) *adj.* Of, pertaining to, or containing chromium, especially with valence 3.

chromic acid. 1. A corrosive, oxidizing acid, H_2CrO_4, known only in solution. **2.** The anhydride of this acid, CrO_3, a purplish crystalline material that reacts explosively with reducing agents and is used in chromium plating, as an oxidizing agent, and to color glass and rubber.

chromic oxide. A bright-green, crystalline powder, Cr_2O_3, used in metallurgy and as a paint pigment.

chro·mite (krō′mīt′) *n.* A widely distributed black to brownish-black chromium ore, $FeCr_2O_4$. [CHROM(O)- + -ITE.]

chro·mi·um (krō′mē-əm) *n. Symbol* **Cr** A lustrous, hard, steel-gray metallic element, resistant to tarnish and corrosion, and found primarily in chromite. It is used as a catalyst, to harden steel alloys, to produce stainless steels, in corrosion-resistant decorative platings, and as pigment in glass. Atomic number 24, atomic weight 51.996, melting point 1,890°C, boiling point 2,482°C, specific gravity 7.18, valences 2, 3, 6. See **element.** [New Latin, from French *chrome,* CHROM(E).]

chromo-, chrom-. Indicates: **1.** Color, colored, staining, or pigment; for example, **chromophore, chromosome. 2.** Chromium or chromic acid; for example, **chromate.** [Greek *khrōma,* color. See **ghrēu-** in Appendix.*]

chro·mo·gen (krō′mə-jən) *n.* **1.** *Chemistry.* A substance capable of chemical conversion into a pigment or dye. **2.** *Biology.* A strongly pigmented or pigment-generating organ or organelle. [CHROMO- + -GEN.] —**chro′mo·gen′ic** *adj.*

chro·mo·lith·o·graph (krō′mō-lĭth′ə-grăf′, -gräf′) *n.* A colored print produced by chromolithography.

chro·mo·li·thog·ra·phy (krō′mō-lĭ-thŏg′rə-fē) *n.* The art or process of printing color pictures from a series of stone or zinc plates by lithography. —**chro′mo·li·thog′ra·pher** *n.* —**chro′mo·lith′o·graph′ic** (-lĭth′ə-grăf′ĭk) *adj.*

chro·mo·mere (krō′mə-mîr′) *n.* One of the serially aligned chromatin granules forming a chromosome. [CHROMO- + -MERE.]

chro·mo·ne·ma (krō′mə-nē′mə) *n., pl.* **-mata** (-mə-tə). The coiled filamentous core of a chromosome. [CHROMO- + Greek *nēma,* thread (see **snē-¹** in Appendix*).] —**chro′mo·ne′mal** (-nē′məl), **chro′mo·ne·mat′ic** (-mō-nĭ-măt′ĭk), **chro′mo·ne′mic** (-nē′mĭk) *adj.*

chro·mo·phore (krō′mə-fôr′, -fōr′) *n.* A molecular group capable of selective light absorption resulting in coloration of aromatic compounds. [CHROMO- + -PHORE.] —**chro′mo·phor′ic** (-fôr′ĭk, -fōr′ĭk) *adj.*

chro·mo·plast (krō′mə-plăst′) *n. Botany.* A colored plastid containing a pigment other than or in addition to chlorophyll. [CHROMO- + -PLAST.]

chro·mo·pro·tein (krō′mō-prō′tēn′, -prō′tē-ĭn) *n.* A substance consisting of a protein and a chromophore or pigment.

chro·mo·some (krō′mə-sōm′) *n.* A DNA-containing linear body of the cell nuclei of plants and animals, responsible for the determination and transmission of hereditary characteristics. [CHROMO- + -SOME (body).] —**chro′mo·so′mal** (-sō′məl), **chro′mo·so′mic** (-sō′mĭk) *adj.* —**chro′mo·so′mal·ly** *adv.*

chro·mo·sphere (krō′mə-sfîr′) *n.* **1.** An incandescent, transparent layer of gas, primarily hydrogen, several thousand miles in depth, that lies above and surrounds the photosphere of the sun but is distinctly separate from the corona. **2.** A similar gaseous layer around a star. [CHROMO- (from its rosy color) + SPHERE.] —**chro′mo·spher′ic** (-sfîr′ĭk, -sfĕr′ĭk) *adj.*

chro·mous (krō′məs) *adj.* Of, pertaining to, or containing chromium, especially with valence 2. [From CHROME.]

chron. chronological; chronology.

Chron. Chronicles (Old Testament).

chro·nax·y (krō′năk′sē) *n., pl.* **-ies.** Also **chro·nax·i·a** (-năk′sē′ə), **chro·nax·ie** (-năk′sē). The time interval necessary to stimulate a muscle or nerve fiber electrically with twice the minimum current needed to elicit a threshold response. [French *chronaxie* : CHRON(O)- + Greek *axia,* value, from *axios,* worthy (see **ag-** in Appendix*).]

chron·ic (krŏn′ĭk) *adj.* **1.** Of long duration; continuing; constant. **2.** Prolonged; lingering, as certain diseases. Compare **acute. 3.** Subject to a disease or habit for a long time; inveterate. [French *chronique,* from Latin *chronicus,* from Greek *khronikos,* pertaining to time, from *khronos*†, time.] —**chron′i·cal·ly** *adv.* —**chro·nic′i·ty** (krō-nĭs′ə-tē) *n.*

chron·i·cle (krŏn′ĭ-kəl) *n.* A chronological record of historical events. —*tr.v.* **chronicled, -cling, -cles.** To record in, or in the form of, a chronicle. [Middle English *cronicle,* from Norman French, from Old French *cronique,* from Latin *chronica,* from Greek *(biblia) khronika,* "chronological (books)," from *khronikos,* chronological. See **chronic.**] —**chron′i·cler** (-klər) *n.*

Chron·i·cles (krŏn′ĭ-kəlz) *pl.n. Abbr.* **Chron.** In the Old Testament, one of two books, I and II Chronicles.

chrono-, chron-. Indicates time; for example, **chronaxy, chronometer.** [From Greek *khronos,* time. See **chronic.**]

chron·o·gram (krŏn′ə-grăm′) *n.* **1.** The record produced by a chronograph. **2.** An inscribed phrase in which certain letters can be read as Roman numerals indicating a specific date. [CHRONO- + -GRAM.] —**chron′o·gram·mat′ic** (-grə-măt′ĭk) *adj.* —**chron′o·gram·mat′i·cal·ly** *adv.*

chron·o·graph (krŏn′ə-grăf′, -gräf′, krō′nə-) *n.* An instrument that registers or graphically records time intervals such as the duration of an event. [CHRONO- + -GRAPH.] —**chron′o·graph′ic** *adj.* —**chron′o·graph′i·cal·ly** *adv.*

chronol. chronological; chronology.

chron·o·log·i·cal (krŏn′ə-lŏj′ĭ-kəl, krō′nə-) *adj.* Also **chron·o·log·ic** (-lŏj′ĭk). *Abbr.* **chron., chronol. 1.** Arranged in order of time of occurrence. **2.** In accordance with or relating to chronology. —**chron′o·log′i·cal·ly** *adv.*

chronological age. *Abbr.* **C.A.** The number of years a person has lived, used in psychometrics as a comparison standard for various performance measures. Compare **mental age.**

chro·nol·o·gy (krə-nŏl′ə-jē) *n., pl.* **-gies.** *Abbr.* **chron., chronol. 1.** The determination of dates and the sequence of events. **2.** The arrangement of events in time. **3.** A chronological list or table. [CHRONO- + -LOGY.] —**chro·nol′o·gist** *n.*

chro·nom·e·ter (krə-nŏm′ə-tər) *n.* An exceptionally precise clock, watch, or other timepiece. [CHRONO- + -METER.] —**chron′o·met′ric** (krŏn′ə-mĕt′rĭk, krō′nə-), **chron′o·met′ri·cal** *adj.* —**chron′o·met′ri·cal·ly** *adv.*

chro·nom·e·try (krə-nŏm′ə-trē) *n.* The scientific measurement of time. [CHRONO- + -METRY.]

chron·o·scope (krŏn′ə-skōp′, krō′nə-) *n.* An optical instrument

ă pat/ā pay/âr care/ä father/b bib/ch church/d deed/ĕ pet/ē be/f fife/g gag/h hat/hw which/ĭ pit/ī pie/îr pier/j judge/k kick/l lid, needle/m mum/n no, sudden/ng thing/ŏ pot/ō toe/ô paw, for/oi noise/ou out/ŏŏ took/ōō boot/p pop/r roar/s sauce/sh ship, dish/

for measuring minute time intervals. [CHRONO- + -SCOPE.] —**chron'o·scop'ic** (krŏn'ə-skŏp'ĭk, krō'nə-) *adj.*

-chroous. Indicates colored; for example, **isochroous.** [From Greek *khrōs,* flesh, complexion, color. See **ghreu-** in Appendix.*]

chrys·a·lid (krĭs'ə-lĭd) *n. Entomology.* A chrysalis. —*adj.* Also **chry·sal·i·dal** (krĭ-săl'ə-dəl). Pertaining to or resembling a chrysalis.

chrys·a·lis (krĭs'ə-lĭs) *n., pl.* **-lises** or **chrysalides** (krĭ-săl'ə-dēz'). *Entomology.* **1.** The third stage in the development of an insect, especially of a moth or butterfly, enclosed in a firm case or cocoon; the **pupa** *(see).* **2.** Anything still in the process of development. [Latin *chrȳsallis,* from Greek *khrusallis,* the golden pupa of a butterfly, from *khrusos,* gold. See **chryso-**.]

chry·san·the·mum (krĭ-săn'thə-məm) *n.* **1.** Any of several plants of the genus *Chrysanthemum,* the cultivated forms especially having showy flowers of various colors and sizes. **2.** The flower of any of these plants. [Latin *chrȳsanthemum,* from Greek *khrusanthemon,* "gold flower" : CHRYS(O)- + *anthemon,* flower, from *anthos,* flower (see **andh-** in Appendix*).]

chrys·a·ro·bin (krĭs'ə-rō'bən) *n.* A medicine obtained from a deposit found in the wood of the araroba tree and used to treat certain chronic skin conditions. [CHRYS(O)- (from its golden color) + (AR)AROB(A) + -IN.]

chrys·el·e·phan·tine (krĭs'ĕl-ə-făn'tēn', -tīn') *adj.* Made of gold and ivory. [Greek *khruselephantinos* : CHRYS(O)- + *elephantinos,* of ivory, from *elephas,* ivory (see **elephant**).]

chryso-, chrys-. Indicates gold or the color of gold; for example, **chrysotile, chrysarobin.** [From Greek *khrusos,* gold, from Semitic, akin to Hebrew *ḥarūz,* gold.]

chrys·o·ber·yl (krĭs'ə-bĕr'əl) *n.* A green to yellow vitreous mineral, $BeAl_2O_4$, used as a gemstone. [Latin *chrȳsobēryllus,* from Greek *khrusobērullos* : CHRYSO- + BERYL.]

chrys·o·lite (krĭs'ə-līt') *n.* A mineral, **olivine** *(see).* [Middle English *crisolite,* from Old French, from Latin *chrȳsolithus,* from Greek *khrusolithos,* "goldstone" : CHRYSO- + -LITE.]

chrys·o·prase (krĭs'ə-prāz') *n.* An apple-green chalcedony used as a gemstone. [Middle English *crisopase,* from Old French *crisopace, crisopras,* from Latin *chrȳsoprasus,* from Greek *khrusoprasos,* "gold green" : CHRYSO- + *prason,* leek (see **praseodymium**).]

Chrys·os·tom (krĭs'əs-təm, krĭ-sŏs'təm), Saint **John.** A.D. 345?–407. Patriarch of Constantinople (398–404).

chrys·o·tile (krĭs'ə-tĭl') *n.* A fibrous mineral variety of serpentine forming part of commercial asbestos. [CHRYSO- + Greek *tilos,* something plucked, fine hair, from *tillein*†, to pluck.]

CHS Airport code for Charleston, South Carolina.

chthon·ic (thŏn'ĭk) *adj.* Also **chtho·ni·an** (thō'nē-ən). Pertaining to the gods and spirits of the underworld. [Greek *khthonios,* under the earth, from *khthōn,* earth. See **dhghem-** in Appendix.*]

chub (chŭb) *n., pl.* **chub** or **chubs. 1.** Any of various freshwater fishes of the family Cyprinidae, related to the carps and minnows; especially, a Eurasian species, *Leuciscus cephalus.* **2.** Any of various other fishes, such as a whitefish of the genus *Coregonus* or a marine fish of the genus *Kyphosus.* [Middle English *chubbe, chobe,* possibly from Scandinavian, akin to Swedish dialectal *kubb,* block, log. See **ku** in Appendix.*]

chub·by (chŭb'ē) *adj.* **-bier, -biest.** Rounded and plump. See Synonyms at **fat.** [Probably from CHUB, from the plumpness of the fish.] —**chub'bi·ness** *n.*

Chu·but (chōō-bōōt', -vōōt'). A river rising in the Andes of southeastern Argentina and flowing 500 miles east across Patagonia to the Atlantic Ocean.

chuck[1] (chŭk) *tr.v.* **chucked, chucking, chucks. 1.** To pat or squeeze fondly or playfully, especially under the chin. **2.** To throw; toss. **3.** *Informal.* To throw out; discard. **4.** *Informal.* To force out; eject. Used with *out.* —*n.* **1.** An affectionate pat or squeeze under the chin. **2.** A throw, toss, or pitch. [Perhaps from Old French *choquer, chuquer,* to strike, SHOCK.]

chuck[2] (chŭk) *n.* **1.** A cut of beef extending from the neck to the ribs and including the shoulder blade. **2.** *Western U.S.* Food. **3.** *Machinery.* A clamp that holds a tool, or the material being worked, in a machine such as a drill or a lathe. [Variant of CHOCK (wedge).]

chuck[3] (chŭk) *intr.v.* **chucked, chucking, chucks.** To make a clucking sound. —*n.* A clucking sound. [Imitative.]

chuck[4] (chŭk) *n. Informal.* A woodchuck.

chuck-a-luck (chŭk'ə-lŭk') *n.* Also **chuck-luck.** A gambling game in which players bet on the possible combinations of three thrown dice. [Probably CHUCK (to throw) + LUCK.]

chuck-full. Variant of **chock-full.**

chuck·hole (chŭk'hōl') *n. Regional.* A rut or mudhole in a road. [Probably from CHUCK (to throw).]

chuck·le (chŭk'əl) *intr.v.* **-led, -ling, -les. 1.** To laugh quietly or to oneself. **2.** To cluck or chuck, as a hen. —*n.* A quiet laugh of mild amusement or satisfaction. [Probably frequentative of CHUCK (to make a clucking sound).] —**chuck'ler** *n.*

chuck·le·head (chŭk'əl-hĕd') *n. Informal.* A stupid and gauche person; blockhead. —**chuck'le·head'ed** *adj.*

chuck wagon. A wagon equipped with food and cooking utensils, as in a lumber camp.

chuck·wal·la (chŭk'wŏl'ə) *n.* A lizard, *Sauromalus obesus,* of the southwestern United States and Mexico, related to the iguana. [Mexican Spanish *chacahuala,* from Shoshonean *tcaxxwal.*]

chuck-will's-wid·ow (chŭk'wilz'wĭd'ō) *n.* A bird, *Caprimulgus carolinensis,* of the southern and central United States, related to and resembling the whippoorwill. [Imitative of its note.]

Chud·sko·ye O·ze·ro. The Russian name for Lake **Peipus.**

chu·fa (chōō'fə) *n.* A sedge, *Cyperus esculentus,* native to the Old World, having edible, nutlike tubers. [Spanish, fluff, nonsense, from Old Spanish, from *chufar, chuflar,* to hiss at, laugh at, from Vulgar Latin *sufilāre* (unattested), variant of Latin *sībilāre,* to whistle at, hiss down. See **swei-[1]** in Appendix.*]

chug (chŭg) *n.* A dull explosive sound, usually short and repeated, made by or as if by a laboring engine. —*intr.v.* **chugged, chugging, chugs. 1.** To make such sounds. **2.** To travel or move while making such sounds. [Imitative.]

Chu·gach Mountains (chōō'găch'). A range of southern Alaska, extending about 300 miles along the coast from Cook Inlet to the St. Elias Mountains to the east. Highest elevation, Mount Marcus Baker (13,250 feet).

chu·kar (chōō'kär') *n.* An Old World partridge, *Alectoris graeca,* introduced into western North America. [Hindi *cakor,* from Sanskrit *cakōra.* See **kau-[1]** in Appendix.*]

Chuk·chi (chŏŏk'chē) *n., pl.* **Chukchi** or **-chis.** Also **Chuk·chee. 1.** A Mongoloid people of northeastern Siberia. **2.** A member of this people. **3.** The language of this people, not related to the Indo-European, Uralic, Altaic, or Eskimo-Aleut language families, and noted for being pronounced differently by men and women.

Chuk·chi Peninsula (chŏŏk'chē). A peninsula of the Soviet Union, in the extreme northeast opposite Alaska.

Chu Kiang (jōō' jăng'). A river in southern Kwangtung Province, flowing 110 miles from Canton to the South China Sea. Also called "Canton River," "Pearl River."

chuk·ka (chŭk'ə) *n.* A short, ankle-length boot, usually made of suede, having two pairs of eyelets. Also called "chukka boot." [From CHUKKER (because polo players wear a kind of chukka boot).]

chuk·ker (chŭk'ər) *n.* Also **chuk·kar.** One of the periods of play, lasting 7½ minutes, in a polo match. [Hindi *cakkar,* circle, turn, from Sanskrit *cakra-.* See **kwel-[1]** in Appendix.*]

Chu·lym (chōō-lĭm'). Also **Chu·lim.** A river rising in the south-central Soviet Union, in Asia, and flowing 700 miles north and then west to the Ob south of Tomsk.

chum[1] (chŭm) *n.* An intimate friend or companion. —*intr.v.* **chummed, chumming, chums. 1.** To be an intimate friend. **2.** To share the same room. [Oxford University slang, said to be from *chamber fellow,* "roommate."]

chum[2] (chŭm) *n.* Bait usually consisting of oily fish ground up and scattered on the water. —*intr.v.* **chummed, chumming, chums.** To fish with chum. [Origin unknown.]

chum·my (chŭm'ē) *adj.* **-mier, -miest.** *Informal.* Intimate; friendly; amicable. See Synonyms at **familiar.** —**chum'mi·ly** *adv.* —**chum'mi·ness** *n.*

chump[1] (chŭmp) *n.* A blockhead; dolt. [Probably a blend of CHUNK and LUMP or STUMP.]

chump[2] (chŭmp) *v.* **chumped, chumping, chumps.** —*tr.* To munch; chew. —*intr.* To make a chewing movement with the jaws. [Variant of CHAMP (to chew).]

Chung·king (chŏŏng'kĭng'). A city in southeastern Szechwan Province, southern China, on the Yangtze River. Formerly the provisional capital of China (1937–46). Population, 2,121,000.

chunk (chŭngk) *n.* **1.** A thick mass or piece of something. **2.** A fair or substantial amount. [Probably a nasalized variant of CHUCK (wedge).]

chunk·y (chŭng'kē) *adj.* **-ier, -iest. 1.** Short and thick; thickset; stocky. **2.** In chunks. —**chunk'i·ness** *n.*

church (chûrch) *n.* Also **Church.** *Abbr.* **Ch., C., ch., c. 1.** *Capital* **C.** The company of all Christians regarded as a mystic spiritual body. **2.** A building for public worship. **3.** A congregation. **4.** Public divine worship in a church; a religious service. **5.** *Usually capital* **C.** A specified Christian denomination: *the Presbyterian Church.* **6.** Ecclesiastical power as distinguished from the secular: *the separation of church and state.* **7.** The clerical profession; clergy. **8.** *Christian Science.* "The structure of Truth and Love." (Mary Baker Eddy). —*tr.v.* **churched, churching, churches.** To conduct church services for; especially, to perform a religious service for (a woman after childbirth). —*adj.* Of or pertaining to the church; ecclesiastical. [Middle English *chirche,* Old English *cirice,* from West Germanic *kirika* (unattested), from Late Greek *kurikon,* variant of *(dōma) kuriakon,* the Lord's (house), from Greek *kuriakos,* of the Lord, from *kurios,* lord. See **keu-[3]** in Appendix.*]

church·go·er (chûrch'gō'ər) *n.* One who attends church regularly. —**church'go'ing** *adj. & n.*

Church·ill (chûr'chĭl). A river rising in northwestern Saskatchewan, Canada, and flowing 1,000 miles generally northeast to Hudson Bay in northeastern Manitoba.

Church·ill (chûr'chĭl), **John.** See First Duke of **Marlborough.**

Church·ill (chûr'chĭl), Sir **Winston (Leonard Spencer).** 1874–1965. Prime minister of the United Kingdom (1940–45 and 1951–55).

church·ly (chûrch'lē) *adj.* Of, pertaining to, or fit for a church. —**church'li·ness** *n.*

church·man (chûrch'mən) *n., pl.* **-men** (-mĭn). **1.** A clergyman; priest. **2.** A member of an established church. —**church'man·ly** *adj.* —**church'man·ship'** *n.*

Church of Christ, Scientist. The official name of the Christian Science Church. See **Christian Science.**

Church of England. *Abbr.* **C. of E.** The episcopal and liturgical national church of England, which withdrew its recognition of papal authority in the 16th century. See **Anglican Church.**

Church of Jesus Christ of Latter-day Saints. The official name of the Mormon Church. See **Mormon.**

Church of Rome. The **Roman Catholic Church** *(see).*

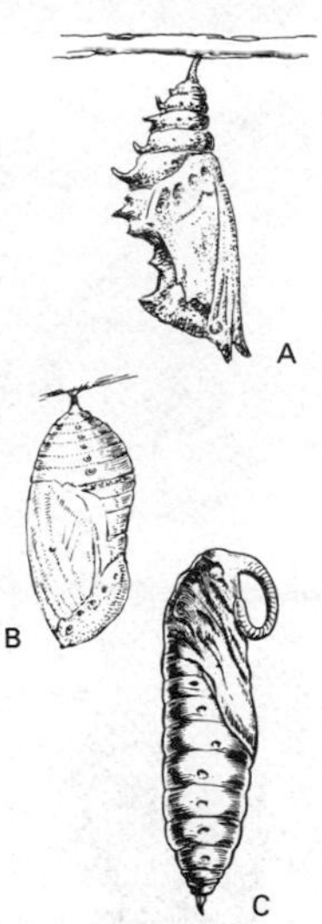

chrysalis
A. Chrysalis of the mourning cloak butterfly
B. Chrysalis of the monarch butterfly
C. Chrysalis of a hawk moth

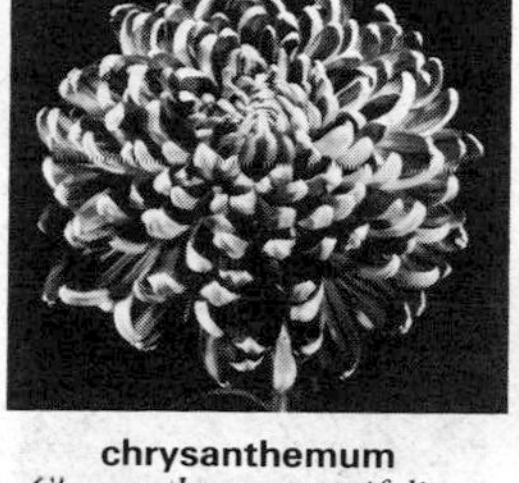

chrysanthemum
Chrysanthemum morifolium

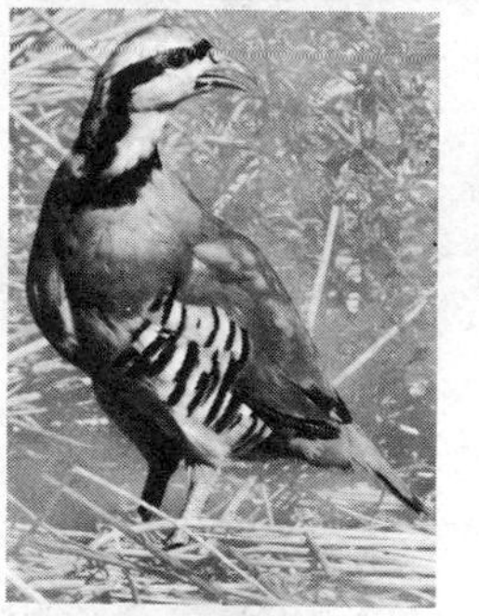

chukar

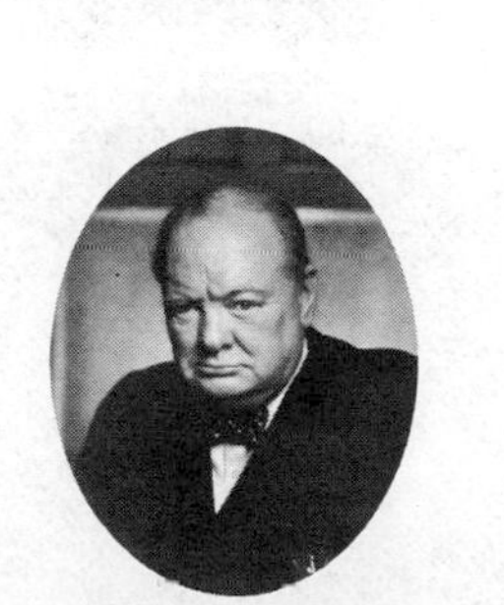

Winston Churchill

Church Slavonic. The literary language of Slavic manuscripts written after the early 11th century and still used as a liturgical language by several churches of the Eastern Orthodoxy in Slavic countries.
church text. *Printing.* **Black letter** *(see).*
church·war·den (chûrch′wôrd′n) *n.* **1.** *Anglican Church.* A lay officer chosen annually by the vicar or the congregation to handle the secular and legal affairs of the parish. **2.** *Episcopal Church.* One of two elected chief lay officers of the vestry.
church·wom·an (chûrch′wŏŏm′ən) *n., pl.* **-women** (-wĭm′ĭn). A female member of a church.
church·yard (chûrch′yärd′) *n.* A yard adjacent to a church, often used as a burial ground.
churl (chûrl) *n.* **1.** A rude, boorish person. **2.** A miser; niggard. **3. a.** A **ceorl** *(see).* **b.** A medieval English peasant. [Middle English *churl, cherl,* man, husband, Old English *ceorl,* man, free man of the lowest rank. See **karlaz** in Appendix.*]
churl·ish (chûr′lĭsh) *adj.* **1. a.** Boorish. **b.** Vulgar. **2.** Difficult to work; intractable. —**churl′ish·ly** *adv.* —**churl′ish·ness** *n.*
churn (chûrn) *n.* A vessel or device in which cream or milk is agitated to separate the oily globules from the caseous and serous parts, used to make butter. —*v.* **churned, churning, churns.** —*tr.* **1.** To stir or agitate (milk or cream) in a churn in order to make butter. **2.** To make by the agitation of milk or cream: *churn butter.* **3.** To shake or agitate vigorously. —*intr.* **1.** To make butter by operating a churn. **2.** To move with great agitation. [Middle English *chirne, cherine,* Old English *cyrin, cyrn,* from Germanic *kernjōn* (unattested).] —**churn′er** *n.*

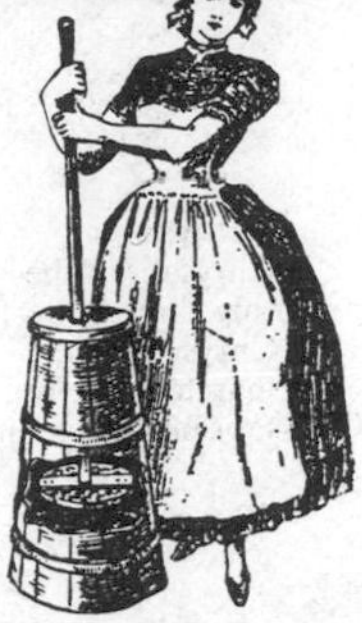

churn

churn·ing (chûr′nĭng) *n.* **1.** The act of operating a churn. **2.** The amount of butter churned at one time.
churr (chûr) *n.* The sharp, whirring or trilling sound made by some insects and birds. —*intr.v.* **churred, churring, churrs.** To make this sound. [Imitative.]
Chur·ri·gue·resque (chŏŏr′ĭ-gə-rĕsk′) *adj.* Of or relating to a style of baroque architecture of Spain and its Latin-American colonies, characterized by elaborate and extravagant decoration. [Spanish *churrigueresco,* after José *Churriguera* (1650–1723), Spanish architect.]
chute (shōōt) *n.* **1.** An inclined trough, passage, or channel down which things may pass. **2.** A waterfall or rapid. **3.** *Informal.* A parachute. [French, a fall, from Old French *cheoite,* feminine past participle of *cheoir,* to fall, from Vulgar Latin *cadēre* (unattested), from Latin *cadere.* See **kad-** in Appendix.*]
Chu Teh (jōō′ dŭ′). Born 1886. Chinese military leader.
chut·ney (chŭt′nē) *n.* Also **chut·nee.** A pungent relish made of fruits, spices, and herbs. [Hindi *catnī*†.]
chutz·pah (KHŏŏts′pə) *n. Slang.* Brazenness; gall. [Yiddish.]
Chu·vash (chōō-väsh′) *n., pl.* **Chuvash** or **-vashes. 1.** One of a Turkic-speaking Tatar people living chiefly in the Chuvash A.S.S.R. **2.** The Turkic language of these people. [Russian, from Chuvash *čăvaš,* akin to Turkish *yavaş,* gentle.]
Chu·vash Autonomous Soviet Socialist Republic (chōō-väsh′). An administrative division, 7,064 square miles in area, of the western Russian S.F.S.R. Population, 1,167,000. Capital, Cheboksary.

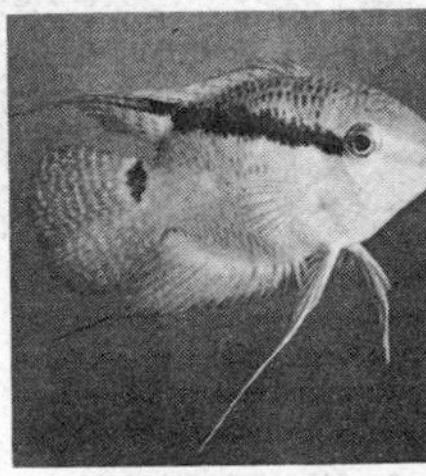

cichlid
Cichlasoma festivum

chyle (kīl) *n.* A thick white or pale-yellow fluid, consisting of lymph and finely emulsified fat, that is taken up by the lacteals from the intestine in digestion. [Latin *chȳlus,* juice, from Greek *khulos,* from *khein,* to pour. See **gheu-** in Appendix.*] —**chy·la′ceous** (kī-lā′shəs), **chy′lous** (kī′ləs) *adj.*
chyme (kīm) *n.* The thick semifluid mass of partly digested food that is passed from the stomach to the duodenum. [Late Latin *chȳmus,* from Greek *khumos,* juice, from *khein,* to pour. See **chyle.**] —**chy′mous** (kī′məs) *adj.*
chy·mo·sin (kī′mə-sĭn) *n.* An enzyme, **rennin** *(see).* [CHYM(E) + -OS(E) + -IN.]
chy·mo·tryp·sin (kī′mə-trĭp′sĭn) *n.* A pancreatic digestive enzyme. [CHYM(E) + TRYPSIN.]
Ci curie.
CIA Central Intelligence Agency.
Cib·ber (sĭb′ər), **Colley.** 1671–1757. English playwright.
Cí·bo·la, Seven Cities of (sē′bō-lä). A legendary land in the North American Southwest, sought by 16th-century Spanish explorers for its rumored treasure.
ci·bo·ri·um (sĭ-bôr′ē-əm, sĭ-bōr′-) *n., pl.* **-boria** (-bôr′ē-ə, -bōr′ē-ə). **1.** A vaulted canopy permanently placed over an altar. **2.** A covered receptacle for holding the consecrated wafers of the Eucharist. [Medieval Latin *cibōrium,* from Latin, drinking vessel, from Greek *kibōrion,* the seed vessel of the Indian lotus, hence, a cup, probably from Semitic.]

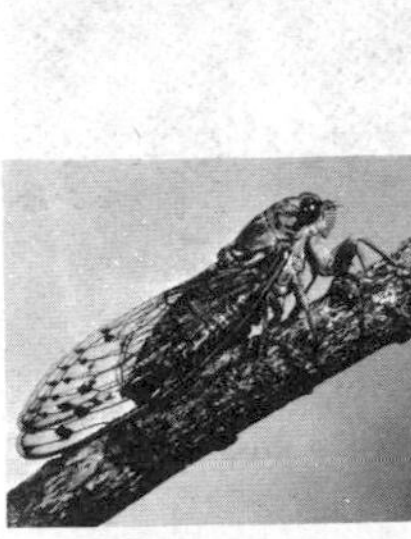

cicada
Cicada hieroglyphica

ci·ca·da (sĭ-kā′də, -kä′də) *n., pl.* **-das** or **-dae** (-dē′). Any of various insects of the family Cicadidae, having a broad head, membranous wings, and, in the male, a pair of resonating organs that produce a characteristic high-pitched, droning sound. [Latin *cicāda,* probably of Mediterranean origin.]
cicada killer. A large wasp, *Sphecius speciosus,* that preys upon cicadas.
cic·a·trix (sĭk′ə-trĭks′, sĭ-kā′trĭks) *n., pl.* **cicatrices** (sĭk′ə-trī′sēz, sĭ-kā′trə-sēz′). **1.** Recently formed connective tissue on a healing wound; scar tissue. **2.** *Botany.* A scar left where a leaf or a branch has been detached. [Middle English *cicatrice,* from Latin *cicātrix*†.] —**cic′a·tri′cial** (sĭk′ə-trĭsh′əl), **ci·cat′ri·cose′** (sĭ-kăt′rĭ-kōs′) *adj.*
cic·e·ly (sĭs′ə-lē) *n., pl.* **-ies.** See **sweet cicely.** [Middle English *ciceli, seseli,* from Latin *seselis,* from Greek *seselis*†.]
Cic·e·ly. Variant of **Cecilia.**
cic·e·ro (sĭs′ə-rō′) *n., pl.* **-ros.** *Printing.* A unit of measurement for type, slightly larger than the pica, used in Europe. [First used in an edition (1458) of Cicero.]
Cic·e·ro (sĭs′ə-rō′). A city of northeastern Illinois and suburb of Chicago. Population, 70,000.
Cic·e·ro (sĭs′ə-rō′), **Marcus Tullius.** 106–43 B.C. Roman statesman and orator.
cic·e·ro·ne (sĭs′ə-rō′nē) *n., pl.* **-nes** or **-ni** (-nē). A guide who conducts sightseers. [Italian *cicerone,* originally "a learned antiquarian," from *Cicerone,* CICERO.]
Cic·e·ro·ni·an (sĭs′ə-rō′nē-ən) *adj.* Of or resembling Cicero or his rhetorical style.
cich·lid (sĭk′lĭd) *n.* Any of various tropical freshwater fishes of the family Cichlidae, many of which are popular as aquarium fish. [New Latin *Cichlidae,* from *Cichla,* type genus, from Greek *kikhlē,* thrush, also, a sea fish. See **ghel-[1]** in Appendix.*]
-cide. Indicates: **1.** Killer of; for example, **regicide, insecticide. 2.** Murder or killing of; for example, **genocide.** [French, from Latin *-cīda,* killer, and *-cīdium,* killing, from *caedere,* to kill. See **skhai-** in Appendix.*]
ci·der (sī′dər) *n.* Also *chiefly British* **cy·der.** The juice pressed from apples or, formerly, from other fruits, used to produce vinegar or as a beverage. The unfermented drink is called *sweet cider,* and the fermented drink *hard cider.* [Middle English *cidre, sidre,* from Old French *sidre, cisdre,* from Medieval Latin *sīcera,* from Greek (Septuagint) *sikera,* strong drink, from Hebrew *shēkār.*]
cider press. A press used for crushing apples.
Cien·fue·gos (syĕn-fwā′gōs). A city and port on the southern coast of western Cuba. Population, 100,000.
ci·gar (sĭ-gär′) *n.* A small, compact roll of tobacco leaves prepared for smoking. [Spanish *cigarro,* possibly from Mayan *sik′ar,* to smoke, from *sik′,* tobacco.]
cig·a·rette (sĭg′ə-rĕt′, sĭg′ə-rĕt′) *n.* Also **cig·a·ret.** A small roll of finely cut tobacco for smoking, usually enclosed in a wrapper of thin paper. [French *cigarette,* diminutive of *cigare,* cigar, from Spanish *cigarro,* CIGAR.]
cig·a·ril·lo (sĭg′ə-rĭl′ō) *n., pl.* **-los.** A small, narrow cigar, somewhat longer than a cigarette. [Spanish, diminutive of *cigarro,* CIGAR.]
ci·gar-store Indian (sĭ-gär′stôr′, -stōr′). A carved and painted figure, a **wooden Indian** *(see).*
ci·lan·tro (sĭ-lăn′trō) *n.* The parsleylike leaves of fresh coriander, used in Oriental cookery. [Origin uncertain.]
cil·i·a (sĭl′ē-ə) *pl.n. Singular* **-ium** (-ē-əm). **1.** Microscopic hairlike processes extending from a cell surface and often capable of rhythmical motion. **2.** The eyelashes. [New Latin, plural of *cilium,* eyelash, hairlike process, from Latin, the lower eyelid. See **kel-[4]** in Appendix.*]
cil·i·ar·y (sĭl′ē-ĕr′ē) *adj.* **1.** Of, pertaining to, or resembling cilia. **2.** Of or pertaining to the ciliary body.
ciliary body. The thickened part of the vascular tunic of the eye that connects the choroid with the iris.
cil·i·ate (sĭl′ē-ĭt, -āt′) *adj.* Also **cil·i·at·ed** (-ā′tĭd). Having cilia. —*n.* Any of various protozoans of the class Ciliata, having numerous cilia. [New Latin *Ciliata,* plural of *ciliatus,* having cilia, from CILIA.]
cil·ice (sĭl′ĭs) *n.* A coarse cloth; haircloth. [French, from Latin *cilicium,* from Greek *kilikion,* coarse cloth made of Cilician goats' hair, from *Kilikia,* Cilicia.]
Ci·li·cia (sĭ-lĭsh′ə). An ancient country and Roman province in southeastern Asia Minor, along the Mediterranean Coast south of the Taurus Mountains. —**Ci·li′cian** *adj. & n.*
Ci·li·cian Gates. The ancient name for **Gülek Bogaz.**
cil·i·o·late (sĭl′ē-ə-lāt′) *adj.* Having minute cilia. [From New Latin *ciliolum,* minute cilium, from *cilium,* singular of CILIA.]
Ci·ma·bu·e (chē′mä-bōō′ā), **Giovanni.** Italian painter of the late 13th century.
Cim·ar·ron (sĭm′ə-rōn′, -rŏn′). A river rising in northeastern New Mexico and flowing 692 miles northeast and southeast to join the Arkansas in northeastern Oklahoma.
ci·mex (sī′mĕks′) *n., pl.* **cimices** (sĭm′ə-sēz′). Any insect of the genus *Cimex,* which includes the bedbugs. [New Latin *Cimex,* from Latin *cīmex*†, bedbug.]
Cim·me·ri·an (sĭ-mîr′ē-ən) *adj.* Gloomy; dark. —*n.* One of a mythical people described by Homer as inhabiting a land of perpetual darkness. [Latin *Cimmerius,* from Greek *Kimmerios,* of the *Kimmerioi*†, the Cimmerians.]
CINC, C in C commander in chief.
cinch[1] (sĭnch) *n.* **1.** A girth for a pack or saddle. **2.** *Informal.* A firm grip. **3.** *Slang.* **a.** Something easy to accomplish. **b.** A sure thing. —*v.* **cinched, cinching, cinches.** —*tr.* **1.** To put a saddle girth on. **2.** *Informal.* To get a tight grip on. **3.** *Slang.* To make certain of: *cinch a victory.* —*intr.* To tighten a saddle girth. Often used with *up.* [Spanish *cincha,* "girdle," from Latin *cingula,* from *cingere,* to gird. See **kenk-[1]** in Appendix.*]
cinch[2] (sĭnch) *n.* A card game, a variety of seven-up. [Obscurely from CINCH (girth).]
cin·cho·na (sĭng-kō′nə, sĭn-chō′nə) *n.* **1.** Any of various trees and shrubs of the genus *Cinchona,* native to South America, whose bark yields quinine and other medicinal alkaloids. **2.** The dried bark of any of these trees. In this sense, also called "Peruvian bark." [New Latin, after Francisca Henriquez de Ribera, countess of *Chinchón* (1576–1639), who introduced it into Europe after recovering from a fever through the use of cinchona bark.] —**cin·chon′ic** (sĭng-kŏn′ĭk, sĭn-chŏn′ĭk) *adj.*
cin·cho·nine (sĭng′kə-nēn′) *n.* An alkaloid, $C_{19}H_{22}N_2O$, derived from the bark of various cinchona trees and used as an antimalarial agent. [French : CINCHON(A) + -INE.]
cin·cho·nism (sĭng′kə-nĭz′əm) *n.* A pathological condition resulting from an overdose of cinchona, marked by deafness, headache, giddiness, and dimming eyesight.

ă pat/ā pay/âr care/ä father/b bib/ch church/d deed/ĕ pet/ē be/f fife/g gag/h hat/hw which/ĭ pit/ī pie/îr pier/j judge/k kick/l lid, needle/m mum/n no, sudden/ng thing/ŏ pot/ō toe/ô paw, for/oi noise/ou out/ŏŏ took/ōō boot/p pop/r roar/s sauce/sh ship, dish/

Cin·cin·nat·i (sĭn′sə-năt′ē, -năt′ə). An industrial city of southwestern Ohio, on the Ohio River. Population, 502,500.
Cin·cin·na·tus (sĭn′sə-nā′təs, -năt′əs), **Lucius Quinctius.** 519?–439? B.C. Roman general; a model of simple virtue.
cinc·ture (sĭngk′chər) *n.* **1.** A belt; girdle. **2.** Something that encompasses or surrounds. —*tr.v.* **cinctured, -turing, -tures.** To gird or encompass. [Latin *cinctūra,* girdle, from *cingere* (past participle *cinctus*), to gird. See **kenk-¹** in Appendix.*]
cin·der (sĭn′dər) *n.* **1.** A burned or partly burned substance, such as coal or wood, that is not reduced to ashes, but is incapable of further combustion. **2.** A partly charred substance that can burn further, but without flame. **3.** *Plural.* Ashes. **4.** *Geology.* Volcanic **scoria** *(see).* **5.** *Metallurgy.* **Slag** *(see).* —*tr.v.* **cindered, -dering, -ders.** To burn or reduce to cinders. [Middle English *cinder, sinder,* Old English *sinder,* (iron) slag, dross. See **sendhro-** in Appendix.*] —**cin′der·y** *adj.*
Cin·der·el·la¹ (sĭn′də-rĕl′ə). The fairy-tale heroine who escapes from a life of drudgery through the intervention of a fairy godmother and marries a handsome prince. [CINDER + *-ella,* feminine diminutive suffix.]
Cin·der·el·la² (sĭn′də-rĕl′ə) *n.* Any girl who achieves recognition or affluence after a period of obscurity and neglect.
cin·e·ma (sĭn′ə-mə) *n.* **1.** A **motion picture** *(see).* **2.** A motion-picture theater. —**the cinema. 1. a.** Motion pictures collectively. **b.** The motion-picture industry. **2.** The art of making motion pictures. [Short for CINEMATOGRAPH.] —**cin′e·mat′ic** (sĭn′ə-măt′ĭk) *adj.* —**cin′e·mat′i·cal·ly** *adv.*
cin·e·mat·o·graph (sĭn′ə-măt′ə-grăf′, -gräf′) *n. British.* A motion-picture camera or projector. [French *cinématographe* : Greek *kinēma* (stem *kinēmat-*), motion, from *kinein,* to move (see **kei-³** in Appendix*) + -GRAPH.] —**cin′e·ma·tog′ra·pher** (sĭn′ə-mə-tŏg′rə-fər) *n.* —**cin′e·mat′o·graph′ic** *adj.* —**cin′e·mat′o·graph′i·cal·ly** *adv.*
cin·e·ma·tog·ra·phy (sĭn′ə-mə-tŏg′rə-fē) *n.* The technique of making motion pictures.
cin·e·ol (sĭn′ē-ōl′) *n.* Also **cin·e·ole. Eucalyptol** *(see).* [New Latin *cina*†, wormseed + Latin *oleum,* OIL.]
cin·e·rar·i·a (sĭn′ə-râr′ē-ə) *n.* A plant, *Senecio cruentis,* native to the Canary Islands but widely cultivated as a house plant, having flat clusters of blue or purplish daisylike flowers. [New Latin, from the feminine of Latin *cinerārius,* of ashes (from the ash-colored down on its leaves). See **cinerarium.**]
cin·e·rar·i·um (sĭn′ə-râr′ē-əm) *n., pl.* **-ia** (ē-ə). A place for keeping the ashes of a cremated body. [Latin, from *cinerārius,* of ashes, from *cinis* (stem *ciner-*), ashes. See **keni-** in Appendix.*] —**cin′er·ar′y** (sĭn′ə-rĕr′ē) *adj.*
ci·ne·re·ous (sĭ-nîr′ē-əs) *adj.* **1.** Consisting of or like ashes. **2.** Of the color of ashes; gray tinged with black. [Latin *cinereus,* from *cinis,* ashes. See **keni-** in Appendix.*]
cin·er·in (sĭn′ə-rĭn) *n.* Either of two compounds, $C_{20}H_{28}O_3$ or $C_{21}H_{28}O_5$, used in insecticides. [Latin *cinis* (stem *ciner-*), ashes (see **cinereous**) + -IN.]
cin·gu·lum (sĭng′gyə-ləm) *n., pl.* **-la** (-lə). *Biology.* A girdlelike structure, band, or marking. [New Latin, from Latin, girdle, from *cingere,* to gird. See **kenk-¹** in Appendix.*] —**cin′gu·late** (sĭng′gyə-lĭt), **cin′gu·la′ted** (-lā′tĭd) *adj.*
cin·na·bar (sĭn′ə-bär′) *n.* **1.** A heavy reddish mercuric sulfide, HgS, that is the principal ore of mercury. Also called "vermilion." **2.** Red mercuric sulfide used as a pigment. [Middle English *cynoper, cynabare,* from Old French *cenobre,* from Latin *cinnābaris,* from Greek *kinnabari,* of Oriental origin.]
cin·na·mon (sĭn′ə-mən) *n.* **1.** Either of two trees, *Cinnamomum zeylanicum* or *C. lourerii,* of tropical Asia, having very aromatic bark. **2.** The yellowish-brown bark of either of these trees, dried and often ground, used as a spice. **3.** Any of several trees yielding a spice similar to this. **4.** Light yellowish brown. See **color.** [Middle English *sinamome, cynamone,* from Old French *cinnamome,* from Latin *cinna(mo)mum, cinnamon,* from Greek *kinna(mō)mon,* from Hebrew *qinnāmown.*] —**cin·nam′ic** (sĭ-năm′ĭk), **cin′na·mon′ic** (sĭn′ə-mŏn′ĭk) *adj.*
cinnamon bear. A reddish-brown color phase of the American black bear.
cinnamon stone. A mineral, **essonite** *(see).*
cin·quain (sĭng-kān′) *n.* A five-line stanza. [French, from *cinq,* five (by analogy with QUATRAIN), from Latin *quīnque.* See **penkwe** in Appendix.*]
cinque (sĭngk, săngk) *n.* The number five, in cards or dice. [Middle English *cink,* from Old French *cinq,* from Latin *quīnque.* See **penkwe** in Appendix.*]
cin·que·cen·to (chĭng′kwĭ-chĕn′tō) *n.* The 16th century, especially in Italian art. [Italian, short for *(mil) cinquecento,* "(one thousand) five hundred" : *cinque,* five, from Latin *quīnque* (see **penkwe** in Appendix*) + *cento,* hundred, from Latin *centum* (see **dekm̥** in Appendix*).]
cinque·foil (sĭngk′foil′, săngk′-) *n.* **1.** Any of various plants of the genus *Potentilla,* having compound leaves, often with five lobes. Also called "five-finger." **2.** *Architecture.* A design having five sides composed of converging arcs, usually used as a frame for glass or a panel. [Middle English *cincfoil,* from Old French *cincfoille,* from Latin *quīnquefolium,* "five leaves" (translation of Greek *pentaphullon*) : *quīnque,* five (see **penkwe** in Appendix*) + *folium,* a leaf (see **bhel-³** in Appendix*).]
Cinque Ports (sĭngk). Five former ports of southeastern England, originally, Hastings, Romney, Hythe, Dover, and Sandwich, on the Strait of Dover and the North Sea, granted special privileges by Edward the Confessor in return for services in defending the coast.
CIO, C.I.O. Congress of Industrial Organizations.
ci·on. *Horticulture.* Variant of **scion.**
Ci·pan·go (sĭ-păng′gō) *n. Poetic.* Japan; the name used by Marco Polo.
ci·pher (sī′fər) *n.* Also **cy·pher. 1.** The mathematical symbol (0) denoting absence of quantity; zero. **2.** Any Arabic numeral or figure; a number. **3.** The Arabic system of numerical notation. **4.** A person or thing without influence or value; a nonentity. **5.** Any cryptographic system in which units of plain text of regular length, usually letters, are arbitrarily transposed or substituted according to a predetermined key. Compare **code. 6. a.** The key to such a system. **b.** A message in cipher. **7.** A design combining or interweaving letters or initials; monogram. —*v.* **ciphered, -phering, -phers.** —*intr.* To solve problems in arithmetic; calculate. —*tr.* **1.** To put (a message) in secret writing; encipher. **2.** To solve (a problem) by means of arithmetic. [Middle English *cifre,* zero, from Old French, from Medieval Latin *cifra,* from Arabic *ṣifr.*]
cir., circ. 1. circular. **2.** circulation. **3.** circumference.
cir·ca (sûr′kə) *prep. Abbr.* **ca, c., C.** About. Used before approximate dates or figures. [Latin *circā,* from *circum,* round about, from *circus,* circle. See **sker-³** in Appendix.*]
cir·ca·di·an (sər-kā′dē-ən) *adj. Biology.* Exhibiting approximately 24-hour periodicity. [Latin *circā,* about, CIRCA + *diēs,* day (see **deiw-** in Appendix*).]
Cir·cas·sia (sər-kăsh′ə, -kăsh′ē-ə). A region of the Soviet Union on the northeastern coast of the Black Sea, north of the Caucasus Mountains.
Cir·cas·sian (sər-kăsh′ən, -kăsh′ē-ən) *n.* Also **Cir·cas·sic** (sər-kăs′ĭk). **1.** An inhabitant of Circassia; especially, a member of a Caucasian people inhabiting Circassia, noted for their striking physical beauty. **2.** The North Caucasian language of this people. —*adj.* Of or pertaining to the people, language, or region of Circassia.
Circassian walnut. The mottled or veined light-brown wood of the **English walnut** *(see),* used especially in decorative cabinetwork.
Cir·ce (sûr′sē). An enchantress described in the *Odyssey* who detains Odysseus for a year and turns his men into swine. —**Cir′ce·an** (sûr′sē-ən, sər-sē′ən) *adj.*
cir·ci·nate (sûr′sə-nāt′) *adj.* **1.** Ring-shaped. **2.** Rolled up from the tip, as a young fern frond or a butterfly's tongue. [Latin *circinātus,* from *circināre,* to make circular, from *circinus,* pair of compasses, from *circus,* CIRCLE.] —**cir′ci·nate′ly** *adv.*
Cir·ci·nus (sûr′sə-nəs) *n.* A constellation in the Southern Hemisphere near Musca and Triangulum Australe. [From Latin *circinus,* a pair of compasses. See **circinate.**]
cir·cle (sûr′kəl) *n.* **1.** A plane curve everywhere equidistant from a given fixed point, the center. **2.** A planar region bounded by such a curve. **3.** Anything shaped like a circle, such as a ring or halo. **4.** A circular course, circuit, or orbit. **5.** A curved section or tier of seats in a theater. **6.** A series or process that finishes at its starting point or continuously repeats itself; cycle. **7.** A group of people sharing an interest, activity, or achievement; a set; club. **8.** In some European countries, a territorial or administrative division, especially of a province. **9.** A sphere of influence or interest; domain. **10.** *Logic.* A fallacy in reasoning in which the premise is used to prove the conclusion, and the conclusion used to prove the premise. Also called "vicious circle." —*v.* **circled, -cling, -cles.** —*tr.* **1.** To make or form a circle around; enclose. **2.** To move in a circle around. —*intr.* To move in circles; revolve: *Crows circled overhead.* —See Synonyms at **turn.** [Middle English *cercle,* from Old French, from Latin *circulus,* diminutive of *circus,* ring. See **sker-³** in Appendix.*] —**cir′cler** (-klər) *n.*
Synonyms: *circle, coterie, set, clique, club, fraternity, society.* These nouns denote a group of associates. *Circle* can describe almost any group having common interests or activities on a scale large or small: *sewing circle; financial circles.* It can also designate the extent of personal relationships: *circle of friends. Coterie* applies to a small, intimate group of congenial persons. *Set* suggests a large, loosely bound group defined either by condition *(younger set)* or preoccupation with fashionable activity *(smart set; jet set). Clique* pertains to an exclusive group, usually social, with activities in which outsiders are denied participation. *Club* can imply exclusiveness but often means only a group devoted to a common interest best pursued in company: *Rotary Club; bridge club. Fraternity* most commonly denotes a Greek letter society of male students. It can also mean a professional group not actually organized: *medical fraternity. Society,* as compared here, is usually a rather large, formally organized group with common interests, often cultural.
cir·clet (sûr′klĭt) *n.* A small circle; especially, a circular ornament. [Middle English *cerclett,* band, from Old French, diminutive of *cercle,* CIRCLE.]
cir·cuit (sûr′kĭt) *n.* **1. a.** A closed, usually circular, curve. **b.** The region enclosed by such a curve. **2. a.** Any path or route, the complete traversal of which without local change of direction requires returning to the starting point. **b.** The act of following such a path. **c.** A journey made on such a path or route. **3.** *Electricity.* **a.** Any closed path followed or capable of being followed by an electric current. **b.** A configuration of electrically or electromagnetically connected components or devices. **4. a.** A regular or accustomed course from place to place, such as that of a judge, salesman, or lecturer; a round. **b.** The area or district thus covered; especially, a territory under jurisdiction of a judge, in which he holds periodic court sessions. **5.** An association of theaters in which plays, acts, or films move from theater to theater for presentation. **6.** An association of teams, clubs, or arenas of competition. —*v.* **circuited, -cuiting, -cuits.** —*tr.* To make a circuit of. —*intr.* To move about in a

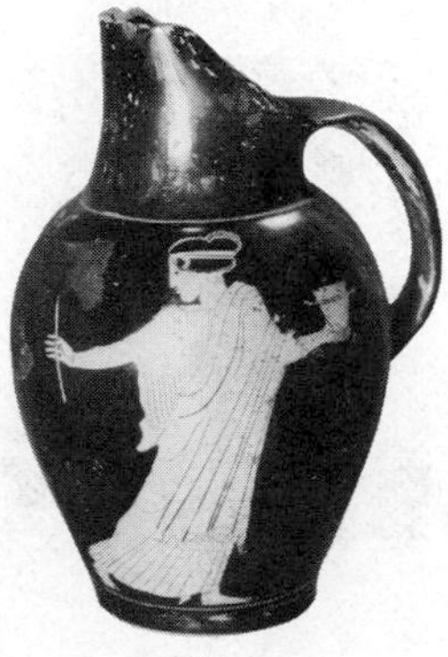

Circe
The enchantress fleeing Odysseus, a painting on an ancient Greek wine vessel

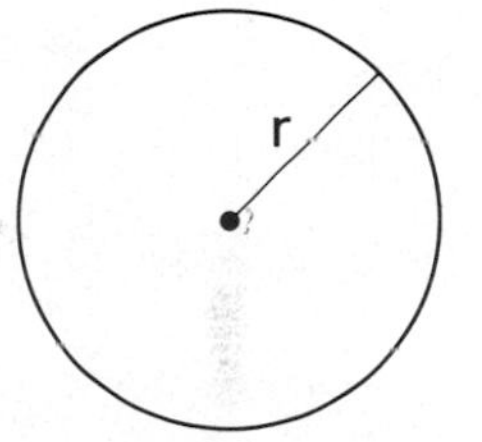

circle
Diameter = $2r$
Area = πr^2 (π = 3.14)
Circumference = $2\pi r$

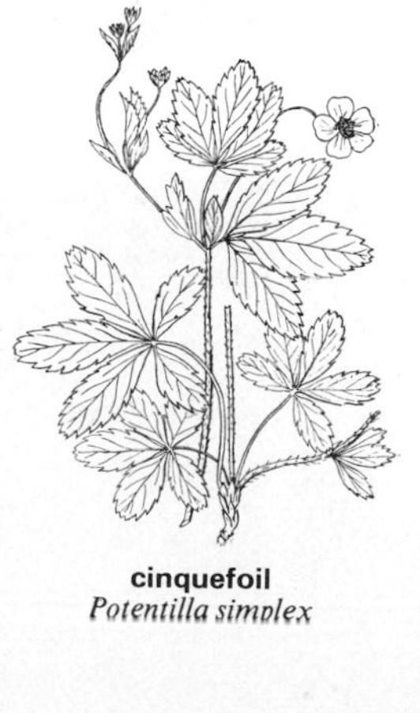

cinquefoil
Potentilla simplex

circuit. [Middle English, from Old French, from Latin *circuitus,* from *circuīre, circumīre,* to go around : *circum-,* around + *īre,* to go (see **ei-**[1] in Appendix*).]
circuit breaker. An automatic switch that stops the flow of electric current in a suddenly overloaded or otherwise abnormally stressed electric circuit.
circuit court. In some states, the lowest court of record, in some instances holding sessions in different places.
cir·cu·i·tous (sər-kyo͞o'ə-təs) *adj.* Being or taking a roundabout, lengthy course. See Synonyms at **indirect.** [Medieval Latin *circuitōsus,* from Latin *circuitus,* CIRCUIT.] —**cir·cu'i·tous·ly** *adv.* —**cir·cu'i·ty, cir·cu'i·tous·ness** *n.*
circuit rider. Formerly, a minister who traveled from church to church in a district.
cir·cuit·ry (sûr'kə-trē) *n.* **1.** The design of or detailed plan for an electric circuit. **2.** Electric circuits collectively.
cir·cu·lar (sûr'kyə-lər) *adj. Abbr.* **cir., circ. 1.** Of or pertaining to a circle. **2. a.** Having the shape of a circle. **b.** Having a shape approximately that of a circle; round. **3.** Moving in or forming a circle. **4.** Circuitous; indirect; roundabout. **5.** Addressed or distributed to a large number of persons. —*n.* A printed advertisement, directive, or notice intended for mass distribution. —**cir'cu·lar'i·ty** *n.* —**cir'cu·lar·ly** *adv.*
cir·cu·lar·ize (sûr'kyə-lə-rīz') *tr.v.* **-ized, -izing, -izes.** To publicize with circulars. —**cir'cu·lar·i·za'tion** *n.* —**cir'cu·lar·iz'er** *n.*
circular measure. The measure of an angle in **radians** *(see).*
circular mil. *Abbr.* **c.m.** A unit of cross-sectional measurement, especially of wire, equal to the area of a circle with a diameter of one mil.
circular saw. An electric saw consisting of a toothed disk rotated at high speed. Also called "buzz saw."

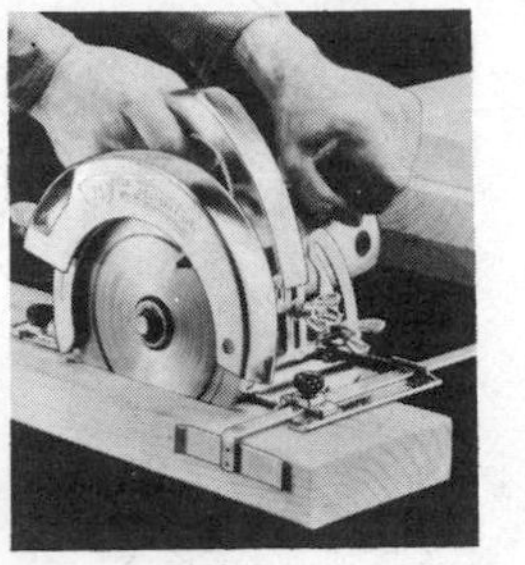

circular saw

cir·cu·late (sûr'kyə-lāt') *v.* **-lated, -lating, -lates.** —*intr.* **1.** To move in or flow through a circle or circuit. **2.** To move around, as from person to person, or place to place. **3.** To move about or flow freely; be diffused, as air. **4.** To spread widely among persons or places; disseminate. —*tr.* To cause to move about or be distributed. [Latin *circulāre,* from *circulus,* CIRCLE.] —**cir'cu·la'tive** (-lā'tĭv) *adj.* —**cir'cu·la'tor** (-lā'tər) *n.* —**cir'cu·la·to'ry** (-lə-tôr'ē, -tōr'ē) *adj.*
circulating decimal. *Mathematics.* A **repeating decimal** *(see).*
circulating medium. Currency or coin that can be exchanged for goods without endorsement.
cir·cu·la·tion (sûr'kyə-lā'shən) *n. Abbr.* **cir., circ. 1.** Movement in a circle or circuit. **2.** The movement of blood through bodily vessels as a result of the heart's pumping action. **3.** Any movement or passage through a system of vessels, as of water through pipes. **4.** Free movement or passage. **5.** The passing of something, as money or news, from place to place or from person to person. **6.** The condition of being passed about and widely known; distribution. **7.** The distribution of printed material, especially copies of newspapers or magazines, among readers. **8.** The number of copies sold or distributed of a given or an average issue of a publication.
circulatory system. The system of structures by which blood and lymph are circulated throughout the body.
circum-. Indicates around or on all sides; for example, **circumscissile, circumlunar.** [Latin, from *circum,* around, from *circus,* circle. See **sker-**[3] in Appendix.*]
circum. circumference.
cir·cum·am·bi·ent (sûr'kəm-ăm'bē-ənt) *adj.* Surrounding; enclosing. [Latin *circumambiēns* : CIRCUM- + AMBIENT.] —**cir'cum·am'bi·ence, cir'cum·am'bi·en·cy** *n.*
cir·cum·cise (sûr'kəm-sīz') *tr.v.* **-cised, -cising, -cises. 1. a.** To remove the prepuce of (a male). **b.** To remove the clitoris of (a female). **c.** To perform the religious rite of circumcision for. **2.** To purify spiritually; cleanse from sin: *"Circumcise yourselves to the Lord"* (Jeremiah 4:4). [Middle English *circumcisen,* from Latin *circumcīdere* (past participle *circumcīsus*), "to cut around" (translation of Greek *peritemnein*) : CIRCUM- + *caedere,* to cut (see **skhai-** in Appendix*).] —**cir'cum·cis'er** *n.*
cir·cum·ci·sion (sûr'kəm-sĭzh'ən) *n.* **1.** *Medicine.* The act of circumcising. **2.** A religious ceremony in which someone is circumcised. **3.** Spiritual purification. **4.** *Capital* **C.** A church festival celebrated on January 1 commemorating the circumcision of Jesus. Usually used with *the.*
cir·cum·fer·ence (sər-kŭm'fər-əns) *n. Abbr.* **cir., circ., circum. 1.** The boundary line of a circle. **2.** The boundary line of any closed curvilinear figure; perimeter. **3.** The length of such a boundary. [Middle English, from Old French, from Latin *circumferentia,* from *circumferēns,* present participle of *circumferre,* to carry around : CIRCUM- + *ferre,* to carry (see **bher-**[1] in Appendix*).] —**cir·cum'fer·en'tial** (-fə-rĕn'shəl) *adj.*
cir·cum·flex (sûr'kəm-flĕks') *n.* A mark (ˆ) used over a vowel in certain languages or in phonetic keys to indicate quality of pronunciation. —*adj.* Marked with a circumflex. —*tr.v.* **circumflexed, -flexing, -flexes.** To mark with a circumflex. [Latin *circumflexus,* "a bending around," from *circumflectere,* to bend around : CIRCUM- + *flectere,* to bend, to FLEX.]
cir·cum·fuse (sûr'kəm-fyo͞oz') *tr.v.* **-fused, -fusing, -fuses. 1.** To pour or diffuse around; spread. **2.** To surround, as with liquid; suffuse. [Latin *circumfundere* (past participle *circumfūsus*), to pour around : CIRCUM- + *fundere,* to pour (see **gheu-** in Appendix*).] —**cir'cum·fu'sion** *n.*
cir·cum·lo·cu·tion (sûr'kəm-lō-kyo͞o'shən) *n.* **1.** The use of prolix and indirect language. **2.** Evasion in speech or writing. **3.** A roundabout expression. [Middle English *circumlocucioun,* from Latin *circumlocūtiō,* from *circumloquī,* "to speak in a roundabout way" : CIRCUM- + *loquī,* to speak (see **tolkw-** in Appendix*).] —**cir'cum·loc'u·to·ry** (-lŏk'yə-tôr'ē, -tōr'ē) *adj.*
cir·cum·lu·nar (sûr'kəm-lo͞o'nər) *adj.* Revolving about or surrounding the moon. [CIRCUM- + LUNAR.]
cir·cum·nav·i·gate (sûr'kəm-năv'ĭ-gāt') *tr.v.* **-gated, -gating, -gates.** To sail completely around. [Latin *circumnāvigāre,* to sail around : CIRCUM- + *nāvigāre,* NAVIGATE.] —**cir'cum·nav'i·ga'tion** *n.* —**cir'cum·nav'i·ga'tor** (-gā'tər) *n.*
cir·cum·nu·tate (sûr'kəm-no͞o'tāt', -nyo͞o'tāt') *intr.v.* **-tated, -tating, -tates.** *Botany.* To exhibit circumnutation; grow or move with an irregular elliptical or spiral motion. [CIRCUM- + Latin *nūtāre,* to nod, sway (see **nutation**).]
cir·cum·nu·ta·tion (sûr'kəm-no͞o-tā'shən, -nyo͞o-tā'shən) *n. Botany.* An elliptical or spiral direction of growth shown by certain plant parts, such as the apex of a growing tendril.
cir·cum·po·lar (sûr'kəm-pō'lər) *adj.* **1.** Located or found in one of the polar regions. **2.** *Astronomy.* Designating a star that from a given observer's latitude does not go below the horizon.
cir·cum·ro·tate (sûr'kəm-rō'tāt') *intr.v.* **-tated, -tating, -tates.** To turn like a wheel; revolve. —**cir'cum·ro·ta'tion** *n.* —**cir'cum·ro'ta·to'ry** (-tə-tôr'ē, -tōr'ē) *adj.*
cir·cum·scis·sile (sûr'kəm-sĭs'əl) *adj. Botany.* Splitting or opening along a transverse circular line: *a circumscissile seed capsule.* [CIRCUM- + Latin *scissilis,* capable of being cut, from *scissus* (see **scission**).]
cir·cum·scribe (sûr'kəm-skrīb') *tr.v.* **-scribed, -scribing, -scribes. 1.** To draw a line around; encircle. **2.** To confine within bounds; to limit; restrict. **3.** To determine the limits of; define. **4.** *Geometry.* **a.** To enclose (a polygon or polyhedron) within a configuration of lines, curves, or surfaces so that every vertex of the enclosed object is incident on the enclosing configuration. **b.** To be erected as such an enclosing configuration. —See Synonyms at **limit.** [Middle English *circumscriben,* from Latin *circumscrībere* : CIRCUM- + *scrībere,* to write (see **skeri-** in Appendix*).] —**cir'cum·scrib'a·ble** *adj.* —**cir'cum·scrib'er** *n.*
cir·cum·scrip·tion (sûr'kəm-skrĭp'shən) *n.* **1. a.** The act of circumscribing. **b.** The state of being circumscribed. **2.** Something that circumscribes. **3.** A circumscribed space; a limited area. **4.** A circular inscription, as on a coin or medallion. —**cir'cum·scrip'tive** *adj.* —**cir'cum·scrip'tive·ly** *adv.*
cir·cum·so·lar (sûr'kəm-sō'lər) *adj.* Revolving about or surrounding the sun.
cir·cum·spect (sûr'kəm-spĕkt') *adj.* Heedful of circumstances or consequences; prudent. [Middle English, from Latin *circumspectus,* past participle of *circumspicere,* to look around, take heed : CIRCUM- + *specere,* to look (see **spek-** in Appendix*).] —**cir'cum·spec'tion** *n.* —**cir'cum·spect'ly** *adv.*
cir·cum·stance (sûr'kəm-stăns') *n.* **1.** One of the conditions or facts attending an event and having some bearing upon it; a determining or modifying factor. **2.** One of the conditions or facts that determine, or that must be considered in the determining of, a course of action. **3.** The sum of determining factors beyond willful control: *a victim of circumstance.* **4.** *Usually plural.* Financial status or means: *"Prior came of a good family, much reduced in circumstances."* (George Sherburn). **5.** Additional or accessory information; detail. **6.** Formal display; ceremony: *pomp and circumstance.* —See Synonyms at **occurrence.** —**under no circumstances.** In no case; never. —**under** (or **in**) **the circumstances.** Given these conditions; such being the case. —*tr.v.* **circumstanced, -stancing, -stances.** To place in particular circumstances or conditions; situate. [Middle English, from Old French, from Latin *circumstantia,* accessory details from *circumstāns,* present participle of *circumstāre,* to stand around, be accessory : CIRCUM- + *stāre,* to stand (see **stā-** in Appendix*).]
cir·cum·stan·tial (sûr'kəm-stăn'shəl) *adj.* **1.** Of, pertaining to, or dependent upon circumstances. **2.** Of no primary significance; incidental; inessential. **3.** Complete and particular; full of detail. —**cir'cum·stan'tial·ly** *adv.*
circumstantial evidence. *Law.* Evidence not bearing directly on the fact in dispute, but on various attendant circumstances from which the judge or jury might infer the occurrence of the fact in dispute.
cir·cum·stan·ti·al·i·ty (sûr'kəm-stăn'shē-ăl'ə-tē) *n., pl.* **-ties. 1.** The quality of being fully or minutely detailed. **2.** A particular detail or circumstance.
cir·cum·stan·ti·ate (sûr'kəm-stăn'shē-āt') *tr.v.* **-ated, -ating, -ates.** To set forth or verify with circumstances; give detailed proof or description of. —**cir'cum·stan'ti·a'tion** *n.*
cir·cum·val·late (sûr'kəm-văl'āt') *tr.v.* **-lated, -lating, -lates.** To surround with a rampart or other defensive barrier. —*adj.* (sûr'kəm-văl'āt', -văl'ĭt). Surrounded by or as if by a rampart. [Latin *circumvallāre* : CIRCUM- + *vallāre,* to wall, from *vallum,* wall (see **walso-** in Appendix*).] —**cir'cum·val'la'tion** *n.*
cir·cum·vent (sûr'kəm-vĕnt') *tr.v.* **-vented, -venting, -vents. 1.** To surround and entrap (an enemy, for example) by craft. **2.** To overcome by artful maneuvering. **3.** To avoid by or as if by passing around. [Latin *circumvenīre* (past participle *circumventus*) : CIRCUM- + *venīre,* to come (see **gwā-** in Appendix*).] —**cir'cum·vent'er, cir'cum·ven'tor** (-tər) *n.* —**cir'cum·ven'tion** *n.* —**cir'cum·ven'tive** *adj.*
cir·cum·vo·lu·tion (sər-kŭm'və-lo͞o'shən, sûr'kəm-vō-) *n.* **1.** A turning, coiling, or folding about a center, core, or axis. **2.** A single turn, coil, or fold; convolution. [Middle English *circumvolucioun,* from Medieval Latin *circumvolūtiō,* from Latin *circumvolvere* (past participle *circumvolūtus*), CIRCUMVOLVE.]
cir·cum·volve (sûr'kəm-vŏlv') *v.* **-volved, -volving, -volves.** —*intr.* To revolve. —*tr.* To cause to revolve. [Latin *circumvolvere* : CIRCUM- + *volvere,* to roll (see **wel-**[3] in Appendix*).]
cir·cus (sûr'kəs) *n.* **1.** A public entertainment consisting typically of a variety of performances by acrobats, clowns, and

trained animals. **2.** A traveling company that performs such entertainments. **3.** A circular arena, surrounded by tiers of seats and often covered by a tent, in which such shows are performed. **4.** A roofless, oval enclosure surrounded by tiers of seats and used in antiquity for public spectacles. **5.** *British.* An open circular place where several streets intersect. **6.** *Informal.* A place or activity given over to rowdy or noisy disorder. [Latin *circus,* ring, CIRCLE.]

cirque (sûrk) *n.* A steep hollow, often containing a small lake, occurring at the upper end of some mountain valleys. Also *Welsh* "cwm." [French, from Latin *circus,* ring, CIRCLE.]

cir·rate (sĭr′āt′) *adj.* Also **cir·rose** (sĭr′ōs′), **cir·rous** (sĭr′əs). *Biology.* Having or of the nature of a cirrus or cirri. [Latin *cirrātus,* curled, from *cirrus,* curl, CIRRUS.]

cir·rho·sis (sĭ-rō′sĭs) *n.* A chronic disease of the liver marked by progressive destruction and regeneration of liver cells and increased connective tissue formation that ultimately results in blockage of portal circulation, portal hypertension, liver failure, and death. [New Latin, "orange-colored disease" (from the color of the diseased liver) : Greek *kirrhos*†, orange tawny + -OSIS.] —**cir·rhot′ic** (sĭ-rŏt′ĭk) *adj.*

cir·ri·ped (sĭr′ə-pĕd′) *n.* Also **cir·ri·pede** (-pēd′). Any of various crustaceans of the order Cirripedia, which includes the barnacles and similar organisms that attach themselves to objects or become parasitic in the adult stage. [New Latin *Cirripedia,* "the cirrus-footed ones" : CIRR(US) + -PED.] —**cir′ri·ped′** *adj.*

cir·ro·cu·mu·lus (sĭr′ō-kyo͞om′yə-ləs) *n.* A high-altitude cloud composed of a series of small, regularly arranged cloudlets in the form of ripples or grains. In nontechnical use, called "mackerel sky." [New Latin : CIRR(US) + CUMULUS.]

cir·ro·stra·tus (sĭr′ō-strā′təs, -străt′əs) *n.* A high-altitude, thin hazy cloud, usually covering the sky and often producing a halo effect. [New Latin : CIRR(US) + STRATUS.]

cir·rus (sĭr′əs) *n., pl.* **cirri** (sĭr′ī′). **1.** A high-altitude cloud composed of narrow bands or patches of thin, generally white, fleecy parts. **2.** *Botany.* A tendril or similar part. **3.** *Zoology.* A slender, flexible appendage, such as a tentacle. [New Latin, from Latin *cirrus*†, curl, filament, tuft.]

cis–. Indicates location on this or the near side; for example, **cislunar.** [Latin, from *cis,* on this side of. See **ko** in Appendix.*]

Cis·al·pine Gaul (sĭs-ăl′pīn′). The part of ancient Gaul south of the Alps of northern Italy.

cis·at·lan·tic (sĭs′ət-lăn′tĭk) *adj.* On this (the speaker's) side of the Atlantic. [CIS- + ATLANTIC.]

Cis·cau·ca·sia (sĭs′kô-kā′zhə, -shə). The part of the Caucasus region north of the principal Caucasus mountain chain.

cis·co (sĭs′kō) *n., pl.* **-coes** or **-cos.** Any of several North American freshwater fishes of the genus *Coregonus* (or *Leucichthys*), related to and resembling the whitefish. [Canadian French *ciscoette,* from Ojibwa *pemitewiskawet,* oily-skinned fish.]

cis·lu·nar (sĭs-lo͞o′nər) *adj.* Between the earth and the moon. [CIS- + LUNAR.]

cis·mon·tane (sĭs-mŏn′tān′) *adj.* On this (the speaker's) side of the mountains. [French *cismontain,* from Latin *cismontānus* : CIS- + *montānus,* of the mountains, MONTANE.]

cist¹ (sĭst) *n.* A wicker receptacle used in ancient Rome for carrying sacred utensils in procession. [Latin *cista,* from Greek *kistē.* See **kistā** in Appendix.*]

cist² (sĭst, kĭst) *n.* Also **kist** (kĭst). A Neolithic stone coffin. [Welsh, "chest," from Latin *cista,* basket, CIST.]

Cis·ter·cian (sĭs-tûr′shən) *n.* A member of a contemplative monastic order founded by reformist Benedictines in France in 1098. —*adj.* Of, pertaining to, or belonging to this order. [French *Cistertien,* from Medieval Latin *Cistercium,* abbey site now called *Cîteaux.*]

cis·tern (sĭs′tərn) *n.* **1.** A receptacle for holding water or other liquid; especially, a tank for catching and storing rainwater. **2.** *Anatomy.* A cisterna. [Middle English *cisterne,* from Old French, from Latin *cisterna,* water tank, from *cista,* box, from Greek *kistē,* basket. See **kistā** in Appendix.*] —**cis·ter′nal** *adj.*

cis·ter·na (sĭs-tûr′nə) *n., pl.* **-nae** (-nē′). Any fluid-containing sac or space in the body of an organism. Also called "reservoir." [New Latin, from Latin, CISTERN.]

cit. **1.** citation. **2.** cited. **3.** citizen.

cit·a·del (sĭt′ə-dəl, -dĕl′) *n.* **1.** A fortress in a commanding position in or near a city. **2.** Any stronghold or fortified place; a bulwark. **3.** The heavily plated central structure of a war vessel. [Old French *citadelle,* from Old Italian *citadella,* from *cittade,* city, from Latin *cīvitās,* citizenry, state, CITY.]

ci·ta·tion (sī-tā′shən) *n. Abbr.* **cit.** **1.** The act of citing. **2.** A quoting of an authoritative source for substantiation. **3.** A source so cited; quotation. **4.** *Law.* A reference to previous court decisions or authoritative writings. **5.** An official commendation for meritorious action, especially in military service. **6.** Enumeration or mention, as of facts. **7.** A summons, especially one calling for appearance in court. —**ci′ta·to′ry** (sī′tə-tôr′ē, -tōr′ē) *adj.*

cite (sīt) *tr.v.* **cited, citing, cites.** **1.** To quote as an authority or example. **2.** To mention or bring forward as support, illustration, or proof. **3.** To commend (a unit or individual in the armed forces) in orders, for meritorious action. **4.** To call to attention or enumerate; to mention. **5.** To summon before a court of law. **6.** To call to action; rouse. [Middle English *citen,* to summon, from Old French *citer,* from Latin *citāre,* frequentative of *ciēre,* to set in motion, summon. See **kei-³** in Appendix.*]

Ci·thae·ron (sĭ-thē′rŏn′). A mountain, 4,622 feet high, in southeastern Greece.

cith·a·ra (sĭth′ə-rə, kĭth′-) *n.* An ancient musical instrument resembling the lyre. [Latin, from Greek *kithara*†.]

cith·er (sĭth′ər, sĭ*th*′-) *n.* Also **cith·ern** (sĭth′ərn, sĭ*th*′-). A musical instrument, a **cittern** *(see).* [French *cithare,* from Latin *cithara,* CITHARA.]

cit·ied (sĭt′ēd) *adj.* Having cities.

cit·i·fied (sĭt′ĭ-fīd′) *adj.* Having customs, manners, fashions, or other characteristics attributed to city people.

cit·i·fy (sĭt′ĭ-fī′) *tr.v.* **-fied, -fying, -fies.** **1.** To cause to become like a city; make urban. **2.** To mark with the styles and manners of the city. —**cit′i·fi·ca′tion** *n.*

cit·i·zen (sĭt′ə-zən) *n. Abbr.* **cit.** **1.** A person owing loyalty to and entitled by birth or naturalization to the protection of a given state. **2.** A resident of a city or town, especially one entitled to vote and enjoy other privileges there. **3.** A civilian, as distinguished from a person employed by the military, the police, or a similar agency. [Middle English *citisein,* from Norman French *citesein,* variant of Old French *citeien,* from *cite,* CITY.] —**cit′i·zen·ly** *adj.*

cit·i·zen·ry (sĭt′ə-zən-rē) *n., pl.* **-ries.** Citizens collectively.

cit·i·zen·ship (sĭt′ə-zən-shĭp′) *n.* The status of a citizen with its attendant duties, rights, and privileges.

Ci·tlal·té·petl. The Aztec name for Pico de **Orizaba.**

cit·ral (sĭt′răl′) *n.* A mobile pale-yellow liquid, $C_{10}H_{16}O$, derived from lemon-grass oil and used in perfume and as a flavoring. Also called "geranial." [CITR(US) + -AL (aldehyde).]

cit·rate (sĭt′rāt′) *n.* A salt or ester of citric acid.

cit·ric (sĭt′rĭk) *adj.* Of or obtained from citrus fruits.

citric acid. A colorless translucent crystalline acid, $C_6H_8O_7 \cdot H_2O$, principally derived by fermentation of carbohydrates or from lemon, lime, and pineapple juices, and used to prepare citrates, in flavorings, and in metal polishes.

cit·ri·cul·ture (sĭt′rĭ-kŭl′chər) *n.* The cultivation of citrus fruits. [CITR(US) + CULTURE.] —**cit′ri·cul′tur·ist** *n.*

cit·rine (sĭt′rĭn, -rēn′) *n.* **1.** A pale-yellow variety of quartz, resembling topaz. **2.** Light to moderate olive. See **color.** [Middle English, from Old French *citrin,* from Medieval Latin *citrinus,* from Latin *citrus,* citron tree, CITRUS.] —**cit′rine** *adj.*

cit·ron (sĭt′rən) *n.* **1.** A tree, *Citrus medica,* native to Asia, having lemonlike fruit with a thick, aromatic rind. **2.** The fruit of this tree. **3.** A variety of watermelon, *Citrullus vulgaris citroides,* having fruit generally considered inedible and a hard rind used as flavoring. In this sense, also called "citron melon." **4.** The preserved or candied rind of either of these fruits, used especially in baking. **5.** Grayish green yellow. See **color.** [French, from Old French, from Latin *citrus,* citron tree. See **citrus.**] —**cit′ron** *adj.*

cit·ron·el·la (sĭt′rə-nĕl′ə) *n.* **1.** A tropical Eurasian grass, *Cymbopogon nardus,* having bluish-green, lemon-scented leaves. Also called "citronella grass." **2.** A light-yellow, aromatic oil obtained from this grass and used in insect repellents and perfumery. Also called "citronella oil." [New Latin, from French *citronnelle,* lemon oil, diminutive of *citron,* CITRON.]

cit·ron·el·lal (sĭt′rə-nĕl′ăl′) *n.* A colorless mixture of isomeric liquids, $C_9H_{17}CHO$, the chief constituent of citronella oil. [CITRONELL(A) + -AL (aldehyde).]

cit·rus (sĭt′rəs) *adj.* Also **cit·rous.** **1.** Of or pertaining to trees or shrubs of the genus *Citrus,* many of which bear edible fruit such as the orange, lemon, lime, and grapefruit. **2.** Of or characteristic of the fruits of these trees or shrubs. —*n., pl.* **citruses** or **citrus.** A citrus tree or shrub. [New Latin, from Latin *citrus*†, citron tree, citrus tree.]

Cit·tà del Va·ti·ca·no. The Italian name for **Vatican City.**

cit·tern (sĭt′ərn) *n.* A 16th-century guitar with a pear-shaped body. Also called "cither," "cithern." [Middle English *giterne,* a Medieval stringed instrument.]

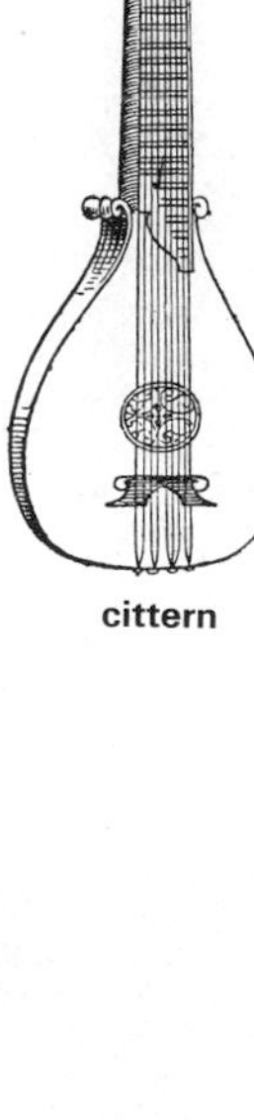

cittern

cit·y (sĭt′ē) *n., pl.* **-ies.** *Abbr.* **c.** **1.** A town of significant size. **2.** In the United States, an incorporated municipality with definite boundaries and legal powers set forth in a charter granted by the state. **3.** In Canada, a municipality of high rank, usually determined by population but varying by province. **4.** In Great Britain, a large incorporated town, usually the seat of a bishop, with its title conferred by the Crown. **5.** The inhabitants of a city as a group. **6.** An ancient Greek city-state. **7.** Formerly, a walled area in the center of a community. —**the City.** The commercial and financial district of London. —*adj.* Of, in, or belonging to a city. [Middle English *cite,* from Old French, from Latin *cīvitās,* citizenry, state, (later) city, from *cīvis,* citizen. See **kei-¹** in Appendix.*]

city desk. The newspaper department handling local news.

city editor. **1.** A newspaper editor responsible for handling local news and reporters' assignments. **2.** In Great Britain, the editor who handles commercial and financial news.

city hall. **1.** The building housing the administrative offices of a municipal government. **2.** The municipal government, especially its officials considered as a group.

city manager. An administrator appointed by a city council to manage the affairs of the municipality.

city slicker. *Informal.* A person exhibiting the smart and sophisticated style traditionally associated by rural people with the manners and mores of the city.

cit·y-state (sĭt′ē-stāt′) *n.* A sovereign state consisting of an independent city and its surrounding territory.

Ciu·dad Bo·lí·var (syo͞o-*th*ä*th*′ bō-lē′vär). A city of east-central Venezuela, a river port on the Orinoco at the head of navigation for oceangoing vessels. Population, 63,000.

Ciu·dad Gua·ya·na (syo͞o-*th*ä*th*′ gwä-yä′nä). A city of Venezuela, on the Orinoco near its delta. Population, 120,000.

Ciu·dad Juá·rez (syo͞o-*th*ä*th*′ hwä′rās). The largest city of Chi-

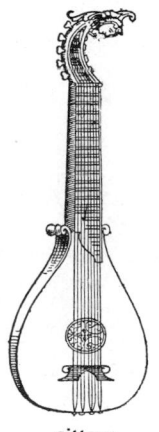

huahua State, Mexico, on the Rio Grande opposite El Paso, Texas. Population, 385,000.

Ciu·dad Tru·jil·lo (syo͞o-*thäth′* tro͞o-hē′yō). The former name for the city of **Santo Domingo**.

Ciu·dad Vic·to·ria (syo͞o-*thäth′* vēk-tō′ryä). The capital of Tamaulipas, eastern Mexico, 150 miles southeast of Monterrey.

civ. civil; civilian.

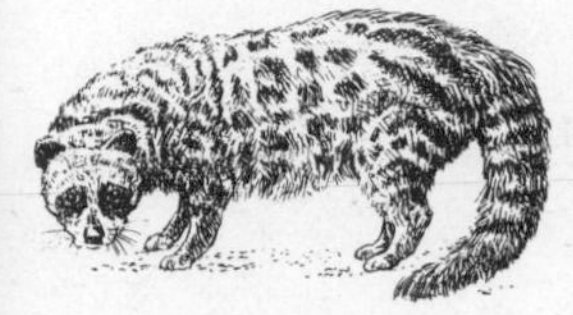

civet
Civettictis civetta

civ·et (sĭv′ĭt) *n.* **1.** Any of various catlike mammals of the family Viverridae, of Africa and Asia, having anal scent glands that secrete a fluid with a musky odor. Also called "civet cat." **2.** This fluid, used in the manufacture of perfumes. **3.** The fur of a civet. [French *civette,* from Old French, from Italian *zibetto,* from Arabic *zabād.*]

civ·ic (sĭv′ĭk) *adj.* Of, pertaining to, or belonging to a city, to a citizen, or to citizenship; municipal or civil. [Latin *cīvicus,* from *cīvis,* citizen. See **kei-**[1] in Appendix.*]

civ·i·cism (sĭv′ə-sĭz′əm) *n.* **1.** The system or principle of government based upon the rights and duties of the individual. **2.** Adherence to the rules and duties of civic government.

civ·ics (sĭv′ĭks) *n.* Plural in form, used with a singular verb. The branch of political science that deals with civic affairs.

civ·ies. Variant of **civvies.**

civ·il (sĭv′əl) *adj. Abbr.* **civ. 1.** Of, pertaining to, or befitting citizens or the citizen as an individual. **2.** Of or pertaining to citizens and their relations with one another or with the state. **3.** Of ordinary citizens or ordinary community life, as distinguished from the military or the ecclesiastical. **4.** Of or in accordance with organized society and government; civilized. **5.** Observing or befitting accepted social usages; proper; polite. **6.** Designating or according to legally recognized divisions of time: *a civil year.* **7.** *Law.* **a.** Of or in accordance with Roman civil law or with its medieval and modern derivatives. **b.** Pertaining to the rights of private individuals and to legal proceedings concerning these rights. Used as a general residual category to distinguish a court, proceeding, or rule which is not criminal, military, or international. —See Synonyms at **polite.** [Middle English, from Old French, from Latin *cīvīlis,* from *cīvis,* citizen. See **kei-**[1] in Appendix.*] —**civ′il·ly** *adv.*

civil day. A **mean solar day** *(see).*

civil death. *Law.* The total deprivation of civil rights resulting from conviction for treason or for some other serious offense.

civil defense. *Abbr.* **C.D.** The ensemble of emergency measures to be taken by an organized body of civilian volunteers for the protection of life and property in the case of a natural disaster or an attack or invasion by an enemy.

civil disobedience. The refusal to obey civil laws that are regarded as unjust, usually by employing methods of passive resistance.

civil engineer. *Abbr.* **C.E.** An engineer trained in the design and construction of public works.

ci·vil·ian (sə-vĭl′yən) *n. Abbr.* **civ. 1.** A person following the pursuits of civil life, as distinguished from one serving in the armed forces. **2.** A student or specialist in Roman or civil law. —*adj.* Of or pertaining to civilians or civil life; nonmilitary. [Middle English, practitioner of civil law, jurist, from *civile,* civil law, from Latin, from *(jūs) cīvīle,* from *cīvīlis,* CIVIL.]

ci·vil·i·ty (sə-vĭl′ə-tē) *n., pl.* **-ties. 1.** Politeness; courtesy. **2.** A courteous act or utterance.

civ·i·li·za·tion (sĭv′ə-lə-zā′shən) *n.* **1.** A condition of human society marked by an advanced stage of development in the arts and sciences and by corresponding social, political, and cultural complexity. **2.** Those nations or peoples regarded as having arrived at this stage. **3.** The type of culture and society developed by a particular group, nation, or region, or by any of these in some particular epoch. **4.** The act or process of civilizing or of reaching a civilized state.

civ·i·lize (sĭv′ə-līz′) *tr.v.* **-lized, -lizing, -lizes.** To bring out of a primitive or savage state; educate or enlighten; refine. —**civ′i·liz′a·ble** *adj.* —**civ′i·liz′er** *n.*

civ·i·lized (sĭv′ə-līzd′) *adj.* **1.** Having a highly developed society and culture. **2.** Of, pertaining to, or characteristic of a people or nation so developed. **3.** Polite or cultured; urbane; refined.

civil law. 1. The body of law dealing with the rights of private citizens in a particular state or nation, as distinguished from criminal law, military law, or international law. **2.** The law of ancient Rome, especially that which applied to private citizens. **3.** Any system of law having its origin in Roman law, as distinguished from common law or canon law.

civil liberty. Liberty legally guaranteeing to the individual the rights of free speech, thought, and action, limited only insofar as their use does not interfere with the rights of others.

civil list. In Great Britain and other countries, the yearly provision by the legislature of funds for the personal and household expenses of the monarch.

civil marriage. A marriage ceremony performed by a civil official, such as a ship's captain.

civil rights. Rights belonging to a person by virtue of his status as a citizen or as a member of civil society. Often used attributively to designate efforts to win political, economic, and social equality for U.S. Negroes: *the civil-rights movement.*

civil servant. A person employed in the civil service.

civil service. *Abbr.* **C.S. 1.** All branches of public service that are not legislative, judicial, military, or naval. **2.** Collectively, the persons employed by these branches of the government. **3.** The body of regulations applied to such service: *He comes under civil service.*

civil time. **Mean time** *(see).*

civil war. A war between factions or regions of one country.

Civil War. 1. In the United States, the war between the Union (the North) and the Confederacy (the South) from 1861 to 1865. Also called "War Between the States," "War of Secession." **2.** In England, the war between the Parliamentarians and the Royalists from 1642 to 1652.

Ci·vi·ta·vec·chia (chē′vē-tä-vĕk′kyä). A seaport of west-central Italy, on the Tyrrhenian Sea, 40 miles northwest of Rome. Population, 38,000.

civ·vies (sĭv′ēz) *pl.n.* Also **civ·ies.** *Slang.* Civilian clothes, as distinguished from military dress. [Short for CIVILIAN.]

C.J. 1. chief justice. **2.** corpus juris.

ck. 1. cask. **2.** check. **3.** cook.

cl centiliter.

Cl The symbol for the element chlorine.

cl. 1. class; classification. **2.** clause. **3.** clearance. **4.** clergyman. **5.** clerk. **6.** closet. **7.** cloth.

c.l. 1. carload. **2.** *Sports.* center line. **3.** common law.

clab·ber (klăb′ər) *n.* Sour, curdled milk. —*v.* **clabbered, -bering, -bers.** —*tr.* To cause to curdle. —*intr.* To become curdled. [Short for earlier *bonnyclabber,* from Irish : *bainne,* milk, from Middle Irish *banne,* a drop (see **band-** in Appendix*) + *clabair*†, thick sour milk.]

clack (klăk) *v.* **clacked, clacking, clacks.** —*intr.* **1.** To make an abrupt, dry sound, as by the collision of two hard surfaces. **2.** To chatter thoughtlessly or at length. **3.** To cackle or cluck, as a hen does. —*tr.* **1.** To cause to make an abrupt, dry sound. **2.** To blab (something). —*n.* **1.** A clacking sound. **2.** Something that makes a clacking sound. **3.** Thoughtless, prolonged talk; chatter. [Middle English *clacken,* from Old Norse *klaka* (imitative).] —**clack′er** *n.*

Clack·man·nan (klăk-măn′ən). **1.** Also **Clack·man·nan·shire** (-shîr, -shər). A county occupying 55 square miles in south-central Scotland. Population, 42,000. **2.** The county seat of this county, in the west near Stirling. Population, 3,000.

clack valve. A hinged valve that permits fluids to flow in only one direction and clacks when the valve closes.

Clac·to·ni·an (klăk-tō′nē-ən) *adj. Archaeology.* Of or pertaining to a lower Paleolithic culture of northwestern Europe. [From *Clacton-on-Sea,* England, site of the discovery of artifacts from which the culture was classified.]

clad[1] (klăd) *tr.v.* **clad, cladding, clads.** To sheathe or cover (a metal) with a metal. [Middle English *cladden,* from *cladde,* past participle of *clathen, clothen,* CLOTHE.]

clad[2]. Alternate past tense and past participle of **clothe.**

clad·ding (klăd′ĭng) *n.* A metal coating bonded onto another metal.

cla·doc·er·an (klə-dŏs′ər-ən) *n.* Any of various small aquatic crustaceans of the order Cladocera, which includes the water fleas. —*adj.* Of or belonging to the Cladocera. [New Latin *Cladocera* : Greek *klados,* branch, shoot (see **kel-**[2] in Appendix*) + *keras,* horn (see **ker-**[1] in Appendix*).]

clad·o·phyll (klăd′ə-fĭl′) *n.* A branch or portion of a stem that resembles and functions as a leaf. Also called "cladode." [New Latin *cladophyllum* : Greek *klados,* twig (see **kel-**[2] in Appendix*) + *phullon,* leaf, -PHYLL.]

clag (klăg) *v.* **clagged, clagging, clags.** —*tr.* To clog. —*intr.* To become clogged. —*n.* A clog or clot. [Middle English *claggen,* to daub with mud, from Scandinavian, akin to Danish *klagge,* mud. See **gel-**[1] in Appendix.*]

claim (klām) *v.* **claimed, claiming, claims.** —*tr.* **1.** To demand as one's due; assert one's right to. **2.** To state to be true; assert or maintain. See Usage note below. **3.** To deserve or call for; require. —*intr.* To make a claim. —*n.* **1.** A demand for something as one's rightful due; affirmation of a right. **2.** A basis for demanding something; title or right. **3.** Something claimed, especially: **a.** A tract of land staked out by a miner or homesteader. **b.** A sum of money demanded in accordance with an insurance policy or other formal arrangement. **4.** A statement of something as a fact; an assertion of truth. —**lay claim to.** To assert one's right to or ownership of. [Middle English *claimen,* from Old French *clamer* (present stem *claim-*), to cry, appeal, from Latin *clāmāre,* to call. See **kel-**[3] in Appendix.*] —**claim′a·ble** *adj.* —**claim′er** *n.*

Usage: *Claim* (verb) is established in the sense of asserting as factual or maintaining a position in the face of possible argument: *The Air Force claims that the battleship is obsolete.* The foregoing example is acceptable in writing to 69 per cent of the Usage Panel. Those who reject this sense as loose suggest *assert, declare,* and *maintain* as suitable alternatives to *claim.*

claim·ant (klā′mənt) *n.* A person making a claim.

claiming race. A horse race in which each entry is available for purchase at a previously fixed price, the right to buy often being limited to those persons entering horses in that race.

clair de lune (klâr′ də lo͞on′; *French* klâr′ də lün′). **1.** A pale, grayish-blue glaze applied to various kinds of Chinese porcelain. **2.** The color of this glaze. [French, "moonlight."] —**clair′-de-lune′** *adj.*

Claire (klâr). A feminine given name. [French, from Old French, from Latin *clāra,* CLARA.]

clair-ob·scure (klâr′əb-skyo͝or′) *n.* **Chiaroscuro** *(see).* [French *clair-obscur,* translation of Italian *chiaroscuro,* CHIAROSCURO.]

clair·schach (klär′shəkh) *n.* An ancient Irish harp. [Middle English *clareschaw,* from Scottish Gaelic *clārsach*†.]

clair·voy·ance (klâr-voi′əns) *n.* **1.** The supposed power to perceive things that are out of the natural range of human senses, attributed to certain individuals. **2.** Acute intuitive insight or perceptiveness. [French, "clear-seeing" : *clair,* clear, from Latin *clārus* (see **kel-**[3] in Appendix*) + *voyant,* present participle of *voir,* to see, from Latin *vidēre* (see **weid-** in Appendix*).] —**clair·voy′ant** *n.* & *adj.*

ă pat/ā pay/âr care/ä father/b bib/ch church/d deed/ĕ pet/ē be/f fife/g gag/h hat/hw which/ĭ pit/ī pie/îr pier/j judge/k kick/l lid, needle/m mum/n no, sudden/ng thing/ŏ pot/ō toe/ô paw, for/oi noise/ou out/o͝o took/o͞o boot/p pop/r roar/s sauce/sh ship, dish/

clam[1] (klăm) *n.* **1.** Any of various usually burrowing marine and freshwater bivalve mollusks of the class Pelecypoda, including members of the genera *Venus, Mya,* and others, many of which are edible. See **quahog. 2.** *Informal.* An uncommunicative person. —*intr.v.* **clammed, clamming, clams.** To hunt for clams. —**clam up.** To cease talking or remain silent. [Shortened from *clamshell,* "bivalve that shuts tight like a clamp," from CLAM (clamp).]

clam[2] (klăm) *n.* **1.** Clamminess. **2.** Something sticky. —*adj.* Sticky; clammy. [Middle English *clam,* probably from Middle Low German *klam.* See **gel-**[1] in Appendix.*]

clam[3] (klăm) *n.* A clamp or vise. [Middle English *clam,* Old English *clamm,* bond, fetter. See **gel-**[1] in Appendix.*]

cla·mant (klā′mənt) *adj.* **1.** Clamorous; loud. **2.** Urgent; compelling. [Latin *clāmāns,* present participle of *clāmāre,* to cry out. See **kel-**[3] in Appendix.*]

clam·a·to·ri·al (klăm′ə-tôr′ē-əl, -tōr′ē-əl) *adj. Ornithology.* Of or relating to the flycatchers, a group of perching and singing birds. [From New Latin *clamatores,* plural of Latin *clāmātor,* shouter, from *clāmāre,* to cry out. See **clamant.**]

clam·bake (klăm′bāk′) *n.* **1.** A seashore picnic where clams, fish, corn, and other foods are baked in layers on buried hot stones. **2.** *Informal.* A party, especially a noisy and lively one.

clam·ber (klăm′ər, klăm′bər) *v.* **-bered, -bering, -bers.** —*intr.* To climb with difficulty, especially on all fours; scramble. —*tr.* To climb (something) in this manner. —*n.* The act of clambering. [Middle English *clambren,* from Old Norse *klembra,* originally, "to grip." See **gel-**[1] in Appendix.*] —**clam′ber·er** *n.*

clam chowder. Any of various soups made of shucked clams, salt pork, potatoes, and onions, as *New England clam chowder,* which is simmered in milk, and *Manhattan clam chowder,* which is made with tomatoes and thyme but contains no milk.

clam·my (klăm′ē) *adj.* **-mier, -miest.** Disagreeably moist and cold. [Middle English, from *clammen,* to stick, smear, Old English *clǣman.* See **gel-**[1] in Appendix.*] —**clam′mi·ly** *adv.* —**clam′mi·ness** *n.*

clam·or (klăm′ər) *n.* Also *chiefly British* **clam·our. 1.** A loud outcry or shouting; hubbub. **2.** A vehement expression of discontent or protest; public outcry. **3.** Any loud and sustained noise; din; blare. —See Synonyms at **noise.** —*v.* **clamored, -oring, -ors.** Also *chiefly British* **clam·our.** —*intr.* **1.** To make a clamor. **2.** To make importunate demands or complaints. —*tr.* **1.** To exclaim insistently and noisily. **2.** To drive or influence by clamor. [Middle English *clamour,* from Old French, from Latin *clāmor,* from *clāmāre,* to cry out. See **kel-**[3] in Appendix.*] —**clam′or·er** *n.*

clam·or·ous (klăm′ər-əs) *adj.* Also *chiefly British* **clam·our·ous.** Making, full of, or characterized by clamor. See Synonyms at **vociferous.** —**clam′or·ous·ly** *adv.* —**clam′or·ous·ness** *n.*

clamp (klămp) *n.* Any of various devices used to join, grip, support, or compress mechanical or structural parts. —*tr.v.* **clamped, clamping, clamps.** To fasten, grip, or support with or as if with a clamp. —**clamp down.** *Informal.* To become more repressive. [Middle English, from Middle Dutch *clampe.* See **gel-**[1] in Appendix.*]

clamp·er (klăm′pər) *n.* A spiked plate attached to the sole of a shoe to prevent slipping on ice. [From CLAMP.]

clam·shell (klăm′shĕl′) *n.* **1.** The shell of a clam. **2.** A dredging bucket made of two hinged jaws.

clam·worm (klăm′wûrm′) *n.* Any of various segmented marine worms of the genus *Nereis.*

clan (klăn) *n.* **1.** A traditional social unit in the Scottish Highlands, consisting of a number of families claiming a common ancestor and following the same hereditary chieftain. **2.** In some tribal societies, a division of a tribe tracing descent from a common ancestor. **3.** Any numerous group of relatives, friends, or associates. [Middle English, from Scottish Gaelic *clann,* children, family, from Latin *planta,* shoot, PLANT.]

clan·des·tine (klăn-dĕs′tən) *adj.* Concealed, usually for some secret or illicit purpose. See Synonyms at **secret.** [French *clandestin,* from Old French, from Latin *clandestīnus,* from *clam,* in secret (after *intestīnus,* inward, INTESTINE). See **kel-**[4] in Appendix.*] —**clan·des′tine·ly** *adv.* —**clan·des′tine·ness** *n.*

clang (klăng) *v.* **clanged, clanging, clangs.** —*intr.* To make a loud, metallic, resonant sound. —*tr.* To cause to clang. —*n.* **1.** A clanging sound. **2.** The strident call of a crane or goose. [Latin *clangere,* to sound. See **klēg-** in Appendix.*]

clan·gor (klăng′ər, klăng′gər) *n.* Also *chiefly British* **clan·gour.** A clang or repeated clanging; loud ringing; din. —*intr.v.* **clangored, -goring, -gors.** Also *chiefly British* **clan·gour.** To make this sound. [Latin, from *clangere,* CLANG.] —**clan′gor·ous** *adj.* —**clan′gor·ous·ly** *adv.*

clank (klăngk) *n.* A metallic sound, sharp and hard but not as resonant as a clang. —*intr.v.* **clanked, clanking, clanks.** To make this sound. [Imitative.]

clan·nish (klăn′ĭsh) *adj.* **1.** Of, pertaining to, or characteristic of a clan. **2.** Inclined to cling together and to exclude outsiders. —**clan′nish·ly** *adv.* —**clan′nish·ness** *n.*

clans·man (klănz′mən) *n., pl.* **-men** (-mĭn). A person belonging to a clan.

clans·wom·an (klănz′wo͝om′ən) *n., pl.* **-women** (-wĭm′ĭn). A woman belonging to a clan.

clap[1] (klăp) *v.* **clapped, clapping, claps.** —*intr.* **1.** To strike the palms of the hands together with a sudden, explosive sound, as in applauding. **2.** To come together suddenly with a sharp noise. —*tr.* **1.** To strike (the hands) together with a brisk movement and an abrupt, loud sound. **2.** To applaud in this manner. **3.** To tap with the open hand, as in greeting. **4.** To put, move, or send promptly or suddenly: *clap in jail.* **5.** To flap (the wings). **6.** *Informal.* To put together hastily. Used with *up* or *together: clap together a plan.* —*n.* **1. a.** The act or sound of clapping the hands. **b.** A loud, sharp, or explosive noise. **2.** A sharp blow with the open hand; a slap. **3.** *Obsolete.* A sudden stroke, especially of bad luck. [Middle English *clappen,* from Old English *clappian,* to throb, beat, from an imitative Germanic root *klap-* (unattested).]

clap[2] (klăp) *n. Vulgar Slang.* Gonorrhea. Often preceded by *the.* [Probably from Old French *clapoir,* venereal sore, from *clapier,* brothel, from Old Provençal *clapier,* "rabbit warren," from *clap*†, heap of stone.]

clap·board (klăb′ərd, klăp′bôrd′, -bōrd′) *n.* A long, narrow board with one edge thicker than the other, overlapped to cover the outer walls of frame houses. —*tr.v.* **clapboarded, -boarding, -boards.** To cover with clapboards. [Partial translation of Middle Dutch *clapholt* : *clappen,* to crack, split, akin to Old English *clappian,* to CLAP + *holt,* board, wood.]

clap·per (klăp′ər) *n.* **1.** A person or thing that claps; especially, the tongue of a bell. **2.** *Plural.* Two flat pieces of wood held between the fingers and struck together rhythmically. **3.** *Slang.* The tongue.

clap·per·claw (klăp′ər-klô′) *tr.v.* **-clawed, -clawing, -claws.** *Archaic.* **1.** To claw or scratch. **2.** To berate or revile. [Probably CLAPPER + CLAW.]

clapper rail. A North American marsh bird, *Rallus longirostris,* having brownish plumage, a long bill, and a clattering cry.

clap·trap (klăp′trăp′) *n.* Pretentious, insincere, or empty language. See Synonyms at **bombast.** [CLAP + TRAP ("a trick to win applause").]

claque (klăk) *n.* **1.** A group of persons hired to applaud at a performance. **2.** Any group of adulating or fawning admirers. [French, from *claquer,* to clap (imitative).]

Clar·a (klăr′ə). A feminine given name. [Middle English, from Latin *clāra,* feminine of *clārus,* bright, beautiful. See **kel-**[3] in Appendix.*]

clar·a·bel·la (klăr′ə-bĕl′ə) *n.* An eight-foot organ stop producing soft, sweet tones. [Latin *clāra,* feminine of *clārus,* CLEAR + *bella,* feminine of *bellus,* pretty (see **deu-**[2] in Appendix*).]

Clare[1] (klâr). A masculine or feminine given name. [Middle English, from Latin *clārus,* bright. See CLARA.]

Clare[2] (klâr). A county, 1,231 square miles in area, in western Ireland. Population, 74,000. County seat, Ennis.

Clare of As·si·si (ə-sē′sē, -zē), **Saint.** 1194–1253. Italian nun, founder with St. Francis of Assisi of the Order of the Poor Clares; canonized 1255.

clar·ence (klăr′əns) *n.* A four-wheeled closed carriage with seats for four passengers. [After the Duke of *Clarence* (1765–1837), later William IV of England.]

clar·en·don (klăr′ən-dən) *n. Printing.* A type similar to roman but with narrower letters and thicker lines. [After the *Clarendon* Press, printing house of the Oxford University Press.]

Clar·en·don (klăr′ən-dən), **Earl of.** Title of Edward Hyde. 1609–1674. English Royalist statesman and historian.

clar·et (klăr′ət) *n.* **1. a.** The dry red table wine of Bordeaux, France. **b.** Any similar wine made elsewhere. **2.** Dark or grayish purplish red to dark purplish pink. See **color.** [Middle English, from Old French, from Medieval Latin *(vīnum) clārātum,* "clarified (wine)," from Latin *clārāre,* to make clear, purify, from *clārus,* CLEAR.] —**clar′et** *adj.*

claret cup. A chilled mixed drink of red wine variously combined with soda and fruit juices.

Cla·re·tian (klə-rē′shən, klă-) *n.* A member of an order, the Congregation of the Missionary Sons of the Immaculate Heart of Mary, founded in Spain in 1849. [After Saint Anthony *Claret* (1807–1870), Spanish priest and founder of the order.] —**Cla·re′tian** *adj.*

clar·i·fy (klăr′ə-fī′) *v.* **-fied, -fying, -fies.** —*tr.* **1.** To make clear or easier to understand; elucidate. **2.** To make clear by removing impurities, often by heating gently: *clarify butter.* —*intr.* To become clear. [Middle English *clarifien,* from Old French *clarifier,* from Late Latin *clārificāre* : Latin *clārus,* CLEAR + *facere,* to make (see **dhē-**[1] in Appendix*).] —**clar′i·fi·ca′tion** *n.* —**clar′i·fi′er** *n.*

clar·i·net (klăr′ə-nĕt′) *n.* Also *rare* **clar·i·o·net** (klăr′ē-ə-nĕt′). **1.** A woodwind instrument having a straight, cylindrical tube with a flaring bell and a single-reed mouthpiece, played by means of finger holes and keys. **2.** An eight-foot organ stop producing a sound suggestive of a clarinet. [French *clarinette,* from Italian *clarinetto,* diminutive of *clarino,* trumpet, from Latin *clārus,* CLEAR.] —**clar′i·net′ist, clar′i·net′tist** *n.*

clar·i·on (klăr′ē-ən) *n.* **1.** A medieval trumpet with a shrill, clear tone. **2.** The sound made by this instrument or any sound resembling it. —*adj.* Shrill and clear. [Middle English *clarioun,* from Medieval Latin *clāriō,* trumpet, from Latin *clārus,* CLEAR.]

clar·i·ty (klăr′ə-tē) *n.* Clearness; lucidity. [Middle English *clarite,* from Latin *clāritās,* from *clārus,* CLEAR.]

Clark (klärk), **Champ.** In full, James Beauchamp Clark. 1850–1921. American political leader.

Clark (klärk), **George Rogers.** 1752–1818. American frontiersman and military leader in the Revolutionary War.

Clark (klärk), **Kenneth Bancroft.** Born 1914. American educator and psychologist.

Clark (klärk), **William.** 1770–1838. American military officer; public official; explorer; commanded overland expedition to the Pacific Ocean (1804–06) with Meriwether **Lewis** *(see).*

Clark Fork River (klärk). A river rising near Butte in southwestern Montana and flowing 360 miles northwest into Pend Oreille Lake in northern Idaho.

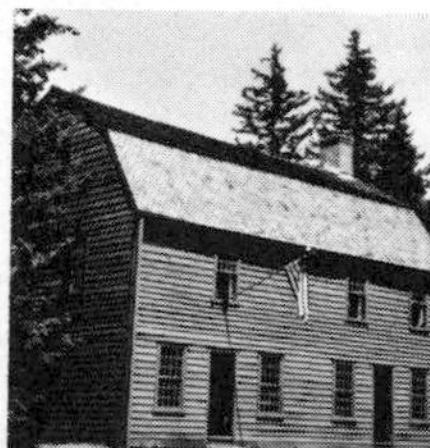

clapboard
Rhode Island house with clapboard siding

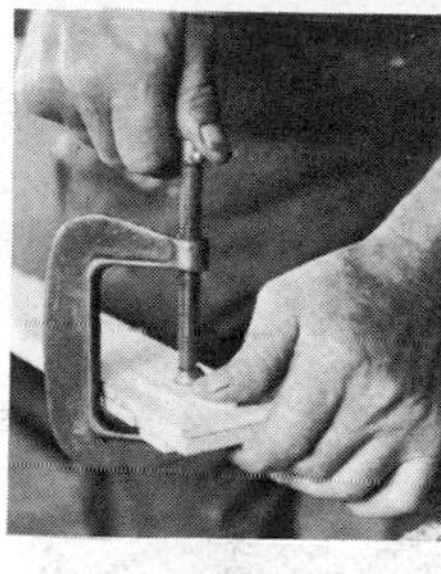

clamp

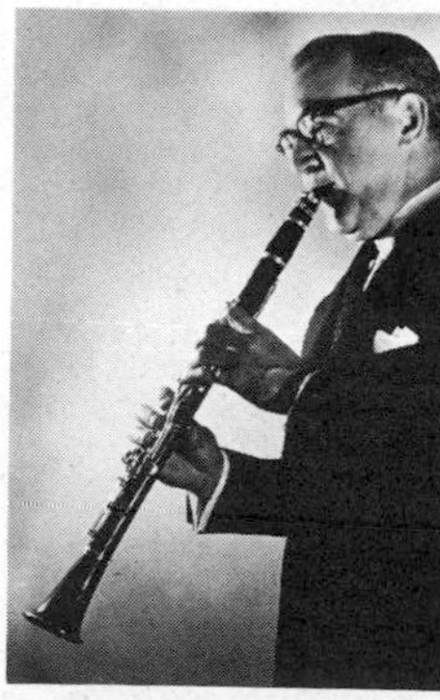

clarinet
Benny Goodman playing clarinet

clark·i·a (klär′kē ə) *n.* Any of several plants of the genus *Clarkia,* of western North America, having red, purple, or pink flowers. [New Latin; discovered by William CLARK.]
cla·ro (klär′ō) *n., pl.* **-ros.** A light-colored, mild cigar. [Spanish, from Latin *clārus,* CLEAR.]
clar·y (klâr′ē) *n., pl.* **-ies.** Any of several European plants of the genus *Salvia,* especially *S. sclarea,* an aromatic herb with bluish-white flowers. Also called "clary sage." [Middle English *clarye, sclarey,* from Old French *sclaree,* from Medieval Latin *sclarea*†.]
-clase. Indicates a mineral with a specified cleavage; for example, **plagioclase.** [French, from Greek *klasis,* a breaking, from *klan,* to break. See **kel-**[2] in Appendix.*]
clash (klăsh) *v.* **clashed, clashing, clashes.** —*intr.* **1.** To collide with a loud, harsh noise. **2.** To conflict or disagree; be in opposition. —*tr.* To strike together with a harsh, metallic noise. —*n.* **1.** A loud, resounding metallic noise, such as that made by two objects colliding. **2.** A conflict, opposition, or disagreement. —See Synonyms at **discord.** [Imitative.]
clasp (klăsp, kläsp) *n.* **1.** A fastening, such as a hook or buckle, used to hold two objects or parts together. **2. a.** An embrace; a hug. **b.** A grip or grasp of the hand. **3.** A small metal bar attached to a military decoration indicating the action for which it was awarded. —*tr.v.* **clasped, clasping, clasps. 1.** To fasten with or as if with a clasp. **2.** To hold in a tight grasp; embrace. **3.** To grip firmly in or with the hand. [Middle English *claspe,* from *claspen, clapsen,* to grip, grasp, perhaps from Old English *clyppan,* to embrace. See **gel-**[1] in Appendix.*] —**clasp′er** *n.*
clasp knife. A pocketknife with a folding blade.
class (klăs, kläs) *n. Abbr.* **cl. 1. a.** A set, collection, group, or configuration containing members having or thought to have at least one attribute in common; kind; sort. **b.** *Statistics.* Any interval in a **frequency distribution** *(see).* **2.** Any division of people or objects by quality, rank, or grade. **3.** A social stratum whose members share similar economic, political, and cultural characteristics. **4. a.** The division of society into relative strata or ranks. **b.** Social rank or caste, especially high rank. **5. a.** A group of students or alumni graduated in the same year. **b.** A group of students meeting to study the same subject. **c.** The period during which such a group meets. **6.** *Biology.* A taxonomic category ranking below a phylum and above an order. **7.** The quality of accommodation on a public vehicle: *travel third class.* **8.** *Slang.* High style in manner or dress: *a girl with class.* —*tr.v.* **classed, classing, classes.** To arrange, group, or rate according to qualities or characteristics; assign to a class; classify. [French *classe,* from Late Latin *classis,* from Latin, one of the six divisions of the Roman people, army, fleet. See **kel-**[3] in Appendix.*]
class. 1. classic; classical. **2.** classification; classified; classify.
class-con·scious (klăs′kŏn′shəs) *adj.* Aware of belonging to a particular socio-economic class. —**class-con′scious·ness.**
clas·sic (klăs′ĭk) *adj.* **1.** Of the highest rank or class. **2.** Serving as an outstanding representative of its kind; model. **3.** Having lasting significance or recognized worth. **4.** *Abbr.* **class.** Pertaining to ancient Greek or Roman literature or art; classical. See Usage note below. **5.** Of or in accordance with established principles and methods in the arts and sciences. **6.** Of lasting historical or literary significance. —*n.* **1.** An artist, author, or work generally considered to be of the highest rank or excellence. **2.** *Plural.* The literature of ancient Greece and Rome. **3.** Something considered to be typical or traditional.
Usage: Classic and *classical* are interchangeable, as adjectives, in some of their senses. Among these are senses pertaining specifically to ancient Greek and Roman culture, though *classical* is more common in that respect. *Classic* is always the choice to indicate, in a general sense, highest rank (and thus to connote respect): *Edward Lear's classic limericks.*
clas·si·cal (klăs′ĭ-kəl) *adj. Abbr.* **class. 1.** Of, pertaining to, or in accordance with the precedents of ancient Greek and Roman art and literature. See Usage note at **classic. 2.** Pertaining to or versed in studies of antiquity. **3.** *Music.* **a.** Pertaining to or designating the European music, as that of Haydn and Mozart, of the latter half of the 18th century. **b.** Designating any music in the educated European tradition, as distinguished from popular or folk music. **4.** Standard and authoritative rather than new or experimental. **5.** Of or pertaining to nonrelativistic or nonquantum physics: *classical mechanics.* [From CLASSIC.] —**clas′si·cal′i·ty, clas′si·cal·ness** *n.* —**clas′si·cal·ly** *adv.*
Classical Greek. The forms of Greek used in classical literature, chiefly Attic-Ionic, Doric, and Aeolic.
Classical Latin. The form of Latin used in classical literature. Compare **Vulgar Latin.**
clas·si·cism (klăs′ə-sĭz′əm) *n.* **1.** Aesthetic attitudes and principles based on the culture, art, and literature of ancient Greece and Rome and characterized by emphasis on form, simplicity, proportion, and restrained emotion. **2.** Classical scholarship. **3.** A Greek or Latin form or idiom.
clas·si·cist (klăs′ə-sĭst) *n.* A student of the classics.
clas·si·fi·a·ble (klăs′ə-fī′ə-bəl) *adj.* Capable of being classified.
clas·si·fi·ca·tion (klăs′ə-fĭ-kā′shən) *n. Abbr.* **cl., class. 1.** The act or result of classifying. **2.** *Biology.* The systematic grouping of organisms into categories based on shared characteristics or traits; taxonomy. **3.** One of a series of degrees of availability for conscription assigned to men by the Selective Service. —**clas′si·fi·ca′to·ry** (-kā′tər-ē, -kə-tôr′ē, -tōr′ē) *adj.*
classified advertisement. An advertisement, usually brief and in small type, printed in a newspaper. Also called "want ad."
clas·si·fy (klăs′ə-fī′) *tr.v.* **-fied, -fying, -fies. 1.** To arrange or organize according to class or category. **2.** To designate (a document, for instance) as secret and available only to authorized persons. [Latin *classis,* CLASS + -FY.] —**clas′si·fi′er** *n.*
clas·sis (klăs′ĭs) *n., pl.* **classes** (klăs′ēz′). *Ecclesiastical.* **1.** In certain Reformed churches, a governing body of pastors and elders having jurisdiction over local churches. **2.** The district or churches governed by such a body. [New Latin, from Latin, division, CLASS.]
class mark. *Statistics.* A **mark** *(see).*
class·mate (klăs′māt′, kläs′-) *n.* A member of the same academic class.
class·room (klăs′ro͞om′, -ro͝om′, kläs′-) *n.* A room in which classes are conducted in a school or college.
class struggle. In Marxist theory, the conflict for economic and political power between an exploiting class, as the bourgeoisie, and an exploited class, as the proletariat.
class·y (klăs′ē, kläs′ē) *adj.* **-ier, -iest.** *Slang.* Stylish; elegant.
-clast. Indicates one that breaks or destroys; for example, **osteoclast.** [Medieval Latin *-clastēs,* from Medieval Greek *-klastēs,* breaker, from *klan,* to break. See **kel-**[2] in Appendix.*]
clas·tic (klăs′tĭk) *adj.* **1.** Separable into parts or having removable sections: *a clastic anatomical model.* **2.** *Geology.* Made up of fragments; fragmental. [Greek *klastos,* broken, from *klan,* to break. See **kel-**[2] in Appendix.*]
clath·rate (klăth′rāt′, klăth′-) *adj.* **1.** *Biology.* Having a latticelike structure or appearance. **2.** *Chemistry.* Of or pertaining to inclusion complexes in which molecules of one substance are completely enclosed within the crystal structure of another. [Latin *clāthrātus,* past participle of *clāthrāre,* to provide with a lattice, from *clāthrī, clātra,* lattice, from Greek *klēithra,* from *klēithron,* door bar, from *kleiein,* to close. See **klēu-** in Appendix.*]
clat·ter (klăt′ər) *v.* **-tered, -tering, -ters.** —*intr.* **1.** To make or move with a rattling sound. **2.** To talk rapidly and noisily; chatter. —*tr.* To cause to make a rattling sound. —*n.* **1.** A rattling sound or sounds. **2.** A loud disturbance; commotion. **3.** Noisy talk; chatter. [Middle English *clatren,* Old English *clatrian* (attested only in gerund *clatrung*). See **gal-**[2] in Appendix.*] —**clat′ter·er** *n.*
Clau·del (klō-dĕl′), **Paul Louis Charles.** 1868–1955. French poet, playwright, and diplomat.
clau·di·ca·tion (klô′dĭ-kā′shən) *n.* A halt in one's walk; a limp; lameness. [Middle English *claudicacioun,* from Latin *claudicātiō,* from *claudicāre,* to limp, from *claudus*†, lame.] —**clau′di·cant** (klô′dĭ-kənt) *adj.*
Clau·di·us I (klô′dē-əs). In full, Tiberius Claudius Drusus Nero Germanicus. 10 B.C.–A.D. 54. Roman emperor (A.D. 41–54).
clause (klôz) *n. Abbr.* **cl. 1.** A group of words containing a subject and a predicate that forms part of a compound or complex sentence. See **dependent clause, independent clause. 2.** A distinct article, stipulation, or provision in a document. [Middle English, from Old French, from Medieval Latin *clausa,* close of a rhetorical period, conclusion of a legal argument, hence section of a law, from *claudere* (past participle *clausus*), to close. See **klēu-** in Appendix.*] —**claus′al** (klô′zəl) *adj.*
Clau·se·witz (klou′zə-vĭts′), **Karl von.** 1780–1831. Prussian military officer and author of works on military strategy.
Clau·si·us (klou′zē-o͝os), **Rudolf Julius Emmanuel.** 1822–1888. German physicist and mathematician.
claus·tral. Variant of **cloistral.**
claus·tro·pho·bi·a (klôs′trə-fō′bē-ə) *n.* A pathological fear of confined spaces. [New Latin : Latin *claustrum,* enclosed place, CLOISTER + -PHOBIA.] —**claus′tro·pho′bic** (-fō′bĭk) *adj.*
cla·vate (klā′vāt′) *adj.* Having one end thickened; club-shaped; claviform. [New Latin *clavatus,* from Latin *clāva,* club. See **klēu-** in Appendix.*] —**cla′vate′ly** *adv.*
clave. *Archaic.* **1.** Past tense of **cleave** (to split). **2.** Past tense of **cleave** (to cling).
cla·ver (klā′vər) *intr.v.* **-vered, -vering, -vers.** *Scottish.* To gossip or talk idly. —*n. Scottish.* Gossip; idle talk. [From Scottish Gaelic *clabaire*†, babbler.]
clav·i·chord (klăv′ĭ-kôrd′) *n.* An early musical keyboard instrument with a soft sound produced by tangents striking horizontal strings. [Medieval Latin *clāvichordium* : Latin *clāvis,* key (see **klēu-** in Appendix*) + *chorda,* CHORD.]
clav·i·cle (klăv′ĭ-kəl) *n.* A bone that links the sternum and the scapula. Also called "collarbone." [New Latin *clavicula,* "small key" (from the shape), from Latin, diminutive of *clāvis,* key. See **klēu-** in Appendix.*] —**cla·vic′u·lar** (klă-vĭk′yə-lər) *adj.* —**cla·vic′u·late′** (-lāt′) *adj.*
clav·i·corn (klăv′ĭ-kôrn′) *adj.* Belonging to or designating a group of beetles of the suborder Polyphaga, having club-shaped antennae. [New Latin *Clavicornia* (family name) : Latin *clāva,* club (see **klēu-** in Appendix*) + Latin *cornū,* horn (see **ker-**[1] in Appendix*).]
cla·vier (klə-vîr′, klā′vē-ər, klăv′ē-ər) *n.* **1.** A keyboard. **2.** Any stringed keyboard instrument, such as a harpsichord. [German *Klavier,* piano, from French *clavier,* keyboard, from Old French *clavier,* key-bearer, from Latin *clāvis,* key. See **klēu-** in Appendix.*]
clav·i·form (klăv′ə-fôrm′) *adj.* Club-shaped; clavate. [Latin *clāva,* club (see **klēu-** in Appendix*) + -FORM.]
claw (klô) *n.* **1.** A sharp, often curved, nail on the toe of a mammal, reptile, or bird. **2. a.** A chela or similar pincerlike structure on the limb of a crustacean or other arthropod. **b.** A limb terminating in such a structure. **3.** Anything resembling a claw, as the cleft end of a hammerhead. **4.** *Botany.* The narrowed basal part of certain petals or sepals. —*v.* **clawed, clawing, claws.** —*tr.* To scratch with or as if with claws. —*intr.* To make scratching or digging motions with or as if with

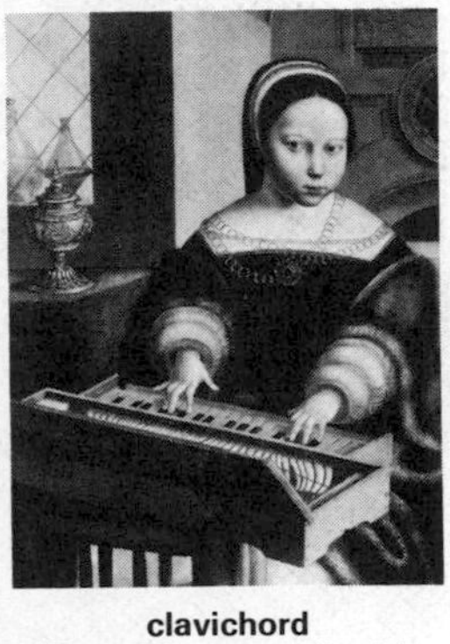

clavichord
Sixteenth-century Flemish painting

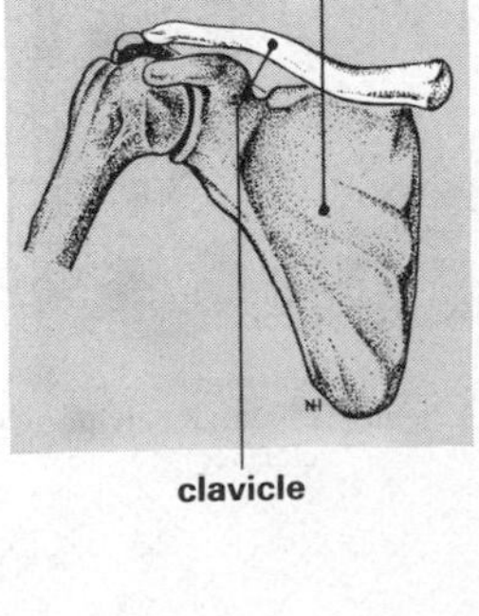

clavicle

claws. [Middle English *clawe,* Old English *clawu.* See **gel-¹** in Appendix.*]
claw hammer. **1.** A hammer having a head with one end forked for removing nails. **2.** A swallow-tailed coat.
claw hatchet. A hatchet having one end of the head forked.
clay (klā) *n.* **1.** A fine-grained, firm natural material, plastic when wet, that consists primarily of hydrated silicates of aluminum and is widely used in making bricks, tiles, and pottery. **2.** Any earth that forms a paste with water and hardens when heated, especially one with grains smaller than 0.002 millimeters in diameter. **3.** Moist earth; mud. **4.** The human body in distinction to the spirit. [Middle English *cley, clay,* Old English *clǣg.* See **gel-¹** in Appendix.*] —**clay′ey** (klā′ē), **clay′ish** (klā′ĭsh) *adj.*
Clay (klā), **Cassius Marcellus.** Also known as "Muhammad Ali." Born 1942. American athlete; world heavyweight boxing champion (1964–67).
Clay (klā), **Henry.** 1777–1852. American statesman; Secretary of State (1825–29).
clay·more (klā′môr′, -mōr′) *n.* A large, double-edged broadsword formerly used by Scottish Highlanders. [Gaelic *claidheamh mōr,* "great sword" : *claidheamh,* sword (see **kel-²** in Appendix*) + *mōr,* great (see **mē-³** in Appendix*).]
clay pigeon. A clay disk thrown as a flying target for skeet and trapshooting. Also called "bird."
clay·to·ni·a (klā-tō′nē-ə) *n.* A plant of the genus *Claytonia,* the **spring beauty** *(see).* [After John *Clayton* (1693–1773), American botanist.]
-cle. Indicates small size; for example, **particle.** [Middle English, from Old French, from Latin *-culus.*]
CLE Airport code for Cleveland, Ohio.
clean (klēn) *adj.* **cleaner, cleanest.** **1.** Free from dirt, stain, or impurities; unsoiled. **2.** Free from foreign matter; unadulterated. **3.** Producing little radioactive fallout or contamination. **4.** Without imperfections or blemishes; regular; perfect: *a clean line.* **5.** Free from clumsiness; clever; deft; adroit: *a clean throw.* **6.** Without restrictions or encumbrances: *a clean bill of health.* **7.** Entire; thorough; complete: *a clean escape.* **8.** Having few alterations or corrections; legible. **9.** Blank: *a clean page.* **10.** Morally pure; unsullied; sinless. **11.** Not ribald or obscene. **12.** Honest; fair, as in sports: *a clean fighter.* **13.** *Slang.* **a.** Free from narcotics addiction, use, or possession. **b.** Innocent of a suspected crime. —**a clean slate.** A fresh start. —*adv.* **1.** In a clean manner; cleanly. **2.** *Informal.* Entirely; wholly. —**come clean.** *Slang.* To admit the truth; confess. —*v.* **cleaned, cleaning, cleans.** —*tr.* **1.** To rid of dirt or other impurities. **2.** To remove (dirt or impurities) from something. **3.** To prepare (fowl or other food) for cooking. —*intr.* To undergo or perform the act of ridding of dirt and impurities. —**clean out.** **1.** To rid of dirt, trash, or impurities. **2.** To rid or empty of contents or occupants. **3.** To drive or force out. **4.** To deprive completely: *The robbery cleaned him out of money.* [Middle English *clene,* Old English *clǣne.* See **gel-²** in Appendix.*] —**clean′a·ble** *adj.* —**clean′ness** *n.*
clean-cut (klēn′kŭt′) *adj.* **1.** Clearly and sharply defined or outlined. **2.** Wholesome; neat and well-dressed.
clean·er (klē′nər) *n.* One that cleans, especially as a business, chemical process, or mechanical function.
clean-hand·ed (klēn′hăn′dĭd) *adj.* Innocent; guiltless.
clean-limbed (klēn′lĭmd′) *adj.* Having well-formed limbs.
clean·ly (klĕn′lē) *adj.* **-lier, -liest.** Habitually and carefully neat and clean. —*adv.* (klēn′lē). In a clean manner. —**clean′li·ness** (klĕn′lē-nĭs) *n.*
cleanse (klĕnz) *tr.v.* **cleansed, cleansing, cleanses.** To free from dirt, defilement, or guilt; purge or clean. [Middle English *clensen,* Old English *clǣnsian.* See **gel-²** in Appendix.*]
Usage: *Cleanse* is largely figurative and literary, with special reference to spiritual and ceremonial matters; *clean* (verb) is literal.
cleans·er (klĕn′zər) *n.* **1.** One that cleans. **2.** A soap, detergent, or other preparation used for cleaning.
clean-shav·en (klēn′shā′vən) *adj.* **1.** Having the beard or hair shaved off. **2.** Having recently shaved.
clean up. **1.** To rid of dirt or disorder. **2.** To make oneself clean, neat, or presentable. **3.** To finish; conclude. **4.** *Informal.* To make a large profit.
clean·up (klēn′ŭp′) *n.* **1.** A thorough cleaning or ordering. **2.** *Informal.* A large profit.
clear (klîr) *adj.* **clearer, clearest.** **1.** Free from anything that dims, obscures, or darkens; unclouded. **2.** Free from flaw, blemish, or impurity. **3.** Free from impediment, obstruction, or hindrance; open. **4.** Plain or evident to the mind. **5.** Easily perceptible to the eye or ear; distinct. **6.** Discerning or perceiving easily; keen: *a clear mind.* **7.** Free from doubt or confusion; certain; sure. **8.** Free from qualification or limitation; absolute. **9.** Resonant; ringing, as certain sounds. **10.** Freed from contact or connection; disengaged. Used with *of: We are now clear of danger.* **11.** Free from roughness or protrusions, as lumber. **12.** Freed from burden or obligation. **13.** Without charges or deductions; net: *He earns a clear $15,000.* —*adv.* **1.** Distinctly; clearly. **2.** *Informal.* All the way; completely; entirely: *She cried clear through the night.* —*v.* **cleared, clearing, clears.** —*tr.* **1.** To make clear, light, or bright. **2.** To rid of impurities, blemishes, muddiness, or foreign matter. **3.** To free from confusion, doubt, or ambiguity; make plain or intelligible. **4.** To rid of obstructions or entanglements: *clear the road of snow.* **5.** To remove or get rid of (obstacles or entanglements): *clear snow from the road.* **6.** To free from a legal charge or imputation of guilt; acquit. **7.** To pass by, under, or over without contact. **8.** To settle (a debt) by paying it. **9.** To gain (a given amount) as net profit or earnings. **10.** To pass (a check or other bill of exchange) through a clearing-house. **11.** To free (a ship or cargo) from legal detention at a harbor by fulfilling the customs and harbor requirements. **12.** To free (the throat) of phlegm by coughing. —*intr.* **1.** To become clean, fair, or bright. **2.** To exchange checks and bills, and to settle accounts, through a clearing-house. **3.** To comply with customs and harbor requirements in discharging a cargo or in leaving or entering a port. Often used with *in* or *out.* —**clear out.** *Informal.* To go away. —**clear the air.** To dispel emotional tensions or differences. —**clear up.** **1.** To make clear. **2.** To become fair and sunny after having been cloudy. **3.** To rid of confusion or mystery; explain. —*n.* **1.** A clear or open space. **2.** Clearance. —**in the clear.** **1.** Free from burdens or dangers. **2.** *Sports.* In a position to receive a pass without interference. [Middle English *clere,* from Old French *cler,* from Latin *clārus,* bright, clear. See **kel-³** in Appendix.*] —**clear′a·ble** *adj.* —**clear′er** *n.* —**clear′ly** *adv.* —**clear′ness** *n.*
clear·ance (klîr′əns) *n.* **1.** The act of clearing. **2.** A space cleared; a clearing. **3.** *Abbr.* **cl.** The amount by which a moving object clears something. **4.** An intervening distance or space enabling free play, as that between machine parts. **5.** Permission for an airplane, ship, or other vehicle to proceed, as after an inspection of equipment or cargo or during certain traffic conditions. **6.** Official certification of blamelessness, trustworthiness, or suitability. **7.** A sale, generally at reduced prices, to dispose of old merchandise. **8.** *Abbr.* **cl.** The passage of checks and other bills of exchange through a clearing-house.
clear-cut (klîr′kŭt′) *adj.* **1.** Distinctly and sharply defined or outlined. **2.** Plain; evident. —See Synonyms at **incisive.**
clear-eyed (klîr′īd′) *adj.* **1.** Having sharp, bright eyes; keen-sighted. **2.** Mentally acute or perceptive.
clear-head·ed (klîr′hĕd′ĭd) *adj.* Having a clear, orderly mind. —**clear′-head′ed·ly** *adv.* —**clear′-head′ed·ness** *n.*
clear·ing (klîr′ĭng) *n.* **1.** A tract of land from which the trees and other obstructions have been removed. **2.** In banking, the exchange among banks of checks, drafts, and notes, and the settlement of differences arising from it. **3.** *Plural.* The total of claims presented daily at a clearing-house.
clear·ing-house (klîr′ĭng-hous′) *n.* Also **clear·ing·house.** *Abbr.* **c.h., C.H.** An office where banks exchange checks and drafts and settle accounts.
clear-sight·ed (klîr′sī′tĭd) *adj.* **1.** Having sharp, clear vision. **2.** Perceptive; discerning. —**clear′-sight′ed·ly** *adv.* —**clear′-sight′ed·ness** *n.*
clear·sto·ry. Variant of **clerestory.**
clear·weed (klîr′wēd′) *n.* A plant, *Pilea pumila,* of eastern North America, having small green flowers and translucent stems and leaves. Also called "richweed."
clear·wing (klîr′wĭng′) *n.* Any of various moths of the family Aegeriidae, having scaleless, transparent wings.
cleat (klēt) *n.* **1.** A strip of wood or iron used to strengthen or support the surface to which it is attached. **2.** A piece of iron, rubber, or leather attached to the underside of a shoe to preserve the sole or prevent slipping. **3.** A piece of metal or wood having projecting arms or ends on which a rope can be wound or secured. **4.** A wedge-shaped piece of wood or other material fastened onto something, such as a spar, to act as a support or to prevent slipping. **5.** A spurlike device used in gripping a tree or pole in climbing. —*tr.v.* **cleated, cleating, cleats.** **1.** To supply, support, or strengthen with a cleat or cleats. **2.** *Nautical.* To secure (rope or other material) to or with a cleat. [Middle English *clete,* Old English *clēat* (unattested), lump, wedge. See **gel-¹** in Appendix.*]
cleav·a·ble (klē′və-bəl) *adj.* Easily cleft or split.
cleav·age (klē′vĭj) *n.* **1.** The act of splitting or cleaving. **2.** The state of being split or cleft; a fissure or division. **3.** *Mineralogy.* The splitting, or the tendency to split, along definite crystalline planes, yielding smooth surfaces. **4.** *Biology.* The process of or any of various stages in cell division that produce a blastula from a fertilized ovum. Also called "segmentation." **5.** *Informal.* The separation between a woman's breasts.
cleave¹ (klēv) *v.* **cleft** (klĕft) or **cleaved** or **clove** (klōv) or *archaic* **clave** (klāv), **cleft** or **cleaved** or **cloven** (klō′vən) or *archaic* **clove, cleaving, cleaves.** —*tr.* **1.** To split or separate, as with an ax. **2.** To make or accomplish as if by cutting: *cleave a path through the forest.* **3.** To pierce or penetrate. —*intr.* **1.** To split or separate, especially along a natural line of division. **2.** To make one's way; penetrate; pass. Used with *through.* —See Synonyms at **tear.** [Cleave, clove, cloven; Middle English *cleven, clave, cloven,* Old English *clēofan, clēaf* (past singular), *clofen.* The weak form *cleft,* Middle English *cleved, cleft,* from the infinitive *cleven.* See **gleubh-** in Appendix.*]
cleave² (klēv) *intr.v.* **cleaved** or *archaic* **clave** (klāv) or **clove** (klōv), **cleaved, cleaving, cleaves.** **1.** To adhere, cling, or stick fast. Used with *to.* **2.** To be faithful. Used with *to: "Cleave to that which is good."* (Romans 12:9). [Middle English *clevien,* Old English *cleofian.* See **gel-¹** in Appendix.*]
cleav·er (klē′vər) *n.* A heavy, axlike knife or hatchet used by butchers.

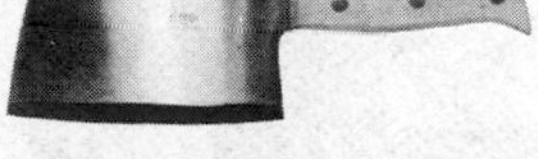
cleaver

cleav·ers (klē′vərz) *n.* Plural in form, usually used with a singular verb. Any of several plants of the genus *Galium;* especially, *G. aparine,* having small white flowers and prickly stems and seeds. This species is also called "goose grass." [Middle English *clivre* (probably influenced by *clivres,* claws), Old English *clīfe,* "the clinging plant," burdock. See **gel-¹** in Appendix.*]
cleek (klēk) *n.* **1.** *Golf.* A number-one iron, having very little

loft to the club face. **2.** *Scottish.* A large hook. [Middle English *cleche, clelke,* "grasping," from *clechen,* to grasp, seize, Old English *clǣcan* (unattested), probably akin to CLUTCH (verb).]

clef (klĕf) *n.* A symbol on a musical staff, indicating the pitch of the notes. [French, key, musical key, from Old French, from Latin *clāvis,* key. See **klēu-** in Appendix.*]

cleft (klĕft). A past tense and past participle of **cleave** (to split). —*adj.* **1.** Divided; split; separated. **2.** *Botany.* Having deeply divided lobes or divisions: *a cleft leaf.* —*n.* **1.** A crack; crevice; split. **2.** A split or indentation between two parts, as of the chin. [Middle English *clift,* rift, fissure, Old English *geclyft.* See **gleubh-** in Appendix.*]

cleft palate. A congenital fissure in the roof of the mouth.

cleis·tog·a·mous (klī-stŏg′ə-məs) *adj.* Also **cleis·to·gam·ic** (klī′stə-găm′ĭk). *Botany.* Characterized by self-fertilization in an unopened, budlike state. [Greek *kleistos,* closed (see **klēu-** in Appendix*) + -GAMOUS.] —**cleis·tog′a·mous·ly** *adv.*

cleis·tog·a·my (klī-stŏg′ə-mē) *n. Botany.* The condition of being cleistogamous.

clem·a·tis (klĕm′ə-tĭs) *n.* Any of various plants or vines of the genus *Clematis,* of eastern Asia and North America, having white or variously colored flowers and plumelike seeds. [New Latin *Clematis,* from Latin *clēmatis,* from Greek *klēmatis,* from *klēma,* twig. See **kel-**[2] in Appendix.*]

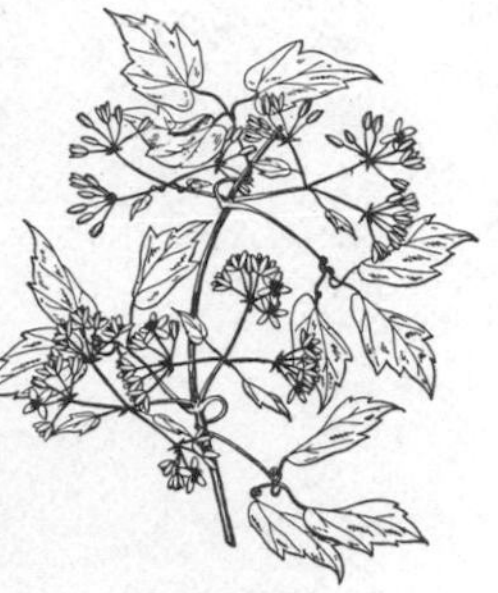

clematis
Clematis virginiana

Cle·men·ceau (klĕm′ən-sō′; *French* klĕ-mäN-sō′), **Georges.** 1841–1929. French statesman; premier (1906–09; 1917).

clem·en·cy (klĕm′ən-sē) *n., pl.* **-cies. 1.** Mildness of temper, especially toward an offender or enemy; leniency; mercy. **2.** A merciful, kind, or lenient act. **3.** Mildness, especially of weather. —See Synonyms at **mercy.**

Clem·ens (klĕm′ənz), **Samuel Langhorne.** Pen name, Mark Twain. 1835–1910. American author and humorist.

clem·ent (klĕm′ənt) *adj.* **1.** Lenient or merciful in disposition. **2.** Mild. Said of weather or climate. [Middle English, from Latin *clēmēns*†, mild, gentle.] —**clem′ent·ly** *adv.*

Clem·ent I (klĕm′ənt), **Saint.** Called "Clement of Rome." Bishop of Rome during the late first century A.D.; reputedly third successor to Saint Peter.

Clem·ent V (klĕm′ənt). Original name, Bertrand de Got. 1264–1314. Pope (1305–14); removed seat of papacy from Rome to Avignon, France (1309).

Clem·ent VII (klĕm′ənt). Original name, Giulio de' Medici. 1478–1534. Pope (1523–34); cousin of Pope Leo X; refused to sanction divorce of Henry VIII (1534).

Clem·ent of Alexandria (klĕm′ənt). Original name, Titus Flavius Clemens. Greek Christian theologian and educator; head of catechetical school in Alexandria (A.D. 190–203).

clench (klĕnch) *tr.v.* **clenched, clenching, clenches. 1.** To bring together (hands or teeth) tightly; close. **2.** To grasp or grip tightly. **3.** To clinch (a nail or bolt, for example). **4.** *Nautical.* To fasten with a clinch. —*n.* **1.** A tight grip or grasp. **2.** Anything that clenches or holds fast, as a mechanical device. **3.** *Nautical.* A kind of knot, a **clinch** *(see).* [Middle English *clenchen,* Old English *beclencan.* See **gel-**[1] in Appendix.*]

Usage: *Clench* and *clinch,* as verbs, both apply to the act of securing or holding. Transitively, either can be used to denote fastening of nails or the like (though *clinch* is more common) and in nautical usage (to fasten by knotting). But one *clenches* an object held, the fingers or fists, and the jaws or teeth. Only *clinch* is used for the securing of a bargain, argument, or verdict. *Clinch,* intransitively, denotes holding in boxing.

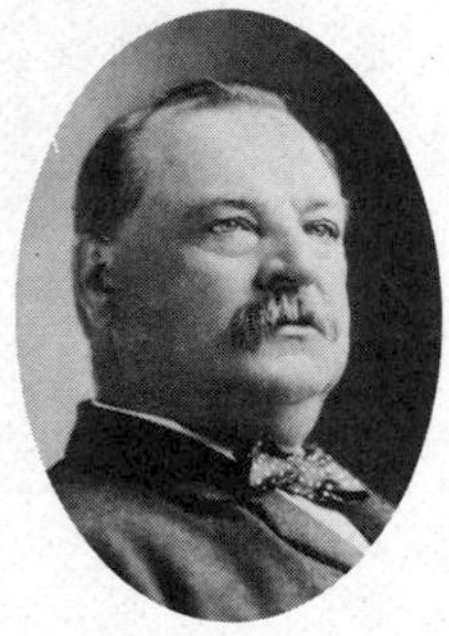

Grover Cleveland

cle·o·me (klē-ō′mē) *n.* Any of various mostly tropical plants of the genus *Cleome;* especially, *C. spinosa,* cultivated for its clusters of white or purplish flowers with long, conspicuous stamens. Also called "spiderflower." [New Latin *Cleome*†.]

Cle·on (klē′ŏn′). Greek political and military leader of Athens in the fifth century B.C.

Cle·o·pat·ra (klē′ə-păt′rə, -pā′trə, -pä′trə). Also known as Cleopatra VI or VII. 69–30 B.C. Queen of Egypt (51–49 B.C. and 48–30 B.C.); wife of Ptolemy III, her brother; mistress of Julius Caesar and Mark Antony.

clepe (klēp) *tr.v.* **cleped** (klēpt, klĕpt) or **clept, cleping, clepes.** Also *past participle* **ycleped** (ĭ-klēpt′, ĭ-klĕpt′) or **yclept.** *Archaic.* To call by the name of; name. [Middle English *clepen,* to speak, call out, Old English *cleopian, clipian*†, to call out, call by name.]

clep·sy·dra (klĕp′sə-drə) *n., pl.* **-dras** or **-drae** (-drē′). An ancient device that measured time by marking the regulated flow of water through a small opening. Also called "water clock." [Latin, from Greek *klepsudra,* "water stealer" (from the "stealthy" flow of the water) : *kleps-,* stem of *kleptein,* to steal (see **klep-** in Appendix*) + *hudōr,* water (see **wed-**[1] in Appendix*).]

clep·to·ma·ni·a. Variant of **kleptomania.**

clere·sto·ry (klîr′stôr′ē, -stōr′ē) *n., pl.* **-ries.** Also **clear·sto·ry. 1.** The upper part of the nave, transepts, and choir of a church, containing windows. **2.** Any similar windowed wall or construction used for light and ventilation. [Middle English : *clere,* lighted, CLEAR + STORY (of a building).]

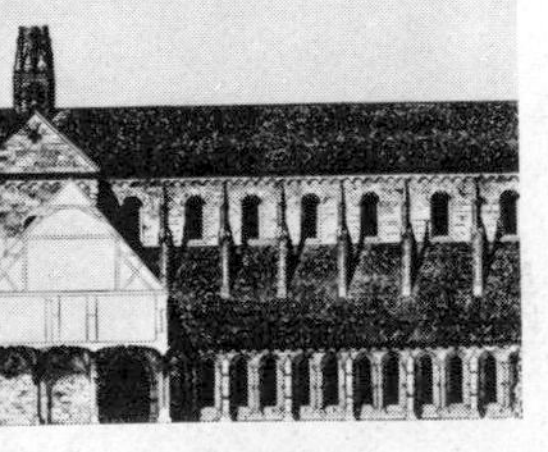

clerestory
Romanesque abbey church at Maulbronn, West Germany

cler·gy (klûr′jē) *n., pl.* **-gies.** The body of men ordained for religious service. Compare **laity.** [Middle English *clergie,* from Old French (influenced by *clerge,* body of clerks), from *clerc,* ecclesiastic, CLERK.]

cler·gy·man (klûr′jē-mən) *n., pl.* **-men** (-mĭn). *Abbr.* **cl.** A member of the clergy.

cler·ic (klĕr′ĭk) *n.* A member of the clergy. —*adj.* Pertaining to the clergy. [Medieval Latin *clēricus,* CLERK.]

cler·i·cal (klĕr′ĭ-kəl) *adj.* **1.** Of or pertaining to clerks or office workers. **2.** Of, relating to, or characteristic of the clergy or a clergyman. **3.** Advocating clericalism. —*n.* **1.** A clergyman. **2.** *Plural.* The distinctive garb of a clergyman. **3.** A person or party advocating clericalism. —**cler′i·cal·ly** *adv.*

cler·i·cal·ism (klĕr′ĭ-kəl-ĭz′əm) *n.* A policy of supporting the power or influence of the clergy in political or secular matters. —**cler′i·cal·ist** *n.*

cler·i·hew (klĕr′ə-hyōō′) *n.* A humorous quatrain about a person who is generally named in the first line. [Invented by Edmund *Clerihew* Bentley (1875–1956), English writer.]

cler·i·sy (klĕr′ə-sē) *n.* Educated people as a class; the literati. [German *Klerisei,* from Medieval Latin *clēricia,* the clergy, from Late Latin *clēricus,* CLERK.]

clerk (klûrk; *British* klärk) *n. Abbr.* **cl., clk. 1.** A person who works in an office performing such tasks as keeping records, attending to correspondence, or filing. **2.** A person who keeps the records and performs the regular business of a court or legislative body. **3.** A salesman or saleswoman in a store. **4.** *Anglican Church.* A lay minister who helps the parish clergyman perform his duties. **5.** *Archaic.* A clergyman. **6.** *Archaic.* **a.** A literate person. **b.** A scholar. —*intr.v.* **clerked, clerking, clerks.** To work or serve as a clerk. [Middle English, from Old English and Old French *clerc,* from Late Latin *clēricus,* a cleric, from Greek *klērikos,* belonging to inheritance, cleric (with reference to the Levites whose only inheritance was the Lord), from *klēros,* allotment, inheritance. See **kel-**[2] in Appendix.*] —**clerk′dom** *n.* —**clerk′ship′** *n.*

clerk·ly (klûrk′lē) *adj.* **-lier, -liest. 1.** Of or pertaining to a clerk or clerks. **2.** *Archaic.* Scholarly. —**clerk′li·ness** *n.*

Cle·ve (klā′və), **Per Teodor.** 1840–1905. Swedish chemist and geologist; discovered rare-earth elements.

Cleve·land (klēv′lənd). A city of northeastern Ohio, a port and industrial center on Lake Erie. Population, 859,000.

Cleve·land (klēv′lənd), **(Stephen) Grover.** 1837–1908. Twenty-second and twenty-fourth President of the United States (1885–89 and 1893–97).

clev·er (klĕv′ər) *adj.* **-er, -est. 1.** Mentally quick and original; bright. **2.** Nimble with the hands; dexterous. **3.** Showing quick-wittedness: *a clever story.* **4.** *Regional.* Handy; suitable. [Probably from Middle English *cliver,* expert to seize, dexterous, perhaps from Scandinavian, akin to Old Norse *kleyfr.* See **gleubh-** in Appendix.*] —**clev′er·ly** *adv.* —**clev′er·ness** *n.*

Synonyms: *clever, cunning, ingenious, shrewd.* These adjectives describe quick-witted action or speech. *Clever,* the most comprehensive, stresses mental quickness or adeptness in handling a situation. *Cunning* adds to *clever* the idea of slyness or craftiness. *Ingenious* implies great originality and invention. *Shrewd* emphasizes mental cleverness and practical understanding.

clev·is (klĕv′ĭs) *n.* A U-shaped metal piece with holes in each end through which a pin or bolt is run, used for attaching a drawbar to a plow. [Probably plural of *clevi,* "cleft instrument," from Scandinavian, akin to Old Norse *klofi,* cleft, fissure. See **gleubh-** in Appendix.*]

clew[1] (klōō) *n.* **1.** A ball of yarn or thread. **2.** *Greek Mythology.* The ball of thread used by Theseus as a guide through the labyrinth of Minos on Crete. **3.** *Plural.* The cords by which a hammock is suspended. **4.** *Nautical.* **a.** One of the two lower corners of a square sail. **b.** The lower aft corner of a fore-and-aft sail. —*tr.v.* **clewed, clewing, clews. 1.** To roll or coil into a ball. **2.** *Nautical.* To raise the lower corners of (a square sail) by means of clew lines. Used with *up.* [Middle English *clewe(n),* Old English *cliewen, clewe(n).* See **gel-**[1] in Appendix.*]

clew[2]. Variant of **clue.**

clew line. A rope used to raise the clew of a sail up to the yard or mast.

cli·ché (klē-shā′) *n.* **1.** A trite or overused expression or idea. **2.** *Printing.* A stereotype or electrotype plate. [French, "stereotyped," from *clicher,* to stereotype (imitative of the sound made when the matrix is dropped into the molten metal to make a stereotype plate).]

Synonyms: *cliché, bromide, truism, commonplace, banality, platitude.* These nouns denote ideas or statements that have lost their originality and force through overuse. *Cliché* specifically describes any expression that once was fresh but has become dull and stereotyped through frequent repetition. A *bromide* is an obvious, dull, hackneyed statement. A *truism* is a statement so self-evident as scarcely to need to be stated. *Commonplace* refers to an idea that is so obvious and generally known that it is dismissed. *Banality* suggests lack of both originality and taste. A *platitude* is a bromide expressed with an air of significance.

Cli·chy (klē-shē′). A city of France, northwest of Paris of which it is a suburb. Population, 56,000.

click (klĭk) *n.* **1.** A brief, sharp, nonresonant sound: *the click of a door latch.* **2.** A mechanical device that snaps into position, such as a detent or pawl. **3.** *Phonetics.* An implosive speech sound, common in some African languages, produced by drawing air into the mouth and clicking the tongue. Also called "suction stop." —*v.* **clicked, clicking, clicks.** —*intr.* **1.** To produce one or a series of clicks. **2.** *Slang.* **a.** To become a success. **b.** To function well together. —*tr.* To cause to click. [Imitative.] —**click′er** *n.*

click beetle. Any of various beetles of the family Elateridae, characterized by the ability to right itself from an overturned position by flipping into the air with a clicking sound. Also called "snapping beetle."

cli·ent (klī′ənt) *n.* **1.** One for whom professional services are rendered. **2.** A customer or patron. **3.** One dependent on the patronage of another. [Middle English, from Old French, from Latin *cliēns,* dependent, follower. See **klei-** in Appendix.*] —**cli·en′tal** (klī-ĕn′təl) *adj.* —**cli′ent·ship′** *n.*

ă pat/ā pay/âr care/ä father/b bib/ch church/d deed/ĕ pet/ē be/f fife/g gag/h hat/hw which/ĭ pit/ī pie/îr pier/j judge/k kick/l lid, needle/m mum/n no, sudden/ng thing/ŏ pot/ō toe/ô paw, for/oi noise/ou out/ŏŏ took/ōō boot/p pop/r roar/s sauce/sh ship, dish/

cli·en·tele (klī′ən-tĕl′; *French* klē-äN-tĕl′) *n.* Also **cli·en·tage** (klī′ən-tĭj). **1.** The clients of a professional person taken collectively. **2.** A body of customers or patrons. [French *clientèle,* from Latin *clientēla,* from *cliēns,* CLIENT.]

cliff (klĭf) *n.* A high, steep, or overhanging face of rock. [Middle English *clif,* Old English *clif,* from Germanic *klibam* (unattested).] **—cliff′fy** *adj.*

cliff dweller. **1.** A member of certain prehistoric Indian tribes of the southwestern United States who lived in caves in the sides of cliffs. **2.** A person who lives in an apartment house, especially in a city. **—cliff dwelling.**

cliff·hang·er (klĭf′hăng′ər) *n.* **1.** A melodramatic serial in which each episode ends in suspense. **2.** A contest so closely matched that the outcome is uncertain until the end. **—cliff′hang′ing** *adj.*

cliff swallow. A North American swallow, *Petrochelidon pyrrhonota,* that builds a bottle-shaped mud nest on the face of a cliff, bluff, or under the eaves of a roof.

Clif·ton (klĭf′tən). A city in northeastern New Jersey. Population, 82,000.

cli·mac·ter·ic (klī-măk′tər-ĭk, klī′măk-tĕr′ĭk) *n.* **1.** A period or year of life when physiological changes supposedly take place in the body. **2.** The **menopause** *(see).* **3.** Any critical period. *—adj.* Also **cli·mac·ter·i·cal** (klī′măk-tĕr′ĭ-kəl). Pertaining to a critical stage, period, or year. [Latin *clīmactēricus,* from Greek *klimaktērikos,* from *klimaktēr,* rung of a ladder, crisis, from *klimax,* ladder. See **climax.**]

cli·mac·tic (klī-măk′tĭk) *adj.* Also **cli·mac·ti·cal** (-tĭ-kəl). Pertaining to or constituting a climax. **—cli·mac′ti·cal·ly** *adv.*

cli·mate (klī′mĭt) *n.* **1.** The meteorological conditions, including temperature, precipitation, and wind, that characteristically prevail in a particular region. **2.** A region manifesting particular meteorological conditions. **3.** A prevailing condition in human affairs: *the political climate.* [Middle English *climat,* from Old French, from Late Latin *clīma,* climate, zone of latitude, from Greek *klima,* sloping surface of the earth. See **klei-** in Appendix.*] **—cli·mat′ic** (klī-măt′ĭk), **cli·mat′i·cal, cli′ma·tal** (-mə-təl) *adj.* **—cli·mat′i·cal·ly** *adv.*

cli·ma·tol·o·gy (klī′mə-tŏl′ə-jē) *n.* The meteorological study of climate. [CLIMAT(E) + -LOGY.] **—cli′ma·to·log′ic** (-tə-lŏj′ĭk), **cli′ma·to·log′i·cal** *adj.* **—cli′ma·tol′o·gist** *n.*

cli·max (klī′măks′) *n.* **1.** The point of greatest intensity in any series or progression of events; culmination. **2.** Orgasm. **3.** *Rhetoric.* **a.** A series of statements or ideas in an ascending order of force or intensity. **b.** The final statement in such a series. **4.** The stage in ecological development or evolution in which the community of organisms becomes stable and begins to perpetuate itself. —See Synonyms at **summit.** *—v.* **climaxed, -maxing, -maxes.** *—intr.* To reach a climax. *—tr.* To bring to a climax. [Latin, rhetorical climax, from Greek *klimax,* ladder. See **klei-** in Appendix.*]

climb (klīm) *v.* **climbed** or, *archaic* **clomb** (klōm), **climbing, climbs.** *—tr.* To move up or mount, especially by using the hands and feet; ascend. See Usage note below. *—intr.* **1.** To rise or move up, especially by using the hands and feet. **2.** To rise slowly or with effort in rank, status, or fortune. **3.** To slant or slope upward. **4.** To grow in an upward direction, as some plants do, by twining about or clinging to another object for support. —See Synonyms at **rise.** **—climb down.** To move downward; descend, especially by means of the hands and feet. See Usage note below. *—n.* **1.** The act of climbing; an ascent. **2.** A place to be climbed. [Climb, clomb; Middle English *climben, clomb,* Old English *climban, clamb* (or *clomb*). See **gel-**[1] in Appendix.*] **—climb′a·ble** (klī′mə-bəl) *adj.*

Usage: *Climb down,* in its literal sense, is established on all levels of usage, though it involves a seeming contradiction. *Climb up* is also standard, though *up* is usually superfluous.

climb·er (clī′mər) *n.* **1.** Something or someone that climbs. **2.** A person seeking to gain a higher social or professional position. **3.** A plant that grows upward by twining about or clinging to something. **4.** *Plural.* **Climbing irons** *(see).*

climbing fumitory. A weak-stemmed, climbing vine, *Adlumia fungosa,* of eastern North America, having spurred pinkish or white flowers. Also called "Allegheny vine."

climbing hempweed. A twining vine, *Mikania scandens,* of eastern and central North America, having clusters of small white flowers.

climbing irons. Iron bars with spikes or spurs attached, which are strapped to a shoe or boot and used in climbing telegraph poles, trees, and the like. Also called "climbers."

climbing perch. A freshwater fish, *Anabas testudineus,* of tropical Asia, capable of moving along the ground with the aid of its gill covers and pectoral fins. Also called "climbing fish."

clime (klīm) *n. Poetic.* Climate. [Middle English, region of the earth, zone, from Late Latin *clīma,* CLIMATE.]

-clinal. Indicates a slope or inclination; for example, **anticlinal, synclinal.** [From CLINE.]

cli·nan·dri·um (klĭ-năn′drē-əm) *n., pl.* **-dria** (-drē-ə). *Botany.* A hollow containing the anther in the upper part of the column of an orchid. [New Latin, "stamen bed" : CLIN(O)- + *-andrium,* "stamen," from Greek *anēr* (stem *andr-*), man (see **ner-**[2] in Appendix*).]

clinch (klĭnch) *v.* **clinched, clinching, clinches.** *—tr.* **1.** To fix or secure (a nail or bolt, for example) by bending down or flattening the end that has been driven through something. **2.** To fasten together in this way. **3.** To settle definitely and conclusively; make final. **4.** *Nautical.* To fasten with a clinch. *—intr.* **1.** To be held together securely. **2.** *Boxing.* To hold the opponent's body with one or both arms to prevent or hinder his punches. **3.** *Slang.* To embrace. —See Usage note at **clench.** *—n.* **1.** The act of clinching. **2.** Something that clinches, such as a clinched nail or clamp. **3.** The clinched part of a nail, bolt, rivet, or the like. **4.** *Boxing.* The act or an instance of clinching. **5.** *Nautical.* A knot in a rope made by a half hitch with the end of the rope fastened back by seizing. Also called "clench." **6.** *Slang.* An amorous embrace. [Variant of CLENCH.]

clinch·er (klĭn′chər) *n.* **1.** A person who clinches. **2.** A nail or bolt for clinching. **3.** A tool for clinching nails or bolts. **4.** *Informal.* A decisive point, fact, or remark, as in an argument.

clinch·er-built. Variant of **clinker-built.**

cline (klīn) *n. Ecology.* A series of differing characteristics within members of a species or population, resulting from gradual changes or transitions in the environment. [From Greek *klinein,* to lean. See **klei-** in Appendix.*]

-cline. Indicates slope; for example, **anticline, syncline.** [From CLINE.]

cling (klĭng) *intr.v.* **clung** (klŭng), **clinging, clings.** **1.** To hold fast or adhere to something, as by grasping, sticking, or entwining. **2. a.** To stay near; remain close. **b.** To resist separation. **3.** To hold on; remain attached: *cling to old-fashioned ideas.* *—n.* A clingstone peach. [Cling, clung (past tense), clung (past participle); Middle English *clingen, clong* (past singular), *clungen* (past plural), *clungen,* Old English *clingan, clang, clungon, clungen.* See **gel-**[1] in Appendix.*] **—cling′er** *n.*

cling·fish (klĭng′fĭsh′) *n., pl.* **clingfish** or **-fishes.** Any of various small marine fishes of the family Gobiesocidae, having an adhesive disk under the front part of the body, by which it fastens itself to rocks and seaweed.

clinging vine. A woman who shows excessive dependence on a man.

Cling·mans Dome (klĭng′mənz). The highest (6,642 feet) of the Great Smoky Mountains.

cling·stone (klĭng′stōn′) *n.* A fruit, especially a peach, having pulp that adheres partially to the stone. Compare **freestone.** **—cling′stone′** *adj.*

clin·ic (klĭn′ĭk) *n.* **1.** A lecture for the instruction of medical students in which patients are examined and treated in their presence. **2.** A class receiving such instruction. **3.** An institution associated with a hospital or medical school and dealing chiefly with outpatients. **4.** A medical establishment run by several specialists working cooperatively. **5.** A center that offers counsel or instruction: *a vocational clinic.* [French *clinique,* originally "a bedridden person," from Greek *klinikē,* medical treatment at sickbed, from *klinikos,* "of a bed," physician who visits bedridden persons, from *klinē,* bed. See **klei-** in Appendix.*]

-clinic. Indicates: **1.** Inclination or slope; for example, **isoclinic.** **2.** A certain number of oblique axial intersections; for example, **triclinic.** [From CLINE.]

clin·i·cal (klĭn′ĭ-kəl) *adj.* **1.** Pertaining to or connected with a clinic. **2.** Of or pertaining to direct observation and treatment of patients. **3.** Analytical; highly objective; rigorously scientific: *clinical details.* **4.** Administered on a deathbed or sickbed: *a clinical sacrament.* **—clin′i·cal·ly** *adv.*

clinical thermometer. A small self-registering glass thermometer used to measure body temperature.

cli·ni·cian (klĭ-nĭsh′ən) *n.* A physician, psychologist, or psychiatrist specializing in clinical studies or practice. [French *clinicien,* from *clinique,* CLINIC.]

clink[1] (klĭngk) *v.* **clinked, clinking, clinks.** *—intr.* **1.** To make a soft, sharp, ringing sound. **2.** *Rare.* To rhyme; jingle. *—tr.* To cause to clink. *—n.* **1.** A soft, sharp, ringing sound. **2.** *Rare.* A rhyme; jingle. **3.** *British.* The shrill cry of some birds, such as the stonechat. [Middle English *clinken,* from Middle Dutch *clinken, klinken*†.]

clink[2] (klĭngk) *n. Slang.* A prison. [After *The Clink,* a prison in London.]

clink·er (klĭng′kər) *n.* **1.** The incombustible residue, fused into an irregular lump, that remains after the combustion of coal. **2.** A partially vitrified brick or a mass of bricks fused together. **3.** An extremely hard burned brick. **4.** Vitrified matter expelled by a volcano. **5.** *Slang.* A mistake or fault, especially in music. *—intr.v.* **clinkered, -ering, -ers.** To create clinkers in burning, as coal does. [Earlier *clincart, klincard,* from obsolete Dutch *klinckaerd,* "one that clinks" (from its clinking sound when struck), from Middle Dutch *klinken, clinken,* CLINK.]

clink·er-built (klĭng′kər-bĭlt′) *adj.* Also **clinch·er-built** (klĭn′chər-). Built with overlapping planks or boards, as a ship. Compare **carvel-built.** [From *clinker,* a fastening or clinching with nails, from Middle English *clinken,* probably variant of *clenchen,* CLENCH.]

clink·stone (klĭngk′stōn′) *n. Mineralogy.* **Phonolite** *(see).*

clino–, clin–. Indicates slope or slant; for example, **clinometer, clinandrium.** [New Latin, from Greek *klinein,* to slope, and *klinē,* bed. See **klei-** in Appendix.*]

cli·nom·e·ter (klī-nŏm′ə-tər, klĭ-) *n.* An instrument for measuring the angle of an incline, as of an embankment. Also called "inclinometer." [CLINO- + -METER.] **—cli′no·met′ric** (-nə-mĕt′rĭk), **cli′no·met′ri·cal** *adj.* **—cli·nom′e·try** *n.*

clin·quant (klĭng′kənt; *French* klăN-käN′) *adj.* Adorned with gold or silver; tinseled; glittering. *—n.* Imitation gold leaf; tinsel. [French, "glistening," from *clinquer,* to glitter, clink, from Middle Dutch *clinken,* CLINK.]

Clin·ton (klĭn′tən), **De Witt.** 1769–1828. American political leader; twice governor of New York State; son of James Clinton.

Clin·ton (klĭn′tən), **George**[1]. 1686?–1761. British admiral and colonial administrator; governor of New York (1743–53); father of Sir Henry Clinton.

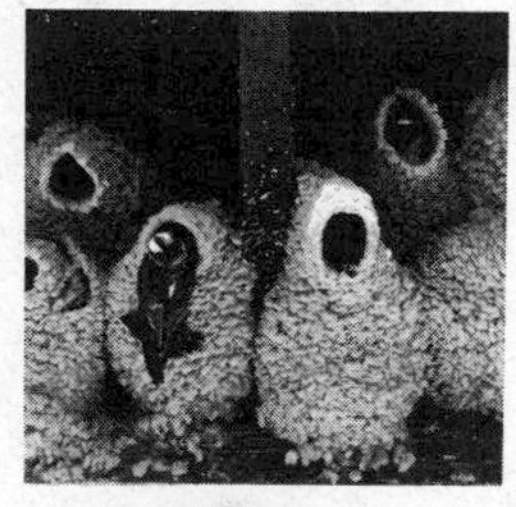

cliff swallow
Bird and nests

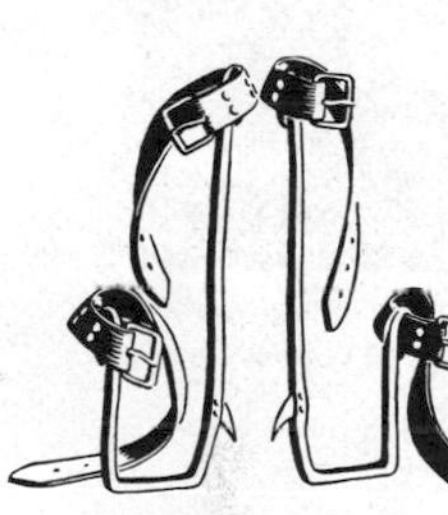

climbing irons

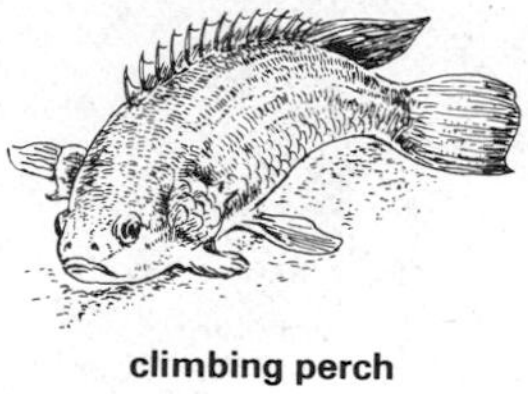

climbing perch

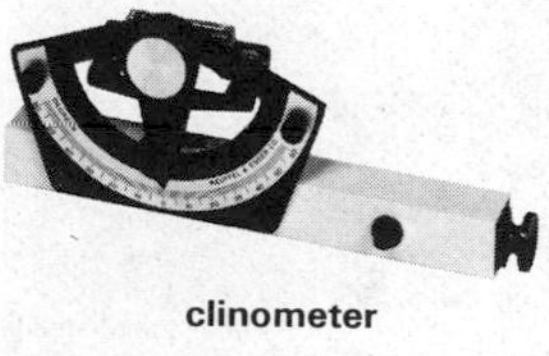

clinometer

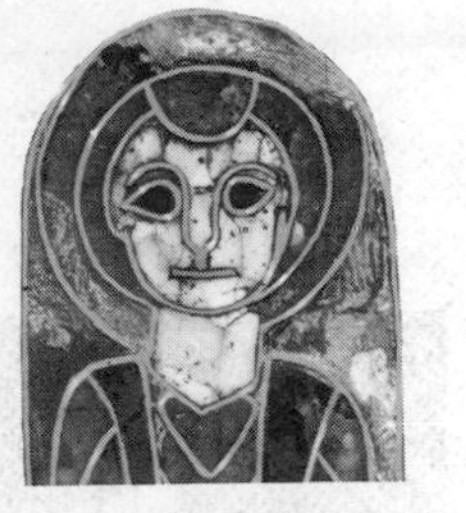

cloisonné
Eleventh-century French cloisonné angel

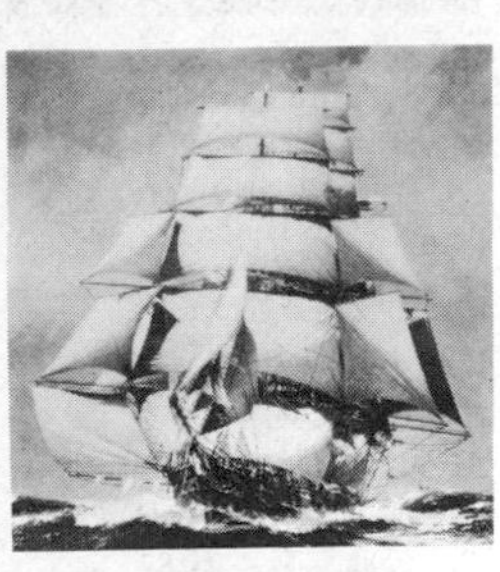

clipper
The clipper *Lightning*

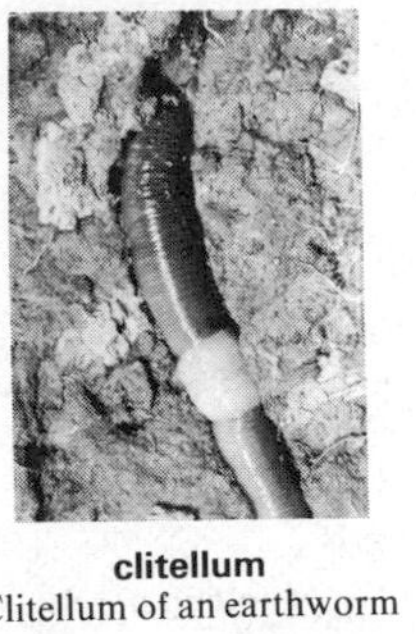

clitellum
Clitellum of an earthworm

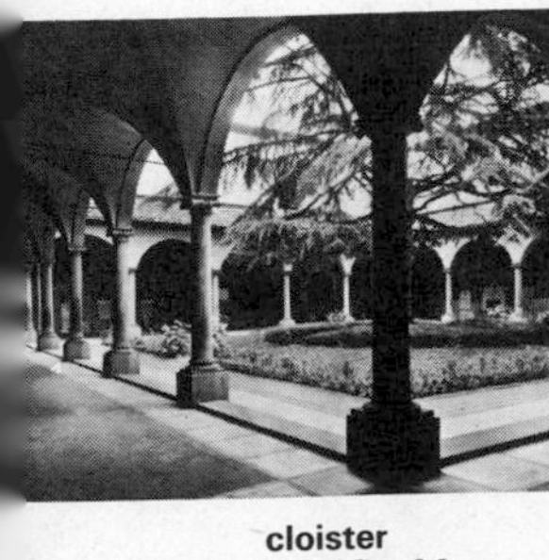

cloister
The cloister of San Marco, Florence, Italy

Clin·ton (klĭn′tən), **George**[2]. 1739–1812. Vice President of the United States under Thomas Jefferson and James Madison (1805–12); first governor of New York State; brother of James Clinton.

Clin·ton (klĭn′tən), Sir **Henry**. 1738?–1795. British general; commander in chief of British forces in Revolutionary War (1778–81); son of Admiral George Clinton.

Clin·ton (klĭn′tən), **James**. 1733–1812. American army officer; brigadier general in Revolutionary War; father of De Witt Clinton; brother of Vice President George Clinton.

clin·to·ni·a (klĭn-tō′nē-ə) *n.* Any plant of the genus *Clintonia*, having broad leaves, white, greenish-yellow, or purplish flowers, and usually blue berries. [New Latin, after De Witt CLINTON.]

Cli·o (klī′ō). *Greek Mythology.* The Muse of history. [Latin *Cliō*, from Greek *Kleiō*, "teller," from *kleiein, kleein*, to tell, praise. See **kleu-**[1] in Appendix.*]

clip[1] (klĭp) *v.* **clipped, clipping, clips.** —*tr.* **1.** To cut off or cut out with shears or scissors. **2.** To make shorter by cutting; trim. **3.** To cut off the edge of: *clip a coin.* **4.** To cut short; curtail. **5.** *Informal.* To hit with a sharp blow. **6.** *Slang.* To cheat or overcharge. —*intr.* **1.** To cut something. **2.** *Informal.* To move rapidly. —*n.* **1.** The act of clipping. **2.** Something clipped off. **3. a.** The wool shorn at one shearing. **b.** A season's shearing. **4.** *Informal.* A quick, sharp blow. **5.** *Informal.* A brisk pace. **6.** *Plural.* A pair of shears. [Middle English *clippen*, from Old Norse *klippa*†, to cut short.]

clip[2] (klĭp) *n.* **1.** A device for gripping; clasp; fastener. **2.** A flange on the top of a horseshoe. **3.** A **cartridge clip** *(see).* —*tr.v.* **clipped, clipping, clips. 1.** To grip securely; fasten. **2.** *Football.* To block (an opponent who is not carrying the ball) illegally from the rear. [Middle English *clipp*, from *clippen*, to embrace, fasten, Old English *clyppan*. See **gel-**[1] in Appendix.*]

clip·board (klĭp′bôrd′, -bōrd′) *n.* A small writing board having at the top a spring clip for holding papers or a writing pad.

clip joint. *Slang.* A restaurant or place of public entertainment where customers are overcharged or otherwise defrauded.

clipped form. A **shortened form** *(see).*

clip·per (klĭp′ər) *n.* **1.** One who cuts, shears, or clips. **2.** *Plural.* An instrument or tool for cutting, clipping, or shearing: *a barber's clippers.* **3.** A sharp-bowed sailing vessel of the mid-19th century, having tall masts and sharp lines and built for great speed. Also called "clipper ship." **4.** Any fast-moving vehicle.

clip·ping (klĭp′ĭng) *n.* Something that is cut off or out; especially, an item from a newspaper.

clip·sheet (klĭp′shēt′) *n.* A sheet of paper containing news items and other newspaper material, usually printed on only one side for convenience in clipping and reprinting.

clique (klēk, klĭk) *n.* An exclusive group of friends or associates. See Synonyms at **circle.** —*intr.v.* **cliqued, cliquing, cliques.** *Informal.* To form, associate in, or act as a clique. [French, from Old French, probably "a group of applauders," from *cliquer*, to click, clap, applaud (imitative).]

cli·quish (klē′kĭsh, klĭk′ĭsh) *adj.* Also **cli·quey, cli·quy** (klē′kē, klĭk′ē). Of, like, or characteristic of a clique; exclusive. —**cli′quish·ly** *adv.* —**cli′quish·ness** *n.*

cli·tel·lum (klī-tĕl′əm, klī-) *n., pl.* **-tella** (-tĕl′ə). A swollen, glandular, saddlelike region in the epidermis of certain annelid worms, such as the earthworm. [New Latin, from Latin *clītellae*, packsaddle. See **klei-** in Appendix.*]

clit·o·ris (klĭt′ə-rĭs, klī′tə-) *n.* A small, erectile organ at the upper end of the vulva, homologous with the penis. [New Latin, from Greek *kleitoris*, "small hill," diminutive of *kleitor-* (unattested), hill, from *klinein*, to lean, incline. See **klei-** in Appendix.*] —**clit′o·ral** (-rəl) *adj.*

Clive (klīv), **Robert.** Baron Clive of Plassey. 1725–1774. British military leader and colonial administrator; founder of the British Indian empire.

clk. clerk.

clm. column.

clo·a·ca (klō-ā′kə) *n., pl.* **-cae** (-sē′). **1.** A sewer. **2.** A latrine. **3.** *Zoology.* **a.** The cavity into which the intestinal, genital, and urinary tracts open in vertebrates such as fish, reptiles, birds, and some primitive mammals. **b.** The posterior part of the intestinal tract in various invertebrates. [Latin *cloāca*, sewer, canal. See **kleu-**[2] in Appendix.*] —**clo·a′cal** (-kəl) *adj.*

cloak (klōk) *n.* **1.** A loose outer garment, usually sleeveless. **2.** Anything that covers or conceals. —*tr.v.* **cloaked, cloaking, cloaks. 1.** To cover with a cloak. **2.** To cover up; hide; conceal. —See Synonyms at **hide.** [Middle English *cloke*, from Old French *cloque*, bell, "bell-shaped garment." See **clock.**]

cloak-and-dagger (klōk′ən-dăg′ər) *adj.* Marked by melodramatic intrigue.

cloak·room (klōk′ro͞om′, -ro͝om′) *n.* A room where coats and other articles may be left temporarily, as in a school or theater.

clob·ber (klŏb′ər) *tr.v.* **-bered, -bering, -bers.** *Slang.* **1.** To strike violently and repeatedly; batter or maul. **2.** To defeat completely. [Origin unknown.]

cloche (klōsh) *n.* **1.** A bell-shaped glass vessel used to cover plants or food. **2.** A close-fitting woman's hat with a bell-like shape. [French, bell, from Old French, bell, CLOCK.]

clock[1] (klŏk) *n.* **1.** Any instrument for measuring or indicating time, especially a mechanical device with a numbered dial and moving hands or pointers. Distinguished from a watch. **2.** *Informal.* A **speedometer** *(see).* **3.** A **time clock** *(see).* **4.** *Botany.* The downy flower head of a dandelion that has gone to seed. —*v.* **clocked, clocking, clocks.** —*tr.* To record the time or speed of, as with a stopwatch. —*intr.* To record working hours with a time clock. Used with *in* for arrival and *out* for departure. [Middle English *clok*, from Middle Dutch *clocke*, bell, clock, from Old French *cloche, cloque*, bell, from Late Latin *clocca* (imitative).] —**clock′er** *n.*

clock[2] (klŏk) *n.* An embroidered or woven decoration on the side of a stocking or sock. [Perhaps originally "a bell-shaped ornament," from Middle Dutch *clocke*, bell, CLOCK.]

clock·wise (klŏk′wīz′) *adv.* In the same direction as the rotating hands of a clock. —**clock′wise′** *adj.*

clock·work (klŏk′wûrk′) *n.* The mechanism of a clock or any similar mechanism. —**like clockwork.** With machinelike regularity and precision; perfectly.

clod (klŏd) *n.* **1.** A lump or chunk, especially of earth or clay. **2.** Earth or soil. **3.** A dull, ignorant, or stupid person; a dolt; an oaf. **4.** A cut of the shoulder of beef. [Middle English *clodde*, Old English *clod-* (only in compounds), variant of *clott*, lump. See **gel-**[1] in Appendix.*] —**clod′dish** *adj.* —**clod′dish·ness** *n.* —**clod′dy** *adj.*

clod·hop·per (klŏd′hŏp′ər) *n.* **1.** A clumsy, coarse person; a lout or bumpkin. **2.** *Plural.* Big, heavy shoes. [Originally "farmer" : CLOD (earth) + HOPPER.]

clog (klŏg) *n.* **1.** An obstacle or hindrance. **2.** A block or other weight attached to the leg of an animal to hinder movement. **3.** A heavy, usually wooden-soled shoe. —*v.* **clogged, clogging, clogs.** —*tr.* **1.** To block up; obstruct. **2.** To impede or encumber; to hamper. —*intr.* **1.** To become obstructed or choked up. **2.** To thicken or stick together; coagulate. **3.** To do a clog dance. [Middle English *clog, clogge*†, block of wood.] —**clog′gi·ness** *n.* —**clog′gy** *adj.*

clog dance. A dance performed with clogs and characterized by heavy, stamping steps.

cloi·son·né (kloi′zə-nā′; *French* klwä-zô-nā′) *n.* **1.** A kind of enamelware in which the surface decoration is formed by different colors of enamel separated by thin strips of metal set on edge. **2.** The process or method of producing such enamelware. —*adj.* Of or denoting this ware or method. [French, past participle of *cloisonner*, to partition, from Old French *cloison*, partition, from Vulgar Latin *clausiō* (unattested), enclosure, from Latin *claudere*, to close. See **klēu-** in Appendix.*]

clois·ter (klois′tər) *n.* **1.** A covered walk with an open colonnade on one side, running along the inside walls of buildings that face a quadrangle. **2.** A place devoted to religious seclusion; especially, a monastery or convent. **3.** Life in a monastery or convent. —*tr.v.* **cloistered, -tering, -ters. 1.** To confine in or as if in a cloister; seclude. **2.** To furnish (a building) with a cloister. [Middle English *cloistre*, from Old French, variant of *clostre* (influenced by *cloison*, partition, CLOISONNÉ), from Medieval Latin *claustrum*, from Latin, enclosed place, from *claudere*, to close. See **klēu-** in Appendix.*]

clois·tral (klois′trəl) *adj.* Also **claus·tral** (klôs′trəl). **1.** Of, resembling, or suggesting a cloister; secluded. **2.** Living in a cloister. [Middle English *claustral*, from Medieval Latin *claustrālis*, from *claustrum*, CLOISTER.]

clomb. *Archaic.* Past tense and past participle of **climb.**

clone (klōn) *n.* Also **clon** (klōn, klŏn). **1.** A group of genetically identical cells descended from a single common ancestor. **2.** A group of organisms descended asexually from a single common ancestor. [Greek *klōn*, twig, shoot. See **kel-**[2] in Appendix.*] —**clon′al** (klō′nəl) *adj.* —**clon′al·ly** *adv.*

clo·nus (klō′nəs) *n., pl.* **-nuses.** A convulsion characterized by rapidly alternating muscular contraction and relaxation. [New Latin, from Greek *klonos*, agitation, turmoil. See **kel-**[5] in Appendix.*] —**clo′nic** (klō′nĭk, klŏn′ĭk) *adj.* —**clo·nic′i·ty** (klō-nĭs′ə-tē, klō-), **clo′nism′** (klō′nĭz′əm, klŏn′ĭz′əm) *n.*

Cloot (klo͞ot) *n.* Also **Cloo·tie** (klo͞o′tē), **Cloots** (klo͞otz). *Scottish.* The devil. [From *cloot*†, cloven foot.]

clop (klŏp) *intr.v.* **clopped, clopping, clops.** To make the drumming sounds of a horse's hoofs against pavement. —*n.* The sound of a horse's hoof striking pavement. [Imitative.]

close (klōs) *adj.* **closer, closest. 1.** Proximate in time, space, or relation; near. **2.** Having all elements or parts near to each other; compact: *a close nap.* **3.** Near the surface; short: *a close shave.* **4.** Nearly equivalent or even, as a contest. **5.** Fitting tightly. **6.** Not deviating from an original: *a close copy.* **7.** Precise; exact, as reasoning. **8.** Complete; thorough: *pay close attention.* **9.** Bound by mutual interests, loyalties, or affections; intimate: *close companions.* **10.** Shut or shut in; not open. **11.** Enclosed or almost enclosed. **12.** Confined or narrow in space; crowded. **13.** Confined to specific persons or groups; restricted. **14.** Confined or guarded, as a prisoner. **15.** Hidden from view; secluded. **16.** Secretive in manner; reticent. **17.** Not giving; miserly. **18.** Not easy to acquire; scarce, as credit or money. **19.** Lacking fresh or circulating air; oppressive; stifling. **20.** *Phonetics.* Uttered with the tongue near the palate. Said of vowels. —See Synonyms at **familiar, stingy.** —See Usage note at **near.** —*v.* (klōz) **closed, closing, closes.** —*tr.* **1.** To shut. **2.** To bar or obstruct; fill up. **3.** To bring together all the elements of; end; finish. **4.** To join or unite; bring into contact: *close a circuit.* **5.** To enclose on all sides; shut in. —*intr.* **1.** To become shut. **2.** To finish or conclude. **3.** To engage in close quarters; to grapple. Used with *with.* **4.** To reach an agreement; come to terms. —See Synonyms at **complete.** —**close down.** To stop or cease entirely. —**close in.** To surround and advance upon, so as to eliminate the possibility of escape. —*n.* (klōz *for senses 1, 2, 3, 4;* klōs *for sense 5*). **1.** The act of closing. **2.** A conclusion; finish. **3.** *Archaic.* A fight at close quarters. **4.** An enclosed place, especially land surrounding or beside a cathedral or other building. **5.** *Scottish & British Regional.* A narrow lane or alley. —*adv.* (klōs). Closely. [Middle English *clos*, from Old French, from Latin *clausus*, past participle of *clau-*

ă pat/ā pay/âr care/ä father/b bib/ch church/d deed/ĕ pet/ē be/f fife/g gag/h hat/hw which/ĭ pit/ī pie/îr pier/j judge/k kick/l lid, needle/m mum/n no, sudden/ng thing/ŏ pot/ō toe/ô paw, for/oi noise/ou out/o͝o took/o͞o boot/p pop/r roar/s sauce/sh ship, dish/

dere, to close. See **klēu-** in Appendix.*] **—close′ly** (klōs′lē) *adv.* **—close′ness** (klōs′nĭs) *n.* **—clos′er** (klō′zər) *n.*

close call (klōs). *Informal.* A narrow escape.

closed (klōzd) *adj.* **1.** Having complete boundaries; enclosed. **2.** Blocked or barred to passage or entry. **3.** Having explicitly limited membership; restricted; exclusive. **4.** Self-contained. **5.** *Geometry.* **a.** Of or pertaining to a curve, such as a circle, having no end points. **b.** Of or pertaining to a surface having no boundary curves.

closed chain. A chemical **ring** *(see).*

closed circuit. 1. A television transmission circuit with a limited number of reception stations and no broadcast facilities. **2.** An electric circuit providing an uninterrupted endless path for the flow of current.

closed corporation. A corporation in which ownership of shares of stock is held by a relatively few persons and is rarely bought or sold on the open market.

closed-end investment company (klōzd′ĕnd′). A company with fixed capitalization whose shares are bought and sold by investors and whose capital is invested in other companies. Compare **mutual fund.**

closed gentian. A plant, the **bottle gentian** *(see).*

closed shop. A **union shop** *(see).*

close-fist·ed (klōs′fĭs′tĭd) *adj.* Stingy; miserly. See Synonyms at **stingy.** **—close′-fist′ed·ness** *n.*

close-grained (klōs′grānd′) *adj.* Dense or compact in structure or texture: *close-grained wood.*

close-hauled (klōs′hôld′) *adv. Nautical.* With sails trimmed flat for sailing as close to the wind as possible. **—close-hauled′** *adj.*

close-mouthed (klōs′mouthd′, -moutht′) *adj.* Not disposed to talking; reticent; taciturn.

close-or·der drill (klōs′ôr′dər). A military drill in marching, maneuvering, and formal handling of arms with the participants performing at close intervals.

close out (klōz). To dispose of (goods) usually at greatly reduced prices.

close-out (klōz′out′) *n.* A sale in which all goods are disposed of, usually at greatly reduced prices.

close shave (klōs). *Informal.* A narrow escape.

close stitch (klōs). The **buttonhole stitch** *(see).*

clos·et (klŏz′ĭt, klô′zĭt) *n. Abbr.* **cl. 1.** A small room, cabinet, or recess for storing linens or supplies, hanging clothes, or the like. **2.** A small private chamber for studying, meditating, praying, or the like. **3.** A water closet; toilet. *—tr.v.* **closeted, -eting, -ets.** To enclose or shut up in a private room, as for discussion or meditation. Usually used reflexively. *—adj.* **1.** Private; concealed; confidential. **2.** Based upon theory and speculation rather than practice: *closet plans.* [Middle English, from Old French, diminutive of *clos,* enclosure, from Medieval Latin *clausum,* from Latin *clausus,* enclosed, CLOSE.]

closet drama. A play to be read rather than performed.

close up. 1. To close entirely. **2.** To come nearer together.

close-up (klōs′ŭp′) *n.* **1.** A picture, such as a motion picture or television shot, taken at close range. **2.** A close or intimate look or view.

clos·trid·i·um (klŏs-trĭd′ē-əm) *n., pl.* **-tridia** (-trĭd′ē-ə). Any of various rod-shaped, spore-forming, chiefly anaerobic bacteria of the genus *Clostridium,* such as the nitrogen-fixing bacteria found in soil and those causing botulism. [New Latin, "small spindle," from Greek *klōstēr,* spindle, from *klōthein,* to spin. See **Clotho.**]

clo·sure (klō′zhər) *n.* **1.** The act of closing or the condition of being closed. **2.** Something that closes or shuts. **3.** A finish; conclusion. **4.** Variant of **cloture.** *—v.* **closured, -suring, -sures.** To end by cloture. [Middle English, from Old French, from Latin *clausūra,* from *clausus,* enclosed, CLOSE.]

clot (klŏt) *n.* A thick, viscous, or coagulated mass or lump. *—v.* **clotted, clotting, clots.** *—intr.* To form into clots. *—tr.* To cause to clot; fill or cover with clots. [Middle English *clot,* Old English *clott,* lump. See **gel-¹** in Appendix.*]

cloth (klôth, klŏth) *n., pl.* **cloths** (klôths, klôthz, klŏths, klŏthz). **1.** *Abbr.* **cl.** Fabric or material formed by weaving, knitting, pressing, or felting of natural or synthetic fibers. **2.** A piece of fabric or material used for a specific purpose, as a tablecloth. **3.** *Nautical.* **a.** Canvas. **b.** A sail. **4.** *Obsolete.* Garments; clothing. **5.** Professional attire or mode of dress. **—the cloth.** The clergy. [Middle English *cloth,* from Germanic.]

cloth·bound (klôth′bound′, klŏth′-) *adj.* Designating a book bound in boards and covered with cloth.

clothe (klōth) *tr.v.* **clothed** or **clad** (klăd), **clothing, clothes. 1.** To put clothes on; dress. **2.** To cover as with clothes; invest. [Middle English *clothen, clathen,* Old English *clāthian,* from *clāth,* CLOTH.]

clothes (klōz, klōthz) *pl.n.* **1.** Articles of dress; wearing apparel; garments. **2. Bedclothes** *(see).* [Middle English, from Old English *clāthas,* plural of *clāth,* CLOTH.]

clothes·horse (klōz′hôrs′, klōthz′-) *n.* **1.** A frame on which clothes are hung to dry or air. **2.** A person considered excessively concerned with dress.

clothes·line (klōz′līn′, klōthz′-) *n.* A cord, rope, or wire on which clothes are hung to dry or air.

clothes moth. Any of various moths of the family Tineidae, of which the larvae feed on wool, hair, fur, and feathers.

clothes·pin (klōz′pĭn, klōthz′-) *n.* A clip of wood or plastic for fastening clothes to a clothesline.

clothes·press (klōz′prĕs′, klōthz′-) *n.* Also **clothes press.** A chest, closet, or wardrobe in which clothes are kept.

clothes tree. An upright pole or stand with hooks or pegs on which to hang garments. Also called "hall tree."

cloth·ier (klōth′yər, klō′thē-ər) *n.* One who makes or sells clothing or cloth.

cloth·ing (klō′thĭng) *n.* **1.** Clothes collectively; wearing apparel; attire. **2.** A covering.

Clo·tho (klō′thō). *Greek Mythology.* One of the three Fates, spinner of the thread of destiny. [Greek *klōthō,* "spinster," from *klōthein,* to spin, akin to *kalathos,* CALATHUS.]

cloth yard. The standard unit of cloth measurement, equal to 36 inches.

clo·ture (klō′chər) *n.* Also **clo·sure** (klō′zhər). A parliamentary procedure by which debate is ended and an immediate vote is taken on the matter under discussion. Compare **previous question.** *—tr.v.* **clotured, -turing, -tures.** To close (a parliamentary debate) by cloture. [French *clôture,* variant of Old French *closure,* CLOSURE.]

cloud (kloud) *n.* **1.** A visible body of very fine droplets of water or particles of ice dispersed in the atmosphere above the earth's surface at various altitudes ranging up to several miles. **2.** Any visible mass in the air, as of steam, smoke, or dust. **3.** A large moving body of things on the ground or in the air; a swarm. **4.** Anything that darkens or fills with gloom. **5.** A dark region or blemish on a polished stone or gem. **6.** An appearance of dimness or milkiness, as in glass or a liquid. **—in the clouds. 1.** Imaginary; unreal; fanciful. **2.** Impractical. **—under a cloud. 1.** Under suspicion. **2.** In a gloomy state of mind; depressed. *—v.* **clouded, clouding, clouds.** *—tr.* **1.** To cover with or as if with clouds; darken; dim. **2.** To make gloomy, sullen, or troubled. **3.** To cast aspersions on; blacken; sully, as a reputation. *—intr.* To become cloudy or overcast. [Middle English *cloud,* hill, mass of earth, cloud, Old English *clūd,* rock, hill. See **gel-¹** in Appendix.*] **—cloud′less** *adj.*

cloud·ber·ry (kloud′bĕr′ē) *n., pl.* **-ries.** A creeping plant, *Rubus chamaemorus,* of northern regions, having white flowers and edible, reddish-orange fruit. Also called "baked-apple berry."

cloud·burst (kloud′bûrst′) *n.* A sudden rainstorm; downpour.

cloud chamber. A device in which the formation of chains of droplets on ions generated by the passage of charged subatomic particles through a supersaturated vapor is used to detect such particles, to infer the presence of neutral particles, and to study certain nuclear reactions. Compare **bubble chamber.**

cloud·land (kloud′lănd′) *n.* A realm of imagination or fantasy.

cloud seeding. A technique of stimulating rainfall, especially by distributing quantities of dry ice crystals or silver iodide smoke through clouds. Also informally called "rainmaking."

cloud·y (klou′dē) *adj.* **-ier, -iest. 1.** *Abbr.* **c.** Full of or covered with clouds; overcast. **2.** Of or like a cloud or clouds. **3.** Marked with indistinct masses or streaks: *cloudy marble.* **4.** Not transparent, as certain liquids. **5.** Obscure; vague. **6.** Troubled; gloomy. **—cloud′i·ly** *adv.* **—cloud′i·ness** *n.*

Clough (klŭf), **Arthur Hugh.** 1819–1861. English poet.

clout (klout) *n.* **1.** A blow, especially with the fist. **2.** A long, powerful hit in baseball. **3.** An archery target. **4.** *Archaic & Regional.* A piece of cloth used for mending; patch. *—tr.v.* **clouted, clouting, clouts. 1.** To hit with the fist. **2.** *Archaic & Regional.* To patch or bandage. [Middle English *clout,* Old English *clūt,* patch. See **gel-¹** in Appendix.*]

clove¹ (klōv) *n.* **1.** An East Indian evergreen tree, *Eugenia aromatica,* of which the aromatic unopened flower buds are used as a spice. **2.** *Often plural.* A spice consisting of the dried flower buds of this tree, used whole or ground. [Middle English *clowe (of gilofre),* "nail-shaped bud (of clove)," from Old French *clou (de girofle)* : *clou,* nail, from Latin *clāvus* (see **klēu-** in Appendix*) + *girofle,* clove tree (see **gillyflower**).]

clove² (klōv) *n.* One of the small sections of a separable bulb, such as that of garlic. [Middle English *clove,* Old English *clufu.* See **gleubh-** in Appendix.*]

clove³. 1. Alternate past tense and *archaic* past participle of **cleave** (to split). **2.** *Archaic.* Past tense of **cleave** (to cling).

clove hitch. *Nautical.* A knot used to secure a line to a spar, post, or other object, consisting of two turns with the second held under the first. [*Clove,* from CLOVEN (split).]

clo·ven (klō′vən). Alternate past participle of **cleave** (to split). *—adj.* Split; divided.

cloven foot. A cloven hoof. **—clo′ven-foot′ed** *adj.*

cloven hoof. 1. A divided or cleft hoof, as in deer or cattle. **2.** The symbol of Satan, usually depicted with such hoofs.

clo·ven-hoofed (klō′vən-ho͝oft′, -ho͞oft′, -ho͝ovd′, -ho͞ovd′) *adj.* **1.** Having cloven hoofs, as cattle do. **2.** Satanic; devilish.

clove pink. A variety of the carnation, *Dianthus caryophyllus,* having flowers with a spicy fragrance.

clo·ver (klō′vər) *n.* **1.** Any plant of the genus *Trifolium,* having compound leaves with three leaflets and tight heads of small flowers. Many species provide valuable pasturage. **2.** Any of several related plants, such as the **bush clover** *(see).* **—in clover.** Living a carefree life of ease, comfort, or prosperity. [Middle English *clover, claver,* Old English *clǣfre,* clover, from Germanic *klaibrōn* (unattested).]

clo·ver·leaf (klō′vər-lēf′) *n., pl.* **-leaves** (-lēvz′). A highway interchange at which two highways crossing each other on different levels are provided with curving access and exit ramps, enabling vehicles to go in any of four directions.

Clo·vis I (klō′vĭs). A.D. 466?–511. King of the Franks (A.D. 481–511) and of most of Gaul; defeated Romans; converted to Christianity.

clown (kloun) *n.* **1.** A buffoon or jester who entertains by jokes, antics, and tricks, in a circus, play, or other presentation. **2.** A coarse, rude, vulgar person; boor. **3.** A rustic or peasant. *—intr.v.* **clowned, clowning, clowns. 1.** To behave like a clown or buffoon. **2.** To perform as a jester or clown. [Probably

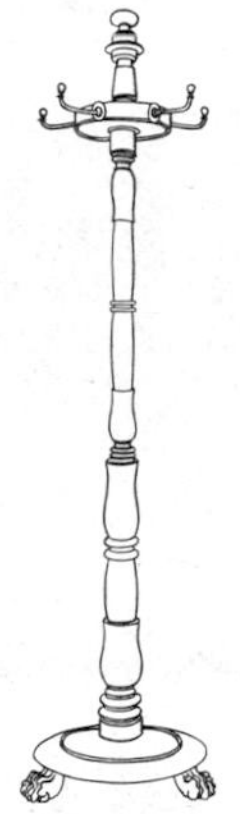

clothes tree

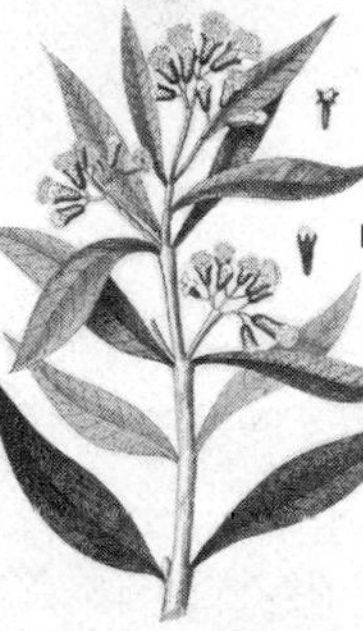

clove¹

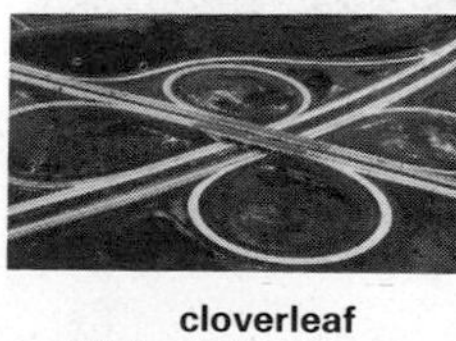

cloverleaf
Highway interchange at Fort Wayne, Indiana

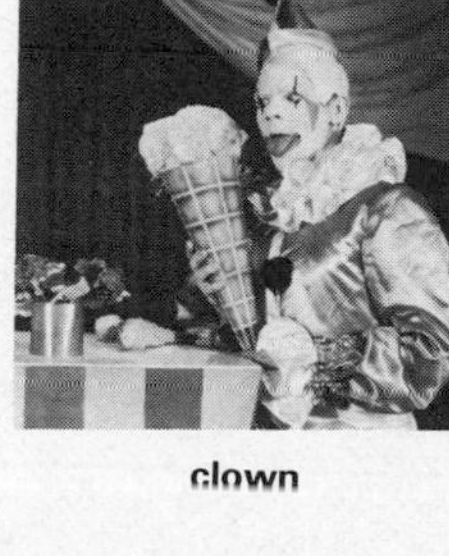

clown

from Scandinavian, akin to Icelandic *klunni*, clumsy person. See **gel-**[1] in Appendix.*] —**clown′ish·ly** *adv.* —**clown′ish·ness** *n.*

cloy (kloi) *v.* **cloyed, cloying, cloys.** —*tr.* To supply with too much of something, especially with something too rich or sweet; surfeit. —*intr.* To cause to feel surfeited. —See Synonyms at **satiate.** [Short for obsolete *accloy*, to nail, hence, to clog, satiate, Middle English *acloien*, to obstruct, hamper, from Old French *encloer*, to nail, from Medieval Latin *inclāvāre* : Latin *in*, in + *clāvāre*, to nail, from *clāvus*, nail (see **klēu-** in Appendix*).] —**cloy′ing·ly** *adv.* —**cloy′ing·ness** *n.*

C.L.U. chartered life underwriter.

club[1] (klŭb) *n.* **1.** A stout, heavy stick, usually thicker at one end than at the other, suitable for use as a weapon; cudgel. **2.** A bat or stick used in certain games to drive a ball; especially, a stick with a curved head used in such games as golf and hockey. **3. a.** A black figure on a playing card, shaped like a trefoil or clover leaf. **b.** A card marked with such figures. **c.** *Plural.* The suit so marked. —*v.* **clubbed, clubbing, clubs.** —*tr.* **1.** To strike or beat with or as with a club. **2.** To use (a rifle or similar firearm) as a club by holding the barrel and hitting with the butt end. **3.** *Archaic.* To gather or combine (hair, for example) into a clublike mass. —*intr. Archaic.* To form or gather into a mass. [Middle English *clubbe*, from Old Norse *klubba*, billet, club. See **gel-**[1] in Appendix.*]

club[2] (klŭb) *n.* **1.** A group of people organized for a common purpose, especially a group that meets regularly. **2.** The room, building, or other facilities used for the meetings of such a group. —See Synonyms at **circle.** —*v.* **clubbed, clubbing, clubs.** —*tr.* To contribute for a joint or common purpose. —*intr.* To join or combine for a common purpose; form a club. Used with *together.* [Probably from CLUB (to gather into a mass).]

club·ba·ble (klŭb′ə-bəl) *adj.* Also **club·a·ble.** *Informal.* Suited to membership in a social club; sociable.

club·by (klŭb′ē) *adj.* **-bier, -biest. 1.** Typical of a club or clubs or their members. **2.** Friendly; sociable. **3.** Clannish; exclusive.

club car. A railroad passenger car equipped with lounge chairs, tables, a buffet or bar, and other extra comforts.

club chair. An upholstered easy chair with arms and a low back.

club·foot (klŭb′fo͝ot′) *n., pl.* **-feet** (-fēt′). **1.** Congenital deformity of the foot, marked by a misshapen appearance often resembling a club. Also called "talipes." **2.** A foot so deformed. —**club′foot′ed** *adj.*

club·house (klŭb′hous′) *n.* A building occupied by a club.

club·man (klŭb′mən, -măn′) *n., pl.* **-men** (-mĭn, -mĕn′). A man who is a member of a fashionable club or clubs, especially one who is active in club life.

club moss. Any of various evergreen, erect or creeping, mosslike plants of the genus *Lycopodium*, having tiny, scalelike, overlapping leaves and reproducing by spores. Some species are also called "ground pine." [From the club-shaped strobiles on some species of this plant.]

club root. A disease of cabbage and related plants, caused by a fungus, *Plasmodiophora brassicae*, and resulting in large, distorted swellings on the roots.

club sandwich. A sandwich, usually of three slices of toast, with a filling of various meats, tomato, lettuce, and dressing.

club soda. An effervescent, unflavored water used in various alcoholic and nonalcoholic drinks.

club steak. A small beefsteak, a **Delmonico steak** *(see).*

club·wom·an (klŭb′wo͝om′ən) *n., pl.* **-women** (-wĭm′ĭn). A female member of a club or clubs.

cluck (klŭk) *v.* **clucked, clucking, clucks.** —*intr.* **1.** To utter the characteristic cry of a hen brooding or calling her chicks. **2.** To make any similar sound, as in coaxing a horse. —*tr.* **1.** To call by making such a sound. **2.** To express by clucking: *He clucked disapproval.* —*n.* **1.** The sound made by, or resembling that made by, a hen when brooding or calling her chicks. **2.** *Informal.* A stupid or foolish person. [Imitative.]

clue (klo͞o) *n.* Also **clew.** Anything that guides or directs in the solution of a problem or mystery. —*tr.v.* **clued, clueing** or **cluing, clues.** Also **clew, clewed, clewing, clews.** To give (someone) guiding information. Used with *in.* [Variant of CLEW.]

Cluj (klo͞ozh). *German* **Klau·sen·burg** (klou′zən-bo͝ork). The second-largest city of Rumania, in the northwest. Population, 167,000.

Clum·ber spaniel (klŭm′bər). Also **clum·ber spaniel.** A dog of a breed developed in England, having short legs and a silky, predominantly white coat. [After *Clumber*, a country estate in Nottinghamshire, England.]

clump (klŭmp) *n.* **1.** A clustered mass; lump. **2.** A thick grouping, as of plants. **3.** A heavy dull sound; a thud, as of footsteps. —*v.* **clumped, clumping, clumps.** —*intr.* **1.** To walk with a heavy dull sound. **2.** To form clumps. —*tr.* To gather into or form clumps of. [Low German *klump*, from Middle Low German *klumpe.* See **gel-**[1] in Appendix.*] —**clump′y** *adj.*

clum·sy (klŭm′zē) *adj.* **-sier, -siest. 1.** Lacking physical coordination, skill, or grace; awkward. **2.** Awkwardly made; unwieldy. **3.** Gauche; inept: *a clumsy excuse.* —See Synonyms at **awkward.** [From obsolete *clumse*, to be numb with cold, Middle English *clumsen*, probably from Scandinavian, akin to Swedish dialectal *klumsen*, benumbed, from Germanic *klum-* (unattested).] —**clum′si·ly** *adv.* —**clum′si·ness** *n.*

clung. Past tense and past participle of **cling.**

clu·pe·id (klo͞o′pē-ĭd) *n.* Any of various oily, soft-finned fishes of the family Clupeidae, which includes the herrings and menhadens. —*adj.* Of or belonging to the Clupeidae. [New Latin *Clupeidae*, from Latin *clupea*†, a kind of small fish.]

clus·ter (klŭs′tər) *n.* **1.** Any configuration of elements gathered or occurring closely together; group; bunch. **2.** Two or more successive consonants in a word; for example, *cl* and *st* in the word *cluster.* —*v.* **clustered, -tering, -ters.** —*intr.* To gather or grow into clusters. —*tr.* To cause to grow or form into clusters. [Middle English *cluster*, Old English *clyster, cluster*†.] —**clus′ter·y** *adj.*

clutch[1] (klŭch) *v.* **clutched, clutching, clutches.** —*tr.* **1.** To grasp and hold tightly. **2.** To seize or snatch. —*intr.* To attempt to grasp or seize. Used with *at.* —See Synonyms at **keep.** —*n.* **1.** The hand, claw, talon, paw, or the like in the act of grasping. **2.** A tight grasp. **3.** *Usually plural.* Control or power: *the clutches of sin.* **4.** A device for gripping and holding. **5.** *Machinery.* **a.** Any of various devices for engaging and disengaging two working parts of a shaft or of a shaft and a driving mechanism. **b.** The lever, pedal, or other apparatus that activates such a device. —**in the clutch.** In a tense or perilous situation. [Middle English *clicchen, clucchen*, Old English *clyccan*, from Germanic *klukjan* (unattested).]

clutch[2] (klŭch) *n.* **1.** The number of eggs produced or incubated at one time. **2.** A brood of chickens. —*tr.v.* **clutched, clutching, clutches.** To hatch (chicks). [Variant of dialectal *cletch*, from Middle English *clecken*, to hatch, give birth, from Old Norse *klekja*†.]

clut·ter (klŭt′ər) *n.* **1.** A confused or disordered state or collection; a litter; a jumble. **2.** A confused noise; clatter. —*v.* **cluttered, -tering, -ters.** —*tr.* To litter or pile in a disordered state. —*intr.* **1.** To run or move with bustle and confusion. **2.** To make a clatter. [Middle English *clotteren*, to clot, coagulate, heap, from *clot*, lump, CLOT.]

Clyde (klīd). A river rising in southern Scotland and flowing north 106 miles to the Firth of Clyde.

Clyde, Firth of (klīd). An inlet of the Atlantic Ocean, extending 64 miles into southwestern Scotland.

Clydes·dale (klīdz′dāl′) *n.* A large, powerful draft horse of a breed developed in the Clyde valley, Scotland.

clyp·e·ate (klĭp′ē-ĭt) *adj.* Also **clyp·e·i·form** (klĭp′ē-ə-fôrm′), **clyp·e·at·ed** (klĭp-ē-ā′tĭd) (for sense 2). **1.** Shaped like a round shield. **2.** Having a clypeus.

clyp·e·us (klĭp′ē-əs) *n., pl.* **-ei** (-ē-ī′). *Biology.* A shieldlike structure, especially a plate on the front of the head of an insect. [New Latin, from Latin *clipeus, clupeus*†, round shield.] —**clyp′e·al** *adj.*

clys·ter (klĭs′tər) *n. Medicine. Rare.* An enema. [Middle English *clister*, from Old French *clistere*, from Latin *clystēr*, from Greek *klustēr*, "liquid for washing out," from *kluzein*, to wash out. See **kleu-**[2] in Appendix.*]

Cly·tem·nes·tra (klī′təm-nĕs′trə). Also **Cly·taem·nes·tra.** *Greek Mythology.* The wife of Agamemnon.

cm centimeter.

Cm The symbol for the element curium.

c.m. 1. circular mil. **2.** center of mass. **3.** court-martial.

Cmdr. commander.

CMH Airport code for Columbus, Ohio.

cml. commercial.

cN centinewton.

C/N credit note.

Cnos·sos. See **Knossos.**

Cnut. See **Canute.**

co-. Indicates: **1.** Joint, jointly, together, or mutually; for example, **co-education, cooperate, copilot. 2.** Same, similar; for example, **coconscious. 3.** Complement of an angle; for example, **cosine, cotangent.** [In borrowed Latin compounds, *co-* is the reduced form of *com-* (see **com-**), used before *h, gn*, and usually before vowels, as in COHERE, COGNATE, and COALESCE.]

Co The symbol for the element cobalt.

CO 1. Colorado (with Zip Code). **2.** conscientious objector.

co. 1. company. **2.** county.

Co. company.

c.o. 1. care of. **2.** *Accounting.* carried over. **3.** cash order.

C.O. 1. commanding officer. **2.** conscientious objector.

c/o care of.

co·ac·er·vate (kō-ăs′ər-vāt′) *n. Chemistry.* A cluster of droplets separated out of a lyophilic colloid. [Latin *coacervātus*, past participle of *coacervāre*, to heap together : *co-*, together + *acervāre*, to heap, ACERVATE.]

co·ac·er·va·tion (kō-ăs′ər-vā′shən) *n.* The process of becoming a coacervate.

coach (kōch) *n.* **1.** A large closed carriage with four wheels. **2.** A closed automobile, usually with two doors. **3.** A motorbus. **4.** A railroad passenger car. **5.** A low-priced class of passenger accommodations on a train or airplane. **6.** A person who trains athletes or athletic teams. **7.** A private tutor employed to prepare a student for an examination. —*v.* **coached, coaching, coaches.** —*tr.* **1.** To teach or train; tutor. **2.** To transport by coach. —*intr.* **1.** To act as a coach. **2.** To ride in a coach. [French *coche*, from German *Kutsche*, from Hungarian *kocsi*, after *Kocs*, a town in Györ, Hungary, where such carriages originated.] —**coach′er** *n.*

coach dog. The **Dalmatian** *(see).* [Formerly trained as a fashionable pet to run behind a coach.]

coach·man (kōch′mən) *n., pl.* **-men** (-mĭn). **1.** A person who drives a coach. **2.** A type of artificial fishing fly.

co·ac·tion (kō-ăk′shən) *n.* An impelling or restraining force; compulsion. [Middle English *coaccioun*, from Old French *coaction*, from Latin *coactiō*, from *cōgere* (past participle *cōactus*), to drive together, force. See **coagulum.**] —**co·ac′tive** *adj.* —**co·ac′tive·ly** *adv.*

co·ad·ju·tant (kō-ăj′o͞o-tənt) *adj.* Helping each other. —*n.* A coworker; assistant. [CO- + ADJUTANT.]

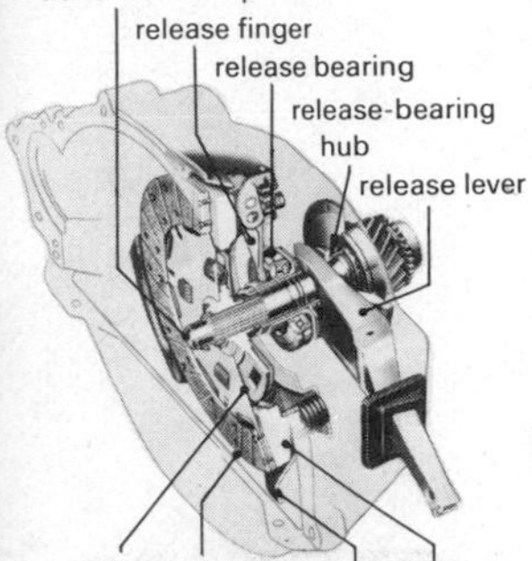
transmission input shaft
release finger
release bearing
release-bearing hub
release lever
clutch disk
pressure plate and cover
clutch[1]
An automotive clutch

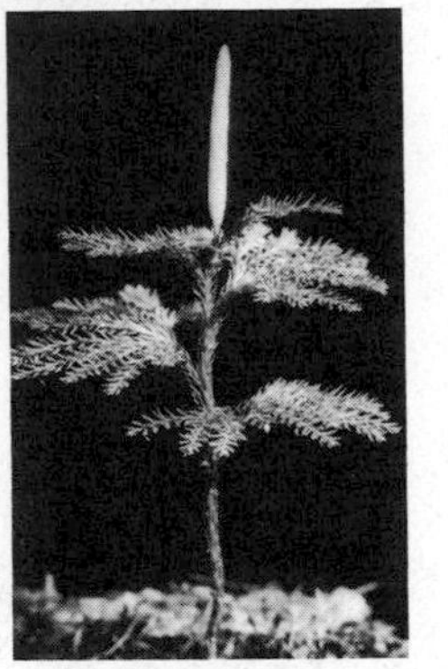
club moss
Lycopodium obscurum

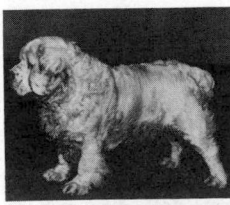

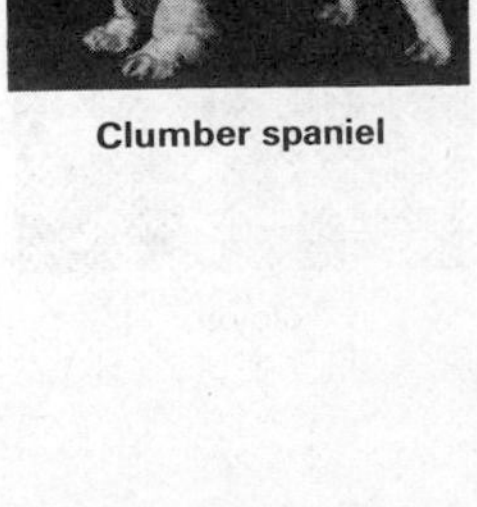
Clumber spaniel

ă pat/ā pay/âr care/ä father/b bib/ch church/d deed/ĕ pet/ē be/f fife/g gag/h hat/hw which/ĭ pit/ī pie/îr pier/j judge/k kick/l lid, needle/m mum/n no, sudden/ng thing/ŏ pot/ō toe/ô paw, for/oi noise/ou out/o͝o took/o͞o boot/p pop/r roar/s sauce/sh ship, dish/

co·ad·ju·tor (kō'ə-jōō'tər, kō-ăj'ə-tər) *n. Abbr.* **coad. 1.** A co-worker; assistant. **2.** The assistant to a bishop. [Middle English *coadjutour*, from Old French *coadjuteur*, from Latin *coadjūtor* : *cō-*, together + *adjūtor*, assistant, from *adjūtāre*, to assist, AID.]

co·ad·u·nate (kō-ăj'ə-nĭt, -nāt') *adj.* Closely joined; united; grown together. [Late Latin *coadūnāre* : *cō-*, together + *adūnāre*, to unite to : Latin *ad-*, to + *ūnāre*, to unite, from *ūnus*, one (see **oino-** in Appendix*).] —**co·ad'u·na'tion** (kō-ăj'ə-nā'shən) *n.* —**co·ad'u·na'tive** *adj.*

co·ag·u·la·ble (kō-ăg'yə-lə-bəl) *adj.* Capable of being coagulated. —**co·ag'u·la·bil'i·ty** *n.*

co·ag·u·lant (kō-ăg'yə-lənt) *n.* An agent that causes coagulation. —**co·ag'u·lant** *adj.*

co·ag·u·lase (kō-ăg'yə-lās', -lāz') *n.* An enzyme, as rennin or thrombin, that causes blood clotting. [COAGUL(ATE) + -ASE.]

co·ag·u·late (kō-ăg'yə-lāt') *v.* **-lated, -lating, -lates.** —*tr.* To cause transformation of (a liquid or sol) into a soft, semisolid, or solid mass. —*intr.* To become such a mass. [Middle English *coagulaten*, from Latin *coāgulāre*, to curdle, from *coāgulum*, COAGULUM.] —**co·ag'u·la'tion** *n.* —**co·ag'u·la'tive** *n.* —**co·ag'u·la'tor** (-lā'tər) *n.*

co·ag·u·lum (kō-ăg'yə-ləm) *n., pl.* **-la** (-lə). A coagulated mass; clot; curd. [Latin *coāgulum*, from *cōgere*, to drive together, condense : *cō-*, together + *agere*, to drive (see **ag-** in Appendix*).]

Co·a·hui·la (kō'ä-wē'lä). A state of Mexico, occupying 58,062 square miles in the northeast. Population, 974,000. Capital, Saltillo.

coal (kōl) *n.* **1.** A natural dark-brown to black solid used as a fuel, formed from fossilized plants, and consisting of amorphous carbon with various organic and some inorganic compounds. **2.** A piece of this substance. **3.** A glowing or charred piece of coal, wood, or other solid fuel; ember. **4.** Charcoal. —**rake (haul, take, drag,** or **call) over the coals.** To reprimand; scold. —*v.* **coaled, coaling, coals.** —*tr.* **1.** To burn a combustible solid to a charcoal residue. **2.** To provide with coal. —*intr.* To take on coal. [Middle English *cole*, Old English *col*, coal, live coal. See **geulo-** in Appendix.*]

coal·er (kō'lər) *n.* **1.** A ship, train, or other means of carrying or supplying coal. **2.** One who sells or supplies coal.

co·a·lesce (kō'ə-lĕs') *intr.v.* **-lesced, -lescing, -lesces. 1.** To grow together; fuse. **2.** To come together so as to form one whole; unite. —See Synonyms at **mix.** [Latin *coalēscere*, to grow together : *cō-*, together + *alēscere*, to grow, inceptive of *alēre*, to nourish (see **al-³** in Appendix*).] —**co'a·les'cence** *n.* —**co'a·les'cent** *adj.*

coal gas. 1. A gaseous mixture produced by the destructive distillation of bituminous coal and used as a commercial fuel. **2.** The gaseous mixture released by burning coal.

co·a·li·tion (kō'ə-lĭsh'ən) *n.* **1.** An alliance, especially a temporary one, of factions, parties, or nations. **2.** A combination or fusion into one body; union. [French, from Medieval Latin *coalitiō*, from Latin *coalēscere*, COALESCE.] —**co'a·li'tion·ist** *n.*

coal measures. *Geology.* **1.** *Capital* **C,** *capital* **M.** A stratigraphic unit equivalent to the Pennsylvanian or Upper Carboniferous periods. **2.** Strata of the Carboniferous period containing coal deposits.

coal oil. Kerosene *(see).*

Coal·sack (kōl'săk') *n.* **1.** A dark nebula near the Southern Cross, appearing as a hole in the Milky Way. **2.** A similar dark region of the sky, the Northern Coalsack, near the Northern Cross.

coal tar. A viscous black liquid obtained by the destructive distillation of coal, used as a raw material for many dyes, drugs, and organic chemicals and for waterproofing, paints, roofing, and insulation materials. —**coal'-tar'** *adj.*

coam·ing (kō'mĭng) *n.* A raised rim or curb around an opening in a ship's deck or the roof of a building, designed to keep out water. [Origin unknown.]

co·arc·tate (kō-ärk'tāt') *adj. Entomology.* **1.** Describing an insect pupa compressed in the larval shell. **2.** Having a constricted separation between the abdomen and thorax. [Latin *coarctātus*, past participle of *coarctāre*, *coartāre*, to press together : *cō-*, together + *artāre*, to press, from *artus*, narrow, tight (see **ar-** in Appendix*).] —**co'arc·ta'tion** *n.*

coarse (kôrs, kōrs) *adj.* **coarser, coarsest. 1.** Of low, common, or inferior quality. **2.** Lacking in delicacy or refinement. **3.** Consisting of large particles; not fine in texture. **4.** Rough; harsh. [Middle English *co(a)rs*, ordinary, coarse, probably from *co(u)rs*, COURSE ("the usual practice").] —**coarse'ly** *adv.* —**coarse'ness** *n.*

Synonyms: *coarse, gross, crass, indelicate, vulgar, obscene, ribald.* These adjectives primarily describe offensive speech or writing and behavior. *Coarse* implies roughness and crudeness in manners, appearance, or expression. *Gross* implies excessive behavior approaching bestiality. *Crass* suggests stupidity combined with rudeness or other manifestation of lack of refinement: *crass ignorance. Indelicate* implies immodesty, tactless behavior, or lack of taste in expression: *an indelicate remark. Vulgar* emphasizes offensiveness to propriety and suggests boorishness and poor breeding. *Obscene* strongly stresses lewdness or indecency, particularly in reference to accepted standards of morality. *Ribald* implies vulgar, coarse, off-color language or behavior intended to provoke laughter.

coarse-grained (kôrs'grānd', kōrs'-) *adj.* **1.** Having a rough or coarse texture. **2.** Not refined; indelicate; crude.

coars·en (kôr'sən, kōr'-) *v.* **-ened, -ening, -ens.** —*intr.* To become coarse. —*tr.* To make coarse.

coast (kōst) *n.* **1.** The land next to the sea; the seashore. **2.** *Obsolete.* The frontier or border of a country. **3.** A hill or other slope down which one may coast, as on a sled. **4.** The act of sliding or coasting; a slide. —**the Coast.** In the United States, the Pacific Coast. —*v.* **coasted, coasting, coasts.** —*intr.* **1.** To slide down an inclined slope, as on a sled. **2.** To move without further acceleration. **3.** To sail near or along a coast. **4.** To act or move aimlessly. —*tr.* To sail or move along the coast or border of. —See Synonyms at **slide.** [Middle English *cost*, from Old French *coste*, from Latin *costa*, rib, side. See **kost-** in Appendix.*] —**coast'al** (kōs'təl) *adj.*

coast artillery. Artillery for protecting coastal areas.

coast·er (kōs'tər) *n.* **1.** One that coasts. **2.** A vessel engaged in coastal trade. **3.** A coasting sled or toboggan. **4.** A disk placed under a bottle, pitcher, or drinking glass to protect a table top or other surface beneath. **5.** A small tray on wheels for passing something, such as a wine decanter, around the table.

coaster brake. A brake and clutch operating on the rear wheel and drive mechanism of a bicycle when pedaling is reversed.

coast guard. Also **Coast Guard.** *Abbr.* **C.G. 1.** The military or naval coastal patrol of a nation, responsible for the protection of life and property at sea, coastal defense, and enforcement of customs, immigration, and navigation laws. **2.** A member of a coast guard; a coastguardsman.

coast·guards·man (kōst'gärdz'mən) *n., pl.* **-men** (-mĭn). A member of a coast guard.

coast·line (kōst'līn') *n.* The shape or boundary of a coast.

Coast Mountains. A continuation of the Cascade Range in extreme western British Columbia, extending northward to Yukon Territory, Canada. Highest elevation, Mount Waddington (13,260 feet) in British Columbia.

Coast Ranges. The mountain ranges along the western coast of North America, extending from southern California to southern Alaska.

coast rhododendron. An evergreen shrub, *Rhododendron californicum* (or *R. macrophyllum*), of the Pacific coast of North America, having rose-purple flowers.

coast·ward (kōst'wərd) *adj.* Directed toward a coast. —*adv.* Also **coast·wards** (-wərdz). Toward the coast.

coast·wise (kōst'wīz') *adj.* Following the coast. —*adv.* Also **coast·ways** (-wāz'). By way of or along the coast.

coat (kōt) *n.* **1.** An outer garment covering the body from the shoulders to the waist or below, worn primarily for protection from cold or inclement weather. **2.** A garment extending to just below the waist and usually forming the top part of a suit. **3.** A natural integument or outer covering, such as the fur of an animal. **4.** A layer of some material covering something else; coating. **5.** *Obsolete.* Traditional garb indicating one's social status. —*tr.v.* **coated, coating, coats. 1.** To provide or cover with a coat. **2.** To cover with a layer, as paint. [Middle English *cote*, from Old French, from Frankish *kotta* (unattested), from West Germanic *kotta* (unattested).]

coat·ed (kō'tĭd) *adj.* **1.** Having an outer layer, coat, or covering. **2.** *Papermaking.* Having a highly polished surface suitable for halftone printing.

co·a·ti (kō-ä'tē) *n.* Any of several omnivorous mammals of the genus *Nasua*, of South and Central America and the southwestern United States, related to and resembling the raccoon but having a longer snout and tail. Also called "coatimundi." [Portuguese *coatí*, from Tupi *coatí*, *coatim*, "belt-nosed" : *cua*, belt, band + *tim*, nose.]

co·a·ti·mun·di (kō-ä'tē-mŭn'dē) *n.* Also **co·a·ti·mon·di.** The coati *(see).* [Tupi.]

coat·ing (kō'tĭng) *n.* **1.** A layer of any substance spread over a surface for protection or decoration; a covering layer. **2.** Cloth for making coats.

coat of arms. 1. A tabard or surcoat blazoned with heraldic bearings. **2.** A representation of such an insigne.

coat of mail *pl.* **coats of mail.** An armored coat made of chain mail, interlinked rings, or overlapping metal plates; a hauberk.

Coats Land (kōts). The region of Antarctica west of Queen Maud Land.

coat·tail (kōt'tāl') *n.* **1.** The loose back part of a coat below the waist. **2.** One half of this part of a coat that is divided at the back. **3.** *Plural.* The skirts of a formal or dress coat.

co·au·thor (kō-ô'thər) *n.* A collaborating or joint author.

coax (kōks) *v.* **coaxed, coaxing, coaxes.** —*tr.* **1.** To persuade or try to persuade by pleading or flattery; cajole; wheedle. **2.** To obtain by persistent persuasion. **3.** *Obsolete.* To caress or fondle. —*intr.* To use persuasion or inducement. —See Synonyms at **urge.** [Earlier *coaks*, *cokes*, to fool, from *cokes*†, fool.] —**coax'er** *n.* —**coax'ing·ly** *adv.*

co·ax·i·al (kō-ăk'sē-əl) *adj.* Having or mounted on a common axis.

coaxial cable. A high-frequency telephone, telegraph, and television transmission cable consisting of a conducting outer metal tube enclosing and insulated from a central conducting core.

cob (kŏb) *n.* **1.** The central core of an ear of corn; corncob. **2.** A male swan. **3.** A thick-set, stocky, short-legged horse. **4.** A small lump or mass, as of coal. **5.** *British Regional.* A great leader. [Middle English *cobbe*†, lump, round object.]

co·balt (kō'bôlt') *n. Symbol* **Co** A hard, brittle metallic element, found associated with nickel, silver, lead, copper, and iron ores and resembling nickel and iron in appearance. It is used chiefly for magnetic alloys, high-temperature alloys, and in the form of its salts for blue glass and ceramic pigments. Atomic number 27, atomic weight 58.9332, melting point 1,495°C, boiling point 2,900°C, specific gravity 8.9, valences 2, 3. See **element.** [German *Kobalt*, *Kobold*, from Middle High German *kobolt*, an un-

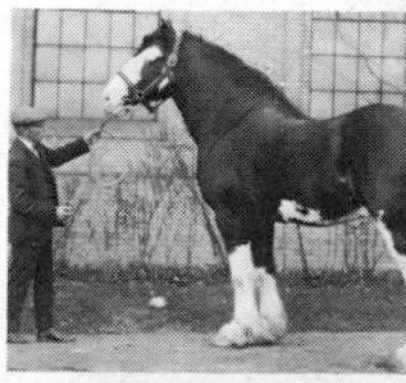

Clydesdale

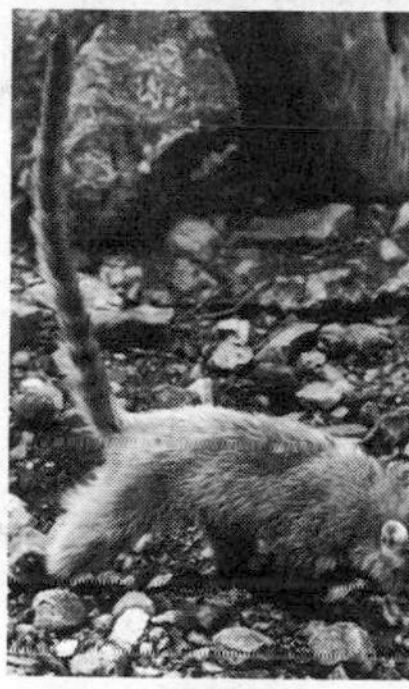

coati

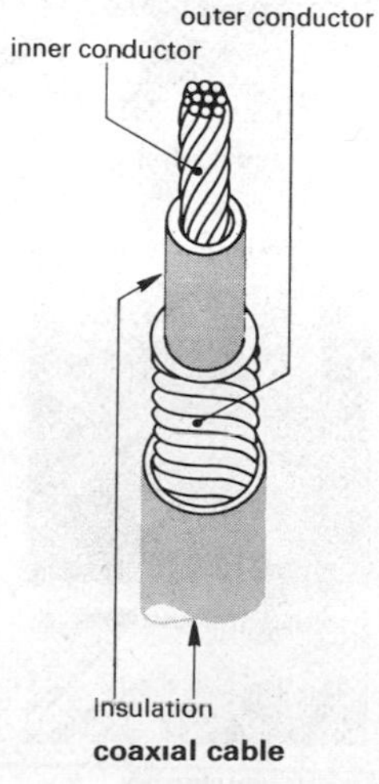

coaxial cable

derground goblin (cobalt was thought to be injurious to silver ores). See **ku-** in Appendix.*]

cobalt 60. A radioactive isotope of cobalt with mass number 60 and exceptionally intense gamma-ray activity, used in radiotherapy, metallurgy, and materials testing.

cobalt blue. **1.** A blue to green pigment consisting of a variable mixture of cobalt and aluminum oxides. **2.** Deep to vivid blue or strong greenish blue. See **color.** —**co′balt-blue′** *adj.*

co·bal·tite (kō′bôl-tīt′) *n.* Also **co·balt·ine** (kō′bôl-tēn′). A silver-white to gray mineral, CoAsS, that is an important cobalt ore and is used in ceramics.

Cobb (kŏb), **Tyrus Raymond ("Ty").** 1886–1961. American baseball player, manager, and holder of many records.

cob·ber (kŏb′ər) *n. Australian.* Comrade. [Origin unknown.]

Cob·bett (kŏb′ĭt), **William.** 1763–1835. English journalist and social reformer.

cob·ble¹ (kŏb′əl) *n.* **1.** A **cobblestone** *(see).* **2.** *Plural.* **Cob coal** *(see).* —*tr.v.* **cobbled, -bling, -bles.** To pave with cobblestones. [Back-formation from COBBLESTONE.]

cob·ble² (kŏb′əl) *tr.v.* **-bled, -bling, -bles. 1.** To make or mend (boots or shoes). **2.** To put together clumsily; bungle. [Probably back-formation from COBBLER.]

cob·bler¹ (kŏb′lər) *n.* **1.** One who mends boots and shoes. **2.** *Archaic.* One who is clumsy at his work; a bungler. [Middle English *cobelere*†.]

cob·bler² (kŏb′lər) *n.* **1.** A deep-dish fruit pie having a thick top crust. **2.** An iced drink made of wine or liqueur, sugar, and citrus fruit. [Perhaps from COBBLER (mender).]

cob·ble·stone (kŏb′əl-stōn′) *n.* A naturally rounded stone, formerly used for paving streets and walls. Also called "cobble." [Middle English *cobelston* : *cobel-*, probably diminutive of *cobbe*, COB (lump) + STONE.]

cob coal. **1.** Coal in rounded lumps of various sizes. **2.** A lump of coal about the size of a cobblestone. Also called "cobbles."

Cob·den (kŏb′dən), **Richard.** 1804–1865. British economist and political leader.

co·bel·lig·er·ent (kō′bə-lĭj′ər-ənt) *n.* A nation associated with another or others in waging war.

co·bi·a (kō′bē-ə) *n.* A large game fish, *Rachycentron canadum,* of tropical and subtropical seas. Also called "sergeant fish." [Origin unknown.]

co·ble (kō′bəl) *n.* **1.** *British.* A small, flat-bottomed fishing boat with a lugsail on a raking mast. **2.** *Scottish.* A kind of flat-bottomed rowboat. [Middle English *cobel,* from Celtic, akin to Old Breton *caubal.* See **keu-**³ in Appendix.*]

Co·blenz (kō′blĕnts′). Also **Ko·blenz.** A city in West Germany, on the Rhine at its junction with the Moselle. Population, 98,000.

cob·nut (kŏb′nŭt′) *n.* **1.** A tree, *Corylus avellana grandis,* related to the hazel. **2.** The large, edible nut of this tree.

co·bra (kō′brə) *n.* **1.** Any of several venomous snakes of the genus *Naja* and related genera, of Asia and Africa, capable of expanding the skin of the neck to form a flattened hood. **2.** Leather made from the skin of a cobra. [Short for Portuguese *cobra (de capello),* "snake (with a hood)," from Latin *colubra,* feminine of *coluber*†, snake.]

cobra plant. A pitcher plant, *Darlingtonia californica,* of the American Pacific coast, having tubular leaves and yellowish-purple flowers. [From its curled hoodlike leaf having a forked, tonguelike appendage at the orifice.]

cob·web (kŏb′wĕb′) *n.* **1.** The web spun by a spider to catch its prey. **2.** A single thread of such a web. **3.** Something resembling a cobweb in gauziness or flimsiness. **4.** An intricate plot; a network of intrigue; a snare. **5.** *Plural.* **a.** Any musty accumulation, especially as a result of disuse or neglect. **b.** Confusion; disorder: *cobwebs in the brain.* —*tr.v.* **cobwebbed, -webbing, -webs.** To cover with or as with cobwebs. [Middle English *coppeweb* : *coppe,* short for *attorcoppe,* spider, Old English *āttorcoppe* (see **ku-** in Appendix*) + WEB.] —**cob′web′by** *adj.*

co·ca (kō′kə) *n.* **1.** A South American tree, *Erythroxylon coca,* having leaves that contain cocaine and related alkaloids. **2.** The dried leaves of this shrub or related plants, chewed by people of the Andes for their stimulating effect. [Spanish, from Quechua *kúka, cuca.*]

co·caine (kō-kān′, kō′kān′) *n.* Also **co·cain.** A colorless or white crystalline narcotic alkaloid, $C_{17}H_{21}NO_4$, extracted from coca leaves and used as a surface anesthetic. [COCA + -INE.]

co·cain·ism (kō-kā′nĭz′əm) *n.* The habitual use of cocaine.

co·cain·ize (kō-kā′nīz′) *tr.v.* **-ized, -izing, -izes.** To anesthetize (a body part) with cocaine. —**co·cain′i·za′tion** *n.*

coc·cid (kŏk′sĭd) *n.* An insect of the family Coccidae, which includes the scale insects and mealybugs. [New Latin *Coccidae,* from *Coccus* (genus), from Greek *kokkos,* kermes berry, pit. See **kokkos** in Appendix.*]

coc·cid·i·o·sis (kŏk-sĭd′ē-ō′sĭs) *n.* A disease of many animals, including cattle, swine, sheep, dogs, cats, and poultry, but rarely of man, resulting from an infection of the digestive tract by parasitic protozoa of the order Coccidia. [New Latin : *Coccidia,* from COCCUS + -OSIS.]

coc·cus (kŏk′əs) *n., pl.* **cocci** (kŏk′sī′, kŏk′ī′). **1.** A bacterium with a spherical or spheroidal shape. **2.** *Botany.* A division that contains a single seed and splits apart from a many-lobed fruit. [New Latin, from Greek *kokkos,* kermes berry, pit. See **kokkos** in Appendix.*] —**coc′coid′, coc′cal** *adj.*

-coccus. Indicates a microorganism that is spheroidal in shape; for example, **streptococcus.** [New Latin, from COCCUS.]

coc·cyx (kŏk′sĭks) *n., pl.* **coccyges** (kŏk-sī′jēz, kŏk′sə-jēz′). A small bone at the base of the spinal column, consisting of several fused rudimentary vertebrae. [New Latin, from Greek *kokkux,* cuckoo, coccyx (bone shaped like the cuckoo's beak) (imitative).] —**coc·cyg′e·al** (kŏk-sĭj′ē-əl) *adj.*

Co·chin¹ (kō′chĭn, kŏch′ĭn). **1.** A region and former state of southwestern India, on the Malabar Coast; part of Kerala State since 1956. **2.** A city of the Republic of India, in the southwest on the Malabar Coast; the first European settlement in India, founded by Vasco da Gama in 1503. Population, 30,000.

Co·chin² (kō′chĭn, kŏch′ĭn) *n.* A large domestic fowl of a breed developed in Asia, having thickly feathered legs. Also called "Cochin China." [After COCHIN CHINA (fowl).]

Co·chin China¹ (kō′chĭn, kŏch′ĭn). The former name for the southernmost region of Vietnam, a part of French Indochina.

Co·chin China² (kō′chĭn, kŏch′ĭn). A fowl, the **Cochin** *(see).*

Co·chin Chinese (kō′chĭn, kŏch′ĭn). A Vietnamese dialect spoken in Cochin China.

coch·i·neal (kŏch′ə-nēl′, kŏch′ə-nēl′) *n.* **1.** A brilliant-red dye made by drying and pulverizing the bodies of the females of a tropical American scale insect, *Dactylopius coccus,* that feeds on certain species of cacti. **2.** Vivid red. See **color.** [French *cochenille,* from Spanish *cochinilla,* from Latin *coccinus,* scarlet, from Greek *kokkinos,* from *kokkos,* kermes berry. See **kokkos** in Appendix.*] —**coch′i·neal′** *adj.*

cochineal plant. A species of **nopal** *(see).*

Co·chise (kō′chēs′, -chēz′). 1815?–1874. American Indian leader; an Apache chief.

coch·le·a (kŏk′lē-ə) *n., pl.* **-leae** (-lē-ē′). A spiral tube of the inner ear resembling a snail shell and containing nerve endings essential for hearing. [New Latin, from Latin, snail shell, from Greek *kokhlias,* from *kokhlos,* land snail. See **konkho-** in Appendix.*] —**coch′le·ar** *adj.*

cochlear nerve. A division of the **acoustic nerve** *(see).*

coch·le·ate (kŏk′lē-ĭt, -āt′) *adj.* Also **coch·le·at·ed** (-ā′tĭd). Shaped like a snail shell; spirally twisted. [Latin *cochleātus,* from *cochlea,* snail. See **cochlea.**]

cock¹ (kŏk) *n.* **1.** The adult male of the domestic fowl; a rooster. **2.** Any male bird. **3.** A weather vane shaped like a rooster; weathercock. **4.** A leader or chief. **5.** A faucet or valve by which the flow of a liquid or gas can be regulated. **6. a.** The hammer in a firearm. **b.** Its position when ready for firing. **7.** A tilting or jaunty turning upward: *the cock of a hat.* **8.** *Vulgar.* The penis. —*v.* **cocked, cocking, cocks.** —*tr.* **1.** To set the hammer of (a firearm) in a position ready for firing. **2.** To tilt or turn up or to one side, usually in a jaunty or alert manner. **3.** To raise in preparation to throw or hit. —*intr.* **1.** To cock the hammer of a firearm. **2.** To turn or stick up. —*adj.* Male. Said of birds and, sometimes, other animals: *a cock lobster.* [Middle English *cok,* Old English *cocc,* from Late Latin *coccus,* from Latin *coco,* cackle (imitative).]

cock² (kŏk) *n.* A cone-shaped pile of straw or hay. —*tr.v.* **cocked, cocking, cocks.** To arrange (straw or hay) in such piles. [Middle English *cok,* Old English *cocc* (attested only in place names). See **ku-** in Appendix.*]

cock·ade (kŏk-ād′) *n.* A rosette or knot of ribbon worn especially on the hat as a badge. [Originally *cockard,* from French *cocarde,* jauntily tilted hat, from Old French *coquard,* strutting, vain, from *coq,* cock, from Late Latin *coccus,* COCK.] —**cock·ad′ed** (kŏk-ā′dĭd) *adj.*

cock-a-doo·dle-doo (kŏk′ə-do͞od′l-do͞o′) *n.* **1.** A representation of the characteristic crow of a rooster. **2.** *Slang.* A rooster or cock. [Imitative.]

cock-a-hoop (kŏk′ə-ho͞op′, -ho͝op′) *adj.* **1.** In a state of elation or exultation. **2.** Boastful. **3.** Askew. [From the expression *set cock a hoop,* perhaps "to set a cock on a hoop or measure of grain."] —**cock′-a-hoop′** *adv.*

Cock·aigne (kŏ-kān′) *n.* An imaginary land of easy and luxurious living. [Middle English *cockayne,* from Old French *(pais de) quoquaigne,* "(land of) delicacies," probably from Middle Low German *kōkenje,* small fancy sugar cake, diminutive of *kōke,* cake. See **kak-**² in Appendix.*]

cock-a-leek·ie (kŏk′ə-lē′kē) *n.* Also **cock·a·leek·ie, cock·ie·leek·ie.** A cream soup made with leeks and chicken.

cock·a·lo·rum (kŏk′ə-lôr′əm, -lōr′əm) *n.* **1.** A little man with an unduly high opinion of himself. **2.** Boastful talk; braggadocio. [Pseudo-Latin : COCK ("strutting leader") + Latin *-orum,* genitive plural ending.]

cock·a·ma·mie (kŏk′ə-mā′mē) *adj.* Also **cock·a·ma·my.** *Slang.* **1.** Trifling; nearly valueless. **2.** Counterfeit; second-rate. **3.** Ludicrous; nonsensical. [Originally "imitation tattoos produced by a decalcomania process," hence, "counterfeit," "worthless," alteration of DECALCOMANIA.]

cock-and-bull story (kŏk′ən-bo͝ol′). An absurd or highly improbable tale. [Originally a rambling animal fable about a cock changed into a bull.]

cock·a·tiel (kŏk′ə-tēl′) *n.* Also **cock·a·teel.** A crested parrot, *Nymphicus hollandicus,* of Australia, having gray and yellow plumage. [From Dutch *kaketielje,* probably from Portuguese *cacatilha,* diminutive of *cacatua,* cockatoo, from Malay *kakatua,* COCKATOO.]

cock·a·too (kŏk′ə-to͞o′) *n., pl.* **-toos.** Any of various parrots of the genus *Kakatoe* and related genera, of Australia and adjacent areas, characterized by a long, erectile crest. [Dutch *kaketoe,* from Malay *kakatua.*]

cock·a·trice (kŏk′ə-trĭs, -trīs′) *n.* A mythical serpent reputed to be hatched from a cock's egg and supposed to have the power of killing by its glance. Compare **basilisk.** [Middle English *cocatrice,* basilisk, crocodile, from Old French *cocatris,* from Medieval Latin *cocātrix,* variant of Late Latin *calcātrix,* "the tracker" (translation of Greek *ikhneumōn,* ICHNEUMON), from *calcāre,* to track, from *calx,* heel. See **calk.**]

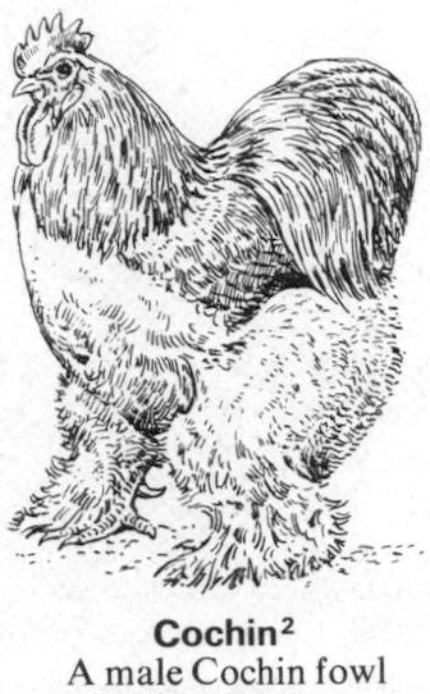

Cochin²
A male Cochin fowl

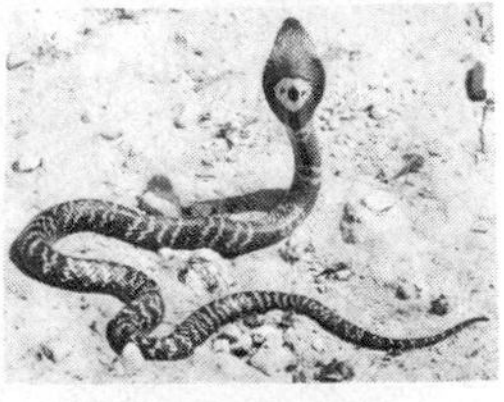

cobra
Naja naja
Indian cobra

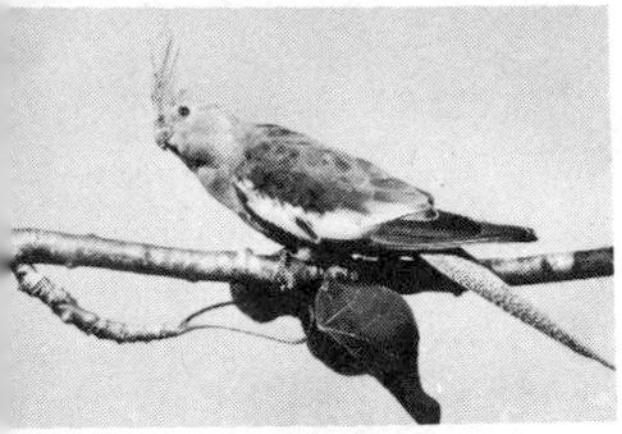

cockatiel

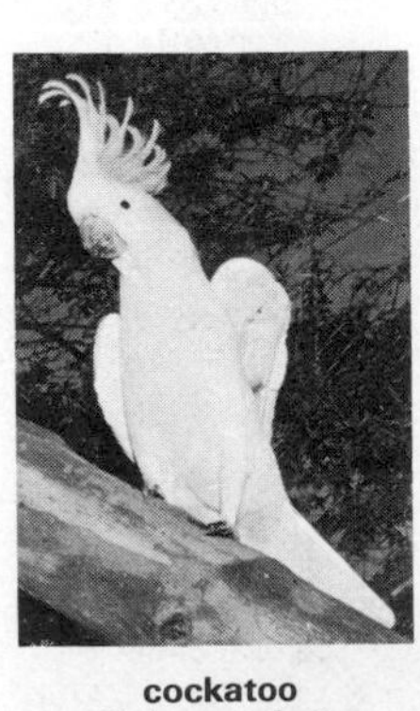

cockatoo
Kakatoe galerita
Sulphur-crested cockatoo

cock·boat (kŏk′bōt′) *n.* A small rowboat kept on a ship, especially one used as a tender. Also called "cockleboat." [Middle English *cokbote* : *cok*, cockboat, from Old French *coque, coche*, probably from Late Latin *caudica*, canoe (made from the trunk of a tree), from Latin *caudex*, trunk of a tree (see **caudex**) + BOAT.]

cock·chaf·er (kŏk′chā′fər) *n.* Any of various Old World beetles of the family Scarabaeidae; especially, *Melolontha melolontha*, a species destructive to plants. [COCK (bird) + CHAFER (so called probably from its large size).]

Cock·croft (kŏk′krôft′, -krŏft′), Sir **John Douglas.** 1897–1967. British physicist.

Cock·croft-Wal·ton accelerator (kŏk′krôft′wôl′tən). *Physics.* A positive-ion accelerator, consisting essentially of several stages of a voltage-doubling circuit together with an ion source and a discharge tube, used in the first purely artificial disintegration of an atomic nucleus. Also called "Cockcroft-Walton machine." [Invented by Sir John Douglas COCKCROFT and Ernest Thomas Sinton WALTON.]

cock·crow (kŏk′krō′) *n.* The time of day when the cock crows; early morning; dawn.

cocked hat. A hat with the brim turned up in two or three places; especially, a three-cornered hat; a tricorn.

cock·er[1] (kŏk′ər) *n.* **1.** A cocker spaniel. **2. a.** A person who keeps or trains gamecocks. **b.** A person who promotes or attends cockfights.

cock·er[2] (kŏk′ər) *tr.v.* **-ered, -ering, -ers.** To pamper, spoil, or coddle. [Middle English *cokeren*, probably "to make a nestle cock of," frequentative formation from *cok*, COCK.]

cock·er·el (kŏk′ər-əl) *n.* A young rooster. [Middle English *cokerelle*, diminutive of COCK.]

cocker spaniel. A dog of a breed originally developed in England, having long, drooping ears and a variously colored silky coat. [Originally used for hunting woodcocks.]

cock·eye (kŏk′ī′) *n.* A squinting eye.

cock·eyed (kŏk′īd′) *adj.* **1.** Cross-eyed. **2.** *Slang.* **a.** Crooked; askew. **b.** Foolish; ridiculous; absurd. **c.** Drunk.

cock·fight (kŏk′fīt′) *n.* A fight between gamecocks that are often fitted with metal spurs. —**cock′fight′ing** *adj.* & *n.*

cock·horse (kŏk′hôrs′) *n.* A rocking horse.

cock·ie·leek·ie. Variant of **cock-a-leekie.**

cock·le[1] (kŏk′əl) *n.* **1.** Any of various bivalve mollusks of the family Cardiidae, having rounded or heart-shaped shells with radiating ribs. **2.** The shell of any of these mollusks; a cockleshell. **3.** A wrinkle or pucker. **4.** A small and shallow boat. —**cockles of one's heart.** One's innermost feelings. —*v.* **cockled, -ling, -les.** —*tr.* To cause to wrinkle or pucker. —*intr.* To become wrinkled or puckered. [Middle English *cokille*, from Old French *coquille*, shell, from Vulgar Latin *conchīllia* (unattested), variant of Latin *conchȳlium*, from Greek *konkhullion*, diminutive of *konkhē*, mussel, conch. See **konkho-** in Appendix.*]

cock·le[2] (kŏk′əl) *n.* Any of several plants often growing as weeds in grain fields. [Middle English *cok(k)el*, Old English *coccel*, from Medieval Latin *cocculus* (unattested), diminutive of Latin *coccus*, kermes berry. See **coccus.**]

cock·le·boat (kŏk′əl-bōt′) *n.* A **cockboat** *(see).*

cock·le·bur (kŏk′əl-bûr′) *n.* **1.** Any of several coarse weeds of the genus *Xanthium*, bearing prickly burs. **2.** The bur of any of these plants.

cock·le·shell (kŏk′əl-shĕl′) *n.* **1. a.** The shell of a cockle. **b.** A shell similar to that of a cockle. **2.** A small, light boat.

cock·loft (kŏk′lôft′, -lŏft′) *n.* A small loft or garret. [So called probably because it often serves as a roosting place.]

cock·ney (kŏk′nē) *n., pl.* **-neys. 1.** *Often capital* **C.** A native of the East End of London. **2.** The dialect or accent of cockneys. —*adj.* Of or like cockneys or their dialect. [Middle English *cokeney*, "cock's egg," pampered brat, effeminate youth, townsman (of London) : *cokene*, genitive plural of *cok*, COCK + *ey*, egg, Old English *ǣg* (see **awi-** in Appendix*).]

cock-of-the-rock (kŏk′əv-*thə*-rŏk′) *n., pl.* **cocks-of-the-rock.** Either of two South American birds, *Rupicola rupicola* or *R. peruviana*, having a distinctive crest and bright-orange or reddish plumage in the male. [From its habit of nesting on rocks.]

cock of the walk. 1. The leader or most important person in a group. **2.** An overbearing or domineering person.

cock·pit (kŏk′pĭt′) *n.* **1.** A pit or enclosed space for cockfights. **2.** A place where many battles have been fought. **3. a.** An apartment in an old warship below the water line, used as quarters for junior officers and as a station for the wounded during a battle. **b.** In small decked vessels, an area toward the stern, lower than the rest of the deck, from which the vessel is steered. **4. a.** The space in the fuselage of a small airplane containing seats for the pilot, copilot, and sometimes passengers. **b.** The space set apart for the pilot and crew in a large airliner.

cock·roach (kŏk′rōch′) *n.* Any of various oval, flat-bodied insects of the family Blattidae, several species of which are common household pests. Also called "roach." [Earlier *cacarootch*, from Spanish *cucaracha*†.]

cocks·comb (kŏks′kōm′) *n.* Also **cox·comb** (for sense 4). **1.** The comb of a rooster. **2.** The cap of a jester, decorated to resemble the comb of a rooster. **3.** Any of several plants of the genus *Celosia*; especially, *C. argentea cristata*, having a showy crested or rolled flower cluster. **4.** A pretentious fop.

cock·shy (kŏk′shī′) *n., pl.* **-shies.** *British.* **1.** A mark aimed at in throwing contests. **2.** The throw itself. [In the earliest form of this game, the contestants shied or threw sticks at a cock to knock it down and carry it away as the prize.]

cock·spur thorn (kŏk′spûr′). A small, thorny North American tree, *Crataegus crus-galli*, having white flowers and small red fruit. [From the resemblance of its thorn to a cock's spur.]

cock·sure (kŏk′shŏŏr′) *adj.* **1.** Completely sure. **2.** Too sure. [Perhaps "as reliable as a cock or faucet (in shutting off water)."] —**cock′sure′ly** *adv.* —**cock′sure′ness** *n.*

cock·swain. Variant of **coxswain.**

cock·tail (kŏk′tāl′) *n.* **1.** Any of various mixed alcoholic drinks, often served chilled, consisting usually of brandy, whiskey, or gin combined with fruit juices or other liquors. **2.** An appetizer, such as seafood, served with a sharp sauce: *a clam cocktail.* —*adj.* **1.** Of or pertaining to cocktails. **2.** Suitable for wear on semiformal occasions: *a cocktail dress.* [Origin unknown.]

cock·up (kŏk′ŭp′) *n.* **1.** A hat or cap with an upturned front. **2.** A turned-up part of anything.

cock·y (kŏk′ē) *adj.* **-ier, -iest.** *Informal.* Cheerfully self-assertive or self-confident; conceited. —**cock′i·ly** *adv.*

co·co (kō′kō) *n., pl.* **-cos. 1.** A tree, the **coconut palm** *(see).* **2.** Its fruit, the coconut. —*adj.* Made of fibers from the coconut shell. [Spanish, from Portuguese *coco*, "goblin," coconut shell, probably of baby-talk origin.]

Co·co (kō′kō). Formerly **Se·go·vi·a** (sĕ-gō′vē-ä), **Wanks** (wăngks). A river rising in southwestern Nicaragua and flowing about 450 miles generally northeast to the Caribbean, forming part of the Nicaragua-Honduras border.

co·coa (kō′kō) *n.* **1.** A powder made from cacao seeds after they have been roasted, ground, and freed of most of their fatty oil. **2.** A beverage made by combining this powder with water or milk and sugar. **3.** Moderate brown to reddish brown. See **color.** [Variant of CACAO, by confusion with COCO (nut).] —**co′coa** *adj.*

cocoa butter. A yellowish-white, waxy solid obtained from cacao seeds and used in the manufacture of pharmaceuticals, confections, and soap. Also called "cacao butter."

co·co·bo·lo (kō′kə-bō′lō) *n., pl.* **-los.** Also **co·co·bo·la** (-bō′lə). **1.** A tropical American tree, *Dahlbergia retusa*, having hard, dark wood banded with light streaks. **2.** The wood of this tree, used in cabinetwork. [Spanish, from Arawakan *kakabali.*]

co·con·scious (kō′kŏn′shəs) *adj.* Being aware or conscious of the same things. —*n.* Also **co·con·scious·ness** (-nĭs). *Psychiatry.* Mental processes outside the realm of conscious activity or awareness, as with schizophrenic individuals.

co·co·nut (kō′kə-nŭt′, -nət) *n.* Also **co·coa·nut.** The fruit of the coconut palm, a large seed with a thick, hard shell that encloses edible white meat and has a milky fluid filling the hollow center. [COCO + NUT.]

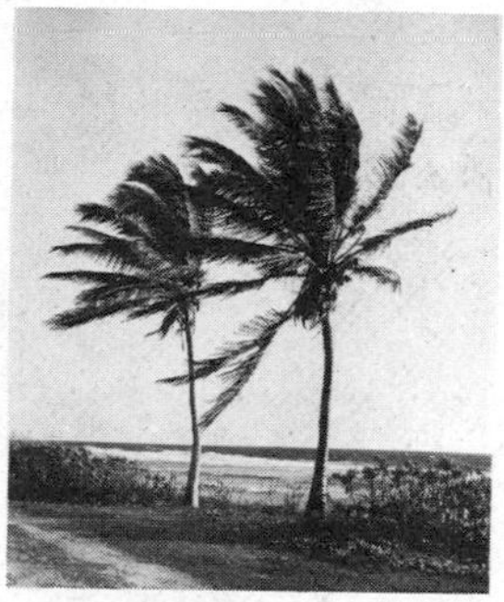

coconut palm

coconut palm. A tall palm tree, *Cocos nucifera*, native to the East Indies, bearing coconuts as fruit. Also called "coco," "coco palm," "coconut tree."

co·coon (kə-kōōn′) *n.* **1.** A covering of silk or similar fibrous material spun by the larvae of moths and other insects as protection for their pupal stage. **2.** Any similar protective covering or structure, such as that of a spider or earthworm. **3.** A protective plastic coating placed over stored inactive military or naval equipment. [French *cocon*, from Provençal *coucoun*, from *coco*, eggshell, hence, cocoon, from Latin *coccum, coccus*, kermes berry, from Greek *kokkos*. See **kokkos** in Appendix.*]

Co·cos Islands (kō′kəs). Also **Kee·ling Islands** (kē′lĭng). A group of 27 islets, about 5 square miles in area, lying in the Indian Ocean about 700 miles southwest of Sumatra, and administered by Australia. Population, 1,000.

co·cotte (kô-kôt′) *n.* A prostitute. [French, originally a baby's word for hen, from *coq*, cock, from Late Latin *coccus*, from Latin *coco*, cackle. See **cock.**]

Coc·teau (kôk-tō′), **Jean.** 1891–1963. French poet.

Co·cy·tus (kō-sī′təs). *Greek Mythology.* One of the six rivers of Hades. [Latin, from Greek *Kōkutos*, "river of lamentation," from *kōkuein*, to wail, lament. See **kau-**[1] in Appendix.*]

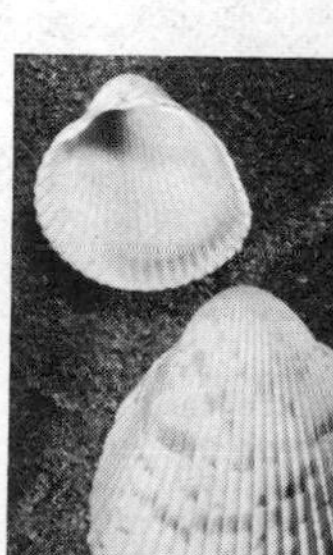

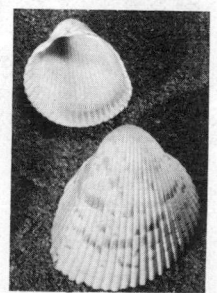

cockleshell
Shells of *Dinocardium robustum*, cockle found off the Atlantic coast of North America

cod[1] (kŏd) *n., pl.* **cod** or **cods.** Any of various marine fishes of the family Gadidae; especially, *Gadus morhua* (or *G. callarias*), an important food fish of Northern Atlantic waters. Also called "codfish." [Middle English, possibly from COD (bag), from its shape.]

cod[2] (kŏd) *n.* **1.** *Regional.* A husk or pod. **2.** *Obsolete.* A bag. **3.** *Archaic.* The scrotum. [Middle English *cod*, Old English *codd*, bag, husk. See **ku-** in Appendix.*]

COD 1. cash on delivery. **2.** collect on delivery.

Cod. codex.

C.O.D. 1. cash on delivery. **2.** collect on delivery.

Cod, Cape (kŏd). A peninsula in southeastern Massachusetts, extending 65 miles to the east and then north and northwest.

co·da (kō′də) *n.* **1.** *Music.* A passage at the end of a movement or composition that brings it to a formal close. **2.** *Choreography.* The closing part of a pas de deux. [Italian, "tail," from Latin *cōda, cauda.* See **caudate.**]

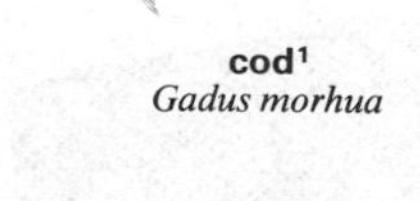

cod[1]
Gadus morhua

cod·dle (kŏd′l) *tr.v.* **-dled, -dling, -dles. 1.** To cook in water just below the boiling point. **2.** To treat indulgently; to baby. —See Synonyms at **pamper.** [Variant of CAUDLE.] —**cod′dler** *n.*

code (kōd) *n.* **1.** A systematically arranged and comprehensive collection of laws. **2.** Any systematic collection of regulations and rules of procedure or conduct: *the military code.* **3.** A system of signals used to represent letters or numbers in transmitting messages. **4.** A system of symbols, letters, or words given certain arbitrary meanings, used for transmitting messages requiring secrecy or brevity. Compare **cipher.** —*tr.v.* **coded, coding, codes. 1.** To systematize and arrange (laws and regulations) into a code. **2.** To convert into code. [Middle English, from Old French, from Latin *cōdex*, CODEX.]

co·deine (kō′dēn′, kō′dē-ĭn) *n.* An alkaloid narcotic, $C_{18}H_{21}$-

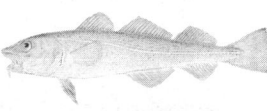

NO$_3$, derived from opium or morphine, used for relieving coughing, as an analgesic, and as a hypnotic. [French *codéine* : Greek *kōdeia*, poppyhead, from *koos*, hollow place, cavity (see **keu-**[3] in Appendix*) + -INE.]

Code Na·po·lé·on (kôd′ nȧ-pô-lā-ôN′). The code of French civil law, prepared under the direction of Napoleon Bonaparte between 1804 and 1807.

co·dex (kō′dĕks′) *n., pl.* **codices** (kō′də-sēz′, kŏd′ə-). *Abbr.* **Cod.** **1.** A manuscript volume, especially of a classic work or of the Scriptures. **2.** *Obsolete.* A code of laws or statutes. [Latin *cōdex*, *caudex*, tree trunk, board, writing tablet, book (of laws). See **caudex**.]

Co·dex Ju·ris Ca·non·i·ci (kō′dĕks′ jŏŏr′ĭs kə-nŏn′ə-sī′). The code of law that has governed the Roman Catholic Church since 1918. [Latin, "book of canon laws."]

cod·fish (kŏd′fĭsh′) *n., pl.* **codfish** or **-fishes.** The **cod** *(see).*

codg·er (kŏj′ər) *n. Informal.* An old man. [Possibly from *cadger*, carrier, peddler, Middle English *cadgear*. See **cadge**.]

cod·i·cil (kŏd′ə-sĭl) *n.* **1.** *Law.* A supplement or appendix to a will. **2.** A supplement or appendix. [Middle English, from Old French *codicille*, from Latin *cōdicillus*, diminutive of *cōdex*, CODEX.] —**cod′i·cil′la·ry** (kŏd′ə-sĭl′ə-rē) *adj.*

cod·i·fy (kŏd′ə-fī′, kō′də-) *tr.v.* **-fied, -fying, -fies. 1.** To reduce to a code: *codify laws.* **2.** To arrange or systematize. —**cod′i·fi·ca′tion** *n.* —**cod′i·fi′er** *n.*

cod·ling[1] (kŏd′lĭng) *n.* Also **cod·lin** (-lĭn). *British.* **1.** A long, tapering apple. **2.** An unripe apple. [Middle English *querdlyng*, possibly from Norman French *querdelyon*, "lion's heart," from its elongated shape.]

cod·ling[2] (kŏd′lĭng) *n., pl.* **-lings** or **codling.** A young cod.

codling moth. Also **codlin moth.** A small grayish moth, *Carpocapsa pomonella*, the larvae of which are destructive to various fruits, especially apples.

cod-liv·er oil (kŏd′lĭv′ər). An oil obtained from the livers of cod and containing a rich supply of vitamins A and D.

co·don (kō′dŏn′) *n. Genetics.* A sequence of three adjacent nucleotides that specifies the insertion of an amino acid in a specific structural position during protein synthesis. [COD(E) + -ON.]

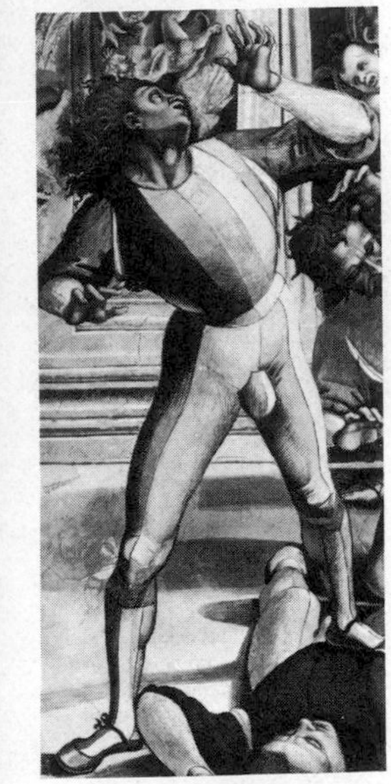

codpiece
Detail of the fresco *il Finimondo* ("The End of the World"), by Luca Signorelli

cod·piece (kŏd′pēs′) *n.* A pouch at the crotch of the tight-fitting breeches worn by men in the 15th and 16th centuries. [Middle English *codpece* : COD (bag, scrotum) + PIECE.]

Co·dy (kō′dē), **William Frederick.** Called "Buffalo Bill." 1846–1917. American frontiersman, scout, and showman.

co-ed, co·ed (kō′ĕd′) *n. Informal.* A woman student attending a co-educational college or university. —*adj. Informal.* Co-educational. [Short for *co-educational student.*]

co-ed·u·ca·tion (kō′ĕj-ŏŏ-kā′shən) *n.* The system of education in which both men and women attend the same institution or classes. —**co′-ed·u·ca′tion·al** *adj.*

co·ef·fi·cient (kō′ə-fĭsh′ənt) *n.* **1.** *Mathematics.* **a.** A numerical factor of an elementary algebraic term, as 4 in the term 4x. **b.** The product of all but one of the factors of an expression, the product being regarded as a distinct entity with respect to the excluded factor and to a designated operation. See **correlation coefficient. 2.** A numerical measure of a physical or chemical property that is constant for a system under specified conditions. [New Latin *coefficiens* : CO- (together) + EFFICIENT.]

coel–. Indicates a cavity within a body or bodily organ; for example, **coelenterate.** [New Latin, from Greek *koilos*, hollow. See **keu-**[3] in Appendix.*]

–coel. Variant of **-cele.**

coe·la·canth (sē′lə-kănth′) *n.* Any of various fishes of the order Coelacanthiformes, known only in fossil form until a living species, *Latimeria chalumnae*, of African marine waters, was identified in 1938. [From New Latin *coelacanthus* (genus), "hollow-spined" : COEL- + Greek *akanthos*, spine, thorn, from *akantha*, thorny plant (see **ak-** in Appendix*).] —**coe′la·can′thine′** (-kăn′thīn′, -thĭn) *adj.* —**coe′la·can′thous** (-thəs) *adj.*

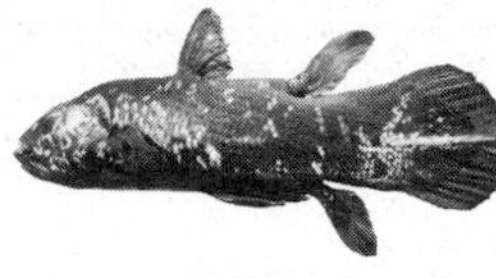

coelacanth

–coele. Variant of **-cele.**

coe·len·ter·ate (sĭ-lĕn′tə-rāt′, -rĭt) *n.* Any invertebrate animal of the phylum Coelenterata, characterized by a radially symmetrical body with a saclike internal cavity, and including the jellyfishes, hydras, sea anemones, and corals. —*adj.* Of or belonging to the Coelenterata. [New Latin *coelenterata*, "hollow-intestined ones" : COEL- + ENTERON + -ATE.] —**coe·len′ter′ic** (sĭ-lĕn′tĕr′ĭk) *adj.*

coe·len·ter·on (sĭ-lĕn′tə-rŏn′, -rən) *n., pl.* **-tera** (-tər-ə). *Zoology.* The saclike body cavity of a coelenterate. [New Latin : COEL- + ENTERON.]

coe·li·ac. Variant of **celiac.**

coe·lom (sē′ləm) *n.* Also **ce·lom, coe·lome.** The body cavity in all animals higher than the coelenterates and certain primitive worms, formed by the splitting of the mesoderm into two layers. [German *Koelom*, from Greek *koilōma*, cavity, from *koilos*, hollow. See **keu-**[3] in Appendix.*]

coeno–, ceno–. Indicates common; for example, **coenurus.** [New Latin, from Greek *koino-*, from *koinos*, common. See **kom** in Appendix*).]

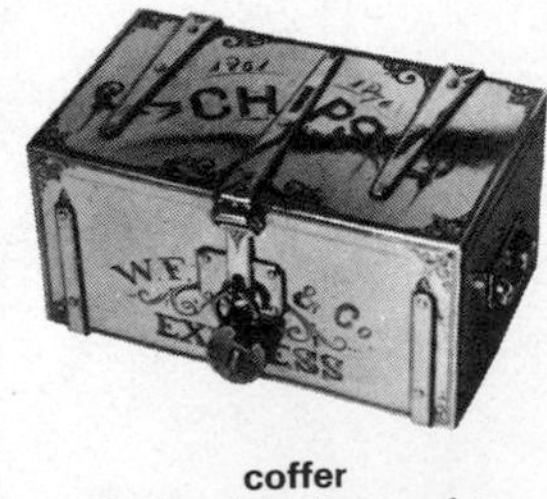

coffer
Coffer of the type used to carry gold bullion and other valuables by stagecoach in the American West

coen·o·bite. Variant of **cenobite.**

coe·no·cyte (sē′nə-sīt′) *n. Botany.* An organism consisting of a multinucleate protoplasmic mass resulting from nuclear division without the formation of a new cell wall or membrane, as in slime molds and certain fungi and algae. [COENO- + -CYTE.] —**coe′no·cyt′ic** (-sĭt′ĭk) *adj.*

coe·no·gen·e·sis. Variant of **cenogenesis.**

coe·nu·rus (sĭ-nyŏŏr′əs) *n., pl.* **-nuri** (-nyŏŏr′ī′). The larval stage of a tapeworm, *Multiceps multiceps* (or *Taenia multiceps*), that attacks the central nervous system of ruminant animals. [New Latin, "having a common tail" (because it has many heads and only one tail) : COEN(O)- + -UR(O)US.]

co·en·zyme (kō-ĕn′zīm′) *n.* A heat-stable organic molecule that must be loosely associated with an enzyme for the enzyme to function.

co·e·qual (kō-ē′kwəl) *adj.* Equal with one another, as in rank or size. —*n.* An equal. —**co′e·qual′i·ty** (kō′ē-kwŏl′ə-tē) *n.* —**co·e′qual·ly** *adv.*

co·erce (kō-ûrs′) *tr.v.* **-erced, -ercing, -erces. 1.** To force to act or think in a given manner; to compel by pressure or threat. **2.** To dominate, restrain, or control forcibly. **3.** To actualize by force. —See Synonyms at **force.** [Middle English *cohercen*, from Old French *cohercier*, from Latin *coercēre*, to enclose together, constrain : *cō-*, together + *arcēre*, to enclose, confine (see **arek-** in Appendix*).] —**co·erc′er** *n.* —**co·er′ci·ble** *adj.*

co·er·cion (kō-ûr′shən) *n.* **1.** The act or practice of coercing. **2.** A coercive power. —**co·er′cion·ar′y** *adj.*

co·er·cive (kō-ûr′sĭv) *adj.* Characterized by or inclined to coercion. —**co·er′cive·ly** *adv.* —**co·er′cive·ness** *n.*

co·es·sen·tial (kō′ĭ-sĕn′shəl) *adj.* Having the same nature or essence. —**co′es·sen′ti·al′i·ty, co′es·sen′tial·ness** *n.* —**co′es·sen′tial·ly** *adv.*

co·e·ta·ne·ous (kō′ĭ-tā′nē-əs) *adj.* Of equal age, duration, or period; contemporary. [Latin *coaetāneus* : *co-*, same + *aetās*, age (see **aiw-** in Appendix*).] —**co′e·ta′ne·ous·ly** *adv.* —**co′e·ta′ne·ous·ness** *n.*

co·e·ter·nal (kō′ĭ-tûr′nəl) *adj.* Equally eternal; eternally existing with one another. —**co′e·ter′nal·ly** *adv.*

co·e·ter·ni·ty (kō′ĭ-tûr′nə-tē) *n.* Existence for eternity with another or others.

Coeur d'A·lene (kôr də-lān′). A lake occupying about 60 square miles in a resort area of northern Idaho.

Coeur de Li·on. See **Richard I.**

co·e·val (kō-ē′vəl) *adj.* Originating or existing during the same period of time; lasting through the same era. —*n.* One of the same era or period. [Latin *coaevus* : *cō-*, same + *aevum*, age (see **aiw-** in Appendix*).] —**co·e′val·ly** *adv.*

co·ex·ist (kō′ĭg-zĭst′) *intr.v.* **-isted, -isting, -ists.** To exist together, at the same time, or in the same place.

co·ex·is·tence (kō′ĭg-zĭs′təns) *n.* **1.** The condition of existing together: *"excitement in coexistence with an overbalance of pleasure"* (Wordsworth). **2.** The concurrent but separate existence of two or more nations of assertedly great ideological disparity. —**co′ex·is′tent** *adj.*

co·ex·tend (kō′ĭk-stĕnd′) *v.* **-tended, -tending, -tends.** —*tr.* To cause to extend through the same space or duration. —*intr.* To reach to or attain the same limit in space or time. —**co′ex·ten′sion** *n.* —**co′ex·ten′sive** *adj.* —**co′ex·ten′sive·ly** *adv.*

C. of C. chamber of commerce.

C. of E. Church of England.

cof·fee (kô′fē, kŏf′ē) *n.* **1.** Any of several trees of the genus *Coffea*, native to eastern Asia and Africa, bearing berries containing beans used in the preparation of a beverage; especially, *C. arabica*, the chief commercial source of these beans. **2.** The seeds or beans of the coffee tree. **3.** An aromatic, mildly stimulating beverage prepared from coffee beans. **4.** Moderate brown to dark or dark grayish yellowish brown. See **color.** [Italian *caffè*, from Turkish *kahve*, from Arabic *qahwah.*]

coffee cake. A cake to be eaten with coffee, made of sweetened yeast dough, often containing nuts or raisins, and topped with powdered sugar or icing.

coffee house. Also **cof·fee·house** (kô′fē-hous′, kŏf′ē-). A restaurant where coffee and other refreshments are served.

coffee klatch, coffee klatsch (klăch, kläch). Also **kaf·fee klatsch** (kô′fē klăch′, kŏf′ē klăch′). A casual gathering for coffee and conversation. [Partial translation of German *Kaffeeklatsch* : *Kaffee*, coffee + *Klatsch*, chat (imitative).]

coffee mill. A device for grinding roasted coffee beans.

cof·fee·pot (kô′fē-pŏt′, kŏf′ē-) *n.* A pot for brewing or serving coffee.

coffee shop. A small restaurant in which light meals are served.

coffee table. A long, low table, often placed before a sofa.

coffee tree. 1. Any tree of the genus *Coffea*, producing coffee beans. **2.** The **Kentucky coffee tree** *(see).*

cof·fer (kô′fər, kŏf′ər) *n.* **1.** A strongbox. **2.** *Plural.* Funds; treasury. **3.** A decorative sunken panel in a soffit, ceiling, dome, or vault. **4.** A canal lock. **5.** A cofferdam. —*tr.v.* **coffered, -fering, -fers. 1.** To put in a coffer. **2.** To supply with decorative sunken panels. [Middle English *cof(f)re*, box, chest, from Old French, from Latin *cophinus*, basket. See **coffin.**]

cof·fer·dam (kô′fər-dăm′, kŏf′ər-) *n. Engineering.* **1.** A temporary watertight enclosure built in the water and pumped dry to expose the bottom so that construction, as of piers, may be undertaken. **2.** A watertight chamber attached to a ship's side to facilitate repairs below the water line.

cof·fin (kô′fən, kŏf′ən) *n.* **1.** An oblong box in which a corpse is buried. **2.** A horse's hoof. —*tr.v.* **coffined, -fining, -fins.** To place in or as if in a coffin. [Middle English, box, basket, from Old French *cofin*, from Latin *cophinus*, from Greek *kophinus*†, basket, measure of capacity.]

coffin bone. The bone inside a horse's hoof.

coffin corner. *Slang.* On a football field, any corner within 10 yards of the defending team's goal line. The ball may be deliberately punted out of bounds in this area, thus placing the receiving team very close to its goal line.

cof·fle (kô′fəl, kŏf′əl) *n.* A file of animals, prisoners, or slaves, chained together in transit. —*tr.v.* **coffled, -fling, -fles.** To fasten together in a coffle. [Arabic *qāfilah*, caravan.]

C. of S. chief of staff.

ă pat/ā pay/âr care/ä father/b bib/ch church/d deed/ĕ pet/ē be/f fife/g gag/h hat/hw which/ĭ pit/ī pie/îr pier/j judge/k kick/l lid, needle/m mum/n no, sudden/ng thing/ŏ pot/ō toe/ô paw, for/oi noise/ou out/ŏŏ took/ōō boot/p pop/r roar/s sauce/sh ship, dish/

cog¹ (kŏg) *n.* **1.** One of a series of teeth on the rim of a wheel which by engagement transmit motive force to a corresponding wheel. **2.** A cogwheel. **3.** A subordinate member within a given organization. [Middle English *cogge,* probably from Scandinavian, akin to Swedish *kugge.* See **ku-** in Appendix.*]
cog² (kŏg) *v.* **cogged, cogging, cogs.** —*tr.* To load or manipulate (dice) fraudulently. —*intr.* To cheat, especially at dice. —*n.* An instance of cheating; a swindle. [Origin unknown.]
cog³ (kŏg) *n.* A tenon projecting from a wooden beam and fitting into an opening in another beam to form a joint. —*tr.v.* **cogged, cogging, cogs.** To join with tenons. [Origin obscure.]
cog. cognate.
co·gent (kōʹjənt) *adj.* Forcibly convincing. [Latin *cōgens,* present participle of *cōgere,* to force, drive together : *cō-,* together + *agere,* to drive (see **ag-** in Appendix*).] —**coʹgen·cy** (-jən-sē) *n.* —**coʹgent·ly** *adv.*
cog·i·tate (kŏjʹə-tātʹ) *v.* **-tated, -tating, -tates.** —*intr.* To take careful and leisurely thought; meditate; ponder. —*tr.* To think carefully about; consider intently. [Latin *cōgitāre* : *cō-* (intensive) + *agitāre,* to turn in mind, consider, AGITATE.] —**cogʹi·ta·ble** (kŏjʹə-tə-bəl) *adj.* —**cogʹi·taʹtor** (-tāʹtər) *n.*
cog·i·ta·tion (kŏjʹə-tāʹshən) *n.* **1.** Thoughtful consideration; meditation. **2.** A serious thought; reflection.
cog·i·ta·tive (kŏjʹə-tāʹtĭv) *adj.* Meditative. —**cogʹi·taʹtive·ly** *adv.* —**cogʹi·taʹtive·ness** *n.*
Cog·lians, Monte. The Italian name for **Kellerwand.**
co·gnac (kōnʹyăk', kŏnʹ-, kônʹ-; *French* kôn-yăkʹ) *n.* **1.** A brandy produced in the vicinity of Cognac in western France. **2.** Any fine brandy.
cog·nate (kŏgʹnātʹ) *adj. Abbr.* **cog. 1.** Related by blood; having a common ancestor. **2.** Related in origin, as certain words in different languages derived from the same root. **3.** Related or analogous in nature, character, or function. —*n. Abbr.* **cog.** A person or thing cognate with another. [Latin *cōgnātus* : *cō-,* same + *gnātus,* born, from *gnāscī, nāscī,* to be born (see **gena-** in Appendix*).] —**cog·naʹtion** (kŏg-nāʹshən) *n.*
cog·ni·tion (kŏg-nĭshʹən) *n.* **1.** The mental process or faculty by which knowledge is acquired. **2.** That which comes to be known, as through perception, reasoning, or intuition; knowledge. [Middle English *cognicioun,* from Latin *cognitiō,* from *cognōscere* (past participle *cognitus*), to get to know, learn : *cō-* (intensive) + *gnōscere,* to know (see **gnō-** in Appendix*).] —**cog·niʹtion·al, cogʹni·tive** (kŏgʹnə-tĭv) *adj.*
cog·ni·za·ble (kŏgʹnə-zə-bəl, kŏg-nīʹ-) *adj.* **1.** Knowable or perceptible. **2.** Judicable. —**cogʹni·za·bly** *adv.*
cog·ni·zance (kŏgʹnə-zəns) *n.* **1.** Conscious knowledge or recognition; apprehension. **2.** The range of what one can know or understand. **3.** *Law.* **a.** The examination of a case by a court. **b.** The right or power of a court's jurisdiction. **c.** Admission of an action or fact; confession. **4.** *Heraldry.* A crest or badge worn to distinguish the bearer. —**take cognizance of.** To take notice of; acknowledge. [Middle English *co(g)nisaunce,* from Old French *conoissance,* from *conoistre,* to know, from Latin *cognōscere,* to learn. See **cognition.**]
cog·ni·zant (kŏgʹnə-zənt) *adj.* Fully informed; conscious. Used with *of.* See Synonyms at **aware.** [From COGNIZANCE.]
cog·no·men (kŏg-nōʹmən) *n., pl.* **-mens** or **-nomina** (-nŏmʹə-nə). **1.** A family name; surname. **2.** The third and usually last name of a citizen of ancient Rome, such as *Caesar* in *Caius Julius Caesar.* **3.** Any name, especially a descriptive nickname acquired through usage. —See Synonyms at **name.** [Latin *cognōmen,* "additional name" (formed after *cognōscere,* to learn) : *cō-,* together + *nōmen,* name (see **nomen-** in Appendix*).] —**cog·nomʹi·nal** (kŏg-nŏmʹə-nəl) *adj.*
co·gno·scen·te (kŏnʹyō-shĕnʹtē) *n., pl.* **-ti** (-tē). A person of superior knowledge or taste; connoisseur. [Obsolete Italian, "the knowing one," from Latin *cognōscēns,* present participle of *cognōscere,* to get to know. See **cognition.**]
cog·no·vit (kŏg-nōʹvĭt) *n. Law.* A written admission by a defendant of his liability, made to avoid the expense of a trial. [Latin, "he has acknowledged," from *cognōscere,* to get to know, recognize, acknowledge. See **cognition.**]
co·gon (kō-gōnʹ) *n.* Any of various tall tropical grasses of the genus *Imperata;* especially, *I. cylindrica* or *I. exaltata,* of the Philippines and adjacent islands, used for thatching. [Spanish *cogón,* from Tagalog *kugon.*]
cog railway. A railway designed to operate on steep slopes, having locomotives with a center cogwheel that engages with a cogged center rail to provide traction. Also called "cogway," "rack railway."
Cogs·well chair (kŏgzʹwĕlʹ, -wəl). Also **Cox·well chair** (kŏksʹ-). An upholstered easy chair, open under the armrests, with a sloping back and cabriole front legs. [Probably from the surname *Cogswell.*]
cog·wheel (kŏgʹhwēlʹ) *n.* One of a set of cogged wheels within a given mechanism.
co·hab·it (kō-hăbʹĭt) *intr.v.* **-ited, -iting, -its.** To live together in a sexual relationship when not legally married. [Late Latin *cohabitāre* : *cō-,* together + *habitāre,* to inhabit (see **habitat**).] —**co·habʹi·taʹtion** *n.*
Co·han (kōʹhănʹ), **George M(ichael).** 1878–1942. American singer, playwright, and songwriter.
co·heir (kō-ârʹ) *n.* A joint heir. [Middle English, from Latin *cohērēs* : *co-,* jointly + *hērēs,* HEIR.]
co·heir·ess (kō-ârʹĭs) *n.* A joint heiress.
co·here (kō-hîrʹ) *v.* **-hered, -hering, -heres.** —*intr.* **1.** To stick or hold together. **2.** To be logically connected. —*tr.* To cause to form a united or orderly whole. [Latin *cohaerēre* : *cō-,* together + *haerere,* to cling to (see **ghais-** in Appendix*).]
co·her·ence (kō-hîrʹəns, kō-hĕrʹ-) *n.* Also **co·her·en·cy** (-ən-sē). The quality or state of logical or orderly relationship of parts; consistency; congruity.
co·her·ent (kō-hîrʹənt, kō-hĕrʹ-) *adj.* **1.** Sticking together; cohering. **2.** Marked by an orderly or logical relation of parts that affords comprehension or recognition: *coherent speech.* **3.** *Physics.* Of or pertaining to waves with a continuous relationship among phases. **4.** *Measurement.* Of or pertaining to a system of units in which a small number of basic units are defined from which all others in the system are derived by multiplication or division only. —**co·herʹent·ly** *adv.*
co·he·sion (kō-hēʹzhən) *n.* **1.** The process or condition of cohering. **2.** *Physics.* The mutual attraction by which the elements of a body are held together. Compare **adhesion. 3.** *Botany.* The congenital joining of two parts. [From Latin *cohaesus,* past participle of *cohaerēre,* COHERE.] —**co·heʹsive** (-sĭv, -zĭv) *adj.* —**co·heʹsive·ly** *adv.* —**co·heʹsive·ness** *n.*
co·hort (kōʹhôrtʹ) *n.* **1.** One of the 10 divisions of a Roman legion, consisting of 300 to 600 men. **2.** A group or band united in some struggle. **3.** *Informal.* A companion or associate. See Usage note. [Middle English, from Old French *cohorte,* from Latin *cohors,* enclosed yard, company of soldiers, multitude. See **gher-²** in Appendix.*]
Usage: *Cohort,* in the sense of an individual companion, associate, or follower, is not appropriate to formal use. It is unacceptable in that sense and on that level to 69 per cent of the Usage Panel.
co·hosh (kōʹhŏshʹ) *n.* Any of several North American plants, such as the **blue cohosh, black cohosh,** and **baneberry** *(all of which see).* [Probably from an Algonquian language of New England.]
co·hune (kō-hōōnʹ) *n.* A tropical American palm tree, *Attalea cohune,* having long featherlike leaves and oily nuts. Also called "cohune palm." [American Spanish, from Mosquito *ókhún.*]
coif (koif) *n.* **1.** A tight-fitting cap worn under a veil, as by nuns. **2. a.** A white skullcap formerly worn by English lawyers and sergeants at law. **b.** The office or rank of sergeant at law. **3.** A heavy skullcap of steel or leather, formerly worn under a helmet or mail hood. —*tr.v.* (koif; *also* kwäf *for sense 2*) **coifed, coifing, coifs. 1.** To cover with or as if with a coif. **2.** To arrange or dress (the hair). [Middle English *coyfe,* from Old French *coiffe, coife,* from Late Latin *cofia*†.]
coif·feur (kwä-fœrʹ) *n. Feminine* **coif·feuse** (kwä-fœzʹ). A hairdresser. [French, from *coiffer,* to coif, from Old French *coiffe,* COIF.]
coif·fure (kwä-fyōōrʹ) *n.* A way of arranging the hair; hair style. —*tr.v.* **coiffured, -furing, -fures.** To arrange or dress (the hair). [French, from *coiffer,* to coif, from Old French *coiffe,* COIF.]
coign of vantage. An advantageous position for observation or action. [*Coign,* obsolete variant of COIN (corner).]
coil¹ (koil) *n.* **1.** A series of connected spirals or concentric rings formed by gathering or winding: *a coil of rope.* **2.** An individual spiral or ring within such a series. **3.** A spiral pipe or series of spiral pipes, as in a radiator. **4.** *Electricity.* **a.** A wound spiral of two or more turns of insulated wire, used to introduce inductance into a circuit. **b.** Any device of which such a spiral is the major component. —*v.* **coiled, coiling, coils.** —*tr.* **1.** To wind in spirals or concentric rings. **2.** To wind into a shape resembling a coil. —*intr.* **1.** To form coils. **2.** To move in a spiral course. [Middle English *coilen,* to collect, cull, from Old French *coillir,* from Latin *colligere* : *com-,* together + *legere,* to gather (see **leg-** in Appendix*).] —**coilʹer** *n.*
coil² (koil) *n. Rare.* A disturbance; fuss. [Origin obscure.]
Coim·ba·tore (koimʹbə-tôrʹ, -tōrʹ). A city of the Republic of India, in southwestern Madras State. Population, 286,000.
coin (koin) *n.* **1.** A small piece of metal, usually flat and circular, authorized by a government for use as money. **2.** Metal money collectively. **3.** *Architecture.* A corner or cornerstone. —*tr.v.* **coined, coining, coins. 1.** To make (coins) from metal; mint; strike: *coin silver dollars.* **2.** To make coins from (metal): *coin gold.* **3.** To invent (a word or phrase). [Middle English *coyne,* wedge, design stamped on a coiner's die, coin, from Old French *coing, coin,* wedge, from Latin *cuneus*†, wedge.] —**coinʹa·ble** *adj.* —**coinʹer** *n.*
coin·age (koiʹnĭj) *n.* **1.** The process or right of making coins. **2. a.** Metal currency. **b.** A system of metal currency. **3. a.** A coined word or phrase. **b.** The invention of new words.
co·in·cide (kōʹĭn-sīdʹ) *intr.v.* **-cided, -ciding, -cides. 1. a.** To occupy the same position simultaneously. **b.** To have identical dimensions. **2.** To happen at the same time or during the same period. **3.** To correspond exactly; be identical. —See Synonyms at **agree.** [Medieval Latin *coincidere* : *cō-,* together + *incidere,* to happen (see **incident**).]
co·in·ci·dence (kō-ĭnʹsə-dəns, -dĕnsʹ) *n.* **1.** The state or fact of coinciding. **2.** An accidental sequence of events that appear to have a causal relationship. —**co·inʹci·dent** *adj.*
co·in·ci·den·tal (kō-ĭnʹsə-dĕnʹtəl) *adj.* Occurring as or resulting from coincidence. —**co·inʹci·denʹtal·ly** *adv.*
co·in·sur·ance (kōʹĭn-shōōrʹəns) *n.* **1.** Insurance held jointly with another or others. **2.** A form of insurance in which a person insures property for less than its full value and agrees to be responsible for the difference.
co·in·sure (kōʹĭn-shōōrʹ) *v.* **-sured, -suring, -sures.** —*intr.* **1.** To take out insurance with another or others. **2.** To take out coinsurance. —*tr.* **1.** To insure jointly. **2.** To insure with coinsurance. —**coʹin·surʹer** *n.*
coir (koir) *n.* The fiber obtained from the husk of a coconut, used in making rope and matting. [Malayalam *kāyar,* cord, from *kāyaru,* to be twisted.]

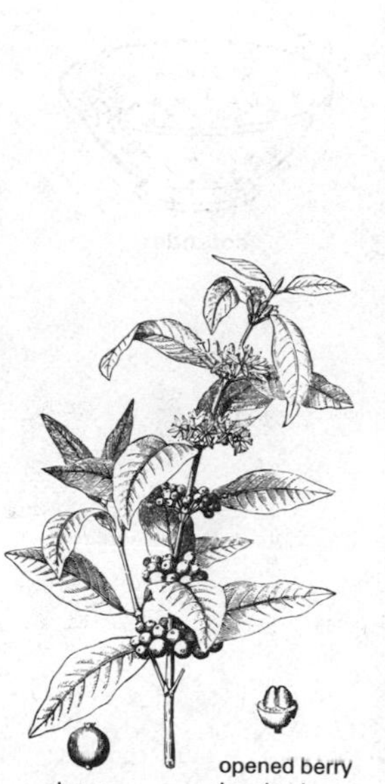
berry — opened berry showing beans
coffee
Coffea arabica

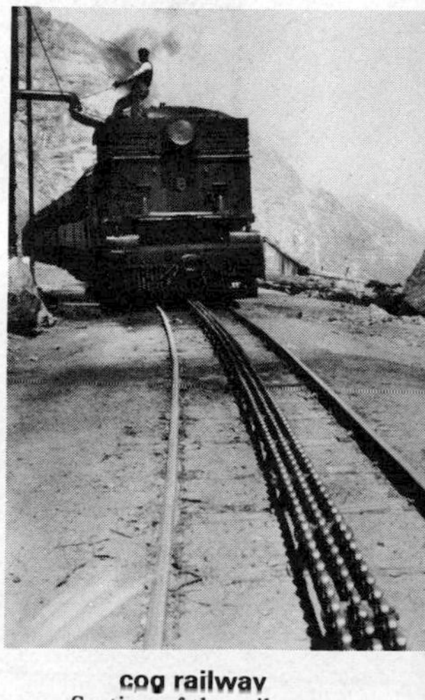
cog railway
Section of the railway over the Andes in Chile

co·i·tus (kō′ə-təs) *n.* Also **co·i·tion** (kō-ĭsh′ən). Sexual intercourse between two human beings. [Latin *coitus,* "meeting," from *coīre,* to come together : *cō-,* together + *īre,* to go (see **ei-**[1] in Appendix*).] —**co′i·tal** *adj.*

co·i·tus in·ter·rup·tus (kō′ə-təs ĭn′tə-rŭp′təs). Sexual intercourse purposely interrupted by withdrawal of the male prior to ejaculation. [Latin, "interrupted intercourse."]

coke[1] (kōk) *n.* The solid carbonaceous residue obtained from coal after removal of volatile material by destructive distillation, used as fuel. —*v.* **coked, coking, cokes.** —*tr.* To convert or change into coke. —*intr.* To become coke. [Middle English *coke*†.]

coke[2] (kōk) *n. Slang.* Cocaine.

Coke (kōk) *n.* A trademark for Coca-Cola, a soft drink.

Coke (ko͝ok), Sir **Edward.** 1552–1634. English jurist.

col (kŏl) *n.* A pass between two peaks or a gap in a ridge. [French, from Old French, neck, from Latin *collum.* See **kwel-**[1] in Appendix.*]

col. **1.** collect; collected; collector. **2.** college; collegiate. **3.** colonial; colony. **4.** color. **5.** column.

Col. **1.** Colombia. **2.** colonel. **3.** Colorado (unofficial). **4.** Colossians (New Testament).

co·la[1] (kō′lə) *n.* A carbonated soft drink containing an extract prepared from kola nuts.

co·la[2]. Alternate plural of **colon.**

co·la[3]. Variant of **kola.**

col·an·der (kŭl′ən-dər, kŏl′-) *n.* Also **cul·len·der** (kŭl′ən-dər). A bowl-shaped kitchen utensil with a perforated bottom for draining off liquids and rinsing food. [Middle English *colyndore, culatre,* from Old Provençal *colador,* from Vulgar Latin *cōlātor* (unattested), from Latin *cōlāre,* to strain, from *cōlum,* sieve, filter. See **kagh-** in Appendix.*]

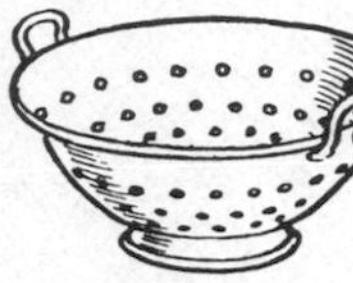

colander

cola nut. Variant of **kola nut.**

Col·bert (kôl-bâr′), **Jean Baptiste.** 1619–1683. French statesman; economic adviser to Louis XIV.

col·can·non (kŏl-kăn′ən) *n.* An Irish dish of mashed potatoes and cabbage. [Irish Gaelic *cal ceannan,* "white-headed cabbage" : *cal,* cabbage, from Old Irish, from Latin *caulis* (see **kaul-** in Appendix*) + *ceannan,* white-headed : *ceann,* head, from Old Irish *cenn,* from Common Celtic *kwenno-* (unattested) + *fionn,* white, from Old Irish *find* (see **weid-** in Appendix*).]

Col·ches·ter (kōl′chĭs-tər). A city of Essex, southeastern England. Population, 65,000.

col·chi·cine (kŏl′chə-sēn′, kŏl′kə-) *n.* A poisonous alkaloid, $C_{22}H_{25}NO_6$, used experimentally to induce chromosome doubling and medicinally to treat gout. [German *Kolchizin,* from New Latin *colchicum,* COLCHICUM.]

col·chi·cum (kŏl′chĭ-kəm, kŏl′kĭ-) *n.* **1.** Any of various bulbous plants of the genus *Colchicum,* such as the **autumn crocus** *(see).* **2.** The dried seeds or corms of *C. autumnale,* a source of colchicine. [New Latin, from Latin, a poisonous root, from Greek *Kolkhikon,* from *Kolkhikos,* of Colchis, belonging to the witch Medea of Colchis, from *Kolkhis,* COLCHIS.]

Col·chis (kŏl′kĭs). *Russian* **Kol·khi·da** (kŏl-KHĒ′də). An ancient region on the Black Sea south of the Caucasus Mountains; the legendary land of the Golden Fleece.

col·co·thar (kŏl′kə-thər, -thär′) *n.* A brownish-red iron oxide obtained as a residue after heating ferrous sulfate, used in glass polishing and as a pigment. [French *colcotar,* from Spanish, from Arabic *qolqoṭār.*]

cold (kōld) *adj.* **colder, coldest. 1. a.** Having a low temperature. **b.** Lacking heat. **c.** Lacking energy. **2.** Having a temperature lower than normal body temperature. **3.** Feeling no warmth; uncomfortably chilled. **4.** Designating a color or tone that suggests little warmth, such as pale gray. **5.** *Informal.* Unconscious; insensible: *knocked cold.* **6.** Not affected by emotion; objective: *cold logic.* **7.** Without appeal to the senses or feelings; depressing: *cold decor.* **8.** Not affectionate or enthusiastic; aloof: *a cold person.* **9.** Without sexual desire; frigid. **10.** Without freshness; faint; weak. **11.** *Informal.* Far removed from the object sought. —**in cold blood.** Without passion or remorse. —*adv. Informal.* Completely; thoroughly: *cold sober.* —*n.* **1.** The relative lack of warmth. **2.** The sensation resulting from lack of warmth. **3.** A viral infection characterized by inflammation of the mucous membranes of the respiratory passages and accompanying fever, chills, coughing, and sneezing. **4.** A condition of low air temperature; cold weather. —**in the cold.** Neglected; ignored. [Middle English *cold, cald,* Old English *ceald.* See **gel-**[3] in Appendix.*] —**cold′ly** *adv.* —**cold′ness** *n.*

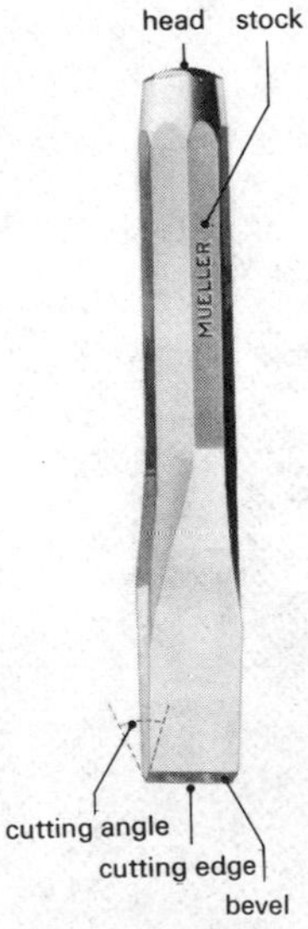
head
stock
MUELLER
cutting angle
cutting edge
bevel

cold chisel
Flat cold chisel

cold-blood·ed (kōld′blŭd′ĭd) *adj.* **1.** Ruthless; unfeeling; heartless. **2.** *Zoology.* Having a body temperature that varies with the external environment; poikilothermous. —**cold′blood′ed·ly** *adv.* —**cold′blood′ed·ness** *n.*

cold chisel. A chisel made of hardened, tempered steel and used for cutting cold metal.

cold cream. An emulsion for cleansing and softening the skin.

cold cuts. Slices of assorted cold meats.

cold-drawn (kōld′drôn′) *adj.* Drawn, as a wire through a die, without prior heating.

cold feet. *Slang.* Failure of nerve.

cold frame. A structure consisting of a wooden frame and a glass top, used for protecting young plants from the cold.

cold front. The leading portion of a cold atmospheric air mass moving against, and eventually replacing, a warm air mass.

Cold Harbor. A place ten miles northeast of Richmond, Virginia, where Confederate victories were won in 1862 and 1864.

cold light. **1.** Light producing little or no heat. **2.** Light emitted by a process other than incandescence.

cold pack. **1.** *Medicine.* A therapeutic pack consisting of a cold, damp sheet. **2.** A canning process in which uncooked food is packed in jars or cans, then sterilized by heat.

cold rubber. A durable strong synthetic rubber polymerized at low temperatures.

cold shoulder. *Informal.* A deliberate slight; a snub.

cold-shoul·der (kōld′shōl′dər) *tr.v.* **-dered, -dering, -ders.** *Informal.* To give (someone) the cold shoulder; to slight; to snub.

cold sore. A small sore on the lips that often accompanies a fever or cold. Also called "fever blister" and, in technical use, "herpes labialis."

cold storage. The protective storage of foods, furs, or the like in a refrigerated place.

cold war. **1.** A state of political tension and military rivalry between nations, stopping short of actual full-scale war. **2.** *Capital* **C,** *capital* **W.** The state of such rivalry existing between the Soviet and American blocs of nations following World War II.

cold wave. **1.** An abrupt onset of unusually cold weather. **2.** A form of permanent wave in which the hair is set by chemicals rather than heat. Compare **permanent wave.**

cole (kōl) *n. Rare.* Any of various plants of the genus *Brassica,* such as the cabbage or rape. Also called "colewort." [Middle English *col, coole,* Old English *cāl, cāul,* from Latin *caulis,* plant stalk, cabbage. See **kaul-** in Appendix.*]

Cole (kōl), **Thomas.** 1801–1848. American landscape painter.

co·lec·to·my (kə-lĕk′tə-mē) *n., pl.* **-mies.** Surgical removal of part or all of the colon. [COL(O)- + -ECTOMY.]

cole·man·ite (kōl′mə-nīt′) *n.* A natural white or colorless hydrated calcium borate, $Ca_2B_6O_{11} \cdot 5H_2O$, a principal source of borax. [After William T. *Coleman* (1824–1893), American pioneer, owner of the mine where it was discovered.]

co·le·op·ter·an (kō′lē-ŏp′tər-ən, kŏl′ē-) *n.* Also **co·le·op·ter·on** (-tə-rŏn′). Any insect of the order Coleoptera, characterized by forewings modified to form tough protective covers for the hind wings, and including the beetles and weevils. —*adj.* Also **co·le·op·ter·ous** (-tər-əs). Of or belonging to the Coleoptera. [From New Latin *Coleoptera,* "sheath-winged ones," from Greek *koleopteros,* sheath-winged : *koleon,* sheath (see **kel-**[4] in Appendix*) + -PTEROUS.]

co·le·op·tile (kō′lē-ŏp′tĭl, kŏl′ē-) *n. Botany.* The first seedling leaf in grasses and similar monocotyledons, forming a protective sheath around the plumule. [New Latin *coleoptilum,* "sheathed plume" : Greek *koleon,* sheath (see **kel-**[4] in Appendix*) + Greek *ptilon,* plume, down (see **pet-**[1] in Appendix*).]

co·le·o·rhi·za (kō′lē-ə-rī′zə, kŏl′ē-) *n., pl.* **-zae** (-zē). *Botany.* A protective sheath around the embryonic root of grasses and similar monocotyledons. [New Latin, "root sheath" : Greek *koleon,* sheath (see **kel-**[4] in Appendix*) + *rhiza,* root (see **wrād-** in Appendix*).]

Cole·ridge (kōl′rĭj), **Samuel Taylor.** 1772–1834. English poet and critic.

cole·slaw (kōl′slô′) *n.* Also **cole slaw.** A salad of finely shredded raw cabbage with a dressing. Also called "slaw." [Dutch *koolsla* : *kool,* cabbage, from Middle Dutch *cōle,* from Latin *caulis* (see **kaul-** in Appendix*) + *sla,* short for *salade,* salad, from French (see **salad**).]

Col·et (kŏl′ĭt), **John.** 1467?–1519. English humanist.

Co·lette (kô-lĕt′). Pen name of Sidonie Gabrielle Claudine Colette. 1873–1954. French novelist and woman of letters.

co·le·us (kō′lē-əs) *n.* Any of various plants of the genus *Coleus,* of Eurasia and Africa, cultivated for their showy leaves, which are often marked with red, yellow, or white. [New Latin *Coleus,* from Greek *koleos, koleon,* sheath (from the way its filaments are joined). See **kel-**[4] in Appendix.*]

cole·wort (kōl′wûrt′, -wôrt′) *n.* A plant, **cole** *(see).*

Col·fax (kōl′făks′), **Schuyler.** 1823–1885. Vice President of the United States under Ulysses S. Grant (1869–73).

col·ic (kŏl′ĭk) *n.* **1.** Acute, paroxysmal pain in the abdomen, caused by spasm, obstruction, or distention of any of the hollow viscera. **2.** Severe abdominal pain in infants, usually resulting from accumulation of gas in the alimentary canal. [Middle English *colike,* from Old French *colique,* from Latin *cōlicus,* from Greek *kōlikos,* suffering in the colon, from *kōlon,* variant of *kolon,* COLON (intestine).] —**col′ick·y** (kŏl′ĭ-kē) *adj.*

col·ic·root (kŏl′ĭk-ro͞ot′, -ro͝ot′) *n.* **1.** A plant, *Aletris farinosa,* of the eastern United States, having a cluster of tubular white flowers and a bitter root formerly used in medicine. Also called "star grass." **2.** Any of various other plants thought to cure or relieve colic.

col·ic·weed (kŏl′ĭk-wēd′) *n.* Any of several plants of the genera *Dicentra* or *Corydalis,* such as the **squirrel corn** *(see).*

co·li·form (kō′lə-fôrm′, kŏl′ə-) *adj.* Of, pertaining to, or resembling the colon bacillus. [COL(ON) + -FORM.]

Co·li·ma (kō-lē′mä). **1.** A state of Mexico, occupying 2,010 square miles in the southwest on the Pacific. Population, 185,000. **2.** The capital and largest city of this state. Population, 44,000. **3.** An active volcano, 12,792 feet high, in Jalisco State, southwestern Mexico.

col·i·se·um (kŏl′ə-sē′əm) *n.* Also **col·os·se·um.** A large amphitheater for public entertainment or assemblies. [After the COLOSSEUM at Rome.]

Col·i·se·um. Variant of **Colosseum.**

co·li·tis (kō-lī′tĭs) *n.* Inflammation of the mucous membrane of the colon. Also called "colonitis." [New Latin : COL(O)- + -ITIS.]

coll. **1.** collateral. **2.** collect; collection; collector. **3.** college; collegiate. **4.** colloquial; colloquialism.

col·lab·o·rate (kə-lăb′ə-rāt′) *intr.v.* **-rated, -rating, -rates. 1.** To work together, especially in a joint intellectual effort. **2.** To

ă pat/ā pay/âr care/ä father/b bib/ch church/d deed/ĕ pet/ē be/f fife/g gag/h hat/hw which/ĭ pit/ī pie/îr pier/j judge/k kick/l lid, needle/m mum/n no, sudden/ng thing/ŏ pot/ō toe/ô paw, for/oi noise/ou out/o͝o took/o͞o boot/p pop/r roar/s sauce/sh ship, dish/

cooperate treasonably, as with an enemy occupying one's country. [Late Latin *collabōrāre* : Latin *com-*, together + *labōrāre*, to work, from *labor*, labor (see **leb-**[1] in Appendix*).] —**col·lab′o·ra′tion** *n.* —**col·lab′o·ra′tor** (-rā′tər) *n.*

col·lab·o·ra·tion·ist (kə-lăb′ə-rā′shən-ĭst) *n.* A person who collaborates with an enemy occupying his country. —**col·lab′o·ra′tion·ism′** *n.*

col·lage (kō-läzh′) *n.* An artistic composition of materials and objects pasted over a surface, often with unifying lines and color. [French, from *coller*, to glue, paste, from *colle*, glue, from Vulgar Latin *colla* (unattested), from Greek *kolla*. See **kolei-** in Appendix.*]

col·la·gen (kŏl′ə-jən) *n.* The fibrous albuminoid constituent of bone, cartilage, and connective tissue. [Greek *kolla*, glue (see **collage**) + -GEN.] —**col′la·gen′ic** (kŏl′ə-jĕn′ĭk), **col·lag′e·nous** (kə-lăj′ə-nəs) *adj.*

col·lapse (kə-lăps′) *v.* **-lapsed, -lapsing, -lapses.** —*intr.* **1.** To fall down or inward suddenly; cave in. **2.** To cease to function; break down suddenly in health or strength. **3.** To fold compactly. —*tr.* To cause to collapse. —*n.* **1.** The act of falling down or inward, as from loss of supports. **2.** An abrupt failure of function, strength, or health; breakdown. [From the past participle *collapsed*, from Latin *collāpsus*, past participle of *collābī*, to fall together, fall in ruin : *com-*, together + *lābī*, slide, fall (see **leb-**[1] in Appendix*).] —**col·laps′i·ble, col·laps′a·ble** *adj.* —**col·laps′i·bil′i·ty** *n.*

col·lar (kŏl′ər) *n.* **1.** The part of a garment that encircles the neck. **2.** A necklace. **3.** A restraining or identifying band of leather or metal put around the neck of an animal. **4.** The cushioned part of a harness that presses against the shoulders of a draft animal. **5.** *Biology.* An encircling structure or bandlike marking suggestive of a collar. **6.** *Machinery.* Any of various ringlike devices used to limit, guide, or secure a part. —*tr.v.* **collared, -laring, -lars. 1.** To furnish with a collar. **2.** *Informal.* To seize or detain. [Middle English *coler*, from Norman French, from Latin *collāre*, necklace, collar, from *collum*, neck. See **kwel-**[1] in Appendix.*]

col·lar·bone (kŏl′ər-bōn′) *n.* *Anatomy.* The **clavicle** *(see).*

collar cell. *Biology.* A **choanocyte** *(see).*

col·lard (kŏl′ərd) *n.* **1.** A variety of kale, *Brassica oleracea acephala*, having a crown of edible leaves. **2.** *Plural.* The leaves of this plant used as a vegetable. [Variant of COLEWORT.]

collat. collateral.

col·late (kə-lāt′, kŏl′āt′, kō′lāt′) *tr.v.* **-lated, -lating, -lates. 1.** To examine and compare carefully (texts) in order to note points of disagreement. **2.** *Bookbinding.* To examine (gathered sheets) in order to arrange them in proper sequence before binding. **3.** *Library Service.* To verify the order and completeness of (the pages of a volume). **4.** To assemble in proper numerical or logical sequence. **5.** *Ecclesiastical.* To admit (a cleric) to a benefice. [Latin *collātus* (past participle of *conferre*, to bring together) : *com-*, together + *lātus*, "carried" (see **tel-**[1] in Appendix*).] —**col·la′tor** (kə-lā′tər, kŏl′ā′tər, kō′lā′-) *n.*

col·lat·er·al (kə-lăt′ər-əl) *adj.* *Abbr.* **coll., collat. 1.** Situated or running side by side; parallel. **2.** Coinciding in tendency or effect; concomitant; accompanying. **3.** Serving to support or corroborate: *collateral evidence.* **4.** Of a secondary nature; subordinate. **5.** *Finance.* Of, designating, or guaranteed by a security pledged against the performance of an obligation: *a collateral loan.* **6.** Having an ancestor in common, but descended from a different line. —*n.* **1.** *Finance.* Property acceptable as security for a loan or other obligation. **2.** A collateral relative. [Middle English, from Medieval Latin *collaterālis* : *com-*, together + *laterālis*, of the side, LATERAL.] —**col·lat′er·al·ly** *adv.*

col·la·tion (kə-lā′shən, kō-, kō-) *n.* **1.** The act or process of collating. **2.** A description of the material aspects of a book. **3.** The appointment of a clergyman to a benefice. **4.** A light meal permitted on fast days. **5.** Any light meal.

col·la·tive (kə-lā′tĭv) *adj.* **1.** Collating. **2.** Presented or held by collation. Said of church benefices.

col·league (kŏl′ēg′) *n.* A fellow member of a profession, staff, or academic faculty; associate. See Synonyms at **partner.** [French *collègue*, from Old French, from Latin *collēga*, one chosen to serve with another : *com-*, together + *lēgāre*, to choose (see **leg-** in Appendix*).] —**col′league·ship′** *n.*

col·lect[1] (kə-lĕkt′) *v.* **-lected, -lecting, -lects.** —*tr.* **1.** To bring together in a group; gather; assemble. **2.** To accumulate as a hobby or for study. **3.** To call for and obtain payment of: *collect taxes.* **4.** To recover control of. —*intr.* **1.** To gather together; congregate; accumulate. **2.** To take in payments or donations. —See Synonyms at **gather.** —*adj.* *Abbr.* **col., coll.** With payment to be made by the receiver. —*adv.* So that the receiver is charged: *send a telegram collect.* [Middle English *collecten*, from Latin *colligere* (past participle *collectus*), to gather together : *com-*, together + *legere*, to gather (see **leg-** in Appendix*).] —**col·lect′i·ble, col·lect′a·ble** *adj.*

col·lect[2] (kŏl′ĭkt, -ĕkt′) *n.* *Ecclesiastical.* A brief formal prayer used in various Western liturgies before the epistle at Mass and varying with the day. [Middle English *collecte*, from Old French, from Medieval Latin *collēcta*, from *ōrātiō ad collēctam*, "prayer at the congregation," from Late Latin *collēcta*, assembly, from Latin *collēctus*, collected. See **collect.**]

col·lec·ta·ne·a (kŏl′ĕk-tā′nē-ə) *pl.n.* A selection of passages from one or more authors; an anthology. [Latin, "things collected," from *collēctāneus*, collected, from *collēctus*. See **collect.**]

col·lect·ed (kə-lĕk′tĭd) *adj.* *Abbr.* **col. 1.** Self-possessed; composed. **2.** Brought or placed together from various sources: *the collected poems of W.H. Auden.* —See Synonyms at **cool.** —**col·lect′ed·ly** *adv.* —**col·lect′ed·ness** *n.*

col·lec·tion (kə-lĕk′shən) *n.* *Abbr.* **coll. 1.** The act or process of collecting. **2.** A group of objects or works to be seen, studied, or kept together. **3.** An accumulation; deposit. **4. a.** A collecting of money, as in church. **b.** The sum collected.

col·lec·tive (kə-lĕk′tĭv) *adj.* **1.** Formed by collecting; assembled or accumulated into a whole. **2.** Of, pertaining to, characteristic of, or made by a number of individuals taken or acting as a group: *a collective decision.* —*n.* **1.** A collective enterprise or the persons working in it. **2.** *Grammar.* A **collective noun** *(see).* —**col·lec′tive·ly** *adv.* —**col·lec′tive·ness** *n.*

collective bargaining. Negotiation between the representatives of organized workers and their employer or employers to determine wages, hours, rules, and working conditions.

collective farm. A farm or a group of farms organized as a unit, managed and worked cooperatively by a group of laborers under governmental supervision. See **kibbutz, kolkhoz.**

collective fruit. *Botany.* A **multiple fruit** *(see).*

collective noun. *Grammar.* A noun that denotes a collection of persons or things regarded as a unit.

Usage: A collective noun takes a singular verb when it refers to the collection as a whole and a plural verb when it refers to the members of the collection as separate persons or things: *The orchestra was playing. The orchestra have all gone home.* A collective noun should not be treated as both singular and plural in the same construction. Thus: *The family is determined to press its* (not *their*) *claim.*

col·lec·tiv·ism (kə-lĕk′tə-vĭz′əm) *n.* The principle or system of ownership and control of the means of production and distribution by the people collectively. —**col·lec′tiv·ist** *adj.* & *n.*

col·lec·tiv·i·ty (kŏl′ĕk-tĭv′ə-tē, kə-lĕk′-) *n.* **1.** The condition or quality of being collective. **2.** The people as a whole.

col·lec·tiv·ize (kə-lĕk′tə-vīz′) *tr.v.* **-ized, -izing, -izes.** To organize (an economy, industry, or enterprise) on the basis of collectivism. —**col·lec′tiv·i·za′tion** *n.*

col·lec·tor (kə-lĕk′tər) *n.* **1.** A person or thing that collects. **2.** *Abbr.* **col., coll.** A person employed to collect taxes, duties, or other payments. **3.** A person who collects something, such as stamps. **4. a.** *Electricity.* A conducting contact between parts of an electric circuit in relative motion. **b.** *Electronics.* The output terminal of a three-terminal semiconducting device, especially of a transistor. —**col·lec′tor·ship′** *n.*

col·leen (kŏl′ēn′, kŏ-lēn′) *n.* An Irish girl. [Irish *cailīn*, diminutive of *caile*, girl, from Old Irish *calé*, probably from Latin *pellex*, concubine, akin to Greek *pallakē*, Sanskrit *pallavaki*, of non-Indo-European origin.]

col·lege (kŏl′ĭj) *n.* *Abbr.* **col., coll. 1.** A school of higher learning that grants the bachelor's degree in liberal arts or science or both. **2.** Any of the undergraduate divisions or schools of a university offering courses and granting degrees in a particular field, such as liberal arts or business administration. **3.** A technical or professional school, often affiliated with a university, offering the bachelor's or master's degree: *Teachers College.* **4.** The building or buildings occupied by any such school. **5.** *British.* A self-governing society of scholars for study or instruction, incorporated within a university. **6.** In France, an institution for secondary education not supported by the state. **7.** A company or assemblage; especially, a body of persons having a common purpose or common duties. **8.** A body of clergymen living together on an endowment. [Middle English, from Old French, from Latin *collēgium*, corporate institution, partnership, from *collēga*, COLLEAGUE.]

College of Arms. Heralds' College *(see).*

College of Cardinals. *Roman Catholic Church.* The body comprising all the cardinals that elects the Pope, assists him in governing the church, and administers the Holy See when vacant. Also called "Sacred College."

College of Heralds. Heralds' College *(see).*

col·le·gian (kə-lē′jən, -jē-ən) *n.* A college student or a recent college graduate.

col·le·giate (kə-lē′jĭt, -jē-ĭt) *adj.* Also **col·le·gi·al** (kə-lē′jē-əl, -jəl). *Abbr.* **col., coll. 1.** Of, pertaining to, or resembling a college. **2.** Of, for, or typical of college students. **3.** Of or pertaining to a collegiate church. [Medieval Latin *collēgiātus*, from Latin *collēgium*, COLLEGE.]

collegiate church. 1. A Roman Catholic or Anglican church other than a cathedral, having a chapter of canons and presided over by a dean or provost. **2. a.** A church in the United States associated with others under a common body of pastors. **b.** An association of such churches. **3.** A church in Scotland served by two or more ministers at the same time.

col·le·gi·um (kə-lē′jē-əm) *n.*, *pl.* **-gia** (-jē-ə) or **-giums.** An executive council or committee of equally empowered members; specifically, one supervising an industry, commissariat, or other organization in the Soviet Union. [Russian *kollegya*, from Latin *collēgium*, COLLEGE.]

col·len·chy·ma (kə-lĕng′kə-mə) *n.* *Botany.* Supportive tissue of plants, consisting of elongated, approximately rectangular cells with cell walls thickened at the corners. [New Latin, "glue tissue" : COLL(O)- + -ENCHYMA.] —**col′len·chym′a·tous** (kŏl′ən-kĭm′ə-təs) *adj.*

col·let (kŏl′ĭt) *n.* **1.** *Machinery.* A cone-shaped sleeve used in a lathe for holding circular or rodlike pieces. **2.** A metal collar used in watchmaking to join one end of a balance spring to the balance staff. **3.** A circular flange or rim, as in a ring, into which a gem is set. —*tr.v.* **colleted, -leting, -lets.** To set in or supply with a collet. [French, diminutive of *col*, neck, collar, from Latin *collum*, neck. See **kwel-**[1] in Appendix.*]

col·lide (kə-līd′) *intr.v.* **-lided, -liding, -lides. 1.** To come together with violent, direct impact. **2.** To meet in opposition;

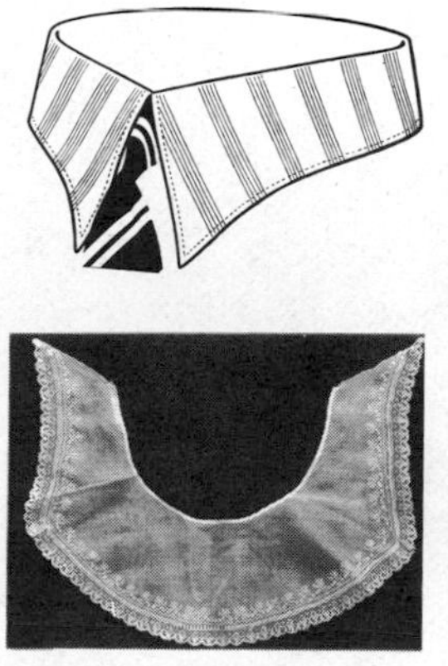

collar
Above: Man's soft collar of the early 20th century
Below: Woman's embroidered collar with bobbin lace, early 19th century

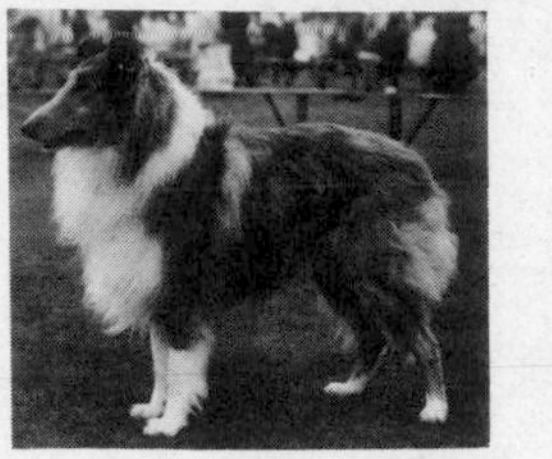
collie

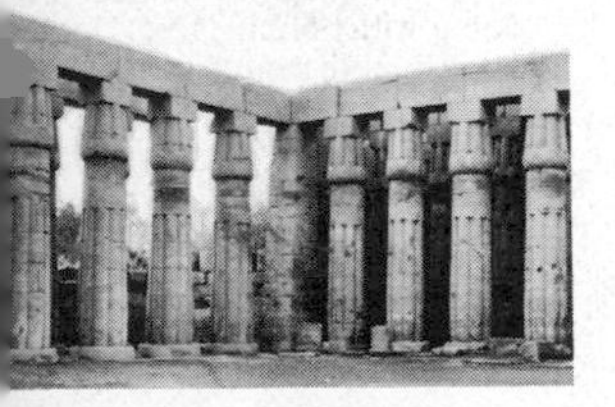
colonnade
Luxor, Egypt

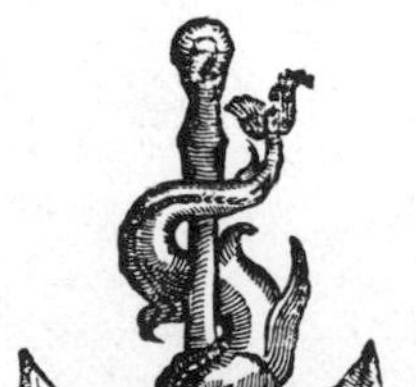
colophon
The colophon of
Aldus Manutius

clash; conflict. [Latin *collīdere* : *com-*, together + *laedere*, to strike, injure (see **lesion**).]

col·lie (kŏl′ē) *n.* A large dog of a breed originating in Scotland as a sheep dog, having long hair and a long, narrow muzzle. [Scottish, possibly from *colly*, "black like coal," from *coll*, variant of COAL.]

col·lier (kŏl′yər) *n. British.* **1.** A coal miner. **2.** A coal ship. [Middle English *colier*, from *col, cole*, COAL.]

col·lier·y (kŏl′yər-ē) *n., pl.* **-ies.** *British.* A coal mine.

col·li·gate (kŏl′ĭ-gāt′) *tr.v.* **-gated, -gating, -gates. 1.** To tie together. **2.** *Logic.* To bring (isolated observations) together by an explanation or hypothesis that applies to them all. [Latin *colligāre* : *com-*, together + *ligāre*, to tie (see **leig-**[1] in Appendix*).] **—col′li·ga′tion** *n.* **—col′li·ga′tive** *adj.*

col·li·mate (kŏl′ə-māt′) *tr.v.* **-mated, -mating, -mates. 1.** To make parallel; line up. **2.** To adjust the line of sight of (a transit, telescope, or other optical device). [New Latin *collimare*, to adjust, misreading of Latin *collīneāre*, to direct in a straight line : *com-* (intensive) + *līneāre*, to make straight, from *līnea*, LINE.] **—col′li·ma′tion** *n.*

col·li·ma·tor (kŏl′ə-mā′tər) *n.* Any device capable of collimating radiation, such as a long narrow tube in which strongly absorbing or reflecting walls permit only radiation traveling parallel to the tube axis to traverse the entire length.

col·lin·e·ar (kŏ′lĭn′ē-ər, kə-) *adj.* **1.** Lying on the same line. **2.** Containing a common line; coaxial. [COM- + LINEAR.] **—col·lin′e·ar·ly** *adv.*

col·lins (kŏl′ənz) *n.* A tall iced drink made with gin, vodka, rum, or other liquor, and lemon or lime juice, carbonated water, and sugar.

Col·lins (kŏl′ənz), **Michael.** 1890–1922. Irish revolutionary.

col·lin·si·a (kə-lĭn′zē-ə) *n.* Any of various North American plants of the genus *Collinsia*, having blue-and-white or purplish flowers. [New Latin, after Zaccheus *Collins* (1764–1831), American botanist.]

col·li·sion (kə-lĭzh′ən) *n.* **1.** A direct, violent striking together; crash. **2.** A clash of ideas or interests; a conflict. **3.** *Physics.* A dynamic event consisting of the interaction between two or more bodies, usually of very brief duration, resulting in a change of momentum of at least one participating body. [Middle English, from Latin *collīsiō*, from *collīdere*, COLLIDE.]

collo-, coll-. Indicates: **1.** Glue; for example, **collenchyma. 2.** Colloid; for example, **collotype.** [New Latin, from Greek *kolla*, glue. See **kolei-** in Appendix.*]

col·lo·cate (kŏl′ō-kāt′) *tr.v.* **-cated, -cating, -cates.** To place together or in proper order; arrange. [Latin *collocāre* : *com-*, together + *locāre*, to place, LOCATE.]

col·lo·ca·tion (kŏl′ō-kā′shən) *n.* **1. a.** The act of collocating. **b.** The state of being collocated. **2.** An arrangement or juxtaposition, especially of words.

Col·lo·di (kōl-lō′dē), **Carlo.** Pen name of Carlo Lorenzini. 1826–1890. Italian author; creator of Pinocchio.

col·lo·di·on (kə-lō′dē-ən) *n.* Also **col·lo·di·um** (kə-lō′dē-əm). A highly flammable, colorless or yellowish syrupy solution of **pyroxylin** *(see)* in ether and alcohol, used to hold surgical dressings, as a coating for certain skin diseases, and for making photographic plates. [New Latin *collodium*, from Greek *kollōdēs*, gluelike, from *kolla*, glue. See **kolei-** in Appendix.*]

col·logue (kə-lōg′) *intr.v.* **-logued, -loguing, -logues.** *British Regional.* To confer secretly; conspire. [Possibly from obsolete verb *colleague*, to be a colleague, ally, conspire (influenced by Latin *colloquī*, to converse), from Old French *colleguer*, from Latin *colligāre*, to tie together, COLLIGATE.]

col·loid (kŏl′oid′, kŏ′loid′) *n.* **1.** *Chemistry.* **a.** A suspension of finely divided particles in a continuous medium, especially a gaseous, liquid, or solid substance, such as an atmospheric fog, a paint, or foam rubber, containing suspended particles that are approximately 5 to 5,000 angstroms in size, do not settle out of the substance rapidly, and are not readily filtered. **b.** The particulate matter so suspended. See **sol, gel, emulsion, foam. 2.** *Physiology.* A clear gelatinous secretion of the thyroid gland. **3.** *Pathology.* Gelatinous material resulting from colloid degeneration or colloid carcinoma. *—adj.* Also **col·loi·dal** (kə-loid′l, kŏ-). Of, relating to, or having the nature of a colloid. [French *colloïde* : COLL(O)- + -OID.]

col·lop (kŏl′əp) *n.* **1.** A small portion or slice, especially of meat. **2.** A roll of flesh on the body. [Middle English *coloppe, colhoppe*†.]

col·lo·qui·al (kə-lō′kwē-əl) *adj. Abbr.* **coll., colloq. 1.** Characteristic of or appropriate to the spoken language or to writing that seeks its effect; informal in diction or style of expression. **2.** Relating to conversation; conversational. [From COLLOQUY.] **—col·lo′qui·al·ly** *adv.* **—col·lo′qui·al·ness** *n.*

col·lo·qui·al·ism (kə-lō′kwē-əl-ĭz′əm) *n. Abbr.* **coll., colloq. 1.** Colloquial style or quality. **2.** A colloquial expression.

col·lo·qui·um (kə-lō′kwē-əm) *n., pl.* **-ums** or **-quia** (-kwē-ə). **1.** An informal meeting for discussion. **2.** An academic seminar on some broad field of study, usually led by a different lecturer at each meeting. [Latin *colloquium*, COLLOQUY.]

col·lo·quy (kŏl′ə-kwē) *n., pl.* **-quies. 1.** A conversation, especially one that is formal or mannered. **2.** A written dialogue. [Latin *colloquium*, conversation, from *colloquī*, to converse : *com-*, together + *loquī*, to speak (see **tolkw-** in Appendix*).]

col·lo·type (kŏl′ə-tīp′) *n.* **1.** A printing process utilizing a glass plate with a gelatin surface carrying the image to be reproduced. Also called "photogelatin process." **2.** A print made by this process. [COLLO- + -TYPE.]

col·lude (kə-lo͞od′) *intr.v.* **-luded, -luding, -ludes.** To be in collusion; act together secretly; connive. [Latin *collūdere* : *com-*, together + *lūdere*, to play, deceive, from *lūdus*, game (see **leid-** in Appendix*).] **—col·lud′er** *n.*

col·lu·sion (kə-lo͞o′zhən) *n.* A secret agreement between two or more persons for a deceitful or fraudulent purpose. See Synonyms at **conspiracy.** [Middle English *collucioun*, from Old French *collusion*, from Latin *collūsiō*, from *collūdere*, COLLUDE.]

col·lu·sive (kə-lo͞o′sĭv, -zĭv) *adj.* Secretly arranged for fraudulent purposes. **—col·lu′sive·ly** *adv.* **—col·lu′sive·ness** *n.*

col·lu·vi·um (kə-lo͞o′vē-əm) *n., pl.* **-via** (-vē-ə) or **-ums.** A loose deposit of rock debris accumulated at the base of a cliff or slope. [Latin *colluvium, colluviō*, collection of filth, washings, from *colluere*, to wash thoroughly, wash out : *com-* (intensive) + *lavere*, to wash (see **lou-** in Appendix*).] **—col·lu′vi·al** *adj.*

col·ly (kŏl′ē) *tr.v.* **-lied, -lying, -lies.** *British Regional.* To blacken; make dirty with or as if with grime. *—n. British Regional.* Soot; grime. [Earlier *colie*, from Middle English *cole*, COAL.]

col·lyr·i·um (kə-lîr′ē-əm) *n., pl.* **-ums** or **-ia** (-ē-ə). A medicinal lotion applied to the eye; eyewash. [Latin, from Greek *kollurion*, poultice, diminutive of *kollura*†, roll of bread.]

col·ly·wob·bles (kŏl′ē-wŏb′əlz) *pl.n. Informal.* A pain in the bowels or stomach; bellyache. [New Latin *cholera morbus*, the disease cholera (influenced by COLIC and WOBBLE) : Latin *cholera*, CHOLERA + *morbus*, disease (see **morbid**).]

Col·mar (kōl′mär′; *French* kôl-mȧr′). *German* **Kol·mar** (kôl′-mär′). A city and industrial center of eastern France between the Vosges Mountains and the Rhine. Population, 52,000.

colo-, col-. Indicates the colon; for example, **colostomy, colitis.** [New Latin, from Latin *colon*, COLON (intestine).]

Colo. Colorado.

col·o·cynth (kŏl′ə-sĭnth′) *n.* **1.** A vine, *Citrullus colocynthis*, of the Mediterranean region, bearing a small, bitter fruit. **2.** The fruit of this plant, used as a cathartic. Also called "bitter apple." [Latin *colocynthis*, from Greek *kolokunthis*, from *kolokunthē*†, round gourd.]

co·logne (kə-lōn′) *n.* A scented liquid made of alcohol and various fragrant oils. Also called "cologne water," "eau de cologne." [French *eau de cologne*, "water of COLOGNE."]

Co·logne (kə-lōn′). *German* **Köln** (kœln). A city of West Germany on the western bank of the Rhine in North Rhine-Westphalia. Population, 848,000.

Co·lom·bi·a (kə-lŭm′bē-ə; *Spanish* kō-lôm′byä). *Abbr.* **Col.** Officially, Republic of Colombia. A republic of northwestern South America, 439,828 square miles in area. Population, 17,432,000. Capital, Bogotá. **—Co·lom′bi·an** *adj. & n.*

Co·lom·bo (kə-lŭm′bō). The capital of Ceylon, a seaport on the western coast. Population, 512,000.

Co·lom·bo, Cristoforo. See Christopher **Columbus.**

co·lon[1] (kō′lən) *n., pl.* **-lons** or **-la** (-lä) (for sense 2). **1. a.** A punctuation mark (:) used after a word introducing a quotation, explanation, example, or series, and after the salutation of a formal letter. **b.** The sign (:) used between numbers or groups of numbers in expressions of time (2:30 A.M.) and ratios (1:2). **2.** A section of a rhythmical period in Greek and Latin verse, consisting of two to six feet and having one principal accent. [Latin *cōlon*, unit of verses, from Greek *kōlon*, "limb." See **skel-**[3] in Appendix.*]

co·lon[2] (kō′lən) *n., pl.* **-lons** or **-la** (-lə). The section of the large intestine extending from the cecum to the rectum. [Middle English, from Latin, from Greek *kolon*†, large intestine.] **—co·lon′ic** (kə-lŏn′ĭk) *adj.*

co·lon[3] (kō-lōn′) *n., pl.* **-lons** (-lōnz′) or *Spanish* **colones** (kō-lō′näs). **1. a.** The basic monetary unit of Costa Rica, equal to 100 centimos. **b.** The basic monetary unit of El Salvador, equal to 100 centavos. See table of exchange rates at **currency. 2.** A coin or note worth one colon. [Spanish *colón*, after *Cristóbal* COLÓN.]

Co·lón (kō-lōn′). A port city of Panama, at the Caribbean entrance to the Panama Canal. Population, 60,000.

Co·lón, Cristóbal. See Christopher **Columbus.**

colon bacillus. A bacillus, *Escherichia coli*, found normally in all vertebrate intestinal tracts and occasionally virulent, causing pyelitis or infantile diarrhea.

colo·nel (kûr′nəl) *n. Abbr.* **Col. 1. a.** An officer in the U.S. Army, Air Force, or Marine Corps ranking immediately above a lieutenant colonel and below a brigadier general. **b.** An officer of similar rank in other military or paramilitary organizations. **2.** An honorary title awarded by some states of the United States. [French, from Old Italian *colonnello*, "commander of a column," diminutive of *colonna*, column (of soldiers), from Latin *columna*. See **kel-**[8] in Appendix.*] **—colo′nel·cy, colo′nel·ship′** *n.*

Colonel Blimp (blĭmp). An elderly, pompous, short-sighted reactionary, especially an army officer or government official. [After *Colonel Blimp*, character in the cartoons by David Low.]

co·lo·ni·al (kə-lō′nē-əl) *adj. Abbr.* **col. 1.** Of, pertaining to, or inhabiting a colony or colonies. **2.** *Often capital* **C. a.** Of or relating to the 13 British colonies that became the original United States of America. **b.** Of or relating to the colonial period in the United States. **3.** *Often capital* **C.** Designating an architectural style prevalent in the American colonies just before and during the Revolution. *—n.* An inhabitant of a colony. **—co·lo′ni·al·ly** *adv.*

co·lo·ni·al·ism (kə-lō′nē-ə-lĭz′əm) *n.* A policy by which a nation maintains or extends its control over foreign dependencies. **—co·lo′ni·al·ist** *n. & adj.*

col·o·nist (kŏl′ə-nĭst) *n.* **1.** An original settler or founder of a colony. **2.** An inhabitant of a colony.

co·lon·i·tis (kō′lə-nī′tĭs) *n. Pathology.* **Colitis** *(see).*

col·o·ni·za·tion (kŏl′ə-nə-zā′shən) *n.* **1.** The act or process of

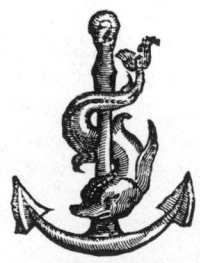

establishing a colony or colonies. **2.** *U.S. History.* The policy or plan of transferring emancipated slaves to Africa.

col·o·nize (kŏl′ə-nīz′) *v.* **-nized, -nizing, -nizes.** —*tr.* **1. a.** To establish a colony or colonies in. **b.** To migrate to and settle in; occupy as a colony. **2.** To establish in a new settlement; form a colony of. —*intr.* **1.** To set up or form a colony. **2.** To settle in a colony or colonies. —**col′o·niz′er** *n.*

col·on·nade (kŏl′ə-nād′) *n. Architecture.* A series of columns placed at regular intervals. [French, from Italian *colonnato,* from *colonna,* column, from Latin *columna.* See **kel-**[8] in Appendix.*] —**col′on·nad′ed** *adj.*

col·o·ny (kŏl′ə-nē) *n., pl.* **-nies. 1.** A group of emigrants or their descendants who settle in a distant land but remain subject to or intimately connected with the parent country. **2.** A territory thus settled. **3.** *Abbr.* **col.** Any region politically controlled by a distant country; dependency. **4.** *Capital* **C.** Any of the 13 British colonies that became the original United States of America and that included Connecticut, Delaware, Georgia, Maryland, Massachusetts, New Hampshire, New Jersey, New York, North Carolina, Pennsylvania, Rhode Island, South Carolina, and Virginia. **5.** A group of people with the same interests or ethnic origin concentrated in a particular area. **6.** The area or place occupied by such a group. **7.** A group of the same kind of animals or plants living or growing together. **8.** *Microbiology.* A visible growth of microorganisms in a nutrient medium. [Middle English *colonie,* from Old French, from Latin *colōnia,* farm, settlement, from *colōnus,* farmer, settler, from *colere,* to cultivate, inhabit. See **kwel-**[1] in Appendix.*]

col·o·phon (kŏl′ə-fŏn′, -fən) *n.* **1.** An inscription placed usually at the end of a book, giving facts pertaining to its publication. **2.** A publisher's emblem or trademark placed usually on the title page of a book. [Latin *colophōn,* from Greek *kolophōn,* summit, finishing. See **kel-**[8] in Appendix.*]

col·or (kŭl′ər) *n. Also chiefly British* **col·our.** *Abbr.* **col. 1.** That aspect of things that is caused by differing qualities of the light reflected or emitted by them. It may be defined in terms of the observer (sense a), or of the light (sense b): **a.** The appearance of objects or light sources described in terms of the individual's perception of them, involving hue, lightness, and saturation for objects, and hue, brightness, and saturation for light sources. **b.** The characteristics of light by which the individual is made aware of objects or light sources through the receptors of the eye, described in terms of dominant wavelength, luminance, and purity. *Note:* The *Explanation of the Color Definitions,* with the accompanying figures, outlines the method of defining colors in this Dictionary. **2.** A dye, pigment, paint, or other substance that imparts color. **3.** Complexion; skin tone. **4. a.** A ruddy complexion. **b.** A reddening of the face; a blush. **5.** The complexion of a person not classed as a Caucasian, especially that of a Negro. **6.** *Plural.* A flag or banner, as of a country, organization, or military unit. **7.** *Plural.* Any distinguishing symbol, badge, ribbon, or mark: *the colors of a college.* **8.** *Plural.* One's opinion or position: *Stick to your colors.* **9.** *Usually plural.* Character or nature: *change colors like a chameleon.* **10.** Outward, often deceptive appearance. **11.** Appearance of truth or authenticity; plausibility. **12.** Variety of effect or expression. **13.** The use of realistic or picturesque detail. **14.** *Painting.* The use or effect of color as distinct from form. **15.** *Music.* Tonal quality. **16.** *Printing.* The amount, shade, or tone of ink used. **17.** *Law.* An apparent or prima-facie right, pretext, or ground. **18.** *Plural.* The salute made during the ceremony of raising or lowering the flag. **19.** A particle or bit of gold found in auriferous gravel or sand. —**change color. 1.** To turn pale. **2.** To become red in the face; to blush. —**lose color.** To become pale. —**with flying colors.** With great success. —*v.* **colored, -oring, -ors.** *Also chiefly British* **col·our.** —*tr.* **1.** To impart color to or change the color of. **2.** To give a distinctive character or quality to; modify or influence. **3.** To misrepresent, especially by distortion or exaggeration. —*intr.* **1.** To take on color or become colored. **2.** To change color. **3.** To become red in the face; to blush. [Middle English *colour,* from Old French, from Latin *color.* See **kel-**[4] in Appendix.*] —**col′or** *adj.* —**col′or·er** *n.*

col·or·a·ble (kŭl′ər-ə-bəl) *adj.* **1.** Capable of being colored. **2.** Seemingly true or genuine; specious. —**col′or·a·bil′i·ty, col′or·a·ble·ness** *n.* —**col′or·a·bly** *adv.*

col·o·ra·do (kŏl′ə-rä′dō) *adj.* Of medium strength and color. Said of cigars. [Spanish, reddish, "colored," from *colorar,* to color, from Latin *colōrāre,* to color. See **COLOR.**]

Col·o·ra·do (kŏl′ə-rä′dō, -răd′ə). *Abbr.* **Colo.** A Rocky Mountain state of the United States, occupying 104,247 square miles in the west-central part of the country; admitted to the Union in 1876. Population, 1,969,000. Capital, Denver. See map at **United States of America.** [After the **COLORADO RIVER.**] —**Col′o·ra′dan** *adj. & n.*

Col·o·ra·do Desert (kŏl′ə-rä′dō, -răd′ə). A hot, arid region in southeastern California and northwestern Mexico.

Colorado potato beetle. The **potato beetle** *(see).*

Col·o·ra·do River (kŏl′ə-rä′dō, -răd′ə). **1.** A river rising in north-central Colorado and flowing 1,450 miles through Utah and Arizona to empty into the northern end of the Gulf of California. **2.** A river rising in northwestern Texas and flowing 970 miles southeast to the Gulf of Mexico. **3.** A river rising in the Andes Mountains of west-central Argentina and flowing 530 miles southeast to the Atlantic Ocean. [Spanish *Rio Colorado,* "reddish river." See **colorado.**]

Col·o·ra·do Springs (kŏl′ə-rä′dō, -răd′ə). A city and resort of central Colorado; the site of the U.S. Air Force Academy. Population, 70,000.

EXPLANATION OF THE COLOR DEFINITIONS

Definitions of color names used in this Dictionary follow the method recommended by the Inter-Society Color Council as it has been developed at the National Bureau of Standards (the ISCC-NBS system). The method is designed to provide a means of designating color sufficiently standardized to be acceptable and usable in science, sufficiently broad for art and industry, and sufficiently familiar to be understood, at least in a general way, by the public.

The method is simple in principle. The terms *light, medium,* and *dark* designate decreasing degrees of lightness, and the adverb *very* extends the lightness scale to *very light* and *very dark.* The adjectives *grayish, moderate, strong,* and *vivid* designate increasing degrees of saturation. These terms with the nouns *white, gray,* and *black,* and a series of hue names used both as nouns and in adjectival form, as shown in the table at the bottom of the column, combine to form names for describing color in terms of its three perceptual attributes: **hue, lightness,** and **saturation** *(all of which see).* Certain adjectives cover combinations of lightness and saturation, as *brilliant* for *light* and *strong; pale* for *light* and *grayish;* and *deep* for *dark* and *strong.*

In the ISCC-NBS system the boundaries of each color name are fixed. These are defined in terms of the Munsell color notation, which specifies colors on numerical scales of hue, **value** *(see),* and **chroma** *(see),* which can be expressed as accurately as desired.

The Munsell system is represented by a collection of color chips, forming an atlas of charts that represent equal visual (not physical) intervals for a gray to white background, so that under set conditions the hue, value, and chroma of the chips correlate closely with the hue, lightness, and saturation of the perceived **color** (sense 1a).

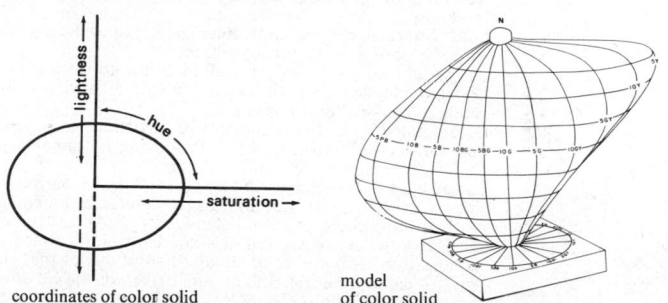

coordinates of color solid   model of color solid

The relationship of these attributes can be explained by reference to what is known as a color solid, in which *hue* extends in a rotary direction clockwise about the neutral axis from red through the hues in spectrum order back to red; *lightness* extends in the vertical direction from black at the bottom through a series of grays to white at the top; and *saturation* extends in a radial direction horizontally from the central neutral axis, at which the saturation is zero, out to the strongest saturation, as far as it may extend from the central axis.

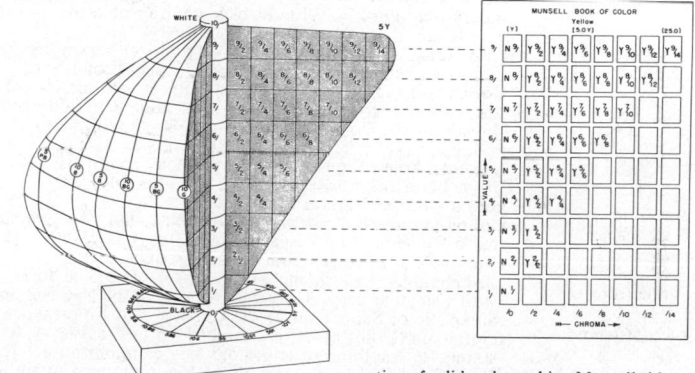

section of solid and matching Munsell chips

In the ISCC-NBS system the color solid is divided into 267 blocks, each of which defines a color name. These vary in size from the smaller and more tightly and irregularly packed blocks in the red, pink, orange, and brown regions to larger and more open blocks in the blue and purple regions. The method makes it possible to describe any color in a way that can be understood, and in a number of color names limited to 267, which cover about all the color differences that can be remembered.

If some of the color-name definitions in this Dictionary seem to cover a wider range than seems familiar, it is because different sources have based standards on different samples representing the same name. For further details on the method, especially with regard to colorimetry, consult National Bureau of Standards Circular 553, *The ISCC-NBS Method of Designating Colors and a Dictionary of Color Names,* and a color-chart supplement, *ISCC-NBS Centroid Color Charts, NBS Standard Sample No. 2106.*

Hue Names used in ISCC-NBS System

red	purple
reddish orange	reddish purple
orange	purplish red
orange yellow	purplish pink
yellow	pink
greenish yellow	yellowish pink
yellow green	brownish pink
yellowish green	brownish orange
green	reddish brown
bluish green	brown
greenish blue	yellowish brown
blue	olive brown
purplish blue	olive
violet	olive green

color-name blocks in purple region of solid

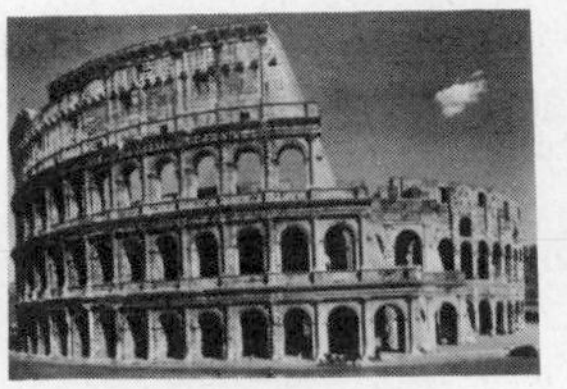

Colosseum

col·or·ant (kŭl′ər-ənt) *n.* Anything that colors or modifies the color of something else, especially a dye, pigment, ink, or paint.
col·or·a·tion (kŭl′ə-rā′shən) *n.* Arrangement of colors.
col·or·a·tu·ra (kŭl′ər-ə-tŏŏr′ə, -tyŏŏr′ə) *n.* **1.** Florid ornamental trills and runs in vocal music. **2.** Music characterized by such ornamentation. **3.** A soprano specializing in this. [Obsolete Italian, "coloring," from Late Latin *colōrātūra,* from Latin *colōrāre,* to color, from *color,* COLOR.]
color bar. **Color line** *(see).*
col·or·blind (kŭl′ər-blīnd′) *adj.* Partially or totally unable to distinguish certain colors. —**col′or·blind′ness** *n.*
col·or·breed (kŭl′ər-brēd′) *tr.v.* **-bred** (-brĕd′), **-breeding, -breeds.** To breed (plants or animals) selectively to produce new or desired colors.
col·or·cast (kŭl′ər-kăst′, -käst′) *v.* **-cast** or **-casted, -casting, -casts.** —*tr.* To broadcast (a television program) in color. —*intr.* To televise in color. —*n.* A broadcast in color. [COLOR + (BROAD)CAST.]
col·ored (kŭl′ərd) *adj.* **1.** Having color. **2.** *Often capital* **C.** Designating a dark-skinned people, especially Negroes. **3.** Distorted or biased, as by irrelevant or incorrect information. —*n.* Also **Col·ored. 1.** A colored person or persons. **2.** A person regarded as the product of mixed racial strains.
col·or·fast (kŭl′ər-făst′, -fäst) *adj.* Having color that will not run or fade with washing or wear. Said of fabrics. —**col′or·fast′ness** *n.*
color filter. A photographic **filter** *(see)* used to increase contrast or take photographs through haze.
col·or·ful (kŭl′ər-fəl) *adj.* **1.** Full of color; abounding in colors. **2.** Characterized by rich variety; vivid; distinctive. —**col′or·ful·ly** *adv.* —**col′or·ful·ness** *n.*
color guard. The flag's ceremonial escort.
col·or·if·ic (kŭl′ə-rĭf′ĭk) *adj.* **1.** Producing or imparting color. **2.** Of or pertaining to color.
col·or·im·e·ter (kŭl′ə-rĭm′ə-tər) *n.* **1.** Any of various instruments used to determine or specify colors, as by comparison with spectroscopic or visual standards. **2.** An instrument that measures the concentration of a known solution constituent by comparison with colors of standard solutions of that constituent. —**col′or·i·met′ric** (kŭl′ər-ə-mĕt′rĭk) *adj.* —**col′or·i·met′ri·cal·ly** *adv.* —**col′or·im′e·try** *n.*
col·or·ing (kŭl′ər-ĭng) *n.* **1.** The art, manner, or process of applying color. **2.** Any substance used to color something. **3.** Appearance with regard to color. **4.** Characteristic aspect, tone, or style. **5.** False or misleading appearance.
col·or·ist (kŭl′ər-ĭst) *n.* A painter skilled in achieving special effects with color. —**col′or·is′tic** *adj.*
col·or·less (kŭl′ər-lĭs) *adj.* **1.** Without color. **2.** Weak or dull in color; pallid. **3.** Lacking animation, variety, or distinction; uninteresting; dull. **4.** Without bias; neutral; objective. —**col′or·less·ly** *adv.* —**col′or·less·ness** *n.*
color line. A social, economic, or political barrier separating nonwhite persons from whites. Also called "color bar."
Co·los·sae (kə-lŏs′ē). An ancient city in central Asia Minor, the seat of a congregation to which Saint Paul addressed the Epistle to the Colossians. —**Co·los′sian** (kə-lŏsh′ən) *adj. & n.*
co·los·sal (kə-lŏs′əl) *adj.* Enormous in size, extent, or degree; gigantic; tremendous. See Synonyms at **enormous.** [French, from Latin *colossus,* COLOSSUS.] —**co·los′sal·ly** *adv.*
col·os·se·um. Variant of **coliseum.**
Col·os·se·um (kŏl′ə-sē′əm). Also **Col·i·se·um.** An amphitheater in Rome built by Vespasian and Titus (A.D. 75–80). [Latin, from *colossēus,* huge, from *colossus,* COLOSSUS.]
Co·los·sians (kə-lŏsh′ənz, -lŏs′ē-ənz) *n.* Plural in form, used with a singular verb. *Abbr.* **Col.** A book of the New Testament, an epistle of Saint Paul to the Christians of Colossae.
co·los·sus (kə-lŏs′əs) *n., pl.* **-lossi** (-lŏs′ī′) or **-suses. 1.** A huge statue. **2.** Anything of enormous size or importance. [Latin, from Greek *kolossos,* probably of Mediterranean origin.]
Colossus of Rhodes. A huge statue, 120 feet high, of Apollo, built about 280 B.C. It was formerly set at the entrance to the harbor of ancient Rhodes. Also called "Colossus."
co·los·to·my (kə-lŏs′tə-mē) *n., pl.* **-mies.** The surgical construction of an artificial excretory opening from the colon. [COLO- + -STOMY.]
co·los·trum (kə-lŏs′trəm) *n.* The first milk secreted by the mammary glands immediately after childbirth, lasting for a few days. Also called "foremilk." [Latin *colostrum, colostra*†.]
col·our. *Chiefly British.* Variant of **color.**
–colous. Indicates habitat in or among; for example, **arenicolous.** [From Latin *-cola,* inhabitant. See **kwel-** in Appendix.*]
col·pi·tis (kŏl-pī′tĭs) *n.* Inflammation of the vaginal mucous membrane. [New Latin : Greek *kolpos,* bosom, womb, vagina (see **kwelp-** in Appendix*) + -ITIS.]
col·por·tage (kŏl′pôr′tĭj, -pōr′tĭj) *n.* The work of a colporteur.
col·por·teur (kŏl′pôr′tər, -pōr′tər) *n.* A peddler of devotional literature. [French, from Old French *comporteur* (influenced by *col,* neck), from *comporter,* to peddle, COMPORT.]
colt (kōlt) *n.* **1.** A young male horse. **2.** A youthful or inexperienced person; a novice or beginner. **3.** A rope whip formerly used for shipboard discipline. [Middle English *colt,* Old English *colt,* young ass or camel, akin to Swedish dialectal *kult, kulter*†, half-grown animal, boy.]
Colt (kōlt) *n.* A trademark for a type of revolver. [Full trademark *Colt's Revolver,* invented by Samuel COLT.]
Colt (kōlt), **Samuel.** 1814–1862. American inventor and manufacturer of firearms.
col·ter (kōl′tər) *n.* Also **coul·ter.** A blade or wheel on a plow for making vertical cuts in the sod. [Middle English *culter, colter,* from Old English *culter* and Old French *coltre,* both from Latin *culter,* knife, plowshare. See **skel-¹** in Appendix.*]

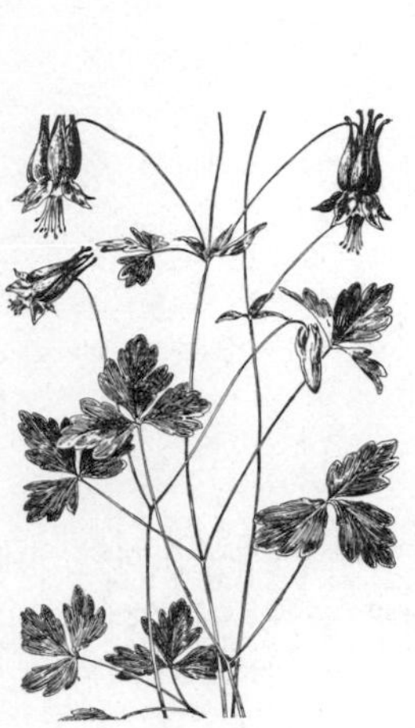

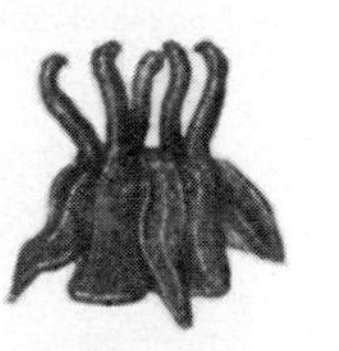

columbine
Above: Aquilegia canadensis
Below: Marginal illustration from *The Hours of Catherine of Cleves*

colt·ish (kōl′tĭsh) *adj.* **1.** Of or like a colt. **2.** Lively and playful; frisky. —**colt′ish·ly** *adv.* —**colt′ish·ness** *n.*
colts·foot (kōlts′fŏŏt′) *n., pl.* **-foots.** A plant, *Tussilago farfara,* native to the Old World, having yellow flowers that appear before the heart-shaped leaves. [From the shape of its leaves.]
col·u·brid (kŏl′ə-brĭd, kŏl′yə-) *n.* Any of numerous chiefly nonvenomous snakes of the family Colubridae, which includes the king snakes and garter snakes. —*adj.* Also **col·u·brine** (-brīn′). Of or belonging to the Colubridae. [New Latin *Colubridae,* from Latin *coluber,* snake. See **cobra.**]
co·lu·go (kə-lōō′gō) *n., pl.* **-gos.** A mammal, the **flying lemur** *(see).* [Malay.]
Col·um (kŏl′əm), **Padraic.** Born 1881. Irish poet and playwright; a founder of Irish theater.
Co·lum·ba (kə-lŭm′bə) *n.* A constellation in the Southern Hemisphere near Caelum and Puppis. Also called the "Dove." [New Latin, from Latin *columba,* dove. See **kel-⁷** in Appendix.*]
Co·lum·ba (kə-lŭm′bə), **Saint.** A.D. 521–597. Irish missionary to the northern Picts.
Co·lum·ban (kə-lŭm′bən), **Saint.** Also **Co·lum·ban·us** (-bən-əs). A.D. 543?–615. Irish missionary and scholar.
col·um·bar·i·um (kŏl′əm-bâr′ē-əm) *n., pl.* **-ia** (-ē-ə). Also **col·um·bar·y** (kŏl′əm-bĕr′ē) *pl.* **-ies. 1. a.** A vault with niches for urns containing ashes of the dead. **b.** One of the niches in such a vault. **2. a.** A dovecote. **b.** A pigeonhole in a dovecote. [Middle English *columba(i)re,* dovecote, from Latin *columbārium,* from *columba,* dove. See **kel-⁷** in Appendix.*]
Co·lum·bi·a¹ (kə-lŭm′bē-ə) *n. Poetic.* A feminine personification of the United States. [After Christopher COLUMBUS.]
Co·lum·bi·a² (kə-lŭm′bē-ə). **1.** The capital of South Carolina, situated in the central part of the state. Population, 97,400. **2.** A river rising in southeastern British Columbia, Canada, and flowing 1,200 miles to the Pacific Ocean, forming most of the Washington-Oregon border along its course.
Co·lum·bi·a, Cape (kə-lŭm′bē-ə). A cape on the northern coast of Ellesmere Island, Canada. It is the northernmost point of Canada.
Co·lum·bi·a, District of. See **District of Columbia.**
Co·lum·bi·an (kə-lŭm′bē-ən) *adj.* **1.** Of or pertaining to the United States. **2.** Of or pertaining to Christopher Columbus.
col·um·bine (kŏl′əm-bīn′) *n.* Any of several plants of the genus *Aquilegia,* having variously colored flowers with five conspicuously spurred petals. —*adj.* Dovelike. [Middle English, from Medieval Latin *(herba) columbīna,* from Latin *columbīnus,* dovelike (from the resemblance of the inverted flower to a cluster of five doves), from *columba,* dove. See **kel-⁷** in Appendix.*]
co·lum·bite (kə-lŭm′bīt′) *n.* A black mineral, essentially (Fe, Mn)(Nb, $Ta)_2O_6$, used as a source of niobium and tantalum. [COLUMB(IUM) + -ITE.]
co·lum·bi·um (kə-lŭm′bē-əm) *n. Symbol* **Cb** The element **niobium** *(see).* [New Latin, after COLUMBIA (United States), because it was discovered in a mineral found in Connecticut.] —**co·lum′bic** *adj.*
Co·lum·bus (kə-lŭm′bəs). **1.** The capital of Ohio and an industrial city on the Scioto River in the central part of the state. Population, 471,000. **2.** An industrial city of western Georgia, on the Chattahoochee River. Population, 116,800.
Co·lum·bus (kə-lŭm′bəs), **Christopher.** *Spanish* **Cristobal Colón** (kō-lôn′); *Italian* **Cristoforo Co·lom·bo** (kō-lōm′bō). 1451–1506. Italian navigator in the service of Spain; opened the New World to exploration.
Columbus Day. October 12, a legal holiday in most of the United States in honor of Christopher Columbus.
col·u·mel·la (kŏl′yə-mĕl′ə, kŏl′ə-) *n., pl.* **-mellae** (-mĕl′ē). Any of several small, columnlike structures in various plants and animals. [New Latin, from Latin, diminutive of *columna,* COLUMN.] —**col′u·mel′lar** (-mĕl′ər) *adj.*
col·umn (kŏl′əm) *n. Abbr.* **col., clm. 1.** A supporting pillar consisting of a base, a cylindrical shaft, and a capital. **2.** Anything resembling a pillar in form or function. **3.** One of two or more vertical sections of typed lines lying side by side on a page and separated by a rule or blank space. **4.** A feature article that appears regularly in a newspaper or other periodical. **5.** A formation, as of troops, vehicles, ships, or aircraft, in which all elements follow one behind the other. **6.** *Botany.* An organ formed by the fusion of stamens, or of stamens and pistils, as in the orchid. [Middle English *columpne,* from Old French *colomne,* from Latin *columna.* See **kel-⁸** in Appendix.*] —**co·lum′nar** (kə-lŭm′nər), **col′umned** (kŏl′əmd) *adj.*
co·lum·ni·a·tion (kə-lŭm′nē-ā′shən) *n.* The use or arrangement of columns in a building.
col·um·nist (kŏl′əm-nĭst, -ə-mĭst) *n.* A writer of a newspaper column.
Col·ville River (kŏl′vĭl′, kōl′-). A river rising in the Brooks Range in northern Alaska and flowing 320 miles east and then north to the Beaufort Sea.
col·za (kŏl′zə, kōl′-) *n.* A plant, **rape** *(see).* [French, from Dutch *koolzaad,* "cabbage seed" : *kool,* cabbage, from Middle Dutch *cōle,* from Latin *caulis,* stalk of plant (see **kaul-** in Appendix*) + *zaad,* seed, from Middle Dutch *saet* (see **sē-¹** in Appendix*).]
com–. *Rare.* Indicates with, together, jointly; for example, **commeasure, commingle.** [In borrowed Latin compounds, *com-* indicates: 1. With, together, joint, jointly, mutually, collectively, as in **compose, compact.** 2. Altogether, comprehensively, inclusively, intensively, as in **comfort, combust.** 3. Same, similar, as in **concord, consubstantial.** 4. Together in mind, mentally, as

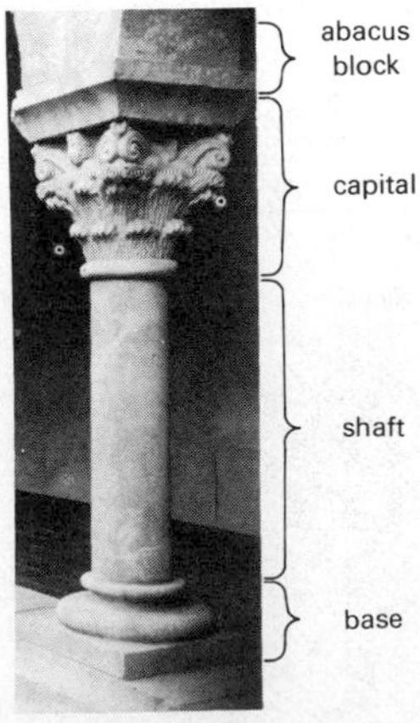
abacus block
capital
shaft
base

column

in **compute, comprehend.** (The semantic function of *com-* is often so indistinct as to be indefinable, as in **concave.**) Before *l* and *r, com-* is assimilated to *col-* and *cor-;* before *h, gn,* and usually before vowels, it is reduced to *co-* (hence English **co-**); before all other consonants except *b, p,* and *m,* it becomes *con-. Com-* is the preverbal form of the Old Latin preposition *com,* which in classical Latin became *cum,* with. See **kom** in Appendix.*]

com. **1.** comedy; comic. **2.** comma. **3.** commentary. **4.** commerce; commercial. **5.** commissioner. **6.** committee. **7.** common. **8.** commune. **9.** communication. **10.** community.

Com. **1.** commander. **2.** commission; commissioner. **3.** committee. **4.** commodore. **5.** Communist.

co·ma[1] (kō′mə) *n., pl.* **-mas.** A deep, prolonged unconsciousness, usually the result of injury, disease, or poison. [New Latin, from Greek *kōma,* deep sleep, lethargy. See **keme-** in Appendix.*]

co·ma[2] (kō′mə) *n., pl.* **-mae** (-mē). **1.** *Astronomy.* The nebulous luminescent cloud containing the nucleus and constituting the major portion of the head of a comet. **2.** *Botany.* A tuft of hairs, as on some seeds. **3.** *Optics.* A diffuse pear-shaped image of a point source. [Latin, hair, from Greek *komē.* See **comet.**] —**co′mal** *adj.*

Co·ma Ber·e·ni·ces (kō′mə bĕr′ə-nī′sēz). A constellation in the northern sky near Boötes and Leo. It contains the coma cluster of galaxies.

Co·man·che (kə-măn′chē) *n., pl.* **Comanche** or **-ches.** **1.** A tribe of Uto-Aztecan-speaking North American Indians, formerly ranging over the western plains from Wyoming to Texas, now living in Oklahoma. **2.** A member of this tribe. **3.** The language of this tribe. [Spanish, from Ute *kimanči,* from *kima-,* "stranger."] —**Co·man′che** *adj.*

Co·man·che·an (kə-măn′chē-ən) *adj.* Of, belonging to, or designating the geologic time, system of rocks, or sedimentary deposits of the Mesozoic era between the Jurassic and the Upper Cretaceous. See **geology.** —*n.* The Comanchean period. Preceded by *the.* Also called "Lower Cretaceous." [After *Comanche,* county in Texas, where limestone rocks of this period were first found.]

co·mate[1] (kō′māt′) *adj.* Also **co·mose** (-mōs′). *Botany.* Having or resembling a tuft of hairs. [Latin *comātus,* from *coma,* hair. See **coma** (cloud).]

co·mate[2] (kō-māt′, kō′māt′) *n.* A mate; companion.

co·ma·tose (kō′mə-tōs′, kŏm′ə-) *adj. Pathology.* **1.** Of, pertaining to, or affected with coma; unconscious. **2.** As if affected with coma; lethargic; torpid. —**co′ma·tose′ly** *adv.*

co·mat·u·lid (kə-măch′ŏŏ-lĭd) *n.* Also **co·mat·u·la** (-lə) *pl.* **-lae** (-lē′). Any of several marine invertebrates of the order Crinoidea, that are attached to a surface by a stalk when young but are free-swimming as adults. [New Latin *Comatulidae* (former designation), from Late Latin *comātulus,* with neatly curled hair, from Latin *comātus,* having hair, COMATE.]

comb (kōm) *n.* **1.** A thin, toothed strip of plastic, bone, rubber, or other material, used to smooth, arrange, or fasten the hair. **2.** Something resembling a comb in shape or use, as a card for dressing and cleansing wool or other fiber. **3.** A currycomb. **4.** The fleshy crest or ridge that grows on the crown of the head of domestic fowl and other birds and is most prominent in the male. **5.** Something suggesting a fowl's comb in appearance or position. **6.** A **honeycomb** *(see).* —*v.* **combed, combing, combs.** —*tr.* **1.** To dress or arrange with or as with a comb. **2.** To card (wool or other fiber). **3.** To search thoroughly; look through. —*intr.* To roll and break. Used of waves. [Middle English *comb,* Old English *comb, camb.* See **gembh-** in Appendix.*]

comb. **1.** combination. **2.** combining.

com·bat (kəm-băt′, kŏm′băt′) *v.* **-bated, -bating, -bats.** Also *chiefly British* **-batted, -batting.** —*tr.* **1.** To fight against; contend with; oppose in battle. **2.** To oppose vigorously; resist. —*intr.* To engage in fighting; contend; struggle. Used with *with* or *against.* —See Synonyms at **oppose.** —*n.* (kŏm′băt′). Fighting, especially armed battle; strife. See Synonyms at **conflict.** [Old French *combattre,* from Vulgar Latin *combattere* (unattested), to fight with : Latin *com-,* with + *battuere,* beat (see **battuere** in Appendix*).]

com·bat·ant (kəm-băt′ənt, kŏm′bə-tənt) *n.* One taking part in armed combat. —*adj.* Engaging in combat.

combat fatigue. A nervous disorder, usually temporary but sometimes leading to a permanent neurosis, brought on by the exhaustion and stress of combat or similar situations, and characterized by deep anxiety, depression, irritability, and other related symptoms. Also called "shell shock."

com·bat·ive (kəm-băt′ĭv) *adj.* Eager or disposed to fight. —**com·bat′ive·ly** *adv.* —**com·bat′ive·ness, com′ba·tiv′i·ty** *n.*

comb·er (kō′mər) *n.* **1.** One that combs. **2.** A long, cresting wave of the sea; breaker.

com·bi·na·tion (kŏm′bə-nā′shən) *n. Abbr.* **comb.** **1. a.** The act of combining. **b.** The state of being combined. **2.** Something resulting from combining; a compound; an aggregate. **3.** An alliance or association of persons or parties for a common purpose; association. **4.** A sequence of numbers or letters used to open a combination lock. **5.** A one-piece undergarment consisting of an undershirt or chemise and drawers. **6.** *Mathematics.* One or more elements selected from a set without regard to order of selection. —See Synonyms at **mixture, monopoly.** —**com′bi·na′tion·al** *adj.*

combination lock. A lock that will open only when its dial is turned through a predetermined sequence of positions identified on the dial face by numbers or letters.

com·bi·na·tive (kŏm′bə-nā′tĭv, kəm-bī′nə-tĭv) *adj.* **1.** Of, pertaining to, or resulting from combination. **2.** Tending, serving, or able to combine.

com·bine (kəm-bīn′) *v.* **-bined, -bining, -bines.** —*tr.* **1.** To bring into a state of unity; join; merge; blend. **2.** To possess or exhibit in combination. —*intr.* **1.** To become united; coalesce. **2.** To join forces for a common purpose; enter into an alliance. **3.** *Chemistry.* To form a chemical compound. —See Synonyms at **join, mix.** —*n.* (kŏm′bīn′). **1.** A harvesting machine that cuts, threshes, and cleans grain. **2.** An association of persons or groups united for the furtherance of commercial or political interests. **3.** A combination. —See Synonyms at **monopoly.** [Middle English *combinen,* from Old French *combiner,* from Late Latin *combīnāre* : Latin *com-,* together + *bīnī,* two at a time (see **dwō-** in Appendix*).] —**com·bin′er** *n.*

comb·ings (kō′mĭngz) *pl.n.* Hairs, wool, or other material removed with a comb.

combining form. *Grammar.* A word element that combines with other word forms to create compounds; for example, **-logy,** as in **gynecology; macro-,** as in **macrochemistry; Sino-,** as in **Sino-Soviet.**

combining weight. **Equivalent weight** *(see).*

comb jelly. A marine organism, a **ctenophore** *(see).*

com·bo (kŏm′bō) *n., pl.* **-bos.** *Informal.* **1.** A small group of musicians. **2.** *Slang.* The result or product of combining; a combination. [Short for COMBINATION.]

com·bust (kəm-bŭst′) *adj. Astrology.* Not visible because of proximity to the sun. Said of a star or planet. [Middle English, "burned," from Old French, from Latin *combustus,* past participle of *combūrere,* to burn up (infixed *b* probably influenced by *ambūrere,* to burn up) : *com-* (intensive) + *ūrere,* to burn (see **eus-** in Appendix*).]

com·bus·ti·ble (kəm-bŭs′tə-bəl) *adj.* **1.** Capable of igniting and burning. **2.** Easily aroused or excited. —*n.* A combustible substance. —**com·bus′ti·bil′i·ty** *n.* —**com·bus′ti·bly** *adv.*

com·bus·tion (kəm-bŭs′chən) *n.* **1.** A burning. **2.** *Chemistry.* A chemical change, especially oxidation, accompanied by the production of heat and light. **3.** Violent anger or agitation: *"the situation which permitted Negro combustion to slowly build up to the revolution point"* (Malcolm X). [Middle English, from Old French, from Late Latin *combustiō,* from Latin *combustus.* See **combust.**] —**com·bus′tive** *adj.*

combustion chamber. An enclosure in which combustion, especially of a fuel or propellant, is initiated and controlled.

comd. command.

comdg. commanding.

Comdr. commander.

Comdt. commandant.

come (kŭm) *intr.v.* **came** (kām), **coming, comes.** **1. a.** To advance toward the speaker or toward a specified place; to approach. **b.** To advance in a specified manner. **2.** To arrive as a result of moving or making progress. **3.** To reach a particular point in a series or as a result of orderly progression. **4.** To move into view; appear. **5.** To occur in time. **6. a.** To arrive at a particular result or end: *come to an understanding.* **b.** To arrive at or reach a particular state or condition. **c.** To move or be brought to a particular position: *The bus came to an abrupt halt.* **7.** To extend; reach: *hair coming to the waist.* **8.** To exist at a particular point or place: *The letter* T *comes before* U. **9. a.** To happen: *How did you come to know that?* **b.** To befall; happen to. **c.** To happen as a result: *This comes of your carelessness.* **10.** To fall to one. **11.** To occur in the mind: *An idea came to him.* **12. a.** To issue from; descend. **b.** To originate; be derived. **13.** To be a native or have been a resident of. **14.** To be moving toward a concluding or culminating stage; develop; evolve: *The project is coming along very well.* **15.** *Vulgar.* To experience orgasm. **16.** To become: *The knot came loose.* **17.** To be available or obtainable: *It comes in two sizes.* **18.** To prove or turn out to be: *His wish came true.* —**come about.** **1.** To occur; take place; happen. **2.** To turn around. **3.** *Nautical.* To change tack. —**come across.** **1.** To meet by chance. **2.** *Slang.* To do or give what is wanted. —**come again.** **1.** To come or go back; return. **2.** *Slang.* To say something once more; to repeat. —**come along.** To achieve success; to advance. —**come around** (or **round**). **1.** To recover; revive. **2.** To change opinion, support, or the like. —**come at.** **1.** To reach. **2.** To obtain; get. **3.** To attack; rush at. —**come between.** To cause separation or estrangement. —**come by.** To acquire; get. —**come down on** (or **upon**). **1.** To descend upon; to attack. **2.** *Informal.* To criticize; scold. —**come forward.** To volunteer one's services. —**come in.** **1.** To enter. **2.** To arrive. —**come in for.** *Informal.* **1.** To be eligible for. **2.** To get; receive; acquire. —**come into.** **1.** To obtain. **2.** To inherit. —**come off.** **1.** To become detached. **2.** To happen; occur. **3.** To reach the end; emerge from trial; acquit oneself. —**come out.** **1.** To be disclosed or made public. **2.** To state publicly. **3.** To make a formal social debut. **4.** To result; end up. —**come out with.** **1.** To disclose publicly; declare. **2.** To put into words; say. —**come over.** **1.** To happen to; seize; possess: *Strange feelings came over me.* **2.** To change sides. **3.** *Informal.* To visit. —**come through.** **1.** To succeed. **2.** *Informal.* To do as expected. **3.** To wear through, as cloth. —**come to.** **1.** To recover consciousness. **2.** To amount to. **3.** *Nautical.* **a.** To bring a ship's bow into the wind. **b.** To anchor. —**come up.** **1.** To manifest itself; arise. **2.** To be regurgitated. —**come upon.** **1.** To meet by accident. **2.** To attack. —**come up to.** **1.** To reach or extend to; meet. **2.** To equal. —**come up with.** *Informal.* To propose; produce. —**how come?** *Informal.* Why? —*interj.* Used to express anger, impatience, or remonstrance: *Come now, that's enough.* [Come, came, come; Middle English

comb

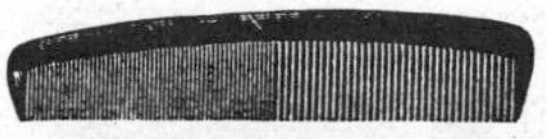

hairdressing comb

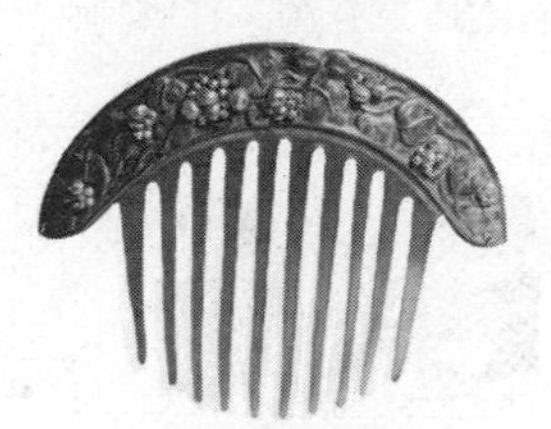

tortoiseshell comb with gold-and-pearl-decorated back

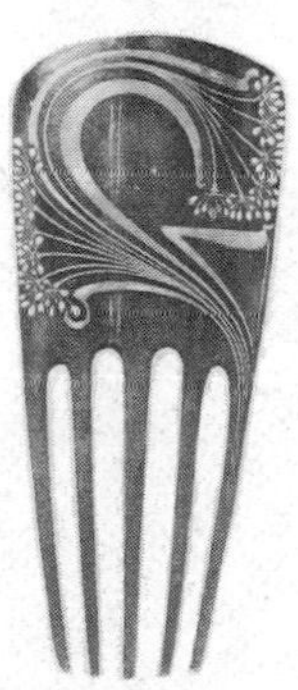

high comb

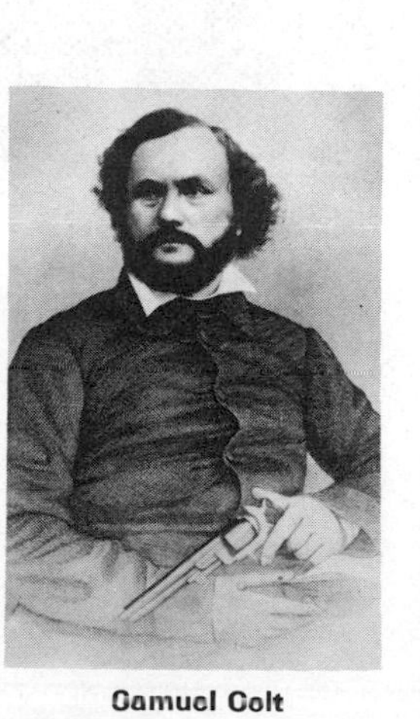

Samuel Colt

comen or *cumen* (infinitive), *com* or *cum* (past singular), *comen* or *camen* (past plural), *comen* or *cumen* (past participle), Old English *cuman, cōm, c(w)ōmon, cumen.* See **gwā-** in Appendix.*]

Usage: *Come* in the subjunctive form occurs in constructions such as these: *Come what will* (or *may*), *I propose to remain here. Our plans will be settled come Friday.*

come back. **1.** To return. **2.** To retort.

come·back (kŭm′băk′) *n.* **1.** A return to former prosperity or status. **2.** A retort; repartee. **3.** A recourse.

co·me·di·an (kə-mē′dē-ən) *n.* **1.** A professional entertainer who tells jokes or does impersonations or performs various other comic acts. **2.** An actor in comedy. **3.** A comedy writer. **4.** A person who amuses or tries to be amusing; clown.

co·me·dic (kə-mē′dĭk) *adj.* Of or relating to comedy.

co·me·di·enne (kə-mē′dē-ĕn′) *n.* A female comedian.

com·e·do (kŏm′ə-dō′) *n., pl.* **-dos** or **comedones** (kŏm′ə-dō′-nēz). A **blackhead** *(see).* [New Latin, from Latin *comedo,* glutton, from *comedere,* to eat up : *com-* (intensive) + *edere,* to eat (see **ed-** in Appendix*).]

come down. **1.** To lose status or wealth. **2.** To become ill. Used with *with: come down with the measles.*

come·down (kŭm′doun′) *n.* A decline or drop to a lower status or level.

com·e·dy (kŏm′ə-dē) *n., pl.* **-dies.** *Abbr.* **com.** **1.** A play, motion picture, or other work that is humorous in its treatment of theme and character and has a happy ending. **2.** Any literary composition with a theme appropriate to comedy or using the methods of comedy. **3.** The branch of literature dealing with comedies. **4.** The art or technique of composing comedy. **5.** A comic element of literature or life. **6.** A comic occurrence. [Middle English *comedie,* from Old French, from Latin *cōmoedia,* from Greek *kōmōidia,* from *kōmōidos,* originally "a singer in the revels" : *kōmos*†, revel + *ōidos, aoidēs,* singer, from *aeidein,* to sing (see **wed-²** in Appendix*).]

comedy of manners. A comedy satirizing fashionable society.

come-hith·er (kŭm′hĭth′ər) *adj.* Seductive; alluring.

come·ly (kŭm′lē) *adj.* **-lier, -liest.** **1.** Having a pleasing appearance; attractive; handsome; graceful. **2.** Suitable; proper; seemly. —See Synonyms at **beautiful.** [Middle English *comli, comeli(ch),* Old English *cȳmlic,* lovely, splendid, from *cȳme*†, beautiful.] —**come′li·ness** *n.*

Co·me·ni·us (kə-mē′nē-əs), **John Amos.** *Czech* **Jan Ko·men·ský** (kô′mən-skē). 1592–1670. Czech theologian and educator.

come on. **1.** To meet by surprise; to find. **2.** To make progress; improve; develop. **3.** To enter, as on a theater stage.

come-on (kŭm′ŏn′, -ôn′) *n.* Something offered to allure or attract; an inducement.

com·er (kŭm′ər) *n.* **1.** One that arrives or comes. **2.** *Informal.* One showing great promise.

co·mes·ti·ble (kə-mĕs′tə-bəl) *adj.* Edible. —*n.* Anything edible. [Old French, from Medieval Latin *comestibilis,* from Latin *comedere* (past participle *comestus*), to eat up : *com-* (intensive) + *edere,* eat (see **ed-** in Appendix*).]

com·et (kŏm′ĭt) *n. Astronomy.* A celestial body, observed only in that part of its orbit that is relatively close to the sun, having a head consisting of a solid nucleus surrounded by a nebulous coma up to 1.5 million miles in diameter, an elongated curved vapor tail arising from the coma when sufficiently close to the sun, and thought to consist chiefly of ammonia, methane, carbon dioxide, and water. [Middle English *comete,* Old English *comēta,* from Latin *comēta, comētēs,* from Greek *(astēr) komētēs,* "long-haired (star)," from *koman,* to wear long hair, from *komē*†, hair.] —**com′et·ar′y** (kŏm′ə-tĕr′ē), **co·met′ic** (kə-mĕt′ĭk) *adj.*

come·up·pance (kŭm′ŭp′əns) *n.* Also **come·up·ance.** *Informal.* Punishment or retribution that one deserves; one's just deserts. [From phrase *come up,* sense development obscured.]

com·fit (kŭm′fĭt, kŏm′-) *n.* A candy; confection; sweetmeat. [Middle English *confit,* from Old French, from Latin *confectum,* "preparation," from Latin *conficere,* to prepare : *com-* (intensive) + *facere,* to make (see **dhē-¹** in Appendix*).]

com·fort (kŭm′fərt) *tr.v.* **-forted, -forting, -forts.** **1.** To soothe in time of grief or fear; to console. **2.** To ease physically; relieve, as of pain. **3.** *Law.* To aid. —See Synonyms at **relieve.** —*n.* **1.** A state of ease or well-being. **2.** Relief; consolation; solace. **3.** Help; assistance. **4.** One that brings ease. **5.** Capacity to give physical ease and well-being: *enjoying the comfort of his favorite chair.* —See Synonyms at **rest.** [Middle English *comforten,* from Old French *conforter,* from Late Latin *confortāre,* to strengthen : Latin *com-* (intensive) + *fortis,* strong (see **bhergh-²** in Appendix*).] —**com′fort·ing·ly** *adv.*

com·fort·a·ble (kŭm′fər-tə-bəl, kŭmf′tər-bəl) *adj.* **1.** Providing or giving comfort. **2.** Being in a state of comfort; at ease. **3.** *Informal.* Sufficient; adequate: *comfortable earnings.* —**com′fort·a·ble·ness** *n.* —**com′fort·a·bly** *adv.*

Synonyms: *comfortable, cozy, snug, restful.* These words mean affording pleasurable ease. *Comfortable* implies the deliberate removal of sources of pain or distress. *Cozy* evokes the image of a warm room in winter and suggests cheerful or reassuring closeness. *Snug* is even closer; the image is of a warm bed. *Restful* suggests a seclusion and quiet conducive to ease. Metaphorically, the terms may acquire ironic overtones. Thus, *comfortable* may suggest lethargy or complacency, and *cozy,* a self-serving closeness of relationship.

com·fort·er (kŭm′fər-tər) *n.* **1.** One that comforts. **2.** *Capital* **C.** The Holy Spirit. **3.** A quilted bedcover. **4.** *Chiefly British.* A woolen neck scarf.

comfort station. A public toilet or rest room.

com·frey (kŭm′frē) *n., pl.* **-freys.** Any of several usually hairy or bristly plants of the genus *Symphytum,* native to the Old World, having clusters of variously colored flowers. [Middle English *conferie,* from Old French *cumfirie, confire,* from Latin *conferva,* a water plant, "healer," from *confervēre,* to boil together, heal : *com-,* together + *fervēre,* to boil (see **bhreu-²** in Appendix*).]

com·fy (kŭm′fē) *adj.* **-fier, -fiest.** *Informal.* Comfortable.

com·ic (kŏm′ĭk) *adj. Abbr.* **com.** **1.** Of, characteristic of, or pertaining to comedy. **2.** Of or pertaining to comic strips. **3.** Amusing; humorous. —*n. Abbr.* **com.** **1.** A person who is comical. **2.** *Plural. Informal.* Comic strips. **3.** *Informal.* A comic book. **4.** Anything that provokes humor in art or life. [Latin *cōmicus,* from Greek *kōmikos,* from *kōmos,* revel, merrymaking. See **comedy.**]

com·i·cal (kŏm′ĭ-kəl) *adj.* **1.** Provoking mirth; funny; amusing. **2.** Of or pertaining to comedy. —**com′i·cal′i·ty** (-kăl′ə-tē), **com′i·cal·ness** *n.* —**com′i·cal·ly** *adv.*

comic book. A booklet of comic strips, sometimes violent or sensational rather than humorous.

comic opera. An opera or operetta with a humorous plot, spoken dialogue, and, usually, a happy ending.

comic strip. A narrative series of cartoons.

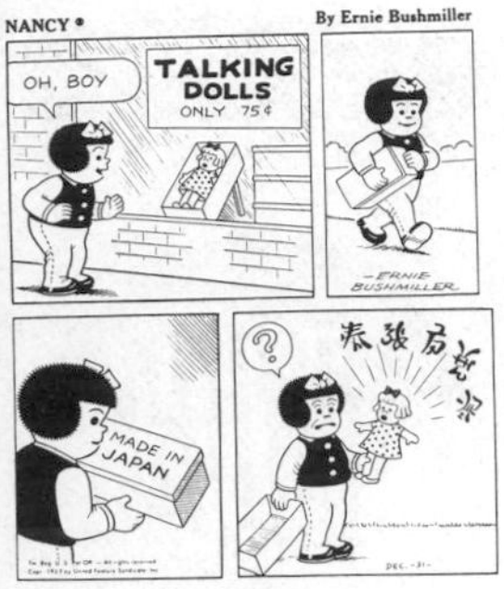

comic strip

Co·mines (kô-mēn′), **Philippe de.** Also **Com·mines.** 1447?–1509? French diplomat and historian; served Louis XI and Charles VIII.

com·ing (kŭm′ĭng) *adj.* **1.** Approaching; next. **2.** *Informal.* Showing promise of fame or success. —*n.* Arrival; advent.

com·ing-out (kŭm′ĭng-out′) *n. Informal.* A social debut.

Com·in·tern (kŏm′ĭn-tûrn) *n.* The Third **International** *(see)* or, especially, its executive committee in Moscow. [COM(MUNIST) INTERN(ATIONAL).]

co·mi·ti·a (kə-mĭsh′ē-ə, -mĭsh′ə) *n., pl.* **comitia.** A popular assembly in ancient Rome having legislative or electoral duties. [Latin, plural of *comitium,* meeting place : *com-,* together + *ire* (past participle *itus*), to go (see **ei-¹** in Appendix*).] —**co·mi′tial** (kə-mĭsh′əl) *adj.*

com·i·ty (kŏm′ə-tē) *n., pl.* **-ties.** Civility; courtesy. [Latin *cōmitās,* from *cōmis,* courteous. See **smei-** in Appendix.*]

comity of nations. **1.** Courteous recognition accorded by one nation to the laws and institutions of another. **2.** The nations observing such courtesy.

comm. **1.** commerce. **2.** commission; commissioner. **3.** commonwealth. **4.** communication.

com·ma (kŏm′ə) *n.* **1.** *Abbr.* **com.** A punctuation mark (,) used to indicate a separation of ideas or of elements within the structure of a sentence. See Usage note below. **2.** Any pause or separation; a caesura. **3.** Any of several butterflies of the genus *Polygonia,* having wings with brownish coloring and irregularly notched edges. [Latin, from Greek *komma,* a cut, section, clause, from *koptein,* to cut. See **skep-** in Appendix.*]

Usage: A comma cannot be used to separate independent clauses not connected by a conjunction, unless they are short and closely related: *I came, I saw, I conquered. It was not only false, it was libelous.* Otherwise, a semicolon or period must be used. When independent clauses are joined by a conjunction, a comma usually precedes the conjunction if the clauses are lengthy, and especially if they have different subjects or if confusion might result from omission of the comma: *It snowed yesterday, and today the road is closed. He was eager to set out, for the woods are splendid in October.* Dependent restrictive, or defining, clauses are never set off by commas: *The book that he requested is still missing.* Nonrestrictive clauses are generally set off: *The book, which was a gift from his teacher, is no longer in print.* Similarly, terms in apposition preceded by the nondefining *a* are separated by a comma: *a Whitman poem, "Song of Myself"*; those preceded by defining terms are often not separated: *the poem "Maud Muller"; my son Joe.* Two adjectives in succession are not separated by commas when the second precedes a noun with which it forms a sort of compound (in which case no pause is felt): *a rare second chance; an ugly old man.* In formal usage, the elements are separated by commas: *colored red, white, and blue.* In less formal contexts, the comma may be omitted before *and* if there is no possibility of resultant confusion. When commas are employed to set off a parenthetical passage, two are necessary: *Mr. Hay, of Montana, is the next speaker.* (Often, in such examples, both commas can be dropped, but not merely one.) Normally a single comma does not appear between the subject and its verb, though subject and verb may be separated by a passage set off by two commas: *The air, heavy with moisture, was like a warm blanket.*

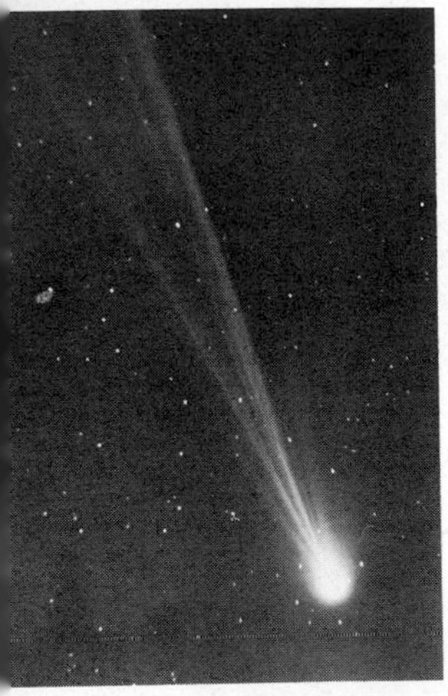
comet
Comet Alcock, photographed September 1, 1959

comma bacillus. A bacillus, *Vibrio comma,* that causes Asiatic cholera. [From its commalike shape.]

comma fault. *Grammar.* Improper use of a comma between independent clauses not joined by a conjunction. See Usage note at **comma.**

Com·ma·ger (kŏm′ə-jər), **Henry Steele.** Born 1902. American historian and educator.

com·mand (kə-mănd′, -mänd′) *v.* **-manded, -manding, -mands.** —*tr.* **1.** To direct with authority; give orders to. **2.** To have control or authority over; rule. **3.** To have at one's disposal: *He commands seven languages.* **4.** To deserve and receive as due; require: *His bravery commanded respect.* **5.** To dominate by position; overlook. —*intr.* **1.** To give commands. **2.** To exercise authority as a commander; be in control. —*n.* **1.** The act of commanding or giving orders. **2.** An order so given. **3.** The authority to command. **4.** The possession and exercising of authority to command. **5.** Ability to control; mastery. **6.** Dominance by location; extent of view. **7.** *Abbr.* **comd.** **a.** The jurisdiction of a commander. **b.** *Military.* A unit, post, district, or region under the control of one officer. **c.** *U.S. Air Force.* A unit consisting of a specified number of wings, generally three or more, under the authority of an officer. **8.** *British.* An invitation from the reigning monarch. [Middle English *com(m)-aunden,* from Old French *comander,* from Vulgar Latin *commandāre* (unattested) : *com-* (intensive) + *mandāre,* to entrust, order (see **man-²** in Appendix*).]

Synonyms: *command, order, bid, enjoin, direct, instruct, charge.* These verbs, with varying degrees of authority, demand obedience on the part of the person or group addressed. *Command* and *order* are similar in emphasizing official authority of the person making the demand: *a general commands; a doctor orders. Bid* suggests an invitation to do something. In an earlier sense, *bid* has the force of *command: I bid you be seated. Enjoin, direct,* and *instruct* do not carry the full authority of *command* or *order. Enjoin* can apply both to demanding the execution of a given act and to demanding the prohibition of something: *Strikers were enjoined from picketing. Direct* implies ordering, but less strongly than *command. Instruct* suggests a mild order directing a person to do something in a specified way. *Charge* adds to *order* the imposition of a moral duty: *charge the commission to find a just solution.*

com·man·dant (kŏm′ən-dănt′, -dänt′) *n. Abbr.* **Comdt.** A commanding officer of a military organization.
com·man·deer (kŏm′ən-dîr′) *tr.v.* **-deered, -deering, -deers. 1.** To force into military service. **2.** To seize (property) for public use; confiscate. **3.** *Informal.* To take arbitrarily or by force. [Afrikaans *kommanderen,* from French *commander,* from Old French *comander,* to COMMAND.]
com·mand·er (kə-măn′dər, kə-män′-) *n.* **1.** A person who commands; leader. **2. a.** *Abbr.* **Comdr., Cdr., Com., Cmdr.** An officer in the U.S. Navy who ranks next above a lieutenant commander and next below a captain. **b.** The chief commissioned officer of a military unit, regardless of his rank. **3.** A chief or an officer in certain knightly orders or of certain contemporary fraternal orders.
commander in chief *pl.* **commanders in chief. 1.** *Often capital* **C,** *capital* **C.** *Abbr.* **CINC, C in C.** The supreme commander of all the armed forces of a nation. **2.** The officer commanding a major armed force.
Com·mand·er Islands. See **Komandorski Islands.**
com·mand·er·y (kə-măn′dər-ē, kə-män′-) *n., pl.* **-ies. 1.** The district or office of a commander, especially of an order of knights. **2.** A lodge or local branch of certain fraternal orders.
com·mand·ing (kə-măn′dĭng, kə-män′-) *adj.* **1.** *Abbr.* **comdg.** Having command; controlling. **2.** Impressive. **3.** Dominating, as by height or position. **—com·mand′ing·ly** *adv.*
commanding officer. *Abbr.* **C.O.** *U.S.Army.* An officer in charge of any unit from company to regiment or of any post, camp, or station.
com·mand·ment (kə-mănd′mənt, kə-mänd′-) *n.* **1.** A command; edict. **2.** *Sometimes capital* **C.** Any of the Ten Commandments.
com·man·do (kə-măn′dō, kə-män′-) *n., pl.* **-dos** or **-does. 1.** A small fighting force specially trained for making quick, destructive raids against enemy-held areas. Compare **ranger. 2.** A member of such a force. **3.** Originally, in South Africa, an organized force of Boer troops. **4.** A raid made by such a force. [Afrikaans *kommando,* from Dutch *commando,* unit of troops, from Spanish *comando,* from *comandar,* to command, from Vulgar Latin *commandāre* (unattested), COMMAND.]
command performance. A performance given at the request of a head of state.
command post. *Abbr.* **C.P.** The field headquarters used by the commander of a military unit.
com·meas·ure (kə-mĕzh′ər) *tr.v.* **-ured, -uring, -ures.** To coincide with; be coextensive with. [COM- + MEASURE.] **—com·meas′ur·a·ble** *adj.*
com·me·dia dell'ar·te (kə-mā′dē-ə dĕl-är′tē). A type of comedy developed in Italy in the 16th century, characterized by improvisation from a plot outline and by the use of stock characters. [Italian, "comedy of art."]
comme il faut (kô mēl fō′). *French.* As it should be; proper.
com·mem·o·rate (kə-mĕm′ə-rāt′) *tr.v.* **-rated, -rating, -rates. 1.** To honor the memory of with a ceremony. **2.** To serve as a memorial to. **—See Synonyms at observe.** [Latin *commemorāre,* to call to mind clearly : *com-* (intensive) + *memorāre,* to remind, speak of, from *memor,* mindful (see **smer-¹** in Appendix*).] **—com·mem′o·ra′tor** (-rā′tər) *n.*
com·mem·o·ra·tion (kə-mĕm′ə-rā′shən) *n.* **1.** The act of commemorating. **2.** Something that commemorates. **3.** A commemorative celebration.
com·mem·o·ra·tive (kə-mĕm′ər-ə-tĭv, -ə-rā′tĭv) *adj.* Also **com·mem·o·ra·to·ry** (-ər-ə-tôr′ē, -tōr′ē). Serving to commemorate. **—n.** Anything that commemorates.
com·mence (kə-mĕns′) *v.* **-menced, -mencing, -mences. —tr.** To begin; start. **—intr.** To come into existence; have a beginning. **—See Synonyms at begin.** [Middle English *commencen,* from Old French *comencer,* from Vulgar Latin *cominitiāre* (unattested) : Late Latin *com-* (intensive) + *initiāre,* to begin, INITIATE.] **—com·menc′er** *n.*
com·mence·ment (kə-mĕns′mənt) *n.* **1.** A beginning; start. **2.** A ceremony at which academic degrees or diplomas are conferred. **3.** The day on which such a ceremony takes place.
com·mend (kə-mĕnd′) *tr.v.* **-mended, -mending, -mends. 1.** To represent as worthy, qualified, or desirable; recommend. **2.** To express approval of; praise. **3.** To commit to the care of another; entrust. **4.** To convey regards to. **—See Synonyms at praise.** [Middle English *commenden,* from Latin *commendāre,*

to commit to one's charge, commend, recommend : *com-* (intensive) + *mandāre,* to entrust (see **man-²** in Appendix*).]
—com·mend′a·ble *adj.* **—com·mend′a·ble·ness** *n.* **—com·mend′a·bly** *adv.*
com·men·da·tion (kŏm′ən-dā′shən) *n.* **1.** The act of commending; recommendation; approval. **2.** Something that commends.
com·mend·a·to·ry (kə-mĕn′də-tôr′ē, -tōr′ē) *adj.* Serving to recommend or praise; approving.
com·men·sal (kə-mĕn′səl) *adj.* **1.** Eating at the same table; sharing meals as table companions. **2.** *Biology.* Pertaining to or characterized by commensalism. **—n. 1.** A mealtime companion. **2.** *Biology.* An organism participating in a commensal relationship. [Middle English, from Medieval Latin *commensālis* : Latin *com-,* together + *mēnsa,* table (see **Mensa**).] **—com·men′sal·ly** *adv.*
com·men·sal·ism (kə-mĕn′səl-ĭz′əm) *n. Biology.* A relationship in which two or more organisms live in close association, and in which one may derive some benefit, but in which neither harms or is parasitic on the other.
com·men·su·ra·ble (kə-mĕn′sər-ə-bəl, -shər-ə-bəl) *adj.* **1.** Able to be measured by a common standard. **2.** Properly proportioned; fitting. **3.** *Mathematics.* Exactly divisible by the same unit an integral number of times. Said of two quantities. [Late Latin *commēnsūrābilis* : *com-,* same + *mēnsūrābilis,* measurable, from *mēnsūrāre,* to measure, from Latin *mēnsūra,* MEASURE.] **—com·men′su·ra·bil′i·ty** *n.* **—com·men′su·ra·bly** *adv.*
com·men·su·rate (kə-mĕn′sə-rĭt, -shə-rĭt) *adj.* **1.** Of the same size, extent, or duration. **2.** Corresponding in scale or measure; proportionate. **3.** Having a common measure or standard; commensurable. [Late Latin *commēnsūrātus* : *com-,* same + *mēnsūrātus,* past participle of *mēnsūrāre,* to measure, from Latin *mēnsūra,* MEASURE.] **—com·men′su·rate·ly** *adv.* **—com·men′su·ra′tion** (-sə-rā′shən, -shə-rā′shən) *n.*
com·ment (kŏm′ĕnt′) *n.* **1.** A written note intended as an explanation, illustration, or criticism of a passage in a book or other writing; annotation. **2. a.** A remark, as in criticism or observation. **b.** A brief statement of fact or opinion, especially one that expresses a personal reaction or attitude. **3.** Talk; gossip. **—v. commented, -menting, -ments. —intr.** To make a comment; remark. **—tr.** To make comments on; annotate. [Middle English, from Latin *commentum,* contrivance, interpretation, from *commentus,* past participle of *comminīscī,* to contrive by thought. See **men-¹** in Appendix.*]
com·men·tar·y (kŏm′ən-tĕr′ē) *n., pl.* **-ies.** *Abbr.* **com. 1.** A series of explanations or interpretations. **2.** *Usually plural.* An expository treatise or series of annotations; exegesis. **3.** Anything that explains or illustrates. **4.** *Usually plural.* A personal narrative; memoir. **—com′men·tar′i·al** (-târ′ē-əl) *adj.*
com·men·tate (kŏm′ən-tāt′) *v.* **-tated, -tating, -tates. —tr.** To make a commentary on. **—intr.** To serve as commentator.
Usage: *Commentate* is objected to by many, largely on the ground that its gracelessness is not compensated for by need. Transitively (*commentate a fashion show*) it is acceptable to only 9 per cent of the Usage Panel; intransitively it is acceptable to 19 per cent of the Panel.
com·men·ta·tor (kŏm′ən-tā′tər) *n.* **1.** An author of commentaries. **2.** A radio or television reporter.
com·merce (kŏm′ərs) *n.* **1.** *Abbr.* **com., comm.** The buying and selling of goods, especially on a large scale, as between cities or nations; business; trade. **2.** Intellectual exchange or social intercourse. **3.** Sexual intercourse. **—See Synonyms at business.** [Old French, from Latin *commercium* : *com-* (collective) + *merx* (stem *merc-*), merchandise (see **merc-** in Appendix*).]
com·mer·cial (kə-mûr′shəl) *adj. Abbr.* **com., cml. 1.** Of, pertaining to, or engaged in commerce. **2.** Designating goods, often unrefined, produced and distributed in large quantities for use by industry. **3.** Of the U.S. government grade of meat, higher than *utility* and lower than *standard.* **4.** Having profit, success, or immediate results as chief aim: *a commercial painter.* **5.** Sponsored by an advertiser: *commercial television.* **—n.** An advertisement on radio or television.
commercial bank. A bank, the principal functions of which are to receive demand deposits and to make short-term loans.
com·mer·cial·ism (kə-mûr′shə-lĭz′əm) *n.* **1.** The practices, methods, aims, and spirit of commerce or business. **2.** An attitude that emphasizes tangible profit or success. **—com·mer′cial·ist** *n.* **—com·mer′cial·is′tic** *adj.*
com·mer·cial·ize (kə-mûr′shə-līz′) *tr.v.* **-ized, -izing, -izes. 1.** To make commercial; apply methods of business to. **2. a.** To exploit, do, or make mainly for financial gain. **b.** To sacrifice the quality of for profit. **—com·mer′cial·i·za′tion** *n.*
commercial paper. Any of various short-term negotiable papers originating in business transactions.
commercial traveler. A traveling salesman.
com·mie (kŏm′ē) *n.* Also **Com·mie.** *Informal.* A Communist.
com·mi·na·tion (kŏm′ə-nā′shən) *n.* A formal denunciation; a threatening. [Middle English *comminacioun,* from Old French *commination,* from Latin *comminātiō,* from *comminārī,* to threaten : *com-* (intensive) + *minārī,* threaten, from *minae,* threats (see **men-²** in Appendix*).] **—com·min′a·to·ry** (kə-mĭn′ə-tôr′ē, -tōr′ē, kŏm′ĭ-nə-) *adj.*
Com·mines, Philippe de. See **Comines.**
com·min·gle (kə-mĭng′gəl) *v.* **-gled, -gling, -gles. —intr.** To blend together; mix. **—tr.** To mix together; combine. [COM- + MINGLE.]
com·mi·nute (kŏm′ə-nōōt′, -nyōōt′) *tr.v.* **-nuted, -nuting, -nutes.** To reduce to powder; pulverize; triturate. [Latin *comminuere* : *com-* (intensive) + *minuere,* to lessen (see **mei-²** in Appendix*).] **—com′mi·nu′tion** *n.*

com·mis·er·ate (kə-mĭz′ə-rāt′) *v.* **-ated, -ating, -ates.** —*tr.* To feel or express sorrow or pity for; sympathize with. —*intr.* To grieve in sympathy. Used with *with.* [Latin *commiserārī* : *com-*, with + *miserārī*, to pity, from *miser*, wretched, pitiable (see **miser** in Appendix*).] —**com·mis′er·a′tive** *adj.* —**com·mis′er·a′tive·ly** *adv.* —**com·mis′er·a′tor** (-ə-rā′tər) *n.*
com·mis·er·a·tion (kə-mĭz′ə-rā′shən) *n.* A feeling or expression of sorrow or sympathy for the distress of another; compassion. See Synonyms at **pity.**
com·mis·sar (kŏm′ə-sär′) *n.* **1.** Formerly, the head of a commissariat in the Soviet Union. **2.** An official of the Communist Party in charge of political indoctrination and the enforcement of party loyalty. [Russian *komissar*, from German *Kommissar*, deputy, commissioner, from Medieval Latin *commissārius*, COMMISSARY.]
com·mis·sar·i·at (kŏm′ə-sâr′ē-ĭt) *n.* **1.** A department of an army in charge of providing food and other supplies for the troops. **2.** The officers in charge of this. **3.** A food supply. **4.** Formerly, any major government department in the Soviet Union. [Russian *komissariat* and New Latin *commissariatus*, from Medieval Latin *commissārius*, COMMISSARY.]
com·mis·sar·y (kŏm′ə-sĕr′ē, -sâr′ē) *n., pl.* **-ies. 1. a.** A store where food and equipment are sold, as in a mining camp. **b.** A supermarket for the personnel of a military post. **2.** A lunchroom or cafeteria, especially one in a motion-picture or television studio. **3.** A person to whom a special duty is given by a higher authority; a representative; deputy. **4.** Formerly, an army officer in charge of supplying provisions. [Middle English *commissarie*, from Medieval Latin *commissārius*, commissioner, agent, from *committere*, to entrust, commission, COMMIT.] —**com′mis·sar′y·ship′** *n.*
com·mis·sion (kə-mĭsh′ən) *n.* **1.** The act of committing or giving authority to carry out a particular task or duty, or granting certain powers; an entrusting. **2.** The authority so granted. **3.** The matter or task so committed. **4.** A document conferring such authorization. **5.** The state of being authorized to perform certain functions. **6.** *Abbr.* **Com., comm.** A group of people lawfully authorized to perform certain duties or functions, as a government agency. **7.** A committing or perpetrating: *commission of a crime.* **8.** The act committed or thing done. **9.** A fee or percentage allowed to a salesman or agent for his services. **10.** *Abbr.* **Com., comm. a.** An official document issued by a government, conferring the rank of a commissioned officer in the armed forces. **b.** The rank and powers so conferred. —**in commission. 1.** In active service, as a ship. **2.** In use or in usable condition. —**out of commission. 1.** Not in active service. **2.** Not in use or not in working condition. —*tr.v.* **commissioned, -sioning, -sions. 1.** To grant a commission to. **2.** To place an order for. **3.** *Nautical.* To put (a ship) into active service. [Middle English *commissioun*, from Old French *commission*, from Latin *commissiō*, from *committere* (past participle *commissus*), COMMIT.] —**com·mis′sion·al, com·mis′sion·ar′y** (kə-mĭsh′ə-nĕr′ē) *adj.*

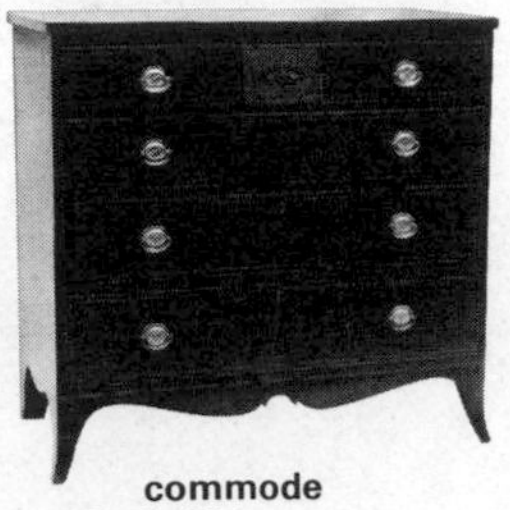
commode
Early 19th-century American

com·mis·sion·aire (kə-mĭsh′ə-nâr′) *n. Chiefly British.* A doorman. [French *commissionnaire*, from Old French *commission*, COMMISSION.]
commissioned officer. Any officer who holds a commission and ranks as a second lieutenant or above in the U.S. Army, Air Force, or Marine Corps, or as an ensign or above in the U.S. Navy or Coast Guard. Compare **noncommissioned officer, warrant officer.**
com·mis·sion·er (kə-mĭsh′ən-ər) *n. Abbr.* **Com., Comr., comm., com. 1.** A person authorized by a commission to perform certain duties. **2.** A member of a commission. **3.** A governmental official in charge of a department: *the commissioner of welfare.* **4.** *Sports.* An official selected by an athletic association or league to exercise judicial or regulatory powers: *a baseball commissioner.* —**com·mis′sion·er·ship′** *n.*
commission merchant. A person who buys and sells goods for others on a commission basis.
commission plan. A type of municipal government in which legislative and administrative functions and powers are vested in an elected commission rather than in a mayor and city council. Also called "Galveston plan."
com·mis·sure (kŏm′ə-shŏŏr′) *n.* **1.** A line or place at which two things are joined; seam; juncture. **2.** *Anatomy.* **a.** A tract of nerve fibers passing from one side to the other of the spinal cord or brain. **b.** The angle or corner of such structures as the lips, eyelids, or cardiac valves. **3.** *Botany.* A surface by which adhering carpels are joined. [Middle English, from Old French, from Latin *commissūra*, from *committere*, COMMIT.] —**com′mis·su′ral** (kŏm′ə-shŏŏr′əl, kə-mĭsh′ər-əl) *adj.*

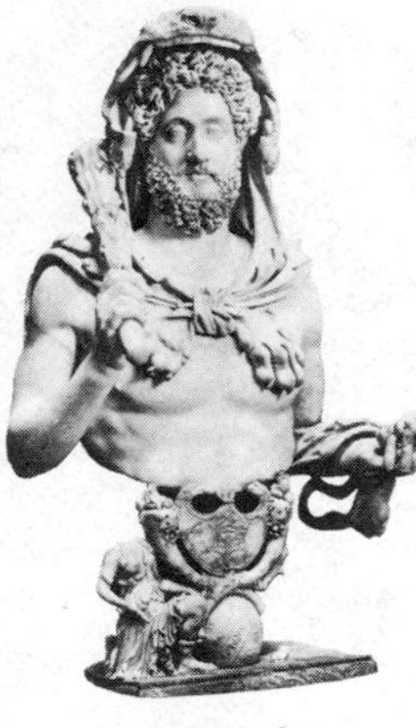
Commodus
Marble bust depicting the emperor with the attributes of Hercules

com·mit (kə-mĭt′) *tr.v.* **-mitted, -mitting, -mits. 1.** To do, perform, or perpetrate: *commit a murder.* **2.** To place in trust or charge; consign; entrust. **3.** To place officially in confinement or custody. **4.** To consign for future use or reference or for preservation: *commit to memory.* **5.** To put in some place to be kept safe or be disposed of: *commit to the flames.* **6. a.** To pledge (oneself) to a position on some issue. **b.** To bind or obligate, as by a pledge. **7.** To refer (a bill, for example) to a committee. [Middle English *committen*, from Latin *committere*, to join, connect, entrust : *com-*, together + *mittere*, to send, put (see **smeit-** in Appendix*).] —**com·mit′ta·ble** *adj.*
Synonyms: *commit, consign, entrust, confide, assign, relegate.* These verbs mean to place a person or thing in custody or safekeeping. *Commit* has the widest application and means to deliver a person or thing, physically or figuratively, into the charge of another. *Consign* states the formal act of transferring or delivering, especially goods or property. *Entrust* and *confide* both stress confidence in another. A child is entrusted to the care of a baby sitter; a secret is confided to a close friend. *Assign* refers to committing someone to a place, position, or task, or to transferring personal property or rights. *Relegate* refers to assigning a person or thing to a specific category or sphere and generally implies debasement or demotion.
com·mit·ment (kə-mĭt′mənt) *n.* Also **com·mit·tal** (kə-mĭt′l) (for senses 1a, 2, 4, 7). **1. a.** The act of committing; a giving in charge or entrusting. **b.** The state of being committed. **2.** Official consignment, as to a prison or mental hospital. **3.** *Law.* A court order authorizing consignment to a prison; mittimus. **4. a.** A pledge to do something. **b.** Something pledged. **5.** An engagement by contract involving financial obligation. **6.** The state of being bound emotionally or intellectually to some course of action: *a deep commitment to liberal policies.* **7.** The act of referring a legislative bill to a committee.
com·mit·tee (kə-mĭt′ē) *n. Abbr.* **com., Com. 1.** A group of people officially delegated to perform a function, as investigating, considering, reporting, or acting on a matter. **2.** *Law.* A person to whom the care of an estate or incompetent person is committed; trustee; guardian. —**in committee.** Under consideration by a committee, as a legislative measure. [Middle English *committe*, trustee, from *committen*, COMMIT.]
com·mit·tee·man (kə-mĭt′ē-mən, -măn′) *n., pl.* **-men** (-mĭn, -mĕn′). A committee member.
committee of the whole. A committee consisting of all the members present of a legislative house.
com·mix (kə-mĭks′, kŏ-) *v.* **-mixed, -mixing, -mixes.** —*tr.* To mix together. —*intr.* To mix; blend. [From Middle English *commixt*, mixed, from Latin *commixtus*, past participle of *commiscēre*, to mix together : *com-*, together + *miscēre*, mix (see **meik-** in Appendix*).]
com·mix·ture (kə-mĭks′chər, kŏ-) *n.* **1.** The act or process of mixing together. **2.** The result of this; a mixture.
com·mode (kə-mōd′) *n.* **1.** A low cabinet or chest of drawers, often elaborately decorated and usually on legs or short feet. **2. a.** A movable stand or cupboard containing a washbowl. **b.** A chair enclosing a chamber pot. **3.** A toilet. **4.** A woman's ornate headdress, fashionable around 1700. [French, "convenient," from Latin *commodus*, COMMODIOUS.]
com·mo·di·ous (kə-mō′dē-əs) *adj.* **1.** Spacious; roomy. **2.** *Archaic.* Convenient; suitable. [Middle English, from Old French *commodieux*, from Medieval Latin *commodiōsus*, from Latin *commodus*, convenient, "(conforming) with (due) measure" : *com-*, with + *modus*, measure (see **med-** in Appendix*).] —**com·mo′di·ous·ly** *adv.* —**com·mo′di·ous·ness** *n.*
com·mod·i·ty (kə-mŏd′ə-tē) *n., pl.* **-ties. 1.** Anything useful or that can be turned to commercial or other advantage. **2.** *Economics.* An article of trade or commerce that can be transported, especially an agricultural or mining product. **3.** *Obsolete.* **a.** Convenience; profit; expediency: *"kings break faith upon commodity"* (Shakespeare). **b.** A quantity of goods. [Middle English *commodite*, profit, income, property, from Old French *commodite*, from Latin *commoditās*, advantage, convenience, from *commodus*, convenient, COMMODIOUS.]
com·mo·dore (kŏm′ə-dôr′, -dōr′) *n. Abbr.* **Com., COMO, Como. 1.** *U.S. Navy.* Formerly, an officer ranking below rear admiral and above captain. This rank was abolished in 1899 but temporarily restored during World War II. **2.** *British Navy.* An unofficial designation for a captain temporarily in command of a fleet division or squadron. **3. a.** The senior captain of a naval squadron or merchant fleet. **b.** The presiding officer of a yacht club. [From Dutch *komandeur*, commander, from French, from Old French *comandeor*, from *comander*, COMMAND.]
Com·mo·dus (kŏm′ə-dəs), **Lucius Aelius Aurelius.** A.D. 161–192. Roman Emperor (180–192); son of Marcus Aurelius.
com·mon (kŏm′ən) *adj.* **-moner, -monest.** *Abbr.* **com. 1.** Belonging equally to two or more; shared by all alike; joint: *common interests.* **2.** Pertaining to the community as a whole; public: *the common good.* **3.** Generally known; notorious: *a common nuisance.* **4.** Widespread; prevalent; general. **5.** Of frequent or habitual occurrence; usual. **6.** Most widely known or occurring most frequently; ordinary: *the common crow.* **7.** Without special designation, status, or rank: *a common sailor.* **8.** Not distinguished by superior or other characteristics; average: *the common spectator.* **9.** Of no special quality; standard; plain: *common courtesy.* **10.** Of mediocre or inferior quality; not costly or rare: *common cloth.* **11.** Vulgar; unrefined; coarse. **12.** *Prosody.* Of variable length; either short or long. Said of a syllable. **13.** *Grammar.* **a.** Either masculine or feminine in gender. **b.** Representing one or all the members of a class; not designating a unique entity. —See Usage note at **mutual.** —*n.* **1.** *Sometimes plural.* A tract of land belonging to or used by a community as a whole. **2.** *Law.* The right of a person to use the lands or waters of another, as for fishing or grazing cattle. **3.** *Sometimes capital* **C.** *Ecclesiastical.* A service used for a particular class of festivals. —**in common.** Equally with or by all; jointly. [Middle English *commun(e)*, from Old French, from Latin *commūnis*. See **mei-¹** in Appendix*.] —**com′mon·ness** *n.*
Synonyms: *common, ordinary, familiar, vulgar, prevalent.* These adjectives describe what is generally known or frequently seen, heard, or the like. *Common* implies that which is customary, takes place daily, is widely used, or is generally known. The term also suggests lack of distinction (*common man*) and can imply coarseness or crudeness. *Ordinary* implies plainness (*ordinary-looking*) or lack of distinctive quality (*ordinary ability*). In the latter sense it is sometimes derogatory. *Familiar* applies to what is well known or quickly recognized through frequent occurrence or regular association. *Vulgar* usually empha-

sizes the coarse sense of *common*. *Prevalent* describes a condition that is widespread.

com·mon·age (kŏm′ə-nĭj) *n.* **1.** The right to pasture animals on common land. **2.** The state of being held in common.

com·mon·al·ty (kŏm′ən-əl-tē) *n., pl.* **-ties.** Also **com·mon·al·i·ty** (kŏm′ə-năl′ə-tē). **1.** The common people, as opposed to the upper classes. **2.** A body corporate; corporation. **3.** The entire group; the universal body. [Middle English *communalte*, from Old French *comunalte*, from Medieval Latin *commūnālitās*, from *commūnālis*, COMMUNAL.]

common carrier. A person or company in the business of transporting the public or goods for a fee.

Common Celtic. 1. The vocabulary of the reconstructed ancestor of the Celtic languages that is attested in the major Celtic subdivisions. **2.** Of or pertaining to Common Celtic.

common cold. A respiratory infection, **coryza** (*see*).

common denominator. A quantity into which all the denominators of a set of fractions may be evenly divided.

common divisor. A quantity that is a factor of two or more quantities. Also called "common measure."

com·mon·er (kŏm′ə-nər) *n.* **1.** One of the common people. **2.** One who is not a noble.

common fraction. A fraction having an integer as a numerator and an integer as a denominator.

common gender. Gender that may refer to either masculine or feminine categories; for example, *child, person*. Compare **natural gender, grammatical gender.**

Common Germanic. 1. The vocabulary of Proto-Germanic that is attested in all the major Germanic subdivisions. **2.** Of or pertaining to Common Germanic.

Common Indic. 1. The vocabulary of the prehistoric ancestor of the Indic languages that is attested in all the major Indic subdivisions. **2.** Of or pertaining to Common Indic.

Common Iranian. 1. The vocabulary of the prehistoric ancestor of the Iranian languages that is attested in all the major Iranian subdivisions. **2.** Of or pertaining to Common Iranian.

common law. *Abbr.* **c.l. 1.** The system of laws originated and developed in England, based on court decisions, on the doctrines implicit in those decisions, and on customs and usages, rather than on codified written laws. Compare **statute law. 2.** The part of a system of laws of any state or nation that is of a general and universal application. —**com′mon-law′** *adj.*

common-law marriage. A marriage existing by mutual agreement between a man and a woman without civil or ecclesiastical ceremony.

common logarithm. A logarithm to the base 10, especially as distinguished from a natural logarithm.

com·mon·ly (kŏm′ən-lē) *adv.* **1.** Generally; ordinarily. **2.** In a common manner.

Common Market. 1. Any customs union. **2.** Official name, European Economic Community. An economic union established in 1958, originally including Belgium, France, Italy, Luxembourg, the Netherlands, and West Germany. In this sense, also called "Euromarket," "Euromart."

common measure. 1. *Music.* **Common time** (*see*). **2.** *Mathematics.* A **common divisor** (*see*).

common multiple. A quantity that is a multiple of each of two or more given quantities.

common noun. *Grammar.* A noun that can be preceded by the definite article and that represents one or all of the members of a class; for example, *book, man.*

com·mon·place (kŏm′ən-plās′) *adj.* Ordinary; uninteresting; common. See Synonyms at **trite.** —*n.* **1.** A trite or obvious remark; platitude. **2.** Something ordinary or common. **3.** A passage in a book marked for reference or a series of such passages entered in a commonplace book. —See Synonyms at **cliché.** [Translation of Latin *locus communis*, translation of Greek *koinos topos*, "common place," literary passage of universal application.] —**com′mon·place′ness** *n.*

commonplace book. A personal journal in which quotable passages, literary excerpts, and comments are written.

common pleas. *Law.* A **Court of Common Pleas** (*see*).

Common Prayer. 1. The liturgy for public worship in the Church of England. **2.** The **Book of Common Prayer** (*see*).

Common Romance. 1. The vocabulary of the reconstructed ancestor of the Romance languages that is attested in all the major Romance subdivisions and that developed from Vulgar Latin in the first century A.D. **2.** Of or pertaining to Common Romance.

com·mons (kŏm′ənz) *n.* Plural in form, used with a singular verb (for senses 3, 4), with a plural verb (for sense 1), or with a singular or plural verb (for senses 2, 5). **1.** The common people; commonalty. **2.** Food provided at meals for a large group, as at a college. **3.** Daily fare; rations: *"He had ate his homely commons"* (Fielding). **4.** A building or hall for dining. **5 a.** The political class comprising the commoners. **b.** *Often capital* **C.** The representatives of this class in Parliament. **c.** *Often capital* **C.** The **House of Commons** (*see*).

common salt. 1. Salt (*see*). **2. Sodium chloride** (*see*). **3. Table salt** (*see*).

common school. A public elementary school.

common sense. 1. Native good judgment; sound ordinary sense. **2.** The set of general unexamined assumptions as distinguished from specially acquired concepts: *Common sense holds that heavier bodies fall faster than lighter ones.* [Translation of Latin *sensus communis* and Greek *koinē aisthēsis*, total perception of the five senses.]

common stock. Ordinary capital shares of a corporation that have exclusive residual claim on the net assets and net income

of the corporation after all prior claims have been paid. Also called "equity stock."

common time. *Music.* A meter having four quarter notes to the measure. Written 4/4. Also called "common measure."

com·mon·weal (kŏm′ən-wēl′) *n.* Also **common weal. 1.** The public good or welfare. **2.** *Archaic.* A commonwealth.

com·mon·wealth (kŏm′ən-wĕlth′) *n.* **1.** The people of a nation or state; body politic. **2.** *Abbr.* **comm.** A nation or state governed by the people; republic. **3.** *Capital* **C. a.** The official title of some U.S. states, including Kentucky, Maryland, Virginia, Massachusetts, and Pennsylvania. **b.** The official title of Puerto Rico, indicating its special status as a self-governing, autonomous political unit voluntarily associated with the United States. **4.** *Obsolete.* The public welfare. Also *archaic* "commonweal." —See Synonyms at **nation.** [Middle English *commun welthe*, "public welfare" : COMMON + WEALTH.]

Commonwealth of Aus·tral·ia. See **Australia.**

Commonwealth of Eng·land (ĭng′glənd). The English government under the protectorships of Oliver and Richard Cromwell (1649–1660). Also called "the Commonwealth."

Commonwealth of Nations. Formerly **British Commonwealth of Nations.** The political community constituted by the former British Empire and consisting of the United Kingdom, its dependencies, and certain former colonies that are now sovereign nations. Also called "the Commonwealth."

com·mo·tion (kə-mō′shən) *n.* **1.** Violent or turbulent motion; agitation. **2.** Political disturbance or insurrection; disorder. [Middle English *commocioun*, from Old French *commotion*, from Latin *commōtiō*, from *commovēre* (past participle *commōtus*), to move violently : *com-* (intensive) + *movēre*, to move (see **mew-** in Appendix*).] —**com·mo′tion·al** *adj.*

com·move (kə-mōōv′) *tr.v.* **-moved, -moving, -moves.** To agitate; disturb; excite. [Middle English *commeven, comm(o)even*, from Latin *commovēre*. See **commotion.**]

com·mu·nal (kə-myōōn′əl, kŏm′yə-nəl) *adj.* **1.** Of or pertaining to a commune or community. **2.** Of, pertaining to, or belonging to the people of a community; public. [French, from Old French *comunal*, from Medieval Latin *commūnālis*, from *commūna, commūnia,* COMMUNE (community).] —**com′mu·nal′i·ty** *n.* —**com·mu′nal·ly** *adv.*

com·mu·nal·ism (kə-myōōn′əl-ĭz′əm, kŏm′yə-nəl-) *n.* **1.** A theory or system of government in which virtually autonomous local communities are loosely bound in a federation. **2.** Belief in or practice of communal ownership, as of goods and property. **3.** Strong devotion to the interests of one's own ethnic group rather than those of society as a whole. —**com·mu′nal·ist** *n.* —**com·mu′nal·is′tic** *adj.*

com·mu·nal·ize (kə-myōōn′əl-īz′, kŏm′yə-nəl-) *tr.v.* **-ized, -izing, -izes.** To convert into municipal or community property.

Com·mu·nard (kŏm′yə-närd′) *n.* A member or advocate of the Commune of Paris (1871). [French, from *commune,* COMMUNE (division).]

com·mune¹ (kə-myōōn′) *intr.v.* **-muned, -muning, -munes. 1.** To converse intimately; exchange thoughts and feelings. **2.** To receive the Eucharist. —*n.* (kŏm′yōōn′). Intimate conversation; communion. [Middle English *communen*, to distribute, share, communicate, from Old French *comuner*, from *comun, commun,* COMMON.]

com·mune² (kŏm′yōōn′) *n.* **1.** *Abbr.* **com.** The smallest local political division of various European countries, such as France, Belgium, Italy, and Switzerland, governed by a mayor and municipal council. **2. a.** A local community organized with a government for promoting local interests. **b.** A municipal corporation in the Middle Ages. **3.** The people of a commune. —**the Commune. 1.** The revolutionary committee that governed Paris from 1789 to 1795. **2.** The revolutionary government of Paris from March 18 to May 28, 1871. Also called "the Commune of Paris." [French, from Medieval Latin *commūnia*, community, from Latin *commūnis*, public, COMMON.]

com·mu·ni·ca·ble (kə-myōō′nĭ-kə-bəl) *adj.* **1.** Able to be communicated or transmitted. **2.** Talkative. —**com·mu′ni·ca·bil′i·ty, com·mu′ni·ca·ble·ness** *n.* —**com·mu′ni·ca·bly** *adv.*

com·mu·ni·cant (kə-myōō′nĭ-kənt) *n.* **1.** A person who receives, or is entitled to receive, Communion. **2.** A person who communicates. —*adj.* Communicating.

com·mu·ni·cate (kə-myōō′nə-kāt′) *v.* **-cated, -cating, -cates.** —*tr.* **1.** To make known; impart: *communicate information.* **2.** To transmit (a disease, for example). —*intr.* **1.** To have an interchange, as of thoughts or ideas. **2.** To receive Communion. **3.** To be connected or form a connecting passage. [Latin *commūnicāre*, "to make common," make known, from *commūnis,* COMMON.] —**com·mu′ni·ca′tor** (-kā′tər) *n.* —**com·mu′ni·ca·to′ry** (-kə-tôr′ē, -kə-tōr′ē) *adj.*

com·mu·ni·ca·tion (kə-myōō′nə-kā′shən) *n. Abbr.* **com., comm. 1.** The act of communicating; transmission. **2.** The exchange of thoughts, messages, or the like, as by speech, signals, or writing. **3.** Something communicated. **4.** *Plural.* A means of communicating, especially: **a.** A system for sending and receiving messages, as by mail, telephone, or television. **b.** *Military.* A network of routes for sending messages and transporting troops and supplies. **5.** Any connective passage or channel. **6.** *Plural.* The art and technology of communicating.

communications satellite. An artificial satellite used to aid communications, as by reflecting or electronically relaying a radio signal.

communication theory. Information theory (*see*).

com·mu·ni·ca·tive (kə-myōō′nə-kā′tĭv, -nĭ-kə-tĭv) *adj.* **1.** Inclined to communicate readily; talkative. **2.** Of communication. —**com·mu′ni·ca′tive·ly** *adv.* **com·mu′ni·ca′tive·ness** *n.*

---

t tight/th thin, path/*th* this, bathe/ŭ cut/ûr urge/v valve/w with/y yes/z zebra, size/zh vision/ə about, item, edible, gallop, circus/ à *Fr.* ami/œ *Fr.* feu, *Ger.* schön/ü *Fr.* tu, *Ger.* über/KH *Ger.* ich, *Scot.* loch/N *Fr.* bon. *Follows main vocabulary. †Of obscure origin.

com·mun·ion (kə-myo͞on′yən) *n.* **1.** A possessing or sharing in common; participation. **2.** A sharing of thoughts or feelings; intimate talk. **3. a.** A religious or spiritual fellowship. **b.** A body of Christians with a common religious faith who practice the same rites; denomination. **4. a.** *Capital* **C.** The **Eucharist** *(see).* **b.** The consecrated elements of the Eucharist. **c.** The part of the Mass in which the sacrament of the Eucharist is received. [Middle English *communioun,* from Old French *communion,* from Late Latin *commūnio,* the Eucharist, from Latin, participation by all, from *commūnis,* COMMON.]

com·mu·ni·qué (kə-myo͞o′nə-kā′, kə-myo͞o′nə-kā′) *n.* An official announcement, such as one issued to the press. [French, from *communiquer,* to inform, announce, from Latin *commūnicāre,* COMMUNICATE.]

com·mu·nism (kŏm′yə-nĭz′əm) *n.* **1.** A social system characterized by the absence of classes and by common ownership of the means of production and subsistence. **2. a.** A political, economic, and social doctrine aiming at the establishment of such a classless society. **b.** *Often capital* **C.** The Marxist-Leninist doctrine of revolutionary struggle toward this goal, the political movement representing it, or, loosely, socialism as practiced in countries ruled by Communist parties. **c.** Communalism. **3.** Leftist activity aiming at revolution. Used loosely. [French *communisme,* from Old French *commun,* COMMON.]

Communism, Mount. Formerly **Sta·lin Peak** (stäl′ən). The highest mountain (24,500 feet) in the Soviet Union, situated in the north-central Tadzhik S.S.R.

Com·mu·nist (kŏm′yə-nĭst) *n. Abbr.* **Com. 1. a.** A member of a Marxist-Leninist party. **b.** A militant supporter of such a party or movement. **2.** *Small* **c.** A communalist. **3.** A Communard. **4.** *Often small* **c.** Any radical viewed as a subversive or revolutionary. —*adj.* Also **com·mu·nist.** Pertaining to, characteristic of, or resembling communism or Communists.

com·mu·nis·tic (kŏm′yə-nĭs′tĭk) *adj.* Of, characteristic of, or inclined to communism. —**com′mu·nis′ti·cal·ly** *adv.*

Communist International. The Third **International** *(see).*

Communist Manifesto. A pamphlet, issued (1848) by Karl Marx and Friedrich Engels, constituting the first statement of the principles of modern Communism.

Communist Party. *Abbr.* **C.P.** A Marxist-Leninist party, usually one originally belonging to the Third **International** *(see).*

com·mu·ni·tar·i·an (kə-myo͞o′nə-târ′ē-ən) *n.* A member or supporter of a communistic community.

com·mu·ni·ty (kə-myo͞o′nə-tē) *n., pl.* **-ties.** *Abbr.* **com. 1. a.** A group of people living in the same locality and under the same government. **b.** The district or locality in which they live. **2.** A social group or class having common interests. **3.** Similarity or identity: *a community of interests.* **4.** Society as a whole; the public. **5.** *Ecology.* **a.** A group of plants and animals living in a specific region under relatively similar conditions. **b.** The region in which they live. **6.** Common possession or participation. [Middle English *communite,* from Old French *comunete,* from Latin *commūnitās,* from *commūnis,* COMMON.]

community center. A meeting place used by members of a community for social, cultural, or recreational purposes.

community chest. A welfare fund financed by private contributions for aiding various charitable organizations.

community property. Property owned jointly by a husband and wife.

com·mu·nize (kŏm′yə-nīz′) *tr.v.* **-nized, -nizing, -nizes. 1.** To make public all the property of a community. **2.** To convert to Communist principles or control. [From Latin *commūnis,* COMMON.] —**com′mu·ni·za′tion** *n.*

com·mut·a·ble (kə-myo͞o′tə-bəl) *adj.* Capable of being commuted; interchangeable. —**com·mut′a·bil′i·ty, com·mut′a·ble·ness** *n.*

com·mu·tate (kŏm′yə-tāt′) *tr.v.* **-tated, -tating, -tates.** To reverse the direction of (an alternating electric current) each half-cycle to produce a unidirectional current. [Back-formation from COMMUTATION.]

com·mu·ta·tion (kŏm′yə-tā′shən) *n.* **1.** A substitution, exchange, or interchange. **2. a.** The substitution of one kind of payment for another. **b.** The payment substituted. **3.** The travel of a commuter. **4.** *Electricity.* **a.** The conversion of alternating to unidirectional current. **b.** The reversing of current direction. **5.** *Law.* A reduction of a penalty to a less severe one. [Middle English, from Old French, from Latin *commūtātiō,* from *commūtāre,* COMMUTE.]

commutation ticket. A ticket issued at a reduced rate by a railroad, bus, or other transportation company for passage over a given route for a specified number of trips.

com·mu·ta·tive (kŏm′yə-tā′tĭv, kə-myo͞o′tə-tĭv) *adj.* **1.** Pertaining to, involving, or characterized by substitution, interchange, or exchange. **2.** Independent of order. Said of a logical or mathematical operation that combines objects two at a time.

commutative group. *Algebra.* A group in which the result of multiplying one member by another is independent of the order of multiplication. Also called "Abelian group."

com·mu·ta·tor (kŏm′yə-tā′tər) *n.* A cylindrical arrangement of insulated metal bars connected to the coils of an electric motor or generator to provide a unidirectional current from the generator or a reversal of current into the coils of the motor.

com·mute (kə-myo͞ot′) *v.* **-muted, -muting, -mutes.** —*tr.* **1.** To substitute; exchange; interchange. **2.** To change (a penalty, debt, or payment) to a less severe one. —*intr.* **1. a.** To make substitution; exchange. **b.** To serve as a substitute. **2.** To pay in gross, usually at a reduced rate, rather than in individual payments. **3.** To travel as a commuter. **4.** *Mathematics & Logic.* To satisfy or engage in a commutative operation. [Middle English *commuten,* from Latin *commūtāre,* to exchange : *com-,* mutually + *mūtāre,* to change (see **mei-**[1] in Appendix*).]

com·mut·er (kə-myo͞o′tər) *n.* A person who travels regularly between his home in one community and his work in another.

Co·mo (kō′mō). **1.** A lake occupying 56 square miles in northern Italy near the Swiss border. **2.** A resort city of northern Italy on this lake. Population, 82,000.

COMO, Como. commodore.

Com·o·rin, Cape (kŏm′ə-rĭn). A cape at the southernmost point of the Republic of India.

Com·o·ro Islands (kŏm′ə-rō′). *French* **Îles Co·mores** (ēl kô-môr′). A group of French islands, 830 square miles in area, at the northern entrance of Mozambique Channel off eastern Africa. Population, 212,000.

co·mose. Variant of **comate** (hairy).

comp (kŏmp) *n. Advertising.* A **comprehensive** *(see).*

comp. 1. companion. **2.** comparative. **3.** compilation; compiled; compiler. **4.** complete. **5.** compose; composer. **6.** composite; composition; compositor. **7.** compound. **8.** comprising.

com·pact[1] (kəm-păkt′, kŏm-, kŏm′păkt′) *adj.* **1.** Closely and firmly united or packed together; solid; dense. **2.** Packed into or arranged within a relatively small space. **3.** Expressed briefly and to the point; concise. —*tr.v.* (kəm-păkt′) **compacted, -pacting, -pacts. 1.** To press or join firmly together; condense; consolidate. **2.** To make or compose by pressing or joining together. —*n.* (kŏm′păkt′). **1.** A small case containing a mirror, face powder, a powder puff, and sometimes rouge. **2.** A relatively small automobile. [Middle English, from Latin *compactus,* past participle of *compingere,* to join together : *com-,* together + *pangere,* to fasten (see **pag-** in Appendix*).] —**com·pact′er** *n.* —**com·pact′ly** *adv.* —**com·pact′ness** *n.*

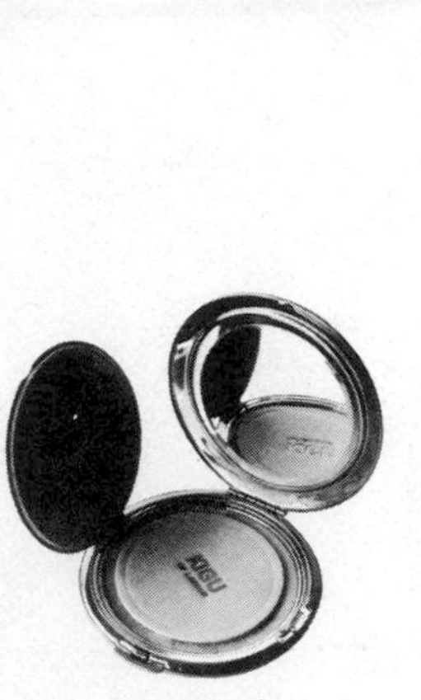

compact[1]
A compact for carrying face powder

com·pact[2] (kŏm′păkt′) *n.* An agreement or covenant. [Latin *compactum,* from *compactus,* past participle of *compacīscī,* to agree together : *com-,* together + *pacīscī,* to agree (see **pag-** in Appendix*).]

com·pac·tion (kəm-păk′shən) *n.* **1.** The process of compacting. **2.** The state of being compacted.

com·pa·dre (kəm-pä′drā) *n. Southwestern U.S.* A friend or close companion. [Spanish, godfather, from Medieval Latin *compater,* "joint father," godfather : Latin *com-,* with + *pater,* father (see **pəter** in Appendix*).]

com·pan·ion[1] (kəm-păn′yən) *n.* **1.** A person who accompanies or associates with another; comrade. **2.** *Abbr.* **comp.** A person employed to assist, live with, or travel with another. **3.** One of a pair or set of things; mate; match. **4.** *Abbr.* **C.** A member of the lowest rank or grade in an order of knighthood. —*tr.v.* **companioned, -ioning, -ions.** To be a companion to; associate with; accompany. [Middle English *compai(g)noun,* from Old French *compaignon,* from Vulgar Latin *compāniō* (unattested), "one who eats bread with another" : Latin *com-,* together + *pānis,* bread (see **pā-** in Appendix*).]

com·pan·ion[2] (kəm-păn′yən) *n.* A companionway.

com·pan·ion·a·ble (kəm-păn′yə-nə-bəl) *adj.* Suited to be a good companion; sociable; friendly. —**com·pan′ion·a·bly** *adv.*

com·pan·ion·ship (kəm-păn′yən-shĭp′) *n.* Association or relationship of companions; fellowship.

com·pan·ion·way (kəm-păn′yən-wā′) *n.* A staircase leading from a ship's deck to the cabins or area below. [Obsolete Dutch *kompanje,* from Old French *compagne,* from Italian *(camera della) campagna,* ship's storeroom, "room (with provisions) for navigation," from *campagna,* open country or sea, navigation, from Latin *Campānia,* CAMPANIA + WAY.]

com·pa·ny (kŭm′pə-nē) *n., pl.* **-nies. 1.** A group of people; assemblage; gathering. **2.** People assembled for a social purpose. **3.** A guest or guests. **4.** Companionship; fellowship. **5.** Society in general. **6.** A business enterprise; firm. **7.** *Abbr.* **co., Co.** A partner or partners not specifically named in a firm's title: *John Rogers and Company.* **8.** A troupe of dramatic or musical performers: *a repertory company.* **9.** A subdivision of a regiment or battalion, the lowest administrative unit, usually under the command of a captain. **10.** A ship's crew and officers. —See Synonyms at **visitor.** —**keep company.** To carry on courtship. —**keep (someone) company.** To accompany. —**part company.** To end an association or friendship. —*v.* **companied, -nying, -nies.** *Rare.* —*tr.* To accompany or associate with. —*intr.* To keep company; associate. [Middle English *compaignie,* from Old French *compagnie,* from *compain,* companion, from Vulgar Latin *compāniō* (unattested), COMPANION.]

Usage: *Company* (noun) usually takes a singular verb in the following senses: a business association, companionship, or society in general *(the company is good),* a military or nautical unit, a theatrical troupe. When *company* refers to any group or assemblage or to a group of guests, it may take a singular verb (with reference to a unified body) or a plural one (members considered individually).

compar. comparative.

com·pa·ra·ble (kŏm′pər-ə-bəl) *adj.* **1.** Able to be compared; having traits or qualities in common; similar or equivalent. **2.** Worthy of comparison. —**com′pa·ra·bil′i·ty, com′pa·ra·ble·ness** *n.* —**com′pa·ra·bly** *adv.*

com·par·a·tist (kəm-păr′ə-tĭst) *n.* A practitioner of comparative linguistics or literature.

com·par·a·tive (kəm-păr′ə-tĭv) *adj. Abbr.* **comp., compar. 1.** Pertaining to, based on, or involving comparison. **2.** Estimated by comparison; relative. **3.** *Grammar.* Designating a degree of comparison of adjectives and adverbs higher than positive and lower than superlative. —*n. Grammar.* **1.** The comparative degree. **2.** An adjective or adverb expressing the comparative degree; for example, *brighter* is the comparative of

ă pat/ā pay/âr care/ä father/b bib/ch church/d deed/ĕ pet/ē be/f fife/g gag/h hat/hw which/ĭ pit/ī pie/îr pier/j judge/k kick/l lid, needle/m mum/n no, sudden/ng thing/ŏ pot/ō toe/ô paw, for/oi noise/ou out/o͝o took/o͞o boot/p pop/r roar/s sauce/sh ship, dish/

bright; more slowly is the comparative of *slowly*. —**com·par′a·tive·ly** *adv.*

com·pa·ra·tor (kŏm′pə-rā′tər, kəm-păr′ə-tər) *n.* Any of various devices for comparing an aspect of an object, such as shape, color, or brightness, with a standard.

com·pare (kəm-pâr′) *v.* **-pared, -paring, -pares.** —*tr.* **1.** To represent as similar, equal, or analogous; liken. Used with *to.* See Usage note below. **2.** *Abbr.* **cf., cp.** To examine in order to note the similarities or differences of. Used with *with.* See Usage note below. **3.** *Grammar.* To form the positive, comparative, or superlative degrees of (an adjective or adverb). —*intr.* **1.** To be worthy of comparison; be considered as similar. Used with *with.* See Usage note below. **2.** To vie; compete. —**compare notes.** To exchange impressions. —*n.* Comparison. Usually used in the phrase *beyond* or *without compare.* [Middle English *comparen,* from Old French *comparer,* from Latin *comparāre,* to pair, match, from *compar,* like, equal : *com-,* mutually + *pār,* equal (see **perə-** in Appendix*).] —**com·par′er** *n.*

Usage: In formal usage, *compare to* is the only acceptable form when *compare* means representing as similar or likening, according to 71 per cent of the Usage Panel: *compare a voice to thunder.* In such comparisons the similarities are often metaphorical rather than real; the things compared are of fundamentally unlike orders, and a general likeness is intended rather than a detailed accounting. *Compare with* is the only acceptable form in the sense of examining in order to note similarities or differences, according to 70 per cent of the Panel: *compare Shelley's poetry with Wordsworth's.* Here the things compared are of like kinds, and specific resemblances and differences are examined in detail. Informally, *to* and *with* are often used interchangeably in the foregoing examples. In formal usage, only *compare with* is acceptable when *compare* intransitively means being worthy of comparison, according to 94 per cent of the Panel: *Promises do not compare with deeds.* In such constructions, *compare to* is infrequent, even in informal usage.

com·par·i·son (kəm-păr′ə-sən) *n.* **1.** A comparing or being compared; a statement or estimate of similarities and differences. **2.** The quality of being capable or worthy of being compared; similarity; likeness. **3.** *Grammar.* The modification or inflection of an adjective or adverb to denote the three degrees (positive, comparative, and superlative). [Middle English *comparisoun,* from Old French *comparaison,* from Latin *comparātiō,* from *comparāre,* COMPARE.]

com·part (kəm-pärt′) *tr.v.* **-parted, -parting, -parts.** To divide into compartments or parts; partition; subdivide. [Italian *compartire,* from Late Latin *compartīrī,* to divide, share with : *com-,* with + *partīrī,* to share, from *pars* (stem *part-*), a part (see **perə-** in Appendix*).]

com·part·ment (kəm-pärt′mənt) *n. Abbr.* **compt. 1.** One of the parts or spaces into which an area is subdivided. **2.** Any separate room, section, or chamber: *a storage compartment.*

com·part·men·tal·ize (kŏm′pärt-mĕn′təl-īz′, kəm-pärt′-) *tr.v.* **-ized, -izing, -izes.** To divide or partition into compartments or categories.

com·pass (kŭm′pəs, kŏm′-) *n.* **1. a.** A device used to determine geographical direction, usually consisting of a magnetic needle or needles horizontally mounted or suspended and free to pivot until aligned with the magnetic field of the earth. **b.** Any other device for determining geographical direction, such as a **radio compass** or a **gyrocompass** *(both of which see).* **2.** *Sometimes plural.* A V-shaped device for drawing circles or circular arcs, consisting of a pair of rigid, end-hinged, and continuously separable arms, one of which is equipped with a pen or pencil and the other with a sharp point providing a central anchor or pivot about which the drawing arm is turned. **3.** An enclosing line or boundary; circumference; girth. **4.** An enclosed space or area. **5.** A range or scope; extent. **6.** *Music.* The range of a voice or instrument; register. —*tr.v.* **compassed, -passing, -passes. 1.** To go around; make a circuit of; circle. **2.** To surround; encircle. **3.** To understand; comprehend. **4.** To achieve; obtain; accomplish. **5.** To scheme; plot. —See Synonyms at **reach.** —*adj.* Circular; round. [Middle English *compas,* measure, circle, compasses, compass, from Old French, from *compasser,* to measure (with compasses), from Vulgar Latin *compassāre* (unattested), "to measure off by steps" : Latin *com-* (intensive) + *passus,* PACE.] —**com′pass·a·ble** *adj.*

compass card. A freely pivoting circular disk carrying the magnetic needles of a compass and marked with the 32 points of the compass and the 360 degrees of the circle. Also called "compass rose," "rose."

com·pas·sion (kəm-păsh′ən) *n.* The deep feeling of sharing the suffering of another in the inclination to give aid or support, or to show mercy. See Synonyms at **pity.** [Middle English *compassioun,* from Old French *compassion,* from Late Latin *compassiō,* from *compatī* (past participle *compassus*), to sympathize with : *com-,* with + *patī,* to suffer (see **pēi-** in Appendix*).]

com·pas·sion·ate (kəm-păsh′ən-ĭt) *adj.* Feeling or showing pity or compassion; sympathetic. See Synonyms at **kind.** —*tr.v.* (kəm-păsh′ə-nāt′) **compassionated, -ating, -ates.** To have compassion for; sympathize; to pity. —**com·pas′sion·ate·ly** *adv.* —**com·pas′sion·ate·ness** *n.*

compass plant. 1. A tall plant, *Silphium laciniatum,* of central North America, having yellow flowers and lower leaves that tend to align in a north-south plane. Also called "rosinweed." **2.** Any of several similar plants.

com·pat·i·ble (kəm-păt′ə-bəl) *adj.* **1.** Capable of living or performing in harmonious, agreeable, or congenial combination with another or others. **2.** Capable of orderly, efficient integration and operation with other elements in a system. **3.** Capable of forming a chemically or biochemically stable system. **4.** Of or pertaining to a television system in which color broadcasts can be received in black and white by sets incapable of color reception. [Middle English, from Old French, from Medieval Latin *compatibilis,* from Late Latin *compatī,* to sympathize with. See **compassion.**] —**com·pat′i·bil′i·ty, com·pat′i·ble·ness** *n.* —**com·pat′i·bly** *adv.*

com·pa·tri·ot (kəm-pā′trē-ət, -ŏt′) *n.* **1.** A fellow countryman. **2.** *Informal.* A colleague. —*adj.* Of the same country. [French *compatriote,* from Late Latin *compatriōta* : *com-,* together + *patriōta,* PATRIOT.]

com·peer (kəm-pîr′, kŏm′pîr′) *n.* **1.** A person of equal status or rank; a peer or equal. **2.** A comrade, companion, or associate. [Middle English *comper,* from Old French, from Latin *compār* : *com-,* with + *pār,* an equal, PEER.]

com·pel (kəm-pĕl′) *tr.v.* **-pelled, -pelling, -pels. 1.** To force, drive, or constrain. **2.** To obtain or bring about by force; to exact. **3.** To force to yield or submit; subdue. **4.** To gather or unite by force; to herd. —See Synonyms at **force.** [Middle English *compellen,* from Old French *compeller,* from Latin *compellere,* "to drive (cattle) together," force : *com-,* together + *pellere,* drive (see **pel-**[6] in Appendix*).] —**com·pel′la·ble** *adj.* —**com·pel′la·bly** *adv.* —**com·pel′ler** *n.*

com·pel·la·tion (kŏm′pə-lā′shən, kŏm-pĕl′ā′shən) *n.* **1.** An addressing or designating by name or title. **2.** The name or title used; appellation. [Latin *compellātiō,* from *compellāre,* to accost, address. See **pel-**[6] in Appendix.*]

com·pen·di·ous (kəm-pĕn′dē-əs) *adj.* Containing or stating briefly and concisely all the essentials of something; terse; succinct. See Synonyms at **concise.** [Middle English, from Latin *compendiōsus,* from *compendium,* COMPENDIUM.] —**com·pen′di·ous·ly** *adv.* —**com·pen′di·ous·ness** *n.*

com·pen·di·um (kəm-pĕn′dē-əm) *n., pl.* **-ums** or **-dia** (-dē-ə). Also **com·pend** (kŏm′pĕnd′). A short, complete summary; an abridgment. [Latin, "that which is weighed together," gain, saving, abridgment, from *compendere,* to weigh together : *com-,* together + *pendere,* to weigh (see **spen-** in Appendix*).]

com·pen·sa·ble (kəm-pĕn′sə-bəl) *adj.* Entitled to compensation; that can be compensated.

com·pen·sate (kŏm′pən-sāt′) *v.* **-sated, -sating, -sates.** —*tr.* **1.** To make up for or offset; counterbalance. **2.** To make equivalent or satisfactory reparation to; recompense or reimburse. **3.** To stabilize the purchasing power of (a monetary unit) by changing the gold content in order to counterbalance price variations. —*intr.* To provide or serve as a substitute or counterbalance. [Latin *compensāre,* to weigh one thing against another, counterbalance : *com-,* mutually, reciprocally + *pensāre,* frequentative of *pendere,* to weigh (see **spen-** in Appendix*).] —**com′pen·sa′tive** (-sā′tĭv, kəm-pĕn′sə-tĭv) *adj.*

Usage: *Compensate* is now established in the extended (psychological) sense of counterbalancing a lack or an unwanted characteristic by cultivating a desirable trait: *Very large men sometimes compensate by being excessively gentle* (acceptable on all levels to 75 per cent of the Usage Panel).

com·pen·sa·tion (kŏm′pən-sā′shən) *n.* **1. a.** The act of compensating or making amends. **b.** The state of being compensated. **2.** Something given or received as an equivalent or as reparation for a loss, service, or debt; a recompense; an indemnity. **3.** *Biology.* The counterbalancing of any functional defect by the supplementary development and activation of another organ or another part of the defective structure. **4.** *Psychology.* Behavior designed to compensate for real or imagined defects. —**com′pen·sa′tion·al** *adj.*

com·pen·sa·tor (kŏm′pən-sā′tər) *n.* One who or that which compensates or produces compensation.

com·pen·sa·to·ry (kəm-pĕn′sə-tôr′ē, -tōr′ē) *adj.* Serving to compensate; affording compensation.

com·pete (kəm-pēt′) *intr.v.* **-peted, -peting, -petes.** To strive or contend with another or others, as for a profit or a prize; vie. See Synonyms at **rival.** [Latin *competere,* "to strive together" : *com-,* together + *petere,* to seek, strive (see **pet-**[1] in Appendix*).]

com·pe·tence (kŏm′pə-təns) *n.* Also **com·pe·ten·cy** (-tən-sē). **1.** The state or quality of being capable or competent; skill; ability. **2.** Sufficient means for a comfortable existence. **3.** *Law.* The quality or condition of being legally qualified, eligible, or admissible; legal authority, qualification, or jurisdiction. —See Synonyms at **ability.**

com·pe·tent (kŏm′pə-tənt) *adj.* **1.** Properly or well qualified; capable. **2.** Adequate for the purpose; suitable; sufficient. **3.** *Law.* Legally qualified or fit; admissible. **4.** Rightly or properly belonging; permissible. Used with *to.* [Middle English, from Old French, from Latin *competēns,* present participle of *competere,* to be competent, COMPETE.] —**com′pe·tent·ly** *adv.*

com·pe·ti·tion (kŏm′pə-tĭsh′ən) *n.* **1.** A striving or vying with another or others for profit, prize, position, or the necessities of life; rivalry. **2.** A contest, match, or other trial of skill or ability. **3.** The rivalry between two or more businesses striving for the same customer or market.

com·pet·i·tive (kəm-pĕt′ə-tĭv) *adj.* Also **com·pet·i·to·ry** (-tôr′ē, -tōr′ē). Of, involving, or determined by competition. —**com·pet′i·tive·ly** *adv.* —**com·pet′i·tive·ness** *n.*

com·pet·i·tor (kəm-pĕt′ə-tər) *n.* A person who competes, as in sports or business; rival. See Synonyms at **opponent.**

Com·piègne (kôɴ-pyĕn′y′). An industrial city of northern France, on the Oise, 45 miles north of Paris, near the site of the signing of the armistice ending World War I (1918) and of the armistice between France and Germany (1940). Population, 24,000.

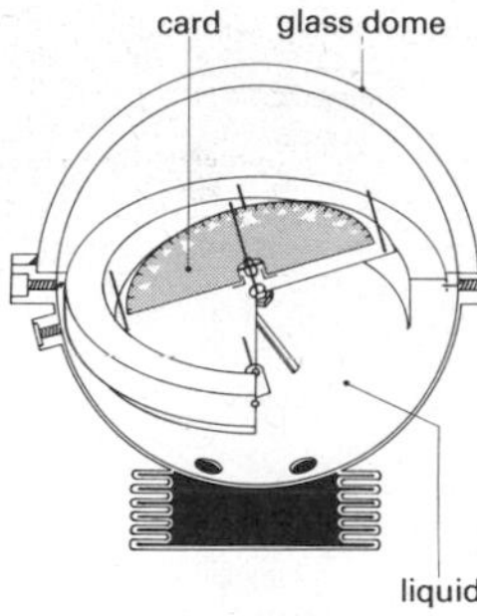
card
glass dome
liquid
compass

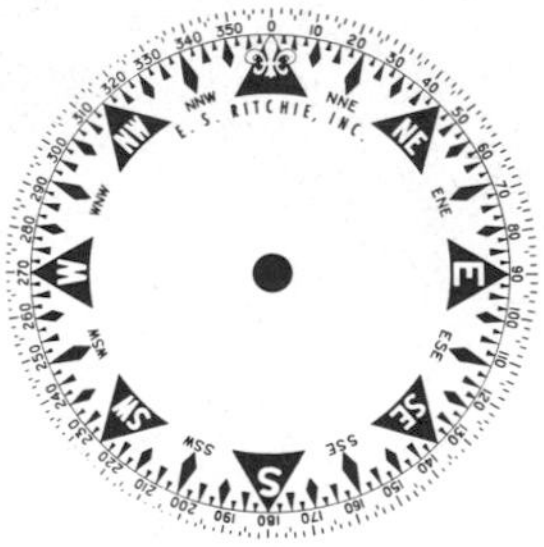
compass card

t tight/th thin, path/*th* this, bathe/ŭ cut/ûr urge/v valve/w with/y yes/z zebra, size/zh vision/ə about, item, edible, gallop, circus/ à *Fr.* ami/œ *Fr.* feu, *Ger.* schön/ü *Fr.* tu, *Ger.* über/KH *Ger.* ich, *Scot.* loch/N *Fr.* bon. ***Follows main vocabulary.** †**Of obscure origin.**

com·pi·la·tion (kŏm′pə-lā′shən) *n. Abbr.* **comp.** **1.** The act of collecting or compiling. **2.** Something compiled, such as a set of data, a report, or an anthology.

com·pile (kəm-pīl′) *tr.v.* **-piled, -piling, -piles.** **1.** To gather (facts, literature, or other material) into one book or corpus. **2.** To put together or compose (a book, outline, or other collection) from materials gathered from several sources. [Middle English *compilen,* from Old French *compiler,* from Latin *compīlāre,* "to heap together," plunder, plagiarize : *com-,* together + *pīlāre,* to plunder, "pile up (booty)," from *pīla,* "pile," PILLAR.] —**com·pil′er** *n.*

com·pla·cen·cy (kəm-plā′sən-sē) *n.* Also **com·pla·cence** (-səns). **1.** A feeling of contentment or satisfaction; gratification. **2.** Self-satisfaction; smugness.

com·pla·cent (kəm-plā′sənt) *adj.* **1.** Contented to a fault; self-satisfied. **2.** Complaisant. [Originally "pleasing," from Latin *complacēns,* present participle of *complacēre,* to please : *com-* (intensive) + *placēre,* to please (see **plāk-**¹ in Appendix*).] —**com·pla′cent·ly** *adv.*

com·plain (kəm-plān′) *intr.v.* **-plained, -plaining, -plains.** **1.** To express feelings of pain, dissatisfaction, or resentment. **2.** To describe one's pains, problems, or dissatisfactions. **3.** To make a formal accusation or bring a formal charge. —See Synonyms at **object.** [Middle English *compleinen,* from Old French *complaindre,* from Vulgar Latin *complangere* (unattested) : Latin *com-* (intensive) + *plangere,* to lament (see **plāk-**² in Appendix*).] —**com·plain′er** *n.*

com·plain·ant (kəm-plā′nənt) *n.* A person who makes a complaint or files a formal charge, as in a court of law; plaintiff.

com·plaint (kəm-plānt′) *n.* **1.** An expression of pain, dissatisfaction, resentment, discontent, or grief. **2.** A cause or reason for complaining; grievance. **3.** A cause of physical pain; malady; illness. **4.** *Law.* The presentation by the plaintiff in a civil action, setting forth the claim on which relief is sought. [Middle English *compleint(e),* from Old French *complainte,* from *complaint,* past participle of *complaindre,* COMPLAIN.]

com·plai·sance (kəm-plā′səns, -zəns) *n.* Willing compliance to the wishes of others; obligingness.

com·plai·sant (kəm-plā′sənt, -zənt, kŏm′plā-zănt′) *adj.* Showing a desire or willingness to please; cheerfully obliging. [French, pleasing, agreeable, from Old French, present participle of *complaire,* to please, from Latin *complacēre.* See **complacent.**] —**com·plai′sant·ly** *adv.*

com·plect (kəm-plĕkt′) *tr.v.* **-plected, -plecting, -plects.** To join by weaving or twining together; interweave. [Latin *complectī, complectere* : *com-,* together + *plectere,* to entwine (see **plek-** in Appendix*).]

com·plect·ed (kəm-plĕk′tĭd) *adj. Regional.* Complexioned. Used only in combination: *light-complected.* [Irregularly from COMPLEXION.]

com·ple·ment (kŏm′plə-mənt) *n.* **1.** Something that completes, makes up a whole, or brings to perfection. **2.** The quantity or number needed to make up a whole. **3.** Either of two parts that complete the whole or mutually complete each other. **4.** The full quantity, allowance, or amount; a complete set. **5.** *Geometry.* An angle related to another so that the sum of their measures is 90 degrees. **6.** A word or words used after a verb to complete a predicate construction. **7.** An interval in music that completes an octave when added to a given interval. **8.** The full crew of officers and men required to man a ship. **9.** *Biochemistry.* The thermolabile substance found in normal blood serum that destroys pathogenic bacteria and materials. In this sense, also formerly called "alexin." —*tr.v.* (kŏm′plə-mĕnt′) **complemented, -menting, -ments.** To add or serve as a complement to. [Middle English, from Latin *complēmentum,* from *complēre,* to COMPLETE.]

com·ple·men·tal (kŏm′plə-mĕn′təl) *adj.* Complementary. —**com′ple·men′tal·ly** *adv.*

com·ple·men·ta·ry (kŏm′plə-mĕn′tə-rē, -mĕn′trē) *adj.* **1.** Forming or serving as a complement; completing. **2.** Supplying needs or lacks. **3.** *Genetics.* Producing effects in concert different from those produced separately. Said of genes. —**com′ple·men′ta·ri·ness** *n.*

complementary angles. Two angles whose sum is 90 degrees.

complementary color. One of two colors which, when ideally mixed in proper proportions, appears white or gray, as the combination of blue-green with red.

complement fixation. *Biochemistry.* The joining of a **complement** *(see)* to the antigen-antibody pair for which it is specific.

com·plete (kəm-plēt′) *adj. Abbr.* **comp.** **1.** Having all necessary or normal parts; entire; whole. See Usage note below and at **replete.** **2.** *Botany.* Having all characteristic floral parts, including sepals, petals, stamens, and a pistil. **3.** Concluded; ended. **4.** Thorough; consummate; perfect. **5.** *Archaic.* Skilled; accomplished. —*tr.v.* **completed, -pleting, -pletes.** **1.** To make whole or complete. **2.** To conclude. [Middle English *complet(e),* from Old French, from Latin *complētus,* past participle of *complēre,* to fill up : *com-* (intensive) + *plēre,* to fill (see **pel-**⁸ in Appendix*).] —**com·plete′ly** *adv.* —**com·plete′ness** *n.* —**com·ple′tive** *adj.*

Synonyms: *complete, close, end, finish, conclude, terminate.* These verbs mean to bring something to, or to arrive at, a stopping point or limit. *Complete* suggests the final stage in assembling parts into a whole: *complete a building,* or bringing a project to fruition: *complete a novel. Close* applies to stopping an action, either when it is completed: *The church service closes with a benediction,* or when it cannot be continued: *Lack of support caused the play to close. End* emphasizes finality: *end a career. Finish,* often interchangeable with *complete,* is especially applicable to what one has set himself to do. *Conclude* adds to *complete* and *close* a sense of formality: *They concluded tariff negotiations. Terminate* more specifically suggests reaching an established limit in time or space.

Usage: *Complete* (adjective) is an absolute term in certain senses and therefore not capable of qualification by *more* or *most.* Such is not the case, however, when the sense relates to comprehensiveness of scope or thoroughness of treatment (where degrees of completeness are felt to exist). Thus: *His book is the most complete treatment of the subject* (acceptable to 67 per cent of the Usage Panel).

com·ple·tion (kəm-plē′shən) *n.* **1.** The act of concluding, perfecting, or making entire. **2.** The state of being completed. **3.** Accomplishment; realization; fulfillment.

com·plex (kəm-plĕks′, kŏm′plĕks′) *adj.* **1.** Consisting of interconnected or interwoven parts; composite; compound. **2.** Involved or intricate, as in structure; complicated. **3.** *Grammar.* Pertaining to or designating a word consisting of at least one bound form, such as *slowly.* —*n.* (kŏm′plĕks′). **1.** A whole composed of intricate or interconnected parts. **2.** *Psychiatry.* A connected group of repressed ideas that compel characteristic or habitual patterns of thought, feeling, and action. **3.** *Informal.* An exaggerated or obsessive concern or fear. [Latin *complexus,* past participle of *complectī, complectere,* to entwine : *com-,* together + *plectere,* to twine braid (see **plek-** in Appendix*).] —**com·plex′ly** *adv.* —**com·plex′ness** *n.*

Synonyms: *complex, complicated, intricate, involved, tangled, knotty.* These adjectives describe things having parts so interconnected as to make the whole difficult to understand. *Complex* and *complicated* are similar in indicating a challenge to the mind. *Complex,* however, often implies many varying parts; *complicated* stresses elaborate relationship of parts rather than number. *Intricate* refers to a pattern of intertwining parts that is difficult to follow. *Involved* stresses confusion arising from the commingling of parts and the consequent difficulty of separating them. *Tangled* strongly emphasizes the random twisting of many parts. *Knotty,* a less formal term applied to problems, stresses difficulty of solution.

complex conjugate. **1.** A complex number that when multiplied by a given complex number yields a real number. **2.** A complex quantity that when multiplied by a given complex quantity yields a product free of imaginary terms.

complex fraction. A fraction in which the numerator or denominator or both contain fractions. Also called "compound fraction."

com·plex·ion (kəm-plĕk′shən) *n.* **1.** The natural color, texture, and appearance of the skin. **2.** General character, aspect, or appearance. **3.** In medieval physiology, the combination of the four humors of cold, heat, moistness, and dryness in specific proportions thought to control the temperament and the constitution of the body. [Middle English *complexioun,* physical constitution, temperament, from Old French *complexion,* from Medieval Latin *complexiō,* "combination of corporeal humors," from Latin, connection, combination, from *complexus.* See **complex.**] —**com·plex′ion·al** *adj.*

com·plex·ioned (kəm-plĕk′shənd) *adj.* Of or having a specified complexion. Used in combination: *fair-complexioned.*

com·plex·i·ty (kəm-plĕk′sə-tē) *n., pl.* **-ties.** **1.** The state or condition of being intricate or complex. **2.** Something intricate or complex.

complex number. A number of the form $a + bi$, where a and b are real numbers and $i^2 = -1$; a member of the set of ordered pairs (a,b) of real numbers in which a pair equals another pair if, and only if, corresponding members of the two pairs are identical, and in which addition and multiplication are defined by $(a,b)+(c,d)=(a+c, b+d)$ and $(a,b)(c,d)=(ac-bd, ad+bc)$, respectively. See **number.**

complex sentence. A sentence containing an independent clause and one or more dependent clauses: *When the rain stops, we'll leave.*

complex variable. An expression of the form $x+iy$, where x and y are real variables and $i^2=-1$.

com·pli·a·ble (kəm-plī′ə-bəl) *adj.* Compliant. —**com·pli′a·ble·ness** *n.* —**com·pli′a·bly** *adv.*

com·pli·ance (kəm-plī′əns) *n.* Also **com·pli·an·cy** (-ən-sē). **1.** A yielding to a wish, request, or demand; acquiescence. **2.** A disposition or tendency to yield to others. **3. a.** The extension or displacement of a loaded structure per unit load. **b.** Flexibility. Not in technical use.

com·pli·ant (kəm-plī′ənt) *adj.* Yielding; submissive. See Synonyms at **obedient.** [COMPL(Y) + -ANT.] —**com·pli′ant·ly** *adv.*

com·pli·ca·cy (kəm-plĭk′ə-sē) *n., pl.* **-cies.** **1.** The state of being complicated. **2.** A complication.

com·pli·cate (kŏm′plĭ-kāt′) *v.* **-cated, -cating, -cates.** —*tr.* **1.** To make complex, intricate, or perplexing. **2.** To twist or twine together. —*intr.* **1.** To become complex, intricate, or difficult. **2.** To become twisted or intertwined. —*adj.* (kŏm′plə-kĭt). **1.** Complex; intricate; involved. **2.** *Biology.* Folded longitudinally one or several times, as certain leaves or the wings of some insects. [Latin *complicāre,* to fold together : *com-,* together + *plicāre,* to fold (see **plek-** in Appendix*).]

com·pli·cat·ed (kŏm′plə-kā′tĭd) *adj.* Containing intricately combined or involved parts; not easily understood or untangled. See Synonyms at **complex.** —**com′pli·cat′ed·ly** *adv.* —**com′pli·cat′ed·ness** *n.*

com·pli·ca·tion (kŏm′plə-kā′shən) *n.* **1.** The act of complicating. **2.** A confused or intricate relationship of parts. **3.** Any factor, condition, or element that complicates. **4.** *Medicine.* A condition occurring during another disease and aggravating it.

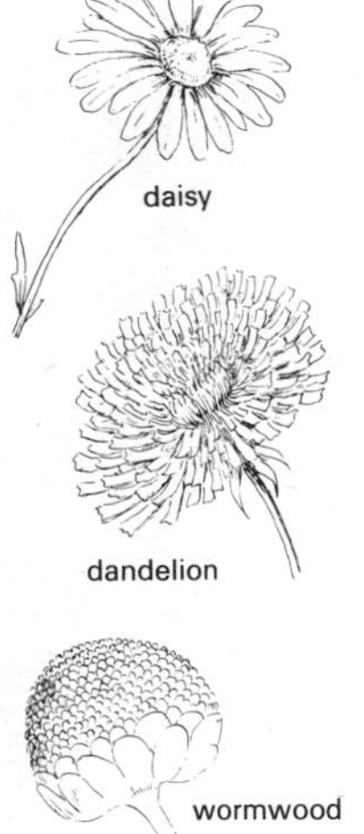
daisy
dandelion
wormwood

composite
Flowers of composite plants

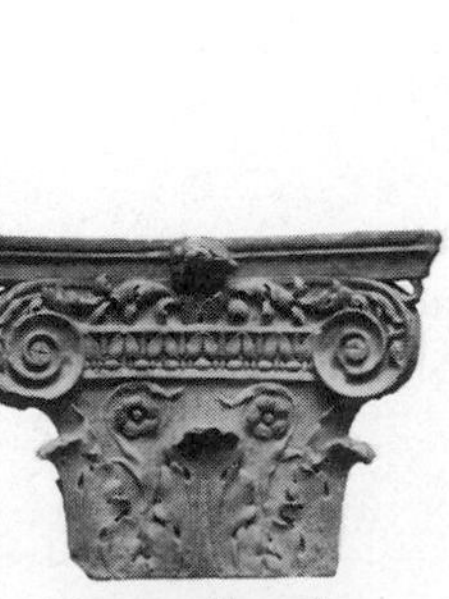

Composite order
Second-century B.C.
marble capital

ă pat/ā pay/âr care/ä father/b bib/ch church/d deed/ĕ pet/ē be/f fife/g gag/h hat/hw which/ĭ pit/ī pie/îr pier/j judge/k kick/l lid, needle/m mum/n no, sudden/ng thing/ŏ pot/ō toe/ô paw, for/oi noise/ou out/ŏŏ took/ōō boot/p pop/r roar/s sauce/sh ship, dish/

com·plice (kŏm′plĭs) *n. Obsolete.* An associate or accomplice. [Middle English, from Old French, from Latin *complex,* closely connected, hence a confederate : *com-,* together + *-plex,* -fold (see **plek-** in Appendix*).]

com·plic·i·ty (kəm-plĭs′ə-tē) *n., pl.* **-ties. 1.** The state of being an accomplice, as in a wrongdoing. **2.** Complexity.

com·pli·er (kəm-plī′ər) *n.* A person who complies or yields.

com·pli·ment (kŏm′plə-mənt) *n.* **1.** An expression of praise, admiration, or congratulation. **2.** A formal act of civility, courtesy, or respect. **3.** *Usually plural.* A formal or ceremonious greeting or remembrance. **4.** *Archaic.* A gift presented for services rendered; gratuity. —*tr.v.* **complimented, -menting, -ments. 1.** To pay a compliment to. **2.** To show fondness, regard, or respect (for someone) by giving a gift or performing a favor. [French, from Spanish *cumplimiento,* from *cumplir,* to complete, behave properly, be courteous, from Latin *complēre,* to fill up : *com-* (intensive) + *plēre,* to fill (see **pel-**⁸ in Appendix*).]

com·pli·men·ta·ry (kŏm′plə-mĕn′tər-ē, -trē) *adj.* **1.** Expressing, using, or resembling a compliment. **2.** Given free to repay a favor or as an act of courtesy. —**com′pli·men′ta·ri·ly** *adv.*

com·plin (kŏm′plĭn) *n.* Also **Com·plin, com·pline** (kŏm′plĭn, -plīn′). *Ecclesiastical.* **1.** The last of the seven **canonical hours** *(see).* **2.** The time of day set aside for this prayer, usually just before retiring. [Middle English *compline,* from Old French *complie,* from Medieval Latin *(hōra) complēta,* "completed (hour)," from Latin *complētus,* past participle of *complēre,* COMPLETE.]

com·ply (kəm-plī′) *intr.v.* **-plied, -plying, -plies. 1.** To act in accordance with a command, request, rule, wish, or the like. Used with *with.* **2.** *Obsolete.* To be courteous or obedient. [Italian *complire,* from Spanish *cumplir,* to complete, do what is proper, be courteous, from Latin *complēre,* to fill up : *com-* (intensive) + *plēre,* to fill (see **pel-**⁸ in Appendix*).]

com·po (kŏm′pō) *n., pl.* **-pos.** Any of various combined substances, such as mortar or plaster, formed by mixing ingredients. [Short for COMPOSITION.]

com·po·nent (kəm-pō′nənt) *n.* **1.** A simple part, or a relatively complex entity regarded as a part, of a system; element; constituent. **2.** A part of a mechanical or electrical complex. **3.** *Mathematics.* One of a set of two or more vectors having a sum equal to a given vector. **4.** *Chemistry.* Any of the minimum number of substances required to completely specify the composition of all phases of a chemical system. —*adj.* Being or functioning as a component; constituent. [Latin *compōnens,* present participle of *compōnere,* to place together : *com-,* together + *pōnere,* to put (see **apo-** in Appendix*).]

com·port (kəm-pôrt′) *v.* **-ported, -porting, -ports.** —*tr.* To conduct or behave (oneself) in a particular manner. —*intr.* To agree, correspond, or harmonize. Used with *with.* [Old French *comporter,* to support, conduct, from Latin *comportāre,* to bring together, later to support : *com-,* together + *portāre,* to carry, bear (see **per-**² in Appendix*).]

com·port·ment (kəm-pôrt′mənt) *n.* Bearing; deportment.

com·pose (kəm-pōz′) *v.* **-posed, -posing, -poses.** —*tr.* **1.** To make up the constituent parts of; constitute or form. See Usage note at **comprise. 2.** To make or create by putting together parts or elements. **3.** To create or produce (a literary or musical piece). **4.** To make (one's mind or body) calm or tranquil; to quiet. **5.** To settle (arguments); reconcile. **6.** To arrange aesthetically or artistically. **7.** *Printing.* To arrange or set (type or matter to be printed). —*intr.* **1.** To create literary or musical pieces. **2.** *Printing.* To set type. [Middle English, from Old French *composer* : *com-,* together, from Latin + *poser,* to place, from Latin *pausāre,* to cease, repose, hence to place, from *pausa,* a pause, from Greek *pausis,* from *pauein,* to stop (see **pauein** in Appendix*).]

com·posed (kəm-pōzd′) *adj.* Calm; serene; self-possessed. See Synonyms at **cool.** —**com·pos′ed·ly** (-pō′zĭd-lē) *adv.* —**com·pos′ed·ness** (-pō′zĭd-nĭs) *n.*

com·pos·er (kəm-pō′zər) *n. Abbr.* **comp.** A person who composes, especially one who composes music.

composing room. *Printing.* A room where typesetting is done.

composing stick. *Printing.* A small shallow tray, usually metal and with an adjustable end, in which a compositor sets type by hand. Also called "job stick."

com·pos·ite (kəm-pŏz′ĭt) *adj. Abbr.* **comp. 1.** Made up of distinct components; compound. **2.** *Mathematics.* Having factors; factorable. **3.** *Botany.* Of, belonging to, or characteristic of the Compositae, a large plant family characterized by flower heads consisting of both **ray flowers** and **disk flowers** *(both of which see),* as in the daisy, of disk flowers only, as in wormwood, or of ray flowers only, as in the dandelion. **4.** *Capital* **C.** *Architecture.* Pertaining to or designating the Composite order. —*n.* **1.** A composite structure or entity. **2.** A complex material, such as wood or fiber glass, in which two or more distinct, structurally complementary substances, especially metals, ceramics, glasses, and polymers, combine to produce some structural or functional properties not present in any individual component. **3.** A composite plant. —See Synonyms at **mixture.** [Latin *compositus,* past participle of *compōnere,* to put together : *com-,* together + *pōnere,* to put (see **apo-** in Appendix*).] —**com·pos′ite·ly** *adv.* —**com·pos′ite·ness** *n.*

composite number. An integer exactly divisible by at least one number other than itself or 1.

Composite order. *Architecture.* A Roman capital formed by superimposing Ionic volutes on a Corinthian capital.

composite photograph. A photograph made by combining two or more separate photographs.

com·po·si·tion (kŏm′pə-zĭsh′ən) *n. Abbr.* **comp. 1.** A putting together of parts or elements to form a whole; a combining. **2.** The manner in which such parts are combined or related; constitution; make-up. **3.** The result or product of composing; mixture; compound. **4.** The arrangement of artistic parts so as to form a unified whole. **5.** The art or act of composing a literary or musical work. **6.** Any work of art, literature, or music, or its structure or organization. **7.** A short essay; especially, one written as a school exercise. **8.** *Law.* **a.** A settlement whereby the creditors of a debtor about to enter bankruptcy agree to accept partial payment in lieu of full payment for debts. **b.** The sum agreed upon. **9.** Settlement by mutual agreement or compromise. **10.** *Linguistics.* The formation of compounds from separate words. **11.** *Printing.* Typesetting. [Middle English *composicioun,* from Old French *composition,* from Latin *compositiō,* from *compōnere,* to put together, arrange : *com-,* together + *pōnere,* to put (see **apo-** in Appendix*).] —**com′po·si′tion·al** *adj.*

composition of forces. The finding or determination of a vector that is the resultant of a given set of forces.

com·pos·i·tive (kəm-pŏz′ə-tĭv) *adj.* Compounded; synthetic.

com·pos·i·tor (kəm-pŏz′ə-tər) *n. Abbr.* **comp.** *Printing.* A typesetter. —**com·pos′i·to′ri·al** (-tôr′ē-əl, -tōr′ē-əl) *adj.*

com·pos men·tis (kŏm′pəs mĕn′tĭs). *Latin.* Of sound mind; sane. Literally, having the mastery of one's mind.

com·post (kŏm′pōst) *n.* **1.** A mixture of decaying organic matter, such as leaves and manure, used as fertilizer. **2.** A composition; mixture. —*tr.v.* **composted, -posting, -posts. 1.** To fertilize with compost. **2.** To change (vegetable matter) to compost. [Middle English, stew, compote, from Old French *composte,* stewed fruit, and *compost,* mixture, respectively from Latin *composita* and *compositum,* feminine and neuter of *compositus,* put together, COMPOSITE.]

com·po·sure (kəm-pō′zhər) *n.* Self-possession; calmness; tranquillity. See Synonyms at **equanimity.** [From COMPOSE.]

com·po·ta·tion (kŏm′pō-tā′shən) *n.* A drinking together; a carouse. [Latin *compōtātiō* (translation of Greek *sumposion,* SYMPOSIUM) : *com-,* together + *pōtātiō,* POTATION.] —**com′po·ta′tor** (-tā′tər) *n.*

com·pote (kŏm′pōt; *French* kôɴ-pôt′) *n.* **1.** Fruit stewed or cooked in syrup. **2.** A long-stemmed dish, used for holding fruit, nuts, or candy. [French, from Old French *composte,* stewed fruit, COMPOST.]

com·pound¹ (kŏm-pound′, kəm-) *v.* **-pounded, -pounding, -pounds.** —*tr.* **1.** To combine; mix. **2.** To produce or create by combining two or more ingredients or parts. **3.** *Pharmacology.* To mix (drugs) according to prescription. **4.** To settle (a debt, for example) by agreeing on an amount less than the claim; adjust. **5.** To compute (interest) on the principal and accrued interest. **6.** *Law.* To agree, for payment or other consideration, not to prosecute: *compound a felony.* **7.** To add to; increase. —*intr.* **1.** To come to terms; agree. **2.** To settle or compromise with a creditor. —See Synonyms at **mix.** —*adj.* (kŏm′pound, kŏm-pound′). Consisting of two or more substances, ingredients, elements, or parts. —*n.* (kŏm′pound). *Abbr.* **comp., cpd. 1.** A combination of two or more elements or parts. **2.** A combination of words or word elements regarded as a unit according to various linguistic analyses, as: **a.** A graphemic unit containing two or more free forms, or one or more free forms with one or more bound forms, with or without hyphenation. **b.** A word containing two or more elements that have perceptible lexical meaning. **c.** An intonational pattern exhibiting a primary stress and a terminal juncture. **d.** A sequence of words not connected by a functional element in surface structure but functioning as a grammatical kernel in deep structure. **3.** *Chemistry.* A pure, macroscopically homogeneous substance consisting of atoms or ions of two or more different elements in definite proportions, and usually having properties unlike those of its constituent elements. —See Synonyms at **mixture.** [Middle English *compounen,* from Old French *compon(d)re,* from Latin *compōnere,* to put together : *com-,* together + *pōnere,* to put (see **apo-** in Appendix*).] —**com·pound′a·ble** *adj.* —**com·pound′er** *n.*

com·pound² (kŏm′pound) *n.* A residence or group of residences set off and enclosed by a barrier, as: **1.** In the Orient, such a group of residences for Europeans. **2.** In Africa, a group of huts for native workers. **3.** Such an enclosure used for confining prisoners of war. [Portuguese *campon* or Dutch *kampoeng,* from Malay *kampong,* village, cluster of buildings.]

com·pound-com·plex sentence (kŏm′pound-kŏm′plĕks). A sentence consisting of at least two coordinate independent clauses and one or more dependent clauses.

compound eye. The eye of most insects and some crustaceans, composed of many light-sensitive elements, each with its own refractive system and each forming a portion of an image.

compound flower. A flower head of a composite plant, consisting of numerous small flowers appearing as a single bloom.

compound fraction. *Mathematics.* A **complex fraction** *(see).*

compound fracture. A fracture in which broken bone lacerates soft tissue.

compound interest. Interest computed on the accumulated unpaid interest as well as on the original principal. Compare **simple interest.**

compound leaf. A leaf consisting of two or more separate leaflets borne on a single leafstalk.

compound microscope. A microscope consisting of an objective and an eyepiece at opposite ends of an adjustable tube.

compound number. A quantity, such as 10 pounds 5 ounces or 3 feet 4 inches, involving different units of measure.

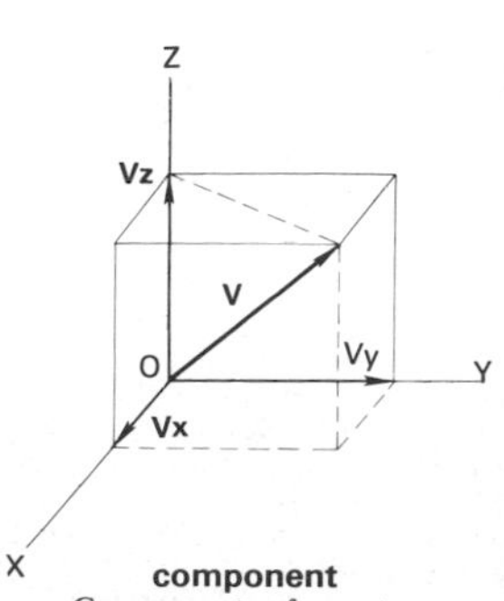

component
Components of a vector **V** along coordinate axes

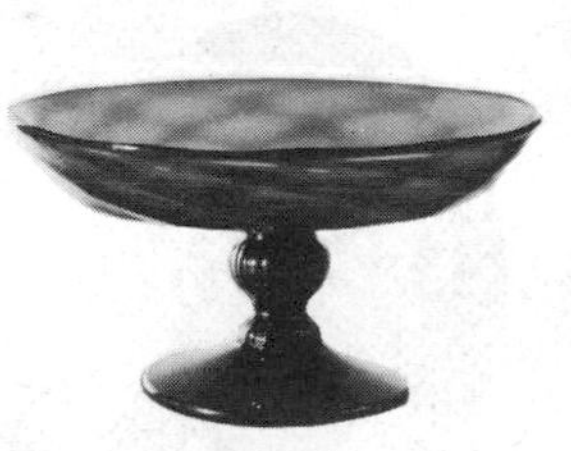

compote
Nineteenth-century American amber glass

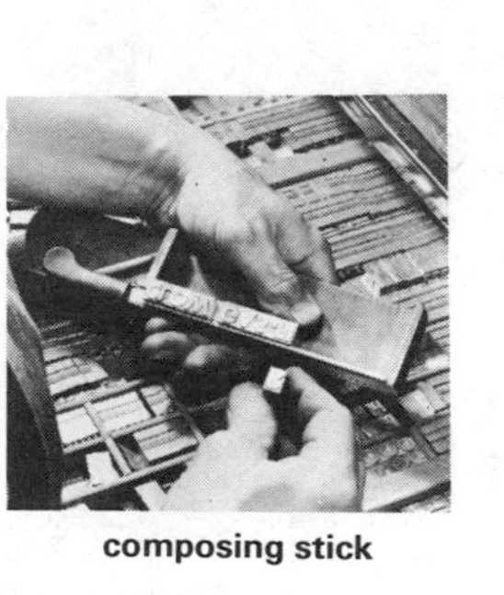

composing stick

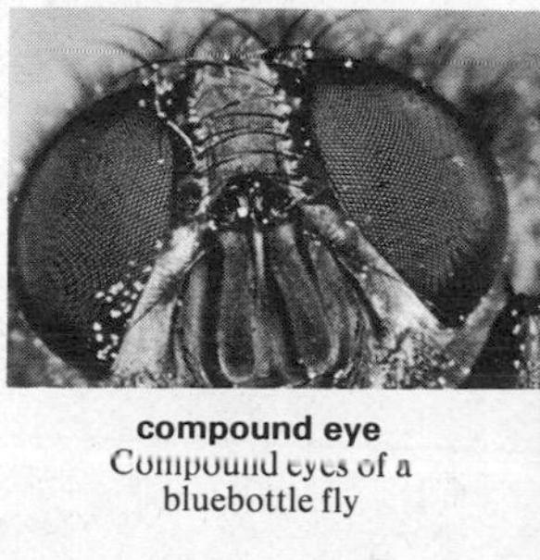

compound eye
Compound eyes of a bluebottle fly

compound sentence. A sentence of two or more coordinate independent clauses, often joined by a conjunction or conjunctions: *The problem was difficult, but I finally found the answer.*

com·pra·dor (kŏm′prə-dôr′) *n.* Also **com·pra·dore.** Formerly, in China and certain other Asian countries, a native agent for a foreign business. [Portuguese, "buyer," from Late Latin *comparātor*, from Latin *comparāre*, provide, buy, prepare : *com-* (collectively) + *parāre*, to prepare (see **per-⁴** in Appendix*).]

com·pre·hend (kŏm′prī-hĕnd′) *tr.v.* **-hended, -hending, -hends.** 1. To grasp mentally; understand or know. 2. To take in, include, or embrace; comprise. —See Synonyms at **apprehend, include.** [Middle English *comprehenden*, from Latin *comprehendere*, to grasp mentally : *com-*, together in mind, mentally + *prehendere*, to seize, grasp (see **ghend-** in Appendix*).]

com·pre·hen·si·ble (kŏm′prī-hĕn′sə-bəl) *adj.* Also **com·pre·hend·i·ble** (-hĕn′də-bəl). Capable of being comprehended or understood; intelligible. —**com′pre·hen′si·bil′i·ty, com′pre·hen′si·ble·ness** *n.* —**com′pre·hen′si·bly** *adv.*

com·pre·hen·sion (kŏm′prī-hĕn′shən) *n.* 1. The act of or capacity for comprehending or understanding. 2. Comprehensiveness. 3. The attributes implied by a term in logic.

com·pre·hen·sive (kŏm′prī-hĕn′sĭv) *adj.* 1. Including or comprehending much; large in scope or content. 2. Capable of understanding or perceiving easily or well. —*n.* 1. *Usually plural. Informal.* Examinations covering the entire field of major study given in the final undergraduate or graduate year. In full, "comprehensive examinations." 2. *Advertising.* A layout showing all the elements planned for an advertisement, but not ready for actual reproduction. Often shortened to "comp." —**com′pre·hen′sive·ly** *adv.* —**com′pre·hen′sive·ness** *n.*

com·press (kəm-prĕs′) *tr.v.* **-pressed, -pressing, -presses.** To press together or force into smaller space; condense; compact. See Synonyms at **contract.** —*n.* (kŏm′prĕs′). 1. *Medicine.* A soft pad of gauze or other material applied to a part of the body to control hemorrhage, or moistened with water or medication, to alleviate pain or reduce infection. 2. A machine or establishment for baling cotton. [Middle English *compressen*, from Old French *compresser*, from Late Latin *compressāre*, frequentative of Latin *comprimere* (past participle *compressus*), to press together : *com-*, together + *premere*, to press (see **per-⁶** in Appendix*).] —**com·press′i·bil′i·ty, com·press′i·ble·ness** *n.* —**com·press′i·ble** *adj.*

com·pressed (kəm-prĕst′) *adj.* 1. Pressed together or into less space; made compact. 2. *Biology.* Flattened laterally or lengthwise, as certain seed pods or the bodies of many fish.

compressed air. Air under greater than atmospheric pressure, especially when used to power a mechanical device or provide a portable supply of oxygen.

com·pres·sion (kəm-prĕsh′ən) *n.* Also **com·pres·sure** (-prĕsh′ər) (for sense 1). 1. a. The act or process of compressing. b. The state of being compressed. 2. a. The process by which the working substance in a heat engine, as the vapor mixture in the cylinder of an internal-combustion engine, is compressed. b. The engine cycle during which this process occurs.

com·pres·sive (kəm-prĕs′ĭv) *adj.* Compressing or capable of compressing. —**com·pres′sive·ly** *adv.*

com·pres·sor (kəm-prĕs′ər) *n.* One that compresses, especially a machine used to compress gases.

com·prise (kəm-prīz′) *tr.v.* **-prised, -prising, -prises.** 1. To consist of; be composed of. 2. To include; contain. —See Synonyms at **include.** [Middle English *comprisen*, from Old French *comprendre* (past participle *compris*), to comprehend, include, from Latin *comprehendere*, to grasp mentally : *com-*, together in mind, mentally + *prehendere*, to seize (see **ghend-** in Appendix*).] —**com·pris′a·ble** *adj.*

Usage: By definition, the whole comprises the parts; the parts do not comprise the whole, nor is the whole comprised of its parts. In strict usage: *The Union comprises 50 states. Fifty states compose* (or *constitute, make up*) *the Union. The Union is composed of 50 states.* This rule restricting *comprise* and *compose* to separate senses is supported by a majority of the Usage Panel, but returns indicate that *comprise* is increasingly used in both senses: *Fifty states comprise the Union* (unacceptable to 61 per cent of the Panel); *the Union is comprised of 50 states* (unacceptable to 53 per cent).

com·pro·mise (kŏm′prə-mīz′) *n.* 1. A settlement of differences in which each side makes concessions. 2. Anything resulting from such a settlement. 3. Something midway between different things or combining certain of their qualities. 4. A laying open to danger, especially one's reputation or character. —*v.* **compromised, -mising, -mises.** —*tr.* 1. To settle by concessions. 2. To expose or make liable to danger, suspicion, or disrepute. 3. To give up (one's interests, principles, or integrity). 4. *Obsolete.* To pledge mutually. —*intr.* To make a compromise. [Middle English *compromis*, from Old French, from Latin *comprōmissum*, from *comprōmittere*, to promise mutually (to abide by an arbiter's decision) : *com-*, mutually + *prōmittere*, to PROMISE.] —**com′pro·mis′er** *n.*

compt. compartment.

Comp·tom·e·ter (kŏmp-tŏm′ə-tər) *n.* A trademark for a high-speed calculating and adding machine. [French *compt*, account, from Old French *compte*, from Late Latin *computus*, from Latin *computāre*, to reckon, COMPUTE + -METER.]

Comp·ton (kŏmp′tən), **Arthur Holly.** 1892–1962. American physicist; discovered the **Compton effect** (*see*).

Compton effect. The increase in wavelength of electromagnetic radiation, especially of an x-ray or gamma-ray photon, scattered by an electron. [Discovered by A.H. COMPTON.]

comp·trol·ler. Variant of **controller.**

com·pul·sion (kəm-pŭl′shən) *n.* 1. The act of compelling or forcing; coercion; constraint. 2. The state of being compelled. 3. *Psychology.* a. An irresistible impulse to act, regardless of the rationality of the motivation. b. An act or acts performed in response to such an impulse. [Middle English *compulsioun*, from Old French *compulsion*, from Late Latin *compulsiō*, from Latin *compellere* (past participle *compulsus*), COMPEL.]

com·pul·sive (kəm-pŭl′sĭv) *adj.* 1. Compelling; compulsory. 2. *Psychology.* Caused or conditioned by compulsion or obsession. —**com·pul′sive·ly** *adv.* —**com·pul′sive·ness** *n.*

com·pul·so·ry (kəm-pŭl′sə-rē) *adj.* 1. Employing or exerting compulsion; coercive; compelling. 2. Obligatory; required. [Medieval Latin *compulsōrius*, from Latin *compellere*, to COMPEL.] —**com·pul′so·ri·ly** *adv.* —**com·pul′so·ri·ness** *n.*

com·punc·tion (kəm-pŭngk′shən) *n.* 1. A strong uneasiness caused by a sense of guilt; remorse. 2. A slight uneasiness or regret. —See Synonyms at **qualm.** [Middle English, from Old French *componction*, from Late Latin *compunctiō*, "prick of conscience," from Latin, puncture, from *compungere*, to prick hard : *com-* (intensive) + *pungere*, to prick, sting (see **peuk-** in Appendix*).] —**com·punc′tious** *adj.* —**com·punc′tious·ly** *adv.*

com·pur·ga·tion (kŏm′pər-gā′shən) *n. Law.* The practice of clearing an accused person of a charge by having a number of people swear to a belief in his innocence. [Late Latin *compurgātiō*, from Latin *compurgāre*, to purify completely : *com-* (intensive) + *purgāre*, to purify (see **peuə-¹** in Appendix*).]

com·pu·ta·tion (kŏm′pyōō-tā′shən) *n.* 1. The act, process, or method of computing. 2. The result of computing.

com·pute (kəm-pyōōt′) *v.* **-puted, -puting, -putes.** —*tr.* To determine by mathematics, especially by numerical methods. —*intr.* To determine an amount or number. —See Synonyms at **calculate.** —*n.* Computation. Used in the phrase *beyond compute.* [Latin *computāre*, to reckon together : *com-*, together in mind, mentally + *putāre*, to think, reckon (see **peuə-²** in Appendix*).] —**com·put′a·bil′i·ty** *n.* —**com·put′a·ble** *adj.*

com·put·er (kəm-pyōō′tər) *n.* 1. A person who computes. 2. A device that computes; especially, an electronic machine that performs high-speed mathematical or logical calculations or that assembles, stores, correlates, or otherwise processes and prints information derived from coded data in accordance with a predetermined **program** (*see*). See **digital computer, analog computer.**

com·put·er·ize (kəm-pyōō′tə-rīz′) *tr.v.* **-ized, -izing, -izes.** 1. To process or store (information) with or in an electronic computer or system of computers. 2. To furnish with a computer or computer system.

computer language. A code used to provide data and instructions to computers.

Comr. commissioner.

com·rade (kŏm′răd, -rĭd, kŭm′-) *n.* 1. A friend, associate, or companion. 2. A person who shares one's interests, occupation, or activities. 3. *Often capital* C. A fellow member, as in a political party or fraternal group; especially, a fellow member of the Communist Party. [Earlier *camerade, cumrade*, from Old French *camarade*, roommate, soldier sharing the same room, from Spanish *camarada*, from *camara*, room, from Late Latin *camera*, from Latin, arched roof, from Greek *kamara*, vault. See **kamer-** in Appendix*.] —**com′rade·ship′** *n.*

Com·stock (kŭm′stŏk, kŏm′-), **Anthony.** 1844–1915. American social reformer and crusader against vice.

Com·stock·er·y (kŭm′stŏk′ə-rē, kŏm′-) *n.* Overzealous censorship of literature and the other arts because of alleged immorality. [After Anthony COMSTOCK.]

Com·stock Lode (kŭm′stŏk, kŏm′-). A gold and silver vein discovered in 1859 at Virginia City, western Nevada, 16 miles southeast of Reno. [Discovered by Henry Comstock (1820–1870), American prospector.]

Comte (kônt), **(Isidore) Auguste (Marie François).** 1798–1857. French mathematician and philosopher; founder of positivism.

Com·tism (kŏm′tĭz-əm) *n.* The philosophy of Auguste Comte; positivism. —**Com′tist** (kŏm′tĭst) *adj. & n.*

Co·mus (kō′məs). A classical deity of revelry. [Latin, from Greek *Kōmos*, personification of *kōmos*, revel, festival procession. See **comedy.**]

con¹ (kŏn) *adv.* Against; in opposition to or disagreement with: *debate pro and con. Compare* **pro.** —*n.* That which weighs against, as an argument, evidence, or a person voting in a group: *the pros and cons.* [Middle English, short for *contra*, against, from Latin *contrā.* See **kom** in Appendix*.]

con² (kŏn) *tr.v.* **conned, conning, cons.** To study, peruse, or examine carefully; learn or commit to memory. [Middle English *connen, cunnen*, to know how, be able, master, Old English *cunnan.* See **gnō-** in Appendix*.] —**con′ner** *n.*

con³ (kŏn) *tr.v.* **conned, conning, cons.** Also **conn.** *Nautical.* To direct the steering or course of (a vessel). —*n. Nautical.* 1. The station or post of the person who cons. 2. The act or process of conning. [Earlier *cond, cund*, from Middle English *conduen, condien*, to guide, from Old French *conduire*, to conduct, from Latin *condūcere*, "to bring together" : *com-*, together + *dūcere*, to lead (see **deuk-** in Appendix*).]

con⁴ (kŏn) *tr.v.* **conned, conning, cons.** *Slang.* To swindle or defraud (a victim) by first winning his confidence; to dupe. —*n. Slang.* A swindle. [Short for CONFIDENCE.]

con⁵ (kŏn) *n. Slang.* A convict.

con. 1. concerto. 2. *Law.* conclusion. 3. connection. 4. consolidate; consolidated. 5. consols. 6. consul. 7. continued. 8. wife (Latin *conjunx*).

Con. 1. conformist. 2. consul.

Anthony Comstock

Con·a·kry (kăn′ə-krē). The capital of the Republic of Guinea, a seaport in the southwest on the Atlantic. Population, 112,000.
con a·mo·re (kōn ä-mō′rā). *Music.* Lovingly; tenderly. Used as a direction. [Italian, "with love."]
Co·nan Doyle, Sir **Arthur.** See Sir Arthur Conan **Doyle.**
Co·nant (kō′nənt), **James Bryant.** Born 1893. American educator and diplomat; president of Harvard (1933–53).
co·na·tion (kō-nā′shən) *n. Psychology.* The aspect of mental processes or behavior directed toward action or change and including impulse, desire, volition, and striving. [Latin *cōnātiō,* endeavor, effort, from *cōnātus,* past participle of *cōnārī,* to endeavor. See **ken-**[1] in Appendix.*] —**co·na′tion·al** *adj.* —**co′-na·tive** (kŏn′ə-tĭv, kō′nə-) *adj.*
co·na·tus (kō-nā′təs) *n., pl.* **conatus.** Any natural tendency, impulse, or directed effort. [Latin *cōnātus,* attempt, effort, from the past participle of *cōnārī,* to endeavor. See **conation.**]
con bri·o (kōn brē′ō). *Music.* With spirit and vigor. Used as a direction. [Italian, "with vigor."]
conc. concentrate.
con·cat·e·nate (kŏn-kăt′ə-nāt′) *tr.v.* **-nated, -nating, -nates.** To connect or link in a series or chain. —*adj.* (-nĭt, -nāt′). Connected or linked in a series. [Late Latin *concatēnāre* : *com-,* together + *catēnāre,* to link, chain, from Latin *catēna,* CATENA.] —**con·cat′e·na′tion** *n.*
con·cave (kŏn-kāv′) *adj.* Curved like the inner surface of a sphere. Compare **convex.** —*n.* A concave surface, structure, or line. —*tr.v.* **concaved, -caving, -caves.** To make concave. [Middle English, from Old French, from Latin *concavus,* vaulted, hollow : *com-* (see **com-**) + *cavus,* hollow (see **keu-**[3] in Appendix*).] —**con·cave′ly** *adv.* —**con·cave′ness** *n.*
con·cav·i·ty (kŏn-kăv′ə-tē) *n., pl.* **-ties. 1.** The condition or state of being concave. **2.** A concave surface or structure.
con·ca·vo-con·cave (kŏn-kā′vō-kŏn-kāv′) *adj.* Concave on both surfaces, as certain lenses.
con·ca·vo-con·vex (kŏn-kā′vō-kŏn-vĕks′) *adj.* **1.** Concave on one side and convex on the other. Also "convexo-concave." **2.** *Optics.* Designating a lens with greater concave than convex curvature.
con·ceal (kən-sēl′) *tr.v.* **-cealed, -cealing, -ceals.** To hide or keep from observation, discovery, or understanding; keep secret. See Synonyms at **hide.** [Middle English *concelen,* from Old French *conceler,* from Latin *concēlāre* : *com-* (intensive) + *cēlāre,* to hide (see **kel-**[4] in Appendix*).] —**con·ceal′a·ble** *adj.* —**con·ceal′er** *n.* —**con·ceal′ment** *n.*
con·cede (kən-sēd′) *v.* **-ceded, -ceding, -cedes.** —*tr.* **1.** To acknowledge as true, just, or proper; admit. **2.** To yield or grant (a privilege or right, for example). —*intr.* To make a concession. —See Synonyms at **acknowledge, grant.** [French *concéder,* from Latin *concēdere,* to yield : *com-* (intensive) + *cēdere,* to go away, withdraw (see **ked-**[1] in Appendix*).] —**con·ced′ed·ly** *adv.* —**con·ced′er** *n.*
con·ceit (kən-sēt′) *n.* **1.** Too high an opinion of one's abilities, worth, or personality; vanity. **2.** An ingenious or witty thought or expression. **3. a.** An elaborate or exaggerated metaphor. **b.** The use of such metaphors. **4.** *Archaic.* A thought or idea; opinion. **5.** *Obsolete.* A fancy article. —*tr.v.* **conceited, -ceiting, -ceits. 1.** *Obsolete.* To imagine or think. **2.** *Regional.* To take a fancy to, think well of. [Middle English *conceite,* concept, notion, from *conceiven,* CONCEIVE (by analogy with DECEIVE, DECEIT).]
con·ceit·ed (kən-sē′tĭd) *adj.* **1.** Holding too high an opinion of oneself; vain. **2.** *Regional.* Inclined to be fanciful or whimsical. —**con·ceit′ed·ly** *adv.* —**con·ceit′ed·ness** *n.*
con·ceive (kən-sēv′) *v.* **-ceived, -ceiving, -ceives.** —*tr.* **1.** To become pregnant with. **2.** To form in the mind; imagine. **3.** To apprehend mentally; understand. **4.** To express in particular words. **5.** To think or believe; hold an opinion. —*intr.* **1.** To form an idea. Used with *of.* **2.** To become pregnant. [Middle English *conceiven,* from Old French *conceivre,* from Latin *concipere,* to take to oneself, hence to be impregnated, to take into the mind : *com-,* comprehensively + *capere,* to take (see **kap-** in Appendix*).] —**con·ceiv′a·bil′i·ty, con·ceiv′a·ble·ness** *n.* —**con·ceiv′a·ble** *adj.* —**con·ceiv′a·bly** *adv.* —**con·ceiv′er** *n.*
con·cel·e·brate (kən-sĕl′ə-brāt′) *intr.v.* **-brated, -brating, -brates.** To take part in a concelebration. [Latin *concelebrāre* : *com-,* together + *celebrāre,* CELEBRATE.]
con·cel·e·bra·tion (kən-sĕl′ə-brā′shən) *n.* The celebration of the Eucharist by two or more clergymen.
con·cen·ter (kŏn-sĕn′tər) *v.* **-tered, -tering, -ters.** —*tr.* To direct toward a common center. —*intr.* To come together at a common center. [Old French *concentrer,* CONCENTRATE.]
con·cen·trate (kŏn′sən-trāt′) *v.* **-trated, -trating, -trates.** —*tr.* **1.** To direct or draw toward a common center; focus. **2.** *Chemistry.* To increase the concentration of (a solution or mixture). —*intr.* **1.** To converge toward a center. **2.** To direct one's thoughts or attention. Often used with *on* or *upon.* —*n. Abbr.* **conc.** *Chemistry.* A product of concentration. —*adj. Abbr.* **conc.** Concentrated. [Probably from Old French *concentrer* : *com-,* same, from Latin + *centre,* CENTER.] —**con′cen·tra′tor** (-trā′tər) *n.*
con·cen·tra·tion (kŏn′sən-trā′shən) *n.* **1.** The act or process of concentrating or the condition of being concentrated. **2.** A thing that has been concentrated. **3.** Close attention. **4.** *Chemistry.* The amount of a specified substance in a unit amount of another substance.
concentration camp. A camp where prisoners of war, enemy aliens, and political prisoners are confined.
con·cen·tra·tive (kŏn′sən-trā′tĭv) *adj.* Tending to concentrate; characterized by concentration. —**con′cen·tra′tive·ly** *adv.*
con·cen·tric (kən-sĕn′trĭk) *adj.* Also **con·cen·tri·cal** (-trĭ-kəl). Having a common center. Compare **eccentric.** [Middle English *concentrik,* from Old French *concentrique,* from Medieval Latin *concentricus* : Latin *com-,* same + *centrum,* CENTER.] —**con·cen′tri·cal·ly** *adv.* —**con′cen·tric′i·ty** *n.*
Con·cep·ción (kôn′sĕp-syôn′). A city of west-central Chile, six miles from the Pacific Ocean. Population, 167,000.
con·cept (kŏn′sĕpt) *n.* **1.** A general idea or understanding, especially one derived from specific instances or occurrences. **2.** A thought or notion. —See Synonyms at **idea.** [Late Latin *conceptus,* a thing conceived, thought, from past participle of *concipere,* to take to oneself, CONCEIVE.]
con·cep·ta·cle (kən-sĕp′tə-kəl) *n.* An external cavity in certain algae and fungi, containing reproductive structures. [French, from Latin *conceptāculum,* from *concipere,* to receive, contain, CONCEIVE.]
con·cep·tion (kən-sĕp′shən) *n.* **1.** *Embryology.* **a.** The formation of a zygote capable of survival and maturation in normal conditions. **b.** The entity so formed; an embryo; zygote. **2.** A beginning; a start. **3.** The ability to form mental concepts; invention. **4.** That which is mentally conceived; a concept, plan, design, idea, or thought. —See Synonyms at **idea.** [Middle English *concepcioun,* from Old French *conception,* from Latin *conceptiō,* from *concipere,* to take to oneself, CONCEIVE.] —**con·cep′tion·al** *adj.*
con·cep·tive (kən-sĕp′tĭv) *adj.* Able to conceive mentally.
con·cep·tu·al (kən-sĕp′chōō-əl) *adj.* Of or pertaining to concepts or conception. —**con·cep′tu·al·ly** *adv.*
con·cep·tu·al·ism (kən-sĕp′chōō-əl-ĭz′əm) *n. Philosophy.* The doctrine, intermediate between nominalism and realism, that universals, or abstract concepts, exist only within the mind and have no external or substantial reality. —**con·cep′tu·al·ist** *n.* —**con·cep′tu·al·is′tic** *adj.*
con·cep·tu·al·ize (kən-sĕp′chōō-əl-īz′) *v.* **-ized, -izing, -izes.** —*tr.* To form concepts or a concept of. —*intr.* To form concepts, theories, or ideas. —**con·cep′tu·al·i·za′tion** *n.*
con·cern (kən-sûrn′) *v.* **-cerned, -cerning, -cerns.** —*tr.* **1.** To pertain or relate to; be of interest or importance to; affect. **2.** To engage or involve the mind or interests of. Used reflexively or in the passive: *concern oneself with trivia.* **3.** To cause anxiety or uneasiness in; to trouble. —*intr. Obsolete.* To be of importance. —*n.* **1.** A matter that relates to or affects one; something of interest or importance. **2.** Regard for or interest in someone or something: *concern for one's well-being.* **3.** Relation; reference. **4.** Anxiety; worry. **5.** A business establishment or enterprise; a company. **6.** *Informal.* A material article or contrivance. —See Synonyms at **anxiety.** [Middle English *concernen,* from Old French *concerner,* from Medieval Latin *concernere,* to relate to, involve with, from Latin, to mix in a sieve (before sifting) : *com-,* together + *cernere,* to sift (see **skeri-** in Appendix*).]
con·cerned (kən-sûrnd′) *adj.* **1.** Interested or affected. **2.** Anxious; troubled; disturbed.
con·cern·ing (kən-sûr′nĭng) *prep.* In reference to; regarding.
con·cern·ment (kən-sûrn′mənt) *n.* **1.** A matter that relates to one's affairs; business. **2.** Reference, relation, or importance. **3.** Participation; involvement. **4.** Anxiety; worry.
con·cert (kŏn′sûrt) *n.* **1.** A musical performance in which a number of vocalists or players participate. **2.** Agreement in purpose, feeling, or action. —**in concert.** All together; in agreement. —*adj.* Pertaining to or designed for concerts. —*v.* (kən-sûrt′) **concerted, -certing, -certs.** —*tr.* **1.** To plan or arrange by mutual agreement. **2.** To contrive or devise. —*intr.* To act or contrive together. [French, from Italian *concerto,* from Old Italian *concertare*†, to bring into agreement, harmonize.]
con·cert·ed (kən-sûr′tĭd) *adj.* **1.** Planned or accomplished together; combined. **2.** *Music.* Arranged in parts for voices or instruments. —**con·cert′ed·ly** *adv.*
concert grand. The largest grand piano, being roughly nine feet in length.
con·cer·ti·na (kŏn′sər-tē′nə) *n.* A small, hexagonal accordion with bellows, and buttons for keys. [CONCERT + Italian *-ina* (feminine diminutive suffix).]
con·cer·ti·no (kŏn′chĕr-tē′nō) *n., pl.* **-nos** or **-ni** (-nē). *Music.* **1.** A short concerto. **2.** The solo instrument group in a concerto grosso. [Italian, diminutive of *concerto,* concerto, CONCERT.]
con·cer·tize (kŏn′sər-tīz′) *intr.v.* **-tized, -tizing, -tizes.** To give, or perform in, concerts.
con·cert·mas·ter (kŏn′sərt-măs′tər, -mäs′tər) *n.* The first violinist and assistant conductor in a symphony orchestra.
con·cer·to (kən-chĕr′tō) *n., pl.* **-tos** or **-ti** (-tē). *Abbr.* **con.** A composition for an orchestra and one or more solo instruments, typically in three movements. [Italian, CONCERT.]
concerto gros·so (kən-chĕr′tō grō′sō) *pl.* **concerti grossi** (kən-chĕr′tē grō′sē). A composition for a small group of solo instruments and a full orchestra. [Italian, "great concerto."]
concert pitch. 1. A pitch to which orchestral instruments are tuned with the A above middle C at 440 cycles per second. **2.** The state of being ready and tensely alert.
con·ces·sion (kən-sĕsh′ən) *n.* **1.** The act of conceding, granting, or yielding. **2.** Any thing or point so conceded. **3.** Something granted by a government or controlling authority, such as a land tract or franchise, to be used for a specific purpose. **4. a.** The privilege of maintaining a subsidiary business within certain premises. **b.** The space allotted for such a business. [Middle English, from Old French, from Latin *concessiō,* from *concēdere* (past participle *concessus*), CONCEDE.]
con·ces·sion·aire (kən-sĕsh′ən-âr′) *n.* Also **con·ces·sion·er** (-sĕsh′ən-ər). The operator or holder of a concession.

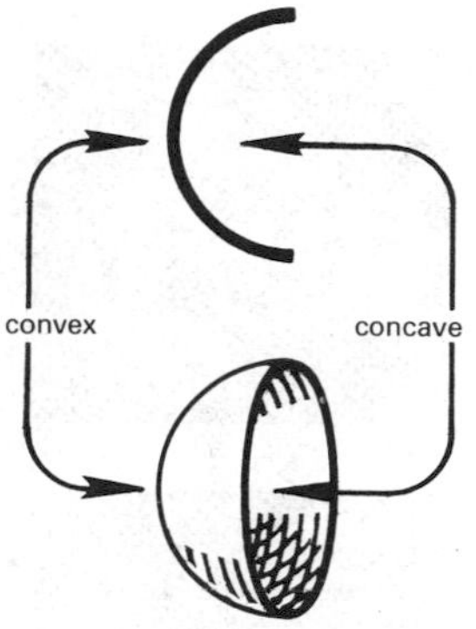

concave

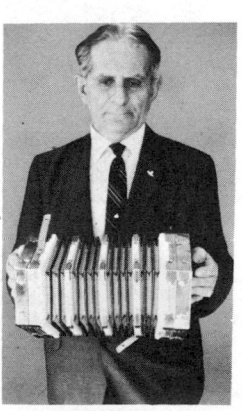

concertina

con·ces·sion·ar·y (kən-sĕsh′ən-ĕr′ē) *adj.* Of or granted by a concession. —*n., pl.* **concessionaries.** A concessionaire.

con·ces·sive (kən-sĕs′ĭv) *adj.* **1.** Of the nature of or containing a concession; tending to concede. **2.** *Grammar.* Expressing concession, as the conjunction *though.* [Latin *concessīvus,* from *concessus,* past participle of *concēdere,* CONCEDE.]

conch (kŏngk, kŏnch) *n., pl.* **conchs** or **conches** (kŏn′chĭz). **1.** Any of various tropical marine gastropod mollusks of the genus *Strombus* and other genera, having large, often brightly colored spiral shells and edible flesh. **2.** The shell of any of these mollusks, used for ornament, in making cameos, or as a horn. **3.** A concha. [Middle English *conche, conk,* from Latin *concha,* from Greek *konkhē.* See **konkho-** in Appendix.*]

con·cha (kŏng′kə) *n., pl.* **-chae** (-kē). **1.** *Anatomy.* A shell-like structure such as the external ear. **2.** *Architecture.* The half dome over an apse. [Latin, CONCH.]

con·chif·er·ous (kŏng-kĭf′ər-əs) *adj.* Having or forming a shell. [CONCH(O)- + -FEROUS.]

concho-, conch-, conchi-. Indicates shell; for example, **conchology.** [Greek *konkho-,* from *konkhē,* shell. See **konkho-** in Appendix.*]

con·choi·dal (kŏng-koid′l) *adj.* Of or pertaining to rocks, such as flint or obsidian, having shell-like surfaces when fractured. [From Greek *konkhoeidēs,* shell-like : CONCH(O)- + -OID.]

con·chol·o·gy (kŏng-kŏl′ə-jē) *n.* The study of mollusks and shells. [CONCHO- + -LOGY.] —**con′cho·log′i·cal** (-kə-lŏj′ĭ-kəl) *adj.* —**con·chol′o·gist** (-kŏl′ə-jĭst) *n.*

Con·chos (kŏn′chəs; *Spanish* kōn′chōs′). A river rising in western Chihuahua, Mexico, and flowing 350 miles east and northeast into the Rio Grande.

con·ci·erge (kŏn′sē-ûrzh; *French* kôN-syârzh′) *n.* **1.** A person who attends the entrance of a building; a janitor. **2.** *Obsolete.* A custodian or warden. [French, from Old French *cumcerges,* from Vulgar Latin *conservius* (unattested), variant of Latin *conservus,* a fellow slave : *com-,* together + *servus,* slave (see **ser-**[1] in Appendix*).]

con·cil·i·ar (kən-sĭl′ē-ər) *adj.* Of or pertaining to a council.

con·cil·i·ate (kən-sĭl′ē-āt′) *tr.v.* **-ated, -ating, -ates. 1.** To overcome the distrust or animosity of; win over; placate; soothe. **2.** To gain, win, or secure (favor, friendship, or good will, for example) by friendly overtures. **3.** To make consistent; reconcile. —See Synonyms at **pacify.** [Latin *conciliāre,* to bring together, unite, from *concilium,* union, gathering, meeting. See **kel-**[3] in Appendix.*] —**con·cil′i·a·ble** (-ə-bəl) *adj.* —**con·cil′i·a′tor** (-ā′tər) *n.* —**con·cil′i·a·to′ry** (-ə-tôr′ē, -tōr′ē) *adj.*

con·cil·i·a·tion (kən-sĭl′ē-ā′shən) *n.* The act or process of conciliating; placation; propitiation. See Synonyms at **mediation.**

con·cin·ni·ty (kən-sĭn′ə-tē) *n., pl.* **-ties. 1.** A skillful, harmonious arrangement of parts. **2.** Elegance of literary style. [Latin *concinnitās,* from *concinnus,* placed fitly together, from *concinnāre,* to place fitly together, arrange in good order : *com-,* together + *cinnus*†, a mixed drink.]

con·cise (kən-sīs′) *adj.* Expressing much in few words; succinct. [Latin *concīsus,* past participle of *concīdere,* to cut up : *com-* (intensive) + *caedere,* to cut (see **skhai-** in Appendix*).] —**con·cise′ly** *adv.* —**con·cise′ness** *n.*

Synonyms: *concise, terse, laconic, pithy, succinct, summary, compendious, epigrammatic.* The idea of stating much in few words is contained in these adjectives. *Concise* implies clarity and compactness through the removal of all unnecessary words. *Terse* adds to *concise* the sense of directness and pointedness. *Laconic* suggests Spartan, almost impolite, brevity and may also indicate consequent lack of clarity. *Pithy* implies pointedness, substance, and telling effect. *Succinct* strongly emphasizes compactness and the elimination of all elaboration. *Summary* implies both condensation and lack of details, and is therefore applicable to anything that covers a broad area concisely, such as an outline. *Compendious* suggests succinctness and condensation, especially of weighty matter. *Epigrammatic* refers to what is brief, well turned, pointed, and witty.

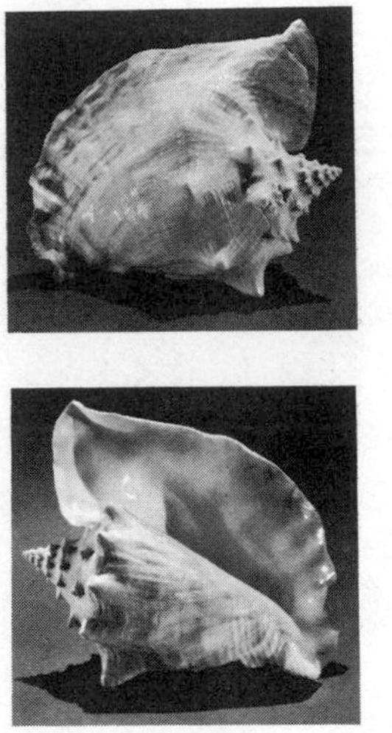

conch
Strombus gigas
Front and back views of the pink conch from the Bahamas

con·ci·sion (kən-sĭzh′ən) *n.* **1.** The quality of being concise; terseness; brevity; succinctness. **2.** *Archaic.* A cutting apart or off; a severing. [Middle English *concisioun,* from Latin *concīsiō,* from *concīsus,* CONCISE.]

con·clave (kŏn′klāv, kŏng′-) *n.* **1.** A confidential or secret meeting. **2. a.** The private rooms in which the cardinals of the Roman Catholic Church meet to elect a pope. **b.** The meeting so held. **3.** The College of Cardinals. [Middle English, from Old French, from Latin *conclāve,* "room locked with a key" : *com-,* together + *clāvis,* key (see **klēu-** in Appendix*).]

con·clude (kən-klo͞od′) *v.* **-cluded, -cluding, -cludes.** —*tr.* **1.** To bring to an end; close; finish. **2.** To come to an agreement or settlement; settle finally: *conclude a peace treaty.* **3.** To reach a decision or form an opinion about; infer or deduce. **4.** To determine; decide; resolve. **5.** *Obsolete.* To confine or enclose. **6.** *Law.* To oblige or bind. Used in the passive. —*intr.* **1.** To come to an end; close. **2.** To form a final judgment; come to a decision or an agreement. —See Synonyms at **complete, decide.** [Middle English *concluden,* from Latin *conclūdere,* to shut up closely : *com-* (intensive) + *claudere,* to shut (see **klēu-** in Appendix*).] —**con·clud′er** *n.*

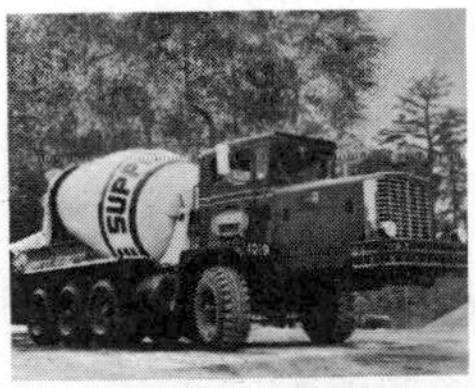

concrete mixer
Concrete mixer mounted on a truck

con·clu·sion (kən-klo͞o′zhən) *n.* **1.** The close or termination of something; the end; the finish. **2.** The closing or last part, as of a discourse, often containing a summing up of the preceding. **3.** The outcome or result of an act or process. **4.** A judgment or decision reached after deliberation. **5.** A final arrangement or settlement, as of a treaty. **6.** *Law. Abbr.* **con. a.** The close of a plea or deed. **b.** An **estoppel** *(see).* **7.** *Logic.* **a.** In a syllogism, the proposition that must follow from the major and minor premises. **b.** The proposition concluded from one or more premises; a deduction. —**in conclusion.** In closing; as a final statement. —**try conclusions with.** To engage (a person) in a contest or argument. [Middle English *conclusioun,* from Old French *conclusion,* from Latin *conclūsiō,* from *conclūdere,* to shut up closely, CONCLUDE.]

con·clu·sive (kən-klo͞o′sĭv) *adj.* Serving to put an end to doubt or question; decisive; final. See Synonyms at **valid.** —**con·clu′sive·ly** *adv.* —**con·clu′sive·ness** *n.*

con·coct (kən-kŏkt′) *tr.v.* **-cocted, -cocting, -cocts. 1.** To prepare by mixing ingredients, as in cookery. **2.** To invent or devise; contrive: *concoct a mystery story.* [Latin *concoquere* (past participle *concoctus*), to cook together : *com-,* together + *coquere,* to cook (see **pekw-** in Appendix*).] —**con·coct′er, con·coc′tor** (-tər) *n.* —**con·coc′tion** *n.* —**con·coc′tive** *adj.*

con·com·i·tance (kən-kŏm′ə-təns) *n.* Also **con·com·i·tan·cy** (-tən-sē) *pl.* **-cies. 1.** Occurrence together or in connection with another; accompaniment. **2.** A concomitant thing or act. **3.** *Roman Catholic Church.* The coexistence of the body and blood of Christ in each element of the Eucharist.

con·com·i·tant (kən-kŏm′ə-tənt) *adj.* Existing or occurring concurrently; accompanying; attendant. See Synonyms at **contemporary.** —*n.* An accompanying state, circumstance, or thing. [Latin *concomitāns,* present participle of *concomitārī,* to accompany : *com-,* together + *comitārī,* to accompany, from *comes* (stem *comit-*), companion (see **ei-**[1] in Appendix*).]

con·cord (kŏn′kôrd, kŏng′-) *n.* **1.** Harmony or agreement of interests or feelings; concurrence; accord. **2.** A treaty establishing peaceful relations. **3.** *Grammar.* Agreement between words in person, number, gender, and case. [Middle English, from Old French *concorde,* from Latin *concordia,* from *concors,* "of the same mind" : *com-,* same, mutually + *cors* (stem *cord-*), the heart, mind (see **kerd-**[1] in Appendix*).]

Con·cord (kŏng′kərd). **1.** A town in eastern Massachusetts, 17 miles northwest of Boston; the site of an early battle (April 19, 1775) of the Revolutionary War. Population, 13,000. **2.** The capital of New Hampshire, situated on the Merrimack River in the south-central part of the state. Population, 30,000.

con·cor·dance (kən-kôr′dəns) *n.* **1.** A state of agreement; harmony; concord. **2.** An alphabetical index of all the words in a text or corpus of texts, showing every contextual occurrence of a word.

con·cor·dant (kən-kôr′dənt) *adj.* Harmonious; agreeing; correspondent. [Middle English *concordaunt,* from Old French *concordant,* from Latin *concordāns,* present participle of *concordāre,* to agree, from *concors,* agreed. See **concord.**] —**con·cor′dant·ly** *adv.*

con·cor·dat (kən-kôr′dăt′) *n.* **1.** A formal agreement; a compact. **2.** An agreement between the pope and a government for the regulation of church affairs. [French, from Medieval Latin *concordātum,* from Latin *concordāre,* to agree. See **concordant.**]

Concord grape. A variety of grape having purple-black fruit with a bluish bloom, used for making jelly, juice, and wine. [Discovered (1846) at CONCORD, Massachusetts.]

con·course (kŏn′kôrs, -kōrs, kŏng′-) *n.* **1.** A great crowd; throng; multitude. **2.** A coming, moving, or flowing together. **3 a.** A large open space for the gathering or passage of crowds, as in a railroad station. **b.** A broad thoroughfare. [Middle English, from Old French *concours,* from Latin *concursus,* from the past participle of *concurrere,* to run together : *com-,* together + *currere,* to run (see **kers-**[2] in Appendix*).]

con·cres·cence (kən-krĕs′əns) *n.* The uniting, especially the growing together, of related parts, as of physical particles or anatomical structures. [Latin *concrēscentia,* from *concrēscēns,* present participle of *concrēscere,* to grow together : *com-,* together + *crēscere,* to grow (see **ker-**[3] in Appendix*).]

con·crete (kŏn-krēt′, kŏn′krēt) *adj.* **1.** Relating to an actual, specific thing or instance; not general; particular. **2.** Existing in reality or in real experience; perceptible by the senses; real. **3.** Designating a thing or group of things as opposed to an abstraction. **4.** Formed by the coalescence of separate particles or parts into one mass; solid. **5.** Made of concrete. —See Synonyms at **real.** —*n.* (kŏn′krēt, kŏn-krēt′). **1.** A construction material consisting of conglomerate gravel, pebbles, broken stone, or slag in a mortar or cement matrix. **2.** A mass formed by the coalescence of particles. —*v.* (kŏn′krēt, kŏn-krēt′) **concreted, -creting, -cretes.** —*tr.* **1.** To form into a mass by coalescence or cohesion of particles. **2.** To build, treat, or cover with concrete. —*intr.* To harden; solidify. [Middle English *concret,* from Old French, from Latin *concrētus,* past participle of *concrēscere,* to grow together, harden : *com-,* together + *crēscere,* to grow (see **ker-**[3] in Appendix*).] —**con·crete′ly** *adv.* —**con·crete′ness** *n.*

concrete mixer. A machine with a revolving drum in which cement, sand, gravel, and water are combined into concrete. Also called "cement mixer."

con·cre·tion (kən-krē′shən) *n.* **1.** The act or process of growing together or becoming united in one mass; coalescence. **2.** A solid or concrete mass. **3.** *Geology.* A rounded mass of mineral matter found in sedimentary rock. **4.** *Pathology.* **a.** A solid mass of inorganic material formed in a cavity or tissue of the body; calculus. **b.** An abnormal fusion of otherwise adjacent parts, as of toes. —**con·cre′tion·ar′y** (-shə-nĕr′ē) *adj.*

con·cre·tize (kŏn′krĭ-tīz′) *tr.v.* **-tized, -tizing, -tizes.** To render concrete; make real or specific.

con·cu·bi·nage (kŏn-kyo͞o′bə-nĭj) *n.* **1.** Cohabitation without legal marriage. **2.** The state of being a concubine.

con·cu·bine (kŏng′kyə-bīn′, kŏn′-) *n.* **1.** A woman who cohabits with a man without being married to him. **2.** In certain polygamous societies, a secondary wife, usually of inferior legal and social status. [Middle English, from Old French, from Latin *concubīna*, "one to sleep with" : *com-*, together + *cubāre*, to lie down (see **keu-²** in Appendix*).]

con·cu·pis·cence (kŏn-kyōō′pə-səns) *n.* **1.** Sexual desire; lust; sensuality. **2.** Any abnormally strong desire. [Latin *concupiscēns*, present participle of *concupiscere*, inceptive of *concupere*, to have a strong desire for : *com-* (intensive) + *cupere*, to desire (see **kwep-** in Appendix*).] —**con·cu′pis·cent** *adj.*

con·cur (kən-kûr′) *intr.v.* **-curred, -curring, -curs. 1.** To have the same opinion; agree. **2.** To act together; cooperate. **3.** To occur at the same time; coincide. **4.** *Rare.* To come together; converge. —See Synonyms at **assent.** [Middle English *concurren*, from Latin *concurrere*, to run together : *com-*, together + *currere*, to run (see **kers-²** in Appendix*).]

Usage: *Concur in* is generally used to express approval or joint action: *concur in a plan. Concur to* (with infinitive) also is used for joint action: *concurred to avert trouble. Concur with* expresses agreement: *concur with him* (or *with his view*).

con·cur·rence (kən-kûr′əns) *n.* Also **con·cur·ren·cy** (-ən-sē) *pl.* **-cies. 1.** Agreement in opinion; accordance. **2.** Cooperation or combination, as of agents, causes, circumstances, or events. **3.** Simultaneous occurrence; coincidence. **4.** *Rare.* Competition. **5.** *Law.* A power or claim jointly held.

con·cur·rent (kən-kûr′ənt) *adj.* **1.** Happening at the same time or place. **2.** Operating in conjunction. **3.** Meeting at or tending to meet at the same point. **4.** In accordance; agreeing; harmonious. —See Synonyms at **contemporary.** —*n.* **1.** One that concurs. **2.** *Rare.* A competitor or rival. [Middle English, from Old French, from Latin *concurrēns*, present participle of *concurrere*, to run together, CONCUR.] —**con·cur′rent·ly** *adv.*

concurrent resolution. A resolution adopted by both houses of a bicameral legislature, that does not have the force of law and does not require the signature of the chief executive. Compare **joint resolution.**

con·cuss (kən-kŭs′) *tr.v.* **-cussed, -cussing, -cusses. 1.** To injure (the brain) by concussion. **2.** *Rare.* To shake or agitate; disturb severely. [Late Latin *concutere* (past participle *concussus*), to shake violently : Latin *com-* (intensive) + *-cutere*, from *quatere*, to shake, dash (see **kwēt-** in Appendix*).]

con·cus·sion (kən-kŭsh′ən) *n.* **1.** A violent jarring; a shock. **2.** An injury of a soft structure, especially of the brain, resulting from a violent blow. —**con·cus′sive** (-kŭs′ĭv) *adj.*

cond. 1. condition. **2.** conductor.

Con·dé (kôN-dā′), **Prince de.** Title of Louis II de Bourbon, Duc d'Enghien. Called "the Great Condé." 1621–1686. French general.

con·demn (kən-dĕm′) *tr.v.* **-demned, -demning, -demns. 1.** To express disapproval of; censure; criticize. **2.** To pronounce judgment against; to sentence; to doom. **3.** To demonstrate the guilt of; to convict. **4.** To judge or declare to be unfit for use or consumption, usually by official order: *condemn an old building.* **5.** *Law.* To declare legally appropriated for public use under the right of eminent domain. —See Synonyms at **criticize.** [Middle English *condem(p)nen*, from Old French *condem(p)ner*, from Latin *condemnāre* : *com-* (intensive) + *damnāre*, to damage, condemn, from *damnum*, damage, fine (see **dap-** in Appendix*).] —**con·dem′na·ble** (-dĕm′nə-bəl) *adj.* —**con·demn′er** *n.*

con·dem·na·tion (kŏn′dĕm-nā′shən) *n.* **1.** The act of condemning. **2.** The state of being condemned. **3.** Severe reproof; strong censure. **4.** A reason or occasion for condemning. —**con·dem′na·to′ry** (-nə-tôr′ē, -tōr′ē) *adj.*

con·den·sa·ble (kən-dĕn′sə-bəl) *adj.* Also **con·den·si·ble.** Capable of being condensed. —**con·den′sa·bil′i·ty** *n.*

con·den·sate (kən-dĕn′sāt′) *adj. Rare.* Condensed. —*n.* A product of condensation. [Latin *condēnsātus*, past participle of *condēnsāre*, CONDENSE.]

con·den·sa·tion (kŏn′dən-sā′shən) *n.* **1.** The act of condensing. **2.** The state of being condensed. **3.** A product of condensing. **4.** *Physics.* **a.** The physical process by which a liquid is removed from a vapor or vapor mixture. **b.** The liquid so removed; a condensate. **5.** *Chemistry.* A chemical reaction in which water or another simple substance is released by the combination of two or more molecules. **6.** *Psychoanalysis.* The process by which a single idea or word is invested with the emotional content of a group of ideas.

con·dense (kən-dĕns′) *v.* **-densed, -densing, -denses.** —*tr.* **1.** To reduce the volume of; compress. **2.** To abridge (a literary work, for example). **3. a.** To form a condensate from (a vapor, for example). **b.** To subject (a vapor, for example) to condensation. —*intr.* **1.** To become more compact. **2.** To undergo condensation. —See Synonyms at **contract.** [Middle English *condensen*, from Old French *condenser*, from Latin *condēnsāre* : *com-* (intensive) + *dēnsāre*, to make dense, from *dēnsus*, dense (see **dens-²** in Appendix*).]

condensed milk. Cow's milk with sugar added, and reduced by evaporation to a thick consistency. Compare **evaporated milk.**

con·dens·er (kən-dĕn′sər) *n.* **1.** One that condenses. **2.** *Physics.* An apparatus used to condense vapor. **3.** *Electricity.* A **capacitor** *(see).* **4.** A mirror, lens, or combination of lenses used to gather light and direct it upon an object or projection lens.

con·de·scend (kŏn′dĭ-sĕnd′) *intr.v.* **-scended, -scending, -scends. 1.** To come down voluntarily to the level of inferiors with whom one is dealing; deign. **2.** To deal with people in a patronizing manner. **3.** *Obsolete.* To yield or assent. [Middle English *condescenden*, from Old French *condescendre*, from Medieval Latin *condēscendere*, to stoop to : Latin *com-* (intensive) + *dēscendere*, to descend : *dē-*, down + *scandere*, to climb (see **skand-** in Appendix*).] —**con′de·scend′er** *n.*

con·de·scen·dence (kŏn′dĭ-sĕn′dəns) *n.* **1.** *Scottish Law.* A list of facts presented by the plaintiff. **2.** Condescension.

con·de·scend·ing (kŏn′dĭ-sĕn′dĭng) *adj.* **1.** Stooping to the level of one's inferiors. **2.** Acting with an air of superiority. —**con′de·scend′ing·ly** *adv.*

con·de·scen·sion (kŏn′dĭ-sĕn′shən) *n.* **1. a.** The act of condescending. **b.** An instance of this. **2.** Patronizing behavior or manner.

con·dign (kən-dīn′) *adj.* **1.** Deserved; adequate; merited. Said of punishment or censure. **2.** *Obsolete.* Worthy; deserving. [Middle English *condigne*, from Old French, from Latin *condignus*, wholly worthy : *com-* (intensive) + *dignus*, worthy (see **dek-¹** in Appendix*).] —**con·dign′ly** *adv.*

con·di·ment (kŏn′də-mənt) *n.* A seasoning for food, such as mustard or various spices. [Middle English, from Old French, from Latin *condīmentum*, from *condīre*, to season, to preserve by pickling, perhaps variant of *condere*, to bring together, store up. See **dhē-¹** in Appendix.*] —**con′di·men′tal** *adj.*

con·di·tion (kən-dĭsh′ən) *n. Abbr.* **cond. 1.** The particular mode or state of being of a person or thing. **2. a.** State of health. **b.** State of readiness or physical fitness. See Usage note at **shape. 3.** *Informal.* A disease or ailment: *a heart condition.* See Usage note below. **4.** Rank or social position: *a person of high condition.* **5.** Something indispensable to the appearance or occurrence of something else; a prerequisite. **6.** Something that restricts or modifies something else; a qualification. **7.** *Usually plural.* The existing circumstances: *poor driving conditions.* **8.** *Grammar.* The dependent clause of a conditional sentence. **9.** *Logic.* A proposition upon which another proposition depends; the antecedent of a conditional proposition. **10.** *Law.* **a.** A provision making the effect of a legal instrument contingent upon the occurrence of some uncertain future event. **b.** The event itself. **11.** An unsatisfactory grade given a student and serving notice that he can make up deficiencies by doing further work. **12.** *Obsolete.* Way; disposition; temper. —See Synonyms at **state.** —*tr.v.* **conditioned, -tioning, -tions. 1.** To make conditional. **2.** To put into a proper condition; render fit. **3.** To accustom (a person) to; adapt. **4.** To give the grade of condition to (a student). **5.** *Psychology.* To cause to respond in a specific manner to a specific stimulus. [Middle English *condicioun*, from Old French *condicion*, from Latin *conditiō*, *condiciō*, agreement, stipulation, probably (irregularly) from *condīcere*, to talk together, agree : *com-*, together + *dīcere*, to talk (see **deik-** in Appendix*).]

Usage: *Condition* (noun), in the sense of disease or ailment *(a liver condition, a nervous condition)*, is not a scientific term, and is sometimes objected to as a euphemism. But it is acceptable to 74 per cent of the Usage Panel in all but scientific writing.

con·di·tion·al (kən-dĭsh′ən-əl) *adj.* **1.** Imposing, depending on, or containing a condition or conditions. **2.** Not certain; tentative. **3.** *Grammar.* Stating or implying a condition. —*n. Grammar.* A mood, tense, clause, or word expressing a condition. —**con·di′tion·al′i·ty** *n.* —**con·di′tion·al·ly** *adv.*

con·di·tioned (kən-dĭsh′ənd) *adj.* **1.** Subject to or dependent upon conditions or stipulations. **2. a.** Physically fit; in good physical condition. **b.** Prepared for a specific action or process. **3.** *Psychology.* Exhibiting or trained to exhibit a conditioned response.

conditioned response. *Psychology.* A new or modified response elicited by a stimulus after conditioning. Also called "conditioned reflex."

conditioned stimulus. *Psychology.* A stimulus rendered capable of eliciting a response like that of a specific **unconditioned stimulus** *(see)* by conditioning.

con·di·tion·er (kən-dĭsh′ən-ər) *n.* **1.** One that conditions: *an air conditioner.* **2.** A worker who conditions a product during manufacture. **3.** An additive or application that improves the quality or usability of a substance: *a soil conditioner.* **4.** A trainer of athletes.

con·di·tion·ing (kən-dĭsh′ən-ĭng) *n. Psychology.* The process of, or the complex of organismic processes resulting from, presenting an initially inadequate stimulus with an unconditioned stimulus until the former is capable of eliciting a response like that elicited by the latter.

con·dole (kən-dōl′) *v.* **-doled, -doling, -doles.** —*intr.* To mourn or express sympathy with one in pain, grief, or misfortune. Used with *with.* —*tr. Rare.* To address words of sympathy to. [Late Latin *condolēre*, to feel another's pain : Latin *com-*, together + *dolēre*, to feel pain, grieve (see **del-³** in Appendix*).] —**con·do′la·to′ry** (-dō′lə-tôr′ē, -tōr′ē) *adj.* —**con·dol′er** *n.*

con·do·lence (kən-dō′ləns) *n.* Also **con·dole·ment** (-dōl′mənt) (for sense 1). **1.** An expression of sympathy with a person in pain, grief, or misfortune. **2.** *Plural.* A formal declaration of such sympathy. —See Synonyms at **pity.** —**con·do′lent** *adj.*

con do·lo·re (kōn dō-lō′rā). *Music.* With sadness; sorrowfully. Used as a direction. [Italian, "with sorrow."]

con·dom (kŏn′dəm) *n.* Also **cun·dum** (kŭn′dəm). A sheath, usually made of thin rubber, designed to cover the penis during sexual intercourse for antivenereal or contraceptive purposes. [Said to have been invented by Dr. *Condom* or *Conton*, 18th-century English physician.]

con·do·min·i·um (kŏn′də-mĭn′ē-əm) *n.* **1. a.** Joint sovereignty; especially, joint rule of a territory by two or more states. **b.** The territory so governed. **2. a.** An apartment building in which the apartments are owned individually. **b.** An apartment in such a building. [New Latin : CON- + DOMINIUM.]

Con·don (kŏn′dən), **Edward Uhler.** Born 1902. American physicist; aided in development of atomic bomb.

con·do·na·tion (kŏn′dō-nā′shən) *n.* **1.** The condoning or overlooking of an offense. **2.** *Law.* A forgiving by a husband or wife of the other's adultery.

con·done (kən-dōn′) *tr.v.* **-doned, -doning, -dones. 1.** To forgive, overlook, or disregard (an offense) without protest or censure. **2.** *Law.* To make condonation of. —See Synonyms at **forgive.** [Latin *condōnāre,* to give up, forgive : *com-* (intensive) + *dōnāre,* to give away, from *dōnum,* gift (see **dō-** in Appendix*).] —**con·don′er** *n.*

con·dor (kŏn′dôr, -dər) *n.* **1.** Either of two very large New World vultures, *Vultur gryphus* of the Andes or *Gymnogyps californianus* of the mountains of California. **2.** Any of several gold coins of some South American countries bearing the figure of a condor. [Spanish *cóndor,* from Quechua *kúntur.*]

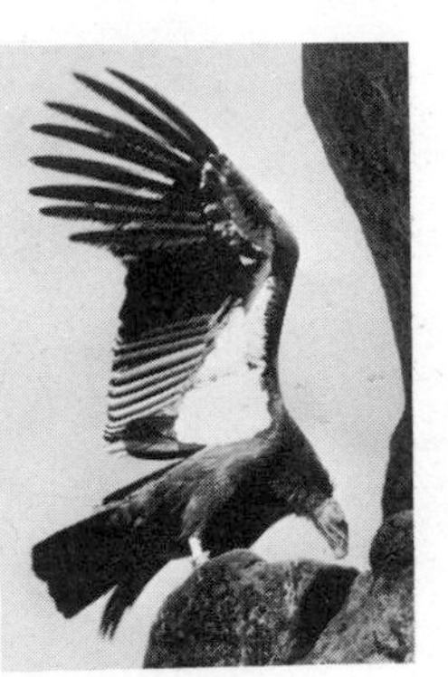

condor
Gymnogyps californianus

con·dot·tie·re (kŏn′dō-tyâr′ā) *n., pl.* **-tieri** (-tyâr′ē). A leader of mercenary soldiers between the 14th and 16th centuries. [Italian, leader, from *condotto,* conduct, leadership, from Latin *conductum,* from *condūcere,* to lead together, CONDUCT.]

con·duce (kən-do͞os′, -dyo͞os′) *intr.v.* **-duced, -ducing, -duces.** To contribute or lead. Used with *to* or *toward.* [Middle English *conducen,* from Latin *condūcere,* to lead together, be useful, contribute : *com-,* together + *dūcere,* to lead (see **deuk-** in Appendix*).] —**con·duc′er** *n.*

con·du·cive (kən-do͞o′sĭv, -dyo͞o′sĭv) *adj.* Conducing; promoting; leading; contributive. Used with *to.* See Synonyms at **favorable.** —**con·du′cive·ness** *n.*

con·duct (kən-dŭkt′) *v.* **-ducted, -ducting, -ducts.** —*tr.* **1.** To direct the course of; manage; control. **2.** To lead or guide: *conduct a tour.* **3.** To lead an orchestra or other musical group. **4.** To serve as a medium or channel for conveying; transmit. **5.** To behave. Used reflexively. —*intr.* **1.** To act as a conductor. **2.** To lead. —See Synonyms at **accompany.** —*n.* (kŏn′dŭkt). **1.** The way a person acts; behavior. **2.** The act of directing or controlling; management; administration. **3.** The act of leading or guiding. **4.** *Obsolete.* A guide or escort. —See Synonyms at **behavior.** [Middle English *conducten,* from Medieval Latin *condūcere,* to escort, from Latin, to lead together : *com-,* together + *dūcere,* to lead (see **deuk-** in Appendix*).] —**con·duct′i·bil′i·ty** *n.* —**con·duct′i·ble** *adj.*

Synonyms: *conduct, direct, manage, control, handle, supervise, oversee.* These verbs refer to forms of authoritative guidance. *Conduct* can apply to the guidance of a single person: *The chairman conducted the hearing.* It can also apply to similar action without stress on individual authority: *conduct elections. Direct* stresses the expert regulation of persons or activities by a leader or small group in authority: *direct a political campaign. Manage* stresses regulation in the sense of manipulation, sometimes of a single person or thing but often of a complex organization: *manage a child; manage a hotel. Control* can imply direction or management but more often suggests regulation in the form of restraint: *police controlling a crowd; control your temper. Handle* also suggests control but implies skillful maneuvering: *handle a delicate affair. Supervise* emphasizes broad authority: *supervise a school system. Oversee* suggests broad authority exercised less directly, as by inspection and observation: *oversee work.*

con·duc·tance (kən-dŭk′təns) *n.* A measure of a material's ability to conduct electric charge, the real part of the complex representation of **admittance** *(see).*

con·duc·tion (kən-dŭk′shən) *n.* The transmission or conveying of something through a medium or passage, especially of electric charge or heat through a conducting medium without perceptible motion of the medium itself.

con·duc·tive (kən-dŭk′tĭv) *adj.* Exhibiting conductivity.

con·duc·tiv·i·ty (kŏn′dŭk-tĭv′ə-tē) *n. Symbol* σ **1.** The ability or power to conduct or transmit. **2.** A measure of the ability of a material to conduct an electric charge, the reciprocal of **resistivity** *(see).*

con·duc·tor (kən-dŭk′tər) *n. Abbr.* **cond. 1.** A person who conducts or leads. **2.** The person in charge of a railroad train, bus, or streetcar. **3.** The director of an orchestra or other musical ensemble. **4.** *Physics.* A substance or medium that conducts heat, light, sound, or, especially, an electric charge. **5.** A lightning rod. —**con·duc′tor·ship′** *n.*

con·duit (kŏn′dĭt, -do͞o-ĭt) *n.* **1.** A channel or pipe for conveying water or other fluids. **2.** A tube or duct for enclosing electric wires or cable. **3.** *Rare.* A fountain. [Middle English, from Old French, conveyance, from Medieval Latin *conductus,* escort, transportation, from Latin, past participle of *condūcere,* to lead together, CONDUCT.]

con·du·pli·cate (kŏn-do͞o′plə-kĭt, kŏn-dyo͞o′-) *adj. Botany.* Folded in half lengthwise. [Latin *conduplicātus,* past participle of *conduplicāre,* to double, fold together : *com-,* together + *duplicāre,* to double, DUPLICATE.] —**con′du·pli·ca′tion** *n.*

con·dyle (kŏn′dīl) *n.* A rounded articulatory prominence at the end of a bone. [French, from Latin *condylus,* knuckle, from Greek *kondulos*†.] —**con′dy·lar** *adj.* —**con′dy·loid′** *adj.*

con·dy·lo·ma (kŏn-də-lō′mə) *n., pl.* **-mas** or **-mata** (-mə-tə). A wartlike growth near the anus or external genitalia. [New Latin, from Greek *kondulōma* : *kondulos,* knuckle, CONDYLE + -OMA.] —**con′dy·lom′a·tous** (-lŏm′ə-təs) *adj.*

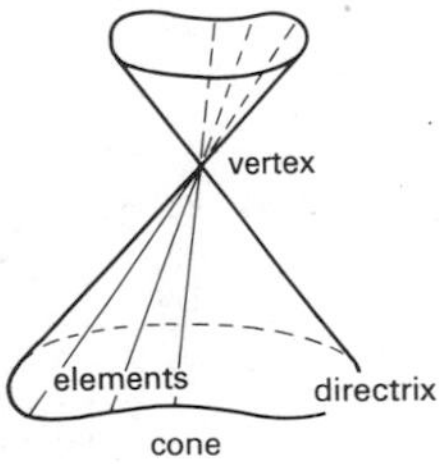

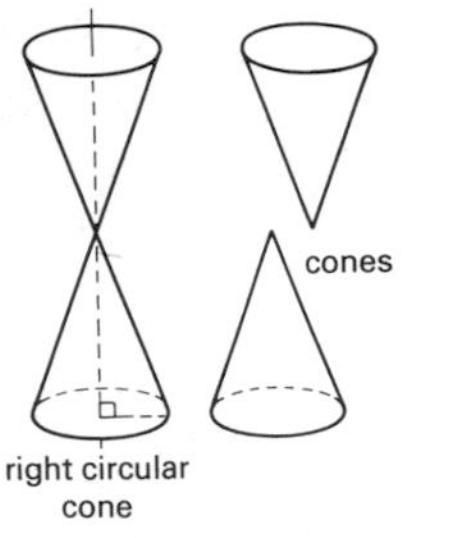

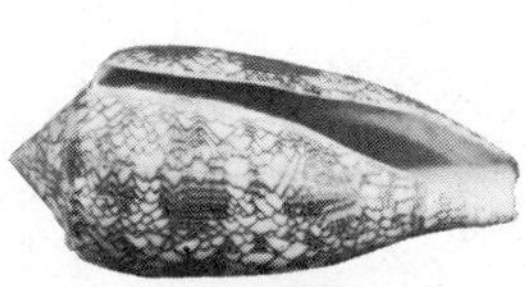

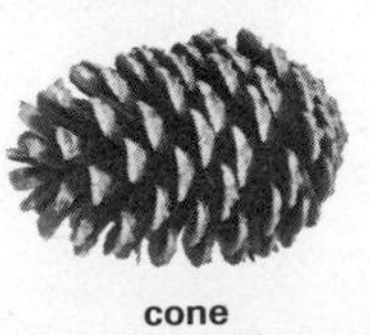

cone
Above: Geometric cones
Center: Shell of *Conus aulicus,* textile cone
Below: Cone of *Pinus taeda,* loblolly pine

cone (kōn) *n.* **1.** *Geometry.* **a.** A surface generated by a straight line, the *generator,* passing through a fixed point, the *vertex,* and moving along the intersection with a fixed curve, the *directrix* **b.** The surface generated by such a generator passing through a vertex lying on the perpendicular axis of a circular directrix. Also called "right circular cone." **2. a.** The figure formed by such a surface bound, or regarded as bound, by its vertex and a plane section taken anywhere above or below the vertex. **b.** Anything having the shape of this figure. **3. a.** A conical, spheroidal, or cylindrical structure borne by certain trees, such as the pines, firs, and hemlocks, consisting of clusters of stiff, overlapping, woody scales, between which are the naked ovules. **b.** Any similar fruit, such as that of the magnolia or hop. **4.** *Physiology.* A photoreceptor in the retina of the eye. **5.** Any of various gastropod mollusks of the family Conidae, of tropical seas, having a conical, often vividly marked shell. —*tr.v.* **coned, coning, cones.** To shape like a cone or cone segment. [French *cône,* from Latin *cōnus,* from Greek *kōnos.* See **kē-** in Appendix.*]

cone·flow·er (kōn′flou′ər) *n.* Any of various North American plants of the genera *Rudbeckia, Ratibida,* and *Echinacea,* having rayed flowers with a conelike center of tubular florets.

Con·el·rad (kŏn′əl-răd) *n.* A system of defense in case of enemy attack on the United States, in which all broadcasting is terminated, allowing only emergency AM stations to broadcast on 640 and 1,240 kilocycles. The purpose is to prevent enemy aircraft from using electromagnetic signals for navigation. [CON(TROL + OF) + EL(ECTROMAGNETIC) + RAD(IATION).]

cone·nose (kōn′nōz′) *n.* Any of several assassin bugs; especially, *Triatoma sanguisuga,* of the southern and western United States and Mexico, having sucking mouth parts and capable of inflicting a painful, toxic bite. Also called "cone-nosed bug."

Con·es·to·ga wagon (kŏn′ĭs-tō′gə). A heavy covered wagon with broad wheels, used by American pioneers for westward travel. Also called "Conestoga." [First built at *Conestoga,* Pennsylvania.]

co·ney. Variant of **cony.**

Co·ney Island (kō′nē). An amusement center in Brooklyn, New York City, on the southwestern tip of Long Island.

conf. 1. conference. **2.** confessor.

con·fab (kŏn′făb′) *n. Informal.* A confabulation. —*intr.v.* (kən-făb′, kŏn′făb′) **confabbed, -fabbing, -fabs.** *Informal.* To talk informally; confabulate.

con·fab·u·late (kən-făb′yə-lāt′) *intr.v.* **-lated, -lating, -lates. 1.** To talk informally; chat. **2.** *Psychiatry.* To replace fact with fantasy in memory. [Latin *confābulārī* : *com-,* together + *fābulārī,* to talk, from *fābula,* story, conversation, from *fārī,* to speak (see **bhā-**[2] in Appendix*).] —**con·fab′u·la′tion** *n.* —**con·fab′u·la′tor** (-lā′tər) *n.* —**con·fab′u·la·to′ry** (-lə-tôr′ē, -tōr′ē) *adj.*

con·fect (kən-fĕkt′) *tr.v.* **-fected, -fecting, -fects. 1.** To prepare by combining ingredients. **2.** To make into a confection or preserve. **3.** To put together; make. —*n.* (kŏn′fĕkt). A candy or other sweet confection; comfit. [Middle English *confecten,* from Latin *conficere* (past participle *confectus*), to prepare : *com-* (intensive) + *facere,* to make (see **dhē-**[1] in Appendix*).]

con·fec·tion (kən-fĕk′shən) *n.* **1.** The act of compounding, mixing, or preparing. **2.** A sweet preparation, such as candy or preserves. **3.** A sweetened medicinal compound; an electuary. **4.** A stylish article of women's clothing. —*tr.v.* **confectioned, -tioning, -tions.** To make into a confection.

con·fec·tion·ar·y (kən-fĕk′shən-ĕr′ē) *adj.* Pertaining to or resembling confections or their preparation. —*n., pl.* **confectionaries.** Variant of **confectionery.**

con·fec·tion·er (kən-fĕk′shən-ər) *n.* One who makes or sells confections.

confectioners' sugar. Finely pulverized sugar with some cornstarch added.

con·fec·tion·er·y (kən-fĕk′shən-ĕr′ē) *n., pl.* **-ies.** Also **con·fec·tion·ar·y** (for sense 3). **1.** Candies and other confections collectively. **2.** The art or occupation of a confectioner. **3.** A confectioner's shop.

confed. confederation.

con·fed·er·a·cy (kən-fĕd′ər-ə-sē) *n., pl.* **-cies. 1.** A union of persons, parties, or states; alliance; league. **2.** A combination for unlawful practices; conspiracy. [Middle English *confederacie,* from Norman French, from Latin *confoederātiō,* union, from *confoederāre,* to unite. See **confederate.**]

con·fed·er·ate (kən-fĕd′ər-ĭt) *n.* **1.** A member of a confederacy; an ally. **2.** One who assists in a plot; an accomplice. **3.** *Capital* **C.** A supporter of the Confederate States of America. —See Synonyms at **partner.** —*adj.* **1.** United in a confederacy; allied. **2.** Of or pertaining to the Confederate States of America. —*v.* (kən-fĕd′ə-rāt′) **confederated, -ating, -ates.** —*tr.* To form into a confederacy. —*intr.* To become part of a confederacy. [Middle English *confederat,* from Latin *confoederātus,* from past participle of *confoederāre,* to unite in a league : *com-,* together + *foederāre,* to unite, from *foedus,* league (see **bheidh-** in Appendix*).] —**con·fed′er·a′tive** *adj.*

Confederate rose. The **cotton rose** *(see).*

Confederate States of America. *Abbr.* **C.S.A.** The confederation of 11 Southern states that seceded from the United States (1860–61), including Alabama, Arkansas, Florida, Georgia, Louisiana, Mississippi, North Carolina, South Carolina, Tennessee, Texas, and Virginia. Also called "the Confederacy," "Southern Confederacy."

Confederate violet. A plant, *Viola priceana,* of the southeastern United States, having streaked pale-blue flowers.

con·fed·er·a·tion (kən-fĕd′ə-rā′shən) *n. Abbr.* **confed. 1.** An act of confederating or a state of being confederated. **2.** A group of confederates, especially of states or nations, united for a common purpose. —**the Confederation. 1.** The union of the American States under the Articles of Confederation (1781–89). **2.** The federal state created in Canada in 1867 by the British North America Act, comprising New Brunswick, Nova Scotia, Ontario, and Quebec, and now including the ten Canadian provinces. —**con·fed′er·a′tion·ism′** *n.* —**con·fed′er·a′tion·ist** *n.*

con·fer (kən-fûr′) *v.* **-ferred, -ferring, -fers.** —*tr.* **1.** To bestow (an honor or degree, for example). Used with *on* or *upon.* **2.** *Obsolete.* To compare. —*intr.* To hold a conference; com-

ă pat/ā pay/âr care/ä father/b bib/ch church/d deed/ĕ pet/ē be/f fife/g gag/h hat/hw which/ĭ pit/ī pie/îr pier/j judge/k kick/l lid, needle/m mum/n no, sudden/ng thing/ŏ pot/ō toe/ô paw, for/oi noise/ou out/o͝o took/o͞o boot/p pop/r roar/s sauce/sh ship, dish/

pare views; consult together. [Latin *conferre*, to bring together, contribute, bestow : *com-*, together + *ferre*, to bring, bear (see **bher-**^{1} in Appendix*).] —**con·fer′ment, con·fer′ral** *n.* —**con·fer′ra·ble** *adj.* —**con·fer′rer** *n.*

con·fer·ee (kŏn′fə-rē′) *n.* Also **con·fer·ree. 1.** A participant in a conference. **2.** One upon whom something is conferred.

con·fer·ence (kŏn′fə-rəns, -frəns) *n. Abbr.* **conf. 1.** A meeting for consultation or discussion. **2.** *Government.* A meeting of committees to settle differences between two legislative bodies. **3.** In various Protestant churches, an assembly of clerical or clerical and lay members from a particular district. **4.** An association, as of schools, for mutual benefit; league. **5.** The act of conferring, as of a degree; a bestowal. [Old French, from Medieval Latin *conferentia*, from Latin *conferēns*, present participle of *conferre*, CONFER.] —**con′fer·en′tial** *adj.*

con·fer·va (kən-fûr′və) *n., pl.* **-vae** (-vē) or **-vas.** Any of various bright-green, threadlike freshwater algae. [New Latin, from Latin *conferva*, COMFREY.] —**con·fer′void′** *n.* & *adj.*

con·fess (kən-fĕs′) *v.* **-fessed, -fessing, -fesses.** —*tr.* **1.** To disclose or acknowledge (something damaging or inconvenient to oneself). **2.** To concede the truth or validity of; admit. **3.** To acknowledge belief or faith in. **4. a.** To make known (one's sins), especially to a priest for absolution. **b.** To hear the confession of. Used of a priest. —*intr.* **1.** To admit or acknowledge a crime or deed. Used with *to.* **2.** To tell one's sins to a priest. —See Synonyms at **acknowledge.** [Middle English *confessen*, from Old French *confesser*, from Late Latin *confessāre*, frequentative of *confitērī* (past participle *confessus*), to acknowledge : *com-* (intensive) + *fatērī*, to confess, admit (see **bhā-**^{2} in Appendix*).] —**con·fess′ed·ly** (-ĭd-lē) *adv.*

con·fes·sion (kən-fĕsh′ən) *n.* **1.** An act of confessing; acknowledgment; avowal; admission. **2.** That which is confessed. **3.** A formal declaration of guilt. **4.** The disclosure of sins to a priest for absolution. **5.** A form of worship in which sins are acknowledged. **6.** An avowal of belief in the doctrines of a particular faith. Also called "confession of faith." **7.** A church or group of worshipers adhering to a particular creed.

con·fes·sion·al (kən-fĕsh′ən-əl) *adj.* Also *rare* **con·fes·sion·ar·y** (-ĕr′ē). Of, pertaining to, or resembling confession. —*n.* Also *rare* **con·fes·sion·ar·y** *pl.* **-ies.** A small enclosed stall in which a priest hears confessions.

con·fes·sor (kən-fĕs′ər) *n.* Also **con·fes·ser.** *Abbr.* **conf. 1.** A priest who hears confession and gives absolution. **2.** One who confesses. **3.** One who confesses faith in Christianity in the face of persecution but does not suffer martyrdom.

con·fet·ti (kən-fĕt′ē) *n.* Plural in form, used with a singular verb. **1.** Small pieces of colored paper scattered around at festive celebrations. **2.** Candies; bonbons. [Italian, plural of *confetto*, confection, candy, from Medieval Latin *confectum*, from Latin *confectus*, past participle of *conficere*, to put together, prepare, CONFECT.]

con·fi·dant (kŏn′fə-dănt′, -dänt′, kŏn′fə-dănt, -dänt) *n.* One to whom secrets or private matters are confided. [French *confident*, from Italian *confidente*, from Latin *confīdēns*, present participle of *confīdere*, CONFIDE.]

con·fi·dante (kŏn′fə-dănt′, -dänt′, kŏn′fə-dănt, -dänt) *n.* A female confidant. [French *confidente*, feminine of *confident*, CONFIDANT.]

con·fide (kən-fīd′) *v.* **-fided, -fiding, -fides.** —*tr.* **1.** To tell (something) in confidence. **2.** To put into another's keeping. —*intr.* To tell private matters in confidence. Used with *in.* —See Synonyms at **commit.** [Middle English *confiden*, from Old French *confider*, from Latin *confīdere* : *com-* (intensive) + *fīdere*, to trust (see **bheidh-** in Appendix*).] —**con·fid′er** *n.*

con·fi·dence (kŏn′fə-dəns) *n.* **1.** Trust in a person or thing. **2.** An intimate and trusting relationship. **3.** Something confided, such as a secret. **4.** A feeling of assurance or certainty, especially concerning oneself. —See Synonyms at **trust.**

Synonyms: *confidence, assurance, aplomb, self-confidence, self-possession, self-reliance.* These nouns imply trust and faith in oneself or in another. *Confidence* indicates a belief in a person or thing. *Assurance* implies a feeling of certainty and can suggest arrogance. *Aplomb* implies poise and self-assurance. *Self-confidence, self-possession,* and *self-reliance* all imply consciousness of one's own powers and abilities. *Self-confidence* stresses trust in one's own self-sufficiency. *Self-possession* implies control over one's own reactions and a tendency to be self-assured. *Self-reliance* stresses self-trust manifested in action and implies independence and self-sufficiency.

confidence game. A swindle in which the victim is defrauded after his confidence has been won. Also *slang* "con game."

confidence man. One who swindles by using a confidence game. Also *slang* "con man."

con·fi·dent (kŏn′fə-dənt) *adj.* **1.** Having assurance or certainty, as of success. **2.** Having confidence in oneself; self-assured. **3.** Very bold; presumptuous. **4.** *Obsolete.* Confiding; trustful. —See Synonyms at **sure.** —*n.* A confidant. [Latin *confīdens*, present participle of *confīdere*, CONFIDE.] —**con′fi·dent·ly** *adv.*

con·fi·den·tial (kŏn′fə-dĕn′shəl) *adj.* **1.** Done or communicated in confidence; told in secret. **2.** Entrusted with the confidence of another; intimate: *a confidential secretary.* **3.** Denoting confidence or intimacy: *a confidential tone of voice.* —See Synonyms at **familiar.** —**con′fi·den′ti·al′i·ty** (-shē-ăl′ə-tē), **con′fi·den′tial·ness** *n.* —**con′fi·den′tial·ly** *adv.*

confidential communication. *Law.* A statement made to someone, such as one's doctor, lawyer, or spouse, who cannot be compelled to divulge the information in court.

con·fid·ing (kən-fī′dĭng) *adj.* Trusting; unsuspicious. —**con·fid′ing·ly** *adv.* —**con·fid′ing·ness** *n.*

con·fig·u·ra·tion (kən-fĭg′yə-rā′shən) *n.* **1. a.** The arrangement of the parts or elements of something. **b.** The form of a figure as determined by the arrangement of its parts; outline; contour. **2.** *Psychology.* A **gestalt** *(see).* —See Synonyms at **form.** [Late Latin *configūrātiō*, from Latin *configūrāre*, "to form together," fashion after : *com-*, together + *figūrāre*, to form, from *figūra*, shape, FIGURE.] —**con·fig′u·ra′tive, con·fig′u·ra′tion·al** *adj.* —**con·fig′u·ra′tion·al·ly** *adv.*

con·fine (kən-fīn′) *v.* **-fined, -fining, -fines.** —*tr.* **1.** To keep within bounds; restrict. **2.** To shut within an enclosure; imprison. **3.** To be undergoing childbirth. Used in the passive. —*intr.* To border; abut. —See Synonyms at **limit.** —*n.* (kŏn′fīn′ *for senses 1, 3;* kən-fīn′ *for sense 2*). **1.** *Usually plural.* A border or limit; boundary; frontier. **2.** *Rare.* Confinement. **3.** *Obsolete.* A prison. —See Synonyms at **boundary.** [Old French *confiner*, from *confin*, boundary, limit, from Latin *confīne*, from *confīnis*, having the same border : *com-*, together + *fīnis*, border, end (see **final**).] —**con·fin′a·ble, con·fine′a·ble** *adj.* —**con·fin′er** *n.*

con·fine·ment (kən-fīn′mənt) *n.* **1.** The act of confining or the state of being confined. **2.** The lying-in of a woman.

con·firm (kən-fûrm′) *tr.v.* **-firmed, -firming, -firms. 1.** To assure the certainty or validity of; corroborate; verify. **2.** To make more firm; strengthen; establish: *She confirmed his suspicions.* **3.** To make valid or binding by a formal or legal act; ratify. **4.** To administer or preside over the religious rite of confirmation. [Middle English *confirmen*, from Old French *confirmer*, from Latin *confirmāre* : *com-* (intensive) + *firmāre*, to make firm, strengthen, from *firmus*, firm (see **dher-**^{2} in Appendix*).] —**con·firm′a·ble** *adj.* —**con·firm′er** *n.*

Synonyms: *confirm, corroborate, substantiate, authenticate, validate, prove, establish, ratify, verify.* These verbs all mean to approve something, principally in the sense of attesting to its truth or vouching for its accuracy or genuineness. *Confirm* generally implies removal of all doubt about a matter heretofore considered uncertain or tentative. *Corroborate* refers to strengthening or supporting something, such as a statement or theory, by means of the evidence of another person or persons. *Substantiate* involves establishing something, such as a truth, claim, or position, by presenting substantial or tangible evidence. *Authenticate* implies doubt about the genuineness of something and the removal of such doubt by the act of an official or the testimony of an expert. *Validate* usually implies formal legal or official action *(validate a deed of sale),* but can refer to establishing any conclusion by detailed evidence or demonstration. *Prove* implies convincing evidence in the form of argument, reasoning, or demonstration. *Establish* adds to *prove* the securing of a position beyond all doubt. *Ratify* involves authoritative sanction, usually legal or official: *Treaties are ratified by the Senate. Verify* implies proving by comparison or by matching a contention against established fact: *verify a signature.*

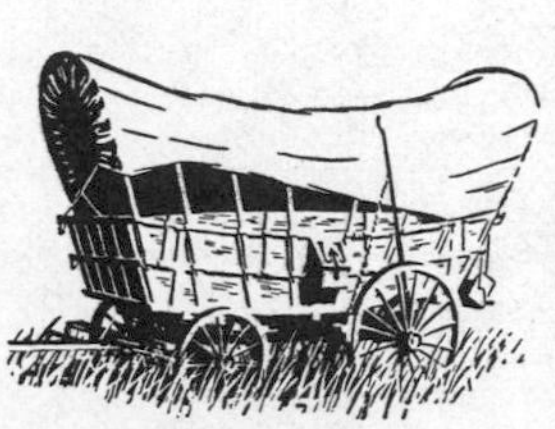

Conestoga wagon

con·fir·ma·tion (kŏn′fər-mā′shən) *n.* **1.** An act of confirming. **2.** That which confirms; verification. **3.** A rite admitting a baptized person to full membership in his church. —**con·firm′a·to′ry** (kən-fûr′mə-tôr′ē, -tōr′ē), **con·firm′a·tive** (-fûr′mə-tĭv) *adj.*

con·firmed (kən-fûrmd′) *adj.* **1.** Ratified; verified. **2.** Habitual; inveterate: *a confirmed bachelor.* **3.** Having received the rite of confirmation. —**con·firm′ed·ly** (-fûr′mĭd-lē) *adv.*

con·fis·ca·ble (kən-fĭs′kə-bəl) *adj.* Subject to confiscation.

con·fis·cate (kŏn′fĭs-kāt′) *tr.v.* **-cated, -cating, -cates. 1.** To seize (private property) for a public treasury, especially by way of penalty. **2.** To seize by or as by authority. —*adj.* **1.** Confiscated; appropriated. **2.** Having lost property through confiscation. [Latin *confiscāre*, to lay up in a chest, confiscate : *com-* (collective) + *fiscus*, chest, the treasury (see **fiscal**).] —**con′fis·ca′tion** *n.* —**con′fis·ca′tor** (-kā′tər) *n.*

Con·fit·e·or (kən-fĭt′ē-ôr) *n. Roman Catholic Church.* A prayer in which confession of sins is made. [Latin, "I confess" (first word of the prayer).]

con·fi·ture (kŏn′fĭ-chŏŏr′) *n.* A confection, preserve, or sweetmeat. [French, from Old French, from *confit*, confection, comfit, from the past participle of *confire*, to preserve, pickle, from Latin *conficere*, to prepare, CONFECT.]

con·fla·grant (kən-flā′grənt) *adj.* Burning intensely; blazing. [Latin *conflagrāns*, present participle of *conflagrāre*, to burn up. See **conflagration.**]

con·fla·gra·tion (kŏn′flə-grā′shən) *n.* A large and destructive fire. [Latin *conflagrātiō*, from *conflagrāre*, to burn up : *com-* (intensive) + *flagrāre*, to burn, blaze (see **bhel-**^{1} in Appendix*).]

con·fla·tion (kən-flā′shən) *n.* **1.** A combining, as of two variant texts into one text. **2.** The result of this. [Middle English *conflacioun*, from Late Latin *conflātiō*, from Latin *conflāre*, "to blow together," combine two readings : *com-*, together + *flāre*, to blow (see **bhlē-**^{2} in Appendix*).]

con·flict (kŏn′flĭkt) *n.* **1.** A prolonged battle; a struggle; clash. **2.** A controversy; disagreement; opposition. **3.** *Psychology.* The opposition or simultaneous functioning of mutually exclusive impulses, desires, or tendencies. **4.** A crashing together; collision. —See Synonyms at **discord.** —*intr.v.* (kən-flĭkt′) **conflicted, -flicting, -flicts. 1.** To come into opposition; collide; differ. **2.** To fight; to struggle; battle. [Middle English, from Latin *conflīctus*, from the past participle of *conflīgere*, to clash together, contend : *com-*, together + *flīgere*, to strike (see **bhlīg-** in Appendix*).] —**con·flic′tion** *n.* —**con·flic′tive** *adj.*

Synonyms: *conflict, contest, combat, fight, affray, melee, scuffle.* These nouns denote struggle between opposing forces. *Conflict* applies both to large-scale physical struggle between hostile forces and to a struggle within a person. *Contest* can mean

either friendly competition or a struggle between hostile forces. In the latter case it is less forceful than *conflict*. *Combat* implies armed encounter between two persons or groups. *Fight* usually refers to a clash, physical or figurative, involving two persons or a small group, or to a struggle for a cause. *Affray, melee,* and *scuffle* all denote generally impromptu and disorderly physical clashes. *Affray* suggests street fighting and disturbing the peace. *Melee* implies confused, hand-to-hand fighting. *Scuffle* suggests hand-to-hand fighting on a small scale.

con·flu·ence (kŏn′flo͞o-əns) *n.* Also **con·flux** (-flŭks). **1.** A flowing together of two or more streams. **2.** The point of juncture of such streams. **3.** A gathering together; crowd.

con·flu·ent (kŏn′flo͞o-ənt) *adj.* **1.** Flowing together; blended into one. **2.** *Pathology.* Merging together so as to form a mass. Said of sores in a rash. **3.** *Anatomy.* Coalesced, as two originally separate bones. —*n.* **1.** One of two or more confluent streams. **2.** A tributary. [Middle English, from Latin *confluēns*, present participle of *confluere*, to flow together : *com-*, together + *fluere*, to flow (see **bhleu-** in Appendix*).]

con·fo·cal (kŏn-fō′kəl) *adj.* Having the same focus or foci.

con·form (kən-fôrm′) *v.* **-formed, -forming, -forms.** —*intr.* **1.** To come to have the same form or character. **2.** To act or be in accord or agreement; comply. Used with *to*. **3.** To act in accordance with current customs or modes. **4.** *English History.* To comply with the usages of the Church of England. —*tr.* **1.** To make similar. **2.** To bring into agreement or correspondence. Often used reflexively —See Synonyms at **agree.** [Middle English *conformen*, from Old French *conformer*, from Latin *conformāre*, "to have the same form," shape after : *com-*, same, similar + *formāre*, to shape, from *forma*, form, shape (see **mer-bh-** in Appendix*).] —**con·form′er** *n.*

con·form·a·ble (kən-fôrm′ə-bəl) *adj.* **1.** In harmony or agreement. Often used with *to*. **2.** In correspondence; similar. **3.** Quick to comply; submissive. **4.** *Geology.* Designating strata that are parallel to each other without interruption. —**con·form′a·bil′i·ty, con·form′a·ble·ness** *n.* —**con·form′a·bly** *adv.*

con·for·mal (kən-fôr′məl) *adj.* **1.** *Mathematics.* Designating a depiction of a surface or region upon another surface so that all angles between intersecting curves remain unchanged. **2.** Of or pertaining to a map projection in which small areas are rendered with true shape. [Late Latin *confōrmālis*, having the same form : Latin *com-*, same, similar + *fōrmālis*, having a form, FORMAL.]

con·for·ma·tion (kŏn′fər-mā′shən) *n.* **1.** The structure or outline of something as determined by the arrangement of its parts. **2.** A symmetrical arrangement of the parts of a thing. **3.** The act of conforming or state of being conformed.

con·form·ist (kən-fôr′mĭst) *n.* **1.** One who conforms to current usages. **2.** *Abbr.* **Con.** One who complies with the usages of the Church of England. Compare **dissenter.**

con·form·i·ty (kən-fôr′mə-tē) *n., pl.* **-ties.** Also **con·form·ance** (-fôr′məns). **1.** Similarity in form or character; correspondence; agreement. **2.** Action or behavior in correspondence with current customs, rules, or styles. **3.** Compliance with the usages of the Church of England.

con·found (kən-found′, kŏn-) *tr.v.* **-founded, -founding, -founds.** **1.** To cause to become confused; bewilder. **2.** To mix up (incompatible elements or ideas); confuse. **3.** To fail to distinguish. **4.** To cause to be ashamed; abash. **5.** To defeat; overthrow. —See Synonyms at **puzzle.** [Middle English *confounden*, from Old French *confondre*, from Latin *confundere*, to pour together, mix up : *com-*, together + *fundere*, to pour (see **gheu-** in Appendix*).] —**con·found′er** *n.*

con·found·ed (kən-foun′dĭd, kŏn-) *adj.* **1.** Confused; befuddled. **2.** Damned. Used as a mild oath: *a confounded fool.* —**con·found′ed·ly** *adv.* —**con·found′ed·ness** *n.*

con·fra·ter·ni·ty (kŏn′frə-tûr′nə-tē) *n., pl.* **-ties.** An association of men united in some common purpose or profession. [Middle English *confraternite*, from Old French, from Medieval Latin *confrāternitās*, from *confrāter*, colleague, CONFRERE.]

con·frere (kŏn′frâr) *n.* A fellow member of a fraternity or profession; colleague. [Middle English, from Old French, from Medieval Latin *confrāter*, colleague, fellow member : Latin *com-*, together + *frāter*, brother (see **bhrāter-** in Appendix*).]

con·front (kən-frŭnt′) *tr.v.* **-fronted, -fronting, -fronts.** **1.** To come face to face with; stand in front of. **2.** To face with hostility; oppose defiantly. **3.** To bring close together for comparison or examination; compare. [Old French *confronter*, from Medieval Latin *confrontāre*, to have a common border : Latin *com-*, together + *frōns* (stem *front-*), forehead, FRONT.] —**con′fron·ta′tion, con·front′ment** *n.* —**con·front′er** *n.*

Con·fu·cian (kən-fyo͞o′shən) *adj.* Of, pertaining to, or characteristic of Confucius, his teachings, or his followers. —*n.* One who adheres to the teachings of Confucius; Confucianist.

Con·fu·cian·ism (kən-fyo͞o′shən-ĭz′əm) *n.* The ethical system based on the teachings of Confucius, emphasizing personal virtue, devotion to family, including the spirits of one's ancestors, and justice. —**Con·fu′cian·ist** *n.*

Con·fu·cius (kən-fyo͞o′shəs). Original name **Kung Chiu** (ko͝ong′ chyo͞o′); long known in China as **Kung Fu-tse** (ko͝ong′ fŭ′dzŭ′). 551–479 B.C. Chinese philosopher and teacher.

con·fuse (kən-fyo͞oz′) *tr.v.* **-fused, -fusing, -fuses.** **1.** To perplex or bewilder; befuddle. **2.** To assemble without order or sense; to jumble. **3.** To mistake one thing for another. [Middle English *confusen*, from *confus*, confused, from Old French, from Latin *confūsus*, past participle of *confundere*, to pour together, mix, confound : *com-*, together + *fundere*, to pour (see **gheu-** in Appendix*).] —**con·fus′ed·ly** (-fyo͞o′zĭd-lē) *adv.* —**con·fus′ed·ness** *n.* —**con·fus′ing·ly** *adv.*

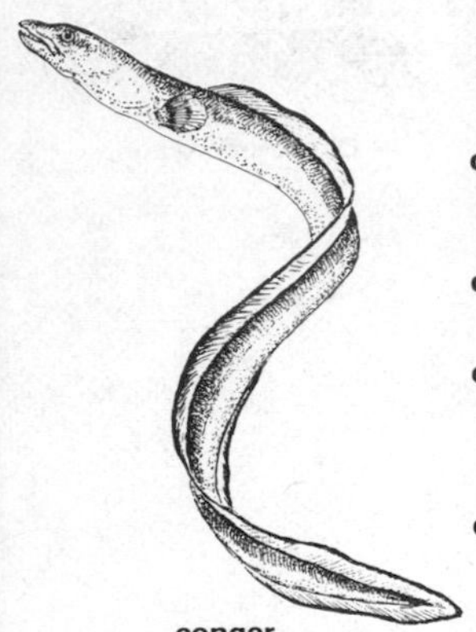

conger
Conger oceanicus

Confucius
Traditional portrayal from a rubbing of an 18th-century engraving

con·fu·sion (kən-fyo͞o′zhən) *n.* **1.** The act of confusing or state of being confused. **2.** Disorder; jumble. **3.** Distraction; bewilderment. **4.** An early stage of psychosis involving mental and emotional disturbances. —**con·fu′sion·al** *adj.*

con·fu·ta·tion (kŏn′fyo͞o-tā′shən) *n.* **1.** An act of confuting. **2.** That which confutes. —**con·fu′ta·tive** (kən-fyo͞o′tə-tĭv) *adj.*

con·fute (kən-fyo͞ot′) *tr.v.* **-futed, -futing, -futes.** **1.** To prove to be wrong or in error. **2.** To cause to come to naught; confound. [Latin *confūtāre*, to check, suppress, restrain. See **bhau-** in Appendix.*] —**con·fut′a·ble** *adj.* —**con·fut′er** *n.*

cong. *Pharmacology.* congius.

Cong. **1.** Congregational. **2.** Congress; Congressional.

con·ga (kŏng′gə) *n.* **1.** A dance of Latin-American origin in which the dancers form a long, winding line. **2.** Music for this dance. —*intr.v.* **congaed, -gaing, -gas.** To dance the conga. [American Spanish *(danza) Conga*, "the Congo (dance)," from Spanish *Congo*, of the CONGO.]

con game. *Slang.* A **confidence game** *(see).*

con·gé (kŏn′zhā, kŏn-zhā′; *also* kŏn′jē *for senses 1, 3; French* kôɴ-zhā′) *n.* Also **con·gee** (kŏn′jē) (for senses 1, 3). **1.** Formal or authoritative permission to depart. **2.** An abrupt dismissal. **3. a.** *Archaic.* A formal bow. **b.** A leave-taking. **4.** *Architecture.* A kind of concave molding. [French, from Old French *congie*, from Latin *commeātus*, "a going to and fro," from *commeāre*, to go to and fro : *com-*, mutually, back and forth + *meāre*, to go (see **mei-**[1] in Appendix*).]

con·geal (kən-jēl′) *v.* **-gealed, -gealing, -geals.** —*intr.* **1.** To solidify, as by freezing. **2.** To coagulate; jell. —*tr.* To cause to solidify or coagulate. [Middle English *congelen*, from Old French *congeler*, from Latin *congelāre*, to freeze solid : *com-*, together + *gelāre*, to freeze (see **gel-**[3] in Appendix*).] —**con·geal′a·ble** *adj.* —**con·geal′er** *n.* —**con·geal′ment** *n.*

con·gee (kŏn′jē) *intr.v.* **-geed, -geeing, -gees.** *Archaic.* **1.** To take ceremonious leave. **2.** To make a formal bow. —*n.* Variant of **congé.** [Middle English *congeien*, from Old French *congier*, from *congie*, leave of absence, CONGÉ.]

con·ge·la·tion (kŏn′jə-lā′shən) *n.* **1.** The process of congealing or the state of being congealed. **2.** A coagulation.

con·ge·ner (kŏn′jə-nər) *n.* **1.** A member of the same kind, class, or group. **2.** An organism belonging to the same genus as another or others. [Latin, of the same race : *com-*, same + *genus* (stem *gener-*), race, kind (see **gene-** in Appendix*).] —**con′ge·ner′ic, con·gen′er·ous** (-jĕn′ə-rəs) *adj.*

con·ge·net·ic (kŏn′jə-nĕt′ĭk) *adj.* Similar in origin.

con·gen·ial (kən-jēn′yəl) *adj.* **1.** Having the same tastes, habits, or temperament; sympathetic. **2.** Suited to one's needs; agreeable. [CON- (same) + GENIAL.] —**con·ge′ni·al′i·ty** (-jē′nē-ăl′ə-tē), **con·gen′ial·ness** *n.* —**con·gen′ial·ly** *adv.*

con·gen·i·tal (kən-jĕn′ə-təl) *adj.* **1.** Existing at birth but not hereditary: *a congenital defect.* **2.** Having a specified character as if by nature: *a congenital thief.* —See Synonyms at **innate.** [From Latin *congenitus*, born together with : *com-*, together + *genitus*, born, past participle of *gignere*, to beget (see **gene-** in Appendix*).] —**con·gen′i·tal·ly** *adv.*

con·ger (kŏng′gər) *n.* Any of various large, scaleless marine eels of the family Congridae; especially, *Conger oceanicus*, of Atlantic waters. Also called "conger eel." [Middle English *congre*, from Old French, from Latin *conger*, *congrus*, from Greek *gongros*, of Mediterranean origin.]

con·ge·ries (kən-jîr′ēz) *n.* Plural in form, usually used with a singular verb. A collection of things heaped together; an aggregation; a heap. [Latin *congeriēs*, heap, pile, from *congerere*, to bring together, CONGEST.]

con·gest (kən-jĕst′) *v.* **-gested, -gesting, -gests.** —*tr.* **1.** To overfill or overcrowd. **2.** *Pathology.* To cause excessive blood accumulation in (a vessel or organ). —*intr.* To become congested. [Latin *congerere* (past participle *congestus*), to bring together, heap up : *com-*, together + *gerere*, to carry (see **gerere** in Appendix*).] —**con·ges′tion** *n.* —**con·ges′tive** *adj.*

con·gi·us (kŏn′jē-əs) *n., pl.* **-gii** (-jē-ī′). **1.** *Abbr.* **c., C., cong.** *Pharmacology.* A gallon. **2.** An ancient Roman measure for liquids, equal to about .84 of the U.S. gallon. [Middle English, from Latin *congius*, possibly from Greek *konkhos*, conch, shell. See **konkho-** in Appendix.*]

con·glo·bate (kŏn-glō′bāt′, kŏng′glō-) *v.* **-bated, -bating, -bates.** Also **con·globe** (kŏn-glōb′), **-globed, -globing, -globes.** —*intr.* To become a globe or globule. —*tr.* To gather into a globe or ball. —*adj.* Shaped like or formed into a ball. [Latin *conglobāre* : *com-*, together + *globāre*, to make into a globe, from *globus*, globe (see **gel-**[1] in Appendix*).] —**con′glo·ba′tion** *n.*

con·glom·er·ate (kən-glŏm′ə-rāt′) *v.* **-ated, -ating, -ates.** —*tr.* To collect into an adhering or rounded mass. —*intr.* To form into an adhering or rounded mass. —*n.* (kən-glŏm′ə-rĭt). **1.** A collected heterogeneous mass; a cluster. **2.** *Geology.* A rock consisting of pebbles and gravel embedded in a loosely cementing material. In this sense, also called "pudding stone." —*adj.* (kən-glŏm′ə-rĭt). **1.** Gathered into a mass; clustered. **2.** *Geology.* Made up of loosely cemented heterogeneous material. [Latin *conglomerāre*, to roll together : *com-*, together + *glomerāre*, to roll into a ball, from *glomus*, ball (see **gel-**[1] in Appendix*).] —**con·glom′er·at′ic** (-ə-răt′ĭk), **con·glom′er·it′ic** (-ə-rĭt′ĭk) *adj.*

con·glom·er·a·tion (kən-glŏm′ə-rā′shən) *n.* **1.** The process of conglomerating or state of being conglomerated. **2.** A collection or mass of miscellaneous things. **3.** A coherent mass; a cluster.

con·glu·ti·nant (kən-glo͞ot′ə-nənt) *adj.* *Medicine.* Promoting adhesion, as of the lips of a wound. [Latin *conglūtināns*, present participle of *conglūtināre*, to glue together, CONGLUTINATE.]

ă pat/ā pay/âr care/ä father/b bib/ch church/d deed/ĕ pet/ē be/f fife/g gag/h hat/hw which/ĭ pit/ī pie/îr pier/j judge/k kick/l lid, needle/m mum/n no, sudden/ng thing/ŏ pot/ō toe/ô paw, for/oi noise/ou out/o͝o took/o͞o boot/p pop/r roar/s sauce/sh ship, dish/

con·glu·ti·nate (kən-glōō′tə-nāt′) *v.* **-nated, -nating, -nates.** —*intr.* **1.** To become stuck or glued together; adhere. **2.** *Medicine.* To become reunited, as bones or tissues. —*tr.* **1.** To stick or glue together. **2.** *Medicine.* To cause to reunite, as bones or tissues. —*adj.* Glued or stuck together. [Middle English *conglutinaten,* from Latin *conglūtināre,* to glue together : *com-,* together + *glūtināre,* to glue, from *glūten,* glue (see **gel-**^{1} in Appendix*).] —**con·glu′ti·na′tion** *n.*

Con·go (kŏng′gō). **1.** The second-longest river in Africa (2,900 miles, including its headstreams), rising as the Chambezi in Zambia and flowing generally north, west, and then southwest through the Congo (Kinshasa) to the Atlantic. **2.** The undefined region in central Africa on both sides of this river.

Con·go, Democratic Republic of the (kŏng′gō). A republic occupying 905,378 square miles in west-central Africa; a former Belgian colony that became independent in 1960. Population, 16,627,000. Capital, Kinshasa. Often referred to as "Congo (Kinshasa)."

Con·go, Republic of (kŏng′gō). A republic occupying 132,000 square miles in west-central Africa; a former French colony that became independent in 1960. Population, 1,013,000. Capital, Brazzaville. Often referred to as "Congo (Brazzaville)."

congo eel. An eellike amphibian, *Amphiuma means,* of the southeastern United States, having two pairs of tiny, nonfunctioning legs. Also called "congo," "congo snake."

Con·go Free State (kŏng′gō). The colonial government in the Congo as established by Leopold II of Belgium until its reorganization in 1908 as the Belgian Congo.

Con·go·lese (kŏng-gə-lēz′) *adj.* Of or pertaining to the region of the Congo and either of the two Congo republics or their inhabitants. —*n., pl.* **Congolese.** An inhabitant of the region of the Congo or of either of the two republics.

Congo red. A brownish-red powder, $C_{32}H_{22}N_6O_6S_2Na_2$, used in medicine and as a dye, indicator, and biological stain.

con·gou (kŏng′gōō) *n.* A variety of black tea from China. [Amoy *kong hu* (*tē*), corresponding to Mandarin Chinese *kung*^{1} *fu*^{1} (*ch'a*^{2}), "(tea) elaborately prepared or brewed," from *kung*^{1} *fu*^{1}, labor, work.]

con·grat·u·late (kən-grăch′ōō-lāt′) *tr.v.* **-lated, -lating, -lates.** To express joy or acknowledgment for the achievement or good fortune of. [Latin *congrātulārī,* to rejoice with someone : *com-,* with + *grātulārī,* to express one's joy, rejoice, from *grātus,* pleasing (see **gwerə-** in Appendix*).] —**con·grat′u·la′tor** (-lā′tər) *n.* —**con·grat′u·la·to′ry** (-lə-tôr′ē, -tōr′ē) *adj.*

con·grat·u·la·tion (kən-grăch′ōō-lā′shən) *n.* **1.** The act of congratulating. **2.** *Plural.* Acknowledgment of the achievement or good fortune of another.

con·gre·gate (kŏng′grə-gāt′) *v.* **-gated, -gating, -gates.** —*intr.* To come together in a crowd; assemble. —*tr.* To bring together in a crowd or an assembly; collect. —See Synonyms at **gather.** —*adj.* (kŏng′grə-gĭt). Gathered; assembled. [Middle English *congregaten,* from Latin *congregāre,* to assemble : *com-,* together + *gregāre,* to flock together, from *grex* (stem *greg-*), herd, flock (see **ger-**^{1} in Appendix*).] —**con′gre·ga′tive** *adj.* —**con′gre·ga′tive·ness** *n.* —**con′gre·ga′tor** (-gā′tər) *n.*

con·gre·ga·tion (kŏng′grə-gā′shən) *n.* **1.** An act of congregating. **2.** A body of assembled people or things; gathering. **3. a.** A group of people gathered for religious worship. **b.** The members of a specific religious group who regularly worship at a common church. **4. a.** In the Old Testament, the Hebrews. **b.** In the New Testament, the Christian church. **5.** *Roman Catholic Church.* **a.** A religious institute in which only simple vows, not solemn vows, are taken. **b.** A division of the **Curia** (*see*). **6.** In colonial New England, a town or settlement considered as a religious community.

con·gre·ga·tion·al (kŏng′grə-gā′shən-əl) *adj.* **1.** Of or pertaining to a congregation. **2.** *Capital* **C.** *Abbr.* **Cong.** Of or pertaining to Congregationalism or Congregationalists.

Congregational Christian Church. An evangelical Protestant denomination practicing Congregationalism and, since 1957, merged with the United Church of Christ. Also called "Congregational Church."

con·gre·ga·tion·al·ism (kŏng′grə-gā′shən-əl-ĭz′əm) *n.* **1.** A type of church government in which each local congregation is self-governing. **2.** *Capital* **C.** The system of government and religious beliefs of the Congregational Christian Churches, in which each member church is self-governing.

Con·gre·ga·tion·al·ist (kŏng′grə-gā′shən-əl-ĭst) *n.* A member of a Congregational Christian Church. —*adj.* Congregational.

Congregation of the Holy Office. The official name for the **Holy Office** (*see*).

con·gress (kŏng′grĭs) *n.* **1.** A formal assembly of representatives, as of various nations, to discuss problems. **2.** The national legislative bodies of certain nations, especially of republics. **3.** *Capital* **C.** *Abbr.* **Cong., C. a.** The national legislative body of the United States, consisting of the Senate and the House of Representatives. **b.** The two-year session of this legislature between elections of the House of Representatives. **4.** A coming together; a meeting. **5.** Sexual intercourse. —*intr.v.* **congressed, -gressing, -gresses.** To meet in or at a congress. [Middle English *congresse,* a coming together, from Latin *congressus,* from *congredī,* to come together : *com-,* together + *gradī,* to go (see **ghredh-** in Appendix*).]

congress boot. An ankle-high shoe with elastic material in the sides. Also called "congress gaiter." [Once popular among members of the U.S. Congress.]

con·gres·sion·al (kən-grĕsh′ən-əl) *adj.* **1.** Of or pertaining to a congress. **2.** *Capital* **C.** *Abbr.* **Cong.** Of or pertaining to the Congress of the United States. [From Latin *congressiō,* a coming together, assembly, from *congredī,* to come together (see **congress**).] —**con·gres′sion·al·ist** *n.*

Congressional district. Any of the districts of each state of the United States, entitled to one representative in Congress.

Congressional Medal of Honor. The **Medal of Honor** (*see*).

Congressional Record. An official U.S. publication containing a daily record of all Congressional activities.

con·gress·man (kŏng′grĭs-mən) *n., pl.* **-men** (-mĭn). Also **Con·gress·man.** A member of the U.S. Congress, especially of the House of Representatives.

Congress of Industrial Organizations. *Abbr.* **CIO, C.I.O.** A former federation of labor unions originally (1935) within the American Federation of Labor, later (1938) separated from it and again (1953) merged with it to form the AFL-CIO.

Congress of Vienna. An international conference of major European powers, held in Vienna (1814–15) after the exile of Napoleon I, to readjust territories and restore monarchies.

con·gress·wom·an (kŏng′grĭs-wŏŏm′ən) *n., pl.* **-women** (-wĭm′ĭn). Also **Con·gress·wom·an.** A female member of the U.S. Congress, especially of the House of Representatives.

Con·greve (kŏn′grēv, kŏng′-), **William.** 1670–1729. English dramatist.

con·gru·ence (kŏng′grōō-əns, kən-grōō′əns) *n.* Also **con·gru·en·cy** (kən-grōō′ən-sē). **1.** Agreement; conformity. **2.** *Mathematics.* **a.** The state of being congruent. **b.** A mathematical statement that two quantities are congruent.

con·gru·ent (kŏng′grōō-ənt, kən-grōō′ənt) *adj.* **1.** Corresponding; congruous. **2.** *Mathematics.* **a.** Coinciding exactly when superimposed: *congruent triangles.* **b.** Having a difference divisible by a modulus: *congruent numbers.* [Middle English, from Latin *congruēns,* present participle of *congruere*†, to meet together, agree.] —**con′gru·ent·ly** *adv.*

con·gru·i·ty (kən-grōō′ə-tē) *n., pl.* **-ties. 1.** The quality or fact of being congruous. **2.** A point of agreement. **3.** *Geometry.* Exact coincidence when superimposed.

con·gru·ous (kŏng′grōō-əs) *adj.* **1.** Corresponding in character or kind; appropriate; harmonious. **2.** *Geometry.* Congruent. [Latin *congruus,* from *congruere,* to meet together, agree. See **congruent.**]

con·ic (kŏn′ĭk) *adj.* Also **con·i·cal** (-ĭ-kəl). **1.** Shaped like a cone. **2.** Pertaining to a cone. —*n. Mathematics.* A conic section. [New Latin *conicus,* from Greek *kōnikos,* from *kōnos,* CONE.]

conic projection. *Cartography.* A method of projecting pictures of parts of the earth's spherical surface on a surrounding cone, which is then flattened to a plane surface having concentric circles as parallels of latitude and radiating lines from the apex as meridians. Also called "conical projection."

conic section. One of a group of plane curves, including the circle, ellipse, hyperbola, and parabola, generated by: **1.** An intersection of a right circular cone and a plane. **2.** The plane locus of a point that moves so that the ratio of its distance to a fixed point to its distance from a fixed line is a positive constant. **3.** A graph of the general quadratic equation in two variables.

co·nid·i·o·phore (kō-nĭd′ē-ə-fôr) *n.* A specialized hyphal filament in fungi, bearing conidia. [CONIDI(UM) + -PHORE.]

co·nid·i·um (kō-nĭd′ē-əm, kə-) *n., pl.* **-ia** (-ē-ə). An asexual fungus spore, usually produced on a specialized sporophore. [New Latin (diminutive), from Greek *konis,* dust. See **keni-** in Appendix.*] —**co·nid′i·al** *adj.*

con·i·fer (kŏn′ə-fər, kō′nə-) *n.* Any of various predominantly evergreen, cone-bearing trees, such as a pine, spruce, hemlock, or fir. [New Latin *Coniferae* (family name), from Latin *cōnifer,* cone-bearing : *cōnus,* CONE + -FER.]

co·nif·er·ous (kō-nĭf′ər-əs) *adj.* **1.** Bearing cones. **2.** Of or composed of conifers. [From Latin *cōnifer.* See **conifer.**]

co·ni·ine (kō′nĭ-ēn′, -nē-ēn) *n.* Also **co·nin** (kō′nĭn), **co·nine** (kō′nēn′). A poisonous, colorless liquid alkaloid, $C_8H_{17}N$, obtained from the poison hemlock and formerly used in the treatment of spasmodic disorders. [German *Koniin* : Late Latin *cōnium,* CONIUM + -IN.]

co·ni·ol·o·gy. Variant of **koniology.**

co·ni·um (kō′nē-əm) *n.* Any of several poisonous plants of the genus *Conium,* including the **poison hemlock** (*see*). [New Latin *Conium,* from Late Latin *cōnium,* poison hemlock, from Greek *kōneion,* possibly from *kōnos,* cone (from its indented, pinnatifid leaves suggesting pine cones). See **kēi-** in Appendix.*]

conj. 1. conjugation. **2.** *Grammar.* conjunction; conjunctive. **3.** *Astronomy.* conjunction.

con·jec·tur·al (kən-jĕk′chər-əl) *adj.* **1.** Involving conjecture. **2.** Inclined to conjecture. —**con·jec′tur·al·ly** *adv.*

con·jec·ture (kən-jĕk′chər) *v.* **-tured, -turing, -tures.** —*tr.* To infer from inconclusive evidence; to guess. —*intr.* To make a conjecture. —*n.* **1.** Inference based on inconclusive or incomplete evidence; guesswork. **2.** An opinion or conclusion based on inference. [Middle English, from Old French, from Latin *conjectūra,* conclusion, interpretation, from *conjicere,* "to throw together," put together mentally, conjecture, interpret : *com-,* together + *jacere,* to throw (see **yē-** in Appendix*).] —**con·jec′tur·a·ble** *adj.* —**con·jec′tur·a·bly** *adv.* —**con·jec′tur·er** *n.*

Synonyms: *conjecture, surmise, guess, speculate, presume, infer.* These verbs mean to reach a conclusion or judgment. *Conjecture* implies that a conclusion is based on incomplete evidence. *Surmise* suggests a conclusion reached by intuition or by interpretation of slender evidence. *Guess,* in formal usage, implies a haphazard attempt to answer or solve a problem and suggests substantial grounds for doubt. Informally the term implies a tentative conclusion reached in the absence of alternatives: *I guess I'll go to the movies. Speculate* implies an

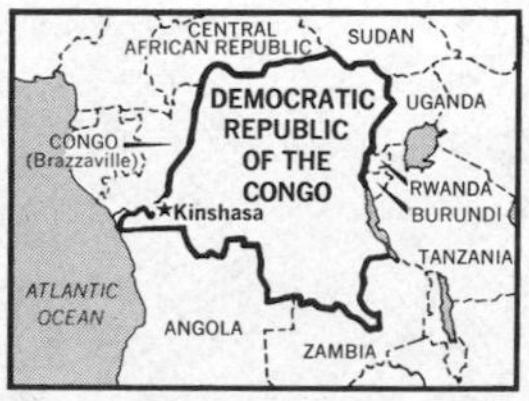

Democratic Republic of the Congo

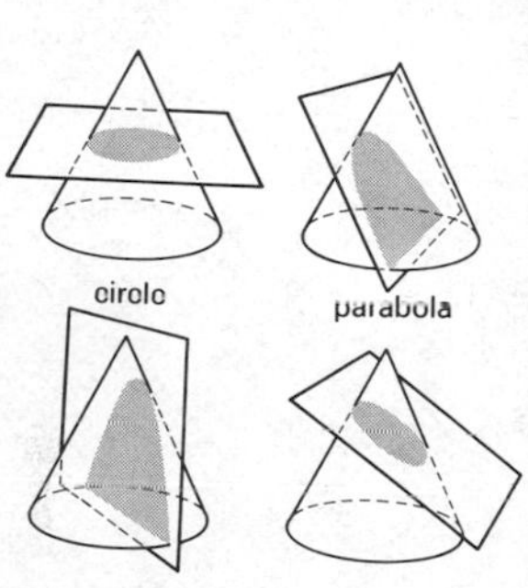

conic section

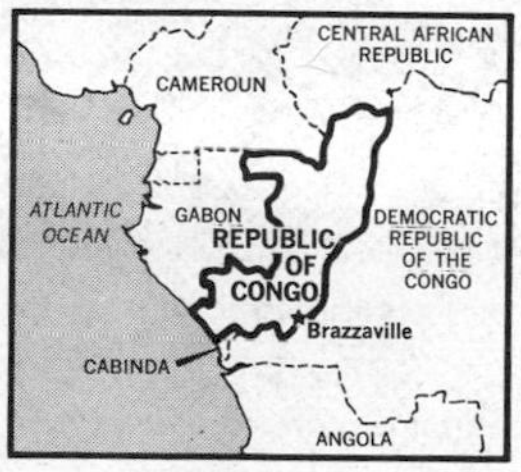

Republic of Congo

orderly process of reasoning based on inconclusive evidence, and is often interchangeable with *conjecture. Presume* and *infer* apply to conclusions about which less doubt is implied. *Presume* involves taking a conclusion for granted. In careful usage it is limited to what is considered worthy of trust; thus the term implies assumption based on experience or knowledge. *Infer* involves reaching a conclusion by reasoning from evidence about which no doubt is necessarily suggested.

con·join (kən-join′) *v.* **-joined, -joining, -joins.** —*tr.* To join together; connect; unite. —*intr.* To become joined or connected. [Middle English *conjoinen,* from Old French *conjoindre,* from Latin *conjungere* : *com-,* together + *jungere,* to join (see **yeug-** in Appendix*).] —**con·join′er** *n.*

con·joint (kən-joint′) *adj.* **1.** Joined together; connected; associated. **2.** Of or pertaining to two or more joined or associated persons or things. [Middle English, from Old French, past participle of *conjoindre,* CONJOIN.] —**con·joint′ly** *adv.*

con·ju·gal (kŏn′jŏŏ-gəl, -jə-gəl) *adj.* Of marriage or the marital relationship. [Old French, from Latin *conjugālis,* from *conjux,* a spouse, from *conjungere,* to join together (in marriage) : *com-,* together + *jungere,* to join (see **yeug-** in Appendix*).] —**con′-ju·gal′i·ty** (-găl′ə-tē) *n.* —**con′ju·gal·ly** *adv.*

con·ju·gant (kŏn′jŏŏ-gənt) *n.* Either of a pair of organisms, cells, or gametes undergoing conjugation. [Latin *conjugāns,* present participle of *conjugāre,* CONJUGATE.]

con·ju·gate (kŏn′jŏŏ-gāt′, -jə-gāt′) *v.* **-gated, -gating, -gates.** —*tr.* **1.** *Grammar.* To inflect (a verb) in the forms corresponding to person, number, tense, mood, and voice. **2.** *Rare.* To join together. —*intr.* **1.** *Biology.* To undergo conjugation. **2.** *Grammar.* To inflect a verb. **3.** To have sexual relations. —*adj.* (kŏn′jŏŏ-gĭt). **1.** Joined together, especially in a pair or pairs; coupled. **2.** *Mathematics & Physics.* Inversely or oppositely related with respect to one of a group of otherwise identical properties; especially, designating either or both of a pair of complex numbers differing only in the sign of the imaginary term. **3.** *Grammar.* Pertaining to words having the same derivation and usually a related meaning. —*n.* (kŏn′jŏŏ-gĭt). **1.** *Grammar.* One of two or more conjugate words. **2.** *Mathematics & Physics.* Either of a pair of conjugate quantities. [Middle English *conjugat,* joined, from Latin *conjugātus,* past participle of *conjugāre,* to yoke or join together : *com-,* together + *jugāre,* to yoke, from *jugum,* yoke (see **yeug-** in Appendix*).] —**con′ju·ga′tive** *adj.* —**con′ju·ga′tor** (-gā′tər) *n.*

conjugated protein. A compound of a protein with a nonprotein.

con·ju·ga·tion (kŏn′jŏŏ-gā′shən, kŏn′jə-) *n. Abbr.* **conj. 1.** The act of conjugating or state of being conjugated; a union. **2.** *Grammar.* **a.** The inflection of a particular verb. **b.** A presentation of the complete set of inflected forms of a verb. **c.** A class of verbs having similar inflected forms. **3. a.** A process of sexual reproduction in which ciliate protozoans of the same species temporarily couple and exchange genetic material. **b.** Chromosome pairing in the first meiotic division. **c.** The fusion of gamete nuclei; karyogamy. **d.** The union of sex cells; syngamy. —**con′ju·ga′tion·al** *adj.* —**con′ju·ga′tion·al·ly** *adv.*

con·junct (kən-jŭngkt′, kŏn′jŭngkt) *adj.* **1.** Joined together; united. **2.** Designating adjacent successive tones of the musical scale. [Middle English, from Latin *conjunctus,* past participle of *conjungere,* to join together : *com-,* together + *jungere,* to join (see **yeug-** in Appendix*).] —**con·junct′ly** *adv.*

con·junc·tion (kən-jŭngk′shən) *n.* **1.** The act of joining or state of being joined; combination. **2.** A simultaneous occurrence; coincidence. **3.** *Abbr.* **conj.** *Grammar.* In some languages, one of the parts of speech comprising words such as, in English, *and, but, because, as,* that connect other words, phrases, clauses, or sentences. See **coordinate conjunction, copulative conjunction, correlative conjunction, subordinate conjunction. 4.** *Abbr.* **conj.** *Astronomy.* The position of two celestial bodies on the celestial sphere when they have the same celestial longitude. —**con·junc′tion·al** *adj.* —**con·junc′tion·al·ly** *adv.*

con·junc·ti·va (kŏn′jŭngk-tī′və, kən-jŭngk′tĭ-və) *n., pl.* **-vas** or **-vae** (-vē). The mucous membrane that lines the inner surface of the eyelid and the exposed surface of the eyeball. [Middle English, from Medieval Latin *(membrāna) conjunctiva,* "the connective (membrane)," from Late Latin *conjunctīvus,* CONJUNCTIVE.] —**con′junc·ti′val** *adj.*

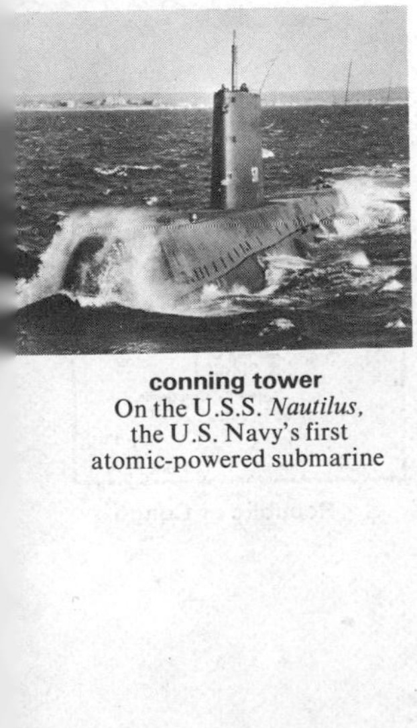
conning tower
On the U.S.S. *Nautilus,* the U.S. Navy's first atomic-powered submarine

con·junc·tive (kən-jŭngk′tĭv) *adj.* **1.** Joining; associative; connective. **2.** Joined together; combined. **3.** *Abbr.* **conj.** *Grammar.* **a.** Of or used as a conjunction. **b.** Serving to connect elements of meaning and construction in a sentence, as *and* and *moreover.* —*n. Abbr.* **conj.** *Grammar.* A connective word, especially a conjunction. [Late Latin *conjunctīvus,* from Latin *conjunctus,* CONJUNCT.] —**con·junc′tive·ly** *adv.*

con·junc·ti·vi·tis (kən-jŭngk′tə-vī′tĭs) *n. Pathology.* Inflammation of the conjunctiva. [New Latin : CONJUNCTIV(A) + -ITIS.]

con·junc·ture (kən-jŭngk′chər) *n.* **1.** A combination of circumstances or events. **2.** A critical set of circumstances; crisis.

con·ju·ra·tion (kŏn′jŏŏ-rā′shən) *n.* **1. a.** The act of conjuring. **b.** A magic spell or incantation. **2.** Magic; legerdemain. **3.** A solemn appeal or invocation.

con·jure (kŏn′jər, kən-jŏŏr′) *v.* **-jured, -juring, -jures.** —*tr.* **1.** To call upon or entreat solemnly, especially by an oath. **2.** To summon (a devil or spirit) by oath or magic spell. **3.** To cause or effect by or as by magic. —*intr.* **1.** To practice magic, especially legerdemain. **2.** To summon a devil by oath, incantation, or magic spell. **3.** *Obsolete.* To conspire. —**conjure up. 1.** To bring into existence as if by magic. **2.** To bring to the mind's eye; evoke. [Middle English *conjuren,* from Old French *conjurer,* from Medieval Latin *conjūrāre,* to invoke with oaths or incantations, from Latin, to swear together, conspire : *com-,* together + *jūrāre,* to swear (see **yewo-**[1] in Appendix*).]

con·jur·er (kŏn′jər-ər, kŭn′-) *n.* Also **con·jur·or. 1.** One who practices magic or legerdemain. **2.** One who entreats.

conk[1] (kŏngk) *n. Slang.* **1.** The head. **2.** The nose. **3.** A blow, especially on the head. —*tr.v.* **conked, conking, conks.** *Slang.* To hit, especially on the head. —**conk out. 1.** To fail suddenly. **2.** To tire after exertion. [Probably alteration of CONCH.]

conk[2] (kŏngk) *n.* A hard, shelflike fruiting body of a fungus, especially of the genera *Polyporus* and *Fomes,* found growing on tree trunks. [Probably variant of CONCH.]

con man. *Slang.* A **confidence man** *(see).*

conn. Variant of **con** (to steer).

Conn. Connecticut.

Con·nacht (kŏn′əKHt, kŏn′ət). Also **Con·naught** (kŏn′ôt). A province of the Republic of Ireland, occupying 6,610 square miles in the northwest and containing the counties of Galway, Leitrim, Mayo, Roscommon, and Sligo. Population, 419,000.

con·nate (kŏn′āt) *adj.* **1.** Part of or existing in someone or something from birth; inborn; innate. **2.** Coexisting since or associated in birth or origin; cognate; related. **3.** *Biology.* Congenitally or firmly united. Said of like parts or organs. [Late Latin *connātus,* past participle of *connascī,* to be born together : *com-,* together + Latin *nascī,* to be born (see **gene-** in Appendix*).] —**con′nate·ly** *adv.* —**con′nate·ness** *n.* —**con·na′tion** (kə-nā′shən) *n.*

con·nat·u·ral (kə-năch′ər-əl) *adj.* **1.** Innate; congenital; natural. **2.** Related or similar in nature; cognate. [Medieval Latin *connātūrālis* : *com-,* together + Latin *nātūrālis,* NATURAL.] —**con·nat′u·ral·ly** *adv.* —**con·nat′u·ral·ness** *n.*

con·nect (kə-nĕkt′) *v.* **-nected, -necting, -nects.** —*tr.* **1.** To join or fasten together; link; unite. **2.** To associate or consider as related. **3.** To establish communication between. Used with *with.* **4.** To join to a communications circuit. —*intr.* **1.** To become joined or united. **2.** To meet so that passengers can easily transfer from one route to another. Used of means of public transportation. **3.** *Informal.* To be successful. **4.** *Informal.* In sports such as baseball, to hit or make contact with the ball. —See Synonyms at **join.** [Middle English *connecten,* from Latin *connectere* : *com-,* together + *nectere,* to bind, tie (see **ned-** in Appendix*).] —**con·nect′ed·ly** *adv.* —**con·nect′i·ble, con·nect′a·ble** *adj.* —**con·nec′tor** (-nĕk′tər), **con·nect′er** *n.*

Con·nect·i·cut (kə-nĕt′ə-kət). **1.** *Abbr.* **Conn.** A New England state of the United States, 5,009 square miles in area, situated along Long Island Sound; one of the original 13 states. Population, 2,832,000. Capital, Hartford. See map at **United States of America. 2.** The largest river in New England, rising in northern New Hampshire and flowing 345 miles south to Long Island Sound.

connecting rod. 1. A rod linking rotating parts of a machine in reciprocating motion. **2.** Such a rod connecting the crankshaft of an automobile to a piston.

con·nec·tion (kə-nĕk′shən) *n.* Also *British* **con·nex·ion.** *Abbr.* **con. 1.** The act of joining or state of being joined; union. **2.** Anything that joins, relates, or connects; a bond; a link. **3.** An association, alliance, or relation. **4.** The logical ordering of words or ideas; coherence. **5.** The relation of a word or idea to the surrounding text; context. **6.** A distant relative. **7.** *Usually plural.* A group of people with whom one is associated. **8.** Sexual intercourse. **9.** *Often plural.* The meeting of various means of transportation for the transfer of passengers. **10.** A line of communication between two points in a telephone or similar wired system. **11.** *Slang.* **a.** A narcotics dealer. **b.** A narcotics purchase. —**con·nec′tion·al** *adj.*

con·nec·tive (kə-nĕk′tĭv) *adj.* Serving or tending to connect. —*n.* **1.** Anything that connects. **2.** *Grammar.* A word, such as a conjunction, that connects words, phrases, clauses, and sentences. **3.** *Botany.* The tissue of a stamen that forms the division between the two lobes of an anther. —**con·nec′tive·ly** *adv.* —**con′nec·tiv′i·ty** *n.*

connective tissue. Tissue arising chiefly from the embryonic mesoderm, including mucous, fibrous, reticular, adipose, cartilage, and bone tissue, characterized by a highly vascular matrix structure and forming the supporting and connecting structures of the body.

Con·ne·ma·ra (kŏn′ĭ-mä′rə). An Atlantic coastal region of the Republic of Ireland, in western County Galway.

conning tower. 1. The armored pilothouse of a warship. **2.** A raised, enclosed observation post in a submarine, also usually used as a means of entrance and exit. [From CON (to steer).]

con·nip·tion (kə-nĭp′shən) *n. Informal.* A fit of anger or other violent emotion; tantrum. [Origin unknown.]

con·niv·ance (kə-nī′vəns) *n.* Also **con·niv·ence. 1.** The act of conniving. **2.** *Law.* Knowledge of, and tacit consent to, the commission of an illegal act by another.

con·nive (kə-nīv′) *intr.v.* **-nived, -niving, -nives. 1.** To feign ignorance of a wrong, thus implying tacit encouragement or consent. Used with *at.* **2.** To cooperate secretly or conspire. Used with *with.* [French *conniver,* from Latin *connivēre, cōnivēre,* to close the eyes, be indulgent. See **kneigwh-** in Appendix.*] —**con·niv′er** *n.*

con·ni·vent (kə-nī′vənt) *adj. Biology.* Converging and touching. Said especially of stamens or an insect's wings. [Latin *connivēns,* present participle of *connivēre,* "to bend together," close the eyes, CONNIVE.]

con·nois·seur (kŏn′ə-sûr′) *n.* A person with informed and astute discrimination, especially concerning the arts or matters of taste. [Obsolete French, from Old French *connoisseor,* from *connoistre,* to know, from Latin *cognōscere,* to get acquainted with, know thoroughly : *co-*, together + *gnōscere, nōscere,* to know (see **gnō-** in Appendix*).] —**con'nois·seur'ship'** *n.*

con·no·ta·tion (kŏn'ə-tā'shən) *n.* **1.** The act or process of connoting. **2.** The configuration of suggestive or associative implications constituting the general sense of an abstract expression beyond its literal, explicit sense. Compare **denotation.** **3.** *Logic.* The total of the attributes constituting the meaning of a term; intension. —**con'no·ta'tive** *adj.* —**con'no·ta'tive·ly** *adv.*

con·note (kə-nōt') *tr.v.* **-noted, -noting, -notes.** **1.** To suggest or imply in addition to literal meaning. **2.** To involve as a condition or consequence. [Medieval Latin *connotāre,* "to mark in addition" : Latin *com-*, together with + *notāre,* to mark, note, from *nota,* a mark, note (see **gnō-** in Appendix*).]

con·nu·bi·al (kə-nōō'bē-əl) *adj.* Of marriage or the married state; conjugal. [Latin *connūbiālis,* from *connūbium,* marriage : *com-*, together + *nūbere,* to marry (see **sneubh-** in Appendix*).] —**con·nu'bi·al'i·ty** (-ăl'ə-tē) *n.* —**con·nu'bi·al·ly** *adv.*

con·quer (kŏng'kər) *v.* **-quered, -quering, -quers.** —*tr.* **1.** To defeat or subdue by force, especially by force of arms. **2.** To gain or secure control of by or as if by force of arms. **3.** To overcome or surmount by physical, mental, or moral force. —*intr.* To be victorious; win. —See Synonyms at **defeat.** [Middle English *conqueren,* from Old French *conquerre,* from Vulgar Latin *conquaerere* (unattested), variant of Latin *conquīrere,* to search for, procure, win : *con-* (intensive) + *quaerere,* to seek (see **quaerere** in Appendix*).] —**con'quer·a·ble** *adj.*

con·quer·or (kŏng'kər-ər) *n.* Someone who conquers. —**the Conqueror. William I** of England *(see).*

con·quest (kŏn'kwĕst, kŏng'-) *n.* **1.** The act or process of conquering. **2.** Something acquired by conquering, as territory. **3.** The act of captivating someone's love or favor. **4.** Someone whose love or favor has been captivated. —See Synonyms at **victory.** —**the Conquest.** The **Norman Conquest** *(see).* [Middle English *conquest(e),* from Old French, from Vulgar Latin *conquaesītus* (unattested), past participle of *conquaerere* (unattested), CONQUER.]

con·qui·an (kŏng'kē-ən) *n.* A card game resembling rummy, for two players. Also called "cooncan." [Mexican Spanish *con quien,* from Spanish *con quién,* with whom? : *con,* with, from Latin *cum* (see **kom** in Appendix*) + *quién,* whom, from Latin *quem* (see **kwo-** in Appendix*).]

con·quis·ta·dor (kŏn-kwĭs'tə-dôr; *Spanish* kōn-kēs-tä-*th*ôr') *n., pl.* **-dors** or *Spanish* **-dores** (-*th*ô'rĕs). A conqueror; especially, any of the Spanish conquerors of Mexico and Peru in the 16th century. [Spanish, from *conquistar,* to conquer, from Medieval Latin *conquestāre,* frequentative of Vulgar Latin *conquaerere* (unattested). See **conquer.**]

Con·rad (kŏn'răd), **Frank.** 1874–1941. American electrical engineer, inventor, and pioneer in radio broadcasting.

Con·rad (kŏn'răd), **Joseph.** Original name, Teodor Józef Konrad Korzeniowski. 1857–1924. Polish-born English novelist and short-story writer.

cons. 1. consigned; consignment. **2.** consonant. **3.** constable. **4.** constitution; constitutional. **5.** construction.

Cons. 1. constable. **2.** consul.

con·san·guin·e·ous (kŏn'săng-gwĭn'ē-əs) *adj.* Also **con·san·guine** (kŏn-săng'gwĭn). Of the same lineage or origin; especially, related by blood. [Latin *consanguineus* : *com-*, joint + *sanguineus,* of blood, SANGUINE.] —**con'san·guin'e·ous·ly** *adv.*

con·san·guin·i·ty (kŏn'săng-gwĭn'ə-tē) *n.* **1.** Blood relationship. **2.** Any close connection or affinity.

con·science (kŏn'shəns) *n.* **1.** The faculty of recognizing the distinction between right and wrong in regard to one's own conduct. **2.** Conformity to one's own sense of right conduct. **3.** *Obsolete.* **a.** Consciousness. **b.** Inner thought. —**in (all) conscience. 1.** In all truth. **2.** Certainly. —**on one's conscience.** Causing remorse. [Middle English, from Old French, from Latin *conscientia,* from *consciēns,* present participle of *conscīre,* to be conscious, know well : *com-* (intensive) + *scīre,* to know (see **skei-** in Appendix*).]

conscience clause. A clause in a law that relieves persons whose conscientious or religious scruples forbid compliance.

conscience money. Money paid to atone for some concealed dishonest act.

con·sci·en·tious (kŏn'shē-ĕn'shəs) *adj.* **1.** Governed by or accomplished according to conscience; scrupulous. **2.** Thorough and painstaking; careful. —See Synonyms at **meticulous.** [French *conscientieux,* from Medieval Latin *conscientiōsus,* from Latin *conscientia,* CONSCIENCE.] —**con'sci·en'tious·ly** *adv.* —**con'sci·en'tious·ness** *n.*

conscientious objector. *Abbr.* **CO, C.O.** One who on the basis of his religious and moral principles refuses to bear arms or participate in military service.

con·scion·a·ble (kŏn'shən-ə-bəl) *adj. Obsolete.* Conscientious. [From *conscions,* obsolete variant of CONSCIENCE + -ABLE.]

con·scious (kŏn'shəs) *adj.* **1. a.** Having an awareness of one's own existence, sensations, and thoughts, and of one's environment. **b.** Capable of complex response to environment. **c.** Not asleep; awake. **2.** Subjectively known: *conscious remorse.* **3.** Intentionally conceived or done; deliberate: *a conscious insult.* **4.** *Rare.* Aware of wrongdoing. —See Synonyms at **aware.** —*n. Psychoanalysis.* That component of waking awareness perceptible by an individual at any given instant; consciousness. [Latin *conscius,* knowing with others, participating in knowledge, aware of : *com-*, with + *scīre,* to know (see **skei-** in Appendix*).] —**con'scious·ly** *adv.*

con·scious·ness (kŏn'shəs-nĭs) *n.* **1.** The state or condition of being conscious. **2.** The essence or totality of attitudes, opinions, and sensitivities held or thought to be held by an individual or group: *national consciousness.* **3.** *Psychoanalysis.* The conscious.

con·script (kŏn'skrĭpt) *n.* One who is compulsorily enrolled for service in the armed forces; a draftee. —*adj.* (kŏn'skrĭpt). Enrolled compulsorily; drafted. —*tr.v.* (kən-skrĭpt') **conscripted, -scripting, -scripts. 1.** To enroll compulsorily for military or naval service; to draft. **2.** To force into service. [Old French, enlisted, from Latin *conscrīptus,* past participle of *conscrībere,* to write together, enter in a list, enroll : *com-*, together + *scrībere,* to write (see **skeri-** in Appendix*).]

conscript fathers. 1. The senators of ancient Rome. **2.** The members of any legislature. [Translation of Latin *patres conscripti,* "fathers elect."]

con·scrip·tion (kən-skrĭp'shən) *n.* **1.** A draft. **2.** A monetary payment exacted by a government in wartime.

con·se·crate (kŏn'sə-krāt') *tr.v.* **-crated, -crating, -crates. 1.** To make, declare, or set apart as sacred: *consecrate a church.* **2.** *Roman Catholic Church.* To change (the elements of bread and wine) into the body and blood of Christ. **3.** *Roman Catholic & Anglican Church.* To initiate (a priest) into the order of bishops. **4.** To dedicate to some service or goal. **5.** To make venerable: *a tradition consecrated by time.* —See Synonyms at **devote.** —*adj. Rare.* Consecrated. [Middle English *consecraten,* from Latin *Consecrāre* : *com-* (intensive) + *sacrāre,* to make sacred, from *sacer,* sacred (see **sak-** in Appendix*).] —**con'se·cra'tive** *adj.* —**con'se·cra'tor** (-krā'tər) *n.* —**con'se·cra·to'ry** (-krə-tôr'ē, -tōr'ē) *adj.*

con·se·crat·ed (kŏn'sə-krā'tĭd) *adj.* **1.** Made holy; sacred. **2.** Honored as holy; hallowed.

con·se·cra·tion (kŏn'sə-krā'shən) *n.* **1.** The act, process, or ceremony of consecrating. **2.** The state of being consecrated.

con·se·cu·tion (kŏn'sə-kyōō'shən) *n.* **1.** A sequence or succession. **2.** *Logic.* The relation of consequent to antecedent; deduction; inference. [Latin *consecūtiō,* sequence, from *consequī,* to follow up. See **consequent.**]

con·sec·u·tive (kən-sĕk'yə-tĭv) *adj.* **1.** Following successively without interruption. **2.** Marked by logical sequence. **3.** *Grammar.* Stating a consequence. [French *consécutif,* Medieval Latin *consecūtīvus,* from Latin *consequī,* to follow up. See **consequent.**] —**con·sec'u·tive·ly** *adv.* —**con·sec'u·tive·ness** *n.*

con·sen·su·al (kən-sĕn'shōō-əl) *adj.* **1.** *Law.* Existing or brought about by consent, as a marriage. **2.** *Physiology.* Of or pertaining to involuntary function; reflex. [From CONSENSUS (after SENSUAL).] —**con·sen'su·al·ly** *adv.*

con·sen·sus (kən-sĕn'səs) *n.* Collective opinion or concord; general agreement or accord. [Latin, from *consentīre,* to agree, CONSENT.]

Usage: *Consensus of opinion* has become a stock expression, but because of its redundancy it should be avoided in writing, according to 69 per cent of the Usage Panel.

con·sent (kən-sĕnt') *intr.v.* **-sented, -senting, -sents. 1.** To give assent; accede; agree. **2.** To agree in opinion; be of the same mind. —See Synonyms at **assent.** —*n.* **1.** Voluntary acceptance or allowance of what is planned or done by another; permission. **2.** Agreement as to opinion or a course of action. [Middle English *consenten,* from Old French *consentir,* from Latin *consentīre,* to feel together, agree : *com-*, together + *sentīre,* to feel (see **sent-** in Appendix*).] —**con·sent'er** *n.*

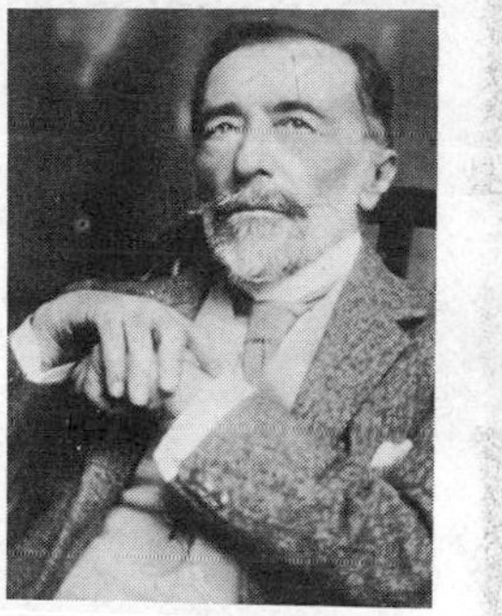

Joseph Conrad

con·sen·ta·ne·ous (kŏn'sĕn-tā'nē-əs) *adj.* **1.** Consistent; accordant. **2.** Unanimous. [Latin *consentāneus,* from *consentīre,* to feel together, CONSENT.] —**con·sen'ta·ne'i·ty** (kən-sĕn'tə-nē'ə-tē), **con'sen·ta'ne·ous·ness** *n.* —**con'sen·ta'ne·ous·ly** *adv.*

con·sen·tience (kən-sĕn'shəns) *n.* The state of being or acting in accord. [From Latin *consentiēns,* present participle of *consentīre,* to feel together, CONSENT.] —**con·sen'tient** *adj.*

con·se·quence (kŏn'sə-kwĕns) *n.* **1.** That which logically or naturally follows from an action or condition; an effect; result. **2.** The relation of a result to its cause. **3.** A logical result or inference. **4.** Distinction or importance in rank: *someone of consequence.* **5.** Significance; importance: *an issue of consequence.* —See Synonyms at **effect, importance.**

con·se·quent (kŏn'sə-kwĕnt, -kwənt) *adj.* **1. a.** Following as a natural effect, result, or conclusion. See Usage note at **consequential. b.** Following as a logical conclusion. **2.** Logically correct or consistent. **3.** *Geology.* Having a position or direction relating to or resulting from the original slope of the earth's surface. —*n.* **1.** Anything that follows something else, with or without causal relation. **2.** An outcome or result. **3.** *Logic.* The conclusion, as of a syllogism. **4.** The second term of a ratio. [Middle English, from Old French, from Latin *consequēns,* present participle of *consequī,* to follow up, accompany : *com-*, together + *sequī,* to follow (see **sekw-**[1] in Appendix*).]

con·se·quen·tial (kŏn'sə-kwĕn'shəl) *adj.* **1.** Following as an effect, result, or conclusion; resultant; consequent. **2.** Having consequence; important; significant. See Usage note. **3.** Conceited; pompous. —**con'se·quen'ti·al'i·ty** (-shē-ăl'ə-tē), **con'se·quen'tial·ness** *n.* —**con'se·quen'tial·ly** *adv.*

Usage: *Consequential,* in the sense of having consequence, importance, or significance, is disputed in modern usage. It is termed unacceptable in that sense (an earlier one) by 66 per cent of the Usage Panel. It is still used to indicate self-importance and conceit, however. *Consequential* and *consequent* (adjectives) also mean following as an effect or result. In that primary sense, *consequent* is more common and is always the choice when *resultant* is meant: *Theft was charged, and the consequent investigation led to his dismissal. Consequential* sometimes implies an indirect or secondary result. Both *consequent* and *consequential* can be used with *to, on,* or *upon.*

con·se·quent·ly (kŏn'sə kwĕnt'lē) *adv.* As a result; therefore.

con·ser·van·cy (kən-sûr′vən-sē) *n., pl.* **-cies. 1.** Conservation, especially of natural resources. **2.** *British.* A commission supervising fisheries, navigation, forests, or the like.

con·ser·va·tion (kŏn′sûr-vā′shən) *n.* **1.** The act of conserving; preservation from loss, waste, or harm. **2.** The official preservation of natural resources, such as topsoil, forests, and waterways. **—con′ser·va′tion·al** *adj.*

con·ser·va·tion·ist (kŏn′sûr-vā′shən-ĭst) *n.* One who practices or advocates preservation of natural resources.

conservation of energy. *Physics.* An exact conservation law stating that the total energy of an isolated system remains constant regardless of changes within the system.

conservation of mass. *Physics.* The classical principle that the total mass of an isolated system is unchanged by interaction of its parts.

conservation of momentum. *Physics.* An exact conservation law stating that the total linear momentum of an isolated system remains constant regardless of changes within the system.

con·ser·va·tism (kən-sûr′və-tĭz′əm) *n.* **1.** The disposition in politics or culture to maintain the existing order and to resist or oppose change or innovation. **2.** The principles and practices of persons or groups so disposed. **3.** *Capital* **C.** The principles and practices of the Conservative Party.

con·ser·va·tive (kən-sûr′və-tĭv) *adj.* **1.** Tending to favor the preservation of the existing order and to regard proposals for change with distrust. **2.** *Capital* **C.** Adhering to or characteristic of the Conservative Party of the United Kingdom. **3.** *Capital* **C.** Adhering to or characteristic of Conservative Judaism. **4.** Moderate; prudent; cautious: *a conservative estimate.* **5.** Traditional in manner or style; not showy: *a conservative suit.* **6.** Tending to conserve; conserving; preservative. *—n.* **1.** A conservative person. **2.** *Capital* **C.** *Abbr.* **C.** A member or supporter of the Conservative Party of the United Kingdom. **3.** *Capital* **C.** *Abbr.* **C.** A member or supporter of the Progressive-Conservative Party of Canada. **4.** A preservative. **—con·ser′va·tive·ly** *adv.* **—con·ser′va·tive·ness** *n.*

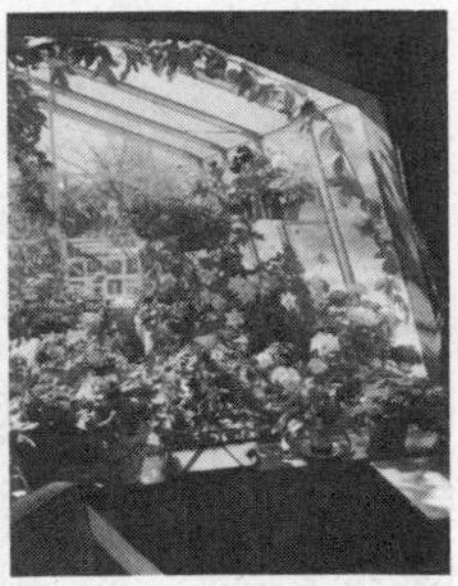

conservatory

Conservative Judaism. The branch of Judaism that holds a modified view of the sanctity of the Torah and is flexible in its submission to the authority of the Rabbinical Law, accepting some liturgical and ritual changes in the light of the needs of modern life. Compare **Orthodox Judaism, Reform Judaism.**

Conservative Party. A major political party of the United Kingdom.

con·ser·va·tor (kən-sûr′və-tər) *n.* **1.** Someone who conserves or preserves from injury, violation, or infraction; a protector. **2.** *Law.* A guardian; keeper.

con·ser·va·to·ry (kən-sûr′və-tôr′ē, -tōr′ē) *n., pl.* **-ries. 1.** A small glass-enclosed room or greenhouse, usually part of a dwelling, in which plants are raised and displayed. **2.** A school of music or dramatic art. *—adj.* Adapted to conserve.

con·serve (kən-sûrv′) *tr.v.* **-served, -serving, -serves. 1.** To protect from loss or depletion; preserve. **2.** To preserve (fruits) with sugar. *—n.* (kŏn′sûrv). A jam made of two or more fruits stewed in sugar. Often used in the plural. [Middle English *conserven*, from Old French *conserver*, from Latin *conservāre* : *com-* (intensive) + *servāre*, to keep, preserve (see **ser-**[1] in Appendix*).] **—con·serv′a·ble** *adj.* **—con·serv′er** *n.*

con·sid·er (kən-sĭd′ər) *v.* **-ered, -ering, -ers.** *—tr.* **1.** To deliberate upon; examine; study. **2.** To regard as; think or deem to be. **3.** To believe after careful deliberation; to judge. **4.** To take into account; make allowance for. **5.** To have regard for; pay attention to. **6.** To regard highly; esteem. **7.** To think about as possible or acceptable. *—intr.* To think carefully; reflect. —See Synonyms at **ponder.** [Middle English *consideren*, from Old French *considerer*, from Latin *considerāre*, to observe (originally a term of augury meaning "to observe the stars carefully"). See **sweid-**[1] in Appendix.*] **—con·sid′er·er** *n.*

Synonyms: *consider, deem, regard, account, reckon.* These verbs refer to holding opinions or views that reflect evaluation of a person or thing. *Consider* suggests objective evaluation based on reflection and reasoning. *Deem* is more subjective through its emphasis on judgment distinguished from analytical thought. *Regard* may imply personal, subjective judgment or, especially in the passive, the sentiment of many. *Account* and *reckon* in this sense are rather literary in flavor and imply calculated judgment. Less formally, *reckon* is used in the related sense of suppose.

Usage: *Consider*, meaning to regard as or think to be or to believe after careful deliberation, is followed by a direct object without *as.* The construction *consider . . . as* is used when *consider* means to study or examine: *The biography considers him as statesman and as writer.*

con·sid·er·a·ble (kən-sĭd′ər-ə-bəl) *adj.* **1.** Fairly large in amount, extent, or degree; respectable: *a man of considerable influence.* **2.** Worthy of consideration; important; significant: *a considerable issue.* *—n. Informal.* A considerable amount or extent; a great deal; much. **—con·sid′er·a·bly** *adv.*

Usage: *Considerable*, used adverbially, is incorrect: *She aided him considerably* (not *considerable*). Its use as an intensive is also incorrect: *She acted considerable strange.*

console table
Louis XVI console table

con·sid·er·ate (kən-sĭd′ər-ĭt) *adj.* **1.** Having regard for the needs or feelings of others. **2.** Characterized by careful thought; deliberate. —See Synonyms at **thoughtful.** [Latin *consīderātus*, past participle of *consīderāre*, to be considerate, CONSIDER.] **—con·sid′er·ate·ly** *adv.* **—con·sid′er·ate·ness** *n.*

con·sid·er·a·tion (kən-sĭd′ə-rā′shən) *n.* **1.** The act or process of considering; deliberation; meditation. **2.** A circumstance to be considered; a factor in forming a judgment or decision. **3.** Thoughtfulness; solicitude. **4.** A thought produced by considering; a thoughtful opinion. **5.** Something given in exchange for a service rendered; a recompense. **6.** *Law.* Something promised, given, or done that has the effect of making an agreement a legally enforceable contract. **7.** High regard. **—in consideration of. 1.** In view of; on account of. **2.** In return for.

con·sid·ered (kən-sĭd′ərd) *adj.* **1.** Reached after deliberation or careful thought. **2.** Regarded; esteemed.

con·sid·er·ing (kən-sĭd′ər-ĭng) *prep.* In view of; taking into consideration. *—adv. Informal.* All things considered.

con·sign (kən-sīn′) *v.* **-signed, -signing, -signs.** *—tr.* **1.** To give over to the care of another; entrust. **2.** To turn over permanently to another's charge or to a lasting condition; commit irrevocably. **3.** To deliver (merchandise, for example) for custody or sale. **4.** To set apart, as for a special use or purpose; assign. **5.** *Obsolete.* To mark with or as if with a seal or stamp; to sign. *—intr. Obsolete.* To submit; consent. —See Synonyms at **commit.** [Middle English *consignen*, to certify by a seal, from Old French *consigner*, from Latin *consignāre* : *com-* (intensive) + *signāre*, to seal, from *signum*, seal, mark (see **sekw-**[1] in Appendix*).] **—con·sign′a·ble** *adj.* **—con′sig·na′tion** (kŏn′sĭg-nā′shən) *n.* **—con·sign′or** (kən-sī′nər, kôn′sī-nôr′), **con·sign′er** (-sī′nər) *n.*

con·sign·ee (kŏn′sī-nē′, kən-sī-) *n.* A person, such as an agent, to whom merchandise is consigned.

con·sign·ment (kən-sīn′mənt) *n. Abbr.* **cons. 1.** The consigning of goods or a cargo, especially to an agent for sale or custody. **2.** That which is consigned. **—on consignment.** Sent to a retailer who is expected to pay following sale. Said of merchandise: *books shipped on consignment.*

con·sist (kən-sĭst′) *intr.v.* **-sisted, -sisting, -sists. 1.** To be made up or composed. Used with *of.* **2.** To have a basis; be inherent; lie; rest. Used with *in.* **3.** To be compatible; to accord. [Old French *consister*, from Latin *consistere*, to stand still, exist : *com-* (intensive) + *sistere*, to cause to stand, place (see **stā-** in Appendix*).]

con·sis·ten·cy (kən-sĭs′tən-sē) *n., pl.* **-cies.** Also **con·sis·tence** (-təns). **1.** Agreement or logical coherence among things or parts. **2.** Compatibility or agreement among successive acts, ideas, or events. **3.** The condition of holding together; firmness. **4.** The degree or texture of firmness or viscosity.

Usage: *Consistency* is more common than *consistence* in all senses and is almost always the form for those dealing with agreement of parts, or harmony or regularity of action.

con·sis·tent (kən-sĭs′tənt) *adj.* **1.** Agreeing; compatible; not contradictory. **2.** Conforming to the same principles or course of action. [Latin *consistens*, present participle of *consistere*, to stand firmly, CONSIST.] **—con·sis′tent·ly** *adv.*

con·sis·to·ry (kən-sĭs′tər-ē) *n., pl.* **-ries. 1.** *Roman Catholic Church.* A gathering, either of cardinals alone, *secret consistory*, or with others present, *public consistory*, presided over by the pope for the solemn promulgation of papal acts, such as the appointment of cardinals or bishops or the canonization of a saint. **2.** In certain Reformed churches, a governing body of a local congregation, composed of the ministers and elders. **3.** In Lutheran state churches, a court appointed to regulate ecclesiastical affairs. **4.** *Anglican Church.* A diocesan court presided over by the bishop's chancellor or commissary. **5.** The meeting place, or the meeting itself, of any such body. **6.** A council or tribunal. [Middle English *consistorie*, from Old French, from Medieval Latin *consistōrium*, from Late Latin, place of assembly, from Latin *consistere*, to take one's place (at a meeting), stand, CONSIST.] **—con′sis·to′ri·al** (kŏn′sĭs-tôr′ē-əl, -tōr′ē-əl), **con′sis·to′ri·an** *adj.*

con·so·ci·ate (kən-sō′shē-āt′) *v.* **-ated, -ating, -ates.** *—tr.* To bring into friendly association. *—intr.* To come into friendly association. *—adj.* (kən-sō′shē-ĭt). Associated; united. *—n.* (kən-sō′shē-ĭt). An associate; a companion; partner. [Middle English *consociat*, associated, from Latin *consociātus*, past participle of *consociāre*, to associate, join : *com-*, together + *sociāre*, to join, from *socius*, ally, companion (see **sekw-**[1] in Appendix*).] **—con·so′ci·a′tion** *n.*

consol. consolidated.

con·so·la·tion (kŏn′sə-lā′shən) *n.* **1. a.** The act or an instance of consoling. **b.** The state of being consoled. **2.** Someone or something that consoles; a comfort.

con·sol·a·to·ry (kən-sŏl′ə-tôr′ē, -tōr′ē) *adj.* Affording or tending to afford consolation; comforting.

con·sole[1] (kən-sōl′) *tr.v.* **-soled, -soling, -soles.** To cheer in time of grief, defeat, or trouble; to comfort; to solace. [French *consoler*, from Old French, from Latin *consōlārī* : *com-* (intensive) + *sōlārī*, to comfort (see **sel-**[2] in Appendix*).] **—con·sol′a·ble** *adj.* **—con·sol′er** *n.* **—con·sol′ing·ly** *adv.*

con·sole[2] (kŏn′sōl) *n.* **1.** A decorative bracket for supporting a cornice, shelf, bust, or other object. **2.** A **console table** *(see).* **3.** The desklike part of an organ that contains the keyboard, stops, and pedals. **4.** A cabinet for a radio, television set, or phonograph, designed to stand on the floor. **5.** A panel housing the controls for electrical or mechanical equipment. [French, short for *consolateur*, a carved human figure used to support cornices, from Latin *consōlātor*, one that consoles, hence a support, from *consōlārī*, CONSOLE. (Possibly also influenced by the use of *Consōlātor*, "Consoler," in Medieval Latin, as a name for Jesus and for certain saints, statues of whom occur as supports for cornices in Gothic architecture.)]

console table. 1. A table supported by decorative consoles fixed to a wall. **2.** A small table, often with curved legs resembling consoles, designed to be set against a wall. Also called "console."

con·sol·i·date (kən-sŏl′ə-dāt′) *v.* **-dated, -dating, -dates.** —*tr.* **1.** To make firm or coherent; form into a compact mass; solidify. **2.** To make internally strong or stable; strengthen: *consolidate an empire.* **3.** *Military.* To strengthen or reorganize (a position). **4.** To unite into one system or body; to combine; merge. —*intr.* To become solidified or united. —See Synonyms at **join.** [Latin *consolidāre* : *com-* (intensive) + *solidāre,* to make solid or firm, from *solidus,* solid (see **sol-** in Appendix*).] —**con·sol′i·da′tor** (-dā′tər) *n.*

consolidated school. A public school, usually rural, for pupils from several adjacent districts.

con·sol·i·da·tion (kən-sŏl′ə-dā′shən) *n.* **1. a.** The act or process of consolidating. **b.** The state of being consolidated. **2.** The merger of two or more commercial interests or corporations.

con·sols (kŏn′sŏlz, kən-sŏlz′) *pl.n. Abbr.* **con.** The perpetual governmental securities of Great Britain. Also called "bank annuities." [Short for *consolidated annuities.*]

con·som·mé (kŏn′sə-mā′) *n.* A clear soup made of meat or vegetable stock or both. [French, "concentrate," from Old French *consommer,* to sum up, from Latin *consummāre* : *com-* (intensive) + *summa,* SUM.]

con·so·nance (kŏn′sə-nəns) *n.* **1.** Agreement; harmony; accord. **2. a.** Correspondence of sounds. **b.** *Prosody.* A similarity of terminal consonants but not of vowels in two or more syllables, words, or lines. **3.** *Music.* A simultaneous combination of sounds conventionally regarded as pleasing and final in effect. Compare **dissonance.**

con·so·nant (kŏn′sə-nənt) *adj.* **1.** In agreement or accord. Often used with *with* or *to.* **2.** Corresponding in sound. Often used with *with* or *to.* **3.** Harmonious in sound. **4.** Consonantal. —*n. Abbr.* **cons.** *Phonetics.* **1. a.** A speech sound produced by a partial or complete obstruction of the air stream by any of various constrictions of the speech organs. **b.** A subordinate or less distinctive sound within a syllable, as a glide in a diphthong. **2.** A letter or character representing such a sound. [Middle English, from Old French, from Latin *(littera) consonāns,* "(letter) sounded with (a vowel)," from the present participle of *consonāre,* to sound at the same time, harmonize, agree : *com-,* together + *sonāre,* to sound (see **swen-** in Appendix*).] —**con′so·nant·ly** *adv.*

con·so·nan·tal (kŏn′sə-năn′təl) *adj.* **1.** Of, relating to, or having the nature of a consonant. **2.** Containing a consonant or consonants. —**con′so·nan′tal·ly** *adv.*

con·sort (kŏn′sôrt) *n.* **1.** A husband or wife; especially, the spouse of a monarch. **2.** A companion or partner. **3.** A ship accompanying another in travel. —*v.* (kən-sôrt′) **consorted, -sorting, -sorts.** —*intr.* **1.** To keep company; to associate. **2.** To be in accord or agreement. —*tr.* **1.** To unite in company; to associate. **2.** *Obsolete.* **a.** To escort; accompany. **b.** To espouse. [Middle English, from Old French, from Latin *consors,* "one who shares the same fate," companion, partner : *com-,* together + *sors,* fate, share (see **ser-**[3] in Appendix*).]

con·sor·ti·um (kən-sôr′shē-əm) *n., pl.* **-tia** (-shē-ə). **1.** An association of financial institutions or capitalists for effecting a venture requiring extensive financial resources, especially in international finance. **2.** Any association or partnership. **3.** *Law.* **a.** A husband's right to the company, help, and affection of his wife. **b.** The right of the wife to the same. [Latin, fellowship, participation, from *consors,* partner, companion, CONSORT.]

con·spe·cif·ic (kŏn′spĭ-sĭf′ĭk) *adj.* Of the same species.

con·spec·tus (kən-spĕk′təs) *n.* **1.** A general survey of a subject. **2.** A synopsis. [Latin, "view," "survey," from the past participle of *conspicere,* to observe (see **conspicuous**).]

con·spic·u·ous (kən-spĭk′yōō-əs) *adj.* **1.** Easy to notice; obvious. **2.** Attracting attention by being unusual or remarkable. [Latin *conspicuus,* from *conspicere,* to look at closely, observe : *com-* (intensive) + *specere,* to look (see **spek-** in Appendix*).] —**con·spic′u·ous·ly** *adv.* —**con·spic′u·ous·ness** *n.*

con·spir·a·cy (kən-spîr′ə-sē) *n., pl.* **-cies. 1.** An agreement to perform together an illegal, treacherous, or evil act. **2.** A combining or acting together, as if by evil design: *a conspiracy of natural forces.* **3.** *Law.* An agreement between two or more persons to commit a crime or to accomplish a legal purpose through illegal action. [Middle English *conspiracie,* from Norman French, variant of Old French *conspiration,* from Latin *conspīrātiō,* from *conspīrāre,* CONSPIRE.]

Synonyms: *conspiracy, plot, machination, collusion, intrigue, cabal.* These nouns denote secret plans or schemes. *Conspiracy* refers to such a plan by a group intent usually on a bold purpose, such as overthrowing a government. *Plot* stresses sinister means and motives but may be small or large in number of participants and scope. *Machination,* usually in the plural, strongly implies crafty, underhand dealing by one or more persons, but is generally less forceful than the preceding terms. *Collusion* refers to secret agreement between persons, usually with intent to defraud others. *Intrigue* denotes a complex, clandestine scheme; usually it implies selfish, petty actions rather than criminal ends. *Cabal* refers to a conspiratorial group or to its actions, which usually are directed against a government or a political leader.

con·spir·a·tor (kən-spîr′ə-tər) *n.* A person engaged in a conspiracy; a plotter.

con·spir·a·to·ri·al (kən-spîr′ə-tôr′ē-əl, -tōr′ē-əl) *adj.* Also **con·spir·a·to·ry** (-spîr′ə-tôr′ē, -tōr′ē). Of or characteristic of conspirators or a conspiracy. —**con·spir′a·to′ri·al·ly** *adv.*

con·spire (kən-spīr′) *v.* **-spired, -spiring, -spires.** —*intr.* **1.** To plan together secretly, especially to commit an illegal or evil act. **2.** To combine or act together. —*tr.* To plan or plot secretly. [Middle English *conspiren,* from Old French *conspirer,* from Latin *conspīrāre,* "to breathe together," agree, unite, plot : *com-,* together + *spīrāre,* to breathe, blow (see **spīrāre** in Appendix*).] —**con·spir′er** *n.* —**con·spir′ing·ly** *adv.*

con spi·ri·to (kŏn spĭ′rĭ-tō′, kōn). *Music.* With spirit and vigor. Used as a direction to the performer.

const. 1. constable. **2.** constant. **3.** constitution. **4.** construction.

Const. 1. constable. **2.** constitution.

con·sta·ble (kŏn′stə-bəl, kŭn′-) *n. Abbr.* **cons., Cons., const., Const. 1.** A peace officer with less authority and smaller jurisdiction than a sheriff, empowered to serve writs and warrants and to make arrests. **2.** In medieval monarchies, an officer of high rank, usually serving as military commander in the ruler's absence. **3.** The governor of a royal castle. **4.** *British.* A policeman. [Middle English, from Old French, from Late Latin *comes stabulī,* "count of the stable" : Latin *comes,* companion, count (see **ei-**[1] in Appendix*) + *stabulī,* genitive of *stabulum,* STABLE.] —**con′sta·ble·ship′** *n.*

Con·sta·ble (kŭn′stə-bəl), **John.** 1776–1837. British painter.

con·stab·u·lar·y (kən-stăb′yə-lĕr′ē) *n., pl.* **-ies. 1.** The body of constables of a district or city. **2.** The district under the jurisdiction of a constable. **3.** An armed police force organized like a military unit. —*adj.* Also **con·stab·u·lar** (-lər). Of or pertaining to constables or to constabularies.

Con·stance[1] (kŏn′stəns). A feminine given name. [French, from Latin *Constantia,* "constancy," from *constāns,* CONSTANT.]

Con·stance[2] (kŏn′stəns). *German* **Kon·stanz** (kōn-stänts′). A city of southwestern West Germany, on the Lake of Constance; the site of the Council of Constance (1414–18) that ended the **Great Schism** *(see).*

Con·stance, Lake of (kŏn′stəns). *German* **Bo·den·see** (bō′dən-zā′). A lake, 207 square miles in area, on the border between southwestern West Germany, western Austria, and northern Switzerland.

con·stan·cy (kŏn′stən-sē) *n.* **1.** Steadfastness in purpose or loyalty; faithfulness. **2.** An unchanging quality or state.

con·stant (kŏn′stənt) *adj.* **1.** Continually recurring; persistent. **2.** Unchanging in nature, value, or extent; invariable. **3.** Steadfast in purpose, loyalty, or affection; faithful. **4.** *Obsolete.* Confident; certain. —See Synonyms at **continual, faithful, steady.** —*n.* **1.** A thing that is unchanging or invariable. **2.** *Abbr.* **const.** *Symbol* **c, C a.** *Mathematics.* A quantity taken to have a fixed value in a specified mathematical context. **b.** An experimental or theoretical condition, factor, or quantity that occurs, is held, or is regarded as invariant in specified circumstances. [Middle English, from Old French, from Latin *constāns,* present participle of *constāre,* to stand together, remain steadfast : *com-,* together + *stāre,* to stand (see **stā-** in Appendix*).] —**con′stant·ly** *adv.*

Con·stan·ța (kôn-stän′tsä). The principal seaport of Rumania in the southeast on the Black Sea. Population, 121,000.

con·stant·an (kŏn′stən-tăn′) *n.* An alloy of equal parts of nickel and copper, used chiefly in electrical instruments because of its constant resistance. [Coined from CONSTANT.]

Con·stan·tine (kŏn′stən-tēn; *French* kôN-stäN-tēn′). A city in Algeria, 200 miles east of Algiers. Population, 223,000.

Con·stan·tine I[1] (kŏn′stən-tēn). Latin name, Flavius Valerius Aurelius Constantinus. Called "The Great." A.D. 280? 337. Roman Emperor (306–337); adopted Christianity.

Con·stan·tine I[2] (kŏn′stən-tēn). 1868–1923. King of Greece (1913–17 and 1920–22); grandfather of Constantine II.

Con·stan·tine II (kŏn′stən-tēn). Born 1940. King of Greece (since 1964); grandson of Constantine I.

Con·stan·tine XI (kŏn′stən-tēn). 1404–1453. Last Byzantine Emperor (1448–53); defeated and killed by Turks.

Con·stan·ti·no·ple. The former name for **Istanbul.**

con·stel·late (kŏn′stə-lāt′) *v.* **-lated, -lating, -lates.** —*tr.* To cause to form a group or cluster. —*intr.* To form a group or cluster. [Back-formation from CONSTELLATION.]

con·stel·la·tion (kŏn′stə-lā′shən) *n.* **1.** *Astronomy.* **a.** Any of 88 stellar groups considered to resemble and named after various mythological characters, inanimate objects, and animals. **b.** An area of the celestial sphere occupied by such a group. **2.** *Astrology.* The position of the stars at the time of one's birth, regarded as determining one's character or fate. **3.** A brilliant gathering or assemblage. **4.** A set or configuration of objects, properties, or individuals, especially a structurally or systematically related grouping. [Middle English *constellacioun,* from Old French *constellation,* from Late Latin *constellātiō,* group of stars : Latin *com-,* together + *stellātus,* starred, from *stella,* star (see **ster-**[3] in Appendix*).] —**con′stel·la′tion·al** *adj.* —**con·stel′la·to′ry** (-stĕl′ə-tôr′ē, -tōr′ē) *adj.*

con·ster·nate (kŏn′stər-nāt′) *tr.v.* **-nated, -nating, -nates.** To cause (someone) to be suddenly and violently confused, amazed, or frustrated. [Latin *consternāre,* to stretch out, overcome, perplex : *com-* (intensifier), with + *sternere,* to spread out (see **ster-**[2] in Appendix*).]

con·ster·na·tion (kŏn′stər-nā′shən) *n.* Sudden confusion, amazement, or frustration. See Synonyms at **fear.**

con·sti·pate (kŏn′stə-pāt′) *tr.v.* **-pated, -pating, -pates.** To cause constipation in. [Latin *constīpāre,* to press or crowd together (in Medieval Latin, "to confine the bowels") : *com-,* together + *stīpāre,* to press, cram (see **steip-** in Appendix*).]

con·sti·pa·tion (kŏn′stə-pā′shən) *n.* Difficult, incomplete, or infrequent evacuation of the bowels.

con·stit·u·en·cy (kən-stĭch′ōō-ən-sē) *n., pl.* **-cies. 1. a.** The body of voters represented by an elected legislator or executive. **b.** The district represented. **2.** Any group of supporters.

con·stit·u·ent (kən-stĭch′ōō-ənt) *adj.* **1.** Serving as part of a whole; component. **2.** Empowered to elect or designate. **3.** Authorized to make or amend a constitution. —*n.* **1.** Someone represented by another; client. **2.** Someone represented by an elected official. **3.** A constituent part; component. **4.** *Grammar.* One of the functional elements into which a construction or compound may be divided by analysis, including: **a.** *Immediate constituent,* one of normally two parts; for example: *He/ works on the railroad.* **b.** *Ultimate constituent:* for example: *He/ work/s/ on/ the/ rail/road.* [Latin *constituēns,* present participle of *constituere,* CONSTITUTE.] —**con·stit′u·ent·ly** *adv.*

con·sti·tute (kŏn′stə-to͞ot,′ -tyo͞ot′) *tr.v.* **-tuted, -tuting, -tutes.** **1.** To be the elements or parts of; make up; compose. **2.** To set up; enact (a law, for example). **3.** To establish formally; found (an institution, for example). **4.** To appoint to an office, dignity, function, or task; designate. **5.** To put together from parts or elements; to form; compose. [Middle English *constituten,* from Latin *constituere,* to cause to stand, set, fix : *com-* (intensive) + *statuere,* to set up (see **stā-** in Appendix*).] —**con′sti·tut′er, con′sti·tu′tor** (-to͞o′tər, -tyo͞o′tər) *n.*

con·sti·tu·tion (kŏn′stə-to͞o′shən, -tyo͞o′shən) *n. Abbr.* **cons., const., Const.** **1.** The act or process of constituting. **2.** The composition of something made of a number of parts; make-up. **3.** A person's prevailing state of health: *"My mother had an excellent constitution: she suckled all her ten children."* (Franklin). **4. a.** The system of fundamental laws and principles that prescribes the nature, functions, and limits of a government or other institution. **b.** The document on which this system is recorded. —**the Constitution.** The Constitution of the United States, adopted in 1787 and put into effect in 1789.

Con·sti·tu·tion (kŏn′stə-to͞o′shən, -tyo͞o′shən) *n.* A 44-gun American frigate active in the War of 1812. Popularly called "Old Ironsides."

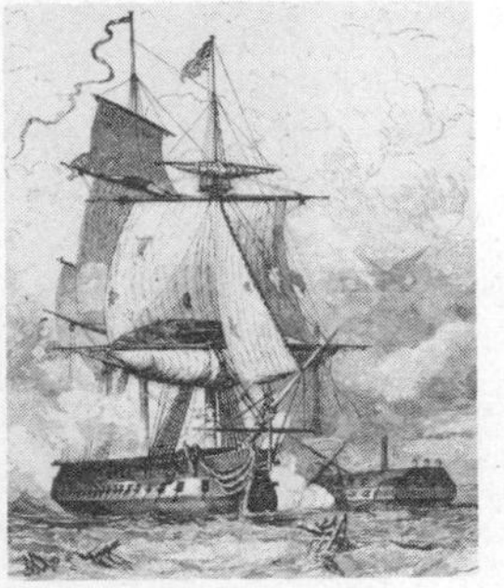

Constitution
"Old Ironsides" defeats H.M.S. *Guerriere*

con·sti·tu·tion·al (kŏn′stə-to͞o′shən-əl, -tyo͞o′shən-əl) *adj. Abbr.* **cons.** **1.** Of or proceeding from the basic structure or nature of a person or thing; essential: *"a constitutional inability to say yes"* (John Dos Passos). **2.** Contained in or consistent with the constitution. **3.** Established by or operating under a constitution. **4.** For the sake of one's general health. —*n.* An exercise, especially a walk, taken regularly for one's health. —**con′sti·tu·tion·al′i·ty** *n.* —**con′sti·tu′tion·al·ly** *adv.*

con·sti·tu·tion·al·ism (kŏn′stə-to͞o′shən-əl-ĭz′əm, kŏn′stə-tyo͞o′-) *n.* **1.** Government in which power is distributed and limited by a system of laws that must be obeyed by the rulers. **2.** Advocacy of such government. —**con′sti·tu′tion·al·ist** *n.*

constitutional monarchy. A monarchy in which the powers of the ruler are restricted to those granted under the constitution and laws of the nation. Also called "limited monarchy."

con·sti·tu·tive (kŏn′stə-to͞o′tĭv, -tyo͞o′tĭv) *adj.* **1.** Making a thing what it is; essential. **2.** Having power to institute, establish, or enact. —**con′sti·tu′tive·ly** *adv.*

constr. construction.

con·strain (kən-strān′) *tr.v.* **-strained, -straining, -strains.** **1.** To compel by physical, moral, or circumstantial force; oblige: *"My poverty had constrained me to mix with the humbler classes"* (T.E. Lawrence). **2.** To keep within close bounds; confine. **3.** To check the freedom or mobility of; restrain. —See Synonyms at **force.** [Middle English *constreinen,* from Old French *constraindre,* from Latin *constringere,* to draw or bind tightly together : *com-,* together + *stringere,* to draw tight (see **streig-** in Appendix*).] —**con·strain′a·ble** *adj.* —**con·strain′er** *n.*

con·strained (kən-strānd′) *adj.* **1.** Resulting from constraint; confined; compelled; restrained. **2.** Forced; unnatural. —**con·strain′ed·ly** (-strā′nĭd-lē) *adv.*

con·straint (kən-strānt′) *n.* **1.** The threat or use of force to prevent, restrict, or dictate the action or thought of others. **2.** The state, quality, or sense of being restricted to a given course of action or inaction. **3.** Something that restricts, limits, or regulates. **4.** A lack of ease; embarrassed reserve or reticence: *"All constraint had vanished between the two, and they began to talk"* (Edith Wharton). [Middle English *constreint(e),* from Old French *constrainte,* from *constraindre,* CONSTRAIN.]

con·strict (kən-strĭkt′) *tr.v.* **-stricted, -stricting, -stricts.** **1.** To make smaller or narrower, as by shrinking or contracting. **2.** To squeeze or compress by or as if by narrowing or tightening. —See Synonyms at **contract.** [Latin *constringere* (past participle *constrictus*), to draw or bind tightly together, CONSTRAIN.] —**con·stric′tive** *adj.* —**con·stric′tive·ly** *adv.*

con·stric·tion (kən-strĭk′shən) *n.* **1. a.** The act or process of constricting. **b.** The condition of being constricted. **2.** A feeling of pressure or tightness. **3.** Something that constricts.

con·stric·tor (kən-strĭk′tər) *n.* **1.** Something that constricts. **2.** *Anatomy.* A muscle that contracts or compresses a part or organ of the body. **3.** Any of various snakes, such as a python or boa, that coil around and crush their prey.

con·stringe (kən-strĭnj′) *tr.v.* **-stringed, -stringing, -stringes.** To cause to contract; constrict. [Latin *constringere,* CONSTRAIN.] —**con·strin′gen·cy** *n.* —**con·strin′gent** *adj.*

con·struct (kən-strŭkt′) *tr.v.* **-structed, -structing, -structs.** **1.** To form by assembling parts; build; erect. **2.** To create (an argument or sentence, for example) by systematically arranging ideas or expressions; devise with the mind. **3.** *Mathematics.* To draw (a geometric figure) that meets specific requirements, usually with instruments limited to a straightedge and compass. —*n.* (kŏn′strŭkt). Something synthesized or constructed from simple elements, especially a concept. [Latin *construere* (past participle *constructus*), to pile up together, build : *com-,* together + *struere,* to pile up (see **ster-**[2] in Appendix*).] —**con·struc′tor** (-strŭk′tər), **con·struct′er** *n.* —**con·struct′i·ble** *adj.*

con·struc·tion (kən-strŭk′shən) *n. Abbr.* **cons., const., constr.** **1. a.** The act or process of constructing. **b.** The condition of being constructed. **c.** The business or work of building. **2.** That which is constructed; a structure or building. **3.** The way in which something is put together. **4.** The interpretation or explanation given an expression or statement. **5.** *Grammar.* **a.** The arrangement of words to form a meaningful phrase, clause, or sentence. **b.** A group of words so arranged. —**con·struc′tion·al** *adj.* —**con·struc′tion·al·ly** *adv.*

con·struc·tion·ist (kən-strŭk′shən-ĭst) *n.* A person who construes a disputed legal text in a specified way.

con·struc·tive (kən-strŭk′tĭv) *adj.* **1.** Serving to advance a good purpose; helpful. **2.** Of or pertaining to construction; structural. **3.** *Law.* Based on an interpretation; not directly expressed. —**con·struc′tive·ly** *adv.* —**con·struc′tive·ness** *n.*

con·struc·tiv·ism (kən-strŭk′tĭv-ĭz′əm) *n.* Also **Con·struc·tiv·ism.** A movement in modern art in which glass, sheet metal, and other industrial materials are used to create nonrepresentational, often geometric objects. —**con·struc′tiv·ist** *adj.* & *n.*

con·strue (kən-stro͞o′) *v.* **-strued, -struing, -strues.** —*tr.* **1.** *Grammar.* **a.** To analyze the structure of (a clause or sentence). **b.** To use syntactically: *The noun "fish" can be construed as singular or plural.* **2.** To discover and apply the meaning of; interpret. **3.** To translate, especially aloud. —*intr.* **1.** To analyze grammatical structure. **2.** To give an explanation or translation. —See Synonyms at **explain** —*n.* (kŏn′stro͞o). An interpretation or translation. [Middle English *construen,* from Late Latin *construere,* from Latin, to CONSTRUCT.] —**con·stru′a·ble** *adj.* —**con·stru′er** *n.*

con·sub·stan·tial (kŏn′səb-stăn′shəl) *adj.* Having the same substance, nature, or essence, as the three persons of the Trinity. [Middle English *consubstancial,* from Late Latin *consubstantiālis* : Latin *com-,* same + *substantiālis,* SUBSTANTIAL.] —**con′sub·stan′ti·al′i·ty** *n.* —**con′sub·stan′tial·ly** *adv.*

con·sub·stan·ti·ate (kŏn′səb-stăn′shē-āt′) *v.* **-ated, -ating, -ates.** —*tr.* **1.** To unite in one common substance, nature, or essence. **2.** To regard as being thus united. —*intr.* To become united in one common substance. [New Latin *consubstantiare* : *com-,* together + SUBSTANTIATE.]

con·sub·stan·ti·a·tion (kŏn′səb-stăn′shē-ā′shən) *n. Theology.* The Lutheran doctrine that the body and blood of Christ coexist with the elements of bread and wine during the Eucharist. Compare **transubstantiation.**

con·sue·tude (kŏn′swĭ-to͞od, -tyo͞od) *n.* Custom; usage; habit. [Middle English, from Latin *consuētūdo,* from *consuēscere,* to accustom : *com-* (intensive) + *suēscere,* to become accustomed (see **seu-**[2] in Appendix*).] —**con′sue·tu′di·nar′y** (kŏn′swĭ-to͞o′də-nĕr′ē, -tyo͞o′də-nĕr′ē) *adj.*

con·sul (kŏn′səl) *n. Abbr.* **c., C., con., Con., Cons.** **1.** Either of the two chief magistrates of the Roman Republic, elected for a term of one year. **2.** Any of the three chief magistrates of the French Republic from 1799 to 1804. **3.** An official appointed by a government to reside in a foreign city and represent its commercial interests and give assistance to its citizens there. —See Usage note at **council.** [Middle English, Roman magistrate, from Old French, from Latin *consul,* possibly akin to *consulere,* to CONSULT.] —**con′su·lar** *adj.*

consular agent. *Abbr.* **C.A.** A consul of the lowest rank.

con·su·late (kŏn′sə-lĭt) *n.* **1. a.** Government by consuls. **b.** The office or term of office of a consul. **2.** The premises occupied by a consul. [Middle English *consulat,* from Old French, from Latin *consulātus,* from *consul,* CONSUL.]

consul general *pl.* **consuls general.** *Abbr.* **c.g., C.G.** A consular officer of the highest rank.

con·sult (kən-sŭlt′) *v.* **-sulted, -sulting, -sults.** —*tr.* **1.** To seek advice or information of. **2.** To have regard for; consider. —*intr.* **1.** To exchange views; confer. **2.** To give expert advice as a professional. [Old French *consulter,* from Latin *consultāre,* frequentative of *consulere*†, to take counsel.] —**con·sult′er, con·sul′tor** (-sŭl′tər) *n.*

con·sult·ant (kən-sŭl′tənt) *n.* **1.** A person who gives expert or professional advice. **2.** A person who consults another.

con·sul·ta·tion (kŏn′səl-tā′shən) *n.* **1.** The act or procedure of consulting. **2.** A conference at which advice is given or views are exchanged.

con·sult·a·tive (kən-sŭl′tə-tĭv) *adj.* Also **con·sul·ta·to·ry** (-tôr′ē, -tōr′ē). Of or pertaining to consultation; advisory.

con·sume (kən-so͞om′, -syo͞om′) *v.* **-sumed, -suming, -sumes.** —*tr.* **1.** To eat or drink up; ingest. **2.** To expend (fuel, for example); use up. **3.** To waste; squander. **4.** To destroy; to level. **5.** To absorb; engross. —*intr.* To be destroyed, expended, or wasted. [Middle English *consumen,* from Old French *consumer,* from Latin *consūmere,* to take completely, consume : *com-* (intensive) + *sūmere,* to take up (see **em-** in Appendix*).] —**con·sum′a·ble** *adj.* & *n.*

con·sum·ed·ly (kən-so͞o′mĭd-lē, kən-syo͞o′-) *adv.* Excessively.

con·sum·er (kən-so͞o′mər, kən-syo͞o′-) *n.* **1.** One that consumes. **2.** *Economics.* One who acquires goods or services; a buyer.

consumer credit. *Economics.* Credit granted to a consumer, permitting him to own or use goods while he is making payments on them.

consumer goods. *Economics.* Goods, such as food and clothing, that satisfy human wants through their consumption or use. Compare **capital goods.**

con·sum·mate (kŏn′sə-māt′) *tr.v.* **-mated, -mating, -mates.** **1.** To bring to completion, perfection, or fulfillment; achieve. **2.** To fulfill (a marriage) with the first act of sexual intercourse after the ceremony. —*adj.* (kən-sŭm′ĭt). **1.** Supremely accomplished or skilled; surpassing. **2.** Complete; utter. [Middle English *consummaten,* from Latin *consummāre,* to bring to-

gether, sum up : com-, together + summa, a SUM.] —con·sum'·mate·ly adv. —con'sum·ma'tive, con·sum'ma·to'ry (-sŭm'ə-tôr'ē, -tōr'ē) adj. —con'sum·ma'tor (kŏn'sə-mā'tər) n.
con·sum·ma·tion (kŏn'sə-mā'shən) n. 1. Completion; fulfillment. 2. An ultimate end or goal. —See Synonyms at effect.
con·sump·tion (kən-sŭmp'shən) n. 1. a. The act or process of consuming. b. The state of being consumed. 2. The amount consumed. 3. Economics. The using up of consumer goods and services. 4. Pathology. a. A wasting of tissue. b. Tuberculosis (see). Not in current technical use. [Middle English consumpcioun, from Old French consumption, from Latin consūmptiō, from consūmere, CONSUME.]
con·sump·tive (kən-sŭmp'tĭv) adj. 1. Tending to consume; wasteful; destructive. 2. Pertaining to or designed for consumption. 3. Pathology. Pertaining to or afflicted with consumption. —n. A person afflicted with consumption. —con·sump'tive·ly adv. —con·sump'tive·ness n.
cont. 1. containing. 2. contents. 3. continent. 4. continue; continued. 5. contract. 6. contraction. 7. control.
con·tact (kŏn'tăkt') n. 1. a. The coming together or touching of two objects or surfaces. b. The fact or relation of touching. 2. The state of being in communication. 3. An acquaintance who might be of use; a connection. See Usage note below. 4. Electricity. a. A connection between two conductors that permits a flow of current. b. A part or device that makes or breaks such a connection. 5. Medicine. A person recently exposed to a contagious disease. 6. Plural. Informal. Contact lenses. —v. (kŏn'tăkt, kən-tăkt') contacted, -tacting, -tacts. —tr. 1. To bring or put in contact. 2. Informal. To get in touch with. See Usage note below. —intr. To be in or come into contact. —adj. (kŏn'tăkt'). 1. Of, sustaining, or making contact. 2. Caused or transmitted by touching: a contact skin rash. [Latin contāctus, from the past participle of contingere, to touch, border upon, attain to : com-, together + tangere, to touch (see tag- in Appendix*).] —con·tac'tu·al (kən-tăk'chōō-əl) adj. —con·tac'tu·al·ly adv.
Usage: Contact, meaning to get in touch with, is widely used but still not appropriate to formal contexts, according to 66 per cent of the Usage Panel. Contact (noun), denoting a person as a source of assistance, is better established and is acceptable to 61 per cent of the Panel in formal usage.
contact flight. Aircraft navigation by visual reference to the horizon or to landmarks. Also called "contact flying."
contact lens. A thin corrective lens fitted over the cornea.
contact print. A print made by exposing a photosensitive surface in direct contact with a photographic negative.
con·ta·gion (kən-tā'jən) n. 1. Disease transmission by direct or indirect contact. 2. A disease that is or may be so transmitted. 3. A contagium. 4. Harmful or corrupting influence. 5. The tendency to spread, as of an influence or emotional state: the contagion of laughter. [Middle English contagioun, from Old French contagion, from Latin contāgiō, from contingere, to touch, touch with pollution, to CONTACT.]
con·ta·gious (kən-tā'jəs) adj. 1. Transmissible by direct or indirect contact. 2. Carrying or capable of carrying disease. 3. Spreading or tending to spread from one to another; catching. —con·ta'gious·ly adv, —con·ta'gious·ness n.
contagious abortion. Brucellosis (see) of cattle.
con·ta·gi·um (kən-tā'jē-əm) n., pl. -gi·a (-jē-ə). The direct cause, as a virus, of an infectious disease. [Latin, from contāgiō, CONTAGION.]
con·tain (kən-tān') tr.v. -tained, -taining, -tains. 1. To have within; enclose. 2. To have as component parts; comprise; include. 3. To be able to hold; have capacity for. 4. Mathematics. To be exactly divisible by. 5. To hold or keep within certain limits; restrain; confine: contain one's emotions. 6. To restrict the strategic power of (a nation or bloc), as by encircling it with hostile alliances. [Middle English conteinen, from Old French contenir, from Latin continēre, to hold together, enclose, restrain, contain : com-, together + tenēre, to hold (see ten- in Appendix*).] —con·tain'a·ble adj. —con·tain'ment n.
Synonyms: contain, hold, accommodate. These verbs mean to have within or to have capacity for. Contain refers to what is actually within at a given time. Hold can be used in that sense, but primarily stresses capacity for enclosing a certain maximum. Accommodate can mean merely to contain but generally refers to capacity for holding comfortably: The auditorium was built to accommodate 500.
con·tain·er (kən-tā'nər) n. A thing in which material is held or carried; receptacle.
container ship. A ship used for carrying cargo that has been previously packaged in uniform metal boxes, trailer vans, or other sealed containers.
con·tam·i·nant (kən-tăm'ə-nənt) n. That which contaminates.
con·tam·i·nate (kən-tăm'ə-nāt') tr.v. -nated, -nating, -nates. To make impure or corrupt by contact or mixture. —adj. Archaic. Contaminated. [Middle English contaminaten, from Latin contāmināre. See tag- in Appendix.*] —con·tam'i·na'tive adj. —con·tam'i·na'tor (-nā'tər) n.
con·tam·i·na·tion (kən-tăm'ə-nā'shən) n. 1. a. The act or process of contaminating. b. The state of being contaminated. 2. One that contaminates; an impurity. 3. Linguistics. The alteration of a form through misunderstood association with another. For example, "miniscule" is a contamination formed from minuscule and miniature.
contd. continued.
conte (kônt) n., pl. contes (kônt). 1. An adventure story; a tale. 2. A short novel. [French, from Old French conter, compter, COUNT (to relate).]

con·temn (kən-tĕm') tr.v. -temned, -temning, -temns. To view with contempt; despise. [Middle English contempnen, from Old French contem(p)ner, from Latin contemnere : com- (intensive) + temnere†, to despise.] —con·temn'er n.
contemp. contemporary.
con·tem·plate (kŏn'təm-plāt') v. -plated, -plating, -plates. —tr. 1. To look at pensively. 2. To ponder or consider thoughtfully. 3. To intend or anticipate: contemplate marriage. 4. To regard as possible; take seriously. —intr. To ponder; meditate. —See Synonyms at see. [Latin contemplārī, to observe carefully (originally a term of augury) : com- (intensive) + templum, open space marked out by augurs for observation (see tem- in Appendix*).] —con'tem·pla'tor (-plā'tər) n.
con·tem·pla·tion (kŏn'təm-plā'shən) n. 1. Thoughtful observation or meditation. 2. Intention or expectation.
con·tem·pla·tive (kən-tĕm'plə-tĭv) adj. Disposed to or characterized by contemplation. See Synonyms at pensive. —n. 1. A person given to contemplation. 2. A member of a religious order dedicated to meditation. —con·tem'pla·tive·ly adv. —con·tem'pla·tive·ness n.
con·tem·po·ra·ne·ous (kən-tĕm'pə-rā'nē-əs) adj. Originating, existing, or happening during the same period of time. See Synonyms at contemporary. [Latin contemporāneus : com-, same + tempus (stem tempor-), time (see temporal).] —con·tem'po·ra·ne'i·ty (-rə-nē'ə-tē), con·tem'po·ra'ne·ous·ness n. —con·tem'po·ra'ne·ous·ly adv.
con·tem·po·rar·y (kən-tĕm'pə-rĕr'ē) adj. Abbr. contemp. 1. Belonging to the same period of time. 2. Of about the same age. 3. Current; modern. —n., pl. contemporaries. 1. One of the same time or age. 2. A person of the present age; a modern. [Medieval Latin contemporārius : Latin com-, together + tempus (stem tempor-), time (see temporal).]
Synonyms: contemporary, contemporaneous, simultaneous, synchronous, concurrent, coincident, concomitant. These adjectives mean existing or occurring at the same time. Contemporary and contemporaneous have this basic sense usually with reference to an age or period; contemporary applies especially to persons, and alone has the sense of modern or present-day. Simultaneous more narrowly specifies occurrence of events at the same point in time. Synchronous generally refers to exact correspondence of events in time or rate of occurrence over a short period: synchronous movements of dancers. Concurrent usually refers to correspondence of events over a longer period; often it implies parallelism in character or length of the events involved: concurrent prison terms. Coincident applies to events occurring at the same time, without implying a relationship between them. Concomitant refers to coincidence in time of events so clearly related that one seems attendant on the other.
Usage: Contemporary calls for care, lest confusion arise over the period meant. When it is used in a context having no other reference to time, it indicates the period of the speaker or writer. When it appears in a context with persons or things of the past, the logical assumption may be that it pertains to the same past period, though often the intended meaning is otherwise. Thus, a Restoration play in modern dress is more explicit than a Restoration play in contemporary dress.
con·tem·po·rize (kən-tĕm'pə-rīz') v. -rized, -rizing, -rizes. —tr. To relate in time; synchronize. —intr. To be contemporary. [From CONTEMPORARY (after TEMPORIZE).]
con·tempt (kən-tĕmpt') n. 1. Reproachful disdain, as for something vile or dishonorable; bitter scorn. 2. The state of being despised or dishonored; disgrace. 3. Open disrespect or willful disobedience of the authority of a court of law or a legislative body. [Middle English, from Latin contemptus, from the past participle of contemnere, CONTEMN.]
con·tempt·i·ble (kən-tĕmp'tə-bəl) adj. 1. Deserving of contempt; despicable. 2. Obsolete. Contemptuous. —con·tempt'i·bil'i·ty, con·tempt'i·ble·ness n. —con·tempt'i·bly adv.
con·temp·tu·ous (kən-tĕmp'chōō-əs) adj. Manifesting or feeling contempt; scornful; disdainful. Often used with of. —con·temp'tu·ous·ly adv. —con·temp'tu·ous·ness n.
con·tend (kən-tĕnd') v. -tended, -tending, -tends. —intr. 1. To strive, as in battle; fight. 2. To strive, as in competition; vie. 3. To strive in controversy or debate; to dispute. —tr. To maintain or assert. —See Synonyms at discuss. [Middle English contenden, from Old French contendre, from Latin contendere, to strain, strive with : com-, with + tendere, to stretch, strain, strive (see ten- in Appendix*).] —con·tend'er n.
con·tent¹ (kŏn'tĕnt) n. 1. Abbr. cont. Usually plural. That which is contained in a receptacle. 2. Sometimes plural. Subject matter, as of a speech or document. 3. The meaning or significance of a literary or artistic work, as distinguished from its form. 4. Ability to receive and hold; capacity. 5. Area or extent; size. 6. The proportion of a specified substance. [Middle English, from Medieval Latin contentum, from Latin contentus, past participle of continēre, CONTAIN.]
con·tent² (kən-tĕnt') adj. 1. Not desiring more than what one has; satisfied. 2. Resigned to circumstances; assenting. —tr.v. contented, -tenting, -tents. To make content or satisfied. Often used reflexively. See Usage note below. —n. 1. Contentment; satisfaction. 2. British. An affirmative vote or voter in the House of Lords. [Middle English, from Old French, from Latin contentus, restrained, satisfied, past participle of continēre, to restrain, CONTAIN.]
Usage: Content (adjective) is now chiefly used predicatively (after a form of the verb to be); contented is both an attributive and predicate adjective. Content (verb) is often used reflexively with by or with to express agency or means: content oneself by working hard or with the thought that work is the best cure for

worry. The construction *content oneself with* also indicates self-limitation: *content oneself with four mugs of ale.*

content analysis. The systematic analysis of the content rather than the structure of a communication; especially, the determination for psychological study of the frequency of occurrence of thematic and symbolic elements, including ideas, feelings, assertions, and personal references, in responses to a test or in another communication.

con·tent·ed (kən-tĕn′tĭd) *adj.* Satisfied with things as they are; content. See Usage note at **content.** —**con·tent′ed·ly** *adv.* —**con·tent′ed·ness** *n.*

con·ten·tion (kən-tĕn′shən) *n.* **1.** A verbal struggling; dispute; controversy. **2.** A striving to win in competition or rivalry. **3.** An assertion put forward in argument. —See Synonyms at **discord.** [Middle English *contencioun,* from Old French *contention,* from Latin *contentiō,* from *contendere,* CONTEND.]

con·ten·tious (kən-tĕn′shəs) *adj.* **1.** Given to contention; quarrelsome. **2.** Involving contention. —See Synonyms at **belligerent.** —**con·ten′tious·ly** *adv.* —**con·ten′tious·ness** *n.*

con·tent·ment (kən-tĕnt′mənt) *n.* The state of being contented.

con·ter·mi·nous (kən-tûr′mə-nəs) *adj.* Also **con·ter·mi·nal** (-nəl), **co·ter·mi·nous** (kō-tûr′mə-nəs). **1.** Having a boundary in common; contiguous. **2.** Contained in the same boundaries; coextensive. [Latin *conterminus* : *com-,* together + *terminus,* boundary, limit (see **ter-**[1] in Appendix*).] —**con·ter′mi·nous·ly** *adv.* —**con·ter′mi·nous·ness** *n.*

con·test (kŏn′tĕst′) *n.* **1.** A struggle for superiority or victory between rivals. **2.** Any competition; especially, one in which entrants perform separately and are rated by judges. —See Synonyms at **conflict.** —*v.* (kən-tĕst′, kŏn′tĕst′) **contested, -testing, -tests.** —*tr.* **1.** To compete or strive for. **2.** To attempt to disprove or invalidate; to dispute; to challenge: *contest a will.* —*intr.* To struggle or compete; contend. Used with *with* or *against.* —See Synonyms at **oppose.** [Old French *conteste,* from *contester,* from Latin *contestārī,* bring in (a lawsuit) by calling witnesses (from both parties) : *com-,* together + *testārī,* to bear witness, from *testis,* a witness (see **trei-** in Appendix*).] —**con·test′a·ble** *adj.* —**con′tes·ta′tion** *n.* —**con·test′er** *n.*

con·test·ant (kən-tĕs′tənt, kŏn′tĕs′tənt) *n.* **1.** One who takes part in a contest; competitor. **2.** One who contests something, such as an election or a will.

con·text (kŏn′tĕkst) *n.* **1.** The part of a written or spoken statement in which a word or passage at issue occurs; that which leads up to and follows and often specifies the meaning of a particular expression. **2.** The circumstances in which a particular event occurs; a situation. [Middle English, from Latin *contextus,* coherence, sequence of words, from the past participle of *contexere,* to join together, weave : *com-,* together + *texere,* to join, weave, plait (see **teks-** in Appendix*).]

con·tex·tu·al (kən-tĕks′cho͞o-əl) *adj.* Of, pertaining to, or depending upon the context. —**con·tex′tu·al·ly** *adv.*

con·tex·ture (kən-tĕks′chər) *n.* **1.** The act of weaving or assembling parts. **2.** An arrangement of interconnected parts; a structure. —**con·tex′tur·al, con·tex′tured** *adj.*

Con·ti (kŏn′tē), **Niccolò de′.** Venetian merchant, traveler, and writer of the 15th century.

con·ti·gu·i·ty (kŏn′tə-gyo͞o′ə-tē, kŏn′tĭ-) *n., pl.* **-ties.** **1.** The state of being contiguous. **2.** A continuous mass or series.

con·tig·u·ous (kən-tĭg′yo͞o-əs) *adj.* **1.** Sharing an edge or boundary; touching. **2.** Nearby; neighboring; adjacent. **3.** Adjacent in time; immediately preceding or following. [Latin *contiguus,* from *contingere,* to touch on all sides, to CONTACT.] —**con·tig′u·ous·ly** *adv.* —**con·tig′u·ous·ness** *n.*

con·ti·nence (kŏn′tə-nəns) *n.* Also **con·ti·nen·cy** (-nən-sē). **1.** Self-restraint; moderation. **2.** Partial or complete abstention from sexual activity. —See Synonyms at **abstinence.**

con·ti·nent[1] (kŏn′tə-nənt) *n.* **1.** *Abbr.* **cont.** One of the principal land masses of the earth, usually regarded as including Africa, Antarctica, Asia, Australia, Europe, North America, and South America. **2.** *Rare.* A thing that holds or retains. —**the Continent.** The mainland of Europe. [Latin *(terra) continēns,* "continuous (land)," from the present participle of *continēre,* to hold together, continue. See **continent** (adjective).]

con·ti·nent[2] (kŏn′tə-nənt) *adj.* **1.** Self-restrained; moderate. **2.** Partially or completely abstaining from sexual activity. [Middle English, from Old French, from Latin *continēns,* present participle of *continēre,* to hold together, CONTAIN.] —**con′ti·nent·ly** *adv.*

con·ti·nen·tal (kŏn′tə-nĕn′təl) *adj.* **1.** Of or like a continent. **2.** *Usually capital* **C.** Of or relating to the mainland of Europe; European. **3.** *Capital* **C.** Of or pertaining to the American colonies during and immediately after the Revolutionary War. —*n.* **1.** *Usually capital* **C.** An inhabitant of the mainland of Europe; a European. **2.** *Capital* **C.** A soldier in the Continental Army during the Revolutionary War. **3.** A piece of paper money issued by the Continental Congress during the Revolutionary War. —**con′ti·nen′tal·ism′** *n.* —**con′ti·nen′tal·ist** *n.* —**con′ti·nen·tal′i·ty** *n.* —**con′ti·nen′tal·ly** *adv.*

continental code. A form of Morse code having no spaces between the dot and dash signals, commonly used for telegraphic communication outside the United States and Canada. Also called "international Morse code."

Continental Congress. Either of two American legislative assemblies that governed the United States during the Revolutionary era. The first convened in 1774 to voice grievances against Great Britain. The second, convening in 1775, established the Continental Army and served both as the legislative and as the executive arm of the government until the Constitution took effect in 1789.

continental divide. **1.** An extensive stretch of high ground from each side of which the river systems of a continent flow in opposite directions. **2.** *Capital* **C,** *capital* **D.** In North America, such a stretch formed by the crests of the Rocky Mountains. In this sense, also called "Great Divide."

continental drift. The theoretical slow shifting of continents due to weakness in the suboceanic crust.

continental shelf. A generally shallow, flat submerged portion of a continent, extending to a point of steep descent to the ocean floor.

con·tin·gence (kən-tĭn′jəns) *n.* **1.** A joining or touching. **2.** Contingency.

con·tin·gen·cy (kən-tĭn′jən-sē) *n., pl.* **-cies.** **1. a.** An event that may occur but that is not likely or intended; a possibility. **b.** A possibility that must be prepared against; future emergency. **2.** The condition of being dependent upon chance; uncertainty; fortuitousness. **3.** Something incidental to something else.

con·tin·gent (kən-tĭn′jənt) *adj.* **1.** Liable to occur, but not with certainty; possible. **2.** Dependent upon conditions or events not yet established; conditional. Often used with *on* or *upon.* **3.** Happening by chance or accident; fortuitous. **4.** *Logic.* Possessing a truth value derived from facts apart from the proposition itself; not necessarily true or false. Said of a proposition. —See Synonyms at **accidental.** —*n.* **1.** A contingent event or condition. **2.** A share or quota contributed to a general effort, as of troops. **3.** A representative group forming part of an assemblage. [Middle English, from Old French, from Latin *contingēns,* present participle of *contingere,* to touch on all sides, happen, to CONTACT.] —**con·tin′gent·ly** *adv.*

con·tin·u·al (kən-tĭn′yo͞o-əl) *adj.* **1.** Repeated regularly and frequently; recurring often. **2.** Continuous in time; incessant: *"These people are under continual disquietudes, never enjoying a minute's peace of mind"* (Swift). —**con·tin′u·al·ly** *adv.*

Synonyms: *continual, continuous, constant, ceaseless, incessant, perpetual, eternal, perennial, interminable.* These adjectives primarily mean occurring over and over during a long period of time or indefinitely. *Continual* can apply to uninterrupted action but is now chiefly restricted to what is intermittent or repeated at intervals: *the continual banging of the shutters. Continuous* implies either action without interruption in time or unbroken extent in space: *a continuous vigil; a continuous slope of terrain. Constant,* applied to action, stresses its steadiness or persistence and unvarying nature. *Ceaseless* and *incessant* pertain to uninterrupted action. *Perpetual* emphasizes both steadfastness and duration of action. *Eternal* refers to what is everlasting, especially to action seemingly without beginning or end in time. *Perennial* describes existence that goes on year after year, often with the suggestion of self-renewal. *Interminable* literally refers to what has no end, but more often is applied to a prolonged and wearisome action.

con·tin·u·ance (kən-tĭn′yo͞o-əns) *n.* **1.** The act or fact of continuing. **2.** The time during which something exists or lasts; duration. **3.** A continuation; sequel. **4.** *Law.* Postponement or adjournment to a future date.

Usage: *Continuance,* except in its legal sense, and *continuation* are sometimes interchangeable. *Continuance,* however, has particular reference to duration of a condition: *a person's continuance in government service; a machine's continuance in working order. Continuation* applies especially to prolongation or resumption of action and to physical extension. *Continuity* has the more special sense of that which is uninterrupted.

con·tin·u·ant (kən-tĭn′yo͞o-ənt) *n. Phonetics.* A consonant, such as *s, z,* or *f,* that may be prolonged as long as the breath lasts without a change in quality. Compare **stop.** [French, from Latin *continuāns,* present participle of *continuāre,* CONTINUE.]

con·tin·u·a·tion (kən-tĭn′yo͞o-ā′shən) *n.* **1. a.** The act or fact of continuing. **b.** The state of being continued. See Usage note at **continuance.** **2.** A part by which something is carried on or extended; supplement; sequel.

con·tin·u·a·tive (kən-tĭn′yo͞o-ā′tĭv) *adj.* Serving to continue or cause continuation. —*n.* Something that expresses or causes continuation. —**con·tin′u·a′tive·ly** *adv.*

con·tin·u·a·tor (kən-tĭn′yo͞o-ā′tər) *n.* One that continues; especially, a person who resumes the work of another.

con·tin·ue (kən-tĭn′yo͞o) *v.* **-ued, -uing, -ues.** —*intr.* **1.** To go on with a particular action or in a particular condition; persist. **2.** To exist over a prolonged period; last. **3.** To remain in the same state, capacity, or place. **4.** To go on after an interruption; resume. —*tr.* **1.** To carry forward; persist in. **2.** To carry further in time, space, or development; extend. **3.** To cause to remain or last; retain. **4.** To carry on after an interruption; resume. **5.** *Law.* To postpone or adjourn. [Middle English *continuen,* from Old French *continuer,* from Latin *continuāre,* from *continuus,* continuous, from *continēre,* to hold together, be continuous, CONTAIN.] —**con·tin′u·a·ble** *adj.* —**con·tin′u·er** *n.*

con·ti·nu·i·ty (kŏn′tə-no͞o′ə-tē, kŏn′tə-nyo͞o′-) *n., pl.* **-ties.** **1.** The state or quality of being continuous. See Usage note at **continuance.** **2.** An uninterrupted succession; unbroken course. **3.** A detailed shooting script consulted to avoid errors and discrepancies from shot to shot in a film. **4.** A script for all the spoken parts of a radio or television program.

con·tin·u·o (kən-tĭn′yo͞o-ō) *n., pl.* **-os.** **1.** A typically keyboard accompaniment for a solo instrument in which numerals indicate the successive chords, the actual notes played being left to the performer. Also called "figured bass." **2.** A full scoring of a part originally written as a continuo. [Italian, "continuous," from Latin *continuus,* CONTINUOUS.]

con·tin·u·ous (kən-tĭn′yo͞o-əs) *adj.* **1.** Extending or prolonged without interruption or cessation; unceasing. **2.** *Mathematics.*

Designating a function of one or more variables in which the variation of its values can be made arbitrarily small in a sufficiently small neighborhood of every point in a given interval. —See Synonyms at **continual.** [Latin *continuus,* from *continēre,* to hold together, CONTINUE.] —**con·tin'u·ous·ly** *adv.* —**con·tin'u·ous·ness** *n.*

continuous spectrum. *Physics.* A spectrum having no breaks, especially a spectrum of radiation distributed over an uninterrupted range of wavelengths.

continuous wave. *Abbr.* **cw, CW** Emitting or capable of emitting continuously; not pulsed. Said especially of lasers.

con·tin·u·um (kən-tĭn'yo͞o-əm) *n., pl.* **-tinua** (-tĭn'yo͞o-ə) or **-ums.** **1.** A continuous extent, succession, or whole, no part of which can be distinguished from neighboring parts except by arbitrary division. **2.** *Mathematics.* A set having the same number of points as all the real numbers in an interval. [Latin, neuter of *continuus,* CONTINUOUS.]

con·to (kŏn'tō) *n., pl.* **-tos. 1.** A money of account in Portugal, equal to 1,000 escudos. **2.** A former money of account in Brazil. [Portuguese, "number," from Late Latin *computus,* computation, from Latin *computāre,* to sum up, COMPUTE.]

con·tort (kən-tôrt') *v.* **-torted, -torting, -torts.** *—tr.* To twist, wrench, or bend severely out of shape. *—intr.* To become twisted into a strained shape or expression. —See Synonyms at **distort.** [Latin *contorquēre* (past participle *contortus*), to twist together : *com-,* together + *torquēre,* to twist (see **terkw-** in Appendix*).] —**con·tor'tion** *n.* —**con·tor'tive** *adj.*

con·tort·ed (kən-tôr'tĭd) *adj.* **1.** Twisted or strained out of shape. **2.** *Botany.* Twisted or bent upon itself. —**con·tort'ed·ly** *adv.* —**con·tort'ed·ness** *n.*

con·tor·tion·ist (kən-tôr'shən-ĭst) *n.* An acrobat who can contort his body and limbs into extraordinary positions. —**con·tor'tion·is'tic** *adj.*

con·tour (kŏn'to͝or) *n.* **1.** The outline of a figure, body, or mass. **2.** A line that represents such an outline. **3.** A surface, especially of a curving form. —See Synonyms at **form.** *—tr.v.* **contoured, -touring, -tours. 1.** To make or shape the outline of; represent in contour. **2.** To build (a road, for example) to follow the contour of the land. *—adj.* **1.** Following the contour lines of uneven terrain to limit erosion of topsoil: *contour plowing.* **2.** Shaped to fit the outline or form of something. [French, from Italian *contorno,* from *contornare,* to go around, draw in outline : *con-* (intensive), from Latin *con-, com-* + *tornare,* to turn in a lathe, from Latin *tornāre,* from *tornus,* lathe, from Greek *tornos* (see **ter-**[2] in Appendix*).]

contour feather. Any of the outermost feathers of a bird, forming the visible body contour and plumage.

contour line. An imaginary line, or its representation on a contour map, joining points of equal elevation.

contour map. A map showing elevations and surface configuration by means of contour lines.

contr. 1. contract. **2.** contraction. **3.** contralto. **4.** control.

contra-. Indicates: **1.** Against, opposing, or contrary; for example, **contraceptive, contradistinction. 2.** Pitched next below a specified musical instrument; for example, **contrabassoon.** [Middle English, from Latin *contrā-,* from *contrā,* against. See **kom** in Appendix.*]

con·tra·band (kŏn'trə-bănd') *n.* **1.** Goods prohibited by law or treaty from being imported or exported. **2. a.** Illegal traffic in such goods; smuggling. **b.** Smuggled goods. **3.** *International Law.* Goods that may be seized and confiscated by a belligerent if shipped to another belligerent by a neutral. Also called "contraband of war." **4.** During the Civil War, an escaped slave who fled to or was taken behind Union lines. *—adj.* Prohibited from being imported or exported. [French *contrebande,* from Italian *contrabbando* : *contra-,* against, from Latin *contrā-* + *bando,* proclamation, from Late Latin *bannus, bannum* (see **bhā-**[2] in Appendix*).] —**con'tra·band'age, con'tra·band'ism'** *n.* —**con'tra·band'ist** *n.*

con·tra·bass (kŏn'trə-bās') *n. Music.* A **double bass** *(see).* *—adj. Music.* Pitched an octave below the normal bass range. [Obsolete Italian *contrabasso* : *contra-,* pitched below, from Latin *contrā-,* against + *basso,* low, bass, from Late Latin *bassus* (see **bassus** in Appendix*).] —**con'tra·bass'ist** *n.*

con·tra·bas·soon (kŏn'trə-bə-so͞on') *n.* The largest and lowest pitched of the double-reed wind musical instruments, sounding an octave below the bassoon. Also called "double bassoon."

con·tra·cep·tion (kŏn'trə-sĕp'shən) *n.* Prevention of conception. [CONTRA- + (CON)CEPTION.]

con·tra·cep·tive (kŏn'trə-sĕp'tĭv) *adj.* Capable of preventing conception. *—n.* A contraceptive agent or device.

con·tra·clock·wise. Variant of **counterclockwise.**

con·tract (kŏn'trăkt') *n. Abbr.* **contr., cont. 1.** An agreement between two or more parties, especially one that is written and enforceable by law. **2.** The writing or document containing such an agreement. **3.** The branch of law dealing with contracts. **4.** Marriage as a formal agreement; betrothal. **5.** In the game of bridge: **a.** The last and highest bid of one hand. **b.** The number of tricks thus bid. **c. Contract bridge** *(see).* *—v.* (kən-trăkt', kŏn'trăkt') **contracted, -tracting, -tracts.** *—tr.* **1.** To enter into by contract; establish or settle by formal agreement. **2.** To acquire or incur. **3.** To reduce in size by drawing together; shrink. **4.** To pull together; wrinkle. **5.** To shorten (a word or words) by omitting or combining some of the letters or sounds; for example, *I'm* for *I am.* *—intr.* **1.** To enter into or make a contract. **2.** To become reduced in size by or as if by being drawn together. [Middle English, from Old French, from Latin *contractus,* from the past participle of *contrahere,* to draw together, bring about, enter into an agreement : *com-,* together + *trahere,* to draw (see **tragh-** in Appendix*).] —**con·tract'i·bil'i·ty, con·tract'i·ble·ness** *n.* —**con·tract'i·ble** *adj.*

Synonyms: *contract, condense, compress, constrict, shrink.* These verbs refer to decrease in size or content of a thing and sometimes to a resultant change in its form. *Contract* applies to internal drawing together that reduces the volume of a thing. *Condense* refers to an increase in compactness produced by the removal or reduction of parts or by a change in physical form of the thing involved, such as a change from gas to liquid or from liquid to solid. *Compress* applies to increased compactness brought about by external force; the term implies reduction of volume and change of form or shape. *Constrict* refers to decreasing the extent of a thing, usually by external pressure. *Shrink* refers to contraction that produces reduction in physical extent.

contract bridge. A form of auction bridge in which tricks in excess of the contract may not count toward game. Also called "contract."

con·trac·tile (kən-trăk'təl) *adj.* Capable of contracting or causing contraction. —**con'trac'til'i·ty** (kŏn'trăk'tĭl'ə-tē) *n.*

con·trac·tion (kən-trăk'shən) *n. Abbr.* **cont., contr. 1.** The act of contracting or the state of being contracted. **2.** *Grammar.* **a.** A shortened word or words formed by omitting or combining some of the letters or sounds; for example, *isn't* for *is not.* **b.** The formation of such a word. **3.** *Physiology.* The shortening, and often thickening, of functioning muscle.

con·trac·tor (kŏn'trăk'tər, kən-trăk'tər) *n.* **1.** One who agrees to furnish materials or perform services at a specified price, especially for construction. **2.** Something that contracts, especially a muscle.

con·trac·tu·al (kən-trăk'cho͞o-əl) *adj.* Of, connected with, or having the nature of a contract.

con·trac·ture (kən-trăk'chər) *n.* **1.** A drawing together, as of muscle or scar tissue, resulting in distortion or deformity. **2.** A deformity resulting from such shortening.

con·tra·dance, con·tra·danse. Variants of **contredanse.**

con·tra·dict (kŏn'trə-dĭkt') *v.* **-dicted, -dicting, -dicts.** *—tr.* **1.** To assert or express the opposite of (a statement). **2.** To deny the statement of. **3.** To be contrary to; be inconsistent with. *—intr.* To utter a contradictory statement. —See Synonyms at **deny.** [Latin *contrādīcere,* to speak against : *contrā-,* against + *dīcere,* to speak (see **deik-** in Appendix*).] —**con'tra·dict'a·ble** *adj.* —**con'tra·dict'er, con'tra·dic'tor** (-dĭk'tər) *n.*

con·tra·dic·tion (kŏn'trə-dĭk'shən) *n.* **1. a.** The act of contradicting. **b.** The state of being contradicted. **2.** A denial. **3.** Inconsistency or discrepancy. **4.** Something that contains contradictory elements.

con·tra·dic·to·ry (kŏn'trə-dĭk'tə-rē) *adj.* **1.** Involving or having the nature of a contradiction; inconsistent. **2.** Given to contradicting. —See Synonyms at **opposite.** *—n., pl.* **contradictories.** *Logic.* Either of two propositions related in such a way that it is impossible for both to be true or both to be false. Compare **contrary.** —**con'tra·dic'to·ri·ly** *adv.* —**con'tra·dic'to·ri·ness** *n.*

con·tra·dis·tinc·tion (kŏn'trə-dĭ-stĭngk'shən) *n.* Distinction by contrast or opposing qualities. —**con'tra·dis·tinc'tive** *adj.* —**con'tra·dis·tinc'tive·ly** *adv.*

con·tra·dis·tin·guish (kŏn'trə-dĭ-stĭng'gwĭsh) *tr.v.* **-guished, -guishing, -guishes.** To distinguish by contrasting qualities.

con·trail (kŏn'trāl') *n.* A visible trail of water droplets or ice crystals sometimes forming in the wake of an aircraft. Also called "vapor trail." [CON(DENSATION) + TRAIL.]

con·tra·in·di·cate (kŏn'trə-ĭn'də-kāt') *tr.v.* **-cated, -cating, -cates.** To indicate the inadvisability of: *Allergic reactions contraindicated the use of penicillin.* —**con'tra·in'di·cant** *n.* —**con'tra·in'di·ca'tion** *n.*

con·tral·to (kən-trăl'tō) *n., pl.* **-tos** or **-ti** (-tē). *Abbr.* **contr.** *Music.* **1.** The lowest female voice or voice part, intermediate in range between soprano and tenor. **2.** A woman having such a voice. [Italian : *contra-,* pitched below, from Latin *contrā-,* against + ALTO.]

con·tra·po·si·tion (kŏn'trə-pə-zĭsh'ən) *n.* An opposite position; opposition; antithesis.

con·trap·tion (kən-trăp'shən) *n.* A contrivance; device. [Humorous blend of CONTRIVE and TRAP + -TION.]

con·tra·pun·tal (kŏn'trə-pŭnt'l) *adj. Music.* Of, pertaining to, or incorporating counterpoint. [From Italian *contrapunto* : *contra-,* from Latin *contrā-,* against + *punto,* point, from Latin *punctus,* POINT.] —**con'tra·pun'tal·ly** *adv.*

con·tra·pun·tist (kŏn'trə-pŭn'tĭst) *n.* A specialist in contrapuntal music.

con·tra·ri·e·ty (kŏn'trə-rī'ə-tē) *n., pl.* **-ties. 1.** The quality or condition of being contrary. **2.** Something contrary; a discrepancy or inconsistency.

con·trar·i·ous (kən-trâr'ē-əs) *adj. Rare.* Perverse; adverse. —**con·trar'i·ous·ly** *adv.*

con·trar·i·wise (kŏn'trĕr'ē-wīz'; *also* kən-trâr'ē-wīz' *for sense 3*) *adv.* **1.** From a contrasting point of view. **2.** In the opposite way or reverse order. **3.** Perversely.

con·tra·ry (kŏn'trĕr'ē) *adj.* **1.** Opposed, as in character or purpose; completely different. **2.** Opposite in direction or position. **3.** Adverse; unfavorable, as winds. **4.** Given to acting or speaking in opposition to others; perverse; willful. —See Synonyms at **opposite.** *—n., pl.* **contraries. 1.** That which is contrary; the opposite. **2.** Either of two contrary or opposing things. **3.** *Logic.* A proposition related to another in such a way that if the latter is true, the former must be false, but if the latter is false, the former is not necessarily true. Compare **contradictory.** —**by contraries.** In opposition to what is expected. —**on the contrary.** From an opposing point of view; conversely. —**to the**

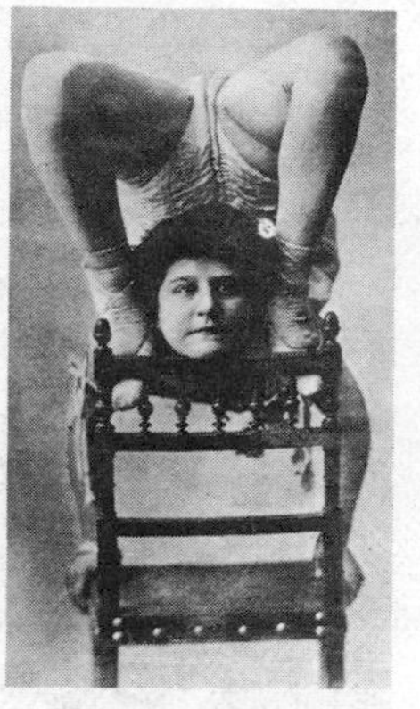

contortionist

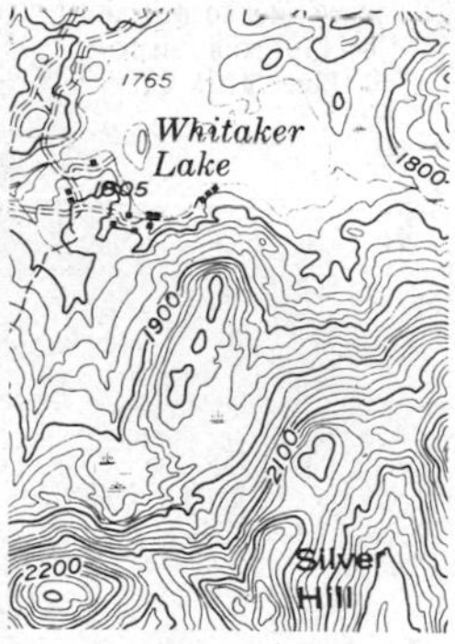

contour map
Map of a section of upper New York State

t tight/th thin, path/*th* this, bathe/ŭ cut/ûr urge/v valve/w with/y yes/z zebra, size/zh vision/ə about, item, edible, gallop, circus/ à *Fr.* ami/œ *Fr.* feu, *Ger.* schön/ü *Fr.* tu, *Ger.* über/KH *Ger.* ich, *Scot.* loch/N *Fr.* bon. ***Follows main vocabulary. †Of obscure origin.**

contrary. To the opposite; to a contrasting effect. —*adv.* In opposition; contrariwise. [Middle English *contrarie*, from Old French *contraire*, from Latin *contrārius*, from *contrā*, against. See **kom** in Appendix.*] —**con'tra·ri·ly** *adv.* —**con'tra·ri·ness** *n.*

Synonyms: *contrary, balky, stubborn, perverse, adverse, wayward, willful.* These adjectives refer to being in opposition to a prevailing order or to prescribed authority. *Contrary* applies especially to a person inherently self-willed and given to resisting authority. *Balky* describes the behavior of an animal that stops short and refuses to proceed, and is also applicable to related human behavior. *Stubborn* stresses inflexibility of mind or will and thus strongly implies resistance to authority. *Perverse* implies native disposition to depart from what is considered proper or morally right. *Adverse* is often applied to opposition, such as personal opinion or unfavorable circumstances, that is antagonistic to the progress or well-being of another person. *Wayward* suggests flouting of authority that leads to erratic, capricious, or morally reprehensible behavior. *Willful* implies headstrong self-determination and lack of susceptibility to either authority or reason.

con·trast (kən-trăst') *v.* **-trasted, -trasting, -trasts.** —*tr.* To set in opposition in order to show or emphasize differences. —*intr.* To show differences when compared. —*n.* (kŏn'trăst'). **1. a.** The act of contrasting. **b.** The state of being contrasted. **2.** A striking dissimilarity between things compared. **3.** Something that shows a striking dissimilarity to something else. **4.** In a work of art, the use of opposing elements, such as colors, forms, or lines, in proximity to produce an intensified effect. [French *contrester, contraster*, to contrast, resist, from Italian *contrastare*, from Medieval Latin *contrāstāre* : Latin *contrā-*, against + *stāre*, to stand (see **stā-** in Appendix*).] —**con·trast'a·ble** *adj.* —**con·trast'ing·ly** *adv.*

Usage: *Contrast* (verb) is usually followed by *with* when a preposition is called for. *Contrast* (noun) often takes *between.* The phrase *in contrast* is followed by *with* or, especially when opposition is stressed, *to.*

con·trast·y (kən-trăs'tē) *adj. Photography.* Having or producing sharp contrasts between light and dark areas.

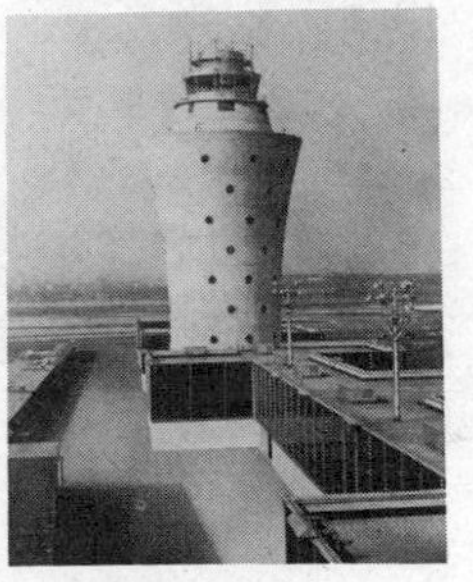

control tower
The control tower and passenger terminal at La Guardia Airport, New York City

con·tra·vene (kŏn'trə-vēn') *tr.v.* **-vened, -vening, -venes. 1.** To act or be counter to; violate; infringe. **2.** To oppose in argument. [Old French *contravenir*, from Late Latin *contrāvenīre*, to come against, oppose : Latin *contrā-*, against + *venīre*, to come (see **gwā-** in Appendix*).] —**con'tra·ven'er** *n.*

con·tra·ven·tion (kŏn'trə-vĕn'shən) *n.* An act of contravening; a violation; infringement.

con·tre·danse (kŏn'trə-dăns', -däns') *n.* Also **con·tre·dance, con·tra·dance, con·tra·danse. 1.** A dance performed in two lines with the partners facing each other. **2.** The music for such a dance. [French, from English COUNTRY-DANCE (influenced by French *contre*, against, opposite, on account of the partners facing each other).]

con·tre·temps (kŏn'trə-tän'; *French* kôɴ-trə-täɴ') *n., pl.* **contretemps.** An inopportune or embarrassing occurrence; a mishap. [French : *contre-*, against, from Latin *contrā-* + *temps*, time, from Latin *tempus* (see **temporal**).]

contrib. contribution; contributor.

con·trib·ute (kən-trĭb'yōōt) *v.* **-uted, -uting, -utes.** —*tr.* **1.** To give or supply in common with others; give to a common fund or for a common purpose. **2.** To submit for publication. —*intr.* **1.** To make a contribution. **2.** To act as a determining factor; share responsibility for something. Used with *to: We have all contributed to his failure.* [Latin *contribuere*, to bring together, unite, collect : *com-*, together + *tribuere*, to allot, grant (see **tribute**).] —**con·trib'ut·a·ble** *adj.* —**con·trib'u·tive** *adj.* —**con·trib'u·tive·ly** *adv.* —**con·trib'u·tive·ness** *n.* —**con·trib'u·tor** (-tər) *n.*

con·tri·bu·tion (kŏn'trĭ-byōō'shən) *n.* **1.** The act of contributing. **2.** *Abbr.* **contrib.** Something contributed, especially a written article contributed to a publication. **3.** An impost or levy for a special purpose.

con·trib·u·to·ry (kən-trĭb'yə-tôr'ē, -tōr'ē) *adj.* **1.** Pertaining to or involving contribution. **2.** Contributing toward a result. **3.** Subject to an impost or levy. —*n., pl.* **contributories.** One that contributes.

con·trite (kən-trīt', kŏn'trīt') *adj.* **1.** Humbled by guilt and repentant for one's sins; penitent. **2.** Arising from contrition: *contrite words.* [Middle English *contrit*, from Old French, from Medieval Latin *contrītus*, "broken in spirit," repentant, from Latin, past participle of *conterere*, to bruise, grind : *com-* (intensive) + *terere*, to rub, grind (see **ter-²** in Appendix*).] —**con·trite'ly** *adv.* —**con·trite'ness** *n.*

con·tri·tion (kən-trĭsh'ən) *n.* **1.** Sincere remorse for wrongdoing. **2.** *Theology.* **a.** Repentance for sin with a sincere desire to amend, arising from pure love of God. **b.** Repentance arising from a motive less than the pure love of God.

con·tri·vance (kən-trī'vəns) *n.* **1. a.** The act or manner of contriving. **b.** The ability to contrive. **2.** Something contrived, as a mechanical device or a clever plan.

con·trive (kən-trīv') *v.* **-trived, -triving, -trives.** —*tr.* **1.** To plan or devise with cleverness or ingenuity. **2.** To plot with evil intent; scheme. **3.** To invent or fabricate, especially by improvisation. **4.** To manage or succeed in, as by scheming. —*intr.* To plot or scheme. [Middle English *contreven, controven*, from Old French *controver*, from Late Latin *contropāre*, to represent figuratively, compare : Latin *com-*, together + *tropus*, figure of speech, trope, from Greek *tropos*, turn, manner, style (see **trep-²** in Appendix*).] —**con·triv'a·ble** *adj.* —**con·triv'ed·ly** *adv.* —**con·triv'er** *n.*

con·trol (kən-trōl') *tr.v.* **-trolled, -trolling, -trols. 1.** To exercise authority or dominating influence over; direct; regulate. **2.** To hold in restraint; to check. **3.** To verify or regulate (a scientific experiment) by conducting a parallel experiment or by comparing with some other standard. **4.** To verify (an account, for example) by using a duplicate register for comparison. —See Synonyms at **conduct.** —*n. Abbr.* **cont., contr. 1.** Authority or ability to regulate, direct, or dominate. **2.** A restraining act or influence; a curb. **3.** A standard of comparison for checking or verifying the results of an experiment. **4.** *Usually plural.* An instrument or set of instruments used to operate, regulate, or guide a machine or vehicle. **5.** *Spiritualism.* A spirit presumed to act through a medium. [Middle English *controllen*, from Old French *cont(r)eroller*, from Medieval Latin *contrārotulāre*, to check by a counter roll or duplicate register, from *contrārotulus*, counter roll, duplicate register : Latin *contrā-*, against, opposite + *rotulus*, roll, "little wheel," from *rota*, wheel (see **ret-** in Appendix*).] —**con·trol'la·bil'i·ty** *n.* —**con·trol'la·ble** *adj.*

control chart. *Statistics.* A graph of a quantitative characteristic of a manufacturing process, usually determined from small, periodically repeated samples and evaluated with respect to control limits rendered as parallel horizontal lines above and below a line representing the expected or average value of the characteristic.

control experiment. An experiment in which the variable factors are controlled so that the effects of changing one at a time can be observed.

controlled response. *Military.* A response to a military attack by limited military means in an effort to avoid nuclear war.

con·trol·ler (kən-trō'lər) *n.* Also **comp·trol·ler** (for sense 2). **1.** One who controls. **2.** An officer who audits accounts and supervises the financial affairs of a corporation or of a governmental body. **3.** A regulating mechanism, as in a vehicle or electric device.

control rocket. *Aviation.* A vernier rocket or similar missile used to change the attitude or trajectory of a rocket or spacecraft.

control stick. A lever used in small aircraft to control the angle of the elevators and ailerons.

control surface. A movable airfoil, especially a rudder, aileron, or elevator, used to control or guide an aircraft, guided missile, or rocket.

control tower. A usually glass-enclosed tower at an airport from which air traffic is controlled by radio.

con·tro·ver·sial (kŏn'trə-vûr'shəl) *adj.* **1.** Of, subject to, or marked by controversy. **2.** Fond of controversy; disputatious. —**con'tro·ver'sial·ist** *n.* —**con'tro·ver'sial·ly** *adv.*

con·tro·ver·sy (kŏn'trə-vûr'sē) *n., pl.* **-sies. 1.** A dispute, especially a lengthy and public one, between sides holding opposing views. **2.** The act or practice of engaging in such disputes. —See Synonyms at **argument.** [Middle English *controversie*, from Latin *contrōversia*, from *contrōversus*, turned against, disputed : *contrō-*, variant of *contrā-*, against + *versus*, past participle of *vertere*, to turn (see **wer-³** in Appendix*).]

con·tro·vert (kŏn'trə-vûrt') *tr.v.* **-verted, -verting, -verts. 1.** To raise arguments against; voice opposition to; deny. **2.** To argue or dispute about; to debate. [From CONTROVERSY (by analogy with CONVERT, REVERT).] —**con'tro·vert'i·ble** *adj.*

con·tu·ma·cious (kŏn'tōō-mā'shəs, kŏn'tyōō-) *adj.* Obstinately disobedient or rebellious; insubordinate. —**con'tu·ma'cious·ly** *adv.* —**con'tu·ma'cious·ness** *n.*

con·tu·ma·cy (kŏn'tōō-mə-sē, kŏn'tyōō-) *n., pl.* **-cies.** Obstinate or contemptuous resistance to authority; stubborn rebelliousness; disobedience; insubordination. [Middle English *contumacie*, from Latin *contumācia*, from *contumāx*, stubborn, disobedient. See **teuə-** in Appendix.*]

con·tu·me·ly (kŏn'tōō-mə-lē, kŏn'tyōō-, -təm-lē) *n., pl.* **-lies. 1.** Rudeness or contempt in behavior or speech; insolence. **2.** An insulting remark or act. [Middle English *contumelie*, from Old French, from Latin *contumēlia*, insult, reproach. See **teuə-** in Appendix.*] —**con'tu·me'li·ous** (-mē'lē-əs) *adj.* —**con'tu·me'li·ous·ly** *adv.*

con·tuse (kən-tōōz', -tyōōz') *tr.v.* **-tused, -tusing, -tuses.** To injure without breaking the skin; to bruise. [Middle English *contusen*, from Old French *contuser*, from Latin *contundere* (past participle *contūsus*), to beat, pound : *com-* (intensive) + *tundere*, to beat (see **steu-** in Appendix*).] —**con·tu'sion** *n.*

co·nun·drum (kə-nŭn'drəm) *n.* **1.** A riddle in which a fanciful question is answered by a pun. **2.** A problem admitting of no satisfactory solution. [Perhaps originally a mock-Latin university slang word.]

con·ur·ba·tion (kŏn'ər-bā'shən) *n.* A predominantly urban region including contiguous administrative areas; metropolitan area. [CON- + Latin *urbs*, city (see **urban**) + -ATION.]

conv. 1. convention. **2.** convertible.

con·va·lesce (kŏn'və-lĕs') *intr.v.* **-lesced, -lescing, -lesces.** To return to health after illness; recuperate. [Latin *convalēscere* : *com-* (intensive) + *valēscere*, to grow strong, from *valēre*, to be strong or well (see **wal-** in Appendix*).]

con·va·les·cence (kŏn'və-lĕs'əns) *n.* **1.** Gradual return to health and strength after illness. **2.** The period needed for this. —**con·va·les'cent** *adj.*

con·vec·tion (kən-vĕk'shən) *n.* **1.** The act or process of transmitting or conveying. **2.** *Physics.* **a.** Heat transfer by fluid motion between regions of unequal density that result from nonuniform heating. **b.** Fluid motion caused by an external force such as gravity. **3.** *Meteorology.* The transfer of heat or other atmospheric properties by massive motion within the atmosphere, especially by such motion directed upward. [Late Latin *convectiō*, from *convehere*, to carry together, bring along :

com-, together + *vehere*, to carry (see **wegh-** in Appendix*).] —**con·vec′tion·al** *adj.* —**con·vec′tive** *adj.* —**con·vec′tive·ly** *adv.*

con·vec·tor (kən-vĕk′tər) *n.* A partly enclosed, directly heated surface from which warm air circulates by convection.

con·vene (kən-vēn′) *v.* **-vened, -vening, -venes.** —*intr.* To assemble, usually for an official or public purpose; meet formally. —*tr.* **1.** To cause to come together or assemble; convoke. **2.** To summon to appear, as before a court of law. [Middle English *convenen*, from Old French *convenir*, to come together, meet, hence agree, be suitable, from Latin *convenīre* : *com-*, together + *venīre*, to come (see **gwā-** in Appendix*).] —**con·ven′a·ble** *adj.* —**con·ven′er** *n.*

con·ven·ience (kən-vēn′yəns) *n.* Also *rare* **con·ven·ien·cy** (-yən-sē) *pl.* **-cies.** **1.** The quality of being convenient; suitability or handiness. **2.** Personal comfort; material advantage. **3.** Anything that increases comfort or makes work less difficult; a convenient appliance, service, condition, or circumstance: *"If one's own car is a convenience, everybody else's is a nuisance."* (Joseph Wood Krutch). **4.** *British.* A lavatory. —**at one's convenience.** When it is convenient.

con·ven·ient (kən-vēn′yənt) *adj.* **1.** Suited or favorable to one's comfort, purpose, or needs. **2.** Easy to reach; accessible. **3.** *Obsolete.* Fitting and proper; appropriate. [Middle English, from Latin *conveniēns*, present participle of *convenīre*, to be suitable. See **convene.**] —**con·ven′ient·ly** *adv.*

con·vent (kŏn′vənt, -vĕnt′) *n.* **1.** A community, especially of nuns, bound by vows to a religious life under a superior. **2.** The building or buildings occupied by such a community; especially, a nunnery. [Middle English *covent*, from Old French, from Medieval Latin *conventus*, from Latin, a coming together, assembly, from *convenīre*, to come together, CONVENE.]

con·ven·ti·cle (kən-vĕn′tĭ-kəl) *n.* A religious meeting, especially a secret or illegal one, such as those held by dissenters in England and Scotland in the 16th and 17th centuries. [Middle English, from Latin *conventiculum*, a place of meeting, diminutive of *conventus*, assembly, CONVENT.] —**con·ven′ti·cler** *n.*

con·ven·tion (kən-vĕn′shən) *n. Abbr.* **conv.** **1.** A formal assembly or meeting of members, representatives, or delegates of a group, such as a political party or fraternal society. **2.** The body of persons attending such an assembly. **3.** An agreement or compact; especially, an international agreement dealing with a specific subject, as the treatment of war prisoners. **4.** General agreement on or acceptance of certain practices or attitudes. **5.** A practice or procedure widely observed in a group, especially to facilitate social intercourse; custom. **6.** A widely used and accepted device or technique, as in drama, literature, or painting: *the theatrical convention of the "aside."* [Middle English *convencioun*, from Old French *convention*, from Latin *conventiō*, assembly, agreement, from *convenīre*, to come together, CONVENE.]

con·ven·tion·al (kən-vĕn′shən-əl) *adj.* **1.** Developed, established, or approved by general usage; customary. **2.** Conforming to established practice or accepted standards. **3.** Marked by or dependent upon conventions, to the point of artificiality. **4.** *Art.* Represented in simplified or abstract form. **5.** *Law.* Based upon consent or agreement; contractual. **6.** Of or having to do with an assembly. **7.** Using means other than nuclear weapons or energy. —**con·ven′tion·al·ism′** *n.* —**con·ven′tion·al·ist** *n.* —**con·ven′tion·al·i·za′tion** *n.* —**con·ven′tion·al·ly** *adv.*

con·ven·tion·al·i·ty (kən-vĕn′shə-năl′ə-tē) *n., pl.* **-ties.** **1.** The state, quality, or character of being conventional. **2.** A conventional act, principle, or practice. —**the conventionalities.** The rules of conventional social behavior.

con·ven·tion·eer (kən-vĕn′shə-nîr′) *n.* One who attends a convention.

con·ven·tu·al (kən-vĕn′cho͞o-əl) *adj.* Of or pertaining to a convent. —*n.* A member of a convent.

Con·ven·tu·al (kən-vĕn′cho͞o-əl) *n.* A member of a branch of the Franciscan order that permits the accumulation and possession of common property.

con·verge (kən-vûrj′) *v.* **-verged, -verging, -verges.** —*intr.* **1.** To approach the same point from different directions; tend toward a meeting or intersection. **2.** To tend or move toward union or toward a common conclusion or result. **3.** *Mathematics.* To approach a limit. Compare **diverge.** —*tr.* To cause to converge. [Late Latin *convergere*, to incline together : Latin *com-*, together + *vergere*, to bend, turn, incline (see **wer-³** in Appendix*).]

con·ver·gence (kən-vûr′jəns) *n.* Also **con·ver·gen·cy** (-jən-sē) *pl.* **-cies.** **1.** The act, condition, quality, or fact of converging. **2.** *Mathematics.* The property or manner of approaching a limit such as a point, line, surface, or value. **3.** The point or degree of converging. **4.** *Physiology.* The coordinated turning of the eyes inward to focus on a nearby point. **5.** *Biology.* The adaptive evolution of superficially similar structures, such as the wings of birds and insects, in unrelated species subjected to similar environments. —**con·ver′gent** *adj.*

con·ver·sance (kŏn′vər-səns) *n.* Also **con·ver·san·cy** (-sən-sē). The state of being conversant; familiarity. Used with *with.*

con·ver·sant (kŏn′vər-sənt, kən-vûr′-) *adj.* Familiar, as by study or experience. Used with *with.* [Middle English *conversaunt*, from Old French *conversant*, from Latin *conversāns*, present participle of *conversārī*, to associate with, CONVERSE.] —**con′ver·sant·ly** *adv.*

con·ver·sa·tion (kŏn′vər-sā′shən) *n.* **1.** An informal spoken exchange of thoughts and feelings; a familiar talk. **2.** Social intercourse; close association. **3.** *Rare.* Close acquaintance, as with an object of study. **4.** *Obsolete.* A circle of acquaintances; one's associates. **5.** *Obsolete.* Manner of life; behavior.

con·ver·sa·tion·al (kŏn′vər-sā′shən-əl) *adj.* **1.** Of, pertaining to, or in the style of conversation. **2.** Adept at or given to conversation. —**con′ver·sa′tion·al·ly** *adv.*

con·ver·sa·tion·al·ist (kŏn′vər-sā′shən-əl-ĭst) *n.* Also **con·ver·sa·tion·ist** (-shən-ĭst). One given to or skilled at conversation.

conversation piece. **1.** A kind of genre painting, especially popular in the 18th century, depicting a group of fashionable people. **2.** An unusual object that arouses comment or interest.

con·ver·sa·zi·o·ne (kŏn′vər-săt′sē-ō′nē; *Italian* kōn′vär-sä′tsyō′nā) *n., pl.* **-nes** or **-ni** (-nē). A meeting for conversation or for discussion, especially of art. [Italian, "conversation," from Latin *conversātiō*, from *conversārī*, to CONVERSE.]

con·verse¹ (kən-vûrs′) *intr.v.* **-versed, -versing, -verses.** **1.** To engage in spoken exchange of thoughts and feelings; talk. **2.** *Rare.* To consort; associate. —See Synonyms at **speak.** —*n.* (kŏn′vûrs′). **1.** Spoken interchange of thoughts and feelings; conversation. **2.** *Rare.* Social intercourse. [Middle English *conversen*, to dwell, associate with, from Old French *converser*, from Latin *conversārī*, to associate with : *com-*, with + *versārī*, to live, occupy oneself, from *versāre*, frequentative of *vertere*, to turn (see **wer-³** in Appendix*).]

con·verse² (kən-vûrs′, kŏn′vûrs′) *adj.* Reversed, as in position, order, or action; contrary. —*n.* (kŏn′vûrs′). **1.** Something that has been reversed; the opposite. **2.** *Logic.* A proposition obtained by conversion. [Latin *conversus*, past participle of *convertere*, to turn around. See **convert.**] —**con·verse′ly** (kən-vûrs′lē) *adv.*

con·ver·sion (kən-vûr′zhən, -shən) *n.* **1.** The act of converting. **2.** The state of being converted. **3.** A change in which one adopts a new religion. **4.** A change from one belief, opinion, or practice to another. **5.** *Law.* **a.** The unlawful appropriation of another's property. **b.** The changing of real property to personal property or vice versa. **6.** *Finance.* The exchange of one type of security or currency for another. **7.** *Logic.* The interchange of the subject and predicate of a proposition. **8.** *Football.* A score made on a try for a point or points after a touchdown. **9.** *Psychiatry.* The symbolic manifestation of repressed ideas or impulses in motor or sensory abnormalities such as paralysis. In this sense, also called "conversion hysteria." [Middle English *conversioun*, from Old French *conversion*, from Latin *conversiō*, from *convertere*, to turn about, CONVERT.] —**con·ver′sion·al, con·ver′sion·ar′y** (-ĕr′ē) *adj.*

con·vert (kən-vûrt′) *v.* **-verted, -verting, -verts.** —*tr.* **1.** To change into another form, substance, state, or product; transform; transmute: *convert water into ice.* **2.** To persuade or induce to adopt a particular religion, faith, or belief. **3.** To change from one use, function, or purpose to another; adapt to a new or different purpose. **4.** To exchange for something of equal value. **5.** *Finance.* To exchange (a security or bond, for example) by substituting an equivalent of another form. **6.** To express (a quantity) in alternative units. **7.** *Logic.* To transform (a proposition) by conversion. **8.** *Law.* **a.** To appropriate without right (another's property) to one's own use. **b.** To change (property) from real to personal, from joint to separate, or vice versa. —*intr.* **1.** To be converted; undergo a change. **2.** *Football.* To make a conversion. —See Synonyms at **change.** —*n.* (kŏn′vûrt′). One who has been converted, especially from one religion or belief to another. [Middle English *converten*, from Old French *convertir*, from Medieval Latin *convertere*, to convert religiously, from Latin, to turn around, transform : *com-* (intensive) + *vertere*, to turn (see **wer-³** in Appendix*).]

con·vert·er (kən-vûr′tər) *n.* Also **con·ver·tor.** **1.** One that converts. **2.** A workman or machine employed in converting raw products into finished products. **3.** A furnace in which pig iron is converted into steel by the Bessemer process. **4. a.** A machine that changes electric current from one kind to another. **b.** A device that changes one frequency to another. **c.** A device that transforms information from one code to another.

con·vert·i·ble (kən-vûr′tə-bəl) *adj.* **1.** Capable of being converted. **2.** Having a top that may be folded back or removed, as an automobile. **3.** *Finance. Abbr.* **conv., cvt.** Capable of being lawfully exchanged for gold or another currency: *dollars convertible into pounds.* —*n.* **1.** A convertible automobile. **2.** That which can be converted. —**con·vert′i·bil′i·ty, con·vert′i·ble·ness** *n.* —**con·vert′i·bly** *adv.*

con·vert·i·plane (kən-vûr′tə-plān′) *n.* Also **con·vert·a·plane.** An airplane built to fly vertically as well as forward. [CONVERT-I(BLE) + (AIR)PLANE.]

con·vex (kŏn′vĕks, kən-vĕks′) *adj.* Having a surface or boundary that curves or bulges outward, as the exterior of a sphere. Compare **concave.** [Latin *convexus*, arched, convex. See **wegh-** in Appendix.*] —**con′vex·ly** *adv.*

con·vex·i·ty (kən-vĕk′sə-tē) *n., pl.* **-ties.** **1.** The state of being convex. **2.** A convex surface, body, part, or line.

con·vex·o-con·cave (kən-vĕk′sō-kən-kāv′) *adj.* **1.** Concavo-convex *(see)*. **2.** *Optics.* Having greater convex than concave curvature. Said of lenses.

con·vex·o-con·vex (kən-vĕk′sō-kən-vĕks′) *adj.* Convex on both sides; doubly convex; biconvex.

con·vey (kən-vā′) *tr.v.* **-veyed, -veying, -veys.** **1.** To take or carry from one place to another; to transport. **2.** To serve as a medium of transmission for; to conduct; transmit. **3.** To communicate or make known; impart: *"a look intended to convey sympathetic comprehension"* (Saki). **4.** *Law.* To transfer ownership of or title to. **5.** *Obsolete.* To steal. [Middle English *conveien*, from Old French *conveier*, from Medieval Latin *conviāre*, to go with, escort : Latin *com-*, with + *via*, way (see **wei-²** in Appendix*).] —**con·vey′a·ble** *adj.*

Synonyms: *convey, carry, bear, transport, transmit, transfer.* These verbs refer to the movement of something from one place

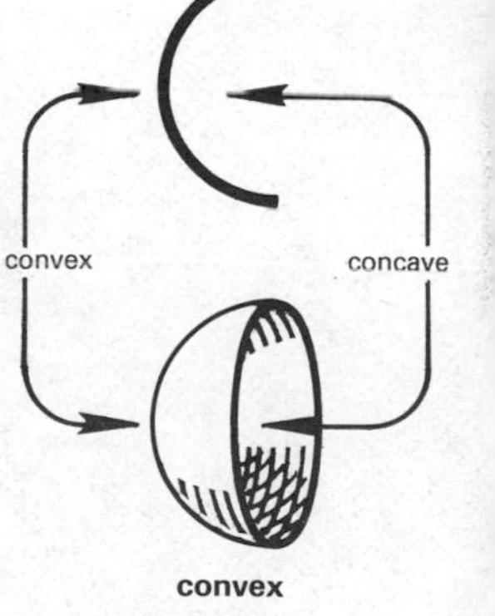

convex

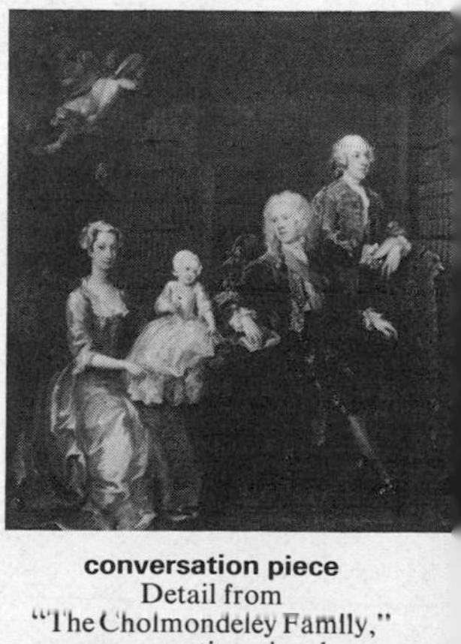

conversation piece
Detail from
"The Cholmondeley Family,"
a conversation piece by
William Hogarth, 1732

t tight/th thin, path/*th* this, bathe/ŭ cut/ûr urge/v valve/w with/y yes/z zebra, size/zh vision/ə about, item, edible, gallop, circus/
à *Fr.* ami/œ *Fr.* feu, *Ger.* schön/ü *Fr.* tu, *Ger.* über/KH *Ger.* ich, *Scot.* loch/N *Fr.* bon. ***Follows main vocabulary.** **†Of obscure origin.**

to another. When applied to physical objects, *convey* often implies continuous, regular movement or flow: *Pipelines convey water.* Figuratively *convey* means to serve as a medium for the movement or delivery of something, such as ideas or messages. *Carry* has broad application but is used principally with reference to movement of physical things. *Bear* has both physical and figurative use. Sometimes it suggests effort or burden; often it implies that the movement involves something important, such as valuable gifts or news. *Transport* is largely limited to movement of persons or material objects, often over a considerable distance. *Transmit* can refer to sending or dispatching material things, but more often applies to communicating (messages, news) or to serving as a medium for passage (of light, electricity, or sound). *Transfer* applies to movement of persons or things. It especially stresses change, as from one locality to another or from one means of travel to another.

con·vey·ance (kən-vā′əns) *n.* **1.** The act of transporting, transmitting, or communicating. **2.** A means of conveying; especially, a vehicle such as a bus. **3.** *Law.* **a.** The transfer of title to property from one person to another. **b.** The document by which this transfer is effected.

con·vey·anc·ing (kən-vā′ən-sĭng) *n.* The branch of legal practice dealing with the conveyance of property or real estate. —**con·vey′anc·er** *n.*

con·vey·er (kən-vā′ər) *n.* Also **con·vey·or** (especially for sense 2). **1.** One that conveys. **2.** Any mechanical contrivance, such as a continuous moving belt, that transports bulk materials or packages from one place to another.

con·vict (kən-vĭkt′) *tr.v.* **-victed, -victing, -victs. 1.** To find or prove (someone) guilty of an offense, especially by the verdict of a court. **2.** To convince of wrongdoing or sinfulness. —*n.* (kŏn′vĭkt′). **1.** A person found or declared guilty of an offense or crime. **2.** A person serving a sentence of imprisonment. —*adj. Rare.* Found guilty; convicted. [Middle English *convicten,* from Latin *convincere* (past participle *convictus*), to prove guilty, CONVINCE.]

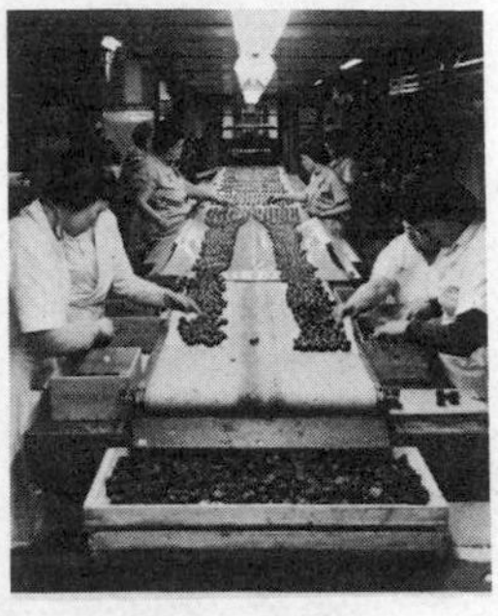

conveyer
Belt for sorting chocolates

con·vic·tion (kən-vĭk′shən) *n.* **1.** The act or process of finding or proving guilty. **2.** The state of being convicted or so proved. **3.** The act or process of convincing. **4.** The state of being convinced or persuaded. **5.** A fixed or strong belief. —See Synonyms at **certainty, opinion.** —**con·vic′tion·al** *adj.*

con·vic·tive (kən-vĭk′tĭv) *adj.* Having power or serving to convince or convict. —**con·vic′tive·ly** *adv.*

con·vince (kən-vĭns′) *tr.v.* **-vinced, -vincing, -vinces. 1.** To bring by argument and evidence to belief; cause to believe something; persuade. Often used with *of.* **2.** *Obsolete.* To convict. **3.** *Obsolete.* To conquer. —See Synonyms at **persuade.** [Latin *convincere,* to overcome, refute, prove guilty : *com-* (intensive) + *vincere,* to conquer, overcome (see **weik-⁵** in Appendix*).] —**con·vince′ment** *n.* —**con·vinc′er** *n.* —**con·vin′ci·ble** *adj.*

Usage: *Convince* is regularly followed by *of* or a clause introduced by *that,* but not by an infinitive with *to. Persuade,* however, can be used with all three constructions. Thus: *He convinced me* (or *I was convinced*) *of his good intentions. He convinced me* (or *I was convinced*) *that I should go. He persuaded* (not *convinced*) *me to go.*

con·vinc·ing (kən-vĭn′sĭng) *adj.* **1.** Persuading or satisfying by evidence or argument. **2.** Believable; plausible. —See Synonyms at **valid.** —**con·vinc′ing·ly** *adv.* —**con·vinc′ing·ness** *n.*

con·viv·i·al (kən-vĭv′ē-əl) *adj.* **1.** Fond of feasting, drinking, and good company; sociable; jovial. **2.** Relating to or of the nature of a feast; festive. —See Synonyms at **jolly.** [Late Latin *convīviālis,* from Latin *convīvium,* "a living together," banquet : *com-,* together + *vīvere,* to live (see **gwei-** in Appendix*).] —**con·viv′i·al′i·ty** *n.* —**con·viv′i·al·ly** *adv.*

con·vo·ca·tion (kŏn′vō-kā′shən) *n.* **1.** The act of convoking or calling together. **2.** A group of people assembled by summons. **3.** *Anglican Church.* A clerical assembly similar to a synod, but assembling only when called. **4.** *Episcopal Church.* **a.** An assembly of the clergy and representative laity of a section of a diocese. **b.** The district represented at such an assembly. —**con′vo·ca′tion·al** *adj.*

con·voke (kən-vōk′) *tr.v.* **-voked, -voking, -vokes.** To cause to assemble; convene. [Old French *convoquer,* from Latin *convocāre,* to call together, summon : *com-,* together + *vocāre,* to call (see **wekw-** in Appendix*).] —**con·vok′er** *n.*

con·vo·lute (kŏn′və-lo͞ot′) *adj.* Rolled or folded together with one part over another; twisted; coiled. —*v.* **convoluted, -luting, -lutes.** —*tr.* To coil around; twist or wind around. —*intr.* To coil up. [Latin *convolūtus,* past participle of *convolvere,* to CONVOLVE.] —**con′vo·lute′ly** *adv.*

con·vo·lut·ed (kŏn′və-lo͞o′tĭd) *adj.* **1.** Exhibiting convolutions; coiled; twisted. **2.** Intricate; complicated.

con·vo·lu·tion (kŏn′və-lo͞o′shən) *n.* **1. a.** A coiling or twisting together. **b.** An entangling or interlacing, so as to make intricate. **2.** One of the convex folds of the surface of the brain.

con·volve (kən-vŏlv′) *v.* **-volved, -volving, -volves.** —*tr.* To roll together; coil up. —*intr.* To form convolutions. [Latin *convolvere,* to roll together, enwrap : *com-,* together + *volvere,* to roll (see **wel-³** in Appendix*).]

con·vol·vu·lus (kən-vŏl′vyə-ləs) *n., pl.* **-luses** or **-li** (-lī′). Any of several trailing or twining plants of the genus *Convolvulus,* which includes the bindweeds. [New Latin *Convolvulus,* from Latin *convolvulus,* bindweed, from *convolvere,* to interweave, CONVOLVE.]

con·voy (kŏn′voi′, kən-voi′) *tr.v.* **-voyed, -voying, -voys.** To accompany on the way for protection, either by sea or land; to escort. —*n.* (kŏn′voi′). **1.** The act of convoying or the state of being convoyed. **2.** An accompanying and protecting force; a convoying vessel, fleet, or troop. **3.** That which is convoyed, such as ships or troops. **4.** A group, as of vehicles, traveling together for convenience. [Middle English *convoyen, conveien,* from Old French *convoier, conveier,* CONVEY.]

con·vulse (kən-vŭls′) *tr.v.* **-vulsed, -vulsing, -vulses. 1.** To shake or agitate violently: *"At that moment Darwin was convulsing society."* (Henry Adams). **2.** To cause to laugh uproariously. **3.** To affect with irregular and involuntary muscular contractions; throw into convulsions. [Latin *convellere* (past participle *convulsus*), to pull violently, wrest : *com-* (intensive) + *vellere,* to pull (see **wel-⁴** in Appendix*).]

con·vul·sion (kən-vŭl′shən) *n.* **1.** *Often plural. Pathology.* An intense paroxysmal involuntary muscular contraction. **2.** An uncontrolled fit of laughter. **3.** A violent turmoil.

con·vul·sion·ar·y (kən-vŭl′shən-ĕr′ē) *adj.* Of, pertaining to, affected with, or of the nature of convulsions. —*n., pl.* **convulsionaries.** A person affected with convulsions, especially as a result of religious fanaticism.

con·vul·sive (kən-vŭl′sĭv) *adj.* **1.** Marked by or of the nature of convulsions. **2.** Having or producing convulsions. —**con·vul′sive·ly** *adv.* —**con·vul′sive·ness** *n.*

co·ny (kō′nē, kŭn′ē) *n., pl.* **-nies.** Also **co·ney** *pl.* **-neys. 1.** A rabbit, especially the Old World species *Oryctolagus cuniculus.* **2.** The fur of a rabbit. **3.** A mammal, the **pika** *(see).* **4.** In the Old Testament, a mammal, the **hyrax** *(see).* Deuteronomy 14:7. **5.** *Archaic.* A dupe. [Middle English *coni(n)g, cunin,* from Old French *conin, conil,* from Latin *cunīculus,* rabbit, probably from Iberian.]

coo (ko͞o) *v.* **cooed, cooing, coos.** —*intr.* **1.** To utter the characteristic murmuring sound of a dove or pigeon, or a sound resembling this. **2.** To talk amorously or fondly in murmurs. Usually used in the phrase *bill and coo.* —*tr.* To express or utter gently or amorously, as with a murmuring sound. —*n., pl.* **coos.** The murmuring sound made by a dove or pigeon, or a sound resembling this. [Imitative.] —**coo′er** *n.*

Cooch Be·har (ko͞och′ bĭ-här′). A former state of northeastern India, now attached to West Bengal State, Republic of India.

coo·ee (ko͞o′ē) *n., pl.* **-ees.** Also **coo·ey** *pl.* **-eys.** A prolonged shrill cry used as a signal by the Australian aborigines and later adopted by the settlers.

cook (ko͝ok) *v.* **cooked, cooking, cooks.** —*tr.* **1.** To prepare for eating by applying heat, as by boiling, frying, or baking. **2.** To prepare or treat by heating. —*intr.* **1.** To prepare food for eating by applying heat. **2.** To undergo cooking. **3.** *Slang.* To happen, develop, or take place. Used chiefly in the phrase *What's cooking?* —**cook up.** *Informal.* To fabricate; concoct. —*n. Abbr.* **ck.** A person who prepares food for eating. [Middle English *coken,* from *cok(e),* a cook, Old English *cōc,* from Vulgar Latin *cōcus* (unattested), from Latin *cocus, coquus,* from *coquere,* to cook. See **pekw-** in Appendix.*]

Cook (ko͝ok), **Frederick Albert.** 1865–1940. American physician and explorer of the Arctic.

Cook (ko͝ok), **James.** Called "Captain Cook." 1728–1779. British mariner and explorer of the Pacific.

Cook, Mount (ko͝ok). **1.** Also **A·o·rang·i** (ä-ō-räng′gē). The highest mountain (12,349 feet) of New Zealand, on South Island in the Southern Alps. **2.** A mountain (13,760 feet high) in the St. Elias Mountains of southeastern Alaska, on the border with the Yukon Territory, Canada.

cook·book (ko͝ok′bo͝ok′) *n.* A book containing recipes and other information about the preparation of food.

Cooke (ko͝ok), **Jay.** 1821–1905. American financier.

cook·er (ko͝ok′ər) *n.* **1.** One that cooks; especially, a utensil or an appliance for cooking: *pressure cooker.* **2.** A person employed to operate cooking apparatuses in the commercial preparation of food and drink.

cook·er·y (ko͝ok′ər-ē) *n., pl.* **-ies. 1.** The art or practice of preparing food. **2.** A place for cooking.

Cook Inlet (ko͝ok). An inlet of the Pacific Ocean, extending 220 miles into southern Alaska.

Cook Islands (ko͝ok). A group of islands, about 90 square miles in area, in the South Pacific, southwest of the Society Islands; annexed to New Zealand in 1901, the group was granted internal self-government in 1965. Population, 21,000. Capital, Avarua, on Rarotonga.

cook·out (ko͝ok′out′) *n.* A meal cooked and served outdoors.

Cook Strait (ko͝ok). The strait between North and South islands, New Zealand.

cook·y, cook·ie (ko͝ok′ē) *n., pl.* **-ies.** Also **cook·ey** *pl.* **-eys. 1.** A small, usually flat cake made from sweet dough. **2.** *Scottish.* A bun. [Dutch *koekje,* diminutive of *koek,* cake, from Middle Dutch *koeke.* See **kak-²** in Appendix.*]

cool (ko͞ol) *adj.* **cooler, coolest. 1.** Moderately cold; neither warm nor very cold. **2.** Reducing discomfort in hot weather; allowing a feeling of coolness: *a cool blouse.* **3.** Not excited; calm; controlled. **4.** Showing dislike, disdain, or indifference; unenthusiastic; not cordial: *a cool greeting.* **5.** Calmly audacious or bold; impudent. **6.** Designating or characteristic of colors, such as blue and green, that produce the impression of coolness. **7.** *Slang.* Having a quiet, indifferent, and aloof attitude. **8.** *Slang.* Excellent; first-rate; superior. **9.** *Informal.* Without exaggeration; entire; full: *He lost a cool million.* —*v.* **cooled, cooling, cools.** —*tr.* **1.** To make less warm. **2.** To make less ardent, intense, or zealous. —*intr.* **1.** To become less warm. **2.** To become calm. —**cool it.** *Slang.* To calm down, slow down, or relax. —**cool one's heels.** *Informal.* To be kept waiting for a long time. —*n.* **1.** Anything that is cool or moderately cold: *the cool of early morning.* **2.** The state or quality of being cool. **3.** *Slang.* Composure: *recover one's cool.* [Middle

English *col,* Old English *cōl.* See **gel-³** in Appendix.*] **—cool′ly** *adv.* **—cool′ness** *n.*

Synonyms: *cool, composed, collected, unruffled, nonchalant, imperturbable, detached.* These adjectives apply to persons to indicate calmness, especially in time of stress. *Cool* has the widest application. Usually it implies merely a high degree of self-control, though it may also indicate aloofness. *Composed* and *collected* more strongly imply conscious display of self-discipline and absence of agitation. *Composed* also often suggests serenity or sedateness, and *collected,* mental concentration. *Unruffled* emphasizes calmness in the face of severe provocation that may have produced agitation in others present. *Nonchalant* describes a casual exterior manner that suggests, sometimes misleadingly, a lack of interest or concern. *Imperturbable* stresses unshakable calmness considered usually as an inherent trait rather than as a product of self-discipline. *Detached* implies aloofness and either lack of active concern or resistance to emotional involvement.

cool·ant (ko͞o′lənt) *n.* An agent that produces cooling; especially, a fluid that draws off heat by circulating through a machine or by bathing a mechanical part.

cool·er (ko͞o′lər) *n.* **1.** A device or container that cools something or keeps it cool. **2.** Anything that makes cool, such as a cold drink. **3.** *Slang.* A jail or prison cell.

cool-head·ed (ko͞ol′hĕd′ĭd) *adj.* Not easily excited or flustered.

Coo·lidge (ko͞o′lĭj), **(John) Calvin.** 1872–1933. Thirtieth President of the United States (1923–29).

coo·lie (ko͞o′lē) *n.* Also **coo·ly** *pl.* **-lies.** An unskilled Oriental laborer. [Hindi *kulī, qulī,* perhaps from *Kulī, Kolī,* an aboriginal tribe of Gujarat, India.]

Coo·mas·sie. The former name for **Kumasi.**

coon (ko͞on) *n.* **1.** *Informal.* A raccoon. **2.** *Slang.* A Negro. An offensive term used derogatorily. [Short for RACCOON.]

coon·can (ko͞on′kăn′) *n.* A card game, **conquian** *(see).*

coon·hound (ko͞on′hound′) *n.* A smooth-coated black and tan hound of a breed developed in the southeastern United States to hunt raccoons.

coon's age. *Slang.* A long time.

coon·skin (ko͞on′skĭn′) *n.* **1.** The pelt of the raccoon. **2.** An article made of coonskin, such as a hat. **—coon′skin′** *adj.*

coon·tie (ko͞on′tē) *n.* An evergreen plant, *Zamia floridana,* of southern Florida, having underground stems that yield a starch resembling arrowroot. [Mikasuki (Seminole) *kuntie,* flour.]

coop (ko͞op) *n.* **1.** An enclosure or cage, as for poultry or small animals. **2.** *Slang.* Any place of confinement. **—fly the coop.** *Slang.* To escape. **—*tr.v.*** **cooped, cooping, coops.** To confine in or as in a coop. Usually used with *in* or *up.* [Middle English *c(o)upe,* wicker basket, chicken coop, probably from Middle Low German *kūpe,* basket, cask, tub, barrel. See **ku-** in Appendix.*]

co-op (kō-ŏp′, kō′ŏp′) *n.* A **cooperative** *(see).*

coop. cooperative.

coop·er (ko͞o′pər) *n.* One who makes wooden tubs and casks. Also called "hooper." **—*v.*** **coopered, -ering, -ers.** **—*tr.*** To repair or make (casks or barrels). **—*intr.*** To work as a cooper. [Middle English *couper,* probably from Middle Low German *kūper,* from *kūpe,* cask, barrel, COOP.]

Coop·er (ko͞o′pər), **James Fenimore.** 1789–1851. American novelist.

coop·er·age (ko͞o′pər-ĭj) *n.* **1.** A cooper's work or products. **2.** A cooper's workshop.

co·op·er·ate (kō-ŏp′ə-rāt′) *intr.v.* **-ated, -ating, -ates.** Also **co-op·er·ate, co·öp·er·ate.** **1.** To work together toward a common end or purpose. **2.** To practice economic cooperation. [Latin *cooperārī* : *co-,* together + *operārī,* to work, from *opus,* work (see **op-¹** in Appendix*).] **—co·op′er·a′tor** (-ā′tər) *n.*

co·op·er·a·tion (kō-ŏp′ə-rā′shən) *n.* Also **co-op·er·a·tion, co·öp·er·a·tion.** **1.** An act of cooperating. **2.** An association of persons for mutual benefit. **—co·op′er·a′tion·ist** *n.*

co·op·er·a·tive (kō-ŏp′rə-tĭv, -ə-rā′tĭv) *adj.* Also **co-op·er·a·tive, co·öp·er·a·tive.** **1.** Working together. **2.** Engaged in joint economic activity. **—*n.*** *Abbr.* **coop.** An enterprise that is collectively owned and operated for mutual benefit. Also called "co-op." **—co·op′er·a·tive·ly** *adv.* **—co·op′er·a·tive·ness** *n.*

co-opt (kō-ŏpt′) *tr.v.* **-opted, -opting, -opts.** **1.** To elect as a fellow member of a board or committee. **2.** To appoint summarily. **3.** To pre-empt; appropriate. [Latin *cooptāre* : *cō-,* together + *optāre,* to choose, elect (see **op-²** in Appendix*).] **—co′-op·ta′tion** (kō′ŏp-tā′shən) *n.* **—co-op′ta·tive** (-tə-tĭv) *adj.*

co·or·di·nate (kō-ôr′də-nāt′, -nĭt) *n.* Also **co-or·di·nate, co·ör·di·nate.** **1.** One that is equal in importance, rank, or degree. **2.** *Mathematics.* One of a set of numbers that determines the location of a point in a space of a given dimension. **3.** *Mathematics.* Any of a set of two or more magnitudes used to determine the position of a point, line, curve, or plane. **—*adj.*** (kō-ôr′də-nĭt, -nāt′). **1.** Of equal importance, rank, or degree; not subordinate. **2.** Of or involving coordination. **3.** Of or based on coordinates. **—*v.*** (kō-ôr′də-nāt′) **coordinated, -nating, -nates.** **—*tr.*** **1.** To place in the same order, class, or rank. **2.** To arrange in the proper relative position. **3.** To harmonize in a common action or effort. **—*intr.*** To work together harmoniously. [Back-formation from COORDINATION.] **—co·or′di·nate·ly** (-nĭt-lē) *adv.* **—co·or′di·nate·ness** (-nĭt-nĭs) *n.* **—co·or′di·na′tive** *adj.* **—co·or′di·na′tor** (-nā′tər) *n.*

coordinate bond. A covalent chemical bond produced when an atom shares a pair of electrons with an atom lacking such a pair. Also called "coordinate covalent bond."

coordinate conjunction. Also **coordinating conjunction, coordinative conjunction.** *Grammar.* A conjunction that connects two identically constructed grammatical elements; for example, *or* in *She doesn't know whether she's coming or going.* Compare **subordinate conjunction.**

co·or·di·na·tion (kō-ôr′də-nā′shən) *n.* Also **co-or·di·na·tion, co·ör·di·na·tion.** **1.** The act of coordinating. **2.** The state of being coordinate; harmonious adjustment or interaction. **3.** *Physiology.* The coordinated functioning of muscles or groups of muscles in the execution of a complex task. [French, from Late Latin *coōrdinātiō,* arrangement in the same order : Latin *cō-,* same + *ōrdinātiō,* arrangement, from *ōrdināre,* to arrange in order, from *ōrdō,* order (see **ar-** in Appendix*).]

coordination compound. A chemical compound formed by joining independent molecules or ions to a central metallic atom.

Coorg (ko͝org). A former state of India, now merged with Mysore State, Republic of India.

Coo·sa River (ko͞o′sə). A navigable river rising in northwestern Georgia and flowing 286 miles south to central Alabama, where it joins the Tallapoosa to form the Alabama River.

Coos Bay (ko͞os). An inlet of the Pacific in Oregon.

coot (ko͞ot) *n.* **1.** Any of several dark-gray aquatic birds of the genus *Fulica;* especially, *F. americana,* of the New World, and *F. atra,* of the Old World. **2.** A duck, the **scoter** *(see).* **3.** *Informal.* A foolish old man. [Middle English *cote,* probably from Middle Dutch *coet, cuut*†.]

coot·ie (ko͞o′tē) *n. Slang.* A body louse. [Probably from Malay *kutu,* louse.]

cop¹ (kŏp) *n.* **1.** A cone-shaped or cylindrical roll of yarn or thread wound on a spindle. **2.** *Archaic.* A summit or crest, as of a hill. [Middle English *cop, coppe,* summit, top, tip, Old English *copp,* from Late Latin *cuppa,* from Latin *cūpa,* tub. See **keu-²** in Appendix.*]

cop² (kŏp) *n. Informal.* A policeman. **—*tr.v.*** **copped, copping, cops.** *Slang.* **1.** To steal. **2.** To seize; catch. **—cop a plea.** *Slang.* To **cop out** *(see).* [Short for *copper,* policeman, "catcher," from *cop, cap,* to catch, probably from Dutch *kapen,* from Old Frisian *cāpia,* to buy (also a euphemism for "to practice piracy"), from Common Germanic *kaupez* (unattested), trader, from Latin *caupō.* See **caupō** in Appendix.*]

cop. copyright.

co·pa·ce·tic, co·pa·se·tic (kō′pə-sĕt′ĭk) *adj.* Also **co·pe·se·tic, co·pe·set·tic.** *Slang.* Excellent; first-rate. [Origin unknown.]

co·pai·ba (kō-pā′bə) *n.* A transparent, yellowish, viscous resin from South American trees of the genus *Copaifera,* used in varnishes and tracing papers and as an expectorant, diuretic, and stimulant. Also called "copaiba balsam." [Spanish, from Portuguese *copaíba,* from Tupi *copaiba.*]

co·pal (kō′pəl) *n.* A brittle, aromatic, yellow to red resin of recent or fossil origin, obtained from various tropical trees and used in varnishes. [Spanish, from Nahuatl *copalli,* resin.]

Co·pán (kō-pän′). In full, **San·ta Ro·sa de Co·pán** (sän′tä rô′sä thä). A ruined city in western Honduras; the southernmost point of the Mayan empire.

co·par·ce·nar·y (kō-pär′sə-nĕr′ē) *n., pl.* **-ies.** Also **co·par·ce·ny** (-sə-nē) (for sense 2). **1.** *Law.* Joint ownership of inherited property. Also called "parcenary." **2.** Any joint ownership. **—*adj.*** Of coparcenary or coparceners.

co·par·ce·ner (kō-pär′sə-nər) *n. Law.* One of two persons sharing an undivided inheritance. Also called "parcener." [CO- + PARCENER.]

co·part·ner (kō-pärt′nər) *n.* Also **co-partner.** A partner, as in a business enterprise; associate. **—co·part′ner·ship′** *n.*

cope¹ (kōp) *intr.v.* **coped, coping, copes.** To contend or strive, especially on even terms or with success. Used with *with.* See Usage note. [Middle English *co(u)pen,* to contend with, join in battle with, strike, from Old French *couper,* to strike, from *coup,* a blow, from Late Latin *colpus,* from Latin *colaphus,* from Greek *kolaphos.* See **kel-²** in Appendix.*]

Usage: *Cope* (intransitive verb) is regularly used with *with: cope with an enemy.* Informally, often humorously, it is not used with *with,* and thus makes no specific reference to the person or thing contended against: *A successful applicant must be able to cope.* As an example in formal written usage, the preceding is unacceptable to 75 per cent of the Usage Panel.

cope² (kōp) *n.* **1.** A long ecclesiastical vestment worn over the alb or surplice. **2.** Any covering resembling a cloak or mantle. **3.** A coping. **—*tr.v.*** **coped, coping, copes.** **1.** To cover or dress in a cope. **2.** To provide with coping, as a wall. [Middle English *cope,* Old English *(cantel)cāp,* from Late Latin *cāpa, cappa,* cloak, hood, head covering, from Latin *caput,* head. See **kaput** in Appendix.*]

co·peck. Variant of **kopeck.**

co·pen·ha·gen (kō′pən-hā′gən) *n.* Grayish blue to purplish blue. See **color.** [From COPENHAGEN.] **—co′pen·ha′gen** *adj.*

Co·pen·ha·gen (kō′pən-hā′gən). *Danish* **Kø·ben·havn** (kœ′bən-houn′). The capital and principal seaport of Denmark, on the eastern coast of Sjaelland just opposite the coast of southern Sweden. Population, 924,000.

co·pe·pod (kō′pə-pŏd′) *n.* Any of numerous small marine and freshwater crustaceans of the order *Copepoda.* [New Latin *Copepoda,* "oar-footed ones" (from the oarlike legs) : Greek *kōpē,* oar handle, oar (see **kap-** in Appendix*) + POD.]

Co·per·ni·can (kō-pûr′nə-kən) *adj.* Pertaining to the theory of Copernicus that the earth rotates on its axis and, with the other planets in the solar system, revolves around the sun.

Co·per·ni·cus (kō-pûr′nə-kəs), **Nicolaus.** Polish name, Mikolaj Kopernik. 1473–1543. Polish astronomer; enunciated the principle of heliocentric planetary motion.

cope·stone. Variant of **capstone.**

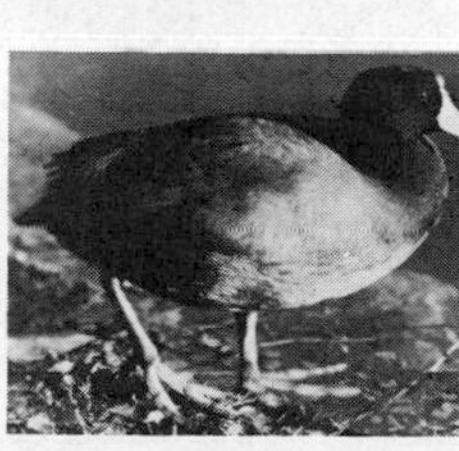

coot
Fulica americana

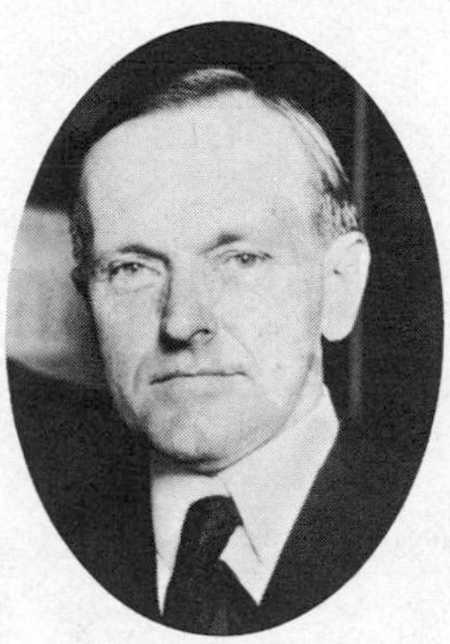

Calvin Coolidge

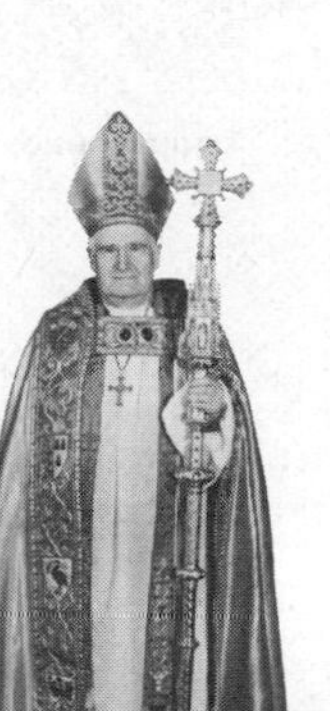

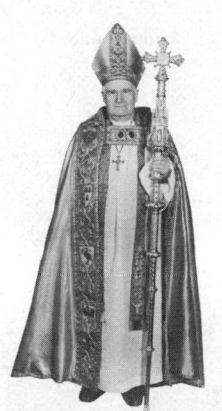

cope²
Arthur Ramsey,
Archbishop of Canterbury

Co·pia·pó (kō'pyä-pō'). A volcano rising to 19,947 feet in north-central Chile.
cop·i·er (kŏp'ē-ər) *n.* **1.** Any of various office machines that make copies. **2.** A copyist or transcriber. **3.** An imitator.
co·pi·lot (kō'pī'lət) *n.* The second or relief pilot of an aircraft.
cop·ing (kō'pĭng) *n.* The top part of a wall or roof, usually slanted. Compare **capstone.** [From COPE (vestment).]
coping saw. A narrow, short-bladed saw set in a recessed handle and used for cutting designs in wood.
co·pi·ous (kō'pē-əs) *adj.* **1.** Yielding or containing plenty; affording ample supply. **2.** Large in quantity; abundant. **3.** Abounding in matter, thoughts, or words; wordy: *"I found our speech copious without order, and energetic without rules"* (Samuel Johnson). [Middle English, from Old French *copieux,* from Latin *cōpiōsus,* from *cōpia,* abundance. See **op-**[1] in Appendix.*] —**co'pi·ous·ly** *adv.* —**co'pi·ous·ness** *n.*
co·pla·nar (kō-plā'nər) *adj.* Lying or occurring in the same plane.
Cop·land (kōp'lənd), **Aaron.** Born 1900. American composer of orchestral and chamber music.
Cop·ley (kŏp'lē), **John Singleton.** 1738–1815. American painter.
co·pol·y·mer (kō-pŏl'ə-mər) *n.* A polymer of two or more different monomers. —**co'pol·y·mer'ic** *adj.*
co·pol·y·mer·ize (kō-pŏl'ə-mə-rīz) *v.* **-ized, -izing, -izes.** —*tr.* To polymerize (different monomers) together. —*intr.* To react to form a copolymer. —**co·pol'y·mer·i·za'tion** *n.*
cop out. *Slang.* **1.** To fail or refuse to commit oneself. **2.** To plead guilty to a lesser charge in order to receive a lighter punishment than if one stands trial. In this sense also "cop a plea." [From *cop a plea,* to plead guilty, from COP, to seize (used here in the rare sense "to give or present").]
cop-out (kŏp'out') *n. Slang.* Failure to commit oneself.
cop·per[1] (kŏp'ər) *n.* **1.** *Symbol* **Cu** A ductile, malleable, reddish-brown metallic element that is an excellent conductor of heat and electricity and is widely used for electrical wiring, water piping, and corrosion-resistant parts either pure or in alloys such as brass and bronze. Atomic number 29, atomic weight 63.54, melting point 1,083°C, boiling point 2,595°C, specific gravity 8.96, valence 1, 2. See **element. 2.** A coin made of copper or a copper alloy. **3.** *Chiefly British.* A large boiler or pot made of copper or often of iron. **4.** Any of various small butterflies of the subfamily Lycaeninae, having predominantly copper-colored wings. —*tr.v.* **coppered, -pering, -pers. 1.** To coat or finish with a layer of copper. **2.** *Slang.* To bet against (in faro, for example). [Middle English *coper,* Old English *coper, copor,* from Common Germanic *kupar* (unattested), from Late Latin *cuprum,* from Latin *Cyprium (aes),* "(copper) of Cyprus" (Cyprus was known in ancient times as the source of the best copper), from *Cyprius,* of Cyprus, from Greek *Kuprios,* from *Kupros,* CYPRUS.] —**cop'per·y** *adj.*
cop·per[2] (kŏp'ər) *n. Slang.* A policeman. [From COP (to seize).]
cop·per·as (kŏp'ər-əs) *n.* A greenish, crystalline, hydrated ferrous sulfate, $FeSO_4 \cdot 7H_2O$, used in the manufacture of fertilizers and inks and in water purification. [Middle English *coperose,* from Old French *co(u)perose,* from Medieval Latin *cup(e)rosa,* probably short for *aqua cup(e)rosa,* "copper water," from Late Latin *cuprum,* COPPER (metal). (*Cuperosa* was later erroneously construed as "rose of copper" by association with Latin *rosa,* ROSE.)]

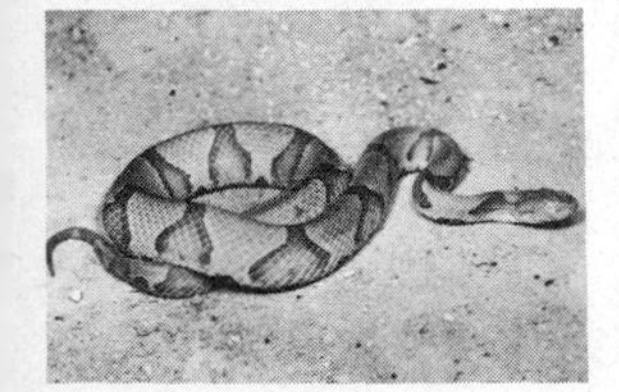
copperhead

cop·per·head (kŏp'ər-hĕd') *n.* **1.** A venomous snake, *Agkistrodon contortrix* (or *Ancistron contortrix*), of eastern United States, having reddish-brown markings. **2.** *Capital* **C.** During the Civil War, a Northerner who sympathized with the South.
Cop·per·mine (kŏp'ər-mīn'). A river rising in central Northwest Territories, Canada, and flowing 525 miles northwest and north to the Beaufort Sea.
cop·per·plate (kŏp'ər-plāt') *n.* **1.** A copper printing plate, engraved or etched to form a recessed pattern of the matter to be printed. **2.** A print or engraving made by using such a plate. **3.** A fine, sharp handwriting style based on copper-plate engraved models.
copper pyrites. A copper ore, **chalcopyrite** *(see).*
cop·per·smith (kŏp'ər-smĭth') *n.* **1.** A worker or manufacturer of objects, especially utensils, in copper. **2.** A brightly colored bird, *Megalaima haemacephala,* of southeastern Asia, having a ringing, metallic call.
copper sulfate. A poisonous blue crystalline copper salt, $CuSO_4 \cdot 5H_2O$, used in agriculture, textile dyeing, leather treatment, electroplating, and the manufacture of germicides. Also called "blue vitriol."
cop·pice (kŏp'ĭs) *n. Chiefly British.* A thicket; copse.
cop·ra (kŏp'rə) *n.* Dried coconut meat from which coconut oil is extracted. [Portuguese, from Malayalam *koppara,* probably from Hindi *khoprā,* coconut, perhaps from Sanskrit *karparah, kharparah,* head, shell. See **sker-**[1] in Appendix.*]

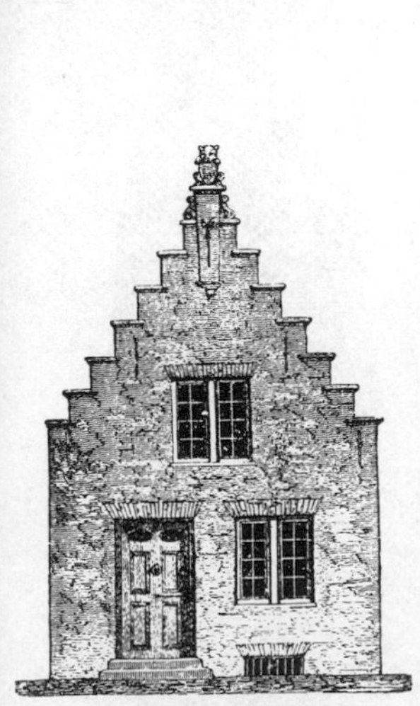
corbie-step

copro–. Indicates dung, excrement, or feces; for example, **coprolite.** [From Greek *kopros,* dung. See **kekw-** in Appendix.*]
cop·ro·lite (kŏp'rə-līt') *n.* Fossilized excrement. [COPRO- + -LITE.] —**cop'ro·lit'ic** (-lĭt'ĭk) *adj.*
cop·rol·o·gy (kŏp-rŏl'ə-jē) *n.* Pornography or scatology. [COPRO- + -LOGY.]
cop·roph·a·gous (kŏp-rŏf'ə-gəs) *adj.* Feeding on excrement: *coprophagous insects.* [New Latin *coprophagus,* from Greek *koprophagos* : COPRO- + -PHAGOUS.] —**coproph'a·gy** (-ə-jē) *n.*
cop·ro·phil·i·a (kŏp'rə-fĭl'ē-ə) *n.* An abnormal attraction to fecal matter. [New Latin : COPRO- + -PHILIA.]
copse (kŏps) *n.* A thicket of small trees or shrubs. [Short for *coppice,* Middle English *copice,* from Old French *co(u)peiz,* "cut wood," thicket for cutting, from *couper,* to cut, strike off. See **cope** (contend).]
Copt (kŏpt) *n.* **1.** A native of Egypt descended from ancient Egyptian stock. **2.** A member of the Coptic Church. [French *Copte,* from New Latin *Coptus,* from Arabic *quft, qubt,* the Copts, from Coptic *gyptios,* from Greek *Aiguptios,* from *Aiguptos,* EGYPT.]
cop·ter (kŏp'tər) *n. Informal.* A helicopter.
Cop·tic (kŏp'tĭk) *n. Abbr.* **Copt.** The Afro-Asiatic language of the Copts, used today only in the liturgy of the Coptic Church. —*adj.* Of or pertaining to the Copts or their language.
Coptic Church. The Christian church of Egypt, adhering to the Monophysite doctrine.
cop·u·la (kŏp'yə-lə) *n., pl.* **-las** or **-lae** (-lē). **1.** A verb that identifies the predicate of a sentence with the subject, usually a form of *be.* In the sentence *The girls are beautiful,* the copula is *are.* **2.** *Logic.* The word or set of words that serves as a link between the subject and predicate of a proposition. [Latin *cōpula,* link, bond. See **ap-**[1] in Appendix.*] —**cop'u·lar** *adj.*
cop·u·late (kŏp'yə-lāt') *intr.v.* **-lated, -lating, -lates.** To engage in coitus. [Latin *cōpulāre,* to fasten together, link, from *cōpula,* link, bond. See **ap-**[1] in Appendix.*] —**cop'u·la'tion** *n.*
cop·u·la·tive (kŏp'yə-lā'tĭv, -lə-tĭv) *adj.* **1.** Joining or uniting; coupling. **2.** *Grammar.* **a.** Serving to connect coordinate words or clauses. Said of a conjunction. **b.** Serving as a copula. Used of a verb. **3.** Of or pertaining to copulation. —*n. Grammar.* A copulative word or group of words. —**cop'u·la'tive·ly** *adv.*
copulative conjunction. Any of various conjunctions that serve to connect words or word groups in a coordinate relationship; for example, the conjunction *and.*
cop·y (kŏp'ē) *n., pl.* **-ies. 1.** An imitation or reproduction of something original; a duplicate. **2.** One specimen or example of a printed text or picture. **3.** *Abbr.* **c., C.** A manuscript or other material to be set in type. **4.** Suitable source material, as for journalism. —*v.* **copied, -ying, -ies.** —*tr.* **1.** To make a copy or copies of; transcribe; reproduce. **2.** To follow as a model or pattern; imitate. —*intr.* **1.** To make one or more copies or reproductions. **2.** To admit of being reproduced. —See Synonyms at **imitate.** [Middle English *copie,* from Old French, from Medieval Latin *cōpia,* transcript, right of reproduction, from Latin, abundance, power. See **op-**[1] in Appendix.*]
cop·y·book (kŏp'ē-bo͝ok') *n.* **1.** A book of models of penmanship for imitation. **2.** A book for copies, as of accounts or documents. —*adj.* Unoriginal; trite: *a copybook phrase.*
copy boy. A boy in a newspaper office who carries copy and runs errands.
cop·y·cat (kŏp'ē-kăt') *n.* A mimic; an imitator.
copy desk. The desk in a newspaper office where copy is edited and prepared for typesetting.
cop·y-ed·it (kŏp'ē-ĕd'ĭt) *tr.v.* **-ited, -iting, -its.** To correct and prepare (a manuscript, for example) for typesetting and printing. —**copy editor.**
cop·y·graph (kŏp'ē-grăf', -gräf') *n.* A **hectograph** *(see).*
cop·y·hold·er (kŏp'ē-hōl'dər) *n.* **1.** An assistant who reads manuscript aloud to a proofreader. **2.** A device that holds copy in place for the typesetter.
cop·y·ist (kŏp'ē-ĭst) *n.* One who makes written copies.
cop·y·read·er (kŏp'ē-rē'dər) *n.* One who edits and corrects newspaper copy for publication.
cop·y·right (kŏp'ē-rīt') *n. Abbr.* **c., C., cop.** The right granted by law to an author, composer, playwright, publisher, or distributor, to exclusive publication, production, sale, or distribution of a literary, musical, dramatic, or artistic work. In the United States, this right extends for a period of 28 years, with the privilege of being renewed for an additional 28 years. —*adj.* Also **cop·y·right·ed** (-rī'tĭd). Protected by copyright. —*tr.v.* **copyrighted, -righting, -rights.** To secure a copyright for. —**cop'y·right'a·ble** *adj.* —**cop'y·right'er** *n.*
cop·y·writ·er (kŏp'ē-rī'tər) *n.* One who writes advertising copy.
coq au vin (kôk ō văN'). *French.* A hearty dish of chicken in red wine, with brandy, mushrooms, salt pork, onions, and a bouquet garni.
co·quet (kō-kĕt') *intr.v.* **-quetted, -quetting, -quets. 1.** To play the coquette; to flirt. **2.** To trifle; dally. [French *coqueter,* to flirt, from *coquet,* flirtatious man. See **coquette.**]
co·quet·ry (kō'kə-trē, kō-kĕt'rē) *n., pl.* **-ries.** Dalliance; flirtation. [French *coquetterie,* from COQUETTE.]
co·quette (kō-kĕt') *n.* A woman who flirts with men. [French, feminine of *coquet,* flirtatious man, diminutive of *coq,* cock, from Old French *coc,* from Late Latin *coccus,* from Latin *coco,* cackle. See **cock.**] —**co·quet'tish** *adj.* —**co·quet'tish·ly** *adv.* —**co·quet'tish·ness** *n.*
co·quil·la nut (kō-kēl'yə, -kē'yə). The nut of a South American palm tree, *Attalea funifera,* having a hard oval shell used for decorative carving or turning. [Portuguese *coquilho,* diminutive of *côco,* COCO.]
co·quille (kō-kēl') *n.* A scallop-shaped dish or a scallop shell in which various seafood dishes are browned and served. [French, variant (influenced by *coque,* shell) of Latin *conchylia,* plural of *conchylium,* mussel, from Greek *konkhulion,* mussel, cockle, diminutive of *konkhē,* CONCH.]
co·qui·na (kō-kē'nə) *n.* **1.** Any of various small bivalve mollusks of warm marine waters, having variously colored, often striped or banded shells. **2.** A soft porous limestone, essentially of shell and coral fragments, used as a construction material. [Spanish, shellfish, cockle, irregular diminutive of *concha,* shell, mussel, from Latin, CONCH.]
co·qui·to (kō-kē'tō) *n., pl.* **-tos.** A Chilean palm tree, *Jubaea*

spectabilis, from the sap of which a sweet edible syrup is obtained. [Spanish, diminutive of *coco,* coco palm, from Portuguese *côco,* COCO.]

cor. **1.** corner. **2.** cornet. **3.** coroner. **4.** corpus. **5.** correction. **6.** correspondence; correspondent; corresponding.

Cor. Corinthians (New Testament).

Co·ra (kôr′ə). A feminine given name. [Latin *Cora,* from Greek *Korē,* "the Maiden" (Persephone), from *korē,* maiden. See **ker-³** in Appendix.*]

cor·a·cle (kôr′ə-kəl, kŏr′-) *n.* A small, rounded boat made of waterproof material stretched over a wicker or wooden frame. Also *Scottish & Irish* "currach." [Earlier *corougle,* from Welsh *corwgl, cwrwgl.* See **currach.**]

cor·a·coid (kôr′ə-koid′, kŏr′-) *n.* A bone or cartilage projecting from the scapula toward the sternum. [New Latin *coracoides,* "(bone) shaped like a crow's beak," from Greek *korakoeidēs,* like a raven : *korax,* raven (see **ker-²** in Appendix*) + -OID.] —**cor′a·coid′** *adj.*

cor·al (kôr′əl, kŏr′əl) *n.* **1.** Any of numerous chiefly colonial marine coelenterates of the class Anthozoa, characterized by calcareous skeletons massed in a wide variety of shapes, and often forming reefs or islands. **2.** The often hard, rocklike structure formed by such organisms. **3.** The material forming such a structure; especially, the red-orange, pinkish, or white stony substance secreted by corals of the genus *Corallium,* used to make jewelry and ornaments. **4.** An object made of coral. **5.** Deep or strong pink to moderate red or reddish orange. See **color.** **6.** The unfertilized eggs of a female lobster, that turn a reddish color when cooked. [Middle English, from Old French, from Latin *corallium,* from Greek *korallion,* probably of Semitic origin, akin to Hebrew *gōrāl,* a pebble.] —**cor′al** *adj.*

cor·al-bells (kôr′əl-bělz′, kŏr′-) *n.* Plural in form, used with a singular or plural verb. A plant, *Heuchera sanguinea,* of the western United States, often cultivated for its clusters of small, bell-shaped, red flowers.

cor·al·ber·ry (kôr′əl-běr′ē, kŏr′-) *n., pl.* **-ries.** **1.** A North American shrub, *Symphoricarpos orbiculatus,* having red or purplish fruit. **2.** The fruit of this shrub. Also called "Indian currant."

Coral Gables. A city of southeastern Florida, on Biscayne Bay, southwest of Miami. Population, 35,000.

cor·al·line (kôr′ə-lĭn, -līn′, kŏr′-) *adj.* **1.** Of, consisting of, or producing coral. **2.** Resembling coral; especially, coral-colored. —*n.* **1.** A corallike animal, such as certain bryozoans or hydrozoans. **2.** Any of various red algae, especially of the genus *Corallina,* covered with a calcareous substance and forming stony deposits. [French *corallin,* from Old French, from Latin *corallīnus,* from *corallium,* CORAL.]

cor·al·loid (kôr′ə-loid′, kŏr′-) *adj.* Resembling coral in appearance or form. [Latin *corallium,* CORAL + -OID.]

coral pink. Moderate to deep or strong yellowish pink. See **color.**

coral reef. An erosion-resistant marine ridge or mound consisting chiefly of compacted coral together with algal material and biochemically deposited magnesium and calcium carbonates.

cor·al·root (kôr′əl-ro͞ot′, -ro͝ot′, kŏr′-) *n.* Any of several orchids of the genus *Corallorhiza,* having small yellow-green or purplish flowers and branched roots that resemble coral.

Coral Sea. A portion of the Pacific Ocean northeast of Queensland, Australia, and southeast of New Guinea; the site of a U.S. naval victory (1942) over the Japanese.

coral snake. Any of various venomous snakes of the genus *Micrurus,* of tropical America and the southern United States, characteristically having brilliant red, black, and yellow banded markings.

coral vine. A climbing woody vine, *Antigonon leptopus,* native to Mexico and cultivated for its red or white flowers.

Co·ran·tijn. The Dutch name for **Courantyne.**

cor·ban (kôr′bən, kôr-băn′) *n.* An offering to God among the ancient Hebrews. [Middle English, from Late Latin, from Greek *korban,* from Hebrew *qorbān.*]

cor·beil (kôr′bəl) *n.* Also **cor·beille** (kôr-bā′). A sculptured basket of flowers or fruits used as an architectural ornament. [French *corbeille,* from Late Latin *corbicula,* diminutive of Latin *corbis,* basket. See **corf.**]

cor·bel (kôr′bəl, -bĕl) *n.* A bracket of stone, wood, brick, or other building material, projecting from the face of a wall and generally used to support a cornice or an arch. —*tr.v.* **corbeled** or **-belled, -beling** or **-belling, -bels.** To provide with or support by a corbel or corbels. [Middle English, from Old French, diminutive of *corp,* raven (early corbels were wedge-shaped, like ravens' beaks), from Latin *corvus.* See **ker-²** in Appendix.*]

cor·bel·ing (kôr′bəl-ĭng, -bĕl-ĭng) *n.* **1.** The building of a corbel. **2.** An overlapping arrangement of bricks or stones in which each course extends farther out from the vertical of the wall than the course below.

cor·bie gable (kôr′bē). A gable roof with corbie-steps.

cor·bie-step (kôr′bē-stĕp′) *n.* Also **cor·bie·step.** One of a series of steps or steplike projections on the top of a gable wall. [From Middle English *corbie,* raven (the steps being accessible only to birds), from Old French *corbin,* from Latin *corvīnus,* ravenlike. See **corbina.**]

cor·bi·na (kôr-bē′nə) *n.* Also **cor·vi·na** (-vē′nə) (especially for sense 2). **1.** A food and game fish, *Menticirrhus undulatus,* of North American Pacific coastal waters. **2.** Any of several related marine fishes of the family Sciaenidae. [Mexican Spanish, from Spanish, from *corvino,* ravenlike (from its color), from Latin *corvīnus,* from *corvus,* raven. See **ker-²** in Appendix.*]

Cor·cy·ra. The ancient name for **Corfu.**

cord (kôrd) *n.* Also **chord** (for sense 5 only). **1.** A string or small rope of twisted strands or fibers. **2.** An insulated, flexible electric wire fitted with a plug or plugs. **3.** A hangman's rope. **4.** Any influence, feeling, or force that binds or restrains. **5.** *Anatomy.* Any structure resembling a cord: *spinal cord.* **6.** A raised rib on the surface of cloth. **7.** A fabric or cloth with such ribs. **8.** *Plural.* Trousers made of corduroy. **9.** A unit of quantity for cut fuel wood, equal to 128 cubic feet in a stack measuring 4 by 4 by 8 feet. —*tr.v.* **corded, cording, cords.** **1.** To fasten or bind with a cord or cords. **2.** To furnish with a cord or cords. **3.** To pile (wood) in cords. [Middle English, from Old French *corde,* from Latin *chorda,* catgut, cord, from Greek *khordē.* See **gher-¹** in Appendix.*] —**cord′er** *n.*

cord·age (kôr′dĭj) *n.* **1.** The ropes in the rigging of a ship. **2.** The amount of wood in an area, as measured in cords.

cor·date (kôr′dāt′) *adj. Biology.* Having a heart-shaped outline: *a cordate leaf.* [New Latin *cordatus,* from Latin *cor* (stem *cord-*), heart. See **kerd-¹** in Appendix.*] —**cor′date′ly** *adv.*

Cor·day (kôr-dā′), **Charlotte.** In full, Marie Anne Charlotte Corday d'Armont. 1768–1793. French Revolutionary patriot; assassin of Marat.

cord·ed (kôr′dĭd) *adj.* **1.** Tied or bound with cords. **2.** Furnished with or made of cords. **3.** Ribbed or twilled, as corduroy. **4.** Stacked in cords, as firewood.

cor·dial (kôr′jəl) *adj.* **1.** Hearty; warm; sincere. **2.** Invigorating; stimulating; reviving. —*n.* **1.** A stimulant. **2.** A **liqueur** (*see*). [Middle English, of the heart, from Medieval Latin *cordiālis,* from Latin *cor* (stem *cord-*), heart. See **kerd-¹** in Appendix.*] —**cor′dial′i·ty** (kôr′jăl′ə-tē, -jē-ăl′ə-tē, -dē-ăl′ə-tē), **cor′dial·ness** *n.* —**cor′dial·ly** *adv.*

cor·di·er·ite (kôr′dē-ə-rīt′) *n.* A dichroic violet-blue to gray mineral silicate of magnesium, aluminum, and sometimes iron. Also called "dichroite." [French, first described by Pierre L.A. *Cordier* (1777–1861), French geologist.]

cor·di·form (kôr′də-fôrm′) *adj.* Heart-shaped. [French *cordiforme* : Latin *cor* (stem *cord-*), heart (see **kerd-¹** in Appendix*) + -FORM.]

cor·dil·le·ra (kôr′dĭl-yâr′ə, kôr-dĭl′ər-ə) *n.* A chain of mountains, especially the principal mountain range or system of a large land mass. [Spanish, from *cordilla,* diminutive of *cuerda,* cord, chain, from Latin *chorda,* CORD.] —**cor′dil·le′ran** *adj.*

Cor·di·lle·ra Cen·tral (kôr′*th*ä-yä′rä sān-träl′). **1.** The central of three ranges of the Andes in western Colombia. Highest elevation, Huila (18,700 feet). **2.** A mountain range in central Dominican Republic. Highest elevation, Pico Duarte (10,115 feet). **3.** A range of the Andes in north-central Peru. **4.** The main mountain range of northern Luzon Island, Republic of the Philippines. Highest elevation, Mount Pulog (9,606 feet). **5.** A mountain range in south-central Puerto Rico. Highest elevation, Cerro de Punta (4,400 feet).

Cor·di·lle·ra de Mé·ri·da (kôr′*th*ä-yä′rä *th*ä mā′rē-*th*ä). Also **Sier·ra Ne·va·da de Mérida** (syĕr′rä nĕ-vä′*th*ä *th*ä mā′rē-*th*ä). A mountain range in western Venezuela. Highest elevation, Pico Bolívar (16,411 feet).

Cor·di·lle·ra Oc·ci·den·tal (kôr′*th*ä-yä′rä ôk′sĕ-*th*ān-täl′). **1.** The western of three ranges of the Andes in western Colombia. **2.** The western range of the Andes along the coast of Peru. Highest elevation, Huascarán (22,205 feet).

Cor·di·lle·ra O·rien·tal (kôr′*th*ä-yä′rä ō′ryān-täl′). **1.** The eastern of three ranges of the Andes in western Colombia. **2.** The eastern range of the Andes in northern Peru. **3.** The eastern range of the Andes in central Bolivia. Highest elevation over 11,000 feet. **4.** The eastern range of the Andes in southeastern Peru. Highest elevation, Salcantay (20,500 feet).

Cor·di·lle·ra Re·al (kôr′*th*ä-yä′rä rē-äl′). **1.** A range of the Andes in western Bolivia. Highest elevations, Ancohuma (21,490 feet), Illampu (21,276 feet), and Illimani (21,185 feet). **2.** A range of the Andes in Ecuador. Highest elevations, Chimborazo (20,561 feet) and Cotopaxi (19,347 feet).

Cor·dil·le·ras (kôr′dĭl-yâr′əz, kôr-dĭl′ər-əz; *Spanish* kôr′*th*ä-yä′räs *for sense 1*). **1.** The Andes range in western South America. **2.** The complex of ranges in western North America embraced between and including the Rocky Mountains and the Sierra Nevada, and their extension north into Canada and Alaska. **3.** The entire complex of mountain ranges on the western side of the Americas, extending from Alaska to Cape Horn. —**Cor′dil·le′ran** *adj.*

cord·ite (kôr′dīt′) *n.* A smokeless explosive powder consisting of nitrocellulose, nitroglycerin, and petrolatum dissolved in acetone, dried, and extruded in cords. [From CORD.]

cord moss. Any moss of the genus *Funaria;* especially, *F. hygrometrica,* usually growing in burned or waste places. [From its cordlike seta.]

cor·do·ba (kôr′də-bə; *Spanish* kôr′dō-vä) *n.* **1.** The basic monetary unit of Nicaragua, equal to 100 centavos. See table of exchange rates at **currency.** **2.** A note worth one cordoba. [After Francisco de *Córdoba* (1475–1526), Spanish explorer.]

Cór·do·ba (kôr′dō-vä *for sense 1;* kôr′*th*ō-vä *for sense 2*). **1.** A city in north-central Argentina. Population, 589,000. **2.** A city in southern Spain, on the Guadalquivir, 73 miles northeast of Seville. Population, 215,000.

cor·don (kôr′dən) *n.* **1.** A line of people, military posts, ships, or the like stationed around an area to enclose or guard it. **2.** A cord or braid worn as a fastening or an ornament. **3.** A ribbon, usually worn diagonally across the breast as a badge of honor or a decoration. **4.** *Architecture.* An ornamental band of stone or masonry, a **stringcourse** (*see*). **5.** *Horticulture.* A fruit tree trained and pruned to grow along wires or other supports. —*tr.v.* **cordoned, -doning, -dons.** To form a cordon around (an

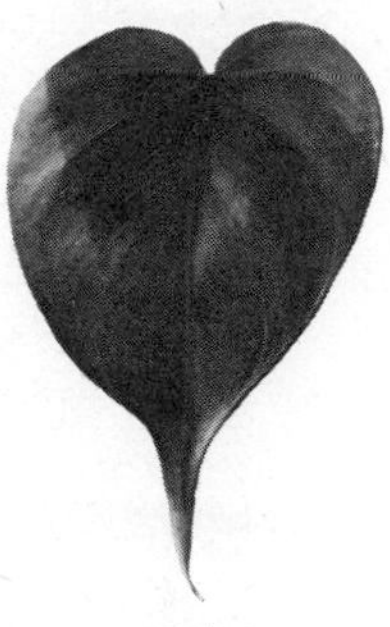

cordate
Cordate leaf of philodendron

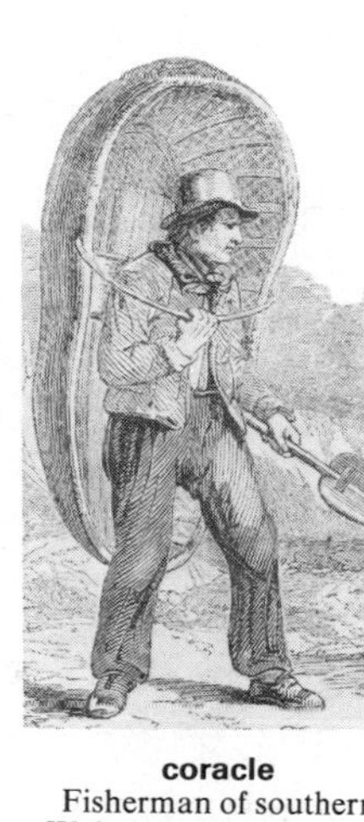

coracle
Fisherman of southern Wales carrying a coracle

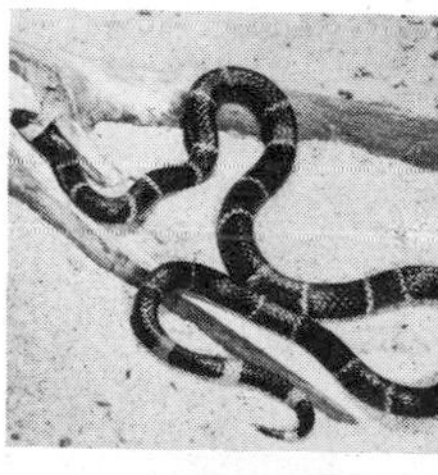

coral snake
Micrurus fulvius
Eastern coral snake

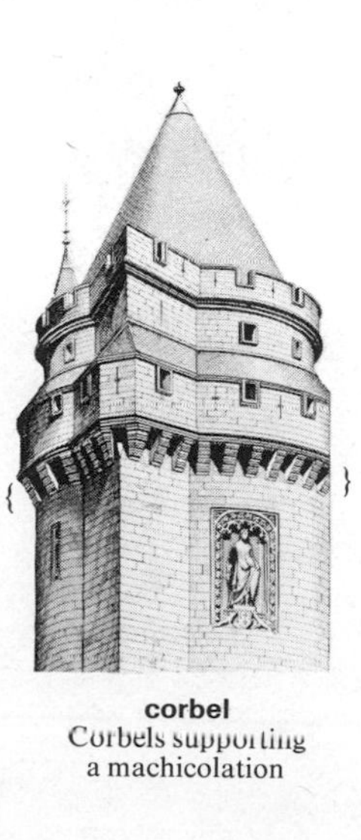

corbel
Corbels supporting a machicolation

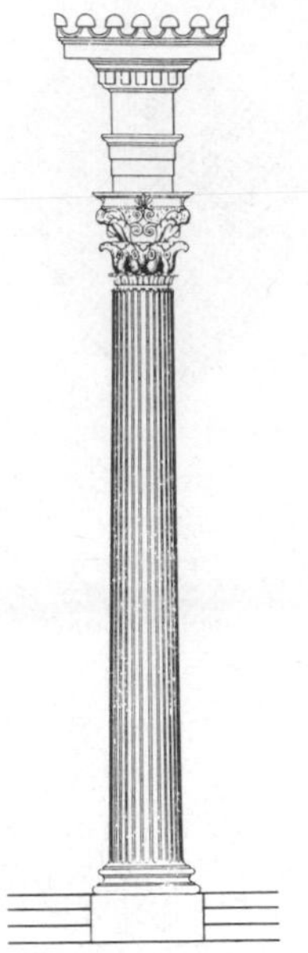

Corinthian order

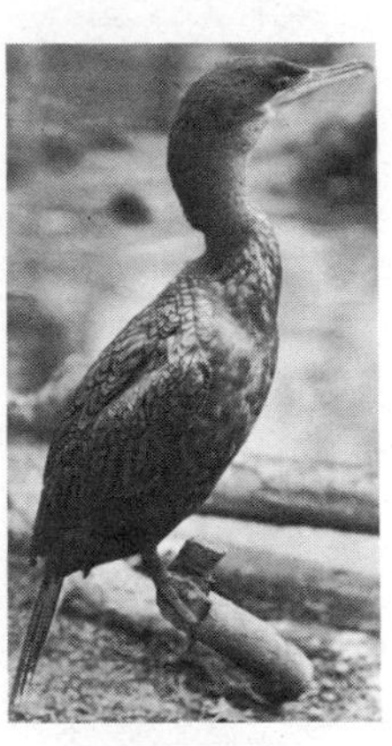

cormorant
Phalacrocorax auritus
Double-crested cormorant

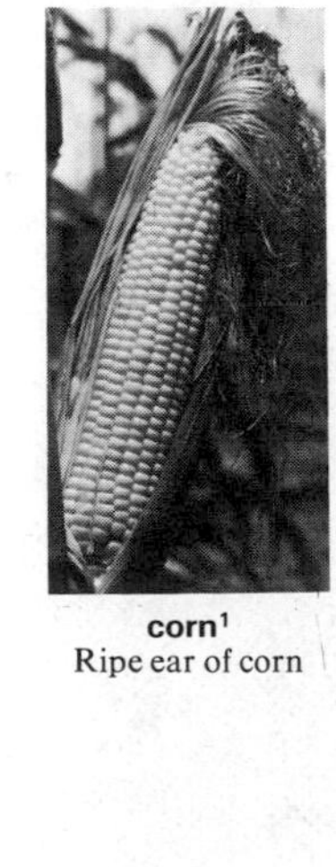

corn[1]
Ripe ear of corn

area) so as to prevent ingress or egress. Often used with *off.* [French, from Old French, diminutive of *corde,* CORD.]

cor·don bleu (kôr-dôN′ blœ′) *pl.* **cordons bleus** (kôr-dôN′ blœ′). **1.** The blue ribbon worn as a decoration by members of the Order of the Holy Ghost, the highest order of French chivalry under the Bourbon monarchy. **2.** A person highly distinguished in his field; especially, a master chef. [French, "blue ribbon."]

cor·don sa·ni·taire (kôr-dôN′ sä-nē-târ′) *pl.* **cordons sanitaires** (kôr-dôN′ sä-nē-târ′). A chain of buffer states organized around a nation considered ideologically dangerous or potentially hostile. [French, "quarantine line."]

cor·do·van (kôr′də-vən) *n.* A fine leather made originally at Córdoba, Spain, first of goatskin but now more frequently of split horsehide. Also called "cordovan leather." —*adj.* Made of this leather. [Spanish *cordobán,* from CÓRDOBA.]

Cor·do·van (kôr′də-vən) *adj.* Of or pertaining to Córdoba, especially Córdoba, Spain. —*n.* An inhabitant or native of Córdoba. [Old Spanish *Cordován,* from *Córdova,* CÓRDOBA.]

cor·du·roy (kôr′də-roi, kôr′də-roi′) *n.* **1.** A durable cut-pile fabric, usually made of cotton, with vertical ribs or wales. **2.** *Plural.* Corduroy trousers. —*adj.* Made of or resembling corduroy. —*tr.v.* **corduroyed, -roying, -roys.** To build (a road) of logs laid together transversely. [Probably from CORD + obsolete *duroy, deroy*†, a coarse woolen fabric.]

cord·wood (kôrd′wo͝od′) *n.* **1.** Wood cut and piled in cords. **2.** Wood sold by the cord.

core (kôr, kōr) *n.* **1.** The hard or fibrous central part of certain fruits, such as the apple or pear, containing the seeds. **2.** The innermost or most important part of anything; heart; center; essence. **3.** *Electricity.* A soft iron rod in a coil or transformer that intensifies and provides a path for the magnetic field produced by the windings. **4.** A mass of dry sand placed within a mold to provide openings or shape to a casting. **5.** The base, usually of soft or inferior wood, to which veneer woods are glued. —*tr.v.* **cored, coring, cores.** To remove the core of: *core apples.* [Middle English *core, coor*†.]

CORE (kôr, kōr) Congress of Racial Equality.

co·re·late. *Chiefly British.* Variant of **correlate.**

co·re·lig·ion·ist (kō′rĭ-lĭj′ə-nĭst) *n.* One having the same religion as another.

Co·rel·li (kō-rĕl′lē), **Arcangelo.** 1653–1713. Italian violinist and composer.

Cor·en·tyn, Cor·en·tyne. See **Courantyne.**

co·re·op·sis (kôr′ē-ŏp′sĭs) *n.* Any of several plants of the genus *Coreopsis,* having daisylike yellow or variegated flowers. Also called "tickseed" and sometimes "calliopsis." [New Latin, "resembling a bedbug" (from the shape of the seed) : Greek *koris,* bedbug (see **sker-**[1] in Appendix*) + -OPSIS.]

cor·er (kôr′ər, kōr′ər) *n.* An implement for coring apples.

co·re·spon·dent (kō′rĭ-spŏn′dənt) *n. Law.* A person charged with having committed adultery with the defendant in a suit for divorce. [CO- + RESPONDENT.] —**co′re·spon′den·cy** *n.*

corf (kôrf, kōrf) *n., pl.* **corves** (kôrvz, kōrvz). *British.* A truck, tub, or basket used in a mine. [Middle English, basket, from Middle Dutch *corf* or Middle Low German *korf,* probably from Latin *corbis*†.]

Cor·fam (kôr′făm) *n.* A trademark for a synthetic leather.

Cor·fu (kôr′fo͞o, kôr′fyo͞o). *Greek* **Ker·ky·ra** (kər-kîr′ə). Ancient name **Cor·cy·ra** (kôr-sī′rə). **1.** One of the Ionian Islands of Greece, 227 square miles in area, lying in the Ionian Sea off the northwestern mainland coast. Population, 99,000. **2.** A seaport and the capital of this island. Population, 31,000.

cor·gi (kôr′gē) *n., pl.* **-gis.** See **Welsh corgi.** [Welsh, "dwarf dog" : *cor*†, dwarf + *ci,* dog (see **kwon-** in Appendix*).]

co·ri·a·ceous (kôr′ē-ā′shəs) *adj.* Of or like leather, especially in texture; tough. [Late Latin *coriāceus,* from Latin *corium,* leather, hide. See **sker-**[1] in Appendix.*]

co·ri·an·der (kôr′ē-ăn′dər, kōr′ē-) *n.* **1.** An herb, *Coriandrum sativum,* widely cultivated for its aromatic seeds. **2.** The dried ripe seeds of this plant, used especially as a condiment. [Middle English *coriandre,* from Old French, from Latin *coriandrum,* from Greek *koriandron, koriannon,* perhaps of Mediterranean origin.]

Cor·inth (kôr′ĭnth, kŏr′-). *Greek* **Ko·rin·thos** (kô′rən-thôs). **1.** A region of ancient Greece, occupying most of the Isthmus of Corinth and part of the northeastern Peloponnesus. **2.** A city of ancient Greece, in the northeastern Peloponnesus, on the Gulf of Corinth. **3.** A modern city three miles northeast of the site of ancient Corinth. Population, 18,000.

Cor·inth, Gulf of (kôr′ĭnth, kŏr′-). An inlet of the Ionian Sea, 80 miles long, between the Peloponnesus and central Greece. Also called "Gulf of Lepanto."

Cor·inth, Isthmus of (kôr′ĭnth, kŏr′-). A neck of land connecting the Peloponnesus to the rest of Greece.

Cor·inth Canal (kôr′ĭnth, kŏr′-). A sea-level canal cut through the Isthmus of Corinth.

Co·rin·thi·an (kə-rĭn′thē-ən) *adj.* **1.** Of or pertaining to ancient Corinth. **2.** Given to luxury; licentious; profligate. **3.** Elegantly or elaborately ornate. **4.** Pertaining to or designating the Corinthian order. —*n.* **1.** A native or inhabitant of Corinth. **2.** A man about town. **3.** A wealthy amateur sportsman, especially an amateur yachtsman. **4.** *Plural. Abbr.* **Cor.** Either of two epistles addressed by Saint Paul to the Christian community at Corinth, each forming a book of the New Testament. In this sense, also called "Epistles to the Corinthians."

Corinthian order. The most ornate of the three classical orders of architecture, characterized by a slender fluted column having an ornate bell-shaped capital decorated with acanthus leaves. Compare **Doric order, Ionic order.**

Cor·i·o·lis force (kôr′ē-ō′lĭs). *Physics.* A fictitious force used mathematically to describe motion, as of aircraft or cloud formations, relative to a noninertial, uniformly rotating frame of reference such as the earth. [After Gaspard G. de *Coriolis* (1792–1843), French mathematician.]

co·ri·um (kôr′ē-əm, kōr′-) *n., pl.* **coria** (kôr′ē-ə, kōr′-). The layer of the skin beneath the epithelium, containing nerve endings, sweat glands, and blood and lymph vessels. Also called "cutis," "derma." [New Latin, from Latin, skin, hide. See **sker-**[1] in Appendix.*]

cork (kôrk) *n.* **1.** The light, porous, elastic outer bark of the **cork oak** *(see),* used widely in industry and the arts. **2.** Something made of cork, especially a bottle stopper. **3.** A bottle stopper made of other material, such as plastic, glass, or rubber. **4.** A small float used on a fishing line or net to buoy up the line or to indicate when a fish bites. **5.** *Botany.* A tissue of dead cells that forms on the outer side of the cambium in the stems of woody plants. —*tr.v.* **corked, corking, corks.** **1.** To stop or seal with or as if with a cork. **2.** To hold back; restrain or check. **3.** To blacken with burnt cork. [Middle English, from Dutch *kurk* or Low German *korck,* from Spanish *alcorque,* cork sole or shoe, probably from Spanish Arabic *al-qūrq.*]

Cork (kôrk). **1.** The largest county (2,880 square miles) of the Republic of Ireland, in the southern part of the republic. Population, 330,000. **2.** The county seat of this county, in the south at the mouth of the Lee River. Population, 78,000.

cork·age (kôr′kĭj) *n.* A charge exacted at a restaurant for every bottle of liquor served that was not bought on the premises.

cork·board (kôrk′bôrd′) *n.* A construction and insulating sheet material made of compressed and baked granules of cork.

cork cambium. *Botany.* A type of plant tissue, **phellogen** *(see).*

corked (kôrkt) *adj.* **1.** Sealed with a cork. **2.** Designating the flavor of wine or spirits that have been tainted by an unsound cork: *corked port.* **3.** Blackened by burnt cork.

cork·er (kôr′kər) *n.* **1.** One that corks. **2.** *Slang.* Someone or something that is remarkable or astounding. **3.** *Slang.* An unanswerable fact or argument.

Cork Harbor (kôrk). An inlet of the Atlantic Ocean on the southeastern coast of County Cork, Republic of Ireland.

cork·ing (kôr′kĭng) *adj. Slang.* Excellent; splendid; fine. [From CORK (verb), probably influenced in meaning by CORKER.]

cork oak. An evergreen oak tree, *Quercus suber,* of the Mediterranean region, having porous outer bark that is the source of cork. Also called "cork tree."

cork·screw (kôrk′skro͞o′) *n.* A device for drawing corks from bottles, consisting of a pointed metal spiral attached to a handle. —*adj.* Resembling a corkscrew in shape; spiral; helical. —*v.* **corkscrewed, -screwing, -screws.** —*tr.* To cause to move in a spiral or winding course. —*intr.* To move spirally; take a winding course.

cork·wood (kôrk′wo͝od′) *n.* **1.** A small tree or shrub, *Leitneria floridiana,* of the southeastern United States, having very light wood. **2.** Any of several other trees having light, porous wood. **3.** The wood of any of these trees or shrubs.

cork·y (kôr′kē) *adj.* **-ier, -iest.** **1.** Of or like cork. **2.** *Informal.* Lively; buoyant. **3.** Tasting of cork; corked. —**cork′i·ness** *n.*

corm (kôrm) *n. Botany.* An underground stem, such as that of the gladiolus, similar to a bulb but without scales. [New Latin *cormus,* from Greek *kormos,* a trimmed tree trunk, from *keirein,* to shear. See **sker-**[1] in Appendix.*]

cor·mel (kôr′məl) *n. Botany.* A young corm that arises at the base of a fully developed corm.

cor·mo·phyte (kôr′mə-fīt′) *n.* Any of a former botanical division, Cormophyta, consisting of plants having roots, stems, and foliage. [New Latin *Cormophyta* : Greek *kormos,* tree trunk (see **corm**) + -PHYTE.] —**cor′mo·phyt′ic** (-fĭt′ĭk) *adj.*

cor·mo·rant (kôr′mər-ənt) *n.* **1.** Any of several widely distributed aquatic birds of the genus *Phalacrocorax,* having dark plumage, webbed feet, a hooked bill, and a distensible pouch. Also called "shag." **2.** A greedy or rapacious person. —*adj.* Greedy; gluttonous; rapacious. [Middle English *cormeraunt,* from Old French *cormoran, cormaran, cormareng* : *corp,* raven, from Latin *corvus* (see **ker-**[2] in Appendix*) + *marenc,* of the sea, from Latin *marīnus,* MARINE.]

corn[1] (kôrn) *n.* **1. a.** Any of several varieties of a tall, widely cultivated cereal plant, *Zea mays,* bearing seeds or kernels on large ears. **b.** The seeds or kernels of this plant, used for food or fodder, and yielding an edible oil. **c.** The ears of this plant. Also called "Indian corn," "maize." **2.** *British.* **a.** Any of several cereal plants producing edible seed, such as wheat, rye, oats, or barley. **b.** The seeds of such a plant or crop; grain. **3. a.** A single seed of a cereal plant; a grain. **b.** A seed or fruit of various other plants. **4.** *Informal.* Corn whiskey. **5.** *Slang.* Anything considered trite, dated, melodramatic, or unduly sentimental. —*tr.v.* **corned, corning, corns.** **1.** To granulate or form into small grains. **2. a.** To preserve and season with granulated salt. **b.** To preserve in brine: *corned beef.* **3.** To feed (animals) with corn or grain. [Middle English *corn,* Old English *corn.* See **gr̥ə-no-** in Appendix.*]

corn[2] (kôrn) *n.* A horny thickening of the skin, usually on or near a toe, resulting from pressure or friction. [Middle English *corne,* from Old French *corne,* corn on the foot, horn, from Latin *cornū,* horn. See **ker-**[1] in Appendix.*]

Corn. Cornwall.

corn·ball (kôrn′bôl′, kōrn′-) *n. Slang.* One who behaves in a mawkish or unsophisticated manner. [Probably CORN (something trite) + (SCREW)BALL.] —**corn′ball′** *adj.*

Corn Belt. A region in the midwestern United States where the chief products are corn and corn-fed livestock.

ă pat/ā pay/âr care/ä father/b bib/ch church/d deed/ĕ pet/ē be/f fife/g gag/h hat/hw which/ĭ pit/ī pie/îr pier/j judge/k kick/l lid, needle/m mum/n no, sudden/ng thing/ŏ pot/ō toe/ô paw, for/oi noise/ou out/o͝o took/o͞o boot/p pop/r roar/s sauce/sh ship, dish/

corn borer. 1. The larva of a moth, *Pyrausta nubilalis,* native to the Old World, that feeds on and destroys corn and other plants. **2.** Any of various similar insect larvae that infest corn.
corn bread. Also **corn·bread** (kôrn′brĕd′). A kind of bread made from cornmeal.
corn·cake (kôrn′kāk′) *n.* Also **corn cake.** A bread made with white cornmeal cooked either as small cakes on a griddle or oven-baked in a pan. Also called "johnnycake."
corn·cob (kôrn′kŏb′) *n.* **1.** The woody core of an ear of corn, on which the kernels grow. **2.** A corncob pipe.
corncob pipe. A pipe with a bowl made of a dried corncob.
corn cockle. A plant, *Agrostemma githago,* native to Europe, having red flowers and growing in fields and by roadsides.
corn·crake (kôrn′krāk′) *n.* A common Old World bird, *Crex crex,* having brownish plumage and frequenting grain fields and meadows.
corn·crib (kôrn′krĭb′) *n.* A structure for storing and drying ears of corn, with slatted sides for ventilation.
corn·dodg·er (kôrn′dŏj′ər) *n.* A corncake either baked, pan-fried, or broiled. [CORN + DODGER.]
cor·ne·a (kôr′nē-ə) *n.* The transparent anterior portion of the outer fibrous tunic of the eye, a uniformly thick, nearly circular, convex structure covering the lens. [Medieval Latin *cornea (tēla),* "horny (tissue)," from Latin, feminine of *corneus,* horny, from *cornū,* horn. See **ker-**[1] in Appendix.*] —**cor′ne·al** *adj.*
corn earworm. The large, destructive larva of a moth, *Heliothis armigera,* that feeds on corn and many other plants. Also called "bollworm."
Cor·neille (kôr-nā′y′), **Pierre.** 1606–1684. French dramatist.
cor·nel (kôr′nəl) *n.* Any of various shrubs, trees, or plants of the genus *Cornus,* which includes the dogwoods; especially, the **dwarf cornel** *(see).* [From German *Kornel(beere), Kornel(baum),* cornel (berry), cornel (tree), from Old High German *kornul-,* from Medieval Latin *corna* (unattested), from Latin *cornus*†, cornel tree.]
cor·nel·ian. Variant of **carnelian.**
cor·nel·ian cherry (kôr-nĕl′yən). A shrub or small tree, *Cornus mas,* native to Eurasia, having very small yellow flowers and bright-red fruit. [From CORNEL.]
cor·ne·ous (kôr′nē-əs) *adj.* Made of horn or a hornlike substance; horny. [Latin *corneus,* from *cornū,* horn. See **ker-**[1] in Appendix.*]
cor·ner (kôr′nər) *n. Abbr.* **cor. 1.** The position at which two lines or surfaces meet. **2.** The immediate interior or exterior region of the angle formed at this position, bounded by the two lines or surfaces. **3.** A vertex, especially the interior region of a vertex, formed by the sides of roads or streets that join, meet, or intersect. **4.** A threatening or embarrassing position, especially one from which escape is difficult or impossible. **5.** Any part, quarter, or region: *the four corners of the earth.* **6.** A remote, secluded, or secret place, area, or part. **7.** A guard or decoration fitted on various kinds of corners, as of a bookbinding. **8.** *Economics.* A speculative monopoly of a stock or commodity, created by purchasing all or most of the available supply, in order to raise its price. —See Synonyms at **monopoly.** —**cut corners.** *Informal.* **1.** To take the shortest route around obstacles, often dangerously or illegally. **2.** To reduce expenses or expenditures; economize. —*v.* **cornered, -nering, -ners.** —*tr.* **1.** To furnish with corners. **2.** To place or drive into a corner. **3.** To form a corner in (a stock or commodity). —*intr.* **1.** To form a corner in a stock or commodity. **2.** To come together or be situated on or at a corner. **3.** To turn, as at a corner. —*adj.* **1.** On or at a corner. **2.** Designed for or used in a corner. [Middle English, from Old French *cornere, corniere,* from Vulgar Latin *cornārium* (unattested), from Latin *cornū,* horn, extremity. See **ker-**[1] in Appendix.*]
cor·ner·back (kôr′nər-băk′) *n.* Also **corner back.** *Football.* Either of two defensive halfbacks stationed a short distance behind the linebackers and relatively near the sidelines.
cor·ner·stone (kôr′nər-stōn′) *n.* Also **corner stone. 1.** A stone at the corner of a building uniting two intersecting walls; quoin. **2.** Such a stone ceremoniously laid and hollowed to contain historical documents or objects, and often inscribed. **3.** The indispensable and fundamental basis of something.
cor·ner·wise (kôr′nər-wīz′) *adv.* Also **cor·ner·ways** (-wāz′). **1.** With a corner toward the front. **2.** So as to form a corner. **3.** From corner to corner; on a diagonal.
cor·net (kôr-nĕt′ *for sense 1;* kôr′nĭt *for senses 2, 3, 4, 5*) *n.* **1.** *Abbr.* **cor.** A musical wind instrument of the trumpet class, having three valves operated by pistons. **2.** A piece of paper twisted into a cone and used to hold small wares such as candy or nuts. **3.** The large white headdress worn by a Sister of Charity. **4.** A headdress, often cone-shaped, worn by women in the 12th and 13th centuries. **5. a.** Formerly, the fifth commissioned officer in a British cavalry troop. **b.** The standard carried by such an officer. [Middle English, from Old French, diminutive of *corn,* horn, from Latin *cornū.* See **ker-**[1] in Appendix.*]
cor·net-à-pis·tons (kôr-nĕt′ə-pĭs′tənz; *French* kôr-nā′ä-pē-stôN′) *n., pl.* **cornets-à-pistons** (kôr-nĕts′ə-pĭs′tənz; *French* kôr-nā′zä-pē-stôN′). A musical instrument, the cornet. [French, "cornet with valves."]
cor·net·cy (kôr′nĭt-sē) *n., pl.* **-cies.** Formerly, the rank or commission of a cornet cavalry officer.
cor·net·ist (kôr-nĕt′ĭst) *n.* Also **cor·net·tist.** One who plays a cornet.
corn-fed (kôrn′fĕd′) *adj.* **1.** Fed on corn. **2.** *Slang.* Healthy and strong, but provincial and unsophisticated.
corn flakes. A crisp, flaky commercially prepared cold cereal made from coarse cornmeal.
corn·flow·er (kôrn′flou′ər) *n.* A garden plant, *Centaurea cyanus,* native to Eurasia, having blue, purple, pink, or white flowers. Also called "bachelor's-button," "bluebottle." [So called because it is found in cornfields.]
corn·husk (kôrn′hŭsk′) *n.* The leafy husk surrounding an ear of corn. Also called "corn shuck."
Corn·husk·er State (kôrn′hŭs′kər). The nickname for Nebraska.
corn·husk·ing (kôrn′hŭs′kĭng) *n.* **1.** The husking of corn. **2.** A social gathering for husking corn. Also called "husking bee." —**corn′husk′er** *n.*
cor·nice (kôr′nĭs) *n.* **1.** *Architecture.* **a.** A horizontal molded projection that crowns or completes a building or wall. **b.** The uppermost part of an entablature. **2.** The molding at the top of the walls of a room, between the walls and ceiling. **3.** Any ornamental horizontal molding or frame used to conceal curtain rods, picture hooks, or the like. —*tr.v.* **corniced, -nicing, -nices.** To supply, decorate, or finish with, or as with, a cornice. [Old French, from Italian, probably from Greek *korōnis,* curved line, flourish with a pen, *korōnē,* anything curved, from *korōnos,* curved. See **sker-**[3] in Appendix.*]
cor·nic·u·late (kôr-nĭk′yə-lāt′, -lĭt) *adj.* Having horns or hornlike projections. [Latin *corniculātus,* from *corniculum,* little horn, diminutive of *cornū,* horn. See **ker-**[1] in Appendix.*]
Cor·ning (kôr′nĭng). A city of New York State, noted for its glass-manufacturing industry, situated in the south, 14 miles northwest of Elmira. Population, 17,000.
Cor·nish (kôr′nĭsh) *adj.* Of or pertaining to Cornwall, England, Cornishmen, or Cornish. —*n.* The Brythonic Celtic language formerly spoken in Cornwall. —**Cor′nish·man** *n.*
Cornish hen. See **Rock Cornish hen.**
Corn Laws. A series of British laws in force before 1846 regulating the grain trade and restricting imports of grain.
corn lily. Any of several bulbous plants of the genus *Ixia,* native to southern Africa, having variously colored lilylike flowers.
corn marigold. A Eurasian plant, *Chrysanthemum segetum,* cultivated for its yellow or white flowers.
corn·meal (kôrn′mēl′) *n.* Also **corn meal. 1.** Meal made from corn. Also called "Indian meal." **2.** *Scottish.* Oatmeal. —**corn′meal′** *adj.*
corn mint. A widely distributed aromatic plant, *Mentha arvensis,* having small white or bluish flowers. Also called "field mint."
Cor·no, Mount (kôr′nō). The highest mountain of the Apennines in Italy, rising to 9,560 feet in the central part of the country.
corn pone (pōn). *Southern U.S.* Corn bread made without milk or eggs. Also called "pone."
corn poppy. An Old World plant, *Papaver rhoeas,* having bright-red flowers, frequently a weed in cultivated fields.
corn rose. *British.* Formerly, any of several red-flowered plants growing in grain fields, as the corn poppy or the corn cockle.
corn salad. Any of several plants of the genus *Valerianella;* especially, *V. locusta* (or *V. olitoria*), native to Europe, having small bluish flowers, and leaves used as salad. Also called "lamb's-lettuce." [So called because it is found in cornfields.]
corn shuck. A **cornhusk** *(see).*
corn silk. The styles and stigmas that appear as a silky tuft or tassel at the tip of an ear of corn.
corn snow. Snow that has melted and refrozen into a rough, granular surface.
corn·stalk (kôrn′stôk′) *n.* Also **corn stalk.** A stalk or stem of corn, especially maize.
corn·starch (kôrn′stärch′) *n.* **1.** Starch prepared from corn. **2.** A purified starchy flour used as a thickener in cooking.
corn sugar. A sugar, **dextrose** *(see).*
corn syrup. A syrup prepared from corn, containing glucose combined with dextrin and maltose.
cor·nu (kôr′nyōō) *n., pl.* **-nua** (-nyōō-ə). A protuberance of bone resembling a horn. [Latin *cornū,* horn. See **ker-**[1] in Appendix.*] —**cor′nu·al** *adj.*
cor·nu·co·pi·a (kôr′nə-kō′pē-ə) *n.* **1.** A goat's horn overflowing with fruit, flowers, and corn, signifying prosperity; horn of plenty. **2.** An overflowing store; abundance. **3.** Any cone-shaped receptacle or ornament. [Late Latin *cornūcōpia,* horn of plenty, from Latin *cornū cōpiae* : *cornū,* horn (see **cornu**) + *cōpiae,* genitive of *cōpia,* plenty (see **op-**[1] in Appendix*).] —**cor′nu·co′pi·an, cor′nu·co′pi·ate′** *adj.*
cor·nute (kôr-nōōt′, -nyōōt′) *adj.* Also **cor·nut·ed** (kôr-nōō′tĭd, -nyōō′tĭd). **1.** Horn-shaped. **2.** Having horns or horn-shaped processes. [Latin *cornūtus,* horned, from *cornū,* horn. See **cornu.**]
Corn·wall (kôrn′wôl; *British* kôrn′wəl). *Abbr.* **Corn.** A county of England, occupying 1,357 square miles in the extreme southwest. Population, 342,000. County seat, Truro.
Corn·wal·lis (kôrn-wŏl′ĭs). An island, 2,596 square miles in area, of the Northwest Territories, Canada; one of the Parry Islands in the Arctic Ocean.
Corn·wal·lis (kôrn-wŏl′ĭs), **Charles.** First Marquis Cornwallis. 1738–1805. British general; a commander of British forces during the American Revolution.
corn whiskey. Whiskey distilled from corn.
corn·y (kôr′nē) *adj.* **-ier, -iest.** *Slang.* Trite, dated, melodramatic, or mawkishly sentimental. [From CORN (from the supposedly unsophisticated humor of farmers).]
corol., coroll. corollary.
co·rol·la (kə-rŏl′ə) *n. Botany.* The outer envelope of a flower, consisting of fused or separate petals. Compare **calyx.** [New Latin, from Latin, diminutive of *corōna,* garland, CORONA.]

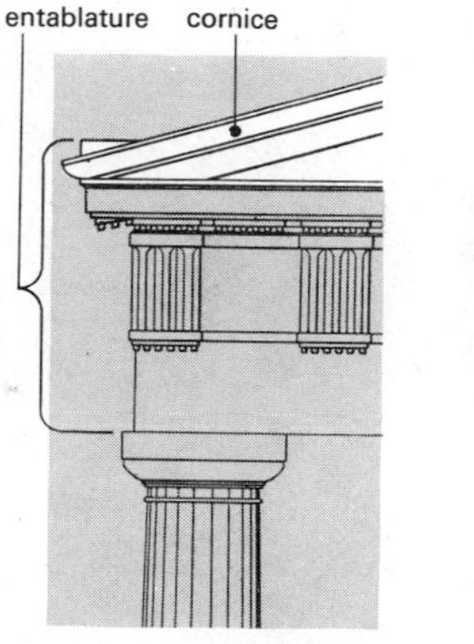

cornice
Detail of cornice on house built in 1810

corolla

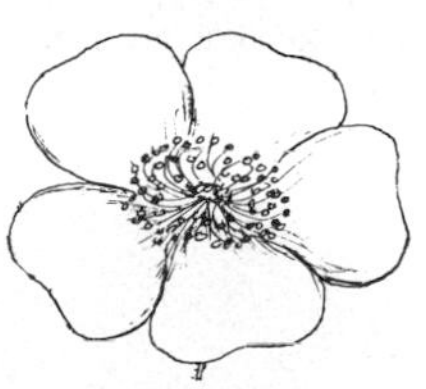

wild rose

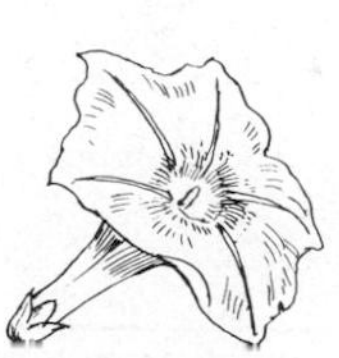

wild potato-vine

cor·ol·lar·y (kôr′ə-lĕr-ē, kŏr′-) *n., pl.* **-ies.** *Abbr.* **corol., coroll.** **1.** A proposition that follows with little or no proof from one already proven. **2.** A deduction or inference. **3.** A natural consequence or effect; a result. —*adj.* Consequent or resultant. [Middle English *corolarie,* from Latin *corollārium,* money paid for a garland, gratuity, a corollary, from *corolla,* small garland, diminutive of *corōna,* garland, CORONA.]

Cor·o·man·del Coast (kôr′ə-măn′dĕl, kŏr′-). The southeastern coast of India, extending north from a point opposite Ceylon to the Kistna River.

co·ro·na (kə-rō′nə) *n., pl.* **-nas** or **-nae** (-nē). **1.** *Astronomy.* **a.** A faintly colored luminous ring around a celestial body visible through a haze or thin cloud, especially such a ring around the moon or sun, caused by diffraction of light from suspended matter in the intervening medium. **b.** The luminous irregular envelope of highly ionized gas outside the chromosphere of the sun. **2.** *Architecture.* The top projecting part of a cornice. **3.** A cigar having a long tapering body and blunt ends. **4.** A circular chandelier hanging from the ceiling of a church. **5.** *Anatomy.* A crownlike or upper part or structure, such as the top of the head. **6.** *Botany.* A crownlike part of a flower, usually between the petals and stamens, but sometimes an appendage of the corolla, as in daffodils. Also called "crown." **7.** *Electricity.* A faint glow enveloping the high-field electrode in a **corona discharge** *(see),* often accompanied by streamers directed toward the low-field electrode. [Latin *corōna,* garland, crown, from Greek *korōnē,* something curved, kind of crown, from *korōnos,* curved. See **sker-**[3] in Appendix.*]

Co·ro·na Aus·tra·lis (kə-rō′nə ôs-trā′lĭs). A constellation in the Southern Hemisphere near Telescopium and Sagittarius. Also called the "Southern Crown."

Corona Bo·re·al·is (bôr′ē-ăl′ĭs, -ā′lĭs, bōr′ē-). A constellation containing the Corona Borealis cluster of galaxies, in the Northern Hemisphere near Hercules and Boötes. Also called the "Northern Crown."

corona discharge. An electrical discharge characterized by a corona and occurring when one of two electrodes in a gas has a shape causing the electric field at its surface to be significantly greater than that between the electrodes.

Co·ro·na·do (kŏr′ä-nä′dō; *Spanish* kō′rō-nä′thō), **Francisco Vásquez de.** 1510–1554. Spanish explorer of the southwestern United States.

co·ro·nal (kə-rō′nəl, kôr′ə-nəl, kŏr′-) *n.* **1.** A garland, wreath, or circlet. **2.** *Anatomy.* The **coronal suture** *(see).* —*adj.* **1.** Of or pertaining to a coronal. **2.** *Anatomy.* Of, designating, or having the direction of the coronal suture. [Middle English, from Old French *coronal,* from Latin *corōnālis,* of a crown, from *corōna,* crown, CORONA.]

coronal suture. The line of union of the two parietal bones with the frontal bone of the skull. Also called "coronal."

cor·o·nar·y (kôr′ə-nĕr-ē, kŏr′-) *adj.* **1.** Encircling, as either of two arteries that originate in the aorta and supply blood directly to the heart tissues. **2.** Of or pertaining to these arteries. **3.** Loosely, of or pertaining to the heart. —*n., pl.* **coronaries.** *Informal.* A **coronary thrombosis** *(see).* [Latin *corōnārius,* of a wreath or garland, from *corōna,* garland, crown, CORONA.]

coronary thrombosis. The occlusion of a coronary artery by a blood clot, often leading to destruction of heart muscle. Also informally called "coronary."

cor·o·na·tion (kôr′ə-nā′shən, kŏr′-) *n.* The act or ceremony of crowning a sovereign or his consort. [Middle English *coronacioun,* from Old French *coronation,* from Medieval Latin *corōnātiō,* from Latin *corōnāre* (past participle *corōnātus*), to crown, from *corōna,* crown, CORONA.]

cor·o·ner (kôr′ə-nər, kŏr′-) *n. Abbr.* **cor.** A public officer whose primary function is to investigate by inquest any death thought to be of other than natural causes. [Middle English, officer charged with maintaining the record of the crown's pleas, from Norman French *corouner,* from Old French *coro(u)ne,* crown, from Latin *corōna,* crown, CORONA.] —**cor′o·ner·ship′** *n.*

coroner's jury. A group of people summoned to attend a coroner's inquest and determine the cause of the death under investigation.

cor·o·net (kôr′ə-nĕt′, -nĭt′, kŏr′-) *n.* **1.** A small crown worn by princes and other nobles below the rank of sovereign. **2.** A chaplet or headband decorated with gold or jewels. **3.** The upper margin of a horse's hoof. [Middle English *coronette,* from Old French, diminutive of *corone,* crown, from Latin *corōna,* crown, CORONA.]

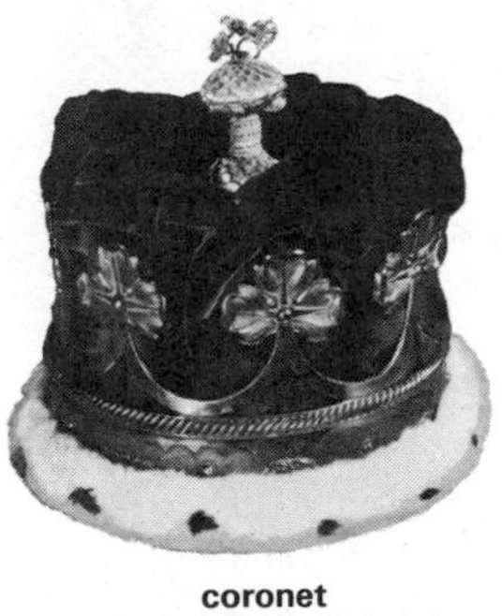

coronet
Coronet of an English duke

Co·rot (kô-rō′), **Jean Baptiste Camille.** 1796–1875. French painter.

corp. corporation.

cor·po·ra. Plural of **corpus.**

cor·po·ral[1] (kôr′pə-rəl) *adj.* Of the body; bodily. [Middle English *corporal, corporel,* from Old French, from Latin *corporālis,* from *corpus* (stem *corpor-*), body. See **krep-** in Appendix.*] —**cor′po·ral′i·ty** (-pə-răl′ə-tē) *n.* —**cor′po·ral·ly** *adv.*

cor·po·ral[2] (kôr′pə-rəl, -prəl) *n. Abbr.* **Cpl.** A noncommissioned officer of the lowest rank in the U.S. Army, Air Force, or Marine Corps. [Obsolete French, variant (probably influenced by *corporal,* bodily, as if meaning "leader of a body of troops") of *caporal.* See **caporal.**]

cor·po·ral[3] (kôr′pə-rəl) *n.* Also **cor·po·ra·le** (kôr′pə-rā′lē). *Ecclesiastical.* A white linen cloth on which the consecrated elements are placed during the celebration of the Eucharist. Also called "corporal cloth." [Middle English *corporale,* from Old French *corporal,* from Medieval Latin *corporāle,* from the neuter of Latin *corporālis,* of the body, CORPORAL (the bread of the Eucharist represents the body of Christ).]

corporal punishment. Physical punishment administered to a convicted offender and including the death penalty.

corporal's guard. **1.** The squad commanded by a corporal. **2.** Any small or barely sufficient number of people.

cor·po·rate (kôr′pə-rĭt) *adj.* **1.** Formed into a corporation; incorporated. **2.** Of a corporation. **3.** United or combined into one body; collective. **4.** Considered as, pertaining to, or shared by a united body. **5.** Variant of **corporative.** [Latin *corporātus,* past participle of *corporāre,* to make into a body, from *corpus* (stem *corpor-*), CORPUS.] —**cor′po·rate·ly** *adv.*

cor·po·ra·tion (kôr′pə-rā′shən) *n. Abbr.* **corp.** **1.** A body of persons granted a charter legally recognizing them as a separate entity having its own rights, privileges, and liabilities distinct from those of its members. Also called "body corporate." **2.** Such a body created for purposes of government. **3.** Any group of people combined into or acting as one body.

cor·po·ra·tive (kôr′pər-ə-tĭv, kôr′pə-rā′tĭv) *adj.* Also **cor·po·rate** (kôr′pə-rĭt). **1.** Of, pertaining to, or associated with a corporation. **2.** Of a government or political system in which the principal economic functions, such as banking, industry, labor, and government, are organized as corporate entities.

cor·po·ra·tor (kôr′pə-rā′tər) *n.* A member of a corporation.

cor·po·re·al (kôr-pôr′ē-əl, -pō′rē-əl) *adj.* **1.** Of, pertaining to, or characteristic of the body. **2.** Of a material nature; tangible. [From Latin *corporeus,* of the body, from *corpus* (stem *corpor-*), CORPUS.] —**cor·po′re·al·ly** *adv.* —**cor·po′re·al·ness** *n.*

cor·po·re·i·ty (kôr′pə-rē′ə-tē) *n.* Also **cor·po·re·al·i·ty** (-rē-ăl′ə-tē). The state of being material or corporeal; physical existence.

cor·po·sant (kôr′pə-zənt) *n.* A luminous electrical phenomenon, **St. Elmo's fire** *(see).* [Portuguese *corpo-santo,* "holy body" : *corpo,* body, from Latin *corpus,* CORPUS + *santo,* holy, from Latin *sanctus,* from the past participle of *sancīre,* to make sacred (see **sak-** in Appendix*).]

corps (kôr, kōr) *n., pl.* **corps** (kôrz, kōrz). **1.** *Abbr.* **c., C.** *Military.* **a.** A separate branch or department of the armed forces having a specialized function. **b.** A tactical unit of ground combat forces between a division and an army commanded by a lieutenant general and composed of two or more divisions and auxiliary service troops. **2.** A body of persons acting together or associated under common direction. [French, from Latin *corpus,* body, CORPUS.]

corps de bal·let (kôr′ də bă-lā′; *French* kôr′ də bȧ-lā′). The dancers in a ballet troupe who perform as a group with no solo parts. [French, "ballet troupe."]

corpse (kôrps) *n.* A dead body, especially of a human being. See Synonyms at **body.** [Middle English *corps, cors,* from Old French, from Latin *corpus,* body, CORPUS.]

corps·man (kôr′mən, kōr′-) *n., pl.* **-men** (-mĭn). *U.S. Navy.* An enlisted man trained as a pharmacist or hospital assistant.

cor·pu·lence (kôr′pyə-ləns) *n.* Fatness; obesity. [Middle English, from Latin *corpulentia,* from *corpulentus,* from *corpus,* body, CORPUS.] —**cor′pu·lent** *adj.* —**cor′pu·lent·ly** *adv.*

cor·pus (kôr′pəs) *n., pl.* **-pora** (-pə-rə). *Abbr.* **cor.** **1.** A human or animal body, especially when dead. **2.** *Anatomy.* A structure constituting the main part of an organ. **3.** The principal or capital, as distinguished from the interest or income, of a fund, estate, investment, or the like. **4.** A large collection of writings of a specific kind or on a specific subject. [Middle English, from Latin, body, substance. See **krep-** in Appendix.*]

corpus cal·lo·sum (kə-lō′səm) *pl.* **corpora callosa** (kə-lō′sə). *Anatomy.* A wide arched band of white matter connecting the cerebral hemispheres at the base of the longitudinal fissure. [New Latin, "callous body."]

Cor·pus Chris·ti[1] (kôr′pəs krĭs′tē, -tī). *Roman Catholic Church.* A festival celebrated in honor of the Eucharist on the first Thursday after Trinity Sunday. [Middle English, from Medieval Latin, "body of Christ" : Latin CORPUS + *Christus,* CHRIST.]

Cor·pus Chris·ti[2] (kôr′pəs krĭs′tē). An industrial city and seaport of southwestern Texas, on the shore of Corpus Christi Bay, an inlet of the Gulf of Mexico. Population, 168,000.

cor·pus·cle (kôr′pəs-əl, -pŭs-əl) *n.* Also **cor·pus·cule** (kôr-pŭs′kyo͞ol). **1.** *Biology.* A cell such as an erythrocyte or leukocyte that is capable of free movement in a fluid or matrix as distinguished from a cell fixed in tissue. **2.** A discrete particle such as a photon or electron. **3.** Any minute globular particle. [Latin *corpusculum,* diminutive of *corpus,* CORPUS.] —**cor·pus′cu·lar** (-kyə-lər) *adj.*

corpus de·lic·ti (dĭl-ĭk′tī). **1.** *Law.* **a.** The material substance upon which a crime has been committed. **b.** The material evidence of the fact that a crime has been committed, such as the discovered corpse of a murder victim. **2.** Loosely, the victim's corpse in a murder case. [New Latin, "body of the crime."]

corpus ju·ris (jo͝or′ĭs). *Abbr.* **C.J.** The collective or comprehensive body of all the laws of a nation or state. [Late Latin, "body of law."]

Corpus Juris Ca·non·i·ci (kə-nŏn′ə-sī′). *Roman Catholic Church.* The body of decrees and canons constituting the standard of ecclesiastical law until replaced in 1918 by Codex Juris Canonici. [Late Latin, "body of canon law."]

Corpus Juris Ci·vi·lis (sĭ-vĭl′ĭs). The body of civil or Roman law comprising the Digest, the Institutes, the Code, and the Novels, assembled and issued (A.D. 528–534) during Justinian's reign and forming the basis of most European law. [Latin, "body of civil law."]

corpus lu·te·um (lo͞o-tē′əm) *pl.* **corpora lutea** (lo͞o′tē-ə). A yellow mass of endocrine cells in a ruptured mature Graafian follicle of the ovary, formed after the release of an ovum. [New Latin, "yellowish body."]

cor·pus stri·a·tum (strī-ā'təm) *pl.* **corpora striata** (strī-ā'tə). Either of two gray-and-white, striated ganglionic masses of the brain stem in the lower lateral wall of each cerebral hemisphere. [New Latin, "striated body."]
corr. **1.** correction. **2.** correspondence; correspondent.
cor·rade (kə-rād') *v.* **-raded, -rading, -rades.** —*tr.* To erode by abrasion with moving objects such as sand and gravel carried in running water, wind, or glaciers. —*intr.* To crumble due to running water. [Latin *corrādere*, to scrape together : *com-*, together + *rādere*, to scrape. See **rēd-** in Appendix.*] —**cor·ra'sion** (kə-rā'zhən) *n.* —**cor·ra'sive** (-sĭv) *adj.*
cor·ral (kə-răl') *n.* **1.** An enclosure for confining livestock. **2.** An enclosure formed by a circle of wagons for defense against attack during an encampment. —*tr.v.* **corralled, -ralling, -rals. 1.** To drive into and hold in a corral. **2.** To arrange (wagons) in a corral. **3.** *Informal.* To seize; capture. [Spanish, probably of Hottentot origin. See also **kraal.**]
cor·rect (kə-rĕkt') *tr.v.* **-rected, -recting, -rects. 1.** To remove the errors or mistakes from. **2.** To indicate or mark the errors in. **3.** To admonish or punish for the purpose of improving: *She corrected him for his rudeness.* **4.** To remove, remedy, or counteract (a malfunction, for example). **5.** To adjust so as to meet a standard or other required condition. —*adj.* **1.** Free from error or fault; true or accurate. **2.** Conforming to standards; proper: *correct behavior.* [Middle English *correcten*, from Latin *corrigere* (past participle *correctus*), to make straight, correct : *com-* (intensifier), with + *regere*, to lead straight, rule (see **reg-**¹ in Appendix*).] —**cor·rect'a·ble, cor·rect'i·ble** *adj.* —**cor·rect'ly** *adv.* —**cor·rect'ness** *n.*
Synonyms: *correct, rectify, remedy, redress, reform, revise, amend.* These verbs mean to make right or to improve. *Correct* can apply broadly to any such act but usually refers to eliminating error or defect. *Rectify* stresses the idea of bringing something into conformity with a standard of what is right. *Remedy* involves repairing or removing something considered a cause of harm or damage. *Redress* usually refers to setting right something considered morally or ethically wrong and involves making reparation to the wronged person. *Reform* implies broad change that improves character, as of a person or institution. *Revise* suggests change as a result of reconsideration of an earlier course. *Amend* adds to revision a more definite implication of improvement through alteration or addition.
cor·rec·tion (kə-rĕk'shən) *n. Abbr.* **cor., corr. 1.** The act or process of correcting. **2.** That which is offered or substituted for a mistake, fault, or abnormality; an improvement. **3.** Punishment. **4.** An amount or quantity that is added or subtracted in making exact or accurate. —**cor·rec'tion·al** *adj.*
cor·rec·ti·tude (kə-rĕk'tə-to͞od, -tyo͞od) *n.* The state or quality of being correct, especially in manners and behavior; propriety.
cor·rec·tive (kə-rĕk'tĭv) *adj.* Tending or intended to correct. —*n.* Something that corrects. —**cor·rec'tive·ly** *adv.*
cor·rec·tor (kə-rĕk'tər) *n.* One that corrects.
Cor·reg·gio (kō-rĕd'jō), **Antonio Allegri da.** 1494–1534. Italian painter; founder of the school of Parma.
Cor·reg·i·dor (kə-rĕg'ə-dôr). An island of the Republic of the Philippines, at the entrance to Manila Bay; the site of a World War II battle (April 9–May 6, 1942) following which the Philippines were surrendered to the Japanese.
correl. correlative.
cor·re·late (kôr'ə-lāt', kŏr'-) *v.* **-lated, -lating, -lates.** Also *chiefly British* **co·re·late.** —*tr.* **1.** To put or bring into causal, complementary, parallel, or reciprocal relation. **2.** To establish or demonstrate as having a correlation. —*intr.* To be related by a correlation. —*adj.* Related by a correlation; especially, having corresponding characteristics. —*n.* Either of two correlate entities; a correlative. [Back-formation from CORRELATION.]
cor·re·la·tion (kôr'ə-lā'shən, kŏr'-) *n.* **1.** A causal, complementary, parallel, or reciprocal relationship, especially a structural, functional, or qualitative correspondence between two comparable entities. **2.** *Statistics.* **a.** The simultaneous increase or decrease in value of two numerically valued random variables. Also called "positive correlation." **b.** The simultaneous increase in the value of one and decrease in the value of the other of two numerically valued random variables. Also called "negative correlation." **3.** The act of correlating or the condition of being correlated. [Medieval Latin *correlātiō* : *com-*, together + *relātiō*, relation, from Latin *relātus*, "carried back" (see **relate**).] —**cor're·la'tion·al** *adj.*
correlation coefficient. *Statistics.* A measure of the interdependence of two random variables that ranges in value from −1 to +1, indicating perfect negative correlation at −1, absence of correlation at 0, and perfect positive correlation at +1.
cor·rel·a·tive (kə-rĕl'ə-tĭv) *adj. Abbr.* **correl. 1.** Related; corresponding. **2.** Reciprocally related. —*n. Abbr.* **correl. 1.** Either of two correlative entities; a correlate. **2.** *Grammar.* A correlative word or expression. —**cor·rel'a·tive·ly** *adv.* —**cor·rel'a·tive·ness, cor·rel'a·tiv'i·ty** *n.*
correlative conjunction. A conjunction indicating a reciprocal or complementary grammatical relation. *Neither* and *nor* are correlative conjunctions.
cor·re·spond (kôr'ə-spŏnd', kŏr'-) *intr.v.* **-sponded, -sponding, -sponds. 1.** To be in agreement, harmony, or conformity; be consistent or compatible. **2.** To be similar, parallel, equivalent, or equal in character, quantity, origin, structure, or function. Used with *to: English "navel" corresponds to Greek "omphalos."* **3.** To communicate by letter, usually over a period of time. —See Synonyms at **agree.** [Old French *correspondre*, from Medieval Latin *correspondēre* : *com-*, together, mutually + *respondēre*, RESPOND.]
cor·re·spon·dence (kôr'ə-spŏn'dəns, kŏr'-) *n.* Also **cor·re·spon·den·cy** (-dən-sē) *pl.* **-cies.** *Abbr.* **cor., corr., corresp. 1.** The act, fact, or state of agreeing or conforming. **2.** Similarity or analogy. **3. a.** Communication by the exchange of letters. **b.** The letters written or received.
correspondence principle. *Physics.* The principle that predictions of quantum theory approach those of classical physics in the limit of large quantum numbers.
correspondence school. A school that offers instruction by mail, sending lessons and examinations to a student.
cor·re·spon·dent (kôr'ə-spŏn'dənt, kŏr'-) *n. Abbr.* **cor., corr. 1.** One who communicates by means of letters. **2.** Someone employed by a newspaper or magazine to supply news or articles from a distant place. **3.** A person who writes letters to a newspaper or magazine. **4.** A person or firm having regular business relations with another, especially at a distance. **5.** A thing that corresponds; a correlative. —*adj.* Corresponding; consistent. —**cor're·spon'dent·ly** *adv.*
correspondent banking. A system of banking under which large banks perform various services for smaller banks in return for balances that the small banks keep with them.
cor·re·spond·ing (kôr'ə-spŏn'dĭng, kŏr'-) *adj. Abbr.* **cor. 1.** Agreeing or conforming; consistent. **2.** Analogous or equivalent. —**cor're·spond'ing·ly** *adv.*
cor·re·spon·sive (kôr'ə-spŏn'sĭv, kŏr'-) *adj.* Corresponding. —**cor're·spon'sive·ly** *adv.*
cor·ri·da (kô-rē'də) *n.* A bullfight. [Spanish, "a running," from the feminine past participle of *correr*, to run, from Latin *currere.* See **corridor.**]
cor·ri·dor (kôr'ĭ-dər, -dôr, kŏr'-) *n.* **1.** A narrow hallway, passageway, or gallery, generally with rooms or apartments opening onto it. **2.** A tract of land forming a passageway, such as that which allows an inland country access to the sea through another country. [Old French, from Old Italian *corridore*, "a run," from *correre*, to run, from Latin *currere.* See **kers-**² in Appendix.*]
cor·rie (kôr'ē, kŏr'ē) *n. Scottish.* A round hollow in a hillside; cirque. [Scottish Gaelic *coire*, cauldron, hollow, whirlpool. See **kwer-**² in Appendix.*]
Cor·ri·en·tes (kôr-ryān'tĕs). A city of northeastern Argentina, on the Paraná near Paraguay. Population, 671,000.
cor·ri·gen·dum (kôr'ə-jĕn'dəm, kŏr'-) *n., pl.* **-da** (-də). **1.** An error to be corrected, especially a printer's error. **2.** *Plural.* A list of errors with their corrections, in a book. [Latin, gerundive of *corrigere*, to CORRECT.]
cor·ri·gi·ble (kôr'ə-jə-bəl) *adj.* Capable of being corrected, reformed, or improved. [Middle English, from Old French, from Medieval Latin *corrigibilis*, from Latin *corrigere*, to CORRECT.] —**cor'ri·gi·bil'i·ty** *n.* —**cor'ri·gi·bly** *adv.*
cor·ri·val (kə-rī'vəl) *n.* A rival or opponent. —*adj.* Rival or opposing. [Old French *corrival*, from Latin *corrīvālis*, joint rival : *com-*, together + *rīvālis*, RIVAL.] —**cor·ri'val·ry** *n.*
cor·rob·o·rant (kə-rŏb'ə-rənt) *adj. Archaic.* Corroborating. —*n. Archaic.* Something that corroborates.
cor·rob·o·rate (kə-rŏb'ə-rāt') *tr.v.* **-rated, -rating, -rates.** To strengthen or support (other evidence); attest the truth or accuracy of. See Synonyms at **confirm.** [Latin *corrōborāre* : *com-* (intensifier), with + *rōborāre*, to strengthen, from *rōbur*, hard kind of oak, strength (see **reudh-** in Appendix*).] —**cor·rob'o·ra'tion** *n.* —**cor·rob'o·ra'tor** (-rā'tər) *n.*
cor·rob·o·ra·tive (kə-rŏb'ə-rā'tĭv, -ər-ə-tĭv) *adj.* Also **cor·rob·o·ra·to·ry** (-ər-ə-tôr'ē, -tōr'ē). Confirming or tending to confirm. —**cor·rob'o·ra'tive·ly** *adv.*
cor·rob·o·ree (kə-rŏb'ə-rē) *n. Australian.* **1.** An aboriginal dance festival held at night to celebrate tribal victories or other events. **2.** Any large or noisy celebration. [Native Australian name *korobra.*]
cor·rode (kə-rōd') *v.* **-roded, -roding, -rodes.** —*tr.* **1.** To dissolve or wear away gradually, especially by chemical action. **2.** To impair; consume; deteriorate. —*intr.* To be eaten or worn away; become corroded. [Middle English *corroden*, from Latin *corrōdere*, to gnaw to pieces : *com-* (intensive) + *rōdere*, to gnaw (see **rēd-** in Appendix*).] —**cor·rod'ent** *n.* —**cor·rod'i·ble, cor·ro'si·ble** (kə-rō'sə-bəl) *adj.*
cor·ro·sion (kə-rō'zhən) *n.* **1.** The act or process of dissolving or wearing away, especially of metals. **2.** A substance, such as rust, resulting from such a process. **3.** The condition produced by such a process. [Middle English *corosioun*, from Old French *corrosion*, from Late Latin *corrōsiō*, from Latin *corrōsus*, past participle of *corrōdere*, to CORRODE.]
cor·ro·sive (kə-rō'sĭv) *adj.* **1. a.** Capable of producing corrosion. **b.** Inclined to produce corrosion. **2.** Spiteful, malicious, or malevolent. —*n.* A corrosive substance. —**cor·ro'sive·ly** *adv.* —**cor·ro'sive·ness** *n.*
corrosive sublimate. *Chemistry.* **Mercuric chloride** *(see).*
cor·ru·gate (kôr'ə-gāt', kôr'yə-, kŏr'-) *v.* **-gated, -gating, -gates.** —*tr.* To shape into folds or parallel and alternating ridges and grooves. —*intr.* To become corrugated. [Latin *corrūgāre*, to make full of wrinkles : *com-*, together + *rūgāre*, to wrinkle, from *rūga*, wrinkle (see **ruk-**² in Appendix*).] —**cor'ru·gate', cor'ru·gat'ed** (-gā'tĭd) *adj.*
corrugated iron. A structural sheet iron, usually galvanized, shaped in parallel furrows and ridges for rigidity.
cor·ru·ga·tion (kôr'ə-gā'shən, kôr'yə-, kŏr'-) *n.* **1.** The act of corrugating. **2.** The state or process of being corrugated. **3.** A groove or ridge on a corrugated surface.
cor·rupt (kə-rŭpt') *adj.* **1.** Immoral; perverted; depraved. **2.** Marked by venality and dishonesty. **3.** Decaying; putrid. **4.** Impure; contaminated; unclean. **5.** Containing errors or al-

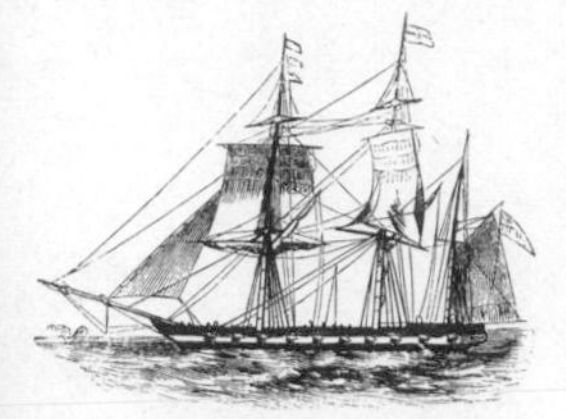

corvette
Early 19th-century
20-gun corvette

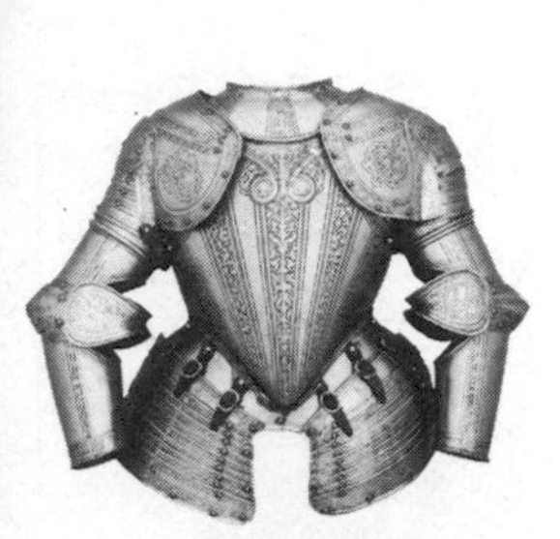

corselet
Sixteenth-century
Italian

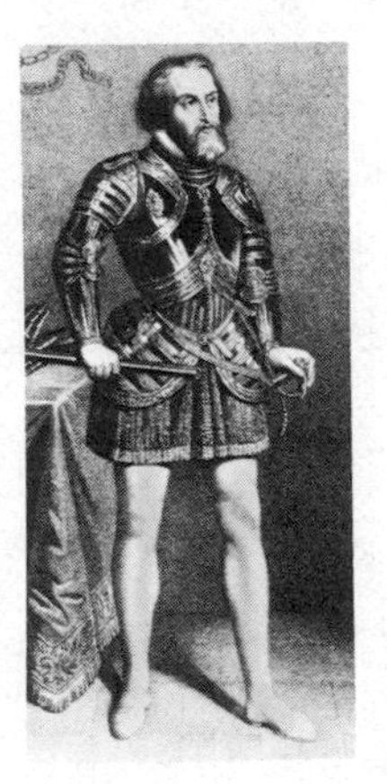

Hernando Cortés

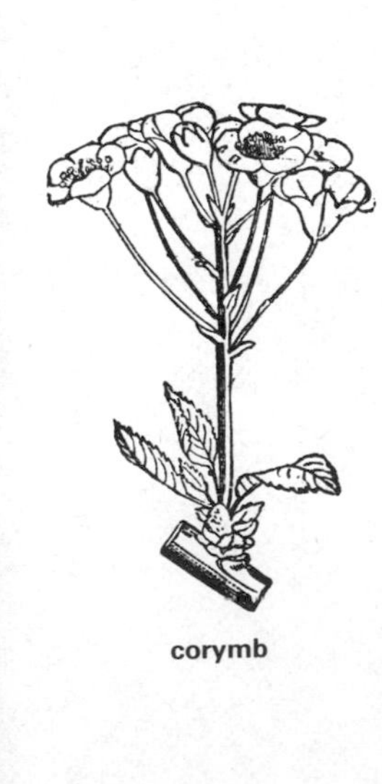

corymb

terations, as a text; debased. —*v.* **corrupted, -rupting, -rupts.** —*tr.* **1.** To destroy or subvert the honesty or integrity of. **2.** To ruin morally; to pervert. **3.** To taint; contaminate; infect. **4.** To cause to become rotten; spoil. **5.** To change the original form of (a text, language, or the like). —*intr.* To become corrupt. [Middle English, from Old French, from Latin *corruptus,* past participle of *corrumpere,* break to pieces, destroy, ruin : *com-,* completely + *rumpere,* to break (see **reup-** in Appendix*).] —**cor·rup′ter, cor·rup′tor** (-rŭp′tər) *n.* —**cor·rup′tive** *adj.* —**cor·rupt′ly** *adv.* —**cor·rupt′ness** *n.*

cor·rupt·i·ble (kə-rŭpt′ə-bəl) *adj.* Able to be corrupted, as by bribery, depravity, or decay. —**cor·rupt′i·bil′i·ty, cor·rupt′i·ble·ness** *n.* —**cor·rupt′i·bly** *adv.*

cor·rup·tion (kə-rŭp′shən) *n.* **1.** The act or result of corrupting. **2.** The state of being corrupt. **3.** Anything that corrupts.

cor·rup·tion·ist (kə-rŭp′shən-ĭst) *n.* One who defends or practices corruption.

cor·sage (kôr-säzh′) *n.* **1.** A small bouquet of flowers worn by a woman at the shoulder, waist, or on the wrist. **2.** The bodice or waist of a dress. [Old French, torso, bust, from *cors, corps,* body, from Latin *corpus,* CORPUS.]

cor·sair (kôr′sâr) *n.* **1.** A privateer, especially along the Barbary Coast. **2.** A swift pirate ship, often operating with official sanction. **3.** A pirate. [Old French *corsaire,* pirate, from Old Provençal *corsari,* from Old Italian *corsaro,* from Medieval Latin *cursārius,* from *cursus,* plunder, from Latin, "a run," course, from the past participle of *currere,* to run. See **corridor.**]

corse (kôrs) *n. Archaic.* Corpse. [Middle English *cors,* CORPSE.]

corse·let (kôrs′lĭt; kôr-sə-lĕt′ *for sense 2*) *n.* Also **cors·let** (kôrs′lĭt) (for sense 1 only). **1.** Body armor; especially, a breastplate. **2.** A light corset with few or no stays. [Old French *corselet,* diminutive of *cors,* CORPSE.]

cor·set (kôr′sĭt) *n.* **1.** A close-fitting undergarment, often reinforced by stays, worn to support and shape the waistline, hips, and breasts. **2.** A medieval outer garment, particularly a laced jacket or bodice. —*tr.v.* **corseted, -seting, -sets.** To enclose in a corset; fit a corset on. [Middle English, from Old French, diminutive of *cors,* CORPSE.]

cor·se·tière (kôr-sə-tyâr′) *n. Masculine* **corsetier** (kôr-sə-tyā′). A maker, fitter, or seller of corsets. [French, from CORSET.]

Cor·si·ca (kôr′sĭ-kə). *French* **Corse** (kôrs). An island of France, 3,367 square miles in area, in the Mediterranean north of the island of Sardinia. Population, 275,000. Capital, Ajaccio. —**Cor′si·can** *adj.* & *n.*

cor·tege (kôr-tĕzh′, -tāzh′) *n.* Also **cor·tège.** **1.** A train of attendants; retinue, as of a distinguished person. **2. a.** A ceremonial procession. **b.** A funeral procession. [French *cortège,* from Italian *corteggio,* from *corteggiare,* to pay honor, to court, from *corte,* court, from Latin *cohors* (stem *cohort-*), enclosure, court. See **gher-²** in Appendix.*]

Cor·tés (kôr-tĕz′; *Spanish* kôr-tās′), **Hernando.** Also **Cor·tez.** Spanish, Hernán Cortés. 1485–1547. Spanish explorer, conqueror of Aztecs, and colonial administrator of New Spain.

cor·tex (kôr′tĕks) *n., pl.* **-tices** (-tə-sēz′) or **-texes.** **1.** *Anatomy.* **a.** The outer layer of an organ or part, as of the kidney, cerebrum, or cerebellum. **b.** The firm outer layer that comprises most of the adrenal gland. **2.** *Botany.* **a.** A layer of tissue in roots and stems lying between the epidermis and the vascular tissue. **b.** An external layer such as bark or rind. [Latin, bark, shell, rind. See **sker-¹** in Appendix.*]

cor·ti·cal (kôr′tĭ-kəl) *adj.* **1.** Of, pertaining to, or consisting of cortex. **2.** Of, pertaining to, associated with, or depending on the cerebral cortex. [New Latin *corticalis,* from Latin *cortex* (stem *cortic-*), bark, shell, CORTEX.] —**cor′ti·cal·ly** *adv.*

cor·ti·cate (kôr′tĭ-kĭt, -kāt) *adj.* Also **cor·ti·cat·ed** (-kāt′ĭd). Having a cortex or similar specialized outer layer. [Latin *corticātus,* covered with bark, from *cortex* (stem *cortic-*), bark, CORTEX.]

cortico-, cortic-. Indicates cortex; for example, **corticotropin, corticoid.** [From Latin *cortex* (stem *cortic-*), CORTEX.]

cor·ti·coid (kôr′tĭ-koid′) *n. Biochemistry.* Any of the steroids of the adrenal cortex. Also called "corticosteroid." [CORTIC(O)- + -OID.]

cor·tic·o·lous (kôr-tĭk′ə-ləs) *adj. Biology.* Growing or living on tree bark: *corticolous mosses.* [From French *corticicole* : CORTI(CO)- + -COLOUS.]

cor·ti·cos·ter·one (kôr′tĭ-kŏs′tə-rōn′) *n.* A corticoid, $C_{21}H_{30}O_4$, that induces hyperglycemia and deposition of glycogen in the liver. [CORTICO- + STER(OL) + -ONE.]

cor·ti·co·tro·pin (kôr′tĭ-kō′trŏp′ən, -trōp′ən) *n.* Also **cor·ti·co·tro·phin** (-trŏf′ən, -trōf′ən). An anterior pituitary hormone, **ACTH** *(see).* [CORTICO- + -TROP(IC) + -IN.]

cor·tin (kôr′tən) *n.* An adrenal cortex extract that contains several hormones and is used in medicine. [CORT(EX) + -IN.]

cor·ti·sone (kôr′tə-sōn, -zōn) *n.* A corticoid, $C_{21}H_{28}O_5$, active in carbohydrate metabolism and used to treat rheumatoid arthritis, adrenal insufficiency, certain allergies, diseases of connective tissue, and gout. [Short for CORTICOSTERONE.]

Co·ru·ña, La. See **La Coruña.**

co·run·dum (kə-rŭn′dəm) *n.* An extremely hard mineral, aluminum oxide, sometimes containing iron, magnesia, or silica, occurring in gem varieties such as ruby and sapphire and in a common gray, brown, or blue form used chiefly in abrasives. [Tamil *kuruntam,* probably ultimately from Sanskrit *kuruvinda*†, ruby.]

co·rus·cant (kə-rŭs′kənt) *adj* Glittering. [Latin *coruscāns,* present participle of *coruscāre,* CORUSCATE.]

cor·us·cate (kôr′əs-kāt′, kŏr′-) *intr.v.* **-cated, -cating, -cates.** To give forth flashes of light; to sparkle; glitter; scintillate. [Latin *coruscāre,* to thrust, vibrate, glitter. See **sker-²** in Appendix.*] —**cor′us·ca′tion** *n.*

cor·vée (kôr-vā′) *n.* **1.** A day of unpaid work required of a vassal by his feudal lord. **2.** Labor exacted by a local authority for little or no pay, or instead of taxes, and used especially in the maintenance of roads. [Middle English *corve,* from Old French, from Late Latin *(opera) corrogāta,* "(works) collected," feminine past participle of Latin *corrogāre,* to summon together, collect : *com-,* together + *rogāre,* to ask (see **reg-¹** in Appendix*).]

corves. Plural of **corf.**

cor·vette (kôr-vĕt′) *n.* Also **cor·vet** (kôr-vĕt′, kôr′vĕt). **1.** A fast, lightly armed warship, smaller than a destroyer. **2.** Formerly, a warship, smaller than a frigate, usually armed with one tier of guns. [French, from Old French, probably from Middle Dutch *corf,* basket, kind of small ship, CORF.]

cor·vi·na. Variant of **corbina.**

cor·vine (kôr′vīn′, -vĭn) *adj.* Of, resembling, or characteristic of crows, ravens, or related birds. [Latin *corvīnus,* from *corvus,* raven. See **ker-²** in Appendix.*]

Cor·vus (kôr′vəs) *n.* A constellation in the Southern Hemisphere near Crater and Virgo. [New Latin, from Latin, raven. See **ker-²** in Appendix.*]

Cor·y·ate (kôr′ē-ĭt), **Thomas.** Also **Cor·y·at.** 1577?–1617. English traveler and court jester.

Cor·y·bant (kôr′ə-bănt, kŏr′-) *pl.* **-bants** or **Corybantes** (kôr′ə-băn′tēz′, kŏr′-). *Greek Mythology.* A priest of the ancient Phrygian goddess Cybele whose rites were celebrated with music and ecstatic dances. [Latin *Corybas* (stem *Corybant-*), from Greek *Korubas,* probably of Phrygian origin.] —**Cor′y·ban′tian** (-băn′tē-ən), **Cor′y·ban′tic** *adj.*

co·ryd·a·lis (kə-rĭd′ə-lĭs) *n.* Any of various plants of the genus *Corydalis,* having finely lobed leaves and spurred yellow or pinkish flowers. [New Latin, from Greek *korudallis,* crested lark (from the shape of the flowers), variant of *korudos.* See **ker-¹** in Appendix.*]

Cor·y·don (kôr′ə-dən, kŏr′-, -dŏn′) *n.* A conventional name for a shepherd in many pastoral poems. [Latin, from Greek *korudōn*†, proper name.]

cor·ymb (kôr′ĭmb, -ĭm, kŏr′-) *n. Botany.* A flat-topped flower cluster in which the individual stalks grow upward from various points of the main stem to approximately the same height. [French *corymbe,* from Latin *corymbus,* cluster, from Greek *korumbos,* uppermost point, cluster of fruits or flowers. See **ker-¹** in Appendix.*] —**co·rym′bose** (kə-rĭm′bōs), **co·rym′bous** (-bəs) *adj.* —**co·rym′bose·ly** *adv.*

cor·y·phae·us (kôr′ə-fē′əs) *n., pl.* **-phaei** (-fē′ī′). **1.** The leader of the chorus in ancient Greek drama. **2.** Any leader or spokesman. [Latin *coryphaeus,* leader, chief, from Greek *koruphaios,* leader, leader of the chorus, from *koruphē,* head, top. See **ker-¹** in Appendix.*]

cor·y·phée (kôr′ə-fā′) *n.* A ballet dancer ranking above the corps de ballet and below the soloists. [French, from Latin *coryphaeus,* leader, CORYPHAEUS.]

co·ry·za (kə-rī′zə) *n.* An acute inflammation of the nasal mucous membrane marked by discharge of mucus, sneezing, and watering of the eyes. Often called "common cold," "head cold." [Late Latin *corȳza,* from Greek *koruza*†, catarrh.]

cos (kôs, kŏs) *n.* A type of lettuce, **romaine** *(see).* [Originally exported from the island of *Cos,* KOS.]

cos cosine.

COS **1.** cash on shipment. **2.** Airport code for Colorado Springs, Colorado.

Cos. The Latin name for **Kos.**

C.O.S. cash on shipment.

Co·sa Nos·tra (kō′sə nōs′trə). A crime syndicate active throughout the United States, hierarchic in structure and comprising locally independent units known as families, the leaders of which make up a supreme commission; it is often believed to have an important relationship with the Sicilian Mafia. [Italian, "our thing," but also rendered "our enterprise," "our property."]

co·se·cant (kō′sē′kənt) *n. Abbr.* **cosec, csc** *Trigonometry.* The **secant** *(see)* of the complement of a directed angle or arc.

co·seis·mal (kō′sĭz′məl, -sīs′məl) *adj.* Also **co·seis·mic** (-mĭk). Pertaining to or designating a line connecting the points on a map that indicate the places simultaneously affected by an earthquake shock. —*n.* A coseismal line. [CO- (together) + SEISM(O)- + -AL.]

Co·sen·za (kō-sĕn′tsä). The capital of Calabria, Italy, about 90 miles northeast of Reggio di Calabria. Population, 79,000.

Cos·grave (kŏz′grāv), **William Thomas.** 1880–1965. Irish political leader; president of Ireland (1922–32).

cosh (kŏsh) *n. British Slang.* **1.** A blackjack. **2.** An attack with a blackjack. —*tr.v.* **coshed, coshing, coshes.** *British Slang.* To bludgeon. [Romany *kosh,* shortened from *koshter*†, stick, skewer.]

cosh hyperbolic cosine.

cosh·er (kŏsh′ər) *tr.v.* **-ered, -ering, -ers.** To coddle; pamper. [Perhaps from Irish *cōisir*†, feast.]

co·sign (kō′sīn′) *tr.v.* **-signed, -signing, -signs.** Also **co-sign.** **1.** To sign (a document) jointly with another or others. **2.** To endorse (a signature), as for a loan or mortgage. —**co′sign′er** *n.*

co·sig·na·to·ry (kō-sĭg′nə-tôr′ē, -tōr′ē) *adj.* Signed jointly with another or others. —*n., pl.* **cosignatories.** One who cosigns.

Co·si·mo, Piero di. See **Piero di Cosimo.**

co·sine (kō′sīn) *n. Abbr.* **cos** **1.** The abscissa of the endpoint of an arc of a unit circle centered at the origin of a Cartesian coordinate system, the arc being of length x and measured counterclockwise from the point (1, 0) if x is positive; or clockwise if x is negative. **2.** In a right triangle, the function of an acute angle that is the ratio of the adjacent side to the hypotenuse. [CO- + SINE.]

cos lettuce. **Romaine** *(see).*

cos·met·ic (kŏz-mĕt′ĭk) *n.* A preparation, such as face powder or skin cream, designed to beautify the body by direct application. —*adj.* Also **cos·met·i·cal** (-ĭ-kəl). Serving to beautify the body. [French *cosmétique,* from adjective, "of adornment," from Greek *kosmētikos,* skilled in arranging, from *kosmētos,* well-ordered, from *kosmein,* to arrange, order, from *kosmos,* order, COSMOS.] —**cos·met′i·cal·ly** *adv.*

cos·me·ti·cian (kŏz′mə-tĭsh′ən) *n.* A person whose occupation is manufacturing, selling, or applying cosmetics.

cos·me·tol·o·gy (kŏz′mə-tŏl′ə-jē) *n.* The study or art of cosmetics and their use. [French *cosmétologie* : *cosmétique,* COSMET(IC) + -LOGY.] —**cos′me·tol′o·gist** *n.*

cos·mic (kŏz′mĭk) *adj.* Also **cos·mi·cal** (-mĭ-kəl). **1.** Of or pertaining to the universe, especially as distinct from the earth or, sometimes, from the solar system. **2.** Infinitely or inconceivably extended in space or time; vast. **3.** *Rare.* Harmonious; orderly. [Greek *kosmikos,* of the universe, from *kosmos,* COSMOS.] —**cos′mi·cal·ly** *adv.*

cosmic dust. Fine solid particles of matter in interstellar space.

cosmic ray. A stream of ionizing radiation of extraterrestrial origin, chiefly of protons, alpha particles, and other atomic nuclei but including some high-energy electrons and photons, that enters the atmosphere and produces secondary radiation, principally pions, muons, electrons, and gamma rays. Also called "primary," "primary radiation."

cosmo–, cosm–. Indicates world or universe; for example, **cosmorama, cosmology.** [From Greek *kosmos,* COSMOS.]

cos·mog·o·ny (kŏz-mŏg′ə-nē) *n., pl.* **-nies. 1.** The astrophysical study of the evolution of the universe. **2.** A specific theory or model of this evolution. [Greek *kosmogonia,* the creation of the world : COSMO- + *gonos,* creation (see **gon-**).] —**cos′mo·gon′ic** (-mə-gŏn′ĭk), **cos′mo·gon′i·cal** *adj.* —**cos·mog′o·nist** *n.*

cos·mog·ra·phy (kŏz-mŏg′rə-fē) *n., pl.* **-phies. 1.** The study of the constitution of nature. **2.** A description of the world or universe. [Greek *kosmographia,* description of the world : COSMO- + -GRAPHY.] —**cos·mog′ra·pher** *n.* —**cos′mo·graph′ic** (-mə-grăf′ĭk), **cos′mo·graph′i·cal** *adj.*

Cos·mo·line (kŏz′mə-lēn) *n.* A trademark for **petrolatum** *(see).* —*tr.v.* **Cosmolined, -lining, -lines.** To coat (firearms) with Cosmoline grease.

cos·mol·o·gy (kŏz-mŏl′ə-jē) *n.* **1.** A branch of philosophy dealing with the origin, processes, and structure of the universe. **2. a.** The astrophysical study of the structure and constituent dynamics of the universe. **b.** A specific theory or model of this structure and dynamics. [New Latin *cosmologia* : COSMO- + -LOGY.] —**cos′mo·log′ic** (-mə-lŏj′ĭk), **cos′mo·log′i·cal** *adj.* —**cos′mo·log′i·cal·ly** *adv.* —**cos·mol′o·gist** *n.*

cos·mo·naut (kŏz′mə-nôt) *n.* An **astronaut** *(see).* [Russian *kosmonavt* : COSMO- + Greek *nautēs,* sailor (see **nau-** in Appendix*).]

cos·mop·o·lis (kŏz-mŏp′ə-lĭs) *n.* A city inhabited by people from all parts of the world. [Back-formation from COSMOPOLITAN.]

cos·mo·pol·i·tan (kŏz′mə-pŏl′ə-tən) *adj.* **1.** Common to the whole world. **2.** At home in all parts of the earth or in many spheres of interest. **3.** *Biology.* Growing or occurring in all or most parts of the world; widely distributed. —*n.* A cosmopolite. [French, *cosmopolitain,* from Old French, from Greek *kosmopolitēs,* COSMOPOLITE.] —**cos′mo·pol′i·tan·ism′** *n.* —**cos′mo·pol′i·tan·ly** *adv.*

cos·mop·o·lite (kŏz-mŏp′ə-līt′) *n.* **1.** A cosmopolitan person. **2.** *Biology.* A cosmopolitan organism. **3.** A butterfly, the **painted lady** *(see).* [Greek *kosmopolitēs,* citizen of the world : COSMO- + *politēs,* citizen, from *polis,* city (see **pele-**[2] in Appendix*).] —**cos·mop′o·lit·ism′** *n.*

cos·mo·ra·ma (kŏz′mə-rä′mə, -răm′ə) *n.* An exhibition of scenes and pictures from all over the world. [COSM(O)- + (PAN)ORAMA.] —**cos′mo·ram′ic** (-răm′ĭk) *adj.*

cos·mos (kŏz′məs, -mŏs) *n.* **1.** The universe regarded as an orderly, harmonious whole. **2.** Any system regarded as ordered, harmonious, and whole. **3.** Harmony and order as distinct from chaos. **4.** Any of various tropical American plants of the genus *Cosmos,* having variously colored rayed flowers; especially, *C. bipinnatus,* widely cultivated as a garden plant. [Greek *kosmos,* order, the universe, the world. See **kosmos** in Appendix.*]

Cos·sack (kŏs′ăk) *n.* A member of a people of the southern Soviet Union in Europe and adjacent parts of Asia, noted as cavalrymen. —*adj.* Of, pertaining to, or characteristic of the Cossacks. [Russian *kazak,* from Central Asian Turkic, adventurer, vagabond.]

cos·set (kŏs′ĭt) *tr.v.* **-seted, -seting, -sets.** To pamper; fondle; pet. —*n.* A pet; especially, a pet lamb. [Origin unknown.]

cost (kôst) *n.* **1.** An amount paid or required in payment for a purchase. **2.** A loss or penalty; detriment. **3.** *Plural. Law.* The charges fixed for litigation, usually payable by the losing party. —See Synonyms at **price.** —*v.* **cost, costing, costs.** —*intr.* To require a specified payment, expenditure, effort, or loss. —*tr.* To estimate or determine the cost of. [Middle English, from Old French, from *coster,* to cost, from Latin *constāre,* to stand with, stand at a particular price : *com-,* with + *stāre,* to stand (see **sta-** in Appendix*).]

cos·ta (kŏs′tə) *n., pl.* **-tae** (-tē). *Biology.* A rib or a riblike part, such as the midrib of a leaf or a thickened anterior vein or margin of an insect's wing. [Latin, rib. See **kost-** in Appendix.*]

Cos·ta Bra·va (kōs′tä brä′vä). A coastal region of northeastern Spain, along the Mediterranean between Barcelona and the French border.

cost accountant. An accountant who keeps records of the costs of production and distribution. —**cost accounting.**

co·star (kō′stär′) *n.* Also **co-star.** A starring actor or actress given equal status with another or others in a play or motion picture. —*v.* (kō′stär′) **costarred, -starring, -stars.** Also **co-star.** —*intr.* To act as a costar. —*tr.* To present as a costar.

cos·tard (kŏs′tərd, kôs′-) *n.* **1.** A large English variety of apple. **2.** *Archaic Slang.* The head. [Middle English, from Norman French, "ribbed one" (from its ribbed appearance), from *coste,* rib, from Latin *costa.* See **kost-** in Appendix.*]

Cos·ta Ri·ca (kŏs′tə rē′kə, kôs′-; *Spanish* kōs′tä rē′kä). A republic of Central America, 19,650 square miles in area, between Panama and Nicaragua. Population, 1,414,000. Capital, San José. —**Costa Rican.**

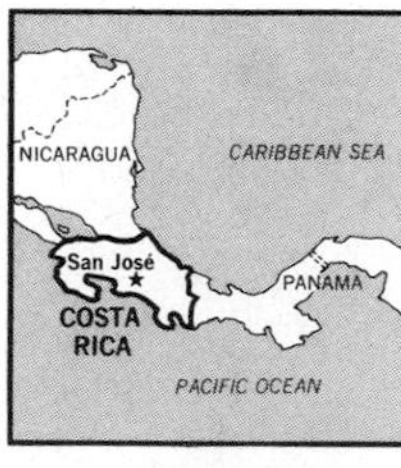

Costa Rica

cos·tate (kŏs′tāt′) *adj.* Having ribs or a ribbed or ridged surface. [Latin *costātus,* from *costa,* rib. See **costard.**]

cos·ter·mon·ger (kŏs′tər-mŭng′gər, -mŏng′gər, kôs′-) *n. British.* One who sells fruit, vegetables, fish, or other goods from a cart, barrow, or stand in the streets, especially in London. Also called "coster." [Originally *costardmonger,* "apple seller" : COSTARD + MONGER.]

cos·tive (kŏs′tĭv) *adj.* **1. a.** Constipated. **b.** Causing constipation. **2.** Slow; sluggish. **3.** Stingy; parsimonious; niggardly. [Middle English *costif,* from Old French *costive,* past participle of *costiver,* to bind, constipate, from Latin *constīpāre,* to CONSTIPATE.]

cost·ly (kôst′lē) *adj.* **-lier, -liest. 1.** Of high price or value; expensive. **2.** Entailing loss or sacrifice. —**cost′li·ness** *n.*

Synonyms: *costly, expensive, dear, valuable, precious, invaluable, priceless.* These adjectives apply to the measure of worth or value of things or, less often, of persons. *Costly, expensive,* and *dear* refer principally to the high price of things on sale. *Costly,* thus used, implies especially high quality or rarity of an object. *Valuable* stresses the quality and importance of the object without specifying the price. *Precious* implies uniqueness and irreplaceability. *Invaluable* and *priceless* describe worth beyond a person's power to estimate.

cost·mar·y (kŏst′mâr-ē, kôst′-) *n.* An herb, *Chrysanthemum balsamita,* native to Asia, having aromatic foliage sometimes used as seasoning. [Middle English *costmarie* : *cost,* costmary, Old English *cost,* from Latin *costum,* from Greek *kostos,* from Sanskrit *kúṣṭhas*† + MARY (so named because regarded as sacred to the Virgin Mary).]

cost of living. The average cost of the basic necessities of life, such as food, shelter, and clothing.

cost-plus (kôst′plŭs′, kŏst′-) *n.* Cost of production plus a fixed rate of profit. Often used as a basis for government contracts.

cos·trel (kŏs′trəl) *n.* A flat, pear-shaped drinking vessel with loops for attachment to the belt of the user. [Middle English, from Old French *costerel,* perhaps from *costier,* "that which is at the side," from *coste,* side, rib, from Latin *costa.* See **kost-** in Appendix.*]

cos·tume (kŏs′to͞om, -tyo͞om, kŏs-to͞om′, -tyo͞om′) *n.* **1.** A style of dress, including garments, accessories, and hair style. **2.** A style of dress characteristic of a particular country, period, or people, often worn in a play or at a masquerade. **3.** A set of clothes appropriate for a particular occasion or season. —*tr.v.* **costumed, -tuming, -tumes. 1.** To put a costume on; to dress. **2.** To furnish a costume or costumes for. [French, from Italian, custom, dress, from Latin *consuētūdō* (stem *consuētūdin-*), CUSTOM.]

cos·tum·er (kŏs-to͞o′mər, -tyo͞o′mər) *n.* Also **cos·tum·i·er** (kŏs-to͞om′yər, -tyo͞om′yər; *French* kôs-tü-myā′). A person who makes or supplies costumes, as for plays or masquerades.

co·sy. Variant of **cozy.**

cot[1] (kŏt) *n.* A narrow bed; especially, one made of canvas stretched on a collapsible frame. [Hindi *khāt,* bedstead, couch, from Sanskrit *khátvā,* from Dravidian, akin to Tamil *kaṭṭil.*]

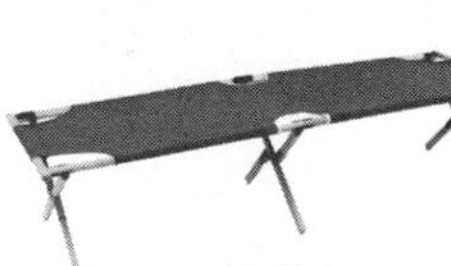
cot[1]

cot[2] (kŏt) *n.* **1.** A small house; cottage. **2.** A small shelter. **3.** A protective covering. [Middle English *cot(e),* Old English *cot.* See **ku-** in Appendix.*]

co·tan·gent (kō-tăn′jənt) *n. Abbr.* **ctn** *Trigonometry.* The **tangent** *(see)* of the complement of a directed angle or arc. —**co′tan·gen′tial** (-jĕn′shəl) *adj.*

cote[1] (kōt) *n.* **1.** A small shed or shelter for sheep or birds. **2.** *Regional.* A cottage; hut. [Middle English *cote,* Old English *cote.* See **ku-** in Appendix.*]

cote[2] (kōt) *tr.v.* **coted, coting, cotes.** *Archaic.* To go around by the side of; to pass. [Origin obscure.]

Côte d'A·zur (kōt′ dá′zür′). The Mediterranean coast of France, especially along the French Riviera.

Côte d'Or (kōt′ dôr′). A chain of hills in eastern France, extending 30 miles southwest of Dijon, and famous for its fine vineyards.

co·ten·ant (kō-tĕn′ənt) *n.* One of two or more tenants sharing common property. [CO- + TENANT.] —**co·ten′an·cy** *n.*

Co·ten·tin Peninsula (kô-täN-täN′). Also **Cher·bourg Peninsula** (shâr′bo͝org, -bo͝or). A peninsula in northwestern France, extending into the English Channel with Cherbourg at its tip.

co·te·rie (kō′tə-rē) *n.* A small group of persons who associate frequently. See Synonyms at **circle.** [French, from Old French, an association of peasant tenants, probably from *cotier,* cot-

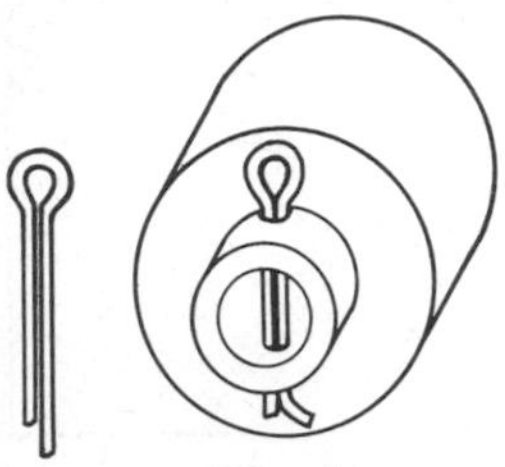

cotter pin
Left: Split cotter pin before use
Right: Cotter pin holding one shaft within another

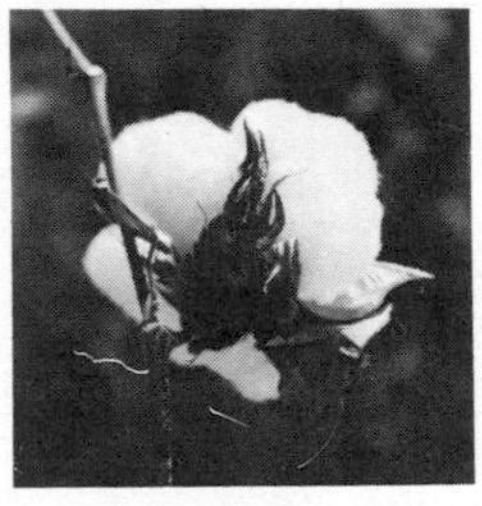

cotton
Cotton in fruit

cotton gin

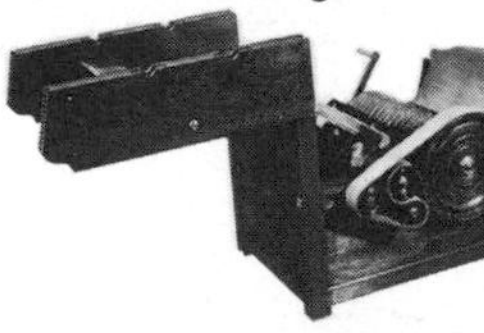

replica of Eli Whitney's original model

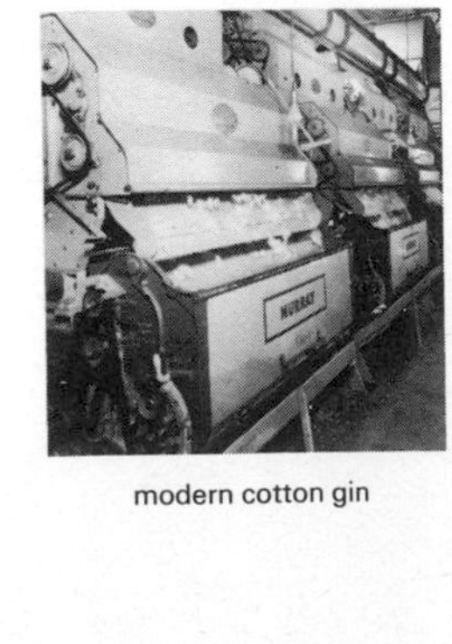

modern cotton gin

tager, from *cote* (unattested), cottage, perhaps from Middle English *cot,* COT (cottage).]
co·ter·mi·nous. Variant of **conterminous.**
coth hyperbolic cotangent.
co·thur·nus (kō-thûr′nəs) *n., pl.* **-ni** (-nī′). Also **co·thurn** (kō′thûrn, kō-thûrn′). **1.** A buskin worn by actors of classical tragedy. **2.** The ancient tragic style. [Latin, from Greek *kothornos,* perhaps from Lydian.]
co·ti·dal (kō-tīd′l) *adj.* **1.** Indicating coincidence of the tides. **2.** Denoting lines on a map that show where high or low tides occur simultaneously.
co·til·lion (kō-tĭl′yən, kə-) *n.* Also **co·til·lon. 1.** A lively dance originating in France in the 18th century, with varied, intricate patterns and steps. **2.** A quadrille. **3.** Music for these dances. **4.** A formal ball at which girls are presented to society. [French *cotillon,* peasant dress, country dance, from Old French, petticoat, diminutive of *cote,* COAT.]
co·to·ne·as·ter (kə-tō′nē-ăs′tər) *n.* Any of various Old World shrubs of the genus *Cotoneaster,* having small white or pinkish flowers and frequently cultivated for ornament. [New Latin *Cotoneaster,* from Latin *cotōneum,* QUINCE.]
Co·to·nou (kō′tə-nōō′). The former capital of Dahomey, a seaport on the Gulf of Guinea. Population, 109,000.
Co·to·pax·i (kō′tō-păk′sē; *Spanish* kō′tō-pä′hē). The highest (19,347 feet) active volcano in the world, in the Cordillera Real, Ecuador, 32 miles southeast of Quito.
cot·quean (kŏt′kwēn′) *n. Archaic.* **1.** A vulgar woman; hussy. **2.** A man who does work regarded suitable only for women. [COT (cottage) + QUEAN.]
Cots·wold (kŏts′wōld, -wəld) *n.* A sheep of a breed, known for its long wool, originally developed in the Cotswold Hills of southwestern England.
cot·ta (kŏt′ə) *n., pl.* **cottae** (kŏt′ē) or **-tas.** A short ecclesiastical surplice, often sleeveless or short-sleeved. [Medieval Latin, from West Germanic *kotta* (unattested), COAT.]
cot·tage (kŏt′ĭj) *n.* **1.** A small, single-storied country house. **2.** A small summer house used during vacations. [Middle English *cotage,* from *cot(e),* COT (cottage).]
cottage cheese. A soft, white cheese made of strained and seasoned curds of skim milk. Also called "Dutch cheese," "pot cheese."
cottage pudding. Plain cake covered with a sweet sauce.
cot·tag·er (kŏt′ĭj-ər) *n.* A person who lives in a cottage.
cottage tulip. A type of tall-stemmed garden tulip, usually having pointed petals.
cot·ter (kŏt′ər) *n.* **1.** A bolt, wedge, key, or pin inserted through a slot in order to hold parts together. **2.** A cotter pin. [Shortened from dialectal *cotterel*†.]
cotter pin. A split cotter inserted through holes in two or more pieces and bent at the ends to fasten and prevent excessive sliding and rotation.
Cot·ti·an Alps (kŏt′ē-ən). The section of the Alps between northwestern Italy and southeastern France. Highest elevation, Mount Viso (12,002 feet).
cot·ti·er (kŏt′ē-ər) *n.* A peasant renting land directly from its owner, the rate having been fixed by public competition. [Middle English, from Old French *cotier,* cottager, from *cote* (unattested), cottage, perhaps from Middle English *cot,* COT (cottage).]
cot·ton (kŏt′n) *n.* **1.** Any of various plants or shrubs of the genus *Gossypium,* cultivated in warm climates for the fiber surrounding their seeds. **2.** The soft, white, downy fiber attached to the seeds of the cotton plant, used in making textiles and other products. **3.** Cotton plants collectively. **4.** The crop of these plants. **5.** Thread or cloth manufactured from cotton fiber. **6.** Any of various soft, downy substances found in other plants. *—adj.* Of, pertaining to, or made from cotton. *—intr.v.* **cottoned, -toning, -tons.** *Informal.* To take a liking; become friendly. Used with *to.* **—cotton up to.** *Informal.* To flatter; make overtures to. [Middle English *cotoun,* from Old French, from Arabic (Spanish dialectal) *qoṭon,* variant of Arabic *quṭn.*]
Cot·ton (kŏt′n), **John.** 1584–1652. English Puritan clergyman and author in America; opposed Roger Williams.
cotton candy. **Spun sugar** *(see).*
cotton flannel. A soft, warm, napped fabric woven of cotton.
cotton gin. A machine that separates the seeds, seed hulls, and other small objects from the fibers of cotton. Also called "gin."
cotton grass. Any of various grasslike bog plants of the genus *Eriophorum,* having densely tufted, cottony flower heads.
cotton leafworm. The larva of a New World moth, *Alabama argillacea,* that feeds on and destroys cotton leaves.
cot·ton·mouth (kŏt′n-mouth′) *n.* A snake, the **water moccasin** *(see).* [Its mouth is lined with a white cottony substance.]
cotton rose. 1. A Chinese shrub, *Hibiscus mutabilis,* cultivated in warm regions for its white or pink flowers that turn deep red. Also called "Confederate rose." **2.** The **cudweed** *(see).*
cot·ton·seed (kŏt′n-sēd′) *n., pl.* **cottonseed** or **-seeds.** The seed of cotton, used as a source of oil and meal.
cottonseed meal. Meal made from the residue of cottonseed after the oil has been removed and used as animal feed and fertilizer.
cottonseed oil. A yellowish to dark-red oil obtained by crushing cottonseed and used in cooking and as salad oil and in the manufacture of paints, soaps, and other products.
cotton stainer. Any of various small, flat, red insects of the genus *Dysdercus,* that pierce cotton bolls and stain the fibers.
cot·ton·tail (kŏt′n-tāl′) *n.* Any of several New World rabbits of the genus *Sylvilagus,* having grayish or brownish fur and a tail with a white underside.
cotton tree. A spiny tropical tree, *Bombax malabaricum,* having seeds surrounded by cottonlike fiber.
cot·ton·weed (kŏt′n-wēd′) *n.* Any of various plants covered with cottony down or having cottonlike tufts.
cot·ton·wood (kŏt′n-wŏŏd′) *n.* Any of several softwood trees of the genus *Populus,* having seeds with cottonlike tufts; especially, *P. deltoides,* of eastern and central North America.
cotton wool. 1. Cotton in its natural or raw state. **2.** *British.* Absorbent cotton.
cot·ton·y (kŏt′n-ē) *adj.* **1.** Of or resembling cotton; downy; fluffy. **2.** Covered with fibers resembling cotton; nappy.
cot·y·le·don (kŏt′ə-lēd′n) *n.* **1.** *Botany.* A leaf of a plant embryo, being the first or one of the first to appear from a sprouting seed. Also called "seed leaf." See **dicotyledon, monocotyledon. 2.** *Anatomy.* A lobule of the placenta, especially of ruminants. [Latin *cotylēdon,* navelwort, from Greek *kotulēdon,* cup-shaped hollow, navelwort, from *kotulē*†, anything hollow, cup.] **—cot′y·le′don·al, cot′y·le′do·nous** *adj.*
cot·y·loid (kŏt′ə-loid′) *adj.* Also **cot·y·loi·dal** (kŏt′ə-loi′dəl). Shaped like a cup. [Greek *kotuloeidēs,* cup-shaped : *kotulē,* anything hollow, cup (see **cotyledon**) + -OID.]
couch (kouch) *n.* **1.** An article of furniture, commonly upholstered and often having a back, on which one may sit or recline; a lounge; sofa. **2. a.** The frame or floor on which grain, usually barley, is spread in malting. **b.** A layer of grain, usually barley, spread to germinate. *—v.* **couched, couching, couches.** *—tr.* **1.** *Archaic.* To cause to lie down. Used passively. **2.** To lower (a spear or lance) to the position of attack. **3.** To embroider by laying thread flat on a surface and fastening it by stitches at regular intervals. **4.** To spread (grain) on a frame or floor to germinate, as in malting. **5.** To place in a certain verbal context. *—intr.* **1.** *Archaic.* To lie down; recline. **2.** To lie in ambush or concealment; lurk. **3.** To be in a heap or pile, as leaves for decomposition or fermentation. [Middle English *couche,* from Old French, from *coucher,* to lay down, from Latin *collocāre,* to place together, put : *com-,* together + *locāre,* to place, LOCATE.] **—couch′er** *n.*
couch·ant (kou′chənt) *adj. Heraldry.* Lying down with the head raised. [Middle English, from Old French, present participle of *coucher,* to lay down, to COUCH.]
couch grass. A grass, *Agropyron repens,* having whitish-yellow rootstocks by means of which it multiplies rapidly, becoming a troublesome weed. Also called "quack grass," "quick grass," "quitch grass," "twitch grass," "witch grass." [Variant of QUITCH GRASS.]
couch·ing (kou′chĭng) *n.* A form of embroidery in which heavy thread is sewn into a material with minute stitches. [Middle English, from *couchen,* to embroider, inlay, from Old French *coucher,* to COUCH.]
Cou·é (kōō-ā′), **Émile.** 1857–1926. French psychotherapist; devised system of autosuggestion; lectured in America.
Coues (kouz), **Elliott.** 1842–1899. American ornithologist, biologist, and editor.
cou·gar (kōō′gər) *n.* The **mountain lion** *(see).* [French *couguar,* from Portuguese *cuguardo,* from Tupi *suasuarana,* "like a deer" (from its color) : *suasú,* deer + *ran, rã,* similar to.]
cough (kôf, kŏf) *v.* **coughed, coughing, coughs.** *—intr.* To expel air from the lungs suddenly and noisily. *—tr.* To expel by coughing. Usually used with *up* or *out.* **—cough up.** *Slang.* To hand over (money) reluctantly. *—n.* **1.** A sudden and noisy effort to expel the air from the lungs. **2.** An illness marked by frequent coughing. [Middle English *coughen,* Old English *cohhian* (unattested), from an imitative root *kokh-.*]
cough drop. A small, often medicated and sweetened lozenge taken to ease coughing or soothe a sore throat.
could. Past tense of **can.**
could·n't (kŏŏd′ənt). Contraction of *could not.*
cou·lee (kōō′lē) *n.* Also *French* **cou·lée** (kōō-lā′) (for sense 2). **1.** *Western U.S.* A deep gulch or ravine formed by rainstorms or melting snow, often dry in summer. **2. a.** A stream of molten lava. **b.** A sheet of solidified lava. [Canadian French *coulée,* from French, a flow, a flow of lava, from the past participle of *couler,* to flow, from Latin *cōlāre,* to strain, filter, from *cōlum,* a sieve. See **kagh-** in Appendix.*]
cou·lisse (kōō-lēs′) *n.* **1.** A grooved timber in which something slides, as one in which the side scenes of a stage run. **2.** *Theater.* **a.** One of the side scenes of the stage. **b.** The space between the side scenes. [French, sliding partition, from the feminine of *coulis,* sliding, from *couler,* to slide, flow. See **coulee.**]
cou·loir (kōōl-wär′) *n.* A deep mountainside gorge or gully, especially in the Alps. [French, colander, passageway, ravine, from *couler,* to slide, flow. See **coulee.**]
cou·lomb (kōō′lŏm′, -lōm′) *n. Abbr.* **C** A meter-kilogram-second unit of electrical charge equal to the quantity of charge transferred in one second by a steady current of one ampere. See **measurement.** [After Charles A. de COULOMB.]
Cou·lomb (kōō-lôN′), **Charles Augustin de.** 1736–1806. French physicist; experimented on elasticity, electricity, and magnetism.
Coulomb field. An electric field equivalent to that produced by a point charge so that the force at every point is described by Coulomb's law.
Coulomb force. An attractive or repulsive electrostatic force described by Coulomb's law.
Coulomb potential. The potential at any point in a Coulomb field.
Coulomb scattering. The scattering of a charged particle from another charged particle, especially from an atomic nucleus, principally or exclusively as a result of Coulomb forces.

Coulomb's law. The fundamental law of electrostatics stating that the force between two charged particles is directly proportional to the product of their charges and inversely proportional to the square of the distance between them. [After Charles A. de COULOMB.]

Couls·don and Pur·ley (kōlz′dən; pûr′lē). A former division of London, England, now part of **Croydon** *(see)*.

coul·ter. Variant of **colter.**

Coul·ter (kōl′tər), **John Merle.** 1851–1928. American botanist.

cou·ma·rin (ko͞o′mə-rĭn) *n.* A fragrant organic compound, $C_9H_6O_2$, extracted from tonka beans or produced synthetically and used in perfumes, flavorings, and soaps. [French *coumarine*, from *coumarou*, tonka bean tree, from Spanish *coumarú*, from Tupi *cumaru, comaru.*] —**cou′ma·ric** *adj.*

coun·cil (koun′səl) *n.* **1.** An assembly of persons called together for consultation, deliberation, or discussion. **2.** A body of people elected or appointed to serve in an administrative, legislative, or advisory capacity. **3.** The discussion or deliberation that takes place in a council. **4.** An assembly of church officials and theologians convened for regulating matters of doctrine and discipline. **5.** The **Sanhedrin** *(see)*. [Middle English *co(u)nceil*, from Norman French *concilie, cuncile*, assembly, from Latin *concilium*, meeting, assembly. See **kel-**[3] in Appendix.*]

Usage: *Council, counsel,* and *consul* are never interchangeable as such, though their meanings are related. *Council* and *councilor* refer principally to a deliberative assembly (such as a city council or student council), its work, and its membership. *Counsel* and *counselor* pertain chiefly to advice and guidance in general and to a person who provides it (such as a lawyer or camp counselor). *Consul* now denotes an officer in the foreign service of a country.

Council Bluffs. A city of southwestern Iowa, on the Missouri. Population, 56,000.

coun·cil·man (koun′səl-mən) *n., pl.* **-men** (-mĭn). A member of a council, especially the local governing body of a city or town.

coun·cil-man·ag·er plan (koun′səl-măn′ə-jər). A type of municipal government in which the chief executive official is a manager selected by the city council.

coun·cil·or (koun′sə-lər) *n.* Also **coun·cil·lor.** A member of a council. See Usage note at **council.**

coun·sel (koun′səl) *n., pl.* **-sels** or **counsel** (for sense 5). **1.** An exchanging of opinions and ideas; a consultation; discussion. **2.** Advice or guidance, especially as solicited from a knowledgeable person. **3.** A deliberate resolution; plan; scheme. **4.** A private purpose or opinion: *keep one's own counsel.* **5.** A lawyer, group of lawyers, or others giving legal advice; especially, an attorney engaged to conduct a cause in court. —See Synonyms at **lawyer.** —See Usage note at **council.** —*v.* **counseled** or **-selled, -seling** or **-selling, -sels.** —*tr.* **1.** To give counsel to; advise. **2.** To urge the adoption of; recommend. —*intr.* To give or take counsel or advice. [Middle English *counseil, conseil*, from Old French *conseil*, from Latin *consilium*, deliberation, consultation, akin to *consulere*, to CONSULT.]

coun·sel·or (koun′sə-lər) *n.* Also **coun·sel·lor.** **1.** A person who gives counsel; an adviser. **2.** An attorney, especially a trial lawyer. Also called "counselor-at-law." **3.** A legal adviser, especially of an embassy or legation. **4.** A person supervising children at a summer camp. —See Synonyms at **lawyer.** —See Usage note at **council.** —**coun′se·lor·ship′** *n.*

count[1] (kount) *v.* **counted, counting, counts.** —*tr.* **1.** To name or list (the units of a group or collection) one by one in order to determine a total; to number. **2.** To recite numerals in ascending order up to and including: *count three before firing.* **3.** To include in a reckoning; take account of: *ten dogs, counting the puppies.* **4.** To believe or consider to be; deem: *He counts himself lucky.* —*intr.* **1.** To recite or list numbers in order or enumerate items by units or groups: *count by tens.* **2.** To have importance; merit consideration. **3.** To have a specified value or importance; to amount. Usually used with *for: His opinions count for little.* **4.** *Music.* To keep time by counting beats. **5.** *Informal.* To have confidence. Used with *on.* —See Synonyms at **rely.** —**count in.** To include. —**count off.** To separate into groups by or as if by counting. —**count out.** To exclude or discount. —*n.* **1.** The act of counting or calculating. **2.** A number reached by counting. **3.** A reckoning; an accounting. **4.** *Law.* Any of the separate and distinct charges in an indictment. **5.** *Boxing.* The counting from one to ten seconds, during which time the fighter who is down must rise or be declared the loser. [Middle English *counten*, from Old French *conter, compter*, from Latin *computāre*, to sum up, reckon : *com-* (collectively) + *putāre*, to clear up, reckon (see **peuə-**[2] in Appendix*).]

count[2] (kount) *n. Abbr.* **Ct.** In some European countries, a nobleman whose rank corresponds to that of an earl in England. [Middle English *counte*, from Old French *conte, comte*, from Late Latin *comes* (stem *comit-*), occupant of any state office, from Latin, companion. See **ei-**[1] in Appendix.*]

count·a·ble (kount′ə-bəl) *adj.* **1.** Capable of being counted. **2.** *Mathematics.* Capable of being put in a one-to-one correspondence with the positive integers.

count·down (kount′doun′) *n.* **1.** The act or process of counting backward aloud to indicate the time elapsing before an imminent deadline that will initiate an event or operation. **2.** *Aerospace.* The act or process of counting backward from an arbitrary starting number while making successive checks during the preparation of a missile or space vehicle scheduled to be launched at the count of zero.

coun·te·nance (koun′tə-nəns) *n.* **1.** Aspect; appearance; especially, the expression of the face. **2.** The face or facial features. **3.** A look or expression of apparent encouragement. **4.** Support or approval in general. **5.** Composure; bearing; self-control. —**out of countenance.** Visibly disconcerted or embarrassed. —*tr.v.* **countenanced, -nancing, -nances.** To give or express tacit approval to; condone. [Middle English *contenaunce*, behavior, demeanor, from Old French *contenance*, from *contenir*, to behave, CONTAIN.] —**coun′te·nanc·er** *n.*

count·er[1] (koun′tər) *adj.* Contrary; opposing. —*n.* **1.** One that is counter; an opposite; a contrary. **2.** *Boxing.* A blow given while receiving or parrying another. **3.** *Fencing.* A parry in which one foil follows the other in a circular fashion. **4.** A stiff piece of leather around the heel of a shoe. **5.** The portion of a ship's stern extending from the water line to the extreme outward swell. **6.** The part of a horse's chest between the shoulders and under the neck. **7.** The depression between the raised lines of a typeface. —*v.* **countered, -ering, -ers.** —*tr.* **1.** To meet or return (a blow) by another blow. **2.** To oppose. —*intr.* **1.** To give a return blow while receiving or parrying one, as in boxing. **2.** To move or act in opposition. —*adv.* In a contrary manner or direction. [Middle English *countre*, from Old French *contre*, from Latin *contrā*, contrary to, against. See **kom** in Appendix.*]

count·er[2] (koun′tər) *n.* **1.** A table or similar flat surface on which money is counted, business is transacted, or food is served. **2.** A piece, as of wood or ivory, used for keeping a count or a place in games. **3. a.** An imitation coin; token. **b.** Any piece of money. [Middle English *contour*, from Old French *comptouer, conteoir*, from Medieval Latin *computātōrium*, place of accounts, from Latin *computāre*, to COUNT.]

count·er[3] (koun′tər) *n.* **1.** A person who counts. **2.** Any electronic or mechanical device that automatically counts occurrences or repetitions of phenomena or events.

counter–. Indicates: **1.** Opposition, as in direction or purpose; for example, **countermarch, counteract. 2.** Reciprocation; for example, **countersign.** ***Note:*** Many compounds other than those entered here may be formed with *counter-*. In forming compounds, *counter-* is normally joined with the following element without space or hyphen: *counterrevolution.* The adjective *counter* is written as a separate word: *Counter Reformation,* but except for that example, it is hardly ever used in attributive position. Rather the preference is for forming a compound with *counter-*, as evidenced by the entries that follow. [Middle English *countre-*, from Norman French, from Old French *contre-*, from Latin *contrā*, opposite to, COUNTER.]

coun·ter·act (koun′tər-ăkt′) *tr.v.* **-acted, -acting, -acts.** To oppose and mitigate the effects of by contrary action; to check. See Synonyms at **neutralize.** —**coun′ter·ac′tion** *n.* —**coun′ter·ac′tive** *adj.* —**coun′ter·ac′tive·ly** *adv.*

coun·ter·at·tack (koun′tər-ə-tăk′) *n.* A return attack. —*v.* **counterattacked, -tacking, -tacks.** —*intr.* To deliver a counterattack. —*tr.* To make a counterattack against.

coun·ter·bal·ance (koun′tər-băl′əns, koun′tər-băl′əns) *n.* **1.** Any force or influence equally counteracting another. **2.** A weight that acts to balance another; a counterpoise. —*tr.v.* (koun′tər-băl′əns, koun′tər-băl′əns) **counterbalanced, -ancing, -ances.** **1.** To act as a counterbalance to; to counterpoise. **2.** To oppose with an equal force; offset.

coun·ter·blast (koun′tər-blăst′, -bläst′) *n.* **1.** A blast that opposes another. **2.** A fervid retort, as in an argument.

coun·ter·change (koun′tər-chānj′) *tr.v.* **-changed, -changing, -changes.** **1.** To exchange; transpose. **2.** To make checkered; diversify; variegate.

coun·ter·charge (koun′tər-chärj′) *n.* A charge in opposition to another charge. —*v.* (koun′tər-chärj′) **countercharged, -charging, -charges.** —*tr.* To bring a charge against (one's accuser). —*intr.* To make a countercharge.

coun·ter·check (koun′tər-chĕk′) *n.* **1.** Something that serves to check something else. **2.** Something that confirms or denies the correctness of a previous check. —*tr.v.* (koun′ter-chĕk′) **counterchecked, -checking, -checks.** **1.** To oppose or check by a counteraction. **2.** To check again.

coun·ter·claim (koun′tər-klām′) *n.* A claim filed in opposition to another claim. —*v.* (koun′tər-klām′) **counterclaimed, -claiming, -claims.** —*tr.* To make a counterclaim against. —*intr.* To plead a counterclaim. —**coun′ter·claim′ant** *n.*

coun·ter·clock·wise (koun′tər-klŏk′wīz′) *adv.* Also **con·tra·clock·wise** (kŏn′trə-). In a direction opposite to that of the movement of the hands of a clock. —**coun′ter·clock′wise′** *adj.*

coun·ter·es·pi·o·nage (koun′tər-ĕs′pē-ə-näzh′, -nĭj) *n.* Espionage undertaken to detect and counteract enemy espionage.

coun·ter·feit (koun′tər-fĭt) *v.* **-feited, -feiting, -feits.** —*tr.* **1.** To make a copy of, usually with the intent to defraud; to forge. **2.** To imitate. **3.** To make a pretense of; feign. —*intr.* **1.** To carry on a deception; feign; dissemble. **2.** To make imitations or counterfeits. —*adj.* **1.** Made in imitation of what is genuine with the intent to defraud. **2.** Simulated; feigned; pretended. —See Synonyms at **artificial.** —*n.* **1.** A fraudulent imitation or facsimile. **2.** *Obsolete.* A portrait; image. [Middle English *countrefeten*, from Old French *contrefaire* (past participle *contrefait*), from Medieval Latin *contrāfacere*, to make in contrast to, hence to make in imitation : Latin *contrā-*, opposite to + *facere*, to make (see **dhē-**[1] in Appendix*).] —**coun′ter·feit·er** *n.*

coun·ter·foil (koun′tər-foil′) *n.* The part of a check or other commerical paper retained by the issuer as a record of the transaction.

coun·ter·glow (koun′tər-glō′) *n.* **Gegenschein** *(see)*.

coun·ter·in·tel·li·gence (koun′tər-ĭn-tĕl′ə-jəns) *n.* The branch of an intelligence service charged with keeping valuable infor-

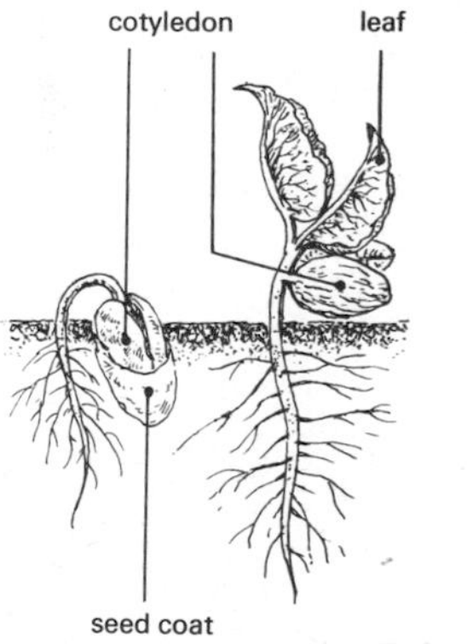

cotyledon
leaf
seed coat

cotyledon
Dicotyledonous bean seedling

mation from an enemy, preventing subversion and sabotage, and gathering political and military information.

coun·ter·ir·ri·tant (koun′tər-ĭr′ə-tənt) *n.* An agent that induces local irritation to counteract general or deep irritation.

coun·ter·man (koun′tər-măn′, -mən) *n., pl.* **-men** (-mĕn′, -mĭn). One who tends a counter, as in a luncheonette.

coun·ter·mand (koun′tər-mănd′, -mänd′) *tr.v.* **-manded, -manding, -mands. 1.** To cancel or reverse (a command or order). **2.** To recall by a contrary order. —*n.* An order or command reversing another. [Middle English *countremaunden,* from Old French *contremander* : COUNTER- + *mander,* to command, from Latin *mandāre* (see **man-²** in Appendix*).]

coun·ter·march (koun′tər-märch′) *n.* **1.** A march back or in a reverse direction. **2.** A complete reversal of method or conduct. —*v.* (koun′tər-märch′) **countermarched, -marching, -marches.** —*tr.* To conduct in a countermarch. —*intr.* To execute a countermarch.

coun·ter·mea·sure (koun′tər-mĕzh′ər) *n.* A measure or action taken in opposition to another.

coun·ter·mine (koun′tər-mīn′) *n.* **1. a.** A mine or tunnel dug by the defenders of a fortress to intercept and destroy a tunnel made by the besiegers. **b.** A mine or charge of explosive placed so as to explode an enemy's mines. **2.** A plot to frustrate another. —*v.* (koun′tər-mīn′) **countermined, -mining, -mines.** —*tr.* **1.** To make or use a countermine against. **2.** To defeat or frustrate by secret and opposite measures. —*intr.* To make or lay down countermines.

coun·ter·move (koun′tər-mōōv′) *n.* A move countering another move. —*v.* (koun′tər-mōōv′) **countermoved, -moving, -moves.** —*intr.* To make a countermove. —*tr.* To move in opposition to. —**coun′ter·move′ment** *n.*

coun·ter·of·fen·sive (koun′tər-ə-fĕn′sĭv) *n.* A large-scale attack by an army, designed to stop the offensive of an enemy force.

coun·ter·pane (koun′tər-pān′) *n.* A coverlet for a bed; bedspread. [Earlier *counterpoint,* from Middle English, from Old French *contrepointe, coultepointe,* from Medieval Latin *culcita puncta,* "stitched quilt" : Latin *culcita,* QUILT + *puncta,* stabbed, stitched, from *pungere,* to stab, prick (see **peuk-** in Appendix*).]

coun·ter·part (koun′tər-pärt′) *n.* **1.** One that closely or exactly resembles another, as in function or relation. **2. a.** One of two parts that fit and complete each other, such as a seal and its impression. **b.** One that is a natural complement to another.

coun·ter·plot (koun′tər-plŏt′) *n.* A plot intended to frustrate another plot. —*v.* (koun′tər-plŏt′) **counterplotted, -plotting, -plots.** —*tr.* To oppose and frustrate by another plot. —*intr.* To devise a counterplot.

coun·ter·point (koun′tər-point′) *n.* **1. a.** Melodic material that is added above or below an existing melody. **b.** The musical technique of combining two or more melodic lines in such a way that they establish a harmonic relationship while retaining their linear individuality. **c.** Music incorporating or consisting of contrapuntal writing. **2.** A contrasting but parallel element, item, or theme.

coun·ter·poise (koun′tər-poiz′) *n.* **1.** A counterbalancing weight. **2.** Any force or influence that balances or equally counteracts another. **3.** The state of being balanced or in equilibrium. —*tr.v.* (koun′tər-poiz′) **counterpoised, -poising, -poises. 1.** To oppose with an equal weight; to counterbalance. **2.** To act against with an equal force or power; to offset.

coun·ter·pro·pos·al (koun′tər-prə-pō′zəl) *n.* A proposal offered to nullify or substitute for a previous one.

coun·ter·ref·or·ma·tion (koun′tər-rĕf′ər-mā′shən) *n.* A reformation in opposition to previous reformation.

Counter Reformation. A reform movement within the Roman Catholic Church during the 16th century and the first half of the 17th century in response to the Protestant Reformation.

coun·ter·rev·o·lu·tion (koun′tər-rĕv′ə-lōō′shən) *n.* A movement arising in opposition to a revolution and aiming to restore the prerevolutionary state. —**coun′ter·rev′o·lu′tion·ar′y** *adj.* & *n.* —**coun′ter·rev′o·lu′tion·ist** *n.*

coun·ter·shaft (koun′tər-shăft′) *n.* A shaft serving as an intermediate between the powered and driven shafts in a belt drive where direct connection is difficult or alternative speed ratios are desired.

coun·ter·sign (koun′tər-sīn′) *tr.v.* **-signed, -signing, -signs.** To sign (a previously signed document), as for authentication. —*n.* **1.** A second or confirming signature, as on a previously signed document; countersignature. **2.** *Military.* A secret sign or signal to be given to a sentry in order to obtain passage; password. **3.** A secret sign or signal given in answer to another.

coun·ter·sig·na·ture (koun′tər-sĭg′nə-chər) *n.* A signature made in countersigning.

coun·ter·sink (koun′tər-sĭngk′) *tr.v.* **-sunk** (-sŭngk′), **-sinking, -sinks. 1.** To enlarge the top part of (a hole) so that a screw or bolthead will lie flush with or below the surface. **2.** To drive a screw or bolt into (such a hole). —*n. Abbr.* **csk. 1.** A tool for making such a hole. In this sense, also called "punch." **2.** A hole so made.

coun·ter·spy (koun′tər-spī′) *n.* A spy working in opposition to enemy espionage. —*intr.v.* **counterspied, -spying, -spys.** To serve as a counterspy.

coun·ter·ten·or (koun′tər-tĕn′ər) *n.* **1.** An adult male voice with a range above that of tenor. **2.** A singer with such a voice. Formerly called "alto."

coun·ter·vail (koun′tər-vāl′, koun′tər-vāl′) *v.* **-vailed, -vailing, -vails.** —*tr.* **1.** To act against with equal force. **2.** To compensate for; offset. —*intr.* To avail. Used with *against.* [Middle English *countrevaillen,* to be equal in value, from Old French *contrevaloir* : COUNTER- + *valoir,* to be worth, from Latin *valēre,* to be strong, be worth (see **wal-** in Appendix*).]

coun·ter·weigh (koun′tər-wā′) *v.* **-weighed, -weighing, -weighs.** —*tr.* To cause to counterbalance; counterpoise. —*intr.* To counterbalance.

coun·ter·weight (koun′tər-wāt′) *n.* A weight used as a counterbalance. —**coun′ter·weight′ed** (-wā′tĭd) *adj.*

counter word. A word commonly used without regard to its precise meaning, as *nice* or *awful.*

count·ess (koun′tĭs) *n., pl.* **-esses. 1. a.** In various European countries, the wife or widow of a count. **b.** In Great Britain, the wife or widow of an earl. **2.** A woman holding the title of count or earl in her own right. [Middle English *countes(se),* from Old French *contesse,* feminine of *conte,* COUNT.]

counting house. Also **count·ing·house** (koun′tĭng-hous′). An office in which a business firm carries on operations such as accounting and correspondence. Also called "counting room."

count·less (kount′lĭs) *adj.* That cannot be counted; infinite; innumerable. See Synonyms at **infinite.**

count palatine. Any of various nobles originally exercising certain royal powers within their own domain, a **palatine** *(see).*

coun·tri·fied (kŭn′trĭ-fīd′) *adj.* Also **coun·try·fied.** Resembling or having the characteristics of country life; rural; rustic.

coun·try (kŭn′trē) *n., pl.* **-tries. 1.** A large tract of land distinguishable by features of topography, biology, or culture. **2.** A district outside of cities and towns; rural area. **3.** The territory of a nation or state; land. **4.** The people of a nation or state. **5.** The land of a person's birth or citizenship or to which a person owes allegiance. **6.** *Law.* A jury. So called from the fact that the jury was originally composed of men from the local area. —See Synonyms at **nation.** —**go to the country.** *British.* To dissolve Parliament and hold a new election. —*adj.* **1.** Of or pertaining to rural areas. **2.** Unsophisticated; rustic. [Middle English *cuntree, contre,* from Old French *contree,* from Medieval Latin *(terra) contrāta,* "(land) lying opposite or before one," from *contrātus,* lying opposite, from Latin *contrā,* against, opposite. See **kom** in Appendix.*]

country club. A suburban club with facilities for golf, other outdoor sports, and social activities.

country cousin. One whose ingenuousness or rustic ways may embarrass or amuse city dwellers.

coun·try-dance (kŭn′trē-dăns′, -däns′) *n.* A folk dance of English origin, in which two lines of dancers face each other.

coun·try·folk (kŭn′trē-fōk′) *pl.n.* People who live in rural areas.

country gentleman. 1. The proprietor of a country estate. **2.** *Often capital* **C,** *capital* **G.** A variety of corn having small, sweet white kernels.

coun·try·man (kŭn′trē-mən) *n., pl.* **-men** (-mĭn). **1.** A man from one's own country. **2.** A man from a particular region. **3.** One who lives in the country; a rustic.

coun·try·seat (kŭn′trē-sēt′) *n.* A mansion in the country.

coun·try·side (kŭn′trē-sīd′) *n.* **1.** A rural region. **2.** The inhabitants of such an area.

coun·try·wom·an (kŭn′trē-wŏŏm′ən) *n., pl.* **-women** (-wĭm′ən). **1.** A woman from one's own country. **2.** A woman from a particular region. **3.** A woman who lives in the country.

coun·ty (koun′tē) *n., pl.* **-ties.** *Abbr.* **co. 1.** In the United States, an administrative subdivision of a state. In Louisiana, also called "parish." **2.** In Great Britain and Ireland, a territorial division exercising administrative, judicial, and political functions. **3.** The people living in a county. **4.** *Obsolete.* **a.** The territory under the jurisdiction of a count or earl. **b.** A count or earl. —*adj.* Of or pertaining to a county. [Middle English *co(u)nte,* from Norman French *counté,* from Medieval Latin *comitātus,* territory of a count, from Late Latin, retinue of a count, from *comes* (stem *comit-*), COUNT.]

county palatine. The domain of a count palatine.

county seat. A town or city that is the center of government in its county.

county town. In Great Britain, a county seat. Also called "shire town."

coup (kōō) *n., pl.* **coups** (kōōz; *French* kōō). **1.** A brilliantly executed stratagem; masterstroke. **2.** A coup d'état. [French, from Old French, from Late Latin *colpus,* from Latin *colaphus,* blow, from Greek *kolaphos,* a blow. See **kel-²** in Appendix.*]

coup de grâce (kōō′ də gräs′). **1.** The mortal or finishing stroke, as delivered to someone mortally wounded. **2.** Any finishing or decisive stroke. [French, "stroke of mercy."]

coup de main (kōō′ də măN′). A sudden action undertaken to surprise an enemy. [French, "stroke of hand."]

coup de maî·tre (kōō′ də mĕt′r′) *French.* A masterstroke.

coup d'é·tat (kōō′ dā-tä′). A sudden stroke of state policy involving deliberate violation of constitutional forms by a group of persons in authority. See Synonyms at **rebellion.** [French, "stroke of state."]

coup de thé·â·tre (kōō′ də tā-ät′r′) *French.* An unexpected and dramatic event that overturns some given situation.

coup d'oeil (kōō′ dœ′y′) *French.* A glance; quick survey.

coupe¹ (kōōp) *n.* **1.** A dessert of ice cream or fruit-flavored ice, variously garnished with nuts, fruit, whipped cream, and the like, served in a special dessert glass. **2. a.** The stemmed glass in which such a dessert is served. **b.** A shallow, bowl-shaped dessert dish. [French, "cup," from Late Latin *cuppa,* CUP.]

coupe². Variant of **coupé** (a two-door automobile).

cou·pé (kōō-pā′) *n.* Also **coupe** (kōōp) (for sense 3). **1.** A closed four-wheel carriage with two seats inside and one outside. **2.** The end compartment in European railway cars. **3.** A closed two-door automobile. [French, short for *(carrosse) coupé,* "cut-off (carriage)," from the past participle of *couper,* to cut off, from Old French *coup,* COUP.]

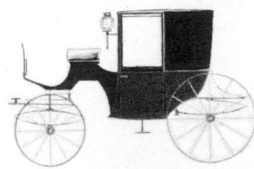

coupé
Square-front coupé

ă pat/ā pay/âr care/ä father/b bib/ch church/d deed/ĕ pet/ē be/f fife/g gag/h hat/hw which/ĭ pit/ī pie/îr pier/j judge/k kick/l lid, needle/m mum/n no, sudden/ng thing/ŏ pot/ō toe/ô paw, for/oi noise/ou out/ŏŏ took/ōō boot/p pop/r roar/s sauce/sh ship, dish/

Cou·pe·rin (kōō-prăN′), **François.** 1668–1733. French composer and organist at the court of Louis XIV.

coup·le (kŭp′əl) *n.* **1.** Two items of the same kind; a pair. **2.** Something that joins two things together; connection; link. **3.** A man and woman united in some way, as by marriage or betrothal or as dancing partners. See Usage note below. **4.** *Informal.* A few; several: *a couple of days.* See Usage note below. **5.** *Physics.* A pair of forces of equal magnitude acting in parallel but opposite directions, capable of causing rotation but not translation. —*v.* **coupled, -ling, -les.** —*tr.* **1.** To link together; attach; join. **2.** To form into pairs. **3.** To join as man and wife; marry. **4.** *Electricity.* To link (two circuits or currents) as by magnetic induction. —*intr.* **1.** To form pairs. **2.** To copulate. [Middle English, pair, bond, from Old French *co(u)ple,* from Latin *cōpula,* bond, link. See **ap-¹** in Appendix.*]

Synonyms: *couple, pair, duo, brace, yoke.* These nouns denote two of something in association. *Couple* refers to two of the same kind or sort not necessarily closely associated, though often it does apply to close relationship. Less formally the term may mean "few." *Pair* stresses close association and often reciprocal dependence of things (as in the case of gloves or pajamas). Sometimes it denotes a single thing with interdependent parts (such as shears or spectacles). *Duo* refers to partners in a duet. *Brace* refers principally to certain game birds, and *yoke* to two joined draft animals.

Usage: *Couple* (noun), referring to a man and woman united, is more often followed by a plural verb, though a singular one is possible. Whatever the choice, the plural or singular sense should be consistent within the context: *The couple are spending their honeymoon* (or *is spending its honeymoon*). *Couple,* meaning several, is followed by *of: a couple of days.*

coup·ler (kŭp′lər) *n.* **1.** A device for coupling two railroad cars. **2.** A device connecting two organ keyboards so that they may be played together.

coup·let (kŭp′lĭt) *n.* **1.** Two successive lines of verse with the same rhyme scheme and the same meter. **2.** Two similar things; a pair. [Old French *couplet,* diminutive of *co(u)ple,* COUPLE.]

coup·ling (kŭp′lĭng) *n.* **1.** The act of forming couples. **2.** A railroad coupler. **3.** The part of the body connecting the hindquarters and forequarters of a four-footed animal.

cou·pon (kōō′pŏn′, kyōō′-) *n.* **1.** One of a number of small, negotiable certificates attached to a bond that represent sums of interest due at stated maturities. **2.** A detachable part of a ticket, advertisement, or other certificate entitling the bearer to certain stated benefits, such as a cash refund or a gift, or for use as an order blank or inquiry form. **3.** One of a number of detachable slips calling for periodic payments, as for merchandise bought on an installment plan. [French, from Old French *colpon,* "a piece cut off," from *colper, couper,* to cut off, from *coup,* a blow. See **coup.**]

cour·age (kûr′ĭj) *n.* **1.** The state or quality of mind or spirit that enables one to face danger with self-possession, confidence, and resolution; bravery; valor. **2.** *Obsolete.* Heart; mind; disposition. [Middle English *corage,* heart as the seat of feeling, courage, from Old French, from Vulgar Latin *corāticum* (unattested), from Latin *cor,* heart. See **kerd-¹** in Appendix.*]

Synonyms: *courage, mettle, fortitude, resolution, tenacity, backbone, guts.* These nouns denote qualities of mind or spirit that enable a person to be steadfast in meeting danger or adversity. *Courage* suggests a reserve of moral strength on which one may draw in time of emergency. *Mettle* implies inherent capacity for rising to a challenge, and is likened to spirit and pluck. *Fortitude* primarily stresses enduring stoutness of mind and heart in time of severe trial. *Resolution* suggests, along with steadfastness of purpose, a positive expression of will directed toward achievement of personal ends. *Tenacity* stresses persistence in resisting adversity. *Backbone* implies inherent steadfastness associated with strength of character. *Guts* less formally refers to physical and moral stamina in the face of hardship or unfavorable odds.

cou·ra·geous (kə-rā′jəs) *adj.* Having or characterized by courage; valiant. See Synonyms at **brave.** —**cou·ra′geous·ly** *adv.* —**cou·ra′geous·ness** *n.*

cou·rante (kōō-ränt′) *n.* **1.** A French dance of the 17th century, characterized by running and gliding steps to an accompaniment in triple time. **2.** The second movement of the classical suite, typically following the allemande. [French, "running (dance)," from *courir,* to run, from Old French *courre,* from Latin *currere.* See **kers-²** in Appendix.*]

Cour·an·tyne (kûr′ən-tīn′). Also **Cor·en·tyn, Cor·en·tyne,** *Dutch* **Co·ran·tijn** (kō′rän-tīn). A river rising in southern Guyana and flowing 300 miles north to the Atlantic Ocean, forming the boundary between Guyana and Surinam.

Cour·bet (kōōr-bē′), **Gustave.** 1819–1877. French painter; a leader of the realists.

cou·ri·er (kōōr′ē-ər, kûr′-) *n.* **1.** A messenger, especially one on urgent or official diplomatic business. **2.** A personal attendant hired to make arrangements for a journey. [Old French *courrier,* from Old Italian *corriere,* from *correre,* to run, from Latin *currere.* See **kers-²** in Appendix.*]

cour·lan (kōōr′lən) *n.* A bird, the **limpkin** *(see).* [French, variant of *courliri,* from Galibi *kurliri.*]

Cour·nand (kōōr-näN′), **André Frédéric.** Born 1895. French-born American physiologist; worked in heart catheterization.

course (kôrs, kōrs, kōōrs) *n.* **1.** Onward movement in a particular direction; progress; advance. **2.** The direction of continuing movement. **3.** The route or path taken by something that moves, as a stream. **4.** A designated area of land or water on which a race is held or a sport played. **5.** Movement in time; duration: *in the course of a year.* **6.** A mode of action or behavior. **7.** A typical or natural manner of proceeding; customary passage from stage to stage; regular development: *The fad ran its course.* **8.** A systematic or orderly succession: *a course of medical treatments.* **9.** *Architecture.* A continuous layer of building material, such as brick or tile, on a wall or roof of a building. **10.** *Education.* **a.** A complete body of prescribed studies constituting a curriculum and leading toward an advanced degree. **b.** A unit of such a curriculum. **11.** A part of a meal served as a unit at one time. **12.** The lowest sail on any mast of a square-rigged ship. **13.** A point on the compass; especially, the one toward which a ship is sailing. —See Synonyms at **way.** —**in due course.** In proper order; at the right time. —**of course. 1.** In the natural order of things; naturally. **2.** Without any doubt; certainly. —*v.* **coursed, coursing, courses.** —*tr.* **1.** To move swiftly through or over; traverse. **2.** To pursue; hunt; especially, to hunt (game) with hounds. **3.** To set (hounds) to chase game; send into pursuit. —*intr.* **1.** To proceed on a course; follow a direction. **2. a.** To move swiftly; race. **b.** To run; flow: *"big tears now coursed down her face"* (Iris Murdoch). **3.** To hunt game with hounds. [Middle English *cours, course,* from Old French, from Latin *cursus,* from the past participle of *currere,* to run. See **kers-²** in Appendix.*]

cours·er¹ (kôr′sər, kōr′-, kōōr′-) *n.* A dog trained for coursing.

cours·er² (kôr′sər, kōr′-, kōōr′-) *n. Poetic.* A swift horse.

cours·ing (kôr′sĭng, kōr′-, kōōr′-) *n.* The sport of hunting with dogs trained to chase game by sight instead of scent.

court (kôrt, kōrt) *n. Abbr.* **C., ct. 1.** An extent of open ground partially or completely enclosed by walls or buildings; courtyard. **2.** A short street; especially, an alley walled by buildings on three sides. **3.** A large, open section of a building, often with a glass roof or skylight. **4.** Formerly, a mansion or other large building standing in a courtyard. Now used only in proper names. **5.** The place of residence of a sovereign or dignitary; a royal mansion or palace. **6.** The retinue of a sovereign, including the royal family and his personal servants, advisers, ministers, and the like. **7.** A sovereign's governing body, including the council of ministers and state advisers. **8.** A formal meeting called for and presided over by a sovereign. **9. a.** A person or body of persons appointed to hear and submit a decision on civil cases. **b.** The building, hall, or room in which cases are heard and determined. **c.** The regular session of a judicial assembly. **10.** Any similar authorized tribunal having military or ecclesiastical jurisdiction. **11.** An open, level area, marked with appropriate lines, upon which tennis, handball, basketball, or another game is played. **12.** The body of directors of a corporation, company, or other organization. —**out of court. 1.** Without a trial. **2.** Too trivial, rash, or ridiculous for discussion or consideration. —**pay court to. 1.** To flatter with solicitous overtures in an attempt to obtain something. **2.** To woo. —*v.* **courted, courting, courts.** —*tr.* **1.** To attempt to gain the favor of by flattery or attention. **2.** To attempt to gain the affections or love of; woo. **3.** To attempt to gain; seek. **4.** To invite, often unwittingly or foolishly: *court disaster.* —*intr.* To pay court; woo. —*adj.* Of, pertaining, or appropriate to a court. [Middle English, from Old French *cort,* from Latin *cohors* (stem *cohort-*), enclosure, court, cohort. See **gher-²** in Appendix.*]

cour·te·ous (kûr′tē-əs) *adj.* Characterized by graciousness; considerate toward others. See Synonyms at **polite.** [Middle English *curteis, corteis,* having manners befitting a courtly gentleman, from Old French, from *cort,* COURT.] —**cour′te·ous·ly** *adv.* —**cour′te·ous·ness** *n.*

cour·te·san (kôr′tə-zən, kōr′-) *n.* Also **cour·te·zan.** A prostitute or kept woman, especially one associating with men of rank or wealth. [Old French *courtisane,* from Old Italian *cortigiana,* "female courtier," from *cortigiano,* courtier, from *corte,* court, from Latin *cohors* (stem *cohort-*), COURT.]

cour·te·sy (kûr′tə-sē) *n., pl.* **-sies. 1.** Polite behavior; gracious manner or manners. **2.** A polite gesture or remark. **3.** Consent or favor; indulgence: *He was called "doctor" by courtesy.* **4.** Variant of **curtsy.** [Middle English *curteisie,* from Old French, from *curteis,* COURTEOUS.]

courtesy title. *British.* A title of nobility having no legal status; for example, the eldest son of the Duke of Bedford is called Marquis of Tavistock during his father's lifetime but is not a peer.

court hand. A style of handwriting formerly used in English legal papers. Also called "Gothic hand."

court·house (kôrt′hous′, kōrt′-) *n. Abbr.* **c.h., C.H.** A building housing judicial courts.

court·i·er (kôr′tē-ər, kōr′-, -tyər) *n.* **1.** An attendant at the court of a sovereign. **2.** One who seeks favor, especially by flattery or obsequious behavior. [Middle English *courteour,* from Norman French, from Old French *corteier,* to be at court, to court, from *cort, court,* COURT.] —**cour′ti·er·ly** *adv.*

court-leet (kôrt′lēt′, kōrt′-) *n.* A former court in Great Britain, a **leet** *(see).*

court·ly (kôrt′lē, kōrt′-) *adj.* **-lier, -liest. 1.** Suitable for a royal court; stately; dignified. **2.** Elegant in manners; polite; refined. **3.** Flattering; obsequious. —*adv.* In a courtly manner; elegant. —**court′li·ness** *n.*

courtly love. A code of chivalrous devotion to a married lady that originated in the mores of Languedoc and developed as a secular counterpart to the cult of the Virgin, exerting an important influence in medieval and Renaissance literature.

court-mar·tial (kôrt′mär′shəl, kōrt′-) *n., pl.* **courts-martial.** *Abbr.* **c.m. 1.** A military or naval court of officers appointed by a commander to try persons for offenses under military law. See **general court-martial, special court-martial, summary court-**

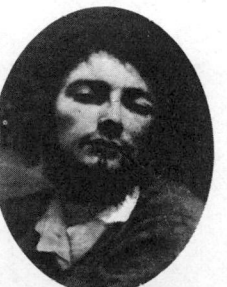

Gustave Courbet
A self-portrait

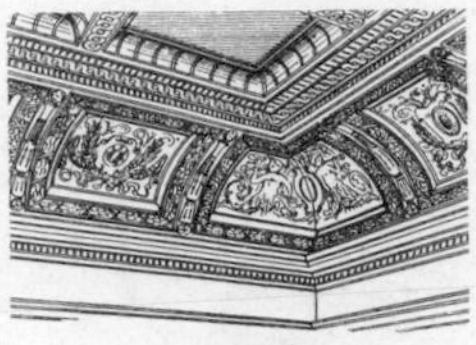

cove¹
Coved ceiling of the Louvre in Paris, France

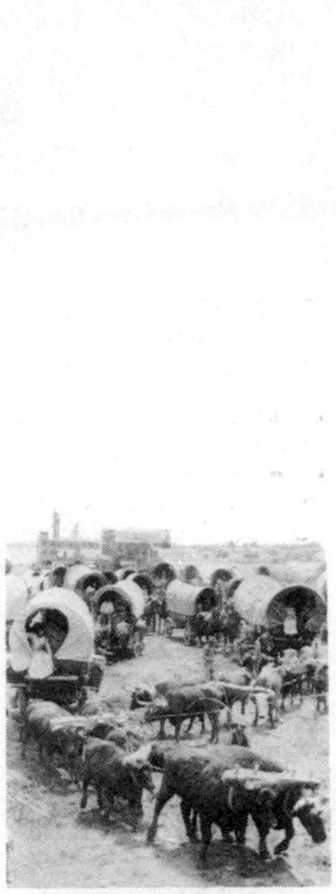

covered wagon

martial. 2. A trial by court-martial. —*tr.v.* **court-martialed** or **-tialled, -tialing** or **-tialling, -tials.** To try by court-martial.

Court of Appeals. A court to which appeals are made on points of law resulting from the judgment of a court of first instance.

court of chancery. A court with jurisdiction in equity, a **chancery** *(see).*

Court of Claims. A U.S. Federal court that determines claims of a specified sort by individuals against the United States.

Court of Common Pleas. 1. In some states of the United States, a court having general jurisdiction. Also called "common pleas." **2.** Formerly, a court in Great Britain to hear civil cases between commoners.

Court of Exchequer. Formerly, a court in Great Britain with jurisdiction in equity and common law, dealing originally with matters of revenue and later all kinds of cases, now merged in the Court of King's Bench. Also called "Exchequer."

Court of King's Bench. A superior court of common law in Great Britain, now merged in the high court of justice as the King's Bench Division. Called during the reign of a queen "Court of Queen's Bench."

Court of St. James's. The British royal court.

court plaster. An adhesive plaster cut into a small piece to cover cuts or scratches on the skin. [Originally, referring to the black silk plaster used by ladies at court to make beauty spots.]

court·room (kôrt′ro͞om′, kōrt′-, -ro͝om′) *n.* A room in which court proceedings are carried on.

court·ship (kôrt′shĭp′, kōrt′-) *n.* **1.** The act or period of wooing a woman. **2.** Solicitations, as of favors.

court tennis. A form of tennis played in a large indoor court having a specially marked-out floor and high cement walls off which the ball may be played.

court·yard (kôrt′yärd′, kōrt′-) *n.* An open space surrounded by walls or buildings, adjoining or within a large building or castle.

cous·cous (ko͞os′ko͞os′) *n.* A North African dish of crushed grain steamed and served with various meats and vegetables. [French, from Arabic *kouskous.*]

cous·in (kŭz′ən) *n.* **1.** Originally, a person related by descent from a common ancestor, but not a brother or sister. **2.** A child of one's aunt or uncle. Also called "cousin-german," "first cousin," "full cousin." **3.** A relative descended from a common ancestor, such as a grandfather, by two or more steps in a diverging line: **a.** Relatives descended the same number of steps; for example, the children of *first cousins* are *second cousins* to each other. **b.** Relatives descended an unequal number of steps; for example, the child of one's first cousin is a *first cousin once removed,* sometimes called *second cousin;* the grandchild of one's first cousin is a *first cousin twice removed;* the child of one's second cousin is a *second cousin once removed,* sometimes called *third cousin.* **4.** Any relative by blood or marriage; kinsman or kinswoman. **5.** A member of a kindred group or country: *our Canadian cousins.* **6.** A title of address used by a sovereign to a nobleman or to another sovereign. [Middle English *cosin(e),* from Old French *cosin, cousin,* from Latin *consōbrīnus,* maternal first cousin : *com-,* together + *sōbrīnus,* maternal cousin (see **swesor-** in Appendix*).] —**cous′in·ly** *adj.*

Cou·sin (ko͞o-zăN′), **Victor.** 1792–1867. French philosopher.

cous·in-ger·man (kŭz′ən-jûr′mən) *n., pl.* **cousins-german.** A first **cousin** *(see).*

Cous·teau (ko͞os-tō′), **Jacques Yves.** Born 1910. French underwater explorer and author.

couth (ko͞oth) *adj.* **1.** Refined; suave; knowledgeable. Used humorously. **2.** *Obsolete.* Friendly; familiar; known. [Middle English *couth,* familiar, known, Old English *cūth.* See **gnō-** in Appendix.*]

cou·ture (ko͞o-to͝or′; *French* ko͞o-tür′) *n.* **1.** The business of a couturier. **2.** Dressmakers and fashion designers collectively. [French, tailoring, sewing, from Old French *cousture,* from Vulgar Latin *consūtūra* (unattested), from the feminine past participle of Latin *consuere,* to sew together : *com-,* together + *suere,* to sew (see **syū-** in Appendix*).]

cou·tu·rier (ko͞o-to͞o-ryā′; *French* ko͞o-tü-ryā′) *n. Feminine* **cou·tu·rière** (ko͞o-to͞o-ryâr′; *French* ko͞o-tü-ryâr′). **1.** One who designs, makes, and sells fashionable, usually custom-made, women's clothing. **2.** An establishment engaged in this business. [French, from COUTURE.]

cou·vade (ko͞o-väd′) *n.* A practice among certain primitive peoples in which the husband of a woman in labor takes to his bed as if he were bearing the child. [Old French, "a hatching," from *couver,* to hatch, sit on (eggs), from Latin *cubāre,* to lie down (on). See **keu-²** in Appendix.*]

co·va·lence (kō-vā′ləns) *n. Chemistry.* The number of electron pairs an atom can share with other atoms. —**co·va′len·cy** *n.* —**co·va′lent** *adj.*

covalent bond. A chemical bond formed by the sharing of one or more electrons, especially pairs of electrons, between atoms.

co·var·i·ance (kō-vâr′ē-əns) *n.* **1.** *Physics.* The principle that the laws of physics have the same form regardless of the system of coordinates in which they are expressed. **2.** *Statistics.* The expected value of the product of the deviations of corresponding values of two variables from their respective means.

co·var·i·ant (kō-var′ē-ənt) *adj.* **1.** *Physics.* Expressing, exhibiting, or pertaining to covariance. **2.** *Mathematics.* Varying with another variable quantity in a manner that leaves a specified relationship unchanged.

cove¹ (kōv) *n.* **1.** A small, sheltered bay in the shoreline of a sea, river, or lake. **2. a.** A recess or small valley in the side of a mountain. **b.** A cave or cavern. **3.** A narrow gap or pass between hills or woods. **4.** A strip of prairie extending into woodland. **5.** *Architecture.* **a.** A concave molding. **b.** A curved surface forming a junction between a ceiling and a wall. In this sense, also called "coving." —*tr.v.* **coved, coving, coves.** To arch over or curve inward. [Middle English *cove,* closet, chamber, cave, Old English *cofa.* See **ku-** in Appendix.*]

cove² (kōv) *n. British Slang.* A fellow. [Probably from Romany *cofe, kova†,* man.]

co·vel·lite (kō-vĕl′īt′, kō′və-līt′) *n.* An indigo-blue mineral, CuS, an important source of copper. [Discovered by Nicholas *Covelli* (died 1829), Italian chemist.]

cov·en (kŭv′ən, kō′vən) *n.* An assembly of 13 witches. [Perhaps from Middle English *covent,* a gathering, CONVENT.]

cov·e·nant (kŭv′ə-nənt) *n.* **1.** A binding agreement made by two or more persons or parties; a compact; contract. **2.** A solemn agreement or vow made by members of a church to defend and support its faith and doctrine. **3.** *Theology.* God's promises to man, as recorded in the Old and New Testaments. **4.** *Law.* **a.** A formal sealed agreement or contract. **b.** A particular clause of such a contract. **c.** A suit to recover damages for violation of such a contract. —*v.* **covenanted, -nanting, -nants.** —*tr.* To promise by a covenant. —*intr.* To enter into a covenant; to contract. [Middle English, from Old French, from the present participle of *co(n)venir,* to agree, CONVENE.] —**cov′e·nant′al** *adj.* —**cov′e·nant′al·ly** *adv.*

cov·e·nant·ee (kŭv′ə-nən-tē′) *n.* The participant in a covenant to whom the promise is made.

cov·e·nant·er (kŭv′ə-nən-tər; *also* kŭv′ə-năn′tər *for sense 2*) *n.* **1.** One who makes a covenant. **2.** *Capital* **C.** A Scottish Presbyterian who supported either of the agreements (National Covenant, 1638, or Solemn League and Covenant, 1643) intended to defend and extend Presbyterianism.

cov·e·nant·or (kŭv′ə-nən-tər) *n.* The party to a covenant by whom the obligation expressed in it is to be performed.

Cov·en·try (kŭv′ən-trē). An industrial city of central Warwickshire, England, 18 miles southeast of Birmingham. Population, 330,000. —**send to Coventry.** To refuse to associate with; ostracize. [*Send to Coventry,* from the sending of Royalist prisoners to Coventry during the English Civil War.]

cov·er (kŭv′ər) *v.* **-ered, -ering, -ers.** —*tr.* **1.** To place something upon, over, or in front of, so as to protect, shut in, or conceal; overlay or spread with something. **2.** To put a covering on; clothe. **3.** To put a cap, hat, or the like on (one's head). **4.** To bring upon or invest (oneself or one's reputation). Used reflexively. **5.** To serve as a covering for; occupy the surface of: *Dust covered the table.* **6.** To extend over; occupy: *a farm covering more than 100 acres.* **7.** To copulate with (a female). Used of animals, especially horses. **8.** To sit on (eggs); incubate; brood. **9.** To hide or screen from view or knowledge; conceal, as a fact or crime. Often used with *up.* **10.** To protect or shield from harm, injury, or danger; to shelter. **11.** To protect by insurance; insure against a specified risk or loss. **12.** To compensate or make up for. **13.** To be sufficient to defray (a charge or expense); meet or offset (a liability). **14.** To make provision for; allow for: *Federal law does not cover all crimes.* **15.** To deal with; treat of. **16.** To travel or pass over; traverse. **17.** To have as one's territory or sphere of work. **18.** To hold within the range and aim of a firearm. **19.** *Military.* **a.** To overlook and dominate from a strategic position; have within range. **b.** To protect (a soldier, unit, or position, for example) by occupying a position from which enemy troops can be fired upon. **c.** To stand or move directly behind (a man or men). **20.** *Journalism.* To be responsible for securing and reporting the details of (an event or situation): *cover a ball game.* **21.** *Sports.* To be responsible for guarding the play of (an opponent) or for defending (an area or position): *cover left field.* **22.** To match (an opponent's stake) in a wager. **23.** *Card Games.* To play a higher-ranking card than (the one previously played). **24.** *Obsolete.* To pardon or remit: *"Thou hast covered all their sins."* (Psalms 85:2). —*intr.* **1.** To spread over a surface to protect or conceal something. **2.** *Informal.* To act as a substitute or replacement during someone's absence. **3.** To hide something in order to save someone from censure or punishment. Often used with *up: cover up for a colleague.* **4.** *Card Games.* To play a higher card than the one previously played. —*n.* **1.** Something that covers or is laid, placed, or spread over or upon something else. **2. a.** Shelter of any kind. **b.** *Military.* Natural or artificial shelter or protection by other armed units: *under a cover of mortar fire.* **3. a.** Vegetation covering an area, often serving to provide shade or prevent erosion. **b.** Underbrush or other vegetation serving as protective concealment for wild animals. **4.** Something that screens, conceals, or disguises, as a pretext. **5.** A table setting for one person. **6.** A **cover charge** *(see).* **7.** *Philately.* **a.** An envelope or wrapper for mail. **b.** An envelope, post card, or the like bearing a stamp and postal markings of special interest to stamp collectors; especially, an envelope or wrapper bearing a newly issued stamp postmarked on the date of issue. **8.** *Finance.* **a.** Funds sufficient to meet an obligation or secure against loss. **b.** Security behind different kinds of paper money. —See Synonyms at **shelter.** —**break cover.** To come out of hiding. —**take cover.** To seek concealment or protection, as from enemy fire. —**under cover. 1.** Operating secretly or under a guise; covert. **2.** Hidden; protected. **3.** Within an envelope. [Middle English *coveren,* from Old French *covrir,* from Latin *cooperīre,* to cover completely : *co-,* completely + *operīre,* to cover (see **wer-⁵** in Appendix*).] —**cov′er·er** *n.*

cov·er·age (kŭv′ər-ĭj) *n.* **1.** *Journalism.* The extent or degree to which something is observed, analyzed, and reported. **2.** The cov·er·alls (kŭv′ər-ôlz′) pl.n. A loose-fitting one-piece garment worn by workmen to protect their clothes.

cover charge. A fixed amount added to the bill, at a nightclub, for entertainment or services. Also called "cover."

cover crop. A temporary crop, such as winter rye or clover, planted to protect the soil from erosion in winter and provide humus or nitrogen when plowed under in the spring.

Cov·er·dale (kŭv′ər-dāl), Miles. 1488–1568. English Protestant clergyman; made first English translation of the entire Bible.

covered wagon. A large wagon covered with an arched canvas top, used by American pioneers for prairie travel.

cover girl. An attractive model whose picture frequently appears on magazine covers.

cov·er·ing (kŭv′ər-ĭng) n. Something that covers for protection, concealment, or warmth.

covering board. Nautical. A plank-sheer (see).

cov·er·let (kŭv′ər-lĭt) n. Also cov·er·lid (-lĭd). An ornamental cloth covering for a bed; a bedspread.

Cov·er·ley (kŭv′ər-lē), Sir Roger de. Also Roger of Coverley. An English country-dance similar, and possibly ancestral, to the Virginia reel. [Origin uncertain. The character created by Addison and Steele was named after the dance.]

covers versed cosine.

co·ver·sine (kō′vûr′sĭn′) n. Trigonometry. Versed cosine (see).

cov·ert (kŭv′ərt, kō′vərt) adj. 1. Covered or covered over; sheltered. 2. Concealed; hidden; secret. 3. Law. Protected by a husband. —See Synonyms at secret. —n. 1. A covering or cover. 2. A covered place or shelter; hiding place. 3. Thick underbrush or woodland affording cover for game; cover. 4. Covert cloth (see). 5. Zoology. One of the feathers covering the bases of the longer main feathers of a bird's wings or tail. 6. A flock of coots. —See Synonyms at flock. [Middle English, from Old French, from the past participle of covrir, to COVER.] —cov′ert·ly adv. —cov′ert·ness n.

covert cloth. A twilled cloth made of woolen or worsted yarn with cotton, silk, or rayon. It has a speckled appearance and is used for suits, coats, or the like. Also called "covert."

cov·er·ture (kŭv′ər-chər) n. 1. A covering; shelter; concealment; disguise. 2. Law. The legal status of a married woman.

cov·et (kŭv′ĭt) tr.v. -eted, -eting, -ets. 1. To desire (that which is another's). 2. To wish for excessively and culpably; crave. —See Synonyms at envy. [Middle English coveiten, from Old French coveitier, from Vulgar Latin cupiditāre (unattested), to desire, from Latin cupiditās, desire, from cupidus, desirous, from cupere, to desire. See kwep- in Appendix.*] —cov′et·a·ble adj. —cov′et·er n.

cov·et·ous (kŭv′ə-təs) adj. 1. Excessively and culpably desirous; avaricious; greedy. 2. Very desirous; eager for acquisition: covetous of learning. —cov′et·ous·ly adv. —cov′et·ous·ness n.

cov·ey (kŭv′ē) n., pl. -eys. 1. A family of partridges. 2. A small party, as of persons. —See Synonyms at flock. [Middle English covei(e), from Old French covee, a brood, from cover, couver, to hatch, sit on (eggs), from Latin cubāre, to lie down (on). See keu-² in Appendix.*]

cov·ing (kō′vĭng) n. Architecture. A molding, a cove (see).

Cov·ing·ton (kŭv′ĭng-tən). A city of northern Kentucky, on the Ohio River opposite Cincinnati, Ohio. Population, 60,000.

cow¹ (kou) n., pl. cows or archaic kine (kīn). 1. The mature female of cattle of the genus Bos. 2. The mature female of other animals, such as whales, elephants, or moose. 3. Broadly, any domesticated bovine. 4. Slang. A fat and slovenly woman. [Cow, kine; Middle English cou, kin, Old English cū, cȳ(e). See gwou- in Appendix.*]

cow² (kou) tr.v. cowed, cowing, cows. To frighten with threats or a show of force. See Synonyms at dismay. [Originally dialectal (as Scottish kow), perhaps ultimately from Old Norse kūga, to oppress. See ku- in Appendix.*]

cow·age (kou′ij) n. Also cow·hage. A tropical vine, Stizolobium pruritum, bearing reddish or blackish pods covered with bristles that cause severe itching. [Hindi Kavāch†.]

cow·ard (kou′ərd) n. One who lacks courage in the face of danger or pain; an ignobly frightened or timid person. [Middle English couherde, coward, from Old French couard, coward, perhaps "one with his tail between his legs," from coue, tail, from Latin cauda, tail. See caudate.]

Cow·ard (kou′ərd), Noël (Pierce). Born 1899. English actor, author, and composer.

cow·ard·ice (kou′ər-dĭs) n. Lack of courage in the face of danger, pain, difficulty, or opposition.

cow·ard·ly (kou′ərd-lē) adj. 1. Lacking courage; ignobly fearful. 2. Showing cowardice; befitting a coward. —adv. In the manner of a coward; basely; meanly. —cow′ard·li·ness n.

cow·bane (kou′bān′) n. 1. A plant, Oxypolis rigidior, of the southeastern and central United States, having poisonous roots and foliage, and clusters of small white flowers. 2. Any of several related plants, such as the water hemlock (see).

cow·bell (kou′bĕl′) n. A bell hung from a collar around a cow's neck to aid in locating her.

cow·ber·ry (kou′bĕr′ē) n., pl. -ries. 1. A creeping evergreen shrub, Vaccinium vitis-idaea, having pink or reddish flowers and edible, slightly acid red berries. 2. A berry of this plant. Also called "mountain cranberry," "lingonberry."

cow·bird (kou′bûrd′) n. Any of various blackbirds of the genus Molothrus and related genera, that lay their eggs in the nests of other birds, especially the common North American species M. ater. [The birds feed on cattle vermin.]

cow·boy (kou′boi′) n. 1. A hired man, especially in the western

United States, who tends cattle and performs many of his duties on horseback. 2. A performer who demonstrates feats of horsemanship, calf roping, and the like, as at a rodeo. 3. Slang. A speedy or reckless driver of a motor vehicle. 4. One of a band of loyalist guerrillas that operated between the British and American lines, mostly in Westchester County, New York, during the Revolutionary War.

cow·catch·er (kou′kăch′ər) n. The iron grille or frame that projects from the front of a locomotive or streetcar and serves to clear the track of obstructions. Also called "pilot."

Cow·ell (kou′əl), Henry (Dixon). 1897–1965. American composer; developed tone cluster and related techniques.

cow·er (kou′ər) intr.v. -ered, -ering, -ers. To cringe or shrink away from cold or in fear. See Synonyms at recoil. [Middle English couren, probably from Scandinavian, akin to Icelandic kūra, to sleep, lie in wait. See ku- in Appendix.*]

Cowes (kouz). A seaport on the northern coast of the Isle of Wight, England, about 12 miles southeast of Southampton. Population, 17,000.

cow·fish (kou′fĭsh′) n., pl. cowfish or -fishes. 1. Any of various small whales, porpoises, or similar aquatic mammals; especially, a whale of the genus Mesopledon, having a pointed snout. 2. A fish, Lactophrys quadricornis, of warm Atlantic waters, having the body encased in a bony covering and hornlike spines over each eye.

cow·hage. Variant of cowage.

cow·hand (kou′hănd) n. A cowboy.

cow·herb (kou′ûrb′, -hûrb′) n. A plant, Saponaria vaccaria, native to Europe, having clusters of deep-pink flowers.

cow·herd (kou′hûrd′) n. A person who herds or tends cattle.

cow·hide (kou′hīd′) n. 1. a. The hide of a cow. b. The leather made from this hide. 2. A strong, heavy, flexible whip, usually made of braided leather. —tr.v. cowhided, -hiding, -hides. To whip with a cowhide.

cow killer. An insect, the velvet ant (see).

cowl (koul) n. 1. a. The hood worn by monks. b. The hooded robe of a monk or a similar garment. 2. A hood-shaped covering used to increase the draft of a chimney. 3. The top portion of the front part of an automobile body, supporting the windshield and dashboard. 4. An aircraft cowling (see). —tr.v. cowled, cowling, cowls. 1. To put a cowl on. 2. To make a monk of. 3. To cover with a cowl. [Middle English coule, Old English cugele, cūle, from Late Latin cuculla, from Latin cucullus†, hood.]

cowled (kould) adj. 1. Wearing or supplied with a cowl; hooded. 2. Having the shape of a cowl.

Cow·ley (kou′lē), Abraham. 1618–1667. English poet.

cow·lick (kou′lĭk′) n. A projecting tuft of hair on the head that will not lie flat. [So called because it appears to have been licked by a cow.]

cowl·ing (kou′lĭng) n. A removable metal covering for an aircraft engine. Also called "cowl."

cow·man (kou′mən) n., pl. -men (-mĭn). 1. The owner of a cattle ranch. 2. British. A man who tends cows.

co·work·er (kō′wûrk′ər) n. A fellow worker.

cow parsnip. Any of several tall, coarse plants of the genus Heracleum, such as H. lanatum, of North America. Also called "masterwort."

cow·pea (kou′pē′) n. 1. A tropical vine, Vigna sinensis, bearing long, hanging pods and grown in the southern United States for soil improvement and as animal feed. 2. The edible, pealike seed of this plant. In this sense, also called "black-eyed pea."

Cow·per (koo′pər), William. 1731–1800. English poet.

Cow·per's glands (kou′pərz, koo′pərz). Either of a pair of small compound racemose glands lying alongside and discharging into the male urethra. [Discovered by William Cowper (1666–1709), English anatomist.]

cow pilot. A fish, the pintano (see).

cow·poke (kou′pōk′) n. Informal. A cowboy.

cow pony. A small, agile horse used in roundups.

cow·pox (kou′pŏks′) n. A contagious skin disease of cattle caused by a virus that is isolated and used to vaccinate humans against smallpox. Also called "vaccinia."

cow·punch·er (kou′pŭn′chər) n. Informal. A cowboy.

cow·ry (kou′rē) n., pl. -ries. Also cow·rie. Any of various tropical marine mollusks of the family Cypraeidae, having glossy, often brightly marked shells, some of which are used as money in the South Pacific and Africa. [Hindi kaurī, from Sanskrit kaparda, from Dravidian, akin to Tamil kōtu, shell.]

cow shark. Any of several sharks of the family Hexanchidae, of warm and temperate seas.

cow·skin (kou′skĭn′) n. 1. The hide of a cow. 2. Leather made from this hide.

cow·slip (kou′slĭp′) n. 1. An Old World primrose, Primula veris, having fragrant yellow flowers. 2. The marsh marigold (see). See Virginia cowslip, shooting star. [Middle English cowslyppe, Old English cūslyppe, "cow dung" (probably because some varieties are found in cow pastures) : cū, cow + slyppe, slypa, slime, paste (see sleubh- in Appendix*).]

cow town. A small town in a cattle-raising area.

cox (kŏks) n. Informal. A coxswain (see). —v. coxed, coxing, coxes. Informal. —tr. To serve as coxswain for (a boat). —intr. To act as coxswain.

cox·a (kŏk′sə) n., pl. cox·ae (kŏk′sē′). 1. Anatomy. The hip or hip joint. 2. Zoology. The first segment of the leg of an insect or other arthropod, adjoining and attached to the body. [Latin coxa, the hip, hipbone. See koks̄ in Appendix.*]

cox·al·gi·a (kŏk-săl′jē-ə) n. Pain in or disease of the hip. [New Latin : cox(a) + -ALGIA.] —cox·al′gic adj.

cowboy
Drawing by
Charles M. Russell

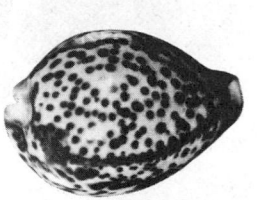
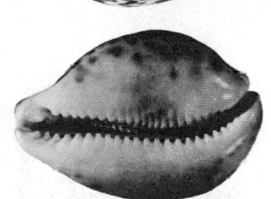
cowry
Cypraea tigris
Tiger cowry of the
Indian and Pacific oceans

cowbane
Oxypolis rigidior

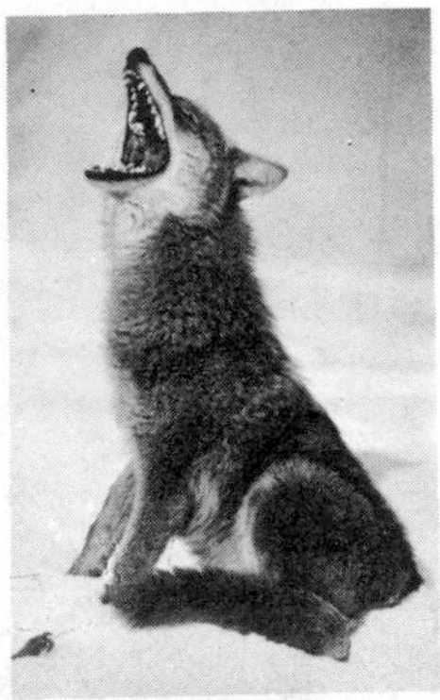

coyote

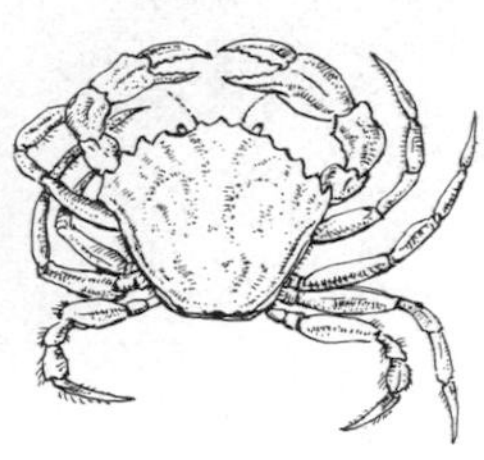

crab[1]
Carcinides maenas

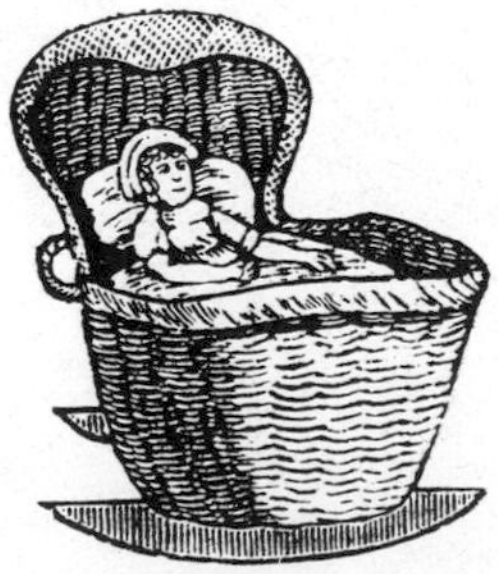

cradle

cox·comb (kŏks′kōm′) *n.* **1.** A conceited dandy; fop. **2.** *Obsolete.* A cap resembling a cockscomb, worn by a professional jester. **3.** Variant of **cockscomb.** [Middle English *cokkes comb,* "cock's comb."]

cox·comb·ry (kŏks′kōm′rē) *n., pl.* **-ries.** Arrogance and pretension in manner or behavior; foolishness; foppery.

Cox·sack·ie virus (kŏŏk-säk′ē). Any of a group of enteroviruses that produce a disease resembling poliomyelitis without paralysis. [The virus was first found in a resident of *Coxsackie,* New York.]

cox·swain (kŏk′sən, kŏk′swān′) *n.* Also **cock·swain.** A person who steers a boat or racing shell or has charge of its crew. Also informally called "cox." [Middle English *cok swain* : *cok,* COCKBOAT + *swain,* servant, SWAIN.]

Cox·well chair. Variant of **Cogswell chair.**

coy (koi) *adj.* **coyer, coyest. 1.** Shy and demure; retiring. **2.** Pretending shyness or modesty; affectedly shy. **3.** Annoyingly unwilling to commit oneself; affectedly devious. —See Synonyms at **shy.** [Middle English, from Old French *coi,* shy, quiet, from Vulgar Latin *quētus* (unattested), variant of Latin *quiētus,* QUIET.] —**coy′ly** *adv.* —**coy′ness** *n.*

coy·o·te (kī-ō′tē, kī′ō-tē′) *n.* **1.** A wolflike carnivorous animal, *Canis latrans,* common in western North America and ranging eastward to Pennsylvania and New York. **2.** *Slang.* A contemptible sneak. [Mexican Spanish, from Nahuatl *coyotl.*]

co·yo·til·lo (kō′yō-tēl′yō, kī′-) *n., pl.* **-los.** A poisonous shrub, *Karwinskia humboldtiana,* of the southwestern United States and Mexico. [Mexican Spanish, diminutive of COYOTE.]

coy·pu (koi′pōō) *n., pl.* **-pus.** A large, beaverlike South American rodent, *Myocaster coypu,* valued for its fur. Also called "nutria." [American Spanish *coipú,* from Araucanian *kóypu.*]

coz (kŭz) *n. Informal.* Cousin.

coz·en (kŭz′ən) *v.* **-ened, -ening, -ens.** —*tr.* To deceive, by means of a petty trick or fraud. —*intr.* To act with intent to deceive. [Possibly from obsolete Italian *cozzonare,* "to be a horse trader," cheat, from *cozzone,* broker, horse trader, from Latin *coctiō,* broker, possibly from Etruscan.] —**coz′en·er** *n.*

coz·en·age (kŭz′ən-ĭj) *n.* **1.** The art or practice of cozening; cheating. **2.** A deception; trickery; fraud.

co·zy (kō′zē) *adj.* **-zier, -ziest.** Also **co·sy. 1.** Snug and comfortable; warm. **2.** Marked by friendly intimacy. **3.** *Informal.* Marked by close association for devious purposes: *a cozy agreement.* —See Synonyms at **comfortable.** —*n., pl.* **cozies.** Also **co·sy.** A padded or knitted covering placed over a teapot to keep the tea hot. Also called "tea cozy." [Scottish *cosie, colsie*†.] —**co′zi·ly** *adv.* —**co′zi·ness** *n.*

Coz·zens (kŭz′ənz), **James Gould.** Born 1903. American author of novels and short stories.

cP centipoise.

cp. compare.

C.P. 1. Cape Province. **2.** command post. **3.** Communist Party.

C.P.A. certified public accountant.

cpd. compound.

CPH Airport code for Copenhagen, Denmark.

Cpl. corporal.

C.P.O. chief petty officer.

cps cycles per second.

CPT Airport code for Cape Town, Republic of South Africa.

CQ Code letters used at the beginning of radio messages intended for all receivers. [C(ALL TO) Q(UARTERS).]

Cr The symbol for the element chromium.

cr. 1. credit; creditor. **2.** creek. **3.** crescendo. **4.** crown.

craal. Variant of **kraal.**

crab[1] (krăb) *n.* **1.** Any of various predominantly marine crustaceans of the section Brachyura within the order Decapoda, characterized by a broad, flattened cephalothorax covered by a hard carapace and having the small abdomen concealed beneath it, and five pairs of legs, of which the anterior pair are large and pincerlike. **2.** Any of various similar related crustaceans, such as the **hermit crab** or the **king crab** *(both of which see).* **3.** The **horseshoe crab** *(see).* **4.** The **crab louse** *(see).* **5.** *Capital* **C.** The constellation and sign of the zodiac, **Cancer** *(see).* **6.** The maneuvering of an aircraft partially into a crosswind in order to compensate for drift. **7.** Any of various machines for handling or hoisting heavy weights. **8.** *Plural.* The lowest cast, usually a two or three, of a pair of dice. —**catch a crab.** In rowing, to strike the water with an oar in recovering a stroke or to miss it in making one. —*v.* **crabbed, crabbing, crabs.** —*intr.* **1.** To hunt or catch crabs. **2.** *Nautical.* To drift diagonally or sidewise. —*tr. Aviation.* To direct (an aircraft) partly into a crosswind to eliminate drift. [Middle English *crab(be),* Old English *crabba.* See **gerebh-** in Appendix.*]

crab[2] (krăb) *n.* **1.** The crab apple or its fruit. **2.** A quarrelsome, ill-tempered person. —*v.* **crabbed** (krăbd), **crabbing, crabs.** —*intr. Informal.* To criticize; find fault. —*tr.* **1.** *Informal.* To interfere with and ruin. **2.** *Informal.* To find fault with. [Middle English *crab(be),* probably from Scandinavian, akin to Swedish *skrabbe*†.]

crab apple. 1. Any of several trees of the genus *Pyrus,* having white, pink, or red flowers and small, applelike fruit. **2.** The tart fruit of any of these trees, used for making jelly.

Crabbe (krăb), **George.** 1754–1832. English poet.

crab·bed (krăb′ĭd) *adj.* **1.** Irritable and perverse in disposition; ill-tempered. **2.** Difficult to understand; complicated. **3.** Difficult to read. Said of handwriting. [Middle English, partly from *crabbe,* CRAB, referring to the perversity of its gait, and partly from *crabbe,* CRAB (apple), referring to its sourness.] —**crab′bed·ly** *adv.* —**crab′bed·ness** *n.*

crab·ber (krăb′ər) *n.* **1.** A person whose occupation is fishing for crabs. **2.** The boat used in fishing for crabs.

crab·by (krăb′ē) *adj.* **-bier, -biest.** Grouchy; ill-tempered.

crab cactus. The **Christmas cactus** *(see).*

crab·grass (krăb′grăs′, -gräs′) *n.* Any of various coarse grasses of the genus *Digitaria,* that tend to spread and displace other grasses in lawns.

Crab Island. See **Vieques Island.**

crab louse. A body louse, *Phthirus pubis,* that generally infests the pubic region and causes severe itching.

crabs (krăbz) *pl.n. Informal.* Infestation by crab lice.

crab·stick (krăb′stĭk′) *n.* A stick made of crab-apple wood.

crack (krăk) *v.* **cracked, cracking, cracks.** —*intr.* **1.** To break with a sharp, snapping sound. **2.** To make such a sound; to snap. **3.** To break without dividing into parts; split slightly. **4.** To change sharply in pitch or timbre, as from hoarseness or emotion. Used of the voice. **5.** To break down; fail; give out. **6.** *Chemistry.* To decompose into simpler compounds. —*tr.* **1.** To cause to make a sharp, snapping sound; to snap: *crack the whip.* **2.** To cause to break or split slightly or completely. **3.** To break with a sharp, snapping sound: *crack an egg.* **4.** To strike with a sudden, sharp sound. **5.** To break open or into. **6.** To discover the solution to, especially after considerable effort: *crack a problem.* **7.** To cause (the voice) to crack. **8.** *Informal.* To tell (a joke). **9.** To impair mentally; render insane. **10.** To impair or diminish (a reputation, for example). **11.** To reduce (petroleum) to simpler compounds by cracking. —See Synonyms at **break.** —**crack a book.** *Slang.* To open a book for studying. —**crack a smile.** *Slang.* To smile. —**cracked up to be.** Praised or lauded as; believed to be. —*n.* **1.** A sharp, snapping sound, such as the report of a firearm. **2.** A partial split or break; flaw; fissure. **3.** A slight, narrow space: *The window was open a crack.* **4.** A sharp, resounding blow. **5.** A mental or physical impairment; a defect. **6.** A cracking vocal tone or sound, as in hoarseness. **7.** An attempt; a chance: *gave him a crack at the job.* **8.** A flippant or sarcastic remark. **9.** A moment; instant: *at the crack of dawn.* —See Synonyms at **joke.** —*adj.* Excelling in skill or achievement; superior; first-rate: *a crack marksman.* [Middle English *craken,* Old English *cracian.* See **ger-**[4] in Appendix.*]

crack·brain (krăk′brān′) *n.* A foolish or insane person. —**crack′brained′** *adj.*

crack down. To become more demanding, severe, or strict. Often used with *on: crack down on student absences.*

crack·down (krăk′doun′) *n.* Sudden punitive action.

crack·er (krăk′ər) *n.* **1.** A thin, crisp wafer or biscuit, usually made of unleavened, unsweetened dough. **2.** A firecracker. **3.** A small cardboard cylinder covered with decorative paper and containing candy or a favor and a weak explosive that makes a sharp popping noise when a paper strip is pulled at one or both ends and torn. Also called "cracker bonbon." **4.** A poor white person of the rural southeastern United States. Used disparagingly. **5.** One that cracks.

crack·er-bar·rel (krăk′ər-băr′əl) *adj.* Resembling or characteristic of the extended informal discussions carried on by persons habitually assembled at a general store: *cracker-barrel theories.* [Cracker barrels were common fixtures in country stores.]

crack·er·jack (krăk′ər-jăk′) *adj.* Also **crack·a·jack** (krăk′ə-). *Slang.* Of excellent quality or ability; fine. —*n.* Also **crack·a·jack.** *Slang.* Someone or something with excellent skills or abilities. [From CRACK (proficient) + JACK (man).]

crack·ers (krăk′ərz) *adj. Chiefly British Slang.* Insane.

crack·ing (krăk′ĭng) *n. Chemistry.* Thermal decomposition, sometimes with catalysis, of a complex substance; especially, such decomposition of petroleum to extract low-boiling fractions such as gasoline.

crack·le (krăk′əl) *v.* **-led, -ling, -les.** —*intr.* To make a succession of slight sharp, snapping noises, as a small fire. —*tr.* **1.** To crush (paper, for example) with such sounds. **2.** To cause (china, for example) to become covered with a network of fine cracks. —*n.* **1.** The act or sound of crackling. **2.** A network of fine cracks on the surface of glazed pottery, china, or glassware. **3.** Ware bearing this network of cracks. Also called "crackleware." [Frequentative of CRACK.]

crack·ling (krăk′lĭng) *n.* **1.** The production of a succession of slight sharp, snapping noises. **2.** The crisp browned rind of roasted pork. **3.** *Plural.* The crisp bits that remain of pork fat after rendering.

crack·ly (krăk′lē) *adj.* Likely to crackle; crisp.

crack·nel (krăk′nəl) *n.* **1.** A hard, crisp biscuit. **2.** *Plural.* Crisp bits of fried pork fat. [Middle English *crak(e)nel,* probably from Old French *craquelin,* from Middle Dutch *krākelinc,* from *krāken,* to crack. See **ger-**[4] in Appendix.*]

crack·pot (krăk′pŏt′) *n.* An eccentric person, especially one espousing bizarre ideas. —**crack′pot′** *adj.*

crack up. *Informal.* **1.** To crash; collide. **2.** To have or be involved in an automobile accident. **3.** To have a mental or physical breakdown. **4.** To laugh boisterously or to cause (a person) to laugh boisterously.

crack·up (krăk′ŭp′) *n.* **1.** A collision, as of an airplane or automobile. **2.** A mental or physical breakdown.

crack·y (krăk′ē) *interj.* Used to express surprise, as in the phrase *by cracky.* [Variant of dialectal *crikey,* perhaps euphemistic variant of *(by) Christ!* or Latin *Christe!*]

Crac·ow. The English name for **Kraków.**

-cracy. Indicates government or rule; for example, **mobocracy.** [Old French *-cratie,* from Late Latin *-cratia,* from Greek *-kratia,* from *kratos,* strength, power. See **kar-**[1] in Appendix.*]

cra·dle (krād′l) *n.* **1.** A small, low bed for an infant, often furnished with rockers. **2.** A place of origin or infancy; birthplace. **3.** A framework of wood or metal used to support something, such as a ship undergoing construction or repair. **4.** A framework used to protect an injured limb. **5.** The part of a telephone that contains the connecting switch upon which the receiver and mouthpiece unit is supported. **6. a.** A frame projecting above a scythe, used to catch grain as it is cut so that it can be laid flat. **b.** A scythe equipped with such a frame. **7.** A low, flat framework that rolls on casters, for use by a mechanic working beneath an automobile. **8.** *Mining.* A boxlike device furnished with rockers, used for washing gold-bearing dirt. **—rob the cradle.** *Informal.* To have as a spouse or sweetheart one much younger than oneself. *—v.* **cradled, -dling, -dles.** *—tr.* **1.** To place into, rock, or hold in or as if in a cradle. **2.** To care for or nurture in infancy. **3.** To reap (grain) with a cradle. **4.** To place or support (a ship) in a cradle. **5.** *Mining.* To wash (gold-bearing dirt) in a cradle. *—intr.* **1.** To lie in or as if in a cradle. **2.** To reap grain with a cradle. [Middle English *cradel,* Old English *cradol, cradel.* See **ger-**[3] in Appendix.*] **—cra′dler** *n.*

cra·dle·song (krād′l-sông′, -sŏng′) *n.* A lullaby.

craft (krăft, kräft) *n., pl.* **crafts** or **craft** (for sense 5). **1.** Skill or ability in something, especially in handwork or the arts; proficiency; expertness. **2.** Skill in evasion or deception; cunning; guile. **3.** An occupation or trade, especially one requiring manual dexterity. **4.** The membership of such an occupation or trade; a guild. **5.** A boat, ship, or aircraft. *—tr.v.* **crafted, crafting, crafts.** To make by hand. [Middle English *craft,* strength, skill, device, Old English *cræft,* from West Germanic *kraftaz, krab-taz* (both unattested), strength.]

-craft. Indicates work, art, or practice of; for example, **woodcraft, stagecraft.** [From CRAFT.]

crafts·man (krăfts′mən, kräfts′-) *n., pl.* **-men** (-mĭn). **1.** A skilled worker who practices a craft by occupation. **2.** An artist as considered with regard to technique. **—crafts′man·ly** *adv.* **—crafts′man·ship′** *n.*

craft union. A labor union limited in membership to workers engaged in the same craft. Also called "horizontal union." Compare **industrial union.**

craft·y (krăf′tē, kräf′-) *adj.* **-ier, -iest. 1.** Skilled in underhandedness and deception; shrewd; cunning. **2.** *Archaic.* Skillful; ingenious; dexterous. —See Synonyms at **sly.** **—craft′i·ly** *adv.* **—craft′i·ness** *n.*

crag (krăg) *n.* A steeply projecting mass of rock forming part of a rugged cliff or headland. [Middle English, from Celtic *kar-n-, kr-ag-* (both unattested). See **cairn.**]

crag·gy (krăg′ē) *adj.* **-gier, -giest.** Also **crag·ged** (krăg′ĭd). Having crags; steep and rugged. **—crag′gi·ly** *adv.* **—crag′gi·ness** *n.*

Craig (krāg), **(Edward) Gordon.** 1872–1966. British theatrical designer, producer, and director; son of Ellen Terry.

Cra·io·va (krä-yō′vä). An industrial city of southern Rumania, 120 miles west of Bucharest. Population, 119,000.

crake (krāk) *n.* Any of several birds of the family Rallidae, such as the **corncrake** *(see),* or a marsh bird of the genus *Porzana.* [Middle English *crak, crake,* crow, raven, from Old Norse *krāka.* See **ger-**[4] in Appendix.*]

cram (krăm) *v.* **crammed, cramming, crams.** *—tr.* **1.** To force, press, or squeeze into an insufficient space; to stuff. **2.** To fill too tightly. **3.** To gorge with food. **4.** *Informal.* To prepare hastily (a person) or review and study (a subject) for an examination. *—intr.* **1.** To gorge oneself with food. **2.** *Informal.* To make a concentrated last-minute review of a given academic subject, as in studying for an examination. *—n.* **1.** The act of, or condition resulting from, cramming. **2.** *Informal.* The knowledge acquired by cramming. [Middle English *crammen,* Old English *crammian.* See **ger-**[1] in Appendix.*] **—cram′mer** *n.*

cram·bo (krăm′bō) *n., pl.* **-bos. 1.** A word game in which a player or team must find and express a rhyme for a word or line presented by the opposing player or team. **2.** Doggerel. A term of contempt. [Obsolete *crambe,* "stale cabbage," tedious repetition, from Latin *crambē (repetīta),* "cabbage (served up again)" (expression used by Juvenal), from Greek *krambē.* See **skerbh-** in Appendix.*]

cramp[1] (krămp) *n.* **1.** A sudden involuntary muscular contraction causing severe pain, often occurring in the leg or shoulder as the result of strain or chill. **2.** A temporary partial paralysis of habitually or excessively used muscles: *writer's cramp.* **3.** *Plural.* Sharp, persistent pains in the abdomen. *—tr.v.* **cramped, cramping, cramps.** To affect or cause to be affected with or as if with a cramp. [Middle English *crampe,* from Old French, probably from Old High German *krampho.* See **ger-**[3] in Appendix.*]

cramp[2] (krămp) *n.* **1.** A bar, usually of iron, with right-angle bends at both ends, used for permanently holding together stones, timber, and other materials used in building. Also called "cramp iron." **2.** A frame with an adjustable part to hold pieces together; a clamp. **3.** Anything that compresses or restrains. **4.** A confined position or part. *—tr.v.* **cramped, cramping, cramps. 1.** To hold together with a cramp. **2.** To confine; restrict; hamper. **3. a.** To steer (the wheels of a vehicle) to make a turn. **b.** To jam (a wheel) by a short turn. **—cramp one's style.** *Slang.* To interfere with or hamper one's usual confidence or skill. *—adj.* **1.** Restricted; contracted; narrowed. **2.** Difficult to read or decipher, as some handwriting. [Middle Dutch *crampe,* hook. See **ger-**[3] in Appendix.*]

cramp·fish (krămp′fĭsh′) *n., pl.* **crampfish** or **-fishes.** The **electric ray** *(see).* [From CRAMP (pain), from its ability to give electric shocks.]

cram·pon (krăm′pən) *n.* Also **cram·poon** (krăm pōōn′). **1.** A hinged pair of curved iron bars for raising heavy objects, such as stones or timber. **2.** *Usually plural.* An iron spike attached to the shoe to prevent slipping when climbing or walking on ice. [Old French *crampon,* perhaps from Frankish *kramp* (unattested), hook. See **ger-**[3] in Appendix.*]

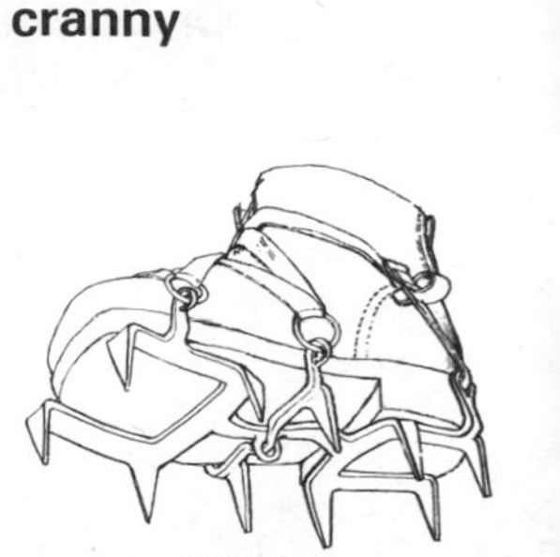

crampon
Boot equipped with crampons

Cra·nach (krăn′ək; *German* krä′näkh), **Lucas.** 1472–1553. German painter and engraver.

cran·ber·ry (krăn′bĕr′ē, -bər-ē) *n., pl.* **-ries. 1.** A slender, trailing North American shrub, *Vaccinium macrocarpon,* growing in damp ground and bearing tart red berries. **2.** The edible berry of this plant, often made into sauce or jelly. **3.** Any of various similar or related plants, especially the European species *V. oxycoccous.* [Partial translation of Low German *kraanbere,* "crane-berry" (from the stamens which resemble a beak) : *kraan,* a crane, from Middle Low German *kran* (see **ger-**[4] in Appendix*) + BERRY.]

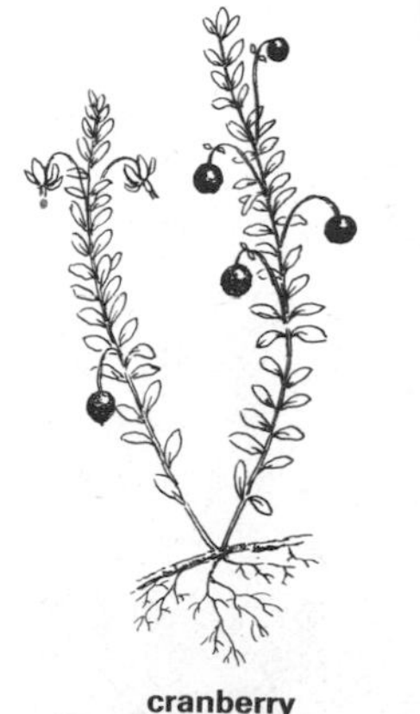

cranberry
Vaccinium macrocarpon

cranberry bush. The **high-bush cranberry** *(see).*

cranberry tree. The **guelder rose** *(see).*

Cran·borne, Viscount. See Robert **Cecil.**

crane (krān) *n.* **1.** Any of various large wading birds of the family Gruidae, having a long neck, long legs, and a long bill. **2.** Loosely, a similar bird, such as a heron. **3.** A machine for hoisting and moving heavy objects by means of cables attached to a movable boom. **4.** Any of various devices with a swinging arm, as one in a fireplace for suspending a pot. *—v.* **craned, craning, cranes.** *—tr.* **1.** To hoist or move with or as if with a crane. **2.** To strain and stretch (the neck). *—intr.* **1.** To stretch one's neck for a better view. **2. a.** To balk and lean forward, as a horse before jumping. **b.** To hesitate. [Middle English *crane,* Old English *cran.* See **ger-**[4] in Appendix.*]

crane

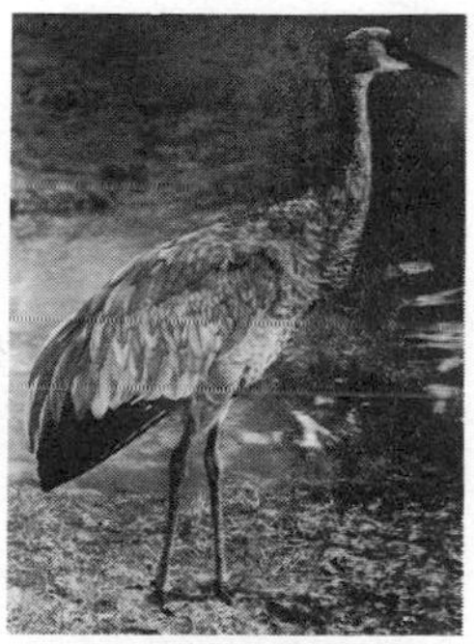

Grus canadensis
Sandhill crane

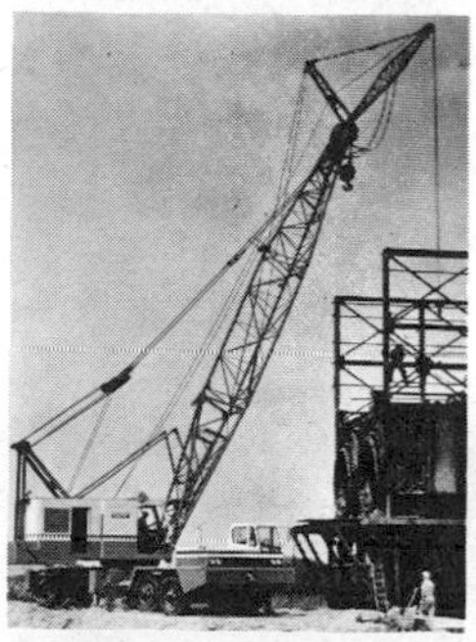

A transit crane

Crane (krān), **(Harold) Hart.** 1899–1932. American poet.

Crane (krān), **Stephen.** 1871–1900. American writer; author of *The Red Badge of Courage.*

crane fly. Any of numerous long-legged, slender-bodied flies of the family Tipulidae, having the general appearance of a large mosquito. Also *chiefly British* "daddy longlegs."

cranes·bill (krānz′bĭl′) *n.* Any of various plants of the genus *Geranium.* See **wild geranium.**

cra·ni·al (krā′nē-əl) *adj.* Of or pertaining to the skull. [From CRANIUM.]

cranial index. The ratio of the maximum width to the maximum length of the cranium, multiplied by 100. Compare **cephalic index.**

cranial nerve. Any of several nerves that arise in pairs from the brainstem and reach the periphery through openings in the skull.

cra·ni·ate (krā′nē-ĭt, -nē-āt′) *adj.* Having a skull. *—n.* Any animal having a skull; a vertebrate. [CRANI(O)- + -ATE.]

cranio-, crani-. Indicates cranium or cranial; for example, **craniology, craniate.** [From CRANIUM.]

cra·ni·ol·o·gy (krā′nē-ŏl′ə-jē) *n.* The scientific study of the characteristics of the skull, such as size and shape, especially in humans. [CRANIO- + -LOGY.] **—cra′ni·o·log′i·cal** (-ə-lŏj′ĭ-kəl) *adj.* **—cra′ni·o·log′i·cal·ly** *adv.* **—cra′ni·ol′o·gist** *n.*

cra·ni·om·e·ter (krā′nē-ŏm′ə-tər) *n.* An instrument for measuring skulls. [CRANIO- + -METER.] **—cra′ni·o·met′ric** (-ə-mĕt′rĭk), **cra′ni·o·met′ri·cal** *adj.* **—cra′ni·om′e·try** *n.*

cra·ni·o·sa·cral system (krā′nē-ō-săk′rəl, -sā′krəl). The **parasympathetic nervous system** *(see).*

cra·ni·ot·o·my (krā′nē-ŏt′ə-mē) *n. pl.* **-mies.** *Surgery.* **1.** The cutting or removal of part of the skull. **2.** The cutting or breaking of the fetal skull to reduce its size for removal when normal delivery is not possible. [CRANIO- + -TOMY.]

cra·ni·um (krā′nē-əm) *n., pl.* **-ums** or **-nia** (-nē-ə). **1.** The skull of a vertebrate. **2.** The portion of the skull enclosing the brain. [Medieval Latin *crānium,* from Greek *kranion.* See **ker-**[1] in Appendix.*]

crank[1] (krăngk) *n.* **1.** A device for transmitting rotary motion, consisting of a handle or arm attached at right angles to a shaft. **2.** A turn of speech; verbal conceit. **3.** A peculiar or eccentric idea or action. **4.** *Informal.* **a.** A grouchy person. **b.** An eccentric. *—v.* **cranked, cranking, cranks.** *—tr.* **1.** To start or operate (an engine, for example) by turning a crank. **2.** To make into the shape of a crank; twist; bend. **3.** To provide with a crank. *—intr.* **1.** To turn a crank. **2.** To twist; wind. [Middle English *crank,* Old English *cranc* (only in *crancstæf,* a weaving instrument). See **ger-**[3] in Appendix.*]

crank[2] (krăngk) *adj. Nautical.* Liable to capsize; unstable. [Short for earlier *crank-sided*†, lopsided.]

crank[3] (krăngk) *adj. Regional.* Lively; cheerful; spirited. [Middle English *cranke*†.]

crank·case (krăngk′kās′) *n.* The metal case enclosing the crankshaft and associated parts in a reciprocating engine.

crank·pin (krăngk′pĭn′) *n.* Also **crank pin.** A bar or cylinder in the arm of a crank to which a reciprocating member or connecting rod is attached.

crank·shaft (krăngk′shăft′, -shäft′) *n.* A shaft that turns or is turned by a crank.

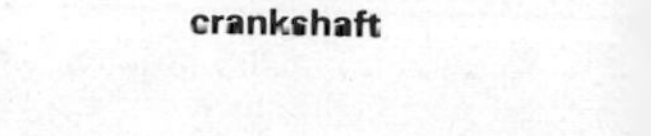

crankshaft

crank·y[1] (krăng′kē) *adj.* **-ier, -iest. 1.** Ill-tempered; peevish. **2.** Odd; eccentric. **3.** Full of bends and turns; crooked. **—crank′i·ly** *adv.* **—crank′i·ness** *n.*

crank·y[2] (krăng′kē) *adj.* **-ier, -iest. 1.** *Nautical.* Liable to capsize. **2.** Rickety; loose; shaky.

Cran·mer (krăn′mər), **Thomas.** 1489–1556. First Protestant Archbishop of Canterbury.

cran·ny (krăn′ē) *n., pl.* **-nies.** A small opening, as in a wall or rock face; crevice; fissure. [Middle English *crani,* from Old French *cran, cren,* notch, perhaps from Late Latin *crēna.* See **crenate.**] **—cran′nied** *adj.*

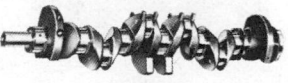

Cran·ston (krăn′stən). A city in the north of Rhode Island near Providence. Population, 67,000.

crap (krăp) *n.* **1.** A losing throw of the dice in the game of **craps** *(see).* **2.** *Vulgar.* Excrement. **3.** *Vulgar Slang.* Nonsense. **4.** *Vulgar Slang.* Something worthless. —*intr.v.* **crapped, crapp·ing, craps.** *Vulgar.* To defecate. —**crap out. 1.** To make a losing throw in the game of craps. **2.** *Slang.* To fail. ["Throw of dice," back-formation from CRAPS. In other senses, Middle English *crappe,* residual rubbish, chaff, from Middle Dutch *crappe,* probably from *crappen*†, to tear off.] —**crap′py** *adj.*

crape. Variant of **crepe.**

crape·hang·er (krāp′hăng′gər) *n.* A morose, gloomy, or pessimistic person.

crape jasmine (krāp). A fragrant shrub, *Tabernaemontana coronaria,* of India, cultivated in warm regions for its white flowers. [From the crinkled lobes of the corolla.]

crape myrtle. Also **crepe myrtle.** An Oriental shrub, *Lagerstroemia indica,* widely cultivated in warm climates for its showy pink, red, or white flowers.

crap·pie (krăp′ē) *n., pl.* **-pies.** Either of two edible North American freshwater fishes, *Pomoxis nigromaculatus,* the *black crappie,* or *P. annularis,* the *white crappie,* related to the sunfishes. [Canadian French *crapet*†.]

craps (krăps) *n.* Plural in form, usually used with a singular verb. A gambling game played with two dice in which a first throw of 7 or 11 wins, a first throw of 2, 3, or 12 loses the bet, and a first throw of any other number (a point) must be repeated to win before a 7 is thrown, which loses both the bet and the dice. [Louisiana French, from French *crabs, craps,* from obsolete English slang *crabs,* the lowest throw at hazard, plural of CRAB.]

crap·shoot·er (krăp′shōō′tər) *n.* One who plays craps.

crap·u·lence (krăp′yŏŏ-ləns) *n.* **1.** Sickness caused by excessive eating or drinking. **2.** Excessive indulgence; intemperance. [From Late Latin *crāpulentus,* drunk, from Latin *crāpula,* intoxication, from Greek *kraipalē*†, hangover, intoxication.] —**crap′u·lent, crap′u·lous** *adj.*

crash¹ (krăsh) *v.* **crashed, crashing, crashes.** —*intr.* **1.** To fall or collide noisily; smash. **2.** To undergo sudden damage or destruction on impact. **3.** To make a sudden loud noise. **4.** To move noisily or so as to cause damage. **5.** To fail suddenly, as a business or an economy. —*tr.* **1.** To cause to crash. **2.** To dash to pieces; smash. **3.** *Informal.* To join or enter without invitation. —*n.* **1.** A sudden loud noise, as of something breaking. **2.** A wrecking; smashing; collision. **3.** A sudden business failure. —*adj. Informal.* Of or characterized by an intensive effort to produce or accomplish something: *a crash program.* [Middle English *crashen,* blend of *crasen,* to shatter, CRAZE, and *dashen,* to DASH.] —**crash′er** *n.*

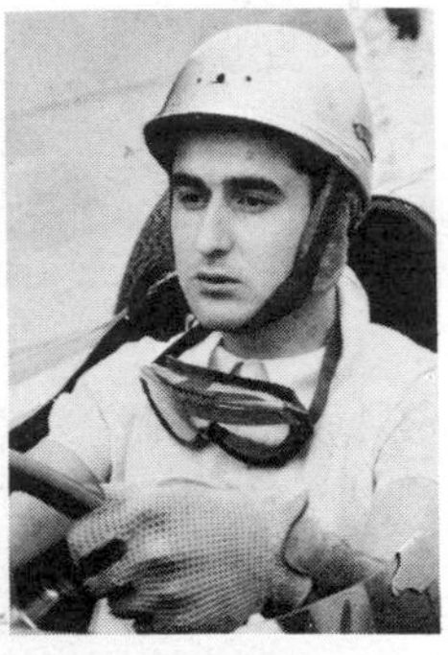

crash helmet
Racing driver wearing a crash helmet

crash² (krăsh) *n.* **1.** A coarse, light, unevenly woven fabric of cotton or linen, used for towels and curtains. **2.** Starched reinforced fabric used to strengthen a book binding or the spine of a bound book. [Russian *krashenina,* a kind of colored linen, from *krashenie,* coloring, from *krasit′,* to color, from *krasa,* beauty. See **kar-²** in Appendix.*]

Crash·aw (krăsh′ô), **Richard.** 1613–1649. English poet.

crash dive. *Naval.* A rapid submerging of a submarine, especially in an emergency.

crash helmet. A padded helmet, as worn by motorcyclists and aviators, to protect the head.

crash-land (krăsh′lănd′) *v.* **-landed, -landing, -lands.** —*tr.* To land and damage (an aircraft) under emergency conditions. —*intr.* To crash-land an aircraft. —**crash landing.**

cra·sis (krā′sĭs) *n., pl.* **-ses** (-sēz′). Vowel contraction in the elision of two adjacent words. [New Latin, from Greek *krasis,* "a mixture." See **kerə-** in Appendix.*]

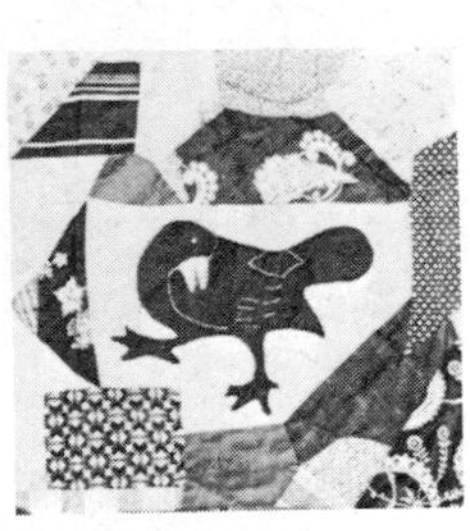

crazy quilt

crass (krăs) *adj.* **crasser, crassest. 1.** Grossly ignorant; coarse; unfeeling; stupid. **2.** *Rare.* Thick; coarse. —See Synonyms at **coarse, stupid.** [Latin *crassus*†, fat, gross, dense.] —**crass′ly** *adv.* —**crass′ness** *n.*

Cras·sus (krăs′əs), **Marcus Licinius.** 115?–53 B.C. Roman general; member of the first triumvirate.

–crat. Indicates a participant or supporter of a class or form of government; for example, **technocrat, Dixiecrat.** [French *-crate,* from Greek *-kratēs,* from *-kratia,* -CRACY.]

crate (krāt) *n.* **1.** A container for storing or shipping things, as: **a.** A slatted wooden case or box. **b.** A wicker basket. **2.** The contents of such containers. **3.** *Slang.* An old, badly used, rickety vehicle, such as an automobile or aircraft. —*tr.v.* **crated, crating, crates.** To pack into a crate. [Latin *crātis,* wickerwork, hurdle. See **kert-** in Appendix.*] —**crat′er** *n.*

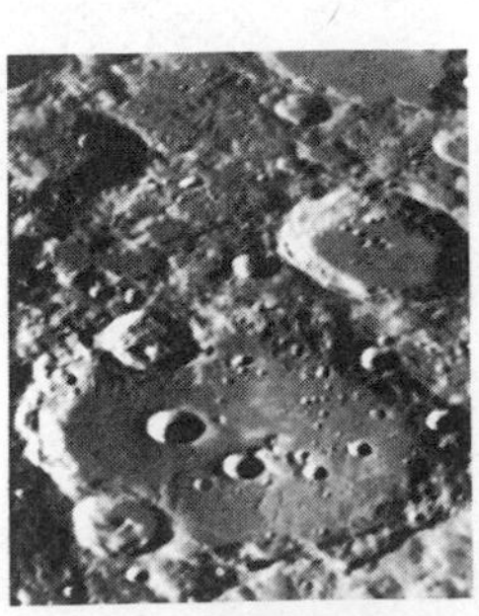

crater
The crater Clavius and surrounding region of the moon

cra·ter (krā′tər) *n.* **1.** A bowl-shaped depression at the mouth of a volcano or geyser. **2.** Any pit resembling this, especially when formed by an explosion or by the impact of a meteor. —See Synonyms at **hole.** [Latin *crātēr,* bowl, crater, from Greek *kratēr,* mixing vessel. See **kerə-** in Appendix.*]

Cra·ter (krā′tər) *n.* A constellation in the Southern Hemisphere near Hydra and Corvus.

Crater Lake. A lake, 20 square miles in area and 2,000 feet deep, in the crater of an extinct volcano at Crater Lake National Park in southwestern Oregon.

Craters of the Moon National Monument. An area of 47,210 acres in south-central Idaho, reserved to protect its many lava formations.

cra·vat (krə-văt′) *n.* A scarf or stock. [French *cravate,* cravat, originally a neckband worn by Croatian mercenaries in the service of France, from *Cravate,* a Croatian, from Flemish *Krawaat,* from Serbo-Croatian *Hrvat,* a CROAT.]

crave (krāv) *v.* **craved, craving, craves.** —*tr.* **1.** To have an intense desire for. **2.** To need urgently; require. **3.** To beg earnestly for; implore. —*intr.* To have an eager or intense desire. —See Synonyms at **beg.** [Middle English *craven,* Old English *crafian,* to beg, demand, from West Germanic *krabjan* (unattested), to demand, from the stem of *krab-taz* (unattested), strength. See **craft.**] —**crav′er** *n.* —**crav′ing·ly** *adv.*

cra·ven (krā′vən) *adj.* Characterized by abject fear; cowardly. —*n.* A coward. [Middle English *cravant,* perhaps from Old French *crevant,* dying, from *crever,* to burst, die, from Latin *crepāre,* to crack, burst. See **ker-²** in Appendix.*] —**cra′ven·ly** *adv.* —**cra′ven·ness** *n.*

crav·ing (krā′vĭng) *n.* A consuming desire; longing; yearning.

craw (krô) *n.* **1.** The crop of a bird. **2.** The stomach of an animal. —**stick in the** (or **one's**) **craw.** To be unacceptable or offensive. [Middle English *crawe,* Old English *craga* (unattested). See **gwerə-²** in Appendix.*]

craw·fish (krô′fĭsh′) *intr.v.* **-fished, -fishing, -fishes.** *Informal.* To withdraw from an undertaking. Usually used with *out.* —*n.* Variant of **crayfish.**

Craw·ford (krô′fərd), **Francis Marion.** 1854–1909. American romantic novelist; son of Thomas Crawford.

Craw·ford (krô′fərd), **Thomas.** 1814–1857. American sculptor.

crawl¹ (krôl) *intr.v.* **crawled, crawling, crawls. 1.** To move slowly on the hands and knees or by dragging the body along the ground; creep. **2.** To advance slowly, feebly, or laboriously: *Time crawls.* **3.** To proceed or act servilely. **4.** To be or feel as if covered with crawling things: *flesh crawling in horror.* **5.** To swim the crawl. —*n.* **1.** The action of crawling. **2.** A rapid swimming stroke consisting of alternating overarm strokes and a flutter kick. See **Australian crawl.** [Middle English *craulen,* from Old Norse *krafla,* to crawl, creep. See **gerebh-** in Appendix.*] —**crawl′er** *n.* —**crawl′ing·ly** *adv.*

crawl² (krôl) *n.* A pen in shallow water, as for confining fish or turtles. [Dutch *kraal,* KRAAL.]

crawl·y (krô′lē) *adj.* **-ier, -iest.** *Informal.* **1.** Creepy. **2.** Feeling as if things are crawling over one's skin.

cray·fish (krā′fĭsh′) *n., pl.* **crayfish** or **-fishes.** Also **craw·fish** (krô′-). **1.** Any of various freshwater crustaceans of the genera *Cambarus* and *Astacus,* resembling a lobster but considerably smaller. **2.** Broadly, a similar crustacean, such as the **spiny lobster** *(see).* [By folk etymology (influenced by FISH) from earlier *crevis, cravis,* Middle English *crevise,* from Old French, from Frankish *krabītja* (unattested). See **gerebh-** in Appendix.*]

Cray·ford (krā′fərd). A former administrative division of London, England, now part of **Bexley** *(see).*

cray·on (krā′ən, -ŏn′) *n.* **1.** A stick of colored wax, charcoal, or chalk, used for drawing. **2.** A drawing made with crayons. —*tr.v.* **crayoned, -oning, -ons.** To draw, color, or decorate with crayons. [French, crayon, pencil, from *craie,* chalk, from Latin *crēta*†. See also **Cretaceous.**] —**cray′on·ist** *n.*

craze (krāz) *v.* **crazed, crazing, crazes.** —*tr.* **1.** To cause to become mentally deranged or obsessed; make insane. **2.** To produce a network of fine cracks in (a ceramic). —*intr.* **1.** To become mentally deranged or obsessed; go insane. **2.** To become covered with fine cracks. —*n.* **1.** A short-lived popular fashion; a rage; fad. **2.** A pattern of fine cracks. [Middle English *crasen,* to shatter, render insane, from Old Norse *krasa* (unattested), to shatter (probably imitative).]

cra·zy (krā′zē) *adj.* **-zier, -ziest. 1.** Affected with or suggestive of madness; insane. **2.** *Informal.* Departing from proportion or moderation, especially: **a.** Possessed by enthusiasm or excitement. **b.** Immoderately fond; infatuated. **c.** Not sensible; impractical. **3.** *Archaic.* Rickety or dilapidated. [From CRAZE.] —**cra′zi·ly** *adv.* —**cra′zi·ness** *n.*

crazy bone. *Informal.* The **olecranon** *(see).*

Cra·zy Horse (krā′zē hôrs, hōrs). Indian name, Tashunca-Uitco. 1849?–1877. American Indian leader; chief of Oglala Sioux; a leader at Little Big Horn; killed while resisting arrest.

crazy quilt. A patchwork quilt of pieces of cloth of various shapes, colors, and sizes, arranged in no definite pattern.

cra·zy·weed (krā′zē-wēd′) *n.* A plant, **locoweed** *(see).* [From its toxic effect on some animals.]

creak (krēk) *v.* **creaked, creaking, creaks.** —*intr.* **1.** To make a grating or squeaking sound. **2.** To move with such a sound or sounds. —*tr.* To cause to make a creaking sound. —*n.* A grating or squeaking sound. [Middle English *creken* (imitative).] —**creak′ing·ly** *adv.*

creak·y (krē′kē) *adj.* **-ier, -iest. 1.** Tending or liable to creak. **2.** Dilapidated; decrepit. —**creak′i·ly** *adv.* —**creak′i·ness** *n.*

cream (krēm) *n.* **1.** The yellowish fatty component of unhomogenized milk that tends to accumulate at the surface. **2.** The color of cream; pale yellow to yellowish white. See **color. 3.** Any of various substances resembling or containing cream, as certain foods or cosmetics. **4.** The choicest part: *the cream of the crop.* —*v.* **creamed, creaming, creams.** —*intr.* **1.** To form cream. **2.** To form foam or scum at the top. —*tr.* **1.** To allow the cream to separate from (milk). **2.** To remove the cream from; to skim. **3.** To select or remove the best part from. **4.** To beat (butter and sugar, for example) into a creamy consistency. **5.** To prepare or cook (a vegetable, for example) in or with a cream sauce. **6.** To add cream to. **7.** *Slang.* To defeat overwhelmingly. [Middle English *creme, creime,* from Old French *cresme, craime,* blends of Late Latin *chrisma,* ointment, CHRISM, and Late Latin *crāmum*†, cream.] —**cream** *adj.*

cream cheese. A soft white cheese made of cream and milk.

cream-col·ored (krēm′kŭl′ərd) *adj.* Of the color of cream; yellowish white.

cream·cups (krēm′kŭps′) *n.* Plural in form, used with a singular or plural verb. A plant, *Platystemon californicus,* of the

ă pat/ā pay/âr care/ä father/b bib/ch church/d deed/ĕ pet/ē be/f fife/g gag/h hat/hw which/ĭ pit/ī pie/îr pier/j judge/k kick/l lid, needle/m mum/n no, sudden/ng thing/ŏ pot/ō toe/ô paw, for/oi noise/ou out/ŏŏ took/ōō boot/p pop/r roar/s sauce/sh ship, dish/

southwestern United States, having long-stalked cream-colored or light-yellow flowers.

cream·er (krē′mər) *n.* **1.** A small jug or pitcher for cream. **2.** A machine or device for separating cream from milk. **3.** A refrigerator in which milk is placed to form cream.

cream·er·y (krē′mə-rē) *n., pl.* **-ies.** An establishment where dairy products are prepared or sold.

cream of tartar. *Chemistry.* **Potassium bitartrate** *(see).*

cream puff. **1.** A shell of light pastry filled with whipped cream, custard, or ice cream. **2.** *Slang.* A sissy.

cream sauce. A white sauce made by heating a mixture of flour and butter in milk or cream.

cream·y (krē′mē) *adj.* **-ier, -iest.** Rich in cream or resembling cream. —**cream′i·ly** *adv.* —**cream′i·ness** *n.*

crease (krēs) *n.* **1.** A line made by pressing, folding, or wrinkling. **2.** *Cricket.* One of the lines marking off the positions of the bowler and batsman or the space between two of these lines. **3.** *Hockey.* A rectangular area marked off in front of the goal cage. —*v.* **creased, creasing, creases.** —*tr.* **1.** To make a fold or wrinkle in. **2.** To graze with a bullet; wound superficially. —*intr.* To become wrinkled. [Earlier *creast,* from Middle English *crest,* ridge, CREST.] —**creas′er** *n.* —**creas′y** *adj.*

cre·ate (krē-āt′) *tr.v.* **-ated, -ating, -ates.** **1.** To cause to exist; bring into being; originate. **2.** To give rise to; bring about; produce: *Her remark created a stir.* **3.** To invest with office or title; appoint. **4.** To be first to portray and give character to (a role or part). —*adj. Poetic.* Created. [Middle English *createn,* from Latin *creāre.* See **ker-³** in Appendix.*]

cre·a·tine (krē′ə-tēn, -tĭn) *n.* Also **cre·a·tin** (-tĭn). A nitrogenous organic acid, $C_4H_9N_3O_2$, found mainly in the muscle tissue of many vertebrates and acting in muscular contraction. [Greek *kreas* (stem *kreat-*), flesh (see **kreu-¹** in Appendix*) + -INE.]

cre·at·i·nine (krē-ăt′ə-nēn) *n.* The creatine anhydride $C_4H_7N_3O$, a normal metabolic waste. [CREATIN(E) + -INE.]

cre·a·tion (krē-ā′shən) *n.* **1. a.** The act of creating. **b.** The fact or process of being created. **2.** *Capital* **C.** God's primal act of bringing the world into existence. Usually preceded by *the.* **3. a.** The world and all things in it. **b.** All creatures or a class of creatures: *all creation.* **4.** An original product of human invention or imagination; a work. **5.** A specially designed garment or other article of fashion. —**cre·a′tion·al** *adj.*

cre·a·tion·ism (krē-ā′shən-ĭz′əm) *n. Theology.* **1.** The doctrine ascribing the origin of all matter and living forms as they now exist to distinct acts of creation by God. Compare **evolutionism.** **2.** The doctrine that each human soul is a distinct and new creation by God. Compare **infusionism.** —**cre·a′tion·ist** *n.*

cre·a·tive (krē-ā′tĭv) *adj.* **1.** Having the ability or power to create things. **2.** Creating; productive. Often used with *of.* **3.** Characterized by originality and expressiveness; imaginative. —**cre·a′tive·ly** *adv.* —**cre′a·tiv′i·ty, cre·a′tive·ness** *n.*

cre·a·tor (krē-ā′tər) *n.* **1.** One that creates. **2.** *Capital* **C.** God.

crea·ture (krē′chər) *n.* **1.** Anything created. **2.** A living being, especially an animal. **3.** A human being. Often used with a suggestion of pity or contempt. **4.** One dependent upon or subservient to another; tool. —**crea′tur·al, crea′ture·ly** *adj.*

creature comforts. Bodily comforts.

crèche (krĕsh) *n.* **1.** A representation of the Nativity scene. **2.** A foundling hospital. **3.** *Chiefly British.* A day nursery. [French, from Old French *creche,* manger, crib, from Frankish *kripja* (unattested). See **ger-³** in Appendix.*]

Cré·cy (krā-sē′). A town of northeastern France; scene of an English victory over the French (1346) during the Hundred Years' War.

cre·dence (krē′dəns) *n.* **1.** Acceptance as true or valid; belief. **2.** Claim to acceptance; trustworthiness. **3.** Recommendation; credential: *a letter of credence.* **4.** *Ecclesiastical.* A small shelf or table to hold the elements of the Eucharist. In this sense, also called "credence table." [Middle English, from Old French, from Medieval Latin *crēdentia,* belief, trust, hence a table holding food for tasting in order to detect poison, from Latin *crēdere,* to believe. See **kerd-¹** in Appendix.*]

cre·den·dum (krē-dĕn′dəm) *n., pl.* **-da** (-də). *Ecclesiastical.* An article or matter of faith. [Latin *crēdundum,* from the neuter gerundive of *crēdere,* to believe. See **kerd-¹** in Appendix.*]

cre·den·tial (krĭ-dĕn′shəl) *n.* **1.** That which entitles one to confidence, credit, or authority. **2.** *Usually plural.* **a.** A letter attesting one's right to credit, confidence, or authority; especially, such a letter given by a government to an ambassador or envoy. **b.** Written evidence of status or qualifications. [From Medieval Latin *crēdentiālis,* giving authority, from *crēdentia,* trust, CREDENCE.]

cre·den·za (krĭ-dĕn′zə) *n.* A buffet or sideboard, especially one without legs. [Italian, from Medieval Latin *crēdentia,* CREDENCE (table).]

cred·i·bil·i·ty (krĕd′ə-bĭl′ə-tē) *n.* Worthiness of belief.

cred·i·ble (krĕd′ə-bəl) *adj.* **1.** Capable of being believed; believable; plausible. **2.** Worthy of confidence; reliable. [Middle English, from Latin *crēdibilis,* from *crēdere,* to believe, entrust. See **kerd-¹** in Appendix.*] —**cred′i·ble·ness** *n.* —**cred′i·bly** *adv.*

cred·it (krĕd′ĭt) *n. Abbr.* **cr.** **1.** Belief or confidence in the truth of something; trust. **2.** The quality or state of being trustworthy or credible: *"one of no less credit than Aristotle"* (Walton). **3.** A reputation for sound character or quality; standing; repute. **4.** A source of honor or distinction: *He is a credit to his family.* **5.** Approval for some act, ability, or quality; praise. **6.** Influence based on the good opinion or confidence of others. **7.** *Usually plural.* An acknowledgment of work done, as in the production of a motion picture, play, or book. **8.** *Education.* **a.** Official certification that a student has successfully completed a course of study. **b.** A unit of study so certified. **9.** Reputation for solvency and integrity, entitling a person to be trusted in buying or borrowing. **10. a.** Confidence in a buyer's ability and intention to fulfill financial obligations at some future time. **b.** The time allowed for payment for anything sold on trust. **11.** *Accounting.* **a.** The acknowledgment of payment by a debtor by entry of the sum in an account. **b.** The right-hand side of an account on which such amounts are entered. Compare **debit.** **c.** An entry on this side. **d.** The sum of such entries. **12.** The positive balance or amount remaining in a person's account. **13.** An amount placed by a bank at the disposal of a client, against which he may draw. —*tr.v.* **credited, -iting, -its.** **1.** To believe; trust: *"she refused steadfastly to credit the reports of his death"* (Agatha Christie). **2.** *Archaic.* To bring honor or distinction to. **3. a.** To give credit to (a person) for something. Used with *with: credit him with the invention.* **b.** To ascribe (something) to a person; attribute to. Used with *to: credit the invention to him.* **4.** *Accounting.* **a.** To give credit for (a sum paid). **b.** To give credit to (a payer). **5.** *Education.* To give or award credits to (a student). —See Synonyms at **attribute.** [Old French, from Old Italian *credito,* from Latin *crēditum,* "something entrusted," loan, from the past participle of *crēdere,* to believe, entrust. See **kerd-¹** in Appendix.*]

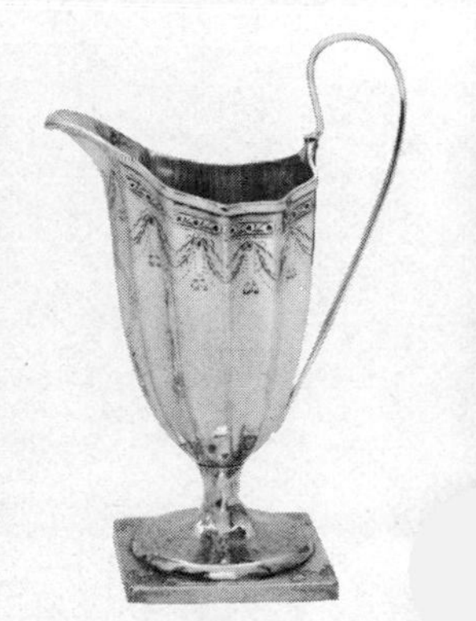

creamer
Silver creamer made by Paul Revere

cred·it·a·ble (krĕd′ĭ-tə-bəl) *adj.* **1.** Deserving commendation. **2.** Capable of being credited or assigned; assignable. —**cred′it·a·bil′i·ty, cred′it·a·ble·ness** *n.* —**cred′it·a·bly** *adv.*

credit bureau. An organization to which business firms apply for credit information on prospective customers. Also called "credit agency."

credit card. A card issued by business concerns authorizing the holder to buy goods or services on credit.

credit line. **1.** A line of copy acknowledging the source or origin of a news dispatch, published article, motion picture, or other work. **2.** The maximum amount of credit to be extended to a customer. In this sense, also called "line of credit."

cred·i·tor (krĕd′ə-tər) *n.* **1.** A person or firm to whom money or its equivalent is owed. Compare **debtor.** **2.** *Abbr.* **cr.** *Accounting.* The credit side of an account.

credit rating. An estimate of the amount of credit that can be extended to a company or individual without undue risk.

credit union. A cooperative organization that makes loans to its members at low interest rates.

cre·do (krē′dō, krā′-) *n., pl.* **-dos.** **1.** A statement of belief; creed. **2.** *Often capital* **C.** **a.** **The Apostles' Creed** or the **Nicene Creed** *(both of which see).* **b.** A musical setting for either of these. [Latin *crēdo,* "I believe," the first word of the Apostles' Creed, from *crēdere,* to believe. See **kerd-¹** in Appendix.*]

cre·du·li·ty (krĭ-do͞o′lə-tē, -dyo͞o′lə-tē) *n.* A disposition to believe too readily; gullibility. [Middle English *credulite,* from Old French, from Latin *crēdulitās,* from *crēdulus,* CREDULOUS.]

cred·u·lous (krĕj′o͞o-ləs, krĕd′yo͞o-) *adj.* **1.** Disposed to believe too readily; gullible. **2.** Arising from or characterized by credulity. [Latin *crēdulus,* from *crēdere,* to believe. See **kerd-¹** in Appendix.*] —**cred′u·lous·ly** *adv.* —**cred′u·lous·ness** *n.*

Cree (krē) *n., pl.* **Cree** or **Crees.** **1.** A tribe of Algonquian-speaking Indians formerly living in Ontario, Manitoba, and Saskatchewan. **2.** A member of this tribe. **3.** The Algonquian language of this tribe. [Shortened from Canadian French *Christianaux,* by folk etymology from Ojibwa *Kenistenoag,* earlier *Kilistino* (unattested), tribal name.]

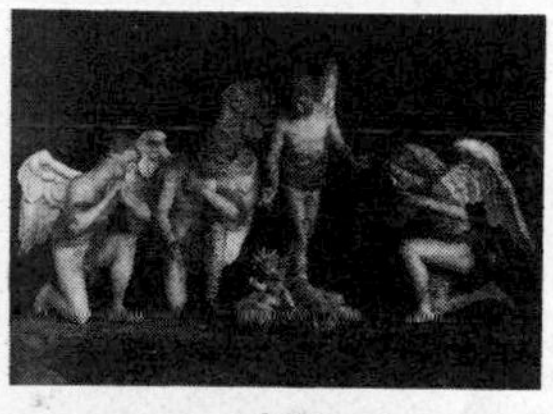

crèche
"Adoration of the Angels," made in Germany about 1800

creed (krēd) *n.* **1.** A formal statement of religious belief; confession of faith. **2.** An authoritative statement of certain articles of Christian faith that are considered essential; for example, the Apostles' Creed and the Nicene Creed. **3.** Any statement or system of belief, principles, or opinions. [Middle English *crede,* Old English *crēda,* from Latin *crēdo,* "I believe." See **credo.**] —**creed′al** *adj.*

creek (krēk, krĭk) *n. Abbr.* **cr.** **1.** A small stream, often a shallow or intermittent tributary to a river; a brook. **2.** *British.* A small inlet in a shoreline. —**up the creek.** *Informal.* In a difficult or unfortunate position. [Middle English *creke, crike,* possibly from Old Norse *kriki,* a bend, nook. See **ger-³** in Appendix.*]

Creek (krēk) *n., pl.* **Creek** or **Creeks.** **1.** A confederacy of several Muskhogean-speaking Indian tribes, formerly inhabiting parts of Georgia, Alabama, and northern Florida. **2.** A member of any of these tribes. **3.** The Muskhogean language of these tribes. [Origin obscure.]

creel (krēl) *n.* **1.** A wicker basket, especially one used by anglers for carrying fish. **2.** A wickerwork trap for fish or lobster. **3.** A frame for holding bobbins or spools in a spinning machine. [Middle English (Scottish) *crel, crelle*†.]

creep (krēp) *intr.v.* **crept** (krĕpt), **creeping, creeps.** **1.** To move with the body close to the ground, as a baby on hands and knees. **2.** To move stealthily, cautiously, or very slowly. **3.** To behave obsequiously; to fawn. **4.** *Botany.* To grow along a surface, rooting at intervals or clinging by means of suckers or tendrils. **5.** To slip out of place from pressure or wear; shift gradually. **6.** To have a tingling sensation: *made my flesh creep.* —*n.* **1.** The action of creeping; a creeping motion or progress. **2.** *Slang.* An obnoxious or insignificant person. **3.** *Metallurgy.* A slow flow of metal when under high temperature or great pressure. **4.** *Geology.* The slow movement of rock debris and soil down a weathered slope. —**the creeps.** *Informal.* A sensation of fear or repugnance, as if things were crawling on one's skin. [Creep: Middle English *crepen,* Old English *crēopan.* Crept: Middle English *creped, crept,* analogous formation from the infinitive *crepen.* See **ger-³** in Appendix.*]

creep·er (krē′pər) *n.* **1.** One that creeps. **2.** *Plural.* A one-piece suit for a baby. **3.** *Botany.* A plant having stems that grow

along a surface, either rooting at intervals or clinging for support. **4.** A grappling device for dragging lakes and the like. **5.** *Usually plural.* A metal frame with spikes, attached to a shoe or boot to prevent slipping.
creeping Char·lie (chär′lē). Any of several creeping or trailing plants, such as **moneywort** *(see).*
creeping eruption. A skin disease caused by larvae burrowing and creeping beneath the skin and characterized by eruptions in the form of reddish lines.
creeping Jen·nie (jĕn′ē). Also **creeping Jenny.** Any of several creeping or trailing plants, especially **moneywort** *(see).*
creeping myrtle. A plant, the **periwinkle** *(see).*
creep·y (krē′pē) *adj.* **-ier, -iest. 1.** Creeping; slow-moving. **2.** *Informal.* Inducing or having a sensation of repugnance or fear, as of things crawling on one's skin. —**creep′i·ness** *n.*
creese. Variant of **kris.**
cre·mate (krē′māt′, krĭ-māt′) *tr.v.* **-mated, -mating, -mates.** To incinerate (a corpse). [Latin *cremāre,* to burn, consume by fire. See **ker-**[4] in Appendix.*] —**cre·ma′tion** (krĭ-mā′shən) *n.*
cre·ma·tor (krē′mā′tər, krĭ-mā′tər) *n.* One that cremates.
cre·ma·to·ri·um (krē′mə-tôr′ē-əm, -tōr′ē-əm) *n., pl.* **-ums** or **-toria** (-tôr′ē-ə, -tōr′ē-ə). A crematory.
cre·ma·to·ry (krē′mə-tôr′ē, -tōr′ē, krĕm′ə-) *n., pl.* **-ries.** A furnace or place for the cremation of corpses. —*adj.* Of or pertaining to cremation. [New Latin *crematorium,* from Latin *cremāre,* CREMATE.]
crème de ca·ca·o (krĕm′ də kə-kā′ō, kə-kä′ō). A sweet liqueur with a chocolate flavor. [French, "cream of cacao."]
crème de la crème (krĕm′ də lä krĕm′). *French.* The essence of excellence. Literally, "cream of the cream."
crème de menthe (krĕm′ də mäNt′). A sweet green or white liqueur, well flavored with mint. [French, "cream of mint."]
Cre·mo·na[1] (krĭ-mō′nə; *Italian* krā-mō′nä). A city of northwestern Italy, situated on the Po about 50 miles southeast of Milan. Population, 74,000.
Cre·mo·na[2] (krĭ-mō′nə; *Italian* krā-mō′nä) *n.* Any of the fine violins made at Cremona, Italy, from the 16th to the 18th century, especially by the Amati family, Antonio Stradivari, or Giuseppe Guarnieri.
cre·nate (krē′nāt′) *adj.* Also **cre·nat·ed** (-nā′tĭd). *Biology.* Having a margin with rounded or scalloped projections: *a crenate leaf.* [New Latin *crenatus,* probably from Late Latin *crēna*†, notch.] —**cre′nate·ly** *adv.*

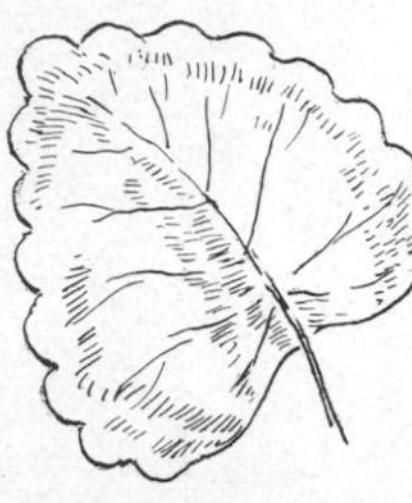

crenate
The crenate leaf of the ground ivy, *Glechoma hederacea*

cre·na·tion (krĭ-nā′shən) *n.* **1.** A rounded projection; crenature. **2.** The condition or fact of being crenate.
cren·a·ture (krĕn′ə-choor, krē′n-) *n.* **1.** A crenation. **2.** A notch between crenations, as on a leaf.
cren·e·lat·ed (krĕn′ə-lā′tĭd) *adj.* Also *chiefly British* **cren·el·lat·ed.** Having battlements. [From French *crenel,* a crenelation, from Old French, perhaps from Vulgar Latin *crenellus* (unattested), diminutive of Late Latin *crēna,* notch. See **crenate.**] —**cren′e·la′tion** *n.*
cren·u·late (krĕn′yə-lĭt, -lāt′) *adj.* Also **cren·u·lat·ed** (-lā′tĭd). Having minutely notched or scalloped projections. [New Latin *crenulatus,* from *crenula,* perhaps diminutive of Late Latin *crēna,* notch. See **crenate.**] —**cren′u·la′tion** *n.*
cre·o·dont (krē′ə-dŏnt′) *n.* Any of various extinct carnivorous mammals of the suborder Creodonta, of the Paleocene to Pliocene epochs. [New Latin *Creodonta,* "flesh-toothed ones" : Greek *kreas,* flesh (see **kreu-**[1] in Appendix*) + -ODONT.]

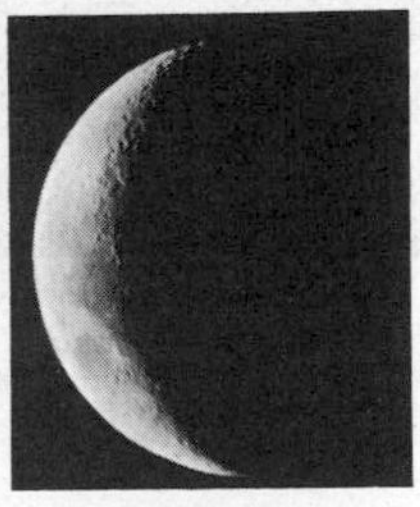

crescent
Crescent moon

Cre·ole (krē′ōl′) *n.* **1.** Any person of European descent born in the West Indies or Spanish America. **2.** A person descended from or culturally related to the original French settlers of the southern United States, especially Louisiana. **3.** The French patois spoken by these people. **4.** A person descended from or culturally related to the Spanish and Portuguese settlers of the Gulf States. **5.** A person of Negro descent born in the Western Hemisphere, as distinguished from a Negro brought from Africa. Also called "Creole Negro." **6.** Any person of mixed European and Negro ancestry who speaks a Creole dialect. **7.** A creolized language. —*adj.* **1.** Of, relating to, or characteristic of the Creoles. **2.** *Small* **c.** Cooked with a spicy sauce containing tomatoes, onions, and peppers. [French *créole,* from Spanish *criollo,* from Portuguese *crioulo,* Negro born in his master's house, from *criar,* to bring up, from Latin *creāre,* to create, beget. See **ker-**[3] in Appendix.*]
cre·o·lized language (krē′ə-līzd′). A type of mixed language that develops when dominant and subordinate groups that speak different languages have prolonged contact, incorporating the basic vocabulary of the dominant language with the grammar and an admixture of words from the subordinate language, and becoming the native tongue of the subordinate group. Compare **pidgin.**
Cre·on (krē′ŏn). *Greek Mythology.* King of Thebes, successor to Oedipus.
cre·o·sol (krē′ə-sōl′) *n.* A colorless to yellow aromatic liquid, $C_8H_{10}O_2$, that is a constituent of creosote and is obtained from beechwood tar. [CREOS(OTE) + -OL.]
cre·o·sote (krē′ə-sōt′) *n.* **1.** A colorless to yellowish oily liquid, obtained by the destructive distillation of wood tar, especially from beechwood, and formerly used to treat tuberculosis and chronic bronchitis. **2.** A yellowish to greenish-brown oily liquid obtained from coal tar and used as a wood preservative and disinfectant. —*tr.v.* **creosoted, -soting, -sotes.** To treat or paint (wood or other material) with creosote. [German *Kreosot,* "flesh preserver" (from its antiseptic qualities) : Greek *kreas,* flesh (see **kreu-**[1] in Appendix*) + *sōtēr,* preserver, from *sōzein,* to preserve, save, from *saos,* safe (see **teue-** in Appendix*).]
creosote bush. A resinous shrub, *Larrea tridentata,* of the western United States and Mexico, exuding an odor like that of creosote. Also called "greasewood."
crepe (krāp) *n.* Also **crape, crêpe** (krĕp). **1.** A light, soft, thin fabric of silk, cotton, wool, or other fiber, with a crinkled surface. **2.** A black band of this fabric displayed or worn on the sleeve or hat as a sign of mourning. **3. Crepe paper** *(see).* **4. Crepe rubber** *(see).* **5.** A very thin pancake. —*tr.v.* **creped, creping, crepes.** Also **crape, crêpe.** To cover or drape with crepe. [French *crêpe,* from Old French *crespe,* crisp, curly, from Latin *crispus.* See **sker-**[3] in Appendix.*]
crêpe de Chine (krāp′ də shēn′, krĕp′). A silk crepe used for women's dresses and blouses. [French, "crepe of China."]
crepe hair. False hair used in theatrical make-up for making artificial beards, sideburns, and the like.
crepe myrtle. Variant of **crape myrtle.**
crepe paper. Crinkled tissue paper, resembling crepe, used for decorations. Also called "crepe."
crepe rubber. Rubber with a crinkled texture, used for shoe soles. Also called "crepe."
crêpe su·zette (krāp sōō-zĕt′; *French* krĕp sü-zĕt′) *pl.* **crêpe suzettes.** A thin dessert pancake usually rolled with hot orange or tangerine sauce and often served with a flaming brandy or curaçao sauce. [French : CREPE (pancake) + *Suzette,* pet form of the name *Suzanne,* SUSAN.]
crep·i·tate (krĕp′ə-tāt′) *intr.v.* **-tated, -tating, -tates.** To make a creaking or rattling sound; crackle. [Latin *crepitāre,* to crackle, frequentative of *crepāre* (past participle *crepitus*), to crack, creak. See **ker-**[2] in Appendix.*] —**crep′i·ta′tion** *n.*
crept. Past tense and past participle of **creep.**
cre·pus·cu·lar (krĭ-pŭs′kyə-lər) *adj.* **1.** Of or like twilight; hazy; dim. **2.** *Zoology.* Becoming active at twilight or before sunrise, as do certain insects and birds. [From Latin *crepusculum,* twilight, from *creper,* dusky, dark, possibly of Sabine origin.]
cres·cen·do (krə-shĕn′dō, -sĕn′dō) *n., pl.* **-dos** or **-di** (-dē). *Abbr.* **cr., cresc., cres. 1.** A gradual increase in the volume or intensity of sound. **2.** A musical passage played in a crescendo. Compare **decrescendo.** —*adj. Abbr.* **cresc., cres.** Gradually increasing in volume or intensity. —*adv. Abbr.* **cresc., cres.** With a crescendo. [Italian, "increasing," from *crescere,* to increase, from Latin *crēscere,* to grow. See **ker-**[3] in Appendix.*]
cres·cent (krĕs′ənt) *n.* **1.** The figure of the moon as it appears in its first quarter, with concave and convex edges terminating in points. **2.** Something shaped like this. **3. a.** The Turkish emblem. **b.** *Capital* **C.** Turkish or Moslem power. —*adj.* **1.** Crescent-shaped. **2.** Increasing; waxing, as the moon. [Middle English *cressaunt,* from Old French *creissant,* "waxing," "increasing," from Latin *crēscēns,* present participle of *crēscere,* to increase, grow. See **ker-**[3] in Appendix.*] —**cres·cen′tic** *adj.*
cre·sol (krē′sōl′) *n.* Any of three isomeric phenols, $CH_3C_6H_4$-OH, used in resins and as a disinfectant. [Variant of CREOSOL.]
cress (krĕs) *n.* Any of various related plants, such as those of the genera *Cardamine* and *Arabis,* having pungent leaves often used in salads and as a garnish. See **watercress.** [Middle English *cresse,* Old English *cresse, cærse.* See **gras-** in Appendix.*]
cres·set (krĕs′ĭt) *n.* A metal cup, often suspended on a pole, containing burning oil or pitch and used as a torch. [Middle English, from Old French *cresset, craisset,* from *craisse,* oil, grease, from Vulgar Latin *crassia* (unattested), animal fat, from Latin *crassus,* fat, thick. See **crass.**]
Cres·si·da (krĕs′ĭ-də). Also **Cri·sey·de.** In medieval romances, a Trojan lady who first returns the love of Troilus but later forsakes him for Diomedes.
crest (krĕst) *n.* **1.** A tuft, ridge, or similar projection on the head of a bird or other animal. **2. a.** A plume used as decoration on top of a helmet. **b.** A helmet. **3.** *Heraldry.* A device placed above the shield on a coat of arms and also used by itself on seals, stationery, and the like. **4. a.** The top of something, as a mountain or wave; peak; summit. **b.** A ridge. **5.** The ridge of an animal's neck or the mane growing on it. **6.** *Architecture.* The ridge on a roof. —*v.* **crested, cresting, crests.** —*tr.* **1.** To decorate or furnish with a crest. **2.** To reach the crest of (a hill, for example). —*intr.* To form into a crest, as a wave. [Middle English *creste,* from Old French, from Latin *crista,* crest, plume. See **sker-**[3] in Appendix.*]
crest·fall·en (krĕst′fô′lən) *adj.* Dejected; dispirited; depressed. —**crest′fall′en·ly** *adv.*
crest·ing (krĕs′tĭng) *n. Architecture.* An ornamental ridge, as on top of a wall or roof.
cre·syl·ic (krĭ-sĭl′ĭk) *adj. Chemistry.* Of or pertaining to creosote or cresol. [CRES(OL) + -YL + -IC.]
Cre·ta·ceous (krĭ-tā′shəs) *adj.* **1.** Of, belonging to, or designating the geologic time, system of rocks, and sedimentary deposits of the third and last period of the Mesozoic era, characterized by the development of flowering plants and the disappearance of dinosaurs. See **geology. 2.** *Small* **c.** Of, containing, or resembling chalk. —*n. Geology.* The Cretaceous period. Preceded by *the.* [Latin *crētāceus* : *crēta*†, chalk, clay (see also **crayon**) + -ACEOUS.]
Cretan mullein. A plant, *Celsia cretica,* native to the Mediterranean region, having hairy foliage and yellow flowers splotched with purple.
Crete (krēt). *Greek* **Kre·te** (krē′tē). An island department of Greece, 3,235 square miles in area, in the Mediterranean off the southeastern coast of Greece. Population, 483,000. Capital, Canea. —**Cre′tan** (krē′tən) *adj. & n.*
Crete, Sea of (krēt). That part of the southern Aegean Sea between Crete and the Cyclades. Also called "Sea of Candia."
cre·tic (krē′tĭk) *n. Prosody.* An **amphimacer** *(see).* [Late Latin

(pēs) crēticus, "Cretan (foot)," amphimacer, from Greek *(pous) krētikos,* from *krētikos,* Cretan, from *Krētē,* CRETE.]

cre·tin (krē'tĭn, krēt'n) *n.* **1.** One afflicted with cretinism. **2.** An idiot. [French *crétin,* idiot, from Swiss French *crestin,* Christian, hence human being, hence deformed idiot (who is nonetheless human), from Latin *Christiānus,* CHRISTIAN.] —**cre'tin·oid'** *adj.* —**cre'tin·ous** *adj.*

cre·tin·ism (krē'tĭn-ĭz'əm) *n.* **Myxedema** *(see),* a thyroid deficiency causing arrested mental and physical development.

cre·tonne (krĭ-tŏn', krē'tŏn') *n.* A heavy unglazed cotton, linen, or rayon fabric, colorfully printed and used for draperies and slipcovers. [French, first made in *Creton,* village in Normandy.]

Cre·ü·sa (krē-o͞o'zə). *Greek Mythology.* **1.** The bride of Jason, killed by Medea. **2.** The daughter of Priam and wife of Aeneas, lost in the flight from Troy.

cre·val·le (krə-văl'ē, -văl'ə) *n.* A food and game fish, *Caranx hippo,* of warm seas, having a laterally compressed silvery body. Also called "crevalle jack." [Variant of CAVALLA.]

cre·vasse (krə-văs') *n.* **1.** A deep fissure, as in a glacier; chasm. **2.** A crack in a dike or levee. —*tr.v.* **crevassed, -vassing, -vasses.** To make crevasses in; fissure. [French, from Old French *crevace,* CREVICE.]

Crève·coeur (krĕv-kœr'), **Michel Guillaume Jean de.** Pen name, J. Hector St. John Crèvecoeur. 1731–1813. French agriculturist, diplomat, and author; worked in America (1759–90).

crev·ice (krĕv'ĭs) *n.* A narrow crack or opening; fissure; cleft. [Middle English *crevice, crevace,* from Old French *crevace,* from *crever,* to split, from Latin *crepāre,* to rattle, crack. See **ker-²** in Appendix.*] —**crev'iced** *adj.*

crew¹ (kro͞o) *n.* **1.** A group of people working together; gang. **2.** *Nautical.* **a.** All personnel manning a ship. **b.** All of a ship's personnel except the officers. **3.** All personnel manning an aircraft in flight. **4.** A company; crowd. **5.** A team of oarsmen. [Middle English *creue,* military reinforcement, from Old French *creue,* an increase, from the feminine past participle of *creistre,* to grow, from Latin *crēscere.* See **ker-³** in Appendix.*]

crew². Alternate past tense of **crow.**

crew cut. A close-cropped man's haircut. [Oarsmen commonly have this kind of haircut.] —**crew'-cut'** *adj.*

crew·el (kro͞o'əl) *n.* A type of loosely twisted worsted yarn used for fancywork and embroidery. [Middle English *crule*†.]

crib (krĭb) *n.* **1.** A child's bed with high sides. **2.** A small building, usually with slatted sides, for storing corn. **3.** A rack or trough for fodder; manger. **4.** A cattle stall. **5.** A small, crude cottage or room. **6.** A framework to support or strengthen a mine or shaft. **7.** A wicker basket. **8.** *Informal.* **a.** A petty theft. **b.** Plagiarism. **9.** *Informal. Chiefly British.* A **pony** *(see).* **10.** *Cribbage.* A set of cards made up from discards by each player, used by the dealer. —*v.* **cribbed, cribbing, cribs.** —*tr.* **1.** To confine in or as in a crib. **2.** To furnish with a crib. **3.** *Informal.* To plagiarize. **4.** *Informal.* To steal. —*intr. Informal.* To use a crib in examinations; cheat. [Middle English *crib,* manger, stall, basket, Old English *cribb,* manger (see **ger-³** in Appendix*).] —**crib'ber** *n.*

crib·bage (krĭb'ĭj) *n.* A card game for from two to four players, in which the score is kept by inserting small pegs into holes arranged in rows on a small board. [Possibly from CRIB (noun), "basket," hence discard pile.]

crib·bing (krĭb'ĭng) *n.* **1.** A supporting framework, as of timber lining a shaft. **2.** **Crib-biting** *(see).*

crib-bite (krĭb'bīt') *intr.v.* **-bit** (-bĭt), **-bitten** (-bĭt'n) or **-bit, -biting, -bites.** To practice crib-biting. —**crib'-bit'er** *n.*

crib-bit·ing (krĭb'bī'tĭng) *n.* An injurious habit of horses of biting at the edge of a feed trough or other object and swallowing air at the same time. Also called "cribbing."

crib·ri·form (krĭb'rə-fôrm') *adj.* Perforated like a sieve. [Latin *crībrum,* sieve (see **skeri-** in Appendix*) + -FORM.]

crib·work (krĭb'wûrk') *n.* A structural framework made of logs stacked one above the other, with the logs in each layer at right angles to those in the layer below.

Crich·ton (krī'tən), **James.** Called "The Admirable Crichton." 1560?–1582. Scottish scholar and adventurer.

crick¹ (krĭk) *n.* A painful cramp or muscle spasm, as in the back or neck. —*tr.v.* **cricked, cricking, cricks.** To cause a crick in by turning or wrenching. [Middle English *crike, crykke*†.]

crick² (krĭk) *n. Regional.* A creek.

Crick (krĭk), **Francis Harry Compton.** Born 1916. British biochemist; discovered molecular structure of DNA with J.D. **Watson** *(see).*

crick·et¹ (krĭk'ĭt) *n.* Any of various insects of the family Gryllidae, having long antennae and legs adapted for leaping. The males of many species produce a shrill, chirping sound by rubbing the front wings together. [Middle English *criket,* from Old French *criquet,* from *criquer,* to click, creak. See **ker-²** in Appendix.*]

crick·et² (krĭk'ĭt) *n.* **1.** An outdoor game, popular in Great Britain, played with bats, a ball, and wickets by two teams of 11 players each. **2.** Good sportsmanship; fair play; gentlemanly conduct: *It's not cricket to cheat at cards.* —*intr.v.* **cricketed, -eting, -ets.** To play cricket. [Probably from Old French *criquet,* wicket or bat in a ball game, probably from *criquer,* to click (from the clicking of the ball against the wood). See **ker-²** in Appendix.*] —**crick'et·er** *n.*

crick·et³ (krĭk'ĭt) *n.* A small, low wooden footstool. [Origin obscure.]

cri·coid (krī'koid) *n. Anatomy.* A ring-shaped cartilage of the lower larynx. [Greek *krikoeidēs,* ring-shaped : *krikos,* ring (see **sker-³** in Appendix*) + -OID.]

cri·er (krī'ər) *n.* **1.** A person who cries. **2.** A person who shouts out public announcements. **3.** A hawker.

crime (krīm) *n.* **1.** An act committed or omitted in violation of a law forbidding or commanding it, and for which punishment is imposed upon conviction. **2.** Unlawful activity in general. **3.** Any serious wrongdoing or offense. **4.** An unjust or senseless act or condition. —See Synonyms at **offense.** [Middle English, from Old French, from Latin *crīmen,* verdict, judgment, crime. See **ker-²** in Appendix.*]

Cri·me·a (krī-mē'ə). Ancient name **Tau·ric Cher·so·nese** (tô'rĭk kûr'sə-nēz'). *Russian* **Krim** (krĭm). A peninsula, 9,900 square miles in area, of the Soviet Union, extending into the Black Sea and constituting part of the Ukrainian S.S.R. —**Cri·me'an** *adj.*

Crimean War. A war (1853–56) fought chiefly in the Crimea, in which Great Britain, France, Turkey, and Sardinia as allies defeated Russia.

crim·i·nal (krĭm'ə-nəl) *adj.* **1.** Of, involving, or having the nature of crime. **2.** Pertaining to the administration of penal law as distinguished from civil law. **3.** Guilty of crime. —*n.* A person who has committed or been legally convicted of a crime. [Middle English, from Old French *criminel,* from Late Latin *crīminālis,* from Latin *crīmen* (stem *crīmin-*), CRIME.] —**crim'i·nal·ly** *adv.*

criminal conversation. *Law.* Adultery.

crim·i·nal·i·ty (krĭm'ə-năl'ə-tē) *n., pl.* **-ties.** **1.** The state, quality, or fact of being criminal. **2.** A criminal action or practice.

criminal law. Law involving crime and its punishment.

crim·i·nate (krĭm'ə-nāt') *tr.v.* **-nated, -nating, -nates.** **1.** To implicate in a crime; incriminate. **2.** To charge with a crime; accuse. **3.** To condemn as criminal; to censure. [Latin *crīminārī,* to accuse, from *crīmen,* accusation, CRIME.] —**crim'i·na'tion** *n.* —**crim'i·na·tive, crim'i·na·to'ry** (-nə-tôr'ē, -tōr'ē) *adj.* —**crim'i·na'tor** (-nā'tər) *n.*

crim·i·nol·o·gy (krĭm'ə-nŏl'ə-jē) *n.* The study of crime, criminals, and criminal behavior. [Italian *criminologia* : Latin *crīmen,* accusation, CRIME + -LOGY.] —**crim'i·no·log'i·cal** (-nə-lŏj'ĭ-kəl) *adj.* —**crim'i·no·log'i·cal·ly** *adv.* —**crim'i·nol'o·gist** *n.*

crimp¹ (krĭmp) *tr.v.* **crimped, crimping, crimps.** **1.** To press into small, regular folds or ridges; to pleat; corrugate. **2.** To bend or mold (leather) into shape. **3.** To gash (the flesh of a raw fish, for example) to make it crisper and firmer when cooked. **4.** To form (hair) into tight curls or waves. —*n.* **1. a.** The act of crimping. **b.** Something that has been crimped. **2.** *Usually plural.* Tightly curled or waved hair. **3.** The natural curliness of wool fibers. **4.** A fold or bend in sheet metal to provide stiffness or form a joint. —**put a crimp in.** *Informal.* To obstruct; hamper: *The blizzard put a crimp in surface traffic.* [Middle English *crimpen,* to wrinkle, shrivel, Old English *gecrympan,* to curl. See **ger-³** in Appendix.*] —**crimp'er** *n.*

crimp² (krĭmp) *n.* A person who procures men to serve as sailors or soldiers by tricking or coercing them. —*tr.v.* **crimped, crimping, crimps.** To procure (sailors or soldiers) by trickery or coercion. [Origin obscure.]

crimp·y (krĭm'pē) *adj.* **-ier, -iest.** Full of crimps; wavy.

crim·son (krĭm'zən) *n.* A deep to vivid purplish red to vivid red. See **color.** —*v.* **crimsoned, -soning, -sons.** —*intr.* To become crimson. —*tr.* To make crimson. [Middle English *cremesin,* from Old Spanish, from Arabic *qirmizī,* from *qirmiz,* kermes insect (from which red dye was obtained). See **kwrmi-** in Appendix.*] —**crim'son** *adj.*

cringe (krĭnj) *intr.v.* **cringed, cringing, cringes.** **1.** To shrink back, as with fear; cower. **2.** To behave in a servile manner; to fawn. —See Synonyms at **recoil.** —*n.* An act or instance of cringing. [Middle English *crengen,* probably ultimately from Old English *cringan,* to fall dead. See **ger-³** in Appendix.*] —**cring'er** *n.* —**cring'ing·ly** *adv.*

crin·gle (krĭng'gəl) *n. Nautical.* A small ring or grommet of rope or metal fastened to the edge of a sail. [Low German *kringel,* diminutive of *kring,* ring, circle, from Middle Low German *krink, kring.* See **ger-³** in Appendix.*]

cri·nite (krī'nīt', krĭ'-) *adj. Biology.* Hairy or having hairlike tufts. [Latin *crīnītus,* past participle of *crīnīre,* to provide with hair, from *crīnis,* hair. See **sker-³** in Appendix.*]

crin·kle (krĭng'kəl) *v.* **-kled, -kling, -kles.** —*intr.* **1.** To form into wrinkles or ripples. **2.** To make a soft, crackling sound; to rustle. —*tr.* To cause to wrinkle or rustle. —*n.* A wrinkle or ripple; a fold. [Middle English *crinkelen,* akin to Middle Dutch *crinkelen.* See **ger-³** in Appendix.*] —**crin'kly** *adj.*

crin·kle·root (krĭng'kəl-ro͞ot', -ro͝ot') *n.* A woodland plant, *Dentaria diphylla,* of eastern North America, having fleshy rootstocks and clusters of white or pinkish flowers. Also called "pepperroot," "toothwort."

cri·noid (krī'noid') *n.* Any of various marine invertebrates of the class Crinoidea, which includes the sea lilies and feather stars, characterized by feathery, radiating arms and a stalk by which they are attached to a surface. —*adj.* Of or belonging to the Crinoidea. [New Latin *Crinoidea* : Greek *krinon,* lily (see **crinum**) + -OID.]

crin·o·line (krĭn'ə-lĭn) *n.* **1.** A coarse, stiff cotton fabric, formerly made of horsehair and linen. It is used to line and stiffen garments. **2.** A petticoat made of this fabric. **3.** A hoop skirt. [French, from Italian *crinolino* : *crino,* horsehair, from Latin *crīnis,* hair (see **sker-³** in Appendix*) + *lino,* flax, from Latin *līnum* (see **lino-** in Appendix*).] —**crin'o·line** *adj.*

cri·num (krī'nəm) *n., pl.* **-nums.** Any of several mostly tropical plants of the genus *Crinum,* having long, strap-shaped leaves and clusters of lilylike flowers. Also called "crinum lily." [New Latin *Crinum,* from Greek *krinon*†, lily.]

cri·o·sphinx (krī'ə-sfĭngks') *n., pl.* **-sphinxes** or **-sphinges** (-sfĭn'-

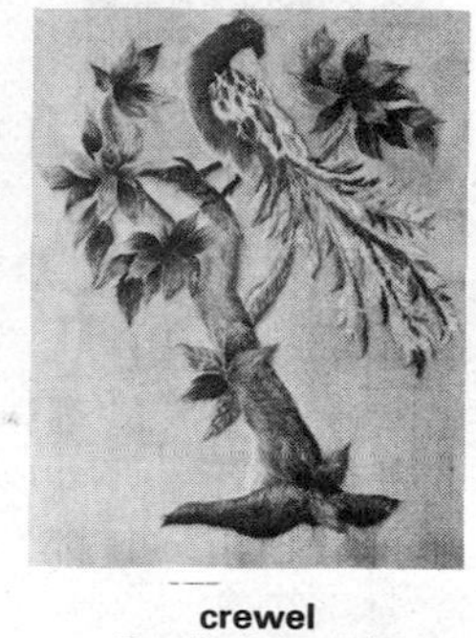

crewel
Detail of a curtain with crewel embroidery

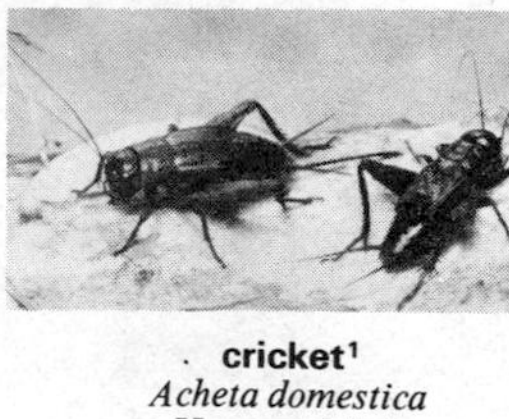

cricket¹
Acheta domestica
House cricket

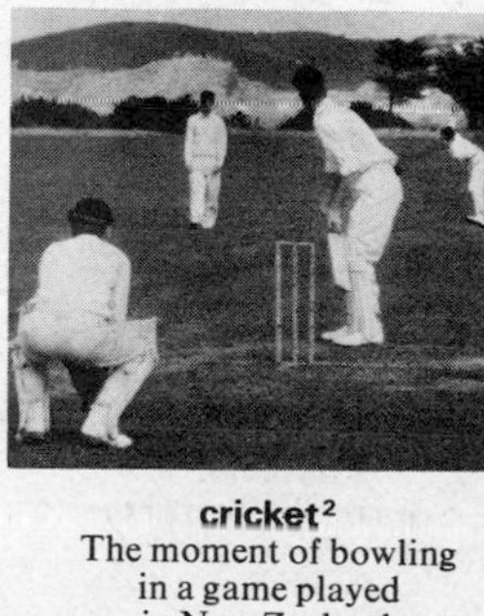

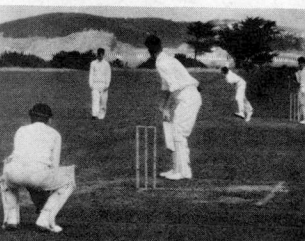

cricket²
The moment of bowling in a game played in New Zealand

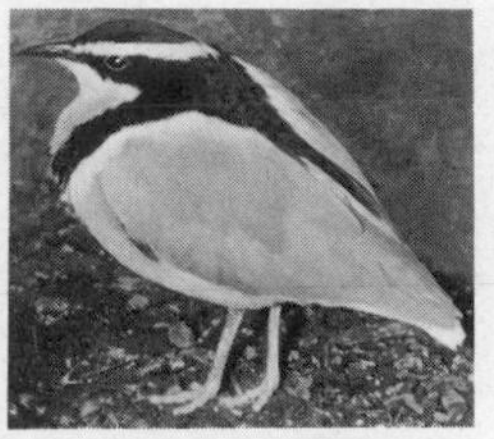

crocodile bird

jēz). A sphinx with the head of a ram. [Greek *krios,* ram (see **ker-**[1] in Appendix*) + SPHINX.]

crip·ple (krĭp′əl) *n.* **1.** One who is partly disabled or lame or deficient in a specified way. **2.** *Regional.* A dense thicket. —*tr.v.* **crippled, -pling, -ples. 1.** To make into a cripple. **2.** To disable or damage. [Middle English *crepel,* Old English *crypel.* See **ger-**[3] in Appendix.*] —**crip′pler** *n.*

Crip·ple Creek (krĭp′əl). A town, once a thriving city and gold-mining center of central Colorado.

cris. Variant of **kris.**

Cri·sey·de. Variant of **Cressida.**

cri·sis (krī′sĭs) *n., pl.* **-ses** (-sēz′). **1. a.** A crucial point or situation in the course of anything; turning point. **b.** An unstable condition in political, international, or economic affairs in which an abrupt or decisive change is impending. **2.** *Pathology.* A sudden change in the course of an acute disease, either toward improvement or deterioration. **3.** The point in a story or drama at which hostile forces are in the most tense state of opposition. [Latin, from Greek *krisis,* turning point, from *krinein,* to separate, decide. See **skeri-** in Appendix.*]

crisp (krĭsp) *adj.* **crisper, crispest. 1.** Firm but easily broken or crumbled; brittle. **2.** Firm and fresh: *crisp celery.* **3.** Brisk; invigorating; bracing. **4.** Animated; stimulating. **5.** Terse; pithy; sharp. **6.** Having small curls, waves, or ripples. —See Synonyms at **incisive.** —*v.* **crisped, crisping, crisps.** —*tr.* To make crisp. —*intr.* To become crisp. —*n. Chiefly British.* A potato chip. [Middle English *crisp,* Old English *crisp,* curly, from Latin *crispus,* crisped, curly. See **sker-**[3] in Appendix.*]

cris·pate (krĭs′pāt′) *adj.* Also **cris·pat·ed** (-pā′tĭd). Crimped, curled, or tightly waved. [Latin *crispātus,* from *crispāre,* to curl, from *crispus,* curly, CRISP.]

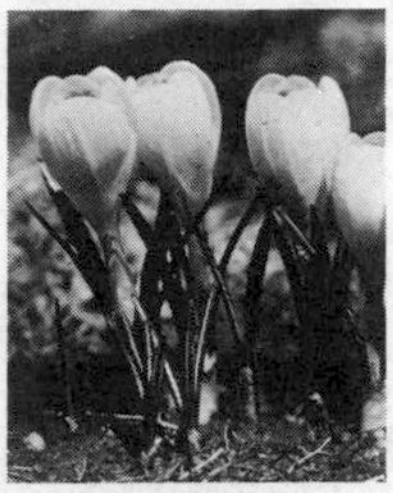

crocus
Crocus vernus

cris·pa·tion (krĭs-pā′shən) *n.* **1. a.** The act of crisping or curling. **b.** The state of being crisped or curled. **2.** A slight involuntary contraction or constriction, as of the skin. **3.** A minute undulation on the surface of a liquid, produced by vibration.

crisp·er (krĭs′pər) *n.* One that crisps; especially, a compartment in a refrigerator, used for storing vegetables to keep them fresh.

Cris·pin (krĭs′pĭn), **Saint.** Roman Christian martyr of the third century A.D.; patron saint of shoemakers.

crisp·y (krĭs′pē) *adj.* **-ier, -iest.** Crisp. —**crisp′i·ness** *n.*

criss·cross (krĭs′krôs′, -krŏs′) *v.* **-crossed, -crossing, -crosses.** —*tr.* **1.** To mark with crossing lines. **2.** To move crosswise through or over. —*intr.* To move crosswise or in crisscrosses. —*n.* **1.** A mark or pattern made of crossing lines. **2.** A game, **ticktacktoe** *(see).* —*adj.* Crossing one another or marked by crossings. —*adv.* In a crisscross manner; in crossing directions. [Variant of CHRISTCROSS.]

cris·sum (krĭs′əm) *n., pl.* **crissa** (krĭs′ə). *Zoology.* The feathers or area surrounding a bird's cloacal opening. [New Latin, from Latin *crissāre, crisāre,* to move the buttocks during intercourse. See **sker-**[3] in Appendix.*] —**cris′sal** *adj.*

cris·tate (krĭs′tāt′) *adj.* Also **cris·tat·ed** (-tā′tĭd). Having or forming a crest. [Latin *cristātus,* from *crista,* tuft, crest. See **sker-**[3] in Appendix.*]

Cris·tó·bal (krĭ-stō′bəl; *Spanish* krēs-tō′väl). A seaport in the Canal Zone, at the Caribbean end of the Panama Canal, adjoining the city of Colón.

crit. critic; critical; criticism.

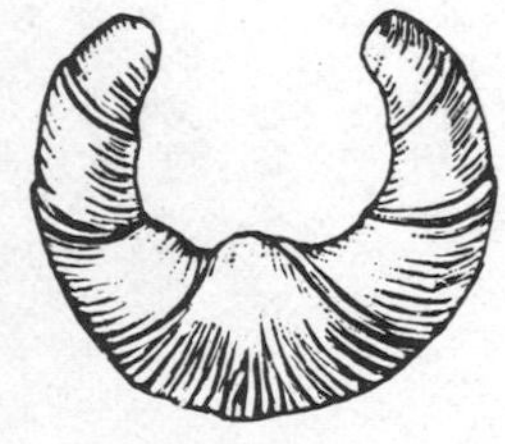

croissant

cri·te·ri·on (krī-tîr′ē-ən) *n., pl.* **-teria** (-tîr′ē-ə) or **-ons.** A standard, rule, or test on which a judgment or decision can be based. [Greek *kritērion,* a means for judging, standard, from *kritēs,* a judge, umpire, from *krinein,* to separate, choose. See **skeri-** in Appendix.*]

Usage: *Criteria* is a plural form only. It cannot properly be used, for *criterion,* in any of the following: *a criterion; one criterion; the only criterion.*

crit·ic (krĭt′ĭk) *n.* **1.** One who forms and expresses judgments of the merits and faults of anything. **2.** *Abbr.* **crit.** A specialist in the explication and judgment of literary or artistic works. **3.** A person who finds fault; a severe judge. **4.** *Obsolete.* A critique. [Latin *criticus,* from adjective, "decisive," from Greek *kritikos,* able to discern, critical, from *kritos,* separated, chosen, from *krinein,* to separate, choose. See **skeri-** in Appendix.*]

crit·i·cal (krĭt′ĭ-kəl) *adj. Abbr.* **crit. 1.** Inclined to judge severely; given to censuring. **2.** Characterized by careful and exact evaluation and judgment. **3.** Of, pertaining to, or characteristic of critics or criticism. **4.** Forming, or of the nature of, a crisis; crucial. **5.** Fraught with danger or risk; perilous. **6.** Designating materials and products essential to some condition or project but in short supply. **7.** *Medicine.* Of or pertaining to a crisis. **8.** *Mathematics.* Of or pertaining to a point at which a curve has a maximum, minimum, or point of inflection. **9.** *Chemistry & Physics.* Of or pertaining to a condition causing an abrupt change in a quality, property, or phenomenon.

Synonyms: *critical, acute, crucial, serious.* These adjectives are applied to conditions or situations to indicate degrees of intensity or significance. *Critical* implies the arrival at a turning point and the imminence of decisive change, usually attended by considerable risk, peril, or suspense. *Acute* is applicable to a somewhat earlier stage, when intensification of unfavorable conditions signals the approach of a crisis. *Crucial* and *critical* may apply to approximately the same point in time, but *crucial* emphasizes change that is likely to shape future events. *Serious* lacks the implication of great significance and immediate concern that is inherent in the other terms.

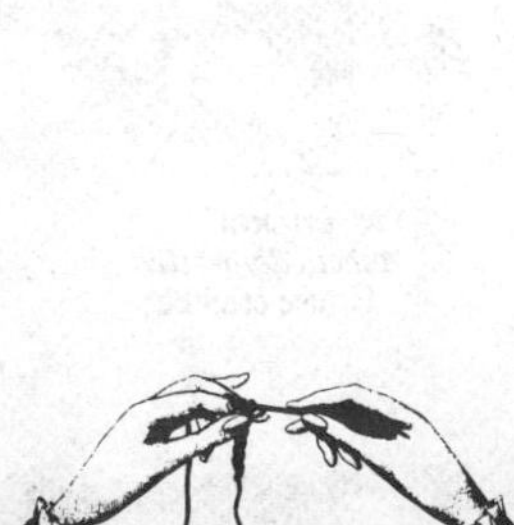

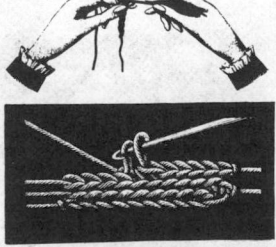

crochet
Above: Position of the hands in crocheting the chain stitch
Below: Chain stitches

critical angle. 1. *Optics.* The smallest angle of incidence at which a light ray passing from one medium to another, less refractive medium can be totally reflected from the boundary between the two. **2.** *Aviation.* The angle of attack of an airfoil at which airflow abruptly changes, causing changes in the lift and drag of an aircraft.

critical mass. The smallest mass of a fissionable material that will sustain a nuclear chain reaction.

critical point. 1. *Physics.* The condition in which the liquid and vapor phases of a pure stable substance have the same density. Also called "critical state." **2.** *Mathematics.* **a.** A maximum, minimum, or point of inflection. **b.** A point at which the derivative of a function is zero or infinite.

critical pressure. The least applied pressure required at the critical temperature to liquefy a gas.

critical temperature. The temperature above which a gas cannot be liquefied, regardless of the pressure applied.

crit·ic·as·ter (krĭt′ĭ-kăs′tər) *n.* A petty or inferior critic.

crit·i·cism (krĭt′ə-sĭz′əm) *n. Abbr.* **crit. 1.** The act of making judgments or criticizing. **2.** A passing of unfavorable judgment; censure; disapproval. **3.** The art, skill, or profession of making discriminating judgments and evaluations, especially of literary or other artistic works. **4.** A review or other article expressing such judgment and evaluation. **5.** The detailed investigation of the origin and history of literary documents.

crit·i·cize (krĭt′ə-sīz′) *v.* **-cized, -cizing, -cizes.** —*tr.* **1.** To judge the merits and faults of; analyze and evaluate. **2.** To judge with severity; find fault with; censure. —*intr.* To act as a critic. —**crit′i·ciz′a·ble** *adj.* —**crit′i·ciz′er** *n.*

Synonyms: *criticize, blame, reprehend, censure, condemn, denounce.* These verbs are compared as they mean to express an unfavorable judgment. *Criticize,* the least specific, can mean merely to evaluate without necessarily finding fault, but usually it does imply detailed expression of disapproval. *Blame* emphasizes the finding of fault and the fixing of responsibility for it. *Reprehend* implies sharp disapproval, usually of the actions or attributes of a person. *Censure* refers to open and strong expression of disapproval; often it implies a reprimand, or formal criticism, of a person or persons by someone in authority. *Condemn* can refer broadly to any expression of severe disapproval or, more narrowly, to an official act of passing judgment, such as sentencing by a court. *Denounce* can apply to any strongly adverse judgment expressed openly and vehemently, or specifically to public proclamation of official criticism or repudiation.

cri·tique (krĭ-tēk′) *n.* **1.** A critical review or commentary, especially one dealing with a literary or other artistic work. **2.** A critical discussion of some specified topic. **3.** The art of criticism. [French, from Greek *kritikē,* the art of criticism, from *kritikos,* critical. See **critic.**]

crit·ter (krĭt′ər) *n. Regional.* **1.** A domestic animal, especially a steer or horse. **2.** Any living creature. [Variant of CREATURE.]

croak (krōk) *v.* **croaked, croaking, croaks.** —*intr.* **1.** To utter the low, hoarse sound characteristic of frogs and crows. **2.** To speak with a low, hoarse voice. **3. a.** To mutter discontentedly; grumble. **b.** To predict evil; talk dolefully. **4.** *Slang.* To die. —*tr.* **1.** To utter by croaking. **2.** *Slang.* To kill. —*n.* A croaking sound. [Middle English *croken* (imitative).] —**croak′i·ly** *adv.* —**croak′y** *adj.*

croak·er (krō′kər) *n.* **1. a.** A croaking animal. **b.** A person who grumbles or habitually predicts evil. **2.** Any of various chiefly marine fishes of the family Sciaenidae, that make croaking or grunting sounds. **3.** *Slang.* A physician or surgeon.

Croat (krōt, krō′ăt′) *n.* **1.** A Slavic native or inhabitant of Croatia. **2.** The language of the Croats; Serbo-Croatian. [New Latin *Croata,* from Serbo-Croatian *Hrvat.*]

Cro·a·tan[1] (krō′ə-tăn′). Also **Cro·a·to·an** (-tō′ən). An island off the coast of North Carolina, between Pamlico Sound and the Atlantic, thought to have been the site to which Raleigh's Roanoke Island colony moved in 1587.

Cro·a·tan[2] (krō′ə-tăn′) *n.* Also **Cro·a·to·an** (-tō′ən). An Indian tribe formerly inhabiting the coastal region of North Carolina, reputedly connected with the disappearance (around 1590) of Sir Walter Raleigh's colony at Roanoke Island.

Cro·a·tia (krō-ā′shə). *Serbo-Croatian* **Hr·vat·ska** (hûr′vät-skä). **1.** A region of southeastern Europe, along the northeastern coast of the Adriatic Sea; an independent kingdom in the Middle Ages, and later a crown land of Austria-Hungary. **2.** A constituent republic of Yugoslavia, occupying 21,611 square miles in the northwest. Population, 4,160,000. Capital, Zagreb.

Cro·a·tian (krō-ā′shən) *adj.* Of or pertaining to Croatia, the Croats, their language, or their culture. —*n.* **1.** A Croat. **2. Serbo-Croatian** *(see).*

Cro·ce (krō′chā), **Benedetto.** 1866–1952. Italian philosopher, critic, and historian.

cro·ce·in (krō′sē-ĭn) *n.* Any of various red or orange acid azo dyes. [Latin *croceus,* saffron-colored, from *crocus,* saffron, CROCUS + -IN.]

cro·chet (krō-shā′) *v.* **-cheted** (-shād′), **-cheting** (-shā′ĭng), **-chets** (-shāz′). —*intr.* To make a piece of needlework by looping thread with a hooked needle. —*tr.* To make or decorate (a fabric) by looping thread with a hooked needle. —*n.* A kind of needlework made by crocheting. [French, a hook, from Old French, diminutive of *croc(he),* a hook, from Frankish *krōk* (unattested). See **ger-**[3] in Appendix.*]

cro·cid·o·lite (krō-sĭd′ə-līt′) *n.* A fibrous, lavender-blue or greenish mineral, a sodium iron silicate that is used as a commercial form of asbestos. [German *Krokydolith,* "fibrous stone" : Greek *krokus* (stem *krokud-*), nap of cloth (see **krek-**[1] in Appendix*) + -LITE.]

crock[1] (krŏk) *n.* **1.** An earthenware vessel. **2.** A broken piece of earthenware; potsherd. [Middle English *crokke,* Old English *crocc(a).* See **ger-**[3] in Appendix.*]

crock[2] (krŏk) *n. British Regional.* **1.** Soot. **2.** Coloring matter

ă pat/ā pay/âr care/ä father/b bib/ch church/d deed/ĕ pet/ē be/f fife/g gag/h hat/hw which/ĭ pit/ī pie/îr pier/j judge/k kick/l lid, needle/m mum/n no, sudden/ng thing/ŏ pot/ō toe/ô paw, for/oi noise/ou out/ŏŏ took/ōō boot/p pop/r roar/s sauce/sh ship, dish/

that rubs off from poorly dyed cloth. —*v.* **crocked, crocking, crocks.** —*tr.* To soil with or as with crock. —*intr.* To give off soot or color. [Possibly from CROCK (pot, hence "soot on a cooking pot").]

crock[3] (krŏk) *n. Chiefly British.* One that is worn-out, decrepit, or impaired. —*intr.v.* **crocked, crocking, crocks.** *Chiefly British Slang.* To get sick; become weak or disabled. [Middle English *crok,* perhaps from Scandinavian, akin to Norwegian *krake,* sickly beast. See **ger-**[3] in Appendix.*]

crocked (krŏkt) *adj. Slang.* Drunk. [Perhaps from CROCK (to disable).]

Crock·er (krŏk′ər), **Charles.** 1822–1888. American railroad financier.

crock·er·y (krŏk′ə-rē) *n.* Crocks collectively; earthenware.

crock·et (krŏk′ĭt) *n. Architecture.* An ornamental device, usually in the form of a cusp or curling leaf, placed along outer angles of pinnacles and gables, especially in the Gothic style. [Middle English *croket,* from Old North French *croquet,* variant of Old French *crochet,* hook. See **crochet.**]

Crock·ett (krŏk′ĭt), **David ("Davy").** 1786–1836. American frontiersman; member U.S. House of Representatives (1827–31 and 1833–35); died at the Alamo.

croc·o·dile (krŏk′ə-dīl′) *n.* **1.** Any of various large aquatic reptiles of the genus *Crocodylus* and related genera, of tropical regions, having thick, armorlike skin and long, tapering jaws. **2.** Broadly, any crocodilian reptile, such as an alligator, caiman, or gavial. **3.** Leather made from crocodile skin. [Middle English *cocodril,* from Old French, from Medieval Latin *cocodrillus,* from Latin *crocodīlus,* from Greek *krokodilos,* "worm of the pebbles" (from its habit of basking in the sun) : *krokē*†, pebbles + *drilos*†, worm.]

Croc·o·dile (krŏk′ə-dīl′). A river, the **Limpopo** *(see).*

crocodile bird. A black and white African bird, *Pluvianus aegyptius,* that feeds on insects that infest crocodiles.

crocodile tears. False tears; an insincere display of grief. [From the belief that crocodiles weep after eating their victims.]

croc·o·dil·i·an (krŏk′ə-dĭl′ē-ən, -dĭl′yən) *n.* Any of various reptiles of the order Crocodylia, which includes the alligators, crocodiles, caimans, and gavials. —*adj.* **1.** Of or pertaining to a crocodile. **2.** Belonging to the order Crocodylia. [New Latin *Crocodylia,* from Latin *crocodīlus,* CROCODILE.]

croc·o·ite (krŏk′ō-īt′, krō′kō-) *n.* A rare orange to reddish mineral of lead chromate, $PbCrO_4$, found in oxidized lead deposits. [Earlier *crocoisite* : French *crocoise,* from Greek *krokoeis,* saffronlike, from *krokos,* saffron, CROCUS + -ITE.]

cro·cus (krō′kəs) *n., pl.* **-cuses** or **-ci** (-sī′). **1.** Any plant of the genus *Crocus,* widely cultivated in gardens, and having showy, variously colored flowers and grasslike leaves. **2.** Grayish to light reddish purple. See **color. 3.** A red variety of iron oxide, Fe_2O_3, used in the form of an abrasive powder for polishing. [New Latin *Crocus,* from Latin *crocus,* saffron, from Greek *krokos,* from Semitic, akin to Hebrew *karkōm.*]

Croe·sus (krē′səs). Died 546 B.C. Last King of Lydia (560–546 B.C.); defeated and killed by the Persians under Cyrus.

croft (krôft, krŏft) *n. British & Scottish.* **1.** A small enclosed field or pasture near a house. **2.** A small farm, especially a tenant farm. [Middle English *croft,* Old English *croft.* See **ger-**[3] in Appendix.*]

croft·er (krôf′tər, krŏf′-) *n. British & Scottish.* A person who rents and cultivates a croft; tenant farmer.

crois·sant (krwä-säN′) *n.* A rich, crescent-shaped roll of leavened dough or puff pastry. [French, from Old French *croissant, creissant,* CRESCENT.]

Croix de Guerre (krwä′ də gâr′). A French military decoration for bravery in battle. [French, "cross of war."]

Cro·ker (krō′kər), **John Wilson.** 1780–1857. English editor, essayist, and political leader.

Cro-Mag·non (krō-măg′nən, -măn′yən) *n.* An early form of modern man, *Homo sapiens,* characterized by a rather robust physique and known from skeletal parts found in the Cro-Magnon cave in southern France. —**Cro-Mag′non** *adj.*

crom·lech (krŏm′lĕk′) *n.* **1.** A prehistoric monument consisting of monoliths encircling a mound. **2.** A **dolmen** *(see).* [Welsh : *crom,* feminine of *crwn,* arched (see **skerbh-** in Appendix*) + *llech,* flat stone (see **lēu-**[1] in Appendix*).]

Crom·well (krŏm′wĕl′, -wəl, krŭm′-), **Oliver.** 1599–1658. English military, political, and religious leader; dictator as Lord Protector of the Commonwealth (1653–58).

Crom·well (krŏm′wĕl′, -wəl, krŭm′-), **Richard.** 1626–1712. English political and military leader; son and successor of Oliver Cromwell; Lord Protector of the Commonwealth (1658–59); abdicated.

Crom·well (krŏm′wĕl′, -wəl, krŭm′-), **Thomas.** Earl of Essex. 1485?–1540. English political leader; adviser to Cardinal Wolsey and Henry VIII; executed for treason.

Crom·well current (krŏm′wĕl′, -wəl). A Pacific Ocean current at the equator, flowing eastward from the Hawaiian to the Galápagos islands. [After Townsend *Cromwell* (1922–1958), American oceanographer.]

Crom·wel·li·an (krŏm-wĕl′ē-ən, krŭm-) *adj.* Of, pertaining to, or characteristic of Oliver Cromwell or his time.

crone (krōn) *n.* A withered, witchlike old woman. [Middle English, from Middle Dutch *caroonje, croonje,* old ewe, dead body, from Old North French *carogne,* carrion, from Vulgar Latin *carōnia* (unattested), from Latin *carō* (stem *carn-*), flesh. See **sker-**[1] in Appendix.*]

Cro·nus (krō′nəs). Also **Kro·nos, Cro·nos** (krō′nŏs). *Greek Mythology.* A Titan who ruled the universe until dethroned by his son Zeus; identified with the Roman god Saturn.

cro·ny (krō′nē) *n., pl.* **-nies.** A close friend or companion. [Earlier *chrony* (Cambridge University slang), "old companion," from Greek *khronios,* long-lasting, from *khronos,* time. See **khronos** in Appendix.*]

crook (krŏŏk) *n.* **1.** Something bent or curved; a hook or hooked part. **2.** An implement or tool with a bent or curved part, such as a bishop's crosier or a shepherd's staff. **3.** A curve or bend; a turn. **4.** *Informal.* A person who makes his living by dishonest methods; a thief. —*v.* **crooked, crooking, crooks.** —*tr.* To give a crook to; curve; bend. —*intr.* To become crooked. [Middle English *crok,* from Old Norse *krōkr,* a hook. See **ger-**[3] in Appendix.*]

Crook (krŏŏk), **George.** 1829–1890. American military leader and Indian fighter; defeated the Sioux and subdued Geronimo.

crook·back (krŏŏk′băk′) *n.* A hunchback. —**crook′backed′** *adj.*

crook·ed (krŏŏk′ĭd) *adj.* **1.** Having bends, curves, or angles; not straight. **2.** Dishonest or unscrupulous; fraudulent. **3.** Misshapen; deformed. —**crook′ed·ly** *adv.* —**crook′ed·ness** *n.*

Crookes (krŏŏks), Sir **William.** 1832–1919. British physicist; discoverer of thallium; studied vacuum-tube discharge.

Crookes tube. A low-pressure discharge tube used to study the properties of cathode rays. [After Sir William CROOKES.]

crook·neck (krŏŏk′nĕk′) *n.* A type of squash having a long, curved neck and yellow flesh. Also called "crookneck squash."

croon (krōōn) *v.* **crooned, crooning, croons.** —*intr.* **1.** To sing or hum softly; murmur. **2.** To sing popular songs in a soft, sentimental manner. **3.** *Scottish & British Regional.* To roar or bellow. —*tr.* To sing by crooning. —*n.* A soft singing, humming, or murmuring. [Middle English *croynen,* to boom, sing, from Middle Dutch *krōnen,* to groan, lament. See **ger-**[4] in Appendix.*] —**croon′er** *n.*

crop (krŏp) *n.* **1.** Cultivated plants or agricultural produce, such as grain, vegetables, or fruit. **2.** The yield of such produce of a particular season, place, or kind. **3.** A seasonal yield of a specified nonagricultural product. **4.** A group, quantity, or supply appearing at one time: *a crop of new ideas.* **5.** A short haircut. **6.** An earmark on an animal. **7. a.** A short whip used in horseback riding, with a loop serving as a lash. **b.** The stock of a whip. **8.** *Zoology.* **a.** A pouchlike enlargement of a bird's esophagus, in which food is stored or partially digested. **b.** A similar organ in earthworms, insects, and other invertebrates. —*v.* **cropped, cropping, crops.** —*tr.* **1.** To cut off the stems or top of (a plant). **2.** To cut (hair, for example) very short. **3.** To clip (an animal's ears, for example). **4.** To reap; harvest. **5.** To cause to grow or yield a crop or crops. —*intr.* To plant, grow, or yield a crop or crops. —**crop up** (or **out**). To appear or develop unexpectedly. [Middle English *crop,* Old English *cropp,* cluster, bunch, ear of corn. See **ger-**[3] in Appendix.*]

crop-eared (krŏp′ĭrd′) *adj.* **1.** Having the ears cropped. **2.** With the hair cut so short that the ears show.

crop·per[1] (krŏp′ər) *n.* **1.** One that crops. **2.** A person who works land in return for a share of the yield; sharecropper.

crop·per[2] (krŏp′ər) *n.* **1.** A heavy fall; tumble. **2.** A disastrous failure; fiasco. —**come a cropper. 1.** To fall heavily. **2.** To fail miserably; come to ruin. [From the phrase *neck and crop,* "completely," perhaps from CROP (to cut off).]

cro·quet (krō-kā′) *n.* **1.** An outdoor game in which the players drive wooden balls through a series of wickets using long-handled mallets. **2.** The act of driving away an opponent's croquet ball by hitting one's own ball when the two are in contact. —*v.* **croqueted** (-kād′), **-queting** (-kā′ĭng), **-quets** (-kāz′). —*tr.* To drive away (an opponent's ball) with a croquet. —*intr.* To croquet an opponent's ball. [Perhaps from French *crochet,* a hook. See **crochet.**]

cro·quette (krō-kĕt′) *n.* A small cake of minced food, often coated with bread crumbs and fried in deep fat. [French, from *croquer,* to crunch, crack (imitative).]

cro·qui·gnole (krō′kĭn-yōl′) *n.* A kind of permanent wave in which the hair is wound around metal rods. [French, a biscuit, perhaps from *croquer,* to crunch. See **croquette.**]

cro·sier (krō′zhər) *n.* Also **cro·zier. 1.** A staff with a crook or cross at the end, carried by or before an abbot, bishop, or archbishop as a symbol of office. **2.** *Botany.* A coiled tip of a plant stalk, as of a young fern frond. [Middle English *crocer,* from Old French *crossier,* staff-bearer, from *crosse,* bishop's staff, from Germanic. See **ger-**[3] in Appendix.*]

cross (krôs, krŏs) *n.* **1.** An upright post with a transverse piece near the top, upon which condemned persons were executed in ancient times. **2.** A symbolic representation of the cross upon which Jesus was crucified. **3.** A crucifix. **4.** A sign made by tracing the outline of a cross with the right hand upon the forehead and chest as a devotional act. **5.** Any trial, affliction, or frustration: *Everyone has his own cross to bear.* **6.** Any of various symbolic or ornamental figures or structures in the form of a cross or modified cross, such as a medal, emblem, or insignia. **7.** A symbol of many pre-Christian religions, consisting of two crossed lines. **8.** Any mark or pattern formed by the intersection of two lines; especially, such a mark (X) used as a signature. **9.** A pipe fitting with four branches in the form of a cross, used as a junction for intersecting pipes. **10.** *Biology.* **a.** A plant or animal produced by crossbreeding; a hybrid. **b.** The process of crossbreeding; hybridization. **11.** A combination of the qualities of two things. **12.** *Slang.* A contest whose outcome has been dishonestly prearranged. —**the Cross.** The cross upon which Jesus was crucified. —*v.* **crossed, crossing, crosses.** —*tr.* **1.** To go or extend across; pass from one side of to the other. **2.** To carry or convey across. **3.** To extend or pass through or over; intersect. **4.** To make or put a line across. **5.** To lay across or over; place crosswise: *cross one's legs.* **6.** To

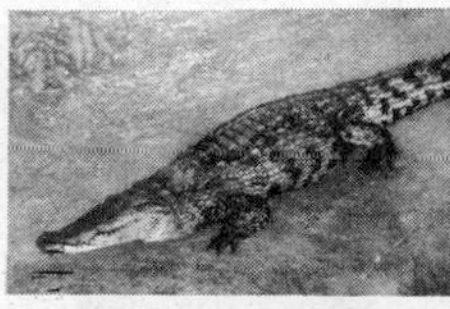

crocodile
Crocodylus acutus
American crocodile

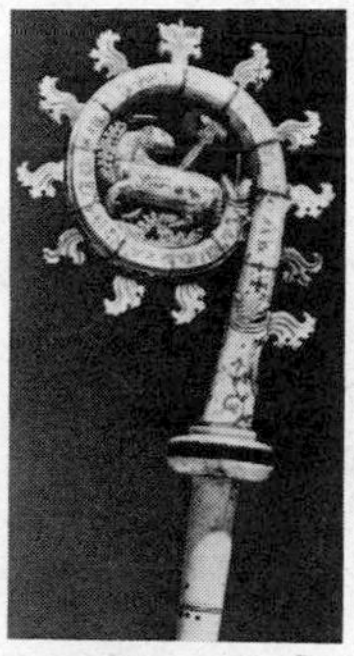

crosier
Thirteenth-century bishop's crosier made in Germany

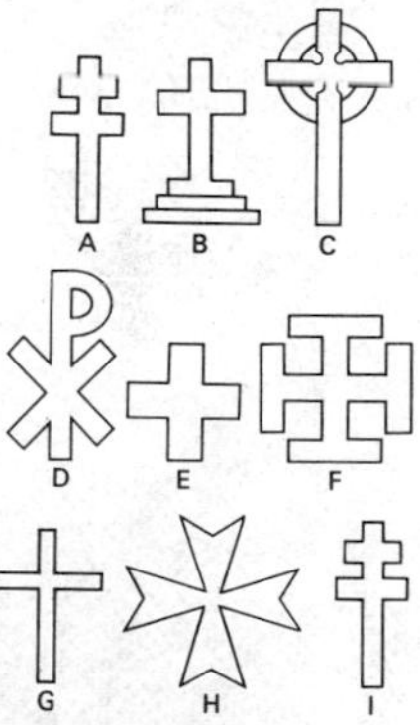

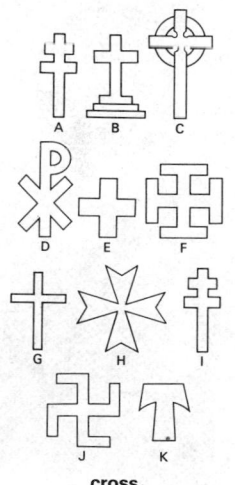

cross
A. Archiepiscopal cross
B. Calvary cross
C. Celtic cross
D. Chi-rho
E. Greek cross
F. Jerusalem cross
G. Latin cross
H. Maltese cross
I. Patriarchal cross
J. Swastika
K. Tau cross

make the sign of the cross upon or over as a sign of devotion. **7.** To encounter in passing: *His path crossed mine.* **8.** *Informal.* To thwart or obstruct; interfere with: *Do not cross me.* **9.** *Biology.* To crossbreed or cross-fertilize (plants or animals). —*intr.* **1.** To lie or pass across; intersect. **2.** To move or extend from one side to another. **3.** To encounter in passing: *Our paths crossed.* **4.** *Biology.* To crossbreed or cross-fertilize. —**cross off** (or **out**). To cancel or eliminate by or as if by drawing a line or lines through. —*adj.* **1.** Lying or passing crosswise; intersecting. **2.** Contrary or counter; opposing. **3.** Showing ill humor; annoyed. **4.** Involving interchange; reciprocal. **5.** Crossbred; hybrid. —*adv.* Crosswise or across. [Middle English *cros,* Old English *cros,* from Old Irish *cross,* from Latin *crux* (stem *cruc-*), perhaps from Phoenician.] —**cross′er** *n.* —**cross′ly** *adv.* —**cross′ness** *n.*

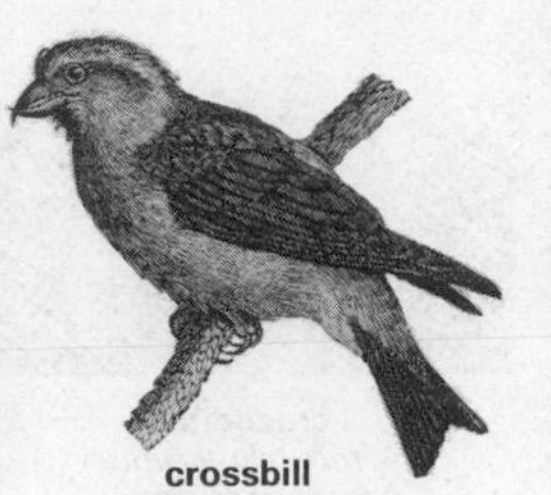

crossbill
Loxia curvirostra
Red crossbill

cross·bar (krôs′bär′, krŏs′-) *n.* A horizontal bar, line, or stripe. —*tr.v.* **crossbarred, -barring, -bars.** To supply, fasten, or mark with crossbars.

cross·bill (krôs′bĭl′, krŏs′-) *n.* Any of several birds of the genus *Loxia,* having curved mandibles with narrow, crossed tips.

cross·bones (krôs′bōnz′, krŏs′-) *n.* A representation of two bones placed crosswise, usually under a skull, symbolizing danger or death.

cross·bow (krôs′bō′, krŏs′-) *n.* A medieval weapon consisting of a bow fixed crosswise on a wooden stock, with grooves on the stock to direct the projectile. —**cross′bow′man** (-mən) *n.*

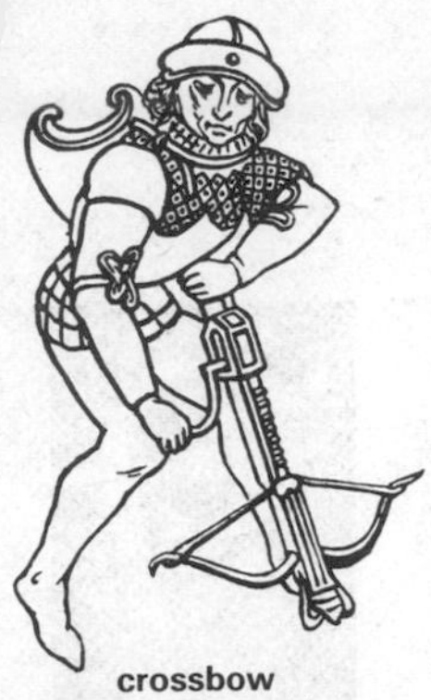

crossbow
Woodcut of an archer cocking his crossbow

cross·breed (krôs′brēd′, krŏs′-) *v.* **-bred** (-brĕd′), **-breeding, -breeds.** —*tr.* To produce (a hybrid) by the mating of individuals of different varieties or breeds; hybridize. —*intr.* To mate so as to produce a hybrid; interbreed. —*n.* A hybrid produced by crossbreeding.

cross bun. A **hot cross bun** *(see).*

cross·check (krôs′chĕk′, krŏs′-) *tr.v.* **-checked, -checking, -checks. 1.** To verify by comparing with parallel or supplementary data. **2.** *Hockey.* To check illegally by thrusting with one's stick at an opponent's arms or stick. —*n.* (krôs′chĕk′, krŏs′-). The act of crosschecking.

cross-coun·try (krôs′kŭn′trē, krŏs′-) *adj.* **1.** Moving or directed across open country, rather than following roads. **2.** From one side of a country to the opposite side.

cross cross·let (krôs′lĭt, krŏs′-). A cross with a smaller cross near the end of each arm.

cross·cur·rent (krôs′kûr′ənt, krŏs′-) *n.* **1.** A current flowing across another current. **2.** A conflicting movement, tendency, or inclination.

cross·cut (krôs′kŭt′, krŏs′-) *v.* **-cut, -cutting, -cuts.** —*tr.* To cut or run across. —*intr.* To cut or run crosswise. —*adj.* **1.** Used or constructed for cutting crosswise: *a crosscut saw.* **2.** Cut on the bias or across the grain. —*n.* **1.** A course or cut going crosswise. **2.** A path more direct than the main path; short cut. **3.** *Mining.* A level driven so that it intersects a vein of ore.

crosse (krôs, krŏs) *n.* A lacrosse stick. [French, from Old French *crosse,* staff. See **crosier.**]

cross-ex·am·ine (krôs′ĭg-zăm′ĭn, krŏs′-) *v.* **-ined, -ining, -ines.** —*tr.* **1.** To question (someone) closely, especially in order to check the resulting answers against answers previously made. **2.** *Law.* To question (a witness already examined by the opposing side). —*intr.* To question a person closely. —**cross′-ex·am′i·na′tion** *n.* —**cross′-ex·am′in·er** *n.*

cross-eye (krôs′ī′, krŏs′ī′) *n.* A form of strabismus in which one or both eyes deviate toward the nose. —**cross′-eyed′** *adj.*

cross-fer·ti·li·za·tion (krôs′fûrt′l-ə-zā′shən, krŏs′-) *n.* **1.** *Biology.* Fertilization by the union of gametes from different individuals, often of different varieties or species. **2.** *Botany.* Fertilization of the ovule of one plant or flower by pollen nuclei from another. In this sense, also called "allogamy." —**cross′-fer′tile** *adj.*

cross-fer·ti·lize (krôs′fûrt′l-īz′, krŏs′-) *v.* **-lized, -lizing, -lizes.** —*tr.* To fertilize by means of cross-fertilization. —*intr.* To be fertilized by means of cross-fertilization.

cross-file (krôs′fīl′, krŏs′-) *intr.v.* **-filed, -filing, -files.** To register as a candidate in the primaries of more than one political party. —**cross′-fil′er** *n.*

cross·fire (krôs′fīr′, krŏs′-) *n.* **1.** *Military.* Lines of fire from two or more positions crossing one another at or near a single objective. **2.** Any situation in which a number of things originating from different sources come together. —*intr.v.* **crossfired, -firing, -fires.** *Military.* To direct crossfire.

Cross-Flor·i·da Barge Canal (krôs′flôr′ə-də, krŏs′flŏr′-). A partially completed canal across Florida, connecting the Gulf of Mexico with the Atlantic by way of the St. Johns River.

Cross-Flor·i·da Waterway. The **Okeechobee Waterway** *(see).*

cross-grained (krôs′grānd′, krŏs′-) *adj.* **1.** Having an irregular, transverse, or diagonal grain. **2.** Stubborn; contrary.

cross hair. Either of two fine strands of wire crossed in the focus of the eyepiece of an optical instrument and used as a calibration or sighting reference.

cross·hatch (krôs′hăch′, krŏs′-) *tr.v.* **-hatched, -hatching, -hatches.** To shade with two or more sets of intersecting parallel lines.

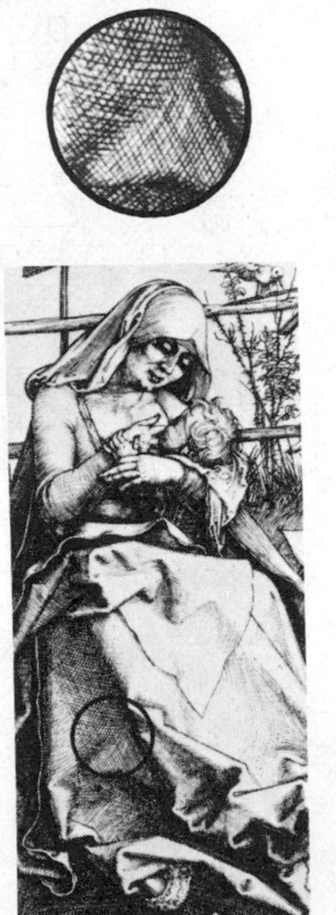

crosshatch
From the "Virgin Seated on a Grassy Bank," engraving by Albrecht Dürer, with enlarged detail above showing crosshatching

cross·head (krôs′hĕd′, krŏs′-) *n.* **1.** *Engineering.* A beam that connects the piston rod to the connecting rod of a reciprocating engine. **2.** Any of the subheads in a newspaper or other article, book, or chapter describing the contents of a section.

cross-in·dex (krôs′ĭn′dĕks, krŏs′-) *v.* **-dexed, -dexing, -dexes.** —*tr.* To furnish (an index) with cross-references. —*intr.* To furnish cross-references.

cross·ing (krôs′ĭng, krŏs′-) *n.* **1.** A place at which roads, lines, or tracks intersect; an intersection. **2.** The place at which something, such as a river or highway, may be crossed. **3.** The intersection of the nave and transept in a cruciform church.

crossing over. The exchange of genetic material between homologous chromosomes. Also called "crossover."

cross·jack (krôs′jăk′, krŏs′-) *n.* The square sail below the lowest mizzenmast spar on a ship. [CROSS + JACK (flag).]

cros·sop·te·ryg·i·an (krŏ-sŏp′tə-rĭj′ē-ən) *adj.* Of or belonging to the Crossopterygii, a group of mostly extinct fishes including the coelacanths, believed to have been the possible ancestors of terrestrial vertebrates. —*n.* A member of the Crossopterygii. [From New Latin *Crossopterygii,* "the fringed-winged ones" : Greek *krossoi*†, fringe + Greek *pterux,* wing, from *pteron,* feather, wing (see **pet-**[1] in Appendix*).]

cross·o·ver (krôs′ō′vər, krŏs′-) *n.* **1.** A place at which or the means by which a crossing is made. **2.** A short connecting track by which a train can be transferred from one line to another. **3.** *Genetics.* **a.** A **crossing over** *(see).* **b.** A character resulting from crossing over.

cross·patch (krôs′păch′, krŏs′-) *n. Informal.* A peevish, irascible person. [CROSS (angry) + obsolete *patch,* jester, probably from Italian *pazzo*†.]

cross·piece (krôs′pēs′, krŏs′-) *n.* A transverse piece, as of a structure.

cross-pol·li·nate (krôs′pŏl′ə-nāt′, krŏs′-) *tr.v.* **-nated, -nating, -nates.** *Botany.* To cross-fertilize (a plant or flower). —**cross′-pol′li·na′tion** *n.*

cross-pur·pose (krôs′pûr′pəs, krŏs′-) *n.* A conflicting or contrary purpose. —**be at cross-purposes.** To have or act under a misunderstanding of each other's purposes.

cross-ques·tion (krôs′kwĕs′chən, krŏs′-) *tr.v.* **-tioned, -tioning, -tions.** To cross-examine; question closely. —*n.* A question asked in the process of cross-examination.

cross-re·fer (krôs′rĭ-fûr′, krŏs′-) *v.* **-ferred, -ferring, -fers.** —*tr.* To refer from one part or passage to another. —*intr.* To make a cross-reference.

cross-ref·er·ence (krôs′rĕf′ər-əns, -rĕf′rəns, krŏs′-) *n.* A reference from one part of a book, index, catalogue, or file to another part containing related information.

Cross River. A river of western Cameroun and southeastern Nigeria, flowing 300 miles into the Gulf of Guinea.

cross·road (krôs′rōd′, krŏs′-) *n.* **1.** A road that intersects another road. **2.** *Plural.* **a.** A place where two or more roads meet. **b.** A place where different cultures meet. **c.** A crucial point or place. Used with a singular verb.

cross·ruff (krôs′rŭf′, -rŭf′, krŏs′-) *n.* A series of plays in games of the whist family where partnership hands alternately ruff suits led by the other partner. —*v.* **crossruffed, -ruffing, -ruffs.** —*intr.* To perform a crossruff or a series of crossruffs. —*tr.* To ruff (one's partner's lead or a lead from the dummy) in alternating plays.

cross section. 1. A section formed by a plane cutting through an object, usually at right angles to an axis. **2.** A piece so cut or a graphic representation of such a piece. **3.** *Physics.* A measure of the probability of occurrence of a particular atomic or nuclear reaction. **4.** A representative sample meant to be typical of the whole. —**cross′-sec′tion·al** *adj.*

cross-stitch (krôs′stĭch′, krŏs′-) *n.* **1.** In sewing and embroidery, a double stitch forming an X. **2.** Needlework made with this stitch. —*v.* **cross-stitched, -stitching, -stitches.** —*tr.* To make or embroider with cross-stitches. —*intr.* To work in cross-stitch.

cross·talk (krôs′tôk′, krŏs′-) *n.* Noise or garbled sounds heard on a telephone or other electronic receiver, caused by interference from another channel.

cross·tie (krôs′tī′, krŏs′-) *n.* **1.** A transverse beam or rod serving as a support or connection. **2.** A wood, concrete, or metal beam that connects and supports the rails of a railroad.

cross-town (krôs′toun′, krŏs′-) *adj.* Running across a city or town: *a cross-town bus.* —*adv.* Across a city or town.

cross·tree (krôs′trē, krŏs′-) *n.* One of the two horizontal crosspieces at the upper ends of the lower masts in fore-and-aft-rigged vessels, serving to spread the shrouds.

cross vault. A vaulting formed by the intersection of two or more simple vaults. Also called "cross vaulting."

cross·vine (krôs′vīn′, krŏs′-) *n.* A woody vine, *Bignonia capreolata,* of the southeastern United States, having large, trumpet-shaped, reddish flowers. [So called because a cross is found in a cross section of the stem.]

cross·walk (krôs′wôk′, krŏs′-) *n.* A path marked off for pedestrians crossing a street.

cross·way (krôs′wā′, krŏs′-) *n.* A crossroad.

cross·wind (krôs′wĭnd′, krŏs′-) *n.* A wind blowing at right angles to a given direction, as to an aircraft's line of flight.

cross·wise (krôs′wīz′, krŏs′-) *adv.* Also **cross·ways** (-wāz′). Across; running transversely.

cross·word puzzle (krôs′wûrd′, krŏs′-). A puzzle in which an arrangement of numbered squares is to be filled with words running both across and down in answer to correspondingly numbered clues.

crotch (krŏch) *n.* **1.** The angle, or region of the angle, formed by the junction of parts or members, as by two branches, limbs, or legs. **2.** The fork of a pole or other support. [Possibly a variant of CRUTCH.] —**crotched** (krŏcht) *adj.*

crotch·et (krŏch′ĭt) *n.* **1.** A small hook or hooklike structure. **2.** An odd, whimsical, or stubborn notion. **3.** *Music.* A **quarter note** *(see).* [Middle English *crochet,* small hook, from Old French. See **crochet.**]

crotch·et·y (krŏch′ĭ-tē) *adj.* Capriciously stubborn or eccentric; perverse. —**crotch′et·i·ness** *n.*

ă pat/ā pay/âr care/ä father/b bib/ch church/d deed/ĕ pet/ē be/f fife/g gag/h hat/hw which/ĭ pit/ī pie/îr pier/j judge/k kick/l lid, needle/m mum/n no, sudden/ng thing/ŏ pot/ō toe/ô paw, for/oi noise/ou out/o͝o took/o͞o boot/p pop/r roar/s sauce/sh ship, dish/

cro·ton (krōt′n) *n.* **1.** Any of various chiefly tropical plants, shrubs, or trees of the genus *Croton.* See **croton oil. 2.** Any of various tropical plants of the genus *Codiaeum;* especially, *C. variegatum pictum,* frequently grown as a house plant for its showy, varicolored foliage. [New Latin *Croton,* from Greek *krotōn*†, castor oil plant.]

Cro·ton bug (krōt′n). A small light-brown cockroach, *Blatella germanica,* that is a common household pest. Also called "German cockroach." [Supposed to have been introduced into New York City in water from the *Croton* River in Westchester County, New York.]

croton oil. A yellowish-brown, violently cathartic oil obtained from the seeds of a tree, *Croton tiglium,* of southeastern Asia.

crouch (krouch) *v.* **crouched, crouching, crouches.** —*intr.* **1.** To stoop with the limbs pulled close to the body. **2.** To bend servilely or timidly; cringe. —*tr.* To cause to bend low, as in fear or humility. —*n.* The act or posture of crouching. [Middle English *cro(u)chen,* from Old French *crochir,* to be bent, from *croc(he),* a hook. See **crochet.**] —**crouch′ing·ly** *adv.*

croup[1] (kro͞op) *n.* A pathological condition affecting the larynx in children, characterized by respiratory difficulty and a harsh cough, and associated with edema, inflammation, and sometimes formation of a fibrinous exudate on the mucous membrane. [Probably imitative of coughing.] —**croup′ous** (kro͞op′əs), **croup′y** *adj.*

croup[2] (kro͞op) *n.* Also **croupe.** The rump of certain animals, especially a horse. [Middle English *croupe,* from Old French, from Frankish *kruppa* (unattested). See **ger-**[3] in Appendix.*]

crou·pi·er (kro͞o′pē-ər, -pē-ā′) *n.* An attendant at a gaming table who collects and pays bets. [French, originally "rider on the rump (behind another rider)," from *croupe,* rump, CROUP.]

crou·ton (kro͞o′tŏn′, kro͞o-tŏn′) *n.* A small crisp piece of toasted or fried bread. [French *croûton,* from *croûte,* crust, from Old French *crouste,* from Latin *crusta,* CRUST.]

crow[1] (krō) *n.* **1.** Any of several large, glossy, black birds of the genus *Corvus,* having a characteristic raucous call; especially, *C. brachyrhynchos,* of North America. **2.** A crowbar. —**as the crow flies.** In a straight line. —**eat crow.** *Informal.* To be forced into a humiliating situation, as from having been in error. [Middle English *croue,* Old English *crāwe.* See **ger-**[4] in Appendix.*]

crow[2] (krō) *intr.v.* **crowed** or **crew** (kro͞o) (for sense 1), **crowing, crows. 1.** To utter the shrill cry characteristic of a cock or rooster. **2.** To boast; exult. **3.** To make a sound expressive of pleasure or well-being, characteristic of an infant. —See Synonyms at **boast.** —*n.* **1.** The shrill cry of a cock. **2.** An inarticulate sound expressive of pleasure or delight. [Middle English *crouen,* Old English *crāwan.* See **ger-**[4] in Appendix.*]

Crow (krō) *n., pl.* **Crow** or **Crows. 1.** A tribe of Siouan-speaking Indians, formerly inhabiting the region between the Platte and Yellowstone rivers and now settled in southeastern Montana. **2.** A member of this tribe. **3.** The language of this tribe.

crow·bar (krō′bär′) *n.* A straight bar of iron or steel, with the working end shaped like a forked chisel, used as a lever. [From the resemblance of the forked end to a crow's foot.]

crow·ber·ry (krō′bĕr′ē) *n., pl.* **-ries. 1.** A low-growing evergreen shrub, *Empetrum nigrum,* of cool regions of the Northern Hemisphere, having small, purplish flowers and black, berrylike fruit. **2.** Any of several similar or related plants, such as the **bearberry** *(see).* **3.** The fruit of any of these plants.

crow blackbird. The **grackle** *(see).*

crowd[1] (kroud) *n.* **1.** A large number of persons gathered together; throng. **2.** The common people; the populace. **3.** A particular social group; clique. **4.** A large number of things grouped or considered together. —*v.* **crowded, crowding, crowds.** —*intr.* **1.** To throng. **2.** To advance by shoving. —*tr.* **1.** To press; shove; push. **2.** To press, cram, or force tightly together. **3.** To fill or occupy to overflowing. **4.** *Informal.* To put pressure on. —**crowd (on) sail.** *Nautical.* To spread a large amount of sail to increase speed. [From Middle English *crouden, crowden,* to crowd, press, Old English *crūdan,* to hasten. See **greut-** in Appendix.*] —**crowd′er** *n.*

crowd[2] (kroud, kro͝od) *n.* An ancient Celtic musical instrument, stringed and played with a bow. [Middle English *croud, crouth,* from Welsh *crwth.* See **krut-** in Appendix.*]

crow·foot (krō′fo͝ot′) *n., pl.* **-foots** (for senses 1, 2) or **-feet** (-fēt′) (for senses 3, 4). **1.** Any of various plants of the genus *Ranunculus,* which includes the buttercups and spearworts; especially, any of several similar plants, such as *R. abortivus* and *R. scleratus,* having small, inconspicuous yellow flowers. **2.** Loosely, any of various other plants having leaves or other parts resembling a bird's foot. **3.** *Military.* A defensive device, **caltrop** *(see).* **4.** *Nautical.* **a.** A block used in supporting the middle section of an awning. **b.** A set of small lines passed through holes of a batten or fitting to help support the backbone of an awning.

crown (kroun) *n. Abbr.* **cr. 1.** An ornamental circlet or head covering, often made of precious metal set with jewels, and worn as a symbol of sovereignty. **2.** The power, position, or empire of a monarch. **3.** A decorative garland or wreath worn on the head as a symbol of victory, honor, or distinction. **4.** Honorary distinction or reward for achievement. **5.** Anything resembling a crown in shape, such as a badge, emblem, or heraldic bearing. **6.** A coin stamped with a crown or crowned head on the reverse side. **7. a.** A former British coin worth five shillings. **b.** Any of several coins with a name that means crown, such as the koruna, krona, and krone. **8. a.** The top or highest part of the head. **b.** The head itself. **9.** The top or upper part of a hat. **10.** The highest point or summit of anything. **11.** The highest or most perfect state or type; acme. **12.** The highest or primary quality or attribute; a chief ornament. **13.** *Dentistry.* **a.** The part of a tooth that is covered by enamel and projects beyond the gum line. **b.** A gold, porcelain, or plastic substitute for the natural crown of a tooth. **14.** The lowest part of the shank of an anchor, where the arms are joined to it. **15. a.** The upper part of a tree, including the leaves and living branches. **b.** The part of a plant, usually at ground level, between the root and the stem. **c.** A flower part, the **corona** *(see).* **16.** The crest of an animal, especially of a bird. **17.** The portion of a cut gem above the girdle. —**the Crown. 1.** The monarch as the head of state or sovereign governing power. **2.** The power, position, or empire of a monarch. —*tr.v.* **crowned, crowning, crowns. 1.** To put a crown or garland upon the head of. **2.** To invest with regal power; make a monarch of; enthrone. **3.** To confer honor, dignity, or reward upon. **4.** To surmount or be the highest part of. **5.** To form the crown, top, or chief ornament of. **6.** To bring to completion or successful conclusion; complete; finish; consummate. **7.** To put a crown on (a tooth). **8.** *Checkers.* To make (a piece that has reached the last row) into a king by placing another piece upon it. **9.** *Informal.* To hit on the head. [Middle English *crowne, coroune,* from Old French *corone,* from Latin *corōna,* garland, wreath, from Greek *korōnē,* anything curved or bent, from *korōnos,* curved. See **sker-**[3] in Appendix.*] —**crown** *adj.*

crown canopy. The canopy or cover formed by the upper branches of trees in a forest. Also called "crown cover."

crown colony. A British colony in which the sovereign has complete control of legislation, usually administered by an appointed governor.

crown gall. A disease of plants caused by a bacterium, *Agrobacterium tumefaciens,* and characterized by warty, usually woody growths on roots and stems, especially near the soil line.

crown glass. 1. A clear soda-lime-silica optical glass with low refraction. Compare **flint glass. 2.** A form of window glass made by whirling a glass bubble to make a flat circular disk with a lump in the center formed by the craftsman's rod.

crown lens. The crown-glass element in an achromatic lens.

crown-of-thorns (kroun′əv-thôrnz′) *n.* A spiny, vinelike desert plant, *Euphorbia splendens,* often grown as a potted plant for its scarlet flowers.

Crown Point. A town of northeastern New York State, on lower Lake Champlain; the site of a strategic fort in the French and Indian and the Revolutionary wars.

crown prince. The heir apparent to a throne.

crown princess. 1. The wife of a crown prince. **2.** A female heir apparent to a throne.

crown roast. A rib section of lamb, veal, or pork, skewered together at the ends to form a circle and roasted as a fancy cut of meat.

crown saw. A cylindrical saw with teeth on the bottom edge of the cylinder.

crown vetch. A sprawling plant, *Coronilla varia,* native to Europe, having compound leaves and clusters of pink flowers. Also called "axseed."

crow's-foot (krōz′fo͝ot′) *n., pl.* **-feet** (-fēt′). **1.** *Usually plural.* Any of the wrinkles at the outer corner of the eye, common in many adults. **2.** A three-pointed embroidery stitch used as finishing, as at the end of a seam.

crow's-nest (krōz′nĕst′) *n.* **1.** A small lookout platform with a high protective railing and wind screen, located near the top of a ship's mast. **2.** Any similar lookout platform located ashore.

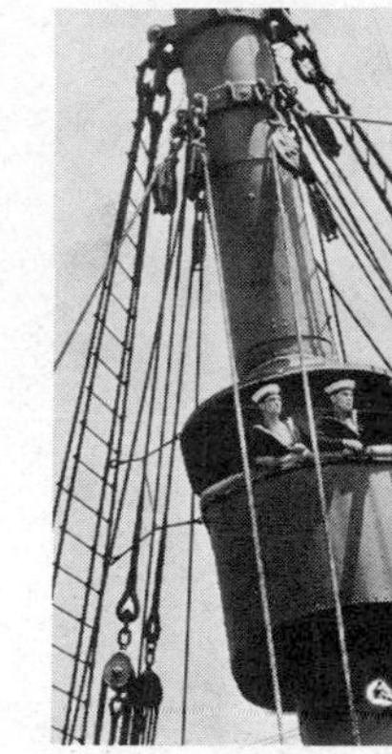

crow's-nest
Crow's-nest of the *Queen Mary*

Croy·don (kroid′n). A borough of London, England, comprising the former administrative divisions of Croydon, and Coulsdon and Purley. Population, 327,000.

croze (krōz) *n.* **1.** The groove at the ends of the staves of a barrel or cask into which the head is set. **2.** A cooper's tool, such as a plane, for making such a groove. [French *creux,* from Old French *crues,* socket, groove, perhaps from Gallo-Roman *crosus*† (unattested).]

cro·zier. Variant of **crosier.**

cru·ces. Alternate plural of **crux.**

cru·cial (kro͞o′shəl) *adj.* **1.** Of supreme importance; critical; decisive: *a crucial election.* **2.** Severe; difficult; trying. **3.** Having the form of a cross; cross-shaped. —See Synonyms at **critical.** [Old French, cross-shaped, from Latin *crux* (stem *cruc-*), CROSS.] —**cru′cial·ly** *adv.*

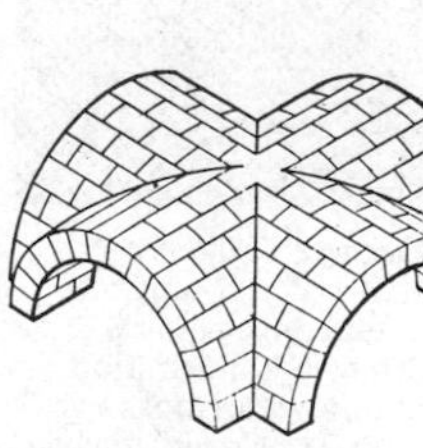

cross vault

cru·ci·ate (kro͞o′shē-āt′) *adj.* **1.** Cross-shaped. **2.** Overlapping or crossing, as the wings of some insects when at rest. [New Latin *cruciatus,* from Latin *crux,* CROSS.]

cru·ci·ble (kro͞o′sə-bəl) *n.* **1.** A vessel made of a refractory substance such as graphite or porcelain, used for melting and calcining materials at high temperatures. **2.** The bottom of an ore furnace, in which the molten metal collects. **3.** A severe test or trial. [Middle English *crusible,* from Medieval Latin *crucibulum,* perhaps originally a lamp kept burning in front of a crucifix, from Latin *crux,* CROSS.]

crucible steel. A high-grade steel made by fusing low-carbon steel with charcoal or cast iron in a graphite crucible and used in tools and dies.

cru·ci·fer (kro͞o′sə-fər) *n.* **1.** One who bears a cross in a religious procession. **2.** *Botany.* Any plant of the family Cruciferae, such as a mustard or cress, having four-petaled flowers suggestive of a cross. [Late Latin : Latin *crux,* CROSS + -FER.] —**cru·cif′er·ous** (-sĭf′ər-əs) *adj.*

cru·ci·fix (kro͞o′sə-fĭks′) *n.* An image of Christ on the cross. [Middle English, from Old French, from Late Latin *crucifixus,* from the past participle of *crucifigere,* CRUCIFY.]

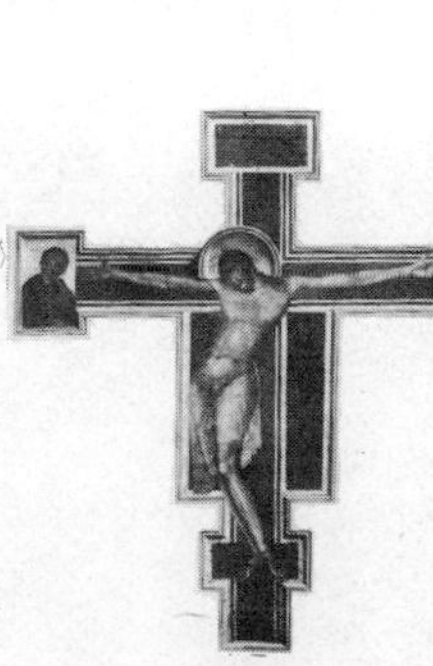

crucifix
"Crucifix of Santa Croce" by Cimabue

cru·ci·fix·ion (kro͞o′sə-fĭk′shən) *n.* **1.** The action of putting to death on a cross. **2.** A representation of Christ on the cross. **—the Crucifixion.** The crucifying of Christ on Calvary.

cru·ci·form (kro͞o′sə-fôrm′) *adj.* Cross-shaped. [Latin *crux* (stem *cruc-*), CROSS + -FORM.]

cru·ci·fy (kro͞o′sə-fī′) *tr.v.* **-fied, -fying, -fies. 1.** To put (a person) to death by nailing or binding to a cross. **2.** To mortify or subdue (the flesh). **3.** To torment; to torture; excruciate. [Middle English *crucifien,* from Old French *crucifier,* from Late Latin *crucifigere* : Latin *crux* (stem *cruc-*), CROSS + *figere,* to fasten (see **dhīgw-** in Appendix*).] **—cru′ci·fi′er** *n.*

crud (krŭd) *n. Slang.* **1.** A coating or incrustation of filth or refuse. **2.** One that is contemptible or disgusting. **3.** Any disease, imaginary or real, especially one affecting the skin. [Middle English *crudde,* CURD.] **—crud′dy** *adj.*

crude (kro͞od) *adj.* **cruder, crudest. 1.** In an unrefined or natural state; raw. **2.** Unripe; immature. **3.** Lacking finish, tact, or taste. **4.** Not carefully or completely made; rough. **5.** Displaying a lack of knowledge or skill. **6.** Undisguised or unadorned; blunt. *—n.* Petroleum in its unrefined state. [Middle English, from Latin *crūdus,* bloody, raw. See **kreu-¹** in Appendix.*] **—crude′ly** *adv.* **—cru′di·ty, crude′ness** *n.*

crude oil. A natural hydrocarbon mixture, **petroleum** *(see).*

cru·el (kro͞o′əl) *adj.* **-eler** or **-eller, -elest** or **-ellest. 1.** Disposed to inflict pain or suffering. **2.** Causing suffering; painful. [Middle English, from Old French, from Latin *crūdēlis,* morally unfeeling, cruel. See **kreu-¹** in Appendix.*] **—cru′el·ly** *adv.*

Synonyms: *cruel, ferocious, barbarous, inhuman, sadistic, vicious, pitiless, ruthless.* These adjectives mean predisposed to inflict violence, pain, or hardship, or to find satisfaction in the suffering of others. *Cruel* implies both disposition to harm and satisfaction in or indifference to suffering. *Ferocious* primarily stresses rough physical treatment and savagery, and *barbarous* adds the suggestion of behavior that befits only primitive or uncivilized men. *Inhuman* means markedly deficient in such qualities as tolerance and sympathy for one's fellow man. *Sadistic* implies the experiencing of satisfaction, especially sexual gratification, from cruelty inflicted on others. *Vicious* suggests native disposition to malicious and destructive behavior, and is sometimes associated with moral depravity. *Pitiless* refers specifically to absence of mercy. *Ruthless* also stresses lack of compassion and often implies relentless pursuit of personal ends regardless of hardship to others.

cru·el·ty (kro͞o′əl-tē) *n., pl.* **-ties. 1.** The quality or condition of being cruel. **2.** Something that causes pain or suffering, such as a cruel action or remark.

cru·et (kro͞o′ĭt) *n.* A small glass bottle for holding vinegar, oil, or other condiments at the table. [Middle English, from Norman French *cruet,* diminutive of Old French *crue,* flask, from Germanic. See **ger-³** in Appendix.*]

Cruik·shank (kro͝ok′shăngk′), **George.** 1792–1878. British illustrator.

cruise (kro͞oz) *v.* **cruised, cruising, cruises.** *—intr.* **1.** To sail or travel about, as for pleasure or reconnaissance. **2.** To travel at a speed providing maximum operating efficiency for a sustained period. *—tr.* To cruise or journey over. *—n.* A sea voyage for pleasure. [Perhaps Dutch *kruisen,* to sail to and fro, from Middle Dutch *crucen,* to cross, from *crūce,* a cross, from Latin *crux,* CROSS.]

cruis·er (kro͞o′zər) *n.* **1.** One of a class of fast warships of medium tonnage with a long cruising radius and less armor and firepower than a battleship. **2.** A large motorboat whose cabin is equipped with living facilities. Also called "cabin cruiser," "cruising yacht." **3.** A police **squad car** *(see).*

cruising radius. The longest distance a ship or aircraft can go and return at cruising speed without refueling.

crul·ler (krŭl′ər) *n.* Also **krul·ler.** A small cake of sweet dough fried in deep fat, usually ring-shaped or twisted. [Dutch *krulle,* from *krullen,* to curl, from *krul,* curly, from Middle Duch *crulle.* See **ger-³** in Appendix.*]

crumb (krŭm) *n.* **1.** A small piece broken or fallen from cake, bread, or other baked goods. **2.** Any small fragment or scrap. **3.** The soft inner portion of bread. Compare **crust. 4.** *Slang.* A contemptible, untrustworthy, or loathsome person. *—v.* **crumbed, crumbing, crumbs.** *—tr.* **1.** To break into small pieces or crumbs; crumble. **2.** *Cooking.* To cover or prepare with bread crumbs; bread. **3.** To brush (a table or cloth) clear of crumbs. *—intr.* To break apart in crumbs. [Middle English *crome,* Old English *cruma.* See **ger-³** in Appendix.*]

crum·ble (krŭm′bəl) *v.* **-bled, -bling, -bles.** *—tr.* To break or cause to break into small parts or crumbs. *—intr.* To fall into tiny pieces; disintegrate. —See Synonyms at **decay.** [Earlier *crimble,* from Middle English *cremelen,* perhaps from Old English *gecrymian,* from *cruma,* CRUMB.]

crum·blings (krŭm′blĭngz) *pl.n.* Crumbled pieces; crumbs.

crum·bly (krŭm′blē) *adj.* **-blier, -bliest.** Easily crumbled; friable.

crum·mie (krŭm′ē) *n. Scottish.* A cow with crooked horns. [From Scottish *crum(b),* crooked, Middle English *croumb,* Old English *crumb.* See **ger-³** in Appendix.*]

crum·my (krŭm′ē) *adj.* **-mier, -miest.** *Slang.* Also **crumb·y. 1.** Miserable; wretched. **2.** Shabby; cheap. [From CRUMB.]

crump (krŭmp) *v.* **crumped, crumping, crumps.** *—tr.* **1.** To crush or crunch with the teeth. **2.** To strike heavily with a crunching sound. *—intr.* To make a crunching sound. *—n.* **1.** A crunching sound. **2.** A heavy blow. [Imitative.]

crum·pet (krŭm′pĭt) *n. Chiefly British.* A light, soft bread similar to a muffin, baked on a griddle and often toasted. [Probably from Middle English *crompid (cake),* "curled cake," from *crampen, crumpen,* to curl, from *crump, crumb,* crooked, Old English *crump.* See **ger-³** in Appendix.*]

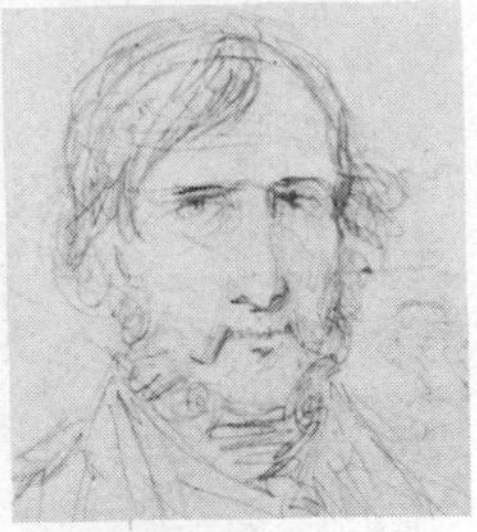

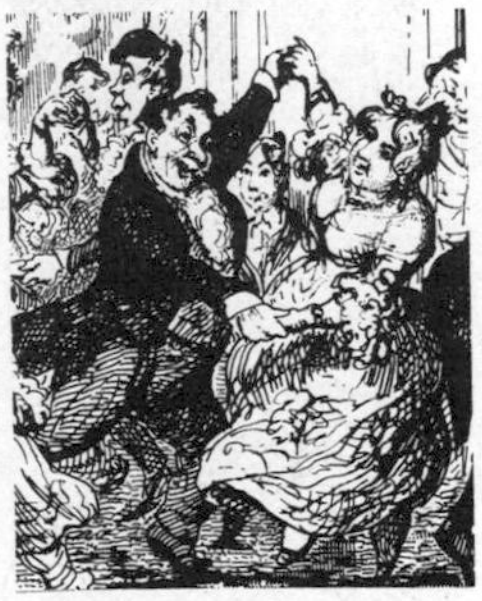

George Cruikshank
Above: A self-portrait at about age forty
Below: His illustration "December-Christmas Eve," done for *The Comic Almanac*

crum·ple (krŭm′pəl) *v.* **-pled, -pling, -ples.** *—tr.* To crush together or press into wrinkles; rumple. *—intr.* **1.** To become wrinkled; shrivel. Often used with *up.* **2.** To fall apart; collapse. *—n.* An irregular fold, crease, or wrinkle. [Probably frequentative of obsolete *crump,* to curl up, from Middle English *crampen.* See **crumpet.**]

crunch (krŭnch) *v.* **crunched, crunching, crunches.** *—tr.* **1.** To chew with a noisy crushing or crackling sound. **2.** To crush, grind, or tread noisily. *—intr.* **1.** To chew noisily with a crushing sound. **2.** To move or proceed with a crushing sound. **3.** To produce or emit a crushing sound. *—n.* The act or sound of crunching. [Imitative.]

cru·node (kro͞o′nōd′) *n. Mathematics.* A point where two branches of a curve intersect, so that each branch has a distinct tangent. [Latin *crux,* CROSS + NODE.]

crup·per (krŭp′ər) *n.* **1.** A leather strap looped under a horse's tail and attached to a harness or saddle to keep it from slipping forward. **2.** The rump of a horse. [Middle English *crouper, cropier,* from Old French *cropiere,* from *croupe,* rump, CROUP.]

cru·ral (kro͝or′əl) *adj.* Of or pertaining to the leg, shank, or thigh. [Latin *crūrālis,* from *crūs* (stem *crūr-*), leg, CRUS.]

crus (kro͞os, krŭs) *n., pl.* **crura** (kro͝or′ə). **1.** The section of the leg or hind limb between the knee and foot; shank. **2.** A leglike part. [Latin *crūs*†, leg.]

cru·sade (kro͞o-sād′) *n.* **1.** *Often capital* **C.** Any of the military expeditions undertaken by European Christians in the 11th, 12th, and 13th centuries to recover the Holy Land from the Moslems. **2.** Any holy war undertaken with papal sanction. **3.** Any vigorous concerted movement for a cause or against an abuse. *—intr.v.* **crusaded, -sading, -sades.** To engage in a crusade. [Earlier forms: (a) *croisade,* from Old French, variant of *croisée,* from the past participle of *croiser,* to bear the cross, from *crois,* cross, from Latin *crux;* (b) *crusado,* from Spanish *cruzada,* from *cruzar,* to bear the cross, from *cruz,* cross, from Latin *crux,* CROSS.] **—cru·sad′er** *n.*

cru·sa·do (kro͞o-sā′dō, -zä′dō) *n., pl.* **-does** or **-dos.** Also **cru·za·do.** An obsolete Portuguese gold or silver coin bearing the figure of a cross on the reverse. [Portuguese *cruzado,* from the past participle of *cruzar,* to bear a cross, from *cruz,* cross, from Latin *crux,* CROSS.]

cruse (kro͞oz, kro͞os) *n.* A small jar or pot for holding water, wine, or oil. [Middle English *crouse,* perhaps from Middle Dutch *cruyse,* pot. See **ger-³** in Appendix.*]

crush (krŭsh) *v.* **crushed, crushing, crushes.** *—tr.* **1.** To press between opposing bodies so as to break or injure; mash; squeeze. **2.** To break, pound, or grind (stone or ore, for example) into small fragments or powder. **3.** To extract or obtain by pressing or squeezing. **4.** To press upon, shove, or crowd. **5.** To put down; overwhelm; subdue. *—intr.* **1.** To be or become crushed or broken. **2.** To proceed or move by crowding or pressing. —See Synonyms at **break.** *—n.* **1.** The act of crushing; extreme pressure; compression. **2.** The state of being crushed. **3.** A great crowd or throng. **4.** A substance prepared by or as if by crushing: *raspberry crush.* **5.** *Informal.* **a.** An infatuation. Usually used with *on.* **b.** The object of it. [Middle English *crushen,* from Old French *croissir,* probably from Vulgar Latin *cruscire*† (unattested).] **—crush′a·ble** *adj.* **—crush′er** *n.*

Cru·soe, Robinson. See **Robinson Crusoe.**

crust (krŭst) *n.* **1.** The hard outer portion or surface area of bread. Compare **crumb. 2.** A piece of bread consisting mostly of this part. **3.** A pastry shell, as of a pie or tart. **4.** Any hard, crisp covering or surface. **5.** A hard deposit produced by maturing wine on the interior of bottles. **6. a.** *Geology.* The exterior portion of the earth that lies above the Mohorovičić discontinuity. **b.** The outermost solid layer of a planet or moon. **7.** The hard outer covering or integument of certain plants and animals, such as lichens and crustaceans. **8.** *Pathology.* A coating or dry outer layer, as of pus or blood; scab. **9.** *Slang.* Insolence; audacity; gall. *—v.* **crusted, crusting, crusts.** *—tr.* **1.** To cover with a crust. **2.** To form (dough) into a crust. *—intr.* **1.** To become covered with a crust. **2.** To harden into a crust. [Middle English *cruste,* from Old French *crouste,* from Latin *crusta*†, shell.]

crus·ta·cean (krŭ-stā′shən) *n.* Any of various predominantly aquatic arthropods of the class Crustacea, including lobsters, crabs, shrimps, and barnacles, characteristically having a segmented body, a chitinous exoskeleton, and paired, jointed limbs. *—adj.* Of or belonging to the Crustacea. [From New Latin *crustacea,* "the shelled ones," from *crustaceus,* CRUSTACEOUS.]

crus·ta·ceous (krŭ-stā′shəs) *adj.* **1.** Having, resembling, or constituting a hard crust or shell. **2.** Crustacean. [New Latin *crustaceus* : Latin *crusta,* shell, CRUST + -ACEOUS.]

crus·tal (krŭs′təl) *adj.* Of or pertaining to a crust, especially that of the earth or the moon.

crust·y (krŭs′tē) *adj.* **-ier, -iest. 1.** Resembling or having a crust. **2.** Harsh; curt; surly. —See Synonyms at **gruff.** **—crust′i·ly** *adv.* **—crust′i·ness** *n.*

crutch (krŭch) *n.* **1.** A staff or support used by the lame or infirm as an aid in walking, usually having a crosspiece to fit under the armpit and often used in pairs. **2.** Any device similar to this in form or function, such as a forked leg rest on a sidesaddle. **3.** A forked support for the boom of a sailing vessel when the sails are furled. **4.** Anything depended upon for support. **5.** The human crotch. *—tr.v.* **crutched, crutching, crutches.** To support on or as on crutches; to prop. [Middle English *crucche,* Old English *crycc.* See **ger-³** in Appendix.*]

crux (krŭks, kro͝oks) *n., pl.* **cruxes** or **cruces** (kro͞o′sēz). **1.** A

crucial or vital moment; critical point. **2.** The basic or essential thing. **3.** A puzzling problem. [Latin, CROSS.]

Crux (krŭks) *n.* A constellation in the Southern Hemisphere near Centaurus and Musca. Also called "Southern Cross."

crux an·sa·ta (krŭks′ ăn-sā′tə). An **ansate cross** *(see).*

cru·za·do. Variant of **crusado.**

cru·zei·ro (kro͞o-zā′rō, -ro͞o) *n., pl.* **-ros. 1.** The basic monetary unit of Brazil, equal to 100 centavos. See table of exchange rates at **currency. 2.** A coin worth one cruzeiro. [Portuguese, "(coin) bearing the figure of a cross," from *cruz,* cross, from Latin *crux,* CROSS.]

CRW Airport code for Charleston, West Virginia.

cry (krī) *v.* **cried, crying, cries.** *—intr.* **1.** To make inarticulate sobbing sounds expressing grief, sorrow, or pain; weep. **2.** To shout. Often used with *out.* **3.** To utter a characteristic sound or call. Used of an animal. *—tr.* **1.** To utter loudly. **2.** To proclaim or announce in public. **3.** To beg for; beseech; implore: *cry forgiveness.* **4.** To bring into a particular condition by weeping: *cry oneself to sleep.* **5.** To belittle or disparage. Used with *down.* **6.** To break or withdraw from a promise, agreement, or undertaking. Used with *off.* **7.** To praise highly; extol. Used with *up.* *—n., pl.* **cries. 1.** A loud utterance of some emotion, such as fear or anger. **2.** Any loud exclamation or utterance; a shout; a call. **3.** A fit of weeping. **4.** An urgent entreaty or appeal. **5.** A public or general demand or complaint; a clamor; an outcry. **6.** An opinion or belief generally held or expressed. **7.** A rumor. **8.** An advertising of wares by calling out. **9.** A rallying call or signal; a call to battle. **10.** A political slogan. **11.** The characteristic call or utterance of an animal or bird. **12.** A pack of hounds. **—a far cry.** A long way. **—in full cry.** In hot pursuit, as hounds hunting. [Middle English *crien,* from Old French *crier,* from Latin *quirītāre,* to cry out, to implore the aid of the Roman citizens, from *Quirītēs,* plural of *Quiris*†, a Roman citizen.]

Synonyms: *cry, weep, wail, keen, moan, whimper, sob, blubber.* These verbs mean to express grief or pain by tears or voice or both. *Cry* and *weep* both involve tear-shedding; *cry* is the more common term and more strongly implies accompanying sound. *Wail* refers primarily to loud, sustained, inarticulate mournful sound. *Keen* suggests wailing associated with funeral dirges. *Moan* refers to sustained, low, inarticulate sound expressive of great suffering or grief. *Whimper* refers to broken or repressed cries in a low, whining voice. *Sob* describes weeping, or a mixture of broken speech and weeping, marked by convulsive breathing or gasping. *Blubber* refers to noisy shedding of tears accompanied by broken or inarticulate speech.

cry·ba·by (krī′bā′bē) *n., pl.* **-bies.** A person who cries or complains frequently with little cause.

cry·ing (krī′ĭng) *adj.* Demanding or requiring immediate action or remedy: *a crying shame; a crying need.*

cryo–. Indicates cold, freezing, or frost; for example, **cryometer.** [From Greek *kruos*†, icy cold, frost.]

cry·o·gen (krī′ə-jən) *n.* A refrigerant used to obtain very low temperatures. [CRYO- + -GEN.]

cry·o·gen·ics (krī′ō-jĕn′ĭks) *n.* The science of low-temperature phenomena. [From CRYO- + -GENIC.]

cry·o·lite (krī′ə-līt′) *n.* A white, vitreous natural fluoride of aluminum and sodium, Na_3AlF_6, used chiefly as an electrolyte in aluminum refining and in electrical insulation. Also called "Greenland spar." [CRYO- + -LITE.]

cry·om·e·ter (krī-ŏm′ə-tər) *n.* A thermometer capable of measuring very low temperatures. [CRYO- + -METER.]

cry·o·plank·ton (krī′ō-plangk′tən) *n.* Minute organisms living in snow, ice, or perpetually icy waters. [CRYO- + PLANKTON.]

cry·o·scope (krī′ə-skōp′) *n.* An instrument used to measure the freezing point of a substance. [Back-formation from CRYOSCOPY.]

cry·os·co·py (krī-ŏs′kə-pē) *n.* The study of the freezing points of solutions. [French *cryoscopie* : CRYO- + -SCOPY.] **—cry′o·scop′ic** (-ə-skŏp′ĭk) *adj.*

cry·o·stat (krī′ə-stăt′) *n.* An apparatus used to maintain constant low temperature. [CRYO- + -STAT.]

cry·o·sur·ger·y (krī′ō-sûr′jə-rē) *n.* Surgery performed by local or general application of extreme cold.

cry·o·ther·a·py (krī′ō-thĕr′ə-pē) *n.* Also **cry·mo·ther·a·py** (krī′-mō-). The use of low temperatures in medical therapy.

crypt (krĭpt) *n.* **1.** An underground vault or chamber, especially one beneath a church that is used as a burial place. **2.** *Anatomy.* Any of various small pits, recesses, glandular cavities, or follicles in the body. [Latin *crypta,* from Greek *kruptē,* from *kruptos,* hidden, from *kruptein,* to hide. See **krāu-** in Appendix.*]

cryp·ta·nal·y·sis (krĭp′tə-năl′ə-sĭs) *n., pl.* **-ses** (-sēz′). The analysis and deciphering of cryptograms, ciphers, codes, or other secret writings. [CRYPT(OGRAM) + ANALYSIS.] **—cryp·tan′a·lyst** (-tăn′ə-lĭst) *n.* **—cryp·tan′a·lyt′ic** (-tăn′ə-lĭt′ĭk) *adj.*

cryp·tes·the·sia, cryp·taes·the·sia (krĭp′təs-thē′zhə, -zhē-ə) *n.* *Psychology.* A term describing the various modes of paranormal perception, such as clairvoyance. [New Latin : CRYPT(O)- + ESTHESIA.]

cryp·tic (krĭp′tĭk) *adj.* Also **cryp·ti·cal** (-tĭ-kəl). **1.** Hidden; concealed. **2.** Secret; mysterious; enigmatic. **3.** Having esoteric or hidden meaning; mystifying. **4.** *Biology.* Tending to conceal or camouflage: *cryptic coloring.* —See Synonyms at **ambiguous.** [Late Latin *crypticus,* from Greek *kruptikos,* from *kruptos,* hidden. See **crypt.**]

crypto–, crypt–. Indicates hidden or secret; for example, **cryptoclastic.** [New Latin, from Greek *kruptos,* hidden, from *kruptein,* to hide. See **krāu-** in Appendix.*]

cryp·to·clas·tic (krĭp′tō-klăs′tĭk) *adj.* Composed of microscopic fragments. Said of rocks. [CRYPTO- + CLASTIC.]

cryp·to·crys·tal·line (krĭp′tō-krĭs′tə-lĭn) *adj.* Having a microscopic crystalline structure.

cryp·to·gam (krĭp′tə-găm′) *n. Botany.* Any of the flowerless and seedless plants that reproduce by spores, such as fungi, algae, mosses, and ferns. Compare **phanerogam.** [French *cryptogame,* from New Latin *cryptogamia* : CRYPTO- + -GAMY.] **—cryp′to·gam′ic, cryp·tog′a·mous** (-tŏg′ə-məs) *adj.*

cryp·to·gen·ic (krĭp′tə-jĕn′ĭk) *adj.* Also **cryp·tog·e·nous** (krĭp-tŏj′ə-nəs). Of obscure or unknown origin. Said of diseases. [CRYPTO- + -GENIC.]

cryp·to·gram (krĭp′tə-grăm′) *n.* **1.** Something written in code or cipher; cryptograph. **2.** A figure having a secret or occult significance. [French *cryptogramme* : CRYPTO- + -GRAM (written).] **—cryp′to·gram′mic** *adj.*

cryp·to·graph (krĭp′tə-grăf′, -gräf′) *n.* **1.** A cryptogram. **2.** A system of secret or cipher writing; cipher. **3. a.** A device for translating plain text into cipher. **b.** A device for deciphering codes and ciphers. [Back-formation from CRYPTOGRAPHY.]

cryp·tog·ra·phy (krĭp-tŏg′rə-fē) *n.* **1.** The art or process of writing in or deciphering secret code. **2.** Any system of secret writing. [New Latin *cryptographia* : CRYPTO- + -GRAPHY.] **—cryp·tog′ra·pher, cryp·tog′ra·phist** *n.* **—cryp′to·graph′ic** (-tə-grăf′ĭk) *adj.* **—cryp′to·graph′i·cal·ly** *adv.*

cryp·to·me·ri·a (krĭp′tə-mîr′ē-ə) *n.* An evergreen tree, *Cryptomeria japonica,* native to Japan, having short, inward-curving needles and soft, durable, fragrant wood. Also called "Japanese cedar." [New Latin : CRYPTO- + Greek *meros,* part, -MERE.]

cryp·to·nym (krĭp′tə-nĭm′) *n.* A secret name. [French *cryptonyme* : CRYPT(O)- + -ONYM.]

cryp·to·zo·ite (krĭp′tə-zō′īt′) *n.* A malaria parasite as it exists in bodily tissue prior to invasion of the red blood cells. [CRYPTO- + (SPORO)ZOITE.]

crys·tal (krĭs′təl) *n.* **1. a.** A three-dimensional atomic, ionic, or molecular structure consisting of periodically repeated, identically constituted, congruent unit cells. **b.** The unit cell of such a structure. **2.** A body, as a piece of quartz, having such a structure, often characterized by external planar faces visible without magnification. **3.** An oscillator, detector, or other electronic device based on crystalline piezoelectricity, magnetism, semiconductivity, or other electric properties. **4. a.** A high-quality clear, colorless glass. **b.** An object, especially a vessel or ornament, made of such glass. **c.** Such objects collectively. **5.** A clear glass or plastic protective cover for the face of a watch or clock. *—adj.* **1.** Of, pertaining to, or based on crystal. **2.** Clear; transparent. [Middle English *cristal,* from Old French, from Latin *crystallum,* rock crystal, crystal, from Greek *krustallos*†.]

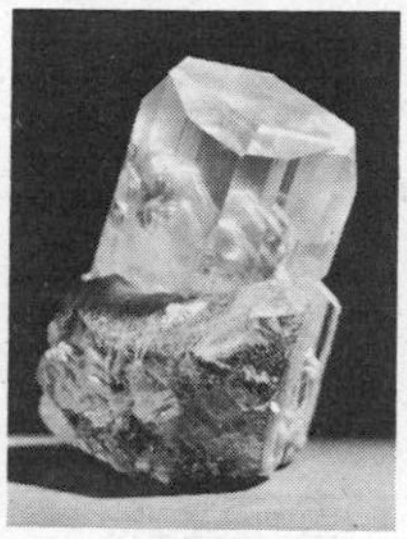

crystal
Topaz crystal

crystal ball. A glass globe used in crystal gazing.

crystal detector. A rectifying detector used especially in early radio receivers and consisting of a semiconducting crystal in point contact with a fine metal wire.

crystal gazing. Divination by gazing into a crystal ball. **—crys′tal-gaz′er** *n.*

crys·tal·lif·er·ous (krĭs′tə-lĭf′ər-əs) *adj.* Also **crys·tal·lig·er·ous** (-lĭj′ər-əs). Producing or containing crystals.

crys·tal·line (krĭs′tə-lĭn) *adj.* **1.** Pertaining to or made of crystal. **2.** Resembling crystal; transparent. [Middle English *cristallin,* from Old French, from Latin *crystallinus,* from Greek *krustallinos,* from *krustallos,* CRYSTAL.] **—crys′tal·lin′i·ty** *n.*

crystalline lens. The **lens** *(see)* of the vertebrate eye.

crys·tal·lite (krĭs′tə-līt′) *n.* Any of numerous minute rudimentary, crystalline bodies found in glassy igneous rocks. [German *Kristallit* : CRYSTALL(O)- + -ITE.] **—crys′tal·lit′ic** (-lĭt′ĭk) *adj.*

crys·tal·lize (krĭs′tə-līz′) *v.* **-lized, -lizing, -lizes.** Also **crys·tal·ize.** *—tr.* **1.** To cause to form crystals or to assume a crystalline structure. **2.** To give a definite and permanent form to. **3.** To coat with sugar. *—intr.* **1.** To assume a crystalline form. **2.** To take on a definite and permanent form. [CRYSTALL(O)- + -IZE.] **—crys′tal·liz′a·bil′i·ty** *n.* **—crys′tal·liz′a·ble** *adj.* **—crys′tal·li·za′tion** *n.* **—crys′tal·liz′er** *n.*

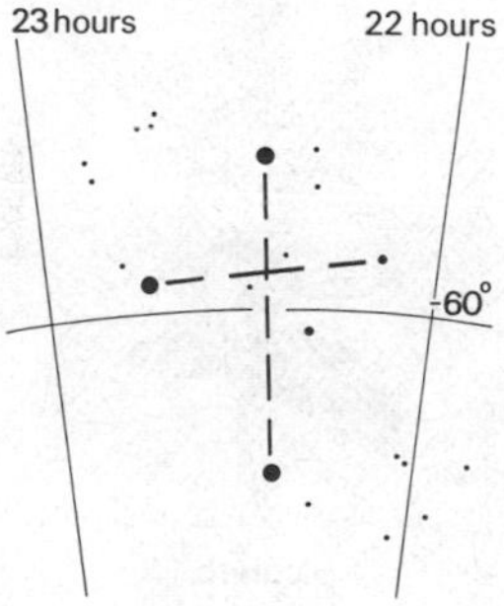
23 hours
22 hours
60°

Crux

crystallo–, crystall–. Indicates crystal; for example, **crystallography, crystalloid.** [From Greek *krustallos,* CRYSTAL.]

crys·tal·log·ra·phy (krĭs′tə-lŏg′rə-fē) *n.* The science of crystal structure and phenomena. [French *crystallographie,* from New Latin *crystallographia* : CRYSTALLO- + -GRAPHY.] **—crys′tal·lo·graph′ic** (-lō-grăf′ĭk), **crys′tal·lo·graph′i·cal** *adj.* **—crys′tal·lo·graph′i·cal·ly** *adv.* **—crys′tal·log′ra·pher** *n.*

crys·tal·loid (krĭs′tə-loid′) *adj.* Also **crys·tal·loi·dal** (krĭs′tə-loid′l). Resembling or having properties of a crystal or crystalloid. *—n.* **1.** *Chemistry.* A water-soluble crystalline substance capable of diffusion through a semipermeable membrane. **2.** *Botany.* Any of various minute crystallike particles consisting of protein, found in certain plant cells, especially oily seeds. [CRYSTALL(O)- + -OID.]

crystal pickup. A phonographic pickup that uses a piezoelectric crystal to convert stylus vibrations into electric impulses. Compare **magnetic pickup.**

crystal set. An early radio receiver using a crystal detector.

crystal violet. A dye derived from rosaniline and used as a general biological stain.

Cs The symbol for the element cesium.

cs. case.

C.S. 1. chief of staff. **2.** Christian Science; Christian Scientist. **3.** civil service.

C.S.A. Confederate States of America.

csc cosecant.

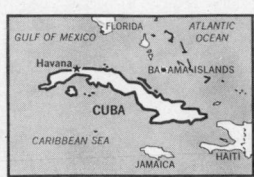

Cuba

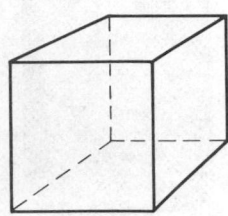

cube

cubeb

cuckoopint

CSC civil service commission.

csch hyperbolic cosecant.

csk. 1. cask. 2. countersink.

CST, C.S.T. Central Standard Time.

CT Connecticut (with Zip Code).

C.T. Central Time.

ct. 1. cent. 2. certificate. 3. court.

Ct. 1. Connecticut (unofficial). 2. count (title).

cte·nid·i·um (tĭ-nĭd′ē-əm) *n., pl.* **-ia** (-ē-ə). *Zoology.* A comblike structure, such as the respiratory apparatus of a mollusk or a row of spines in some insects. [New Latin : Greek *kteis* (stem *kten-*), a comb (see *pek-²* in Appendix*) + *-idium*, diminutive suffix.]

cten·oid (tĕn′oid′, tē′noid′) *adj. Biology.* Having narrow segments or spines resembling the teeth of a comb; comblike: *fishes with ctenoid scales.* [Greek *ktenoeidēs*, like a comb : *kteis* (stem *kten-*), comb (see *pek-²* in Appendix*) + -OID.]

cten·o·phore (tĕn′ə-fôr′, -fōr′) *n.* Any of various marine animals of the phylum Ctenophora, having transparent, gelatinous bodies bearing eight rows of comblike cilia used for locomotion. Also called "comb jelly." [New Latin *Ctenophora* : Greek *kteis* (stem *kten-*), a comb (see *pek-²* in Appendix*) + -PHORE.] —**cte·noph′o·ran** (tĭ-nŏf′ər-ən) *adj.*

ctf. certificate.

ctge. cartage.

ctn cotangent.

ctn. carton.

ctr. center.

Cu The symbol for the element copper. [Latin *cuprum.*]

cu. cubic.

Cuan·za (kwän′zə). A river of Africa, rising in south-central Angola and flowing 500 miles northwest to the Atlantic Ocean near Luanda.

cub (kŭb) *n.* 1. The young of certain carnivorous animals, such as the bear, wolf, or lion. 2. An inexperienced, awkward, or ill-mannered youth. 3. A novice or learner, particularly in newspaper reporting. 4. *Capital* C. A Cub Scout *(see).* [Origin unknown.]

Cu·ba (kyōō′bə; *Spanish* kōō′vä). An island republic, 44,218 square miles in area, in the Caribbean off the southern coast of Florida. Population, 7,256,000. Capital, Havana. —**Cu′ban** *adj. & n.*

Cu·ba li·bre (kyōō′bə lē′brə). Also **cu·ba li·bre.** An iced drink consisting of rum, a cola beverage, and lemon or lime juice. [American Spanish, "free Cuba."]

Cu·ban·go. The Portuguese name for the **Okovanggo.**

cu·ba·ture (kyōō′bə-choor′) *n.* Also **cub·age** (kyōō′bĭj). 1. The determination of the cubic contents of a solid. 2. Cubic contents. [CUB(E) + (QUADR)ATURE.]

cub·by (kŭb′ē) *n., pl.* **-bies.** A small room; cubbyhole. [From obsolete English *cub,* a stall, perhaps from Dutch *kub, kubbe,* trap, basket, from Middle Dutch *cubbe.* See **ku-** in Appendix.*]

cub·by·hole (kŭb′ē-hōl′) *n.* 1. A snug or cramped space or room. 2. A small compartment. 3. A small cupboard or closet.

cube (kyōōb) *n.* 1. *Geometry.* A regular solid having six congruent square faces. 2. Anything having such a shape. 3. *Mathematics.* The third power of a number or quantity. —*tr.v.* **cubed, cubing, cubes.** 1. To raise (a quantity or number) to the third power. 2. To determine the cubic contents of. 3. To form or cut into cubes or the shape of a cube; dice. 4. To tenderize (meat) by breaking the fibers with superficial cuts in a pattern of squares. [Old French, from Latin *cubus,* a die, cube, from Greek *kubos.* See **keu-²** in Appendix.*]

cu·bé (kyōō′bā′, kyōō-bā′) *n.* Also **cu·be.** 1. Any of various tropical American shrubs or plants, especially of the genus *Lonchocarpus,* whose roots yield rotenone. 2. An extract from the roots of these plants, used as a fish poison and insecticide. [American Spanish *cubé†.*]

cu·beb (kyōō′bĕb′) *n.* 1. A treelike woody vine, *Piper cubeba,* of southeastern Asia, bearing brownish berries. 2. The dried, unripe, spicy fruit of this plant, used as a stimulant and diuretic and sometimes smoked in cigarettes. [Middle English *cubibe,* from Old French *cubebe,* from Medieval Latin *cubēba,* from Arabic *kabābah.*]

cube steak. A thin, round or square slice of beef made tender by cubing and usually pan-broiled.

cu·bic (kyōō′bĭk) *adj.* 1. a. Having the shape of a cube. b. Having a shape similar to or approximating that of a cube. 2. *Abbr.* **c, cu. a.** Having three dimensions. b. Having a volume equal to a cube whose edge is of a stated length: *a cubic foot.* 3. *Mathematics.* Of the third power, order, or degree. 4. *Crystallography.* Isometric. —*n. Mathematics.* A cubic expression, curve, or equation.

cu·bi·cal (kyōō′bĭ-kəl) *adj.* 1. Cubic. 2. Of or pertaining to volume. —**cu′bi·cal·ly** *adv.* —**cu′bi·cal·ness** *n.*

cu·bi·cle (kyōō′bĭ-kəl) *n.* 1. A small sleeping compartment. 2. Any small compartment. [Latin *cubiculum,* sleeping chamber, from *cubāre,* to lie down, to sleep. See **keu-²** in Appendix.*]

cubic measure. A unit, as a cubic foot, or a system of units used to measure volume or capacity.

cu·bi·form (kyōō′bə-fôrm′) *adj.* Having the shape of a cube.

cub·ism (kyōō′bĭz′əm) *n.* A school of painting and sculpture developed in Paris in the early 20th century, tending through the geometrical reduction of natural forms to establish the work itself as a plastic fact independent of all imitative or representational intention. [French, from CUBE (from a remark by Henri Matisse concerning the "small cubes" which predominated in a painting by Georges Braque).] —**cub′ist** *adj. & n.* —**cu·bis′tic** *adj.* —**cu·bis′ti·cal·ly** *adv.*

cu·bit (kyōō′bĭt) *n.* An ancient unit of linear measure, originally equal to the length of the forearm from the tip of the middle finger to the elbow, or from 17 to 22 inches. [Middle English *cubite,* from Latin *cubitum,* cubit, elbow. See **keu-²** in Appendix.*]

cu·bi·tal (kyōō′bĭ-təl) *adj.* 1. Of or pertaining to the forearm or ulna. 2. Of or pertaining to measurement by cubits.

cu·boid (kyōō′boid′) *adj.* Also **cu·boi·dal** (kyōō-boid′l). 1. Having the shape or approximate shape of a cube. 2. *Anatomy.* Designating the cuboid bone. —*n.* 1. *Anatomy.* A bone on the side of the tarsus between the calcaneus and the fourth and fifth metatarsal bones of the foot. 2. *Geometry.* A rectangular parallelepiped.

Cub Scout. A member of the junior division of the Boy Scouts.

Cu·chul·ain (kōō-kŭl′ĭn). Also **Cu·chul·ainn.** *Celtic Mythology.* A tribal hero of Ulster who single-handedly defended it against the rest of Ireland.

cuck·ing stool (kŭk′ĭng). A former instrument of punishment for prostitutes or dishonest tradesmen, consisting of a chair in which the offender was tied and exposed to public derision or ducked in water. Compare **ducking stool.** [Middle English *cucking stol,* "excreting stool" : *cucking,* present participle of *cukken,* to defecate, from (unattested) Old Norse *kūka* (see **kakka-** in Appendix*) + *stol,* STOOL.]

cuck·old (kŭk′əld) *n.* A man whose wife has committed adultery. —*tr.v.* **cuckolded, -olding, -olds.** To make a cuckold of. Said of a husband. [Middle English *cukeweld, cokewold,* from Norman French *cucuald* (unattested), variant of Old French *cucualt,* from *cucu,* cuckoo (perhaps because cuckoos leave their eggs in the nests of other birds) (imitative).] —**cuck′old·ry** (kŭk′əl-drē) *n.*

cuck·oo (kōō′kōō, kŏŏk′ōō) *n.* 1. a. An Old World bird, *Cuculus canorus,* having grayish plumage and a characteristic two-note call. b. Any of various related birds of the family Cuculidae, including several New World species. 2. The call or cry of a cuckoo. 3. A foolish person; simpleton. —*v.* **cuckooed, -ooing, -oos.** —*tr.* To repeat again and again. —*intr.* To utter or imitate a cuckoo's call. —*adj.* Demented; foolish. [Middle English *cuccu* (imitative).]

cuck·oo-bud (kōō′kōō-bŭd′, kŏŏk′ōō-) *n. Archaic.* A yellow-flowered plant, probably the buttercup: *"cuckoo-buds of yellow hue/Do paint the meadows with delight"* (Shakespeare).

cuckoo clock. A wall clock having a mechanical cuckoo announcing intervals of time.

cuck·oo-flow·er (kōō′kōō-flou′ər, kŏŏk′ōō-) *n.* 1. A plant, *Cardamine pratensis,* of the North Temperate Zone, having white or rose-pink flowers. Also called "lady's-smock." 2. A plant, the ragged robin *(see).*

cuck·oo-pint (kōō′kōō-pint′, kŏŏk′ōō-) *n.* A European plant, *Arum maculatum,* having arrow-shaped leaves and a spadix enclosed in a purple-spotted spathe. Also called "lords-and-ladies." [Short for obsolete *cuckoo-pintle,* from Middle English *cokkupyntel* : *cokku, cuccu,* CUCKOO + *pintel,* penis, PINTLE (from the shape of the spadix).]

cuckoo spit. A frothy mass of liquid secreted on plant stems as a protective covering by nymphs of the **spittlebug** *(see).* Also called "frog spit," "toad spit."

cu·cu·li·form (kyōō′kə-lə-fôrm′) *adj.* Of or belonging to the order Cuculiformes, which includes the cuckoos and related birds. [New Latin *Cuculiformes* : Latin *cuculus,* cuckoo (imitative) + -FORM.]

cu·cul·late (kyōō′kə-lāt′, kyōō-kŭl′āt′) *adj.* Also **cu·cul·lat·ed.** Having the shape of a cowl or hood: *cucullate sepals.* [Medieval Latin *cucullātus,* from Latin *cucullus,* cap, hood. See **cowl.**] —**cu′cul·late·ly** *adv.*

cu·cum·ber (kyōō′kŭm′bər) *n.* 1. A vine, *Cucumis sativus,* cultivated for its edible fruit. 2. The usually cylindrical fruit of this vine, having a hard green rind and white succulent flesh. [Middle English *cucumer, cocumber,* from Old French *cocombre,* from Latin *cucumis,* of Mediterranean origin.]

cu·cum·ber-root (kyōō′kŭm-bər-rōōt′, -rŏŏt′) *n.* See **Indian cucumber-root.**

cucumber tree. 1. A tree, *Magnolia acuminata,* of eastern and central North America, having cup-shaped greenish-yellow flowers and brown or scarlet cucumber-shaped fruit. 2. A tree, *Averrhoa bilimbi,* of eastern Asia, having reddish-purple flowers and edible fruit that resemble small cucumbers.

cu·cu·mi·form (kyōō′kyōō-mə-fôrm′) *adj.* Having the shape of a cucumber. [Latin *cucumis,* CUCUMBER + -FORM.]

cu·cur·bit (kyōō-kûr′bĭt) *n.* 1. A gourd-shaped flask forming the body of an alembic, formerly used in distillation. 2. Any of various vines of the family Cucurbitaceae, which includes the squash, pumpkin, and cucumber. [Middle English *cucurbite,* from Old French, from Latin *cucurbita,* GOURD.]

Cú·cu·ta (kōō′kōō-tä). A city of northeastern Colombia, near the border of Venezuela. Population, 175,000.

cud (kŭd) *n.* 1. Food regurgitated from the first stomach to the mouth of a ruminant and chewed again. 2. Something suitable to be held in the mouth and chewed, such as a quid of tobacco. —**chew the cud.** To meditate. [Middle English *cud(de),* Old English *cwudu, cudu.* See **gwet-¹** in Appendix.*]

cud·bear (kŭd′bâr′) *n.* A purplish-red coloring substance derived from certain lichens, especially of the genera *Rocella* and *Lecanora.* [From the name of Dr. *Cuthbert* Gordon, 18th-century Scottish chemist who patented the substance.]

cud·dle (kŭd′l) *v.* **-dled, -dling, -dles.** —*tr.* To fondle in the arms; hug. —*intr.* To nestle; snuggle. —*n.* A hug. [Origin obscure.] —**cud′dle·some** *adj.* —**cud′dly** *adj.*

cud·dy (kŭd′ē) *n., pl.* **-dies.** 1. A small cabin or the cook's galley

on a ship. **2.** A small room or cupboard. [Origin obscure.]
cudg·el (kŭj′əl) *n.* A short, heavy club. **—take up the cudgels.** To join in a dispute, especially in defense of a participant. Often used with *for.* **—***tr.v.* **cudgeled, -eling, -els.** Also *chiefly British* **-elled, -elling.** To beat or strike with a cudgel. **—cudgel one's brains.** To think hard. [Middle English *cuggel,* Old English *cycgel.* See **ku-** in Appendix.*] **—cudg′el·er** *n.*
cudg·el-play (kŭj′əl-plā′) *n.* **1.** A sporting contest with cudgels. **2.** The art of fighting with cudgels.
cud·weed (kŭd′wēd′) *n.* **1.** Any of various woolly plants of the genus *Gnaphalium,* having clusters of whitish or yellow buttonlike flowers. **2.** Any of several similar or related plants, especially a European plant, *Filago germanica.* This species is also called "cotton rose."
cue[1] (kyo͞o) *n.* **1.** *Billiards.* The long, tapered rod used to propel the ball. **2.** A queue of hair. **—***tr.v.* **cued, cuing, cues. 1.** To strike (a ball) with a cue. **2.** To braid or twist (hair) into a cue. [French *queue,* "tail" (from the shape of the cue), from Old French *coue,* from Latin *cauda,* tail. See **caudate.**]
cue[2] (kyo͞o) *n.* **1.** *Theater.* A word or bit of stage business signaling the beginning of another action or speech. **2.** A hint or reminder; a prompting. **3.** *Psychology.* A perceived signal for action, especially one that produces an operant response. **—***tr.v.* **cued, cuing, cues.** *Theater.* To give (an actor) a cue. [Origin obscure.]
cue[3] (kyo͞o) *n.* The letter *q.*
cue ball. *Billiards.* The ball that is propelled with the cue.
Cuer·na·va·ca (kwĕr′nä-vä′kä). The capital of Morelos State, south-central Mexico; a residential suburb of Mexico City. Population, 37,000.
cues·ta (kwĕs′tə) *n. Southwestern U.S.* A land elevation with a gentle slope on one side and a cliff on the other. [Spanish, sloping side, from Latin *costa,* side. See **kost-** in Appendix.*]
cuff[1] (kŭf) *n.* **1.** A fold or band used as trimming at the bottom of a sleeve. **2.** The turned-up fold at the bottom of a trouser leg. **3.** A band of linen, lace, or other fabric attached about the wrist, either under or over a sleeve. **4.** The part of a gauntlet that extends over the wrist. **5.** A **handcuff** *(see).* **—off the cuff.** *Informal.* Extemporaneously. **—on the cuff.** *Informal.* **1.** Without immediate payment; on credit. **2.** Without payment; gratis. [Middle English *cuffe*†, glove, mitten.]
cuff[2] (kŭf) *tr.v.* **cuffed, cuffing, cuffs.** To strike with the open hand; slap. **—***n.* A blow or slap with the open hand. [Origin obscure.]
cuff links. A pair of linked buttons or a similar device used to fasten the cuffs of a shirt.
Cu·fic. Variant of **Kufic.**
Cu·ia·bá (ko͞o′yə-bä′). The capital of Mato Grosso, Brazil, in the center of the state. Population, 43,000.
cui·rass (kwĭ-răs′) *n.* **1.** A piece of armor for protecting the breast and back. **2.** The breastplate alone. **3.** *Zoology.* A protective covering of bony plates or scales. **—***tr.v.* **cuirassed, -rassing, -rasses.** To protect with a cuirass. [Middle English *curace,* cuirass (especially one of leather), from Old French *cuirasse,* from Vulgar Latin *coriācea* (unattested), "leather buckler," from Latin *coriāceus,* of leather, from *corium,* hide, skin. See **sker-**[1] in Appendix.*]
cui·ras·sier (kwĭr′ə-sîr′) *n.* A horse soldier in European armies whose equipment included the cuirass.
cui·sine (kwĭ-zēn′) *n.* A characteristic manner or style of preparing food. [French, from Late Latin *coquīna,* a kitchen, cookery, from *coquere,* to cook. See **pekw-** in Appendix.*]
cuisse (kwĭs) *n.* Also **cuish** (kwĭsh). Plate armor worn to protect the thigh. [Back-formation from Middle English *cussues, cushies,* from Old French *cuissaux,* plural of *cuissel,* from *cuisse,* thigh, from Latin *coxa,* thigh, hip. See **koksā** in Appendix.*]
culch (kŭlch) *n.* Also **cultch. 1.** A natural bed for oysters, consisting of gravel or crushed shells to which oyster spawn may adhere. **2.** The spawn of the oyster. **3.** Rubbish or refuse. [Possibly from Old French *culche, couche,* bed, COUCH.]
cul-de-sac (kŭl′dĭ-săk′, ko͝ol′-) *n., pl.* **cul-de-sacs. 1.** A dead-end street; impasse. **2.** *Anatomy.* A saclike cavity or tube open only at one end. [French, "bottom of the sack," blind alley.]
-cule. Indicates smallness; for example, **molecule.** [French, from New Latin *-cula,* diminutive suffix from Latin *-culus, -cula, -culum.* See also **-cle.**]
cu·let (kyo͞o′lĭt) *n.* **1.** The flat face of a gem cut as a brilliant. **2.** One of the plates of medieval armor covering the lower back. [French, diminutive of *cul,* the rump, anus, from Latin *cūlus.* See **skeu-** in Appendix.*]
cu·lex (kyo͞o′lĕks′) *n., pl.* **-lices** (-lə-sēz′). Any of various mosquitoes of the genus *Culex,* which includes the common house mosquito, *C. pipiens.* [New Latin, from Latin *culex*†, gnat.]
Cu·lia·cán (ko͞o′lyä-kän′). The capital of Sinaloa, Mexico, a commercial city in the center of the state. Population, 85,000.
cu·li·nar·y (kyo͞o′lə-nĕr′ē, kŭl′ə-) *adj.* Of or pertaining to a kitchen or to cookery. [Latin *culīnārius,* from *culīna,* kitchen, deformed variant of *coquīna,* female cook. See **cuisine.**] **—cu′li·nar′i·ly** *adv.*
cull (kŭl) *tr.v.* **culled, culling, culls. 1.** To pick out from others; select. **2.** To gather; collect. **—***n.* **1.** The act of culling. **2.** Something picked out from others, especially something rejected because of inferior quality. [Middle English *coilen,* from Old French *cuillir,* from Latin *colligere,* to COLLECT.] **—cull′er** *n.*
Cul·len (kŭl′ən), **Countee.** 1903–1946. American poet.
cul·len·der. Variant of **colander.**
cul·let (kŭl′ĭt) *n.* Scraps of broken or waste glass gathered for remelting. [Perhaps variant of earlier *collet,* from French *collet,* "little neck" (the neck of glass broken off a newly blown vessel), diminutive of *col,* neck, from Old French, from Latin *collum.* See **kwel-**[1] in Appendix.*]
cul·lis (kŭl′ĭs) *n., pl.* **-lises.** A gutter or groove in a roof. [Middle English *colis,* from Old French *coleïs,* channel, from *coler,* to pour, strain, from Latin *cōlāre,* to filter, strain, from *cōlum,* a sieve. See **kagh-** in Appendix.*]
culm[1] (kŭlm) *n.* The jointed stem of a grass or sedge. [Latin *culmus,* stalk. See **kolәm-** in Appendix.*]
culm[2] (kŭlm) *n.* **1.** Waste from anthracite coal mines, consisting of fine coal, coal dust, and dirt. **2. a.** Carboniferous shale. **b.** Inferior anthracite coal. [Middle English *colme,* coal dust, perhaps akin to *col,* coal. See **geulo-** in Appendix.*]
cul·mi·nant (kŭl′mə-nənt) *adj.* Culminating; highest.
cul·mi·nate (kŭl′mə-nāt′) *intr.v.* **-nated, -nating, -nates. 1.** To reach the highest point or degree; come to full effect; climax. Used with *in.* **2.** *Astronomy.* To cross the meridian of the observer; reach the highest point above an observer's horizon. Used of stars and other celestial bodies. [Late Latin *culmināre,* from Latin *culmen* (stem *culmin-*), top, summit. See **kel-**[8] in Appendix.*] **—cul′mi·na′tion** *n.*
cu·lottes (ko͞o-lŏts′, kyo͞o-) *pl.n.* Also **cu·lotte.** A woman's full trousers cut to resemble a skirt; a divided skirt. [French, breeches, diminutive of *cul,* backside, from Latin *cūlus.* See **skeu-** in Appendix.*]
cul·pa (kŭl′pə; *Latin* ko͝ol′pä) *n. Law.* Fault; misconduct. [Latin *culpa*†, fault.]
cul·pa·ble (kŭl′pə-bəl) *adj.* Responsible for wrong or error; deserving censure; blameworthy. [Middle English *coupable,* from Old French, from Latin *culpābilis,* from *culpāre,* to blame, from *culpa,* CULPA.] **—cul′pa·bil′i·ty** *n.* **—cul′pa·bly** *adv.*
Cul·pep·er (kŭl′pĕp′ər), **Thomas.** Second Baron Culpeper of Thoresway. 1635–1689. English colonial administrator; governor of Virginia (1680–83).
cul·prit (kŭl′prĭt) *n.* **1.** A person charged with an offense or crime. **2.** A person guilty of a fault or crime. [From the 17th-century legal phrase "*Culprit,* how will you be tryed?" perhaps a mistake for Norman French "*Culpable. Prit d'averrer . . . ,*" "Guilty. (I am) ready to prove . . . ," the prosecutor's response to a plea of not guilty, which might have been abbreviated as "*Cul. prit, etc.*" : CULPABLE + *prit, prist,* ready, from Latin *praestus* (see **presto**).]

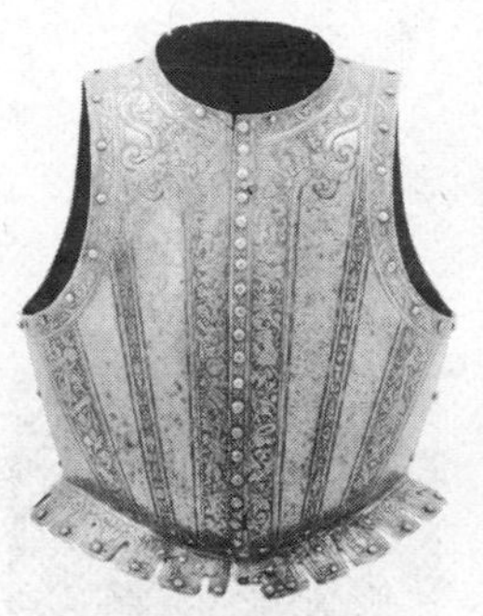
cuirass
Sixteenth-century Italian cuirass

cult (kŭlt) *n.* **1.** A system or community of religious worship and ritual, especially one focusing upon a single deity or spirit. **2. a.** Obsessive devotion or veneration for a person, principle, or ideal. **b.** The object of such devotion. **3.** An exclusive group of persons sharing an esoteric interest. [French *culte,* from Latin *cultus,* cultivation, a laboring, worship, from the past participle of *colere,* to CULTIVATE.] **—cul′tic** *adj.* **—cult′ism′** *n.* **—cult′ist** *n.*
cultch. Variant of **culch.**
cul·ti·gen (kŭl′tə-jən) *n.* An organism, especially a cultivated plant, such as maize, of a kind not known to have a wild or uncultivated counterpart. [CULTI(VATED) + -GEN.]
cul·ti·va·ble (kŭl′tə-və-bəl) *adj.* Also **cul·ti·vat·a·ble** (-vā′tə-bəl). Capable of being cultivated. **—cul′ti·va·bil′i·ty** *n.*
cul·ti·var (kŭl′tə-vär′, -vâr′) *n.* A horticulturally or agriculturally derived variety of a plant, as distinguished from a natural variety. [CULTI(VATED) + VAR(IETY).]
cul·ti·vate (kŭl′tə-vāt′) *tr.v.* **-vated, -vating, -vates. 1. a.** To improve and prepare (land), as by plowing or fertilizing, for raising crops; to till. **b.** To loosen or dig (soil) around growing plants. **2.** To grow or tend (a plant or crop). **3.** To promote the growth of (a biological culture, for example). **4.** To nurture; foster. **5.** To form and refine, as by education. **6.** To seek the acquaintance or good will of. [Medieval Latin *cultīvāre,* from *(terra) cultīva,* tilled (land), from *cultīvus,* tilled, from Latin *cultus,* past participle of *colere,* to till, cultivate. See **kwel-**[1] in Appendix.*]

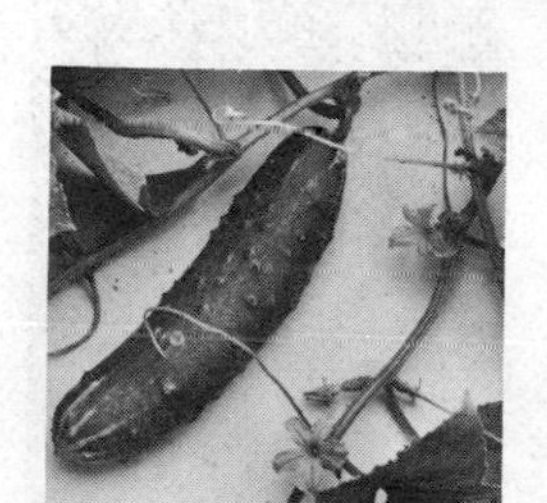
cucumber
Vine and fruit

cul·ti·vat·ed (kŭl′tə-vā′tĭd) *adj.* Cultured; refined.
cul·ti·va·tion (kŭl′tə-vā′shən) *n.* **1. a.** The act of cultivating. **b.** The state of being cultivated. **2.** Refinement; social polish. —See Synonyms at **culture.**
cul·ti·va·tor (kŭl′tə-vā′tər) *n.* **1.** One who cultivates. **2.** An implement or machine for loosening the earth and destroying weeds around growing plants.
cul·trate (kŭl′trāt′) *adj.* Also **cul·trat·ed** (-trā′tĭd). Sharp-edged and pointed; knifelike. [Latin *cultrātus,* knifelike, from *culter* (stem *cultr-*), knife. See **skel-**[1] in Appendix.*]
cul·tur·al (kŭl′chər-əl) *adj.* **1.** Of or relating to culture. **2.** Obtained by specialized breeding, as certain plant varieties.
cultural anthropology. The scientific study of human culture based on archaeological, ethnologic, ethnographic, linguistic, social, and psychological data and methods of analysis. Compare **physical anthropology.**

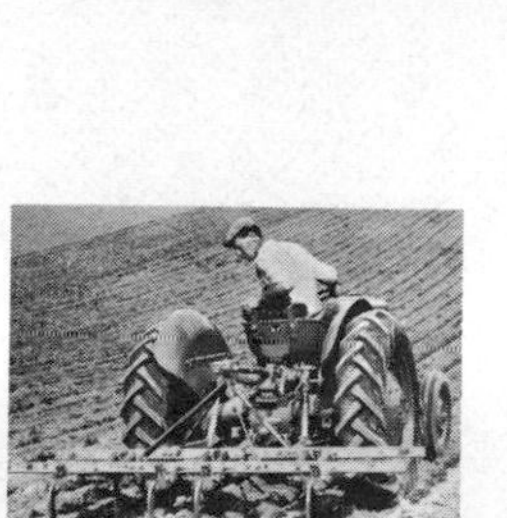
cultivator

cul·ture (kŭl′chər) *n.* **1.** The cultivation of the soil; tillage. **2.** The breeding of animals or growing of plants, especially to produce improved stock. **3.** *Biology.* **a.** The growing of microorganisms in a nutrient medium. **b.** Such a growth or colony, as of bacteria. **4.** Social and intellectual formation. **5.** The totality of socially transmitted behavior patterns, arts, beliefs, institutions, and all other products of human work and thought characteristic of a community or population. **6.** A style of social and artistic expression peculiar to a society or class. **7.** Intellectual and artistic activity. **—***tr.v.* **cultured, -turing, -tures. 1.** To cultivate. **2.** To develop (microorganisms or tissues, for example) in a culture medium. [Middle English, cultivation, tillage, from Old French, from Latin *cultūra,* from *cultus,* cultivation. See **cultivate.**]

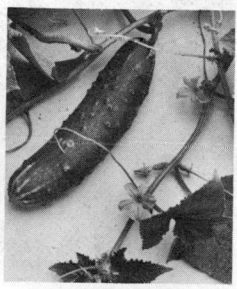

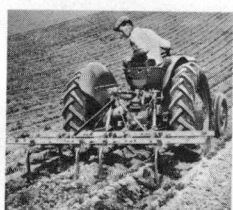

Synonyms: *culture, cultivation, breeding, refinement, gentility, taste.* These nouns are applied to personal achievement in the development of intellect, manners, and aesthetic appreciation. *Culture,* which overlaps the others, implies enlightenment attained through close association with and appreciation of the highest level of civilization. *Cultivation* usually refers to the self-improvement or self-development by which a person acquires culture. *Breeding* is the development of good character and behavior, and is especially revealed in manners, poise, and sensitivity to the feelings of others. *Refinement,* the highest product of breeding, stresses aversion to coarseness; sometimes it may imply a delicacy of feeling associated with fastidiousness. *Gentility* is sometimes still synonymous with refinement or good birth; in modern usage it may suggest extreme elegance in behavior or manners. *Taste* is the capacity for recognizing and appreciating what is aesthetically superior.

cul·tured (kŭl′chərd) *adj.* **1.** Cultivated. **2.** Produced under artificial and controlled conditions: *cultured pearls.*

cul·tus (kŭl′təs) *n., pl.* **-tuses** or **-ti** (-tī′). A religious cult. [New Latin, from Latin *cultus,* worship, CULT.]

cul·ver (kŭl′vər) *n. Poetic.* A dove; pigeon. [Middle English *culver,* Old English *culufre,* from Vulgar Latin *columbra* (unattested), from Latin *columbula,* diminutive of *columba,* dove. See **kel-**[7] in Appendix.*]

cul·ver·in (kŭl′vər-ĭn) *n.* **1.** A type of early musket. **2.** A heavy cannon used in the 16th and 17th centuries. [Middle English, from Old French *coulevrine,* "serpentine," from *couleuvre,* snake, from Vulgar Latin *colobra* (unattested), from Latin *colubra,* feminine of *coluber,* snake. See **cobra.**]

Cul·ver's root (kŭl′vərz). **1.** A North American plant, *Veronicastrum virginicum,* having spikes of small white or purplish flowers. **2.** The root of this plant, formerly used as a cathartic and emetic. [After a Dr. *Culver,* 18th-century American physician.]

cul·vert (kŭl′vərt) *n.* A sewer or drain crossing under a road or embankment. [Origin unknown.]

cum (ko͝om, kŭm) *prep.* Together with; plus. Used in combination: *her attic-cum-studio.* [Latin. See **kom** in Appendix.*]

Cu·mae (kyo͞o′mē). An ancient town and the earliest Greek colony in Italy, on the coast of Campania, west of Naples. —**Cu·mae′an** *adj.*

Cu·ma·ná (ko͞o′mä-nä′). A city of northeastern Venezuela on the Caribbean; the oldest permanent Spanish settlement in South America (founded in 1523). Population, 70,000.

Cumb Cumberland (English county).

cum·ber (kŭm′bər) *tr.v.* **-bered, -bering, -bers. 1.** To weigh down; burden. **2.** To hamper; obstruct. —*n.* A hindrance; encumbrance. [Middle English *combren,* perhaps from Old French *combrer,* from *combre*†, hindrance.] —**cum′ber·er** *n.*

Cum·ber·land (kŭm′bər-lənd) **1.** *Abbr.* **Cumb** A county of England occupying 1,520 square miles in the northwest. Population, 294,000. County seat, Carlisle. **2.** A city of northwestern Maryland on the Potomac. Population, 33,000. **3.** A river rising in southeastern Kentucky and flowing 690 miles through Kentucky and Tennessee to the Ohio in western Kentucky.

Cum·ber·land Gap (kŭm′bər-lənd). A pass through the Cumberland Mountains at the junction of the borders of Kentucky, Virginia, and Tennessee.

Cum·ber·land Mountains (kŭm′bər-lənd). Also **Cum·ber·land Plateau.** The western section of the Appalachian Mountains, extending along the Virginia-Kentucky border and into central Tennessee. Average elevation, 2,000 feet.

Cum·ber·land Road (kŭm′bər-lənd). The first national highway in the United States, constructed during the early 19th century and extending originally from Cumberland, Maryland, to central Illinois. Also called "National Road."

cum·ber·some (kŭm′bər-səm) *adj.* **1.** Clumsy; unwieldy. **2.** Burdensome. —See Synonyms at **heavy.** —**cum′ber·some·ly** *adv.* —**cum′ber·some·ness** *n.*

cum·brance (kŭm′brəns) *n.* **1.** Encumbrance; burden. **2.** Trouble. [Middle English *cumbraunce,* from *cumbren,* to CUMBER.]

Cum·bri·a (kŭm′brē-ə). The southern portion of the ancient kingdom of **Strathclyde and Cumbria** *(see).* [Medieval Latin, from Welsh *Cymry,* CAMBRIA.]

Cum·bri·an Mountains (kŭm′brē-ən). A range of hills in northwestern England, west of the Pennine Chain. Highest elevation, Scafell Pike (3,210 feet).

cum·brous (kŭm′brəs) *adj.* Cumbersome. [Middle English, from *cumbren,* to CUMBER.]

cum gra·no sa·lis (ko͝om grä′nō sä′lĭs, kŭm grā′nō sā′lĭs). *Latin.* With a grain of salt; with skepticism.

cum·in (kŭm′ĭn) *n.* Also **cum·min. 1.** An Old World plant, *Cuminum cyminum,* having finely divided leaves and small white or pinkish flowers. **2.** The aromatic seeds of this plant, used as a condiment. [Middle English *comin,* from Old French *cumin,* from Latin *cuminum,* from Greek *kuminon,* from Semitic, akin to Hebrew *kammōn,* Akkadian *kamūnu.*]

cum lau·de (ko͝om lou′də, lou′dē, kŭm lô′dē). With honor. Used on diplomas as a mark of high standing. Compare **magna cum laude, summa cum laude.** [New Latin, "with praise."]

cum·mer·bund (kŭm′ər-bŭnd′) *n.* Also **kum·mer·bund.** A broad, pleated sash worn as an article of men's formal dress. [Hindi *kamarband,* from Persian, loinband, waistband : *kamar,* loins, waist (see **kamer-** in Appendix*) + *band,* band (see **bhendh-** in Appendix*).]

Cum·mings (kŭm′ĭngz), **Edward Estlin ("e e cummings").** 1894–1962. American poet, playwright, and artist.

cum·quat. Variant of **kumquat.**

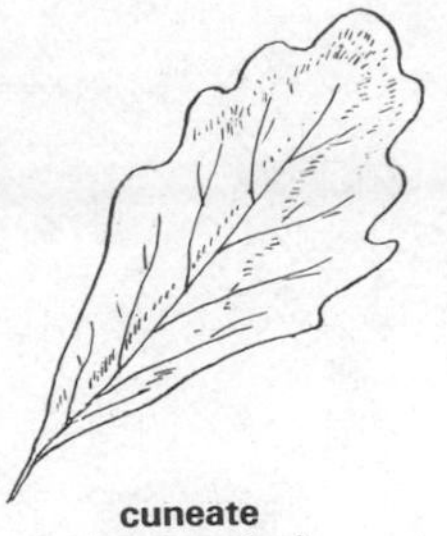
cuneate
A cuneate leaf

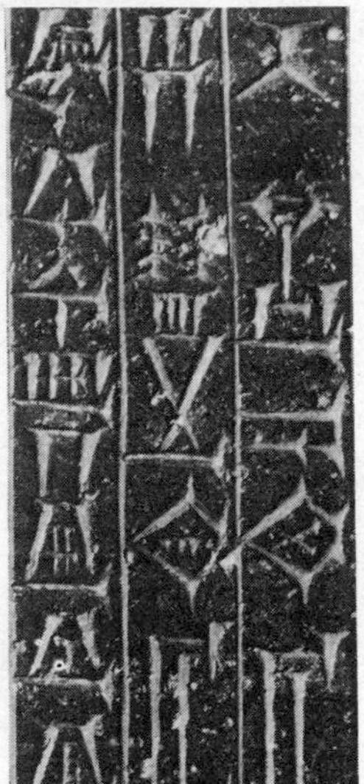
cuneiform

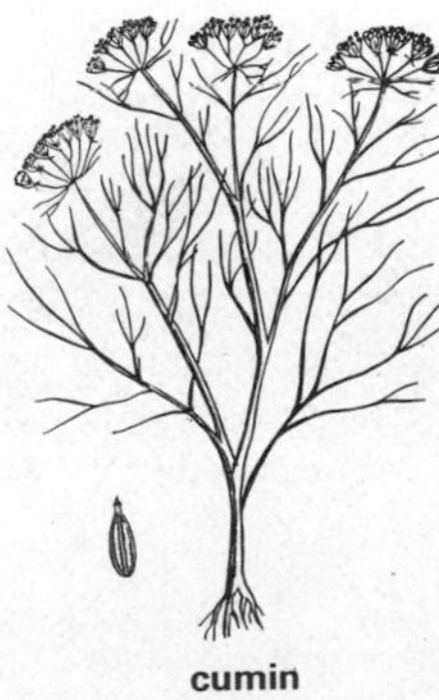
cumin

cum·shaw (kŭm′shô′) *n.* A tip; gratuity; present. [Pidgin English, from Amoy *kam sia,* from Mandarin Chinese *kan*[3] *hsieh*[4], to thank, gratitude : *kan*[3], to feel + *hsieh*[4], to thank, gratitude.]

cu·mu·late (kyo͞om′yə-lāt′) *tr.v.* **-lated, -lating, -lates.** To accumulate. [Latin *cumulāre,* from *cumulus,* heap. See **keu-**[3] in Appendix.*] —**cu′mu·la′tion** *n.*

cu·mu·la·tive (kyo͞om′yə-lā′tĭv, -yə-lə-tĭv) *adj.* **1.** Increasing or enlarging by successive addition. **2.** Acquired by or resulting from accumulation. **3.** *Finance.* Of or pertaining to interest or a dividend that increases if not paid when due. **4.** *Law.* Designating additional or supporting evidence. **5.** *Statistics.* **a.** Of or pertaining to the sum of the frequencies of experimentally determined values of a random variable that are less than or equal to a specified value. **b.** Of or pertaining to experimental error that increases in magnitude with each successive measurement. —**cu′mu·la′tive·ly** *adv.*

cu·mu·li·form (kyo͞om′yə-lə-fôrm′) *adj. Meteorology.* Having the shape of a cumulus. [CUMUL(US) + -FORM.]

cu·mu·lo·nim·bus (kyo͞om′yə-lō-nĭm′bəs) *n., pl.* **-buses** or **-bi** (-bī′). *Meteorology.* An extremely dense, vertically developed cumulus with a relatively hazy outline and a glaciated top, usually producing heavy rains, thunderstorms, or hailstorms. [New Latin : CUMUL(US) + NIMBUS.]

cu·mu·lus (kyo͞om′yə-ləs) *n., pl.* **-li** (-lī′). **1.** *Meteorology.* A dense, white, fluffy, flat-based cloud with a multiple rounded top and a well-defined outline, usually formed by the ascent of thermally unstable air masses. **2.** A pile, mound, or heap. [New Latin, from Latin, heap, mass. See **keu-**[3] in Appendix.*] —**cu′mu·lous** *adj.*

Cu·nax·a (kyo͞o-năk′sə). A town of ancient Babylonia, about 90 miles northwest of Babylon; site of the defeat of the army of Cyrus the Younger of Persia by his brother (401 B.C.).

cunc·ta·tion (kŭngk-tā′shən) *n.* A delay. [Latin *cūnctātiō,* from *cūnctātus,* past participle of *cūnctārī,* to delay. See **konk-** in Appendix.*] —**cunc′ta′tive** *adj.* —**cunc′ta′tor** (-tā′tər) *n.*

cun·dum. Variant of **condom.**

cu·ne·al (kyo͞o′nē-əl) *adj.* Wedge-shaped. [New Latin *cunealis,* from Latin *cuneus,* wedge. See **coin.**]

cu·ne·ate (kyo͞o′nē-ĭt, -āt′) *adj.* Also **cu·ne·at·ed** (-nē-ā′tĭd). Wedge-shaped. Said especially of leaves that are narrow and triangular, and taper toward the base. [Latin *cuneātus,* from *cuneus,* wedge. See **coin.**] —**cu′ne·ate′ly** *adv.*

cu·ne·i·form (kyo͞o′nē-ə-fôrm′, kyo͞o-nē′-) *adj.* **1.** Wedge-shaped. **2.** Designating: **a.** The wedge-shaped characters used in ancient Sumerian, Akkadian, Assyrian, Babylonian, and Persian writing. **b.** Documents or inscriptions written in such characters. **3.** *Anatomy.* Denoting any of the three wedge-shaped bones in the tarsus of the foot. —*n.* **1.** Cuneiform writing. **2.** A cuneiform bone. [French *cunéiforme* : Latin *cuneus,* wedge (see **coin**) + -FORM.]

Cu·ne·ne (ko͞o-nā′nə). Also **Ku·ne·ne.** A river of Africa, rising in east-central Angola and flowing 700 miles first south and then west to the Atlantic, forming part of the border between Angola and South-West Africa on its western course.

Cun·ha (ko͞o′nyə), **Tristão da.** 1460?–1540? Portuguese navigator and explorer.

cun·ner (kŭn′ər) *n.* A marine fish, *Tautogolabrus adspersus,* of North American Atlantic waters. [Origin unknown.]

cun·ni·lin·gus (kŭn′ə-lĭng′gəs) *n.* Also **cun·ni·linc·tus** (-lĭngk′-təs). Oral stimulation of the clitoris or vulva. [From Latin *cunnilingus,* "he who licks the vulva" : *cunnus,* vulva (see **skeu-** in Appendix*) + *lingere,* to lick (see **leigh-** in Appendix*).]

cun·ning (kŭn′ĭng) *adj.* **1.** Shrewd; crafty; artful. **2.** Executed with or exhibiting ingenuity. **3.** *Regional.* Delicately pleasing; pretty; cute. —See Synonyms at **clever, sly.** —*n.* **1.** Skill in deception; craftiness; guile. **2.** Skill or adeptness in performance; expertness; adroitness; dexterity. [Middle English *conning,* perhaps from the present participle of *connen,* to know, Old English *cunnan.* See **gnō-** in Appendix.*] —**cun′ning·ly** *adv.* —**cun′ning·ness** *n.*

cunt (kŭnt) *n.* **1.** *Vulgar.* The female pudendum. **2.** *Vulgar Slang.* A woman regarded as a sexual object. [Middle English *cunte,* perhaps of Low German origin, akin to Middle Low German *kunte.* See **ku-** in Appendix.*]

cup (kŭp) *n.* **1.** A small, open container, usually with a flat bottom and a handle, used for drinking. **2.** Such a container and its contents. **3.** *Abbr.* **c.** A measure of capacity equal to ½ pint, 8 ounces, or 16 tablespoons. **4.** The bowl of a drinking vessel. **5.** The chalice or the wine used in the celebration of the Eucharist. **6.** An ornamented cup-shaped vessel given to commemorate an event or as a prize or trophy. **7.** *Golf.* A hole or the metal container inside a hole. **8.** Any of various beverages, usually combining wine, fruit, and spices. **9.** Anything resembling a cup. **10.** *Biology.* A cuplike structure or organ. **11.** A lot or portion to be suffered or enjoyed. —*tr.v.* **cupped, cupping, cups. 1.** To place in or as in a cup. **2.** To shape like a cup: *cup one's hand.* [Middle English *cuppe,* Old English *cuppe,* from Late Latin *cuppa,* drinking vessel. See **keu-**[2] in Appendix.*]

cup·bear·er (kŭp′bâr′ər) *n.* One who serves wine, as in a royal household.

cup·board (kŭb′ərd) *n.* A closet or cabinet, usually with shelves for storing food, crockery, and the like.

cup·cake (kŭp′kāk′) *n.* A small cake baked in a cup-shaped container.

cu·pel (kyo͞o′pəl, kyo͞o-pĕl′) *n.* **1.** A small, shallow, porous vessel used in assaying to separate precious metals from less valuable elements such as lead. **2.** The bottom or receptacle in a silver-refining furnace. —*tr.v.* **cupeled** or **-pelled; -peling** or **-pelling, -pels.** To assay or separate from base metals in a cupel. [French *coupelle,* diminutive of *coupe,* cup, from Late Latin *cuppa,* CUP.] —**cu′pel·er** *n.*

cu·pel·la·tion (kyo͞o′pə-lā′shən) *n.* A refining process for nonoxidizing metals, such as silver and gold, in which the components of a metallic mixture oxidized at high temperatures are separated by absorption into the walls of a cupel.

cup·ful (kŭp′fo͝ol′) *n., pl.* **-fuls.** **1.** The amount a cup will hold. **2.** *Cooking.* A measure of capacity equal to ½ pint, 8 ounces, or 16 tablespoons.

Cu·pid (kyo͞o′pĭd). The Roman god of love, identified with the Greek Eros. [Latin *Cupīdō,* personification of *cupīdō,* desire, from *cupere,* to desire. See **kwēp-** in Appendix.*]

cu·pid·i·ty (kyo͞o-pĭd′ə-tē) *n.* Avarice; greed. [Middle English *cupidite,* from Old French, from Latin *cupiditās,* from *cupidus,* desiring, from *cupere,* to desire. See **kwēp-** in Appendix.*]

cup of tea. *Informal.* That which or one who is suitable.

cu·po·la (kyo͞o′pə-lə) *n.* **1. a.** A domed roof or ceiling. **b.** A small, usually domed structure surmounting a roof. **2.** A cylindrical shaft type of blast furnace used for remelting metals, usually iron, before casting. Also called "cupola furnace." [Italian *cupola,* from Late Latin *cūpula,* diminutive of Latin *cūpa,* tub, vat. See **keu-²** in Appendix.*]

cup·ping (kŭp′ĭng) *n.* A therapeutic process, rarely used in modern medicine, in which glass cups, partially evacuated by heating, are locally applied to the skin in order to draw blood toward or through the surface.

cup plant. A coarse North American plant, *Silphium perfoliatum,* having yellow-rayed flowers. Also called "rosinweed." [From the cup formed around its stem by its leaves.]

cu·pre·ous (kyo͞o′prē-əs) *adj.* Of, concerning, resembling, or containing copper; coppery. [Late Latin *cupreus,* from *cuprum,* COPPER.]

cu·pric (kyo͞o′prĭk) *adj.* Of or containing divalent copper. [From Late Latin *cuprum,* COPPER.]

cu·prif·er·ous (kyo͞o-prĭf′ər-əs) *adj.* Containing copper. [Late Latin *cuprum,* COPPER + -FEROUS.]

cu·prite (kyo͞o′prīt′) *n.* A natural red copper ore, essentially Cu_2O. [German *Kuprit* : Late Latin *cuprum,* COPPER + -ITE.]

cu·prous (kyo͞o′prəs) *adj.* Of, pertaining to, or containing univalent copper. [From Late Latin *cuprum,* COPPER.]

cu·pu·la (kyo͞o′pyə-lə) *n., pl.* **-lae** (-lē′). *Anatomy.* A cup-shaped or domed cap over a structure, such as the apex of the cochlea. [New Latin, CUPULE.]

cu·pu·late (kyo͞o′pyə-lāt′, -lĭt) *adj.* Also **cu·pu·lar** (-lər). **1.** Resembling a small cup; cup-shaped. **2.** Having or bearing a cupule.

cu·pule (kyo͞o′pyo͞ol) *n. Biology.* A cup-shaped part, structure, or indentation; especially, the involucre of an acorn. [New Latin *cupula,* from Late Latin *cūpula,* little cask or tub, diminutive of Latin *cūpa,* a tub, vat. See **keu-²** in Appendix.*]

cur (kûr) *n.* **1.** A dog considered to be inferior or undesirable; a mongrel. **2.** A base or cowardly person. [Middle English *curre,* short for *kur(dogge),* "growling dog," perhaps from Old Norse *kurra,* to growl. See **ger-⁴** in Appendix.*]

cur. **1.** currency. **2.** current.

cur·a·ble (kyo͝or′ə-bəl) *adj.* Capable of being healed or cured. —**cur′a·bil′i·ty, cur′a·ble·ness** *n.* —**cur′a·bly** *adv.*

cu·ra·çao (kyo͝or′ə-sō′) *n.* Also **cu·ra·çoa** (kyo͝or′sō′ə). A liqueur flavored with the peel of the sour orange. [From CURAÇAO.]

Cu·ra·çao (kyo͝or′ə-sou′, -sō′, ko͞or′ə-). An island of the Netherlands Antilles, 210 square miles in area in the Caribbean, 60 miles off the northwestern coast of Venezuela. Population, 132,000.

cu·ra·cy (kyo͝or′ə-sē) *n., pl.* **-cies.** The office, duties, or term of office of a curate. [CURA(TE) + -CY.]

cur·agh. Variant of **currach.**

cu·ra·re (ko͞o-rär′ē, kyo͞o-) *n.* Also **cu·ra·ri, u·ra·ri** (o͞o-rär′ē, yo͞o-). **1.** Any of various resinous extracts of uncertain and variable chemical composition, obtained from several species of South American trees of the genera *Chondodendron* and *Strychnos.* It is used medicinally as a muscle relaxant and by some South American Indians as an arrow poison. **2.** Any of the trees from which these substances are obtained. [Portuguese and Spanish, from Cariban *kurari.*]

cu·ra·rine (kyo͞o-rär′ĭn, -ēn′) *n.* A poisonous alkaloid, $C_{19}H_{26}N_2O$, obtained from curare. [CURAR(E) + -INE.]

cu·ra·rize (kyo͞o-rär′īz′) *tr.v.* **-rized, -rizing, -rizes.** **1.** To poison with curare. **2.** To treat with curare so as to paralyze the motor nerves. —**cu·ra′ri·za′tion** *n.*

cu·ras·sow (kyo͝or′ə-sō′) *n.* Any of several long-tailed, crested tropical American birds of the family Cracidae, related to the pheasants and domestic fowl. [Variant of CURAÇAO (island).]

cu·rate (kyo͝or′ĭt) *n.* **1.** A clergyman who has charge of a parish. **2.** A clergyman who assists a rector or vicar. [Middle English *curat,* from Medieval Latin *cūrātus,* "one having a (spiritual) cure or charge," from *cūra,* CURE.]

cur·a·tive (kyo͝or′ə-tĭv) *adj.* **1.** Serving or tending to cure. **2.** Of or relating to the cure of disease. —*n.* Something that cures; a remedy. —**cur′a·tive·ly** *adv.* —**cur′a·tive·ness** *n.*

cu·ra·tor (kyo͞o-rā′tər, kyo͝or′ə-tər) *n.* The administrative director of a museum, library, or other similar institution. [Middle English *curatour,* from Old French *curateur,* from Latin *cūrātor,* overseer, manager, from *cūrāre,* to take care of, from *cūra,* care, CURE.] —**cu′ra·to′ri·al** (kyo͝or′ə-tôr′ē-əl, -tōr′ē-əl) *adj.* —**cu·ra′tor·ship′** *n.*

curb (kûrb) *n.* Also *British* **kerb** (for sense 2). **1.** Anything that checks or restrains. **2.** A concrete border or row of joined stones forming part of a gutter along the edge of a street. **3.** A chain or strap serving in conjunction with the bit to restrain a horse. **4.** A hard swelling on the hind leg of a horse, causing lameness. **5.** A **curb exchange** (*see*). —*tr.v.* **curbed, curbing, curbs.** **1.** To check, restrain, or control; rein in. **2.** To furnish with a curb. —See Synonyms at **restrain.** [Old French *courbe,* a curved object, horse's bit, from Latin *curvus,* curved. See **sker-³** in Appendix.*] —**curb′a·ble** *adj.* —**curb′er** *n.*

curb broker. A broker on a curb exchange.

curb exchange. A market dealing in securities not listed on the regular stock exchange. Also called "curb."

curb·ing (kûr′bĭng) *n.* **1.** The material used to construct a curb. **2.** A row of curbstones; a curb.

curb roof. A roof having two slopes on each side.

curb·stone (kûrb′stōn′) *n.* A stone or row of stones that constitutes a curb.

cur·cu·li·o (kər-kyo͞o′lē-ō′) *n., pl.* **-os.** Any of several weevils of the family Curculionidae, many of which are destructive to fruit, vegetables, and other plants. [New Latin, from Latin *curculiō*†, weevil.]

cur·cu·ma (kûr′kyə-mə) *n.* Any of various Old World tropical plants of the genus *Curcuma,* having thick, aromatic rootstocks. *C. longa* is the source of **turmeric** (*see*). [New Latin, from Arabic *kurkum,* saffron.]

curd (kûrd) *n.* **1.** *Often plural.* The coagulated part of milk, used to make cheese. **2.** Any coagulation resembling this. **3.** The edible whitish flower head of the cauliflower. —*v.* **curded, curding, curds.** —*tr.* To form into curd; cause to thicken; curdle. —*intr.* To become curd; curdle; coagulate. [Middle English *curd, crudde*†.] —**curd′y** *adj.*

curd cheese. *Chiefly British.* Cottage cheese.

cur·dle (kûrd′l) *v.* **-dled, -dling, -dles.** —*intr.* To become curd; coagulate; thicken. —*tr.* To cause to change into curd. [Frequentative of CURD.]

cure (kyo͝or) *n.* **1.** Restoration of health; recovery from disease. **2.** A method or course of medical treatment used to restore health. **3.** An agent, such as a drug, that restores health; a remedy. **4.** *Ecclesiastical.* Spiritual charge or care of souls, as of a priest for his congregation. Also called "cure of souls." **5.** The office or duties of a curate. **6.** The act or process of preserving a product, such as fish, meat, and tobacco. —*v.* **cured, curing, cures.** —*tr.* **1.** To restore to health. **2.** To get rid of; to remedy: *cure an evil.* **3.** To preserve (meat, fish, or the like), as by salting, smoking, or aging. **4.** To prepare, preserve, or finish (a substance) by a chemical or physical process. **5.** To vulcanize (rubber). —*intr.* **1.** To effect a cure or recovery. **2.** To be prepared, preserved, or finished by a chemical or physical process. [Middle English, care, spiritual charge, cure, from Old French, from Latin *cūra,* care, charge, healing. See **cūra** in Appendix.*] —**cure′less** *adj.* —**cur′er** *n.*

cu·ré (kyo͞o-rā′, kyo͝or′ā′) *n. French.* A parish priest.

cure-all (kyo͝or′ôl′) *n.* That which cures all diseases or evils; panacea.

cu·ret·tage (kyo͝or′ə-täzh′, kyo͞o-rĕt′ĭj) *n.* Surgical scraping of a bodily cavity, as of the uterus, with a curette. Also called "curettement."

cu·rette (kyo͞o-rĕt′) *n.* Also **cu·ret.** A surgical instrument shaped like a scoop or spoon, used to remove dead tissue or growths from a bodily cavity. [French, from *curer,* to cure, from Old French, from Latin *cūrāre,* from *cūra,* CURE.]

cur·few (kûr′fyo͞o) *n.* **1.** An order or regulation enjoining specified classes of the population to retire from the streets at a prescribed hour. **2.** A similar medieval regulation requiring fires to be extinguished. **3. a.** The period during which any such regulation is in effect. **b.** The signal, as a bell, announcing it. [Middle English *curfeu, coeverfu,* from Old French *cuevrefeu,* "a covering of the fire" : *co(u)vrir,* to COVER + *feu,* fire, from Latin *focus,* hearth (see **fuel**).]

cu·ri·a (kyo͝or′ē-ə) *n., pl.* **curiae** (kyo͝or′ē-ē′). **1. a.** One of the ten primitive subdivisions of a tribe in early Rome, consisting of ten gentes and corresponding to the Attic phratry. **b.** Its place of assembly. **2. a.** The Senate or any of the various buildings in which it met in republican Rome. **b.** The place of assembly of high councils in various Italian cities under Roman administration. **3.** The ensemble of central administrative and governmental services in imperial Rome. **4.** *Often capital* **C.** The central administration governing the Roman Catholic Church. **5.** In medieval Europe: **a.** A feudal assembly or council. **b.** A royal court of justice. [Latin *cūria,* curia, council. See **wiros** in Appendix.*] —**cu′ri·al** *adj.*

cu·rie (kyo͝or′ē, kyo͞o-rē′), *n. Abbr.* **Ci** A unit of radioactivity, the amount of any nuclide that undergoes exactly 3.7 x 10^{10} radioactive disintegrations per second. [After Marie CURIE.]

Cu·rie, Irène. See **Joliot-Curie.**

Curie law. The law that the magnetic susceptibility varies inversely with absolute temperature in a paramagnetic substance with negligible interactions among magnetic carriers. Also called "Curie's law." [After Pierre CURIE.]

Cu·rie (kyo͝or′ē, kyo͞o-rē′) **Marie.** Original name, Marja Sklodowska. 1867–1934. Polish-born French chemist; discovered radioactivity of thorium; discovered polonium and radium and isolated radium from pitchblende; awarded Nobel Prize in physics (1903) with husband, Pierre Curie, and in chemistry (1911); mother of Irène Joliot-Curie.

Cu·rie (kyo͝or′ē, kyo͞o-rē′), **Pierre.** 1859–1906. French chemist; shared Nobel Prize in physics (1903) for work on radioactivity with his wife, Marie Curie; father of Irène Joliot-Curie.

Curie point. A transition temperature marking a change in the magnetic properties of a substance, especially the change from

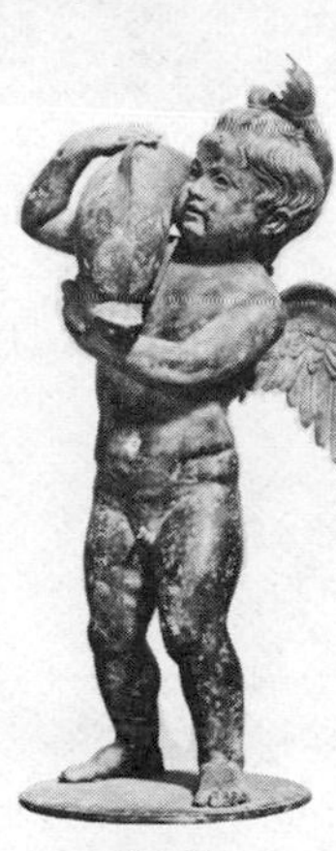

Cupid
Bronze statue
from Pompeii

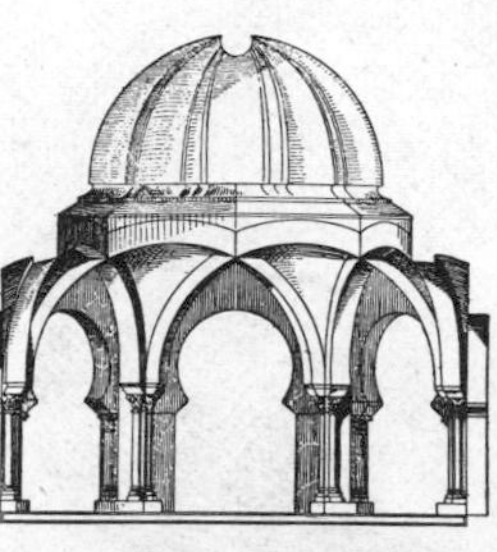

cupola
A cupola of the mosque
at Córdoba, Spain

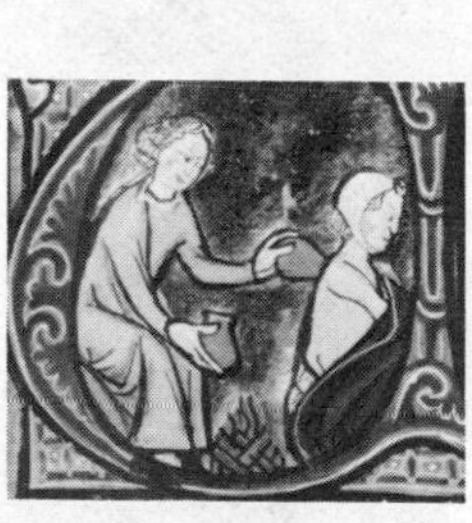

cupping
Illustration from a
13th-century French
manuscript

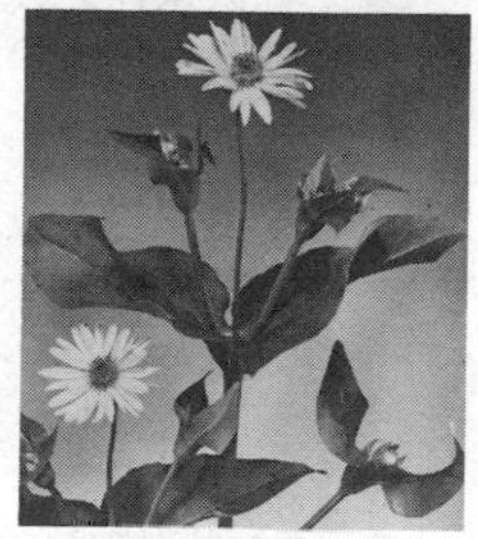

cup plant

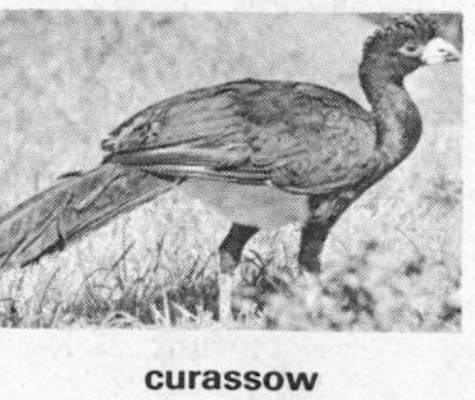

curassow
Crax alector

t tight/th thin, path/*th* this, bathe/ŭ cut/ûr urge/v valve/w with/y yes/z zebra, size/zh vision/ə about, item, edible, gallop, circus/ à *Fr.* ami/œ *Fr.* feu, *Ger.* schön/ü *Fr.* tu, *Ger.* über/KH *Ger.* ich, *Scot.* loch/N *Fr.* bon. ***Follows main vocabulary.** **†Of obscure origin.**

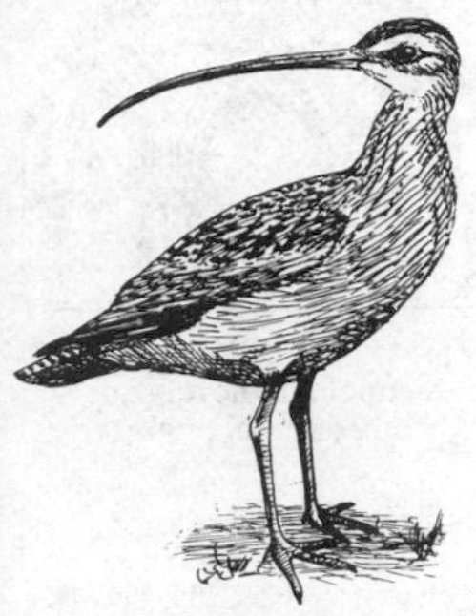

curlew
Numenius americanus

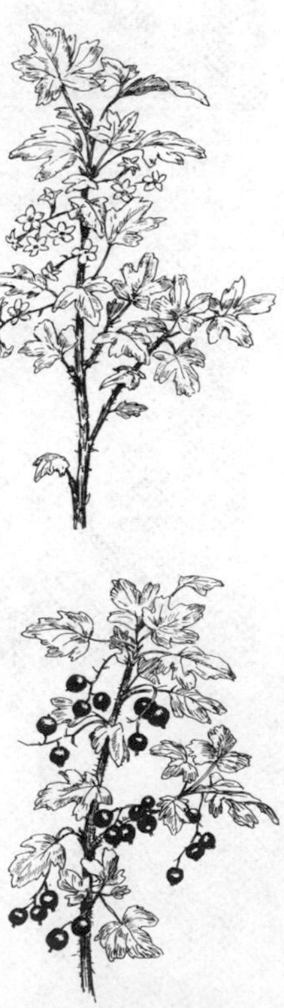

currant
Ribes lacustre
Above: The plant in flower
Below: The plant in fruit

ferromagnetism to paramagnetism. Also called "Curie temperature." [After Pierre CURIE.]

Cu·rie-Weiss law (kyŏŏr′ē-wīs′, -vīs′, kyŏŏ-rē′-). The law that the magnetic susceptibility of a paramagnetic substance above the Curie point varies inversely with the excess of temperature above that point. [After Pierre CURIE and Pierre-Ernest *Weiss* (died 1940), French physicist.]

cu·ri·o (kyŏŏr′ē-ō′) *n., pl.* **-os.** A curious or unusual object of art or bric-a-brac. [Short for CURIOSITY.]

cu·ri·o·sa (kyŏŏr′ē-ō′sə, -zə) *pl.n.* Books or other writings dealing with unusual, especially pornographic, topics. [New Latin, from Latin *cūriōsa*, neuter plural of *cūriōsus*, CURIOUS.]

cu·ri·os·i·ty (kyŏŏr′ē-ŏs′ə-tē) *n., pl.* **-ties. 1.** A desire to know or learn, especially about something new or strange. **2.** That which arouses interest, as by being novel or extraordinary. **3.** *Obsolete.* Fastidiousness.

cu·ri·ous (kyŏŏr′ē-əs) *adj.* **1.** Eager to acquire information or knowledge. **2.** Unduly inquisitive; prying; nosy. **3.** Interesting because of novelty or rarity; singular; odd. **4.** *Obsolete.* **a.** Accomplished with skill or ingenuity. **b.** Extremely careful or scrupulous. [Middle English, from Old French *curios*, from Latin *cūriōsus*, careful, diligent, inquisitive, from *cūra*, care, CURE.] **—cu′ri·ous·ly** *adv.* **—cu′ri·ous·ness** *n.*

Synonyms: *curious, inquisitive, snoopy, nosy, intrusive.* These adjectives apply to persons who show a marked desire for information or knowledge. *Curious* more often implies a legitimate desire to enlarge one's knowledge, but can suggest a less commendable urge to concern oneself in others' affairs. *Inquisitive* frequently suggests excessive curiosity and the asking of many questions. *Snoopy* implies an unworthy motive and underhandedness in implementing it. *Nosy* suggests excessive curiosity and impertinence in an adult; applied to a child, it may refer less unfavorably to habitual curiosity. *Intrusive* stresses unwarranted and unwelcome concern with another's affairs.

Cu·ri·ti·ba (kŏŏ′rē-tē′bä). The capital of Paraná, Brazil, in the northeastern part of the state. Population, 361,000.

cu·ri·um (kyŏŏr′ē-əm) *n. Symbol* **Cm** A silvery, metallic synthetic radioactive transuranic element having 13 isotopes with mass numbers from 238 to 250 and half-lives from 64 minutes to 16.4 million years. Atomic number 96. See **element.** [New Latin; named for Marie and Pierre CURIE.]

curl (kûrl) *v.* **curled, curling, curls.** *—tr.* **1.** To twist (the hair, for example) into ringlets or coils. **2.** To form into the spiral shape of a ringlet or coil. **3.** To decorate with curls. *—intr.* **1.** To form ringlets or coils. **2.** To assume a spiral or curved shape. **3.** To move in a curve or spiral. **4.** To play the game of curling. **—curl up. 1.** To assume a position with the legs drawn up. **2.** To make oneself comfortable. *—n.* **1.** Something with a spiral or coiled shape. **2.** A coil or ringlet of hair. **3. a.** The act of curling. **b.** The state of being curled. **4.** *Mathematics.* The vector product of the del operator and a vector function. Compare **divergence.** [Middle English *curlen, crullen*, from *crulle*, curly, from Middle Dutch. See **ger-³** in Appendix.*]

curl·er (kûr′lər) *n.* **1.** One that curls. **2.** A pin, roller, or the like on which hair is wound for curling. **3.** A player of curling.

cur·lew (kûrl′yŏŏ, kûr′lŏŏ) *n.* Any of several brownish, long-legged shore birds of the genus *Numenius*, having long, slender, downward-curving bills. [Middle English *curleu*, from Old French *courlieu* (imitative).]

Cur·ley (kûr′lē), **James Michael.** 1874–1958. American political leader; five times mayor of Boston.

curl·i·cue (kûr′lĭ-kyŏŏ′) *n.* Also **curl·y·cue.** A fancy twist or curl, such as a flourish made with a pen. [CURLY + CUE (rod).]

curl·ing (kûr′lĭng) *n.* A Scottish game played on ice, in which two four-man teams slide heavy, oblate stones toward a fixed mark in the center of a circle at either end.

curling iron. Also **curling irons.** A pair of rod-shaped metal tongs used when heated to curl the hair.

curl paper. A piece of soft paper on which a lock of hair is rolled up for curling.

curl·y (kûr′lē) *adj.* **-ier, -iest. 1.** Having curls. **2.** Having the tendency to curl. **3.** Having a wavy grain. Said of wood: *curly maple.* **—curl′i·ly** *adv.* **—curl′i·ness** *n.*

curly top. A disease of plants caused by a virus, *Ruga verrucosans*, and resulting in severe stunting of plants.

cur·mudg·eon (kər-mŭj′ən) *n.* **1.** A cantankerous person. **2.** *Rare.* A miser. [Origin obscure.] **—cur·mudg′eon·ly** *adj.*

cur·rach (kûr′əKH, kûr′ə) *n.* Also **cur·agh, cur·ragh.** *Scottish & Irish.* A kind of boat, a **coracle** *(see).* [Middle English *currok*, from Scottish Gaelic *curach* and Irish Gaelic *currach*, akin to Welsh *corwgl, cwrwgl*†.]

cur·rant (kûr′ənt) *n.* **1.** Any of various usually prickly shrubs of the genus *Ribes*, bearing clusters of red, black, or greenish fruit. **2.** The small, sour fruit of any of these plants, used chiefly for making jelly. **3.** A small, dried seedless grape of the Mediterranean region, used in cooking. [Middle English *(raysons of) coraunte*, (raisins of) Corinth, from Norman French *Corauntz*, from Old French *Corinthe*, CORINTH.]

cur·ren·cy (kûr′ən-sē) *n., pl.* **-cies. 1.** *Abbr.* **cur.** Any form of money in actual use as a medium of exchange. **2.** A passing from hand to hand; circulation. **3.** Common acceptance; prevalence. [Medieval Latin *currentia*, "a flowing," from Latin *currēns*, present participle of *currere*, to run. See **current.**]

cur·rent (kûr′ənt) *adj.* **1.** *Abbr.* **cur.** Belonging to the time now passing; now in progress: *the current issue.* **2.** Passing from one to another; circulating, as money. **3.** Commonly accepted; prevalent. **4.** *Rare.* Running; flowing. —See Synonyms at **prevailing.** *—n.* **1.** A steady and smooth onward movement, as of water. **2.** The part of any body of liquid or gas that has a continuous onward movement: *a river current.* **3.** A general tendency, movement, or course. **4.** *Symbol* **i, I** *Electricity.* **a.** A flow of electric charge. **b.** The amount of electric charge flowing past a specified circuit point per unit time. In this sense, also called "electric current." —See Synonyms at **tendency.** [Middle English *curraunt*, from Old French *corant*, present participle of *courre*, to run, from Latin *currere.* See **kers-²** in Appendix.*] **—cur′rent·ly** *adv.* **—cur′rent·ness** *n.*

current assets. Cash or other assets convertible into cash at short notice.

current density. *Symbol* **J 1.** *Electricity.* The ratio of the magnitude of current flowing in a conductor to the cross-sectional area perpendicular to the current flow. **2.** *Physics.* The number of subatomic particles per unit time crossing a unit area in a designated plane perpendicular to the direction of motion of the particles.

cur·ri·cle (kûr′ĭ-kəl) *n.* A light, open two-wheeled carriage, drawn by two horses abreast. [Latin *curriculum*, a running, racecourse, racing chariot. See **curriculum.**]

cur·ric·u·lum (kə-rĭk′yə-ləm) *n., pl.* **-la** (-lə) or **-lums. 1.** All the courses of study offered by an educational institution. **2.** A particular course of study, often in a special field. [New Latin, from Latin, a running, course, from *currere*, to run. See **kers-²** in Appendix.*] **—cur·ric′u·lar** (-lər) *adj.*

cur·ric·u·lum vi·tae (kə-rĭk′yə-ləm vī′tē, kŏŏ-rĭk′ŏŏ-lŏŏm wē′-tī′). A short résumé of one's career, as for an employer. [Latin, the course of one's life.]

cur·ri·er (kûr′ē-ər) *n.* One who curries, especially leather. [Middle English *curr(e)iour*, from Old French, from Latin *coriārius*, a tanner, from *corium*, leather. See **sker-¹** in Appendix.*]

Cur·ri·er and Ives (kûr′ē-ər; īvz). An American lithographing firm operated by Nathaniel Currier (1813–1888) and James Merritt Ives (1824–1895), specializing in scenes of American life, manners, and history.

cur·ri·er·y (kûr′ē-ə-rē) *n., pl.* **-ies.** The trade, work, or shop of a leather currier.

cur·rish (kûr′ĭsh) *adj.* Of or like a cur; snarling; bad-tempered.

cur·ry¹ (kûr′ē) *tr.v.* **-ried, -rying, -ries. 1.** To groom (a horse) with a currycomb. **2.** To prepare (tanned hides) for use by soaking, coloring, or other processes. **—curry favor.** To seek or gain favor by fawning or flattery. [Middle English *curreien*, from Old French *co(n)reer*, to prepare, equip, from Vulgar Latin *conrēdāre* (unattested) : *com-* (intensifier), with + *rēdāre* (unattested), to prepare, from Germanic (see **reidh-** in Appendix*). Sense 2 is partly a back-formation from CURRIER.]

cur·ry² (kûr′ē) *n., pl.* **-ries.** Also **cur·rie. 1.** A condiment, **curry powder** *(see).* **2.** A heavily spiced sauce or relish made with curry powder and eaten with rice, meat, fish, or other food. **3.** A dish seasoned with curry powder. *—tr.v.* **curried, -rying, -ries.** To season with curry. [Tamil *kari*, relish, sauce.]

Cur·ry (kûr′ē), **John Steuart.** 1897–1946. American painter.

cur·ry·comb (kûr′ē-kōm′) *n.* A comb with metal teeth, used for grooming horses. *—tr.v.* **currycombed, -combing, -combs.** To groom with a currycomb.

curry powder. A blended condiment prepared from cumin, coriander, turmeric, and other pungent spices.

curse (kûrs) *n.* **1.** An appeal to a supernatural power for evil or injury to befall someone or something. **2.** The evil or injury thus invoked. **3.** Someone or something accursed. **4.** That which brings or causes evil; a scourge. **5.** Any profane oath. **6.** *Ecclesiastical.* A censure, ban, or anathema. **7.** *Slang.* Menstruation. Used with *the.* *—v.* **cursed** or **curst, cursing, curses.** *—tr.* **1.** To invoke evil, calamity, or injury upon; to damn. **2.** To swear at; abuse profanely. **3.** To bring evil upon; afflict. **4.** *Ecclesiastical.* To put under ban or anathema; excommunicate. *—intr.* To utter curses; swear. [Middle English *curs(e)*, Old English *curs*†.] **—curs′er** *n.*

curs·ed (kûr′sĭd, kûrst) *adj.* Also **curst** (kûrst) (for sense 1). **1.** Deserving to be cursed; wicked; detestable. **2.** *Regional.* Variant of **curst. —curs′ed·ly** *adv.* **—curs′ed·ness** *n.*

cur·sive (kûr′sĭv) *adj.* Designating writing or printing in which the letters are joined together; flowing. *—n.* **1.** A cursive character or letter. **2.** A manuscript written in cursive characters. **3.** *Printing.* A kind of type that imitates handwriting. [Medieval Latin *(scripta) cursīva*, "flowing (script)," from Latin *cursus*, past participle of *currere*, to run. See **kers-²** in Appendix.*]

cur·so·ri·al (kûr-sôr′ē-əl, -sōr′ē-əl) *adj. Zoology.* Adapted to or specialized for running: *cursorial birds; cursorial legs.* [From Late Latin *cursōrius*, of running. See **cursory.**]

cur·so·ry (kûr′sə-rē) *adj.* Hasty and superficial; not thorough. See Synonyms at **superficial.** [Late Latin *cursōrius*, of running, from Latin *cursor*, a runner, from *cursus.* See **cursive.**] **—cur′so·ri·ly** *adv.* **—cur′so·ri·ness** *n.*

curst (kûrst) *adj.* Also **curs·ed** (kûr′sĭd, kûrst) (for sense 1). **1.** *Regional.* Cantankerous; ill-tempered. **2.** Variant of **cursed.**

curt (kûrt) *adj.* **1.** Rudely brief or abrupt, as in speech or manner. **2.** Terse; concise. **3.** Shortened. —See Synonyms at **gruff.** [Latin *curtus*, cut short. See **sker-¹** in Appendix.*] **—curt′ly** *adv.* **—curt′ness** *adj.*

cur·tail (kər-tāl′) *tr.v.* **-tailed, -tailing, -tails.** To cut short; abbreviate. [Variant of obsolete *curtal*, to dock the tail of a horse, from CURTAL.] **—cur·tail′er** *n.* **—cur·tail′ment** *n.*

curtail step. The widened step or steps at the foot of a flight of stairs. [Origin obscure.]

ă pat/ā pay/âr care/ä father/b bib/ch church/d deed/ĕ pet/ē be/f fife/g gag/h hat/hw which/ĭ pit/ī pie/îr pier/j judge/k kick/l lid, needle/m mum/n no, sudden/ng thing/ŏ pot/ō toe/ô paw, for/oi noise/ou out/ŏŏ took/ōō boot/p pop/r roar/s sauce/sh ship, dish/ t tight/th thin, path/*th* this, bathe/ŭ cut/ûr urge/v valve/w with/y yes/z zebra, size/zh vision/ə about, item, edible, gallop, circus/ à *Fr.* ami/œ *Fr.* feu, *Ger.* schön/ü *Fr.* tu, *Ger.* über/KH *Ger.* ich, *Scot.* loch/N *Fr.* bon. *Follows main vocabulary. †Of obscure origin.

CURRENCY
TABLE OF EXCHANGE RATES

Country	Basic Unit	Standard Subdivision	*	†
Afghanistan	afghani	100 puls	Af.	0.013
Albania	lek	100 quintars	L	0.200
Algeria	dinar	100 centimes	DA	0.202
Argentina	peso	100 centavos	M$N	0.003
Australia	dollar	100 cents	$A	1.120
Austria	schilling	100 groschen	S	0.038
Belgium	franc	100 centimes	BF	0.020
Bolivia	peso	100 centavos	$b	0.084
Brazil	cruzeiro	100 centavos	Cr$	0.260
Bulgaria	lev	100 stotinki	LV	0.850
Burma	kyat	100 pyas	K	0.210
Burundi	franc	100 centimes	FBu	0.011
Cambodia	riel	100 sen	CR	0.028
Cameroun	franc	100 centimes	CFAF	0.004
Canada	dollar	100 cents	Can$	0.925
Central African Republic	franc	100 centimes	CFAF	0.004
Ceylon	rupee	100 cents	Cey Rs	0.168
Chad	franc	100 centimes	CFAF	0.004
Chile	escudo	100 centesimos	E°	0.112
China, People's Republic of	yuan	10 chiao, 100 fen	$	0.405
China, Republic of (Taiwan)	yuan	100 cents	N.T.$	0.025
Colombia	peso	100 centavos	Col$	0.060
Congo (Brazzaville)	franc	100 centimes	CFAF	0.004
Congo (Kinshasa)	zaire	100 makuta	Z	2.000
Costa Rica	colon	100 centimos	₡	0.128
Cuba	peso	100 centavos	$	1.000
Cyprus	pound	1000 mils	£C	2.400
Czechoslovakia	koruna	100 halers	Kčs	0.139
Dahomey	franc	100 centimes	CFAF	0.004
Denmark	krone	100 øre	DKr	0.132
Dominican Republic	peso	100 centavos	RD$	1.000
East Germany	ostmark	100 pfennigs	OM	0.450
Ecuador	sucre	100 centavos	S/	0.045
El Salvador	colon	100 centavos	₡	0.400
Ethiopia	dollar	100 cents	Eth$	0.400
Finland	markka	100 pennis	Fmk	0.240
France	franc	100 centimes	Fr	0.202
Gabon	franc	100 centimes	CFAF	0.004
Gambia	pound	20 shillings, 240 pence	£G	2.400
Ghana	cedi	100 pesewa	N₡	0.980
Greece	drachma	100 lepta	Dr	0.033
Guatemala	quetzal	100 centavos	Q	1.000
Guinea	franc	100 centimes	GF	0.004
Guyana	dollar	100 cents	G$	0.500
Haiti	gourde	100 centimes	G	0.200
Honduras	lempira	100 centavos	L	0.500
Hong Kong	dollar	100 cents	HK$	0.164
Hungary	forint	100 fillér	Ft	0.041
Iceland	krona	100 aurar	IKr	0.011
India	rupee	100 paise	Rs	0.133
Indonesia	rupiah	100 sen	Rp	0.003
Iran	rial	100 dinars	Rls	0.013
Iraq	dinar	1000 fils	ID	2.800
Ireland, Republic of	pound	20 shillings, 240 pence	£Ir.	2.400
Israel	pound	100 agorot	I£	0.285
Italy	lira	100 centesimi	Lit	0.002
Ivory Coast	franc	100 centimes	CFAF	0.004
Jamaica	pound	20 shillings, 240 pence	£J	2.400
Japan	yen	100 sen	¥	0.003
Jordan	dinar	1000 fils	JD	2.800
Kenya	shilling	100 cents	K Sh.	0.140
Kuwait	dinar	1000 fils	KD	2.800
Laos	kip	100 at	K	0.001
Lebanon	pound	100 piasters	LL	0.310
Liberia	dollar	100 cents	$	1.000
Libya	pound	100 piasters	£L	2.800
Luxembourg	franc	100 centimes	Lux.F.	0.020
Malagasy Republic	franc	100 centimes	FMG	0.004
Malawi	pound	20 shillings, 240 pence	£M	2.400
Malaysia	dollar	100 cents	M$	0.320
Mali	franc	100 centimes	MF	0.002
Malta	pound	20 shillings, 240 pence	£	2.280
Mauritania	franc	100 centimes	CFAF	0.004
Mauritius	rupee	100 cents	MRps	0.210
Mexico	peso	100 centavos	Mex$	0.080
Morocco	dirham	100 francs	DH	0.190
Nepal	rupee	100 pice	NRs	0.100
Netherlands	guilder	100 cents	f	0.276
Netherlands Antilles	guilder	100 cents	Ant f	0.530
New Zealand	dollar	100 cents	$NZ	1.120
Nicaragua	cordoba	100 centavos	C$	0.142
Niger	franc	100 centimes	CFAF	0.004
Nigeria	pound	20 shillings, 240 pence	£N	2.800
North Korea	won	100 jun	W	0.388
North Vietnam	dong	100 xu	D	0.676
Norway	krone	100 øre	NKr	0.138
Pakistan	rupee	100 paisas	PRs	0.210
Panama	balboa	100 centesimos	B	0.800
Paraguay	guarani	100 centimos	G	0.010
Peru	sol	100 centavos	S/	0.024
Philippines, Republic of the	peso	100 centavos	₱	0.250
Poland	zloty	100 groszy	Zl	0.041
Portugal	escudo	100 centavos	Esc	0.034
Rhodesia	pound	20 shillings, 240 pence	£R	2.800
Rumania	leu	100 bani	L	0.160
Rwanda	franc	100 centimes	RF	0.005
Saudi Arabia	riyal	20 qurush	SRls	0.222
Senegal	franc	100 centimes	CFAF	0.004
Sierra Leone	leone	100 cents	Le	1.200
Singapore	dollar	100 cents	S$	0.330
Somali Republic	shilling	100 cents	So. Sh.	0.140
South Africa, Republic of	rand	100 cents	R	1.400
Southern Yemen, People's Republic of	dinar	1000 fils	SA£	2.400
South Korea	won	100 chon	W	0.004
South Vietnam	piaster	100 cents	VN$	0.012
Spain	peseta	100 centimos	Pts	0.014
Sudan	pound	100 piasters	SdL	1.700
Surinam	guilder	100 cents	Sur.f	0.530
Sweden	krona	100 øre	SKr	0.192
Switzerland	franc	100 centimes	SwF	0.231
Syria	pound	100 piasters	L. S.	0.260
Tanzania	shilling	100 cents	T. Sh.	0.140
Thailand	baht	100 satangs	B	0.046
Togo	franc	100 centimes	CFAF	0.004
Trinidad & Tobago	dollar	100 cents	TT$	0.500
Tunisia	dinar	1000 milliemes	D	1.904
Turkey	pound	100 piasters	LT	0.110
Uganda	shilling	100 cents	U. Sh.	0.140
Union of Soviet Socialist Republics	rouble	100 kopecks	R	1.111
United Arab Republic	pound	100 piasters	LE	2.300
United Kingdom of Great Britain and Northern Ireland	pound	100 new pence	£	2.400
United States of America	dollar	100 cents	$	1.000
Uruguay	peso	100 centesimos	UR$	0.004
Upper Volta	franc	100 centimes	CFAF	0.004
Venezuela	bolivar	100 centimos	Bs	0.220
Western Samoa	dollar	100 cents	$	0.750
West Germany	Deutsche mark	100 pfennigs	DM	0.250
Yemen	riyal	40 bugshas	R	0.930
Yugoslavia	dinar	100 paras	Din	0.800
Zambia	kwacha	100 ngwee	KW	1.400

* Abbreviation or Symbol   †Equivalence in U.S. Dollars, March 1969

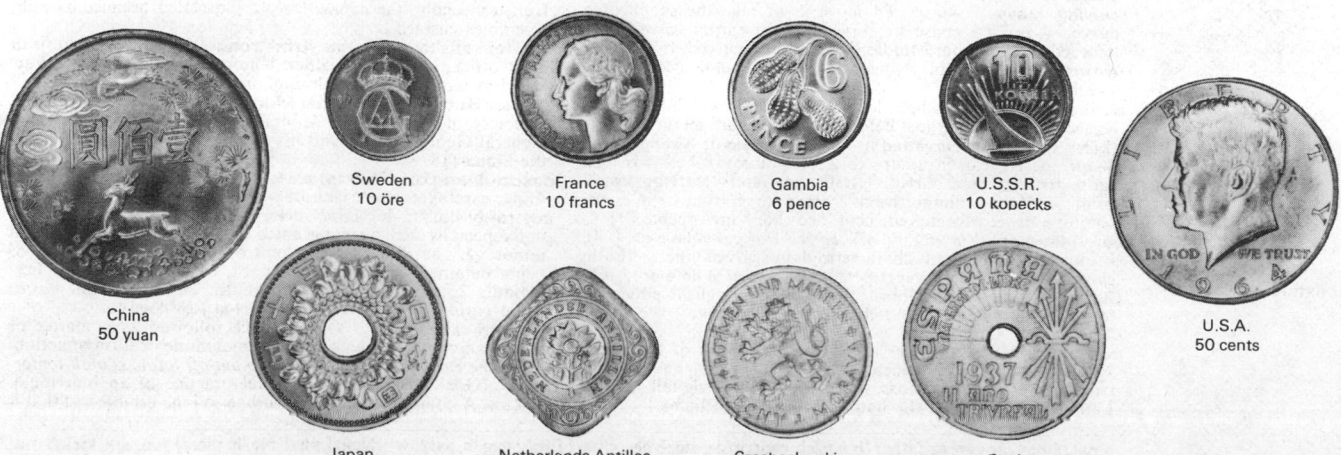

China 50 yuan

Sweden 10 öre

France 10 francs

Gambia 6 pence

U.S.S.R. 10 kopecks

U.S.A. 50 cents

Japan 50 yen

Netherlands Antilles 5 cents

Czechoslovakia 1 koruna

Spain 25 centimos

cur·tain (kûrt′n) *n.* **1.** A piece of cloth or similar material hanging in a window or other opening as a decoration, shade, or screen. **2.** *Theater.* A line, speech, or situation in a play that occurs at the very end or just before the curtain falls. **3.** The part of a rampart or parapet connecting two bastions or gates. **4.** *Architecture.* An enclosing wall connecting two towers or similar structures. **5.** Any barrier, such as a restriction on communication. **6.** *Plural. Slang.* The end; ruin; death. —*tr.v.* **curtained, -taining, -tains.** To provide or shut off with or as if with a curtain. [Middle English *curtin(e)*, from Old French, from Late Latin *cortīna*, enclosure, curtain, from Latin *cohors* (stem *cohort-*), enclosure. See **gher-**[2] in Appendix.*]

curtain call. The appearance of a performer or performers at the end of a performance in response to applause.

curtain lecture. A private reprimand given to a husband by his wife, so called from the curtained beds in which such scoldings once took place.

curtain raiser. 1. A short play presented before the principal dramatic production. **2.** Any preliminary event.

curtain speech. 1. A talk given in front of the curtain at the conclusion of a theatrical performance. **2.** The final speech of a play or of an act of a play.

cur·tal (kûr′təl) *n. Obsolete.* **1.** An animal with a docked tail. **2.** Anything cut short or docked. —*adj. Obsolete.* **1.** Cut short or docked, as an animal's tail. **2.** Wearing a short frock. [Old French *courtault*, horse with a cropped tail or mane, from *court*, short, from Latin *curtus*, shortened. See **sker-**[1] in Appendix.*]

curtal ax. *Archaic.* A cutlass. [Variant (influenced by CURTAL and AX) of earlier *curtelace*, *coutelace*, CUTLASS.]

cur·tate (kûr′tāt′) *adj.* Shortened; abbreviated. [Latin *curtātus*, past participle of *curtāre*, to shorten, from *curtus*, short, CURT.]

cur·te·sy (kûr′tə-sē) *n., pl.* **-sies.** The life tenure which by common law is held by a man over the property of his deceased wife if children with rights of inheritance were born during the marriage. [Middle English *courteisie*, curtesy, COURTESY.]

cur·ti·lage (kûr′tə-lĭj) *n. Law.* The enclosed land surrounding a house or dwelling. [Middle English, from Old French *courtillage*, from *courtil*, little court, diminutive of *cort*, COURT.]

Cur·tis (kûr′tĭs), **Charles.** 1860–1936. Vice President of the United States under Herbert Hoover (1929–33).

Cur·tiss (kûr′tĭs), **Glenn Hammond.** 1878–1930. American pioneer aviator; designer and manufacturer of airplanes.

curt·sy (kûrt′sē) *n., pl.* **-sies.** Also **curt·sey** *pl.* **-seys, cour·te·sy** (kûr′tə-sē) *pl.* **-sies.** A gesture of respect or reverence made by women by bending the knees with one foot forward and lowering the body. —*intr.v.* **curtsied, -sying, -sies.** Also **curt·sey, -seyed, -seying, -seys** or **cour·te·sy** (kûr′tə-sē), **-sied, -sying, -sies.** To make a curtsy. [Variant of COURTESY.]

cu·rule (kyŏŏr′ōōl) *adj.* Privileged to sit in a curule chair; of superior rank. [Latin *curūlis*, "of a chariot," of a curule chair (originally a throne mounted on a chariot), from *currus*, a chariot, from *currere*, to run. See **kers-**[2] in Appendix.*]

curule chair. A seat with heavy, curved legs and no back, reserved for the use of the highest officials in ancient Rome. Also called "curule seat."

cur·va·ceous (kûr-vā′shəs) *adj.* Having a full or voluptuous figure; shapely. [CURV(E) + -ACEOUS.] —**cur·va′ceous·ly** *adv.*

cur·va·ture (kûr′və-chŏŏr) *n.* **1. a.** An act of curving. **b.** The state of being curved. **2.** *Mathematics.* **a.** The ratio of the change in tangent inclination over a given arc to the length of the arc. Also called "average curvature." **b.** The limit of this ratio as the length of the arc approaches zero. **3.** *Medicine.* A curving or bending, especially an abnormal one: *curvature of the spine.* [Latin *curvātūra*, from *curvātus*, past participle of *curvāre*, to bend, from *curvus*, curved. See **sker-**[3] in Appendix.*]

curve (kûrv) *n.* **1. a.** A line that deviates from straightness in a smooth, continuous fashion. **b.** A surface that deviates from planarity in a smooth, continuous fashion. **2.** A curved part, object, or region, as: **a.** The female bosom, hips, or buttocks. **b.** A relatively smooth bend or connected series of bends in a course or route, especially in a road. **3. a.** A line representing data on a graph. **b.** A trend derived from or as if from such a graph. **4.** *Mathematics.* **a.** The graph of a function on a coordinate plane. **b.** The intersection of two surfaces in three dimensions. **5.** *Baseball.* A pitched ball that veers to one side as it approaches the batter. Also called "curve ball." —*v.* **curved, curving, curves.** —*intr.* To move in or take the shape of a curve. —*tr.* To cause to curve. [From earlier *curve (line)*, "curved (line)," from Middle English *curve*, curved, from Latin *curvus.* See **sker-**[3] in Appendix.*] —**curv′ed·ly** (-ĭd-lē) *adv.* —**curv′ed·ness** *n.*

cur·vet (kûr′vĭt) *n.* A light leap by a horse, in which both hind legs leave the ground just before the forelegs are set down. —*v.* (kûr-vĕt′, kûr′vĭt) **curvetted** or **-veted, -vetting** or **-veting, -vets.** —*intr.* **1.** To leap in a curvet. **2.** To prance; frolic. —*tr.* To cause to leap in a curvet. [Italian *corvetta*, "curving leap," from Old Italian, diminutive of *corva*, a curve, from Latin *curva*, feminine of *curvus*, curved, bent. See **sker-**[3] in Appendix.*]

cur·vi·lin·e·ar (kûr′və-lĭn′ē-ər) *adj.* Also **cur·vi·lin·e·al** (-əl). Formed, bounded, or characterized by curved lines. [Latin *curvus*, curved (see **curve**) + LINEAR.] —**cur′vi·lin′e·ar·ly** *adv.*

Cur·wen (kûr′wən), **John.** 1816–1880. English educator; founder of tonic sol-fa system of music teaching.

Cus·co. See **Cuzco.**

cus·cus (kŭs′kəs) *n.* Any of several marsupials of the genus *Phalanger*, of New Guinea and adjacent areas, having protruding eyes, a yellow nose, and a long, prehensile tail. [New Latin, probably from the native New Guinean name.]

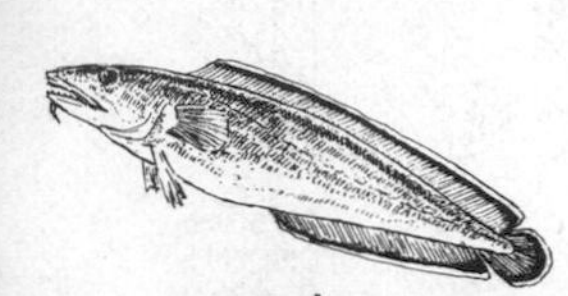

cusk

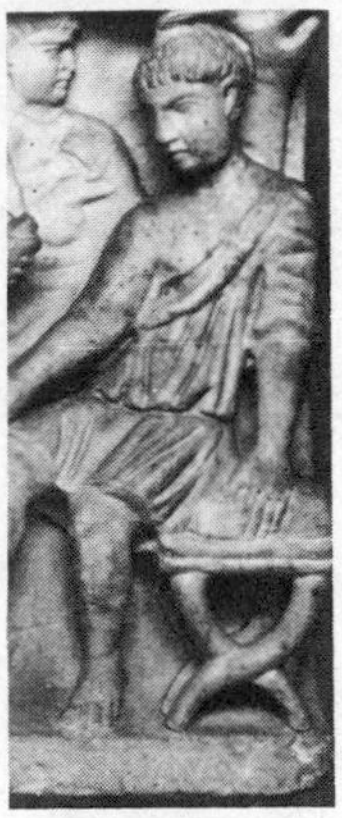

curule chair
Detail from the sarcophagus of Junius Bassus, fourth century A.D.

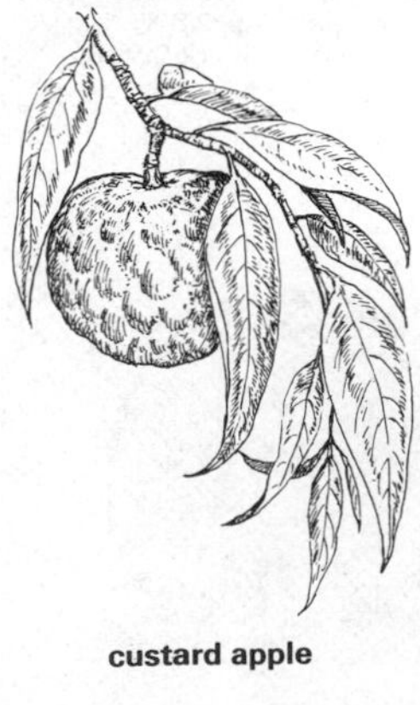

custard apple

cu·sec (kyōō′sĕk) *n.* A unit of volumetric flow of liquids, equal to one cubic foot per second. [CU(BIC) + SEC(OND).]

Cush[1] (kŭsh, kŏŏsh). The eldest son of Ham. Genesis 10:6.

Cush[2] (kŭsh, kŏŏsh). Also **Kush.** A legendary ancient region of northeastern Africa where the Biblical descendants of Cush settled, often identified with Ethiopia.

cu·shaw (kə-shô′) *n.* Also **ca·shaw.** A squash, *Cucurbita moschata*, having variably shaped, often crook-necked fruit. [Earlier *coscushaw*, from some Algonquian language of North Carolina or Virginia.]

Cush·ing (kŏŏsh′ĭng), **Caleb.** 1800–1879. American diplomat and political leader.

Cush·ing (kŏŏsh′ĭng), **Harvey Williams.** 1869–1939. American neurologist; pioneer in brain surgery.

Cushing's disease (kŏŏsh′ĭngz). A disease caused by an overgrowth of basophilic cells of the pituitary, characterized by obesity and muscular weakness. Also called "Cushing's syndrome." [After Harvey CUSHING.]

cush·ion (kŏŏsh′ən) *n.* **1.** A pad or pillow with a soft filling, used for resting or reclining. **2.** Anything resilient used as a rest, support, or shock absorber. **3.** The rim bordering a billiard table. **4.** A pillow used in lacemaking. —*tr.v.* **cushioned, -ioning, -ions. 1.** To provide with a cushion. **2.** To place or seat on a cushion. **3.** To cover or hide with or as if with a cushion. **4.** To protect against or absorb the shock of. [Middle English *cuisshen*, from Old French *coissin*, from Vulgar Latin *coxīnus* (unattested), "hip rest," cushion, from Latin *coxa*, hip. See **koksā** in Appendix.*] —**cush′ion·y** *adj.*

cushion pink. A plant, the **moss campion** *(see).*

Cush·it·ic (kŏŏ-shĭt′ĭk) *n.* Also **Kush·it·ic.** A group of Hamitic languages, including Somali and other languages spoken in Somaliland and Ethiopia. —*adj.* Also **Kush·it·ic.** Of or pertaining to this group of languages.

Cush·man (kŏŏsh′mən), **Charlotte Saunders.** 1816–1876. American actress; appeared extensively in Great Britain.

cush·y (kŏŏsh′ē) *adj.* **-ier, -iest.** *Slang.* Comfortable; undemanding: *a cushy job.* [Anglo-Indian, from Hindi *khush*, from Persian *khōsh*†, pleasant.]

cusk (kŭsk) *n., pl.* **cusk** or **cusks.** A food fish, *Brosme brosme*, of North Atlantic coastal waters. [Probably variant of earlier *tusk*, from Norn. See **ters-** in Appendix.*]

cusk eel. Any of various eellike, chiefly marine fishes of the family Ophidiidae.

cusp (kŭsp) *n.* **1.** A point or pointed end. **2.** *Anatomy.* **a.** A prominence or projection on the chewing surface of a tooth. **b.** A fold or flap of a heart valve. **3.** *Geometry.* A point at which a curve crosses itself and at which the two tangents to the curve coincide. **4.** *Architecture.* The pointed figure formed by two intersecting arcs or foils. **5.** *Astronomy.* Either point of a crescent moon. **6.** *Astrology.* The transitional first or last part of a house or sign. [Latin *cuspis*†, a point, spear.]

cus·pate (kŭs′pāt′) *adj.* Also **cus·pat·ed** (-pāt′ĭd), **cusped** (kŭspt). **1.** Having a cusp or cusps. **2.** Shaped like a cusp.

cus·pid (kŭs′pĭd) *n.* A tooth having one point; canine tooth. [Back-formation from BICUSPID.]

cus·pi·date (kŭs′pə-dāt′) *adj.* Also **cus·pi·dat·ed** (-dā′tĭd), **cus·pi·dal** (kŭs′pə-dəl). **1.** Having a cusp or cusps. **2.** *Biology.* Terminating in or tipped with a sharp point: *a cuspidate leaf.* [Latin *cuspidātus*, from the past participle of *cuspidāre*, to make pointed, from *cuspis* (stem *cuspid-*), point, CUSP.]

cus·pi·da·tion (kŭs′pə-dā′shən) *n. Architecture.* Decoration with cusps.

cus·pi·dor (kŭs′pə-dôr′) *n.* A **spittoon** *(see).* [Portuguese, from *cuspir*, to spit, from Latin *conspuere*, to spit upon : *com-* (intensifier), with + *spuere*, to spit (see **spyeu-** in Appendix*).]

cuss (kŭs) *v.* **cussed, cussing, cusses.** *Informal.* —*intr.* To curse. —*tr.* To shout curses at. —*n. Informal.* **1.** A curse. **2.** An odd or perverse creature. [Variant of CURSE.]

cuss·ed (kŭs′ĭd) *adj. Informal.* **1.** Cursed. **2.** Perverse; vexatious. —**cuss′ed·ly** *adv.* —**cuss′ed·ness** *n.*

cus·tard (kŭs′tərd) *n.* A dessert of milk, sugar, eggs, and flavoring, boiled or baked until set. [Middle English *crustade*, a kind of pie, probably from Old Provençal *croustado*, from *crosta*, crust, from Latin *crusta*, CRUST.]

custard apple. 1. A tropical American tree, *Annona reticulata*, bearing large, heart-shaped fruit. **2.** The fruit of this tree, having edible, fleshy pulp. **3.** Any of several related trees or fruit; especially, the **papaw** *(see).* [So called because its pulp resembles custard.]

Cus·ter (kŭs′tər), **George Armstrong.** 1839–1876. American army officer and Indian fighter; Union general in the Civil War; killed at battle of the Little Bighorn.

Cus·ter Battlefield National Monument (kŭs′tər). A national cemetery in southeastern Montana, marking the scene where General George Custer and his command were annihilated by the Sioux (1876).

cus·to·di·an (kŭs-tō′dē-ən) *n.* **1.** One who has charge of something; caretaker. **2.** A janitor. —**cus·to′di·an·ship′** *n.*

cus·to·dy (kŭs′tə-dē) *n., pl.* **-dies. 1.** The act or right of guarding, especially such a right granted by a court to a guardian of a minor. **2.** The state of being kept or guarded. **3.** The state of being detained or held under guard, especially by the police. [Middle English *custodie*, from Latin *custōdia*, from *custōs* (stem *custōd-*), CUSTOS.] —**cus·to′di·al** (-tō′dē-əl) *adj.*

cus·tom (kŭs′təm) *n.* **1.** A practice followed as a matter of course among a people; a conventional mode or form of action: *"It is the custom in Spain always to put off business until tomorrow."* (G.B. Shaw). **2.** A habitual practice of an individual. **3.** *Law.* A common tradition or usage so long established that it has the force or validity of law. **4.** Habitual patronage, as of a store. **5.** *Plural.* **a.** A duty or tax imposed on imported and, less commonly, exported goods. **b.** The governmental agency authorized to collect these duties. Used with a singular verb. **c.** The procedure for inspecting goods and baggage entering a country. Used with a singular verb. **6.** Tribute, service, or rent paid by a feudal tenant to his lord. —See Synonyms at **habit.** —*adj.* **1.** Made to the specifications of an individual purchaser. **2.** Specializing in the making or selling of made-to-order goods. [Middle English *custume,* from Old French *costume,* from Latin *consuētūdō,* a being accustomed, from *consuēscere,* to accustom : *com-* (intensifier), with + *suēscere,* to become accustomed (see **seu-**[2] in Appendix*).]

cus·tom·a·ble (kŭs′təm-ə-bəl) *adj.* Subject to tariffs.

cus·tom·ar·y (kŭs′tə-mĕr′ē) *adj.* **1.** Commonly practiced or used as a matter of course; usual. **2.** Based on custom or tradition rather than written law or contract. —See Synonyms at **usual.** —**cus′tom·ar′i·ly** *adv.* —**cus′tom·ar′i·ness** *n.*

cus·tom-built (kŭs′təm-bĭlt′) *adj.* Built according to the specifications of the buyer.

cus·tom·er (kŭs′təm-ər) *n.* **1.** A person who buys goods or services, especially on a regular basis. **2.** *Informal.* A person with whom one must deal: *a tough customer.*

cus·tom·house (kŭs′təm-hous′) *n., pl.* **-houses** (-hou′zĭz). Also **custom house.** *Abbr.* **c.h., C.H.** A governmental building or office where customs are collected and ships are cleared for entering or leaving the country.

cus·tom·ize (kŭs′tə-mīz′) *tr.v.* **-ized, -izing, -izes.** To alter (a standard car model, for example) to the tastes of the buyer.

cus·tom-made (kŭs′təm-mād′) *adj.* Made according to the specifications of an individual purchaser.

customs union. An international association organized to eliminate customs restrictions on goods exchanged between member nations and to establish a uniform tariff policy toward nonmember nations.

cus·tos (kŭs′tŏs) *n., pl.* **custodes** (kŭs-tō′dēz). **1.** A guardian or keeper; custodian. **2.** A superior in certain monastic orders. [Middle English, from Latin *custōs*†, guard, protector.]

cus·tu·mal (kŭs′cho͞o-məl, -tyo͞o-məl) *n.* A written record of the customs of a monastery or community. [Medieval Latin *custumāle,* from the neuter of *custumālis,* customary, from Old French *custumel,* from *custome,* CUSTOM.]

cut (kŭt) *v.* **cut, cutting, cuts.** —*tr.* **1.** To penetrate with a sharp edge; strike a narrow opening in. **2.** To separate into parts with, or as if with, a sharp-edged instrument; sever: *cut cloth with scissors.* **3.** To sever the edges or outer extensions of; shorten; trim. **4.** To reap; harvest. **5.** To fell by sawing; hew. **6.** To have (a new tooth) grow through the gums. **7.** To form or shape by severing or incising: *a doll cut from paper.* **8.** To form by penetrating, probing, or digging. **9.** To separate or dissociate from a main body; detach: *cut off a drumstick.* **10.** To pass through or across; to cross. **11.** *Card Games.* To divide (a deck of cards) in two, as before dealing. **12.** To reduce or curtail the size, extent, or duration of. **13.** To lessen the strength of; dilute: *cut whiskey.* **14.** To dissolve by breaking down the fat of: *Soap cuts grease.* **15.** To injure the feelings of; hurt keenly. **16.** *Informal.* To fail to attend purposely: *cut a class.* **17.** *Informal.* To cease; stop. **18.** *Sports.* To strike (the ball) so that it spins irregularly or is deflected. **19.** To perform: *cut a caper.* **20.** To terminate (a scene in a film). **21.** To record a performance on (a phonograph record). **22.** To edit (film or audio tape). —*intr.* **1.** To make an incision or separation. **2.** To allow incision or severing: *Butter cuts easily.* **3.** To use a sharp-edged instrument. **4.** To grow through the gums. Used of teeth. **5.** To penetrate injuriously. **6.** To change direction abruptly: *cut to the left.* **7.** To go directly and often hastily: *cut across the field.* **8.** To divide a pack of cards into two parts. —*n.* **1.** The act of incising, severing, or separating. **2.** The result of cutting; an incision. **3.** A part that has been severed from a main body: *a cut of beef.* **4.** A passage resulting from excavating or probing. **5.** An elimination or excision of a part: *a cut in a speech.* **6.** A reduction: *a salary cut.* **7.** The style in which a garment is cut. **8.** *Informal.* A share of profits or earnings. **9.** *Informal.* A wounding remark; an insult. **10.** *Informal.* An unexcused absence, as from school or a class. **11.** *Printing.* **a.** An engraved block or plate. **b.** A print made from such a block. **12.** *Sports.* A stroke that causes a ball to spin irregularly or to deflect. **13.** *Card Games.* The act of dividing a deck of cards into two parts, as before dealing. **14.** A sharp transition between shots or scenes in a film. **15.** One of the objects used in drawing lots. —**a cut above.** A little better than. [Middle English *cutten, kitten,* probably from late Old English *cyttan* (unattested), akin to Icelandic *kuta,* to cut with a knife, of North Germanic origin.]

cut-and-dried (kŭt′ən-drīd′) *adj.* **1.** Prepared and arranged in advance; settled. **2.** Ordinary; routine; lacking spontaneity.

cu·ta·ne·ous (kyo͞o-tā′nē-əs) *adj.* Of, pertaining to, or affecting the skin. [New Latin *cutaneus,* from Latin *cutis,* skin. See **skeu-** in Appendix.*] —**cu·ta′ne·ous·ly** *adv.*

cut·a·way (kŭt′ə-wā′) *n.* A man's formal daytime coat, with front edges sloping diagonally from the waist and forming tails at the back. Also called "cutaway coat."

cut·back (kŭt′băk′) *n.* **1.** A decrease; curtailment: *a cutback in production.* **2.** A **flashback** *(see).* **3.** A sharp reversal of direction, as of a ballcarrier in football.

cutch (kŭch) *n.* A resinous substance, **catechu** *(see).* [Malay *kachu,* CATECHU.]

Cutch (kŭch). Also **Kutch. 1.** A region of northwestern India on the Arabian Sea north of the Gulf of Cutch, now part of Gujarat State of the Republic of India. **2.** See **Rann of Cutch.**

cute (kyo͞ot) *adj.* **cuter, cutest. 1.** Delightfully pretty or dainty. **2.** Obviously contrived to charm; precious. **3.** *Archaic.* Shrewd; clever. [Short for ACUTE.] —**cute′ly** *adv.* —**cute′ness** *n.*

cut glass. Glassware shaped or decorated by cutting instruments or abrasive wheels.

cut·grass (kŭt′grăs′, -gräs′) *n.* Any of several swamp grasses of the genus *Leersia;* especially, *L. oryzoides,* having leaves with very rough margins.

Cuth·bert (kŭth′bərt), **Saint.** A.D. 635?–687. English monk; bishop of Lindisfarne.

cu·ti·cle (kyo͞o′tĭ-kəl) *n.* **1.** The epidermis. **2.** The strip of hardened skin at the base of a fingernail or toenail. **3.** *Zoology.* The noncellular, often horny protective outer covering in many invertebrates. **4.** *Botany.* The layer of cutin covering the epidermis of plants. [Latin *cutīcula,* diminutive of *cutis,* skin. See **skeu-** in Appendix.*] —**cu·tic′u·lar** (-tĭk′yə-lər) *adj.*

cu·tie (kyo͞o′tē) *n.* Also **cu·tey.** *Slang.* A cute person.

cut in. 1. To move into a line of people out of turn. **2.** To interrupt. **3.** To interrupt a dancing couple in order to dance with one of them.

cut-in (kŭt′ĭn′) *n.* An inserted shot, often a still close-up, interrupting the continuity of the main action of a film.

cu·tin (kyo͞o′tĭn) *n.* *Botany.* A waxlike, water-repellent material present in the walls of some plant cells, and forming the cuticle which covers the epidermis. [Latin *cut(is),* skin (see **skeu-** in Appendix*) + -IN.]

cu·tin·ize (kyo͞o′tə-nīz′) *v.* **-ized, -izing, -izes.** *Botany.* —*tr.* To coat or impregnate with cutin. —*intr.* To become coated or impregnated with cutin. —**cu′tin·i·za′tion** *n.*

cu·tis (kyo͞o′tĭs) *n.* *Anatomy.* The **corium** *(see).* [Latin *cutis,* skin. See **skeu-** in Appendix.*]

cut·lass (kŭt′ləs) *n.* Also **cut·las.** A short, heavy sword with a curved single-edged blade, once used as a weapon by sailors. [Variant of earlier *coutelace,* from Old French *coutelas,* from *coutel,* knife, from Latin *cultellus,* diminutive of *culter,* knife. See **skel-**[1] in Appendix.*]

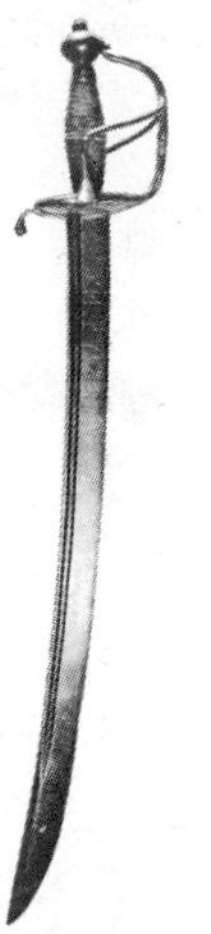

cutlass
Dated 1743

cutlass fish. Any of several marine fishes of the genus *Trichiurus,* having a long, narrow body and a pointed tail.

cut·ler (kŭt′lər) *n.* A person who makes, repairs, or sells knives or other cutting instruments. [Middle English, from Old French *coutelier,* from *coutel,* knife. See **cutlass.**]

cut·ler·y (kŭt′lĕr-ē) *n.* **1.** Cutting instruments and tools. **2.** Implements used as tableware. **3.** The occupation of a cutler.

cut·let (kŭt′lĭt) *n.* **1.** A thin slice of meat, usually veal or lamb, cut from the leg or ribs of an animal, and suitable for broiling or frying. **2.** A flat croquette of chopped meat or fish. [French *côtelette,* from Old French *costelette,* diminutive of *coste,* rib, from Latin *costa,* rib. See **kost-** in Appendix.*]

cut off. 1. To detach by severing. **2.** To discontinue; stop. **3.** To interrupt.

cut·off (kŭt′ôf′, -ŏf′) *n.* **1.** A designated limit or point of termination. **2.** A short cut or by-pass. **3.** A new channel cut by a river across the neck of an oxbow. **4. a.** A checking or cutting off of a flow of steam, water, or other fluid. **b.** The device that cuts off. **5.** *Music.* A conductor's signal indicating a stop or break in singing or playing.

cut out. 1. To be fitted or suited: *not cut out for city life.* **2.** *Slang.* To leave; depart. **3.** To cease; stop doing.

cut·out (kŭt′out′) *n.* **1.** Something cut out or intended to be cut out. **2.** *Electricity.* A device that interrupts, by-passes, or disconnects a circuit or circuit element.

cut·o·ver (kŭt′ō′vər) *adj.* Cleared of trees.

cut·purse (kŭt′pûrs′) *n.* *Archaic.* A pickpocket. [Originally one who cut off purses that were attached to a girdle.]

cut-rate (kŭt′rāt′) *adj.* Sold or on sale at a reduced price.

Cut·tack (kŭt′ək). A city of the Republic of India, in east-central Orissa. Population, 161,000.

cut·ter (kŭt′ər) *n.* **1.** One who cuts, especially in tailoring. **2.** A device or machine that cuts. **3.** *Nautical.* **a.** A single-masted fore-and-aft-rigged sailing vessel with a running bowsprit, a mainsail, and two or more headsails which are usually set flying. Compare **sloop. b.** A ship's boat, powered by a motor or oars, and used for transporting stores or passengers. **c.** A small, lightly armed motorboat used by the Coast Guard. **4.** A small sleigh, usually seating one person and drawn by a single horse.

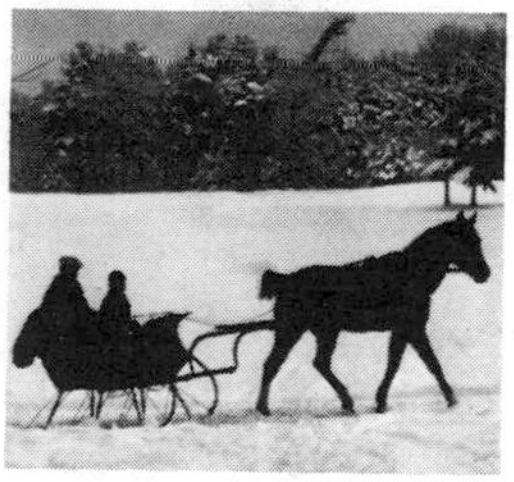

cutter

cut·throat (kŭt′thrōt′) *n.* One who cuts throats; a murderer. —*adj.* **1.** Cruel; murderous. **2.** Relentless or merciless in competition. **3.** *Games & Sports.* Of or designating a form of a game in which each of three players acts and scores for himself.

cut time. *Music.* A kind of measure, **alla breve** *(see).*

cut·ting (kŭt′ĭng) *adj.* **1.** Capable of or designed for incising, shearing, or severing. **2.** Sharply penetrating; piercing and cold: *a cutting wind.* **3.** Bitterly sarcastic or insulting: *a cutting remark.* —See Synonyms at **incisive.** —*n.* **1.** A part cut off from a main body. **2.** An excavation made through high ground in the construction of a road, railway, or the like. **3.** *Chiefly British.* A clipping, as from a newspaper. **4.** The editing of film or audio tape. **5.** *Horticulture.* A twig or similar plant part removed to form roots and propagate a new plant.

cut·tle (kŭt′l) *n.* *Rare.* A cuttlefish. [Middle English *codel,* Old English *cudele.* See **ku-** in Appendix.*]

cut·tle·bone (kŭt′l-bōn′) *n.* The calcareous internal shell of a cuttlefish, used as a dietary supplement for cage birds or ground into powder for use as a polishing agent.

cut·tle·fish (kŭt′l-fĭsh′) *n., pl.* **cuttlefish** or **-fishes.** Any of various squidlike cephalopod marine mollusks of the genus *Sepia,* having ten arms, a calcareous internal shell, and secreting a dark, inky fluid.

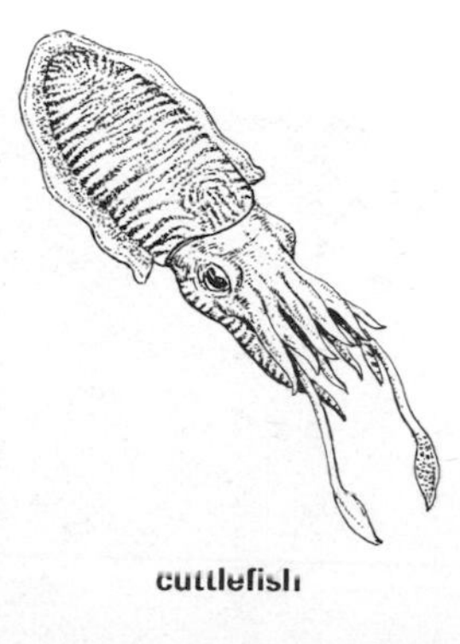

cuttlefish

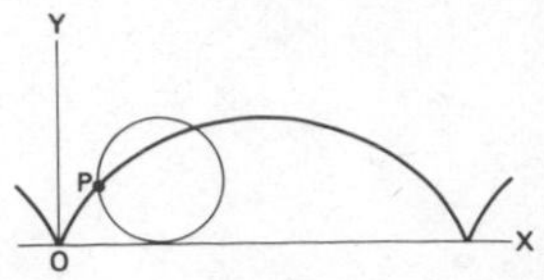

cycloid

cut up. **1.** To divide into pieces. **2.** To inflict lacerations upon. **3.** *Informal.* To behave mischievously. **4.** *Informal.* To criticize.
cut·up (kŭt′ŭp′) *n. Informal.* A mischievous person; prankster.
cut·wa·ter (kŭt′wô′tər) *n.* **1.** The forward part of a ship's prow. **2.** The wedge-shaped end of a bridge pier, designed to divide the current and break up ice floes.
cut·work (kŭt′wûrk′) *n.* Openwork embroidery in which the ground fabric is cut away from the design.
cut·worm (kŭt′wûrm′) *n.* The larva of any of various moths of the family Noctuidae, feeding on a wide variety of plants. [So called because many species eat through stems of plants.]
Cu·vi·er (ko͞o′vē-ā, kyo͞o′-; *French* kü-vyā′), Baron **Georges Léopold.** 1769–1832. French naturalist; founder of comparative anatomy and vertebrate paleontology.
Cuz·co (ko͞os′kō). Also **Cus·co.** A city and the former capital of the Inca Empire, in south-central Peru, 350 miles southeast of Lima. Population, 78,000.
CVG Airport code for Cincinnati, Ohio.
cvt. *Finance.* convertible.
cw, CW continuous wave.
cwm (ko͞om) *n. Welsh.* A steep hollow, a **cirque** *(see).*
CWO chief warrant officer.
c.w.o. **1.** cash with order. **2.** chief warrant officer.
CWS Chemical Warfare Service.
cwt. hundredweight.
-cy. Indicates: **1.** A quality or condition; for example, **bankruptcy.** **2.** Office or rank; for example, **baronetcy.** [Middle English *-cie,* from Old French, from Latin *-cia, -tia,* and Greek *-kiā, -tiā,* both abstract noun suffixes.]
cy·an (sī′ăn) *n.* Greenish blue; one of the subtractive primary colors; a complement of red. See **color, primary color.** [Greek *kuanos,* CYANO-.]
cy·an·am·ide (sī-ăn′ə-mĭd) *n.* Also **cy·an·am·id.** **1.** An irritating caustic acidic crystalline compound, $NCNH_2$, prepared by treating calcium cyanamide with sulfuric acid. **2.** A compound, **calcium cyanamide** *(see).* **3.** A salt or ester of cyanamide. [French : CYAN(O)- + AMIDE.]
cy·a·nate (sī′ə-nāt′, -nət) *n.* A salt or ester of cyanic acid. [CYAN(O)- + -ATE.]
cy·an·ic (sī-ăn′ĭk) *adj.* **1.** Pertaining to or containing cyanogen. **2.** Blue or bluish. [CYAN(O)- + -IC.]
cyanic acid. A poisonous, unstable, highly volatile organic acid, HOCN, used to prepare certain cyanates.
cy·a·nide (sī′ə-nīd′) *n.* Also **cy·an·id** (-nĭd). Any of various salts or esters of hydrogen cyanide containing a CN group; especially, the extremely poisonous compounds **potassium cyanide** and **sodium cyanide** *(both of which see).* —*tr.v.* **cyanided, -niding, -nides.** **1.** To treat (a metal surface) with cyanide to produce a hard surface. **2.** To treat (an ore) with cyanide to extract gold or silver. [CYAN(O)- + -IDE.]
cyanide process. A process of extracting gold or silver from ores treated with a solution of sodium or calcium cyanide.
cy·a·nine (sī′ə-nīn) *n.* Any of various blue dyes, used to extend the range of color sensitivity of photographic emulsions. [CYAN(O)- + -INE.]
cy·a·nite. *Mineralogy.* Variant of **kyanite.**
cyano-, cyan-. Indicates: **1.** A blue or dark-blue coloring; for example, **cyanine, cyanic.** **2.** *Chemistry.* Cyanide or cyanogen; for example, **cyanate, cyanotype.** [German *zyan-,* from Greek *kuanos,* dark-blue enamel, the color blue, from an unknown language of Asia Minor.]
cy·a·no·co·bal·a·min (sī′ə-nō′kō-bô′lə-mĭn) *n.* A form of vitamin B_{12}. [CYANO- + COBAL(T) + (VIT)AMIN.]
cy·an·o·gen (sī-ăn′ə-jən) *n. Chemistry.* **1.** A colorless, flammable, highly poisonous gas, C_2N_2, used as a rocket propellant, fumigant, military weapon, and in welding. **2.** The univalent radical CN found in simple and complex cyanide compounds. [French *cyanogène* : CYANO- + -GEN.]
cy·a·nosed (sī′ə-nōzd′) *adj. Pathology.* Afflicted with cyanosis. [From CYANOSIS.]
cy·a·no·sis (sī′ə-nō′sĭs) *n. Pathology.* A bluish discoloration of the skin, resulting from inadequate oxygenation of the blood. [New Latin, from Greek *kuanōsis,* dark-blue color : CYAN(O)- + -OSIS.] —**cy′a·not′ic** (-nŏt′ĭk) *adj.*
cy·an·o·type (sī-ăn′ə-tīp′) *n.* A **blueprint** *(see).*
cy·a·nu·ric acid (sī′ə-no͝or′ĭk, -nyo͝or′ĭk). A white crystalline acid, $C_3N_3(OH)_3$, that decomposes with heating to form cyanic acid. [CYAN(O)- + URIC ACID.]
Cyb·e·le (sĭb′ə-lē, kĭb′ə-lā) *n.* The Phrygian goddess of nature, the consort of Attis.
cy·ber·nate (sī′bər-nāt′) *v.* **-nated, -nating, -nates.** —*tr.* To control (an industrial process) automatically by computer. —*intr.* To become so controlled. [From CYBERNET(ICS) + -ATE.] —**cy′ber·na′tion** *n.*
cy·ber·net·ics (sī′bər-nĕt′ĭks) *n.* Plural in form, used with a singular verb. The theoretical study of control processes in electronic, mechanical, and biological systems, especially the mathematical analysis of the flow of information in such systems. [Coined by Norbert Wiener from Greek *kubernētēs,* pilot, governor, from *kubernan,* to steer, guide, GOVERN.] —**cy′ber·net′ic** *adj.* —**cy′ber·net′i·cist** *n.*
cy·cad (sī′kăd) *n.* Any seed-bearing plant of the family Cycadaceae, resembling a palm tree but surmounted by fernlike leaves. [New Latin *Cycas* (stem *Cycad-*), genus name, from Greek *kukas,* manuscript error for *koïkas,* accusative plural of *koïx,* doom palm, perhaps from Egyptian.]
Cyc·la·des (sĭk′lə-dēs). *Greek* **Ky·kla·des** (kē-klä′thez), **Ki·kla·dhes.** A group of Greek islands, 1,023 square miles in area, in the southern Aegean Sea, constituting a department of Greece. Population, 100,000. Capital, Hermoupolis, on Syros.

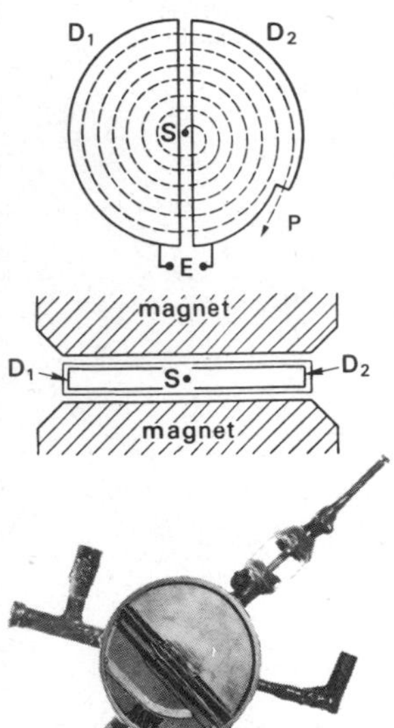

cyclotron
Above: Top view: D_1, D_2 form a hollow disk within which particles P from source S are accelerated outward by potential E
Center: Side view showing field magnets
Below: First cyclotron, 4½ inches in diameter, built at the University of California in 1930

cyc·la·men (sī′klə-mən, sĭk′lə-, -mĕn) *n.* Any of several plants of the genus *Cyclamen,* having showy white, pink, or red flowers with reflexed petals. Also called "sowbread." [New Latin, from Greek *kuklaminos,* probably from *kuklos,* a circle (from the bulbous roots). See **kwel-¹** in Appendix.*]
cy·cle (sī′kəl) *n.* **1.** A time interval in which a characteristic, especially a regularly repeated, event or sequence of events occurs. **2. a.** A single complete execution of a periodically repeated phenomenon. **b.** A periodically repeated sequence of events. **3.** The orbit of a celestial body. **4.** A long period of time; an age; eon. **5. a.** The aggregate of traditional poems or stories organized around a central theme or hero: *the Arthurian cycle.* **b.** A series of poems or songs on the same theme: *Schubert's song cycles.* **6.** A bicycle or motorcycle. **7.** *Botany.* A circular arrangement of flower parts such as petals or sepals. —*intr.v.* **cycled, -cling, -cles.** **1.** To occur in or pass through a cycle. **2.** To move in, or as if in, a circle. **3.** To ride a bicycle or motorcycle. [French, from Late Latin *cyclus,* from Greek *kuklos,* circle. See **kwel-¹** in Appendix.*]
cycle car. A light vehicle resembling a motorcycle but having three or four wheels.
cy·clic (sī′klĭk, sĭk′lĭk) *adj.* Also **cy·cli·cal** (-kəl). **1. a.** Of, relating to, or characterized by cycles. **b.** Recurring or moving in cycles. **2.** *Chemistry.* Of or pertaining to compounds having atoms arranged in a ring or closed-chain structure. **3.** *Botany.* **a.** Having parts arranged in a whorl. **b.** Forming a whorl. —**cy′cli·cal·ly** *adv.*
cy·clist (sī′klĭst) *n.* Also **cy·cler** (-klər). One who rides or races a bicycle, motorcycle, or similar vehicle.
cyclo-, cycl-. Indicates: **1.** Circle; for example, **cyclometer, cyclorama.** **2.** A cyclic compound; for example, **cyclohexane.** [From Greek *kuklos,* circle, CYCLE.]
cy·clo·hex·ane (sī′klō-hĕk′sān′) *n.* An extremely flammable, colorless, mobile liquid, C_6H_{12}, obtained from petroleum and benzene and used as a solvent, paint and varnish remover, and in the manufacture of nylon.
cy·cloid (sī′kloid′) *adj.* **1.** Resembling a circle. **2.** *Zoology.* Thin, rounded, and smooth-edged; disklike. Said of fish scales. **3.** *Psychiatry.* Designating a person afflicted with cyclothymia. —*n. Geometry.* The curve traced by a point on the circumference of a circle that rolls on a straight line. [French *cycloïde,* from Greek *kukloeidēs* : CYCL(O) + -OID.] —**cy·cloi′dal** *adj.*
cy·clom·e·ter (sī-klŏm′ə-tər) *n.* **1.** An instrument that records the revolutions of a wheel in order to indicate distance traveled. **2.** An instrument that measures circular arcs. [CYCLO- + -METER.] —**cy′clo·met′ric** (-klō-mĕt′rĭk) *adj.* —**cy·clom′e·try** *n.*
cy·clone (sī′klōn′) *n.* **1.** *Meteorology.* A type of atmospheric disturbance characterized by masses of air rapidly circulating clockwise in the southern and counterclockwise in the northern hemisphere, about a low-pressure center, usually accompanied by stormy, often destructive, weather. **2.** Loosely, any violent, rotating windstorm, such as a **tornado** *(see).* —See Synonyms at **wind.** [Probably from Greek *kuklōma,* coil, wheel, from *kuklos,* circle, CYCLE.] —**cy·clon′ic** (-klŏn′ĭk), **cy·clon′i·cal** *adj.* —**cy·clon′i·cal·ly** *adv.*
cyclone cellar. An underground shelter in or adjacent to a house, used for protection from cyclones, tornadoes, or the like. Also called "storm cellar."
cy·clo·par·af·fin (sī′klō-păr′ə-fĭn) *n.* Any of a class of hydrocarbons, including cyclopropane, cyclopentane, and cyclohexane, in which at least three carbon atoms per molecule are joined in a ring structure and each such carbon in the ring is bonded to two hydrogen atoms or alkyl groups.
cy·clo·pe·an (sī′klə-pē′ən, sī-klō′pē-ən) *adj.* **1.** *Often capital* **C.** Pertaining to or suggestive of the Cyclopes. **2.** Pertaining to or designating a primitive style of masonry characterized by the use of massive stones of irregular shape and size.
cy·clo·pe·di·a (sī′klə-pē′dē-ə) *n.* Also **cy·clo·pae·di·a.** An encyclopedia. [Short for ENCYCLOPEDIA.]
cy·clo·pe·dic (sī′klə-pē′dĭk) *adj.* Also **cy·clo·pae·dic.** Encyclopedic. —**cy′clo·pe′di·cal·ly** *adv.*
cy·clo·pe·dist (sī′klə-pē′dĭst) *n.* Also **cy·clo·pae·dist.** One who compiles or contributes to an encyclopedia.
cy·clo·pen·tane (sī′klə-pĕn′tān, sĭk′lə-) *n.* A colorless flammable liquid, C_5H_{10}, derived from petroleum and used as a solvent and motor fuel.
cy·clo·ple·gi·a (sī′klə-plē′jē-ə) *n.* Loss of visual accommodation because of paralysis of the ciliary muscles of the eye. [New Latin : CYCLO- + -PLEGIA.]
cy·clo·pro·pane (sī′klə-prō′pān) *n.* A highly flammable, explosive, colorless gas, C_3H_6, used as an anesthetic.
Cy·clops (sī′klŏps) *pl.* **Cyclopes** (sī-klō′pēz). *Greek Mythology.* **1.** Any of the three one-eyed Titans who forged thunderbolts for Zeus. **2.** Any of a race of one-eyed giants, reputedly descended from these Titans, inhabiting the island of Sicily. [Latin *Cyclōps,* from Greek *Kuklōps*†.]
cy·clo·ram·a (sī′klə-răm′ə, -rä′mə) *n.* **1.** A large composite picture placed on the interior walls of a cylindrical room so as to appear in natural perspective to a spectator standing in the center. **2.** A large curtain or wall, usually concave, placed or hung at the rear of a stage. [CYCL(O)- + (PAN)ORAMA.] —**cy′clo·ram′ic** *adj.*
cy·clo·sis (sī-klō′sĭs) *n., pl.* **-ses** (-sēz). The streaming circulatory motion of protoplasm within certain cells and cell structures. [New Latin, from Greek *kuklōsis,* a surrounding, from *kukloun,* to surround, from *kuklos,* a circle, CYCLE.]
cy·clo·stome (sī′klə-stōm′) *n.* Any of various primitive eellike vertebrates of the class Agnatha, such as a lamprey, lacking

jaws and true teeth and having a circular, sucking mouth. [New Latin *Cyclostomi*, "round-mouths" and *Cyclostomata*, "round-mouthed" : CYCLO- + -STOME.] —**cy·clos′to·mate′** (sī-klŏs′tə-māt′), **cy′clo·stom′a·tous** (sī′klō-stŏm′ə-təs) *adj.*

cy·clo·thyme (sī′klə-thīm′) *n. Psychiatry.* A person afflicted with cyclothymia.

cy·clo·thy·mi·a (sī′klə-thī′mē-ə) *n. Psychiatry.* A form of manic-depressive psychosis characterized by alternating periods of activity and excitement and periods of inactivity and depression. [New Latin, from German *Zyklothymie* : CYCLO- + -THYMIA.]

cy·clo·thy·mic (sī′klə-thī′mĭk) *adj.* Of or characterized by cyclothymia. —*n.* A cyclothyme.

cy·clo·tron (sī′klə-trŏn′) *n. Physics.* A circular accelerator capable of generating particle energies between a few million and several tens of millions of electron volts, in which charged particles generated at a central source are accelerated spirally outward in a plane at right angles to a fixed magnetic field by an alternating electric field. [CYCLO- + -TRON.]

cy·der. *Chiefly British.* Variant of **cider.**

Cy·do·ni·a. The ancient name for **Canea.**

cy·e·sis (sī-ē′sĭs) *n., pl.* **-ses** (-sēz). Pregnancy; gestation. [New Latin, from Greek *kuēsis*, from *kuein*, to be pregnant, to swell. See **keu-**[3] in Appendix.*]

cyg·net (sĭg′nĭt) *n.* A young swan. [Middle English *sygnett*, diminutive of Old French *cygne*, swan, from Latin *cycnus*, *cygnus*, from Greek *kuknos*. See **keuk-** in Appendix.*]

Cyg·nus (sĭg′nəs) *n.* A constellation in the Northern Hemisphere near Lacerta and Lyra, containing the star Deneb. Also called "Northern Cross," "Swan." [Latin *cygnus*, swan. See **cygnet.**]

cyl·in·der (sĭl′ən-dər) *n. Abbr.* **cyl. 1.** *Geometry.* **a.** A surface generated by a straight line moving parallel to a fixed straight line and intersecting a plane curve. **b.** The portion of such a surface bounded by two parallel planes and the regions of the planes bounded by the surface. **c.** A solid bounded by two parallel planes and such a surface having a closed curve, especially a circle, as a directrix. **2.** Any cylindrical container or object. **3.** *Engineering.* **a.** The chamber in which a piston of a reciprocating engine moves. **b.** The chamber of a pump from which fluid is expelled by a piston. **4.** The rotating chamber of a revolver that holds the cartridges. **5.** Any of the rotating cylinders in a printing press that carry the paper or the curved printing plate, or receive the ink or impression. **6.** *Archaeology.* A cylindrical stone or clay object with an engraved design or inscription. —*tr.v.* **cylindered, -dering, -ders.** To press or furnish with a cylinder. [Old French *cylindre*, from Latin *cylindrus*, from Greek *kulindros*, roller, cylinder, from *kulindein*, to revolve, roll. See **skel-**[3] in Appendix.*]

cylinder head. The closed, often detachable, end of a cylinder or cylinders in an internal-combustion engine.

cy·lin·dri·cal (sə-lĭn′drĭ-kəl) *adj. Abbr.* **cyl.** Also **cy·lin·dric** (-drĭk). **1.** Having the shape of a cylinder, especially of a circular cylinder. **2.** Of or pertaining to a cylinder. **3.** Of or pertaining to the coordinate system, or to any of three coordinates in it, formed by two polar coordinates in a plane and a rectangular coordinate measured perpendicularly from the plane. —**cy·lin′dri·cal′i·ty** (-kăl′ə-tē) *n.* —**cy·lin′dri·cal·ly** *adv.*

cyl·in·droid (səl′ĭn-droid′) *n.* A cylindrical surface or solid all of whose sections perpendicular to the elements are elliptical. —*adj.* Resembling a cylinder.

cy·lix. Variant of **kylix.**

Cym. Cymric.

cy·ma (sī′mə) *n., pl.* **-mae** (-mē′) or **-mas.** *Architecture.* A molding for a cornice, having a partly concave and partly convex curve in profile, used especially in classical architecture. [Greek *kuma*, anything swollen, waved molding, from *kuein*, to swell, be pregnant. See **keu-**[3] in Appendix.*]

cy·ma·ti·um (sī-mā′shē-əm) *n., pl.* **-tia** (-shē-ə). **1.** A cyma. **2.** The topmost molding of a classical cornice. [Latin *cȳmatium*, from Greek *kumation*, diminutive of *kuma*, molding, CYMA.]

cym·bal (sĭm′bəl) *n.* **1.** One of a pair of concave brass plates that are struck together as percussion instruments. **2.** A single brass plate, sounded by hitting with a drumstick and often part of a set of drums. [Middle English, from Old French *symbale*, from Latin *cymbalum*, from Greek *kumbalon*, from *kumbē*, hollow of a vessel, a cup. See **keu-**[2] in Appendix.*] —**cym′bal·eer′, cym′bal·er, cym′bal·ist** *n.*

cyme (sīm) *n. Botany.* An often flat-topped flower cluster that blooms from the center toward the edges, and whose main axis is always terminated by a flower. [New Latin *cyma*, from Latin *cȳma*, young cabbage sprout, from Greek *kuma*, anything swollen, CYMA.] —**cy·mif′er·ous** (sī-mĭf′ər-əs) *adj.*

cy·mene (sī′mēn′) *n. Chemistry.* Any of three colorless isomeric liquid hydrocarbons, $C_{10}H_{14}$, obtained chiefly from the essential oils of various plants and used in the manufacture of synthetic resins. [French *cymène*, from Greek *kuminon*, CUMIN.]

cym·ling (sĭm′lĭng) *n.* Also **cym·lin** (-lĭn), **sim·lin.** A greenish-white, flat, round squash with a scalloped edge. Also called "pattypan squash." [Probably variant of SIMNEL.]

cy·mo·gene (sī′mə-jēn′) *n.* A flammable gaseous fraction of petroleum, chiefly butane. [CYM(ENE) + -GENE.]

cy·mo·graph. Variant of **kymograph.**

cy·moid (sī′moid′) *adj.* Resembling a cyma or cyme. [CYM(E) or CYM(A) + -OID.]

cy·mo·phane (sī′mə-fān′) *n.* A variety of chrysoberyl having an undulating luster. [French : Greek *kuma*, undulation, CYMA + -PHANE.]

cy·mose (sī′mōs′, sī-mōs′) *adj.* Also **cy·mous** (sī′məs). *Botany.* **1.** Pertaining to or resembling a cyme. **2.** Bearing a cyme or cymes. [CYM(E) + -OSE.] —**cy′mose′ly** *adv.*

Cym·ric (kĭm′rĭk, sĭm′rĭk) *adj.* Also **Kym·ric** (kĭm′rĭk). *Abbr.* **Cym.** Of or pertaining to the Cymry; Brythonic. —*n.* The Brythonic branch of the Celtic languages, including Welsh, Breton, and Cornish.

Cym·ry (kĭm′rē, sĭm′rē) *n.* Also **Cym·ri, Kym·ry.** The branch of the Celtic people to which the Welsh, the Cornish, and the Bretons belong. [Welsh *Cymry*, the Welsh, Wales, CAMBRIA.]

Cyn·e·wulf (kĭn′ə-wo͝olf). Also **Cyn·wulf, Kyn·e·wulf.** Anglo-Saxon poet of the late eighth century A.D.

cyn·ic (sĭn′ĭk) *n.* **1.** *Capital* **C.** A member of a sect, founded by Antisthenes of Athens, of ancient Greek philosophers who believed virtue to be the only good and self-control to be the only means of achieving virtue. **2.** A person who believes all men are motivated by selfishness. —*adj.* **1.** *Capital* **C.** Of or pertaining to the Cynics or their doctrines. **2.** Cynical. [Latin *cynicus*, from Greek *kunikos*, "doglike," currish (perhaps mistaken by the Greeks from the first part of *kunosarge*, the gymnasium where Antisthenes taught), from *kuōn* (stem *kun-*), dog. See **kwon-** in Appendix.*]

cyn·i·cal (sĭn′ĭ-kəl) *adj.* **1.** Scornful of the motives or virtue of others; bitterly mocking; sneering. **2.** *Capital* **C.** Of or pertaining to the Cynics or their doctrines. —**cyn′i·cal·ly** *adv.* —**cyn′i·cal·ness** *n.*

cyn·i·cism (sĭn′ə-sĭz′əm) *n.* **1.** A cynical attitude or character. **2.** A cynical comment or act. **3.** *Capital* **C.** The beliefs and doctrines of the Cynics.

cy·no·sure (sī′nə-sho͝or′, sĭn′ə-) *n.* **1.** An object that serves as a focal point of attention and admiration; a center of interest or attraction. **2.** Anything that serves to guide. [French, Ursa Minor, "the guiding star," from Latin *cynosūra*, from Greek *kunosoura*, "the dog's tail," Ursa Minor : *kunos*, genitive of *kuōn*, dog (see **kwon-** in Appendix*) + *-ura*, plural of *-urus*, -UROUS.] —**cy′no·sur′al** *adj.*

Cyn·thi·a[1] (sĭn′thē-ə). A feminine given name. [Latin, from Greek *Kunthia*, title of Artemis (who was born on Mount *Cynthus*, on the island of Delos, Greece).]

Cyn·thi·a[2] (sĭn′thē-ə). *Greek Mythology.* Artemis, goddess of the moon.

Cyn·thi·a[3] (sĭn′thē-ə) *n. Poetic.* The moon or its personification.

CYO Catholic Youth Organization.

cy·pher. Variant of **cipher.**

cy·press (sī′prəs) *n.* **1.** Any evergreen tree of the genus *Cupressus*, growing in warm climates, and having small, compressed needles. **2.** Any of several similar or related trees, such as one of the genus *Chamaecyparis*, or the **bald cypress** *(see)*. **3.** The wood of any of these trees. **4.** Cypress branches used as a symbol of mourning. [Middle English *cipres*, from Old French, from Late Latin *cypressus*, from Greek *kuparissos*, of Mediterranean origin.]

cypress spurge. A plant, *Euphorbia cyparissias*, native to Eurasia, having densely crowded, narrow leaves and clusters of yellow-green flowers. [Probably because its narrow leaves suggest the needles of the cypress.]

cypress vine. A tropical American vine, *Quamoclit pennata*, having finely divided compound leaves and scarlet flowers.

Cyp·ri·an (sĭp′rē-ən) *adj.* **1.** Of or pertaining to Cyprus, its people, their customs, or their language. **2.** Characteristic of or resembling the ancient worship of Aphrodite on Cyprus; licentious; wanton; lewd. —*n.* **1.** A **Cypriot** *(see)*. **2.** *Obsolete.* A wanton person, especially a prostitute.

cy·pri·nid (sĭp′rə-nĭd) *n.* Any of numerous often small freshwater fishes of the family Cyprinidae, which includes the minnows, carps, and shiners. —*adj.* Of, relating to, or belonging to the family Cyprinidae. [New Latin *Cyprinidae* : *Cyprinus* (genus name), from Latin *cyprīnus*, a carp, from Greek *kuprinos*, from *kupros*, "the henna plant," from Semitic, akin to Hebrew *kōpher* + -ID.]

cy·prin·o·dont (sĭ-prĭn′ə-dŏnt′, sĭ-prī′nə-) *n.* Any of various small, soft-finned fishes of the family Cyprinodontidae, which includes the killifishes, topminnows, and many species popular in home aquariums. [New Latin *Cyprinodon* : Latin *cyprinus*, carp (see **cyprinid**) + -ODONT.]

cyp·ri·noid (sĭp′rə-noid′, sĭ-prī′-) *adj.* Of, pertaining to, or resembling a carp or related fish. —*n.* A cyprinoid fish. [New Latin *Cyprinoidea* : *Cyprinus*, genus (see **cyprinid**) + -OID.]

Cyp·ri·ot (sĭp′rē-ōt) *n.* Also **Cyp·ri·ote. 1.** A native or inhabitant of Cyprus. Also called "Cyprian." **2.** The ancient Greek dialect of Cyprus, belonging to the Arcado-Cyprian. —*adj.* Also **Cyp·ri·ote. 1.** Of or pertaining to Cyprus. **2.** Of or pertaining to the Cypriot language. [French, from CYPRUS.]

cyp·ri·pe·di·um (sĭp′rə-pē′dē-əm) *n.* Any orchid of the genus *Cypripedium*, which includes the lady's-slippers. [New Latin, probably "Venus' slipper" : Late Latin *Cypris*, Venus, from Greek *Kupris*, Aphrodite, from *Kupros*, CYPRUS (supposedly her birthplace) + New Latin *-pedium*, probably a variant of Greek *pedilon*, sandal (see **ped-**[1] in Appendix*).]

Cy·prus (sī′prəs). An island republic, 3,572 square miles in area, in the Mediterranean off southern Turkey; a former British colony, independent since 1961, and a member of the Commonwealth of Nations. Population, 588,000. Capital, Nicosia. [Latin, from Greek *Kupros*†. See also **copper.**]

cyp·se·la (sĭp′sə-lə) *n., pl.* **-lae** (-lē′). *Botany.* An achene that does not separate from its calyx, characteristic of composite plants. [New Latin, from Greek *kupselē*, hollow vessel, chest. See **keu-**[2] in Appendix.*]

Cyr·a·no de Ber·ge·rac (sîr′ə-nō də bûr′zhə răk; *French* sē

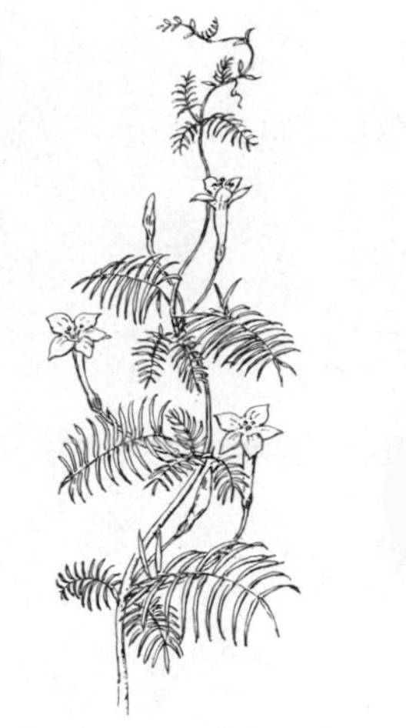

cypress vine

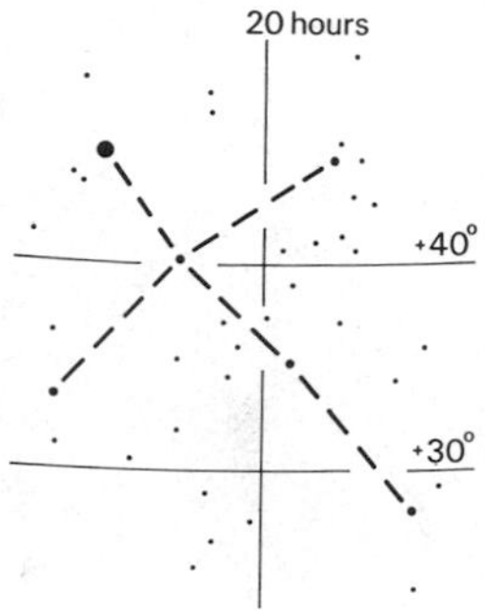

Cygnus

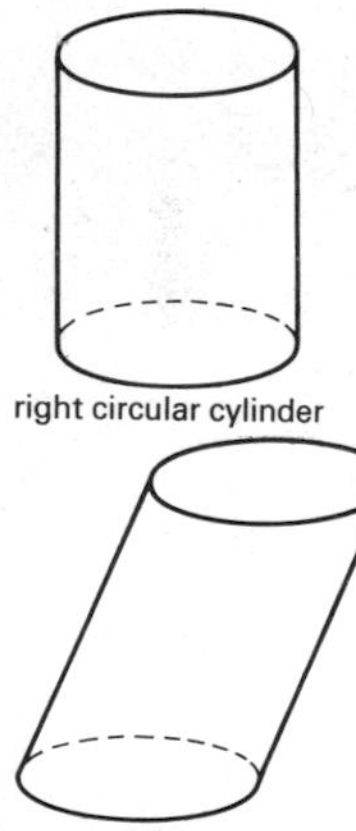

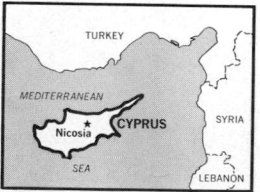

right circular cylinder

oblique circular cylinder

cylinder

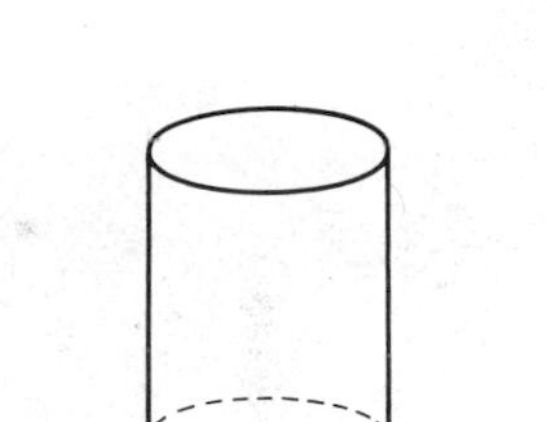

Cyprus

rä-nō′ də bĕr-zhə-räk′), **Savinien de.** 1619–1655. French author of satirical prose; fought over 1,000 duels.

Cyr·e·na·ic (sîr′ə-nā′ĭk, sîr′-) *adj.* **1.** Of or pertaining to Cyrenaica or its major city, Cyrene. **2.** Of or pertaining to the hedonistic school of philosophy founded in Cyrene by Aristippus, who believed that pleasure is the only good in life. —*n.* **1.** A native or inhabitant of Cyrenaica or Cyrene. **2.** A disciple of the Cyrenaic school of philosophy.

Cyr·e·na·i·ca (sîr′ə-nā′ĭ-kə, sîr′-). A region of northeastern Libya, first settled by the Greeks around 630 B.C.

Cy·re·ne (sî-rē′nē). An ancient Greek city of Cyrenaica.

Cyril (sîr′əl). A masculine given name. [Greek *Kurillos,* probably from *kurios,* master, lord. See **keu-**³ in Appendix.*]

Cyril (sîr′əl), **Saint.** A.D. 827–869. Greek Christian theologian; with his brother, **Saint Methodius** (A.D. 826–885), missionary to the Moravians; regarded as inventor of Cyrillic alphabet.

Cy·ril·lic (sə-rĭl′ĭk) *adj.* **1.** Of or pertaining to Saint Cyril, the ninth-century missionary to the Moravians. **2.** Of or designating the Cyrillic alphabet.

Cyrillic alphabet. An old Slavic alphabet ascribed to Saint Cyril, presently used in modified form for Russian, Bulgarian, certain other Slavic languages, and other languages of the Soviet Union.

Cy·rus¹ (sî′rəs). A masculine given name. [Greek *Kuros,* from Persian *kuru†.*]

Cy·rus² (sî′rəs). Called "the Elder," "the Great." 600?–529 B.C. King of Persia (550–529 B.C.); founder of the Persian Empire.

Cy·rus³. The ancient name for **Kura.**

CYS Airport code for Cheyenne, Wyoming.

cyst (sĭst) *n.* **1.** *Pathology.* An abnormal membranous sac containing a gaseous, liquid, or semisolid substance. **2.** *Anatomy.* Any sac or vesicle in the body. **3.** *Biology.* A capsulelike membrane of certain organisms in a resting stage. **4.** *Botany.* Any of various cells of nonsexual origin in green algae, that germinate and produce new plants after a resting period. [New Latin *cystis,* from Greek *kustis,* bladder, pouch. See **kwes-** in Appendix.*]

cys·tec·to·my (sĭ-stĕk′tə-mē) *n., pl.* **-mies. 1.** Surgical removal of a cyst. **2.** Surgical excision of the gall bladder or of a portion of the urinary bladder. [CYST + -ECTOMY.]

cys·te·ine (sĭs′tē-ēn′, -tē-ĭn) *n.* An amino acid, C₃H₇NO₂S, found in most proteins, especially in keratin. [From CYSTINE.]

cys·tic (sĭs′tĭk) *adj.* **1.** Of, pertaining to, or like a cyst. **2.** Having or containing a cyst or cysts. **3.** Enclosed in a cyst. **4.** *Anatomy.* Pertaining to the gall bladder or urinary bladder.

cys·ti·cer·coid (sĭs′tə-sûr′koid) *n.* The larval stage of certain tapeworms, like a cysticercus but having the scolex completely filling the enclosing sac. [CYSTICERC(US) + -OID.]

cys·ti·cer·cus (sĭs′tə-sûr′kəs) *n., pl.* **-ci** (-sī′). The larval stage of many tapeworms, consisting of a scolex enclosed in a fluid-filled sac. [New Latin, "bladder tail" : CYST(O)- + Greek *kerkos,* tail (see **ker-**² in Appendix*).]

cystic fibrosis. A congenital disease of mucous glands throughout the body, usually developing during childhood and causing pancreatic insufficiency and pulmonary disorders.

cys·tine (sĭs′tēn) *n.* A white crystalline compound, C₆H₁₂N₂O₄S₂, the principal sulfur-containing amino acid of protein. [CYST(O)- + -INE.]

cys·ti·tis (sĭs-tī′tĭs) *n.* Inflammation of the urinary bladder. [New Latin : CYST(O)- + -ITIS.]

cysto-, cyst-. Indicates a bladder or cyst; for example, **cystocele, cystoid.** [From Greek *kustis,* bladder. See **skeu-** in Appendix.*]

cys·to·carp (sĭs′tə-kärp′) *n. Botany.* A structure consisting of fertile filaments and carpospores, developed after fertilization of the carpogonium in red algae. [CYSTO- + -CARP.]

cys·to·cele (sĭs′tə-sēl) *n.* Hernia of the bladder. [CYSTO- + -CELE (hernia).]

cys·toid (sĭs′toid′) *adj.* Formed like or resembling a cyst. —*n.* A cystoid structure. [CYST(O)- + -OID.]

cys·to·lith (sĭs′tə-lĭth) *n.* **1.** *Botany.* A mineral concretion, usually calcium carbonate, formed in the cellulose wall of plant cells. **2.** *Pathology.* A urinary calculus. [CYSTO- + -LITH.]

cys·to·scope (sĭs′tə-skōp′) *n.* A tubular instrument fitted with a light and used to examine the urinary bladder and ureter. [CYSTO- + -SCOPE.] —**cys·to·scop·ic** (-skŏp′ĭk) *adj.*

–cyte. Indicates a cell; for example, **leukocyte.** [New Latin -*cyta,* from Greek *kutos,* hollow vessel. See **kwes-** in Appendix.*]

Cy·the·ra (sə-thîr′ə). *Modern Greek* **Ki·thi·ra** (kē′thē-rä). A Greek island situated between the Peloponnesus and Crete; chief center of the Aphrodite cult in antiquity.

Cyth·e·re·a. See **Aphrodite.**

cyto-, cyt-. Indicates cell; for example, **cytokinesis, cytosine.** [From Greek *kutos,* hollow vessel. See **skeu-** in Appendix.*]

cy·to·chem·is·try (sī′tō-kĕm′ĭs-trē) *n.* The chemistry of plant and animal cells. —**cy′to·chem′i·cal** *adj.*

cy·to·chrome (sī′tō-krōm′) *n.* Any of a class of iron-containing proteins important in cell metabolism. [CYTO- + -CHROME.]

cy·to·gen·e·sis (sī′tō-jĕn′ə-sĭs) *n.* Also **cy·tog·e·ny** (sī′tŏj′ə-nē). The formation and development of cells. [CYTO- + -GENESIS.] —**cy′to·ge·net′ic** (sī′tō-jə-nĕt′ĭk) *adj.*

cy·to·ge·net·ics (sī′tō-jə-nĕt′ĭks) *n.* Plural in form, used with a singular verb. The study of heredity by cytological and genetic methods. —**cy′to·ge·net′i·cal** *adj.* —**cy′to·ge·net′i·cal·ly** *adv.* —**cy′to·ge·net′i·cist** *n.*

cy·to·ki·ne·sis (sī′tō-kĭ-nē′sĭs, -kī-nē′sĭs) *n.* The cleavage of cytoplasm during cell division. [New Latin : CYTO- + -KINESIS.]

cy·tol·o·gy (sī-tŏl′ə-jē) *n. Abbr.* **cytol.** The branch of biology dealing with the study of the formation, structure, and function of cells. [CYTO- + -LOGY.] —**cy′to·log′ic** (-tə-lŏj′ĭk), **cy′to·log′i·cal** *adj.* —**cy′tol′o·gist** *n.*

cy·tol·y·sin (sī-tŏl′ə-sĭn) *n.* An antibody capable of destroying an animal cell partially or completely. [CYTOLYS(IS) + -IN.]

cy·tol·y·sis (sī-tŏl′ə-sĭs) *n.* The dissolution of a cell. [New Latin : CYTO- + -LYSIS.] —**cy′to·lyt′ic** (sī′tə-lĭt′ĭk) *adj.*

cy·toph·a·gy (sī-tŏf′ə-jē) *n.* The devouring of other cells by the phagocytes. [CYTO- + -PHAGY.] —**cy′to·phag′ic** (sī′tə-făj′ĭk), **cy·toph′a·gous** *adj.*

cy·to·plasm (sī′tə-plăz′əm) *n.* The protoplasm outside a cell nucleus. [CYTO- + -PLASM.] —**cy′to·plas′mic** *adj.* —**cy′to·plas′mi·cal·ly** *adv.*

cy·to·plast (sī′tə-plăst′) *n.* The cytoplasm within a single cell. [CYTO- + -PLAST.] —**cy′to·plas′tic** *adj.*

cy·to·sine (sī′tō-sēn′, -zēn′, -sən) *n.* A pyrimidine base, C₄H₅N₃O, that is an essential constituent of both ribonucleic and deoxyribonucleic acids. [CYT(O)- + -OS(E) + -INE.]

cy·to·tax·on·o·my (sī′tō-tăk-sŏn′ə-mē) *n.* The classification of organisms based on cellular structure, especially on the comparative morphology of chromosomes. —**cy′to·tax′o·nom′ic** (-tăk′sə-nŏm′ĭk) *adj.* —**cy′to·tax·on′o·mist** *n.*

CZ Canal Zone (with Zip Code).

C.Z. Canal Zone.

czar (zär) *n.* Also **tsar, tzar. 1.** A king or emperor; especially, one of the former emperors of Russia. **2.** A tyrant; autocrat. **3.** *Informal.* One in authority; leader: *a czar of finance.* [Polish, from Russian *tsar′,* from Old Russian *tsĭsarĭ,* from Gothic *kaisar,* from Latin *Caesar,* emperor, CAESAR.] —**czar′dom** *n.*

Usage: *Czar* is the most common form in American usage and virtually the only one employed in the extended senses (*any tyrant* or, informally, *one in authority*). But *tsar* is preferred by most scholars of Slavic studies as a more accurate transliteration of the Russian, and is often found in scholarly writing with reference to one of the Russian emperors.

czar·das (chär′däsh) *n.* **1.** An intricate Hungarian dance characterized by variations in tempo. **2.** Music for this dance. [Hungarian *csárdás.*]

czar·e·vitch (zär′ə-vĭch) *n.* The eldest son of a czar. [Polish, from Russian *tsarevich* : *tsar′,* CZAR + -*evich,* masculine patronymic suffix.]

cza·rev·na (zä-rĕv′nə) *n.* **1.** The daughter of a czar. **2.** The wife of a czarevitch. [Polish, from Russian *tsarevna* : *tsar′,* CZAR + -*evna,* feminine patronymic suffix.]

cza·ri·na (zä-rē′nə) *n.* Also **cza·rit·za** (zä-rĭt′sə). The wife of a czar; an empress of Russia. [Polish, from Russian *tsarina* : *tsar′,* CZAR + -*ina,* feminine suffix.]

czar·ism (zär′ĭz′əm) *n.* The system of government in Russia under the czars; absolute monarchy; autocracy. —**czar′ist** *adj.*

Czech (chĕk) *n.* **1.** A native or inhabitant of Czechoslovakia; especially, a Bohemian, Moravian, or Slovak. **2.** The West Slavic language of these people. Formerly called "Bohemian." [Polish, from Czech *Čechy.*] —**Czech** *adj.*

Czech·o·slo·va·ki·a (chĕk′ə-slō-vä′kē-ə, -văk′ē-ə). *Czech* **Čes·ko·slo·ven·sko** (chĕs′kō-slō′vĕn-skō). *Abbr.* **Czech.** A socialist republic of central Europe, 49,366 square miles in area, formed in 1918 by the Czechs and Slovaks from territories which were part of the Austro-Hungarian Empire. Population, 14,107,000. Capital, Prague. [From CZECH + SLOVAK.] —**Czech′o·slo′vak, Czech′o·slo·vak′i·an** *adj. & n.*

Czer·no·witz. The German name for **Chernovtsy.**

Czer·ny (chĕr′nē), **Karl.** 1791-1857. Austrian pianist, teacher, and composer of piano exercises.

Czę·sto·cho·wa (chĕN′stô-KHO′vä). *Russian* **Chen·sto·khov** (chĕn-stə-KHôf′). A city of south-central Poland, on the Warta River. Population, 173,000.

ă pat/ā pay/âr care/ä father/b bib/ch church/d deed/ĕ pet/ē be/f fife/g gag/h hat/hw which/ĭ pit/ī pie/îr pier/j judge/k kick/l lid, needle/m mum/n no, sudden/ng thing/ŏ pot/ō toe/ô paw, for/oi noise/ou out/ŏŏ took/ōō boot/p pop/r roar/s sauce/sh ship, dish/

Czechoslovakia

Dd

Around 1000 B.C. the Phoenicians and other Semites of Syria and Palestine began to use a graphic sign in the form of a triangle (1,2). They gave it the name dāleth, *meaning "door," and used it for the consonant* d. *After 900 B.C. the Greeks borrowed the sign from the Phoenicians, using different forms of the triangle (3,5,6) and also a semicircular form (4). They also changed its name to* delta. *The semicircular form (4) passed via Etrusean to the Roman alphabet (7). The Roman Monumental Capital (8) is the prototype of our modern capital, printed (11) and written (12). The written Roman form (7) developed into the late Roman and medieval Uncial (9) and Cursive (10), in which the semicircular part was prolonged upward and the originally vertical line was curved. These are the bases of our modern small letter, printed (13) and written (14).*

d, D (dē) *n., pl.* **d's** *or rare* **ds, D's** *or* **Ds. 1.** The fourth letter of the modern English alphabet. See **alphabet. 2.** Any of the speech sounds represented by this letter.
d, D, d., D. *Note:* As an abbreviation or symbol, *d* may be a small or a capital letter, with or without a period. Established forms or those generally preferred precede the definition. When no form is given, all four forms are in general use in that sense. **1. d.** *Genealogy.* dam. **2. d.** date. **3. d.** daughter. **4. d** day. **5. D.** December. **6. d** deci-. **7. D, D.** democrat; democratic. **8. D.** department. **9. d., D.** deputy. **10. D.** Deus. **11. D** deuterium. **12. d** *Physics.* deuteron. **13. d** dextro-. **14. d.** died. **15. D.** *Optics.* diopter. **16. D.** doctor (in academic degrees). **17. D.** Dominus. **18. D.** Don (title). **19. d., D.** dose. **20. d., D.** drachma. **21. D.** duchess. **22. D.** duke. **23. D.** Dutch. **24. D** The Roman numeral for 500. **25. d.** *British.* penny (Latin *denarius*). **26.** The fourth in a series. **27. D** The lowest passing grade given to a student in a school or college. **28. D** *Music.* **a.** The second tone in the scale of C major, or the fourth tone in the relative minor scale. **b.** The key or a scale in which D is the tonic. **c.** A written or printed note representing this tone. **d.** A string, key, or pipe tuned to the pitch of this tone.
–'d. 1. Contraction of *had, should, would,* or *did,* as in *Who'd you see?* **2.** Contraction of *-ed,* as in *martyr'd.*
da deca-.
Da. Danish.
D.A. district attorney.
dab¹ (dăb) *v.* **dabbed, dabbing, dabs.** *—tr.* **1.** To apply with short, poking strokes. **2.** To cover lightly with or as with a moist substance. **3.** To strike or hit lightly, as with a quick pat of the hand. *—intr.* **1.** To peck at something; to poke. **2.** To tap gently; to pat. *—n.* **1. a.** A small amount. **b.** A small mass or lump of substance: *a dab of jelly.* **2.** A quick, light pat, as with the hand. [Middle English *dabben*, probably from Middle Dutch *dabben†*, to tap.]
dab² (dăb) *n.* Any of various flatfishes, chiefly of the genera *Limanda* and *Hippoglossoides*, related to and resembling the flounders. [Middle English *dabbe*, perhaps originally "a soft flattish mass," from *dabbe*, light stroke, from *dabben*, DAB (verb).]
dab³ (dăb) *n. British Informal.* An expert. [Originally school slang, perhaps from DAB (verb).] **—dab** *adj.*
D.A.B. Dictionary of American Biography.
dab·ber (dăb'ər) *n.* **1.** One that dabs. **2.** *Printing.* A cushioned pad used with a brayer by printers and engravers to apply ink.
dab·ble (dăb'əl) *v.* **-bled, -bling, -bles.** *—tr.* **1.** To splash or spatter, as with a liquid: *"the moon hung over the harbour dabbling the waves with gold"* (Katherine Mansfield). *—intr.* **1.** To splash liquid gently and playfully. **2.** To undertake something

superficially or without serious intent. **3.** To bob forward and under in shoal water so as to feed off the bottom. [Probably from Dutch *dabbelen*, frequentative of *dabben*, to strike, tap, from Middle Dutch, to DAB.] **—dab'bler** *n.*
dab·chick (dăb'chĭk') *n.* Any of various small grebes of the genus *Podiceps*. [Earlier *dapchick, dopchick* ; *dop-*, probably from Middle English *doppe*, diving bird, Old English *-doppa* (see **dub-** in Appendix*) + CHICK.]
da ca·po (dä kä'pō, də). *Abbr.* **D.C.** *Music.* From the beginning. Used as a direction to repeat a passage. [Italian.]
Dac·ca (dăk'ə). The capital of East Pakistan, situated in the east-central part of this province. Population, 557,000.
dace (dās) *n., pl.* **dace** *or* **daces.** Any of various small freshwater fishes of the family Cyprinidae, related to and resembling the minnows. [Middle English *dars, dase*, from Old French *dars*, probably from *dart*, DART (from its swift motion).]
da·cha (dä'chə) *n.* A Russian country house; villa. [Russian *dacha*, gift, portion, land (granted by a prince). See **dō-** in Appendix.*]
Da·chau (dä'кноu). A city, ten miles northwest of Munich, Bavaria, West Germany; the site of a Nazi concentration camp. Population, 29,000.
dachs·hund (däks'hoŏnt', däks'hoŏnd') *n.* A small dog of a breed native to Germany, having a long body with a usually short-haired brown or black and brown coat, drooping ears, and very short legs. [German *Dachshund* : *Dachs*, badger, from Old High German *dahs* (see **teks-** in Appendix*) + *Hund*, dog, from Old High German *hunt* (see **kwon-** in Appendix*).]
Da·cia (dä'shə). The ancient name for the part of Europe corresponding to modern Rumania. **—Da'cian** *adj. & n.*
da·coit (də-koit') *n.* Also **da·koit.** A member of one of the robber bands that were formerly prevalent in India and Burma. [Hindi *dakait*, from *ḍākā*, "gang-robbery," from Sanskrit *dasṭaka†*, crowded.]
Da·cron (dä'krŏn', dăk'rŏn') *n.* A trademark for a synthetic polyester textile fiber resistant to stretching and wrinkling.
dac·tyl (dăk'təl) *n.* Also **dac·ty·lus** (-tə-ləs) *pl.* **-li** (-lī') (for sense 2). **1.** *Prosody.* In accentual verse, a metrical foot consisting of one accented syllable followed by two unaccented, and in quantitative verse, of one long syllable followed by two short. **2.** *Zoology.* A finger, toe, or similar part or structure; digit. [Middle English *dactil*, from Latin *dactylus*, from Greek *daktulos†*, finger, hence dactyl (the three syllables of which correspond to the three joints of a finger).] **—dac·tyl'ic** *adj. & n.* **—dac·tyl'i·cal·ly** *adv.*
dactylo–. Indicates finger or toe; for example, **dactylogram.** [From Greek *daktulos*, finger, DACTYL.]
dac·tyl·o·gram (dăk-tĭl'ə-grăm') *n.* A fingerprint. [DACTYLO- + -GRAM.]
dac·ty·log·ra·phy (dăk'tə-lŏg'rə-fē) *n.* The study of fingerprints as a method of identification. [DACTYLO- + -GRAPHY.] **—dac'-ty·lo·graph'ic** (-lō-grăf'ĭk) *adj.*
dac·ty·lol·o·gy (dăk'tə-lŏl'ə-jē) *n.* The use of the fingers and hands to convey ideas, as in the manual alphabet used by deafmutes. [DACTYLO- + -LOGY.]
dad (dăd) *n. Informal.* Father. [Of baby-talk origin. See **tata-** in Appendix.*]
Da·da (dä'dä) *n.* Also **da·da, Da·da·ism** (-ĭz'əm). A western European artistic and literary movement (1916–23) having as its program the discovery of authentic reality through the abolition of traditional cultural and aesthetic forms by a technique of comic derision in which irrationality, chance, and intuition were the guiding principles. [French *dada*, pet theme, hobbyhorse,

dachshund
Smooth dachshund

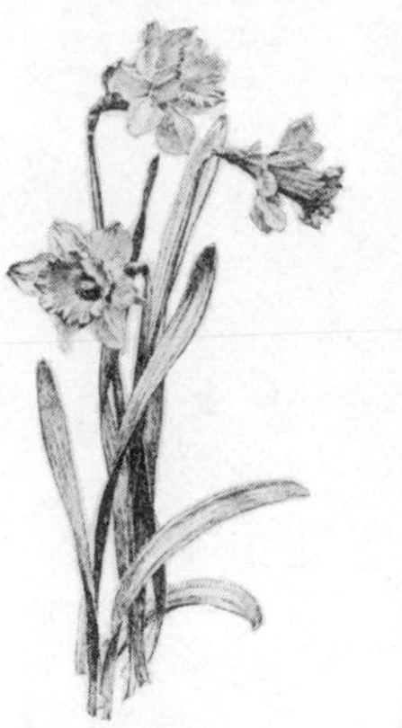
daffodil

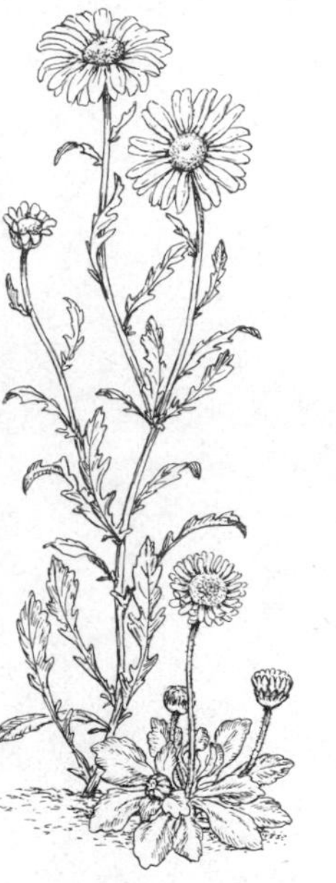
daisy
Chrysanthemum leucanthemum (left) and *Bellis perennis*

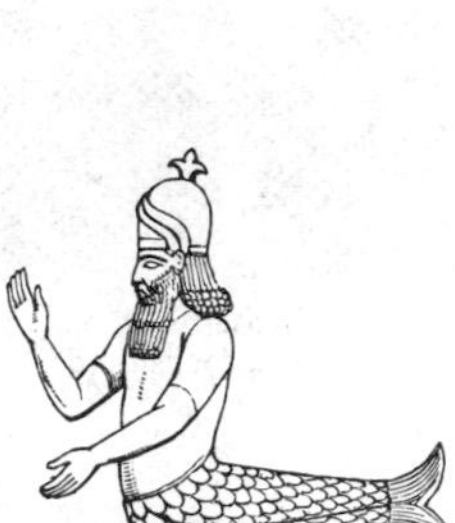
Dagon

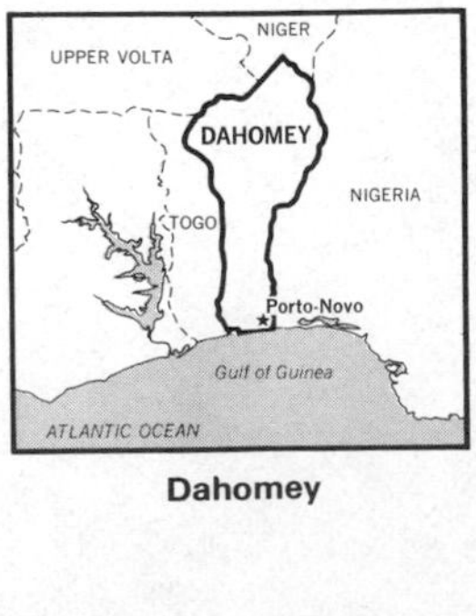

Dahomey

from baby talk (a name arbitrarily adopted by leading members of the movement).] —**Da′da·ist** *n.* —**Da′da·ist′ic** *adj.*

dad·dle. Variant of **diddle** (to waste time).

dad·dy (dăd′ē) *n., pl.* **-dies.** Diminutive of **dad.**

daddy long·legs (lông′lĕgz′, lŏng′-) *pl.* **daddy longlegs. 1.** Any of various arachnids of the order Phalangida, having a small, rounded body and long, slender legs. Also called "harvestman." **2.** *Chiefly British.* An insect, the **crane fly** *(see).*

da·do (dā′dō) *n., pl.* **-does. 1.** *Architecture.* The section of a pedestal between the base and crown. **2.** The lower portion of the wall of a room, decorated differently from the upper section, as with panels. [Italian, a die, cube, probably from Latin *datum,* gift, pawn (chessman), from the neuter of *datus,* past participle of *dare,* to give. See **dō-** in Appendix.*]

Daed·a·lus (dĕd′l-əs; *British* dēd′l-əs). *Greek Mythology.* A legendary artist and inventor, builder of the Labyrinth. —**Dae·da′li·an** (dĭ-dā′lē-ən, -dāl′yən), **Dae·da′le·an** *adj.*

dae·mon. Variant of **demon.**

daf·fa·dil·ly (dăf′ə-dĭl′ē) *n., pl.* **-lies.** Also **daf·fo·dil·ly.** *Regional.* A daffodil. Also called "daffadowndilly," "daffydowndilly."

daf·fo·dil (dăf′ə-dĭl) *n.* **1.** A bulbous plant, *Narcissus pseudonarcissus,* having showy, usually yellow flowers with a trumpet-shaped central crown. **2.** Its flower. **3.** Brilliant to vivid yellow. See **color.** [Probably from Dutch *de affodil,* the asphodel : *de,* the, from Middle Dutch (see **to-** in Appendix*) + *affodil,* from Old French *affrodille,* from Latin *asphodelus,* ASPHODEL.]

daf·fy (dăf′ē) *adj.* **-fier, -fiest.** *Informal.* Silly; foolish; zany. [From obsolete English *daff,* fool, Middle English *daffe,* probably related to *dafte,* gentle, foolish, DAFT.]

daft (dăft, däft) *adj.* **1.** Mad; crazy: *"He thinks young Wilson a likely lad, though daft/On education"* (Robert Frost). **2.** Foolish; stupid. **3.** *Scottish.* Frolicsome. [Middle English *dafte,* gentle, modest, foolish, Old English *gedæfte,* mild, meek. See **dhabh-** in Appendix.*] —**daft′ly** *adv.* —**daft′ness** *n.*

dag (dăg) *n.* **1.** A lock of matted or dung-coated wool. **2.** *Archaic.* A pendent end or shred. [Middle English *dagge*†, shred, tag.]

dag decagram.

Da·gan (dä′gän′). The Babylonian god of the earth, considered by some to be identified with Baal. [Akkadian *Dagān.*]

Da·gen·ham (dăg′nəm). A former administrative division of London, England, now part of **Barking** *(see).*

Da·ge·stan Autonomous Soviet Socialist Republic (dăg′ə-stăn′, däg′ə-stän′). Also **Dag·he·stan.** An administrative division, 19,416 square miles in area, of the southwestern Russian S.F.S.R. Population, 1,299,000. Capital, Makhachkala.

dag·ger (dăg′ər) *n.* **1.** A short pointed weapon with sharp edges. **2.** Something that agonizes, torments, or wounds. **3.** *Printing.* **a.** An **obelisk** *(see).* **b.** A **double dagger** *(see).* —**look daggers at.** To glare at angrily or hatefully. —*tr.v.* **daggered, -gering, -gers. 1.** To stab with a dagger. **2.** To mark with a dagger. [Middle English *daggere,* from Old French *dague,* from Old Provençal or Old Italian *daga,* perhaps from Vulgar Latin *daca* (unattested), "Dacian knife," feminine of Latin *Dācus,* Dacian, from DACIA.]

dagger fern. An evergreen North American fern, *Polystichum acrostichoides,* having dense clusters of lance-shaped fronds. Also called "Christmas fern."

da·go (dā′gō) *n., pl.* **-gos** or **-goes.** Also **Da·go.** *Slang.* An Italian, Spaniard, or Portuguese. An offensive term, used derogatorily. [Alteration of common Spanish given name *Diego,* from Latin *Jacōbus,* JACOB.]

Da·gon (dā′gŏn′). The chief god of the ancient Philistines and later the Phoenicians, represented as half-man and half-fish. [Middle English, from Latin, from Greek *Dagōn,* from Hebrew *Dāgōn,* "small fish," diminutive of *dāg,* fish.]

Da·guerre (də-gâr′), **Louis Jacques Mandé.** 1787–1851. French scenic artist; invented (1839) the daguerreotype, an early photographic process.

da·guerre·o·type (də-gâr′ə-tīp′) *n.* **1.** An early photographic process with the impression made on a light-sensitive silver-coated metallic plate and developed by mercury vapor. **2.** A photograph made by this process. —*tr.v.* **daguerreotyped, -typing, -types.** To photograph by this process. [Invented by Louis J. M. DAGUERRE.] —**da·guerre′o·typ′er** *n.* —**da·guerre′o·typ′y** *n.*

dah (dä′) *n.* A dash in Morse code. Compare **dit.**

dahl·ia (dăl′yə, däl′-, dāl′-) *n.* **1.** Any of several plants of the genus *Dahlia,* native to Mexico and Central America, having tuberous roots and showy, variously colored flowers; especially, any of the horticultural forms derived from *D. pinnata.* **2.** The flower of any of these plants. [New Latin *Dahlia;* named in honor of Anders *Dahl,* 18th-century Swedish botanist.]

Dah·na (dä′nä′). Also **Da·ha·na.** A desert region in east-central Arabia, part of the **Rub al Khali** *(see).*

Da·ho·mey (də-hō′mē; *French* dȧ-ô-mā′). A republic of western Africa, 44,696 square miles in area, formerly an overseas territory of French West Africa; independent since 1960. Population, 2,300,000. Capital, Porto-Novo.

da·hoon (də-ho͞on′) *n.* An evergreen shrub or small tree, *Ilex cassine,* of the southeastern United States, having red fruit. [Origin unknown.]

Dai·do. The Japanese name for **Taedong.**

Dail Ei·reann (dô′əl ā′rən). The lower legislative house of the Irish **Oireachtas** *(see).* [Irish : *dail,* assembly, from Old Irish *dāl* (see **dhē-**[1] in Appendix*) + *Eireann,* genitive of *Eire,* Ireland, from Old Irish *Ēriu,* "land" (see **Iveriū** in Appendix*).]

dai·ly (dā′lē) *adj.* Of, pertaining to, occurring, or published every day or every weekday. —*n., pl.* **dailies.** A daily publication, especially a newspaper. —*adv.* Each day; day after day. [Middle English *daili,* Old English *dæglīc,* from *dæg,* DAY.]

daily double. *Horse Racing.* A bet won by choosing both winners of two specified races on one day.

dai·mio (dī′myō) *n., pl.* **daimio** or **-mios.** Also **dai·myo.** A hereditary nobleman in feudal Japan. [Japanese *daimyō,* from Ancient Chinese *d′âi miăng,* great name (whence Mandarin Chinese *ta*^{4} *ming*^{2}) : *d′âi,* great + *miăng,* name.]

Daim·ler (dĭm′lĕr), **Gottlieb.** 1834–1900. German engineer and automotive pioneer; invented early internal-combustion engine.

dai·mon. Variant of **demon.**

dain·ty (dān′tē) *adj.* **-tier, -tiest. 1.** Delicately beautiful or charming; exquisite: *"No dainty rhymes or sentimental love verses for you, terrible year"* (Walt Whitman). **2.** Delicious; choice. **3.** Of refined taste; discriminating. **4.** Too fastidious; squeamish. —*n., pl.* **dainties.** Something delicious; a delicacy. [Middle English *deinte,* delicious, pleasant, from *deinte,* dignity, pleasure, delicacy, from Old French *deintie,* from Latin *dīgnitās,* dignity, worth, from *dīgnus,* worthy. See **dek-**[1] in Appendix.*] —**dain′ti·ly** *adv.* —**dain′ti·ness** *n.*

dai·qui·ri (dī′kə-rē, dăk′ə-rē) *n., pl.* **-ris.** An iced cocktail of rum, lime or lemon juice, and sugar. [Originally made with rum from *Daiquirí,* Cuba.]

Dai·ren. The former name for **Talien.**

dair·y (dâr′ē) *n., pl.* **-ies. 1.** A commercial establishment that processes or sells milk and milk products. **2.** A place where milk and cream are stored and processed, such as a specially equipped building on a farm. **3. a.** A dairy farm. **b.** The herd of cattle on a dairy farm. **4.** The dairy business; dairying. **5.** Dairy products, as distinguished from meat, with reference to Jewish religious dietary laws. [Middle English *daierie,* from *daie,* dairymaid, Old English *dæge,* female breadmaker. See **dheigh-** in Appendix.*] —**dair′y** *adj.*

dairy cattle. Cows bred and raised for milk rather than meat.

dairy farm. A farm for producing milk and milk products.

dair·y·ing (dâr′ē-ĭng) *n.* The business of a dairy.

dair·y·maid (dâr′ē-mād′) *n.* A female dairy worker.

dair·y·man (dâr′ē-mən) *n., pl.* **-men** (-mĭn). **1.** A dairy manager or owner. **2.** A male dairy worker.

da·is (dā′ĭs, dās) *n., pl.* **-ises** (-ĭ-sĭz). A raised platform, as in a lecture hall or dining hall, upon which honored guests or speakers sit or stand. [Middle English *deis,* from Old French, table, platform, from Latin *discus,* dish, quoit, DISK.]

dai·sy (dā′zē) *n., pl.* **-sies. 1.** Any of several related plants having rayed flowers; especially, in North America, a widely naturalized Eurasian plant, *Chrysanthemum leucanthemum,* having flowers with a yellow center and white rays. This species is also called "oxeye daisy," "white daisy." **2.** A low-growing European plant, *Bellis perennis,* having flowers with pink or white rays. This species is the daisy of literary tradition. Also called "English daisy," "bachelor's-button." **3.** The flower of any of these plants. **4.** *Slang.* Something excellent or notable. [Middle English *daisie, dayeseye,* Old English *dægesēage,* "day's eye" (the flower of some species opens to reveal a yellow disk in the morning and closes again in the evening) : *dæges,* genitive of *dæg,* DAY + *ēage,* eye (see **okw-** in Appendix*).]

daisy fleabane. Any of several plants of the genus *Erigeron,* especially *E. annuus,* a weedy North American plant having numerous small flowers with white or pinkish rays.

Da·kar (dä-kär′, də-). The capital of Senegal, a seaport on Cape Verde in the west. Population, 298,000.

Da·kin's solution (dā′kənz). A dilute sodium hypochlorite solution used as a surgical disinfectant. [Developed by Henry Drysdale *Dakin* (1880–1952), British chemist.]

Da·ko·ta[1] (də-kō′tə). **1.** A former U.S. territory, now consisting of North and South Dakota. **2.** See **James River.** —**the Dakotas.** North and South Dakota.

Da·ko·ta[2] (də-kō′tə) *n., pl.* **Dakota** or **-tas. 1.** A large group of Siouan-speaking tribes of North American Plains Indians, commonly called Sioux, now living on reservations in North and South Dakota, Minnesota, and Montana. **2.** The Siouan language of these Indians. **3.** A member of any of these tribes. —**Da·ko′tan** *adj.* & *n.*

DAL Airport code for Dallas, Texas.

Da·la·dier (dȧ-lȧ-dyā′), **Édouard.** Born 1884. French statesman; premier (1933, 1934, and 1938–40).

Da·lai La·ma[1] (dä-lī′ lä′mə). The traditional governmental ruler and highest priest of the Lamaist religion in Tibet and Mongolia. Also called "Grand Lama." [Tibetan : Mongolian *dalai,* ocean + Tibetan *bla-ma,* a Buddhist monk, LAMA.]

Da·lai La·ma[2] (dä-lī′ lä′mə). Original name, La-mu-tan-chu. Born 1934. Fourteenth Dalai Lama, 1940; exiled, 1959.

Da Lat (dä lät′). A city of east-central South Vietnam, 140 miles northeast of Saigon. It was the former summer capital of Vietnam. Population, 49,000.

dale (dāl) *n.* A valley. [Middle English *dale,* Old English *dæl.* See **dhel-** in Appendix.*]

Dale (dāl), Sir **Henry Hallet.** Born 1875. British biologist; worked on chemical transmission of nerve impulses.

Dale (dāl), Sir **Thomas.** English colonial administrator of the early 17th century; governor of Virginia (1611 and 1614–16).

dales·man (dālz′mən) *n., pl.* **-men** (-mĭn). A person who lives in a dale, especially in northern Yorkshire, England.

da·leth (dä′ləth) *n.* The fourth letter of the Hebrew alphabet. See **alphabet.** [Hebrew *dāleth,* from *dālt,* door, daleth.]

Dal·hou·sie (dăl-ho͞o′zē), **Tenth Earl and First Marquis of.** Title of James Andrew Broun Ramsay. 1812–1860. British colonial administrator; governor general of India (1847–56).

Da·li (dä′lē; *Spanish* dä-lē′), **Salvador.** Born 1904. Spanish artist; a leader of surrealist school; resident of United States since 1940.

Dal·las (dăl′əs). The second-largest city in Texas, in the northeast. Population, 680,000.

Dal·las (dăl′əs), **George Mifflin.** 1792–1864. Vice President of the United States under James K. Polk (1845–49).

dalles (dălz) *pl.n.* The steep precipices forming the sides of a gorge or narrow valley, usually having rapids at the bottom. [French, plural of *dalle,* gutter, drain, from Old French, from Old Norse *dæla.* See **dhel-** in Appendix.*]

dal·li·ance (dăl′ē-əns) *n.* **1.** Frivolous spending of time; dawdling. **2.** Amorous play; flirtation.

Dal·lis grass (dăl′əs, -ĭs). A South American grass, *Paspalum dilatatum,* grown for pasturage in the southern United States. [*Dallis,* probably alteration of DALLAS.]

dal·ly (dăl′ē) *v.* **-lied, -lying, -lies.** —*intr.* **1.** To play amorously; flirt: *"Sylvester dallied about Lena until he began to make mistakes in his work"* (Willa Cather). **2.** To trifle; toy. **3.** To waste time; dawdle. —*tr.* To waste (time). Used with *away.* [Middle English *dalien,* from Norman French *dalier*†.] —**dal′li·er** *n.* —**dal′ly·ing·ly** *adv.*

Dal·ma·ti·a (dăl-mā′shə). *Serbo-Croatian* **Dal·ma·ci·ja** (däl′mä-tsə-yä); *Italian* **Dal·ma·zi·a** (däl-mä′tsyä). A region of Croatia, Yugoslavia, along the eastern coast of the Adriatic Sea; a former Austrian crownland.

Dal·ma·tian (dăl-mā′shən) *n.* **1.** A dog of a breed believed to have originated in Dalmatia, having a short, smooth white coat covered with black or dark-brown spots. Also called "coach dog," "carriage dog." **2.** A native or inhabitant of Dalmatia. —*adj.* Of or pertaining to Dalmatia or its inhabitants.

dal·mat·ic (dăl-măt′ĭk) *n.* **1.** *Roman Catholic Church.* A wide-sleeved garment worn over the alb by a deacon, cardinal, bishop, or abbot at the celebration of Mass. **2.** A similar garment worn by an English monarch at his coronation. [Middle English *dalmatik,* from Old French *dalmatique,* from Late Latin *dalmatica (vestis),* "Dalmatian (garment)" (originally made of white wool from Dalmatia), from *dalmaticus,* of DALMATIA.]

dal se·gno (däl sān′yō) *Abbr.* **d.s., D.S.** *Music.* A direction to repeat from a place marked by the sign (§) to a designated point. [Italian, "from the sign."]

Dal·ton (dôlt′n), **John.** 1766–1844. British physicist and chemist; formulated first practical atomic theory and table of atomic weights.

dal·to·ni·an (dôl-tō′nē-ən) *adj.* Also **Dal·to·ni·an. 1.** Of or pertaining to John Dalton or his atomic theory. **2.** Of or pertaining to daltonism.

dal·ton·ism (dôlt′n-ĭz′əm) *n.* Also **Dal·ton·ism.** Red-green colorblindness. [After John DALTON, who was colorblind.] —**dal·ton′ic** (-tŏn′ĭk) *adj.*

Da·ly (dā′lē), **(John) Augustin.** 1838–1899. American theatrical manager and playwright.

dam¹ (dăm) *n.* **1.** A barrier constructed across a waterway to control the flow or raise the level of water. **2.** A body of water controlled by such a barrier. **3.** Any obstruction or hindrance. —*tr.v.* **dammed, damming, dams. 1.** To construct a dam across; hold back by means of a dam. **2.** To obstruct or restrain; confine. Usually used with *in* or *up.* —See Synonyms at **hinder.** [Middle English, probably from Middle Low German *dam,* Germanic *dammjan* (unattested), to impede, dam.]

dam² (dăm) *n.* **1.** *Abbr.* **d.** A female parent. Said of a quadruped. **2.** *Archaic.* A mother. [Middle English, variant of DAME.]

dam decameter.

DAM Airport code for Damascus, Syria.

Dam (däm), **(Carl Peter) Henrik.** Born 1895. Danish biochemist.

dam·age (dăm′ĭj) *n.* **1.** Impairment of the usefulness or value of person or property; loss; harm. **2.** *Plural. Law.* Money paid or ordered to be paid as compensation for injury or loss. **3.** *Usually plural. Informal.* Cost; price. —*v.* **damaged, -aging, -ages.** —*tr.* To cause injury to; impair; harm. —*intr.* To suffer or be susceptible to damage. —See Synonyms at **injure, ruin.** [Middle English, from Old French, from *dam(me),* loss, damage, from Latin *damnum,* loss, harm, fine. See **dap-** in Appendix.*] —**dam′age·a·ble** *adj.* —**dam′ag·ing·ly** *adv.*

da·man (dăm′ən) *n. Rare.* The hyrax, a small mammal of Africa and Asia Minor. [Arabic *damān (Isrā′īl),* "sheep of Israel."]

Da·man·hûr (dä′män-hŏŏr′). A city of northeast-central Egypt, in the western Nile delta area. Population, 133,000.

Da·mão (dä-mouN′). Also **Da·man** (də-män′). A former Portuguese territory consisting of three enclaves in southern Gujarat, Republic of India.

dam·ar. Variant of **dammar.**

dam·as·cene (dăm′ə-sēn′, dăm′ə-sēn′) *tr.v.* **-cened, -cening, -cenes.** Also **dam·as·keen** (dăm′ə-skēn′, dăm′ə-skēn′), **-keened, -keening, -keens.** To decorate (metal) with wavy patterns of inlay or etching. —*n.* Work decorated by damascening. —*adj.* Of or pertaining to damascening or damask. [Middle English, from Old French *damasquiner,* "to decorate in the manner of Damascus blades or steel," from *damasquin,* of Damascus, from Italian *damaschino,* from Latin *Damascēnus,* from Greek *Damaskēnos,* from *Damaskos,* DAMASCUS.] —**dam′a·scen′er** *n.*

Dam·a·scene (dăm′ə-sēn′) *adj.* Of or pertaining to Damascus or its inhabitants. —*n.* A native or inhabitant of Damascus.

Dam·a·sce·nus, Johannes. See **John of Damascus.**

Da·mas·cus (də-măs′kəs). *Arabic* **Es sham** (ăsh shăm′). The capital of Syria, an ancient city in the southwestern part of the country. Population, 545,000. [Latin, from Greek *Damaskos,* from Arabic *Damišqu, Dimišqu.*]

Damascus steel. An early form of steel having wavy markings, developed in Near Eastern countries, especially Persia, and used chiefly in sword blades. Also called "damask steel."

dam·ask (dăm′əsk) *n.* **1.** A rich patterned fabric of cotton, linen, silk, or wool. **2.** A fine, twilled table linen. **3.** Damascus steel. **4.** The wavy pattern on Damascus steel. —*tr.v.* **damasked, -asking, -asks. 1.** To damascene. **2.** To decorate or weave with rich patterns. —*adj.* **1.** Of or from Damascus. **2.** Made from damask or damask steel. [Middle English *damask (cloth),* from Medieval Latin *(pannus de) damasco,* "(cloth of) Damascus," from Latin *Damascus,* DAMASCUS.]

damask rose. A rose, *Rosa damascena,* native to Asia, having fragrant red or pink flowers used as a source of attar. [Medieval Latin *rosa Damascēna,* from Latin *Damascēnus,* of Damascus, from *Damascus,* DAMASCUS, its supposed place of origin.]

dame (dām) *n.* **1.** A title formerly given to a woman in authority or to the mistress of a household. Now only used in expressions such as *Dame Fortune.* **2.** A married woman; matron. **3.** *Slang.* A woman; female. **4.** *British.* **a.** *Archaic.* The legal title of the wife or widow of a knight or baronet. **b.** A title of a woman, equivalent to that of a knight. **5.** *Obsolete.* A schoolmistress. [Middle English, from Old French, from Latin *domina,* feminine of *dominus,* master, lord. See **demə-¹** in Appendix.*]

dame's rocket. A plant, *Hesperis matronalis,* native to Europe, having clusters of fragrant purple or white flowers. Also called "dame's violet," "damewort."

Da·mien (dȧ-myăN′), **Father.** Original name, Joseph de Veuster. 1840–1888. Belgian Roman Catholic priest; missionary to leper colony on Molokai, Hawaii.

Dam·i·et·ta (dăm′ē-ĕt′ə). *Arabic* **Dum·yat** (dŏŏm-yät′). A city in northeastern Egypt on the Nile delta. Population, 72,000.

dam·mar, da·mar (dăm′ər) *n.* Also **dam·mer.** Any of various hard resins obtained from Indo-Malayan trees of the genera *Shorea, Balanocarpus,* and *Hopea,* and used in varnishes and lacquers. [Malay *damar,* resin.]

damn (dăm) *v.* **damned, damning, damns.** —*tr.* **1.** To pronounce an adverse judgment upon; criticize adversely. **2.** To bring about the failure of; ruin. **3.** To condemn as harmful, illegal, or immoral: *damn gambling and strong drink.* **4.** *Theology.* To condemn to everlasting punishment or a similar fate; doom. **5.** To swear at by using the word "damn"; curse. —*intr.* To swear; curse. —*interj.* Used to express anger, irritation, contempt, or disappointment. —*n.* **1.** The saying of "damn"; a curse. **2.** *Informal.* The least valuable bit; a jot: *don't give a damn; not worth a damn.* —*adj.* Damned. —*adv.* Damned. [Middle English *dam(p)nen,* from Old French *dam(p)ner,* from Latin *damnāre,* to inflict loss upon, to condemn, from *damnum,* loss, damage. See **dap-** in Appendix.*] —**damn′ing·ly** *adv.*

dam·na·ble (dăm′nə-bəl) *adj.* Deserving condemnation; odious; hateful. —**dam′na·ble·ness** *n.* —**dam′na·bly** *adv.*

dam·na·tion (dăm-nā′shən) *n.* **1.** The act of damning or condition of being damned. **2.** *Theology.* **a.** Condemnation to everlasting punishment; doom. **b.** Everlasting punishment. **3.** Failure or ruination incurred by adverse criticism. —*interj.* Used to express anger or annoyance.

dam·na·to·ry (dăm′nə-tôr′ē, -tōr′ē) *adj.* Threatening with damnation; condemning; damning.

damned (dămd) *adj.* Superlative **damndest** or **damnedest. 1.** Condemned, especially to eternal punishment; doomed. **2.** *Informal.* **a.** Deserving condemnation; detestable. Used as an expression of irritation or disappointment: *this damned weather.* **b.** Absolute; utter. Used as an intensive: *a damned fool.* —*adv. Informal.* Very; extremely: *a damned poor excuse.* —*n. Theology.* Souls doomed to eternal punishment. Preceded by *the.*

dam·ni·fy (dăm′nə-fī′) *tr.v.* **-fied, -fying, -fies.** *Law.* To cause loss or damage to. [Old French *damnifier,* from Late Latin *damnificāre,* from Latin *damnificus,* causing loss, harmful : *damnum,* loss, harm (see **dap-** in Appendix*) + *-ficus,* -FIC.] —**dam′ni·fi·ca′tion** *n.*

Dam·o·cles (dăm′ə-klēz′). A member of the court of Dionysius the Elder, tyrant of Syracuse, who assertedly forced Damocles to sit at a banquet under a sword suspended by a single hair, to demonstrate the precariousness of a king's fortunes. See **Sword of Damocles.** —**Dam′o·cle′an** (-klē′ən) *adj.*

Da·mo·dar (dä′mə-där′). A river of northeastern India, rising in Bihar and flowing 368 miles southeast through West Bengal to the Hooghly River near Calcutta.

Da·mon and Pyth·i·as (dā′mən; pĭth′ē-əs). *Roman Mythology.* Two friends so devoted that Damon pledged his life as a hostage for the condemned Pythias.

dam·o·sel (dăm′ə-zĕl′) *n.* Also **dam·oi·selle** (dăm′ə-zĕl′), **dam·o·zel.** *Archaic.* A damsel. [Variant of DAMSEL.]

damp (dămp) *adj.* **damper, dampest. 1.** Slightly wet; moist; humid. **2.** *Archaic.* Dejected. —See Synonyms at **wet.** —*n.* **1.** Moisture; humidity; mist. **2.** Foul or poisonous gas that sometimes pollutes the air in mines. **3.** Lowness of spirits; depression. **4.** A restraint or check; discouragement. —*tr.v.* **damped, damping, damps. 1.** To make damp or moist; moisten. **2.** To extinguish (a fire, for example) by cutting off air. **3.** To restrain or check; discourage. **4.** To provide (the strings of a keyboard instrument) with dampers as a means of reducing the dynamic level. **5.** *Physics.* To decrease the amplitude of (a wave). —**damp off.** *Botany.* To be affected by **damping off** *(see).* [Middle English, poison gas, choke-damp, from Middle Low German and Middle Dutch, smoke, vapor, from Germanic *damp-* (unattested).] —**damp′ish** *adj.* —**damp′ly** *adv.* —**damp′ness** *n.*

damp·en (dăm′pən) *v.* **-ened, -ening, -ens.** —*tr.* **1.** To moisten;

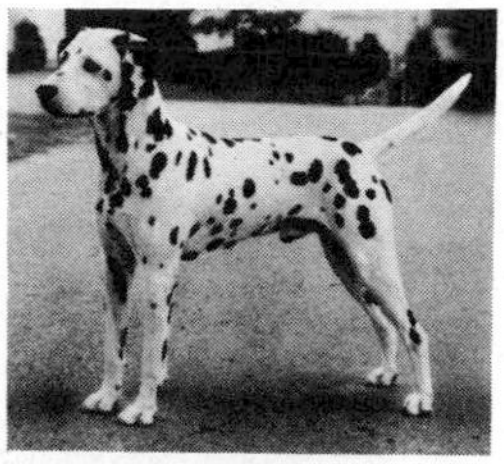

Dalmatian

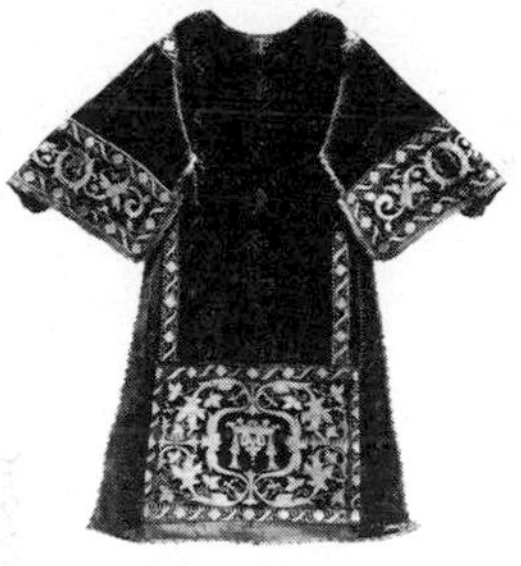

dalmatic
Early 16th-century dalmatic of embroidered velvet

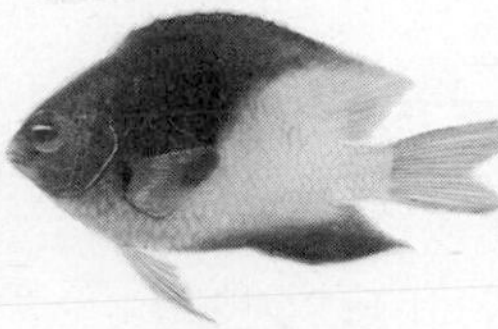

damselfish
Eupomacentrus partitus

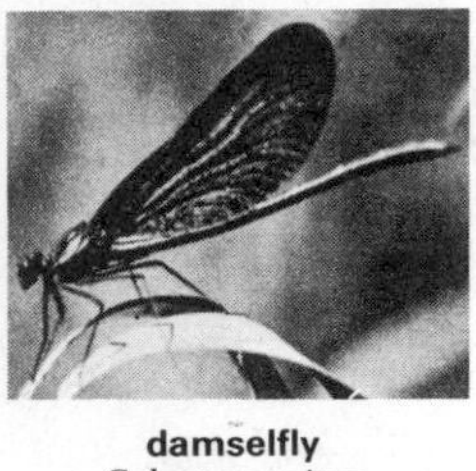

damselfly
Colopteryx virgo

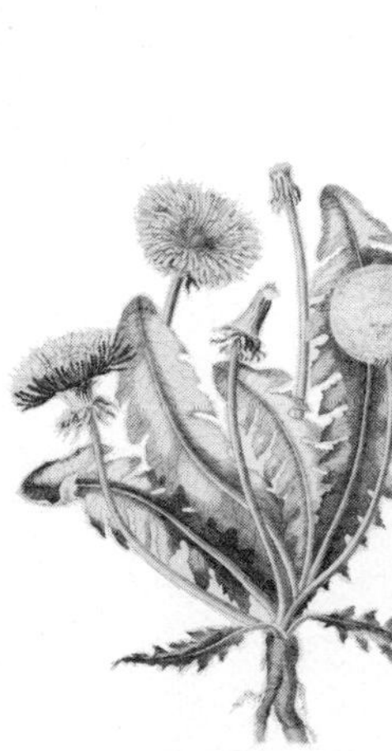

dandelion
Taraxacum officinale

make damp. **2.** To deaden; depress: *dampen one's spirits.* —*intr.* To become wet or moist. —**damp'en·er** *n.*

damp·er (dăm'pər) *n.* **1.** One that damps, restrains, or depresses. **2.** An adjustable plate in the flue of a furnace or stove for controlling the draft. **3.** *Music.* **a.** A device in various keyboard instruments for deadening the vibrations of the strings. **b.** A mute for various brass instruments. **4.** Any device that eliminates or progressively diminishes oscillations.

Dam·pi·er (dăm'pē-ər, -pyər), **William.** 1652–1715. English explorer, pirate, and author; twice circumnavigated the globe.

damping off. A disease of planted seeds or very young seedlings caused by fungi and resulting in death of the newly sprouted plants.

Dam·rosch (dăm'rŏsh'), **Walter Johannes.** 1862–1950. German-born American composer and conductor.

dam·sel (dăm'zəl) *n.* A young woman or girl; maiden. [Middle English *damisele,* from Old French *dameisele,* from Vulgar Latin *dominicella* (unattested), diminutive of Latin *domina,* lady, DAME.]

dam·sel·fish (dăm'zəl-fĭsh') *n., pl.* **damselfish** or **-fishes.** Any of various small tropical marine fishes of the family Pomacentridae, having laterally compressed, usually brightly colored bodies.

dam·sel·fly (dăm'zəl-flī') *n., pl.* **-flies.** Any of various slender-bodied, often brightly colored insects of the order Odonata, related to the dragonflies but differing in having wings that are folded together over the back when at rest.

dam·son (dăm'zən, -sən) *n.* **1.** A plum tree, *Prunus institia,* native to Eurasia, cultivated since ancient times for its edible fruit. Sometimes called "bullace." **2.** The oval, bluish-black, juicy plum borne by this tree. Also called "damson plum." [Middle English *damascene, damson,* from Latin *(prūnum) Damascēnum,* "(plum) of Damascus," from *Damascēnus,* from *Damascus,* DAMASCUS.]

Dan¹ (dăn). A masculine given name. [Short for DANIEL.]

Dan² (dăn). **1.** The fifth son of Jacob. Genesis 30:6. **2.** One of the 12 tribes of Israel, descended from Dan.

Dan³ (dăn) *n. Obsolete.* A title of honor equivalent to *master* or *sir: "Dan Chaucer, well of English undefiled"* (Spenser). [Middle English *Dan, Daunz,* "master," "mister," originally a title of respect for a monk or priest, from Old French *Dan, Danz,* from Medieval Latin *Domnus,* contracted from Latin *dominus,* master, lord. See **demə-¹** in Appendix.*]

Dan. 1. Daniel (Old Testament). **2.** Danish.

Da·na (dā'nə), **Richard Henry.** 1815–1882. American lawyer and sailor; author of *Two Years Before the Mast.*

Dan·a·e (dăn'ə-ē'). Also **Dan·a·ë.** *Greek Mythology.* The mother of Perseus by Zeus, who visited her in the form of a shower of gold during her imprisonment.

Dan·a·id (dăn'ē-ĭd) *n.* Also **Dan·a·ïd.** Any of the Danaides.

Da·na·i·des (də-nā'ə-dēz') *pl.n.* Also **Da·na·ï·des.** *Greek Mythology.* The daughters of Danaus who at their father's command murdered their bridegrooms on the wedding night and were condemned in Hades to pour water eternally into a bottomless vessel. [Greek, from *Danaos,* DANAUS.] —**Dan'a·id'e·an** (dăn'ē-ĭd'ē-ən) *adj.*

Da Nang (də năng', dä näng'). Formerly **Tou·rane** (tōō-rän'). A city and port of northeastern South Vietnam on the South China Sea, the site of a U.S. military air base established in 1965. Population, 111,000.

Dan·a·us (dăn'ē-əs). Also **Dan·a·üs.** *Greek Mythology.* A king of Argos, father of the **Danaides** *(see).*

dance (dăns, däns) *v.* **danced, dancing, dances.** —*intr.* **1.** To move rhythmically to music, using prescribed or improvised steps and gestures. **2.** To leap or skip about excitedly; caper; frolic. **3.** To bob up and down. —*tr.* **1.** To engage in or perform (a dance). **2.** To cause to dance. **3.** To bring to a particular state or condition by dancing: *He danced her to exhaustion.* —**dance attendance.** To wait upon another attentively; lavish attentions on someone. —*n.* **1.** A series of rhythmical motions and steps, usually to music. **2.** A particular set of such prescribed movements. **3.** The art of dancing. Often preceded by *the.* **4.** A party or gathering of people for dancing; ball. **5.** One round or turn of dancing. **6.** An act of dancing; a dance performance. **7.** A musical or rhythmical accompaniment composed or played for dancing. [Middle English *dansen, dauncen,* from Old French *danser, dancier,* probably from Frankish *dintjan*† (unattested).] —**danc'er** *n.* —**danc'ing·ly** *adv.*

dance·able (dăns'ə-bəl, däns'-) *adj.* Suitable for dancing. Said of music.

dan·de·li·on (dăn'də-lī'ən) *n.* **1.** A plant, *Taraxacum officinale,* native to Eurasia, widely naturalized as a weed in North America, and having many-rayed yellow flowers and deeply notched basal leaves, sometimes used in salads. **2.** Any of several similar, related plants. **3.** Brilliant to vivid yellow. See **color.** [Middle English *dent-de-lion,* from Old French, translation of Medieval Latin *dēns leōnis,* "lion's tooth" (from its sharply indented leaves) : Latin *dēns,* tooth (see **dent-** in Appendix*) + *leōnis,* genitive of *leō,* LION.] —**dan'de·li'on** *adj.*

dan·der¹ (dăn'dər) *n. Informal.* Temper. —**get one's dander up.** *Informal.* To become angry or roused to vigorous action. [Origin unknown.]

dan·der² (dăn'dər) *n.* Scurf from the coat of various animals, such as dogs, cats, or horses, often of an allergenic nature. [Short for DANDRUFF.]

Dan·die Din·mont (dăn'dē dĭn'mŏnt'). A small terrier of a breed developed in England, having a rough grayish or brownish coat and short legs. [After *Dandie Dinmont,* owner of two such dogs in *Guy Mannering,* a novel by Sir Walter Scott.]

dan·di·fy (dăn'də-fī') *tr.v.* **-fied, -fying, -fies.** To dress up or make resemble a dandy or fop. —**dan'di·fi·ca'tion** *n.*

dan·di·prat (dăn'dē-prăt') *n.* **1.** *Archaic.* A little, insignificant, or contemptible fellow. **2.** A small 16th-century English coin. [Origin unknown.]

dan·dle (dănd'l) *tr.v.* **-dled, -dling, -dles.** To move (a small child) up and down on the knees or in the arms: *"somebody who was dandled on Queen Victoria's knee must appear an old fogy"* (Duke of Windsor). [Possibly related to Italian *dandolare,* to dandle, swing (expressive formation).] —**dan'dler** *n.*

dan·druff (dăn'drəf) *n.* A scaly scurf formed on and shed from the scalp, often caused by seborrhea. [*Dand-*† + *-ruff,* perhaps from Middle English *roufe,* scab, from Old Norse *hrufa* (see **kreup-** in Appendix*).]

dan·dy¹ (dăn'dē) *n., pl.* **-dies. 1.** A man who affects extreme elegance in his clothes and manners. **2.** *Informal.* Something very good or agreeable. **3.** *Nautical.* A **yawl** *(see).* —*adj.* **dandier, -diest. 1.** Like or dressed like a dandy; foppish. **2.** *Informal.* Fine; good. [Perhaps short for *jack-a-dandy,* pert person, fop : JACK (person) + A- (of) + *dandy,* probably from *Dandy,* Scottish nickname for ANDREW.] —**dan'dy·ism'** *n.*

dan·dy² (dăn'dē) *n. Pathology.* **Dengue** *(see).* Also called "dandy fever." [West Indian, variant of DENGUE.]

dandy roll. Also **dandy roller.** A cylinder of wire gauze pressed on drained but moist paper pulp before it starts through the rollers. It produces watermarks in the paper. [From DANDY (fine, hence neat).]

Dane (dān) *n.* A native or inhabitant of Denmark or a person of Danish ancestry. [Middle English *Dan* (replacing *Dene,* from Old English *Dene,* the Danes), from Old Norse *Danr.* See **dan-** in Appendix.*]

Dane·geld (dān'gĕld') *n.* Also **Dane·gelt** (-gĕlt'). A tax levied in England from the 10th to the 12th century to finance protection against Danish invasion. [Middle English (modeled upon some Scandinavian compound such as Old Danish *Danegjeld*) : *Dane,* genitive plural of *Dan,* DANE + *geld,* tribute, payment, Old English *gield* (see **ghelt-** in Appendix*).]

Dane·law (dān'lô') *n.* Also **Dane·lagh. 1.** The body of law established by the Danish invaders and settlers in northeastern England in the ninth and tenth centuries. **2.** The sections of England under jurisdiction of this law. [Middle English *Dene laue,* Old English *Dena lagu,* "Danes' law" : *Dena,* genitive of *Dene,* the Danes (see **dan-** in Appendix*) + *lagu,* law (see **legh-** in Appendix*).]

dan·ger (dān'jər) *n.* **1.** Exposure or vulnerability to harm or evil; risk; peril. **2.** A source or instance of risk or peril. **3.** *Obsolete.* Power, especially power to harm. [Middle English *daunger,* power, dominion, peril, damage, from Old French *dangier, dongier,* from Vulgar Latin *dom(i)niārium* (unattested), authority, from Latin *dominium,* sovereignty, from *dominus,* lord, master. See **demə-¹** in Appendix.*]

Synonyms: *danger, peril, hazard, risk.* These nouns refer to exposure to harm or loss. *Danger,* the least specific, is applicable to any potentially harmful situation. *Peril* is much stronger through its suggestions of great potential for harm and of immediacy, or imminence, of the threat involved. *Hazard* less forcefully suggests the threat posed by chance or something largely beyond one's control. *Risk* also stresses chance or uncertainty, but often from the standpoint of one who weighs them against possible gain; the term therefore may imply voluntary exposure to harm or loss.

dan·ger·ous (dān'jər-əs) *adj.* **1.** Involving or fraught with danger; perilous. **2.** Able or apt to do harm. —**dan'ger·ous·ly** *adv.* —**dan'ger·ous·ness** *n.*

dan·gle (dăng'gəl) *v.* **-gled, -gling, -glings.** —*intr.* **1.** To hang loosely and swing or sway to and fro. **2.** To hover after someone; be a hanger-on. —*tr.* To cause to dangle. —*n.* **1.** The act of dangling. **2.** Something that is dangled. [Perhaps from Danish *dangle* or Swedish *dangla,* from Germanic *dang-* (unattested).] —**dan'gler** *n.*

dan·gle·ber·ry (dăng'gəl-bĕr'ē) *n., pl.* **-ries. 1.** A shrub, *Gaylussacia frondosa,* of eastern North America, having small, greenish-purple flowers and bluish-black fruit. **2.** The sweet, edible fruit of this shrub. Also called "tangleberry."

dangling participle. *Grammar.* A participle that lacks clear connection with the word it modifies. In the sentence *Working at my desk, the sudden noise startled me, Working at my desk* is a dangling participle. See Usage note at **participle.**

Dan·iel¹ (dăn'yəl). A masculine given name. [Hebrew *Dānī'ēl,* "God is my judge."]

Dan·iel² (dăn'yəl). In the Old Testament, a Hebrew prophet during the Babylonian captivity.

Dan·iel³ (dăn'yəl) *n. Abbr.* **Dan.** The book in the Old Testament containing the story and prophecies of Daniel.

da·ni·o (dā'nē-ō') *n., pl.* **-os.** Any of various small, often brightly colored freshwater fishes of the genera *Danio* and *Brachydanio,* native to Asia and popular as aquarium fish. [New Latin *Danio*†.]

Dan·ish (dā'nĭsh) *adj. Abbr.* **Dan., Da.** Of or pertaining to Denmark, the Danes, their language, or their culture. —*n. Abbr.* **Dan., Da. 1.** The North Germanic language of the Danes. **2.** *Informal.* Danish pastry. [Middle English *Danish,* Old English *Denisc,* from *Dene,* the Danes. See **dan-** in Appendix.*]

Danish pastry. A sweet, buttery pastry made with raised dough. Also informally called "Danish."

Danish West In·dies (ĭn'dēz). The former possessions of Denmark in the Lesser Antilles, including St. Thomas, St. Croix, and St. John, sold to the United States in 1917, and since known as the Virgin Islands of the United States.

ă pat/ā pay/âr care/ä father/b bib/ch church/d deed/ĕ pet/ē be/f fife/g gag/h hat/hw which/ĭ pit/ī pie/îr pier/j judge/k kick/l lid, needle/m mum/n no, sudden/ng thing/ŏ pot/ō toe/ô paw, for/oi noise/ou out/ŏŏ took/ōō boot/p pop/r roar/s sauce/sh ship, dish/

Dan·ite (dăn′īt′) *n.* A descendant of Dan. Judges 13:2. —*adj.* Of or pertaining to the Hebrew tribe descended from Dan.

dank (dăngk) *adj.* **danker, dankest.** Uncomfortably damp; chilly and wet: "*Nothing would sleep in that cellar, dank as a ditch.*" (Theodore Roethke). See Synonyms at **wet.** [Middle English *dank*†.] —**dank′ly** *adv.* —**dank′ness** *n.*

Dan·mark. The Danish name for **Denmark.**

D'An·nun·zio (dä-no͞on′tsyō), **Gabriele.** 1863–1938. Italian poet, playwright, and novelist.

Da·no-Nor·we·gian (dā′nō-nôr-wē′jən) *n.* A form of the Norwegian language, **Riksmål** *(see).*

danse ma·ca·bre (däns mȧ-kȧ′br′). *French.* Dance of death.

dan·seur (däN-sœr′) *n., pl.* **-seurs** (-sœr′). *Feminine* **dan·seuse** (däN-sœz′) *pl.* **-seuses** (-sœz′). A ballet dancer. [French, from Old French, from *danser,* to DANCE.]

Dan·te A·li·ghie·ri (dän′tā ä′lē-gyā′rē). Original surname, Durante. 1265–1321. Italian poet; author of *Divine Comedy.*

Dan·te·an (dăn′tē-ən, dăn-tē′ən) *adj.* **1.** Of or pertaining to Dante or his writings: *Dantean scholarship.* **2.** Dantesque. —*n.* A scholar specializing in the life and writings of Dante.

Dan·tesque (dăn-tĕsk′) *adj.* Characterized by or having the exalted, visionary style of Dante.

Dan·ton (däN-tôN′), **Georges Jacques.** 1759–1794. French lawyer and revolutionary leader.

Da·nu (*th*ä′no͞o). *Irish Mythology.* The goddess of death and mother of the gods. [Irish, akin to Welsh *Don*†.]

Dan·ube (dăn′yo͞ob). *German* **Do·nau** (dō′nou′); *Hungarian* **Du·na** (do͞o′nô); *Rumanian* **Du·nă·rea** (do͞o′nə-ryä); *Serbo-Croatian & Bulgarian* **Du·nav** (do͞o′näf). The major river of southeastern Europe, rising in the Black Forest of southwestern West Germany and flowing 1,750 miles generally eastward to the Black Sea coast of Rumania. [Latin *Dānuvius,* from Celtic. See **dānu-** in Appendix.*] —**Dan·u′bi·an** (dăn-yo͞o′bē-ən) *adj.*

Dan·zig. The German name for **Gdańsk.**

Dan·zig Free City (dăn′sĭg, -zĭg; *German* dän′tsĭκ). A former state, established by the treaty of Versailles (1919), occupying 731 square miles on the Gulf of Danzig and including Gdańsk (then Danzig).

Dan·zig, Gulf of (dăn′sĭg, -zĭg; *German* dän′tsĭκ). An inlet of the Baltic Sea between northern Poland and the northwestern Soviet Union.

dap (dăp) *intr.v.* **dapped, dapping, daps. 1.** To fish by letting a baited hook fall gently on the water. **2.** To dip lightly or quickly into water, as a bird does. **3.** To skip or bounce, especially over the surface of water. [Probably alteration of DAB (to strike lightly), influenced by DIP.]

daph·ne (dăf′nē) *n.* Any of several shrubs of the genus *Daphne,* native to Eurasia, often cultivated for their glossy evergreen foliage and clusters of small, bell-shaped flowers. [New Latin *Daphne,* from Latin *daphnē,* laurel, from Greek. See **Daphne.**]

Daph·ne (dăf′nē). *Greek Mythology.* A personification of the laurel as a nymph choosing this metamorphosis as an escape from Apollo. [Latin *Daphnē,* from Greek, from *daphnē,* laurel, probably related to Latin *laurus,* LAUREL.]

daph·ni·a (dăf′nē-ə) *n., pl.* **daphnia.** Any of various small fresh-water crustaceans of the genus *Daphnia,* some species of which are commonly used as food for aquarium fish. [New Latin *Daphnia,* perhaps from Latin *Daphnē,* DAPHNE.]

dap·per (dăp′ər) *adj.* **1.** Neatly dressed; trim. **2.** Small and active. [Middle English *dapyr,* elegant, probably from Middle Low German or Middle Dutch *dapper,* quick, nimble. See **dheb-** in Appendix.*] —**dap′per·ly** *adv.* —**dap′per·ness** *n.*

dap·ple (dăp′əl) *n.* **1. a.** Mottled or spotted marking, as on a horse's skin. **b.** An individual spot. **2.** An animal with a mottled or spotted skin or coat. —*tr.v.* **dappled, -pling, -ples.** To mark or mottle with spots. —*adj.* Also **dap·pled** (-əld). Spotted or mottled. [Probably from DAPPLE-GRAY.]

dap·ple-gray (dăp′əl-grā′) *adj.* Gray with a mottled pattern of darker gray markings. —*n.* A dapple-gray horse. [Middle English *dappel-grey,* perhaps alteration (influenced by Old Norse *depill,* a spot) of *appel-gray* (unattested), "apple-gray," probably from Old Norse *apalgrār* : *apall-, epli,* apple (see **abel-** in Appendix*) + *grār,* gray (see **gher-**[4] in Appendix*).]

Dap·sang. See **Godwin Austen.**

DAR 1. Airport code for Dar es Salaam, Tanzania. **2.** Daughters of the American Revolution.

D.A.R. Daughters of the American Revolution.

darb (därb) *n. Canadian Slang.* Something considered especially excellent or outstanding. [Perhaps variant of DAB (expert).]

Dar·by and Joan (där′bē). An elderly married couple who live a placid, harmonious life together and are seldom seen apart: "*When we travel together, we must go Darby and Joan fashion, as man and wife.*" (Trollope). [After the elderly couple in a popular 18th-century English ballad.]

Dard (därd) *n., pl.* **Dard** or **Dards.** Also **Dar·dic** (där′dĭk). The Indic languages of the upper Indus River valley.

Dar·dan (därd′n) *n.* Also **Dar·da·ni·an** (där-dā′nē-ən). A Trojan. [After DARDANUS.] —**Dar′dan** *adj.*

Dar·da·nelles (därd′n-ĕlz′). Ancient name **Hel·les·pont** (hĕl′ĭs-pŏnt′). A strait 37 miles long and up to 4 miles wide, linking the Sea of Marmara and the Aegean Sea.

Dar·da·nus (därd′n-əs). *Greek Mythology.* Eponymous hero of the Dardans and founder of Troy.

dare (dâr) *v.* **dared** or *archaic* **durst** (dûrst), **daring, dare** or **dares.** See Usage note below. —*tr.* **1.** To have the courage required for: *He dared a voyage round the world.* **2.** To challenge (someone) to do something requiring boldness: *I dare you to climb that tree.* —*intr.* To be courageous or bold enough to do or try something. —**dare say.** Also **dare·say.** To consider (it) very likely or almost certain. See Usage note below. —*n.* A challenge; an act of taunting or defying. [*Dare, durst;* Middle English *dar, dorste* (also *durste*), Old English *dear, dorste* (also *durste*), first and third person present and past indicative of *durran,* to venture, dare. See **dhers-** in Appendix.*] —**dar′er** *n.*

Usage: *Dare* is often followed by an infinitive (sometimes an infinitive without *to*). In the third person singular, present indicative, two forms of this verb exist: the regular (inflected) *dares* (*He dares to speak up*) and the uninflected *dare.* The latter occurs principally in interrogative and negative constructions employing the infinitive without *to* or the unstated but understood infinitive: *Dare he speak up? He dare not.* The form *dare say* (or *daresay*) is typically followed by a clause without an introductory conjunction: *I dare say he tried hard.*

Dare (dâr), **Virginia.** Born 1587. First child born in America of English parents (on Roanoke Island).

dare·dev·il (dâr′dĕv′əl) *n.* One who is recklessly bold. —*adj.* Recklessly bold. —**dare′dev′il·ry, dare′dev′il·try** *n.*

Dar-el-Bei·da. The Arabic name for **Casablanca.**

Dar es Sa·laam (där′ ĕs sə-läm′). The capital, principal port, and largest city of Tanzania, in the northeast on the mainland coast. Population, 129,000.

Dar·fur (där-fo͝or′). **1.** A former kingdom in the western Sudan, conquered by Egypt in 1874 and incorporated into the Anglo-Egyptian Sudan in 1898. **2.** A province of Sudan, occupying 191,650 square miles in the northwest. Population, 1,329,000. Capital, El Fasher.

dar·ic (dăr′ĭk) *n.* A gold coin of ancient Persia. [Greek *Dār(e)ikos,* probably after *Dāreîos,* DARIUS I.]

Dar·ién (dä-ryĕn′). A region of eastern Panama between the Gulf of Darién and the Gulf of Panama.

Da·rién, Gulf of (dä-ryĕn′). A wide bay of the Caribbean Sea between northeastern Panama and northwestern Colombia.

Da·rién, Isthmus of. The former name for the Isthmus of **Panama.**

dar·ing (dâr′ĭng) *adj.* Willing to take risks; fearless; bold; adventurous. See Synonyms at **brave, reckless.** —*n.* Active bravery; boldness; intrepidity. —**dar′ing·ly** *adv.* —**dar′ing·ness** *n.*

dar·i·ole (dâr′ē-ōl′) *n.* **1.** A small cream tart made with puff pastry in a circular mold. **2.** The mold itself. [French, from Old French, perhaps a diminutive formation from *dorer,* to gild, from Latin *deaurāre* : *dē-* (intensive) + *aurāre,* to gild, from *aurum,* gold (see **aurum** in Appendix*).]

Da·ri·us I (də-rī′əs). Surname, Hystaspis. Called "the Great." 558?–486 B.C. King of Persia (521–486 B.C.); made war against Greece until defeat at Marathon (490 B.C.). [Latin, from Greek *Dāreîos* (for *Dāreiaîos*), from Old Persian *Dārayavauš,* "holding firm the good" : *dārayat,* he holds, from *dār-,* to hold (see **dher-**[2] in Appendix*) + *vahu*†, good.]

Da·ri·us III (də-rī′əs). Surname, Codomannus. 380?–330 B.C. Last Achaemenid king of Persia (336–330 B.C.); defeated by Alexander the Great.

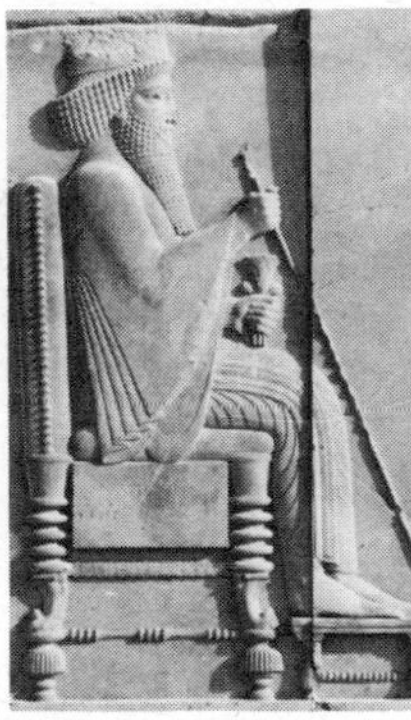

Darius I
Relief from the ancient treasury at Persepolis, Iran, showing Darius seated on his throne

Dar·jee·ling[1] (där-jē′lĭng). A district capital and resort city in northern West Bengal, Republic of India, 305 miles north of Calcutta in the Himalayan foothills. Population, 41,000.

Dar·jee·ling[2] (där-jē′lĭng) *n.* A fine variety of black tea from Darjeeling, India. Also called "Darjeeling tea."

dark (därk) *adj.* **darker, darkest.** *Abbr.* **dk. 1.** With very little or no light. **2.** Reflecting only a small fraction of the incident light. See **color. 3.** Lacking light or brightness; shaded; obscure: *a dark day.* **4.** Of a shade tending toward black or brown by comparison with *light, pale,* or *white: dark hair; dark meat.* **5.** Characterized by or producing gloom; dreary; dismal. **6.** Sullen; threatening: *a dark scowl.* **7.** Hard to understand; obscure. **8.** Concealed; secret; mysterious. **9.** Unenlightened; uncivilized: *a dark era in history.* **10.** Evil or wicked; sinister: *a dark purpose.* —*n.* **1.** Absence of light. **2.** A place having little light. **3.** Night; nightfall. **4.** A dark hue or color. —**in the dark. 1.** In secret: *things done in the dark.* **2.** In a state of ignorance; uninformed. [Middle English *derk,* Old English *deorc.* See **dher-**[1] in Appendix.*] —**dark′ish** *adj.*

Synonyms: *dark, dim, murky, dusky, obscure, opaque, shady, shadowy.* These adjectives indicate the absence of light or clarity. *Dark,* the most widely applicable, can refer to insufficiency of illumination for seeing, to deepness of shade of a color, as *dark brown,* or figuratively to absence of cheer or rectitude: *dark day; dark mood; dark comedy; dark deeds. Dim* suggests lack of clarity of outline of physical things or mental ones, such as memories or recollections, and can also apply to the source of light to indicate insufficiency. *Murky* usually implies darkness such as that produced by smoke or fog; less often it refers to extreme darkness or, figuratively, to unclear, sullen thoughts. *Dusky* applies principally to the dimness characteristic of twilight or to deepness of shade of a color. *Obscure* usually means unclear to the mind or senses but can refer to physical darkness. *Opaque* means incapable of being penetrated by light; figuratively it applies to what is incapable of perceiving reason and to what is unintelligible. *Shady* refers to what is sheltered from light, especially sunlight, or, figuratively, to what is covertly dishonest. *Shadowy* also implies obstructed light but suggests shifting illumination and indistinct vision.

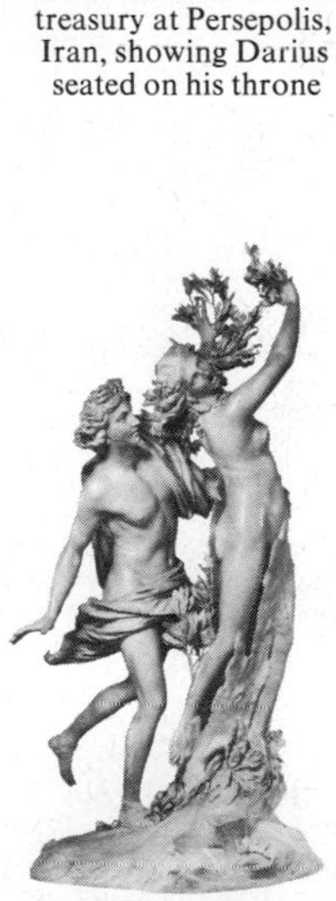

Daphne
"Apollo and Daphne," a sculpture by Bernini

dark adaptation. The physical and chemical adjustments of the eye, including dilation of the pupil, that make vision possible in relative darkness. —**dark′-a·dapt′ed** (därk′ə-dăp′tĭd) *adj.*

Dark Ages. 1. The early part of the Middle Ages. **2.** The entire period from the end of classical civilization to the revival of learning in the West.

Dark Continent. Africa. [So called because its hinterland was largely unknown until the late 19th century.]

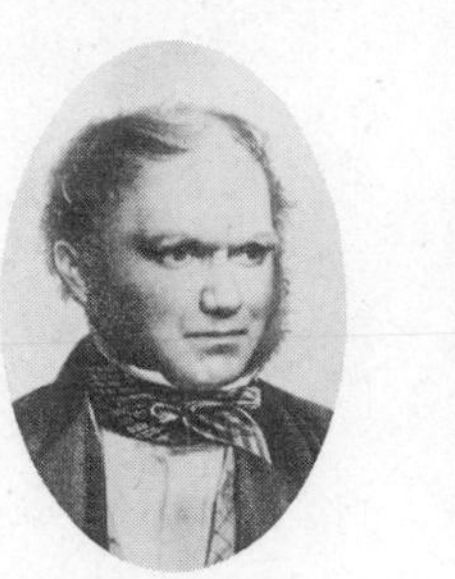

Charles Darwin

dark·en (där′kən) *v.* **-ened, -ening, -ens.** —*tr.* **1.** To shut out the light of; make dark or darker. **2.** To impart a darker hue to; render less white or clear. **3.** To fill with sadness; make gloomy. **4.** To obscure or cloud the meaning of; render vague. **5.** To strike with blindness. —*intr.* **1.** To become dark or darker. **2.** To become dark in color. **3.** To become obscure, vague, or uncertain. **4.** To grow clouded, gloomy, or sullen. **5.** To become blind. —**darken one's door.** To come to one's house as an ominous or unwelcome visitor. —**dark′en·er** *n.*

dark-field microscope (därk′fēld′). An **ultramicroscope** *(see).*

dark horse. **1.** A little-known entrant in a horse race, contest, or the like. **2.** One who receives unexpected support as a candidate for the nomination in a political convention.

dark lantern. A lantern whose light can be blocked by a panel or other device.

dar·kle (där′kəl) *intr.v.* **-kled, -kling, -kles.** **1.** To appear darkly or indistinctly. **2.** To grow dark. [From DARKLING.]

dark·ling (därk′lĭng) *adv. Poetic.* In the dark. —*adj. Poetic.* **1.** Being or happening in the dark or the night. **2.** Dim; obscure. [Middle English *derkeling* : DARK + -LING (becoming).]

dark·ly (därk′lē) *adv.* **1.** So as to appear dark; in a dark manner. **2. a.** Mysteriously. **b.** In a sinister manner. **3.** Dimly; obscurely; faintly: *"For now we see through a glass, darkly."* (I Corinthians 13:12).

dark·ness (därk′nĭs) *n.* **1.** Total or almost total absence of light. **2.** The quality of being dark in color. **3.** Blindness. **4.** Lack of enlightenment; ignorance. **5.** Evil; wickedness. **6.** Secrecy; concealment. **7.** Lack of clearness; obscurity.

dark·room (därk′rōōm′, -rŏŏm′) *n.* A room in which photographic materials are processed, either in complete darkness or illuminated by sources of light to which the materials are not sensitive.

dark·some (därk′səm) *adj. Poetic.* Dark; darkish; somber.

dark star. A star that is normally obscured or too faint for direct visual observation, especially the component of an eclipsing binary detectable by spectral analysis or in the eclipse of the bright component.

dark·y (där′kē) *n., pl.* **-ies.** Also **dark·ey** *pl.* **-eys, dark·ie.** A Negro. An offensive term used derogatorily.

dar·ling (där′lĭng) *n.* **1.** One who is very dear; a much-loved person. Often used as a term of address. **2.** One that is greatly liked or preferred; a favorite. —*adj.* **1.** Regarded with great affection and tenderness; very dear; beloved. **2.** Regarded with special favor; favorite: *"Metaphysics and poetry . . . are my darling studies."* (Coleridge). **3.** *Informal.* Charming; amusing; pleasing: *a darling hat.* [Middle English *dereling,* Old English *dēorling* : DEAR + -LING (diminutive).]

Darling Range. An upland area of Australia, stretching about 200 miles parallel to the southwestern coast.

Darling River. A river of Australia, formed by headstreams at the Queensland-New South Wales border and flowing 1,702 miles generally southwest through New South Wales to the Murray River.

Darm·stadt (därm′stăt′; *German* därm′shtät′). A city of west-central West Germany, 17 miles south of Frankfurt; the former capital of Hesse. Population, 140,000.

darn¹ (därn) *v.* **darned, darning, darns.** —*tr.* To mend by weaving thread or yarn across a gap or hole. —*intr.* To mend or repair a hole or garment by darning. —*n.* **1.** A place repaired by darning. **2.** The act of darning. [French (Channel Islands dialect) *darner,* probably from Norman French *darne,* piece, from Breton *darn*†.] —**darn′er** *n.*

darn² (därn). Euphemism for **damn.**

dar·nel (där′nəl) *n.* Any of several grasses of the genus *Lolium,* native to the Old World; especially, *L. tementulum* or *L. perenne.* [Middle English, akin to French dialectal *darnelle*†, cockle.]

darning egg. An egg-shaped object used to hold the shape of material being darned.

darning needle. **1.** A long, large-eyed needle used in darning. **2.** *Informal.* A **dragonfly** *(see).*

Darn·ley (därn′lē), **Lord.** Title of Henry Stuart or Stewart. 1545–1567. Scottish nobleman; second husband of Mary, Queen of Scots; father of James I; murdered.

Dar·row (dăr′ō), **Clarence Seward.** 1857–1938. American criminal lawyer and social reformer.

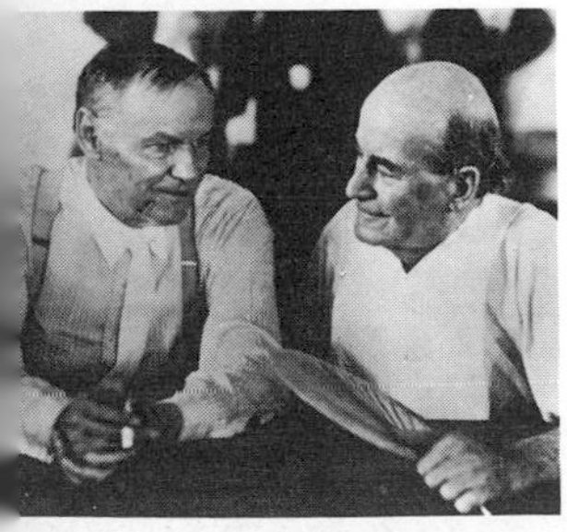

Clarence Darrow
With William Jennings Bryan *(right)* at the 1925 Scopes trial in Dayton, Tennessee

dart (därt) *n.* **1.** A slender, pointed missile, often having tail fins, to be thrown by the hand or shot from a blowgun, crossbow, or the like. **2.** Anything like a dart in shape, use, or effect. **3.** An insect's stinger. **4.** *Plural.* A game in which darts are thrown at a target. Used with a singular verb. **5.** A rapid, sudden movement. **6.** In sewing, a tapered tuck to adjust the fit of a garment. —*v.* **darted, darting, darts.** —*intr.* To move suddenly and swiftly. —*tr.* To throw or thrust suddenly or swiftly; emit; shoot. [Middle English, from Old French, from Germanic *darōdhaz* (unattested), spear.]

dar·ter (där′tər) *n.* **1.** One that moves suddenly and swiftly. **2.** Any of several long-necked, long-billed birds of the genus *Anhinga,* such as the **water turkey** *(see).* **3.** Any of various small, often brightly colored freshwater fishes of the family Percidae, of eastern North America.

dar·tle (därt′l) *tr.v.* **-tled, -tling, -tles.** To thrust or shoot out repeatedly. [Frequentative of *dart,* to pierce with a dart, from Middle English *darten,* from DART.]

Dart·moor (därt′mŏŏr′). **1.** A barren heath in southern Devonshire, England. **2.** A prison located on this heath.

Dart·mouth (därt′məth). A town and port in southern Devonshire, England, on the English Channel; seat of the Royal Naval College. Population, 6,000.

Dar·win (där′wĭn). The capital and a port of the Northern Territory, Australia, on the Timor Sea. Population, 13,000.

Dar·win (där′wĭn), **Charles Robert.** 1809–1882. British naturalist; expounded theory of evolution by natural selection in *On the Origin of Species* (1859); grandson of Erasmus Darwin; father of Sir George Darwin.

Dar·win (där′wĭn), **Erasmus.** 1731–1802. British physiologist and poet; grandfather of Charles Darwin.

Dar·win (där′wĭn), Sir **George Howard.** 1845–1912. British astronomer and mathematician; son of Charles Darwin.

Dar·win·ism (där′wə-nĭz′əm) *n.* A theory of biological evolution developed by Charles Darwin and others. It states that species of plants and animals develop through **natural selection** *(see)* of variations that increase the organism's ability to survive and reproduce. —**Dar·win′i·an** (-wĭn′ĭ-ən) *adj.* —**Dar′win·ist** *adj.* & *n.* —**Dar′win·is′tic** *adj.*

Darwin tulip. A type of garden tulip having squarish flowers in a wide variety of colors. [After Charles DARWIN.]

dash¹ (dăsh) *v.* **dashed, dashing, dashes.** —*tr.* **1.** To break or smash by striking violently. **2.** To hurl, knock, or thrust with sudden violence. Usually used with *away, down,* or *out.* **3.** To splash; bespatter. **4.** To complete hastily; finish off. Used with *off* or *down.* **5.** To add an enlivening or altering element to; mix; adulterate: *"Some truth there was, but dash'd and brew'd with lies."* (Dryden). **6.** To destroy; frustrate: *His dreams were dashed.* **7.** To confound; abash. —*intr.* **1.** To strike violently; smash. **2.** To move with haste; rush; race. —*n.* **1.** A swift, violent blow or stroke. **2.** A splash. **3.** A small amount of an added ingredient: *a dash of salt.* **4.** A quick stroke, as with a pencil or brush. **5.** A sudden movement; a rush. **6.** A foot race run at top speed from the outset, usually less than a quarter-mile long. **7.** Spirited action or style; vigor; verve. **8.** A punctuation mark (—) used in writing and printing. See Usage note below. **9.** *Telecommunications.* In Morse code and similar codes, the long sound or signal used in combination with the dot, a shorter sound, and silent intervals to represent letters or numbers. [Middle English *daschen, dashen,* from Scandinavian, akin to Danish *daske,* to beat, from North Germanic *daskanan* (unattested).]

Usage: The dash as a mark of punctuation has the following uses: 1. To set off a parenthetical clause: *Her face—or so it seemed to me—was never more radiant.* 2. To indicate a break in thought: *Then he ran—the fool.* 3. To mark an omission: *She doesn't give a d——.* 4. To mark a summing up: *Study and practice—these are the only solution.* 5. To do the work of a colon: *Ten were chosen—five girls and five boys.* In modern writing, the dash is not used in combination with the colon or comma, though it can be followed immediately by a period at the end of a sentence. Indiscriminate use of the dash often leads to choppiness and confusion of expression.

dash² (dăsh). Euphemism for **damn.**

dash·board (dăsh′bôrd′, -bōrd′) *n.* A panel under the windshield of an automobile, containing indicator dials, compartments, and sometimes control instruments.

da·sheen (dă-shēn′) *n.* A plant, **taro** *(see).* [Origin unknown.]

dash·er (dăsh′ər) *n.* **1.** One that dashes. **2.** The plunger of a churn or ice-cream freezer. **3.** *Informal.* A spirited person.

dash·ing (dăsh′ĭng) *adj.* **1.** Audacious and gallant; bold; spirited. **2.** Marked by showy elegance; splendid: *a dashing sport coat.* —**dash′ing·ly** *adv.*

Dasht-i-Ka·vir (dăsht′ē-kä-vîr′). Also **Dasht-e-Ka·vir.** The great salt desert of the central plateau of Iran. Also called "Kavir Desert."

Dasht-i-Lut (dăsht′ē-lōōt′). Also **Dasht-e-Lut.** A large sand and stone desert in eastern Iran. Also called "Lut Desert."

dash·y (dăsh′ē) *adj.* **-ier, -iest.** Stylishly showy; dashing.

das·sie (dăs′ē) *n.* A mammal, the **hyrax** *(see).* [Afrikaans, diminutive of *das,* badger, hyrax, from Middle Dutch. See **teks-** in Appendix.*]

das·tard (dăs′tərd) *n.* A base, sneaking coward. [Middle English, perhaps from Old Norse *dæstr,* exhausted, past participle of *dæsa,* to languish, decay. See **dhē-²** in Appendix.*]

das·tard·ly (dăs′tərd-lē) *adj.* Cowardly and mean-spirited; base. —**das′tard·li·ness** *n.*

Usage: *Dastardly* is employed most precisely when it refers to acts involving cowardice. It is loosely used when it applies to any reprehensible or risky act.

das·y·ure (dăs′ē-yŏŏr′) *n.* Any of various marsupial mammals of the family Dasyuridae, of Australia and adjacent regions, ranging in size and appearance from that of a mouse to that of a dog. [New Latin *Dasyurus* (genus), "hairy-tailed" : Greek *dasus,* hairy, shaggy (see **dens-²** in Appendix*) + -UROUS.]

dat. dative.

da·ta (dā′tə, dăt′ə, dä′tə) *pl.n. Singular* **datum** (dā′təm, dăt′əm, dä′təm). See Usage note below. **1.** Information, especially information organized for analysis or used as the basis for a decision. **2.** Numerical information in a form suitable for processing by computer. [Latin, plural of DATUM.]

Usage: *Data* is now used both as a plural and as a singular collective: *These data are inconclusive. This data is inconclusive.* The plural construction is the more appropriate in formal usage. The singular is acceptable to 50 per cent of the Usage Panel.

data processing. **1.** The preparation of information for processing by computers. **2.** The storing or processing of raw data by a computer. —**data processor.**

da·ta·ry (dā′tə-rē) *n., pl.* **-ries.** *Roman Catholic Church.* **1.** The duty, formerly an official office of the curia, of investigating the fitness of candidates for papal benefices. **2.** A cardinal assum-

ă pat/ā pay/âr care/ä father/b bib/ch church/d deed/ĕ pet/ē be/f fife/g gag/h hat/hw which/ĭ pit/ī pie/îr pier/j judge/k kick/l lid, needle/m mum/n no, sudden/ng thing/ŏ pot/ō toe/ô paw, for/oi noise/ou out/ŏŏ took/ōō boot/p pop/r roar/s sauce/sh ship, dish/

ing the duty of datary. Called in full "cardinal datary." [Medieval Latin *datārius,* official who dated all papal letters, from Late Latin *data,* DATE (time).]

date[1] (dāt) *n. Abbr.* **d. 1.** A particular point or period of time at which something happened or existed or is to happen. **2.** The time during which something lasts; duration. **3.** The time or historical period to which something belongs: *artifacts of a later date.* **4.** *Plural.* The years of a person's birth and death. **5.** The day of the month. **6.** An inscription or statement, as on a coin or letter, indicating when it was made or written. **7.** *Informal.* **a.** An appointment to meet socially at a particular time; especially, one with a member of the opposite sex. **b.** A person so met. —**to date.** Up to the present time; as yet. —*v.* **dated, dating, dates.** —*tr.* **1.** To mark or supply (a letter, for example) with a date. **2.** To assign a date to; determine the date of. **3.** To betray the age of. **4.** *Informal.* To make or have a social engagement with (a person of the opposite sex). —*intr.* **1.** To have origin in a particular time in the past. Usually used with *from: This statue dates from 500* B.C. **2.** To become old-fashioned. **3.** *Informal.* To have social engagements with persons of the opposite sex. [Middle English, from Old French, from Medieval Latin *data,* "given," "issued" (used for Latin *datum* in the letter-dating formula *datum Romae prīdiē Kalendās Māiās,* issued at Rome on the day before the first day of May), from Latin *datus,* past participle of *dare,* to give. See **dō-** in Appendix.*] —**dat′able, date′able** *adj.* —**dat′er** *n.*

date[2] (dāt) *n.* **1.** The sweet, oblong, edible fruit of the **date palm** *(see),* containing a narrow, hard seed. **2.** The date palm. [Middle English, from Old French, from Old Provençal *datil,* from Latin *dactylus,* from Greek *daktulos,* "finger" (from the shape of the fruit). See **dactyl.**]

dat·ed (dā′tĭd) *adj.* **1.** Marked with or displaying a date. **2.** Old-fashioned; antiquated; out-of-date. —**dat′ed·ness** *n.*

date line. An imaginary line through the Pacific Ocean roughly corresponding to 180 degrees longitude, to the east of which, by international agreement, the calendar date is one day earlier than to the west. Called in full "International Date Line."

date·line (dāt′līn′) *n.* A phrase at the beginning of a newspaper or magazine article that gives the date and place of its origin.

date palm. A tree, *Phoenix dactylifera,* of tropical regions, having featherlike leaves and bearing clusters of dates as fruit.

da·tive (dā′tĭv) *adj.* Also **da·ti·val** (dā-tī′vəl). *Abbr.* **dat.** Designating or belonging to a grammatical case in Latin, Russian, and other inflected Indo-European languages that marks the indirect object of a verb and the object of any of certain verbs and prepositions. —*n. Abbr.* **dat. 1.** The dative case. **2.** A word or form in the dative case. [Middle English *datif,* from Latin *(cāsus) datīvus,* "(case) of giving" (translation of Greek *dotikos ptōsis*), from *dare,* to give. See **dō-** in Appendix.*] —**da′tive·ly** *adv.*

dat·to (dä′tō) *n., pl.* **-tos.** Also **da·to. 1.** The chief of a Moslem Moro tribe in the Philippines. **2.** The head man of a barrio or Malay tribe. [Spanish *dato,* from Tagalog *datò,* from Malay *dato(′),* "grandfather."]

da·tum (dā′təm, dăt′əm, dä′təm) *n., pl.* **-ta** (-tə) or **-tums** (for sense 3). **1.** An assumed, given, measured, or otherwise determined fact or proposition used to draw a conclusion or make a decision. See Usage note at **data. 2.** The real or assumed point from which any reckoning or scale begins. **3.** A point, line, or surface used as a reference, as in surveying, mapping, or geology. [Latin, "something given," from the neuter past participle of *dare,* to give. See **dō-** in Appendix.*]

da·tu·ra (də-to͝or′ə, -tyo͝or′ə) *n.* Any of several plants of the genus *Datura,* having large trumpet-shaped flowers. [New Latin *Datura,* from Hindi *dhatūrā,* from Sanskrit *dhattūrā*†.]

daub (dôb) *v.* **daubed, daubing, daubs.** —*tr.* **1.** To cover, coat, or smear with an adhesive substance, such as plaster, mud, or grease. **2.** To apply paint to with hasty or crude strokes. —*intr.* To apply paint or coloring with crude, unskillful strokes. —*n.* **1.** The act or a stroke of daubing. **2.** Any soft adhesive coating material, such as plaster or mud. **3.** A crude or amateurishly inferior painting: *"A job-lot of horrid art-student daubs covered the walls."* (Anthony Burgess). [Middle English *dauben,* from Old French *dauber,* from Latin *dēalbāre,* to whitewash : *dē-,* completely + *albāre,* to whiten, from *albus,* white (see **albho-** in Appendix*).] —**daub′er** *n.* —**daub′er·y** (dô′bə-rē) *n.* —**daub′ing·ly** *adv.* —**daub′y** *adj.*

daube (dōb) *n.* **1.** A method of cooking in which meat, usually beef, is braised in red wine. **2.** A stew so prepared. [French, from Spanish *doba* (unattested), from *dobar*†, to stew.]

Dau·bi·gny (dō-bē-nyē′), **Charles François.** 1817–1878. French landscape painter; a leader of the Barbizon school.

Dau·det (dō-dā′), **Alphonse.** 1840–1897. French author.

Dau·ga·va. The Lettish name for the **Dvina.**

daugh·ter (dô′tər) *n. Abbr.* **d. 1.** One's female child. **2.** A female descendant. **3.** A girl or woman considered as if in a relationship of child to parent: *a daughter of the nation.* **4.** Anything personified or regarded as a female descendant: *"Culturally Japan is a daughter of Chinese civilization"* (Edwin Reischauer). [Middle English *doughter,* Old English *dohtor.* See **dhugheter-** in Appendix.*] —**daugh′ter·ly** *adj.*

daugh·ter-in-law (dô′tər-ĭn-lô′) *n., pl.* **daughters-in-law.** The wife of one's son.

Daughters of the American Revolution. *Abbr.* **DAR, D.A.R.** A society of women descended from American patriots of the Revolutionary War, organized in 1890.

Dau·mier (dō-myā′), **Honoré.** 1808–1879. French painter, lithographer, and cartoonist.

daunt (dônt, dänt) *tr.v.* **daunted, daunting, daunts. 1.** To intimidate. **2.** To discourage; dishearten. —See Synonyms at **dismay.** [Middle English *daunten,* from Old French *danter, donter,* from Latin *domitāre,* frequentative of *domāre,* to tame, subdue. See **deme-**[2] in Appendix.*] —**daunt′er** *n.* —**daunt′ing·ly** *adv.*

daunt·less (dônt′lĭs, dänt′-) *adj.* That cannot be intimidated or discouraged; fearless; bold. See Synonyms at **brave.** —**daunt′less·ly** *adv.* —**daunt′less·ness** *n.*

dau·phin (dô′fĭn; *French* dō-făN′) *n.* The eldest son of the king of France. Used as a title from 1349 to 1830. [French, from Old French *dalphin, dalfin,* DOLPHIN. This title (originally borne by the lords of Viennois, France, whose coat of arms bore three dolphins) was adopted by the French crown princes as a condition when the Viennois province Dauphiné was ceded to the crown.]

Dau·phi·né (dō-fē-nā′). A region and former province of southeastern France.

dau·phin·ess (dô′fĭ-nĭs) *n.* Also **dau·phine** (dô-fēn′; *French* dō-fēn′). The wife of the dauphin.

DAV, D.A.V. Disabled American Veterans.

Da·vao (dä′vou). A seaport in southeastern Mindanao, Republic of the Philippines, on Davao Gulf. Population, 83,000.

Da·vao Gulf (dä′vou). A large inlet on the southeastern coast of Mindanao, Republic of the Philippines.

Da·ve·nant (dăv′ə-nənt), Sir **William.** Also **D′Av·e·nant.** 1606–1668. English dramatist; poet laureate (1638–68).

dav·en·port (dăv′ən-pôrt′, -pōrt′) *n.* **1.** A large sofa, often convertible into a bed. **2.** *British.* A small desk. [Said to be from *Davenport,* name of the original manufacturer of the desk.]

Dav·en·port (dăv′ən-pôrt′, -pōrt′). A city and river port of eastern Iowa, on the Mississippi. Population, 89,000.

Dav·en·port (dăv′ən-pôrt′, -pōrt′), **John.** 1597–1670. English Puritan clergyman and colonist in America; a founder of the New Haven colony.

Da·vid[1] (dā′vĭd). A masculine given name. [Hebrew *Dāwid,* possibly from root *dwd,* beloved.]

Da·vid[2] (dā′vĭd). Second king of Judah and Israel (1010?–970? B.C.), successor to Saul; father of King Solomon; reputed author of many of the Psalms. —**Da·vid′ic** *adj.*

Da·vid (dä-vēd′), **Jacques Louis.** 1748–1825. French painter; founder of French classical school; court painter to Louis XVI and Napoleon I.

Da·vid (dā′vĭd), **Saint.** Christian Bishop of Menevia in the sixth century A.D.; patron saint of Wales; canonized 1120.

David, Star of. A symbol of Judaism, the **Magen David** *(see).*

Da·vid·son (dā′vĭd-sən), **Jo.** 1883–1952. American sculptor.

da Vin·ci, Leonardo. See **Leonardo da Vinci.**

Da·vis (dā′vĭs), **Jefferson.** 1808–1889. American military officer and political leader; president of the Confederate States of America (1861–65).

Da·vis, John. See **Davys.**

Da·vis (dā′vĭs), **Richard Harding.** 1864–1916. American war correspondent, editor, and novelist.

Davis Cup. A trophy awarded to the nation whose team is the winner of the International Lawn Tennis Championship. [Donated in 1900 by Dwight F. *Davis* (1879–1945), American civic leader and government official.]

Da·vis·son (dā′vĭ-sən), **Clinton Joseph.** 1881–1958. American physicist; worked on diffraction of electrons.

Da·vis Strait (dā′vĭs). An arm of the North Atlantic Ocean, 400 miles long and 180 to 400 miles wide, between southeastern Baffin Island and southwestern Greenland.

dav·it (dăv′ĭt, dā′-) *n.* Any of various types of small cranes, usually made of shaped steel tubing and used on ships to hoist boats, anchors, and cargo. [Middle English *daviot,* from Old French *daviot, daviet,* diminutive of *David,* DAVID, also the name given to a carpenter's tool.]

Da·vy (dā′vē), Sir **Humphry.** 1778–1829. British chemist; discovered 12 chemical elements.

Da·vy Jones (dā′vē jōnz′). The spirit of the sea. [Perhaps *Davy,* nickname for DAVID + *Jones,* alteration of *Jonas, Jonah* (the prophet, with allusion to the whale in Jonah 1:17).]

Davy Jones's locker. The bottom of the sea, especially as the grave of all who perish at sea.

Davy lamp. An early safety oil lamp used by coal miners. Also called "davy." [Invented by Sir Humphry DAVY.]

Da·vys (dā′vĭs), **John.** Also **Da·vis.** 1550?–1605. English navigator; searched for Northwest Passage; discovered Falkland Islands (1592).

daw (dô) *n.* A bird, the **jackdaw** *(see).* [Middle English *dawe,* probably from Old English *dāwe* (unattested), from West Germanic *dǣgw-* (unattested).]

daw·dle (dôd′l) *v.* **-dled, -dling, -dles.** —*intr.* To waste time by trifling or loitering; linger. —*tr.* To waste (time) in this manner. Usually used with *away: dawdling away the hours.* [Probably variant of DADDLE (influenced by DAW, simpleton, hence sluggard).] —**daw′dler** *n.* —**daw′dling·ly** *adv.*

Dawes (dôz), **Charles Gates.** 1865–1931. Vice President of the United States under Calvin Coolidge (1925–29).

dawn (dôn) *n.* **1.** The time each morning when daylight first appears. **2.** The first appearance; emergence; beginning: *the dawn of history.* —*intr.v.* **dawned, dawning, dawns. 1.** To begin to become light in the morning. **2.** To begin to appear or develop; emerge. **3.** To begin to be perceived or understood. Used with *on* or *upon: "the suspicion dawning on him that he was not a welcome visitor"* (Maugham). [Middle English *daunen,* probably back-formation from *dauninge,* daybreak, alteration of *dauinge,* Old English *dagung,* from *dagian,* to dawn. See **agh-**[2] in Appendix.*]

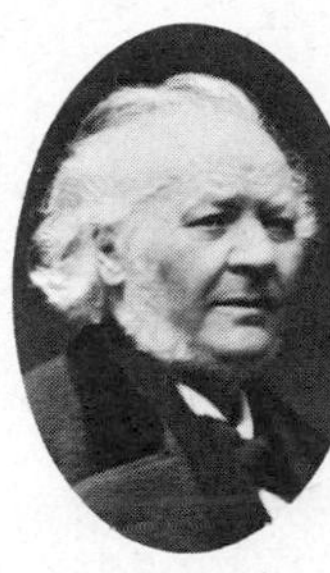

Honoré Daumier

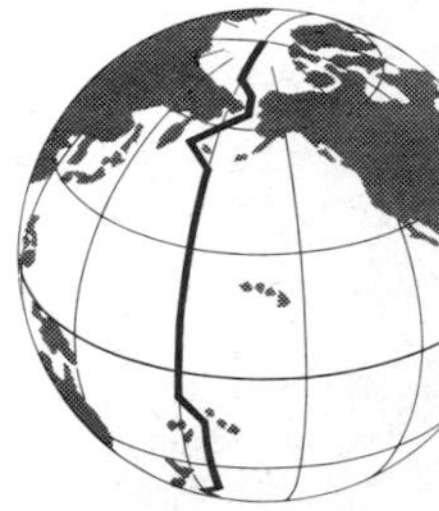

date line

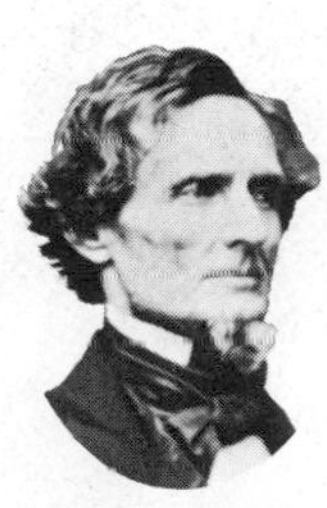

Jefferson Davis

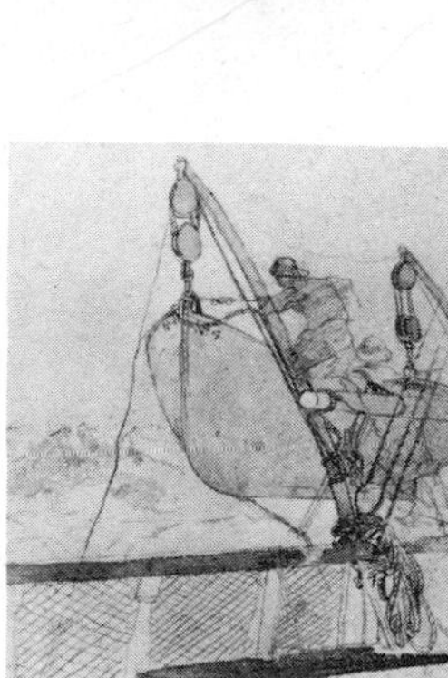

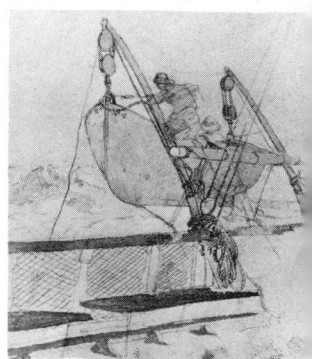

davit
Lifeboat on davits in a drawing by Winslow Homer

dawn redwood. A Chinese coniferous tree, *Metasequoia glyptostroboides,* discovered as an extant species after having long been considered extinct.
Daw·son Creek (dô′sən). The southern terminus of the Alaska Highway in eastern British Columbia. Population, 11,000.
day (dā) *n. Abbr.* **d 1.** The period of light between dawn and nightfall; the interval from sunrise to sunset. **2.** The 24-hour period during which the earth completes one rotation on its axis. See **mean solar day. 3.** The portion of a day devoted to work: *the eight-hour day.* **4.** A day reserved for a certain activity: *assembly day; the day of rest.* **5.** *Usually capital* **D.** A particular day connected with a special event or observance: *Mother's Day.* **6. a.** The period of activity or prominence in one's lifetime: *a writer who has had his day.* **b.** A period of opportunity: *Every dog has his day.* **7.** *Often plural.* A period of time; age; era: *in Napoleon's day; in days of old.* **8.** A unit of distance traveled in an ordinary day's journey. **9.** The contest or issue at hand: *carry the day.* **10.** *Astronomy.* The period during which a heavenly body completes one turn on its axis. **—call it a day.** *Informal.* **1.** To stop one's work or activity for the day. **2.** To terminate after any period of time. **—day after day.** Continuously; for many days. **—day in, day out.** Every day without fail; continuously. [Middle English *dai, day,* Old English *dæg.* See **agh-**[2] in Appendix.*]
Day (dā), **Benjamin Henry.** 1810–1889. American journalist; published New York *Sun* as first one-cent newspaper (1833); grandfather of Clarence Day.
Day (dā), **Clarence Shepard.** 1874–1935. American humorist; author of *Life with Father;* grandson of B.H. Day.
DAY Airport code for Dayton, Ohio.
Day·ak. Variant of **Dyak.**
day bed. A couch or sofa convertible into a bed.
day blindness. *Pathology.* **Hemeralopia** *(see).*
day·book (dā′bo͝ok′) *n.* **1.** *Abbr.* **D.B.** *Bookkeeping.* A book in which daily transactions are recorded. **2.** A diary.
day·break (dā′brāk′) *n.* The time each morning when light first appears; dawn.
day coach. An ordinary passenger car of a railroad train, as distinguished from other cars with special accommodations.
day·dream (dā′drēm′) *n.* A dreamlike musing or fantasy while awake; idle reverie, especially of the fulfillment of wishes or hopes. *—intr.v.* **daydreamed** or **-dreamt** (-drĕmt′), **-dreaming, -dreams.** To have daydreams. **—day′dream′er** *n.*
day·flow·er (dā′flou′ər) *n.* Any of various plants of the genus *Commelina,* having blue or purplish flowers that wilt quickly.
day·fly (dā′flī′) *n., pl.* **-flies.** An insect, the **mayfly** *(see).*
day labor. Labor hired and paid by the day. **—day laborer.**
day letter. A telegram sent during the day, usually less expensive but slower than a regular telegram.
day·light (dā′līt′) *n.* **1.** The light of day; direct light of the sun. **2. a.** Daybreak. **b.** Daytime. **3.** Exposure to public notice. **4.** Understanding or insight into what was formerly obscure. **—see daylight.** To approach the end of a difficult endeavor.
day·lights (dā′līts′) *pl.n. Slang.* Life; sense; wits: *scare the daylights out of him.*
day·light-sav·ing time (dā′līt′sā′vĭng). *Abbr.* **DST, D.S.T.** Time during which clocks are set one hour or more ahead of standard time to provide more daylight at the end of the working day during late spring, summer, and early fall.
day lily. 1. Any of various plants of the genus *Hemerocallis,* native to Eurasia, having sword-shaped leaves and orange, yellow, or red funnel-shaped flowers. **2.** The **plantain lily** *(see).*
day·long (dā′lông′, -lŏng′) *adj.* Lasting the whole day. *—adv.* Through the whole day.
day nursery. A nursery providing daytime care for children of preschool age, especially while their mothers are at work.
Day of Atonement. Yom Kippur *(see).*
Day of Judgment. The **Judgment Day** *(see).*
day school. 1. A private school for pupils living at home. Compare **boarding school. 2.** A school that holds classes during the day.
days·man (dāz′mən) *n., pl.* **-men** (-mĭn). *Rare.* An arbiter or mediator. [Middle English *dayesman* : *dayes,* genitive of DAY (appointed for settlement of dispute) + MAN.]
days of grace. Extra days, usually three, allowed for payment of a note or bill after it has fallen due. [Translation of Latin *diēs grātiae.*]
day·spring (dā′sprĭng′) *n. Poetic.* The early dawn; daybreak.
day·star (dā′stär′) *n.* **1.** The morning star. **2.** *Poetic.* The sun.
day·time (dā′tīm′) *n.* The time between dawn and dark; day. *—adj.* During the day.
Day·ton (dāt′n). **1.** A city and manufacturing center of southwestern Ohio on the Miami River. Population, 262,000. **2.** A town in southeast-central Tennessee, scene of the Scopes trial (1925). Population, 3,500.
Day·to·na Beach (dā-tō′nə). A city of east-central Florida, a winter resort on the Atlantic. Population, 37,000.
daze (dāz) *tr.v.* **dazed, dazing, dazes. 1.** To stun, as with a heavy blow or shock; stupefy. **2.** To dazzle, as with strong light. *—n.* A stunned or bewildered condition: *wandering about in a daze.* [Middle English *dasen,* from Old Norse *dasa* (attested in the reflexive form *dasask,* to become weary). See **dhē-**[2] in Appendix.*] **—daz′ed·ly** *adv.*
daz·zle (dăz′əl) *v.* **-zled, -zling, -zles.** *—tr.* **1.** To dim the vision of; blind with intense light. **2.** To bewilder, amaze, or overwhelm with spectacular display. *—intr.* **1.** To become blinded: *"thy sight is young,/ And thou shalt read when mine begin to dazzle"* (Shakespeare). **2.** To inspire admiration or wonder. *—n.* The act or quality of dazzling: *"the dazzle of league after league of featureless sand"* (T.E. Lawrence). [Frequentative of DAZE.] **—daz′zler** *n.* **—daz′zling·ly** *adv.*

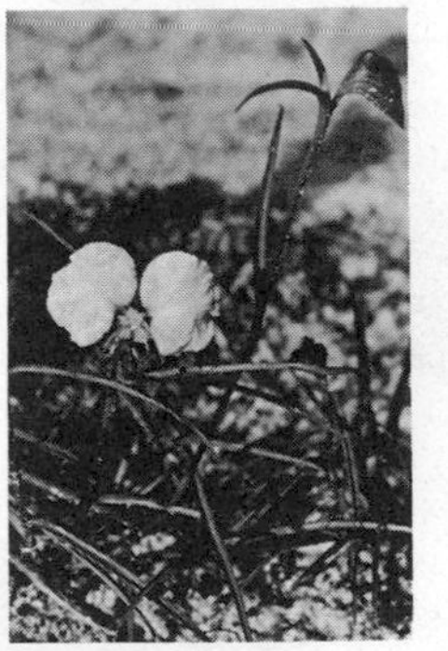

dayflower
Commelina erecta

dB decibel.
D.B. daybook.
d.b.a. doing business as.
D.B.E. Dame of the British Empire.
d.b.h. *Forestry.* diameter at breast height.
D.Bib. Douay Bible.
dbl. double.
dc direct current.
DC District of Columbia (with Zip Code).
D.C. 1. *Music.* da capo. **2.** District of Columbia.
DCA Airport code for Washington, D.C.
D.C.M. Distinguished Conduct Medal.
D.D. 1. demand draft. **2.** dishonorable discharge. **3.** Doctor of Divinity (Latin *Divinitatis Doctor*).
D-day (dē′dā′) *n.* The unnamed day on which a military offensive is to be launched; specifically, June 6, 1944, the day on which the Allied forces invaded France during World War II. [*D* (abbreviation for DAY) + DAY.]
D.D.S. Doctor of Dental Science; Doctor of Dental Surgery.
DDT A colorless contact insecticide, $(ClC_6H_4)_2CHCCl_3$, toxic to man and animals when swallowed or absorbed through the skin. [Abbreviation of *d(ichloro)d(iphenyl)t(richloroethane)* : DI- + CHLORO- + DI- + PHENYL + TRI- + CHLORO- + ETHANE.]
de, De (də) *prep. French.* Of; from. Used in personal names, originally to show place of origin: *Guy de Maupassant.* [French, from Latin *dē,* from. See **de-** in Appendix.*]
de–. Indicates: **1.** Reversal or undoing; for example, **deactivate, decode. 2.** Removal; for example, **deaminate, delouse. 3.** Degradation, reduction; for example, **declass. 4.** Disparagement; for example, **demean.** ***Note:*** Many compounds other than those entered here may be formed with *de-.* In forming compounds, *de-* is normally joined with the following element without space or hyphen: *decarbonize.* However, if the second element begins with *e,* it is separated with a hyphen: *de-escalate.* It is also preferable to use the hyphen if the compound brings together three or more vowels: *de-aerate.* In the rare case that the second element begins with a capital letter, it is separated with a hyphen: *de-Americanize.* [In borrowed Latin and French compounds, Latin *dē-* (French *dé-,* Old French *des-*) indicates: 1. Down, downward, as in **declivity, deject.** 2. Away, away from, off, as in **decide, deprecate.** 3. Reversal, undoing, as in **decrease, destroy.** 4. Removal, riddance, as in **defoliate, decapitate.** 5. Completely, carefully, intensively, as in **denominate, declare.** 6. Pejorative sense, as in **deride, deceive.** Latin *dē-,* from *dē,* from. See **de-** in Appendix.*]
DE Delaware (with Zip Code).
dea·con (dē′kən) *n.* **1.** In the Anglican, Greek Orthodox, and Roman Catholic churches, a clergyman ranking just below a priest. **2.** In various other Christian churches, a layman who assists the minister in various functions. *—tr.v.* **deaconed, -coning, -cons.** *Informal.* **1.** To read aloud lines or verses of (a hymn) to help the congregation in singing. **2.** To arrange (produce) for sale so that inferior items are concealed. **3.** To adulterate. [Middle English *dek(e)n,* Old English *dīacon,* from Late Latin *diāconus,* from Greek *diakonos,* "servant." See **ken-**[1] in Appendix.*]
dea·con·ess (dē′kə-nĭs) *n.* A woman appointed or elected to serve as an assistant in a church.
dea·con·ry (dē′kən-rē) *n., pl.* **-ries. 1.** The office or position of a deacon. **2.** Deacons collectively.
de·ac·ti·vate (dē-ăk′tə-vāt′) *tr.v.* **-vated, -vating, -vates. 1.** To render inactive; make harmless or ineffective. **2.** *Military.* To remove from active status. **—de·ac′ti·va′tion** *n.*
dead (dĕd) *adj.* Sometimes **deader, deadest. 1.** No longer alive; lifeless. **2.** Not having the capacity to live; inanimate: *as dead as a stone.* **3.** Lacking feeling or sensitivity; unresponsive. **4.** No longer in existence, use, force, or operation: *a dead language.* **5.** Devoid of animation, interest, or excitement. **6.** Not productive; idle: *dead capital.* **7.** *Informal.* Weary and worn-out; exhausted. **8.** Without brightness or luster. Said of colors. **9.** Without resonance. Said of sounds. **10.** Extinguished: *a dead flame.* **11.** Lacking elasticity or resilience. **12.** Suggestive of the finality or absoluteness of death, especially: **a.** Abrupt: *dead stop.* **b.** Complete; utter: *dead silence.* **c.** Exact; unerring: *the dead center.* **13.** *Sports.* Out of play. Said of a ball. **14. a.** Lacking connection to a source of electric current. **b.** Drained of electric charge, as a battery; discharged. **15.** *Printing.* No longer needed for use. Said of type. *—n.* **1.** A person who has died, or those who have died collectively. Preceded by *the.* **2.** The period of greatest intensity, as of cold or darkness: *the dead of winter.* *—adv.* **1.** Absolutely; altogether. **2.** Directly; exactly: *dead ahead.* [Middle English *ded,* Old English *dēad.* See **dheu-**[3] in Appendix.*] **—dead′ness** *n.*
Synonyms: *dead, deceased, departed, extinct, lifeless, inanimate.* These adjectives all mean without life. *Dead,* which has the widest use, applies in general to whatever once had physical life, function, or usefulness but no longer does. *Deceased* refers only to nonliving human beings, as does *departed,* a euphemistic term. *Extinct* can refer to what has no living successors, such as an animal species, or to what is extinguished or inactive, such as a volcano. *Lifeless* applies to what no longer has physical life and to persons or things that lack animation or spirit. *Inanimate* is limited to what has never had physical life.
dead-air space (dĕd′âr′). An unventilated space.
dead·beat[1] (dĕd′bēt′) *adj. Machinery.* **1.** Lacking recoil. **2.** Stopping without oscillation. [DEAD + BEAT (oscillation).]
dead·beat[2] (dĕd′bēt′) *n. Slang.* **1.** A person who does not pay

his debts. **2.** A lazy or lethargic person; loafer. [Probably DEAD (completely) + BEAT (exhausted).]

dead center. Either of two points in the path of a moving crank and connecting rod at the ends of a stroke when the two lie in a straight line. Also called "dead point."

dead duck. *Slang.* A person or thing doomed to failure.

dead·en (dĕd'n) *v.* **-ened, -ening, -ens.** —*tr.* **1.** To render less sensitive, intense, or vigorous. **2.** To make soundproof. **3.** To make less colorful. —*intr.* To become dead or as if dead. —**dead'en·er** *n.*

dead end. **1.** An end of a passage, such as a street or pipe, that affords no outlet. **2.** Any point beyond which no movement or progress can be made; impasse. —**dead'-end'** *adj.*

dead·en·ing (dĕd'n-ĭng) *n.* Material used for soundproofing.

dead·eye (dĕd'ī') *n.* **1.** *Nautical.* A flat hardwood disk with a grooved perimeter, pierced by three holes through which the lanyards are passed, used to fasten the shrouds. **2.** *Slang.* An expert marksman. [Perhaps because the holes on the disk resemble the empty sockets in a human skull.]

dead·fall (dĕd'fôl') *n.* **1.** A trap for large animals, in which a heavy weight is arranged to fall on and kill or disable the prey. **2.** A mass of fallen timber and tangled brush.

dead hand. *Law.* **Mortmain** *(see).* [Middle English *dede hond,* translation of Old French *mortemain,* MORTMAIN.]

dead·head (dĕd'hĕd') *n. Informal.* **1.** A person who uses a free ticket for admittance, accommodation, or entertainment. **2.** A vehicle, such as a railroad car or airplane, carrying no passengers or freight. **3.** A dull-witted or sluggish person. —*tr.v.* **deadheaded, -heading, -heads.** *Informal.* To drive (a railroad car, bus, or truck) carrying no passengers or freight. —*adv. Informal.* Without passengers or freight; empty.

dead heat. A race in which two or more contestants finish at the same time; a tie.

dead letter. **1.** An unclaimed or undelivered letter that after a period of time is destroyed or returned to the sender by the post office. **2.** A law, directive, or factor still formally in effect but no longer valid or enforced.

dead·light (dĕd'līt') *n.* **1.** *Nautical.* **a.** A strong shutter or plate fastened over a ship's porthole or cabin window in stormy weather. **b.** A thick window set in a ship's side or deck. **2.** A skylight made so that it cannot be opened.

dead·line (dĕd'līn') *n.* **1.** A time limit, as for payment of a debt or completion of an assignment. **2.** A boundary line in a prison that prisoners can cross only at the risk of being shot.

dead load. The fixed weight of a structure or piece of equipment, such as a bridge on its supports. Also called "dead weight." Compare **live load.**

dead·lock (dĕd'lŏk') *n.* A stoppage or standstill resulting from the opposition of two unrelenting forces. —*v.* **deadlocked, -locking, -locks.** —*tr.* To bring to a deadlock. —*intr.* To come to a deadlock.

dead·ly (dĕd'lē) *adj.* **-lier, -liest.** **1.** Causing or tending to cause death; lethal. **2.** Suggestive of death: *deadly white.* **3.** Implacable; mortal: *deadly enemies.* **4.** Destructive in effect. **5.** Absolute; unqualified: *deadly accuracy.* —See Synonyms at **fatal.** —*adv.* **1.** So as to suggest death. **2.** To an extreme: *deadly earnest.* —**dead'li·ness** *n.*

Usage: *Deadly* (adjective) and *deathly* (adjective) overlap in meaning. But in modern usage *deadly* is largely confined to what causes death or extreme distress (such as disease or boredom), and *deathly* to what resembles or suggests death (such as silence or pallor).

deadly nightshade. **1.** A poisonous plant, *Solanum nigrum,* having small white flowers and black fruit. Also called "black nightshade." **2.** A Eurasian plant, the **belladonna** *(see).*

deadly sins. The **seven deadly sins** *(see).*

dead march. A slow, solemn march played for a funeral.

dead nettle. Any of several weedy plants of the genus *Lamium,* native to the Old World, having clusters of small purplish, white, or yellow flowers. [Because it does not sting.]

dead·pan (dĕd'păn') *adj. Slang.* Characterized by a blank or expressionless face or manner. —*adv. Slang.* With an emotionless face or manner.

dead point. *Machinery.* **Dead center** *(see).*

dead reckoning. **1.** *Navigation.* A method of estimating the position of an aircraft or ship without astronomical observations, as by applying to a previously determined position the course and distance traveled since. **2.** Calculation based on inference or guesswork. [From DEAD (probably "complete," "exact," because it is the closest estimate possible).]

Dead Sea. *Arabic* **Bah·ret Lut** (bäh'rĕt lo͞ot'); *Hebrew* **Yam ham Me·lah** (yäm' häm mĕ-läKH'). A salt lake occupying 404 square miles between Israel and Jordan, 1,302 feet below sea level.

Dead Sea Scrolls. A number of parchment scrolls, commonly dated from about 100 B.C. to about A.D. 100, containing Hebrew and Aramaic Scriptural texts and liturgical and communal writings. The first scrolls were found in 1947 in caves near the Dead Sea.

dead weight. **1.** The unrelieved weight of a heavy, motionless mass. **2.** An oppressive burden or difficulty affording no advantage whatever. **3.** *Engineering.* A **dead load** *(see).*

dead·wood (dĕd'wo͝od') *n.* **1.** Dead branches or wood on a tree. **2.** Anything burdensome or superfluous. **3.** *Nautical.* The vertical planking between the keel of a vessel and the sternpost, serving merely as a reinforcement.

deaf (dĕf) *adj.* **deafer, deafest.** **1.** Partially or completely incapable of hearing. **2.** Unwilling or refusing to listen; heedless. [Middle English *de(a)f,* Old English *dēaf.* See **dheu-¹** in Appendix.*] —**deaf'ly** *adv.* —**deaf'ness** *n.*

deaf·en (dĕf'ən) *tr.v.* **-ened, -ening, -ens.** **1.** To make deaf, especially momentarily by a loud noise. **2.** To make soundproof.

deaf·en·ing (dĕf'ən-ĭng) *adj.* Stunning to the ears; resoundingly loud. —**deaf'en·ing·ly** *adv.*

deaf-mute (dĕf'myo͞ot') *n.* Also **deaf mute.** A person who can neither speak nor hear. —*adj.* (dĕf'myo͞ot'). Unable to speak or hear.

deal¹ (dēl) *v.* **dealt** (dĕlt), **dealing, deals.** —*tr.* **1.** To give to someone as his share; apportion. **2.** To distribute or pass out among several people. **3.** To administer; deliver (a blow, for example). **4.** *Card Games.* **a.** To distribute (playing cards) among players. **b.** To give (a specific card) to a player while so distributing. —*intr.* **1.** To be occupied or concerned; treat. Used with *in* or *with: a book dealing with the Middle Ages.* **2.** To behave in a specified way toward another or others; have transactions. Used with *with: deal honestly with competitors.* **3.** To take action. Used with *with: The committee will deal with this complaint.* **4.** To do business; to trade: *dealing in diamonds.* **5.** *Card Games.* To distribute playing cards. —See Synonyms at **distribute.** —*n.* **1.** The act or a round of apportioning or distributing. **2.** *Card Games.* **a.** The distribution of the playing cards. **b.** The cards so distributed; a hand. **c.** The right or turn of a player to distribute the cards. **d.** The playing of one hand. **3.** *Informal.* An indefinite quantity, extent, or degree: *a great deal of experience.* **4.** An agreement arranged secretly, as in business or politics. **5.** *Informal.* Any agreement or business transaction. **6.** *Informal.* A bargain or favorable sale. **7.** *Informal.* Treatment received; especially as the result of an agreement. **8.** *Slang.* An important issue: *make a big deal out of nothing.* **9.** A program, such as a political platform, that offers some specified treatment for those participating: *Truman's Fair Deal.* [Middle English *delen,* Old English *dǣlan,* to divide, distribute. See **dail-** in Appendix.*]

deal² (dēl) *n.* **1.** A fir or pine board cut to standard dimensions. **2.** Such boards or planks collectively. **3.** Fir or pine wood. [Middle English *dele,* from Middle Low German or Middle Dutch *dele.* See **tel-²** in Appendix.*]

deal·er (dē'lər) *n. Abbr.* **dlr.** **1.** A person or group engaged in buying and selling: *a used-car dealer.* **2.** *Card Games.* The person who distributes the cards.

deal·fish (dēl'fĭsh') *n., pl.* **dealfish** or **-fishes.** A marine fish, *Trachipterus arcticus,* of Atlantic waters, resembling the ribbonfishes. [DEAL (plank), from its long, thin body + FISH.]

deal·ing (dē'lĭng) *n.* **1.** *Usually plural.* Transactions or relations with others, usually in business. **2.** Method or manner of conduct in relation to others; treatment: *honest dealing.*

de·am·i·nate (dē-ăm'ə-nāt') *tr.v.* **-nated, -nating, -nates.** To remove an amino group from (an organic compound). —**de·am'i·na'tion** *n.*

de·am·i·nize (dē-ăm'ə-nīz') *tr.v.* **-nized, -nizing, -nizes.** To deaminate. —**de·am'i·ni·za'tion** *n.*

dean (dēn) *n.* **1. a.** An administrative officer in charge of a college, faculty, or division in a university. **b.** An officer of a college or high school who counsels students and supervises the enforcement of rules. **2.** *Ecclesiastical.* The head of the chapter of canons governing a cathedral or collegiate church. **3.** *Chiefly British.* A priest appointed to oversee a group of parishes within a diocese. **4.** The senior member of any body. [Middle English *deen, den,* from Norman French, from Late Latin *decānus,* "(one) set over ten," from Greek *dekanos,* from *deka,* ten. See **dekm̥** in Appendix.*] —**dean'ship** *n.*

Deane (dēn), **Silas.** 1737–1789. American diplomat and lawyer; enlisted foreign aid in revolutionary cause.

dean·er·y (dē'nə-rē) *n., pl.* **-ies.** **1.** The office, jurisdiction, or authority of a dean. **2.** A dean's official residence.

dean's list. A list, issued periodically, of students in a college or university who have attained high academic rank.

dear¹ (dîr) *adj.* **dearer, dearest.** **1.** Beloved; loved; precious. **2.** Highly esteemed or regarded. Used in direct address, especially in salutations: *Dear Sir.* **3. a.** High-priced; expensive. **b.** Charging high prices. **4.** Earnest; ardent: *"this good man was a dear lover and constant practiser of angling"* (Walton). **5.** *Obsolete.* Noble; worthy. —See Synonyms at **costly.** —*n.* A greatly loved person; a darling. Often used as a term of affectionate address: *my dear.* —*adv.* **1.** Fondly or affectionately. **2.** At a high cost. —*interj.* Used as a polite exclamation, chiefly of surprise or distress: *oh dear; dear me.* [Middle English *dere,* Old English *dēore,* from Common Germanic *deuriaz* (unattested), worthy, costly, dear.] —**dear'ness** *n.*

dear² (dîr) *adj.* Also **dere.** *Obsolete.* Severe; grievous; dire. [Middle English *dere,* Old English *dēor*†.]

Dear·born (dîr'bôrn'). A city and automobile-manufacturing center of southeastern Michigan, ten miles west of Detroit. Population, 112,000.

dear·ly (dîr'lē) *adv.* **1.** With deep affection; fondly. **2.** At great cost or price. **3.** Earnestly; ardently.

dearth (dûrth) *n.* **1.** Scarcity; lack; paucity. **2.** Shortage of food; famine: *"Sometimes such signs in heaven are presages of miserable dearths and scarcity."* (Increase Mather). [Middle English *dearth(e),* costliness, scarcity, from *dere,* DEAR (expensive).]

dear·y (dîr'ē) *n., pl.* **-ies.** Also **dear·ie.** *Informal.* Darling; dear.

death (dĕth) *n.* **1.** The act of dying; termination of life. **2.** The state of being dead. **3.** *Often capital* **D.** A personification of the destroyer of life, usually represented as a skeleton holding a scythe. **4.** Termination; extinction: *the death of imperialism.* **5.** The cause of dying. **6.** A manner of dying: *a hero's death.* **7.** Loss or absence of spiritual life. **8.** *Law.* **Civil death** *(see).* **9.** *Christian Science.* The product of human belief of life in

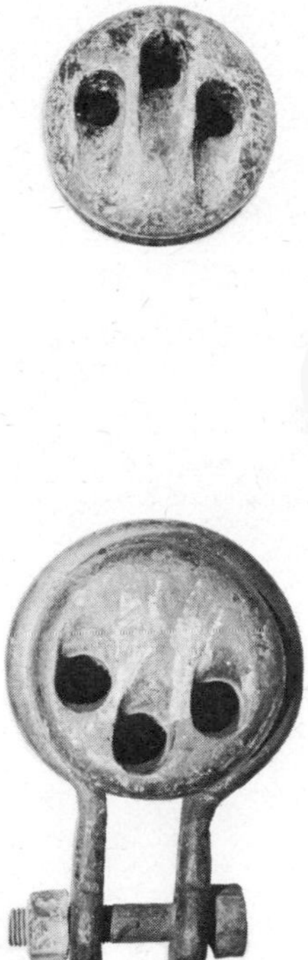

deadeye
Pair of deadeyes

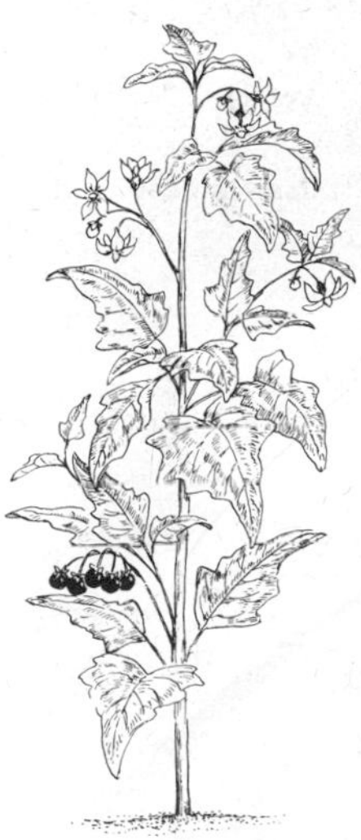

deadly nightshade
Solanum nigrum

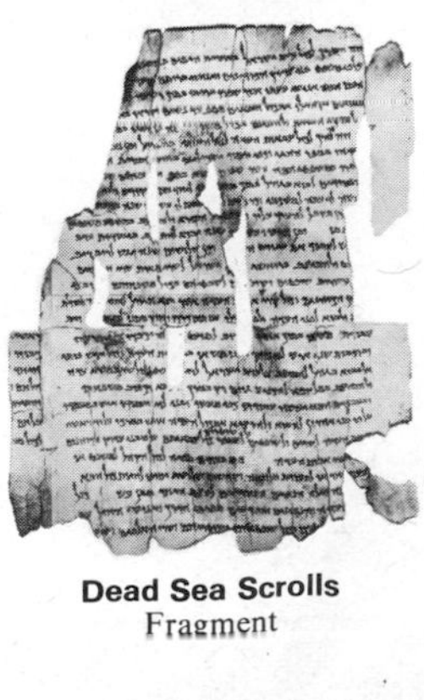

Dead Sea Scrolls
Fragment

matter. —**do** (or **put**) **to death.** To kill or execute. —**to death.** To an intolerable degree: *worried to death.* [Middle English *de(e)th,* Old English *dēath.* See **dheu-**[3] in Appendix.*]

death·bed (dĕth'bĕd') *n.* **1.** The bed on which a person dies. **2.** The last hours before death.

death bell. A bell tolled to announce a death. Also called "passing bell."

death·blow (dĕth'blō') *n.* **1.** A blow or stroke that causes death. **2.** Any fatal event or occurrence.

death camas. Also **death camass.** Any of several plants of the genus *Zygadenus,* of western North America, having grasslike leaves and clusters of greenish-white flowers. [So called because they are poisonous to livestock.]

death cup. A poisonous, usually white mushroom, *Amanita phalloides,* having a prominent bulbous base. Also called "death angel."

death duty. *British.* An inheritance tax.

death·ful (dĕth'fəl) *adj.* **1.** Fatal; deadly. **2.** Deathly.

death house. A cell-block or other part of a prison in which prisoners condemned to death await execution.

death·less (dĕth'lĭs) *adj.* Not subject to death; immortal. —**death'less·ly** *adv.* —**death'less·ness** *n.*

death·ly (dĕth'lē) *adj.* **1.** Resembling or characteristic of death. **2.** Causing death; fatal; deadly. **3.** *Poetic.* Of death. —*adv.* **1.** In the manner of death. **2.** Extremely; very. —See Usage note at **deadly.** —**death'li·ness** *n.*

death mask. A cast of a person's face taken after death.

death point. An environmental limit, as of temperature, moisture, or radiation, beyond which a specified life form cannot survive.

death rate. **1.** The ratio of total deaths to total population, usually expressed as deaths per 1,000, 10,000, or 100,000 population, in a specified community. Also called "mortality rate." **2.** The number of deaths per 100 persons having the same disease. In this sense, also called "fatality rate."

death rattle. A rare respiratory gurgling or rattling in the throat of a dying person, caused by loss of the cough reflex and passage of breath through accumulating mucus in the throat.

death's-head (dĕths'hĕd') *n.* The human skull or a representation of it, symbolizing mortality or death.

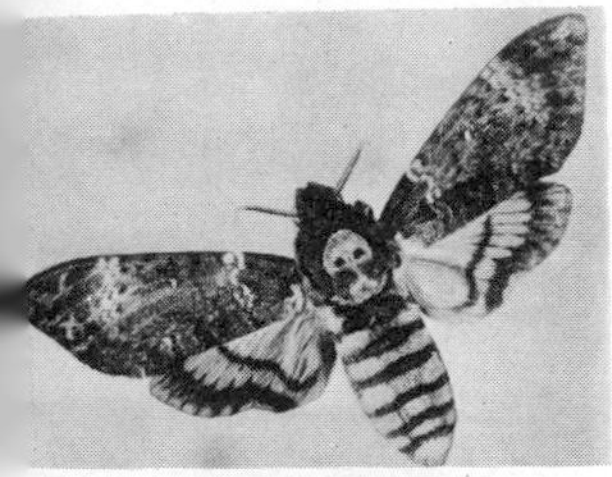

death's-head moth

death's-head moth. A large Old World moth, *Acherontia atropos,* having a skull-like marking on the upper part of the thorax.

deaths·man (dĕths'mən) *n., pl.* **-men** (-mĭn). *Archaic.* An executioner.

death tax. An **inheritance tax** *(see).*

death·trap (dĕth'trăp') *n.* **1.** An unsafe building or structure, especially one susceptible to fire. **2.** Any perilous circumstance or situation.

Death Valley. A desert basin, 1,500 square miles in area, in eastern California and western Nevada, containing the lowest point in the Western Hemisphere (280 feet below sea level).

Death Valley National Monument. A major resort and tourist area occupying 2,906 square miles in eastern California and containing most of Death Valley.

death warrant. **1.** *Law.* An official order authorizing a person's execution. **2.** Anything that destroys hope, joy, or expectation.

death·watch (dĕth'wŏch') *n.* **1.** A vigil kept beside a dying or dead person. **2.** One who guards a condemned person before his execution. **3. a.** Any of several beetles of the family Anobiidae that strike their heads against the wood into which they burrow with a hollow, clicking sound. Also called "deathwatch beetle." **b.** A booklouse that makes a similar sound.

death·y (dĕth'ē) *adj. Rare.* Deathly. —*adv. Rare.* Deathly.

deave (dēv) *tr.v.* **deaved, deaving, deaves.** *British Regional.* To deafen or confuse with noise. [Middle English *deven,* Old English *ādēafian,* from *dēaf,* DEAF.]

deb. debenture.

de·ba·cle (dĭ-bä'kəl, -băk'əl) *n.* **1.** A sudden, disastrous overthrow or collapse; rout; ruin. **2.** The breaking up of ice in a river. **3.** A violent flood. —See Synonyms at **disaster.** [French *débâcle,* from *débâcler,* to unbar, from Old French *desbacler* : *des-,* from Latin *dē-* (removal) + *bacler,* to bar, from Old Provençal *baclar,* from Vulgar Latin *bacclāre* (unattested), from Latin *baculum,* rod, stick (see **bak-** in Appendix*).]

De Ba·key (dĭ bā'kē), **Michael Ellis.** Born 1908. American surgeon and educator.

de·bar (dē-bär') *tr.v.* **-barred, -barring, -bars.** **1.** To exclude or bar; shut out. Usually used with *from.* **2.** To forbid, hinder, or prevent. [Middle English *debarren,* from Old French *desbarrer,* to unbar : *des-,* from Latin *dē-* (removal) + *barrer,* to bar, from *barre,* a rod, BAR.] —**de·bar'ment** *n.*

de·bark (dĭ-bärk') *v.* **-barked, -barking, -barks.** —*tr.* To unload, as from a ship. —*intr.* To disembark. [French *débarquer,* from Old French *debarquer* : *de-,* from Latin *dē-* (removal) + *barque,* ship, BARK.] —**de'bar·ka'tion** (dē'bär-kā'shən) *n.*

de·base (dĭ-bās') *tr.v.* **-based, -basing, -bases.** **1.** To lower in character, quality, or value; degrade; adulterate: *"language is continually being debased and reduced to nonspeech"* (W.H. Auden). **2.** *Obsolete.* To lower in rank, dignity, or estimation. [DE- (down) + BASE (low).] —**de·base'ment** *n.* —**de·bas'er** *n.*

de·bat·a·ble (dĭ-bā'tə-bəl) *adj.* **1.** Capable of being argued or discussed. **2.** In dispute; questionable. —**de·bat'a·bly** *adv.*

de·bate (dĭ-bāt') *v.* **-bated, -bating, -bates.** —*intr.* **1.** To deliberate; consider. **2.** To engage in argument; discuss opposing points. **3.** To engage in a formal discussion or argument. **4.** *Obsolete.* To fight; quarrel. —*tr.* **1.** To dispute or argue about. **2.** To discuss or argue (a question, for example) formally. **3.** To deliberate upon; consider. **4.** *Obsolete.* To fight or argue for or over. —See Synonyms at **discuss.** —*n.* **1.** A discussion involving opposing points; argument; dispute. **2.** Deliberation; consideration. **3.** A formal contest of argumentation in which two opposing teams defend and attack a given proposition. **4.** *Obsolete.* Conflict; strife; contention. [Middle English *debaten,* from Old French *debattre* : *de-, des-,* from Latin *dis-,* apart, against each other + *battre,* to fight, beat, from Latin *battere, battuere* (see **battuere** in Appendix*).] —**de·bat'er** *n.*

de·bauch (dĭ-bôch') *v.* **-bauched, -bauching, -bauches.** —*tr.* **1.** To corrupt morally; seduce; pervert: *"riches debauched one class with idleness of mind and body"* (Edward Bellamy). **2.** *Obsolete.* To cause to forsake allegiance. —*intr.* To indulge in dissipation. —*n.* An act or period of dissipation. [French *débaucher,* from Old French *desbaucher,* "to roughhew (timber) into a beam," separate, lead away from : *des-,* from Latin *dē-* (removal) + *bauch,* beam, from (unattested) Frankish *balk* (see **bhelg-** in Appendix*).] —**de·bauch'ed·ly** *adv.* —**de·bauch'er** *n.*

deb·au·chee (dĕb'ô-chē', -shē', dĭ-bô'chē) *n.* A person who habitually indulges in dissipation or debauchery; libertine.

de·bauch·er·y (dĭ-bô'chə-rē) *n., pl.* **-ies.** **1.** Extreme indulgence in sensual pleasures; intemperance; dissipation. **2.** *Archaic.* Seduction from morality, allegiance, or duty.

de Beau·voir, Simone. See **Beauvoir.**

de·ben·ture (dĭ-bĕn'chər) *n. Abbr.* **deb., deben.** **1.** A certificate or voucher acknowledging a debt. **2.** An unsecured bond, issued by a civil or governmental corporation or agency and backed only by the credit standing of the issuer. Also called "debenture bond." **3.** A customhouse certificate providing for the payment of a drawback. [Middle English *debentur,* from Latin *dēbentur,* "they are due," from *dēbēre,* to owe. See **ghabh-** in Appendix.*]

de·bil·i·tate (dĭ-bĭl'ə-tāt') *tr.v.* **-tated, -tating, -tates.** To make feeble; enervate. [Latin *dēbilitāre,* from *dēbilis,* weak. See **bel-** in Appendix.*] —**de·bil'i·ta'tion** *n.* —**de·bil'i·ta'tive** *adj.*

de·bil·i·tat·ed (dĭ-bĭl'ə-tā'tĭd) *adj.* Tired; worn-out. See Synonyms at **weak.**

de·bil·i·ty (dĭ-bĭl'ə-tē) *n.* The state of abnormal bodily weakness; feebleness. [Middle English *debilite,* from Old French, from Latin *dēbilitās,* from *dēbilis,* weak. See **bel-** in Appendix.*]

deb·it (dĕb'ĭt) *n. Abbr.* **dr.** **1.** An item of debt as recorded in an account. **2. a.** An entry of a sum in the debit or left-hand side of an account. **b.** The sum of such entries. Compare **credit.** **3.** The left-hand side of an account or an accounting ledger where bookkeeping entries are made. —*tr.v.* **debited, -iting, -its.** **1.** To enter (a sum) on the left-hand side of an account or accounting ledger. **2.** To charge with a debt. [Middle English *debite,* from Old French, from Latin *dēbitum,* DEBT.]

deb·o·nair (dĕb'ə-nâr') *adj.* Also **deb·o·naire, deb·on·naire.** **1.** Suave; nonchalant; urbane. **2.** Affable; gracious; genial. **3.** Carefree; gay; jaunty. [Middle English *debonaire,* from Old French, from *de bon aire,* "of good disposition" : *de,* of, from Latin *dē* + *bon,* good, from Latin *bonus* (see **deu-**[2] in Appendix*) + *aire,* disposition, AIR.] —**deb'o·nair'ly** *adv.* —**deb'o·nair'ness** *n.*

Deb·o·rah[1] (dĕb'ər-ə, dĕb'rə). A feminine given name. [Hebrew *dəvōrā,* bee.]

Deb·o·rah[2] (dĕb'ər-ə). A prophetess and judge of Israel who helped the Israelites free themselves from the Canaanites. Judges 4:4.

de·bouch (dĭ-bo͞osh') *v.* **-bouched, -bouching, -bouches.** —*intr.* **1.** *Military.* To march from a narrow or confined area into the open. **2.** To emerge or issue. —*tr.* To cause to emerge or issue. [French *déboucher* : *dé-,* from Latin *dē-,* out of + *bouche,* mouth, opening, from Old French, from Latin *bucca,* puffed-out cheek, mouth (see **beu-**[1] in Appendix*).]

dé·bou·ché (dā'bo͞o-shā') *n.* **1.** An opening in military works for the passage of troops. **2.** An outlet, as for goods. [French, from *déboucher,* DEBOUCH.]

de·bouch·ment (dĭ-bo͞osh'mənt) *n.* **1.** The act or an instance of emerging or debouching. **2.** Debouchure.

de·bou·chure (dā'bo͞o-sho͝or') *n.* A mouth or opening, especially of a river or channel.

De·bre·cen (dĕb'rĕt-sĕn'). A city and marketing center in an agricultural area of east-central Hungary. Population, 137,000.

dé·bride·ment (dā-brēd-mäɴ', dĭ-brēd'mənt) *n.* The surgical excision of dead and devitalized tissue and the removal of all foreign matter from a wound. [French, from *débrider,* "to unbridle," from Old French *desbrider* : *des-,* from Latin *dē-* (removal) + *bride,* bridle, from Middle High German *brīdel* (see **bherək-** in Appendix*).]

de·brief (dē'brēf') *tr.v.* **-briefed, -briefing, -briefs.** **1.** *Military.* To question or interrogate to obtain knowledge or intelligence gathered on a mission. **2.** To instruct (a government agent or similar employee) not to reveal classified or secret information after the employment has ceased. [DE- (reversal) + BRIEF.]

de·brief·ing (dē-brē'fĭng) *n.* **1.** The act or process of being debriefed. **2.** The information conveyed during this procedure.

de·bris (də-brē', dā'brē') *n.* Also **dé·bris** (dā'brē'). **1.** The scattered remains of something broken or destroyed; ruins; rubble; fragments: *"The whole library groaned with the accumulated debris of centuries of recorded folly."* (Jack Kerouac). **2.** *Geology.* An accumulation of relatively large rock fragments, especially as distinguished from pulverized rock waste. [French *débris,* from Old French *de(s)brisier,* to break to pieces : *des-,* from Latin *dē-* (intensive) + *brisier,* to break, from (unattested) Vulgar Latin *brīsāre* (see **bhrēi-** in Appendix*).]

de Brog·lie, Louis Victor. See **Broglie.**

Debs (dĕbz), **Eugene Victor.** 1855–1926. American labor leader; five times (1900–20) Socialist candidate for President.

debt (dĕt) *n.* **1.** Something owed, such as money, goods, or services. **2.** An obligation or liability to pay or render something to someone else. **3.** The condition of having such an obligation. Usually used with *in.* **4.** *Theology.* An offense requiring forgiveness or reparation; sin; trespass. [Middle English *det(te),* from Old French *dette,* from Vulgar Latin *dēbita* (unattested), feminine of Latin *dēbitum,* debt, from *dēbitus,* past participle of *dēbēre,* to owe. See ghabh- in Appendix.*]

Debt·ford (dĕt′fərd). A former administrative division of London, now part of **Lewisham** *(see).*

debt·or (dĕt′ər) *n. Abbr.* **dr. 1.** One who owes something to another. Compare **creditor. 2.** One guilty of a trespass or sin; sinner. [Middle English *det(t)our,* from Old French *det(t)or,* from Latin *dēbitor,* from *dēbēre,* to owe. See **debt.**]

de·bug (dē′bŭg′) *tr.v.* **-bugged, -bugging, -bugs. 1.** To remove insects from. **2.** To search for and eliminate malfunctioning elements in. **3.** To search for and eliminate sources of error in (a computer program, for example).

de·bunk (dĭ-bŭngk′) *tr.v.* **-bunked, -bunking, -bunks.** *Informal.* To expose or ridicule the falseness, sham, or exaggerated claims of. [DE- + BUNK (nonsense).] —**de·bunk′er** *n.*

De·bus·sy (də-byōō′sē; *French* də-bü-sē′), **Claude Achille.** 1862–1918. French composer.

de·but (dĭ-byōō′, dā-, dā′byōō′) *n.* Also **dé·but. 1.** A first public appearance, as of an actor on the stage. **2.** The formal presentation of a girl to society. **3.** The beginning of a career or other course of action. [French *début,* from *débuter,* to make one's debut, "give the first stroke in a game" : *dé-,* from Latin *dē-,* away + *but,* BUTT (target).]

Usage: Debut is not established as a verb, though it is sometimes so used, both intransitively in the sense of making a first appearance *(The singer debuts here tonight)* and transitively in the sense of presenting (something) for the first time *(The company will debut its new models at the auto show).* The intransitive construction is unacceptable to 93 per cent of the Usage Panel, and the transitive to 97 per cent.

deb·u·tante (dĕb′yōō-tänt′, dĕb′yōō-tänt′, dā′byōō-) *n.* Also **dé·bu·tante.** A young woman making a debut into society. [French *débutante,* from *débuter,* to make one's DEBUT.]

De·bye (də-bī′), **Peter Joseph Wilhelm.** 1884–1966. Dutch-born American physicist; developed the theory of specific heat.

dec. 1. deceased. **2.** declaration. **3.** declension. **4.** declination. **5.** decrease.

Dec. December.

deca-, dec-, deka-. *Abbr.* **da** Indicates ten; for example, **decahedron, decane.** [Greek *deka-.* from *deka,* ten. See **dekm̥** in Appendix.*]

de·cade (dĕk′ād′, dĕ-kād′) *n.* **1.** A period of ten years. **2.** A group or series of ten. [Middle English, from Old French, from Late Latin *decas,* from Greek *dekas,* from *deka,* ten. See **dekm̥** in Appendix.*]

de·ca·dence (dĭ-kā′dəns, dĕk′ə-dəns) *n.* Also **de·ca·den·cy** (-dən-sē) *pl.* **-cies.** A process, condition, or period of deterioration or decline, as in morals or art; decay. [Old French, from Medieval Latin *dēcadentia,* from Vulgar Latin *dēcadere* (unattested), to DECAY.]

de·ca·dent (dĭ-kā′dənt, dĕk′ə-dənt) *adj.* **1.** In a state or condition of decline or decay. **2.** Of or pertaining to the decadents. —*n.* **1.** A person in a condition or process of mental or moral decay. **2.** A member of a group of French and English writers of the 19th century who often sought inspiration in the morbid, neurotic, or macabre and tended toward overrefinement of style. [From DECADENCE.] —**de·ca′dent·ly** *adv.*

dec·a·gon (dĕk′ə-gŏn′) *n.* A polygon with ten angles and ten sides. [New Latin *decagonum,* from Greek *dekagōnon,* "(one) having ten angles" : DECA- + -GON.] —**de·cag′o·nal** (dĭ-kăg′ə-nəl) *adj.* —**de·cag′o·nal·ly** *adv.*

dec·a·gram (dĕk′ə-grăm′) *n. Abbr.* **dag** Ten grams. See **measurement.** [French *décagramme* : DECA- + GRAM.]

dec·a·he·dron (dĕk′ə-hē′drən) *n., pl.* **-drons** or **-dra** (-drə). A polyhedron with ten faces. [New Latin : DECA- + -HEDRON.] —**dec′a·he′dral** *adj.*

de·cal (dē′kăl′) *n.* A picture or design transferred by the process of **decalcomania** *(see).*

de·cal·ci·fy (dē-kăl′sə-fī′) *tr.v.* **-fied, -fying, -fies.** To remove calcium or calcareous matter from (bones or teeth, for example). —**de·cal′ci·fi·ca′tion** *n.* —**de·cal′ci·fi′er** *n.*

de·cal·co·ma·ni·a (dē′kăl-kə-mā′nē-ə) *n.* **1.** The process of transferring pictures or designs printed on specially prepared paper to glass, metal, or other material. **2.** A picture so transferred; a decal. [French *décalcomanie,* from *décalquer,* to transfer by tracing : *dé-,* from, from Latin *dē-* + *calquer,* to trace, from Italian *calcare,* to trace, trample, from Latin, to tread, from *calx,* heel (see **calk**) + *manie,* madness, from Late Latin *mania,* MANIA (from its mid-19th-century popularity).]

de·ca·les·cence (dē′kə-lĕs′əns) *n.* In a metal being heated, a sudden slowing in the rate of temperature increase, as a result of endothermic structural changes. [DE- + Latin *calescere,* to become warm, from *calēre,* to be warm (see **kel-¹** in Appendix*).] —**de′ca·les′cent** *adj.*

Dec·a·logue (dĕk′ə-lôg′, -lŏg′) *n.* Also **Dec·a·log, dec·a·logue, dec·a·log.** The **Ten Commandments** *(see).* [Middle English *decalog,* from Old French *decalogue,* from Late Latin *decalogus,* from Greek *dekalogos* : DECA- + *logos,* speech, word (see **leg-¹** in Appendix*).]

dec·a·me·ter, dek·a·me·ter (dĕk′ə-mē′tər) *n. Abbr.* **dam** Ten meters. See **measurement.**

de·camp (dĭ-kămp′) *intr.v.* **-camped, -camping, -camps. 1.** To depart from a camping ground; break camp. **2.** To depart

secretly or suddenly; run away. [French *décamper,* from Old French *descamper* : *des-,* from Latin *dē-* (reversal) + *camper,* to camp, from *camp,* CAMP.] —**de·camp′ment** *n.*

dec·a·nal (dĕk′ə-nəl, dĭ-kā′nəl) *adj.* Of or pertaining to a dean or deanery: *decanal authority.* [From Late Latin *decānus,* DEAN.] —**dec′a·nal·ly** *adv.*

dec·ane (dĕk′ān′) *n.* Any of various liquid isomers, $C_{10}H_{22}$, of the methane series. [DEC(A)- + -ANE.]

de·ca·no·ic acid (dĕk′ə-nō′ĭk). *Chemistry.* **Capric acid** *(see).* [DECAN(E) + -OIC.]

de·cant (dĭ-kănt′) *tr.v.* **-canted, -canting, -cants. 1.** To pour off (wine, for example) without disturbing the sediment. **2.** To pour (a liquid) from one container into another. [Medieval Latin *dēcanthāre* : Latin *dē-,* from + *canthus,* rim of a vessel, from, rim of a wheel, tire (see **kantho-** in Appendix*).] —**de′can·ta′tion** (dē′kăn-tā′shən) *n.*

de·cant·er (dĭ-kăn′tər) *n.* **1.** A decorative bottle used for serving liquids, as wine. **2.** A vessel used for decanting.

de·cap·i·tate (dĭ-kăp′ə-tāt′) *tr.v.* **-tated, -tating, -tates.** To cut off the head of; behead. [Late Latin *dēcapitāre* : Latin *dē-* (removal) + *caput,* head (see **kaput** in Appendix*).] —**de·cap′i·ta′tion** *n.* —**de·cap′i·ta′tor** (-tā′tər) *n.*

dec·a·pod (dĕk′ə-pŏd′) *n.* **1.** Any crustacean of the order Decapoda, such as a crab, lobster, or shrimp, characteristically having five pairs of locomotor appendages, each joined to a segment of the thorax. **2.** A cephalopod mollusk, such as a squid or cuttlefish, having ten armlike tentacles. —*adj.* Of or pertaining to the Decapoda or a decapod. [New Latin *Decapoda,* "the ten-footed ones" : DECA- + -POD.] —**de·cap′o·dal** (dĭ-kăp′ə-dəl), **de·cap′o·dan, de·cap′o·dous** *adj.*

De·cap·o·lis (dĭ-kăp′ə-lĭs). A confederacy of ten cities in the northeastern part of ancient Palestine, established in 62 B.C. and governed by Rome. [Greek *Dekapolis* : DECA- + *polis,* city (see **pele-²** in Appendix*).]

de·car·bon·ate (dē-kär′bə-nāt′) *tr.v.* **-ated, -ating, -ates.** To remove carbon dioxide or carbonic acid from.

de·car·bon·ize (dē-kär′bə-nīz′) *tr.v.* **-ized, -izing, -izes.** To remove carbon from; decarburize. —**de·car′bon·i·za′tion** *n.* —**de·car′bon·iz′er** *n.*

de·car·box·y·la·tion (dē′kär-bŏk′sə-lā′shən) *n.* The removal of a carboxyl group from a chemical compound, with hydrogen usually replacing it.

de·car·bu·rize (dē-kär′byə-rīz′) *tr.v.* **-rized, -rizing, -rizes.** To decarbonize. —**de·car′bu·ri·za′tion** *n.*

dec·a·syl·la·ble (dĕk′ə-sĭl′ə-bəl) *n.* A line of verse having ten syllables. —**dec′a·syl·lab′ic** (-sə-lăb′ĭk) *adj.*

de·cath·lon (dĭ-kăth′lən, -lŏn′) *n.* An athletic contest in which each contestant participates in ten different track and field events. [French *décathlon* : DECA- + Greek *athlon,* contest (see **athlete**).]

De·ca·tur (dĭ-kā′tər). A city and manufacturing center of east-central Illinois. Population, 78,000.

De·ca·tur (dĭ-kā′tər), **Stephen.** 1779–1820. American naval officer.

de·cay (dĭ-kā′) *v.* **-cayed, -caying, -cays.** —*intr.* **1.** *Biology.* To decompose; rot. **2.** *Physics.* To disintegrate or diminish by radioactive decay. **3.** *Aerospace.* To decrease in orbit, as an artificial satellite. **4.** To become a ruin; fall into ruin. **5.** *Pathology.* To decline in health or vigor; waste away. **6.** To decline from a state of normality, excellence, or prosperity. —*tr.* To cause to decay. —*n.* **1.** The destruction or decomposition of organic matter as a result of bacterial or fungal action; rot. **2.** *Physics.* **Radioactive decay** *(see).* **3.** The decrease in orbital altitude of an artificial satellite due to conditions such as atmospheric drag. **4.** A gradual deterioration to an inferior state, as of health or mental capability. [Middle English *decayen,* from Old North French *decair,* from Vulgar Latin *dēcadere* (unattested), to fall down, decay : Latin *dē-,* down + *cadere,* to fall (see **kad-** in Appendix*).]

Synonyms: decay, rot, putrefy, spoil, crumble, molder, disintegrate, decompose. These verbs all refer to gradual change marked by destruction or dissolution. *Decay,* which can apply to physical change or figuratively to breakdown of the mind, morals, or the like, usually implies a stage in deterioration short of destruction. *Rot* has both physical and figurative use, and *putrefy* largely physical; both stress later stages of deterioration marked, in physical contexts, by offensiveness to smell and sight. *Spoil* can refer to organic decay or figuratively (and transitively) to impairment of character of a person. *Crumble* and *molder* apply mostly to physical breakdown of a substance into small pieces or, in the case of *molder,* into dust. *Disintegrate,* which has physical and figurative use, refers to complete breakdown into component parts; it implies as well the destruction of usefulness or integrity. *Decompose* is largely restricted to the breakdown of substances into their chemical components.

Dec·can Plateau (dĕk′ən). A triangular plateau extending over most of peninsular India.

decd. deceased.

de·cease (dĭ-sēs′) *intr.v.* **-ceased, -ceasing, -ceases.** To die. —*n.* Death. [Middle English *decesen,* to die, from *deces,* death, from Old French, from Latin *dēcessus,* "departure," death, from the past participle of *dēcēdere,* to depart : *dē-,* away + *cēdere,* to go (see **ked-¹** in Appendix*).]

de·ceased (dĭ-sēst′) *adj. Abbr.* **dec., decd.** No longer living; dead. See Synonyms at **dead.** —*n.* A dead person or persons.

de·ce·dent (dĭ-sē′dənt) *n. Law.* The deceased. [Latin *dēcēdēns,* present participle of *dēcēdere,* to die, DECEASE.]

de·ceit (dĭ-sēt′) *n.* **1.** Misrepresentation; deception. **2.** A stratagem; trick; wile. **3.** Falseness; deceitfulness. [Middle English *deceit(e)*, from Old French, from Latin *dēcepta*, feminine of *dēceptus*, past participle of *dēcipere*, DECEIVE.]

de·ceit·ful (dĭ-sēt′fəl) *adj.* **1.** Given to cheating or deceiving. **2.** Misleading; deceptive. —See Synonyms at **dishonest**. —**de·ceit′ful·ly** *adv.* —**de·ceit′ful·ness** *n.*

de·ceive (dĭ-sēv′) *v.* **-ceived, -ceiving, -ceives.** —*tr.* **1.** To delude; mislead. **2.** *Archaic.* To catch by guile; ensnare: *"is it not an art to deceive a trout with an artificial fly?"* (Walton). —*intr.* To practice deceit. [Middle English *deceiven*, from Old French *deceivre, decevoir*, from Latin *dēcipere*, to take in, deceive : *dē-* (pejorative) + *capere*, to take, seize (see **kap-** in Appendix*).] —**de·ceiv′er** *n.* —**de·ceiv′ing·ly** *adv.*

Synonyms: *deceive, betray, mislead, beguile, delude, dupe, hoodwink, bamboozle, outwit, double-cross.* These verbs mean to victimize persons, for the most part by underhand means. *Deceive* involves falsehood or the deliberate concealment or misrepresentation of truth with intent to lead another into error or to disadvantage. *Betray* implies faithlessness or treachery that brings another to grave disadvantage or into danger. *Mislead* means to lead into error and does not invariably imply intent to harm. *Beguile* suggests deceiving or misleading by means of allurement. *Delude* refers to deceiving or misleading to the point of rendering a person unable to detect falsehood or make sound judgment. *Dupe* means to delude by playing upon another's susceptibilities or naiveté. *Hoodwink* refers to deluding by trickery such as mental blinding or dazzling. *Bamboozle* less formally means to delude by trickery such as hoaxing, befuddling, or artful persuasion. *Outwit* means to frustrate another person by ingenuity and cunning and is less forceful in its suggestion of bad faith. *Double-cross*, a slang term, implies betrayal of a confidence or the willful breaking of a pledge.

de·cel·er·ate (dē-sĕl′ə-rāt′) *v.* **-ated, -ating, -ates.** —*tr.* To decrease the velocity of. —*intr.* To decrease in velocity. [DE- + (AC)CELERATE.] —**de·cel′er·a′tor** (-ə-rā′tər) *n.*

de·cel·er·a·tion (dē-sĕl′ə-rā′shən) *n.* Decrease in velocity.

de·cel·er·on (dē-sĕl′ə-rŏn′) *n.* An aileron speed brake used primarily on jet aircraft. [DECELER(ATE) + (AILER)ON.]

De·cem·ber (dĭ-sĕm′bər) *n. Abbr.* **Dec., D.** The 12th and last month of the year according to the Gregorian calendar. December has 31 days. See **calendar**. [Middle English *decembre*, from Old French, from Latin *December*, "the tenth month," from *decem*, ten. See **dekm** in Appendix.*]

de·cem·vir (dĭ-sĕm′vər) *n., pl.* **-virs** or **-viri** (-və-rī′). One of a body of ten Roman magistrates; especially, a member of one of two such bodies appointed in 451 and 450 B.C. to draw up a code of laws. [Middle English, from Latin, singular of *decemvirī*, from *decem virī*, ten men : *decem*, ten (see **dekm** in Appendix*) + *virī*, plural of *vir*, man (see **wiros** in Appendix*).] —**de·cem′vi·ral** *adj.* —**de·cem′vi·rate′** *n.*

de·cen·a·ry (dĭ-sĕn′ə-rē) *adj.* Also **de·cen·na·ry**. Of or pertaining to a tithing. —*n., pl.* **decenaries**. Also **de·cen·na·ry**. A tithing. [Middle English *decennare*, tithing man, from Medieval Latin *decennārius*, from *decenna*, tithing, from Latin *decem*, ten. See **dekm** in Appendix.*]

de·cen·cy (dē′sən-sē) *n., pl.* **-cies.** **1.** The state or condition of being decent; propriety. **2.** Conformity to prevailing standards of propriety or modesty. **3.** *Plural.* The proprieties.

de·cen·na·ry¹ (dĭ-sĕn′ə-rē) *adj.* Of or pertaining to a ten-year period. —*n., pl.* **decennaries**. A decennium; decade. [From Latin *decennis*, of ten years. See **decennium**.]

de·cen·na·ry². Variant of **decenary**.

de·cen·ni·al (dĭ-sĕn′ē-əl) *adj.* **1.** Pertaining to or lasting for ten years. **2.** Occurring every ten years. —*n.* **1.** An anniversary celebrated every ten years. **2.** The celebration itself. [From Latin *decennium*, DECENNIUM.] —**de·cen′ni·al·ly** *adv.*

de·cen·ni·um (dĭ-sĕn′ē-əm) *n., pl.* **-ums** or **-cennia** (-sĕn′ē-ə). A period of ten years; decade. [Latin, from *decennis*, of ten years : *decem*, ten (see **dekm** in Appendix*) + *annus*, year (see **at-** in Appendix*).]

de·cent (dē′sənt) *adj.* **1.** Characterized by conformity to recognized standards of propriety. **2.** Free from indelicacy; modest. **3.** Adequate; passable; tolerable: *a decent salary.* **4.** Kind; obliging; generous. **5.** *Informal.* Properly or modestly dressed. [Latin *decēns*, present participle of *decēre*, to be fitting, suit. See **dek-¹** in Appendix.*] —**de′cent·ly** *adv.* —**de′cent·ness** *n.*

de·cen·tral·ize (dē-sĕn′trə-līz′) *tr.v.* **-ized, -izing, -izes.** **1.** To distribute the administrative functions or powers of (a central authority) among several local authorities. **2.** To cause to withdraw from an area of concentration: *decentralize an industry.* —**de·cen′tral·i·za′tion** *n.*

de·cep·tion (dĭ-sĕp′shən) *n.* **1.** The use of deceit. **2.** The fact or state of being deceived. **3.** A ruse; imposture. [Middle English *decepcioun*, from Old French *deception*, from Late Latin *dēceptiō*, from Latin *dēcipere* (past participle *dēceptus*), DECEIVE.]

de·cep·tive (dĭ-sĕp′tĭv) *adj.* Intended or tending to deceive; disingenuous. See Synonyms at **misleading**. —**de·cep′tive·ly** *adv.* —**de·cep′tive·ness** *n.*

deci-. *Symbol* **d** Indicates one-tenth; for example, **decimeter**. [French *déci-*, from Latin *decimus*, tenth, from *decem*, ten. See **dekm** in Appendix.*]

dec·i·bel (dĕs′ĭ-bəl, -bĕl′) *n. Abbr.* **dB.** A unit used to express relative difference in power, usually between acoustic or electric signals, equal to one-tenth the common logarithm of the ratio of the two levels. [DECI- + BEL.]

de·cide (dĭ-sīd′) *v.* **-cided, -ciding, -cides.** —*tr.* **1.** To conclude or settle. **2.** To influence or determine the conclusion of. **3.** To cause to make or reach a decision. —*intr.* **1.** To pronounce a judgment; announce a verdict. **2.** To make up one's mind. [Middle English *deciden*, from Old French *decider*, from Latin *dēcīdere*, to cut off, determine : *dē-*, off + *cædere*, to cut (see **skhai-** in Appendix*).] —**de·cid′a·ble** *adj.* —**de·cid′er** *n.*

Synonyms: *decide, determine, settle, rule, conclude, resolve.* These verbs are compared in the sense of making decisions or judgments. *Decide*, the least specific, overlaps the other terms without conveying their more special meanings. *Determine* differs in that it often involves somewhat narrower issues and more detailed solutions. *Settle* stresses finality of decision, and *rule* implies that the decision is handed down by someone having recognized authority. *Conclude* suggests decision or judgment produced by careful consideration of all pertinent matters. *Resolve* implies formal deliberation and finality of decision or determination.

de·cid·ed (dĭ-sī′dĭd) *adj.* **1.** Unquestionable; definite. **2.** Resolute; unhesitating. —**de·cid′ed·ly** *adv.* —**de·cid′ed·ness** *n.*

de·cid·u·a (dĭ-sĭj′o͞o-ə, -sĭd′yo͞o-ə) *n.* A mucous membrane of the uterus, modified during pregnancy and cast off during menstruation or at parturition. [New Latin *(membrana) decidua*, "(membrane) that falls off," from Latin *dēcidua*, feminine of *dēciduus*, DECIDUOUS.] —**de·cid′u·al** *adj.*

de·cid·u·ate (dĭ-sĭj′o͞o-ĭt, -sĭd′yo͞o-ĭt) *adj.* **1.** Characterized by or having a decidua. **2.** Characterized by shedding.

de·cid·u·ous (dĭ-sĭj′o͞o-əs, -sĭd′yo͞o-əs) *adj.* **1.** Falling off or shed at a specific season or stage of growth; not permanent or persistent: *deciduous antlers; deciduous leaves.* **2.** Shedding or losing foliage at the end of the growing season: *deciduous trees.* Compare **evergreen**. **3.** Not lasting; temporary. [Latin *dēciduus*, from *dēcidere*, to fall off : *dē-*, off + *cadere*, to fall (see **kad-** in Appendix*).] —**de·cid′u·ous·ly** *adv.* —**de·cid′u·ous·ness** *n.*

dec·i·gram (dĕs′ĭ-grăm′) *n. Abbr.* **dg** One-tenth (10^{-1}) of a gram. See **measurement**.

dec·i·li·ter (dĕs′ə-lē′tər) *n. Abbr.* **dl** One-tenth (10^{-1}) of a liter. See **measurement**.

de·cil·lion (dĭ-sĭl′yən) *n.* **1.** The cardinal number represented by 1 followed by 33 zeros, usually written 10^{33}. **2.** *British.* The cardinal number represented by 1 followed by 60 zeros, usually written 10^{60}. See **number**. [Latin *decem*, ten (see **dekm** in Appendix*) + (M)ILLION.] —**de·cil′lion** *adj.*

de·cil·lionth (dĭ-sĭl′yənth) *n.* **1.** The ordinal number decillion in a series. **2.** One of a decillion equal parts. See **number**. —**de·cil′lionth** *adj.* & *adv.*

dec·i·mal (dĕs′ə-məl) *n.* **1.** A linear array of integers that represents a fraction, every **decimal place** *(see)* indicating a multiple of a positive or negative power of 10. For example, the decimal .1 = $^{1}/_{10}$, .12 = $^{12}/_{100}$, .003 = $^{3}/_{1000}$. Also called "decimal fraction." **2.** Any number written using base 10; a number containing a decimal point. In this sense, also called "decimal number." —*adj.* **1.** Expressed or expressible as a decimal. **2. a.** Based on ten. **b.** Numbered or ordered by tens. **3.** Loosely, not integral; fractional. [Medieval Latin *decimālis*, of tithes, from Latin *decimus*, tenth, from *decem*, ten. See **dekm** in Appendix.*] —**dec′i·mal·ly** *adv.*

dec·i·mal·ize (dĕs′ə-mə-līz′) *tr.v.* **-ized, -izing, -izes.** To change to a decimal system. —**dec′i·mal·i·za′tion** *n.*

decimal place. The position of a digit to the right of a decimal point, usually identified by successive ascending ordinal numbers with the digit immediately to the right of the decimal point being first.

decimal point. A period placed to the left of a decimal.

decimal system. **1.** A number system using the base 10. **2.** A system of measurement in which all derived units are multiples of ten of fundamental units. See **measurement**.

dec·i·mate (dĕs′ĭ-māt′) *tr.v.* **-mated, -mating, -mates.** **1.** To destroy or kill a large part of. **2.** To select by lot and kill one in every ten of: *decimate a cohort.* [Latin *decimāre*, from *decimus*, tenth, from *decem*, ten. See **dekm** in Appendix.*] —**dec′i·ma′tion** *n.* —**dec′i·ma′tor** (-mā′tər) *n.*

dec·i·me·ter (dĕs′ə-mē′tər) *n. Abbr.* **dm** One-tenth (10^{-1}) of a meter. See **measurement**. [French *décimètre* : DECI- + METER.]

de·ci·pher (dĭ-sī′fər) *tr.v.* **-phered, -phering, -phers.** **1.** To read or interpret (something ambiguous, obscure, or illegible). **2.** To convert from a code or cipher to plain text; decode. [DE- (reversal) + CIPHER (after Old French *deschiffrer*).] —**de·ci′pher·a·ble** *adj.* —**de·ci′pher·ment** *n.*

de·ci·sion (dĭ-sĭzh′ən) *n.* **1.** The passing of judgment on an issue under consideration. **2.** The act of reaching a conclusion or making up one's mind. **3.** A conclusion or judgment reached or pronounced; verdict. **4.** Firmness of character or action; determination. **5.** *Boxing.* A victory won on points when no knockout has occurred. [Middle English *decisioun*, from Old French *decision*, from Latin *dēcisiō*, from *dēcīdere*, DECIDE.]

de·ci·sive (dĭ-sī′sĭv) *adj.* **1.** Having the power to settle a dispute or doubt; conclusive. **2.** Characterized by decision and firmness; resolute; determined. **3.** Beyond doubt; unmistakable; unquestionable. —**de·ci′sive·ly** *adv.* —**de·ci′sive·ness** *n.*

deck¹ (dĕk) *n. Abbr.* **dk.** **1. a.** A platform extending horizontally from one side of a ship to the other. **b.** The space between two such platforms. **2.** Any similar platform or surface. **3.** A pack of playing cards. —**clear the deck.** To prepare for action. —**hit the deck.** *Slang.* **1.** To get out of bed. **2.** To prepare for action. **3.** To fall or drop to a prone position. —**on deck.** *Slang.* **1.** On hand; present. **2.** Waiting to take one's turn. —*tr.v.* **decked, decking, decks.** To furnish (a ship) with a deck. [Middle English *dekke*, from Middle Dutch *dec, decke*, roof, covering. See **steg-¹** in Appendix.*]

deck² (dĕk) *tr.v.* **decked, decking, decks.** To clothe with finery; decorate; adorn. Often used with *out: decked out for a party.* [Middle Dutch *dekken*, to cover. See **steg-¹** in Appendix.*]

deck chair. A folding chair, usually with arms and a leg rest, as those on the decks of a ship for use by passengers.
deck hand. A member of a ship's crew who works on deck.
deck·house (dĕk′hous′) *n.* A superstructure on the upper deck of a ship.
deck·le (dĕk′əl) *n.* Also **deck·el.** **1.** A frame used in making paper by hand to form paper pulp into sheets of a desired size. **2.** A deckle edge. [German *Deckel,* diminutive of *Decke,* "a cover," from Old High German *decchī,* from *decchen,* to cover. See **steg-¹** in Appendix.*]
deckle edge. The rough edge of handmade paper formed in a deckle. Also called "featheredge." **—deck′le-edged′** *adj.*
decl. declension.
de·claim (dĭ-klām′) *v.* **-claimed, -claiming, -claims.** *—intr.* **1.** To deliver an elocutionary recitation. **2.** To speak loudly and vehemently; inveigh. *—tr.* To utter or recite with rhetorical effect. [Middle English *declamen,* from Latin *dēclāmāre* : *dē-* (intensive) + *clāmāre,* to cry out (see **kel-³** in Appendix*).] **—de·claim′er** *n.*
dec·la·ma·tion (dĕk′lə-mā′shən) *n.* **1.** An elocutionary recitation. **2. a.** Vehement oratory. **b.** A harangue; tirade. **3. a.** Correct and expressive delivery of words set to music. **b.** The art or action of reading or reciting a literary text with the proper intonation and expression. —See Synonyms at **bombast.** [Middle English *declamacioun,* from Latin *dēclāmātiō,* from *dēclāmāre,* DECLAIM.]
de·clam·a·to·ry (dĭ-klăm′ə-tôr′ē, -tōr′ē) *adj.* **1.** Having the quality of a declamation; loudly demanding attention: *"the effect of a declamatory beauty spot on her chin"* (Samuel Beckett). **2.** Pretentiously rhetorical; meaninglessly bombastic. **—de·clam′a·to′ri·ly** *adv.*
de·clar·a·ble (dĭ-klâr′ə-bəl) *adj.* Such as can or should be declared, as for payment of customs duty.
de·clar·ant (dĭ-klâr′ənt) *n.* One who has signed a declaration of intention of becoming a U.S. citizen.
dec·la·ra·tion (dĕk′lə-rā′shən) *n. Abbr.* **dec.** **1.** An explicit or formal statement or announcement. **2.** Such a statement in written form. **3.** The act or process of declaring. **4.** A statement of taxable goods or of properties subject to duty. **5.** *Law.* **a.** A formal statement by a plaintiff specifying the facts and circumstances constituting his cause of action. **b.** An unsworn statement of facts that is admissible as evidence. **6.** *Card Games.* **a.** A bid, especially the final bid of a hand. **b.** An announcement by a player of points made.
Declaration of Independence. A proclamation by the Second Continental Congress declaring the 13 American colonies politically independent from Great Britain, formally adopted July 4, 1776.
de·clar·a·tive (dĭ-klâr′ə-tĭv) *adj.* Also **de·clar·a·to·ry** (-tôr′ē, -tōr′ē). Serving to declare or state. **—de·clar′a·tive·ly** *adv.*
de·clare (dĭ-klâr′) *v.* **-clared, -claring, -clares.** *—tr.* **1.** To state officially or formally. **2.** To state with emphasis or authority; affirm. **3.** To reveal or manifest; prove. **4.** To make a full statement of (dutiable goods, for example). **5.** *Bridge.* To designate (a trump suit or no-trump) with the final bid of a hand. *—intr.* **1.** To make a declaration. **2.** To proclaim one's choice, opinion, or resolution; to act. Used with *for* or *against.* —See Synonyms at **assert.** [Middle English *declaren,* from Old French *declarer,* from Latin *dēclārāre,* to make clear : *dē-* (intensive) + *clārāre,* to make clear, from *clārus,* clear (see **kel-³** in Appendix*).] **—de·clar′er** *n.*
de·class (dē-klăs′, kläs′) *tr.v.* **-classed, -classing, -classes.** To lower in class or status; degrade; debase.
dé·clas·sé (dā-klà-sā′) *adj.* Also **de·classed** (dē-klăst′). Lowered in social class. [French, from *déclasser,* to lower in class : *dé-,* from Latin *dē-,* down + *classe,* CLASS.]
de·clas·si·fy (dē-klăs′ə-fī′) *tr.v.* **-fied, -fying, -fies.** To remove official security classification from (a document). **—de·clas′si·fi′a·ble** *adj.* **—de·clas′si·fi·ca′tion** *n.*
de·clen·sion (dĭ-klĕn′shən) *n.* **1.** *Abbr.* **dec., decl.** *Linguistics.* **a.** In certain languages, the inflection of nouns, pronouns, and adjectives in such categories as case, number, and gender. **b.** A class of words of one language with the same or a similar system of inflections, as the first declension in Latin. **2.** A descending slope; descent. **3.** A decline or decrease; deterioration: *"states and empires have their periods of declension"* (Sterne). **4.** A deviation, as from a standard or practice. [Learned respelling of Middle English *declinson,* from Old French *declinaison,* from Late Latin *dēclīnātiō,* grammatical declension, from Latin, DECLINATION.] **—de·clen′sion·al** *adj.*
dec·li·na·tion (dĕk′lə-nā′shən) *n. Abbr.* **dec.** **1.** A sloping or bending downward. **2.** A falling off, especially from prosperity or vigor; a decline. **3.** A deviation, as from a specific direction or standard. **4.** A refusal to accept. **5. Magnetic declination** *(see).* **6.** *Astronomy.* The angular distance to a point on the celestial sphere, measured north or south from the celestial equator along the **hour circle** *(see)* to the point. [Middle English *declinacioun,* from Old French *declination,* from Latin *dēclīnātiō,* from *dēclīnāre,* DECLINE.] **—dec′li·na′tion·al** *adj.*
de·cli·na·to·ry (dĭ-klī′nə-tôr′ē, -tōr′ē) *adj.* Involving or conveying declination; expressing refusal.
de·cline (dĭ-klīn′) *v.* **-clined, -clining, -clines.** *—intr.* **1.** To refuse to do or accept something. **2.** To slope downward. **3.** To degrade or lower oneself; condescend. **4.** To deteriorate gradually; fail. **5.** To draw to a gradual close; wane. *—tr.* **1.** To refuse (something). **2.** To cause to slope downward. **3.** *Linguistics.* In certain languages, to give the inflected forms of (a noun, pronoun, or adjective). —See Synonyms at **refuse.** *—n.* **1.** The process or result of declining; especially, gradual deterioration. **2.** A downward movement. **3.** The period when something is tending toward an end. **4.** A downward slope. **5.** Any disease, such as tuberculosis, that gradually weakens or wastes the body or a bodily part. [Middle English *declinen,* from Old French *decliner,* from Latin *dēclīnāre,* to turn aside, go down, inflect grammatically : *dē-,* away, aside + *-clīnāre,* to bend (see **klei-** in Appendix*).] **—de·clin′a·ble** *adj.* **—de·clin′er** *n.*
dec·li·nom·e·ter (dĕk′lə-nŏm′ə-tər) *n.* An instrument for measuring magnetic declination. [DECLIN(ATION) + -METER.]
de·cliv·i·tous (dĭ-klĭv′ə-təs) *adj.* Rather steep.
de·cliv·i·ty (dĭ-klĭv′ə-tē) *n., pl.* **-ties.** A descending slope, as of a hill. [Latin *dēclīvitās,* from *dēclīvis,* sloping down : *dē-,* down + *clīvus,* a slope (see **klei-** in Appendix*).]
de·coct (dĭ-kŏkt′) *tr.v.* **-cocted, -cocting, -cocts.** **1. a.** To extract (the flavor or active principle of) by boiling. **b.** To steep in hot water. **2.** To concentrate by boiling; boil down. [Middle English *decocten,* from Latin *dēcoquere* (past participle *dēcoctus*), to boil down to the dregs : *dē-* (intensive) + *coquere,* to cook (see **pekw-** in Appendix*).] **—de·coc′tion** *n.*
de·code (dē-kōd′) *tr.v.* **-coded, -coding, -codes.** To convert from code into plain text. **—de·cod′er** *n.*
dé·colle·tage (dā′kôl-täzh′) *n.* **1.** A low neckline on a garment. **2.** A décolleté garment. [French, from DÉCOLLETÉ.]
dé·colle·té (dā′kôl-tā′) *adj.* **1.** Having a low neckline: *a décolleté dress.* **2.** Wearing a garment with a low neckline. [French, past participle of *décolleter,* to uncover the neck, cut a low neckline : *dé-,* from Latin *dē-* (removal) + *collet,* collar, diminutive of *col,* neck, collar, from Old French, from Latin *collum,* neck (see **kwel-¹** in Appendix*).]
de·col·or (dē-kŭl′ər) *tr.v.* **-ored, -oring, -ors.** To deprive of color; bleach. **—de′col·or·a′tion** *n.*
de·col·or·ant (dē-kŭl′ər-ənt) *adj.* Able to remove color or to bleach. *—n.* A bleaching agent.
de·col·or·ize (dē-kŭl′ə-rīz′) *tr.v.* **-ized, -izing, -izes.** To decolor. **—de·col′or·i·za′tion** *n.* **—de·col′or·iz′er** *n.*
de·com·pose (dē′kəm-pōz′) *v.* **-posed, -posing, -poses.** *—tr.* **1.** To separate into component parts or basic elements. **2.** To cause to rot. *—intr.* **1.** To break down into component parts; disintegrate. **2.** To decay; putrefy. —See Synonyms at **decay.** [French *décomposer* : *dé-,* from Latin *dē-* (reversal) + *composer,* to compose, from Old French, COMPOSE.] **—de′com·pos′a·ble** *adj.* **—de′com·pos′er** *n.*
de·com·po·si·tion (dē′kŏm-pə-zĭsh′ən) *n.* **1.** The act or result of decomposing. **2. a.** *Chemistry.* Separation into constituents by chemical reaction. **b.** *Biology.* Organic decay.
de·com·pound¹ (dē′kəm-pound′) *tr.v.* **-pounded, -pounding, -pounds.** To compound (compounded things). *—adj.* **1.** Compounded or consisting of things or parts already compound. **2.** Having or consisting of subdivided or compound leaflets: *a decompound leaf.* [DE- (from) + COMPOUND (noun).]
de·com·pound² (dē′kəm-pound′) *tr.v.* **-pounded, -pounding, -pounds.** To decompose. [DE- (reversal) + COMPOUND (verb).]
de·com·press (dē′kəm-prĕs′) *tr.v.* **-pressed, -pressing, -presses.** **1.** To relieve of pressure. **2.** To bring (a person working in compressed air) back to normal air pressure by means of an air lock or a decompression chamber.
de·com·pres·sion (dē′kəm-prĕsh′ən) *n.* **1.** The act or process of decompressing. **2.** Any surgical procedure used to relieve pressure on an organ or part.
decompression sickness. *Pathology.* **Caisson disease** *(see).*
de·con·tam·i·nate (dē′kən-tăm′ə-nāt′) *tr.v.* **-nated, -nating, -nates.** **1.** To eliminate contamination in. **2.** To make safe by eliminating poisonous or otherwise harmful substances, such as noxious chemicals or radioactive material. **—de′con·tam′i·nant** *n.* **—de′con·tam′i·na′tion** *n.*
de·con·trol (dē′kən-trōl′) *tr.v.* **-trolled, -trolling, -trols.** To free from control, especially from governmental control.
dé·cor (dā′kôr′, dā′kôr′) *n.* Also **de·cor.** **1.** A decorative style or scheme, as of a room, home, stage setting, or the like. **2.** A stage setting; scenery. [French, from *décorer,* to decorate, from Latin *decorāre,* DECORATE.]
dec·o·rate (dĕk′ə-rāt′) *tr.v.* **-rated, -rating, -rates.** **1.** To furnish or adorn with fashionable or beautiful things; embellish; ornament. **2.** To confer a medal or other honor upon; present with a decoration. [Latin *decorāre,* from *decus* (stem *decor-*), ornament. See **dek-¹** in Appendix.*]
dec·o·ra·tion (dĕk′ə-rā′shən) *n.* **1.** The act, process, technique, or art of decorating. **2.** An object or group of objects used to decorate; ornament; embellishment. **3.** A medal, badge, or other emblem of honor.
Decoration Day. **Memorial Day** *(see).*
dec·o·ra·tive (dĕk′ər-ə-tĭv) *adj.* Serving to decorate; ornamental. **—dec′o·ra·tive·ly** *adv.* **—dec′o·ra·tive·ness** *n.*
dec·o·ra·tor (dĕk′ə-rā′tər) *n.* An **interior decorator** *(see).*
dec·o·rous (dĕk′ər-əs, dĭ-kôr′əs) *adj.* Characterized by or exhibiting decorum; proper. [Latin *decōrus,* from *decor,* seemliness, elegance, beauty. See **dek-¹** in Appendix.*] **—dec′o·rous·ly** *adv.* **—dec′o·rous·ness** *n.*
de·cor·ti·cate (dĭ-kôr′tĭ-kāt′) *tr.v.* **-cated, -cating, -cates.** **1.** To remove the cortex from (an organ or structure), especially as a surgical procedure. **2.** To remove the bark, husk, or outer layer from; to strip; peel. [Latin *dēcorticāre* : *dē-* (removal) + *cortex* (stem *cortic-*), bark (see **sker-¹** in Appendix*).] **—de·cor′ti·ca′tion** *n.* **—de·cor′ti·ca′tor** (-kā′tər) *n.*
de·co·rum (dĭ-kôr′əm, dĭ-kōr′əm) *n.* Conformity to social conventions; propriety: *"the rigid decorum of the English"* (Havelock Ellis). —See Synonyms at **etiquette.** [Latin *decōrum,* from *decōrus,* DECOROUS.]
de·cou·page (dā′ko͞o-päzh′) *n.* Also **dé·cou·page** (dā′ko͞o-päzh′;

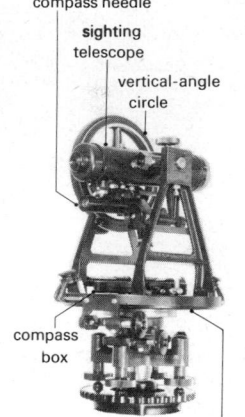

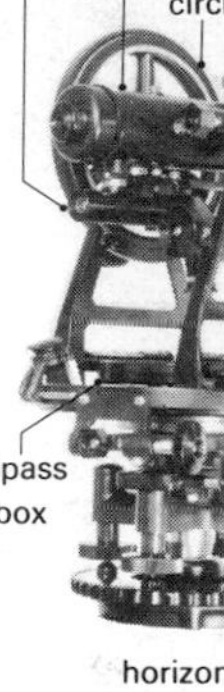
microscope for observing compass needle
sighting telescope
vertical-angle circle
compass box
horizontal-angle circle
declinometer
Transit declinometer

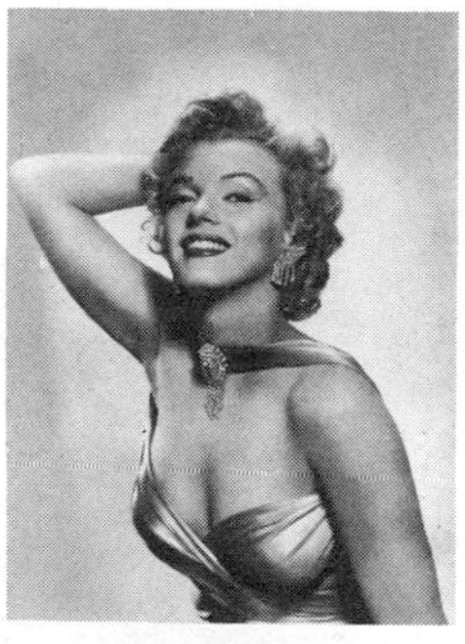
décolletage
Actress Marilyn Monroe

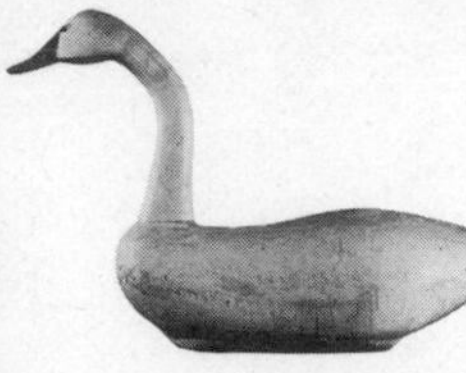
decoy
Painted wooden decoy of a whistling swan

French dā-ko͞o-pȧzh′). **1.** The technique of decorating a surface with paper cutouts. **2.** Something produced by decoupage. [French, from Old French *decouper,* to cut out : *de-,* from Latin *dē-,* away + *couper,* to cut, strike, from *coup,* stroke, COUP.]

de·coy (dē′koi′, dĭ-koi′) *n.* **1.** An enclosed place, such as a pond, into which wildfowl are lured for capture. **2.** A living or artificial bird or other animal used to entice game into a trap or within shooting range. **3.** One who leads another into danger, deception, or a trap. **4.** Any means used to mislead or lead into danger. —*v.* (dĭ-koi′) **decoyed, -coying, -coys.** —*tr.* To lure into danger or a trap; entrap by or as if by a decoy. —*intr.* To be lured by or as if by a decoy; fall into a trap. —See Synonyms at **lure.** [Possibly from Dutch *de kooi,* "the cage" : *de,* the, from Middle Dutch (see **to-** in Appendix*) + *kooi,* cage, from Middle Dutch *cōie,* from Latin *cavea,* from *cavus,* hollow (see **keu-³** in Appendix*).] —**de·coy′er** *n.*

de·crease (dĭ-krēs′) *v.* **-creased, -creasing, -creases.** —*intr.* To grow or become gradually less or smaller; diminish gradually; dwindle. —*tr.* To cause to grow or become less or smaller; make less; reduce. —*n.* (dē′krēs′). *Abbr.* **dec.** The act or process of decreasing, or the resulting condition. [Middle English *decresen,* from Old French *de(s)creistre* (present stem *decreiss-*), from Vulgar Latin *discrēscere* (unattested), variant of Latin *dēcrēscere* : *dē-* (reversal) + *crēscere,* to grow, increase (see **ker-³** in Appendix*).] —**de·creas′ing·ly** *adv.*

Synonyms: *decrease, reduce, lessen, dwindle, abate, diminish, shrink, subside.* These verbs mean to become smaller or less or to make something smaller. *Decrease* refers to gradual decline or making steadily smaller. *Reduce* emphasizes cutting down in size, time, cost, or rank. *Lessen* usually refers to decrease in number. *Dwindle* suggests decreasing bit by bit to a vanishing point. *Abate* stresses a decrease in quantity or strength and suggests there was originally too much. *Diminish* implies taking away or making or becoming perceptibly smaller by removal. *Shrink* applies specifically to reduction in original physical size. *Subside* implies decreasing to a more normal condition.

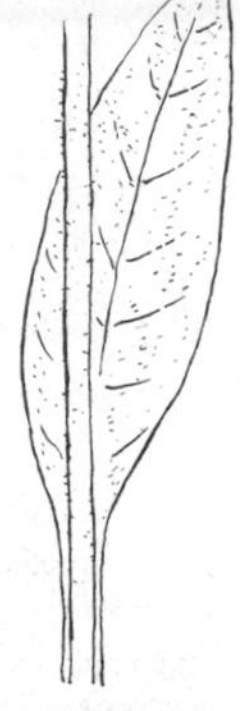
decurrent
A decurrent leaf

de·cree (dĭ-krē′) *n.* **1.** An authoritative order having the force of law. **2.** The judgment of a court of equity, admiralty, probate, or divorce. **3.** *Roman Catholic Church.* **a.** A doctrinal or disciplinary act of an ecumenical council. **b.** An administrative act applying or interpreting articles of canon law. —*v.* **decreed, -creeing, -crees.** —*tr.* To ordain, establish, or decide by decree. —*intr.* To issue a decree. [Middle English *decre(t),* from Old French, from Latin *dēcrētum,* from *dēcrētus,* past participle of *dēcernere,* to decide : *dē-* (removal) + *cernere,* to sift (see **skeri-** in Appendix*).] —**de·cree′a·ble** *adj.* —**de·cre′er** *n.*

de·cree-law (dĭ-krē′lô′) *n.* A decree having the force of a law enacted by a legislature, but usually issued on the sole authority of an absolute ruler or the executive branch of a government.

dec·re·ment (dĕk′rə-mənt) *n.* **1.** The act or process of decreasing or becoming gradually less; waste. **2.** The amount lost by gradual diminution or waste. **3.** *Mathematics.* The amount by which a variable is decreased; a negative increment. [Latin *dēcrēmentum,* from *dēcrēscere,* to DECREASE.]

de·crep·it (dĭ-krĕp′ĭt) *adj.* Weakened by old age, illness, or hard use; broken-down. See Synonyms at **weak.** [Middle English, from Old French, from Latin *dēcrepitus,* probably "cracked," "broken" : *dē-* (intensive) + *crepitus,* past participle of *crepāre,* to crack, creak (see **ker-²** in Appendix*).] —**de·crep′it·ly** *adv.*

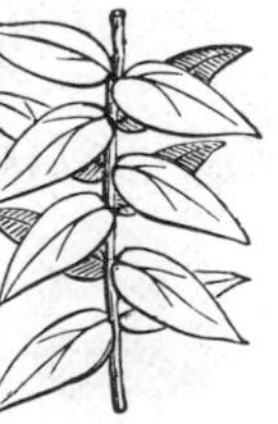
decussate
Decussate leaves

de·crep·i·tate (dĭ-krĕp′ĭ-tāt′) *v.* **-tated, -tating, -tates.** —*tr.* To roast or calcine (crystals or salts) until they emit a crackling sound or until this sound stops. —*intr.* To make a crackling sound when roasted. [Medieval Latin *dēcrepitāre* : Latin *dē-* (intensive) + *crepitāre,* frequentative of *crepāre,* to creak, crack (see **ker-²** in Appendix*).] —**de·crep′i·ta′tion** *n.*

de·crep·i·tude (dĭ-krĕp′ĭ-to͞od′, -tyo͞od′) *n.* The state of being decrepit; weakness; infirmity.

de·cre·scen·do (dē′krə-shĕn′dō) *n., pl.* **-dos.** *Abbr.* **decresc. 1.** A gradual decrease in force or loudness. **2.** A musical passage marked or performed in a decrescendo. Also called "diminuendo." —*adj. Abbr.* **decresc.** Gradually diminishing in force or loudness. Also "diminuendo." —*adv. Abbr.* **decresc.** With a decrescendo. Also "diminuendo." [Italian, from Latin *dēcrescendum,* gerund of *dēcrēscere,* to DECREASE.]

de·cres·cent (dĭ-krĕs′ənt) *adj.* **1.** Decreasing; diminishing. **2.** Of, or similar to, the waning moon. [Latin *dēcrescēns,* present participle *dēcrescere,* to DECREASE.] —**de·cres′cence** *n.*

de·cre·tal (dĭ-krēt′l) *n. Roman Catholic Church.* **1.** A decree; especially, a letter from the pope giving a decision on some point or question of canon law. **2.** *Capital* **D.** *Plural.* The body of papal laws and decrees forming a part of canon law. [Middle English, from Old French, from Medieval Latin *(epistola) dēcrētālis,* (letter) of decree, from Latin *dēcrētum,* DECREE.] —**de·cre′tal** *adj.* —**de·cre′tal·ist** *n.*

de·cre·tive (dĭ-krē′tĭv) *adj.* Having the force of a decree.

dec·re·to·ry (dĕk′rə-tôr′ē, -tōr′ē) *adj.* Of or resulting from a decree.

de·cry (dĭ-krī′) *tr.v.* **-cried, -crying, -cries. 1.** To belittle or disparage openly; to censure. **2.** To depreciate or devalue (currency, for example) by official proclamation or by rumor. [French *décrier,* from Old French *descrier,* "to cry down" : *des-,* from Latin *dē-,* down + *crier,* to CRY.] —**de·cri′er** *n.*

Synonyms: *decry, disparage, belittle.* These verbs mean to express a low valuation of something or someone. *Decry* implies making public objection by condemnation. *Disparage* means to express slight regard for another's accomplishments, often by indirection. *Belittle* implies open depreciation.

de·cum·bence (dĭ-kŭm′bəns) *n.* Also **de·cum·ben·cy** (-bən-sē). The position or state of lying down.

de·cum·bent (dĭ-kŭm′bənt) *adj.* **1.** Reclining; prostrate. **2.** *Botany.* Lying or growing along the ground but erect at or near the apex: *decumbent stems.* [Latin *dēcumbēns,* present participle of *dēcumbere,* to lie down : *dē-,* down + *-cumbere,* to lie down (see **keu-²** in Appendix*).]

dec·u·ple (dĕk′yə-pəl) *adj.* Ten times as great; tenfold. [Middle English, from Old French, from Late Latin *decuplus* : Latin *decem,* ten (see **dekm̥** in Appendix*) + *-plus,* -fold (see **pel-³** in Appendix*).]

de·cur·rent (dĭ-kûr′ənt) *adj. Botany.* Extending downward from the base along a stem: *decurrent leaves.* [Latin *dēcurrēns,* present participle of *dēcurrere,* to run down : *dē-,* down + *currere,* to run (see **kers-²** in Appendix*).] —**de·cur′rent·ly** *adv.*

de·cus·sate (dĭ-kŭs′āt′) *v.* **-sated, -sating, -sates.** —*tr.* To cross or intersect so as to form an X. —*intr.* To cross each other; intersect. —*adj.* **1.** Intersected or crossed in the form of an X. **2.** *Botany.* Arranged on a stem in opposite pairs at right angles to those above or below. [Latin *decussāre,* from *decussis,* number ten, symbol X, coin worth ten asses : *decem,* ten (see **dekm̥** in Appendix*) + *ās,* AS (coin).] —**de·cus′sate′ly** *adv.*

dec·us·sa·tion (dē′kə-sā′shən) *n.* **1.** A crossing in the shape of an X. **2.** An X-shaped crossing of nerve fibers connecting dissimilar parts on the two sides of the spinal cord or brain.

de·dans (dē′dəns) *n., pl.* **dedans. 1.** A screened gallery for spectators at the service end of the court. **2.** The spectators at a court-tennis match. [French, "inside," "interior," from Old French, "from within" : *de,* from, from Latin *dē* + *dans,* in, within, from Late Latin *deintus* : Latin *dē,* from + *intus,* within (see **en** in Appendix*).]

De·de·kind (dā′dĕ-kĭnt), **Julius Wilhelm Richard.** 1831–1916. German mathematician; contributed to analysis and theory of functions.

Dedekind cut. A subdivision of the rational numbers into two nonempty sets satisfying the condition that any member of the first set is less than any member of the second and the condition that the first set has no largest member, used as a theoretical device for defining the system of real numbers. [After J.W.R. DEDEKIND.]

ded·i·cate (dĕd′ə-kāt′) *tr.v.* **-cated, -cating, -cates. 1.** To set apart for a deity or for religious purposes; consecrate. **2.** To set apart for some special use; to appropriate; devote. **3.** To address or inscribe (a literary work or artistic performance, for example) to someone as a mark of respect or affection. **4.** To commit (oneself) to a particular course of thought or action. **5.** To open (a building, for example) for public use or unveil (a monument), especially with a ceremony. —See Synonyms at **devote.** —*adj.* Devoted; dedicated. [Middle English *dedicaten,* from Latin *dēdicāre,* to give out tidings, proclaim : *dē-,* away from oneself + *dicāre,* to say, proclaim (see **deik-** in Appendix*).] —**ded′i·ca·tee′** *n.* —**ded′i·ca′tor** (-kā′tər) *n.*

ded·i·ca·tion (dĕd′ə-kā′shən) *n.* **1. a.** The act of dedicating. **b.** The state of being dedicated. **2.** A note prefixed to a literary, artistic, or musical composition dedicating it to someone in token of affection or esteem. **3.** A rite or ceremony of dedicating. —**ded′i·ca′tive, ded′i·ca·to′ry** (-kə-tôr′ē, -tōr′ē) *adj.*

de·dif·fer·en·ti·a·tion (dē′dĭf-ə-rĕn′shē-ā′shən) *n. Biology.* The loss of specialized cellular form, especially prior to redifferentiation.

de·duce (dĭ-do͞os′, -dyo͞os′) *tr.v.* **-duced, -ducing, -duces. 1.** To reach (a conclusion) by reasoning. **2.** To infer from a general principle; reason deductively. **3.** To trace the origin or derivation of. [Middle English *deducen,* from Latin *dēdūcere,* to lead away, infer logically : *dē-,* away + *dūcere,* to lead (see **deuk-** in Appendix*).] —**de·duc′i·ble** *adj.*

de·duct (dĭ-dŭkt′) *v.* **-ducted, -ducting, -ducts.** —*tr.* **1.** To take away (a quantity from another); subtract. **2.** To derive by deduction; deduce. —*intr.* To detract; diminish. Usually used with *from: Bad plumbing deducts from the value of his house.* [Latin *dēdūcere* (past participle *dēductus*), to lead or take away, DEDUCE.]

de·duct·i·ble (dĭ-dŭk′tə-bəl) *adj.* **1.** Capable of being deducted. **2.** Allowable as a tax deduction.

de·duc·tion (dĭ-dŭk′shən) *n.* **1.** The act of deducting; subtraction. **2.** That which is or may be deducted: *Certain business expenses are legitimate tax deductions.* **3. a.** The act of deducing; drawing of a conclusion by reasoning. **b.** *Logic.* The process of reasoning in which a conclusion follows necessarily from the stated premises; inference by reasoning from the general to the specific. **c.** *Logic.* A conclusion reached by this process. In this sense, compare **induction.**

de·duc·tive (dĭ-dŭk′tĭv) *adj.* **1.** Of or based on deduction. **2.** Involving deduction in reasoning. —**de·duc′tive·ly** *adv.*

dee (dē) *n.* The letter *d.*

Dee (dē). **1.** A river of northeast-central Scotland, rising in the Cairngorm Mountains and flowing about 90 miles east to the North Sea at Aberdeen. **2.** A river rising in northern Wales and flowing 70 miles generally north and northeast through western England to the Irish Sea.

deed (dēd) *n.* **1.** An act. **2.** A feat; exploit. **3.** Action or performance in general, especially as distinguished from words: *bold in deed as well as in speech.* **4.** *Law.* A document sealed as an instrument of bond, contract, or conveyance, especially pertaining to property. —*tr.v.* **deeded, deeding, deeds.** To transfer by means of a deed. [Middle English *dede,* Old English *dǣd.* See **dhē-¹** in Appendix.*]

deem (dēm) *v.* **deemed, deeming, deems.** —*tr.* To judge; consider; think: *We deem it advisable to wait.* —*intr.* To have an opinion; suppose. —See Synonyms at **consider.** [Middle English *demen,* Old English *dēman.* See **dhē-¹** in Appendix.*]

ă pat/ā pay/âr care/ä father/b **bib**/ch **church**/d **deed**/ĕ pet/ē be/f **fife**/g **gag**/h **hat**/hw **which**/ĭ pit/ī pie/îr pier/j **judge**/k **kick**/l **lid,** needle/m **mum**/n **no,** sudden/ng **thing**/ŏ pot/ō toe/ô paw, for/oi noise/ou out/o͝o took/o͞o boot/p **pop**/r **roar**/s **sauce**/sh **ship, dish**/

deep (dēp) *adj.* **deeper, deepest. 1.** Extending to or located at: **a.** An unspecified distance below a surface. **b.** A specified distance below a surface. **2.** Extending from front to rear, or inward from the outside, for: **a.** An unspecified distance. **b.** A specified distance. **3.** Arising from or penetrating to a depth. **4.** Far distant. **5. a.** Difficult to fathom or understand; obscure. **b.** Learned; understanding; wise. **c.** Cunning; crafty; sly. **6. a.** Profound; intense; extreme. **b.** Profoundly absorbed or immersed. **7.** Dark rather than pale in shade. See **color. 8.** Low in pitch; resonant. **—go off the deep end.** *Informal.* To act recklessly or hysterically. **—in deep water.** In trouble. *—n.* **1.** Any deep place on land or in a body of water, especially in the ocean and over 3,000 fathoms in depth: *the Mindanao Deep.* **2.** The most intense or extreme part. **3.** A distance estimated in fathoms between successive marks on a sounding line: *by the deep, 11.* **—the deep.** *Poetic.* The ocean. *—adv.* **1.** Deeply; profoundly. **2.** Well on in time; late: *worked deep into the night.* **—in deep.** *Informal.* Completely committed. [Middle English *dep,* Old English *dēop.* See **dheub-** in Appendix.*] **—deep′ly** *adv.* **—deep′ness** *n.*

deep-dyed (dēp′dīd′) *adj.* Unmitigated; absolute.

deep·en (dē′pən) *v.* **-ened, -ening, -ens.** *—tr.* To make deep or deeper. *—intr.* To become deep or deeper. **—deep′en·er** *n.*

Deep·freeze (dēp′frēz′) *n.* **1.** A trademark for a refrigerator designed to freeze and store food for long periods. **2.** *Often small* **d.** *Informal.* Storage in, or as if in, a Deepfreeze.

deep-fry (dēp′frī′) *tr.v.* **-fried, -frying, -fries.** To fry by immersing in a deep pan of fat or oil.

deep-root·ed (dēp′rōō′tĭd, -rŏŏt′ĭd) *adj.* Firmly implanted.

deep-sea (dēp′sē′) *adj.* Pertaining to deep parts of the sea.

deep-seat·ed (dēp′sē′tĭd) *adj.* Deeply rooted; ingrained.

Deep South. Also **deep South.** The southeasternmost part of the United States; especially, the Confederate heartland of South Carolina, Georgia, Alabama, and Mississippi.

deep space. The regions beyond the moon, encompassing interplanetary, interstellar, and intergalactic space.

deer (dîr) *n., pl.* **deer** or **deers. 1.** Any of various hoofed ruminant mammals of the family Cervidae, characteristically having deciduous antlers borne only by the males. **2.** Any of various smaller deerlike mammals, such as the mouse deer. [Middle English *der,* animal, beast, deer, Old English *dēor.* See **dheu-[1]** in Appendix.*]

deer fly. Any of various blood-sucking flies of the genus *Chrysops,* having dark bars or spots on the wings.

deer grass. A plant, the **meadow beauty** *(see).*

deer·hound (dîr′hound′) *n.* A dog of a breed developed in Scotland, resembling a greyhound but larger and having a wiry coat. Also called "Scottish deerhound."

deer mouse. Any of various New World mice of the genus *Peromyscus,* having large ears, white feet and underparts, and a long tail. Also called "white-footed mouse." [From its deerlike agility.]

deer·skin (dîr′skĭn′) *n.* **1.** Leather made from the hide of a deer. **2.** A garment made from such leather.

deer's-tongue (dîrz′tŭng′) *n.* A tall plant, *Frasera speciosa,* of western North America, having whorls of greenish flowers.

deer·weed (dîr′wēd′) *n.* Any of several bushlike, yellow-flowered plants of the genus *Lotus,* of southwestern North America, sometimes used as forage in arid regions.

de-es·ca·late (dē′ĕs′kə-lāt′) *tr.v.* **-lated, -lating, -lates.** To decrease the scope or intensity of (a war). **—de′-es′ca·la′tion** *n.*

def. 1. defective. **2.** defendant. **3.** defense. **4.** deferred. **5.** definite. **6.** definition.

de·face (dĭ-fās′) *tr.v.* **-faced, -facing, -faces. 1.** To spoil or mar the surface or appearance of; disfigure. **2.** To impair the usefulness, value, or influence of. **3.** To efface or obliterate. [Middle English *defacen,* from Old French *desfacier* : *des-,* from Latin *dē-* (undoing, ruin) + *face,* FACE.] **—de·face′a·ble** *adj.* **—de·face′ment** *n.* **—de·fac′er** *n.*

de fac·to (dē făk′tō). **1.** In reality or fact; actually. **2. a.** Actual. **b.** Actually exercising power. Compare **de jure.** [Latin, "from the fact."]

de·fal·cate (dĭ-făl′kāt′, dĭ-fôl′kāt′, dĕf′əl-kāt′) *intr.v.* **-cated, -cating, -cates.** To misuse funds; embezzle. [Medieval Latin *dēfalcāre,* to cut off : Latin *dē-,* off + *falx* (stem *falc-*), sickle (see **falcate**).] **—de′fal·ca′tion** *n.* **—de·fal′ca′tor** (-kā′tər) *n.*

def·a·ma·tion (dĕf′ə-mā′shən) *n.* Calumny; slander or libel. **—de·fam′a·to′ry** (-tôr′ē, -tōr′ē) *adj.*

de·fame (dĭ-fām′) *tr.v.* **-famed, -faming, -fames.** To attack the good name of by slander or libel. —See Synonyms at **malign.** [Middle English *diffamen, defamen,* from Old French *diffamer, defamer,* from Latin *diffāmāre* : *dis-* (undoing, ruin) + *fāma,* report, fame (see **bhā-[2]** in Appendix*).] **—de·fam′er** *n.*

de·fault (dĭ-fôlt′) *n.* **1.** A failure to perform a task or fulfill an obligation; especially, failure to meet a financial obligation. **2.** Failure to make a required appearance in court. **3.** The failure of one or more competitors or teams to participate in a contest: *win by default.* **—in default of.** Through the failure, absence, or lack of. *—v.* **defaulted, -faulting, -faults.** *—intr.* **1.** To fail to do that which is required. **2.** To fail to pay money when it is due. **3.** *Law.* **a.** To fail to appear in court when summoned. **b.** To lose a case by not appearing. **4.** *Sports.* To fail to compete in or complete a scheduled contest. *—tr.* **1.** To fail to perform or pay. **2.** To fail to take part in or complete, as a contest. **3.** *Law.* To lose (a case) by failing to take part in it. [Middle English *defaut(e),* from Old French *defaute,* from Vulgar Latin *dēfallita* (unattested), from *dēfallīre* (unattested), to fail : *de-* (intensive) + *fallire* (unattested), variant of Latin *fallere,* to fail (see **fail**).] **—de·fault′er** *n.*

de·fea·sance (dĭ-fē′zəns) *n.* **1.** An annulment or rendering void. **2.** The voiding of a contract or deed. **3.** A clause within a contract or deed providing for annulment. [Middle English *defesaunce,* from Old French *de(s)fesance,* from *de(s)fesant,* present participle of *de(s)faire,* to destroy, DEFEAT.]

de·fea·si·ble (dĭ-fē′zə-bəl) *adj.* Of that which may be annulled or terminated. **—de·fea′si·bil′i·ty, de·fea′si·ble·ness** *n.*

de·feat (dĭ-fēt′) *tr.v.* **-feated, -feating, -feats. 1.** To win victory over; vanquish. **2.** To prevent the success of; thwart. **3.** *Law.* To annul or make void. *—n.* **1.** The act of defeating or state of being defeated. **2.** Failure to win; overthrow. **3.** A coming to naught; frustration. **4.** *Law.* A making null and void. [Middle English *defeten,* from Old French *de(s)faire* (past participle *desfait*), from Medieval Latin *disfacere,* to undo, destroy : Latin *dis-* (reversal) + *facere,* to do, make (see **dhē-[1]** in Appendix*).] **—de·feat′er** *n.*

Synonyms: *defeat, conquer, vanquish, beat, rout, subdue, subjugate, overcome.* These verbs mean to get the better of an adversary. *Defeat,* the most general, does not necessarily imply finality of outcome. *Conquer* suggests decisive wide-scale victory. *Vanquish* emphasizes total and final mastery. *Beat,* less formal, is often the equivalent of *defeat,* though *beat* may convey greater emphasis. *Rout* implies not only complete victory but also putting an adversary to flight. *Subdue* suggests mastery and control by suppression or taming. *Subjugate* more strongly implies making an opponent subservient. *Overcome* stresses the importance of the conquest to the victor's well-being and often implies courage and perseverance.

de·feat·ism (dĭ-fē′tĭz′əm) *n.* Acceptance of, or resignation to, the prospect of defeat. **—de·feat′ist** *n.*

def·e·cate (dĕf′ə-kāt′) *v.* **-cated, -cating, -cates.** *—intr.* To void feces from the bowels. *—tr.* To clarify (a chemical solution). [Latin *dēfaecāre* : *dē-* (removal) + *faex,* dregs, FECES.] **—def′e·ca′tion** *n.* **—def′e·ca′tor** (-kā′tər) *n.*

de·fect (dē′fĕkt′, dĭ-fĕkt′) *n.* **1.** The lack of something necessary or desirable; deficiency. **2.** An imperfection; a failing; fault. —See Synonyms at **blemish.** *—intr.v.* (dĭ-fĕkt′) **defected, -fecting, -fects.** To leave, without consent or permission, an allegiance which one had espoused or acknowledged. [Middle English, from Old French, from Latin *dēfectus,* deficiency, lack, from the past participle of *dēficere,* to remove from, desert, fail, be wanting : *dē-,* away from + *facere,* to do, set (see **dhē-[1]** in Appendix*).] **—de·fec′tion** *n.* **—de·fec′tor** (-fĕk′tər) *n.*

de·fec·tive (dĭ-fĕk′tĭv) *adj. Abbr.* **def. 1.** Lacking perfection; having a defect; faulty. See Usage note below. **2.** *Grammar.* Lacking one or more of the inflected forms normal for a particular category of word. In English, *may* is a defective verb. **3.** Of subnormal intelligence. *—n.* **1.** Something imperfect or damaged. **2.** Someone mentally incapacitated. **—de·fec′tive·ly** *adv.* **—de·fec′tive·ness** *n.*

Usage: *Defective* applies especially to what has a discernible fault and is therefore primarily concerned with quality. *Deficient* refers to insufficiency or incompleteness and is therefore basically a quantitative term associated with *deficit.*

de·fend (dĭ-fĕnd′) *v.* **-fended, -fending, -fends.** *—tr.* **1.** To protect from danger, attack, or harm; to shield; guard. **2.** To support or maintain, as by argument or action; justify. **3.** *Law.* **a.** To represent (the defendant) in a civil or criminal case. **b.** To contest (a legal action or claim). *—intr.* To make a defense. [Middle English *defenden,* from Old French *defendre,* from Latin *dēfendere,* to ward off. See **gwhen-[1]** in Appendix.*] **—de·fend′a·ble** *adj.* **—de·fend′er** *n.*

Synonyms: *defend, protect, guard, preserve, shield, safeguard.* These verbs mean to make safe from danger or attack. *Defend* implies use of countermeasures in repelling an actual attack. *Protect* suggests providing a cover to repel discomfort, injury, or attack. *Guard* suggests keeping watch over a person or thing. *Preserve* implies protective measures to maintain something as it is for an extended period. *Shield* suggests protection in the form of something or someone placed between the threat and the threatened. *Safeguard* stresses protection against potential or less imminent danger, often by preventive action.

de·fen·dant (dĭ-fĕn′dənt) *n. Abbr.* **def.** *Law.* A person against whom an action is brought. Compare **plaintiff.**

Defender of the Faith. *Abbr.* **D.F.** A title of English sovereigns, originally conferred upon Henry VIII by Pope Leo X (1521).

de·fen·es·tra·tion (dē-fĕn′ə-strā′shən) *n.* An act of throwing something or someone out of a window. [DE- + FENESTRA.]

de·fense (dĭ-fĕns′) *n.* Also *chiefly British* **de·fence.** *Abbr.* **def. 1.** The act of defending against attack, danger, or injury; protection. **2.** Anything that defends or protects. **3.** *Psychoanalysis.* An unconsciously acquired, involuntarily operating mental attribute, mechanism, or dynamism, such as regression, repression, reaction-formation, or projection, that protects the individual from shame, anxiety, or loss of self-esteem. **4.** An argument in support or justification of something. **5.** *Law.* **a.** The action of the defendant in opposition to complaints against him. **b.** The defendant and his legal counsel. **6.** The science or art of defending oneself; self-defense. **7.** *Sports.* The team or those players on the team attempting to stop the opposition from scoring. *—tr.v.* **defensed, -fensing, -fenses.** *Football.* To act as defense: *defense a play.* [Middle English *defens(e),* from Old French, from Latin *dēfensa,* from the feminine past participle of *dēfendere,* DEFEND.] **—de·fense′less** *adj.* **—de·fense′less·ly** *adv.* **—de·fense′less·ness** *n.*

defense mechanism. 1. *Biology.* Any reaction of an organism used in self-defense, as against germs. **2.** *Psychoanalysis.* Loosely, a defense; especially, the psychic structure or mechanism underlying a defense.

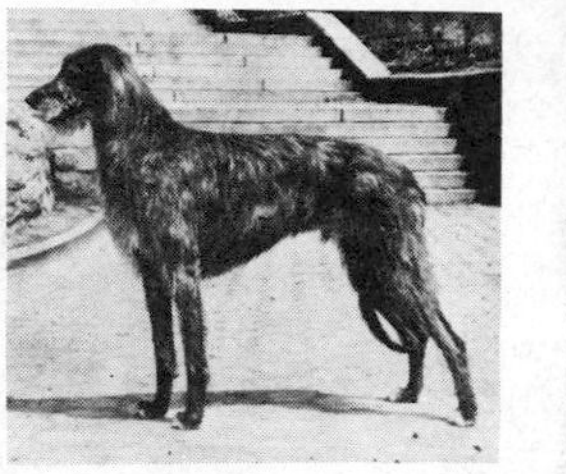

deerhound

de·fen·si·ble (dĭ-fĕn′sə-bəl) *adj.* Capable of being defended, protected, or justified. —**de·fen′si·bil′i·ty, de·fen′si·ble·ness** *n.* —**de·fen′si·bly** *adv.*

de·fen·sive (dĭ-fĕn′sĭv) *adj.* **1.** Intended or appropriate for defense. **2.** Done for defense; defending. **3.** Of or pertaining to defense. —*n.* **1.** A means of defense. **2.** An attitude of defense. —**de·fen′sive·ly** *adv.* —**de·fen′sive·ness** *n.*

de·fer[1] (dĭ-fûr′) *v.* **-ferred, -ferring, -fers.** —*tr.* **1.** To put off until a future time; postpone: *"against my wishes I deferred writing to you until now"* (Emily Dickinson). **2.** To postpone the induction of (one eligible for the military draft). —*intr.* To procrastinate; delay. [Middle English *differen,* from Old French *differer,* from Latin *differre* : *dis-,* away + *ferre,* to carry (see **bher-**[1] in Appendix*).] —**de·fer′rer** *n.*

de·fer[2] (dĭ-fûr′) *intr.v.* **-ferred, -ferring, -fers.** To comply with or submit to the opinion or decision of another; be deferential. Used with *to: "Defer, defer, / To the Lord High Executioner."* (W.S. Gilbert). See Synonyms at **yield.** [Middle English *deferen,* from Old French *def(f)erer,* from Latin *dēferre,* to carry away, bring to, submit : *dē-,* away + *ferre,* to carry (see **bher-**[1] in Appendix*).] —**de·fer′rer** *n.*

def·er·ence (dĕf′ər-əns) *n.* **1.** Submission or courteous yielding to the opinion, wishes, or judgment of another: *"Reason is to practise some vague and unassignable amount of deference to instinct."* (John Stuart Mill). **2.** Courteous respect. —See Synonyms at **honor.**

def·er·ent[1] (dĕf′ər-ənt) *adj.* Showing deference; deferential.

def·er·ent[2] (dĕf′ər-ənt) *adj.* **1.** Carrying down or away. **2.** Adapted to carry or transport. [Latin *dēferēns,* present participle of *dēferre,* to bring to, DEFER (to comply).]

def·er·en·tial (dĕf′ə-rĕn′shəl) *adj.* Marked by courteous respect: *"Mr. Bulstrode had also a deferential, bending attitude in listening."* (George Eliot). —**def′er·en′tial·ly** *adv.*

de·fer·ment (dĭ-fûr′mənt) *n.* Also **de·fer·ral** (-fûr′əl). The act of delaying or putting off; postponement.

de·fer·ra·ble (dĭ-fûr′ə-bəl) *adj.* **1.** Suitable for being postponed: *deferrable plans.* **2.** Eligible for deferment, especially from military service. —**de·fer′ra·ble** *n.*

de·ferred (dĭ-fûrd′) *adj. Abbr.* **def. 1.** Postponed; delayed. **2.** With benefits or payments withheld until a future date. **3.** Having had one's compulsory military service postponed.

de·fi·ance (dĭ-fī′əns) *n.* **1.** The disposition to defy or resist an opposing force or authority; resolute resistance. **2.** Intentionally provocative behavior or attitude; a challenge. [Middle English *defiaunce,* from Old French *desfiance,* from *desfier,* DEFY.]

de·fi·ant (dĭ-fī′ənt) *adj.* Marked by defiance. —**de·fi′ant·ly** *adv.*

de·fi·cien·cy (dĭ-fĭsh′ən-sē) *n., pl.* **-cies.** Also *rare* **de·fi·cience** (dĭ-fĭsh′əns). **1.** The quality or condition of being deficient. **2.** A lack; shortage; insufficiency.

de·fi·cient (dĭ-fĭsh′ənt) *adj.* **1.** Lacking an essential quality or element; incomplete; defective. **2.** Inadequate in amount or degree; insufficient. —See Usage note at **defective.** [Latin *dēficiēns,* present participle of *dēficere,* to remove from, desert, fail, lack : *dē-,* away + *facere,* to make, do (see **dhē-**[1] in Appendix*).] —**de·fi′cient·ly** *adv.*

def·i·cit (dĕf′ə-sĭt) *n.* The amount by which a sum of money falls short of the required or expected amount; a shortage. [French *déficit,* from Latin *dēficit,* it is lacking, from *dēficere,* to lack. See **deficient.**]

deficit spending. The spending of money obtained by borrowing.

def·i·lade (dĕf′ə-lād′) *tr.v.* **-laded, -lading, -lades.** *Military.* To arrange (fortifications) so as to give protection from enfilading and other fire. —*n.* The act or procedure of defilading. [DE- + (EN)FILADE.]

de·file[1] (dĭ-fīl′) *tr.v.* **-filed, -filing, -files. 1.** To make filthy or dirty; befoul. **2.** To tarnish the luster of; render impure; corrupt. **3.** To profane or sully (a good name or reputation, for example). **4.** To make unclean or unfit for ceremonial use; desecrate. **5.** To violate the chastity of. [Middle English *defilen,* probably alteration (influenced by *filen,* to sully) of *defoulen,* to trample down, injure, from Old French *defouler* : *de-,* from Latin *dē-,* down + *fouler,* to trample, FULL (verb).] —**de·file′ment** *n.* —**de·fil′er** *n.* —**de·fil′ing·ly** *adv.*

de·file[2] (dĭ-fīl′) *intr.v.* **-filed, -filing, -files. 1.** To march in single file. **2.** To march in files or columns. —*n.* **1.** A narrow gorge, valley, or other feature of the terrain that restricts lateral movement, as of troops. **2.** A marching in line or lines. [French *défiler* : *dé-,* from Latin *dē-,* off, away + *filer,* to march by files, from Old French, to spin, from Late Latin *filāre,* from Latin *filum,* thread (see **gwhī-** in Appendix*).]

de·fine (dĭ-fīn′) *v.* **-fined, -fining, -fines.** —*tr.* **1.** To state the precise meaning of (a word or sense of a word, for example). **2.** To describe the nature or basic qualities of; explain: *define the properties of a new drug.* **3.** To delineate the outline or form of; make clear: *a shape defined by a line.* **4.** To specify distinctly; fix definitely: *define the weapons to be used in limited warfare.* **5.** To serve to distinguish; characterize. —*intr.* To make a definition. [Middle English *diffinen,* from Old French *definer,* from Vulgar Latin *dēfināre* (unattested), variant of Latin *dēfinīre,* to set bounds to : *dē,* off + *finis,* end, boundary (see **final**).] —**de·fin′a·bil′i·ty** *n.* —**de·fin′a·ble** *adj.* —**de·fin′a·bly** *adv.* —**de·fine′ment** *n.* —**de·fin′er** *n.*

de·fin·i·en·dum (dĭ-fĭn′ē-ĕn′dəm) *n., pl.* **-da** (-də). That which is defined by a definiens. [Latin, neuter of *dēfīniendus,* gerundive of *dēfīnīre,* to set bounds to, DEFINE.]

de·fin·i·ens (dĭ-fĭn′ē-ĕnz′) *n., pl.* **definientia** (dĭ-fĭn′ē-ĕn′shē-ə, -shə). The word or words serving to define another word or expression, as in a dictionary entry. [Latin *dēfīniēns,* present participle of *dēfīnīre,* DEFINE.]

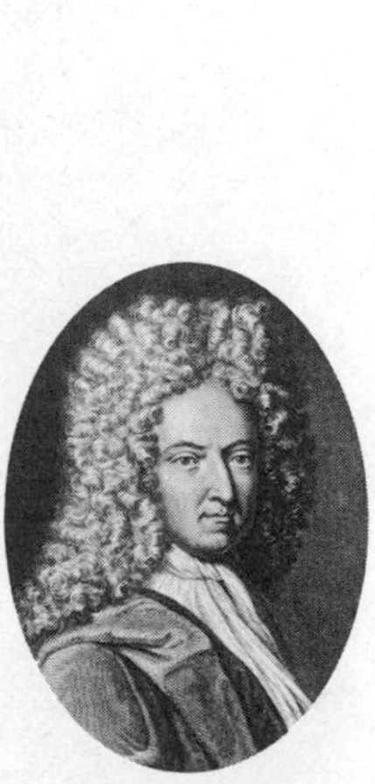

Daniel Defoe

def·i·nite (dĕf′ə-nĭt) *adj.* **1.** Having distinct limits: *definite restrictions on liquor sales.* **2.** Known positively; for certain; sure: *a definite victory.* **3.** Clearly defined; precise; explicit: *a definite statement of the terms of the will.* **4.** *Abbr.* **def.** *Grammar.* Limiting or particularizing. **5.** *Botany.* **a.** Of a specified number not exceeding 20. Said of floral organs, especially stamens. **b.** Cymose; determinate. [Middle English *diffinite,* from Latin *dēfīnītus,* past participle of *dēfīnīre,* to determine, DEFINE.] —**def′i·nite·ly** *adv.* —**def′i·nite·ness** *n.*

Usage: *Definite* and *definitive* both apply to what is precisely defined or explicitly set forth. But *definitive* more often refers, in addition, to what is unalterably final (a sense that *definite* does not have). The terms therefore are not usually interchangeable. For example, a *definite* decision is clear-cut and unequivocal; a *definitive* decision is generally also beyond change or appeal. Usage has established *definitely* in another sense, *for certain, assuredly,* though the sense is sometimes disputed or downgraded. But the following typical example, employing this sense, is acceptable on all levels to 71 per cent of the Usage Panel: *They will definitely arrive on Friday.*

definite article. *Grammar.* The article *the,* which restricts or particularizes the noun or noun phrase following it. Compare **indefinite article.**

definite integral. The limit of sums with terms of the form $f(x_i)\triangle x_i$, where f is a function defined in the interval between two numbers a and b, $\triangle x_i$ is the length of one of several intervals into which the interval from a to b is divided, x_i is a number in that interval, and the limit is taken as the lengths of the subintervals become smaller.

def·i·ni·tion (dĕf′ə-nĭsh′ən) *n. Abbr.* **def. 1.** The act of stating a precise meaning or significance, as of a word, phrase, or term. **2.** The statement of the meaning of a word, phrase, or term. **3.** The act of making clear and distinct: *a definition of one's intentions.* **4.** The state of being closely outlined or determined: *"A way of liberation can have no positive definition."* (Alan W. Watts). **5.** A determining of outline, extent, or limits: *the definition of a nation's authority.* **6.** *Telecommunications.* The degree of clarity with which a televised image is received or a radio receives a given station. **7.** *Optics.* The clarity of detail in an optically produced image, as in a photograph, produced by a combination of resolution and contrast. [Middle English *diffinicioun,* from Old French *definition,* from Latin *dēfīnītiō,* from *dēfīnīre,* DEFINE.] —**def′i·ni′tion·al** *adj.*

de·fin·i·tive (dĭ-fĭn′ə-tĭv) *adj.* **1.** Precisely defining or outlining; explicit. **2.** Determining finally; conclusive; decisive: *"Addison's authority has been influential, but fortunately not definitive."* (Richard Kain). **3.** Designating a statement, such as a scholarly work, that can stand as the most complete and authoritative on its subject: *"I do not pretend to have written the definitive biography of Lawrence."* (Richard Aldington). —See Usage note at **definite.** —*n. Grammar.* A word that defines or limits, such as the definite article or a demonstrative pronoun. —**de·fin′i·tive·ly** *adv.* —**de·fin′i·tive·ness** *n.*

de·fin·i·tude (dĭ-fĭn′ə-to͞od′, -tyo͞od′) *n.* The quality of being definite or exact; precision.

def·la·grate (dĕf′lə-grāt′) *v.* **-grated, -grating, -grates.** —*tr.* To cause to burn with great heat and intense light. —*intr.* To burn with great heat and intense light. [Latin *dēflagrāre* : *dē-* (intensive) + *flagrāre,* to burn (see **bhel-**[1] in Appendix*).] —**def′la·gra′tion** *n.*

de·flate (dĭ-flāt′) *v.* **-flated, -flating, -flates.** —*tr.* **1. a.** To release contained air or gas from. **b.** To collapse by releasing contained air or gas. **2.** To reduce or lessen the confidence, pride, self-esteem, or certainty of. **3.** *Economics.* To reduce the value or amount of (currency), effecting a decline in prices. —*intr.* To be or become deflated. [DE- (reversal) + (IN)FLATE.] —**de·fla′tor** (-flā′tər) *n.*

de·fla·tion (dĭ-flā′shən) *n.* **1. a.** The act of deflating. **b.** The state of being deflated. **2.** *Economics.* A reduction in the general price level, brought on by a decrease in the amount of money in circulation or by a decrease in the total volume of spending. In this sense, compare **inflation.** —**de·fla′tion·ar′y** *adj.* —**de·fla′tion·ist** *n.*

de·flect (dĭ-flĕkt′) *v.* **-flected, -flecting, -flects.** —*tr.* To cause to swerve or turn aside. —*intr.* To swerve or turn aside. [Latin *dēflectere* : *dē-,* away + *flectere,* to bend, FLEX.] —**de·flec′ta·ble** *adj.* —**de·flec′tive** *adj.* —**de·flec′tor** (-flĕk′tər) *n.*

de·flec·tion (dĭ-flĕk′shən) *n.* Also *British* **de·flex·ion. 1. a.** The act of deflecting. **b.** The condition of being deflected. **2.** Deviation or the amount of deviation. **3.** The deviation from zero shown by the indicator of a measuring instrument. **4.** The movement of a structure or structural part as a result of stress.

de·flexed (dĭ-flĕkst′, dē′flĕkst′) *adj. Botany.* Bent or turned downward at a sharp angle: *deflexed petals.* [Latin *dēflexus,* past participle of *dēflectere,* DEFLECT.]

def·lo·ra·tion (dĕf′lə-rā′shən) *n.* The act of deflowering.

de·flow·er (dē-flou′ər) *tr.v.* **-ered, -ering, -ers. 1.** To strip of flowers. **2.** To rupture the hymen of (a virgin) by sexual intercourse. **3.** To spoil the appearance or nature of; mar. **4.** To destroy the innocence of; violate. [Middle English *deflouren,* from Old French *deflorer,* from Late Latin *dēflōrāre* : Latin *dē-* (removal) + *flōs* (stem *flōr-*), flower (see **bhel-**[3] in Appendix*).] —**de·flow′er·er** *n.*

De·foe (dĭ-fō′), **Daniel.** 1660?–1731. English novelist.

de·fo·li·ant (dĭ-fō′lē-ənt) *n.* A chemical sprayed or dusted on plants to cause the leaves to fall off.

de·fo·li·ate (dĭ-fō′lē-āt′) *v.* **-ated, -ating, -ates.** —*tr.* **1.** To

deprive (a tree or other plant) of leaves. **2.** To cause the leaves of (a tree or other plant) to fall off, especially by the use of a chemical spray or dust. —*intr.* To lose foliage. [Late Latin *dēfoliāre* : Latin *dē*, removal + *folium*, leaf (see **bhel-³** in Appendix*).] —**de·fo′li·ate** (-ĭt) *adj.* —**de·fo′li·a′tion** *n.* —**de·fo′li·a′tor** (-ā′tər) *n.*

de·force (dē-fôrs′) *tr.v.* **-forced, -forcing, -forces.** *Law.* To withhold (something) by force from the rightful owner. [Middle English *deforcen*, from Norman French *deforcer*, variant of Old French *de(s)forcier* : *des-*, from Latin *dē-* (reversal) + *forcier*, to force, from Vulgar Latin *fortiāre* (unattested), from Latin *fortis*, strong (see **bhergh-²** in Appendix*).] —**de·force′ment** *n.*

de·for·ciant (dē-fôr′shənt, dĭ-fôr′-) *n.* *Law.* One who deforces a rightful owner.

de·for·est (dī-fôr′ĭst, dĭ-fŏr′-) *tr.v.* **-ested, -esting, -ests.** To cut down and clear away the trees or forests from. —**de·for′es·ta′tion** *n.* —**de·for′est·er** *n.*

De For·est (dĭ fôr′ĭst), **Lee.** 1873–1961. American inventor; received more than 300 patents in electronics and communications.

de·form (dī-fôrm′) *v.* **-formed, -forming, -forms.** —*tr.* **1.** To spoil the natural form of; misshape: *"poverty twists and deforms the spirit"* (Michael Harrington). **2.** To deface; disfigure. **3.** *Physics.* To alter the shape of by pressure or stress. —*intr.* To become deformed. —See Synonyms at **distort.** [Middle English *deformen*, from Old French *deformer*, from Latin *dēformāre* : *dē-* (reversal) + *formāre*, to form, from *forma*, form (see **mer-bh-** in Appendix*).] —**de·form′a·bil′i·ty** *n.* —**de·form′a·ble** *adj.* —**de·for′ma′tion** (dī-fôr-mā′shən, dĕf′ər-) *n.*

de·formed (dĭ-fôrmd′) *adj.* Misshapen.

de·form·i·ty (dĭ-fôr′mĭ-tē) *n.*, *pl.* **-ties. 1.** The state or condition of being deformed. **2.** A bodily malformation, such as a clubfoot or humpback. **3.** A deformed person or thing. **4.** Gross ugliness or distortion, especially in art or morals.

de·fraud (dĭ-frôd′) *tr.v.* **-frauded, -frauding, -frauds.** To take from or deprive of by fraud; to swindle. [Middle English *defrauden*, from Old French *defrauder*, from Latin *dēfraudāre* : *dē-* (intensive) + *fraudāre*, to cheat, from *fraus* (stem *fraud-*), FRAUD.] —**de·fraud·a′tion** *n.* —**de·fraud′er** *n.*

de·fray (dī-frā′) *tr.v.* **-frayed, -fraying, -frays.** To meet or satisfy by payment (costs or expenses); pay: *defray the cost of a trip.* [French *défrayer*, from Old French *deffrayer, desfrayer* : *des-*, from Latin *dē-* (removal) + *frai* (attested only in the plural *frais*), expense, cost, "damage," from Latin *fractum*, from *fractus*, past participle of *frangere*, to break (see **bhreg-** in Appendix*).] —**de·fray′a·ble** *adj.* —**de·fray′al** *n.*

de·frock (dē-frŏk′) *tr.v.* **-frocked, -frocking, -frocks.** To unfrock.

de·frost (dē-frôst′, -frŏst′) *v.* **-frosted, -frosting, -frosts.** —*tr.* **1.** To remove ice or frost from. **2.** To cause to thaw. —*intr.* **1.** To become free of ice or frost. **2.** To become unfrozen; thaw.

de·frost·er (dē-frôs′tər, dē-frŏs′-) *n.* A heating device designed to remove ice or frost or prevent its formation, as on a windshield, aircraft wing, or refrigerator.

deft (dĕft) *adj.* Skillful; adroit. See Synonyms at **dexterous.** [Middle English *defte*, originally "gentle," "meek," variant of *dafte*, DAFT.] —**deft′ly** *adv.* —**deft′ness** *n.*

de·funct (dĭ-fŭngkt′) *adj.* Having ceased to live or exist; extinct; dead. [Latin *dēfunctus*, past participle of *dēfungī*, to discharge, finish, die : *dē-* (intensive) + *fungī*, to discharge (see **bheug-²** in Appendix*).] —**de·func′tive** *adj.* —**de·funct′ness** *n.*

de·fy (dĭ-fī′) *tr.v.* **-fied, -fying, -fies. 1.** To confront or stand up to; to challenge: *"Andrew Jackson was a Democrat,/Defying Kings in his old cocked hat"* (Vachel Lindsay). **2.** To resist successfully; withstand: *"so the plague defied all medicines"* (Defoe). **3.** To challenge or dare (someone) to perform something deemed impossible. [Middle English *defien, diffien*, from Old French *desfier*, from Vulgar Latin *disfīdāre* (unattested), to renounce one's faith : *dis-* (reversal) + *fīdāre* (unattested), variant of Latin *fīdere*, to trust (see **bheidh-** in Appendix*).] —**de·fi′er** *n.*

deg, deg. degree (thermometric).

dé·ga·gé (dā-gà-zhā′) *adj.* Free and relaxed in manner; casual. [French, past participle of *dégager*, to disengage, release, from Old French *desgagier*, "to redeem a pledge" : *des-*, from Latin *dē-* (reversal) + *gage*, a pledge, gage, from Frankish (unattested) *wadi* (see **wadh-** in Appendix*).]

de·ga·me (də-gä′mə) *n.* Also **de·ga·mi** (-mē). **1.** A tree, *Calycophyllum candidissimum*, of tropical America, having hard, close-grained, yellowish wood. **2.** The wood of this tree. Also called "lemonwood." [American Spanish *dagame*, a native name.]

de·gas (dē-găs′) *tr.v.* **-gassed, -gassing, -gasses** or **-gases. 1.** To remove poisonous gases from (a place or person). **2.** To evacuate gas from (a substance or device). —**de·gas′ser** *n.*

De·gas (də-gä′), **(Hilaire Germain) Edgar.** 1834–1917. French painter and sculptor.

De Gaulle (də gōl′), **Charles.** Born 1890. French general and statesman; president (1945–46; 1959–69).

de·gauss (dē′gous′) *tr.v.* **-gaussed, -gaussing, -gausses.** To neutralize the magnetic field of, as of a ship or television receiver. [DE- + GAUSS.]

de·gen·er·a·cy (dĭ-jĕn′ər-ə-sē) *n.*, *pl.* **-cies. 1.** The state or condition of being degenerate. **2.** The process of degenerating.

de·gen·er·ate (dĭ-jĕn′ə-rāt′) *intr.v.* **-ated, -ating, -ates.** To deteriorate. —*adj.* (dĭ-jĕn′ər-ĭt). **1.** Characterized by deterioration. **2.** Marked by or exhibiting degeneracy. **3.** *Physics.* Taking on several discrete or distinct values or states. —*n.* (dĭ-jĕn′ər-ĭt). **1.** A morally degraded person. **2. a.** A person lacking or having progressively lost normative biological or psychological char-

acteristics. **b.** A person exhibiting antisocial, especially sexually deviant, behavior. [Latin *dēgenerāre*, to fall from one's ancestral quality : *dē-*, away from + *genus* (stem *gener-*), race (see **gene-** in Appendix*).] —**de·gen′er·ate·ly** *adv.* —**de·gen′er·ate·ness** *n.* —**de·gen′er·a·tive** (-ə-tĭv) *adj.*

de·gen·er·a·tion (dī-jĕn′ə-rā′shən) *n.* **1.** The process of degenerating. **2.** The state or condition of being degenerate. **3.** *Biology.* The usually irreversible deterioration of specific cells or organs with corresponding functional impairment, caused by injury or disease and often resulting in necrosis or death. **4.** *Electronics.* Negative feedback of output power to an input signal in an amplifying circuit.

de·glu·ti·nate (dī-glōōt′n-āt′) *tr.v.* **-nated, -nating, -nates.** To extract the gluten from (wheat flour, for example). [Latin *dēglūtināre* : *dē* (expressing removal) + *glūtināre*, to glue, from *glūten*, glue (see **gel-¹** in Appendix*).] —**de·glu′ti·na′tion** *n.*

de·glu·ti·tion (dē′glōō-tĭsh′ən) *n.* The process or act of swallowing. [French, from Latin *dēglūtīre*, to swallow down : *dē-*, down + *glūtīre*, to swallow (see **gwel-⁵** in Appendix*).] —**de·glu′ti·to′ry** (dī-glōō′tə-tôr′ē, -tōr′ē) *adj.*

deg·ra·da·tion (dĕg′rə-dā′shən) *n.* **1.** The act or process of degrading, specifically: **a.** A deposition, removal, or dismissal from rank or office. **b.** A reduction in worth or standing. **2.** A process of transition from a higher to a lower quality or level. **3.** The state or condition of being degraded; deterioration; degeneration. **4.** *Geology.* A general lowering of the earth's surface by erosion or transportation in running water. **5.** *Chemistry.* Decomposition of a compound by stages, exhibiting well-defined intermediate products. —See Synonyms at **disgrace.**

de·grade (dī-grād′) *tr.v.* **-graded, -grading, -grades. 1.** To reduce in grade, rank, or status; especially, to deprive of an office or dignity. **2.** To lower in moral or intellectual character; debase; corrupt. **3.** To reduce, divert, or pervert. **4.** To expose to contempt, dishonor, or disgrace. **5.** *Geology.* To lower or wear by erosion. **6.** *Chemistry.* To decompose (a compound) by stages. [Middle English *degraden*, from Old French *degrader*, from Late Latin *dēgradāre* : Latin *dē-*, down + *gradus*, rank, step (see **ghredh-** in Appendix*).] —**de·grad′er** *n.*

Synonyms: degrade, abase, demean, humble, humiliate, discredit, mortify. These verbs mean to cast down persons by reducing in dignity, respect, or rank. *Degrade* implies reduction to a state that incurs shame, disgrace, and contempt, or to a state of actual corruption. *Abase* refers principally to loss of rank or prestige. *Demean* suggests placing a person in an inferior social position. *Humble* can refer to lowering in rank or estate or, more often, to driving out undue self-esteem. *Humiliate* involves subjecting one to shame, usually in public, and causing feelings of inferiority and loss of self-respect. *Discredit* refers to lowering of reputation or professional status. *Mortify* suggests causing extreme humiliation, chagrin, and embarrassment.

de·grad·ed (dī-grā′dĭd) *adj.* **1.** Reduced in rank, honor, or position. **2.** Reduced in quality or value; distorted; vulgarized: *a degraded level of art.* **3.** Having declined in moral qualities; depraved; degenerate. **4.** Considered as below normal standards of civilization. —**de·grad′ed·ly** *adv.* —**de·grad′ed·ness** *n.*

de·grad·ing (dī-grā′dĭng) *adj.* **1.** Debasing. **2.** *Geology.* Eroding to a lower level; wearing down. —**de·grad′ing·ly** *adv.*

de·grease (dē-grēs′, -grēz′) *tr.v.* **-greased, -greasing, -greases.** To remove the grease from.

de·gree (dĭ-grē′) *n.* **1.** One of a series of steps or stages in a process, course of action, progression, or retrogression. **2.** The relative distance, or a step, in a direct hereditary line of descent or ascent. **3.** Relative social or official rank, dignity, or position. **4.** Relative intensity or amount of a quality, attribute, or the like. **5.** Relative condition or extent; capacity; manner. **6.** The extent or measure of a being, action, or the like. **7.** *Abbr.* **deg, deg.** *Symbol* ° A unit division of a temperature scale. **8.** *Geometry. Symbol* ° A unit of angular measure equal in magnitude to the central angle subtended by ¹⁄₃₆₀ of the circumference of a circle. **9.** *Geography.* A unit of latitude or longitude, ¹⁄₃₆₀ of a great circle. **10.** *Algebra.* **a.** The greatest sum of the exponents of the variables in a term of a polynomial or polynomial equation. **b.** The exponent of the derivative of highest order in a differential equation in standard form. Compare **order. 11.** *Education.* **a.** An academic title given by a college or university to a student who has completed a course of study. **b.** A similar title conferred as an honorary distinction. **12.** *Law.* A division or classification of a specific crime according to its seriousness. **13.** *Grammar.* One of the forms used in the comparison of adjectives and adverbs. See **positive, comparative, superlative. 14.** *Music.* **a.** One of the seven notes of a diatonic scale. **b.** A space or line of the staff. —**by degrees.** Little by little; gradually. —**to a degree. 1.** To a great extent. **2.** Somewhat. [Middle English *degre*, from Old French, from Vulgar Latin *dēgradus* (unattested), "a step down" : Latin *dē-*, down + *gradus*, a step (see **ghredh-** in Appendix*).]

de·gree-day (dĭ-grē′dā′) *n.* **1.** An indication of the extent of departure from a standard of mean daily temperature. **2.** A unit used in estimating quantities of fuel and power consumption, based on a daily ratio of consumption and the mean temperature below 65°F.

degree of freedom. 1. *Statistics.* Any of the unrestricted, independent random variables that constitute a statistic. **2. a.** *Mechanics.* Any of the minimum number of coordinates required to specify completely the motion of a mechanical system. **b.** *Thermodynamics.* Any of the independent variables, such as pressure, temperature, or composition, required to specify a system with a given number of phases and components. See **phase rule.**

Degas
A self-portrait

Charles De Gaulle
Photograph taken in 1965 with a World War II portrait behind

ă pat/ā pay/âr care/ä father/b bib/ch church/d deed/ĕ pet/ē be/f fife/g gag/h hat/hw which/ĭ pit/ī pie/îr pier/j judge/k kick/l lid, needle/m mum/n no, sudden/ng thing/ŏ pot/ō toe/ô paw, for/oi noise/ou out/ŏŏ took/ōō boot/p pop/r roar/s sauce/sh ship, dish/t tight/th thin, path/*th* this, bathe/ŭ cut/ûr urge/v valve/w with/y yes/z zebra, size/zh vision/ə about, item, edible, gallop, circus/ à Fr. ami/œ Fr. feu, Ger. schön/ü Fr. tu, Ger. über/KH Ger. ich, Scot. loch/N Fr. bon. *Follows main vocabulary. †Of obscure origin.

de·gres·sion (dĭ-grĕsh′ən, dē′-) *n.* A going down by steps; descent. [Middle English *digressioun*, from Medieval Latin *dēgressiō*, from Latin *dēgredī* (past participle *dēgressus*), to step down : *dē-*, down + *gradī*, to go, step (see **ghredh-** in Appendix*).]

de·gum (dē-gŭm′) *tr.v.* **-gummed, -gumming, -gums.** To free from gum.

de·gust (dĭ-gŭst′, dē′-) *v.* **-gusted, -gusting, -gusts.** —*tr.* To taste with relish or care. —*intr.* To have a taste; be relishing. [Latin *dēgustāre* : *dē-* (intensive) + *gustāre*, to taste (see **geus-** in Appendix*).] —**de′gus·ta′tion** (dē′gŭs-tā′shən) *n.*

de·hisce (dĭ-hĭs′) *intr.v.* **-hisced, -hiscing, -hisces.** To burst or split open along a line or slit, as do the ripe capsules or pods of some plants. [Latin *dēhiscere* : *dē-*, off + *hiscere*, to open, split, inceptive of *hiāre*, to be open, gape (see **ghei-** in Appendix*).]

de·his·cent (dĭ-hĭs′ənt) *adj.* Opening at pores or by splitting to release seeds within a fruit or pollen from an anther. Compare **indehiscent.** —**de·his′cence** *n.*

de·horn (dē-hôrn′) *tr.v.* **-horned, -horning, -horns.** **1.** To remove the horns from. **2.** To prevent growth in the horns of, as by cauterization.

Deh·ra Dun (dâr′ə do͞on′). A city of northern Uttar Pradesh, Republic of India; site of India's Armed Forces Academy. Population, 130,000.

de·hu·man·ize (dē-hyo͞o′mə-nīz′) *tr.v.* **-ized, -izing, -izes.** **1.** To deprive of human qualities or attributes. **2.** To render mechanical and routine. —**de·hu′man·i·za′tion** *n.*

de·hu·mid·i·fy (dē′hyo͞o-mĭd′ə-fī′) *tr.v.* **-fied, -fying, -fies.** To remove atmospheric moisture from; decrease the humidity of. —**de′hu·mid′i·fi·ca′tion** *n.* —**de·hu·mid′i·fi′er** *n.*

de·hy·drate (dē-hī′drāt′) *v.* **-drated, -drating, -drates.** —*tr.* **1.** *Chemistry.* To eliminate water from or make anhydrous. **2.** To remove water from (fruits or vegetables, for example) for preservation. —*intr.* To lose water or moisture; become dry. —**de·hy′dra·tor** (-drā′tər) *n.*

de·hy·dra·tion (dē′hī-drā′shən) *n.* **1.** The process of removing water from a substance or compound. **2.** *Pathology.* Excessive loss of water from the body or from an organ or bodily part.

de·hy·dro·gen·ase (dē′hī′drŏj′ə-nās′) *n.* An enzyme that removes hydrogen from a substrate.

de·hy·dro·ge·nate (dē′hī′drŏj′ə-nāt′) *tr.v.* **-nated, -nating, -nates.** *Chemistry.* To remove hydrogen from; dehydrogenize. —**de·hy′dro·ge·na′tion** *n.*

de·hy·dro·ge·nize (dē′hī-drŏj′ə-nīz′, dē-hī′drə-jə-nīz′) *tr.v.* **-nized, -nizing, -nizes.** To dehydrogenate. —**de′hy·dro·ge′ni·za′tion** *n.*

de·hyp·no·tize (dē-hĭp′nə-tīz′) *tr.v.* **-tized, -tizing, -tizes.** To arouse from a hypnotic state.

de·ice (dē-īs′) *tr.v.* **-iced, -icing, -ices.** To keep free of ice; melt ice from.

de·ic·er (dē-ī′sər) *n.* **1.** Any device used on an aircraft in flight to keep certain surfaces free from ice or remove ice after it has formed. **2.** Any compound used to prevent the formation of ice on windows, windshields, and the like.

de·i·cide (dē′ə-sīd′) *n.* **1.** The killing of a god. **2.** One who kills a god. [New Latin *deicīda* : Latin *deus*, god, DEITY + -CIDE.]

deic·tic (dīk′tĭk) *adj.* *Logic.* Directly proving by argument. Compare **elenctic.** [Greek *deiktikos*, from *deiktos*, able to show directly, from *deiknunai*, to show. See **deik-** in Appendix.*] —**deic′ti·cal·ly** *adv.*

de·if·ic (dē-ĭf′ĭk) *adj.* **1.** Making or tending to make divine. **2.** Divine; godlike. [Old French *deifique*, from Late Latin *deificus* : Latin *deus*, god, DEITY + -FIC.]

de·i·fi·ca·tion (dē′ə-fĭ-kā′shən) *n.* **1. a.** The act or process of deifying. **b.** The condition of having been deified. **2.** One who embodies the qualities of a god.

de·i·fy (dē′ə-fī′) *tr.v.* **-fied, -fying, -fies.** **1.** To raise to divine rank. **2.** To worship or revere as a god. **3.** To idealize; exalt. [Middle English *deifien*, from Old French *deifier*, from Late Latin *deificāre*, from *deificus*, DEIFIC.] —**de′i·fi′er** *n.*

deign (dān) *v.* **deigned, deigning, deigns.** —*intr.* To think it appropriate or suitable to one's dignity to do something. —*tr.* To condescend to give or grant. [Middle English *deinen*, from Old French *deignier*, to regard as worthy, from Latin *dignārī*, from *dignus*, worthy. See **dek-¹** in Appendix.*]

Dei·mos (dī′mŏs) *n.* The smaller and more distant from the primary of the two moons of Mars. [After *Deimos*, a son of Ares, from *deimos*, fear. See **dwei-** in Appendix.*]

Deir·dre¹ (dîr′drə, -drē). A feminine given name. [Old Irish *De(i)dru*, "the raging one," from *derdethar*†, he rages.]

Deir·dre² (dîr′drə, -drē). *Irish Mythology.* A princess of Ulster who killed herself after her husband, Naoise, was murdered.

de·ism (dē′ĭz′əm) *n.* The belief, claiming foundation solely upon the evidence of reason, in the existence of God as the creator of the universe who after setting it in motion abandoned it, assumed no control over life, exerted no influence on natural phenomena, and gave no supernatural revelation. Compare **pantheism, theism.** [French *déisme*, from Latin *deus*, god, DEITY.] —**de′ist** *n.* —**de·is′tic** *adj.* —**de·is′ti·cal·ly** *adv.*

de·i·ty (dē′ə-tē) *n., pl.* **-ties.** **1.** A god or goddess. **2.** Divinity. —**the Deity.** God. [Middle English *deite*, from Old French, from Late Latin *deitās*, from Latin *deus*, god. See **deiw-** in Appendix.*]

dé·jà vu (dā-zhä vü′). The illusion of having already experienced something actually being experienced for the first time. [French, "already seen."]

de·ject (dĭ-jĕkt′) *tr.v.* **-jected, -jecting, -jects.** To dishearten; dispirit. [Middle English *dejecten*, from Latin *dējicere* (past participle *dējectus*), to cast down : *dē-*, down + *jacere*, to throw (see **yē-** in Appendix*).]

de·jec·ta (dĭ-jĕk′tə) *pl.n.* Excremental matter; feces. [New Latin, from Latin, neuter plural of *dējectus*, past participle of *dējicere*, to cast down, DEJECT.]

de·ject·ed (dĭ-jĕk′tĭd) *adj.* Depressed; disheartened. See Synonyms at **sad.** —**de·ject′ed·ly** *adv.* —**de·ject′ed·ness** *n.*

de·jec·tion (dĭ-jĕk′shən) *n.* **1.** A state of depression; melancholy. **2.** *Medicine.* **a.** Evacuation of the bowels. **b.** Excrement. —See Synonyms at **despair.**

de ju·re (dē jo͞or′ē, dā yo͞o′rā). *Latin.* According to law; by right. Compare **de facto.**

deka-. Variant of **deca-.**

de·ka·me·ter. Variant of **decameter.**

Dek·ker (dĕk′ər), **Thomas.** 1572?-1632. English dramatist.

del (dĕl) *n.* *Mathematics.* The vector differential operator, having as components in three-dimensional Cartesian coordinates the first partial derivative operators with respect to each coordinate direction. [Short for DELTA (because it appears like an inverted delta).]

del. **1.** delegate; delegation. **2.** delete.

Del. Delaware.

De·la·croix (də-là-krwä′), **Ferdinand Victor Eugène.** 1799-1863. French painter.

Delacroix
A self-portrait

de·laine (də-lān′) *n.* A light dress fabric of wool or cotton and wool. [French (*mousseline*) *de laine*, "(muslin) of wool," from Latin *lāna*, wool. See **wel-⁵** in Appendix.*]

De la Mare (də lə mâr′, dĕl′ə mâr′), **Walter (John).** 1873-1956. English poet and novelist.

de·lam·i·nate (dē-lăm′ĭ-nāt′) *intr.v.* **-nated, -nating, -nates.** To split into thin layers. [DE- (reversal) + LAMINATE.]

de·lam·i·na·tion (dē-lăm′ĭ-nā′shən) *n.* **1.** A splitting or separating into layers. **2.** *Embryology.* The splitting of the blastoderm into two layers of cells.

Del·a·ware¹ (dĕl′ə-wâr′) *n., pl.* **Delaware** or **-wares.** **1.** A group of Algonquian-speaking North American Indian tribes, formerly inhabiting the Delaware River valley. **2.** A member of any of these tribes. **3.** Their language. Also called "Lenape," "Leni-Lenape," "Lenni-Lenape." —**Del′a·war′e·an** *adj.*

Del·a·ware² (dĕl′ə-wâr′) *n.* A variety of grape having sweet, light-red fruit. [After the state of DELAWARE.]

Del·a·ware³ (dĕl′ə-wâr′). *Abbr.* **Del.** The second-smallest state (2,057 square miles) of the United States, in the east on Delaware Bay and the Atlantic. It was one of the original 13 states and first to ratify the Constitution. Population, 505,000. Capital, Dover. See map at **United States of America.**

Del·a·ware Bay (dĕl′ə-wâr′). An inlet of the Atlantic, extending 52 miles north between Delaware and New Jersey.

Del·a·ware River (dĕl′ə-wâr′). A river flowing 315 miles generally southeast and south from the Catskill Mountains, New York State, to Delaware Bay, and forming the New York-Pennsylvania, Pennsylvania-New Jersey, and New Jersey-Delaware borders on its course.

Del·a·ware Water Gap (dĕl′ə-wâr′). **1.** A gorge in eastern Pennsylvania, cut through the Kittatinny Mountains by the Delaware River. **2.** A resort town nearby.

De La Warr (dĕl′ə wâr′), **Baron.** Title of Thomas West. Known as Lord Delaware. 1577-1618. English colonial administrator in America; first governor of Virginia (1610-11); rescuer of Jamestown colony.

de·lay (dĭ-lā′) *v.* **-layed, -laying, -lays.** —*tr.* **1.** To postpone until a later time; defer. **2.** To cause to be late or detained; hinder. —*intr.* To procrastinate or tarry; linger. —*n.* **1.** The act of delaying; postponement. **2.** The condition of being delayed; detainment. **3.** The period of time during which one is delayed. **4.** The time interval between any two events. [Middle English *delaien*, from Old French *delaier*, *deslaier* : *des-*, from Latin *dē-*, off + *laier*, variant of *laissier*, to leave, let, from Latin *laxāre*, to slacken, undo, from *laxus*, slack, loose (see **slēg-** in Appendix*).] —**de·lay′er** *n.*

Synonyms: *delay, slow, retard, detain, check.* These verbs mean, transitively, to hold back and thus hinder or prevent action or progress. *Delay* applies either to putting behind schedule or to postponing or deferring action. *Slow* means to decrease in pace, often deliberately. *Retard* also stresses slackening of pace, intentional or otherwise; in the latter case it often refers to frustration of progress or development. *Detain* stresses holding at a particular point in time or place and thus preventing action. *Check* implies sudden impeding of action or progress in mid-course, usually by restraint.

de·layed-ac·tion (dĭ-lād′ăk′shən) *adj.* Also **de·lay-ac·tion** (dĭ-lā′-). **1.** Acting only after a predetermined time interval elapses. **2.** Detonating after impact.

delayed neutron. A neutron emitted by a product of nuclear fission several seconds or minutes after the fission occurs. Compare **prompt neutron.**

de·le (dē′lē) *n.* A sign indicating that something is to be removed from typeset matter. See table of Proofreaders' Marks at **proofread.** —*tr.v.* **deled, -leing, -les.** **1.** To take out or delete. **2.** To mark with a dele. Compare **stet.** [Latin *dēle*, imperative singular of *dēlēre*, DELETE.]

de·lec·ta·ble (dĭ-lĕk′tə-bəl) *adj.* Greatly pleasing; enjoyable; delightful. [Middle English, from Old French, from Latin *dēlectābilis*, from *dēlectāre*, to please, DELIGHT.] —**de·lec′ta·bil′i·ty, de·lec′ta·ble·ness** *n.* —**de·lec′ta·bly** *adv.*

de·lec·ta·tion (dē′lĕk-tā′shən) *n.* Pleasure; delight.

del·e·ga·cy (dĕl′ə-gə-sē) *n., pl.* **-cies.** **1.** The authority, office, or position of a delegate. **2.** The act of delegating or being delegated. **3.** A body of delegates; delegation.

del·e·gate (dĕl′ə-gāt′, -gĭt) *n. Abbr.* **del. 1.** A person authorized to act as representative for another or others; deputy; agent. **2. a.** An elected or appointed representative of a Territory in the House of Representatives who is entitled to speak but not vote. **b.** A member of the House of Delegates, the lower house of the Maryland, Virginia, and West Virginia legislatures. —*tr.v.* (dĕl′ə-gāt′) **delegated, -gating, -gates. 1.** To authorize and send (a person) as one's representative. **2.** To commit to one's agent or representative. **3.** *Law.* To appoint (one's debtor) as a debtor to one's creditor to replace oneself in satisfying a claim. [Middle English *delegat,* from Medieval Latin *dēlēgātus,* from Latin, past participle of *dēlēgāre,* to send away, dispatch : *dē-,* away + *lēgāre,* to send (see **leg-** in Appendix*).]

del·e·ga·tion (dĕl′ə-gā′shən) *n.* **1. a.** The act of delegating. **b.** The condition of being delegated; appointment; deputation. **2.** *Abbr.* **del.** A person or group of persons officially elected or appointed to represent another or others.

de Les·seps, Vicomte **Ferdinand Marie.** See **Lesseps.**

de·lete (dĭ-lēt′) *tr.v.* **-leted, -leting, -letes.** *Abbr.* **del.** To strike out or cancel; omit. See Synonyms at **erase.** [Latin *dēlēre*†, to wipe out, efface.]

del·e·te·ri·ous (dĕl′ə-tîr′ē-əs) *adj.* Injurious; harmful. [Medieval Latin *dēlētērius,* from Greek *dēlētērios,* from *dēleisthai*†, to harm, injure.] —**del′e·te′ri·ous·ly** *adv.* —**del′e·te′ri·ous·ness** *n.*

de·le·tion (dĭ-lē′shən) *n.* **1.** An act of deleting; an omission or erasing. **2.** A word, passage, or the like that has been deleted from written or printed matter.

delft (dĕlft) *n.* Also **delf** (dĕlf). **1.** A style of glazed earthenware, usually blue and white, originally made in Delft. **2.** A piece of pottery of this style. **3.** Any pottery made in imitation of this style. Also called "delftware."

Delft (dĕlft). A city of the southwest-central Netherlands, five miles southeast of The Hague. Population, 72,000.

Del·hi (dĕl′ē) **1.** A Union Territory of the Republic of India, 573 square miles in area, in the northeast. Population, 2,659,000. **2.** The capital of this territory, and of India from 1912 to 1931, on the Jumna River adjacent to New Delhi. Population, 2,299,000. Also called "Old Delhi."

Del·ia (dēl′yə). A feminine given name. [Latin *Dēlia,* "Delian" (epithet of Artemis), feminine of *Dēlius,* of Delos, from Greek *Dēlios,* from *Dēlos,* DELOS.]

De·li·an (dē′lē-ən) *adj.* Of or pertaining to Delos or its inhabitants. —*n.* A native or inhabitant of Delos.

de·lib·er·ate (dĭ-lĭb′ə-rāt′) *v.* **-ated, -ating, -ates.** —*intr.* **1.** To take careful thought; reflect. **2.** To consult with another or others as a process in reaching a decision. —*tr.* To consider (a matter) by carefully weighing alternatives or the like. —See Synonyms at **ponder.** —*adj.* (dĭ-lĭb′ər-ĭt). **1.** Premeditated; intentional. **2. a.** Careful and slow in deciding or determining. **b.** Not rashly or hastily determined: *a deliberate choice.* **3.** Leisurely or slow in motion or manner; not hurried or impulsive. —See Synonyms at **slow, voluntary.** [Latin *dēlīberāre,* to weigh well, ponder : *dē-,* completely + *librāre,* to weigh, from *lībra,* a scale, pound (see **līthrā** in Appendix*).] —**de·lib′er·ate·ly** *adv.* —**de·lib′er·ate·ness** *n.*

de·lib·er·a·tion (dĭ-lĭb′ə-rā′shən) *n.* **1.** The process of deliberating; thoughtful and lengthy consideration. **2.** *Often plural.* Formal discussion and debate of all sides of an issue. **3.** Thoughtfulness in decision or action.

de·lib·er·a·tive (dĭ-lĭb′ə-rā′tĭv, -ər-ə-tĭv) *adj.* **1.** Assembled or organized for deliberation or debate: *a deliberative legislature.* **2.** Characterized by or for use in deliberation or debate. —**de·lib′er·a·tive·ly** *adv.* —**de·lib′er·a′tive·ness** *n.*

del·i·ca·cy (dĕl′ĭ-kə-sē) *n., pl.* **-cies. 1.** The quality of being delicate. **2.** Frailty of bodily constitution or health. **3.** Sensitivity of perception, feeling, appreciation, or the like; refinement. **4. a.** Consideration of the feelings of others. **b.** Aversion to what is considered morally distasteful or injurious. **5.** A need of taste and tact in treating or handling: *a topic of some delicacy.* **6.** Softness or fineness of touch. **7.** Fineness or keenness of response or reaction. **8.** Something pleasing and appealing, especially a choice food. [Middle English *delicacie,* from *delicat,* DELICATE.]

del·i·cate (dĕl′ĭ-kĭt) *adj.* **1.** Exquisitely or pleasingly fine. **2.** Frail in constitution or health. **3.** Easily broken or damaged. **4.** Requiring tasteful and tactful treatment. **5.** Keen in sense discrimination or perception. **6.** Manifesting sensitivity and attentiveness to the proprieties. **7.** Regardful of the feelings of others. **8.** Keenly accurate in response or reaction. **9.** Soft or gentle in touch or skill. **10.** Very subtle in difference or distinction. —See Synonyms at **fragile.** [Middle English *delicat,* from Latin *dēlicātus*†, alluring, charming, dainty.] —**del′i·cate·ly** *adv.* —**del′i·cate·ness** *n.*

del·i·ca·tes·sen (dĕl′ĭ-kə-tĕs′ən) *n.* A shop that sells cooked or prepared foods ready for serving. [German *Delikatessen,* plural of *Delikatesse,* delicacy, from French *délicatesse,* from Italian *delicatezza,* from *delicato,* delicate, dainty, from Latin *dēlicātus,* DELICATE.]

de·li·cious (dĭ-lĭsh′əs) *adj.* **1.** Highly pleasing or agreeable to the senses of taste or smell. **2.** Very pleasant; enjoyable; delightful. [Middle English, from Old French, from Late Latin *dēliciōsus,* pleasing, delightful, from Latin *dēlicia,* pleasure, from *dēlicere,* to entice away, DELIGHT.] —**de·li′cious·ly** *adv.* —**de·li′cious·ness** *n.*

De·li·cious (dĭ-lĭsh′əs) *n.* A variety of apple having sweet fruit often streaked with yellow and red.

de·lict (dĭ-lĭkt′) *n.* In civil law, a misdemeanor; tort; an offense. [Latin *dēlictum,* from *dēlictus,* past participle of *dēlinquere,* to fail in duty, offend. See **delinquent.**]

de·light (dĭ-līt′) *n.* **1.** Great pleasure; gratification; joy. **2.** Something that gives great pleasure or enjoyment. —See Synonyms at **pleasure.** —*v.* **delighted, -lighting, -lights.** —*intr.* **1.** To take great pleasure or joy. **2.** To give great pleasure or joy. —*tr.* To please greatly. [Middle English *deliten,* from Old French *deleitier,* from Latin *dēlectāre,* frequentative of *dēlicere,* to allure, entice away : *dē-,* away + *lacere*†, to allure.]

de·light·ed (dĭ-lī′tĭd) *adj.* **1.** Filled with delight. **2.** *Obsolete.* Delightful. —**de·light′ed·ly** *adv.* —**de·light′ed·ness** *n.*

de·light·ful (dĭ-līt′fəl) *adj.* Affording keen satisfaction; greatly pleasing. —**de·light′ful·ly** *adv.* —**de·light′ful·ness** *n.*

de·light·some (dĭ-līt′səm) *adj.* Delightful. —**de·light′some·ly** *adv.* —**de·light′some·ness** *n.*

De·li·lah (dĭ-lī′lə). A Philistine woman who betrayed Samson, her lover, to the Philistines by having his hair shorn as he slept, thus depriving him of his strength. Judges 16.

de·lim·it (dĭ-lĭm′ĭt) *tr.v.* **-ited, -iting, -its.** Also **de·lim·i·tate** (dĭ-lĭm′ə-tāt′) **-tated, -tating, -tates.** To establish the limit or boundaries of; demarcate. [French *délimiter,* from Latin *dēlīmitāre* : *dē-,* completely + *līmitāre,* to limit, from *līmes* (stem *līmit-*), LIMIT.] —**de·lim′i·ta′tion** *n.* —**de·lim′i·ta′tive** *adj.*

de·lin·e·ate (dĭ-lĭn′ē-āt′) *tr.v.* **-ated, -ating, -ates. 1.** To draw or trace the outline of; sketch out. **2.** To represent pictorially; depict. **3.** To depict in words or gestures; portray. [Latin *dēlīneāre* : *dē-,* completely + *līnea,* thread, LINE.] —**de·lin′e·a′tion** *n.* —**de·lin′e·a′tive** *adj.*

de·lin·e·a·tor (dĭ-lĭn′ē-ā′tər) *n.* **1.** One that delineates. **2.** An adjustable pattern used by tailors for cutting garments of various sizes.

de·lin·quen·cy (dĭ-lĭng′kwən-sē) *n., pl.* **-cies. 1.** Negligence or failure in doing what is required. **2.** An offense or misdemeanor; misdeed. **3. Juvenile delinquency** *(see).*

de·lin·quent (dĭ-lĭng′kwənt) *adj.* **1.** Failing to do what is required by law or obligation. **2.** Overdue in payment: *a delinquent account.* —*n.* **1.** A person who neglects or fails to do what law or obligation requires. **2.** A **juvenile delinquent** *(see).* [Latin *dēlinquēns,* present participle of *dēlinquere,* to fail in duty, offend, "leave undone" : *dē-* (intensive) + *linquere,* to leave (see **leikw-** in Appendix*).] —**de·lin′quent·ly** *adv.*

del·i·quesce (dĕl′ə-kwĕs′) *intr.v.* **-quesced, -quescing, -quesces. 1.** To melt away or disappear as if by melting. **2.** *Chemistry.* To dissolve and become liquid by absorbing moisture from the air. **3.** *Botany.* **a.** To branch out into numerous subdivisions that lack a main axis. **b.** To become fluid or soft on maturing, as do certain fungi. —See Synonyms at **melt.** [Latin *dēliquēscere* : *dē-,* completely + *liquēscere,* to melt, from *liquēre,* to be liquid (see **wleik-** in Appendix*).]

del·i·ques·cence (dĕl′ə-kwĕs′əns) *n.* **1.** The act or process of deliquescing. **2.** The liquid resulting from the process of deliquescing. —**del′i·ques′cent** *adj.*

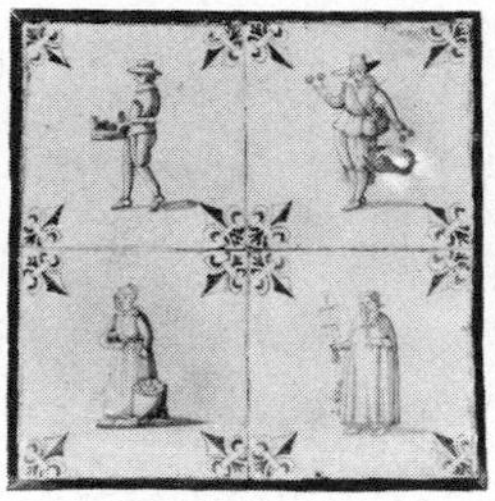
delft
Four 17th century tiles

del·i·ra·tion (dĕl′ə-rā′shən) *n.* Madness; delirium. [Latin *dēlīrātiō,* from *dēlīrāre,* to be deranged. See **delirium.**]

de·lir·i·ous (dĭ-lîr′ē-əs) *adj.* **1.** Suffering from delirium. **2.** Characteristic of or pertaining to delirium: *a delirious speech.* —**de·lir′i·ous·ly** *adv.* —**de·lir′i·ous·ness** *n.*

de·lir·i·um (dĭ-lîr′ē-əm) *n., pl.* **-ums** or **-ia** (-ē-ə). **1.** A state of temporary mental confusion and clouded consciousness resulting from high fever, intoxication, or shock, and characterized by anxiety, tremors, hallucinations, delusions, and incoherence. **2.** A state of uncontrolled excitement or emotion. [Latin *dēlīrium,* from *dēlīrāre,* to deviate from a straight line, be deranged : *dē-,* away from + *līra,* a furrow (see **leis-** in Appendix*).] —**de·lir′i·ant** *adj.*

delirium tre·mens (trē′mənz). An acute delirium caused by alcohol poisoning. Also shortened to "D.T.'s." [New Latin, "trembling delirium."]

del·i·tes·cence (dĕl′ə-tĕs′əns) *n.* **1.** The unexpected disappearance or subsidence of disease symptoms. **2.** An incubation period of an infectious disease. [From Latin *dēlitēscens,* present participle of *dēlitēscere,* to hide away, lurk : *dē-,* away + *latēscere,* inceptive of *latēre,* to be concealed (see **lādh-** in Appendix*).] —**del′i·tes′cent** *adj.*

De·li·us (dē′lē-əs), **Frederick.** 1862–1934. British composer.

de·liv·er (dĭ-lĭv′ər) *tr.v.* **-ered, -ering, -ers. 1.** To release or rescue from bondage, danger, or evil of any kind; set free: *deliver one from slavery.* **2. a.** To assist (a female) in giving birth. Often used with *of: The doctor delivered her of twins.* **b.** To assist or aid in the birth of: *The midwife delivered the twins.* **3.** To put into another's possession or power; surrender; hand over. **4.** To take to the intended recipient: *deliver groceries.* **5.** To send forth (a blow, for example) by releasing, discharging, or throwing. **6.** To utter (a lecture, for example). **7.** To secure (votes, for example) for a candidate or party. —See Synonyms at **save.** —**deliver oneself of.** To pronounce; utter. —**deliver the goods.** *Slang.* To perform as desired or promised. [Middle English *deliv(e)ren,* from Old French *delivrer,* from Late Latin *dēlīberāre* : Latin *dē-,* completely + *līberāre,* to set free, from *līber,* free (see **leudh-**[2] in Appendix*).] —**de·liv′er·a·bil′i·ty** *n.* —**de·liv′er·a·ble** *adj.* —**de·liv′er·er** *n.*

de·liv·er·ance (dĭ-lĭv′ər-əns) *n.* **1.** The act of delivering; especially, rescue from bondage or danger. **2.** The state of being so delivered. **3.** A publicly expressed opinion or judgment, such as the verdict of a jury.

de·liv·er·y (dĭ-lĭv′ə-rē) *n., pl.* **-ies.** *Abbr.* **dlvy 1.** The act of delivering or conveying. **2.** That which is delivered. **3.** The act of releasing or rescuing. **4.** The act of giving birth; parturition. **5.** The act of transferring to another. **6.** A giving up; surrender. **7. a.** Utterance. **b.** Manner of speaking or singing. **8.** The act of manner of throwing or discharging

delivery room. A room in a hospital equipped for delivering babies.

dell (dĕl) *n.* A small, secluded wooded valley. [Middle English *del,* Old English *dell.* See **dhel-** in Appendix.*]

del·la Rob·bia (dĕl′lä rôb′byä). An Italian family of Florentine sculptors, including **Luca** (1400?–1482); his nephew **Andrea** (1437–1528); and his grandnephew **Giovanni** (1469–1529?).

dells (dĕlz) *pl.n.* The rapids of a river.

Del·mar·va Peninsula (dĕl-mär′və). A peninsula between Chesapeake Bay and the Atlantic, comprising most of Delaware and parts of Maryland and Virginia. [DEL(AWARE) + MAR(YLAND) + V(IRGINI)A.]

Del·mon·i·co steak (dĕl-mŏn′ĭ-kō′) *n.* A small, often boned steak from the front section of the short loin of beef. Also called "club steak." [After the *Delmonico* Restaurant, New York City, which was founded by Lorenzo *Delmonico* (1813–1881).]

de·lo·cal·ize (dē-lō′kə-līz′) *tr.v.* **-ized, -izing, -izes.** **1.** To remove (something) from its native or usual locality. **2.** To broaden the range or scope of. **—de·lo′cal·i·za′tion** *n.*

De Long (də lông′, lŏng′), **George Washington.** 1844–1881. American naval officer and explorer of the Arctic.

De·lorme (də-lôrm′), **Philibert.** Also **de l'Orme.** 1515?–1570. French court architect of the Tuileries.

De·los (dē′lŏs). The smallest island of the Cyclades, Greece; the traditional birthplace of Apollo and Artemis.

de·louse (dē-lous′) *tr.v.* **-loused, -lousing, -louses.** To rid of parasitic infestation by physical or chemical means.

Del·phi (dĕl′fī′). An ancient town of central Greece, on the southern slope of Mount Parnassus; seat of an oracle of Apollo.

Del·phic (dĕl′fĭk). Also **Del·phi·an** (-fē-ən). **1.** Of or pertaining to Delphi or to the oracle of Apollo at Delphi. **2.** Ambiguous; obscure in meaning; oracular.

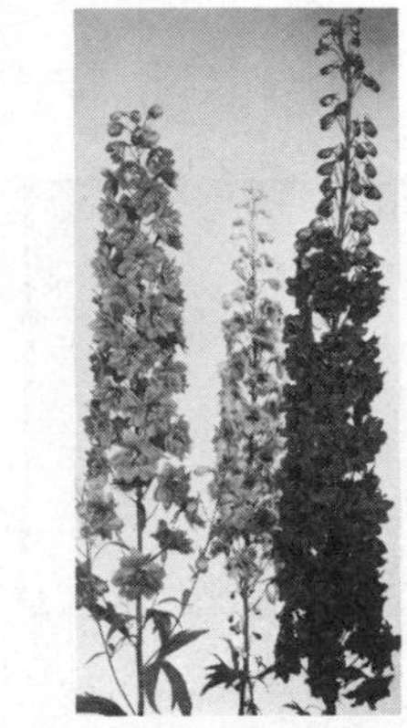

delphinium

del·phin·i·um (dĕl-fĭn′ē-əm) *n.* Any plant of the genus *Delphinium;* especially, any of several tall cultivated varieties having spikes of showy, variously colored spurred flowers. See **larkspur.** [New Latin *Delphinium* (genus), from Greek *delphinion,* larkspur, diminutive of *delphis* (stem *delphin-*), DOLPHIN (from the shape of the nectary).]

Del·phi·nus (dĕl-fī′nəs) *n.* A constellation in the Northern Hemisphere near Pegasus and Aquila. [New Latin, from Latin *delphīnus,* DOLPHIN.]

del·ta (dĕl′tə) *n.* **1.** The fourth letter in the Greek alphabet, written Δ, δ. Transliterated in English as *d, D.* See **alphabet.** **2. a.** A usually triangular alluvial deposit at the mouth of a river. **b.** A similar deposit at the mouth of a tidal inlet, caused by tidal currents. **3.** Anything resembling the shape of a triangle. **4.** *Mathematics.* A finite increment in a variable. [Middle English, from Greek, from Semitic, akin to Hebrew *dāleth.*] **—del·ta′ic** (-tā′ĭk), **del′tic** *adj.*

delta ray. **1.** An electron ejected from matter by ionizing radiation. **2.** The track of such an electron in a nuclear emulsion or cloud-chamber photograph.

delta wing. An aircraft with sweptback wings that give it the appearance of an isosceles triangle.

del·toid (dĕl′toid′) *n.* A thick, triangular muscle covering the shoulder joint, used to raise the arm from the side. *—adj.* **1.** Triangular. **2.** Pertaining to the deltoid. [New Latin *deltoides,* from Greek *deltoeidēs,* triangular : DELTA + -OID.]

de·lude (dĭ-lo͞od′) *tr.v.* **-luded, -luding, -ludes.** **1.** To deceive the mind or judgment of; mislead. **2.** *Obsolete.* To elude or evade. **3.** *Obsolete.* To frustrate the hopes or plans of. —See Synonyms at **deceive.** [Middle English *deluden,* from Latin *dēlūdere,* to play false, deceive : *dē-* (pejorative) + *lūdere,* to play, from *lūdus,* game (see **leid-** in Appendix*).] **—de·lud′a·ble** *adj.* **—de·lud′er** *n.* **—de·lud′ing·ly** *adv.*

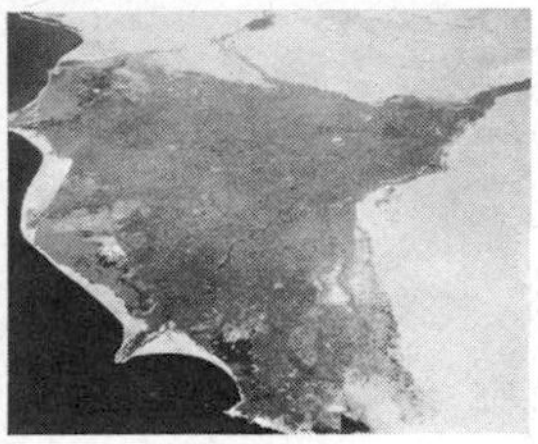

delta
The delta of the Nile photographed from a Gemini space flight

del·uge (dĕl′yo͞oj) *tr.v.* **-uged, -uging, -uges.** **1.** To overrun with water. **2.** To inundate in overwhelming numbers. *—n.* **1.** A great flood; heavy downpour. **2.** Anything that overwhelms as if by a great flood. **—the Deluge.** The great flood that occurred in the time of Noah. Genesis 7–10. [Middle English, from Old French, from Latin *dīluvium,* flood, from *dīluere,* to wash away : *dis-,* apart + *-luere,* from *lavere,* to wash (see **lou-** in Appendix*).]

de·lu·sion (dĭ-lo͞o′zhən, dĭ-lyo͞o′-) *n.* **1. a.** The act or process of deluding; deception. **b.** The state of being deluded. **2.** A false belief held in spite of invalidating evidence. See Usage note below. [Middle English *delusioun,* from Latin *dēlūsio,* from *dēlūdere* (past participle *dēlūsus*), DELUDE.] **—de·lu′sion·al** *adj.*

Usage: *Delusion* and *illusion* are seldom interchangeable, though closely related. *Delusion* refers to false belief held without reservation as a result of self-deception, the imposition of another, or mental disorder. It is the stronger term, often associated with harm. *Illusion* is applicable to a false impression, frequently based on fancy or on wishful thinking, or to a false perception (such as an optical illusion) that one eventually recognizes as false.

de·lu·sive (dĭ-lo͞o′sĭv) *adj.* Also **de·lu·so·ry** (-lo͞o′sə-rē). **1.** Tending to deceive or mislead; deceptive. **2.** Having the nature of a delusion; false. —See Synonyms at **misleading.** **—de·lu′sive·ly** *adv.* **—de·lu′sive·ness** *n.*

de luxe (dĭ lo͝oks′, dĭ lŭks′). Also **de·luxe.** **1.** Of special elegance or luxury; sumptuous: *a de luxe model.* **2.** In an elegant or luxurious manner; sumptuously. [French, "of luxury."]

delve (dĕlv) *v.* **delved, delving, delves.** *—intr.* **1.** To search deeply and laboriously. **2.** *Archaic.* To dig the ground, as with a spade. *—tr. Archaic.* To dig (ground) with a spade. [Middle English *delven,* to dig, Old English *delfan.* See **dhelbh-** in Appendix.*] **—delv′er** *n.*

Dem. Democrat; Democratic.

de·mag·net·ize (dē-măg′nə-tīz′) *tr.v.* **-ized, -izing, -izes.** To remove magnetic properties from. **—de·mag′net·i·za′tion** *n.* **—de·mag′net·iz′er** *n.*

dem·a·gog·ic (dĕm′ə-gŏj′ĭk) *adj.* Also **dem·a·gog·i·cal** (-ĭ-kəl). Relating to, of the nature of, or characteristic of a demagogue. **—dem′a·gog′i·cal·ly** *adv.*

dem·a·gogue (dĕm′ə-gôg′, -gŏg′) *n.* Also **dem·a·gog.** **1.** A leader who obtains power by means of impassioned appeals to the emotions and prejudices of the populace. **2.** A leader of the common people in ancient times. [Greek *dēmagōgos,* popular leader : *dēmos,* common people (see **dā-** in Appendix*) + *agōgos,* leading, from *agein,* to lead (see **ag-** in Appendix*).]

dem·a·gogu·er·y (dĕm′ə-gô′gə-rē, -gŏg′ə-rē) *n.* The practices or rhetoric of a demagogue. Also called "demagogism."

dem·a·go·gy (dĕm′ə-gō′jē, -gô′jē, -gŏj′ē) *n.* The quality or character of demagogues.

de·mand (dĭ-mănd′, -mänd′) *v.* **-manded, -manding, -mands.** *—tr.* **1.** To ask for urgently or firmly, leaving no chance for refusal or denial. **2.** To claim as just or due. **3.** To ask to be informed of: *demand the cause of his action.* **4.** To need or require as useful, just, proper, or necessary. **5.** *Law.* **a.** To summon to court. **b.** To claim formally; lay legal claim to. *—intr.* To make a demand. —See Usage note below. *—n.* **1.** The act of demanding. **2.** Something that is demanded. **3. a.** The state of being sought after. **b.** An urgent requirement, need, or claim: *an increased demand for capital goods.* **4.** *Archaic.* An emphatic question or inquiry. **5.** *Law.* A formal claim. **6.** *Economics.* **a.** The desire to possess something combined with the ability to purchase it. **b.** The amount of any commodity that people are ready and able to buy at a given time for a given price. **—on demand.** On presentation. [Middle English *demaunden,* from Old French *demander,* to ask, charge with doing, from Latin *dēmandāre,* to give in charge, entrust : *dē-* (intensive) + *mandāre,* to entrust (see **man-**[2] in Appendix*).] **—de·mand′a·ble** *adj.* **—de·mand′er** *n.*

Usage: *Demand* (verb) is commonly followed by a direct object in the form of a word *(demand payment)* or clause *(demand that he go),* or by an infinitive *(demand to know why).* The object is often followed by *of* or *from: demand much of* (or *from*) *him.* In a parallel construction, *demand* (noun) is followed by *on: make a demand on him.*

demand deposit. A bank deposit that can be withdrawn by the depositor immediately and without advance notice.

de·mand·ing (dĭ-măn′dĭng, dĭ-män′-) *adj.* **1.** Making rigorous or trying demands. **2.** Involving or requiring careful attention or constant effort. —See Synonyms at **burdensome.** **—de·mand′ing·ly** *adv.*

demand note. A bill or draft payable in lawful money on presentation or demand.

de·man·toid (dĭ-măn′toid′) *n.* A transparent, green variety of garnet, used as a gem. [German *Demantoid* : *Demant* (obsolete), diamond, from Middle High German *diemant,* from Old French *diamant,* DIAMOND + -OID.]

de·mar·cate (dĭ-mär′kāt′, dē′mär-kāt′) *tr.v.* **-cated, -cating, -cates.** **1.** To set the boundaries of; delimit. **2.** To separate clearly as if by boundaries; discriminate. [Back-formation from DEMARCATION.] **—de·mar′ca′tor** (-kā′tər) *n.*

de·mar·ca·tion (dē′mär-kā′shən) *n.* Also **de·mar·ka·tion.** **1.** The setting or marking of boundaries or limits. **2.** A separation; distinction. Usually used in the phrase *line of demarcation.* [Spanish *demarcación,* from *demarcar,* to mark out the boundary : *de-,* completely + *marcar,* to mark, from Italian *marcare,* from Old Italian, from Germanic (see **merg-** in Appendix*).]

dé·marche (dā-màrsh′) *n. French.* **1.** A proceeding; maneuver; step. **2.** A diplomatic representation or protest. **3.** A statement or protest addressed by citizens to public authorities.

de·mark (dĭ-märk′) *tr.v.* **-marked, -marking, -marks.** To demarcate.

de·ma·te·ri·al·ize (dē′mə-tîr′ē-ə-līz′) *v.* **-ized, -izing, -izes.** *—tr.* To divest of material qualities or characteristics. *—intr.* To lose material character or form. **—de′ma·te′ri·al·i·za′tion** *n.*

Dem·a·vend, Mount (dĕm′ə-vĕnd′). The highest elevation (18,600 feet) of the Elburz Mountains, northern Iran.

deme (dēm) *n.* **1.** One of the townships of ancient Attica. **2.** *Ecology.* A local, usually stable population of organisms of the same kind or species. [Greek *dēmos,* common people, deme. See **dā-** in Appendix.*]

de·mean[1] (dĭ-mēn′) *tr.v.* **-meaned, -meaning, -means.** To conduct or behave (oneself) in a particular manner. *—n. Archaic.* Behavior; demeanor. [Middle English *demeinen,* from Old French *demener* : *de-,* completely + *mener,* to lead, conduct, from Latin *mināre,* to drive (herds), from *minārī,* to threaten, from *minae,* threats (see **men-**[2] in Appendix*).]

de·mean[2] (dĭ-mēn′) *tr.v.* **-meaned, -meaning, -means.** **1.** To debase in dignity or stature. **2.** To humble (oneself). —See Synonyms at **degrade.** [DE- (pejorative) + MEAN (base).]

de·mean·or (dĭ-mē′nər) *n.* Also *British* **de·mean·our.** The way in which a person behaves or conducts himself; deportment; manner. See Synonyms at **bearing.**

de·ment (dĭ-mĕnt′) *tr.v.* **-mented, -menting, -ments.** To make insane. [Late Latin *dēmentāre,* from Latin *dēmēns,* mad : *dē-* (undoing) + *mēns,* mind (see **men-**[1] in Appendix*).]

de·ment·ed (dĭ-mĕn′tĭd) *adj.* **1.** Insane. **2.** Afflicted with dementia. **—de·ment′ed·ly** *adv.* **—de·ment′ed·ness** *n.*

de·men·tia (dĭ-mĕn′shə, -shē-ə) *n.* Irreversible deterioration of intellectual faculties with concomitant emotional disturbance resulting from organic brain disorder. See Synonyms at **insanity.** [Latin *dēmentia,* madness, from *dēmēns,* mad. See **dement.**]

dementia prae·cox (prē′kŏks′). **Schizophrenia** *(see).* [New Latin, "premature dementia."]

Dem·e·rar·a (dĕm′ə-râr′ə, -rä′rə). The principal river of Guyana, rising in the center of the country and flowing 200 miles generally north to the Atlantic Ocean.

de·mer·it (dĭ-mĕr′ĭt) *n.* **1. a.** A quality or characteristic that deserves blame or censure; fault. **b.** Absence of merit. **2.** A mark made against one's record by a superior and implying some loss of status or privileges for bad conduct or failure. —*tr.v.* **demerited, -iting, -its.** To penalize (an inferior) with a demerit. [Middle English *demerite,* offense, guilt, originally "merit," "desert," from Old French, probably from Latin *dēmerēre,* to deserve : *dē-* (intensive) + *merēre, merērī,* to deserve, MERIT.] —**de·mer′i·to′ri·ous** (-tôr′ē-əs, -tōr′ē-əs) *adj.* —**de·mer′i·to′ri·ous·ly** *adv.*

Dem·e·rol (dĕm′ə-rōl′, -rôl′) *n.* A trademark for a synthetic morphine, **meperidine hydrochloride** *(see).*

de·mesne (dĭ-mān′, -mēn′) *n.* **1.** *Law.* Possession and use of one's own land. **2.** Lands retained by a feudal lord for his own use. **3.** The grounds belonging to a mansion or country house. **4.** An extensive piece of landed property; estate. **5.** Any district; territory. **6.** A realm; domain. [Middle English *demesne, demeine,* from Old French *demaine,* DOMAIN.]

De·me·ter (dĭ-mē′tər). *Greek Mythology.* The goddess of agriculture, fertility, and marriage. Identified with the Roman goddess Ceres. [Greek *Dēmētēr.* See **māter-** in Appendix.*]

demi–. Indicates: **1.** Half; for example, **demisemiquaver. 2.** Less than full status; for example, **demigod.** [French, from *demi,* half, from Medieval Latin *dīmedius,* from Latin *dīmidius,* half, divided in half : *dis-,* apart + *medius,* half (see **medhyo-** in Appendix*).]

dem·i·god (dĕm′ē-gŏd′) *n.* **1. a.** A mythological semidivine being, such as the offspring of a god and a mortal. **b.** An inferior deity; minor god. **2.** A man with godlike attributes.

dem·i·god·dess (dĕm′ē-gŏd′ĭs) *n.* A female demigod.

dem·i·john (dĕm′ē-jŏn′) *n.* A large, narrow-necked bottle made of glass or earthenware, usually encased in wickerwork. [Probably a variant of French *dame-Jeanne,* "Lady Jane."]

de·mil·i·ta·rize (dē-mĭl′ə-tə-rīz′) *tr.v.* **-rized, -rizing, -rizes. 1.** To eliminate the military character of. **2.** To prohibit military forces or installations in. **3.** To replace military control of with civilian control. —**de·mil′i·ta·ri·za′tion** *n.*

demilitarized zone. *Abbr.* **DMZ** A region, defined by diplomatic or political agreement, wherein military forces and installations may not be established.

De Mille (də mĭl′), **Agnes.** Born 1909. American choreographer; niece of Cecil B. De Mille.

De Mille (də mĭl′), **Cecil B(lount).** 1881–1959. American motion-picture producer and director.

dem·i·lune (dĕm′ē-lo͞on′) *n.* **1.** A crescent or half-moon. **2.** *Military.* A crescent-shaped outwork to defend the entrance of a fort. **3.** A crescent-shaped granular mass of protoplasm found in salivary glands. [French *demi-lune* : DEMI- + *lune,* moon, from Latin *lūna* (see **leuk-** in Appendix*).]

dem·i·mon·daine (dĕm′ē-mŏn′dān′) *n.* A woman belonging to the demimonde. Also called "demirep."

dem·i·monde (dĕm′ē-mŏnd, dĕm′ē-mŏnd′) *n.* **1.** The social class of those who are kept by wealthy lovers or protectors. **2.** Any group existing on the margin of success or respectability: *the literary demimonde.* [French *demi-monde,* "half-world," coined (1855) by Alexandre Dumas fils to designate "the class of the déclassé."]

dem·i·pique (dĕm′ē-pēk′) *n.* A military saddle used during the 18th century, having a pommel about half the height of those on earlier saddles. [Earlier *demipeak* : DEMI- + PEAK.]

dem·i·re·lief (dĕm′ē-rĭ-lēf′) *n. Sculpture.* **Half relief** *(see).*

dem·i·rep (dĕm′ē-rĕp′) *n.* A woman of low repute; a harlot.

de·mise (dĭ-mīz′) *n.* **1.** Death. **2.** The transfer of an estate by lease or will. **3.** The transfer of a ruler's authority by death or abdication. —*v.* **demised, -mising, -mises.** —*tr.* **1.** To transfer (an estate) by will or lease. **2.** To transfer (sovereignty) by abdication or will. —*intr.* **1.** To be transferred by will or descent. **2.** To die. [Middle English *dimise, demise,* transfer of property, from Old French, from feminine past participle of *demettre,* DEMIT.] —**de·mis′a·ble** *adj.*

dem·i·sem·i·qua·ver (dĕm′ē-sĕm′ē-kwā′vər) *n. Chiefly British.* A **thirty-second note** *(see).* [DEMI- + SEMI- + QUAVER (eighth note).]

de·mis·sion (dĭ-mĭsh′ən) *n.* The relinquishment of an office or function. [Middle English *dimissioun,* from Latin *dīmissiō,* dismissal, from *dimittere* (past participle *dīmissus*), to send away, DEMIT.]

de·mit (dĭ-mĭt′) *v.* **-mitted, -mitting, -mits.** —*tr.* **1.** To relinquish (an office or function). **2.** *Obsolete.* To dismiss. —*intr.* To resign. [Middle English *dimitten,* to release, deliver, Old French *demettre,* from Latin *dīmittere,* to dismiss, renounce, send away : *dis-,* away + *mittere,* to send (see **smeit-** in Appendix*).]

dem·i·tasse (dĕm′ē-tăs′, -täs′) *n.* **1.** A small cup of strong black coffee. **2.** The cup itself. [French : DEMI- + *tasse,* cup, from Old French, from Arabic *ṭast,* basin, from Persian *tast*†.]

dem·i·urge (dĕm′ē-ûrj′) *n.* **1.** *Often capital* **D.** The name used by Plato to designate the deity who fashions the material world. **2.** *Often capital* **D.** The Gnostic creator of the material world. **3.** A public magistrate in some ancient Greek states. [Late Latin *dēmiūrgus,* from Greek *dēmiourgos,* "public craftsman" : *dēmios,* public, from *dēmos,* people (see **dā-** in Appendix*) + *ergon,* work (see **werg-**¹ in Appendix*).] —**de′mi·ur′geous, dem′i·ur′gic, dem′i·ur′gi·cal** *adj.* —**dem′i·ur′gi·cal·ly** *adv.*

dem·i·vierge (dĕm′ē-vyĕrzh′) *n.* A virgin whose sexual activities stop short of intercourse. [French, "half virgin."]

de·mob (dē-mŏb′) *tr.v.* **-mobbed, -mobbing, -mobs.** *British Informal.* To demobilize. —*n. British Informal.* Demobilization.

de·mo·bil·ize (dē-mō′bə-līz′) *tr.v.* **-ized, -izing, -izes.** To discharge from military service or use; disband or dismiss, as an army or troops. —**de·mo′bil·i·za′tion** *n.*

de·moc·ra·cy (dĭ-mŏk′rə-sē) *n., pl.* **-cies. 1.** Government by the people, exercised either directly or through elected representatives. **2.** A political or social unit based upon this form of rule. **3.** A social condition of equality and respect for the individual within the community. [Old French *democratie,* from Late Latin *dēmocratia,* from Greek *dēmokratia* : *dēmos,* common people (see **dā-** in Appendix*) + -CRACY.]

dem·o·crat (dĕm′ə-krăt′) *n.* **1.** An advocate of democracy. **2.** *Capital* **D.** *Abbr.* **D., D., Dem.** A member of the Democratic Party. [French *démocrate,* back-formation from *democratie,* DEMOCRACY.]

dem·o·crat·ic (dĕm′ə-krăt′ĭk) *adj.* **1.** Of, characterized by, or advocating democracy. **2.** Pertaining to, encompassing, or promoting the interests of the people. **3.** Persuaded of or practicing social equality; not snobbish: *"a proper democratic scorn for bloated dukes and lords"* (George Du Maurier). **4.** *Capital* **D.** *Abbr.* **D, D., Dem.** Pertaining to or characteristic of the Democratic Party. —**dem′o·crat′i·cal·ly** *adv.*

Democratic Party. One of the two major political parties in the United States. It owes its origin to a split in the Democratic-Republican Party under Andrew Jackson in 1828.

Dem·o·crat·ic-Re·pub·li·can Party (dĕm′ə-krăt′ĭk-rĭ-pŭb′lĭ-kən). A U.S. political party opposed to the Federalist Party, founded by Thomas Jefferson in 1792 and dissolved in 1828.

de·moc·ra·tize (dĭ-mŏk′rə-tīz′) *tr.v.* **-tized, -tizing, -tizes.** To make democratic. —**de·moc′ra·ti·za′tion** *n.*

De·moc·ri·tus (dĭ-mŏk′rə-təs). Greek philosopher of the late fifth century B.C.; proposed a primitive atomic theory.

dé·mo·dé (dā-mō-dā′) *adj. French.* Outmoded.

de·mod·u·late (dē-mŏd′jo͞o-lāt′, -yo͞o-lāt′) *tr.v.* **-lated, -lating, -lates.** To extract (information) from a modulated carrier wave. —**de·mod′u·la′tion** *n.* —**de·mod′u·la′tor** (-lā′tər) *n.*

de·mog·ra·phy (dĭ-mŏg′rə-fē) *n.* The study of the characteristics of human populations, as size, growth, density, distribution, and vital statistics. [French *démographie* : Greek *dēmos,* people (see **dā-** in Appendix*) + -GRAPHY.] —**de·mog′ra·pher** *n.* —**dem′o·graph′ic** (dĕm′ə-grăf′ĭk), **dem′o·graph′i·cal** *adj.* —**dem′o·graph′i·cal·ly** *adv.*

dem·oi·selle (dĕm′wa-zĕl′) *n.* **1.** A young lady. **2.** An Old World crane, *Anthropoides virgo,* having gray and black plumage and white plumes at the sides of the head. Usually called "demoiselle crane." **3.** *Rare.* A damselfly. [French, from Old French *dameisele,* DAMSEL.]

De·moi·vre (də-moi′vər, dĭ-; *French* də-mwä′vr′), **Abraham.** 1667–1754. French mathematician and author.

de·mol·ish (dĭ-mŏl′ĭsh) *tr.v.* **-ished, -ishing, -ishes. 1.** To tear down completely; wreck; level. **2.** To do away with completely; put an end to. —See Synonyms at **ruin.** [Old French *demolir* (present stem *demoliss-*), from Latin *dēmōlīrī,* to throw down, demolish : *dē-* (reversal) + *mōlīrī,* to endeavor, strive, build, from *mōlēs,* mass (see **mō-** in Appendix*).]

dem·o·li·tion (dĕm′ə-lĭsh′ən) *n.* **1.** The act or process of wrecking or destroying; specifically, destruction, as of a building, by explosives. **2.** *Plural.* Explosives used to demolish. [Old French, from Latin *dēmōlītiō,* from *dēmōlīrī,* DEMOLISH.] —**dem′o·li′tion·ist** *n.*

de·mon (dē′mən) *n.* Also **dae·mon, dai·mon** (dī′mōn′) (for senses 3, 4). **1.** A devil or evil being; especially, in the New Testament, an unclean spirit that possesses and afflicts a person. **2.** A persistently tormenting person, force, or passion. **3.** *Greek Mythology.* An inferior divinity, such as a deified hero. **4.** An attendant spirit; a genius. **5.** One who is extremely zealous, skillful, or engrossed in a given activity. [Middle English, from Late Latin *daemōn,* evil spirit, from Latin, spirit, from Greek *daimōn,* divine power, fate, god. See **dā-** in Appendix*.]

demon. *Grammar.* demonstrative.

de·mon·e·tize (dĭ-mŏn′ə-tīz′, dĭ-mŭn′-) *tr.v.* **-tized, -tizing, -tizes. 1.** To divest (a coin, for example) of monetary value. **2.** To stop using (a metal) as a monetary standard. [French *démonétiser* : *dé-,* from Latin *dē-,* away from + *monēta,* coin, MONEY.] —**de·mon′e·ti·za′tion** *n.*

de·mo·ni·ac (dĭ-mō′nē-ăk′) *adj.* Also **de·mo·ni·a·cal** (dē′mə-nī′ə-kəl). **1.** Arising or seeming to arise from possession by a demon. **2.** Befitting or suggestive of a devil; fiendish; frenzied. —*n.* One who is or seems to be possessed by a demon. [Middle English *demoniak,* from Late Latin *daemoniācus,* from Greek *daimoniakos,* from *daimonios,* of a spirit, from *daimōn,* DEMON.] —**de′mo·ni′a·cal·ly** *adv.*

de·mon·ic (dĭ-mŏn′ĭk) *adj.* **1.** Befitting a demon; fiendish. **2.** Motivated by a spiritual force or genius; inspired.

de·mon·ize (dē′mə-nīz′) *tr.v.* **-ized, -izing, -izes. 1.** To turn into or as if into a demon. **2.** To possess by a demon.

de·mon·ol·o·gy (dē′mə-nŏl′ə-jē) *n.* **1.** The study of demons. **2.** A treatise on demons or demon worship. [DEMON + -LOGY.] —**de′mon·ol′o·gist** *n.*

de·mon·stra·ble (dĭ-mŏn′strə-bəl) *adj.* Capable of being shown or proved. —**de·mon′stra·bil′i·ty, de·mon′stra·ble·ness** *n.* —**de·mon′stra·bly** *adv.*

de·mon·strant (dĭ-mŏn′strənt) *n.* One who participates in a public demonstration.

dem·on·strate (dĕm′ən-strāt′) *v.* **-strated, -strating, -strates.**

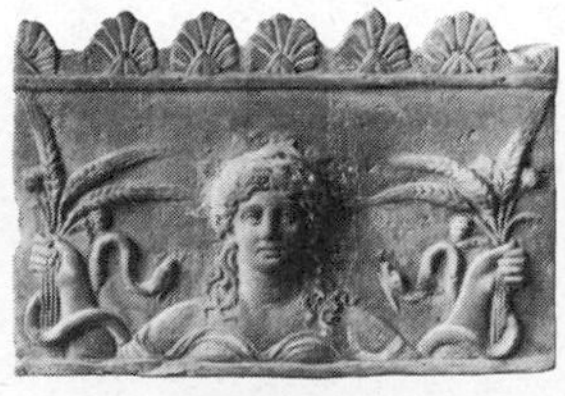
Demeter
Head of Demeter
in terra-cotta relief

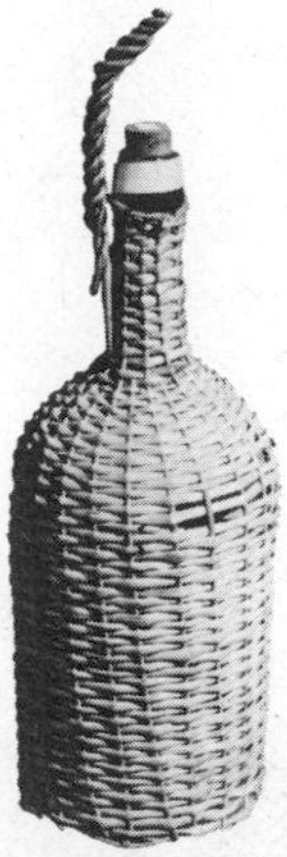
demijohn

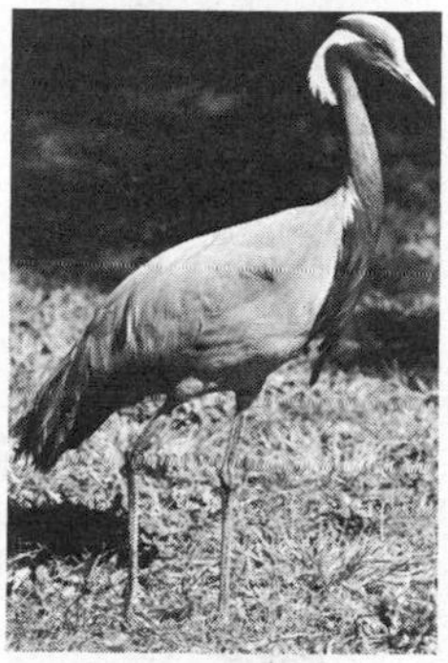
demoiselle

—*tr.* **1.** To prove or make manifest by reasoning or adducing evidence. **2.** To describe or illustrate by experiment or practical application. **3.** To manifest or reveal. **4.** To display, operate, and explain (a product). —*intr.* To present or participate in a demonstration. [Latin *dēmonstrāre,* to point out : *dē-,* completely + *monstrāre,* to show, from *mōnstrum,* divine portent, from *monēre,* to warn (see **men-**[1] in Appendix*).]

dem·on·stra·tion (dĕm′ən-strā′shən) *n.* **1.** The act of making evident or proving. **2.** Conclusive evidence; proof. **3.** An illustration or explanation, as of a theory or product, by exemplification or practical application. **4.** A manifestation, as of one's feelings. **5.** A public display of group opinion, as by a rally or march. **6.** A show of military strength.

de·mon·stra·tive (dĭ-mŏn′strə-tĭv) *adj.* **1.** Serving to manifest or prove. **2.** Involving or characterized by demonstration. **3.** Given to or marked by the open expression of emotion, especially affection. **4.** *Abbr.* **demon.** *Grammar.* Specifying or singling out the person or thing referred to; for example, *these* is a demonstrative pronoun. —*n. Abbr.* **demon.** *Grammar.* A demonstrative pronoun or adjective. —**de·mon′stra·tive·ly** *adv.* —**de·mon′stra·tive·ness** *n.*

dem·on·stra·tor (dĕm′ən-strā′tər) *n.* **1.** One who demonstrates something. **2.** A sample used in such a demonstration. **3.** One who takes part in a public demonstration.

dem·o·pho·bi·a (dĕm′ō-fō′bē-ə) *n.* Abnormal fear of crowds. [Greek *dēmos,* people, DEMOS + -PHOBIA.] —**dem′o·pho′bic** *adj.*

de·mor·al·ize (dĭ-môr′əl-īz′, dĭ-mŏr′-) *tr.v.* **-ized, -izing, -izes. 1.** To debase the morals of; corrupt. **2.** To undermine the confidence or morale of; dishearten. **3.** To put into disorder; confuse. —**de·mor′al·i·za′tion** *n.* —**de·mor′al·iz′er** *n.*

de·mos (dē′mŏs) *n.* **1.** The people of an ancient Greek state, considered as a social class or as a political entity. **2.** The common people; populace. [Greek *dēmos,* district, people. See **dā-** in Appendix.*]

De·mos·the·nes (dĭ-mŏs′thə-nēz′). 384?–322 B.C. Greek orator and political leader.

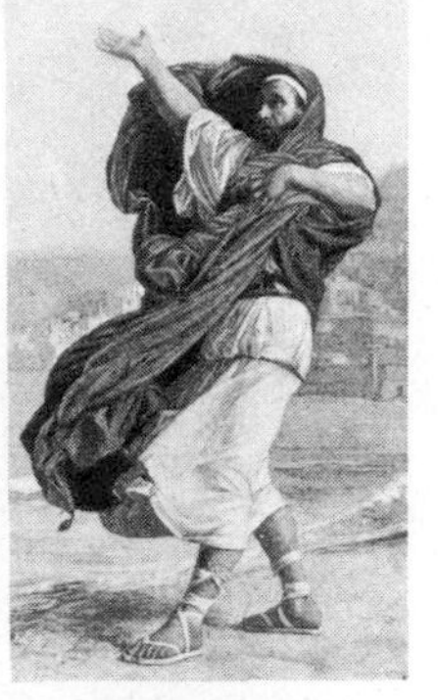

Demosthenes
Practicing oratory on the seashore

de·mote (dĭ-mōt′) *tr.v.* **-moted, -moting, -motes.** To lower in rank or grade. [DE- (reversal) + (PRO)MOTE.] —**de·mo′tion** *n.*

de·mot·ic (dĭ-mŏt′ĭk) *adj.* **1.** Of or pertaining to the common people; in common use; popular. **2.** Of, pertaining to, or written in the simplified form of ancient Egyptian hieratic writing. **3.** *Often capital* **D.** Of or pertaining to **Dhimotiki** *(see).* [Greek *dēmotikos,* from *dēmotēs,* commoner, from *dēmos,* common people, DEMOS.] —**de·mot′ist** *n.*

De·mot·ic (dĭ-mŏt′ĭk) *n.* **Dhimotiki** *(see).*

de·mount (dē-mount′) *tr.v.* **-mounted, -mounting, -mounts.** To remove (a gun or motor, for example) from a position on a mounting or other support. —**de·mount′a·ble** *adj.*

Demp·sey (dĕmp′sē), **William Harrison ("Jack").** Born 1895. American athlete; world heavyweight boxing champion (1919–26).

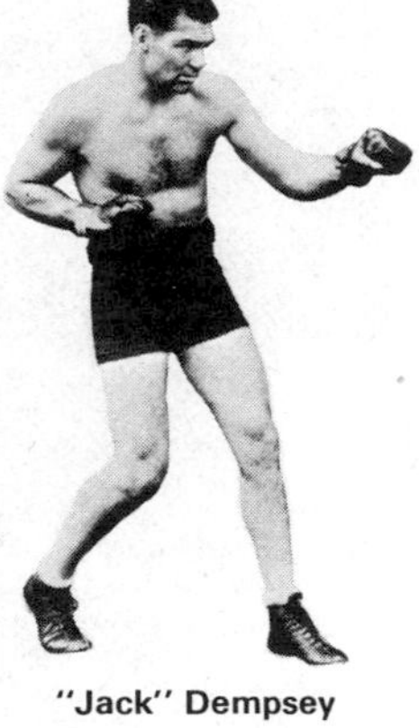

"Jack" Dempsey

Demp·ster (dĕmp′stər), **Arthur Jeffrey.** 1886–1950. Canadian-born American physicist; discovered the isotope uranium 235.

de·mul·cent (dĭ-mŭl′sənt) *adj.* Soothing. —*n.* A soothing, usually mucilaginous or oily substance, used especially to relieve pain in inflamed or irritated mucous surfaces. [Latin *dēmulcēns,* present participle of *dēmulcēre,* to stroke down, caress, soothe : *dē-,* down + *mulcēre*†, to stroke.]

de·mur (dĭ-mûr′) *intr.v.* **-murred, -murring, -murs. 1.** To take exception; raise objections; object. **2.** *Law.* To enter or interpose a demurrer. **3.** To delay. —See Synonyms at **object.** —*n.* Also **de·mur·ral** (dĭ-mûr′əl). **1.** The act of demurring. **2.** An objection. **3.** A delay. [Middle English *demeoren, demuren,* to delay, linger, from French *demorer, demurer,* from Latin *dēmorārī* : *dē-* (intensive) + *morārī,* to delay, from *mora,* delay (see **merə-** in Appendix*).] —**de·mur′ra·ble** *adj.*

de·mure (dĭ-myŏŏr′) *adj.* **-murer, -murest. 1.** Sedate in manner or behavior; reserved. **2.** Feigning modesty or shyness. —See Synonyms at **shy.** [Middle English, from Old French *demore,* quiet, sedate, "settled," past participle of *demorer,* to stay, delay, DEMUR.] —**de·mure′ly** *adv.* —**de·mure′ness** *n.*

de·mur·rage (dĭ-mûr′ĭj) *n.* **1.** The detention of a ship, freight car, or other cargo conveyance during loading or unloading beyond the scheduled time of departure. **2.** The compensation paid for this detention.

de·mur·rer (dĭ-mûr′ər) *n.* **1.** A person who demurs; objector. **2.** *Law.* A plea to dismiss a lawsuit on the grounds that although the opposition's statements may be true, they are insufficient to sustain the claim. Compare **plea. 3.** An objection.

De·muth (dĭ-myŏŏth′), **Charles.** 1883–1935. American painter, illustrator, and water colorist.

de·my (dĭ-mī′) *n., pl.* **-mies. 1.** Any of several standard sizes of paper, especially: **a.** In England, paper measuring 15½ by 20 inches or 17½ by 22½ inches. **b.** In the United States, paper measuring 16 by 21 inches. **2.** A size of book, 8¾ by 5⅝ inches. Also called "demy octavo." **3.** A size of book, 11¼ by 8¾ inches. In this sense, also called "demy quarto." [From DEMI-.]

den (dĕn) *n.* **1.** The shelter or retreat of a wild animal; lair. **2.** A cave considered as a refuge or hiding place. **3.** A residence or abode, especially if hidden or squalid; haunt: *a den of thieves.* **4.** A small secluded room for study or relaxation. **5.** A unit of about eight to ten Cub Scouts. —*intr.v.* **denned, denning, dens.** To inhabit or hide in a den. [Middle English *den(ne),* Old English *denn.* See **dan-** in Appendix.*]

DEN Airport code for Denver, Colorado.

Den. Denmark.

de·nar·i·us (dĭ-nâr′ē-əs) *n., pl.* **-narii** (-nâr′ē-ī′). **1.** An ancient Roman silver coin, originally equivalent to ten bronze asses. **2.** An ancient Roman gold coin valued at 25 silver denarii. [Middle English, from Latin *dēnārius,* from adjective, "consisting of ten," from *dēnī,* by tens. See **dekm-** in Appendix.*]

den·a·ry (dĕn′ə-rē) *adj.* **1.** Tenfold. **2.** Divided or counted by tens; decimal. [Latin *dēnārius.* See **denarius.**]

de·na·tion·al·ize (dē-năsh′ən-ə-līz′) *tr.v.* **-ized, -izing, -izes. 1.** To deprive of national rights, status, or characteristics. **2.** To return (a nationalized industry or function) to private ownership. —**de·na′tion·al·i·za′tion** *n.*

de·nat·u·ral·ize (dē-năch′ər-ə-līz′) *tr.v.* **-ized, -izing, -izes. 1.** To make unnatural. **2.** To deprive of the rights of naturalization or citizenship. —**de·nat′u·ral·i·za′tion** *n.*

de·na·ture (dē-nā′chər) *tr.v.* **-tured, -turing, -tures.** Also **de·na·tur·ize** (-chə-rīz′), **-ized, -izing, -izes. 1.** To change the nature or natural qualities of. **2.** To render unfit to eat or drink; especially, to add methanol to ethyl alcohol for this purpose. **3.** *Physics.* To add nonfissionable matter to (fissionable material) to prevent use in an atomic weapon. —**de·na′tur·ant** *n.* —**de·na′tur·a′tion** *n.*

denatured alcohol. Ethyl alcohol made unfit for drinking by the addition of a substance, such as methanol.

Den·bigh (dĕn′bē). Also **Den·bigh·shire** (dĕn′bē-shîr, -shər). A county occupying 668 square miles of northeastern Wales. Population, 177,000.

den·dri·form (dĕn′drə-fôrm′) *adj.* Having the characteristic form or structure of a tree. [DENDR(I)- + -FORM.]

den·drite (dĕn′drīt′) *n.* **1. a.** A mineral crystallizing in another mineral in the form of a branching or treelike mark. **b.** A rock or mineral bearing such a mark or marks. **2.** A branched part of a nerve cell that transmits impulses toward the cell body. In this sense, also called "dendron." [DENDR(O)- + -ITE.]

den·drit·ic (dĕn-drĭt′ĭk) *adj.* Also **den·drit·i·cal** (-ĭ-kəl). **1.** Of, pertaining to, or resembling a dendrite. **2.** Tree-shaped; dendriform. —**den·drit′i·cal·ly** *adv.*

dendro-, dendri-, dendr-. Indicates tree; for example, **dendrology, dendriform, dendrite.** [New Latin, from Greek, from *dendron,* tree. See **deru-** in Appendix.*]

den·dro·chro·nol·o·gy (dĕn′drō-krə-nŏl′ə-jē) *n.* The study of the growth rings in trees to determine and date past events. —**den′dro·chron′o·log′i·cal** (-krŏn′ə-lŏj′ĭ-kəl) *adj.*

den·droid (dĕn′droid′) *adj.* Also **den·droi·dal** (dĕn-droid′l). Shaped like a tree. [Greek *dendroeidēs* : DENDR(O)- + -OID.]

den·drol·o·gy (dĕn-drŏl′ə-jē) *n.* The botanical study of trees. [DENDRO- + -LOGY.] —**den′dro·log′ic** (-drə-lŏj′ĭk), **den′dro·log′i·cal** *adj.* —**den·drol′o·gist** *n.*

De·neb (dĕn′ĕb) *n.* The brightest star in the constellation Cygnus, approximately 1,630 light years from Earth. [Arabic *dhanab,* tail.]

De·neb·o·la (dĭ-nĕb′ə-lə) *n.* The second-brightest star in the constellation Leo. [Arabic *dhanab al-(asad),* "tail of the (lion)." See **Deneb.**]

den·e·ga·tion (dĕn′ə-gā′shən) *n.* A denial. [Middle English *denegacioun,* from Old French *denegation,* from Latin *dēnegātiō,* from *dēnegātus,* past participle of *dēnegāre,* DENY.]

den·gue (dĕng′gē, dĕng′gā; *Spanish* dĕng′gĕ) *n.* An infectious, virulent, tropical and subtropical epidemic disease transmitted by mosquitoes and characterized by fever, rash, and severe pains in the joints. Also called "breakbone fever," "dandy." [Spanish, of African origin, akin to Swahili *kidinga.*]

de·ni·a·ble (dĭ-nī′ə-bəl) *adj.* Capable of being denied; questionable. —**de·ni′a·bly** *adv.*

de·ni·al (dĭ-nī′əl) *n.* **1.** A negative reply, as to a request; a refusal to comply or satisfy. **2.** Refusal to grant the truth of a statement or allegation; contradiction. **3.** A rejection, as of a doctrine or belief. **4.** A disowning or disavowal; repudiation. **5.** Abstinence; self-denial. [From DENY.]

de·nic·o·tin·ize (dē-nĭk′ə-tĭ-nīz′) *tr.v.* **-ized, -izing, -izes.** Also **de·nic·o·tine** (dē-nĭk′ə-tēn′), **-tined, -tining, -tines.** To remove nicotine from (tobacco, for example).

de·ni·er[1] (dĭ-nī′ər) *n.* One who denies.

den·ier[2] (də-nyā′; *also* dĕn′yər *for sense 1; also* də-nîr′ *for sense 2*) *n.* **1.** A unit of fineness for rayon, nylon, and silk yarns, based on a standard of 50 milligrams per 450 meters of yarn. **2. a.** A small coin of varying composition and value current in France and western Europe from the eighth century until the French Revolution. **b.** *Archaic.* A small or trifling sum. [Middle English *denere,* a small coin, from Old French *denier,* from Latin *dēnārius,* DENARIUS.]

den·i·grate (dĕn′ĭ-grāt′) *tr.v.* **-grated, -grating, -grates. 1.** To belittle or calumniate the character or reputation of; defame. **2.** *Rare.* To blacken. [Latin *dēnigrāre,* to blacken : *dē-,* completely + *nigrāre,* blacken, from *niger,* black (see **niger** in Appendix*).] —**den′i·gra′tion** *n.* —**den′i·gra′tor** (-grā′tər) *n.*

den·im (dĕn′əm) *n.* **1. a.** A coarse twilled cloth used for overalls and work uniforms. **b.** *Plural.* Garments made of coarse denim. **2.** A finer grade of material used in draperies and upholstery. [French *(serge) de Nîmes,* serge of *Nîmes,* city in southern France.]

Den·is (dĕn′ĭs; *French* dĕ-nē′), **Saint.** Also **Den·ys.** Apostle to the Gauls in the third century A.D.; first Bishop of Paris; patron saint of France.

de·ni·tri·fy (dē-nī′trə-fī′) *tr.v.* **-fied, -fying, -fies.** To remove nitrogen from (a material or chemical compound), as by bacterial action on soil. —**de·ni′tri·fi·ca′tion** *n.*

den·i·zen (dĕn′ə-zən) *n.* **1.** An inhabitant; resident. **2.** *British.* A foreigner permitted certain rights and privileges of citizenship. **3.** *Ecology.* An animal or plant naturalized in a region to which it is not indigenous. —*tr.v.* **denizened, -zening, -zens.**

ă pat/ā pay/âr care/ä father/b **bib**/ch **church**/d **deed**/ĕ pet/ē be/f **fife**/g **gag**/h **hat**/hw **which**/ĭ pit/ī pie/îr pier/j **judge**/k **kick**/l **lid,** needle/m **mum**/n **no,** sudden/ng **thing**/ŏ pot/ō toe/ô paw, for/oi noise/ou out/ŏŏ took/ōō boot/p **pop**/r **roar**/s **sauce**/sh **ship,** dish/

British. To make a denizen of; naturalize. [Middle English *denisein,* from Old French *denzein,* from *deinz,* within, from Late Latin *dēintus,* from within : Latin *dē-,* from + *intus,* within (see **en** in Appendix*).] —**den'i·zen·a'tion** *n.*

Den·mark (dĕn'märk'). *Danish* **Dan·mark** (dăn'märk'). *Abbr.* **Den.** A kingdom of northern Europe, 16,576 square miles in area, consisting of a peninsula and an archipelago between the North and Baltic seas. Population, 4,684,000. Capital, Copenhagen.

Den·mark Strait (dĕn'märk'). A sea passage, 300 miles long and 130 miles wide, between Greenland and Iceland, connecting the Arctic Ocean with the Atlantic.

den mother. A woman who supervises a den of Cub Scouts.

Den·ner (dĕn'ər), **Johann Christoph.** 1655–1707. German maker of woodwind instruments; inventor of the clarinet.

Den·nis (dĕn'ĭs). Also **Den·is.** A masculine given name. [Middle English *Denes, Dionisius,* from Latin *Dionȳsius,* DIONYSUS.]

denom. denomination (religious sect).

de·nom·i·nate (dĭ-nŏm'ə-nāt') *tr.v.* **-nated, -nating, -nates.** To give a name to; designate. [Latin *dēnōmināre* : *dē-,* completely + *nōmināre,* to name, from *nōmen,* name (see **nomen-** in Appendix*).] —**de·nom'i·na·ble** (-nə-bəl) *adj.*

de·nom·i·nate number (dĭ-nŏm'ə-nĭt). A number that designates a quantity as a multiple of a unit. In the expression *12 pounds, 12* is a denominate number.

de·nom·i·na·tion (dĭ-nŏm'ə-nā'shən) *n.* **1.** The act of naming. **2.** A name; designation. **3.** The name of a class or group; classification. **4.** A class of units having specified values, as in a system of currency or weights. **5.** *Abbr.* **denom.** An organized group of religious congregations. —See Synonyms at **name.** —**de·nom'i·na'tion·al** *adj.* —**de·nom'i·na'tion·al·ly** *adv.*

de·nom·i·na·tion·al·ism (dĭ-nŏm'ə-nā'shən-ə-lĭz'əm) *n.* **1.** The tendency to separate into religious sects or denominations. **2.** Advocacy of such separation. **3.** Strict adherence to a denomination; sectarianism. —**de·nom'i·na'tion·al·ist** *n.*

de·nom·i·na·tive (dĭ-nŏm'ə-nā'tĭv, -nə-tĭv) *adj.* **1.** Giving or constituting a name; naming; appellative. **2.** *Grammar.* Formed from a noun or adjective. —*n.* A word, especially a verb, that is derived from a noun or adjective, such as the verb *to bus* from the noun *bus.*

de·nom·i·na·tor (dĭ-nŏm'ə-nā'tər) *n.* The quantity below the line indicating division in a fraction; the quantity that divides the numerator. Compare **numerator.**

de·no·ta·tion (dē'nō-tā'shən) *n.* **1.** The act of denoting; indication. **2.** A sign, symbol, or reference that denotes; indicator. **3.** Something signified or referred to; a particular meaning of a symbol. **4.** The explicit meaning of a word, as opposed to its connotation.

de·no·ta·tive (dĭ-nō'tə-tĭv, dē'nō-tā'-) *adj.* **1.** Able to denote; designative. **2.** Explicit. —**de·no'ta·tive·ly** *adv.*

de·note (dĭ-nōt') *tr.v.* **-noted, -noting, -notes. 1.** To reveal or indicate; mark. **2.** To serve as a symbol or name for; signify. **3.** To refer to specifically; mean explicitly. —See Synonyms at **mean** (convey sense). [Old French *denoter,* from Latin *dēnotāre* : *dē-,* completely + *notāre,* mark, from *nota,* NOTE.] —**de·not'a·ble** *adj.* —**de·no'tive** *adj.*

dé·noue·ment (dā-nōō-mäN') *n.* Also **de·noue·ment. 1.** The solution, clarification, or unraveling of the plot of a play or novel. **2.** Any outcome or final solution. [French, "an untying," from Old French *desnouement,* from *desno(u)er,* undo : *des-, de-,* reversing + *no(u)er,* to tie, from Latin *nōdāre,* from *nōdus,* knot (see **ned-** in Appendix*).]

de·nounce (dĭ-nouns') *tr.v.* **-nounced, -nouncing, -nounces. 1.** To condemn openly; censure, especially as evil. **2.** To accuse formally; inform against. **3.** To give formal announcement of the ending of (a treaty). —See Synonyms at **criticize.** [Middle English *denouncen,* from Old French *denoncier,* announce, from Latin *dēnūntiāre,* make an official announcement of : *dē-,* completely + *nūntiāre,* announce, from *nūntius,* messenger (see **neu-**¹ in Appendix*).] —**de·nounce'ment** *n.* —**de·nounc'er** *n.*

dense (dĕns) *adj.* **denser, densest. 1. a.** Having relatively high density. **b.** Crowded closely together; compact. **2.** Thick; impenetrable. **3.** Thickheaded; dull. **4.** *Photography.* Opaque, with good contrast between light and dark areas. Said of a developed negative. —See Synonyms at **stupid.** [Latin *dēnsus.* See **dens-**² in Appendix.*] —**dense'ly** *adv.* —**dense'ness** *n.*

den·sim·e·ter (dĕn-sĭm'ə-tər) *n.* An instrument used to determine density. [Latin *dēnsus,* DENSE + METER.] —**den'si·met'ric** (-sə-mĕt'rĭk) *adj.*

den·si·tom·e·ter (dĕn'sə-tŏm'ə-tər) *n.* An apparatus for measuring the optical density of a material, such as a negative. [DENSIT(Y) + METER.]

den·si·ty (dĕn'sə-tē) *n., pl.* **-ties. 1.** The degree or a measure of the degree to which anything is filled or occupied. **2.** *Physics.* **a.** The amount of something per unit measure, especially per unit length, area, or volume. See **charge density, current density, energy density. b.** The mass per unit volume of a substance under specified or standard conditions of pressure and temperature. Also called "mass density." **3.** The number of inhabitants per unit geographical region. Also called "population density." **4.** The degree of optical opacity of a medium or material, as of a photographic negative. **5.** Thickness of consistency; impenetrability. **6.** Stupidity; dullness.

dent (dĕnt) *n.* A depression in a surface made by pressure or a blow. —*v.* **dented, denting, dents.** —*tr.* To make a dent in. —*intr.* To become dented. [Middle English *dent,* variant of *dint,* strike, blow, Old English *dynt,* from Germanic *dunti-* (unattested).]

dent. dental; dentist; dentistry.

den·tal (dĕnt'l) *adj.* **1.** *Abbr.* **dent.** Of, pertaining to, or for the teeth. **2.** *Abbr.* **dent.** Of, pertaining to, or for dentistry. **3.** *Phonetics.* Produced with the tip of the tongue near or against the upper front teeth; alveolar. —*n. Phonetics.* A dental consonant. [New Latin *dentalis,* from Latin *dēns* (stem *dent-*), tooth. See **dent-** in Appendix.*]

dental floss. A strong waxed thread used to clean areas between the teeth.

dental plate. A **denture** *(see).*

den·tate (dĕn'tāt') *adj.* Edged with toothlike projections; toothed. [Latin *dentātus,* from *dēns* (stem *dent-*), tooth. See **dent-** in Appendix.*] —**den'tate'ly** *adv.*

den·ta·tion (dĕn-tā'shən) *n.* **1.** The condition of being dentate. **2.** A toothlike part or projection.

dent corn. A tall-growing variety of corn, *Zea mays indentata,* having yellow or white kernels that are indented at the tip.

denti-, dent-. Indicates tooth; for example, **dentiform, dentoid.** [From Latin *dēns* (stem *dent-*), tooth. See **dent-** in Appendix.*]

den·ti·cle (dĕn'tĭ-kəl) *n.* A small tooth or toothlike projection. [Middle English, from Latin *denticulus,* diminutive of *dēns* (stem *dent-*), tooth. See **dent-** in Appendix.*]

den·tic·u·late (dĕn-tĭk'yə-lĭt) *adj.* Also **den·tic·u·lat·ed** (-lā'tĭd). **1.** Finely toothed; minutely dentate. **2.** *Architecture.* Having dentils. [Latin *denticulātus,* from *denticulus,* DENTICLE.] —**den·tic'u·late·ly** *adv.* —**den·tic'u·la'tion** *n.*

den·ti·form (dĕn'tə-fôrm') *adj.* Shaped like a tooth. [DENTI- + -FORM.]

den·ti·frice (dĕn'tə-frĭs) *n.* A substance, such as a powder or paste, for cleaning the teeth. [Old French, from Latin *dentifricium* : DENTI- + *fricāre,* to rub (see **bhrēi-** in Appendix*).]

den·til (dĕn'tĭl) *n. Architecture.* One of a series of small rectangular blocks forming a molding or projecting beneath a cornice. [Obsolete French *dentille,* from Old French, diminutive of *dent,* tooth, from Latin *dēns* (stem *dent-*), tooth. See **denti-.**]

den·ti·la·bi·al (dĕn'tĭ-lā'bē-əl) *adj. Phonetics.* Labiodental. [DENTI- + LABIAL.] —**den'ti·la'bi·al** *n.*

den·ti·lin·gual (dĕn'tĭ-lĭng'gwəl) *adj. Phonetics.* Interdental. [DENTI- + LINGUAL.] —**den'ti·lin'gual** *n.*

den·tine (dĕn'tēn') *n.* Also **den·tin** (-tĭn). The calcareous part of a tooth, beneath the enamel, containing the pulp chamber and root canals. [DENT(I)- + -INE.] —**den'ti·nal** *adj.*

den·tist (dĕn'tĭst) *n. Abbr.* **dent.** A person whose profession is dentistry. [French *dentiste,* from *dent,* tooth. See **dentil.**]

den·tist·ry (dĕn'tĭ-strē) *n. Abbr.* **dent.** The diagnosis, prevention, and treatment of diseases of the teeth and related structures, including the repair or replacement of defective teeth.

den·ti·tion (dĕn-tĭsh'ən) *n.* **1.** *Biology.* The type, number, and arrangement of teeth, especially in animals. **2.** The cutting of teeth; a teething. [Latin *dentītiō,* from *dentītus,* past participle of *dentīre,* teethe, from *dēns* (stem *dent-*), tooth. See **denti-.**]

den·toid (dĕn'toid') *adj.* Toothlike. [DENT(I)- + -OID.]

D'En·tre·cas·teaux Islands (däN'trə-kăs'tō'). An island group, about 1,200 square miles in area, in the southwestern Pacific, administered as part of the Trust Territory of New Guinea.

den·tu·lous (dĕn'chə-ləs) *adj.* Possessing teeth; toothed.

den·ture (dĕn'chər) *n.* A set of artificial teeth. Also called "dental plate." [French, from Old French, from *dent,* tooth. See **dentil.**]

de·nu·date (dĭ-nōō'dāt', dĭ-nyōō'-) *tr.v.* **-dated, -dating, -dates.** To denude. —*adj.* Bare; denuded. [Latin *dēnūdāre,* DENUDE.]

de·nude (dĭ-nōōd', -nyōōd') *tr.v.* **-nuded, -nuding, -nudes. 1.** To divest of covering; make bare. **2.** *Geology.* To expose (rock strata) by erosion. —See Synonyms at **strip.** [Latin *dēnūdāre* : *dē-,* thoroughly + *nūdāre,* to make bare, from *nūdus,* NUDE.] —**den'u·da'tion** (dĕn'yōō-dā'shən) *n.*

de·nu·mer·a·ble (dĭ-nōō'mər-ə-bəl, dĭ-nyōō'-) *adj.* Capable of being put into one-to-one correspondence with the positive integers; countable. —**de·nu'mer·a·bly** *adv.*

de·nun·ci·ate (dĭ-nŭn'sē-āt', -shē-āt') *tr.v.* **-ated, -ating, -ates.** To denounce. [Latin *dēnūntiāre,* to DENOUNCE.]

de·nun·ci·a·tion (dĭ-nŭn'sē-ā'shən, -shē-ā'shən) *n.* **1.** The act of denouncing; open condemnation or censure. **2.** The act of accusing another of a crime before a public prosecutor. **3.** A formal declaration of the termination of a treaty.

Den·ver (dĕn'vər). The capital of Colorado, in the north-central part of the state. Population, 494,000.

de·ny (dĭ-nī') *tr.v.* **-nied, -nying, -nies. 1.** To declare untrue; assert the contrary of; contradict. **2.** To refuse to believe; reject. **3.** To refuse to recognize or acknowledge; disavow; disown. **4.** To refuse to grant; withhold. —**deny oneself.** To abstain from indulging oneself in. [Middle English *denien,* from Old French *denier,* from Latin *dēnegāre* : *dē-,* completely + *negāre,* say no (see **ne** in Appendix*).]

Synonyms: *deny, gainsay, contradict, refute.* These verbs mean to dispute the truthfulness of a statement or speaker. *Deny,* the most general, usually implies an open declaration that something is untrue. *Gainsay* more often appears in the negative to stress the unlikelihood or impossibility of opposing or rejecting. *Contradict* involves an assertion that the opposite of a statement is true. *Refute* emphasizes the marshaling of evidence to disprove something.

Den·ys. See Saint **Denis.**

de·o·dar (dē'ə-där') *n.* A tall cedar, *Cedrus deodara,* native to the Himalayas, having drooping branches and wood valued as timber. [Hindi *dē'odār,* from Sanskrit *devadāru* : *devás,* divine (see **deiw-** in Appendix*) + *dāru,* wood (see **deru-** in Appendix*).]

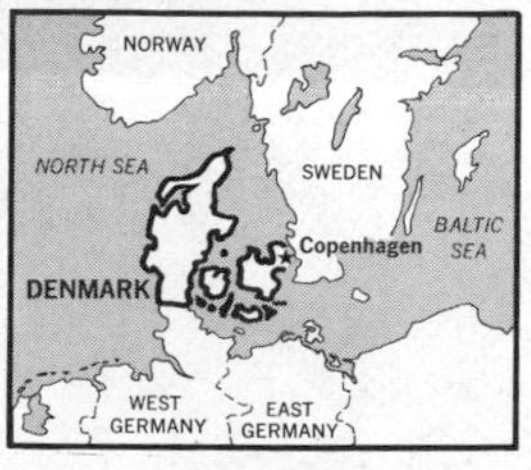

Denmark

t tight/th thin, path/*th* this, bathe/ŭ cut/ûr urge/v valve/w with/y yes/z zebra, size/zh vision/ə about, item, edible, gallop, circus/ à *Fr.* ami/œ *Fr.* feu, *Ger.* schön/ü *Fr.* tu, *Ger.* über/KH *Ger.* ich, *Scot.* loch/N *Fr.* bon. ***Follows main vocabulary. †Of obscure origin.**

de·o·dor·ant (dē-ō'dər-ənt) n. **1.** A substance applied to counteract body odors. **2.** A chemical exposed to or sprayed into the air to counteract staleness. —adj. Capable of destroying or disguising odors. [DE- (removal) + ODOR + -ANT.]

de·o·dor·ize (dē-ō'də-rīz') tr.v. -ized, -izing, -izes. To disguise or absorb the odor of. —de·o'dor·i·za'tion n. —de·o'dor·iz'er n.

de·on·tol·o·gy (dē'ŏn-tŏl'ə-jē) n. The theory or study of moral obligation or commitment; ethics. [Greek deon (stem deont-), that which is binding or needful (influenced in meaning by dein, to bind), from dei, it is necessary, from dein, to need, want, lack (see deu-¹ in Appendix*) + -LOGY.] —de·on'to·log'i·cal (-tə-lŏj'ĭ-kəl) adj. —de'on·tol'o·gist n.

De·o vo·len·te (dē'ō vō-lĕn'tē, dā'ō vō-lĕn'tā). Abbr. **D.V.** Latin. God willing.

de·ox·i·dize (dē-ŏk'sə-dīz') tr.v. -dized, -dizing, -dizes. To remove oxygen, especially chemically combined oxygen, from. —de·ox'i·di·za'tion n. —de·ox'i·diz'er n.

deoxy-. Indicates that a molecule contains less oxygen than another to which it is related; for example, **deoxyribonucleic acid.**

de·ox·y·cor·ti·co·ster·one (dē-ŏk'sē-kôr-tē-kŏs'tə-rōn) n. A steroid hormone, $C_{21}H_{30}O_3$, derived from the adrenal cortex and used to treat adrenal insufficiency.

de·ox·y·gen·ate (dē-ŏk'sə-jə-nāt') tr.v. -ated, -ating, -ates. To remove oxygen from. —de·ox'y·gen·a'tion n.

de·ox·y·ri·bo·nu·cle·ic acid (dē-ŏk'sē-rī-bō-noo-klē'ĭk, -nyoō-klē'ĭk). Abbr. **DNA** A polymeric chromosomal constituent of living cell nuclei, consisting of two long chains of alternating phosphate and deoxyribose units twisted into a double helix and joined by hydrogen bonds between the complementary bases adenine and thymine or cytosine and guanine, each of which projects toward the axis of the helix from one of the strands where it is bonded in a sequence that determines individual hereditary characteristics. [DEOXY- + RIBONUCLEIC ACID.]

de·oxy·ri·bose (dē-ŏk'sĭ-rī'bōs) n. A sugar, $C_5H_{10}O_4$, that is a constituent of deoxyribonucleic acid.

dep. **1.** depart; departure. **2.** department. **3.** deponent. **4.** deposed. **5.** deposit. **6.** depot. **7.** deputy.

Dep. dependency (territorial).

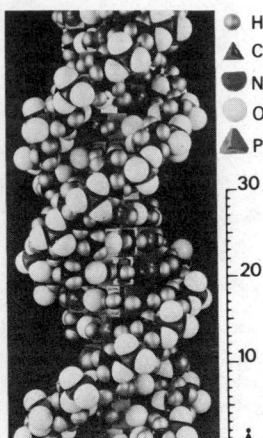

H
C
N
O
P

deoxyribonucleic acid
Structural model of DNA

de·part (dĭ-pärt') v. -parted, -parting, -parts. —intr. **1.** To go away; set forth; leave. **2.** To vary, as from a regular course; deviate: depart from custom. —tr. To leave. Used especially in the phrase depart this life. [Middle English departen, divide, from Old French departir : de-, away + partir, go, divide, from Latin partīre, from pars (stem part-), PART.]

de·part·ed (dĭ-pär'tĭd) adj. **1.** Bygone; past. **2.** Dead. —See Synonyms at dead.

de·part·ment (dĭ-pärt'mənt) n. Abbr. **D., dep., dept., dpt.** **1.** A distinct division of a large organization, such as a government, company, or store, having a specialized function and personnel and often housed separately. **2.** Usually capital **D.** One of the principal executive divisions of the Federal government of the United States, headed by a cabinet officer. **3.** An administrative district in the government of France. **4.** A division of a school or college dealing with a particular field of knowledge: the physics department. **5.** Informal. An area of special knowledge or activity; sphere. [French département, from Old French, departure, from departir, divide, DEPART.]

de·part·men·tal (dē'pärt·mĕn'təl) adj. Pertaining to a department or departments. —de'part·men'tal·ly adv.

de·part·men·tal·ize (dē-pärt'mĕn'təl-īz') tr.v. -ized, -izing, -izes. To organize into departments. —de'part·men'tal·i·za'tion n.

department store. A large retail establishment offering a wide variety of merchandise and services, and organized into departments according to the kinds of goods sold.

de·par·ture (dĭ-pär'chər) n. Abbr. **dep.** **1.** The act of leaving; a going away. **2.** A starting out, as on a trip or a new course of action. **3.** A deviation or divergence, as from an established rule, plan, or procedure. **4.** Nautical. **a.** The distance sailed due east or west by a ship on its course. **b.** A ship's bearing at the start of a voyage, used as a basis for dead reckoning.

de·pend (dĭ-pĕnd') intr.v. -pended, -pending, -pends. **1.** To rely, as for support or aid. Used with on or upon. **2.** To be assured; to place trust. Used with on or upon. **3.** To be determined, conditioned, or dependent. Used with on or upon: "Whether Ann is good-looking or not depends upon your taste" (G.B. Shaw). **4.** To hang down. Used with from. **5.** To be pending or undecided. —See Synonyms at rely. [Middle English dependen, from Old French dependre, hang down, from Latin dēpendēre : dē-, down + pendēre, to hang (see spen- in Appendix*).]

Usage: Depend. indicating condition or contingency, is always followed by on or upon in examples such as: It depends upon who is in charge. Omission of the prepositions is typical of casual speech.

de·pend·a·ble (dĭ-pĕn'də-bəl) adj. Capable of being depended upon; trustworthy. —de·pend'a·bil'i·ty, de·pend'a·ble·ness n. —de·pend'a·bly adv.

de·pen·dence (dĭ-pĕn'dəns) n. Also **de·pen·dance.** **1.** The state of being dependent, as for support. **2.** Subordination to someone or something needed or greatly desired. **3.** The state of being determined, influenced, or controlled by something else. **4.** Trust; reliance. —See Synonyms at trust.

de·pen·den·cy (dĭ-pĕn'dən-sē) n., pl. -cies. Also **de·pen·dan·cy.** **1.** Dependence. **2.** Anything dependent or subordinate. **3.** Abbr. A territory or state under the jurisdiction of another country from which it is separated geographically.

de·pen·dent (dĭ-pĕn'dənt) adj. Also **de·pen·dant.** **1.** Contingent upon something or someone else: "The past is not dependent on us for its existence, but exists in its own right." (Henry Steele Commager). **2.** Subordinate. **3.** Unable to exist or function satisfactorily without the aid or use of another: "He is a man dependent to the point of childishness on his money" (Erik Erikson). **4.** Hanging down. —n. Also **de·pen·dant.** One who relies on another for support. —de·pend'ent·ly adv.

dependent clause. Grammar. A clause that cannot stand alone as a full sentence and that functions as a noun, adjective, or adverb within a sentence. Also called "subordinate clause."

dependent variable. Mathematics. A variable restricted to one or more of a set of values for every value assumed by an independent variable.

de·per·son·al·ize (dē-pûr'sə-nə-līz') tr.v. -ized, -izing, -izes. **1.** To deprive of personal or individual character. **2.** To render impersonal. —de·per'son·al·i·za'tion n.

de·phleg·ma·tor (dē-flĕg'mā'tər) n. A device used in distillation to condense the higher boiling constituents of a mixed vapor. [From DE- + PHLEGM.]

de·pict (dĭ-pikt') tr.v. -picted, -picting, -picts. **1.** To represent in a picture or sculpture. **2.** To represent in words; describe. [Latin dēpingere (past participle dēpictus) : dē-, completely + pingere, to picture (see peig-¹ in Appendix*).] —de·pic'tion n.

dep·i·late (dĕp'ə-lāt') tr.v. -lated, -lating, -lates. To remove hair from (the body). [Latin dēpilāre : dē-, completely + pilāre, deprive of hair, from pilus, hair (see pilo- in Appendix*).] —dep'i·la'tion n. —dep'i·la·tor (-lā'tər) n.

de·pil·a·to·ry (dĭ-pĭl'ə-tôr'ē, -tōr'ē) adj. Able to remove hair. —n., pl. depilatories. A liquid or cream used to remove unwanted hair from the body.

de·plane (dē-plān') intr.v. -planed, -planing, -planes. To disembark from an airplane.

de·plete (dĭ-plēt') tr.v. -pleted, -pleting, -pletes. To use up or exhaust. [Latin dēplēre (past participle dēplētus), to empty : dē- (reversal) + plēre, fill (see pel-⁸ in Appendix*).] —de·plet'a·ble adj. —de·ple'tion n.

Synonyms: deplete, drain, exhaust, impoverish, enervate. These verbs all signify depletion of strength or resources to the point of functional impairment. Deplete refers to using up gradually, and only hints at harmful consequences. Drain suggests reduction by gradually drawing off, and is stronger in implying harm. Exhaust stresses reduction to a point of no further usefulness in a given activity. Impoverish refers to severe reduction of resources or qualities essential to adequate functioning. Enervate refers to weakening of vitality or moral strength.

de·plor·a·ble (dĭ-plôr'ə-bəl, dĭ-plōr'ə-) adj. **1.** Worthy of severe reproach. **2.** Lamentable; grievous. **3.** Wretched; bad. —de·plor'a·ble·ness, de·plor'a·bil'i·ty n. —de·plor'a·bly adv.

de·plore (dĭ-plôr', -plōr') tr.v. -plored, -ploring, -plores. **1.** To feel or express deep sorrow over; to lament. **2.** To feel or express strong disapproval of; to censure: "American educators have long deplored our use of bargain-basement prices for education." (L.M. Kable). [Old French deplorer, from Latin dēplōrāre : dē-, completely + plōrāre†, to wail.]

de·ploy (dĭ-ploi') v. -ployed, -ploying, -ploys. —tr. **1.** To station (persons or forces) systematically over an area. **2.** Military. To spread out (troops) to form an extended front. —intr. To be or become deployed. [French déployer, from Latin displicāre, to scatter : dis- (reversal) + plicāre, to fold (see plek- in Appendix*).] —de·ploy'ment n.

de·plume (dē-ploōm') tr.v. -plumed, -pluming, -plumes. **1.** To pluck the feathers from. **2.** To deprive of honor or pride. [Middle English deplumen, from Old French deplumer, from Medieval Latin dēplumāre : Latin dē-, removal + plūma, feather (see pleus- in Appendix*).] —de'plu·ma'tion n.

de·po·lar·ize (dē-pō'lə-rīz') tr.v. -ized, -izing, -izes. To eliminate or counteract the polarization. —de·po'lar·i·za'tion n.

de·pone (dĭ-pōn') v. -poned, -poning, -pones. Archaic. —tr. To testify or declare under oath. —intr. To give testimony. [Medieval Latin dēpōnere, from Latin, to put down : dē-, down + pōnere, put (see apo- in Appendix*).]

de·po·nent (dĭ-pō'nənt) adj. Abbr. **dep.** Grammar. Denoting a verb of active meaning but passive form, as certain Latin and Greek verbs. —n. Abbr. **dep., dpt.** **1.** A deponent verb. **2.** Law. A person who testifies under oath, especially in writing. [Late Latin dēpōnēns, "laying aside," from Latin, present participle of dēpōnere, to put down, lay aside. See depone.]

de·pop·u·late (dē-pŏp'yə-lāt') tr.v. -lated, -lating, -lates. To reduce sharply the population of, as by expulsion or massacre. [Latin dēpopulāre, ravage : dē-, completely + populāre, to ravage, from populus, people (see populus in Appendix*).] —de·pop'u·la'tion n. —de·pop'u·la·tor (-lā'tər) n.

de·port (dĭ-pôrt', -pōrt') tr.v. -ported, -porting, -ports. **1.** To expel from a country. **2.** To behave or conduct (oneself). —See Synonyms at banish. [Old French deporter, behave, from Latin dēportāre, carry off, carry away : dē-, away, off + portāre, carry (see per-² in Appendix*).]

de·por·ta·tion (dē'pôr-tā'shən, dē'pōr-) n. Banishment from a country; specifically, the expulsion of an undesirable alien.

de·por·tee (dē'pôr-tē', -pōr-tē') n. A deported person.

de·port·ment (dĭ-pôrt'mənt, dĭ-pōrt'-) n. Conduct; demeanor. See Synonyms at bearing, behavior.

de·pos·al (dĭ-pō'zəl) n. The act of deposing one from office.

de·pose (dĭ-pōz') v. -posed, -posing, -poses. —tr. **1.** To remove from office or a position of power. **2.** Law. To declare under oath, especially in writing. —intr. Law. To testify, especially in writing. [Middle English deposen, from Old French deposer : de-, away + poser, to put, POSE.] —de·pos'a·ble adj.

de·pos·it (dĭ-pŏz′ĭt) *v.* **-ited, -iting, -its.** *—tr.* **1.** To place carefully or safely in the proper repository. **2.** To put down or place, especially in a layer or layers, by a natural process. **3.** To give (money) as partial payment or security. **4.** To entrust (money) to a bank. *—intr.* To become deposited; to precipitate; settle. *—n. Abbr.* **dep. 1.** Something entrusted for safekeeping, such as a sum of money in a bank. **2.** The condition of being entrusted for safekeeping. Usually used in the phrase *on* (or *in*) *deposit.* **3.** A partial or initial payment of a cost or debt. **4.** A sum of money given as security for an item acquired for temporary use. **5.** A depository. **6.** Something deposited, especially by a natural process, as: **a.** *Geology.* Mineral or sandy matter settled out of water or accumulated in a vein. **b.** *Physiology.* A sediment in a bodily fluid or a localized bodily accretion, as of calcium. [Latin *dēpōnere* (past participle *dēpositus*), to put aside : *dē-*, aside + *pōnere*, put (see **apo-** in Appendix*).] —**de·pos′i·tor** (-pŏz′ə-tər) *n.*

de·pos·i·tar·y (dĭ-pŏz′ə-tĕr′ē) *n., pl.* **-ies. 1.** A person or group entrusted with the preservation or safekeeping of something. **2.** A repository; depository.

dep·o·si·tion (dĕp′ə-zĭsh′ən) *n.* **1.** The act of deposing, as from high office. **2.** The act of depositing. **3.** Something deposited; a deposit. **4.** *Law.* Testimony under oath; especially, a written statement by a witness for use in court in his absence. **5.** *Capital* **D.** The taking down of Christ from the cross, or a work of art depicting this scene.

de·pos·i·to·ry (dĭ-pŏz′ə-tôr′ē, -tōr′ē) *n., pl.* **-ries. 1.** A place where something is deposited for safekeeping; repository. **2.** A depositary: *"I know of no safe depository of the ultimate powers of the society but the people"* (Jefferson).

de·pot (dē′pō) *n. Abbr.* **dep. 1.** A railroad or bus station. **2.** A warehouse or storehouse. **3.** *Military.* **a.** A centrally located installation for the storage, repair, or distribution of military equipment and materials. **b.** A station for receiving, classifying, and assembling personnel. [French *dépôt*, from Old French *depost*, from Latin *dēpositum*, deposit, from the neuter past participle of *dēpōnere*, to DEPOSIT.]

de·prave (dĭ-prāv′) *tr.v.* **-praved, -praving, -praves.** To deprive of rectitude; debase morally; corrupt. [Middle English *depraven*, from Old French *depraver*, to pervert, from Latin *dēprāvāre* : *dē-*, completely + *prāvus*†, distorted, crooked.] —**dep′ra·va′tion** (dĕp′rə-vā′shən) *n.* —**de·prav′er** *n.*

de·praved (dĭ-prāvd′) *adj.* Morally corrupt; debased; perverted.

de·prav·i·ty (dĭ-prăv′ə-tē) *n., pl.* **-ties. 1.** Moral corruption. **2.** A wicked or perverse act.

dep·re·cate (dĕp′rĭ-kāt′) *tr.v.* **-cated, -cating, -cates. 1.** To express disapproval of; protest or plead against. **2.** To depreciate; belittle. See Usage note below. [Latin *dēprecārī*, to ward off by prayer : *dē-*, away + *precārī*, pray (see **perk-²** in Appendix*).] —**dep′re·ca′tion** *n.* —**dep′re·ca′tor** *n.*

Usage: *Deprecate* is now sometimes employed in the approximate sense of *depreciate* (*to belittle, make to seem less*), frequently with reference to mild self-belittlement: *modestly deprecated his own contribution; self-deprecating* (or *self-deprecatory*) *manner.* The practice probably is traceable to the similarity in appearance (although not in basic meaning) between *deprecate* and *depreciate*, and it is not well established. The preceding examples are acceptable (in the sense of *depreciate*) to 52 per cent of the Usage Panel.

dep·re·ca·to·ry (dĕp′rə-kə-tôr′ē, -tōr′ē) *adj.* Also **dep·re·ca·tive** (-kā′tĭv). Expressing deprecation; disapproving.

de·pre·ci·a·ble (dĭ-prē′shē-ə-bəl) *adj.* Capable of depreciation in value.

de·pre·ci·ate (dĭ-prē′shē-āt′) *v.* **-ated, -ating, -ates.** *—tr.* **1.** To lessen the price or value of. **2.** To make to seem less; belittle: *"Contemporary liberalism does not depreciate emotion in the abstract"* (Lionel Trilling). *—intr.* To diminish in value or price. [Medieval Latin *dēpreciāre*, manuscript error for Late Latin *dēpretiāre* : *dē-*, down from + *pretium*, price (see **per¹** in Appendix*).] —**de·pre′ci·a′tor** (-ā′tər) *n.*

de·pre·ci·a·tion (dĭ-prē′shē-ā′shən) *n.* **1.** A decrease or loss in value because of wear, age, or other cause. **2.** *Accounting.* An allowance made for this loss. **3.** A reduction in the purchasing value of money. **4.** A disparaging; a belittling.

de·pre·ci·a·to·ry (dĭ-prē′shē-ə-tôr′ē, -tōr′ē) *adj.* Also **de·pre·ci·a·tive** (-ā′tĭv). **1.** Tending to diminish in value. **2.** Disparaging; slighting.

dep·re·date (dĕp′rə-dāt′) *v.* **-dated, -dating, -dates.** *—tr.* To prey upon; to plunder. *—intr.* To commit plunder. [Late Latin *dēpraedārī* : Latin *dē-*, completely + *praedārī*, to plunder, to make booty, from *praeda*, booty (see **ghend-** in Appendix*).] —**dep′re·da′tion** *n.* —**dep′re·da′tor** (-dā′tər) *n.* —**dep′re·da′to·ry** (-dā′tə-rē) *adj.*

De·prés. See **des Prés.**

de·press (dĭ-prĕs′) *tr.v.* **-pressed, -pressing, -presses. 1.** To dispirit; sadden. **2.** To press down; lower: *depress a pedal.* **3.** To lower prices in (a stock market). [Middle English *depressen*, from Old French *depresser*, from Latin *deprimere* (past participle *depressus*) : *de-*, down + *premere*, to press (see **per-⁶** in Appendix*).]

de·pres·sant (dĭ-prĕs′ənt) *adj.* Serving to lower the rate of vital activities. *—n.* A depressant drug.

de·pressed (dĭ-prĕst′) *adj.* **1.** In low spirits; dejected. **2.** *Botany.* Flattened downward, as if pressed from above. **3.** *Zoology.* Flattened along the dorsal and ventral surfaces. **4.** Sunk below the surrounding region: *the depressed center of a crater.* **5.** Economically and socially below standard; troubled with widespread poverty and unemployment. —See Synonyms at **sad.**

de·pres·sion (dĭ-prĕsh′ən) *n.* **1. a.** The act of depressing. **b.** The condition of being depressed. **2.** An area that is sunk below its surroundings; a hollow: *"Their home was a long, shallow, grassy depression"* (J.H. Parry). **3.** *Meteorology.* A region or reading of low barometric pressure. **4.** The angular distance below the horizontal plane through the point of observation. **5.** *Astronomy.* The angular distance of a celestial body below the horizon. **6.** *Economics.* A period of drastic decline in the national economy, characterized by decreasing business activity, falling prices, and unemployment. **7.** Despondency; melancholy; dejection. —See Synonyms at **despair.**

de·pres·sive (dĭ-prĕs′ĭv) *adj.* **1.** Causing depression. **2.** Psychologically characterized by the inability to respond to all or selected stimuli, by low initiative, and by sullen or despondent attitudes. —**de·pres′sive·ly** *adv.* —**de·pres′sive·ness** *n.*

de·pres·sor (dĭ-prĕs′ər) *n.* **1.** Something that depresses or is used to depress. **2.** A **depressor nerve** *(see).* **3.** Any of several muscles that cause depression or contraction of a part. **4.** Any instrument, such as a tongue depressor, used to depress a part. *—adj. Physiology.* Of or pertaining to a nerve that depresses.

depressor nerve. A nerve that lowers arterial blood pressure. Also called "depressor."

dep·ri·va·tion (dĕp′rə-vā′shən) *n.* Also **de·priv·al** (dĭ-prī′vəl). **1. a.** The act of depriving. **b.** The condition of being deprived. **2.** Privation. **3.** A taking away of rank or office.

de·prive (dĭ-prīv′) *tr.v.* **-prived, -priving, -prives. 1.** To take something away from; dispossess; divest. **2.** To keep from the possession or enjoyment of something; deny. **3.** To take a position from; depose from office. [Middle English *depriven*, from Old French *depriver*, from Medieval Latin *dēprīvāre* : Latin *dē-*, completely + *prīvāre*, deprive, from *prīvus*, individual, private (see **per¹** in Appendix*).] —**de·priv′a·ble** *adj.*

dept. 1. department. **2.** deputy.

Dept·ford (dĕt′fərd). A former administrative division of London, England, now part of **Lewisham** *(see).*

depth (dĕpth) *n.* **1.** The condition or quality of being deep; deepness. **2.** The extent, measurement, or dimension downward, backward, or inward. **3.** *Often plural.* A deep part of or place in something. **4.** *Often plural.* The middle, inner, or most remote or inaccessible part. **5.** The most profound or intense part or stage: *the depth of despair.* **6.** The severest or worst part: *in the depth of winter.* **7.** Intellectual penetration; profundity. **8.** The range of one's understanding or competence: *beyond one's depth.* **9.** Richness; intensity; darkness: *depth of color.* **10.** Lowness in pitch. —**in depth.** With thorough coverage of matters likely to be overlooked: *a study in depth.* [Middle English *depthe*, probably from *dep*, DEEP.]

depth charge. Any charge designed for explosion under water, especially such a charge dropped or catapulted from a ship's deck and used against submarines.

depth perception. Perception of spatial relationships, especially of distances between objects, in three dimensions.

depth psychology. 1. Any psychology of the unconscious, especially as distinguished from the psychology of conscious behavior. **2.** Loosely, psychoanalysis.

dep·u·rate (dĕp′yə-rāt′) *v.* **-rated, -rating, -rates.** *—tr.* To cleanse or purify. *—intr.* To become cleansed or purified. [Medieval Latin *dēpūrāre* : Latin *dē-*, removal + *pūrāre*, purify, from *pūrus*, pure (see **peuə-¹** in Appendix*).] —**dep′u·ra′tion** *n.* —**dep′u·ra′tor** (-rā′tər) *n.*

dep·u·ta·tion (dĕp′yə-tā′shən) *n.* **1. a.** The act of deputing. **b.** The state of being deputed. **2.** A person or group appointed to represent another or others; delegation.

de·pute (dĭ-pyo͞ot′) *tr.v.* **-puted, -puting, -putes. 1.** To appoint or authorize as an agent or representative. **2.** To assign (authority or duties) to another or others; delegate. [Middle English *deputen*, from Old French *deputer*, from Late Latin *dēputāre*, allot, from Latin, "to cut off," consider : *dē-*, off + *putāre*, to prune, cut, esteem (see **peuə-²** in Appendix*).]

dep·u·tize (dĕp′yə-tīz′) *v.* **-tized, -tizing, -tizes.** *—tr.* To appoint as a deputy. *—intr.* To serve as a deputy.

dep·u·ty (dĕp′yə-tē) *n., pl.* **-ties.** *Abbr.* **d., D., dep., dept. 1.** A person named or empowered to act for another. **2.** An assistant exercising full authority in the absence of his superior and equal authority in emergencies. **3.** A representative in a legislative body in certain countries, such as France. *—adj.* Acting as deputy. [Middle English *depute*, from Old French, from the past participle of *deputer*, DEPUTE.]

De Quin·cey (dĭ kwĭn′sē), **Thomas.** 1785–1859. English essayist and critic.

der. derivation; derivative.

de·rac·i·nate (dĭ-răs′ə-nāt′) *tr.v.* **-nated, -nating, -nates. 1.** To pull out by the roots; uproot. **2.** To displace from a natural environment; dislocate. [From French *déraciner*, from Old French *desraciner* : *des-*, *de-* (sense of undoing) + *racine*, root, from Late Latin *radīcīna*, from Latin *rādix* (stem *rādīc-*) (see **werād-** in Appendix*).] —**de·rac′i·na′tion** *n.*

de·rail (dē-rāl′) *v.* **-railed, -railing, -rails.** *—tr.* To cause (a train) to run off the rails. *—intr.* To run off the rails. [French *dérailler* : *dé-*, off + *rail*, RAIL.] —**de·rail′ment** *n.*

De·rain (də-răN′), **André.** 1880–1954. French painter.

de·range (dĭ-rānj′) *tr.v.* **-ranged, -ranging, -ranges. 1.** To disturb the order or arrangement of; disorder; disarrange. **2.** To disturb the normal condition or functioning of; upset. **3.** To unbalance mentally; make insane. [French *déranger*, from Old French *desrengier* : *de-* (sense of undoing) + *reng*, *renc*, line, from (unattested) Frankish *hring* (see **sker-³** in Appendix*).]

de·range·ment (dĭ-rānj′mənt) *n.* **1.** Severe mental disorder; insanity. **2.** Disarrangement; confusion; disorder.

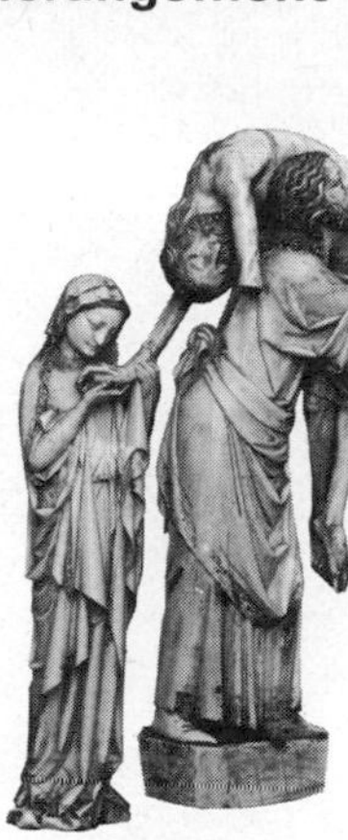

Deposition

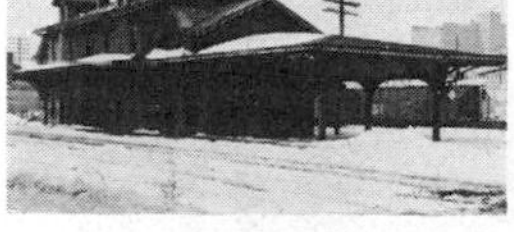

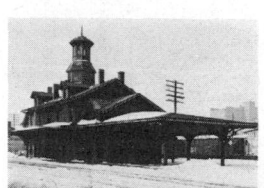

depot
A depot at Wilkes-Barre, Pennsylvania

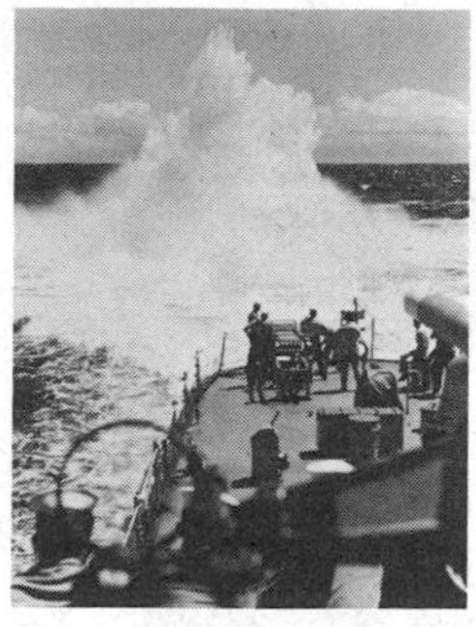

depth charge
Explosion of a depth charge off the U.S.S. *Philip*

der·by (dûr′bē) *n., pl.* **-bies.** A stiff felt hat with a round crown and a narrow, curved brim. Also called "bowler." [After DERBY (race).]

Der·by¹ (där′bē *for sense 1;* dûr′bē *for senses 2, 3*) *n.* **1.** A horse race for three-year-olds, held annually at Epsom Downs in Surrey, England. **2.** Any of various other horse races, especially the Kentucky Derby. **3.** *Small* **d.** Any formal race with a more or less open field of contestants: *a soapbox derby.* [Founded in 1780 by the 12th Earl of *Derby* (died 1834).]

Der·by² (där′bē). **1.** Also **Der·by·shire** (där′bē-shîr, -shər). A county occupying 1,006 square miles in central England. Population, 901,000. **2.** The seat of this county, a mining and manufacturing center in the south. Population, 130,000.

dere. Variant of **dear** (dire).

der·e·lict (dĕr′ə-lĭkt) *adj.* **1.** Neglectful of duty or obligation; remiss; delinquent. **2.** Deserted by an owner or guardian; abandoned; forsaken. —*n.* **1.** Abandoned property; especially, a ship abandoned at sea. **2.** A social outcast; vagrant. **3.** *Law.* Land left dry by a permanent recession of the water line. [Latin *dērelictus,* past participle of *dērelinquere,* abandon : *dē-,* completely + *relinquere,* leave behind : *re-,* behind + *linquere,* leave (see **leikw-** in Appendix*).]

der·e·lic·tion (dĕr′ə-lĭk′shən) *n.* **1.** Willful neglect, as of duty. **2.** Abandonment. **3.** *Law.* **a.** A gaining of land by the permanent recession of the water line. **b.** The land so gained.

de·ride (dĭ-rīd′) *tr.v.* **-rided, -riding, -rides.** To speak of or treat with contemptuous mirth; scoff at: *"eminent scientists continue to deride the rocket pioneers"* (Arthur C. Clarke). See Synonyms at **ridicule.** [Latin *dērīdēre* : *dē-* (pejorative) + *rīdēre,* to laugh at (see **wer-³** in Appendix*).] —**de·rid′er** *n.*

de ri·gueur (də rē-gœr′). *French.* Required by the current fashion or custom; socially obligatory.

der·in·ger. Variant of **derringer.**

de·ri·sion (dĭ-rĭzh′ən) *n.* **1. a.** Scoffing; ridicule. **b.** A state of being derided. **2.** An object of ridicule; laughingstock. [Middle English *derisioun,* from Old French *derision,* from Late Latin *dērīsiō,* from Latin *dērīsus,* past participle of *dērīdēre,* DERIDE.] —**de·ris′i·ble** *adj.*

de·ri·sive (dĭ-rī′sĭv) *adj.* Also **de·ri·so·ry** (-sə-rē). Mocking; scoffing. —**de·ri′sive·ly** *adv.* —**de·ri′sive·ness** *n.*

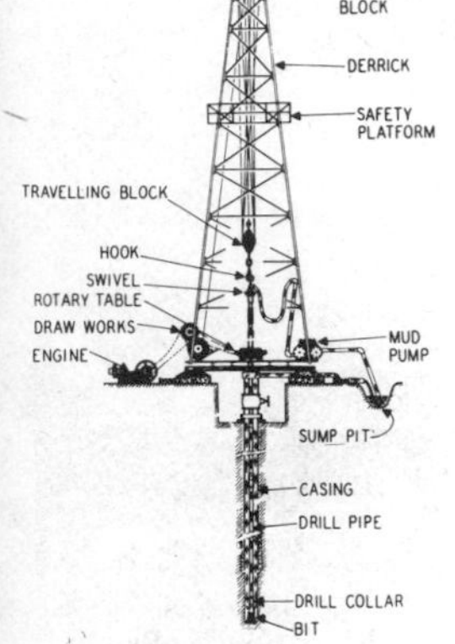

CROWN BLOCK
DERRICK
SAFETY PLATFORM
TRAVELLING BLOCK
HOOK
SWIVEL
ROTARY TABLE
DRAW WORKS
ENGINE
MUD PUMP
SUMP PIT
CASING
DRILL PIPE
DRILL COLLAR
BIT

derrick
Rotary drilling rig

der·i·va·tion (dĕr′ə-vā′shən) *n. Abbr.* **der., deriv. 1.** The act or process of deriving. **2.** The condition or fact of being derived. **3.** Something derived; a derivative. **4.** The form or source from which something is derived; origin; descent. **5.** The historical origin and development of a word; etymology. **6.** *Linguistics.* The morphological process by which new words are formed from existing words, chiefly by the addition of affixes to roots, stems, or words. **7.** *Mathematics.* A logical or mathematical process indicating through a sequence of statements that a result such as a theorem or a formula necessarily follows from the initial assumptions. —**der′i·va′tion·al** *adj.*

de·riv·a·tive (dĭ-rĭv′ə-tĭv) *adj.* Also **der·i·vate** (dĕr′ə-vāt′). *Abbr.* **der. 1.** Resulting from derivation; derived. **2.** Copied or adapted from others: *"My merits, whatever they are, are original and personal; his are derivative."* (Burke). —*n.* **1.** Something derived. **2.** *Linguistics.* A word formed from another by derivation. Compare **primitive. 3.** *Mathematics.* The limit, as the increment in the argument of a function approaches zero, of the ratio of the increment in its value to the corresponding increment in the argument; loosely, the instantaneous rate of change of a function with respect to a variable. Also called "differential coefficient." **4.** *Chemistry.* Any compound derived or obtained from known or hypothetical substances and containing essential elements of the parent substance. —**de·riv′a·tive·ly** *adv.*

de·rive (dĭ-rīv′) *v.* **-rived, -riving, -rives.** —*tr.* **1.** To obtain or receive from a source. **2.** To arrive at by reasoning; deduce; infer: *derive a conclusion from facts.* **3.** To trace the origin or development of (a word, for example). **4.** *Chemistry.* To produce or obtain (a compound) from another substance by chemical reaction. —*intr.* To issue from a source; originate: *"Modern science derives from Rome as well as from Greece."* (A.N. Whitehead). [Middle English *deriven,* conduct water from a source, spring from, from Old French *deriver,* from Latin *dērīvāre,* draw off, derive : *dē-,* away, off + *rīvus,* stream (see **er-¹** in Appendix*).] —**de·riv′a·ble** *adj.* —**de·riv′er** *n.*

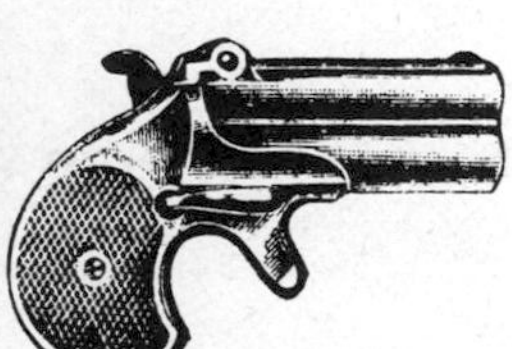
derringer

-derm. *Biology.* Indicates skin; for example, **endoderm, echinoderm.** [French *-derme,* from Greek *derma,* skin. See **der-²** in Appendix.*]

der·ma¹ (dûr′mə) *n.* Also **derm** (dûrm), **der·mis** (dûr′mĭs). *Anatomy.* A layer of skin, the **corium** *(see).* [New Latin *derma, dermis,* from Greek *derma,* skin. See **der-²** in Appendix.*]

der·ma² (dûr′mə) *n.* Beef casing stuffed with a seasoned mixture of matzo meal or flour, onion, and suet, prepared by boiling, then roasting. Also called "stuffed derma," "kishke." [Yiddish *derme,* plural of *darm,* intestine, from Middle High German, from Old High German. See **ter-²** in Appendix.*]

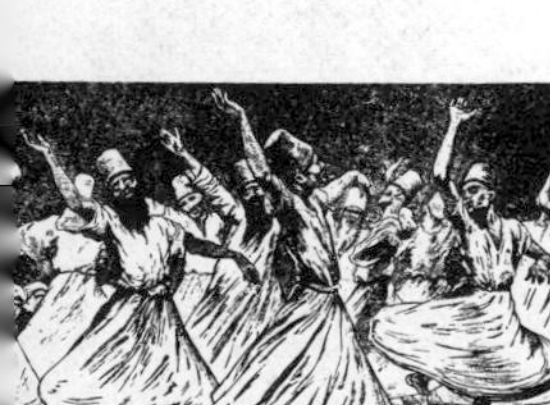
dervish

-derma. Indicates skin or skin disease; for example, **scleroderma.** [New Latin, from Greek *derma,* skin. See **der-²** in Appendix.*]

der·mal (dûr′məl) *adj.* Also **der·mic** (-mĭk). Of or pertaining to the skin. [DERM(ATO)- + -AL.]

der·ma·ti·tis (dûr′mə-tī′tĭs) *n.* Inflammation of the skin. [New Latin : DERMAT(O)- + -ITIS.]

dermato-, derm-, derma-, dermat-. Indicates skin; for example, **dermatology, dermal, dermatome, dermatoid.** [Greek, from *derma,* skin. See **der-²** in Appendix.*]

der·mat·o·gen (dûr-măt′ə-jən) *n. Botany.* The outer layer of **meristem** *(see),* from which the epidermis is formed. [DERMATO- + -GEN.]

der·ma·toid (dûr′mə-toid′) *n.* Also **der·moid** (dûr′moid′). Resembling skin; skinlike. [DERMAT(O)- + -OID.]

der·ma·tol·o·gy (dûr′mə-tŏl′ə-jē) *n.* The medical study of the physiology and pathology of the skin. [DERMATO- + -LOGY.] —**der′ma·to·log′i·cal** *adj.* —**der′ma·tol′o·gist** *n.*

der·ma·tome (dûr′mə-tōm′) *n.* **1.** An area of skin with sensory fibers from a single spinal nerve. **2.** An instrument used in cutting thin slices of the skin, as in skin grafting. **3.** *Embryology.* The lateral wall of a somite. [DERMA(TO)- + -TOME.]

der·ma·to·phyte (dûr′mə-tō-fīt′) *n.* Any of various fungi that cause skin disease. [DERMATO- + -PHYTE.]

der·ma·to·phy·to·sis (dûr′mə-tō-fī-tō′sĭs) *n.* **Athlete's foot** *(see).* [DERMATOPHYT(E) + -OSIS.]

der·ma·to·plas·ty (dûr′mə-tō-plăs′tē) *n.* The use of skin grafts in plastic surgery to correct defects or replace skin loss. [DERMATO- + -PLASTY.]

der·ma·to·sis (dûr′mə-tō′sĭs) *n., pl.* **-ses** (-sēz). A skin disease. [New Latin : DERMAT(O)- + -OSIS.]

der·nier cri (dĕr-nyā krē′). *French.* The latest thing; newest fashion. Literally, "last cry."

der·o·gate (dĕr′ə-gāt′) *v.* **-gated, -gating, -gates.** —*intr.* **1.** To detract; take away. Used with *from.* **2.** To deviate from a standard or expectation; go astray. Used with *from.* —*tr.* To disparage; belittle. [Latin *dērogāre,* repeal, restrict, disparage : *dē-,* away + *rogāre,* ask (see **reg-¹** in Appendix*).] —**der′o·ga′tion** *n.* —**de·rog′a·tive** (dĭ-rŏg′ə-tĭv) *adj.*

de·rog·a·to·ry (dĭ-rŏg′ə-tôr′ē, -tōr′ē) *adj.* Detracting or disparaging. —**de·rog′a·to′ri·ly** *adv.* —**de·rog′a·to′ri·ness** *n.*

der·rick (dĕr′ĭk) *n.* **1.** A large crane for hoisting and moving heavy objects, consisting of a movable boom equipped with cables and pulleys and connected to the base of an upright stationary beam. **2.** A tall framework over the opening of an oil well or other drilled hole, used to support boring equipment or to hoist and lower pipe lengths. [Originally, a gallows, after *Derick,* noted hangman at Tyburn, England, circa 1600.]

der·ri·ère (dĕr′ē-âr′; *French* dĕ-ryâr′) *n.* The buttocks; the rear. [French, "the rear."]

der·ring-do (dĕr′ĭng-dōō′) *n.* Daring spirit and action; valor. [Middle English *durring don,* daring to do (taken as a noun phrase) : *durring,* present participle of *durren,* Old English *durran,* to DARE + *don,* to DO.]

der·rin·ger (dĕr′ĭn-jər) *n.* Also **der·in·ger.** A short-barreled pistol with a large bore. [Invented by Henry *Deringer,* 19th-century American gunsmith.]

der·ris (dĕr′ĭs) *n.* Any of various woody vines of the genus *Derris,* of tropical Asia, whose roots yield rotenone. [New Latin, from Greek, covering, skin. See **der-²** in Appendix.*]

der·ry (dĕr′ē) *n., pl.* **-ries.** A meaningless word used as a refrain or chorus in old songs.

Der·ry. See **Londonderry.**

der·vish (dûr′vĭsh) *n.* A member of any of various Moslem orders of ascetics, some of which practice the achievement of collective ecstasy through whirling dances and the chanting of religious formulas. [Turkish *dervis,* mendicant, from Persian *dārvīsh*†.]

Der·went (dûr′wənt). A river rising in south-central Tasmania and flowing 107 miles through Hobart to the Tasman Sea.

Des·a·gua·de·ro (dās′ä-gwä-*thā*′rō). The upper reaches of the **Salado** *(see).*

de·sal·i·nate (dē-săl′ə-nāt′) *tr.v.* **-nated, -nating, -nates.** To desalinize. —**de·sal′i·na′tion** *n.*

de·sal·in·ize (dē-săl′ə-nīz′) *tr.v.* **-ized, -izing, -izes.** To remove (salts and other chemicals) from sea water or saline water. —**de·sal′i·ni·za′tion** *n.*

de·salt (dē-sôlt′) *tr.v.* **-salted, -salting, -salts.** To desalinize.

des·cant (dĕs′kănt) *n.* Also **dis·cant** (dĭs′-) (for sense 1). **1.** *Music.* **a.** An ornamental melody or counterpoint sung or played above a musical theme. **b.** The highest part sung in part music. **2.** A discussion or discourse on a theme. —*intr.v.* (dĕs-kănt′) **descanted, -canting, -cants.** Also **dis·cant** (dĭs-kănt′) (for sense 2). **1.** To comment at length; discourse. Used with *on* or *upon: "I have now descanted at some length on what I am going to talk about"* (William Dean Howells). **2. a.** To sing or play a descant. **b.** To sing melodiously. [Middle English *discant,* from Old North French *descant,* from Medieval Latin *discantus,* refrain : *dis-,* apart + *cantus,* song, from the past participle of *canere,* to sing (see **kan-** in Appendix*).] —**des·cant′er** *n.*

Des·cartes (dā-kärt′), **René.** 1596–1650. French philosopher and mathematician.

de·scend (dĭ-sĕnd′) *v.* **-scended, -scending, -scends.** —*intr.* **1.** To move from a higher to a lower place; come or go down. **2.** To slope, extend, or incline downward: *"a rough path descended like a steep stair into the plain"* (J.R.R. Tolkien). **3.** To be derived from ancestors; be inherited. **4.** To have hereditary derivation. **5.** To lower oneself in behavior; to stoop: *"she, the conqueror, had descended to the level of the conquered"* (James Bryce). **6.** To arrive in an overwhelming manner. Used with *on* or *upon.* —*tr.* To move from a higher to a lower part of; go down. [Middle English *descenden,* from Old French *descendre,* from Latin *dēscendere* : *dē-,* down + *scandere,* climb (see **skand-** in Appendix*).] —**de·scend′i·ble, de·scend′a·ble** *adj.*

de·scen·dant (dĭ-sĕn′dənt) *n.* A person or animal descended from another or others; an immediate or remote offspring. —*adj.* Descendent.

de·scen·dent (dĭ-sĕn′dənt) *adj.* Also **de·scen·dant. 1.** Moving downward; descending. **2.** Proceeding by descent from an ancestor. Often used with *from.*

de·scend·er (dĭ-sĕn′dər) *n.* **1.** One that descends. **2.** *Printing.* **a.** The part of certain letters, such as *g, p,* or *y,* that extends

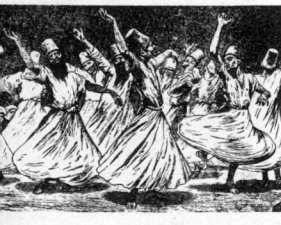

below the bottom of most lower-case letters. **b.** Any such letter.

de·scent (dĭ-sĕnt′) *n.* **1.** The act or an instance of descending; a coming or going down. **2.** A way down; downward incline or passage. **3.** Hereditary derivation; ancestral extraction; lineage. **4.** A generation of a specific lineage. **5.** A lowering or decline, as in status or level. **6.** A sudden attack; onslaught. **7.** *Law.* Transference of property by inheritance. [Middle English *descent*, from Old French, from *descendre*, DESCEND.]

Des·chutes (dā-sho͞ot′). A river rising in west-central Oregon and flowing 250 miles north to the Columbia.

de·scribe (dĭ-skrīb′) *tr.v.* **-scribed, -scribing, -scribes. 1.** To give a verbal account of; tell about in detail. **2.** To transmit a mental image or impression of with words; picture verbally. **3.** To trace or draw the figure of; outline: *describe a circle with a compass.* [Latin *dēscrībere*, to copy off, write down : *dē-*, down + *scrībere*, to write (see **skeri-** in Appendix*).] —**de·scrib′a·ble** *adj.* —**de·scrib′er** *n.*

de·scrip·tion (dĭ-skrĭp′shən) *n.* **1.** The act, process, or technique of describing; verbal representation. **2.** A statement or account describing something. **3.** The act of drawing or tracing a figure. **4.** A kind; sort: *costumes of every description.* [Middle English *descripcioun*, from Old French *description*, from Latin *dēscriptiō*, from *dēscriptus*, past participle of *dēscrībere*, DESCRIBE.]

de·scrip·tive (dĭ-skrĭp′tĭv) *adj.* **1.** Involving or characterized by description; serving to describe. **2.** Concerned with description or classification rather than explanation: *descriptive science.* **3.** *Grammar.* Expressing an attribute of the modified noun; for example, *green* in *green grass*. Said of an adjective or adjectival clause. —**de·scrip′tive·ly** *adv.* —**de·scrip′tive·ness** *n.*

descriptive geometry. The collection of mathematical techniques used to describe geometrical relationships among three-dimensional structures on a plane surface.

descriptive linguistics. The study of a language or languages as they exist, or as they existed at a specific stage of development, with emphasis on constructing a complete grammar rather than on historical development or comparison with other languages. Also called "synchronic linguistics." Compare **historical linguistics.**

de·scry (dĭ-skrī′) *tr.v.* **-scried, -scrying, -scries. 1.** To discern (something difficult to catch sight of): *"through the mists they could descry the long arm of the mountains"* (J.R.R. Tolkien). **2.** To discover by careful observation or investigation. —See Synonyms at **see.** [Middle English *descrien*, cry out, proclaim, catch sight of, from Old French *descrier*, decry : *des-*, used in pejorative sense, DIS- + *crier*, to CRY.] —**de·scri′er** *n.*

des·e·crate (dĕs′ə-krāt′) *tr.v.* **-crated, -crating, -crates.** To abuse the sacredness of; subject to sacrilege; profane. [DE- (reversal) + (CON)SECRATE.] —**des′e·crat′er, des′e·cra′tor** (-krā′tər) *n.* —**des′e·cra′tion** *n.*

de·seg·re·gate (dē-sĕg′rə-gāt′) *v.* **-gated, -gating, -gates.** —*tr.* To abolish racial segregation in (a public school, for example). —*intr.* To become desegregated. —**de′seg·re·ga′tion** *n.* —**de·seg′re·ga′tion·ist** *adj.* & *n.*

de·sen·si·tize (dē-sĕn′sə-tīz′) *tr.v.* **-tized, -tizing, -tizes.** To render less sensitive or insensitive, as to light or pain. —**de·sen′si·ti·za′tion** *n.* —**de·sen′si·tiz′er** *n.*

Des·e·ret (dĕz′ə-rĕt′). A state proposed by the Mormons in 1849 as an independent state or, failing that, a state of the Union, including much of the southwestern United States with a capital in Salt Lake City. [From *deseret*, the Jaredite word for honeybee in the Book of Mormon.]

des·ert¹ (dĕz′ərt) *n.* A region rendered barren or partially barren by environmental extremes, especially by low rainfall. —*adj.* Of, pertaining to, or characteristic of a desert; barren and uninhabited; desolate: *a desert island.* [Middle English, from Old French, from Late Latin *dēsertum*, from Latin, neuter past participle of *dēserere*, to abandon, DESERT.]

de·sert² (dĭ-zûrt′) *n.* **1.** *Usually plural.* That which is deserved or merited, especially a punishment: *received his just deserts.* **2.** The state or fact of deserving reward or punishment. **3.** *Obsolete.* A good deed. [Middle English *deserte*, from Old French, from *desert*, from *deservir*, DESERVE.]

de·sert³ (dĭ-zûrt′) *v.* **-serted, -serting, -serts.** —*tr.* **1.** To forsake or leave; abandon: *"his set smile did not once desert him"* (Willa Cather). **2.** To forsake in violation of orders or oath, as a post. —*intr.* To forsake one's duty or post; especially, to be absent without leave from the armed forces with no intention of returning. [French *déserter*, from Late Latin *dēsertāre*, from Latin *dēsertus*, past participle of *dēserere*, to abandon : *dē-*, reversal + *serere*, join (see **ser-³** in Appendix*).] —**de·sert′er** *n.*

de·ser·tion (dĭ-zûr′shən) *n.* **1. a.** The act of deserting. **b.** The state of being deserted. **2.** *Law.* Willful abandonment of one's spouse or children, or both, without their consent and with the intention of forsaking all legal obligation.

de·serve (dĭ-zûrv′) *v.* **-served, -serving, -serves.** —*tr.* To be worthy of; have a right to; merit: *"An American girl of college age . . . deserved instant inspection"* (Kingsley Amis). —*intr.* To be worthy. [Middle English *deserven*, to be entitled to in return for services, deserve, from Old French *deservir*, from Latin *dēservīre*, serve well : *dē-*, completely + *servīre*, to SERVE.]

de·served (dĭ-zûrvd′) *adj.* Merited or earned: *a deserved vacation.* —**de·serv′ed·ly** (dĭ-zûr′vĭd-lē) *adv.* —**de·serv′ed·ness** *n.*

de·serv·ing (dĭ-zûr′vĭng) *adj.* Worthy of reward or praise; meritorious. —*n.* Merit or demerit. —**de·serv′ing·ly** *adv.* —**de·serv′ing·ness** *n.*

de·sex (dē-sĕks′) *tr.v.* **-sexed, -sexing, -sexes.** To remove part or all of the reproductive organs of; spay or castrate.

des·ha·bille. Variant of **dishabille.**

des·ic·cant (dĕs′ĭ-kənt) *n.* A substance, such as calcium oxide or sulfuric acid, that has a high affinity for water and is used to absorb moisture. [Latin *dēsiccāns*, present participle of *dēsiccāre*, DESICCATE.] —**des′ic·cant** *adj.*

des·ic·cate (dĕs′ĭ-kāt′) *v.* **-cated, -cating, -cates.** —*tr.* **1.** To make thoroughly dry; dry out. **2.** To preserve (foods) by removing the moisture. **3.** To divest of spirit, spontaneity, or animation; make dry or uninteresting. —*intr.* To become dry. —*adj.* Also **des·ic·cat·ed** (-kā′tĭd). Lacking spirit, spontaneity, or animation; arid: *"there was only the sun-bruised and desiccate feeling in his mind"* (J.R. Salamanca). [Latin *dēsiccāre* : *dē-*, completely + *siccāre*, dry up, from *siccus*, dry (see **seikw-** in Appendix*).] —**des′ic·ca′tion** *n.* —**des′ic·ca′tive** *adj.*

des·ic·ca·tor (dĕs′ə-kā′tər) *n.* One that desiccates, especially an apparatus used to desiccate a substance.

de·sid·er·ate (dĭ-sĭd′ə-rāt′) *tr.v.* **-ated, -ating, -ates.** To long for. [Latin *dēsīderāre*, DESIRE.]

de·sid·er·a·tive (dĭ-sĭd′ə-rā′tĭv) *adj.* **1.** Of or pertaining to desire. **2.** Designating a category of verbs in some Indo-European languages expressing a wish to perform the action denoted by the given verb.

de·sid·er·a·tum (dĭ-sĭd′ə-rā′təm) *n., pl.* **-ta** (-tə). Something needed and desired: *"A journalist of spirit is a desideratum in a revolution."* (Hugh H. Brackenridge). [Latin *dēsīderātum*, neuter past participle of *dēsīderāre*, DESIRE.]

de·sign (dĭ-zīn′) *v.* **-signed, -signing, -signs.** —*tr.* **1.** To conceive; invent; contrive. **2.** To form a plan for. **3.** To draw a sketch of. **4.** To have as a goal or purpose; intend. —*intr.* **1.** To make or execute plans. **2.** To create designs. —*n.* **1.** A drawing or sketch. **2.** The invention and disposition of the forms, parts, or details of something according to a plan. **3.** A decorative or artistic work. **4.** A visual composition; pattern. **5.** The art of creating designs. **6.** A plan; project; an undertaking. **7.** A reasoned purpose; intention. **8.** *Often plural.* A sinister or hostile scheme; crafty plot. Used with *on, upon,* or *against.* [Old French *designer*, from Latin *dēsignāre*, DESIGNATE.] —**de·sign′a·ble** *adj.* —**de·sign′er** *n.*

des·ig·nate (dĕz′ĭg-nāt′) *tr.v.* **-nated, -nating, -nates. 1.** To indicate or specify; point out. **2.** To give a name or title to; characterize. **3.** To select for a particular duty, office, or purpose; appoint. —*adj.* (dĕz′ĭg-nĭt). Appointed but not yet installed in office. [Latin *dēsignāre*, designate, mark out : *dē-*, out + *signāre*, mark, from *signum*, sign (see **sekw-¹** in Appendix*).] —**des′ig·na′tive, des′ig·na·to′ry** (-nə-tôr′ē, -tōr′ē) *adj.* —**des′ig·na′tor** (-nā′tər) *n.*

des·ig·na·tion (dĕz′ĭg-nā′shən) *n.* **1.** The act of designating; a marking or pointing out. **2.** Nomination or appointment. **3.** A distinguishing name or mark; title. —See Synonyms at **name.**

de·sign·ed·ly (dĭ-zī′nĭd-lē) *adv.* On purpose; intentionally.

des·ig·nee (dĕz′ĭg-nē′) *n.* A person who has been designated.

de·sign·ing (dĭ-zī′nĭng) *adj.* **1.** Conniving; artful; crafty. **2.** Showing or exercising forethought. —**de·sign′ing·ly** *adv.*

des·i·nence (dĕs′ə-nəns) *n.* **1.** Termination; finishing. **2.** *Grammar.* An inflectional ending. [Old French, from Medieval Latin *dēsinentia*, from Latin *dēsinēns*, present participle of *dēsinere*, cease, leave off : *dē-*, off + *sinere*, leave (see **site**).]

de·sir·a·ble (dĭ-zīr′ə-bəl) *adj.* **1.** Worth seeking or meriting preference; pleasing; fine. **2.** Arousing desire. **3.** Worth wanting or doing; advantageous; advisable: *a desirable reform.* —*n.* A desirable person or thing. —**de·sir′a·bil′i·ty, de·sir′a·ble·ness** *n.* —**de·sir′a·bly** *adv.*

de·sire (dĭ-zīr′) *tr.v.* **-sired, -siring, -sires. 1.** To wish or long for; want; crave. **2.** To express a wish for. —*n.* **1.** A wish, longing, or craving. **2.** A request as expressed; a petition. **3.** Something or someone longed for. **4.** Sexual appetite; passion. [Middle English *desiren*, from Old French *desirer*, from Latin *dēsīderāre*. See **sweid-¹** in Appendix.*] —**de·sir′er** *n.*

de·sir·ous (dĭ-zīr′əs) *adj.* Having, expressing, or characterized by desire; desiring. —**de·sir′ous·ly** *adv.* —**de·sir′ous·ness** *n.*

de·sist (dĭ-zĭst′) *intr.v.* **-sisted, -sisting, -sists.** To cease doing something; forbear; abstain. Often used with *from.* [Old French *desister*, from Latin *dēsistere*, cease, stand off : *dē-*, from + *sistere*, stop, stand (see **stā-** in Appendix*).]

desk (dĕsk) *n.* **1.** A piece of furniture typically having a flat top for writing and accessory drawers or compartments. **2.** A table, counter, or booth at which specified, typically public services or functions are performed: *an information desk.* **3.** A department of a large organization, such as a governmental agency or newspaper, in charge of a specified operation: *city desk.* **4. a.** A music stand in an orchestra. **b.** Two string players using the same music stand in an orchestra. **c.** A particular position in an orchestra. [Middle English *deske*, from Medieval Latin *desca*, variant of Italian *desco*, table, from Latin *discus*, quoit, DISK.]

desk·man (dĕsk′măn′, -mən) *n., pl.* **-men** (-mĕn′, -mĭn). A person who works at a desk, especially a newspaper writer.

des·man (dĕs′mən) *n., pl.* **-mans.** Either of two aquatic, insectivorous, molelike mammals, *Desmana moschata* of eastern Europe and western Asia, or *Galemys pyrenaicus* of southwestern Europe, having dense, brownish fur, a long snout, and a flattened, scaly tail. [Short for Swedish *desman(sråtta)*, musk(rat), from Middle Low German *desem*, musk, from West Germanic *dessem* (unattested), from Medieval Latin *bisamum*, from Semitic, akin to Hebrew *beśem*, mild odor.]

des·mid (dĕs′mĭd) *n.* Any of various green, unicellular freshwater algae of the family Desmidiaceae, often forming chainlike colonies. [New Latin *Desmidiaceae*, from *Desmidium* (genus) : Greek *desmos*, bond, from *dein*, to bind (see **dē-** in Appendix*) + *-idium*, diminutive suffix.]

Des Moines (də moin′, moinz′). **1.** The capital of Iowa, in the

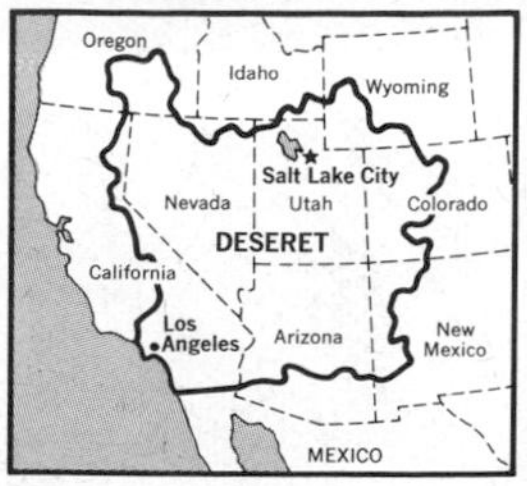

Deseret

desk
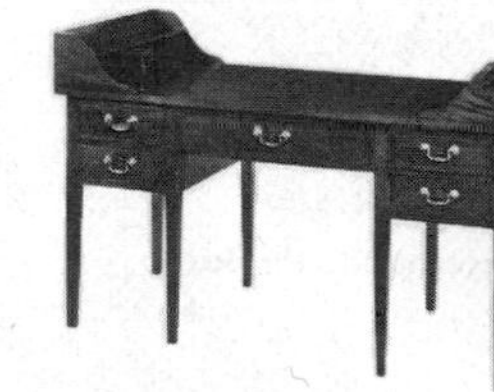
Hepplewhite

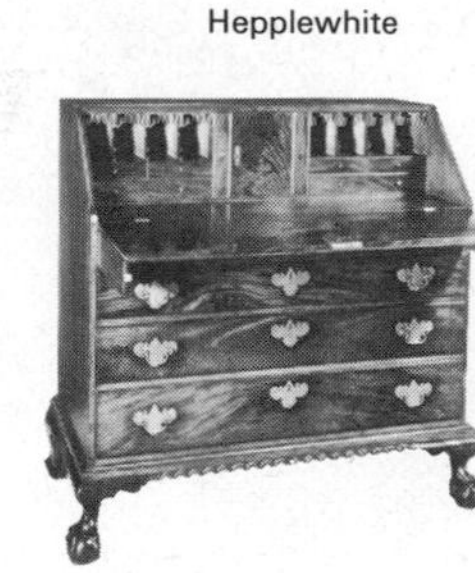
18th-century American

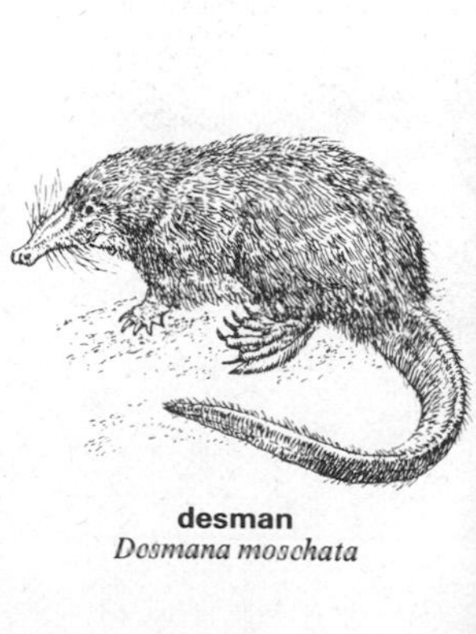
desman
Desmana moschata

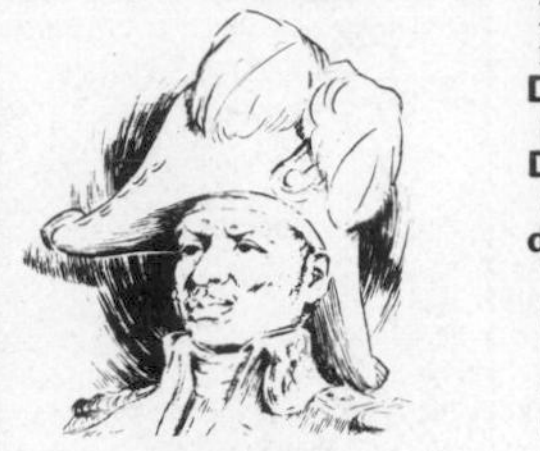
Jean Jacques Dessalines

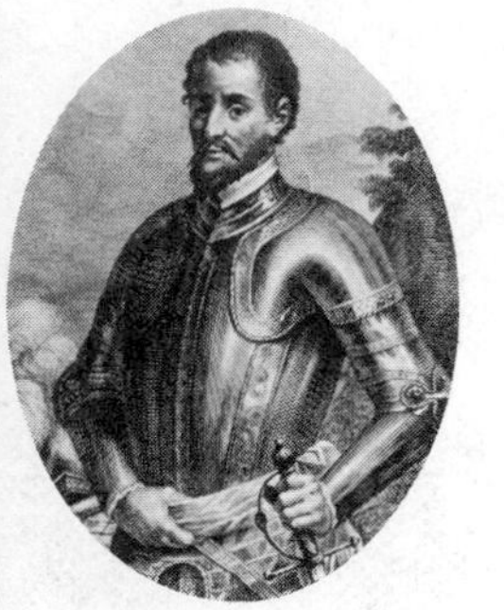
Hernando de Soto

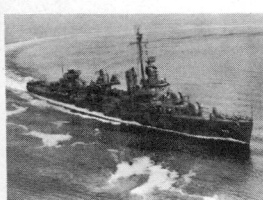

destroyer
U.S.S. *Fletcher*
in July 1942

south-central part on the Des Moines River. Population, 209,000. **2.** A river rising in southwestern Minnesota and flowing 535 miles southeast to the Mississippi in Iowa.

Des·mou·lins (dā-mōō-lăN′), **(Lucie Simplice) Camille (Benoît).** 1760–1794. French revolutionary leader.

Des·na (dyə-snä′). A river of the western Soviet Union, rising near Smolensk and flowing 737 miles south to the Dnieper.

des·o·late (dĕs′ə-lĭt) *adj.* **1.** Devoid of inhabitants; deserted: *"streets which were usually so thronged now grown desolate"* (Defoe). **2.** Rendered unfit for habitation; laid waste; devastated. **3.** Dreary; dismal; gloomy. **4.** Without friends or hope; forlorn; lonely. —See Synonyms at **sad.** —*tr.v.* (dĕs′ə-lāt′) **desolated, -lating, -lates. 1.** To rid or deprive of inhabitants. **2.** To devastate: *"Here we have no wars to desolate our fields"* (St. John de Crèvecoeur). **3.** To forsake; abandon. **4.** To make lonely, forlorn, or wretched. [Middle English *desolat,* from Latin *dēsōlātus,* from the past participle of *dēsōlāre,* abandon : *dē-,* completely + *sōlus,* alone (see **seu-**[2] in Appendix*).] —**des′o·late·ly** *adv.* —**des′o·late·ness** *n.* —**des′o·lat′er, des′o·la′tor** (-lā′tər) *n.*

des·o·la·tion (dĕs′ə-lā′shən) *n.* **1.** The act of rendering desolate. **2.** The state of being desolate; ruin. **3.** A wasteland. **4.** Loneliness or misery; wretchedness: *"an air of tranquil and unwitting desolation . . . as if she had never lived at all"* (Faulkner).

de So·to (dĕ sō′tō), **Hernando.** 1500?–1542. Spanish explorer; discoverer of the Mississippi (1541).

de·spair (dĭ-spâr′) *intr.v.* **-spaired, -spairing, -spairs.** To lose all hope; to be overcome by a sense of futility or defeat. —*n.* **1.** Utter lack of hope. **2.** That which destroys all hope. [Middle English *despeiren,* from Old French *desperer,* from Latin *dēspērāre* : *dē-* (reversal) + *spērāre,* to hope (see **spēi-** in Appendix*).] —**de·spair′ing·ly** *adv.*

Synonyms: *despair, hopelessness, desperation, despondency, depression, discouragement, dejection.* These nouns denote emotional states marked by lowness of spirits or loss of hope. *Despair* and *hopelessness* stress the utter absence of hope and often imply a sense of powerlessness or resignation. *Desperation* implies absence of grounds for hope, but adds the idea of fighting back, often blindly or recklessly. *Despondency* and *depression* emphasize lowness of spirits; *despondency* is usually stronger in suggesting cessation of hope, courage, or effort to recoup. *Discouragement* suggests loss of confidence or courage in the face of obstacles, but is generally the weakest of these terms. *Dejection* is lowness of spirits, often of short duration and generally traceable to an external cause.

des·patch. Variant of **dispatch.**

des·per·a·do (dĕs′pə-rä′dō, -rā′dō) *n., pl.* **-does** or **-dos.** A desperate, dangerous criminal, especially of the western U.S. frontier. [Pseudo-Spanish variant of DESPERATE.]

des·per·ate (dĕs′pər-ĭt) *adj.* **1.** Reckless or violent because of despair; driven to take any risk. **2.** Undertaken as a last resort. **3.** Nearly hopeless; critical; grave: *a desperate illness.* **4.** Marked by, arising from, or showing despair; despairing: *the desperate look of hunger.* **5.** In an unbearable situation because of need or anxiety: *desperate for recognition.* **6.** Extreme because of fear, danger, or suffering; very great: *in desperate need.* [Latin *dēspērātus,* past participle of *dēspērāre,* to DESPAIR.] —**des′per·ate·ly** *adv.* —**des′per·ate·ness** *n.*

des·per·a·tion (dĕs′pə-rā′shən) *n.* **1.** The condition of being desperate. **2.** Recklessness arising from despair. —See Synonyms at **despair.**

des·pi·ca·ble (dĕs′pĭ-kə-bəl, dĭ-spĭk′-) *adj.* Deserving of contempt or disdain; mean; vile. [Late Latin *dēspicābilis,* from Latin *dēspicārī,* despise. See **spek-** in Appendix.*] —**des′pi·ca·bil′i·ty, des′pi·ca·ble·ness** *n.* —**des′pi·ca·bly** *adv.*

de·spise (dĭ-spīz′) *tr.v.* **-spised, -spising, -spises.** To regard with contempt or disdain. [Middle English *despisen,* from Old French *despire* (present stem *despis-*), from Latin *dēspicere,* to look down on : *dē-,* down + *specere,* to look (see **spek-** in Appendix*).] —**de·spis′er** *n.*

de·spite (dĭ-spīt′) *prep.* In spite of: *win despite overwhelming odds.* See Synonyms at **notwithstanding.** —*n.* **1.** Contemptuous defiance. **2.** An act of such defiance; insult; offense. —**in despite of.** In spite of. [Short for *in despite of,* from Middle English *despit,* spite, from Old French, from Latin *dēspectus,* past participle of *dēspicere,* to DESPISE.]

de·spite·ful (dĭ-spīt′fəl) *adj. Archaic.* Full of malice; spiteful. —**de·spite′ful·ly** *adv.* —**de·spite′ful·ness** *n.*

des·pit·e·ous (dĕs-pĭt′ē-əs) *adj. Obsolete.* Full of spite or malice; despiteful. —**des·pit′e·ous·ly** *adv.*

Des Plaines (dĕs plānz′). A river rising in southeastern Wisconsin and flowing 110 miles south into Illinois to join the Kankakee and form the Illinois River.

de·spoil (dĭ-spoil′) *tr.v.* **-spoiled, -spoiling, -spoils.** To deprive of possessions by force; plunder; ravage. [Middle English *despoilen,* from Old French *despoiller,* from Latin *dēspoliāre* : *dē-,* sense of undoing + *spoliāre,* plunder, from *spolium,* booty, spoil (see **spel-**[1] in Appendix*).] —**de·spoil′er** *n.* —**de·spoil′ment** *n.*

de·spo·li·a·tion (dĭ-spō′lē-ā′shən) *n.* The act of despoiling or the condition of being despoiled; plunder. [Late Latin *dēspoliātiō,* from Latin *dēspoliātus,* past participle of *dēspoliāre,* DESPOIL.]

de·spond (dĭ-spŏnd′) *intr.v.* **-sponded, -sponding, -sponds.** To become disheartened. [Latin *dēspondēre,* despond, promise to give, give up : *dē-,* away + *spondēre,* promise (see **spend-** in Appendix*).] —**de·spond′ing·ly** *adv.*

de·spon·den·cy (dĭ-spŏn′dən-sē) *n., pl.* **-cies.** Also **de·spon·dence** (-dəns). Depression of spirits from loss of hope, confidence, or courage; dejection. See Synonyms at **despair.**

de·spon·dent (dĭ-spŏn′dənt) *adj.* Feeling or expressing despondency; disheartened; dejected. [Latin *dēspondēns,* present participle of *dēspondēre,* DESPOND.] —**de·spon′dent·ly** *adv.*

des·pot (dĕs′pət) *n.* **1.** Lord; a Greek title borne by Byzantine emperors and princes, by Christian rulers in the Balkans under the Turks, and by Eastern Orthodox bishops. **2.** An autocratic ruler. [Old French, from Greek *despotēs.* See **deme-**[1] in Appendix.*] —**des·pot′ic** (dĭ-spŏt′ĭk) *adj.* —**des·pot′i·cal·ly** *adv.*

des·pot·ism (dĕs′pə-tĭz′əm) *n.* **1.** Rule by or as if by a despot; absolute power or authority. **2.** The actions of a despot; tyranny. **3. a.** A government or political system in which the ruler exercises absolute power. **b.** A state so ruled.

des Prés (dā prā′), **Josquin.** Also **De·prés** (də-prĕ′). 1450?–1521. Flemish composer of masses, motets, and chansons.

des·qua·mate (dĕs′kwə-māt′) *intr.v.* **-mated, -mating, -mates.** *Pathology.* To shed, peel, or scale off. Used of skin. [Latin *dēsquāmāre* : *dē-,* removal + *squāma,* scale (see **squama**).] —**des′qua·ma′tion** *n.*

Des·sa·lines (dā-sà-lēn′), **Jean Jacques.** 1758–1806. Haitian revolutionary leader; emperor (1804–06).

des·sert (dĭ-zûrt′) *n.* **1.** The last course of a lunch or dinner, consisting of a serving of a sweet food, such as fruit, ice cream, or pastry. **2.** *British.* Fresh fruit, nuts, or sweetmeats served after the sweet course of a dinner. [Old French, from *desservir,* clear the table : *des-, de-,* reversal + *servir,* to SERVE.]

des·sert·spoon (dĭ-zûrt′spōōn′) *n.* A spoon intermediate in size between a tablespoon and a teaspoon, used for eating dessert. —**des·sert′spoon′ful** *n.*

de·ster·i·lize (dē-stĕr′ə-līz′) *tr.v.* **-lized, -lizing, -lizes.** To release (gold) from an inactive status and return it to use as a backing for credit and new currency.

de Stijl (də stīl′, stāl′). A school of art originated in the Netherlands in 1917 and characterized by the use of rectangular shapes and primary colors. [Dutch, "the style."]

des·ti·na·tion (dĕs′tə-nā′shən) *n.* **1.** The place or point to which someone or something is going or directed. **2.** The ultimate goal or purpose for which anything is created or intended.

des·tine (dĕs′tĭn) *tr.v.* **-tined, -tining, -tines. 1.** To determine beforehand; preordain to or as if to an inevitable outcome. Usually used with the infinitive: *"Modigliani's paintings were destined to attract more attention than his sculpture"* (Herbert Read). **2.** To assign for a specific end, use, or purpose. **3.** To direct toward a given destination. [Middle English *destinen,* from Old French *destiner,* from Latin *dēstināre,* determine, destine, make firm. See **stā-** in Appendix.*]

des·ti·ny (dĕs′tə-nē) *n., pl.* **-nies. 1.** The inevitable or necessary fate to which a particular person or thing is destined; one's lot: *"The destiny of mankind is not decided by material computation."* (Winston Churchill). **2.** The preordained or inevitable course of events considered as something beyond the power or control of man: *"Marriage and hanging go by destiny"* (Robert Burton). **3.** The power or agency thought to predetermine events; fate. **4.** *Capital* **D.** This power personified or regarded as a goddess. [Middle English *destine,* from Old French *destinee,* from the feminine past participle of *destiner,* to DESTINE.]

des·ti·tute (dĕs′tə-tōōt′, -tyōōt′) *adj.* **1.** Altogether lacking; devoid. Used with *of: destitute of experience.* **2.** Utterly impoverished. **3.** *Obsolete.* Abandoned; deserted. —See Synonyms at **poor.** [Middle English *destitut,* from Latin *dēstitūtus,* past participle of *dēstituere,* to set down, desert : *dē-,* down, away from + *statuere,* to place (see **stā-** in Appendix*).]

des·ti·tu·tion (dĕs′tə-tōō′shən, -tyōō′shən) *n.* **1.** Extreme want of resources or the means of subsistence; complete poverty. **2.** Any deprivation or lack; deficiency.

des·tri·er (dĕs′trē-ər, -trĭr) *n. Archaic.* A war horse; charger. [Middle English, from Old French, from Vulgar Latin *dextrārius* (unattested), from Latin *dexter,* right (the squire managed his own horse with his left hand and led his knight's horse with his right). See **deks-** in Appendix.*]

de·stroy (dĭ-stroi′) *v.* **-stroyed, -stroying, -stroys.** —*tr.* **1.** To ruin completely; spoil so that restoration is impossible; consume: *ancient manuscripts destroyed by fire.* **2.** To tear down or break up; raze; demolish. **3.** To do away with; get rid of; put an end to: *"In crowded populations, poverty destroys the possibility of cleanliness"* (G.B. Shaw). **4.** To kill. **5.** To render useless or ineffective. **6.** To subdue or defeat completely; crush. —*intr.* To be destructive or harmful: *"Too much money destroys as surely as too little"* (John Simon). —See Synonyms at **ruin.** [Middle English *destruyen,* from Old French *destruire,* from Vulgar Latin *dēstrūgere* (unattested), from Latin *dēstruere* (past participle *dēstructus*) : *dē-* (reversal) + *struere,* pile up (see **ster-**[2] in Appendix*).]

de·stroy·er (dĭ-stroi′ər) *n.* **1.** One that destroys. **2.** A small, fast warship armed with guns, torpedos, and depth charges, and noted for its high maneuverability.

destroyer escort. A warship, usually smaller than a destroyer, used to convoy merchant vessels.

destroying angel. Any of several poisonous mushrooms of the genus *Amanita,* especially *A. verna.*

de·struct (dĭ-strŭkt′) *n.* The intentional destruction of a space vehicle, rocket, or missile after launching. [Back-formation from DESTRUCTION.]

de·struc·ti·ble (dĭ-strŭk′tə-bəl) *adj.* Subject to destruction; capable of being destroyed: *destructible machine parts.* —**de·struc′ti·bil′i·ty, de·struc′ti·ble·ness** *n.*

de·struc·tion (dĭ-strŭk′shən) *n.* **1.** The act of destroying. **2.** The condition or fact of being destroyed: *the destruction of the cathedral during the war.* **3.** The cause or means of destroying. [Middle English *destruccioun,* from Old French *destruction,* from Latin *dēstructiō,* from *dēstructus,* past participle of *dēstruere,* DESTROY.]

de·struc·tion·ist (dĭ-strŭk′shən-ĭst) *n.* A person who favors destruction, especially of existing social institutions.

de·struc·tive (dĭ-strŭk′tĭv) *adj.* **1.** Tending to destroy; causing or wreaking destruction; ruinous. Often used with *of* or *to:* *destructive to national safety.* **2.** Designed or tending to disprove or discredit; not constructive: *destructive criticism.* —**de·struc′tive·ly** *adv.* —**de·struc′tive·ness** *n.*

destructive distillation. *Chemistry.* The simultaneous decomposition by heat and distillation of substances such as wood, coal, and oil shale to produce useful by-products such as coke, charcoal, oils, and gases.

des·ue·tude (dĕs′wə-to͞od′, -tyo͞od′) *n.* The state or condition of disuse: *words fallen into desuetude.* [French *désuétude,* from Latin *dēsuētūdō,* from *dēsuēcere,* to put out of use, become unaccustomed : *dē-* (reversal) + *suēscere,* become accustomed (see **seu-**[2] in Appendix*).]

de·sul·fur·ize (dē-sŭl′fə-rīz′) *tr.v.* **-ized, -izing, -izes.** To eliminate sulfur from. —**de·sul′fu·ri·za′tion** *n.*

des·ul·to·ry (dĕs′əl-tôr′ē, -tōr′ē) *adj.* **1.** Moving or jumping from one thing to another; disconnected; rambling. **2.** Occurring haphazardly; random. —See Synonyms at **chance.** [Latin *dēsultōrius,* of a leaper, from *dēsultor,* a leaper, from *dēsultus,* past participle of *dēsilīre,* to leap down : *dē-,* down + *salīre,* to jump (see **sel-**[4] in Appendix*).] —**des′ul·to′ri·ly** *adv.* —**des′ul·to′ri·ness** *n.*

det. 1. *Military.* detachment. **2.** detail.

de·tach (dĭ-tăch′) *tr.v.* **-tached, -taching, -taches. 1.** To separate, usually without violence or damage; disconnect. **2.** *Military.* To send (troops or ships, for example) on a special mission. [French *détacher,* from Old French *destachier* : *des-, de-,* apart + *atachier,* variant of *estachier,* to ATTACH.] —**de·tach′a·bil′i·ty** *n.* —**de·tach′a·ble** *adj.* —**de·tach′a·bly** *adv.*

de·tached (dĭ-tăcht′) *adj.* **1.** Standing apart from others; disconnected; separate: *a detached house.* **2.** Free from emotional, intellectual, social, or other involvement; disinterested. —See Synonyms at **cool, indifferent.**

de·tach·ment (dĭ-tăch′mənt) *n.* **1.** The act or process of disconnecting or detaching; separation. **2.** The state or condition of being separate or apart. **3.** Dissociation from surroundings, the concerns of others, or wordly affairs; aloofness. **4.** Absence of prejudice or bias; disinterest. **5.** *Military.* **a.** The dispatch of troops or ships selected from a larger unit for a special duty or mission. **b.** *Abbr.* **det.** The unit of troops or ships so dispatched. **c.** *Abbr.* **det.** A permanent unit, usually smaller than a platoon, organized for special duties.

de·tail (dĭ-tāl′, dē′tāl) *n. Abbr.* **det. 1.** An individually considered portion or item; a particular. **2.** Particulars considered separately and in relation to a whole: *careful attention to detail.* **3.** The act of dealing with particulars or treating things item by item. **4.** A small or secondary part of a painting, statue, building, or other work of art, especially when considered or represented in isolation. **5.** *Military.* **a.** The selection of one or more troops for a particular duty, usually a fatigue duty. **b.** The personnel so selected. **c.** The duty assigned. —**in detail.** With particulars; item by item. —*tr.v.* (dĭ-tāl′) **detailed, -tailing, -tails. 1.** To report or relate minutely or in particulars. **2.** *Military.* To select and dispatch for a particular duty. [French *détail,* from Old French *detail,* piece cut off, from *detailler,* to cut up : *de-,* thoroughly + *tailler,* cut, from Vulgar Latin *tāliāre* (unattested), to cut off (see **tailor**).]

detail man. A representative of a manufacturer of drugs or medical supplies who calls on doctors, pharmacists, and other professional users to promote new drugs and supplies.

de·tain (dĭ-tān′) *tr.v.* **-tained, -taining, -tains. 1.** To keep from proceeding; delay or retard. **2.** To keep in custody; confine. **3.** *Obsolete.* To retain or withhold. —See Synonyms at **delay.** [Middle English *deteynen,* from Old French *detenir,* from Latin *dētinēre,* to keep back : *dē-,* away + *tenēre,* to hold (see **ten-** in Appendix*).] —**de·tain′ment** *n.*

de·tain·er (dĭ-tā′nər) *n. Law.* **1. a.** The unlawful withholding of the property of another. **b.** The detention of a person, especially in custody or confinement. **2.** A writ authorizing the further detention of a person in custody pending action.

de·tect (dĭ-tĕkt′) *tr.v.* **-tected, -tecting, -tects. 1.** To discover or discern the existence, presence, or fact of. **2.** To find out the true nature of. **3.** *Electronics.* To demodulate. [Middle English *detecten,* from Latin *dētegere* (past participle *dētectus*), uncover : *dē-* (reversal) + *tegere,* to cover (see **steg-**[1] in Appendix*).] —**de·tect′a·ble, de·tect′i·ble** *adj.* —**de·tect′er** *n.*

de·tec·tion (dĭ-tĕk′shən) *n.* **1.** The act of finding out or the fact of being found out; discovery, as of something hidden or obscure. **2.** *Electronics.* Demodulation.

de·tec·tive (dĭ-tĕk′tĭv) *n.* A person, usually a policeman, whose work is investigating crimes, obtaining evidence, and performing similar duties. —*adj.* **1.** Of or pertaining to detectives or their work. **2.** Suited for or used in detection.

de·tec·tor (dĭ-tĕk′tər) *n.* One that detects, especially a mechanical, electrical, or chemical device that automatically identifies and records or registers a stimulus such as an environmental change in pressure or temperature, an electric signal, or radiation from a radioactive material.

de·tent (dĭ-tĕnt′) *n. Machinery.* A **pawl** *(see).* [French *détente,* a loosening, a trigger, from Old French *destente,* from *destendre,* to release : *des-, de-,* apart + *tendre,* stretch, from Latin *tendere* (see **ten-** in Appendix*).]

dé·tente (dā-tänt′) *n.* A relaxing or easing, as of tension between nations. [French, a loosening, a DETENT.]

de·ten·tion (dĭ-tĕn′shən) *n.* **1. a.** The act of detaining. **b.** The state of being detained. **2.** Retention. **3.** A keeping in custody or confinement; especially, a period of temporary custody while awaiting trial. [Old French, from Late Latin *dētentiō,* from Latin *dētentus,* past participle of *dētinēre,* DETAIN.]

de·ter (dĭ-tûr′) *tr.v.* **-terred, -terring, -ters.** To prevent or discourage (someone) from acting by means of fear, doubt, or the like. [Latin *dēterrēre,* frighten from : *dē-,* away from + *terrēre,* frighten (see **tres-** in Appendix*).] —**de·ter′ment** *n.*

de·terge (dĭ-tûrj′) *tr.v.* **-terged, -terging, -terges.** To wash or wipe off; cleanse. [French *déterger,* cleanse, from Latin *dētergēre,* wipe off : *dē-,* off, away + *tergēre*†, to wipe.]

de·ter·gen·cy (dĭ-tûr′jən-sē) *n.* Also **de·ter·gence** (-jəns). Cleansing power or quality.

de·ter·gent (dĭ-tûr′jənt) *n.* A cleansing substance, especially one that acts as a wetting agent and emulsifier and is made from chemical compounds rather than from fats and lye. —*adj.* Having cleansing power. [Latin *dētergēns,* present participle of *dētergēre,* to DETERGE.]

de·te·ri·o·rate (dĭ-tîr′ē-ə-rāt′) *v.* **-rated, -rating, -rates.** —*tr.* To lower in quality, character, or value. —*intr.* To degenerate. [Late Latin *dēteriōrāre,* from Latin *dēterior,* worse, comparative of *dēter* (unattested). See **de-** in Appendix.*] —**de·te′ri·o·ra′tion** *n.* —**de·te′ri·o·ra′tive** *adj.*

de·ter·mi·na·ble (dĭ-tûr′mə-nə-bəl) *adj.* **1.** Capable of being settled, fixed, or determined. **2.** *Law.* Liable to be terminated. —**de·ter′mi·na·bly** *adv.*

de·ter·mi·nant (dĭ-tûr′mə-nənt) *adj.* Tending or serving to determine; determinative. —*n.* **1.** An influencing or determining factor. **2.** *Mathematics.* A square array of quantities, or elements, having a value determined by a rule of combination for the elements and used especially in solving certain classes of simultaneous equations.

de·ter·mi·nate (dĭ-tûr′mə-nĭt) *adj.* **1.** Precisely limited or defined. **2.** Settled; final. **3.** Firm in purpose; resolute. **4.** *Botany.* **a.** Terminating in a flower, and blooming in a sequence beginning with the uppermost or central flower: *a determinate inflorescence.* **b.** Not continuing indefinitely at the tip of an axis: *determinate growth.* [Middle English *determinat,* from Latin *dēterminātus,* past participle of *dēterminãre,* DETERMINE.] —**de·ter′mi·nate·ly** *adv.* —**de·ter′mi·nate·ness** *n.*

de·ter·mi·na·tion (dĭ-tûr′mə-nā′shən) *n.* **1. a.** The act of making or arriving at a decision. **b.** The decision arrived at; a strong resolve. **2.** The quality of being resolute or firm in purpose; resoluteness. **3. a.** The act of settling a dispute, suit, or other question by an authoritative decision or pronouncement. **b.** The decision or pronouncement made. **4. a.** The ascertaining or establishing of the extent, quality, position, or character of anything. **b.** The result of such ascertaining. **5.** A fixed movement or tendency toward some object or end. **6.** *Logic.* **a.** The rendering of a concept or proposition more definite by further qualification. **b.** The factor or factors that so qualify. **c.** The defining of a concept through its constituent elements.

de·ter·mi·na·tive (dĭ-tûr′mə-nā′tĭv, -nə-tĭv) *adj.* Tending, able, or serving to determine or settle; limiting; deciding. —*n.* **1.** Something that determines. **2.** *Grammar.* A word belonging to a group of noun modifiers generally considered to include articles, demonstratives, possessive adjectives, and a few other words such as *any, both, several,* and *whose,* that occupies the first position in a noun phrase or the second or third position after another determinative. For example, in the phrase *he knows both girls, both* is a determinative. Some determinatives may be used in the place of the noun phrase that they introduce: *several people have left* or *several have left.* In this sense, also called "determiner." —**de·ter′mi·na′tive·ness** *n.*

de·ter·mine (dĭ-tûr′mĭn) *v.* **-mined, -mining, -mines.** —*tr.* **1. a.** To decide or settle (a dispute, for example) conclusively and authoritatively. **b.** To end or decide by judicial or other final action. **2.** To establish or ascertain definitely, as after consideration, investigation, or calculation. **3.** To cause (someone) to come to a conclusion or resolution. **4.** To be the cause of; influence; regulate. **5.** To give direction to; decide the course of. **6.** To limit in scope or extent; fix the bounds of. **7.** *Geometry.* To fix or define the position, form, or configuration of. **8.** *Logic.* To explain or limit by adding differences. **9.** *Law.* To put an end to; terminate. —*intr.* **1.** To reach a decision; to resolve. **2.** *Law.* To come to an end. —See Synonyms at **decide.** [Middle English *determinen,* from Old French *determiner,* from Latin *dēterminãre,* to limit : *dē-,* off + *termināre,* to limit, from *terminus,* boundary line (see **ter-**[1] in Appendix*).]

de·ter·mined (dĭ-tûr′mĭnd) *adj.* Marked by or showing determination or fixed purpose; resolute; unwavering; firm. —**de·ter′mined·ly** *adv.* —**de·ter′mined·ness** *n.*

de·ter·min·er (dĭ-tûr′mə-nər) *n.* **1.** One that determines. **2.** *Grammar.* A **determinative** *(see).*

de·ter·min·ism (dĭ-tûr′mə-nĭz′əm) *n.* The philosophical doctrine that every event, act, and decision is the inevitable consequence of antecedents, such as physical, psychological, or environmental conditions, that are independent of the human will.

de·ter·rence (dĭ-tûr′əns) *n.* **1.** The action or a means of deterring. **2.** Measures taken by a state or an alliance of states to prevent hostile action by another state. —**de·ter′rent** *adj.* & *n.* —**de·ter′rent·ly** *adv.*

de·test (dĭ-tĕst′) *tr.v.* **-tested, -testing, -tests.** To dislike intensely; abhor; loathe. [Latin *dētestārī,* curse, execrate : *dē-* (pejorative) + *testārī,* to invoke, call to witness, from *testis,* a witness (see **trei-** in Appendix*).] —**de·test′er** *n.*

de·test·a·ble (dĭ-tĕs′tə-bəl) *adj.* Deserving abhorrence or execration; odious; abominable. See Synonyms at hateful. —de·test′a·bil′i·ty, de·test′a·ble·ness *n.* —de·test′a·bly *adv.*

de·tes·ta·tion (dē′tĕ-stā′shən) *n.* 1. Strong dislike; hatred or abhorrence. 2. Someone or something that is detested.

de·throne (dē-thrōn′) *tr.v.* -throned, -throning, -thrones. To remove from the throne; depose. —de·throne′ment *n.*

det·i·nue (dĕt′ĭ-nyōō′) *n.* *Law.* 1. a. An action to recover possession or the value of property wrongfully detained. b. The writ authorizing such action. 2. *Obsolete.* The act of unlawfully detaining personal property. [Middle English detenewe, from Old French detenue, detention, from the past participle of detenir, DETAIN.]

det·o·na·ble (dĕt′n-ə-bəl) *adj.* Also det·o·nat·a·ble (dĕt′n-ā′tə-bəl). Capable of being detonated.

det·o·nate (dĕt′n-āt′) *v.* -nated, -nating, -nates. —*tr.* To cause to explode. —*intr.* To explode suddenly and violently. [Latin dētonāre, to thunder down : dē-, down + tonāre, to thunder (see stenə- in Appendix*).]

det·o·na·tion (dĕt′n-ā′shən) *n.* 1. The act of detonating or exploding. 2. A violent explosion.

det·o·na·tor (dĕt′n-ā′tər) *n.* 1. A device, such as a fuse or percussion cap, used to set off explosives. 2. An explosive.

de·tour (dē′tŏŏr′, dĭ-tŏŏr′) *n.* 1. A roundabout way or course; especially, a byroad used temporarily instead of a main route. 2. Deviation from the direct or shortest road, route, or course of action. —*v.* detoured, -touring, -tours. —*tr.* To cause to go by a roundabout way or detour. —*intr.* To go by a roundabout way. [French détour, from Old French destor, from destorner, to turn away : des-, de-, away + torner, TURN.]

de·tox·i·fy (dē-tŏk′sə-fī′) *tr.v.* -fied, -fying, -fies. Also de·tox·i·cate (-kāt′), -cated, -cating, -cates. 1. To counteract or destroy the toxic properties of. 2. To remove the effects of poison from. [DE- (reversal) + TOXI(C) + -FY.] —de·tox′i·fi·ca′tion *n.*

de·tract (dĭ-trăkt′) *v.* -tracted, -tracting, -tracts. —*intr.* To take away a desirable part; diminish. Used with *from.* —*tr.* To distract. [Middle English detracten, from Latin dētrahere (past participle dētractus), to pull down, draw away : dē-, away + trahere, pull (see tragh- in Appendix*).]

de·trac·tion (dĭ-trăk′shən) *n.* 1. Disparagement; slander. 2. The act of detracting or taking away. —de·trac′tive *adj.* —de·trac′tor (-tər) *n.*

de·train (dē-trān′) *v.* -trained, -training, -trains. *Chiefly British Military.* —*tr.* To cause to leave a railroad train. —*intr.* To leave a railroad train. —de·train′ment *n.*

de·trib·al·ize (dē-trī′bə-līz′) *tr.v.* -ized, -izing, -izes. To cause to lose tribal customs. —de·trib′al·i·za′tion *n.*

det·ri·ment (dĕt′rə-mənt) *n.* 1. Damage, harm, or loss. 2. Something that causes damage, harm, or loss. [Middle English, from Old French, from Latin dētrīmentum, from dēterere, to wear away : dē-, away + terere, to rub (see ter-² in Appendix*).]

det·ri·men·tal (dĕt′rə-mĕnt′l) *adj.* Causing damage or harm; injurious. —det′ri·men′tal·ly *adv.*

de·tri·tion (dĭ-trĭsh′ən) *n.* The act of wearing away by friction or rubbing. [Medieval Latin dētrītiō, from Latin dētrītus, past participle of dēterere, to rub away. See detriment.]

de·tri·tus (dĭ-trī′təs) *n.* 1. Loose fragments, particles, or grains that have been formed by the disintegration of rocks. 2. Any disintegrated matter; debris. [French détritus, from Latin dētrītus, past participle of dēterere, to wear away. See detriment.]

De·troit (dĭ-troit′). A city, port, and automobile-manufacturing center in southeastern Michigan, on the Detroit River, opposite Windsor, Ontario, Canada. Population, 1,670,000.

De·troit River (dĭ-troit′). A river flowing about 32 miles between Lake St. Clair and Lake Erie and forming part of the U.S.-Canadian border.

de trop (də trō′). *French.* Too much; too many; superfluous.

de·tu·mes·cence (dē′tōō-mĕs′əns, -tyōō-mĕs′əns) *n.* Contraction following expansion, especially restoration of a swollen organ or part to normal size. [Latin dētumescere, cease swelling : dē- (reversal) + tumescere, swell up, from tumēre, be swollen (see teuə- in Appendix*).]

Deu·ca·li·on (dōō-kā′lē-ən, dyōō-). *Greek Mythology.* A son of Prometheus who, with his wife Pyrrha, survived a deluge sent by Zeus and became the ancestor of the renewed human race.

deuce¹ (dōōs, dyōōs) *n.* 1. a. A playing card or side of a die bearing two spots. b. A cast of the dice totaling two. 2. *Tennis.* A score in which each player or side has 40 points (or 5 or more games each) and either player or side must win 2 successive points (or games) to win the game (or set). [Old French deus, two, from Latin duōs, accusative of duo. See dwō in Appendix*.]

deuce² (dōōs, dyōōs) *n.* *Informal.* Bad luck; the devil. Used as a mild oath or exclamation of annoyance, impatience, or surprise. [Probably from Low German duus, deuce, two at dice (from the exclamation of the player making the lowest throw), ultimately from Latin duōs, two. See deuce (card with two spots).]

deu·ced (dōō′sĭd, dyōō′sĭd) *adj.* *Informal.* Darned; confounded; extreme. [From DEUCE (devil).] —deu′ced, deu′ced·ly *adv.*

deuces wild. A variation of certain card games, such as poker, in which each deuce may represent any card the holder chooses.

De·us (dē′əs, dā′ŏŏs) *n.* *Abbr.* D. *Latin.* God.

de·us ex mach·i·na (dā′ŏŏs ĕks mä′kē-nä′, dē′əs ĕks măk′ə-nə). 1. A deity in Greek and Roman drama who was brought in by stage machinery to intervene in a difficult situation. 2. Any unexpected, artificial, or improbable character, device, or event suddenly introduced to resolve a situation or untangle a plot.

Eamon de Valera
Photographed in 1955

[New Latin, "god from a machine" (translation of Greek *theos ek mēkhanēs*).]

Deut. Deuteronomy (Old Testament).

deu·ter·a·no·pi·a (dōō′tər-ə-nō′pē-ə, dyōō′-) *n.* A form of color-blindness characterized by confusion of green, bluish red, and neutral. [New Latin : DEUTER(O)- + AN- (lack of) + -OPIA.] —deu′ter·a·nope′ *n.*

deu·te·ri·um (dōō-tîr′ē-əm) *n.* *Symbol* D An isotope of hydrogen having an atomic weight of 2.0141. Also called "heavy hydrogen." [New Latin : DEUTER(O)- (because it is the second in the series of possible hydrogen isotopes) + -IUM.]

deuterium oxide. An isotopic form of water with composition D₂O, present in natural water as approximately 1 part in 6,500 and isolated for use as a moderator in certain nuclear reactors. Also called "heavy water."

deutero-, deuter-, deuto-. Indicates second or secondary; for example, deuterocanonical, deuteranopia, deutoplasm. [From Greek deuteros, second. See deu-¹ in Appendix.*]

deu·ter·o·ca·non·i·cal (dōō′tə-rō-kə-nŏn′ĭ-kəl, dyōō′-) *adj.* 1. Pertaining to books or sections of books in the New Testament whose authority was once contested but later accepted. 2. Pertaining to books or sections of books in the Old Testament, considered canonical by the Eastern Orthodox and Roman Catholics, and apocryphal by many Protestants. See Apocrypha. [DEUTERO- + CANONICAL.]

deu·ter·og·a·my (dōō′tə-rŏg′ə-mē, dyōō′-) *n.* A second legal marriage, after the death or divorce of a first spouse. [Late Greek deuterogamia : DEUTERO- + -GAMY.]

Deu·ter·o-I·sa·iah (dōō′tə-rō-ī-zā′ə, dyōō′-). The name given to the author of chapters 40–66 of Isaiah, who was a Hebrew writer during the Babylonian captivity (586–539 B.C.).

deu·ter·on (dōō′tə-rŏn, dyōō′-) *n.* *Symbol* d The nucleus of a deuterium atom, a composite of a proton and a neutron, regarded as a subatomic particle with unit positive charge. [DEUTER(IUM) + -ON.]

Deu·ter·on·o·my (dōō′tə-rŏn′ə-mē, dyōō′-) *n.* *Abbr.* Deut. The fifth book of the Old Testament, in which the law of Moses is stated completely for the second time. [Late Latin deuteronomium, from Greek deuteronomion, from the Septuagint mistranslation (Deuteronomy 16:18) of Hebrew mishnēh hattôrah hazzō'th, "a copy of this law," as deuteronomion (touto), "(this) second law" : DEUTERO- + nomos, law (see nem-² in Appendix*).]

deu·to·plasm (dōō′tə-plăz′əm, dyōō′-) *n.* Also deu·ter·o·plasm (-tə-rō-plăz′əm). Food substance or yolk in the cytoplasm of an ovum or other cell. [DEUT(ERO)- + -PLASM.]

Deut·sche mark (doi′chə märk′). Also deut·sche·mark. *Abbr.* DM 1. The basic monetary unit of West Germany, equal to 100 pfennigs. See table of exchange rates at currency. 2. A coin worth one Deutsche mark. See mark (money). [German, "German mark."]

Deutsch·land. The German name for Germany.

deut·zi·a (dōōt′sē-ə, dyōōt′-) *n.* Any of various shrubs of the genus *Deutzia*, cultivated for their clusters of white or pinkish flowers. [New Latin *Deutzia*, after Jean Deutz (died 1784?), Dutch patron of botany.]

de Va·le·ra (dĕv′ə-lâr′ə, -lîr′ə), Eamon. Born 1882. American-born prime minister of Ireland (1937–48, 1951–54, and 1957–59); president of Ireland (since 1959).

de·val·u·ate (dē-văl′yōō-āt′) *tr.v.* -ated, -ating, -ates. Also de·val·ue (dē-văl′yōō), -ued, -uing, -ues. 1. To lessen or annul the value of. 2. To lower the exchange value of (currency) by lowering its gold equivalency. —de·val′u·a′tion *n.*

De·va·na·ga·ri (dā′və-nä′gə-rē) *n.* The alphabet in which Sanskrit and many modern Indian languages are written. [Sanskrit devanāgarī, "the divine script of the city" : deváh, god (see deiw- in Appendix*) + nāgarī, (script) of the city, from nāgaram, town, city, probably from Dravidian.]

dev·as·tate (dĕv′ə-stāt′) *tr.v.* -tated, -tating, -tates. 1. To lay waste. 2. *Informal.* To defeat; confound. —See Synonyms at ruin. [Latin dēvāstāre : dē- (intensive) + vāstāre, to lay waste, from vāstus, waste (see eu-² in Appendix*).] —dev′as·tat′ing·ly *adv.* —dev′as·ta′tion *n.* —dev′as·ta′tor (-ə-stā′tər) *n.*

de Ve·ga, Lope. See Vega.

de·vel·op (dĭ-vĕl′əp) *v.* -oped, -oping, -ops. Also de·vel·ope. —*tr.* 1. To expand or realize the potentialities of; bring gradually to a fuller, greater, or better state. 2. To elaborate or enlarge. 3. *Music.* To unfold (a theme) with rhythmic and harmonic variations. 4. To disclose gradually. 5. To bring into being; make active; generate. 6. To make more available; put to use. 7. To convert (a tract of land) to a specific purpose, as by building extensively. 8. To come to have gradually; acquire. 9. To become affected with; contract. See Usage note below. 10. *Photography.* To process (a photosensitive material), especially with chemicals, in order to render a recorded image visible. —*intr.* 1. To grow; expand. 2. To come gradually into existence or activity. 3. To be disclosed. 4. *Biology.* a. To progress from earlier to later stages of individual maturation. b. To progress from earlier to later or from simpler to more complex stages of evolution. [French développer, from Old French desvoluper : des-, from Latin dis- (reversal) + voluper, to wrap up, perhaps from Celtic vol- (unattested), to roll (see wel-³ in Appendix*).] —de·vel′op·a·ble *adj.*

Usage: Develop has been established in the sense of contract, with reference to illness: He developed tuberculosis. This is acceptable to 67 per cent of the Usage Panel.

de·vel·op·er (dĭ-vĕl′ə-pər) *n.* 1. One that develops. 2. *Photography.* A chemical used to render visible the image recorded on a photosensitive surface.

de·vel·op·ment (dĭ-vĕl′əp-mənt) *n.* **1.** The act of developing. **2.** A developed state, condition, or form. **3.** Something that has been developed; a product or result of developing. **4.** An event, occurrence, or happening: *a development in the war.* **5.** A group of dwellings built by the same contractor. **—de·vel′op·men′tal** *adj.* **—de·vel′op·men′tal·ly** *adv.*

de·verb·a·tive (dĭ-vûr′bə-tĭv) *adj. Grammar.* **1.** Designating a word derived from a verb. *Worker* is a deverbative noun derived from the verb *work.* **2.** Designating an element used in derivation from a verb. The suffix *-er* in *teacher* is deverbative. *—n. Grammar.* A deverbative word or element.

Dev·er·eux, Robert. See **Essex.**

de·vest (dĭ-vĕst′) *tr.v.* **-vested, -vesting, -vests.** *Law.* To take (a title, estate, or right, for example) away from. [Old French *desvestir,* to undress, from Vulgar Latin *disvestire* (unattested) : Latin *dis-* (reversal) + *vestīre,* to dress, from *vestis,* garment (see **wes-**[4] in Appendix*).]

De·vi (dā′vē). *Hinduism.* A general appellation for all feminine deities, especially in their demoniac aspects. Used mainly of the **Shakti** *(see)* of Shiva. [Sanskrit *devī,* feminine of *devah,* god. See **deiw-** in Appendix.*]

de·vi·ant (dē′vē-ənt) *adj.* Differing from a norm or from the accepted standards of society; deviating. *—n.* A **deviate** *(see).* [Middle English *deviaunt,* from Late Latin *dēviāns,* present participle of *dēviāre,* DEVIATE.] **—de′vi·ance** *n.*

de·vi·ate (dē′vē-āt′) *v.* **-ated, -ating, -ates.** *—intr.* To oscillate about or move increasingly away from a designated norm, as from a specified course or prescribed mode of behavior. *—tr.* To cause to turn aside or differ. *—n.* (dē′vē-ĭt). **1.** A person whose attitude or behavior differs from the norm or from the accepted social or moral standards. **2.** A sexual pervert. Also called "deviant." [Late Latin *dēviāre* : Latin *dē-,* away from + *via,* road, way (see **wei-**[2] in Appendix*).] **—de′vi·a′tor** (-ā′tər) *n.*

de·vi·a·tion (dē′vē-ā′shən) *n.* **1.** The act of deviating or turning aside. **2.** An abnormality; departure: *"vice was a deviation from our nature . . . as deformity of the body is"* (Fielding). **3.** *Statistics.* **a.** The difference, especially the absolute difference, between one of a set of numbers and their mean. **b.** Any variation from a trend. **4.** Divergence from an accepted policy or norm. **—de′vi·a′tion·ism′** *n.* **—de′vi·a′tion·ist** *n.*

de·vice (dĭ-vīs′) *n.* **1.** Something devised or constructed for a particular purpose; especially, a machine used to perform one or more relatively simple tasks. **2.** An artistic contrivance in a literary work used to achieve a particular effect. **3.** A plan or scheme, especially a malign one. **4.** A decorative design, figure, or pattern, as one used in embroidery. **5.** A graphic symbol or motto, especially in heraldry. **6.** *Archaic.* The act, state, or power of devising. **—leave to one's own devices.** To allow to do as one pleases. [Middle English *devis, devise,* from Old French *devis,* division, contrivance, invention, and *devise,* difference, design, plan, both from *deviser,* to divide, DEVISE.]

dev·il (dĕv′əl) *n.* **1.** *Often capital* **D.** *Theology.* The major spirit of evil, ruler of Hell, and foe of God, often depicted as a man with horns, a tail, and cloven hoofs; Satan. **2.** A subordinate evil spirit. **3.** A wicked, malevolent, or ill-tempered person. **4.** An unfortunate person; wretch: *poor devil.* **5.** A person who is energetic, mischievous, daring, or clever. **6.** The personification of something evil or undesirable: *"I have said my prayers and devil Envy say Amen"* (Shakespeare). **7.** A **printer's devil** *(see).* **8.** Any of various mechanical devices with sharp teeth or spikes, as for tearing up rags. **9.** *Informal.* Anything difficult or hard to manage: *"the poor dear sufferer had the very devil of a time"* (Ford Madox Ford). **10.** *Christian Science.* The opposite of Truth; error; a lie. **—give the devil his due.** To acknowledge the ability or success of an evil or disliked person. **—the devil.** *Informal.* An exclamation or expletive used to express surprise, anger, disgust, vexation, or the like. **—the devil to pay.** Trouble to be faced as a result of some action. *—v.* **deviled** or **-villed, -viling** or **-villing, -vils.** *—tr.* **1.** To prepare (food) with pungent seasoning or condiments, such as mustard or cayenne pepper. **2.** To tear up (cloth or rags) in a toothed machine. **3.** To annoy, torment, or harass. *—intr.* To serve as a printer's devil. [Middle English *devel,* Old English *dēofol,* from Late Latin *diabolus,* from Late Greek *diabolos,* from Greek, slanderer, from *diaballein,* to slander, set at variance, "throw across" : *dia-,* across + *ballein,* to throw (see **gwel-**[1] in Appendix*).]

dev·il·fish (dĕv′əl-fĭsh′) *n., pl.* **devilfish** or **-fishes. 1.** The **manta** *(see).* **2.** An **octopus** *(see),* or a similar cephalopod.

dev·il·ish (dĕv′ə-lĭsh) *adj.* **1.** Of, resembling, or characteristic of a devil; fiendish: *"that's the devilish side of a woman's fascination: she makes you will your own destruction"* (G.B. Shaw). **2.** *Informal.* Excessive; extreme: *devilish heat.* *—adv. Informal.* Extremely; very. **—dev′il·ish·ly** *adv.* **—dev′il·ish·ness** *n.*

dev·il-may-care (dĕv′əl-mā-kâr′) *adj.* Careless; reckless.

dev·il·ment (dĕv′əl-mənt) *n.* Devilish mischief.

devil's advocate. 1. *Roman Catholic Church.* An official appointed to present arguments against a proposed canonization or beatification. **2.** A person who opposes an argument with which he does not necessarily disagree, as to determine its validity. **3.** An adverse critic, especially of a good cause.

devil's bit. A plant, the **blazing star** *(see).* [From its bitter taste.]

devil's club. A spiny shrub, *Oplopanax horridus,* of western North America, having greenish-white flowers and scarlet fruit.

devil's darning needle. *Informal.* A **dragonfly** *(see).*

dev·il's-food cake (dĕv′əlz-fo͝od′). A rich chocolate cake. [From the contrast with the white color of ANGEL FOOD CAKE.]

Devil's Island. *French* **Île du Dia·ble** (ēl dü dyä′bl′). An islet, eight miles off the coast of French Guiana; site of a former French penal colony.

devil's paintbrush. A plant, the **orange hawkweed** *(see).*

devil's walking stick. A shrub, **Hercules'-club** *(see).*

dev·il·try (dĕv′əl-trē) *n., pl.* **-tries.** Also **dev·il·ry** (-əl-rē). **1.** Wanton or reckless mischief. **2.** Wickedness. **3.** Evil magic.

dev·il·wood (dĕv′əl-wo͝od′) *n.* A tree, *Osmanthus americanus,* of the southeastern United States, having fragrant greenish flowers and hard wood. [Because it is extremely difficult to cut.]

de·vi·ous (dē′vē-əs) *adj.* **1.** Straying or deviating from the usual, straight, or direct course or way; swerving; roundabout. **2.** Straying or departing from the correct or proper way; erring. **3.** Done, used, or acting in an underhand manner; not straightforward; shifty: *a devious person.* [Latin *dēvius,* off the main road : *dē-,* away from + *via,* way (see **wei-**[2] in Appendix*).] **—de′vi·ous·ly** *adv.* **—de′vi·ous·ness** *n.*

de·vis·a·ble (dĭ-vī′zə-bəl) *adj.* **1.** *Law.* Capable of being transmitted **by** will. Said of real property. **2.** Capable of being invented or contrived.

de·vi·sal (dĭ-vī′zəl) *n.* The act of devising.

de·vise (dĭ-vīz′) *v.* **-vised, -vising, -vises.** *—tr.* **1.** To form or arrange in the mind; plan; invent; contrive. **2.** *Law.* To transmit or give (real property) by will. **3.** *Obsolete.* To guess; imagine; conceive. *—intr.* To form a plan; contrive. *—n. Law.* **1.** The act of transmitting or giving real property by will. **2.** The property or lands so transmitted. **3.** A will or clause in a will devising real property. [Middle English *devisen,* to divide, distinguish, examine, design, from Old French *deviser,* from Vulgar Latin *dīvīsāre* (unattested), frequentative of Latin *dīvidere* (past participle *dīvīsus*), to divide. See **weidh-** in Appendix.*] **—de·vis′er** *n.*

de·vi·see (dĭ-vī′zē′) *n. Law.* One to whom a devise is made.

de·vi·sor (dĭ-vī′zər) *n. Law.* One who makes a devise.

de·vi·tal·ize (dē-vīt′l-īz′) *tr.v.* **-ized, -izing, -izes.** To lower or destroy the vitality of.

de·vit·ri·fy (dē-vĭt′rə-fī′) *tr.v.* **-fied, -fying, -fies. 1.** To deprive of or destroy the glassy quality of. **2.** To treat (material such as glass) so as to cause crystallization, brittleness, and loss of transparency. [French *dévitrifier* : *dé-,* from Latin *dē-* (reversal) + *vitrifier,* VITRIFY.] **—de·vit′ri·fi·ca′tion** *n.*

de·vo·cal·ize (dē-vō′kə-līz′) *tr.v.* **-ized, -izing, -izes.** *Phonetics.* To unvoice. **—de·vo′cal·i·za′tion** *n.*

de·voice (dē-vois′) *tr.v.* **-voiced, -voicing, -voices.** *Phonetics.* To unvoice (a speech sound).

de·void (dĭ-void′) *adj.* Completely lacking; destitute; empty; without. Used with *of.* [Middle English *devoide,* from Middle English *devoiden,* from Old French *desvuidier* : *des-,* from Latin *dē-,* completely + *vuidier,* to empty, from Vulgar Latin *vocitāre* (unattested), from *vocitus* (unattested), empty, from Latin *vacāre,* to be empty (see **eu-**[2] in Appendix*).]

de·voir (də-vwär′, dĕv′wär′) *n.* **1.** *Usually plural.* Courteous attentions; compliments; respects: *pay one's devoirs to the hostess.* **2.** *Archaic.* Duty. [Middle English *dever, devoir,* duty, from Old French *devoir,* "that which is due," from *devoir,* to owe, from Latin *dēbēre.* See **ghabh-** in Appendix.*]

dev·o·lu·tion (dĕv′ə-lo͞o′shən) *n.* **1.** A passing down through successive stages. **2.** The passing to a successor of anything, such as properties, rights, and qualities. **3.** A delegating of authority or duties to a subordinate or substitute. **4.** Biological degeneration, as distinguished from evolution. [Medieval Latin *dēvolūtiō,* from Latin *dēvolvere* (past participle *dēvolūtus*), to roll down, DEVOLVE.] **—dev′o·lu′tion·ar′y** *adj.*

de·volve (dĭ-vŏlv′) *v.* **-volved, -volving, -volves.** *—tr.* To pass on or delegate (duty or authority, for example) to a successor or substitute. *—intr.* To be passed on to a substitute or successor; be conferred. Used with *on, to,* or *upon: "With this high honor devolves upon you also a corresponding responsibility."* (Lincoln). [Middle English *devolven,* from Latin *dēvolvere,* to roll down : *dē-,* down + *volvere,* to roll (see **wel-**[3] in Appendix*).] **—de·volve′ment** *n.*

Dev·on[1] (dĕv′ən). **1.** An island, 21,606 square miles in area, of the Northwest Territories, Canada, south of Ellesmere Island. **2.** See **Devonshire.**

Dev·on[2] (dĕv′ən) *n.* Any of a breed of reddish cattle developed in Devonshire, England, and raised primarily for beef.

De·vo·ni·an (dĭ-vō′nē-ən) *adj.* **1.** Of or pertaining to Devon or Devonshire, England. **2.** Of, belonging to, or designating the geologic time, system of rocks, or sedimentary deposits of the fourth period of the Paleozoic era, preceded by the Silurian and followed by the Mississippian or Carboniferous period, and characterized by the appearance of forests and amphibians. See **geology.** *—n. Geology.* The Devonian period or system of deposits. Preceded by *the.*

Dev·on·shire (dĕv′ən-shîr, -shər). Also **Dev·on** (dĕv′ən). A county, 2,611 square miles in area, of southwestern England. Population, 851,000. County seat, Exeter.

de·vote (dĭ-vōt′) *tr.v.* **-voted, -voting, -votes. 1.** To give or apply (one's time, attention, or self) entirely to a particular activity, pursuit, cause, or person. **2.** To set apart by or as if by a vow or solemn act; dedicate; consecrate. **3.** *Rare.* To doom to destruction; to curse. [Latin *dēvovēre* (past participle *dēvōtus*), to vow, devote : *dē-,* completely + *vovēre,* to vow (see **wegwh-** in Appendix*).] **—de·vote′ment** *n.*

Synonyms: *devote, dedicate, consecrate, pledge.* These verbs are compared primarily in the sense of giving oneself or one's effort for a particular end. *Devote,* the most general, implies loyal and close attention to a cause, a job, another person, or the like. *Dedicate* adds the idea of a solemn and often formal commitment; in a related sense it means to set something apart,

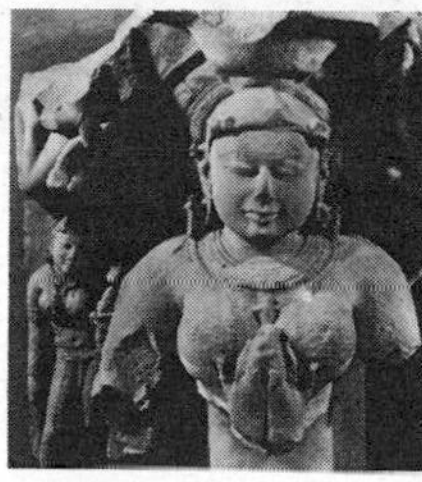

Devi
Tenth-century sandstone figure of a Devi, from central India

such as land or a structure, for special use. *Consecrate* stresses sacred commitment, as of a person to a cause or of a physical thing to religious use. *Pledge* refers to personal commitment backed by a solemn promise.

de·vot·ed (dĭ-vō′tĭd) *adj.* **1.** Feeling or displaying strong affection or attachment; selflessly loyal; ardent. **2.** Consecrated; dedicated. **3.** *Archaic.* Doomed. —See Synonyms at **faithful.** —**de·vot′ed·ly** *adv.* —**de·vot′ed·ness** *n.*

dev·o·tee (dĕv′ə-tē′, -tā′) *n.* **1.** One ardently devoted or attached to anything: *a devotee of sports.* **2.** One ardently or fanatically devoted to a religion. —See Synonyms at **votary.**

de·vo·tion (dĭ-vō′shən) *n.* **1.** Ardent attachment or affection, as to a person or cause; faithfulness; loyalty. **2.** Religious ardor or zeal; piety. **3.** *Usually plural.* An act of religious observance or prayer, especially when private. **4.** The act of devoting or the state of being devoted. —See Synonyms at **love, fidelity.**

de·vo·tion·al (dĭ-vō′shən-əl) *adj.* **1.** Of or pertaining to devotion. **2.** Used in worship. —*n.* A short service of worship. —**de·vo′tion·al·ly** *adv.*

de·vour (dĭ-vour′) *tr.v.* **-voured, -vouring, -vours. 1.** To swallow or eat up greedily. **2.** To destroy, consume, or waste. **3.** To take in greedily with the senses or mind: *devour a novel.* **4.** To swallow up; engulf; absorb. [Middle English *devouren,* from Old French *devourer,* from Latin *dēvorāre* : *dē-,* completely + *vorāre,* to swallow, devour (see **gwerə-**[2] in Appendix*).] —**de·vour′er** *n.* —**de·vour′ing·ly** *adv.*

de·vout (dĭ-vout′) *adj.* **1.** Deeply religious; pious. **2.** Displaying reverence or piety. **3.** Sincere; earnest; devoted. —See Synonyms at **religious.** [Middle English *devo(u)t,* from Old French *devot,* from Late Latin *dēvōtus,* from Latin, past participle of *dēvovēre,* to vow, DEVOTE.] —**de·vout′ly** *adv.* —**de·vout′ness** *n.*

De Vries (də vrēs′), **Hugo.** 1848–1935. Dutch botanist; rediscovered Mendel's laws; developed mutation theories.

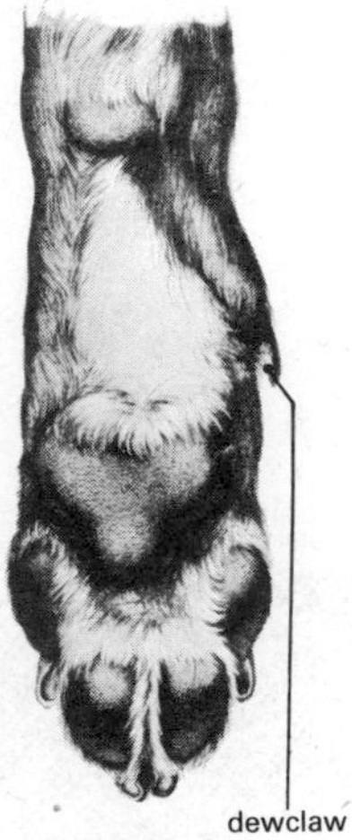

dewclaw
Paw of a dog

dew (dōō, dyōō) *n.* **1.** Water droplets condensed from the air, usually at night, onto cool surfaces, as of grass. **2.** Anything resembling or suggestive of dew; something moist, refreshing, or pure. **3.** Any moisture appearing in small drops, as tears. —*tr.v.* **dewed, dewing, dews.** To wet with or as with dew; moisten; bedew. [Middle English *deu, de(a)w,* Old English *dēaw.* See **dheu-**[2] in Appendix.*]

de·wan (dĭ-wän′, -wôn′) *n.* Also **di·wan.** Any of certain governmental officials, especially a prime minister, in India. [Hindi *dīwān,* from Persian *dīvān*†, register, account book, hence office of accounts, council of state. See also **divan.**]

Dew·ar flask (dōō′ər, dyōō′-). An insulated container used especially to store liquefied gases, having a double wall with evacuated space between the walls and silvered surfaces. [Invented by Sir James *Dewar* (1842–1923), Scottish physicist.]

dew·ber·ry (dōō′bĕr′ē, dyōō′-) *n., pl.* **-ries. 1.** Any of several trailing forms of the blackberry, such as *Rubus hispidus,* of North America, and *R. caesius,* of Europe. **2.** The fruit of any of these plants.

dew·claw (dōō′klô′, dyōō′-) *n.* A vestigial digit, claw, or hoof on the foot of certain mammals. [Because it reaches only the dewy surface of the ground.]

dew·drop (dōō′drŏp′, dyōō′-) *n.* **1.** A drop of dew. **2.** A North American plant, *Dalibarda repens,* having rounded leaves and white flowers.

Dew·ey (dōō′ē, dyōō′ē), **George.** 1837–1917. American naval officer; commander of Asiatic fleet.

Dew·ey (dōō′ē, dyōō′ē), **John.** 1859–1952. American philosopher, educator, and author.

Dew·ey (dōō′ē, dyōō′ē), **Thomas Edmund.** Born 1902. American political leader; twice Presidential candidate (1944 and 1948).

Dew·ey decimal system (dōō′ē, dyōō′ē). *Library Service.* A system of classification of books and other publications into ten major categories, each category being further subdivided by number. Also called "Dewey classification." [Devised in 1876 by Melvil *Dewey* (1851–1931), American librarian.]

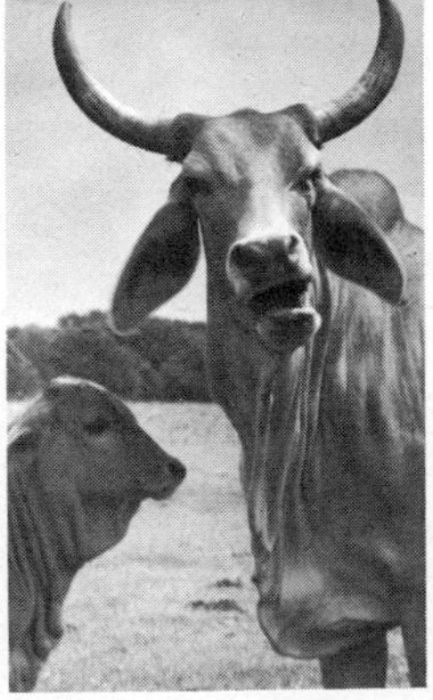

dewlap
Brahman cow and calf

dew·fall (dōō′fôl′, dyōō′-) *n.* **1.** The formation of dew. **2.** The time of evening when dew begins to form. [From the erroneous assumption that dew falls like rain.]

dew·lap (dōō′lăp′, dyōō′-) *n.* **1.** A fold of loose skin hanging from the neck region of certain animals. **2.** A similar pendulous part, such as the wattle of a bird or a fold of skin hanging from the throat of an aged person. [Middle English *dewlappe* : DEW + *lappe,* LAP (loose flap).]

DEW line (dōō, dyōō). A line of radar stations at about the 70th parallel across the North American continent, designed to give advance warning of approaching aircraft and missiles.

dew point. The temperature at which air becomes saturated and produces dew.

dew·worm (dōō′wûrm′, dyōō′-). Any earthworm found on or near the surface of the ground and used as fishing bait.

dew·y (dōō′ē, dyōō′ē) *adj.* **-ier, -iest. 1.** Wet or moist with or as if with dew. **2.** Pertaining to, resembling, or forming dew. **3.** *Poetic.* Suggestive of dew. —**dew′i·ly** *adv.* —**dew′i·ness** *n.*

dew·y-eyed (dōō′ē-īd′, dyōō′-) *adj.* Characterized by childlike innocence and faith.

dex·ter (dĕk′stər) *adj.* **1.** Of or located on the right side. **2.** *Heraldry.* Located on the wearer's right and the observer's left. Compare **sinister. 3.** *Obsolete.* Auspicious; favorable. [Latin, on the right side. See **deks-** in Appendix.*]

dex·ter·i·ty (dĕk-stĕr′ə-tē) *n.* **1.** Skill in the use of the hands or body; adroitness. **2.** Mental skill or adroitness; cleverness: *"He admired the dexterity with which their host directed the conversation."* (Joyce). **3.** *Rare.* Right-handedness. [Old French *dexterite,* from Latin *dexteritās,* from *dexter,* skillful, DEXTER.]

dex·ter·ous (dĕk′strəs) *adj.* Also **dex·trous. 1.** Adroit or skillful in the use of the hands, body, or mind; artful; clever. **2.** Done with dexterity. [From Latin *dexter,* skillful, DEXTER.] —**dex′ter·ous·ly** *adv.* —**dex′ter·ous·ness** *n.*

Synonyms: *dexterous, deft, adroit, handy, nimble.* These adjectives refer to skill and ease in performance. *Dexterous* usually applies to manual ability. *Deft* suggests quickness, sureness, and lightness of touch in physical or mental activity. *Adroit* implies ease and natural skill, especially in meeting difficult situations. *Handy* implies a more modest aptitude, principally in manual work. *Nimble* stresses quickness and liveliness in physical or mental performance.

dex·tral (dĕk′strəl) *adj.* **1.** Of, pertaining to, or located on the right side; right. **2.** Right-handed. Compare **sinistral. 3.** *Zoology.* Designating or pertaining to a gastropod shell that has its aperture to the right when facing the observer with the apex upward. [Medieval Latin *dextralis,* from Latin *dexter,* DEXTER.] —**dex·tral′i·ty** (-străl′ə-tē) *n.* —**dex′tral·ly** *adv.*

dex·tran (dĕk′strən) *n.* Any of various heavy long-chain polymers of glucose that are used, depending on molecular weight, as a blood-plasma substitute, in confections, lacquers, and food additives. [DEXTR(O)- + -AN.]

dex·trin (dĕk′strĭn) *n.* Also **dex·trine** (dĕk′strĭn, -strēn′). A white or yellow powder formed by the hydrolysis of starch, having colloidal properties, and used mainly as an adhesive and thickening agent. [DEXTR(O)- + -IN.]

dex·tro (dĕk′strō) *adj. Chemistry.* Dextrorotatory.

dextro-, dextr-. *Abbr.* **d** Indicates on or toward the right-hand side; for example, **dextrorotatory, dextran.** [Latin, from *dexter,* on the right side. See **deks-** in Appendix.*]

dex·tro·glu·cose (dĕk′strō-glōō′kōs) *n.* **Dextrose** *(see).*

dex·tro·ro·ta·tion (dĕk′strō-rō-tā′shən) *n. Optics.* A turning to the right. Said especially of the plane of polarization of light.

dex·tro·ro·ta·to·ry (dĕk′strō-rō′tə-tôr′ē, -tōr′ē) *adj.* Also **dex·tro·ro·ta·ry** (-tə-rē). **1.** *Optics.* Turning or rotating the plane of polarization of light to the right or clockwise: *dextrorotatory crystals.* **2.** *Chemistry.* Of or pertaining to a solution that so rotates the plane of polarized light. In this sense, also "dextrogyrate." Compare **levorotatory.**

dex·trorse (dĕk′strôrs′, dĕk-strôrs′) *adj.* Growing upward in a spiral that turns from left to right: *a dextrorse vine.* Compare **sinistrorse.** [New Latin *dextrorsus,* from Latin, turned toward the right side : DEXTRO- + *versus,* past participle of *vertere,* to turn (see **wer-**[3] in Appendix*).] —**dex′trorse·ly** *adv.*

dex·trose (dĕk′strōs′) *n.* A dextrorotatory sugar, $C_6H_{12}O_6 \cdot H_2O$, found in animal and plant tissue and derived synthetically from starch. Also called "corn sugar," "dextroglucose," "grape sugar," "glucose." [DEXTR(O)- + -OSE.]

dey (dā) *n.* **1.** The title of the governor of Algiers before the French conquest in 1830. **2.** Formerly, a title held by a ruler of Tunis or Tripoli. [French, from Turkish *dayı,* maternal uncle.]

Dezh·nev, Cape (dĕzh′nəf). Formerly **East Cape.** A cape forming the northeastern extremity of Asia, on the Bering Strait in the Russian S.F.S.R.

D.F. 1. Defender of the Faith. **2.** Distrito Federal.

DFC, D.F.C. Distinguished Flying Cross.

dg decigram.

dhak (däk, dôk) *n.* A tree, *Butea frondosa,* of tropical Asia, that yields a red resin used as an astringent. [Hindi *ḍhāk*†.]

dhar·ma (där′mə, dŭr′-) *n. Hinduism & Buddhism.* **1.** The ultimate law of all things. **2.** Individual right conduct in conformity to this law. [Sanskrit, law. See **dher-**[2] in Appendix.*]

Dhau·la·gi·ri (dou′lə-gîr′ē). A peak rising to 26,810 feet in the Himalayas of north-central Nepal.

Dhe·gi·ha (dā′jē-hä′) *n., pl.* **Dhegiha** or **-has. 1.** A Siouan language of the Osage, Omaha, and other neighboring tribes. **2.** The tribes speaking this language. **3.** A member of any of these tribes.

Dhi·mo·ti·ki (*th*ē-mō′tē-kē) *n.* The colloquial form of Modern Greek. Also called "Demotic."

dhole (dōl) *n.* A doglike, carnivorous mammal, *Cuon alpinus,* of Asia, having yellowish fur, and often hunting in packs. [Of Anglo-Indian origin, akin to Kanarese *tōla,* wolf.]

dho·ti (dō′tē) *n., pl.* **-tis.** Also **dhoo·ti** (dōō-). A loincloth worn by Hindu men in India. [Hindi *dhōtī*†.]

dhow (dou) *n.* A lateen-rigged Arabian vessel. [Arabic *dāw*†.]

Dhul-Hij·ja (dŭl′hĭj′ä) *n.* Also **Dul·heg·gia.** The 12th month of the Moslem year. Dhul-Hijja has 29 days. See **calendar.** [Arabic *dhū'l-ḥijja,* "the one of the pilgrimage."]

Dhul-Qa·dah (dŭl′käd′ä) *n.* Also **Dul·kaa·da.** The 11th month of the Moslem year. Dhul-Qadah has 30 days. See **calendar.** [Arabic *dhū'l-qa'dah,* "the one of the sitting."]

di-. Indicates: **1.** Twice, double, or two; for example, **dicotyledon. 2.** *Chemistry.* Having two atoms, molecules, or radicals; for example, **diacetylmorphine.** [From Greek *di-,* two, twice. See **dwō** in Appendix.*]

Di The symbol for didymium.

dia-, di-. Indicates: **1.** Through or throughout; for example, **diachronic. 2.** Across or by transmission; for example, **diapophysis, diactinic. 3.** *Botany.* Over, across, or at right angles; for example, **diatropism. 4.** In opposite or different directions; for example, **diamagnetic.** [In borrowed Greek compounds, *dia-* indicates: 1. Through, throughout, as in **diapason.** 2. Across, as in **diagonal.** 3. Between, as in **diapause.** 4. Apart, as in **dialysis.** 5. From one to another, mutually, as in **dialogue.** 6. In different directions, as in **diathesis.** 7. Completely, as in **diaphragm.** 8. Made of, as in **diatessaron.** Greek *dia-* is the preverbal form of *dia*†, through.]

dia. diameter.

di·a·base (dī′ə-bās′) *n.* Dark-gray to black, fine-textured igneous rock, composed mainly of feldspar and pyroxene, and used for monuments and as crushed stone. [French, from Greek *diabasis*, a crossing over, from *diabainein*, to cross over : *dia-*, across + *bainein*, to go (see **gwā-** in Appendix*).]

di·a·be·tes (dī′ə-bē′tĭs, -tēz) *n.* Any of several metabolic disorders marked by excessive discharge of urine and persistent thirst, especially **diabetes mellitus** *(see)*. [Middle English *diabete*, from Medieval Latin *diabētēs*, from Greek *diabētēs*, "a crossing over or passing through" (from the symptomatic excessive urination), from *diabainein*, to cross over : *dia-*, across + *bainein*, to go (see **gwā-** in Appendix*).]

diabetes in·sip·i·dus (ĭn-sĭp′ə-dəs). A disease characterized by intense thirst and excessive urination, caused by a disorder of the pituitary gland. [New Latin, "insipid diabetes."]

diabetes mel·li·tus (mə-lī′təs). A chronic disease of pancreatic origin, characterized by insulin deficiency, subsequent inability to utilize carbohydrates, excess sugar in the blood and urine, excessive thirst, hunger, and urination, weakness, emaciation, imperfect combustion of fats resulting in acidosis, and, without injection of insulin, eventual coma and death. [New Latin, "honey-sweet diabetes."]

di·a·bet·ic (dī′ə-bĕt′ĭk) *adj.* Of, relating to, or having diabetes. —*n.* One afflicted with diabetes mellitus.

di·a·ble·rie (dē-ä′blə-rē; *French* dyä-blə-rē′) *n.* Also **di·a·ble·ry** *pl.* **-ries.** **1.** Dealings with demons or the devil; sorcery; witchcraft. **2.** The representation of devils or demons, as in paintings or fiction. **3.** Devilish conduct; deviltry. [French, from *diable*, devil, from Late Latin *diabolus*, DEVIL.]

di·a·bol·ic (dī′ə-bŏl′ĭk) *adj.* Also **di·a·bol·i·cal** (-ĭ-kəl). **1.** Of, concerning, proceeding from, or having the characteristics of the devil; satanic; hellish. **2.** Appropriate to a devil; extremely wicked; fiendishly cruel. [Middle English *deabolik*, from Old French *diabolique*, from Late Latin *diabolicus*, from *diabolus*, DEVIL.] —**di′a·bol′i·cal·ly** *adv.* —**di′a·bol′i·cal·ness** *n.*

di·ab·o·lism (dī-ăb′ə-lĭz′əm) *n.* **1.** Dealings with or worship of the devil or demons; sorcery; witchcraft. **2.** Devilish conduct or character. —**di·ab′o·list** *n.*

di·ab·o·lize (dī-ăb′ə-līz′) *tr.v.* **-lized, -lizing, -lizes.** **1.** To cause to be diabolic or devilish. **2.** To bring under the influence of the devil. **3.** To represent as diabolic.

di·ac·e·tyl·mor·phine (dī-ăs′ə-təl-môr′fēn′) *n.* A narcotic, **heroin** *(see)*. [DI- (two) + ACETYL + MORPHINE.]

di·a·chron·ic (dī′ə-krŏn′ĭk) *adj.* **1.** Considering phenomena as they occur or develop through time. **2.** *Linguistics.* Pertaining to the study of language and linguistic phenomena as they change with time. Compare **synchronic.** [DIA- (through) + Greek *khronos*, time (see **chronic**).]

di·ac·id (dī-ăs′ĭd) *adj.* **1.** Capable of combining with two monoprotic acid molecules or one diprotic acid molecule to form a salt or ester. Said especially of bases. **2.** Possessing two hydrogen atoms replaceable by metal atoms. Said of a salt. —*n.* An acid possessing two readily replaceable hydrogen atoms.

di·ac·o·nal (dī-ăk′ə-nəl) *adj.* Of or concerning a deacon or the diaconate. [Late Latin *diācōnālis*, from *diāconus*, DEACON.]

di·ac·o·nate (dī-ăk′ə-nĭt) *n.* **1.** The rank or office of a deacon. **2.** Deacons. [Late Latin *diācōnātus*, from *diāconus*, DEACON.]

di·a·crit·ic (dī′ə-krĭt′ĭk) *adj.* **1.** Diacritical. **2.** *Medicine.* Diagnostic or distinctive. —*n.* A diacritical mark.

di·a·crit·i·cal (dī′ə-krĭt′ĭ-kəl) *adj.* Marking a distinction; distinguishing. [Greek *diakritikos*, distinguishing, from *diakrinein*, to distinguish : *dia-*, apart + *krinein*, to separate (see **skeri-** in Appendix*).] —**di′a·crit′i·cal·ly** *adv.*

diacritical mark. A mark added to a letter to indicate a special phonetic value; for example, in French *façon*, the cedilla indicates that the *c* does not have its regular prevocalic value (k), but a sibilant value (s).

di·ac·tin·ic (dī′ăk-tĭn′ĭk) *adj.* Capable of transmitting chemically active, or actinic, radiation. [DI(A)- (across) + ACTINIC.] —**di·ac′tin·ism′** (-ăk′tə-nĭz′əm) *n.*

di·a·del·phous (dī′ə-dĕl′fəs) *adj.* *Botany.* **1.** Having the filaments united so as to form two groups. Said of stamens. **2.** Having stamens thus united. Compare **monadelphous.** [DI- (two) + -ADELPHOUS.]

di·a·dem (dī′ə-dĕm′) *n.* **1.** A crown or cloth headband, worn as a sign of royalty. **2.** Royal power or dignity. —*tr.v.* **diademed, -deming, -dems.** To adorn with or as with a diadem. [Middle English *diademe*, from Old French, from Latin *diadēma*, from Greek *diadēma*, from *diadein*, to bind on either side : *dia-*, across + *dein*, to bind (see **dē-** in Appendix*).]

di·aer·e·sis. Variant of **dieresis.**

diag. **1.** diagonal. **2.** diagram.

di·a·ge·ot·ro·pism (dī′ə-jē-ŏt′rə-pĭz′əm) *n.* *Botany.* The tendency of growing parts to become oriented at right angles to the direction of gravitational force. [DIA- (over across) + GEOTROPISM.] —**di′a·ge′o·trop′ic** (-ə-trŏp′ĭk) *adj.*

Dia·ghi·lev (dyä′gə-lĕf′), **Sergei Pavlovich.** 1872–1929. Russian ballet producer.

di·ag·nose (dī′əg-nōs′, -nōz′) *v.* **-nosed, -nosing, -noses.** —*tr.* **1.** To distinguish or identify by diagnosis, as a disease. **2.** To perform an examination of (a person or thing). —*intr.* To make a diagnosis. [Back-formation from DIAGNOSIS.]

di·ag·no·sis (dī′əg-nō′sĭs) *n.*, *pl.* **-ses** (-sēz). **1.** *Medicine.* **a.** The act or process of identifying or determining the nature of a disease through examination. **b.** The opinion derived from such an examination. **2. a.** An analysis of the nature of something. **b.** The conclusion reached by such analysis. **3.** *Biology.* A precise and detailed description of the characteristics of an organism for taxonomic classification. [New Latin, from Greek *diagnōsis*, discernment, from *diagignōskein*, to distinguish, discern : *dia-*, apart + *gignōskein*, to perceive (see **gnō-** in Appendix*).]

di·ag·nos·tic (dī′əg-nŏs′tĭk) *adj.* Of, pertaining to, or used in a diagnosis. —*n.* *Medicine.* A symptom serving as supporting evidence in a diagnosis. [Greek *diagnōstikos*, from *diagnōstos*, to be distinguished, from *diagignōskein*, to distinguish. See **diagnosis.**] —**di′ag·nos′ti·cal·ly** *adv.*

di·ag·nos·ti·cian (dī′əg-nŏ-stĭsh′ən) *n.* A person who diagnoses; especially, a physician specializing in medical diagnostics.

di·ag·nos·tics (dī′əg-nŏs′tĭks) *n.* Plural in form, used with a singular verb. Diagnosis, especially medical diagnosis.

di·ag·o·nal (dī-ăg′ə-nəl) *adj.* *Abbr.* **diag.** **1.** *Geometry.* **a.** Joining two nonadjacent vertices of a polygon. **b.** Joining two vertices of a polyhedron not in the same face. **2.** Having a slanted or oblique direction. **3.** Having oblique lines or markings. —*n.* *Abbr.* **diag.** **1.** *Geometry.* A diagonal line or plane. **2.** Anything arranged obliquely, such as a row, course, or part. **3.** A fabric woven with diagonal lines. [Latin *diagōnālis*, from Greek *diagōnios*, from angle to angle : *dia-*, across + *gōnia*, angle (see **genu-**[1] in Appendix*).] —**di·ag′o·nal·ly** *adv.*

di·a·gram (dī′ə-grăm′) *n.* *Abbr.* **diag.** **1.** A plan, sketch, drawing, or outline, not necessarily representational, designed to demonstrate or explain something or clarify the relationship existing between the parts of a whole. **2.** *Mathematics.* A graphic representation of an algebraic or geometric relationship. **3.** A chart or graph. —*tr.v.* **diagrammed** or **-gramed, -gramming** or **-graming, -grams.** To indicate or represent by or as if by a diagram. [Latin *diagramma*, from Greek, from *diagraphein*, to mark out : *dia-*, apart + *graphein*, write (see **gerebh-** in Appendix*).] —**di′a·gram·mat′ic, di′a·gram·mat′i·cal** *adj.* —**di′a·gram·mat′i·cal·ly** *adv.*

di·a·ki·ne·sis (dī′ə-kə-nē′sĭs) *n.*, *pl.* **-ses** (-sēz). *Genetics.* The final stage of the prophase in meiosis, characterized by the shortening, thickening, and dispersion of the chromosomes and the disappearance of the nucleolus. [DIA- (across) + -KINESIS (division).]

di·al (dī′əl) *n.* **1.** Any graduated circular face or disk on which some measurement, as of speed or temperature, is indicated by a moving needle or pointer. **2. a.** The face of a clock. **b.** A **sundial** *(see)*. **3. a.** The panel or face on a radio or television receiver on which the frequencies or channels are indicated. **b.** The control on a radio or television receiver used to change the frequency. **4.** A rotatable disk on a telephone with numbers and letters used to make connections. **5.** A miner's compass with sights, a spirit level, and a vernier, used for underground surveying. —*v.* **dialed** or **-alled, -aling** or **-alling, -als.** —*tr.* **1.** To measure or survey with or as with a dial. **2.** To point to, indicate, or register by means of a dial. **3.** To call on a telephone by means of a dial. **4.** To select (a station or program) on a radio or television receiver by means of a dial. —*intr.* To use a dial, as on a telephone. [Middle English *diall*, from Medieval Latin *diāle*, from *diālis*, daily, from Latin *diēs*, day. See **deiw-** in Appendix.*] —**di′al·er, di′al·ler** *n.*

dial. **1.** dialect; dialectal. **2.** dialectic; dialectical. **3.** dialogue.

di·a·lect (dī′ə-lĕkt′) *n.* *Abbr.* **dial.** **1.** A regional variety of a language, distinguished from other varieties by pronunciation, grammar, or vocabulary, especially: **a.** A variety of speech differing from the standard literary language or speech pattern of the culture in which it exists. **b.** A variety of language that, with other varieties, constitutes a single language of which no single variety is standard: *the dialects of Ancient Greek.* **2.** The spoken language peculiar to the members of an occupational or professional group, a foreign-born or minority group, or a particular social class. **3.** The manner or style of expressing oneself in language or the arts. **4.** A language considered as part of a larger family of languages or a linguistic branch: *Spanish and French are Romance dialects.* [Old French *dialecte*, from Latin *dialectus*, from Greek *dialektos*, speech, language, dialect, from *dialegesthai*, to converse : *dia-*, one with another + *legesthai*, middle voice of *legein*, to tell (see **leg-** in Appendix*).]

Synonyms: *dialect, vernacular, jargon, cant, argot, lingo, patois.* These nouns denote forms of language that vary from the accepted standard. *Dialect* applies to the words, usage, and pronunciation characteristic of specific localities. The *vernacular* is the colloquial language of a people. *Jargon* is the specialized language used in particular fields of activity, and is often not understandable by persons outside those fields. *Cant* now usually refers to the specialized language of a group or trade, and is often marked by stock phrases. *Cant* can also mean "insincere expression of piety." *Argot* is the language of the underworld or, by extension, that of any specific group. *Lingo* is applied humorously or contemptuously to language foreign to one or so specialized that it is difficult to understand. *Patois* refers to the dialect of a bilingual region and especially to a hybrid language used by the rustic or uneducated.

di·a·lec·tal (dī′ə-lĕk′təl) *adj.* *Abbr.* **dial.** Pertaining to or characteristic of a dialect. —**di′a·lec′tal·ly** *adv.*

di·a·lec·tic (dī′ə-lĕk′tĭk) *n.* **1.** The art of arriving at the truth by disclosing the contradictions in an opponent's argument and overcoming them. **2. a.** The Hegelian process of change whereby an ideational entity (thesis) is transformed into its opposite (antithesis) and preserved and fulfilled by it, the combination of the two being resolved in a higher form of truth (synthesis). **b.** Hegel's critical method for the investigation of this process. **3. a.** *Often plural.* The Marxian process of change through the conflict of opposing forces, whereby any given contradiction is characterized by a primary and a secondary aspect, the secondary succumbing to the primary, which is then transformed

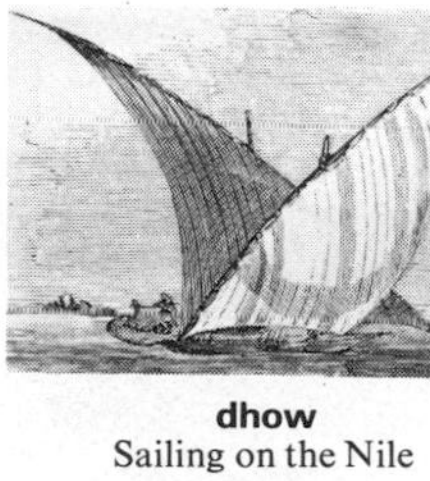

dhow
Sailing on the Nile

into an aspect of a new contradiction. Used with a singular verb. **b.** The Marxian critique of this process. **4.** *Plural.* Any method of argument or exposition that systematically weighs contradictory facts or ideas with a view to the resolution of their real or apparent contradictions. Used with a singular verb. **5.** The contradiction between two conflicting forces viewed as the determining factor in their continuing interaction. [Middle English *dialetik,* from Old French *dialetique,* from Latin *dialectica,* from Greek *dialektikē (tekhnē),* "(the art) of debate," from *dialektikos,* of conversation or discussion, from *dialektos,* discussion, debate, DIALECT.] —**di′a·lec′ti·cal, di′a·lec′tic** *adj.* —**di′a·lec·ti′cian** (-lĕk-tĭsh′ən) *n.*

dialectical materialism. The Marxian interpretation of reality, viewing matter as the sole subject of change and all change as the product of a constant conflict between opposites arising from the internal contradictions inherent in all things.

di·a·lec·tol·o·gy (dī′ə-lĕk-tŏl′ə-jē) *n.* The study of dialects. —**di′a·lec′to·log′i·cal** *adj.* —**di′a·lec′to·log′i·cal·ly** *adv.* —**di′a·lec·tol′o·gist** *n.*

di·a·log·ic (dī′ə-lŏj′ĭk) *adj.* Also **di·a·log·i·cal** (-ĭ-kəl). Of, pertaining to, or written in dialogue. —**di′a·log′i·cal·ly** *adv.*

di·al·o·gism (dī-ăl′ə-jĭz′əm) *n.* **1.** *Obsolete.* A dialogue. **2.** *Logic.* A conclusion inferred from a single premise.

di·al·o·gist (dī-ăl′ə-jĭst) *n.* **1.** One who writes dialogue. **2.** One who speaks in a dialogue. —**di′a·lo·gis′tic** (dī′ə-lō-jĭs′tĭk), **di′a·lo·gis′ti·cal** *adj.*

di·al·o·gize (dī-ăl′ə-jīz′) *intr.v.* **-gized, -gizing, -gizes.** To carry on a dialogue.

di·a·logue (dī′ə-lôg′, -lŏg′) *n.* Also **di·a·log.** *Abbr.* **dial. 1.** A conversation between two or more people. **2.** A conversational passage in a play or narrative. **3.** The lines spoken by the characters in a play or narrative. **4.** A literary work written in the form of a conversation: *the dialogues of Galileo.* **5.** An exchange of ideas or opinions. —*v.* **dialogued, -loguing, -logues.** Also **di·a·log, -logged, -logging, -logs.** —*tr.* To express as or in a dialogue. —*intr.* To converse in a dialogue. [Middle English *dialog(ue),* from Old French *dialogue,* from Latin *dialogus,* from *dialegesthai,* to converse : *dia-,* one with another + *legesthai,* middle voice of *legein,* to tell, talk (see **leg-** in Appendix*).] —**di′a·log′uer** *n.*

dial tone. A low, steady tone in a telephone receiver that indicates to the user that a telephone number may be dialed.

di·al·y·sis (dī-ăl′ə-sĭs) *n., pl.* **-ses** (-sēz′). The separation of smaller molecules from larger molecules, or of crystalloid particles from colloidal particles, in a solution by selective diffusion through a semipermeable membrane. [New Latin, from Greek *dialusis,* from *dialuein,* to tear apart : *dia-,* apart + *luein,* to loosen (see **leu-**[1] in Appendix*).] —**di′a·lyt′ic** (-ə-lĭt′ĭk) *adj.* —**di′a·lyt′i·cal·ly** *adv.*

di·a·lyze (dī′ə-līz′) *v.* **-lyzed, -lyzing, -lyzes.** —*tr.* To subject to dialysis; separate by dialysis. —*intr.* To undergo dialysis. [Back-formation from DIALYSIS.]

diam diameter.

di·a·mag·net (dī′ə-măg′nət) *n.* A diamagnetic substance. [From DIAMAGNETIC.]

di·a·mag·net·ic (dī′ə-măg-nĕt′ĭk) *adj.* Of or pertaining to a substance in which an induced magnetic field is in the opposite direction to, and much weaker than, the magnetizing field [DIA- (in different directions) + MAGNETIC.] —**di′a·mag′ne·tism′** (-nə-tĭz′əm) *n.*

di·am·e·ter (dī-ăm′ə-tər) *n. Abbr.* **dia., diam 1.** *Mathematics.* **a.** A straight line segment passing through the center of a figure, especially of a circle or sphere, and terminating at the periphery. **b.** The length of such a segment. **2.** Loosely, the thickness or width of anything. [Middle English *diametre,* from Old French, from Latin *diametros,* from Greek *diametros (grammē),* "(line) which measures through" : *dia-,* through + *metron,* measure (see **mē-**[2] in Appendix*).]

di·a·met·ri·cal (dī′ə-mĕt′rĭ-kəl) *adj.* Also **di·am·e·tral** (dī-ăm′ə-trəl) (for sense 1), **di·a·met·ric** (-rĭk) (for sense 2). **1.** Of, pertaining to, or along a diameter. **2.** Exactly opposite; contrary.

di·a·met·ri·cal·ly (dī′ə-mĕt′rĭk-lē) *adv.* **1.** Along a diameter; straight across a circle or other figure. **2.** Absolutely; irreconcilably: *"a lesson diametrically opposite to the one I'd been trying to teach"* (Anthony Burgess).

di·am·ine (dī-ăm′ēn, -ĭn, dī′ə-mēn′, -mĭn) *n.* Any of various chemical compounds containing two amino groups, especially **hydrazine** *(see).* [DI- (two) + -AMINE.]

dia·mond (dī′mənd, dī′ə-) *n.* **1.** An extremely hard, highly refractive, colorless or white crystalline allotrope of carbon, used when pure as a gemstone and chiefly in abrasives otherwise. **2.** A figure with four equal sides forming two inner obtuse angles and two inner acute angles; a rhombus or lozenge. **3. a.** A red, lozenge-shaped figure on certain playing cards. **b.** A playing card with this figure. **c.** *Plural.* The suit of cards represented by this figure. **4.** *Sports.* **a.** A baseball infield. **b.** The whole playing field. **5.** *Printing.* A small type size, 4½-point. —*adj.* Of, resembling, or made with diamonds. —*tr.v.* **diamonded, -monding, -monds.** To adorn with or as with diamonds. [Middle English *diamaunt,* from Old French *diamant,* from Late Latin *diamas* (stem *diamant-*), variant of Vulgar Latin *adimas* (unattested), variant of Latin *adamas,* from Greek. See **adamant.**]

dia·mond·back (dī′mənd-băk′, dī′ə-) *n.* **1.** Any of several large, venomous rattlesnakes of the genus *Crotalus,* of the southern and western United States and Mexico, having diamond-shaped markings. Also called "diamondback rattlesnake." **2.** Any of several turtles of the genus *Malaclemys,* of the southern Atlantic and Gulf coasts of the United States, having edible flesh and a carapace with roughly diamond-shaped, ridged or knobbed markings. In this sense, also called "diamondback terrapin."

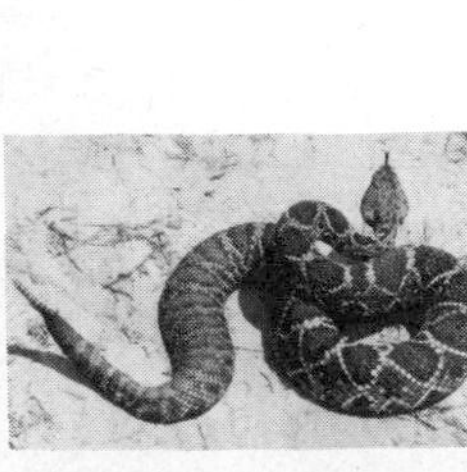

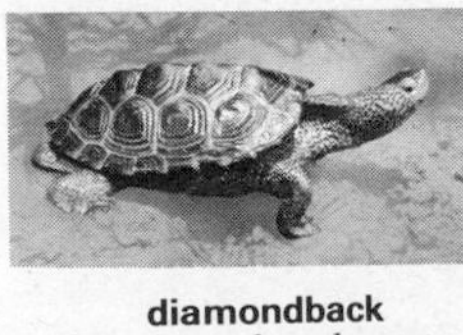

diamondback
Above: Crotalus adamanteus, diamondback rattlesnake
Below: Malaclemys terrapin, diamondback terrapin

Diamond, Cape. A promontory at the confluence of the St. Lawrence and Charles rivers in southern Quebec, at the eastern end of the city of Quebec.

Diamond Head. A promontory, 760 feet high on the southeastern coast of Oahu, Hawaii.

dia·mond·if·er·ous (dī′mən-dĭf′ər-əs, dī′ə-) *adj.* Bearing or yielding diamonds.

Di·an·a[1] (dī-ăn′ə). A feminine given name. [From DIANA (goddess).]

Di·an·a[2] (dī-ăn′ə). *Roman Mythology.* The goddess of chastity, hunting, and the moon; identified with the Greek goddess Artemis. [Middle English, from Latin *Diāna,* moon goddess. See **deiw-** in Appendix.*]

Di·an·a[3] (dī-ăn′ə) *n. Poetic.* The moon. [From DIANA (moon goddess).]

di·an·drous (dī-ăn′drəs) *adj. Botany.* Having two stamens. [DI- (two) + -ANDROUS.]

di·a·no·et·ic (dī′ə-nō-ĕt′ĭk) *adj.* Of or pertaining to reasoning; intellectual. [Greek *dianoētikos,* from *dianoia,* thought, process of thinking : *dia-,* through + *nous,* mind (see **nous** in Appendix*).]

di·an·thus (dī-ăn′thəs) *n.* Any plant of the genus *Dianthus,* which includes carnations and pinks. [New Latin *Dianthus* : DI- (two) + Greek *anthos,* flower (see **andh-** in Appendix*).]

di·a·pa·son (dī′ə-pā′sən, -zən) *n. Music.* **1.** Either of the two principal stops on a pipe organ, the *open diapason* and the *closed diapason,* which form the tonal basis for the entire scale of the instrument. **2.** The interval, and the consonance, of an octave. **3.** A standard indication of pitch. In this sense, also called "diapason normal." [Middle English *dyapason,* from Latin *diapāsōn,* from Greek *(hē) dia pasōn (khordōn sumphonia),* (concord) through all (the notes) : *dia-,* through + *pasōn,* feminine genitive plural of *pas,* all (see **keu-**[3] in Appendix*).]

di·a·pause (dī′ə-pôz′) *n. Biology.* A period during which growth or development is suspended, as in certain insects. [Greek *diapausis,* pause, from *diapauein,* to rest between times, pause : *dia-,* between + *pauein,* to stop, cease (see **pauein** in Appendix*).]

di·a·pe·de·sis (dī′ə-pə-dē′sĭs) *n.* The passing of blood or any constituents, especially erythrocytes, through intact blood-vessel walls. [New Latin, from Greek *diapēdēsis,* "a leaping through," from *diapēdan,* to leap through, ooze : *dia-,* through + *pēdan,* to leap (see **ped-**[1] in Appendix*).] —**di′a·pe·det′ic** (-dĕt′ĭk) *adj.*

di·a·per (dī′ə-pər, dī′pər) *n.* **1.** A baby's garment consisting of a folded cloth or other absorbent material, used to cover the genitals and anus. **2.** A white cotton or linen fabric patterned with small, duplicative diamond-shaped figures. **3.** A piece of such cloth, or such a pattern. —*tr.v.* **diapered, -pering, -pers. 1.** To put a diaper on (a baby). **2.** To weave or decorate in a diamond-shaped pattern. [Middle English *diapre,* linen cloth with diamond pattern, from Old French, from Medieval Latin *diasprum,* from Medieval Greek *diaspros,* made of diaper, pure white : *dia-,* thoroughly + *aspros,* white, shining, newly minted (see **asper.**)]

di·aph·a·nous (dī-ăf′ə-nəs) *adj.* **1.** Allowing light to show through; transparent or translucent. **2.** Characterized by delicacy of form. [Medieval Latin *diaphanus,* from Greek *diaphanēs,* from *diaphanein,* to show through : *dia-,* through + *phainein,* to show (see **bhā-**[1] in Appendix*).] —**di·a·pha·ne·i·ty** (dī′ə-fə-nē′ə-tē), **di·aph′a·nous·ness** *n.* —**di·aph′a·nous·ly** *adv.*

di·aph·o·ny (dī-ăf′ə-nē) *n., pl.* **-nies. 1.** Organum. **2.** *Obsolete.* Dissonance. [Medieval Latin *diaphonia,* from Greek *diaphōnia,* discord, dissonance, from *diaphōnos,* dissonant : *dia-,* apart + *phōnē,* sound (see **bhā-**[2] in Appendix*).] —**di′a·phon′ic** *adj.*

di·a·pho·re·sis (dī′ə-fə-rē′sĭs) *n.* Perspiration, especially when copious and medically induced. [Late Latin *diaphorēsis,* from Greek, from *diaphorein,* to disperse abroad, dissipate (by perspiration) : *dia-,* in different directions + *phorein,* frequentative of *pherein,* to carry (see **bher-**[1] in Appendix*).]

di·a·pho·ret·ic (dī′ə-fə-rĕt′ĭk) *adj.* Producing perspiration. —*n.* A diaphoretic medicine or agent.

di·a·phragm (dī′ə-frăm′) *n.* **1.** *Anatomy.* A muscular membranous partition separating the abdominal and thoracic cavities and functioning in respiration. **2.** Any similar membranous part that divides or separates. **3.** A thin disk, especially in a microphone or telephone receiver, the vibrations of which convert electric to acoustic signals or acoustic to electric signals. **4.** A contraceptive consisting of a flexible disk that covers the uterine cervix. **5.** *Optics.* A disk having a fixed or variable opening used to restrict the amount of light traversing a lens or optical system. —*tr.v.* **diaphragmed, -phragming, -phragms.** To supply with or act upon a diaphragm. [Middle English *diafragma,* from Late Latin *diaphragma,* from Greek, from *diaphrassein,* to barricade : *dia-,* completely + *phrassein,* to enclose (see **bhrekw-** in Appendix*).] —**di′a·phrag·mat′ic** (-frăg-măt′ĭk) *adj.* —**di′a·phrag·mat′i·cal·ly** *adv.*

di·aph·y·sis (dī-ăf′ə-sĭs) *n., pl.* **-ses** (-sēz′). The shaft of a long bone, especially as distinguished from extremities and outgrowths. [New Latin, from Greek *diaphusis,* spinous process of the tibia, from *diaphuesthai,* to grow between : *dia-,* between + *phuesthai,* middle voice of *phuein,* to bring forth, beget (see **bheu-** in Appendix*).] —**di′a·phys′i·al** (dī′ə-fĭz′ē-əl) *adj.*

di·a·poph·y·sis (dī′ə-pŏf′ə-sĭs) *n., pl.* **-ses** (-sēz′). The superior or articular surface of a transverse vertebral process. [New Latin : DI(A)- (across) + APOPHYSIS.] —**di′ap·o·phys′i·al** (-ăp-ə-fĭz′ē-əl) *adj.*

di·ar·chy (dī′är′kē) *n., pl.* **-chies.** Also **dy·ar·chy.** Government by two joint rulers. [DI- (two) + -ARCHY.]

di·a·rist (dī′ə-rĭst) *n.* A person who keeps a diary.

di·ar·rhe·a (dī′ə-rē′ə) *n.* Also **di·ar·rhoe·a.** Pathologically excessive evacuation of watery feces. [Middle English *diaria,* from Late Latin *diarrhœa,* from Greek *diarrhoia,* "a flowing through," from *diarrhein,* to flow through : *dia-,* through + *rhein,* to flow (see **sreu-** in Appendix*).] —**di′ar·rhe′al, di′ar·rhe′ic, di′ar·rhet′ic** (-rĕt′ĭk) *adj.*

di·ar·thro·sis (dī′är-thrō′sĭs) *n., pl.* **-ses** (-sēz). Any of several types of bone articulation permitting free motion in a joint. [New Latin, from Greek *diarthrōsis,* from *diarthroun,* to fasten by a joint, articulate : *dia-,* between + *arthroun,* to fasten, from *arthron,* joint (see **ar-** in Appendix*).] —**di′ar·thro′di·al** *adj.*

di·a·ry (dī′ə-rē) *n., pl.* **-ries. 1.** A daily record, especially a personal record of events, experiences, and observations. **2.** A book for keeping such a record; journal. [Latin *diārium,* daily allowance, (later) journal, from *diēs,* day. See **deiw-** in Appendix.*] —**di′a·rist** *n.*

Di·as (dē′əs; *Portuguese* dē′äsh), **Bartholomeu.** Also **Di·az.** 1450?–1500. Portuguese navigator; discovered Cape of Good Hope; perished off the cape in a later voyage.

Di·as·po·ra (dī-ăs′pər-ə) *n.* **1.** The aggregate of Jews or Jewish communities outside of Palestine. **2.** The body of Jews living dispersed among the Gentiles after the Babylonian captivity. **3.** In the New Testament, the body of Christians living outside of Palestine. **4.** A dispersion, as of any originally homogeneous people. [Greek, "dispersion" (Deuteronomy 28:25), from *diaspeirein,* to disperse : *dia-,* apart + *speirein,* to scatter (see **sper-**[4] in Appendix*).]

di·a·spore (dī′ə-spôr′, -spōr′) *n.* A white to greenish, pearly hydrous aluminum oxide, $Al_2O_3 \cdot H_2O$, found in bauxite, corundum, and dolomite, and used as a refractory and abrasive. [Greek *diaspora,* scattering, DIASPORA (from the strong decrepitation of the mineral before the blowpipe).]

di·a·stal·sis (dī′ə-stôl′sĭs, -stăl′sĭs) *n., pl.* **-ses** (-sēz). The peristaltic contraction of the small intestine in digestion. [New Latin : DIA- (through) + (PERI)STALSIS.] —**di′a·stal′tic** *adj.*

di·a·stase (dī′ə-stās′) *n.* An amylase or a mixture of amylases that converts starch to maltose, found in certain germinating grains such as malt. [French, from Greek *diastasis,* separation, DIASTASIS.] —**di′a·sta′sic, di′a·stat′ic** (-stăt′ĭk) *adj.*

di·as·ta·sis (dī-ăs′tə-sĭs) *n., pl.* **-ses** (-sēz′). **1.** *Pathology.* Separation of normally adjacent, unjoined bones without fracture or of certain muscles during pregnancy. **2.** *Physiology.* The last stage of diastole in the heart, occurring prior to contraction and during which little blood enters the filled ventricle. [New Latin, from Greek, separation, from *diistanai,* to set apart : *dia-,* apart + *histanai,* to cause to stand, set (see **stā-** in Appendix*).] —**di′a·stat′ic** (dī′ə-stăt′ĭk) *adj.*

di·a·ste·ma (dī′ə-stē′mə) *n., pl.* **-mata** (-mə-tə). **1.** *Pathology.* Any bodily fissure or cleft, especially if congenital. **2.** *Dentistry.* An abnormally large space between teeth. [New Latin, from Late Latin *diastēma,* interval, from Greek, interval, aperture, from *diistanai,* to set apart. See **diastasis.**]

di·as·ter (dī′ăs-tər) *n. Obsolete.* **Anaphase** *(see).* [DI- (two) + Greek *astēr,* star (see **ster-**[3] in Appendix*).] —**di·as′tral** *adj.*

di·as·to·le (dī-ăs′tə-lē) *n.* **1.** *Physiology.* The normal rhythmically occurring relaxation and dilatation of the heart cavities during which the cavities are filled with blood. **2.** *Greek & Latin Prosody.* The lengthening of a normally short syllable. [Greek *diastolē,* dilatation, separation, from *diastellein,* to expand, separate : *dia-,* apart + *stellein,* to put (see **stel-**[1] in Appendix*).] —**di′a·stol′ic** (dī′ə-stŏl′ĭk) *adj.*

di·as·tro·phism (dī-ăs′trə-fĭz′əm) *n.* The process or series of processes by which the major features of the earth's crust, including continents, mountains, ocean beds, folds, and faults, are formed. [From Greek *diastrophē,* twisting, distortion, from *diastrephein,* to twist different ways, distort : *dia-,* in different directions + *strephein,* to turn, twist (see **strebh-** in Appendix*).] —**di′a·stroph′ic** (dī′ə-strŏf′ĭk) *adj.*

di·a·tes·sa·ron (dī′ə-tĕs′ər-ən) *n.* In Greek and medieval music, the interval of a fourth. [Middle English *diatessaron,* from Late Latin *diatessarōn,* from Greek *dia tessarōn,* consisting of four : *dia-,* made out of + *tessarōn,* genitive of *tessares,* four (see **kwetwer** in Appendix*).]

di·a·ther·my (dī′ə-thûr′mē) *n.* The therapeutic generation of local heat in body tissues by high-frequency electromagnetic waves. [DIA-, across, by transmission + Greek *thermē,* heat (see **therm**).]

di·ath·e·sis (dī-ăth′ə-sĭs) *n., pl.* **-ses** (-sēz′). A congenital, often hereditary, predisposition of the body to a disease, group of diseases, or structural or metabolic abnormality. [New Latin, from Greek, disposition, bodily state, condition, from *diatithenai,* to distribute, treat, dispose : *dia-,* in different directions + *tithenai,* to put, set (see **dhē-**[1] in Appendix*).] —**di′a·thet′ic** (dī′ə-thĕt′ĭk) *adj.*

di·a·tom (dī′ə-tŏm′, -təm) *n.* Any of various minute, unicellular or colonial algae of the class Bacillariophyceae, having siliceous cell walls consisting of two overlapping, symmetrical parts. [New Latin *diatoma,* from Greek *diatomē,* feminine of *diatomos,* cut in half, from *diatemnein,* to cut through, cut in half : *dia-,* through + *temnein,* to cut (see **tem-** in Appendix*).]

di·a·to·ma·ceous (dī′ə-tə-mā′shəs) *adj.* Consisting of diatoms or their siliceous skeletons.

diatomaceous earth. A white or cream-colored siliceous earth composed of the shells of diatoms. See **diatomite.**

di·a·tom·ic (dī′ə-tŏm′ĭk) *adj.* **1.** Made up of two atoms. Said of a molecule. **2.** Having two replaceable atoms or radicals.

di·at·o·mite (dī-ăt′ə-mīt′) *n.* A fine, powdered diatomaceous earth used in industry as a filler, filtering agent, absorbent, clarifier, and insulator. Also called "kieselguhr."

di·a·ton·ic (dī′ə-tŏn′ĭk) *adj. Music.* Of or using only the eight tones of a standard major or minor scale without chromatic variations. [Old French *diatonique,* from Late Latin *diatonicus,* from Greek *diatonikos,* from *diatonos,* "at the interval of a tone" : *dia-,* throughout, at the interval of + *tonos,* TONE.] —**di′a·ton′i·cal·ly** *adv.* —**di′a·ton′i·cism′** (-ə-sĭz′əm) *n.*

di·a·tribe (dī′ə-trīb′) *n.* A bitter and abusive criticism or denunciation; invective. [Latin *diatriba,* learned discourse, from Greek *diatribē,* "a wearing away," "pastime," from *diatribein,* to rub hard, rub away, consume (time) : *dia-,* completely + *tribein,* to rub, wear out (see **ter-**[2] in Appendix*).]

di·at·ro·pism (dī-ăt′rə-pĭz′əm) *n.* The tendency of certain plants or their parts to arrange themselves at right angles to the line of force of a stimulus. [DIA- (over across, at right angles) + -TROPISM.] —**di′a·trop′ic** (dī′ə-trŏp′ĭk) *adj.*

Di·az, Bartholomeu. See **Dias.**

Dí·az (dē′äs), **(José de la Cruz) Porfirio.** 1830–1915. Mexican general; president of Mexico (1877–80 and 1884–1911).

di·a·zine (dī′ə-zēn′, -zĭn, dī-ăz′ĭn) *n.* Also **di·a·zin** (dī′ə-zĭn, dī-ăz′ĭn). A compound containing a benzene ring in which two of the carbon atoms have been replaced by nitrogen atoms, especially any of three compounds so structured and having the composition $C_4H_4N_2$. [DIAZ(O) + -INE.]

di·az·o (dī-ăz′ō) *adj.* Of or relating to a pair of nitrogen atoms bonded together and to an organic compound. [DI- (two) + A- (not) + Greek *zoē,* life (see **gwei-** in Appendix*).]

di·a·zo·ni·um (dī′ə-zō′nē-əm) *adj.* Of or pertaining to the univalent cation RN_2, where R is an aromatic hydrocarbon. [DIAZ(O) + (AMM)ONIUM.]

di·ba·sic (dī-bā′sĭk) *adj. Chemistry.* **1.** Containing two replaceable hydrogen atoms. **2.** Designating salts, or acids forming salts, with two atoms of a univalent metal. [DI- + BASIC.]

dib·ble[1] (dĭb′əl) *n.* Also **dib·ber** (dĭb′ər). A pointed gardening implement used to make holes in soil, especially for planting bulbs or seedlings. —*tr.v.* **dibbled, -bling, -bles. 1.** To make holes in (soil) with a dibble. **2.** To plant by means of a dibble. [Middle English *debyllet*†.] —**dib′bler** *n.*

dib·ble[2] (dĭb′əl) *intr.v.* **-bled, -bling, -bles.** Also **dib** (dĭb), **dibbed, dibbing, dibs.** *British Regional.* **1.** In angling, to dip bait gently up and down in the water. **2.** To dabble. [Probably variant of obsolete *dib,* to tap, dip, variant of DAB.]

di·bran·chi·ate (dī-brăng′kē-ĭt) *n.* Any of various cephalopod mollusks of the order Dibranchiata, which includes the octopuses, cuttlefish, and squids. —*adj.* Of or belonging to the Dibranchiata. [New Latin *Dibranchiata,* "two-gilled ones" : DI- (two) + BRANCHIATE.]

di·bro·mide (dī-brō′mīd′, -mĭd) *n.* A binary chemical compound containing two bromine atoms per molecule.

Di·bru·garh (dĭb′ro͞o-gär′). A town, rail terminus, and head of navigation on the Brahmaputra River, in northeastern Assam, Republic of India. Population, 58,000.

dibs (dĭbz) *pl.n. Slang.* Money, especially in small amounts. —**dibs on (something).** *Slang.* A claim on (something); rights. [Short for *dibstones,* a children's game played with knucklebones, hence knucklebones, counters used in a game, money, probably from *dib,* to tap, dip, variant of DAB.]

di·car·box·yl·ic (dī-kär′bŏk-sĭl′ĭk) *adj.* Containing two carboxyl groups per molecule.

di·cast (dī′kăst′, dĭk′əst) *n.* In ancient Athens, one of the 6,000 citizens chosen each year to sit in the law courts, with functions resembling those of a judge and juror. [Greek *dikastēs,* judge, from *dikazein,* to judge, from *dikē,* custom, right, lawsuit. See **deik-** in Appendix.*] —**di·cas′tic** *adj.*

dice (dīs) *pl.n. Singular* **die** (dī). **1.** Small cubes, as of ivory, bone, or plastic, marked on each side with a number of small dots, varying from one to six, and used in games of chance. **2.** Any game of chance using dice. Usually used with a singular verb. **3.** Any small cubes. —**no dice.** *Slang.* No luck or success. —*v.* **diced, dicing, dices.** —*intr.* To play or gamble with dice. —*tr.* **1.** To win or lose (money) by gambling with dice. **2.** To cut (food) into small cubes. **3.** To decorate with dicelike figures. [Plural of DIE (cube).]

di·cen·tra (dī-sĕn′trə) *n.* Any plant of the genus *Dicentra,* which includes the bleeding-heart and Dutchman's-breeches. [New Latin *Dicentra,* "two-spurred" (from its dissected leaves) : *di-* (two) + Greek *kentron,* spur, point, center, from *kentein,* to prick (see **kent-** in Appendix*).]

di·ceph·a·lous (dī-sĕf′ə-ləs) *adj.* Having two heads, as a monster. [DI- + -CEPHALOUS.]

dic·er (dī′sər) *n.* **1.** A device used for dicing food. **2.** One who gambles with dice.

di·cha·si·um (dī-kā′zhē-əm) *n., pl.* **-sia** (-zhē-ə). *Botany.* A cyme having two lateral stems branching from the main axis. [New Latin, from Greek *dikhasis,* division, from *dikhazein,* to divide in two, from *dikha,* in two. See **dwō** in Appendix.*] —**di·cha′si·al** *adj.* —**di·cha′si·al·ly** *adv.*

di·chlo·ride (dī-klôr′īd, -ĭd, dī-klōr′-) *n.* A binary chemical compound containing two chloride atoms per molecule. Also called "bichloride."

di·chlor·o·di·phen·yl·tri·chlor·o·eth·ane (dī-klôr′ō-dī-fĕn′əl-trī-klôr′ō-ĕth′ān′, -klōr′ō-ĕth′ān′, dī-klōr′-) *n.* An organic compound, **DDT** *(see).*

dicho-. Indicates two parts or a division into two parts; for example, **dichotomy, dichogamous.** [Late Latin, from Greek *dikho-,* from *dikha,* in two. See **dwō** in Appendix.*]

di·chog·a·mous (dī-kŏg′ə-məs) *adj. Botany.* Having pistils and

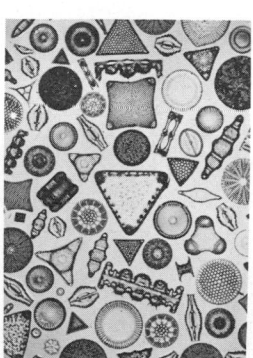

diatom
Cell walls of diatoms

stamens that mature at different times, thus ensuring cross-fertilization rather than self-pollination. [DICHO- + -GAMOUS.]
—di·chog'a·my n.

di·chot·o·mize (dī-kŏt'ə-mīz') v. -mized, -mizing, -mizes. —tr. To separate into two parts or classifications. —intr. To be or become divided into parts or branches; to fork. —di·chot'o·mist n. —di·chot'o·mi·za'tion n.

di·chot·o·mous (dī-kŏt'ə-məs) adj. Also di·cho·tom·ic (dī'kə-tŏm'ĭk). 1. Divided or dividing into two parts or classifications. 2. Characterized by dichotomy. —di·chot'o·mous·ly adv.

di·chot·o·my (dī-kŏt'ə-mē) n., pl. -mies. 1. Division into two usually contradictory parts or opinions; schism. 2. Logic. The division or subdivision of a class into two mutually exclusive groups: the dichotomy of truth and falsehood. 3. Astronomy. Rare. The phase of the moon, Mercury, or Venus when half of the disk is illuminated. 4. Botany. Branching characterized by successive forking into two approximately equal divisions. [Greek dikhotomia, from dikhotomos, divided : DICHO- + temnein, to cut (see tem- in Appendix*).]

di·chro·ic (dī-krō'ĭk) adj. Also di·chro·it·ic (dī'krō-ĭt'ĭk). 1. Manifesting dichroism. 2. Dichromatic. [From Greek dikhroos, two-colored : DI- (two) + -CHROOUS.]

di·chro·ism (dī'krō-ĭz'əm) n. 1. Chemistry. The property of showing different colors depending on the thickness of the medium or the relative concentration of coloring matter in it. 2. Crystallography. The property possessed by some crystals of exhibiting different colors, especially two different colors, when viewed along different axes. Compare pleochroism. [From Greek dichroos, two-colored, DICHROIC.]

di·chro·ite (dī-krō'īt') n. A mineral, cordierite (see). [DICHRO(IC) + -ITE.]

di·chro·mate (dī-krō'māt') n. A chemical compound with two chromium atoms per anion, usually having a characteristic orange-red color. Also called "bichromate."

di·chro·mat·ic (dī'krō-măt'ĭk) adj. 1. Possessing or exhibiting two colors. 2. Zoology. Having two distinct color phases in the adult, as do certain species of birds. 3. Pathology. Capable of distinguishing only two colors. Also "dichroic," "dichromic."

di·chro·ma·tism (dī-krō'mə-tĭz'əm) n. Also di·chro·mism (-mĭz'əm). The quality or condition of being dichromatic.

di·chro·mic (dī-krō'mĭk) adj. 1. Dichromatic. 2. Chemistry. Containing two chromium atoms per molecule.

dichromic acid. An acid, $H_2Cr_2O_7$, known only in solution.

dick[1] (dĭk) n. Slang. A detective. [Shortened from DETECTIVE.]

dick[2] (dĭk) n. 1. British Slang. A fellow; guy. 2. Vulgar Slang. The penis. [From Dick, nickname for Richard.]

dick·cis·sel (dĭk-sĭs'əl) n. A sparrowlike bird, Spiza americana, of central North America, of which the male has a yellow breast marked with black. [Imitative of its note.]

dick·ens (dĭk'ənz) interj. Deuce; devil: "I cannot tell what the dickens his name is." (Shakespeare) [Possibly a euphemistic alteration of (OLD) NICK.]

Dick·ens (dĭk'ənz), Charles (John Huffam). Pen name, "Boz." 1812–1870. English novelist.

Dick·en·si·an (dĭ-kĕn'zē-ən) adj. Of or characteristic of Charles Dickens, his novels and characters, or his literary style.

dick·er (dĭk'ər) v. -ered, -ering, -ers. —intr. 1. To bargain; barter. 2. In politics, to make or attempt to make a deal by bargaining and barter. —tr. To trade or exchange. —n. The act or process of dickering. [Probably from dicker, ten, ten hides, Middle English dike, Old English dicor (unattested), from West Germanic dicura (unattested), from Latin dicuria, set of ten, from decem, ten. See dekm in Appendix.*]

dick·ey (dĭk'ē) n., pl. -eys. Also dick·ie, dick·y pl. -ies. 1. A woman's blouse front worn under a suit jacket or low-necked garment. 2. A man's detachable shirt front. 3. A collar for a shirt. 4. A child's bib or pinafore. 5. A donkey. 6. Any small bird. Also called "dickeybird," "dickybird." 7. Either of two seats on a carriage, the forward outside driver's seat or a rear seat for servants. [From Dick, nickname for Richard.]

Dick·in·son (dĭk'ən-sən), Emily (Elizabeth). 1830–1886. American poet; works published posthumously.

Emily Dickinson

Dick test (dĭk). A test of susceptibility to scarlet fever. [After George Dick (born 1881), American physician.]

di·cli·nous (dī-klī'nəs) adj. Botany. 1. Having stamens and pistils in separate flowers: a diclinous plant. 2. Having pistils but not stamens, or stamens but not pistils: diclinous flowers. [DI- (two) + Greek klinē, bed (see klei- in Appendix*).] —di'cli·ny (dī'klī-nē) n.

di·cot·y·le·don (dī'kŏt'l-ēd'n) n. Also di·cot (dī'kŏt). Botany. Any plant of the Dicotyledonae, one of the two major divisions of angiosperms, characterized by a pair of embryonic seed leaves that appear at germination. Compare monocotyledon. [DI- (two) + COTYLEDON.] —di'cot·y·le'don·ous adj.

di·cro·tism (dī'krə-tĭz'əm) n. A pathological doubling of the pulse with each beat of the heart. [From Greek dikrotos, double-beating : DI- (two) + krotein, to strike (see kret-² in Appendix*).] —di·crot'ic (-krŏt'ĭk) adj.

dict. 1. dictation. 2. dictionary.

dic·ta. Plural of dictum.

Dic·ta·phone (dĭk'tə-fōn') n. A trademark for a phonographic apparatus that records and reproduces dictation for transcription. [DICTA(TE) + -PHONE.]

dic·tate (dĭk'tāt, dĭk-tāt') v. -tated, -tating, -tates. —tr. 1. To say or read aloud (something) to be recorded or written by another. 2. To prescribe expressly and with authority: dictate a command. —intr. 1. To say or read aloud material to be recorded by another. 2. To issue orders or commands. —n. (dĭk'tāt'). A directive or command: the dictates of common

sense. [Latin dictāre, frequentative of dīcere, to say, tell. See deik- in Appendix.*]

dic·ta·tion (dĭk-tā'shən) n. Abbr. dict. 1. The process of dictating material to another for transcription. 2. The material dictated. 3. Any authoritative command or order; a dictate.

dic·ta·tor (dĭk'tā-tər) n. 1. A ruler having absolute authority and supreme jurisdiction over the government of a state; especially, one who is considered tyrannical or oppressive. 2. One who dictates. 3. In ancient Rome, a magistrate appointed temporarily to deal with an immediate crisis or emergency.

dic·ta·to·ri·al (dĭk'tə-tôr'ē-əl, -tōr'ē-əl) adj. 1. Tending to dictate; overbearing; domineering. 2. Characteristic of or pertaining to a dictator; autocratic. —dic'ta·to'ri·al·ly adv. —dic'ta·to'ri·al·ness n.

Synonyms: dictatorial, arbitrary, dogmatic, doctrinaire, imperious, authoritative, overbearing. These adjectives mean tending to or disposed to assert authority or to impose one's will on other persons. Dictatorial stresses the idea of great power in the hands of one person, who usually exercises it in a highhanded, absolute manner. Arbitrary implies improper use of power by one motivated by selfishness, a hasty judgment, or anything other than sound reasoning. Dogmatic suggests the imposition of one's will or opinion as though these were beyond challenge. Doctrinaire implies belief in the theoretical rather than the practical; usually it also implies imposition of such theory or doctrine on others. Imperious suggests the manner of one accustomed to commanding. Authoritative can apply to exercise of official authority or authority based on acknowledged merit. Less often it implies unwarranted assumption of power. Overbearing implies a tendency to be domineering and arrogant.

dic·ta·tor·ship (dĭk-tā'tər-shĭp', dĭk'tā-) n. 1. The office or tenure of office of a dictator. 2. A state or government under dictatorial rule. 3. Absolute or despotic control or power.

dic·tion (dĭk'shən) n. 1. Choice and use of words in speech or writing. 2. The degree of clarity of enunciation; distinctness of speech. [Latin dictiō, from dictus, past participle of dīcere, to say. See deik- in Appendix.*]

Synonyms: diction, wording, vocabulary, articulation, enunciation. These nouns refer to choice, arrangement, and expression of words. Diction refers to the selection and use of words in relation to effective written or oral expression. More narrowly it means quality of delivery of speech. Wording stresses style of expression with reference to choice and arrangement of words, especially in writing. Vocabulary is the aggregate of the words a person understands or uses. Articulation refers rather broadly to sound (clarity) and flow (coherence and organization) of speech, whereas enunciation refers to sound judged principally on the basis of distinctness of pronunciation.

dic·tion·ar·y (dĭk'shə-nĕr'ē; chiefly British dĭk'shən-ə-rē) n., pl. -ies. Abbr. dict. 1. A reference book containing an explanatory alphabetical list of words, as: a. A book listing a comprehensive or restricted selection of the words of a language, identifying usually the phonetic, grammatical, and semantic value of each word, often with etymology, citations, and usage guidance, and other information. b. Such a book listing the words of a particular category within a language. 2. A book listing the words of a language with translations into another language. 3. A book listing words or other linguistic items, with specialized information about them: a medical dictionary. [Medieval Latin dictiōnārium, from Latin dictiō, DICTION.]

Dic·to·graph (dĭk'tə-grăf', -gräf') n. A trademark for a telephonic instrument that reproduces or records sounds from a transmitter by means of a small, often concealed microphone. [Latin dictum, saying, DICTUM + -GRAPH.]

dic·tum (dĭk'təm) n., pl. dicta (dĭk'tə) or -tums. 1. A dogmatic and authoritative pronouncement. 2. Law. An obiter dictum (see). 3. A popular saying; maxim. [Latin, from dictus, past participle of dīcere, say. See deik- in Appendix.*]

did. Past tense of do.

Did·a·che (dĭd'ə-kē) n. An anonymous church treatise of the second century or possibly the first century A.D., known as "The Teaching of the Twelve Apostles." [Greek didakhē, "a teaching," from didaskein, to teach. See dens-¹ in Appendix.*]

di·dac·tic (dī-dăk'tĭk) adj. Also di·dac·ti·cal (-tĭ-kəl). 1. Intended to instruct; expository. 2. Morally instructive. 3. Inclined to teach or moralize too much; pedantic. [Greek didaktikos, skillful in teaching, from didaktos, taught, from didaskein, to teach. See dens-¹ in Appendix.*] —di·dac'ti·cal·ly adv. —di·dac'ti·cism' (-tə-sĭz'əm) n.

di·dac·tics (dī-dăk'tĭks) n. Plural in form, used with a singular verb. The art or science of teaching or instruction; pedagogy.

di·dap·per (dī'dăp'ər) n. A small grebe, such as the dabchick. [Middle English didopper, variant of divedap, dovedop, Old English dūfedoppa, pelican : dūfan, DIVE + -doppa, dapper (see dub- in Appendix*).]

did·dle[1] (dĭd'l) v. -dled, -dling, -dles. Also dad·dle (dăd'l). —tr. To cheat; swindle. —intr. To waste time; dawdle. [Probably back-formation from Jeremy Diddler, a dawdling, swindling character in Raising the Wind (1803), a farce by James Kenney, perhaps ultimately related to Old English dydrian, to delude, deceive. See dud- in Appendix.*] —did'dler n.

did·dle[2] (dĭd'l) v. -dled, -dling, -dles. —tr. To jerk up and down or back and forth. —intr. To shake rapidly; jiggle. [Perhaps variant of dialectal didder, to quiver, tremble, Middle English dideren, probably variant of doderen, perhaps from Middle Low German. See dud- in Appendix.*]

Di·de·rot (dēd-rō'), Denis. 1713–1784. French philosopher, encyclopedist, playwright, and critic.

did·n't (dĭd'ənt). Contraction of did not.

ă pat/ā pay/âr care/ä father/b bib/ch church/d deed/ĕ pet/ē be/f fife/g gag/h hat/hw which/ĭ pit/ī pie/îr pier/j judge/k kick/l lid, needle/m mum/n no, sudden/ng thing/ŏ pot/ō toe/ô paw, for/oi noise/ou out/ŏŏ took/ōō boot/p pop/r roar/s sauce/sh ship, dish/

di·do (dī′dō) *n., pl.* **-dos** or **-does.** *Informal.* A mischievous prank or antic; caper. [Origin unknown.]
Di·do (dī′dō). *Roman Mythology.* A Tyrian princess, founder and queen of Carthage.
didst (dĭdst). *Archaic.* Second person singular, past tense, of **do.** Used with *thou.*
di·dy (dī′dē) *n., pl.* **-dies.** *Informal.* A diaper. [Variant of DIAPER.]
di·dym·i·um (dī-dĭm′ē-əm) *n. Symbol* **Di 1.** A metallic mixture, once considered an element, composed of neodymium and praseodymium. **2.** A mixture of rare-earth elements and oxides used chiefly in manufacturing and coloring various forms of glass. [New Latin, from Greek *didumos,* twin. See **didymous.**]
did·y·mous (dĭd′ə-məs) *adj.* Arranged or occurring in pairs; twin. [Greek *didumos,* twin. See **dwō** in Appendix.*]
Did·y·mus (dĭd′ə-məs). See Saint **Thomas.**
di·dyn·a·mous (dī-dĭn′ə-məs) *adj. Botany.* Having four stamens arranged in pairs that differ from one another, especially in length. [From New Latin *Didynamia,* a former class of didynamous plants, "having two stamens stronger than the others" : DI- (two) + Greek *dunamis,* power (see **dynamic**).]
die¹ (dī) *intr.v.* **died, dying, dies. 1.** To cease living; become dead; expire. See Usage note below. **2.** To cease existing, especially by degrees; fade or pass away: *The sunlight died in the west.* **3.** To lose vitality, activity, or force; become faint or weak. Often used with *away, out,* or *down*: *The storm died down.* **4.** To cease existing completely; become extinct. Often used with *off* or *out.* **5.** To experience an agony or suffering similar to that of death. **6.** To become apathetic or indifferent. Used with *to.* **7.** *Informal.* To desire greatly, as if pining away: *dying to go to the party.* **8.** *Theology.* To experience spiritual death. [Middle English *d(e)ien, deighen,* from late Old English *diegan,* from Old Norse *deyja.* See **dheu-³** in Appendix.*]
Usage: *Die,* in its primary sense of *cease living,* is usually followed by *of* or *as a result of,* in expressing cause: *He died of* (not *from*) *a heart attack.*
die² (dī) *n., pl.* **dies** (for senses 1, 2) or **dice** (dīs) (for senses 3, 4). **1.** Any of various devices used for cutting out, forming, or stamping material, especially: **a.** An engraved metal piece used for impressing a design upon a softer metal, as in coining money. **b.** Any of several component pieces that are fitted into a diestock to cut threads on screws or bolts. **c.** A part on a machine that punches shaped holes in, cuts, or forms sheet metal, cardboard, or other stock. **d.** A metal block containing small conical holes through which plastic, metal, or other ductile stock is extruded or drawn. **2.** *Architecture.* The dado of a pedestal, especially when cube-shaped. **3.** One of a pair of **dice** *(see).* **4.** Any small block or cube. *—tr.v.* **died, dieing, dies.** To cut, form, or stamp with or as with a die. [Middle English *dee,* from Old French *de,* from Vulgar Latin *datum* (unattested), "playing piece," from Latin, neuter past participle of *dare,* to give, "play." See **dō-** in Appendix.*]
die back. To be affected by dieback.
die·back (dī′băk′) *n.* The gradual dying of plant shoots, starting at the tips, as a result of various diseases or climatic conditions.
di·e·cious. Variant of **dioecious.**
die-hard (dī′härd′) *n.* Also **die·hard.** One who stubbornly refuses to abandon a position or resists apparently inevitable change. *—***die′-hard′** *adj.* *—***die′-hard′ism′** *n.*
di·e·lec·tric (dī′ə-lĕk′trĭk) *n.* A nonconductor of electricity, especially a substance with electrical conductivity less than a millionth (10^{-6}) of a mho. [DI(A)- (through) + ELECTRIC.] *—***di′e·lec′tric** *adj.* *—***di′e·lec′tri·cal·ly** *adv.*
dielectric constant. *Electricity.* **Permittivity** *(see).*
dielectric heating. The heating of electrically nonconducting materials by a rapidly varying electromagnetic field, widely used in the manufacture of furniture, plastics, foam rubber, and other products.
Dien Bien Phu (dyĕn′ byĕn′ fo͞o′). A town in northwestern North Vietnam, near the Laos border; site of the decisive victory of Vietminh forces over the French army (1954).
di·en·ceph·a·lon (dī′ĕn-sĕf′ə-lŏn′) *n.* The posterior part of the forebrain that connects the midbrain with the cerebral hemispheres, encloses the third ventricle, and contains the pituitary gland. Also called "thalamencephalon." [New Latin : DI(A)- (between) + ENCEPHALON.]
-diene. *Chemistry.* Indicates a compound containing two double bonds; for example, **butadiene.** [DI- (two) + -ENE.]
Di·eppe (dē-ĕp′; *French* dyĕp). A port of northwestern France, on the English Channel; site of cross-channel raid in World War II. Population, 30,000.
di·er·e·sis (dī-ĕr′ə-sĭs, dī-îr′-) *n., pl.* **-ses** (-sēz′). Also **di·aer·e·sis. 1.** A mark (¨) placed over the second of two adjacent vowels to indicate that two separate sounds are to be pronounced. **2.** The separation of two adjacent vowels into separate syllables. **3.** In poetry, a slight pause at the end of a line that occurs when the end of a word and the end of a metric foot coincide. Compare **syneresis.** [Late Latin *diaeresis,* from Greek *diairesis,* separation, from *diairein,* to divide : *dia-,* apart + *hairein,* to take (see **heresy**).]
Die·sel (dē′zəl, -səl), **Rudolf.** 1858–1913. German mechanical engineer and inventor.
diesel engine. Also **Diesel engine.** An internal-combustion engine that uses the heat of highly compressed air to ignite a spray of fuel introduced after the start of the compression stroke. Also called "diesel motor," "diesel." [Invented by Rudolf DIESEL.]
die·sel·ize (dē′zə-līz′, -sə-līz′) *tr.v.* **-ized, -izing, -izes.** To equip with a diesel engine or machinery using diesel engines.
Di·es I·rae (dī′ēz ī′rē; *Latin* dē′ās ē′rī). A medieval Latin hymn describing the Day of Judgment, used in some Masses for the dead. [Latin, "day of ire."]
di·e·sis (dī′ə-sĭs) *n., pl.* **-ses** (-sēz′). *Printing.* The **double dagger** *(see).* [Middle English, semitone, interval of a semitone (often indicated by a double dagger), from Latin, quarter tone, from Greek, "a letting through," from *diienai,* send through, discharge : *dia-,* through + *hienai,* to send (see **yē-** in Appendix*).]
di·es non ju·rid·i·cus (dī′ēz nŏn jo͞o-rĭd′ĭ-kəs). *Law.* A day on which courts may not convene nor any legal business be transacted. Also "dies non." [Latin, "day without courts."]
die·stock (dī′stŏk′) *n.* An apparatus for holding dies that cut threads on screws, bolts, pipes, or rods.
di·et¹ (dī′ət) *n.* **1.** The usual food and drink of a person or animal; daily sustenance. **2.** A regulated selection of foods, especially as prescribed by a doctor for gaining or losing weight or for other medical reasons. **3.** Anything taken or provided regularly. *—v.* **dieted, -eting, -ets.** *—tr.* To regulate or prescribe food and drink for. *—intr.* **1.** To eat and drink according to a prescribed regimen. **2.** To eat or feed. [Middle English *diete,* from Old French, from Latin *diaeta,* from Greek *diaita,* mode of life, regimen, diet, from *diaitan,* to lead one's life. See **ai-¹** in Appendix.*] *—***di′et·er** *n.*
di·et² (dī′ət) *n.* **1.** A deliberative assembly; legislature. **2.** *Scottish.* **a.** A single daily session of a court or local legislature. **b.** A day upon which a court convenes. [Middle English *diete, dyet,* day's journey, day for meeting, from Medieval Latin *diēta,* from Latin *diēs,* day. See **deiw-** in Appendix.*]
Di·et (dī′ət) *n.* **1.** The general legislative assembly of certain countries, such as Japan. **2.** The semiannual general assembly of the estates of the former Holy Roman Empire.
diet. dietetics.
di·e·tar·y (dī′ə-tĕr′ē) *adj.* Of or pertaining to diet. *—n., pl.* **dietaries. 1.** A system or regimen of dieting. **2.** A regulated daily food allowance.
dietary laws. *Judaism.* A body of regulations prescribing the kinds and combinations of food that may be eaten.
di·e·tet·ic (dī′ə-tĕt′ĭk) *adj.* Also **di·e·tet·i·cal** (-tĭ-kəl). **1.** Of or pertaining to diet or its regulation. **2.** Specially prepared or processed for restrictive diets. [Late Latin *diaetēticus,* from Greek *diaitētikos,* from *diaita,* DIET.] *—***di′e·tet′i·cal·ly** *adv.*
di·e·tet·ics (dī′ə-tĕt′ĭks) *n.* Plural in form, used with a singular verb. *Abbr.* **diet.** The study of diet and dieting as it relates to health and hygiene.
di·eth·y·lene glycol (dī-ĕth′ə-lēn′). A clear, colorless, extremely hygroscopic, syrupy liquid, $CH_2OHCH_2OCH_2CH_2OH$, widely used as an antifreeze, solvent, softening agent, and herbicide. [DI- (two) + ETHYLENE.]
di·eth·yl ether (dī′ĕth′əl). **Ether** *(see).* [DI- (two) + ETHYL.]
di·eth·yl·stil·bes·trol (dī′ĕth′əl-stĭl-bĕs′trōl′) *n.* A synthetic estrogen, $C_{18}H_{20}O_2$, used as an estrogen substitute, especially in the treatment of menstrual disorders. Also called "stilbestrol." [DI- (two) + ETHYL + STILBESTROL.]
di·e·ti·tian (dī′ə-tĭsh′ən) *n.* Also **di·e·ti·cian.** A person specializing in dietetics.
dif., diff. difference; different.
dif·fer (dĭf′ər) *intr.v.* **-fered, -fering, -fers. 1.** To be unlike or dissimilar in nature, quality, amount, or form. Often used with *from.* **2.** To be of a different opinion; disagree; dissent. Often used with *with.* **3.** To quarrel; dispute. [Middle English *differen,* from Old French *differer,* from Latin *differre,* to carry in different directions, be different : *dis-,* apart + *ferre,* to carry (see **bher-¹** in Appendix*).]
dif·fer·ence (dĭf′ər-əns, dĭf′rəns) *n. Abbr.* **dif., diff. 1.** The condition or degree of being unlike, dissimilar, or diverse; disparity; variation. **2.** A specific point of disparity or unlikeness; an instance of variation. **3.** *Archaic.* A distinct mark or peculiarity. **4.** A disagreement; controversy; quarrel. **5.** Discrimination; distinction. **6.** *Mathematics.* **a.** The amount by which one quantity is greater or less than another. **b.** The amount that remains after one quantity is subtracted from another. Also called "remainder." **7.** *Logic.* Differentia. **8.** *Heraldry.* A distinguishing mark on a coat of arms to differentiate branches of the same family. *—tr.v.* **differenced, -encing, -ences. 1.** To make or cause to make a difference between or in; distinguish. **2.** *Heraldry.* To add a distinguishing mark to (a coat of arms).
Synonyms: *difference, dissimilarity, unlikeness, divergence, variation, distinction, discrepancy.* These nouns refer to lack of correspondence, agreement, or equality, as revealed by comparison. *Difference,* the most general, applies to any such condition. *Dissimilarity* points up difference between things otherwise alike or capable of close comparison. *Unlikeness* usually implies greater and more obvious difference. *Divergence* implies a gradually developing difference between things originally similar or alike. *Variation* is difference between things of the same class or species; often it refers to modification of something original, prescribed, or typical. *Distinction* usually means a slight difference in detail between like or related things, determined only by close inspection. The difference is also subjectively determined rather than palpable or factual. *Discrepancy* stresses the idea of difference, such as conflict or contradiction, that should not exist, as discrepancies in two accounts of an incident or between financial statements.
dif·fer·ent (dĭf′ə-rənt, dĭf′rənt) *adj. Abbr.* **dif., diff. 1.** Characterized by a difference; unlike. **2.** Distinct; separate. **3.** Differing from others; peculiar; unusual. [Middle English, from Old French, from Latin *differēns,* present participle of *differre,* DIFFER.] *—***dif′fer·ent·ly** *adv.* *—***dif′fer·ent·ness** *n.*
Usage: *Different from* and *different than* are both widely used,

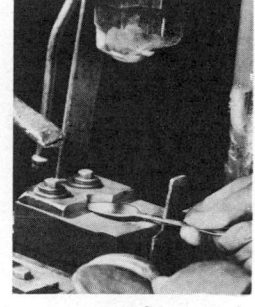

die²
Contour die used for stamping the bowl of a spoon

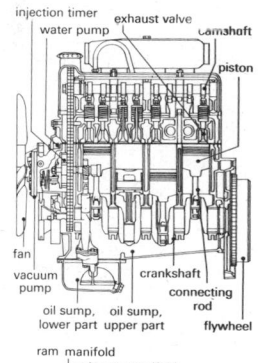

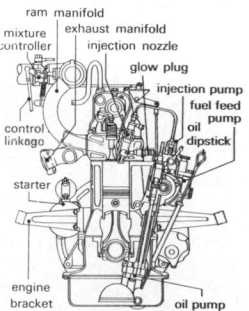

diesel engine
Above: Side view, cross section
Below: Front view, cross section

but the Usage Panel has a strong preference for *different from.* This is especially marked when *different from* can be used without inducing wordiness (when it is followed by a single noun or pronoun or by a short phrase or clause): *This illustration is different from that. This was different from what we expected.* In the first example, only 11 per cent of the Panel consider the alternative *different than* acceptable; in the second only 17 per cent would accept *different than.* But *different than* has wider acceptance, as an aid to conciseness, when the passage that follows is a clause (frequently a shortened or elliptical clause): *How different things seem now than yesterday* (acceptable to 44 per cent). Here *different from* could not be used except ponderously; consequently the alternative to *different than* is to rephrase completely. *Different to,* a third form, is principally British. In an unrelated but common construction, *different* is superfluous: *Three different doctors examined him.*

dif·fer·en·ti·a (dĭf'ər-ĕn'shē-ə) *n., pl.* **-tiae** (-shē-ē', -shē-ī'). *Logic.* An attribute that characterizes and distinguishes a species from others of the same genus. [Latin, difference, diversity, species, from *differēns,* DIFFERENT.]

dif·fer·en·ti·a·ble (dĭf'ə-rĕn'shē-ə-bəl) *adj.* **1.** Capable of being differentiated. **2.** *Mathematics.* Possessing a derivative. —**dif'fer·en'ti·a·bil'i·ty** *n.*

dif·fer·en·tial (dĭf'ə-rĕn'shəl) *adj.* **1.** Pertaining to or showing a difference or differences. **2.** Constituting or making a difference; distinctive. **3.** Dependent on or making use of a difference or distinction. **4.** *Mathematics.* Of or pertaining to differentiation. **5.** Involving differences in speed or direction of motion: *differential gear.* —*n.* **1.** *Mathematics.* **a.** An infinitesimal increment in a variable. **b.** The product of the derivative of a function of one variable multiplied by the independent variable increment. **2.** A **differential gear** *(see).* **3.** A **differential rate** *(see).*

differential analyzer. A mechanical or electronic analog computer used to solve especially complicated differential equations.

differential calculus. The mathematics of the variation of a function with respect to changes in independent variables; loosely, the study of slopes of curves, accelerations, maxima, and minima by means of derivatives and differentials.

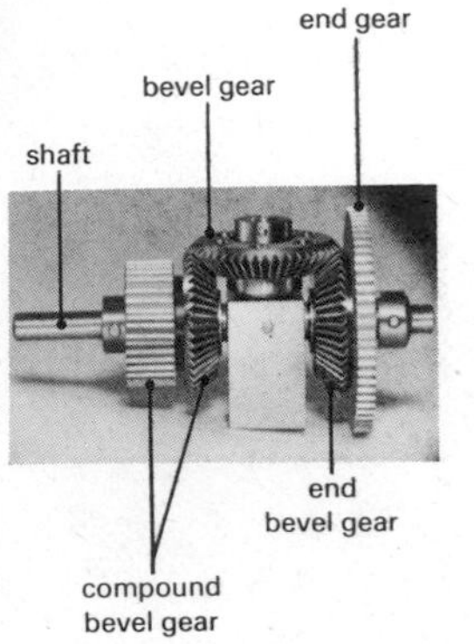
end gear
bevel gear
shaft
end
bevel gear
compound
bevel gear
differential gear

differential coefficient. *Mathematics.* A **derivative** *(see).*

differential equation. An equation containing derivatives or differentials of an unknown function.

differential gear. An arrangement of gears in an epicycle train permitting the rotation of two shafts at different speeds, used on the rear axle of automotive vehicles to allow different rates of wheel rotation on curves.

differential rate. **1.** A difference in wage rate paid for the same work because of differing conditions. **2. a.** A difference in transportation rates to the same destination over different routes, to equalize traffic. **b.** A rate difference over the same route owing to differences in the commodities being shipped.

differential windlass. A hoisting device that has two drums of different sizes on the same axis. A line wound on the larger and unwound from the smaller provides extra lifting power. Also called "Chinese windlass."

dif·fer·en·ti·ate (dĭf'ə-rĕn'shē-āt') *v.* **-ated, -ating, -ates.** —*tr.* **1.** To constitute the difference in or between; serve to make a distinction between: *subspecies differentiated by the markings on their wings.* **2.** To perceive or show the difference in or between; discriminate; distinguish. **3.** To develop differences in by alteration or modification. **4.** *Mathematics.* To calculate the derivative or differential of. —*intr.* **1.** To become distinct or specialized; acquire a different character. **2.** To make distinctions; to discriminate. **3.** *Biology.* To develop into specialized organs. Used especially of embryonic cells or tissues. —**dif'fer·en'ti·a'tion** *n.*

dif·fi·cult (dĭf'ĭ-kŭlt', -kəlt) *adj.* **1.** Hard to do or achieve: *a difficult task.* **2.** Hard to comprehend or solve. **3.** Hard to please, satisfy, or manage: *a difficult child.* **4.** Hard to persuade or convince; stubborn; obstinate. —See Synonyms at **hard.** [Middle English, back-formation from *difficulte,* DIFFICULTY.] —**dif'fi·cult'ly** *adv.*

dif·fi·cul·ty (dĭf'ĭ-kŭl'tē, -kəl-tē) *n., pl.* **-ties.** **1.** The condition, fact, or quality of being difficult. **2.** Something not easily done, accomplished, comprehended, or solved. **3.** *Usually plural.* Troublesome or embarrassing state of affairs. **4.** A trouble; a worry. **5.** A disagreement; a dispute. **6.** An objection or reluctance; unwillingness. [Middle English *difficulte,* from Latin *difficultās,* from *difficilis* (earlier *difficul*), difficult : *dis-,* not + *facilis,* easy (see **dhē-**[1] in Appendix*).]

dif·fi·dence (dĭf'ə-dəns, -dĕns') *n.* The quality or state of being diffident.

dif·fi·dent (dĭf'ə-dənt, -dĕnt') *adj.* Lacking self-confidence; timid. See Synonyms at **shy.** [Middle English, from Latin *diffidens,* present participle of *diffīdere,* to mistrust : *dis-,* not + *fīdere,* to trust (see **bheidh-** in Appendix*).] —**dif'fi·dent·ly** *adv.*

dif·fract (dĭ-frăkt') *v.* **-fracted, -fracting, -fracts.** —*tr.* To cause to undergo diffraction. —*intr.* To undergo diffraction. [Back-formation from DIFFRACTION.] —**dif·frac'tive** *adj.* —**dif·frac'tive·ly** *adv.* —**dif·frac'tive·ness** *n.*

dif·frac·tion (dĭ-frăk'shən) *n.* **1.** Modification of the behavior of light or of other waves resulting from limitation of their lateral extent, as by an obstacle or aperture. **2.** The class of phenomena resulting from such modification. [New Latin *diffractio,* "a breaking up," from Latin *diffractus,* past participle of *diffringere,* to break to pieces : *dis-,* apart + *frangere,* to break (see **bhreg-**[1] in Appendix*).]

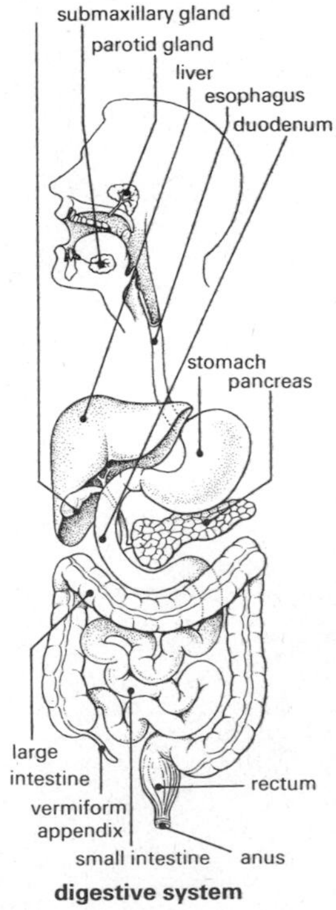
gallbladder
submaxillary gland
parotid gland
liver
esophagus
duodenum
stomach
pancreas
large
intestine
rectum
vermiform
appendix
small intestine
anus
digestive system

diffraction grating. A usually glass or polished metal surface having a large number of very fine parallel grooves or slits cut in the surface and used to produce optical spectra by diffraction of transmitted or reflected light.

dif·fuse (dĭ-fyōōz') *v.* **-fused, -fusing, -fuses.** —*tr.* **1.** To pour out and cause to spread or disperse, as a gas or liquid. **2.** To spread about or scatter; disseminate. **3.** To make less brilliant; soften. —*intr.* **1.** To spread out or soften. **2.** *Physics.* To undergo diffusion. —*adj.* (dĭ-fyōōs'). **1.** Characterized by profusion or excess of words; verbose; long-winded. **2.** Widely spread or scattered; dispersed. [Middle English, dispersed, from Old French *diffus,* from Latin *diffūsus,* past participle of *diffundere,* to pour out, spread : *dis-,* apart + *fundere,* to pour (see **gheu-** in Appendix*).] —**dif·fuse'ly** (dĭ-fyōōs'lē) *adv.* —**dif·fuse'ness** (dĭ-fyōōs'nĭs) *n.* —**dif·fus'i·ble** *adj.*

dif·fus·er (dĭ-fyōō'zər) *n.* Also **dif·fu·sor** (-zər). **1.** That which diffuses. **2.** A lighting fixture, such as a frosted globe or optically rough reflector, that diffuses light. **3.** A flow passage in a wind tunnel that decelerates a stream of gas or liquid from a high to a low velocity.

dif·fu·sion (dĭ-fyōō'zhən) *n.* **1.** The process of diffusing or the condition of being diffused. **2.** *Physics.* The angular redistribution of radiation by a scattering, reflecting, or refracting system, ideally producing an isotropic distribution of intensity. **3.** *Physics.* The gradual mixing of the molecules of two or more substances, as a result of random thermal motion. **4.** Needless profusion of words in verbal expression; verbosity.

dif·fu·sive (dĭ-fyōō'sĭv, -zĭv) *adj.* Characterized by diffusion; tending to diffuse. —**dif·fu'sive·ly** *adv.* —**dif·fu'sive·ness** *n.*

dig (dĭg) *v.* **dug** (dŭg) or *archaic* **digged** (dĭgd), **digging, digs.** —*tr.* **1.** To break up, turn over, or remove (earth or sand, for example) with a spade, the hands, or the like; excavate. **2.** To make (an excavation) by or as by digging. **3.** To obtain by digging: *dig coal.* **4.** To learn or discover by careful research or investigation. Often used with *up* or *out.* **5.** To force or thrust against. Used with *into.* **6.** *Slang.* To comprehend, appreciate, or enjoy. —*intr.* **1.** To loosen or turn over the earth. **2.** To proceed along one's way by or as by digging. Used with *through, into,* or *under.* **3.** *Informal.* To study or work hard and diligently. —**dig in.** **1.** *Military.* To dig holes or trenches. **2.** To entrench oneself. **3.** *Informal.* To begin to work intensively. —*n.* **1.** A poke; a punch: *a dig in the ribs.* **2.** A sarcastic, taunting remark; a gibe. **3.** An archaeological excavation. **4.** *Plural. Chiefly British.* **Diggings** *(see).* [Middle English *diggen,* from Old French *diguer,* "to make a dike or ditch," from *digue,* ditch, from Germanic. See **dhīgw-** in Appendix.*]

dig. digest (compilation).

di·ga·met·ic (dī'gə-mĕt'ĭk) *adj. Biology.* Having two types of gametes, one producing males and the other producing females.

di·gam·ma (dī-găm'ə) *n.* A letter occurring in certain early forms of Greek. Transliterated in English as *w.* See **alphabet.** [Latin, from Greek : DI- (two) + GAMMA (from its resemblance to two capital gammas placed one above the other).]

dig·a·my (dĭg'ə-mē) *n.* Remarriage after the death or divorce of one's first husband or wife. [Late Latin *digamia,* from Late Greek : DI- (two) + -GAMY.] —**dig'a·mous** *adj.*

di·gas·tric (dī-găs'trĭk) *adj.* Having two fleshy ends connected by a thinner tendonous portion. Said of certain muscles. —*n.* A lower jaw muscle that assists in lowering the jaw. [New Latin *digastricus,* "having two bellies" : DI- (two) + GASTRIC.]

di·gen·e·sis (dī-jĕn'ə-sĭs) *n. Biology.* **Metagenesis** *(see).*

di·gest (dĭ-jĕst', dī-) *v.* **-gested, -gesting, -gests.** —*tr.* **1.** To transform (food) into an assimilable condition, as by chemical and muscular action in the alimentary canal. **2.** To absorb or assimilate mentally. **3.** To organize into a systematic arrangement, usually by summarizing or classifying. **4.** To endure or bear patiently. **5.** *Chemistry.* To soften or disintegrate by means of chemical action, heat, or moisture. —*intr.* **1.** To become assimilated into the body. **2.** To assimilate food substances. **3.** *Chemistry.* To undergo exposure to heat, liquids, or chemical agents. —*n.* (dī'jĕst'). **1.** *Abbr.* **dig.** A systematic organization or arrangement of summarized literary, scientific, or statistical materials or data; synopsis. **2.** *Law.* A systematic arrangement of statutes or court decisions. —**the Digest.** The **Pandects** *(see).* [Middle English *digesten,* from Latin *dīgerere* (past participle *dīgestus*), to divide, distribute, digest : *di-,* apart + *gerere,* to bear, carry (see **gerere** in Appendix*).]

di·gest·er (dĭ-jĕs'tər, dī-) *n.* **1.** A person who organizes a digest or synopsis. **2.** A digestant. **3.** *Chemistry.* An autoclave or other vessel in which substances are softened or decomposed, usually for further processing.

di·gest·i·ble (dĭ-jĕs'tə-bəl, dī-) *adj.* Capable of being digested. —**di·gest'i·bil'i·ty, di·gest'i·ble·ness** *n.* —**di·gest'i·bly** *adv.*

di·ges·tion (dĭ-jĕs'chən, dī-) *n.* **1.** *Physiology.* **a.** The primarily enzymatic bodily process by which foodstuffs are decomposed into simple, assimilable substances. **b.** The ability to digest food. **c.** The result of this process. **2.** The process of decomposing organic matter in sewage by bacteria. **3.** The assimilation of ideas; understanding.

di·ges·tive (dĭ-jĕs'tĭv, dī-) *adj.* **1.** Pertaining to or aiding digestion. **2.** Functioning to digest food. —*n.* Any substance that aids digestion. —**di·ges'tive·ly** *adv.*

digestive gland. Any of various endocrine and exocrine glands that secrete enzymes necessary for digestion.

digestive system. The alimentary canal together with accessory glands including the salivary glands, liver, and pancreas, regarded as an integrated system responsible for digestion.

dig·ger (dĭg'ər) *n.* **1.** One that digs or excavates. **2.** *Informal.* A soldier from New Zealand or Australia. [Sense 2, with allusion to Australian gold-miners.]

Dig·ger (dĭg′ər) *n.* A small group of Indians of southwestern Utah and California. [So called presumably because they lived on roots dug up from the ground.]

digger wasp. Any of various wasps of the family Sphecidae, that burrow into the ground to build their nests.

dig·gings (dĭg′ĭngz) *pl.n.* **1.** An excavation site. **2.** Materials dug out. **3.** *Chiefly British.* Rooms; lodgings. In this sense, also called "digs."

dight (dīt) *tr.v.* **dight** or **dighted, dighting, dights.** *Archaic.* To dress; adorn. [Middle English *dighten,* Old English *dihtan,* to arrange, compose, from Latin *dictāre,* DICTATE.]

dig·it (dĭj′ĭt) *n.* **1.** A finger or toe. **2.** The breadth of a finger, used as a unit of length, equal to about ¾ inch. **3.** Any one of the ten Arabic number symbols, 0 through 9. [Middle English, from Latin *digitus.* finger. See **deik-** in Appendix.*]

dig·i·tal (dĭj′ə-təl) *adj.* **1.** Of, relating to, or resembling a digit, especially a finger. **2.** Having digits —*n.* Any key played with the finger, as on a piano. —**dig′i·tal·ly** *adv.*

digital computer. A computer that performs operations with quantities represented electronically as digits, usually in the binary system. Compare **analog computer.**

dig·i·tal·in (dĭj′ə-tăl′ĭn) *n.* A poisonous white powder, $C_{36}H_{56}O_{14}$, used in treatment of heart disease. [DIGITAL(IS) + -IN.]

dig·i·tal·is (dĭj′ə-tăl′ĭs) *n.* **1.** Any plant of the genus *Digitalis,* which includes the foxgloves. **2.** A drug prepared from the seeds and dried leaves of this plant, used as a cardiac stimulant. [New Latin, from Latin *digitālis,* digital (from the finger-shaped corollas of foxglove), from *digitus,* DIGIT.]

dig·i·tal·ize (dĭj′ə-tə-līz′) *tr.v.* **-ized, -izing, -izes.** To treat with digitalis until the desired medical or physiological effect has been obtained. —**dig′i·tal·i·za′tion** *n.*

dig·i·tate (dĭj′ə-tāt′) *adj.* Also **dig·i·tat·ed** (-tā′tĭd). **1.** Having digits or fingerlike parts. **2.** *Botany.* Having radiating fingerlike lobes or leaflets. [From DIGIT.] —**dig′i·tate·ly** *adv.*

dig·i·ta·tion (dĭj′ə-tā′shən) *n.* **1.** Division into fingerlike parts; the condition of being digitate. **2.** A fingerlike part or process.

dig·i·ti·grade (dĭj′ə-tə-grād′) *adj.* Walking so that only the toes touch the ground, as do horses, cats, and dogs. —*n.* A digitigrade animal. Compare **plantigrade.** [Latin *digitus,* finger, toe, DIGIT + -GRADE.]

dig·i·tox·in (dĭj′ə-tŏk′sĭn) *n.* A highly active glycoside, $C_{41}H_{64}O_{13}$, derived from digitalis. [DIGI(TALIS) + TOXIN.]

dig·ni·fied (dĭg′nə-fīd′) *adj.* Having or expressing dignity. —**dig′ni·fied′ly** (dĭg′nə-fīd′lē, -fī′ĭd-lē) *adv.*

dig·ni·fy (dĭg′nə-fī′) *tr.v.* **-fied, -fying, -fies. 1.** To add to the prestige of. **2.** To impart an air of dignity to; elevate with the semblance of dignity. [Middle English *dignifien,* from Old French *dignifier,* from Late Latin *dignificāre* : Latin *dignus,* worthy (see **dek-¹** in Appendix*) + *facere,* to make, do (see **dhē-¹** in Appendix*).]

dig·ni·tar·y (dĭg′nə-tĕr′ē) *n., pl.* **-ies.** A person of high rank. [From DIGNITY.]

dig·ni·ty (dĭg′nə-tē) *n., pl.* **-ties. 1. a.** The presence of poise and self-respect in one's deportment to a degree that inspires respect. **b.** Inherent nobility and worth: *the dignity of labor.* **2.** The respect and honor associated with an important position. **3.** A high office or rank. **4.** *Plural.* The ceremonial symbols and observances attached to high office. Used chiefly in the phrase *the dignities of office.* [Middle English *dignite,* from Old French, from Latin *dignitās,* from *dignus,* worthy. See **dek-¹** in Appendix*]

di·graph (dī′grăf) *n.* **1.** A pair of letters that represents a single speech sound, such as the *ph* in *pheasant* or the *ea* in *beat.* **2.** Two letters run together to represent a special sound, such as Old English *æ.* [DI- + -GRAPH.] —**di′graph·ic** *adj.*

di·gress (dī-grĕs′, dĭ-) *intr.v.* **-gressed, -gressing, -gresses.** To stray from the main subject in writing or speaking; turn aside. [Latin *dīgredī* (past participle *dīgressus*), to go aside : *dis-,* apart, aside + *gradī,* to go (see **ghredh-** in Appendix*).]

di·gres·sion (dĭ-grĕsh′ən, dī-) *n.* **1.** The act of digressing. **2.** An instance of digressing; an excursive passage within a discussion or piece of writing. —**di·gres′sion·al** *adj.*

di·gres·sive (dĭ-grĕs′ĭv, dī-) *adj.* Characterized by digression; rambling. —**di·gres′sive·ly** *adv.* —**di·gres′sive·ness** *n.*

Di·gul (dē′gool). Also **Di·goel.** A river of Indonesia, rising in the mountains of east-central West Irian and flowing 400 miles south and then east to the Arafura Sea.

di·he·dral (dī-hē′drəl) *adj.* **1.** Formed by or having two plane faces; two-sided. **2.** Relating to, having, or forming a dihedral angle. —*n.* **1.** A dihedral angle. **2.** *Aviation.* The upward or downward inclination of an aircraft wing from true horizontal. [DI- + -HEDRAL.]

dihedral angle. 1. *Geometry.* The angle formed by two intersecting planes. **2.** The acute angle between an aircraft wing and true horizontal. In this sense, also called "dihedral."

di·hy·brid (dī-hī′brĭd) *n. Genetics.* An individual heterozygous for two pairs of genes.

di·hy·dric (dī-hī′drĭk) *adj.* Containing two hydroxyl radicals.

Di·jon (dē-zhôn′). A city of eastern France, 160 miles southeast of Paris. Population, 113,000.

dik-dik (dĭk′dĭk′) *n.* Any of several very small African antelopes of the genus *Madoqua.* [Native name in East Africa, imitative of its cry.]

dike (dīk) *n.* Also **dyke. 1.** An embankment of earth and rock, especially: **a.** A levee built to prevent floods. **b.** *British.* A low wall, often of sod, dividing or enclosing lands. **c.** A barrier blocking a passage, especially for protection. **d.** A causeway. **2.** A ditch or channel. **3.** *Geology.* A long mass of igneous rock that cuts across the structure of adjacent rock. **4.** *Slang.* A les-

bian. —*tr.v.* **diked, diking, dikes.** Also **dyke. 1.** To protect, enclose, or provide with a dike. **2.** To drain with ditches. [Middle English *dike,* Old English *dic,* moat, ditch (possibly influenced in sense by Middle Low German *dīk,* ditch). See **dhīgw-** in Appendix.*] —**dik′er** *n.*

dik·tat (dĭk-tät′) *n.* A unilaterally imposed settlement that deals harshly with a defeated party. [From German, "dictation," "command," from Latin *dictātum,* neuter past participle of *dictāre,* DICTATE.]

dil. dilute (weak).

Di·lan·tin (dī-lăn′tĭn) *n.* A trademark for diphenylhydantoin sodium, used to treat epilepsy. [From DI(PHENY)L(HYD)ANT(O)IN (SODIUM).]

di·lap·i·date (dĭ-lăp′ə-dāt′) *v.* **-dated, -dating, -dates.** —*tr.* To bring into a state of ruin, decay, or disrepair. —*intr.* To fall into partial ruin or decay. [Latin *dīlapidāre,* to throw away, destroy : *dis-,* apart + *lapidāre,* to throw stones, from *lapis,* stone (see **lapidary**).] —**di·lap′i·da′tion** *n.*

di·lap·i·dat·ed (dĭ-lăp′ə-dā′tĭd) *adj.* Fallen into a state of disrepair; broken-down.

di·la·tan·cy (dĭ-lāt′n-sē, dĭ-) *n.* **1.** The increase in volume of a fixed amount of certain materials, as of wet sand, subjected to a deformation that alters the interparticle distances of its constituents from their minimum-value configuration. **2.** Any of various related phenomena, such as increase in viscosity or solidification, resulting from such deformation.

di·la·tant (dĭ-lāt′ənt, dĭ-) *adj.* **1.** Tending to dilate; dilating. **2.** Exhibiting dilatancy. —*n.* A dilator.

di·la·ta·tion (dĭl′ə-tā′shən, dī′lə-) *n.* **1.** The act or process of dilating; expansion; dilation. **2.** The state or condition of being dilated or stretched. **3.** *Medicine.* **a.** The condition of being abnormally enlarged or dilated. **b.** Dilation. **4.** Expatiation in writing or speech. —**dil′a·ta′tion·al** *adj.*

di·late (dī-lāt′, dī′lāt′, dĭ-lāt′) *v.* **-lated, -lating, -lates.** —*tr.* To make wider or larger; cause to expand. —*intr.* **1.** To become wider or larger; expand. **2.** To expatiate. [Middle English *dilaten,* from Old French *dilater,* from Latin *dīlātāre,* to enlarge, extend : *dis-,* apart + *lātus,* wide (see **stel-²** in Appendix*).] —**di·lat′a·ble** *adj.* —**di·la′tion** *n.* —**di·la′tive** *adj.*

di·lat·ed (dī-lā′tĭd, dī′lā′tĭd, dĭ-lā′tĭd) *adj.* **1.** Widened; expanded. **2.** Distended.

dil·a·tom·e·ter (dĭl′ə-tŏm′ə-tər, dī′lə-) *n.* An instrument used to measure thermal expansion in solids, liquids, and gases. [DILATE + -METER.] —**dil′a·to·met′ric** (-tə-mĕt′rĭk) *adj.* —**dil′a·tom′e·try** *n.*

di·la·tor (dī-lā′tər, dĭ′lā′tər, dĭ-lā′tər) *n.* Also **di·la·ter, dil·a·ta·tor** (dĭl′ə-tā′tər, dī′lə-). Something that dilates an object, organ, or part, especially a drug, surgical instrument, or muscle that produces dilation.

dil·a·to·ry (dĭl′ə-tôr′ē, -tōr′ē) *adj.* **1.** Tending or intended to delay. **2.** Characterized by procrastination. —See Synonyms at **slow, tardy.** [Middle English *dilatorie,* from Latin *dīlātōrius,* from *dīlātor,* delayer, from *dīlātus* (past participle of *differre,* to postpone, DEFER) : *dis-,* apart + *-lātus,* "carried" (see **tel-¹** in Appendix*).] —**dil′a·to′ri·ly** *adv.* —**dil′a·to′ri·ness** *n.*

dil·do (dĭl′dō) *n., pl.* **-dos.** Also **dil·doe.** *Vulgar.* An object used as a substitute for an erect penis. [Origin unknown.]

di·lem·ma (dĭ-lĕm′ə) *n.* **1. a.** A situation that requires one to choose between two equally balanced alternatives. **b.** A predicament that seemingly defies a satisfactory solution. **2.** *Logic.* An argument in which a choice of two or more alternatives, each being conclusive and fatal, is presented to an antagonist. —See Synonyms at **predicament.** [Latin, from Greek *dilēmma,* ambiguous proposition : DI- (double) + *lēmma,* proposition, LEMMA.] —**dil′em·mat′ic** (dĭl′ə-măt′ĭk) *adj.*

Usage: Dilemma is loosely used when the predicament in question does not involve some idea of choice and when it does not suggest reasonably well-defined alternative courses: *Juvenile delinquency represents the dilemma of our time.* In this example, unacceptable to 79 per cent of the Usage Panel, a more general term (*predicament* or *leading problem*) is called for. *Dilemma* is less often applied to a hard choice between attractive courses, but is acceptable to 82 per cent of the Panel in an example involving a choice between equally able political candidates.

dil·et·tante (dĭl′ə-tänt′, -tän′tē, -tänt′, -tăn′tē, dĭl′ə-tänt′) *n., pl.* **-tantes** or **-tanti** (-tän′tē, -tăn′tē). **1.** A dabbler in the arts. **2.** *Rare.* A lover of the fine arts; connoisseur. —*adj.* Superficial or amateurish. [Italian *dilettante,* "amateur," from *dilettarsi,* to take pleasure in, from Latin *dēlectāre,* to DELIGHT.] —**dil′et·tan′tish** *adj.* —**dil′et·tan′tism** *n.*

Di·li (dĭl′ē). Also **Dil·li, Dil·ly.** The capital of Portuguese Timor, a port town on the northern coast. Population, 10,000.

dil·i·gence¹ (dĭl′ə-jəns) *n.* **1.** Long, steady application to one's occupation or studies; persistent effort; assiduity. **2.** Attentive care; heedfulness.

dil·i·gence² (dĭl′ə-jəns; French dē-lē-zhäns′) *n.* A stagecoach. [French, from *diligence,* "speed," from *diligent,* DILIGENT.]

dil·i·gent (dĭl′ə-jənt) *adj.* **1.** Industrious; assiduous. **2.** Done with persevering, painstaking effort. —See Synonyms at **busy.** [Middle English, from Old French, from Latin *dīligēns,* "loving," attentive, careful, from *dīligere,* "to single out," "choose," esteem highly, love : *dis-,* apart + *legere,* to choose, gather (see **leg-** in Appendix*).] —**dil′i·gent·ly** *adv.*

dill (dĭl) *n.* **1.** An aromatic herb, *Anethum graveolens,* native to the Old World, having finely dissected leaves and small yellow flowers. **2.** The leaves or seeds of this plant, used as seasoning. [Middle English *dile,* from Old English *dile,* from West Germanic *dilja* (unattested).]

dill pickle. A cucumber pickled and flavored with dill.

digitate
Digitate leaf

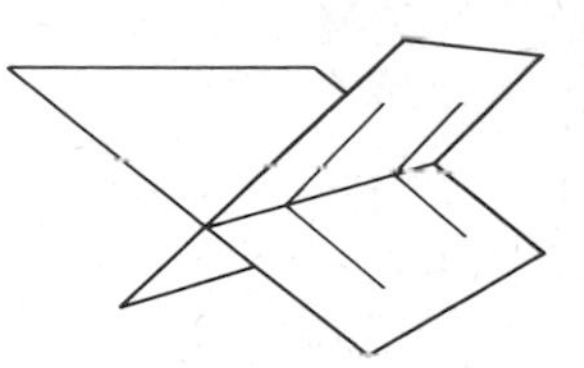

dihedral angle

dike
The dike between the Ijsselmeer and the Waddenzee in the Netherlands

dill

ǎ pat/ā pay/âr care/ä father/b bib/ch church/d deed/ĕ pet/ē be/f fife/g gag/h hat/hw which/ĭ pit/ī pie/îr pier/j judge/k kick/l lid, needle/m mum/n no, sudden/ng thing/ŏ pot/ō toe/ô paw, for/oi noise/ou out/ŏo took/ōo boot/p pop/r roar/s sauce/sh ship, dish/t tight/th thin, path/th this, bathe/ŭ cut/ûr urge/v valve/w with/y yes/z zebra, size/zh vision/ə about, item, edible, gallop, circus/ à *Fr.* ami/œ *Fr.* feu, *Ger.* schön/ü *Fr.* tu, *Ger.* über/KH *Ger.* ich, *Scot.* loch/N *Fr.* bon. *Follows main vocabulary. †Of obscure origin.

dil·ly (dĭl′ē) *n., pl.* **-lies.** *Slang.* Something remarkable or startling. [Possibly from DELIGHTFUL.]

dilly bag. A bag or basket woven of rushes or bark and used in Australia. [From *dillī*, a native word in Queensland.]

dil·ly-dal·ly (dĭl′ē-dăl′ē) *intr.v.* **-lied, -lying, -lies. 1.** To dawdle. **2.** To vacillate. [Reduplication of DALLY.]

dil·u·ent (dĭl′yo͞o-ənt) *adj.* Capable of diluting. —*n.* A substance used to dilute. [Latin *diluēns*, present participle of *dīluere*, DILUTE.]

di·lute (dī-lo͞ot′, dĭ-) *tr.v.* **-luted, -luting, -lutes. 1.** To thin or reduce the concentration of (a solute). **2.** To lessen the potency, strength, purity, or brilliance of by admixture. —*adj. Abbr.* **dil.** Weakened; diluted. [Latin *dīluere* (past participle *dīlūtus*), to wash away, dilute, dissolve : *dis-*, apart + *-luere*, from *lavere*, to wash (see **lou-** in Appendix*).] —**di·lut′er** *n.*

di·lu·tion (dī-lo͞o′shən, dĭ-) *n.* **1. a.** The process of diluting. **b.** A dilute or weakened condition. **2.** A diluted substance.

di·lu·vi·al (dĭ-lo͞o′vē-əl) *adj.* Also **di·lu·vi·an** (-ən). Of or produced by a flood. [Late Latin *dīluviālis*, from Latin *dīluvium*, flood, from *dīluere*, to wash away, DILUTE.]

dim (dĭm) *adj.* **dimmer, dimmest. 1. a.** Faintly lighted. **b.** Shedding a small amount of light; faint. **c.** Negative or unpromising; gloomy. **2.** Lacking brightness or luster; subdued; dull. **3.** Faintly outlined; indistinct; obscure. **4.** Lacking keenness or vigor. —See Synonyms at **dark.** —*v.* **dimmed, dimming, dims.** —*tr.* **1.** To make dim. **2.** To put on low beam: *dim headlights of an automobile.* —*intr.* To become dim. —*n. Plural.* The parking lights on an automobile. [Middle English *dim(me)*, Old English *dimm*, from Germanic *dim-* (unattested).] —**dim′ly** *adv.* —**dim′ness** *n.*

dim. 1. dimension. **2.** diminished. **3.** *Music.* diminuendo. **4.** diminutive.

dime (dīm) *n.* **1.** A U.S. coin worth ten cents or 1/10 of a dollar. **2.** A similar coin in Canadian currency. [Middle English, a tenth part, tithe, from Old French *dime, disme*, from Latin *decima (pars)*, tenth (part), tithe, from *decimus*, tenth, from *decem*, ten. See **dekm̥** in Appendix.*]

di·men·hy·dri·nate (dī′mĕn-hī′drə-nāt′) *n.* An antihistamine, $C_{24}H_{28}ClN_5O_3$, used to treat motion sickness and allergic disorders. [DIME(THYL) + (AMI)N(E) + HYDR(O)- + -IN + -ATE.]

dime novel. 1. Formerly, a romance or adventure story cheaply produced in book form to sell for ten cents. **2.** Any cheap novel.

di·men·sion (dĭ-mĕn′shən) *n. Abbr.* **dim. 1.** A measure of spatial extent, especially width, height, or length. **2.** *Often plural.* Extent; magnitude; size; scope. **3.** *Mathematics.* **a.** Any of the least number of independent coordinates required to specify a point in space uniquely. **b.** The range of any of these coordinates. **4.** *Physics.* A physical property, often mass, length, time, or some combination thereof, regarded as a fundamental measure, or as one of a set of fundamental measures, of a physical quantity: *Velocity has the dimensions of length divided by time.* —*tr.v.* **dimensioned, -sioning, -sions.** To cut or shape to specified dimensions. —*adj.* Cut to given dimensions. [Middle English *dimensio(u)n*, from Old French *dimension*, from Latin *dīmēnsiō*, "a measuring," from *dīmētīrī* (past participle *dīmēnsus*), to measure carefully : *dis-* (intensive) + *mētīrī*, to measure (see **mē-**[2] in Appendix*).] —**di·men′sion·al** *adj.* —**di·men′sion·al′i·ty** *n.* —**di·men′sion·al·ly** *adv.*

di·mer (dī′mər) *n. Chemistry.* **1.** A molecule consisting of two identical simpler molecules. **2.** A chemical compound consisting of such molecules. [DI- + Greek *meros*, part (see **smer-**[2] in Appendix*).]

di·mer·ic (dī-mĕr′ĭk) *adj. Biology.* Composed of two parts or divisions.

dim·er·ous (dĭm′ər-əs) *adj.* **1.** Consisting of two parts or segments, as the tarsus in certain insects. **2.** *Botany.* Having flower parts, such as petals, sepals, and stamens, in sets of two. Also written *2-merous.* [New Latin *dimerus* : DI- + -MEROUS.] —**dim′er·ism** *n.*

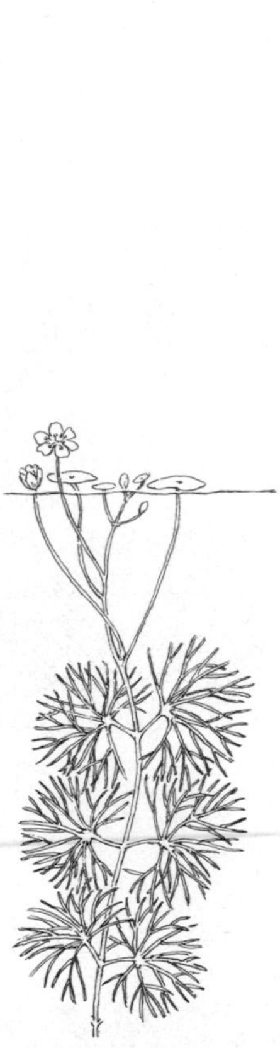

dimorphism
Exhibited in the distinction between the submerged and floating leaves of *Cabomba caroliniana*

dime store. A **five-and-ten-cent store** *(see).*

dim·e·ter (dĭm′ə-tər) *n. Prosody.* A verse consisting of two metrical feet or of two dipodies. [Late Latin, (verse) of two measures or meters, from Greek *dimetros*, having two meters : DI- + *metron*, METER.]

di·meth·yl (dī-mĕth′əl) *n. Chemistry.* **Ethane** *(see).* [DI- + METHYL.]

di·meth·yl·sulf·ox·ide (dī-mĕth′əl-sŭl-fŏk′sīd′) *n. Abbr.* **DMSO** A colorless hygroscopic liquid, $(CH_3)_2SO$, obtained from lignin, used as a solvent and in medicine as a skin penetrant to convey medications into the tissues.

dimin. 1. *Music.* diminuendo. **2.** diminutive.

di·min·ish (dĭ-mĭn′ĭsh) *v.* **-ished, -ishing, -ishes.** —*tr.* **1. a.** To reduce the apparent or actual size of; make smaller or less. **b.** To detract from the authority, rank, or prestige of. **2.** To cause to taper. **3.** *Music.* To reduce (a perfect or minor interval) by a semitone. —*intr.* **1.** To become smaller or less. **2.** To become narrower; to taper. —See Synonyms at **decrease.** [Middle English *deminishen*, blend of (a) *diminuen*, to reduce, lessen, from Old French *diminuer*, from Latin *dīminuere*, variant of *dēminuere* : *dē-*, from + *minuere*, to lessen (see **mei-**[2] in Appendix*), and (b) *minishen, minuisen*, to make smaller, from Old French *menuiser*, from Vulgar Latin *minūtiāre* (unattested), from Latin *minūtia*, smallness, from *minūtus*, small, from the past participle of *minuere*, to lessen.] —**di·min′ish·a·ble** *adj.* —**di·min′ish·ment** *n.*

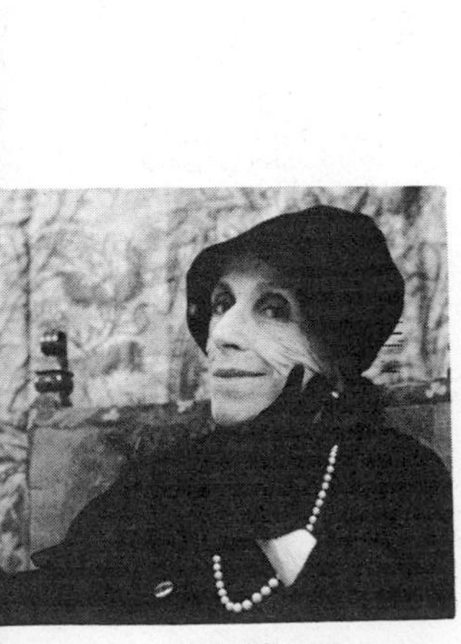

Isak Dinesen

diminishing returns, law of. The observation that after a certain point, profits diminish in proportion to the amount of further investment.

di·min·u·en·do (dĭ-mĭn′yo͞o-ĕn′dō) *n., pl.* **-dos** or **-does.** *Abbr.* **dim., dimin.** *Music.* **Decrescendo** *(see).* [Italian, "diminishing," from Latin *dīminuendum*, gerund of *dīminuere*, DIMINISH.] —**di·min′u·en′do** *adj.* & *adv.*

dim·i·nu·tion (dĭm′ə-no͞o′shən, -nyo͞o′shən) *n.* **1. a.** The act or process of diminishing. **b.** The resulting reduction; decrease. **2.** *Music.* The repetition of a theme in notes one-quarter or one-half the duration of the original. [Middle English *diminucioun*, from Old French *diminution*, from Latin *dīminūtiō*, *dēminūtiō*, from *dēminuere*, DIMINISH.]

di·min·u·tive (dĭ-mĭn′yə-tĭv) *adj. Abbr.* **dim., dimin. 1.** Of small size; tiny. **2.** Designating certain suffixes that denote smallness, youth, familiarity, or affection, as *-let* in *booklet* or *-kin* in *lambkin.* —See Synonyms at **small.** —*n. Abbr.* **dim., dimin.** A diminutive suffix, word, or name. [Middle English *diminutif*, from Old French, from Latin *dīminūtīvus, dēminūtīvus*, from *dēminūtus*, past participle of *dēminuere*, DIMINISH.] —**di·min′u·tive·ly** *adv.* —**di·min′u·tive·ness** *n.*

dim·is·so·ry (dĭm′ə-sôr′ē, -sōr′ē) *adj.* **1.** Formerly, designating a letter from a bishop granting a clergyman permission to depart for another diocese. **2.** Designating a bishop's letter certifying the eligibility of the bearer for ordination. [From Late Latin *dīmissōrius* (used in *dīmissōriae litterae*, "letter of dismissal," letter granting leave), from Latin *dīmittere* (past participle *dīmissus*), to send away, DISMISS.]

dim·i·ty (dĭm′ə-tē) *n., pl.* **-ties.** A sheer, crisp cotton fabric, usually corded or checked, used chiefly for curtains and dresses. [Middle English *demyt*, from Medieval Latin *dimitum*, from Medieval Greek *dimitos*, double-threaded : DI- + *mitos*, thread (see **mei-**[4] in Appendix*).]

dim·mer (dĭm′ər) *n.* **1.** A rheostat or other device used to reduce the intensity of illumination continuously. **2.** *Plural.* Parking lights on an automobile.

di·morph (dī′môrf′) *n.* Either of two dimorphic forms. [From DIMORPHISM.]

di·mor·phic (dī-môr′fĭk) *adj.* Also **di·mor·phous** (-fəs). Having two distinct forms.

di·mor·phism (dī-môr′fĭz′əm) *n.* **1.** *Botany.* The occurrence of two distinct forms of the same parts, such as leaves, flowers, or stamens, in a single plant or in plants of the same kind. **2.** *Chemistry & Physics.* Dimorphic crystallization. **3.** *Zoology.* The state of having two distinct forms in the same species when the sexes differ in secondary as well as primary sexual characteristics. [From Greek *dimorphos*, having two forms : DI- + -MORPHOUS.]

dim-out (dĭm′out′) *n.* **1.** The restricted use or exposure of lights at night, especially to lessen the chance of air attack. **2.** The semidarkness resulting from this. Compare **blackout.**

dim·ple (dĭm′pəl) *n.* **1.** A small natural indentation in the flesh on a part of the human body, especially on a chin or cheek. **2.** Any slight depression in a surface: *the dimples of a mattress.* —*v.* **dimpled, -pling, -ples.** —*tr.* To produce dimples in. —*intr.* To form dimples by smiling. [Middle English *dimple*, Old English *dympel* (unattested), pool, dimple. See **dub-** in Appendix.*] —**dim′ply** *adj.*

dim·wit (dĭm′wĭt′) *n. Slang.* A stupid person. —**dim′wit′ted** *adj.* —**dim′wit′ted·ly** *adv.* —**dim′wit′ted·ness** *n.*

din (dĭn) *n.* A medley of resounding and discordant noises; a continuing cacophony. See Synonyms at **noise.** —*v.* **dinned, dinning, dins.** —*tr.* **1.** To stun with deafening noise. **2.** To impress by wearying repetition. Usually used with *into: din an idea into one's head.* —*intr.* To make a din. [Middle English *dine, dune*, Old English *dyne.* See **dhwen-** in Appendix.*]

din. dinar.

Di·nah (dī′nə). A feminine given name. [Hebrew *Dīnah*, judgment, from *dīn*, to judge.]

di·nar (dĭ-när′, dē′när′) *n. Abbr.* **din. 1. a.** The basic monetary unit of Iraq, Jordan, Kuwait, and Southern Yemen, equal to 1,000 fils. **b.** The basic monetary unit of Algeria, equal to 100 centimes. **c.** The basic monetary unit of Tunisia, equal to 1,000 milliemes. **d.** The basic monetary unit of Yugoslavia, equal to 100 paras. See table of exchange rates at **currency. 2.** A monetary unit equal to 1/100 of the rial of Iran. See table of exchange rates at **currency. 3.** A coin or note worth one dinar. **4.** Any of several units of gold and silver currency used in the Middle East from the 8th to 19th century. [Arabic *dīnār*, from Late Greek *dēnarion*, denarius, from Latin *dēnārius*, DENARIUS.]

Di·nar·ic Alps (dĭ-năr′ĭk). The southeastern range of the Alps, extending along the Adriatic coast of Yugoslavia into northern Albania. Highest elevation, 8,714 feet.

dine (dīn) *v.* **dined, dining, dines.** —*intr.* To take dinner. —*tr.* To entertain at dinner; give dinner to. —**dine on** (or **upon** or **off**). To eat for dinner: *"They dined upon mince and slices of quince"* (Edward Lear). [Middle English *dinen*, from Old French *di(s)ner*, to dine, breakfast, from Vulgar Latin *disjējūnāre* (unattested), to break one's fast : Latin *dis-* (reversal) + Latin *jējūnus*†, fasting, hungry, hence poor, meager.]

din·er (dī′nər) *n.* **1.** A person taking dinner. **2.** A railroad dining car. **3.** A restaurant with a long counter and booths, originally shaped like a railroad car.

di·ne·ro (dĭ-nâr′ō) *n., pl.* **-ros.** *Slang.* Money. [Spanish, from Latin *dēnārius*, DENARIUS.]

Din·e·sen (dĭn′ə-sən), **Isak.** Pen name of Baroness Karen Dinesen Blixen. 1885–1962. Danish author of stories in Danish and English.

di·nette (dī-nĕt′) *n.* **1.** A nook or alcove for informal meals. **2.** The table and chairs used in a dinette. [From DINE.]

ding (dĭng) *v.* **dinged, dinging, dings.** —*intr.* **1.** To ring; clang. **2.** To speak persistently and repetitiously. —*tr.* **1.** To cause to

ă pat/ā pay/âr care/ä father/b bib/ch church/d deed/ĕ pet/ē be/f fife/g gag/h hat/hw which/ĭ pit/ī pie/îr pier/j judge/k kick/l lid, needle/m mum/n no, sudden/ng thing/ŏ pot/ō toe/ô paw, for/oi noise/ou out/o͝o took/o͞o boot/p pop/r roar/s sauce/sh ship, dish/

clang, as by striking. **2.** To hammer into or at with repetitious talk. *—n.* A ringing sound. [Probably imitative, but influenced by *ding,* to strike. See **dingbat.**]

ding·bat (dĭng′băt′) *n. Informal.* **1.** A small object, such as a stick or stone, suitable for hurling at another object. **2.** Any unspecified gadget or other article. **3.** *Printing.* Any typographical ornament not further specified. [Probably *ding,* to strike, Middle English *dingen,* probably from Old Norse *dengja,* to cudgel, from Germanic *ding-* (unattested) + BAT (cudgel).]

ding-dong (dĭng′dông′, -dŏng′) *n.* **1.** The peal of a bell. **2.** Any similar repeating sound. *—intr.v.* **ding-donged, -donging, -dongs.** To ring; jingle. *—adj.* Characterized by a hammering exchange, as of blows. [Imitative.]

din·ghy (dĭng′ē) *n., pl.* **-ghies.** Also **din·gy, din·gey** *pl.* **-eys.** Any small rowboat. [Hindi *ḍiṅgī, dēṅgī,* diminutive of *dēṅgā*†, boat.]

din·gle (dĭng′gəl) *n.* A small, wooded valley; dell. [Middle English *dingle*†.]

din·go (dĭng′gō) *n., pl.* **-goes.** A wild dog, *Canis dingo,* of Australia, having a yellowish-brown coat. [Native Australian name.]

ding·us (dĭng′əs) *n. Slang.* A gadget or other article whose name eludes one or is not known. [From Dutch *dinges,* probably from German *Dinges,* genitive of *Ding,* thing, from Old High German *ding.* See **tenk-¹** in Appendix.*]

Ding·wall (dĭng′wôl′, -wəl). The county seat of Ross and Cromarty, Scotland. Population, 4,000.

din·gy¹ (dĭn′jē) *adj.* **-gier, -giest.** **1.** Darkened with smoke and grime; dirty. **2.** Drab. **3.** Shabby; worn. [Possibly from Middle English *dinge,* rare variant of *dung, dong,* DUNG.] **—din′gi·ly** *adv.* **—din′gi·ness** *n.*

din·gy². Variant of **dinghy.**

dining car. A railroad car in which meals are served.

dining room. A room in which meals are served.

di·ni·tro·ben·zene (dī-nī′trō-bĕn′zēn′, -bĕn-zēn′) *n.* Any of three isomeric compounds, $C_6H_4(NO_2)_2$, made from a mixture of nitric acid, sulfuric acid, and heated benzene and used in celluloid manufacture, in dyes, and in organic syntheses. [DI- (two) + NITRO- + BENZENE.]

Din·ka (dĭng′kä) *n., pl.* **Dinka** or **-kas.** **1.** A member of a group of Nilotic tribes of the southern Sudan. **2.** The East Sudanic language of this people. [Dinka *jieng,* "people."]

dink·ey (dĭng′kē) *n., pl.* **-eys.** Also **dink·y** *pl.* **-ies.** *Informal.* A small locomotive used in a railroad yard. [From DINKY.]

dink·y (dĭng′kē) *adj.* **-ier, -iest.** **1.** *Informal.* Of small size or consequence; insignificant. **2.** *British Informal.* Dainty; cute. *—n., pl.* **dinkies.** A dinkey. [Probably from Scottish *dink*†, trim, neat.]

Din·mont (dĭn′mŏnt′) *n.* See **Dandie Dinmont.**

din·ner (dĭn′ər) *n.* **1.** The chief meal of the day, eaten at the noon hour or in the evening. **2.** A banquet or formal meal in honor of some person or commemorating an occasion. [Middle English *diner,* from Old French *di(s)ner,* from *di(s)ner,* DINE.]

dinner jacket. A **tuxedo** *(see).*

din·ner·ware (dĭn′ər-wâr′) *n.* **1.** The dishes, serving bowls, platters, or the like used in serving a meal. **2.** A set of dishes.

di·no·flag·el·late (dī′nō-flăj′ə-lĭt, -lāt′, -flə-jĕl′ĭt) *n.* Any of numerous minute, chiefly marine protozoans of the class Dinoflagellata, characteristically having two flagella and a cellulose outer envelope, and forming one of the chief constituents of plankton. [New Latin *Dinoflagellata,* "ones having whirling flagella" : Greek *dinos,* whirlpool, eddy, from *dinein*†, to whirl + FLAGELLUM.]

di·no·saur (dī′nə-sôr′) *n.* Any of various extinct, often gigantic reptiles of the orders Saurischia and Ornithischia, that existed during the Mesozoic era. [New Latin : Greek *deinos,* fearful, monstrous (see **dwei-** in Appendix*) + -SAUR.] **—di′no·sau′ri·an** *adj. & n.* **—di′no·sau′ric** *adj.*

Dinosaur National Monument. An area of 298 square miles in northeastern Utah, reserved to protect the extensive fossil remains of prehistoric animals.

di·no·there (dī′nə-thîr′) *n.* Any of various extinct elephantlike mammals of the genus *Dinotherium,* that existed during the Miocene, Pliocene, and Pleistocene epochs. [New Latin *dinotherium* : Greek *deinos,* fearful, monstrous (see **dwei-** in Appendix*) + -THERE.]

dint (dĭnt) *n.* **1.** Force or effort; power; exertion. Used in the phrase *by dint of.* **2.** A dent. *—tr.v.* **dinted, dinting, dints.** **1.** To put a dent or dents in. **2.** To impress or drive in forcibly. [Middle English *dint, dunt,* Old English *dynt.* See **dent.**]

di·oc·e·san (dī-ŏs′ə-sən) *adj. Abbr.* **dioc.** Of or pertaining to a diocese. *—n. Abbr.* **dioc.** A bishop of a diocese.

di·o·cese (dī′ə-sĭs, -sēs′, -sēz′) *n. Abbr.* **dioc.** The district or churches under the jurisdiction of a bishop; a bishopric. [Middle English *diocise,* from Old French, from Late Latin *diocēsis,* from Latin *dioecēsis,* jurisdiction, district, from Greek *dioikesis,* "housekeeping," administration, from *dioikein,* to keep house, manage, administer : *dia-,* completely + *oikein,* to inhabit, possess, from *oikos,* house (see **weik-¹** in Appendix*).]

Di·o·cle·tian (dī′ə-klē′shən). Full name, Gaius Aurelius Valerius Diocletianus. A.D. 245–313. Roman emperor (284–305).

di·ode (dī′ōd′) *n.* **1.** Any electronic device that restricts current flow chiefly to one direction. **2.** A vacuum tube having two electrodes, a cathode, and an anode. **3.** A two-terminal semiconductor device used chiefly as a rectifier. [DI- + -ODE.]

di·oe·cious (dī-ē′shəs) *adj.* Also **di·e·cious.** *Botany.* Having male and female flowers borne on separate plants. Compare **monoecious.** [From New Latin *Dioecia* : DI- + Greek *oikia,* dwelling, from *oikos,* house (see **weik-¹** in Appendix*).] **—di·oe′cious·ly** *adv.*

Di·og·e·nes (dī-ŏj′ə-nēz′). 412?–323 B.C. Greek Cynic philosopher; exponent of asceticism.

di·oi·cous (dī-oi′kəs) *adj. Botany.* Having antheridia and archegonia on separate plants; unisexual. Said of mosses and related plants. [New Latin *dioecus,* "having two houses" : DI- (two) + Greek *oikos,* house (see **weik-¹** in Appendix*).]

Di·o·mede Islands (dī′ə-mēd′). Two islands in the center of the Bering Strait, one, Little Diomede, belonging to the United States and the other, Big Diomede, to the Soviet Union.

Di·o·me·des (dī′ə-mē′dēz). Also **Di·o·med** (dī′ə-mĕd′), **Di·o·mede** (-mēd′). *Greek Mythology.* A prince of Argos and, in the Homeric poems, one of the chief heroes at Troy.

Di·o·ne (dī-ō′nē). *Greek Mythology.* The mother of Aphrodite by Zeus.

Di·o·nys·i·a (dī′ə-nĭsh′ē-ə, -nĭzh′ē-ə, -nĭs′ē-ə) *pl.n.* Any of various festivals of ancient Attica in honor of the god Dionysus, as: **a.** The lesser festival, held in the fall, in which the tragedy is thought to have had its origin. **b.** The great spring festival in Athens, at which competing plays were presented from the time of Pisistratus.

Di·o·nys·i·ac (dī′ə-nĭs′ē-ăk′) *adj.* **1.** Of or relating to Dionysus or the Dionysia. **2.** *Sometimes small* **d.** Dionysian, as opposed to Apollonian. **—Di′o·ny·si′a·cal·ly** (-nĭ-sī′ĭk-lē) *adv.*

Di·o·nys·i·an (dī′ə-nĭsh′ən, -nĭzh′ən, -nĭs′ē-ən) *adj.* **1.** Of or relating to any of several historical persons named Dionysius. **2.** Of or relating to Dionysus or the Dionysia. **3.** *Often small* **d.** **a.** Of an ecstatic, orgiastic, or irrational character. **b.** Filled with tremendous creative energy. **4.** *Sometimes small* **d.** In the philosophy of Nietzsche, characteristic of the acquisition of the creative-imaginative power, as opposed to the critical-rational power embodied by the **apollonian** *(see).*

Di·o·ny·si·us (dī′ə-nĭsh′ē-əs, -nĭsh′əs, -nī′sē-əs). Called "The Elder." 430?–367 B.C. Greek tyrant of Syracuse; proverbial for cruelty.

Di·o·ny·si·us of Halicarnassus (dī′ə-nĭsh′ē-əs, -nĭsh′əs, -nī′sē-əs). Greek historian of the first century B.C.; author of a history of Rome.

Di·o·ny·sus (dī′ə-nī′səs). Also **Di·o·ny·sos.** *Greek Mythology.* The god of wine and of an orgiastic religion celebrating the power and fertility of nature. Also called "Bacchus."

Di·o·ny·sus Za·gre·us (dī′ə-nī′səs zā′grē-əs). *Greek Mythology.* A god, **Zagreus** *(see).*

di·o·phan·tine analysis (dī′ə-făn′tīn, -tēn, -tən). *Mathematics.* A method for determining integral solutions of certain algebraic equations. [After *Diophantus,* Greek mathematician of the third century B.C.]

di·op·side (dī-ŏp′sīd′) *n.* A monoclinic pyroxene mineral, $CaMgSi_2O_6$, used as a gemstone and as a refractory. [French : DI- (two) + Greek *opsis* (stem *opsid-*), appearance, sight (see **okw-** in Appendix*).]

di·op·ter (dī-ŏp′tər) *n. Optics.* A unit, equal to a reciprocal meter, of curvature and of the power of lenses, refracting surfaces, and other optical systems. [From Latin *dioptra,* an optical instrument for measuring angles and altitudes, from Greek : *dia-,* through + *optos,* seen, visible (see **okw-** in Appendix*).] **—di·op′tral** *adj.*

di·op·tom·e·ter (dī′ŏp-tŏm′ə-tər) *n.* An instrument for measuring ocular refraction. [DI- + Greek *optos,* visible (see **optic**) + -METER.] **—di′op·tom′e·try** *n.*

di·op·tric (dī-ŏp′trĭk) *adj.* Also **di·op·tri·cal** (-trĭ-kəl). *Optics.* **1.** Of or relating to dioptrics. **2.** Pertaining to optical refraction; refractive.

di·op·trics (dī-ŏp′trĭks) *n.* Plural in form, used with a singular verb. *Optics.* The study of the refraction of light. [From Greek *dioptrikos,* from *dioptra,* optical instrument. See **diopter.**] **—di·op′tric, di·op′tri·cal** *adj.*

di·o·ram·a (dī′ə-răm′ə, -rä′mə) *n.* **1.** A three-dimensional miniature scene with painted modeled figures and background. **2.** A scene reproduced on cloth transparencies with various lights shining through the cloths to produce changes in effect, and viewed through a small aperture. [French : DI(A)- (through) + (PAN)ORAMA.] **—di′o·ram′ic** *adj.*

di·o·rite (dī′ə-rīt′) *n.* Any of various granite-textured, crystalline dark rocks rich in plagioglase and having little quartz. [French, from Greek *diorizein,* to distinguish : *dia-,* apart + *horizein,* to divide, from *horos,* boundary (see **horizon**).] **—di′o·rit′ic** (-rĭt′ĭk) *adj.*

Di·os·cu·ri (dī-ŏs′kyə-rī′, dī′ə-skyŏŏr′ī′). *Greek Mythology.* **Castor and Pollux** *(see).* [Greek *Dioskouroi,* "sons of Zeus" : *Dios,* genitive of ZEUS + *kouroi,* plural of *kouros,* boy, son (see **ker-³** in Appendix*).]

di·ox·ane (dī-ŏk′sān′) *n.* A flammable, potentially explosive, colorless liquid, $C_4H_8O_2$, used as a solvent for fats, greases, and resins and in various products including paints, lacquers, glues, cosmetics, and fumigants. [DI- + OX(A)- + -ANE.]

di·ox·ide (dī-ŏk′sīd′) *n.* An oxide with two oxygen atoms per molecule.

dip (dĭp) *v.* **dipped, dipping, dips.** *—tr.* **1.** To plunge briefly in or into a liquid, usually in order to wet, coat, or saturate. **2.** To color or dye in this manner: *dip Easter eggs.* **3.** To immerse (cattle or sheep, for example) in a disinfectant solution. **4.** To make (a candle) by repeatedly immersing a wick in melted wax or tallow. **5.** To galvanize or plate (metal) by immersion. **6.** To scoop up by plunging the hand or a container into and out of a liquid; to bail; ladle. **7.** To lower and raise (a flag) in salute. *—intr.* **1.** To plunge into water or other liquid and come out quickly. **2.** To plunge the hand or a container into a liquid,

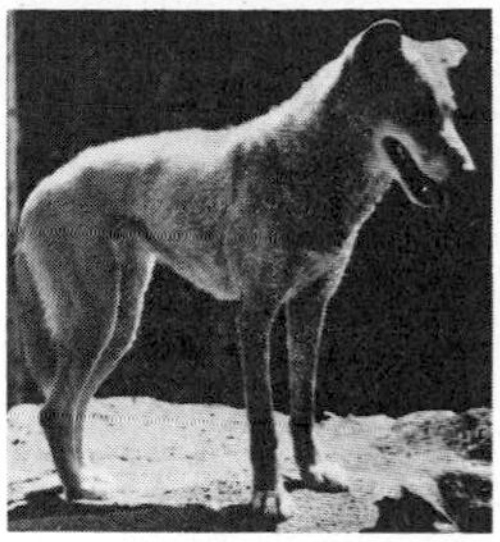

dingo

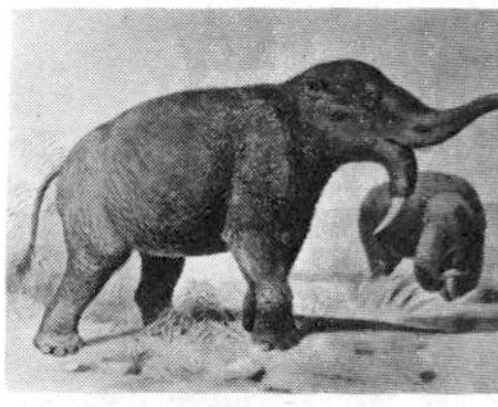

dinothere

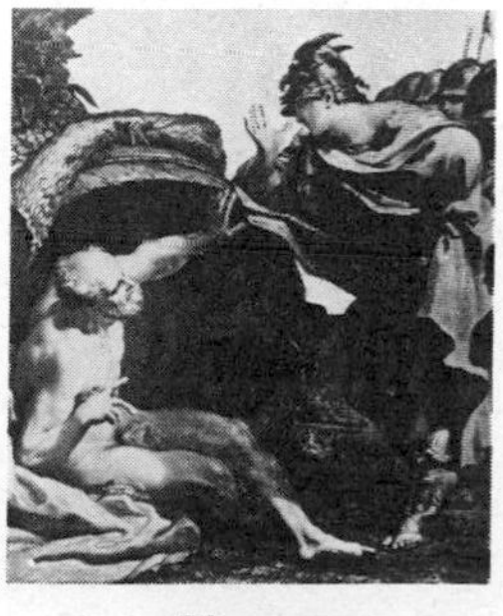

Diogenes
With Alexander the Great

t tight/th thin, path/*th* this, bathe/ŭ cut/ûr urge/v valve/w with/y yes/z zebra, size/zh vision/ə about, item, edible, gallop, circus/ à *Fr.* ami/œ *Fr.* feu, *Ger.* schön/ü *Fr.* tu, *Ger.* über/KH *Ger.* ich, *Scot.* loch/N *Fr.* bon. ***Follows main vocabulary.** †**Of obscure origin.**

especially for the purpose of taking something up or out. **3.** To drop or sink suddenly. **4.** To appear to sink. **5.** To slope downward; decline. **6.** *Geology.* To lie at an angle to the horizontal plane, as a rock stratum or vein. **7.** To read here and there in a book or magazine; browse. Used with *into.* **8.** To investigate a subject superficially; dabble. —*n.* **1.** A brief plunge or immersion. **2.** A liquid into which something is dipped. **3.** A smooth creamed preparation, as of softened cheese or seasoned sour cream, into which crackers may be dipped. **4.** An amount taken up by dipping. **5.** A container for dipping. **6.** A candle made by repeated dipping in tallow or wax. **7.** A downward slope or sloping; a decline. **8.** *Geology.* The downward inclination of a rock stratum or vein in reference to the plane of the horizon. **9.** *Surveying.* The angular difference between eye level and the lower level of the horizon. **10. Magnetic dip** *(see).* **11.** A hollow; depression. **12.** *Gymnastics.* An exercise on the parallel bars in which the body is lowered by bending the elbows until the chin reaches the level of the bars and then is raised by straightening the arms. [Middle English *dippen,* Old English *dyppan.* See **dheub-** in Appendix.*]

di·pet·al·ous (dī-pĕt′l-əs) *adj. Botany.* Having two petals.

di·phase (dī′fāz′) *adj.* Also **di·pha·sic** (dī-fā′zĭk). Having two phases.

di·phen·yl (dī-fĕn′əl, -fē′nəl) *n. Chemistry.* Biphenyl *(see).*

di·phen·yl·a·mine (dī-fĕn′əl-ə-mēn′, -ăm′ĭn, dī-fē′nəl-) *n.* A colorless crystalline compound, $(C_6H_5)_2NH$, used as a stabilizer for plastics and in the manufacture of dyes, explosives, pesticides, and pharmaceuticals. [DIPHENYL + AMINE.]

di·phen·yl·a·mine·chlor·ar·sine (dī-fĕn′əl-ə-mēn′klôr-är′sēn′, -klôr-är′sēn′, dī-fĕn′əl-ăm′ĭn-, dī-fē′nəl-) *n. Chemistry.* **Phenarsazine chloride** *(see).*

di·phen·yl·chlor·ar·sine (dī-fĕn′əl-klôr-är′sēn′, -klôr-är′sēn′, dī-fē′nəl-) *n.* A dark-brown liquid organic compound, $(C_6H_5)_2AsCl$, used as a poison gas, especially during World War I. [DIPHENYL + CHLOR(O)- + ARSINE.]

di·phen·yl·hy·dan·to·in sodium (dī-fĕn′əl-hī-dăn′tō-ĭn, dī-fē′nəl-). A white powder, $C_{15}H_{11}N_2O_2Na$, used as an anticonvulsant. [DIPHENYL + HYDANTOIN.]

di·phen·yl·ke·tone (dī-fĕn′əl-kē′tōn′, dī-fē′nəl-) *n. Chemistry.* **Benzophenone** *(see).* [DIPHENYL + KETONE.]

di·phos·gene (dī-fŏz′jĕn′) *n.* A colorless mobile liquid, $ClCOOCCl_3$, with a vapor used as a military poison gas. [DI- + PHOSGENE.]

diph·the·ri·a (dĭf-thîr′ē-ə, dĭp-) *n.* An acute contagious disease caused by infection with the bacillus *Corynebacterium diphtheriae,* and characterized by the formation of false membranes in the throat and other air passages, causing difficulty in breathing, high fever, and weakness. [New Latin, from French *diphthérie,* from Greek *diphthera,* piece of leather (from the rough false membrane). See **deph-** in Appendix.*] —**diph′the·rit′ic** (-thə-rĭt′ĭk), **diph·ther′ic** (-thĕr′ĭk), **diph·the′ri·al** *adj.*

diph·thong (dĭf′thŏng′, -thŏng′, dĭp′-) *n. Phonetics.* **1.** A complex speech sound beginning with one vowel sound and moving to another vowel or semivowel position within the same syllable. For example, *oy* in the word *boy* is a diphthong. **2.** Either of the two ligatures æ or œ, originally pronounced as diphthongs in Classical Latin but now pronounced as single vowels. [Middle English *diptonge,* from Old French *diptongue,* from Late Latin *dipthongus,* from Greek *diphthongos* : DI- (two) + *phthongos†,* voice, sound. See also **monophthong, apothegm.**]

diph·thong·ize (dĭf′thŏng-īz′, dĭf′thŏng-, dĭp′-) *v.* **-ized, -izing, -izes.** —*tr.* To pronounce as a diphthong. —*intr.* To become a diphthong. —**diph′thong·i·za′tion** *n.*

di·phy·cer·cal (dĭf′ĭ-sûr′kəl) *adj. Zoology.* Designating or having a tail fin in which the vertebral column extends to the tip, with symmetrical upper and lower parts. [From Greek *diphuēs,* double, twofold (see **diphyodont**) + *kerkos,* tail (see **ker-²** in Appendix*).]

di·phy·let·ic (dī′fī-lĕt′ĭk) *adj.* Descended from two ancestral lines or individuals. [DI- + PHYLETIC.]

di·phyl·lous (dī-fĭl′əs) *adj. Botany.* Having two leaves. [New Latin *diphyllus* : DI- + -PHYLLOUS.]

di·phy·o·dont (dī-fī′ə-dŏnt′) *adj. Zoology.* Having two successive sets of teeth, as do most mammals. [From Greek *diphuēs,* double, twofold : DI- (two) + *phuein,* to bring forth, grow (see **bheu-** in Appendix*) + -ODONT.]

dipl. diplomat; diplomatic.

di·ple·gia (dī-plē′jə, -jē-ə) *n.* Paralysis of corresponding parts on both sides of the body. [DI- + -PLEGIA.]

di·plex (dī′plĕks′) *adj.* Capable of simultaneous transmission or reception of two messages in the same radio channel. [DI- + (DU)PLEX.]

diplo-, dipl-. Indicates double; for example, **diplococcus, diploid.** [Greek, from *diploos,* double : DI- (two) + *-ploos,* "-fold" (see **dwò** in Appendix*).]

dip·lo·blas·tic (dĭp′lō-blăs′tĭk) *adj.* Having two distinct cellular layers. Said of embryos and lower invertebrate animals such as sponges and coelenterates. [DIPLO- + -BLASTIC.]

dip·lo·car·di·ac (dĭp′lō-kär′dē-ăk′) *adj.* Having or characterizing a heart in which the two sides are distinctly separated, as in birds and mammals. [DIPLO- + Greek *kardia,* heart (see **kerd-¹** in Appendix*).]

dip·lo·coc·cus (dĭp′lō-kŏk′əs) *n., pl.* **-cocci** (-kŏk′sī′, -kŏk′ī′). Any of various paired spherical bacteria of the genus *Diplococcus,* some of which are pathogenic. [New Latin *Diplococcus* : DIPLO- + -COCCUS.] —**dip′lo·coc′cal** (dĭp′lō-kŏk′əl), **dip′lo·coc′cic** (-kŏk′sĭk, -kŏk′ĭk) *adj.*

di·plod·o·cus (dĭ-plŏd′ə-kəs, dī-) *n.* A very large extinct, herbivorous dinosaur of the genus *Diplodocus,* that existed during the Jurassic period. [New Latin : DIPLO- + Greek *dokos,* beam (see **dek-¹** in Appendix*).]

dip·lo·e (dĭp′lō-ē′) *n.* The spongy, bony tissue between the outer and inner bone layers of the cranium. [New Latin, from Greek *diploē,* "doubling," "fold," from *diploos,* double. See **diplo-.**]

dip·loid (dĭp′loid′) *adj.* **1.** Double or twofold. **2.** *Genetics.* Having a homologous pair of chromosomes for each characteristic except sex, the total number of chromosomes being twice that of a gamete. In this sense, compare **haploid.** —*n. Genetics.* **1.** A diploid cell. **2.** An individual characterized by a diploid chromosome number. [DIPL(O)- + -OID.]

di·plo·ma (dĭ-plō′mə) *n.* **1. a.** A document issued by a university or other school testifying that a student has earned a degree and conferring upon him the rights and privileges of that degree. **b.** Any certificate indicating that a particular course of study has been successfully completed. **2.** A certificate conferring a privilege or honor. **3.** An official document or charter. [Latin, from Greek *diplōma,* something doubled, folded paper, document, from *diploos,* double. See **diplo-.**]

di·plo·ma·cy (dĭ-plō′mə-sē) *n., pl.* **-cies. 1.** The art or practice of conducting international relations, as in negotiating alliances, treaties, and agreements. **2.** Tact or skill in dealing with people. —See Synonyms at **tact.**

dip·lo·mat (dĭp′lə-măt′) *n.* **1.** *Abbr.* **dipl.** One appointed to represent his government in its relations with other governments. **2.** One who possesses skill or tact in dealing with others. [French *diplomate,* back-formation from *diplomatique,* DIPLOMATIC.]

dip·lo·mate (dĭp′lə-māt′) *n.* A physician certified as a specialist by a board of examiners.

dip·lo·mat·ic (dĭp′lə-măt′ĭk) *adj.* **1.** *Abbr.* **dipl.** Of, pertaining to, or involving diplomacy. **2.** Characterized by tact and sensitivity in dealing with people; discreet; politic. —See Synonyms at **suave.** [French *diplomatique,* connected with the documents that regulate international relations, from New Latin *diplomaticus,* connected with documents or diplomatics, from Latin *diplōma,* document. See **diploma.**] —**dip′lo·mat′i·cal·ly** *adv.*

diplomatic corps. The body of diplomatic personnel in residence at the capital of a nation.

diplomatic immunity. Exemption from ordinary processes of law afforded to diplomatic personnel in a foreign country.

dip·lo·mat·ics (dĭp′lə-măt′ĭks) *n.* Plural in form, used with a singular verb. **1.** Diplomacy. **2.** The branch of paleography devoted to the study of ancient documents and the determination of their age and authenticity.

di·plo·ma·tist (dĭ-plō′mə-tĭst) *n.* A diplomat.

dip·lont (dĭp′lŏnt) *n. Biology.* An organism having somatic cells with diploid chromosomes. [DIPLO- + *-ont,* cell, from Greek *ōn* (stem *ont-*), present participle of *einai,* to be (see **es-** in Appendix*).]

di·plo·pi·a (dĭ-plō′pē-ə) *n. Pathology.* A disorder of vision which causes objects to appear double. [New Latin : DIPL(O)- + -OPIA.] —**di·plo′pic** (dĭ-plō′pĭk, -plŏp′ĭk) *adj.*

dip·lo·pod (dĭp′lə-pŏd′) *n.* Any of various segmented, cylindrical arthropods of the class Diplopoda, which includes the millipedes. [New Latin *Diplopoda* : DIPLO- + -POD.]

di·plo·sis (dĭ-plō′sĭs) *n.* The formation of the full number of chromosomes found in a somatic cell by the fusion of gamete nuclei containing haploid sets in fertilization. [New Latin, from Greek *diplōsis,* a doubling, from *diploun,* to double, from *diploos,* double. See **diplo-.**]

dip needle. 1. *Physics.* A magnetic needle vertically balanced and pivoted to rotate freely in order to indicate the local inclination of the earth's magnetic field. **2.** An instrument; the **inclinometer** *(see).*

dip·no·an (dĭp′nō-ən) *n.* Any of various fishes of the group Dipnoi, which includes the lungfishes, characterized by modified lungs that enable them to breathe atmospheric air. —*adj.* Of or belonging to the Dipnoi. [From New Latin *Dipnoi,* from *dipnous,* having two apertures for breathing, from Greek *dipnoos* : DI- + *pnoē,* breath, from *pnein,* to breathe (see **pneu-** in Appendix*).]

dip·o·dy (dĭp′ə-dē) *n., pl.* **-dies.** A prosodic unit consisting of two feet. [Late Latin *dipodia,* from Greek, having two feet, from *dipous* (stem *dipod-*), two-footed : DI- + -POD.]

di·po·lar (dī′pō′lər) *adj.* Of, pertaining to, or having a dipole.

di·pole (dī′pōl′) *n.* **1.** *Physics.* A pair of electric charges or magnetic poles, of equal magnitude but of opposite sign or polarity, separated by a small distance. **2.** *Electronics.* An antenna, usually fed from the center, consisting of two equal rods extending outward in a straight line. In this sense, also called "dipole antenna."

dipole moment. 1. The product of either charge in an electric dipole with the distance separating them. Also called "electric dipole moment." **2.** The product of the strength of either pole in a magnetic dipole with the distance separating them. Also called "magnetic dipole moment."

dip·per (dĭp′ər) *n.* **1.** One that dips. **2.** A container used for dipping, such as a long-handled cup for taking up water. **3.** *Capital* **D.** Either of two dipper-shaped star groups, the Big Dipper in **Ursa Major** *(see)* or the Little Dipper in **Ursa Minor** *(see).* **4.** A bird, the **water ouzel** *(see).*

dip·py (dĭp′ē) *adj.* **-pier, -piest.** *Slang.* Foolish; not sensible. [Origin unknown.]

di·pro·pel·lant (dī′prə-pĕl′ənt) *n.* A bipropellant *(see).*

dip·sas (dĭp′səs) *n., pl.* **-sades** (-sə-dēz′). A serpent whose bite was fabled to produce a great thirst. [Middle English, from Latin, from Greek, from *dipsa†,* thirst.]

dipper

dip·so·ma·ni·a (dĭp′sə-mā′nē-ə, -mān′yə) *n.* An insatiable, often periodic craving for alcoholic liquors. [New Latin : Greek *dipsa,* thirst (see **dipsas**) + -MANIA.] —**dip′so·ma′ni·ac, dip′so·ma·ni′a·cal** (-mə-nī′ĭ-kəl) *adj.* —**dip′so·ma′ni·ac** *n.*
dip·stick (dĭp′stĭk′) *n.* A graduated rod for measuring the depth or amount of liquid in a container, as of oil in a crankcase.
dip·ter·an (dĭp′tər-ən) *n.* Also **dip·ter·on** (-tə-rŏn′). A dipterous insect. —*adj.* Of or belonging to the order Diptera; dipterous. [From New Latin *Diptera,* plural of *dipterus,* DIPTEROUS.]
dip·ter·ous (dĭp′tər-əs) *adj.* **1.** Of, pertaining to, or belonging to the Diptera, a large order of insects which includes the true flies and mosquitoes, characterized by a single pair of membranous wings and a pair of club-shaped balancing organs called halteres. **2.** *Botany.* Having two winglike parts: *the dipterous fruit of the maple.* [New Latin *dipterus,* from Greek *dipteros,* having two wings : DI- + -PTEROUS.]
dip·tych (dĭp′tĭk) *n.* **1.** An ancient writing tablet having two leaves hinged together. **2.** A pair of painted or carved panels hinged together. [Late Latin *diptycha,* from Greek *diptukha,* from *diptukhos,* double-folded : DI- + *ptukhē,* a fold, from *ptussein,* to fold (see **epi** in Appendix*).]
dir. director.
Di·rac (dĭ-răk′), **Paul Adrien Maurice.** Born 1902. British theoretical physicist; a founder of quantum electrodynamics.
dire (dīr) *adj.* **direr, direst.** Having dreadful or terrible consequences; calamitous; disastrous. See Synonyms at **sinister.** [Latin *dīrus,* fearful, ill-omened. See **dwei-** in Appendix.*] —**dire′ly** *adv.* —**dire′ness** *n.*
di·rect (dĭ-rĕkt′, dī-) *v.* **-rected, -recting, -rects.** —*tr.* **1.** To conduct the affairs of; manage; regulate. **2.** To take charge of with authority; control. **3.** To conduct (musicians) in a musical rehearsal or performance. **4.** To move (something or someone) toward a goal; aim; point. **5.** To give instructions to (someone) for finding a place. **6.** To address to a destination. **7.** To address to a person or audience. **8. a.** To give guidance and instruction to (actors) in the rehearsal and performance of a play or the filming of a motion picture. **b.** To supervise the performance of actors in. —*intr.* **1.** To give commands or directions. **2.** To conduct a performance or rehearsal. —See Synonyms at **command, conduct.** —*adj.* **1.** Proceeding or lying in a straight course or line; not deviating or swerving. **2.** Straightforward; candid; frank. **3.** Without intervening persons, conditions, or agencies; immediate. **4.** By action of the voters, rather than through elected representatives or delegates. **5.** Of unbroken descent; lineal. **6.** Consisting of the exact words of the writer or speaker. **7.** Absolute; total: *direct opposites.* **8.** *Mathematics.* Varying in the same manner as another quantity; especially, increasing if another quantity increases or decreasing if it decreases. Compare **inverse.** **9.** *Astronomy.* Designating a west-to-east motion of a planet in the same direction as the sun's movement among the stars. —*adv.* In a direct manner; straight; directly. See Usage note below. [Middle English *directen,* from Latin *dīrigere* (past participle *dīrectus*), to arrange in distinct lines, direct : *dis-,* apart + *regere,* to guide (see **reg-**[1] in Appendix*).]
Usage: *Direct* (adverb) and *directly* are interchangeable in the senses of in a direct line or manner, or straight *(went direct,* or *directly, to Atlanta),* and in the sense of without anyone or anything intervening *(direct,* or *directly, from manufacturer to buyer).* In all other senses of *directly,* listed at that word, the use of *direct* is not possible.
direct action. The use of strikes, demonstrations, and sabotage to achieve an end. —**direct actionist.**
di·rect-ac·tion (dĭ-rĕkt′ăk′shən, dī-rĕkt′-) *adj.* Operating without intermediate ingredients, components, stages, or processes.
direct current. *Abbr.* **dc** An electric current flowing in one direction.
directed angle. An angle having an indicated positive sense.
directed distance. A segment of a line having an indicated positive sense.
di·rec·tion (dĭ-rĕk′shən, dī-) *n.* **1.** The act or function of directing. **2.** Management, supervision, or guidance of some action or operation. **3.** The art or action of musical or theatrical directing. **4.** A word or phrase in a musical score indicating how a particular passage is to be played or sung. **5.** *Usually plural.* An instruction or series of instructions for doing something. **6.** An order or command; authoritative indication. **7. a.** The distance-independent relationship between two points that specifies the angular position of either with respect to the other; the relationship by which the alignment or orientation of any position with respect to any other position is established. **b.** A position to which motion or another position is referred. **c.** A line leading to a place or point. **d.** The line or course along which a person or thing moves. **8.** The statement, in degrees, of the angle measured between due north and a given line or course on a compass. **9.** A course or area of development; tendency toward a particular end or goal. [Middle English, arrangement, management, from Old French, from Latin *dīrectiō,* from *dīrigere,* to DIRECT.]
di·rec·tion·al (dĭ-rĕk′shən-əl, dī-) *adj.* Of or pertaining to spatial direction, especially a single specified direction. —**di·rec′tion·al′i·ty** *n.*
directional antenna. An antenna adapted for receiving signals from or sending signals in a particular direction.
directional signal. One of two flashing lights on an automobile that indicates the direction of a turn. Also called "directionals."
direction finder. A device for determining the source of a transmitted signal, consisting mainly of a radio receiver and a coiled rotating antenna. Often called "radio direction finder."
direction indicator. A compass used in airplane navigation to compare an intended heading to the actual heading.
di·rec·tive (dĭ-rĕk′tĭv, dī-) *n.* An order or instruction, especially one issued by a government or military unit. —*adj.* Serving to direct, indicate, or point out; directing.
di·rect·ly (dĭ-rĕkt′lē, dī-) *adv.* **1.** In a direct line or manner; straight. See Usage note at **direct.** **2.** Without anyone or anything intervening; immediately. See Usage note at **direct.** **3.** Exactly; totally; absolutely. **4.** At once; instantly. —See Synonyms at **immediately.** —*conj. Chiefly British.* As soon as: *We'll go, directly he's ready.*
direct object. In English and some other languages, the word or words in a sentence designating the person or thing receiving the action of a transitive verb. The direct object in English is usually a noun, nominal clause or phrase, or pronoun and generally follows a verb. In *The boy broke the dish,* the direct object is *the dish.* See **object.**
Di·rec·toire (dē-rĕk-twär′) *n.* The **Directory** *(see).* —*adj.* Of or in the style characteristic of the Directory period in France.
di·rec·tor (dĭ-rĕk′tər, dī-) *n. Abbr.* **dir. 1.** One who supervises, controls, or manages. **2.** A member of a board of persons who control or govern the affairs of an institution or corporation. **3. a.** One whose profession is the supervision and instruction of the actors in a dramatic production. **b.** The conductor of an orchestra or chorus. —**di·rec′tor·ship′** *n.*
di·rec·tor·ate (dĭ-rĕk′tər-ĭt, dī-) *n.* **1.** The office or position of a director. **2.** A board of directors.
di·rec·to·ri·al (dĭ-rĕk′tôr′ē-əl, -tōr′ē-əl, dī-) *adj.* **1.** Of or pertaining to a director or directorate. **2.** Serving to direct; directive. —**di·rec′to′ri·al·ly** *adv.*
di·rec·to·ry (dĭ-rĕk′tə-rē, dī-) *n., pl.* **-ries. 1.** One that directs. **2.** A book listing names, addresses, and other data about a specific group of persons or organizations. **3.** A book of rules or directions, especially for use in church worship. **4.** A group or body of directors; directorate. —*adj.* Serving to direct.
Di·rec·to·ry (dĭ-rĕk′tə-rē, dī-) *n.* The executive body in charge of the French government from 1795 to 1799. Also called "Directoire."
direct primary. A preliminary election in which a party's candidates for public office are nominated by popular vote.
di·rec·tress (dĭ-rĕk′trĭs, dī-) *n.* A female director.
di·rec·trix (dĭ-rĕk′trĭks, dī-) *n., pl.* **-trixes** or **directrices** (dĭ′rĕk-trī′sēz). **1.** *Geometry.* The fixed curve traversed by a generatrix in generating a conic or a cylinder. **2.** *Military.* The median line in the trajectory of fire. [New Latin, "directress," from Late Latin *dīrector,* DIRECTOR.]
direct tax. A tax, such as an income or property tax, levied directly on the taxpayer.
dire·ful (dīr′fəl) *adj.* Dreadful; frightful; dire. —**dire′ful·ly** *adv.* —**dire′ful·ness** *n.*
dirge (dûrj) *n.* **1.** A funeral hymn or lament. **2.** *Ecclesiastical.* The office for the dead; a funeral service that is sung. [Middle English *dirige, derge,* from the first word in Medieval Latin *dīrige, Domine, Deus meus, in conspectu tuo viam meam,* "Direct, O Lord, my God, my way in thy sight" (an antiphon in the office of the dead, adopted from Psalms 5:9), from Latin, singular imperative of *dīrigere,* to DIRECT.] —**dirge′ful** *adj.*
dir·ham (də-răm′) *n.* The basic monetary unit of Morocco, equal to 100 francs. See table of exchange rates at **currency.** [Arabic *dirham,* from Greek *drakhmē,* DRACHMA.]
dir·i·gi·ble (dĭr′ə-jə-bəl, dĭ-rĭj′ə-bəl) *n.* An early steerable lighter-than-air craft. —*adj.* Able to be guided or steered. [From Latin *dīrigere,* to guide, DIRECT.] —**dir′i·gi·bil′i·ty** *n.*
dir·i·ment (dĭr′ə-mənt) *adj.* Rendering totally void; nullifying. Used especially in the phrase *diriment impediment of marriage* to signify any sufficient cause for voiding a marriage in the Roman Catholic Church. [From Latin *dīrimēns,* present participle of *dīrimere,* to take apart, separate, interrupt : *dis-,* apart + *emere,* to take, buy (see **em-** in Appendix*).]
dirk (dûrk) *n.* A dagger. —*tr.v.* **dirked, dirking, dirks.** To stab with a dirk. [Earlier *durk, dork,* probably related to or altered from German *Dolch,* dagger. See **dhelg-** in Appendix.*]
dirn·dl (dûrnd′l) *n.* **1.** A full-skirted dress with a tight bodice, patterned after Tyrolean peasant wear. **2.** A skirt of a similar cut. [German, short for *Dirndlkleid* : *Dirndl,* diminutive of *Dirne,* girl, from Old High German *thiorna,* maid (see **tek-**[1] in Appendix*) + *Kleid,* dress.]
dirt (dûrt) *n.* **1.** Earth or soil. **2.** A filthy or soiling substance, such as mud, dust, or excrement. **3.** Something mean, contemptible, or vile. **4.** Obscene language. **5.** Malicious or scandalous gossip. **6.** Gravel, slag, or other material from which metal is extracted in mining. —*adj.* Made of dirt. [Middle English *dirt,* variant of *drit,* excrement, mud, filth, from Old Norse *drit,* from Germanic *drit-* (unattested).]
dirt-cheap (dûrt′chēp′) *adj.* Very cheap. —**dirt′-cheap′** *adv.*
dirt farmer. *Informal.* A farmer who does all his own work.
dirt·y (dûr′tē) *adj.* **-ier, -iest. 1.** Soiled, as with dirt; grimy; unclean. **2.** Obscene or scatological. **3.** Contemptibly contrary to honor or rules. **4.** Of a clouded or muddy appearance. **5.** Designating a nuclear weapon that produces an excessive amount of radioactive fallout. **6.** Stormy; rough: *dirty weather.* —*v.* **dirtied, -ying, -ies.** —*tr.* To make soiled; stain; tarnish. —*intr.* To become dirty. [Middle English *dritti, dirti,* from *drit,* DIRT.] —**dirt′i·ly** *adv.* —**dirt′i·ness** *n.*
Synonyms: *dirty, filthy, foul, nasty, squalid, soiled, grimy, slovenly, slatternly.* These adjectives apply to what is unclean, impure, or unkempt. *Dirty,* the most general, describes anything physically unclean or offensive to propriety by being off-color. *Filthy* intensifies these senses, as does *foul,* which suggests

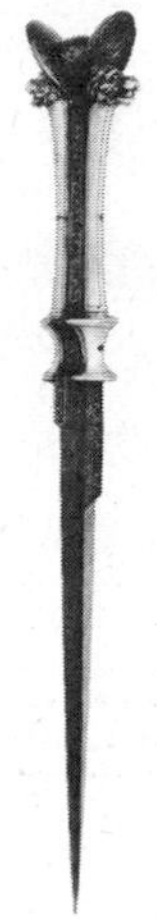

dirk

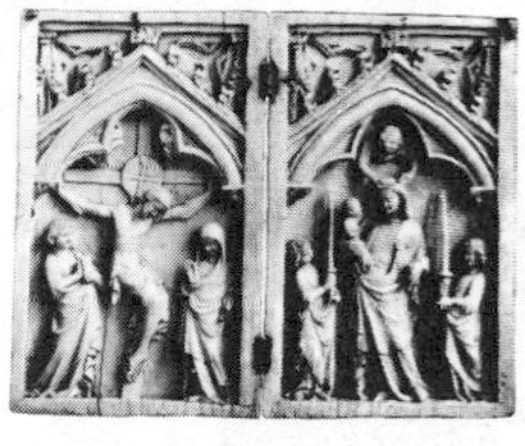

diptych
Fourteenth-century Italian ivory

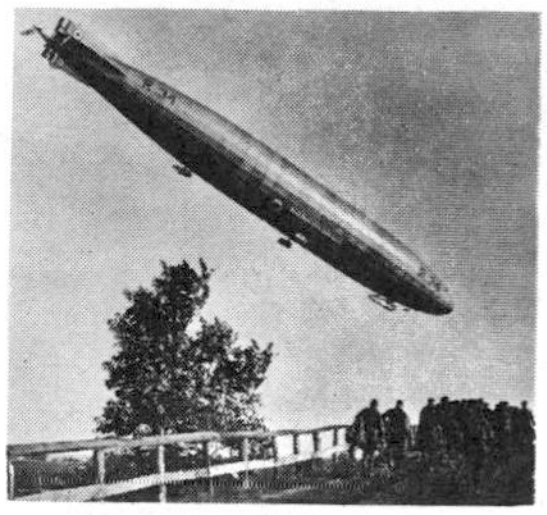

dirigible
Landing at Mineola, New York, in July 1919

that which is revolting, particularly to the sense of smell or, figuratively, to decency. *Nasty* can mean offensive to good taste, but often is applied to what is merely unpleasant. *Squalid* suggests, besides dirtiness, the neglect and untidiness characteristic of extreme poverty; figuratively it implies sordidness. *Soiled* suggests something stained or partly dirtied, and *grimy*, something whose surface is smudged with soot or other dirt. *Slovenly* and *slatternly* describe personal appearance. Both stress unkemptness and disorderliness, but *slatternly* is restricted to women.

dirty work. *Informal.* **1.** Foul play; deceit. **2.** A difficult or distasteful chore or task.

dis–. Indicates: **1.** Negation, lack, invalidation, or deprivation; for example, **distrust, disuse. 2.** Reversal; for example, **disunite, disapprove. 3.** Removal or rejection; for example, **disbud, disbar, discard. 4.** Intensification or completion of negative action; for example, **disannul.** [In borrowed Latin and French compounds, Latin *dis-* (Old French *des-*) indicates: 1. Apart, asunder, aside, as in **distrain, digress.** 2. Away, abroad, in different directions, as in **dismiss, divulge, disseminate.** 3. Negation, deprivation, as in **diffident, disparage.** 4. Reversal, as in **dissimulate.** 5. Removal, as in **dismantle.** 6. Intensification or completion of divisive action, as in **disturb, dissever.** 7. Pejoration, as in **disaster.** Latin *dis-* (sometimes *di-*) is the preverbal form of *dis*†, apart, asunder.]

dis. 1. discount. **2.** distance; distant.

dis·a·bil·i·ty (dĭs′ə-bĭl′ə-tē) *n., pl.* **-ties. 1.** A disabled state or condition; incapacity. **2.** Something that disables; a handicap. **3.** A legal incapacity or disqualification.

dis·a·ble (dĭs-ā′bəl) *tr.v.* **-bled, -bling, -bles. 1.** To weaken or destroy the normal physical or mental abilities of; to cripple; incapacitate. **2.** To render legally disqualified: *disabled from inheriting the estate.*

dis·a·buse (dĭs′ə-byo͞oz′) *tr.v.* **-bused, -busing, -buses.** To free from a falsehood or misconception; undeceive. [French *désabuser* : *dés-*, from Latin *dis-* (reversal) + *abuser*, to delude, from Old French, to ABUSE.]

di·sac·cha·ride (dī-săk′ə-rīd′) *n. Chemistry.* Any of a class of carbohydrates, including lactose and sucrose, that yield two monosaccharides on hydrolysis.

dis·ac·cord (dĭs′ə-kôrd′) *n.* Lack of accord; disagreement. —*intr.v.* **disaccorded, -cording, -cords.** To disagree. [Middle English *disaccorden*, to disagree, from Old French *desacorder* : *des-*, from Latin *dis-*, not + *acorder*, to ACCORD.]

dis·ac·cus·tom (dĭs′ə-kŭs′təm) *tr.v.* **-tomed, -toming, -toms.** To cause to become unaccustomed: *disaccustomed to wearing vests by his years in the tropics.* [Old French *desacostumer* : *des-*, from Latin *dis-* (reversal) + *acostumer*, ACCUSTOM.]

dis·ad·van·tage (dĭs′əd-văn′tĭj, -vän′tĭj) *n.* **1.** An unfavorable condition or circumstance; handicap. **2.** Detriment. —*tr.v.* **disadvantaged, -taging, -tages.** To put at a disadvantage; set back. [Middle English *disavauntage*, from Old French *desavantage* : *des-*, from Latin *dis-* (negative) + *avantage*, ADVANTAGE.]

dis·ad·van·taged (dĭs′əd-văn′tĭjd, -vän′tĭjd) *adj.* Subjected to severe economic and social disadvantage.

dis·ad·van·ta·geous (dĭs-ăd′vən-tā′jəs, dĭs′ăd-vən-) *adj.* Detrimental; unfavorable; injurious. **—dis·ad′van·ta′geous·ly** *adv.* **—dis·ad′van·ta′geous·ness** *n.*

dis·af·fect (dĭs′ə-fĕkt′) *tr.v.* **-fected, -fecting, -fects.** To cause to lose affection or loyalty; alienate. See Synonyms at **estrange.** [DIS- + AFFECT (to be fond of).]

dis·af·fect·ed (dĭs′ə-fĕk′tĭd) *adj.* No longer contented and loyal; alienated. **—dis′af·fect′ed·ly** *adv.*

dis·af·fec·tion (dĭs′ə-fĕk′shən) *n.* Absence or withdrawal of affection or loyalty.

dis·af·fil·i·ate (dĭs′ə-fĭl′ē-āt′) *v.* **-ated, -ating, -ates.** —*tr.* To disassociate from an alliance or affiliation. —*intr.* To sever an affiliation or association. **—dis′af·fil′i·a′tion** *n.*

dis·af·firm (dĭs′ə-fûrm′) *tr.v.* **-firmed, -firming, -firms. 1.** To deny or contradict. **2.** *Law.* **a.** To repudiate. **b.** To set aside; reverse. **—dis′af·fir′mance** (dĭs′ə-fûr′məns), **dis′af·fir·ma′tion** (dĭs′ăf-ər-mā′shən) *n.*

dis·a·gree (dĭs′ə-grē′) *intr.v.* **-greed, -greeing, -grees. 1.** To be different or inconsistent; fail to correspond. **2.** To have a different opinion; fail to agree; dissent. **3.** To dispute; to quarrel. **4.** To cause adverse effects; be incompatible. [Middle English *disagreen*, from Old French *desagreer* : *des-*, from Latin *dis-*, not + *agreer*, AGREE.]

dis·a·gree·a·ble (dĭs′ə-grē′ə-bəl) *adj.* **1.** Unpleasant; offensive; distasteful. **2.** Quarrelsome; bad-tempered. **—dis′a·gree′a·ble·ness** *n.* **—dis′a·gree′a·bly** *adv.*

dis·a·gree·ment (dĭs′ə-grē′mənt) *n.* **1.** A failure or refusal to agree. **2.** Disparity; inconsistency. **3.** A conflict or difference of opinion.

dis·al·low (dĭs′ə-lou′) *tr.v.* **-lowed, -lowing, -lows. 1.** To refuse to allow. **2.** To reject as invalid, untrue, or improper. [Middle English *disallowen*, from Old French *desalouer*, to refuse praise, reprimand : *des-*, from Latin *dis-* (negative) + *al(l)ouer*, to approve, ALLOW.] **—dis′al·low′a·ble** *adj.* **—dis′al·low′ance** *n.*

dis·an·nul (dĭs′ə-nŭl′) *tr.v.* **-nulled, -nulling, -nuls.** To annul completely; make void; cancel. [DIS- (completely) + ANNUL.] **—dis′an·nul′ment** *n.*

dis·ap·pear (dĭs′ə-pîr′) *intr.v.* **-peared, -pearing, -pears. 1.** To pass out of sight either suddenly or gradually; vanish. **2.** To die out; become extinct. **—dis′ap·pear′ance** *n.*

dis·ap·point (dĭs′ə-point′) *tr.v.* **-pointed, -pointing, -points. 1.** To fail to satisfy the hope, desire, or expectation of. **2.** To frustrate; thwart. [Middle English *disappointen*, to remove from office, dispossess, from Old French *desapointier* : *des-*, from Latin *dis-* (reversal) + *apointier*, APPOINT.] **—dis′ap·point′er** *n.* **—dis′ap·point′ing·ly** *adv.*

dis·ap·point·ed (dĭs′ə-poin′tĭd) *adj.* Made unhappy by the failure of one's hopes; frustrated. **—dis′ap·point′ed·ly** *adv.*

dis·ap·point·ment (dĭs′ə-point′mənt) *n.* **1. a.** The act of disappointing. **b.** The condition or feeling of being disappointed. **2.** One that disappoints.

dis·ap·pro·ba·tion (dĭs-ăp′rə-bā′shən) *n.* Moral disapproval; condemnation.

dis·ap·prov·al (dĭs′ə-pro͞o′vəl) *n.* The act of disapproving; condemnation; censure.

dis·ap·prove (dĭs′ə-pro͞ov′) *v.* **-proved, -proving, -proves.** —*tr.* **1.** To have an unfavorable opinion of; to censure; condemn. **2.** To refuse to approve. —*intr.* To have an unfavorable opinion. Used with *of.* **—dis′ap·prov′ing·ly** *adv.*

dis·arm (dĭs-ärm′) *v.* **-armed, -arming, -arms.** —*tr.* **1.** To deprive of weapons; divest of arms. **2.** To deprive of the means of attack or defense; render helpless or harmless. **3.** To overcome or allay the suspicion, hostility, or antagonism of; win the confidence of. —*intr.* **1.** To lay down arms. **2.** To reduce or abolish one's stock of weapons, armaments, or armed forces. [Middle English *disarmen*, from Old French *desarmer* : *des-*, from Latin *dis-* (reversal) + *armer*, to arm, from Latin *armāre*, from *arma*, tools, weapons (see **ar-** in Appendix*).]

dis·ar·ma·ment (dĭs-är′mə-mənt) *n.* **1.** The act of laying down arms; especially, the reduction or abolition of military forces and armaments by a national government. **2.** The condition of being disarmed.

dis·arm·ing (dĭs-är′mĭng) *adj.* Tending to remove suspicion or hostility; winning; endearing. **—dis·arm′ing·ly** *adv.*

dis·ar·range (dĭs′ə-rānj′) *tr.v.* **-ranged, -ranging, -ranges.** To upset the arrangement of; to disorder. **—dis′ar·range′ment** *n.*

dis·ar·ray (dĭs′ə-rā′) *n.* **1.** A state of disorder; disarrangement; confusion. **2.** Disordered or insufficient dress. —*tr.v.* **disarrayed, -raying, -rays.** To throw into confusion; to upset. [Middle English *disaraien*, from Old French *desareer* : *des-*, from Latin *dis-* (reversal) + *areer*, ARRAY.]

dis·ar·tic·u·late (dĭs′är-tĭk′yə-lāt′) *v.* **-lated, -lating, -lates.** —*tr.* To separate at the joints; disjoint. —*intr.* To come apart at the joints; become disjointed. **—dis′ar·tic′u·la′tion** *n.* **—dis′ar·tic′u·la′tor** (-lā′tər) *n.*

dis·as·sem·ble (dĭs′ə-sĕm′bəl) *tr.v.* **-bled, -bling, -bles.** To take apart. **—dis′as·sem′bly** *n.*

dis·as·so·ci·ate (dĭs′ə-sō′shē-āt′, -sē-āt′) *tr.v.* **-ated, -ating, -ates.** To dissociate. **—dis′as·so′ci·a′tion** *n.*

dis·as·ter (dĭ-zăs′tər, -zäs′tər) *n.* **1. a.** An occurrence inflicting widespread destruction and distress. **b.** A grave misfortune. **2.** A total failure. **3.** *Obsolete.* An evil influence of a celestial body. [French *désastre*, from Italian *disastro*, back-formation from *disastrato*, "ill-starred" : *dis-*, from Latin (pejorative) + *astro*, star, from Latin *astrum*, from Greek *astron* (see **ster-**[3] in Appendix*).]

Synonyms: *disaster, calamity, catastrophe, cataclysm, debacle, holocaust.* These nouns refer to grave occurrences having destructive results. *Disaster* generally implies great destruction, hardship, or loss of life, while *calamity* emphasizes distress, grief, and the sense of loss more than widespread destruction. *Catastrophe* especially stresses the sense of tragic outcome with irreparable loss. *Cataclysm* refers to a sudden upheaval that brings an earth-shaking change, physical, as an earthquake, or social, as a revolution. *Debacle* usually implies overwhelming defeat or sudden, chaotic collapse. *Holocaust* refers, in strict usage, to widespread destruction and loss of life caused by fire.

dis·as·trous (dĭ-zăs′trəs, -zäs′trəs) *adj.* Calamitous; ruinous. **—dis·as′trous·ly** *adv.* **—dis·as′trous·ness** *n.*

dis·a·vow (dĭs′ə-vou′) *tr.v.* **-vowed, -vowing, -vows.** To disclaim knowledge of, responsibility for, or association with; disown. [Middle English *disavowen*, from Old French *desavouer* : *des-*, from Latin *dis-* (negative) + *avouer*, AVOW.] **—dis′a·vow′er** *n.*

dis·a·vow·al (dĭs′ə-vou′əl) *n.* The act or an instance of disavowing; repudiation.

dis·band (dĭs-bănd′) *v.* **-banded, -banding, -bands.** —*tr.* To break up; dissolve. —*intr.* To become disbanded; disperse. **—dis·band′ment** *n.*

dis·bar (dĭs-bär′) *tr.v.* **-barred, -barring, -bars.** To expel (a lawyer) from the legal profession by official action or procedure. **—dis·bar′ment** *n.*

dis·be·lief (dĭs′bĭ-lēf′) *n.* Refusal or reluctance to believe.

dis·be·lieve (dĭs′bĭ-lēv′) *v.* **-lieved, -lieving, -lieves.** —*tr.* To refuse to believe in; reject. —*intr.* To withhold belief. Used with *in.* **—dis′be·liev′er** *n.* **—dis′be·liev′ing·ly** *adv.*

dis·branch (dĭs-brănch′, -bränch′) *tr.v.* **-branched, -branching, -branches. 1.** To cut or break a branch or branches from (a tree). **2.** To remove (a limb or branch).

dis·bud (dĭs-bŭd′) *tr.v.* **-budded, -budding, -buds. 1.** *Horticulture.* To remove buds from (a plant) to promote better blooms from remaining buds or to control the shape of the plant. **2.** To remove newly developing horns from (livestock).

dis·bur·den (dĭs-bûrd′n) *v.* **-dened, -dening, -dens.** —*tr.* **1.** To relieve of a burden. **2.** To unload or remove (a burden). —*intr.* To remove or unload a burden. **—dis·bur′den·ment** *n.*

dis·burse (dĭs-bûrs′) *tr.v.* **-bursed, -bursing, -burses.** To pay out; expend, as from a fund. [Old French *desbourser* : *des-*, from Latin *dis-* (reversal) + *bourse*, purse, from Medieval Latin *bursa*, from Greek (see **bursa** in Appendix*).] **—dis·burs′a·ble** *adj.* **—dis·burs′er** *n.*

dis·burse·ment (dĭs-bûrs′mənt) *n.* Also **dis·bur·sal** (-bûr′səl). **1.** The act of disbursing. **2.** Money paid out; expenditure.

ă pat/ā pay/âr care/ä father/b bib/ch church/d deed/ĕ pet/ē be/f fife/g gag/h hat/hw which/ĭ pit/ī pie/îr pier/j judge/k kick/l lid, needle/m mum/n no, sudden/ng thing/ŏ pot/ō toe/ô paw, for/oi noise/ou out/o͝o took/o͞o boot/p pop/r roar/s sauce/sh ship, dish/

disc (dĭsk) *n.* Also **disk.** **1.** *Informal.* A phonograph record. **2.** Variant of **disk.**
disc. **1.** discount. **2.** discovered.
dis·calced (dĭs-kălst′) *adj.* Barefooted. Said of certain orders of monks. [From Latin *discalceātus* : *dis-*, not + *calceātus*, shod, from *calceus*, shoe (see **calceolate**).]
dis·cant. Variant of **descant.**
dis·card (dĭs-kärd′) *v.* **-carded, -carding, -cards.** —*tr.* **1.** To throw away; reject; dismiss. **2.** *Card Games.* **a.** To throw out (an undesired card or cards) from one's hand. **b.** To play (a card other than a trump and different in suit from the card led). —*intr. Card Games.* To discard a card. —*n.* (dĭs′kärd′). **1.** The act of discarding. **2.** A person or thing discarded; especially, the card or cards discarded in a card game. [DIS- (removal) + CARD.] —**dis·card′er** *n.*
dis·cern (dĭ-sûrn′, -zûrn′) *v.* **-cerned, -cerning, -cerns.** —*tr.* **1.** To perceive (something obscure or concealed); detect. **2.** To perceive the distinctions of; to discriminate. —*intr.* To perceive differences; make distinctions. —See Synonyms at **see.** [Middle English *discernen*, from Old French *discerner*, from Latin *discernere*, "to separate by sifting," distinguish between : *dis-*, apart + *cernere*, to sift, separate, perceive (see **skeri-** in Appendix*).] —**dis·cern′er** *n.*
dis·cern·i·ble (dĭ-sûr′nə-bəl, dĭ-zûr′-) *adj.* Perceptible; distinguishable. See Synonyms at **perceptible.** —**dis·cern′i·bly** *adv.*
dis·cern·ing (dĭ-sûr′nĭng, dĭ-zûr′-) *adj.* Astute; perceptive. —**dis·cern′ing·ly** *adv.*
dis·cern·ment (dĭ-sûrn′mənt, dĭ-zûrn′-) *n.* **1.** The act or process of discerning. **2.** Keenness of discrimination; perspicacity. —See Synonyms at **reason.**
dis·charge (dĭs-chärj′) *v.* **-charged, -charging, -charges.** —*tr.* **1.** To relieve of a burden or of contents; unload. **2.** To unload or empty (contents). **3.** To release, as from confinement or duty. **4.** To dismiss from employment. **5.** To send or pour forth; emit. **6.** To shoot or fire (a projectile or weapon). **7.** To perform the obligations or demands of (an office, duty, or task). **8.** To acquit oneself of (a debt or promise); comply with the terms of. **9.** *Law.* **a.** To release (a defendant, for example). **b.** To set aside; dismiss; annul: *discharge a court order.* **10.** *Textiles.* To remove (color) from cloth, as by chemical bleaching. **11.** *Electricity.* To cause electrical discharge in (a battery, for example). **12.** *Architecture.* **a.** To apportion (weight) evenly, as over a door. **b.** To relieve (a part) of excess weight by distribution of pressure. —*intr.* **1.** To get rid of a burden, load, or weight. **2.** To fire. **3.** To pour forth contents. **4.** To become blurred; run. **5.** To undergo electrical discharge. —See Synonyms at **perform.** —*n.* (dĭs′chärj′, dĭs-chärj′). **1.** The act of removing a load or burden; an unloading. **2.** The act of shooting or firing a projectile or weapon. **3.** A pouring forth; an emission; ejection. **4.** The amount or rate of emission or ejection. **5.** Something that is discharged, released, or emitted. **6.** A relieving from or elimination of an obligation, burden, or responsibility. **7.** Fulfillment or performance. **8. a.** Dismissal or release from employment, service, or confinement. **b.** A document certifying such release, especially from military service. **9.** A legal annulment or acquittal; dismissal, as of a court order. **10.** *Electricity.* **a.** The release of stored energy in a capacitor by the flow of electric current between its terminals. **b.** The conversion of chemical energy to electric energy in a storage battery. **c.** A flow of electricity in a dielectric, especially in a rarefied gas. **d.** Loosely, the elimination of net electric charge from any charged body. [Middle English *dischargen*, from Old French *deschargier*, from Vulgar Latin *discarricāre* (unattested), to unload : *dis-* (reversal) + *carricāre* (unattested), to load, CHARGE.] —**dis·charge′a·ble** *adj.* —**dis·charg′er** *n.*
discharge lamp. A lamp that generates light by means of an internal electrical discharge.
discharge tube. A closed insulating vessel fitted with electrodes and containing a gas in which an electrical discharge is induced by high applied potentials.
dis·ci. Alternate plural of **discus.**
dis·ci·ple (dĭ-sī′pəl) *n.* **1. a.** A person who subscribes to the teachings of a master and assists in spreading them. **b.** Any active adherent, as of a movement or philosophy. **2.** One of the companions of Christ. **3.** *Capital* **D.** A member of the **Disciples of Christ** *(see).* [Middle English *disciple*, Old English *discipul*, from Latin *discipulus*, pupil, from *discere*, to learn. See **dek-**[1] in Appendix.*] —**dis·ci′ple·ship′** *n.*
Disciples of Christ. A Christian denomination, founded in 1809 by Thomas and Alexander Campbell, that accepts the Bible as the only rule of Christian faith and practice, rejects denominational creeds in a desire for the union of all Christian sects, and practices baptism by immersion.
dis·ci·plin·a·ble (dĭs′ə-plĭn′ə-bəl, dĭs′ə-plĭn′-) *adj.* **1.** Deserving of or subject to discipline. **2.** Responsive to training.
dis·ci·plin·ant (dĭs′ə-plə-nənt, -plĭn′ənt) *n.* **1.** A person who practices self-discipline. **2.** *Capital* **D.** A member of a former religious order of flagellants in Spain.
dis·ci·pli·nar·i·an (dĭs′ə-plə-nâr′ē-ən) *n.* A person who enforces or believes in strict discipline. —*adj.* Disciplinary.
dis·ci·pli·nar·y (dĭs′ə-plə-nĕr′ē) *adj.* Also **dis·ci·pli·nal** (-plə-nəl, -plĭn′əl). Of, pertaining to, or used for discipline.
dis·ci·pline (dĭs′ə-plĭn) *n.* **1.** Training that is expected to produce a specified character or pattern of behavior, especially that which is expected to produce moral or mental improvement. **2.** Controlled behavior resulting from such training. **3.** A systematic method to obtain obedience: *a military discipline.* **4.** A state of order based upon submission to rules and authority. **5.** Punishment intended to correct or train. **6.** A set of rules or methods, as those regulating the practice of a church or monastic order. **7.** A branch of knowledge or of teaching. —*tr.v.* **disciplined, -plining, -plines.** **1.** To train by instruction and control; teach to obey rules or accept authority. **2.** To punish or penalize. —See Synonyms at **teach, punish.** [Middle English, from Old French, from Latin *disciplīna*, *discipulīna*, instruction, knowledge, from *discipulus*, pupil, DISCIPLE.] —**dis′ci·plin′er** *n.*
disc jockey. Also **disk jockey.** *Abbr.* **DJ** A radio announcer who presents and comments on popular phonograph records.
dis·claim (dĭs-klām′) *v.* **-claimed, -claiming, -claims.** —*tr.* **1.** To deny or renounce any claim to or connection with; disown. **2.** To deny the validity of; repudiate. **3.** *Law.* To renounce one's right or claim to. —*intr. Law.* To renounce a legal right or claim. [Middle English *discla(i)men*, from Old French *desclamer* : *des-*, from Latin *dis-* (reversal) + *clamer*, to CLAIM.]
dis·claim·er (dĭs-klā′mər) *n.* A repudiation or denial of a claim.
dis·cla·ma·tion (dĭs′klə-mā′shən) *n.* Disavowal; renunciation.
dis·cli·max (dĭs-klī′măks′) *n.* An ecological community, normally stable under certain climatic conditions, that has been altered by man or other influences.
dis·close (dĭs-klōz′) *tr.v.* **-closed, -closing, -closes.** **1.** To expose to view, as by removing a cover; uncover. **2.** To make known; divulge. —See Synonyms at **reveal.** [Middle English *disclosen*, from Old French *desclore* (present stem *desclos-*) : *des-*, from Latin *dis-* (reversal) + *clore*, to CLOSE.] —**dis·clos′er** *n.*
dis·clo·sure (dĭs-klō′zhər) *n.* **1.** The act or process of disclosing. **2.** Something that is disclosed; a revelation.
disco–. Indicates a phonograph record; for example, **discophile.** [From *disc*, variant of DISK.]
dis·cob·o·lus (dĭs-kŏb′ə-ləs) *n., pl.* **-li** (-lī′). A discus-thrower. [Latin, from Greek *diskobolos* : *diskos*, quoit, DISK + *-bolos*, thrower, from *ballein*, to throw (see **gwel-**[1] in Appendix*).]
dis·cog·ra·phy (dĭs-kŏg′rə-fē) *n., pl.* **-phies.** A catalogue of phonograph records; especially, a comprehensive list of the recordings made by a particular performer or of a particular composer's works. [French *discographie* : DISCO- + -GRAPHY.] —**dis·cog′ra·pher** *n.*
dis·coid (dĭs′koid′) *adj.* Also **dis·coi·dal** (dĭs-koid′l). **1.** Having the shape of a disk. **2.** *Botany.* Having disk flowers but no ray flowers. Said of a composite flower head. —*n.* A disk or an object shaped like a disk. [Late Latin *dīscoides*, disk-shaped, from Greek *diskoeidēs* : *diskos*, DISK + -OID.]
dis·col·or (dĭs-kŭl′ər) *v.* **-ored, -oring, -ors.** —*tr.* To alter or spoil the proper color of; to stain. —*intr.* To become changed or spoiled in color. [Middle English *discolouren*, from Old French *descolourer*, from Late Latin *discolōrāre* : Latin *dis-* (reversal) + *colōrāre*, to color, from *color*, COLOR.]
dis·col·or·a·tion (dĭs-kŭl′ə-rā′shən) *n.* **1. a.** The act of discoloring. **b.** The condition of being discolored. **2.** A stain.
dis·com·bob·u·late (dĭs′kəm-bŏb′yə-lāt′) *tr.v.* **-lated, -lating, -lates.** *Slang.* To throw into a state of confusion; disconcert; upset. [Mock-Latin formation.]
dis·com·fit (dĭs-kŭm′fĭt) *tr.v.* **-fited, -fiting, -fits.** **1.** To thwart the plans or purposes of; frustrate; foil. **2.** To defeat in battle; rout; vanquish. **3.** To make uneasy or perplexed; disconcert; distress. See Usage note below. [Middle English *discomfiten*, from Old French *desconfire* (past participle *disconfit*), to defeat, from Vulgar Latin *disconficere* (unattested) : Latin *dis-* (reversal) + *conficere*, to prepare, accomplish : *com-*, together + *facere*, to make (see **dhē-**[1] in Appendix*).]
Usage: *Discomfit* and *discomfiture* were earlier confined largely to the strong senses of defeat and frustration, and some writers still restrict them accordingly. But the terms are now often used to convey the milder senses of discomfort, disconcert, uneasiness, and confusion, and they are acceptable as such to 80 per cent of the Usage Panel.
dis·com·fi·ture (dĭs-kŭm′fĭ-cho͝or′) *n.* **1.** Frustration; disappointment. **2.** Defeat. **3.** Lack of ease; discomfort; embarrassment. —See Usage note at **discomfit.**
dis·com·fort (dĭs-kŭm′fərt) *n.* **1.** The condition of being uncomfortable in body or mind; mild distress. **2.** Something that disturbs one's comfort; an annoyance. —*tr.v.* **discomforted, -forting, -forts.** To make uncomfortable. [Middle English, from Old French *desconfort*, from *desconforter* : *des-*, from Latin *dis-* (reversal) + *conforter*, to COMFORT.]
dis·com·fort·a·ble (dĭs-kŭmf′tə-bəl, -kŭm′fər-tə-bəl) *adj. Rare.* Not comfortable; distressed or distressing.
dis·com·mend (dĭs′kə-mĕnd′) *tr.v.* **-mended, -mending, -mends.** **1.** To show or voice disapproval of. **2.** To bring into disfavor or ill regard. —**dis′com·mend′a·ble** *adj.*
dis·com·mode (dĭs′kə-mōd′) *tr.v.* **-moded, -moding, -modes.** To put to inconvenience; disturb. [French *discommoder* : Latin *dis-* (reversal) + *commode*, convenient (see **commode**).]
dis·com·pose (dĭs′kəm-pōz′) *tr.v.* **-posed, -posing, -poses.** **1.** To disturb the composure or calm of; agitate; perturb. **2.** To put into a state of disorder; disarrange. —**dis′com·pos′ed·ly** (-pō′zĭd-lē) *adv.* —**dis′com·pos′ing·ly** *adv.*
dis·com·po·sure (dĭs′kəm-pō′zhər) *n.* Absence of composure.
dis·con·cert (dĭs′kən-sûrt′) *tr.v.* **-certed, -certing, -certs.** **1.** To upset the self-possession of; perturb; ruffle. **2.** To frustrate by throwing into disorder; upset; rout. [Obsolete French *disconcerter*, from Old French *desconcerter* : *des-*, from Latin *dis-* (reversal) + *concerter*, to bring into agreement, from Italian *concertare* (see **concert**).] —**dis′con·cert′ing·ly** *adv.*
dis·con·cert·ed (dĭs′kən-sûr′tĭd) *adj.* Bereft of composure; perturbed. —**dis′con·cert′ed·ly** *adv.* —**dis′con·cert′ed·ness** *n.*
dis·con·form·i·ty (dĭs′kən-fôr′mə-tē) *n., pl.* **-ties.** *Geology.* An interruption of sedimentation caused by erosion and forming two parallel strata.

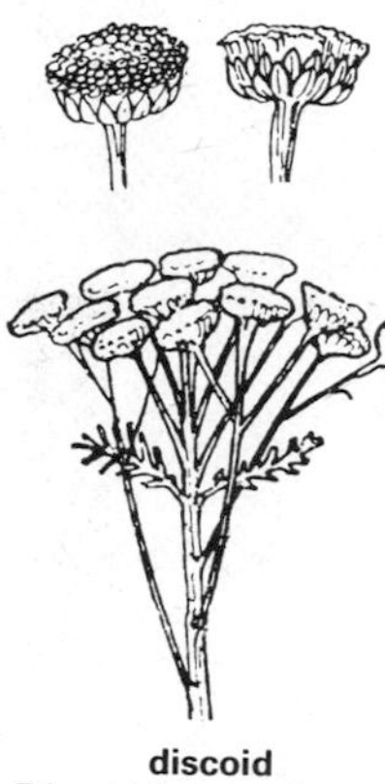

discoid
Discoid flowers of tansy, with detail *(above)* of individual flower heads

dis·con·nect (dĭs′kə-nĕkt′) *tr.v.* **-nected, -necting, -nects. 1.** To sever, interrupt, or dissolve the connection of or between. **2.** To shut off the current in (an electrical appliance) by removing its connection with the power source. —**dis′con·nec′tion** *n.*
dis·con·nect·ed (dĭs′kə-nĕk′tĭd) *adj.* **1.** Not connected; detached. **2.** Consisting of or marked by unrelated parts; incoherent. —**dis′con·nect′ed·ly** *adv.* —**dis′con·nect′ed·ness** *n.*
dis·con·so·late (dĭs-kŏn′sə-lĭt) *adj.* **1.** Beyond consolation; hopelessly sad. **2.** Cheerless; gloomy; dismal. [Middle English, from Medieval Latin *disconsōlātus* : Latin *dis-* (negative) + *consōlātus*, past participle of *consōlārī*, CONSOLE.] —**dis·con′so·late·ly** *adv.* —**dis·con′so·late·ness, dis·con′so·la′tion** *n.*
dis·con·tent (dĭs′kən-tĕnt′) *n.* **1.** Absence of contentment; dissatisfaction. **2.** A sense of resentment and grievance. —*adj.* Discontented. —*tr.v.* **discontented, -tenting, -tents.** To cause dissatisfaction in; make discontented.
dis·con·tent·ed (dĭs′kən-tĕn′tĭd) *adj.* Restlessly unhappy; dissatisfied. —**dis′con·tent′ed·ly** *adv.* —**dis′con·tent′ed·ness** *n.*
dis·con·tin·u·ance (dĭs′kən-tĭn′yo͞o-əns) *n.* **1.** The act of discontinuing or the condition of being discontinued; cessation. **2.** *Law.* The termination of an action by the plaintiff.
dis·con·tin·u·a·tion (dĭs′kən-tĭn′yo͞o-ā′shən) *n.* Discontinuance; cessation.
dis·con·tin·ue (dĭs′kən-tĭn′yo͞o) *v.* **-ued, -uing, -ues.** —*tr.* **1.** To cause to cease; put a stop to; terminate. **2.** To cease from; give up; abandon. **3.** *Law.* To terminate (an action) by discontinuance. —*intr.* To come to an end. [Middle English *discontinuen*, from Old French *descontinuer*, from Medieval Latin *discontinuāre* : Latin *dis-* (negative) + *continuāre*, CONTINUE.] —**dis′con·tin′u·er** *n.*
dis·con·ti·nu·i·ty (dĭs′kŏn-tĭ-no͞o′ə-tē, -nyo͞o′ə-tē) *n., pl.* **-ties. 1.** A lack of continuity, logical sequence, or cohesion. **2.** A break or gap. **3.** *Mathematics.* **a.** The property of being discontinuous. **b.** A point at which a function is defined but is not continuous. **c.** A point at which a function is undefined.
dis·con·tin·u·ous (dĭs′kən-tĭn′yo͞o-əs) *adj.* **1.** Marked by breaks or interruptions; intermittent. **2.** *Mathematics.* Possessing one or more discontinuities. —**dis′con·tin′u·ous·ly** *adv.* —**dis′con·tin′u·ous·ness** *n.*
disc·o·phile (dĭsk′ə-fīl′) *n.* A collector of or specialist in phonograph records. [DISCO- + -PHILE.]
dis·cord (dĭs′kôrd′) *n.* **1.** Lack of agreement among persons, groups, or things; dissension. **2.** A confused or harsh mingling of sounds; a din. **3.** *Music.* Inharmonious combination of simultaneously sounded tones; dissonance. —*intr.v.* (dĭs-kôrd′) **discorded, -cording, -cords.** To fail to agree or harmonize; to clash. [Middle English, from Old French *descorde*, Latin *discordia*, strife, from *discors*, disagreeing : *dis-*, apart + *cor* (stem *cord-*), heart (see **kerd-**[1] in Appendix*).]
Synonyms: *discord, strife, contention, dissension, conflict, clash, dissonance, variance.* These nouns can all mean a condition marked by disagreement. *Discord* in general implies sharply opposing positions within a group, preventing united action. *Strife* usually implies outright fighting, often a destructive struggle between rivals or factions. *Contention* is largely limited to dispute in the form of heated debate or quarreling. *Dissension* implies rebellious unrest that disrupts unity within a group. *Conflict*, as compared here, suggests antagonism of ideas or interests that results in open hostility or divisiveness. *Clash* suggests sharp conflict involving ideas or interests that are irreconcilable. *Dissonance*, in this context, also stresses harsh disagreement between strongly opposed or incongruous positions. *Variance*, used chiefly in *at variance with*, usually suggests discrepancy or incompatibility between persons or things.
dis·cor·dant (dĭs-kôr′dənt) *adj.* **1.** Not in accord; conflicting. **2.** Disagreeable in sound; harsh or dissonant. —See Synonyms at **inconsistent.** —**dis·cor′dance, dis·cor′dan·cy** *n.* —**dis·cor′dant·ly** *adv.*
Dis·cor·di·a (dĭs-kôr′dē-ə). *Roman Mythology.* The goddess of strife, identified with the Greek goddess Eris. [Latin, from *discordia*, DISCORD.]
dis·co·theque (dĭs′kə-tĕk′, dĭs′kə-tĕk′) *n.* Also **dis·co·thèque.** A nightclub featuring dancing to amplified recorded music. [French : DISCO- + *(biblio)thèque*, library, from Latin *bibliothēca*, BIBLIOTHECA.]
dis·count (dĭs′kount′, dĭs-kount′) *v.* **-counted, -counting, -counts.** —*tr.* **1.** To deduct or subtract (a specified sum or percentage) from a cost or price. **2. a.** To purchase or sell (a bill, note, or other commercial paper) after deducting the amount of interest that will accumulate before it matures. **b.** To advance money as a loan on (a commercial paper not immediately payable) after deducting the interest. **3.** To reduce in cost, quantity, or value. **4.** To leave out of account as being untrustworthy or exaggerated; disregard; ignore. **5.** To anticipate and make allowance for. —*intr.* To lend money after deduction of interest. —*n.* (dĭs′kount). *Abbr.* **dis., disc. 1.** A reduction from the full or standard amount of a price or debt. **2.** The interest deducted in advance in purchasing, selling, or lending a bill, note, or other commercial paper. **3.** The rate of interest deducted in such a transaction. Also called "discount rate." **4.** The act or an instance of discounting a bill of exchange, note, or the like. —*adj.* Selling at prices below those set by manufacturers: *discount store; discount merchandise.* [Old French *desconter, descompter*, from Medieval Latin *discomputāre* : Latin *dis-* (reversal) + *computāre*, to add, sum up, COMPUTE.] —**dis′count′a·ble** *adj.* —**dis′count′er** *n.*
dis·coun·te·nance (dĭs-koun′tə-nəns) *tr.v.* **-nanced, -nancing, -nances. 1.** To view or treat with disfavor. **2.** To put out of countenance; abash; disconcert. —*n.* Disfavor; disapproval.
dis·cour·age (dĭs-kûr′ĭj) *tr.v.* **-aged, -aging, -ages. 1.** To deprive of confidence, hope, or spirit; dishearten; daunt. **2.** To dissuade or deter. Used with *from.* **3.** To hamper; hinder. **4.** To try to prevent by expressing disapproval or raising objections: *"My father discouraged me, by ridiculing my performances, and telling me versemakers were always beggars."* (Franklin). [Middle English *discoragen*, from Old French *descoragier* : *des-*, from Latin *dis-* (reversal) + *corage*, COURAGE.] —**dis·cour′ag·er** *n.* —**dis·cour′ag·ing·ly** *adv.*
dis·cour·age·ment (dĭs-kûr′ĭj-mənt) *n.* **1. a.** The act of discouraging. **b.** The condition of being discouraged. **2.** Something that discourages; a deterrent. —See Synonyms at **despair.**
dis·course (dĭs′kôrs′, -kōrs′) *n.* **1.** Verbal expression in speech or writing. **2.** Verbal exchange; conversation. **3.** A formal and lengthy discussion of a subject, either written or spoken. **4.** *Archaic.* The process or power of reasoning. —*v.* (dĭs-kôrs′, -kōrs′) **discoursed, -coursing, -courses.** —*intr.* **1.** To speak or write formally and at length. Used with *on* or *upon.* **2.** To engage in conversation or discussion; converse: *"he discourses as well as ever I heard man, in few words and handsome"* (Pepys). —*tr. Archaic.* **1.** To narrate or discuss. **2.** To give forth (musical sounds); perform. —See Synonyms at **speak.** [Middle English *discours*, from Late Latin *discursus*, conversation, from Latin, "a running back and forth," from the past participle of *discurrere*, to run back and forth, speak at length : *dis-*, in different directions + *currere*, to run (see **kers-**[2] in Appendix*).] —**dis·cours′er** *n.*
dis·cour·te·ous (dĭs-kûr′tē-əs) *adj.* Lacking courtesy; impolite; rude. —**dis·cour′te·ous·ly** *adv.* —**dis·cour′te·ous·ness** *n.*
dis·cour·te·sy (dĭs-kûr′tə-sē) *n., pl.* **-sies. 1.** Lack of courtesy; rudeness. **2.** A discourteous act or statement.
dis·cov·er (dĭs-kŭv′ər) *tr.v.* **-ered, -ering, -ers. 1.** To obtain knowledge of; arrive at through search or study: *"I have been endeavouring to discover a better sonnet stanza than we have."* (Keats). **2.** To be the first to find, learn of, or observe. **3.** *Archaic.* To reveal; expose. [Middle English *discoveren*, from Old French *descovrir*, from Late Latin *discooperīre*, to uncover, disclose : Latin *dis-* (reversal) + *cooperīre*, to COVER.] —**dis·cov′er·a·ble** *adj.* —**dis·cov′er·er** *n.*
dis·cov·ert (dĭs-kŭv′ərt) *adj. Law.* Having no husband, and therefore not subject to coverture. Said of a woman.
dis·cov·er·y (dĭs-kŭv′ə-rē) *n., pl.* **-ies. 1.** The act or an instance of discovering. **2.** Something that has been discovered.
Discovery Bay. An inlet of the Indian Ocean in southeastern Australia, between Victoria and South Australia.
dis·cred·it (dĭs-krĕd′ĭt) *tr.v.* **-ited, -iting, -its. 1.** To damage in reputation; to disgrace; dishonor. **2.** To cast doubt on; cause to be distrusted. **3.** To give no credence to; disbelieve. —See Synonyms at **degrade.** —*n.* **1.** Loss of or damage to one's reputation; dishonor; disgrace. **2.** Lack or loss of trust or belief; doubt. **3.** Anything damaging to one's reputation or stature. —See Synonyms at **disgrace.**
dis·cred·it·a·ble (dĭs-krĕd′ĭ-tə-bəl) *adj.* Deserving of or resulting in discredit; blameworthy. —**dis·cred′it·a·bly** *adv.*
dis·creet (dĭs-krēt′) *adj.* **1.** Having or showing a judicious reserve in one's speech or behavior; respectful of propriety. **2.** Lacking ostentation or pretension; unobtrusive; modest. [Middle English, from Old French *discret*, from Medieval Latin *discrētus*, "showing good judgment," from Latin, past participle of *discernere*, to separate, DISCERN.] —**dis·creet′ly** *adv.* —**dis·creet′ness** *n.*
dis·crep·an·cy (dĭs-krĕp′ən-sē) *n., pl.* **-cies.** Also **dis·crep·ance** (-əns). **1.** Divergence or disagreement, as between facts or claims; inconsistency. **2.** An instance of such disagreement. —See Synonyms at **difference.**
dis·crep·ant (dĭs-krĕp′ənt) *adj.* Marked by discrepancy; not consistent or matching; disagreeing. [Middle English *discrepaunt*, from Latin *discrepāns*, present participle of *discrepāre*, to sound different, vary : *dis-*, apart + *crepāre*, to rattle, sound (see **ker-**[2] in Appendix*).] —**dis·crep′ant·ly** *adv.*
dis·crete (dĭs-krēt′) *adj.* **1.** Constituting a separate thing; individual; distinct. **2.** Consisting of unconnected distinct parts. [Middle English, from Latin *discrētus*, separate. See **discreet.**] —**dis·crete′ly** *adv.* —**dis·crete′ness** *n.*
dis·cre·tion (dĭs-krĕsh′ən) *n.* **1.** The quality of being discreet; prudent or cautious reserve. **2.** Freedom to act or judge on one's own; latitude of choice and action: *"a general discretion was given to Endicott . . . to make grants to particular persons"* (Charles W. Upham). —See Synonyms at **prudence.** —**at one's discretion.** In accordance with one's wishes or judgment.
dis·cre·tion·al (dĭs-krĕsh′ən-əl) *adj.* Discretionary. —**dis·cre′tion·al·ly** *adv.*
dis·cre·tion·ar·y (dĭs-krĕsh′ə-nĕr′ē) *adj.* Left to or regulated by one's own discretion or judgment. —**dis·cre′tion·ar′i·ly** *adv.*
dis·crim·i·nate (dĭs-krĭm′ə-nāt′) *v.* **-nated, -nating, -nates.** —*intr.* **1.** To make a clear distinction; distinguish; differentiate. **2.** To act on the basis of prejudice. —*tr.* **1.** To perceive the distinguishing features of; recognize as distinct. **2.** To serve to mark; differentiate. —*adj.* (dĭs-krĭm′ə-nĭt). Discriminating. [Latin *discrīmināre*, to divide, distinguish, from *discrīmen*, distinction. See **skeri-** in Appendix.*] —**dis·crim′i·nate·ly** *adv.*
dis·crim·i·nat·ing (dĭs-krĭm′ə-nā′tĭng) *adj.* **1.** Able or tending to draw fine distinctions; perceptive. **2.** Fastidiously selective. **3.** Serving to differentiate; distinctive. **4.** Showing favoritism; differential, as a tariff. —**dis·crim′i·nat′ing·ly** *adv.*
dis·crim·i·na·tion (dĭs-krĭm′ə-nā′shən) *n.* **1.** The act of discriminating. **2.** The ability or power to see or make fine distinctions; discernment. **3.** An act based on prejudice.
dis·crim·i·na·tive (dĭs-krĭm′ə-nā′tĭv, -ə-nə-tĭv) *adj.* **1.** Drawing

distinctions; discriminating. **2.** Discriminatory. **—dis·crim′i·na′tive·ly** *adv.*

dis·crim·i·na·tor (dĭs-krĭm′ə-nā′tər) *n.* **1.** One who or that which discriminates. **2.** *Electronics.* A device that converts a property of a signal, such as frequency or phase, into an amplitude variation.

dis·crim·i·na·to·ry (dĭs-krĭm′ə-nə-tôr′ē, -tōr′ē) *adj.* **1.** Marked by or showing prejudice; biased. **2.** Discriminating. **—dis·crim′i·na·to′ri·ly** *adv.*

dis·crown (dĭs-kroun′) *tr.v.* **-crowned, -crowning, -crowns.** To deprive of a crown; dethrone; depose.

dis·cur·sive (dĭs-kûr′sĭv) *adj.* **1.** Covering a wide field of subjects; rambling; digressive. **2.** Proceeding to a conclusion through reason rather than intuition. [Medieval Latin *discursīvus,* from Latin *discursus,* "a running back and forth." See **discourse.**] **—dis·cur′sive·ly** *adv.* **—dis·cur′sive·ness** *n.*

dis·cus (dĭs′kəs) *n., pl.* **-cuses** or **disci** (dĭs′ī). **1.** A disk, typically wooden with a metal rim and weighing about 4½ pounds, thrown for distance in athletic competitions. **2.** The field event in which this disk is thrown. **3.** A small, brilliantly colored South American freshwater fish, *Symphysodon discus,* that has a disk-shaped body and is popular in home aquariums. [Latin, DISK.]

dis·cuss (dĭs-kŭs′) *tr.v.* **-cussed, -cussing, -cusses. 1.** To speak or write about; treat of. **2.** To speak together about; talk over. **3.** *Rare.* To consume (food or drink) with relish. [Middle English *discussen,* from Late Latin *discutere* (past participle *discussus*), to investigate, discuss, from Latin, to break up, scatter : *dis-,* apart + *quatere,* to shake, strike (see **kwēt-** in Appendix*).] **—dis·cuss′er** *n.* **—dis·cuss′i·ble** *adj.*

Synonyms: *discuss, argue, debate, dispute, contend.* These verbs mean to speak with others in an effort to reach agreement, to ascertain truth, or to convince. *Discuss* involves close examination of a subject with interchange of opinions, and need not imply disagreement. *Argue* emphasizes the presentation of facts and reasons in support of a position opposed by others. *Debate* involves formal and often public argument. *Dispute* implies wide differences of opinion and sharp argument. *Contend* suggests a heated competition of arguments.

dis·cuss·ant (dĭs-kŭs′ənt) *n.* A person who participates in a discussion.

dis·cus·sion (dĭs-kŭsh′ən) *n.* **1.** The consideration of a subject by a group; an earnest conversation. **2.** A discourse by one person upon a topic; an exposition.

dis·dain (dĭs-dān′) *tr.v.* **-dained, -daining, -dains. 1.** To regard or treat with haughty contempt; despise. **2.** To consider unworthy of oneself; reject with scorn. *—n.* A feeling, attitude, or show of scornful superiority; aloof contempt: *"a cold stare of lionlike disdain"* (Bram Stoker). [Middle English *desdeynen,* from Old French *desdeignier,* from Vulgar Latin *disdignāre* (unattested), variant of Latin *dēdignārī,* to scorn : *dē-* (reversal) + *dignāre,* to deem worthy, from *dignus,* worthy (see **dek-¹** in Appendix*).]

dis·dain·ful (dĭs-dān′fəl) *adj.* Feeling or showing disdain; scornful and haughty. See Synonyms at **proud. —dis·dain′ful·ly** *adv.* **—dis·dain′ful·ness** *n.*

dis·ease (dĭ-zēz′) *n.* **1.** An abnormal condition of an organism or part, especially as a consequence of infection, inherent weakness, or environmental stress, that impairs normal physiological functioning. **2.** A condition or tendency, as of society, regarded as abnormal and pernicious. **3.** *Obsolete.* Lack of ease. *—tr.v.* **diseased, -easing, -eases.** To cause a disease in; sicken. [Middle English *disese,* from Old French *desaise,* discomfort : *des-,* from Latin *dis-* (reversal) + *aise,* EASE.]

dis·eased (dĭ-zēzd′) *adj.* **1.** Affected with disease. **2.** Unhealthy; unsound; disordered.

dis·em·bark (dĭs′ĭm-bärk′) *v.* **-barked, -barking, -barks.** *—intr.* To go ashore from a ship. *—tr.* To put or cause to go ashore from a ship. **—dis·em′bar·ka′tion** *n.*

dis·em·bar·rass (dĭs′ĭm-băr′əs) *tr.v.* **-rassed, -rassing, -rasses.** To free from something embarrassing, bothersome, or encumbering; relieve. **—dis′em·bar′rass·ment** *n.*

dis·em·bod·y (dĭs′ĭm-bŏd′ē) *tr.v.* **-ied, -ying, -ies.** To free (the soul or spirit) from the body. **—dis′em·bod′i·ment** *n.*

dis·em·bogue (dĭs′ĭm-bōg′) *v.* **-bogued, -boguing, -bogues.** *—intr.* To empty at the mouth. Used of a river. *—tr.* To discharge (waters) at the mouth. Used of a river. [Alteration of Spanish *desembocar* : *des-,* from Latin *dis-* (reversal) + *embocar,* to put into the mouth : *em-,* from Latin *in-,* in + *boca,* mouth, from Latin *bucca,* cheek (see **beu-¹** in Appendix*).] **—dis′em·bogue′ment** *n.*

dis·em·bow·el (dĭs′ĭm-bou′əl) *tr.v.* **-eled, -eling, -els.** Also *chiefly British* **-elled, -elling.** To remove the entrails from. [DIS- (intensive) + EMBOWEL.] **—dis′em·bow′el·ment** *n.*

dis·em·broil (dĭs′ĭm-broil′) *tr.v.* **-broiled, -broiling, -broils.** To free from a condition of complexity or confusion; resolve.

dis·en·a·ble (dĭs′ĭn-ā′bəl) *tr.v.* **-bled, -bling, -bles.** To render unable; incapacitate. **—dis′en·a′ble·ment** *n.*

dis·en·chant (dĭs′ĭn-chănt′, -chänt′) *tr.v.* **-chanted, -chanting, -chants.** To free from enchantment or illusion; undeceive. **—dis′en·chant′er** *n.* **—dis′en·chant′ment** *n.*

dis·en·cum·ber (dĭs′ĭn-kŭm′bər) *tr.v.* **-bered, -bering, -bers.** To relieve of encumbrances. **—dis′en·cum′ber·ment** *n.*

dis·en·gage (dĭs′ĭn-gāj′) *v.* **-gaged, -gaging, -gages.** *—tr.* **1.** To release from something that holds fast, connects, or entangles; unfasten; detach. **2.** To release from an engagement, pledge, or obligation. *—intr.* To free oneself; get loose.

dis·en·gage·ment (dĭs′ĭn-gāj′mənt) *n.* **1. a.** The act of disengaging. **b.** The condition of being disengaged. **2.** Freedom from work or obligation; leisure.

dis·en·tail (dĭs′ĭn-tāl′) *tr.v.* **-tailed, -tailing, -tails.** *Law.* To release (an estate) from entail. **—dis′en·tail′ment** *n.*

dis·en·tan·gle (dĭs′ĭn-tăng′gəl) *v.* **-gled, -gling, -gles.** *—tr.* **1.** To extricate from entanglement or involvement; to free. **2.** To clear up or resolve (a plot, for example). *—intr.* To become free of entanglement. **—dis′en·tan′gle·ment** *n.*

dis·en·tomb (dĭs′ĭn-to͞om′) *tr.v.* **-tombed, -tombing, -tombs.** To remove from or as if from a tomb. **—dis′en·tomb′ment** *n.*

dis·en·twine (dĭs′ĭn-twīn′) *v.* **-twined, -twining, -twines.** *—tr.* To disentangle; untwine. *—intr.* To become untwined.

dis·e·qui·lib·ri·um (dĭs′ē-kwə-lĭb′rē-əm) *n.* Loss or lack of equilibrium or stability.

dis·es·tab·lish (dĭs′ĭ-stăb′lĭsh) *tr.v.* **-lished, -lishing, -lishes. 1.** To alter the status of (something established by authority or general acceptance). **2.** To deprive (a church) of official governmental support. **—dis′es·tab′lish·ment** *n.*

dis·es·teem (dĭs′ĭ-stēm′) *tr.v.* **-teemed, -teeming, -teems.** To have little regard for; hold in disfavor. *—n.* Lack of esteem.

dis·fa·vor (dĭs-fā′vər) *n.* **1.** Unfavorable opinion or regard; disapproval. **2.** The condition of being regarded with disapproval. *—tr.v.* **disfavored, -voring, -vors.** To view or treat with dislike or disapproval.

dis·fea·ture (dĭs-fē′chər) *tr.v.* **-tured, -turing, -tures.** To spoil the features of; disfigure. **—dis·fea′ture·ment** *n.*

dis·fig·ure (dĭs-fĭg′yər) *tr.v.* **-ured, -uring, -ures.** To blemish or spoil the appearance or shape of; deform. [Middle English *disfiguren,* from Old French *desfigurer,* from Vulgar Latin *disfigūrāre* (unattested) : Latin *dis-* (destruction) + *figūra,* FIGURE.] **—dis·fig′ur·er** *n.*

dis·fig·ure·ment (dĭs-fĭg′yər-mənt) *n.* Also **dis·fig·u·ra·tion** (-fĭg′yə-rā′shən). **1. a.** The act of disfiguring. **b.** The condition of being disfigured. **2.** A deformity; flaw.

dis·for·est (dĭs-fôr′ĭst, -fŏr′ĭst) *tr.v.* **-ested, -esting, -ests.** To clear the forest from; deforest. **—dis·for′es·ta′tion** *n.*

dis·fran·chise (dĭs-frăn′chīz′) *tr.v.* **-chised, -chising, -chises.** Also **dis·en·fran·chise** (dĭs′ĕn-frăn′chīz′). **1.** To deprive (an individual) of a right of citizenship, especially of the right to vote. **2.** To deprive (a corporation, for example) of a privilege or franchise. **—dis·fran′chise′ment** (-chīz′mənt, -chĭz-mənt) *n.* **—dis·fran′chis′er** *n.*

dis·frock (dĭs-frŏk′) *tr.v.* **-frocked, -frocking, -frocks.** To unfrock.

dis·gorge (dĭs-gôrj′) *v.* **-gorged, -gorging, -gorges.** *—tr.* **1.** To bring up and expel from the throat or stomach; to vomit. **2.** To discharge violently; spew. *—intr.* To discharge or pour forth contents. **—dis·gorge′ment** *n.*

dis·grace (dĭs-grās′) *n.* **1.** Loss of honor, respect, or reputation; shame. **2.** The condition of being out of favor or in ill repute. **3.** Something that brings shame, dishonor, or disfavor: *"He held it a disgrace to die rich."* (E.M. Forster). *—tr.v.* **disgraced, -gracing, -graces. 1.** To bring shame or dishonor upon. **2.** To put (someone) out of grace or favor. [French *disgrâce,* from Italian *disgrazia* : *dis-,* from Latin *dis-* (negative) + *grazia,* grace, from Latin *grātia,* charm, favor, GRACE.] **—dis·grac′er** *n.*

Synonyms: *disgrace, dishonor, shame, infamy, ignominy, odium, scandal, obloquy, opprobrium, disrepute, discredit, degradation.* These nouns refer to the condition of being held in low regard. In current usage *disgrace* implies strong disfavor or ostracism. *Dishonor* implies loss of esteem or respect or loss of a good reputation. *Shame* suggests loss of status as a result of a moral offense. *Infamy* is public disgrace or notoriety. *Ignominy* often implies public contempt. *Odium* adds to disgrace the sense of being widely detested. *Scandal* in this comparison suggests open public disapproval in response to improper conduct. *Obloquy* implies being subjected to abuse and vilification. *Opprobrium* is the condition of being condemned with scorn. *Disrepute* involves lack of or loss of a good name but is weaker than dishonor in suggesting descent from previous high regard. *Discredit* implies doubt or distrust and applies to loss of professional status more often than to loss of esteem resulting from personal misconduct. *Degradation* involves reduction to a rank so low that it demoralizes or at least incurs extreme humiliation and contempt.

dis·grace·ful (dĭs-grās′fəl) *adj.* Bringing or warranting disgrace; shameful. **—dis·grace′ful·ly** *adv.* **—dis·grace′ful·ness** *n.*

dis·grun·tle (dĭs-grŭnt′l) *tr.v.* **-tled, -tling, -tles.** To make discontented or cross; put in a disagreeable mood: *disgruntled by his meager share.* [DIS- (intensive) + dialectal *gruntle,* to grumble, Middle English *gruntlen,* frequentative of *grunten,* to GRUNT.] **—dis·grun′tle·ment** *n.*

dis·guise (dĭs-gīz′) *tr.v.* **-guised, -guising, -guises. 1.** To modify the manner or appearance of in order to prevent recognition. **2.** To conceal or obscure by dissemblance or false show; misrepresent: *disguise one's interest.* *—n.* **1. a.** The act of disguising. **b.** The condition of being disguised. **2.** Something that serves to disguise, as a mask, costume, or pretense. [Middle English *disg(u)isen,* from Old French *desguisier* : *des-,* from Latin *dis-* (reversal) + *guise,* manner, GUISE.] **—dis·guis′er** *n.*

dis·gust (dĭs-gŭst′) *tr.v.* **-gusted, -gusting, -gusts. 1.** To excite nausea or loathing in; sicken. **2.** To offend the taste or moral sense of; repel. *—n.* Profound aversion or repugnance excited by something offensive. [Old French *desgouster* : *des-,* from Latin *dis-* (negative) + *goust,* taste, from Latin *gustus* (see **geus-** in Appendix*).]

dis·gust·ed (dĭs-gŭs′tĭd) *adj.* Filled with disgust or irritated impatience. **—dis·gust′ed·ly** *adv.*

Usage: *Disgusted* is often followed by *with* (a person or his action), *at* (an action or behavior), or *by* (a personal quality, action, or behavior).

dis·gust·ful (dĭs-gŭst′fəl) *adj.* **1.** Causing disgust; repugnant. **2.** Full of or marked by disgust. —**dis·gust′ful·ly** *adv.*
dis·gust·ing (dĭs-gŭs′tĭng) *adj.* Acutely repugnant; loathsome; repellent. —**dis·gust′ing·ly** *adv.*
dish (dĭsh) *n.* **1.** An open container, generally shallow and concave, for holding or serving food. **2. a.** The food served or contained in a dish. **b.** A particular variety or preparation of food. **c.** The portion a dish holds. **3. a.** A concavity or depression like that in a dish. **b.** The degree of such a concavity. **4.** *Informal.* Something one especially likes or excels in: *Mathematics is not my dish.* **5.** *Slang.* A good-looking girl or woman. —*tr.v.* **dished, dishing, dishes. 1.** To serve (food) in or as if in a dish. Usually used with *up* or *out.* **2.** To hollow out; make concave. Used with *out.* **3.** *British Slang.* To foil; cheat; ruin. **4.** *Informal.* To give out; dispense; distribute. Used with *out.* —**dish it out.** *Slang.* To abuse verbally or physically. [Middle English *dish,* Old English *disc,* plate, bowl, platter, from West Germanic *diskaz* (unattested), from Latin *discus,* quoit, DISK.]
dis·ha·bille (dĭs′ə-bēl′, -bē′) *n.* Also **des·ha·bille** (dĕs′-). **1.** The state of being partially or very casually dressed; a state of undress. **2.** Casual or lounging attire. [French *déshabillé,* from the past participle of *déshabiller,* to undress : *dés-,* from Latin *dis-* (reversal) + *habiller,* to dress (see **habiliment**).]
dis·hal·low (dĭs-hăl′ō) *tr.v.* **-lowed, -lowing, -lows.** To defile; desecrate; profane.
dis·har·mo·ny (dĭs-här′mə-nē) *n., pl.* **-nies.** Lack of harmony; discord. —**dis′har·mo′ni·ous** (-mō′nē-əs) *adj.*
dish·cloth (dĭsh′klôth′, -klŏth′) *n., pl.* **-cloths** (-klôths′, -klô*thz*′, -klŏths′, -klŏ*thz*′). A cloth or rag used for washing dishes. Also called "dishrag."
dishcloth gourd. A plant, the **loofa** *(see),* or its fruit. [Its fibrous interior is dried and used as a sponge.]
dis·heart·en (dĭs-härt′n) *tr.v.* **-ened, -ening, -ens.** To shake or destroy the courage or resolution of; dispirit. —**dis·heart′en·ing·ly** *adv.* —**dis·heart′en·ment** *n.*
dished (dĭsht) *adj.* Slanting toward one another at the bottom. Said of a pair of wheels.
di·shev·el (dĭ-shĕv′əl) *tr.v.* **-eled, -eling, -els.** Also *chiefly British* **-elled, -elling. 1.** To loosen and let fall (hair or clothing) in disarray. **2.** To disarrange the hair or clothing of (a person). [Back-formation from DISHEVELED.] —**di·shev′el·ment** *n.*
di·shev·eled (dĭ-shĕv′əld) *adj.* **1.** Hanging in loose disarray; unkempt, as hair. **2.** Disarranged; untidy. [Middle English *discheveled,* from Old French *deschevele,* past participle of *descheveler,* to disarrange the hair : *des-,* from Latin *dis-,* apart + *chevel,* hair, from Latin *capillus* (see **capillary**).]
dis·hon·est (dĭs-ŏn′ĭst) *adj.* **1.** Disposed to lie, cheat, defraud, or deceive. **2.** Proceeding from, gained by, or betokening falseness or improbity. [Middle English *dishoneste,* from Old French *deshoneste* : *des-,* from Latin *dis-* (negative) + *honeste,* HONEST.] —**dis·hon′est·ly** *adv.*
Synonyms: *dishonest, lying, untruthful, deceitful, mendacious, tricky, shady, underhand.* These adjectives mean lacking honesty or truthfulness. *Dishonest* is the least specific. *Lying,* applicable principally to persons, conveys a blunt accusation of untruth. *Untruthful* is a softer but closely related term applied to persons and even more to their statements. *Deceitful* implies misleading by falsehood or by concealment of truth. *Mendacious* suggests chronic inclination toward untruth. *Tricky* implies the use of cunning to fool a person. *Shady* suggests impropriety or illegality. *Underhand* is associated with unfairness and secrecy.
dis·hon·es·ty (dĭs-ŏn′ĭ-stē) *n., pl.* **-ties. 1.** Want of integrity; improbity. **2.** A dishonest act or statement.
dis·hon·or (dĭs-ŏn′ər) *n.* **1.** Loss of honor, respect, or reputation; disgrace; shame. **2.** Something that causes loss of honor. **3.** Failure to pay a note, bill, or other commercial obligation. —See Synonyms at **disgrace.** —*tr.v.* **dishonored, -oring, -ors. 1.** To deprive of honor; to disgrace. **2.** To fail to pay (a note, for example). [Middle English *dishonour,* from Old French *deshonor,* from Vulgar Latin *dishonor* (unattested) : Latin *dis-* (negative) + *honor,* HONOR.] —**dis·hon′or·er** *n.*
dis·hon·or·a·ble (dĭs-ŏn′ər-ə-bəl) *adj.* **1.** Characterized by or causing dishonor or discredit. **2.** Lacking integrity; unprincipled. —**dis·hon′or·a·ble·ness** *n.* —**dis·hon′or·a·bly** *adv.*
dish·pan (dĭsh′păn′) *n.* A basin or tub in which to wash dishes.
dish·rag (dĭsh′răg′) *n.* A **dishcloth** *(see).*
dish·tow·el (dĭsh′tou′əl) *n.* A towel for drying dishes.
dish·wash·er (dĭsh′wŏsh′ər, -wô′shər) *n.* **1.** A person who washes dishes; specifically, one hired to wash dishes in a restaurant. **2.** A machine that washes dishes.

dishwasher

dish·wa·ter (dĭsh′wô′tər, -wŏt′ər) *n.* Water in which dishes are being or have been washed.
dis·il·lu·sion (dĭs′ĭ-lōō′zhən) *tr.v.* **-sioned, -sioning, -sions.** To free or deprive of illusion; disenchant. —*n.* **1.** The act of disenchanting. **2.** The condition or fact of being disenchanted. —**dis′il·lu′sion·ment** *n.* —**dis′il·lu′sive** (-sĭv, -zĭv) *adj.*
dis·in·cli·na·tion (dĭs-ĭn′klə-nā′shən) *n.* Lack of willingness or disposition; reluctance; aversion.
dis·in·cline (dĭs′ĭn-klīn′) *v.* **-clined, -clining, -clines.** —*tr.* To make reluctant or averse. —*intr.* To be reluctant or averse.
dis·in·clined (dĭs′ĭn-klīnd′) *adj.* Unwilling; reluctant.
dis·in·fect (dĭs′ĭn-fĕkt′) *tr.v.* **-fected, -fecting, -fects.** To cleanse or rid of pathogenic microorganisms. —**dis′in·fec′tion** *n.* —**dis′in·fec′tor** (-fĕk′tər) *n.*
dis·in·fec·tant (dĭs′ĭn-fĕk′tənt) *n.* An agent that disinfects by destroying, neutralizing, or inhibiting the growth of pathogenic microorganisms. —*adj.* Serving to disinfect.
dis·in·fest (dĭs′ĭn-fĕst′) *tr.v.* **-fested, -festing, -fests.** To rid of vermin. —**dis′in·fes·ta′tion** *n.*

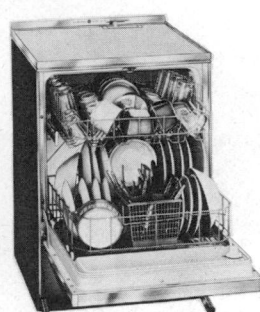

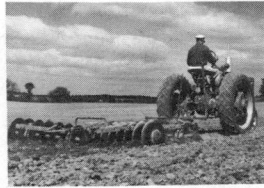

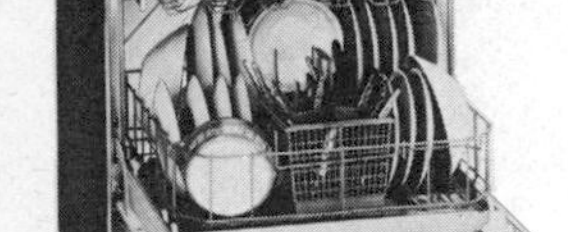
disk harrow

dis·in·fla·tion (dĭs′ĭn-flā′shən) *n.* The downward movement of inflated prices to a more normal level.
dis·in·gen·u·ous (dĭs′ĭn-jĕn′yōō-əs) *adj.* Not straightforward; crafty. —**dis′in·gen′u·ous·ly** *adv.* —**dis′in·gen′u·ous·ness** *n.*
dis·in·her·it (dĭs′ĭn-hĕr′ĭt) *tr.v.* **-ited, -iting, -its.** To exclude from inheritance or the right to inherit. —**dis′in·her′i·tance** *n.*
dis·in·te·grate (dĭs-ĭn′tə-grāt′) *v.* **-grated, -grating, -grates.** —*intr.* To separate into components; fragment. —*tr.* To cause (a body) to separate into components; destroy. —See Synonyms at **decay.** —**dis·in′te·gra′tor** (-grā′tər) *n.*
dis·in·te·gra·tion (dĭs-ĭn′tə-grā′shən) *n.* **1.** The process of disintegrating or the state of being disintegrated. **2.** *Physics.* The natural or induced transformation of an atomic nucleus from a more massive to a less massive configuration by the emission of radiation, an electron, or a nuclear fragment.
dis·in·ter (dĭs′ĭn-tûr′) *tr.v.* **-terred, -terring, -ters. 1.** To dig up or remove, as from a grave or tomb; exhume. **2.** To remove from obscurity; expose. —**dis′in·ter′ment** *n.*
dis·in·ter·est (dĭs-ĭn′trĭst, -ĭn′tər-ĭst) *n.* **1.** Freedom from selfish bias or self-interest; impartiality. **2.** Lack of interest. —See Usage note at **disinterested.** —*tr.v.* **disinterested, -esting, -ests.** *Rare.* To rid of interest.
dis·in·ter·est·ed (dĭs-ĭn′trĭ-stĭd, -ĭn′tə-rĕs′tĭd) *adj.* **1.** Free of bias and self-interest; impartial: *"The pupil is fully worthy of the praises bestowed by the disinterested instructor."* (Thackeray). **2.** *Nonstandard.* Uninterested; indifferent. See Usage note. —See Synonyms at **indifferent.** —**dis·in′ter·est·ed·ly** *adv.* —**dis·in′ter·est·ed·ness** *n.*
Usage: *Disinterested* differs from *uninterested* to the degree that lack of self-interest differs from lack of any interest. *Disinterested* is synonymous with *impartial, unbiased. Uninterested* has the sense of *indifferent, not interested.* According to 93 per cent of the Usage Panel, *disinterested* is not acceptable in the sense of *uninterested,* though it is often thus employed.
dis·ject (dĭs-jĕkt′) *tr.v.* **-jected, -jecting, -jects.** To split or disperse with force; scatter. [Latin *disjicere* (past participle *disjectus*) : *dis-,* apart + *jacere,* to throw (see **yē-** in Appendix*).]
dis·join (dĭs-join′) *v.* **-joined, -joining, -joins.** —*tr.* To undo the joining of; separate. —*intr.* To become disconnected. [Middle English *disjoinen,* from Old French *desjoindre,* from Latin *disjungere* : *dis-* (reversal) + *jungere,* JOIN.]
dis·joint (dĭs-joint′) *v.* **-jointed, -jointing, -joints.** —*tr.* **1.** To put out of joint; dislocate. **2.** To take apart at the joints. **3.** To destroy the coherence or connections of. **4.** To separate; disjoin. —*intr.* **1.** To come apart at the joints. **2.** To become dislocated. —*adj. Mathematics.* Having no elements in common. [Middle English *disjointen,* from Old French *desjoindre* (past participle *desjoint*), DISJOIN.]
dis·joint·ed (dĭs-join′tĭd) *adj.* **1.** Separated at the joints. **2.** Out of joint; dislocated. **3.** Lacking order or coherence; disconnected. —**dis·joint′ed·ly** *adv.* —**dis·joint′ed·ness** *n.*
dis·junct (dĭs-jŭngkt′) *adj.* **1.** Separated; disconnected. **2.** *Music.* Pertaining to progression by intervals larger than major seconds. **3.** *Zoology.* Having the head, thorax, and abdomen separated by deep constrictions. Said of insects. [Middle English *disjuncte,* from Latin *disjunctus,* past participle of *disjungere,* DISJOIN.]
dis·junc·tion (dĭs-jŭngk′shən) *n.* Also **dis·junc·ture** (-chər) (for sense 1). **1.** The act of disjoining or the condition of being disjointed. **2.** *Logic.* A proposition that presents two or more alternative terms, with the assertion that only one is true.
dis·junc·tive (dĭs-jŭngk′tĭv) *adj.* **1.** Serving to separate or divide. **2.** *Grammar.* Serving to establish a relationship of contrast or opposition. The conjunction *but* in the phrase *poor but comfortable* is disjunctive. **3.** *Logic.* **a.** Presenting two or more alternative terms. Said of a proposition. **b.** Containing a disjunction as one premise. Said of a syllogism. —*n. Grammar.* A disjunctive conjunction.
disk (dĭsk) *n.* Also **disc. 1.** Any thin, flat, circular plate. **2.** Anything resembling such a plate, as an astronomical body or an anatomical structure. **3.** *Botany.* The enlarged receptacle containing numerous tiny flowers in the flower head of many composite plants, such as the daisy and the coneflower. **4.** Variant of **disc.** —*tr.v.* **disked, disking, disks.** To work (soil) with a disk harrow. [Latin *discus,* quoit, from Greek *diskos,* quoit, from *dikein,* to throw. See **deik-** in Appendix.*]
disk brake. A brake in which the retarding friction is generated by contact between disks attached to a stationary frame and corresponding disks attached to a rotating part.
disk flower. Any of the tiny tubular flowers forming the center of the flower head of certain composite plants, such as the daisy. Also called "disk floret." Compare **ray flower.**
disk harrow. A harrow equipped with a series of disks set on edge or at an angle on one or more axles.
disk jockey. Variant of **disc jockey.**
Dis·ko (dĭs′kō). An island, 3,312 square miles in area, in Davis Strait off the western coast of Greenland.
disk wheel. A wheel having a solid structure, instead of spokes, extending from the hub to the rim.
dis·like (dĭs-līk′) *tr.v.* **-liked, -liking, -likes.** To regard with distaste or aversion. —*n.* An attitude or feeling of distaste or aversion; antipathy.
dis·lo·cate (dĭs′lō-kāt′, dĭs-lō′kāt′) *tr.v.* **-cated, -cating, -cates. 1.** To put out from the usual or proper relationship with contiguous parts; displace; shift. **2.** *Pathology.* To displace (a limb or organ) from the normal position; especially, to displace (a bone) from the socket or joint. **3.** To throw into confusion or disorder; upset; disturb. [Medieval Latin *dislocāre* : Latin *dis-* (reversal) + *locāre,* to place, LOCATE.] —**dis′lo·ca′tion** *n.*

ă pat/ā pay/âr care/ä father/b bib/ch church/d deed/ĕ pet/ē be/f fife/g gag/h hat/hw which/ĭ pit/ī pie/îr pier/j judge/k kick/l lid, needle/m mum/n no, sudden/ng thing/ŏ pot/ō toe/ô paw, for/oi noise/ou out/ŏŏ took/ōō boot/p pop/r roar/s sauce/sh ship, dish/

dis·lodge (dĭs-lŏj′) *v.* **-lodged, -lodging, -lodges.** —*tr.* To remove or force out from a dwelling or position previously occupied. —*intr.* To move or go from a dwelling or former position. [Middle English *disloggen,* from Old French *deslogier* : *des-,* from Latin *dis-* (reversal) + *logier,* to lodge, from *loge,* shed, LODGE.] —**dis·lodg′ment, dis·lodge′ment** *n.*

dis·loy·al (dĭs-loi′əl) *adj.* Lacking in loyalty. See Synonyms at **faithless.** —**dis·loy′al·ly** *adv.*

dis·loy·al·ty (dĭs-loi′əl-tē) *n., pl.* **-ties. 1.** The quality of being disloyal; faithlessness. **2.** A disloyal act.

dis·mal (dĭz′məl) *adj.* **1.** Causing gloom or depression; dreary: *"For two rainy dismal days they were . . . storm-bound at Ouchy"* (Peter Quennell). **2.** Causing dread or dismay; dire: *"We beheld the dismal spectacle, the whole city in dreadful flames"* (John Evelyn). —See Synonyms at **boring.** —*n.* **1.** *Plural.* Low spirits: *in the dismals.* **2.** *Southern U.S.* An area of swampland. [Middle English, unlucky days (two days in each month that were considered unpropitious), from Medieval Latin *diēs malī* : Latin *diēs,* plural of *diēs,* day (see **deiw-** in Appendix*) + *malī,* plural of *malus,* evil (see **mel-[5]** in Appendix*).] —**dis′mal·ly** *adv.* —**dis′mal·ness** *n.*

Dismal Swamp. A swamp extending some 20 miles from northeastern North Carolina into southeastern Virginia.

dis·man·tle (dĭs-măn′tl) *tr.v.* **-tled, -tling, -tles. 1.** To strip (a house, for example) of furnishings or equipment. **2.** To take apart; tear down. **3.** To strip of clothing or covering. [Old French *desmanteler* : *des-,* from Latin *dis-* (removal) + *mantel,* MANTLE.] —**dis·man′tle·ment** *n.*

dis·mast (dĭs-măst′, -mäst′) *tr.v.* **-masted, -masting, -masts.** *Nautical.* To remove or break off the mast or masts of.

dis·may (dĭs-mā′) *tr.v.* **-mayed, -maying, -mays. 1.** To fill with dread or apprehension; make anxious or afraid. **2.** To discourage or trouble greatly; daunt; dishearten. —*n.* A sudden or complete loss of courage or confidence in the face of trouble or danger; consternation. See Synonyms at **fear.** [Middle English *dismayen,* from Old French *desmayer* (attested only in past participle *dismaye*) : *des-,* from Latin *dis-* (intensive) + *esmayer,* to frighten, be frightened, from Vulgar Latin *exmagāre* (unattested), to deprive of power, from Germanic (see **magh-[1]** in Appendix*).]

Synonyms: *dismay, appall, daunt, horrify, intimidate, cow.* These verbs mean to fill a person with fear. Usually they imply reducing him to inaction. *Dismay* can mean as little as to frighten or dishearten or as much as to overwhelm. *Appall* implies a sense of helplessness caused by an awareness of an enormity or a difficulty. *Daunt* suggests subduing by removing the courage necessary for action. *Horrify,* the strongest term, implies literally causing dread or revulsion; in a weaker sense it means to shock by some impropriety. *Intimidate* involves making a person fearful as a means of bringing about his submission or discouraging him from action. *Cow* stresses the breaking down of all resistance in another by a show of force.

dis·mem·ber (dĭs-mĕm′bər) *tr.v.* **-bered, -bering, -bers. 1.** To cut, tear, or pull off the limbs of. **2.** To divide into pieces: *"Frescobaldi permitted organists to dismember his toccatas"* (Donald Jay Grout). [Middle English *dismembren,* from Old French *desmembrer,* from Vulgar Latin *dismembrāre* (unattested) : Latin *dis-* (removal) + *membrum,* MEMBER.] —**dis·mem′ber·er** *n.* —**dis·mem′ber·ment** *n.*

dis·miss (dĭs-mĭs′) *tr.v.* **-missed, -missing, -misses. 1.** To discharge, as from employment. **2.** To direct or allow to leave: *dismiss troops.* **3.** To rid one's mind of; dispel. **4.** To reject; repudiate: *"unanimous in dismissing the claim as highly improbable"* (Richard Aldington). **5.** To discontinue consideration of; to drop. **6.** *Law.* To put (a claim or action) out of court without further hearing. —See Synonyms at **eject.** [Middle English *dismissen,* from Medieval Latin *dismittere* (past participle *dismissus*), variant of Latin *dīmittere* : *dīs-,* away + *mittere,* to send (see **smeit-** in Appendix*).] —**dis·miss′i·ble** *adj.*

dis·miss·al (dĭs-mĭs′əl) *n.* Also *rare* **dis·mis·sion** (-mĭsh′ən). **1. a.** The act of dismissing. **b.** The condition of being dismissed. **2.** An order or notice of discharge.

dis·mount (dĭs-mount′) *v.* **-mounted, -mounting, -mounts.** —*intr.* To get off or down, as from a horse or bicycle; alight. —*tr.* **1.** To remove (a thing) from its support, setting, or mounting. **2.** To unseat, as from a horse. **3.** To take apart (a mechanism); disassemble. —*n.* The act or manner of dismounting from a horse. —**dis·mount′a·ble** *adj.*

Dis·ney (dĭz′nē), **Walter Elias ("Walt").** 1901–1966. American cartoonist, motion-picture producer, and showman.

dis·o·be·di·ence (dĭs′ə-bē′dē-əns) *n.* The condition or fact of not obeying; insubordination. —**dis′o·be′di·ent** *adj.* —**dis′o·be′di·ent·ly** *adv.*

dis·o·bey (dĭs′ə-bā′) *v.* **-beyed, -beying, -beys.** —*intr.* To refuse or fail to follow an order or rule. —*tr.* To refuse or fail to obey. [Middle English *disobeien,* from Old French *desobeir,* from Vulgar Latin *disobēdīre* (unattested) : Latin *dis-* (negative) + *oboedīre,* OBEY.] —**dis′o·bey′er** *n.*

dis·o·blige (dĭs′ə-blīj′) *tr.v.* **-bliged, -bliging, -bliges. 1.** To refuse or neglect to act in accord with the wishes of. **2.** To slight; offend. **3.** *Regional.* To inconvenience. —**dis′o·blig′ing·ly** *adv.*

dis·or·der (dĭs-ôr′dər) *n.* **1.** A lack of order or regular arrangement; confusion. **2.** A breach of civic order or peace; public disturbance. **3.** An upset of health or functioning. —*tr.v.* **disordered, -dering, -ders. 1.** To throw into disorder; muddle; disarrange. **2.** To disturb the normal physical or mental health of; to derange.

dis·or·dered (dĭs-ôr′dərd) *adj.* **1.** In a condition of disorder; disarranged. **2.** Physically or mentally ill; deranged.

dis·or·der·ly (dĭs-ôr′dər-lē) *adj.* **1.** Lacking regular or logical order or arrangement; irregular; unsystematic. **2.** Undisciplined; unruly; riotous. **3.** *Law.* Disturbing the public peace or decorum. —**dis·or′der·li·ness** *n.*

disorderly conduct. *Law.* Any of various petty offenses involving a disturbance of public peace and decorum.

disorderly house. *Law.* Any house whose inmates regularly violate the public order or decency, as a house of prostitution or a gambling house.

dis·or·gan·i·za·tion (dĭs-ôr′gə-nə-zā′shən) *n.* **1.** A destroying or dissolving of order, unity, or system. **2.** The condition of being disorganized; disorder.

dis·or·gan·ize (dĭs-ôr′gə-nīz′) *tr.v.* **-ized, -izing, -izes.** To destroy the organization, systematic arrangement, or unity of; throw into confusion. —**dis·or′gan·iz′er** *n.*

dis·o·ri·ent (dĭs-ôr′ē-ĕnt′, dĭs-ōr′-) *tr.v.* **-ented, -enting, -ents.** To cause to lose one's sense of direction or location, as by removing from a familiar environment. —**dis·o′ri·en·ta′tion** *n.*

dis·own (dĭs-ōn′) *tr.v.* **-owned, -owning, -owns.** To refuse to acknowledge or accept as one's own; repudiate.

disp. dispensary.

dis·par·age (dĭs-păr′ĭj) *tr.v.* **-aged, -aging, -ages. 1.** To belittle; slight. **2.** To reduce in esteem or rank. —See Synonyms at **decry.** [Middle English *disparagen,* to degrade, disgrace, humble, from Old French *desparager,* "to deprive one of his rank" : *des-,* from Latin *dis-* (privative) + *parage,* rank, from *per,* PEER.] —**dis·par′ag·er** *n.* —**dis·par′ag·ing·ly** *adv.*

dis·par·age·ment (dĭs-păr′ĭj-mənt) *n.* **1.** The act of disparaging; derogation; detraction. **2.** A lowering of dignity or esteem; discredit. **3.** Something that lowers dignity or esteem.

dis·pa·rate (dĭs′pər-ĭt, dĭs-păr′ĭt) *adj.* Completely distinct or different in kind; entirely dissimilar. [Latin *disparātus,* past participle of *disparāre,* to separate : *dis-,* apart + *parāre,* to prepare (see **per-[4]** in Appendix*).] —**dis′pa·rate·ly** *adv.* —**dis′pa·rate·ness** *n.*

dis·par·i·ty (dĭs-păr′ə-tē) *n., pl.* **-ties. 1.** The condition or fact of being unequal in age, rank, or degree; difference. **2.** Unlikeness; incongruity; dissimilarity. [Old French *disparite,* from Late Latin *disparitās* : Latin *dis-* (negative) + *paritās,* PARITY.]

dis·pas·sion (dĭs-păsh′ən) *n.* Freedom from passion, bias, or emotion; objectivity.

dis·pas·sion·ate (dĭs-păsh′ən-ĭt) *adj.* Devoid of or unaffected by passion, emotion, or bias; impartial; calm: *"a language which constantly tempts the user away from dispassionate exposition into sarcasm and diatribe"* (T.S. Eliot). See Synonyms at **fair.** —**dis·pas′sion·ate·ly** *adv.* —**dis·pas′sion·ate·ness** *n.*

dis·patch (dĭs-păch′) *tr.v.* **-patched, -patching, -patches.** Also **des·patch. 1.** To send off to a specific destination or on specific business. **2.** To complete or dispose promptly of. **3.** To put to death summarily. —*n.* **1.** The act of dispatching or sending off. **2.** A putting to death. **3.** Efficient speed or promptness; expeditious performance. **4.** A written message, particularly an official communication, sent with speed. **5.** A news item sent to a newspaper, as by a correspondent. [Spanish *despachar* or Italian *dispacciare,* from Old French *despeechier,* to set free, unshackle : *des-,* from Latin *dis-* (reversal) + *(em)peechier,* to hinder, from Late Latin *impedicāre,* to entangle : Latin *in-* + *pedica,* shackle (see **ped-[1]** in Appendix*).]

dis·patch·er (dĭs-păch′ər) *n.* **1.** One that dispatches. **2.** A person employed by a transportation company to send out trains, buses, or trucks according to a schedule.

dis·pel (dĭs-pĕl′) *tr.v.* **-pelled, -pelling, -pels.** To rid of by or as if by driving away or scattering; dispense with: *"the effect of his tone was to dispel her shyness"* (Henry James). See Synonyms at **scatter.** [Middle English *dispellen,* from Latin *dispellere* : *dis-,* away + *pellere,* to push, drive, strike (see **pel-[6]** in Appendix*).] —**dis·pel′ler** *n.*

dis·pend (dĭs-pĕnd′) *tr.v.* **-pended, -pending, -pends.** *Obsolete.* To spend, especially lavishly; squander. [Middle English *dispenden,* from Old French *despendre,* from Latin *dispendere,* to weigh out. See **dispense.**]

dis·pen·sa·ble (dĭs-pĕn′sə-bəl) *adj.* **1.** Capable of being dispensed with; unimportant. **2.** Capable of being dispensed, administered, or distributed. **3.** Subject to dispensation, as a sin; condonable. —**dis·pen′sa·bil′i·ty, dis·pen′sa·ble·ness** *n.*

dis·pen·sa·ry (dĭs-pĕn′sə-rē) *n., pl.* **-ries.** *Abbr.* **disp. 1.** An office in a hospital, school, or other institution from which medical supplies and preparations are dispensed. **2.** A public institution that dispenses medicines or medical aid.

dis·pen·sa·tion (dĭs′pən-sā′shən, dĭs′pĕn-) *n.* **1.** The act of dispensing or giving out; distribution; apportionment. **2.** Something that is dispensed or given out. **3.** A specific arrangement or system by which something is dispensed or administered. **4.** Any exemption or release from an obligation or rule, granted by or as if by an authority. **5. a.** An exemption from a church law, a vow, or other similar obligation granted in a particular case by an ecclesiastical authority. **b.** The document containing this exemption. **6.** *Theology.* **a.** The divine ordering of worldly affairs. **b.** A religious system or code of commands considered to have been divinely revealed or appointed: *the Moslem dispensation.* —**dis′pen·sa′tion·al** *adj.*

dis·pen·sa·to·ry (dĭs-pĕn′sə-tôr′ē, -tōr′ē) *adj.* Of, pertaining to, or granted by dispensation. —*n., pl.* **dispensatories. 1.** A book in which the preparation, uses, and contents of medicines are described; a pharmacopoeia. **2.** *Archaic.* A dispensary.

dis·pense (dĭs-pĕns′) *v.* **-pensed, -pensing, -penses.** —*tr.* **1.** To deal out or distribute in parts or portions: *"Queen Alexandra dispensed carrots to the thoroughbred from a basket"* (Duke of Windsor). **2.** To prepare and give out (medicines). **3.** To ad-

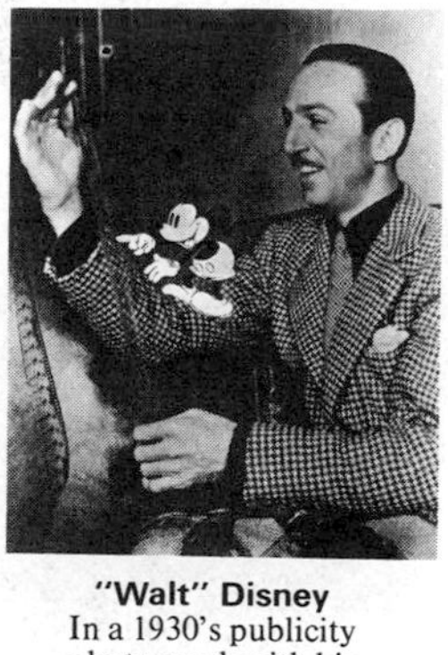

"Walt" Disney
In a 1930's publicity photograph with his creation Mickey Mouse

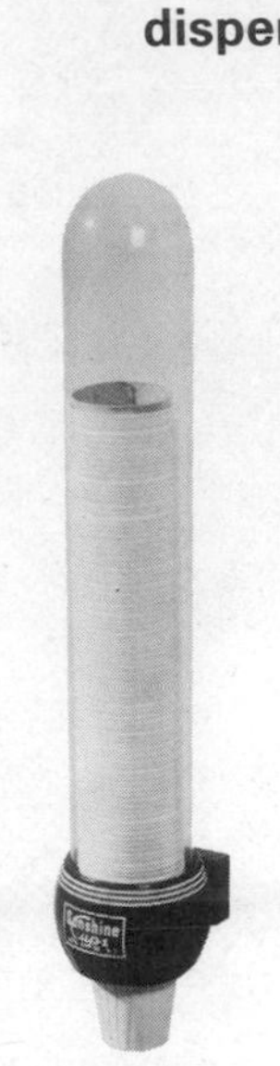

dispenser
Paper-cup dispenser

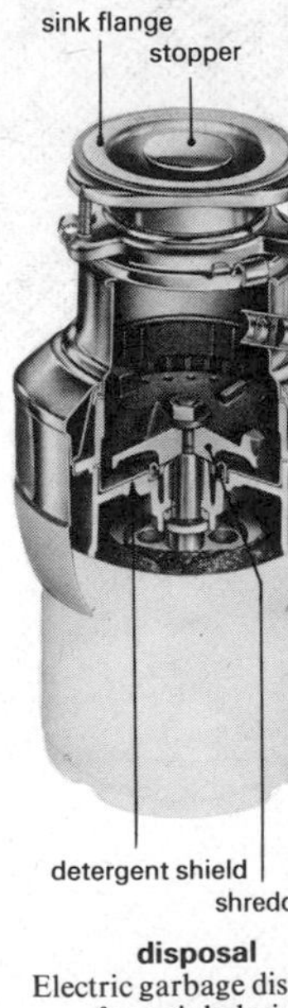
sink flange
stopper
detergent shield
shredder

disposal
Electric garbage disposal for a sink drain

minister (laws, for example). **4.** To exempt or release, as from a duty or religious obligation. —*intr.* To grant dispensation or exemption. —**dispense with. 1.** To manage without; forgo. **2.** To dispose of. —See Synonyms at **distribute.** [Middle English *dispensen,* from Medieval Latin *dispensāre,* to grant dispensation to, exempt, condone, from Latin, to pay out, distribute, frequentative of *dispendere,* to weigh out : *dis-,* away + *pendere,* to weigh (see **spen-** in Appendix*).]

dis·pens·er (dĭs-pĕn′sər) *n.* One that dispenses or gives out: *a paper-cup dispenser.*

dis·per·sal (dĭs-pûr′səl) *n.* The act or process of dispersing or the condition of being dispersed; distribution.

dis·perse (dĭs-pûrs′) *v.* **-persed, -persing, -perses.** —*tr.* **1.** To scatter in various directions; distribute widely. **2.** To cause to vanish or disappear; dispel. **3.** To disseminate (knowledge, for example). **4.** To separate (light) into spectral rays. —*intr.* To move or scatter in different directions. —See Synonyms at **scatter.** [Middle English *dispersen,* from Old French *disperser,* from Latin *dispergere* (past participle *dispersus*), to scatter on all sides : *dis-,* in different directions + *spargere,* to strew, scatter (see **sphereg-** in Appendix*).] —**dis·pers′ed·ly** (-pûr′sĭd-lē) *adv.* —**dis·pers′er** *n.* —**dis·pers′i·ble** *adj.*

disperse system. Any continuous medium containing dispersed entities of any size or state.

dis·per·sion (dĭs-pûr′zhən, -shən) *n.* **1. a.** The act or process of dispersing. **b.** The state of being dispersed. **2.** *Statistics.* The degree of scatter of data, usually about some mean or median value. **3.** *Physics.* **a.** The separation of a complex wave into component parts according to some characteristic, such as frequency or wavelength. **b.** The separation of visible light into its color components by refraction or diffraction. **4.** *Chemistry.* A suspension, such as smog or homogenized milk, of solid, liquid, or gaseous particles, of colloidal size or larger, in a liquid, solid, or gaseous medium.

dis·per·sive (dĭs-pûr′sĭv, -zĭv) *adj.* **1.** Tending to become dispersed. **2.** Tending to produce dispersion.

dis·pir·it (dĭs-pĭr′ĭt) *tr.v.* **-ited, -iting, -its.** To lower in spirit; dishearten. [DI(S)- (negative) + SPIRIT.]

dis·pir·it·ed (dĭs-pĭr′ĭt-ĭd) *adj.* Characterized by low spirits; dejected. —**dis·pir′it·ed·ly** *adv.*

dis·place (dĭs-plās′) *tr.v.* **-placed, -placing, -places. 1.** To change the place or position of. **2.** To take the place of; supplant. **3.** To discharge from an office or position. **4.** To cause a displacement of (a body, for example). —See Synonyms at **replace.** —**dis·place′a·ble** *adj.* —**dis·plac′er** *n.*

displaced person. *Abbr.* **DP, D.P.** A person living in a foreign country who has been driven from his homeland by war.

dis·place·ment (dĭs-plās′mənt) *n.* **1. a.** The act of displacing. **b.** The condition of being displaced. **2.** *Chemistry.* A reaction in which one kind of atom, molecule, or radical is removed from combination and replaced by another. **3.** *Physics.* **a.** The weight or volume of a fluid displaced by a floating body, used especially as a measurement of the weight or bulk of ships. **b.** A vector, or the magnitude of a vector, from the initial position to a subsequent position assumed by a body. **4.** *Psychoanalysis.* The shifting of an emotional affect, as of anger, from an appropriate to an inappropriate object.

displacement ton. *Nautical.* A unit for measuring the displacement of a ship afloat, equivalent to one long ton or about 35 cubic feet of salt water.

dis·play (dĭs-plā′) *tr.v.* **-played, -playing, -plays. 1.** To hold up to view; make visible; expose; exhibit. **2.** To make manifest or noticeable; show evidence of. **3.** To exhibit ostentatiously or prominently; show off; parade; flaunt. **4.** To spread out; unfurl. **5.** *Printing.* To give prominence to (printed letters or words, for example), as by using large type. —See Synonyms at **show.** —*n.* **1.** The act of displaying; exhibition. **2.** Anything that is exhibited or displayed. **3.** A vulgar ostentation: *She made quite a display of herself.* **4.** *Printing.* **a.** An arrangement or style of type designed to give prominence to printed matter. **b.** Printed matter that is set off prominently. **5.** Designating an advertisement designed to catch the eye, as distinguished from a classified advertisement. [Middle English *displayen,* to unfold, unfurl, exhibit, from Norman French *despleier,* from Medieval Latin *displicāre,* from Latin, to scatter : *dis-* (reversal) + *plicāre,* to fold (see **plek-** in Appendix*).]

dis·please (dĭs-plēz′) *v.* **-pleased, -pleasing, -pleases.** —*tr.* To cause annoyance or vexation to; offend. —*intr.* To cause annoyance or displeasure. [Middle English *displesen,* from Old French *desplaisir,* from Vulgar Latin *displacēre* (unattested), variant of Latin *displicēre* : *dis-* (reversal) + *placēre,* PLEASE.] —**dis·pleas′ing·ly** *adv.*

dis·pleas·ure (dĭs-plĕzh′ər) *n.* **1.** The condition or fact of being displeased or dissatisfied; annoyance; anger. **2.** *Archaic.* Discomfort; uneasiness. **3.** *Archaic.* An annoying or injurious offense. —*tr.v.* **displeasured, -uring, -ures.** *Archaic.* To displease.

dis·plode (dĭs-plōd′) *v.* **-ploded, -ploding, -plodes.** *Archaic.* —*tr.* To explode (something). —*intr.* To explode. [Latin *displōdere,* to spread out, burst asunder : *dis-,* apart + *plaudere,* to beat, strike (see **explode**).]

dis·port (dĭs-pôrt′, -pōrt′) *v.* **-ported, -porting, -ports.** —*intr.* To play; to sport. —*tr.* To occupy (oneself) with diversion or amusement. —*n.* Diversion; play; sport. [Middle English *disporten,* from Old French *desporter,* "to carry away," divert : *des-,* from Latin *dis-,* apart + *porter,* to carry, PORT.]

dis·pos·a·ble (dĭs-pō′zə-bəl) *adj.* **1.** Designed to be disposed of after use. **2.** Subject to use; available. —**dis·pos′a·bil′i·ty** *n.*

dis·pos·al (dĭs-pō′zəl) *n.* **1.** A particular order, distribution, or placement: *a pleasing disposal of window trimming.* **2.** A particular method of attending to or settling matters. **3.** The transference of something by gift or sale. **4.** A throwing out or away. **5.** An apparatus or device for disposing of something, as garbage. **6.** The liberty or power to dispose of or use someone or something: *funds at our disposal.*

dis·pose (dĭs-pōz′) *v.* **-posed, -posing, -poses.** —*tr.* **1.** To place or set in a particular order; arrange. **2.** To put (business affairs, for example) into correct, definitive, or conclusive form. **3.** To make willing or receptive for; to incline: *"I'm a cheerful sort of man and very disposed to laughter."* (P.L. Travers). —*intr.* To settle or decide a matter. —**dispose of. 1.** To attend to; arrange; settle. **2.** To transfer or part with, as by giving or selling. **3.** To get rid of; throw out or away. **4.** To eat or drink (food). —*n. Obsolete.* **1.** Disposal. **2.** Disposition; demeanor. [Middle English *disposen,* from Old French *disposer,* reshaped (after *poser,* to POSE), from Latin *dispōnere,* to place here and there, arrange : *dis-,* in different directions + *pōnere,* to put (see **apo-** in Appendix*).] —**dis·pos′er** *n.*

dis·po·si·tion (dĭs′pə-zĭsh′ən) *n.* **1.** One's customary manner of emotional response; temperament: *"She had a lively, playful disposition, which delighted in anything ridiculous."* (Jane Austen). **2.** A tendency or inclination, especially when habitual: *"A disposition to the drink and aversion to humdrum toil was no novelty in early Kenya."* (Robert Ruark). **3. a.** The act or manner of disposing. **b.** The condition or fact of being disposed. **4.** The power or liberty to control, direct, or dispose: *"some bishops interpreted canon law as giving them disposition of the parish tithes"* (Marshall W. Baldwin).

Synonyms: *disposition, temperament, character, personality, nature.* These nouns refer to the sum of traits that identify a person. *Disposition* is approximately equivalent to habitual frame of mind. *Temperament* applies broadly to the sum of one's emotional characteristics. *Character* emphasizes moral and ethical qualities. *Personality* is the sum of distinctive traits or characteristics of a person that give him individuality, especially in his relationships with other persons. *Nature* suggests those inherent qualities that determine characteristic behavior or emotional response in people.

dis·pos·sess (dĭs′pə-zĕs′) *tr.v.* **-sessed, -sessing, -sesses.** To deprive (someone) of the possession of something, such as real property. —**dis′pos·ses′sion** *n.* —**dis′pos·ses′sor** (-zĕs′ər) *n.* —**dis′pos·ses′so·ry** (-zĕs′ə-rē) *adj.*

dis·po·sure (dĭs-pō′zhər) *n. Rare.* Disposal.

dis·praise (dĭs-prāz′) *tr.v.* **-praised, -praising, -praises.** To express disapproval of; disparage; censure. —*n.* Reproach; censure. [Middle English *dispreisen,* from Old French *despreiser,* from Vulgar Latin *dispretiāre* (unattested), variant of Latin *dēpretiāre,* DEPRECIATE.] —**dis·prais′er** *n.* —**dis·prais′ing·ly** *adv.*

dis·prize (dĭs-prīz′) *tr.v.* **-prized, -prizing, -prizes.** *Archaic.* To hold or regard in low esteem; to disdain. [Middle English *disprisen, dispreisen,* DISPRAISE.]

dis·proof (dĭs-pro͞of′) *n.* **1.** The act of disproving or refuting. **2.** Evidence that disproves or refutes.

dis·pro·por·tion (dĭs′prə-pôr′shən, -pōr′shən) *n.* **1.** The absence of due proportion; disparity. **2.** An instance of a disproportionate relation, as in size. —*tr.v.* **disproportioned, -tioning, -tions.** To make disproportionate.

dis·pro·por·tion·al (dĭs′prə-pôr′shən-əl, -pōr′shən-əl) *adj.* Disproportionate. —**dis′pro·por′tion·al·ly** *adv.*

dis·pro·por·tion·ate (dĭs′prə-pôr′shən-ĭt, -pōr′shən-ĭt) *adj.* Not proportionate; out of proportion, as in relative size, shape, or amount. —**dis′pro·por′tion·ate·ly** *adv.* —**dis′pro·por′tion·ate·ness** *n.*

dis·prove (dĭs-pro͞ov′) *tr.v.* **-proved, -proving, -proves.** To prove to be false, invalid, or in error; refute. [Middle English *dispreven, disproven,* from Old French *desprover* : *des-,* from Latin *dis-* (reversal) + *prover,* PROVE.] —**dis·prov′a·ble** *adj.* —**dis·prov′al** *n.*

dis·put·a·ble (dĭs-pyo͞o′tə-bəl, dĭs′pyo͝o-) *adj.* Capable of being disputed; debatable. —**dis·put′a·bil′i·ty** *n.* —**dis·put′a·bly** *adv.*

dis·pu·tant (dĭs-pyo͞o′tənt, dĭs′pyo͝o-tənt) *adj.* Engaged in argument or dispute. —*n.* A person who disputes; debater.

dis·pu·ta·tion (dĭs′pyo͝o-tā′shən) *n.* **1.** The act of disputing; a debate. **2.** An academic exercise consisting of a formal debate or an oral defense of a thesis.

dis·pu·ta·tious (dĭs′pyo͝o-tā′shəs) *adj.* Inclined to dispute; contentious. —**dis′pu·ta′tious·ly** *adv.* —**dis′pu·ta′tious·ness** *n.*

dis·pute (dĭs-pyo͞ot′) *v.* **-puted, -puting, -putes.** —*tr.* **1.** To argue about; to debate. **2.** To question the truth or validity of; to doubt. **3.** To strive to win (a prize, for example); contest for. **4.** To strive against; oppose; resist. —*intr.* **1.** To argue; discuss; to debate. **2.** To quarrel vehemently. —See Synonyms at **discuss.** —*n.* **1.** A verbal controversy; an argument; a debate. **2.** A quarrel. —See Synonyms at **argument.** [Middle English *disputen,* from Old French *desputer,* from Late Latin *disputāre,* from Latin, to reckon, discuss : *dis-,* separately + *putāre,* to clean, prune, settle an account, hence to reckon, think (see **peue-**[2] in Appendix*).] —**dis·put′er** *n.*

dis·qual·i·fi·ca·tion (dĭs-kwŏl′ə-fĭ-kā′shən) *n.* **1.** The act of disqualifying, or the condition of being disqualified. **2.** Something that disqualifies.

dis·qual·i·fy (dĭs-kwŏl′ə-fī′) *tr.v.* **-fied, -fying, -fies. 1.** To render unfit or unqualified; disable. **2.** To declare ineligible or unqualified. **3.** To deprive of legal rights, powers, or privileges.

dis·qui·et (dĭs-kwī′ĭt) *tr.v.* **-eted, -eting, -ets.** To deprive of peace or rest; to trouble. —*n.* The absence of mental peace or rest; restlessness; anxiety. —*adj. Rare.* Uneasy; restless. —**dis·qui′et·ing·ly** *adv.* —**dis·qui′et·ly** *adv.* —**dis·qui′et·ness** *n.*

ă pat/ā pay/âr care/ä father/b bib/ch church/d deed/ĕ pet/ē be/f fife/g gag/h hat/hw which/ĭ pit/ī pie/îr pier/j judge/k kick/l lid, needle/m mum/n no, sudden/ng thing/ŏ pot/ō toe/ô paw, for/oi noise/ou out/o͝o took/o͞o boot/p pop/r roar/s sauce/sh ship, dish/

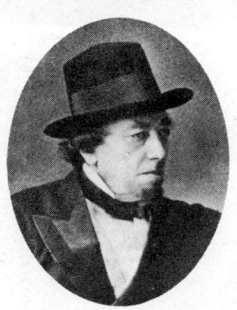

dis·qui·e·tude (dĭs-kwī′ə-to͞od′, -tyo͞od′) *n.* A state of worry or uneasiness; anxiety.
dis·qui·si·tion (dĭs′kwə-zĭsh′ən) *n.* A formal discourse or treatise, often in writing; dissertation. [Latin *disquīsītiō*, inquiry, from *disquīrere*, to inquire diligently : *dis-* (intensive) + *quaerere*, to search for (see **quaerere** in Appendix*).]
Dis·rae·li (dĭz-rā′lē), **Benjamin.** First Earl of Beaconsfield. 1804–1881. British statesman, author, and diplomat; prime minister (1868 and 1874–80).
dis·rate (dĭs-rāt′) *tr.v.* **-rated, -rating, -rates.** To reduce in rating or rank; demote.
dis·re·gard (dĭs′rĭ-gärd′) *tr.v.* **-garded, -garding, -gards. 1.** To pay no attention or heed to; fail to consider; ignore. **2.** To treat without proper respect or attentiveness. —*n.* The lack of thoughtful attention or due regard, especially when willful. **—dis′re·gard′er** *n.* **—dis′re·gard′ful** *adj.*
dis·rel·ish (dĭs-rĕl′ĭsh) *tr.v.* **-ished, -ishing, -ishes.** To have distaste for; dislike: *"Disrelishing the dust of the Avenida, he directed his steps towards the park."* (Ronald Firbank). —*n.* Distaste; aversion.
dis·re·mem·ber (dĭs′rĭ-mĕm′bər) *v.* **-bered, -bering, -bers.** *Regional.* —*tr.* To fail to remember. —*intr.* To forget.
dis·re·pair (dĭs′rĭ-pâr′) *n.* The condition of being in need of repairs; state of neglect; dilapidation: *a house in disrepair.*
dis·rep·u·ta·ble (dĭs-rĕp′yə-tə-bəl) *adj.* **1.** Lacking a good reputation; not esteemed. **2.** Not respectable in character or appearance. **3.** Disgraceful; discreditable. **—dis·rep′u·ta·bil′i·ty, dis·rep′u·ta·ble·ness** *n.* **—dis·rep′u·ta·bly** *adv.*
dis·re·pute (dĭs′rĭ-pyo͞ot′) *n.* Also *archaic* **dis·rep·u·ta·tion** (dĭs-rĕp′yə-tā′shən). The absence or loss of reputation; discredit; disgrace. See Synonyms at **disgrace.**
dis·re·spect (dĭs′rĭ-spĕkt′) *n.* Lack of respect, esteem, or courteous regard; rudeness. —*tr.v.* **disrespected, -specting, -spects.** To show a lack of respect for.
dis·re·spect·a·ble (dĭs′rĭ-spĕk′tə-bəl) *adj.* Lacking respectability; not worthy of respect. **—dis′re·spect′a·bil′i·ty** *n.*
dis·re·spect·ful (dĭs′rĭ-spĕkt′fəl) *adj.* Having or demonstrating a lack of respect; rude; discourteous. **—dis′re·spect′ful·ly** *adv.* **—dis′re·spect′ful·ness** *n.*
dis·robe (dĭs-rōb′) *v.* **-robed, -robing, -robes.** —*tr.* To remove the clothing from. —*intr.* To undress oneself. **—dis·robe′ment** *n.* **—dis·rob′er** *n.*
dis·rupt (dĭs-rŭpt′) *v.* **-rupted, -rupting, -rupts.** —*tr.* **1.** To upset the order of; throw into confusion or disorder. **2.** To interrupt or impede the progress, movement, or procedure of. **3.** To break or burst; rupture. —*intr. Rare.* To burst into pieces. [Latin *disrumpere* (past participle *disruptus*), to break asunder : *dis-*, asunder + *rumpere*, to break (see **reup-** in Appendix*).] **—dis·rupt′er, dis·rup′tor** (-rŭp′tər) *n.* **—dis·rup′tion** *n.*
dis·rup·tive (dĭs-rŭp′tĭv) *adj.* Pertaining to, causing, or produced by disruption. **—dis·rup′tive·ly** *n.*
diss. dissertation.
dis·sat·is·fac·tion (dĭs-săt′ĭs-făk′shən) *n.* **1.** The condition or feeling of being displeased or not satisfied; discontent. **2.** Anything that causes discontent.
dis·sat·is·fac·to·ry (dĭs-săt′ĭs-făk′tə-rē) *adj.* Unsatisfactory.
dis·sat·is·fied (dĭs-săt′ĭs-fīd′) *adj.* Affected by a sense of inadequacy, discontent, or displeasure, or by an insufficiency of something; not content. **—dis·sat′is·fied′ly** *adv.*
dis·sat·is·fy (dĭs-săt′ĭs-fī′) *tr.v.* **-fied, -fying, -fies.** To fail to meet the expectations or fulfill the desires of; to disappoint.
dissd. dissolved.
dis·seat (dĭs-sēt′) *tr.v.* **-seated, -seating, -seats.** To unseat.
dis·sect (dĭ-sĕkt′, dī-, dĭ′sĕkt′) *tr.v.* **-sected, -secting, -sects. 1.** To cut apart or separate (tissue), especially for anatomical study or in surgery. **2.** To examine, analyze, or criticize in minute detail: *dissected the plan afterward to learn why it had failed.* [Latin *dissecāre* (past participle *dissectus*), to cut apart : *dis-*, apart + *secāre*, to cut (see **sek-** in Appendix*).] **—dis·sec′ti·ble** *adj.* **—dis·sec′tor** (-sĕk′tər) *n.*
dis·sect·ed (dĭ-sĕk′tĭd, dī-) *adj. Botany.* Divided into numerous narrow segments or lobes: *dissected leaves.*
dis·sec·tion (dĭ-sĕk′shən, dī-) *n.* **1.** The act of dissecting. **2.** Something that has been dissected, as tissue under study. **3.** A detailed examination or analysis: *"Dead scandals form good subjects for dissection."* (Byron).
dis·seize (dĭs-sēz′) *tr.v.* **-seized, -seizing, -seizes.** Also **dis·seise.** *Law.* To dispossess unlawfully of real property. [Middle English *disseisen*, from Norman French *disseisir*, variant of Old French *dessaisir* : *des-*, from Latin *dis-* (reversal) + *saisir*, SEIZE.] **—dis·sei′zor** (dĭs-sē′zər, -zôr′) *n.*
dis·sei·zee (dĭs′sē-zē′, dĭs-sē′zē′) *n.* Also **dis·sei·see.** *Law.* A person who is disseized.
dis·sei·zin (dĭs-sē′zĭn) *n.* Also **dis·sei·sin, dis·sei·zure** (dĭs-sē′zhər). *Law.* Wrongful usurpation of the powers and privileges of ownership. [Middle English *dysseysyne*, from Norman French *disseisine*, variant of Old French *dessaisine* : *des-*, from Latin *dis-* (reversal) + SEIZIN.]
dis·sem·blance (dĭ-sĕm′bləns) *n.* **1.** The act of dissembling or disguising; dissimulation. **2.** *Archaic.* Absence of resemblance; dissimilarity.
dis·sem·ble (dĭ-sĕm′bəl) *v.* **-bled, -bling, -bles.** —*tr.* **1.** To disguise the real nature of; hide with a specious appearance or semblance: *dissemble one's fears with laughter.* **2.** To make a false show of; feign. **3.** *Obsolete.* To pretend not to recognize or notice; ignore. —*intr.* To conceal one's real motives, nature, or feelings under a pretense. —See Synonyms at **pretend.** [Middle English *dissemblen*, from Old French *dessembler*, to be different (influenced by *dissimuler*, to pretend, dissimulate) : *des-*, from Latin *dis-* (reversal) + *sembler*, to be like, appear, seem (see **semblance**).] **—dis·sem′bler** *n.* **—dis·sem′bling·ly** *adv.*
dis·sem·i·nate (dĭ-sĕm′ə-nāt′) *v.* **-nated, -nating, -nates.** —*tr.* **1.** To scatter widely, as in sowing seed; distribute; disperse. **2.** To spread abroad; promulgate widely. —*intr. Rare.* To become diffused; to spread. [Latin *dissēmināre* : *dis-*, in different directions + *sēmināre*, to sow, from *sēmen*, seed (see **sē-**[1] in Appendix*).] **—dis·sem′i·na′tion** *n.* **—dis·sem′i·na′tive** *adj.* **—dis·sem′i·na′tor** (-nā′tər) *n.*
dis·sem·i·nule (dĭ-sĕm′ə-nyo͞ol′) *n.* A reproductive plant part, such as a seed, fruit, or spore, that is modified for dispersal. [DISSEMIN(ATE) + -ULE.]
dis·sen·sion (dĭ-sĕn′shən) *n.* A difference of opinion, especially one that leads to contention or strife. See Synonyms at **discord.** [Middle English *dissencioun*, from Old French *dissension*, from Latin *dissensiō*, from *dissentīre*, to DISSENT.]
dis·sent (dĭ-sĕnt′) *intr.v.* **-sented, -senting, -sents. 1.** To think or feel differently; disagree; differ. Often used with *from, in,* or *with*: *"When misfortunes happen to such as dissent from us in matters of religion, we call them judgements."* (William Shenstone). **2.** To withhold assent or approval. —See Synonyms at **object** (verb). —*n.* **1.** Difference of opinion or feeling; disagreement. **2.** The refusal to conform to the authority or doctrine of an established church; nonconformity. [Middle English *dissenten*, from Latin *dissentīre* : *dis-*, apart + *sentīre*, to feel (see **sent-** in Appendix*).] **—dis·sent′ing·ly** *adv.*
dis·sent·er (dĭ-sĕn′tər) *n.* **1.** One who dissents. **2.** *Often capital* **D.** One who refuses to accept the doctrines or usages of an established or national church, especially a Protestant who dissents from the Church of England. Compare **conformist.**
dis·sen·tient (dĭ-sĕn′shənt) *adj.* Dissenting, especially from the sentiment or policies of a majority. —*n.* One who dissents. **—dis·sen′tience** *n.*
dis·sen·tious (dĭ-sĕn′shəs) *adj.* Given to dissension.
dis·sep·i·ment (dĭ-sĕp′ə-mənt) *n.* A membranous or calcareous partition between organs or parts; septum. [Latin *dissaepīmentum*, partition, from *dissaepīre*, to separate, divide : *dis-*, apart + *saepīre*, to fence in, enclose, from *saepes*, fence, hedge (see **septum**).] **—dis·sep′i·men′tal** (-mĕnt′l) *adj.*
dis·ser·tate (dĭs′ər-tāt′) *intr.v.* **-tated, -tating, -tates.** Also **dis·sert** (dĭ-sûrt′), **-serted, -serting, -serts.** *Rare.* To discourse formally, learnedly, or at some length. [Latin *dissertāre*, frequentative of *disserere*, to discuss (translation of Greek *dialegesthai*, to discuss, converse, "pick out," "separate"; see **dialogue**) : *dis-*, apart + *serere*, to connect, join (in speech), discuss (see **ser-**[3] in Appendix*).] **—dis′ser·ta′tor** (-tā′tər) *n.*
dis·ser·ta·tion (dĭs′ər-tā′shən) *n. Abbr.* **diss.** A lengthy and formal treatise or discourse, especially one written by a candidate for the doctoral degree at a university; thesis.
dis·serve (dĭs-sûrv′) *tr.v.* **-served, -serving, -serves.** To treat badly; do a disservice to; harm.
dis·ser·vice (dĭs-sûr′vĭs) *n.* A harmful action; an ill turn.
dis·sev·er (dĭ-sĕv′ər) *v.* **-ered, -ering, -ers.** —*tr.* **1.** To separate; break away; sever. **2.** To divide into parts; break up. —*intr.* To become separated or disunited. [Middle English *dis(s)everen*, from Old French *des(s)evrer*, from Late Latin *dissēparāre* : Latin *dis-* (intensive) + *sēparāre*, to SEPARATE.] **—dis·sev′er·ance, dis·sev′er·ment** *n.*
dis·si·dence (dĭs′ə-dəns) *n.* Disagreement, as of opinion or belief; difference; dissent.
dis·si·dent (dĭs′ə-dənt) *adj.* Disagreeing, as in opinion or belief; differing; dissenting. —*n.* One who disagrees; a dissenter. [Latin *dissidēns*, present participle of *dissidēre*, "to sit apart," dissent : *dis-*, apart + *sedēre*, to sit (see **sed-**[1] in Appendix*).]
dis·sil·i·ent (dĭ-sĭl′ē-ənt) *adj.* Bursting apart, as some seed pods do when ripe. [Latin *dissiliēns*, present participle of *dissilīre*, to leap asunder, burst apart : *dis-*, apart + *salīre*, to leap (see **sel-**[4] in Appendix*).]
dis·sim·i·lar (dĭ-sĭm′ə-lər) *adj.* Distinct; unlike; different. **—dis·sim′i·lar·ly** *adv.*
dis·sim·i·lar·i·ty (dĭ-sĭm′ə-lăr′ə-tē) *n., pl.* **-ties. 1.** The quality of being distinct or unlike; difference. **2.** A point of distinction or difference. —See Synonyms at **difference.**
dis·sim·i·late (dĭ-sĭm′ə-lāt′) *v.* **-lated, -lating, -lates.** —*tr.* **1.** To make dissimilar or unlike. **2.** *Linguistics.* To cause to undergo dissimilation. —*intr.* **1.** To become dissimilar. **2.** *Linguistics.* To undergo dissimilation. [DIS- + (AS)SIMILATE.]
dis·sim·i·la·tion (dĭ-sĭm′ə-lā′shən) *n.* **1.** The act or process of making or becoming dissimilar. **2.** *Linguistics.* The process by which one of two similar phonemes is displaced or changed by the other; for example, the English form *marble* from French *marbre.*
dis·si·mil·i·tude (dĭs′ĭ-mĭl′ə-to͞od′, -tyo͞od′) *n.* **1.** Lack of resemblance; difference. **2.** A point of difference; dissimilarity. [Middle English, from Latin *dissimilitūdō*, from *dissimilis*, different : *dis-*, not + *similis*, like, SIMILAR.]
dis·sim·u·late (dĭ-sĭm′yə-lāt′) *v.* **-lated, -lating, -lates.** —*tr.* To disguise (one's intentions, for example) under a feigned appearance. —*intr.* To conceal one's true feelings or intentions. [Middle English *dissimulaten*, from Latin *dissimulāre* : *dis-* (reversal) + *simulāre*, SIMULATE.] **—dis·sim′u·la′tion** *n.* **—dis·sim′u·la′tive** *adj.* **—dis·sim′u·la′tor** (-lā′tər) *n.*
dis·si·pate (dĭs′ə-pāt′) *v.* **-pated, -pating, -pates.** —*tr.* **1.** To drive away or dispel by or as if by dispersing; rout; scatter. **2.** To exhaust or expend intemperately; to waste; squander. —*intr.* **1.** To vanish by dispersion; scatter; disappear. **2.** To indulge in intemperate pursuit of pleasure; carouse: *"He could dissipate without going to pieces"* (F. Scott Fitzgerald). —See Synonyms at **scatter.** [Middle English *dissipaten*, from Latin

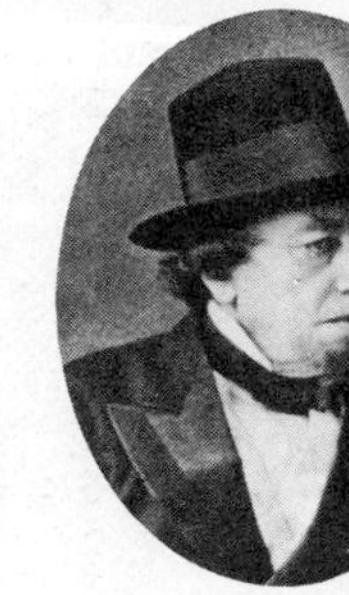

Disraeli

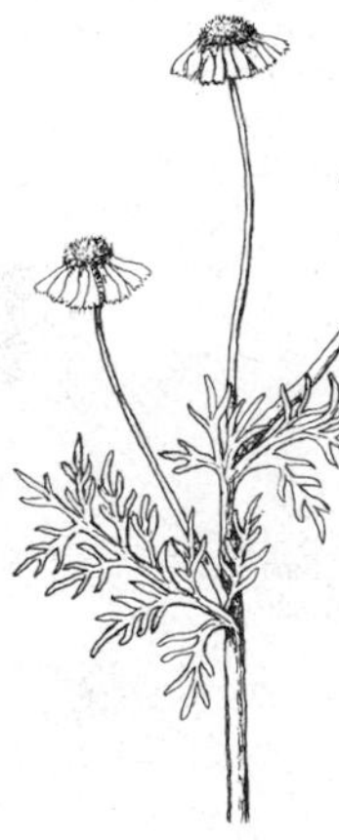

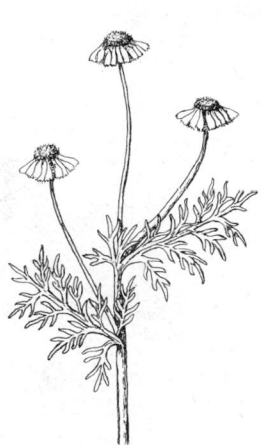

dissected
Dissected leaves of mayweed

dissipāre, to disperse, squander. See **swep-²** in Appendix.*] **—dis′si·pat′er, dis′si·pa′tor** (-pā′tər) *n.* **—dis′si·pa′tive** *adj.*

dis·si·pat·ed (dĭs′ə-pā′tĭd) *adj.* **1.** Intemperate in the pursuit of pleasure; dissolute. **2.** Wasted; squandered. **—dis′si·pat′ed·ly** *adv.* **—dis′si·pat′ed·ness** *n.*

dis·si·pa·tion (dĭs′ə-pā′shən) *n.* **1. a.** The act of scattering. **b.** The condition of being scattered; dispersion. **2.** Wasteful consumption or expenditure. **3.** Dissolute indulgence in pleasure; intemperance. **4.** An amusement; a diversion.

dis·so·cia·ble (dĭ-sō′shə-bəl, -shē-ə-bəl) *adj.* Capable of being dissociated; separable. **—dis·so′cia·bil′i·ty, dis·so′cia·ble·ness** *n.* **—dis·so′cia·bly** *adv.*

dis·so·ci·ate (dĭ-sō′shē-āt′, -sē-āt′) *v.* **-ated, -ating, -ates.** *—tr.* **1.** To remove from association; to separate: *"Marx never dissociated man from his social environment"* (Sidney Hook). **2.** *Chemistry.* To cause to undergo dissociation. *—intr.* **1.** To cease associating; to part. **2.** *Chemistry.* To undergo dissociation. [Latin *dissociāre* : *dis-* (reversal) + *sociāre,* to join, associate, from *socius,* companion (see **sekw-¹** in Appendix*).] **—dis·so′ci·a′tive** *adj.*

dis·so·ci·a·tion (dĭ-sō′sē-ā′shən, -shē-ā′shən) *n.* **1. a.** The act of dissociating. **b.** The condition of being dissociated; separation. **2.** *Chemistry.* **a.** The chemical process by means of which a change in physical condition, as in pressure or temperature, or the action of a solvent causes a molecule to split into simpler groups of atoms, single atoms, or ions. **b.** The separation of an electrolyte into ions of opposite sign. **3.** *Psychiatry.* The separation of a group of related psychological activities into autonomously functioning units, as in the generation of multiple personalities.

dis·sol·u·ble (dĭ-sŏl′yə-bəl) *adj.* Capable of being dissolved. [Latin *dissolūbilis,* from *dissolvere,* DISSOLVE.] **—dis′sol·u·bil′i·ty, dis·sol′u·ble·ness** *n.*

dis·so·lute (dĭs′ə-lōōt′) *adj.* Lacking in moral restraint; abandoned; debauched. [Middle English, from Latin *dissolūtus,* loose, licentious, past participle of *dissolvere,* DISSOLVE.] **—dis′so·lute′ly** *adv.* **—dis′so·lute′ness** *n.*

dis·so·lu·tion (dĭs′ə-lōō′shən) *n.* **1.** Decomposition into fragments or parts; disintegration. **2.** Termination or extinction by deconcentration or dispersion. **3.** Extinction of life; death. **4.** Annulment or termination of a formal or legal bond, tie, or contract. **5.** Formal dismissal of an assembly or legislature. **6.** Reduction to a liquid form; liquefaction. **—dis′so·lu′tive** *adj.*

dis·solve (dĭ-zŏlv′) *v.* **-solved, -solving, -solves.** *—tr.* **1.** To cause to pass into solution. **2.** To reduce to liquid form; melt. **3.** To cause to disappear or vanish; dispel. **4.** To break into component parts; disintegrate. **5.** To bring to an end by or as if by breaking up; terminate. **6.** To dismiss (a meeting or parliament, for example). **7.** To cause to give way emotionally or psychologically; to upset. **8.** To cause to lose definition; to blur; confuse: *"Morality has finally been dissolved in pity."* (Leslie Fiedler). **9.** *Law.* To render null; abrogate; annul. *—intr.* **1.** To pass into solution. **2.** To become liquid; melt. **3.** To break up or disperse. **4.** To become disintegrated; disappear. **5.** To collapse emotionally or psychologically. **6.** To lose clarity or definition; fade away. **7.** *Motion Pictures & Television.* To shift scenes by having one scene fade out while the next appears behind it and grows clearer as the first dims. —See Synonyms at **melt.** *—n. Motion Pictures & Television.* A scene transition made by dissolving. [Middle English *dissolven,* from Latin *dissolvere* : *dis-,* apart + *solvere,* to loosen, untie (see **leu-¹** in Appendix*).] **—dis·solv′a·ble** *adj.* **—dis·solv′er** *n.*

dis·sol·vent (dĭ-zŏl′vənt) *adj.* Capable of dissolving. *—n.* A solvent.

dis·so·nance (dĭs′ə-nəns) *n.* Also **dis·so·nan·cy** (-nən-sē). **1.** A harsh or disagreeable combination of sounds; discord. **2.** Want of agreement or consistency; disparity; variance. **3.** *Music.* A combination of tones conventionally considered to suggest unrelieved tension and to require resolution. Compare **consonance.** —See Synonyms at **discord.**

dis·so·nant (dĭs′ə-nənt) *adj.* **1.** Harsh or inharmonious in sound; discordant. **2.** Disagreeing or at variance: *"Jerome's new presumption, so dissonant from his former meekness"* (Horace Walpole). **3.** *Music.* Constituting or producing a dissonance. [Middle English *dissonaunt,* from Old French *dissonant,* from Latin *dissonāns,* present participle of *dissonāre,* to disagree in sound, be inharmonious : *dis-,* apart + *sonāre,* to sound (see **swen-** in Appendix*).] **—dis′so·nant·ly** *adv.*

dis·suade (dĭ-swād′) *tr.v.* **-suaded, -suading, -suades.** To discourage or deter (a person) from a purpose or course of action by persuasion or exhortation. Used with *from.* [Latin *dissuādēre* : *dis-* (reversal) + *suādēre,* to advise, persuade (see **swād-** in Appendix*).] **—dis·suad′er** *n.*

dis·sua·sion (dĭ-swā′zhən) *n.* The act or an instance of dissuading; exhortation against a course of action. [Latin *dissuāsiō,* from *dissuādēre,* DISSUADE.] **—dis·sua′sive** *adj.* **—dis·sua′sive·ly** *adv.* **—dis·sua′sive·ness** *n.*

dis·syl·la·ble (dĭs′sĭl′ə-bəl, dĭ-sĭl′-, dĭ′sĭl′-) *n.* Also **di·syl·la·ble** (dĭ′sĭ-). A word with two syllables. **—dis′syl·lab′ic** (dĭs′ĭ-lăb′ĭk, dĭ′sĭ-) *adj.*

dis·sym·me·try (dĭs-sĭm′ə-trē) *n., pl.* **-tries.** Lack or absence of symmetry. **—dis′sym·met′ric** (dĭ′sĭ-mĕt′rĭk), **dis′sym·met′ri·cal** (-rĭ-kəl) *adj.* **—dis′sym·met′ri·cal·ly** *adv.*

dist. **1.** distance; distant. **2.** distinguish; distinguished. **3.** district.

dis·taff (dĭs′tăf′, -täf′) *n., pl.* **-taffs** or *rare* **-taves** (-tāvz′). **1.** A staff that holds on its cleft end the unspun flax, wool, or tow from which thread is drawn in spinning by hand. **2.** A woman's work and concerns. **3.** Woman, or women in general. [Middle English *distaf,* Old English *distæf* : *dis-,* bunch of flax, akin to Middle Low German *dise* (see **dizen**) + STAFF.]

distaff side. The female line or maternal branch of a family. Compare **spear side.**

dis·tal (dĭs′təl) *adj.* Anatomically located far from the origin or line of attachment. Compare **proximal.** [DIST(ANT) + -AL.] **—dis′tal·ly** *adv.*

dis·tance (dĭs′təns) *n. Abbr.* **dis., dist.** **1.** The fact or condition of being apart in space or time. **2.** *Geometry.* **a.** A nonnegative number designating the magnitude of a path along a straight line or curve. **b.** The length of a line segment joining two points. **c.** The length of the perpendicular from a given point to a given line. **3.** The interval separating any two specified instants in time. **4. a.** The degree of deviation or difference that separates two things in relationship. **b.** The degree of progress between two points in a trend or course. **5.** A stretch of linear space without designation of limit. **6.** A point removed in space or time. **7.** Chilliness of manner; aloofness. **8.** The section of the track that a horse must reach in a given heat before the winner crosses the finish line in order to qualify for later heats. **—keep one's distance.** To remain reserved or aloof. *—tr.v.* **distanced, -tancing, -tances.** **1.** To place or keep at a distance. **2.** To cause to appear at a distance. **3.** To leave behind, as at a race; outrun; outstrip. [Middle English *distaunce,* from Old French *destance,* from Latin *distantia,* from *distāns,* DISTANT.]

dis·tant (dĭs′tənt) *adj. Abbr.* **dis., dist.** **1.** Separate or apart in space or time. **2.** Far removed in space or time. **3.** Located at, coming from, or going to a distance. **4.** Far apart in relationship; remote: *a distant cousin.* **5.** Far removed from the present situation: *distant thoughts.* **6.** Aloof or chilly in manner: *"his manner I think is distant, his handshake cool"* (Frank Budgen). [Middle English *distaunt,* from Old French, from Latin *distāns,* present participle of *distāre,* to be remote : *dis-,* apart + *stāre,* to stand (see **stā-** in Appendix*).] **—dis′tant·ly** *adv.*

Synonyms: *distant, far, far-off, faraway, remote, removed.* These adjectives mean to be widely apart in space or, less often, in time. *Distant* can be used (with a figure) to indicate a specific separation, or it can indicate an indefinite but sizable interval. *Far* implies a wide but indefinite interval, principally in space. *Far-off* and *faraway* imply a wider interval in either time or space. *Remote* not only means faraway but suggests isolation from the speaker's locality or point in time. *Removed* implies distinct separation in place, time, kind, or character with respect to the speaker.

dis·taste (dĭs-tāst′) *n.* Dislike or aversion. Used with *for.* *—tr.v.* **distasted, -tasting, -tastes.** *Archaic.* **1.** To feel repugnance for; dislike. **2.** To offend; displease.

dis·taste·ful (dĭs-tāst′fəl) *adj.* Unpleasant; disagreeable. **—dis·taste′ful·ly** *adv.* **—dis·taste′ful·ness** *n.*

Dist. Atty. district attorney.

dis·tem·per¹ (dĭs-tĕm′pər) *n.* **1. a.** An infectious virus disease occurring in certain mammals, especially dogs, characterized by loss of appetite, a catarrhal discharge from the eyes and nose, and often partial paralysis and death. **b.** Any of various similar mammalian diseases. **2.** Any illness or disease; an ailment: *"He died . . . of a broken heart, a distemper which kills many more than is generally imagined."* (Fielding). **3.** Ill humor; testiness. **4.** Disorder or disturbance, especially of a social or political nature. *—tr.v.* **distempered, -pering, -pers.** To upset or disturb; to disorder. [Middle English *distemperen,* to upset the proper balance of the humors, to anger, be ill, from Old French *destemprer,* from Medieval Latin *distemperāre* : Latin *dis-* (reversal) + *temperāre,* to mingle in due proportion, TEMPER.]

dis·tem·per² (dĭs-tĕm′pər) *n.* **1.** A process of painting in which pigments are mixed with water and a glue-size or casein binder, used for flat wall decoration or for scenic and poster painting. **2.** The paint used in this process. **3.** A painting done in distemper. **4.** *British.* **Calcimine** *(see).* *—tr.v.* **distempered, -pering, -pers.** **1.** To mix (powdered pigments or colors) with water and size. **2.** To paint in distemper. [Middle English *distemperen,* to dissolve, dilute, mix, from Medieval Latin *distemperāre* : Latin *dis-* (intensive) + *temperāre,* to mingle, TEMPER.]

dis·tend (dĭs-tĕnd′) *v.* **-tended, -tending, -tends.** *—intr.* To become bloated and turgid from or as if from internal pressure; swell out. *—tr.* **1.** To cause to expand by or as by internal pressure; dilate. **2.** To blow up, as in importance; magnify; exaggerate. **3.** To stretch out; extend in all directions. [Middle English *distenden,* from Latin *distendere* : *dis-,* apart + *tendere,* to stretch (see **ten-** in Appendix*).]

dis·ten·si·ble (dĭs-tĕn′sə-bəl) *adj.* Capable of being distended. **—dis·ten′si·bil′i·ty** *n.*

dis·ten·tion (dĭs-tĕn′shən) *n.* Also **dis·ten·sion.** The act of distending or the condition of being distended. [Middle English *distensioun,* from Latin *distentiō,* from *distendere* (past participle *distentus*), DISTEND.]

dis·tich (dĭs′tĭk) *n., pl.* **-tichs.** *Prosody.* A couplet; especially, one used in a Latin or Greek elegiac. [Latin *distichon,* from Greek *distikhon,* neuter of *distikhos,* having two rows or verses : DI- + *stikhos,* row, line, verse (see **steigh-** in Appendix*).]

dis·ti·chous (dĭs′tĭ-kəs) *adj. Botany.* Arranged in two vertical rows or ranks on opposite sides of an axis. Said of leaves. [Late Latin *distichus,* with two rows, from Greek *distikhos.* See **distich.**] **—dis′ti·chous·ly** *adv.*

dis·till (dĭs-tĭl′) *v.* **-tilled, -tilling, -tills.** Also *chiefly British* **dis·til, -tilled, -tilling, -tils.** *—tr.* **1.** To subject (a substance) to distillation. **2.** To extract (a distillate) by distillation. **3.** To purify or refine by or as if by distillation. **4.** To separate (a thought or motif, for example) from the unrelated or attenuating factors of

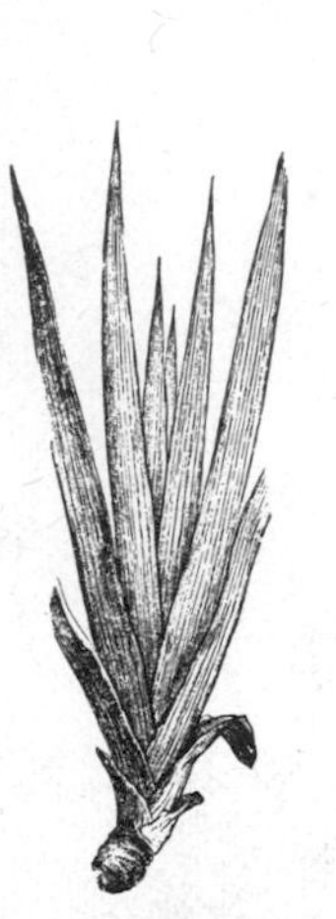

distichous
Distichous leaves of iris

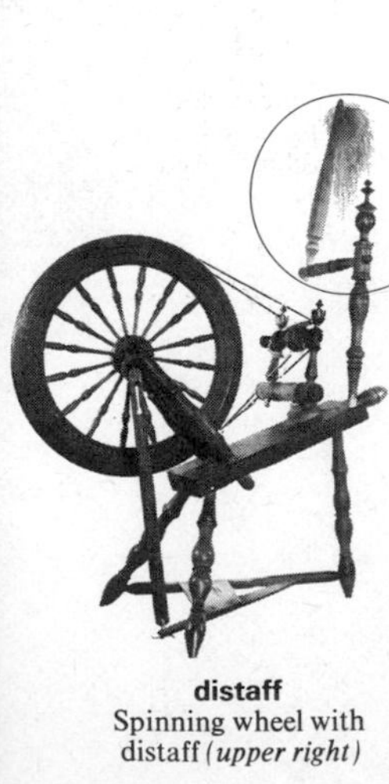

distaff
Spinning wheel with distaff *(upper right)*

ă pat/ā pay/âr care/ä father/b bib/ch church/d deed/ĕ pet/ē be/f fife/g gag/h hat/hw which/ĭ pit/ī pie/îr pier/j judge/k kick/l lid, needle/m mum/n no, sudden/ng thing/ŏ pot/ō toe/ô paw, for/oi noise/ou out/ŏŏ took/ōō boot/p pop/r roar/s sauce/sh ship, dish/

its context. **5.** To exude or give off in drops or small quantities. —*intr.* **1.** To undergo or be produced by distillation. **2.** To fall or exude in drops or small quantities. [Middle English *distillen,* to trickle, drip, distill, from Old French *distiller,* from Latin *dēstillāre, dīstillāre* : *dē-,* down + *stillāre,* to drip, from *stilla*†, drop.] —**dis·till'a·ble** *adj.*

dis·til·late (dĭs'tə-lāt', dĭs-tĭl'ĭt) *n.* **1.** The liquid condensed from vapor in distillation. **2.** Anything regarded as an essence or purified form. Also called "distillation."

dis·til·la·tion (dĭs'tə-lā'shən) *n.* **1.** Any of various heat-dependent processes used to purify or separate a fraction of a relatively complex substance; especially, the vaporization of a liquid mixture with subsequent collection of components by differential cooling to condensation. **2.** A distillate.

distillation column. A tall cylindrical metal shell internally fitted with perforated horizontal plates used to promote separation of miscible liquids ascending in the shell as vapor.

dis·till·er (dĭs-tĭl'ər) *n.* **1.** One that distills, as a condenser; a still. **2.** A producer or maker of alcoholic liquors by the process of distillation.

dis·till·er·y (dĭs-tĭl'ə-rē) *n., pl.* **-ies.** An establishment or plant for distilling, especially alcoholic liquors.

dis·tinct (dĭs-tĭngkt') *adj.* **1.** Not identical; individual; discrete. **2.** Not similar; different; unlike. **3.** Easily perceived by the senses or intellect; clear. **4.** Well-defined; explicit; unquestionable. —See Synonyms at **evident.** —See Usage note at **distinctive.** [Middle English, separated, different, from Old French, from Latin *distinctus,* past participle of *distinguere,* DISTINGUISH.] —**dis·tinct'ly** *adv.* —**dis·tinct'ness** *n.*

dis·tinc·tion (dĭs-tĭngk'shən) *n.* **1.** The action of distinguishing; discrimination; differentiation. **2.** The condition or fact of being dissimilar or distinct; a difference. **3.** A distinguishing factor, attribute, or characteristic. **4.** Excellence or eminence, as of performance, character, or reputation: *a man of distinction.* **5.** Recognition of achievement or superiority; honor: *graduate with distinction.* —See Synonyms at **difference.**

dis·tinc·tive (dĭs-tĭngk'tĭv) *adj.* **1.** Serving to identify; distinguishing: *distinctive tribal tattoos.* **2.** Characteristic: *distinctive habits.* **3.** *Linguistics.* Phonemically relevant. —See Synonyms at **characteristic.** —**dis·tinc'tive·ly** *adv.* —**dis·tinc'tive·ness** *n.*

Usage: *Distinctive* and *distinct* are related but seldom interchangeable without difference of meaning. A *distinctive* odor sets something apart; a *distinct* odor is an unmistakable one. A *distinctive* manner of speaking sharply characterizes a person; a *distinct* manner emphasizes clarity. Two *distinctive* groups are, again, individualistic (with respect to all others); two *distinct* groups are separate ones (primarily with respect to each other).

dis·tin·gué (dĭs'tăng-gā', dĭ-stăng'gā; *French* dēs-tăN-gā') *adj.* Distinguished in appearance, manner, or bearing. [French, "distinguished."]

dis·tin·guish (dĭs-tĭng'gwĭsh) *v.* **-guished, -guishing, -guishes.** —*tr.* **1.** To recognize as being different or distinct. **2.** To perceive distinctly; discern; make out. **3.** To detect or recognize; pick out. **4.** To make noticeable or different; set apart. **5.** To cause to be eminent or recognized. Usually used in the reflexive: *He distinguished himself as a statesman.* —*intr.* To perceive or indicate differences; discriminate. Usually used with *among* or *between.* [Middle English *distinguen,* from Old French *distinguer* (present stem *distinguiss-*), from Latin *distinguere,* to separate, distinguish. See **steig-** in Appendix.*] —**dis·tin'guish·a·ble** *adj.* —**dis·tin'guish·a·bly** *adv.*

dis·tin·guished (dĭs-tĭng'gwĭsht) *adj. Abbr.* **dist. 1.** Characterized by excellence or distinction; eminent; renowned. **2.** Dignified in conduct or appearance.

Distinguished Conduct Medal. *Abbr.* **D.C.M.** A British military decoration for distinguished conduct in the field.

Distinguished Flying Cross. *Abbr.* **DFC, D.F.C. 1.** A U.S. military decoration awarded for heroism or extraordinary achievement in aerial combat. **2.** A similar British decoration awarded to officers of the Royal Air Force.

Distinguished Service Cross. *Abbr.* **DSC, D.S.C. 1.** A U.S. Army decoration awarded for exceptional heroism in combat. **2.** A British decoration awarded to officers of the Royal Navy for gallantry in action.

Distinguished Service Medal. *Abbr.* **DSM, D.S.M. 1.** A U.S. military decoration awarded for distinguished performance in a duty of great responsibility. **2.** A British decoration awarded to noncommissioned officers and men in the Royal Navy and Royal Marines for distinguished conduct in war.

Distinguished Service Order. *Abbr.* **D.S.O.** A British military decoration for gallantry in action.

dis·tort (dĭs-tôrt') *tr.v.* **-torted, -torting, -torts. 1.** To twist out of a proper or natural relation of parts; misshape; contort. **2.** To cast false light on; alter misleadingly; misrepresent. **3.** To cause to work in a twisted or disorderly manner; to pervert. [Latin *distorquēre* (past participle *distortus*) : *dis-,* apart, aside + *torquēre,* to twist (see **terkw-** in Appendix*).] —**dis·tort'er** *n.*

Synonyms: *distort, twist, deform, contort, warp, gnarl.* These verbs mean to change the form or character of something, usually to its disadvantage. *Distort* applies to physical change in shape, as by bending, wrenching, or exaggerating certain features; to verbal or pictorial misrepresentation; and to alteration or perversion of meaning of something spoken or written. *Twist* has similar application but intensifies the idea of marked and deliberate change. *Deform* refers only to physical change that disfigures and usually deprives the object of attractiveness or capacity for normal functioning. *Contort* implies violent physical change that produces unnatural or grotesque effects. *Warp* can refer to physical turning or twisting out of shape or, figuratively, to turning something, such as the human mind or judgment, from a true course. *Gnarl* usually refers to making twisted or knotty in a physical sense.

dis·tor·tion (dĭs-tôr'shən) *n.* **1.** The act or an instance of distorting. **2.** The condition of being distorted. **3.** *Optics.* A distorted image resulting from imperfections in an optical system, such as a lens. **4.** *Electronics.* **a.** An undesired change in the waveform of a signal. **b.** Any consequence of such a change; especially, diminished clarity in reception or reproduction. **5.** *Psychoanalysis.* The modification of unconscious impulses into forms acceptable by conscious or dreaming perception. —**dis·tor'tion·al** *adj.*

distr. distributor.

dis·tract (dĭs-trăkt') *tr.v.* **-tracted, -tracting, -tracts. 1.** To cause to turn away from the original focus of attention or interest; to sidetrack; divert: *"Do not allow any temporary excitement to distract you from the real business."* (C.S. Lewis). **2.** To pull in conflicting directions; unsettle; bewilder. [Middle English *distracten,* from Latin *distrahere* (past participle *distractus*), to pull apart, draw away, perplex : *dis-,* apart, aside + *trahere,* to draw (see **tragh-** in Appendix*).] —**dis·trac'tive** *adj.* —**dis·tract'ing·ly** *adv.*

dis·tract·ed (dĭs-trăk'tĭd) *adj.* **1.** Having the attention diverted. **2.** Suffering conflicting emotions; distraught. See Synonyms at **forgetful.** —**dis·tract'ed·ly** *adv.*

dis·trac·tion (dĭs-trăk'shən) *n.* **1.** The act of distracting or the condition of being distracted; a diversion from an original focus. **2.** Anything that compels attention or distracts; especially, an amusement. **3.** Extreme mental or emotional disturbance; obsession: *"I loved Dora Spenlow to distraction!"* (Dickens).

dis·train (dĭs-trān') *v.* **-trained, -training, -trains.** *Law.* —*tr.* **1.** To seize and hold (property) to compel payment or reparation, as of debts. **2.** To seize the property of (a person) in order to compel payment of debts; to distress. —*intr.* To levy a distress. [Middle English *distreinen,* to seize, compel, detain, from Old French *destreindre* (present stem *destreign-*), from Medieval Latin *distringere,* to seize, compel, from Latin, to draw apart, detain, hinder : *dis-,* apart + *stringere,* to draw tight (see **streig-** in Appendix*).] —**dis·train'a·ble** *adj.* —**dis·train'ment** *n.* —**dis·trai'nor** (-trā'nər), **dis·train'er** *n.*

dis·train·ee (dĭs'trā-nē') *n. Law.* One who has been distrained.

dis·traint (dĭs-trānt') *n. Law.* The act or process of distraining; a distress. [From DISTRAIN (after RESTRAIN, RESTRAINT).]

dis·traught (dĭs-trôt') *adj.* **1.** Anxious or agitated; harried; worried. **2.** Crazed; mad. —See Synonyms at **abstracted.** [Middle English, alteration of *distract,* distracted, from Latin *distractus,* past participle of *distrahere,* to perplex, DISTRACT.]

dis·tress (dĭs-três') *tr.v.* **-tressed, -tressing, -tresses. 1.** To cause anxiety or suffering to; to worry or upset. **2.** To bring into difficult circumstances, especially financial. **3.** *Archaic.* To constrain by harassment. **4.** *Law.* To hold the property of (a person) against the payment of debts; to distrain. —*n.* **1.** Anxiety or suffering; sorrow; unhappiness. **2.** Severe strain resulting from exhaustion, accident, or the like. **3.** The condition of being in need of immediate assistance: *a damsel in distress; a ship in distress.* **4.** *Law.* **a.** The act of distraining or seizing, as goods. **b.** The goods thus seized. [Middle English *distressen, destressen,* from Old French *destresser,* from *destresse,* "narrow passage," strait, constraint, from Vulgar Latin *districtia* (unattested), narrowness, from Latin *districtus,* past participle of *distringere,* "to draw tight," detain, hinder. See **distrain.**] —**dis·tress'ing·ly** *adv.*

dis·tress·ful (dĭs-três'fəl) *adj.* **1.** Causing distress. **2.** Experiencing distress. —**dis·tress'ful·ly** *adv.* —**dis·tress'ful·ness** *n.*

dis·trib·u·tar·y (dĭs-trĭb'yə-tĕr'ē) *n., pl.* **-ies.** A branch of a river that flows away from the main stream and does not return to it; especially, such a branch on the delta of a large river. Compare **tributary.**

dis·trib·ute (dĭs-trĭb'yo͞ot) *tr.v.* **-uted, -uting, -utes. 1.** To divide and dispense in portions; parcel out. **2.** To deliver or pass out: *distributing handbills on the street.* **3.** To spread or diffuse over an area. Often used in the passive: *a widely distributed species.* **4.** To separate into categories; classify. **5.** *Logic.* To use (a term) so as to include all individuals or entities of a given class. **6.** *Printing.* To separate (type) and replace in the proper boxes. [Middle English *distributen,* from Latin *distribuere* : *dis-,* apart + *tribuere,* to allot, grant (see **tribute**).]

Synonyms: *distribute, divide, dispense, dole, deal, ration.* These verbs mean to give something as a portion or share. *Distribute* is the least specific. *Divide* implies giving out portions determined by plan and purpose, often equal parts or portions based on what is due or deserved. *Dispense* stresses even more the sense of careful determination of portions according to what is considered due or proper. *Dole* (usually followed by *out*) implies careful and scant measurement of portions; often it applies to distribution of charity or something given reluctantly. *Deal* suggests orderly and equitable distribution, piece by piece. *Ration* refers to equitable division of scarce items, often necessities, by a system that limits individual portions.

dis·tri·bu·tion (dĭs'trə-byo͞o'shən) *n.* **1.** The act of distributing or the condition of being distributed; apportionment. **2.** Something distributed; an allotment. **3.** The act of dispersing or the condition of being dispersed; a diffusion. **4.** The geographical occurrence or range of an organism. **5.** Division into categories; classification. **6.** *Law.* The division of an estate or property among rightful heirs. **7.** *Commerce.* The process of marketing and merchandising goods. **8.** Any spatial or temporal array of objects or events: *the distribution of theaters on Broad-*

way. **9.** *Statistics.* A set of numbers collected from a well-defined universe of possible measurements arising from a property or relationship under study. See **frequency distribution.** —**dis′tri·bu′tion·al** *adj.*

dis·trib·u·tive (dĭs-trĭb′yə-tĭv) *adj.* **1.** Of or pertaining to distribution. **2.** Serving to distribute. **3.** *Grammar.* Referring to each individual or entity of a group separately rather than collectively; for example, *every* in the sentence *every employee attended the meeting.* **4.** *Mathematics.* Valid, equivalent, or having the same effect whether performed on a set combined in a specified manner or on elements of the set with subsequent combination in the same manner. For example, in the equation $a(b + c) = ab + ac$, multiplication is *distributive* to the right over addition. —*n.* A distributive word or term. —**dis·trib′u·tive·ly** *adv.* —**dis·trib′u·tive·ness** *n.*

dis·trib·u·tor (dĭs-trĭb′yə-tər) *n.* Also **dis·trib·ut·er.** *Abbr.* **distr.** **1.** One that distributes. **2.** One that markets or sells merchandise; especially, a wholesaler. **3.** In the ignition system of an internal-combustion engine, a device for applying electric current in proper sequence to the spark plugs.

dis·trict (dĭs′trĭkt) *n. Abbr.* **dist.** A division of an area or geographical unit either created arbitrarily, as for administrative purposes, or existing as a division by virtue of a characteristic: *a school district; an electoral district; a residential district.* See Synonyms at **area.** —*tr.v.* **districted, -tricting, -tricts.** To mark off or divide into districts. [French, from Medieval Latin *districtus,* (area of) jurisdiction, distraint, from Latin, past participle of *distringere,* to detain, hinder. See **distrain.**]

district attorney. *Abbr.* **D.A., Dist. Atty.** The prosecuting officer of a given judicial district.

district court. **1.** A U.S. Federal trial court serving a judicial district. **2.** In some states, a state court of general jurisdiction.

District of Columbia. *Abbr.* **D.C.** The Federal District of the United States, occupying 69 square miles formerly in Maryland and coextensive with the capital city of Washington. Population, 764,000.

Dis·tri·to Fe·de·ral (dēs-trē′tō fā′*th*ā-räl′). *Abbr.* **D.F.** *Spanish.* Federal District.

dis·trust (dĭs-trŭst′) *n.* Lack of trust; doubtfulness or misgiving; suspicion. —*tr.v.* **distrusted, -trusting, -trusts.** To lack confidence in; doubt or suspect.

dis·trust·ful (dĭs-trŭst′fəl) *adj.* Doubting; suspicious. —**dis·trust′ful·ly** *adv.* —**dis·trust′ful·ness** *n.*

dis·turb (dĭs-tûrb′) *tr.v.* **-turbed, -turbing, -turbs.** **1.** To break up or destroy the tranquillity or settled state of: *"Subterranean fires and deep unrest disturb the whole area."* (Rachel Carson). **2.** To trouble emotionally or mentally; to upset. **3.** To intrude upon; interrupt: *disturb one's sleep.* **4.** To disarrange; put out of order. [Middle English *destourben,* from Old French *destorber,* from Latin *disturbāre* : *dis-* (intensive) + *turbāre,* to throw into disorder, disturb, from *turba,* confusion, probably from Greek *turbē,* disorder (see **twer-¹** in Appendix*).] —**dis·turb′er** *n.* —**dis·turb′ing·ly** *adv.*

dis·tur·bance (dĭs-tûr′bəns) *n.* **1.** The act of disturbing or the condition of being disturbed. **2.** Something that disturbs; an interruption; intrusion. **3.** A commotion or scuffle; especially, a public tumult. **4.** Unbalance or disorder, as of the mind. **5.** A variation in a normal course or condition.

di·sul·fide (dī-sŭl′fīd′) *n.* A chemical compound containing two sulfur atoms combined with other elements or radicals. Also called "bisulfide."

dis·un·ion (dĭs-yōōn′yən) *n.* **1.** The state of being disunited; separation. **2.** Lack of unity; discord.

dis·un·ion·ist (dĭs-yōōn′yə-nĭst) *n.* **1.** One who advocates disunion. **2.** During the Civil War period, a secessionist.

dis·u·nite (dĭs′yōō-nīt′) *v.* **-nited, -niting, -nites.** —*tr.* **1.** To disrupt the union of; to separate. **2.** To estrange; put at odds. —*intr.* To become separate.

dis·u·ni·ty (dĭs-yōō′nə-tē) *n., pl.* **-ties.** Lack of unity; dissension.

dis·use (dĭs-yōōs′) *n.* The state of not being used or of being no longer in use; desuetude.

dis·u·til·i·ty (dĭs′yōō-tĭl′ə-tē) *n.* **1.** Uselessness. **2.** Harmfulness.

dis·val·ue (dĭs-văl′yōō) *tr.v.* **-ued, -uing, -ues.** *Rare.* To regard as of little or no value; disparage. —*n.* Disesteem.

di·syl·la·ble. Variant of **dissyllable.**

dit (dĭt) *n.* The oral representation of the dot in radio and telegraphic code. Compare **dah.** [Imitative.]

ditch (dĭch) *n.* A long narrow trench or furrow dug in the ground, as for irrigation, drainage, or a boundary line. —*tr.v.* **ditched, ditching, ditches.** **1.** To dig or make a ditch in. **2.** To surround with a ditch. **3. a.** To drive (a vehicle) into a ditch. **b.** To derail (a train). **4.** *Slang.* To throw aside; to discard; desert. **5.** *Slang.* To escape from or avoid; to quit. **6.** *Slang.* To bring (a land-based aircraft) down on water. [Middle English *dich,* Old English *dīc,* moat, ditch. See **dhīgw-** in Appendix.*] —**ditch′er** *n.*

dith·er (dĭ*th*′ər) *n.* A state of agitation or indecision. —*intr.v.* **dithered, -ering, -ers.** To be in a dither. [Earlier *didder,* Middle English *didderen* (expressive).]

dith·y·ramb (dĭth′ĭ-răm′, -rămb′) *n.* **1.** A frenzied and impassioned choric hymn and dance of ancient Greece in honor of Dionysus. **2.** An irregular poetic expression suggestive of the ancient Greek dithyramb. [Latin *dīthyrambus,* from Greek *dithurambos,* of non-Indo-European origin, akin to *thriambos,* TRIUMPH, and *iambos,* IAMBUS.] —**dith′y·ramb′ic** *adj.*

dit·ta·ny (dĭt′n-ē) *n., pl.* **-nies.** **1.** An aromatic Old World plant, *Origanum dictamnus,* formerly believed to have magical powers. **2.** A plant, the **stone mint** *(see).* **3.** The **gas plant** *(see).* [Middle English *ditane, diteyne,* from Old French *ditan, ditain,* from Medieval Latin *di(p)tamnus,* variant of Latin *dictamnus,* from Greek *diktamnon,* perhaps after *Diktē,* mountain in Crete.]

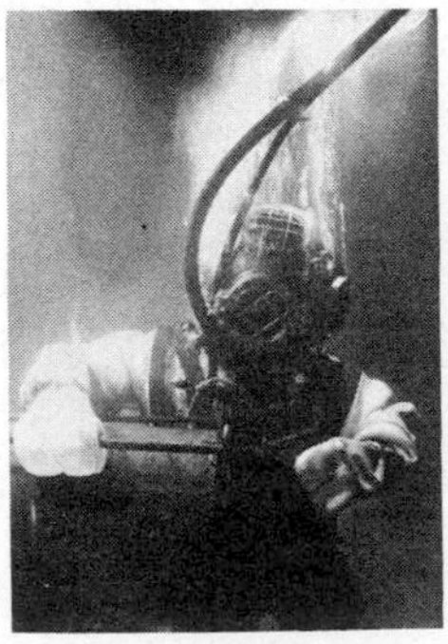

diver
Deep-sea diver

dit·to (dĭt′ō) *n., pl.* **-tos.** *Abbr.* **do.** **1.** The aforesaid; the above; the same as before. Used to avoid repetition and indicated by a pair of small marks (″) placed under the word that would otherwise be repeated. **2.** A duplicate or copy. —*adv.* As before. —*tr.v.* **dittoed, -toing, -tos.** To duplicate or repeat. —*interj.* Used to express sameness or agreement. [Italian dialectal (Tuscan) *ditto,* "said," from Latin *dictus,* past participle of *dīcere,* to say. See **deik-** in Appendix.*]

dit·ty (dĭt′ē) *n., pl.* **-ties.** **1.** A simple song. **2.** The lyrics for such a song. [Middle English *dite, ditti,* from Old French *ditie,* "composition," from Latin *dictātum,* "thing dictated," from *dictāre,* to dictate, compose, frequentative of *dīcere,* to say. See **deik-** in Appendix.*]

ditty bag. A bag used by sailors to carry small items such as sewing implements. [Possibly from obsolete *duttv,* coarse calico, from Hindi *dhōtī,* loincloth, DHOTI.]

ditty box. A box used like a ditty bag.

di·u·re·sis (dī′yōō-rē′sĭs) *n.* Excessive discharge of urine. [New Latin, from Late Latin *diūrēticus,* DIURETIC.]

di·u·ret·ic (dī′yōō-rĕt′ĭk) *adj.* Tending to increase the discharge of urine. —*n.* A diuretic drug. [Middle English *diuretik,* from Late Latin *diūrēticus,* from Greek *diourētikos,* from *diourein,* to pass urine : *dia-,* through + *ourein,* to urinate, from *ouron,* urine (see **wer-⁷** in Appendix*).]

di·ur·nal (dī-ûr′nəl) *adj.* **1.** Pertaining to or occurring in a day or each day; daily. **2.** Occurring or active during the daytime rather than at night. **3.** *Botany.* Opening during daylight hours and closing at night. —*n. Archaic.* **1.** A diary. **2.** A daily newspaper. [Middle English, from Latin *diurnālis,* from *diurnus,* of a day, daily : *diēs,* day (see **deiw-** in Appendix*) + adjective suffix *-urnus.*] —**di·ur′nal·ly** *adv.*

div. **1.** divergence. **2.** diversion. **3.** divided; division; divisor. **4.** dividend. **5.** divorced.

di·va (dē′və) *n., pl.* **-vas** or *Italian* **-ve** (-vā). An operatic prima donna. [Italian, "goddess," from Latin, feminine of *dīvus,* god. See **deiw-** in Appendix.*]

di·va·gate (dī′və-gāt′, dĭv′ə-) *intr.v.* **-gated, -gating, -gates.** **1.** To wander or drift about. **2.** To ramble; digress. [Late Latin *dīvagārī* : Latin *dis-,* apart + *vagārī,* to wander, from *vagus,* wandering, VAGUE.] —**di′va·ga′tion** *n.*

di·va·lent (dī-vā′lənt) *adj.* Having a valence of 2; bivalent.

di·van (dĭ-văn′, dī′văn′ *for sense 1;* dĭ-văn′, -vän′, dī-văn′ *for senses 2, 3, 4*) *n.* Also **di·wan** (dĭ-wän′) (for senses 2, 4). **1.** A long backless couch, especially one against a wall with pillows. **2.** In Moslem countries: **a.** A counting room, tribunal, or public audience room. **b.** The seat used by an administrator when holding audience. **c.** A government bureau or council chamber. **3.** A coffee house or smoking lounge with divans. **4.** In the Middle East, a book of poems by one author. [French, from Turkish *dīvān,* from Persian *dīvān*†, register, account, hence office of accounts, council of state.]

di·var·i·cate (dī-văr′ə-kāt′, dĭ-) *intr.v.* **-cated, -cating, -cates.** To diverge at a wide angle; branch off; spread apart. —*adj.* (dī-văr′ə-kĭt, -kāt′, dĭ-). *Biology.* Branching or spreading widely from a point or axis; diverging. [Latin *dīvāricāre,* to spread apart : *dis-,* apart + *vāricāre,* to straddle, from *vāricus,* with the feet spread apart, from *vārus,* bent, knock-kneed (see **wā-¹** in Appendix*).] —**di·var′i·cate′ly** *adv.*

di·var·i·ca·tion (dī-văr′ə-kā′shən, dĭ-) *n.* **1.** The act of divaricating; a branching off. **2.** A divergence of opinion. **3.** The point at which branching occurs.

dive (dīv) *v.* **dived** or **dove** (dōv), **dived, diving, dives.** See Usage note below. —*intr.* **1. a.** To plunge headfirst into water, often as a sport. **b.** To go toward the bottom of a body of water: *dive for pearls.* **c.** To submerge under power. Used of a submarine. **d.** To fall head down through the air. **e.** To descend nose down at an acceleration usually exceeding that of free fall. Used of an airplane. **f.** To engage in the sport of skydiving. **g.** To drop sharply and rapidly; plummet. **2. a.** To rush headlong and vanish into: *dive into a crowd.* **b.** To plunge one's hand into: *dive into a cooky jar.* **3.** To lunge. Used with *at* or *for.* **4.** To plunge into some question, activity, or study with vigor and gusto. —*tr.* To cause (an aircraft or a submarine, for example) to dive. —*n.* **1. a.** A headlong plunge into water, especially one executed with athletic skill and form. **b.** A nearly vertical descent at an accelerated speed through water or space. **c.** A quick, pronounced drop. **2.** *Slang.* A disreputable or run-down bar or nightclub. **3.** *Slang.* A knockout feigned by prearrangement between prize fighters. [Middle English *diven, duven,* to dive, to submerge, Old English *dȳfan* (transitive), to dip, immerse, and *dūfan* (intransitive), to sink, dive. See **dheub-** in Appendix.*]

Usage: *Dove* is less formal than *dived,* but is not confined to usage that is expressly informal. It is acceptable in writing to 49 per cent of the Usage Panel in the following typical example: *The airplane dove into the sea.*

dive-bomb (dīv′bŏm′) *tr.v.* **-bombed, -bombing, -bombs.** *Aviation.* To bomb at the end of a steep dive toward the target. —**dive bomber.**

div·er (dī′vər) *n.* **1.** One who dives into water. **2.** One who works under water, especially one equipped with breathing apparatus and weighted clothing. **3.** Any of several diving birds, especially the **loon** *(see).*

di·verge (dĭ-vûrj′, dī-) *v.* **-verged, -verging, -verges.** —*intr.* **1.** To tend in different directions from a common point: *"Two roads diverged in a wood, and I—/I took the one less traveled by"* (Robert Frost). **2.** To differ, as in opinion or manner. **3.** To depart from a set course or norm; to deviate. **4.** *Mathematics.* To fail to approach a limit. Compare **converge.** —*tr.* To cause to diverge; deflect. —See Synonyms at **separate.** [Late Latin *dīvergere,* to turn aside : Latin *dis-,* apart + *vergere,* to bend, turn (see **wer-**[3] in Appendix*).]

di·ver·gence (dĭ-vûr′jəns, dī-) *n.* Also **di·ver·gen·cy** (-jən-sē) *pl.* **-cies.** *Abbr.* **div.** **1. a.** The act of diverging. **b.** The state of being divergent. **c.** The degree by which things diverge. **2.** Departure from a norm; deviation. **3.** Difference, as of opinion. **4.** *Mathematics.* **a.** The property or manner of diverging; failure to approach a limit. **b.** The scalar product of the del operator and a vector function. In this sense, compare **curl.** **5.** *Meteorology.* A condition characterized by the uniform expansion in volume of a mass of air over a region, usually accompanied by fine dry weather. —See Synonyms at **difference.**

di·ver·gent (dĭ-vûr′jənt, dī-) *adj.* **1. a.** Drawing apart from a common point; diverging. **b.** Causing divergence of radiation. **2.** Departing from convention; deviant. **3.** Differing: *a divergent opinion.* **4.** *Mathematics.* Failing to approach a limit; not convergent. —**di·ver′gent·ly** *adv.*

di·vers (dī′vərz) *adj.* Various; several; sundry. [Middle English *divers(e).* See **diverse.**]

di·verse (dī-vûrs′, dĭ-, dī′vûrs′) *adj.* **1.** Distinct in kind; disparate; unlike. **2.** Having variety in form; diversified; multiform. [Middle English *divers(e),* from Old French *divers,* from Latin *dīversus,* contrary, diverse, from the past participle of *dīvertere,* to turn aside, DIVERT.] —**di·verse′ly** *adv.* —**di·verse′ness** *n.*

di·ver·si·form (dĭ-vûr′sə-fôrm′, dī-) *adj.* Having a variety of forms; variform.

di·ver·si·fy (dĭ-vûr′sə-fī′, dī-) *v.* **-fied, -fying, -fies.** —*tr.* **1. a.** To make diverse; give variety to; vary. **b.** To extend (activities) into disparate fields. Used of a business enterprise. **2.** To distribute (investments) among several companies in order to average the risk of loss. —*intr.* To spread out activities or investments. Used of a business. [Middle English *diversifien,* from Old French *diversifier,* from Medieval Latin *dīversificāre* : Latin *dīversus,* DIVERSE + *facere,* to make (see **dhē-**[1] in Appendix*).] —**di·ver′si·fi·ca′tion** (-fĭ-kā′shən) *n.*

di·ver·sion (dĭ-vûr′zhən, -shən, dī-) *n. Abbr.* **div. 1.** An act or instance of diverting; a turning aside. **2.** Something that distracts the mind and relaxes or entertains. **3.** In military strategy, a maneuver that draws the attention of the enemy away from the planned point of attack. **4.** A temporary rerouting of traffic. —**di·ver′sion·ar′y** *adj.*

di·ver·sion·ist (dĭ-vûr′zhən-ĭst, -shən-ĭst, dī-) *n.* One engaged in diversionary, disruptive, or subversive activities.

di·ver·si·ty (dĭ-vûr′sə-tē, dī-) *n., pl.* **-ties. 1. a.** The fact or quality of being diverse; difference. **b.** A point or respect in which things differ. **2.** Variety; multiformity: *a healthy diversity in one's diet.*

di·vert (dĭ-vûrt′, dī-) *v.* **-verted, -verting, -verts.** —*tr.* **1.** To turn aside from a course or direction; deflect. **2.** To distract. **3.** To amuse or entertain. —*intr.* To turn aside. —See Synonyms at **amuse.** [Middle English *diverten,* to turn aside, digress, escape, from Old French *divertir,* from Latin *dīvertere,* to turn aside : *dis-,* aside + *vertere,* to turn (see **wer-**[3] in Appendix*).] —**di·vert′er** *n.* —**di·vert′ing·ly** *adv.*

di·ver·tic·u·li·tis (dī′vûr-tĭk′yə-lī′tĭs) *n. Pathology.* Inflammation of a diverticulum.

di·ver·tic·u·lum (dī′vûr-tĭk′yə-ləm) *n., pl.* **-la** (-lə). A pouch or sac branching out from a hollow organ or structure, such as the intestine. [New Latin, from Latin *dēverticulum,* bypath, from *dēvertere,* to turn aside : *dē-,* away + *vertere,* to turn (see **wer-**[3] in Appendix*).] —**di′ver·tic′u·lar** *adj.*

di·ver·ti·men·to (dĭ-vĕr′tĭ-mĕn′tō) *n., pl.* **-ti** (-tē). *Music.* A chiefly 18th-century form of instrumental chamber music having several short movements. [Italian, "diversion," "amusement," from *divertire,* to divert, amuse, from Old French *divertir,* DIVERT.]

di·ver·tisse·ment (dē-vĕr-tēs-mäN′) *n.* **1.** A short ballet or other performance given as an interlude in the opera or theater. **2.** *Music.* A divertimento. **3.** A diversion; an amusement. [French, from *divertir,* DIVERT.]

Di·ves (dī′vēz) *n.* A man of wealth. [Middle English, from Latin *Dīves,* the rich man in the parable of Lazarus, Luke 16:19–31, from *dīves,* rich, costly. See **deiw-** in Appendix.*]

di·vest (dĭ-vĕst′, dī-) *tr.v.* **-vested, -vesting, -vests. 1.** To strip, as of clothes. **2.** To deprive, as of rights or property; dispossess. **3.** *Law.* To devest. —See Synonyms at **strip.** [Alteration of DEVEST.]

di·vide (dĭ-vīd′) *v.* **-vided, -viding, -vides.** —*tr.* **1. a.** To separate into parts, sections, groups, or branches. **b.** To sector into units of measurement; graduate. **c.** To separate and group according to kind; classify. **2. a.** To separate into opposing factions; disunite. **b.** *British.* To cause (Parliamentary members) to vote by separating into groups, as pro and con. **3.** To separate from; cut off. **4.** To apportion among a number. **5.** *Mathematics.* **a.** To subject to the process of division. **b.** To be an exact divisor of. —*intr.* **1. a.** To become separated into parts. **b.** To branch out, as a river. **c.** To form into factions; take sides. **d.** *British.* To vote by dividing. **2.** To perform the mathematical operation of division. —See Synonyms at **distribute, separate.** —*n.* **1.** A dividing point or line. **2.** A ridge of land; watershed. **3.** See **Great Divide.** [Middle English *dividen,* from Latin *dīvidere.* See **weidh-** in Appendix.*] —**di·vid′a·ble** *adj.*

di·vid·ed (dĭ-vī′dĭd) *adj. Abbr.* **div. 1.** Separated into parts or pieces. **2.** In disagreement; disunited. **3.** Pulled by conflicting interests or activities. **4.** Having the lanes for opposing traffic separated. Said of a highway. **5.** *Botany.* Having indentations extending to the midrib or base and forming distinct divisions: *divided leaves.*

div·i·dend (dĭv′ə-dĕnd′) *n. Abbr.* **div. 1.** *Mathematics.* A quantity to be divided. **2. a.** A share of profits received by a stockholder or by a policyholder in a mutual insurance society. **b.** A payment pro rata to a creditor of a person adjudged bankrupt. **c.** *Informal.* A share of a surplus; bonus. —See Synonyms at **bonus.** [French, from Latin *dīvidendum,* "thing to be divided," neuter gerundive of *dīvidere,* DIVIDE.]

di·vid·er (dĭ-vī′dər) *n.* **1. a.** One that divides. **b.** A screen or other partition. **2.** *Plural.* A device resembling a compass, used for dividing lines and transferring measurements.

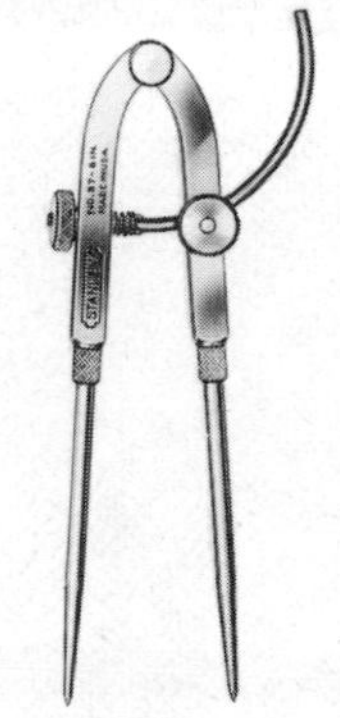
dividers

div·i·div·i (dĭv′ē-dĭv′ē) *n., pl.* **-is. 1.** A tropical American tree, *Caesalpina coriaria,* having compound leaves and long pods. **2.** The dried pods of this tree, yielding an extract used in tanning leather. [Spanish *dividivi,* from Cariban.]

div·i·na·tion (dĭv′ə-nā′shən) *n.* **1.** The art or act of foretelling future events or revealing occult knowledge by means of augury or alleged supernatural agency. **2.** An inspired guess or a presentiment. **3.** That which has been divined. —**di·vin′a·to′ry** (dĭ-vĭn′ə-tôr′ē, -tōr′ē) *adj.*

di·vine[1] (dĭ-vīn′) *adj.* **-viner, -vinest. 1. a.** Being or having the nature of a deity. **b.** Of, relating to, emanating from, or being the expression of a deity. **c.** In the service or worship of a deity or god; sacred; holy. **2.** Superhuman; godlike. **3.** Supremely good; magnificent. **4.** *Informal.* Heavenly; perfect. —*n.* **1.** A clergyman. **2.** A religious. [Middle English, from Old French *devin,* from Latin *dīvīnus,* from *dīvus,* divine, god. See **deiw-** in Appendix.*] —**di·vine′ly** *adv.* —**di·vine′ness** *n.*

di·vine[2] (dĭ-vīn′) *v.* **-vined, -vining, -vines.** —*tr.* **1.** To foretell or reveal through the art of divination. **2. a.** To know by inspiration, intuition, or reflection: *"if we can divine the future, out of what we can collect from the past"* (Burke). **b.** To guess. **3.** To locate (water) with a divining rod. —*intr.* **1.** To practice divination. **2.** To guess. —See Synonyms at **foretell.** [Middle English *divinen,* from Old French *deviner,* from Latin *dīvīnāre,* from *dīvīnus,* soothsayer, "(one) inspired by the gods," DIVINE (adjective).] —**di·vin′er** *n.*

Divine Liturgy. The Eastern Orthodox Eucharistic rite.

Divine Office. *Roman Catholic Church.* The office of the breviary; the canonical hours.

diving beetle. Any of various predatory aquatic beetles of the family Dytiscidae.

diving bell. A large vessel for underwater work, open on the bottom and supplied with air under pressure.

diving board. A flexible board from which a dive may be executed, secured at one end and projecting over water at the other. Also called "springboard."

diving suit. A heavy waterproof garment with a detachable air-fed helmet, used for underwater work.

divining rod. A forked branch or stick that allegedly indicates subterranean water or minerals by bending downward when held over a source. Also called "dowsing rod."

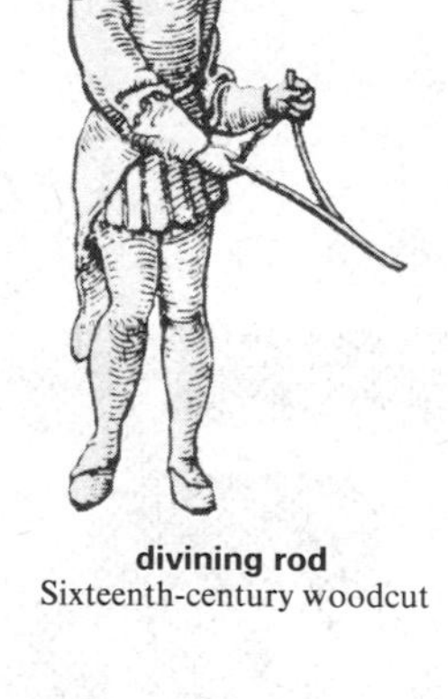
divining rod
Sixteenth-century woodcut

di·vin·i·ty (dĭ-vĭn′ə-tē) *n., pl.* **-ties. 1.** The state or quality of being divine; especially, the state of being a deity. **2. a.** *Capital* **D.** God; the godhead. **b.** A god or goddess; a deity. **3.** Godlike character. **4.** Theology.

div·i·nize (dĭv′ə-nīz′) *tr.v.* **-nized, -nizing, -nizes.** To treat as divine; deify. —**div′i·ni·za′tion** *n.*

di·vis·i·ble (dĭ-vĭz′ə-bəl) *adj.* Capable of being divided, especially of being divided evenly with no remainder. —**di·vis′i·bil′i·ty, di·vis′i·ble·ness** *n.* —**di·vis′i·bly** *adv.*

di·vi·sion (dĭ-vĭzh′ən) *n. Abbr.* **div 1. a.** The act or process of dividing. **b.** The state of being divided. **2.** The proportional distribution of a quantity or entity. **3.** Something that serves to divide or keep separate, as a boundary or partition. **4.** One of the parts, sections, or groups into which something is divided. **5. a.** An area of government or business activity organized as an administrative or functional unit. **b.** A territorial section marked off for political or governmental purposes. **6. a.** *Military.* An administrative and tactical unit that is smaller than a corps but is self-contained and equipped for prolonged combat activity. **b.** *U.S. Navy.* A group of several ships of similar type forming a tactical unit under a single command. **c.** *U.S. Air Force.* An air combat group of two or more combat wings and required service units. **7.** A major taxonomic category corresponding approximately to a phylum, used especially in botany. **8. a.** Variance of opinion; disagreement. **b.** A splitting into factions; disunion. **9.** *British.* The physical separation and regrouping of members of Parliament according to their stand on an issue put to vote. **10.** *Mathematics.* The operation of determining how many times one quantity is contained in another. Compare **multiplication. 11.** A type of propagation characteristic of plants that spread by means of newly formed parts such as bulbs, suckers, or rhizomes. [Middle English *divisioun,* from Old French *division,* from Latin *dīvīsiō,* from *dīvidere* (past participle *dīvīsus*), DIVIDE.] —**di·vi′sion·al** *adj.*

di·vi·sion·ism (də-vĭzh′ə-nĭz′əm) *n.* A branch of neo-impressionism in which colors are divided into their components and mechanically arranged so that the eye organizes the shape. —**di·vi′sion·ist** *n. & adj.*

division sign. The symbol (÷) placed between two quantities to indicate the division of the first by the second.

di·vi·sive (dĭ-vī′sĭv) *adj.* Creating discord or dissension. —**di·vi′sive·ly** *adv.* —**di·vi′sive·ness** *n.*

di·vi·sor (dĭ-vī′zər) *n. Abbr.* **div.** The quantity by which another quantity, the dividend, is to be divided.

di·vorce (dĭ-vôrs′, -vōrs′) *n.* **1.** The dissolution of a marriage by law, or in primitive societies, by established custom. **2.** A complete or radical separation of things closely connected. In this sense, also called "divorcement." —*v.* **divorced, -vorcing, -vorces.** —*tr.* **1.** To dissolve the marriage bond between. **2.** To shed (one's spouse) by legal divorce. **3.** To separate or remove; disunite. —*intr.* To obtain a divorce. —See Synonyms at **separate.** [Middle English, from Old French, from Latin *dīvortium,* separation, divorce, fork in a road, from *dīvortere, dīvertere,* to turn aside, separate, DIVERT.]

di·vor·cée (dǐ-vôr'sā', -vōr'sā', -vôr'sā', -vōr'sā') *n.* A divorced woman. [French, "divorced."]

div·ot (dǐv'ət) *n.* **1.** *Golf.* A piece of turf torn up by the club in striking a ball. **2.** *Scottish.* A thin square of turf or sod used for roofing. [Scottish *deva(i)t, dewot, duvat†.*]

di·vulge (dǐ-vŭlj') *tr.v.* **-vulged, -vulging, -vulges. 1.** To disclose (a secret); reveal; make known. **2.** *Archaic.* To proclaim publicly. —See Synonyms at **reveal.** [Middle English *divulgen,* from Latin *dīvulgāre,* to spread abroad among the people : *dis-,* abroad + *vulgāre,* to make common, publish, from *vulgus,* multitude, public. See **vulgar.**] —**di·vul'gence, di·vulge'ment** *n.* —**di·vulg'er** *n.*

di·vul·sion (dǐ-vŭl'shən) *n.* A tearing apart; violent separation. [Latin *dīvulsiō,* from *dīvellere* (past participle *dīvulsus*), to tear apart : *dis-,* apart + *vellere,* to tear, pluck (see **wel-**⁴ in Appendix*).] —**di·vul'sive** *adj.*

div·vy (dǐv'ē) *n., pl.* **-vies.** *Slang.* A share or portion. —*tr.v.* **divvied, -vying, -vies.** *Slang.* To divide. Usually used with *up.* [Short for DIVIDEND.]

di·wan. 1. Variant of **dewan. 2.** Variant of **divan.**

Dix (dǐks), **Dorothea Lynde.** 1802–1887. American social reformer, philanthropist, and author of children's books.

Dix (dǐks), **Dorothy.** Pen name of Elizabeth Meriwether Gilmer. 1870–1951. American journalist; author of column of advice to the lovelorn.

Dix·ie (dǐk'sē). Those states that joined the Confederacy during the Civil War; the Southern states. Also called "Dixie Land." [Originally a nickname for New Orleans, from *dixie,* a ten-dollar bill issued by a New Orleans bank prior to the Civil War, with a large *Dix* printed on each side, from French *dix,* ten, from Latin *decem.* See **dekm̥** in Appendix.*]

Dix·ie·crat (dǐk'sē-krăt') *n.* A member of a dissenting group of Democrats in the South who formed the States' Rights Party in 1948. —**Dix'ie·crat'ic** *adj.*

Dix·ie·land (dǐk'sē-lănd') *n.* A style of instrumental jazz associated with New Orleans and characterized by a relatively fast, strongly accented two-beat rhythm and by polyphonic group improvisation, as well as improvised solos.

di·zen (dī'zən, dǐz'ən) *tr.v.* **-ened, -ening, -ens.** *Archaic.* To deck out in fine clothes or adornments; bedizen. [Earlier *disen,* to dress a distaff with flax, from (unattested) Middle English, from Middle Dutch, possibly from Middle Low German *dise†,* bunch of flax on a distaff.] —**di'zen·ment** *n.*

di·zy·got·ic (dī'zī-gŏt'ĭk) *adj.* Derived from two separate and separately fertilized ova. Said especially of fraternal twins. [DI- (two) + ZYGOTE.]

diz·zy (dǐz'ē) *adj.* **-zier, -ziest. 1.** Having a sensation of whirling or feeling a tendency to fall; giddy. **2.** Bewildered or confused. **3. a.** Producing or tending to produce giddiness. **b.** Caused by giddiness; reeling. **4.** Characterized by precipitation: *"the American language had begun its dizzy onward march before the Revolution"* (H.L. Mencken). **5.** *Informal.* Scatterbrained; silly; foolish. —*tr.v.* **dizzied, -zying, -zies.** To make dizzy; confuse; bewilder. [Middle English *dusie,* foolish, giddy, from Old English *dysig,* foolish, stupid. See **dheu-**¹ in Appendix.*] —**diz'zi·ly** *adv.* —**diz'zi·ness** *n.*

dj *Library Service.* dust jacket.

DJ disc jockey.

Djai·lo·lo. The Dutch name for **Halmahera.**

Dja·kar·ta (jə-kär'tə). Also **Ja·kar·ta.** Formerly **Ba·ta·vi·a** (bə-tā'vĭ-ə.) The capital of Indonesia, a seaport on the northwestern coast of Java. Population, 2,907,000.

Djeb·el Toub·kal (jĕb'əl tōōb'kăl). The highest peak (13,665 feet) of the Atlas mountains, in southwest-central Morocco.

Dji·bou·ti (jĭ-bōō'tē). Also **Ji·bu·ti.** The capital of French Somaliland, a port city near the southern entrance to the Red Sea. Population, 40,000.

djin·ni, djin·ny. Variants of **jinni.**

Djok·ja·kar·ta (jŏk'yə-kär'tə). Also **Jok·ja·kar·ta.** A city and seaport of Indonesia, on the south-central coast of Java. Population, 313,000.

dk. 1. dark. **2.** deck. **3.** dock.

DKR Airport code for Dakar, Senegal.

dl deciliter.

D/L demand loan.

D layer. The lowest area of the ionosphere, existing only during the day as a layer in the **D region** (*see*).

D.Lit., D.Litt. Doctor of Letters; Doctor of Literature (Latin *Doctor Lit(t)erarum*).

dlr. dealer.

dlvy delivery.

dm decimeter.

DM 1. *Chemistry.* adamsite. **2.** Deutsche mark.

DMSO dimethylsulfoxide.

DMZ demilitarized zone.

dn. down.

DNA deoxyribonucleic acid.

DNB Dictionary of National Biography.

Dne·pro·dzer·zhinsk (nĕp'rō-dər-zhĭnsk'). A city of the Soviet Union, on the Dnieper in the central Ukrainian S.S.R. Population, 207,000.

Doberman pinscher

dobson fly
Larva (*left*) and adult

Dne·pro·pe·trovsk (nĕp'rō-pə-trôfsk'). Formerly **Ye·ka·te·ri·no·slav** (yĭ-kăt'ə-rē'nə-slăf', -släv'). A city of the Soviet Union, on the Dnieper in east-central Ukraine. Population, 738,000.

Dnie·per (nē'pər). *Russian* **Dne·pr** (dnyĕ'pər). A river of the Soviet Union, the third longest in Europe, rising near Smolensk and flowing 1,420 miles generally southwest to the Black Sea.

Dnies·ter (nēs'tər). *Russian* **Dnes·tr** (dnyĕs'tər). A river rising in the Carpathian Mountains and flowing 850 miles generally southeast through the Ukrainian S.S.R. to the Black Sea.

do¹ (dōō) *v.* **did** (dǐd) or *archaic* **didst** (dǐdst), **done** (dŭn), **doing, does** (dŭz). Present tense, first person, **do;** second person, **do** or *archaic* **doest** (dōō'əst), **dost** (dŭst); third person singular, **does** or *archaic* **doeth** (dōō'əth), **doth** (dŭth); third person plural, **do.** —*tr.* **1.** To perform or execute (an action or procedure). **2.** To carry out the requirements of; fulfill; complete. **3.** To create, invent, or compose (a piece or amount of work); make. **4.** To bring about; effect; cause: *It won't do any good.* **5.** To bring or put forth; put into action; exert: *I'll do what I can.* **6.** To attend to or handle the requirements of; deal with as is necessary. **7.** To render or give: *"I leave you to do equal justice to the drawbacks of the alternative establishment."* (G.B. Shaw). **8.** To have for a living (an occupation or profession); work at. **9.** To work out the details of; solve (a problem). **10.** To present (a play or dramatic reading, for example); perform; to stage. **11.** To have the role of; play. **12.** To cover (a specified distance) in traveling: *do a mile in four minutes.* **13.** To travel about; to visit; tour: *do Europe on five dollars a day.* **14.** To meet the needs of sufficiently; be suitable or convenient for; suffice: *This room will do us very nicely.* **15.** To set or style (the hair). **16.** *Informal.* To serve (an amount of time), as a prison term. **17.** *Slang.* To cheat or swindle: *do someone out of his inheritance.* —*intr.* **1.** To behave or conduct oneself; to act: *"They will do as they have been done by."* (Joseph Wood Krutch). **2.** To act effectively or energetically; strive: *Do or die.* **3.** To get along; fare: *doing well at school.* **4.** To be adequate to meet a situation; serve the purpose: *This coat will do for another season.* **5.** Used as an auxiliary in the past or present tense followed by a simple infinitive, or, in reply to a question or suggestion, with the infinitive understood. Its function can be: **a.** To indicate the tense of the infinitive in questions, negative statements, and inverted phrases: *Do you understand? I did not sleep well. Little did I suspect.* **b.** To intensify or emphasize the infinitive: *I do want to be sure. Do be still!* **c.** To represent an antecedent verb, and thus avoid its repetition: *She tries as hard as they do.* **d.** To serve as an expletive, in verse or poetic prose, or in the expression of certain nuances of irony or humor: *There will be some changes made around here, I do believe.* —**do away with. 1.** To dispose of; eliminate. **2.** To destroy; kill. —**do by.** To behave with respect to; deal with. —**do for.** To care or provide for; take care of. —**do in.** *Slang.* **1.** To tire completely; exhaust. **2.** To kill. —**do over.** *Informal.* To redecorate. —**do up. 1.** To adorn or dress lavishly. **2.** To wrap and tie (a package). **3.** To tie up or arrange (the hair) so that it is off the neck. **4.** To launder, mend, or iron (clothing): *do up the week's wash.* —**do without.** To manage easily without; be able to dispense with. —**have to do with. 1.** To have a relation to or relationship with. **2.** To be concerned with; have as subject matter: *a book having to do with religion.* —**make do.** To manage (with whatever one has or whatever is available). —*n., pl.* **do's** or **dos. 1.** *Informal.* A hoax or swindle; a cheat. **2.** *Regional.* Commotion; ado; bustle. **3.** *Informal.* An entertainment; party. **4.** A statement of what should be done: *do's and don'ts.* **5.** *Archaic.* Duty. Used chiefly in the phrase *to do the week's work.* [Do, did, done, dost, does (or doth), didst; Middle English *don, did(d)e, idon, dost; does* (regularly *doth*), *diddest,* Old English *dōn, dyde, gedōn, dēst, dēth* (plural *dōth*), *dydest.* See **dhē-**¹ in Appendix.*]

do² (dō) *n. Music.* The first tone of the diatonic scale in solfeggio. [Italian, variant of *du,* perhaps inverted variant of *ut.* See **gamut.**]

do. ditto.

D.O. 1. Doctor of Optometry. **2.** Doctor of Osteopathy.

D.O.A. *Medicine.* dead on arrival.

do·a·ble (dōō'ə-bəl) *adj.* Able to be done.

do·all (dōō'ôl') *n.* A person employed to do all kinds of work; factotum.

doat. Variant of **dote.**

dob·bin (dŏb'ĭn) *n.* A horse, especially a workhorse. [From *Dobbin,* alteration of *Robin,* pet form for ROBERT.]

Do·bell's solution (dō'bĕlz'). An aqueous solution of sodium borate, sodium bicarbonate, glycerol, and phenol, used as an antiseptic and astringent for the mucous membranes, especially of the nose and throat. [After Horace B. *Dobell* (1828–1917), British physician.]

Do·ber·man pin·scher (dō'bər-mən pǐn'shər). A fairly large dog of a breed originating in Germany, having a smooth, short, usually black coat. [German *Dobermann,* after Ludwig *Dobermann,* 19th-century German dog-breeder + *Pinscher,* terrier, probably from English PINCH (in allusion to its cropped ears and bobtail).]

do·bie (dō'bē) *n., pl.* **-bies.** Also **do·by.** *Western U.S.* Adobe. [Shortened from ADOBE.]

Do·bie (dō'bē), **J(ames) Frank.** 1888–1964. American historian and folklorist.

dob·son (dŏb'sən) *n.* The larva of the dobson fly. Usually called "hellgrammite." [Probably from the family name *Dobson.*]

dobson fly. An insect, *Corydalus cornutus,* having four large, many-veined wings and long, pincerlike mandibles. See **hellgrammite.**

doc. document.

do·cent (dō′sənt, dō-sĕnt′) *n.* A teacher or lecturer at certain universities who is not a regular faculty member. [Obsolete German *Docent,* from Latin *docēns,* present participle of *docēre,* to teach. See **dek-¹** in Appendix.*]

Do·ce·tism (dō-sē′tĭz′əm, dō′sə-tĭz′əm) *n.* The doctrine, espoused by a sect considered heretical in the early Christian Church, that Christ had no human body and only appeared to have died on the cross. [From Late Latin *Docētae,* the sect advocating this doctrine, from Late Greek *Dokētai,* from Greek *dokein,* to seem, appear. See **dek-¹** in Appendix.*]

doc·ile (dŏs′əl; *British* dō′sīl′) *adj.* **1.** Capable of being taught; ready and willing to receive training; teachable. **2.** Submissive to training or management; tractable. **3.** Yielding to handling or treatment; easily shaped or formed: *"metal is so docile that it will submit to any formal conception a sculptor may have"* (Herbert Read). —See Synonyms at **obedient.** [Latin *docilis,* from *docēre,* to teach. See **dek-¹** in Appendix.*] —**doc′ile·ly** *adv.* —**do·cil′i·ty** (dŏ-sĭl′ə-tē, dō-) *n.*

dock¹ (dŏk) *n. Abbr.* **dk. 1.** The area of water between two piers or alongside a pier that receives a ship for loading, unloading, or repairs. **2.** A pier or wharf. **3.** *Often plural.* A group of piers on a protected basin or other waterway serving as a general landing area for ships or boats. **4.** A platform at which trucks or trains discharge or pick up cargo. —*v.* **docked, docking, docks.** —*tr.* **1.** To maneuver (a vessel or other vehicle) into or next to a dock. **2.** *Aerospace.* To couple (two or more spacecraft, for example) in space. —*intr.* To move or come into a dock. [Middle Low German and Middle Dutch *docke,* probably from Vulgar Latin *ductia* (unattested), conduit, aqueduct, from Latin *dūcere,* to lead. See **deuk-** in Appendix.*]

dock² (dŏk) *n.* **1.** The solid or fleshy part of an animal's tail. **2.** The tail of an animal after it has been bobbed or clipped. —*tr.v.* **docked, docking, docks. 1.** To clip short or cut off (an animal's tail, for example). **2.** To withhold a part of the wages or salary of (an employee). **3.** To deduct a part from (one's salary or wages). [Middle English *dok,* trimmed hair (of a tail), perhaps Old English *docca* (attested only in *fingerdocca,* finger muscle), from Common Germanic *dukk-* (unattested), bundle. See also **doxy.**]

dock³ (dŏk) *n.* An enclosed place where the defendant stands or sits in a criminal court. [Flemish *docke, dok*†, cage, pen.]

dock⁴ (dŏk) *n.* Any of various weedy plants of the genus *Rumex,* having clusters of small greenish or reddish flowers. [Middle English *dock, docke,* Old English *docce.* See **dheu-¹** in Appendix.*]

dock·age (dŏk′ĭj) *n.* **1.** A charge for docking privileges. **2.** Facilities for docking vessels. **3.** The docking of ships.

dock·er¹ (dŏk′ər) *n.* One that docks something, such as the tail of an animal, for example.

dock·er² (dŏk′ər) *n.* A dock laborer; longshoreman.

dock·et (dŏk′ĭt) *n.* **1.** A summary or other brief statement of the contents of a document; an abstract. **2.** *Law.* **a.** A brief entry of the proceedings in a court of justice. **b.** The book containing such entries. **c.** A calendar of the cases awaiting action in a court. **3.** Any list of things to be done; an agenda. **4.** A label on or ticket affixed to a package listing the contents or directions for assembling or operating. —*tr.v.* **docketed, -eting, -ets. 1.** To provide with a brief identifying statement. **2.** To enter in a docket. **3.** To label or ticket (a parcel). [Middle English *doggette*†.]

dock·hand (dŏk′hănd′) *n.* A dock worker; longshoreman.

dock·mack·ie (dŏk′măk′ē) *n.* A shrub, *Viburnum acerifolium,* of eastern North America, having clusters of white flowers. Also called "arrow-wood." [Probably from Dutch, probably from Delaware *dogekumak.*]

dock·yard (dŏk′yärd′) *n.* **1.** An area, often bordering a body of water, with facilities for building, repairing, or dry-docking ships. **2.** *British.* A navy yard.

doc·tor (dŏk′tər) *n.* **1.** *Abbr.* **D.** A person who holds the highest academic degree awarded by a college or university in any specified discipline: *a Doctor of Music.* **2.** *Abbr.* **Dr.** A person trained in the healing arts and licensed to practice; especially, a physician, surgeon, dentist, or veterinarian. **3.** *Abbr.* **Dr.** The title used in addressing a person who holds the degree of doctor. **4.** *Obsolete.* A learned person; teacher. **5.** Any rig or device contrived for remedying an emergency situation or for doing a special task. **6.** Any of several brightly colored artificial flies used in fly fishing: *a silver doctor.* —*v.* **doctored, -toring, -tors.** *Informal.* —*tr.* **1.** To give medical treatment to; serve as physician to. **2.** To repair, especially in a makeshift manner. **3.** To change or falsify (evidence) so as to make it favorable to oneself. Often used with *up.* **4.** To add ingredients to (food) in order to improve its taste or appearance. Often used with *up.* —*intr.* **1.** To practice medicine. **2.** To receive medical treatment. [Middle English, church father, theologian, canonist, medical doctor, scholar, from Old French *docteur,* from Medieval Latin *doctor,* from Latin, teacher, *docēre,* to teach. See **dek-¹** in Appendix.*] —**doc′tor·al** *adj.*

doc·tor·ate (dŏk′tər-ĭt) *n.* The degree or status of a doctor as conferred by a university.

Doctor of Philosophy. *Abbr.* **Ph.D., D.Ph., D.Phil.** The highest academic degree granted in most arts and sciences.

doc·tri·naire (dŏk′trə-nâr′) *n.* A person inflexibly attached to certain practices or theories without regard to practicality, applicability, or the like. —*adj.* Pertaining to or characteristic of a doctrinaire; obstinately devoted to speculative, impractical doctrines. See Synonyms at **dictatorial.** —**doc′tri·nair′ism′** *n.* **doc′tri·nar′i·an** *n.*

doc·tri·nal (dŏk′trə-nəl; *British* dŏk-trī′nəl) *adj.* Belonging to, characterized by, or concerning doctrine. —**doc′tri·nal·ly** *adv.*

doc·trine (dŏk′trĭn) *n.* **1.** Something that is taught; a principle or body of principles taught or advocated in instruction: *"the schoolma'am to this day clings to the doctrine that there is such a thing as 'correct English' "* (H.L. Mencken). **2.** A principle or creed of principles presented for acceptance or belief, as by a religious, political, scientific, or philosophic group; dogma; theory. [Middle English, from Old French, from Latin *doctrīna,* teaching, learning, from *doctor,* teacher, DOCTOR.]

doc·u·ment (dŏk′yə-mənt) *n.* **1.** *Abbr.* **doc.** A written or printed paper bearing the original, official, or legal form of something, and which can be used to furnish decisive evidence or information. **2.** Anything serving as evidence or proof, as a material substance bearing a revealing symbol or mark. —*tr.v.* **documented, -menting, -ments. 1.** To furnish with a document or documents. **2.** To support (an assertion or claim, for example) with evidence or decisive information. **3.** To support (statements in a book, for example) with written references or citations; annotate. [Middle English, precept, instruction, from Old French, from Latin *documentum,* lesson, example, warning, from *docēre,* to teach. See **dek-¹** in Appendix.*]

doc·u·men·ta·ry (dŏk′yə-mĕn′tə-rē) *adj.* Also **doc·u·men·tal** (-mĕnt′l). **1.** Consisting of, concerning, or based upon documents. **2.** Presenting facts objectively without editorializing or inserting fictional matter, as in a book, newspaper account, or film. —*n., pl.* **documentaries.** A television or motion-picture presentation of factual, political, social, or historical events or circumstances, often consisting of actual news films accompanied by narration.

doc·u·men·ta·tion (dŏk′yə-mĕn-tā′shən) *n.* **1.** The supplying of documents or supporting references or records. **2.** The documents or references supplied.

dod·der¹ (dŏd′ər) *intr.v.* **-dered, -dering, -ders. 1.** To shake or tremble, as from old age; totter. **2.** To progress in a feeble, unsteady manner. [Alteration of earlier *dadder,* from Middle English *dadiren,* perhaps from Scandinavian, akin to Norwegian *dudra,* to quiver. See **dud-** in Appendix.*]

dod·der² (dŏd′ər) *n.* Any of various parasitic vines of the genus *Cuscuta,* having slender, twining yellow or reddish stems with a few minute, scalelike leaves, and small whitish flowers. [Middle English *doder,* perhaps from Scandinavian, akin to Norwegian *dudra,* to quiver. See **dud-** in Appendix.*]

dod·dered (dŏd′ərd) *adj.* **1.** Lacking the top branches as a result of age or decay. **2.** Infirm or feeble. [Alteration of *doddard* : *dod,* to lop off, Middle English *doden*† + -ARD.]

dod·der·ing (dŏd′ər-ĭng) *adj.* Feeble-minded from age; senile.

do·dec·a·gon (dō-dĕk′ə-gŏn′) *n.* A polygon with 12 sides. [Greek *dōdekagōnon* : *dōdeka, duōdeka,* twelve : *duo,* two (see **dwō** in Appendix*) + *deka,* ten (see **dekm̥** in Appendix*) + -GON.] —**do′de·cag′o·nal** (dō′dĕ-kăg′ə-nəl) *adj.*

do·dec·a·he·dron (dō′dĕk-ə-hē′drən) *n., pl.* **-drons** or **-dra** (-drə). A polyhedron with 12 faces. [Greek *dōdekaedron,* having 12 surfaces : *dōdeka,* twelve (see **dodecagon**) + -HEDRON.] —**do′dec·a·he′dral** *adj.*

Do·dec·a·nese (dō-dĕk′ə-nēs′, -nēz′). A group of Greek islands, 1,044 square miles in area, in the Aegean Sea between Turkey and Crete. Capital, Rhodes, on the island of Rhodes.

do·dec·a·phon·ic (dō′dĕk-ə-fŏn′ĭk) *adj.* Pertaining to, composed in, or consisting of 12-tone music. [Greek *dōdeka,* twelve (see **dodecagon**) + PHONIC.] —**do·dec′a·phon·ist** (dō-dĕk′ə-fə-nĭst, dō′də-kăf′ə-) *n.* —**do·dec′a·phon′y** (-fō′nē, dō′-də-kăf′ə-), **do·dec′a·phon·ism′** *n.*

dodge (dŏj) *v.* **dodged, dodging, dodges.** —*tr.* **1.** To avoid (a blow, for example) by moving or shifting quickly aside. **2.** To evade (an obligation or issue, for example) by cunning, trickery, or deceit. —*intr.* **1.** To move aside quickly; shift or twist suddenly. **2.** To practice trickery or cunning; prevaricate. —*n.* **1.** An act of dodging; a quick move or shift. **2.** A clever or evasive plan or device; stratagem. —See Synonyms at **artifice.** [Origin unknown.]

Dodge (dŏj), **Mary (Elizabeth) Mapes.** 1831–1905. American editor and author of books for children.

Dodge City (dŏj). A city of Kansas, on the Arkansas River in the southwest; a former frontier town on the Santa Fe Trail. Population, 13,000.

dodg·er (dŏj′ər) *n.* **1.** A person who dodges or evades. **2.** A shifty or dishonest person; a cheat; trickster. **3.** A small printed handbill. **4.** *Southern U.S.* A corndodger.

Dodg·son, Charles Lutwidge. See Lewis **Carroll.**

do·do (dō′dō) *n., pl.* **-does** or **-dos. 1.** A large flightless bird, *Raphus cucullatus,* of the island of Mauritius in the Indian Ocean, that has been extinct since the late 17th century. **2.** *Informal.* One whose ideas, dress, or manner of living is hopelessly passé. [Portuguese *doudo,* from *doudo*†, stupid (from its clumsy appearance).]

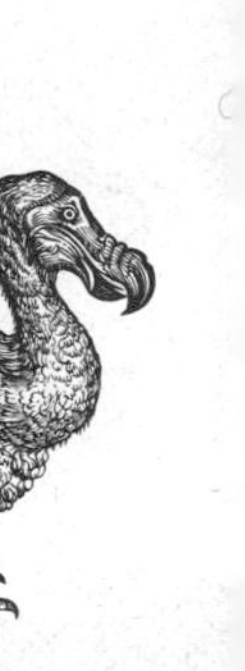

dodo

doe (dō) *n., pl.* **does** or **doe. 1.** The female of a deer or related animal. **2.** The female of certain other animals, such as the hare or kangaroo. [Middle English *do,* Old English *dā,* akin to German dialectal *te*†.]

do·er (do͞o′ər) *n.* **1.** A person who does something, as an agent. **2.** A particularly active and energetic person.

does. Present tense, third person singular of **do.**

doe·skin (dō′skĭn′) *n.* **1.** The skin of a doe, deer, or goat. **2.** Leather made from this and used especially for gloves. **3.** A fine, soft, smooth woolen fabric. **4.** A densely napped finish for certain woolen fabrics, such as flannel.

does·n't (dŭz′ənt). Contraction of *does not.*

doest. *Archaic.* Second person singular, present tense of **do.**

doeth. *Archaic.* Third person singular, present tense of **do.**

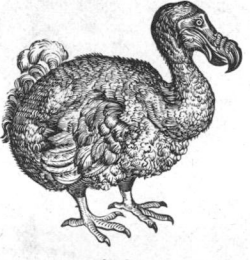

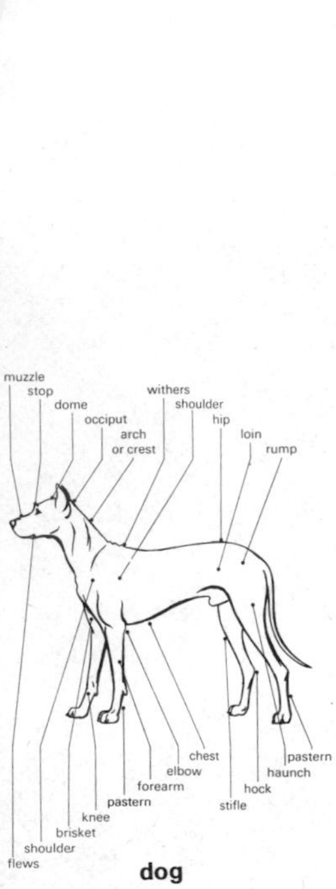

dog

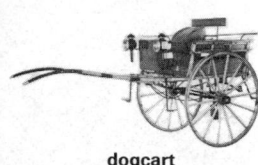

dogcart
Horse-drawn dogcart

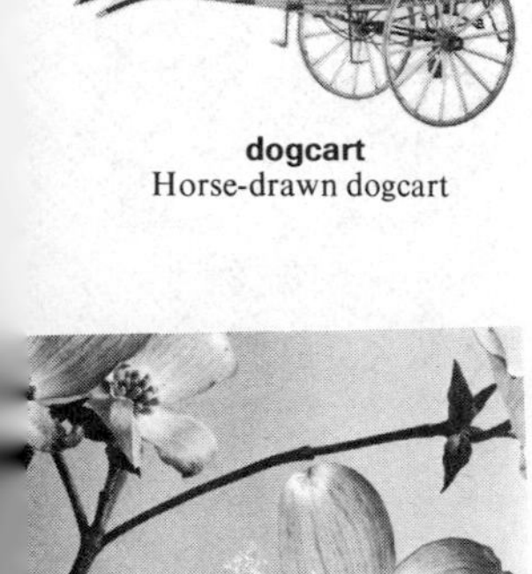
dogwood
Flowers of the pink dogwood

doff (dôf, dŏf) *tr.v.* **doffed, doffing, doffs. 1.** To remove or take off: *doff one's clothes.* **2.** To lift or remove (one's hat) in salutation; to tip. **3.** To throw out or away; discard. [Middle English *doffen,* from *don off* : *don,* to DO + OFF.]

dog (dôg, dŏg) *n.* **1.** A domesticated carnivorous mammal, *Canis familiaris,* raised in a wide variety of breeds and probably originally derived from several wild species. **2.** Any of various other animals of the family Canidae, such as the dingo. **3.** A male canine animal, especially of a domesticated breed or of the fox. **4.** Any of various other animals, such as the prairie dog. **5.** *Informal.* A fellow: *you lucky dog.* **6.** *Slang.* **a.** An uninteresting, unattractive, or unresponsive person: *a date with a real dog.* **b.** A hopelessly inferior product or creation: *That play was some dog!* **7.** A contemptible, wretched fellow. **8.** *Plural. Slang.* The feet. **9.** A firedog; andiron. **10.** Any of various hooked or U-shaped metallic devices used for gripping or holding heavy objects. **11.** *Astronomy.* **Sun dog** *(see).* **—go to the dogs.** *Informal.* To go to ruin; to degenerate. **—put on the dog.** *Informal.* To make an ostentatious display of elegance, wealth, or culture; feign refinement. *—adj.* Inferior; undesirable; not genuine: *dog Latin.* *—adv.* Totally; completely. Used in combination: *dog-tired.* *—tr.v.* **dogged, dogging, dogs. 1.** To follow after like a dog; track or trail persistently: *"a stranger then is still dogging us"* (Arthur Conan Doyle). **2.** To hold or fasten with a mechanical dog. [Middle English *dog, dogge,* Old English *docga*†.]

dog-ape (dôg′āp′, dŏg′-) *n.* Broadly, a baboon or similar monkey.

dog·bane (dôg′bān′, dŏg′-) *n.* Any of several plants of the genus *Apocynum,* having milky juice and bell-shaped white or pink flowers. [Said to be poisonous to dogs.]

dog·ber·ry (dôg′bĕr′ē, dŏg′-) *n., pl.* **-ries. 1.** A wild gooseberry, *Ribes cynosbati,* of eastern North America, bearing large, prickly berries. **2.** Any of several other plants or shrubs bearing berrylike fruit. **3.** The fruit of any of these plants.

dog·cart (dôg′kärt′, dŏg′-) *n.* **1.** A vehicle drawn by one horse and accommodating two persons seated back to back. **2.** A small cart pulled by dogs.

dog·catch·er (dôg′kăch′ər, dŏg′-) *n.* One appointed or elected to impound stray dogs.

dog collar. 1. A collar for a dog. **2.** *Slang.* A clerical collar. **3.** A **choker** *(see).*

dog days. The hot, sultry period between mid-July and September. [Translation of Late Latin *diēs caniculārēs,* "Dog Star days" (so called because Sirius rises and sets with the sun during this time).]

doge (dōj) *n.* The elected chief magistrate of the former republics of Venice and Genoa. [French, from Italian (Venetian dialect), from Latin *dux* (stem *duc-*), leader, from *dūcere,* to lead. See **deuk-** in Appendix.*]

dog-ear (dôg′îr′, dŏg′-) *n.* Also **dog's-ear** (dôgz′îr′, dŏgz′-). A turned-down corner of the page of a book. *—tr.v.* **dog-eared, -earing, -ears. 1.** To turn down the corner of (a book page). **2.** To make worn or shabby from overuse.

dog-eat-dog (dôg′ēt-dôg′, dŏg′ēt-dŏg′) *adj.* Ruthlessly competitive or acquisitive: *a dog-eat-dog society.*

dog·face (dôg′fās′, dŏg′-) *n. Slang.* An infantryman in the U.S. Army in World War II.

dog fennel. 1. Any of various strong-smelling plants of the genus *Anthemis,* such as the **mayweed** *(see).* **2.** A weedy plant, *Eupatorium capillifolium,* of the southeastern United States, having divided leaves and long clusters of greenish flowers.

dog·fight (dôg′fīt′, dŏg′-) *n.* **1.** A violent fight between or as if between dogs; a brawl. **2.** An aerial battle, especially between fighter planes.

dog·fish (dôg′fĭsh′, dŏg′-) *n., pl.* **dogfish** or **-fishes. 1.** Any of various small sharks, chiefly of the family Squalidae, of Atlantic and Pacific coastal waters. Also called "grayfish." **2.** The **bowfin** *(see).*

dog·ged (dô′gĭd, dŏg′ĭd) *adj.* Not yielding readily; willful; stubborn: *"his manner displayed a kind of dogged self-assertion which had nothing aggressive in it"* (Conrad). See Synonyms at **obstinate.** **—dog′ged·ly** *adv.* **—dog′ged·ness** *n.*

Dog·ger Bank (dô′gər, dŏg′ər). A submerged sand bank and fishing area in the North Sea between Denmark and England.

dog·ger·el (dô′gər-əl, dŏg′ər-) *n.* Also **dog·grel** (dôg′rəl, dŏg′-). Verse of a loose, irregular rhythm or of a trivial nature. *—adj.* Also **dog·grel.** Pertaining to or written in such verse. [Middle English *dogerel,* poor, worthless, perhaps from *dogge,* DOG.]

dog·ger·y (dô′gə-rē, dŏg′ə-) *n., pl.* **-ies. 1.** Surly behavior; meanness. **2.** Dogs collectively.

dog·gish (dô′gĭsh, dŏg′ĭsh) *adj.* **1.** Pertaining to or suggestive of a dog. **2.** Surly. **3.** *Informal.* Stylish.

dog·gone (dôg′gôn′, -gŏn′, dŏg′-). Euphemism for **damn.**

dog·gy, dog·gie (dô′gē, dŏg′ē) *n., pl.* **-gies.** A dog, especially a small one. *—adj.* **doggier, -giest.** Of or like a dog.

dog·house (dôg′hous′, dŏg′-) *n.* A small house or shelter for a dog. **—in the doghouse.** *Slang.* In disfavor; in trouble. Used chiefly of husbands.

do·gie (dō′gē) *n.* Also **do·gy** *pl.* **-gies.** *Western U.S.* A motherless or stray calf. [Origin unknown.]

dog in the manger. One who prevents others from enjoying what he himself has no use for. [From a fable of Aesop.]

dog·leg (dôg′lĕg′, dŏg′-) *n.* Something that has a sharp bend; especially, a golf hole in which the fairway is abruptly angled. **—dog′leg′ged** (-lĕg′ĭd, -lĕgd′) *adj.*

dog·ma (dôg′mə, dŏg′-) *n., pl.* **-mas** or **-mata** (-mə-tə). **1.** *Theology.* A system of doctrines proclaimed true by a religious sect: *Christian dogma.* **2.** A principle, belief, or statement of idea or opinion, especially one formally or authoritatively considered to be absolute truth: *"the battle-cry of freedom may become a dogma which crushes the soul"* (John Jay Chapman). **3.** A system of such principles or beliefs: *"The dogmas of the quiet past are inadequate to the stormy present."* (Lincoln). [Latin, from Greek, opinion, belief, public decree, from *dokein,* to seem, to think. See **dek-**[1] in Appendix.*]

dog·mat·ic (dôg-măt′ĭk, dŏg-) *adj.* Also **dog·mat·i·cal** (-ĭ-kəl). **1.** Pertaining to or characteristic of dogma. **2.** Characterized by an authoritative, arrogant assertion of unproved or unprovable principles; overpositive. —See Synonyms at **dictatorial.** [Late Latin *dogmaticus,* from Greek *dogmatikos,* from *dogma* (stem *dogmat-*), DOGMA.] **—dog·mat′i·cal·ly** *adv.*

dog·mat·ics (dôg-măt′ĭks, dŏg-) *n.* Plural in form, used with a singular verb. The study of religious dogmas, especially those of the Christian church. Also called "dogmatic theology."

dog·ma·tism (dôg′mə-tĭz′əm, dŏg′-) *n.* Dogmatic assertion of opinion or belief.

dog·ma·tist (dôg′mə-tĭst, dŏg′-) *n.* **1.** An arrogantly assertive person. **2.** One who expresses or sets forth dogma.

dog·ma·tize (dôg′mə-tīz′, dŏg′-) *v.* **-tized, -tizing, -tizes.** *—intr.* To express oneself dogmatically in writing or speech. *—tr.* To proclaim as dogma. **—dog′ma·ti·za′tion** *n.*

do-good·er (do͞o′go͝od′ər) *n. Informal.* One who is impractical and naively idealistic in supporting philanthropic or humanitarian reforms. **—do′-good′ism′** *n.*

dog paddle. A prone swimming stroke in which the arms and legs remain submerged and each limb paddles in alternation.

dog rose. A prickly wild rose, *Rosa canina,* native to Europe, having fragrant pink or white flowers.

dog's age. *Informal.* A long time.

dog's-ear. Variant of **dog-ear.**

dog sled. Also **dog sledge.** A sled pulled by one or more dogs.

dog's life. *Informal.* An unhappy, slavish existence.

dog's mercury. A creeping, ill-smelling Old World weed, *Mercurialis perennis,* having small greenish flowers.

dog's-tail (dôgz′tāl′, dŏgz′-) *n.* Any grass of the genus *Cynosurus,* native to Europe; especially, *C. cristatus,* having spikelets in a densely crowded, narrow cluster.

Dog Star. 1. The star **Sirius** *(see).* **2.** The star **Procyon** *(see).*

dog tag. 1. A metal identification disk attached to a dog's collar. **2.** A military identification tag worn in duplicate on a chain around the neck.

dog-tired (dôg′tīrd′, dŏg′-) *adj.* Extremely tired; exhausted.

dog·tooth (dôg′to͞oth′, dŏg′-) *n., pl.* **teeth** (-tēth′). Also **dog tooth** (for sense 1). **1.** A canine tooth; an eyetooth. **2.** *Architecture.* A medieval architectural ornament consisting of four leaflike projections radiating from a raised center.

dogtooth violet. Any of several plants of the genus *Erythronium;* especially, *E. americanum,* of North America, having leaves with reddish blotches and nodding, lilylike yellow flowers. Also called "adder's-tongue," "trout lily."

dog·trot (dôg′trŏt′, dŏg′-) *n.* A steady trot like that of a dog.

dog·watch (dôg′wŏch′, dŏg′-) *n. Nautical.* Either of two short periods of watch duty, from 4 to 6 P.M. or from 6 to 8 P.M.

dog·wood (dôg′wo͝od′, dŏg′-) *n.* **1.** A tree, *Cornus florida,* of eastern North America, having small greenish flowers surrounded by showy white or sometimes pink bracts that resemble petals. Also called "flowering dogwood." **2.** Any of several other trees or shrubs of the genus *Cornus.*

do·gy. Variant of **dogie.**

Do·ha (dō′hə, -hă). The capital and chief commercial center of Qatar, a port on the Persian Gulf. Population, 45,000.

doi·ly (doi′lē) *n., pl.* **-lies.** Also **doy·ly, doy·ley** *pl.* **-leys. 1.** A small ornamental mat made of lace, linen, or the like, and used to protect or adorn furniture. **2.** A small table napkin. [After *Doyly* or *Doily,* a London draper, circa 1712.]

Doi·sy (doi′zē), **Edward Adelbert.** Born 1893. American biochemist; worked on vitamins.

doit (doit) *n.* **1.** A former Dutch coin worth about ¼ cent. **2.** Any small part of something; a bit. [Dutch *duit,* from Middle Dutch. See **twei-** in Appendix.*]

do-it-your·self (do͞o′ĭt-yər-sĕlf′) *adj. Informal.* Of or designed to be done by an amateur without professional help.

dol (dŏl) *n.* A unit used to measure pain, or by inference analgesia, based on application of heat to the skin. See **dolorimetry.** [From Latin *dolor,* pain, DOLOR.]

dol. 1. dollar. **2.** *Music.* dolce.

do·lab·ri·form (dō-lăb′rə-fôrm′) *adj.* Also **do·lab·rate** (-rāt′). *Biology.* Having the shape of the head of an ax. [Latin *dolābra,* pickax, from *dolāre,* to hew (see **del-**[3] in Appendix*) + -FORM.]

dol·ce (dōl′chā′) *adv. Abbr.* **dol.** *Music.* Gently and sweetly. Used as a direction. [Italian, "sweet," from Latin *dulcis.* See **dlku-** in Appendix.*] **—dol′ce** *adj.*

dol·ce far nien·te (dōl′chā fär nyĕn′tā). *Italian.* Delicious inactivity. Literally, sweet to do nothing.

dol·drums (dōl′drəmz′, dôl′-, dŏl′-) *n.* Plural in form, used with a singular verb and usually preceded by *the.* **1. a.** Ocean regions near the equator, characterized by calms or light winds. **b.** The calms characteristic of these areas. **2.** A period of inactivity, listlessness, or depression. [British dialect, perhaps ultimately from Old English *dol,* dull (probably influenced in form by TANTRUM). See **dheu-**[1] in Appendix.*]

dole[1] (dōl) *n.* **1.** The distribution or dispensing of goods, especially of money, food, or clothing as charity. **2.** A gift or share of money, food, or clothing distributed as charity. **3.** *Chiefly British.* The distribution by the government of relief payments to the unemployed. **4.** *Archaic.* One's fate. **—on the dole.**

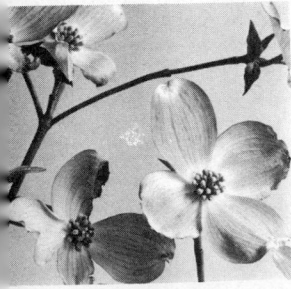

Chiefly British. Receiving regular relief payments from the government. *—tr.v.* **doled, doling, doles.** To distribute in small portions; give out sparingly. Usually used with *out.* See Synonyms at **distribute.** [Middle English *dol(e),* part, division, Old English *dāl,* share, portion. See **dail-** in Appendix.*]
dole² (dōl) *n. Archaic.* Grief; sorrow; dolor. [Middle English *dol,* from Old French *dol, duel,* from Late Latin *dolus,* pain, grief, from Latin *dolēre,* to feel pain, grieve for. See **del-³** in Appendix.*]
Dole (dōl), **Sanford Ballard.** 1844–1926. American jurist; president of Republic of Hawaii (1894–98); first governor of Territory of Hawaii (1900–03).
dole·ful (dōl′fəl) *adj.* Filled with grief; mournful; melancholy. See Synonyms at **sad.** **—dole′ful·ly** *adv.* **—dole′ful·ness** *n.*
dol·er·ite (dŏl′ə-rīt′) *n.* **1.** *Chiefly British.* A coarse variety of basalt; diabase. **2.** Any dark igneous rock with macroscopically indeterminate composition. [French *dolérite* : Greek *doleros,* deceitful, from *dolos,* bait, trick (so named from the difficulty in analyzing it) (see **del-²** in Appendix*) + -ITE.]
dol·i·cho·ce·phal·ic (dŏl′ə-kō-sə-făl′ĭk) *adj.* Also **dol·i·cho·ceph·a·lous** (-sĕf′ə-ləs). Having a relatively long head; designating a skull that is longer than it is broad, with a cephalic index of 75.9 or less. [From New Latin *dolichocephalus* : Greek *dolikhos,* long (see **del-¹** in Appendix*) + -CEPHALOUS.] **—dol′i·cho·ceph′a·lism′** (-sĕf′ə-lĭz′əm), **dol′i·cho·ceph′a·ly** (-sĕf′ə-lē) *n.*
doll (dŏl) *n.* **1.** A child's toy representing a baby or other human being. **2.** A pretty child. **3.** *Slang.* An attractive woman of dubious intelligence. **4.** Any person regarded with fond familiarity: *My boss is a living doll.* *—v.* **dolled, dolling, dolls.** *Slang. —intr.* To dress up or adorn oneself smartly, as for a special occasion. Used with *up.* *—tr.* To dress (oneself) up smartly, especially for ostentation. [From *Doll,* pet name for DOROTHEA.]
dol·lar (dŏl′ər) *n. Abbr.* **dol.** *Symbol* $ **1.** The basic monetary unit of the United States, Australia, Canada, Ethiopia, Guyana, Liberia, Malaysia, New Zealand, Trinidad and Tobago, Western Samoa, and of Hong Kong and Singapore, equal to 100 cents. See table of exchange rates at **currency.** **2.** A coin or note worth one dollar. [Low German *daler,* from German *Taler,* taler, short for *Joachimstaler,* a coin made with metal from *Joachimsthal,* Jachymov, town in the Erzgebirge Mountains, Czechoslovakia.]
dol·lar-a-year (dŏl′ər-ə-yîr′) *adj.* Designating U.S. Federal employment or employees considered on the basis of patriotic service rather than financial reward or career: *a dollar-a-year government consultant.*
dollar diplomacy. **1.** A policy aimed at furthering the interests of the United States abroad by encouraging the investment of U.S. capital in foreign countries. **2.** A policy designed to safeguard such investments.
dol·lar·fish (dŏl′ər-fĭsh′) *n., pl.* **dollarfish** or **-fishes.** Any of several rounded silvery fishes, such as the **moonfish** *(see).*
dollar sign. The symbol ($) for a dollar or dollars when placed before a numeral. Also called "dollar mark."
Doll·fuss (dôl′fo͞os′), **Engelbert.** 1892–1934. Austrian statesman; proclaimed dictatorship (1933); assassinated.
dol·lop (dŏl′əp) *n.* A large lump, helping, or portion, as of ice cream or brandy. [Origin obscure.]
dol·ly (dŏl′ē) *n., pl.* **-lies.** **1.** A child's term for a doll. **2. a.** A low mobile platform that rolls on casters, used for moving heavy loads. **b.** Such a platform as used by one working underneath an automobile or the like. **3.** A similar wheeled apparatus used to move a motion-picture or television camera about a set. **4.** A small locomotive for use in a railroad yard, construction site, or the like. **5.** A tool used to hold one end of a rivet while the opposite end is being hammered to form a head. **6.** A small piece of wood or metal placed on the head of a pile to prevent damage while the pile is being driven. *—intr.v.* **dollied, -lying, -lies.** To move the dolly on which a motion-picture or television camera is mounted toward or away from the scene of action. Often used with *in* or *out.* [From DOLLY.]
Dol·ly (dŏl′ē). A feminine given name. [Pet form of DOROTHY.]
Dol·ly Var·den (dŏl′ē värd′n) *n.* **1.** A 19th-century ladies' costume consisting of a dress with a tight bodice and a flowered skirt draped over a brightly colored petticoat. **2.** A colorfully spotted trout, *Salvelinus malma,* of northwestern North America. [After *Dolly Varden,* a character who wore such a dress in Dickens' *Barnaby Rudge.*]
dol·man (dŏl′mən) *n.* **1.** A long Turkish outer robe. **2.** A woman's cloak or coat with capelike arm pieces. **3.** A jacket, usually elaborately decorated, often worn like a cape as part of a hussar's uniform. [French, from German *Dolman,* from Turkish *dolaman,* "a winding," from *dolamak,* to wind.]
dolman sleeve. A full sleeve that is very wide at the armhole and narrow at the wrist.
dol·men (dŏl′mən) *n.* Any prehistoric megalithic structure consisting of two or more upright stones with a capstone, typically forming a chamber. Also called "cromlech." Compare **menhir.** [French, probably coined from Breton *tol,* table, from Old Breton, from Latin *tabula,* TABLE + *men,* stone, from (unattested) Common Celtic *magino-* (compare **menhir**).]
dol·o·mite (dŏl′ə-mīt′) *n.* **1.** A light-tinted, especially gray, pink, or white mineral, essentially $CaMg(CO_3)_2$, used as a furnace refractory, construction, and ceramic material, and in fertilizer. **2.** A magnesia-rich sedimentary rock, resembling limestone. [French, after Déodat de *Dolomieu* (1705–1801), French geologist.]
Do·lo·mites (dŏl′ə-mīts′). Also **Do·lo·mite Alps** (-mīt′). *Italian* **Do·lo·mi·ti** (dō-lō-mē′tē). A section of the eastern Alps in northern Italy. Highest elevation, Marmolada (10,964 feet).
do·lor (dō′lər) *n.* Also *British* **do·lour.** *Poetic.* Sorrow; grief. [Middle English *dolour,* pain, suffering, grief, from Old French, from Latin *dolor,* from *dolēre,* to feel pain, grieve. See **del-³** in Appendix.*]
dol·or·im·e·try (dŏl′ə-rĭm′ə-trē) *n.* A technique for measuring the intensity of pain perception in degrees, ranging from unpleasant to unbearable, by means of heat applied to the skin. [DOLOR + -METRY.]
do·lo·ro·so (dō′lə-rō′sō) *adj. Music.* Mournful; plaintive. *—adv. Music.* With a mournful or plaintive tempo or quality. Used as a direction to the performer. [Italian, from Latin *dolōrōsus,* DOLOROUS.]
do·lor·ous (dō′lə-rəs, dŏl′-) *adj.* **1.** Sorrowful; sad. **2.** Painful. [Middle English, from Late Latin *dolōrōsus,* from Latin *dolor,* DOLOR.] **—do′lor·ous·ly** *adv.* **—do′lor·ous·ness** *n.*
dol·phin (dŏl′fĭn, dôl′-) *n.* **1.** Any of various marine mammals, chiefly of the family Delphinidae, related to the whales but generally smaller and having a beaklike snout; especially, the common, widely distributed species *Delphinus delphis.* Sometimes called "porpoise." **2.** Either of two marine fishes, *Coryphaena hippurus* or *C. equisetis,* having iridescent coloring. [Middle English *dolphin, dalphin,* from Old French *daufin, dalfin,* from Vulgar Latin *dalfīnus* (unattested), from Latin *delphīnus,* from Greek *delphis* (stem *delphin-*). See **gwelbh-** in Appendix.*]

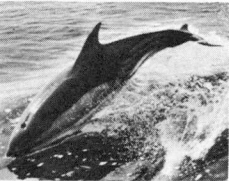

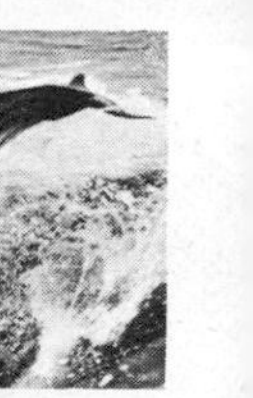
dolphin
Delphinus delphis

dolt (dōlt) *n.* A dullard; blockhead. [Perhaps a variant of DULL.] **—dolt′ish** *adj.* **—dolt′ish·ly** *adv.* **—dolt′ish·ness** *n.*
Dom (dŏm; *Portuguese* dôN) *n.* **1.** A title formerly bestowed in Portugal and Brazil. **2.** *Roman Catholic Church.* A title used before the names of monks of certain orders. [Portuguese, from Latin *dominus,* lord. See **demə-¹** in Appendix.*]
-dom. Indicates: **1.** The condition of being; for example, **boredom.** **2.** The domain, position, or rank of; for example, **saintdom.** [Middle English *-dom,* Old English *-dōm.* See **dhē-¹** in Appendix.*]
dom. **1.** domestic. **2.** dominant. **3.** dominion.
Dom. Dominican.
Do·magk (dō′mäk′), **Gerhard.** 1895–1964. German biochemist; discovered first sulfonamide.
do·main (dō-mān′) *n.* **1.** A territory or range of rule or control; realm. **2.** A sphere of concern or function; field: *the domain of history.* **3.** *Physics.* Any of numerous contiguous regions in a ferromagnetic material in which the direction of spontaneous magnetization is uniform and different from that in neighboring regions. Also called "magnetic domain." **4.** *Law.* **a.** The ownership and right of disposal of property. **b.** The right of **eminent domain** *(see).* **5.** *Mathematics.* **a.** The set of possible values of an independent variable of a function. Compare **range.** **b.** Any open connected set that contains at least one point. [French *domaine,* from Old French *demaine,* from Latin *dominium,* property, ownership rights, from *dominus,* lord. See **demə-¹** in Appendix.*]
dome (dōm) *n.* **1.** A generally hemispherical roof or vault. **2.** Any object or structure resembling the shape of this. **3.** *Poetic.* A large, stately building. **4.** *Slang.* The head. **5.** *Crystallography.* A form of crystal in which two similarly inclined faces intersect in a line parallel to the horizontal axis. *—v.* **domed, doming, domes.** *—tr.* **1.** To cover with or as with a dome. **2.** To shape like a dome. *—intr.* To assume the shape of a dome by rising or swelling. [French *dôme,* from Italian *duomo,* (domed) cathedral, from Latin *domus,* house. See **demə-¹** in Appendix.*]
domes·day. Variant of **doomsday.**
Domes·day Book (do͞omz′dā′, dōmz′-). Also **Dooms·day Book** (do͞omz′-). The written record of a census and survey of English landowners and their property made by order of William the Conqueror in 1085–86.
do·mes·tic (də-mĕs′tĭk) *adj. Abbr.* **dom.** **1.** Of or pertaining to the family or household: *domestic chores.* **2.** Fond of home life and household affairs. **3.** Tame; domesticated. Said of animals. **4.** Of or pertaining to a country's internal affairs: *"foreign attachments are the fruit of domestic misrule"* (Macaulay). **5.** Produced in or indigenous to a particular country: *domestic wine.* *—n. Abbr.* **dom.** **1.** A household servant. **2.** Cotton cloth as distinguished from linen. **3.** *Plural.* Household linens. [Old French *domestique,* from Latin *domesticus,* from *domus,* house. See **demə-¹** in Appendix.*] **—do·mes′ti·cal·ly** *adv.*
do·mes·ti·cate (də-mĕs′tĭ-kāt′) *v.* **-cated, -cating, -cates.** Also **do·mes·ti·cize** (də-mĕs′tə-sīz′), **-cized, -cizing, -cizes.** *—tr.* **1.** To train to live with and be of use to man; to tame. **2.** To cause to feel comfortable at home; make domestic. **3.** To accommodate to surroundings or an environment. *—intr.* To become domestic. [DOMESTIC + -ATE.] **—do·mes′ti·ca′tion** *n.*
do·mes·tic·i·ty (dō′mĕ-stĭs′ə-tē) *n., pl.* **-ties.** **1.** The quality or condition of being domestic. **2.** Home life or devotion to it. **3.** *Plural.* Household affairs.
domestic science. Home economics.
do·mi·cal (dō′mĭ-kəl, dŏm′ĭ-) *adj.* Also **do·mic** (dō′mĭk, dŏm′ĭk). Pertaining to, having, or shaped like a dome. **—do′mi·cal·ly** *adv.*
dom·i·cile (dŏm′ə-sīl′, -səl, dō′mə-) *n.* Also **dom·i·cil** (-səl). **1.** A residence; home. **2.** One's legal residence. *—v.* **domiciled, -ciling, -ciles.** Also **dom·i·cil·i·ate** (dŏm′ə-sĭl′ē-āt′, dō′mə-), **-ated, -ating, -ates.** *—tr.* To establish (a person or oneself) in a residence. *—intr.* To reside or dwell. [Old French, from Latin *domicilium,* habitation, abode. See **demə-¹** in Appendix.*] **—dom′i·cil′i·ar′y** (-ə-sĭl′ē-ĕr′ē) *adj.*

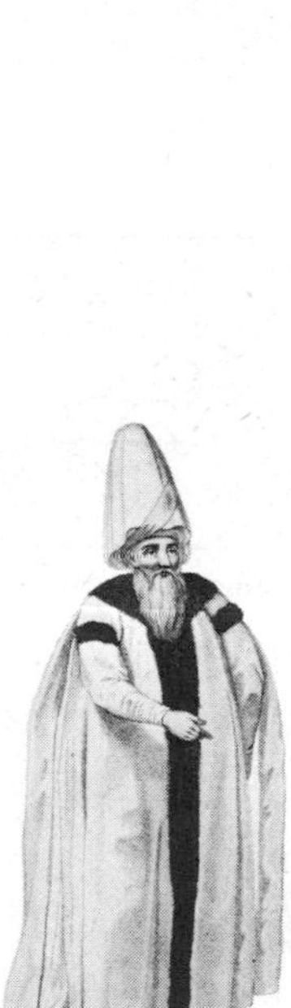
dolman
A grand vizier of Turkey wearing dolman

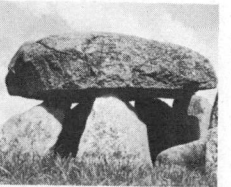

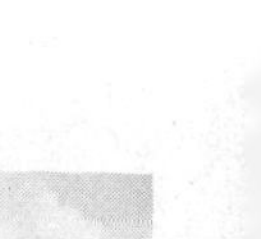
dolmen

dom·i·nance (dŏm′ə-nəns) *n.* Also **dom·i·nan·cy** (-nən-sē). The condition or fact of being dominant; ascendancy.

dom·i·nant (dŏm′ə-nənt) *adj. Abbr.* **dom. 1.** Exercising the most influence or control; governing. **2.** Pre-eminent in position or prevalence; ascendant. **3.** *Genetics.* Producing the same phenotypic effect whether paired with an identical or a dissimilar gene. Compare **recessive. 4.** *Ecology.* Designating or pertaining to the species that is most characteristic of a habitat and that may determine the presence and type of other species. **5.** *Music.* Relating to or based upon the fifth tone of a diatonic scale. *—n. Abbr.* **dom. 1.** *Genetics.* A dominant character. **2.** *Ecology.* A dominant species. **3.** *Music.* The fifth tone of a diatonic scale. [Old French, from Latin *dominans,* present participle of *dominārī,* to DOMINATE.] **—dom′i·nant·ly** *adv.*

Synonyms: *dominant, predominant, preponderant, paramount, pre-eminent.* These adjectives mean surpassing all others in power, influence, or the like. *Dominant* applies to what exercises principal control or is unmistakably outstanding. *Predominant* is often nearly identical with the preceding term but can mean uppermost at a particular time or for the time being. *Preponderant* implies superiority as the result of outweighing or outnumbering all others. *Paramount* means first in importance, rank, or regard. *Pre-eminent* especially suggests esteem and general recognition of supremacy in a given area.

dominant wavelength. The wavelength of the light that when combined in specific proportions with an achromatic standard light matches a given color. See **color.**

dom·i·nate (dŏm′ə-nāt′) *v.* **-nated, -nating, -nates.** *—tr.* **1.** To control, govern, or rule by superior authority or power. **2.** To occupy the pre-eminent position in or over. **3.** To overlook from a height. *—intr.* To be dominant in position or authority. [Latin *dominārī,* to be lord and master, from *dominus,* master, lord. See **demə-¹** in Appendix.*] **—dom′i·na′tive** *adj.* **—dom′i·na′tor** (-nā′tər) *n.*

dom·i·na·tion (dŏm′ə-nā′shən) *n.* **1.** The act of dominating or the condition of being dominated; rule; control. **2.** *Plural. Theology.* The fourth of the nine orders of angels. Also called "dominions." See **angel.**

dom·i·neer (dŏm′ə-nîr′) *v.* **-neered, -neering, -neers.** *—tr.* To rule over arbitrarily or arrogantly; tyrannize. *—intr.* To govern tyrannically. [Dutch *domineren,* from French *dominer,* from Latin *dominārī,* to DOMINATE.] **—dom′i·neer′ing·ly** *adv.*

Dom·i·nic (dŏm′ə-nĭk), **Saint.** 1170–1221. Spanish-born Roman Catholic priest; active in France; founded Dominican order.

Dom·i·ni·ca (dŏm′ə-nē′kə, də-mĭn′ĭ-kə). An island and former British colony, 304 square miles in area, in the West Indies; a member of the West Indies Associated States since 1967. Population, 67,000. Capital, Roseau.

do·min·i·cal (də-mĭn′ĭ-kəl) *adj.* **1.** Of or associated with the Lord (Christ). **2.** Pertaining to Sunday as the Lord's day. [Medieval Latin *dominicālis,* from Latin *dominicus,* of a lord, from *dominus,* lord. See **demə-¹** in Appendix.*]

dominical letter. One of the first seven letters of the alphabet applied to Sundays in the ecclesiastical calendar for a given year, the letter being the one that corresponds with the first Sunday in January when the first seven days of the month are lettered in order; for example, if the first Sunday is January 2, *B* will be the dominical letter for the year.

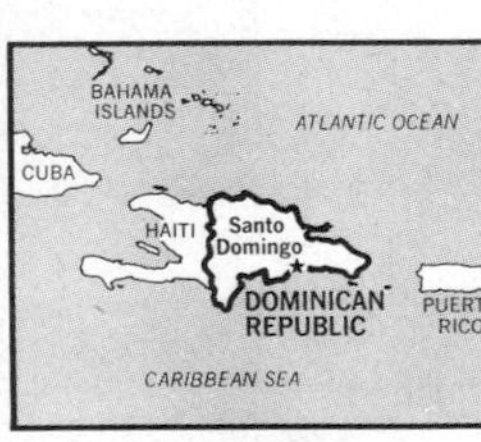

Dominican Republic

Do·min·i·can (də-mĭn′ĭ-kən) *adj. Abbr.* **Dom. 1.** Of or pertaining to the order of preaching friars established in 1215 by Saint Dominic. **2.** Of or pertaining to the Dominican Republic. *—n. Abbr.* **Dom. 1.** A friar of the order of Saint Dominic. **2.** A native or inhabitant of the Dominican Republic.

Dominican Republic. A country occupying the eastern two-thirds (19,129 square miles) of the Caribbean island of Hispaniola. Population, 3,573,000. Capital, Santo Domingo.

dom·i·nie (dŏm′ə-nē′, dō′mə-) *n.* **1.** A clergyman of the Dutch Reformed Church. **2.** *Informal.* Any minister. **3.** *Chiefly Scottish.* A schoolmaster. [From obsolete *domine,* form of address to ministers and schoolmasters, from Latin *domine,* vocative of *dominus,* lord, master. See **demə-¹** in Appendix.*]

do·min·ion (də-mĭn′yən) *n. Abbr.* **dom. 1.** Control or the exercise of control; rule; sovereignty: *"The devil . . . has their souls in his possession, and under his dominion"* (Jonathan Edwards). **2.** A territory or sphere of influence or control; realm; domain. **3.** *Often capital* **D.** One of the self-governing nations within the British Commonwealth. **4.** *Law.* **Dominium** *(see).* **5.** *Plural. Theology.* An order of angels, **dominations** *(see).* [Middle English *dominioun,* from Old French *dominion,* from Medieval Latin *dominiō,* from Latin *dominium,* property, ownership rights, lordship, from *dominus,* lord, master. See **demə-¹** in Appendix.*]

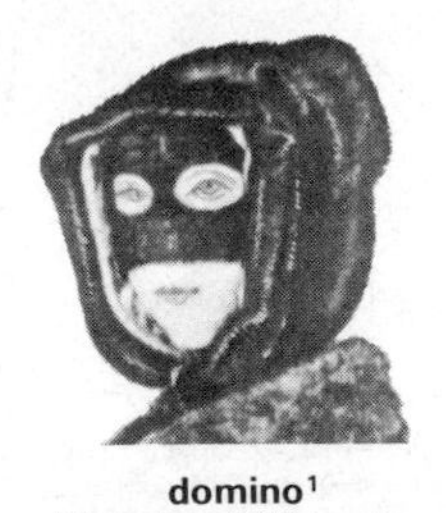

domino¹
Worn by a 17th-century English woman

Dominion Day. July 1, a legal holiday in Canada, the anniversary of the Dominion's formation in 1867.

Dom·i·nique (dŏm′ə-nēk′, dŏm′ə-nĭk) *n.* Also **Dom·i·nick** (dŏm′ə-nĭk). An American breed of domestic fowl having gray, barred plumage, yellow legs, and a rose-colored comb. [From the island DOMINICA.]

do·min·i·um (də-mĭn′ē-əm) *n. Law.* Ownership of property, especially of land, and the right to its disposition. Also called "dominion." [Latin, property, DOMINION.]

dom·i·no¹ (dŏm′ə-nō′) *n., pl.* **-noes** or **-nos. 1.** A hooded cape worn by clergymen. **2. a.** A hooded robe worn with an eye mask at a masquerade. **b.** The mask itself. **3.** One wearing such a robe or mask. [French, from Latin *(benedicamos) domino,* "(let us bless) the Lord," from the dative or ablative of *dominus,* master, lord. See **demə-¹** in Appendix.*]

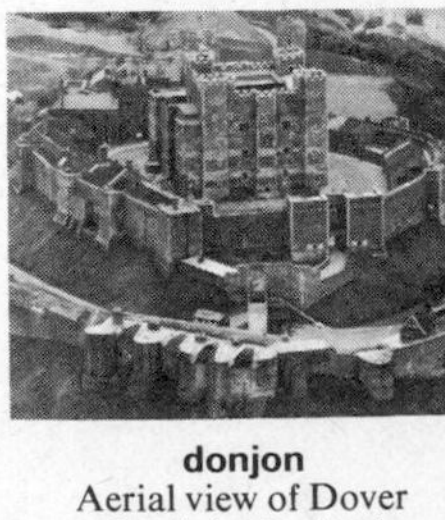

donjon
Aerial view of Dover Castle in England

dom·i·no² (dŏm′ə-nō′) *n., pl.* **-noes** or **-nos. 1.** A small, rectangular block, the face of which is divided into halves. Each half is marked by one to six dots or is blank. **2.** *Plural.* The game played with a set, generally 28, of these pieces. Used with a singular verb. [French, obscurely from *domino,* DOMINO (priest's robe).]

Do·mi·nus (dō′mĭ-no͝os′, dŏm′ə-nəs) *n. Abbr.* **D.** *Latin.* The Lord. Used with reference to God or Christ.

Do·mi·tian (də-mĭsh′ən). Full name, Titus Flavius Domitianus Augustus. A.D. 51–96. Roman emperor (81–96).

don¹ (dŏn) *n.* **1.** *Capital* **D.** *Abbr.* **D.** Sir. A title formerly affixed to the Christian name of a Spaniard of high rank, now used generally as a courtesy title. **2.** A Spanish gentleman. **3.** *British.* A head, tutor, or fellow at a college of Oxford or Cambridge. [Spanish, from Latin *dominus,* lord, master. See **demə-¹** in Appendix.*]

don² (dŏn) *tr.v.* **donned, donning, dons.** To put on; dress in. [Contraction of *do on.*]

Don (dŏn). **1.** A river of the Soviet Union, rising near Tula, Russian S.F.S.R., and flowing 1,222 miles southward and then westward to the Sea of Azov. **2.** A river in England, flowing 70 miles across southern Yorkshire to join the Ouse. **3.** A river in Scotland, flowing 82 miles eastward across central Aberdeen to the North Sea. [Sense 1, Russian *Don.* Senses 2 and 3, Middle English *Don,* Old English *Don,* from Celtic. See **dānu-** in Appendix.*]

do·ña (dō′nyä) *n.* **1.** A Spanish gentlewoman. **2.** *Capital* **D.** Lady. A title of courtesy used with a woman's given name in Spanish-speaking countries. [Spanish, "lady," from Latin *domina.* See **dame.**]

Don·ald (dŏn′əld). A masculine given name. [Gaelic *Domhnall*†, "world-mighty."]

do·nate (dō′nāt′, dō-nāt′) *tr.v.* **-nated, -nating, -nates.** To present as a gift to a fund or cause; contribute. [Back-formation from DONATION.] **—do′na·tor** (dō′nā′tər, dō-nā′tər) *n.*

Do·na·tel·lo (dŏn′ə-tĕl′ō). Original name, Donato di Niccolò di Betto Bardi. 1386?–1466. Italian sculptor.

do·na·tion (dō-nā′shən) *n.* **1.** The act of giving something to a fund or cause. **2.** A gift or grant; contribution. [Middle English *donacioun,* from Old French, from Latin *dōnātiō,* from *dōnātus,* past participle of *dōnāre,* to give, from *dōnum,* gift. See **dō-** in Appendix.*]

Don·a·tist (dŏn′ə-tĭst, dō′nə-) *n.* A member of a schismatic Christian sect that arose in North Africa in the fourth century A.D. *—adj.* Of or pertaining to the Donatists. [Medieval Latin *Dōnātista,* from *Dōnātus,* probably the bishop of Carthage in the fourth century.] **—Don′a·tism** *n.*

don·a·tive (dō′nə-tĭv, dŏn′ə-) *n.* **1.** A bounty or largess. **2.** A benefice. *—adj.* Constituting a benefice. [Latin *dōnātīvum,* neuter of *dōnātīvus,* of a donation, from *dōnātus.* See **donation.**]

Do·nau. The German name for the **Danube.**

Don·cas·ter (dŏng′kə-stər). A city of England, in southern Yorkshire. Population, 87,000.

done (dŭn). Past participle of **do.** *—adj.* **1.** Finished. See Usage note below. **2.** Cooked adequately. **3.** Socially acceptable: *not done in polite society.* *—interj.* Used to express concurrence. **—done for. 1.** Doomed; dying. **2.** Exhausted.

Usage: *Done,* in the sense of completely accomplished, finished, is found often, but not exclusively, in casual or informal usage. It is termed acceptable in writing in the following example by 53 per cent of the Usage Panel: *The entire project will not be done until next year.* Where *done* can readily be misconstrued as a form of *do* without the express sense of completed or finished *(The work will be done next week),* a more specific term, such as *finished,* is preferable.

do·nee (dō-nē′) *n.* A recipient of a gift. [DON(OR) + -EE.]

Don·e·gal (dŏn′ĭ-gôl′, dŭn′-). A county of the Republic of Ireland, occupying 1,865 square miles in the extreme northwest. Population, 114,000. County seat, Lifford.

Do·nets (də-nĕts′). A river of the Soviet Union, rising in southwestern Russian S.F.S.R. and flowing 631 miles generally southeast to the Don near Rostov.

Do·nets Basin (də-nĕts′). Also **Don·bas, Don·bass** (dŏn′băs′). A major coal-mining and industrial region of the Soviet Union, lying southwest of the lower Donets River.

Do·netsk (də-nĕtsk′). Originally **Yu·zov·ka** (yo͞o′zôf-kə). Formerly **Sta·li·no** (stä′lĭ-nō′, stăl′ĭ-). The major industrial city of the Donets Basin, in the Ukrainian S.S.R. Population, 774,000.

dong (dŏng) *n.* Symbol **D 1.** The basic monetary unit of North Vietnam, equal to 100 xu. See table of exchange rates at **currency. 2.** A coin or note worth one dong. [Vietnamese.]

Don·go·la (dŏng′gə-lə, dŏng-gō′lə). A town in northern Sudan, on the west bank of the Nile; the capital of the former Christian Kingdom of Dongola from the 6th to the 14th century.

don·go·la leather (dŏng′gə-lə, dŏng-gō′lə). Goatskin, sheepskin, or calfskin tanned into a leather that resembles kid. Also called "dongola kid." [From DONGOLA.]

Don·i·phan (dŏn′ə-fən), **Alexander William.** 1808–1887. American army officer, lawyer, and frontiersman; led 5,000-mile march during Mexican War.

Don·i·zet·ti (dŏn′ə-zĕt′ē; *Italian* dō′nē-dzāt′tē), **Gaetano.** 1797–1848. Italian composer of more than 60 operas.

don·jon (dŏn′jən, dŭn′-) *n.* The massive, heavily fortified main tower of a castle; a keep. Also called "dungeon." [Variant of DUNGEON.]

Don Juan (dŏn′ wän′). **1.** A libertine; profligate. **2.** A man obsessed with seducing women. [After *Don Juan,* legendary Spanish nobleman and libertine.] **—Don Juanism.**

don·key (dŏng′kē, dŭng′-, dông′-) *n., pl.* **-keys. 1.** The domesticated ass, probably descended from the wild ass *Equus asinus.*

2. An obstinate, sluggish, or stupid fellow. [Perhaps blend of DUN (dark) + diminutive suffix *-ey* (influenced by MONKEY).]
donkey engine. A small auxiliary steam engine used for hoisting or pumping, especially aboard ship.
don·na (dŏn′ə; *Italian* dôn′nä) *n.* **1.** An Italian gentlewoman. **2.** *Capital* **D.** Lady. A title of courtesy used with a woman's given name in Italian-speaking countries. [Italian, "lady," from Latin *domina.* See **dame.**]
Don·na (dŏn′ə). A feminine given name. [Italian, DONNA.]
Donne (dŭn), **John.** 1573–1631. English poet and theologian.
don·nish (dŏn′ĭsh) *adj.* Resembling or characteristic of a university don; bookish; pedantically erudite: "The Times *printed valedictory lines which donnish readers turned into Latin and Greek*" (Reginald Pound).
don·ny·brook (dŏn′ē-brŏŏk′) *n.* A brawl or uproar; free-for-all. [After the annual *Donnybrook* fair, held at *Donnybrook,* near Dublin, Ireland, at which such uproars are common.]
do·nor (dō′nər) *n.* **1.** One who contributes something, such as money to a cause or fund. **2.** One who donates blood, tissue, or an organ for use in a transfusion or transplant. [Old French *doneur,* from Latin *dōnātor,* from *dōnātus.* See **donation.**]
do-no·thing (dōō′nŭth′ĭng) *adj.* Offering no initiative for change, especially in politics.
do-no·thing·ism (dōō′nŭth′ĭng-ĭz-əm) *n.* A political policy that offers no initiative for change. Used disparagingly.
Don Qui·xo·te (dŏn′ kē-hō′tē, kwĭk′sət). An impractical idealist bent on righting incorrigible wrongs. [After *Don Quixote,* hero of a satirical chivalric romance by Miguel de Cervantes, published 1605–15.]
don't (dōnt). Contraction of *do not.*
Usage: *Don't* is nonstandard for *doesn't* (third person singular): *He doesn't* (not *don't*) *go often.*
do·nut. Variant of **doughnut.**
doo·dad (dōō′dăd′) *n. Informal.* Any unnamed or nameless gadget or trinket. Also called "doohickey."
doo·dle (dōōd′l) *v.* **-dled, -dling, -dles.** *Informal.* —*intr.* To scribble mechanically while thinking about something else. —*tr.* To draw (figures) while preoccupied. —*n. Informal.* A figure, design, or scribble drawn or written absent-mindedly. [English dialect *doodle*†, to trifle, fritter away time.]
doo·dle·bug (dōōd′l-bŭg′) *n.* **1. a.** An insect, the **ant lion** *(see),* especially in its larval stage. **b.** Loosely, any of various other insects or insect larvae. **2.** A divining rod. [Perhaps English dialect *doodle,* to waste time (see **doodle**) + BUG.]
doo·hick·ey (dōō′hĭk′ē) *n., pl.* **-eys.** *Informal.* **1.** A **doodad** *(see).* **2.** A pimple. [Perhaps DOO(DAD) + HICKEY (device).]
Doo·ley (dōō′lē), **Mr.** See Finley Peter **Dunne.**
Doo·lit·tle (dōō′lĭt′l), **Hilda.** Pen name, H. D. 1886–1961. American imagist poet.
doom (dōōm) *n.* **1.** Condemnation to a severe penalty. **2.** The Last Judgment. **3.** A predestined end in ruin or tragedy; a terrible fate. **4.** Disaster; ruin; extinction. —*tr.v.* **doomed, dooming, dooms. 1.** To condemn to ruination or death. **2.** To destine to an unhappy end. [Middle English *doom,* Old English *dōm.* See **dhē-**[1] in Appendix.*]
doom palm (dōōm). Also **doum palm.** An African palm tree, *Hyphaene thebaica,* having fanlike foliage and fruit that tastes like gingerbread. Also called "gingerbread palm." [From French *doum,* from Arabic *dawm.*]
dooms·day (dōōmz′dā′) *n.* Also **domes·day** (dōōmz′dā′, dōmz′-). **1.** The day of the Last Judgment. **2.** Any dreaded day of judgment or reckoning. [Middle English *domesday,* Old English *dōmes dæg* : *dōmes,* genitive of *dōm,* DOOM + *dæg,* DAY.]
Doomsday Book. Variant of **Domesday Book.**
door (dôr, dōr) *n.* **1.** Any movable structure used to close off the entrance to a room, building, vehicle, or covered enclosure, typically consisting of a panel of wood, glass, or metal that swings on hinges. **2.** The entranceway to a room, building, or passage: *Go through that door and turn left.* **3.** Any means of approach or access. **4.** The room or building to which a door belongs: *three doors down the hall.* [Middle English *dor,* Old English *dor, duru,* gate, door. See **dhwer-** in Appendix.*]
door·bell (dôr′bĕl′, dōr′-) *n.* A buzzer or bell outside a door, used as a signal for admission.
door·jamb (dôr′jăm′, dōr′-) *n.* Either of the two vertical pieces framing a doorway and supporting the lintel. Also called "doorpost."
door·keep·er (dôr′kē′pər, dōr′-) *n.* **1.** A person employed to guard an entrance or gateway. **2.** *Roman Catholic Church.* One of the **minor orders** *(see).*
door·knob (dôr′nŏb′, dōr′-) *n.* A knob-shaped handle for opening and closing a door.
door·man (dôr′măn′, -mən, dōr′-) *n., pl.* **-men** (-mĕn′, -mĭn). A man employed to attend the entrance of a hotel, apartment house, or building.
door·mat (dôr′măt′, dor′-) *n.* **1.** A mat placed before a doorway for wiping the shoes. **2.** *Slang.* A person who unprotestingly allows himself to be mistreated by others.
door·nail (dôr′nāl′, dōr′-) *n.* A large-headed nail formerly used as a stud on doors. —**dead as a doornail.** Undoubtedly dead.
door·sill (dôr′sĭl′, dōr′-) *n.* The threshold of a doorway.
door·step (dôr′stĕp′, dōr′-) *n.* A step leading to a door.
door·stop (dôr′stŏp′, dōr′-) *n.* **1.** A wedge inserted beneath a door to hold it open at a desired position. **2.** A weight or spring that prevents a door from slamming. **3.** A rubber-tipped projection attached to a wall to protect it from the impact of an opening door.
door·way (dôr′wā′, dōr′-) *n.* The entranceway to a room or building.
door·yard (dôr′yärd′, dōr′-) *n.* A yard in front of the door of a house.
dop·ant (dō′pənt) *n.* A small quantity of a substance, such as phosphorus, added to another substance, such as a semiconductor, to alter the latter's properties. [DOP(E) + -ANT.]
dope (dōp) *n.* **1.** Any viscid substance or liquid; especially: **a.** A lubricant, such as axle grease. **b.** An absorbent material, such as nitroglycerin, used in manufacturing dynamite. **c.** Any of various preparations resembling varnish formerly used to protect, waterproof, and tauten the cloth surfaces of airplane wings. **2.** *Informal.* A narcotic, especially one used by an addict. See Usage note below. **3.** *Slang.* A very stupid person. **4.** *Slang.* Factual information. —*tr.v.* **doped, doping, dopes. 1.** To add or apply dope to. **2.** *Informal.* To administer a narcotic to; to drug. See Usage note below. **3.** *Informal.* To figure out (an outcome or puzzle) by calculation and guesswork. Often used with *out.* **4.** *Informal.* To make a rough plan of; sketch out. Used with *out.* [Dutch *doop,* sauce, from *doopen,* to dip, to mix, from Middle Dutch *dōpen.* See **dub-** in Appendix.*]
Usage: *Dope,* in senses dealing with narcotics, is common in slang and informal usage, but is not restricted to those levels. As a noun, it is acceptable in writing to 86 per cent of the Usage Panel in the following example: *A man who peddles dope has no claim to our sympathy.* As a verb *(The horse was doped),* it is acceptable in written usage to 92 per cent of the Panel.
dope sheet. *Slang.* A publication giving information on the horses running in the day's races. Also called "scratch sheet."
do·pey (dō′pē) *adj.* **-ier, -iest.** Also **do·py.** *Slang.* **1.** Dazed or lethargic, as if drugged. **2.** Stupid. **3.** Silly.
Dop·pel·gäng·er (dŏp′əl-găng′ər; *German* dôp′əl-gĕng′ər) *n.* A ghostly double of a living person, especially one that haunts its own fleshly counterpart. [German, "double-goer."]
Dopp·ler (dŏp′lər), **Christian Johann.** 1803–1853. Austrian physicist; experimented with sound waves.
Doppler effect. An apparent change in the frequency of waves, as of sound or light, occurring when the source and observer are in motion relative to one another, the frequency increasing when the source and observer approach one another and decreasing when they move apart. [After Christian DOPPLER.]
dor (dôr) *n.* Any of various insects that fly with a droning sound, as a dorbeetle. [Middle English *dorre, dore,* Old English *dora,* bumblebee. See **dher-**[3] in Appendix.*]
Dor. Dorian; Doric.
Do·ra·do (də-rä′dō) *n.* A constellation of the Southern Hemisphere near Reticulum and Pictor, containing a great portion of the larger **Magellanic Cloud** *(see).*
dor·bee·tle (dôr′bēt′l) *n.* An Old World dung beetle, *Geotrupes stercorarius,* that flies with a droning sound.
Dor·cas society (dôr′kəs). A women's auxiliary group, often sponsored by a church, that provides clothes for the poor. [After *Dorcas,* Christian disciple mentioned in Acts 9:36.]
Dor·dogne (dôr-dôn′y′). A river flowing 300 miles generally west from south-central France to the Garonne near Bordeaux.
Dor·drecht (dôr′drĕKHt′). Also **Dort** (dôrt). A city of the Netherlands, in the southwest on the Meuse. Population, 81,000.
Do·ré (dô-rā′), **(Paul) Gustave.** 1833–1883. French graphic artist, painter, and illustrator.
Do·ri·an (dôr′ē-ən, dōr′-) *n. Abbr.* **Dor.** One of a Hellenic people that invaded Greece around 1100 B.C. and remained culturally and linguistically distinct within the Greek world, especially in Sparta, Corinth, and Argos. —**Do′ri·an** *adj.*
Dor·ic (dôr′ĭk, dŏr′-) *n. Abbr.* **Dor.** The Greek dialect of the Dorians, spoken chiefly in the Peloponnesus, in various Aegean islands, and in Magna Graecia. —*adj. Abbr.* **Dor. 1.** Belonging to, characteristic of, or designating this dialect. **2.** In the style of or designating the Doric order. **3.** *Rare.* Dialectally rustic. [Latin *Dōricus,* from Greek *Dōrikos,* from *Dōris,* area of Ancient Greece. See **Doris.**]
Doric order. The oldest and simplest of the three orders of classical Greek architecture, characterized by heavy, fluted columns having no base, plain, saucer-shaped capitals, and a bold, simple cornice. Compare **Corinthian order, Ionic order.**
Dor·is (dôr′ĭs, dŏr′-). A feminine given name. [Latin *Dōris,* from Greek, name of a Greek sea nymph, also an area of Ancient Greece, the traditional home of the Dorians.]
Dor·king (dôr′kĭng) *n.* A domestic fowl of a breed having a heavy body and raised chiefly for table use. [From *Dorking,* town in Surrey, England.]
dorm (dôrm) *n. Informal.* A dormitory.
dor·mant (dôr′mənt) *adj.* **1.** Asleep or lying as if asleep; not awake or active. **2.** Latent but capable of being activated: *"a harrowing experience which . . . lay dormant but still menacing"* (Charles Jackson). **3.** Temporarily quiescent: *a dormant volcano.* **4.** *Biology.* In a relatively inactive or resting condition in which some processes are slowed down or suspended. —See Synonyms at **inactive, latent.** [Middle English *dormaunt,* from Old French *dormant,* from the present participle of *dormir,* to sleep, from Latin *dormīre.* See **drem-** in Appendix.*] —**dor′man·cy** *n.*
dor·mer (dôr′mər) *n.* **1.** A window set vertically in a small gable projecting from a sloping roof. Also called "dormer window." **2.** The gable holding such a window. [Old French *dormeor,* "bedroom window," from *dormir,* to sleep. See **dormant.**]
dor·mi·to·ry (dôr′mə-tôr′ē, -tōr′ē) *n., pl.* **-ries. 1.** A room providing sleeping quarters for a number of persons. **2.** A building for housing a number of persons, as at a school or resort. [Latin *dormītōrium,* from *dormītōrius,* of sleep, from *dormītus,* past participle of *dormīre,* to sleep. See **drem-** in Appendix.*]

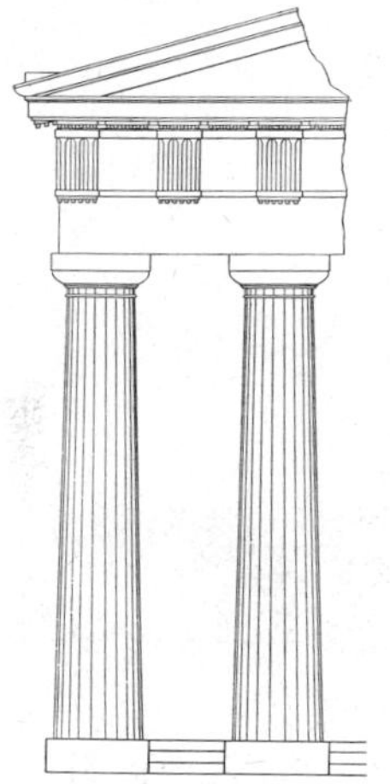
Doric order

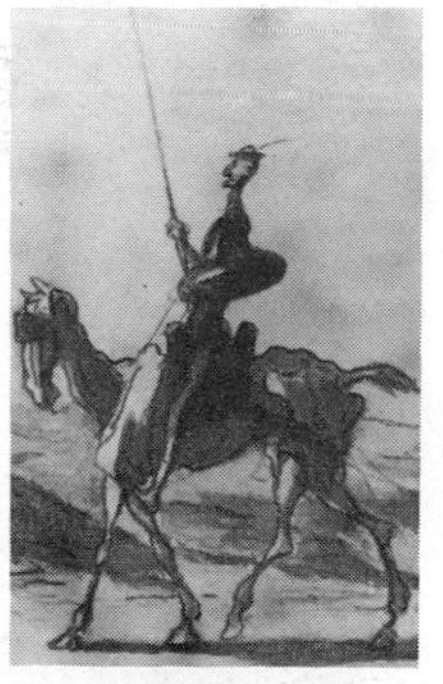
Don Quixote
A drawing by Daumier

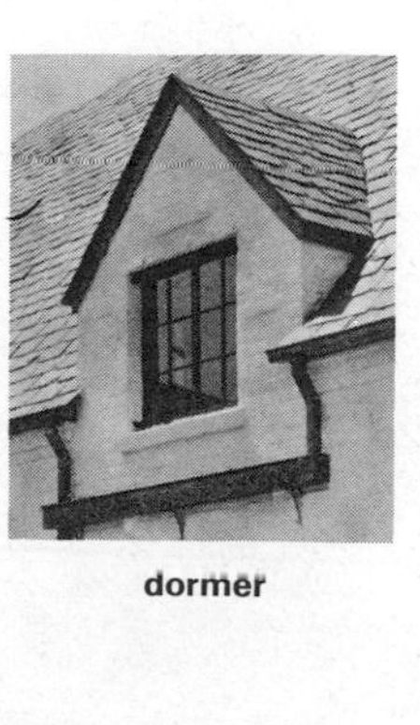
dormer

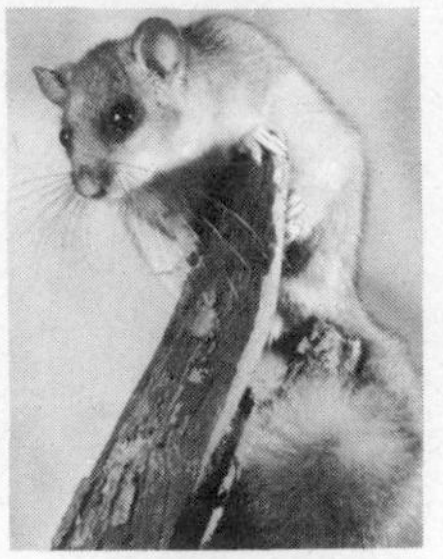

dormouse
Glis glis

dor·mouse (dôr′mous′) *n., pl.* **-mice** (-mīs′). Any of various small, squirrellike Old World rodents of the family Gliridae; especially, *Glis glis*, of Europe and Asia Minor. [Middle English *dormowse*, probably named from the fact that being nocturnal and hibernatory, it is often found sleeping : Northern dialectal *dorm*, sleep, probably from Old French *dormir*, to sleep (see **dormant**) + *mowse, mous*, MOUSE.]

dor·my (dôr′mē) *adj.* Also **dor·mie**. *Golf.* Ahead of an opponent by as many holes as remain to be played. [Origin obscure.]

dor·nick[1] (dôr′nĭk) *n.* A coarse damask cloth. [Middle English *dornewick*, first manufactured in *Doornik* (French *Tournai*), city in Belgium.]

dor·nick[2] (dôr′nĭk) *n. Regional.* A small chunk of rock; a stone. [Origin obscure.]

do·ron·i·cum (də-rŏn′ĭ-kəm) *n.* A plant of the genus *Doronicum*, which includes the leopard's-bane. [New Latin, from Arabic *dorūnaj*.]

Dor·o·thy (dôr′ə-thē, dŏr′-). Also **Dor·o·thee, Dor·o·the·a** (dôr′ə-thē′ə, dŏr′-). A feminine given name. [Latin *Dōrothea*, from Greek : *dōron*, gift (see **dō-** in Appendix*) + *theos*, god (see **dhēs-** in Appendix*).]

dor·sad (dôr′săd′) *adv. Anatomy.* In the direction of the back. [DORS(O)- + -AD (toward).]

dor·sal (dôr′səl) *adj. Anatomy.* **1.** Of, toward, on, in, or near the back. **2.** *Botany.* Of or on the outer surface, underside, or back of an organ. [Late Latin *dorsālis*, from Latin *dorsuālis*, from *dorsum*, back. See **dorsum** in Appendix.*] —**dor′sal·ly** *adv.*

dorsal fin. The main fin on the dorsal surface of fishes or certain marine mammals.

Dor·set, Earl of. See Thomas **Sackville**.

Dor·set Horn (dôr′sĭt) *n.* A domestic sheep of a breed having large horns and fine-textured wool. [From DORSET(SHIRE).]

Dor·set·shire (dôr′sĭt-shîr′, -shər). Also **Dor·set** (dôr′sĭt). A county occupying 973 square miles in southwestern England. Population, 327,000. County seat, Dorchester.

dor·si·ven·tral (dôr′sĭ-vĕn′trəl) *adj.* Having distinct upper and lower surfaces, as most leaves do. [DORSI- + VENTRAL.]

dorso–, dorsi–, dors–. Indicates the dorsal area; for example, **dorsoventral, dorsiventral, dorsad.** [From Latin *dorsum*, back. See **dorsum** in Appendix.*]

dor·so·ven·tral (dôr′sō-vĕn′trəl) *adj.* Extending from a dorsal to a ventral surface. [DORSO- + VENTRAL.]

dor·sum (dôr′səm) *n., pl.* **-sa** (-sə). *Anatomy.* **1.** The back. **2.** Any part of an organ analogous to the back: *the dorsum of the foot.* [Latin, back. See **dorsum** in Appendix.*]

Dort. See **Dordrecht.**

Dort·mund (dôrt′mənd; *German* dôrt′mŏŏnt′). An industrial city in central North Rhine-Westphalia, West Germany. Population, 650,000.

Dort·mund-Ems Canal (dôrt′mənd-ĕmz′; *German* dôrt′-mŏŏnt′-ĕmz). A canal in northwest West Germany linking the Ruhr with the Ems.

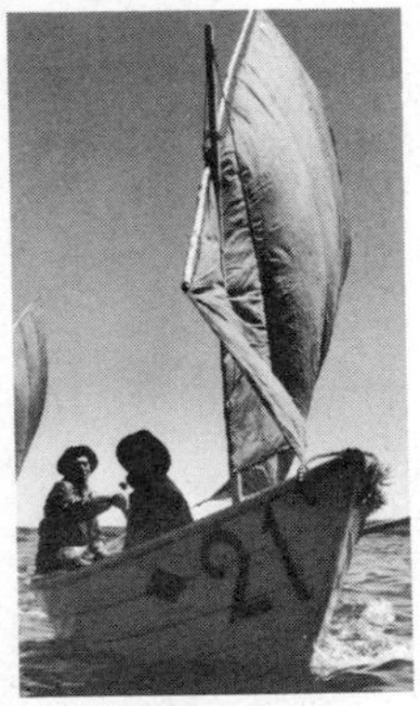

dory[1]

do·ry[1] (dôr′ē, dōr′ē) *n., pl.* **-ries.** A small, narrow, flat-bottomed fishing boat with high sides and a sharp prow. [Mosquito *dóri*, dugout.]

do·ry[2] (dôr′ē, dōr′ē) *n., pl.* **-ries. 1.** Any of various marine fishes of the family Zeidae; especially, the **John Dory** *(see)*. **2.** A fish, the **walleye** *(see)*. [Middle English *dorre*, from Old French *doree*, gilded (from its metallic shine), from the feminine past participle of *dorer*, to gild, from Late Latin *dēaurāre* : Latin *dē-*, thoroughly + *aurum*, gold (see **aurum** in Appendix*).]

dos-à-dos (dō-zà-dō′) *n., pl.* **dos-à-dos** (-dōz′; *French* -dō′). Also **do-si-do** (dō′sē-dō′) (for sense 2) *pl.* **-dos. 1.** A sofa or carriage that accommodates two people seated back to back. **2. a.** A movement in square dancing in which two dancers approach each other and circle back to back, then return to their original positions. **b.** The call given for such a movement. [French, "back to back."]

dos·age (dō′sĭj) *n.* **1.** The administration of a therapeutic agent in prescribed amounts. **2.** The amount administered.

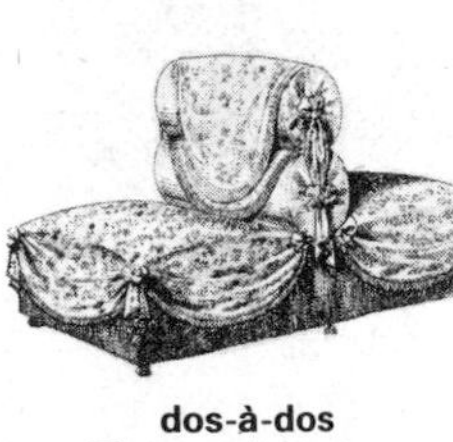

dos-à-dos
Nineteenth-century double chair

dose (dōs) *n.* **1.** *Abbr.* **d., D.** A specified quantity of a therapeutic agent prescribed to be taken at one time or at stated intervals. **2.** *Informal.* An amount, especially of something unpleasant, to which one is subjected: *his dose of hard luck.* **3.** An ingredient added to wine to impart flavor or strength. **4.** *Slang.* A venereal infection. —*tr.v.* **dosed, dosing, doses. 1.** To give (someone) a dose, as of medicine. **2.** To give or prescribe (medicine) in doses. [French, from Late Latin *dosis*, from Greek, a giving, dose, from *didonai*, to give. See **dō-** in Appendix.*] —**dos′er** *n.*

do·sim·e·ter (dō-sĭm′ə-tər) *n.* A device that measures and indicates the amount of x rays or radioactivity absorbed. [DOS(E) + -METER.]

do·sim·e·try (dō-sĭm′ə-trē) *n. Medicine.* The accurate measurement of doses. [DOS(E) + -METRY.]

Dos Pas·sos (dəs păs′əs), **John (Roderigo).** Born 1896. American novelist.

doss (dŏs) *n. British Slang.* **1.** A makeshift or crude bed. **2.** A cheap lodging house; flophouse. Also called "doss house." **3.** Sleep. —*intr.v.* **dossed, dossing, dosses.** *British Slang.* To bed down; sleep. [Variant of earlier *dorse*, from Latin *dorsum*, back. See **dorsum** in Appendix.*]

dos·sal (dŏs′əl) *n.* Also **dos·sel. 1.** An ornamental hanging of rich fabric, as behind an altar or at the sides of a chancel. **2.** An ornamental covering for the back of a chair or throne. In this sense, also called "dosser." [Medieval Latin *dossāle*, neuter of *dossālis*, of the back, from Late Latin *dorsālis*, DORSAL.]

dos·ser (dŏs′ər) *n.* **1.** A large pack basket; pannier. **2.** A **dossal** *(see)*. [Middle English *doser*, from Old French *dossier*, from Medieval Latin *dorsārium*, from Latin *dorsum*, back. See **dorsum** in Appendix.*]

dos·si·er (dŏs′ē-ā′, dôs′yā′) *n.* A collection of papers or documents pertaining to a particular person or subject; a file. [French, from Old French, bundle of papers having a label on the back, from *dos*, back, from Latin *dorsum*. See **dorsum** in Appendix.*]

dost. *Archaic.* Second person singular, present tense of **do**.

Dos·to·ev·ski (dôs′tô-yĕf′skē), **Feodor Mikhailovich.** 1821–1881. Russian novelist.

dot[1] (dŏt) *n.* **1. a.** A tiny round mark made by or as if by a pointed instrument; a spot; point. **b.** Such a mark used in orthography, as the *dot* above an *i*. **2.** A tiny amount. **3.** In Morse and similar codes, a short sound or signal used in combination with the dash and written as a dot to represent letters, numbers, or punctuation. **4.** *Mathematics.* **a.** A decimal point. **b.** A symbol of multiplication. **5.** *Music.* A mark after a note indicating an increase in time value by half. —**on the dot.** *Informal.* Absolutely punctual; on time. —*v.* **dotted, dotting, dots.** —*tr.* **1.** To mark with a dot. **2.** To form or make with dots. **3.** To cover with or as if with dots: *"Campfires, like red, peculiar blossoms, dotted the night."* (Stephen Crane). —*intr.* To make a dot or dots. [Middle English *dot* (unattested), lump, dot, Old English *dott*, head of a boil, possibly akin to Old English *titt*, teat, TIT.] —**dot′ter** *n.*

dot[2] (dŏt; *French* dō) *n.* A woman's marriage portion; dowry. [French, from Latin *dōs* (stem *dōt-*), dowry. See **dō-** in Appendix.*] —**do′tal** (dōt′l) *adj.*

do·tage (dō′tĭj) *n.* **1.** Second childhood; senility. **2.** Foolish or excessive fondness. [Middle English, from *doten*, DOTE.]

do·tard (dō′tərd) *n.* A senile person. [Middle English, from *doten*, DOTE.]

dote (dōt) *intr.v.* **doted, doting, dotes.** Also **doat. 1.** To lavish excessive love or fondness. Used with *on* or *upon*: *"His parents ne'er agreed except in doting / Upon the most inquiet imp on earth."* (Byron). **2.** To be foolish or feeble-minded, especially as a result of senility. —See Synonyms at **like**. [Middle English *doten*, from Middle Dutch, to be silly. See **dud-** in Appendix.*] —**dot′er** *n.*

doth. *Archaic.* Third person singular, present tense of **do**.

dot product. *Mathematics.* **Scalar product** *(see)*. [So called because it is written $x \cdot y$.]

dot-se·quen·tial (dŏt′sĭ-kwĕn′shəl) *adj.* Pertaining to a color-television system in which the primary colors red, green, and blue are transmitted as dots in sequence and exhibited in the same sequence to produce a complete color image.

dotted swiss. A crisp cotton fabric, embellished with woven, flocked, or embroidered dots.

dot·ter·el (dŏt′ər-əl) *n.* Also **dot·trel** (dŏt′rəl). **1.** A Eurasian plover, *Eudromias morinellus*, having predominantly reddish-brown and black plumage. **2.** Any of several similar or related birds. [Middle English *dotrelle* : *dot(en)*, DOTE + *(coke)relle*, COCKEREL.]

dot·tle (dŏt′l) *n.* Also **dot·tel.** The plug of tobacco ash left in the bowl of a pipe after it has been smoked. [From DOT (in the obsolete sense of a lump).]

dot·ty (dŏt′ē) *adj.* **-tier, -tiest. 1.** Having a feeble or unsteady gait; shaky. **2. a.** Daft; crazy: *a dotty old lady.* **b.** Infatuated. Used with *about*. [Variant of Scottish *dottle*, silly, from Middle English *doten*, DOTE.]

Dou·ai (dōō′ā; *French* dwā). Formerly **Dou·ay.** A city of France, in the northwest, 18 miles south of Lille. Population, 46,000.

Dou·a·la (dōō-ä′lə). Also **Du·a·la.** A city of Cameroun, a seaport in the west on the Bight of Biafra. Population, 128,000.

Dou·ay Bible (dōō′ā). Also **Douai Bible.** *Abbr.* **D.Bib., D.V.** An English translation of the Latin Vulgate Bible by Roman Catholic scholars. Also called "Douay Version."

dou·ble (dŭb′əl) *adj. Abbr.* **dbl. 1.** Twice as much in size, strength, number, or amount: *a double dose.* **2.** Composed of two like parts; in a pair: *double doors.* **3.** Composed of two unlike parts; combining two; dual: *a double meaning.* **4.** Accommodating or designed for two: *a double sleeping bag.* **5. a.** Acting two parts: *a double agent.* **b.** Characterized by duplicity; deceitful: *speak with a double tongue.* **6.** *Botany.* Having many more than the usual number of petals, usually in a crowded or overlapping arrangement: *a double chrysanthemum.* **7.** *Music.* Producing pitches one octave lower than the notes written on the score: *a double bass.* —*n. Abbr.* **dbl. 1.** Something increased twofold. **2. a.** A duplicate; counterpart. **b.** An apparition; a wraith. **3.** An actor's understudy. **4. a.** A sharp turn in running; reversal. **b.** An evasive reversal or shift in argument. **5.** *Plural.* A game, such as tennis or handball, having two players on each side. **6.** *Baseball.* A two-base hit. **7.** *Bridge.* **a.** A bid indicating strength to one's partner; request for a bid. **b.** A bid doubling one's opponent's bid, thus increasing the penalty for failure to fulfill the contract. **c.** A hand justifying such a bid. —**on** (or **at**) **the double.** *Informal.* **1.** In double time. **2.** Immediately. —*v.* **doubled, -bling, -bles.** —*tr.* **1.** To make twice as great. **2.** To be twice as much as. **3.** To fold in two. **4.** To duplicate; repeat. **5.** *Bridge.* To challenge (an opponent's bid) with a double. **6.** *Music.* To duplicate (another part or voice) an octave higher or lower or in unison. **7.** *Nautical.* To sail around: *double a cape.* —*intr.* **1.** To be increased twofold. **2.** To turn sharply backward; reverse. Often used with *back*: *double back on one's trail.* **3.** To serve in an additional capacity. **4.** To replace an actor in the execution of a given action or in the actor's absence: *doubled for the star in the chase scene.* **5.** *Baseball.* To make a two-base hit. **6.** *Bridge.* To announce a double. —**double in brass.** *Slang.* **1.** To be capable in more than one specialty. **2.** Originally, to be able to play an additional instrument. —*adv.* **1. a.** To twice the extent; doubly. **b.** To twice the amount: *double your money back.* **2.** Two together: *sleeping double.* **3.** In two: *bent double.* —**see double.** To see two images of a single object, usually as a result of visual aberration. [Middle English, from Old French, from Latin *duplus,* twofold, double. See **dwō** in Appendix.*] —**dou'ble·ness** *n.* —**dou'bler** *n.*

double bar. A double vertical or heavy black line drawn through a staff to indicate the end of any of the main sections of a musical composition.

doub·le-bar·reled (dŭb'əl-băr'əld) *adj.* **1.** Having two barrels mounted side by side: *a double-barreled shotgun.* **2.** Serving two purposes; twofold.

double bass. The largest member of the violin family, shaped like a cello, played usually with a bow, and having a deep range of about three octaves. Also called "bass viol," "bull fiddle," "contrabass," "string bass."

double bassoon. The **contrabassoon** *(see).*

double bed. A bed accommodating two people.

double boiler. A cooking utensil consisting of two nested pans, designed to allow slow, even cooking or heating of food in the upper pan by the action of the water boiling in the lower.

dou·ble-breast·ed (dŭb'əl-brĕs'tĭd) *adj.* **1.** Fastened by lapping one half over the other, and usually having a double row of buttons with a single row of buttonholes: *a double-breasted jacket.* **2.** Having a coat of this type: *a double-breasted suit.*

double chin. A fold of fatty flesh beneath the chin.

double coconut. **1.** A tall palm tree, *Lodoica maldivia,* of the Seychelles Islands, having broad, fanlike foliage and large fruit. **2.** The two-lobed fruit of this tree, containing seeds sometimes weighing 40 pounds each. Also called "sea coconut."

dou·ble-cross (dŭb'əl-krôs', -krŏs') *tr.v.* **-crossed, -crossing, -crosses.** *Slang.* To betray by acting in contradiction to an agreed course of action. See Synonyms at **deceive.** —*n. Slang.* An instance of such betrayal; treachery. —**doub'le-cross'er** *n.*

double dagger. In writing and printing, a reference mark (‡). Sometimes shortened to "dagger." Also called "diesis."

Dou·ble·day (dŭb'əl-dā'), **Abner.** 1819–1893. American Army officer; reputed inventor of the game of baseball.

dou·ble-deal·ing (dŭb'əl-dē'lĭng) *adj.* Characterized by duplicity; deceitful; treacherous. —*n.* An act of treachery or duplicity. —**doub'le-deal'er** *n.*

dou·ble-deck·er (dŭb'əl-dĕk'ər) *n.* **1.** A vehicle having two decks or tiers for passengers. **2.** Two beds, one built above the other. **3.** *Informal.* A sandwich having three slices of bread and two layers of filling.

double decomposition. A chemical reaction between two compounds in which the first and second parts of one reactant are united, respectively, with the second and first parts of the other reactant. Also called "metathesis."

double dome. *Slang.* An intellectual; a highbrow.

double Dutch. Language that cannot be understood; gibberish.

double eagle. A U.S. gold coin withdrawn from circulation in 1934 and having a face value of 20 dollars.

doub·le-edged (dŭb'əl-ĕjd') *adj.* **1.** Having two cutting edges, as a sword or razor blade. **2.** Capable of being effective or interpreted in two ways: *double-edged praise.*

doub·le-en·ten·dre (dŭb'əl-än-tän'drə; *French* dōō-blän-täɴ'dr') *n.* **1.** A word or phrase having a double meaning, especially when the second meaning is risqué. **2.** The use of such expressions. [French, "double meaning."]

double entry. A method of bookkeeping in which a transaction is entered both as a debit to one account and a credit to another account, so that the totals of debits and credits are equal.

doub·le-faced (dŭb'əl-fāst') *adj.* **1.** Having two faces, aspects, or sides. **2.** Characterized by duplicity; hypocritical.

double feature. A motion-picture program consisting of two full-length films.

doub·le-head·er (dŭb'əl-hĕd'ər) *n.* **1.** Two baseball games played by two teams in succession on the same day. **2.** A train pulled by two locomotives. [From DOUBLE + HEAD.]

doub·le-joint·ed (dŭb'əl-join'tĭd) *adj.* Having unusually flexible joints permitting connected parts, such as limbs or fingers, to be bent at unusual angles.

double negative. **1.** A syntactic construction that employs two negatives, especially to express a single negation. **2.** A similar construction in which the repetition of negation produces an affirmative.

Usage: The form of double negative now considered clearly nonstandard is that which employs two negatives in a single statement, usually a brief construction: *He didn't say nothing. We aren't going, neither.* In modern usage this is considered illiteracy or dialect, and as such is to be avoided. Formerly, such constructions were common even in written English as a form of intensified negation, and they still survive in literary works. An example is Hamlet's advice to the players: *"Be not too tame neither, but let your own discretion be your tutor."* Two other constructions employing more than one negative are generally accepted at present, however. One of these employs *not* before an adjective having a negative sense: *a not infrequent visitor; a not uncommon experience.* These form conditional, or weak, positives, whose meanings express a shade of distinction not contained in the forthrightly positive *frequent* and *common.* The other construction employs a second, reinforcing negative as a reminder of the prevailing negative sense. This type is often found in long sentences in which emphasis of the negative is sought: *He would not surrender, not even in the face of impossible odds.* This is approved by 71 per cent of the Usage Panel.

doub·le-park (dŭb'əl-pärk') *v.* **-parked, -parking, -parks.** —*tr.* To park (a car or vehicle) alongside another vehicle already parked parallel to the curb. —*intr.* To park a vehicle in such a manner.

double play. *Baseball.* A play in which two players are put out.

double pneumonia. Pneumonia afflicting both lungs.

doub·le-quick (dŭb'əl-kwĭk') *adj.* Very quick; rapid. —*n.* A marching cadence, **double time** *(see).* —*intr.v.* **double-quicked, -quicking, -quicks.** To double-time.

doub·le-reed (dŭb'əl-rēd') *adj.* Pertaining to any of a group of wind instruments that have a mouthpiece formed of two joined reeds that vibrate against each other.

double refraction. *Optics.* **Birefringence** *(see).*

double salt. *Chemistry.* A salt consisting, or regarded as consisting, of a molecular combination of two simple salts.

doub·le-space (dŭb'əl-spās') *v.* **-spaced, -spacing, -spaces.** —*intr.* To type so that there is a full space between lines. —*tr.* To type (copy) in this way.

double standard. A set of principles permitting greater opportunity or liberty to one than to another, especially the granting of greater sexual freedom to men than to women.

double star. A **binary star** *(see).*

doub·let (dŭb'lĭt) *n.* **1.** A close-fitting jacket, with or without sleeves, worn by men between the 15th and 17th centuries. **2.** A counterfeit gem made of a piece of colored glass covered with crystal or with a thin face of real gemstone. **3. a.** A pair of similar things. **b.** One of a pair. **c.** *Physics.* A multiplet with two members. **4.** *Linguistics.* One of two words derived from the same source by different routes of transmission. **5.** *Plural.* A throw of two dice in which the same number of dots appears on the upper face of each. [Middle English, from Old French, from *double,* DOUBLE.]

double take. A delayed reaction to an unusual remark or circumstance, often used as a comic device.

double talk. **1.** Meaningless speech that consists of nonsense syllables mixed with intelligible words; gibberish. **2.** Ambiguous or evasive language.

doub·le·think (dŭb'əl-thĭngk') *n.* The belief in two contradictory ideas or points of view at the same time.

double time. *Abbr.* **d.t.** **1.** *U.S. Army.* A marching pace of 180 three-foot steps per minute. Also called "double-quick." **2.** *Music.* Duple time. **3.** A wage rate that is double the normal rate.

doub·le-time (dŭb'əl-tīm') *v.* **-timed, -timing, -times.** —*tr.* To march (troops) in double time. —*intr.* **1.** To march in double time. **2.** To jog or run.

doub·le-tongue (dŭb'əl-tŭng') *intr.v.* **-tongued, -tonguing, -tongues.** To play a rapidly repeated series of notes on a wind instrument by placing the tongue alternately between the positions for *t* and *k.*

doub·le·tree (dŭb'əl-trē') *n.* A crossbar on a wagon or coach to which two whiffletrees are attached for harnessing two animals abreast.

doub·le-u (dŭb'əl-yōō') *n.* The letter *w.*

dou·bloon (dŭ-blōōn') *n.* An obsolete Spanish gold coin. [Spanish *doblón,* augmentative of *dobla,* Spanish coin, from Latin *dupla,* feminine of *duplus,* DOUBLE.]

dou·blure (dōō-blŏŏr') *n.* An ornamental lining, as of vellum or leather, on the inside face of a book cover. [French, lining, from Old French, from *doubler,* to double, to line, from Latin *duplāre,* to double, from *duplus,* DOUBLE.]

doub·ly (dŭb'lē) *adv.* **1.** To a double degree; twice. **2.** In a twofold manner.

doubt (dout) *v.* **doubted, doubting, doubts.** —*tr.* **1.** To be uncertain or skeptical about; be undecided about. **2.** To tend to disbelieve; distrust: *"It is hard for those who live near a bank/To doubt the security of their money."* (T.S. Eliot). **3.** *Archaic.* To suspect; fear: *"we doubted our cables and anchors would scarcely hold until morning"* (John White). —*intr.* To be undecided, unconvinced, or skeptical. —*n.* **1. a.** A lack of conviction or certainty. **b.** An instance of this; a point about which one is uncertain or skeptical. Usually used in the plural. **2.** An uncertain condition or state of affairs: *an outcome still in doubt.* —See Synonyms at **uncertainty.** —**beyond doubt.** Unquestionably; definitely. —**no doubt.** **1.** Certainly. **2.** Probably. See Usage note at **doubtless.** —**without doubt.** Certainly. See Usage note at **doubtless.** [Middle English *d(o)uten,* from Old French *douter,* from Latin *dubitāre,* to waver, vibrate. See **dwō** in Appendix.*] —**doubt'er** *n.*

Usage: *Doubt* and *doubtful* are often followed by clauses introduced by *that, whether,* or *if.* A choice among the three is guided by the nature of the sentence involved, but considerable leeway often exists. The clearest choice occurs when an outright negative or interrogative sense is expressed (in effect, a denial of doubt), in which case *that* is almost invariably used: *There is no doubt that you are right. Do you doubt that I believe you?* In positive statements intended to convey real doubt or uncertainty, *whether* is the most widely accepted choice, especially in formal contexts: *We doubt whether they can succeed. It is doubtful whether he will come.* According to 58 per cent of the Usage Panel, *whether* is the only acceptable choice in these examples; the remainder would also accept *if* (which is more informal in tone) and *that.* With respect to *that* in positive statements, the majority (58 per cent) recommend that it be restricted to sentences in which unbelief rather than genuine doubt is conveyed: *I doubt that he will come* (intended meaning: *I don't think he will come*). Thus *that* is especially appropriate to denial of doubt and to implied unbelief, but cannot be ruled out where real doubt is intended. See Usage note at **but.**

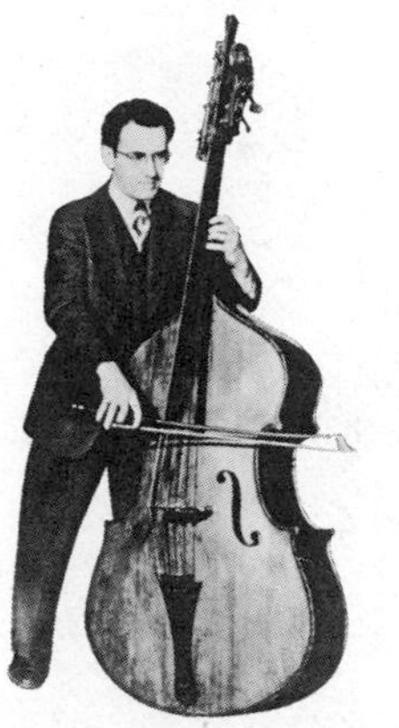

double bass

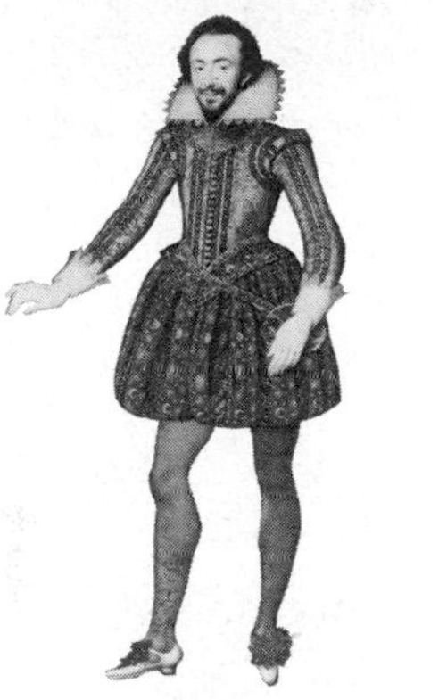

doublet
Portrait of Richard Sackville, Earl of Dorset, wearing a doublet

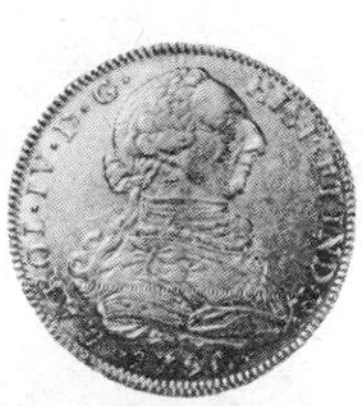

doubloon
Doubloon of Charles IV, dated 1790

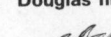

Douglas fir

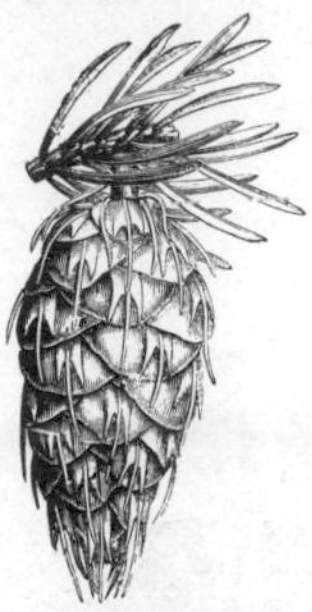

cone

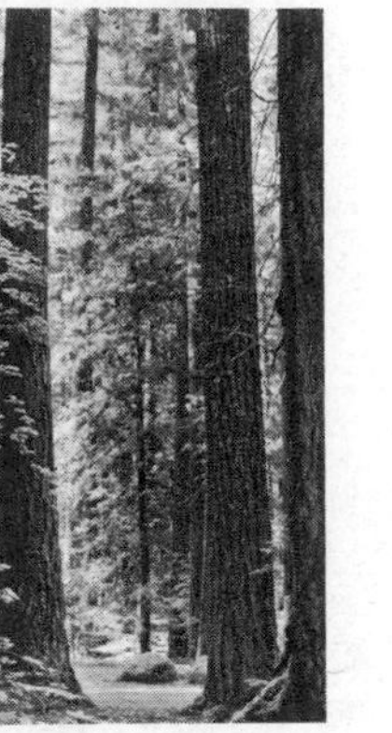

stand of Douglas firs

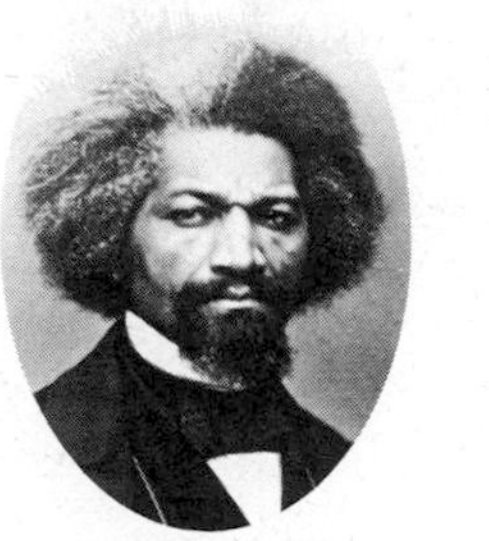

Frederick Douglass

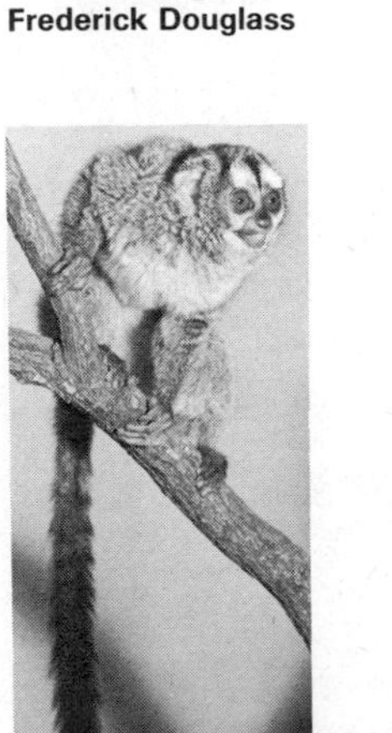

douroucouli

doubt·ful (dout′fəl) *adj.* **1.** Subject to or tending to cause doubt; uncertain; unclear. **2.** Experiencing doubt. **3.** Of uncertain outcome; undecided. **4.** Questionable; suspicious: *a man with a doubtful past.* —See Usage note at **doubt**. —**doubt′ful·ly** *adv.* —**doubt′ful·ness** *n.*

Synonyms: *doubtful, dubious, questionable.* These adjectives express a degree of uncertainty (as to the occurrence of something, for example), or they can imply reservations about persons or their attributes. *Doubtful* suggests pronounced uncertainty as to such an occurrence or as to the worth or fitness of a person. *Dubious* expresses uncertainty less directly and less forcefully; often it suggests hesitancy based on suspicion or mistrust rather than on something more tangible, such as fact or past performance. *Questionable* can mean uncertain in the sense of being open to doubt or debate, or it can imply, more strongly than the other terms, that the person or thing specified is not worthy of confidence or trust.

doubting Thomas. One who habitually expresses or feels doubts. [After SAINT THOMAS, who doubted Jesus' resurrection until he had proof.]

doubt·less (dout′lĭs) *adj.* Certain; assured: *doubtless of ultimate victory.* —*adv.* **1.** Certainly. **2.** Presumably; probably. —**doubt′less·ly** *adv.*

Usage: *Doubtless* and *no doubt* are relatively weak in expressing certainty (absence of doubt), since they also can indicate mere presumption or probability: *He will doubtless go;* or concession: *You are no doubt right in some details.* In contrast, *undoubtedly* and *without doubt* express only certainty and conviction.

dou·ceur (do͞o-sûr′) *n.* Money given as a tip, gratuity, or bribe. [French, "sweetness," from Late Latin *dulcor,* from Latin *dulcis,* sweet. See **dḷku-** in Appendix.*]

douche (do͞osh) *n.* **1.** A stream of water or air applied to a part or cavity of the body for cleansing or medicinal purposes. **2.** The application of a douche. **3.** A syringe or other instrument for applying a douche. —*v.* **douched, douching, douches.** —*tr.* To cleanse or treat by means of a douche. —*intr.* To be cleansed or treated by a douche. [French, douche, shower, from Italian *doccia,* conduit pipe, shower, douche, probably from *doccione,* pipe, tube, from Latin *ductiō* (stem *ductiōn-*), a leading away, from *ductus,* past participle of *dūcere,* to lead. See **deuk-** in Appendix.*]

dough (dō) *n.* **1.** A soft, thick mixture of flour or meal, liquids, and various dry ingredients that is baked as bread, pastry, or the like. **2.** Any similar pasty mass. **3.** *Slang.* Money. [Middle English *dogh,* Old English *dāg.* See **dheigh-** in Appendix.*]

dough·boy (dō′boi′) *n.* **1.** Bread dough that is rolled thin and cut into various shapes, then fried in deep fat. **2.** An infantryman in World War I. [Sense 2, origin obscure.]

dough·nut (dō′nŭt′, -nət) *n.* Also **do·nut.** A small, ring-shaped cake made of rich, light dough that is fried in deep fat.

dough·ty (dou′tē) *adj.* **-tier, -tiest.** Stouthearted; courageous. See Synonyms at **brave.** [Middle English *doughty,* Old English *dohtig, dyhtig.* See **dheugh-** in Appendix.*] —**dough′ti·ly** *adv.* —**dough′ti·ness** *n.*

dough·y (dō′ē) *adj.* **-ier, -iest.** Having the consistency or appearance of dough.

Doug·las[1] (dŭg′ləs). A masculine given name. [Gaelic *dubhglas*†, dark, gray.]

Doug·las[2] (dŭg′ləs). The capital of the Isle of Man, a seaport in the southeast. Population, 19,000.

Doug·las (dŭg′ləs), **Stephen Arnold.** 1813–1861. American political leader; debated Abraham Lincoln (1858).

Douglas fir. A tall evergreen timber tree, *Pseudotsuga taxifolia* (or *P. menziesii*), of northwestern North America, having short needles and egg-shaped cones. Also called "Oregon fir." [After David *Douglas* (1798–1834), Scottish botanist, who traveled in North America.]

Doug·las-Home (dŭg′ləs-hyo͞om′), Sir **Alexander Frederick.** Formerly, 14th Earl of Home. Born 1903. Prime Minister of the United Kingdom (1963–64).

Doug·lass (dŭg′ləs), **Frederick.** Original name, Frederick Augustus Washington Bailey. 1817?–1895. American Negro abolitionist.

Dou·kho·bors. Variant of **Dukhobors.**

Dou·ma. Variant of **Duma.**

doum palm. Variant of **doom palm.**

dour (do͝or, dour) *adj.* **1.** Marked by intractable sternness or harshness; forbidding. **2.** Silently ill-humored; gloomy. —See Synonyms at **glum.** [Middle English, perhaps from Latin *dūrus,* hard. See **deru-** in Appendix.*]

dou·ra, dou·rah. Variants of **durra.**

dou·rine (do͞o-rēn′) *n.* A contagious venereal disease of horses, asses, and mules, caused by the microorganism *Trypanosoma equiperdum,* which is transmitted during copulation. [French, from Arabic *darina,* to be dirty.]

Dou·ro (dō′ro͞o). *Spanish* **Due·ro** (dwā′rō). A river rising in north-central Spain and flowing 475 miles generally west to the Atlantic near Oporto, Portugal.

dou·rou·cou·li (do͞o′ro͞o-ko͞o′lē) *n., pl.* **-lis.** Also **dou·ro·cou·li** (do͞o′rō-). A small nocturnal monkey, *Aotus trivigatus,* of Central and South America, having very large, round eyes. [Native South American name.]

douse[1] (dous) *v.* **doused, dousing, douses.** Also **dowse.** —*tr.* **1.** To plunge into liquid; immerse. **2.** To wet thoroughly; drench. —*intr.* To become thoroughly wet; soak. —*n.* Also **dowse.** A drenching. [Perhaps from earlier *douse*†, to strike, smite.] —**dous′er** *n.*

douse[2] (dous) *tr.v.* **doused, dousing, douses.** To put out (a light or fire); extinguish. [Perhaps from earlier *douse,* to strike, smite. See **douse.**]

douse[3]. Variant of **dowse** (to use a divining rod).

DOVAP (dō′văp′). *Electronics.* A system for determining the velocity and position of a long-range missile using the **Doppler effect** *(see).* [DO(PPLER) V(ELOCITY) A(ND) P(OSITION).]

dove[1] (dŭv) *n.* **1.** Any of various birds of the family Columbidae, which also includes the pigeons; especially, an undomesticated species, such as the **mourning dove** *(see).* **2.** A gentle or innocent child or woman. Used especially as a term of endearment. **3.** A messenger of peace or deliverance from care by allusion to the dove of Genesis 8:8–12. **4.** A member of a group promoting or adhering to a cause of peace. Compare **hawk.** **5.** *Capital* **D.** The constellation **Columba** *(see).* [Middle English *do(u)ve,* Old English *dūfe* (unattested). See **dheu-**[1] in Appendix.*]

dove[2]. Alternate past tense of **dive.** See Usage note at **dive.**

dove·cote (dŭv′kōt′, -kŏt′) *n.* Also **dove·cot** (-kŏt′). A roost for domesticated pigeons.

dove·kie (dŭv′kē) *n.* Also **dove·key.** A small black-and-white sea bird, *Plautus alle,* of arctic and northern Atlantic regions. Also called "little auk." [Diminutive of DOVE.]

Do·ver (dō′vər). **1.** A port city of England, in eastern Kent. Population, 36,000. **2.** The capital of Delaware, in the east-central part of the state. Population, 7,000.

Do·ver, Strait of (dō′vər). A strait between England and France, 21 miles wide at its narrowest point, connecting the eastern end of the English Channel with the North Sea.

Do·ver's powder (dō′vərz). A powdered drug, made essentially of ipecac and opium, formerly used to relieve pain and induce perspiration. [After Thomas *Dover* (1660–1742), English physician.]

dove·tail (dŭv′tāl′) *n.* **1.** A fan-shaped tenon that forms a tight interlocking joint when fitted into a corresponding mortise. **2.** A joint formed by interlocking one or more such tenons and mortises. In this sense, also called "dovetail joint." —*v.* **dove-tailed, -tailing, -tails.** —*tr.* **1.** To cut into or join by means of dovetails. **2.** To connect or combine precisely or harmoniously. —*intr.* To combine or interlock into a unified whole. [From its supposed resemblance to a dove's tail.]

dow·a·ger (dou′ə-jər) *n.* **1.** A widow who holds a title or property derived from her dead husband. Often used in combination with the title. **2.** An elderly woman of high social station. [Old French *douagiere,* from *douage,* dower, from *douer,* to portion, endow, from Latin *dōtāre,* from *dōs* (stem *dōt-*), dowry. See **dō-** in Appendix.*]

dow·dy (dou′dē) *adj.* **-dier, -diest.** Lacking in stylishness or neatness; shabby: *dowdy clothes.* See Synonyms at **sloppy.** —*n., pl.* **dowdies.** A dowdy woman; frump. [From Middle English *doude*†, slut.] —**dow′di·ly** *adv.* —**dow′di·ness** *n.*

dow·el (dou′əl) *n.* **1.** A usually round pin that fits tightly into a corresponding hole to fasten or align two adjacent pieces. **2.** A round stick or rod from which dowels are cut. **3.** A piece of wood driven into a wall to act as an anchor for nails. —*tr.v.* **doweled** or **-elled, -eling** or **-elling, -els.** **1.** To fasten or align with dowels. **2.** To equip with dowels. [Middle English *dowle,* from Middle Low German *dōvel,* peg, block, nail. See **dheubh-** in Appendix.*]

dow·er (dou′ər) *n.* **1.** The part or interest of a deceased man's real estate allotted by law to his widow for her lifetime. Also *archaic* "dowry." **2.** A marriage portion, **dowry** *(see).* **3.** A sum of money required of a postulant at a convent; dowry. **4.** A natural endowment or gift; dowry. —*tr.v.* **dowered, -ering, -ers.** To assign a dower to; endow. [Middle English *dowere,* from Old French *douaire,* from Medieval Latin *dōtārium,* from Latin *dōs* (stem *dōt-*), dowry. See **dō-** in Appendix.*]

dow·itch·er (dou′ĭ-chər) *n.* Either of two shore birds, *Limnodromus griseus* or *L. scolopaeus,* of northern regions, having brownish plumage and a long, straight bill. [Of Iroquoian origin.]

down[1] (doun) *adv. Abbr.* **dn.** **1. a.** From a higher to a lower place or position. **b.** Downstairs. **c.** Toward, to, or on the ground, floor, or bottom. **2. a.** Into a lower posture. **b.** In or into a prostrate position. **3.** Out of one's grasp. **4.** Toward or in the south or in a southerly direction. **5. a.** Toward or in a center of activity: *going down to the office.* **b.** Away from the present place: *down on the farm.* **6.** To the source: *tracking a rumor down.* **7.** Toward or at a low or lower point on a scale. **8.** To or in a quiescent or subdued state. **9.** To or in a low status, as of subjection or disgrace. **10.** To an extreme degree; heavily. **11.** Seriously; vigorously: *get down to work.* **12.** From earlier times or people. **13.** To a reduced form; to a finer consistency: *boiling down maple syrup.* **14.** In writing; on paper: *taking a statement down.* **15.** In partial payment at the time of purchase: *five dollars down.* —**down with.** **1.** To a lower or inferior position. **2.** Away with; put down or overthrow. —**go down.** *Vulgar Slang.* To have sexual intercourse. —**go down on.** *Vulgar Slang.* To perform fellatio or cunnilingus upon. —*adj.* **1. a.** Moving or directed downward: *a down elevator.* **b.** In a low position; not up. **c.** At a reduced level. **2. a.** Sick. **b.** Low in spirit; depressed: *feel down.* **3. a.** In games, trailing an opponent by a specified number of points, goals, or strokes: *down two.* **b.** *Football.* Not in play. Said of the ball. **c.** *Baseball.* Put out. **4.** Being the first installment. —**down and out.** Lacking friends or resources; destitute. —**down in the mouth.** Discouraged; sad. —**down on.** *Informal.* Hostile or negative toward; out of patience with. —*prep.* **1.** In a descending direction along, upon, into, or through. **2.** Along the course of. **3.** Toward the mouth of a river. —*n.* **1.** A downward move-

ment; descent. **2.** *Football.* Any of a series of four plays during which a team must advance at least ten yards to retain possession of the ball. —*v.* **downed, downing, downs.** —*tr.* **1.** To bring, put, strike, or throw down. **2.** To swallow hastily; to gulp. —*intr.* To go or come down; descend. [Middle English *doun,* Old English *dūne,* short for *adūne,* reduced form of *ofdūne,* "from the hill" : *of,* OFF + *dūne,* dative of *dūn,* hill (see **dhūno-** in Appendix*).]

down² (doun) *n.* **1.** Fine, soft, fluffy feathers forming the first plumage of a young bird and underlying the contour feathers in adult birds. **2.** *Botany.* A covering of soft, short fibers, as on some leaves. **3.** Any soft, silky, or feathery substance, such as the first growth of human beard. [Middle English *doun, downe,* from Old Norse *dūnn.* See **dheu-¹** in Appendix.*]

down³ (doun) *n.* **1.** *Usually plural.* An expanse of rolling, grassy upland used for grazing, especially in southern England. **2.** *Often capital* **D.** Any of several breeds of sheep having short wool, developed in the downs of England. [Middle English *doun, dun,* hill, Old English *dūn.* See **dhūno-** in Appendix.*]

Down (doun). A county occupying 951 square miles in southeastern Northern Ireland. Population, 277,000. County seat, Downpatrick.

down·beat (doun'bēt') *n. Music.* The downward stroke made by a conductor to indicate the first beat of a measure.

down·bow (doun'bō') *n. Music.* A stroke made by drawing a bow from handle to tip across the strings of a violin or other bowed instrument.

down·cast (doun'kăst', -käst') *adj.* **1.** Directed downward. **2.** Depressed; dejected; sad. —See Synonyms at **sad.**

Down East. Also **down East.** New England, especially Maine.

Down Easter. Also **Down-East·er** (doun'ē'stər), **down-East·er.** One that lives in or comes from New England, especially Maine.

Down·ey (dou'nē). A city of southern California, southeast of Los Angeles. Population, 83,000.

down·fall (doun'fôl') *n.* **1. a.** A sudden loss of wealth, rank, reputation, or happiness; ruin. **b.** Something causing this. **2.** A fall of rain or snow, especially a heavy or unexpected one.

down·fall·en (doun'fô'lən) *adj.* Fallen, as from high estate; ruined.

down·grade (doun'grād') *n.* A descending slope in a road. —**on the downgrade.** Declining, as in influence, reputation, or wealth; losing status. —*tr.v.* **downgraded, -grading, -grades. 1.** To lower the status and salary of one. **2.** To lower or minimize the importance or reputation of.

down·haul (doun'hôl') *n.* A rope or set of ropes for hauling down or securing a sail or spar.

down·heart·ed (doun'här'tĭd) *adj.* Low in spirit; depressed; discouraged. —**down'heart'ed·ly** *adv.* —**down'heart'ed·ness** *n.*

down·hill (doun'hĭl') *adv.* Down the slope of a hill; in a downward direction. —**go downhill.** To decline, as in one's career or health. —*adj.* (doun'hĭl'). Sloping downward; descending.

Down·ing Street (dou'nĭng). The British government. [From the location of the Prime Minister's residence at No. 10 Downing Street, London.]

down·pour (doun'pôr', -pōr') *n.* A heavy fall of rain.

down·range (doun'rānj') *adv.* In a direction away from the launch site and along the flight line of a missile test range. —*adj.* (doun'rānj'). Designating the area and airspace along the flight line of a missile test range.

down·right (doun'rīt') *adj.* **1.** Thoroughgoing; unequivocal. **2.** Forthright; candid. —*adv.* Thoroughly; absolutely.

Downs, The (dounz). **1.** Two parallel hill ranges in southern England. **2.** A roadstead in the English Channel, off the southeastern coast of Kent, England.

down·stage (doun'stāj') *adv.* Toward or at the front part of a stage. —*adj.* (doun'stāj'). Relating to the front part of a stage. —*n.* (doun'stāj'). The front half of a stage.

down·stairs (doun'stârz') *adv.* **1.** Down the stairs. **2.** To or on a lower floor. —*adj.* (doun'stârz'). Also **down·stair** (-stâr'). Located on a lower or main floor. —*n.* (doun'stârz'). Plural in form, used with a singular verb. The lower or main floor of a building.

down·stream (doun'strēm') *adj.* In the direction of a stream's current. —*adv.* (doun'strēm'). Down a stream.

down·swing (doun'swĭng') *n.* **1.** A swing downward. **2.** A business decline.

down·time (doun'tīm') *n.* The period of time when a factory or its machinery is inactive.

down-to-earth (doun'tə-ûrth') *adj.* Realistic; sensible.

down·town (doun'toun') *adv.* To, toward, or in the lower part or the business center of a city or town. —*adj.* (doun'toun'). Of, relating to, or located downtown. —*n.* (doun'toun'). The business hub or lower part of a city or town.

down·trod·den (doun'trŏd'n) *adj.* Oppressed; tyrannized.

down under. *Informal* Australia or New Zealand.

down·ward (doun'wərd) *adv.* Also **down·wards** (-wərdz). **down·ward·ly** (-wərd-lē). **1.** From a higher to a lower place, point, level, or condition. **2.** From an earlier to a more recent time. —*adj.* **1.** Descending from a higher to a lower place, point, level, character, or condition. **2.** Descending from a source or origin.

down·wind (doun'wĭnd') *adv.* In the direction in which the wind blows; leeward. —**down'wind'** *adj.*

down·y (dou'nē) *adj.* **-ier, -iest. 1.** Made of or covered with down. **2. a.** Resembling down. **b.** Quietly soothing; soft.

downy mildew. A disease of plants caused by fungi of the order Peronosporales and characterized by gray, velvety patches of spores on the lower surfaces of leaves.

dow·ry (dour'ē) *n., pl.* **-ries. 1.** Money or property brought by a bride to her husband at marriage. Also called "dower." **2.** *Archaic.* A widow's inheritance, a **dower** (*see*). **3.** A sum of money required of a postulant at a convent; dower. **4.** A natural endowment or gift; dower. [Variant of DOWER.]

dowse¹ (douz) *intr.v.* **dowsed, dowsing, dowses.** Also **douse.** To use a divining rod to find underground water or minerals. [Origin unknown.] —**dows'er** *n.*

dowse². Variant of **douse** (to drench).

dowsing rod. A divining rod (*see*).

Dow·son (dou'sən), **Ernest.** 1867–1900. English poet.

dox·ol·o·gy (dŏk-sŏl'ə-jē) *n., pl.* **-gies. 1.** A liturgical formula of praise to God. See **Gloria in excelsis Deo, Gloria Patri. 2.** Any formula beginning "Praise God from whom all blessings flow." [Medieval Latin *doxologia,* from Greek, laudation : *doxa,* opinion, judgment + -LOGY.] —**dox'o·log'i·cal** (-sə-lŏj'ə-kəl) *adj.* —**dox'o·log'i·cal·ly** *adv.*

dox·y (dŏk'sē) *n., pl.* **-ies.** *Slang.* **1.** A loose woman; prostitute. **2.** A paramour. [Perhaps from obsolete Dutch *docke,* doll, from Middle Dutch, from Common Germanic *dukk-* (unattested), bundle. See also **dock** (doll).]

doy·en (doi-ĕn', doi'ən; *French* dwä-yăɴ') *n.* *Feminine* **doy·enne** (doi-ĕn'; *French* dwä-yĕn'). The eldest or senior member of a group. [French, from Late Latin *decānus,* chief of ten, a kind of officer, from Greek *dekanos,* from *deka,* ten. See **dekm̥** in Appendix.*]

Doyle (doil), Sir **Arthur Conan.** 1859–1930. English physician and novelist; creator of Sherlock Holmes.

doy·ley, doy·ly. Variants of **doily.**

D'Oy·ly Carte, Richard. See **Carte.**

doz. dozen.

doze (dōz) *intr.v.* **dozed, dozing, dozes.** To sleep lightly and intermittently; nod sleepily; nap. —**doze off.** To fall into a light sleep. —*n.* A short, light sleep; a nap. [Originally transitive, to make dull, stupefy, drowse, probably of Scandinavian origin, akin to Danish *døse.* See **dheu-¹** in Appendix.*] —**doz'er** *n.*

doz·en (dŭz'ən) *n., pl.* **dozen** (for sense 1) or **-ens** (for sense 2). *Abbr.* **doz., dz. 1.** A set of 12. **2.** An indefinite number; a great many. —*adj.* Twelve. [Middle English *dozeine,* from Old French, from *doze,* twelve, from Latin *duodecim* : *duo,* two (see **dwō** in Appendix*) + *decem,* ten (see **dekm̥** in Appendix*).] —**doz'enth** *adj.*

Usage: **Dozen** is usually not followed by *of,* in current usage, except with reference to a quantity that is part of a larger, specified quantity: *a dozen eggs, two dozen large oranges;* but *a dozen of his friends, two dozen of those oranges.* The plural *dozens,* representing an indefinitely large quantity of something specified, is followed by *of: dozens of examples.*

doz·er (dō'zər) *n.* A bulldozer.

do·zy (dō'zē) *adj.* **-zier, -ziest.** Drowsy; half asleep. —**doz'i·ly** *adv.* —**do'zi·ness** *n.*

DP, D.P. displaced person.

D.Ph., D.Phil. Doctor of Philosophy.

dpt. 1. department. **2.** deponent.

dr dram.

dr. 1. debit. **2.** debtor.

Dr. 1. doctor. **2.** drive (in street names).

drab¹ (drăb) *adj.* **drabber, drabbest. 1. a.** Of a dull light brown. **b.** Of a light olive brown or khaki color. **2.** Faded and dull in appearance. **3.** Of a commonplace character; dreary. —*n.* **1.** Cloth of a light dull brown or grayish brown or unbleached natural color; especially, a heavy woolen or cotton fabric. **2.** Moderate to grayish or light grayish yellowish brown or light olive brown. See **color. 3.** See **drape.** [Variant of obsolete *drap,* cloth, from Old French *drape.*] —**drab'ly** *adv.* —**drab'ness** *n.*

drab² (drăb) *n.* **1.** A slattern. **2.** A whore. —*intr.v.* **drabbed, drabbing, drabs.** To consort with whores: *"Even amid his drabbing, he himself retained some virginal airs"* (Stanislaus Joyce). [From Celtic, akin to Scottish Gaelic *drabag,* slattern, Middle Irish *drab,* dregs. See **dher-¹** in Appendix.*]

drab·ble (drăb'əl) *v.* **-bled, -bling, -bles.** —*intr.* To draggle. —*tr.* To bedraggle. [Middle English *drabelen,* of Low German origin, akin to Low German *drabbelen,* to paddle in water or mire. See **dher-¹** in Appendix.*]

dra·cae·na (drə-sē'nə) *n.* Any of several tropical plants of the genera *Dracaena* and *Cordyline,* some species of which are cultivated as house plants for their decorative foliage. [New Latin *Dracaena,* from Late Latin, from Greek *drakaina,* feminine of *drakōn,* serpent, DRAGON.]

drachm (drăm) *n.* **1.** *British.* A dram. **2.** A drachma.

drach·ma (drăk'mə) *n., pl.* **-mas** or **-mae** (-mē). *Abbr.* **d., D. 1. a.** The basic monetary unit of Greece, equal to 100 lepta. See table of exchange rates at **currency. b.** A coin worth one drachma. **2.** A silver coin of ancient Greece. **3.** One of several modern units of weight, especially the dram. **4.** A unit of weight of ancient Greece. [Latin, from Greek *drakhmē.* See **dergh-** in Appendix.*]

Dra·co (drā'kō) *n.* A constellation in the polar region of the Northern Hemisphere near Cepheus and Ursa Major. Also called "Dragon." [Latin *draco,* DRAGON.]

dra·co·ni·an (drā-kō'nē-ən) *adj.* Also **dra·con·ic** (drā-kŏn'ĭk). **1.** *Often capital* **D.** Designating a law or code of extreme severity. **2.** Harsh; rigorous: *a draconian penalty.* [After *Draco,* Athenian lawgiver, whose code (621 B.C.) was proverbially harsh.] —**dra·co'ni·al·ly** *adv.*

dra·con·ic¹ (drā-kŏn'ĭk) *adj.* Of or pertaining to a dragon. [From Latin *draco* (stem *dracōn-*), DRAGON.]

dra·con·ic². Variant of **draconian.**

draff (drăf) *n.* Refuse from brewing or distilling; dregs; lees of

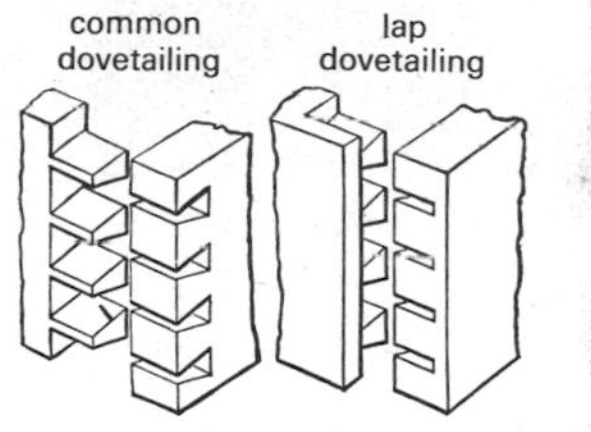

common dovetailing   lap dovetailing

dovetail

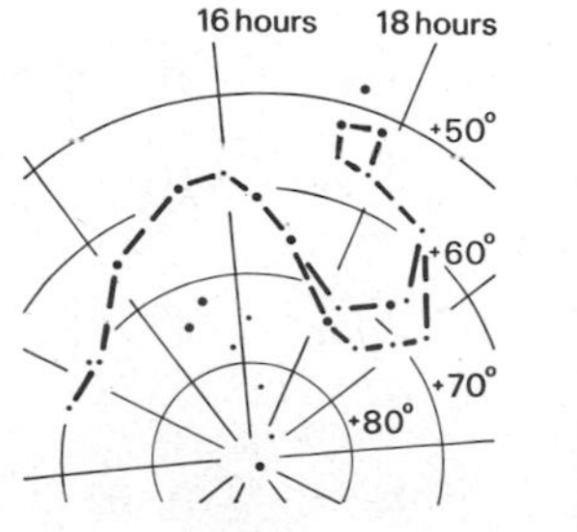

Draco

ă pat/ā pay/âr care/ä father/b bib/ch church/d deed/ĕ pet/ē be/f fife/g gag/h hat/hw which/ĭ pit/ī pie/îr pier/j judge/k kick/l lid, needle/m mum/n no, sudden/ng thing/ŏ pot/ō toe/ô paw, for/oi noise/ou out/σ̄σ took/σ̄σ boot/p pop/r roar/s sauce/sh ship, dish/t tight/th thin, path/th this, bathe/ŭ cut/ûr urge/v valve/w with/y yes/z zebra, size/zh vision/ə about, item, edible, gallop, circus/ à *Fr.* ami/œ *Fr.* feu, Ger. schön/ü *Fr.* tu, Ger. über/κʜ Ger. ich, Scot. loch/ɴ *Fr.* bon. *Follows main vocabulary. †Of obscure origin.

malt. [Middle English *draf,* Old English *dræf* (unattested). See **dher-¹** in Appendix.*]

draft (drăft, dräft) *n.* Also *chiefly British* **draught** (dräft). **1. a.** A current of air in an enclosed area. **b.** A current of air induced by artificial means. **c.** A device in a flue controlling the circulation of air. **2. a.** A pull or traction of a load. **b.** That which is pulled or drawn. **c.** *British.* The traction power or duty of a locomotive. **3.** The depth of a vessel's keel below the water line. **4.** A heavy demand upon resources. **5.** A documentary instrument for transferring money. **6. a.** A gulp, swallow, or inhalation. **b.** The amount taken in by a single act of drinking or inhaling. **c.** A measured portion; dose. **7.** The drawing of a liquid, as from a cask or keg. **8. a.** A selection of personnel from a group for some particular purpose or duty. **b.** Conscription for military service. **c.** The body of a people selected or conscripted. **9. a.** The drawing in of a fishnet. **b.** The catch. **10. a.** A preliminary outline of a plan, document, or picture. **b.** A representation of something to be constructed. **11.** *Masonry.* A narrow line chiseled on a stone to guide the stonecutter in leveling its surface. **12.** *Metallurgy.* A slight taper given a die to facilitate the removal of a casting. **13.** *Commerce.* An allowance made for loss in weight of merchandise. **—on draft.** Tapped from the keg; not bottled. *—tr.v.* **drafted, drafting, drafts.** Also *chiefly British* **draught. 1.** To select and draw from a group for some usually compulsory assignment, as military service. **2. a.** To draw up a preliminary version of or plan for. **b.** To compose. *—adj.* Also *chiefly British* **draught. 1.** Suited for or used for drawing heavy loads. **2.** Drawn from a cask or tap. [Middle English *draught,* a pulling, a drawing, perhaps from Old Norse *drāttr.* See **dhragh-** in Appendix.*] **—draft'er** *n.*

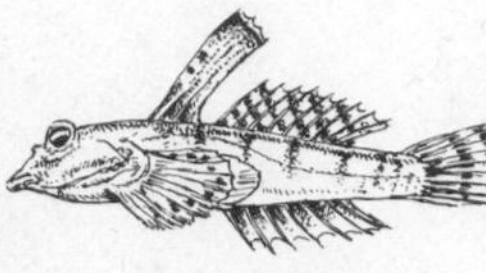

dragonet
Callionymus bairdi

draft board. A local board of civilians in charge of the selection of men for compulsory military service.

draft·ee (drăf-tē', dräf-) *n.* One drafted for military service.

draft·ing (drăf'tĭng, dräf'-) *n.* The systematic representation and dimensional specification of mechanical and architectural structures. Also called "mechanical drawing."

drafts·man (drăfts'mən, dräfts'-) *n., pl.* **-men** (-mĭn). **1.** One who draws plans or designs. **2.** One who draws up documents. **3.** One who excels in drawing. [Drafts, genitive of DRAFT + MAN.] **—drafts'man·ship'** *n.*

draft·y (drăf'tē, dräf'-) *adj.* **-ier, -iest.** Having or exposed to drafts of air. **—draft'i·ly** *adv.* **—draft'i·ness** *n.*

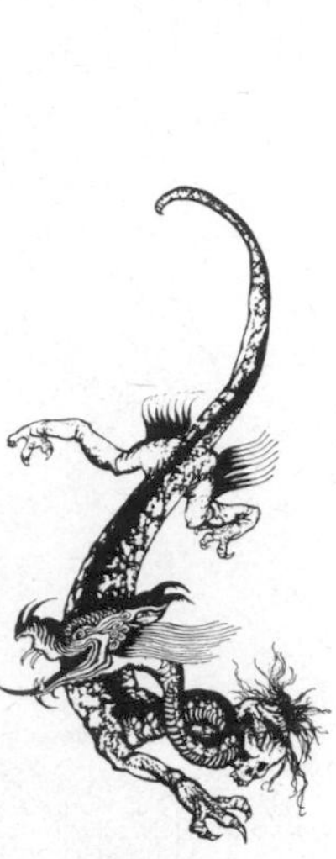

dragon
Arthur Rackham cover design for Edgar Allan Poe's *Tales of Mystery and Imagination*

drag (drăg) *v.* **dragged** or *nonstandard* **drug** (drŭg) (for transitive sense 8. See Usage note below.), **dragging, drags.** *—tr.* **1. a.** To pull or draw along the ground by force; to haul. **b.** To cause to trail along the ground. **2. a.** To search or sweep the bottom of (a body of water), as with a grappling hook or dragnet. **b.** To bring up or catch by such means. **3.** To bring forcibly to or into. **4.** To move with great reluctance, weariness, or difficulty. **5.** To break (land) with a harrow. **6.** To prolong tediously. Used with *out.* **7.** To introduce gratuitously into a discussion. Used with *in.* **8.** *Slang.* To bore or annoy. See Usage note below. *—intr.* **1.** To trail along the ground. **2.** To move slowly or with effort. **3.** To lag behind. **4.** To pass or proceed slowly, tediously, or laboriously. **5.** To search or dredge the bottom of a body of water. **6.** *Slang.* To draw on a cigarette. **—drag one's feet.** To act, work, or move with intentional slowness. *—n.* **1.** The act of dragging. **2.** Something that is dragged along the ground, as a harrow or an implement for spreading manure. **3.** A device for dragging under water, as a grappling hook, dredge, or dragnet. **4.** A heavy sledge or cart for conveying loads. **5.** A large four-horse coach with seats inside and on top. **6.** Something that retards motion, as a sea anchor, or a brake on a fishing reel. **7.** A person or thing that holds one back or hinders progress; a drawback. **8.** The degree of resistance involved in dragging or hauling. **9.** *Aviation.* The retarding force exerted on a moving body by a fluid medium. **10.** *Billiards.* A backspin given to the cue ball to prevent it from continuing onward after hitting another ball. **11.** A slow, laborious motion or movement. **12.** *Hunting.* **a.** The scent or trail of a fox or other animal. **b.** Something that provides an artificial scent. **13.** *Slang.* Something or someone that is obnoxiously tiresome: *"What a drag it is to be criminally handsome"* (S.J. Perelman). **14.** *Slang.* A puff on a cigarette, pipe, or cigar. **15.** *Slang.* A girl accompanying her escort. **16.** *Slang.* Women's clothing worn by a man. [Middle English *draggen,* from Old English *dragan* or Old Norse *draga.* See **dhragh-** in Appendix.*]

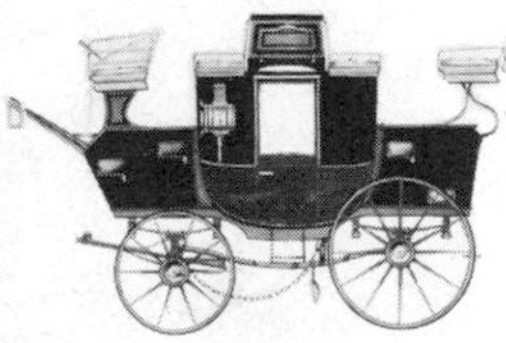

drag
A park drag built in 1877

Usage: *Drug* is nonstandard as the past tense and past participle of *drag,* and its occasional use, usually facetiously, by literate speakers since about 1960 is restricted to transitive sense 8 (to bore, annoy).

drag anchor. *Nautical.* A **sea anchor** *(see).*

dra·gée (drȧ-zhā') *n.* A small, often medicated candy. [French, "sweetmeat," from Old French *dragee*†.]

drag·ger (drăg'ər) *n.* **1.** One that drags. **2.** A fishing vessel, smaller than a trawler, that makes its catch in nets dragged along the bottom.

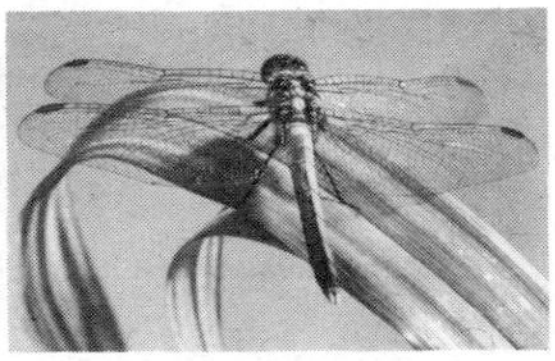

dragonfly
Anax junius

drag·gle (drăg'əl) *v.* **-gled, -gling, -gles.** *—tr.* To make wet and dirty by dragging in mud. *—intr.* **1.** To become muddy by being trailed. **2.** To follow slowly; to lag; straggle. [DRAG + *-le,* diminutive suffix.]

drag·gle·tail (drăg'əl-tāl') *n.* A bedraggled or slatternly woman.

drag·gle·tailed (drăg'əl-tāld') *adj.* Bedraggled.

drag·gy (drăg'ē) *adj.* **-gier, -giest. 1.** Dull and listless. **2.** *Slang.* Obnoxiously tiresome.

drag·line (drăg'līn') *n.* **1.** A line used for dragging. **2.** A kind of dredging machine.

drag link. A link for transmitting rotary motion between cranks on two parallel but slightly offset shafts, as the rod connecting the lever of the steering gear to the steering arm in an automobile.

drag·net (drăg'nĕt') *n.* **1. a.** A net for trawling; a trawl. **b.** A net for catching small game. **2.** The system of interrelated police procedures used in the apprehension of criminal suspects.

drag·o·man (drăg'ə-mən) *n., pl.* **-mans** or **-men** (-mĭn). An interpreter or guide in countries where Arabic, Turkish, or Persian is spoken. [Middle English *drogman,* from Old French *drugeman,* from Medieval Latin *dragumannus,* from Middle Greek *dragoumanos,* from Arabic *targumān,* from Aramaic *tūrgemānā,* from Akkadian *targumānu,* "interpreter," from *ragāmu,* to call, akin to Mishnaic Hebrew *targūm,* TARGUM.]

drag·on (drăg'ən) *n.* **1. a.** A fabulous monster represented as a gigantic reptile having a lion's claws, the tail of a serpent, wings, and a scaly skin. **b.** A figure or other representation of this creature. **2.** *Archaic.* A large snake or serpent. **3.** A fiercely vigilant or intractable woman. **4.** Any of various lizards, such as one of the genus *Draco,* or the **Komodo dragon** *(see).* **5.** A plant, the **green dragon** *(see).* **6.** *Capital* **D.** The constellation **Draco** *(see).* [Middle English *drago(u)n,* from Old French *dragon,* from Latin *dracō,* dragon, serpent, from Greek *drakōn,* serpent. See **derk-** in Appendix.*]

drag·on·et (drăg'ə-nĭt) *n.* Any of various small, often brightly colored marine fishes of the family Callionymidae, having a slender body and a flattened head. [Middle English, from DRAGON.]

drag·on·fly (drăg'ən-flī') *n., pl.* **-flies.** Any of various large insects of the order Odonata, having two pairs of narrow, net-veined wings and a long, slender body. Sometimes called "darning needle," "devil's darning needle."

drag·on·head (drăg'ən-hĕd') *n.* Any of several plants of the genera *Dracocephalum* or *Physostegia,* having terminal spikes of rose-pink or purplish flowers.

drag·on·root (drăg'ən-rōōt', -rŏŏt') *n.* A plant, the **green dragon** *(see).*

dragon's blood. 1. A red, resinous substance obtained from the fruit of a tree, *Daemonorops draco,* of tropical Asia, formerly used in the manufacture of varnishes and lacquers. **2.** Any of several similar resins.

dragon tree. A tree, *Dracaena draco,* of the Canary Islands, having a thick trunk, clusters of sword-shaped leaves, and orange fruit. [So called because it was once thought to be the source of DRAGON'S BLOOD.]

dra·goon (drə-gōōn', dră-) *n.* A heavily armed trooper in some European armies of the 17th and 18th centuries. *—tr.v.* **dragooned, -gooning, -goons. 1.** To persecute by the use of troops. **2.** To coerce by violent measures; harass. [French *dragon,* carbine, "fire-breather," from Old French, DRAGON.]

drag race. A race between cars to determine which can accelerate faster from a standstill.

drain (drān) *v.* **drained, draining, drains.** *—tr.* **1.** To draw off (a liquid) by a gradual process. **2.** To cause liquid substance to go out from; to empty; to dry. **3.** To drink all the contents of. **4. a.** To consume totally; exhaust. **b.** To fatigue or spend emotionally or physically. *—intr.* **1.** To flow off or go out of. **2.** To become empty or dry by the drawing off of liquid. **3.** To discharge surface waters in a given tract of land or region, through natural drainage channels. —See Synonyms at **deplete.** *—n.* **1.** A pipe or channel by which liquid is drawn off. **2.** *Surgery.* A device, such as a tube, inserted into the opening of a wound or cavity to facilitate discharge of fluid. **3.** The action or process or an instance of exhausting; consumption. [Middle English *dreinen,* Old English *drēahnian.* See **driug-** in Appendix.*] **—drain'a·ble** *adj.*

drain·age (drā'nĭj) *n.* **1.** The action or a given method of draining. **2.** A natural or artificial system of drains. **3.** That which is drained off. **4.** *Pathology.* The draining of fluids from wounds or body cavities.

drainage basin. The area drained by a river system.

drai·ner (drā'nər) *n.* One that drains, especially a device to hold objects being drained and specifically a wire basket to hold table utensils for drying.

drain·pipe (drān'pīp') *n.* A pipe for carrying off rainwater or sewage.

drake¹ (drāk) *n.* A male duck. [Middle English, perhaps from Low German, from West Germanic *drako* (unattested), male.]

drake² (drāk) *n.* A mayfly used as fishing bait. Also called "drake fly." [Middle English *drake,* dragon, drake fly, Old English *draca,* from West Germanic *drako* (unattested), from Latin *dracō,* DRAGON.]

Drake (drāk), Sir **Francis.** 1540?–1596. English navigator; sailed around the world (1577–80); commander at defeat of Spanish Armada (1588).

Dra·kens·berg (drä'kənz-bûrg'). A mountain range of southeastern Africa, extending about 700 miles from Swaziland northwestward through South Africa and Lesotho. Highest elevation, Thabantshonyana (11,425 feet) in Lesotho.

Drake Passage (drāk). A strait in Antarctica, extending about 500 miles between the South Atlantic and the South Pacific oceans south of Cape Horn.

dram (drăm) *n.* **1.** *Abbr.* **dr a.** A unit of weight in the U.S. Customary System, an avoirdupois unit equal to 27.344 grains or 0.0625 ounce. **b.** A unit of apothecary weight, equal to 60 grains. See **measurement. 2. a.** A small draft: *a dram of cordial.* **b.** A bit: *not a dram of compassion.* [Middle English *dragme, drame,* dram, drachma, from Old French, from Medieval Latin *dragma,* from Latin *drachma,* DRACHMA.]

dram. dramatic; dramatist.

dra·ma (drä'mə, drăm'ə) *n.* **1.** A prose or verse composition written for or as if for performance by actors; a play. **2.** The dramatic art or a particular dramatic repertory: *Elizabethan drama.* **3.** A situation or succession of events in real life having the dramatic progression or emotional content characteristic of a play. **4.** The quality or condition of being dramatic. [Late Latin *drāma,* from Greek *drama,* deed, action on the stage, drama, from *dran,* to do. See **derə-** in Appendix.*]

Dram·a·mine (drăm′ə-mēn′) *n.* A trademark for dimenhydrinate, used to treat motion sickness.

dra·mat·ic (drə-măt′ĭk) *adj.* Also *rare* **dra·mat·i·cal** (-ĭ-kəl). *Abbr.* **dram.** **1.** Of or pertaining to drama or the theater. **2.** Resembling a drama in emotional content or progression. **3.** Striking in appearance or forcefully effective. [Late Latin *drāmaticus,* from Greek *dramatikos,* from *drama* (stem *dramat-*), DRAMA.] —**dra·mat′i·cal·ly** *adv.*

dra·mat·ics (drə-măt′ĭks) *n.* Plural in form, used with a singular or plural verb. **1.** The art of acting. **2.** The art and practice of staging plays. **3.** Dramatic or histrionic behavior.

dram·a·tis per·so·nae (drăm′ə-tĭs pər-sō′nē, drä′mə-tĭs pər-sō′nī′). **1.** The characters in a play or story. **2.** A list of these characters, printed at the beginning of the text. [New Latin, "characters of the drama."]

dram·a·tist (drăm′ə-tĭst, drä′mə-) *n. Abbr.* **dram.** A playwright.

dram·a·ti·za·tion (drăm′ə-tə-zā′shən, drä′mə-) *n.* **1.** The act or art of transforming into a play or drama. **2.** A dramatic version of something.

dram·a·tize (drăm′ə-tīz′, drä′mə-) *v.* **-tized, -tizing, -tizes.** —*tr.* **1.** To adapt for presentation as a drama. **2.** To present or view in a dramatic or melodramatic way. **3.** To bring home strikingly; emphasize. —*intr.* **1.** To be adaptable to dramatic form. **2.** To indulge in self-dramatization.

dram·a·turge (drăm′ə-tûrj′, drä′mə-) *n.* A playwright. [French, from Greek *dramatourgos,* contriver, dramatist : *drama* (stem *dramat-*), DRAMA + *ergon,* work, deed (see **werg-**[1] in Appendix*).]

dram·a·tur·gy (drăm′ə-tûr′jē, drä′mə-) *n.* The art of the theater. —**dram′a·tur′gic, dram′a·tur′gi·cal** *adj.*

drank. Past tense of **drink.**

dr ap apothecaries' dram.

drape (drāp) *v.* **draped, draping, drapes.** —*tr.* **1.** To dress or hang with or as if with cloth in loose folds. **2.** To arrange or let fall in loose folds. **3.** To hang or rest limply: *He draped his legs over the chair.* —*intr.* To fall or hang in loose folds. —*n.* **1.** *Often plural.* **a.** A drapery. **b.** *Surgery.* A cloth or cloths arranged in an operating room to keep the site of maximum sterility as small as possible. **2.** The way in which cloth falls or hangs. [Middle English *drapen,* to weave, drape, from Old French *draper,* from *drap,* cloth, from Late Latin *drappus,* from Celtic. See **der-**[2] in Appendix.*]

drap·er (drā′pər) *n. British.* A dealer in cloth or clothing and dry goods. [Middle English, from Norman French, from Old French *drap,* DRAPE.]

Dra·per (drā′pər), **John William.** 1811–1882. British-born American chemist; did research in photochemistry, radiant energy, and photomicrography.

drap·er·y (drā′pə-rē) *n., pl.* **-ies.** **1.** Cloth or clothing arranged in loose folds; especially, clothing draped on figures in sculpture and painting. **2.** *Often plural.* Curtains, usually of heavy fabric, that hang straight in loose folds. **3.** Cloth; fabric. **4.** *British.* The business of a draper.

dras·tic (drăs′tĭk) *adj.* **1.** Violently effective. **2.** Especially severe; extreme. [Greek *drastikos,* active, efficient, from *drān,* to do. See **derə-** in Appendix.*] —**dras′ti·cal·ly** *adv.*

drat (drăt) *interj.* Used to express annoyance. [Short for earlier *'od rot,* euphemism for *God rot.*]

draught. *Chiefly British.* Variant of **draft.**

draughts (drăfts, dräfts) *n.* Plural in form, used with a singular verb. *Chiefly British.* The game of **checkers** *(see).* [Middle English *draughtes,* plural of *draught,* a move at chess, DRAFT.]

Dra·va (drä′və). Also **Dra·ve** (-və). *German* **Drau** (drou). A river of south-central Europe, rising in southern Austria and flowing 450 miles east and then southeast to the Danube in Yugoslavia.

dr avdp avoirdupois dram.

drave. *Archaic.* Past tense of **drive.**

Dra·vid·i·an (drə-vĭd′ē-ən) *n.* **1.** A large family of languages spoken mainly in southern India and northern Ceylon, and including Tamil, Telegu, Malayalam, and Kanarese. **2.** A member of any of the peoples that speak one of the Dravidian languages; especially, a member of the aboriginal population of southern India. —*adj.* Also **Dra·vid·ic** (-vĭd′ĭk). Of or pertaining to Dravidian or the Dravidians. [From Sanskrit *Drāviḍaḥ,* a Dravidian. See also **Tamil.**]

draw (drô) *v.* **drew** (dro͞o), **drawn, drawing, draws.** —*tr.* **1.** To pull (something) toward or after one. **2.** To pull or move (something) in a given direction or to a given position. **3.** To take or pull out, as from a scabbard or holster. **4.** To cause to flow forth: *a pump drawing water.* **5.** To suck or take in (air). **6.** To displace (a specified depth of water) in floating: *a boat drawing 18 inches.* **7.** To cause to move, as by leading. **8.** To induce to act. **9.** To attract. **10.** To extract from evidence at hand; formulate: *draw conclusions.* **11. a.** To earn; bring in: *draw interest.* **b.** To withdraw (money). **12.** To evoke; elicit. **13.** To force (a card) to be played. **14.** To take or accept as a chance: *draw lots.* **15.** To get or receive by chance. **16.** To end (a game) in a draw. **17.** To distort; contract. **18.** To stretch taut. **19.** To shape (wire or candles, for example). **20.** To eviscerate. **21. a.** To describe (a line or figure) with a drafting implement. **b.** To draft or sketch (a picture). **22.** To portray by lines, words, or imitative actions. **23.** To compose or write up in set form, as a will or contract. —*intr.* **1.** To proceed; to move. **2.** To describe forms and figures; to sketch. **3.** To be an attraction. **4.** To take in a draft of air: *The flue isn't drawing.* **5.** To use or call upon part of a fund or store. Used with *on* or *upon.* **6.** To cause suppuration. **7.** To steep in the manner of tea. **8.** To pull out a weapon for use. —**draw a blank. 1.** To be unsuccessful; lose. **2.** To fail to find something; especially, to forget something completely. —**draw and quarter. 1.** To execute (a prisoner) by tying each limb to a horse and driving the horses in different directions. **2.** To disembowel and dismember after hanging. —**draw on.** To approach; move along. —**draw oneself up.** To stiffen or bridle, as with indignation. —**draw out. 1.** To cause to converse easily. **2.** To prolong; drag out. —**draw the line.** To set a limit, as of acceptable behavior. —**draw up. 1.** To write up in set form; to draft; compose. **2.** To pull up to a halt. —*n.* **1.** An act of drawing: *quick on the draw.* **2.** A special advantage; edge: *have the draw on one's enemies.* **3.** A contest ending in a tie. **4.** A natural drainage basin; gully. [Draw, drew, drawn; Middle English *drawen, drow, drawen,* Old English *dragan, drōh, dragen,* drag, draw. See **dhragh-** in Appendix.*]

draw·back (drô′băk′) *n.* **1.** A disadvantage or inconvenience. **2.** A refund or remittance, such as a discount on duties or taxes for goods destined for favored uses.

draw·bar (drô′bär′) *n.* **1.** A bar across the rear of a tractor for hitching machinery. **2.** A railroad coupler.

draw·bore (drô′bôr′, -bōr′) *n.* A hole bored in a tenon such that a pin driven into the hole will tighten the joint.

draw·bridge (drô′brĭj′) *n.* A bridge that can be raised or drawn aside either to prevent access or to permit passage beneath it.

draw·ee (drô′ē′) *n.* A person on whom an order for the payment of money is drawn.

draw·er (drô′ər; drôr *for sense 2;* drôrz *for sense 3*) *n.* **1.** One who draws, specifically: **a.** A draftsman. **b.** A person who draws an order for the payment of money. **2.** A boxlike compartment in furniture that can be drawn on slides. **3.** *Plural.* Underpants.

draw·ing (drô′ĭng) *n.* **1.** The act or an instance of drawing. **2.** The art of depicting forms or figures on a surface by lines. **3.** A portrayal in lines on a surface of a form or figure.

drawing account. An account recording cash payments to a partner or employee to cover expenses or as advances on commissions.

drawing card. An attraction drawing large audiences.

drawing pin. *British.* A thumbtack.

drawing room. 1. A formal reception room. **2.** A ceremonial reception. **3.** A private room on a railroad sleeping car. [Originally, a room to which one retired for rest, short for *withdrawing room.*]

draw·knife (drô′nīf′) *n., pl.* **-knives** (-nīvz′). A knife with a handle at each end of the blade, used with a drawing motion to shave a surface. Also called "drawshave," "spokeshave."

drawl (drôl) *v.* **drawled, drawling, drawls.** —*intr.* In natural speech, to lengthen or add vowels or to make diphthongs of vowels in syllables that are simpler in the dialect regarded as standard. —*tr.* To utter with a drawl. —*n.* The speech or manner of speaking of one who drawls: *A Southern drawl.* [Possibly a frequentative of DRAW.] —**drawl′er** *n.*

drawn (drôn). Past participle of **draw.** —*adj.* **1.** Pulled out of a sheath. Said of a sword. **2.** Haggard, as from fatigue or ill health. **3.** Eviscerated, as an oven-ready chicken.

drawn butter. The clarified butter that separates from the salt and curds after melting, often used with herbs as a sauce.

draw·plate (drô′plāt′) *n.* A die with conical holes through which wire is drawn to regulate its thickness.

draw·string (drô′strĭng′) *n.* A cord or ribbon run through a hem or casing and pulled to tighten or close an opening.

draw·tube (drô′to͞ob′, -tyo͞ob′) *n.* A tube that slides within another tube.

dray (drā) *n.* A low, heavy cart without sides, used for haulage. —*tr.v.* **drayed, draying, drays.** To haul by dray. [Middle English *draye,* probably Old English *dræge,* dragnet. See **dhragh-** in Appendix.*]

dray·age (drā′ĭj) *n.* **1.** Transport by dray. **2.** A charge for transport by dray.

dray horse. A horse suited for hauling heavy loads; draft horse.

dray·man (drā′mən) *n., pl.* **-men** (-mĭn). A driver of a dray.

Dray·ton (drāt′n), **Michael.** 1563–1631. English poet.

dread (drĕd) *v.* **dreaded, dreading, dreads.** —*tr.* **1.** To be in terror of; fear greatly. **2.** To hold in awe or reverence. **3.** To anticipate with alarm, anxiety, or reluctance. —*intr.* To be very afraid. —*n.* **1.** Profound fear; terror. **2.** Awe; reverence. **3.** Anxious or fearful anticipation. **4.** The object of fear, awe, or reverence. —See Synonyms at **fear.** —*adj.* **1.** Terrifying; fearsome; dreadful. **2.** Awesome; revered. [Middle English *drēden,* Old English *drǣdan*†.]

dread·ful (drĕd′fəl) *adj.* **1.** Inspiring dread; terrible. **2.** Extremely unpleasant; distasteful or shocking. —**dread′ful·ly** *adv.* —**dread′ful·ness** *n.*

dread·nought (drĕd′nôt′) *n.* A heavily armed battleship.

dream (drēm) *n.* **1.** A series of images, ideas, and emotions occurring in certain stages of sleep. **2.** A daydream; reverie. **3.** A state of abstraction; a trance; bemusement. **4.** A wild fancy or hope. **5.** An aspiration; ambition. **6.** Anything extremely beautiful, fine, or pleasant. —*v.* **dreamed** or **dreamt** (drĕmt), **dreaming, dreams.** —*intr.* **1.** To experience a dream or dreams in sleep. **2.** To daydream. **3.** To have a deep aspiration; hope for something. Used with *of.* **4.** To consider something feasible or practical; conceive even remotely. Used with *of: I wouldn't*

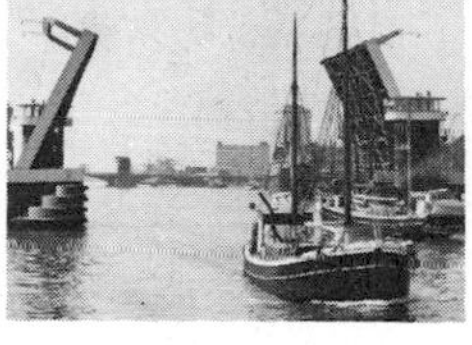

drawbridge
Bascule drawbridge in Copenhagen Harbor

drawknife

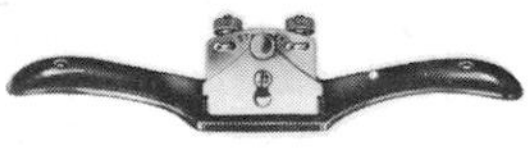

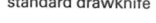

standard drawknife

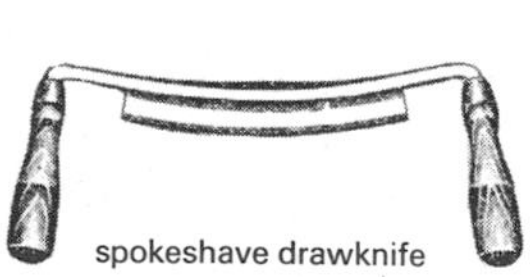

spokeshave drawknife

t tight/th thin, path/*th* this, bathe/ŭ cut/ûr urge/v valve/w with/y yes/z zebra, size/zh vision/ə about, item, edible, gallop, circus/ à *Fr.* ami/œ *Fr.* feu, *Ger.* schön/ü *Fr.* tu, *Ger.* über/KH *Ger.* ich, *Scot.* loch/N *Fr.* bon. ***Follows main vocabulary.** **†Of obscure origin.**

dream of going. —*tr.* **1.** To experience an image sequence of in sleep. **2.** To conceive of; imagine. **3.** To pass idly or in reverie. Used with *away.* —**dream up.** To invent; concoct. [Middle English *drem, dreem,* Old English *drēam,* joy, gladness, music. See **dhreugh-** in Appendix.*]

dream·er (drē′mər) *n.* **1.** One who dreams. **2.** A person habitually inclined to interpret experience imaginatively without strict regard to practical concerns; a visionary.

dream·land (drēm′lănd′) *n.* An ideal or imaginary land.

dream·y (drē′mē) *adj.* **-ier, -iest. 1.** Resembling a dream; vague. **2.** Given to daydreams or reverie. **3.** Soothing; quiet; serene. **4.** *Informal.* Inspiring delight; wonderful. —**dream′i·ness** *n.* —**dream′i·ly** *adv.*

drear·y (drîr′ē) *adj.* **-ier, -iest.** Also *poetic* **drear** (drîr). **1.** Gloomy; dismal. **2.** Boring; dull. **3.** Discouraging; depressing. —See Synonyms at **boring.** [Middle English *dreri,* Old English *drēorig,* bloody, grievous, sad, from *drēor,* blood. See **dhreu-** in Appendix.*] —**drear′i·ly** *adv.* —**drear′i·ness** *n.*

dreck (drĕk) *n.* Also **drek. 1.** *Vulgar.* Excrement. **2.** *Slang.* Trash; disgusting stuff, especially inferior merchandise made to cheat the buyer. [Yiddish *drek* or German *Dreck,* from Middle High German *drēc.* See **sker-^{4}** in Appendix.*]

dredge^{1} (drĕj) *n.* **1.** Any of various machines equipped with scooping or suction devices used in deepening harbors and waterways and in underwater mining. **2.** A boat or barge equipped with such a machine. **3.** An implement consisting of a net on a frame, used for gathering shellfish. —*v.* **dredged, dredging, dredges.** —*tr.* **1.** To clean, deepen, or widen with a dredge. **2.** To bring up with a dredge. Used with *up.* —*intr.* To use a dredge. —**dredge up.** To come up with; unearth. [Perhaps Middle English *dreg-,* perhaps ultimately from Old English *dragan,* to DRAG.]

dredge^{2} (drĕj) *tr.v.* **dredged, dredging, dredges.** To coat (food) by sprinkling with a powder, such as flour or powdered sugar. [Origin unknown.]

dredg·er^{1} (drĕj′ər) *n.* A barge or boat equipped with a dredge.

dredg·er^{2} (drĕj′ər) *n.* A container with a perforated lid used for coating food with a powder, such as flour.

D region. *Meteorology.* The region of the ionosphere approximately 25 to 40 miles above the earth.

dregs (drĕgz) *pl.n.* **1.** The sediment of a liquid; lees. **2.** The basest or least desirable portion. **3.** A small amount; residue. [From Middle English *dreg* (singular), from Old Norse *dregg.* See **dher-^{1}** in Appendix.*]

Drei·bund (drī′bo͝ont′) *n.* An alliance of three powers, especially the Triple Alliance of Germany, Austria, and Italy formed in 1882. [German, "triple bund."]

Drei·ser (drī′sər), **Theodore (Herman Albert).** 1871–1945. American novelist.

drench (drĕnch) *tr.v.* **drenched, drenching, drenches. 1.** To wet through and through; saturate. **2.** To administer a dose of liquid medicine to (an animal). —*n.* **1.** The act of drenching. **2.** A large dose of liquid medicine. [Middle English *drenchen,* to drown, from Old English *drencan,* to give to drink, to soak. See **dhreg-** in Appendix.*] —**drench′er** *n.*

Dren·the (drĕn′tə). Also **Dren·te.** A province of the Netherlands, occupying 1,010 square miles in the northeast. Population, 312,000. Capital, Assen.

Drep·a·num. The ancient name for **Trapani.**

Dres·den (drĕz′dən; *German* drāz′dən). A city of East Germany, on the Elbe, 100 miles south of Berlin. Population, 495,000.

Dres·den china (drĕz′dən). **Meissen ware** *(see).* [From DRESDEN.]

dress (drĕs) *v.* **dressed, dressing, dresses.** —*tr.* **1.** To put clothes on; clothe. **2.** To trim; adorn. Sometimes used with *up.* **3.** To arrange a display in: *dress a store window.* **4.** To arrange (troops) in ranks; align. **5.** To apply therapeutic materials to (a wound). **6.** To do up (the hair); to comb. **7.** To groom (an animal); curry. **8.** To cultivate (land or plants). **9.** To clean (fish or fowl) for cooking or sale. **10.** To put a finish on. —*intr.* **1.** To put on clothes. **2.** To wear clothes. **3.** To wear formal clothes. **4.** To get into proper alignment. —**dress down.** To scold; reprimand. —**dress ship.** To display the ensign, signal flags, and bunting on a ship. —**dress up. 1.** To wear formal clothes, or clothing more formal than usual, as for a special occasion. **2.** To arrange in ranks. —*n.* **1.** Clothing; apparel. **2.** A one-piece, skirted outer garment for women and children. **3.** Outer covering or appearance. **4.** *Obsolete.* A setting right; redress. —*adj.* **1.** For or relating to a dress. **2. a.** Suitable for a formal occasion: *a dress coat; dress uniform.* **b.** Requiring formal clothing: *a dress dinner.* [Middle English *dressen,* to place, put, prepare, from Old French *drecier, dresser,* from Vulgar Latin *dīrectiāre* (unattested), from Latin *dīrigere* (past participle *dīrectus*), to DIRECT.]

dres·sage (drĕs′ĭj, drĕ-säzh′) *n.* **1.** The guiding of a horse through a series of complex maneuvers by slight movements of the hands, legs, and weight. **2.** The training of a horse in deportment and obedience. [French, preparation, from *dresser,* to DRESS.]

dress circle. A section of seats in a theater or opera house, usually the first tier above the orchestra. [Originally reserved for persons in formal dress.]

dress·er^{1} (drĕs′ər) *n.* **1.** One that dresses. **2.** A wardrobe assistant, as for an actor; valet. **3.** One who dresses well or in some specified way.

dress·er^{2} (drĕs′ər) *n.* **1.** A chest of drawers with a mirror. **2.** A cupboard or set of shelves for dishes or kitchen utensils. [Middle English *dressour,* kitchen sideboard on which food was prepared, from Old French *dreceur,* from *drecier,* prepare, to DRESS.]

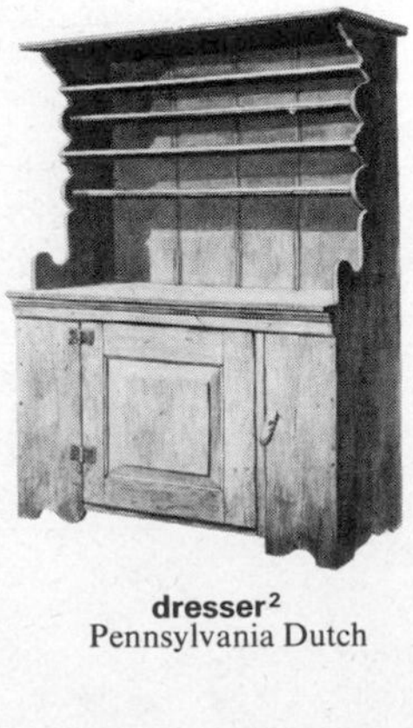

dresser^{2}
Pennsylvania Dutch

dress·ing (drĕs′ĭng) *n.* **1.** The act of one that dresses. **2.** Therapeutic material applied to a wound. **3.** A sauce for certain dishes, such as salads. **4.** A stuffing, as for poultry or fish. **5.** Manure used to dress soil.

dress·ing-down (drĕs′ĭng-doun′) *n.* A severe scolding.

dressing gown. A robe worn for lounging or before dressing.

dressing room. A room in a theater or a home for changing costumes or clothes, and making up.

dressing table. A low table with a mirror at which one sits while making up. Also called "vanity."

dress·mak·er (drĕs′mā′kər) *n.* One who makes women's dresses. —*adj.* Having soft rather than tailored lines. Said of women's clothing. —**dress′mak′ing** *n.*

dress parade. A military parade in dress uniform.

dress rehearsal. A final, uninterrupted run-through, as of a play with costumes and stage properties.

dress·y (drĕs′ē) *adj.* **-ier, -iest. 1.** Having a penchant for fancy or elegant clothing. **2.** Smart; stylish. **3.** Suitable for more formal occasions: *too dressy to wear to the office.* —**dress′i·ly** *adv.* —**dress′i·ness** *n.*

drew. Past tense of **draw.**

Drew (dro͞o), **John.** 1853–1927. American actor.

Drey·fus (drā′fəs, drī′-; *French* drĕ-füs′), **Alfred.** 1859–1935. French army officer; convicted of treason and imprisoned (1895); retried (1899); acquitted (1906).

drib·ble (drĭb′əl) *v.* **-bled, -bling, -bles.** —*intr.* **1.** To flow or fall in drops or an unsteady stream; to trickle. **2.** To drool; slobber. **3.** *Sports.* To dribble a ball. —*tr.* **1.** To let flow or fall in drops or an unsteady stream. **2.** *Sports.* To move (a ball) by repeated light bounces or kicks, as in basketball or soccer. —*n.* **1.** A trickle; a drip. **2.** A small quantity; a bit. **3.** *Sports.* The act of moving a ball by dribbling. [Frequentative of earlier *drib,* variant of DRIP.] —**drib′bler** *n.*

drib·let (drĭb′lĭt) *n.* **1.** A tiny falling drop of liquid. **2.** A small amount or portion. [From earlier *drib,* drop, from *drib,* to dribble, variant of DRIP.]

dribs and drabs (drĭbz′; drăbz′). Small and sporadic amounts. [From earlier *drib,* a drop (see **driblet**) + *drab,* perhaps variant of *drib.*]

dri·er^{1} (drī′ər) *n.* Also **dry·er** (preferred for sense 2). **1.** One that dries. **2.** An appliance that removes moisture by heating or some other process: *a hair dryer.* **3.** A substance added to paint, varnish, ink, or the like, to speed drying.

dri·er^{2}. Comparative of **dry.**

drift (drĭft) *v.* **drifted, drifting, drifts.** —*intr.* **1.** To be carried along by or as by currents of air or water. **2.** To proceed without resistance; move unhurriedly and smoothly. **3.** To move from place to place without regular employment and with no particular goal. **4. a.** To wander from a set course or point of attention; to stray. **b.** To vary from or oscillate randomly about a fixed setting, position, or mode of operation. **5.** To be piled up in banks or heaps by the force of a current. **6.** To skid; sideslip. Used of a motor vehicle. **7.** To continue in motion for a while after a switching off of power. —*tr.* To carry along by or as by a current; cause to drift. —*n.* **1.** The act or condition of drifting. **2.** Something moving along on a current of air or water. **3.** A bank or pile, as of sand or snow, heaped up by currents of air or water. **4.** *Geology.* Rock debris transported and deposited by or from ice, especially by or from a glacier. **5. a.** A trend or general bearing; direction. **b.** General meaning or purport; tenor. **6. a.** Lateral displacement or deviation of an object or vehicle from a planned course, especially as a result of wind, ocean current, or other disturbance in the medium of travel. **b.** Variation or random oscillation about a fixed setting, position, or mode of behavior. **7.** The rate of flow of a water current. **8.** *Machinery.* **a.** A tool for ramming or driving something down. **b.** A tapered steel pin for enlarging and aligning holes. **9.** *Mining.* **a.** A horizontal or nearly horizontal passageway running through or parallel to a vein. **b.** A secondary passageway between two main shafts or tunnels. **10.** A drove or herd, especially of swine. In this sense, see Synonyms at **flock.** —See Synonyms at **tendency.** [From Middle English, a driving, snowdrift, a drove, both from Old Norse *drift,* snowdrift, and from Middle Dutch *drift,* herd, course. See **dhreibh-** in Appendix.*] —**drift′y** *adj.*

drift·age (drĭf′tĭj) *n.* **1.** Deviation from a set course caused by drifting. **2.** Anything that has been carried along or deposited by air or water currents.

drift anchor. A **sea anchor** *(see).*

drift·er (drĭf′tər) *n.* **1.** One that drifts, especially: **a.** One who moves from place to place or from job to job. **b.** A vagabond. **2.** A fishing boat with a net that drifts with the current.

drift·wood (drĭft′wo͝od′) *n.* **1.** Wood floating in or washed up by the water. **2.** A collection of worthless or trivial elements.

drill^{1} (drĭl) *n.* **1. a.** An implement with cutting edges or a pointed end for boring holes in hard materials, usually by a rotating abrasion or by repeated blows. Also called "drill bit." **b.** The hand-operated or hand-powered holder for this tool. **2.** Disciplined, repetitious exercise as a means of teaching and perfecting a skill or procedure, especially as part of military training. **3.** A specific task or exercise designed to develop a skill or familiarity with a procedure. **4.** Any of several marine gastropod mollusks, chiefly of the genus *Urosalpinx,* that drill holes into the shells of bivalve mollusks; especially, *U. cinerea,* a species destructive to oysters. —*v.* **drilled, drilling, drills.** —*tr.* **1.** To make a hole in (a hard material) with a drill. **2. a.** To instruct thoroughly and by repetition in a skill or procedure.

b. To infuse knowledge of or skill in by repetitious instruction. *—intr.* **1.** To make a hole with a drill. **2.** To perform an exercise; complete a drill. —See Synonyms at **teach.** [Probably Dutch *dril,* from Middle Dutch, from *drillen,* to drill. See **ter-**[2] in Appendix.*]

drill[2] (drĭl) *n.* **1.** A trench or furrow in which seeds are planted. **2.** A row of planted seeds. **3.** A machine or implement for planting seeds in holes or furrows. *—tr.v.* **drilled, drilling, drills. 1.** To sow (seeds) in rows. **2.** To plant (a field) in drills. [Origin obscure.]

drill[3] (drĭl) *n.* Strong cotton or linen twill of varying weights, generally used for work clothes. Also called "drilling." [Back-formation from drilling, variant of German *Drillich,* from Old High German *drilīch,* from Latin *trilīx,* triple-twilled : *tri-,* three + *līcium,* thread (see **trellis**).]

drill[4] (drĭl) *n.* A monkey, *Mandrillus leucophaeus,* of western Africa, related to and resembling the mandrill. [Native West African name.]

drill bit. A boring tool, a **drill** *(see).*

drill·mas·ter (drĭl′măs′tər, -mäs′tər) *n.* **1.** A military drill instructor. **2.** An instructor given to severely rigorous training.

drill press. A powered vertical drilling machine, used mainly on metals, in which the drill is pressed to the metal by a hand lever or automatically.

drill·stock (drĭl′stŏk′) *n.* The part of a drilling tool or machine that holds the shank of a drill or bit.

drink (drĭngk) *v.* **drank** (drăngk) or *archaic* **drunk** (drŭngk), **drunk** or *obsolete* **drunken** (drŭng′kən), **drinking, drinks.** *—tr.* **1.** To take into the mouth and swallow (a liquid). **2.** To soak up (liquid or moisture); absorb; imbibe. **3.** To take in eagerly through the senses or intellect; receive with pleasure. Often used with *in.* **4.** To swallow the liquid contents of (a vessel). **5. a.** To give or make (a toast). **b.** To toast (a person or occasion, for example). *—intr.* **1.** To swallow liquid. **2.** To imbibe alcoholic liquors, especially excessively or habitually. **3.** To salute a person or occasion with a toast. Used with *to.* *—n.* **1.** Any liquid that is fit for drinking; a beverage. **2.** An alcoholic beverage, such as a cocktail. **3.** An amount of liquid swallowed, as a cupful or glassful. **4.** Alcoholic liquor. **5.** Excessive or habitual indulgence in alcoholic liquor. **6.** *Slang.* A body of water; the sea. Preceded by *the.* [Drink, drank or drunk, drunk or drunken; Middle English *drinken, drank* or *dronk, drunke* or *drunken,* Old English *drincan, dranc* or *druncon* (plural), *druncen.* See **dhreg-** in Appendix.*]

drink·a·ble (drĭng′kə-bəl) *adj.* Suitable for drinking; potable. *—n.* A beverage. Usually used in the plural.

drink·er (drĭng′kər) *n.* **1.** One who drinks. **2.** One who enjoys alcoholic liquors; especially, one who drinks to excess.

Drink·wat·er (drĭngk′wô′tər, -wŏt′ər), **John.** 1882–1937. English poet and playwright.

drip (drĭp) *v.* **dripped** or *rare* **dript** (drĭpt), **dripping, drips.** *—intr.* **1.** To fall in drops. **2.** To shed drops. *—tr.* To let fall in or as if in drops. *—n.* **1.** The process of forming and falling in drops; trickling. **2.** Liquid or moisture that falls in drops. **3.** The sound made by dripping liquid. **4.** A projection on a cornice or sill that protects the area below from rainwater. **5.** *Slang.* An unpleasant or tiresomely dull person. [Middle English *drippen,* perhaps from Middle Danish *drippe.* See **dhreu-** in Appendix.*]

drip-dry (drĭp′drī′) *adj.* Made of a fabric that will not wrinkle when hung dripping wet for drying.

drip pan. Also **dripping pan.** A pan for catching the drippings from roasting meat.

drip·ping (drĭp′ĭng) *n.* **1.** The act of something that drips. **2.** *Usually plural.* The fat and juice exuded from roasting meat, often used in making gravy. *—adv.* Completely; thoroughly. Used in the phrase *dripping wet.*

drip·py (drĭp′ē) *adj.* **-pier, -piest. 1.** Very wet; drizzly. **2.** *Slang.* Mawkishly sentimental.

drip·stone (drĭp′stōn′) *n.* **1.** A drip made of stone, as on a cornice over a door or window. **2.** Calcium carbonate in the form of stalactites or stalagmites.

drive (drīv) *v.* **drove** (drōv) or *archaic* **drave** (drāv), **driven** (drĭv′ən), **driving, drives.** *—tr.* **1.** To push, propel, or press onward forcibly; urge forward. **2.** To force to work, usually excessively; overtask or overwork. **3.** To force or thrust into or from a particular act or state. **4.** *Sports.* To throw, strike, or cast (a ball, for example) hard or rapidly. **5.** To force to go through or penetrate. **6.** To create or produce by penetrating forcibly. **7.** To guide, control, or direct (a vehicle). **8.** To convey or transport in a vehicle. **9.** To supply the motive force to and cause to function. **10.** To carry through vigorously to a conclusion. **11.** *Hunting.* **a.** To chase (game) into the open or into traps or nets. **b.** To search (an area) for game in this manner. *—intr.* **1.** To move along or advance quickly as if pushed by an impelling force. **2.** To rush, dash, or advance violently against an obstruction. **3.** To hit, throw, or impel a ball or other missile forcibly. **4.** To operate a car or other vehicle. **5.** To go or be transported in a car or other vehicle. **6.** To make an effort to reach or achieve a particular objective; to aim. **—drive at.** To mean to do or say. **—drive home. 1.** To force in completely. **2.** To cause to be evident or obvious through force or emphasis. **—let drive.** To aim or hurl forth. *—n.* **1.** The act of driving. **2.** *Abbr.* **Dr.** A road for automobiles and other vehicles; a driveway or highway. **3.** A trip or journey in a vehicle. **4. a.** The means or apparatus for transmitting motion to a machine or machine part. **b.** The means by which automotive power is applied to a roadway: *four-wheel drive.* **c.** The means or apparatus for controlling and directing an automobile: *right-hand drive.* **5.** An organized effort to accomplish some purpose, such as raising money; a campaign. **6.** Energy; push; aggressiveness; initiative. **7.** *Psychoanalysis.* A strong motivating tendency or instinct, especially of sexual or aggressive origin, that prompts activity toward a particular end. **8.** A massive and sustained military offensive. **9.** *Sports.* **a.** The hitting, knocking, or thrusting of the ball very swiftly. **b.** The stroke or thrust by which the ball is driven. **10. a.** A rounding-up and driving of cattle to new pastures or to market. **b.** A similar gathering and driving of logs down a river. **c.** The cattle or logs thus driven. [Drive, drove or drave, driven; Middle English *driven, drof* or *draf, driven,* Old English *drīfan, drāf, drifon.* See **dhreibh-** in Appendix.*]

drive-in (drīv′ĭn′) *n.* A retail establishment, such as a restaurant or motion-picture theater, designed to permit customers to remain in their automobiles. *—adj.* Designating or pertaining to an establishment so equipped: *a drive-in bank.*

driv·el (drĭv′əl) *v.* **-eled** or **-elled, -eling** or **-elling, -els.** *—intr.* **1.** To slobber; drool. **2.** To flow like spittle or saliva. **3.** To talk stupidly or childishly. *—tr.* **1.** To allow to flow from the mouth. **2.** To say (something) stupidly. *—n.* **1.** Saliva flowing from the mouth; slaver. **2.** Stupid, childish, or senseless talk; twaddle. [Middle English *drivelen, drevelen,* Old English *dreflian.* See **dher-**[1] in Appendix.*] **—driv′el·er** *n.*

driv·er (drī′vər) *n.* **1.** One who drives, especially: **a.** A chauffeur. **b.** A coachman. **c.** *British.* The operator of a locomotive; engineer. **d.** A drover on a cattle drive. **2.** An employer who demands hard work of his subordinates. **3.** A tool or device used for driving, as a hammer or mallet. **4.** Any machine part that transmits motion or force to another part. **5.** *Golf.* A wooden-headed club with a long shaft, used for making long shots from the tee. **6.** *Nautical.* A **spanker** *(see).*

driver ant. Any of various rapacious tropical Old World ants of the subfamily Dorylinae, that move from place to place in huge groups.

driver's seat. 1. The seat occupied by the driver of a vehicle. **2.** Any position of control, authority, or superiority.

drive shaft. A rotating shaft that transmits mechanical power to a point or region of application.

drive·way (drīv′wā′) *n.* A private road connecting a house, garage, or other building with the street.

driv·ing (drī′vĭng) *adj.* **1.** Transmitting or communicating power or motion. **2.** Violent, intense, or forceful. **3.** Capable of eliciting work or participation from others; energetic; active.

driz·zle (drĭz′əl) *v.* **-zled, -zling, -zles.** *—intr.* To rain gently in fine, mistlike drops. *—tr.* **1.** To let fall in fine drops or particles. **2.** To moisten with fine drops. *—n.* A fine, gentle rain. [Perhaps a frequentative of Middle English *dresen,* to fall, Old English *drēosan.* See **dhreu-** in Appendix.*] **—driz′zly** *adj.*

drogue (drōg) *n.* **1.** A **sea anchor** *(see).* **2.** A **drogue parachute** *(see).* **3.** A funnel- or cone-shaped device towed behind an aircraft as a target. **4.** A funnel-shaped device at the end of the hose of a tanker aircraft, used as a stabilizer and receptacle for the probe of a receiving aircraft. **5.** A device for indicating wind direction, a **windsock** *(see).* [Perhaps a dialectal form ultimately from Old English *dragan,* to DRAW.]

drogue parachute. 1. A parachute used in decelerating a fast-moving object, especially a small parachute used to slow down a re-entering spacecraft or satellite prior to deployment of the main parachute. Also called "drogue." **2.** A small parachute used to pull a main parachute from its storage pack.

droit (droit; *French* drwȧ) *n.* A legal right; also, that to which one has legal right. [Old French, from Late Latin *dīrectum,* from *dīrectus,* right, correct, from Latin, past participle of *dīregere,* to DIRECT.]

droll (drōl) *adj.* Amusingly odd; whimsically comical. *—n. Archaic.* A buffoon. *—intr.v.* **drolled, drolling, drolls.** To clown. [French *drôle,* from noun, buffoon, from Middle Dutch *drol*†, "little man."] **—drol′ly** *adv.* **—droll′ness** *n.*

droll·er·y (drō′lə-rē) *n., pl.* **-ies. 1.** A droll quality; quaint comedy. **2.** A droll way of acting, talking, or behaving. **3. a.** The act of joking; clowning. **b.** Something droll, as a story.

-drome. Indicates: **1.** A racecourse or a running; for example, **acrodrome. 2.** A large field or arena; for example, **airdrome.** [Old French, from Latin *-dromos,* from Greek *dromos,* race, course. See **der-**[1] in Appendix.*]

drom·e·dar·y (drŏm′ə-dĕr′ē, drŭm′-) *n., pl.* **-ies.** The one-humped domesticated camel, *Camelus dromedarius,* widely used as a beast of burden in northern Africa and eastern Asia. Also called "Arabian camel." Compare **Bactrian camel.** [Middle English *dromedarie,* from Old French *dromedaire,* from Late Latin *dromedārius,* from Greek *dromas* (stem *dromad-*), dromedary, runner. See **der-**[1] in Appendix.*]

drom·ond (drŏm′ənd, drŭm′-) *n.* Also **drom·on** (-ən). A large medieval galley. [Middle English *dromon(d),* from Old French *dromon,* from Late Latin *dromō* (stem *dromōn-*), a kind of fast ship, from Late Greek *dromōn,* from *dromos,* a running. See **der-**[1] in Appendix.*]

-dromous. Indicates running or moving; for example, **catadromous.** [New Latin *-dromus,* from Greek *-dromos,* from *dromos,* a running. See **der-**[1] in Appendix.*]

drone[1] (drōn) *n.* **1.** A male bee, especially a honeybee, characteristically stingless, performing no work, and producing no honey. **2.** A loafer; sluggard. **3.** A pilotless aircraft operated by remote control. [Middle English *drane, drone,* Old English *drān, drǣn.* See **dher-**[3] in Appendix.*]

drone[2] (drōn) *v.* **droned, droning, drones.** *—intr.* **1.** To make a continuous low, dull humming sound: *"Somewhere an electric*

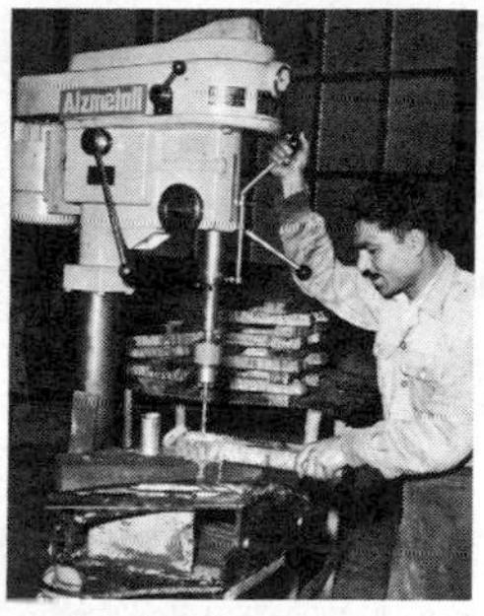

drill press

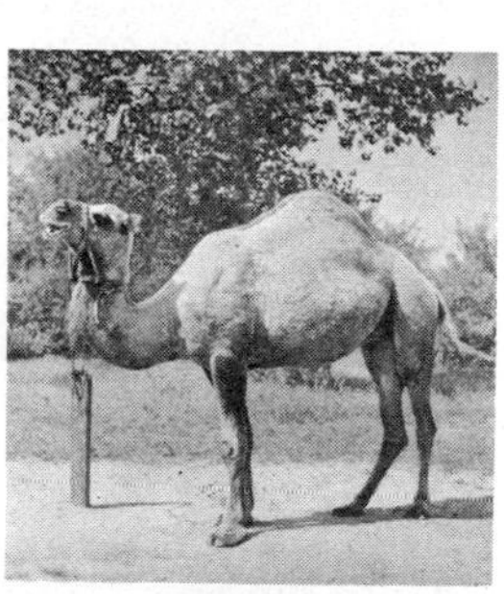

dromedary

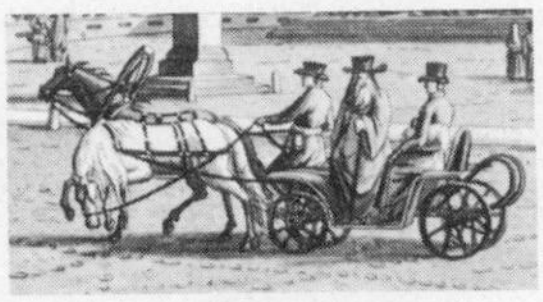

droshky
Detail from a painting of St. Petersburg in 1809

fan droned without end" (William Styron). **2.** To speak in a monotonous tone. *—tr.* To utter in a monotonous low tone: *"the mosquitoes droned their angry chant"* (Maugham). *—n.* **1.** A continuous low humming or buzzing sound. **2.** Any of the pipes of a bagpipe tuned to produce a single tone. Also called "drone pipe." **3.** *Music.* A single sustained tone. [From the sound of the DRONE (bee).]

dron·go (drŏng′gō) *n., pl.* **-gos.** Any of various tropical Old World birds of the family Dicruridae, characteristically having glossy black plumage and a forked tail. [Native name in Madagascar.]

drool (dro͞ol) *v.* **drooled, drooling, drools.** *—intr.* **1.** To let saliva run from the mouth; to drivel. **2.** *Informal.* To make an extravagant show of appreciation. **3.** *Informal.* To talk nonsense. *—tr.* To let run from the mouth. *—n.* **1.** Saliva; drivel. **2.** *Informal.* Silly talk; nonsense. [Perhaps variant of DRIVEL.]

droop (dro͞op) *v.* **drooped, drooping, droops.** *—intr.* **1.** To bend or hang downward; sag: *"his mouth drooped sadly, pulled down, no doubt, by the plump weight of his jowls"* (Gore Vidal). **2.** To sag in dejection, exhaustion, or lifelessness: *"the roses drooped in the heat, their petals scattering"* (Herman Wouk). *—tr.* To let bend or hang down: *"He drooped his body over the rail"* (Norman Mailer). *—n.* The act or condition of drooping. [Middle English *droupen,* from Old Norse *drūpa.* See **dhreu-** in Appendix.*] **—droop′i·ly, droop′ing·ly** *adv.* **—droop′y** *adj.*

drop (drŏp) *n.* **1.** The smallest quantity of liquid heavy enough to fall in a spherical or pear-shaped mass; a globule. **2.** A minute quantity of any substance. **3.** *Plural.* Liquid medicine administered in such quantity. **4.** A trace or hint of something abstract. **5. a.** Anything shaped or hanging like a drop. **b.** A small globular piece of hard candy. **6.** The act of falling; a rapid descent. **7.** A swift decline or decrease, as in quality, quantity, intensity, or the like. **8. a.** The vertical distance from a higher to a lower level. **b.** The distance through which something falls or drops. **9.** A sheer incline, such as the face of a cliff; a steep slope. **10.** Men and equipment landed by means of parachute. **11.** Something arranged to fall or be lowered, specifically: **a.** An unframed curtain that forms part of the scenery on a stage. **b.** A theater curtain that can be lowered or raised. Also called "drop curtain." **c.** A trap door on a gallows. **12.** A slot through which something is deposited in a receptacle. **—at the drop of a hat.** Immediately and willingly. **—get** (or **have**) **the drop on.** To get (or have) a distinct advantage over. *—v.* **dropped** or *archaic* **dropt, dropping, drops.** *—intr.* **1.** To fall in drops. **2.** To fall from a higher to a lower place or position. **3.** To become less in number, intensity, volume, or the like; decrease; decline. **4.** To descend from one level to another. **5.** To fall or sink into a state of exhaustion or death. **6.** To pass or slip into some specified state or condition. **7.** To cease; come to an end. **8.** To crouch. Used of a hunting dog. *—tr.* **1.** To let fall by releasing hold of. **2.** To let fall in drops. **3.** To cause to become less; decrease; reduce. **4.** To cause to fall, as by hitting or shooting. **5.** To give birth to. Used of animals. **6.** To say or offer casually. **7.** To write and send off (a note, for example) at leisure. **8.** To cease consideration or treatment of; have done with. **9.** To terminate an association or relationship. **10.** To leave out (a letter, for example) in speaking or writing. **11.** To leave or set down at a particular place. **12.** To parachute. **13.** To lower the level of (the voice). **14.** To lose (a game or contest, for example). **—drop behind.** To fall behind. **—drop by** (or **in**). To stop in for a short visit. **—drop off. 1.** To fall asleep. **2.** To decrease. [Middle English *drop(e),* Old English *dropa.* See **dhreu-** in Appendix.*]

drop·forge (drŏp′fôrj′, -fōrj′) *tr.v.* **-forged, -forging, -forges.** To forge (a metal) between dies by the force of a drop hammer.

drop hammer. A machine used to forge or stamp metal, consisting of an anvil or base aligned with a hammer that is forced down upon the molten metal. Also called "drop press."

drop kick. *Football.* A kick made by dropping the ball and kicking it just as it starts to rebound.

drop-kick (drŏp′kĭk′) *v.* **-kicked, -kicking, -kicks.** *—intr.* To make a drop kick. *—tr.* To kick with a drop kick.

drop leaf. A wing on a table, hinged for folding down when not in use. **—drop′-leaf′** *adj.*

drop·let (drŏp′lĭt) *n.* A tiny drop.

drop letter. A letter mailed and picked up at or delivered from the same post office.

drop·light (drŏp′līt′) *n.* A hanging lamp that can be lowered and raised on its cord.

drop out. To withdraw from participation in a game, club, school, or organized society.

drop·out (drŏp′out′) *n.* **1.** A person who quits school before completing a course of instruction. **2.** One who has withdrawn from a given social group.

Usage: *Dropout* is well established in its educational sense. According to 97 per cent of the Usage Panel, it is acceptable in writing and speech on all levels, though some members feel that it is most appropriate to journalism.

drop·per (drŏp′ər) *n.* **1.** One that drops. **2.** A small tube with a suction bulb at one end for drawing in a liquid and releasing it in drops. In this sense, also called "eyedropper."

drop·ping (drŏp′ĭng) *n.* **1.** The act of one that drops. **2.** That which has fallen in drops. **3.** *Plural.* The dung of animals.

drop·sy (drŏp′sē) *n.* Pathological accumulation of diluted lymph in body tissues and cavities. [Middle English *dropesie,* short for *ydropesie,* from Old French, from Latin *hydrōpisis,* from Greek *hudrōpisis,* from *hudrōps,* from *hudōr,* water. See **wed-¹** in Appendix.*] **—drop′si·cal** *adj.* **—drop′si·cal·ly** *adv.*

dropt. *Archaic.* Past tense and past participle of **drop.**

drop·wort (drŏp′wûrt′) *n.* A plant, *Filipendula hexapetala,* native to Eurasia, having finely divided leaflets and clusters of small white flowers.

drosh·ky (drŏsh′kē) *n., pl.* **-kies.** Also **dros·ky** (drŏs′kē). An open, four-wheeled, horse-drawn carriage formerly common in Russia. [Russian *drozhki,* diminutive of *drogi,* wagon, plural formation from *droga,* beam of the wagon. See **dhragh-** in Appendix.*]

dro·soph·i·la (drō-sŏf′ə-lə) *n., pl.* **-las.** A small fly of the genus *Drosophila;* especially, the fruit fly *D. melanogaster,* used extensively in genetic studies. [New Latin : Greek *drosos*†, dew + *-philos,* loving, -PHILOUS.]

dross (drôs, drŏs) *n.* **1.** Waste product or impurities formed on the surface of molten metal during smelting. **2. a.** Worthless stuff as opposed to valuables or value. **b.** Stultifying rubbish: *"He was wide-awake, and his mind worked clearly, purged of all dross"* (Vladimir Nabokov). [Middle English *dros,* Old English *drōs,* dregs. See **dher-¹** in Appendix.*] **—dross′i·ness** *n.* **—dross′y** *adj.*

drought (drout) *n.* Also **drouth** (drouth). **1.** A long period with no rain, especially during a planting season. **2.** A dearth of anything; scarcity. [Middle English *drought,* Old English *drūgath.* See **driug-** in Appendix.*] **—drought′y** *adj.*

drove¹. Past tense of **drive.**

drove² (drōv) *n.* **1.** A flock or herd being driven in a body. **2.** A large mass of people moving or acting as a body. **3.** A stonemason's broad-edged chisel used for rough hewing. **4.** A stone surface dressed with a drove. —See Synonyms at **flock.** *—tr.v.* **droved, droving, droves. 1.** *British.* To herd (animals). **2.** To dress (stone) with a drove. [Middle English *drove,* Old English *drāf,* from *drīfan,* to drive. See **dhreibh-** in Appendix.*]

drov·er (drō′vər) *n.* A driver of cattle or sheep.

drown (droun) *v.* **drowned, drowning, drowns.** *—intr.* To die by suffocating in water or other liquid. *—tr.* **1.** To kill by submerging and suffocating in water or other liquid. **2.** To drench thoroughly or cover with a liquid. **3.** To deaden one's awareness of, as by immersion : *drowned his troubles in drink.* **4.** To overwhelm and blur (a sound) by a louder sound. Often used with *out.* [Middle English *dr(o)unen,* from Scandinavian *drunkna* (unattested), variant of *drugna* (unattested). See **dhreg-** in Appendix.*]

drowse (drouz) *v.* **drowsed, drowsing, drowses.** *—intr.* To be half-asleep; to doze: *"Stuffed to the eyes, McTeague drowsed over his pipe"* (Frank Norris). *—tr.* **1.** To make drowsy: *"on a half-reaped furrow sound asleep,/drowsed with the fume of poppies"* (Keats). **2.** To pass (time) drowsing. Used with *away.* *—n.* The condition of being sleepy. [Perhaps ultimately from Old English *drūsian,* to be sluggish. See **dhreu-** in Appendix.*]

drow·sy (drou′zē) *adj.* **-sier, -siest. 1.** Dull with sleepiness. **2.** Produced or characterized by sleepiness. **3.** Inducing sleepiness; soporific. **—drow′si·ly** *adv.* **—drow′si·ness** *n.*

dr t troy dram.

drub (drŭb) *v.* **drubbed, drubbing, drubs.** *—tr.* **1.** To thrash with a stick. **2.** To instill or rout (an idea, for example) forcefully. Used with *into* or *out of.* **3.** To defeat emphatically. **4.** To stamp (the feet). *—intr.* **1.** To beat the ground; to stamp. **2.** To pound; throb. *—n.* A blow with a stick. [Arabic *dáraba,* to beat.] **—drub′ber** *n.*

drub·bing (drŭb′ĭng) *n.* **1.** A severe thrashing. **2.** A total defeat.

drudge (drŭj) *n.* Also **drudg·er** (drŭj′ər). A person who does tedious, menial, or unpleasant work: *"The Drudge expends her life in mopping, /In emptying and filling pails"* (Edward Gorey). *—intr.v.* **drudged, drudging, drudges.** To do the work of a drudge. [Perhaps from Middle English *druggen,* to labor, perhaps Old English *drycgean* (unattested). See **dher-²** in Appendix.*] **—drudg′ing·ly** *adv.*

drudg·er·y (drŭj′ə-rē) *n., pl.* **-ies.** Tedious, menial, or unpleasant work: *"the drudgery of penning definitions and marking quotations for transcription"* (Macaulay). See Synonyms at **work.**

drug¹. *Nonstandard.* Past tense and past participle of **drag.** See Usage note at **drag.**

drug² (drŭg) *n.* **1.** A substance used as medicine in the treatment of disease. **2.** A narcotic, especially one that is addictive. **3.** *Obsolete.* A chemical or dye. **—drug on the market.** A commodity for which there is no demand. *—tr.v.* **drugged, drugging, drugs. 1.** To administer a drug to. **2.** To poison or mix (food or drink, for example) with drugs. **3.** To stupefy or dull with or as if with a drug. [Middle English *drogge,* from Old French *drogue,* chemical material, possibly from Middle Low German *droge*†, dry (goods). See **drug.**]

drug addict. A person addicted to narcotics.

drug·get (drŭg′ĭt) *n.* **1.** A heavy felted fabric of wool or wool and cotton, having characteristic colored designs, used for floor covering. **2.** A coarse rug of this fabric, made in India. **3.** A fabric woven wholly or partly of wool, formerly used for clothing. [Old French *droguet,* diminutive of *drogue,* stuff, perhaps from Middle Low German *droge,* dry (goods).]

drug·gist (drŭg′ĭst) *n.* **1.** A pharmacist. **2.** One who sells drugs.

drug·store (drŭg′stôr′, -stōr′) *n.* Also **drug store.** A store where prescriptions are filled and drugs and other articles are sold.

dru·id (dro͞o′ĭd) *n.* Also **Dru·id.** A member of an order of priests in ancient Gaul and Britain, who appear in Welsh and Irish legend as prophets and sorcerers. [Latin *druides,* druids, from Gaulish. See **deru-** in Appendix.*] **—dru·id′ic, dru·id′i·cal** *adj.* **—dru′id·ism′** *n.*

drum (drŭm) *n.* **1.** A percussion instrument consisting of a hollow cylinder or hemisphere with a membrane stretched tightly over one or both ends, played by beating with the hands or sticks. **2.** A sound produced by such an instrument. **3.** Something resembling a drum in shape or structure, especially: **a.** A metal cylinder or spool, wound with cable, wire, or heavy rope. **b.** A cylindrical or barrellike metal container. **4.** *Architecture.* **a.** A cylindrical block or section forming the shaft of a stone pillar. **b.** A circular or polygonal wall or other structure, as that supporting a dome. **5.** Any of various marine and freshwater fishes of the family Sciaenidae, that make a drumming sound. —*v.* **drummed, drumming, drums.** —*intr.* **1.** To play the drum. **2.** To thump or tap rhythmically or continually. **3.** To produce a booming, reverberating sound by beating the wings, as certain birds do. —*tr.* **1.** To perform (a piece or tune) on or as if on a drum. **2.** To summon by or as if by beating a drum. **3.** To make known to or force upon (a person) by constant repetition. Used with *into.* **4.** To obtain, create, or work up (business or trade, for example) by canvassing, soliciting, or advertising. Often used with *up.* **5.** To expel or dismiss in disgrace, originally to the beat of a drum. Used with *out.* [Perhaps Dutch *trom,* from Middle Dutch *tromme* (imitative).]

drum·beat (drŭm′bēt′) *n.* The sound produced by beating a drum.

drum·fire (drŭm′fīr′) *n.* **1.** Heavy, continuous gunfire. **2.** A sound suggestive of this.

drum·head (drŭm′hĕd′) *n.* **1.** The membrane stretched over the open end of a drum. **2.** *Nautical.* The circular top part of a capstan, used to hold bars for turning.

drumhead court-martial. A court-martial held for the summary trial of an offense committed during military operations. [So called because it was sometimes held around a drumhead.]

drum·lin (drŭm′lĭn) *n.* A streamlined hill or ridge composed of glacial drift. [Irish Gaelic *druim,* ridge, from Old Irish *druim†* + -LIN(G).]

drum major. A person who leads a marching band or drum corps, often prancing before it and twirling a baton.

drum majorette. A costumed girl who prances and twirls a baton at the head of a marching band.

drum·mer (drŭm′ər) *n.* **1.** One who plays a drum, as in a band. **2.** A traveling salesman.

drum·stick (drŭm′stĭk) *n.* **1.** A stick for beating a drum. **2.** The lower part of the leg of a cooked fowl.

drunk (drŭngk). Past participle and *archaic* past tense of **drink.** —*adj.* **1.** Intoxicated with alcoholic liquor to the point of impairment of physical and mental faculties; inebriated. **2.** Overcome by strong feeling or emotion: *drunk with power.* —*n.* **1.** A drunken person; especially, a drunkard. **2.** A bout of drinking; spree; binge: *"The drunk . . . began in Liguria and lasted well past Naples"* (Thomas Pynchon).

Usage: Drunk (adjective) is used predicatively after a verb for the most part: *He was drunk.* In contrast, *drunken* (adjective) is largely used attributively before a noun: *a drunken driver.* The attributive use of *drunk,* as in *drunk driving* and *drunk driver,* is unacceptable in writing to 83 per cent of the Usage Panel.

drunk·ard (drŭng′kərd) *n.* One who is habitually drunk.

drunk·en (drŭng′kən). *Obsolete.* Alternate past participle of **drink.** —*adj.* **1.** Delirious with or as with strong drink; intoxicated. **2.** Habitually intoxicated; chronically drunk: *a drunken wastrel.* **3.** Pertaining to or occurring during intoxication: *drunken driving.* —See Usage note at **drunk.** —**drunk′en·ly** *adv.* —**drunk′en·ness** *n.*

drunk·o·me·ter (drŭng′kə-mē′tər, drŭng-kŏm′ə-tər) *n.* A device for determining the alcoholic content of the blood by analysis of the breath. [DRUNK + -METER.]

dru·pa·ceous (drōō-pā′shəs) *adj. Botany.* **1.** Pertaining to or consisting of a drupe: *drupaceous fruit.* **2.** Producing drupes: *a drupaceous tree.* [DRUP(E) + -ACEOUS.]

drupe (drōōp) *n. Botany.* A fleshy fruit, such as the peach, plum, or cherry, usually having a single hard stone that encloses a seed. [New Latin *drupa,* from Latin *drūpa, druppa,* overripe olive, from Greek *druppa,* from *drupepēs,* "ripened on a tree," overripe : *drus,* tree (see **deru-** in Appendix*) + *peptein,* to cook, to ripen (see **pekw-** in Appendix*).]

drupe·let (drōōp′lĭt) *n. Botany.* A small drupe, such as one of the many subdivisions of the raspberry or the blackberry.

druse (drōōz) *n.* **1.** A crust of tiny crystals lining a rock cavity. **2.** A cavity lined by such a crust. [German *Druse,* "weathered ore," from Old High German *druos†,* bump, gland.]

Druse (drōōz) *n.* Also **Druze.** A member of a sect in Syria and Lebanon, whose primarily Moslem religion contains some elements of Christianity. [From Arabic *Durūz,* plural of *darazi,* a Druse, after Ismail al-Darazi (died 1019), Moslem religious leader.] —**Dru′si·an, Dru′se·an** *adj.*

DRV Democratic Republic of Vietnam (North Vietnam).

dry (drī) *adj.* **drier** or **dryer, driest** or **dryest. 1.** Free from liquid or moisture; not wet, damp, or moistened. **2.** Having or characterized by little or no rain: *a dry climate.* **3.** Marked by the absence of natural or normal moisture: *a dry month.* **4.** Not under water: *dry land.* **5.** Having all or almost all the water drained away, evaporated, or exhausted: *a dry river.* **6.** No longer yielding liquid, especially milk: *a dry cow.* **7.** Lacking a mucous or watery discharge: *a dry cough.* **8.** Needing or desiring drink; thirsty. **9.** Of or pertaining to solid rather than liquid substances or commodities. **10.** Not sweet as a result of the decomposition of sugar during fermentation. Said of wines. **11.** Having a large proportion of strong liquor to other ingredients. Said of a cocktail, such as a martini. **12.** Plain; bare; bald; unadorned. **13.** Matter-of-fact; cold: *"he would deal you out facts in a dry mechanical way"* (W.H. Hudson). **14.** Humorous or sarcastic in a shrewd, impersonal way: *dry wit.* **15.** *Informal.*

Prohibiting or opposed to the sale or consumption of alcoholic beverages. —*v.* **dried, drying, dries.** —*tr.* **1.** To make dry; free from moisture. **2.** To preserve (meat or other foods, for example) by extracting the moisture. —*intr.* To become dry or lose moisture. —**dry up. 1.** To become intellectually unproductive. **2.** *Slang.* To stop talking; shut up. Often used as a command. —*n., pl.* **drys.** *Informal.* A prohibitionist. [Middle English *dry, drye,* Old English *drȳge.* See **driug-** in Appendix.*] —**dry′ly, dri′ly** *adv.* —**dry′ness** *n.*

dry·ad (drī′əd, -ăd′) *n.* Also **Dry·ad.** *Greek Mythology.* A nature divinity inhabiting or presiding over forests and trees; wood nymph. [Latin *dryas* (stem *dryad-*), from Greek *druas,* from *drus,* tree. See **deru-** in Appendix.*] —**dry·ad′ic** *adj.*

dry·as·dust (drī′əz-dŭst′) *n.* A dull, pedantic speaker or writer. [After Dr. Jonas *Dryasdust,* a fictitious character to whom Sir Walter Scott dedicated some of his novels.] —**dry′·as·dust′** *adj.*

dry battery. An electric battery consisting of two or more dry cells.

dry-bone ore (drī′bōn′). *Mining.* **Smithsonite** *(see).*

dry cell. A primary cell having an electrolyte in the form of moist paste. Compare **wet cell.** [So called because its contents are not spillable.]

dry-clean (drī′klēn′) *tr.v.* **-cleaned, -cleaning, -cleans.** To clean (clothing or fabrics) with chemical solvents having little or no water. —**dry cleaner.** —**dry cleaning.**

Dry·den (drīd′n), **John.** 1631–1700. English poet, dramatist, and critic.

dry dock. A large floating or stationary dock in the form of a basin from which the water can be emptied, used for maintaining, repairing, and altering a ship below the water line.

dry-dock (drī′dŏk′) *v.* **-docked, -docking, -docks.** —*tr.* To place in a dry dock. —*intr.* To go into a dry dock. Used of a ship.

dry·er. 1. Alternate comparative of **dry. 2.** Variant of **drier.**

dry·est. Alternate superlative of **dry.**

dry-eyed (drī′īd′) *adj.* Not weeping: *dry-eyed mourners.*

dry farming. A type of farming practiced in arid areas without irrigation by maintaining a fine surface tilth or mulch which protects the natural moisture of the soil from evaporation. —**dry farm.** —**dry farmer.**

dry fly. An artificial fly used in fishing that floats on the water's surface when cast.

dry goods. Textiles, clothing, and related articles of trade. Also called "soft goods."

Dry Ice. A trademark for solid carbon dioxide, which evaporates directly to gas at −78.5°C (−110°F) at normal atmospheric pressure and is used primarily as a refrigerant.

drying oil. Any of various oily organic liquids, such as linseed oil, soybean oil, or dehydrated castor oil, that form a tough plastic layer on exposure to air in thin films and are used as binders in paints and varnishes.

dry kiln. A heated chamber in which cut lumber is dried and seasoned.

dry law. A law prohibiting the sale of alcoholic liquors.

dry measure. A system of units for measuring dry quantities such as grains, fruits, and vegetables. See **measurement.**

dry nurse. A nurse employed to care for an infant without breast-feeding it.

dry·o·pith·e·cine (drī′ō-pĭth′ə-sēn′) *n.* An extinct ape of the genus *Dryopithecus,* known from Old World fossil remains of the Miocene and Pliocene epochs, and believed to be an ancestor of the chimpanzees, gorillas, and man. —*adj.* Of or belonging to the genus *Dryopithecus.* [From New Latin *Dryopithecus* : Greek *drus,* tree (see **deru-** in Appendix*) + *pithēkos,* ape (see **Pithecanthropus**).]

dry point. 1. A technique of intaglio engraving in which a hard steel needle is used to incise lines in the metal plate, with the burr at the side of the furrows retained. **2.** An engraving or print made with this technique.

dry rot. 1. A fungous disease of timber, causing it to become brittle and crumble into powder. **2.** Any plant disease in which the plant tissue remains relatively dry while fungi invade and ultimately decay bulbs, fruit, or woody tissue.

dry run. 1. *Military.* A test exercise in bombing, attacking, or other combat skills without the use of live ammunition. **2.** A trial run; rehearsal.

dry-salt (drī′sôlt′) *tr.v.* **-salted, -salting, -salts.** To preserve (meats or hides, for example) by salting and drying.

dry socket. A painful inflamed condition of a tooth socket after the tooth has been extracted.

Dry Tor·tu·gas (tôr-tōō′gəz). A group of small islands belonging to Florida, 65 miles west of Key West.

dry wash. Laundry washed and dried but not ironed.

d.s. 1. *Music.* dal segno. **2.** *Commerce.* days after sight. **3.** document signed.

D.S. dal segno.

DSC, D.S.C. Distinguished Service Cross.

DSM 1. Airport code for Des Moines, Iowa. **2.** Distinguished Service Medal.

D.S.M. Distinguished Service Medal.

D.S.O. Distinguished Service Order.

d.s.p. died without issue (Latin *decessit sine prole*).

DST, D.S.T. daylight-saving time.

d.t. double time.

D.T.'s (dē′tēz′) *pl.n.* Delirium tremens *(see).*

DTT Airport code for Detroit, Michigan.

Du. 1. duke (title). 2. Dutch.

du·ad (dōō′ăd′, dyōō′-) *n.* A unit of two objects; a pair. [Greek *duas* (stem *duad-*), the number two, a pair, from *duo,* two. See **dwo** in Appendix.*]

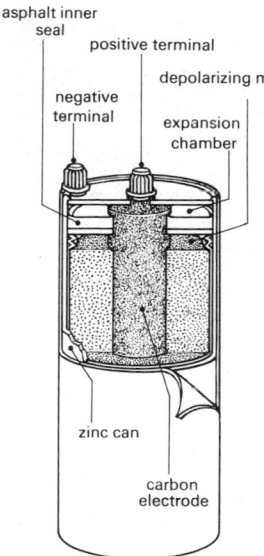

dry cell

dry dock
A ship undergoing repairs in a floating dry dock

du·al (dōō′əl, dyōō′-) *adj.* **1.** Composed of two parts; double; twofold: *dual controls on an automobile.* **2.** Pertaining or relating to two. **3.** *Grammar.* Designating or pertaining to a number category that indicates two persons or things, as in Greek, Sanskrit, and Old English. Compare **plural.** —*n. Grammar.* **1.** The dual number. **2.** A word or expression in the dual number. [Latin *duālis,* from *duo,* two. See **dwo** in Appendix.*] —**du′al·ly** *adv.*

Du·a·la. See **Douala.**

du·al·ism (dōō′ə-lĭz′əm, dyōō′-) *n.* **1.** The condition of being twofold; duality. **2.** *Philosophy.* The view that the world consists of or is explicable as two fundamental entities, such as mind and matter. Compare **monism, pluralism. 3.** *Psychology.* The view that there is a phenomenal distinction between mental and physical processes. **4.** *Theology.* **a.** The concept that the world is ruled by the antagonistic forces of good and evil. **b.** The concept that man has two basic natures, the physical and the spiritual. —**du′al·ist** *n.*

du·al·is·tic (dōō′ə-lĭs′tĭk, dyōō′-) *adj.* **1.** Pertaining to or having the nature of dualism. **2.** Dual. —**du′al·is′ti·cal·ly** *adv.*

du·al·i·ty (dōō-ăl′ə-tē, dyōō-) *n.* The quality or character of being twofold; dichotomy.

du·al-pur·pose (dōō′əl-pûr′pəs, dyōō′-) *adj.* Having two functions or designed to serve two purposes.

dub¹ (dŭb) *tr.v.* **dubbed, dubbing, dubs. 1.** To tap lightly on the shoulder by way of conferring knighthood. **2.** To honor with a new title or description; to style. **3.** To name facetiously or playfully; to nickname. **4.** To strike, cut, or rub (timber or leather, for example) so as to make even or smooth. **5.** To dress (a fowl). **6.** *Slang.* To execute (a golf stroke, for example) poorly; to bungle. —*n. Slang.* An awkward, unskillful person or player; a bungler. [Middle English *dubben,* Old English *dubbian.* See **dheubh-** in Appendix.*]

dub² (dŭb) *v.* **dubbed, dubbing, dubs.** —*tr.* **1.** To thrust at; poke. **2.** To beat (a drum). —*intr.* **1.** To make a thrust. **2.** To beat on a drum. —*n.* **1.** The act of dubbing. **2.** A drumbeat. [Perhaps from Low German *dubben,* to hit, strike. See **dheubh-** in Appendix.*]

dub³ (dŭb) *tr.v.* **dubbed, dubbing, dubs. 1.** To make a new recording from the original of (a record or tape) in order to make changes, cuts, or additions. **2.** To insert a new sound track, often a synchronized translation of the original dialogue, into (a film). **3.** To insert (sound) into a film or tape. Often used with *in.* —*n.* The new sounds so added. [Short for DOUBLE.]

DUB Airport code for Dublin, Ireland.

Dub. Dublin.

Du Bar·ry (dōō băr′ē, dyōō; *French* dü bà-rē′), **Comtesse.** Original name, Marie Jeanne Bécu. 1746?–1793. French courtesan; last mistress of Louis XV.

dub·bin (dŭb′ĭn) *n.* Also **dub·bing** (-ĭng). An application of tallow and oil for dressing leather. [From DUB (to dress, trim).]

du Bel·lay, Joachim. See **Bellay.**

du·bi·e·ty (dōō-bī′ə-tē, dyōō-) *n., pl.* **-ties.** Also **du·bi·os·i·ty** (dōō′bē-ŏs′ə-tē, dyōō′-). **1.** The quality of being dubious. **2.** A matter of doubt; an uncertainty. —See Synonyms at **uncertainty.** [Late Latin *dubietās,* from Latin *dubius,* DUBIOUS.]

du·bi·ous (dōō′bē-əs, dyōō′-) *adj.* **1.** Fraught with uncertainty or doubt; not yet determined; undecided. **2.** Arousing doubt as to validity, quality, or propriety; questionable: *"the dubious distinction of becoming California's first suicide"* (Irving Stone). **3.** Reluctant to concur; skeptical; doubtful. —See Synonyms at **doubtful.** [Latin *dubius,* dubious, fluctuating, moving in two directions. See **dwo** in Appendix.*] —**du′bi·ous·ly** *adv.* —**du′bi·ous·ness** *n.*

du·bi·ta·ble (dōō′bə-tə-bəl, dyōō′-) *adj.* Subject to doubt or question; uncertain. [Latin *dubitābilis,* from *dubitāre,* to DOUBT.] —**du′bi·ta·bly** *adv.*

du·bi·ta·tion (dōō′bə-tā′shən, dyōō′-) *n.* Doubt.

du·bi·ta·tive (dōō′bə-tā′tĭv, dyōō′-) *adj.* Feeling or expressing doubt or hesitancy; doubting. —**du′bi·ta′tive·ly** *adv.*

Dub·lin (dŭb′lĭn). *Irish* **Baile Átha Cliath** (blä′klē′ə). *Abbr.* **Dub. 1.** The capital of the Republic of Ireland, a port on the Irish Sea. Population, 537,000. **2.** A county occupying 356 square miles in eastern Ireland, of which Dublin is the seat. Population, 718,000.

Dub·lin Bay (dŭb′lĭn). An inlet of the Irish Sea in east-central Ireland.

Du·bois (dü-bwä′), **Eugène.** 1858–1940. Dutch paleontologist; discovered *Pithecanthropus erectus* (1891).

Du Bois (dōō bois′), **W(illiam) E(dward) B(urghardt).** 1868–1963. American educator and sociologist; a founder (1910) of the NAACP.

Du·bon·net (dōō′bə-nā′; *French* dü-bô-ně′) *n.* A trademark for a fortified French sweet wine, often used as an apéritif.

Du·bos (dü-bō′), **René Jules.** Born 1901. French-born American bacteriologist.

Du·brov·nik (dōō-brôv′nĭk). *Italian* **Ra·gu·sa** (rä-gōō′sä). A port city and resort of Yugoslavia, on the Dalmatian coast. Population, 24,000.

Du·buf·fet (dü-bü-fě′), **Jean.** Born 1901. French painter and sculptor.

Du·buque (də-byōōk′). A city on the Mississippi in eastern Iowa. Population, 57,000.

du·cal (dōō′kəl, dyōō′-) *adj.* Of or pertaining to a duke or dukedom. [Old French, from Late Latin *ducālis,* from Latin *dux* (stem *duc-*), leader, DUKE.] —**du′cal·ly** *adv.*

duc·at (dŭk′ət) *n.* **1.** Any of various gold coins formerly used in European countries. **2.** *Slang.* A piece of money. **3.** *Slang.* An

ducking stool

dudeen
A woman of Galway, Ireland, smoking a dudeen

admission ticket. [Middle English, from Old French, from Old Italian *ducato,* from Medieval Latin *ducātus,* DUCHY (word used on one of the early ducats).]

Duc·cio di Buo·nin·se·gna (dōōt′chō dē bwô-nēn-sā′nyä). Italian painter of late 13th and early 14th centuries; founder of Sienese school.

du·ce (dōō′chā) *n. Italian.* A leader or commander; chief. —**il Duce.** Benito Mussolini as Fascist leader of Italy.

Du·champ (dü-shän′), **Marcel.** 1887–1968. French painter; a founder of Dada.

duch·ess (dŭch′ĭs) *n. Abbr.* **D. 1.** The wife or widow of a duke. **2.** A woman holding title to a duchy in her own right. [Middle English *duchesse,* from Old French, from Medieval Latin *ducissa,* from Latin *dux* (stem *duc-*), leader, DUKE.]

duch·y (dŭch′ē) *n., pl.* **-ies.** The territory ruled by a duke or duchess; a dukedom. [Middle English *duchie,* from Old French *duche,* from Medieval Latin *ducātus,* from Latin *dux* (stem *duc-*), leader, DUKE.]

duck¹ (dŭk) *n.* **1.** Any of various wild or domesticated aquatic birds of the family Anatidae, characteristically having a broad, flat bill, short legs, and webbed feet. **2.** The female of one of these birds, as distinguished from a drake. **3.** The flesh of this bird used as food. **4.** *Slang.* A person, especially a peculiar one. **5.** *British Informal.* Dear. Used as a term of familiarity. In this sense, also "ducks." [Middle English *doke,* Old English *dūce,* from *dūcan* (unattested), to dive, DUCK.]

duck² (dŭk) *v.* **ducked, ducking, ducks.** —*tr.* **1.** To lower quickly, especially so as to avoid something: *He ducked his head as he went below deck.* **2.** To evade; dodge. **3.** To push suddenly under water. —*intr.* **1.** To lower the head or body. **2.** To move swiftly, especially so as to escape being seen. **3.** To submerge the head or body briefly in water. —*n.* **1.** A quick lowering of the head or body. **2.** A plunge into water; a dip. [Middle English *douken,* Old English *dūcan* (unattested), to dive, from West Germanic *dukjan* (unattested).] —**duck′er** *n.*

duck³ (dŭk) *n.* **1.** A very durable, closely woven heavy cotton or linen fabric. **2.** *Plural.* Clothing made of this fabric; especially, white trousers. [Dutch *doek,* from Middle Dutch *doek, doec,* akin to Old Norse *dūkr*†.]

duck⁴ (dŭk) *n.* An amphibious military truck used during World War II. [Variant of *DUKW,* its code designation.]

duck·bill (dŭk′bĭl′) *n.* A mammal, the **platypus** *(see).* Also called "duck-billed platypus."

duck blind. A structure of wood or canvas, often camouflaged with reeds and grasses, behind which a duck hunter can hide and shelter himself from winds while awaiting a flight of ducks.

duck·board (dŭk′bôrd′, -bōrd′) *n.* A board or boardwalk laid across wet or muddy ground or flooring.

duck hawk. The peregrine falcon *(see).*

ducking stool. A device formerly used in Europe and New England for punishment, consisting of a chair in which an offender was tied and ducked into water. Compare **cucking stool.**

duck·ling (dŭk′lĭng) *n.* A young duck.

duck·pin (dŭk′pĭn′) *n.* **1.** A bowling pin, shorter and squatter than a tenpin. **2.** *Plural.* A bowling game played with these pins and small balls. Used with a singular verb. [From its squat appearance.]

ducks and drakes. The game of skipping flat stones along the surface of water. —**make ducks and drakes of** or **play ducks and drakes with.** To squander; waste.

duck soup. *Slang.* Something easy to accomplish.

duck·weed (dŭk′wēd′) *n.* Any of various small, free-floating, stemless aquatic plants of the genus *Lemna,* having a rounded or oval leaflike form.

duck·y (dŭk′ē) *adj.* **-ier, -iest.** *Slang.* Excellent; fine. Often used ironically. —*n., pl.* **duckies.** Dear. Used as a term of familiarity. [From DUCK (darling).]

duct (dŭkt) *n.* **1.** Any tubular passage through which a substance, especially a fluid, is conveyed. **2.** A bodily passage, especially one for secretion. **3.** *Electricity.* A tube or pipe for carrying cables or wires. [Latin *ductus,* a leading, from *ducere,* to lead. See **deuk-** in Appendix.*]

duc·tile (dŭk′tĭl) *adj.* **1.** Capable of being drawn into wire or hammered thin. Said of metal. **2.** Capable of being easily molded or shaped; plastic. **3.** Readily persuaded or influenced; tractable. —See Synonyms at **flexible.** [Old French, from Latin *ductilis,* from *ductus,* DUCT.] —**duc·til′i·ty** *n.*

duct·less gland (dŭkt′lĭs). An endocrine gland *(see).*

dud (dŭd) *n. Informal.* **1.** A bomb, shell, or round that fails to explode when it should. **2.** Someone or something disappointingly ineffective or unsuccessful. [Middle English *dudde†,* article of clothing, thing.]

dude (dōōd, dyōōd) *n.* **1.** *Informal.* An Easterner or city person who vacations on a Western ranch. **2.** *Informal.* A conspicuously overdressed man; a dandy. **3.** *Slang.* A fellow; chap. [Origin unknown.]

du·deen (dōō-dēn′) *n.* A short-stemmed clay pipe. [Irish *dúidín,* diminutive of *dúd,* pipe. See **dheu-**¹ in Appendix.*]

dude ranch. A resort patterned after a Western ranch, featuring camping, horseback riding, and other outdoor activities.

dudg·eon¹ (dŭj′ən) *n.* A sullen, angry, or indignant humor: *"Slamming the door in Meg's face, Aunt March drove off in high dudgeon."* (Louisa May Alcott). [Origin unknown.]

dudg·eon² (dŭj′ən) *n.* **1.** *Obsolete.* A kind of wood used in making knife handles. **2.** *Archaic.* **a.** A dagger with a hilt made of this wood. **b.** The hilt of a dagger. [Middle English *dogeon,* from Norman French *digeon†.*]

Dud·ley (dŭd′lē), **Joseph.** 1647–1720. British colonial admin-

istrator; governor of Massachusetts; son of Thomas Dudley.
Dud·ley, Robert. See Earl of **Leicester.**

Dud·ley (dŭd′lē), **Thomas.** 1576–1653. British colonial administrator; four times governor of Massachusetts Bay Colony; father of Joseph Dudley and Anne Bradstreet.

duds (dŭdz) *pl.n. Informal.* 1. Clothes; clothing. 2. Personal belongings. [Plural of earlier *dud*, article of clothing, from Middle English *dudde.* See **dud.**]

due (dōō, dyōō) *adj.* 1. Payable immediately or on demand. 2. Owed as a debt; owing: *the amount still due.* 3. Owed by right, convention, or courtesy; fitting or appropriate: *due esteem.* 4. Meeting special requirements; sufficient; adequate: *We have due cause to honor him.* 5. Expected or scheduled; especially, appointed to arrive. **—due to.** 1. Attributable to; caused by. 2. Because of. See Usage note below. **—n.** 1. Something that is owed or deserved: *"The leading position came to him as a kind of natural due."* (Haakon Chevalier). 2. *Plural.* A charge or fee for membership, as in a club or organization. **—adv.** 1. Straight; directly: *due west.* 2. *Archaic.* Duly. [Middle English, from Old French *deu,* from Vulgar Latin *dēbūtus* (unattested), "owed," from Latin *dēbitus,* past participle of *dēbēre,* to owe. See **ghabh-** in Appendix.*]

Usage: The phrase *due to* is always acceptable when *due* functions as a predicate adjective following a linking verb: *His hesitancy was due to fear.* But objection is often made when *due to* introduces an adverbial phrase that assigns the reason for, or cause of, the action denoted by a nonlinking verb: *He hesitated due to fear.* The adverbial construction typified by the second example is termed unacceptable in writing by 84 per cent of the Usage Panel, though it is widely employed informally. Generally accepted alternatives to *due to,* in such examples, are *because of, on account of, through,* and *owing to.*

due bill. A written acknowledgment of indebtedness to a particular party, but not payable to his order or transferable by endorsement.

du·el (dōō′əl, dyōō′-) *n.* 1. A prearranged combat between two persons, fought according to formal procedure with deadly weapons, typically to settle a point of honor. 2. Any struggle for ascendancy between two contending persons, groups, or ideas. **—v. dueled** or **-elled, -eling** or **-elling, -els.** **—tr.** To fight with in a duel. **—intr.** To fight a duel. [Medieval Latin *duellum,* from Latin, war. See **duellum** in Appendix.*] **—du′el·er, du′el·ist** *n.*

du·el·lo (dōō-ĕl′ō, dyōō-) *n.* The art of the duel. [Italian, from Latin *duellum,* war. See **duel.**]

du·en·na (dōō-ĕn′ə, dyōō-) *n.* 1. An elderly woman retained by a Spanish or Portuguese family to act as governess and companion to the daughters. 2. Any chaperon. [Spanish *dueña,* from Latin *domina,* lady, feminine of *dominus,* lord, master. See **deme-¹** in Appendix.*]

Due·ro. The Spanish name for the **Douro.**

du·et (dōō-ĕt′, dyōō-) *n.* 1. A musical composition written for two voices or two instruments. 2. The two performers presenting such a composition. [Italian *duetto,* diminutive of *duo,* duet, from Latin, two. See **dwō** in Appendix.*]

Du·fay (dü-fā′), **Guillaume.** 1400?–1474. Flemish composer; pioneer contrapuntist.

duff¹ (dŭf) *n.* A stiff flour pudding boiled in a cloth bag or steamed; *plum duff.* [English dialectal variant of DOUGH.]

duff² (dŭf) *n.* 1. Decaying leaves and branches covering a forest floor. 2. Fine coal; coal dust; slack. [Back-formation from DUFFER (considered useless).]

duf·fel (dŭf′əl) *n.* Also **duf·fle.** 1. A blanket fabric made of low-grade woolen cloth with a nap on both sides. 2. Clothing and other personal gear carried by a camper. [Dutch, from *Duffel,* town near Antwerp, Belgium.]

duffel bag. A large cloth bag of canvas or duck for carrying personal belongings, used especially by soldiers and sailors.

duf·fer (dŭf′ər) *n.* 1. *Informal.* An incompetent or dull-witted person. 2. *Slang.* A peddler of cheap merchandise. 3. *Slang.* Something worthless or useless. [Origin obscure.]

Du·fy (dü-fē′), **Raoul.** 1877–1953. French painter, illustrator, and lithographer.

dug¹ (dŭg) *n.* An udder, breast, or teat of a female animal. [Origin obscure.]

dug². Past tense and past participle of **dig.**

du·gong (dōō′gŏng′) *n.* A herbivorous marine mammal, *Dugong dugon,* of tropical coastal waters of the Old World, having flipperlike forelimbs and a deeply notched tail fin. [Variant of Malay *duyong.*]

dug·out (dŭg′out′) *n.* 1. A boat or canoe made by hollowing out a log. 2. A pit dug into the ground or on a hillside and used as a shelter. 3. A long sunken shelter at the side of a baseball field where the players stay while not on the field.

dui. Alternate plural of **duo.**

dui·ker (dī′kər) *n.* Any of various small African antelopes, chiefly of the genus *Cephalopus,* having short, backward-pointing horns. [Afrikaans, "diver," from Dutch *duiken,* to dive, from Middle Dutch *dūken,* from West Germanic *dukjan* (unattested), to DUCK.]

Duis·burg (düs′bŏŏrKH′). Formerly **Duis·burg-Ham·born** (-häm-bŏrn, -häm′bŏrn). An industrial city and river port of West Germany, at the junction of the Rhine and Ruhr rivers. Population, 501,000.

Du·kas (dü-kà′), **Paul.** 1865–1935. French composer.

duke (dōōk, dyōōk) *n. Abbr.* **D., Du.** 1. A nobleman with the highest hereditary rank; especially, in Great Britain, a man of the highest grade of the peerage. 2. A prince who rules an independent duchy. 3. A type of cherry intermediate between a

sweet and a sour cherry. [Middle English, from Old French *duc,* from Latin *dux* (stem *duc-*), leader, from *dūcere,* to lead. See **deuk-** in Appendix.*]

Duke (dōōk, dyōōk), **James Buchanan.** 1856–1925. American industrialist and philanthropist; with his brother, **Benjamin Newton** (1855–1929), established American Tobacco Company.

duke·dom (dōōk′dəm, dyōōk′-) *n.* 1. The state or territory ruled by a duke; a duchy. 2. The office, rank, or title of a duke.

dukes (dōōks, dyōōks) *pl.n. Slang.* The fists: *Put up your dukes!* [From *Duke of Yorks,* rhyming slang for "forks" (i.e., fingers).]

Du·kho·bors (dōō′kə-bôrz′) *pl.n.* Also **Dou·kho·bors.** The members of a Christian religious sect of Russia, many of whom migrated to Canada in the 1890's to escape persecution. [Russian *dukhoborets,* "spirit-wrestlers" : *dukh,* spirit (see **dheu-¹** in Appendix*) + *borets,* wrestler, from *borot',* to overcome (see **bher-²** in Appendix*).]

dul·cet (dŭl′sĭt) *adj.* 1. Pleasing to the ear; gently melodious; quieting: *"subdued and dulcet sound . . . of that melting flute-like quality"* (W.H. Hudson). 2. *Archaic.* Sweet to the taste. **—n.** An organ stop pitched an octave higher than the dulciana. [Learned respelling of Middle English *doucet,* from Old French, from *doux* (feminine *douce*), sweet, from Latin *dulcis.* See **dḷku-** in Appendix.*]

dul·ci·an·a (dŭl′sē-ăn′ə) *n.* An organ stop with a sweet, somewhat thin tone suggestive of a stringed instrument. [New Latin, from Medieval Latin, bassoon, perhaps from Latin *dulcis,* sweet. See **dḷku-** in Appendix.*]

dul·ci·fy (dŭl′sə-fī′) *tr.v.* **-fied, -fying, -fies.** 1. To make agreeable or gentle; mollify. 2. *Rare.* To sweeten. [Late Latin *dulcificāre,* to sweeten : Latin *dulcis,* sweet (see **dḷku-** in Appendix*) + *facere,* to do (see **dhē-¹** in Appendix*).] **—dul′ci·fi·ca′tion** *n.*

dul·ci·mer (dŭl′sə-mər) *n.* A musical instrument with wire strings of graduated lengths stretched over a sound box, played with two padded hammers or by plucking. [Middle English *dowcemere,* from Old French *doulcemer, doulcemele* : probably Latin *dulcis,* sweet (see **dḷku-** in Appendix*) + *melos,* song, from Greek (see **mel-³** in Appendix*).]

Dul·heg·gia. Variant of **Dhul-Hijja.**

Dul·kaa·da. Variant of **Dhul-Qadah.**

dull (dŭl) *adj.* **duller, dullest.** 1. Lacking mental agility; slow to learn; stupid. 2. Lacking responsiveness or alertness; insensitive. 3. Dispirited; depressed. 4. Not brisk or rapid; sluggish. 5. Not sharp or keen; blunt. 6. Not intensely or keenly felt: *a dull ache.* 7. Arousing no interest or curiosity; unexciting; boring. 8. Not bright or vivid; dim: *a dull brown.* 9. Cloudy; gloomy. 10. Muffled; indistinct. **—See Synonyms at stupid.** **—v. dulled, dulling, dulls.** **—tr.** 1. To make less sharp; to blunt. 2. To make less bright or distinct. 3. To make (the senses, for example) less keen or receptive. **—intr.** To become dull. [Middle English *dul, dulle,* from Middle Low German *dul.* See **dheu-¹** in Appendix.*] **—dul′ly** *adv.* **—dull′ness, dul′ness** *n.*

Synonyms: dull, blunt, obtuse. These adjectives are compared as they apply to the absence of sharpness. In general usage only *dull* and *blunt* describe absence of physical sharpness. *Dull* implies loss of sharpness through use; *blunt* more often refers to what is thick-edged by design. Figuratively, *dull* implies lack of intelligence or slowness of perception, while *blunt* refers to unrefined manner. *Obtuse* implies marked insensitivity to what is directed to the intellect or emotions.

dull·ard (dŭl′ərd) *n.* A mentally dull person; dolt.

Dul·les (dŭl′əs), **John Foster.** 1888–1959. American lawyer and diplomat; Secretary of State (1953–59).

Du·long (dü-lôN′), **Pierre Louis.** 1785–1838. French chemist and physician; studied specific heat.

dulse (dŭls) *n.* A coarse, reddish-brown seaweed, *Rhodymenia palmata,* sometimes eaten as a vegetable. [Irish Gaelic *duileasg,* from Old Irish *duilesc,* "seaweed." See **dhal-** in Appendix.*]

Du·luth (də-lōōth′, dōō-). A city of Minnesota, a major port at the western end of Lake Superior. Population, 107,000.

Du·luth (də-lōōth′; French dü-lüt′), **Daniel Greysolon.** Also **Du·hut** (dü-lüt′). 1636–1710. French explorer of Canada and Great Lakes area.

du·ly (dōō′lē, dyōō′-) *adv.* 1. In a proper manner; rightfully; fittingly: *duly consecrate a church.* 2. At the expected time; punctually. [Middle English *duely,* from DUE.]

Du·ma (dōō′mə) *n.* Also **Dou·ma.** A Russian national parliament, convened and dissolved four times between 1905 and 1917. [Russian *duma,* thought, from Gothic *dōms,* judgment. See **dhē-¹** in Appendix.*]

Du·mas (dü-mà′), **Alexandre¹.** Known as Dumas père. 1802–1870. French author of romantic plays and novels; father of Dumas fils.

Du·mas (dü-mà′), **Alexandre².** Known as Dumas fils. 1824–1895. French author of plays of social realism; natural son of Dumas père.

Du·mas (dü-ma′), **Jean-Baptiste.** 1800–1884. French chemist; studied vapor density and molecular weight.

du Mau·ri·er (dōō môr′ē-ā′), Sir **Gerald.** 1873–1934. British actor and theatrical manager.

dumb (dŭm) *adj.* **dumber, dumbest.** 1. Lacking the power or faculty of speech; mute. 2. Temporarily speechless with shock or fear. 3. Unwilling to speak. 4. Not producing or accompanied by speech or sound. 5. *Nautical.* Not self-propelling. 6. *Informal.* Ignorant or stupid. **—See Synonyms at stupid.** [Middle English *dumb,* Old English *dumb.* See **dheu-¹** in Appendix.*] **—dumb′ly** *adv.* **—dumb′ness** *n.*

Synonyms: dumb, mute, speechless, voiceless. These adjectives refer to the absence of speech. *Dumb* applies chiefly to animals.

duel
Nineteenth-century
illustration of the duel
between Burr and Hamilton

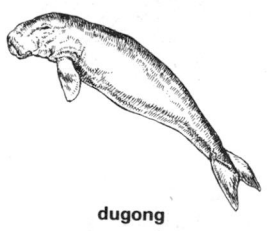

dugong

With reference to human beings, *dumb* and *mute* both can mean permanently incapable of speech because of physical defects, with *mute* usually reserved for those with a congenital incapacity. Both terms also apply to persons rendered speechless from surprise or emotion. *Dumb* in addition applies to action without speech, as in *dumb show,* and *mute* to expression without speech, as in *mute entreaty. Speechless* implies temporary and usually abrupt loss of speech by a person. *Voiceless* generally specifies absence of the right or power of self-expression.

dumb ague. Subacute malaria lacking intense chills and exhibiting only slight periodicity.

Dum·bar·ton (dŭm-bärt′n). **1.** The county seat of Dunbarton, Scotland. Population, 26,000. **2.** See **Dunbarton.**

dumb·bell (dŭm′bĕl′) *n.* **1.** A weight lifted for muscular exercise, consisting of a short bar with a metal ball at each end. **2.** *Slang.* A dull, stupid person; dolt.

dumb cane. Any of several tropical plants of the genus *Dieffenbachia,* some of which have an acrid juice that temporarily inhibits speech when a part of the plant is chewed.

dumb show. 1. A part of a dramatic performance unaccompanied by speech; a pantomime. **2.** Communication by means of gestures.

dumb·wait·er (dŭm′wā′tər) *n.* **1.** A small elevator used to convey food or other goods from one floor to another. **2.** *Chiefly British.* A portable serving table.

dum-dum bullet (dum′dum′). A small-arms bullet with a soft nose designed to expand upon contact, inflicting a gaping wound. [Once made in *Dum-Dum,* town near Calcutta, India.]

dum·found (dŭm′found′) *tr.v.* **-founded, -founding, -founds.** Also **dumb·found.** To strike dumb with astonishment or amazement; stun; nonplus. See Synonyms at **surprise.** [DUM(B) + (CON)FOUND.]

Dum·fries (dŭm-frēs′). **1.** Also **Dum·fries·shire** (-shîr, -shər). A county occupying 1,073 square miles in southern Scotland. Population, 88,000. **2.** Its county seat. Population, 28,000.

dum·my (dŭm′ē) *n., pl.* **-mies. 1.** An imitation of a real or original object, intended to be used as a practical substitute. **2.** A figure imitating the human form, especially: **a.** A mannequin used in designing and displaying clothes. **b.** A stuffed or pasteboard figure used as a target. **c.** A figure of a person or an animal manipulated by a ventriloquist. **3.** *Military.* A blank round. **4.** A mute person. Usually considered offensive. **5.** A blockhead; dolt. **6.** A person or agency secretly in the service of another; a front. **7.** *Printing.* **a.** A model of a work being published, indicating its general appearance and dimensions. **b.** A model page with text and illustrations pasted into place to direct the printer; a layout. **8. a.** In the game of bridge, the partner who exposes his hand to be played by the declarer. **b.** The hand thus exposed. —*adj.* **1.** Simulating something but lacking its function; artificial: *a dummy pocket.* **2.** Silent; mute. **3.** Secretly serving another. —*tr.v.* **dummied, -mying, -mies.** *Printing.* To make a dummy of (a publication or page). Often used with *up.* [Earlier *dummie, dumbie,* dumb person, from DUMB.]

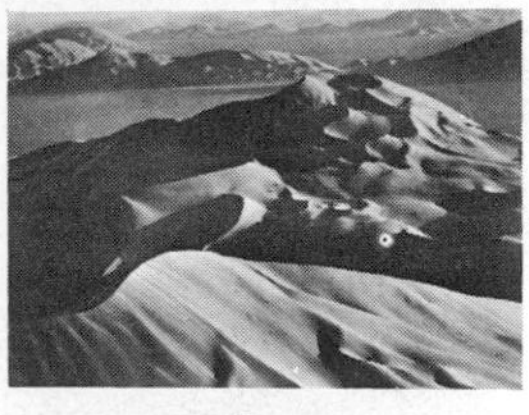

dune
Desert terrain in Saudi Arabia

Du·mont d'Ur·ville (dü-môɴ dür-vē′y′), **Jules Sébastien César.** 1790–1842. French naval commander and explorer of Pacific Ocean and Antarctica.

du·mor·ti·er·ite (dōō-môr′tē-ə-rīt′, dyōō-) *n.* A greenish-blue aluminum borosilicate mineral, used in spark-plug porcelain and in special refractories. [French; discovered by Eugène *Dumortier,* 19th-century French paleontologist.]

dump (dŭmp) *v.* **dumped, dumping, dumps.** —*tr.* **1.** To release or throw down in a large mass; drop heavily. **2.** To empty (material) out of a container or vehicle. **3.** To empty out (a container or vehicle), as by overturning or tilting. **4.** To get rid of (rubbish, for example); dispose of. **5.** To discard or reject (a burden or a problem, for example) unceremoniously. **6.** To place (goods) on the market, especially in a foreign country, in large quantities and at a low price. **7.** *Slang.* To knock down or knock out. —*intr.* **1.** To fall or drop abruptly, especially in a mass. **2.** To discharge cargo or contents; unload. —*n.* **1.** A place where refuse is dumped. **2.** A storage place for goods or supplies; depot. **3.** An unordered accumulation; pile. **4.** *Slang.* A poorly maintained or disreputable place. [Middle English *dompen, dumpen,* to drop, fall, plunge, probably of Scandinavian origin, akin to Norwegian *dumpa,* to fall suddenly. See **dub-** in Appendix.*] —**dump′er** *n.*

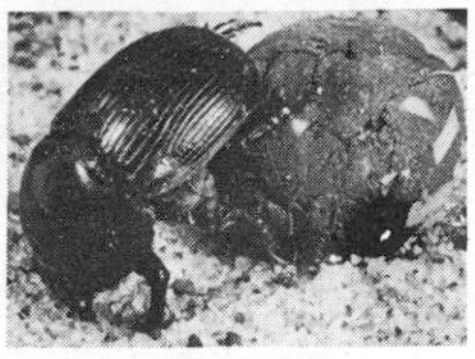

dung beetle
Canthon pilularius

dump·ling (dŭmp′lĭng) *n.* **1.** A small ball of dough cooked with stew or soup. **2.** Sweetened dough wrapped around an apple or other fruit, baked and served as a dessert. **3.** *Informal.* A short, chubby creature. [Origin obscure.]

dumps (dŭmps) *pl.n. Informal.* A gloomy, melancholy state of mind: *"as I was musing in the midst of my dumps"* (Bunyan). Usually preceded by *the.* [From Dutch *domp,* haze, exhalation, "hazy or gloomy state of mind," from Middle Dutch *domp, damp.* See **damp.**]

dump truck. A truck bearing a cargo bin that can be mechanically tilted, allowing the load to be dumped.

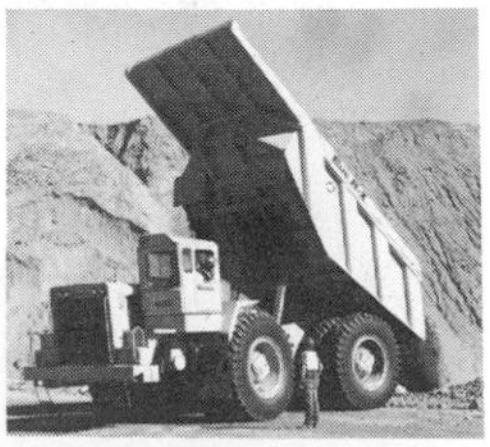

dump truck

dump·y[1] (dŭm′pē) *adj.* **-ier, -iest.** Short and stout; squat. [From archaic *dump,* a shapeless mass, lump, perhaps a back-formation from DUMPLING.] —**dump′i·ly** *adv.* —**dump′i·ness** *n.*

dump·y[2] (dŭm′pē) *adj.* **-ier, -iest.** Depressed or discontented.

dumpy level. A surveyor's instrument having a short telescope fixed rigidly to a horizontally rotating table.

Dum·yat. The Arabic name for **Damietta.**

dun[1] (dŭn) *tr.v.* **dunned, dunning, duns.** To importune (a debtor) persistently for payment. —*n.* **1.** One who importunes debtors for payment; a bill collector. **2.** An importunate demand for payment. [Origin unknown.]

dun[2] (dŭn) *n.* **1.** A color ranging from almost neutral brownish gray to dull grayish brown. **2.** A dun-colored fishing fly. **3.** A dun-colored horse. [Middle English *dun,* Old English *dunn.* See **dheu-**[1] in Appendix.*]

Du·na. The Hungarian name for the **Danube.**

Dü·na. The German name for the **Dvina.**

Du·nant (dü-näɴ′), **Jean Henri.** 1828–1910. Swiss philanthropist and man of letters; founder of the Red Cross.

Du·nă·rea. The Rumanian name for the **Danube.**

Du·nav. The Serbo-Croatian and Bulgarian name for the **Danube.**

Dun·bar (dŭn′bär′), **Paul Lawrence.** 1872–1906. American poet and novelist.

Dun·bar (dŭn-bär′), **William.** 1460?–1520. Scottish poet and cleric.

Dun·bar·ton (dŭn-bärt′n). Also **Dum·bar·ton** (dŭm-), **Dun·bar·ton·shire** (-shîr′, -shər). A county of Scotland, occupying 244 square miles in the west. Population, 197,000. County seat, Dumbarton.

Dun·can (dŭng′kən). A masculine given name. [Gaelic *Donnceann,* "brown head" : *donn,* brown, from Middle Irish, brown, dark (see **dheu-**[1] in Appendix*) + *ceann,* from Common Celtic *gwenno-* (unattested), head (see **pendragon**).]

Dun·can (dŭng′kən), **Isadora.** 1878–1927. American dancer.

dunce (dŭns) *n.* A stupid person; numbskull. [Originally *Duns men,* a contemptuous reference to the disciples of John DUNS SCOTUS, used by their philosophical opponents.]

dunce cap. Also **dunce's cap.** A cone-shaped paper cap, formerly placed upon the head of a slow or lazy pupil.

Dun·dalk (dŭn-dôk′, -dôlk′). An urban area of central Maryland, constituting a suburb of Baltimore. Population, 82,000.

Dun·dee (dŭn-dē′). A major industrial and commercial city on the Firth of Tay in eastern Scotland. Population, 185,000.

Dun·dee (dŭn-dē′), **First Viscount.** Title of John Graham of Claverhouse. 1649?–1689. Scottish Royalist and Jacobite leader.

dun·der·head (dŭn′dər-hĕd′) *n.* A numbskull; dunce. [Perhaps "one stunned by a thunderstroke" : Dutch *donder,* thunder, from Middle Dutch (see **stene-** in Appendix*) + HEAD.]

dun·drear·ies (dŭn-drîr′ēz) *pl.n.* Long side whiskers with a clean-shaven chin. Also called "Dundreary whiskers." [From Lord *Dundreary,* a character in the play *Our American Cousin* (1858) by Tom Taylor (1817–1880), English dramatist.]

dune (dōōn, dyōōn) *n.* A hill or ridge of wind-blown sand, especially one barren of vegetation. [French, from Old French, from Middle Dutch *dūne.* See **dhūno-** in Appendix.*]

Dun·e·din (dŭn-ēd′n). **1.** A city of New Zealand, a seaport on the southeastern shore of South Island. Population, 78,000. **2.** The Scottish Gaelic name for **Edinburgh.**

Dunes State Park. See **Indiana Dunes National Lakeshore.**

dung (dŭng) *n.* **1.** The excrement of animals. **2.** Manure. **3.** Anything foul or abhorrent. —*tr.v.* **dunged, dunging, dungs.** To fertilize with manure. [Middle English *d(o)ung,* from Old English *dung,* akin to Old Norse *dyngja,* heap, from Germanic *dung-* (unattested).] —**dung′y** *adj.*

dun·ga·ree (dŭng′gə-rē′) *n.* **1.** A sturdy, usually blue denim fabric. **2.** *Plural.* Overalls or trousers made from this fabric; blue jeans. [Hindi *dungrī,* from *Dungrī,* name of a section of Bombay where it originated.]

dung beetle. Any of various beetles of the family Scarabaeidae, that form balls of dung on which they feed and in which they lay their eggs.

dun·geon (dŭn′jən) *n.* **1.** A dark, often underground chamber or cell used to confine prisoners. **2.** A donjon *(see).* [Middle English *donjon,* from Old French, "keep of the lord's castle," from Medieval Latin *dominiō,* lordship, dominion, from Latin *dominus,* lord, master. See **demə-**[1] in Appendix.*]

dung·hill (dŭng′hĭl′) *n.* **1.** A heap of animal excrement. **2.** A foul, degraded place or condition.

dunk (dŭngk) *v.* **dunked, dunking, dunks.** —*tr.* **1.** To plunge into liquid; immerse. **2.** To dip (a doughnut, for example) into coffee or other liquid before eating it. **3.** *Informal.* To shoot (a basketball) through the basket from above. —*intr.* To go under water; submerge oneself briefly. [Pennsylvania Dutch *dunke,* from Middle High German *dunken, tunken,* from Old High German *dunkōn.* See **teng-** in Appendix.*] —**dunk′er** *n.*

Dun·ker (dŭng′kər) *n.* Also **Dun·kard** (-kərd). A member of the German Baptist Brethren, a sect of German-American Baptists opposed to military service and the taking of legal oaths. [Pennsylvania Dutch, from *dunke,* DUNK (from their baptism by triple immersion).]

Dun·kerque (dœɴ-kĕrk′). *English* **Dun·kirk** (dŭn′kûrk′). An industrial city of northern France, on the North Sea coast; scene of British troop evacuation of May–June 1940.

dun·lin (dŭn′lĭn) *n.* A brown and white sandpiper, *Erolia* (or *Calidris*) *alpina,* of northern regions. [DUN (color) + -LIN(G), diminutive suffix.]

Dun·lop (dŭn′lŏp′, dŭn-lŏp′), **John Boyd.** 1840–1921. Scottish inventor; credited with invention of pneumatic tire.

Dun·more (dŭn′môr′,-mōr′), **Fourth Earl of.** Title of John Murray. 1732–1809. British colonial administrator; governor of Virginia (1771–75); governor of New York (1770).

dun·nage (dŭn′ĭj) *n.* **1.** Loose packing material protecting a ship's cargo from damage during transport. **2.** Personal belongings or baggage. [Middle English *dennage, donage,* perhaps from Middle Low German *dünne,* thin, hence "loose, light stuff." See **ten-** in Appendix.*]

Dunne (dŭn), **Finley Peter.** 1867–1936. American journalist and humorist; creator of the character "Mr. Dooley."

ă pat/ā pay/âr care/ä father/b bib/ch church/d deed/ĕ pet/ē be/f fife/g gag/h hat/hw which/ĭ pit/ī pie/îr pier/j judge/k kick/l lid, needle/m mum/n no, sudden/ng thing/ŏ pot/ō toe/ô paw, for/oi noise/ou out/ŏŏ took/ōō boot/p pop/r roar/s sauce/sh ship, dish/

Du·nois (dü-nwä′), **Jean.** Comte de Dunois. Called "the Bastard of Orleans." 1402?–1468. Capetian prince; companion of Joan of Arc.
Duns (dŭnz). The county seat of Berwick, in southeastern Scotland. Population, 2,000.
Dun·sa·ny (dŭn-sā′nē), **18th Baron.** Title of Edward John Moreton Drax Plunkett. 1878–1957. Irish poet, playwright, and writer of short stories.
Duns Sco·tus (dŭnz skō′təs), **John.** Called "Doctor Subtilis." 1265?–1308. Scottish philosopher and theologian.
Dun·sta·ble (dŭn′stə-bəl), **John.** 1370?–1453. English composer, astronomer, and mathematician.
Dun·stan (dŭn′stən), **Saint.** A.D. 925?–988. English prelate; archbishop of Canterbury (959–78).
du·o (dōō′ō, dyōō′ō) *n., pl.* **-os** (-ōz) or **dui** (dōō′ē, dyōō′ē) (for senses 1, 2). **1.** *Music.* A duet. **2.** *Music.* Two performers singing or playing together. **3.** Two people in close association; a pair. —See Synonyms at **couple.** [Italian, "two," from Latin. See **dwō** in Appendix.*]
duo–. Indicates two; for example, **duopsony.** [Latin, from *duo,* two. See **dwō** in Appendix.*]
du·o·dec·i·mal (dōō′ō-dĕs′ə-məl, dyōō′-) *adj.* **1.** Of, pertaining to, or based on the number 12: *the duodecimal system.* **2.** Of or pertaining to twelfths. —*n.* A twelfth. [From Latin *duodecimus,* twelfth, from *duodecim,* twelve : DUO- + *decem,* ten (see **dekm̥** in Appendix*).]
du·o·dec·i·mo (dōō′ō-dĕs′ə-mō′, dyōō′-) *n., pl.* **-mos. 1.** The page size (5 by 7¾ inches) of a book, formed by folding a single printer's sheet into 12 leaves. **2.** A book composed of pages of this size. Also called "twelvemo." Also written *12mo., 12°.* —*adj.* Having pages of this size. [Latin, ablative of *duodecimus,* twelfth, from *duodecim,* twelve. See **duodecimal.**]
du·o·de·ni·tis (dōō′ə-də-nī′tĭs, dyōō′-) *n.* Inflammation of the duodenum. [New Latin : DUODEN(UM) + -ITIS.]
du·o·de·num (dōō′ə-dē′nəm, dyōō′-, dōō-ŏd′n-əm, dyōō-) *n., pl.* **-odena** (-ŏd′n-ə). The beginning portion of the small intestine, starting at the lower end of the stomach and extending to the jejunum. [Middle English, from Medieval Latin, short for *intestinum duodenum digitōrum,* "intestine of twelve digits" (translation of the Greek *dodekadaktulon,* "twelve fingers long," the duodenum), from Latin *duodēni,* twelve each, from *duodecim,* twelve. See **duodecimal.**] —**du′o·de′nal** (dōō′ə-dē′nəl, dyōō′-, dōō-ŏd′n-əl, dyōō-) *adj.*
du·op·so·ny (dōō-ŏp′sə-nē, dyōō-) *n., pl.* **-nies.** *Economics.* A stock-market condition wherein two rival buyers exert a controlling influence on numerous sellers. [DUO- + Greek *opsōnia,* purchasing of victuals, catering, from *opsōnes,* victualer, caterer : *opson,* food, relish, delicacy (see **opsonin**) + *ōnē,* buying (see **wes-¹** in Appendix*).]
du·o·tone (dōō′ō-tōn′, dyōō′-) *n. Printing.* **1.** A process for printing halftone illustrations in two tones of the same color or black and one color. **2.** A picture in duotone. —*adj. Printing.* Having a two-toned effect or appearance.
dup. duplicate.
dupe (dōōp, dyōōp) *n.* **1.** A person who is easily deceived or used. **2.** A person who is the tool of another person or a power: *a dupe of Communism.* —*tr.v.* **duped, duping, dupes.** To make a dupe of. See Synonyms at **deceive.** [French, from Old French *dupe,* dupe, probably jocular use of *dupe,* the hoopoe (from the supposed stupid appearance of the bird), contraction of *de huppe* : *de,* of + *huppe,* HOOPOE.] —**dup′a·bil′i·ty** *n.* —**dup′a·ble** *adj.* —**dup′er** *n.*
dup·er·y (dōō′pə-rē, dyōō′-) *n., pl.* **-ies. 1.** The action of duping. **2.** The state of being duped: *"we must think so as to avoid dupery"* (William James). [French *duperie,* from *dupe,* DUPE.]
du·ple (dōō′pəl, dyōō′-) *adj.* Double; consisting of two. [Latin *duplus,* twofold, double. See **dwō** in Appendix.*]
Du·pleix (dü-plĕks′), Marquis **Joseph-François.** 1697–1763. French colonial administrator in India.
du·plex (dōō′plĕks′, dyōō′-) *adj.* **1.** Twofold. **2.** *Machinery.* Having two identical units operating in a single frame, each capable of operating independently. **3.** *Electronics.* Able to transmit two messages simultaneously in the same or opposite directions over a single wire. —*n.* A duplex apartment or house. [Latin, twofold, double. See **dwō** in Appendix.*] —**du·plex′i·ty** *n.*
duplex apartment. An apartment having rooms on two adjoining floors connected by an inner staircase.
duplex house. A house divided into two living units.
du·pli·cate (dōō′plĭ-kĭt, dyōō′-) *adj. Abbr.* **dup. 1.** Identically copied from an original. **2.** Existing or growing in two corresponding parts; double. **3.** *Card Games.* Designating a manner of play in which two partners exchange their original hands and replay them, to compare scores. —*n. Abbr.* **dup. 1.** An identical copy; facsimile. **2.** Anything that corresponds exactly to something else, especially an original; a double. **3.** A duplicate card game. See **bridge.** —*tr.v.* (dōō′plĭ-kāt′, dyōō′-) **duplicated, -cating, -cates. 1.** To make an identical copy of; reproduce. **2.** To double; make twofold. **3.** To make or perform again. [Middle English, from Latin *duplicātus,* past participle of *duplicāre,* to make twofold, from *duplex,* twofold, DUPLEX.] —**du′pli·cate·ly** *adv.*
du·pli·ca·tion (dōō′plĭ-kā′shən, dyōō′-) *n.* **1. a.** The act or procedure of duplicating. **b.** The condition of being duplicated. **2.** A duplicate; replica. —**du′pli·ca′tive** *adj.*
du·pli·ca·tor (dōō′plĭ-kā′tər, dyōō′-) *n.* A machine that reproduces printed or written material, especially one designed for large-quantity reproduction using ink and a master plate.
du·plic·i·ty (dōō-plĭs′ə-tē, dyōō-) *n., pl.* **-ties.** Deliberate deceptiveness in behavior or speech; double-dealing. [Middle English *duplicite,* from Old French, from Late Latin *duplicitās,* from Latin *duplex* (stem *duplic-*), twofold, DUPLEX.]
Du Pont (dōō pŏnt′, dyōō; *French* dü pôN′), **Éleuthère Irénée.** 1771–1834. French-born American industrialist; son of Pierre Samuel Du Pont de Nemours.
Du Pont de Ne·mours (dōō pŏnt′ də nə-mŏŏr′, dyōō-; *French* dü pôN′ də nə-mōōr′), **Pierre Samuel.** 1739–1817. French author, economist, and political leader; adviser to President Jefferson (1799–1802); father of Éleuthère Irénée Du Pont.
Du·que de Ca·xi·as (dōō′kĕ dĕ kä-shē′äs). A city of southeastern Brazil, a suburb of Rio de Janeiro. Population, 170,000.
Dur. Durham.
du·ra·ble (dŏŏr′ə-bəl, dyŏŏr′-) *adj.* Able to withstand wear and tear or decay; lasting. [Middle English, from Old French, from Latin *dūrābilis,* from *dūrāre,* to last, endure. See **deu-⁴** in Appendix.*] —**du′ra·bil′i·ty, du′ra·ble·ness** *n.*
durable goods. Manufactured products capable of long utility, as refrigerators and automobiles; hard goods.
du·ral (dŏŏr′əl, dyŏŏr′-) *adj.* Pertaining to the dura mater.
Du·ral·u·min (dōō-răl′yə-mĭn, dyōō-) *n.* A trademark for an alloy of aluminum containing copper, manganese, magnesium, iron, and silicon. It is resistant to corrosion by acids and sea water. [First made at *Düren,* Germany (1910).]
du·ra ma·ter (dŏŏr′ə mā′tər, dyŏŏr′-). A tough fibrous membrane, lying over the arachnoid and the pia mater, that covers the brain and the spinal cord. Also called "endocranium." [Middle English, from Medieval Latin *dūra mater (cerebri),* "hard mother (of the brain)" (translation from Arabic *umm al-dimāgh aṣ-ṣafīqah*) : Latin *dūra,* feminine of *dūrus,* hard (see **duramen**) + *mater,* mother (see **mater**).]
du·ra·men (dōō-rā′mən, dyōō-) *n. Botany.* **Heartwood** *(see).* [New Latin, from Latin, hardness, from *dūrāre,* to harden, from *dūrus,* hard. See **deru-** in Appendix.*]
dur·ance (dŏŏr′əns, dyŏŏr′-) *n.* Forced confinement; imprisonment. [Middle English *duraunce,* duration, "prison term," from Old French, from *durer,* to last, from Latin *dūrāre.* See **deu-⁴** in Appendix.*]
Du·rand (dyōō-rănd′), **Asher Brown.** 1796–1886. American painter and engraver.
Du·ran·go (dōō-răng′gō). **1.** A landlocked state of Mexico, occupying 47,641 square miles in the northwest. Population, 781,000. **2.** Officially, Victoria de Durango. The capital of this state, in the central southern region. Population, 119,000.
Du·rant (dyōō-rănt′), **Will(iam James).** Born 1885. American educator and, with his wife, **Ariel** (born 1898), author of works popularizing history and philosophy.
du·ra·tion (dōō-rā′shən, dyōō-) *n.* **1.** Continuance or persistence in time. **2.** The period of time during which something exists or persists. [Medieval Latin *dūrātiō,* from Latin *dūrāre,* to last. See **deu-⁴** in Appendix.*]
Dur·ban (dûr′bən). A port city on the east coast of the Republic of South Africa. Population, 560,000.
dur·bar (dûr′bär′) *n.* **1.** A state reception given formerly by an Indian prince or by a British governor in India. **2.** The reception hall. **3.** The court of an Indian prince. [Hindi *darbār,* from Persian, "court" : *dar,* door (see **dhwer-** in Appendix*) + *bār,* admission, audience, time (see **wel-³** in Appendix*).]
Dü·rer (dü′rər), **Albrecht.** 1471–1528. German painter and engraver; regarded as inventor of etching.
du·ress (dōō-rĕs′, dyōō-, dŏŏr′ĭs, dyŏŏr′-) *n.* **1.** Constraint by threat; coercion: *confessed under duress.* **2.** *Law.* **a.** Coercion illegally applied. **b.** Forcible confinement; durance. [Middle English *duresse,* hardness, restraint, confinement, from Old French *dure(s)ce,* hardness, from Latin *dūritia,* from *dūrus,* hard. See **deru-** in Appendix.*]
Dur·ham¹ (dûr′əm). **1.** *Abbr.* **Dur.** A county occupying 1,015 square miles in northeastern England. Population, 1,533,000. **2.** The county seat of this county. Population, 23,000. **3.** A city of north-central North Carolina. Population, 78,000.
Dur·ham² (dûr′əm) *n.* One of a breed of beef cattle, a **shorthorn** *(see).* [Originally bred in DURHAM (county).]
du·ri·an (dŏŏr′ē-ən) *n.* **1.** A tree, *Durio zibethinus,* of southeastern Asia, bearing edible fruit. **2.** The fruit of this tree, having a hard, prickly rind and soft pulp with an offensive odor but a pleasant taste.
dur·ing (dŏŏr′ĭng, dyŏŏr′-) *prep.* **1.** Throughout the course or duration of. **2.** Within the time of; at some time in. [Middle English (after Old French *durant,* "lasting"), from *duren,* to last, from Old French *durer,* from Latin *dūrāre.* See **deu-⁴** in Appendix.*]
dur·mast (dûr′măst′, -mäst′) *n.* A European oak, *Quercus petraea,* having tough, elastic wood. [Probably alteration of *dun mast* : DUN (grayish brown) + MAST (nut, acorn).]
du·ro (dōō′rō) *n., pl.* **-ros.** The silver dollar of Spain and Spanish America. [Spanish *(peso) duro,* "hard (peso)," from Latin *dūrus,* hard. See **deru-** in Appendix.*]
du·roc (dōō-rŏk′, dyōō-) *n.* Also **Du·roc.** A large red hog of a breed developed during the 19th century in the United States. [After *Duroc,* a horse owned by the developer of the breed.]
dur·ra (dŏŏr′ə) *n.* Also **dou·ra, dou·rah.** A cereal grain, *Sorghum vulgare durra,* of Asia and northern Africa, much cultivated in dry regions. Also called "Egyptian corn." [Arabic *dhurah,* "grain."]
Dur·rell (dûr′əl), **Lawrence (George).** Born 1912. English novelist and poet.
Dürr·en·matt (dü′rən-mät′), **Friedrich.** Born 1921. Swiss dramatist and novelist.
durst. *Archaic.* Past tense of **dare.**

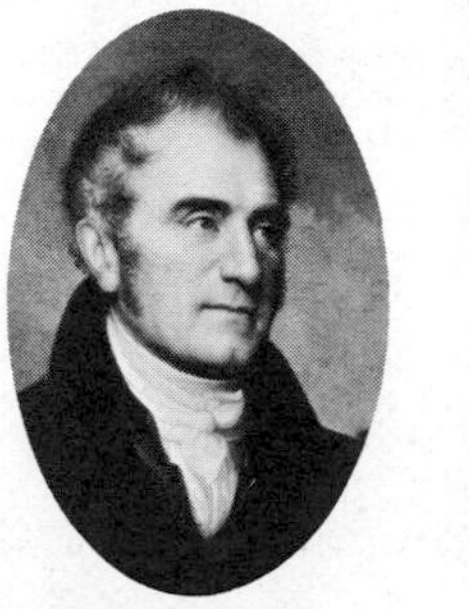

Éleuthère Irénée Du Pont
Contemporary portrait
by Rembrandt Peale

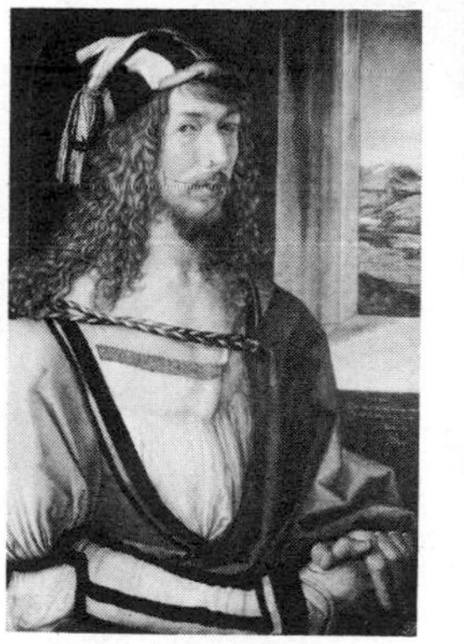

Dürer
A self-portrait

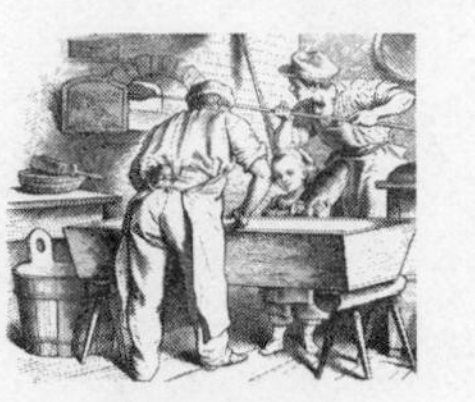

Dutch oven
Baking bread in a Dutch oven

du·rum (do͝or′əm, dyo͝or′-) *n.* A hardy wheat, *Triticum aestivum durum*, used chiefly in making macaroni, spaghetti, and similar products. Also called "durum wheat." [New Latin, from Latin, neuter of *dūrus*, hard. See **deru-** in Appendix.*]
Dur·yea (do͝or′yā), **Charles Edgar.** 1862–1938. American industrialist and inventor; with his brother **J(ames) Frank** (1869–1967) constructed first successful automobile in 1893.
Du·se (do͞o′zā), **Eleonora.** 1859–1924. Italian actress.
Du·shan·be (do͞o-shän′bə, dyo͞o-). Also **Dyu·shan·be.** Formerly **Sta·lin·a·bad** (stä′lĭn-ə-băd′). The capital of the Tadzhik S.S.R. Population, 226,000.
dusk (dŭsk) *n.* The darker stage of twilight, especially in the evening. *—adj.* Tending to darkness. *—v.* **dusked, dusking, dusks.** *—intr.* To become dark or dusky. *—tr.* To darken. [Middle English *dosc, dusk*, dusky, from Old English *dox*, dark, dusky. See **dheu-**[1] in Appendix.*]
dusk·y (dŭs′kē) *adj.* **-ier, -iest. 1.** Dark; shadowy. **2.** Rather dark in color, especially in skin color. **3.** Gloomy. —See Synonyms at **dark.** **—dusk′i·ly** *adv.* **—dusk′i·ness** *n.*
dusky grouse. A bird, the **blue grouse** *(see).*
Düs·sel·dorf (dü′səl-dôrf′). The capital of North Rhine-Westphalia, an industrial city on the Rhine north of Cologne. Population, 704,000.
dust (dŭst) *n.* **1.** Fine particulate matter. **2.** A cloud of such matter. **3.** Such matter regarded as the result of disintegration. **4.** Disturbance; confusion; excitement. **5. a.** Earth, especially when regarded as the substance of the grave: *"Dust thou art, and shalt to dust return."* (Milton). **b.** The surface of the ground. **6.** A debased or despised condition. **7.** Something of no worth. **8.** *British.* Ashes, household dirt, or rubbish. **9.** Pollen. *—v.* **dusted, dusting, dusts.** *—tr.* **1.** To remove dust from by wiping, brushing, or beating. **2.** To sprinkle with a powdery substance. **3.** To strew like dust: *Freckles dusted her nose.* **4.** *Baseball.* To deliver a pitch so close to (the batter) as to make him back away. **5.** To restore to use. Used with *off.* **6.** *Archaic.* To cover with dust. *—intr.* **1.** To clean by removing dust. **2.** To cover itself with dust. Used of a bird. [Middle English *dust, doust*, Old English *dūst*. See **dheu-**[1] in Appendix.*]
dust·bin (dŭst′bĭn′) *n. British.* A can for trash or garbage.
dust bowl. 1. A region reduced to aridity by drought and dust storms. **2.** *Capital* **D,** *capital* **B.** A semiarid region in the south-central United States where the topsoil was lost by wind erosion in the mid-1930's.
dust devil. A small transient whirlwind that swirls dust, debris, and sand to great heights.
dust·er (dŭs′tər) *n.* **1.** One that dusts. **2.** A cloth or brush used to remove dust. **3.** A device for sifting or scattering a powdered substance. **4.** A smock worn to protect one's clothing from dust. **5.** A woman's loose dress-length housecoat.
dust jacket. *Abbr.* **dj** A removable paper cover used to protect the binding of a book. Also called "book jacket," "dust cover."
dust·man (dŭst′mən) *n., pl.* **-men** (-mĭn). *British.* A man employed to remove trash.
dust·pan (dŭst′păn′) *n.* A short-handled, shovellike pan into which dust is swept.
dust storm. A severe windstorm that sweeps clouds of dust across an extensive area, especially in an arid region.
dust·up (dŭst′ŭp′) *n. Informal.* A row; argument.
dust·y (dŭs′tē) *adj.* **-ier, -iest. 1.** Covered or filled with dust. **2.** Consisting of or resembling dust; powdery. **3.** Tinged with gray; subdued; dull. **—dust′i·ly** *adv.* **—dust′i·ness** *n.*
dusty miller. Any of various plants having leaves and stems covered with dustlike down, such as the **beach wormwood** and the **rose campion** *(both of which see).*
Dutch (dŭch) *adj. Abbr.* **D., Du. 1.** Of or pertaining to the Netherlands, its inhabitants, or their language. **2.** *Archaic.* German. *—n. Abbr.* **D., Du. 1. a.** The people of the Netherlands. Preceded by *the.* **b.** *Archaic.* The Germans. **2. a.** The West Germanic language of the Netherlands. Sometimes called "Low Dutch." **b.** The German language. Now used only in the term *High Dutch.* **3. Pennsylvania Dutch** *(see).* **4.** *Slang.* Anger; temper. *—adv.* So that each person pays his own way: *go Dutch for lunch.* **—in Dutch.** *Informal.* In trouble; in disfavor. [Middle English *Duch(e)*, German, Dutch, Low German, from Middle Dutch, *duutsch.* See **teutā-** in Appendix.*]
Dutch auction. *Informal.* An auction in which the auctioneer opens with a high price and lowers it until a buyer is found.
Dutch bargain. *Informal.* A transaction settled while both parties are drinking.
Dutch Bor·ne·o. A former name for **Kalimantan.**
Dutch cheese. 1. A small, round, firm cheese made from skim milk, produced in the Netherlands. **2. Cottage cheese** *(see).*
Dutch clover. The **white clover** *(see).*
Dutch courage. *Informal.* Courage from drinking liquor.
Dutch door. A door divided in half horizontally so that either part may be left open or closed.
Dutch East In·dies. A former name for **Indonesia.**
Dutch elm disease. A disease of elm trees caused by a fungus, *Ceratocystis ulmi*, and resulting in brown streaks in the wood and eventual death of the tree.
Dutch Gui·a·na. A former name for **Surinam.**
dutch·man (dŭch′mən) *n., pl.* **-men** (-mĭn). Something used to conceal faulty construction. [Playful use of DUTCHMAN.]
Dutch·man (dŭch′mən) *n., pl.* **-men** (-mĭn). **1. a.** A native or inhabitant of the Netherlands. **b.** A person of Dutch descent. **2.** *Archaic.* A German.
Dutch·man's-breech·es (dŭch′mənz-brĭch′ĭz) *n.* Plural in form, used with a singular or plural verb. A woodland plant, *Dicentra cucullaria*, of eastern North America, having finely divided leaves and yellowish-white flowers with two spurs. [From its breeches-shaped blossoms.]

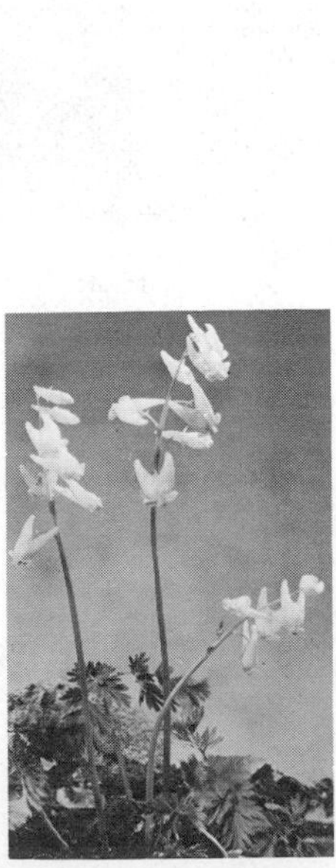

Dutchman's-breeches

Dutch·man's-pipe (dŭch′mənz-pīp′) *n.* The **pipe vine** *(see).*
Dutch metal. An alloy of copper and zinc used in thin sheets as a cheap imitation of gold leaf. Also called "Dutch foil," "Dutch gold," "Dutch leaf." [Originally imported from Holland.]
Dutch New Guin·ea. A former name for **West Irian.**
Dutch oven. 1. A large, heavy pot or kettle, usually of cast iron and with a tight lid, used for slow cooking. **2.** A metal utensil open on one side and equipped with shelves, that is placed before an open fire for baking or roasting food. **3.** A wall oven in which food is baked by means of preheated brick walls.
Dutch treat. *Informal.* An outing, as for dinner or a movie, for which each person pays his own expenses.
Dutch uncle. *Informal.* A stern and candid critic or adviser.
Dutch West In·dies. The former name for the **Netherlands Antilles.**
du·te·ous (do͞o′tē-əs, dyo͞o′-) *adj.* **1.** Obedient; dutiful. **2.** Laborious. [From DUTY.] **—du′te·ous·ly** *adv.* **—du′te·ous·ness** *n.*
du·ti·a·ble (do͞o′tē-ə-bəl, dyo͞o′-) *adj.* Subject to import tax.
du·ti·ful (do͞o′tĭ-fəl, dyo͞o′-) *adj.* **1.** Careful to perform duties. **2.** Expressing or filled with a sense of duty. —See Synonyms at **obedient.** **—du′ti·ful·ly** *adv.* **—du′ti·ful·ness** *n.*
du·ty (do͞o′tē, dyo͞o′-) *n., pl.* **-ties. 1.** An act or a course of action that is exacted of one by position, social custom, law, or religion. **2. a.** Moral obligation. **b.** The compulsion felt to meet such obligation. **3. a.** A service assigned or demanded of one, especially in the armed forces. **b.** Function; work. **4.** A tax charged by a government, especially on imports. **5.** *Machinery.* **a.** The work capability of a machine under specified conditions. **b.** A measure of efficiency expressed as work per unit energy input. **6.** *Agriculture.* The amount of water required to irrigate a given area for the cultivation of some crop. **—off duty.** Not engaged in one's assigned work. —See Synonyms at **obligation.** **—on duty.** At one's post or work. [Middle English *duete*, from Norman French, from Old French *deu*, DUE.]
du·ty-free (do͞o′tē-frē′, dyo͞o′-) *adj.* Exempt from customs duties. **—du′ty-free′** *adv.*
du·um·vir (do͞o-ŭm′vər, dyo͞o-) *n., pl.* **-virs** or **-viri** (-və-rē′). A member of a duumvirate. [Latin, variant of *duovir* : *duo*, two (see **dwō** in Appendix*) + *vir*, man (see **wiros** in Appendix*).]
du·um·vi·rate (do͞o-ŭm′vər-ĭt, dyo͞o-) *n.* **1.** Any of various two-man executive boards in the Roman Republic. **2.** Any regime or partnership of two men.
Du·va·lier (dü-vȧ-lyā′), **François.** Called "Papa Doc." Born 1907? President and dictator of Haiti (since 1957).
du·ve·tyn (do͞o′və-tēn′, dyo͞o′-, do͞o′və-tēn′, dyo͞o′-) *n.* Also **du·ve·tine, du·ve·tyne.** A soft, short-napped fabric with a twill weave, made of wool, cotton, rayon, or silk. [French *duvetine*, from *duvet*, down, from Old French *duvet*, alteration of *dumet*, diminutive of *dum*, alteration (probably influenced by *plume*, PLUME) of *dun*, from Old Norse *dūnn.* See **dheu-**[1] in Appendix.*]
du Vi·gneaud (do͞o vēn′yō, dyo͞o), **Vincent.** Born 1901. American biochemist; first to synthesize a protein hormone.
D.V. 1. Deo volente. **2.** Douay Version (of the Bible).
Dvi·na (dvē′nə; *Russian* dvĭ-nä′). **1.** *Russian* **Se·ver·na·ya Dvi·na** (sā′vər-nə-yə). A river of the Soviet Union, flowing 455 miles from north-central Russian S.F.S.R. north to the White Sea at Archangel. Also called "Northern Dvina." **2.** *Russian* **Za·pad·na·ya Dvi·na** (zä′pəd-nə-yə); *German* **Dü·na** (dü′nä); *Lettish* **Dau·ga·va** (dou′gä-vä). A river rising in western Russian S.F.S.R. and flowing 633 miles generally southwest to the Gulf of Riga. Also called "Western Dvina."
D.V.M. Doctor of Veterinary Medicine.
Dvoř·ák (dvôr′zhäk), **Antonín.** Known as Anton Dvořák. 1841–1904. Czech composer.
D/W dock warrant.
dwarf (dwôrf) *n., pl.* **dwarfs** or **dwarves** (dwôrvz). **1. a.** A very small person, especially one afflicted with dwarfism. **b.** An atypically small animal or plant. **2.** A diminutive, often ugly, manlike creature of fairy tales and legend. **3.** A **dwarf star** *(see).* *—v.* **dwarfed, dwarfing, dwarfs.** *—tr.* **1.** To check the natural growth or development of; to stunt: *"the oaks were dwarfed from lack of moisture"* (Steinbeck). **2.** To cause to appear small by comparison: *"Together these two big men dwarfed the tiny Broadway office"* (Saul Bellow). *—intr.* To become stunted or grow smaller. *—adj.* **1.** Diminutive; undersized; stunted. **2.** *Biology.* Much smaller than the usual or typical kind: *dwarf gourami; dwarf zinnias.* [Middle English *dwerf, dwergh*, Old English *dweorg, dweorh*, from Germanic *dwerg-* (unattested).]
dwarf cornel. A woody plant, *Cornus canadensis*, of northern North America, having inconspicuous greenish flowers surrounded by white, petallike bracts, and scarlet fruit. Also called "bunchberry."
dwarf·ism (dwôr′fĭz′əm) *n.* A pathological condition of arrested growth having various causes.
dwarf star. A star such as the sun having relatively low mass and average or below average luminosity. Also called "dwarf."
dwell (dwĕl) *intr.v.* **dwelt** (dwĕlt) or **dwelled, dwelling, dwells. 1.** To live as a resident; reside. **2.** To exist in some place or state. **3. a.** To fasten one's attention. **b.** To expatiate. [Middle English *dwellen*, to delay, linger, remain, reside, Old English *dwellan*, deceive, hinder, delay (meaning influenced by Old Norse *dvelja*, "sojourn," "dwell"). See **dheu-**[1] in Appendix.*] **—dwell′er** *n.*
dwell·ing (dwĕl′ĭng) *n.* A place to live in; residence; abode.
Dwight (dwīt), **Timothy.** 1752–1817. American Congregational clergyman and author; grandson of Jonathan Edwards.
dwin·dle (dwĭnd′l) *v.* **-dled, -dling, -dles.** *—intr.* To become

gradually less until little remains; waste away; diminish. —*tr.* To make smaller or less; cause to shrink. —See Synonyms at **decrease.** [Frequentative of obsolete *dwine,* to waste away, diminish, languish, Middle English *dwinen,* Old English *dwīnan.* See **dheu-³** in Appendix.*]

dwt. pennyweight. [D(ENARIUS) + W(EIGH)T.]

Dy The symbol for the element dysprosium.

dy·ad (dī′ăd′) *n.* **1.** Two units regarded as a pair. **2.** *Biology.* One pair of chromosomes separated from a tetrad in meiosis. **3.** *Chemistry.* A divalent atom or radical. **4.** A mathematical operator represented as a pair of vectors juxtaposed without multiplication. —*adj.* Made up of two units. [From Greek *duas* (stem *duad-*), pair, from *duo,* two. See **dwō** in Appendix.*]

dy·ad·ic (dī-ăd′ĭk) *adj.* **1.** Twofold. **2.** Of or relating to a dyad. —*n. Mathematics.* The direct product *(B·C) AD* of two dyads *AB* and *CD.*

Dy·ak (dī′ăk′) *n.* Also **Day·ak.** A member of any of various Indonesian peoples of Borneo and the Sulu Sea islands. [Malay *Dayak,* "upcountry," from *darat,* land.]

dy·ar·chy. Variant of **diarchy.**

dye (dī) *n.* **1.** Any substance used to color materials. **2.** A color imparted by dyeing. —*v.* **dyed, dyeing, dyes.** —*tr.* To color (a material) with or as if with a dye, especially by soaking in a coloring solution. —*intr.* To take on or impart color. —**of the deepest dye.** Of the most extreme sort. [Middle English *deie,* Old English *dēah, dēag*†, hue, tinge.] —**dy′er** *n.*

dyed-in-the-wool (dīd′ĭn-*th*ə-wo͝ol′) *adj.* **1.** Dyed before being woven into cloth. **2.** Thoroughgoing; out-and-out.

dyer's greenweed. A small shrub, *Genista tinctoria,* native to Eurasia, having clusters of yellow flowers. Also called "dyer's broom," "woadwaxen," "woodwaxen." [So called because it yields a green dye.]

dyer's rocket. A plant, *Reseda luteola,* native to Europe, having long spikes of small, yellowish-green flowers and yielding a yellow dye. Also called "weld," "yellowweed."

dy·er's-weed (dī′ərz-wēd′) *n.* Any of various plants yielding coloring matter used as dye.

dye·stuff (dī′stŭf′) *n.* Any material used as or yielding a dye. [Probably translation of German *Farbstoff.*]

dye·wood (dī′wo͝od′) *n.* Any wood used as a dyestuff.

dy·ing (dī′ĭng) *adj.* **1.** About to die. **2.** Drawing to an end; declining. **3.** Done or uttered just before death.

dyke. Variant of **dike.**

dyn *Physics.* dyne.

dy·nam·ic (dī-năm′ĭk) *adj.* Also **dy·nam·i·cal** (-ĭ-kəl). **1.** Of or pertaining to energy, force, or motion in relation to force. **2.** Characterized by or tending to produce continuous change or advance. **3.** Energetic; vigorous; forceful. **4.** Of or pertaining to variation of intensity, as in musical sound. —See Synonyms at **active.** [French *dynamique,* from Greek *dunamikos,* powerful, from *dunamis,* power, from *dunasthai,* to be able. See **deu-²** in Appendix.*] —**dy·nam′i·cal·ly** *adv.*

dy·nam·ics (dī-năm′ĭks) *pl.n.* **1. a.** The study of the relationship between motion and the forces affecting motion. **b.** The combined study of **kinetics** and **kinematics** *(both of which see).* Used with a singular verb. **2.** The physical or moral forces that produce motion and change in any field or system. **3.** Variation in force or intensity, especially in musical sound. Used with a singular verb. **4.** *Psychoanalysis.* **a.** The action of psychic forces or mechanisms. **b.** The psychological aspect or conduct of an interpersonal relationship. Used with a singular verb.

dy·na·mism (dī′nə-mĭz′əm) *n.* **1.** Any of various theories or philosophical systems that explain the universe in terms of force or energy. **2.** A process or mechanism responsible for the development or motion of a system. **3.** The quality of being dynamic. [French *dynamisme* : DYNAM(O)- + -ISM.] —**dy′na·mist** *n.* —**dy′na·mis′tic** *adj.*

dy·na·mite (dī′nə-mīt′) *n.* A powerful explosive composed of nitroglycerin or ammonium nitrate dispersed in an absorbent medium with a combustible dope such as wood pulp and an antacid such as calcium carbonate. —*tr.v.* **dynamited, -miting, -mites.** **1.** To blow up, shatter, or destroy with or as with dynamite. **2.** To charge with dynamite. [Swedish *dynamit* : DYNAM(O)- + -ITE.] —**dy′na·mit′er** *n.*

dy·na·mo (dī′nə-mō′) *n., pl.* **-mos.** **1.** A generator, especially one for producing direct current. **2.** *Informal.* An extremely energetic and forceful person. [Short for *dynamo(electric) machine,* translation of German *dynamoelektrische Maschine.*]

dynamo–. Indicates power; for example, **dynamoelectric.** [Greek *dunamo-,* from *dunamis,* power, from *dunasthai,* to be able. See **deu-²** in Appendix.*]

dy·na·mo·e·lec·tric (dī′nə-mō′ə-lĕk′trĭk) *adj.* Also **dy·na·mo·e·lec·tri·cal** (-trĭ-kəl). Relating to the interconversion of mechanical energy and electrical energy.

dy·na·mom·e·ter (dī′nə-mŏm′ə-tər) *n.* Any of several instruments used to measure force or power. [French *dynamomètre* : DYNAMO- + -METER.]

dy·na·mom·e·try (dī′nə-mŏm′ə-trē) *n.* Measurement by means of a dynamometer. —**dy′na·mo·met′ric** (-mō-mĕt′rĭk), **dy′na·mo·met′ri·cal** *adj.*

dy·na·mo·tor (dī′nə-mō′tər) *n.* A rotating electric machine with two armatures, used to convert alternating to direct current. [DYNA(MO)- + MOTOR.]

dy·nast (dī′năst′, -nəst) *n.* A lord or ruler; especially, a hereditary ruler. [Latin *dynastēs,* from Greek *dunastēs,* lord, master, from *dunasthai,* to be able. See **deu-²** in Appendix.*]

dy·nas·ty (dī′nə-stē) *n., pl.* **-ties.** **1.** A succession of rulers from the same family or line. **2.** A family or group that maintains power for several generations. [French *dynastie,* from Greek *dunasteia,* domination, lordship, from *dunastēs,* ruler, DYNAST.] —**dy·nas′tic** (dī-năs′tĭk) *adj.* —**dy·nas′ti·cal·ly** *adv.*

dy·na·tron (dī′nə-trŏn′) *n. Electronics.* A tetrode with grid and plate potentials so arranged that plate current decreases when plate potential increases. [DYNA(MO)- + -TRON.]

dyne (dīn) *n. Abbr.* **dyn** *Physics.* A centimeter-gram-second unit of force, equal to the force required to impart an acceleration of one centimeter per second per second to a mass of one gram. See **measurement.** [French, from Greek *dunamis,* power. See **dynamic.**]

Dy·nel (dī-nĕl′) *n.* **1.** A trademark for a copolymer of vinyl chloride and acrylonitrile, used to make fire-resistant, insect-resistant, and easily dyed textile fiber. **2.** A fiber or fabric made from this compound.

dy·node (dī′nōd′) *n.* An electrode used in certain electron tubes to provide secondary emission. [DYN(AMO)- + -ODE.]

dys–. Indicates diseased, difficult, faulty, or bad; for example, **dysplasia, dyslexia.** [Middle English *dis-,* from Old French, from Latin *dys-,* from Greek *dus-.* See **dus-** in Appendix.*]

dys·cra·si·a (dĭs-krā′zhē-ə, -zhə) *n. Rare.* Loosely, a morbid condition caused by poisons in the blood. [New Latin, from Medieval Latin, disease, distemper, "disproportionate mixture of the humors," from Greek *duskrasia* : DYS- + *krasis,* mixing (see **kerə-** in Appendix*).]

dys·en·ter·y (dĭs′ən-tĕr′ē) *n.* An infection of the lower intestinal tract producing pain, fever, and severe diarrhea, often with blood and mucus. [Middle English *dissenterie,* from Latin *dysenteria,* from Greek *dusenteria* : DYS- + *enteron,* intestine (see **en** in Appendix*).] —**dys′en·ter′ic** *adj.*

dys·func·tion (dĭs-fŭngk′shən) *n.* Disordered or impaired functioning of a bodily system or organ.

dys·gen·ic (dĭs-jĕn′ĭk) *adj.* Pertaining to or causing the deterioration of hereditary qualities. [DYS- + -GENIC.]

dys·gen·ics (dĭs-jĕn′ĭks) *n.* Plural in form, used with a singular verb. The biological study of the factors producing degeneration in offspring. Also called "cacogenics."

dys·lex·i·a (dĭs-lĕk′sē-ə) *n.* Impairment of the ability to read; incomplete alexia. [New Latin : DYS- + Greek *lexis,* speech, from *legein,* to speak (see **leg-** in Appendix*).] —**dys·lec′tic** (-lĕk′tĭk) *adj.* & *n.* —**dys·lex′ic** *adj.*

dys·lo·gis·tic (dĭs′lō-jĭs′tĭk) *adj.* Conveying censure; disapproving. [DYS- + (EU)LOGISTIC.] —**dys′lo·gis′ti·cal·ly** *adv.*

dys·men·or·rhe·a (dĭs-mĕn′ə-rē′ə) *n.* Also **dys·men·or·rhoe·a.** Difficult or painful menstruation. [New Latin : DYS- + Greek *mēn* (stem *mēno-*), month (see **mē-²** in Appendix*) + -RRHEA.]

dys·pep·sia (dĭs-pĕp′shə, -sē-ə) *n.* Disturbed digestion; indigestion. [Latin, from Greek *duspepsia* : DYS- + *-pepsia,* digestion (see **pekw-** in Appendix*).]

dys·pep·tic (dĭs-pĕp′tĭk) *adj.* Also **dys·pep·ti·cal** (-tĭ-kəl). **1.** Pertaining to or having dyspepsia. **2.** Morose. —*n.* One who suffers from dyspepsia. —**dys·pep′ti·cal·ly** *adv.*

dys·pha·gi·a (dĭs-fā′jē-ə) *n.* Difficulty in swallowing. [New Latin : DYS- + -PHAGIA.] —**dys·phag′ic** (-făj′ĭk) *adj.*

dys·pha·sia (dĭs-fā′zhə, -zhē-ə) *n.* Impairment of speech and verbal comprehension, especially when associated with brain injury. [New Latin : DYS- + -PHASIA.] —**dys·pha′sic** (-zĭk) *adj.*

dys·pho·ni·a (dĭs-fō′nē-ə) *n.* Difficulty in speaking, usually evidenced by hoarseness. [New Latin : DYS- + Greek *-phōnia,* -PHONY.] —**dys·phon′ic** (-fŏn′ĭk) *adj.*

dys·pho·ri·a (dĭs-fôr′ē-ə, -fōr′ē-ə) *n.* An emotional state characterized by anxiety, depression, and restlessness. [New Latin, from Greek *dusphoria,* distress, from *dusphoros,* hard to bear : DYS- + -PHOROUS.] —**dys·phor′ic** (-fôr′ĭk, -fŏr′ĭk) *adj.*

dys·pla·sia (dĭs-plā′zhə, -zhē-ə) *n.* Abnormal development of tissues, organs, or cells. [New Latin : DYS- + Greek *plasis,* formation, from *plassein,* to mold (see **pelə-¹** in Appendix*).] —**dys·plas′tic** (-plăs′tĭk) *adj.*

dysp·ne·a (dĭsp-nē′ə) *n.* A sense of difficulty in breathing, often associated with lung or heart disease. [New Latin, from Greek *duspnoia,* from *duspnoos,* short of breath : DYS- + *-pnoos,* from *pnoē,* breathing, from *pnein,* to breathe (see **pneu-** in Appendix*).] —**dysp·ne′ic** *adj.*

dys·pro·si·um (dĭs-prō′zē-əm) *n. Symbol* **Dy** A soft, silvery rare-earth metal used in nuclear research. Atomic number 66, atomic weight 162.50, melting point 1,407°C, boiling point 2,600°C, specific gravity 8.536, valence 3. See **element.** [New Latin, from Greek *dusprositos,* difficult to approach : DYS- + *prositos,* approachable, from *prosienai,* to approach : *pros-,* toward + *ienai,* to go (see **ei-¹** in Appendix*).]

dys·tel·e·ol·o·gy (dĭs′tĕl-ē-ŏl′ə-jē, dĭs′tē-lē-) *n.* **1.** The doctrine of purposelessness in nature. Compare **teleology.** **2.** Purposelessness in natural structures, as manifested by the existence of vestigial or nonfunctional organs or parts. [German *Dysteleologie* : DYS- + New Latin *teleologia,* TELEOLOGY.] —**dys′tel·e·o·log′i·cal** (-ə-lŏj′ĭ-kəl) *adj.* —**dys′tel·e·ol′o·gist** *n.*

dys·tro·phy (dĭs′trə-fē) *n.* Also **dys·tro·phi·a** (dĭs-trō′fē-ə). **1.** Defective nutrition. **2.** Any disorder caused by defective nutrition. [New Latin *dystrophia* : DYS- + -TROPHY.] —**dys·troph′ic** (-trŏf′ĭk, -trō′fĭk) *adj.*

dys·u·ri·a (dĭs-yo͝or′ē-ə) *n.* Painful or difficult urination. [New Latin, from Greek *dusouria* : DYS- + -URIA.] —**dys·u′ric** *adj.*

Dyu·shan·be. See **Dushanbe.**

dz. dozen.

Dzau·dzhi·kau. The former name for **Ordzhonikidze.**

Dzer·zhinsk (dzĕr-zhĭnsk′). An industrial city of the Soviet Union, just west of Gorkiy. Population, 180,000.

Dzhu·ga·shvi·li, Iosif. See Joseph **Stalin.**

Dzun·gar·i·a (zŭn-găr′ē-ə, dzŭn-). Also **Zun·gar·i·a.** A vast arid region of northwestern China, north of the Tien Shan.

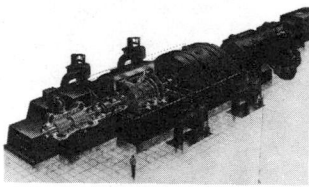

dynamo
Nuclear-powered steam turbine generator

t tight/th thin, path/*th* this, bathe/ŭ cut/ûr urge/v valve/w with/y yes/z zebra, size/zh vision/ə about, item, edible, gallop, circus/ à *Fr.* ami/œ *Fr.* feu, *Ger.* schön/ü *Fr.* tu, *Ger.* über/KH *Ger.* ich, *Scot.* loch/N *Fr.* bon. *Follows main vocabulary. †Of obscure origin.

Ee

Around 1000 B.C. the Phoenicians and other Semites of Syria and Palestine began to use a graphic sign in the forms (1,2). They gave it the name hē *and used it for the consonant* h. *After 900 B.C. the Greeks borrowed the sign from the Phoenicians, gradually simplifying it and reversing its orientation (3,4,5,6). They also changed its name to* ē *and used it for the vowel* e. *Later they renamed the sign* epsilon, *"the short* e," *to differentiate it from* ēta, *which was reserved for the long* ē. *The Greek forms passed unchanged via Etruscan to the Roman alphabet (7,8). The Roman Monumental Capital (9) is the prototype of our modern capital, printed (12) and written (13). The written Roman form (8) developed into the late Roman and medieval Uncial (10) and Cursive (11), replacing linear with rounded shapes. These are the bases of our modern small letter, printed (14) and written (15).*

e, E (ē) *n., pl.* **e's** or *rare* **es, E's** or **Es. 1.** The fifth letter of the modern English alphabet. See **alphabet. 2.** Any of the speech sounds represented by this letter.

e, E, e., E. *Note:* As an abbreviation or symbol, *e* may be a small or a capital letter, with or without a period. Established forms or those generally preferred precede the definition. When no form is given, all four forms are in general use in that sense. **1. E.** earl. **2. E** Earth. **3.** east; eastern. **4.** e electron. **5. e.**, **E.** engineer; engineering. **6. E, E.** English. **7. e, e.** *Baseball.* error. **8. E** excellent. **9. e** *Mathematics.* The base of the natural system of logarithms, having a numerical value of approximately 2.718... . **10.** The fifth in a series.

each (ēch) *adj. Abbr.* **ea.** One of two or more persons, objects, or things considered individually or one by one; every: *Each man cast a vote.* —*pron.* Every one of a group of objects, persons, or things considered individually; each one. Usually regarded as singular: *Each presented his gift.* —*adv.* For or to each one; apiece: *ten cents each.* [Middle English *ech, ælc,* Old English *ælc, æghwile.* See **līk-** in Appendix.*]

Usage: Each (pronoun), employed as subject, takes a singular verb and related pronouns or pronominal adjectives in formal usage: *Each has his own job to perform.* This is true also when *each* is followed by *of* and a plural noun or pronoun: *Each of the boys has his own job.* Informally, especially in speech, such sentences sometimes take the form *Each . . . have their own job.* The plural construction is especially common when *each* refers to members of a group of men and women or boys and girls, and *their* is consequently felt to be more appropriate than *his.* On a formal level, however, a singular verb is required: *Each of them has a large following.* The alternative, *Each have large followings,* is termed unacceptable by 95 per cent of the Usage Panel. When *each* occurs after a plural subject with which it is in apposition, the verb is usually plural: *We each require much attention. O'Brien and Loeb each have large followings.* In examples involving compound subjects, such as the second, however, a singular verb sometimes occurs. Thus, the alternative construction, *O'Brien and Loeb each has a large following,* is acceptable to 69 per cent of the Panel, though most grammarians prescribe a plural verb. The phrase *each and every* is redundant and preferably replaced by either *each* or *every,* used singly. When it is used, however, *each and every* governs a singular verb and related words: *Each and every girl has an obligation to do her share.* See Usage note at **between.**

each other. 1. Each the other. Used as a compound reciprocal pronoun: *They met each other* (each met the other). **2.** One another. See Usage note.

Usage: Each other occurs most often when the reference is to only two persons or things. Some grammarians recommend its restriction to such examples and prescribe *one another* in examples where more than two are involved. The distinction is not observed rigidly, however. Thus, the following is acceptable to 55 per cent of the Usage Panel: *The four partners regarded each other with suspicion.* Similarly, the construction *husband and wife should confide in one another* is acceptable to 54 per cent. The possessive forms are invariably written *each other's* (not *others'*) and *one another's.*

Eads (ēdz), **James Buchanan.** 1820–1887. American civil engineer and inventor.

ea·ger¹ (ē'gər) *adj.* **-gerer, -gerest. 1.** Intensely desirous of something; impatiently expectant: *an eager search for a familiar face in the crowd.* **2.** *Obsolete.* Tart; sharp; cutting. —See Usage note at **anxious.** [Middle English *egre,* sharp, keen, eager, from Old French *aigre,* from Latin *ācer.* See **ak-** in Appendix.*] —**ea'ger·ly** *adv.* —**ea'ger·ness** *n.*

Synonyms: eager, avid, keen, anxious, earnest, fervid, zealous. These adjectives describe a condition of mind marked by great interest, desire, or concern, or a manifestation of such a condition. *Eager* primarily suggests strong interest or desire. *Avid,* an intensification of *eager,* implies enthusiasm and unbounded craving. *Keen* suggests acuteness or intensity of interest or emotional drive. *Anxious* applies to interest or desire tinged by concern or fear. *Earnest* stresses seriousness of purpose and sincerity of motivation. *Fervid* emphasizes intensity of interest or desire, expressed in behavior that may be compulsive or overwrought. *Zealous* makes an even stronger implication of unbridled enthusiasm or concern, sometimes verging on fanaticism and unrestrained behavior. The term generally suggests dedication to a cause or pursuit.

ea·ger². Variant of **eagre.**

eager beaver. *Informal.* An industrious, overzealous person.

ea·gle (ē'gəl) *n.* **1.** Any of various large birds of prey of the family Accipitridae, including members of the genera *Aquila, Haliaeetus,* and other genera, characterized by a powerful hooked bill, long broad wings, and strong, soaring flight. **2.** A representation of an eagle used as an emblem, insignia, seal, or the like. **3.** A former gold coin of the United States having a face value of ten dollars. **4.** *Golf.* A score of two below par on any hole. [Middle English *egle,* from Old French *egle, aigle,* from Latin *aquila†.*]

ea·gle-eyed (ē'gəl-īd') *adj.* Having keen eyesight.

eagle owl. A large Eurasian owl, *Bubo bubo,* having brownish plumage and prominent ear tufts.

Eagle Scout. The highest rank in the Boy Scouts.

ea·gle·stone (ē'gəl-stōn') *n.* A nodule of ironstone roughly the size of a walnut. [From the popular belief that such stones were kept by eagles in their nests to facilitate hatching.]

ea·glet (ē'glĭt) *n.* A young eagle.

ea·gre (ē'gər, ā'-) *n.* Also **eag·er.** A tidal flood, a **bore** *(see).* [Perhaps ultimately from Old English *ēagor,* flood tide. See **akwā-** in Appendix.*]

Ea·kins (ā'kĭnz), **Thomas.** 1844–1916. American painter.

eal·dor·man (ôl'dər-mən) *n., pl.* **-men** (-mĭn). The chief magistrate of a shire in Anglo-Saxon England. [Old English *ealdormann,* prince. See **alderman.**]

Ea·ling (ē'lĭng). A borough of London, England, comprising the former administrative divisions of Acton, Ealing, and Southall. Population, 300,000.

-ean. Indicates of or pertaining to or derived from. Used chiefly with proper names; for example, **Caesarean, Tyrolean.** [Variant of -IAN.]

ear¹ (îr) *n.* **1.** *Anatomy.* **a.** The vertebrate organ of hearing,

eagle
Haliaeetus leucocephalus
Bald eagle

ă pat/ā pay/âr care/ä father/b bib/ch church/d deed/ĕ pet/ē be/f fife/g gag/h hat/hw which/ĭ pit/ī pie/îr pier/j judge/k kick/l lid, needle/m mum/n no, sudden/ng thing/ŏ pot/ō toe/ô paw, for/oi noise/ou out/ŏŏ took/ōō boot/p pop/r roar/s sauce/sh ship, dish/

responsible, in general, for maintaining equilibrium as well as sensing sound, and divided in man into the **external ear**, the **middle ear**, and the **internal ear** *(all of which see)*. **b.** The part of this organ that is externally visible. **2.** An analogous organ in invertebrates, as insects. **3.** The sense of hearing. **4.** Aural sensitivity, as to differences in musical pitch. **5.** Attention; especially, favorable attention; heed: *"I shall beg your patient ear a little longer"* (Walton). **6.** Anything resembling or suggestive of the shape or position of the external ear, such as one of the tufts of feathers on the head of some owls or a projecting handle on a vase or pitcher. **7.** *Journalism.* A small box appearing in either of the upper corners of the front page of a newspaper. **—all ears.** Acutely attentive: *If you want to tell your story, we're all ears.* **—fall on deaf ears.** To be ignored: *His advice fell on deaf ears.* **—give** (or **lend**) **an ear.** To pay close attention to; listen attentively. **—have** (or **keep**) **an ear to the ground.** To give attention to or watch the trends of public opinion. **—in one ear and out the other.** Heard but without influence or effect. **—play by ear.** To perform music without reference to or memorization of a score. **—play it by ear.** To act without plan; improvise. **—turn a deaf ear.** To be unwilling to listen or pay heed. **—up to one's** (or **the**) **ears.** Deeply involved or committed: *up to one's ears in debt.* [Middle English *ere,* Old English *ēare.* See **ous-** in Appendix.*] **—ear'less** *adj.*

ear² (îr) *n.* The seed-bearing spike of a cereal plant, as corn. *—intr.v.* **eared, earing, ears.** To form or grow ears, as corn. [Middle English *ere, er,* Old English *ēar.* See **ak-** in Appendix.*]

ear·ache (îr'āk') *n.* Pain in the ear.

ear·drop (îr'drŏp') *n.* A pendent earring.

ear·drum (îr'drŭm') *n. Anatomy.* The **tympanic membrane** *(see).*

eared (îrd) *adj.* **1.** Having ears or earlike projections. **2.** Having a specified kind or number of ears. Often used in combination: *a crop-eared puppy.*

eared seal. Any of various seals of the family Otariidae, which includes the sea lions and fur seals, characterized by external ears, oarlike front flippers, and hind flippers that can be turned forward for walking on land.

ear·flap (îr'flăp') *n.* Also **ear·lap** (-lăp'). Either of two cloth or fur appendages to a cap that may be turned down over the ears.

ear·ful (îr'fo͝ol') *n.* A flow of information or gossip.

Ear·hart (âr'härt'), **Amelia.** 1898–1937? American aviator; first woman to fly the Atlantic; lost on Pacific flight.

ear·ing (îr'ĭng) *n. Nautical.* A short line attaching an upper corner of a sail to the yard. [Perhaps from EAR (part of body).]

earl (ûrl) *n. Abbr.* **E.** A British peer next in rank above a viscount and below a marquis. [Middle English *erl,* Old English *eorl,* warrior, chief, nobleman, from Common Germanic *erilaz* (unattested).]

Earl (ûrl) *n.* A masculine given name. [From EARL.]

ear·lap (îr'lăp') *n.* **1. a.** The lobe of the external ear. **b.** The external ear. **2.** Variant of **earflap.**

earl·dom (ûrl'dəm) *n.* **1.** The rank or title of an earl. **2.** The territory under the jurisdiction of an earl. [Middle English *erldom,* Old English *eorldōm* : EARL + -DOM.]

ear lobe. The soft, fleshy tissue at the lowest portion of the external ear.

ear·ly (ûr'lē) *adj.* **-lier, -liest.** **1.** Near the beginning of a given series, period of time, or course of events: *in the early evening.* **2.** In or belonging to a distant or remote period or stage of development; primitive: *Early man discovered fire.* **3.** Occurring, developing, or appearing before the expected or usual time. **4.** Occurring in the near future: *Experts foresee an early strike of workers.* *—adv.* **1.** Near the beginning of a given series, period of time, or course of events: *He campaigned early in the senate race.* **2.** Far back in time. **3.** Before the expected or arranged time: *They left early.* [Middle English *erly, erliche,* Old English *ǣrlīce,* from *ǣr,* before (after Old Norse *ārliga*). See **ayer-** in Appendix.*] **—ear'li·ness** *n.*

Ear·ly (ûr'lē), **Jubal Anderson.** 1816–1894. American military leader; commanded Confederate troops in Civil War.

early bird. A person who habitually arises early or arrives before others.

ear·mark (îr'märk') *n.* **1.** An identifying mark on the ear of a domestic animal. **2.** Any identifying mark, feature, or characteristic. *—tr.v.* **earmarked, -marking, -marks.** **1.** To mark the ear of (a domestic animal) for identification. **2.** To place an identifying or distinctive mark on. **3.** To reserve or set aside for some purpose: *earmark merchandise for special customers.*

ear·muff (îr'mŭf') *n.* Either of a pair of fur or warm cloth ear coverings often attached to an adjustable headband and worn to protect against the cold.

earn¹ (ûrn) *tr.v.* **earned, earning, earns.** **1.** To gain or deserve (salary, wages, or other reward) for one's service, labor, or performance. **2.** To acquire or deserve as a result of behavior: *He has earned the disapproval of his peers.* **3.** To produce (interest or return) as profit. [Middle English *ernen,* Old English *earnian,* to earn, merit. See **esen-** in Appendix.*] **—earn'er** *n.*

earn² (ûrn) *intr.v.* **earned, earning, earns.** *Obsolete.* To yearn. [Variant of YEARN.]

ear·nest¹ (ûr'nĭst) *adj.* **1.** Determined; eager; zealous: *an earnest attempt.* **2.** Showing deep sincerity or feeling; serious: *an earnest gesture of good will.* **3.** Of an important or vital nature; not trivial or petty: *an earnest conference affecting world peace.* —See Synonyms at **eager, serious.** **—in earnest.** With a purposeful or serious intent. [Middle English *ernest,* Old English *eornost,* zeal, seriousness. See **er-¹** in Appendix.*] **—ear'nest·ly** *adv.* **—ear'nest·ness** *n.*

ear·nest² (ûr'nĭst) *n.* **1.** Money paid in advance as part payment to bind a contract or bargain. Also called "earnest money." **2.** A token of something to come; a promise or assurance. [Middle English *ernest, ernes,* from Old French *erres,* plural of *erre,* pledge, earnest money, from Latin *arra, arrha,* short for *arrabō, arrhabō,* pledge, from Greek *arrabon,* from Hebrew *'ērābhōn,* security, pledge, from *'ārabh,* he pledged.]

earn·ings (ûr'nĭngz) *pl.n.* Something earned, especially: **a.** The salary or wages of a person. **b.** The profits of a business enterprise. **c.** Gains from investment.

Earp (ûrp), **Wyatt.** 1849–1929. American frontier law officer.

ear·phone (îr'fōn') *n.* A device that converts electric signals, as from a telephone or radio receiver, to audible sound and that is worn or listened to in contact with the ear.

ear·ring (îr'rĭng, -ĭng) *n.* An ornament or jewel worn on or pendent from the ear lobe.

ear shell. The shell of the abalone.

ear·shot (îr'shŏt') *n.* The range within which sound can be heard; hearing distance.

ear·split·ting (îr'splĭt'ĭng) *adj.* Loud and shrill enough to hurt the ears; deafening.

earth (ûrth) *n.* **1.** The land surface of the world, as distinguished from the oceans and air. **2.** The softer, friable part of land; soil; especially, productive soil. **3.** The dwelling place of mortal men, as distinguished from heaven and hell; the temporal world. **4.** All of the human inhabitants of the world: *The earth received the news with joy.* **5.** Worldly affairs; temporal matters, as distinguished from spiritual concerns: *the temptations of the earth.* **6.** The material body of the human being considered as made of dust or clay. **7.** The lair of a burrowing animal. **8.** *Chiefly British. Electricity.* The ground of a circuit. **9.** *Chemistry.* Any of several metallic oxides that are difficult to reduce, as alumina or zirconia, formerly regarded as elements. **—down to earth.** Sensible; realistic. **—run to earth.** To hunt and run down (a fox, for example). *—v.* **earthed, earthing, earths.** *—tr.* **1.** To cover or heap up (plants, seeds, or roots) with soil for protection. **2.** To chase (an animal) into an underground lair. *—intr.* To burrow or hide in the ground, as a fox. [Middle English *erthe,* Old English *eorthe.* See **er-³** in Appendix.*]

Earth (ûrth) *n. Abbr.* **E** The third planet from the sun, having a sidereal period of revolution about the sun of 365.26 days at a mean distance of 92.96 million miles, an axial rotation period of 23 hours 56.07 minutes, an average radius of 3,959 miles, and a mass of 13.17 x 10^{24} pounds. See **solar system.** [From EARTH.]

earth·born (ûrth'bôrn') *adj.* **1.** Springing from or born on the earth. **2.** Human; mortal.

earth·bound (ûrth'bound') *adj.* Also **earth-bound.** **1. a.** Attached or confined to or by the earth and earthly interests. **b.** Unimaginative; ordinary. **2.** Headed for the earth: *an earthbound meteor.*

earth·en (ûr'thən) *adj.* **1. a.** Made of dirt, soil, or earth: *an earthen fortification.* **b.** Made of baked clay: *an earthen vase.* **2.** Earthly; worldly.

earth·en·ware (ûr'thən-wâr') *n.* **1.** A variety of coarse, porous baked clay. **2.** Ware made from such clay, such as dishes, pots, and tableware. *—adj.* Made of earthenware.

earth·ling (ûrth'lĭng) *n.* **1.** One who inhabits the earth; a human being. **2.** A person devoted to the world; a worldling.

earth·ly (ûrth'lē) *adj.* **1.** Of the earth, specifically: **a.** Not heavenly or divine; secular. **b.** Terrestrial. **2.** Conceivable; feasible; possible: *no earthly meaning whatever.* **—earth'li·ness** *n.*

Synonyms: *earthly, terrestrial, worldly, mundane, earthy.* These adjectives all indicate relationship to the earth, but are not always interchangeable. *Earthly* is used principally in opposition or contrast to heavenly. *Terrestrial* is in opposition to celestial or specifies Earth distinguished from other planets or land distinguished from water. *Worldly,* in opposition to spiritual, describes the actions and concerns of men, especially as they pertain to this life (distinguished from afterlife); the term is associated with the pursuit of pleasure, wealth, or success. *Mundane* likewise refers to what is secular rather than spiritual or eternal and especially to the more ordinary, routine aspects of life on the earth. *Earthy,* in opposition to spiritual, suggests what is down to earth, especially the satisfaction of material wants and the more primitive human instincts.

earth·nut (ûrth'nŭt') *n.* **1. a.** An Old World plant, *Conopodium denudatum,* having edible, nutlike tubers. **b.** The tuber of this plant. Also called "pignut." **2.** Any of various other plants having similar edible tubers or underground parts.

earth·quake (ûrth'kwāk') *n.* A series of elastic waves in the crust of the earth, caused by sudden relaxation of strains accumulated along geologic faults and by volcanic action, and resulting in movements in the earth's surface. Also called "seism."

earth satellite. A satellite that orbits the earth.

earth science. Any of several essentially geologic sciences concerned with the origin, structure, and physical phenomena of the earth.

earth·shak·ing (ûrth'shā'kĭng) *adj.* Of enormous consequence or fundamental importance.

earth·shine (ûrth'shīn') *n.* The sunlight reflected from the earth's surface that illuminates part of the moon not directly lighted by the sun. Also called "earthlight."

earth·star (ûrth'stär') *n.* A fungus of the genus *Geastrum,* related to and resembling the puffballs and having an outer covering that splits open in a starlike form.

earth·ward (ûrth'wərd) *adv.* Also **earth·wards** (-wərdz). To or toward the earth. *—adj.* Heading toward the earth; earthbound.

earth·work (ûrth'wûrk') *n.* **1.** An earthen embankment especially when used as a military fortification. **2.** *Engineering.* Ex-

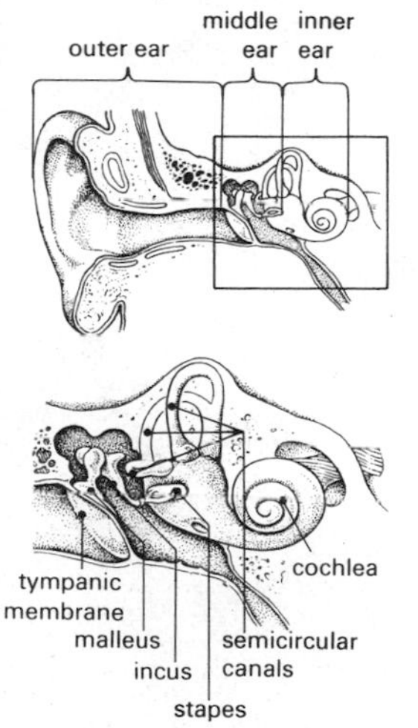

middle
inner
outer ear
ear
ear
cochlea
tympanic
membrane
malleus
semicircular
incus
canals
stapes

ear¹
The human ear

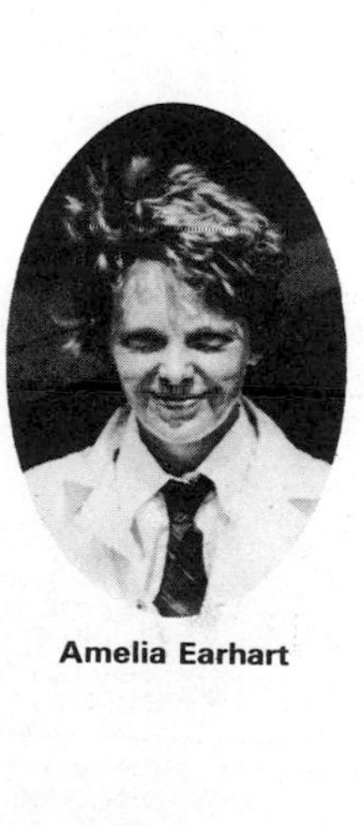

Amelia Earhart

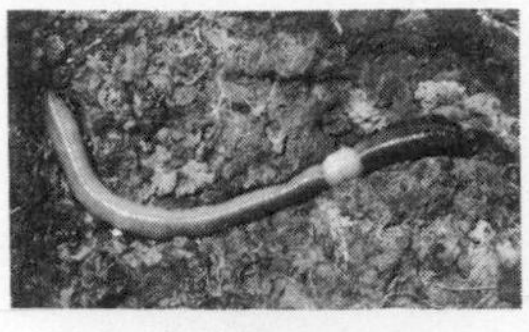

earthworm
Lumbricus terrestris

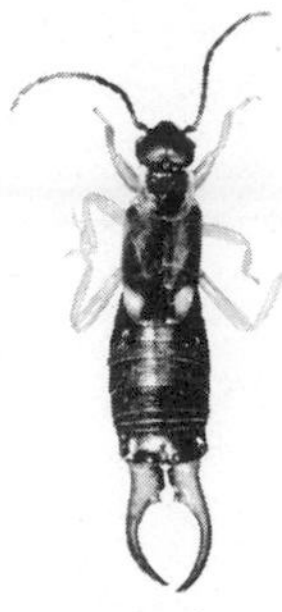

earwig

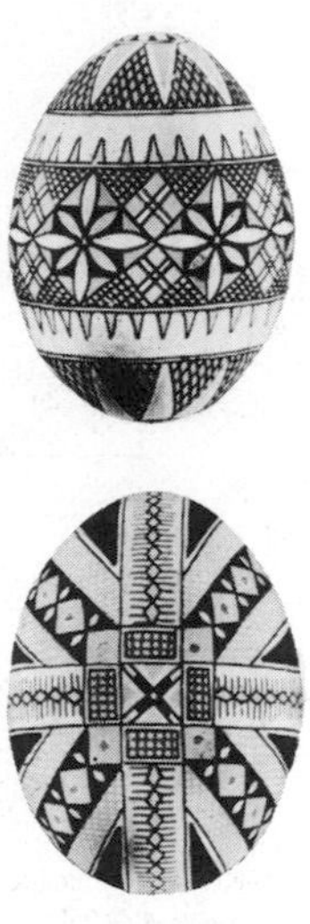

Easter egg
Easter eggs decorated with Ukrainian designs

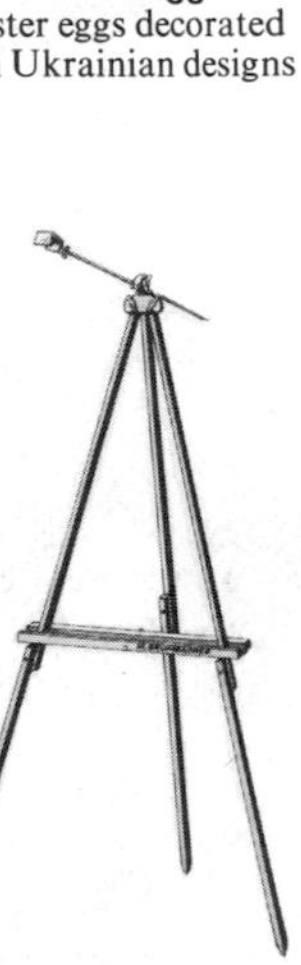

easel

cavation and embankment of earth. —See Synonyms at **bulwark.**

earth·worm (ûrth′wûrm′) *n.* Any of various terrestrial annelid worms of the class Oligochaeta and especially of the family Lumbricidae, that burrow into and help aerate and enrich soil.

earth·y (ûr′thē) *adj.* **-ier, -iest. 1.** Consisting of or resembling earth or soil. **2.** Pertaining to or characteristic of this world; worldly. **3.** Crude or coarse; unrefined. **4.** Uninhibited; hearty: *an earthy woman.* —See Synonyms at **earthly.** —**earth′i·ness** *n.*

ear trumpet. A horn-shaped instrument formerly used to direct sound into the ear of a partially deaf person.

ear·wax (îr′wăks′) *n.* The waxlike secretion of certain glands lining the canal of the outer ear; cerumen.

ear·wig (îr′wĭg′) *n.* Any of various insects of the order Dermaptera, having pincerlike appendages protruding from the rear of the abdomen. —*tr.v.* **earwigged, -wigging, -wigs.** To attempt to influence by insinuation or subterfuge. [Middle English *erwigge,* Old English *ēarwicga,* "ear insect" (thought to be able to penetrate a person's head through the ear) : EAR + *wicga,* insect (see **wegh-** in Appendix*).]

ear·worm (îr′wûrm′) *n.* See **corn earworm.** [From EAR (of corn).]

ease (ēz) *n.* **1.** The condition of being without discomfort; freedom from pain, worry, or agitation: *watch a sunset with a sense of ease.* **2.** Freedom from constraint, embarrassment, or awkwardness; poise; naturalness: *the ease of his approach to a stranger.* **3.** Freedom from difficulty, hard work, or great effort; readiness; facility: *play tennis with ease.* **4.** Freedom from financial difficulty; affluence. —See Synonyms at **rest.** —*v.* **eased, easing, eases.** —*tr.* **1.** To free from pain, worry, agitation, or trouble; soothe; comfort. **2.** To alleviate or lighten (discomfort); mitigate; lessen. **3.** To slacken the strain, pressure, tension, or stress of; loosen. Often used with *away, down, up,* or *off: ease off a cable.* **4.** To move or fit into place or position slowly and carefully: *ease the pie into the oven.* —*intr.* To lessen in discomfort, stress, pressure, or the like. Often used with *up* or *off.* —**ease the helm** (or **rudder**). *Nautical.* To bring the helm somewhat toward midships in order to reduce the strain on the rudder. [Middle English *ese,* from Old French *aise,* comfort, convenience, from Latin *adjacēns,* nearby, adjacent, from *adjacēre,* to lie near : *ad-,* near to + *jacēre,* to lie, from *jacere,* to throw (see **yē-** in Appendix*).]

ease·ful (ēz′fəl) *adj.* Affording or characterized by comfort and peace; restful. —**ease′ful·ly** *adv.* —**ease′ful·ness** *n.*

ea·sel (ē′zəl) *n.* A frame, usually in the form of an upright tripod, upon which something may be displayed or which may support an artist's canvas. [Dutch *ezel,* "ass," from Middle Dutch *esel,* from Common Germanic *asiluz* (unattested), from Latin *asinus.* See **asinus** in Appendix.*]

ease·ment (ēz′mənt) *n.* **1.** The act of easing or the condition of being eased. **2.** Something that affords ease or comfort. **3.** *Law.* A right afforded a person to make limited use of another's real property, as the right of way.

eas·i·ly (ē′zə-lē) *adv.* **1.** Without difficulty or stress: *a problem easily solved.* **2.** Without doubt or question; certainly: *easily the best play this season.* **3.** Likely; possibly: *That may easily have been a mistake.*

eas·i·ness (ē′zĭ-nĭs) *n.* **1.** The condition or quality of being easy to accomplish, acquire, or the like. **2.** Ease of manner; nonchalance; poise.

east (ēst) *n. Abbr.* **e, E, e., E. 1. a.** The direction of the earth's axial rotation. **b.** The cardinal point on the mariner's compass 90 degrees clockwise from north and directly opposite west. See **compass card. 2.** Any area or region lying in this direction. **3.** *Often capital* **E. a.** The eastern part of any country or region. **b.** The eastern part of the earth, especially Asia and its neighboring islands; the Orient. —**the East.** In the United States: **1.** The region east of the Mississippi and north of the Mason-Dixon line. **2.** The region east of the Alleghenies and north of the Mason-Dixon line. —*adj.* **1.** To, toward, of, facing, or in the east. **2.** Coming from or originating in the east, as a wind. **3.** *Capital* **E.** Officially designating the eastern part of a country, continent, or other geographical area: *East Germany.* —*adv.* In, from, or toward the east. [Middle English *e(a)st,* Old English *ēast.* See **awes-** in Appendix.*]

East An·gli·a (ăng′glē-ə). **1.** An Anglo-Saxon kingdom of southeastern England, in the area now occupied by Norfolk and Suffolk. **2.** An ill-defined area of southeastern England, between Greater London and the Thames in the south and the Wash in the north.

East Bar·net (bär′nĭt). A former administrative division of London, England, now part of **Barnet** *(see).*

East Ben·gal (bĕn-gôl′, bĕng-, bĕn′gəl). That part of Bengal now in East Pakistan.

East Ber·lin (bûr-lĭn′). The sector of Berlin constituting the capital of the German Democratic Republic. Population, 1,071,000.

east·bound (ēst′bound′) *adj.* Going toward the east.

East·bourne (ēst′bôrn, -bərn). A seaside resort in southeastern Sussex, England. Population, 61,000.

east by north. *Abbr.* **EbN** The direction or point on the mariner's compass halfway between due east and east-northeast. It is 78 degrees 45 minutes east of due north. See **compass card.**

east by south. *Abbr.* **EbS** The direction or point on the mariner's compass halfway between due east and east-southeast. It is 101 degrees 15 minutes east of due north. See **compass card.**

East Cape. 1. The easternmost point of New Guinea. **2.** The easternmost point of New Zealand, on North Island. **3.** The former name for Cape **Dezhnev.**

East Chi·ca·go (shə-kä′gō, -kô′gō, -kä′gə). A port in northwestern Indiana, on Lake Michigan. Population, 58,000.

East Chi·na Sea (chī′nə). An arm of the Pacific Ocean extending about 600 miles between the eastern coast of China and the Ryukyu Islands.

East End. A densely populated section of London containing slums and industrial and dock areas.

East·er (ē′stər) *n.* **1.** A festival in the Christian Church commemorating the Resurrection of Christ, celebrated on the first Sunday following the full moon that occurs on or next after March 21. **2.** The Sunday on which this festival is held. In this sense, also called "Easter Sunday." [Middle English *ester, estre,* Old English *ēastre* (usually in plural *ēastron*). See **awes-** in Appendix.*]

Easter egg. A dyed or painted hard-boiled egg, eggshell, or other egg-shaped object used as an Easter gift.

Easter Island. *Spanish* **Is·la de Pas·cu·a** (ēz′lä *thä* päs′kwä). An island of Chile in the South Pacific Ocean, 2,350 miles west of the Chilean mainland. It is the site of a number of ancient massive sculptured heads.

Easter lily. Any of various white-flowered lilies that bloom around Easter, such as the **Bermuda lily** *(see).*

east·er·ly (ē′stər-lē) *adj.* **1.** Situated toward the east. **2.** From the east. Said of wind. —*n., pl.* **easterlies.** A storm or wind from the east. —**east′er·ly** *adv.*

Easter Monday. The Monday following Easter.

east·ern (ē′stərn) *adj. Abbr.* **e, E, e., E. 1.** Situated toward, in, or facing the east. **2.** Coming from the east. Said of wind. **3.** Growing in the east. **4.** *Often capital* **E.** Of, pertaining to, or characteristic of eastern regions or the East. **5.** *Capital* **E.** Of, pertaining to, or characteristic of the eastern part of the earth, especially Asia and its neighboring islands; Oriental: *Eastern philosophy.* **6.** *Capital* **E.** Of or pertaining to the Eastern churches, especially the Eastern Orthodox Church, as distinguished from the Roman Catholic Church. [Middle English *esterne,* Old English *ēasterne.* See **awes-** in Appendix.*]

Eastern Algonquian. The eastern division of the Algonquian family of languages.

Eastern Az·er·bai·jan. See **Azerbaijan.**

Eastern Church. 1. The church of the Eastern Roman Empire, as distinguished from the Western Church, including the patriarchates of Constantinople, Antioch, Alexandria, and Jerusalem. Also called "Greek Church." **2.** The **Eastern Orthodox Church** *(see).* **3.** The Uniat Church.

Eastern Empire. See **Byzantine Empire.**

east·ern·er (ē′stər-nər) *n.* Also **East·ern·er.** A native or inhabitant of the east, especially of the eastern United States.

Eastern Ghats. See **Ghats.**

Eastern Hemisphere. The part of the earth including the continents of Europe, Africa, Asia, and Australia.

Eastern Highlands. A mountain range, from about 100 to 200 miles wide, extending along the entire eastern coast of Australia. Highest elevation, Mount Kosciusko (7,316 feet). Also called "Great Dividing Range."

east·ern·most (ē′stərn-mōst′) *adj.* Farthest east.

Eastern Orthodox Church. The body of modern churches, including the Greek and Russian Orthodox, derived from the church of the Byzantine Empire and acknowledging the Byzantine rite and primacy of the patriarch of Constantinople. Also called "Eastern Church," "Orthodox Church," "Greek Church."

Eastern Region. A region of Nigeria that seceded in 1967, proclaiming itself the Republic of Biafra.

Eastern Roman Empire. See **Byzantine Empire.**

Eastern Ru·me·lia (rōō-mēl′yə, -mē′lē-ə). A former autonomous province of the Ottoman Empire, now comprising a region of Bulgaria.

Eastern Shore. The sectors of Maryland and Virginia lying east of Chesapeake Bay.

Eastern Standard Time. *Abbr.* **EST, E.S.T.** Time at the 75th meridian west of Greenwich, England, and in the fifth time zone based on it in North America. It is five hours earlier than Greenwich time. See **standard time.**

Eastern Thrace. See **Thrace.**

East·er·tide (ē′stər-tīd′) *n.* **1.** The Easter season, extending in different churches from Easter to Ascension Day, Whitsunday, or Trinity Sunday. **2.** The week following Easter Sunday.

East Flan·ders (flăn′dərz). A province, 1,147 square miles in area, situated in northwestern Belgium. Population, 1,289,000. Capital, Ghent.

East Fries·land (frēz′lənd, -lănd′). A historic region of northwestern Germany, on the North Sea, extending east from the Ems estuary to that of the Weser.

East Fri·sians. See **Frisian Islands.**

East Germanic. A subdivision of the Germanic languages, represented only by Gothic.

East Ger·ma·ny. The unofficial name for the German Democratic Republic. See **Germany.**

East Greek. A principal dialectal division of Ancient Greek, comprising Mycenaean Greek, Arcado-Cyprian, Attic-Ionic, and Aeolic.

East India Company. Any of several European companies organized in the 17th and 18th centuries to trade with the East Indies; especially, such companies as formed by the English, Dutch, and French.

East In·dies (ĭn′dēz). *Abbr.* **E.I. 1.** Historically, India. **2.** Sometimes, Southeast Asia. **3.** The Malay Archipelago. **4.** Formerly **Neth·er·lands East In·dies** (nĕth′ər-ləndz). The islands comprising Indonesia. —**East Indian.**

ă pat/ā pay/âr care/ä father/b bib/ch church/d deed/ĕ pet/ē be/f fife/g gag/h hat/hw which/ĭ pit/ī pie/îr pier/j judge/k kick/l lid, needle/m mum/n no, sudden/ng thing/ŏ pot/ō toe/ô paw, for/oi noise/ou out/ŏŏ took/ōō boot/p pop/r roar/s sauce/sh ship, dish/

east·ing (ē′stĭng) *n.* **1.** *Nautical.* **a.** The distance sailed by a ship on an easterly course. **b.** The longitudinal distance from a given meridian on an easterly course. **2.** An easterly direction.

East Lon·don (lŭn′dən). A seaport and industrial center of South Africa, in southeastern Cape of Good Hope Province, on the Indian Ocean. Population, 116,000.

East Los An·ge·les (lôs ăn′jə-ləs, ăng′gə-ləs, lŏs). A suburb of Los Angeles, California. Population, 104,000.

East Lo·thi·an (lō′*thē*-ən). Formerly **Had·ding·ton·shire** (hăd′ĭng-tən-shîr, -shər). A county occupying 267 square miles in eastern Scotland. Population, 53,000. County seat, Haddington.

East·main (ēst′mān′). A river rising in central Quebec, Canada, and flowing 375 miles generally west to James Bay.

East·man (ēst′mən), **George.** 1854–1932. American inventor, industrialist, and philanthropist.

east-north·east (ēst′nôrth-ēst′; *Nautical* -nôr-ēst′). *Abbr.* **ENE** The direction or point on the mariner's compass halfway between due east and northeast. It is 67 degrees 30 minutes east of due north. See **compass card.** —*adj.* Situated toward, facing, or in this direction. —*adv.* In, from, or toward this direction.

East Or·ange (ôr′ĭnj, ŏr′-). A city in northeastern New Jersey near Newark, of which it is a suburb. Population, 77,000.

East Pak·i·stan (pä′kĭ-stän′, păk′ĭ-stăn′). The eastern province of Pakistan, 54,501 square miles in area and over 900 miles east of West Pakistan. Population, 50,844,000. Capital, Dacca.

East·port (ēst′pôrt′, -pōrt′). The easternmost city in the United States, in Maine on an island in Passamaquoddy Bay. Population, 3,000.

East Prov·i·dence (prŏv′ə-dəns). A suburb of Providence, Rhode Island. Population, 45,000.

East Prus·sia (prŭsh′ə). *German* **Ost·preus·sen** (ōst′proi′sən). A former province of Prussia, divided after 1945 between Poland and the Russian S.F.S.R.

East Rid·ing (rī′dĭng). An administrative division of southeastern Yorkshire, England. Population, 527,000.

East River. A narrow strait connecting Upper New York Bay with Long Island Sound and separating Manhattan Island from Long Island.

East Siberian Sea. An arm of the Arctic Ocean, extending from Wrangel Island to the New Siberian Islands.

East Slavic. The eastern division of the Slavic languages, consisting of Russian, Ukrainian, and Byelorussian.

east-south·east (ēst′south′ēst′) *n. Abbr.* **ESE** The direction or point on the mariner's compass halfway between due east and southeast. It is 112 degrees 30 minutes east of due north. See **compass card.** —*adj.* Situated toward, facing, or in this direction. —*adv.* In, from, or toward east-southeast.

East St. Lou·is (sānt lo͞o′ĭs, -lo͞o′ē). An industrial city in Illinois on the Mississippi, opposite St. Louis, Missouri. Population, 82,000.

East Sudanic. The eastern division of the Sudanic languages.

east·ward (ēst′wərd) *adv.* Also **east·wards** (-wərdz), **east·ward·ly** (-wərd-lē). Toward the east. —*adj.* Toward, facing, or in the east. —*n.* An eastward direction, point, or region.

eas·y (ē′zē) *adj.* **-ier, -iest. 1.** Capable of being accomplished or acquired with ease; posing no difficulty: *"How easy is success to those who will only be true to themselves"* (Trollope). **2.** Free from worry, anxiety, trouble, or pain: *"Now as I was young and easy under the apple boughs"* (Dylan Thomas). **3.** Conducive to rest or comfort; pleasant and relaxing. **4.** Relaxed; easygoing; informal: *an easy, sociable manner.* **5.** Not strict or severe; lenient: *an easy teacher.* **6.** Readily persuaded or influenced; compliant. **7.** Not strained, hurried, or forced; moderate: *an easy walk around the block.* **8.** *Economics.* **a.** Small in demand and therefore readily obtainable: *Commodities are easier.* **b.** Plentiful and therefore obtainable at low interest rates: *easy money.* **9.** Evenly distributed between opponents. Said of cards: *easy aces.* —*adv.* In a cautious, restrained manner: *"She bid me take love easy, as the leaves grow on the tree"* (Yeats). See Usage note below. **—go easy on.** *Informal.* **1.** To use moderately or carefully: *go easy on the liquor.* **2.** To be indulgent or lenient with: *go easy on a tardy student.* **3.** To be delicate or tactful about: *go easy on the family scandal.* **—take it easy.** *Informal.* **1.** To refrain from exertion; relax. **2.** To refrain from anger or violence; stay calm. [Middle English *esy,* from Old French *aisie,* past participle of *aisier,* to put at ease, from *aise,* EASE.]

Synonyms: *easy, simple, facile, effortless, smooth, light.* These adjectives mean not requiring much effort or not reflecting effort or difficulty in performance. *Easy* applies both to tasks that require little effort and to persons who are not demanding. *Simple* describes tasks that are not complex and hence not demanding intellectually. *Facile* and *effortless* apply to performance and stress readiness and fluency of execution. *Facile,* however, sometimes has unfavorable connotations, as of haste or lack of care in action, glibness or lack of sincerity in speech, or superficiality of thought. *Effortless* can imply actual lack of effort but often refers to performance in which application of great strength or skill makes the execution seem easy. *Smooth* describes performance whose progress is even and unimpeded. *Light* refers to tasks or impositions that involve no taxing burdens or responsibilities.

Usage: *Easy* is used as an adverb principally in the constructions *easy come, easy go* and the informal *go easy on, take it easy,* and *easier said than done.* It is not customarily interchangeable with *easily.* Thus, *easy* and the comparative *easier* are not possible in such typical examples as these: *The handle turns easily. This is more easily recognized than the other.*

easy chair. A large, comfortable, well-upholstered chair.

eas·y·go·ing (ē′zē-gō′ĭng) *adj.* Also **eas·y-go·ing. 1. a.** Living without intense concern; placid. **b.** Lazy and careless. **c.** Lax in moral attitude. **d.** Undemanding: *an easygoing life.* **2.** Having or moving at an even gait. Said of a horse.

easy street. Also **Easy Street.** *Slang.* A condition of financial security or independence: *A substantial inheritance put them on easy street.*

eat (ēt) *v.* **ate** (āt; *British* ĕt) or *regional* **eat** (ĕt), **eaten** (ēt′n), **eating, eats.** —*tr.* **1.** To take into the mouth, chew, and swallow (food). **2.** To consume, ravage, or destroy by or as if by eating. Usually used with *away* or *up.* **3.** To erode or corrode. **4.** *Vulgar Slang.* To perform fellatio or cunnilingus upon. —*intr.* **1.** To consume food; have or take a meal or meals. **2.** To wear away or corrode by or as if by eating or gnawing. **—eat one's heart out.** To undergo bitter, hopeless anguish or longing. **—eat one's words.** To retract something that one has said. **—eat up.** *Slang.* To delight in: *He eats up old movies.* [Eat, ate, eaten; Middle English *eten, et, eten,* Old English *etan, ǣt, eten.* See **ed-** in Appendix.*] **—eat′er** *n.*

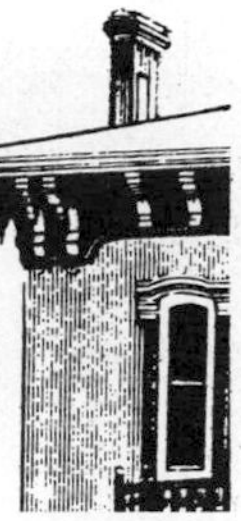

eaves

eat·a·ble (ē′tə-bəl) *adj.* Fit to be eaten; edible. —*n.* Something fit to be eaten; food. Often used in the plural.

eat·er·y (ē′tə-rē) *n., pl.* **-ies.** *Informal.* A lunchroom; diner.

eat·ing (ē′tĭng) *n.* **1.** The act of one that eats. **2.** Food: *The peaches were not only beautiful, they were good eating.* —*adj.* Suitable for eating raw: *These are eating apples.*

Ea·ton (ēt′n), **Theophilus.** 1590–1658. English founder and governor (1638–58) of New Haven colony.

eats (ēts) *pl.n. Slang.* Food.

eau de co·logne (ō′ də kə-lōn′) *pl.* **eaux de cologne** (ō′, ōz′). A toilet water, **cologne** *(see).*

eau de vie (ō′ də vē′) *pl.* **eaux de vie** (ō′, ōz′). Brandy. [French, "water of life."]

eaves (ēvz) *n.* Plural in form, usually used with a plural verb. The projecting overhang at the lower edge of a roof. [Middle English *eves,* Old English *yfes, efes,* eaves, edge, border. See **upo** in Appendix.*]

eaves·drop (ēvz′drŏp′) *intr.v.* **-dropped, -dropping, -drops.** To listen secretly to the private conversation of others. [Back-formation from *eavesdropper,* Middle English *evesdropper,* from *evesdrop,* water from the eaves, probably from Old English *yfesdrype* (influenced by Old Norse *upsardropi*). See **upo** in Appendix.*] **—eaves′drop′per** *n.*

ebb (ĕb) *n.* **1.** Ebb tide. **2.** A period of fading away, declining, or diminishing: *"insistence upon rules of conduct marks the ebb of religious fervor"* (A.N. Whitehead). —*intr.v.* **ebbed, ebbing, ebbs. 1.** To fall back or recede: *"that sea of horror ebbing and flowing around the edges of the world"* (Elizabeth Bowen). **2.** To waste or fall away. [Middle English *ebbe,* Old English *ebba,* low tide. See **apo-** in Appendix.*]

ebb tide. The period of a tide between high water and a succeeding low water. Compare **flood tide.**

Eb·bw Vale (ĕb′o͞o vāl′). An urban district and coal-mining and steel-producing region in southern Wales.

Eb·lis (ĕb′lĭs). Also **Ib·lis** (ĭb′lēs). The principal evil spirit or devil of Islamic mythology. [Arabic *Iblīs,* from Greek *diabolos,* slanderer. See **devil.**]

EbN east by north.

eb·on (ĕb′ən) *adj. Poetic.* **1.** Made of ebony. **2.** Black. —*n.* Ebony. [Middle English *eban, ebenus,* ebony, from Latin *ebenus,* from Greek *ebenos.* See **ebony.**]

eb·on·ite (ĕb′ə-nīt′) *n.* A **hard rubber** *(see),* especially when colored black. [EBON + -ITE.]

eb·on·ize (ĕb′ə-nīz′) *tr.v.* **-ized, -izing, -izes.** To finish with an ebony stain.

eb·on·y (ĕb′ə-nē) *n., pl.* **-ies. 1.** Any of several chiefly tropical trees of the genus *Diospyros;* especially, *D. ebenum,* of southern Asia, having hard, dark-colored heartwood. **2.** The wood of such a tree, used in cabinetwork and for piano keys. **3. a.** Black. **b.** Dark olive or olive gray to dark gray. See **color.** —*adj.* Made of or suggesting ebony. [Middle English *hebenyf,* from Late Latin *ebeninus,* (made) of ebony, from Greek *ebeninos,* from *ebenos,* ebony tree, from Egyptian *hebni.*]

e·brac·te·ate (ē-brăk′tē-āt′) *adj. Botany.* Without bracts. [New Latin *ebracteatus* : EX- (out, without) + BRACTEATE.]

E·bro (ē′brō; *Spanish* ā′vrō). Ancient name **I·ber·us** (ī-bîr′əs). The longest river of Spain, rising in the Cantabrian Mountains in the north and flowing about 575 miles generally southeast to the Mediterranean Sea.

EbS east by south.

e·bul·lient (ĭ-bŭl′yənt) *adj.* **1.** Boiling. Said of a liquid. **2.** Overflowing with excitement, enthusiasm, or exuberance. [Latin *ēbulliēns,* present participle of *ēbullīre,* to boil over : *ex-,* completely + *bullīre,* to boil (see **beu-**[1] in Appendix*).] **—e·bul′lience, e·bul′lien·cy** *n.* **—e·bul′lient·ly** *adv.*

eb·ul·li·tion (ĕb′ə-lĭsh′ən) *n.* **1.** The bubbling or effervescence of a liquid; a boiling. **2.** A sudden, violent outpouring, as of emotion or violence: *"did not . . . give way to any ebullitions of private grief"* (Thackeray). [Late Latin *ēbullītiō,* from Latin *ēbullīre,* to boil over. See **ebullient.**]

eb·ur·na·tion (ĕb′ər-nā′shən) *n.* The degeneration of bone into a hard, ivorylike mass. [From Latin *eburnus,* (made) of ivory, from *ebur,* IVORY.]

E.C. Established Church.

Ec·bat·a·na. The ancient name for **Hamadan.**

ec·ce ho·mo (ĕk′sē hō′mō, ĕk′ē). Also **Ec·ce Ho·mo.** A picture depicting Christ wearing the crown of thorns. [Late Latin, "Behold the Man," words used by Pontius Pilate to present Christ crowned with thorns to his accusers. John 19:5.]

ec·cen·tric (ĕk sĕn′trĭk, ĭk-) *adj.* **1. a.** Departing or deviating

from the conventional or established norm, model, or rule. **b.** Departing from a direct or charted course; erratic; irregular: *"The day seemed to be running in jagged rhythms, eccentric and aimless"* (Ross Lockridge, Jr.). **2.** Deviating from a circular form, as in an elliptical orbit. **3.** Not situated at or in the center. **4.** Not having the same center. Said of figures such as circles, cylinders, and spheres. Compare **concentric**. —See Synonyms at **strange**. —*n.* **1.** One that deviates markedly from a normal, conventional, or expected course or pattern; an odd or erratic person or thing. **2.** *Machinery.* A disk or wheel having its axis of revolution displaced from its center so that it is capable of imparting reciprocating motion. [Middle English *excentryke*, not having the same center (said of planets), from Late Latin *eccentricus*, from Greek *ekkentros* : *ex-*, out + *kentron*, point, center, from *kentein*, to prick (see **kent-** in Appendix*).] —**ec·cen'tri·cal·ly** *adv.*

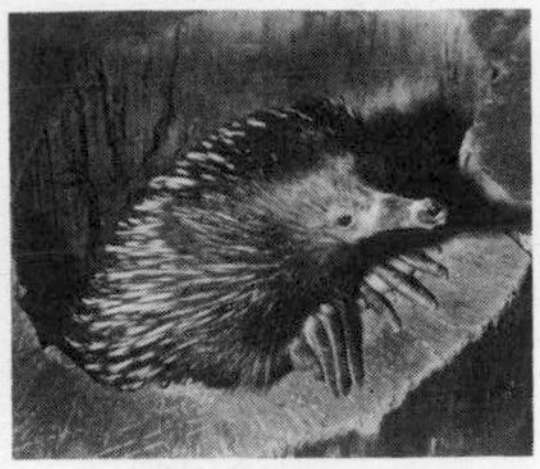

echidna
Tachyglossus aculeatus

ec·cen·tric·i·ty (ĕk'sĕn-trĭs'ə-tē) *n., pl.* **-ties. 1.** Deviation from the normal, conventional, or expected. **2. a.** The quality of being eccentric. **b.** The degree of being off center or not concentric: *an eccentric orbit.* **3.** *Machinery.* The distance between the center of an eccentric and its axis; the throw. **4.** *Mathematics.* The ratio of the distance of any point on a conic section from a focus to its distance from the corresponding directrix.

Synonyms: *eccentricity, idiosyncrasy, quirk.* These nouns refer to peculiarity of behavior. *Eccentricity* implies divergence from the usual or customary that, in extreme form, may suggest a disordered mind. *Idiosyncrasy* more often refers to such divergence viewed as peculiar to the temperament of a ruggedly individualistic person and serving as an identifying trait. *Quirk,* a milder term, suggests an odd trait or mannerism.

ec·chy·mo·sis (ĕk'ĭ-mō'sĭs) *n.* **1.** The passage of blood from ruptured blood vessels into subcutaneous tissue, marked by a purple discoloration of the skin. **2.** The resultant skin discoloration. [New Latin, from Greek *ekkhumōsis*, from *ekkhumousthai*, to pour out : *ex-*, out of + *khumos*, juice, from *khein*, to pour (see **gheu-** in Appendix*).] —**ec'chy·mot'ic** (-mŏt'ĭk) *adj.*

eccl., eccles. ecclesiastic; ecclesiastical.

Eccles. Ecclesiastes (Old Testament).

ec·cle·si·a (ĭ-klē'zhē-ə, -zē-ə) *n., pl.* **-siae** (-zhē-ē', -zē-ē'). **1.** The political assembly of citizens of an ancient Greek state. **2.** A church or congregation. [Latin *ecclēsia*, from Greek *ekklēsia*, duly summoned assembly, from *ekkalein*, to call out, summon : *ex-*, out + *kalein*, to call (see **kel-³** in Appendix*).]

Ec·cle·si·as·tes (ĭ-klē'zē-ăs'tēz) *n. Abbr.* **Eccles.** A book of the Old Testament traditionally attributed to Solomon. [Latin *Ecclēsiastēs*, from Greek *ekklēsiastēs*, member of the assembly of citizens, from *ekklēsia*, ECCLESIA.]

ec·cle·si·as·tic (ĭ-klē'zē-ăs'tĭk) *adj. Abbr.* **eccl., eccles.** Ecclesiastical. —*n. Abbr.* **eccl., eccles.** A clergyman; priest.

ec·cle·si·as·ti·cal (ĭ-klē'zē-ăs'tĭ-kəl) *adj. Abbr.* **eccl., eccles. 1.** Of or pertaining to a church, especially as an organized institution; clerical. **2.** Churchly.

ecclesiastical calendar. See **calendar.**

ec·cle·si·as·ti·cism (ĭ-klē'zē-ăs'tə-sĭz'əm) *n.* **1.** Ecclesiastical principles, practices, and activities. **2.** Excessive adherence to ecclesiastical principles and forms.

Ec·cle·si·as·ti·cus (ĭ-klē'zē-ăs'tĭ-kəs) *n.* A book of the Apocrypha. Also called "Wisdom of Jesus, the Son of Sirach."

ec·cle·si·ol·a·try (ĭ-klē'zē-ŏl'ə-trē) *n.* Worship of the church, especially extreme devotion to its principles or traditions. [From ECCLESI(A) + -LATRY.] —**ec·cle'si·ol'a·ter** *n.*

ec·cle·si·ol·o·gy (ĭ-klē'zē-ŏl'ə-jē) *n.* The study of ecclesiastical art, especially in relation to the architecture and decoration of churches. [ECCLESI(A) + -LOGY.]

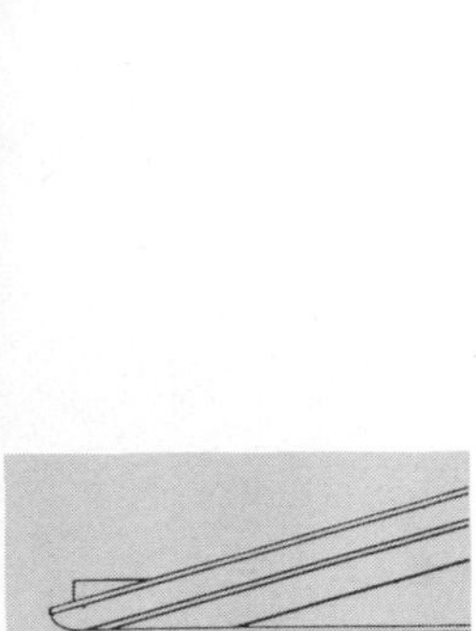

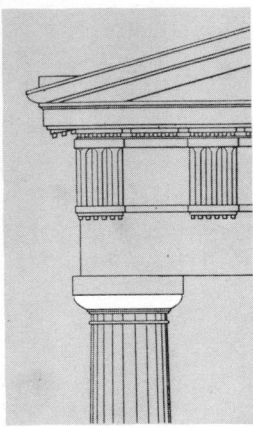

echinus
Echinus of
a Doric column

ec·crine (ĕk'rĭn, -rīn', -rēn') *adj.* **1.** Secreting externally; especially, pertaining to an eccrine gland or its secretion. **2. Exocrine** *(see).* [From Greek *ekkrinein*, to exude, secrete : *ex-*, out + *krinein*, to separate (see **skeri-** in Appendix*).]

eccrine gland. Any of the small sweat glands distributed over the body's surface.

ec·crin·ol·o·gy (ĕk'rə-nŏl'ə-jē) *n.* The study of eccrine secretions and secretory organs. [ECCRINE + -LOGY.]

ec·dys·i·ast (ĕk-dĭz'ē-ăst', -əst) *n.* A stripteaser. [From ECDYSIS; coined by Henry L. MENCKEN.]

ec·dy·sis (ĕk'də-sĭs) *n., pl.* **-ses** (-sēz'). The shedding of an outer integument or layer of skin, as in insects, crustaceans, and snakes. [New Latin, from Greek *ekdusis*, a stripping, from *ekduein*, to take off : *ex-*, out + *duein*, to get into, put on, enter (see **adytum**).]

e·ce·sis (ĭ-sē'sĭs) *n.* The successful establishment of an organism in a new environment. [Greek *oikēsis*, habitation, from *oikein*, to dwell, from *oikos*, house. See **weik-¹** in Appendix.*]

ec·hard (ĕk'härd') *n. Ecology.* Soil water not available for absorption by plants. [From Greek *ekhein*, to hold, hold back (see **segh-** in Appendix*) + *ardein*†, to water, irrigate.]

ech·e·lon (ĕsh'ə-lŏn') *n.* **1. a.** A formation of troops in which units are parallel but unaligned in a steplike fashion. **b.** A similar formation of groups, units, or individuals. **c.** A flight formation or arrangement of vessels in this manner. **2.** A subdivision of a military or naval force: *command echelon.* **3.** A level of command or authority: *the lowest echelon of the business office.* **4.** *Optics.* A specialized form of diffraction grating consisting of parallel glass plates of successively varying sizes, used to examine extremely fine structures. —*v.* **echeloned, -loning, -lons.** —*tr.* To arrange in echelon. —*intr.* To form, march, or move in echelon. [French *échelon*, "rung of a ladder," from Old French *eschelon*, from *eschile*, ladder, from Latin *scālae*, ladder, stairs. See **skand-** in Appendix.*]

ech·e·ve·ri·a (ĕch'ə-və-rē'ə) *n.* Any of various tropical American plants of the genus *Echeveria*, having thick, succulent leaves often clustered in a rosette. [New Latin *Echeveria*, after *Echevería*, 19th-century Mexican botanical illustrator.]

e·chid·na (ĭ-kĭd'nə) *n.* Any of several burrowing, egg-laying mammals of the genera *Tachyglossus* and *Zaglossus*, of Australia, New Zealand, and New Guinea, having a spiny coat and a slender snout. Also called "spiny anteater." [New Latin, from Latin, viper, from Greek *ekhidna*. See **angwhi-** in Appendix.*]

ech·i·nate (ĕk'ə-nāt') *adj.* Bearing or covered with spines; prickly; spiny. [Latin *echinātus*, from *echinus*, hedgehog. See **echino-**.]

echino–, echin–. Indicates prickly, covered with spines; for example, **echinoderm, echinoid.** [New Latin, from Latin *echinus*, hedgehog, sea urchin, from Greek *ekhinos*. See **angwhi-** in Appendix.*]

e·chi·no·coc·cus (ĭ-kī'nə-kŏk'əs) *n., pl.* **-cocci** (-kŏk'sī'). Any of several parasitic tapeworms of the genus *Echinococcus*, the larvae of which infect mammals and form large, spherical cysts, causing serious or fatal disease. [New Latin *Echinococcus* : ECHINO- + COCCUS.]

e·chi·no·derm (ĭ-kī'nə-dûrm') *n.* Any of numerous radially symmetrical marine invertebrates of the phylum Echinodermata, which includes the starfishes, sea urchins, and sea cucumbers, having a body often covered with spines. [ECHINO- + -DERM.] —**e·chi'no·der'mal, e·chi'no·der'ma·tous** *adj.*

e·chi·noid (ĭ-kī'noid') *n.* Any echinoderm of the class Echinoidea, which includes the sand dollars and sea urchins. [ECHIN(O)- + -OID.]

e·chi·nus (ĭ-kī'nəs) *n., pl.* **-ni** (-nī'). *Architecture.* A curved molding just below the abacus of a Doric capital. [Latin, "hedgehog," "sea urchin" (from the shape). See **echino-**.]

Ech·mi·a·dzin (ĕch'mē-ä-dzēn'). Formerly **Va·gar·sha·pat** (vä'gär-shä-pät', -shä-bäd'). A city in central Armenian S.S.R., site of the founding of the Armenian Church (A.D. 309) and, as Vagarshapat, the capital of Armenia (second to fourth century A.D.).

ech·o (ĕk'ō) *n., pl.* **-oes. 1.** Repetition of a sound by reflection of sound waves from a surface. **2.** The sound produced in this manner. **3.** Any repetition or imitation of something, as of the opinions, speech, or dress of another: *Mod fashion is an echo of Edwardian style.* **4.** One who imitates another, as in opinions, speech, or dress. **5.** A sympathetic response. **6.** The repetition of certain sounds or syllables in poetry. **7.** The repetition of a musical note or phrase in a softer tone. **8.** A signal to a partner at bridge or whist that the same suit is to be continued. **9.** *Electronics.* A reflected wave received by a radio or radar. **10.** *Capital* **E.** *Aerospace.* One of a series of U.S. passive satellites that are often visible at night. —*v.* **echoed, -oing, -oes.** —*tr.* **1.** To repeat by or as by an echo; send back the sound of: *The canyon echoed her cry.* **2.** To repeat or imitate: *followers echoing the thoughts of the leader.* —*intr.* **1.** To be repeated by or as if by an echo. **2.** To resound with or emit an echo; reverberate: *woods echoing with hunting cries.* [Middle English *ecco, ecko*, from Old French *echo*, from Latin *ēchō*, from Greek *ēkhō*. See **swagh-** in Appendix.*] —**ech'o·er** *n.*

Ech·o (ĕk'ō). *Greek Mythology.* A nymph whose unrequited love for Narcissus caused her to pine away until nothing but her voice remained.

e·cho·ic (ĕ-kō'ĭk) *adj.* **1.** Being like or resembling an echo. **2.** Imitative of sounds; onomatopoeic.

ech·o·ism (ĕk'ō-ĭz'əm) *n.* The formation of words in imitation of sounds; onomatopoeia.

ech·o·la·li·a (ĕk'ō-lā'lē-ə) *n.* Involuntary repetition of words or phrases just spoken by others. [ECHO + Greek *lalia*, talk, from *lalos*, talkative (see **lā-** in Appendix*).]

ech·o·lo·ca·tion (ĕk'ō-lō-kā'shən) *n.* **1.** The ability of an animal that emits high-frequency sounds, as a bat or dolphin, to orient itself by means of the reflected sound waves. **2.** *Electronics.* Ranging by acoustical echo analysis.

Eck (ĕk), **Johann.** Original surname, Mayer. 1486–1543. German theologian; opposed Reformation.

Eck·hart (ĕk'härt), **Johannes.** Called "Meister Eckhart." 1260?-1327? German philosopher and mystic.

é·clair (ā'klâr', ĭ-klâr') *n.* A light, tubular pastry with cream or custard filling and usually iced with chocolate. [French, "lightning," from Old French *esclair*, from *esclairier*, to light, flash, from Vulgar Latin *exclāriāre* (unattested), variant of Latin *exclārāre* : *ex-*, completely + *clārāre*, to brighten, clarify, from *clārus*, bright, clear (see **kel-³** in Appendix*).]

é·clair·cisse·ment (ā-klâr-sēs-mäN') *n.* A clarification; enlightenment; explanation. [French, from Old French *esclarcir*, to clarify, from Vulgar Latin *exclāriciāre* : Latin *ex-*, completely + *clārus*, clear (see **kel-³** in Appendix*).]

ec·lamp·si·a (ĭ-klămp'sē-ə) *n.* Coma and convulsions arising from any of several conditions during or immediately after pregnancy. [New Latin, from Greek *eklampsis*, a shining forth, brightness, from *eklampein*, to shine forth : *ex-*, out + *lampein*, to shine (see **lāp-** in Appendix*).]

é·clat (ā-klä') *n.* **1.** Great brilliance, as of performance or achievement. **2.** Conspicuous success or acclaim. **3.** *Archaic.* Notoriety; scandal. [French, explosion, from *éclater*, to burst, explode, from Old French *esclater*, from Germanic *slītan* (unattested), to tear, SLIT.]

ec·lec·tic (ĭ-klĕk'tĭk) *adj.* **1.** Choosing what appears to be the best from diverse sources, systems, or styles. **2.** Consisting of that which has been selected from diverse sources, systems, or styles. —*n.* One whose opinions and beliefs are drawn from

ă pat/ā pay/âr care/ä father/b bib/ch church/d deed/ĕ pet/ē be/f fife/g gag/h hat/hw which/ĭ pit/ī pie/îr pier/j judge/k kick/l lid, needle/m mum/n no, sudden/ng thing/ŏ pot/ō toe/ô paw, for/oi noise/ou out/o͝o took/o͞o boot/p pop/r roar/s sauce/sh ship, dish/

several sources: *"Nominally a Moslem, he was really an eclectic"* (Maurice Collis). [Greek *eklektikos,* from *eklektos,* selected, from *eklegein,* to single out : *ex-,* out + *legein,* to choose (see **leg-** in Appendix*).] —**ec·lec'ti·cal·ly** *adv.*

ec·lec·ti·cism (ĭ-klĕk'tə-sĭz'əm) *n.* **1.** An eclectic system or method. **2.** Free selection and borrowing, as of ideas or styles, from diverse sources.

e·clipse (ĭ-klĭps') *n.* **1. a.** The partial or complete obscuring, relative to a designated observer, of one celestial body by another. **b.** The period of time during which such an obscuring occurs. **2.** Any temporary or permanent dimming or cutting off of light. **3.** Any diminution into obscurity or disuse; a decline; downfall. —*tr.v.* **eclipsed, eclipsing, eclipses. 1.** To cause an eclipse or obscuring of; darken. **2.** To obscure or overshadow the importance, fame, or reputation of; reduce in importance by comparison. [Middle English *eclipse,* from Old French, from Latin *eclipsis,* from Greek *ekleipsis,* cessation, abandonment, from *ekleipein,* to leave out, abandon : *ek-, ex-,* out + *leipein,* to leave (see **leikw-** in Appendix*).]

e·clip·sis. An **ellipsis** *(see).* [Greek *ekleipsis,* abandonment. See **eclipse.**]

e·clip·tic (ĭ-klĭp'tĭk) *n.* **1.** The apparent path of the sun among the stars; the intersection plane of the earth's solar orbit with the celestial sphere. **2.** A great circle on a terrestrial globe inclined at an approximate angle of 23 degrees 27 minutes to the equator. [Middle English *ecliptik,* from Late Latin *eclīpticus,* from Latin, of an eclipse, from Greek *ekleiptikos,* from *ekleipein,* to abandon. See **eclipse.**]

ec·logue (ĕk'lôg', -lŏg') *n.* A bucolic poem, typically a pastoral dialogue. [French *éclogue,* from Old French *eglogue,* from Latin *ecloga,* "selection," from Greek *eklogē,* from *eklegein,* to single out. See **eclectic.**]

e·clo·sion (ĭ-klō'zhən) *n.* The emergence of an adult insect from a pupal case or of an insect larva from an egg. [French *éclosion,* from *éclore,* to open, be hatched, from Vulgar Latin *exclaudere* (unattested), variant of Latin *exclūdere,* to shut out : *ex-,* out + *claudere,* to shut, close (see **klēu-** in Appendix*).]

ecol. ecological; ecology.

e·col·o·gist (ĭ-kŏl'ə-jĭst) *n.* One who specializes in ecology.

e·col·o·gy (ĭ-kŏl'ə-jē) *n. Abbr.* **ecol.** The science of the relationships between organisms and their environments. Also called "bionomics." [German *Ökologie* : Greek *oikos,* house (see **weik-**[1] in Appendix*) + -LOGY.] —**ec'o·log'i·cal** (ĕk'ə-lŏj'ĭ-kəl) *adj.* —**ec'o·log'i·cal·ly** *adv.*

econ. economics; economist; economy.

ec·o·nom·ic (ĕk'ə-nŏm'ĭk, ē'kə-) *adj.* **1.** Of or pertaining to the production, development, and management of material wealth, as of a country, household, or business enterprise. **2.** Of or pertaining to economics. **3.** Of or pertaining to matters of finance. **4.** Of or pertaining to the necessities of life; utilitarian.

ec·o·nom·i·cal (ĕk'ə-nŏm'ĭ-kəl, ē'kə-) *adj.* **1.** Not wasteful or extravagant; prudent in management; reserved in quantity. **2.** Economic. —See Synonyms at **sparing.** —**ec'o·nom'i·cal·ly** *adv.*

economic rent. Rent *(see).*

ec·o·nom·ics (ĕk'ə-nŏm'ĭks, ē'kə-) *n.* Plural in form, used with a singular verb. *Abbr.* **econ.** The science that deals with the production, distribution, and consumption of commodities.

e·con·o·mist (ĭ-kŏn'ə-mĭst) *n. Abbr.* **econ. 1.** A specialist in economics. **2.** One who is economical.

e·con·o·mize (ĭ-kŏn'ə-mīz') *v.* **-mized, -mizing, -mizes.** —*intr.* To be frugal; reduce expenses. —*tr.* To use or manage with thrift; practice economy. —**e·con'o·miz'er** *n.*

e·con·o·my (ĭ-kŏn'ə-mē) *n., pl.* **-mies.** *Abbr.* **econ. 1.** The careful or thrifty use or management of resources, as of income, materials, or labor. **2.** An example of this; a saving. **3.** The management of the resources of a country, community, or business: *the American economy.* **4. a.** A system for the management and development of resources: *an agricultural economy.* **b.** The economic system of a country or area: *"the milch cow is the center round which this economy revolves"* (Conrad M. Arensberg). **5.** The functional arrangement of elements within a structure or system: *the economy of an organism.* **6.** *Theology.* The divine plan or system for the government of the world. **7.** *Theology.* Divine dispensation, especially for a specific period or nation. [Old French *economie,* management of a household, from Latin *oeconomia,* from Greek *oikonomia,* from *oikonomos,* manager of a household : *oikos,* house (see **weik-**[1] in Appendix*) + *-nomos,* managing (see **-nomy**).]

economy class. The least expensive and luxurious category of airline accommodations. Also called "coach class."

e·co·spe·cies (ē'kō-spē'shēz, -sēz, ĕk'ə-) *n.* A taxonomic species considered in terms of its ecological characteristics and usually including several subpopulations, or ecotypes. [ECO(LOGY) + SPECIES.]

ec·o·sys·tem (ĕk'ō-sĭs'təm) *n.* An ecological community together with its physical environment, considered as a unit. [ECO(LOGY) + SYSTEM.]

e·co·tone (ē'kə-tōn', ĕk'ə-) *n.* An ecological community of mixed vegetation formed by the overlapping of adjoining communities. [ECO(LOGY) + Greek *tonos,* tension, TONE.]

e·co·type (ē'kə-tīp', ĕk'ə-) *n.* The smallest taxonomic subdivision of an ecospecies, consisting of subspecies or varieties adapted to a particular set of environmental conditions. [ECO(LOGY) + TYPE.]

ec·ru (ĕk'rōō, ā'krōō) *n.* Grayish to pale yellow or light grayish yellowish brown. See **color.** [French *écru* : *é-,* completely, from Latin *ex* + *cru,* crude, raw, from Latin *crudus* (see **kreu-**[1] in Appendix*).] —**ec'ru** *adj.*

ec·sta·sy (ĕk'stə-sē) *n., pl.* **-sies. 1.** A state of exalted delight in which normal understanding is felt to be surpassed: *"allay thy ecstasy; In measure rein thy joy"* (Shakespeare). **2.** A state of any emotion so intense that rational thought and self-control are obliterated: *an ecstasy of anger.* **3.** The trance, frenzy, or rapture associated with mystic or prophetic exaltation. [Middle English *extasie,* from Old French, from Late Latin *extasis, ecstasis,* from Greek *ekstasis,* from *existanai,* to displace, drive out of one's senses : *ex-,* out + *histanai,* to place (see **stā-** in Appendix*).]

Synonyms: *ecstasy, rapture, transport, exaltation, euphoria, bliss.* These nouns all have reference to extremely strong emotion. The first four are now often used interchangeably in the approximate sense of joy. Even in general usage, however, *ecstasy* retains some of its original sense of a trancelike condition marked by loss of orientation toward rational experience and by concentration on a single emotion, and *rapture* that of attainment of an elevated state permitting superhuman sensory or emotional experience. *Transport* implies violence of feeling and sometimes of accompanying action. *Exaltation* and *euphoria* both involve a sense of extreme personal well-being, but *exaltation* is the stronger and more elevated term. *Bliss* is extreme happiness or joy, considered usually as a relatively tranquil state.

ec·stat·ic (ĕk-stăt'ĭk) *adj.* **1.** Of, relating to, induced by, or inducing ecstasy. **2.** In a state of ecstasy; enraptured. —*n.* **1.** One subject to ecstasies. **2.** *Plural.* Fits of ecstasy; raptures. —**ec·stat'i·cal·ly** *adv.*

ecto-. Indicates outside or external part or surface; for example, **ectoderm, ectoplasm.** [Greek *ekto-,* from *ektos,* outside (after *entos,* inside), from *ek, ex,* out. See **eghs** in Appendix.*]

ec·to·blast (ĕk'tə-blăst') *n. Biology. Rare.* Ectoderm. [ECTO- + -BLAST.]

ec·to·derm (ĕk'tə-dûrm') *n.* The outermost of the three primary germ layers of an embryo, developing the epidermis, nervous tissue, and, in vertebrates, sense organs. Also called "exoderm." [ECTO- + -DERM.]

ec·tog·e·nous (ĕk-tŏj'ə-nəs) *adj.* Able to live and develop outside a host. Said of certain pathogenic microorganisms. [ECTO- + -GENOUS.]

ec·to·mere (ĕk'tə-mîr') *n. Embryology.* A blastomere that develops into ectoderm. [ECTO- + -MERE.]

ec·to·morph (ĕk'tə-môrf') *n.* An ectomorphic individual. Compare **mesomorph.**

ec·to·mor·phic (ĕk'tə-môr'fĭk) *adj.* Lean and slightly muscular. [ECTO(DERM) + -MORPHIC.] —**ec'to·mor'phy** *n.*

-ectomy. Indicates removal of a part by surgery; for example, **tonsillectomy.** [New Latin *-ectomia* : Greek *ek-, ex-,* out + -TOMY.]

ec·to·par·a·site (ĕk'tō-păr'ə-sīt') *n.* A parasite, such as a flea, that lives on the exterior of another organism.

ec·to·pi·a (ĕk-tō'pē-ə) *n.* Congenital positional abnormality of an organ or part. [New Latin, from Greek *ektopos,* away from a place : *ex-,* out of + *topos,* place (see **topic**).] —**ec·top'ic** (-tŏp'ĭk) *adj.*

ectopic pregnancy. *Pathology.* Gestation outside the uterus, often in a Fallopian tube.

ec·to·plasm (ĕk'tə-plăz'əm) *n.* **1.** *Biology.* A portion of the continuous phase of cytoplasm distinguishable in some cells as a relatively rigidly gelled cortex limited on the outside by the cell membrane. Compare **endoplasm. 2.** The alleged emanation from a spiritualistic medium. [ECTO- + -PLASM.]

ec·to·sarc (ĕk'tə-särk') *n. Rare.* The relatively clear outermost layer of protoplasm of certain protozoans, such as the amoeba. [ECTO- + Greek *sarx,* flesh (see **twerk-** in Appendix*).]

ec·type (ĕk'tīp') *n.* A reproduction of an original; imitation; copy. [Greek *ektupos,* worked in relief : *ex-,* out of + *tupos,* impression, mold, TYPE.] —**ec'ty·pal** (-tə-pəl) *adj.*

é·cu (ā-kü') *n., pl.* **écus** (ā-kü'). Any of various French gold or silver coins; especially, a silver five-franc piece. [French, from Old French *escu,* from Latin *scūtum,* shield (from the shield stamped on the coin). See **skei-** in Appendix.*]

Ec·ua·dor (ĕk'wə-dôr'; *Spanish* ā-kwä-*th*ôr'). *Abbr.* **Ecua.** Officially, Republic of Ecuador. A country of South America, occupying 108,478 square miles in the northwest. Population, 4,485,000. Capital, Quito.

ec·u·men·i·cal (ĕk'yŏŏ-mĕn'ĭ-kəl) *adj.* Also **oec·u·men·i·cal, ec·u·men·ic** (-mĕn'ĭk). **1.** Universal; worldwide; general. **2.** Of or pertaining to the worldwide Christian church, especially in regard to unity. [From Late Latin *oecūmenicus,* from Greek *oikoumenikos,* of the whole world, from *oikoumenē,* the inhabited world, from *oikein,* to inhabit, from *oikos,* house. See **weik-**[1] in Appendix.*] —**ec'u·men'i·cal·ism'** *n.* —**ec'u·men'i·cal·ly** *adv.*

ecumenical patriarch. A **patriarch** *(see)* of the Eastern Orthodox Church.

ec·ze·ma (ĕk'sə-mə, ĕg'zə-, ĕg-zē'-, ĭg-zē'-) *n.* A noncontagious inflammation of the skin, marked mainly by redness, itching, and the outbreak of lesions that discharge serous matter and become encrusted and scaly. Also called "salt rheum." [New Latin, from Greek *ekzema,* eruption : *ex-,* out + *zema,* fermentation, boiling, from *zeein,* boil (see **yes-** in Appendix*).] —**ec·zem'a·tous** (ĕg-zĕm'ə-təs, -zē'mə-təs, ĭg-) *adj.*

-ed[1]. Used to form the past tense of most verbs; for example, **removed.** [Middle English *-ede,* Old English *-ode, -ede, -ade.*]

-ed[2]. Used to form past participles of most verbs; for example, **robed, hoped.** [Middle English *-ed,* Old English *-od, -ed, -ad.*]

-ed[3]. Used to form adjectives from nouns and phrases to indicate possessing, characterized by, or provided with; for

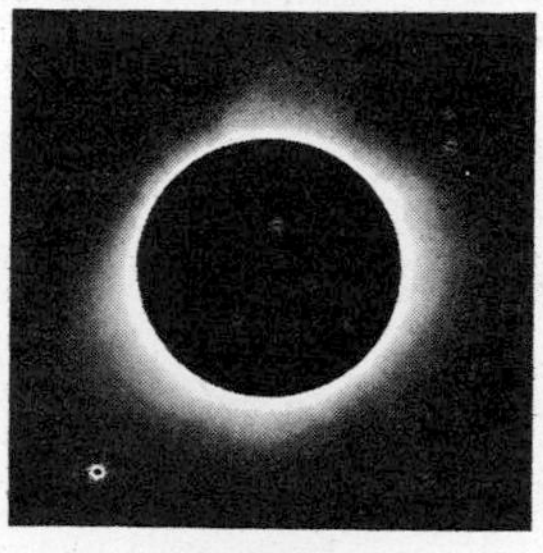

eclipse
Total solar eclipse photographed near Cañaguas, Peru, November 12, 1966

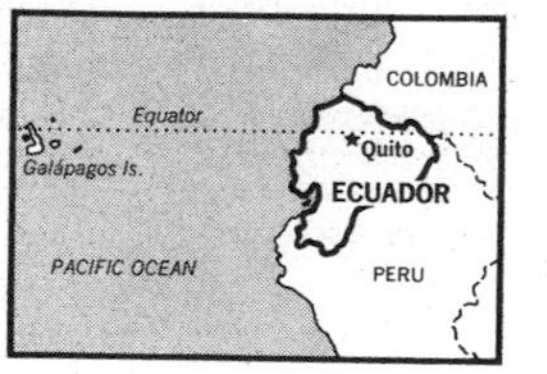

Ecuador

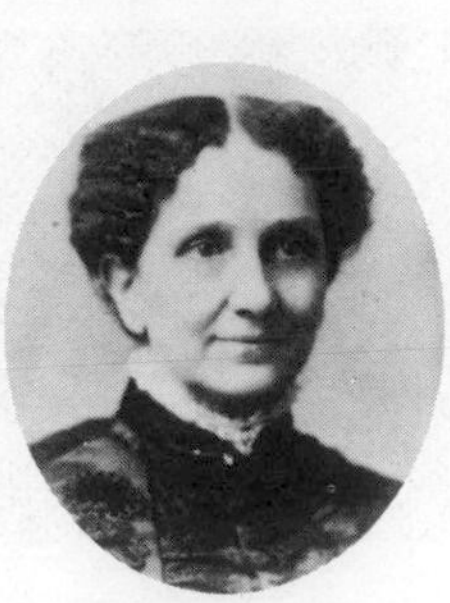
Mary Baker Eddy

ð
edh

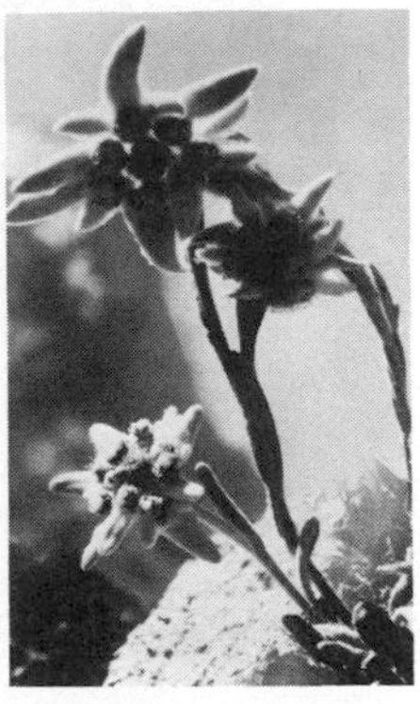
edelweiss

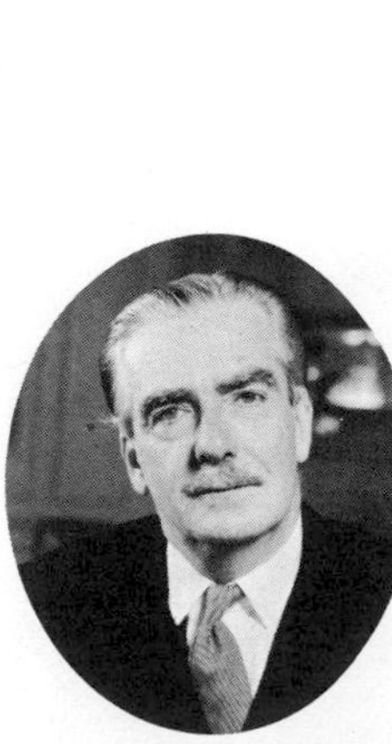
Sir Anthony Eden

example, **forked, gray-haired.** [Middle English *-ede, -de,* Old English *-ede.*]
ed. **1.** edition; editor. **2.** education.
E.D. election district.
e·da·cious (ĭ-dā′shəs) *adj.* Gluttonous; voracious. Used humorously. [From Latin *edax,* gluttonous, from *edere,* to eat. See **ed-** in Appendix.*] —**e·dac′i·ty** (ĭ-dăs′ə-tē) *n.*
E·dam (ē′dəm, ĕ′dăm). A town in the Netherlands, in the northwest on the Ijsselmeer. It is a major center of the cheese industry. Population, 4,000.
Edam cheese. A mild, yellow Dutch cheese, pressed into balls and usually covered with red paraffin.
e·daph·ic (ĭ-dăf′ĭk) *adj.* Of or pertaining to soil, especially as it affects living organisms. [From Greek *edaphos,* ground, foundation, soil. See **sed-¹** in Appendix.*]
Ed·da (ĕd′ə) *n.* **1.** A collection of Old Norse poems called the Elder or Poetic Edda, assembled in the early 13th century. **2.** A manual of Icelandic poetry, called the Younger or Prose Edda, compiled a generation later. [Old Norse *edda*†.]
Ed·ding·ton (ĕd′ĭng-tən), Sir **Arthur Stanley.** 1882–1944. British astronomer and physicist.
ed·do (ĕd′ō) *n., pl.* **-does.** A plant, **taro** *(see).* [From an African word, akin to Twi *o¹de³,* yam.]
ed·dy (ĕd′ē) *n., pl.* **-dies. 1.** A current, as of water or air, moving contrary to the direction of the main current, especially in a circular motion: *"little eddies of wind were whirling dust and torn paper into spirals"* (George Orwell). **2.** A current that runs contrary to the main current or tradition, as of life, art, or philosophy; a byway. —*v.* **eddied, -dying, -dies.** —*intr.* To move against the main current, as in an eddy: *"A whirlpool can exist only as long as the water continues to eddy"* (Fritz Kahn). —*tr.* To cause to move against the main current, as in an eddy. —See Synonyms at **turn.** [Middle English *ydy,* from Old Norse *idha,* "that which flows back," whirlpool, from *idh-,* again. See **eti** in Appendix.*]
Ed·dy (ĕd′ē), **Mary Baker.** 1821–1910. American religious leader; founder of the Church of Christ, Scientist.
Ed·dy·stone Rocks (ĕd′ē-stōn′). A dangerous reef capped by a historic lighthouse in the English Channel off southeastern Cornwall, England.
E·de¹ (ā′də). A city of the Netherlands, in western Gelderland Province. Population, 58,000.
E·de² (ā′dā). A city and center of the Yoruba people in the Western Region of Nigeria. Population, 135,000.
e·del·weiss (ā′dəl-vīs′) *n.* A plant, *Leontopodium alpinum,* of mountainous regions, especially the Alps, having leaves covered with whitish down and small flowers surrounded by conspicuous whitish bracts. [German *Edelweiss,* "noble white" : *edel,* noble, from Old High German *edili* (see **athal-** in Appendix*) + *weiss,* white, from Old High German *wīz, hwīz* (see **kweit-** in Appendix*).]
e·de·ma (ĭ-dē′mə) *n., pl.* **-mas** or **-mata** (-mə-tə). Also **oe·de·ma. 1.** *Pathology.* An excessive accumulation of serous fluid in the tissues. **2.** *Botany.* Extended swellings in plant organs caused primarily by an excessive accumulation of water. [New Latin, from Greek *oidēma,* tumor, swelling, from *oidein,* to swell. See **oid-** in Appendix.*]
E·den (ēd′n) *n.* **1.** In the Bible, the first home of Adam and Eve; Paradise. Also called "Garden of Eden." **2.** Any delightful place or dwelling; paradise. **3.** A state of bliss or ultimate happiness. [Middle English, from Late Latin *Ēden,* from Greek *Ēdēn,* from Hebrew *'ēdhen,* "the place of pleasure."]
E·den (ēd′n), Sir **(Robert) Anthony.** Earl of Avon. Born 1897. Prime Minister of the United Kingdom (1955–57).
e·den·tate (ē-dĕn′tāt′) *adj. Biology.* **1.** Lacking teeth. **2.** Of or belonging to the order Edentata, which includes mammals, such as anteaters, armadillos, and sloths, having few or no teeth. —*n.* A member of the Edentata. [Latin *edentātus,* toothless, from the past participle of *edentāre,* to take out the teeth : *ex-,* out + *dēns* (stem *dent-*), tooth (see **dent-** in Appendix*).]
E·des·sa (ĭ-dĕs′ə). **1.** A town in western Macedonia, Greece, the original capital of ancient Macedonia. **2.** The ancient name for **Urfa.**
Ed·fu. See **Idfu.**
Ed·gar (ĕd′gər). A masculine given name. [Middle English *Edgar,* Old English *Ēadgār* : *ēad,* happiness, riches (see **audaz** in Appendix*) + *gār,* spear (see **ghaiso-** in Appendix*).]
edge (ĕj) *n.* **1. a.** The usually thin, sharpened side of the blade of a cutting instrument, weapon, or tool. **b.** The degree of sharpness of a cutting blade. **2.** Keenness, as of desire or enjoyment; zest: *"His simplicity sets off the satire, and gives it a finer edge"* (William Hazlitt). **3.** A rim, brink, or crest, as of a cliff or ridge of hills. **4.** A dividing line or point of transition; a margin; a border: *"an edge of wintery chill"* (John Knowles). **5.** The line of intersection of two surfaces of a solid: *the edge of a brick.* **6.** A margin of superiority; an advantage: *a slight edge over the opposition.* —See Synonyms at **border.** —**on edge. 1.** Highly tense or nervous; irritable. **2.** Eagerly anticipatory; impatient. —**set one's teeth on edge.** *Informal.* **1.** To give one an unpleasant nervous reaction or sensation, as of tingling. **2.** To provoke strong feelings of irritation or annoyance. —**take the edge off.** To soften or dull, as the pleasure, excitement, or force of. —*v.* **edged, edging, edges.** —*tr.* **1.** To give an edge to; sharpen. **2.** To put a border or edge on. **3.** To advance or push gradually. —*intr.* To move gradually or hesitantly: *"She smiled almost slyly as she edged toward the mescal barrel"* (Malcolm Lowry). [Middle English *egge,* Old English *ecg,* edge, point, sword. See **ak-** in Appendix.*]
Edge·hill (ĕj′hĭl′). A ridge, part of the limestone uplands, in southern Warwickshire, England; site of the first battle between Charles I and the Parliamentarian army (1642).
edge tool. Any tool having a cutting edge, such as a chisel.
edge·wise (ĕj′wīz′) *adv.* Also **edge·ways** (-wāz′). **1.** Having the edge foremost. **2.** On, by, with, or toward the edge. —**get a word in edgewise.** To manage to intrude a remark into a long conversation or monologue.
edg·ing (ĕj′ĭng) *n.* Something that forms or serves as an edge; a trimming; a border.
edg·y (ĕj′ē) *adj.* **-ier, -iest. 1.** On edge; tense; nervous. **2.** With a sharp edge. **3.** With excessively sharp definition, as in painting or sculpture. —**edg′i·ness** *n.*
edh (ĕth) *n.* Also **eth. 1.** An old Germanic letter appearing in Old (and Middle) English, Old Saxon, Old Norse, and modern Icelandic. In the Scandinavian languages, it represents the interdental voiced fricative (transliterated as *dh* in the etymologies), and is distinguished from the voiceless thorn. In Old English, this distinction between edh and thorn (both transliterated as *th*) was not observed. **2.** The letter in the International Phonetic Alphabet representing the interdental voiced fricative, as in *the, with.*
EDI Airport code for Edinburgh, Scotland.
ed·i·ble (ĕd′ə-bəl) *adj.* **1. a.** Capable of being eaten. **b.** Fit to eat; nonpoisonous. **2.** Ready to be eaten. —*n.* Something fit to be eaten; food. Usually used in the plural. [Late Latin *edibilis,* from Latin *edere,* to eat. See **ed-** in Appendix.*] —**ed′i·bil′i·ty, ed′i·ble·ness** *n.*
e·dict (ē′dĭkt′) *n.* **1.** A decree or proclamation issued by an authority: *"The edict . . . extended to all natives . . . the rights of Roman citizenship"* (James Bryce). **2.** Any formal proclamation, command, or decree. [Latin *ēdictum,* from *ēdīcere,* to speak out, proclaim : *ex-,* out + *dīcere,* speak (see **deik-** in Appendix*).]
ed·i·fi·ca·tion (ĕd′ĭ-fə-kā′shən) *n.* Intellectual, moral, or spiritual improvement; enlightenment: *"this very day, in which I am now writing this book for the edification of the world"* (Sterne).
ed·i·fice (ĕd′ə-fĭs) *n.* A building, especially one of imposing appearance or size. See Synonyms at **building.** [Middle English, from Old French, from Latin *aedificium,* from *aedificāre,* to build : *aedēs,* building, house (see **aidh-** in Appendix*) + *fac(e)re,* to make (see **dhē-¹** in Appendix*).]
ed·i·fy (ĕd′ə-fī′) *tr.v.* **-fied, -fying, -fies.** To instruct or enlighten so as to encourage moral or spiritual improvement. [Middle English *edifien,* from Old French *edifier,* from Latin *aedificāre,* to build, instruct. See **edifice.**]. —**ed′i·fi′er** *n.*
Ed·in·burgh (ĕd′n-bûr′ə). *Scottish Gaelic* **Dun·e·din** (dun-ēd′n). The capital of Scotland, in the east on the Firth of Forth. Population, 472,000.
Ed·in·burgh, Duke of. See Prince **Philip.**
E·dir·ne (ĕ-dîr′nĕ). Formerly **A·dri·a·no·ple** (ā′drē-ə-nō′pəl). A town in extreme western Turkey, in Europe, noted for its mosques. Population, 39,000.
Ed·i·son (ĕd′ə-sən), **Thomas Alva.** 1847–1931. American inventor; obtained 1,100 patents in such fields as telegraphy, phonography, electric lighting, and photography.
ed·it (ĕd′ĭt) *tr.v.* **-ited, -iting, -its. 1. a.** To make (written material) suitable for publication or presentation. **b.** To prepare an edition of for publication: *edit a collection of short stories.* **2.** To supervise the publication of (a newspaper or magazine, for example). **3.** To omit or eliminate; delete. Usually used with *out.* **4.** To integrate the component parts of (film, electronic tape, or sound track) by cutting, combining, and splicing. [Back-formation from EDITOR.]
edit. edition; editor.
E·dith (ē′dĭth). A feminine given name. [Middle English *Edithe, Editha,* Old English *Eadgyth,* "possession-battle" (one who fights for the family possessions) : *ēad,* possessions, riches (see **audaz** in Appendix*) + *gūth,* war, battle (see **gwhen-¹** in Appendix*).]
E·dith Cav·ell Mountain (ē′dĭth kăv′əl, kə-vĕl′). A mountain rising to 11,033 feet, in the Rocky Mountains of western Alberta, Canada.
e·di·tion (ĭ-dĭsh′ən) *n. Abbr.* **ed., edit. 1. a.** The entire number of copies of a publication printed from a single type setting or other form of reproduction. Compare **printing. b.** A single copy from this group. **c.** A facsimile of an earlier publication having substantial changes or additions. **2. a.** Any of the various forms in which something is issued or produced, as publications, music, or stamps. **b.** Any of the forms in which a publication is produced: *a leather-bound edition.* **c.** One closely similar to an original; a version: *The boy was a smaller edition of his father.* **3.** An issue of a work identified by its editor or publisher: *the Oxford edition of Shakespeare.* **4.** All the copies of a single press run of a newspaper: *the morning edition.* [Old French, from Latin *ēditiō,* a bringing forth, publication, from *ēdere* (past participle *ēdictus*), to bring forth, publish : *ex-,* out + *dāre,* to give (see **dō-** in Appendix*).]
e·di·ti·o prin·ceps (ĭ-dĭsh′ē-ō′ prĭn′sĕps). *Latin.* First edition.
ed·i·tor (ĕd′ə-tər) *n. Abbr.* **ed., edit. 1.** A person who edits a literary, artistic, or musical work for publication or public presentation. **2.** A person who supervises the policies or production of a publication. **3.** A person in charge of a department of a publication: *a sports editor.* **4.** One who writes editorials. **5.** A device for editing film, consisting basically of a splicer and viewer. [Late Latin, publisher, from Latin *ēdere,* to bring forth, publish. See **edition.**]
ed·i·to·ri·al (ĕd′ə-tôr′ē-əl, -tōr′ē-əl) *n.* An article in a publication expressing the opinion of its editors or publishers. —*adj.* **1. a.** Of or pertaining to an editor or editors: *an editorial staff.*

ă pat/ā pay/âr care/ä father/b bib/ch church/d deed/ĕ pet/ē be/f fife/g gag/h hat/hw which/ĭ pit/ī pie/îr pier/j judge/k kick/l lid, needle/m mum/n no, sudden/ng thing/ŏ pot/ō toe/ô paw, for/oi noise/ou out/ŏŏ took/ōō boot/p pop/r roar/s sauce/sh ship, dish/

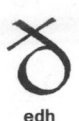

b. Prepared by an editor or editorial department: *the editorial content of a magazine.* **2.** Characteristic of an editorial; opinionated; slanted.

ed·i·to·ri·al·ize (ĕd′ə-tôr′ē-ə-līz′, -tōr′ē-ə-līz′) *intr.v.* **-ized, -izing, -izes. 1.** To express an opinion in or as if in an editorial. **2.** To present a supposedly objective report in a way intended to implant an opinion. —**ed′i·to′ri·al·i·za′tion** *n.* —**ed′i·to′ri·al·i′zer** *n.*

editor in chief *pl.* **editors in chief.** The editor having final responsibility for the operations and policies of a publication.

ed·i·tor·ship (ĕd′ə-tər-shĭp′) *n.* The position, functions, authority, or guidance of an editor.

Ed·mon·ton (ĕd′mən-tən). **1.** A former administrative division of London, England, now part of **Enfield** *(see).* **2.** The capital of Alberta, Canada, on the North Saskatchewan River in the south-central part of the province. Population, 372,000.

Ed·mund (ĕd′mənd). A masculine given name. [Middle English *Edmund, Edmond,* Old English *Ēadmund,* "protector of (family) possessions" : *ēad,* riches, property (see **audaz** in Appendix*) + *mund,* protector (see **man-**[2] in Appendix*).]

Ed·na (ĕd′nə). A feminine given name. [Greek, from Hebrew *'ēdnāh,* delight, akin to *'ēdhen,* EDEN.]

E·do. A former name for **Tokyo.**

E·dom (ē′dəm). Also **Id·u·mae·a** (ĭd′yo͞o-mē′ə), **Id·u·me·a.** An ancient country of southwestern Asia, south of the Dead Sea.

E·dom·ite (ē′də-mīt′) *n.* **1.** An inhabitant of Edom. **2.** A descendant of Esau. —**E′dom·it′ish** *adj.*

EDP electronic data processing.

E.D.T. Eastern Daylight Time.

educ. education; educational.

ed·u·ca·ble (ĕj′o͝o-kə-bəl) *adj.* Capable of being educated. [EDUC(ATE) + -ABLE.]

ed·u·cate (ĕj′o͝o-kāt′) *v.* **-cated, -cating, -cates.** —*tr.* **1.** To provide with knowledge or training, especially through formal schooling; teach. **2.** To provide with training for some particular purpose: *educate someone for the priesthood.* **3.** To provide with information; inform. **4.** To discipline, train, or develop (taste or skill, for example). —*intr.* To teach or instruct a person or group: *Their purpose is to educate through the use of visual aids.* —See Synonyms at **teach.** [Middle English *educaten,* from Latin *ēducāre,* to bring up, educate. See **deuk-** in Appendix.*]

ed·u·cat·ed (ĕj′o͝o-kā′tĭd) *adj.* **1.** Having an education, especially one above the average. **2.** Showing evidence of having been taught or instructed; cultivated; cultured. **3.** Based primarily on experience and some factual knowledge: *His estimation of the test results was an educated guess.*

ed·u·ca·tion (ĕj′o͝o-kā′shən) *n. Abbr.* **ed., educ. 1.** The act or process of imparting knowledge or skill; systematic instruction; teaching. **2.** The obtaining of knowledge or skill through such a process; schooling. **3. a.** The knowledge or skill obtained or developed by such a process; learning. **b.** A program of instruction of a specified kind or level: *driver education; a college education.* **4.** The field of study that is concerned with teaching and learning; the theory of teaching; pedagogy.

ed·u·ca·tion·al (ĕj′o͝o-kā′shən-əl) *adj. Abbr.* **educ. 1.** Of or relating to education. **2.** Serving to impart knowledge or skill: *an educational television program.* —**ed′u·ca′tion·al·ly** *adv.*

ed·u·ca·tion·al·ist (ĕj′o͝o-kā′shən-ə-lĭst) *n.* Also **ed·u·ca·tion·ist** (-shən ĭst). **1.** *Chiefly British.* An educator. **2.** An educational theorist. Usually used disparagingly.

ed·u·ca·tive (ĕj′o͝o-kā′tĭv) *adj.* Educational.

ed·u·ca·tor (ĕj′o͝o-kā′tər) *n.* **1.** One trained in teaching; a teacher. **2.** A specialist in the theory and practice of education.

e·duce (ĭ-do͞os′, ĭ-dyo͞os′) *tr.v.* **educed, educing, educes. 1.** To draw or bring out; elicit; evoke; evolve. **2.** To assume or work out from given facts; deduce. [Latin *ēdūcere* : *ex-,* out + *dūcere,* to lead (see **deuk-** in Appendix*).] —**e·duc′i·ble** *adj.*

e·duc·tion (ĭ-dŭk′shən) *n.* **1.** An act or the process of educing. **2.** The result of an educing; an inference. [Middle English *educcion,* from Late Latin *ēductiō,* from Latin *ēdūcere,* EDUCE.]

Ed·ward[1] (ĕd′wərd). A masculine given name. [Middle English *Edward,* Old English *Ēadweard,* "guardian of (family) possessions" : *ēad,* riches, property (see **audaz** in Appendix*) + *weard,* ward, guardian (see **wer-**[4] in Appendix*).]

Ed·ward[2] (ĕd′wərd). Called "the Confessor." 1004?–1066. Last Anglo-Saxon king of the English (1043–66).

Ed·ward[3] (ĕd′wərd). Called "the Black Prince." 1330–1376. Prince of Wales; son of Edward III.

Ed·ward I (ĕd′wərd). 1239–1307. King of England (1272–1307); son of Henry III; conquered Wales and warred with Scotland.

Ed·ward II (ĕd′wərd). 1284–1327. King of England (1307–27); son of Edward I; defeated by Robert the Bruce; murdered.

Ed·ward III (ĕd′wərd). 1312–1377. King of England (1327–77); son of Edward II.

Ed·ward IV (ĕd′wərd). 1442–1483. King of England (1461 83); secured crown from Henry VI.

Ed·ward V (ĕd′wərd). 1470–1483. King of England (1483); son of Edward IV; murdered.

Ed·ward VI (ĕd′wərd). 1537–1553. King of England (1547–53); son of Henry VIII and Jane Seymour.

Ed·ward VII (ĕd′wərd). 1841–1910. King of the United Kingdom and Emperor of India (1901–10); son of Queen Victoria.

Ed·ward VIII (ĕd′wərd). Born 1894. King of England (1936); son of George V; abdicated and was created Duke of Windsor; married Wallis Warfield Simpson (1937).

Ed·ward, Lake (ĕd′wərd). Also **Ed·ward Ny·an·za** (nē-ăn′zə, nyän′zä). A lake in the Great Rift Valley, in Africa, occupying 830 square miles between the Congo (Kinshasa) and Uganda.

Ed·ward·i·an (ĕd-wôr′dē-ən, ĕd-wär′-) *adj.* Of, relating to, or characteristic of the reign or person of any of several kings of England named Edward, especially Edward VII, during whose reign the styles and views of the cultured were generally regarded as opulent, ornate, overrefined, and pompous.

Ed·wards (ĕd′wərdz), **Jonathan.** 1703–1758. American Puritan theologian.

Ed·wards Plateau (ĕd′wərdz). An extension of the Great Plains in southwestern Texas.

Ed·win (ĕd′wĭn). A masculine given name. [Middle English *Edwin,* Old English *Ēadwine,* "friend of (family) possessions" : *ēad,* riches, property (see **audaz** in Appendix*) + *wine,* friend (see **wen-** in Appendix*).]

-ee[1]. Indicates: **1.** The recipient of an action; for example, **addressee, endorsee. 2.** One who is in a condition specified by the main element; for example, **standee.** Used to form nouns from verbs. [Middle English *-e,* from Old French *-e,* from past participial ending *-e,* from Latin *-ātus,* -ATE.]

-ee[2]. Indicates: **1.** A particular type of, especially when small; for example, **bootee. 2.** Something resembling or suggestive of; for example, **goatee.** [Originally *-ie,* variant of -Y.]

e.e. errors excepted.

E.E. electrical engineer; electrical engineering.

EEG electroencephalogram.

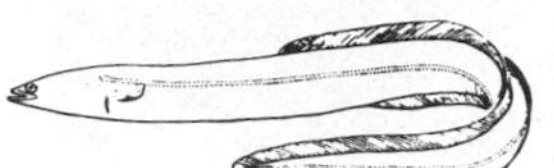

eel
Anguilla rostrata

eel (ēl) *n., pl.* **eel** or **eels. 1.** Any of various long, snakelike marine or freshwater fishes of the order Anguilliformes (or Apodes); especially, *Anguilla rostrata,* of eastern North America, or *A. anguilla,* of Europe, characteristically migrating from fresh water to the Sargasso Sea to spawn. **2.** Any of several similar or related fishes. **3.** Any of several animals having an elongated body, such as the congo eel. [Middle English *ele,* Old English *ǣl,* from Common Germanic *ǣlaz*† (unattested).]

eel·grass (ēl′grăs′, -gräs′) *n.* **1.** Any of several submerged aquatic plants of the genus *Zostera,* of coastal areas, having narrow, grasslike leaves and growing in dense masses. **2.** Any of several similar or related plants, such as **tape grass** *(see).*

eel·pout (ēl′pout′) *n., pl.* **eelpout** or **-pouts.** Any of various marine fishes of the family Zoarcidae, having an elongated body and a large head. One species, *Macrozoarces americanus,* is sometimes called "muttonfish." [Middle English *elepout* (unattested), Old English *ǣlepūte* : EEL + POUT (fish).]

eel·worm (ēl′wûrm′) *n.* Any of various, often parasitic nematode worms, such as the **vinegar eel** *(see).*

e'en[1] (ēn) *n. Poetic.* Evening.

e'en[2] (ēn) *adv. Poetic.* Even.

E.E.N.T. eye, ear, nose, and throat.

-eer. Indicates: **1.** One who works with or is concerned with; for example, **auctioneer, rocketeer. 2.** One who makes or composes; for example, **profiteer, balladeer.** [Old French *-ier,* from Latin *-ārius,* -ARY.]

e'er (âr) *adv. Poetic.* Ever.

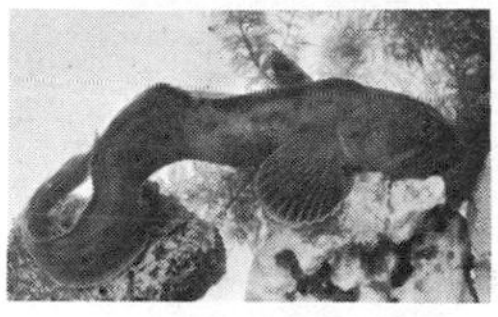

eelpout
Zoarces anguillaris

ee·rie (îr′ē) *adj.* **-rier, -riest.** Also **ee·ry. 1. a.** Inspiring fear or dread without being openly threatening; peculiarly unsettling; weird. **b.** Supernatural in aspect or character; uncanny; mysterious. **2.** *Archaic.* Frightened or intimidated by superstition. —See Synonyms at **weird.** [Middle English *eri,* fearful, cowardly, Old English *earg,* cowardly, timid, from Common Germanic *arg-* (unattested).]

Ees·ti. The Estonian name for **Estonia.**

E·fa·te (ā-fä′tē). An island, 200 square miles in area, of the New Hebrides, in the southwestern Pacific Ocean. It is the site of the capital, Vila.

eff, ef (ĕf) *n.* The letter *f.*

eff. efficiency.

ef·fa·ble (ĕf′ə-bəl) *adj. Archaic.* Capable of being expressed in words. [Latin *effābilis,* from *effārī,* to speak out : *ex-,* out + *fārī,* to speak (see **bhā-**[2] in Appendix*).]

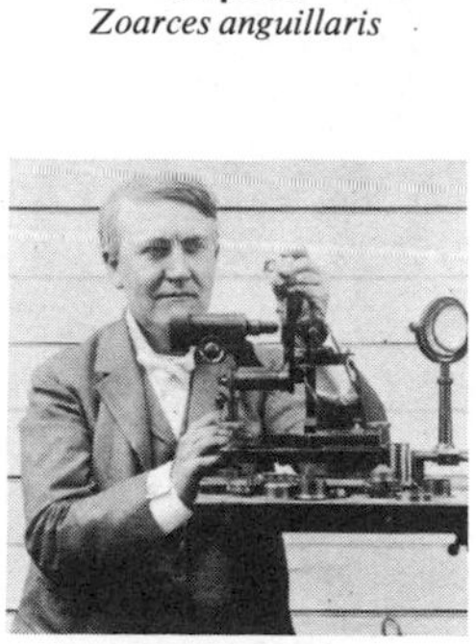

Thomas Alva Edison
Photographed in his laboratory in West Orange, New Jersey, in 1893

ef·face (ĭ-fās′) *tr.v.* **-faced, -facing, -faces. 1.** To rub or wipe out; obliterate; erase. **2.** To make faded or indistinct as if by rubbing out: *"five years' absence had done nothing to efface the people's memory of his firmness"* (Allan Moorehead). **3.** To conduct (oneself) inconspicuously or humbly: *"When the two women went out together, Anna deliberately effaced herself and played to the dramatic Molly."* (Doris Lessing). —See Synonyms at **erase.** [Old French *effacer,* "to remove the face" : *ef-,* out, from Latin *ex-* + *face,* FACE.] —**ef·face′a·ble** *adj.* —**ef·face′ment** *n.* —**ef·fac′er** *n.*

ef·fect (ĭ-fĕkt′) *n.* **1.** Something brought about by a cause or agent; result: *"Fortunately in England, at any rate, education produces no effect whatsoever."* (Oscar Wilde). **2.** The way in which something acts upon or influences an object: *the effect of a drug on the nervous system.* **3.** The final or comprehensive result; an outcome. **4.** The power or capacity to achieve the desired result; efficacy; influence. **5.** The condition of being in full force or execution; being; realization: *come into effect tomorrow.* **6. a.** An artistic technique or element that produces a specific impression or supports a general design or intention. Often used in the plural with regard to audiovisual techniques: *The effectiveness of this animated cartoon depends on special effects.* **b.** The impression produced by an artifice or manner of presentation: *She cries just for effect.* **7.** The basic meaning or tendency of something said or written; purport: *He said he approved, or something to that effect.* —**in effect. 1.** In fact; actually. **2.** In essence; virtually. **3.** In active force; in operation. —**take effect.** To become operative; gain active force. —*tr.v.* **effected, -fecting, -fects. 1.** To produce as a result; cause to occur; bring about: *"If he is taught to fear and tremble, enough has been effected."* (De Quincey). **2.** To execute; make: *"im-*

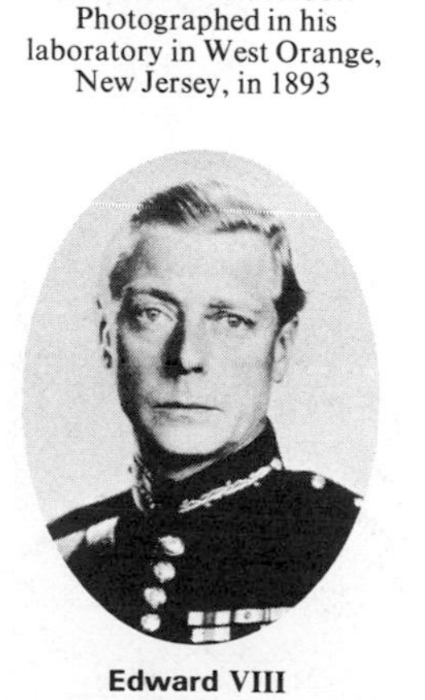

Edward VIII

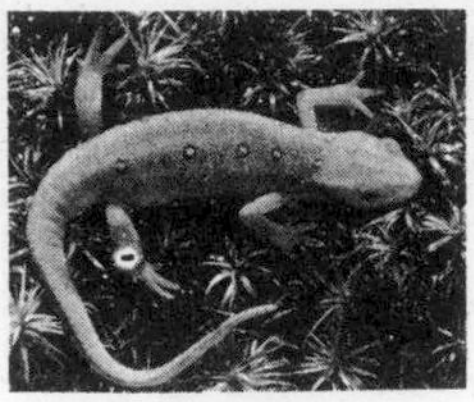

eft
Diemictylus viridescens

portant change of ancient custom can only be effected by Act of Parliament" (Winston Churchill). —See Synonyms at **perform**. —See Usage note at **affect**. [Middle English, from Old French, from Latin *effectus*, past participle of *efficere*, to accomplish, perform, work out : *ex-*, out + *facere*, to do (see **dhē-¹** in Appendix*).] —**ef·fect'er** *n.* —**ef·fect'i·ble** *adj.*

Synonyms: *effect, consequence, result, outcome, upshot, sequel, consummation.* These nouns denote occurrences, situations, or conditions that are traceable to something antecedent. An *effect* is that which is produced by the action of an agent or cause and follows it in time, either immediately or shortly. A *consequence* also follows the action of an agent and is traceable to it, but the relationship between them is less sharply definable and less immediate than that between a cause and its effect. A *result* is an effect, or the last in a series of effects, that follows a cause and that is viewed as the end product of the operation of the cause. An *outcome* is a result that has clear definition; the term is even stronger than *result* in implying finality, and may suggest operation of a cause over a relatively long period. An *upshot* is a decisive result, often arrived at abruptly or in the nature of a climax. A *sequel* is a logical but relatively long-range consequence of an antecedent action. *Consummation* refers to the final, decisive stage of an action directed toward achievement of a specific end.

ef·fec·tive (ĭ-fĕk'tĭv) *adj.* **1.** Having the intended or expected effect; serving the purpose. **2.** Producing or adapted to produce the desired impression or response; striking: *an effective speech.* **3.** Operative; in effect: *The law is effective immediately.* **4.** Prepared for use or action in warfare: *We have eight effective troop divisions.* —*n.* **1.** A member of a military force or a piece of equipment that is ready for action. **2.** The total number of men prepared and available for military action. —**ef·fec'tive·ly** *adv.* —**ef·fec'tive·ness** *n.*

Synonyms: *effective, efficacious, effectual, efficient.* These adjectives mean having the capacity to produce an effect or a result. The first three are often interchangeable. Where they are distinguished, *effective* and *effectual* may imply proven capacity for doing the job in question and *efficacious* may suggest having the potential to do it. *Efficient* implies proven capability based on productiveness in operation, and especially stresses ability to perform well and economically. Inherent in such performance are the absence of waste of time, energy, or material and the demonstration of skillful management of means and technical expertness suggested by the term "know-how."

ef·fec·tor (ĭ-fĕk'tər) *n.* An organ at the end of a nerve that activates either gland secretion or muscular contraction.

ef·fects (ĭ-fĕkts') *pl.n.* Physical belongings; goods; properties. See Synonyms at **asset**.

ef·fec·tu·al (ĭ-fĕk'cho͞o-əl) *adj.* **1.** Producing, or sufficient to produce, a desired effect; fully adequate: *"Aurelian was a stern but effectual handler of both would-be barbarian invaders and domestic rebels"* (Stringfellow Barr). **2.** Valid or legally binding. —See Synonyms at **effective**. —**ef·fec'tu·al'i·ty, ef·fec'tu·al·ness** *n.* —**ef·fec'tu·al·ly** *adv.*

ef·fec·tu·ate (ĭ-fĕk'cho͞o-āt') *tr.v.* **-ated, -ating, -ates.** To cause; to make happen; bring about; effect; accomplish. [Medieval Latin *effectuāre*, from Latin *efficere*, to accomplish, EFFECT.] —**ef·fec'tu·a'tion** *n.*

ef·fem·i·na·cy (ĭ-fĕm'ə-nə-sē) *n.* The quality or condition of being effeminate: *"Their pursuit of truth and beauty . . . has not led them into effeminacy or decadence"* (Christopher Morris).

ef·fem·i·nate (ĭ-fĕm'ə-nĭt) *adj.* **1.** Having the qualities associated with women; not characteristic of or befitting a man; unmanly. **2.** Characterized by softness, weakness, or lack of force; not dynamic or vigorous. —See Synonyms at **feminine**. [Middle English *effeminat*, from Latin *effēminātus*, past participle of *effēmināre*, "to make a woman out of," to make effeminate : *ex-*, out of + *fēmina*, woman (see **dhēi-** in Appendix*).] —**ef·fem'i·nate·ly** *adv.* —**ef·fem'i·nate·ness** *n.*

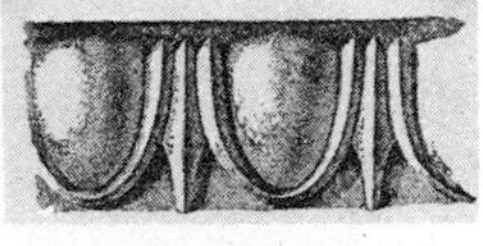

egg-and-dart

ef·fen·di (ĭ-fĕn'dē) *n.* Sir. Used as a title of respect in Turkey. [Turkish *efendi*, "master," from Medieval Greek *aphentē*, vocative of *aphentēs*, lord, master, from Greek *authentēs*. See **authentic**.]

ef·fer·ent (ĕf'ər-ənt) *adj.* Directed away from a central organ or section; especially, carrying impulses from the central nervous system to an effector. Compare **afferent**. —*n.* An efferent organ or part. [French *efférent*, from Latin *efferēns*, present participle of *efferre*, to carry away : *ex-*, away from + *ferre*, to carry (see **bher-¹** in Appendix*).]

ef·fer·vesce (ĕf'ər-vĕs') *intr.v.* **-vesced, -vescing, -vesces.** **1.** To emit small bubbles of gas, as a carbonated or fermenting liquid. **2.** To appear and come out of a liquid in bubbles; bubble forth. **3.** To show high spirits; be lively or vivacious. [Latin *effervēscere*, to boil over : *ex-*, completely + *fervēscere*, to start to boil, from *fervēre*, to be hot, boil (see **bhreu-²** in Appendix*).]

ef·fer·ves·cence (ĕf'ər-vĕs'əns) *n.* Also **ef·fer·ves·cen·cy** (-ən-sē). **1.** The act of bubbling up out of liquid; bubbling. **2.** Bubbles of gas formed in liquid. **3.** Sparkling high spirits; spontaneous liveliness; vivacity.

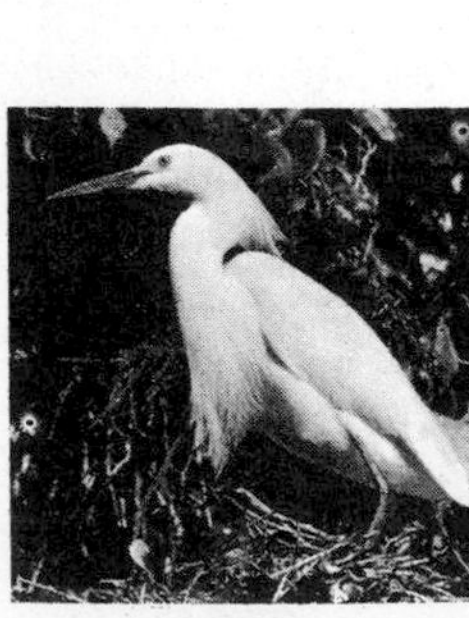

egret
Leucophoyx thula
Snowy egret

ef·fer·ves·cent (ĕf'ər-vĕs'ənt) *adj.* **1.** Emitting a profusion of small bubbles of gas; bubbling. **2.** Produced by effervescence: *effervescent gas.* **3.** High-spirited; ebullient; vivacious.

ef·fete (ĭ-fēt') *adj.* **1.** Unable to produce further offspring or fruit; barren. **2.** Exhausted of vitality, force, or effectiveness; depleted of vigor; worn-out; spent: *effete romanticism.* **3.** Characterized by unproductive self-indulgence, self-absorption, or decadence: *effete manners.* [Latin *effētus*, worn out by childbearing : *ex-*, out + *fētus*, childbearing, offspring (see **dhēi-** in Appendix*).] —**ef·fete'ly** *adv.* —**ef·fete'ness** *n.*

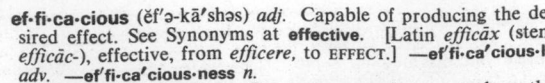

ef·fi·ca·cious (ĕf'ə-kā'shəs) *adj.* Capable of producing the desired effect. See Synonyms at **effective**. [Latin *efficāx* (stem *efficāc-*), effective, from *efficere*, to EFFECT.] —**ef'fi·ca'cious·ly** *adv.* —**ef'fi·ca'cious·ness** *n.*

ef·fi·ca·cy (ĕf'ə-kə-sē) *n.* Power or capacity to produce the desired effect; ability to achieve results; effectiveness: *"he was a firm believer in the efficacy of prayer"* (Samuel Butler). [Latin *efficācia*, from *efficāx*, EFFICACIOUS.]

ef·fi·cien·cy (ĭ-fĭsh'ən-sē) *n., pl.* **-cies.** **1. a.** The quality or property of being efficient. **b.** The degree to which this quality is exercised. **2.** *Abbr.* **eff.** The ratio of the effective or useful output to the total input in any system; especially, the ratio of the energy delivered by a machine to the energy supplied for its operation. **3.** *Informal.* A furnished apartment with cooking facilities for short-term rental, especially one in a resort area. In this sense, also called "efficiency apartment."

efficiency expert. An expert in the analysis and improvement of industrial efficiency and productivity.

ef·fi·cient (ĭ-fĭsh'ənt) *adj.* **1.** Having a direct effect; causative. **2. a.** Acting or producing effectively with a minimum of waste, expense, or unnecessary effort. **b.** Exhibiting a high ratio of output to input. —See Synonyms at **effective**. [Middle English, from Old French, from Latin *efficiēns*, present participle of *efficere*, to EFFECT.] —**ef·fi'cient·ly** *adv.*

ef·fi·gy (ĕf'ə-jē) *n., pl.* **-gies.** **1.** A painted or sculptured representation of a person, as on a stone wall or monument. **2.** A crude image or dummy fashioned in the likeness of a person, often as an expression of hatred for him. —**hang** (or **burn**) **in effigy.** To hang or burn in public the image of a leader or other public figure held in contempt or derision. [Middle English *effigie*, from Latin *effigiēs*, likeness, image, from *effingere*, to form, portray : *ex-*, out of + *fingere*, fashion, shape (see **dheigh-** in Appendix*).]

ef·flo·resce (ĕf'lô-rĕs') *intr.v.* **-resced, -rescing, -resces.** **1.** To blossom; flower; bloom. **2.** *Chemistry.* **a.** To become a powder by losing water of crystallization. **b.** To become covered with a powdery deposit, as by evaporation. [Latin *efflōrēscere*, to blossom out : *ex-*, out + *flōrēscere*, inceptive of *flōrēre*, to blossom, from *flōs*, flower (see **bhel-³** in Appendix*).]

ef·flo·res·cence (ĕf'lô-rĕs'əns) *n.* **1.** A flowering or blooming forth. **2.** The culmination or fulfillment of something, as of an artistic career. **3.** *Chemistry.* **a.** The process of efflorescing. **b.** The deposit that results from this process. **c.** A growth of salt crystals on surfaces, such as wells, due to evaporation of salt-laden water. —**ef'flo·res'cent** *adj.*

ef·flu·ence (ĕf'lo͞o-əns) *n.* **1.** The act or an instance of flowing out. **2.** Something that flows out or forth; an emanation.

ef·flu·ent (ĕf'lo͞o-ənt) *adj.* Flowing out or forth. —*n.* Something that flows out or forth; especially: **a.** A stream flowing out of a lake or other body of water. **b.** An outflow of a sewer, storage tank, irrigation canal, or other channel. [Middle English, from Latin *effluēns*, present participle of *effluere*, to flow out : *ex-*, out + *fluere*, to flow (see **bhleu-** in Appendix*).]

ef·flu·vi·um (ĭ-flo͞o'vē-əm) *n., pl.* **-via** (-vē-ə) or **-ums.** **1.** An outflow or rising vapor of invisible or barely visible gas or particles. **2.** Foul-smelling vapor or fumes emanating from decaying matter. **3.** An imaginary outflow of imponderable radiation or invisible vapor; aura. [Latin, from *effluere*, to flow out. See **effluent**.] —**ef·flu'vi·al** *adj.*

ef·flux (ĕf'lŭks') *n.* Also **ef·flux·ion** (ĭ-flŭk'shən). **1.** An outward flowing; an emanating. **2.** Something that flows out or forth; an emanation. [Latin *effluxus*, past participle of *effluere*, to flow out. See **effluent**.]

ef·fort (ĕf'ərt) *n.* **1.** The use of physical or mental energy to do something; exertion. **2.** A difficult or tiring exertion of the strength or will: *It was an effort to get up.* **3.** An attempt; especially, an earnest attempt: *Make an effort to arrive promptly.* **4.** Something done or produced through exertion; achievement; creation. **5.** *Physics.* Loosely, force applied against inertia. [Old French *effort, esfort*, from *esforcier*, to force (reflexive *s'esforcier*, to exert oneself), from Vulgar Latin *exfortiāre* (unattested), to show strength : Latin *ex-*, out + *fortis*, strong (see **bhergh-²** in Appendix*).]

Synonyms: *effort, exertion, endeavor, application, strain.* These nouns refer to the expenditure of physical or mental power as a means to an end. *Effort* can apply to any such act, great or small; where it is not qualified, the term usually implies a substantial expenditure of one's time, strength, or faculties. *Exertion* always implies great expenditure, usually of physical strength. *Endeavor* suggests earnest striving to achieve a serious goal. *Application* refers to devoting one's full attention to the mastery of something; it is closely associated with diligence, persistence, and hard work. *Strain* can denote excessive effort or exertion or a by-product of this, such as tension or muscular pain.

ef·fort·less (ĕf'ərt-lĭs) *adj.* Calling for, requiring, or showing little or no effort. See Synonyms at **easy**. —**ef'fort·less·ly** *adv.*

ef·front·er·y (ĭ-frŭn'tə-rē) *n., pl.* **-ies.** Impudent and insulting boldness; presumptuous self-assertion; audacity. See Synonyms at **temerity**. [French *effronterie*, from *effronté*, shameless, from Vulgar Latin *exfrontātus* (unattested), from Late Latin *effrōns*, shameless, "barefaced" : *ex-*, out of + *frōns*, forehead (see **front**).]

ef·ful·gence (ĭ-fo͝ol'jəns) *n.* A resplendent radiance.

ef·ful·gent (ĭ-fo͝ol'jənt) *adj.* Shining forth brilliantly; resplendent: *"Till, in the western sky, the downward sun looks out effulgent"* (James Thomson). See Synonyms at **bright**. [Latin *effulgēns*, present participle of *effulgēre*, to shine out : *ex-*, out + *fulgēre*, to shine (see **bhel-¹** in Appendix*).]

ă pat/ā pay/âr care/ä father/b bib/ch church/d deed/ĕ pet/ē be/f fife/g gag/h hat/hw which/ĭ pit/ī pie/îr pier/j judge/k kick/l lid, needle/m mum/n no, sudden/ng thing/ŏ pot/ō toe/ô paw, for/oi noise/ou out/o͝o took/o͞o boot/p pop/r roar/s sauce/sh ship, dish/

ef·fuse (ĭ-fyōōs′) *adj. Botany.* Spreading out loosely on a surface. —*v.* (ĭ-fyōōz′) **effused, -fusing, -fuses.** —*tr.* To pour or spread out; disseminate. —*intr.* **1.** To spread out. **2.** To exude. **3.** To flow out. [Latin *effūsus,* past participle of *effundere,* to pour out : *ex-,* out + *fundere,* to pour (see **gheu-** in Appendix*).]

ef·fu·sion (ĭ-fyōō′zhən) *n.* **1. a.** The act or an instance of pouring forth. **b.** Something that is poured forth. **2.** An unrestrained outpouring of feeling, as in speech or writing: *"The devout effusions of sacred eloquence"* (Burke). **3.** *Pathology.* **a.** The seeping of serous, purulent, or bloody fluid into a cavity. **b.** The effused fluid.

ef·fu·sive (ĭ-fyōō′sĭv) *adj.* **1.** Irrepressibly demonstrative. **2.** Unrestrained in emotional expression; gushy. —See Synonyms at **talkative.** —**ef·fu′sive·ly** *adv.* —**ef·fu′sive·ness** *n.*

Ef·ik (ĕf′ĭk) *n.* **1.** One of a people of southern Nigeria. **2.** The Ibibio language of this people. —**Ef′ik** *adj.*

eft (ĕft) *n.* A newt; especially, the reddish-orange immature terrestrial form of a North American species, *Diemictylus viridescens.* [Middle English *evete,* Old English *efeta*†, lizard.]

eft·soons (ĕft-sōōnz′) *adv.* Also **eft·soon** (-sōōn′). *Archaic.* **1.** Soon afterward; presently. **2.** Once again. [Middle English *eftsōne,* Old English *eftsōna* : *eft,* again (see **apo-** in Appendix*) + *sōna,* SOON.]

e.g. exempli gratia.

Eg. Egypt; Egyptian.

e·gad (ĭ-găd′, ē-găd′) *interj.* By God! Used as a mild oath expressing surprise or enthusiasm. [Euphemism for *oh God* or *ah God.*]

Eg·a·di Islands (ĕg′ə-dē). Also **Ae·ga·de·an Islands** (ē-gā′dē-ən). *Italian* **I·so·le E·ga·di** (ē′zō-lā ĕ-gä′dē). Ancient name **Aeg·a·tes** (ē-gā′tēz). An island group in the Mediterranean off the western coast of Sicily; site of the defeat of the Carthaginian fleet by the Romans, marking the end of the First Punic War (241 B.C.).

e·gal·i·tar·i·an (ĭ-găl′ə-târ′ē-ən) *adj.* **1.** Advocating the doctrine of equal political, economic, and legal **rights** for all citizens. **2.** Pertaining to or arising from this doctrine. —*n.* One who holds or advances egalitarian opinions. [French *égalitaire,* from *égalité,* equality, from Latin *aequālitās,* from *aequālis,* EQUAL.] —**e·gal′i·tar′i·an·ism′** *n.*

E·ger (ā′gər). **1.** A city in northern Hungary, an ecclesiastical center known as "The Rome of Hungary." Population, 40,000. **2.** The German name for the **Ohře.**

E·ge·ri·a (ĭ-jîr′ē-ə) *n.* A woman counselor or adviser. [By allusion to *Egeria,* mythical companion and adviser of Numa, legendary second king of Rome.]

e·gest (ē-jĕst′) *tr.v.* **egested, egesting, egests.** To discharge or excrete from the body. [Latin *ēgerere* (past participle *ēgestus*), to carry out, expel : *ex-,* out + *gerere,* to carry (see **gerere** in Appendix*).] —**e·ges′tion** *n.* —**e·ges′tive** *adj.*

e·ges·ta (ē-jĕs′tə) *pl.n.* Egested matter, especially excrement. [Latin *ēgesta,* neuter plural of Latin *ēgestus.* See **egest.**]

egg[1] (ĕg) *n.* **1.** Any female gamete; an ovum. **2.** One of the female reproductive cells of various animals, consisting usually of an embryo surrounded by nutrient material with a protective covering, and often deposited externally. **3.** The oval, thin-shelled ovum of a bird, especially that of a domestic fowl, used as food. **4.** Something having the characteristically ovoid shape of a hen's egg. **5.** *Slang.* A fellow; a person: *a good egg.* —**lay an egg.** To fail completely; fall flat, especially before an audience. —**put (or have) all one's eggs in one basket.** To risk everything on a single venture, method, act, or the like. —*tr.v.* **egged, egging, eggs. 1.** To mix or cover with beaten egg, as in cooking. **2.** *Informal.* To throw eggs at. [Middle English *egge,* from Old Norse *egg.* See **awi-** in Appendix.*]

egg[2] (ĕg) *tr.v.* **egged, egging, eggs.** To encourage or incite (another) with taunts, dares, or similar verbal appeals; to urge; spur. Used with *on.* [Middle English *eggen,* Old English *eggian,* from Old Norse *eggja.* See **ak-** in Appendix.*]

egg-and-dart (ĕg′ən-därt′) *n.* A decorative molding common in classical architecture consisting of a series of egg-shaped figures alternating with dart, anchor, or tongue-shaped figures. Also called "egg-and-anchor," "egg-and-tongue."

egg·beat·er (ĕg′bē′tər) *n.* A kitchen utensil with rotating blades for beating eggs, whipping cream, or mixing together cooking ingredients.

eg·ger (ĕg′ər) *n.* Also **eg·gar.** Any of various moths of the family Lasiocampidae, of which the larvae often construct tent-like webs. [From EGG, from its egg-shaped cocoon.]

egg·head (ĕg′hĕd′) *n. Slang.* **1.** An intellectual; theorist: *"The 'egghead' label is more commonly reserved for the college teacher"* (Mary Anne Raywid). **2.** A sophisticate; highbrow. [Said to be originally applied to an intellectual who supported the Presidential candidacy (1952) of Adlai Stevenson with reference to Stevenson's baldness.]

egg·nog (ĕg′nŏg′) *n.* A drink consisting of milk and beaten eggs, commonly mixed with rum, brandy, or wine. Also called "nog." [EGG + NOG (original sense "ale").]

egg·plant (ĕg′plănt′, -plänt′) *n.* **1. a.** A tropical Old World plant, *Solanum melongena,* cultivated for its edible fruit, cooked and eaten as a vegetable. **b.** The ovoid fruit of this plant, having glossy, dark-purple skin. Also called "aubergine." **2.** Blackish purple. See **color.** [From the shape of its fruit.] —**egg′plant′** *adj.*

egg roll. A Chinese-American dish consisting of an egg pastry rolled around minced vegetables, sometimes with seafood, and fried.

eggs Ben·e·dict (bĕn′ə-dĭkt′). A dish consisting of poached eggs on slices of toast and ham, and covered with hollandaise sauce. [Invented by Commodore E.C. *Benedict* (1834–1920), American banker and yachtsman.]

egg·shell (ĕg′shĕl′) *n.* **1.** The thin, brittle, exterior covering of a bird's egg. **2.** Pale yellow to yellowish white. See **color.** —**egg′-shell** *adj.*

egg white. The albumen of an egg.

e·gis. Variant of **aegis.**

eg·lan·tine (ĕg′lən-tīn′, -tēn′) *n.* A rose, the **sweetbrier** *(see).* [Middle English *eglentyn,* from Old French *aiglantine,* from *aiglent,* from Vulgar Latin *aquilentum* (unattested), "prickly," irregularly from Latin *aculeus,* diminutive of *acus,* needle. See **ak-** in Appendix.*]

Eg·mont (ĕg′mŏnt). An extinct volcano with an elevation of 8,260 feet on North Island, New Zealand.

e·go (ē′gō, ĕg′ō) *n.* **1.** The conscious subject, as designated by the first person singular pronoun; the self: *"A human being, thus, is at all times an organism, an ego, and a member of a society"* (Erik Erikson). **2.** *Psychoanalysis.* The personality component that is conscious, most immediately controls behavior, and is most in touch with external reality. **3.** Self-love; conceit; egotism. **4.** *Christian Science.* The divine Mind, the source of eternal individuality. [New Latin, from Latin, I. See **eg** in Appendix.*]

e·go·cen·tric (ē′gō-sĕn′trĭk, ĕg′ō-) *adj.* **1.** Thinking or acting with the view that one's self is the center, object, and norm of all experience. **2.** Individualistic; selfish. **3.** *Philosophy.* Real or valid only as perceived or conceived by the individual mind. —*n.* An egocentric person. [EGO + CENTRIC.] —**e′go·cen·tric′i·ty** (-trĭs′ə-tē) *n.*

ego ideal. *Psychoanalysis.* The entirety of an individual's positive identifications with loving, reassuring parents or parental substitutes, regarded as a differentiated component of the mature ego.

e·go·ism (ē′gō-ĭz′əm, ĕg′ō-) *n.* **1.** The quality of thinking or acting with only oneself and one's own interests in mind; preoccupation with one's own welfare and advancement. **2.** *Ethics.* **a.** The doctrine that morality has its foundations in self-interest. **b.** The belief that self-interest is the just and proper motive for all human conduct. **3.** Conceit; egotism.

e·go·ist (ē′gō-ĭst, ĕg′ō-) *n.* **1.** One devoted to his own interests and advancement; an egocentric person: *"The Egoist is the Son of Himself"* (Meredith). **2.** *Ethics.* An adherent of egoism; one who acts according to self-interest on principle. **3.** An egotist. [French *égoiste,* from *égo,* from Latin *ego,* EGO.] —**e′go·is′tic, e′go·is′ti·cal** *adj.* —**e′go·is′ti·cal·ly** *adv.*

e·go·ma·ni·a (ē′gō-mā′nē-ə, -mān′yə, ĕg′ō-) *n.* Obsessive or pathological preoccupation with the self; extreme egotism. [New Latin : EGO + -MANIA.] —**e′go·ma′ni·ac′** (-nē-ăk′) *n.*

e·go·tism (ē′gə-tĭz′əm, ĕg′ə-) *n.* **1.** The tendency to speak or write of oneself excessively and boastfully. **2.** An inordinately large sense of self-importance; egoism: *"The people of this world moved about in an armor of egotism, drunk with self-gazing, athirst for compliments"* (Thornton Wilder). [EGO + -ISM (by analogy with nouns such as NEPOTISM).]

e·go·tist (ē′gə-tĭst, ĕg′ə-) *n.* **1.** A conceited, boastful person. **2.** A person who acts selfishly; an egoist. —**e′go·tis′tic, e′go·tis′ti·cal** *adj.* —**e′go·tis′ti·cal·ly** *adv.*

e·gre·gious (ĭ-grē′jəs, -jē-əs) *adj.* Outstandingly bad; blatant; outrageous. [Latin *ēgregius,* "standing out from the herd" : *ex-,* out of + *grex* (stem *greg-*), herd, flock (see **ger-**[1] in Appendix*).] —**e·gre′gious·ly** *adv.* —**e·gre′gious·ness** *n.*

e·gress (ē′grĕs) *n.* **1.** The act of going out; emergence. **2.** The path or opening by means of which one goes out; exit. **3.** The right of going out: *deny egress.* **4.** *Astronomy.* The emergence of a celestial body from eclipse or occultation. Also called "egression." [Latin *ēgressus,* from the past participle of *ēgredī,* to go out : *ex-,* out + *gradī,* to go, step (see **ghredh-** in Appendix*).]

e·gret (ē′grĭt, ĕg′rĭt) *n.* Any of several usually white wading birds of the genera *Bubulcus, Casmerodius, Leucophoyx,* and related genera, characteristically having long, showy, drooping plumes during the breeding season. [Middle English *egrete,* from Old French *aigrette,* from Old Provençal *aigreta,* from *aigron,* heron, from Germanic. See **ker-**[2] in Appendix.*]

E·gypt (ē′jĭpt). *Arabic* **Mirs** (mĭrz). Officially, United Arab Republic. *Abbr.* **Eg.** A country of northeastern Africa, 386,110 square miles in area, bounded on the north by the Mediterranean Sea and on the east by the Red Sea. Population, 29,059,000. Capital, Cairo. [Middle English *Egipte,* Old English *Egypte,* from Latin *Aegyptus,* from Greek *Aiguptos,* from Egyptian dialectal *Hikuptah,* variant of *Hat-kaptah,* one of the names for the city *Memphis.* See also **Copt, gyp** (swindler), and **gypsy.**]

E·gyp·tian (ĭ-jĭp′shən) *adj. Abbr.* **Eg. 1.** Of or pertaining to Egypt, its people, or its culture. **2.** *Obsolete.* Of or pertaining to the gypsies. —*n.* **1.** A native or citizen of Egypt. **2.** The extinct Hamitic language spoken by the ancient Egyptians. **3.** *Obsolete.* A gypsy.

Egyptian clover. A plant, **berseem** *(see).*

Egyptian corn. A grain, **durra** *(see).*

Egyptian cotton. A long-staple, fine cotton grown chiefly in northern Africa.

E·gyp·tol·o·gy (ē′jĭp-tŏl′ə-jē) *n.* The study of the culture and artifacts of the ancient Egyptian civilization. —**E·gyp′to·log′i·cal** (ĭ-jĭp′tə-lŏj′ĭ-kəl) *adj.* —**E′gyp·tol′o·gist** *n.*

eh (ā, ĕ) *interj.* **1.** Used interrogatively: *Eh? What was that?* **2.** Used in asking for confirmation or agreement: *She's a bit of a flirt, eh?*

EHF extremely high frequency.

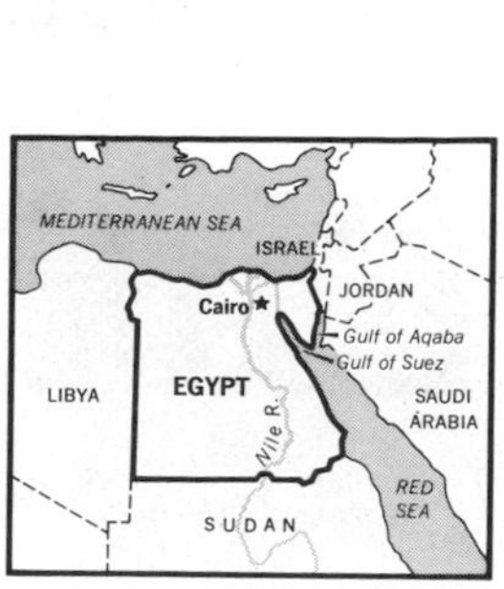

Egypt

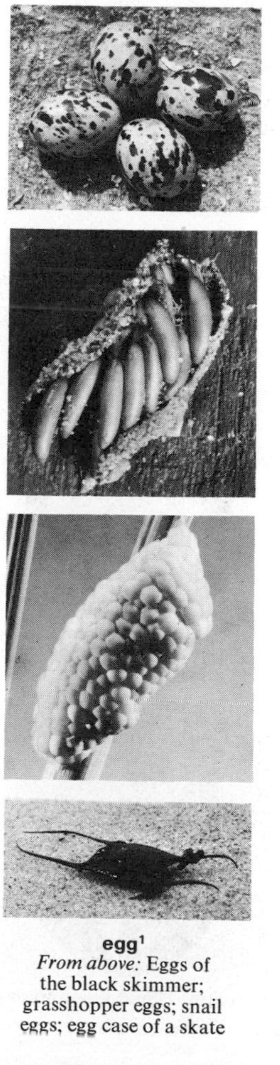

egg[1]
From above: Eggs of the black skimmer; grasshopper eggs; snail eggs; egg case of a skate

t tight/th thin, path/*th* this, bathe/ŭ cut/ûr urge/v valve/w with/y yes/z zebra, size/zh vision/ə about, item, edible, gallop, circus/ à *Fr.* ami/œ *Fr.* feu, *Ger.* schön/ü *Fr.* tu, *Ger.* über/KH *Ger.* ich, *Scot.* loch/N *Fr.* bon. ***Follows main vocabulary.** †**Of obscure origin.**

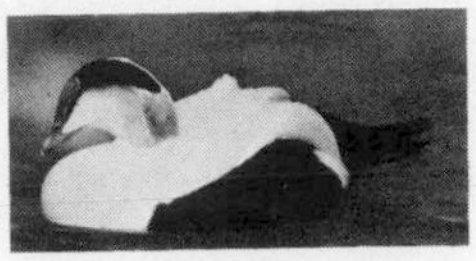

eider
Somateria mollissima
A male of the species

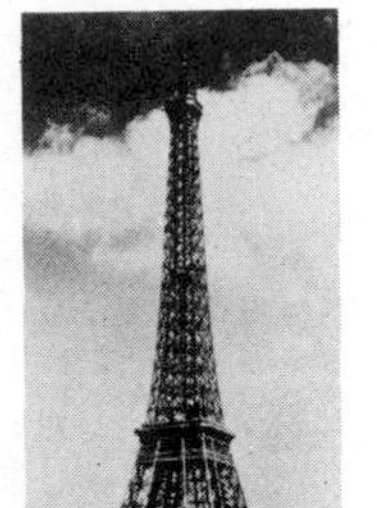

Eiffel Tower

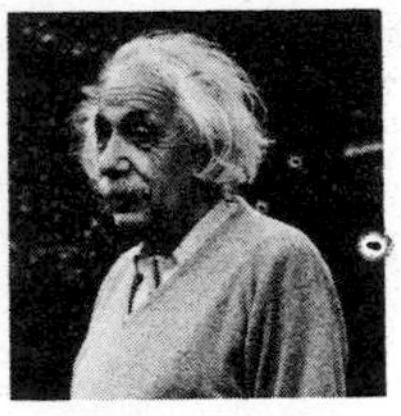

Albert Einstein

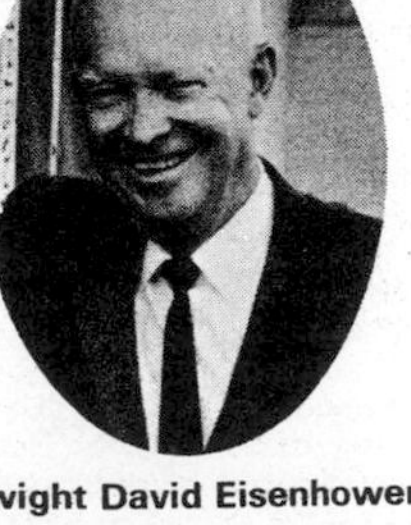

Dwight David Eisenhower

Eh·ren·burg (ā′rən-bŏŏrk′, ĕr′ən-bŏŏrg), **Ilya Grigorievich.** 1891–1967. Soviet novelist and essayist.

Ehr·lich (âr′lĭKH), **Paul.** 1854–1915. German bacteriologist; pioneer in bacteriology, immunology, and chemotherapy.

E.I. East Indian; East Indies.

Eich·mann (īKH′män′), **(Karl) Adolf.** 1906–1962. German Nazi leader; convicted and executed in Israel for war crimes.

ei·der (ī′dər) *n.* Any of several sea ducks of the genus *Somateria* and related genera, of northern regions, having soft, commercially valuable down and predominantly black and white plumage in the males. [Icelandic *ǣdhur* (genitive *ǣdhar*), from Old Norse *ǣdhr.* See **ēti-** in Appendix.*]

Ei·der (ī′dər). A river flowing about 115 miles in northern West Germany, the historic boundary between Schleswig and Holstein.

ei·der·down (ī′dər-doun′) *n.* Also **eider down.** **1.** The down of the eider duck, used as stuffing for quilts and pillows. **2.** A quilt stuffed with this down. **3.** A warm cotton fabric with a woolen nap. [Probably from German *Eiderdaune,* from Icelandic *ǣdhardúnn* : *ǣdhar,* genitive of *ǣdhur,* EIDER + *dúnn,* down, from Old Norse *dūnn,* down (see **dheu-**[1] in Appendix*).]

ei·det·ic (ī-dĕt′ĭk) *adj.* Especially vivid but unreal. Said of images experienced especially in childhood. [German *eidetisch,* from Greek *eidētikos,* relating to images or knowledge, from *eidēsis,* knowledge, from *eidos,* form, shape. See **weid-** in Appendix.*] —**ei·det′i·cal·ly** *adv.*

ei·do·lon (ī-dō′lən) *n., pl.* **-lons** or **-la** (-lə). **1.** A phantom; apparition: *"The putrid, dripping eidolon of unwholesome revelation"* (H.P. Lovecraft). **2.** An image of an ideal. [Greek *eidōlon,* from *eidos,* form, shape. See **weid-** in Appendix.*]

Eids·voll (āts′vôl). Also **Eids·vold** (-vôl). A village in southeastern Norway, site of the proclamation of the Norwegian constitution in 1814.

Ei·fel (ī′fəl). A volcanic plateau in West Germany, bounded by the Rhine River in the east, the Moselle River in the south, and the Ardennes in the west.

Eif·fel (ī′fəl; *French* ā-fĕl′), **Alexandre Gustave.** 1832–1923. French civil and aeronautic engineer.

Eif·fel Tower (ī′fəl; *French* ā-fĕl′). A tower, 984 feet high, in Paris, France, designed by A.G. Eiffel and originally erected for the Paris Exposition (1889).

Ei·ger (ī′gər). A peak, 13,036 feet high, in the Bernese Alps of south-central Switzerland.

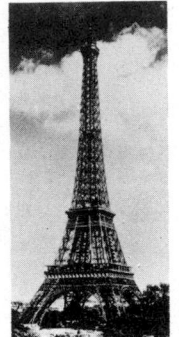

eight (āt) *n.* **1.** The cardinal number written 8 or in Roman numerals VIII. See **number.** **2.** The eighth in a set or sequence. **3.** Something having eight parts, units, or members, especially: **a.** An eight-oared racing shell. **b.** An eight-cylinder engine. **c.** An automobile having such an engine. **4.** A **figure eight** *(see).* [Middle English *eighte, eihte,* Old English *eahta.* See **oktō** in Appendix.*] —**eight** *adj. & pron.*

eight ball. A black pool ball bearing the number eight. In a popular form of pool, the player who pockets the eight ball while other object balls remain on the table loses the game. —**behind the eight ball.** *Slang.* In an unfavorable or uncomfortable position; in trouble.

eight·een (ā-tēn′) *n.* The cardinal number written 18 or in Roman numerals XVIII. See **number.** [Middle English *eightetene, eihtene,* Old English *eahtatīene* : EIGHT + -TEEN.] —**eight·een′** *adj. & pron.*

eight·een·mo (ā-tēn′mō) *n., pl.* **-mos.** A size of book, **octodecimo** *(see).* [EIGHTEEN + -MO.] —**eight·een′mo** *adj.*

eight·eenth (ā-tēnth′) *n.* **1.** The ordinal number 18 in a series. **2.** One of 18 equal parts. See **number.** [Middle English *eigh(te)tenthe, eigh(te)tethe,* Old English *eah(te)tēotha,* from *eahtatīene,* EIGHTEEN.] —**eight·eenth′** *adj. & adv.*

Eighteenth Amendment. An amendment to the Constitution of the United States, ratified in 1920 and repealed in 1933, that prohibited the manufacture and sale of alcoholic beverages. Also called "Prohibition Amendment."

eighth (ātth, āth) *n.* **1.** The ordinal number eight in a series. Also written 8th. **2.** One of eight equal parts. See **number.** [Middle English *eigh(te)the, eighthe,* Old English *eahtotha,* from *eahta,* EIGHT.] —**eighth** *adj. & adv.*

eighth note. *Music.* A note having one-eighth the time value of a whole note. Also *chiefly British* "quaver."

eight·i·eth (ā′tē-ĭth) *n.* **1.** The ordinal number 80 in a series. Also written 80th. **2.** One of 80 equal parts. See **number.** [Middle English *eigh(te)tithe,* shortened from Old English *(hund)eahtatigotha,* from *(hund)eahtatig,* EIGHTY.] —**eight′i·eth** *adj. & adv.*

eight·vo (āt′vō) *n., pl.* **-vos.** A page size and a book, **octavo** *(see).* [EIGHT + (OCTA)VO.] —**eight′vo** *adj.*

eight·y (ā′tē) *n.* The cardinal number written 80 or in Roman numerals LXXX. See **number.** [Middle English *eigh(te)ty,* Old English *(hund)eahtatig* : *hund,* HUNDRED + *eahta,* EIGHT + *-tig,* -TY (ten).] —**eight′y** *adj. & pron.*

eight·y-nin·er (ā′tē-nī′nər) *n.* One of the homesteaders who settled in Oklahoma in 1889.

Eijk·man (īk′män), **Christiaan.** 1858–1930. Dutch hygienist.

ei·kon. Variant of **icon.**

Ei·lat. The Arabic name for **Elath.**

Ei·leen (ī-lēn′). A feminine given name. [Irish *Eibhilin, Eibhlin*†.]

-ein. Variant of **-in.**

Eind·ho·ven (īnt′hō′vən). A city and major science and engineering center in the southern Netherlands. Population, 178,000.

ein·korn (īn′kôrn′) *n.* A one-seeded wheat, *Triticum monococcum,* grown in arid regions. [German *Einkorn* : *ein,* one, from Old High German *ein* (see **oino-** in Appendix*) + *Korn,* corn, grain, from Old High German *korn* (see **g̑ṛə-no-** in Appendix*).]

Ein·stein (īn′stīn′), **Albert.** 1879–1955. German-born American theoretical physicist; explained Brownian motion and the photoelectric effect, contributed to the theory of atomic spectra, and formulated the theories of special and general relativity.

Ein·stein·i·an (īn-stī′nē-ən) *adj.* Pertaining or relating to Albert Einstein or his theories.

ein·stein·i·um (īn-stī′nē-əm) *n.* *Symbol* **Es** A synthetic transuranic element first produced by neutron irradiation of uranium in a thermonuclear explosion. It has 12 known isotopes with half-lives ranging between 1.2 minutes and 270 days and mass numbers from 245 to 256. Atomic number 99. See **element.** [New Latin, after Albert EINSTEIN.]

Eir·e (âr′ə). The Gaelic name for the Republic of **Ireland.** [Irish Gaelic *Éire,* from Old Irish *Ériu.* See **Erin.**]

Ei·sen·ach (ī′zə-näKH′). A city of East Germany, in the southwest near the West German border. It is the birthplace of Johann Sebastian Bach. Population, 48,000.

Ei·sen·how·er (ī′zən-hou′ər), **Dwight David.** 1890–1969. Thirty-fourth President of the United States (1953–61).

Ei·sen·stein (ī′zən-stīn′), **Sergei Mikhailovich.** 1898–1948. Soviet director and producer of motion pictures.

Eis·le·ben (īz′lā′bən). A city of East Germany, in the southwest, 19 miles west of Halle; site of the birth and death of Martin Luther. Population, 34,000.

eis·tedd·fod (ā-stĕth′vŏd, ĕs-tĕth′-) *n., pl.* **-fods** or **eisteddfodau** (ā′stĕth-vŏd′ī, ĕs′tĕth-). An annual assembly of Welsh poets and musicians. [Welsh, "session," "a sitting" : *eistedd,* to sit, from *sedd,* seat (see **sed-**[1] in Appendix*) + *-fod,* from *bod,* to be (see **bheu-** in Appendix*).]

ei·ther (ē′thər, ī′thər) *pron.* One or the other: *Choose either. Either will serve the purpose.* —*conj.* Used before the first of two or more stated alternatives, the following alternatives being signaled by *or: Either we go now, or remain here forever.* —*adj.* **1.** One or the other; any one (of two): *Wear either coat.* **2.** One and the other; each: *She wore rings on either hand.* —*adv.* Likewise; any more so; also. Used as an intensifier following negative statements: *If you don't order a dessert, I won't either.* [Middle English *aither, either,* Old English *ǣgther, ǣghwæther.* See **kwo-** in Appendix.*]

Usage: *Either* (pronoun), as subject, takes a singular verb and related pronouns or pronominal adjectives in formal usage: *Either is capable of discharging its payload in flight.* Informally, *either* sometimes occurs with a plural verb, particularly when *either* is followed by *of* and a plural noun or pronoun in negative or interrogative constructions. In formal written usage, however, the verb is invariably singular: *I doubt whether either of them is available. Is either of them available?* The plural *are* is unacceptable in both examples, according to 92 per cent of the Usage Panel. As pronoun and adjective, *either* is now usually limited to constructions involving two persons or things: *Choose either* (one of two). *Either book* (of two) *is suitable.* Although *either* sometimes occurs in examples involving more than two, most grammarians consider *any* or *any one* (written as two words) preferable to *either.* Similarly, the conjunction *either,* when used in combination with *or,* is most appropriate to statements involving two alternative elements. In *either . . . or* constructions, the two conjunctions properly introduce parallel elements; that is, *either* and *or* are followed by like parts of speech or by phrasing that corresponds structurally: *It is either yours or his. Either he obeys or he leaves* (not *He either obeys or he leaves*). *You may have either the ring or the bracelet* (not *You may either have* or *You either may have*). *It concludes with either a song or a recitation* (or *concludes either with a song or with a recitation*). When *either* and *or* join subjects that differ in number, grammatically, the number of the verb is determined according to the procedure that governs *neither . . . nor* constructions, as set forth in the Usage note at **neither.** —See also Usage note at **or.**

e·jac·u·late (ĭ-jăk′yə-lāt′) *v.* **-lated, -lating, -lates.** —*tr.* **1.** To eject or discharge abruptly; especially, to discharge (semen) in orgasm. **2.** To utter suddenly and passionately; exclaim. —*intr.* To emit semen. —*n.* (ĭ-jăk′yə-lĭt, -lāt′). Semen ejaculated in orgasm. [Latin *ējaculārī* : *ex-,* out + *jaculārī,* to throw, shoot, from *jaculum,* dart, from *jacere,* to throw (see **yē-** in Appendix*).] —**e·jac′u·la′tor** (-lā′tər) *n.*

e·jac·u·la·tion (ĭ-jăk′yə-lā′shən) *n.* **1.** The act of ejaculating. **2.** An abrupt discharge of fluid; especially, an emission of seminal fluid. **3. a.** A sudden, emphatic utterance; an exclamation. **b.** A brief, pious utterance or prayer.

e·jac·u·la·to·ry (ĭ-jăk′yə-lə-tôr′ē, -tōr′ē) *adj.* Also **e·jac·u·la·tive** (-lā′tĭv). **1.** Of or pertaining to ejaculation. **2.** Pertaining to or constituting a sudden, brief utterance; exclamatory.

e·ject (ĭ-jĕkt′) *v.* **ejected, ejecting, ejects.** —*tr.* **1.** To throw out forcefully; expel. **2.** To compel to leave; evict: *"ejected from his pulpit for overvehemence"* (Tucker Brooke). —*intr.* To make an emergency exit by ejection capsule or seat: *He ejected at 20,000 feet.* [Middle English *ejecten,* from Latin *ēicere* (past participle *ējectus*) : *ex-,* out + *jacere,* to throw (see **yē-** in Appendix*).]

Synonyms: *eject, expel, evict, dismiss, oust, throw out.* These verbs refer in various senses to removing things or persons. *Eject* applies principally to the hurling out of things or to the forcible physical removal of persons. *Expel* usually refers to permanent removal of a person from membership in a group; with reference to things, it is frequently interchangeable with *eject. Evict* generally refers to the dispossessing of persons, or putting them out of property by legal means. *Dismiss* refers to

sending persons away as a matter of routine, as a teacher dismisses pupils, or to exercise the power to discharge subordinates from service or office. *Dismiss* also can refer to putting a person or thing out of one's mind or, in law, to refusing him or it further consideration. *Oust* is applied chiefly to the removal of persons from office by means lawful or otherwise. *Throw out* refers literally to the discarding of things; with reference to persons it is sometimes used as an informal substitute for any of the foregoing terms that imply forcible removal.

e·jec·ta (ĭ-jĕk′tə) *pl.n.* Ejected matter, as that from an erupting volcano. [New Latin, from Latin *ējectus*, ejected. See **eject**.]
e·jec·tion (ĭ-jĕk′shən) *n.* 1. The act of ejecting or the condition of being ejected. 2. Ejected matter.
ejection capsule. A compartment, especially a cabin or cockpit, in an aircraft or spacecraft that can be ejected and parachuted to the ground in an emergency.
ejection seat. A seat designed to eject clear of an aircraft and parachute to the ground in an emergency.
e·ject·ment (ĭ-jĕkt′mənt) *n.* 1. The act of ejecting; eviction; dispossession. 2. An action to regain possession of real estate held by another.
e·jec·tor (ĭ-jĕk′tər) *n.* 1. A person or thing that ejects. 2. A device in a gun that ejects the empty shell after each firing.
E·ka·te·rin·burg. The former name for Sverdlovsk.
E·ka·te·ri·no·dar. The former name for Krasnodar.

ejection seat
Ejection seat of a
fighter aircraft

eland
Taurotragus oryx

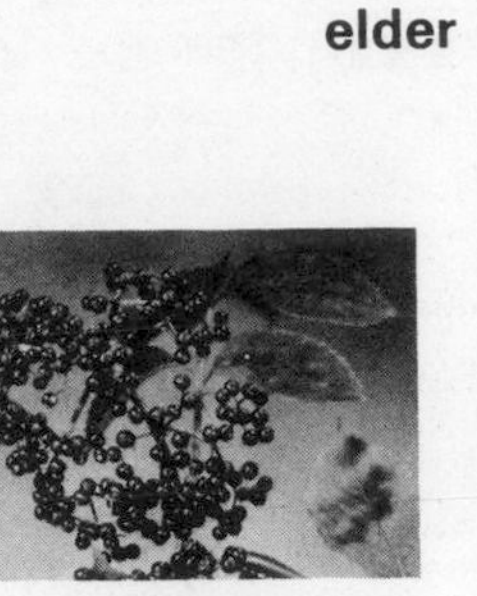

elderberry
Fruit of
Sambucus canadensis

dicate age or seniority. Typical examples are *the elder Smith; my eldest brother; the elder partner;* but *He is older than Frank.*

el·der[2] (ĕl′dər) *n.* **1.** Any of various shrubs or small trees of the genus *Sambucus,* having clusters of small white flowers and red or blackish berrylike fruit. Also called "elderberry." **2.** Any of several similar trees or shrubs. [Middle English *eller, eldre,* Old English *ellaern, ellen.* See **el-**[2] in Appendix.*]

el·der·ber·ry (ĕl′dər-bĕr′ē) *n., pl.* **-ries. 1.** The small, edible fruit of an elder, sometimes used to make wine or preserves. **2.** A shrub or tree producing such fruit; an elder.

eld·er·ly (ĕl′dər-lē) *adj.* Approaching old age; rather old. See Synonyms at **old.** —**el′der·li·ness** *n.*

elder statesman. An elderly man, usually a retired statesman, who acts as an unofficial adviser on national problems.

eld·est. Alternate superlative of **old.** See Usage note at **elder.** [Middle English *eldest,* Old English *ieldesta, eldesta.* See **al-**[3] in Appendix.*]

El Do·ra·do (ĕl də-rä′dō; *Spanish* ĕl dō-rä′thō). **1.** A legendary kingdom or city in Spanish America rich in precious metals and jewels, sought after by 16th-century explorers. **2.** Any place of fabulous wealth or opportunity; especially, California in the gold-rush days. [Spanish, "the gilded (land)" : *el,* the, from Latin *ille,* that (see **al-**[1] in Appendix*) + *dorado,* past participle of *dorar,* to gild, from Latin *dēaurāre* : *de-,* thoroughly + *aurum,* gold (see **aurum** in Appendix*).]

el·dritch (ĕl′drĭch) *adj. Archaic.* Strange or unearthly; weird. [Possibly from Old English *ælfrīce* (unattested), fairyland : *ælf,* elf (see **albho-** in Appendix*) + *rīce,* rule, kingdom (see **reg-**[1] in Appendix*).]

E·le·a (ē-lē′ə). An ancient town in southern Italy, site of the founding of the Eleatic school of philosophy.

El·ea·nor, El·i·nor (ĕl′ə-nər, -nôr′). A feminine given name. [Middle English *Eleanore,* from Old French *Elienor, Alienor,* variants of *Helene,* HELEN.]

El·ea·nor of Aquitaine (ĕl′ə-nər, -nôr′). 1122?–1204. Queen of France and later wife of Henry II of England; mother of two kings of England, Richard I and John.

El·e·at·ic (ĕl′ē-ăt′ĭk) *adj.* Of or characteristic of Elea or the school of philosophy founded there in the sixth and fifth centuries B.C. by Xenophanes and Parmenides. —*n.* **1.** A resident of Elea. **2.** An adherent of the Eleatic school, which held immutable being to be the only knowable reality and change to be the subject of mere opinion. —**El′e·at′i·cism′** *n.*

elec. electric; electrical; electrician; electricity.

el·e·cam·pane (ĕl′ĭ-kăm-pān′) *n.* A tall, coarse plant, *Inula helenium,* native to Eurasia, having rayed yellow flowers. [Middle English *elycampane,* from Old French *enule campane,* from Medieval Latin *enula campāna* : *enula,* from Latin *inula,* elecampane, from Greek *helenion* (see **wel-**[3] in Appendix*) + *campāna,* variant of Latin *campānea,* feminine of *campāneus,* of the field, from *campus,* field (see **camp**).]

e·lect (ĭ-lĕkt′) *v.* **elected, electing, elects.** —*tr.* **1.** To select by vote for an office, usually by a majority or plurality over other candidates. **2.** To choose; pick out: *elect an art course.* **3.** *Theology.* To predestine for salvation. Used in the passive voice. —*intr.* To make a choice, especially with deliberation; decide: *"Twenty-seven hardy men elected to remain with Champlain at the Habitation for the winter"* (Gerald L. Berry). —See Synonyms at **choose.** —*adj.* **1.** Chosen deliberately; singled out. **2.** Elected but not yet installed in office. Used in combination: *the governor-elect.* **3.** *Theology.* Selected by the divine will for salvation. —*n.* **1.** A person who is chosen or selected. **2.** *Theology.* Those selected by the divine will for salvation. Preceded by *the.* [Middle English *electen,* from Latin *ēligere* (past participle *ēlectus*), to pick out, select : *ex-,* out + *legere,* to gather, choose (see **leg-** in Appendix*).]

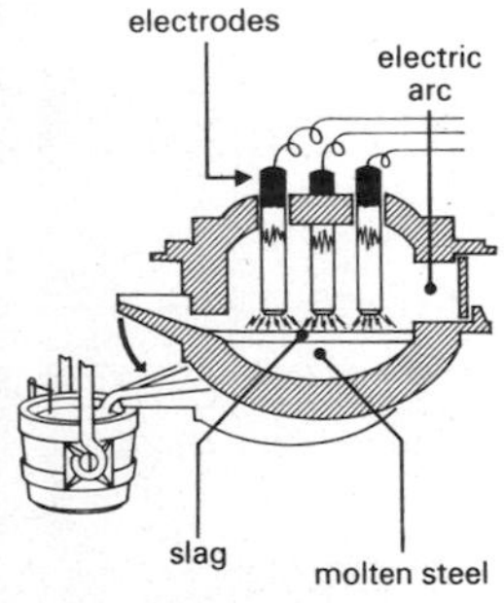
electrodes
electric arc
slag
molten steel

electric furnace

e·lec·tion (ĭ-lĕk′shən) *n.* **1.** The act or power of choosing. **2. a.** The act or process of choosing by vote among candidates to fill an office or position. **b.** The fact of being so chosen. **3.** *Theology.* Predestined salvation, especially as conceived by Calvinists. —See Synonyms at **choice.**

e·lec·tion·eer (ĭ-lĕk′shə-nîr′) *intr.v.* **-eered, -eering, -eers.** To work actively for a particular candidate or political party, as by canvassing.

e·lec·tive (ĭ-lĕk′tĭv) *adj.* **1.** Of or pertaining to a selection by vote. **2.** Filled or obtained by election: *elective office.* **3.** Having the power or authority to elect; electoral. **4.** Capable of being chosen; optional. —*n.* An optional, rather than prerequisite or obligatory, course or class in an academic curriculum. —**e·lec′tive·ly** *adv.*

e·lec·tor (ĭ-lĕk′tər) *n.* **1.** A person who elects; a qualified voter. **2.** A member of the Electoral College of the United States. **3.** *Usually capital* **E.** One of the German princes in the Holy Roman Empire entitled to elect the emperor.

e·lec·tor·al (ĭ-lĕk′tər-əl) *adj.* **1.** Of, pertaining to, or composed of electors. **2.** Having the power or duty to elect.

Electoral College. A popularly elected body of electors chosen by the States and the District of Columbia to elect the President and Vice President of the United States.

e·lec·tor·ate (ĭ-lĕk′tər-ĭt) *n.* **1.** The body of qualified voters. **2.** A district or division of voters. **3.** The dignity or territory of an Elector of the Holy Roman Empire.

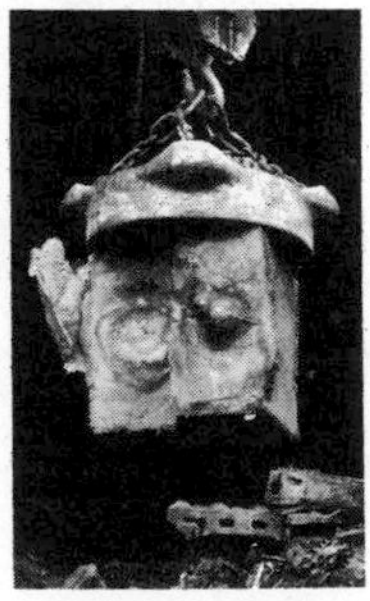

electromagnet
Industrial electromagnet lifting scrap iron

E·lec·tra[1] (ĭ-lĕk′trə). Also **E·lek·tra.** *Greek Mythology.* A daughter of Clytemnestra and Agamemnon. With her brother Orestes she avenged the murder of Agamemnon by killing their mother and her lover, Aegisthus.

E·lec·tra[2] (ĭ-lĕk′trə). Also **E·lek·tra.** *Greek Mythology.* One of the **Pleiades** *(see).* [Latin *Ēlectra,* from Greek *Ēlektra,* shining, bright. See **wlek** in Appendix.*]

E·lec·tra[3] (ĭ-lĕk′trə) *n.* A star in the constellation Pleiades. [After *Electra,* daughter of Atlas.]

Electra complex. *Psychoanalysis.* Unconscious libidinal feelings for the father generally manifesting itself first in girls between the ages of three and five. Compare **Oedipus complex.**

e·lec·tret (ĭ-lĕk′trĭt) *n.* A solid dielectric that exhibits persistent dielectric polarization. [ELECTR(ICITY) + (MAGN)ET.]

e·lec·tric (ĭ-lĕk′trĭk) *adj.* Also **e·lec·tri·cal** (-trĭ-kəl). *Abbr.* **elec. 1.** Of, pertaining to, producing, derived from, produced, powered, or operated by electricity. **2. a.** Emotionally exciting; thrilling. **b.** Exceptionally tense; charged with emotion: *"In 1916 and 1917, on the eve of war, the atmosphere . . . was electric with dissent"* (Matthew Josephson). —*n. Rare.* An electrically powered machine, especially a vehicle or conveyance. [New Latin *electricus,* "like amber," because amber produces sparks when rubbed, from Latin *ēlectrum,* amber, from Greek *ēlektron.* See **wlek** in Appendix.*] —**e·lec′tri·cal·ly** *adv.*

electrical engineering. *Abbr.* **E.E.** The scientific technology of electricity; especially, the design and application of circuitry and equipment for power generation and distribution, machine control, and communications. —**electrical engineer.**

electric chair. 1. A chair used to restrain and electrocute an individual sentenced to death. **2.** Execution by means of electrocution. **3.** The sentence of death by electrocution.

electric charge. *Electricity.* **Charge** *(see).*

electric current. *Electricity.* **Current** *(see).*

electric displacement. The product of electric intensity and permittivity. Also called "electric flux density."

electric eel. A long, eellike freshwater fish, *Electrophorus electricus,* of northern South America, having organs capable of producing a powerful electric discharge.

electric eye. A **photoelectric cell** *(see),* especially when used as a sensor for an automatic switch.

electric field. A region of space characterized by the existence of a detectable electric intensity at every point.

electric flux. The integral over a designated surface of the component of electric displacement normal to the surface.

electric flux density. Electric displacement *(see).*

electric furnace. An industrial or laboratory furnace heated by an electric arc, electric induction, or electric resistance.

electric guitar. A guitar that transmits tones to an amplifier by means of an electronic pickup placed under the strings.

e·lec·tri·cian (ĭ-lĕk′trĭsh′ən) *n. Abbr.* **elec.** A person whose occupation is the installation, repair, or operation of electric equipment and circuitry.

electric intensity. The ratio of the electrostatic force exerted on a body to the charge on the body.

e·lec·tric·i·ty (ĭ-lĕk′trĭs′ə-tē, ē′lĕk-) *n. Abbr.* **elec. 1.** The class of physical phenomena arising from the existence and interactions of electric charge. **2.** The physical science of such phenomena. **3.** Electric current used or regarded as a source of power. **4.** Intense emotional excitement.

electric lamp. A lamp that uses electricity to produce light.

electric light. 1. An electric lamp. **2.** Light produced electrically.

electric moment. The **dipole moment** *(see)* of an electric dipole.

electric motor. A motor powered by electricity.

Electric Peak. The highest point (11,155 feet) of the Gallatin Range, in Yellowstone National Park, southwestern Montana.

electric ray. Any of various fishes of the family Torpedinidae, having a rounded body and a pair of organs capable of producing a fairly strong electric discharge. Also called "cramp-fish," "numbfish."

e·lec·tri·fy (ĭ-lĕk′trə-fī′) *tr.v.* **-fied, -fying, -fies. 1.** To produce electric charge on or in (a conductor). **2. a.** To wire or otherwise equip (a building, for example) for the use of electric power. **b.** To provide with electric power. **3.** To thrill, startle greatly, or shock. [ELECTRI(C) + -FY.] —**e·lec′tri·fi′a·ble** *adj.* —**e·lec′tri·fi·ca′tion** *n.* —**e·lec′tri·fi′er** *n.*

electro–, electr–. Indicates: **1.** Electric; for example, **electromagnet, electrode. 2.** Electrically; for example, **electrocute. 3.** Electrolysis; for example, **electrolyte.** [New Latin, from Latin *ēlectrum,* amber, from Greek *ēlektron.* See **wlek** in Appendix.*]

e·lec·tro·a·cous·tics (ĭ-lĕk′trō-ə-kōō′stĭks) *n.* Plural in form, used with a singular verb. The science of the interaction or interconversion of electric and acoustic phenomena. —**e·lec′tro·a·cous′tic** *adj.* —**e·lec′tro·a·cous′tic·al·ly** *adv.*

e·lec·tro·a·nal·y·sis (ĭ-lĕk′trō-ə-năl′ə-sĭs) *n., pl.* **-ses** (-sēz′). Chemical analysis using electrolytic techniques. —**e·lec′tro·an′a·lyt′ic** (-trō-ăn′ə-lĭt′ĭk), **e·lec′tro·an·a·lyt′i·cal** *adj.*

e·lec·tro·car·di·o·gram (ĭ-lĕk′trō-kär′dē-ə-grăm′) *n. Abbr.* **EKG** The curve traced by an electrocardiograph, used to diagnose heart disease.

e·lec·tro·car·di·o·graph (ĭ-lĕk′trō-kär′dē-ə-grăf′, -gräf′) *n. Abbr.* **EKG** An instrument used to record electric potentials associated with the electric currents that traverse the heart. —**e·lec′tro·car′di·og′ra·phy** (-kär′dē-ŏg′rə-fē) *n.*

e·lec·tro·chem·is·try (ĭ-lĕk′trō-kĕm′ĭs-trē) *n.* The science of the interaction or interconversion of electric and chemical phenomena. —**e·lec′tro·chem′i·cal** (-kĕm′ĭ-kəl) *adj.* —**e·lec′tro·chem′i·cal·ly** *adv.* —**e·lec′tro·chem′ist** *n.*

e·lec·tro·cute (ĭ-lĕk′trə-kyōōt′) *tr.v.* **-cuted, -cuting, -cutes.** To kill with electricity; especially, to execute by passing a high-voltage electric current through the body of. [ELECTRO- + (EXE)CUTE.] —**e·lec′tro·cu′tion** (-kyōō′shən) *n.*

e·lec·trode (ĭ-lĕk′trōd′) *n.* **1.** A solid electric conductor through which an electric current enters or leaves a medium such as an electrolyte, a nonmetallic solid, a molten metal, a gas, or a vacuum. **2.** Broadly, a collector or emitter of electric charge or electric-charge carriers, as in a semiconducting device. [ELEC-TR(O)- + -ODE.]

e·lec·tro·de·pos·it (ĭ-lĕk′trō-dĭ-pŏz′ĭt) *tr.v.* **-ited, -iting, -its.** To deposit (a dissolved or suspended substance) on an electrode by electrolysis. —*n.* The substance so deposited. —**e·lec′tro·dep′-o·si′tion** (-dĕp′ə-zĭsh′ən, -dē′pə-zĭsh′ən) *n.*

e·lec·tro·di·al·y·sis (ĭ-lĕk′trō-dī-ăl′ə-sĭs) *n.,* *pl.* **-ses** (-sēz′). Dialysis at a rate speeded by the application of an electric potential across the dialysis membrane, used especially to remove electrolytes from a colloidal suspension.

e·lec·tro·dy·nam·ics (ĭ-lĕk′trō-dī-năm′ĭks) *n.* Plural in form, used with a singular verb. The physics of the relationship between electric, magnetic, and mechanical phenomena. —**e·lec′tro·dy·nam′ic** *adj.*

e·lec·tro·dy·na·mom·e·ter (ĭ-lĕk′trō-dī′nə-mŏm′ə-tər) *n.* An instrument that uses the interaction of the magnetic fields of fixed and moving sets of coils to measure current, voltage, or power.

e·lec·tro·en·ceph·a·lo·gram (ĭ-lĕk′trō-ĕn-sĕf′ə-lə-grăm) *n. Abbr.* **EEG** A graphic record of the electrical activity of the brain as recorded by the electroencephalograph. Also called "encephalogram."

e·lec·tro·en·ceph·a·lo·graph (ĭ-lĕk′trō-ĕn-sĕf′ə-lə-grăf′, -grăf′) *n.* An instrument that records the electrical activity of the brain. —**e·lec·tro·en·ceph′a·lo·graph′ic** *adj.* —**e·lec′tro·en·ceph′a·log′ra·phy** (-ĕn-sĕf′ə-lŏg′rə-fē) *n.*

e·lec·tro·form (ĭ-lĕk′trə-fôrm′) *tr.v.* **-formed, -forming, -forms.** To produce or reproduce by electrodeposition in a mold. [ELECTRO- + -FORM.]

e·lec·tro·graph (ĭ-lĕk′trə-grăf′, -grăf′) *n.* **1.** Any electrically produced graph or tracing. **2.** Equipment used to produce such graphs or tracings in facsimile transmission. [ELECTRO- + -GRAPH.]

e·lec·tro·kin·et·ics (ĭ-lĕk′trō-kĭ-nĕt′ĭks) *n.* Plural in form, used with a singular verb. The electrodynamics of heating effects and of current distribution in electric networks.

e·lec·tro·lu·mi·nes·cence (ĭ-lĕk′trō-lōō′mə-nĕs′əns) *n.* **1.** The direct conversion of electric energy to light by a solid phosphor subjected to an alternating electric field. **2.** The emission of light caused by electric discharge in a gas. —**e·lec′tro·lu′mi·nes′cent** *adj.*

e·lec·trol·y·sis (ĭ-lĕk′trŏl′ə-sĭs, ē′lĕk-) *n.* **1.** Chemical change, especially decomposition, produced in an electrolyte by an electric current. **2.** Destruction of living tissue, as of hair roots, by an electric current. [New Latin : ELECTRO- + -LYSIS.]

e·lec·tro·lyte (ĭ-lĕk′trə-līt′) *n.* A substance that dissociates into ions in solution or when fused, thereby becoming electrically conducting. [ELECTRO- + -LYTE.]

e·lec·tro·lyt·ic (ĭ-lĕk′trə-lĭt′ĭk) *adj.* **1. a.** Of or pertaining to electrolysis. **b.** Produced by electrolysis. **2.** Of or pertaining to an electrolyte.

electrolytic cell. 1. A cell containing an electrolyte through which an externally generated electric current is passed by a system of electrodes in order to produce an electrochemical reaction. **2.** A cell containing an electrolyte in which an electrochemical reaction produces an electromotive force.

e·lec·tro·lyze (ĭ-lĕk′trə-līz′) *tr.v.* **-lyzed, -lyzing, -lyzes.** To decompose by electrolysis. [Back-formation from ELECTROLYSIS.]

e·lec·tro·mag·net (ĭ-lĕk′trō-măg′nĭt) *n.* A magnet consisting essentially of a soft-iron core wound with a current-carrying coil of insulated wire, the current in which produces the magnetization of the core.

e·lec·tro·mag·net·ic (ĭ-lĕk′trō-măg′nĕt′ĭk) *adj.* Of or exhibiting electromagnetism. —**e·lec′tro·mag·net′i·cal·ly** *adv.*

electromagnetic field. The field of force associated with electric charge in motion, having both electric and magnetic components and containing a definite amount of electromagnetic energy.

electromagnetic spectrum. The entire range of radiation extending in frequency approximately from 10^{23} cycles per second to 0 cycles per second (or, in corresponding wavelengths, from 10^{-13} centimeter to infinity) and including, in order of decreasing frequency, cosmic-ray photons, gamma rays, x rays, ultraviolet radiation, visible light, infrared radiation, microwaves, radio waves, heat, and electric currents.

electromagnetic unit. *Abbr.* **emu** Any of a system of units for electricity and magnetism based on a system of equations in which the permeability of free space is taken as unity and by means of which the **abampere** *(see)* is defined as the fundamental unit of current.

electromagnetic wave. A wave propagating as a periodic disturbance of the electromagnetic field and having a frequency in the electromagnetic spectrum.

e·lec·tro·mag·net·ism (ĭ-lĕk′trō-măg′nə-tĭz′əm) *n.* **1.** Magnetism arising from electric charge in motion. **2.** The physics of electricity and magnetism.

e·lec·tro·met·al·lur·gy (ĭ-lĕk′trō-mĕt′ə-lûr′jē) *n.* The use of electricity to purify metals or to reduce metallic compounds to metals. —**e·lec′tro·met′al·lur′gi·cal** (-mĕt′ə-lûr′jə-kəl) *adj.*

e·lec·trom·e·ter (ĭ-lĕk′trŏm′ə-tər) *n.* An instrument for detecting or measuring potential differences, electric charge, or, indirectly, electric current by means of mechanical forces exerted between electrically charged bodies. [ELECTRO- + -METER.]

e·lec·tro·mo·tive (ĭ-lĕk′trō-mō′tĭv) *adj.* Of, pertaining to, or producing electric current.

electromotive force. *Abbr.* **emf, EMF** The energy per unit charge that is converted reversibly from chemical, mechanical, or other forms of energy into electrical energy in a conversion device such as a battery or dynamo.

e·lec·tron (ĭ-lĕk′trŏn′) *n. Symbol* **e** A subatomic particle in the lepton family having a rest mass of 9.1066×10^{-28} gram and a unit negative electric charge of approximately 1.602×10^{-19} coulomb. See **particle.** [ELECTR(O)- + -ON.]

e·lec·tro·neg·a·tive (ĭ-lĕk′trō-nĕg′ə-tĭv) *adj.* **1.** Having a negative electric charge. **2.** Tending to attract electrons to form a chemical bond.

electron gun. An electron-emitting electrode and associated elements, especially in a cathode-ray tube, that produce a beam of accelerated electrons.

e·lec·tron·ic (ĭ-lĕk′trŏn′ĭk, ē′lĕk-) *adj.* **1.** Of or pertaining to electrons. **2.** Of, pertaining to, based on, operated by, or otherwise involving the controlled conduction of electrons or other charge carriers, especially in a vacuum, gas, or semiconducting material. **3.** Pertaining to electronics. —**e·lec′tron′i·cal·ly** *adv.*

electronic flash. A strobe light *(see).*

electronic music. Music produced entirely or in part by manipulating natural or artificial sounds with tape recorders or other electronic devices.

e·lec·tron·ics (ĭ-lĕk′trŏn′ĭks, ē′lĕk-) *n.* Plural in form, used with a singular verb. **1.** The science and technology of electronic phenomena. **2.** The commercial industry of electronic devices and systems.

electron lens. Any of various devices that use an electric or a magnetic field to focus a beam of electrons.

electron micrograph. A micrograph made by an electron microscope.

electron microscope. Any of a class of microscopes that use electrons rather than visible light to produce magnified images, especially of objects having dimensions smaller than the wavelengths of visible light, with linear magnification up to or exceeding a million (10^6).

electron multiplier. A vacuum tube in which a single electron produces a large number of secondary electrons by collision with an anode, the process generally being repeated through a number of stages to achieve great amplification.

electron optics. The science of the control of electron motion by electron lenses, in systems or under conditions analogous to those involving or affecting visible light.

electron pair. 1. Any two electrons functioning or regarded as functioning in concert; especially, two electrons shared by two atoms joined by a covalent chemical bond. **2.** The combination of an electron and a positron as produced by a high-energy photon. Also called "pair." See **pair production.**

electron tube. A sealed enclosure, either highly evacuated or containing a controlled quantity of gas, in which electrons can be made sufficiently mobile to act as the principal carriers of current between at least one pair of electrodes, often under the control of one or more additional electrodes.

electron volt. *Abbr.* **eV** A unit of energy equal to the energy acquired by an electron falling through a potential difference of one volt, approximately 1.602×10^{-19} joule. See **measurement.**

e·lec·tro·pho·re·sis (ĭ-lĕk′trō-fə-rē′sĭs) *n.* The motion of charged particles, especially colloidal particles, through a relatively stationary liquid under the influence of an applied electric field provided, in general, by immersed electrodes. Also called "cataphoresis." [New Latin : ELECTRO- + -PHORESIS.]

e·lec·troph·o·rus (ĭ-lĕk′trŏf′ər-əs, ē′lĕk-) *n., pl.* **-ori** (-ə-rī′). An apparatus for generating static electricity, consisting of a disk that is given a negative charge by friction and a metal plate that is charged by induction when in contact with the disk. [New Latin : ELECTRO- + -PHOROUS.]

e·lec·tro·plate (ĭ-lĕk′trə-plāt′) *tr.v.* **-plated, -plating, -plates.** To coat or cover with a thin layer of metal by electrodeposition.

e·lec·tro·pos·i·tive (ĭ-lĕk′trō-pŏz′ə-tĭv) *adj.* **1.** Having a positive electric charge. **2.** Tending to release electrons to form a chemical bond.

e·lec·tro·scope (ĭ-lĕk′trə-skōp′) *n.* An instrument used to detect the presence, sign, and in some configurations the magnitude of an electric charge by the mutual attraction or repulsion of metal foils or pith balls. [ELECTRO- + -SCOPE.] —**e·lec′tro·scop′ic** (-skŏp′ĭk) *adj.*

e·lec·tro·shock (ĭ-lĕk′trō-shŏk′) *n.* A form of **shock therapy** *(see)* in which an electric current is passed through the brain.

e·lec·tro·stat·ic (ĭ-lĕk′trō-stăt′ĭk) *adj.* **1. a.** Of or pertaining to stationary electric charges. **b.** Produced or caused by such charges. **2.** Of or pertaining to electrostatics. —**e·lec′tro·stat′i·cal·ly** *adv.*

electrostatic generator. Any of various devices, including the electrophorus, the Wimshurst machine, and especially the Van de Graaff generator *(see),* that generate high voltages by accumulating large quantities of electric charge.

electrostatic precipitation. The removal of particles suspended in a gas by electrostatic charging and subsequent precipitation onto a collector in a strong electric field.

e·lec·tro·stat·ics (ĭ-lĕk′trō-stăt′ĭks) *n.* Plural in form, used with a singular verb. The physics of electrostatic phenomena.

electrostatic unit. *Abbr.* **esu** Any of a system of units for electricity and magnetism based on a system of equations in which the permittivity of empty space is defined as unity and by means of which a fundamental unit of charge is defined.

e·lec·tro·ther·a·peu·tics (ĭ-lĕk′trō-thĕr′ə-pyōō′tĭks) *n.* Plural in form, used with a singular verb. Electrotherapy.

e·lec·tro·ther·a·py (ĭ-lĕk′trō-thĕr′ə-pē) *n.* Medical therapy using electric currents.

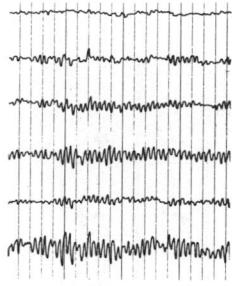

electroencephalogram

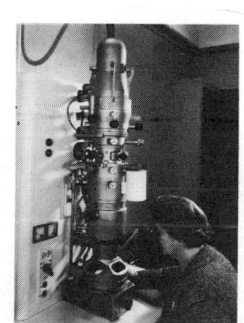

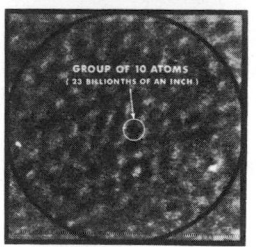

electron microscope
Above: Electron microscope
Below: Micrograph of the hexagonal cell of carbon, 23 billionths of an inch across

ă pat/ā pay/âr care/ä father/b bib/ch church/d deed/ĕ pet/ē be/f fife/g gag/h hat/hw which/ĭ pit/ī pie/îr pier/j judge/k kick/l lid, needle/m mum/n no, sudden/ng thing/ŏ pot/ō toe/ô paw, for/oi noise/ou out/ōō took/ōō boot/p pop/r roar/s sauce/sh ship, dish/
t tight/th thin, path/*th* this, bathe/ŭ cut/ûr urge/v valve/w with/y yes/z zebra, size/zh vision/ə about, item, edible, gallop, circus/ à *Fr.* ami/œ *Fr.* feu, *Ger.* schön/ü *Fr.* tu, *Ger.* über/KH *Ger.* ich, *Scot.* loch/N *Fr.* bon. ***Follows main vocabulary.** **†Of obscure origin.**

PERIODIC TABLE OF THE ELEMENTS

KEY

Atomic Number — 1
H — Symbol
Hydrogen
1.00797
Atomic Weight (or Mass Number of most stable isotope if in parentheses)

1a																	0
1 **H** Hydrogen 1.00797	2a											3a	4a	5a	6a	7a	2 **He** Helium 4.0026
3 **Li** Lithium 6.939	4 **Be** Beryllium 9.0122											5 **B** Boron 10.811	6 **C** Carbon 12.01115	7 **N** Nitrogen 14.0067	8 **O** Oxygen 15.9994	9 **F** Fluorine 18.9984	10 **Ne** Neon 20.183
11 **Na** Sodium 22.9898	12 **Mg** Magnesium 24.312	3b	4b	5b	6b	7b	8			1b	2b	13 **Al** Aluminum 26.9815	14 **Si** Silicon 28.086	15 **P** Phosphorus 30.9738	16 **S** Sulfur 32.064	17 **Cl** Chlorine 35.453	18 **Ar** Argon 39.948
19 **K** Potassium 39.102	20 **Ca** Calcium 40.08	21 **Sc** Scandium 44.956	22 **Ti** Titanium 47.90	23 **V** Vanadium 50.942	24 **Cr** Chromium 51.996	25 **Mn** Manganese 54.9380	26 **Fe** Iron 55.847	27 **Co** Cobalt 58.9332	28 **Ni** Nickel 58.71	29 **Cu** Copper 63.546	30 **Zn** Zinc 65.37	31 **Ga** Gallium 69.72	32 **Ge** Germanium 72.59	33 **As** Arsenic 74.9216	34 **Se** Selenium 78.96	35 **Br** Bromine 79.904	36 **Kr** Krypton 83.80
37 **Rb** Rubidium 85.47	38 **Sr** Strontium 87.62	39 **Y** Yttrium 88.905	40 **Zr** Zirconium 91.22	41 **Nb** Niobium 92.906	42 **Mo** Molybdenum 95.94	43 **Tc** Technetium (97)	44 **Ru** Ruthenium 101.07	45 **Rh** Rhodium 102.905	46 **Pd** Palladium 106.4	47 **Ag** Silver 107.868	48 **Cd** Cadmium 112.40	49 **In** Indium 114.82	50 **Sn** Tin 118.69	51 **Sb** Antimony 121.75	52 **Te** Tellurium 127.60	53 **I** Iodine 126.9044	54 **Xe** Xenon 131.30
55 **Cs** Cesium 132.905	56 **Ba** Barium 137.34	57–71* Lanthanides	72 **Hf** Hafnium 178.49	73 **Ta** Tantalum 180.948	74 **W** Tungsten 183.85	75 **Re** Rhenium 186.2	76 **Os** Osmium 190.2	77 **Ir** Iridium 192.2	78 **Pt** Platinum 195.09	79 **Au** Gold 196.967	80 **Hg** Mercury 200.59	81 **Tl** Thallium 204.37	82 **Pb** Lead 207.19	83 **Bi** Bismuth 208.980	84 **Po** Polonium (210)	85 **At** Astatine (210)	86 **Rn** Radon (222)
87 **Fr** Francium (223)	88 **Ra** Radium (226)	89–103** **Actinides															

*Lanthanides	57 **La** Lanthanum 138.91	58 **Ce** Cerium 140.12	59 **Pr** Praseodymium 140.907	60 **Nd** Neodymium 144.24	61 **Pm** Promethium (145)	62 **Sm** Samarium 150.35	63 **Eu** Europium 151.96	64 **Gd** Gadolinium 157.25	65 **Tb** Terbium 158.924	66 **Dy** Dysprosium 162.50	67 **Ho** Holmium 164.930	68 **Er** Erbium 167.26	69 **Tm** Thulium 168.934	70 **Yb** Ytterbium 173.04	71 **Lu** Lutetium 174.97
**Actinides	89 **Ac** Actinium (227)	90 **Th** Thorium 232.038	91 **Pa** Protactinium (231)	92 **U** Uranium 238.03	93 **Np** Neptunium (237)	94 **Pu** Plutonium (244)	95 **Am** Americium (243)	96 **Cm** Curium (247)	97 **Bk** Berkelium (247)	98 **Cf** Californium (251)	99 **Es** Einsteinium (254)	100 **Fm** Fermium (257)	101 **Md** Mendelevium (256)	102 **No** Nobelium (254)	103 **Lw** Lawrencium (257)

---

e·lec·tro·ther·mal (ĭ-lĕk′trō-thûr′məl) *adj.* Of, pertaining to, or involving both electricity and heat; especially, producing heat electrically.

e·lec·trot·o·nus (ĭ-lĕk′trŏt′ə-nəs, ē′lĕk-) *n.* The alteration in excitability and conductivity of a nerve caused by the passage of an electric current. [New Latin : ELECTRO- + TONUS.] **—e·lec′tro·ton′ic** (-trə-tŏn′ĭk) *adj.*

e·lec·tro·type (ĭ-lĕk′trə-tīp′) *n.* **1.** A duplicate metal plate used in letterpress printing, made by electroplating a lead or plastic mold of the original plate. **2.** The process of making such a plate. —*tr.v.* **electrotyped, -typing, -types.** To make an electrotype of. [ELECTRO- + TYPE.] **—e·lec′tro·typ′er** *n.* **—e·lec′tro·typ′ic** (-trō-tĭp′ĭk) *adj.*

e·lec·tro·va·lence (ĭ-lĕk′trō-vā′ləns) *n.* Also **e·lec·tro·va·len·cy** (-lən-sē). **1.** Valence characterized by the transfer of electrons from atoms of one element to atoms of another. **2.** The number of electric charges lost or gained by an atom in such a transfer. **—e·lec′tro·va′lent** *adj.*

electrovalent bond. *Chemistry.* An ionic bond (*see*).

e·lec·trum (ĭ-lĕk′trəm) *n.* An alloy of varying proportions of silver and gold, especially one used in ancient metallurgy. [Middle English *electrum*, from Latin *electrum*, amber, from Greek *ēlektron*. See **wlek** in Appendix.*]

e·lec·tu·ar·y (ĭ-lĕk′chōō-ĕr′ē) *n., pl.* **-ies.** A drug mixed with sugar and water or honey into a pasty mass suitable for oral administration. [Middle English *electuarie*, from Late Latin *ēlectuārium*, something that melts in the mouth, probably alteration of Greek *ekleikton*, from *ekleikhein*, to lick up, lick out : *ex-*, out + *leikhein*, to lick (see **leigh-** in Appendix*).]

el·ee·mos·y·nar·y (ĕl′ə-mŏs′ə-nĕr′ē, ĕl′ē-ə-) *adj.* **1.** Of or pertaining to alms or the giving of alms; charitable. **2.** Dependent upon or supported by alms. **3.** Contributed as alms; gratuitous. [Medieval Latin *eleēmosynārius*, from Late Latin *eleēmosyna*, ALMS.]

el·e·gance (ĕl′ə-gəns) *n.* Also **el·e·gan·cy** (-gən-sē) *pl.* **-cies.** **1. a.** Refinement and grace in movement, appearance, or manners. **b.** Tasteful opulence in form, decoration, or presentation. **2.** Something that is elegant.

el·e·gant (ĕl′ə-gənt) *adj.* **1.** Characterized by or exhibiting elegance. **2.** Excellent. [Old French, from Latin *ēlegāns*, choice, fine, from *ēligere*, to choose out, select : *ex-*, out + *legere*, to choose (see **leg-** in Appendix*).] **—el′e·gant·ly** *adv.*

el·e·gi·ac (ĕl′ə-jī′ək, ĭ-lē′jē-ăk′) *adj.* **1. a.** Pertaining to an elegy or elegies. **b.** Expressing sorrow; mournful. **2.** Composed in classical distichs, having the first line a dactylic hexameter and the second a pentameter. —*n.* **1.** A distich in elegiac form. **2.** *Usually plural.* Poetry written in elegiac form. [French *élégiaque*, from Late Latin *elegīacus*, from Greek *elegeiakos*, from *elegeia*, ELEGY.]

el·e·gist (ĕl′ə-jĭst) *n.* The composer of an elegy or elegies.

el·e·git (ĭ-lē′jĭt) *n. Law.* A writ of execution against a debtor by which the plaintiff is delivered of the debtor's goods or property until the debtor can settle his debt. [Latin *ēlēgit*, "he has chosen" (the first word in a phrase often used in such writs), from *ēligere*, to choose out. See **elegant**.]

el·e·gize (ĕl′ə-jīz′) *v.* **-gized, -gizing, -gizes.** —*intr.* To compose an elegy. —*tr.* To compose an elegy upon or for.

el·e·gy (ĕl′ə-jē) *n., pl.* **-gies. 1.** A poem composed in elegiac distichs. **2.** A mournful poem; especially, a poem composed to lament one who is dead. **3.** A mournful musical composition. [French *élégie*, from Latin *elegīa*, from Greek *elegeia*, from *elegos*, lament, probably from Phrygian.]

E·lek·tra. *Greek Mythology.* **1.** Variant of **Electra** (daughter of Agamemnon). **2.** Variant of **Electra** (Pleiad).

el·e·ment (ĕl′ə-mənt) *n.* **1.** A fundamental, essential, or irreducible constituent of a composite entity. **2.** A basic assumption or proposition. **3.** *Mathematics.* **a.** A member of a set. **b.** A point, line, or plane. **c.** A part of a geometric configuration, as an angle in a triangle. **d.** The generatrix of a geometric figure. **e.** Any of the terms in the rectangular array of terms that constitute a matrix or determinant. **4.** *Chemistry & Physics.* A substance composed of atoms having an identical number of protons in each nucleus. **5.** Earth, air, fire, or water regarded as a fundamental constituent of the universe in ancient and medieval cosmologies. **6.** *Plural.* The forces that collectively constitute the weather: especially, cold, wind, rain, or other inclement influences. **7.** An environment naturally occupied, preferred, or regarded as being preferred by an individual. **8.** *Plural.* The bread and wine of the Eucharist. [Middle English, from Old French, from Latin *elementum*, rudiment, first principle, possibly from Etruscan.]

el·e·men·tal (ĕl′ə-mĕnt′l) *adj.* **1.** Of, pertaining to, or being an element. **2.** Fundamental or essential; basic. **3.** Resembling a force of nature in power or effect. **—el′e·men′tal·ly** *adv.*

el·e·men·ta·ry (ĕl′ə-mĕn′tə-rē, -trē) *adj.* **1.** Fundamental, essential, or irreducible. **2.** Of, involving, or introducing the fundamental or simplest aspects of a subject: *an elementary text.* **—el′e·men·ta′ri·ly** (-tĕr′ə-lē) *adv.* **—el′e·men′ta·ri·ness** *n.*

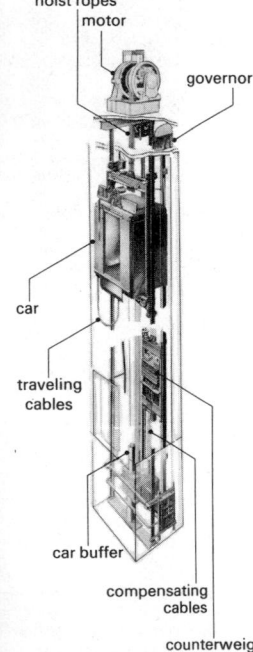

hoist ropes
motor
governor
car
traveling cables
car buffer
compensating cables
counterweight
elevator

ă pat/ā pay/âr care/ä father/b bib/ch church/d deed/ĕ pet/ē be/f fife/g gag/h hat/hw which/ĭ pit/ī pie/îr pier/j judge/k kick/l lid,
needle/m mum/n no, sudden/ng thing/ŏ pot/ō toe/ô paw, for/oi noise/ou out/ōŏ took/ōō boot/p pop/r roar/s sauce/sh ship, dish/

elementary particle. A subatomic **particle** *(see)* hypothesized or regarded as an irreducible constituent of matter. Also called "fundamental particle."

elementary school. 1. The first six to eight years of a child's formal education. **2.** A school in which this instruction is given. Also called "grade school," "grammar school."

el·e·mi (ĕl'ə-mē) *n., pl.* **-mis.** Any of various oily resins derived from certain tropical trees, especially *Canarium luzonicum,* of the Philippines, and used in making varnishes and inks. [Spanish *elemí,* from Arabic *elemī,* dialectal variant of *al-lāmī,* the elemi.]

e·len·chus (ĭ-lĕng'kəs) *n., pl.* **-chi** (-kī', -kē'). **1.** *Logic.* A refutation that disproves an opponent's conclusion or establishes a proposition contrary to his. **2.** A syllogistic refutation. [Latin, from Greek *elenkhos,* refutation, from *elenkhein,* to refute. See **lengh-** in Appendix.*]

e·lenc·tic (ĭ-lĕngk'tĭk) *adj. Logic.* Refuting by proving the opposite. Compare **deictic.** [Greek *elenktikos,* from *elenkhein,* to refute. See **elenchus.**]

el·e·phant (ĕl'ə-fənt) *n.* Either of two very large herbivorous mammals, *Elephas maximus,* of south-central Asia, or *Loxodonta africana,* of Africa, having thick, almost hairless skin, a long, flexible, prehensile trunk, upper incisors forming long, curved tusks, and, in the African species, large, fan-shaped ears. [Middle English *elifaunt, elephan,* from Old French *olifant, elifant,* from Vulgar Latin *olifantus* (unattested), from Latin *elephantus,* from Greek *elephas* (stem *elephant-*) : *el-,* akin to Hamitic *elu,* elephant + *-ephas,* akin to Egyptian *abu,* elephant, ivory (see **ivory**).]

Elephant Butte Dam. A dam across the Rio Grande in southwestern New Mexico, 1,674 feet long and over 300 feet high, forming Elephant Butte Reservoir.

el·e·phant-ear (ĕl'ə-fənt-ĭr') *n.* Also **el·e·phant's-ear** (ĕl'ə-fənts-). **1.** A plant, *Colocasia antiquorum,* native to the East Indies, having stout stems and large leaves resembling an elephant's ears. **2.** A similar or related plant, such as the taro.

elephant folio. A book or other publication of the largest size, often approximately two feet in height.

el·e·phan·ti·a·sis (ĕl'ə-fən-tī'ə-sĭs) *n.* A chronic, often extreme enlargement and hardening of the cutaneous and subcutaneous tissue, especially of the legs and the scrotum, resulting from lymphatic obstruction, and usually caused by a nematode worm, *Wuchereria bancrofti.* [Latin *elephantiăsis* : Greek *elephas,* ELEPHANT (so called because the affected skin resembles an elephant's hide) + -IASIS.]

el·e·phan·tine (ĕl'ə-făn'tĭn, -tēn', -tīn') *adj.* **1.** Of or pertaining to an elephant. **2.** Like an elephant; ponderous and heavy-footed.

elephant seal. Either of two large seals, *Mirounga angustirostris* or *M. leonina,* of Pacific coastal waters of North and South America, having a trunklike proboscis. Also called "sea elephant."

Eleusinian mysteries. The ancient religious rites of spring celebrated at Eleusis in honor of Demeter.

E·leu·sis (ĭ-lo͞o'sĭs). A town in east-central Greece ten miles east of Athens, site of the Eleusinian mysteries and birthplace of Aeschylus. **—El'eu·sin'i·an** (ĕl'yo͞o-sĭn'ē-ən) *n. & adj.*

elev. elevation.

el·e·vate (ĕl'ə-vāt') *tr.v.* **-vated, -vating, -vates. 1.** To raise to a higher place or position; lift up. **2.** To increase the amplitude, intensity, or volume of. **3.** To promote to a higher rank. **4.** To raise to a higher moral, cultural, or intellectual level: *"I know of no more encouraging fact than the . . . ability of man to elevate his life by a conscious endeavor"* (Thoreau). **5.** To lift the spirits of; elate: *"Drink itself does not seem to elevate him"* (Lamb). —See Synonyms at **lift.** [Middle English *elevaten,* from Latin *ēlevāre* : *ex-,* up + *levāre,* to lighten, raise (see **legwh-** in Appendix*).]

el·e·vat·ed (ĕl'ə-vā'tĭd) *adj.* **1.** Raised above a given level: *an elevated scaffold.* **2.** Exalted; lofty: *elevated praise.* **3.** Elated; high-spirited; joyful. —See Synonyms at **high.** *—n. Informal.* An elevated railway.

elevated railway. A railway that operates on a raised structure in order to permit passage of vehicles or pedestrians beneath it. Also called "elevated railroad" and *informal* "el."

el·e·va·tion (ĕl'ə-vā'shən) *n. Abbr.* **el., elev. 1.** The act of elevating or the condition of being elevated. **2.** An elevated place or position. **3.** The height to which something is elevated above a reference datum, especially above the **ground. 4.** Loftiness of thought or feeling. **5.** A scale drawing of the side, front, or rear of a given structure. **6.** *Geography.* **Altitude** *(see).* **7.** The technique enabling a ballet dancer to remain in midair during the execution of a movement. —See Synonyms at **height.**

el·e·va·tor (ĕl'ə-vā'tər) *n.* **1. a.** A platform or enclosure raised and lowered in a vertical shaft to transport freight or people. **b.** The enclosure or platform with its operating equipment, motor, cables, and accessories. Also *chiefly British* "lift." **2.** A mechanism used to hoist grain, usually consisting of buckets or scoops attached to a conveyor. **3.** A granary equipped with devices for hoisting and discharging grain. **4.** *Aviation.* A movable control surface, usually attached to the horizontal stabilizer, and used to make an aircraft go up or down.

e·lev·en (ĭ-lĕv'ən) *n.* The cardinal number written 11 or in Roman numerals XI. See **number.** [Middle English *ellevene, enlevene,* Old English *endleofan.* See **oino-** in Appendix.*] **—e·lev'en** *adj. & pron.*

e·lev·en·fold (ĭ-lĕv'ən-fōld') *adj.* **1.** Having 11 parts. **2.** Eleven times as many or as much. **—e·lev'en·fold'** *adv.*

e·lev·ens·es (ĭ-lĕv'ən-zəs) *pl.n. British.* A snack with beverage taken at midmorning, usually around 11 o'clock.

e·lev·enth (ĭ-lĕv'ənth) *n.* **1.** The ordinal number 11 in a series. Also written 11th. **2.** One of 11 equal parts. See **number. —e·lev'enth** *adj. & adv.*

eleventh hour. The latest possible time. [By allusion to the parable (Matthew 20:1–16) in which the workers hired at the eleventh hour received the same wages as those hired earlier.]

el·e·von (ĕl'ə-vŏn') *n.* An airplane control surface combining the functions of an elevator and an aileron. [ELEV(ATOR) + (AILER)ON.]

elf (ĕlf) *n., pl.* **elves** (ĕlvz). **1.** One of a kind of small magic-wielding people, regarded in early Germanic belief as powerful and terrifying, being sometimes beneficent and sometimes maleficent to man, but in later medieval folklore regarded as merely mischievous. **2.** A mischievous child. **3.** A dwarf. [Middle English *elf,* Old English *ælf.* See **albho-** in Appendix.*]

El Fai·yum (ăl fā-yo͞om', fī-). Also **El Fa·yum.** A city of northern Egypt, center of a region abundant in archaeological finds. Population, 118,000.

El Fa·sher (ăl fă'shər). A city of western Sudan, capital of Darfur. Population, 26,000.

elf·in (ĕl'fĭn) *adj.* **1.** Pertaining to or of the nature of an elf; elfish. **2. a.** Small and sprightly; mischievous. **b.** Fairylike. [Probably from Middle English *elvene,* genitive plural of ELF.]

elf·ish (ĕl'fĭsh) *adj.* Also **elv·ish** (ĕl'vĭsh). **1.** Of or pertaining to elves; elfin. **2.** Supernatural; weird. **3.** Prankish; mischievous. **—elf'ish·ly** *adv.* **—elf'ish·ness** *n.*

elf·lock (ĕlf'lŏk') *n.* A lock of hair tangled as if by elves.

El·gar (ĕl'gär), Sir **Edward William.** 1857–1934. British composer.

El·gin (ĕl'gĭn). Also **El·gin·shire** (ĕl'gĭn-shĭr, -shər). Former names for **Moray.**

El Gi·zeh. See **Giza.**

El·gon, Mount (ĕl'gŏn). An extinct volcano on the border between Kenya and Uganda in Africa, 14,178 feet high and having a five-mile-wide crater.

El Gre·co. See **Greco.**

El Ha·sa. See **Hasa.**

el·hi (ĕl'hī') *adj.* Elementary and high-school. [EL(EMENTARY) + HI(GH-SCHOOL).]

E·li (ē'lī). A judge of Israel; teacher of Samuel. I Samuel 3. [Hebrew *'Ēlī,* high, from *'ālāh,* he went up.]

E·li·a. Pen name of Charles **Lamb** *(see).*

E·li·as. See **Elijah.**

e·lic·it (ĭ-lĭs'ĭt) *tr.v.* **-ited, -iting, -its. 1.** To bring out; draw forth; evoke. **2.** To bring to light; call forth or educe. [Latin *ēlicere* (past participle *ēlicitus*) : *ex-,* out + *lacere,* to allure, deceive (see **delight**).] **—e·lic'i·ta'tion** *n.* **—e·lic'i·tor** (-ĭ-tər) *n.*

e·lide (ĭ-līd') *tr.v.* **elided, eliding, elides. 1.** To omit or slur over (a vowel or syllable) in pronunciation. **2. a.** To eliminate or leave out. **b.** To suppress. [Latin *ēlīdere,* to strike out : *ex-,* out + *laedere,* to strike, hurt (see **lesion**).]

el·i·gi·ble (ĕl'ə-jə-bəl) *adj.* **1.** Qualified for an office, position, or other function. **2.** Worthy of choice, acceptance, adoption, or the like. **3.** Qualified and desirable, especially for marriage: *"Algernon is an extremely, I may almost say an ostentatiously, eligible young man"* (Oscar Wilde). *—n.* An eligible person. [Middle English, from Old French, from Late Latin *ēligibilis,* from Latin *ēligere,* to choose, ELECT.] **—el'i·gi·bil'i·ty** *n.* **—el'i·gi·bly** *adv.*

E·li·jah (ĭ-lī'jə). Also **E·li·as** (ĭ-lī'əs). Hebrew prophet of the ninth century B.C.

e·lim·i·nate (ĭ-lĭm'ə-nāt') *tr.v.* **-nated, -nating, -nates. 1.** To get rid of; remove: *"The teacher may be eliminated, the student being instructed . . . entirely by machine"* (Denis Baly). **2. a.** To leave out or omit from consideration; reject. **b.** To remove from consideration by defeating, as in a contest. **3.** *Algebra.* To remove (an unknown quantity) by combining equations. **4.** *Physiology.* To excrete (waste products). [Latin *ēlīmināre,* "to drive outside of the threshold" : *ex-,* out + *līmen,* threshold (see **limen**).] **—e·lim'i·na'tion** *n.* **—e·lim'i·na'tive, e·lim'i·na·to'ry** (-nə-tôr'ē, -tōr'ē) *adj.* **—e·lim'i·na'tor** (-nā'tər) *n.*

El·i·nor. Variant of **Eleanor.**

El·i·ot (ĕl'ē-ət), **Charles William** 1834–1926. American educator and editor.

El·i·ot (ĕl'ē-ət), **George.** Pen name of Mary Ann Evans. 1819–1880. English novelist.

El·i·ot (ĕl'ē-ət), **John.** 1604–1690. English Puritan missionary to North American Indians.

El·i·ot (ĕl'ē-ət), **T(homas) S(tearns).** 1888–1965. American-born English poet, critic, and playwright.

E·lis (ē'lĭs). **1.** A plain of the northwest Peloponnesus whose original capital in Olympia was the main sanctuary of Zeus in Greece and site of the Olympic games. **2.** A town founded in 471 B.C., supplanting Olympia as capital of this region.

E·lis·a·beth·ville. The former name for **Lubumbashi.**

E·li·sha (ĭ-lī'shə). Hebrew prophet of the ninth century B.C. [Hebrew *'Ělīshā',* "God (is) salvation" : *Ēl,* God + *yesha',* salvation.]

e·li·sion (ĭ-lĭzh'ən) *n.* **1.** The action of eliding. **2.** The omission of an unstressed vowel or syllable, as in scanning a verse. [Latin *ēlīsiō,* from *ēlīdere* (past participle *ēlīsus*), ELIDE.]

E·lis·ta (ə-lĭs'tə). Formerly **Step·noi** (stĕp-noi'). A city of the southern U.S.S.R., capital of the Kalmuck A.S.S.R. Population, 22,000.

e·lite (ĭ-lēt') *n.* Also **é·lite** (ā-lēt'). **1. a.** The best or most skilled members of a given social group. Used with a plural verb: *"Poets may easily conceive of themselves as an elite entitled*

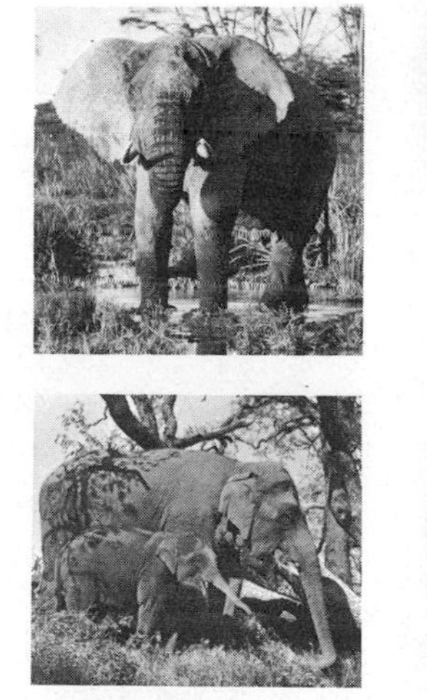

elephant
Above: Loxodonta africana
Below: Elephas maximus

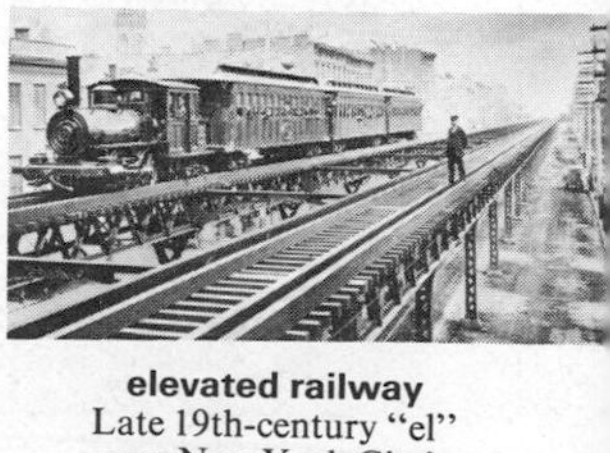

elevated railway
Late 19th-century "el" over New York City's Third Avenue, razed in the 1950's

to spurn the masses" (Christopher Morris). **b.** A narrow and powerful clique: *"Twentieth-century show business has a small and incomparable elite"* (Kenneth Tynan). **2.** A size of type on a typewriter, equal to ten points. [French *élite,* from Old French *eslite,* feminine past participle of *eslire,* to choose, from Vulgar Latin *exlegere* (unattested), variant of Latin *ēligere,* ELECT.] —**e·lite′** *adj.*

e·lix·ir (ĭ-lĭk′sər) *n.* **1.** A sweetened aromatic solution of alcohol and water, containing or serving as a vehicle for medicine. **2.** Any medicinal potion thought to have generalized curative or restorative powers. **3.** *Alchemy.* **a.** A substance believed to have the power to transmute base metals to gold. Also called "philosopher's stone." **b.** A substance believed to have the power to cure all human disorders. Also called "panacea." **c.** A substance believed to maintain life indefinitely. Also called "elixir of life." The three substances were often regarded as one. **4.** The quintessence or underlying principle of anything. [Middle English *elixir,* from Medieval Latin, from Arabic *al-iksīr,* "the elixir" : *al-,* the + *iksīr,* perhaps from Greek *xērion,* dry powder medicine, from *xēros,* dry (see **ksero-** in Appendix*).]

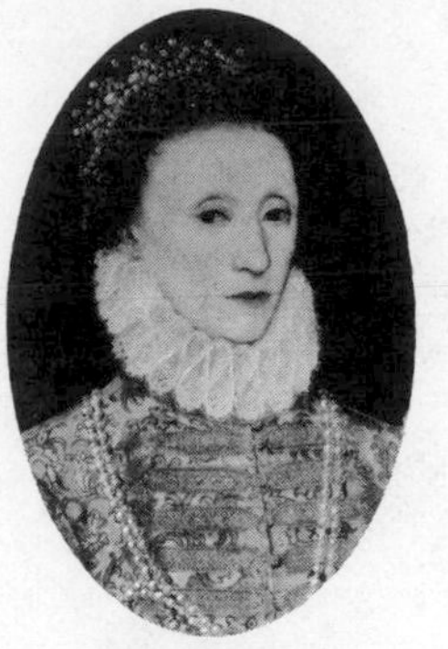

Elizabeth I
Detail from a portrait by an unknown artist, painted about 1575

E·liz·a·beth¹ (ĭ-lĭz′ə-bəth). Also **E·lis·a·beth.** A feminine given name. [Middle English, from Late Latin, from Greek *Eleisabeth, Elisabet,* from Hebrew *'Elīshebha',* probably "one to whom God is an oath" : *'Ēl,* God + *shebha',* oath, related to *shībhə'āh,* seven, and *nishəbā',* he swore (because seven was a sacred number upon which oaths were taken).]

E·liz·a·beth² (ĭ-lĭz′ə-bəth). The mother of John the Baptist and wife of Zacharias, and a kinswoman of Mary. Luke 1.

E·liz·a·beth³ (ĭ-lĭz′ə-bəth). A city in northeastern New Jersey, on Newark Bay. It was the first provincial capital of New Jersey (1668–86). Population, 108,000.

E·liz·a·beth I (ĭ-lĭz′ə-bəth). 1533–1603. Queen of England and Ireland (1558–1603).

E·liz·a·beth II (ĭ-lĭz′ə-bəth). Full name, Elizabeth Alexandra Mary. Born 1926. Queen of Great Britain and Northern Ireland (since 1952).

E·liz·a·be·than (ĭ-lĭz′ə-bē′thən, -bĕth′ən) *adj.* Pertaining to or characteristic of the reign of Elizabeth I: *Elizabethan drama.* —*n.* An Englishman of the second half of the 16th century.

Elizabethan sonnet. A **Shakespearean sonnet** *(see).*

E·liz·a·beth Islands (ĭ-lĭz′ə-bəth). An island chain of Massachusetts, extending 15 miles southwest from southwestern Cape Cod.

E·liz·a·beth River (ĭ-lĭz′ə-bəth). A short river of Virginia, entering Hampton Roads between Norfolk and Portsmouth.

El Je·zi·ra. The Arabic name for **Gezira.**

El Jib. The modern name for **Gibeon.**

elk (ĕlk) *n., pl.* **elks** or **elk.** **1.** A North American deer, the **wapiti** *(see).* **2.** A large deer, *Alces alces,* of northern regions, having large, palmate antlers, and called "moose" in North America. **3.** A light, pliant leather of horsehide or calfskin, tanned and finished to resemble elk hide. [Middle English *elke,* from Old Norse *elgr.* See **el-²** in Appendix.*]

El Kha·lil. The Arabic name for **Hebron.**

elk·hound (ĕlk′hound′) *n.* A hunting dog of an ancient breed developed in Scandinavia, having a thick, grayish coat and a tail curled up over the back. Also called "Norwegian elkhound."

Elk Mountains. A range of the Rocky Mountains in west-central Colorado. Highest elevation, 14,259 feet.

ell¹ (ĕl) *n.* A wing of a building at right angles to the main structure.

ell² (ĕl) *n.* An English linear measure equal to 45 inches, formerly used in measuring cloth. [Middle English *elle, eln,* Old English *eln,* forearm, ell (originally about the length from the elbow to tip of the middle finger). See **el-¹** in Appendix.*]

ell³. Variant of **el** (letter).

El·las. The Modern Greek name for **Greece.**

El·len (ĕl′ən). A feminine given name. [Variant of HELEN.]

Elles·mere Island (ĕlz′mîr). The largest (82,119 square miles) of the Queen Elizabeth Islands, Northwest Territories, Canada, constituting at its tip the northernmost point in North America.

El·lice Islands (ĕl′ĭs). Formerly **Lagoon Islands.** A group of atolls in the southwestern Pacific Ocean, part of the British Western Pacific High Commission Protectorate of Gilbert and Ellice Islands.

Ell·ing·ton (ĕl′ĭng-tən), **Edward Kennedy ("Duke").** Born 1899. American jazz composer, pianist, and conductor.

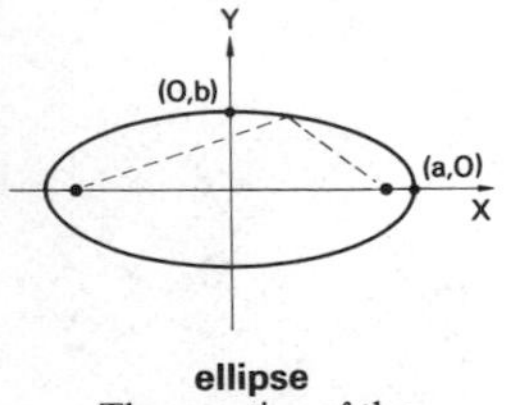

ellipse
The equation of the ellipse shown is $\frac{x^2}{a^2}+\frac{y^2}{b^2}=1$

el·lipse (ĭ-lĭps′) *n.* A plane curve formed by: **a.** A conic section taken neither parallel to an element nor parallel to the axis of the intersected cone. **b.** The locus of points the sum of the distances of each of which from two fixed points is the same constant. [Back-formation from ELLIPSIS; when an ellipse is formed from a conic section the angle made by the base of the cone and the intersecting plane is less than, or "falls short of," the angle made by the intersecting plane which forms a parabola.]

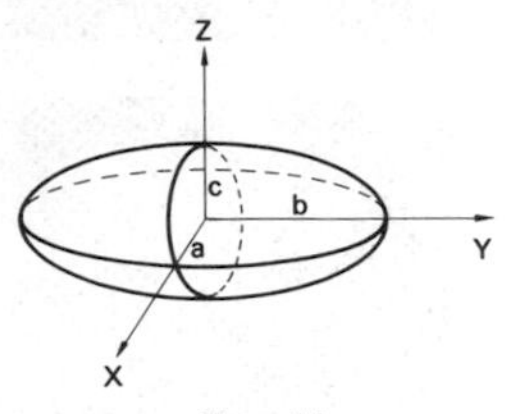

ellipsoid
The equation of the ellipsoid shown is $\frac{x^2}{a^2}+\frac{y^2}{b^2}+\frac{z^2}{c^2}=1$

el·lip·sis (ĭ-lĭp′sĭs) *n., pl.* **-ses** (-sēz′). **1.** *Grammar.* The omission of a word or words necessary for the complete syntactical construction of a sentence but not necessary for understanding it; for example, *Stop laughing* for *You stop laughing.* **2.** A mark or series of marks (. . . or ***) used in writing or printing to indicate an omission of a word or words. Also called "eclipsis." [Latin *ellīpsis,* from Greek *elleipsis,* a falling short, defect, from *elleipein,* to leave in or behind, leave out : *en-,* in + *leipein,* to leave (see **leikw-** in Appendix*).]

el·lip·soid (ĭ-lĭp′soid′) *n.* A geometric surface whose plane sections are all either ellipses or circles. [ELLIPS(E) + -OID.] —**el′lip·soi′dal** *adj.*

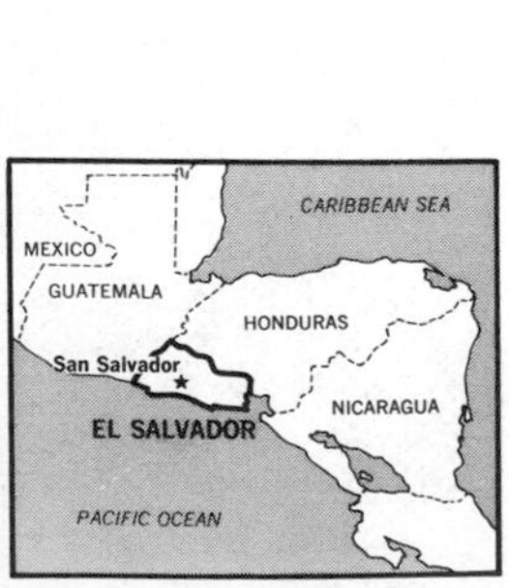

El Salvador

el·lip·tic (ĭ-lĭp′tĭk) *adj.* Also **el·lip·ti·cal** (-tĭ-kəl). **1. a.** Of, pertaining to, or having the shape of an ellipse. **b.** Resembling or having the approximate shape of an ellipse. **2.** *Grammar.* Containing or characterized by ellipsis; having a word or words omitted. [Greek *elleiptikos,* defective, from *elleipein,* to fall short. See **ellipsis.**] —**el·lip′ti·cal·ly** *adv.*

elliptic geometry. Riemannian geometry *(see).*

el·lip·tic·i·ty (ĭ-lĭp′tĭs′ə-tē) *n.* **1.** Deviation from perfect circular or spherical form toward elliptic or ellipsoidal form. **2.** The degree of such deviation.

El·lis (ĕl′ĭs), **(Henry) Havelock.** 1859–1939. British psychologist and man of letters.

El·lis Island (ĕl′ĭs). An island, about 27 acres in area, in Upper New York Bay, the former leading U.S. immigration center (1892–1943) and now part of the Statue of Liberty National Monument.

El·li·son (ĕl′ĭ-sən), **Ralph (Waldo).** Born 1914. American author.

Ells·worth (ĕlz′wûrth′), **Lincoln.** 1880–1951. American explorer of the Arctic and Antarctic.

Ells·worth Land (ĕlz′wûrth′). A high plateau of Antarctica, between Marie Byrd Land and the west coast of Weddell Sea.

El·lul. Variant of **Elul.**

elm (ĕlm) *n.* **1.** Any of various deciduous trees of the genus *Ulmus,* characteristically having arching or curving branches and widely planted as shade trees. **2.** The wood of any of these trees. [Middle English *elm,* Old English *elm.* See **el-²** in Appendix.*] —**elm′y** *adj.*

El Man·su·ra (ĕl măn-so͝or′ə). A city of southern Egypt; site of the defeat of Louis IX of France by the Mamelukes in 1250. Population, 147,000.

El·mi·ra (ĕl-mī′rə). A city of southwestern New York State; the site of Mark Twain's home and burial place. Population, 47,000.

El Mis·ti (ĕl mēs′tə). A volcano, 19,166 feet high, in southern Peru, northeast of Arequipa.

El Mor·ro National Monument (ĕl mŏr′ō). An area occupying 240 acres in western New Mexico, reserved to protect its cliff-dweller ruins and a sandstone rock bearing inscriptions by early Spanish and other later explorers.

El O·beid (ĕl ō-bād′). The capital of Kordofan Province, Republic of Sudan, and an important transportation and trade center. Population, 52,000.

el·o·cu·tion (ĕl′ə-kyo͞o′shən) *n.* **1.** The art of public speaking, emphasizing gesture and vocal production and delivery. **2.** The style or manner of public speaking. **3.** An artificial, forced manner of speaking. [Middle English *elocucion,* from Latin *ēlocūtiō,* from *ēloquī* (past participle *ēlocūtus*), to speak out : *ex-,* out + *loquī,* to speak (see **tolkw-** in Appendix*).] —**el′o·cu′tion·ar′y** *adj.* —**el′o·cu′tion·ist** *n.*

E·lo·him (ĕ-lō′hĭm, ĕl′ō-hēm′). The Hebrew name for God most frequently encountered in the Old Testament. Compare **Yahweh.** [Hebrew *'Elōhim,* plural of *'Elōah,* God, possibly enlarged from *'Ēl,* God.] —**E·lo′hism′** *n.*

E·lo·hist (ĕ-lō′hĭst) *n.* The author of the passages of the Hexateuch in which the name *Elohim* is used to designate God rather than the name *Yahweh.* —**El′o·his′tic** *adj.*

e·loign (ĭ-loin′) *tr.v.* **eloigned, eloigning, eloigns.** *Archaic.* To remove or carry away (property). [Middle English *eloynen,* from Old French *esloignier,* from Vulgar Latin *exlongāre* (unattested), variant of Late Latin *ēlongāre* : Latin *ex-,* away + *longē,* far away, distant, from *longus,* long (see **del-¹** in Appendix*).]

El·o·ise (ĕl′ō-wēz′, ĕl′ō-wēz′). A feminine given name. [French *Héloïse,* from Germanic. See **kailo-** in Appendix.*]

e·lon·gate (ĭ-lông′gāt′, ĭ-lŏng′-) *v.* **-gated, -gating, -gates.** —*tr.* To lengthen or extend. —*intr.* To grow in length. —*adj.* **1.** Lengthened; extended. **2.** Slender. [Late Latin *ēlongāre* : Latin *ex-,* out + *longus,* long (see **del-¹** in Appendix*).]

e·lon·ga·tion (ĭ-lông′gā′shən, ĭ-lŏng′-, ē′lông-, ē′lŏng-) *n.* **1.** The act of elongating or the condition of being elongated. **2.** Something that elongates; an extension.

e·lope (ĭ-lōp′) *intr.v.* **eloped, eloping, elopes.** **1.** To run away with a lover, especially with the intention of getting married, usually without parental consent. **2.** To run away; abscond. [Norman French *aloper,* legal term applied to a wife who ran away with her lover, from Middle English *alopen* (unattested), past participle of *alepen* (unattested), to run away : a- (away) + *lepen,* to run, leap, Old English *hlēopan* (see **klou-** in Appendix*).] —**e·lope′ment** *n.* —**e·lop′er** *n.*

el·o·quence (ĕl′ə-kwəns) *n.* **1.** Persuasive and fluent discourse. **2.** The ability or power to persuade with such discourse.

el·o·quent (ĕl′ə-kwənt) *adj.* **1.** Persuasive, fluent, and graceful in discourse. **2.** Vividly or movingly expressive of an emotion: *"Each face eloquent of polite misgiving"* (Evelyn Waugh). [Middle English, from Old French, from Latin *ēloquēns,* present participle of *ēloquī,* to speak out. See **elocution.**] —**el′o·quent·ly** *adv.* —**el′o·quent·ness** *n.*

El Pas·o (ĕl păs′ō). A city of Texas, in the west on the Rio Grande opposite Ciudad Juárez, Mexico. Population, 277,000.

El Sal·va·dor (ĕl săl′və-dôr′; *Spanish* ĕl säl′vä-thôr′). Officially, Republic of El Salvador. A country of Central America, in the west on the Pacific Coast. Population, 2,859,000. Capital, San Salvador.

El·sass-Lo·thring·en. The German name for **Alsace-Lorraine.**

else (ĕls) *adj.* **1.** Other; different: *somebody else.* **2.** In addition; additional; more: *Would you like anything else?* —*adv.* **1.** In a different time, place, or manner; differently: *How else could it be done?* **2.** If not; otherwise: *Be careful, or else you will make a*

ă pat/ā pay/âr care/ä father/b bib/ch church/d deed/ĕ pet/ē be/f fife/g gag/h hat/hw which/ĭ pit/ī pie/îr pier/j judge/k kick/l lid, needle/m mum/n no, sudden/ng thing/ŏ pot/ō toe/ô paw, for/oi noise/ou out/o͝o took/o͞o boot/p pop/r roar/s sauce/sh ship, dish/

mistake. [Middle English *elles,* Old English *elles,* otherwise, else. See **al-¹** in Appendix.*]

Usage: The possessive forms of combinations employing *else* are now usually written *anyone* (or *anybody*) *else's, everyone* (or *everybody*) *else's, no one* (or *nobody*) *else's, someone* (or *somebody*) *else's.* Both *who else's* (followed by a noun) and *whose else* are used, but not *whose else's: Who else's book could it have been? Whose else could it have been?*

else·where (ĕls'hwâr') *adv.* Somewhere or anywhere else.

El Sham. The Arabic name for **Syria.**

El·si·nore (ĕl'sə-nôr, -nōr). *Danish* **Hel·sing·or** (hĕl'sĭng-œr'). The scene in Denmark of Shakespeare's *Hamlet.*

e·lu·ci·date (ĭ-lōō'sə-dāt') *v.* **-dated, -dating, -dates.** —*tr.* To make clear or plain; clarify: *"an incomparable gift for elucidating the most obscure questions"* (Ernst Cassirer). —*intr.* To clarify something. —See Synonyms at **explain.** [Late Latin *ēlūcidāre* : Latin *ex-*, completely + *lūcidus,* bright, clear, from *lūcēre,* to shine (see **leuk-** in Appendix*).] —**e·lu'ci·da'tion** *n.* —**e·lu'ci·da'tive** *adj.* —**e·lu'ci·da'tor** (-dā'tər) *n.*

e·lude (ĭ-lōōd') *tr.v.* **eluded, eluding, eludes. 1.** To avoid or escape from, as by cunning, daring, or artifice; evade: *elude capture.* **2.** To escape understanding or detection by; baffle: *The meaning of her glance eluded him.* —See Synonyms at **escape.** [Latin *ēlūdere,* "to take away from (someone) at play," to cheat, deceive : *ex-*, away + *lūdere,* to play, from *lūdus,* play (see **leid-** in Appendix*).]

E·lul, El·lul (ĕ-lōōl', ĕl'ŏŏl) *n.* The 12th month of the year of the Hebrew calendar. See **calendar.** [Hebrew *'Elūl,* from Akkadian *ulūlu, elūlu,* "(time when harvest is) brought in."]

e·lu·sion (ĭ-lōō'zhən) *n. Rare.* The action of eluding or evading; escape or avoidance. [Medieval Latin *ēlūsiō,* from Latin *ēlūdere* (past participle *ēlūsus*), ELUDE.]

e·lu·sive (ĭ-lōō'sĭv) *adj.* Tending to elude grasp, perception, or mental retention: *"the edge of the sea remains an elusive and indefinable boundary"* (Rachel Carson). —**e·lu'sive·ly** *adv.* —**e·lu'sive·ness** *n.*

e·lu·tri·ate (ĭ-lōō'trē-āt') *tr.v.* **-ated, -ating, -ates.** To purify, separate, or remove (ore, for example) by washing, decanting, and settling. [Latin *ēlūtriāre,* from *ēluere,* to wash out. See **eluvium.**] —**e·lu'tri·a'tion** (ĭ-lōō'trē-ā'shən) *n.*

e·lu·vi·a·tion (ĭ-lōō'vē-ā'shən) *n.* Internal movement of soil from place to place when rainfall exceeds evaporation. [ELUVI(UM) + -ATION.]

e·lu·vi·um (ĭ-lōō'vē-əm) *n.* Residual deposits of soil, dust, and rock particles at a specific site, produced by the action of the wind. [New Latin, from Latin *ēluere,* to wash out : *ex-*, out + *lavere,* to wash (see **lou-** in Appendix*).]

el·ver (ĕl'vər) *n.* A young or immature eel. [Variant of *eelfare,* originally "the passage of young eels up a river" : EEL + FARE.]

elves. Plural of **elf.**

elv·ish. Variant of **elfish.**

E·ly (ē'lē). A town in Isle of Ely, England, 15 miles northeast of Cambridge. Population, 10,000.

E·ly, Isle of (ē'lē). An administrative county occupying 375 square miles in eastern England. Population, 89,000. County seat, March.

E·ly·sée (ā-lē-zā'). The residence of the president of France, in Paris on the Champs Elysées.

E·ly·sian (ĭ-lĭzh'ən, -ē-ən) *adj.* **1.** Pertaining to or suggestive of Elysium. **2.** Blissful; delightful.

E·ly·si·um (ĭ-lĭzh'ē-əm, ĭ-lĭz'-) *n.* **1.** *Greek Mythology.* The abode of the blessed after death. Also called "Elysian Fields." **2.** A place or condition of ideal happiness. [Latin *Ēlysium,* from Greek *Ēlusion*† *(pedion),* Elysian (fields).]

el·y·tron (ĕl'ə-trŏn') *n., pl.* **-tra** (-trə). One of the leathery or chitinous forewings of a beetle or related insect, serving to encase the thin, membranous hind wings used in flight. [New Latin, from Greek *elutron,* covering, sheath. See **wel-³** in Appendix.*] —**el'y·troid'** *adj.*

El·ze·vir (ĕl'zə-vîr') *adj.* Pertaining to the Elzevir family of 17th-century Dutch printers. —*n.* **1.** A book printed by the Elzevir family. **2.** *Printing.* A compact typeface.

em (ĕm) *n.* **1.** The letter *m.* **2.** *Printing. Abbr.* **m, M** The square of the body size of any type, used as a unit of measure; especially, of a pica M. Originally, an em was equivalent to the space occupied by the letter M in any given font.

em (əm) *pron. Informal.* Them. [Originally from Middle English *hem,* Old English *him, heom,* dative and accusative plural of *hē,* HE; but now felt as a shortened form of *them.*]

em-¹. Variant of **en-** (put into).

em-². Variant of **en-** (into).

EM enlisted man.

e·ma·ci·ate (ĭ-mā'shē-āt') *tr.v.* **-ated, -ating, -ates.** To make thin, as by starvation or illness. [Latin *ēmaciāre* : *ex-*, completely + *maciāre,* to make thin, from *macer,* thin (see **māk-** in Appendix*).] —**e·ma'ci·a'tion** *n.*

em·a·nate (ĕm'ə-nāt') *v.* **-nated, -nating, -nates.** —*intr.* To come forth or proceed, as from a source or origin; issue; originate: *"there was no light of any kind emanating from lamp or candle"* (Poe). —*tr.* To send forth; emit. [Latin *ēmānāre,* flow out : *ex-*, out + *mānāre,* to flow (see **mā-³** in Appendix*).] —**em'a·na'tive** *adj.*

em·a·na·tion (ĕm'ə-nā'shən) *n.* **1.** An act or instance of emanating; a coming or flowing forth. **2. a.** Something that emanates or issues from a source; an effluence. **b.** *Chemistry.* A gaseous product of radioactive disintegration.

e·man·ci·pate (ĭ-măn'sə-pāt') *tr.v.* **-pated, -pating, -pates. 1.** To free from oppression, bondage, or authority; liberate. **2.** To free from restraint. **3.** *Law.* To release (a child) from the control of his parents. [Latin *ēmancipāre,* "to release from slavery or tutelage" : *e-*, out of, EX- + *mancipium,* ownership, purchase, from *manceps,* purchaser (see **man-²** in Appendix*).] —**e·man'ci·pa'tive** *adj.* —**e·man'ci·pa'tor** (-pā'tər) *n.*

e·man·ci·pa·tion (ĭ-măn'sə-pā'shən) *n.* **1.** The act of emancipating. **2.** The condition of being emancipated; freedom; liberation.

Emancipation Proclamation. A proclamation issued by President Abraham Lincoln, effective January 1, 1863, declaring the freedom of all slaves in territory still at war with the Union.

e·mar·gi·nate (ĭ-mär'jə-nĭt, -nāt') *adj.* Having a notched tip, as a leaf or petal. [Latin *ēmarginātus,* past participle of *ēmargināre,* to take the edge away : *ex-*, away + *margō* (stem *margin-*), MARGIN.]

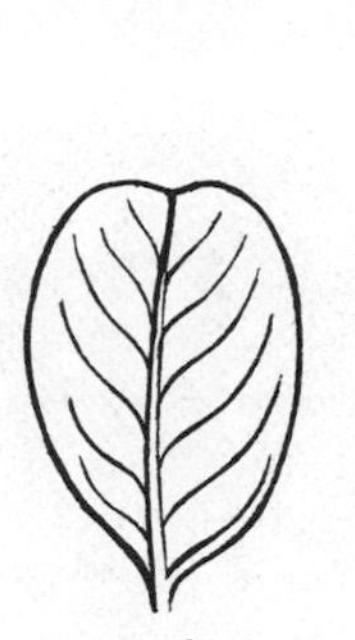

emarginate
An emarginate leaf

e·mas·cu·late (ĭ-măs'kyə-lāt') *tr.v.* **-lated, -lating, -lates. 1.** To castrate. **2.** To deprive of manly strength or vigor; make weak or effeminate. —*adj.* (ĭ-măs'kyə-lĭt, -lāt'). Emasculated; effeminate; ineffectual. [Latin *ēmasculāre* : *ex-* (removal) + *masculus,* male, manly (see **mas** in Appendix*).] —**e·mas'cu·la'tion** *n.* —**e·mas'cu·la'tive, e·mas'cu·la·to'ry** (-lə-tôr'ē, -tōr'ē) *adj.* —**e·mas'cu·la'tor** (-lā'tər) *n.*

em·balm (ĕm-bäm', ĭm-) *tr.v.* **-balmed, -balming, -balms. 1.** To prevent the decay of (a corpse) by treatment with preservatives. **2.** To preserve or cherish the memory of. **3.** To impart fragrance to. [Middle English *embaumen, embalmen,* from Old French *embaumer, embasmer* : *en-*, to put on + *basme,* BALM.] —**em·balm'er** *n.* —**em·balm'ment** *n.*

em·bank (ĕm-băngk', ĭm-) *tr.v.* **-banked, -banking, -banks.** To confine, support, or protect with a bank or banks.

em·bank·ment (ĕm-băngk'mənt, ĭm-) *n.* **1.** The act of embanking. **2.** A mound of earth or stone built to hold back water or to support a roadway.

em·bar (ĕm-bär', ĭm-) *tr.v.* **-barred, -barring, -bars. 1.** To put behind bars; imprison. **2. a.** To stop; to bar. **b.** To put under embargo. [Middle English *embarren,* from Old French *embarrer* : *en-*, in + *barre,* BAR.] —**em·bar'ment** *n.*

em·bar·go (ĕm-bär'gō, ĭm-) *n., pl.* **-goes. 1.** An order by a government prohibiting the movement of merchant ships into or out of its ports. **2.** A governmental suspension of foreign trade or of foreign trade in a particular commodity. **3.** An injunction by a state agency or common carrier against accepting specified freight for shipment. **4.** Any prohibition. —*tr.v.* **embargoed, -going, -goes.** To impose an embargo upon. [Spanish, from *embargar,* to impede, restrain, from Vulgar Latin *imbarricāre* (unattested), "to place behind bars" : Latin *in-*, in + *barra* (unattested), BAR.]

em·bark (ĕm-bärk', ĭm-) *v.* **-barked, -barking, -barks.** —*tr.* **1.** To cause to board a vessel. **2.** To enlist or invest in an enterprise. —*intr.* **1.** To go aboard a vessel, especially at the start of a journey. **2.** To set out on a venture; commence. [Old French *embarquer,* from Late Latin *imbarcāre* : *in-*, in + *barca,* BARK.] —**em'bar·ka'tion, em·bark'ment** *n.*

em·bar·rass (ĕm-băr'əs, ĭm-) *tr.v.* **-rassed, -rassing, -rasses. 1.** To cause to feel self-conscious or ill at ease; disconcert. **2.** To involve in or hamper with financial difficulties. Used in the passive. **3.** To beset with difficulties; impede. **4.** To complicate. [French *embarrasser,* from Spanish *embarazar,* from Italian *imbarazzare,* from *imbarrare,* "to put in bars," impede : *in-*, in, from Latin + *barra* (unattested), BAR.] —**em·bar'rass·ing·ly** *adv.*

em·bar·rass·ment (ĕm-băr'əs-mənt, ĭm-) *n.* **1.** The state of being embarrassed. **2.** The act or an instance of embarrassing one. **3.** Something that embarrasses. **4.** An overabundance. Used chiefly in the phrase *an embarrassment of riches.*

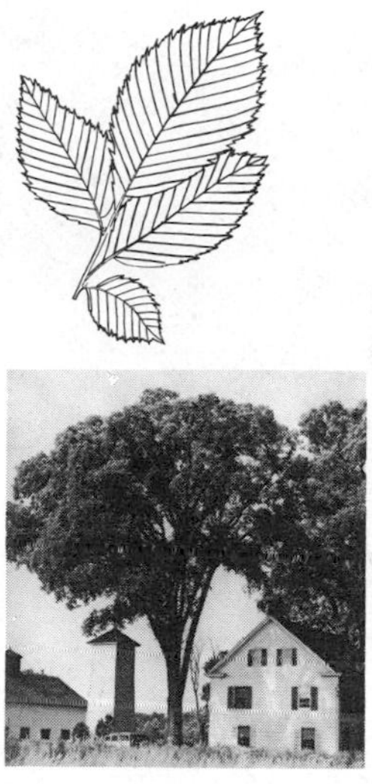

elm
Ulmus americana
American elm,
with view of leaf *(above)*

em·bas·sage (ĕm'bə-sĭj) *n. Archaic.* Embassy. [Middle English *ambassage,* perhaps variant of *ambassade,* ambassador's mission, from Old French, from Old Italian *ambasciata,* EMBASSY.]

em·bas·sy (ĕm'bə-sē) *n., pl.* **-sies. 1.** The position, function, or assignment of an ambassador. **2.** A mission to a foreign government headed by an ambassador. **3.** An ambassador and his staff. **4.** The official headquarters of an ambassador and his staff. [Middle English, from Old French *ambassee,* from Old Italian *ambasciata,* from Old Provençal *ambaissada,* from *ambaissa* (unattested), service, from Medieval Latin *ambactia.* See **ambassador.**]

em·bat·tle¹ (ĕm-băt'l, ĭm-) *tr.v.* **-tled, -tling, -tles. 1.** To prepare or array for battle. **2.** To dispose to struggle or resist. [Middle English *embatailen,* from Old French *embataillier* : *en-*, in + *batailler,* to battle, from *bataille,* BATTLE.]

em·bat·tle² (ĕm-băt'l, ĭm-) *tr.v.* **-tled, -tling, -tles.** To furnish with battlements for defense. [Middle English *embatailen* : *en-*, in + *batailen,* to build, fortify, from Old French *bataillier,* from *bataille,* battlement, BATTLE.]

em·bat·tled (ĕm-băt'əld, ĭm-) *adj. Architecture.* Crenelated.

em·bat·tle·ment (ĕm-băt'l-mənt, ĭm-) *n.* A battlement.

em·bay (ĕm-bā', ĭm-) *tr.v.* **-bayed, -baying, -bays. 1.** To put or force (a vessel) into a bay; to shelter or detain in a bay. **2.** To enclose in or as if in a bay.

em·bay·ment (ĕm-bā'mənt, ĭm-) *n.* **1.** A bay or baylike shape. **2.** The formation of a bay.

em·bed (ĕm-bĕd', ĭm-) *v.* **-bedded, -bedding, -beds.** Also **im·bed** (ĭm-). —*tr.* **1.** To fix firmly in a surrounding mass. **2.** To enclose snugly or firmly. **3.** To fix in the memory. —*intr.* To become embedded. [EM- + BED.] —**em·bed'ment** *n.*

em·bel·lish (ĕm-bĕl'ĭsh, ĭm-) *tr.v.* **-lished, -lishing, -lishes. 1.** To make more beautiful, as by ornamentation; adorn. **2.** To add fanciful or fictitious details to (a statement or narrative). [Middle English *embellisshen,* from Old French *embellir* (present

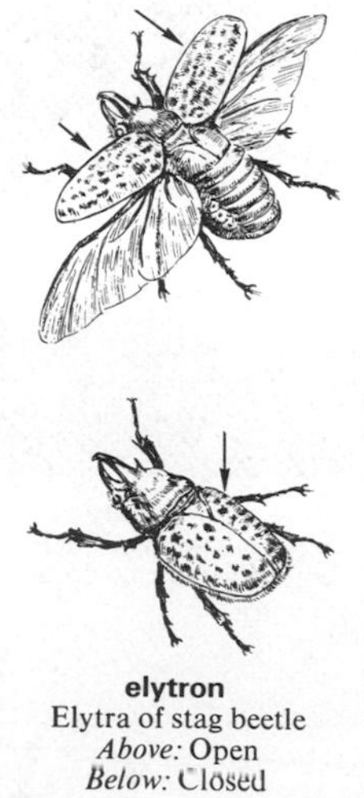

elytron
Elytra of stag beetle
Above: Open
Below: Closed

stem *embelliss-*) : *en-* (causative) + *bel*, beautiful, from Latin *bellus* (see **deu-**[2] in Appendix*).]
em·bel·lish·ment (ĕm-bĕl′ĭsh-mənt, ĭm-) *n.* **1.** An act of embellishing. **2.** The state of being embellished. **3.** That which results from embellishing, especially ornamentation.
em·ber (ĕm′bər) *n.* **1.** A small piece of live coal or wood, as in a dying fire. **2.** *Plural.* The smoldering coal or ash of a dying fire. [Middle English *embre, emere*, Old English *ǣmerge*, embers, ashes. See **eus-** in Appendix.*]

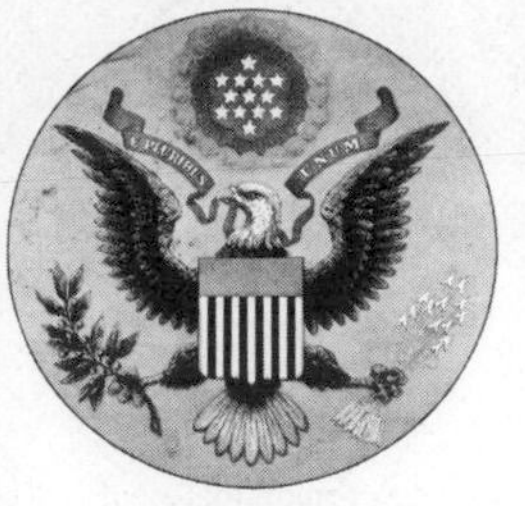

emblem
The Great Seal
of the United States

Ember days. Three days out of each calendar season reserved for prayer and fasting by some Christian churches, observed on the Wednesday, Friday, and Saturday after the first Sunday of Lent, after Whitsunday, after September 14, and after December 13. [Middle English *Ymber Dayes*, Old English *Ymbrendagas*, plural of *Ymbrendæg*, "recurring day" : *ymbryne*, "a running around," circuit : *ymbe*, around (see **ambhi** in Appendix*) + *ryne*, a running (see **er-**[1] in Appendix*) + *dæg*, DAY.]
Ember week. A week in which Ember days fall. [Middle English *Ymber Weke*, Old English *Ymbrenwuce* : *ymbryne*, a running around (see **Ember days**) + *wuce, wice*, WEEK.]
em·bez·zle (ĕm-bĕz′əl, ĭm-) *tr.v.* **-zled, -zling, -zles.** To take (money or property) for one's own use in violation of a trust. [Middle English *embesilen*, from Norman French *enbesiler* : Old French *en-* (intensive) + *besiller*†, to do away with, destroy.] **—em·bez′zle·ment** *n.* **—em·bez′zler** *n.*
em·bit·ter (ĕm-bĭt′ər, ĭm-) *tr.v.* **-tered, -tering, -ters. 1.** To make bitter. **2.** To arouse bitter feelings in; make resentful or hostile. **—em·bit′ter·ment** *n.*
em·blaze[1] (ĕm-blāz′, ĭm-) *tr.v.* **-blazed, -blazing, -blazes. 1.** To set on fire. **2.** To cause to glow or glitter.
em·blaze[2] (ĕm-blāz′, ĭm-) *tr.v.* **-blazed, -blazing, -blazes.** *Obsolete.* To emblazon.
em·bla·zon (ĕm-blā′zən, ĭm-) *tr.v.* **-zoned, -zoning, -zons. 1.** To ornament richly, especially with heraldic devices or armorial bearings: *"he unfolded the banner upon which was emblazoned the Cross"* (Maurice Collis). **2.** To make resplendent with brilliant colors. **3.** To render illustrious; exalt. [EM- + BLAZON.] **—em·bla′zon·er** *n.* **—em·bla′zon·ment** *n.*
em·bla·zon·ry (ĕm-blā′zən-rē, ĭm-) *n.* **1.** The art of emblazoning. **2.** Heraldic devices collectively.
em·blem (ĕm′bləm) *n.* **1.** An object or a depiction of an object that comes to represent something else, usually by suggesting its nature or history; a symbol linked pictorially with its referent. **2.** A distinctive badge, design, or device. **3.** An allegorical picture usually inscribed with a verse or motto presenting a moral lesson. [Middle English *emblem*, from Latin *emblēma*, inlaid work, from Greek, insertion, from *emballein*, to throw in, insert : *en-*, in + *ballein*, to throw (see **gwel-**[1] in Appendix*).]
em·blem·at·ic (ĕm′blə-măt′ĭk) *adj.* Also **em·blem·at·i·cal** (-ĭ-kəl). Of, relating to, or serving as an emblem; symbolic: *"The very patterns of Stendhal's prose seem emblematic of his political situation."* (Irving Howe). **—em′blem·at′i·cal·ly** *adv.*
em·blem·a·tize (ĕm-blĕm′ə-tīz′) *tr.v.* **-tized, -tizing, -tizes.** Also **em·blem·ize** (ĕm′blə-mīz′). To represent with an emblem.
em·ble·ments (ĕm′blə-mənts) *pl.n. Law.* The right of a tenant farmer to the crops or products of land he has cultivated. [Middle English *emblayment*, from Old French *emblaement*, land sown with wheat, from *emblaer*, to sow with wheat, from Medieval Latin *imblādāre* : *in-*, in + Frankish *blād* (unattested), produce of the land (see **bhel-**[3] in Appendix*).]
em·bod·i·er (ĕm-bŏd′ē-ər, ĭm-) *n.* One that embodies.
em·bod·i·ment (ĕm-bŏd′ĭ-mənt, ĭm-) *n.* **1.** The act of embodying or the condition of being embodied. **2.** That which embodies something: *"The flag is the embodiment, not of sentiment, but of history."* (Woodrow Wilson).
em·bod·y (ĕm-bŏd′ē, ĭm-) *tr.v.* **-bodied, -bodying, -bodies. 1.** To invest with or as if with bodily form; make corporeal; to incarnate: *"the whole purpose of Nature embodied in a woman can enslave a man"* (G.B. Shaw). **2.** To represent in bodily form; personify: *"As John Adams embodied the old style, Andrew Jackson embodied the new"* (Richard Hofstadter). **3.** To make part of a united whole.

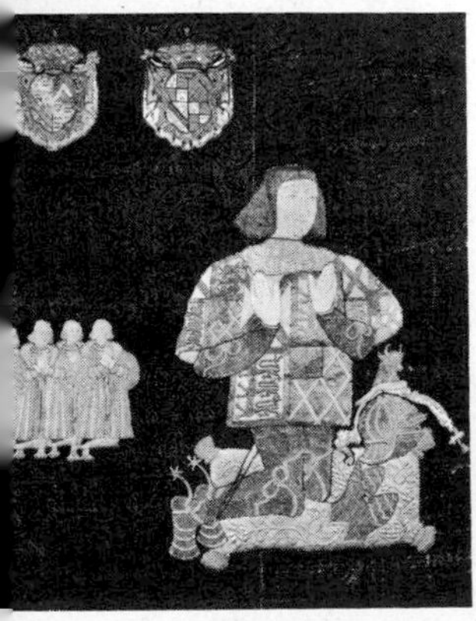
embroidery
Fifteenth-century English
embroidered altar frontal

em·bold·en (ĕm-bōl′dən, ĭm-) *tr.v.* **-ened, -ening, -ens.** To foster boldness in; encourage.
em·bo·lec·to·my (ĕm′bə-lĕk′tə-mē) *n., pl.* **-mies.** The removal of an embolus. [EMBOL(US) + -ECTOMY.]
em·bol·ic (ĕm-bŏl′ĭk, ĭm-) *adj. Pathology.* Of or relating to an embolus or an embolism.
em·bo·lism (ĕm′bə-lĭz′əm) *n.* **1.** Obstruction or occlusion of a blood vessel by an embolus. **2.** The insertion of a period of time into a calendar; intercalation. [Middle English *embolisme*, from Medieval Latin *embolismus*, from Late Latin, insertion, from Greek *embolismos*, from *emballein*, "to throw in," insert. See **emblem.**] **—em′bo·lis′mic** *adj.*
em·bo·lus (ĕm′bə-ləs) *n., pl.* **-li** (-lī′). An air bubble, detached clot, mass of bacteria, or other foreign body that occludes a blood vessel. [New Latin, from Latin, piston, from Greek *embolos*, "something inserted," stopper, from *emballein*, to throw in, insert. See **emblem.**]
em·bo·ly (ĕm′bə-lē) *n. Embryology.* Development of a gastrula from a blastula by invagination. [Greek *embolē*, insertion, entrance, from *emballein*, to insert. See **emblem.**]
em·bon·point (äN-bôN-pwăN′) *n. French.* A well-fed appearance; plumpness. Literally, in good condition.
em·bor·der (ĕm-bôr′dər, ĭm-) *tr.v.* **-dered, -dering, -ders.** To provide with a border; to edge.
em·bos·om (ĕm-bŏŏz′əm, -bōō′zəm, ĭm-) *tr.v.* **-omed, -oming, -oms. 1.** To clasp to or hold in the bosom; cherish; embrace. **2.** To envelop or enclose protectively; to shelter.
em·boss (ĕm-bôs′, -bŏs′, ĭm-) *tr.v.* **-bossed, -bossing, -bosses. 1.** To represent, mold, or carve (a design) in relief. **2.** To cover with or as if with bosses or a raised design; raise the surface of in relief: *"The whole buoy was embossed with barnacles"* (Melville). **3.** To ornament lavishly. [Middle English *embosen*, from Old French *embocer*, "to put a knob in" : *en-*, in + *boce*, BOSS (knob).] **—em·boss′er** *n.* **—em·boss′ment** *n.*
em·bou·chure (äm′bōō-shŏŏr′) *n.* **1. a.** The mouth of a river. **b.** The opening out of a valley into a prairie or plain. **2. a.** The mouthpiece of a wind instrument. **b.** The manner in which the lips and tongue are applied to such a mouthpiece. [French, from Old French *emboucher*, "to put in one's mouth" : *en-*, in + *bouche*, mouth, from Latin *bucca*, puffed-out cheek (see **beu-**[1] in Appendix*).]
em·bow (ĕm-bō′, ĭm-) *tr.v.* **-bowed, -bowing, -bows.** To curve into the shape of a bow or arch. **—em·bow′ment** *n.*
em·bowed (ĕm-bōd′, ĭm-) *adj.* **1.** Bent or curved like a bow. **2.** *Architecture.* **a.** Arched. **b.** Protruding in an outward curve so as to form a recess.
em·bow·el (ĕm-bou′əl, ĭm-) *tr.v.* **-eled** or **-elled, -eling** or **-elling, -els. 1.** To disembowel. **2.** *Obsolete.* To put in the bowels; bury deeply: *emboweled in the earth.*
em·bow·er (ĕm-bou′ər, ĭm-) *tr.v.* **-ered, -ering, -ers.** To enclose in a bower; surround, as with sheltering foliage.
em·brace[1] (ĕm-brās′, ĭm-) *v.* **-braced, -bracing, -braces.** *—tr.* **1.** To clasp or hold to one with the arms, usually as a display of affection. **2. a.** To encircle or surround. **b.** To twine around. **3.** To include within its bounds; encompass: *"Nor can conventional narrative history really embrace the complexities of cultural change."* (Crane Brinton). **4.** To take up; adopt (a cause or doctrine, for example). **5.** To avail oneself of; accept eagerly: *embrace an opportunity.* **6.** To take in with the eyes or mind. **7.** To submit to with dignity or fortitude: *embrace misfortune.* *—intr.* To clasp each other in the arms; join in an embrace. —See Synonyms at **include.** *—n.* **1.** An act of embracing; an affectionate hug. **2.** An enclosure or encirclement. **3.** Eager acceptance. [Middle English *embracen*, from Old French *embracer*, from Vulgar Latin *imbracchiāre* (unattested) : Latin *in-* + *bracchium*, arm, from Greek *brakhiōn* (see **mreghu-** in Appendix*).] **—em·brace′ment** *n.* **—em·brac′er** *n.*
em·brace[2] (ĕm-brās′, ĭm-) *tr.v.* **-braced, -bracing, -braces.** *Law.* To try to influence (a judge or jury) by corrupt means. [Back-formation from EMBRACER.] **—em·brac′er·y** *n.*
em·brac·er (ĕm-brā′sər, ĭm-) *n.* Also **em·brace·or.** *Law.* One guilty of attempting to influence a court illegally. [Middle English *embracer*, from Old French *embraseor*, instigator, from *embraser*, "to set on fire," instigate : *en-*, in + *brese*, embers (see **bhreu-**[2] in Appendix*).]
em·branch·ment (ĕm-brănch′mənt, ĕm-bränch′-, ĭm-) *n.* **1.** A branching out or off, as of a mountain range or river. **2.** A subdivision; ramification.
em·bran·gle (ĕm-brăng′gəl, ĭm-) *tr.v.* **-gled, -gling, -gles.** To entangle; embroil; confuse. [EN- + dialectal *brangle*†, to wrangle.] **—em·bran′gle·ment** *n.*
em·bra·sure (ĕm-brā′zhər, ĭm-) *n.* **1.** *Architecture.* An opening in a wall for a door or window, slanted so that its interior dimensions are larger than those of its exterior. **2.** An opening for a gun in a wall or parapet. [French, from *embraser*, to set on fire, fire a gun. See **embracer.**]
em·bro·cate (ĕm′brō-kāt′) *tr.v.* **-cated, -cating, -cates.** To moisten and rub (an afflicted part of the body) with a lotion. [Medieval Latin *embrocāre*, from Late Latin *embrocha*, lotion, from Greek *embrokhē*, from *embrekhein*, to moisten with a lotion : *en-*, in + *brekhein*, to wet (see **meregh-** in Appendix*).]
em·bro·ca·tion (ĕm′brō-kā′shən) *n.* **1.** The action of embrocating. **2.** A liniment.
em·broi·der (ĕm-broi′dər, ĭm-) *v.* **-dered, -dering, -ders.** *—tr.* **1.** To ornament (fabric) with needlework. **2.** To work (a design) into fabric with a needle and yarn. **3.** To embellish (a narrative, for example) with fictitious details or exaggerations. *—intr.* To make embroidery. [Middle English *embroderen*, from Norman French *enbrouder* : Old French *en-*, in + *brouder, brosder*, to embroider, from (unattested) Frankish *bruzdon* (see **bhar-** in Appendix*).] **—em·broi′der·er** *n.*
em·broi·der·y (ĕm-broi′də-rē, ĭm-) *n., pl.* **-ies. 1.** The art, act, or practice of embroidering. **2.** Ornamentation of fabric with needlework. **3.** A piece of embroidered fabric. **4.** Any additional or lavish ornamentation; an embellishment.
em·broil (ĕm-broil′, ĭm-) *tr.v.* **-broiled, -broiling, -broils. 1.** To involve in argument, contention, or hostile actions: *"These considerations are additional admonitions to avoid . . . any step that may embroil us with Great Britain."* (Alexander Hamilton). **2.** To throw into confusion or disorder; entangle. [French *embrouiller* : Old French *en-*, in + *brouiller*, to mix, confuse, probably from *breu*, broth, from Germanic (see **bhreu-**[2] in Appendix*).] **—em·broil′ment** *n.*
em·brown (ĕm-broun′, ĭm-) *tr.v.* **-browned, -browning, -browns.** To make brown or dusky; darken.
em·brue. Variant of **imbrue.**
em·bry·ec·to·my (ĕm′brē-ĕk′tə-mē) *n., pl.* **-mies.** The surgical removal of an extrauterine embryo. [EMBRY(O) + -ECTOMY.]
em·bry·o (ĕm′brē-ō′) *n., pl.* **-os. 1.** *Biology.* **a.** An organism in its early stages of development, especially before it has reached a distinctively recognizable form. **b.** Such an organism at any time before full development, birth, or hatching. **2. a.** The fertilized egg of a vertebrate animal. **b.** In man, the prefetal product of conception up to the beginning of the third month of pregnancy. **3.** *Botany.* The minute, rudimentary plant contained within a seed or archegonium. **4.** A rudimentary or

ă pat/ā pay/âr care/ä father/b bib/ch church/d deed/ĕ pet/ē be/f fife/g gag/h hat/hw which/ĭ pit/ī pie/îr pier/j judge/k kick/l lid, needle/m mum/n no, sudden/ng thing/ŏ pot/ō toe/ô paw, for/oi noise/ou out/ŏŏ took/ōō boot/p pop/r roar/s sauce/sh ship, dish/

beginning stage: *"The flame, which had before lain in embryo, now burst forth."* (Fielding). —*adj.* Incipient; rudimentary. [Medieval Latin *embryo* (stem *embryon-*), from Greek *embroun*, "something that grows in the body" : *en-*, in + *bruein*, to grow (see **gweru-** in Appendix*).]

em·bry·o·gen·e·sis (ĕm'brē-ō-jĕn'ə-sĭs) *n.* Also **em·bry·og·e·ny** (-ŏj'ə-nē). The development and growth of an embryo. —**em'bry·o·gen'ic** (-ō-jĕn'ĭk), **em'bry·o·ge·net'ic** (-ō-jə-nĕt'ĭk) *adj.*

em·bry·ol·o·gy (ĕm'brē-ŏl'ə-jē) *n.* The science dealing with the formation, early growth, and development of living organisms. —**em'bry·o·log'ic** (-ə-lŏj'ĭk), **em'bry·o·log'i·cal** *adj.* —**em'bry·o·log'i·cal·ly** *adv.* —**em'bry·ol'o·gist** *n.*

em·bry·on·ic (ĕm'brē-ŏn'ĭk) *adj.* Also **em·bry·on·al** (ĕm'brē-ə-nəl). **1.** Of, pertaining to, or in the state of being an embryo. **2.** Incipient; rudimentary; undeveloped.

embryo sac. A structure formed by the female gametophyte of a seed plant, in which the embryo develops.

em·cee (ĕm'sē') *n. Informal.* **A master of ceremonies** (see). —*v.* **emceed, -ceeing, -cees.** *Informal.* —*tr.* To serve as master of ceremonies of. —*intr.* To act as master of ceremonies. [Short for M(ASTER OF) C(EREMONIES).]

–eme. Indicates an irreducible linguistic unit; for example, **semanteme, morpheme.** [French *-ème*, from *phonème*, PHONEME.]

e·meer. Variant of **emir.**

e·mend (ĭ-mĕnd') *tr.v.* **emended, emending, emends. 1.** To improve (a text) by critical editing. **2.** *Rare.* To free from faults; to correct. [Middle English *emenden*, from Latin *ēmendāre* : *ex-* (removal) + *mendum*, fault (see **mend-** in Appendix*).]

e·men·date (ē'mĕn-dāt', ĭ-mĕn'-) *tr.v.* **-dated, -dating, -dates.** To emend (a text). —**e'men·da'tor** (-dā'tər) *n.*

e·men·da·tion (ĭ-mĕn'dā'shən, ē'mĕn-) *n.* **1.** The act of emending. **2.** An alteration that improves something, especially a literary work. —**e·men'da·to'ry** (-də-tôr'ē, -tōr'ē) *adj.*

em·er·ald (ĕm'ər-əld, ĕm'rəld) *n.* **1.** A brilliant, transparent green beryl used as a gemstone. **2.** Strong yellowish green. See **color.** —*adj.* **1.** Of, pertaining to, or similar to an emerald. **2.** Of a strong yellowish-green color. [Middle English *emeraude*, from Old French *esmeraude*, from Vulgar Latin *smaralda* (unattested), variant of Latin *smaragdus*, SMARAGDITE.]

Emerald Isle. The island of Ireland.

e·merge (ĭ-mûrj') *intr.v.* **emerged, emerging, emerges. 1.** To rise up or come forth from or as if from immersion; come into sight. **2.** To become evident or obvious. **3.** To issue, as from obscurity or an unfortunate condition: *"We have seen how the Church emerged from this welter of barbarism."* (G.G. Coulton). **4.** To crop up; come into existence. [Latin *ēmergere* : *ex-*, out of + *mergere*, to dip, immerse (see **mezg-¹** in Appendix*).]

e·mer·gence (ĭ-mûr'jəns) *n.* **1.** The act or process of emerging. **2.** *Botany.* A superficial outgrowth of plant tissue, as a thorn. **3.** The unpredicted appearance of new characteristics or phenomena in the course of biological or social evolution.

e·mer·gen·cy (ĭ-mûr'jən-sē) *n., pl.* **-cies.** A situation or occurrence of a serious nature, developing suddenly and unexpectedly, and demanding immediate action.

emergency brake. A separate brake system in an automobile, usually set by hand, for use in case of failure of the service brakes and commonly used as a parking brake.

e·mer·gent (ĭ-mûr'jənt) *adj.* **1.** Coming into existence, view, or attention; issuing forth. **2.** Demanding prompt action.

emergent evolution. A theory holding that completely new types of organisms, modes of behavior, and consciousness appear at certain stages of the evolutionary process, usually as a result of an unpredictable rearrangement of the pre-existing elements.

e·mer·i·tus (ĭ-mĕr'ə-təs) *adj.* Retired but retaining an honorary title corresponding to that held immediately before retirement: *a professor emeritus.* —*n., pl.* **emeriti** (-tī'). One who is emeritus. [Latin *ēmeritus*, past participle of *ēmerērī*, to earn by service : *ex-*, out of + *merērī, merēre*, to earn, deserve (see **smer-²** in Appendix*).]

e·mersed (ĭ-mûrst') *adj. Botany.* Rising above the surface of the water, as leaves or stems of aquatic plants.

e·mer·sion (ĭ-mûr'zhən, -shən) *n.* The act of emerging; emergence. [From Latin *ēmergere* (past participle *ēmersus*), EMERGE.]

Em·er·son (ĕm'ər-sən), **Ralph Waldo.** 1803–1882. American essayist and poet.

em·er·y (ĕm'ə-rē, ĕm'rē) *n.* A fine-grained impure corundum used for grinding and polishing. [Middle English *emery*, from Old French *emeri, esmeril*, from Vulgar Latin *smericulum* (unattested), from Medieval Greek *smēri*, variant of Greek *smuris*†, emery powder.]

emery board. A small, flat strip of cardboard or thin wood coated with powdered emery, used to file fingernails.

emery cloth. Cloth coated with powdered emery, used as a fine abrasive.

Em·e·sa. The ancient name for **Homs.**

em·e·sis (ĕm'ə-sĭs) *n.* Vomiting. [New Latin, from Greek, from *emein*, to vomit. See **emetic.**]

e·met·ic (ĭ-mĕt'ĭk) *adj.* Causing vomiting. —*n.* An emetic agent or medicine. [Latin *emeticus*, from Greek *emetikos*, inclined to vomit, from *emetos*, vomiting, from *emein*, to vomit. See **wem-** in Appendix*.] —**e·met'i·cal·ly** *adv.*

em·e·tine (ĕm'ə-tēn') *n.* A bitter-tasting, crystalline alkaloid, $C_{29}H_{40}O_4N_2$, derived from ipecac root, and used as an emetic. [French *émétine* : *émétique*, causing vomiting, from Latin *emeticus* (see **emetic**) + -INE.]

e·meu. Variant of **emu.**

é·meute (ā-mœt') *n., pl.* **émeutes** (ā-mœt'). *French.* A popular uprising; a riot.

emf, EMF electromotive force.

–emia, –aemia, –hemia. Indicates blood; for example, **leukemia, polycythemia.** [New Latin *-emia, -aemia*, from Greek *-aimiā*, from *haima*, blood. See **hemo-.**]

em·i·grant (ĕm'ĭ-grənt) *n.* One who emigrates. —*adj.* **1.** Emigrating. **2.** Of or pertaining to emigration.

em·i·grate (ĕm'ĭ-grāt') *intr.v.* **-grated, -grating, -grates.** To leave one country or region to settle in another. See Usage note at **migrate.** [Latin *ēmigrāre*, to move away from : *ex-*, away + *migrāre*, to move (see **mei-¹** in Appendix*).]

em·i·gra·tion (ĕm'ĭ-grā'shən) *n.* **1.** The action of emigrating; the departure of persons from their native land. **2.** Emigrants collectively.

é·mi·gré (ĕm'ĭ-grā'; *French* ā-mē-grā') *n.* An emigrant, especially one who has fled his country during a revolution. [French, past participle of *émigrer*, to emigrate, from Latin *ēmigrāre.* See **emigrate.**]

Em·i Kous·si (ā'mē kōō'sē). The highest mountain (11,204 feet) of the Tibesti Massif, in north-central Chad.

E·mil (ā'məl). A masculine given name. [German, from French *Émile*, from Latin *Aemilius*, name of a Roman gens, from *aemulus*, emulating, imitating. See **emulate.**]

E·mi·lia-Ro·ma·gna (ā-mē'lyä-rō-män'yä). Formerly **E·mi·lia.** A region, 8,542 square miles in area, in north-central Italy. Population, 3,647,000. Capital, Bologna.

Em·i·ly (ĕm'ə-lē). A feminine given name. [Middle English *Emelye*, from Old French *Emilie*, from Latin *Aemilia*, feminine of *Aemilius*, EMIL.]

em·i·nence (ĕm'ə-nəns) *n.* Also **em·i·nen·cy** (-nən-sē) *pl.* **-cies. 1.** A position of great distinction or superiority in achievement, position, rank, or character. **2.** A rise of ground; hill: *"The palace stood on an eminence raised about thirty paces above the surface of the lake."* (Samuel Johnson). **3.** *Capital* **E.** A title of honor given to cardinals in the Roman Catholic Church. —See Synonyms at **fame.**

em·i·nent (ĕm'ə-nənt) *adj.* **1.** Towering above others; projecting; prominent: *the Empire State Building, eminent among the skyscrapers.* **2. a.** Outstanding in performance or character; distinguished: *an eminent historian.* **b.** Of high rank or station. **3.** Possessed or shown to a remarkable degree; noteworthy: *a man esteemed for his eminent achievements.* [Middle English, from Old French, from Latin *ēminēns*, present participle of *ēminēre*, to stand out : *ex-*, out + *-minēre*, to stand, project (see **men-²** in Appendix*).] —**em'i·nent·ly** *adv.*

eminent domain. *Law.* The right of a government to appropriate private property for public use, usually with compensation to the owner.

e·mir (ĕ-mîr') *n.* Also **e·meer, a·mir, a·meer. 1.** An Arabian prince, chieftain, or governor. **2.** A title of honor given to the descendants of Mohammed. [French *émir*, from Spanish *emir*, from Arabic *'umir*, commander, from *amara*, he commanded.]

e·mir·ate (ĕ-mîr'ĭt, -āt') *n.* The office or jurisdiction of an emir.

em·is·sar·y (ĕm'ĭ-sĕr'ē) *n., pl.* **-ies.** A messenger or agent sent to represent or advance the interests of another. [Latin *emissārius*, from *ēmittere* (past participle *ēmissus*), to send out, EMIT.]

e·mis·sion (ĭ-mĭsh'ən) *n.* **1.** The action of emitting. **2.** Something that is emitted. **3.** An issuance, as of paper money or shares. [From Latin *ēmittere* (past participle *ēmissus*), EMIT.]

emission spectrum. The spectrum of bright lines, bands, or continuous radiation characteristic of and determined by a specific emitting substance subjected to a specific kind of excitation. Compare **absorption spectrum.**

e·mis·sive (ĭ-mĭs'ĭv) *adj.* **1.** Sending forth; emitting. **2.** Sent forth; emitted.

em·is·siv·i·ty (ĕm'ə-sĭv'ə-tē) *n.* The ratio of radiation intensity from a surface to the radiation intensity at the same wavelength from a blackbody at the same temperature.

e·mit (ĭ-mĭt') *tr.v.* **emitted, emitting, emits. 1.** To release or send forth (radiation, for example). **2. a.** To utter: *"she emitted her small strange laugh"* (Edith Wharton). **b.** To express; vent, as an opinion or emotion. **3.** To issue with authority; especially, to put into circulation (paper currency or shares of stock, for example). [Latin *ēmittere*, to send out : *ex-*, out + *mittere*, to send (see **smeit-** in Appendix*).] —**e·mit'ter** *n.*

Em·ma (ĕm'ə). A feminine given name. [Middle English, from Old High German *Emma, Imma*, from *Erma*, short for names such as *Ermenhilde*, from *Ermin-*, "whole," "universal." See **er-¹** in Appendix*.]

em·men·a·gogue (ĭ-mĕn'ə-gôg', -gŏg') *n.* A medicine that induces or hastens the menstrual flow. [Greek *emmēna*, the menses, from *emmēnos*, monthly : *en-*, in + *mēnē, mēn*, month (see **mē-²** in Appendix*) + -AGOGUE.]

em·mer (ĕm'ər) *n.* A Eurasian wheat, *Triticum dicoccum*, cultivated as a cereal grain and as livestock feed. [German *Emmer*, from Old High German *amaro.* See **yellowhammer.**]

em·met (ĕm'ĭt) *n. Archaic.* An ant. [Middle English *emete, emet*, Old English *æmette.* See **mai-¹** in Appendix*.]

Em·met (ĕm'ĭt), **Robert.** 1778–1803. Irish patriot.

em·me·tro·pi·a (ĕm'ə-trō'pē-ə) *n.* The condition of the normal eye when parallel rays are focused exactly on the retina and vision is perfect. [New Latin : Greek *emmetros*, in measure : *en-*, in + *metron*, measure (see **mē-²** in Appendix*) + -OPIA.] —**em'me·trop'ic** (-trŏp'ĭk) *adj.*

Em·mett (ĕm'ĭt), **Daniel Decatur.** 1815–1904. American songwriter; organized first minstrel show.

Em·my (ĕm'ē) *n., pl.* **-mys** or **-mies.** One of the statuettes

Ralph Waldo Emerson

presented annually by the Academy of Television Arts and Sciences for outstanding performances and productions. [Variation of *Immy,* short for *im(age orthicon tube).*]

e·mol·lient (ĭ-mŏl′yənt, -ē-ənt) *adj.* Having softening and soothing qualities, especially for the skin. —*n.* **1.** An agent that softens or soothes the skin. **2.** Anything that assuages or mollifies: *"The great emollient of the common ills of life, the humanitarian movement"* (G.M. Trevelyan). [Latin *ēmolliēns,* present participle of *ēmollīre,* to soften, soothe : *ex-,* completely + *mollīre,* to soften, from *mollis,* soft (see **mel-**[1] in Appendix*).]

e·mol·u·ment (ĭ-mŏl′yə-mənt) *n.* Profit derived from one's office or employment; payment for services rendered. [Middle English, from Latin *ēmolumentum,* originally "miller's fee for grinding grain," from *ēmolere,* to grind out : *ex-,* out + *molere,* to grind (see **mele-** in Appendix*).]

e·mote (ĭ-mōt′) *intr.v.* **emoted, emoting, emotes.** *Informal.* To express emotion or sentiment in an effusive and theatrical manner. [Back-formation from EMOTION.]

e·mo·tion (ĭ-mō′shən) *n.* **1.** Agitation of the passions or sensibilities often involving physiological changes. **2.** Any strong feeling, as of joy, sorrow, reverence, hate, or love, arising subjectively rather than through conscious mental effort. —See Synonyms at **feeling.** [French *émotion,* earlier *esmocion,* from Old French *esmovoir,* to excite, from Vulgar Latin *exmovēre* (unattested), variant of Latin *ēmovēre,* to move out, stir up, excite : *ex-,* out + *movēre,* to move (see **mew-** in Appendix*).]

e·mo·tion·al (ĭ-mō′shən-əl) *adj.* **1.** Of or pertaining to emotion. **2.** Readily affected with or stirred by emotion. **3.** Capable of stirring the emotions: *an emotional appeal.* **4.** Revealing emotion; agitated; excited. —**e·mo′tion·al·ly** *adv.*

e·mo·tion·al·ism (ĭ-mō′shən-ə-lĭz′əm) *n.* **1.** An inclination to encourage or yield to emotion: *the emotionalism of adolescent girls.* **2.** Undue display of emotion. **3.** An ethical or aesthetic attitude basing conduct or value on emotion.

e·mo·tion·al·ist (ĭ-mō′shən-ə-lĭst) *n.* **1.** One whose conduct, thought, or rhetoric is governed by emotion rather than reason, often as a matter of policy. **2.** An excessively emotional person. —**e·mo′tion·al·is′tic** (ĭ-mō′shən-ə-lĭs′tĭk) *adj.*

e·mo·tion·al·i·ty (ĭ-mō′shə-năl′ə-tē) *n.* The quality or state of being emotional.

e·mo·tion·al·ize (ĭ-mō′shən-ə-līz′) *tr.v.* **-ized, -izing, -izes.** To impart an emotional character to.

e·mo·tion·less (ĭ-mō′shən-lĭs) *adj.* Devoid of apparent emotion. —**e·mo′tion·less·ness** *n.*

e·mo·tive (ĭ-mō′tĭv) *adj.* Pertaining to, expressing, or tending to excite emotion. [From EMOTION.] —**e·mo′tive·ly** *adv.* —**e·mo′tive·ness, e′mo·tiv′i·ty** (ē′mō-tĭv′ə-tē) *n.*

Emp. emperor; empire; empress.

em·pale. Variant of **impale.**

em·pan·el. Variant of **impanel.**

em·path·ic (ĕm-păth′ĭk, ĭm-) *adj.* Also **em·pa·thet·ic** (ĕm′pə-thĕt′ĭk). Of, pertaining to, or characterized by empathy. —**em·path′i·cal·ly** *adv.*

em·pa·thize (ĕm′pə-thīz′) *intr.v.* **-thized, -thizing, -thizes.** To feel or experience empathy. Often used with *with.*

em·pa·thy (ĕm′pə-thē) *n.* **1.** The attribution of feelings aroused by an object in nature or art to the object itself, as when one speaks of a painting full of love. **2.** Understanding so intimate that the feelings, thoughts, and motives of one are readily comprehended by another. —See Synonyms at **pity.** [EN- (in) + -PATHY (translation of German *Einfühlung,* "a feeling in"), after Greek *empatheia,* passion.]

em·pen·nage (ĕm′pĭ-nĭj; *French* äɴ-pĕ-näzh′) *n. Aviation.* The **tail** *(see).* [French, originally "the feathers on an arrow," from *empenner,* to put feathers on an arrow : *en-,* in + *penne,* feather, from Latin *pinna* (see **pet-**[1] in Appendix*).]

em·per·or (ĕm′pər-ər) *n.* **1.** *Abbr.* **Emp.** The ruler of an empire, having power either absolute or subject to constitutional restrictions. **2. a.** Any of several brightly colored butterflies of the family Nymphalidae, such as *Asterocampa clyton,* having orange-tawny wings with dark markings. Also called "emperor butterfly." **b.** Any of several moths of the family Saturniidae; especially, an Old World species, *Saturnia pavonia,* having distinctively patterned wings. Also called "emperor moth." [Middle English *emperour,* from Old French *empereor,* from Latin *imperātor,* emperor, commander, from *imperāre* (stem *imperāt-*), "to prepare against (an occasion)," hence to command : *in-,* against + *parāre,* to prepare (see **per-**[4] in Appendix*).] —**em′per·or·ship′** *n.*

emperor penguin. A large penguin, *Aptenodytes forsteri,* of Antarctic regions.

em·per·y (ĕm′pə-rē) *n., pl.* **-ies.** **1.** Absolute dominion; sovereignty; empire. **2.** *Archaic.* The domain of an emperor. [Middle English *emperie,* from Old French, EMPIRE.]

em·pha·sis (ĕm′fə-sĭs) *n., pl.* **-ses** (-sēz′). **1.** Special importance or significance placed upon or imparted to something. **2.** Stress applied to a syllable, word, or passage by the use of a gesture, italics, or other indication. **3.** Force or intensity of expression, feeling, or action. **4.** Sharpness or vividness of outline; prominence. [Latin, from Greek, reflection, meaning, significance, from *emphainein,* to exhibit, indicate : *en-,* in + *phainein,* to show (see **bhā-**[1] in Appendix*).]

em·pha·size (ĕm′fə-sīz′) *tr.v.* **-sized, -sizing, -sizes.** To impart emphasis to; to stress: *"A flash of yellow light emphasized the darkness which had succeeded the twilight."* (Gore Vidal). [From EMPHASIS.]

em·phat·ic (ĕm-făt′ĭk) *adj.* **1.** Expressed or performed with emphasis. **2.** Bold and definite in expression or action; positive. **3.** Accentuated; sharply delineated; striking; definite: *an emphatic victory.* [Late Latin *emphaticus,* from Greek *emphatikos,* exhibited, hence emphatic, from *emphainein,* to exhibit. See **emphasis.**] —**em·phat′i·cal·ly** *adv.*

em·phy·se·ma (ĕm′fə-sē′mə) *n.* **1.** A condition of the lungs in which there is dilation of the air vesicles following atrophy of the septa, resulting in labored breathing and increased susceptibility to infection. **2.** Any distention of connective tissues due to retention of air. [New Latin, from Greek *emphusēma,* swelling, inflation, from *emphusan,* to blow in : *en-,* in + *phusan,* to blow, from *phusai,* bellows (see **pu-**[1] in Appendix*).] —**em′phy·sem′a·tous** (-sĕm′ə-təs) *adj.*

em·pire (ĕm′pīr′) *n. Abbr.* **Emp.** **1.** A political unit, usually larger than a kingdom and often comprising a number of territories or nations, ruled by a single supreme authority. **2.** The territory included in such a unit. **3. a.** Imperial dominion. **b.** The period during which such dominion exists. **4.** An extensive enterprise maintained by a unified authority: *a publishing empire.* [Middle English *empire,* from Old French *empire, emperie,* from Latin *imperium,* dominion, empire, from *imperāre,* to command. See **emperor.**]

Em·pire (ĕm′pīr′ *for sense 1;* ŏm-pīr′ *for sense 2*) *adj.* **1.** Of or characteristic of the first Empire of France (1804–15). **2.** Designating a décolleté gown with a high waistline and straight loose skirt worn during the first French Empire. **3.** Designating a neoclassic style of art, architecture, and decor, and especially a style of furniture in hard woods with massive members, Egyptian motifs, and gilded ornamentation.

Empire State. The nickname for New York.

em·pir·ic (ĕm-pîr′ĭk, ĭm-) *n.* **1.** One who believes that practical experience is the sole source of knowledge. **2.** A charlatan: *"we must not . . . prostitute our past-cure malady / To empirics"* (Shakespeare). [Latin *empiricus,* from Greek *empeirikos,* from *empeirā,* experience, from *empeiros,* experienced in : *en-,* in + *peira,* experiment, trial (see **per-**[5] in Appendix*).]

em·pir·i·cal (ĕm-pîr′ĭ-kəl, ĭm-) *adj.* **1.** Relying upon or derived from observation or experiment: *empirical methods; an empirical conclusion.* **2.** Guided by practical experience and not theory, especially in medicine. —**em·pir′i·cal·ly** *adv.*

empirical formula. A type of chemical formula that indicates the ratio of the elements rather than the total number of atoms in a molecule.

em·pir·i·cism (ĕm-pîr′ə-sĭz′əm, ĭm-) *n.* **1.** The view that experience, especially of the senses, is the only source of knowledge. **2. a.** The employment of empirical methods, as in an art or science. **b.** An empirical conclusion. **3.** The practice of medicine without scientific knowledge. —**em·pir′i·cist** *n.*

em·place (ĕm-plās′, ĭm-) *tr.v.* **-placed, -placing, -places.** To put in place or position.

em·place·ment (ĕm-plās′mənt, ĭm-) *n.* **1.** A prepared position, such as a mounting or platform, for guns within a fortification. **2.** A setting in position; placement. **3.** *Rare.* Position; location. [French, place, situation, from (obsolete) *emplacer,* to place in (a position) : *em-,* in, from Old French, from Latin *in* + *placer,* to place, from *place,* from Old French, PLACE.]

em·plane. Variant of **enplane.**

em·ploy (ĕm-ploi′, ĭm-) *tr.v.* **-ployed, -ploying, -ploys.** **1.** To use in some process or effort; put to service. **2.** To devote or apply (one's time or energies, for example) to some activity. **3. a.** To engage the services of; put to work. **b.** To provide with a job and livelihood. —See Synonyms at **use.** —*n.* **1.** The state of being employed. **2.** *Archaic.* Occupation. [Middle English *emploien,* from Old French *employer, emplier,* from Latin *implicāre,* to infold, involve : *in-,* in + *plicāre,* to fold (see **plek-** in Appendix*).] —**em·ploy′a·bil′i·ty** *n.* —**em·ploy′a·ble** *adj.*

em·ploy·ee (ĕm-ploi′ē, ĭm-, ĕm′ploi-ē′) *n.* Also **em·ploy·e, em·ploy·é.** A person who works for another in return for financial or other compensation.

em·ploy·er (ĕm-ploi′ər, ĭm-) *n.* A person or concern that employs persons for wages or salary.

em·ploy·ment (ĕm-ploi′mənt, ĭm-) *n.* **1. a.** The act of employing; a putting to use or work. **b.** The state of being employed. **2.** The work in which one is engaged; business; profession. **3.** An activity to which one devotes time.

em·poi·son (ĕm-poi′zən, ĭm-) *tr.v.* **-soned, -soning, -sons.** **1.** To fill with venom; embitter. **2.** *Archaic.* To poison. [Middle English *empoysonen,* from Old French *empoisoner* : *en-,* in + *poison,* POISON.]

em·po·ri·um (ĕm-pôr′ē-əm, ĕm-pōr′-, ĭm-) *n., pl.* **-ums** or **-poria** (-pôr′ē-ə, -pōr′ē-ə). **1.** A place, town, or city that is an important trade center; marketplace. **2.** A large retail store carrying a wide variety of merchandise. [Latin, from Greek *emporion,* market, from *emporos,* merchant, traveler : *en-,* in + *poros,* path, journey (see **per-**[2] in Appendix*).]

em·pow·er (ĕm-pou′ər, ĭm-) *tr.v.* **-ered, -ering, -ers.** Also **im·pow·er** (ĭm-). **1.** To invest with legal power; authorize. **2.** To enable or permit. [EM- + POWER.]

em·press (ĕm′prĭs) *n. Abbr.* **Emp.** **1.** A female sovereign of an empire. **2.** The wife or widow of an emperor. [Middle English *emperesse,* from Old French, feminine of *empereor,* EMPEROR.]

em·presse·ment (äɴ-prĕs-mäɴ′) *n.* Effusive cordiality or regard. [French, from *s'empresser,* to be eager : Old French *en-,* in + *presser,* to PRESS.]

empress tree. A tree, *Paulownia tomentosa,* native to China, having large, hairy leaves and clusters of lavender flowers.

em·prise (ĕm-prīz′, ĭm-) *n.* Also **em·prize.** **1.** An undertaking, especially one of a chivalrous or adventurous nature; enterprise; adventure. **2.** Chivalrous daring or prowess. [Middle English *emprise,* from Old French, from the feminine past participle of *emprendre,* to undertake, from Vulgar Latin *imprendere* (unat-

ă pat/ā pay/âr care/ä father/b bib/ch church/d deed/ĕ pet/ē be/f fife/g gag/h hat/hw which/ĭ pit/ī pie/îr pier/j judge/k kick/l lid, needle/m mum/n no, sudden/ng thing/ŏ pot/ō toe/ô paw, for/oi noise/ou out/ŏŏ took/ōō boot/p pop/r roar/s sauce/sh ship, dish/

tested) : Latin *in-*, in + *prendere, prehendere,* to take, seize (see **ghend-** in Appendix*).]

emp·ty (ĕmp′tē) *adj.* **-tier, -tiest. 1.** Void of content; containing nothing: *an empty bottle.* **2.** Having no occupants or inhabitants; vacant; unoccupied: *an empty chair.* **3.** Having no load or cargo: *an empty railroad car.* **4.** Lacking purpose or substance; meaningless: *an empty life.* **5.** Idle: *empty hours.* **6.** Vacuous; inane: *an empty mind.* **7.** Needing nourishment; hungry. **8.** Devoid; destitute. Used with *of: empty of pity.* —*v.* **emptied, -tying, -ties.** —*tr.* **1.** To remove the contents of; make empty: *empty one's pockets.* **2.** To transfer or pour off: *empty the ashes into a pail.* **3.** To unburden; relieve. Used with *of: empty oneself of doubt.* —*intr.* **1.** To become empty. **2.** To discharge or flow. Used with *into: The river empties into a bay.* —*n., pl.* **empties.** An empty container, carrier, or the like. [Middle English *empty, emptie,* Old English *ǣmettig, ǣmtig,* empty, unoccupied, from *ǣmetta,* rest, leisure. See **med-** in Appendix.*] —**emp′ti·ly** *adv.* —**emp′ti·ness** *n.*

Synonyms: *empty, vacant, blank, void, vacuous, bare, barren.* These adjectives describe that which has nothing in it or on it and inferentially lacks what it could or should have. *Empty* applies physically and figuratively to what is without contents, content (substance), or occupants (persons): *an empty box; empty promises; an empty room. Vacant,* in physical usage, is largely limited to what is without an occupant or incumbent; in this sense, much more than *empty,* it suggests a condition of some duration. Figuratively *vacant* refers to absence of intellectual content, sometimes momentary: *a vacant stare; a vacant mind. Blank* stresses absence of something on a surface that would convey meaning or content: *a blank page; a blank expression. Void* appears principally in the expression *void of,* to indicate absence of the object specified, or in the legal sense of lacking force or validity. *Vacuous* means containing a vacuum, literally or, more often, figuratively in the sense of being silly or inane. *Bare* refers to lack of surface covering or detail or to the condition of being stripped of contents or furnishings. *Barren* stresses lack of productivity in both literal and figurative applications: *barren land; a barren scheme; barren ideas.*

emp·ty-hand·ed (ĕmp′tē-hăn′dĭd) *adj.* **1.** Bearing no gift, possessions, or impedimenta: *They arrived empty-handed.* **2.** Having received or gained nothing.

emp·ty-head·ed (ĕmp′tē-hĕd′ĭd) *adj.* Lacking sense or discretion; foolish; scatterbrained.

Empty Quarter. See **Rub al Khali.**

em·pur·ple (ĕm-pûr′pəl, ĭm-) *tr.v.* **-pled, -pling, -ples.** To color or tinge with purple.

em·py·e·ma (ĕm′pī-ē′mə) *n., pl.* **-mata** (-mə-tə). Pus in a body cavity, such as the pleural cavity or gall bladder. [Medieval Latin, from Greek *empuēma,* from *empuein,* to suppurate. See **pu-²** in Appendix.*] —**em′py·e′mic** *adj.*

em·pyr·e·al (ĕm′pī-rē′əl) *adj.* **1.** Empyrean. **2.** Of or pertaining to the sky; celestial. **3.** Formed of pure fire or light; fiery. [Middle English *imperyale,* from Late Latin *empyrius, empyreus,* from Greek *empurios, empuros,* fiery : *en-,* in + *pur,* fire (see **pūr-** in Appendix*).]

em·py·re·an (ĕm′pī-rē′ən) *n.* **1.** The highest reaches of heaven, believed by the ancients to be a realm of pure fire and by early Christians to be the abode of God and the angels. **2.** The sky; space. —*adj.* Of or pertaining to the empyrean of ancient belief: *"he ascends the empyrean heaven, and is not intoxicated"* (Lamb). [From Late Latin *empyreus,* EMPYREAL.]

Ems (ĕms, ĕmz). A river of West Germany, rising in northeastern North Rhine-Westphalia and flowing 250 miles generally north to the North Sea.

Ems·land (ĕms′länt′). A former swamp region, now a major petroleum-producing area, in northwestern West Germany, between the Ems River and the Netherlands border.

e·mu (ē′myōō) *n.* Also **e·meu.** A large, flightless Australian bird, *Dromiceius novaehollandiae,* related to and resembling the ostrich. [Portuguese *ema,* possibly from Moluccan *eme.*]

emu electromagnetic unit.

em·u·late (ĕm′yə-lāt′) *tr.v.* **-lated, -lating, -lates. 1.** To strive to equal or excel, especially through imitation. **2.** To compete with or rival successfully: *"Korea emulates Japan in its geographical regionalization and its paradoxical homogeneity of culture."* (Walter A. Fairservis). —See Synonyms at **rival.** —*adj. Obsolete.* Ambitious; emulous. [Latin *aemulārī,* from *aemulus,* EMULOUS.] —**em′u·la′tive** *adj.* —**em′u·la′tive·ly** *adv.* —**em′u·la′tor** (-lā′tər) *n.*

em·u·la·tion (ĕm′yə-lā′shən) *n.* **1.** Effort or ambition to equal or surpass another. **2.** Imitation of another. **3.** *Obsolete.* Jealous rivalry.

em·u·lous (ĕm′yə-ləs) *adj.* **1.** Eager or ambitious to equal or surpass another. **2.** Characterized or prompted by a spirit of rivalry. **3.** *Obsolete.* Covetous of power or honor; envious. [Latin *aemulus,* imitating, probably related to *imitārī,* IMITATE.] —**em′u·lous·ly** *adv.* —**em′u·lous·ness** *n.*

e·mul·si·fy (ĭ-mŭl′sə-fī′) *tr.v.* **-fied, -fying, -fies.** To make into an emulsion. [EMULSI(ON) + -FY.] —**e·mul′si·fi·ca′tion** *n.* —**e·mul′si·fi′er** *n.*

e·mul·sion (ĭ-mŭl′shən) *n.* **1.** *Chemistry.* A suspension of small globules of one liquid in a second liquid with which the first will not mix, such as milk fats in milk. **2.** *Photography.* A light-sensitive coating, usually of silver halide grains in a thin gelatin layer, on photographic film, paper, or glass. [New Latin, from Latin *ēmulgēre* (past participle *ēmulsus*), to drain out, milk out : *ex-,* out + *mulgēre,* to milk (see **melg-** in Appendix*).] —**e·mul′sive** *adj.*

e·munc·to·ry (ĭ-mŭngk′tə-rē) *adj.* Serving to carry waste matter out of the body; excretory. —*n., pl.* **emunctories.** An emunctory organ or passage. [Middle English *emunctorie,* from Medieval Latin *ēmunctorius,* from Latin *ēmongere* (past participle *ēmunctus*), to blow the nose : *ex-,* completely + *mungere,* to blow the nose (see **meug-²** in Appendix*).]

en (ĕn) *n.* **1.** The letter *n.* **2.** *Printing. Abbr.* **n, N** A space equal to half the width of an **em** *(see).*

en-¹. Also **em-** before *b, p,* and sometimes *m.* **1.** Used to form verbs from nouns to indicate: **a.** To put into or on; for example, **encompass, enthrone. b.** To go into or on; for example, **entrain. c.** To cover or imbue with; for example, **enrobe, empurple. d.** To provide with; for example, **empower. 2.** Used to form verbs from nouns and adjectives to indicate causing to become or resemble; for example, **endanger.** [Middle English, from Old French, from Latin *in-, im-.* See **en** in Appendix.*]

en-². Also **em-** before *b, m, p,* or *ph.* Used to form nouns and adjectives to indicate in, into, or within; for example, **enzootic, empathy.** [Middle English *en-,* from Latin, from Greek. See **en** in Appendix.* In borrowed Greek compounds, *en-* also becomes *el-* before *l,* as in **ellipsis.**]

-en¹. 1. Used to form verbs from adjectives to indicate being, becoming, or causing to be; for example, **cheapen, redden. 2.** Used to form verbs from nouns to indicate causing to have or gain; for example, **lengthen, hearten.** [Middle English *-nen, -nien,* Old English *-nian.*]

-en². Used to form adjectives from nouns to indicate made of, composed of, or resembling; for example, **wooden, earthen, ashen.** [Middle English *-en,* Old English *-en.*]

en·a·ble (ĕn-ā′bəl) *tr.v.* **-bled, -bling, -bles. 1. a.** To supply with the means, knowledge, or opportunity to be or do something. **b.** To make feasible or possible. **2.** To give legal power, capacity, or sanction to; permit.

en·act (ĕn-ăkt′) *tr.v.* **-acted, -acting, -acts. 1.** To make (a bill) into an act; decree by legislative process; pass. **2.** To act out as on a stage; represent. —**en·act′a·ble** *adj.* —**en·ac′tor** *n.*

en·ac·tive (ĕn-ăk′tĭv) *adj.* Having capacity or force to enact.

en·act·ment (ĕn-ăkt′mənt) *n.* **1.** The act of enacting. **2.** The state of being enacted. **3.** A law or statute.

en·am·el (ĭ-năm′əl) *n.* **1.** A vitreous, usually opaque, protective or decorative coating baked on metal, glass, or ceramic ware. **2.** An object with an enameled surface, such as a piece of cloisonné. **3.** A paint that dries to a hard, glossy surface. **4.** Any glossy, hard coating resembling enamel: *nail enamel.* **5.** *Anatomy.* The hard, calcareous substance covering the exposed portion of a tooth. —*tr.v.* **enameled** or **-elled, -eling** or **-elling, -els. 1.** To coat, inlay, or decorate with enamel. **2.** To give a glossy or brilliant surface to. **3.** To adorn, as with bright colors or cosmetics. [Middle English *enamelen,* from Norman French *enameler, enamailler* : *en-,* in + *amail,* enamel, from Old French *esmail,* from Germanic (see **mel-¹** in Appendix*).] —**en·am′el·er, en·am′el·ist** *n.*

en·am·el·ing (ĭ-năm′əl-ĭng) *n.* Also **en·am·el·ling. 1.** The art, craft, or occupation of a person who enamels. **2.** A coating or decoration of enamel.

en·am·el·ware (ĭ-năm′əl-wâr′) *n.* Ware coated with enamel.

en·am·or (ĭ-năm′ər) *tr.v.* **-ored, -oring, -ors.** Also *chiefly British* **en·am·our** To inspire with love; charm; captivate. Usually used in the passive with *of* or *with: enamored of his surroundings.* [Middle English *enamouren,* from Old French *enamourer* : *en-,* in + *amour,* love, from Latin *amor,* from *amāre,* to love (see **amma** in Appendix*).]

en·an·ti·o·morph (ĕn-ăn′tē-ə-môrf′) *n. Crystallography.* Either of a pair of crystals that are similar in form but cannot be superimposed, one crystal being the mirror image of the other. [Greek *enantios,* opposite : *en-,* in + *antios,* opposite, from *anti,* over against (see **anti** in Appendix*) + -MORPH.] —**en·an′ti·o·morph′ism′** *n.* —**en·an′ti·o·mor′phous, en·an′ti·o·mor′phic** *adj.*

en·ar·thro·sis (ĕn′är-thrō′sĭs) *n., pl.* **-ses** (-sēz′). *Anatomy.* A ball-and-socket joint. [New Latin, from Greek *enarthrōsis,* from *enarthros,* jointed : *en-,* in + *arthron,* joint (see **ar-** in Appendix*).]

e·nate (ē′nāt′, ĭ-nāt′) *adj.* Also **e·nat·ic** (ĭ-năt′ĭk) (for sense 2). **1.** Growing outward. **2.** Related on the mother's side. —*n.* A relative on one's mother's side. [Latin *ēnātus,* past participle of *ēnāscī,* to be born from : *ex-,* out of + *nāscī,* to be born (see **genə-** in Appendix*).]

en bro·chette (äN brô-shĕt′). *French.* Broiled on a skewer.

enc. enclosed; enclosure.

en·cage (ĕn-kāj′, ĭn-) *tr.v.* **-caged, -caging, -cages.** Also **in·cage** (ĭn-). To confine in or as if in a cage.

en·camp (ĕn-kămp′, ĭn-) *v.* **-camped, -camping, -camps.** —*intr.* To set up or live in a camp. —*tr.* To provide quarters for in a camp.

en·camp·ment (ĕn-kămp′mənt, ĭn-) *n.* **1.** The act of setting up a camp. **2.** A camp or campsite.

en·cap·su·late (ĕn kăp′sə-lāt′, ĭn-) *v.* **-lated, -lating, -lates.** Also **in·cap·su·late** (ĭn-). —*tr.* To encase in or as if in a capsule. —*intr.* To become encapsulated. —**en·cap′su·la′tion** *n.*

en·case (ĕn-kās′, ĭn-) *tr.v.* **-cased, -casing, -cases.** Also **in·case** (ĭn-). To enclose in or as if in a case. —**en·case′ment** *n.*

en·caus·tic (ĕn-kô′stĭk, ĭn-) *adj.* Pertaining to a painting process in which colored beeswax is applied and fixed with heat. —*n.* **1.** The art of painting in this way. **2.** An encaustic painting. [Latin *encausticus,* from Greek *enkaustikos,* from *enkaiein,* to burn in : *en-,* in + *kaiein,* to burn (see **kēu-** in Appendix*).]

-ence, -ency. Used to form nouns from adjectives ending in *-ent* to indicate action, state, quality, or condition; for example,

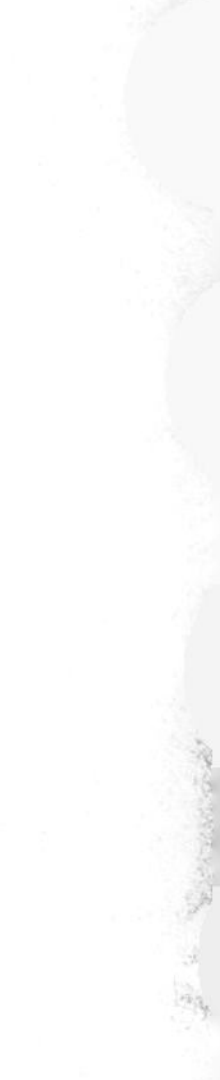

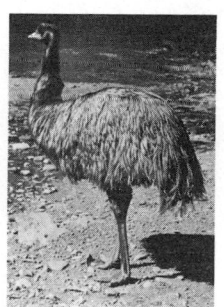

emu

reference. [Middle English *-ence,* from Old French, from Latin *-entia,* from *-ēns,* present participial suffix.]

en·ceinte¹ (ĕn-sānt′; *French* äN-săNt′) *adj.* Being with child; pregnant. [French, from Late Latin *incincta,* without a girdle : Latin *in-,* without + *cinta,* feminine past participle of *cingere,* to gird (see **kenk-¹** in Appendix*).]

en·ceinte² (ĕn-sānt′; *French* äN-săNt′) *n.* **1.** An encircling fortification around a fort, castle, or town. **2.** The structures or area protected by such a fortification. [French, from Latin *incinta,* feminine past participle of *incingere,* to gird in : *in-,* in + *cingere,* to gird (see **kenk-¹** in Appendix*).]

En·cel·a·dus (ĕn-sĕl′ə-dəs). *Greek Mythology.* A giant who rebelled against the gods and as a consequence was struck down and buried under Mount Etna.

en·ce·phal·ic (ĕn′sə-făl′ĭk) *adj.* **1.** Of or pertaining to the brain. **2.** Located within the cranial cavity. [French *encéphalique* : ENCEPHAL(O)- + -IC.]

en·ceph·a·li·tis (ĕn-sĕf′ə-lī′tĭs, ĕn′sĕf-) *n.* Inflammation of the brain. Also called "brain fever." [New Latin : ENCEPHAL(O)- + -ITIS.] —**en·ceph′a·lit′ic** (-lĭt′ĭk) *adj.*

encephalitis le·thar·gi·ca (lə-thär′jĭ-kə). A viral epidemic encephalitis often associated with influenza and marked by apathy, double vision, and extreme muscular weakness. Also called "lethargic encephalitis," "sleeping sickness."

encephalo-, encephal-. Indicates the brain; for example, **encephalogram, encephalitis.** [New Latin, from Greek *(muelos) enkephalos,* "(marrow) in the head," the brain : *en-,* in + *kephalē,* head (see **ghebhel-** in Appendix*).]

en·ceph·a·lo·gram (ĕn-sĕf′ə-lō-grăm′) *n.* **1.** An x-ray picture of the brain taken by encephalography. **2.** An **electroencephalogram** *(see).* [ENCEPHALO- + -GRAM.]

en·ceph·a·log·ra·phy (ĕn-sĕf′ə-lŏg′rə-fē) *n.* Roentgenography of the brain. [ENCEPHALO- + -GRAPHY.] —**en·ceph′a·lo·graph′** (-lō-grăf′, -gräf′) *n.* —**en·ceph′a·lo·graph′ic** *adj.* —**en·ceph′a·lo·graph′i·cal·ly** *adv.*

en·ceph·a·lo·ma (ĕn-sĕf′ə-lō′mə) *n., pl.* **-mas** or **-mata** (-mə-tə). A tumor of the brain. [ENCEPHAL(O)- + -OMA.]

en·ceph·a·lo·my·e·li·tis (ĕn-sĕf′ə-lō-mī′ə-lī′tĭs) *n.* Any of several viral diseases causing inflammation of the brain and the spinal cord.

en·ceph·a·lon (ĕn-sĕf′ə-lŏn′) *n., pl.* **-la** (-lə). The brain of a vertebrate. [New Latin, from Greek *enkephalon, enkephalos.* See **encephalo-.**] —**en·ceph′a·lous** *adj.*

en·chain (ĕn-chān′, ĭn-) *tr.v.* **-chained, -chaining, -chains. 1.** To bind with or as if with chains; fetter: *enchained by superstition.* **2.** To hold fast; rivet (the attention, for example). [Middle English *encheynen,* from Old French *enchaeiner* : *en-,* in + *chaeine,* CHAIN.] —**en·chain′ment** *n.*

en·chant (ĕn-chănt′, -chänt′, ĭn-) *tr.v.* **-chanted, -chanting, -chants. 1.** To cast under a spell; bewitch: *"A savage place! as holy and enchanted/As e'er beneath a waning moon was haunted"* (Coleridge). **2.** To delight completely; charm; enrapture. [Middle English *enchanten,* Old French *enchanter,* from Latin *incantāre,* to chant (magic words) : *in-* (intensive) + *cantāre,* frequentative of *canēre,* to sing (see **kan-** in Appendix*).]

en·chant·er (ĕn-chăn′tər, ĭn-) *n.* One that enchants; a sorcerer or magician.

enchanter's nightshade. Any of several plants of the genus *Circaea,* having small white flowers and bristly, clinging fruit.

en·chant·ing (ĕn-chăn′tĭng, -chän′tĭng, ĭn-) *adj.* Having the power to enchant or enrapture. —**en·chant′ing·ly** *adv.*

en·chant·ment (ĕn-chănt′mənt, -chänt′mənt, ĭn-) *n.* **1. a.** An act of enchanting. **b.** The state of being enchanted. **2.** Something that enchants; an irresistible charm.

en·chant·ress (ĕn-chăn′trĭs, -chän′trĭs, ĭn-) *n.* **1.** A woman of unusual allure or fascination. **2.** A sorceress.

en·chase (ĕn-chās′, ĭn-) *tr.v.* **-chased, -chasing, -chases. 1.** To set (a gem, for example) in some material. **2.** To set with or as if with gems. **3.** To decorate or ornament (a surface) by inlaying, engraving, or chasing. [Middle English *enchasen,* from Old French *enchasser* : *en-,* in + *chasse,* case, from Latin *capsa,* box (see **kap-** in Appendix*).]

en·chi·la·da (ĕn′chə-lä′də) *n.* A tortilla rolled and stuffed usually with a mixture containing meat or cheese and served with a sauce spiced with chili. [American Spanish, feminine past participle of *enchilar,* to put chili in : *en-,* in, from Latin *in-* + *chile,* CHILI.]

en·chi·rid·i·on (ĕn′kī-rĭd′ē-ən) *n., pl.* **-ons** or **-ia** (-ē-ə). A handbook; manual. [Late Latin, from Greek *enkheiridion* : *en-,* in + *-kheiridion,* diminutive of *kheir,* hand (see **ghesor-** in Appendix*).]

en·chon·dro·ma (ĕn′kən-drō′mə) *n., pl.* **-mata** (-mə-tə) or **-mas.** A benign cartilaginous tumor in a part of the body usually free from cartilage. [New Latin : EN- + CHONDR(O)- + -OMA.] —**en′chon·drom′a·tous** (-drŏm′ə-təs) *adj.*

en·cho·ri·al (ĕn-kôr′ē-əl, -kōr′ē-əl, ĭn-) *adj.* Also **en·chor·ic** (-kôr′ĭk, -kŏr′ĭk). Belonging or native to a particular region or people; especially, demotic: *Egyptian enchorial writing.* [From Greek *enkhōrios,* indigenous, native : *en-,* in + *khōra,* country, place (see **ghē-** in Appendix*).]

-enchyma. Indicates cellular tissue; for example, **collenchyma.** [New Latin, from (PAR)ENCHYMA.]

en·ci·na (ĕn-sē′nə) *n.* An evergreen oak, *Quercus agrifolia,* of southwestern North America often cultivated as a shade tree. [Spanish, holm oak, from Late Latin *īlicīna,* from *īlicīnus,* of holm oak, from Latin *īlex* (stem *īlic-*), holm oak, perhaps of Mediterranean origin.]

en·ci·pher (ĕn-sī′fər, ĭn-) *tr.v.* **-phered, -phering, -phers.** To put (a message) into cipher.

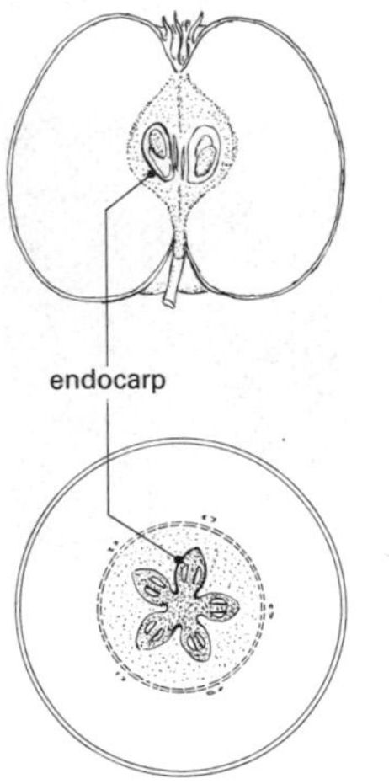

endocarp
Longitudinal section *(above)* and cross section of an apple

en·cir·cle (ĕn-sûr′kəl, ĭn-) *tr.v.* **-cled, -cling, -cles. 1.** To form a circle around; surround. **2.** To move or go around; make a circuit of. —**en·cir′cle·ment** *n.*

encl. enclosed; enclosure.

en·clasp (ĕn-klăsp′, -kläsp′, ĭn-) *tr.v.* **-clasped, -clasping, -clasps.** Also **in·clasp** (ĭn-). To hold in or as if in a clasp; embrace.

en·clave (ĕn′klāv′, än′-) *n.* **1.** A country or part of a country lying wholly within the boundaries of another. Compare **exclave. 2.** Any distinctly bounded area enclosed within a larger area. [French, from Old French *enclaver,* to enclose, from Vulgar Latin *inclāvāre* (unattested), to lock in with a key : Latin *in-,* in + *clāvis,* key (see **klēu-** in Appendix*).]

en·clit·ic (ĕn-klĭt′ĭk, ĭn-) *adj. Linguistics.* Having no independent accent in a sentence and forming an accentual and sometimes also graphemic unit with the preceding word. Said of a word or particle; for example, *'em* in informal English: *Give 'em the works;* or *-que* in Latin: *Senatus populusque Romanus* ("The senate and people of Rome"). Compare **proclitic.** —*n.* An enclitic word or particle. [Late Latin *encliticus,* from Greek *enklitikos,* "leaning (on the preceding word for accent)," from *enklinein,* to lean on : *en-,* in + *klinein,* to lean (see **klei-** in Appendix*).]

en·close (ĕn-klōz′, ĭn-) *tr.v.* **-closed, -closing, -closes.** Also **inclose** (ĭn-). **1.** To surround on all sides; fence in; close in. **2. a.** To place within a container. **b.** To insert in the same envelope or package with the main letter. **3.** To contain, especially so as to shelter or hide: *"every one of those darkly clustered houses encloses its own secret"* (Dickens). [Middle English *enclosen,* from Old French *enclore* (past participle *enclose*), from Vulgar Latin *inclaudere* (unattested), variant of Latin *inclūdere,* INCLUDE.]

en·clo·sure (ĕn-klō′zhər, ĭn-) *n. Abbr.* **enc., encl. 1.** The act of enclosing. **2.** The state of being enclosed. **3.** An area, object, or item that is enclosed. **4.** Something that encloses, such as a wall or fence.

en·code (ĕn-kōd′, ĭn-) *tr.v.* **-coded, -coding, -codes.** To put (a message) into code. —**en·cod′er** *n.*

en·co·mi·ast (ĕn-kō′mē-ăst′) *n.* A person who delivers or writes encomiums; eulogist. [Greek *enkōmiastēs,* from *enkōmiazein,* to praise, from *enkōmion,* ENCOMIUM.]

en·co·mi·as·tic (ĕn-kō′mē-ăs′tĭk) *adj.* Also **en·co·mi·as·ti·cal** (-tĭ-kəl). Pertaining to, containing, or being an encomium.

en·co·mi·um (ĕn-kō′mē-əm) *n., pl.* **-ums** or **-mia** (-mē-ə). A formal expression of lofty praise; tribute; eulogy. [Latin *encōmium,* from Greek *enkōmion (epos),* "(speech) in praise of a conqueror," from *enkōmios,* belonging to revels : *en-,* in + *kōmos,* celebration, revel (see **comedy**).]

en·com·pass (ĕn-kŭm′pəs, ĭn-) *tr.v.* **-passed, -passing, -passes. 1.** To form a circle or ring about; surround. **2.** To enclose; envelop. **3.** To comprise; include. [EN- + COMPASS.] —**en·com′pass·ment** *n.*

en·core (äng′kôr′, -kōr′, än′-) *n.* **1.** A demand by an audience, expressed by extended applause for an additional performance. **2.** An additional performance in response to such a demand. —*tr.v.* **encored, -coring, -cores.** To demand an encore of. —*interj.* Used to demand an additional performance. [French, still, yet, again, probably from Latin *hinc ad hōram,* from that to this hour : *hinc,* from here, from *hic,* this (see **ko-** in Appendix*) + *ad,* to (see **ad-** in Appendix*) + *hōram,* accusative of *hōra,* hour, from Greek *hōra* (see **yēro-¹** in Appendix*).]

en·coun·ter (ĕn-koun′tər, ĭn-) *n.* **1.** A meeting, especially when casual and unplanned. **2.** A hostile confrontation; a contest. —*v.* **encountered, -tering, -ters.** —*tr.* **1.** To meet or come upon, especially casually or unexpectedly. **2.** To confront in battle or contention. **3.** To come up against; be faced with or exposed to: *encounter numerous obstacles.* —*intr.* To meet, especially in conflict. [Middle English *encountre,* from Old French *encontre,* from *encontrer,* to meet, from Vulgar Latin *incontrāre* (unattested) : Latin *in-,* in + *contrā,* opposite, against (see **kom** in Appendix*).]

en·cour·age (ĕn-kûr′ĭj, ĭn-) *tr.v.* **-aged, -aging, -ages. 1.** To inspire to continue on a chosen course; impart courage or confidence to; embolden; hearten. **2.** To give support to; foster. [Middle English *encoragen,* from Old French *encorager* : *en-* (causative) + *corage,* COURAGE.] —**en·cour′ag·er** *n.*

en·cour·age·ment (ĕn-kûr′ĭj-mənt, ĭn-) *n.* **1.** The act of encouraging. **2.** The state of being encouraged. **3.** One that encourages; an inspiration or incentive.

en·cour·ag·ing (ĕn-kûr′ə-jĭng, ĭn-) *adj.* Permitting one to be confident or hopeful. —**en·cour′ag·ing·ly** *adv.*

en·croach (ĕn-krōch′, ĭn-) *intr.v.* **-croached, -croaching, -croaches. 1.** To intrude gradually or insidiously upon the domain, possessions, or rights of another; trespass. Used with *on* or *upon.* **2.** To advance beyond proper or prescribed limits: *"Freud has . . . no desire to encroach upon the artist's autonomy"* (Lionel Trilling). [Middle English *encroachen,* from Old French *encrochier,* "to catch in a hook," seize : *en-,* in + *croc,* hook, from (unattested) Frankish *krōk* (see **ger-³** in Appendix*).]

en·croach·ment (ĕn-krōch′mənt, ĭn-) *n.* The act or an instance of encroaching. See Synonyms at **breach.**

en·crust (ĕn-krŭst′, ĭn-) *tr.v.* **-crusted, -crusting, -crusts.** Also **in·crust** (ĭn-). To cover or surmount with a crust or crustlike layer: *a scepter encrusted with diamonds.* [Probably from French *incruster,* from Latin *incrustāre* : *in-* (causative) + *crusta,* CRUST.] —**en′crust·a′tion** *n.*

en·cum·ber (ĕn-kŭm′bər, ĭn-) *tr.v.* **-bered, -bering, -bers. 1.** To weigh down unduly; lay too much upon. **2.** To hinder, impede, or clutter, as with useless articles or unwanted additions. **3.** To handicap or burden, as with obligations or legal claims. —See Synonyms at **hinder.** [Middle English *encombren,* from Old French *encombrer,* to block up : *en-,* in + *combre,* hindrance, from Gaulish *comboros*† (unattested).]

en·cum·brance (ĕn-kŭm′brəns, ĭn-) *n.* **1.** One that encumbers; a burden, impediment, or obstacle. **2.** *Law.* A lien or claim upon property. —See Synonyms at **obstacle.**

en·cum·branc·er (ĕn-kŭm′brən-sər, ĭn-) *n. Law.* A person who holds an encumbrance.

-ency. Variant of **-ence.**

ency., encyc., encycl. encyclopedia.

en·cyc·li·cal (ĕn-sĭk′lĭ-kəl, ĭn-) *adj.* Intended for general or wide circulation. Said of letters. —*n. Roman Catholic Church.* A papal letter on a specific subject addressed to the ordinaries of the Church or to the hierarchy of a particular country. [Late Latin *encyclicus,* from Greek *enkuklios,* in a circle, circular : *en-,* in + *kuklos,* circle (see **kwel-¹** in Appendix*).]

en·cy·clo·pe·di·a (ĕn-sī′klə-pē′dē-ə, ĭn-) *n.* Also **en·cy·clo·pae·di·a.** *Abbr.* **ency., encyc., encycl.** A comprehensive, often multivolume, reference work containing articles on a wide range of subjects or on numerous aspects of a particular field, usually arranged alphabetically. [Medieval Latin *encyclopaedia,* general education course, from Greek *enkuklopaideiā,* a mistaken transcription of *enkuklios paideia,* general education : *enkuklios,* circular, general (see **encyclical**) + *paideia,* education, training, from *pais* (stem *paid-*), child (see **pou-** in Appendix*).]

en·cy·clo·pe·dic (ĕn-sī′klə-pē′dĭk, ĭn-) *adj.* Also **en·cy·clo·pae·dic, en·cy·clo·pe·di·cal** (-dĭ-kəl). **1.** Of, pertaining to, or characteristic of an encyclopedia. **2.** Embracing many subjects; comprehensive: *"An ignorance almost as encyclopedic as his erudition"* (William James). —**en·cy′clo·pe′di·cal·ly** *adv.*

en·cy·clo·pe·dism (ĕn-sī′klə-pē′dĭz′əm, ĭn-) *n.* Also **en·cy·clo·pae·dism.** Encyclopedic learning.

en·cy·clo·pe·dist (ĕn-sī′klə-pē′dĭst, ĭn-) *n.* Also **en·cy·clo·pae·dist.** **1.** A person who writes for or compiles an encyclopedia. **2.** *Capital E.* One of the writers of the French *Encyclopédie* (1751–72), including its editors, Diderot and d'Alembert.

en·cyst (ĕn-sĭst′, ĭn-) *v.* **-cysted, -cysting, -cysts.** —*tr.* To enclose in a cyst. —*intr.* To take the form of or become enclosed in a cyst. —**en·cyst′ment, en′cys·ta′tion** *n.*

end (ĕnd) *n.* **1.** Either extremity of something that has length. **2.** The outside or extreme edge or limit of a space, form, or area; a boundary. **3.** The point in time at which an action, event, or phenomenon ceases or is completed; conclusion: *the end of a day.* **4.** A result; outcome. **5.** The termination of life or existence; death. **6.** An ultimate extent; a limit: *the end of one's patience.* **7.** That toward which one strives; a goal: *"The end of Poetry is to produce excitement in coexistence with an overbalance of pleasure"* (Wordsworth). **8.** *Usually plural.* A remainder or remnant. **9.** *Informal.* A share of a responsibility or obligation; duty; part: *your end of the bargain.* **10.** *Football.* **a.** Either of the players in the outermost position at the line of scrimmage. **b.** The position played by such a player. —See Synonyms at **boundary, intention.** —**go off the deep end.** *Informal.* To behave or proceed in an impulsive, reckless, or distraught manner. —**make (both) ends meet.** To manage to live within one's means. —**no end.** *Informal.* A great deal: *no end of stories to tell.* —*v.* **ended, ending, ends.** —*tr.* **1.** To bring to an end; finish; conclude. **2.** To form the end or concluding part of. **3.** To bring about the extinction of; destroy. —*intr.* **1.** To come to an end; cease. **2.** To die. —See Synonyms at **complete.** —*adj.* At a position on the end; final; concluding: *end man; end point.* [Middle English *ende,* Old English *ende.* See **anti** in Appendix*.]

en·da·moe·ba, en·da·me·ba. Variants of **entamoeba.**

en·dan·ger (ĕn-dān′jər, ĭn-) *tr.v.* **-gered, -gering, -gers.** To expose to danger or harm; imperil. —**en·dan′ger·ment** *n.*

end·brain (ĕnd′brān′) *n. Anatomy.* The **telencephalon** *(see).*

en·dear (ĕn-dîr′, ĭn-) *tr.v.* **-deared, -dearing, -dears. 1.** To cause to be held dear; make beloved or esteemed. **2.** *Obsolete.* To increase the cost or value of.

en·dear·ing (ĕn-dîr′ĭng, ĭn-) *adj.* Inspiring affection or warm sympathy: *endearing qualities.* —**en·dear′ing·ly** *adv.*

en·dear·ment (ĕn-dîr′mənt, ĭn-) *n.* **1.** The act of endearing. **2.** An expression of affection; a loving word or caress: *"the promise of such kisses and dazed endearments as we could now exchange"* (Lawrence Durrell).

en·deav·or (ĕn-dĕv′ər, ĭn-) *n.* Also *chiefly British* **en·deav·our.** A conscientious or concerted effort toward a given end; an earnest attempt. See Synonyms at **effort.** —*intr.v.* **endeavored, -oring, -ors.** Also *chiefly British* **en·deav·our.** To make an earnest attempt; strive. Usually used with an infinitive: *endeavor to keep abreast of events.* [Middle English *endevour,* from *endeveren,* to exert oneself, from the phrase *putten in dever,* to put in duty, make it one's duty : IN + *dever,* duty, from Old French *devoir,* DEVOIR.] —**en·deav′or·er** *n.*

En·de·cott (ĕn′dĭ-kət, -kŏt′), **John.** Also **En·di·cott.** 1589?–1665. English colonial administrator; first governor of Massachusetts Bay Colony.

en·dem·ic (ĕn-dĕm′ĭk) *adj.* Also **en·de·mi·al** (-dē′mē-əl), **en·dem·i·cal** (-dĕm′ĭ-kəl). **1.** Prevalent in or peculiar to a particular locality or people: *"Disorder in some sense appears to be endemic in all societies"* (Crane Brinton). **2.** *Ecology.* Native or confined to a certain region; having a comparatively restricted distribution. **3.** *Medicine.* Peculiar to and recurring in a particular locality. Said of a disease. —See Synonyms at **native.** —*n. Ecology.* An endemic plant or animal. [French *endémique,* from Greek *endēmios, endēmos,* dwelling in a place,

indigenous : *en-,* in + *dēmos,* people (see **dā-** in Appendix*).] —**en·dem′i·cal·ly** *adv.* —**en·dem′ism** *n.*

En·der·by Land (ĕn′dər-bē). A region of Antarctica, at about the same longitude as Madagascar.

en·der·mic (ĕn-dûr′mĭk) *adj.* Acting medicinally by absorption through the skin. [EN- + -DERM + -IC.]

end·ing (ĕn′dĭng) *n.* **1.** A conclusion or termination. **2.** The concluding part, especially of a book, play, or film; finale: *a happy ending.* **3.** The letter or letters added to a word or word part, especially to make a derivative or inflectional form.

en·dive (ĕn′dīv′, än′dēv′) *n.* **1.** A plant, *Cichorium endivia,* cultivated for its crown of crisp, succulent leaves, used in salads. See **escarole.** **2.** A variety of the common chicory, *Cichorium intybus,* cultivated to produce a narrow, pointed cluster of whitish leaves used in salads. In this sense, also called "witloof." [Middle English, from Old French, from Medieval Latin *endiva,* variant of Latin *entubus, entibus,* chicory, from Greek *entubioi,* possibly from Egyptian *tybi,* January, because the plant grows in this month.]

end leaf. An endpaper *(see).*

end·less (ĕnd′lĭs) *adj.* **1.** Being or seeming to be without an end; infinite; boundless. **2.** Incessant; interminable: *an endless conversation.* **3.** Formed with the ends joined; continuous: *"They looked out across the endless acres of Gerald O'Hara's newly plowed cotton fields"* (Margaret Mitchell). —**end′less·ly** *adv.* —**end′less·ness** *n.*

end·long (ĕnd′lông′, -lŏng′) *adv. Archaic.* Lengthwise.

end man. **1.** The person at the end of a line or row. **2.** The man in a minstrel show who sits at one end of the company and engages in banter with the interlocutor.

end matter. Material, often including an index, appendix, bibliography, or notes, that follows the main body of a book. Also called "back matter." Compare **front matter.**

end·most (ĕnd′mōst′) *adj.* Being at or closest to the end; last.

endo-, end-. Indicates inside or within; for example, **endocarp, endomorph.** [Greek, from *endon,* within. See **en** in Appendix*.]

en·do·blast (ĕn′də-blăst′) *n.* Also **en·to·blast** (ĕn′tə-). *Embryology.* The inner layer of the blastoderm. Also called "hypoblast." [ENDO- + -BLAST.] —**en′do·blas′tic** *adj.*

en·do·car·di·tis (ĕn′dō-kär-dī′tĭs) *n.* Inflammation of the endocardium. [ENDOCARD(IUM) + -ITIS.] —**en′do·car·dit′ic** (-dĭt′ĭk) *adj.*

en·do·car·di·um (ĕn′dō-kär′dē-əm) *n., pl.* **-dia** (-dē-ə). The thin, endothelial, serous membrane that lines the interior of the heart. [New Latin : ENDO- + Greek *kardia,* heart (see **kerd-¹** in Appendix*).] —**en′do·car′di·al** *adj.*

en·do·carp (ĕn′də-kärp′) *n. Botany.* The often hard or leathery inner layer of the pericarp of many fruits. [ENDO- + -CARP.]

en·do·cra·ni·um (ĕn′dō-krā′nē-əm) *n., pl.* **-nia** (-nē-ə). A membrane, the **dura mater** *(see).*

en·do·crine (ĕn′də-krĭn, -krēn′, -krīn′) *adj.* Also **en·do·crin·ic** (-krĭn′ĭk), **en·doc·ri·nous** (ĕn-dŏk′rə-nəs). **1.** Secreting internally. **2.** Of or pertaining to any of the ductless or endocrine glands. —*n.* **1.** The internal secretion of a gland. **2.** An endocrine gland. [ENDO- + Greek *krīnein,* to separate, "secrete" (see **skeri-** in Appendix*).]

endocrine gland. Any of the ductless glands, such as the thyroid or adrenal, the secretions of which pass directly into the blood stream from the cells of the gland. Also called "ductless gland."

en·do·cri·nol·o·gy (ĕn′də-krə-nŏl′ə-jē) *n.* The physiology of the endocrine glands. [ENDOCRIN(E) + -LOGY.] —**en′do·cri·no·log′ic** (-krĭn′ə-lŏj′ĭk) *adj.* —**en′do·cri·nol′o·gist** *n.*

en·do·derm (ĕn′də-dûrm′) *n.* Also **en·to·derm** (ĕn′tə-). The innermost of the three primary germ layers of an embryo, developing into the intestinal tract and associated structures. [ENDO- + -DERM.] —**en′do·der′mal** *adj.*

en·do·der·mis (ĕn′dō-dûr′mĭs) *n. Botany.* The innermost layer of the cortex in many plants. [ENDO- + Greek *derma,* skin, DERMA.]

en·do·don·tics (ĕn′dō-dŏn′tĭks) *n.* Plural in form, used with a singular verb. Also **en·do·don·ti·a** (-shə, -shē-ə). The branch of dentistry dealing with diseases of the tooth pulp. [ENDO- + -ODONT.] —**en′do·don′tic** *adj.* —**en′do·don′tist** *n.*

en·do·en·zyme (ĕn′dō-ĕn′zīm′) *n.* An enzyme that acts inside the cell that produces it.

en·dog·a·my (ĕn-dŏg′ə-mē) *n.* **1.** Marriage within a particular group, caste, class, or tribe in accordance with set custom or law; inbreeding. Compare **exogamy.** **2.** *Botany.* Fertilization in which pollen is transferred to another flower of the same plant. [ENDO- + -GAMY.] —**en·dog′a·mous** *adj.*

en·dog·e·nous (ĕn-dŏj′ə-nəs) *adj.* **1.** Produced from within. **2.** *Biology.* Originating within an organ or part. [ENDO- + -GENOUS.] —**en·dog′e·nous·ly** *adv.* —**en·dog′e·ny** *n.*

en·do·lymph (ĕn′də-lĭmf′) *n.* The fluid in the cochlear duct of the labyrinth of the ear. [ENDO- + LYMPH.]

en·do·me·tri·um (ĕn′dō-mē′trē-əm) *n., pl.* **-tria** (-trē-ə). The mucous membrane lining the uterus. [ENDO- + METR(O)- (uterus) + -IUM.]

en·do·morph (ĕn′də-môrf′) *n.* **1.** *Mineralogy.* A mineral found as an inclusion in another, as rutile or tourmaline in quartz. Compare **perimorph.** **2.** *Physiology.* An endomorphic person. Compare **mesomorph.** [ENDO- + -MORPH.]

en·do·mor·phic (ĕn′də-môr′fĭk) *adj.* **1.** *Mineralogy.* **a.** Of or pertaining to an endomorph. **b.** Created through endomorphism. **2.** *Physiology.* Characterized by relative prominence of the abdomen and other soft body parts developed from the embryonic endodermal layer. —**en′do·mor′phy** *n.*

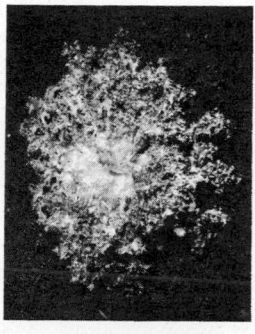

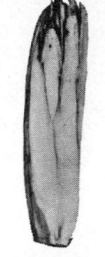

endive
Above: *Cichorium endivia*
Below: *Cichorium intybus*

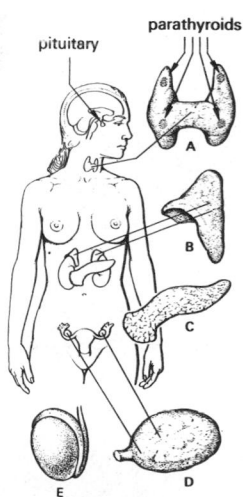

endocrine gland
A. Thyroid
B. Adrenal gland
C. Islands of Langerhans
  in pancreas
D. Ovary
E. Testis (in male)

parathyroids
pituitary

ă pat/ā pay/âr care/ä father/b bib/ch church/d deed/ĕ pet/ē be/f fife/g gag/h hat/hw which/ĭ pit/ī pie/îr pier/j judge/k kick/l lid, needle/m mum/n no, sudden/ng thing/ŏ pot/ō toe/ô paw, for/oi noise/ou out/ōō took/ōō boot/p pop/r roar/s sauce/sh ship, dish/t tight/th thin, path/th this, bathe/ŭ cut/ûr urge/v valve/w with/y yes/z zebra, size/zh vision/ə about, item, edible, gallop, circus/à Fr. ami/œ Fr. feu, Ger. schön/ü Fr. tu, Ger. über/KH Ger. ich, Scot. loch/N Fr. bon. *Follows main vocabulary. †Of obscure origin.

en·do·morph·ism (ĕn′dō-môr′fĭz′əm) n. The metamorphism of igneous rock as it cools, resulting from contact with and the assimilation of the wall rock.

en·do·par·a·site (ĕn′dō-păr′ə-sīt′) n. An organism, such as a tapeworm, that lives parasitically within another organism.

en·do·phyte (ĕn′də-fīt′) n. A plant, such as certain fungi, growing within another plant. [ENDO- + -PHYTE.] —**en′do·phyt′ic** (-dō-fĭt′ĭk) adj.

en·do·plasm (ĕn′dō-plăz′əm) n. A low-viscosity portion of the continuous phase of cytoplasm distinguishable within some cells. Compare **ectoplasm**. [ENDO- + -PLASM.]

end organ. The expanded functional termination of a sensory nerve or of a motor nerve in tissue.

en·dorse (ĕn-dôrs′, ĭn-) tr.v. -**dorsed**, -**dorsing**, -**dorses**. Also **in·dorse** (ĭn-). **1.** To write one's signature on the back of (a check, money order, or stock certificate) as evidence of the legal transfer of its ownership, especially in return for the cash or credit indicated on its face. **2.** To place (one's signature) on a contract or other instrument to indicate approval of its contents or terms. **3.** To acknowledge (receipt of payment) by signing the bill, draft, or other instrument. **4.** To give approval of or support to; sanction. —See Synonyms at **approve**. [Middle English endosen, from Old French endosser, "to put on the back of" : en-, to put on + dos, back, from Latin dorsum (see **dorsum** in Appendix*).] —**en·dors′a·ble** adj. —**en·dors′er**, **en·dor′sor** (-dôr′sər) n.

en·dor·see (ĕn-dôr′sē′, ĭn-) n. One to whom ownership of a negotiable document is transferred by endorsement.

en·dorse·ment (ĕn-dôrs′mənt, ĭn-) n. **1.** An act of endorsing. **2.** Something that endorses or validates, as a signature or voucher. **3.** Approbation; sanction; support. **4.** An amendment to a contract, such as an insurance policy, permitting a change in the original terms.

endorsement in blank. A blank endorsement (see).

en·do·scope (ĕn′də-skōp′) n. An instrument for examining the interior of a bodily canal or hollow organ. [ENDO- + -SCOPE.]

en·do·skel·e·ton (ĕn′dō-skĕl′ə-tən) n. An internal supporting skeleton characteristic of vertebrates. Compare **exoskeleton**. —**en′do·skel′e·tal** adj.

en·dos·mo·sis (ĕn′dŏz-mō′sĭs, ĕn′dŏs-) n. Osmosis toward the interior of a cell or cavity. Compare **exosmosis**. [END(O)- + OSMOSIS.] —**en′dos·mot′ic** (-mŏt′ĭk) adj.

en·do·some (ĕn′də-sōm′) n. A discrete, cellular particle of chromatin situated near the center of a nucleus.

en·do·sperm (ĕn′də-spûrm′) n. Botany. The nutritive tissue of a plant seed, surrounding and absorbed by the embryo. [ENDO- + -SPERM.]

en·do·spore (ĕn′də-spôr′, -spōr′) n. **1.** A small asexual spore, as that formed by some bacteria. **2.** The inner layer of the wall of a spore.

en·dos·te·um (ĕn-dŏs′tē-əm) n., pl. -**tea** (-tē-ə). The membrane that lines the medullary cavity of a bone. [New Latin : END(O)- + Greek osteon, bone (see **osth-** in Appendix*).] —**en·dos′te·al** adj.

en·do·the·ci·um (ĕn′dō-thē′sē-əm, -shē-əm) n., pl. -**cia** (-sē-ə, -shē-ə). Botany. The inner tissue of an anther or a moss capsule. [New Latin : ENDO- + Greek thēkion, diminutive of thēkē, chest (see **dhē-¹** in Appendix*).]

en·do·the·li·o·ma (ĕn′dō-thē′lē-ō′mə) n., pl. -**mata** (-mə-tə) or -**mas**. Any of various neoplasms derived from endothelial tissue. [ENDOTHELI(UM) + -OMA.]

en·do·the·li·um (ĕn′dō-thē′lē-əm) n., pl. -**lia** (-lē-ə). A thin layer of flat cells that lines serous cavities, lymph vessels, and blood vessels. [New Latin : ENDO- + Greek thēlē, nipple (see **dhēi-** in Appendix*).] —**en′do·the′li·al**, **en′do·the′li·oid′** adj.

en·do·ther·mic (ĕn′dō-thûr′mĭk) adj. Also **en·do·ther·mal** (-məl). Characterized by or causing the absorption of heat. Compare **exothermic**. [ENDO- + THERM + -IC.]

en·do·tox·in (ĕn′dō-tŏk′sən) n. A toxin produced within a microorganism and released upon destruction of the cell in which it is produced.

en·dow (ĕn-dou′, ĭn-) tr.v. -**dowed**, -**dowing**, -**dows**. **1.** To provide with property, income, or a source of income. **2.** To equip with a talent or quality. **3.** To invest with qualities or characteristics: "He endows the world with poetic beauty." (Walter Sutton). **4.** Obsolete. To provide with a dower. [Middle English endowen, from Norman French endouer : Old French en- (intensive) + douer, to provide with a dowry, from Latin dōtāre, from dōs (stem dōt-), dowry (see **dō-** in Appendix*).]

en·dow·ment (ĕn-dou′mənt, ĭn-) n. **1.** An act of endowing. **2.** Funds or property donated to an institution, individual, or group as a source of income. **3.** A natural gift or quality; an attribute, as beauty or talent.

endowment insurance. A form of life insurance in which the policy matures within a specified period after issuance and becomes a claim payable to the insured at that time, or to his beneficiary upon the death of the insured prior to that time.

end·pa·per (ĕnd′pā′pər) n. Also **end paper**. Either of two folded sheets of heavy paper having one half pasted to the inside front or back cover of a book and the other half pasted to the base of the first or last page to form a flyleaf. Also called "end leaf."

end·plate (ĕnd′plāt′) n. A motor nerve terminal that transmits nerve impulses to muscle.

end table. A small table, usually placed at either end of a couch or beside a chair.

en·due (ĕn-dōō′, -dyōō′, ĭn-) tr.v. -**dued**, -**duing**, -**dues**. Also **in·due** (ĭn-). **1.** To provide with some quality or trait. **2.** Rare. **a.** To put on; dress in. **b.** To clothe. [Sense 1, Middle English enduen, endeuen, from Old French enduire, to lead in, induct

(meaning influenced by Middle English endowen, endow), from Latin indūcere, INDUCE. Sense 2, Middle English induen, from Latin induere, to don. See **eu-¹** in Appendix.*]

en·dur·a·ble (ĕn-dŏor′ə-bəl, -dyŏor′ə-bəl, ĭn-) adj. Capable of being endured; tolerable; bearable. —**en·dur′a·bly** adv.

en·dur·ance (ĕn-dŏor′əns, -dyŏor′əns, ĭn-) n. **1.** The act, quality, or power of withstanding hardship or stress. **2.** The state or fact of persevering; continuing survival.

en·dure (ĕn-dŏor′, -dyŏor′, ĭn-) v. -**dured**, -**during**, -**dures**. —tr. **1.** To carry on through, despite hardships; undergo: endure an Arctic winter. **2.** To bear with tolerance; put up with: "they were too free-minded to endure command" (T.E. Lawrence). —intr. **1.** To continue in existence; remain; to last: buildings that endure for centuries. **2.** To suffer patiently without yielding; persevere; hold out. —See Synonyms at **bear**. [Middle English enduren, from Old French endurer, from Late Latin indūrāre, "to harden one's heart against," bear, from Latin, to harden : in- (intensive) + dūrāre, to harden, from dūrus, hard (see **deru-** in Appendix*).]

en·dur·ing (ĕn-dŏor′ĭng, -dyŏor′ĭng, ĭn-) adj. **1.** Lasting; durable. **2.** Chronic; unresolved: an enduring problem. **3.** Longsuffering. —**en·dur′ing·ly** adv. —**en·dur′ing·ness** n.

end·wise (ĕnd′wīz′) adv. Also **end·ways** (-wāz′). **1.** On end. **2.** With the end foremost. **3.** Lengthwise. **4.** End to end.

En·dym·i·on (ĕn-dĭm′ē-ən). Greek Mythology. A handsome young man who was loved by a moon goddess and whose youth was preserved by eternal sleep. [Latin, from Greek Endumiōn, "diver" (so called perhaps because Endymion was originally a sun god), from enduein, to dive into : en-, into + duein†, to dive, sink, set (as the sun).]

-ene. Chemistry. Indicates unsaturation of an organic compound, especially one having a double bond; for example, ethylene. [From Greek -ēnē, feminine patronymic suffix.]

ENE east-northeast.

en·e·ma (ĕn′ə-mə) n. **1.** The injection of liquid into the rectum for cleansing, laxative, or other therapeutic purposes; an anal douche. **2.** The fluid so injected. [Late Latin, from Greek, from enienai, to throw in, inject : en-, in + hienai, to send, throw (see **yē-** in Appendix*).]

en·e·my (ĕn′ə-mē) n., pl. -**mies**. **1.** One who manifests malice or hostility toward, or opposes the purposes or interests of, another; a foe; an opponent. **2.** A hostile power or force, as a nation, or a member or unit of such a force. **3.** Something destructive or injurious in its effects: Fear is our chief enemy. —adj. Of or pertaining to a hostile power or force. [Middle English enemi, from Old French, from Latin inimīcus : in-, not + amīcus, friend (see **amma** in Appendix*).]

enemy alien. An alien living in a country at war with his own country.

en·er·get·ic (ĕn′ər-jĕt′ĭk) adj. Possessing, exerting, or displaying energy; vigorous. See Synonyms at **active**. [Greek energētikos, active, from energein, to be active, from energos, active. See **energy**.] —**en′er·get′i·cal·ly** adv.

en·er·get·ics (ĕn′ər-jĕt′ĭks) n. Plural in form, used with a singular verb. The physics of energy and its transformations.

en·er·gid (ĕn′ər-jĭd′) n. Biology. A unit consisting of a nucleus surrounded by cytoplasm, with or without a cell wall, that does not constitute a cell. [ENERG(Y) + -ID.]

en·er·gize (ĕn′ər-jīz′) v. -**gized**, -**gizing**, -**gizes**. —tr. To give energy to; activate; charge. —intr. To release or put out energy. —**en′er·giz′er** n.

en·er·gu·men (ĕn′ər-gyōō′mən) n. **1.** One believed to be possessed by an evil spirit; a demoniac. **2.** A zealot; fanatic. [Late Latin energūmenus, from Greek energoumenos, worked on, "possessed," from energein, to be active, effect, from energos, active. See **energy**.]

en·er·gy (ĕn′ər-jē) n., pl. -**gies**. **1. a.** Vigor or power in action. **b.** Vitality and intensity of expression. **2.** The capacity for action or accomplishment: lacked energy to finish the job. **3.** Usually plural. Power exercised with vigor and determination: devote one's energies to a worthy cause. **4.** Physics. The work that a physical system is capable of doing in changing from its actual state to a specified reference state, the total including, in general, contributions of **potential energy, kinetic energy,** and **rest energy** (all of which see). —See Synonyms at **strength**. [Late Latin energīa, from Greek energeia, coined by Aristotle from energēs, energos, active, at work : en-, at + ergon, work (see **werg-¹** in Appendix*).]

energy density. The energy per unit volume of a region of space.

energy level. 1. The energy characteristic of a stationary state of any quantum mechanical system. **2.** The state characterized by such an energy.

en·er·vate (ĕn′ər-vāt′) tr.v. -**vated**, -**vating**, -**vates**. To deprive of strength or vitality; debilitate; weaken: "the luxury which enervates and destroys nations" (Thoreau). See Synonyms at **deplete**. —adj. (ĭ-nûr′vĭt). Deprived of strength; devitalized. [Latin ēnervāre, "to remove the sinews from" : ex- (removal) + nervus, sinew, nerve (see **sneu-** in Appendix*).] —**en′er·va′tion** n.

en·face (ĕn-fās′, ĭn-) tr.v. -**faced**, -**facing**, -**faces**. To write on the face of (a check or draft). [EN- + FACE.] —**en·face′ment** n.

en fa·mille (äN fà-mē′y′). French. In or with the family; at home.

en·fant ter·ri·ble (äN-fäN′ tĕ-rē′bl′) pl. **enfants terribles** (äN-fäN′ tĕ-rē′bl′). **1.** A child who habitually causes embarrassment by his conduct or remarks. **2.** A person whose startlingly unconventional behavior and ideas are a source of embarrassment or dismay to a cause, group, or profession: "Cocteau, the ever

---

ă pat/ā pay/âr care/ä father/b bib/ch church/d deed/ĕ pet/ē be/f fife/g gag/h hat/hw which/ĭ pit/ī pie/îr pier/j judge/k kick/l lid/ needle/m mum/n no, sudden/ng thing/ŏ pot/ō toe/ô paw, for/oi noise/ou out/ŏŏ took/ōō boot/p pop/r roar/s sauce/sh ship, dish/

unpredictable perennial enfant terrible of the French cinema" (John R. Taylor). [French, "terrible child."]

en·fee·ble (ĕn-fē′bəl, ĭn-) *tr.v.* **-bled, -bling, -bles.** To make feeble; deprive of strength. [Middle English *enfeblen,* from Old French *enfebler* : *en-* (causative) + *feble,* FEEBLE.] **—en·fee′ble·ment** *n.* **—en·fee′bler** *n.*

en·feoff (ĕn-fĕf′, -fēf′, ĭn-) *tr.v.* **-feoffed, -feoffing, -feoffs. 1.** To invest with a feudal estate or fee. **2.** To surrender or give into vassalage. [Middle English *enfeffen, enfeoffen,* from Norman French, from Old French : *en-,* to put in + *fief,* fee, FIEF.] **—en·feoff′ment** *n.*

en·fet·ter (ĕn-fĕt′ər, ĭn-) *tr.v.* **-tered, -tering, -ters.** To bind in fetters; enchain; enslave.

En·field (ĕn′fēld′). A borough of London, England, comprising the former administrative divisions of Edmonton, Enfield, and Southgate. Population, 274,000.

Enfield rifle. Any of several rifles of varying calibers used formerly by British and American troops, especially the .30 or .303 bolt-action, breechloading model. Also called "Enfield." [From ENFIELD, England, where it was first made.]

en·fi·lade (ĕn′fə-lād′) *n.* **1.** The firing of a gun or guns so as to sweep the length of a target, such as a column of troops. **2.** A position or emplacement under enfilade. *—tr.v.* **enfiladed, -lading, -lades.** To rake with gunfire. [French, "series," from *enfiler,* to thread, from Old French : *en-,* in + *fil,* thread, from Latin *filum* (see **gwhī-** in Appendix*).]

en·fleu·rage (äN-flœ-räzh′) *n.* A process in the making of perfume by which odorless fats or oils are exposed to the exhaled fragrance of fresh flowers. [French, from *enfleurer,* to cause to take in the fragrance of flowers : Old French *en-,* in + *fleur, flor,* flower, from Latin *flōs* (stem *flōr-*) (see **bhel-**³ in Appendix*).]

en·fold (ĕn-fōld′, ĭn-) *tr.v.* **-folded, -folding, -folds.** Also **in·fold** (ĭn-). **1.** To cover with or as if with folds; envelop. **2.** To hold within limits; enclose. **3.** To embrace. **—en·fold′er** *n.*

en·force (ĕn-fôrs′, -fōrs′, ĭn-) *tr.v.* **-forced, -forcing, -forces. 1.** To compel observance of or obedience to: *enforce a regulation.* **2.** To impose (specified action or behavior); compel: *"A formal and unnatural position, enforcing an erect carriage of the body."* (Ambrose Bierce). **3.** To give force to; stress; underline; reinforce: *"enforces its plea with a description of the pains of hell"* (Albert C. Baugh). [Middle English *enforcen,* from Old French *enforcier,* from Vulgar Latin *infortiāre* (unattested), to make strong : Latin *in-* (causative) + *fortis,* strong (see **bhergh-**² in Appendix*).] **—en·force′a·ble** *adj.* **—en·force′ment** *n.* **—en·forc′er** *n.*

en·fran·chise (ĕn-frăn′chīz′, ĭn-) *tr.v.* **-chised, -chising, -chises. 1.** To bestow a franchise upon. **2.** To endow with the rights of citizenship, especially the right to vote. **3.** To free, as from bondage. [Middle English *enfraunchisen,* from Old French *enfranchir* (present stem *enfranchiss-*) : *en-* (causative) + *franche, franc,* free (see **franchise**).]

eng (ĕng) *n.* A phonetic symbol (ŋ) representing in some pronunciation alphabets the velar nasal consonantal sound of *ng,* as in bri*ng* or lo*ng,* or of *n,* as in li*n*k.

eng. 1. engine. **2.** engineer; engineering.

Eng. England; English.

En·ga·dine (ĕng′gə-dēn′). A valley, about 60 miles long, of the Inn River and a resort area in eastern Switzerland.

en·gage (ĕn-gāj′, ĭn-) *v.* **-gaged, -gaging, -gages.** *—tr.* **1.** To obtain or contract for the services of; employ: *engage a carpenter.* **2.** To contract for the use of; reserve: *engage a room.* **3.** To obtain and hold the attention of; engross: *The project engaged her interest for months.* **4.** To require the use of; occupy: *Studying engages most of a student's time.* **5.** To pledge; especially, to promise to marry; betroth. Usually used in the passive: *She is engaged to Harry.* **6.** To enter or bring into conflict with: *We have engaged the enemy.* **7.** To interlock or cause to interlock; mesh. **8.** To please or attract; win. **9.** To entangle; involve: *engage someone in idle chatter.* **10.** *Archaic.* To give or take as security; attach. *—intr.* **1.** To involve oneself or become occupied; participate: *engage in conversation.* **2.** To assume an obligation; pledge; agree. **3.** To enter into conflict or battle. **4.** To become meshed or interlocked. [Middle English *engagen,* from Old French *engager* : *en-,* in + *gage,* pledge, from (unattested) Frankish *wadi* (see **wadh-** in Appendix*).] **—en·gag′er** *n.*

en·gaged (ĕn-gājd′, ĭn-) *adj.* **1.** Employed; occupied; busy. **2.** Contracted for; pledged. **3.** Betrothed; affianced: *an engaged couple.* **4.** Involved in conflict or battle. **5.** Being in gear; meshed; interlocked. **6.** Partly sunk, built into, or attached to another part, as columns on a wall.

en·gage·ment (ĕn-gāj′mənt, ĭn-) *n.* **1.** An act of engaging or the state of being engaged. **2.** Betrothal. **3.** A person or thing that engages. **4.** A promise, pledge, or obligation; especially, a commitment to appear at a certain time, as for business or social activity; an appointment. **5. a.** Employment, especially for a specified time. **b.** The period of employment. **6.** A battle or encounter. **7.** The condition of being in gear. **8.** *Usually plural.* Financial obligations or commitments.

en·gag·ing (ĕn-gā′jĭng, ĭn-) *adj.* Tending to attract; charming; pleasing. **—en·gag′ing·ly** *adv.*

En·ga·ño, Cape (ĕn-gä′nyō). A cape on northeastern Luzon, Republic of the Philippines, near the site of a naval battle (1944) in which Japanese forces were defeated by a U.S. fleet.

en garde (äN gärd′). Used to warn a fencer to assume the first position preparatory to a match. [French, on guard.]

en·gar·land (ĕn-gär′lənd, ĭn-) *tr.v.* **-landed, -landing, -lands.** To encircle or deck with or as if with a garland or garlands.

Eng·els (ĕng′əls), **Friedrich.** 1820–1895. German socialist leader and writer; collaborated with Karl Marx.

en·gen·der (ĕn-jĕn′dər, ĭn-) *v.* **-dered, -dering, -ders.** *—tr.* **1.** To bring into existence; give rise to; produce: *"Special needs . . . engender special deities to provide for them"* (Edward Conze). **2.** To procreate; propagate. *—intr.* To come into existence; be born; be produced. [Middle English *engenderen,* from Old French *engenderer,* from Latin *ingenerāre* : *in-,* in + *generāre,* GENERATE.]

engin. engineering.

en·gine (ĕn′jən) *n. Abbr.* **eng. 1. a.** A machine that converts energy into mechanical motion. **b.** Such a machine distinguished from an electric, spring-driven, or hydraulic motor by its consumption of a fuel. **c.** Any mechanical appliance, instrument, or tool. **2.** A locomotive. **3.** *Archaic.* Any agent, instrument, or means of accomplishment: *"Huddled in the dirt, the reasoning engine lies"* (John Wilmot). [Middle English *engin,* from Old French, skill, invention, from Latin *ingenium,* inborn talent, skill. See **gene-** in Appendix.*]

engine block. The cast metal block containing the cylinders of an internal-combustion engine. Also called "block."

en·gi·neer (ĕn′jə-nîr′) *n. Abbr.* **E., e., eng., engr. 1.** A person trained in, skilled at, or professionally engaged in a branch of engineering: *a mining engineer.* **2.** A person who skillfully or shrewdly manages an enterprise. **3.** A person who operates an engine. *—tr.v.* **engineered, -neering, -neers. 1.** To plan, construct, and manage as an engineer; act as engineer. **2.** To plan, manage, and put through by skillful acts or contrivance; maneuver: *"Claudius's murder was engineered by his wife Agrippina"* (Robert Graves). [Middle English *enginer,* from Old French *engigneor,* from Medieval Latin *ingeniātor,* contriver, from *ingeniāre,* to contrive, from Latin *ingenium,* talent. See **engine.**]

en·gi·neer·ing (ĕn′jə-nîr′ĭng) *n. Abbr.* **E., e., eng., engin. 1.** The application of scientific principles to practical ends as the design, construction, and operation of efficient and economical structures, equipment, and systems. **2.** The profession of or the work performed by an engineer.

en·gine·ry (ĕn′jən-rē) *n.* **1.** Machines and tools; machinery. **2.** Engines or instruments of war. **3.** Skillful management; maneuvering.

en·gird (ĕn-gûrd′) *tr.v.* **-girt** (-gûrt′) or **-girded, -girding, -girds.** Also **en·gird·le** (-gûrd′l). To encircle; gird.

en·gla·ci·al (ĕn-glā′shəl, ĭn-) *adj.* Located or occurring within a glacier: *an englacial stream.*

Eng·land (ĭng′glənd). *Abbr.* **Eng. 1.** The largest (50,874 square miles) political division of the United Kingdom of Great Britain and Northern Ireland, in southern Great Britain. Population, 43,461,000. Capital, London. **2.** Popularly, Great Britain. **3.** Popularly, the United Kingdom of Great Britain and Northern Ireland. [Middle English *Engeland,* Old English *Engla land,* "land of the Angles" : *Engla,* genitive of *Engle,* the Angles (see **ank-** in Appendix*) + LAND.]

Eng·lish (ĭng′glĭsh) *adj.* **1. a.** Of, pertaining to, derived from, or characteristic of England and its inhabitants. **b.** Of a type or style predominant in England: *English breakfast.* **2.** Of, belonging to, or spoken or written in the English language. **3.** British. *—n. Abbr.* **E, E., Eng. 1.** The people of England collectively. Used with *the.* **2.** The West Germanic language of the English divided historically into Old English, Middle English, and Modern English and now spoken in the British Isles, the United States, and numerous other countries. **3.** The English language as spoken or written at a particular time, in a particular region, or by a particular person or group of people: *American English; Shakespeare's English.* **4.** A translation into or an equivalent in the English language. **5.** A course or individual class in the study of English literature, language, or composition. **6.** *Printing.* A size of type, 14-point. **7.** *Often small* **e.** The spin given to a ball by striking it on one side or releasing it with a sharp twist. *—tr.v.* **Englished, -lishing, -lishes. 1.** To translate into English. **2.** To adapt into English; Anglicize. **3.** *Often small* **e.** To cause (a ball) to spin, as in billiards or bowling. [Middle English *English,* Old English *Englisc,* from *Engle,* the Angles. See **England.**]

English Channel. *French* **La Manche** (lä mäNsh′). An arm of the Atlantic varying in width between 20 and 100 miles and extending 350 miles between England and France, and connected with the North Sea by the Strait of Dover.

English daisy. See **daisy.**

English finish. A smooth, nonglossy finish for paper.

English horn. A double-reed woodwind musical instrument similar to but larger than the oboe and pitched lower by a fifth.

Eng·lish·ism (ĭng′glĭsh-ĭz′əm) *n.* **1.** Something characteristic of England or the English people. **2.** A fondness for or attachment to anything English. **3.** An idiom of British English; an Anglicism or Briticism.

Eng·lish·man (ĭng′glĭsh-mən) *n., pl.* **-men** (-mĭn). A native or inhabitant of England.

Englishman's tie. *Nautical.* A **fisherman's knot** *(see).* Also called "Englishman's knot."

English muffin. A griddle-baked muffin made with yeast dough, and usually split and toasted for eating.

English plantain. A plant, **ribgrass** *(see).*

English Revolution. The sequence of events occurring in England during the latter part of the 17th century, including the execution of Charles I, the rise of the Commonwealth and Cromwell, the dethronement of James II, and the accession of William and Mary.

English setter. A dog of a breed developed in England, having

English horn

en garde
Fencer in first position

English setter

a silky white coat usually with black or brownish markings.
English sheepdog. See **Old English sheepdog.**
English sonnet. A **Shakespearean sonnet** *(see).*
English sparrow. The **house sparrow** *(see),* especially as naturalized in North America.
English walnut. A Eurasian tree, *Juglans regia,* cultivated in southern Europe and California for its large edible nuts. Also called "Persian walnut."
Eng·lish·wom·an (ĭng′glĭsh-wo͝om′ən) *n., pl.* **-women** (-wĭm′ĭn). A woman who is English by birth, descent, or naturalization.
en·glut (ĕn-glŭt′, ĭn-) *tr.v.* **-glutted, -glutting, -gluts.** To gulp down; swallow greedily. [EN- + GLUT.]
en·gorge (ĕn-gôrj′, ĭn-) *v.* **-gorged, -gorging, -gorges.** —*tr.* **1.** To devour greedily. **2.** To gorge; to glut. **3.** To congest or fill to excess, as with blood or other fluid. Usually used in the passive. —*intr.* To feed ravenously. [Old French *engorgier* : *en-,* in + *gorge,* throat, GORGE.] —**en·gorge′ment** *n.*
engr. **1.** engineer. **2.** engraved; engraver; engraving.
en·graft (ĕn-grăft′, -gräft′, ĭn-) *tr.v.* **-grafted, -grafting, -grafts.** Also **in·graft** (ĭn-). **1.** To graft (a scion) onto or into another tree or plant for propagation. **2.** To plant firmly; establish; root. —**en·graft′ment** *n.*
en·grail (ĕn-grāl′, ĭn-) *tr.v.* **-grailed, -grailing, -grails.** **1.** To indent (the edge of something) with small curves. **2.** To decorate the edge of by adding a series of curved indentations. [Middle English *engrelen,* from Old French *engresler* : *en-,* in + *gresle,* slender, from Latin *gracilis,* slender (see **gracile**).]
en·grain (ĕn-grān′, ĭn-) *tr.v.* **-grained, -graining, -grains.** To treat, dye, or color so as to suggest the grain of wood. [Middle English *engreinen,* from Old French *engrainer,* to dye in grain, from *en graine,* in grain : *en-,* in + *graine,* cochineal dye, kermes, from Latin *grāna,* plural of *grānum,* GRAIN.]
en·gram (ĕn′grăm′) *n.* Also **en·gramme.** A persistent protoplasmic alteration hypothesized to occur on stimulation of living neural tissue and to account for memory. [EN- + -GRAM.]
en·grave (ĕn-grāv′, ĭn-) *tr.v.* **-graved, -graving, -graves.** **1.** To carve, cut, or etch (a design or letters) into a material. **2. a.** To carve, cut, or etch (a design or letters) into a block or surface used for printing. **b.** To print from a block or plate made by such a process. **3.** To impress deeply; fix permanently. [EN- + GRAVE (to carve).] —**en·grav′er** *n.*
en·grav·ing (ĕn-grā′vĭng, ĭn-) *n. Abbr.* **engr.** **1.** The art or technique of one that engraves. **2.** An engraved surface for printing. **3.** A print made from an engraved plate or block.
en·gross (ĕn-grōs′, ĭn-) *tr.v.* **-grossed, -grossing, -grosses.** **1.** To occupy the complete attentions of; absorb wholly. **2.** To acquire most or all of a commodity; monopolize a market. Compare **forestall.** **3. a.** To write or transcribe in a large, clear hand. **b.** To prepare the text of (an official document) by an officially prescribed process, such as handwriting or printing. [Senses 1 and 2, Middle English *engrossen,* from Norman French *engrosser,* from Old French *en gros,* in large quantity : *en-,* in + *gros,* GROSS. Sense 3, Middle English *engrossen,* from Medieval Latin *ingrossāre* : Latin *in-,* in + Latin *grossus,* GROSS.] —**en·gross′er** *n.*
en·gross·ing (ĕn-grō′sĭng, ĭn-) *adj.* Occupying one's complete attention; wholly absorbing. —**en·gross′ing·ly** *adv.*
en·gross·ment (ĕn-grōs′mənt, ĭn-) *n.* **1.** The state of being completely absorbed, occupied, or monopolized. **2.** A document, such as a deed or will, that has been engrossed.
en·gulf (ĕn-gŭlf′, ĭn-) *tr.v.* **-gulfed, -gulfing, -gulfs.** Also **in·gulf.** **1.** To surround completely. **2.** To swallow up or overwhelm by or as if by overflowing and enclosing: *"In crossing the moor . . . they were all three engulfed in a treacherous piece of bog"* (Saki). [EN- + GULF.] —**en·gulf′ment** *n.*
en·hance (ĕn-hăns′, -häns′, ĭn-) *tr.v.* **-hanced, -hancing, -hances.** To increase or make greater, as in value, cost, beauty, or reputation; augment: *"The effect of this forceful poem is enhanced by contrast"* (Tucker Brooke). See Synonyms at **improve.** [Middle English *enhauncen,* from Norman French *enhauncer,* variant of Old French *enhaucer,* from Vulgar Latin *inaltiāre* (unattested), to raise : Latin *in-* (intensive) + *altus,* high (see **al-**[3] in Appendix*).] —**en·hance′ment** *n.* —**en·hanc′er** *n.* —**en·hanc′ive** *adj.*
en·har·mon·ic (ĕn′här-mŏn′ĭk) *adj. Music.* Of, relating to, or involving a tone whose written representation is altered, as from C♯ to D♭, as a conventional means of visually preparing for a new key that has a key signature distinctly different from that of the original. [Late Latin *enharmonicus,* from Greek *enarmonikos,* "in harmony" : *en-,* in + *harmonia,* HARMONY.] —**en′har·mon′i·cal·ly** *adv.*
E·nid[1] (ē′nĭd). A feminine given name. [Middle English *Enid,* from Middle Welsh, from *eneit,* soul. See **ane-** in Appendix.*]
E·nid[2] (ē′nĭd). The loyal wife of Geraint in Arthurian legend.
E·nid[3] (ē′nĭd). A city in northern Oklahoma. Population, 39,000.
e·nig·ma (ĭ-nĭg′mə) *n.* **1.** An obscure riddle. **2.** An obscure speech or writing. **3.** One that is puzzling, ambiguous, or inexplicable. [Latin *aenigma,* from Greek *ainigma,* from *ainissesthai,* to speak in riddles, hint, from *ainos,* tale, story (see **ai-**[2] in Appendix*).]
en·ig·mat·ic (ĕn′ĭg-măt′ĭk) *adj.* Also **en·ig·mat·i·cal** (-ĭ-kəl). Of or resembling an enigma; puzzling: *"a smile that was at once worldly, wan, and enigmatic"* (J.D. Salinger). See Synonyms at **ambiguous, mysterious.** —**en′ig·mat′i·cal·ly** *adv.*
E·ni·sei. See **Yenisei.**
en·isle (ĕn-īl′, ĭn-) *tr.v.* **-isled, -isling, -isles.** **1.** To make into an island. **2.** To set apart from others; isolate.
E·ni·we·tok (ĕn′ĭ-wē′tŏk′, ĕ-nē′wə-tŏk′). An atoll in the Marshall Islands in the west-central Pacific Ocean; site of U.S. atomic tests (1948).
en·jamb·ment, en·jambe·ment (ĕn-jăm′mənt, -jămb′mənt, ĭn-) *n.* The continuation of a sentence or idea from one line or couplet of a poem to the next. [French, from Old French *enjamber,* to straddle : *en-,* in + *jambe,* leg (see **jamb**).]
en·join (ĕn-join′, ĭn-) *tr.v.* **-joined, -joining, -joins.** **1.** To direct with authority and emphasis; command; impose: *"The regulations enjoin the attendance of almost the entire ship's company."* (Melville). **2.** To prohibit or forbid, especially by legal action: *The court enjoined him from visiting his children.* —See Synonyms at **command.** [Middle English *enjoinen,* from Old French *enjoindre,* from Latin *injungere,* to join to, impose : *in-,* in, to + *jungere,* join (see **yeug-** in Appendix*).] —**en·join′er** *n.* —**en·join′ment** *n.*
en·join·der (ĕn-join′dər, ĭn-) *n.* An authoritative request or injunction: *"in Zen . . . the enjoinder to put aside desires and perturbations"* (Ernest Becker). [From ENJOIN (after REJOINDER).]
en·joy (ĕn-joi′, ĭn-) *tr.v.* **-joyed, -joying, -joys.** **1.** To experience joy in; receive pleasure from; relish: *enjoy good food.* **2.** To have the use of; benefit from; have as one's lot: *"at one time the white elephant enjoyed immense symbolic importance in the East"* (Richard Carrington). —See Synonyms at **like.** —**enjoy oneself.** To have a pleasant time. [Middle English *enjoien,* from Old French *enjoïr* : *en-,* in + *joïr,* to rejoice, from Latin *gaudēre* (see **gāu-** in Appendix*).] —**en·joy′er** *n.*
en·joy·a·ble (ĕn-joi′ə-bəl, ĭn-) *adj.* Capable of being enjoyed; giving enjoyment; pleasurable; agreeable. —**en·joy′a·ble·ness** *n.* —**en·joy′a·bly** *adv.*
en·joy·ment (ĕn-joi′mənt, ĭn-) *n.* **1.** The act or state of experiencing joy or pleasure in something. **2.** The use or possession of something beneficial or pleasurable: *enjoyment of the right to vote.* **3.** Something that is enjoyed. **4.** Pleasure; joy. —See Synonyms at **pleasure.**
en·kin·dle (ĕn-kĭnd′l, ĭn-) *tr.v.* **-dled, -dling, -dles.** **1.** To set afire; light; kindle. **2.** To incite; arouse. **3.** To make luminous and glowing. —**en·kin′dler** *n.*
enl. **1.** enlarged. **2.** enlisted.
en·lace (ĕn-lās′, ĭn-) *tr.v.* **-laced, -lacing, -laces.** Also **in·lace.** **1.** To wrap or wind about with or as if with a lace or laces; encircle. **2.** To interlace; entangle; entwine. —**en·lace′ment** *n.*
en·large (ĕn-lärj′, ĭn-) *v.* **-larged, -larging, -larges.** —*tr.* **1.** To make larger; add to; magnify. **2.** To give greater scope to; expand: *"the tourist anywhere is rarely interested in enlarging his mental boundaries"* (Gordon K. Lewis). —*intr.* **1.** To become larger; grow. **2.** To speak or write at greater length or in greater detail. Used with *on* or *upon.* —See Synonyms at **increase.** [Middle English *enlargen,* from Old French *enlargier* : *en-,* in + *large,* LARGE.] —**en·larg′er** *n.*
en·large·ment (ĕn-lärj′mənt, ĭn-) *n.* **1.** An act of enlarging or the state of being enlarged. **2.** Something that enlarges another thing, as an addition, expansion, or increase. **3.** A reproduction or copy larger than the original; especially, an optically magnified print of a photographic negative.
en·light·en (ĕn-līt′n, ĭn-) *tr.v.* **-ened, -ening, -ens.** **1.** To give knowledge or truth to; endow with spiritual understanding; edify; instruct. **2.** To acquaint (someone) with information; inform. [EN- + LIGHTEN.] —**en·light′en·er** *n.*
en·light·en·ment (ĕn-līt′n-mənt, ĭn-) *n.* **1.** An act or means of enlightening. **2.** The state of being enlightened. —See Synonyms at **knowledge.** —**the Enlightenment.** A philosophical movement of the 18th century, concerned with the critical examination of previously accepted doctrines and institutions from the point of view of rationalism.
en·list (ĕn-lĭst′, ĭn-) *v.* **-listed, -listing, -lists.** —*tr.* **1.** To persuade to enter the armed forces. **2.** To engage the assistance or cooperation of; secure on one's behalf. —*intr.* **1.** To enter the armed forces voluntarily. **2.** To participate actively in some cause or enterprise. [EN- + LIST (roster).] —**en·list′ment** *n.*
enlisted man. *Abbr.* **EM** A man who has enlisted in the armed forces without an officer's commission or warrant.
en·li·ven (ĕn-lī′vən, ĭn-) *tr.v.* **-vened, -vening, -vens.** To make lively or spirited; to animate; invigorate. [EN- + LIVE (adjective).] —**en·liv′en·er** *n.* —**en·liv′en·ment** *n.*
en masse (ĕn măs′). In one group or body; all together. [French : Old French *en,* in + *masse,* MASS (body).]
en·mesh (ĕn-mĕsh′, ĭn-) *tr.v.* **-meshed, -meshing, -meshes.** Also **im·mesh** (ĭ-mĕsh′). **1.** To entangle, involve, or catch in or as if in a mesh. **2.** To cover with mesh: *"Her neck was enmeshed in black netting"* (William Golding).
en·mi·ty (ĕn′mə-tē) *n., pl.* **-ties.** Deep-seated hatred, as between rivals or opponents; antagonism: *"The mind of man . . . is full of enmity against the doctrines of the gospel"* (Jonathan Edwards). [Middle English *enemite,* from Old French *enemiste,* from Vulgar Latin *inimīcitās* (unattested), from Latin *inimīcus,* ENEMY.]
Synonyms: *enmity, hostility, antagonism, animosity, rancor, antipathy, animus.* These nouns refer to the feeling or expression of ill will. *Enmity* and *hostility* both denote the ill will of one person or group toward another or, more often, mutual bad feeling. *Hostility,* in addition, can refer to clear expression of this in the form of threats or violent acts. The remaining terms denote conditions of ill will likely to produce such acts. *Antagonism* makes the strongest implication of active opposition or combat or the imminence of it. *Animosity* and, to a greater degree, *rancor* suggest the harboring of hatred and resentment; such feelings typically trace to past differences that have pro-

duced grievances and the desire for revenge. *Antipathy* is deep-seated aversion or repugnance. *Animus* is ill will of a distinctively personal and sometimes irrational nature, based on one's prejudices or peculiarity of character or temperament.

en·ne·ad (ĕn′ē-ăd′) *n.* Any group or set of nine. [Greek *enneas* (stem *ennead-*), from *ennea,* nine. See **newn̥** in Appendix.*]

En·nis (ĕn′ĭs). The county seat of County Clare, Republic of Ireland. Population, 6,000.

En·nis·kil·len (ĕn′ĭs-kĭl′ən). The county seat of County Fermanagh, Northern Ireland, 65 miles southwest of Belfast. Population, 7,000.

en·no·ble (ĕn-nō′bəl, ĭn-) *tr.v.* **-bled, -bling, -bles. 1.** To invest with nobility; add to the honor of: *"That name he [Nelson] had ennobled beyond all addition of nobility"* (Southey). **2.** To raise to the rank of nobleman; confer nobility upon. [Middle English *ennoblen,* from Old French *ennoblir* : *en-,* in + NOBLE.] **—en·no′ble·ment** *n.* **—en·no′bler** *n.*

en·nui (än′wē′) *n.* Listlessness and dissatisfaction resulting from lack of interest; boredom: *"the servants relieved their ennui with gambling and gossip about their masters"* (John Barth). [French, from Old French *enui,* from Latin *in odiō,* "in hate," odious : *in,* in + *odium,* hate (see **od-**[2] in Appendix*).]

E·noch[1] (ē′nək). The eldest son of Cain. Genesis 4:17. [Late Latin, from Greek *Enōkh,* from Hebrew *Ḥanōkh,* "consecrated," "initiated," from *hānakh,* he initiated. See also **Chanukah.**]

E·noch[2] (ē′nək). The father of Methuselah. Genesis 5:21.

e·nol (ē′nôl′, ē′nōl′, ē′nŏl′) *n.* An organic compound containing a hydroxyl group bonded to a carbon atom which in turn is doubly bonded to another carbon atom. [*En(e)-,* from -ENE + -OL.] **—e·nol′ic** (ē-nŏl′ĭk) *adj.*

e·nol·o·gy. Variant of **oenology.**

e·nor·mi·ty (ĕ-nôr′mə-tē) *n., pl.* **-ties. 1.** The quality of passing all moral bounds; excessive wickedness; outrageousness. **2.** A monstrous offense or evil; an outrage.

Usage: *Enormity* is not used acceptably when it is applied to indicate mere size, without the accompanying sense of outrageousness, wickedness, or evil. In the following example, termed unacceptable by 93 per cent of the Usage Panel, it refers merely to physical extent: *The enormity of Latin America is readily apparent from these maps.* The desired sense would be conveyed by *immensity, hugeness,* or *enormousness.*

e·nor·mous (ĕ-nôr′məs) *adj.* **1.** Very great in size, extent, number, or degree; immense; vast. **2.** *Archaic.* Very wicked; heinous. [Middle English *enorme,* from Latin *ēnormis,* unusual, immense : *ex-,* out of + *norma,* pattern, rule (see **gnō-** in Appendix*).] **—e·nor′mous·ly** *adv.* **—e·nor′mous·ness** *n.*

Synonyms: *enormous, immense, huge, gigantic, colossal, mammoth, tremendous, stupendous, gargantuan, vast.* These adjectives describe what is extraordinarily large or great in some respect. *Enormous* specifies a marked excess beyond the norm in size, amount, or degree. *Immense* literally means infinite and generally refers to size or extent that is beyond the usual means of measurement. *Huge* especially implies greatness of physical size or capacity. *Gigantic* implies abnormal deviation from the usual physical size or capacity of a given kind. *Colossal* suggests hugeness that creates awe or taxes belief. *Mammoth* is applied to anything on an extremely large or extravagant scale. *Tremendous,* in careful usage, refers to what inspires awe or fear; less strictly it describes greatness of quantity, extent, or degree. *Stupendous* implies size that astounds or defies description. *Gargantuan* stresses greatness of capacity, especially for food or pleasure. *Vast* often makes reference to greatness of extent or scope; less frequently it refers to quantity or amount.

E·nos (ē′nəs). A son of Seth. Genesis 4:26. [Greek *Enōs,* from Hebrew *Enōsh,* "man."]

e·nough (ĭ-nŭf′) *adj.* Sufficient to meet a need or satisfy a desire; adequate. See Synonyms at **sufficient.** *—n.* An adequate quantity: *He ate enough for two.* *—adv.* **1.** To a satisfactory amount or degree; sufficiently. **2.** Very; fully; quite: *We were glad enough to leave.* **3.** Tolerably; rather: *She sang well enough, but the show was a failure.* [Middle English *ynough, inough,* Old English *genōg.* See **nek-**[2] in Appendix.*]

e·nounce (ĭ-nouns′) *tr.v.* **enounced, enouncing, enounces. 1.** To declare publicly or formally; state; announce. **2.** To pronounce; enunciate. [French *énoncer,* from Latin *ēnuntiāre,* ENUNCIATE.] **—e·nounce′ment** *n.*

e·now (ĭ-nou′) *adj. Archaic.* Enough. **—e·now′** *adv.*

en pas·sant (äɴ pä-säɴ′). **1.** *French.* In passing; by the way. **2.** *Chess.* The capture of a pawn that has made an initial move of two squares by an opponent's pawn that occupies the adjacent square on the forward diagonal to the square that is crossed.

en·phy·tot·ic (ĕn′fī-tŏt′ĭk) *adj.* Designating or characterizing a plant disease that causes a relatively constant amount of damage each year. [EN- + -PHYT(E) + -OTIC.]

en·plane (ĕn-plān′) *intr.v.* **-planed, -planing, -planes.** Also **em·plane** (ĕm-). To board an airplane. [EN- + PLANE (airplane).]

en·quire. Variant of **inquire.**

en·rage (ĕn-rāj′, ĭn-) *tr.v.* **-raged, -raging, -rages.** To put in a rage; infuriate; anger.

en·rapt (ĕn-răpt′, ĭn-) *adj.* Enraptured; enthralled. [EN- + RAPT.]

en·rap·ture (ĕn-răp′chər, ĭn-) *tr.v.* **-tured, -turing, -tures.** To move to rapture; transport with delight.

en·rav·ish (ĕn-răv′ĭsh, ĭn-) *tr.v.* **-ished, -ishing, -ishes.** To enrapture. [EN- + RAVISH.]

en·reg·is·ter (ĕn-rĕj′ĭ-stər, ĭn-) *tr.v.* **-tered, -tering, -ters.** To enter in a register; put on record.

en·rich (ĕn-rĭch′, ĭn-) *tr.v.* **-riched, -riching, -riches. 1.** To make rich or richer. **2.** To make fuller, more meaningful, or more rewarding: *"The English language was enriched with thousands of French words."* (Albert C. Baugh). **3.** To add fertilizer to (soil) to increase its productivity. **4.** To add nutrients to (foodstuffs) during processing. **5.** To add to the beauty or character of; embellish or adorn: *"Glittering tears enriched her eyes."* (Arnold Bennett). **6.** *Physics.* To increase the ratio of radioactive isotopes in. [Middle English *enrichen,* from Old French *enricher* : *en-* (causative) + *riche,* RICH.] **—en·rich′er** *n.*

en·rich·ment (ĕn-rĭch′mənt, ĭn-) *n.* **1. a.** The act of enriching. **b.** The state of being enriched. **2.** Anything that enriches.

en·robe (ĕn-rōb′, ĭn-) *tr.v.* **-robed, -robing, -robes.** To dress richly in or as if in a robe.

en·roll (ĕn-rōl′, ĭn-) *v.* **-rolled, -rolling, -rolls.** Also **en·rol, -rolled, -rolling, -rols.** *—tr.* **1.** To enter the name of in a register, record, or roll. **2.** To put on record; to record. **3.** To roll or wrap up. *—intr.* To place one's name on a roll or register. [Middle English *enrollen,* from Old French *enroller* : *en-,* in + *rolle,* ROLL.]

en·roll·ment (ĕn-rōl′mənt, ĭn-) *n.* Also **en·rol·ment. 1. a.** The action of enrolling. **b.** The state or process of being enrolled. **2.** A record or entry. **3.** The number enrolled.

en·root (ĕn-ro͞ot′, -ro͝ot′, ĭn-) *tr.v.* **-rooted, -rooting, -roots.** To establish firmly by or as if by roots; implant.

en route (än ro͞ot′; *French* äɴ ro͞ot′). On the route; on or along the way. [French.]

ens (ĕnz) *n., pl.* **entia** (ĕn′shē-ə). *Philosophy.* **1.** Existence or being as an abstract concept. **2.** An entity as opposed to an attribute. [Medieval Latin, from Latin, irregular present participle of *esse,* to be. See **es-** in Appendix.*]

ENS, Ens. ensign.

en·sam·ple (ĕn-săm′pəl, ĭn-) *n. Archaic.* An example.

en·san·guine (ĕn-săng′gwĭn) *tr.v.* **-guined, -guining, -guines. 1.** To cover or stain with blood. **2.** To make crimson.

En·sche·de (ĕn′sᴋʜə-dā′). A city and industrial center of the eastern Netherlands. Population, 134,000.

en·sconce (ĕn-skŏns′, ĭn-) *tr.v.* **-sconced, -sconcing, -sconces. 1.** To settle (oneself) securely or comfortably: *"She was ensconced in a ponderous fauteuil of figured velvet."* (Ronald Firbank). **2.** To place, fix, or conceal in a secure place. [EN- + SCONCE.]

en·sem·ble (än-säm′bəl; *French* äɴ-säɴ′bl′) *n.* **1.** A unit or group of complementary parts that contribute to a single effect, as: **a.** A coordinated outfit or costume. **b.** A set, as of furniture. **c.** A group of musicians, singers, dancers, or a troupe of players who perform together. **2. a.** Music for two or more vocalists or instrumentalists. **b.** The quality of performance by a group of actors or musicians, especially as judged in regard to their success in achieving a unity and balance of style and technique. [French, "together," from Vulgar Latin *insemul* (unattested), from Latin *insimul,* at the same time : *in-,* in + *simul, semul,* at the same time (see **sem-**[1] in Appendix*).]

en·shrine (ĕn-shrīn′, ĭn-) *tr.v.* **-shrined, -shrining, -shrines.** Also **in·shrine** (ĭn-). **1.** To enclose in or as if in a shrine. **2.** To cherish as sacred. **—en·shrine′ment** *n.*

en·shroud (ĕn-shroud′, ĭn-) *tr.v.* **-shrouded, -shrouding, -shrouds.** To shroud; to veil or conceal.

en·si·form (ĕn′sə-fôrm′) *adj.* Sword-shaped, as the leaf of an iris or gladiolus. [French *ensiforme* : from Latin *ēnsis,* sword (see **n̥si-** in Appendix*) + -FORM.]

ensiform
Ensiform leaves of an iris

en·sign (ĕn′sən; *also* ĕn′sīn′ *for senses 1, 2, 3, 5*) *n.* **1.** A national flag displayed on ships and aircraft, often with the special insignia of a branch or unit of the armed forces: *the naval ensign.* **2.** Any standard or banner, as of a military unit. **3.** A standard-bearer. **4.** *Abbr.* **ENS, Ens.** A commissioned officer of the lowest rank in the U.S. Navy or Coast Guard. **5. a.** A badge; emblem. **b.** A sign; token. [Middle English *ensigne,* from Old French *enseigne,* from *insignia,* INSIGNIA.]

en·si·lage (ĕn′sə-lĭj) *n.* **1.** The process of storing and fermenting green fodder in a silo. **2.** Fodder thus preserved; silage. *—tr.v.* **ensilaged, -laging, -lages.** To ensile. [French, from *ensiler,* ENSILE.]

en·sile (ĕn-sīl′, ĭn-) *tr.v.* **-siled, -siling, -siles. 1.** To store (fodder) in a silo for preservation. **2.** To convert (green fodder) into silage. [French *ensiler* : *en-,* in + *silo,* silo, from Old Spanish (see **silo**).]

en·slave (ĕn-slāv′, ĭn-) *tr.v.* **-slaved, -slaving, -slaves.** To make a slave of; reduce to slavery, bondage, or dependence. **—en·slave′ment** *n.* **—en·slav′er** *n.*

en·snare (ĕn-snâr′, ĭn-) *tr.v.* **-snared, -snaring, -snares.** Also **in·snare** (ĭn-). To catch in or as if in a snare. **—en·snare′ment** *n.* **—en·snar′er** *n.*

en·sor·cel (ĕn-sôr′səl, ĭn-) *tr.v.* **-celed, -celing, -cels.** Also **en·sor·cell, -celled, -celling, -cells.** To bewitch; enchant. [Old French *ensorceler, ensorcerer* : *en-,* in + *sorcier,* SORCERER.]

en·soul (ĕn-sōl′, ĭn-) *tr.v.* **-souled, -souling, -souls.** Also **in·soul** (ĭn-). To endow with a soul.

en·sphere (ĕn-sfîr′, ĭn-) *tr.v.* **-sphered, -sphering, -spheres.** Also **in·sphere** (ĭn-). **1.** To enclose in or as if in a sphere. **2.** To give spherical form to.

en·sta·tite (ĕn′stə-tīt′) *n.* A variety of orthorhombic pyroxene having a magnesium silicate base, mainly $Mg_2Si_2O_6$, usually found embedded in igneous rocks. [German *Enstatit* : Greek *enstatēs,* adversary (from its refractory nature) : *en-,* in, at, near + *-statēs,* standing (see **stā-** in Appendix*).]

en·sue (ĕn-so͞o′, ĭn-) *intr.v.* **-sued, -suing, -sues. 1.** To follow immediately afterward; take place subsequently. **2.** To follow as a consequence; result. —See Synonyms at **follow.** [Middle

English *ensuen,* from Old French *ensuivre* (stem *ensu-*), from Vulgar Latin *insequere* (unattested), variant of Latin *insequī,* to follow after or on : *in-,* in, onward + *sequī,* to follow (see **sekw-¹** in Appendix*).]

en suite (äN swēt′). *French.* In a series or set; in succession.

en·sure. Variant of **insure.**

-ent. 1. Used to form adjectives having the quality of the main element of the word; for example, **effervescent. 2.** Used to form nouns of agency; for example, **referent.** [Middle English *-ent,* from Old French, from Latin *-ens* (stem *-ent-*). Compare **-ant.**]

E.N.T. ear, nose, and throat.

en·tab·la·ture (ĕn-tăb′lə-chŏŏr′, ĭn-) *n. Architecture.* **1.** The upper section of a classical order, resting on the capital and including the architrave, frieze, and cornice. **2.** Any raised, horizontal architectural member. [Obsolete French, from Italian *intavolatura,* from *intavolare,* to put on the table : *in-,* in, from Latin + *tavola,* table, from Latin *tabula,* board, TABLE.]

en·ta·ble·ment (ĕn-tā′bəl-mənt, ĭn-) *n.* The platform supporting a statue, above the base and the dado. [French, from Old French : *en-,* in + TABLE.]

en·tail (ĕn-tāl′, ĭn-) *tr.v.* **-tailed, -tailing, -tails. 1.** To have as a necessary accompaniment or consequence: *"they did eat in disobedience; and disobedience to God entails death."* (Jaroslav Pelikan). **2.** To limit the inheritance of (property) to a specified, unalterable succession of heirs. **3.** To impose (a duty, expense, or the like) upon a person. —*n.* **1. a.** The act of entailing, especially property. **b.** The state of being entailed. **2.** An entailed estate. **3.** A predetermined order of succession, as to an estate or to an office. **4.** Anything transmitted as if by unalterable inheritance. [Middle English *entaillen, entailen* : EN- + *taille,* TAIL (limitation).] —**en·tail′ment** *n.*

en·ta·moe·ba, en·ta·me·ba (ĕn′tə-mē′bə) *n., pl.* **-bas** or **-bae** (-bē). Also **en·da·moe·ba, en·da·me·ba** (ĕn′də-). Any of several parasitic amoebas of the genus *Entamoeba;* especially, *E. histolytica,* causing dysentery and ulceration of the colon and liver. [New Latin *Entamoeba* : ENT(O)- + AMOEBA.]

en·tan·gle (ĕn-tăng′gəl, ĭn-) *tr.v.* **-gled, -gling, -gles. 1.** To twist together so that disengagement is difficult; make tangled; snarl. **2.** To complicate; confuse. **3.** To involve inextricably, as in complications or difficulties: *"The President became entangled in his own contradictions."* (John Dos Passos). —**en·tan′gle·ment** *n.* —**en·tan′gler** *n.*

En·teb·be (ĕn-tĕb′ə). The former capital of Uganda (1896-1962), in the south on Lake Victoria.

en·tel·e·chy (ĕn-tĕl′ə-kē) *n., pl.* **-chies. 1.** In the philosophy of Aristotle, the condition of a thing whose essence is fully realized; actuality as distinguished from potentiality. **2.** In various philosophical systems, a vital force urging an organism toward self-fulfillment: *"Courage is the affirmation of one's essential nature, one's inner aim or entelechy."* (Paul Tillich). [Late Latin *entelechia,* from Greek *entelekheia,* complete reality : *enteles,* complete, full : *en-,* in + *telos,* perfection, end (see **kwel-¹** in Appendix*) + *ekhein,* to have (see **segh-** in Appendix*).]

en·tente (än-tänt′; *French* äN-tänt′) *n.* **1.** An agreement, usually unformalized, between two or more governments or powers for cooperative action or policy. **2.** The parties to such an agreement. [French, "understanding," from Old French *entendre,* to understand, INTEND.]

en·ter (ĕn′tər) *v.* **-tered, -tering, -ters.** —*tr.* **1.** To come or go into. **2.** To penetrate; pierce. **3.** To introduce; insert. **4.** To become an element in or a part of. **5.** To begin (an age or era); embark upon: *"America was entering the period of the Missile Gap"* (Theodore H. White). **6. a.** To obtain admission to (a school, for example). **b.** To procure the admission of. **c.** To enroll. **7. a.** To submit or register as an entry in an exhibition or competition: *enter dahlias in a flower show.* **b.** To become a participant or a contestant in: *enter a primary.* **8.** To take up; embrace (a profession or career): *Their son entered the priesthood.* **9.** *Law.* **a.** To place formally before a court or upon the records: *enter a plea.* **b.** To go upon or into (real property) as a trespasser or with felonious intent: *break and enter.* **c.** To go upon (land) to take possession of it. **10.** To report (a ship's arrival or cargo) for the record at a customhouse. —*intr.* **1.** To come or go in; make an entry. **2.** To gain entry; penetrate. **3.** To become a member. —**enter into. 1.** To participate in; take an active interest in. **2.** To be a component of; form a part of. **3.** To consider; delve into. **4.** To become party to (a contract). —**enter on** (or **upon**). **1.** To set out upon; embark upon. **2.** To take legal possession of (land). **3.** To begin to consider or deal with (a subject). [Middle English *entren,* from Old French *entrer,* from Latin *intrāre,* from *intrā,* within. See **en-** in Appendix*.]

en·ter·al (ĕn′tər-əl) *adj.* Enteric. —**en′ter·al·ly** *adv.*

en·ter·ic (ĕn-tĕr′ĭk) *adj.* Of or within the intestine. [Greek *enterikos,* from *enteron,* ENTERON.]

enteric fever. *Pathology.* Typhoid fever *(see).*

en·ter·i·tis (ĕn′tə-rī′tĭs) *n.* Inflammation of the intestinal tract. [New Latin : ENTER(O)- + -ITIS.]

entero-, enter-. Indicates intestine; for example, **enterostomy, enteritis.** [New Latin, from Greek *enteron,* intestines. See **en** in Appendix*.]

en·ter·o·gas·trone (ĕn′tə-rō-găs′trōn′) *n.* A hormone found in the upper intestinal mucosa that inhibits gastric motility and secretion. [ENTERO- + GASTR(O)- + (HORM)ONE.]

en·ter·o·ki·nase (ĕn′tə-rō-kī′nās′, -kĭn′ās′) *n.* An enzyme found in intestinal juice that converts trypsinogen to trypsin. [ENTERO- + KINASE.]

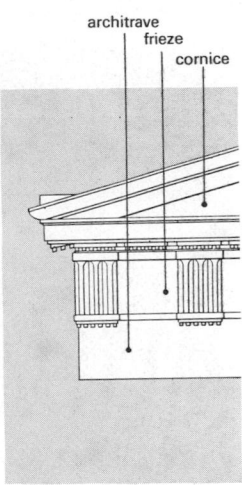

architrave
frieze
cornice

entablature

en·ter·on (ĕn′tə-rŏn′) *n.* The intestine. [New Latin, from Greek, intestine, entrails. See **en** in Appendix.*]

en·ter·os·to·my (ĕn′tə-rŏs′tə-mē) *n., pl.* **-mies.** Surgical formation of an opening into the intestine through the abdominal wall. [ENTERO- + -STOMY.]

en·ter·ot·o·my (ĕn′tə-rŏt′ə-mē) *n., pl.* **-mies.** Surgical incision into the intestine. [ENTERO- + -TOMY.]

en·ter·prise (ĕn′tər-prīz′) *n.* **1.** An undertaking, especially one of some scope, complication, and risk: *"One generation abandons the enterprises of another like stranded vessels."* (Thoreau). **2.** A business. **3.** Industrious effort, especially when directed toward making money. **4.** Readiness to venture; boldness; initiative. [Middle English, from Old French *entreprise,* from the feminine past participle of *entreprendre,* to undertake : *entre-,* between, from Latin *inter-* + *prendre,* to take, from Latin *prendere, prehendere* (see **ghend-** in Appendix*).] —**en′ter·pris′er** *n.*

en·ter·pris·ing (ĕn′tər-prī′zĭng) *adj.* Showing imagination, initiative, and readiness to undertake the adventurous or risky. See Synonyms at **ambitious.** —**en′ter·pris′ing·ly** *adv.*

en·ter·tain (ĕn′tər-tān′) *v.* **-tained, -taining, -tains.** —*tr.* **1.** To hold the attention of; amuse. **2.** To extend hospitality toward: *entertain friends at dinner.* **3.** To mull over; contemplate: *"wrong as she was even to entertain such an idea, she could not help feeling . . . his death would mean great relief"* (James Agee). **4.** To hold in mind; harbor: *"he could entertain no more illusions about the ship's magnificence"* (John Barth). **5.** *Archaic.* To continue with; maintain. —*intr.* **1.** To have guests, as for dinner or a party. **2.** To provide entertainment. —See Synonyms at **amuse.** [Middle English *entertinen,* to maintain, from Old French *entretenir,* from Vulgar Latin *intertenēre* (unattested), "to hold between" : Latin *inter-,* between + *tenēre,* to hold (see **ten-** in Appendix*).] —**en′ter·tain′er** *n.*

en·ter·tain·ing (ĕn′tər-tā′nĭng) *adj.* Serving to entertain; agreeably diverting; amusing. —**en′ter·tain′ing·ly** *adv.*

en·ter·tain·ment (ĕn′tər-tān′mənt) *n.* **1.** The act of entertaining. **2.** The art or field of entertaining. **3.** Something that entertains; especially, a performance or show designed to amuse or divert. **4.** The pleasure afforded by being entertained; amusement. **5.** Hospitality extended toward guests. **6.** *Obsolete.* **a.** Maintenance; support. **b.** Employment.

en·thal·py (ĕn′thăl′pē, ĕn-thăl′-) *n.* A thermodynamic function of a system, equivalent to the internal energy plus the product of the pressure and the volume. [From Greek *enthalpein,* to heat in : *en-,* in + *thalpein†,* to warm, heat.]

en·thrall (ĕn-thrôl′, ĭn-) *tr.v.* **-thralled, -thralling, -thralls.** Also **en·thral, in·thrall** (ĭn-). **1.** To hold spellbound; captivate; charm. **2.** To reduce to thralldom; enslave. [Middle English *enthrallen* : EN- + THRALL.] —**en·thrall′ment** *n.*

en·throne (ĕn-thrōn′, ĭn-) *tr.v.* **-throned, -throning, -thrones.** Also **in·throne** (ĭn-). **1. a.** To seat on a throne. **b.** To invest with sovereign power or with the authority of high office. **2.** To raise to a lofty position; revere; exalt. —**en·throne′ment** *n.*

en·thuse (ĕn-thōōz′, ĭn-) *v.* **-thused, -thusing, -thuses.** *Informal.* —*tr.* To stimulate enthusiasm in. —*intr.* To show enthusiasm. —See Usage note. [Back-formation from ENTHUSIASM.]

Usage: Enthuse is not well established in writing on a serious level. The following typical examples are termed unacceptable by substantial majorities of the Usage Panel. *The majority leader enthused over his party's gains* is disapproved by 76 per cent. *He was considerably less enthused by signs of factionalism* is disapproved by 72 per cent. Alternative phrasing might be *became* (or *waxed*) *enthusiastic* or *was less enthusiastic over.*

en·thu·si·asm (ĕn-thōō′zē-ăz′əm, ĭn-) *n.* **1. a.** Rapturous interest or excitement. **b.** Ardent fondness or eagerness; zeal. **2.** A subject or activity that inspires a lively interest. **3.** *Archaic.* **a.** Ecstasy arising from supposed possession by a god. **b.** A fanatic religious ardor. —See Synonyms at **passion.** [Late Latin *enthūsiasmus,* from Greek *enthousiasmos,* inspiration, from *enthousiazein,* to be inspired by a god, from *enthous, entheos,* possessed, inspired : *en-,* in + *theos,* god (see **dhēs-** in Appendix*).]

en·thu·si·ast (ĕn-thōō′zē-ăst′, ĭn-) *n.* **1.** A person filled with enthusiasm; one ardently preoccupied with a particular subject: *a baseball enthusiast.* **2.** A religious zealot, fanatic, or visionary. —See Synonyms at **fanatic.** [Greek *enthousiastēs,* from *enthousiazein,* to be inspired. See **enthusiasm.**]

en·thu·si·as·tic (ĕn-thōō′zē-ăs′tĭk, ĭn-) *adj.* Having or demonstrating enthusiasm; eager; ardent. —**en·thu′si·as′ti·cal·ly** *adv.*

en·thy·meme (ĕn′thə-mēm′) *n. Logic.* A syllogism with one of the premises implicit. [Latin *enthȳmēma,* from Greek *enthumēma,* from *enthumeisthai,* "to have in mind," consider : *en-,* in + *thūmos,* mind (see **dheu-¹** in Appendix*).]

en·ti·a. Plural of **ens.**

en·tice (ĕn-tīs′) *tr.v.* **-ticed, -ticing, -tices.** To attract by arousing hope or desire; lure. See Synonyms at **lure.** [Middle English *enticen,* from Old French *enticier,* from Vulgar Latin *intītiāre* (unattested), to set on fire : Latin *in-,* in + *tītiō†,* firebrand.] —**en·tice′ment** *n.* —**en·tic′er** *n.* —**en·tic′ing·ly** *adv.*

en·tire (ĕn-tīr′, ĭn-) *adj.* **1.** Having no part missing or excepted; whole: *an entire set of the encyclopedia; the entire country.* **2.** Without reservation or limitation; total; complete: *entire freedom; my entire approval; his entire attention.* **3.** All in one piece; unbroken; intact: *The ship was still entire after the typhoon.* **4.** Of one piece; continuous. **5.** Not castrated. **6.** *Botany.* Not indented or toothed, as the margin of a leaf. **7.** *Obsolete.* Unmixed or unalloyed; pure. —*n.* **1.** The whole of something; entirety. **2.** An uncastrated horse. [Middle English *entier,* from Old French, from Latin *integrum,* accusative of *integer,* intact. See **tag-** in Appendix.*] —**en·tire′ness** *n.*

en·tire·ly (ĕn-tīr′lē, ĭn-) *adv.* **1.** Wholly; completely: *"This did not entirely satisfy me; I wanted to be taken seriously."* (James Weldon Johnson). **2.** Solely or exclusively: *"In men of his class, vigor and resolution are entirely a physical matter"* (Harriet Beecher Stowe).

en·tire·ty (ĕn-tī′rə-tē, ĭn-) *n., pl.* **-ties. 1.** The state or condition of being entire or complete; completeness. **2.** Something that is entire; a whole. **3.** The entire amount or extent; the sum total.

en·ti·tle (ĕn-tīt′l, ĭn-) *tr.v.* **-tled, -tling, -tles. 1.** To give a name or title to; to designate: *"Because one expresses oneself and entitles/it wisdom, one is not a fool."* (Marianne Moore). **2.** To bestow a title of nobility, rank, honor, or dignity upon. **3. a.** To give (one) a right to do or have something; allow; qualify. **b.** To give (one) a legal right or claim to something. [Middle English *entitlen,* from Old French *entiteler,* from Late Latin *intitulāre* : *in-,* in + *titulus,* TITLE.] —**en·ti′tle·ment** *n.*

en·ti·ty (ĕn′tə-tē) *n., pl.* **-ties. 1.** The fact of existence; being. **2.** Something that exists independently, not relative to other things. **3.** A particular and discrete unit; an entirety: *Persons and corporations are equivalent entities under the law.* [Medieval Latin *entitās,* from Latin *ēns* (stem *ent-*), irregular present participle of *esse,* to be. See **es-** in Appendix.*]

ento-. Indicates within, inside; for example, **entozoa.** [New Latin, from Greek *entos,* within. See **en** in Appendix.*]

en·to·blast. Variant of **endoblast.**

en·to·derm. Variant of **endoderm.**

en·toil (ĕn-toil′, ĭn-) *tr.v.* **-toiled, -toiling, -toils.** *Obsolete.* To ensnare; entrap. [EN- + TOIL (trap).] —**en·toil′ment** *n.*

entom. entomological; entomology.

en·tomb (ĕn-tōōm′, ĭn-) *tr.v.* **-tombed, -tombing, -tombs. 1.** To place in or as if in a tomb or grave; bury. **2.** To serve as a tomb for. [Middle English *entoumben,* from Old French *entomber* : *en-,* in + *tombe,* tomb, from Late Latin *tumba,* TOMB.] —**en·tomb′ment** *n.*

entomo-. Indicates insect; for example, **entomology, entomophagous.** [French, from Greek *entomon,* insect, "one whose body is cut into segments," from *entomos,* cut up, from *entemnein,* to cut in, cut up : *en-,* in + *temnein,* to cut (see **tem-** in Appendix*).]

entomol. entomology.

en·to·mol·o·gize (ĕn′tə-mŏl′ə-jīz′) *intr.v.* **-gized, -gizing, -gizes.** To study or collect insects.

en·to·mol·o·gy (ĕn′tə-mŏl′ə-jē) *n. Abbr.* **entom., entomol.** The scientific study of insects. [ENTOMO- + -LOGY.] —**en′to·mo·log′ic** (-mə-lŏj′ĭk), **en′to·mo·log′i·cal** *adj.* —**en′to·mo·log′i·cal·ly** *adv.* —**en′to·mol′o·gist** *n.*

en·to·moph·a·gous (ĕn′tə-mŏf′ə-gəs) *adj. Rare.* Feeding on insects; insectivorous. [ENTOMO- + -PHAGOUS.]

en·to·moph·i·lous (ĕn′tə-mŏf′ə-ləs) *adj.* Pollinated by insects. [ENTOMO- + -PHILOUS.] —**en′to·moph′i·ly** *n.*

en·tou·rage (än′tōō-räzh′; *French* äN-tōō-ràzh′) *n.* **1.** A train of attendants, followers, or associates. **2.** One's environment or surroundings. [French, from *entourer,* to surround, from Old French *entour,* surroundings : *en-,* in + *tour,* circuit, TOUR.]

en·to·zo·a (ĕn′tə-zō′ə) *pl.n. Singular* **-zoan** (-zō′ən) or **-zoon** (-zō′ŏn). Any of various animals, such as tapeworms, that live within other animals, usually as parasites. [New Latin : ENTO- + -ZOA.] —**en′to·zo′ic** *adj.*

en·tr'acte (än-träkt′; *French* äN-tràkt′) *n.* **1.** The interval between two successive acts of a theatrical performance. **2.** An entertainment provided during this interval. [French : Old French *entr(e)-,* between, from Latin *inter-* + *acte,* ACT.]

en·trails (ĕn′trālz′, -trəlz) *pl.n.* The internal organs, especially the intestines; viscera. [Middle English *entrailles,* from Old French, from Medieval Latin *intrālia,* variant of Latin *interānea,* from the neuter plural of *interāneus,* internal, from *inter,* within. See **en** in Appendix.*]

en·train[1] (ĕn-trān′, ĭn-) *tr.v.* **-trained, -training, -trains.** To pull or draw along after itself. [Old French *entrainer* : *en-,* in + *trainer,* to draw (see **train**).]

en·train[2] (ĕn-trān′, ĭn-) *v.* **-trained, -training, -trains.** —*tr.* To put on a train. —*intr.* To board a train. —**en·train′ment** *n.*

en·trance[1] (ĕn′trəns) *n.* **1.** The act or an instance of entering; especially, the entry of an actor into the performing area. **2.** Any passage or opening that affords entry. **3.** The permission, power, or liberty to enter; admission. **4.** The point in a script or musical score at which a performer is to begin: *The soprano made her usual dramatic entrance.* [Middle English *entraunce,* from Old French *entrance,* from *entrer,* ENTER.]

en·trance[2] (ĕn-trăns′, -träns′, ĭn-) *tr.v.* **-tranced, -trancing, -trances. 1.** To put into a trance. **2.** To fill with great pleasure, wonder, or enchantment; fascinate: *a child entranced by his own reflection.* —**en·trance′ment** *n.* —**en·tranc′ing·ly** *adv.*

en·trant (ĕn′trənt) *n.* **1.** One who enters; especially, one who enters into a competition: *Ten girls were entrants in the beauty contest.* **2.** A new member, as of a profession, organization, university, or the like. [French, from the present participle of *entrer,* ENTER.]

en·trap (ĕn-trăp′, ĭn-) *tr.v.* **-trapped, -trapping, -traps. 1.** To catch in or as if in a trap. **2.** To lure into danger, difficulty, or self-incrimination. [Old French *entraper* : *en-,* in + *trape,* trap (see **der-**[1] in Appendix*).] —**en·trap′ment** *n.*

en·treat (ĕn-trēt′, ĭn-) *v.* **-treated, -treating, -treats.** Also **in·treat** (ĭn-). —*tr.* **1.** To ask (someone) earnestly; beseech; implore; beg. **2.** To ask for (something) earnestly; petition for. **3.** *Archaic.* To treat. —*intr.* To make an earnest request or petition; plead. —See Synonyms at **beg.** [Middle English *entreten,* to deal with, plead with, from Old French *entraitier* : *en-,* in + *traitier, traiter,* to TREAT.] —**en·treat′ing·ly** *adv.* —**en·treat′ment** *n.*

en·treat·y (ĕn-trē′tē, ĭn-) *n., pl.* **-ies.** An earnest request; plea.

en·tre·chat (äN-trə-shä′) *n.* A leap in ballet during which the dancer crosses his feet a number of times, often beating them together. [French, earlier *entrecha(se),* by folk etymology (influenced by *chasse,* chase) from Italian *(capriola) intrecciata,* "interlaced (caper)," from the feminine past participle of *intrecciare,* to interlace, entwine : *in-,* in, from Latin + *treccia,* tress, akin to Old French *tresse,* TRESS.]

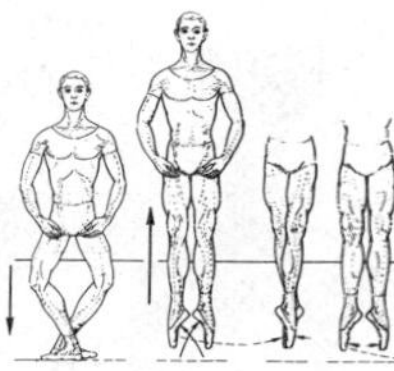

entrechat

en·tre·côte (än′trə-kōt′) *n.* A cut of steak taken from between the ribs. [French, "between the ribs."]

en·trée (än′trā; *French* äN-trā′) *n.* Also **en·tree** (än′trā). **1. a.** The power, permission, or liberty to enter; admittance. **b.** Access by special privilege to a place normally inaccessible. **2. a.** The main course of an ordinary meal. **b.** A dish served in formal dining immediately before the main course or between any two principal courses. [French, from Old French *entree,* ENTRY.]

en·tre·mets (än′trə-mā′; *French* äN-trə-mĕ′) *n., pl.* **-mets** (-māz′; *French* -mĕ′). A side dish or dishes; especially, a dish served between principal courses or as a dessert. [French, earlier *entremes* : Old French *entre-,* between, from Latin *inter-* + *mes,* dish, MESS.]

en·trench (ĕn-trĕnch′, ĭn-) *v.* **-trenched, -trenching, -trenches.** Also **in·trench** (ĭn-). —*tr.* **1.** To provide with a trench or trenches for the purpose of draining, fortifying, defending, or supporting. **2.** To fix firmly or securely: *The accident was entrenched in his memory.* —*intr.* **1.** To dig a trench or trenches. **2.** *Rare.* To encroach, infringe, or trespass.

en·trench·ment (ĕn-trĕnch′mənt, ĭn-) *n.* **1.** The act of entrenching or the condition of being entrenched. **2.** A fortification; especially, a series of banked trenches.

en·tre nous (än′trə nōō′; *French* äN-tr′ nōō′). Between ourselves; confidentially. [French, "between ourselves."]

en·tre·pôt (än′trə-pō′; *French* äN-trə-pō′) *n.* **1.** A place where goods are stored or deposited and from which they are distributed. **2.** A trading or market center. [French, from *entreposer,* to put in, to store : Old French *entre-,* in, between, from Latin *inter-* + *poser,* to put, POSE.]

en·tre·pre·neur (än′trə-prə-nûr′) *n.* A person who organizes, operates, and assumes the risk for business ventures, especially an impresario. [French, from Old French, from *entreprendre,* to undertake. See **enterprise.**]

En·tre Rí·os (ĕn′trā rē′ōs). A province of Argentina, occupying 29,427 square miles in the east, between the Paraná and Uruguay rivers. Population, 991,000. Capital, Paraná.

en·tre·sol (ĕn′tər-sŏl′, ĕn′trə-; *French* äN-trə-sôl′) *n.* The floor just above the ground floor; mezzanine. [French, "between floors," *entre-,* between, from Latin *inter-* + *sol,* floor, ground, from Latin *solum* (see **sel-**[1] in Appendix*).]

en·tro·py (ĕn′trə-pē) *n.* **1.** A measure of the capacity of a system to undergo spontaneous change, thermodynamically specified by the relationship $dS = dQ/T$, where dS is an infinitesimal change in the measure for a system absorbing an infinitesimal quantity of heat dQ at absolute temperature T. **2.** A measure of the randomness, disorder, or chaos in a system specified in statistical mechanics by the relationship $S = k\ln P + c$, where S is the value of the measure for a system in a given state, P is the probability of occurrence of that state, and k is a fixed and c an arbitrary constant. [German *Entropie* : Greek *en-,* in + *tropē,* a turning, change (see **trep-**[2] in Appendix*).]

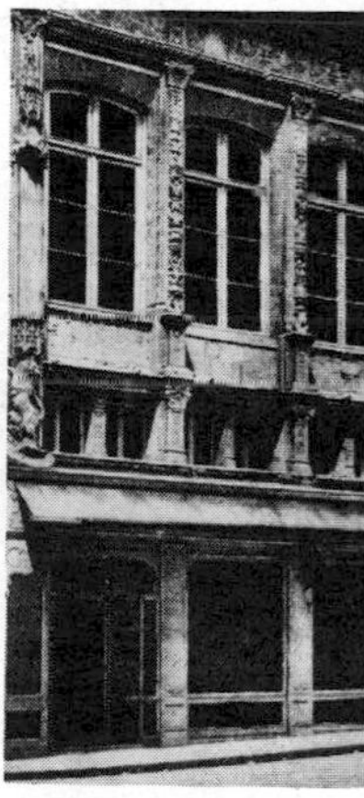

entresol

en·trust (ĕn-trŭst′, ĭn-) *tr.v.* **-trusted, -trusting, -trusts.** Also **in·trust** (ĭn-). **1.** To give over to another for care, protection, or performance: *entrusted the task to his aides.* **2.** To commit something trustfully to; place a trust upon: *entrusted his aides with the task.* —See Synonyms at **commit.**

en·try (ĕn′trē) *n., pl.* **-tries. 1.** The act, right, or an instance of entering. **2.** A passage or opening affording entrance. **3. a.** The inclusion or insertion of an item in a diary, register, list, or other record. **b.** An item thus entered. **4. a.** A word, term, or phrase defined or identified in a dictionary and often set apart typographically from the text of the definitions. **b.** Such an item along with the text related to it. **5.** One registered as a participant in a competition. [Middle English *entre,* from Old French *entree,* from Vulgar Latin *intrāta* (unattested), from the feminine past participle of Latin *intrāre,* ENTER.]

en·try·way (ĕn′trē-wā′) *n.* A passage or opening serving as an entrance.

en·twine (ĕn-twīn′, ĭn-) *v.* **-twined, -twining, -twines.** Also **in·twine** (ĭn-). —*tr.* To twine or twist around or about: *Ivy entwined the pillar.* —*intr.* To twine or twist together.

en·twist (ĕn-twĭst′, ĭn-) *tr.v.* **-twisted, -twisting, -twists.** Also **in·twist** (ĭn-). To twist together, around, or about.

e·nu·cle·ate (ĭ-nōō′klē-āt′, ĭ-nyōō′-) *tr.v.* **-ated, -ating, -ates. 1.** *Archaic.* To explain or elucidate. **2.** *Surgery.* To remove (a tumor or eyeball, for example) from its enveloping cover or sac. **3.** *Biology.* To remove the nucleus of (a cell). —*adj.* (-ĭt, -āt′). Lacking a nucleus. [Latin *ēnucleāre,* to take out the kernel : *ex-,* out + *nucleus,* kernel, NUCLEUS.] —**e·nu′cle·a′tion** *n.* —**e·nu′cle·a′tor** (-ā′tər) *n.*

E·nu·gu (ā-nōō′gōō). A city of Nigeria, the capital of the Eastern Region before its secession as the Republic of Biafra. Population, 138,000.

e·nu·mer·ate (ĭ-nōō′mə-rāt′, ĭ-nyōō′-) *tr.v.* **-ated, -ating, -ates. 1.** To count off or name one by one; to list: *"he began humorously to enumerate some of his difficulties"* (Edgar Snow). **2.** To determine the number of; to count. [Latin *ēnumerāre,* to count out : *ex-,* out + *numerus,* number (see **nem-**[2] in Appendix*).]

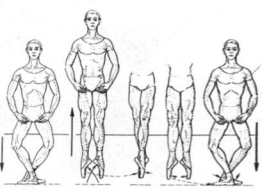

—**e·nu′mer·a′tive** *adj.* —**e·nu′mer·a′tor** (-mə-rā′tər) *n.*

e·nu·mer·a·tion (ĭ-nōō′mə-rā′shən, ĭ-nyōō′-) *n.* **1.** The act of enumerating. **2.** A detailed list of items; a catalogue.

e·nun·ci·a·ble (ĭ-nŭn′sē-ə-bəl, -shē-ə-bəl) *adj.* Capable of being enunciated. —**e·nun′ci·a·bil′i·ty** *n.*

e·nun·ci·ate (ĭ-nŭn′sē-āt′, -shē-āt′) *v.* **-ated, -ating, -ates.** —*tr.* **1.** To pronounce or articulate (speech sounds); especially, to pronounce with clarity or in another specified manner. **2.** To state or set forth precisely or systematically: *"Wordsworth enunciated an anti-democratic doctrine of leadership"* (Samuel Chew). **3.** To announce; proclaim. —*intr.* To pronounce words, especially distinctly. [Latin *ēnuntiāre, ēnunciāre* : *ex-*, out + *nuntiāre*, to announce, from *nuncius, nuntius*, message, messenger (see **neu-**[1] in Appendix*).] —**e·nun′ci·a′tive, e·nun′ci·a·to′ry** (-ə-tôr′ē, -tōr′ē) *adj.* —**e·nun′ci·a′tive·ly** *adv.* —**e·nun′ci·a′tor** (-ā′tər) *n.*

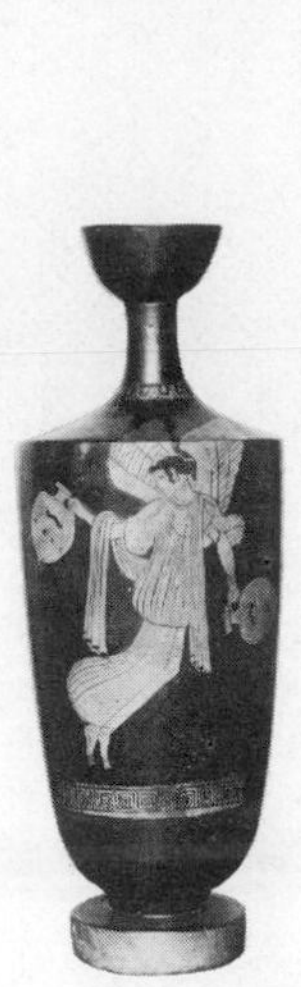

Eos
Ancient Greek vase painting of Eos sprinkling the earth with dew

e·nun·ci·a·tion (ĭ-nŭn′sē-ā′shən, ĭ-nŭn′shē-) *n.* **1.** The act of enunciating or the condition of being enunciated. **2.** The manner in which a speaker articulates words or speech sounds. **3.** An announcement, declaration, or similar official statement. —See Synonyms at **diction.**

en·ure. Variant of **inure.**

en·u·re·sis (ĕn′yə-rē′sĭs) *n.* Involuntary urination. [New Latin, from Greek *enourein*, to urinate in : *en-*, in + *ourein*, to urinate, from *ouron*, urine (see **wer-**[7] in Appendix*).]

env. envelope.

en·vel·op (ĕn-vĕl′əp, ĭn-) *tr.v.* **-oped, -oping, -ops.** **1.** To enclose or encase with or as if with a covering or wrapping. **2.** To serve as a covering or wrapping for. **3.** To surround; encircle. [Middle English *enveloupen*, from Old French *enveloper* : *en-*, in + *voloper, veloper*, to wrap up (see **develop**).] —**en·vel′op·er** *n.*

en·ve·lope (ĕn′və-lōp′, än′-) *n. Abbr.* **env.** **1.** Something that envelops; an enclosing or surrounding cover, coat, or wrapping. **2.** A flat, folded paper container for a letter or similar object, usually rectangular and having a gummed sealing flap. **3.** *Biology.* Any enclosing covering, membrane, or structure. **4.** The bag containing the gas in a balloon. **5.** *Mathematics.* A curve or surface that is tangent to all curves or surfaces of a family of curves or surfaces. [French *enveloppe*, from Old French *envelope*, from *enveloper*, ENVELOP.]

en·vel·op·ment (ĕn-vĕl′əp-mənt) *n.* **1.** The act of enveloping or the condition of being enveloped. **2.** Material that serves to cover, wrap, or surround. **3.** *Military.* An attack on an enemy's flank or rear.

en·ven·om (ĕn-vĕn′əm, ĭn-) *tr.v.* **-omed, -oming, -oms.** **1.** To put venom into or on; make poisonous or noxious. **2.** To fill with malice; embitter. [Middle English *envenimen*, from Old French *envenimer* : *en-*, in + *venim*, VENOM.]

en·vi·a·ble (ĕn′vē-ə-bəl) *adj.* Arousing strong envy; highly desirable: *"the enviable English quality of being able to be mute without unrest"* (Henry James). —**en′vi·a·bly** *adv.*

en·vi·ous (ĕn′vē-əs) *adj.* **1.** Feeling, expressing, or characterized by envy. **2.** *Obsolete.* Eager to emulate; emulous. —**en′vi·ous·ly** *adv.* —**en′vi·ous·ness** *n.*

en·vi·ron (ĕn-vī′rən, ĭn-) *tr.v.* **-roned, -roning, -rons.** To encircle; surround. [Middle English *envirounen*, from Old French *environer*, from *environ*, around : *en-*, in + *viron*, circle, from *virer*, to turn, VEER.]

en·vi·ron·ment (ĕn-vī′rən-mənt, ĭn-) *n.* **1.** Something that surrounds; surroundings. **2.** The total of circumstances surrounding an organism or group of organisms, specifically: **a.** The combination of external or extrinsic physical conditions that affect and influence the growth and development of organisms. **b.** The complex of social and cultural conditions affecting the nature of an individual or community. Compare **heredity.** —**en·vi′ron·men′tal** (-mĕnt′l) *adj.* —**en·vi′ron·men′tal·ly** *adv.*

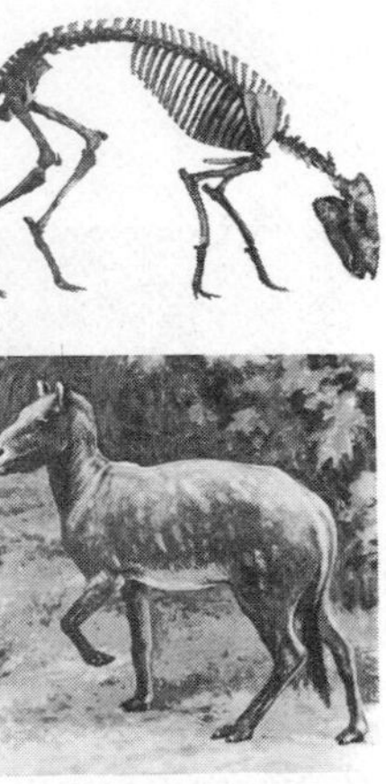

eohippus
Above: The skeleton of *Hyracotherium resartus*
Below: A reconstruction

en·vi·rons (ĕn-vī′rənz, ĭn-) *pl.n.* **1.** A surrounding area, especially of a city; suburbs; outskirts. **2.** Surroundings; environment.

en·vis·age (ĕn-vĭz′ĭj, ĭn-) *tr.v.* **-aged, -aging, -ages.** To have an image of; conceive of, especially as a future possibility or goal: *"they envisaged a society ruled by a learned and therefore enlightened aristocracy"* (George L. Mosse). [French *envisager* : Old French *en-*, in + *visage*, face, VISAGE.]

en·vi·sion (ĕn-vĭzh′ən) *tr.v.* **-sioned, -sioning, -sions.** To picture in the mind; foresee. [EN- + VISION.]

en·voi (ĕn′voi, än′-) *n.* Also **en·voy.** A short concluding stanza of certain French verse forms, such as the ballade, originally serving as a postscript dedicating the poem to a patron and later as a pithy summation of the poem. [Middle English *envoie*, from Old French *envoy*, "a sending away," conclusion, from *envoier*, to send. See **envoy.**]

en·voy[1] (ĕn′voi, än′-) *n.* **1.** A messenger or other agent sent on a mission. **2.** A representative of a government or faction sent on a special diplomatic mission. **3.** A minister plenipotentiary assigned to a foreign embassy, ranking next below the ambassador. [From French *envoyé*, one who is sent, from past participle of *envoyer*, to send, from Old French *envoier, enveier*, from Late Latin *inviāre*, to put on the way : Latin *in-*, in + *via*, way (see **wei-**[2] in Appendix*).]

en·voy[2]. Variant of **envoi.**

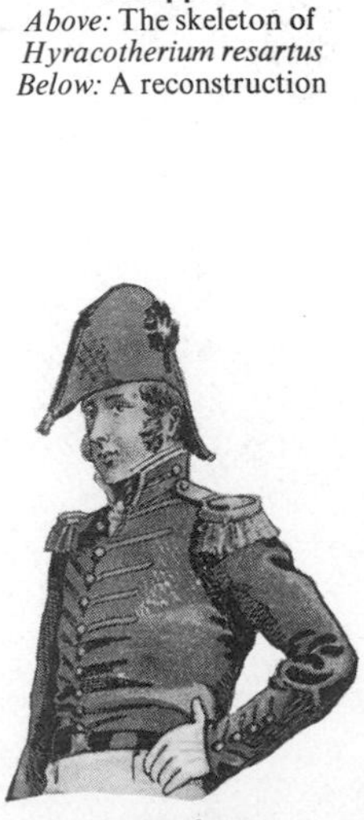

epaulet
On an early 19th-century U.S. Army uniform

en·vy (ĕn′vē) *n., pl.* **-vies.** **1.** A feeling of discontent and resentment aroused by contemplation of another's desirable possessions or qualities, with a strong desire to have them for oneself. **2. a.** A possession of another that is strongly desired. **b.** One who possesses what another strongly desires. **3.** *Obsolete.* Malevolence. —*v.* **envied, -vying, -vies.** —*tr.* To feel envy for; regard with envy. —*intr.* To be filled with envy. [Middle English *envie*, from Old French, from Latin *invidia*, from *invidēre*, to look at with malice : *in-*, in, upon + *vidēre*, to see (see **weid-** in Appendix*).] —**en′vi·er** *n.* —**en′vy·ing·ly** *adv.*

Synonyms: *envy, begrudge, covet.* These verbs mean to resent another's good fortune or to desire to have what is his. *Envy* is wider in range than the others, since it combines both resentment and desire. *Begrudge* stresses resentment toward the possessor and unwillingness to acknowledge his right or claim. *Covet* stresses desire for another's possession, especially when the desire is a secret or shameful longing.

en·wind (ĕn-wīnd′, ĭn-) *tr.v.* **-wound** (-wound′), **-winding, -winds.** Also **in·wind** (ĭn-). To wind around or about; encircle.

en·womb (ĕn-wōōm′, ĭn-) *tr.v.* **-wombed, -wombing, -wombs.** *Archaic & Poetic.* To hold in the womb or a womblike enclosure.

en·wrap (ĕn-răp′, ĭn-) *tr.v.* **-wrapped, -wrapping, -wraps.** Also **in·wrap** (ĭn-). **1.** To wrap up; enclose; enfold. **2.** To engross; preoccupy.

en·wreathe (ĕn-rēth′, ĭn-) *tr.v.* **-wreathed, -wreathing, -wreathes.** Also **in·wreathe** (ĭn-). To enclose or surround with or as if with a wreath.

en·zo·ot·ic (ĕn′zō-ŏt′ĭk) *adj.* Affecting or peculiar to animals of a specific area or limited district. Said of diseases. —*n.* An enzootic disease. [EN- (within) + ZO(O)- + -OTIC.]

en·zyme (ĕn′zīm′) *n.* Any of numerous proteins or conjugated proteins produced by and functioning as biochemical catalysts in living organisms. [German *Enzym*, from Medieval Greek *enzumos*, leavened : Greek *en-*, in + *zumē*, leaven (see **yeu-**[1] in Appendix*).] —**en′zy·mat′ic** (-zə-măt′ĭk) *adj.*

en·zy·mol·o·gy (ĕn′zə-mŏl′ə-jē) *n.* The biochemistry of enzymes. [ENZYM(E) + -LOGY.] —**en′zy·mol′o·gist** *n.*

eo–. Indicates: **1.** An early period of time; for example, **Eocene. 2.** An early form or representative; for example, **eohippus.** [Greek *ēō-*, from *ēōs*, dawn. See **awes-** in Appendix.*]

e.o. ex officio.

E·o·cene (ē′ə-sēn′) *adj.* Of, pertaining to, or designating the geologic time, rock series, sedimentary deposits, and fossils of the second oldest of the five major epochs of the Cenozoic era or Tertiary period, extending from the end of the Paleocene to the beginning of the Oligocene, and characterized by the rise of mammals. See **geology.** —*n. Geology.* The Eocene epoch. Preceded by *the.* [EO- + -CENE.]

e·o·hip·pus (ē′ō-hĭp′əs) *n.* An extinct, small, herbivorous mammal of the genus *Hyracotherium* (or *Eohippus*), of the Eocene epoch, having four-toed front feet and three-toed hind feet, and related ancestrally to the horse. [New Latin : EO- + Greek *hippos*, horse (see **ekwo-** in Appendix*).]

e·o·li·an (ē-ō′lē-ən) *adj.* Also **ae·o·li·an.** Pertaining to, caused by, or carried by the wind. [From AEOLUS (god of the winds).]

e·o·lith (ē′ə-lĭth′) *n. Anthropology.* Any of the alleged stone artifacts characterizing the Eolithic. [EO- + -LITH.]

E·o·lith·ic (ē′ə-lĭth′ĭk) *adj. Anthropology.* Of or relating to the postulated earliest period of human culture preceding the Lower Paleolithic. —*n. Anthropology.* The Eolithic period. Preceded by *the.* [EO- + -LITHIC.]

e.o.m. end of month.

e·on (ē′ŏn′, ē′ən) *n.* Also **ae·on.** **1.** An indefinitely long period of time; an age; eternity. **2.** *Geology.* The longest division of geologic time, containing two or more eras. [Late Latin *aeōn*, age, from Greek *aiōn*. See **aiw-** in Appendix.*]

e·o·ni·an (ē-ō′nē-ən) *adj.* Also **ae·o·ni·an.** Lasting for eons; eternal; ageless.

E·os (ē′ŏs′). *Greek Mythology.* The goddess of the dawn, identified with the Roman goddess Aurora. [Greek *Ēōs*, from *ēōs*, dawn. See **awes-** in Appendix.*]

e·o·sin (ē′ə-sən) *n.* A red crystalline powder, $C_{20}H_8Br_4O_5$, used in textile dyeing, ink manufacturing, and in coloring gasoline. [Greek *ēōs*, dawn (see **awes-** in Appendix*) + -IN. (So called from its color.)]

e·o·sin·o·phil (ē′ə-sĭn′ə-fĭl′) *n.* Also **e·o·sin·o·phile** (-fīl′). **1.** *Physiology.* A type of leukocyte in vertebrate blood that accepts an eosin stain. **2.** *Biochemistry.* Any microorganism, cell, or histological element easily stained by eosin dye. [EOSIN + -PHILE.] —**e′o·sin′o·phil′, e′o·sin′o·phil′ic, e′o·si·noph′i·lous** (ē′ō-sĭ-nŏf′ə-ləs) *adj.*

-eous. Indicates having the nature of or akin to; for example, **gaseous, beauteous.** [Latin *-eus.*]

EP extended play.

e·pact (ē′păkt′) *n.* **1.** The excess of time, about 11 days, of the solar year over the lunar year. **2.** The age of the moon at the beginning of the calendar year. **3.** The excess of time of a calendar month over a lunar month. [Old French *epacte*, from Late Latin *epacta*, from Greek *epaktai (hēmerai)*, "(days) brought in," from *epaktos*, brought in from abroad, from *epagein*, to lead on, bring in : from *epi-*, on + *agein*, to lead (see **ag-** in Appendix*).]

ep·arch (ĕp′ärk′) *n.* **1.** The chief administrator of an eparchy. **2.** *Greek Orthodox Church.* A bishop or metropolitan. [Greek *eparkhos*, commander, governor : *epi-*, on, over + -ARCH.] —**e·par′chi·al** *adj.*

ep·ar·chy (ĕp′är′kē) *n., pl.* **-chies.** **1.** An administrative subdivision of Greece. **2.** *Greek Orthodox Church.* An ecclesiastical district; diocese.

ep·au·let (ĕp′ə-lĕt′, ĕp′ə-lĕt′) *n.* Also **ep·au·lette.** A shoulder ornament; especially, either of two fringed straps on certain dress uniforms. [French *épaulette*, diminutive of *épaule*, shoulder, from Old French *espaule*, from Latin *spatula.* See **spatula.**]

é·pée (ā-pā′) *n.* Also **e·pee.** **1.** A fencing sword with a bowl-shaped guard and a long, narrow, fluted blade that has no cutting edge and tapers to a blunted point. **2.** The art of fencing

ă pat/ā pay/âr care/ä father/b bib/ch church/d deed/ĕ pet/ē be/f fife/g gag/h hat/hw which/ĭ pit/ī pie/îr pier/j judge/k kick/l lid, needle/m mum/n no, sudden/ng thing/ŏ pot/ō toe/ô paw, for/oi noise/ou out/ōō took/ōō boot/p pop/r roar/s sauce/sh ship, dish/

with the épée. [French, from Latin *spatha,* sword, blade. See **spatula.**] —**é·pée′ist** *n.*

ep·ei·rog·e·ny (ĕp′ī-rŏj′ə-nē) *n.* The deformation of the crust of the earth by which continents and oceanic basins, or parts of these, are formed. [Greek *ēpeiros,* continent (see **apero-** in Appendix*) + -GENY.] —**e·pei′ro·gen′ic** (ĭ-pī′rō-jĕn′ĭk) *adj.*

ep·en·the·sis (ĕ-pĕn′thə-sĭs) *n., pl.* **-ses** (-sēz′). *Linguistics.* The insertion of an excrescent phoneme into a word; for example: (fĭl′əm), nonstandard pronunciation for *film* (fĭlm). [Late Latin, from Greek, from *epentithenai,* to insert : *epi-,* in addition to + *entithenai,* to put in : *en-,* in + *tithenai,* to place (see **dhē-**[1] in Appendix*).] —**ep′en·thet′ic** (ĕp′ĭn-thĕt′ĭk) *adj.*

e·pergne (ĭ-pûrn′, ā-pârn′) *n.* A large silver or glass serving dish, usually compartmented or branched and used as a table centerpiece. [Probably from French *épargne,* saving, from *épargner,* to save, from Old French *espargnier,* from Germanic *sparōjan* (unattested), to SPARE.]

É·per·nay (ā-pĕr-nā′). A town and champagne-producing center on the Marne in northeastern France. Population, 21,000.

ep·ex·e·ge·sis (ĕp′ĕk′sə-jē′sĭs) *n.* **1.** The addition of an explanation or clarification to a text. **2.** The additional material itself. [Greek *epexēgēsis,* from *epexēgeisthai,* to explain in detail : *epi-,* in addition to + *exēgeisthai,* to explain (see **exegesis**).] —**ep′ex′e·get′ic** (-jĕt′ĭk), **ep′ex′e·get′i·cal** *adj.* —**ep′ex′e·get′i·cal·ly** *adv.*

Eph. Ephesians (New Testament).

e·phah (ē′fə) *n.* Also **e·pha.** A unit of dry measure equal to slightly more than a bushel, used by the ancient Hebrews. [Hebrew *'ephāh,* probably from Egyptian *'pt.*]

e·phebe (ĕf′ēb′, ĭ-fēb′) *n.* *Latin* **e·phe·bus** (ĭ-fē′bəs) *pl.* **-bi** (-bī′). In ancient Greece, a youth between eighteen and twenty years of age. [Latin *ephēbus,* from Greek *ephēbos* : *epi-,* at + *hēbē,* youth (see **yēgwā** in Appendix*).] —**e′phe′bic** *adj.*

e·phed·rine (ĭ-fĕd′rĭn, ĕf′ə-drēn′) *n.* A white, odorless, powdered or crystalline alkaloid, $C_{10}H_{15}NO$, isolated from the mahuang shrub or made synthetically, used to treat allergies and asthma and as a vasoconstrictor. [New Latin *Ephedra,* genus name of mahuang, from Latin *ephedra,* horsetail, from Greek *ephedros,* sitting upon : *epi-,* upon + *hedra,* seat (see **sed-**[1] in Appendix*) + -INE.]

e·phem·er·a (ĭ-fĕm′ər-ə) *n., pl.* **-as** or **-erae** (-ə-rē′). **1.** Something short-lived or transitory. **2.** *Plural.* Printed matter of current and passing interest, such as periodicals, handbills, and topical pamphlets. [From the plural of EPHEMERON.]

e·phem·er·al (ĭ-fĕm′ər-əl) *adj.* **1.** Lasting for a brief time; short-lived; transitory. **2.** Living or lasting only one day, as certain flowers or adult insects. —See Synonyms at **transient.** —*n.* An ephemeral thing or organism. [Greek *ephēmeros* : *epi-,* on + *hēmera,* day (see **āmer-** in Appendix*).] —**e·phem′er·al′i·ty** *n.* —**e·phem′er·al·ly** *adv.*

e·phem·er·id (ĭ-fĕm′ər-ĭd) *n.* An insect of the order Ephemeroptera, which includes the mayflies. [New Latin *Ephemeridae,* former name of the order, from Greek *ephēmeros,* EPHEMERAL.]

e·phem·er·is (ĭ-fĕm′ər-ĭs) *n., pl.* **ephemerides** (ĕf′ə-mĕr′ə-dēz′). **1.** A table giving the coordinates of one or a number of celestial bodies at a number of specific times during a given period. **2.** A publication that presents a collection of such tables; an astronomical almanac. **3.** *Obsolete.* **a.** A calendar. **b.** A diary or journal. [Late Latin *ephēmeris,* diary, from Greek, from *ephemeros,* EPHEMERAL.]

ephemeris time. A highly accurate astronomical sytem for the measurement of time based on the period of the earth's orbit, but in practice relying on lunar observations and an accurate lunar ephemeris to calculate corrections to be applied to clocks. The unit is the ephemeris second equal to 1/31,556,925.9747 of the tropical year for epoch 1900 January 0.

e·phem·er·on (ĭ-fĕm′ə-rŏn′) *n., pl.* **-era** (-ər-ə) or **-ons.** A short-lived thing or organism. [New Latin, from Greek *ephemēron,* mayfly, from the neuter of *ephemēros,* EPHEMERAL.]

E·phe·sian (ĭ-fē′zhən) *adj.* Of or relating to Ephesus or its people. —*n.* A native or inhabitant of Ephesus.

E·phe·sians (ĭ-fē′zhənz) *n.* Plural in form, used with a singular verb. *Abbr.* **Eph.** A book of the New Testament consisting of the Apostle Paul's epistle to the Christians of Ephesus.

Eph·e·sus (ĕf′ə-səs). An ancient Greek city, one of the most prosperous in Ionia, in Asia Minor near the Aegean Sea. It was the site of the famed Temple of Artemis.

eph·od (ĕf′ŏd′, ē′fŏd′) *n.* An embroidered vestment worn by ancient Hebrew priests. [Hebrew *ēphōdh.*]

eph·or (ĕf′ôr′, -ər) *n., pl.* **-ors** or **-ori** (-ə-rī′). One of a body of five elected magistrates exercising a supervisory power over the kings of Sparta. [Latin *ephorus,* from Greek *ephoros,* from *ephoran,* to oversee : *epi-,* over + *horan,* to see (see **wer-**[4] in Appendix*).]

E·phra·im[1] (ē′frē-əm, ē′frəm). The younger son of Joseph. Genesis 41:52.

E·phra·im[2] (ē′frē-əm, ē′frəm) *n.* A tribe of Israel descended from the younger son of Joseph.

E·phra·im[3] (ē′frē-əm, ē′frəm). **1.** A range of low hills in northwestern Israel. Also called "Mount Ephraim." **2.** The Kingdom of Israel.

E·phra·im·ite (ē′frē-ə-mīt′) *n.* A member of the tribe of Ephraim. —**E′phra·im·ite′** *adj.*

epi–. Indicates: **1.** On, upon; for example, **epiphyte. 2.** Over, above; for example, **epicenter. 3.** Around, covering; for example, **epineurium, epicardium. 4.** To, toward, close to, next to; for example, **epicalyx. 5.** Besides, in addition; for example, **epiphenomenon. 6.** After; for example, **epigenesis. 7.** Among; for example, **epizootic.** [Greek *epi-* (before a vowel, *ep-*), from *epi,* upon, over, at, after. See **epi** in Appendix.*]

e·pib·o·ly (ĭ-pĭb′ə-lē) *n.* Gastrulation by the differential growth of the cells of one embryonic part over and around another. [Greek *epibolē,* a throwing on, from *epiballein,* to throw on : *epi-,* on + *ballein,* to throw (see **gwel-**[1] in Appendix*).] —**ep′i·bol′ic** (ĕp′ə-bŏl′ĭk) *adj.*

ep·ic (ĕp′ĭk) *n.* **1.** An extended narrative poem, such as *Beowulf* or the *Iliad,* celebrating episodes of a people's heroic tradition, typically developed by oral composition within a standard formulaic diction and set of metrical and narrative conventions, a final version being transcribed after the introduction of writing. **2.** The genre represented by such poems; epos. **3.** A formal poem, such as the *Aeneid,* composed in literary imitation of these conventions. Also called "literary epic." **4.** *Capital* **E.** The form of Ancient Greek used in epic poetry, essentially Attic-Ionic with elements of Aeolic. **5.** A literary or dramatic composition thought to embody the qualities characteristic of epic poetry. **6.** A historical event or movement likened to the epos, as in grandeur and sweep: *the epic of the Old West.* —*adj.* **1.** Of or designating an epic: *epic poem.* **2.** Occurring in or characteristic of epics: *epic simile.* **3.** Resembling the epos in grandeur, scope, or theme; heroic: *"Theresa's passionate, ideal nature demanded an epic life"* (George Eliot). [Latin *epicus,* from Greek *epikos,* from *epos,* song, word. See **wekw-** in Appendix.*]

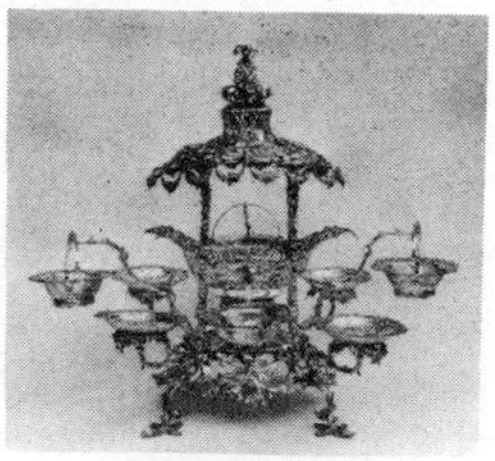

epergne
Eighteenth-century English silver epergne

ep·i·ca·lyx (ĕp′ĭ-kā′lĭks, -kăl′ĭks) *n., pl.* **-lyxes** or **-calyces** (-kā′lə-sēz′, -kăl′ə-sēz′). *Botany.* A set of bracts close to and resembling a calyx. Sometimes called "calycle." [EPI- + CALYX.]

ep·i·can·thic fold (ĕp′ĭ-kăn′thĭk). A fold of skin of the upper eyelid that tends to cover the inner corner of the eye, characteristic of many Mongolian peoples. Also called "epicanthus." [EPI- + CANTHUS.]

ep·i·car·di·um (ĕp′ĭ-kär′dē-əm) *n., pl.* **-dia** (-dē-ə). The inner layer of the pericardium that is in actual contact with the heart. [New Latin : EPI- + Greek *kardia,* heart (see **kerd-**[1] in Appendix*).]

ep·i·carp (ĕp′ĭ-kärp′) *n.* *Botany.* An **exocarp** *(see).* [French *épicarpe* : EPI- + -CARP.]

ep·i·ce·di·um (ĕp′ə-sē′dē-əm) *n., pl.* **-dia** (-dē-ə). A funeral hymn or dirge. [Latin *epicēdium,* from Greek *epikēdeion,* from the neuter of *epikēdeios,* funeral : *epi-,* at + *kēdos,* sorrow, grief (see **kād-** in Appendix*).]

ep·i·cene (ĕp′ə-sēn′) *adj.* **1. a.** Belonging to, or having the characteristics of both the male and the female: *an epicene statue; an epicene angel.* **b.** Effeminate; womanish. **c.** Sexless; neuter. **2.** *Linguistics.* Capable of being applied to both the male and the female without a change in form, as Greek *pais,* child (*ho pais,* the boy; *hē pais,* the girl). —*n.* **1.** *Linguistics.* An epicene word. **2.** An epicene person or object. [Middle English *epicene,* from Latin *epicoenus,* from Greek *epikoinos,* common to many, promiscuous : *epi-,* to + *koinos,* common (see **kom** in Appendix*).]

ep·i·cen·ter (ĕp′ə-sĕn′tər) *n.* Also **ep·i·cen·trum** (ĕp′ə-sĕn′trəm) *pl.* **-tra** (-trə). **1.** The part of the earth's surface directly above the origin of an earthquake. **2.** A focal point. [New Latin *epicentrum* : EPI- + Latin *centrum,* CENTER.]

ep·i·cot·yl (ĕp′ĭ-kŏt′l) *n.* *Botany.* The part of the stem of a seedling or embryonic plant that is above the cotyledons and below the first true leaves. [EPI- + COTYL(EDON).]

e·pic·ri·sis[1] (ĭ-pĭk′rĭ-sĭs) *n., pl.* **-ses** (-sēz). A detailed critique of a literary work. [New Latin, from Greek *epikrisis,* selection, judgment, from *epikrinein,* to decide, select : *epi-,* over + *krinein,* to judge (see **skerī-** in Appendix*).]

ep·i·cri·sis[2] (ĕp′ĭ-krī′sĭs, ĕp′ē-) *n., pl.* **-ses** (-sēz). *Pathology.* A crisis that occurs after the primary crisis of a disease. [EPI- (after) + CRISIS.]

ep·i·crit·ic (ĕp′ĭ-krĭt′ĭk) *adj.* Pertaining to sensory nerve fibers that enable acute thermal and tactile sensitivity. Compare **protopathic.** [Greek *epikritikos,* decisive, from *epikritos,* decided on, from *epikrinein,* to decide. See **epicrisis.**]

Ep·ic·te·tus (ĕp′ĭk-tē′təs). Greek Stoic philosopher of the first century A.D.

ep·i·cure (ĕp′ĭ-kyŏŏr′) *n.* **1.** A person with refined taste in food and wine. **2.** *Archaic.* A person devoted to sensuous pleasure and luxurious living. [After EPICURUS, who supposedly advocated sensuous pleasure as the highest good.]

Ep·i·cu·re·an (ĕp′ĭ-kyŏŏ-rē′ən) *adj.* **1.** Of or associated with the philosophy of Epicureanism. **2.** *Small* **e.** Devoted to the pursuit of pleasure; fond of good food, comfort, and ease; hedonistic. **3.** *Small* **e.** Suited to the tastes of an epicure: *an epicurean repast.* —See Synonyms at **sensuous.** —*n.* **1.** A follower of Epicurus. **2.** *Small* **e.** An epicure.

Ep·i·cu·re·an·ism (ĕp′ĭ-kyŏŏ-rē′ə-nĭz′əm) *n.* The philosophy advanced by Epicurus who sought freedom from pain and emotional disturbances, rejected the afterlife and the influence of gods in human affairs, and subscribed to the atomic theory of Democritus.

ep·i·cur·ism (ĕp′ĭ-kyŏŏ-rĭz′əm) *n.* Also **ep·i·cu·re·an·ism** (ĕp′ĭ-kyŏŏ-rē′ə-nĭz′əm). The beliefs, tastes, or manner of living of an epicure.

Ep·i·cu·rus (ĕp′ĭ-kyŏŏr′əs). 342?–270 B.C. Greek founder of Epicureanism.

ep·i·cy·cle (ĕp′ə-sī′kəl) *n.* In Ptolemaic cosmology, a small circle, the center of which moves on the circumference of a larger circle at whose center is the earth, and the circumference of which describes the orbit of one of the planets around the earth. [Middle English *epicicle,* from Late Latin *epicyclus,* from Greek *epikuklos* : *epi-*, on + *kuklos*, circle, CYCLE.] —**ep′i·cy′clic** (-sī′klĭk, -sĭk′lĭk) *adj.*

epicyclic train. A system of gears in which at least one wheel axis revolves about another.

ep·i·cy·cloid (ĕp′ə-sī′kloid′) *n.* The curve described by a point fixed on the circumference of a circle as it rolls on the outside of the circumference of a fixed circle. [EPICYCL(E) + -OID.] —**ep′i·cy′cloid′al** (-kloid′l) *adj.*

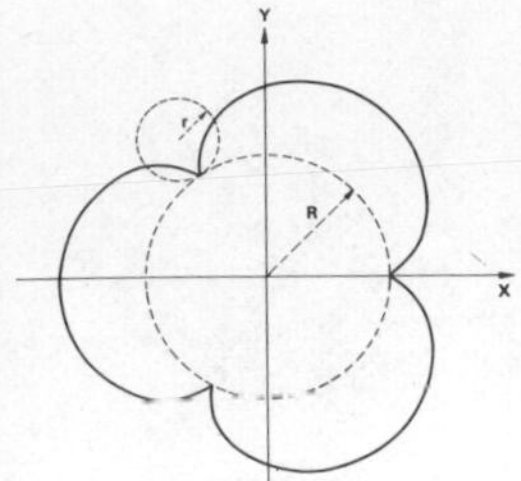

epicycloid
An epicycloid of three cusps; $r = \frac{R}{3}$

epicycloidal wheel. A wheel in an epicyclic train.

Ep·i·dau·rus (ĕp′ə-dôr′əs). An ancient town of Greece, near the eastern shore of the Peloponnesus; the site of the best preserved ancient Greek theater.

ep·i·dem·ic (ĕp′ə-dĕm′ĭk) *adj.* Also **ep·i·dem·i·cal** (-ĭ-kəl). Spreading rapidly and extensively among many individuals in an area. Said especially of contagious diseases. —*n.* **1.** A contagious disease that spreads rapidly. **2.** A temporary, widespread popularity, as of a fashion or a fad. **3.** A rapid spread, growth, or development. [French *épidémique*, from *épidémie*, from Old French *espydymie*, from Late Latin *epidēmia*, from Greek *epidēmia (nosos)*, "(illness) prevalent among people," from *epidēmos*, prevalent, common : *epi-*, on, "among" + *dēmos*, people (see **dā-** in Appendix*).] —**ep′i·dem′i·cal·ly** *adv.*

ep·i·de·mi·ol·o·gy (ĕp′ə-dē′mē-ŏl′ə-jē, -dĕm′ē-ŏl′ə-jē) *n.* The study of epidemics and epidemic diseases. [Late Latin *epidēmia*, an EPIDEM(IC) + -LOGY.] —**ep′i·de′mi·o·log′ic** (-ə-lŏj′ĭk), **ep′i·de′mi·o·log′i·cal** *adj.* —**ep′i·de′mi·ol′o·gist** *n.*

ep·i·der·mis (ĕp′ə-dûr′mĭs) *n.* **1. a.** *Anatomy.* The outer, protective, nonvascular layer of the skin. **b.** An integument or outer layer of various organisms. **2.** *Botany.* The outermost layer of cells or protective covering of a plant or plant part. [Late Latin, from Greek : *epi-*, over + *derma*, skin (see **der-**[2] in Appendix*).] —**ep′i·der′mal** *adj.*

ep·i·der·moid (ĕp′ə-dûr′moid′) *adj.* Also **ep·i·der·moid·al** (ĕp′ə-dûr′moid′l). Having the characteristics of or relating to the epidermis. [EPIDERM(IS) + -OID.]

ep·i·di·a·scope (ĕp′ə-dī′ə-skōp′) *n.* A machine for projecting the images of opaque objects or transparencies upon a screen. [EPI- + DIA- + -SCOPE.]

ep·i·did·y·mis (ĕp′ə-dĭd′ə-mĭs) *n., pl.* **-mides** (-mə-dēz′). A long, narrow, flattened convoluted body that is part of the spermatic duct system, lying on the lateral edge of the posterior border of the testis. [New Latin, from Greek : *epi-*, at, near + *didumos*, testicle (see **dwō** in Appendix*).] —**ep′i·did′y·mal** *adj.*

ep·i·dote (ĕp′ə-dōt′) *n.* A natural, yellow, green, or black mineral consisting mainly of a silicate of calcium, aluminum, and iron, commonly found in metamorphic rock. [French *épidote*, from Greek *epididonai*, to give additionally, increase (so called because two sides of the mineral's base are longer than the other two) : *epi-*, in addition + *didonai*, to give (see **dō-** in Appendix*).] —**ep′i·dot′ic** (-dŏt′ĭk) *adj.*

ep·i·gas·tri·um (ĕp′ĭ-găs′trē-əm) *n., pl.* **-tria** (-trē-ə). The upper middle region of the abdomen. [New Latin, from Greek *epigastrion* : *epi-*, above + *gastrium*, diminutive of *gastēr*, stomach (see **gras-** in Appendix*).] —**ep′i·gas′tric** *adj.*

ep·i·ge·al (ĕp′ə-jē′əl) *adj.* Also **e·pi·ge·an** (-ən), **e·pi·ge·ous** (-əs). **1.** *Biology.* Living or occurring on or near the surface of the ground. **2.** *Botany.* Designating or characterized by cotyledons that appear above the surface of the ground. [Greek *epigaios*, on the earth : *epi-*, on + *gaia*, *gē*, earth (see **gē** in Appendix*).]

ep·i·gene (ĕp′ə-jēn′) *adj.* **1.** Formed, originating, or occurring on or just below the surface of the earth. **2.** Foreign; not natural to the material in which found. Said of crystals. [French *épigène*, from Greek *epigenēs*, arising after, from *epigignesthai*, to be born after : *epi-*, after + *gignesthai*, to be born (see **gene-** in Appendix*).]

ep·i·gen·e·sis (ĕp′ə-jĕn′ə-sĭs) *n.* **1.** *Biology.* The theory that the individual is developed by structural elaboration of the unstructured egg rather than by a simple enlarging of a preformed entity. **2.** *Geology.* Change in the mineral characteristics of a rock due to outside influence. [New Latin : EPI- + -GENESIS.] —**ep′i·ge·net′ic** (-jə-nĕt′ĭk) *adj.*

e·pig·e·nous (ĭ-pĭj′ə-nəs) *adj. Botany.* Developing or growing on an upper surface, as fungi on leaves. [EPI- + -GENOUS.]

ep·i·glot·tis (ĕp′ĭ-glŏt′ĭs) *n., pl.* **-tises** or **-glottides** (-glŏt′ĭ-dēz′). An elastic cartilage located at the root of the tongue that folds over the glottis to prevent food from entering the windpipe during the act of swallowing. [New Latin, from Greek *epiglōttis* : *epi-*, over + *glōttis*, GLOTTIS.]

ep·i·gone (ĕp′ə-gōn′) *n.* A second-rate imitator or follower, as of an artist or philosopher. [Greek *Epigonoi*, sons of the Seven against Thebes who imitated their fathers by attacking Thebes, from the plural of *epigonos*, born after : EPI- + *gonos*, child (see **gene-** in Appendix*).] —**ep′i·gon′ic** (-gŏn′ĭk) *adj.*

ep·i·gram (ĕp′ĭ-grăm′) *n.* **1.** A short poem expressing a single thought or observation with terseness and wit. **2.** A concisely and cleverly worded statement, making a pointed observation and often concluding with a satirical twist. **3.** Discourse or expression by means of such statements. —See Synonyms at **saying.** [Old French *epigramme*, from Latin *epigramma*, from Greek, inscription, from *epigraphein*, to write on : *epi-*, on + *graphein*, to write (see **gerebh-** in Appendix*).]

ep·i·gram·mat·ic (ĕp′ĭ-grə-măt′ĭk) *adj.* **1.** Of or having the nature of an epigram. **2.** Full of or given to the use of epigrams. —See Synonyms at **concise.** —**ep′i·gram·mat′i·cal·ly** *adv.*

ep·i·gram·ma·tism (ĕp′ĭ-grăm′ə-tĭz′əm) *n.* Literary style marked by the use of epigrams. —**ep′i·gram′ma·tist** *n.*

ep·i·gram·ma·tize (ĕp′ĭ-grăm′ə-tīz′) *v.* **-tized, -tizing, -tizes.** —*tr.* To express (a thought or sentiment) in an epigram or epigrams. —*intr.* To speak or write in epigrams.

ep·i·graph (ĕp′ĭ-grăf′, -gräf′) *n.* **1.** An inscription, as on a statue or building. **2.** A motto or quotation at the beginning of a book or chapter. [Greek *epigraphē*, from *epigraphos*, written on, from *epigraphein*, to write on. See **epigram.**] —**ep′i·graph′ic, ep′i·graph′i·cal** *adj.* —**ep′i·graph′i·cal·ly** *adv.*

e·pig·ra·phy (ĭ-pĭg′rə-fē) *n.* **1.** Inscriptions collectively. **2. a.** The study of inscriptions. **b.** The interpretation of ancient inscriptions. Compare **paleography.** —**e·pig′ra·pher, e·pig′ra·phist** *n.*

e·pig·y·nous (ĭ-pĭj′ə-nəs) *adj. Botany.* Having or characterizing floral parts or organs attached to or near the summit of the ovary. [EPI- + -GYNOUS.] —**e·pig′y·ny** *n.*

ep·i·lep·sy (ĕp′ə-lĕp′sē) *n.* A nervous disorder characterized by recurring attacks of motor, sensory, or psychic malfunction with or without unconsciousness or convulsive movements. Also called "falling sickness." [Old French *epilepsie*, from Late Latin *epilēpsia*, from Greek, from *epilambanein* (stem *epilab-*), to take besides, seize upon : *epi-*, besides, in addition to + *lambanein*, to take hold of (see **slagw-** in Appendix*).]

ep·i·lep·tic (ĕp′ə-lĕp′tĭk) *adj.* **1.** Affected with epilepsy. **2.** Of, characteristic of, or associated with epilepsy. —*n.* One who has epilepsy.

ep·i·lep·toid (ĕp′ə-lĕp′toid′) *adj.* Resembling epilepsy or any of its symptoms. [EPILEPT(IC) + -OID.]

ep·i·logue (ĕp′ə-lôg′, -lŏg′) *n.* Also **ep·i·log. 1. a.** A short poem or speech spoken directly to the audience following the conclusion of a play. **b.** The performer or performers who speak this. **2.** A short addition or concluding section at the end of any literary work, often dealing with the future of its characters. [Middle English *epiloge*, from Old French *epilogue*, from Latin *epilogus*, from Greek *epilogos*, from *epilegein*, to say more, to add : *epi-*, in addition + *legein*, to say (see **leg-** in Appendix*).]

ep·i·mor·pho·sis (ĕp′ə-môr′fə-sĭs, -môr-fō′sĭs) *n.* Regeneration of a part of an organ characterized by proliferation of new tissue. Compare **metamorphosis.** [EPI- + MORPHOSIS.]

e·pi·my·si·um (ĕp′ə-mĭz′ē-əm, -mĭzh′ē-əm) *n., pl.* **-mysia** (-mĭz′ē-ə, -mĭzh′ē-ə). The fibrous sheath enclosing a muscle. [New Latin : EPI- + Greek *mus*, muscle (see **mū-**[1] in Appendix*).]

ep·i·nas·ty (ĕp′ə-năs′tē) *n., pl.* **-ties.** A downward bending of leaves or other plant parts, resulting from excessive growth of the upper side. [EPI- + -NASTY.] —**e′pi·nas′tic** *adj.*

ep·i·neph·rine (ĕp′ə-nĕf′rĕn′, -rĭn) *n.* Also **ep·i·neph·rin** (-rĭn). **1.** An adrenal hormone that stimulates autonomic nerve action. **2.** A white to brownish crystalline compound, $C_9H_{13}NO_3$, isolated from adrenal glands of certain mammals or synthesized, and used as a heart stimulant, vasoconstrictor, and in the treatment of asthma. Also called "adrenalin." [EPI- + NEPHR(O)- + -INE.]

ep·i·neu·ri·um (ĕp′ə-nŏŏr′ē-əm, -nyŏŏr′ē-əm) *n., pl.* **-neuria** (-nŏŏr′ē-ə, -nyŏŏr′ē-ə). The connective tissue sheath surrounding a nerve trunk that contains blood and lymph vessels. [New Latin : EPI- + NEUR(O)- + -IUM.] —**ep′i·neu′ri·al** *adj.*

e·piph·a·ny (ĭ-pĭf′ə-nē) *n., pl.* **-nies. 1.** A revelatory manifestation of a divine being. **2.** A spiritual event in which the essence of a given object of manifestation appears to the subject, as in a sudden flash of recognition. [Greek *epiphaneia*, appearance, from *epiphanēs*, appearing, manifest, from *epiphainein*, to manifest : *epi-*, to + *phainein*, to show (see **bhā-**[1] in Appendix*).]

E·piph·a·ny (ĭ-pĭf′ə-nē) *n.* A Christian festival held on January 6 in celebration of the manifestation of the divine nature of Christ to the Gentiles as represented by the Magi. Also called "Twelfth-day." [Middle English *epiphanie*, from Old French *epiphanie*, from Late Latin *epiphania*, from Late Greek *(hiera) epiphania*, "(the feast) of the manifestation," from the neuter plural of *epiphanios* (unattested), "pertaining to manifestation," from Greek *epiphainein*, to manifest. See **epiphany.**]

ep·i·phe·nom·e·nal·ism (ĕp′ə-fĭ-nŏm′ə-nə-lĭz′əm) *n. Philosophy.* The doctrine that mental activities are simply epiphenomena of the neural processes of the brain and have no causal influence.

ep·i·phe·nom·e·non (ĕp′ə-fĭ-nŏm′ə-nŏn′) *n., pl.* **-na** (-nə). **1.** A secondary phenomenon overlapping and resulting from another. **2.** *Pathology.* An additional condition in the course of a disease, not necessarily connected with the disease. [EPI- + PHENOMENON.] —**ep′i·phe·nom′e·nal** *adj.*

e·piph·y·sis (ĭ-pĭf′ə-sĭs) *n., pl.* **-ses** (-sēz′). *Anatomy.* A part of a bone, often an end of a long bone, that initially develops separated from the main portion by cartilage. [New Latin, from Greek *epiphusis*, a growth upon : *epi-*, upon + *phusis*, growth, from *phuein*, to grow (see **bheu-** in Appendix*).] —**ep′i·phys′i·al** (ĕp′ə-fĭz′ē-əl), **ep′i·phys′e·al** *adj.*

ep·i·phyte (ĕp′ə-fīt′) *n.* A plant, such as certain orchids or ferns, that grows on another plant or object upon which it depends for mechanical support but not as a source of nutrients. Also called "air plant," "aerophyte." [EPI- + -PHYTE.] —**ep′i·phyt′ic** (-fĭt′ĭk), **ep′i·phyt′i·cal** *adj.*

e·pi·phy·tot·ic (ĕp′ə-fī-tŏt′ĭk) *adj.* Of, pertaining to, or characterizing a sudden or abnormally destructive outbreak of a plant disease, usually over an extended geographical area. —*n.* An outbreak of such a disease. [EPI- + PHYT(O)- + -OTIC.]

E·pi·rus (ĭ-pī′rəs). **1.** An administrative division of Greece, occupying 3,573 square miles in the northwest. Population, 353,000. Capital, Ioannina. **2.** An ancient country including this division and part of southern Albania.

Epis. 1. Episcopal; Episcopalian. **2.** Epistle.

Episc. Episcopal; Episcopalian.

e·pis·co·pa·cy (ĭ-pĭs′kə-pə-sē) *n., pl.* **-cies. 1.** An episcopate. **2.** The system of church government in which bishops are the chief ministers. [From EPISCOPATE.]

e·pis·co·pal (ĭ-pĭs′kə-pəl) *adj.* **1.** Of or pertaining to a bishop or bishops. **2.** Of or advocating church government by bishops. **3.** *Capital* **E.** *Abbr.* **Epis., Episc.** Designating or pertaining to the Anglican Church, or a branch of it. [Middle English, from Old French, from Late Latin *episcopālis,* from *episcopus,* bishop, from Greek *episkopos,* overseer : *epi-,* over + *skopos,* watcher, seer (see **spek-** in Appendix*).] —**e·pis′co·pal·ly** *adv.*

Episcopal Church. The **Protestant Episcopal Church** *(see).*

e·pis·co·pa·li·an (ĭ-pĭs′kə-pā′lē-ən, -pāl′yən) *adj.* Of or advocating church government by bishops; episcopal. —*n.* An advocate of church government by bishops.

E·pis·co·pa·li·an (ĭ-pĭs′kə-pā′lē-ən, -pāl′yən) *adj. Abbr.* **Epis., Episc.** Of, pertaining to, or belonging to the Protestant Episcopal Church. —*n. Abbr.* **Epis., Episc.** A member or adherent of the Protestant Episcopal Church. —**E·pis′co·pa′li·an·ism′** *n.*

e·pis·co·pal·ism (ĭ-pĭs′kə-pə-lĭz′əm) *n.* The belief that the power to govern the church should rest with an episcopal or pastoral body, rather than with any supreme individual.

e·pis·co·pate (ĭ-pĭs′kə-pĭt, -pāt′) *n.* **1.** The position or term of office of a bishop. **2.** The area of jurisdiction of a bishop; a bishopric. **3.** Bishops collectively. [Late Latin *episcopātus,* from *episcopus,* bishop. See **episcopal.**]

ep·i·sode (ĕp′ə-sōd′) *n.* **1.** An incident or series of related events in the course of a continuous experience: *an episode from her childhood.* **2.** A portion of a narrative that relates an event or series of connected events and forms a coherent story in itself; an incident: *an episode of a picaresque novel.* **3.** A separately presented portion of a serialized novel, play, radio or television drama, or the like; an installment. **4.** A section of a classic Greek tragedy that occurs between two choric songs. **5.** *Music.* A passage between statements of a main subject or theme, as in a rondo or fugue. —See Synonyms at **occurrence.** [Greek *epeisodion,* "addition," from *epeisodios,* coming in besides : *epi-,* besides + *eisodios,* coming in : *eis,* into (see **en** in Appendix*) + *hodos,* way, road (see **sed-**[2] in Appendix*).]

ep·i·sod·ic (ĕp′ə-sŏd′ĭk) *adj.* Also **ep·i·sod·i·cal** (-ĭ-kəl). **1.** Pertaining to or resembling an episode; incidental. **2.** Proceeding by a series of episodes; segmented: *an episodic narrative.* —**ep′i·sod′i·cal·ly** *adv.*

ep·i·spas·tic (ĕp′ə-spăs′tĭk) *adj.* Causing blisters. —*n.* A blistering agent; vesicatory. [Greek *epispastikos,* drawing after (because blisters were thought to be humors drawn toward the skin), from *epispatos,* drawn, from *epispan,* to draw after one, attract : *epi-,* after + *span,* to draw (see **spasm**).]

Epist. Epistle.

e·pis·ta·sis (ĭ-pĭs′tə-sĭs) *n., pl.* **-ses** (-sēz′). **1.** *Genetics.* A nonreciprocal interaction between nonalternative forms of gene in which one gene suppresses the expression of another affecting the same part of an organism. **2.** *Medicine.* Matter that rises to the surface of a body discharge. [New Latin, from Greek, stoppage, stopping, from *ephistanai,* to place upon, stop : *epi-,* upon + *histanai,* to place, set (see **stā-** in Appendix*).] —**ep′i·stat′ic** (ĕp′ə-stăt′ĭk) *adj.*

ep·i·stax·is (ĕp′ə-stăk′sĭs) *n. Pathology.* **Nosebleed** *(see).* [New Latin, from Greek, "dropping," from *epistazein,* to let fall in drops upon : *epi-,* upon + *stazein,* to drip (see **stag-** in Appendix*).]

e·pis·te·mol·o·gy (ĭ-pĭs′tə-mŏl′ə-jē) *n., pl.* **-gies. 1.** The division of philosophy that investigates the nature and origin of knowledge. **2.** A theory of the nature of knowledge. [Greek *epistēmē,* knowledge, understanding, from *epistanai,* "to stand upon," understand : *epi-,* upon + *histanai,* to stand, place (see **stā-** in Appendix*) + -LOGY.] —**e·pis′te·mo·log′i·cal** (-mə-lŏj′ĭ-kəl) *adj.* —**e·pis′te·mo·log′i·cal·ly** *adv.* —**e·pis′te·mol′o·gist** *n.*

e·pis·tle (ĭ-pĭs′əl) *n.* **1.** A letter, especially a formal one. **2.** *Usually capital* **E.** *Abbr.* **Epis., Epist. a.** One of the letters written by an Apostle and included in the New Testament. **b.** An excerpt from one of these letters, read as part of a religious service. **3.** A verse letter of the genre invented by Horace and imitated by poets of the 17th and 18th centuries. **4.** A prefatory dedication in epistolary form. [Middle English, from Old French, from Latin *epistola,* from Greek *epistolē,* from *epistellein,* to send to : *epi-,* to + *stellein,* to send (see **stel-**[1] in Appendix*).]

e·pis·tler (ĭ-pĭs′lər) *n.* Also **e·pis·to·ler** (ĭ-pĭs′tə-lər). **1.** A writer of epistles. **2.** *Usually capital* **E.** The person who reads the Epistle in a religious service.

e·pis·to·lar·y (ĭ-pĭs′tə-lĕr′ē) *adj.* **1.** Of or associated with letters or letter writing. **2.** In the form of a letter or letters. **3.** Carried on by or made up of letters: *an epistolary friendship.* [Latin *epistolāris,* from *epistola,* EPISTLE.]

ep·i·style (ĕp′ə-stīl′) *n. Architecture.* An **architrave** *(see).* [Latin *epistylium,* from Greek *epistulion* : *epi-,* upon + *stulos,* pillar (see **stā-** in Appendix*).]

ep·i·taph (ĕp′ə-tăf′, -täf′) *n.* **1.** An inscription on a tombstone or monument in memory of the one or ones buried there. **2.** A brief literary piece summarizing or epitomizing a deceased person. [Middle English *epitaphe,* from Old French, from Latin *epitaphium,* funeral oration, from Greek *epitaphion,* neuter of *epitaphios,* "over a tomb" : *epi-,* over + *taphos,* tomb (see **dhembh-** in Appendix*).] —**ep′i·taph′ic** *adj.*

e·pit·a·sis (ĭ-pĭt′ə-sĭs) *n., pl.* **-ses** (-sēz′). In Alexandrian criticism, the part of a play in which the plot thickens. [Greek, a stretching over, intensification, from *epiteinein,* to stretch over : *epi-,* over + *teinein,* to stretch (see **ten-** in Appendix*).]

ep·i·tha·la·mi·um (ĕp′ə-thə-lā′mē-əm) *n., pl.* **-ums** or **-mia** (-mē-ə). Also **ep·i·tha·la·mi·on** (-ŏn′). A lyric ode in honor of a bride and bridegroom. [Latin, from Greek *epithalamion,* from the neuter of *epithalamios,* belonging to a wedding : *epi-,* at + *thalamos,* bridal chamber (see **thalamus**).]

ep·i·the·li·oid (ĕp′ə-thē′lē-oid′) *adj.* Resembling epithelium. [EPITHELI(UM) + -OID.]

ep·i·the·li·o·ma (ĕp′ə-thē′lē-ō′mə) *n., pl.* **-mata** (-mə tə) or **-mas.** A carcinoma derived from the epithelium. [New Latin : EPITHEL(IUM) + -OMA.] —**ep′i·the′li·om′a·tous** (-ŏm′ə-təs) *adj.*

ep·i·the·li·um (ĕp′ə-thē′lē-əm) *n., pl.* **-ums** or **-lia** (-lē-ə). Membranous tissue, usually in a single layer, composed of closely arranged cells separated by very little intercellular substance and forming the covering of most internal surfaces and organs and the outer surface of an animal body. [New Latin : EPI- + Greek *thēlē,* nipple (see **dhēi-** in Appendix*).] —**ep′i·the′li·al** *adj.*

ep·i·thet (ĕp′ə-thĕt′) *n.* **1.** A term used to characterize the nature of a person or thing: *"that seemingly unending war to which we have given the curious epithet 'cold'"* (John F. Kennedy). **2.** An adjective or descriptive phrase that comes to form part of or to substitute for a person's name or title: *"The Lion-Hearted" is an epithet for Richard I.* **3.** An abusive or contemptuous word or phrase used to describe a person. See Usage note below. [Latin *epitheton,* from Greek, "an addition," from *epitithenai,* to put on, add : *epi-,* on + *tithenai,* to place, put (see **dhē-**[1] in Appendix*).] —**ep′i·thet′ic, ep′i·thet′i·cal** *adj.*

Usage: *Epithet,* construed strictly, refers to a word or phrase that describes, characterizes, or serves as an appellation. The word or phrase need not be derogatory. Employment of *epithet* in a narrower sense, as the equivalent of *term of abuse or contempt,* is therefore disputed though increasingly common. According to 53 per cent of the Usage Panel, *epithet* is acceptably used in that narrower sense and conveys it fully without need for elaboration: *shaking his fist and shouting epithets.* The intended sense would be conveyed even more unmistakably by *shouting abuse* or the like.

e·pit·o·me (ĭ-pĭt′ə-mē) *n.* **1.** A summary of a book, article, event, or the like; an abridgment; abstract. **2.** One that is consummately representative or expressive of an entire class or type; embodiment: *"Paul's . . . experience was an epitome of the revolution which Christ wrought in religion"* (C.H. Dodd). [Latin *epitomē,* from Greek, from *epitemnein,* to cut upon the surface, cut short : *epi-,* upon + *temnein,* to cut (see **tem-** in Appendix*).]

e·pit·o·mize (ĭ-pĭt′ə-mīz′) *tr.v.* **-mized, -mizing, -mizes. 1.** To make an epitome of; sum up. **2.** To typify eminently an entire class, type, or quality; capture the essence or extreme of: *"the boy . . . epitomizes for all human creatures in all times the moment when masks are laid aside"* (James Agee).

ep·i·zo·ic (ĕp′ə-zō′ĭk) *adj.* Living or growing on the exterior of a living animal: *epizoic fungi.* [EPI- + -ZOIC.]

ep·i·zo·ot·ic (ĕp′ə-zō-ŏt′ĭk) *adj.* **1.** Attacking a large number of animals simultaneously. Said of a disease. **2.** Prevalent among a group of animals. Said of a disease. —*n.* An epizootic disease. [EPI- + ZO(O)- + -OTIC.]

e plu·ri·bus u·num (ē plo͝or′ə-bəs yo͞o′nəm). *Latin.* One out of many. The motto of the United States.

ep·och (ĕp′ək; *British* ē′pŏk′) *n.* **1.** A particular period of history; especially, one regarded as being in some way characteristic, remarkable, or memorable; an era: *"New epochs emerge with comparative suddenness"* (A.N. Whitehead). **2.** A point in time or progress that marks the beginning of such a period; milestone; breakthrough: *The addition of sound was an epoch in motion-picture history.* **3.** *Geology.* A unit of geologic time that is a division of a period. See **geology. 4.** *Astronomy.* An instant in time that is arbitrarily selected as a reference datum. —See Synonyms at **period.** [New Latin *epocha,* from Greek *epokhē,* pause. See **segh-** in Appendix.*]

ep·och·al (ĕp′ə-kəl) *adj.* **1.** Of, pertaining to, or characteristic of an epoch. **2.** Marking an epoch; epoch-making.

ep·och-mak·ing (ĕp′ək-mā′kĭng; *British* ē′pŏk-) *adj.* Highly significant or important; momentous.

ep·ode (ĕp′ōd′) *n.* **1.** The last strophe of the triad (*strophe, antistrophe,* and *epode*) that forms the basic compositional unit of the lyric ode. **2.** A type of lyric composition invented by Archilochus and used by Horace, characterized by couplets formed by a long line followed by a shorter one. [Latin *epōdos,* from Greek *epōidos,* "a singing after," from *epaidein,* to sing after : *epi-,* after + *aidein,* to sing (see **wed-**[2] in Appendix*).]

ep·o·nym (ĕp′ə-nĭm′) *n.* **1.** A real or mythical person whose name is or is thought to be the source of the name of a city, country, era, institution, or the like: *"Romulus" is the eponym of Rome.* **2.** A real or fictitious person whose name has become synonymous with an era, event, object, practice, or the like. [Greek *epōnumos,* from *epōnumos,* EPONYMOUS.]

e·pon·y·mous (ĭ-pŏn′ə-məs) *adj.* Also **ep·o·nym·ic** (ĕp′ə-nĭm′ĭk). **1.** Of or constituting an eponym. **2.** Giving one's name to something, as a city, country, era, or institution. [Greek *epōnumos* : *epi-,* to + *onoma,* name (see **nomen-** in Appendix*).]

e·pon·y·my (ĭ-pŏn′ə-mē) *n.* The derivation of the name of a city, country, era, institution, or the like, from that of a person.

ep·o·pee (ĕp′ə-pē′, ĕp′ə-pē′) *n.* **1.** Epic poetry, especially as a literary genre. **2.** An epic poem. [French *épopée,* from Greek *epopoiia,* from *epopoios,* epic poet : *epos,* word, EPIC + *poiein,* to make (see **poet**).]

ep·os (ĕp′ŏs′) *n.* **1.** Oral epic poetry. **2.** An epic poem. [Latin, from Greek, word, poem. See **wekw-** in Appendix.*]

ep·ox·y (ĭ-pŏk′sē) *n., pl.* **-ies.** Any of various usually thermosetting resins capable of forming tight cross-linked polymer structures characterized by toughness, strong adhesion, and high corrosion and chemical resistance, used especially in surface coatings and adhesives. Also called "epoxy resin." [EP(I)- + OXY-.]

Ep·ping Forest (ĕp′ĭng). A forest that once included all of Essex, England, and is now a royal park occupying 5,600 acres in the western part of the county.

ep·si·lon (ĕp′sə-lŏn′) *n.* The fifth letter in the Greek alphabet, written Ε, ϵ. Transliterated in English as *E, e.* See **alphabet**. [Greek *e psilon,* "simple *e,*" from *psilos,* mere, simple. See **bhes-**[1] in Appendix.*]

Ep·som (ĕp′səm). A town in north-central Surrey, England, noted for its nearby racetrack, Epsom Downs, where the Derby and other horse races are run.

Epsom salts. Also **Epsom salt.** Hydrated **magnesium sulfate** *(see)* used as a cathartic. [First obtained from the mineral springs in EPSOM.]

Ep·stein (ĕp′stīn), Sir **Jacob.** 1880–1959. American-born British sculptor.

eq. **1.** equal. **2.** equation. **3.** equivalent.

E.Q. educational quotient.

eq·ua·bil·i·ty (ĕk′wə-bĭl′ə-tē, ē′kwə-) *n.* Also **eq·ua·ble·ness** (-bəl-nĭs). The quality or state of being uniform, even, or tranquil; equanimity.

eq·ua·ble (ĕk′wə-bəl, ē′kwə-) *adj.* **1.** Unvarying; steady; even: *"The West Indian climate is . . . the most equable in the world"* (Alec Waugh). **2.** Tranquil; serene; even-tempered. —See Synonyms at **steady.** [Latin *aequābilis,* from *aequāre,* to make even, from *aequus,* level, even, EQUAL.] —**eq′ua·bly** *adv.*

e·qual (ē′kwəl) *adj. Abbr.* **eq. 1.** Having the same capability, quantity, or effect as another: *equal strength, equal weight, equal damage.* **2.** *Mathematics.* Related by a reflexive, symmetric, and transitive relationship; broadly, alike or in agreement in a specified sense with respect to specified properties. **3.** Having the same privileges, status, or rights; deserving or worthy: *equal before the law.* **4. a.** Having the requisite strength, ability, determination, or the like; qualified or disposed: *"Elizabeth found herself quite equal to the scene"* (Jane Austen). **b.** Adequate in extent, amount, or degree. **5.** *Archaic.* Impartial; just; equitable. **6.** *Archaic.* Tranquil; calm; equable. **7.** *Archaic.* Flat, level, and smooth. —See Synonyms at **same.** —*n.* A person or thing that is equal to another; worthy substitute or rival: *I am his equal in every respect.* —*tr.v.* **equaled** or **equalled, equaling** or **equalling, equals. 1.** To be equal to, especially in value. **2.** To do, make, or produce something equal to: *He equaled the world's record in the mile run.* —**equal out.** To reach a point of equilibrium. [Latin *aequālis,* from *aequus*†, even, level.] —**e′qual·ly** *adv.*

Usage: *Equal* (adjective) is sometimes preceded by *more* and less often by *most,* even though *equal* is not capable of comparison in its literal sense: *Our aim is a more equal distribution of the burden.* The example is acceptable to 71 per cent of the Usage Panel, and is typical of constructions in which *more equal* is applied in the sense of "more nearly equal" or "more equitable," either of which would also be appropriate and even more precise. The following illustrate *equal* in constructions that often cause difficulty: *It is the equal of any of his earlier novels, if not better* (or *is the equal of, if not better than, any*). *It is equal to, if not better than, any of the others* (or *is equal to any of the others, if not better*). The adverb *equally* is redundant in combination with *as,* and the following examples employing *equally as* are termed unacceptable by 63 per cent of the Panel: *Experience is equally as valuable as theory. Equally as important is the desire to learn.* In the first, delete *equally;* in the second, delete *as.* The solution usually involves using *as* alone when a comparison is explicit and *equally* alone when it is not.

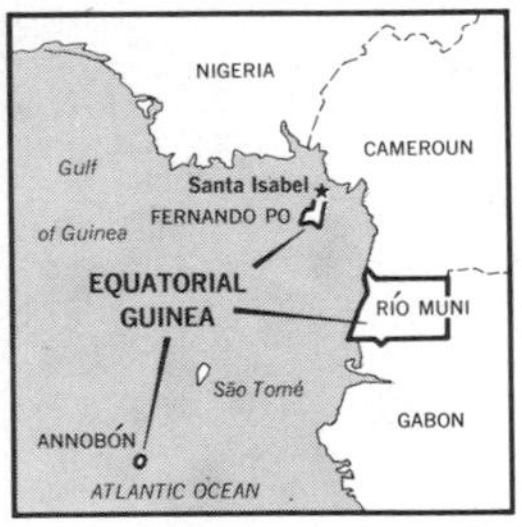

Equatorial Guinea

e·qual·i·tar·i·an (ĭ-kwŏl′ə-târ′ē-ən) *adj.* Egalitarian.

e·qual·i·ty (ĭ-kwŏl′ə-tē) *n., pl.* **-ties. 1.** The state or instance of being equal; especially, the state of enjoying equal rights, as political, economic, and social. **2.** A mathematical statement, usually an equation, that one thing equals another. [Middle English *equalite,* from Old French, from Latin *aequālitās,* from *aequālis,* EQUAL.]

e·qual·ize (ē′kwə-līz′) *v.* **-ized, -izing, -izes.** —*tr.* **1.** To make equal. **2.** To make uniform. —*intr.* To constitute or induce equality, equilibrium, or balance.

e·qual·iz·er (ē′kwə-lī′zər) *n.* **1.** One that equalizes, as a device for equalizing pressure or strain. **2.** *Slang.* A weapon; especially, a revolver.

equal sign. Also **equals sign, equality sign.** The symbol (=) used, especially in an equation, to indicate that one thing is logically or mathematically equal to another.

equal temperament. *Music.* The modification of the intervals of just intonation in the tuning of instruments of fixed intonation to permit the modulation of harmony. Also called "temperament."

e·qua·nim·i·ty (ē′kwə-nĭm′ə-tē, ĕk′wə-) *n.* The quality or characteristic of being calm and even-tempered; composure. [Latin *aequanimitās,* from *aequanimis,* even-tempered : *aequus,* even, EQUAL + *animus,* mind (see **ane-** in Appendix*).]

Synonyms: *equanimity, composure, sang-froid, serenity, nonchalance.* These nouns are closely related to calmness and self-control. *Equanimity* implies mental balance and evenness of temperament, usually as a characteristic state. *Composure* is calmness that suggests the exercise of self-control and maintenance of dignity. *Sang-froid* is coolness, especially in trying circumstances. *Serenity* is tranquillity of nature that suggests imperviousness to agitation or turmoil. *Nonchalance* is the absence not only of agitation but of close interest, customarily manifested by an indifference or casual air.

e·quate (ĭ-kwāt′) *v.* **equated, equating, equates.** —*tr.* **1.** To make, treat, or regard as equal or equivalent: *Many people equate wisdom with old age.* **2.** To reduce to a standard or average; equalize or stabilize; balance: *equate profit and loss.* **3.** To show or state the equality of; express in or as if in an equation. —*intr.* To be or seem to be equal; correspond; accord: *She equates easily with our conception of classic beauty.* [Middle English *equaten,* from Latin *aequāre,* from *aequus,* EQUAL.]

e·qua·tion (ĭ-kwā′zhən, -shən) *n. Abbr.* **eq. 1.** The process or act of equating or of being equated. **2.** The state of being equal; a balanced state; equilibrium. **3.** *Mathematics.* A linear array of mathematical symbols separated into left and right sides that are designated at least conditionally equal by an equal sign. **4.** *Chemistry.* A symbolic representation of a chemical reaction as a linear array of symbols for the reacting atomic and molecular species, separated into left and right sides by an equal sign, arrow, or opposing arrows. **5.** A **personal equation** *(see).* —**e·qua′tion·al** *adj.* —**e·qua′tion·al·ly** *adv.*

e·qua·tor (ĭ-kwā′tər) *n.* **1.** The great circle circumscribing the earth's surface, the reckoning datum of latitudes and dividing boundary of Northern and Southern hemispheres, formed by the intersection of a plane passing through the earth's center perpendicular to its axis of rotation. **2.** Any similar great circle drawn on the surface of a celestial body at right angles to the axis of rotation. **3.** This area or belt of earth as, most often, a warm or torrid region: *The passengers swelter as we approach the equator.* **4.** *Astronomy.* The **celestial equator** *(see).* [Middle English, from Medieval Latin *(circulus) aequator (diei et noctis),* (circle) equalizing (day and night), from Latin *aequāre,* EQUATE.]

e·qua·to·ri·al (ē′kwə-tôr′ē-əl, -tōr′ē-əl, ĕk′wə-) *adj.* **1.** Of, relating to, or like the equator. **2.** Pertaining to conditions that exist at the earth's equator: *equatorial heat.* **3.** Having a support with two perpendicular axes, one of which is parallel to the earth's rotational axis. Said of a telescope. —*n. Astronomy.* An equatorial telescope. —**e′qua·to′ri·al·ly** *adv.*

Equatorial Current. One of the surface currents drifting westward through the oceans at the equator.

Equatorial Guin·ea (gĭn′ē). Formerly **Spanish Guin·ea.** A country, about 10,800 square miles in area, of western Africa, comprising the island of Fernando Po and smaller islands in the Gulf of Guinea and mainland Río Muni. A former Spanish colony, it became independent in 1968. Population, 267,000. Capital, Santa Isabel.

Equatorial Islands. See **Line Islands.**

eq·uer·ry (ĕk′wə-rē) *n., pl.* **-ries. 1.** An officer charged with supervision of the horses belonging to a royal or noble household. **2.** An attendant to the English royal household. [Earlier *escurie,* from Old French, from *escuier,* riding master, squire. See **esquire.**]

e·ques·tri·an (ĭ-kwĕs′trē-ən) *adj.* **1.** Of or pertaining to horsemanship: *"pony rides at childhood carnivals were the limit of my equestrian experience"* (Truman Capote). **2.** Depicted or represented on horseback: *the equestrian statue of General Grant.* **3.** Of, pertaining to, or composed of knights, horsemen, cavalry, or the like: *equestrian troops.* —*n.* One who rides a horse or performs on horseback. [From Latin *equester,* from *equus,* horse. See **ekwo-** in Appendix.*]

e·ques·tri·enne (ĭ-kwĕs′trē-ĕn′) *n.* A female equestrian.

equi-. Indicates equality; for example, **equiangular.** [Middle English *equi-,* from Latin *aequi-,* from *aequus,* EQUAL.]

e·qui·an·gu·lar (ē′kwē-ăng′gyə-lər) *adj.* Having all angles equal. [EQUI- + ANGULAR.]

e·qui·dis·tant (ē′kwə-dĭs′tənt) *adj.* Equally distant. [Old French *equidistant,* from Late Latin *aequidistāns* : EQUI- + *distāns,* DISTANT.] —**e′qui·dis′tance** *n.* —**e′qui·dis′tant·ly** *adv.*

e·qui·lat·er·al (ē′kwə-lăt′ər-əl) *adj.* Having all sides or faces equal. —*n.* **1.** A side exactly equal to others. **2.** A geometric figure having equal sides. [Late Latin *aequilaterālis* : EQUI- + *laterālis,* LATERAL.] —**e′qui·lat′er·al·ly** *adv.*

e·quil·i·brant (ĭ-kwĭl′ə-brənt) *n.* A force capable of balancing a system of forces to produce equilibrium. [EQUILIBR(ATE) + -ANT.]

e·qui·li·brate (ē′kwə-lī′brāt′, ĭ-kwĭl′ə-) *v.* **-brated, -brating, -brates.** —*intr.* To be in or bring about equilibrium. —*tr.* To maintain in or bring into equilibrium. [Latin *aequilibrāre,* to balance, from *aequilībris,* in perfect balance, from *aequilibrium,* EQUILIBRIUM.] —**e′qui·li·bra′tion** *n.*

e·qui·li·bra·tor (ē′kwə-lī′brā′tər, ĭ-kwĭl′ə-) *n.* A device that brings about and helps maintain equilibrium.

e·quil·i·brist (ĭ-kwĭl′ə-brĭst) *n.* A person who performs feats of balance, such as tightrope walking. [French *équilibriste,* from Latin *aequilībrium,* EQUILIBRIUM.] —**e·quil′i·bris′tic** *adj.*

e·qui·lib·ri·um (ē′kwə-lĭb′rē-əm) *n.* **1.** Any condition in which all acting influences are cancelled by others resulting in a stable, balanced, or unchanging system. **2.** *Physics.* The condition of a system in which the resultant of all acting forces is zero and the sum of all torques about any axis is zero. **3.** *Chemistry.* The state of a reaction in which its forward and reverse reactions occur at equal rates so that the concentration of the reactants does not change with time. **4.** Mental or emotional balance; psychological stability. [Latin *aequilībrium,* even balance : EQUI- + *lībra,* balance (see **līthrā** in Appendix*).]

e·quine (ē′kwīn′) *adj.* **1.** Of, pertaining to, or characteristic of a horse. **2.** Of or belonging to the family Equidae, which includes the horses, asses, and zebras. —*n.* A member of the Equidae. [Latin *equīnus,* from *equus,* horse. See **ekwo-** in Appendix.*]

e·qui·noc·tial (ē′kwə-nŏk′shəl, ĕk′wə-) *adj.* **1.** Pertaining to an equinox. **2.** Relating to the celestial equator. **3.** *Botany.* Having or characterizing flowers that open and close at specific times. —*n.* **1.** *Meteorology.* A violent storm of wind and rain occurring, supposedly, at or near the time of the equinox. **2.** The **equinoctial circle** *(see).* [Middle English *equinoxial,* from Old French, from Latin *aequinoctiālis,* from *aequinoctium,* EQUINOX.]

equinoctial circle. The celestial equator. Also called "equinoctial," "equinoctial line."

e·qui·nox (ē′kwə-nŏks′, ĕk′wə-) *n.* **1.** Either of two points on the celestial sphere where the ecliptic intersects the celestial equator. **2.** Either of the two times during a year when the sun crosses the celestial equator and when the length of day and night are approximately equal: the **vernal equinox** and the **autumnal equinox** *(both of which see).* [Middle English *equinox,* from Old French, from Medieval Latin *aequinoxium,* variant of Latin *aequinoctium* : EQUI- + *nox* (stem *noct-*), night (see **nekwt-** in Appendix*).]

e·quip (ĭ-kwĭp′) *tr.v.* **equipped, equipping, equips. 1.** To supply with material necessities such as tools, gear, provisions, or furnishings. **2.** To supply with intellectual, emotional, or spiritual essentials: *College equipped him for such problems.* —See Synonyms at **furnish.** [Old French *eschiper, e(s)quiper,* to put to sea, embark, from Germanic. See **skipam** in Appendix.*]

equip. equipment.

eq·ui·page (ĕk′wə-pĭj) *n.* **1.** Equipment or furnishings, as of a military unit or ship; accouterments. **2.** A carriage that is elegantly equipped, as with caparisoned horses and liveried footmen. **3.** Any carriage. **4.** *Archaic.* A retinue, as of a person of royalty or nobility. **5.** *Archaic.* A set of household articles, as for dining or personal adornment. **6.** *Archaic.* A case for storing such articles.

e·quip·ment (ĭ-kwĭp′mənt) *n. Abbr.* **equip. 1.** The act of equipping or the state of being equipped. **2.** Something with which a person, organization, or thing is equipped; furnishings. **3.** The rolling or unstationary stock of a transportation system; especially, the cars, engines, and the like of a railroad.

e·qui·poise (ē′kwə-poiz′, ĕk′wə-) *n.* **1.** Equality in distribution, as of weight, relationship, or emotional forces; balance; equilibrium: *"And if he has not the balance of the critic, he has some other equipoise of his own"* (T.S. Eliot). **2.** A counterpoise; counterbalance. [EQUI- + POISE.]

e·qui·pol·lence (ē′kwə-pŏl′əns) *n.* Also **e·qui·pol·len·cy** (-pŏl′ən-sē). Equality, as in effectiveness or validity; equivalence.

e·qui·pol·lent (ē′kwə-pŏl′ənt) *adj.* **1.** Equal in power, effectiveness, significance, or the like. **2.** *Logic.* Validly derived from each other; deducible. Said of two propositions. **3.** Equivalent. —*n.* An equivalent. [Middle English *equipollent,* from Old French, from Latin *aequipollēns* : EQUI- + *pollēns,* present participle of *pollēre*†, to be powerful.]

e·qui·pon·der·ance (ē′kwə-pŏn′dər-əns) *n.* Also **e·qui·pon·der·an·cy** (-ən-sē). Equality of weight; equipoise. [Medieval Latin *aequiponderāns,* present participle of *aequiponderāre,* EQUIPONDERATE.]

e·qui·pon·der·ate (ē′kwə-pŏn′də-rāt′) *tr.v.* **-ated, -ating, -ates. 1.** To counterbalance. **2.** To give equal balance or weight to. [Medieval Latin *aequiponderāre* : EQUI- + Latin *ponderāre,* to weigh (see **spen-** in Appendix*).]

e·qui·po·ten·tial (ē′kwə-pə-tĕn′shəl) *adj.* **1.** Having equal potential. **2.** *Physics.* Having the same potential at every point: *equipotential surface.*

eq·ui·se·tum (ĕk′wə-sē′təm) *n.* Any of the flowerless, seedless plants of the genus *Equisetum,* which includes the horsetails. [New Latin, from Latin *equisaetum,* the horsetail : *equus,* horse (see **ekwo-** in Appendix*) + *saeta,* bristle, SETA.]

eq·ui·ta·ble (ĕk′wə-tə-bəl) *adj.* **1.** Exhibiting or characterized by equity; impartial or reasonable in judgment or dispensation; just. **2.** *Law.* Concerned with or valid in equity, as distinguished from statute and common law. —See Synonyms at **fair.** [French *équitable,* from Old French, from *equite,* EQUITY.] —**eq′ui·ta·ble·ness** *n.* —**eq′ui·ta·bly** *adv.*

eq·ui·tant (ĕk′wə-tənt) *adj. Botany.* Overlapping at the base to form a flat, fanlike arrangement, as the leaves of some irises. [Latin *equitāns,* present participle of *equitāre,* to ride, from *eques* (stem *equit-*), horseman, from *equus,* horse. See **ekwo-** in Appendix.*]

eq·ui·ta·tion (ĕk′wə-tā′shən) *n.* The learning and practice of riding a horse; horsemanship. [Old French, from Latin *equitātiō,* riding, from *equitāre,* to ride. See **equitant.**]

eq·ui·ty (ĕk′wə-tē) *n., pl.* **-ties. 1.** The state, ideal, or quality of being just, impartial, and fair. **2.** Something that is just, impartial, and fair. **3.** The residual value of a business or property beyond any mortgage thereon and liability therein. **4.** *Law.* **a.** Justice applied in circumstances not covered by law. **b.** A system of jurisprudence supplementing common law. **c.** An equitable right or claim. **5.** *Law.* **Equity of redemption** *(see).* [Middle English *equite,* from Old French, from Latin *aequitās,* from *aequus,* EQUAL.]

equity of redemption. *Law.* The right of one who has mortgaged his property to redeem that property upon payment of the sum due within a reasonable amount of time after the due date. Also called "equity."

equity stock. Common stock *(see).*

equiv. equivalent.

e·quiv·a·lence (ĭ-kwĭv′ə-ləns) *n.* Also **e·quiv·a·len·cy** (-lən-sē) *pl.* **-cies. 1.** The state or condition of being equivalent; equality. **2.** *Mathematics.* A reflexive, symmetric, and transitive relation between elements of a set that establishes any two elements in the set as equivalent or nonequivalent. In this sense, also called "**equivalence relationship.**"

e·quiv·a·lent (ĭ-kwĭv′ə-lənt; ē′kwə-vā′lənt *for sense 1 only*) *adj. Abbr.* **eq., equiv. 1. a.** Equal in substance, degree, value, force, or meaning. **b.** Having similar or identical effects. **2.** To the extent or degree of; practically equal; tantamount: *"Pancoast knew that a Hearst request was equivalent to an order"* (W.A. Swanberg). **3.** *Mathematics.* **a.** Capable of being put into a one-to-one relationship. Said of two sets. **b.** Broadly, having identical corresponding parts. **c.** Equal. **4.** *Chemistry.* Having the same ability to combine. —See Synonyms at **same.** —*n. Abbr.* **eq., equiv. 1.** That which is equivalent. **2.** *Chemistry.* **Equivalent weight** *(see).* [Middle English, from Old French, from Late Latin *aequivalēns,* present participle of *aequivalēre,* to be equal in value : EQUI- + *valēre,* to be strong, be worth (see **wal-** in Appendix*).] —**e·quiv′a·lent·ly** *adv.*

equivalent weight. The number of parts by weight of any element combining with or replacing the equivalent of half the atomic weight of oxygen or with one atomic weight of hydrogen. Also called "combining weight," "equivalent."

e·quiv·o·cal (ĭ-kwĭv′ə-kəl) *adj.* **1.** Capable of two interpretations; cryptic; evasive; ambiguous: *an equivocal statement.* **2.** Of uncertain outcome, origin, or worth; indeterminate: *an equivocal result.* **3.** Of doubtful nature, as categorically or ethically; questionable; not genuine: *"He struck me as a smooth, smiling, equivocal sort of person"* (G.K. Chesterton). —See Synonyms at **ambiguous.** [Late Latin *aequivocus* : EQUI- + Latin *vōx* (stem *vōc-*), voice (see **wekw-** in Appendix*).] —**e·quiv′o·cal·ly** *adv.* —**e·quiv′o·cal·ness** *n.*

e·quiv·o·cate (ĭ-kwĭv′ə-kāt′) *intr.v.* **-cated, -cating, -cates.** To use equivocal language intentionally; speak in ambiguities; to hedge. [Middle English *equivocaten,* from Medieval Latin *aequivocāre,* from Late Latin *aequivocus,* EQUIVOCAL.]

e·quiv·o·ca·tion (ĭ-kwĭv′ə-kā′shən) *n.* **1.** The use of equivocal language. **2.** An instance of this; an equivocal statement or expression. **3.** *Logic.* A fallacy arising in a formally correct statement from the ambiguity or multiplicity of possible interpretations of a repeated word or phrase.

eq·ui·voque (ĕk′wə-vōk′) *n.* Also **eq·ui·voke. 1.** An equivocal word, phrase, or expression. **2.** A pun. **3.** Double meaning. [French *équivoque,* from adjective, "equivocal," from Late Latin *aequivocus,* EQUIVOCAL.]

E·quu·le·us (ĭ-kwo͞o′lē-əs) *n.* A constellation in the equatorial region of the Northern Hemisphere near Delphinus and Pegasus. [Latin, diminutive of *equus,* horse. See **ekwo-** in Appendix.*]

-er[1]. **1.** Indicates: **a.** Someone who or something that performs the action indicated by the root verb; for example, **helper, blender. b.** Someone performing or involved with an occupation or some other function; for example, **photographer, bookkeeper. c.** Geographical origin or residence; for example, **Vermonter, westerner. 2.** Used to form informal shortenings for certain phrases; for example, **homer** instead of **home run.** [Middle English *-ere, -er,* Old English *-ere,* from Common Germanic *-ārjaz* (unattested), from Latin *-ārius.* See **-ary.**]

-er[2], **-r.** Used to form the comparative degree of adjectives and adverbs; for example, **whiter, slower.** [Middle English *-ere, -re,* Old English *-re, -ra.*]

-er[3]. Used to form verbs indicating frequent or recurrent action or sound; for example, **quaver.** [Middle English *-rien, -ren,* Old English *-rian, -erian.*]

Er The symbol for the element erbium.

e·ra (ĭr′ə, ĕr′ə) *n.* **1.** A period of time that utilizes a specific point in history as the basis of its chronology: *"from this date, 1492, a new era in the history of mankind takes its beginning"* (Winston Churchill). **2.** A period of time that is distinctive or notable because of its new or different aspects, events, or personages: *the Colonial era of U.S. history.* **3.** The beginning or onset of such a period of time; turning point or milestone; epoch. **4.** *Geology.* The longest division of geologic time comprising one or more periods. —See Synonyms at **period.** [Late Latin *aera,* era, from Latin, "counters for calculating," a number as a basis for calculating, an era from which time is reckoned, from *aes* (stem *aer-*), brass, copper, money. See **ayos-** in Appendix.*]

e·ra·di·ate (ĭ-rā′dē-āt′) *v.* **-ated, -ating, -ates.** —*tr.* To emanate (radiation); radiate. —*intr.* To emanate. [EX- + RADIATE.] —**e·ra′di·a′tion** *n.*

e·rad·i·cate (ĭ-răd′ĭ-kāt′) *tr.v.* **-cated, -cating, -cates. 1.** To remove all traces of; annihilate; erase: *"What the Ice Age did was to eradicate the abundant mammalian life in the northern hemisphere"* (Willy Ley). **2.** To pull or tear up by the roots; uproot. —See Synonyms at **abolish.** [Latin *ērādicāre,* to pluck up by the roots, to root out : *ē-,* out, from *ex-* + *rādix* (stem *rādic-*), root (see **werād-** in Appendix*).] —**e·rad′i·ca·ble** *adj.* —**e·rad′i·ca′tion** *n.* —**e·rad′i·ca′tive** *adj.* —**e·rad′i·ca′tor** *n.*

e·rase (ĭ-rās′) *tr.v.* **erased, erasing, erases. 1.** To remove; rub, wipe, scrape, or blot out; efface. **2.** To remove all traces of: *"What was it in him that made him desire to recreate something that time had erased?"* (J.P. Marquand). **3.** *Slang.* To get rid of (a person) by murder. [Latin *ērādere* (past participle *ērāsus*), to scrape out, scrape off : *ex-,* out + *radere,* to scrape (see **rēd-** in Appendix*).] —**e·ras′a·ble** *adj.*

Synonyms: *erase, expunge, efface, delete, cancel, blot.* These verbs mean to remove or eliminate, especially what is written down or otherwise recorded. Though related, they are not always interchangeable. *Erase* refers to rubbing out, literally or figuratively. *Expunge* implies thoroughgoing removal that leaves no trace, as by wiping away something written down or by putting a thing out of mind or memory. *Efface* also can refer to removal of every trace, or it can mean to remove gradually and partially by making indistinct, as lettering on a tombstone is worn away. *Delete* is used principally in the sense of removing

autumnal equinox
September 22

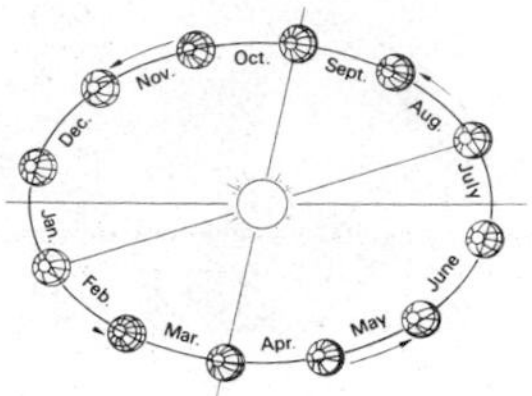

vernal equinox
March 22

equinox

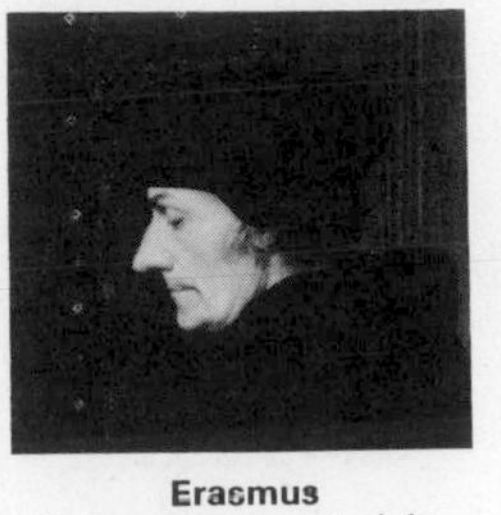

Erasmus
Contemporary portrait by Hans Holbein the Younger

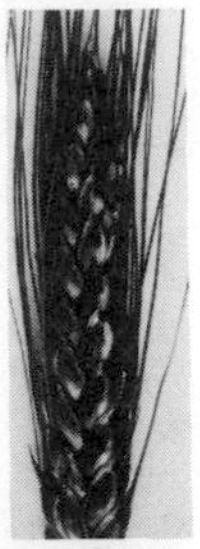

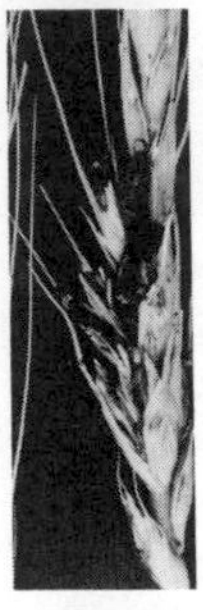

ergot
Above: Normal grain head
Below: Grain head infected with ergot

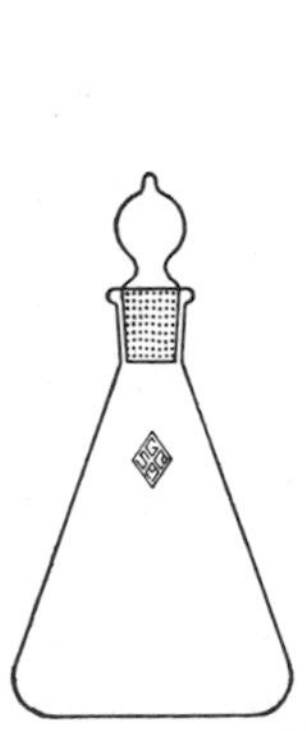

Erlenmeyer flask

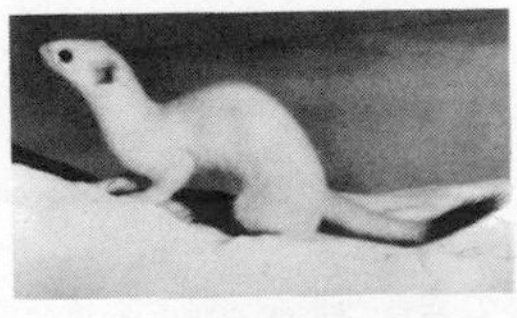

ermine
Winter color phase

a passage from a manuscript. *Cancel* refers to invalidating, by drawing lines through something written or marking it in a way that indicates that its force or effect has been terminated. *Blot,* usually followed by *out,* refers literally to rendering illegible by covering over or smearing a written passage. In extended senses it means to remove by covering, as *Night blots out a view,* or by putting something out of mind. In every usage it implies complete removal.

e·ras·er (ĭ-rā′sər) *n.* Something that erases, as a piece of rubber, cloth, or felt: *a blackboard eraser.*

e·ra·sion (ĭ-rā′zhən) *n.* **1.** An act of erasing. **2.** *Surgery.* The removal of tissue, especially from bone, by scraping.

Er·a·sis·tra·tus (ĕr′ə-sĭs′trə-təs). Greek physician and anatomist of the third century B.C.

E·ras·mus (ĭ-răz′məs), **Desiderius.** Original name, Geert Geerts. 1466?–1536. Dutch theologian, scholar, humanist, and traveler.

E·ras·tian·ism (ĭ-răs′chə-nĭz′əm, -tē-ə-nĭz′əm) *n.* A doctrine attributed to Thomas Erastus stressing the submission of the church to civil authority in all matters. —**E·ras′tian** *adj.* & *n.*

E·ras·tus (ĭ-răs′təs), **Thomas.** Original surname, Lieber. 1524–1583. Swiss theologian; follower of Zwingli.

e·ra·sure (ĭ-rā′shər) *n.* **1.** An act of erasing. **2.** Something that has been erased; a deletion. **3.** The trace or mark remaining on a surface from which something has been erased.

Er·a·to (ĕr′ə-tō′). *Greek Mythology.* The Muse of lyric poetry and mime. [Latin *Eratō,* from Greek, from *eratos,* loved, from *eran,* to love, akin to *erōs,* love. See **Eros** (god).]

Er·a·tos·the·nes (ĕr′ə-tŏs′thə-nēz′). Greek mathematician and astronomer of the third century B.C.; accurately estimated the circumference of the earth.

Er·bil. The modern name for **Arbela.**

er·bi·um (ûr′bē-əm) *n. Symbol* **Er** A soft, malleable, silvery rare-earth element, used in metallurgy, nuclear research, and to color glass and porcelain. Atomic number 68, atomic weight 167.26, melting point 1,497°C, boiling point 2,900°C, specific gravity 9.051, valence 3. See **element.** [New Latin, first discovered in *Ytterby,* Sweden.]

Er·ci·yas Da·ği (ĕr′jē-yäs′ dä-ĭ′). An extinct volcanic peak, 12,848 feet high, in central Turkey.

ere (âr) *prep. Archaic.* Previous to; before. —*conj. Archaic.* **1.** Before. **2.** Sooner than; rather than. [Middle English *ar, er,* Old English *ǣr,* before. See **ayer-** in Appendix.*]

Er·e·bus (ĕr′ə-bəs). *Greek Mythology.* The dark region beneath the earth through which the dead must pass before they reach Hades. [Latin, from Greek *Erebos.* See **regwos-** in Appendix.*]

Er·e·bus, Mount (ĕr′ə-bəs). An active volcano, 13,202 feet high, on Ross Island, Antarctica.

E·rech·the·us (ĭ-rĕk′thē-əs, -thyōōs′). A legendary founder and early king of Athens. [Latin, from Greek *Erekhtheus,* "(Earth) Shaker," from *erekhthein*†, to rend, break.]

e·rect (ĭ-rĕkt′) *adj.* **1.** Directed or pointing upward; standing upright; vertical: *erect posture.* **2.** Being in a stiff, rigid condition: *every hair erect.* **3.** *Archaic.* Wide-awake; alert. —*v.* **erected, erecting, erects.** —*tr.* **1.** To raise (a building, for example); construct: *erect a skyscraper.* **2.** To raise upright; set on end; lift up: *erect a Christmas tree for decorating.* **3.** To put together; fashion; assemble: *erect a child's model airport.* **4.** To set up; establish: *erect a dynasty.* **5.** *Geometry.* To construct (an altitude, for example) from or upon a given base. —*intr. Physiology.* To become rigid and upright. [Middle English, from Latin *ērectus,* past participle of *ērigere,* to raise up, set up, erect : *ē-,* out, up, from *ex-* + *regere,* to direct, to set (see **reg-**[1] in Appendix*).] —**e·rect′ly** *adv.* —**e·rect′ness** *n.*

e·rec·tile (ĭ-rĕk′təl) *adj.* **1.** Able to be erected or raised upright. **2.** *Physiology.* Of or pertaining to vascular tissue, as in the nasal cavities, the penis, and the clitoris, that is capable of filling with blood and becoming rigid.

e·rec·tion (ĭ-rĕk′shən) *n.* **1.** The act of erecting, building, or raising upright. **2.** The state of being erected or raised upright. **3.** Something erected; a construction or edifice; a building. **4.** *Physiology.* **a.** The condition of erectile tissue when filled with blood. **b.** An erect penis.

e·rec·tive (ĭ-rĕk′tĭv) *adj.* Tending to erect.

e·rec·tor (ĭ-rĕk′tər) *n.* Also **e·rect·er. 1.** Something that or someone who erects. **2.** *Anatomy.* Any muscle that holds up or causes the erection of a body part.

E region. A layer of the ionosphere, the **E layer** *(see).*

ere·long (âr-lông′, -lŏng′) *adv. Archaic.* Before much time passes; before long; soon.

er·e·mite (ĕr′ə-mīt′) *n.* A person who isolates himself from society, especially as a religious recluse. [Middle English *(h)ermite,* HERMIT.] —**er′e·mit′ic** (-mĭt′ĭk), **er′e·mit′i·cal, er′e·mit′ish** (ĕr′ə-mī′tĭsh) *adj.*

ere·now (âr-nou′) *adv. Archaic.* Before this particular moment; before now; heretofore.

e·rep·sin (ĭ-rĕp′sən) *n.* A mixture of peptidases in the small intestines that acts to produce amino acids. [Probably Latin *ēr(ipere),* to snatch away : *ē-,* away, from *ex-* + *rapere,* to snatch (see **rep-** in Appendix*) + (P)EPSIN.]

er·e·thism (ĕr′ə-thĭz′əm) *n.* Abnormal irritability and sensibility to stimulation in any part of the body. [French *éréthisme,* from Greek *erethismos,* irritation, annoyance, from *erethizein, eretheinn*†, to irritate, stir.] —**er′e·this′mic** *adj.*

E·re·tri·a (ĭ-rē′trĭ-ə, ĭ-rĕt′rĭ-ə). An ancient coastal city on Euboea, Greece, about 15 miles south of Chalcis, destroyed by the Persians about 490 B.C.

E·re·van. See **Yerevan.**

ere·while (âr-hwīl′) *adv.* Also **ere·whiles** (-hwīlz′). *Archaic.* Some time ago; formerly.

Er·furt (âr′fŏŏrt′). An industrial city in south-central East Germany, 65 miles southwest of Leipzig. Population, 190,000.

erg (ûrg) *n.* A centimeter-gram-second unit of energy or work equal to the work done by a force of one dyne acting over a distance of one centimeter. See **measurement.** [Greek *ergon,* work. See **werg-**[1] in Appendix.*]

er·go (ûr′gō, âr′-) *conj.* Consequently; therefore. —*adv.* Consequently; hence. [Latin *ergō,* therefore. See **reg-**[1] in Appendix.*]

er·go·cal·cif·er·ol (ûr′gō-kăl-sĭf′ə-rôl′, -rōl′, -rŏl′) *n.* **Vitamin D_2** *(see).* [ERGO(T) + CALCIFEROL.]

er·go·graph (ûr′gə-grăf′, -gräf′) *n.* A device for determining the work capacity of a muscle or group of muscles by measuring the extent of movement. [From Greek *ergon,* work (see **erg**) + -GRAPH.]

er·gom·e·ter (ûr′gŏm′ə-tər) *n.* An apparatus for measuring the amount of work done by a group of muscles under control conditions. [From Greek *ergon,* work (see **erg**) + -METER.]

er·gos·ter·ol (ûr′gŏs′tə-rôl′, -rōl′, -rŏl′) *n.* A crystalline sterol, $C_{28}H_{44}O$, synthesized by yeast from sugars or derived from ergot and converted under ultraviolet irradiation to vitamin D_2. [ERGO(T) + STEROL.]

er·got (ûr′gət, -gŏt′) *n.* **1.** Any fungus of the genus *Claviceps,* infecting various cereal plants, and forming black sclerotia, or compact masses of branching filaments, that replace many of the seeds of the host plant. **2.** The disease caused by such a fungus. **3.** The dried sclerotia of such a fungus, usually obtained from rye seed, and used as a source of several medicinally important alkaloids and as the basic source of lysergic acid. [French, "cock's spur," which the fungus resembles, from Old French *argor, argot*†.]

er·got·ism (ûr′gə-tĭz′əm) *n.* Poisoning by ergot-infected grain or grain products, characterized by lameness and necrosis of the extremities.

Er·hard (ĕr′härt′), **Ludwig.** Born 1897. Chancellor of West Germany (1963–66).

ERI Airport code for Erie, Pennsylvania.

Er·ic, Er·ik (ĕr′ĭk). A masculine given name. [Old Norse *Eirīkr.* See **reg-**[1] in Appendix.*]

Er·ic·son (ĕr′ĭk-sən), **Leif.** Norwegian navigator; discovered Vinland (A.D. 1000), probably the coast of North America; son of Eric the Red.

Er·ics·son (ĕr′ĭk-sən), **John.** 1803–1889. Swedish-born American inventor; builder of the first ironclad warship, the *Monitor.*

Er·ic the Red (ĕr′ĭk). Norwegian navigator of the tenth century A.D.; discovered and named Greenland; father of Leif Ericson.

E·rid·a·nus (ĭ-rĭd′n-əs) *n.* A constellation located in the Southern Hemisphere near Orion and Fornax and containing the star Achernar. [Greek *Ēridanos,* a mythical river associated with the myth of Phaethon.]

E·rie[1] (ĭr′ē) *n., pl.* **Erie** or **Eries. 1.** A tribe or member of a tribe of North American Indians of Iroquoian stock formerly inhabiting the region around Lake Erie. **2.** The language of this tribe.

E·rie[2] (ĭr′ē). A shipping and industrial center in Pennsylvania, on Lake Erie in the northwest. Population, 138,000.

E·rie, Lake (ĭr′ē). The fourth largest (9,940 square miles) of the Great Lakes, in east-central North America on the boundary between the United States and Canada.

E·rie Canal (ĭr′ē). A historic American waterway, extending 363 miles through central New York State, from Albany to Buffalo on Lake Erie, and now part of the extensive New York State Barge Canal system.

E·rig·e·na (ĕ-rĭj′ə-nə), **Johannes Scotus.** 815?–877. Irish-born theologian and scholar.

Er·i·ka, Er·i·ca (ĕr′ĭ-kə). A feminine given name. [Feminine of ERIC.]

Er·in (ĕr′ĭn). *Poetic.* Ireland. [Middle English *Erin,* from Old Irish *Ērinn,* dative of *Ēriu,* Ireland. See **Iveriū** in Appendix.*]

e·rin·go. Variant of **eryngo.**

E·rin·y·es (ĭ-rĭn′ē-ēz′). *Greek Mythology.* The Furies. [Latin *Erīnyes,* from Greek *Erinues,* plural of *Erinus*†, a Fury.]

E·ris (ĭr′ĭs, ĕr′-). *Greek Mythology.* The goddess of discord. [Greek, from *eris*†, strife, discord.]

e·ris·tic (ĭ-rĭs′tĭk) *adj.* **1.** Of or relating to argument, controversy, or discord. **2.** Given to argument or dispute; discordant. —*n.* **1.** One given to or expert in argument or dispute. **2.** The art or practice of debate. [Greek *eristikos,* eager for strife, from *erizein,* to strive, wrangle, from *eris,* strife, discord. See **Eris.**]

Er·ith (ĕr′ĭth, ĭr′-). A former administrative division of London, England, now part of **Bexley** *(see).*

E·ri·tre·a (ĕr′ə-trē′ə). An autonomous unit of Ethiopia, occupying 45,754 square miles in the north along the Red Sea. It was an Italian colony (1890–1941), and then under British administration (1941–52), until federated with Ethiopia in 1952. Population, 1,422,000. Capital, Asmara. —**Er′i·tre′an** *adj.* & *n.*

E·ri·van. See **Yerevan.**

Er·len·mey·er flask (ûr′lən-mī′ər, âr′-). A conical laboratory flask with a narrow neck and flat, broad bottom. [Originated by Emil *Erlenmeyer* (1825–1909), a German chemist.]

erl·king (ûrl′kĭng′) *n.* An evil spirit of Germanic mythology and folklore, typically represented as a perpetrator of cruel tricks on children. [Partial translation of German *Erlkönig,* "king of alders," coined by Herder in a misunderstanding of Danish *ellerkonge,* variant of *elverkonge,* elf-king : *elver,* elf (see **albho-** in Appendix*) + *konge,* king.]

er·mine (ûr′mĭn) *n.* **1.** A weasel, *Mustela erminea,* of northern regions, having brownish fur that in winter turns to white with a black tail tip. **2.** The valuable white fur of this animal. [Middle English *ermin*, from Old French, from Medieval Latin *(mūs) Armenius*, "Armenian (mouse)."]

Er·mine Street (ûr′mĭn). An ancient, partially excavated Roman road in England, between London and Lincoln.

erne (ûrn) *n.* Also **ern.** Any of several sea eagles; especially, *Haliaeetus albicella*, of the Old World. [Middle English *ern*, eagle, Old English *earn*. See **er-**[2] in Appendix.*]

Er·nest (ûr′nĭst). A masculine given name. [German *Ernst*, from Old High German *Ernust*, "earnestness," "vigor," from *ernust*, struggle. See **er-**[1] in Appendix.*]

Ernst (ĕrnst), **Max.** Born 1891. German-born American surrealist painter.

e·rode (ĭ-rōd′) *v.* **eroded, eroding, erodes.** —*tr.* **1.** To wear away by or as if by abrasion, dissolution, and transportation. **2.** Loosely, to corrode. **3.** To make or form by wearing away. —*intr.* To become eroded or worn. [Latin *ērōdere*, to gnaw off, eat away : *ē-*, off, from *ex-* + *rōdere*, to gnaw (see **rēd-** in Appendix*).]

e·ro·dent (ĭ-rō′dənt) *adj.* Causing to erode; erosive.

e·rog·e·nous (ĭ-rŏj′ə-nəs) *adj.* Also **er·o·gen·ic** (ĕr′ə-jĕn′ĭk). Arousing sexual desire; especially, indicating or pertaining to zones of the body sensitive to sexual stimulation. [Greek *erōs*, desire, sexual love (see **Eros**) + -GENOUS.]

Er·os[1] (îr′ŏs′, ĕr′-). *Greek Mythology.* The god of love, son of Aphrodite. [Latin *Erōs*, from Greek *erōs*†, love, desire.]

Er·os[2] (îr′ŏs′, ĕr′-) *n. Psychoanalysis.* **1.** The sum of all self-preservative, as contrasted with self-destructive, instincts. **2.** Sexual drive; libido. [From EROS.]

e·rose (ĭ-rōs′) *adj.* Irregularly notched, toothed, or indented, as if gnawed; jagged: *erose leaves.* [Latin *ērōsus*, past participle of *ērōdere*, to ERODE.]

e·ro·sion (ĭ-rō′zhən) *n.* **1.** The state of being eroded or the process of eroding. **2.** The group of natural processes including weathering, dissolution, abrasion, corrosion, and transportation by which earthy or rock material is removed from any part of the earth's surface.

e·ro·sive (ĭ-rō′sĭv) *adj.* Serving to erode; causing erosion; eroding: *"the sea waves have battered the coastlines of the world with erosive effect"* (Rachel Carson).

e·rot·ic (ĭ-rŏt′ĭk) *adj.* **1.** Of or concerning sexual love and desire; amatory. **2.** Tending to arouse sexual desire. **3.** Dominated by sexual love or desire. —*n.* **1.** *Rare.* **a.** An amatory poem. **b.** A doctrine of love. **2.** An erotic person. [Greek *erōtikos*, of or caused by love, from *erōs* (stem *erōt-*), love, desire. See **Eros.**] —**e·rot′i·cal·ly** *adv.*

e·rot·i·ca (ĭ-rŏt′ĭ-kə) *pl.n.* Literature or art concerning or intended to arouse sexual desire. [New Latin, from Greek *erōtika*, plural of *erōtikos*, EROTIC.]

e·rot·i·cism (ĭ-rŏt′ə-sĭz′əm) *n.* Also **er·o·tism** (ĕr′ə-tĭz′əm). **1.** Erotic quality or character. **2.** Sexual excitement. **3. a.** Abnormally persistent sexual excitement. **b.** Preoccupation with sex, especially in literature and art.

e·ro·to·ma·ni·a (ĭ-rō′tə-mā′nē-ə, ĭ-rŏt′ə-) *n.* Abnormal desire for the opposite sex; nymphomania or satyriasis. [New Latin : Greek *erōs* (stem *erōt-*), love (see **Eros**) + -MANIA.]

err (ûr, ĕr) *intr.v.* **erred, erring, errs. 1.** To deviate from the proper course or aim; go astray: *"He erred on the side of brilliance, of overenergetic compulsion"* (Louis Untermeyer). **2.** To make an error or mistake; be incorrect. **3.** To violate accepted moral standards; to sin. [Middle English *erren*, to wander about, from Old French *errer*, from Latin *errāre*. See **ers-**[1] in Appendix.*]

er·ran·cy (ĕr′ən-sē) *n., pl.* **-cies. 1.** A state or instance of going astray. **2.** The condition of being in doctrinal error.

er·rand (ĕr′ənd) *n.* **1.** A short trip taken to convey a message or perform a specified task. **2.** The purpose or object of such a trip: *His errand was to mail a letter.* [Middle English *erend*, business, message, Old English *ǣrende*, message, from Germanic *arundjam* (unattested).]

er·rant (ĕr′ənt) *adj.* **1.** Roving, especially in search of adventure. **2.** Straying from the proper course or standards; erring. [Middle English *erraunt*, from Old French *errant*, present participle of both *errer*, to travel, to look for an adventure, from Vulgar Latin *iterāre* (unattested), from Late Latin *itinerārī*, to ITINERATE, and *errer*, to ERR.] —**er′rant·ly** *adv.*

er·rant·ry (ĕr′ən-trē) *n.* The condition of being errant; especially, the conduct or attitudes characteristic of a knight errant.

er·rat·ic (ĭ-răt′ĭk) *adj.* **1.** Without a fixed or regular course; straying; wandering: *"The tears coursed their erratic way down her cheeks"* (Elizabeth Bowen). **2.** Lacking consistency, regularity, or uniformity. **3.** Deviating from the customary course in conduct or opinion; unconventional; eccentric: *erratic behavior.* [Middle English *erratik*, from Old French *erratique*, from Latin *errāticus*, wandering, straying, from *errāre*, to wander. See **ers-**[1] in Appendix.*] —**er·rat′i·cal·ly** *adv.*

er·ra·tum (ĭ-rä′təm, ĭ-rā′-) *n., pl.* **-ta** (-tə). **1.** An error in printing or writing; especially, such an error noted in a list of corrections appended to a book. **2.** Corrigenda. [Latin *errātum*, neuter past participle of *errāre*, to wander, ERR.]

Usage: The plural form *errata* is often employed in the collective sense of a list of errors, but is nevertheless construed as plural when preceded by an inflected adjective, as in *these errata*, and when used as subject: *the errata are.* According to 91 per cent of the Usage Panel the plural verb *are* is the only acceptable one in the following typical example: *The errata are (not is) noted in an appendix.* According to 92 per cent of the Panel, *erratas* is not an acceptable alternative plural form.

er·rhine (ĕr′īn′, -ĭn) *adj.* Promoting nasal discharge. —*n.* An errhine medicine. [Greek *errhinos* : *en-*, in + *rhis* (stem *rhin-*), nose (see **rhino-**).]

Er Rif, Er Riff. See **Rif.**

err·ing (ûr′ĭng, ĕr′-) *adj.* Being in error, especially as to opinions or conduct. —**err′ing·ly** *adv.*

er·ro·ne·ous (ĭ-rō′nē-əs) *adj. Abbr.* **erron.** Containing or derived from error; mistaken; false. [Middle English, from Old French *erroneus*, or Latin *errōneus*, wandering, from *errāre*, to wander, ERR.] —**er·ro′ne·ous·ly** *adv.* —**er·ro′ne·ous·ness** *n.*

er·ror (ĕr′ər) *n.* **1.** An act, assertion, or belief that unintentionally deviates from what is correct, right, or true. **2.** The condition of having incorrect or false knowledge. **3.** The act or an instance of deviation from the accepted code of behavior; a transgression; wrongdoing. **4.** A mistake: *"the errors of civilization stand bare to the scorn of the fields"* (Lord Dunsany). **5.** The difference between a computed or measured value and a correct value. **6.** *Abbr.* **e, e.** *Baseball.* A defensive fielding or throwing misplay by a player when a play normally should have resulted in an out or prevented an advance by a base runner. —See Synonyms at **offense.** [Middle English *errour*, from Old French, from Latin *error*, from *errāre*, to ERR.]

Synonyms: *error, mistake, oversight.* These nouns refer to what is not in accordance with truth, accuracy, right, or propriety. In many examples *error* and *mistake* may be used interchangeably. *Error* is clearly preferable to indicate belief in untruth or departure from what is morally or ethically right or proper. *Mistake* often implies misunderstanding, misinterpretation, and resultant poor judgment, and is usually weaker than *error* in imputing blame or censure. *Oversight* refers to an omission or a faulty act that results from one's lack of attention.

er·satz (ĕr-zäts′, ĕr′zäts′) *adj.* Substitute; artificial: *ersatz mink.* See Synonyms at **artificial.** —*n.* A substitute; especially, an inferior imitation. [German, from *Ersatz*, compensation, replacement, from *ersetzen*, to replace, from Old High German *irsezzen* : *ir-* (perfective prefix) (see **ud-** in Appendix*) + *sezzen*, to set (see **sed-**[1] in Appendix*).]

Erse (ûrs) *n.* The Gaelic language, especially **Irish Gaelic** *(see).* —*adj.* Of or pertaining to the Scottish or Irish Celts or their language. [Middle English (Scottish) *Erisch*, variant of IRISH.]

erst (ûrst) *adv. Archaic.* **1.** At first. **2.** Formerly. —*adj. Archaic.* First. [Middle English *erest*, formerly, first, earliest, Old English *ǣrest*. See **ayer-** in Appendix.*]

erst·while (ûrst′hwīl′) *adj.* Former. —*adv. Archaic.* Formerly.

er·u·bes·cence (ĕr′o͞o-bĕs′əns) *n.* A reddening of the skin; a flushing; blush. [Latin *ērubēscentia*, from *ērubēscēns*, present participle of *ērubēscere*, to blush, to grow red : *ē-*, out, "completely," from *ex-* + *rubēscere*, to grow red, from *rubēre*, to be red (see **reudh-** in Appendix*).] —**er′u·bes′cent** *adj.*

e·ruct (ĭ-rŭkt′) *v.* **eructed, eructing, eructs.** —*intr.* To belch. —*tr.* **1.** To belch (gas from the stomach). **2.** To emit (fumes) violently. Said of a volcano. [Latin *ēructāre* : *ē-*, out, from *ex-* + *ructāre*, to belch (see **reug-** in Appendix*).]

e·ruc·ta·tion (ĭ-rŭk′tā′shən, ē′rŭk-) *n.* **1.** The act or an instance of eructing or belching. **2.** Matter belched forth. —**e·ruc′ta·tive** (ĭ-rŭk′tə-tĭv) *adj.*

er·u·dite (ĕr′yo͝o-dīt′, ĕr′o͝o-) *adj.* **1.** Deeply learned. **2.** Characterized by erudition. [Middle English *erudit*, from Latin *ērudītus*, past participle of *ērudīre*, "to take the roughness out of," polish, teach : *ē-*, out of, from *ex-* + *rudis*, rough, RUDE.] —**er′u·dite′ly** *adv.* —**er′u·dite′ness** *n.*

er·u·di·tion (ĕr′yo͝o-dĭsh′ən, ĕr′o͝o-) *n.* Deep and extensive learning. See Synonyms at **knowledge.**

e·ru·go. Variant of **aerugo.**

e·rum·pent (ĭ-rŭm′pənt) *adj.* Bursting through or as if through a surface or covering. [Latin *ērumpens*, present participle of *ērumpere*, to ERUPT.]

e·rupt (ĭ-rŭpt′) *v.* **erupted, erupting, erupts.** —*intr.* **1.** To emerge violently from limits or restraint; explode. **2.** To become violently active. **3.** To force out or release suddenly, as something enclosed or pent up: *The geyser erupts periodically.* **4. a.** To pierce the gum. Used of a tooth. **b.** To appear on the skin. Used of a skin blemish. —*tr.* To eject violently (steam, lava, or other confined matter). [Latin *ērumpere* (past participle *ēruptus*), to erupt, to break out, to burst : *ē-*, out, from *ex-* + *rumpere*, to break (see **reup-** in Appendix*).]

e·rup·tion (ĭ-rŭp′shən) *n.* **1.** An act, process, or instance of erupting, especially the discharge of lava from a volcano, or of water or mud from a geyser. **2.** A sudden, often violent outburst. **3. a.** Redness, spotting, or other blemishing of the skin or mucosa, especially as a local manifestation of a general disease. **b.** The passage of a tooth through the gum. —**e·rup′tive** *adj.* —**e·rup′tive·ly** *adv.*

-ery, -ry. Used to form nouns from verbs or other nouns to indicate: **1.** A certain activity; for example, **bakery, hatchery. 2.** Certain things or persons; for example, **nunnery. 3.** A collection or class of objects; for example, **finery. 4.** A craft, study, or practice; for example, **husbandry. 5. a.** Certain characteristics; for example, **snobbery. b.** A kind of behavior; for example, **knavery. 6.** Condition or status; for example, **slavery.** [Middle English *-erie*, from Old French : *-er*, *-ier*, from Latin *-ārius* (see **-ary**) + *-ie*, from Latin *-ia* (see **-ia**).]

Er·y·man·thus, Mount (ĕr′ə-măn′thəs). *Greek* **Er·y·man·thos** (-thŏs). A mountain massif, rising to 7,294 feet in the northwestern Peloponnesus, Greece.

e·ryn·go (ĭ-rĭng′gō) *n., pl.* **-goes.** Also **e·rin·go** (for sense 2). **1.** Any of several plants of the genus *Eryngium*, having spiny leaves and dense clusters of small bluish flowers. **2.** *Obsolete.*

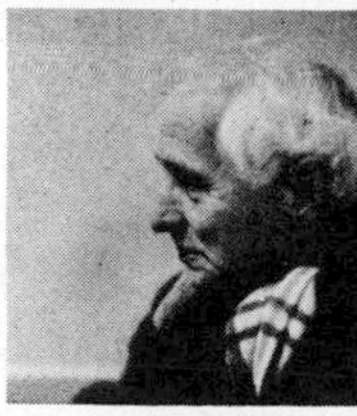

Max Ernst

The candied root of *E. maritimum*, the sea holly, formerly considered an aphrodisiac. [Latin *ēryngion*, from Greek *ērungion*, diminutive of *ērungos*, eryngo, sea holly, possibly from *ēr*, ear, spring, in the sense of "spring flower." See **wesr** in Appendix.*]

er·y·sip·e·las (ĕr′ə-sĭp′ə-ləs, ĭr′ə-) *n.* An acute disease of the skin and subcutaneous tissue caused by a streptococcus and marked by spreading inflammation. Also called "St. Anthony's fire." [Middle English *erisipila, herisipila*, from Latin *erysipelas*, from Greek *erusipelas*, "red skin" : *eruthros*, red (see **reudh-** in Appendix*) + *-pelas*, skin (see **pel-⁴** in Appendix*).] —**er′y·si·pel′a·tous** (-sĭ-pĕl′ə-təs) *adj.*

er·y·sip·e·loid (ĕr′ə-sĭp′ə-loid′, ĭr′ə-) *n.* An infectious disease of the hands characterized by red lesions, and caused by the bacterium *Erysipelothrix rhusiopathiae*, found in infected meat or fish. [ERYSIPEL(AS) + -OID.]

er·y·the·ma (ĕr′ə-thē′mə) *n.* A redness of the skin, as caused by chemical poisoning or sunburn. [New Latin, from Greek *eruthēma*, from *eruthainein*, to be red, from *eruthros*, red. See **reudh-** in Appendix.*] —**er′y·them′a·tous** (-thĕm′ə-təs, -thē′mə-təs), **er′y·the·mat′ic** (-thĭ-măt′ĭk), **er′y·the′mic** *adj.*

e·ryth·rism (ĭ-rĭth′rĭz′əm) *n.* Unusual redness of pigmentation, as of hair or plumage. [ERYTHR(O)- + -ISM.] —**er′y·thris′mal** *adj.*

e·ryth·rite (ĭ-rĭth′rīt′) *n.* A reddish hydrated arsenate of cobalt found in veins bearing cobalt and arsenic and used in coloring glass. [ERYTHR(O)- + -ITE.]

erythro-, erythr-. Indicates red; for example, **erythrocyte, erythrite.** [From Greek *eruthros*, red. See **reudh-** in Appendix.*]

e·ryth·ro·blast (ĭ-rĭth′rə-blăst′) *n.* Any of the nucleated cells in bone marrow that develop into erythrocytes. [ERYTHRO- + -BLAST.] —**e·ryth′ro·blas′tic** *adj.*

e·ryth·ro·cyte (ĭ-rĭth′rə-sīt′) *n.* The yellowish, nonnucleated, disk-shaped blood cell that contains hemoglobin and is responsible for the color of blood. Also called "red blood cell." [ERYTHRO- + -CYTE.] —**e·ryth′ro·cyt′ic** (-sĭt′ĭk) *adj.*

e·ryth·ro·cy·tom·e·ter (ĭ-rĭth′rō-sī-tŏm′ə-tər) *n.* A **hemacytometer** *(see)*. [ERYTHROCYT(E) + -METER.]

e·ryth·ro·my·cin (ĭ-rĭth′rə-mī′sĭn) *n.* An antibiotic agent from cultures of the bacterium *Streptomyces erythreus*, effective especially against Gram-positive bacteria. [ERYTHRO- + -MYCIN.]

Erz·ge·bir·ge (ĕrts′gə-bîr′gə). *Czech* **Kruš·né Ho·ry** (kro͝osh′nə hô′rĭ). A mountain range, rich in mineral resources, on the border between East Germany and Czechoslovakia. Also called "Ore Mountains."

Er·zu·rum (ĕr′zə-ro͞om′). Ancient name **The·o·do·si·op·o·lis** (thē′ə-dō′shē-ŏp′ə-lĭs). A city in Turkey, 540 miles east of Ankara; a strategic Armenian fortress in the 19th-century Russo-Turkish conflicts. Population, 90,000.

Es The symbol for the element einsteinium.

-es¹. Indicates the plural form, for which it is used in nouns ending in a sibilant or an affricate and in some nouns ending in a vowel or a postconsonantal *y*; for example, **trusses, switches, Negroes, ladies.** Compare **-s** (in nouns). [Middle English *-es, -s*, -s (plural).]

-es². Indicates the third person singular form of the present indicative, for which it is used in most verbs ending in a sibilant, an affricate, a vowel, or a postconsonantal *y*; for example, **guesses, rushes, does, defies.** Compare **-s** (in verbs). [Middle English *-es, -s*, -s (third person singular indicative suffix).]

E·sar·had·don (ē′sär-hăd′n). King of Assyria (681–669 B.C.); conquered Egypt and rebuilt Babylon.

E·sau (ē′sô′). The son of Isaac and Rebecca, who sold his birthright to his brother Jacob. Genesis 25:25. [Late Latin *Ēsau*, from Greek, from Hebrew *'Ēsāw*, "hairy."]

Es·bjerg (ĕs′bē-ĕrg′). A major fishing and North Sea port of Denmark, in southwestern Jutland. Population, 55,000.

es·ca·drille (ĕs′kə-drĭl′; *French* ĕs-kȧ-drē′y′) *n.* A unit of an air command, especially in France during World War I. [French, from Spanish *escuadrilla*, diminutive of *escuadra*, squadron, from *escuadrar*, to square, from Vulgar Latin *exquadrāre* (unattested), to SQUARE.]

es·ca·lade (ĕs′kə-lād′) *n.* The act of scaling a fortified wall or rampart by means of ladders, especially during an assault. Also called "scalade." —*tr.v.* **escaladed, -lading, -lades.** To climb up and over (a wall or fortified place). [French, from Italian *scalata*, from *scalare*, to climb, from *scala*, ladder, from Late Latin *scāla*, from Latin *scālae*, steps. See **skand-** in Appendix.*]

es·ca·late (ĕs′kə-lāt′) *v.* **-lated, -lating, -lates.** —*tr.* To increase, enlarge, or intensify; especially, to intensify a war. —*intr.* To increase in intensity or extent. [Back-formation from ESCALATOR.] —**es′ca·la′tion** *n.*

Usage: *Escalate* is established as both a transitive and intransitive verb. It was at first principally intransitive: *The conflict escalated.* Later it was used transitively, as in *Both sides have escalated the war*, and is acceptably used in the preceding example, according to 75 per cent of the Usage Panel. The antonym is *de-escalate* (not *descalate*).

es·ca·la·tor (ĕs′kə-lā′tər) *n.* A moving stairway consisting of steps attached to a continuously circulating belt, for moving passengers up and down between floors. Also called "moving staircase." [Originally a trademark : possibly ESCAL(ADE) + (ELEV)ATOR.]

escalator clause. A provision in a contract between an employer and a labor union stipulating an increase or decrease in wages under certain conditions, such as changes in the cost of living.

es·cal·lop. Variant of **scallop.**

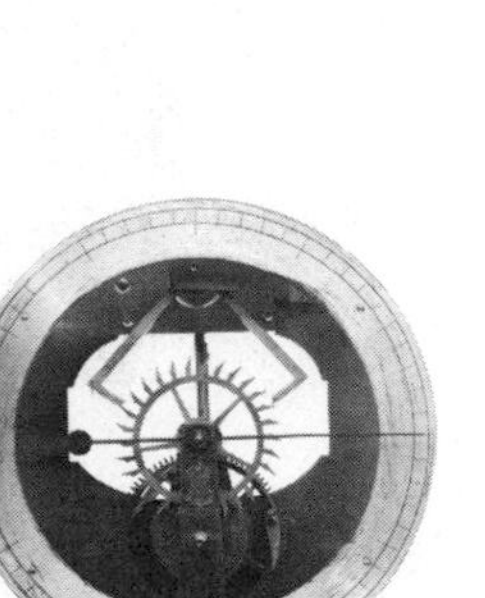

escapement

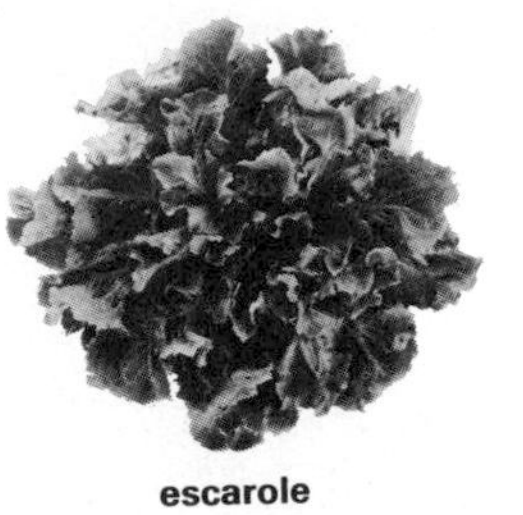

escarole

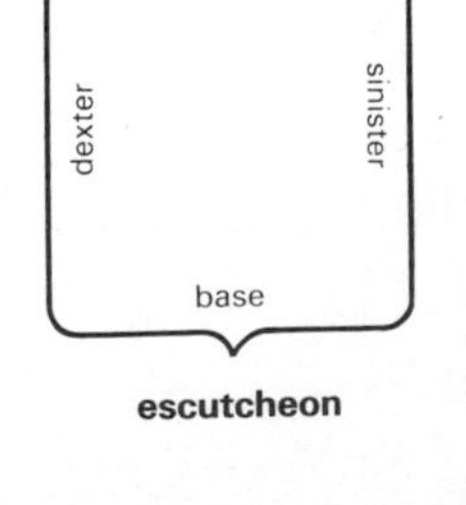

chief
dexter
sinister
base

escutcheon

es·ca·pade (ĕs′kə-pād′) *n.* **1.** A breaking loose from restraint; flight from confining rules. **2.** A carefree or reckless adventure; a fling; caper. [French, from Old French, from Old Italian *scappata*, from the feminine past participle of *scappare*, to escape, from Vulgar Latin *excappāre* (unattested), to ESCAPE.]

es·cape (ĕ-skāp′, ĭ-skāp′) *v.* **-caped, -caping, -capes.** Also *archaic* **scape** (skāp). —*intr.* **1.** To break loose from confinement; get free. **2.** To issue from confinement or an enclosure; leak or seep out. **3.** To succeed in avoiding capture, danger, or harm. **4.** To elude the memory or sight; slip away; vanish. **5.** To grow beyond a cultivated area or a condition of cultivation. Used of plants. —*tr.* **1.** To break loose from; get free of (confinement or restraint). See Usage note below. **2.** To succeed in avoiding (capture, danger, or harm). **3.** To be unnoticed or not recallable or obvious to: *The meaning of this cryptic note escapes me.* **4.** To issue involuntarily from: *A regretful sigh escaped her lips.* —*n.* **1.** The act or an instance of escaping. **2.** A means of escaping. **3. a.** Temporary freedom from worry, care, or unpleasantness. **b.** A means of obtaining this: *Television is his escape from worry.* **4.** A gradual effusion from an enclosure; a leakage. **5.** A cultivated plant that has become established away from cultivation. —*adj.* **1.** Affording a means of escape: *an escape hatch.* **2.** Providing a legal basis for avoiding liability or responsibility: *an escape clause.* [Middle English *escapen*, from Old North French *escaper*, "to take off one's cloak," to emerge from restraint, escape, from Vulgar Latin *excappāre* (unattested) : *ex-*, out, off + Late Latin *cappa*, cloak, hood (see **cape**).] —**es·cap′a·ble** *adj.* —**es·cap′er** *n.*

Synonyms: *escape, avoid, shun, eschew, evade, elude.* These verbs mean to get away from or keep away from persons or things. *Escape* can mean to get free from confinement by fleeing or to remain untouched or unaffected by something unwanted, such as death, punishment, or notice. The second sense does not invariably imply flight or even conscious effort to keep away. *Avoid*, in contrast, always involves such an effort to keep away from persons or things considered a source of danger or difficulty. *Shun* involves deliberately keeping clear of persons or things one dislikes. *Eschew* refers to staying clear of things because to do otherwise would be unwise or morally wrong. *Evade* applies both to getting clear of persons by adroit maneuvering and avoiding distasteful things by similar means. In the latter sense the term sometimes implies dishonesty or irresponsibility. To *elude* is to get away from artfully or by a small margin, or, metaphorically, to escape another's understanding by being perplexing.

Usage: *Escape* (verb), in the sense of breaking out of confinement, is used with *from: Three prisoners escaped from the penitentiary.* In modern usage, *escape* in that sense is not followed by a direct object, though it is used transitively in other senses. The preceding example, with *from* deleted *(escaped the penitentiary)*, is unacceptable to 74 per cent of the Usage Panel.

es·cap·ee (ĕs-kā′pē′, ĕ-skā′pē, ĭ-skā′pē) *n.* One that has escaped; especially, an escaped prisoner.

es·cape·ment (ĕ-skāp′mənt, ĭ-skāp′-) *n.* **1.** An escape, or a means of escape. **2.** A mechanism consisting in general of an escape wheel and anchor, used especially in timepieces to control the wheel movement and to provide periodic energy impulses to a pendulum or balance. **3.** The mechanism in a typewriter that controls the lateral movement of the carriage.

escape velocity. The minimum velocity that a body must attain to overcome the gravitational attraction of another body, such as the earth.

escape wheel. The rotating notched wheel periodically engaged and disengaged by the anchor in an escapement.

es·cap·ism (ĕ-skā′pĭz′əm, ĭ-skā′-) *n.* The habit or tendency of escaping from unpleasant realities in self-deceiving fantasy or entertainment.

es·cap·ist (ĕ-skā′pĭst, ĭ-skā′-) *adj.* Indulging in or characterized by escapism. —*n.* One whose conduct or thought is characterized by escapism.

es·car. Variant of **esker.**

es·car·got (ĕs-kär-gō′) *n., pl.* **-gots** (-gō′). An edible snail, especially when cooked. [French, a snail, from Old French, from Old Provençal *escaragol*†.]

es·ca·role (ĕs′kə-rōl′) *n.* A variety of *Cichorium endivia*, having leaves with irregular, frilled edges, used in salads. [French, from Old French *scariole*, from Late Latin *escariola*, from Latin *escārius*, of food, from *esca*, food, from *edere*, to eat. See **ed-** in Appendix.*]

es·carp (ĕ-skärp′, ĭ-skärp′) *n.* **1.** A steep slope or cliff; an escarpment. **2.** The inner wall of a ditch or trench dug around a fortification. —*tr.v.* **escarped, -carping, -carps. 1.** To cause to form a steep slope. **2.** To furnish with an escarp or escarps. [French *escarpe*, from Old French, from Italian *scarpa*, SCARP.]

es·carp·ment (ĕ-skärp′mənt, ĭ-skärp′-) *n.* **1.** A steep slope or long cliff resulting from erosion or faulting and separating two relatively level areas of differing elevations. **2.** A steep slope in front of a fortification.

Es·caut. The French name for the **Scheldt.**

-escence. Indicates a beginning or continuing state; for example, **opalescence, luminescence.** [Old French, from Latin *-ēscentia*, from *-ēscēns* (stem *-ēscent-*), -ESCENT.]

-escent. Indicates beginning to be or exhibit; for example, **luminescent, phosphorescent.** [Old French, from Latin *-ēscēns* (stem *-ēscent-*), present participial suffix of *-ēscere*, chiefly inceptives of verbs in *-ēre*. See **-ent.**]

esch·a·lot (ĕsh′ə-lŏt′, ĕsh′ə-lŏt′) *n. Rare.* A shallot. [French *eschalote*, from obsolete French *eschalotte*, SHALLOT.]

ă pat/ā pay/âr care/ä father/b bib/ch church/d deed/ĕ pet/ē be/f fife/g gag/h hat/hw which/ĭ pit/ī pie/îr pier/j judge/k kick/l lid, needle/m mum/n no, sudden/ng thing/ŏ pot/ō toe/ô paw, for/oi noise/ou out/o͝o took/o͞o boot/p pop/r roar/s sauce/sh ship, dish/

es·char (ĕs′kär′, -kər) *n.* A dry scab or slough formed on the skin as a result of a burn or by the action of a corrosive or caustic substance. [Middle English *escare,* scab, SCAR.]
es·cha·rot·ic (ĕs′kə-rŏt′ĭk) *adj.* Producing or capable of producing an eschar; caustic; corrosive. —*n.* A caustic or corrosive substance or drug.
es·cha·tol·o·gy (ĕs′kə-tŏl′ə-jē) *n.* The branch of theology that is concerned with the ultimate or last things, such as death, judgment, heaven, and hell. [Greek *eskhatos,* last, extreme (see **eghs** in Appendix*) + -LOGY.] **—es′cha′to·log′i·cal** (-tə-lŏj′ĭ-kəl) *adj.* **—es′cha·tol′o·gist** *n.*
es·cheat (ĕs-chēt′) *n.* **1.** The reversion of land held under feudal tenure to the manor in the absence of legal heirs or claimants. **2.** The reversion of property to the state in the absence of legal heirs or claimants. **3. a.** Property reverted to the state when no legal heirs or claimants exist. **b.** The right of the state to acquire such property. —*v.* **escheated, -cheating, -cheats.** —*intr.* To revert to the state by escheat. —*tr.* To cause (property) to revert to the state by escheat. [Middle English *eschete,* from Old French *eschete, escheoite,* from *escheoit,* past participle of *escheoir,* to fall out, from Vulgar Latin *excadēre* (unattested) : Latin *ex-,* out + *cadere,* to fall (see **kad-** in Appendix*).] **—es·cheat′a·ble** *adj.*
es·cheat·age (ĕs-chē′tĭj) *n.* The right of the state to acquire property by escheat.
es·chew (ĕs-cho͞o′) *tr.v.* **-chewed, -chewing, -chews.** To take care to avoid; shun. See Synonyms at **escape.** [Middle English *escheuen, eschiuen,* from Old French *eschiver, eschiuver,* to shun, to avoid, from Vulgar Latin *scivāre* (unattested), from Germanic *skiuhwan* (unattested), from *skiuhwaz* (unattested), SHY.] **—es·chew′al** *n.*
Es·cof·fier (ĕs-kô-fyā′), **Auguste.** 1847?–1935. French chef and author.
es·co·lar (ĕs′kə-lär′) *n., pl.* **-lars** or **escolar.** Any of several slender fishes of the family Gempylidae; especially, *Lepidocybium flavobrunneum,* of warm marine waters. [Spanish, "scholar" (from the spectaclelike rings around its eyes), from Late Latin *scholāris,* SCHOLAR.]
Es·co·ri·al (ĕ-skôr′ē-əl, -skōr′ē-əl, ĭ-skôr′-, ĭ-skōr′-; *Spanish* ĕs′kō-ryäl′). Also **Es·cu·ri·al** (ĕs-kyo͝or′ē-əl). A monastery, historic royal residence, and major architectural complex, in central Spain, 36 miles northwest of Madrid.
es·cort (ĕs′kôrt′) *n.* **1.** One or more persons accompanying another to give guidance or protection or to pay honor. **2.** One or more guards, often armed, traveling with important persons or goods. **3.** A man who acts as the companion of a woman in public. **4.** One or more vehicles accompanying another vehicle to guide, protect, or honor its passengers. —*tr.v.* (ĕs-kôrt′) **escorted, -corting, -corts.** To accompany as an escort: *"He used to escort flies and moth millers out the door as if they were guests"* (John Cheever). See Synonyms at **accompany.** [French *escorte,* from Old French *(e)scorte,* from Old Italian *scorta,* guide, an escorting, from the feminine past participle of *scorgere,* to show, to guide, from Vulgar Latin *excorrigere* (unattested), to conduct, guide, escort : Latin *ex-,* out + *corrigere,* to set right, CORRECT.]
es·cri·toire (ĕs′krĭ-twär′) *n.* A desk or table suitable for writing; a secretary. [French, from Old French *escriptoire,* a study, from Medieval Latin *scriptorium,* SCRIPTORIUM.]
es·crow (ĕs′krō, ĕ-skrō′, ĭ-skrō′) *n.* **1.** A written agreement, such as a deed or bond, put into the custody of a third party and not in effect until certain conditions are fulfilled by the grantee. **2.** The condition of being ineffective until certain conditions are fulfilled: *a deed held in escrow until the heir reaches his twenty-first birthday.* [Old French *escroe,* strip of parchment, scroll, from Frankish *scrōda* (unattested), piece. See **skeru-** in Appendix.*]
es·cu·do (ĕ-sko͞o′dō, ĭ-sko͞o′-; *Portuguese* ĭsh-ko͞o′tho͞o; *Spanish* ĕs-ko͞o′thō) *n.* **1. a.** The basic monetary unit of Portugal, equal to 100 centavos. **b.** The basic monetary unit of Chile, equal to 100 centesimos. See table of exchange rates at **currency. 2.** A coin worth one escudo. [Portuguese and Spanish, "shield," from Latin *scūtum,* shield. See **skei-** in Appendix.*]
es·cu·lent (ĕs′kyə-lənt) *adj.* Suitable for eating; edible. —*n.* Something edible, as a vegetable. [Latin *esculentus,* from *esca,* food, from *edere,* to eat. See **ed-** in Appendix.*]
es·cutch·eon (ĕ-skŭch′ən, ĭ-) *n.* Also **scutch·eon** (skŭch′ən). **1.** A shield or shield-shaped emblem bearing a coat of arms. **2.** Any ornamental shield-shaped emblem; especially, a plate surrounding the keyhole of a door, or a plate on which the door knocker is mounted. **3.** *Nautical.* The ornamented plate on the stern of a ship inscribed with the ship's name and home port. **—a blot on one's escutcheon.** A disgrace to one's reputation. [Middle English *escochon,* from Old French *escuchon, escusson,* from Vulgar Latin *scūtiō* (unattested), from Latin *scūtum,* shield. See **skei-** in Appendix.*] **—es·cutch′eoned** *adj.*
Esd. Esdras.
Es·dra·e·lon. See Plain of **Jezreel.**
Es·dras (ĕz′drəs) *n. Abbr.* **Esd. 1.** Either of the first two books of the Apocrypha, I Esdras and II Esdras, called in the Douay Bible III Esdras and IV Esdras. **2.** Either of two books of the Douay Bible Old Testament, I Esdras and II Esdras, corresponding to the books Ezra and Nehemiah in the King James Bible and other versions.
-ese. Indicates: **1.** A native or inhabitant; for example, **Sudanese. 2.** A language or dialect; for example, **Japanese. 3.** A literary style or diction; for example, **journalese.** [Old French *-eis* and Italian *-ese,* from Latin *ēnsis,* "originating in."]
ESE east-southeast.
es·er·ine (ĕs′ə-rēn′, -rĭn) *n. Biochemistry.* **Physostigmine** *(see).* [*Eser-,* native African name + -INE.]
Es·fa·han. See **Isfahan.**
Esh·kol (ĕsh′kôl, ĕsh-kôl′), **Levi.** Original surname, Shkolnik. 1895–1969. Russian-born premier of Israel (1963–69).
Esk. Eskimo.
es·ker (ĕs′kər) *n.* Also **es·car** (ĕs′kär, -kər). A long, narrow ridge of coarse gravel deposited by a stream flowing in an ice-walled valley or tunnel in a decaying glacial ice sheet. Also called "os." [Irish *eiscir,* ridge, from Old Irish *escir*†.]
Es·ki·mo (ĕs′kə-mō′) *n., pl.* **-mos** or **Eskimo.** Also **Es·qui·mau** *pl.* **-maux** (-mōz′). *Abbr.* **Esk. 1.** One of a people native to the Arctic coastal regions of North America and to parts of Greenland and northeastern Siberia. **2.** The language spoken by these people. —*adj.* Also **Es·qui·mau.** *Abbr.* **Esk.** Of, pertaining to, or concerning the Eskimos or their language. [Earlier *Esquimawes,* perhaps from Micmac *eskameege,* to eat raw fish : Proto-Algonquian *ašk-* (unattested), "raw" + *-amekw-* (unattested), "fish."]
Es·ki·mo-Al·e·ut (ĕs′kə-mō-ăl′ē-o͞ot′) *n.* A family of languages spoken chiefly among peoples native to the Arctic coastal regions of North America, Greenland, the Aleutian Islands, and the northeastern tip of Siberia.
Es·ki·mo·an (ĕs′kə-mō′ən) *adj.* Eskimo.
Eskimo dog. A large dog of a breed used in Arctic regions as a sled dog, having a thick coat and a plumed tail.
Es·ki·se·hir (ĕs′kĭ-shĕ-hîr′). A city in west-central Turkey, an early capital of the Ottoman Turks; site of the defeat of the Turks by the crusaders in 1097. Population, 153,000.
e·soph·a·gus (ĭ-sŏf′ə-gəs) *n., pl.* **-gi** (-jī′). Also **oe·soph·a·gus.** A muscular, membranous tube for the passage of food from the pharynx to the stomach; gullet. [Middle English *ysophagus,* from Greek *oisophagos*†, gullet.] **—e′so·phag′e·al** (ē′sō-făj′ē-əl, ĭ-sŏf′ə-jē′əl) *adj.*
es·o·ter·ic (ĕs′ə-tĕr′ĭk) *adj.* **1.** Intended for or understood by only a small group: *To the esoteric Hellenic mystery cults, Christianity opposed an exoteric religion.* Compare **exoteric. 2.** Difficult to understand; abstruse: *The theory remained esoteric despite efforts to popularize it.* **3.** Not publicly disclosed; confidential. —See Synonyms at **mysterious.** [Late Latin *esōtericus,* from Greek *esōterikos,* from *esōterō,* comparative of *esō,* within. See **en** in Appendix.*] **—es′o·ter′i·cal·ly** *adv.*
ESP extrasensory perception.
esp. especially.
es·pa·drille (ĕs′pə-drĭl′) *n.* A sandal having a rope sole and a canvas upper part. [French, variant of *espardille,* from Provençal *espardilho,* diminutive of *espart,* esparto, from Latin *spartum,* ESPARTO.]
es·pal·ier (ĕ-spăl′yər, -yā′, ĭ-spăl′-) *n.* **1.** A fruit tree or ornamental shrub that is trained to grow in a flat plane against a wall, often in a symmetrical pattern. **2.** A trellis or other framework upon which such a plant is grown. —*tr.v.* **espaliered, -iering, -iers. 1.** To train (a plant) on an espalier. **2.** To provide with an espalier or espaliers. [French, from Italian *spalliera,* applied to shoulder supports, hence stakes of that height, from *spalla,* shoulder, from Latin *spatula,* broad piece, flat piece. See **spatula.**]
Es·pa·ña. The Spanish name for **Spain.**
Es·pa·ño·la. The Spanish name for **Hispaniola.**
es·par·to (ĕ-spär′tō, ĭ-spär′-) *n.* A tough, wiry grass, *Stipa tenacissima,* of northern Africa, yielding a fiber used in making paper and as cordage. Also called "esparto grass." [Spanish, from Latin *spartum,* from Greek *sparton,* rope, cable, esparto. See **sper-²** in Appendix.*]
es·pe·cial (ĕ-spĕsh′əl, ĭ-spĕsh′-) *adj.* **1.** Standing above or apart from others; exceptional. **2.** Pertaining uniquely to one person or thing; particular. —See Usage note at **special.** [Middle English, from Old French, from Latin *speciālis,* from *speciēs,* a view, appearance. See **spek-** in Appendix.*]
es·pe·cial·ly (ĕ-spĕsh′əl-ē, ĭ-spĕsh′-) *adv. Abbr.* **esp.** To an extent or degree deserving of special emphasis; particularly. See Usage note at **special.**
es·per·ance (ĕs′pər-əns) *n. Obsolete.* Hope. [Middle English *esperaunce,* from Old French *esperance,* from Vulgar Latin *sperantia* (unattested), from Latin *sperāns,* present participle of *spērāre,* to hope. See **spēi-** in Appendix.*]
Es·pe·ran·to (ĕs′pə-răn′tō, -rän′tō) *n.* An artificial international language invented in 1887, characterized by a vocabulary based on word roots common to many European languages, a single, unvarying ending for each principal part of speech, and a regularized system of conjugation and inflection. [Invented by Dr. L.L. Zamenhof (died 1917), Polish philologist, who wrote under the name of Dr. *Esperanto,* "one who hopes."]
es·pi·al (ĕ-spī′əl, ĭ-spī′-) *n.* **1.** The act of catching sight of something. **2.** The act of watching, especially in secret. **3.** The fact of being seen or noticed. [Middle English *espiaille,* from Old French, from *espier,* to watch, to SPY.]
es·pi·o·nage (ĕs′pē-ə-näzh′, -nĭj) *n.* **1.** The act or practice of spying on others. **2.** The use of spies by a government to obtain secret military or political information from another government. [French, from Old French, from *espionner,* to spy, from *espion,* spy, from Old Italian *spione,* from *spia,* from Germanic. See **spek-** in Appendix.*]
Es·pí·ri·to San·to (ĭs-pē′rē-to͞o sän′to͞o). A state of Brazil, occupying 15,780 square miles in the southeast. Population, 1,189,000. Capital, Vitória.
Es·pí·ri·tu San·to (ĕs-pē′rē-to͞o sän′tō). The largest (1,875 square miles) and westernmost of the New Hebrides islands in the southwestern Pacific Ocean.

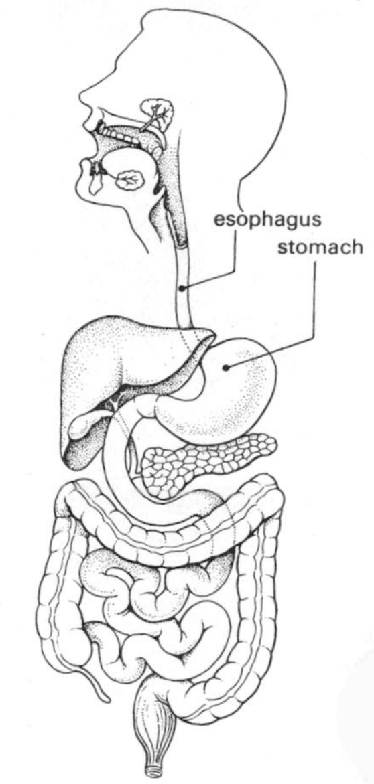

esophagus

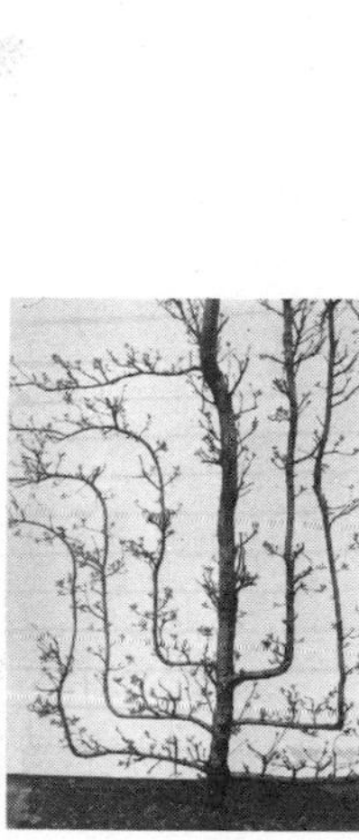
espalier

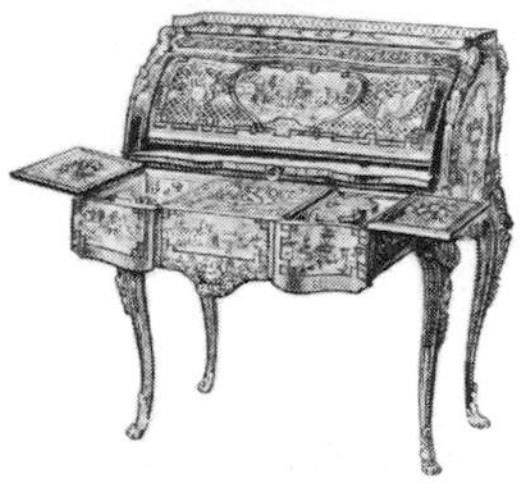
escritoire
Louis XVI marquetry escritoire

es·pla·nade (ĕs′plə-nād′, -näd′) *n.* A flat, open stretch of pavement or grass used as a promenade; especially, such a promenade along the shore. [French, from Italian *spianala,* from *spianare,* to level, from *explānāre,* to flatten, EXPLAIN.]

es·pou·sal (ĕ-spou′zəl, ĭ-spou′-) *n.* **1.** *Sometimes plural.* A betrothal or wedding ceremony. **2.** An espousing of an idea or cause; adoption; a support.

es·pouse (ĕ-spouz′, ĭ-spouz′) *tr.v.* **-poused, -pousing, -pouses.** **1.** To take in marriage; marry. **2.** To give (a woman) in marriage. **3.** To give one's loyalty or support to; adopt. [Middle English *espousen,* from Old French *espouser,* from Late Latin *spōnsāre,* from Latin *spondēre* (past participle *spōnsus*), to promise solemnly. See **spend-** in Appendix.*]

es·pres·so (ĕ-sprĕs′ō, ĭ-sprĕs′-) *n., pl.* **-sos.** A strong coffee brewed by forcing steam under pressure through long-roasted, powdered beans. [Italian *(caffè) espresso,* "pressed out (coffee)," from the past participle of *esprimere,* to press out, express, from Latin *exprimere* : *ex-,* out + *premere,* to PRESS.]

es·prit (ĕ-sprē′) *n.* **1.** Spirit. **2.** Liveliness of mind and expression; wit. [French, from Latin *spiritus,* SPIRIT.]

es·prit de corps (ĕ-sprē′ də kôr′). A spirit of devotion and enthusiasm among members of a group for one another, their group, and its purposes.

es·py (ĕ-spī′, ĭ-spī′) *tr.v.* **-pied, -pying, -pies.** To catch sight of; glimpse (something distant or partly obscured): *"Through one of the rents of his gown, you espied a fat capon hung round the monk's waist"* (Henry James). See Synonyms at **see.** [Middle English *(e)spien,* from Old French *espier,* to SPY.]

Esq. Esquire (title).

–esque. Indicates possession of a specified manner or quality; for example, **statuesque, Lincolnesque.** [French, from Italian *-esco,* from Germanic *-iskaz* (unattested). See also **-ish.**]

Es·qui·line (ĕs′kwə-līn′). One of the Seven Hills of Rome.

Es·qui·mau. Variant of **Eskimo.**

es·quire (ĕs′kwīr′) *n.* **1.** A candidate for knighthood in medieval times, serving a knight as attendant and shield-bearer. **2.** A member of the English gentry ranking just below a knight. **3.** *Archaic.* An English country gentleman; a squire. **4.** *Capital* **E.** *Abbr.* **Esq.** Used as a title of courtesy after a man's full name: *Martin Chuzzlewit, Esq.* **5.** *Rare.* A woman's escort. —*tr.v.* **esquired, -quiring, -quires.** **1.** To serve (a knight) as esquire. **2.** To promote to the rank of esquire. **3.** To address as "Esquire." **4.** *Rare.* To accompany (a woman) as her escort. [Middle English *esquier, esquire,* from Old French *esquier, escuier,* squire, "shield-carrier," from Late Latin *scūtārius,* from Latin *scūtum,* shield. See **skei-** in Appendix.*]

ess, es (ĕs) *n.* The letter *s.*

–ess. Indicates a female; for example, **heiress, lioness.** [Middle English *-esse,* from Old French *-esse,* from Late Latin *-issa,* from Greek.]

Ess. Essex.

Es·sa·oui·ra (ĕs′ə-wîr′ə). Formerly **Mo·ga·dor** (mŏg′ə-dôr). A city in Morocco on the Atlantic Ocean west of Marrakesh. Population, 22,000.

es·say (ĕ-sā′) *tr.v.* **-sayed, -saying, -says.** **1.** To make an attempt at; try: *"The Lieutenant essayed a few initial pleasantries"* (S.J. Perelman). **2.** To subject to a test; try out. —*n.* (ĕs′ā, ĕ-sā′ *for senses 1, 2; only* ĕs′ā *for sense 3*). **1.** An attempt; endeavor. **2.** A testing or trial of the value or nature of a thing: *an essay of his capabilities.* **3.** A short literary composition on a single subject, usually presenting the personal views of the author. [Old French *essaier, assaier,* from *essai, assai,* a trial, from Vulgar Latin *exagiāre* (unattested), to weigh out, from Late Latin *exagium,* a weighing, balance, from Latin *exigere,* to weigh out, examine. See **exact.**] —**es·say′er** *n.*

es·say·ist (ĕs′ā′ĭst) *n.* A writer of essays.

Es·sen (ĕs′ən). A steel-producing city in the heart of the Ruhr industrial region of West Germany. Population, 728,000.

es·sence (ĕs′əns) *n.* **1.** The quality or qualities of a thing that give it its identity; the intrinsic or indispensable properties of a thing: *"Government and Law, in their very essence, consist of restrictions on freedom"* (Bertrand Russell). **2.** The most important or effectual ingredient; crucial element. **3.** *Philosophy.* The inherent, unchanging nature of a thing or class of things, as distinguished from its attributes or its existence. **4. a.** An extract of a substance that retains its fundamental or most desirable properties in concentrated form. **b.** Such an extract in a solution of alcohol. **c.** A perfume or scent. **5.** An existing thing; especially, a spiritual or incorporeal entity. [Middle English *essence, essencia,* from Old French *essence,* from Latin *essentia,* from *esse,* to be. See **es-** in Appendix.*]

Es·sene (ĕs′ēn′, ĕ-sēn′) *n.* A member of an ascetic Jewish sect that existed in ancient Palestine from the second century B.C. to the third century A.D. —**Es·se′ni·an** (ĕ-sē′nē-ən), **Es·sen′ic** (ĕ-sĕn′ĭk) *adj.*

es·sen·tial (ĭ-sĕn′shəl) *adj.* **1.** Constituting or part of the essence of something; basic or indispensable: *"since wine was essential for the drinking of David's health, he added a half bottle of . . . Burgundy"* (A.A. Milne). **2.** Of the fullest degree or extent; absolute; undiluted: *the essential beauty of a sunrise.* **3.** Constituting or containing an essence of a plant, liquid, or other substance. —See Synonyms at **necessary.** —*n.* A fundamental, necessary, or indispensable part, item, or principle. —**es·sen′ti·al′i·ty** (-shē-ăl′ə-tē), **es·sen′tial·ness** *n.* —**es·sen′tial·ly** *adv.*

essential oil. A volatile oil, usually having the characteristic odor or flavor of the plant from which it is obtained, used to make perfumes and flavorings.

Es·se·qui·bo River (ĕs′ə-kwē′bō). The largest river in Guyana, rising in the Guiana Highlands and flowing some 600 miles to the Atlantic, north of Georgetown.

Es·sex (ĕs′ĭks). *Abbr.* **Ess.** A county of England, occupying 1,528 square miles in the southeast. Population, 2,288,000. County seat, Chelmsford. [Middle English *Essex,* Old English *East Seaxe,* "East Saxons" : EAST + *Seaxe, Seaxan,* SAXON(S).]

Es·sex (ĕs′ĭks), **Second Earl of.** Title of Robert Devereux. 1566–1601. English military and naval leader and favorite of Elizabeth I; executed for treason.

Es sham. The Arabic name for **Damascus.**

Ess·ling (ĕs′lĭng). A town just east of Vienna, Austria, where Napoleon was defeated by Archduke Charles Louis (1809).

es·so·nite (ĕs′ə-nīt′) *n.* Also **hes·son·ite** (hĕs′ə-nīt′). A brown or yellowish-brown variety of garnet. Also called "cinnamon stone." [French, from Greek *hēssōn,* inferior to, less than (it is less hard than true hyacinth), from *hēka,* a little, slightly. See **sēk-** in Appendix.*]

–est¹. Indicates the superlative degree of adjectives and adverbs; for example, **greatest, earliest.** [Middle English *-est,* Old English *-est, -ost,* from Common Germanic *-istaz* (unattested).]

–est², –st. Indicates the archaic second person singular form of the present and past indicative tenses, with the pronoun *thou;* for example, *comest, seest.* [Middle English *-est,* Old English *-est, -ast.*]

EST Eastern Standard Time.

est. **1.** established. **2.** *Law.* estate. **3.** estimate.

E.S.T. Eastern Standard Time.

es·tab·lish (ĕ-stăb′lĭsh, ĭ-stăb′-) *tr.v.* **-lished, -lishing, -lishes.** Also *archaic* **stab·lish** (stăb′lĭsh). **1.** To make firm or secure; fix in a stable condition. **2.** To settle securely in a position or condition; install: *"he established me in the firm which thereafter bore my name"* (Louis Auchincloss). **3.** To cause to be recognized and accepted without question: *His flight established Lindbergh as a national hero.* **4.** To originate on a firm, lasting basis; to found. **5.** To create a state institution of (a church or religion). **6.** To introduce as a permanent entity; promulgate: *ordinances established by the king.* **7.** To prove the validity or truth of. **8.** *Card Games.* To gain control of (a suit) so that all remaining tricks can be won. —See Synonyms at **confirm.** [Middle English *establissen,* from Old French *establir* (stem *establiss-*), from Latin *stabilīre,* to make firm, from *stabilis,* firm. See **stā-** in Appendix.*] —**es·tab′lish·er** *n.*

established church. **1.** A church that is officially recognized and given support as a national institution by a government. **2.** *Capital* **E,** *capital* **C.** *Abbr.* **E.C.** The Church of England.

es·tab·lish·ment (ĕ-stăb′lĭsh-mənt, ĭ-stăb′-) *n.* **1.** The act of establishing. **2.** The condition or fact of being established. **3. a.** A business firm, club, institution, or residence, including its members or occupants. **b.** A place of business, including the possessions and employees. **c.** Any organized group, such as a government, political party, or military force. **4.** *Capital* **E.** An established church. **5.** *Usually capital* **E. a.** An exclusive group of powerful people who rule a government or society by means of private agreements and decisions. **b.** A powerful group that tacitly controls a given field of activity, usually in a conservative manner: *the literary Establishment.*

es·ta·mi·net (ĕs-tå-mē-nā′) *n. French.* A small café.

es·tan·cia (ĕs-tän′syä) *n.* A large estate or cattle ranch in Spanish America. [American Spanish, from Spanish, room, enclosure, from Vulgar Latin *stantia* (unattested), a standing (thing), from Latin *stāns,* present participle of *stāre,* to stand. See **stā-** in Appendix.*]

es·tate (ĕ-stāt′, ĭ-stāt′) *n.* **1.** A sizable piece of rural land, usually with a large house. **2.** The whole of one's possessions; especially, all of the property and debts left by a deceased or bankrupt person. **3.** *Abbr.* **est.** *Law.* The nature and extent of an owner's rights with respect to his property and its use. **4.** A stage in one's development or maturation: *A child's estate gives way to man's estate.* **5. a.** A condition of life, wealth, or status; a rank. **b.** High rank or status: *gentlemen of estate.* **6.** *Archaic.* Display of wealth or power; pomp. **7.** A class of citizens within a nation with distinct political rights. Often called Estates of the Realm. [Middle English *estat,* state, condition, from Old French, STATE.]

Es·tates-Gen·e·ral (ĕ-stāts′jĕn′ər-əl, ĭ-stāts′-) *n.* The **States-General** *(see).* [Translation of French *états généraux.*]

Es·te (ĕs′tā). Italian family of rulers of Ferrara (1208–1598) and patrons of the Renaissance.

es·teem (ĕ-stēm′, ĭ-stēm′) *tr.v.* **-teemed, -teeming, -teems.** **1.** To regard as of a high order; think of with respect; prize: *"Oysters were not too much esteemed in the Baltimore of my youth"* (H.L. Mencken). **2.** To judge to be; regard as; consider. —See Synonyms at **appreciate.** —*n.* **1.** Favorable regard; respect: *He is held in high esteem.* **2.** *Archaic.* Judgment; opinion. —See Synonyms at **regard.** [Middle English *estemen,* from Old French *estimer,* from Latin *aestimāre,* to ESTIMATE.]

Es·telle (ĕ-stĕl′, ĭ-stĕl′). A feminine given name. [French, from Spanish *Estella,* "star," from Latin *stella,* star. See **ster-³** in Appendix.*]

es·ter (ĕs′tər) *n.* Any of a class of organic compounds corresponding to the inorganic salts formed from an acid by the replacement of hydrogen by an alkyl radical. [German *Ester,* short for *Essigäther,* "vinegar ether" : *Essig,* vinegar, from Middle High German *ezzich,* from Old High German *ezzīh,* from Latin *acētum* (see **ak-** in Appendix*) + *Äther,* ether, from Latin *aethēr,* ETHER.]

es·ter·ase (ĕs′tə-rās′) *n.* Any enzyme that catalyzes the hydrolysis of an ester. [ESTER + -ASE.]

ă pat/ā pay/âr care/ä father/b bib/ch church/d deed/ĕ pet/ē be/f fife/g gag/h hat/hw which/ĭ pit/ī pie/îr pier/j judge/k kick/l lid, needle/m mum/n no, sudden/ng thing/ŏ pot/ō toe/ô paw, for/oi noise/ou out/ŏŏ took/ōō boot/p pop/r roar/s sauce/sh ship, dish/

es·ter·i·fi·ca·tion (ĕ-stĕr′ə-fə-kā′shən, ĭ-stĕr′-) *n.* Any reaction resulting in the formation of at least one ester product.

es·ter·i·fy (ĕ-stĕr′ə-fī′, ĭ-stĕr′-) *v.* **-fied, -fying, -fies.** —*intr.* To change to an ester. —*tr.* To change (a compound) into an ester. [ESTER + -FY.]

Es·ther¹ (ĕs′tər). A feminine given name. [Greek *Esthēr*, from Hebrew *'Estēr*, from Persian *sitareh*, star. See **ster-³** in Appendix.*]

Es·ther² (ĕs′tər) *n.* A book of the Old Testament recounting the story of Esther, the Jewish queen of Persia who saved her people from massacre.

es·the·sia (ĕs-thē′zhə, -zhē-ə) *n.* The ability to receive sense impressions. [New Latin, back-formation from ANESTHESIA.]

es·thet·ics (ĕs-thĕt′ĭks) *n.* **Aesthetics** *(see).* —**es′thete′** (-thēt′) *n.* —**es·thet′ic** *adj.* —**es′the·ti′cian** *n.* —**es·thet′i·cism′** *n.*

Es·tho·ni·a. See **Estonia.**

Es·tho·ni·an. Variant of **Estonian.**

Es·tienne (ĕs-tyĕn′). French family of printers and publishers, including **Henri** (1460?–1520) and his sons, **François** (1502–1550), **Robert** (1503–1559), and **Charles** (1504–1564).

es·ti·ma·ble (ĕs′tə-mə-bəl) *adj.* **1.** Capable of being estimated or evaluated; calculable. **2.** Deserving of esteem; admirable. —**es′ti·ma·ble·ness** *n.* —**es′ti·ma·bly** *adv.*

es·ti·mate (ĕs′tə-māt′) *tr.v.* **-mated, -mating, -mates. 1.** To make a judgment as to the likely or approximate cost, quantity, or extent of; calculate approximately. **2.** To form a tentative opinion about; evaluate: *"While an author is yet living we estimate his powers by his worst performance"* (Samuel Johnson). —See Synonyms at **calculate.** —*n.* (ĕs′tə-mĭt). *Abbr.* **est. 1.** A tentative evaluation or rough calculation. **2. a.** A preliminary calculation submitted by a contractor or workman of the cost of work to be undertaken. **b.** The written statement of such a calculation. **3.** A judgment based upon one's impressions; an opinion. [Latin *aestimāre*†.] —**es′ti·ma′tive** *adj.* —**es′ti·ma′tor** (-mā′tər) *n.*

Synonyms: *estimate, appraise, assess, assay, evaluate, rate.* These verbs mean to form a judgment of worth or significance. *Estimate* may imply judgment based on rather rough calculation. In general it lacks the definitiveness of the other terms, especially *appraise,* which stresses expert judgment. *Assess* implies authoritative judgment; it involves setting a monetary value on something as a basis for taxation. *Assay* likewise refers to careful examination, such as chemical analysis of ore to determine its content. In extended senses, *appraise, assess,* and *assay* can refer to any critical analysis or appraisal. *Evaluate* implies considered judgment in setting a value on a person or thing. *Rate* involves determining the rank of a person or thing when he or it is judged in relation to others of the same kind.

es·ti·ma·tion (ĕs′tə-mā′shən) *n.* **1.** The act or an instance of estimating. **2.** An opinion reached by estimating; judgment: *"No man ever stood the lower in my estimation for having a patch in his clothes"* (Thoreau). **3.** Favorable regard; esteem.

es·ti·val. Variant of **aestival.**

es·ti·vate. Variant of **aestivate.**

es·ti·va·tion. Variant of **aestivation.**

Es·to·ni·a (ĕs-tō′nē-ə). *Estonian* **Ees·ti** (ās′tĭ). Also **Es·tho·ni·a.** Officially, Estonian Soviet Socialist Republic. A constituent republic of the Soviet Union, occupying 17,400 square miles in northeastern Europe, along the Baltic Sea. Population, 1,273,000. Capital, Tallinn.

Es·to·ni·an (ĕs-tō′nē-ən) *adj.* Also **Es·tho·ni·an.** Pertaining to or characteristic of Estonia, its people, or their language. —*n.* Also **Es·tho·ni·an. 1.** A native or inhabitant of Estonia. **2.** The Finno-Ugric language of Estonia.

es·top (ĕs-tŏp′) *tr.v.* **-topped, -topping, -tops. 1.** *Law.* To prohibit, preclude, or impede by estoppel. **2.** *Archaic.* To stop up; plug up. [Middle English *estoppen*, from Old French *estoper, estouper*, from Late Latin *stuppāre*, to stop up. See **stop.**] —**es·top′page** (ĕs-tŏp′ĭj) *n.*

es·top·pel (ĕs-tŏp′əl) *n. Law.* A restraint on a person to prevent him from contradicting his own previous assertion. Also called "conclusion." [Old French *estoupail, estouppail*, from *estouper*, to ESTOP.]

es·to·vers (ĕs-tō′vərz) *pl.n.* Necessaries granted by law, as wood from a landlord to a tenant, alimony from a husband to a wife, or subsistence income from an estate to a beneficiary. [Middle English, from Norman French *estover*, from Old French *estoveir*, to be necessary, from Latin *est opus*, it is necessary : *est*, (it) is, from *esse*, to be (see **es-** in Appendix*) + *opus*, need, necessity (see **op-¹** in Appendix*).]

es·tra·di·ol (ĕs′trə-dī′əl) *n.* An estrogenic hormone, $C_{18}H_{24}O_2$, found in the follicle cells of ovaries and isolated commercially from sow ovaries or the urine of pregnant mares for use in treating estrogen deficiency. [ESTR(US) + DI- + -OL.]

es·tra·gon (ĕs′trə-gŏn; *French* ĕs-trà-gôN′) *n. French.* Tarragon.

es·trange (ĕs-trānj′) *tr.v.* **-tranged, -tranging, -tranges. 1.** To remove from an accustomed place or relation; put at a distance, especially a psychological distance. **2.** To alienate the affections of; make hostile or unsympathetic. [Old French *estranger, estrangier*, from Medieval Latin *extrāneāre*, from Latin *extrāneus*, STRANGE.] —**es·trange′ment** *n.* —**es·trang′er** *n.*

Synonyms: *estrange, alienate, disaffect.* These verbs refer to the disrupting of love, friendship, loyalty, or a similar bond. *Estrange* and *alienate* are often used with reference to two persons, typically a husband and wife or partners or coworkers, whose harmonious relationship has been replaced by hostility or indifference. *Estrange* generally implies separation. *Alienate* sometimes refers to a break caused by a third person. Both terms also can apply to disruption of a bond that existed between one or more persons and a group or institution. *Disaffect* usually refers to the disruption of loyalty or allegiance within the membership of a group.

es·tray (ĕ-strā′, ĭ-strā′) *n.* **1.** *Archaic.* A stray. **2.** *Law.* A stray domestic animal. —*intr.v.* **estrayed, -traying, -trays.** *Archaic.* To stray. [Norman French *estray*, from Old French *estraie*, stray, wandering, from *estraier*, to STRAY.]

Es·tre·cho de Ma·ga·lla·nes. The Spanish name for the Strait of **Magellan.**

Es·tre·ma·du·ra (ĕs′trə-mə-do͝or′ə; *Portuguese* ĕsh′trə-mə-do͞o′-rə). **1.** A province occupying 2,065 square miles in central Portugal. Population, 1,760,000. Capital, Lisbon. **2.** *Spanish* **Ex·tre·ma·du·ra** (ĕs′trä-mä-*th*o͞o′rä). A historic region of western Spain, once part of Roman Lusitania, along the Portuguese border.

es·tri·ol (ĕs′trē-ōl′) *n.* An estrogenic hormone, $C_{18}H_{24}O_3$, found in the ovaries of mammals, obtained commercially from the urine of pregnant animals, and used in treating estrogen deficiency. [ES(TRUS) + TRI- + -OL.]

es·tro·gen (ĕs′trə-jən) *n.* Also **oes·tro·gen** (ĕs′-, ēs′-). Any of several steroid hormones produced chiefly by the ovary and responsible for promoting estrus and the development and maintenance of female secondary sex characteristics. Compare **androgen.** [ESTR(US) + -GEN.] —**es′tro·gen′ic** (-jĕn′ĭk) *adj.* —**es′tro·gen′i·cal·ly** *adv.*

es·trone (ĕs′trōn′) *n.* An estrogenic hormone, $C_{18}H_{22}O_2$, found in the mammalian ovary and isolated commercially from the urine of pregnant females for use in treating estrogen deficiency. Also called "theelin." [ESTR(US) + -ONE.]

es·trous (ĕs′trəs) *adj.* **1.** Of or pertaining to estrus. **2.** In heat. Said of an animal.

estrous cycle. The series of chemical and physiological changes in female mammals from one period of estrus to the next.

es·trus (ĕs′trəs) *n.* Also **oes·trus** (ĕs′-, ē′strəs). A regularly recurrent period of ovulation and sexual excitement in female mammals other than humans. Also called "heat." [New Latin, from Latin *oestrus*, gadfly, frenzy, from Greek *oistros*. See **eis-¹** in Appendix.*]

es·tu·a·rine (ĕs′cho͞o-ə-rĭn, -rīn′) *adj.* Of, pertaining to, or found in an estuary.

es·tu·ar·y (ĕs′cho͞o-ĕr′ē) *n., pl.* **-ies. 1.** The part of the wide lower course of a river where its current is met and influenced by the tides. **2.** An arm of the sea that extends inland to meet the mouth of a river. [Latin *aestuārium*, estuary, tidal channel, from *aestus*, heat, swell, surge, tide. See **aidh-** in Appendix.*] —**es′tu·ar′i·al** *adj.*

esu electrostatic unit.

e·su·ri·ent (ĭ-so͝or′ē-ənt) *adj.* Hungry; greedy: *"an esurient unprovided advocate: Danton"* (Carlyle). [Latin *ēsuriēns*, present participle of *ēsurīre*, to want food, to be hungry, desiderative of *edere* (past participle *ēsus*), to eat. See **ed-** in Appendix.*] —**e·su′ri·ence, e·su′ri·en·cy** *n.* —**e·su′ri·ent·ly** *adv.*

-et. Indicates smallness; for example, **falconet, spinneret.** [Middle English *-et*, from Old French *-et*, from Common Romance *-itta, -ētto* (both unattested).]

E.T. Eastern Time.

e·ta (ā′tə, ē′tə) *n.* The seventh letter in the Greek alphabet, written Η, η. Transliterated in English as long *e*. See **alphabet.** [Late Latin *ēta*, from Greek, from a Phoenician source, akin to Hebrew *hēth*, HETH.]

e.t.a. estimated time of arrival.

é·ta·gère (ā-tà-zhâr′) *n.* Also **e·ta·gere.** A piece of furniture with open shelves for ornaments or bric-a-brac; whatnot. [French, from Old French *estagiere, estage*, floor of a building, position. See **stage.**]

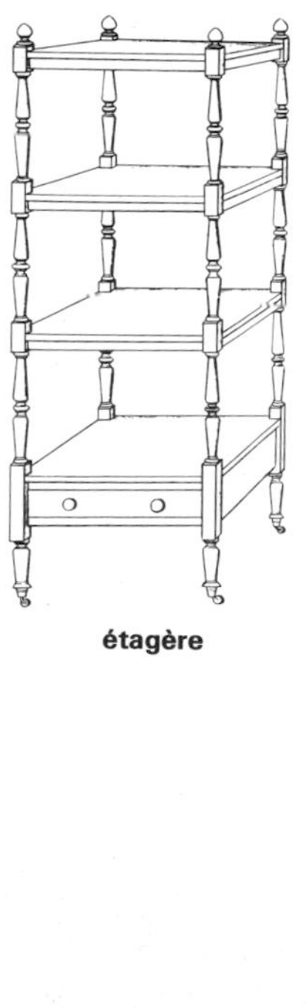

étagère

et al. and others (Latin *et alii*).

etc. et cetera.

Usage: *Etc.* is principally appropriate to informal writing or to special areas such as technical reporting or business correspondence. It is not appropriate to formal writing in general.

et cet·er·a (ĕt sĕt′ər-ə, -sĕt′rə). Also **et·cet·er·a, et caet·er·a.** *Abbr.* **etc.** And other unspecified things of the same class; and so forth. [Latin, "and other (things)" : *et*, and (see **eti** in Appendix*) + *cētera*, the rest, from the neuter plural of *cēterus*, remaining (see **ko-** in Appendix*).]

et·cet·er·as (ĕt-sĕt′ər-əz, -sĕt′rəz) *pl.n.* A miscellany of extras; additional odds and ends.

etch (ĕch) *v.* **etched, etching, etches.** —*tr.* **1.** To wear away (metal or glass, for example) with or as if with acid. **2.** To make (a pattern) on a metal plate or other surface with acid. **3.** To impress or imprint clearly. —*intr.* To practice etching. [Dutch *etsen*, from German *ätzen*, to etch, to bite, to feed, from Old High German *ezzen*, to feed. See **ed-** in Appendix.*]

etch·ing (ĕch′ĭng) *n.* **1.** The art of preparing etched metal plates and printing designs and pictures with them. **2.** A design etched on a plate. **3.** An impression made from an etched plate.

e.t.d. estimated time of departure.

E·te·o·cles (ĭ-tē′ə-klēz′). *Greek Mythology.* A son of Oedipus and Jocasta.

e·ter·nal (ĭ-tûr′nəl) *adj.* **1.** Without beginning or end; existing outside of time: *God, the eternal Father.* **2.** Having a beginning but without interruption or end: *an eternal flame.* **3.** Unaffected by time; lasting; timeless. **4.** Seemingly endless; interminable. **5.** Of or relating to existence after death: *one's eternal reward.* —See Synonyms at **continual, infinite.** —*n.* Something eternal. —**the Eternal.** God. [Middle English, from Old French, from Late Latin *aeternālis*, from Latin *aeternus*, eternal. See **aiw-** in Appendix.*] —**e′ter·nal′i·ty, e·ter′nal·ness** *n.* —**e·ter′nal·ly** *adj.*

Eternal City. A name for Rome, Italy.

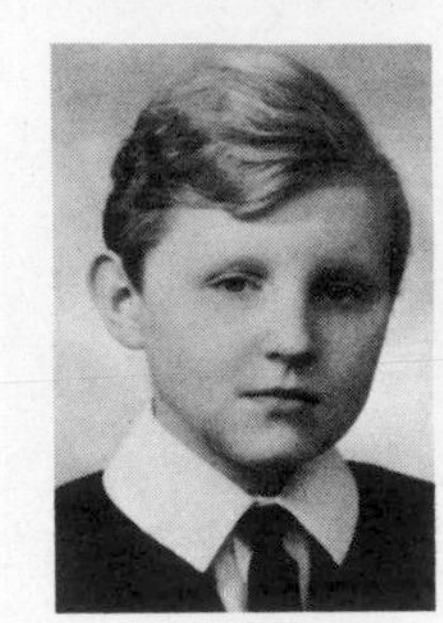
Eton collar

e·terne (ĭ-tûrn′) *adj. Archaic.* Eternal. [Middle English, from Old French, from Latin *aeternus*, ETERNAL.]

e·ter·ni·ty (ĭ-tûr′nə-tē) *n., pl.* **-ties.** **1.** The totality of time without beginning or end; infinite time. **2.** The state or quality of being eternal; everlastingness. **3. a.** The endless period of time following death. **b.** The afterlife; immortality. **4.** A very long or seemingly very long time. [Middle English *eternite*, from Old French, from Latin *aeternitās*, from *aeternus*, ETERNAL.]

e·ter·nize (ĭ-tûr′nīz′) *tr.v.* **-nized, -nizing, -nizes.** Also **e·ter·na·lize** (-nə-līz′). **1.** To make eternal. **2.** To make perpetually famous; immortalize. [Old French *eterniser*, from ETERNE.]

e·te·sian (ĭ-tē′zhən) *adj.* Recurring annually. Said of prevailing northerly summer winds of the Mediterranean. [From Latin *etēsius*, from Greek *etēsios*, from *etos*, year. See **wet-** in Appendix.*]

eth. Variant of **edh.**

-eth¹, -th. Indicates the archaic third person singular form of the present indicative tense; for example, *leadeth, praiseth.* [Middle English *-eth*, Old English *-eth, -th.*]

-eth². Variant of -th (in ordinal numbers).

eth·ane (ĕth′ān′) *n.* A colorless, odorless gas, C_2H_6, occurring as a constituent of natural gas and used as a fuel and refrigerant. Also called "dimethyl." [ETH(YL) + -ANE.]

eth·a·nol (ĕth′ə-nôl′, -nōl′, -nŏl′) *n. Chemistry.* An **alcohol** *(see).* [ETHAN(E) + -OL.]

Eth·el (ĕth′əl). A feminine given name. [Back-formation from names such as *Ethelred.*]

Eth·el·red II (ĕth′əl-rĕd′). Also **Aeth·el·red.** Called "the Unready." 968?–1016. King of England (978–1016). [Old English *Æthelrǣd, Ethelrēd,* "noble counsel" : *æthele*, noble (see **athal-** in Appendix*) + *rǣd*, counsel (see **ar-** in Appendix*).]

eth·ene (ĕth′ēn′) *n. Chemistry.* **Ethylene** *(see).* [ETH(YL) + -ENE.]

e·ther (ē′thər) *n.* Also **ae·ther.** **1.** Any of a class of organic compounds in which two hydrocarbon groups are linked by an oxygen atom. **2.** A volatile, highly flammable liquid, $C_4H_{10}O$, derived from the distillation of ethyl alcohol with sulfuric acid, and widely used in industry and as an anesthetic. Also called "diethyl ether," "ethyl ether." **3.** The regions of space beyond the earth's atmosphere; the clear sky; the heavens. **4.** *Physics.* An all-pervading, infinitely elastic, massless medium formerly postulated as the medium of propagation of electromagnetic waves. [Middle English, from Latin *aethēr*, the upper or bright air, ether, from Greek *aithēr.* See **aidh-** in Appendix.*] —**e·ther′ic** (ē-thĕr′ĭk) *adj.*

e·the·re·al (ĭ-thîr′ē-əl) *adj.* Also **ae·the·re·al** (for sense 4). **1.** Resembling ether in lightness; impalpable; intangible. **2.** Highly refined; delicate; exquisite. **3. a.** Of the celestial spheres; heavenly: *"Him the almighty power/Hurl'd headlong flaming from th' Ethereal Sky"* (Milton). **b.** Unearthly; spiritual. **4.** *Chemistry.* Of or pertaining to ether. [From Latin *aetherius, aethereus*, from Greek *aitherios*, from *aithēr*, ETHER.] —**e·the′re·al′i·ty, e·the′re·al·ness** *n.* —**e·the′re·al·ly** *adv.*

e·the·re·al·ize (ĭ-thîr′ē-ə-līz′) *v.* **-ized, -izing, -izes.** —*tr.* To make, or treat as being, ethereal; spiritualize. —*intr.* To become ethereal. —**e·the′re·al·i·za′tion** *n.*

Eth·er·ege (ĕth′ər-ĭj), Sir **George.** 1635?–1691. English Restoration dramatist.

e·ther·i·fy (ĭ-thĕr′ə-fī′) *tr.v.* **-fied, -fying, -fies.** To convert (an alcohol) into ether. —**e·ther′i·fi·ca′tion** *n.*

e·ther·ize (ē′thə-rīz′) *tr.v.* **-ized, -izing, -izes.** **1.** To subject to the fumes of ether; anesthetize. **2.** *Chemistry.* To etherify. —**e′ther·i·za′tion** *n.* —**e′ther·iz′er** *n.*

eth·ic (ĕth′ĭk) *n.* A principle of right or good conduct, or a body of such principles. [Middle English *et(h)ik*, the science of ethics, from Old French *ethique*, from Late Latin *ēthica* and Latin *ēthicē*, from Greek *ēthikē*, from *ēthikos*, ethical, from *ēthos*, moral custom. See **seu-²** in Appendix.*]

eth·i·cal (ĕth′ĭ-kəl) *adj.* **1.** Of, pertaining to, or dealing with ethics: *an ethical dilemma.* **2.** In accordance with the accepted principles of right and wrong governing the conduct of a group. **3.** Designating a medicinal preparation dispensed solely through the medical profession. —See Synonyms at **moral.** —**eth′i·cal·ly** *adv.* —**eth′i·cal·ness, eth′i·cal′i·ty** *n.*

eth·i·cize (ĕth′ə-sīz′) *tr.v.* **-cized, -cizing, -cizes.** To make ethical; assign ethical attributes to.

eth·ics (ĕth′ĭks) *pl.n.* **1. a.** The study of the general nature of morals and of the specific moral choices to be made by the individual in his relationship with others; the philosophy of morals. Also called "moral philosophy." **b.** The moral sciences as a whole, including moral philosophy and customary, civil, and religious law. Used with a singular verb: *"Jurisprudence . . . is the principal and most perfect branch of ethics."* (Blackstone). **2.** The rules or standards governing the conduct of the members of a profession: *"all citizens share in blame for lax municipal ethics."* (Christian Science Monitor). **3.** Any set of moral principles or values. **4.** The moral quality of a course of action; fitness; propriety: *I question the ethics of his decision.*

E·thi·op (ē′thē-ŏp′) *n.* Also **E·thi·ope** (-ōp′). *Archaic.* A dark-skinned African. [Latin *Aethiops*, from Greek *Aithiops*†.]

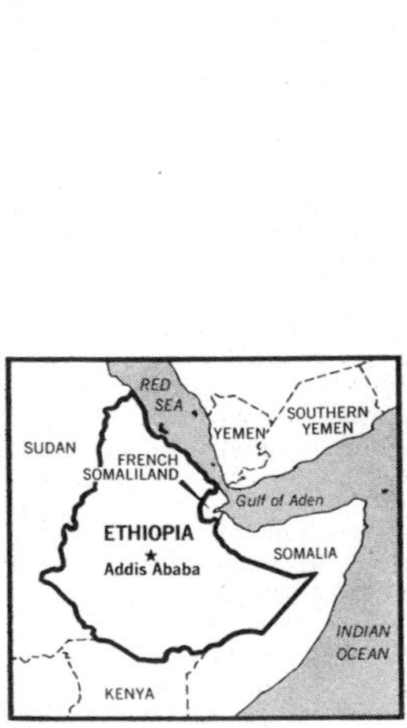

Ethiopia

E·thi·o·pi·a (ē′thē-ō′pē-ə). Also **Ae·thi·o·pi·a.** Formerly **Ab·ys·sin·i·a** (ăb′ə-sĭn′ē-ə). Officially, Empire of Ethiopia. An empire occupying some 400,000 square miles in eastern Africa. Population, 21,462,000. Capital, Addis Ababa.

E·thi·o·pi·an (ē′thē-ō′pē-ən) *adj.* **1.** Of or pertaining to Ethiopia or its people. **2.** *Ecology.* Of or designating the zoogeographic region that includes Africa and most of Arabia. **3.** *Archaic.* Black African; Negro. —*n.* **1.** A native or inhabitant of Ethiopia. **2.** *Archaic.* A member of the ancient Greek classification of dark-skinned Africans from the lands beyond Egypt; a Negro. **3.** Ethiopic.

E·thi·op·ic (ē′thē-ŏp′ĭk, -ō′pĭk) *n.* The Semitic language of ancient Ethiopia or Abyssinia, having a Christian literature, and still used for liturgical purposes in Ethiopia. Also called "Geez." —*adj.* **1.** Pertaining to this language. **2.** Ethiopian.

eth·moid (ĕth′moid′) *adj.* Also **eth·moi·dal** (ĕth′moid′l). Of or pertaining to a light spongy bone located between the orbits, that forms part of the walls of the superior nasal cavity. —*n.* The ethmoid bone. [French *ethmoïde*, from Old French, from Greek *ēthmoeidēs*, perforated (the bone contains many perforations) : *ēthmos*, strainer, from *ēthein*, to strain, to sift (see **sē-³** in Appendix*) + -OID.]

eth·narch (ĕth′närk′) *n.* The ruler of a province or a people. [Greek *ethnarkhēs*, ruler of the people : ETHN(O)- + *arkhos*, -ARCH.] —**eth′nar·chy** *n.*

eth·nic (ĕth′nĭk) *adj.* Also **eth·ni·cal** (-nĭ-kəl). **1.** Of or pertaining to a social group within a cultural and social system that claims or is accorded special status on the basis of complex, often variable traits including religious, linguistic, ancestral, or physical characteristics. **2.** Broadly, characteristic of a religious, racial, national, or cultural group. **3.** Pertaining to a people not Christian or Jewish; heathen; pagan: *"These are ancient ethnic revels, / Of a faith long since forsaken"* (Longfellow). [Late Latin *ethnicus*, heathen, foreign, from Greek *ethnikos*, of a national group, foreign, from *ethnos*, people, nation. See **seu-²** in Appendix.*] —**eth′ni·cal·ly** *adv.*

ethno-, ethn-. Indicates race or people; for example, **ethnocentrism.** [French, from Late Greek, from Greek *ethnos*, people. See **seu-²** in Appendix.*]

eth·no·cen·trism (ĕth′nō-sĕn′trĭz′əm) *n.* **1.** Belief in the superiority of one's own ethnic group. **2.** Overriding concern with race. [ETHNO- + CENTR(O)- + -ISM.] —**eth′no·cen′tric** *adj.*

eth·nog·e·ny (ĕth-nŏj′ə-nē) *n., pl.* **-nies.** The ethnology of racial and ethnic origins. [French *ethnogénie* : ETHNO- + -GENY.] —**eth′no·gen′ic** (ĕth′nō-jĕn′ĭk) *adj.*

eth·nog·ra·phy (ĕth-nŏg′rə-fē) *n., pl.* **-phies.** **1.** The descriptive anthropology of technologically primitive societies. **2.** Ethnology. [French *ethnographie* : ETHNO- + -GRAPHY.] —**eth·nog′ra·pher** *n.* —**eth′no·graph′ic** (ĕth′nə-grăf′ĭk), **eth′no·graph′i·cal** *adj.* —**eth′no·graph′i·cal·ly** *adv.*

eth·nol·o·gy (ĕth-nŏl′ə-jē) *n.* The anthropological study of socio-economic systems and cultural heritage, especially of cultural origins and of factors influencing cultural growth and change, in technologically primitive societies. [ETHNO- + -LOGY.] —**eth′no·log′ic** (ĕth′nə-lŏj′ĭk), **eth′no·log′i·cal** *adj.* —**eth′no·log′i·cal·ly** *adv.* —**eth·nol′o·gist** *n.*

e·thol·o·gy (ĕ-thŏl′ə-jē, ē-) *n.* The scientific study of animal behavior. [Latin *ēthologia*, the art of depicting character, from Greek *ēthologia* : *ēthos*, ETHOS + -LOGY.] —**eth′o·log′i·cal** (ĕth′ə-lŏj′ĭ-kəl) *adj.* —**e·thol′o·gist** *n.*

e·thos (ē′thŏs′) *n.* **1.** The disposition, character, or attitude peculiar to a specific people, culture, or group that distinguishes it from other peoples or groups; fundamental values or spirit; mores. **2.** The governing or central principle in a movement, work of art, mode of expression, or the like: *"the revolutionary ethos had become corrupted"* (Irving Howe). [New Latin, from Greek *ēthos*, custom, usage, trait. See **seu-²** in Appendix.*]

eth·yl (ĕth′əl) *n.* **1.** A univalent organic radical, C_2H_5. **2.** *Capital* **E. a.** A trademark for a gasoline containing an antiknock substance, tetraethyl lead. **b.** A trademark for any of various additives for hydrocarbon fuels and lubricants and for other products, used as antiknock compounds, metal deactivators, ignition control compounds, and antioxidants. [ETH(ER) + -YL.] —**eth·yl′ic** *adj.*

ethyl acetate. A colorless, volatile, flammable liquid, $CH_3COOC_2H_5$, used in perfumes, flavorings, lacquers, pharmaceuticals, and rayon, and as a general solvent.

ethyl alcohol. *Chemistry.* An **alcohol** *(see).*

eth·yl·a·mine (ĕth′ə-lə-mēn′) *n.* A colorless, volatile liquid, $C_2H_5NH_2$, used in petroleum refining, detergents, and organic synthesis. [ETHYL + AMINE.]

eth·yl·ate (ĕth′ə-lāt′) *tr.v.* **-lated, -lating, -lates.** *Chemistry.* To introduce the ethyl group into (a compound). [ETHYL + -ATE.] —**eth′yl·a′tion** (ĕth′ə-lā′shən) *n.*

ethyl chloride. A chemical compound, C_2H_5Cl, a gas at ordinary temperatures and a colorless, volatile, flammable liquid when compressed, used as a solvent, refrigerant, and in the manufacture of tetraethyl lead.

eth·yl·ene (ĕth′ə-lēn′) *n.* **1.** A colorless, flammable gas, C_2H_4, derived from natural gas and petroleum and used as a source of many organic compounds, in welding and cutting metals, to color citrus fruits, and as an anesthetic. **2.** The bivalent organic radical C_2H_4. Also called "ethene." [ETHYL + -ENE.]

ethylene glycol. A colorless, syrupy alcohol, $C_2H_6O_2$, used as an antifreeze in cooling and heating systems.

ethyl ether. *Chemistry.* **Ether** *(see).*

ethyl mercaptan. *Chemistry.* **Mercaptan** *(see).*

e·ti·o·late (ē′tē-ə-lāt′) *v.* **-lated, -lating, -lates.** —*tr.* To cause (a plant) to develop without normal green coloring by preventing exposure to sunlight; blanch; whiten. —*intr.* To become blanched or whitened, as when grown without sunlight. [French *étioler*, from *eteule*, a stalk, from Old French *estuble*, from Latin *stipula*, stalk, straw, stubble. See **steibh-** in Appendix.*] —**e′ti·o·la′tion** *n.*

e·ti·ol·o·gy (ē′tē-ŏl′ə-jē) *n., pl.* **-gies.** Also **ae·ti·ol·o·gy.** **1.** The study of causes, origins, or reasons. **2.** That part of medicine that deals with the causation of disease. **3. a.** The assignment of a cause, origin, or reason for something. **b.** The cause of a disease or disorder as determined by medical diagnosis. [Late Latin *aetiologia*, from Greek *aitiologia*, a giving the cause of : *aitia*, responsibility, cause (see **ai-**[1] in Appendix*) + -LOGY.] —**e'ti·o·log'ic** (-ə-lŏj'ĭk), **e'ti·o·log'i·cal** *adj.* —**e'ti·o·log'i·cal·ly** *adv.* —**e'ti·ol'o·gist** *n.*

et·i·quette (ĕt'ə-kĕt', -kĭt) *n.* **1.** The body of prescribed social usages. **2.** Any special code of behavior or courtesy: *"In the code of military etiquette, silence and fixity are forms of deference"* (Ambrose Bierce). [French *etiquette*, prescribed routine, label, ticket, from Old French *estiqu(i)er*, to attach, from Middle Dutch *steken*. See **steig-** in Appendix.*]

Synonyms: *etiquette, propriety, decorum, protocol.* These nouns refer to codes governing correct behavior. *Etiquette* consists of the prescribed forms of conduct in polite society, a code also denoted by the plural form *the proprieties.* The singular *propriety* and *decorum* are usually interchangeable with the foregoing terms, both implying in a more general way the standards to be observed by one who makes claim to good breeding. *Protocol* refers to etiquette as it relates to affairs of state; especially to diplomatic exchange.

Et·na, Mount (ĕt'nə). Also **Aet·na.** The highest (10,705 feet) active volcano in Europe, in eastern Sicily.

E·ton (ēt'n). A town in southern Buckinghamshire, England, on the Thames opposite Windsor; the site of Eton College, a public school for boys.

Eton collar. A broad white collar worn, overlapping the lapels, with an Eton jacket.

E·to·ni·an (ē-tō'nē-ən) *adj.* Of or pertaining to Eton College. —*n.* A boy who is or has been a student at Eton College.

Eton jacket. 1. A waist-length jacket with wide lapels and cut square at the hips, usually worn with a wide, stiff collar, or Eton collar, and originally worn by pupils of Eton College. **2.** A similar short jacket worn by women and girls.

E·tru·ri·a (ĭ-trŏŏr'ē-ə). An ancient country of west-central Italy, now comprising Tuscany and parts of Umbria.

E·trus·can (ĭ-trŭs'kən) *adj.* Also **E·tru·ri·an** (ĭ-trŏŏr'ē-ən). Of or pertaining to Etruria, its inhabitants, their language or culture. —*n.* Also **E·tru·ri·an. 1.** A person who lived in ancient Etruria. **2.** The pre-Roman, now extinct language of the Etruscans, of undetermined linguistic affiliation.

et se·quens (ĕt sē'kwənz) *pl.* **et sequentia** (ĕt sĭ-kwĕn'shē-ə). *Abbr.* **et seq.** *Latin.* And the following.

-ette. Indicates: **1.** Small or diminutive; for example, **kitchenette. 2.** An imitation of or a substitute for; for example, **leatherette. 3.** Female or feminine; for example, **usherette.** [Middle English *-ette*, from Old French, feminine of -ET.]

e·tude (ā'tōōd', -tyōōd'; *French* ā-tüd') *n.* **1.** A study piece of music for the development of a given point of technique. **2.** A composition embodying some point of technique but intended for performance. [French *étude*, study, from Old French *estudie*, STUDY.]

é·tui (ā-twē') *n.*, *pl.* **étuis** (ā-twēz'). Also **e·twee** (ĕ-twē', ĕt'wē). A case for holding small articles, as needles or toiletries. [French, from Old French *estui*, container, prison, from *estuier*, to shut up, guard, probably from Vulgar Latin *estudiāre* (unattested), to take care of, from Latin *studium*, STUDY.]

etym., etymol. etymological; etymology.

et·y·mo·log·i·cal (ĕt'ə-mə-lŏj'ĭ-kəl) *adj.* Also **et·y·mo·log·ic** (-lŏj'ĭk). *Abbr.* **etym., etymol.** Of or pertaining to etymology, or based upon the principles of etymology. —**et'y·mo·log'i·cal·ly** *adv.*

et·y·mol·o·gist (ĕt'ə-mŏl'ə-jĭst) *n.* A specialist in the principles of etymology and their application.

et·y·mol·o·gize (ĕt'ə-mŏl'ə-jīz') *v.* **-gized, -gizing, -gizes.** —*tr.* To trace and state the etymology of (a word or words). —*intr.* To give or suggest the etymology of a word or words.

et·y·mol·o·gy (ĕt'ə-mŏl'ə-jē) *n.*, *pl.* **-gies.** *Abbr.* **etym., etymol. 1.** The origin and historical development of a word, as evidenced by study of its basic elements, earliest known use, and changes in form and meaning; semantic derivation and evolution. **2.** An account of the history of a specific word. **3.** The branch of linguistics that studies the derivation of words. [Learned respelling of Middle English *ethimologie*, from Old French, from Medieval Latin *ethimologia*, from Latin *etymologia*, from Greek *etumologiā* : *etumon*, ETYMON + -LOGY.]

et·y·mon (ĕt'ə-mŏn', -mən) *n.*, *pl.* **-mons** or **-ma** (-mə). The earliest form of a word that can be discovered, from which its modifications are derived. [Latin, origin of a word, from Greek *etumon*, true sense of a word, etymology, from *etumos*, true, real, akin to *eteos*†, true.]

eu-. Indicates: **1.** Well, pleasant, or beneficial; for example, **eudemon. 2.** Derivative of a specified substance; for example, **eucaine.** [Middle English *eu-*, from Latin, from Greek, from *eus*, good. See **esu-** in Appendix.*]

Eu The symbol for the element europium.

Eu·boe·a (yōō-bē'ə). *Modern Greek* **Ev·voi·a** (ĕv'yä). The largest Greek island in the Aegean Sea (1,457 square miles), lying northeast of Attica and Boeotia across the Gulf of Euboea, an arm of the Aegean; the site of ancient Chalcis and Eretria. Population, 166,000. Capital, Khalkis.

eu·caine (yōō'kān') *n.* A crystalline substance, $C_{15}H_{21}NO_2$, formerly used as a local anesthetic. [EU- + -CAINE.]

eu·ca·lyp·tol (yōō'kə-lĭp'tôl', -tōl') *n.* Also **eu·ca·lyp·tole** (-tōl'). A colorless oily liquid, $C_{10}H_{18}O$, derived from eucalyptus oil and used in pharmaceuticals, flavoring, and perfumery. Also called "cineol." [EUCALYPT(US) + -OL.]

eu·ca·lyp·tus (yōō'kə-lĭp'təs) *n.*, *pl.* **-tuses** or **-ti** (-tī'). Also *rare* **eu·ca·lypt** (yōō'kə-lĭpt'). Any of numerous tall trees of the genus *Eucalyptus*, native to Australia, having in many species aromatic leaves that yield an oil used medicinally and wood valued as timber. [New Latin : EU- + Greek *kaluptos*, covered (from the flower which is covered before it opens), from *kaluptein*, to cover, hide (see **kel-**[4] in Appendix*).]

Eu·cha·rist (yōō'kər-ĭst) *n.* **1.** The Christian sacrament commemorating Christ's Last Supper. Also called "Communion," "Holy Communion." **2.** The consecrated elements of bread and wine used in this sacrament. **3.** *Christian Science.* "Our Eucharist is spiritual communion with the one God." (Mary Baker Eddy). [Middle English *eukarist*, from Old French *eucariste*, from Late Latin *eucharistia*, from Greek *eukharistia*, gratitude, from *eukharistos*, grateful : *eu-*, well, good + *kharizesthai*, to show favor, from *kharis*, favor, grace (see **gher-**[6] in Appendix*).] —**Eu'cha·ris'tic, Eu'cha·ris'ti·cal** *adj.*

eu·chre (yōō'kər) *n.* **1.** A card game played with the 32 highest cards of the deck in which each player is dealt 5 cards; the player making the trump is required to take at least 3 tricks to win. **2.** The action of euchring an opponent. —*tr.v.* **euchred, -chring, -chres. 1.** To prevent (an opponent) from taking 3 tricks in euchre. **2.** *Informal.* To outwit. Often used with *out: He euchred him out of the contest.* [Origin unknown.]

Eu·clid[1] (yōō'klĭd). Greek mathematician of the third century B.C.; author of *Elements*, in which the earliest systematic geometry is developed from the essentially undefined concepts of point, line, and plane.

Eu·clid[2] (yōō'klĭd). A city of Ohio, in the north on Lake Erie, near Cleveland. Population, 63,000.

Eu·clid·e·an (yōō-klĭd'ē-ən) *adj.* Also **Eu·clid·i·an.** Of or pertaining to Euclid's geometric principles.

Eu·clid of Meg·a·ra (yōō'klĭd; mĕg'ər-ə). Also **Eu·cli·des** (-klə-dēz'). 450?–374 B.C. Greek philosopher.

eu·de·mon (yōō-dē'mən) *n.* Also **eu·dae·mon.** A good or benevolent spirit. [EU- + DEMON.]

eu·de·mo·ni·a (yōō'dĭ-mō'nē-ə) *n.* Also **eu·dae·mo·ni·a.** Happiness or well-being; especially, in Aristotelian philosophy, happiness resulting from an active, rational life. [Greek *eudaimonia*, from *eudaimōn*, lucky, with a good spirit : *eu-*, good + *daimōn*, spirit (see **dā-** in Appendix*).]

eu·de·mon·ics (yōō'dĭ-mŏn'ĭks) *n.* Also **eu·dae·mon·ics.** Plural in form, used with a singular verb. **1.** The art or theory of happiness. **2.** Eudemonism. —**eu'de·mon'ic** *adj.*

eu·de·mon·ism (yōō-dē'mə-nĭz'əm) *n.* Also **eu·dae·mon·ism.** A system of ethics that evaluates the morality of actions in terms of their capacity to produce happiness. —**eu·de'mon·ist** *n.* —**eu·de'mon·is'tic, eu·de'mon·is'ti·cal** *adj.*

Eu·gene[1] (yōō-jēn', yōō'jēn'). A masculine given name. [French *Eugène*, from Latin *Eugenius*, from Greek *Eugenios*, from *eugenēs*, well-born, noble : EU- + -GEN.]

Eu·gene[2] (yōō-jēn'). A city and industrial center on the Willamette River in western Oregon. Population, 70,000.

eu·gen·i·cist (yōō-jĕn'ə-sĭst) *n.* Also **eu·gen·ist** (yōō'jə-nĭst). An advocate of or specialist in eugenics.

eu·gen·ics (yōō-jĕn'ĭks) *n.* Plural in form, used with a singular verb. The study of hereditary improvement, especially of human improvement by genetic control. Compare **euthenics.** [From Greek *eugenēs*, well-born : EU- + -GEN.] —**eu·gen'ic** *adj.*

Eu·gé·nie (œ-zhā-nē'). Full name, Eugénie Marie de Montijo de Guzmán. 1826–1920. Empress of France (1853–71) as wife of Napoleon III.

eu·ge·nol (yōō'jə-nôl', -nōl', -nŏl') *n.* A colorless aromatic oil, $C_{10}H_{12}O_2$, found in cloves and used in perfumes and germicides. [New Latin *Eugenia*, genus of the clove, after *Eugene*, Prince of Savoy (died 1736) + -OL.]

eu·gle·na (yōō-glē'nə) *n.* Any of various minute unicellular freshwater organisms of the genus *Euglena*, characterized by the presence of chlorophyll, a reddish eyespot, and a single anterior flagellum. [New Latin : EU- + Greek *glēnē*, eyeball (see **gel-**[2] in Appendix*).]

eu·he·mer·ism (yōō-hē'mə-rĭz'əm, -hĕm'ə-rĭz'əm) *n.* **1.** A theory attributing the origin of the gods to the deification of historical heroes. **2.** Any similar theory linking mythology or folklore with real persons or events. [Developed by *Euhemerus* (circa 300 B.C.), Greek philosopher.] —**eu·he'mer·ist** *n.* —**eu·he'mer·is'tic** *adj.* —**eu·he'mer·is'ti·cal·ly** *adv.*

eu·he·mer·ize (yōō-hē'mə-rīz', -hĕm'ə-rīz') *tr.v.* **-ized, -izing, -izes.** To explain or interpret (myths) euhemeristically.

eu·la·chon (yōō'lə-kŏn') *n.*, *pl.* **eulachon** or **-chons.** The **candlefish** *(see).* [Chinook *vlâkân.*]

Eu·ler-Chel·pin (oi'lər-kĕl'pĭn), **Hans von.** 1873–1964. Swedish-born German chemist; worked on enzymes.

eu·lo·gize (yōō'lə-jīz') *tr.v.* **-gized, -gizing, -gizes.** To write or deliver a eulogy about or for; praise highly; extol. —**eu'lo·gist** (-jĭst), **eu'lo·giz'er** *n.*

eu·lo·gy (yōō'lə-jē) *n.*, *pl.* **-gies. 1.** A public speech or written tribute extolling the virtues or achievements of a person or thing; especially, an oration honoring one recently deceased. **2.** Great praise or commendation: *"The amount of sugary eulogy which James and Elizabeth could absorb was marvelous"* (Catherine Drinker Bowen). [Middle English *euloge*, from Medieval Latin *eulogium*, probably variant of *eulogia*, from Greek, praise, eulogy : EU- + -LOGY.] —**eu'lo·gis'tic** *adj.*

Eu·men·i·des (yōō-mĕn'ə-dēz') *pl.n.* *Greek Mythology.* The Furies. [Latin, from Greek, "well-minded (ones)," euphemism for the Furies, from *eumenēs*, kindly, well-disposed : *eu-*, well + *menos*, spirit, soul (see **men-**[1] in Appendix*).]

Eu·nice (yōō'nĭs). A feminine given name. [Latin, from Greek *Eunikē*, "good victory" : *eu-*, good + *nikē*, victory (see **nikē** in Appendix*).]

eu·nuch (yōō'nək) *n.* A castrated man; especially, one of those

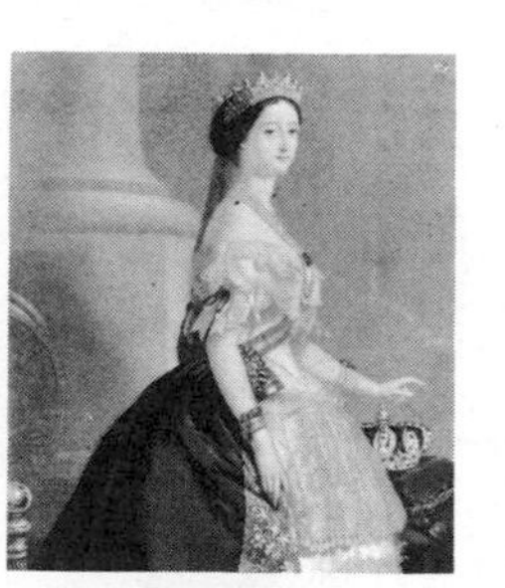
Eugénie

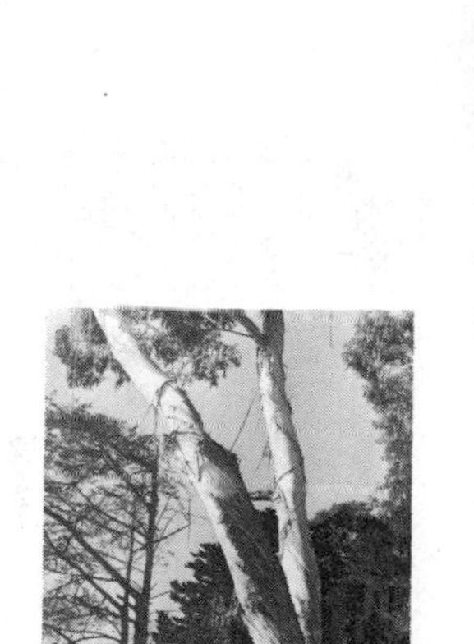

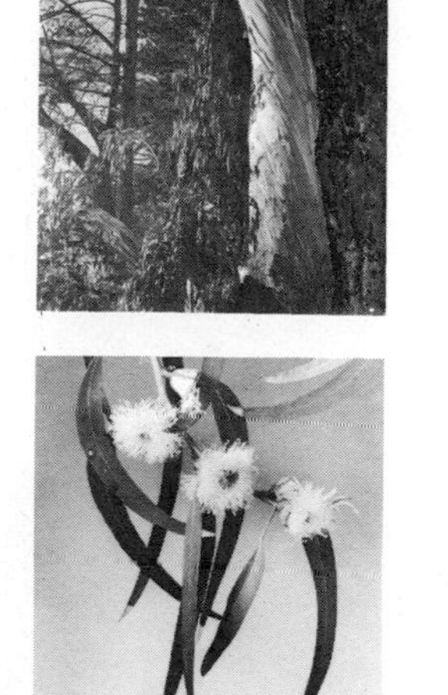
eucalyptus
Above: Eucalyptus globulus
Below: Flowers and leaves

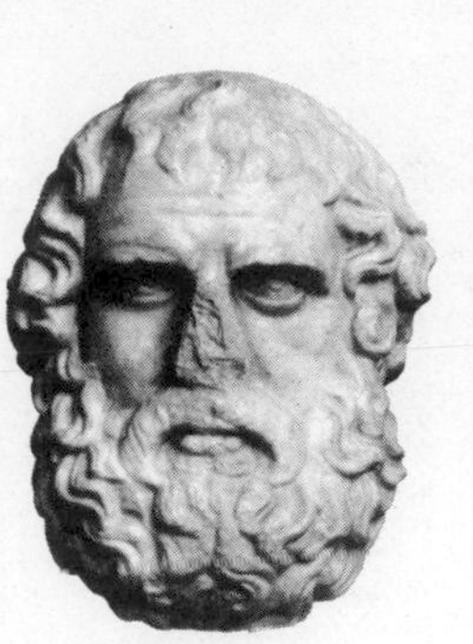
Euripides
Hellenistic sculpture

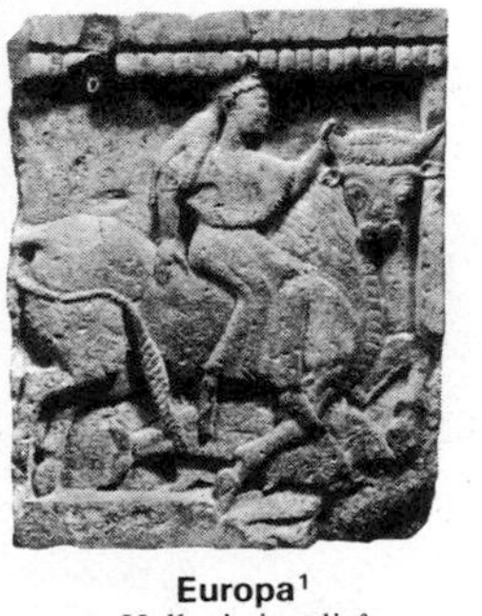
Europa[1]
Hellenistic relief

who were employed as harem attendants or functionaries in certain Oriental courts and under the Roman emperors. **2.** A man whose testes have not developed. [Middle English *eunuke,* from Latin *eunūchus,* from Greek *eunoukhos,* "bed-watcher," eunuch : *eunē*†, bed + *ekhein,* to have, to hold (see **segh-** in Appendix*).]

eu·on·y·mus (yōō-ŏn′ə-məs) *n.* Any of various trees, shrubs, or vines of the genus *Euonymus,* many of which are cultivated for their decorative foliage or fruits. [New Latin, from Latin *euōnymus,* spindle, tree, from Greek *euōnumos,* of good name : *eu-,* good + *onoma,* name (see **nomen-** in Appendix*).]

eu·pat·rid (yōō-păt′rĭd, yōō′pə-trĭd) *n., pl.* **-patridae** (-păt′rə-dē′) or **-rids.** Also **Eu·pat·rid.** A member of the hereditary aristocracy of ancient Athens. [Greek *eupatridēs,* of noble family : *eu-,* well + *patēr* (stem *patr-*), father (see **peter** in Appendix*) + *-idēs,* patronymic suffix.] —**eu′pat·rid** *adj.*

eu·pep·si·a (yōō-pĕp′sē-ə, -shə) *n.* Good digestion. [New Latin, from Greek, from *eupeptos,* EUPEPTIC.]

eu·pep·tic (yōō-pĕp′tĭk) *adj.* **1.** Pertaining to or having good digestion. **2.** Conducive to digestion. [From Greek *eupeptos,* having good digestion : *eu-,* well + *peptein,* to digest, cook (see **pekw-** in Appendix*).]

eu·phe·mism (yōō′fə-mĭz′əm) *n.* **1.** The substitution of an inoffensive term for one considered offensively explicit. **2.** The term thus substituted: *"Euphemisms such as 'slumber room' . . . abound in the funeral business"* (Jessica Mitford). [Greek *euphēmismos,* from *euphēmizein,* to speak with good words, from *euphēmia,* use of good words : *eu-,* good + *phēmē,* speech, saying (see **bhā-²** in Appendix*).] —**eu′phe·mist** *n.* —**eu′phe·mis′tic** (-mĭs′tĭk) *adj.* —**eu′phe·mis′ti·cal·ly** *adv.*

eu·phe·mize (yōō′fə-mīz′) *v.* **-mized, -mizing, -mizes.** —*tr.* To speak of or refer to euphemistically. —*intr.* To speak with euphemisms.

eu·phon·ic (yōō-fŏn′ĭk) *adj.* **1.** Pertaining or relating to euphony. **2.** Euphonious. —**eu·phon′i·cal·ly** *adv.*

eu·pho·ni·ous (yōō-fō′nē-əs) *adj.* Pertaining to or characterized by euphony; agreeable to the ear: *"Nevil Shute was quite a good euphonious name for an author"* (Nevil Shute). —**eu·pho′ni·ous·ly** *adv.*

eu·pho·ni·um (yōō-fō′nē-əm) *n.* A brass wind instrument, similar to the tuba, but having a somewhat higher pitch and a mellower sound. [From Greek *euphōnos,* sweet-voiced. See **euphony.**]

eu·pho·nize (yōō′fə-nīz′) *tr.v.* **-nized, -nizing, -nizes.** To make euphonious.

eu·pho·ny (yōō′fə-nē) *n., pl.* **-nies. 1.** Agreeable sound, especially in the phonetic quality of words. **2.** *Phonetics.* The tendency to change speech sounds for the sake of easier pronunciation. [French *euphonie,* from Late Latin *euphōnia,* from Greek, from *euphōnos,* sweet-voiced, euphonious : *eu-,* good + *phōnē,* sound (see **bhā-²** in Appendix*).]

eu·phor·bi·a (yōō-fôr′bē-ə) *n.* Any plant of the genus *Euphorbia,* which includes the spurges. [New Latin, from Latin *euphorbea,* from *Euphorbus,* Greek physician of the first century A.D.]

eu·pho·ri·a (yōō-fôr′ē-ə, -fōr′ē-ə) *n.* **1.** A feeling of great happiness or well-being; bliss. **2.** *Psychiatry.* An exaggerated sense of well-being in pathological cases involving sympathetic delusions. —See Synonyms at **ecstasy.** [New Latin, from Greek, from *euphoros,* easy to bear, well-borne : *eu-,* well + *pherein,* to bear (see **bher-¹** in Appendix*).] —**eu·phor′ic** *adj.*

eu·pho·ri·ant (yōō-fôr′ē-ənt, -fōr′ē-ənt) *adj.* Tending to produce euphoria. —*n.* An agent that produces euphoria.

eu·phot·ic (yōō-fŏt′ĭk) *adj.* Pertaining to, designating, or characterizing the uppermost layer of a body of water, receiving sufficient light for photosynthesis and the growth of green plants. [EU- + PHOTIC.]

eu·phra·sy (yōō′frə-sē′) *n. Archaic.* A plant of the genus *Euphrasia;* eyebright. [Middle English *eufrasie,* from Medieval Latin *eufrasia,* from Greek *euphrasia,* good cheer, from *euphrainein,* to cheer, gladden : *eu-,* good + *phrēn,* mind (see **gwhren-** in Appendix*).]

Eu·phra·tes (yōō-frā′tēz). A river of southwestern Asia, flowing some 2,235 miles from east-central Turkey, through northeastern Syria and central Iraq, to the Tigris River with which it forms the Shatt-al-Arab. [Latin *Euphrātes,* from Greek *Euphratēs,* from Avestan *hupərəthwa,* "good to cross over," the Euphrates. See **per-²** in Appendix.*]

eu·phroe (yōō′frō′) *n.* Also **u·phroe. 1.** *Nautical.* A perforated batten through which the lines of a crowfoot are reeved to suspend an awning. **2.** A piece of wood having holes through which a tent rope, for example, is passed, and by means of which tension on the rope can be adjusted. [Dutch *juffrouw,* maiden, euphroe, from Middle Dutch *joncfrouwe.* See **per¹** in Appendix.*]

Eu·phros·y·ne (yōō-frŏz′ə-nē′). *Greek Mythology.* One of the three Graces. [Latin *Euphrosynē,* from Greek *Euphrosunē,* "mirth," from *euphrōn,* of good mind, cheerful : *eu-,* good + *phrēn,* mind (see **gwhren-** in Appendix*).]

eu·phu·ism (yōō′fyōō-ĭz′əm) *n.* **1.** An affectedly elegant style of speech or writing, especially the literary style used by imitators of John Lyly in the late 16th and early 17th centuries, characterized by elaborate alliteration, antitheses, and similes. **2.** Any affectation of elegance or style: *"Among his contemporaries, Willie's euphuisms only raised a laugh"* (Aldous Huxley). [After *Euphues,* a character in two works by John Lyly, from Greek *euphuēs,* shapely, well-grown : *eu-,* well + *phuein,* to grow, to bring forth (see **bheu-** in Appendix*).] —**eu′phu·ist** *n.* —**eu′phu·is′tic, eu′phu·is′ti·cal** *adj.* —**eu′phu·is′ti·cal·ly** *adv.*

eu·plas·tic (yōō-plăs′tĭk) *adj.* Healing readily. [EU- + PLASTIC.]

eup·ne·a (yōōp-nē′ə, yōōp′nē-ə) *n.* Normal, unlabored breathing. [New Latin, from Greek *eupnoia,* from *eupnoos,* breathing well : *eu-,* good + *pnoē, pnoiē,* a breathing, from *pnein,* to breathe (see **pneu-** in Appendix*).]

Eur. Europe; European.

Eur·a·sia (yōō-rā′zhə). The continents of Europe and Asia, and their offshore islands. [EUR(OPE) + ASIA.]

Eur·a·sian (yōō-rā′zhən) *adj.* **1.** Of, pertaining to, or originating in Eurasia. **2.** Of mixed European and Asian ancestry. —*n.* A person of mixed European and Asian ancestry.

EURATOM (yōōr′ăt′əm) European Atomic Energy Commission.

eu·re·ka (yōō-rē′kə) *interj.* Used to express triumph upon finding or discovering something. [Greek *heurēka,* "I have found (it)" (exclaimed by Archimedes when, while bathing, he discovered the means of measurement of volume of an irregular solid by the displacement of water, and thus was able to determine the purity of a gold crown belonging to the tyrant of Syracuse), perfect indicative of *heuriskein,* to find. See **wer-¹** in Appendix.*]

eu·rhyth·mics. Variant of **eurythmics.**

eu·rhyth·my. Variant of **eurythmy.**

Eu·rip·i·des (yōō-rĭp′ə-dēz′). 480?–406 B.C. Greek dramatist; author of 19 extant plays.

eu·ri·pus (yōō-rī′pəs) *n., pl.* **-pi** (-pī′). A sea channel characterized by turbulent and unpredictable currents in either direction. [Latin, from Greek *euripos,* strait, place where the current is violent : *eu-,* thoroughly (well) + *ripē,* rush, force, from *rīptein,* to throw (see **wer-³** in Appendix*).]

eu·ro (yōōr′ō) *n., pl.* **-ros.** A kangaroo, the **wallaroo** *(see).* [From a native name in Australia.]

Eur·o·mar·ket (yōōr′ō-mär′kĭt) *n.* The **Common Market** *(see).* [EURO(PE) + MARKET.]

Eur·o·mart (yōōr′ō-märt′) *n.* The **Common Market** *(see).*

Eu·ro·pa¹ (yōō-rō′pə). *Greek Mythology.* A Phoenician princess abducted to Crete by Zeus, in the guise of a white bull.

Eu·ro·pa² (yōō-rō′pə) *n.* A female form representing Europe.

Eu·rope (yōōr′əp). *Abbr.* **Eur.** A continent, about 3,700,000 square miles in area, consisting of the section of the Eurasian land mass that extends westward from a line marked unofficially by the Dardanelles, the Black Sea, the Ural River, and the Ural Mountains. [Latin *Eurōpa,* from Greek *Eurōpē,* Europe, possibly of Semitic origin and originally meaning "land of the setting sun."]

Eu·ro·pe·an (yōōr′ə-pē′ən) *adj. Abbr.* **Eur. 1.** Of or derived from the continent of Europe, its peoples, cultures, or languages. **2.** Indigenous to or native to Europe. —*n.* **1.** A native or inhabitant of Europe. **2.** One of European ancestry.

European Economic Community. The official name for the **Common Market** *(see).*

Eu·ro·pe·an·ize (yōōr′ə-pē′ə-nīz′) *tr.v.* **-ized, -izing, -izes.** To make European. —**Eu′ro·pe′an·i·za′tion** *n.*

European plan. A system of hotel management in which a guest pays for his room and services separately from his payment for meals. Distinguished from **American plan.**

European Recovery Program. An American economic aid program to European nations following World War II, initiated by George C. Marshall. Also called "Marshall Plan."

eu·ro·pi·um (yōō-rō′pē-əm) *n. Symbol* **Eu** A silvery-white, soft, rare-earth element occurring in monazite and bastnaesite and used as a laser dopant and to absorb neutrons in research. Atomic number 63, atomic weight 151.96, melting point 826°C, boiling point 1,439°C, specific gravity 5.259, valences 2, 3. See **element.** [New Latin, from EUROPE.]

Eu·rus (yōōr′ĭs). *Greek Mythology.* The god of the east or southeast wind. [Latin, from Greek *Euros,* possibly from *heuein,* to burn, to singe. See **eus-** in Appendix.*]

eury–. Indicates wide or broad; for example, **eurypterid.** [New Latin, from Greek *euru-,* from *eurus,* wide. See **wer-⁸** in Appendix.*]

Eu·ry·a·le (yōō-rī′ə-lē). *Greek Mythology.* One of the Gorgons.

Eu·ryd·i·ce (yōō-rĭd′ə-sē′). *Greek Mythology.* The wife of Orpheus, who was permitted by Pluto to follow her husband out of Hades, provided that he refrain from looking back at her; Orpheus did look back, and Eurydice was doomed to return. [Latin, from Greek *Eurudikē,* "wide justice" : *euru-,* EURY- + *dikē,* justice, custom, law (see **deik-** in Appendix*).]

eu·ryp·ter·id (yōō-rĭp′tər-ĭd) *n.* Any of various large, extinct, segmented aquatic arthropods of the order Eurypterida, existing from the Ordovician to the Permian period. [New Latin *Eurypterida,* from *Eurypterus* (genus) : EURY- + -PTEROUS.]

Eu·rys·the·us (yōō-rĭs′thē-əs, -thōōs). *Greek Mythology.* The Argos king who imposed the 12 labors upon Hercules.

eu·ry·ther·mal (yōōr-ə-thûr′məl) *adj.* Also **eu·ry·ther·mic** (-mĭk), **eu·ry·ther·mous** (-məs). Adaptable to a wide range of temperatures. Said of an organism.

eu·ryth·mics (yōō-rĭth′mĭks) *n.* Also **eu·rhyth·mics.** Plural in form, used with a singular verb. The choreographic art of interpreting musical composition by a rhythmical, free-style graceful movement of the body in response to the rhythm of the music. [From EURYTHMY.] —**eu·ryth′mic** *adj.*

eu·ryth·my (yōō-rĭth′mē) *n.* Also **eu·rhyth·my. 1.** Harmony of proportion in architecture. **2.** Rhythmical or graceful movement. **3.** A system of rhythmical body movements in harmony with the rhythm of the spoken word, used in a form of dance training. [Latin *eurythmia,* from Greek *eurūthmia,* from *eurūthmos,* well-rhythmed : *eu-,* good + *ruthmos,* RHYTHM.]

Eu·sta·chian tube (yo͞o-stā′shən, -stā′kē-ən, -stā′shē-ən). A bony and cartilaginous tube through which the tympanic cavity communicates with the nasal part of the pharynx. [After Bartolommeo *Eustachio* (died 1517), Italian anatomist.]
eu·tax·y (yo͞o′tăk′sē) *n. Rare.* Good and fitting order or arrangement. [Greek *eutaxia*, from *eutaktos*, well-ordered : *eu-*, well + *taktos*, in order, from *tattein*, to put in order, to arrange (see **tāg-** in Appendix*).]
eu·tec·tic (yo͞o-tĕk′tĭk) *adj.* **1.** Of, pertaining to, or formed at the lowest possible temperature of solidification for any mixture of specified constituents. Said especially of alloys. **2.** Exhibiting the constitution or properties of a solid so formed. —*n.* **1.** A eutectic mixture, solution, or alloy. **2.** The eutectic temperature. [From Greek *eutēktos*, easily melted : *eu-*, well + *tēktos*, melted, from *tēkein*, to melt (see **tā-** in Appendix*).]
Eu·ter·pe (yo͞o-tûr′pē). *Greek Mythology.* The Muse of lyric poetry and music.
eu·tha·na·sia (yo͞o′thə-nā′zhə, -shə) *n.* **1.** The action of inducing the painless death of a person for reasons assumed to be merciful. **2.** An easy or painless death. [Greek : *eu-*, good + *thanatos*, death (see **dhwenə-** in Appendix*).]
eu·then·ics (yo͞o-thĕn′ĭks) *n.* Plural in form, often used with a singular verb. The study of the improvement of human functioning and well-being by adjustment of environment. Compare **eugenics.** [From Greek *euthenein*, to flourish, thrive. See **gwhen-[2]** in Appendix.*]
eu·troph·ic (yo͞o-trŏf′ĭk, -trō′fĭk) *n.* Designating a body of water in which the increase of mineral and organic nutrients has reduced the dissolved oxygen, producing an environment that favors plant over animal life. [Probably from German *eutroph*, from Greek *eutrophos*, well-nourished, from *eutrophein*, to thrive : *eu-*, well + *trephein*, to nourish (see **threph-** in Appendix*).] —**eu·troph′i·ca′tion** *n.*
eux·e·nite (yo͞ok′sə-nīt′) *n.* A lustrous blackish-brown mineral consisting primarily of cerium, erbium, titanium, uranium, and yttrium. [German *Euxenit*, from Greek *euxenos*, kind to strangers (it contains many rare or "strange" elements) : *eu-*, good + *xenos*, stranger (see **xenos** in Appendix*).]
eV electron volt.
EVA extravehicular activity.
e·vac·u·ant (ĭ-văk′yo͞o-ənt) *adj.* Causing evacuation of an organ, especially of the bowels. —*n.* An evacuant medicine or agent; purgative; emetic.
e·vac·u·ate (ĭ-văk′yo͞o-āt′) *v.* **-ated, -ating, -ates.** —*tr.* **1. a.** To cause to be empty by removing the contents of. **b.** To create a vacuum in. **2.** To excrete or discharge (waste matter), especially from the bowels. **3.** *Military.* **a.** To relinquish possession or occupation of (a town, fortress, or encampment, for example). **b.** To withdraw or send away (troops or inhabitants) from a threatened area. **4.** To withdraw or depart from; vacate. —*intr.* To withdraw from or vacate any place or area, especially a threatened area. [Latin *ēvacuāre*, to empty out, to evacuate : *ē-*, out, from *ex-* + *vacuus*, empty, from *vacāre*, to be empty (see **eu-[2]** in Appendix*).] —**e·vac′u·a′tor** (-ā′tər) *n.*
e·vac·u·a·tion (ĭ-văk′yo͞o-ā′shən) *n.* **1.** The act of evacuating, or the condition of being evacuated. **2.** *Physiology.* **a.** The excretion of waste materials from the excretory passages, especially from the bowels. **b.** The material thus discharged.
e·vac·u·ee (ĭ-văk′yo͞o-ē′) *n.* A person withdrawn or sent away from a threatened or dangerous area.
e·vade (ĭ-vād′) *v.* **evaded, evading, evades.** —*tr.* **1.** To escape or avoid by cleverness or deceit: *evade arrest.* **2.** To avoid fulfilling, answering, or performing: *evade responsibility.* **3.** To baffle or elude: *The accident evades explanation.* —*intr.* To use cleverness or deceit in avoiding or escaping. —See Synonyms at **escape.** [Old French *evader*, from Latin *ēvādere*, to evade, to go out, escape : *ē-*, out, from *ex-* + *vādere*, to go (see **wādh-** in Appendix*).] —**e·vad′a·ble, e·vad′i·ble** *adj.* —**e·vad′er** *n.*
e·vag·i·nate (ĭ-văj′ə-nāt′) *v.* **-nated, -nating, -nates.** —*intr.* To turn inside out by eversion of an inner surface of a part or organ. —*tr.* To cause (a body part) to turn inside out; protrude by inversion. [Latin *ēvāgināre*, to unsheath : *ē-* (indicating removal), from *ex-* + *vāgīna*, sheath (see **wag-** in Appendix*).] —**e·vag′i·na′tion** *n.*
e·val·u·ate (ĭ-văl′yo͞o-āt′) *tr.v.* **-ated, -ating, -ates.** **1.** To ascertain or fix the value or worth of. **2.** To examine and judge; appraise; estimate: *"Plato has been evaluated as having one of the finest minds the world has produced"* (S.E. Frost, Jr.). **3.** *Mathematics.* To calculate or set down the numerical value of; express numerically. —See Synonyms at **estimate.** [Back-formation from evaluation, from French *évaluation*, from Old French *evaluation*, from *evaluer*, to evaluate : *e-*, out, from Latin *ex-* + VALUE.] —**e·val′u·a′tion** *n.*
evan. evangelical; evangelist.
ev·a·nesce (ĕv′ə-nĕs′) *intr.v.* **-nesced, -nescing, -nesces.** To dissipate like vapor; disappear gradually; fade away; vanish. [Latin *ēvānēscere*, to vanish : *ē-*, completely, from *ex-* + *vānēscere*, to pass away, from *vānus*, empty, vain (see **eu-[2]** in Appendix*).] —**ev′a·nes′cence** *n.*
ev·a·nes·cent (ĕv′ə-nĕs′ənt) *adj.* Vanishing or likely to vanish; transitory; fleeting: *"Seeking permanence in the midst of what was only perpetually evanescent"* (Malcolm Lowry). See Synonyms at **transient.** —**ev′a·nes′cent·ly** *adv.*
evang. evangelical; evangelist.
e·van·gel (ĭ-văn′jəl) *n.* **1.** *Usually capital* **E.** The Christian gospel; especially, any of the four Gospels of the New Testament. **2.** Any glad tidings. **3.** An evangelist. [Middle English *evangelie*, from Old French *evangile*, from Late Latin *evangelium*, from *euangelion*, good news, reward for bringing good news, from *euangelos*, bringing good news : *eu-*, good + *angelos*, messenger (see **angelos** in Appendix*).]
e·van·gel·i·cal (ē′văn-jĕl′ĭ-kəl) *adj.* Also **e·van·gel·ic** (-jĕl′ĭk). *Abbr.* **evan., evang. 1.** Of, pertaining to, or in accordance with the Christian gospel, especially the four Gospels of the New Testament. **2.** *Often capital* **E.** Protestant. **3.** Of, pertaining to, or being a Protestant group emphasizing the authority of the Gospel and holding that salvation is from faith and grace rather than from good works and sacraments alone. **4.** Of or pertaining to the Evangelical Church in Germany. **5.** Pertaining or belonging to the Low Church party in the Church of England. —*n. Abbr.* **evan., evang.** A member of an evangelical church or party. —**e′van·gel′i·cal·ly** *adv.*
Evangelical and Reformed Church. A Protestant denomination organized in 1934 and a part of the United Church of Christ since 1957.
e·van·gel·i·cal·ism (ē′văn-jĕl′ĭ-kə-lĭz′əm) *n.* **1.** Evangelical beliefs or doctrines. **2.** Adherence to the churches or party professing such beliefs or doctrines.
Evangelical United Brethren. A former Protestant denomination created in 1947 by a merging of the Evangelical Church and the United Brethren and now forming a part of the **United Methodist Church** *(see).*
e·van·gel·ism (ĭ-văn′jə-lĭz′əm) *n.* **1.** The zealous preaching and dissemination of the gospel, as through missionary work. **2.** Militant zeal for any cause.
e·van·gel·ist (ĭ-văn′jə-lĭst) *n. Abbr.* **evan., evang. 1.** *Usually capital* **E.** Any of the authors of the four New Testament Gospels; Matthew, Mark, Luke, or John. **2.** One who practices evangelism, especially a Protestant preacher or missionary. **3.** A dignitary of the Mormon Church, a **patriarch** *(see).* —**e·van′gel·is′tic** *adj.* —**e·van′gel·is′ti·cal·ly** *adv.*
e·van·gel·ize (ĭ-văn′jə-līz′) *v.* **-ized, -izing, -izes.** —*tr.* **1.** To preach the gospel to. **2.** To convert to Christianity. —*intr.* To preach the gospel; be an evangelist. —**e·van′gel·i·za′tion** *n.* —**e·van′gel·iz′er** *n.*
Ev·ans, Mary Ann. See George **Eliot.**
Ev·ans (ĕv′ənz), **Oliver.** 1755–1819. American inventor of the high-pressure steam engine.
Ev·ans·ton (ĕv′ən-stən). A city in Illinois, on Lake Michigan, north of Chicago. Population, 79,000.
Ev·ans·ville (ĕv′ənz-vĭl, -vəl). A major city of Indiana, in the southwest on the Ohio River. Population, 102,000.
e·vap·o·ra·ble (ĭ-văp′ər-ə-bəl) *adj.* Capable of being evaporated. —**e·vap′o·ra·bil′i·ty** *n.*
e·vap·o·rate (ĭ-văp′ə-rāt′) *v.* **-rated, -rating, -rates.** —*tr.* **1. a.** To convert or change into a vapor. **b.** To draw off in the form of vapor. **2.** To draw moisture from, leaving only the dry solid portion. **3.** To deposit (a metal) on a substrate by vacuum sublimation. —*intr.* **1. a.** To change into vapor. **b.** To pass off in or as vapor. **2.** To produce vapor. **3.** To disappear; vanish: *His fears evaporated.* [Middle English *evaporaten*, from Latin *ēvapōrāre* (past participle *ēvapōrātus*), "to go out in vapor," evaporate : *ē-*, out of, from *ex-* + *vapor*, steam, vapor (see **kwēp-** in Appendix*).] —**e·vap′o·ra′tion** *n.* —**e·vap′o·ra′tive** *adj.* —**e·vap′o·ra′tor** (-rā′tər) *n.*
evaporated milk. Concentrated, unsweetened milk made by evaporating some of the water from whole milk. Compare **condensed milk.**
e·va·sion (ĭ-vā′zhən) *n.* **1.** The act of avoiding, evading, or escaping; dodging. **2.** A means of evading; an excuse; subterfuge. [Middle English *evasioun*, from Old French *evasion*, from Late Latin *ēvāsiō*, from Latin *ēvāsus*, past participle of *ēvādere*, to EVADE.]
e·va·sive (ĭ-vā′sĭv) *adj.* **1.** Characterized by or exhibiting evasion. **2.** Intentionally vague or ambiguous; equivocal: *an evasive statement.* —**e·va′sive·ly** *adv.* —**e·va′sive·ness** *n.*
eve (ēv) *n.* **1.** *Often capital* **E.** The evening or day preceding a special day, such as a saint's day or holiday. **2.** The period immediately preceding a certain event: *the eve of war.* **3.** *Poetic.* Evening. [Middle English *eve*, variant of EVEN (evening).]
Eve[1] (ēv). A feminine given name. [Middle English *Eve*, Old English *Ēfe, Ēve*, from Late Latin *Ēva*, from Hebrew *Ḥawwah*, "living," from *ḥāwa, ḥāya*, to live.]
Eve[2] (ēv). In the Bible, the first woman and wife of Adam. Genesis 3:20.
e·vec·tion (ĭ-vĕk′shən) *n.* Solar perturbation of the lunar orbit. [Latin *ēvectiō*, a going up, from *ēvectus*, past participle of *ēvehere*, to carry out : *ē-*, out, upward, from *ex-* + *vehere*, to carry (see **wegh-** in Appendix*).] —**e·vec′tion·al** *adj.*
Ev·e·lyn (ĕv′ə-lĭn; *British* ēv′lĭn). A feminine or masculine given name. [Middle English *Avelyn*, from Norman French *Aveline*, from Old High German *Avelina*, from *Avi*†, a given name.]
Eve·lyn (ēv′lĭn), **John.** 1620–1706. English diarist.
e·ven[1] (ē′vən) *adj.* **1. a.** Having a horizontal surface; flat: *an even floor.* **b.** Having no irregularities, roughness, or indentations; smooth. **2.** Having the same plane or line; at the same height or depth; parallel; level: *The picture is even with the window.* **3.** Having no variations or fluctuations; uniform; steady; regular: *an even rate of speed.* **4.** Of uniform thickness; uniformly distributed: *an even application of varnish.* **5.** Tranquil; calm; peaceful: *an even temper.* **6.** Equally matched or balanced. Said of a competition: *an even fight.* **7.** Equal or identical in degree, extent, or amount: *even amounts of wine and water.* **8.** Having equal probability. Said of alternatives, possibilities, or events: *an even chance of winning or losing.* **9. a.** Having an equal score: *The teams are even.* **b.** Being equal for each opponent. Said of a score. **10.** Neither owing nor being owed; having nothing due: *Give him five dollars, and you*

will be even. **11.** Having exacted full revenge. **12. a.** *Mathematics.* Exactly divisible by 2. **b.** Characterized or indicated by a number exactly divisible by 2. Compare **odd.** **13. a.** Having an even number in a series. **b.** Having an even number of members. **14.** Having an exact amount, extent, or number: *an even pound.* —See Synonyms at **steady, level.** —*adv.* **1.** To a higher degree or extent; yet; still. Used as an intensive: *an even worse condition.* **2.** At the same time as; just: *Even as we watched, the building collapsed.* **3.** In spite of; nevertheless; notwithstanding: *Even with his head start, I soon overtook him.* **4.** Indeed; in fact; moreover. Used as an intensive: *unhappy, even weeping.* **5.** To a degree that extends to: *loyal even unto death.* **6.** *Archaic.* The same as; identical with: *It is I, even I.* **7.** *Nonstandard.* Smoothly; evenly. —**break even.** *Informal.* To have neither losses nor gains. —**get even.** To exact one's full measure of revenge. —*v.* **evened, evening, evens.** —*tr.* **1.** To make even, smooth, or level. **2.** To settle or balance (accounts, debts, or the like); to square. Used with *off* or *up.* —*intr.* To become even or smooth. Used with *up* or *off.* [Middle English *even,* Old English *ef(e)n,* even, level, from Common Germanic *ibnaz* (unattested).] —**e'ven·ly** *adv.* —**e'ven·ness** *n.*

e·ven[2] (ē'vən) *n. Archaic.* **1.** Evening. **2.** The eve preceding an event. [Middle English *eve, even,* Old English *ǣfen.* See **apo-** in Appendix.*]

e·ven·fall (ē'vən-fôl') *n. Poetic.* The beginning of evening; twilight; dusk.

e·ven·hand·ed (ē'vən-hăn'dĭd) *adj.* Dealing equitably with all; impartial. —**e'ven·hand'ed·ly** *adv.* —**e'ven·hand'ed·ness** *n.*

eve·ning (ēv'nĭng) *n. Abbr.* **evg.** **1.** The period of decreasing daylight during the decline and setting of the sun between afternoon and nightfall. **2. a.** The period between the termination of one's daily activities and bedtime. **b.** This period occupied in a given manner: *an evening at home.* **3.** Any latter period or time of decline: *in the evening of his life.* [Middle English *evening,* Old English *ǣfnung,* evening, from *ǣfnian,* to become evening, from *ǣfen,* evening. See **apo-** in Appendix.*]

evening dress. Clothing, especially formal clothing, such as a man's tuxedo, worn for evening social events. Also called "evening clothes."

evening gown. A woman's formal dress, usually long, and worn especially in the evening.

Evening Prayer. *Anglican Church.* An evening prayer service which is read or sung. Also called "evensong," "vespers."

evening primrose. Any of various North American plants of the genus *Oenothera,* characteristically having four-petaled yellow flowers that open in the evening.

evening star. Any planet that crosses the local meridian before midnight, especially Mercury or Venus when either is prominent in the west shortly after sunset. Also, especially referring to Venus, formerly called "Vesper."

evening stock. A plant, *Mathiola bicornis,* native to Eurasia, having fragrant purple flowers that bloom at night. Also called "night-scented stock."

e·ven·song (ē'vən-sông', -sŏng') *n.* **1.** A song sung in the evening. **2.** A vesper service. **3.** *Archaic.* Evening. **4.** *Anglican Church.* **Evening Prayer** *(see).*

e·vent (ĭ-vĕnt') *n.* **1.** An occurrence, incident, or experience, especially one of some significance. **2.** The actual outcome or final result. **3.** One of the items in a program of sports. **4.** *Physics.* A coincidence of two or more point objects at a particular position in space at a particular instant of time, regarded as the fundamental observational entity in relativity theory. —See Synonyms at **occurrence.** —**in the event.** If it should happen; in case. [Latin *ēventus,* a coming out, event, from the past participle of *ēvenīre,* to come out, happen : *ē-,* out, from *ex-* + *venīre,* to come (see **gwā-** in Appendix*).]

e·vent·ful (ĭ-vĕnt'fəl) *adj.* **1.** Full of or abounding in events: *an eventful week.* **2.** Important; momentous: *an eventful decision.* —**e·vent'ful·ly** *adv.* —**e·vent'ful·ness** *n.*

e·ven·tide (ē'vən-tīd') *n. Poetic.* Evening. [Middle English *eventide,* Old English *ǣfentīd* : *ǣfen,* EVEN (evening) + *tīd,* time, season (see **dā-** in Appendix*).]

e·ven·tu·al (ĭ-vĕn'cho͞o-əl) *adj.* **1.** Occurring at an unspecified time in the future; ultimate: *his eventual death.* **2.** Dependent on circumstance; possible; contingent. —See Synonyms at **last.** [From EVENT.] —**e·ven'tu·al·ly** *adv.*

e·ven·tu·al·i·ty (ĭ-vĕn'cho͞o-ăl'ə-tē) *n., pl.* **-ties.** Something that may occur; contingency; possibility.

e·ven·tu·ate (ĭ-vĕn'cho͞o-āt') *intr.v.* **-ated, -ating, -ates.** To result ultimately: *Their debate eventuated in an agreement.*

ev·er (ĕv'ər) *adv.* **1. a.** At all times; always; constantly: *He is ever courteous.* **b.** Repeatedly. **2.** At any time: *Have you ever seen a circus?* **3.** By any chance; in any possible way or case; at all. Used frequently for emphasis: *How could you ever treat him so?* —**ever and ever** (or **anon**). Now and then; occasionally. —**ever so.** *Informal.* To an extreme extent or degree; very: *ever so glad.* —**ever so often.** Frequently. See Usage note below. —**for ever and a day.** Always; forever. [Middle English *ever,* Old English *ǣfre.* See **aiw-** in Appendix.*]

Usage: *Ever so often* is equivalent to *frequently* or *repeatedly.* It is distinguished from, and not interchangeable with, *every so often,* which is equivalent to *occasionally* or *now and then. Ever so often* is sometimes employed in the senses appropriate to the other expression, but not acceptably so, according to 74 per cent of the Usage Panel. See also Usage note at **rarely.**

Ev·er·est, Mount (ĕv'ər-ĭst, ĕv'rĭst). *Tibetan* **Cho·mo·lung·ma** (chō'mə-lo͞ong'mə). A mountain in the Himalayas on the border of Nepal and Tibet, the highest peak in the world (29,028 feet).

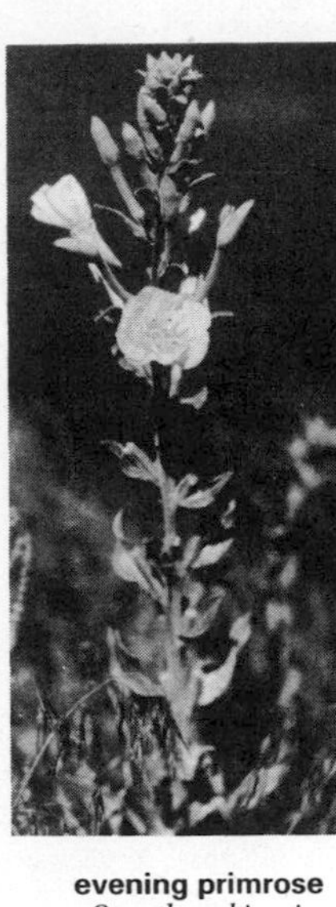

evening primrose
Oenothera biennis

Ev·er·ett (ĕv'rĭt, ĕv'ər-ĭt). A city and port in Washington, on Puget Sound, 25 miles north of Seattle. Population, 51,000.

Ev·er·ett (ĕv'ər-ĭt, ĕv'rĭt), **Edward.** 1794–1865. American Unitarian minister, orator, and educator.

ev·er·glade (ĕv'ər-glād') *n.* A tract of marsh land, usually under water and covered in places with tall grass; a swamp. [Perhaps EVER ("interminable") + GLADE (open space).]

Everglades, The. A subtropical swamp on a limestone plateau in southern Florida, including the Everglades National Park, an area occupying 1,719 square miles and reserved to protect the abundant wildlife and tropical plants.

ev·er·green (ĕv'ər-grēn') *adj.* **1. a.** Having foliage that persists and remains green throughout the year: *evergreen trees.* **b.** Persisting and remaining green throughout the year: *evergreen foliage.* Compare **deciduous.** **2.** Remaining fresh. —*n.* **1.** An evergreen tree, shrub, or plant. **2.** *Plural.* Twigs or branches of evergreen plants used as decorations.

ev·er·last·ing (ĕv'ər-lăs'tĭng, -läs'tĭng) *adj.* **1.** Lasting forever; eternal. **2.** Continuing indefinitely or for a long period of time; perpetual. **3.** Retaining color and form for a long time when cut or dried, as certain plants. —*n.* **1.** *Capital* **E.** God. Preceded by *the.* **2.** Eternal duration; eternity. **3.** Any of various plants, such as the strawflower or one of the genus *Anaphalis,* that retain form and color long after they are dry.

ev·er·more (ĕv'ər-môr', -mōr') *adv.* **1.** Forever. Obsolete except in the phrase *for evermore.* **2.** Constantly; always.

e·ver·sion (ĭ-vûr'zhən, -shən) *n.* **1.** The act of everting. **2.** The state of being everted. [Middle English *eversioun,* from Old French *eversion,* from Latin *ēversiō,* from *ēversus,* past participle of *ēvertere,* to EVERT.] —**e·ver'si·ble** *adj.*

e·vert (ĭ-vûrt') *tr.v.* **everted, everting, everts.** To turn inside out or outward. [Latin *ēvertere,* to turn out, overturn : *ē-,* out, from *ex-* + *vertere,* to turn (see **wer-**[3] in Appendix*).]

eve·ry (ĕv'rē, -ə-rē) *adj.* **1.** Each and all single members of an aggregate; each without exception: *every student in the class.* **2.** Each particular member of a series. Used where a qualification is involved: *every third seat; every two hours.* **3.** Each thing or all possible things without exception; no matter which or when: *arrive late at every party.* **4.** The highest degree or expression of; the utmost; the greatest: *gave him every care.* —*adv.* More or less; periodically. Used as an intensifier with idioms indicating indefinite or occasional recurrence: *every once in a while.* —**every bit.** *Informal.* In all ways; quite; equally: *He is every bit as mean as she is.* —**every other.** Each alternate; each second: *Leave every other door unmarked.* —**every so often.** Occasionally. See Usage note at **ever.** —**every which way.** *Informal.* In complete disorder; chaotic. [Middle English *every, everich, everulch,* Old English *ǣfre ǣlc,* "ever each," every, each one : *ǣfre,* EVER + *ǣlc,* EACH.]

eve·ry·bod·y (ĕv'rē-bŏd'ē) *pron.* Every person; everyone. See Usage note at **everyone.**

eve·ry·day (ĕv'rē-dā') *adj.* **1.** Suitable for ordinary days or routine occasions: *an everyday suit.* **2.** Commonplace; usual; ordinary: *everyday worries.*

every one. Each person or thing comprising a group: *Every one of my geraniums died.* See Usage note at **everyone.**

eve·ry·one (ĕv'rē-wŭn') *pron.* Every person; everybody.

Usage: *Everyone* and *everybody* as subjects take singular verbs. Especially in formal usage, accompanying pronouns and pronominal adjectives are also singular: *Everyone* (or *everybody*) *has the right to speak his mind.* Frequently in speech and less often in writing, *their* is substituted for the singular *his* in such examples, on the ground that *their* has a more natural sound, since it has a sense that corresponds with *all* and takes into account the possibility of the presence of both sexes. *His* is still more frequent in formal writing, however, and is appropriate to such examples despite its masculine form, since it refers to an indefinite pronoun. An alternative possibility is *his or her,* for either *his* or *their,* but many writers and speakers would regard this as a cumbersome choice. In usage, *everyone* and the two-word form *every one* occupy separate roles. *Everyone* is the choice when *everybody* can be substituted for it; that is, when the sense is that of *every person,* considered indefinitely: *Everyone knew what he meant. Every one* refers to each person or thing of a specific group; it is typically followed by *of,* or else *of* and an object are implied: *Every one of them is at fault* (or *Every one is at fault*). *There are six possibilities, every one of which involves difficulty.*

eve·ry·place (ĕv'rē-plās') *adv. Informal.* Everywhere.

Usage: *Everyplace* and *every place,* used adverbially for *everywhere,* are appropriate principally to informal writing or dialogue or to casual speech. *Everywhere* is preferable on a formal level. This does not apply to the phrase *every place,* used as adjective and noun and always written as two words, which is acceptable on all levels in examples such as: *Every place is occupied. I searched in every place that he mentioned.*

eve·ry·thing (ĕv'rē-thĭng') *pron.* **1.** All things or factors that exist or pertain to a given instance; the entirety or totality: *everything in this room.* **2.** All relevant items or factors: *Tell him everything.* **3.** The most important fact or consideration, especially for success or happiness; principal concern: *Her children mean everything to her.* **4.** All aspects of something; life in general: *everything went wrong.*

eve·ry·where (ĕv'rē-hwâr') *adv.* In any or every place; in all places. See Usage note at **everyplace.**

evg. evening.

e·vict (ĭ-vĭkt') *tr.v.* **evicted, evicting, evicts.** **1.** To expel (a tenant, for example) by legal process; put out. **2.** To force out; eject; dispossess: *"We have allowed the Communists to evict us* *from our rightful estate"* (John F. Kennedy). **3.** To recover (property, for example) by a superior claim or legal process. —See Synonyms at **eject.** [Middle English *evicten,* from Latin *ēvincere* (past participle *ēvictus*), to conquer, overcome : *ē-,* completely, from *ex-* + *vincere,* to conquer (see **weik-**[5] in Appendix*).] —**e·vic′tion** *n.* —**e·vic′tor** (-tər) *n.*

ev·i·dence (ĕv′ə-dəns) *n.* **1.** The data on which a judgment or conclusion may be based, or by which proof or probability may be established: *fossilized evidence of climatic change.* **2.** That which serves to indicate or suggest: *His reaction was evidence of guilt.* **3.** *Law.* The documentary or verbal statements and the material objects admissible as testimony in a court of law. —**in evidence.** Present and plainly visible; conspicuous: *He was very much in evidence at the convention.* —**turn state's evidence.** To testify in court for the prosecution and against one's former accomplices. —*tr.v.* **evidenced, -dencing, -dences. 1.** To indicate clearly; exemplify or prove. **2.** To support by testimony; attest. [Middle English, from Old French, from Late Latin *ēvidentia,* from Latin *ēvidēns,* EVIDENT.]

ev·i·dent (ĕv′ə-dənt) *adj.* Easily recognizable or perceived; clear; obvious. [Middle English, from Old French, from Latin *ēvidēns,* evident, clear : *ē-,* completely, from *ex-* + *vidēns,* present participle of *vidēre,* to see (see **weid-** in Appendix*).]

Synonyms: *evident, apparent, obvious, plain, distinct, manifest.* These adjectives mean easily perceived or grasped. *Evident* and *apparent* are often interchangeable and imply the presence of visible signs or circumstances that make the thing in question clear to the eye or, by inference, to the mind. *Apparent* stresses the idea of openness to view. The remaining terms are intensifications of the first two. What is *obvious* is not only readily seen or understood but almost impossible to conceal or to misunderstand. What is *plain* is readily accessible to the mind because it is simple or permits but one interpretation. Something termed *distinct* is clearly seen and not easily confused with something else. Something *manifest* is revealed clearly and openly by outward display; the term therefore stresses visual perception.

ev·i·den·tial (ĕv′ə-dĕn′shəl) *adj.* Pertaining to, providing, or having the nature of evidence. —**ev′i·den′tial·ly** *adv.*

ev·i·dent·ly (ĕv′ə-dənt-lē, ĕv′ə-dĕnt′lē) *adv.* **1.** Obviously; perceptibly; clearly: *He was quite evidently dead.* **2.** Apparently or seemingly; probably: *She's evidently going to be late.*

e·vil (ē′vəl) *adj.* **1.** Morally bad or wrong; wicked; malevolent; sinful: *an evil tyrant.* **2.** Causing an undesirable condition, as ruin, injury, or pain; harmful; injurious: *an evil suggestion.* **3.** Characterized by or boding misfortune; foreboding; ominous: *evil omens.* **4.** Purportedly bad or blameworthy; undesirable; infamous: *an evil reputation.* **5.** Characterized by anger or spite; malicious: *an evil temper.* —See Synonyms at **bad.** —*n.* **1.** *Sometimes capital* **E.** That which is destructive, corruptive, or fallible whether from natural circumstances, or by human ignorance, error, or design: *"The evil that men do lives after them"* (Shakespeare). **2.** *Sometimes capital* **E. a.** That which is morally bad or wrong; wickedness; sin. **b.** That which causes or constitutes misfortune, suffering, difficulty, or the like; woe. **3.** *Often plural.* Anything that is undesirable because of its injurious nature or effect: *the evils of war.* **4.** An evil thing or an act or instance of being evil. —*adv. Archaic.* In an evil manner. [Middle English *evel, ivel,* Old English *yfel.* See **upo** in Appendix.*] —**e′vil·ly** *adv.* —**e′vil·ness** *n.*

e·vil·do·er (ē′vəl-dōō′ər) *n.* One who does evil. —**e′vil·do′ing** *n.*

evil eye. A look or a stare superstitiously believed to cause injury or misfortune to others.

e·vil-mind·ed (ē′vəl-mīn′dĭd) *adj.* Having evil thoughts, opinions, or intentions. —**e′vil-mind′ed·ly** *adv.* —**e′vil-mind′ed·ness** *n.*

e·vince (ĭ-vĭns′) *tr.v.* **evinced, evincing, evinces.** To show or demonstrate clearly or convincingly; manifest; exhibit: *"To evince surprise at her husband's statement was part of her wifely amiability"* (Stephen Crane). [Latin *ēvincere,* to conquer, to prove. See **evict.**] —**e·vin′ci·ble** *adj.*

e·vis·cer·ate (ĭ-vĭs′ə-rāt′) *v.* **-ated, -ating, -ates.** —*tr.* **1.** To remove the entrails of; disembowel. **2.** To take away a vital or essential part of. **3.** *Surgery.* **a.** To remove the contents of (an eyeball). **b.** To remove an organ, such as an eye, from (a patient). —*intr. Surgery.* To protrude through an incision of a part after an operation. —*adj.* Disemboweled. [Latin *ēviscerāre,* "to remove the viscera from," to disembowel : *ē-,* indicating removal, from *ex-* + VISCERA.] —**e·vis′cer·a′tion** *n.*

ev·i·ta·ble (ĕv′ə-tə-bəl) *adj. Rare.* Avoidable. [Latin *ēvītābilis,* from *ēvītāre,* to avoid : *ē-,* away, from *ex-* + *vītāre*†, to shun.]

ev·o·ca·tion (ĕv′ə-kā′shən) *n.* **1.** The act of calling forth or conjuring up: *an evocation of childhood memories.* **2.** *Law.* The power of a higher court to try all the aspects of a case that has been appealed. —**ev′o·ca′tor** (-kā′tər) *n.*

e·voc·a·tive (ĭ-vŏk′ə-tĭv) *adj.* Tending or having the power to evoke. —**e·voc′a·tive·ly** *adv.*

e·voke (ĭ-vōk′) *tr.v.* **evoked, evoking, evokes. 1.** To summon or call forth (memories, for example); reawaken; inspire. **2.** To produce or elicit (a reaction, emotion, or response): *"Every slight movement in the street evoked a casual curiosity in him"* (Richard Wright). [Latin *ēvocāre,* to call forth, to call out, summon : *ē-,* out, from *ex-* + *vocāre,* to call (see **wekw-** in Appendix*).] —**ev′o·ca·ble** (ĕv′ə-kə-bəl, ĭ-vō′kə-) *adj.*

ev·o·lute (ĕv′ə-lōōt′) *n.* The locus of the centers of curvature of a given curve. [Back-formation from EVOLUTION.]

ev·o·lu·tion (ĕv′ə-lōō′shən) *n.* **1.** A gradual process in which something changes into a significantly different, especially more complex or more sophisticated, form. **2.** *Biology.* **a.** The theory that groups of organisms, as species, may change with passage of time so that descendants differ morphologically and physiologically from their ancestors. **b.** The historical development of a related group of organisms; phylogeny. **3.** The developmental or historical process of something, as of a social institution, geographical division, or system of thought. **4.** *Often plural.* A movement which is part of a larger movement, as: **a.** A wheeling motion in a dance. **b.** A tactical or parade-ground maneuver. **5.** *Mathematics.* The extraction of a root of a quantity. In this sense, compare **involution.** [Latin *ēvolūtiō,* an opening, an unrolling, from *ēvolūtus,* past participle of *ēvolvere,* to roll out, to open, EVOLVE.]

ev·o·lu·tion·al (ĕv′ə-lōō′shən-əl) *adj.* Evolutionary.

ev·o·lu·tion·ar·y (ĕv′ə-lōō′shə-nĕr′ē) *adj.* **1.** Of, pertaining to, or resulting from evolution: *"The present state of the universe resulted from a continuous evolutionary process"* (George Gamow). **2.** In accord with the theory of biological evolution; Darwinian. **3.** Developing or evolving as a slow or historical process; gradually changing or progressing; evolutional. **4.** Of, pertaining to, or characterized by military evolutions.

ev·o·lu·tion·ism (ĕv′ə-lōō′shə-nĭz′əm) *n.* **1.** Acceptance of a theory of biological evolution, especially of the formulation by Charles Darwin. Compare **creationism. 2.** Any belief in an evolutionary process. —**ev′o·lu′tion·ist** *n.*

e·volve (ĭ-vŏlv′) *v.* **evolved, evolving, evolves.** —*tr.* **1.** To develop or achieve gradually; devise; formulate: *"Not one of the schemes he evolved to line his purse materialized"* (S.J. Perelman). **2.** *Biology.* To develop by evolutionary processes from a primitive to a more highly organized form. **3.** To yield, give, or throw off (gas, vapor, or heat, for example); set free. —*intr.* **1.** To be part of or subject to the process of natural, temporal, or biological evolution, as in an organism, plant, or rock stratum. **2.** To be developed, disclosed, or unfolded; come forth; emerge: *The plot evolves in many subtle ways.* **3.** To undergo change or transformation; develop; lead. [Latin *ēvolvere,* to roll out, unfold : *ē-,* out, from *ex-* + *volvere,* to roll (see **wel-**[3] in Appendix*).] —**e·volv′a·ble** *adj.* —**e·volve′ment** *n.*

e·vul·sion (ĭ-vŭl′shən) *n.* A pulling out or plucking; forcible extraction. [Latin *ēvulsiō,* a pulling out, from *ēvulsus,* past participle of *ēvellere,* to pull out : *ē-,* out, from *ex-* + *vellere,* to pull (see **wel-**[4] in Appendix*).]

Ev·voi·a. The Modern Greek name for **Euboea.**

ev·zone (ev′zōn′) *n.* An infantryman of a special corps of the Greek army. [Modern Greek *euzōnos,* from Greek, well-girdled, active : *eu-,* well + *zōnē,* girdle (see **yōs-** in Appendix*).]

E·wab Islands (ē′wôb). Formerly **Kai Islands** (kī). An island group of Indonesia, occupying 565 square miles southwest of West Irian.

ewe (yōō) *n.* A female sheep, especially when full-grown. [Middle English *ewe,* Old English *ēowu.* See **owi-** in Appendix.*]

E·we (ā′vā, ā′wā) *n.* **1. a.** A Negro people of Togo, Ghana, and parts of Dahomey. **b.** A member of this people. **2.** The Niger-Congo language of this people.

ewe-neck (yōō′nĕk′) *n.* A horse's neck that is thin and hollowed rather than arched. —**ewe′-necked′** *adj.*

ew·er (yōō′ər) *n.* A large, wide-mouthed pitcher or jug. [Middle English, from Norman French, from Old North French *eviere,* from Vulgar Latin *aquāria* (unattested), from Latin *aquārius,* relating to water, from *aqua,* water. See **akwā-** in Appendix.*]

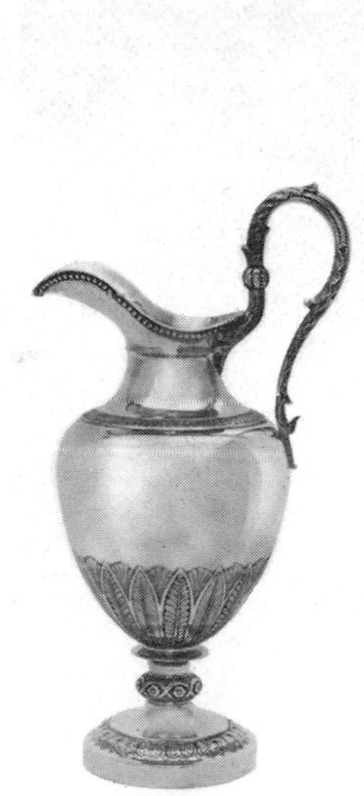

ewer
Mid-19th-century American silver ewer

Ew·ing (yōō′ĭng), **William Maurice.** Born 1906. American geophysicist and oceanographer.

EWR Airport code for Newark, New Jersey.

ex[1] (ĕks) *prep. Abbr.* **x. 1.** *Finance.* Without; not including; not participating in: *ex dividend; ex rights.* **2.** *Commerce.* Free of charge to the purchaser until he removes it from (a particular place or thing). [Latin *ex,* out of, from. See **eghs** in Appendix.*]

ex[2] (ĕks) *n., pl.* **exes.** The letter *x.*

ex[3] (ĕks) *n. Slang.* A former wife or husband.

ex-[1]. Indicates: **1.** Removal out of or from; for example, **explant. 2.** Former; for example, *ex-president.* [Middle English, from Old French, from Latin. In borrowed Latin compounds *ex-* indicates: 1. out or out of, as in **expire.** 2. away from or removed away from, as in **expropriate.** 3. up; as in **elevate.** 4. completely or intensively, as in **execute.** 5. opposing; as in **execrate.** *Ex-* becomes *ef-* before *f.* Latin *ex-,* from *ex,* out, out of. See **eghs** in Appendix.*]

ex-[2]. Indicates out of; for example, **exergue.** [In borrowed Greek compounds *ex-* indicates: 1. out of, as in **exegesis.** 2. away from, as in **exorcise.** Greek *ex-,* from *ex,* out of. See **eghs** in Appendix.*]

ex. 1. examination. **2.** example. **3.** except; excepted; exception. **4.** exchange. **5.** executive. **6.** express. **7.** extra.

Ex. Exodus (Old Testament).

ex·ac·er·bate (ĕg-zăs′ər-bāt′, ĭg-, ĕk-săs′-, ĭk-) *tr.v.* **-bated, -bating, -bates. 1.** To increase the severity of; aggravate. Used of a pain, emotion, disease, or the like. **2.** To embitter or irritate (a person): *"with his exacerbated nerves he was constantly receiving impressions"* (Allen Tate). [Latin *exacerbāre,* aggravate, make harsh : *ex-,* completely + *acerbus,* bitter, harsh (see **ak-** in Appendix*).] —**ex·ac′er·ba′tion** *n.*

ex·act (ĕg-zăkt′, ĭg-) *adj.* **1.** Accurate and precise. **2.** Strictly and completely in accord with fact. **3.** Meticulously observing or adhering to a standard. —*tr.v.* **exacted, -acting, -acts. 1.** To force the payment or yielding of; extort. **2.** To call for; require; to demand. [Latin *exactus,* past participle of *exigere,* "to drive out," require, examine : *ex-,* out + *agere,* to lead, to drive (see ag- in Appendix*).] —**ex·act′a·ble** *adj.* —**ex·act′ness** *n.* —**ex·ac′tor** (-zăk′tər), **ex·act′er** *n.*

ex·act·ing (ĕg-zăk′tĭng, ĭg-) *adj.* **1.** Making severe or unremitting demands: *an exacting taskmaster.* **2.** Requiring great care, effort, or attention: *an exacting task.* —See Synonyms at **burdensome, severe.** —**ex·act′ing·ly** *adv.* —**ex·act′ing·ness** *n.*

ex·ac·tion (ĕg-zăk′shən, ĭg-) *n.* **1.** The act of exacting. **2.** Something that is exacted, as a sum of money or act of obedience.

ex·act·i·tude (ĕg-zăk′tə-to͞od, -tyo͞od′, ĭg-) *n.* The state or quality of being exact.

ex·act·ly (ĕg-zăkt′lē, ĭg-) *adv.* **1.** In an exact manner; accurately. **2.** In all respects; just: *Do exactly as you please.*

ex·ag·ger·ate (ĕg-zăj′ə-rāt′, ĭg-) *v.* **-ated, -ating, -ates.** —*tr.* **1.** To enlarge (something) disproportionately; increase to an abnormal degree. **2.** To make (something) greater than is actually the case; magnify beyond the truth: *"He began to exaggerate the endurance, the skill, and the valor of those who were coming"* (Stephen Crane). —*intr.* To distort through emphasis; overstate. [Latin *exaggerāre,* to pile up, exaggerate : *ex-,* completely + *aggerāre,* to pile up, from *agger,* pile, heap.] —**ex·ag′ger·a′tive, ex·ag′ger·a·to′ry** (-ə-tôr′ē, -tōr′ē) *adj.* —**ex·ag′ger·a′tor** (-ā′tər) *n.*

ex·ag·ger·at·ed (ĕg-zăj′ə-rā′tĭd, ĭg-) *adj.* **1.** Unduly emphasized or magnified; going beyond truth, fact, or reality; overstated. **2.** Physically enlarged; abnormally or disproportionately developed. —**ex·ag′ger·at′ed·ly** *adv.*

ex·ag·ger·a·tion (ĕg-zăj′ə-rā′shən, ĭg-) *n.* **1.** The act of exaggerating. **2.** An instance of exaggerating; an overstatement.

ex·alt (ĕg-zôlt′, ĭg-) *tr.v.* **-alted, -alting, -alts. 1.** To raise in position, character, status, or the like; elevate: *"Do away with masters, exalt the will of the people"* (D.H. Lawrence). **2.** To glorify; praise; honor; extol. **3.** To fill with an intensified feeling such as joy, pride, delight, or the like; elate. **4.** To increase the effect or intensity of, as colors; heighten. [Middle English *exalten,* from Old French *exalter,* from Latin *exaltāre,* to lift up, exalt : *ex-,* up + *altus,* high (see **al-**[3] in Appendix*).] —**ex·alt′er** *n.*

ex·al·ta·tion (ĕg′zôl-tā′shən) *n.* **1.** The act of exalting. **2.** The state of being exalted; elevation. **3.** The state or feeling of intense, often excessive exhilaration and well-being; rapture; elation. See Synonyms at **ecstasy. 4.** *British.* A flight of larks. See Synonyms at **flock.**

ex·alt·ed (ĕg-zôl′tĭd, ĭg-) *adj.* **1.** Elevated in rank, character, position, or the like. **2.** Lofty; sublime; noble: *"That provision should be made for continuing the race of . . . so exalted . . . a Being as man — I am far from denying"* (Sterne). —**ex·alt′ed·ly** *adv.* —**ex·alt′ed·ness** *n.*

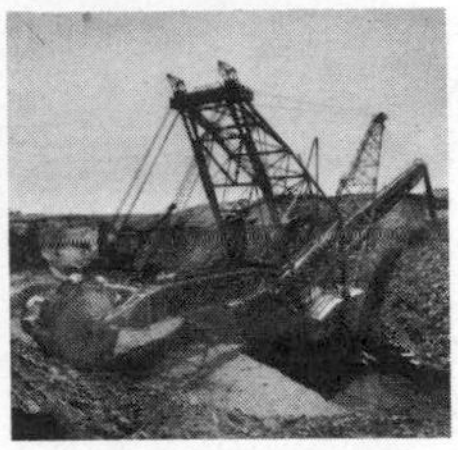

excavator

ex·am (ĕg-zăm′, ĭg-) *n. Informal.* An examination.

exam. examination.

ex·a·men (ĕg-zā′mən, ĭg-) *n. Ecclesiastical.* A usually daily examination of one's conscience. [Latin *exāmen,* consideration, examination, from *exigere,* to EXAMINE.]

ex·am·i·nant (ĕg-zăm′ə-nənt, ĭg-) *n.* One who examines.

ex·am·i·na·tion (ĕg-zăm′ə-nā′shən, ĭg-) *n. Abbr.* **ex., exam. 1.** The act of examining or the state or result of being examined; an inspection; analysis. **2.** A set of questions or exercises testing knowledge or skills; a written, practical, or oral test. **3.** Formal interrogation; official inquiry. —**ex·am′i·na′tion·al** *adj.*

ex·am·ine (ĕg-zăm′ĭn, ĭg-) *tr.v.* **-ined, -ining, -ines. 1.** To inspect or scrutinize (a person, thing, or situation) in detail; observe or analyze carefully. **2.** To study the state of health of. **3.** To determine the qualifications, aptitude, memory, or the like by subjecting to questions or exercises. **4.** To interrogate or question formally to elicit facts, information, or the like. **5.** To consider or test introspectively; reflect upon: *"The time has come, God knows, for us to examine ourselves"* (James Baldwin). —See Synonyms at **ask.** [Middle English *examinen,* from Old French *examiner,* from Latin *exāmināre,* to weigh accurately, examine, from *exāmen,* a weighing, consideration, from *exigere,* to examine, to lead out : *ex-,* out + *agere,* to lead (see **ag-** in Appendix*).] —**ex·am′in·a·ble** *adj.* —**ex·am′in·er** *n.*

ex·am·in·ee (ĕg-zăm′ə-nē′, ĭg-) *n.* One who is examined.

ex·am·ple (ĕg-zăm′pəl, -zäm′pəl, ĭg-) *n. Abbr.* **ex. 1.** One that is representative of a group as a whole; a sample; specimen. **2.** Someone or something worthy of imitation or duplication; a model; a pattern; exemplar. **3.** A previous case or situation that is the same or similar to one at hand; precedent. **4.** One that serves as a warning, as a punishment or a punished person. **5.** An illustrative problem or exercise with its solution. —**for example.** Serving as an illustration, a model, or an instance. —**set an example.** To be or provide a model of behavior capable and worthy of imitation. [Middle English *exaumple,* from Old French *example, essample,* from Latin *exemplum,* "(something) taken out," example, sample, from *eximere,* to take out : *ex-,* out + *emere,* to take (see **em-** in Appendix*).]

Synonyms: *example, instance, case, illustration, sample, specimen.* Each of these nouns refers to what is representative of, or serves to explain, something larger. The first four are sometimes interchangeable. An *example* represents, usually typically and concretely, something of which it is a part, and thereby demonstrates the nature or operation of what it represents. An *instance* is an action, occurrence, event, or, less often, a person that is representative of a general subject and that is cited in some way bearing on the subject. A *case* is an action, occurrence, event, or condition that constitutes a specific instance: *a typical case of child neglect.* An *illustration* demonstrates or explains in detail all or part of a broad subject of which it is itself a part. *Sample* and *specimen* are often interchangeable. A *sample* is an actual part of something larger, presented as evidence of the quality of the whole. A *specimen* is either such a part of a whole or an individual and representative member of a group or class of persons or things.

ex·an·the·ma (ĕg′zăn-thē′mə) *n., pl.* **-mata** (-mə-tə) or **-mas.** Also **ex·an·them** (ĕg-zăn′thəm, ĭg-). **1.** A skin eruption. **2.** A disease, such as measles or scarlet fever, accompanied by a skin eruption. [New Latin, from Late Latin *exanthēma,* from Greek, "a blooming out," eruption, from *exanthein,* to bloom out, burst forth : *ex-,* out + *anthein,* to bloom, from *anthos,* flower (see **andh-** in Appendix*).] —**ex·an′the·mat′ic** (-thə-măt′ĭk), **ex′an·them′a·tous** (-thĕm′ə-təs) *adj.*

ex·arch (ĕk′särk) *n.* **1.** The ruler of a province in the Byzantine Empire. **2.** *Eastern Orthodox Church.* **a.** The deputy of a patriarch. **b.** A bishop ranking immediately below a patriarch. [Late Latin *exarchus,* from Greek *exarkhos,* leader, from *exarkhein,* to initiate, lead out : *ex-,* out + *arkhein,* rule, lead (see **arkhein** in Appendix*).]

ex·ar·chate (ĕk′sär-kāt′) *n.* Also **ex·ar·chy** (ĕk′sär′kē). The office, rank, jurisdiction, or province of an exarch.

ex·as·per·ate (ĕg-zăs′pə-rāt′, ĭg-) *tr.v.* **-ated, -ating, -ates. 1.** To make very angry or irritated; tax the patience of; provoke; irk. **2.** *Obsolete.* To increase the gravity or intensity of (a passion or pain, for example): *"He speaks of a scene in* Pelleas et Melisande *that exasperates his rose fever and makes him sneeze"* (Samuel Beckett). [Latin *exasperāre,* to exasperate, irritate, make rough : *ex-,* entirely + *asperāre,* to make rough, from *asper,* rough (see **asper**).] —**ex·as′per·at′er** *n.*

ex·as·per·a·tion (ĕg-zăs′pə-rā′shən, ĭg-) *n.* **1.** An act or instance of exasperating. **2.** The state of being exasperated; extreme annoyance or irritation: *"It brought his despair of her up to a point of exasperation"* (Ford Madox Ford).

exc. 1. excellent. **2.** except; excepted; exception.

Exc. Excellency.

Ex·cal·i·bur (ĕk-skăl′ə-bər). The name of King Arthur's sword. [Middle English *Excalibur,* from Old French *Escalibor,* from Medieval Latin *Caliburnus,* from Welsh *Caledvwlch,* from Celtic *kaleto-* (unattested), hard.]

ex ca·the·dra (ĕks kə-thē′drə). *Latin.* With authority; from the seat of authority. Said especially of official or solemn papal pronouncements.

ex·cau·date (ĕks-kô′dāt) *adj.* Tailless; without a tail. [EX- + CAUDATE.]

ex·ca·vate (ĕk′skə-vāt′) *v.* **-vated, -vating, -vates.** —*tr.* **1.** To make a cavity or hole in; dig out; hollow out. **2.** To form (a tunnel, for example) by such hollowing out; dig. **3.** To remove (soil) by digging or scooping out. **4.** To expose or uncover by digging. —*intr.* To engage in digging, hollowing out, or removing. [Latin *excavāre,* to hollow out : *ex-,* out + *cavāre,* to hollow, from *cavus,* hollow (see **keu-**[3] in Appendix*).]

ex·ca·va·tion (ĕk′skə-vā′shən) *n.* **1.** The act or condition of excavating. **2.** A cavity formed by excavating. **3.** Something revealed by excavating, as ruins. —See Synonyms at **hole.**

ex·ca·va·tor (ĕk′skə-vā′tər) *n.* A person or device, such as a steam shovel, that excavates.

ex·ceed (ĕk-sēd′, ĭk-) *tr.v.* **-ceeded, -ceeding, -ceeds. 1.** To be greater than; surpass. **2.** To go beyond the prior or proper limits of. —See Synonyms at **excel.** [Middle English *exceden,* from Old French *exceder,* from Latin *excēdere,* to depart, to go out, surpass : *ex-,* out + *cēdere,* to go (see **ked-**[1] in Appendix*).]

ex·ceed·ing (ĕk-sē′dĭng, ĭk-) *adj.* Extreme; extraordinary. —*adv. Archaic.* Exceedingly.

ex·ceed·ing·ly (ĕk-sē′dĭng-lē, ĭk-) *adv.* To an advanced or unusual degree; extremely.

ex·cel (ĕk-sĕl′, ĭk-) *v.* **-celled, -celling, -cels.** —*tr.* To be better than; surpass; outdo: *excels his class in English.* —*intr.* To surpass others; be better or do better than others: *She excels in wit.* [Middle English *excellen,* from Latin *excellere,* to excel, raise up. See **kel-**[8] in Appendix.*]

Synonyms: *excel, surpass, exceed, transcend, outdo, outstrip.* These verbs mean to go beyond a limit or standard, usually in the sense of being superior. *Excel* and *surpass* are generally applied to performance or achievement in things that reflect credit on a person. To *excel* is to be pre-eminent in a general sense or to be or perform at a level higher than that of another or others specified. To *surpass* another is to be superior in performance, quality, or degree. *Exceed* can also refer to superiority in quality, but more often applies to what is greater in sheer size or quantity: *He surpasses* (or *excels*) *me in knowledge, but my wealth exceeds his.* In a related sense *exceed* means to go beyond a proper limit: *exceed one's authority; exceed the speed limit. Transcend* usually refers to marked superiority in quality or degree; often it implies attainment of a level so high that comparison is hardly possible: *Great art transcends mere rules of composition. The national interest must transcend regional goals. Outdo* and *outstrip* refer to superiority in performance. *Outstrip,* the stronger, implies obvious superiority.

ex·cel·lence (ĕk′sə-ləns) *n.* Also *archaic* **ex·cel·len·cy** (-lən-sē) *pl.* **-cies. 1.** The state, quality, or condition of excelling; superiority; pre-eminence. **2.** Something in which a person or thing excels; a surpassing feature or virtue. **3.** *Capital* **E.** Variant of **Excellency.** [From EXCEL.]

Ex·cel·len·cy (ĕk′sə-lən-sē) *n., pl.* **-cies.** Also **Ex·cel·lence** (ĕk′sə-ləns). **1.** *Abbr.* **Exc.** A title or form of address for certain high officials, such as ambassadors, bishops, or governors. Usually preceded by *His, Her,* or *Your.* **2.** *Small* **e.** *Archaic.* Variant of **excellence.**

ex·cel·lent (ĕk′sə-lənt) *adj.* **1.** *Abbr.* **E, exc.** Being of the highest or finest quality; exceptionally good; superb: *"Her voice was ever soft, / Gentle and low, an excellent thing in woman."* (Shakespeare). **2.** *Archaic.* Surpassing; superior. [Middle English, from Old French, from Latin *excellens,* present participle of *excellere,* to EXCEL.] —**ex′cel·lent·ly** *adv.*

ex·cel·si·or (ĕk-sĕl′sē-ər, ĭk-) *n.* Slender, curved wood shavings used for packing, stuffing, or the like. [Originally a trade name, from Latin, comparative of *excelsus,* high, from the past participle of *excellere,* to EXCEL.]

ex·cept (ĕk-sĕpt′, ĭk-) *prep. Abbr.* **ex., exc.** With the exclusion of; other than; but: *All the eggs except one broke.* —*conj.* **1.** If it were not for the fact that; only. Often used with *that: He would buy the suit, except that it costs too much.* **2.** Otherwise than; with any purpose or manner other than. Usually used with an adverb, a clause, or a phrase: *He would not open his mouth except to yell.* **3.** *Archaic.* Unless. —*v.* **excepted, -cepting, -cepts.** —*tr.* To leave out; exclude; excuse. —*intr.* To object. Usually used with *to* or *against.* [Middle English, from Latin *exceptus,* past participle of *excipere,* to take out, except : *ex-,* out + *capere,* to take (see **kap-** in Appendix*).]
  Usage: Except, in the sense of *with the exclusion of, other than,* or *but,* is usually construed as a preposition (as it is defined above) rather than as a conjunction. When a pronoun follows *except* in this sense, therefore, it is in the objective case: *No one except me knew it. Every member of the original cast was signed except her.* In this sense *except* is much more common than *excepting,* in modern usage. *Excepting* appears principally in negative constructions: *All money received, not excepting bonuses, must be reported.*

ex·cept·ing (ĕk-sĕp′tĭng, ĭk-) *prep.* Excluding; except. See Usage note at **except.** —*conj. Archaic.* Except; unless.

ex·cep·tion (ĕk-sĕp′shən, ĭk-) *n. Abbr.* **ex., exc. 1.** The act of excepting or state of being excepted; exclusion. **2.** One that is excepted; a case which does not conform to normal rules, general principles, or the like: *"Americans want to be liked — and Senators are no exception"* (John F. Kennedy). **3.** An objection or criticism; opposition: *open to exception.* **4.** *Law.* A formal objection taken in the course of an action or proceeding. —**take exception. 1.** To object to; take issue with. Usually used with *to: I take exception to your remarks.* **2.** *Archaic.* To take offense; resent. Often used with *at.*

ex·cep·tion·a·ble (ĕk-sĕp′shən-ə-bəl, ĭk-) *adj.* Open or liable to objection or exception. —**ex·cep′tion·a·bly** *adv.*
  Usage: Exceptionable and exceptional, often confused, are not interchangeable. *Exceptionable* alone is synonymous with *objectionable* and *debatable,* and *exceptional* with *uncommon* and *extraordinary.*

ex·cep·tion·al (ĕk-sĕp′shən-əl, ĭk-) *adj.* **1.** Being an exception; uncommon; extraordinary. See Usage note at **exceptionable. 2.** *Education.* Pertaining to or describing a child whose endowments or intelligence are unusually high or low; precocious or retarded. —**ex·cep′tion·al·ly** *adv.*

ex·cep·tive (ĕk-sĕp′tĭv, ĭk-) *adj. Rare.* **1.** Of, being, or containing an exception. **2.** Tending to object or criticize; captious; faultfinding.

ex·cerpt (ĕk′sûrpt′) *n.* A passage or scene selected from a speech, book, film, play, or the like. —*tr.v.* (ĭk-sûrpt′) **excerpted, -cerpting, -cerpts.** To select, quote, or take out (a passage or scene) from a book, speech, play, film, or the like. [Latin *excerptum,* "something picked out," excerpt, from the neuter past participle of *excerpere,* to pick out, excerpt : *ex-,* out + *carpere,* to pick, pluck (see **kerp-** in Appendix*).]

ex·cess (ĕk-sĕs′, ĭk-, ĕk′sĕs′) *n.* **1.** The state of exceeding what is normal or sufficient. **2.** An amount or quantity beyond what is requisite; superfluity. **3.** The amount or degree by which one quantity exceeds another; remainder. **4.** Intemperance; overindulgence: *"Not at all, if you please, an oversexed person: that is a vital defect, not a true excess"* (G.B. Shaw). —**in excess of.** Greater than; more than. —**to excess.** To an extreme degree or extent; too much. —*adj.* Being more than is required or usual: *"Skim the excess fat from the soup"* (Craig Claiborne). [Middle English, from Old French *exces,* from Latin *excessus,* past participle of *excēdere,* to EXCEED.]

excess baggage. 1. Baggage, as on airplanes, in excess of the amount carried free, and for which the passenger pays an extra charge. **2.** Anything useless or hampering; something unnecessary.

ex·ces·sive (ĕk-sĕs′ĭv, ĭk-) *adj.* Exceeding a reasonable degree of propriety, necessity, or the like; extreme; inordinate: *excessive charges.* —**ex·ces′sive·ly** *adv.*
  Synonyms: excessive, exorbitant, extravagant, immoderate, inordinate, extreme, unreasonable. These adjectives mean beyond a normal or proper limit. *Excessive,* which has the widest range, describes a quantity, amount, or degree that is beyond what is specified, required, reasonable, or just. *Exorbitant* usually refers to a quantity or amount that far exceeds what is customary, right, or just. *Extravagant* sometimes specifies excessive or unwise expenditure of money; in a more general sense it means beyond the bounds of truth, sound judgment, proper conduct, or the like: *extravagant claims. Immoderate* suggests what violates reason or good taste. *Inordinate* implies lack of balance and an overstepping of bounds imposed by authority or implied by good sense. *Extreme* implies great departure from a norm governing behavior, speech, or quality or degree in general. *Unreasonable* applies to what exceeds a limit set by custom, good judgment, fairness, or decent regard for others.

exch. 1. exchange. **2.** exchequer.

ex·change (ĕks-chānj′, ĭks-) *v.* **-changed, -changing, -changes.** —*tr.* **1.** To give and receive in a reciprocal manner; interchange: *exchange ideas.* **2.** To relinquish (one thing for another); give over. **3.** To replace (something unsatisfactory) with

something else: *exchange defective merchandise.* **4.** To provide or transfer (goods or services, for example) in return for something of equal value. —*intr.* **1.** To make an exchange of something; reciprocate. **2.** To be taken as an equivalent for; pass in exchange. —*n. Abbr.* **ex., exch. 1.** An act or instance of exchanging. **2.** One that is exchanged. **3.** A place where things are exchanged; especially, a center where securities and commodities are bought and sold: *a stock exchange.* **4.** A telephone **exchange** *(see).* **5.** A system of payments using negotiable drafts, bills of exchange, or the like, instead of money. **6.** The fee or percentage charged for participating in such a system of payment. **7.** A bill of exchange. **8.** Rate of exchange. **9.** The amount of difference in the actual value of two or more currencies, or between values of the same currency at two or more places. **10.** *Usually plural.* The checks, bills, drafts, or the like, presented to a clearing-house for settlement or exchange. [Middle English *eschaungen,* from Norman French *eschaunge,* from Old French *eschangier,* from Vulgar Latin *excambiāre* (unattested) : Late Latin *ex-,* indicating change + *cambiāre,* to exchange, barter (see **skamb-** in Appendix*).] —**ex·chang′er** *n.*

ex·change·a·ble (ĕks-chān′jə-bəl, ĭks-) *adj.* Able to be exchanged; remittable. —**ex·change′a·bil′i·ty** *n.*

exchange rate. Rate of exchange *(see).*

ex·cheq·uer (ĕks-chĕk′ər, ĭks-, ĕks′chĕk′ər) *n.* **1.** *Capital* E. The British governmental department charged with the collection and care of the national revenue. **2.** *Capital* E. A law court, the **Court of Exchequer** *(see).* **3.** *Abbr.* **exch.** A treasury, as of a nation or an organization. **4.** *Informal.* The total of one's financial resources; funds. [Middle English *escheker,* from Norman French, from Old French *eschequier,* chessboard, a counting table usually covered with a checkered cloth, from *eschec,* CHECK (at chess).]

ex·cip·i·ent (ĕk-sĭp′ē-ənt, ĭk-) *n.* Any inert substance used as a diluent or vehicle for a drug. [Latin *excipiēns,* present participle of *excipere,* to EXCEPT.]

ex·cis·a·ble (ĕk-sī′zə-bəl, ĭk-) *adj.* Subject to an excise.

ex·cise¹ (ĕk′sīz′, ĕk-sīz′, ĭk-) *n.* **1.** An indirect tax levied on the production, sale, or consumption of certain commodities, such as tobacco or liquor, within a country. Also called "excise tax." **2.** A license fee paid to allow a person to pursue certain types of employment or amusement, such as operating a gambling casino. **3.** *British.* A branch of the civil service that is responsible for the inland revenue taxes and duties. —*tr.v.* **excised, -cising, -cises.** To levy an excise on. [Obsolete Dutch *excijs,* from Middle Dutch, probably from Old French *acceis,* from Vulgar Latin *accēnsum* (unattested) : Latin *ad-,* against, to + *cēnsus,* tax, CENSUS.]

ex·cise² (ĕk-sīz′, ĭk-) *tr.v.* **-cised, -cising, -cises.** To remove by or as if by cutting; especially, to remove surgically (an organ or part). [Latin *excīdere* (past participle *excīsus*), to cut out : *ex-,* out + *caedere,* to cut (see **skhai-** in Appendix*).] —**ex·ci′sion** (ĕk-sĭzh′ən, ĭk-) *n.*

ex·cise·man (ĕk-sīz′mən, ĭk-) *n., pl.* **-men** (-mĭn). *British.* An officer who collects excise taxes or enforces excise laws.

ex·cit·a·ble (ĕk-sī′tə-bəl, ĭk-) *adj.* **1. a.** Capable of being excited. **b.** Easily excited; sensitive or volatile. **2.** Capable of responding to stimuli. —**ex·cit′a·bil′i·ty, ex·cit′a·ble·ness** *n.* —**ex·cit′a·bly** *adv.*

ex·ci·tant (ĕk-sī′tənt, ĭk-) *adj.* Also **ex·ci·ta·tive** (ĕk-sī′tə-tĭv, ĭk-), **ex·ci·ta·to·ry** (-tə-tôr′ē, -tōr′ē). Capable of exciting or stimulating. —**ex′ci·tant** *n.*

ex·ci·ta·tion (ĕk-sī-tā′shən) *n.* **1.** The act or process of exciting something. **2.** An agent or means used to excite or stimulate. **3.** The state or condition of being excited.

ex·cite (ĕk-sīt′, ĭk-) *tr.v.* **-cited, -citing, -cites. 1.** To stir to activity; put into motion. **2.** To elicit, as a reaction or emotion; induce: *excite a response.* **3. a.** To arouse strong feeling in (a person); provoke: *She excited him to anger.* **b.** To stir the sexual passions of (a person); arouse. **4.** *Biology.* To produce increased activity in (an organism or part); stimulate. **5.** *Physics.* **a.** To increase the energy of. **b.** To raise (an atom, for example) to a higher energy level. —See Synonyms at **provoke.** [Middle English *exciten,* from Old French *exciter,* from Latin *excitāre,* to excite, arouse, frequentative of *exciēre* (past participle *excitus*), to call or bring out : *ex-,* out + *ciēre, cīre,* to call, to put in motion (see **kei-³** in Appendix*).]

ex·cit·ed (ĕk-sī′tĭd, ĭk-) *adj.* **1.** In a state of excitement; emotionally aroused; stirred. **2.** *Physics.* At an energy level higher than the ground state. —**ex·cit′ed·ly** *adv.*

ex·cite·ment (ĕk-sīt′mənt, ĭk-) *n.* **1.** The state or condition of being excited; agitation. **2.** Something that excites.

ex·cit·er (ĕk-sī′tər, ĭk-) *n.* **1.** One that excites. **2.** *Electricity.* **a.** An auxiliary generator used to provide field current for a larger generator or alternator. **b.** An oscillator for generating the carrier frequency of a transmitter.

ex·cit·ing (ĕk-sī′tĭng, ĭk-) *adj.* Creating excitement or agitation; rousing. —**ex·cit′ing·ly** *adv.*

ex·ci·ton (ĕk-sī′tŏn) *n.* An electrically neutral excited state of a crystal, often regarded as a bound state of an electron and a hole. [EXCIT(ATION) + -ON.]

ex·ci·tor (ĕk-sī′tər, ĭk-) *n.* A stimulant.

excl. 1. exclamation. **2.** exclusive.

ex·claim (ĕks-klām′, ĭks-) *v.* **-claimed, -claiming, -claims.** —*intr.* To cry out or speak suddenly or vehemently, as from surprise or emotion. —*tr.* To cry out or speak suddenly or vehemently. [Old French *exclamer,* from Latin *exclāmāre,* to call out, exclaim : *ex-,* out + *clāmāre,* to call (see **kel-³** in Appendix*).] —**ex·claim′er** *n.*

ex·cla·ma·tion (ĕks′klə-mā′shən) *n.* **1.** An abrupt, forceful utterance; an outcry. **2.** *Abbr.* **excl., exclam.** An interjection. **3.** An exclamation point.

exclamation point. A punctuation mark (!) used after an exclamation. Also called "exclamation," "exclamation mark."

ex·clam·a·to·ry (ĕks-klăm′ə-tôr′ē, -tōr′ē, ĭks-) *adj.* Constituting, containing, relating to, or using exclamation.

ex·clave (ĕks′klāv′) *n.* A portion of a country which is isolated in alien territory: *Cabinda, in the Congo (Kinshasa), is an exclave of Angola.* Compare **enclave.** [EX- + (EN)CLAVE.]

ex·clude (ĕks-klo͞od′, ĭks-) *tr.v.* **-cluded, -cluding, -cludes. 1.** To prevent or keep from entering a place, group, or the like; to bar; reject. **2.** To omit noticing or considering; leave out; disregard. **3.** To put out (someone or something); expel. [Middle English *excluden,* from Latin *exclūdere* : *ex-,* out + *claudere,* shut (see **kleu-** in Appendix*).] **—ex·clud′a·bil′i·ty** *n.* **—ex·clud′a·ble, ex·clud′i·ble** *adj.* **—ex·clud′er** *n.*

ex·clu·sion (ĕks-klo͞o′zhən, ĭks-) *n.* **1.** The act of excluding; rejection. **2.** The state of being excluded. [Latin *exclūsiō,* from *exclūsus,* past participle of *exclūdere,* to EXCLUDE.]

ex·clu·sion·ist (ĕks-klo͞o′zhən-ĭst, ĭks-) *n.* One who favors or practices excluding others from rights or privileges. **—ex·clu′sion·ism′** *n.* **—ex·clu′sion·ist** *adj.*

exclusion principle. The principle that no two particles of a given type, such as electrons, protons, or neutrons, can occupy a particular quantum state.

ex·clu·sive (ĕks-klo͞o′sĭv, ĭks-) *adj.* *Abbr.* **excl. 1.** Pertaining to, characterized by, or requiring exclusion. **2.** Not divided or shared with others: *exclusive publishing rights.* **3.** Single or independent; sole: *your exclusive function.* **4.** Regarded as unrelated or autonomous; separate; incompatible: *mutually exclusive roles in life.* **5.** Concentrated on the matter at hand; undivided; undistracted. **6.** Admitting only certain people to membership, participation, or the like; select: *"It's a very exclusive war at present"* (Evelyn Waugh). **7.** Catering to a wealthy clientele; expensive; chic: *exclusive shops.* **—exclusive of.** Not including or considering: *exclusive of other factors.* **—***n.* A news item granted to or obtained by only one person or source. **—ex·clu′sive·ly** *adv.* **—ex·clu′sive·ness** *n.*

ex·cog·i·tate (ĕks-kŏj′ə-tāt′, ĭks-) *tr.v.* **-tated, -tating, -tates.** To think out in great detail; devise; contrive. [Latin *excōgitāre,* to find out by thinking : *ex-,* out + *cōgitāre,* to COGITATE.] **—ex·cog′i·ta′tion** *n.* **—ex·cog′i·ta′tive** *adj.*

ex·com·mu·ni·ca·ble (ĕks′kə-myo͞o′nĭ-kə-bəl) *adj.* Liable to, meriting, or punishable by excommunication.

ex·com·mu·ni·cate (ĕks′kə-myo͞o′nĭ-kāt′) *tr.v.* **-cated, -cating, -cates.** To cut off from the rites, privileges, or fellowship of a church by ecclesiastical authority; exclude from religious membership. **—***n.* (ĕks′kə-myo͞o′nĭ-kĭt). A person who has been excommunicated. **—***adj.* (ĕks′kə-myo͞o′nĭ-kĭt, -kāt′). Excommunicated. [Middle English *excommunicaten,* from Late Latin *excommūnicāre* (past participle *excommūnicātus*), to put out of the (church) community : Latin *ex-,* out + *commūnicāre,* to COMMUNICATE.] **—ex′com·mu′ni·ca′tor** (-kā′tər) *n.*

ex·com·mu·ni·ca·tion (ĕks′kə-myo͞o′nĭ-kā′shən) *n.* **1.** The act of excommunicating. **2.** The state of being excommunicated; exclusion. **3.** The formal ecclesiastical censure or motion by which one is excommunicated.

ex·com·mu·ni·ca·tive (ĕks′kə-myo͞o′nĭ-kā′tĭv, -kə-tĭv) *adj.* Also **ex·com·mu·ni·ca·to·ry** (-kə-tôr′ē, -tōr′ē). Pertaining to, disposed to, or effecting excommunication.

ex·co·ri·ate (ĕk-skôr′ē-āt′, ĕk-skōr′-, ĭk-) *tr.v.* **-ated, -ating, -ates. 1.** To tear or wear off the skin of; abrade; chafe. **2.** To censure strongly; denounce severely; upbraid. [Middle English *excoriaten,* from Latin *excoriāre* (past participle *excoriātus*), to strip of its skin : *ex-,* removal from + *corium,* skin, hide, leather (see **sker-¹** in Appendix*).]

ex·co·ri·a·tion (ĕk-skôr′ē-ā′shən, ĕk-skōr′-, ĭk-) *n.* **1. a.** The act of excoriating. **b.** The state of being excoriated. **2.** A scratch on the skin, usually covered with a scab; an abrasion; a sore.

ex·cre·ment (ĕk′skrə-mənt) *n.* Waste material expelled from the body after digestion; especially, fecal matter. [Latin *excrēmentum,* from *excrētus,* past participle of *excernere,* to sift out : *ex-,* out + *cernere,* to sift (see **skeri-** in Appendix*).] **—ex′cre·men′tal** (ĕk′skrə-mĕn′təl) *adj.*

ex·cres·cence (ĕk-skrĕs′əns, ĭk-) *n.* **1.** An abnormal, disfiguring outgrowth or enlargement: *"a weird horny excrescence that had detached itself from the ceremonious big toe"* (John C. Powys). **2.** A normal outgrowth or appendage, such as a beard or toenail. [Middle English, from Latin *excrēscentia,* from *excrēscens,* present participle of *excrēscere,* to grow out : *ex-,* out + *crēscere,* to grow (see **ker-³** in Appendix*).]

ex·cres·cen·cy (ĕk-skrĕs′ən-sē, ĭk-) *n., pl.* **-cies. 1.** The state of being excrescent. **2.** An excrescence.

ex·cres·cent (ĕk-skrĕs′ənt, ĭk-) *adj.* **1.** Growing out abnormally, excessively, or superfluously. **2.** *Linguistics.* Intrusive; epenthetic: *an excrescent vowel sound.* **—ex·cres′cent·ly** *adv.*

ex·cre·ta (ĕk-skrē′tə, ĭk-) *pl.n.* Waste matter, such as sweat, urine, or feces, excreted from the body. [New Latin, from Latin *excrēta,* from the neuter plural past participle of *excernere,* to sift out. See **excrement.**] **—ex·cre′tal** *adj.*

ex·crete (ĕk-skrēt′, ĭk-) *tr.v.* **-creted, -creting, -cretes.** To eliminate (waste matter) from the blood, tissues, or organs. [Latin *excernere* (past participle *excrētus*), to sift out. See **excrement.**]

ex·cre·tion (ĕk-skrē′shən, ĭk-) *n.* **1.** The process or act of excreting undigested food residues or metabolic wastes. **2.** The matter so excreted.

ex·cre·to·ry (ĕk′skrə-tôr′ē, -tōr′ē) *adj.* Also **ex·cre·tive** (-tĭv). **1.** Of or pertaining to excretion. **2.** Having the function of excreting: *excretory organs.*

ex·cru·ci·ate (ĕk-skro͞o′shē-āt′, ĭk-) *tr.v.* **-ated, -ating, -ates.** To inflict with severe pain; torture; torment. [Latin *excruciāre,* to torment : *ex-,* completely + *cruciāre,* to torment, crucify, from *crux,* CROSS.] **—ex·cru′ci·a′tion** *n.*

ex·cru·ci·at·ing (ĕk-skro͞o′shē-ā′tĭng, ĭk-) *adj.* Intensely painful; agonizing: *an excruciating headache.* **—ex·cru′ci·at′ing·ly** *adv.*

ex·cul·pate (ĕk′skŭl-pāt′, ĕk-skŭl′-, ĭk-) *tr.v.* **-pated, -pating, -pates.** To clear of a charge; prove guiltless or blameless; exonerate. [Medieval Latin *exculpāre* : Latin *ex-* (removal away from) + *culpa,* guilt, blame (see **culpa**).] **—ex·cul′pa·ble** (-pə-bəl) *adj.* **—ex′cul·pa′tion** *n.*

ex·cul·pa·to·ry (ĕk-skŭl′pə-tôr′ē, -tōr′ē, ĭk-) *adj.* Proving or tending to prove guiltless; exculpating.

ex·cur·rent (ĕk-skûr′ənt, ĭk-) *adj.* **1. a.** Running or flowing in an outward direction. **b.** Having an outward flow, as a duct, tube, or anatomical passage. **2.** *Botany.* **a.** Having a single, undivided trunk with lateral branches, as many coniferous trees. **b.** Extending beyond the apex of a leaf, as a midrib or vein. [Latin *excurrens,* present participle of *excurrere,* to run out. See **excursion.**]

ex·cur·sion (ĕk-skûr′zhən, ĭk-) *n.* **1.** A short journey made with the intention of returning to the starting point; an outing. **2. a.** A pleasure tour, especially one of limited duration and at a special low fare. **b.** The party on such a tour. **3.** A rambling from the main topic; digression. **4.** *Obsolete.* A military raid; sortie. **5. a.** A movement from a mean position or axis in an oscillating or alternating motion. **b.** The distance traversed in such a movement. [Latin *excursiō,* from *excursus,* past participle of *excurrere,* to run out, make an excursion : *ex-,* out + *currere,* to run (see **kers-²** in Appendix*).]

ex·cur·sion·ist (ĕk-skûr′zhə-nĭst, ĭk-) *n.* A person who goes on an excursion.

ex·cur·sive (ĕk-skûr′sĭv, ĭk-) *adj.* **1.** Given to digression; rambling: *an excursive lecturer.* **2.** Unmethodical; desultory: *excursive reading habits.* [From Latin *excursus.* See **excursion.**] **—ex·cur′sive·ly** *adv.* **—ex·cur′sive·ness** *n.*

ex·cur·sus (ĕk-skûr′səs, ĭk-) *n., pl.* **-suses. 1.** A lengthy, appended exposition of some point raised in a text. **2.** A digression. [Latin, from the past participle of *excurrere,* to run out. See **excursion.**]

ex·cus·a·to·ry (ĕk-skyo͞o′zə-tôr′ē, -tōr′ē, ĭk-) *adj.* Tending or serving to excuse; apologetic.

ex·cuse (ĕk-skyo͞oz′, ĭk-) *tr.v.* **-cused, -cusing, -cuses. 1.** To grant pardon to; forgive: *She excused him for his clumsiness.* **2.** To make allowance for (a shortcoming); overlook; condone. **3.** To serve as apology for; justify; vindicate: *Her brilliance does not excuse her rudeness.* **4.** To free, as from an obligation or duty; exempt. **5.** To give (someone) permission to leave; dismiss or release. **6.** To refrain from exacting; remit: *excuse taxes.* —See Synonyms at **forgive. —excuse oneself. 1.** To request forgiveness; seek indulgence; apologize. **2.** To request exemption, as from an obligation or duty. **3.** To request permission to leave. **—***n.* (ĕk-skyo͞os′, ĭk-) **1.** A plea or explanation offered to elicit pardon. **2.** The reason or ground for excusing. **3.** An act of excusing; forgiveness; pardon; indulgence. **4.** *Informal.* One that falls short of certain standards or expectations: *He is a poor excuse for a poet.* [Middle English *excusen,* from Old French *excuser,* from Latin *excūsāre* : *ex-,* removal from + *causa,* accusation, CAUSE.] **—ex·cus′a·ble** *adj.* **—ex·cus′a·ble·ness** *n.* **—ex·cus′a·bly** *adv.* **—ex·cus′er** *n.*

exec. 1. executive. **2.** executor.

ex·e·cra·ble (ĕk′sĭ-krə-bəl) *adj.* **1.** Deserving of detestation; abominable; abhorrent. **2.** Extremely inferior; very bad. [Middle English, from Old French, from Latin *ex(s)ecrābilis,* from *ex(s)ecrārī,* to EXECRATE.] **—ex′e·cra·bly** *adv.*

ex·e·crate (ĕk′sĭ-krāt′) *tr.v.* **-crated, -crating, -crates. 1.** To inveigh against; denounce. **2.** To abominate; abhor. **3.** *Archaic.* To invoke a curse upon; curse. [Latin *ex(s)ecrārī,* to curse, execrate : *ex-,* opposing + *sacrāre,* to be sacred, from *sacer,* sacred (see **sak-** in Appendix*).] **—ex′e·cra′tive** *adj.* **—ex′e·cra′tor** (-krā′tər) *n.* **—ex′e·cra·to′ry** (-krə-tôr′ē, -tōr′ē) *adj.*

ex·e·cra·tion (ĕk′sĭ-krā′shən) *n.* **1.** The act of execrating. **2.** A curse. **3.** Detestation; abhorrence. **4.** That which is execrated; something that is loathed.

ex·ec·u·tant (ĕg-zĕk′yə-tənt, ĭg-) *n.* One who performs or carries out; especially, a musical performer.

ex·e·cute (ĕk′sĭ-kyo͞ot′) *tr.v.* **-cuted, -cuting, -cutes. 1.** To carry out; put into effect: *execute a law.* **2.** To perform; do. **3.** To carry out (a work of art, for example) in accordance with a prescribed design. **4.** To make valid; legalize, as by signing and sealing: *execute a deed.* **5.** To perform or carry out what is required by: *execute a will.* **6.** To subject to capital punishment. —See Synonyms at **perform.** [Middle English *executen,* from Old French *executer,* from Medieval Latin *executāre,* from Latin *ex(s)equī* (past participle *ex(s)ecūtus*), execute, follow to the end : *ex-,* completely + *sequī,* to follow (see **sekw-¹** in Appendix*).] **—ex′e·cut′a·ble** *adj.* **—ex′e·cut′er** *n.*

ex·e·cu·tion (ĕk′sĭ-kyo͞o′shən) *n.* **1.** The act of executing. **2.** The state of being executed. **3.** The manner, style, or result of performance. **4.** A putting or being put to death as a legal penalty. **5.** *Law.* **a.** The carrying into effect of a court judgment. **b.** A writ empowering an officer to enforce a judgment. **6.** *Law.* The validating of a legal document by the performance of certain formalities, such as signing or sealing. **7.** Military destruction or decimation. Usually used with *do.*

ex·e·cu·tion·er (ĕk′sĭ-kyo͞o′shən-ər) *n.* **1.** One who administers capital punishment. **2.** One who puts another to death.

ex·ec·u·tive (ĕg-zĕk′yə-tĭv, ĭg-) *n.* *Abbr.* **ex., exec. 1.** A person or group having administrative or managerial authority in an organization. **2.** The chief officer of a government, state, or political division. **3.** The branch of government charged with putting into effect the country's laws; the administration. *—adj. Abbr.* **ex., exec. 1.** Of, pertaining to, capable of, or suited for carrying out plans, duties, or the like. **2.** Of or pertaining to the branch of government charged with the execution and administration of the nation's laws. Compare **legislative, judicial. 3.** Of or pertaining to an executive.

executive agreement. An agreement made between heads of state without senatorial ratification.

executive officer. 1. The officer second in command of a military unit smaller than a division. **2.** The officer second in command of a naval unit. **3.** A person holding executive power in an organization.

executive session. A legislative session, usually one closed to the public.

ex·ec·u·tor (ĕg-zĕk'yə-tər, ĭg-; *also* ĕk'sə-kyōō'tər *for sense 1*) *n. Abbr.* **exec., exr. 1.** A person who carries out or performs something. **2.** *Law.* A person who is appointed by a testator to execute his will. **—ex·ec'u·tor'i·al** (ĕg-zĕk'yə-tôr'ē-əl, -tōr'ē-əl) *adj.* **—ex·ec'u·tor·ship'** *n.*

ex·ec·u·to·ry (ĕg-zĕk'yə-tôr'ē, -tōr'ē, ĭg-) *adj.* **1.** Administrative. **2.** Operative; in effect. **3.** *Law.* Intended to go into effect, or having the potential of becoming effective at some future time; contingent.

ex·ec·u·trix (ĕg-zĕk'yə-trĭks', ĭg-) *n., pl.* **-trixes** or **executrices** (ĕg-zĕk'yə-trī'sēz', ĭg-). *Law.* A woman acting as executor.

ex·e·dra (ĕk'sĭ-drə, ĕk-sē'-) *n.* **1.** In classical architecture, a portico with a curved continuous bench where discussions were held. **2.** A usually curved outdoor bench of masonry with a high back. **3.** A bishop's throne. [Latin, from Greek *exedra,* out(doors) seat, bench : *ex-,* out + *hedra,* seat (see **sed-**[1] in Appendix*).]

ex·e·ge·sis (ĕk'sə-jē'sĭs) *n., pl.* **-ses** (-sēz). Critical explanation or analysis; especially, interpretation of the Scriptures. [New Latin, from Greek *exēgēsis,* from *exēgeisthai,* to show the way, expound : *ex-,* out of + *hēgeisthai,* lead (see **sāg-** in Appendix*).]

ex·e·gete (ĕk'sə-jēt') *n.* Also **ex·e·ge·tist** (ĕk'sə-jĕt'ĭst). A person skilled in exegesis. [Greek *exēgētes,* from *exēgeisthai,* to expound. See **exegesis.**]

ex·e·get·ic (ĕk'sə-jĕt'ĭk) *adj.* Also **ex·e·get·i·cal** (-ĭ-kəl). Of or pertaining to exegesis; analytic. **—ex'e·get'i·cal·ly** *adv.*

ex·e·get·ics (ĕk'sə-jĕt'ĭks) *n.* Plural in form, used with a singular verb. The science of exegesis.

ex·em·plar (ĕg-zĕm'plär', -plər, ĭg-) *n.* **1.** One that is worthy of being copied; a model: *"To name a man Blessed was to declare him . . . an exemplar and an intercessor for the faithful."* (Morris L. West). **2.** One considered typical or representative; example; specimen. **3.** An original, whether real or ideal; archetype. **4.** A copy, as of a book. —See Synonyms at **ideal.** [Middle English, from Old French *exemplaire,* from Late Latin *exemplārium,* from Latin *exemplum,* EXAMPLE.]

ex·em·pla·ry (ĕg-zĕm'plə-rē, ĭg-) *adj.* **1.** Worthy of being imitated; commendable: *exemplary behavior.* **2.** Serving as a model or archetype. **3.** Serving as an illustration; typical. **4.** Serving as a warning: *exemplary punishment.* **—ex'em·plar'i·ly** (ĕg'zəm-plâr'ə-lē) *adv.* **—ex·em'pla·ri·ness** *n.*

ex·em·pli·fi·ca·tion (ĕg-zĕm'plə-fĭ-kā'shən, ĭg-) *n.* **1.** The act of exemplifying. **2.** One that exemplifies; an example. **3.** *Law.* An official and certified copy of a document from public records.

ex·em·pli·fi·ca·tive (ĕg-zĕm'plə-fĭ-kā'tĭv, ĭg-) *adj.* Serving to exemplify; providing an example.

ex·em·pli·fy (ĕg-zĕm'plə-fī', ĭg-) *tr.v.* **-fied, -fying, -fies. 1. a.** To illustrate by example. **b.** To serve as an example of. **2.** *Law.* To make a certified copy of (a document from public records). [Middle English *exemplifien,* from Old French *exemplifier,* from Medieval Latin *exemplificāre* : Latin *exemplum,* EXAMPLE + *facere,* to make (see **dhē-**[1] in Appendix*).] **—ex·em'pli·fi'a·ble** *adj.* **—ex·em'pli·fi'er** *n.*

ex·em·pli gra·ti·a (ĕg-zĕm'plī' grā'shē-ə, ĭg-). *Abbr.* **e.g.** *Latin.* For the sake of example; for example.

ex·empt (ĕg-zĕmpt', ĭg-) *tr.v.* **-empted, -empting, -empts.** To free from an obligation or duty required of others; to excuse; release. *—adj.* **1.** Freed from an obligation or duty required of others; excused; released. **2.** *Obsolete.* Isolated; set apart. *—n.* One who is exempted from an obligation. [Middle English *exempten,* from Latin *eximere* (past participle *exemptus*), to take out, exempt. See **example.**] **—ex·empt'i·ble** *adj.*

ex·emp·tion (ĕg-zĕmp'shən) *n.* **1.** An act of exempting. **2.** The state of being exempt; immunity. **3. a.** An amount allowed for each of the persons dependent upon a taxpayer's income, including himself, and deductible from his gross annual income in the calculation of income tax. **b.** A person represented by such a deduction.

ex·en·ter·ate (ĕk-sĕn'tə-rāt') *tr.v.* **-ated, -ating, -ates. 1.** To disembowel; eviscerate. **2.** *Surgery.* To remove the contents of (an organ). [Latin *exenterāre* (past participle *exenterātus*), to take the insides out of, to disembowel : *ex,* from, out of + Greek *enteron,* insides, intestines (see **en** in Appendix*).] **—ex·en'ter·a'tion** *n.*

ex·e·qua·tur (ĕk'sə-kwā'tər) *n.* **1.** An official document recognizing a consul or commercial agent, granted by the country to which he is assigned. **2.** Authorization by a secular authority for the publication of ecclesiastical documents, or for the performance by a bishop of his duties. [Latin, "let him perform," third person singular present subjunctive of *exequī,* to EXECUTE.]

ex·e·quies (ĕk'sə-kwēz) *pl n.* Funeral rites. [Middle English *exequies,* from Old French, from Latin *exsequiae,* funeral ceremonies, from *ex(s)equī,* to follow, EXECUTE.]

ex·er·cise (ĕk'sər-sīz') *n.* **1.** An act of employing or putting into play; use: *"the demand for orthodoxy is stifling to any free exercise of intellect"* (Bertrand Russell). **2.** The discharge of (a duty, function, or office). **3.** Activity that requires physical or mental exertion, especially when performed to develop or maintain fitness. **4.** A lesson, composition, problem, or the like, designed to increase one's skill, discipline, or fitness in some capacity: *a piano exercise.* **5.** *Usually plural.* A ceremony, either religious or secular, including speeches, awards, and other traditional rites: *graduation exercises.* *—v.* **exercised, -cising, -cises.** *—tr.* **1.** To put into play or operation; employ. **2.** To bring to bear; exert: *"the desire to be re-elected exercises a strong brake on independent courage."* (John F. Kennedy). **3.** To subject to forms of practice or exertion in order to train, strengthen, condition, or the like; put through exercises: *exercise the memory; exercise a platoon.* **4.** To carry out the functions of; execute; perform: *exercise the role of disciplinarian.* **5.** To absorb the attentions of; especially, to worry, upset, or make anxious: *He was greatly exercised by his wife's illness.* *—intr.* To take exercise or do exercises. [Middle English, from Old French *exercice,* from Latin *exercitium,* exercise, from *exercitus,* past participle of *exercēre,* to drive on, drill, practice : *ex-,* out of, from + *arcēre,* enclose, restrain (see **arek-** in Appendix*).] **—ex'er·cis'a·ble** *adj.*

ex·er·cis·er (ĕk'sər-sī'zər) *n.* **1.** A person who exercises or performs exercises. **2.** A device for exercising the body.

ex·er·ci·ta·tion (ĕg-zûr'sə-tā'shən, ĭg-) *n.* **1.** *Often plural.* Exercises, as of some specified faculty or powers: *intellectual exercitations.* **2.** Practice, as of an art, with a view to improvement: *rhetorical exercitation.* **3.** A display of oratorical skill: *the exercitations of Demosthenes.* [Middle English *exercitacioun,* from Latin *exercitātiō,* from *exercitāre,* to exercise often, frequentative of *exercēre* (past participle *exercitus*), to EXERCISE.]

ex·ergue (ĕk'sûrg', ĕg'zûrg') *n.* **1.** The space on the reverse of a coin or medal, below the central design, often giving the date and place of engraving. **2.** The inscription in this space. [French, from New Latin *exergum* : *ex-,* out of + *ergon,* work (see **werg-**[1] in Appendix*).] **—ex·ergu'al** (ĕk-sûr'gəl) *adj.*

ex·ert (ĕg-zûrt', ĭg-) *tr.v.* **-erted, -erting, -erts. 1.** To put into vigorous action; put forth (strength, ability, or the like): *"Educators need not fear that a child will fail to exert learning effort when that effort is required for survival."* (Gertrude Hildreth). **2.** To bring to bear; exercise: *exert influence.* **3.** To put (oneself) into strenuous effort. [Latin *ex(s)erere* (past participle *ex(s)ertus*), to stretch out : *ex-,* out + *serere,* to join, put in a row, unite (see **ser-**[3] in Appendix*).]

ex·er·tion (ĕg-zûr'shən, ĭg-) *n.* An act or instance of exerting; especially, a strenuous effort. See Synonyms at **effort.**

Ex·e·ter (ĕk'sə-tər). The county seat of Devonshire, England. Population, 82,000.

ex·e·unt (ĕk'sē-ənt, -ōōnt'). *Latin.* They go out. Used as a stage direction to indicate that two or more actors leave the stage.

ex·e·unt om·nes (ĕk'sē-ənt ŏm'nēz', -ōōnt'). *Latin.* They all go out. Used as a stage direction.

ex·fo·li·ate (ĕks-fō'lē-āt') *v.* **-ated, -ating, -ates.** *—tr.* **1.** To remove (skin or bark, for example) in flakes or scales; peel. **2.** To cast off in scales, flakes, or the like. *—intr.* To come off or separate, as scales, flakes, sheets, or layers. [Latin *exfoliāre,* to strip of leaves : *ex-,* removal from + *folium,* leaf (see **bhel-**[3] in Appendix*).] **—ex·fo'li·a'tion** *n.* **—ex·fo'li·a'tive** *adj.*

ex·ha·lant (ĕks-hā'lənt, ĕk-sā'-, ĭk-sā'-) *adj.* Also **ex·ha·lent.** Capable of or functioning in exhalation.

ex·ha·la·tion (ĕks'hə-lā'shən, ĕk'sə-) *n.* **1.** An act of exhaling. **2.** That which is exhaled, such as air or vapor.

ex·hale (ĕks-hāl', ĕk-sāl', ĭk-sāl') *v.* **-haled, -haling, -hales.** *—intr.* **1. a.** To breathe out. **b.** To emit air or vapor. **2.** To be given off or emitted. *—tr.* **1.** To blow forth or breathe out (air, vapor, smoke, or the like). **2.** To give off; emit: *"The moon-speckled landscape exhaled its night rustlings, its truffle-odor of swamps."* (John Howard Griffin). **3.** To draw out or off; evaporate. [Middle English *exalen,* from Old French *exhaler,* from Latin *exhālāre,* to breathe out : *ex-,* out + *hālāre,* to breathe (see **halitosis.**)] **—ex·hal'a·ble** *adj.*

ex·haust (ĕg-zôst', ĭg-) *v.* **-hausted, -hausting, -hausts.** *—tr.* **1.** To let out or draw off (air or fumes). **2.** To draw out the contents of; drain; empty: *exhaust the oil from a storage tank.* **3.** To use up; expend; consume: *exhaust one's money.* **4.** To wear out completely; tire: *"Like all people who try to exhaust a subject, he exhausted his listeners."* (Oscar Wilde). **5.** To drain of resources or properties; deplete: *"Art . . . did not exhaust itself in . . . photographic records of reality"* (Siegfried Kracauer). **6.** To study or deal with comprehensively: *exhaust a topic.* *—intr.* To escape or pass out, as steam. —See Synonyms at **deplete.** *—n.* **1.** The escape or release of vaporous waste material, as from an engine. **2.** The fumes or gases released. **3.** A device or part, such as a pipe, through which such waste material escapes. **4.** An apparatus for drawing out noxious air or waste material by means of a partial vacuum. [Latin *exhaurīre* (past participle *exhaustus*), to draw out, exhaust : *ex-,* out + *haurīre,* to draw up (see **aus-** in Appendix*).] **—ex·haust'er** *n.* **—ex·haust'i·bil'i·ty** *n.* **—ex·haust'i·ble** *adj.*

ex·haus·tion (ĕg-zôs'chən, ĭg-) *n.* **1.** An act or instance of exhausting. **2.** The state of being exhausted.

ex·haus·tive (ĕg-zôs'tĭv, ĭg-) *adj.* **1.** Tending to exhaust. **2.** Comprehensive; thorough: *an exhaustive survey.* **—ex·haus'tive·ly** *adv.* **—ex·haus'tive·ness** *n.*

t tight/th thin, path/*th* this, bathe/ŭ cut/ûr urge/v valve/w with/y yes/z zebra, size/zh vision/ə about, item, edible, gallop, circus/ à *Fr.* ami/œ *Fr.* feu, *Ger.* schön/ü *Fr.* tu, *Ger.* über/KH *Ger.* ich, *Scot.* loch/N *Fr.* bon. ***Follows main vocabulary.** †**Of obscure origin.**

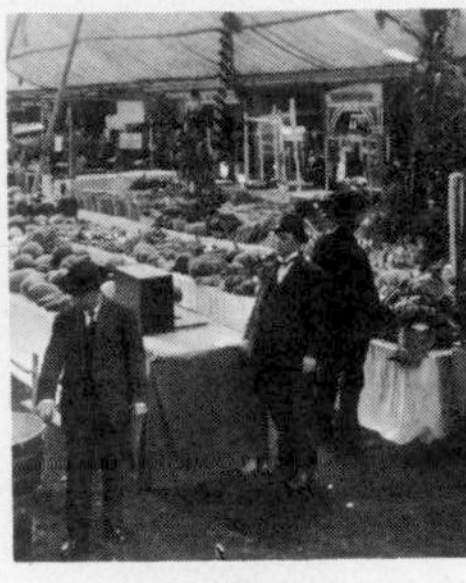

exhibition
At a fair in Danbury, Connecticut, about 1910

ex·haust·less (ĕg-zôst′lĭs, ĭg-) *adj.* Impossible to exhaust; inexhaustible. —**ex·haust′less·ly** *adv.* —**ex·haust′less·ness** *n.*

ex·hib·it (ĕg-zĭb′ĭt, ĭg-) *v.* **-ited, -iting, -its.** —*tr.* **1.** To show; display: *"The Middle Ages exhibit life and color and change"* (Charles H. Haskins). **2. a.** To present for the public to view. **b.** To enter or show in an exhibition or contest. **3.** To give an instance or evidence of; demonstrate: *The specimen exhibits a cancerous condition.* **4.** *Law.* To submit (evidence or documents) in a court; introduce officially. —*intr.* To put something on display; have an exhibition. —See Synonyms at **show.** —*n.* **1.** An act of exhibiting. **2.** That which is exhibited. **3.** *Law.* Something, such as a document, formally introduced as evidence in court. [Middle English *exhibiten,* from Latin *exhibēre* (past participle *exhibitus*), to hold forth, exhibit : *ex-,* out + *habēre,* to hold (see **ghabh-** in Appendix*).]

ex·hi·bi·tion (ĕk′sə-bĭsh′ən) *n.* **1.** An act of exhibiting. **2.** Something exhibited. **3.** A display for the public, as of art objects, industrial achievements, or agricultural products. **4.** *British.* A fixed allowance given to scholars by a school or university.

ex·hi·bi·tion·er (ĕk′sə-bĭsh′ən-ər) *n. British.* A student who receives an exhibition.

ex·hi·bi·tion·ism (ĕk′sə-bĭsh′ə-nĭz′əm) *n.* **1.** The act or practice of flaunting oneself in order to attract attention. **2.** *Psychology.* Compulsive exposure of the sexual organs in public. —**ex′hi·bi′tion·ist** *n.* & *adj.* —**ex′hi·bi′tion·is′tic** *adj.*

ex·hib·i·tive (ĕg-zĭb′ə-tĭv, ĭg-) *adj.* Tending to exhibit; serving as an exhibition. Usually used with *of: His behavior was exhibitive of his lack of interest.* —**ex·hib′i·tive·ly** *adv.*

ex·hib·i·tor (ĕg-zĭb′ə-tər, ĭg-) *n.* Also **ex·hib·i·ter. 1.** One that exhibits; especially, a person or group exhibiting articles in a show. **2.** A motion-picture theater or its manager.

ex·hil·a·rant (ĕg-zĭl′ər-ənt, ĭg-) *adj.* Exhilarating. —*n.* A stimulant or euphoriant.

ex·hil·a·rate (ĕg-zĭl′ə-rāt′, ĭg-) *tr.v.* **-rated, -rating, -rates. 1.** To make cheerful; elate. **2.** To invigorate; stimulate. [Latin *exhilarāre* : *ex-,* completely + *hilarāre,* to make happy, from *hilaris,* cheerful, happy, from Greek *hilaros* (see **sel-**[2] in Appendix*).] —**ex·hil′a·rat′ive** *adj.* —**ex·hil′a·ra′tor** (-rā′tər) *n.*

ex·hil·a·rat·ing (ĕg-zĭl′ə-rā′tĭng, ĭg-) *adj.* **1.** Cheering; gladdening. **2.** Invigorating; stimulating. —**ex·hil′a·rat′ing·ly** *adv.*

ex·hil·a·ra·tion (ĕg-zĭl′ə-rā′shən, ĭg-) *n.* **1.** The state of being exhilarated: *"Few Yosemite visitors ever see snow avalanches and fewer still know the exhilaration of riding on them."* (John Muir). **2.** An act of exhilarating.

ex·hort (ĕg-zôrt′, ĭg-) *v.* **-horted, -horting, -horts.** —*tr.* To urge or incite by strong argument, advice, or appeal; admonish earnestly: *"He exhorted his crews to take a good night's rest, wind up their family affairs, and make their wills"* (Washington Irving). —*intr.* To make urgent appeal. —See Synonyms at **urge.** [Middle English *exhorten,* from Old French *exhorter,* from Latin *exhortārī* : *ex-,* completely + *hortārī,* to encourage (see **gher-**[6] in Appendix*).] —**ex·hort′er** *n.*

ex·hor·ta·tion (ĕg′zôr-tā′shən, ĕk′sôr-) *n.* **1.** An act of exhorting. **2.** The practice of exhorting. **3.** A speech or discourse intended to advise, incite, or encourage.

ex·hor·ta·tive (ĕg-zôr′tə-tĭv, ĭg-) *adj.* Also **ex·hor·ta·to·ry** (-tôr′ē, -tōr′ē). **1.** Pertaining to exhortation. **2.** Serving to exhort; intended to incite or advise.

ex·hume (ĕg-zyōōm′, ĭg-, ĕks-hyōōm′) *tr.v.* **-humed, -huming, -humes. 1.** To remove from a grave; disinter. **2.** To bring to light; uncover: *"the most ancient superstitions have been exhumed"* (Harold Rosenberg). [French *exhumer,* from Medieval Latin *exhumāre* : Latin *ex-,* out of + *humus,* earth (see **dhghem-** in Appendix*).] —**ex′hu·ma′tion** *n.* —**ex·hum′er** *n.*

ex·i·gen·cy (ĕk′sə-jən-sē) *n., pl.* **-cies.** Also **ex·i·gence** (-jəns). **1.** The state or quality of being exigent. **2.** A situation demanding swift attention; a pressing state. **3.** *Usually plural.* Urgent requirements; pressing needs. —See Synonyms at **need.**

ex·i·gent (ĕk′sə-jənt) *adj.* **1.** Requiring immediate attention or remedy; urgent. **2.** Excessively demanding; exacting. [Latin *exigēns,* present participle of *exigere,* to demand. See **exact.**] —**ex′i·gent·ly** *adv.*

ex·i·gi·ble (ĕk′sə-jə-bəl) *adj.* Able to be exacted; demandable; requirable. [French, from *exiger,* to demand, from Latin *exigere.* See **exact.**]

ex·i·gu·i·ty (ĕk′sə-gyōō′ə-tē) *n.* Scantiness; meagerness: *"their resources were of such exiguity that they could not afford the conveniences of modern civilization"* (Ford Madox Ford).

ex·ig·u·ous (ĕg-zĭg′yōō-əs, ĭg-, ĕk-sĭg′-, ĭk-) *adj.* Scanty; meager. [Latin *exiguus,* from *exigere,* to weigh exactly, demand. See **exact.**] —**ex·ig′u·ous·ly** *adv.* —**ex·ig′u·ous·ness** *n.*

ex·ile (ĕg′zīl′, ĕk′sīl′) *n.* **1. a.** Enforced removal from one's native country by authoritative decree; banishment. **b.** Self-imposed separation from one's country. **2. a.** The state or circumstance of being exiled. **b.** The period of time in exile. **3.** One who is or has been separated from his country. —*tr.v.* **exiled, -iling, -iles.** To send (someone) into exile; banish. See Synonyms at **banish.** [Middle English *exil,* from Old French, from Latin *exilium,* from *exul,* one who is exiled. See **al-**[2] in Appendix.*] —**ex·il′ic** (ĕg-zĭl′ĭk, -sĭl′ĭk, ĭg-), **ex·il′i·an** (ĕg-zĭl′ē-ən, -zĭl′yən, ĭg-, ĭk-, ĕk-sĭl′ē-ən, -sĭl′yən, ĭg-) *adj.*

ex·ist (ĕg-zĭst′, ĭg-) *intr.v.* **-isted, -isting, -ists. 1.** To have being or actuality; to be. **2. a.** To have life; live. **b.** To continue to live. **3.** To be present under certain circumstances or in a specified place; occur. [Latin *ex(s)istere,* to exist, emerge, come forth : *ex-,* out + *sistere,* to take a position, stand firm (see **stā-** in Appendix*).]

ex·is·tence (ĕg-zĭs′təns, ĭg-) *n.* **1.** The fact or state of existing; being. **2.** The fact or state of continued being; life. **3. a.** All that exists. **b.** A thing that exists; an entity. **4.** A mode or manner of existing: *a meager existence.* **5.** Occurrence; specific presence: *the existence of life on other planets.*

ex·is·tent (ĕg-zĭs′tənt, ĭg-) *adj.* **1.** Having life or being; existing. **2.** Occurring or present at the moment; current. —See Synonyms at **real.** —*n.* One that exists.

ex·is·ten·tial (ĕg′zĭ-stĕn′shəl, ĕk′sĭ-) *adj.* **1.** Of, pertaining to, or dealing with existence: *"anxiety is existential in . . . that it belongs to existence as such and not to an abnormal state of mind"* (Paul Tillich). **2.** Based on experience; empirical. **3.** Pertaining to existentialism. —**ex′is·ten′tial·ly** *adv.*

ex·is·ten·tial·ism (ĕg′zĭ-stĕn′shə-lĭz′əm, ĕk′sĭ-) *n.* A body of ethical thought, current in the 19th and 20th centuries, centering about the uniqueness and isolation of individual experience in a universe indifferent or even hostile to man, regarding human existence as unexplainable, and emphasizing man's freedom of choice and responsibility for the consequences of his acts. —**ex′is·ten′tial·ist** *adj.* & *n.*

ex·it[1] (ĕg′zĭt, ĕk′sĭt). *Latin.* He (or she) goes out. Used as a stage direction for a specified actor to leave the stage.

ex·it[2] (ĕg′zĭt, ĕk′sĭt) *n.* **1.** The departure of a performer from the stage. **2. a.** The act of going away or out. **b.** Death; demise. **3.** A passage or way out. —*intr.v.* **exited, -iting, -its.** To make one's exit. [Latin *exitus,* exit, departure, from the past participle of *exīre,* to go out : *ex-,* out + *īre,* to go (see **ei-**[1] in Appendix*).]

ex li·bris (ĕks lī′brĭs, lē′-). *Abbr.* **ex lib.** *Latin.* From the library of. A phrase used on bookplates before the owner's name.

Ex·moor (ĕks′mŏŏr′). A moorland plateau occupying about 30 square miles in Somerset and Devonshire, England.

exo-. Indicates outside of, external, or beyond; for example, **exocarp, exoskeleton.** [Greek *exō,* outside of, outside, from *ex,* out of. See **eghs** in Appendix.*]

ex·o·bi·ol·o·gy (ĕk′sō-bī-ŏl′ə-jē) *n.* **1.** A branch of biology that deals with the search for and study of extraterrestrial living organisms. Also called "astrobiology." **2.** A branch of biology that deals with the effects of extraterrestrial space on living organisms. In this sense, also called "space biology."

ex·o·carp (ĕk′sə-kärp′) *n. Botany.* The outermost layer of the pericarp of fruit. Also called "epicarp." [EXO- + -CARP.]

ex·o·crine (ĕk′sə-krĭn′, -krēn, -krīn′) *adj.* **1.** Having or secreting through a duct. Said of a gland. **2.** Of or pertaining to the secretion of a gland having a duct. Also "eccrine." [EXO- + Greek *krinein,* to separate (see **skeri-** in Appendix*).]

Exod. Exodus (Old Testament).

ex·o·derm (ĕk′sə-dûrm′) *n.* An embryonic germ layer, the **ectoderm** *(see).* [EXO- + -DERM.]

ex·o·don·tia (ĕk′sō-dŏn′shə, -shē-ə) *n.* Dentistry involving the extraction of teeth. [New Latin : EX- + *-odontia,* from -ODONT.] —**ex′o·don′tist** *n.*

ex·o·dus (ĕk′sə-dəs) *n.* **1.** A movement away; a departure, usually of a large number of people: *"At the turn of the century most Negroes still lived in rural areas of the South, but by 1914 the largest exodus began."* (LeRoi Jones). **2.** *Capital* **E.** The departure of the Israelites from Egypt. Used with *the.* [Late Latin, from Greek *exodos,* a going out, a way out : *ex-,* out + *hodos,* way (see **sed-**[2] in Appendix*).]

Ex·o·dus (ĕk′sə-dəs) *n. Abbr.* **Ex., Exod.** The second book of the Old Testament, which recounts the Exodus of the Israelites.

ex·o·en·zyme (ĕk′sō-ĕn′zīm′) *n.* An enzyme, such as a digestive enzyme, that functions outside a cell.

ex of·fi·ci·o (ĕks′ ə-fĭsh′ē-ō′). *Abbr.* **e.o., ex off.** *Latin.* By virtue of office or position.

ex·og·a·my (ĕk-sŏg′ə-mē) *n.* **1.** The custom of marrying outside the tribe, family, clan, or other social unit. Compare **endogamy.** **2.** *Biology.* Reproduction by the fusion of gametes of different ancestries. [EXO- + -GAMY.] —**ex′o·gam′ic** (ĕk′sō-găm′ĭk), **ex·og′a·mous** (ĕk-sŏg′ə-məs) *adj.*

ex·og·e·nous (ĕk-sŏj′ə-nəs) *n.* **1.** *Biology.* Derived or developed from external causes. **2.** *Botany.* Characterized by the addition of layers of woody tissue. **3.** Having a cause external to the body. Said of diseases. [From French *exogène,* having additional layers : EXO- + -GEN.] —**ex·og′e·nous·ly** *adv.*

ex·on·er·ate (ĕg-zŏn′ə-rāt′, ĭg-) *tr.v.* **-ated, -ating, -ates. 1.** To free from a charge; declare blameless; exculpate. **2.** To free from a responsibility, obligation, or task. [Middle English *exoneraten,* from Latin *exonerāre* (past participle *exonerātus*), to free from a burden : *ex-,* removal from + *onus* (stem *oner-*), load, burden (see **enos-** in Appendix*).] —**ex·on′er·a′tion** *n.*

exophthalmic goiter. A disease caused by the excessive production of thyroid hormone and characterized by an enlarged thyroid gland, protrusion of the eyeballs, tachycardia, and nervous excitability. Also called "Graves' disease." [From EXOPHTHALMOS.]

ex·oph·thal·mos (ĕk′sŏf-thăl′məs) *n.* Also **ex·oph·thal·mus.** Abnormal protrusion of the eyeball. [New Latin, from Greek, with prominent eyes : *ex-,* out of + *ophthalmos,* eye (see **okw-** in Appendix*).] —**ex′oph·thal′mic** *adj.*

ex·o·ra·ble (ĕk′sər-ə-bəl) *adj. Rare.* Responsive to entreaty. [Latin *exōrābilis,* from *exōrāre,* to move : *ex-,* completely + *ōrāre,* to plead (see **ōr-** in Appendix*).] —**ex′o·ra·bil′i·ty** *n.*

ex·or·bi·tance (ĕg-zôr′bə-təns, ĭg-) *n.* Also **ex·or·bi·tan·cy** (-tən-sē). **1.** Excessiveness, as of price, demand, or need; extravagance. **2.** *Archaic.* Legal or moral irregularity of conduct.

ex·or·bi·tant (ĕg-zôr′bə-tənt, ĭg-) *adj.* **1.** Out of all bounds; extravagant; immoderate. **2.** *Law.* Exceeding the established limits of right or propriety. —See Synonyms at **excessive.** [Middle English, from Old French, from Late Latin *exorbitāns,*

present participle of *exorbitāre*, to deviate : Latin *ex-*, out of + *orbita*, route, ORBIT.] —**ex·or′bi·tant·ly** *adv.*
ex·or·cise (ĕk′sôr-sīz′, ĕk′sər-) *tr.v.* **-cised, -cising, -cises.** Also **ex·or·cize. 1.** To expel (an evil spirit) by or as if by incantation or adjuration. **2.** To free from evil spirits. [Middle English *exorcisen*, from Old French *exorciser*, from Late Latin *exorcīzāre*, from Greek *exorkizein*, to exorcise (an evil spirit) with an oath : *ex-*, away + *horkos*†, oath.] —**ex′or·cis′er** *n.*
ex·or·cism (ĕk′sôr-sĭz′əm, ĕk′sər-) *n.* **1.** The act of exorcising. **2.** A formula used in exorcising. —**ex′or·cist′** *n.*
ex·or·di·um (ĕg-zôr′dē-əm, ĭg-, ĕk-sôr′-, ĭk-) *n., pl.* **-ums** or **-dia** (-dē-ə). A beginning or introductory part, especially of a speech, treatise, or the like. [Latin, from *exōrdīrī*, to begin : *ex-*, completely + *ōrdīrī*, to begin (see **ar-** in Appendix*).] —**ex·or′di·al** *adj.*
ex·o·skel·e·ton (ĕk′sō-skĕl′ə-tən) *n.* An external protective or supporting structure of many invertebrates, such as insects and crustaceans. Compare **endoskeleton.** [EXO- + SKELETON.]
ex·os·mo·sis (ĕk′sŏz-mō′sĭs) *n.* The flow of a fluid through a permeable membrane into a less dense fluid. Compare **endosmosis.** [EX(O)- + OSMOSIS.] —**ex′os·mot′ic** (-mŏt′ĭk) *adj.*
ex·o·sphere (ĕk′sō-sfîr′) *n.* The outermost portion of the atmosphere, estimated to begin 300 to 600 miles above the earth, and characterized by the ability of constituent molecules with appropriate velocities to escape from the earth without colliding with other molecules. [EXO- + -SPHERE.]
ex·o·spore (ĕk′sō-spôr′, -spōr′) *n. Botany.* The outermost layer of a spore in some algae and fungi. [EXO- + SPORE.]
ex·os·to·sis (ĕk′sŏ-stō′sĭs) *n., pl.* **-ses** (-sēz). A bony tumor on the surface of a bone. [New Latin, from Greek *exostōsis* : *ex-*, out of + *osteon*, bone (see **osth-** in Appendix*).]
ex·o·ter·ic (ĕk′sə-tĕr′ĭk) *adj.* **1.** Not belonging only to an inner circle of disciples or initiates. **2.** Comprehensible to or suited to the public; popular. Compare **esoteric. 3.** Pertaining to the outside; external. [Latin *exōtericus*, external, from Greek *exōterikos*, from *exōterō*, comparative of *exō*, outside, from *ex*, out (see **eghs** in Appendix*).] —**ex′o·ter′i·cal·ly** *adv.*
ex·o·ther·mic (ĕk′sō-thûr′mĭk) *adj.* Also **ex·o·ther·mal** (-məl). Releasing, as opposed to absorbing, heat. Compare **endothermic.** [EXO- + THERM(O)- + -IC.]
ex·ot·ic (ĕg-zŏt′ĭk, ĭg-) *adj.* **1.** From another part of the world; not indigenous; foreign. **2.** Having the charm of the unfamiliar; strikingly and intriguingly unusual or beautiful. —See Synonyms at **fantastic.** —*n.* One that is exotic. [Latin *exōticus*, from Greek *exōtikos*, from *exō*, outside, from *ex*, out (see **eghs** in Appendix*).] —**ex·ot′i·cal·ly** *adv.* —**ex·ot′ic·ness** *n.*
ex·o·tox·in (ĕk′sō-tŏk′sĭn) *n.* A toxin excreted by a microorganism into a surrounding medium and recoverable from a culture without destruction of the producing agent. See **toxin.** [EXO- + TOXIN.]
exp *Mathematics.* exponential.
exp. 1. expenses. **2.** experiment; experimental. **3.** expiration; expired. **4.** export; exported; exporter. **5.** express.
ex·pand (ĕk-spănd′, ĭk-) *v.* **-panded, -panding, -pands.** —*tr.* **1.** To open up or out; spread out; unfold. **2.** To increase the dimensions of; cause to swell; distend: *"One's perceptions blow out rapidly like air balls expanded by some rush of air"* (Virginia Woolf). **3.** To increase the scope of; extend; develop. **4.** To make relaxed and better disposed: *"Like a kitten she was expanded with warmth and food and drink"* (Michael Gilbert). **5.** *Mathematics.* To write (a quantity) as a sum of terms, as a continued product, or as another extended form. —*intr.* **1.** To open up; unfold. **2.** To become larger or wider. **3.** To speak or write at length; expatiate. **4.** To feel expansive. —See Synonyms at **increase.** [Middle English *expanden*, from Latin *expandere* : *ex-*, out + *pandere*, to spread (see **pet-²** in Appendix*).] —**ex·pand′er** *n.*
expanding universe theory. 1. The interpretation of the shifts of the lines in the spectra of galaxies as resulting from a Doppler effect, with the experimental results that all galaxies are retreating from each other at speeds proportional to the distance separating them and that the universe is expanding. **2.** The cosmological theory in which violent eruption from a point source leads to the formation of elementary particles, the subsequent formation of hydrogen and helium, and the dispersion of the galaxies that develop from this matter. In this sense, also called "big bang theory."
ex·panse (ĕk-spăns′, ĭk-) *n.* **1.** A wide and open extent, as of land, sky, or water. **2.** Expansion. [Latin *expansum*, from the neuter participle of *expandere*, to EXPAND.]
ex·pan·si·ble (ĕk-spăn′sə-bəl, ĭk-) *adj.* Capable of expanding or of being expanded. —**ex·pan′si·bil′i·ty** *n.*
ex·pan·sile (ĕk-spăn′səl, ĭk-) *adj.* Of, pertaining to, or adapted for expansion.
ex·pan·sion (ĕk-spăn′shən, ĭk-) *n.* **1.** The act or process of expanding. **2.** The state of being expanded. **3.** A part produced by expanding. **4.** The extent or amount by which something has expanded. **5.** An enlargement, increase, or extension, as of business, currency, or territory. **6.** Increase in the dimensions of a body. **7.** *Mathematics.* **a.** A quantity written in an extended form, as a sum of terms or as a continued product. **b.** The process of obtaining this form. **8.** An expanse.
ex·pan·sion·ar·y (ĕk-spăn′shə-nĕr′ē, ĭk-) *adj.* Tending toward expansion.
expansion bolt. A bolt having an attachment that expands as the bolt is driven into a surface.
ex·pan·sion·ism (ĕk-spăn′shə-nĭz′əm, ĭk-) *n.* The practice or policy of territorial or economic expansion, as by a nation. —**ex·pan′sion·ist** *n.* & *adj.*
ex·pan·sive (ĕk-spăn′sĭv, ĭk-) *adj.* **1.** Capable of expanding or tending to expand. **2.** Wide; sweeping; comprehensive. **3.** Disposed to be open and generous; outgoing. **4.** Marked by euphoria and delusions of grandeur. **5.** Grand in scale: *expansive living.* —**ex·pan′sive·ly** *adv.* —**ex·pan′sive·ness** *n.*
ex par·te (ĕks pär′tē). *Latin.* **1.** *Law.* From or on one side only. **2.** One-sided; partisan.
ex·pa·ti·ate (ĕk-spā′shē-āt′, ĭk-) *intr.v.* **-ated, -ating, -ates. 1.** To speak or write at length on a subject; dilate: *"He expatiated freely, more for his own edification than that of the crew"* (John Barth). **2.** *Rare.* To wander freely. [Latin *ex(s)patiārī*, to spread out, digress, expatiate : *ex-*, out + *spatiārī*, to walk, to spread, from *spatium*, SPACE.] —**ex·pa′ti·a′tion** *n.*
ex·pa·tri·ate (ĕks-pā′trē-āt′) *v.* **-ated, -ating, -ates.** —*tr.* **1.** To banish (a person) from his native land; to exile. **2.** To banish (oneself) from one's native land. —*intr.* To leave one's homeland, and often renounce one's citizenship, to reside in another country. —See Synonyms at **banish.** —*n.* (ĕks-pā′trē-ĭt, -āt′). An expatriated person: *"The example of the famous expatriate Henry James haunted the mind of Ezra Pound."* (Matthew Josephson). —*adj.* Expatriated. [Medieval Latin *expatriāre* : Latin *ex-*, out of + *patria*, native land, from *pater* (stem *patr-*), father (see **peter** in Appendix*).] —**ex·pa′tri·a′tion** *n.*
ex·pect (ĕk-spĕkt′, ĭk-) *tr.v.* **-pected, -pecting, -pects. 1.** To look forward to the probable occurrence or appearance of. **2.** To consider likely or certain. **3.** To consider reasonable or due: *I expect an apology.* **4.** To consider obligatory; require. **5.** *Informal.* To presume; suppose. —**be expecting.** To be pregnant. [Latin *ex(s)pectāre*, to look out (for), expect : *ex-*, out + *spectāre*, look at, frequentative of *specere*, to see, look at (see **spek-** in Appendix*).]
Synonyms: *expect, anticipate, hope, await, foresee.* These verbs are related in various ways to the idea of looking ahead to something in the future. To *expect* is to look forward to the occurrence of something with little reservation as to its likelihood. To *anticipate* usually involves something more than expectation. In some contexts it refers to taking appropriate action in advance of something expected, so as to forestall or prevent its occurrence, or so as to meet an order or request: *anticipate trouble; anticipate one's wishes.* The term can also refer to looking forward to something and experiencing it beforehand: *anticipate pleasure.* To *hope* is to desire, usually with confidence in the likelihood of gaining what is desired. To *await*, in this comparison, is to look forward to without doubt as to occurrence. To *foresee* is to know of an occurrence in advance of its coming into existence, by means of insight, intuition, study, or inference.
ex·pec·tan·cy (ĕk-spĕk′tən-sē, ĭk-) *n., pl.* **-cies.** Also **ex·pec·tance** (-təns). **1.** The act or state of expecting; expectation. **2.** The state of being expected. **3. a.** Something expected. **b.** That which one can look forward to having; prospect: *a life expectancy of seventy years.*
ex·pec·tant (ĕk-spĕk′tənt, ĭk-) *adj.* **1.** Having or marked by expectation: *an expectant pause.* **2.** Waiting in confident expectation. Used with *of: expectant of praise.* **3.** Awaiting the birth of a child: *an expectant mother.* —*n.* A person who is expecting something. —**ex·pec′tant·ly** *adv.*
ex·pec·ta·tion (ĕk′spĕk-tā′shən) *n.* **1. a.** The act or state of expecting. **b.** Eager anticipation: *"Ten boys sat before him, their hands folded, their eyes bright with expectation."* (Evelyn Waugh). **2.** The state of being expected. **3.** *Plural.* Prospects, especially of inheritance. **4.** Something expected. **5.** The expected value of a random variable, especially the **mean** *(see).* —See Synonyms at **prospect.**
ex·pec·ta·tive (ĕk-spĕk′tə-tĭv, ĭk-) *adj.* Of, relating to, or characterized by expectation.
ex·pec·to·rant (ĕk-spĕk′tər-ənt, ĭk-) *adj.* Promoting or facilitating secretion or expulsion from the mucous membrane of the air passages. —*n.* An expectorant medicine.
ex·pec·to·rate (ĕk-spĕk′tə-rāt′, ĭk-) *v.* **-rated, -rating, -rates.** —*tr.* **1.** To eject from the mouth; spit. **2.** To cough up and eject by spitting. —*intr.* **1.** To spit. **2.** To clear out the chest and lungs by coughing up and spitting out matter. [Latin *expectorāre*, to drive from the breast : *ex-*, from, out of + *pectus* (stem *pector-*), breast (see **peg-** in Appendix*).] —**ex·pec′to·ra′tion** *n.*
ex·pe·di·en·cy (ĕk-spē′dē-ən-sē) *n., pl.* **-cies.** Also **ex·pe·di·ence** (-dē-əns). **1.** Appropriateness to the purpose at hand. **2.** Adherence to self-serving means. **3.** An expedient. **4.** *Obsolete.* Speed: *"making hither with all due expedience"* (Shakespeare).
ex·pe·di·ent (ĕk-spē′dē-ənt) *adj.* **1.** Appropriate to the purpose at hand. **2.** Serving to promote one's interest; politic though perhaps unprincipled. **3.** *Obsolete.* Expeditious. —*n.* **1.** That which answers the immediate purpose; a means to an end: *"Advertisers regard acting merely as a sales expedient."* (Charles Marowitz). **2.** A contrivance adopted to meet an urgent need; a device; recourse. [Middle English, from Old French, from Latin *expediēns*, present participle of *expedīre*, to free, make ready. See **expedite.**] —**ex·pe′di·ent·ly** *adv.*
ex·pe·di·en·tial (ĕk-spē′dē-ĕn′shəl, ĭk-) *adj.* Of, pertaining to, or concerned with what is expedient. —**ex·pe′di·en′tial·ly** *adv.*
ex·pe·dite (ĕk′spə-dīt′) *tr.v.* **-dited, -diting, -dites. 1.** To speed up the progress of; help along; assist; facilitate: *"a broad way now is pav'd/To expedite your glorious march"* (Milton). **2.** To perform quickly and efficiently. **3.** *Rare.* To issue officially; dispatch. —See Synonyms at **speed.** —*adj. Obsolete.* **1.** Expeditious; prompt. **2.** Unimpeded. [Latin *expedīre* (past participle *expeditus*), to free the feet, to extricate. See **ped-¹** in Appendix.*] —**ex′pe·dit′er, ex′pe·di′tor** (-tər) *n.*

ex·pe·di·tion (ĕk'spə-dĭsh'ən) *n.* **1. a.** A journey undertaken by an organized group of people with a definite objective. **b.** A long march or voyage made by military forces to a scene of battle. **2.** The force sent out, with its retinue, conveyances, and equipment. **3.** Speed in performance; dispatch; promptness. [Middle English *expediciοun,* from Old French *expedition,* from Latin *expeditiō,* from *expedītus,* past participle of *expedīre,* to extricate. See **expedite.**]

ex·pe·di·tion·ar·y (ĕk'spə-dĭsh'ə-nĕr'ē) *adj.* Relating to or constituting an expedition, especially military.

ex·pe·di·tious (ĕk'spə-dĭsh'əs) *adj.* Acting or done with speed and efficiency. See Synonyms at **fast.** —**ex'pe·di'tious·ly** *adv.* —**ex'pe·di'tious·ness** *n.*

ex·pel (ĕk-spĕl', ĭk-) *tr.v.* **-pelled, -pelling, -pels. 1.** To force or drive out; eject forcefully. **2.** To discharge, as from the body or some receptacle: *"Frau Hutton expelled an enormous charge of breath"* (Katherine Anne Porter). **3.** To dismiss from a school or society by official decision; turn out. —See Synonyms at **eject.** [Middle English *expellen,* from Latin *expellere* : *ex-,* out + *pellere,* to drive (see **pel-⁶** in Appendix*).] —**ex·pel'la·ble** *adj.*

ex·pel·lant (ĕk-spĕl'ənt, ĭk-) *adj.* Also **ex·pel·lent.** Expelling or tending to expel; expulsive. —**ex·pel'lant** *n.*

ex·pend (ĕk-spĕnd', ĭk-) *tr.v.* **-pended, -pending, -pends. 1.** To put out or lay out; spend. **2.** To use up; consume: *"every effort seemed to expend her spirit's force"* (Meredith). [Middle English *expenden,* from Latin *expendere,* to pay out : *ex,* out + *pendere,* weigh, pay (see **spen-** in Appendix*).]

ex·pend·a·ble (ĕk-spĕn'də-bəl, ĭk-) *adj.* **1.** Subject to use or consumption. **2.** Suitable for sacrifice if required; not essential to preserve: *"that most expendable commodity, a former leader."* (Paul Goodman). —*n.* That which is expendable.

ex·pen·di·ture (ĕk-spĕn'də-chər, ĭk-) *n.* **1.** The act or process of expending; outlay. **2. a.** The amount expended. **b.** An expense. —See Synonyms at **price.**

ex·pense (ĕk-spĕns', ĭk-) *n.* **1.** The cost involved in some activity; a sacrifice; a price: *"Every attempt at a system is made at the expense of facts"* (Bernard Berenson). **2.** *Plural. Abbr.* **exp. a.** Charges incurred while performing one's job. **b.** *Informal.* Money allotted for payment of such charges. **3.** Something requiring the expenditure of money. **4.** *Archaic.* An act of expending; expenditure. —See Synonyms at **price.** [Middle English, from Old French *espense,* from Late Latin *expensa,* from the feminine past participle of Latin *expendere,* to EXPEND.]

ex·pen·sive (ĕk-spĕn'sĭv, ĭk-) *adj.* Involving a large expenditure; high-priced; costly. See Synonyms at **costly.**

ex·pe·ri·ence (ĕk-spîr'ē-əns, ĭk-) *n.* **1.** The apprehension of an object, thought, or emotion through the senses or mind: *"the experience of art has always been taken to be 'recreation'"* (Paul Goodman). **2.** Active participation in events or activities, leading to the accumulation of knowledge or skill. **3.** The knowledge or skill so derived. **4.** An event or series of events participated in or lived through. **5.** The totality of such events in the past of an individual or group. —*tr.v.* **experienced, -encing, -ences.** To participate in or partake of personally; undergo: *"everyone experiences this feeling of loneliness, of not belonging."* (Brendan Behan). [Middle English, from Old French, from Latin *experientia,* from *experiēns,* present participle of *experīrī,* to try, test. See **per-⁵** in Appendix.*]

ex·pe·ri·enced (ĕk-spîr'ē-ənst, ĭk-) *adj.* **1.** Skilled through frequent use or practice: *"knit all the Greekish ears / To his experienced tongue"* (Shakespeare). **2.** Knowledgeable from long or wide experience: *an experienced teacher.*

experience table. A table compiled from life-insurance statistics to indicate expectation of life.

ex·pe·ri·en·tial (ĕk-spîr'ē-ĕn'shəl, ĭk-) *adj.* Pertaining to or derived from experience. —**ex·pe'ri·en'tial·ly** *adv.*

ex·per·i·ment (ĕk-spĕr'ə-mənt, -mĕnt', ĭk-) *n. Abbr.* **exp., expt. 1.** A test made to demonstrate a known truth, to examine the validity of a hypothesis, or to determine the efficacy of something previously untried: *a laboratory experiment.* **2.** The conducting of such a test. —*intr.v.* **experimented, -menting, -ments.** To conduct an experiment or experiments; to try or test. [Middle English, from Old French, from Latin *experīmentum,* from *experīrī,* to try, test. See **experience.**]

ex·per·i·men·tal (ĕk-spĕr'ə-mĕnt'l, ĭk-) *adj. Abbr.* **exp., exptl. 1. a.** Pertaining to or based upon experiment. **b.** Given to experimenting. **2.** Provisional; tentative. **3.** Founded upon experience; empirical. —**ex·per'i·men'tal·ly** *adv.*

ex·per·i·men·tal·ism (ĕk-spĕr'ə-mĕnt'l-ĭz'əm, ĭk-) *n.* The use of or reliance upon experimentation. —**ex·per'i·men'tal·ist** *n.*

ex·per·i·men·ta·tion (ĕk-spĕr'ə-mĕn-tā'shən, ĭk-) *n.* The act, process, or practice of experimenting: *"in the arts as in the sciences a certain freedom for experimentation is necessary"* (Edmund Wilson).

experiment station. An establishment in which scientific experiments are conducted in a specific field, such as agriculture, and practical uses are developed.

ex·pert (ĕk'spûrt') *n.* **1.** A person with a high degree of skill in or knowledge of a certain subject. **2.** *Military.* **a.** The highest grade that can be achieved in marksmanship. **b.** A person who has achieved this grade. Compare **sharpshooter, marksman.** —*adj.* (ĭk-spûrt', ĕk'spûrt). Having or demonstrating impressive skill, dexterity, or knowledge. [Middle English, from Old French, from Latin *expertus,* past participle of *experīrī,* to try. See **per-⁵** in Appendix.*] —**ex·pert'ly** *adv.* —**ex·pert'ness** *n.*

ex·per·tise (ĕk'spûr-tēz') *n.* **1.** Expert advice or opinion. **2.** Specialized knowledge; expertness. [French, survey, evaluation, from Old French, expertness, from EXPERT.]

ex·pi·a·ble (ĕk'spē-ə-bəl) *adj.* Capable of being expiated.

ex·pi·ate (ĕk'spē-āt') *v.* **-ated, -ating, -ates.** —*tr.* To make atonement for; redress. —*intr.* To make expiation. [Latin *expiāre* : *ex-,* completely + *piāre,* appease, atone, from *pius,* devout (see **pius** in Appendix*).] —**ex'pi·a'tor** (-ā'tər) *n.*

ex·pi·a·tion (ĕk'spē-ā'shən) *n.* **1.** The act of expiating; an atonement: *"tragedy is a formalized ritual of expiation"* (Stanley E. Hyman). **2.** The means of redress or atonement; amends. —**ex'pi·a·to'ry** (-ə-tôr'ē, -tōr'ē) *adj.*

ex·pi·ra·tion (ĕk'spə-rā'shən) *n. Abbr.* **exp. 1.** A coming to a close; termination; an ending. **2.** The act of breathing out.

ex·pir·a·to·ry (ĕk-spīr'ə-tôr'ē, -tōr'ē, ĭk-) *adj.* Of, pertaining to, or involving the expiration of air from the lungs.

ex·pire (ĕk-spīr', ĭk-) *v.* **-pired, -piring, -pires.** —*intr.* **1.** To come to an end; terminate; cease to be effective: *His membership expired.* **2.** To breathe one's last breath; die. **3.** To exhale; breathe out. —*tr.* **1.** To breathe out. **2.** *Archaic.* To give off, as moisture; exude. [Middle English *expiren,* from Old French *exspirer,* from Latin *ex(s)pīrāre,* to breathe out, to expire : *ex-,* out + *spīrāre,* to breathe (see **spirāre** in Appendix*).]

ex·pi·ry (ĕk-spīr'ē, ĭk-) *n., pl.* **-ries.** An expiration, especially of a contract or agreement. [From EXPIRE.]

ex·plain (ĕk-splān', ĭk-) *v.* **-plained, -plaining, -plains.** —*tr.* **1.** To make plain or comprehensible; remove obscurity from; elucidate: *"It was the economists who undertook to explain this puzzle"* (Robert L. Heilbroner). **2.** To define; explicate; expound: *He explained his plan.* **3.** To offer reasons for or a cause of; answer for; justify: *explain an error.* —*intr.* To give an explanation. —**explain away.** To minimize or nullify by explanation. [Middle English *explanen,* from Latin *explānāre,* to explain, to spread out : *ex-,* completely + *plānus,* plain, flat (see **pele-¹** in Appendix*).] —**ex·plain'a·ble** *adj.*

Synonyms: *explain, elucidate, expound, explicate, interpret, construe.* These verbs mean to make the nature or meaning of something clear. *Explain* is most widely applicable, since it has the fewest special implications. *Elucidate* is used most appropriately in contexts that suggest an attempt to throw light in some way on a complex subject. *Expound* and *explicate* imply detailed and usually learned and lengthy exploration or analysis of such a subject. *Interpret* can refer to translation of a foreign tongue or, by extension, to translation of complexities into understandable terms. It often also implies the disclosure of underlying meaning by the application of special knowledge or insight. *Construe* involves putting a construction or interpretation on something: *a law construed strictly by the Supreme Court; construe silence as a sign of disapproval.*

ex·pla·na·tion (ĕk'splə-nā'shən) *n.* **1.** The act or process of making plain or comprehensible; elucidation; clarification: *His plan requires explanation.* **2.** That which serves to explain or to account for something: *He always has a ready explanation.* **3.** A mutual clarification of misunderstandings; reconciliation.

ex·plan·a·to·ry (ĕk-splăn'ə-tôr'ē, -tōr'ē) *adj.* Also **ex·plan·a·tive** (-ə-tĭv). Serving or intended to explain. —**ex·plan'a·to'ri·ly** *adv.*

ex·plant (ĕks-plănt', -plänt', ĭks-) *tr.v.* **-planted, -planting, -plants.** To take (living tissue) from the natural site of growth and place in a medium or culture. —*n.* The material explanted. [EX- + PLANT.] —**ex'plan·ta'tion** *n.*

ex·ple·tive (ĕks'plə-tĭv) *adj.* Also **ex·ple·to·ry** (-tôr'ē, -tōr'ē). Added or inserted in order to fill out something; especially, a word added to a sentence. —*n.* **1.** An exclamation or oath, especially one that is profane or obscene. **2.** *Grammar.* A word or phrase added to a sentence in order to ease syntax or rhythm, as the word *there* in the sentence *There are many reasons given,* or *it* in the sentence *It is nice to see you.* [Late Latin *explētīvus,* from Latin *explētus,* past participle of *explēre,* to fill out : *ex-,* out + *plēre,* fill (see **pel-⁸** in Appendix*).]

ex·pli·ca·ble (ĕks'plĭ-kə-bəl) *adj.* Capable of being explained; explainable: *"Perhaps now 'stories' have become too sane, too explicable, too commonplace"* (Pauline Kael).

ex·pli·cate (ĕks'plĭ-kāt') *tr.v.* **-cated, -cating, -cates.** To make clear the meaning of; explain. See Synonyms at **explain.** [Latin *explicāre,* to unfold, explicate : *ex-* (reversal) + *plicāre,* to fold (see **plek-** in Appendix*).] —**ex'pli·ca'tor** (-kā'tər) *n.*

ex·pli·ca·tion (ĕks'plĭ-kā'shən) *n.* **1.** An explanation. **2.** Exhaustive exposition and elucidation: *"He took a naive delight in explication, and loved to give accounts of things in verse"* (Mark Van Doren). **3. a.** Critical exposition and interpretation, as of literary texts. **b.** An **explication de texte** *(see).*

ex·pli·ca·tion de texte (ĕk-splē-kä-syôɴ də tĕkst') *pl.* **explications de texte** (ĕk-splē-kä-syôɴ də tĕkst'). *French.* **1.** A method of literary criticism in which a detailed reading and analysis of a given text in each of its linguistic, compositional, and expressive parts and aspects is followed by a synthesizing exposition of these with relation to each other and to the whole work. **2.** An analysis in accordance with this method. **3.** A classroom lecture or oral report embodying this as a method of instruction. [French, "textual exposition."]

ex·pli·ca·tive (ĕks'plə-kā'tĭv) *adj.* Also **ex·pli·ca·to·ry** (-kə-tôr'ē, -tōr'ē). Serving to explain; explanatory.

ex·plic·it¹ (ĕk-splĭs'ĭt, ĭk-) *adj.* **1.** Expressed with precision; clearly defined; specific: *"But if you are really innocent and ignorant, I must be more explicit"* (Jane Austen). **2.** Forthright in expression; unreserved; outspoken. [French *explicite,* from Latin *explicitus,* past participle of *explicāre,* to EXPLICATE.] —**ex·plic'it·ly** *adv.* —**ex·plic'it·ness** *n.*

ex·plic·it² (ĕks'plĭk-ĭt) *n.* A word formerly used to indicate the close of a manuscript or book. [Late Latin, short for *explicitus (est liber),* "(the book is) unrolled," from Latin *explicitus,* EXPLICIT.]

ex·plode (ĕk-splōd', ĭk-) *v.* **-ploded, -ploding, -plodes.** —*intr.*

ă pat/ā pay/âr care/ä father/b bib/ch church/d deed/ĕ pet/ē be/f fife/g gag/h hat/hw which/ĭ pit/ī pie/îr pier/j judge/k kick/l lid, needle/m mum/n no, sudden/ng thing/ŏ pot/ō toe/ô paw, for/oi noise/ou out/ŏŏ took/ōō boot/p pop/r roar/s sauce/sh ship, dish/

1. To release mechanical, chemical, or nuclear energy in an explosion. **2.** To burst and be destroyed by explosion. **3.** To burst forth or break out suddenly: *explode into action.* **4.** To fly into a sudden rage. **5.** To increase suddenly, sharply, and without control. *—tr.* **1.** To cause to explode or burst violently and noisily; detonate. **2.** To expose as false, unreliable, or irrelevant; confute: *explode a hypothesis.* **3.** *Obsolete.* To hoot (an actor or play) off the stage. **4.** *Phonetics.* To pronounce as a plosion. [Latin *explōdere,* drive out by clapping : *ex-,* out + *plaudere*†, to clap.] **—ex·plod'er** *n.*

exploded view. An illustration or diagram of a construction, showing its parts separately, but in positions indicating their proper relationships to the whole.

ex·ploit (ĕks'ploit') *n.* An act or deed, especially a brilliant or heroic feat. *—tr.v.* (ĕk-sploit', ĭk-) **exploited, -ploiting, -ploits. 1.** To employ to the greatest possible advantage; utilize: *exploit an advantage.* **2.** To make use of selfishly or unethically: *exploit peasant labor.* **3.** To publicize (a theatrical production, popular song, or the like). [Middle English *esploit, expleit,* from Old French *exploit, esplait,* achievement, from Gallo-Romance *explictum* (unattested), from Latin *explicitus,* EXPLICIT.] **—ex·ploit'a·ble, ex·ploit'a·tive** *adj.* **—ex·ploit'er** *n.*

ex·ploi·ta·tion (ĕks'ploi-tā'shən) *n.* **1.** The act of exploiting: *"Deterrence is concerned with the exploitation of potential force."* (Thomas Schelling). **2.** The utilization of another person for selfish purposes. **3.** A program of publicity for a theatrical performance, popular song, or the like.

ex·plo·ra·tion (ĕk'splə-rā'shən) *n.* **1.** The act or instance of exploring (a region). **2.** *Medicine.* A digital, instrumental, or surgical diagnostic examination of an organ or part, especially of one hidden from sight. **3.** An investigation or search. **—ex·plor'a·to'ry** (ĕk-splôr'ə-tôr'ē, -splōr'ə-tōr'ē, ĭk-) *adj.*

ex·plore (ĕk-splôr', -splōr', ĭk-) *v.* **-plored, -ploring, -plores.** *—tr.* **1.** To investigate systematically; examine; to study: *explore the possibility of a just peace.* **2.** To search into or range over (a country) for the purpose of discovery. **3.** *Medicine.* To examine for diagnostic purposes. *—intr.* To make an examination; to study. [Latin *explōrāre,* to search out, explore : *ex-,* out + *plōrāre,* cry aloud (see **deplore**).]

ex·plor·er (ĕk-splôr'ər, -splōr'ər, ĭk-) *n.* **1.** One who explores; especially, one who explores a geographical area. **2.** An implement or tool used for exploring; a probe. **3.** *Capital* **E.** A member of the exploring program of Boy Scouts of America, including boys between fourteen and seventeen years of age. **4.** *Usually capital* **E.** *Aerospace.* Any of a series of early U.S. satellites, two of which were instrumental in the discovery of the **Van Allen belts** *(see).*

ex·plo·sion (ĕk-splō'zhən, ĭk-) *n.* **1.** A sudden rapid violent release of mechanical, chemical, or nuclear energy from a confined region; especially, such a release that generates a radially propagating shock wave accompanied by a loud, sharp report, flying debris, heat, light, and fire. **2.** The loud, sharp sound accompanying such a release. **3.** Anything regarded as having the characteristics or destructive potential of such a release. **4.** A sudden vehement expression: *"she was given to abrupt explosions of speech after long intervals of silence"* (Edith Wharton). **5.** A sudden and great increase: *the cultural explosion.* **6.** *Phonetics.* A **plosion** *(see).* [Latin *explōsiō,* from *explōsus,* past participle of *explōdere,* to EXPLODE.]

ex·plo·sive (ĕk-splō'sĭv, ĭk-) *adj.* **1.** Pertaining to or of the nature of an explosion: *an explosive subject.* **2.** Tending to explode. **3.** Increasing without limit. **4.** *Phonetics.* Pertaining to a plosion; plosive. *—n.* **1.** A substance, especially a prepared chemical, that explodes or causes explosion. **2.** *Phonetics.* A **plosive** *(see).* [Old French *explosif,* from Latin *explōsus.* See **explosion.**] **—ex·plo'sive·ly** *adv.* **—ex·plo'sive·ness** *n.*

ex·po·nent (ĕk-spō'nənt, ĭk-) *n.* **1.** One that defines, expounds, or interprets. **2.** One that speaks for, represents, or advocates: *an exponent of international cooperation.* **3.** *Mathematics.* Any number or symbol, as *3* in $(x+y)^3$, placed to the right of and above another number, symbol, or expression, denoting the power to which the latter is to be raised. In this sense, also called "power." *—adj.* Expository; explanatory. [Latin *expōnēns,* present participle of *expōnere,* to EXPOUND.]

ex·po·nen·tial (ĕk'spō-nĕn'shəl) *adj.* **1.** *Mathematics.* **a.** Containing, involving, or expressed as an exponent. **b.** *Symbol* **exp** Expressed in terms of a designated power of *e,* the base of natural logarithms. **2.** Of or pertaining to an exponent. **—ex'po·nen'tial·ly** *adv.*

ex·po·ni·ble (ĕk-spō'nə-bəl, ĭk-) *adj.* Requiring or admitting of explanation or definition. Said especially of an obscure logical proposition. *—n.* An exponible proposition. [Medieval Latin *expōnibilis,* from Latin *expōnere,* to EXPOUND.]

ex·port (ĕk-spôrt', -spōrt', ĭk-, ĕks'pôrt', -pōrt') *v.* **-ported, -porting, -ports.** *—tr.* To send or carry (as a commodity) abroad, especially for trade or sale: *We export woolens.* *—intr.* To send or carry abroad merchandise, especially for sale or trade: *We export to Europe.* *—n.* (ĕks'pôrt, -pōrt). Also **ex·por·ta·tion** (ĕk'spôr-tā'shən, ĕk'spōr-). *Abbr.* **exp. 1.** The act of exporting. **2.** That which is exported. [Latin *exportāre,* to carry out or away : *ex-,* out + *portāre,* to carry (see **per-**[2] in Appendix*).] **—ex·port'a·bil'i·ty** *n.* **—ex·port'a·ble** *adj.* **—ex·port'er** *n.*

ex·pose (ĕk-spōz', ĭk-) *tr.v.* **-posed, -posing, -poses. 1.** To lay open, as to something undesirable or injurious. **2.** To subject (a photographic film or plate) to the action of light. **3.** To make visible or known; make manifest; display, reveal, or exhibit: *Cleaning exposed the grain of the wood.* **4.** To disclose or unmask, as a crime; lay bare; make known. **5.** *Roman Catholic Church.* To leave (the Host) displayed on the altar for veneration. **6.** To put out or abandon (an infant, for example) without food or shelter. —See Synonyms at **reveal, show.** [Middle English *exposen,* from Old French *exposer,* from Latin *expōnere,* to expose, EXPOUND.] **—ex·pos'er** *n.*

ex·po·sé (ĕk'spō-zā') *n.* **1.** An exposure or revelation of something discreditable. **2.** An exposition of facts. [French, from the past participle of *exposer,* to EXPOSE.]

ex·po·si·tion (ĕk'spə-zĭsh'ən) *n.* **1.** A setting forth of meaning or intent. **2.** A precise statement or definition; explication; elucidation. **3.** *Music.* The first part of a sonata or fugue that introduces the themes. **4.** The part of a play that introduces the theme and chief characters. **5.** The act of exposing or the condition of being exposed. **6.** A public exhibition or show, as of artistic or industrial developments. **7.** *Roman Catholic Church.* The display of the Host on the altar for public veneration. **8.** *Archaic.* Exposure. [Middle English *exposicioun,* from Old French *exposition,* from Latin *expositiō,* from *expositus,* past participle of *expōnere,* to EXPOUND.] **—ex·pos'i·tive** (ĕk-spŏz'ə-tĭv, ĭk-), **ex·pos'i·to'ry** (-tôr'ē, -tōr'ē) *adj.* **—ex·pos'i·tor** (-tər) *n.*

ex post fac·to (ĕks' pōst' făk'tō). *Latin.* Formulated, enacted, or operating retroactively. Said especially of a law.

ex·pos·tu·late (ĕk-spŏs'cho͝o-lāt', ĭk-) *intr.v.* **-lated, -lating, -lates.** To reason earnestly with someone in an effort to dissuade or correct; remonstrate. See Synonyms at **object.** [Latin *expostulāre,* to demand strongly : *ex-,* entirely + *postulāre,* to demand (see **perk-**[2] in Appendix*).] **—ex·pos'tu·la'tor** (-lā'tər) *n.* **—ex·pos'tu·la·to'ry** (-lə-tôr'ē, -tōr'ē), **ex·pos'tu·la'tive** *adj.*

ex·pos·tu·la·tion (ĕk-spŏs'cho͝o-lā'shən, ĭk-) *n.* The act or instance of expostulating; remonstrance: *"Anna's voice was sharply raised in strong rebuke and worn expostulation"* (Gertrude Stein).

ex·po·sure (ĕk-spō'zhər, ĭk-) *n.* **1.** The act or instance of exposing. **2.** The condition of being exposed. **3.** A position in relation to climatic or weather conditions or points of the compass: *a room with a southern exposure.* **4.** *Photography.* **a.** The act of exposing sensitized photographic film or plate. **b.** A film or plate so exposed. **c.** The amount of radiant energy needed to expose a photographic film. **d.** A part of a film for individual pictures: *A 35-millimeter film often has 36 exposures.* **5.** *Law.* Indecent public display of one's body.

exposure meter. A photoelectric instrument that measures light intensity in a given area and, in photographic use, indicates the proper exposure for each of several shutter speeds. Also called "light meter."

ex·pound (ĕk-spound', ĭk-) *v.* **-pounded, -pounding, -pounds.** *—tr.* **1.** To give a detailed statement of; set forth. **2.** To elucidate or explain; interpret. *—intr.* To make a detailed statement; explain a point of view. Usually used with *on: He was expounding on his favorite sport.* —See Synonyms at **explain.** [Middle English *expoun(d)en,* from Old French *espondre,* from Latin *expōnere,* to put forth, expose : *ex-,* out + *pōnere,* place, put (see **apo-** in Appendix*).] **—ex·pound'er** *n.*

ex·press (ĕk-sprĕs', ĭk-) *tr.v.* **-pressed, -pressing, -presses. 1.** To make known or set forth in words; state; utter: *express one's wishes.* **2.** To manifest or communicate, as by a gesture; show; exhibit: *His posture expressed his exhaustion.* **3.** To make one's feelings or opinions known. **4.** To make or suggest a representation of; depict: *His poems express a sense of wonder.* **5.** To represent by a sign or symbol; symbolize: *The* ∞ *sign expresses infinity.* **6.** To squeeze or press out, as juice from a fruit. **7.** To send by special courier or rapid transport. —See Synonyms at **vent. —express oneself. 1.** To communicate one's thoughts through words or gestures. **2.** To communicate one's feelings or imagination, especially through artistic activity. *—adj. Abbr.* **ex., exp. 1.** Definitely and unmistakably stated; explicit: *an express wish.* **2. a.** Sent out with or moving at high speed. **b.** Direct, rapid, and usually nonstop: *express mail delivery.* **3.** Pertaining to or handling that which is express: *an express office.* *—adv.* By express delivery or transport. *—n. Abbr.* **ex., exp. 1. a.** A special courier. **b.** A message delivered by special courier. **2. a.** A rapid, efficient system for the delivery of goods and mail. **b.** Goods and mail conveyed by such a system. **3. a.** A train, bus, or other means of transportation that is rapid and nonstop. **b.** A company that deals in such transport. **4.** An express rifle. [Middle English *expressen,* from Old French *expresser,* from Vulgar Latin *expressāre* (unattested), to press out, express : Latin *ex-,* out + *pressāre,* to press, from *premere* (past participle *pressus*), press (see **per-**[6] in Appendix*).] **—ex·press'er** *n.* **—ex·press'i·ble** *adj.*

ex·press·age (ĕk-sprĕs'ĭj, ĭk-) *n.* **1.** The conveyance of goods by express. **2.** The amount charged for such conveyance.

ex·pres·sion (ĕk-sprĕsh'ən, ĭk-) *n.* **1.** The act of expressing, conveying or representing in words, art, music, or movement; manifestation: *the expression of an idea.* **2.** That which communicates, indicates, embodies, or symbolizes something; a symbol; a sign; token. **3.** *Mathematics.* A designation of any symbolic mathematical form, such as an equation. **4.** The means by which something is expressed: *His expression is through music.* **5.** The manner in which one expresses oneself, especially in speaking, depicting, or performing. **6.** A particular word or phrase: *a slang expression.* **7.** The outward manifestation of an inner mood or disposition: *Her tears were an expression of her grief.* **8.** A facial aspect or look that conveys a special feeling: *an expression of scorn in his eyes.* **9.** The act of removing a liquid from a solid by squeezing.

ex·pres·sion·ism (ĕk-sprĕsh'ə-nĭz'əm, ĭk-) *n.* A movement in the fine arts during the latter part of the 19th and early part of the 20th centuries that originated in Europe and emphasized the

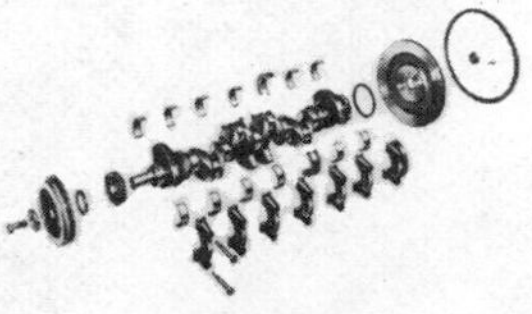

exploded view
Exploded view of a crankshaft and its related parts

t tight/th thin, path/*th* this, bathe/ŭ cut/ûr urge/v valve/w with/y yes/z zebra, size/zh vision/ə about, item, edible, gallop, circus/ à *Fr.* ami/œ *Fr.* feu, *Ger.* schön/ü *Fr.* tu, *Ger.* über/KH *Ger.* ich, *Scot.* loch/N *Fr.* bon. ***Follows main vocabulary.** †**Of obscure origin.**

objective expression of inner experience through the use of conventional characters and symbols, especially in art and drama. —**ex·pres′sion·ist** *n. & adj.* —**ex·pres′sion·is′tic** *adj.*

ex·pres·sion·less (ĕk-sprĕsh′ən-lĭs, ĭk-) *adj.* **1.** Lacking expression. **2.** Having a fixed expression.

ex·pres·sive (ĕk-sprĕs′ĭv, ĭk-) *adj.* **1.** Pertaining to, related to, or characterized by expression: *expressive hands.* **2.** Serving to express or indicate: *His actions are expressive of frustration.* **3.** Containing forceful expression; significant: *an expressive glance.* —**ex·pres′sive·ly** *adv.* —**ex·pres′sive·ness** *n.*

ex·pres·siv·i·ty (ĕk-sprĕs-ĭv′ə-tē) *n.* The quality of being aesthetically expressive: *a work of great expressivity.*

ex·press·ly (ĕk-sprĕs′lē, ĭk-) *adv.* **1.** In an express or definite manner; explicitly: *I expressly order you to leave.* **2.** Especially; particularly: *These candies are expressly for you.*

ex·press·man (ĕk-sprĕs′mən, ĭk-) *n., pl.* **-men** (-mĭn). A worker employed by an express agency.

express rifle. A hunting rifle having low trajectory, high velocity, and a long pointblank range.

express train. A passenger or freight train that travels at high speed and makes a minimum of stops.

ex·press·way (ĕk-sprĕs′wā′, ĭk-) *n.* A major divided highway designed for fast travel.

ex·pro·pri·ate (ĕks-prō′prē-āt′) *tr.v.* **-ated, -ating, -ates. 1.** To deprive of (ownership or property, for example); especially, to acquire for public use. **2.** To transfer (someone's property) to another or to oneself. [Medieval Latin *expropriāre* : Latin *ex-* (removal away from) + *proprius*, one's own (see **per¹** in Appendix*).] —**ex·pro′pri·a′tion** *n.* —**ex·pro′pri·a′tor** (-ā′tər) *n.* —**ex·pro′pri·a·to·ry** (-ə-tôr′ē, -tōr′ē) *adj.*

expt. experiment.

exptl. experimental.

ex·pug·na·ble (ĕk-spyōō′nə-bəl, ĭk-) *adj.* Capable of being defeated or taken by force.

ex·pul·sion (ĕk-spŭl′shən, ĭk-) *n.* The act of expelling or the state of being expelled.

ex·punc·tion (ĕk-spŭngk′shən, -spŭng′shən, ĭk-) *n.* The act of expunging, or the condition of being expunged; a deletion, erasure, or cancellation. [Latin *expunctus*, past participle of *expungere*, to EXPUNGE + -ION.]

ex·punge (ĕk-spŭnj′, ĭk-) *tr.v.* **-punged, -punging, -punges. 1.** To omit, erase, strike out, or obliterate (a word or sentence, for example): *"I have corrected some factual slips, expunged some repetitions"* (Kenneth Tynan). **2.** To eliminate physically; annihilate: *"Detestable race, continue to expunge yourself, die out"* (Edna St. Vincent Millay). —See Synonyms at **erase.** [Latin *expungere*, to prick out, erase : *ex-*, out + *pungere*, to prick (see **peuk-** in Appendix*).] —**ex·pung′er** *n.*

ex·pur·gate (ĕks′pər-gāt′, -pûr-gāt′) *tr.v.* **-gated, -gating, -gates. 1.** To amend (a published work) by removing obscene, objectionable, or erroneous passages from the text. **2.** To cleanse or clean; purge. [Latin *expurgāre*, to purge out, purify : *ex-*, out + *purgāre*, to purge (see **peue·¹** in Appendix*).] —**ex′pur·ga′tion** *n.* —**ex′pur·ga′tor** (-gā′tər) *n.*

ex·pur·ga·to·ry (ĕk-spûr′gə-tôr′ē, -tōr′ē, ĭk-) *adj.* Also **ex·pur·ga·to·ri·al** (-tôr′ē-əl, -tōr′ē-əl). **1.** Of or pertaining to expurgation or an expurgator. **2.** Serving or tending to expurgate.

ex·qui·site (ĕks′kwĭ-zĭt) *adj.* **1.** Beautifully made or designed: *an exquisite chalice.* **2.** Of such beauty or delicacy as to arouse delight: *an exquisite sunset.* **3.** Acutely perceptive or discriminating: *an exquisite sense of color.* **4.** Intense; keen: *an exquisite pain.* **5.** *Obsolete.* Carefully sought or selected. —*n.* One who is extremely sensitive and fastidious in dress, manners, or taste; a dandy; fop. [Middle English *exquisit*, from Latin *exquīsītus*, chosen, exquisite, from the past participle of *exquīrere*, to search out : *ex-*, out + *quaerere*, to seek (see **quaerere** in Appendix*).] —**ex′qui·site·ly** *adv.* —**ex′qui·site·ness** *n.*

exr. executor.

ex·san·gui·nate (ĕks-săng′gwə-nāt′) *tr.v.* **-nated, -nating, -nates.** To drain of blood. [From Latin *exsanguinātus*, bloodless : *ex-*, without + *sanguis* (stem *sanguin-*), blood (see **sanguine**).] —**ex·san′gui·na′tion** *n.*

ex·san·guine (ĕks-săng′gwĭn) *adj.* Also **ex·san·gui·nous** (-gwĭ-nəs). Lacking blood; anemic. [Latin *exsanguis*, deprived of blood : *ex-*, without + *sanguis* (stem *sanguin-*), blood (see **sanguine**).]

ex·scind (ĕk-sĭnd′, ĭk-) *tr.v.* **-scinded, -scinding, -scinds.** To excise or cut out; extirpate. [Latin *exscindere* : *ex-*, out + *scindere*, to cut (see **skei-** in Appendix*).]

ex·sect (ĕk-sĕkt′, ĭk-) *tr.v.* **-sected, -secting, -sects.** To cut out. [Latin *exsecāre* (past participle *exsectus*) : *ex-*, out + *secāre*, to cut (see **sek-** in Appendix*).] —**ex·sec′tion** *n.*

ex·sert (ĕk-sûrt′, ĭk-) *tr.v.* **-serted, -serting, -serts.** To thrust out or forth; cause to protrude. —*adj.* Also **ex·sert·ed** (-sûr′tĭd). *Biology.* Thrust outward; protruding. [Latin *ex(s)erere* (past participle *ex(s)ertus*), to EXERT.] —**ex·ser′tion** *n.*

ex·sic·cate (ĕk′sĭ-kāt′) *v.* **-cated, -cating, -cates.** —*tr.* To make dry; remove the moisture from; dehydrate. —*intr.* To dry up. [Latin *exsiccāre*, to dry out : *ex-*, out + *siccāre*, to dry, from *siccus*, dry (see **seikw-** in Appendix*).] —**ex′sic·ca′tion** *n.* —**ex′sic·ca′tive** *adj.* —**ex′sic·ca′tor** (-kā′tər) *n.*

ex·stip·u·late (ĕks-stĭp′yə-lĭt, -lāt′) *adj. Botany.* Having no stipules. [From EX- + STIPULE.]

ext. 1. extension. **2.** external; externally. **3.** extinct. **4.** extra. **5.** extract.

ex·tant (ĕk′stənt, ĕk-stănt′, ĭk-) *adj.* **1.** Still in existence; not destroyed, lost, or extinct: *extant manuscripts; extant species of mammals.* **2.** *Archaic.* Conspicuously outstanding; manifest. —See Synonyms at **living.** [Latin *ex(s)tāns*, present participle

of *ex(s)tāre*, to stand out, exist, be prominent : *ex-*, out + *stāre*, to stand (see **stā-** in Appendix*).]

ex·tem·po·ral (ĕk-stĕm′pə-rəl, ĭk-) *adj. Archaic.* Extempore.

ex·tem·po·ra·ne·ous (ĕk-stĕm′pə-rā′nē-əs, ĭk-) *adj.* **1.** Done, made, spoken, or otherwise performed with little or no preparation or practice; impromptu: *an extemporaneous recital.* **2.** Prepared in advance, but delivered without notes or text: *an extemporaneous sermon.* **3.** Skilled at or given to unrehearsed speech or performance. **4.** Provided, made, or adapted as an expedient; improvised; makeshift. [Late Latin *extemporāneus*, from Latin *ex tempore*, EXTEMPORE.] —**ex·tem′po·ra′ne·ous·ly** *adv.* —**ex·tem′po·ra′ne·ous·ness** *n.*

Synonyms: extemporaneous, impromptu, offhand, unrehearsed, unpremeditated, ad lib. These adjectives mean without formal preparation and sometimes without previous thought or study. They principally describe a form of expression or action. *Extemporaneous* is applied most often to public speaking without a written text. *Impromptu* even more strongly suggests lack of preparation, as in action or expression that comes on the spur of the moment to fill an unforeseen need. *Offhand* implies not only a spontaneous response but also an unceremonious or even casual manner of delivery. *Unrehearsed* describes performance without formal preparation, though it does not rule out forethought. *Unpremeditated* applies to action taken without prior thought or plan; often the term implies impulsiveness prompted by strong feeling. *Ad lib* refers to expression that is spontaneous and improvised and therefore not part of a prepared script or score.

ex·tem·po·rar·y (ĕk-stĕm′pə-rĕr′ē, ĭk-) *adj.* Extemporaneous. [From Latin *ex tempore*, EXTEMPORE.] —**ex·tem′po·rar′i·ly** *adv.* —**ex·tem′po·rar′i·ness** *n.*

ex·tem·po·re (ĕk-stĕm′pə-rē, ĭk-) *adj.* Extemporaneous. —*adv.* Without advance preparation; extemporaneously: *"which he could command at all times extempore"* (Smollett). [Latin *ex tempore* : *ex-*, out of + *tempore*, ablative of *tempus*, time (see **temporal**).]

ex·tem·po·rize (ĕk-stĕm′pə-rīz′, ĭk-) *v.* **-rized, -rizing, -rizes.** —*tr.* To perform, utter, or do extemporaneously: *"he smiled to himself at the idea of his extemporizing a lecture"* (Henry James). —*intr.* To perform or make extemporaneously; improvise. —**ex·tem′po·ri·za′tion** *n.* —**ex·tem′po·riz′er** *n.*

ex·tend (ĕk-stĕnd′, ĭk-) *v.* **-tended, -tending, -tends.** —*tr.* **1.** To open or straighten out to full length; unbend: *extend the leg.* Compare **flex. 2.** To stretch out or spread to fullest length: *The ladder was fully extended.* **3. a.** To exert (oneself) vigorously or to full capacity. **b.** To cause (a horse, for example) to move at full gallop. **4.** To increase the quantity or bulk of (a product or substance) by the addition of a less pure or cheaper substance; adulterate. **5. a.** To enlarge the area or scope of; widen; spread out; expand: *extend our boundaries.* **b.** To expand the influence, range, or meaning of; make more comprehensive or inclusive; broaden: *extend his responsibilities.* **6.** To offer to give or grant; afford: *extend one's greetings.* **7.** *Finance.* To cause to be longer, especially to prolong the time of payment of (a debt, for example). **8.** *Law.* **a.** *British.* To appraise or assess; value. **b.** To seize or make a levy upon (land or property) for the purpose of settling a debt. —*intr.* To be or become extended; stretch or reach, as in a certain direction: *His influence extended to other continents.* —See Synonyms at **prolong, increase.** [Middle English *extenden*, from Latin *extendere* : *ex-*, out + *tendere*, to stretch (see **ten-** in Appendix*).] —**ex·tend′i·bil′i·ty** *n.* —**ex·tend′i·ble** *adj.*

ex·tend·ed (ĕk-stĕn′dĭd, ĭk-) *adj.* **1.** Stretched or pulled out. **2.** Continued for a long period of time; prolonged; protracted. **3.** Enlarged or extensive in meaning, scope, or influence; widespread: *extended television coverage.* **4.** *Printing.* Having a longer width than height. Said of type. —**ex·tend′ed·ly** *adv.*

ex·ten·der (ĕk-stĕn′dər, ĭk-) *n.* A substance added to another substance to modify, dilute, or adulterate.

ex·ten·si·bil·i·ty (ĕk-stĕn′sə-bĭl′ə-tē, ĭk-) *n.* The capability of being extended, especially without breaking.

ex·ten·si·ble (ĕk-stĕn′sə-bəl, ĭk-) *adj.* **1.** Capable of being extended or protruded. **2.** Extensile. [From Latin *extensus*, past participle of *extendere*, to EXTEND.] —**ex·ten′si·bil′i·ty** *n.*

ex·ten·sile (ĕk-stĕn′sĭl, ĭk-) *adj.* Capable of being stretched out or protruded; extensible.

ex·ten·sion (ĕk-stĕn′shən, ĭk-) *n. Abbr.* **ext. 1. a.** The act of extending or the condition of being extended. **b.** That which is extended. **2.** The amount, degree, or range to which something extends or can extend; compass: *an extension of 40 miles to the highway.* **3. a.** The act of straightening or extending a limb. **b.** The position assumed by an extended limb. **4.** *Surgery.* Application of traction to a fractured or dislocated limb to restore the normal position. **5.** Any part added to or extended from a main structure to form an addition; a prolongation: *an extension to a hospital.* **6.** An additional telephone connected to the main line. **7. a.** A granting of extra time, especially to allow payment of a debt or compliance with a legal formality. **b.** The period of this extra time. **8.** That property of something by which it occupies space; spatial magnitude. **9.** *Logic.* The class of objects designated by a specific term or concept; denotation. In this sense, compare **intension.** [Middle English *extensioun*, from Old French *extension*, from Late Latin *extensiō*, from Latin *extensus*, past participle of *extendere*, to EXTEND.]

ex·ten·si·ty (ĕk-stĕn′sə-tē, ĭk-) *n.* **1.** The quality of having extension or being extensive. **2.** The attribute of sensation that enables one to perceive space or size.

ex·ten·sive (ĕk-stĕn′sĭv, ĭk-) *adj.* **1.** Having a great extent; vast; broad: *an extensive meadow.* **2.** Having a wide range; inclusive;

ă pat/ā pay/âr care/ä father/b bib/ch church/d deed/ĕ pet/ē be/f fife/g gag/h hat/hw which/ĭ pit/ī pie/îr pier/j judge/k kick/l lid/ needle/m mum/n no, sudden/ng thing/ŏ pot/ō toe/ô paw, for/oi noise/ou out/ŏŏ took/ōō boot/p pop/r roar/s sauce/sh ship, dish/

comprehensive: *an extensive library.* **3.** Considerable in amount: *Extensive capital was invested.* **4.** Pertaining to or characterized by extension: *an extensive addition to a school.* **5.** Designating or pertaining to the agricultural cultivation of vast areas of land with a minimum of labor or expense. **6.** *Physics.* Having a value that is the sum of the values for subdivisions of a thermodynamic system. Said of volume, for example. —**ex·ten′sive·ly** *adv.* —**ex·ten′sive·ness** *n.*

ex·ten·som·e·ter (ĕk′stĕn-sŏm′ə-tər) *n.* An instrument used to measure minute deformations in a test specimen of a material. [EXTENS(ION) + -METER.]

ex·ten·sor (ĕk-stĕn′sər, ĭk-) *n.* Any muscle that extends or stretches a limb. Also called "protractor." [New Latin, from Latin *extensus,* past participle of *extendere,* EXTEND.]

ex·tent (ĕk-stĕnt′, ĭk-) *n.* **1.** The range over which something extends; scope; comprehensiveness. **2. a.** The dimensions to which something is extended; magnitude; spread. **b.** The distance over which a thing extends or the space it occupies. **3.** Any extensive space or area: *an extent of desert.* **4.** *British History.* An assessment or valuation, as of land, especially for taxation. **5.** *Law.* **a.** *British.* A writ allowing a creditor to seize temporarily a debtor's property or land. **b.** *British.* A seizure in execution of such a writ. **c.** In the United States, a writ allowing a creditor to assume temporary ownership of a debtor's property or land. [Middle English *extente,* from Norman French, from Medieval Latin *extenta,* from Latin, feminine past participle of *extendere,* to EXTEND.]

ex·ten·u·ate (ĕk-stĕn′yo͞o-āt′, ĭk-) *tr.v.* **-ated, -ating, -ates. 1.** To lessen or attempt to lessen the magnitude of (an offense or guilt) by providing partial excuses: *"Speak of me as I am; nothing extenuate"* (Shakespeare). **2.** To cause to appear less serious or blameworthy: *circumstances extenuating the error.* **3.** *Archaic.* To belittle. **4.** *Archaic.* To make thin or emaciated. **5.** *Archaic.* To reduce the strength of. [Latin *extenuāre,* to thin out, lessen : *ex-,* out + *tenuāre,* to make thin, from *tenuis,* thin (see **ten-** in Appendix*).] —**ex·ten′u·a′tor** (-ā′tər) *n.*

ex·ten·u·at·ing (ĕk-stĕn′yo͞o-ā′tĭng, ĭk-) *adj.* Serving to qualify guilt or blame: *extenuating circumstances.*

ex·ten·u·a·tion (ĕk-stĕn′yo͞o-ā′shən) *n.* **1.** The act of extenuating or the condition of being extenuated; partial justification. **2.** That which serves to extenuate; a partial excuse: *"The jury brought it in a killing, but with every provocation and extenuation known to God or man"* (Kipling). —**ex·ten′u·a′tive** *adj.* & *n.* —**ex·ten′u·a·to′ry** (-ə-tôr′ē, -tōr′ē) *adj.*

ex·te·ri·or (ĕk-stîr′ē-ər, ĭk-) *adj.* **1.** Outer; external. **2.** Originating or acting from the outside. **3.** Suitable for use outside: *an exterior paint.* —*n.* **1.** A part or surface that is outside. **2.** An external or outward appearance; aspect: *a friendly exterior.* [Latin, comparative of *exterus,* outward, outside. See **eghs** in Appendix.*] —**ex·te′ri·or·ly** *adv.*

exterior angle. 1. The angle between any side of a polygon and an extended adjacent side. **2.** Any of the four angles that do not include a region of the space between two lines intersected by a transversal.

ex·te·ri·or·ize (ĕk-stîr′ē-ə-rīz′, ĭk-) *tr.v.* **-ized, -izing, -izes.** To externalize.

ex·ter·mi·nate (ĕk-stûr′mə-nāt′, ĭk-) *tr.v.* **-nated, -nating, -nates.** To get rid of by destroying completely; extirpate: *a new spray to exterminate insects.* See Synonyms at **abolish.** [Latin *extermināre,* to drive out : *ex-,* out of + *termināre,* to limit, end (see **ter-**¹ in Appendix*).] —**ex·ter′mi·na′tion** *n.* —**ex·ter′mi·na′tive, ex·ter′mi·na·to′ry** (-nə-tôr′ē, -tōr′ē) *adj.*

ex·ter·mi·na·tor (ĕk-stûr′mə-nā′tər, ĭk-) *n.* One that exterminates; especially, one whose occupation is the extermination of rodents, cockroaches, or other vermin.

ex·tern (ĕk′stûrn′) *n.* Also **ex·terne.** A person associated with, but not officially residing in, an institution; especially, a nonresident doctor on a hospital staff. [Old French *externe,* from Latin *externus,* EXTERNAL.]

ex·ter·nal (ĕk-stûr′nəl, ĭk-) *adj. Abbr.* **ext. 1.** Pertaining to, existing on, or connected with the outside or an outer part; exterior. **2.** Affecting or capable of affecting the outside: *a salve for external use only.* **3.** *Philosophy.* Existing independently of the mind; objective; phenomenal: *external objects.* **4.** Acting or coming from the outside: *external pressures.* **5.** Of or pertaining to the outward appearance; superficial. **6.** Of or pertaining to foreign affairs or foreign countries; international. —*n.* **1.** An exterior part or surface. **2.** *Plural.* External circumstances; appearances. [Middle English, from Latin *externus,* from *exterus,* outward. See **eghs** in Appendix.*] —**ex·ter′nal·ly** *adv.*

ex·ter·nal-com·bus·tion engine (ĕk-stûr′nəl-kəm-bŭs′chən, ĭk-). An engine, such as a steam engine, in which the fuel is burned outside the engine cylinder.

external ear. The portion of the ear including the auricle and the external acoustic meatus. See **ear.**

ex·ter·nal·ism (ĕk-stûr′nə-lĭz′əm, ĭk-) *n.* **1.** The doctrine that only objects perceived by the senses are capable of being judged real; phenomenalism. **2.** Devotion to externals or to matters of form or procedure, as in religion. —**ex·ter′nal·ist** *n.*

ex·ter·nal·i·ty (ĕk′stər-năl′ə-tē) *n., pl.* **-ties. 1.** The condition or quality of being external or externalized. **2.** *Philosophy.* The quality of being external to the perceiving subject.

ex·ter·nal·ize (ĕk-stûr′nə-līz′, ĭk-) *tr.v.* **-ized, -izing, -izes. 1.** To make external; give external existence to. **2.** To attribute (a feeling or opinion) to others or to one's environment: *externalize one's problems.* —**ex·ter′nal·i·za′tion** *n.*

ex·ter·o·cep·tor (ĕk′stə-rō-sĕp′tər) *n.* A sense organ receiving and responding to external stimuli. [New Latin : Latin *exter, exterus,* EXTERIOR + (RE)CEPTOR.] —**ex′ter·o·cep′tive** *adj.*

ex·ter·ri·to·ri·al (ĕks′tĕr-ə-tôr′ē-əl, -tōr′ē-əl) *adj.* Beyond the territorial limits; extraterritorial. [EX- + TERRITORIAL.] —**ex′ter·ri·to′ri·al′i·ty** *n.* —**ex′ter′ri·to′ri·al·ly** *adv.*

ex·tinct (ĕk-stĭngkt′, ĭk-) *adj. Abbr.* **ext. 1.** Extinguished or inactive, as a fire or volcano. **2.** No longer existing in living form; having died out: *extinct birds such as the dodo and moa.* **3.** Lacking a claimant; void: *an extinct title.* **4.** No longer in use; superseded: *an extinct custom.* —See Synonyms at **dead.** [Middle English, from Latin *ex(s)tinctus,* past participle of *ex(s)tinguere,* to EXTINGUISH.]

ex·tinc·tion (ĕk-stĭngk′shən, ĭk-) *n.* **1.** The act of extinguishing or making extinct: *"They aim at the extinction of the belief in individuality"* (Edward Conze). **2.** The fact or condition of being extinguished or extinct. —**ex·tinc′tive** *adj.*

ex·tin·guish (ĕk-stĭng′gwĭsh, ĭk-) *tr.v.* **-guished, -guishing, -guishes. 1.** To put out (a fire or light); quench: *"the bright centres of the brain extinguished one by one like lamps"* (Joyce). **2.** To put an end to (hope, for example); destroy. **3.** To obscure; to eclipse. **4.** *Law.* **a.** To settle or discharge (a debt). **b.** To nullify. —See Synonyms at **abolish.** [Latin *ex(s)tinguere* : *ex-,* out + *stinguere,* to quench (see **steig-** in Appendix*).] —**ex·tin′guish·a·ble** *adj.* —**ex·tin′guish·ment** *n.*

ex·tin·guish·er (ĕk-stĭng′gwĭ-shər, ĭk-) *n.* One that extinguishes, especially: **a.** A small metal cone on a long handle, used for snuffing out candles. **b.** Any of various portable mechanical apparatuses capable of spraying fire-extinguishing chemicals.

ex·tir·pate (ĕk′stər-pāt′, ĕk-stûr′-, ĭk-) *tr.v.* **-pated, -pating, -pates. 1.** To pull up by the roots; root up or out. **2.** To destroy the whole of; exterminate. **3.** To remove by surgery. —See Synonyms at **abolish.** [Latin *ex(s)tirpāre,* to pluck up by the roots : *ex-,* out + *stirps,* root, stem (see **stirps**).] —**ex′tir·pa′tion** *n.* —**ex′tir·pa′tive** *adj.* —**ex′tir·pa′tor** (-pā′tər) *n.*

ex·tol (ĕk-stōl′, ĭk-) *tr.v.* **-tolled, -tolling, -tols.** Also **ex·toll.** To praise lavishly; laud; eulogize: *"Highland verse, which Mr. Macpherson extolled very highly"* (Hume). See Synonyms at **praise.** [Middle English *extollen,* to lift up, praise, from Latin *extollere* : *ex-,* up + *tollere,* to lift, raise (see **tel-**¹ in Appendix*).] —**ex·tol′ler** *n.* —**ex·tol′ment** *n.*

ex·tort (ĕk-stôrt′, ĭk-) *tr.v.* **-torted, -torting, -torts.** To obtain (money or information) from another by coercion or intimidation; to exact; wring: *"If greatness is thrust upon certain men, thought is extorted from others"* (Norman Mailer). [Latin *extorquēre* (past participle *extortus*), to twist out : *ex-,* out + *torquēre,* to twist (see **terkw-** in Appendix*).] —**ex·tort′er** *n.* —**ex·tor′tive** *adj.*

ex·tor·tion (ĕk-stôr′shən, ĭk-) *n.* **1.** The act or an instance of extorting. **2.** The criminal offense of using one's official position or powers to obtain property, funds, or patronage to which one is not entitled. **3.** The exaction of an exorbitant price. **4.** Something extorted. —**ex·tor′tion·ar′y, ex·tor′tion·ate** (-ĭt) *adj.* —**ex·tor′tion·ate·ly** *adv.*

ex·tor·tion·ist (ĕk-stôr′shə-nĭst, ĭk-) *n.* Also **ex·tor·tion·er** (-nər). A person who commits extortion.

ex·tra (ĕk′strə) *adj. Abbr.* **ex., ext. 1.** More or beyond what is usual, normal, expected, or necessary; additional; supplementary. **2.** Better than ordinary; superior: *extra fineness.* —*n.* **1.** Something more than what is usual or necessary. **2.** *Often plural.* Something, as an accessory on an automobile, for which an additional charge is made. **3.** A special edition of a newspaper. **4.** An additional or alternate worker. **5.** An actor hired to play a minor part, as in a crowd scene. **6.** Something of exceptional quality. —*adv.* Exceptionally; unusually: *extra dry.* [Probably short for EXTRAORDINARY.]

extra-. Indicates outside a boundary or scope; for example, **extragalactic.** ***Note:*** Many compounds other than those entered here may be formed with *extra-.* In forming compounds, *extra-* is normally joined with the following element without space or hyphen: *extracurricular.* However, if the second element begins with a capital letter or with the letter *a,* it is separated with a hyphen: *extra-Biblical, extra-alimentary.* Note that the adjective *extra* in its various senses of "additional" may be joined to another word with a hyphen when the two words are used as a unit modifier: *extra-base hit.* [Middle English, from Latin *extrā,* outside, above, beyond, without, short for *extera,* ablative feminine of *exterus,* outward. See **eghs** in Appendix.*]

ex·tra-base hit (ĕk′strə-bās′). A double, triple, or home run.

ex·tra·ca·non·i·cal (ĕk′strə-kə-nŏn′ĭ-kəl) *adj.* Not included in any ecclesiastical canon of Scripture; noncanonical.

ex·tra·cel·lu·lar (ĕk′strə-sĕl′yə-lər) *adj.* Located or occurring outside a cell. —**ex′tra·cel′lu·lar·ly** *adv.*

ex·tract (ĕk-străkt′, ĭk-) *tr.v.* **-tracted, -tracting, -tracts. 1.** To draw out or forth forcibly; pull out: *extract a tooth.* **2.** To obtain despite resistance, as by contrivance or extortion: *extract a promise.* **3.** To obtain from a substance by chemical or mechanical action, as by pressure, distillation, or evaporation: *extract juice from an orange.* **4.** To remove (a literary passage, for example) for separate consideration or publication. **5.** *Mathematics.* To determine or calculate (the root of a number). —*n.* (ĕk′străkt). *Abbr.* **ext. 1.** Something drawn or pulled out. **2.** A passage from a literary work; an excerpt. **3.** A concentrated preparation of the essential constituents of a food, flavoring, or other substance; essence; concentrate: *maple extract.* [Middle English *extracten,* from Latin *extrahere* (past participle *extractus*), to draw out : *ex-,* out + *trahere,* to draw (see **tragh-** in Appendix*).] —**ex·tract′a·ble, ex·tract′i·ble** *adj.*

ex·trac·tion (ĕk-străk′shən, ĭk-) *n.* **1.** The act of extracting or the condition of being extracted. **2.** Something obtained by extracting; an extract. **3.** Origin; descent; lineage: *of Asian extraction; of noble extraction.*

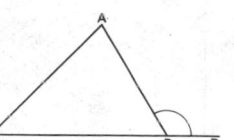

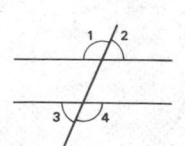

exterior angle
Above: Exterior angle of a triangle (angle ABD)
Below: Exterior angles of parallel lines (angles 1, 2, 3, and 4)

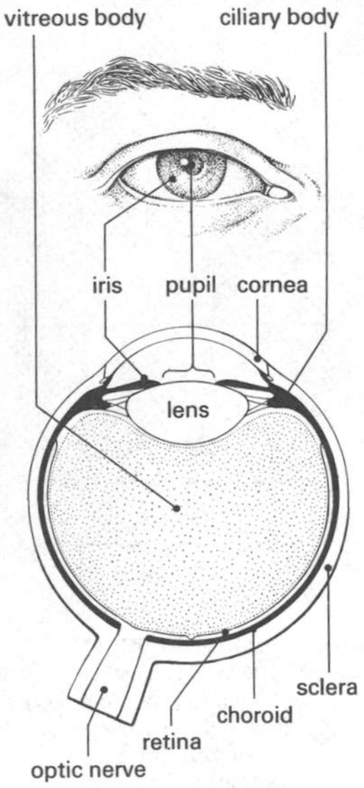
vitreous body
ciliary body
iris
pupil
cornea
lens
sclera
choroid
retina
optic nerve

eye
Anterior view and cross section of the human eye

ex·trac·tive (ĕk-străk′tĭv, ĭk-) *adj.* **1.** Used in or obtained by extraction. **2.** Capable of being extracted. —*n.* **1.** Something that may be extracted. **2.** The insoluble portion of an extract.
ex·trac·tor (ĕk-străk′tər, ĭk-) *n.* One that extracts; especially, a device such as forceps used for extracting teeth.
ex·tra·cur·ric·u·lar (ĕk′strə-kə-rĭk′yə-lər) *adj.* **1.** Carried on outside the curriculum or regular course of study in school or college life. **2.** Outside the usual duties of a job or profession.
ex·tra·dit·a·ble (ĕk′strə-dī′tə-bəl) *adj.* Subject to or making one liable to extradition: *an extraditable crime.*
ex·tra·dite (ĕk′strə-dīt′) *tr.v.* **-dited, -diting, -dites. 1.** To surrender (an alleged criminal) to another authority for trial. **2.** To obtain (an alleged criminal held by another authority) for trial. —See Synonyms at **banish**. [Back-formation from EXTRADITION.]
ex·tra·di·tion (ĕk′strə-dĭsh′ən) *n.* The legal surrender of an alleged criminal to the jurisdiction of another state, country, or government for trial. [French : Latin *ex-*, out + *trāditiō*, a surrendering (see **tradition**).]
ex·tra·dos (ĕk′strə-dŏs′, -dōs′) *n., pl.* **extrados** (-dōz′) or **-doses**. The upper or exterior curve of an arch. [French : Latin *extrā*, outside (see **extra-**) + French *dos*, back, from Latin *dorsum* (see **dorsum** in Appendix*).]
ex·tra·ga·lac·tic (ĕk′strə-gə-lăk′tĭk) *adj.* Located or originating beyond the Galaxy.
ex·tra·ju·di·cial (ĕk′strə-jo͞o-dĭsh′əl) *adj.* **1.** Outside of the authority of a court. **2.** Outside of usual judicial proceedings. —**ex′tra·ju·di′cial·ly** *adv.*
ex·tra·mar·i·tal (ĕk′strə-măr′ə-təl) *adj.* Adulterous.
ex·tra·mun·dane (ĕk′strə-mŭn′dān′, -mŭn′dān′) *adj.* Occurring or existing outside of the physical world or universe.
ex·tra·mu·ral (ĕk′strə-myo͝or′əl) *adj.* **1.** Occurring or situated outside of the walls or boundaries, as of a fortress or city: *extramural skirmishes.* **2.** Interscholastic: *extramural sports.*
ex·tra·ne·ous (ĕk-strā′nē-əs, ĭk-) *adj.* **1.** Coming from without; foreign: *extraneous interference.* **2.** Present but not essential or vital; accidental. **3.** Irrelevant. —See Synonyms at **extrinsic**. [Latin *extrāneus*, strange, from *extrā*, outward (see **extra-**).] —**ex·tra′ne·ous·ly** *adv.* —**ex·tra′ne·ous·ness** *n.*
ex·tra·nu·cle·ar (ĕk′strə-no͞o′klē-ər, -nyo͞o′klē-ər) *adj.* Located or occurring outside a nucleus.
ex·traor·di·nar·y (ĕk-strôr′də-nĕr′ē, ĭk-, ĕk′strə-ôr′-) *adj.* **1.** Beyond what is ordinary, usual, or commonplace: *extraordinary authority.* **2.** Exceeding the ordinary degree, amount, or extent; exceptional; remarkable: *an extraordinary feat.* **3.** Used for a special service or occasion. —**ex·traor′di·nar′i·ly** *adv.*
ex·trap·o·late (ĕk-străp′ə-lāt′, ĭk-) *v.* **-lated, -lating, -lates.** —*tr.* **1.** *Mathematics.* To estimate (a value or values of a function) for values of the argument not used in the process of estimation; broadly, to infer (a value or values) from known values. **2.** To infer or estimate (unknown information) by extending or projecting known information. —*intr.* To engage in the process of extrapolation. [EXTRA- + (INTER)POLATE.] —**ex·trap′o·la′tion** *n.* —**ex·trap′o·la′tive** *adj.*
ex·tra·sen·so·ry (ĕk′strə-sĕn′sə-rē) *adj.* **1.** Not perceptible by the normal senses. **2.** Perceptible by supernatural means. **3.** Supernatural. [EXTRA- + SENSORY.]
extrasensory perception. *Abbr.* **ESP** Perception by supernatural or other extraordinary means.
ex·tra·ter·res·tri·al (ĕk′strə-tə-rĕs′trē-əl) *adj.* Originating, located, or occurring outside the earth or its atmosphere.
ex·tra·ter·ri·to·ri·al (ĕk′strə-tĕr′ə-tôr′ē-əl, -tōr′ē-əl) *adj.* **1.** Located outside territorial boundaries. **2.** Of or pertaining to persons exempt from the legal jurisdiction of the country in which they reside. —**ex′tra·ter′ri·to′ri·al·ly** *adv.*
ex·tra·ter·ri·to·ri·al·i·ty (ĕk′strə-tĕr′ə-tôr′ē-ăl′ə-tē, -tōr′ē-ăl′ə-tē) *n.* **1.** Exemption from local legal jurisdiction, such as is granted to foreign diplomats. **2.** The jurisdiction of a country over its nationals abroad.
ex·tra·u·ter·ine (ĕk′strə-yo͞o′tər-ĭn, -tə-rēn′, -rīn′) *adj.* Located or occurring outside the uterus: *extrauterine pregnancy.*
ex·trav·a·gance (ĕk-străv′ə-gəns, ĭk-) *n.* Also **ex·trav·a·gan·cy** (-gən-sē) *pl.* **-cies. 1.** The quality of being extravagant; immoderation to the point of wastefulness. **2.** An immoderate expense or display. **3.** Something costly and self-indulgent.
ex·trav·a·gant (ĕk-străv′ə-gənt, ĭk-) *adj.* **1.** Given to lavish or imprudent expenditure; prodigal: *"The poor are also extravagant, even at the cost of burdensome debts"* (Jawaharlal Nehru). **2.** Exceeding reasonable bounds; excessive; unrestrained: *extravagant demands on one's patience.* **3.** Extremely abundant; profuse: *extravagant vegetation.* **4.** Unreasonably high; exorbitant. **5.** *Obsolete.* Straying beyond limits or bounds; wandering. —See Synonyms at **excessive**. [Middle English *extravagaunt*, from Old French *extravagant*, from Medieval Latin *extrāvagāns*, present participle of *extrāvagārī*, to wander beyond : Latin *extrā*, beyond + *vagārī*, to wander, akin to *vagus*, VAGUE.] —**ex·trav′a·gant·ly** *adv.* —**ex·trav′a·gant·ness** *n.*
ex·trav·a·gan·za (ĕk-străv′ə-găn′zə, ĭk-) *n.* **1.** A light orchestral composition marked by freedom and diversity of form, often with burlesque elements. **2.** Any elaborate, spectacular entertainment. [Italian *(e)stravaganza*, from *(e)stravagant*, extravagant, from Medieval Latin *extrāvagāns*, EXTRAVAGANT.]
ex·trav·a·gate (ĕk-străv′ə-gāt′, ĭk-) *intr.v.* **-gated, -gating, -gates. 1.** To wander or roam at will; stray. **2.** To exceed reasonable limits or bounds. [From EXTRAVAGANT.]
ex·trav·a·sate (ĕk-străv′ə-sāt′, ĭk-) *v.* **-sated, -sating, -sates.** —*tr.* **1.** *Pathology.* To force the flow of (blood or lymph) out into surrounding tissue. **2.** *Geology.* To cause (molten lava or the like) to pour forth from a volcanic vent. —*intr.* **1.** *Pathology.* To exude into the surrounding tissues. Used of blood or lymph. **2.** *Geology.* To erupt. [EXTRA- + VAS + -ATE.]
ex·trav·a·sa·tion (ĕk-străv′ə-sā′shən, ĭk-) *n.* **1.** The act of extravasating or the condition of being extravasated. **2.** The matter extravasated.
ex·tra·vas·cu·lar (ĕk′strə-văs′kyə-lər) *adj.* **1.** Located or occurring outside a blood vessel or the vascular system. **2.** Lacking vessels; nonvascular.
ex·tra·ve·hic·u·lar activity (ĕk′strə-vē-hĭk′yə-lər). *Abbr.* **EVA** Activity or maneuvers performed by an astronaut outside a spacecraft in space.
ex·tra·ver·sion. Variant of **extroversion**.
ex·tra·vert. Variant of **extrovert**.
Ex·tre·ma·du·ra. The Spanish name for **Estremadura**.
ex·treme (ĕk-strēm′, ĭk-) *adj.* **1.** Outermost or farthest; most remote in any direction: *the extreme edge of the field.* **2.** Final; last. **3.** Being in or attaining the greatest or highest degree; very intense: *extreme pleasure; extreme degradation.* **4.** Extending far beyond the norm; radical: *an extreme conservative.* **5.** Of the greatest severity; drastic. —See Synonyms at **excessive**. —*n.* **1.** The greatest or utmost degree or point: *eager to the extreme.* **2.** Either of the two things situated at the ends of a spectrum or range: *the extremes of boiling and freezing.* **3.** An extreme condition. **4.** A drastic or immoderate expedient. **5.** *Mathematics.* The first or last term of a ratio or series. **6.** *Logic.* The major or minor term of a syllogism. [Middle English, from Old French, from Latin *extrēmus*. See **eghs** in Appendix.*] —**ex·treme′ly** *adv.* —**ex·treme′ness** *n.*
extremely high frequency. *Abbr.* **EHF** A radio-frequency band with a range of 30,000 to 300,000 megahertz.
extreme unction. *Roman Catholic Church.* The sacrament in which a priest anoints and prays for one in danger of death.
ex·trem·ist (ĕk-strē′mĭst, ĭk-) *n.* A person who advocates or resorts to extreme measures, especially in politics; a radical. See Synonyms at **fanatic**. —*adj.* Belonging or pertaining to extremists. —**ex·trem′ism′** *n.*
ex·trem·i·ty (ĕk-strĕm′ə-tē, ĭk-) *n., pl.* **-ties. 1.** The outermost or farthest point or portion; an end; an edge. **2.** The greatest or utmost degree: *the extremity of despair.* **3.** Grave danger, necessity, or distress. **4.** The moment at which the end, as of life, is imminent. **5.** An extreme or severe measure: *"drought that compelled the people to live on their famine store, an alarming extremity"* (Willa Cather). **6.** A bodily limb or appendage. **7.** *Plural.* The hands or feet.
ex·tri·cate (ĕk′strĭ-kāt′) *tr.v.* **-cated, -cating, -cates. 1.** To release from an entanglement or difficulty; disengage. **2.** To cause to be liberated or emitted: *extricate gas from a solution.* **3.** To distinguish from something related; discriminate; differentiate. [Latin *extrīcāre* : *ex-*, out + *trīcae*†, perplexities.] —**ex′tri·ca·ble** *adj.* —**ex′tri·ca′tion** *n.*
ex·trin·sic (ĕk-strĭn′sĭk, -zĭk, ĭk-) *adj.* **1.** Not forming an essential part of a thing; extraneous; inessential. **2.** Not inherent; accessory; adventitious. **3.** Originating from the outside; external. [Late Latin *extrinsecus*, outer, from Latin, outwardly : *exterus*, EXTERIOR + *secus*, alongside (see **sekw-**[1] in Appendix*).] —**ex·trin′si·cal·ly** *adv.*
Synonyms: *extrinsic, extraneous, foreign, alien.* These adjectives mean not inherently part of a thing or not compatible with it. What is *extrinsic* is either literally apart from the thing in question or derived from something external to it: *Sympathy is extrinsic to impartial judgment.* What is *extraneous* is not an integral part and is inessential or harmful: *extraneous matter in foodstuffs; an issue extraneous to the debate.* Something *foreign* is markedly different from the thing in question or out of place: *a technique foreign to classical ballet.* What is *alien* is generally irreconcilably different or adverse: *an economic theory alien to the spirit of capitalism.*
ex·trorse (ĕk′strôrs′) *adj. Botany.* Facing outward; turned away from the axis. Said especially of anthers. [Late Latin *extrōrsus*, outward : *extrā*, outside + *introrsus*, INTRORSE.]
ex·tro·ver·sion (ĕk′strə-vûr′zhən) *n.* Also **ex·tra·ver·sion. 1.** Interest in environment or others as opposed to, or to the exclusion of, oneself. Compare **introversion**. **2.** A turning inside out, as of an organ or part. [From *extro-*, variant of EXTRA- + Latin *versus*, past participle of *vertere*, to turn (see **wer-**[3] in Appendix*).] —**ex′tro·ver′sive** *adj.* —**ex′tro·ver′sive·ly** *adv.*
ex·tro·vert (ĕk′strə-vûrt′) *n.* Also **ex·tra·vert.** An individual interested in others or in the environment as opposed to, or to the exclusion of, self. Compare **introvert**. [*Extro-*, variant of EXTRA- + Latin *vertere*, to turn (see **wer-**[3] in Appendix*).] —**ex′tro·vert′ed** *adj.*
ex·trude (ĕk-stro͞od′, ĭk-) *v.* **-truded, -truding, -trudes.** —*tr.* **1.** To push or thrust out. **2.** To shape (metal or plastic, for example) by forcing through a die. —*intr.* To protrude or project. [Latin *extrūdere*, thrust out : *ex-*, out + *trūdere*, to thrust (see **treud-** in Appendix*).]
ex·tru·sion (ĕk-stro͞o′zhən, ĭk-) *n.* **1.** The act or process of extruding. **2.** Material that has been extruded. [Medieval Latin *extrūsiō*, from Latin *extrūsus*, past participle of *extrūdere*, EXTRUDE.]
ex·tru·sive (ĕk-stro͞o′sĭv, -zĭv, ĭk-) *adj.* **1.** Tending to extrude. **2.** *Geology.* Derived from magma. Said of rock.
ex·u·ber·ance (ĕg-zo͞o′bər-əns, ĭg-) *n.* **1.** The condition or quality of being exuberant. **2.** An exuberant act or manifestation.
ex·u·ber·ant (ĕg-zo͞o′bər-ənt, ĭg-) *adj.* **1.** Full of unrestrained high spirits; abandonedly joyous. **2.** Lavish; effusive; overflowing. **3.** Growing or producing abundantly; luxuriant. [Middle English, from Old French, from Latin *exūberāns*, present participle of *exūberāre*, to EXUBERATE.] —**ex·u′ber·ant·ly** *adv.*

ex·u·ber·ate (ĕg-zōō′bə-rāt′, ĭg-) *intr.v.* **-ated, -ating, -ates.** To be exuberant; to abound or overflow. [Latin *exūberāre* : *ex-*, completely + *ūberāre*, to be fruitful, from *über*, fertile (see eudh- in Appendix*).]

ex·u·date (ĕks′yōō-dāt′) *n.* An exuded substance; exudation. [From EXUDE.]

ex·u·da·tion (ĕks′yōō-dā′shən) *n.* **1.** The act or an instance of exuding. **2.** Something that is exuded; exudate: *an exudation of sweat.* —**ex′u·da′tive** *adj.*

ex·ude (ĕg-zōōd′, ĭg-, ĕk-sōōd′, ĭk-) *v.* **-uded, -uding, -udes.** —*intr.* To ooze forth; come gradually through an opening: *sap exudes from the pine bark.* —*tr.* **1.** To discharge or emit gradually. **2.** To emit as if through the pores; give off copiously: *"he exuded about as much menace as boiled haddock"* (S.J. Perelman). [Latin *ex(s)ūdāre*, to sweat out, exude : *ex-*, out + *sūdāre*, to sweat, ooze (see sweid-² in Appendix*).]

ex·ult (ĕg-zŭlt′, ĭg-) *intr.v.* **-ulted, -ulting, -ults. 1.** To rejoice greatly; be jubilant or triumphant. **2.** *Obsolete.* To leap upward, especially for joy. [Latin *ex(s)ultāre*, frequentative of *exsilīre*, to leap up, rejoice : *ex-*, up + *salīre*, to leap (see sel-⁴ in Appendix*).] —**ex·ult′ing·ly** *adv.*

ex·ul·tant (ĕg-zŭl′tənt, ĭg-) *adj.* Joyful; jubilant; triumphant. —**ex·ul′tant·ly** *adv.*

ex·ul·ta·tion (ĕg′zŭl-tā′shən) *n.* Also **ex·ul·tance** (ĕg-zŭl′təns, ĭg-), **ex·ul·tan·cy** (-tən-sē). The act or condition of exulting.

ex·ur·ban·ite (ĕk-sûr′bə-nīt, ĕg-zûr′-) *n.* A regular commuter living in a small community, usually a well-to-do town, beyond the suburbs of a major city. [EX- + (SUB)URBANITE.]

ex·ur·bi·a (ĕk-sûr′bē-ə, ĕg-zûr′-) *n.* A semirural residential area situated beyond the suburbs of a city. Also called "exurb." [EX- + (SUB)URBIA.]

ex·u·vi·ae (ĕg-zōō′vē-ē′) *pl.n.* Also **ex·u·vi·a** (-vē-ə) *singular* **ex·u·vi·um** (-vē-əm). The cast skins of coverings of various animals, especially the larvae and nymphs of insects. [Latin, stripped-off clothing, spoils, from *exuere*, to take off. See eu-¹ in Appendix.*] —**ex·u′vi·al** *adj.*

ex·u·vi·ate (ĕg-zōō′vē-āt′, ĭg-) *v.* **-ated, -ating, -ates.** —*tr.* To shed or cast off (a covering, such as a skin or shell). —*intr.* To shed or cast off exuviae. [From EXUVIAE.] —**ex·u′vi·a′tion** *n.*

-ey¹. Variant of **-y** (existence or possession).

-ey². Variant of **-y** (smallness).

ey·as (ī′əs) *n.* A nestling hawk or falcon, especially one to be trained for falconry. [Middle English, variant (by incorrect division of *a nias*) of *niyas*, from Old French *niais*, bird taken from the nest, from Vulgar Latin *nidiāx* (unattested), from Latin *nīdus*, nest. See nizdo- in Appendix.*]

Eyck. See van Eyck.

eye (ī) *n.* **1. a.** An organ of vision or of light sensitivity. **b.** The vertebrate organ of vision, either of a pair of hollow structures located in fixed bony sockets of the skull, functioning together or independently, each having a lens capable of focusing incident light on an internal photosensitive retina. **2.** The external, visible portion of this organ together with its associated structures, such as the eyelids, eyelashes, and eyebrows. **3.** The pigmented iris of this organ. **4.** The faculty of seeing; sight; vision. **5.** The ability to make mental perceptions; discernment: *a good eye for fashion.* **6. a.** A look; gaze: *"Cast a cold eye/On life, on death."* (Yeats). **b.** A way of regarding something; point of view. **7.** Anything suggestive of an eye in appearance, as an opening in a needle, a marking on a peacock feather, or a hole in cheese. **8.** A loop, as in a hook. **9.** *Botany.* **a.** A bud on a twig or tuber: *the eye of a potato.* **b.** The often differently colored center of the corolla of some flowers. **10.** *Meteorology.* The circular area of relative calm at the center of a cyclone. **11.** Anything construed as a center or focal point. **12.** *Informal.* A detective. —**an eye for an eye.** Punishment requiring that the offender suffer what he has caused another to suffer. —**catch one's eye.** *Informal.* To attract one's attention. —**give (someone) the eye.** *Informal.* To look at with admiration or invitation. —**in a pig's eye.** *Slang.* Never; under no condition. —**in the eye of the wind.** *Nautical.* In the direction opposite to that of the wind; close to the wind. —**make eyes at.** To gaze at flirtatiously. —**see eye to eye.** To be in agreement. —**with an eye to.** With a view to. —*tr.v.* **eyed, eyeing** or **eying, eyes. 1.** To concentrate the eyes on; to stare at. **2.** To supply with an eye or eyes. [Middle English *eie, eighe,* Old English *ēage.* See okw- in Appendix.*]

eye·ball (ī′bôl′) *n.* **1.** The ball-shaped portion of the eye enclosed by the socket and eyelids. **2.** The eye itself.

eye bank. A place at which corneas taken from human cadavers immediately after death are stored and preserved for subsequent transplantation to individuals with corneal defects.

eye·bolt (ī′bōlt′) *n.* A bolt having a looped head designed to receive a hook or rope.

eye·bright (ī′brīt′) *n.* Any of several plants of the genus *Euphrasia;* especially, *E. officinalis,* native to the Old World, having small white and purplish flowers.

eye·brow (ī′brou′) *n.* **1.** The bony ridge extending over the eye. **2.** The arch of short hairs covering this ridge.

eyebrow pencil. A cosmetic in pencil form used for extending or darkening the eyebrows.

eye·cup (ī′kŭp′) *n.* A small cup with a rim contoured to fit the orbit of the eye, used for applying a liquid medicine or wash to the eye. Also called "eye bath."

eyed (īd) *adj.* **1.** Having an eye or eyes, as a sail. **2.** Having eyes of a specified number or kind. Used in combination: *one-eyed; blue-eyed.* **3.** Having markings that resemble eyes.

eye·drop·per (ī′drŏp′ər) *n.* A dropper *(see)* for administering liquid eye medicines.

eye·ful (ī′fŏŏl′) *n.* **1.** An amount of something that covers the eye: *an eyeful of salt water.* **2.** All that the eye can encompass at one time; a good look. **3.** A sight to please the eyes; especially, a beautiful woman. **4. a.** Sufficient observation to reveal more than expected or enough to satisfy: *The inspector got an eyeful of petty corruption.* **b.** Something striking to see; a satisfying sight: *In her bikini, she was an eyeful.*

eye·glass (ī′glăs′, -gläs′) *n.* **1. a.** *Plural.* A pair of lenses used to correct faulty vision and worn in front of the eyes supported by a light frame that passes over the nose and around the ears. Also called "glasses," "spectacles." **b.** A monocle. **2.** An eyepiece. **3.** An eyecup.

eye·hole (ī′hōl′) *n.* **1.** The orbit of the eye. **2.** A peephole. **3.** An eye for the insertion of a rope, pin, hook, or the like.

eye·hook (ī′hŏŏk′) *n.* A hook attached to a ring at the end of a rope or chain.

eye·lash (ī′lăsh′) *n.* **1.** One of a row of short hairs fringing the edge of the eyelid. **2.** A row of these hairs.

eye·let (ī′lĭt) *n.* **1. a.** A small hole or perforation, usually rimmed with metal, cord, fabric, or leather, used for fastening with a cord or hook. **b.** A metal ring designed to reinforce such a hole; grommet. **2. a.** A small hole edged with fine embroidered stitches as part of a design. **b.** A piece of embroidery so worked. Also called "eyelet embroidery." **c.** Cloth that is ornamented with machine-produced eyelet embroidery. **3.** An aperture or peephole. **4.** A small eye. —*tr.v.* **eyeletted, -letting, -lets.** To make eyelets in. [Middle English *oilet,* from Old French *oillet,* diminutive of *oil,* eye, from Latin *oculus,* eye. See okw- in Appendix.*]

eye·let·eer (ī′lə-tîr′) *n.* A pointed instrument for piercing eyelets in cloth; bodkin; stiletto.

eye·lid (ī′lĭd′) *n.* Either of two folds of skin and muscle that can be closed over an eye.

eye opener. 1. A revelation that serves to open the eyes as by startling or shocking. **2.** A drink of liquor, especially one taken as a stimulant early in the day.

eye·piece (ī′pēs′) *n.* The lens or lens group closest to the eye in a microscope, telescope, or other optical instrument; ocular.

eye rhyme. A false rhyme consisting of words with similar spellings but different sounds; for example, *lint* and *pint.*

eye shadow. A cosmetic available in various colors or tints and applied to the eyelids to enhance the eyes.

eye·shot (ī′shŏt′) *n.* The range of vision; view; sight.

eye·sight (ī′sīt′) *n.* **1.** The faculty of sight; vision. **2.** The range of vision; view.

eye·sore (ī′sôr′, -sōr′) *n.* **1.** Something offensive to look at. **2.** An enduring cause of vexation or disgust.

eye splice. *Nautical.* A loop formed at the end of a rope by turning it back and splicing in the end strands.

eye·spot (ī′spŏt′) *n.* **1.** A light-sensitive, pigmented area in certain algae, protozoans, and other organisms. **2.** A rounded, eyelike marking, as on the tail of a peacock.

eye·stalk (ī′stôk′) *n.* A movable, stalklike structure bearing at its tip one of the eyes of a crab, shrimp, or similar crustacean.

eye·strain (ī′strān′) *n.* Fatigue of the ciliary muscle or of the extrinsic muscles of the eyeball caused by refractive errors or imbalance of the ocular muscles and characterized by pain in the eyes, lacrimation, headache, nausea, dizziness, or other reflex symptoms.

eye·tooth (ī′tōōth′) *n., pl.* **-teeth** (tēth′). A canine *(see)* of the upper jaw. —**cut one's eyeteeth.** To gain experience. —**give one's eyeteeth.** To be willing to give up a great deal to acquire something much desired. [Perhaps so called because it lies immediately under the eye.]

eye·wash (ī′wŏsh′, -wôsh′) *n.* **1.** A medicated solution applied as a wash for the eyes. **2.** Nonsense; meaningless talk.

eye·wink (ī′wĭngk′) *n.* **1.** A wink of the eye. **2.** An instant. **3.** *Obsolete.* A glance.

eye·wit·ness (ī′wĭt′nəs) *n.* A person who has personally seen someone or something and can bear witness to the fact.

ey·ra (âr′ə) *n.* A reddish-brown color phase of the jaguarondi, a wild cat of tropical America. [American Spanish, from Tupi *irara, eirara.*]

eyre (âr) *n. Obsolete.* **1.** A circuit; itineration. **2.** A circuit court held by itinerant justices in medieval England. —**justices in eyre.** Justices who traveled periodically to hold court in various shires. [Middle English *eire,* from Old French, from Latin *iter,* journey, trip. See ei-¹ in Appendix.*]

Eyre, Lake (âr). A shallow salt lake, occupying about 3,700 square miles at nearly 40 feet below sea level in central South Australia, Australia.

Eyre Peninsula (âr). A peninsula extending for about 200 miles between the Great Australian Bight and Spencer Gulf, in southern South Australia, Australia.

ey·rie. Variant of **aerie.**

ey·rir (ā′rîr′) *n., pl.* **aurar** (œ′rär′). A coin equal to ¹/₁₀₀ of the krona of Iceland. See table of exchange rates at **currency.** [Icelandic, from Old Norse, an ounce, probably from Latin *aureus,* gold coin, from *aurum,* gold. See aurum in Appendix.*]

ey·ry. Variant of **aerie.**

Eze., Ezek. Ezekiel (Old Testament).

Ez·e·chi·as, Ez·e·ki·as. See Hezekiah.

E·ze·ki·el¹ (ĭ-zē′kē-əl). A major Hebrew prophet of the sixth century B.C., author of the Book of Ezekiel.

E·ze·ki·el² (ĭ-zē′kē-əl) *n. Abbr.* **Ezek., Eze.** The Old Testament book bearing the name of the prophet Ezekiel.

Ez·ra¹ (ĕz′rə). Hebrew high priest of the fifth century B.C.

Ez·ra² (ĕz′rə) *n.* A book of the Old Testament bearing the name of the priest Ezra. Also called "Esdras" in the Douay Bible.

eyestalks

eyestalk
Eyestalks of a
fiddler crab

ă pat/ā pay/âr care/ä father/b bib/ch church/d deed/ĕ pet/ē be/f fife/g gag/h hat/hw which/ĭ pit/ī pie/îr pier/j judge/k kick/l lid/m mum/n no, sudden/ng thing/ŏ pot/ō toe/ô paw, for/oi noise/ōō took/ōō boot/ou out/p pop/r roar/s sauce/sh ship, dish/
t tight/th thin, path/th this, bathe/ŭ cut/ûr urge/v valve/w with/y yes/z zebra, size/zh vision/ə about, item, edible, gallop, circus/
à *Fr.* ami/œ *Fr.* feu, *Ger.* schön/ü *Fr.* tu, *Ger.* über/кн *Ger.* ich, *Scot.* loch/N *Fr.* bon. *Follows main vocabulary. †Of obscure origin.

Ff

Y Y F F F F F F f F f f

The letter F is ultimately a descendant of the letter **V** *(see). Around 1000* B.C. *the Phoenicians and other Semites of Syria and Palestine began to use a graphic sign in the forms (1,2). They gave it the name* wāw *and used it for a semiconsonant* w, *as in English* know, knows. *After 900* B.C., *when the Greeks borrowed the alphabet from the Phoenicians, they developed two signs from* wāw. *One sign (3), which they called* digamma, *they used for the semiconsonant* w, *which disappeared in later Greek. (For the other sign, see* V.) *The* digamma *passed via Etruscan to the Roman alphabet (4,5), in which it was used for the consonant* f. *The Roman Monumental Capital (6) is the prototype of our modern capital, printed (9) and written (10). The written Roman form (5) developed into the late Roman and medieval Uncial (7) and Cursive (8), which are the bases of our modern small letter, printed (11) and written (12).*

f, F (ĕf) *n., pl.* **f's** *or rare* **fs, F's** *or* **Fs. 1.** The sixth letter of the modern English alphabet. See **alphabet. 2.** Any of the speech sounds represented by this letter.

f, F, f., F. Note: As an abbreviation or symbol, *f* may be a small or a capital letter, with or without a period. Established forms or those generally preferred precede the definition. When no form is given, all four forms are in general use in that sense. **1.** F Fahrenheit. **2.** F farad. **3.** f. farthing. **4.** F. February (unofficial). **5.** F, F. fellow (of a university or other institution). **6.** female. **7.** f., F. *Grammar.* feminine. **8.** f *Physics.* femto-. **9.** f., F. *Metallurgy.* fine. **10.** F The symbol for the element fluorine. **11.** f., F. folio. **12.** f. following. **13.** F *Physics.* force. **14.** f, F *Music.* forte. **15.** f. *Sports.* foul. **16.** f. franc. **17.** F. French. **18.** F. Friday (unofficial). **19.** The sixth in a series. **20.** F A failing grade in schoolwork. **21.** F *Music.* **a.** The fourth tone in the scale of C major, or the sixth tone in the relative minor scale. **b.** The key or a scale in which F is the tonic. **c.** A written or printed note representing this tone. **d.** A string, key, or pipe tuned to the pitch of this tone.

fa (fä) *n.* The fourth tone of the diatonic scale in solmization. [Middle English, from Medieval Latin, short for *famuli*, servants, word sung to this note in a hymn to Saint John the Baptist (see **gamut**), plural of Latin *famulus*, servant. See **family.**]

FA 1. field artillery. **2.** fine art.

f.a. fire alarm.

F.A. fine art.

FAA Federal Aviation Administration.

Fa·ber·gé (făb'ər-jā', -zhā'; *French* fȧ-bĕr-zhā'), **Peter Carl.** 1846–1920. Russian court jeweler; resident in France (1918–20); noted for his gold and enamel objects of virtu.

Fa·bi·an (fā'bē-ən) *adj.* **1.** Using or characterized by a cautious strategy of gradual social progress and avoidance of direct confrontation with the state. **2.** Of or relating to the Fabian Society. —*n.* A member or supporter of the Fabian Society. [Latin *Fabiānus*, after Quintus *Fabius* Maximus (died 203 B.C.), Roman general who defeated Hannibal by avoiding direct conflict.] —**Fa'bi·an·ism'** *n.* —**Fa'bi·an·ist** *n. & adj.*

Fabian Society. An organization founded in Great Britain in 1884 to promote the gradual spread of socialism.

fa·ble (fā'bəl) *n.* **1.** A concise narrative making an edifying or cautionary point and often employing as characters animals that speak and act like human beings. **2. a.** A story about legendary persons and exploits. **b.** A literary genre consisting of such stories: *"the origin of the Peruvian empire . . . is lost in the mists of fable"* (William H. Prescott). **3.** A falsehood; lie. —*v.* **fabled, -bling, -bles.** —*tr.* To recount as if true. —*intr. Archaic.* To compose fables. [Middle English, from Old

French, from Latin *fābula*, narration, account, story, from *fāri*, to speak. See **bhā-²** in Appendix.*] —**fa'bler** *n.*

fa·bled (fā'bəld) *adj.* **1.** Made known or famous by fable; legendary. **2.** Existing only in fable; fictitious.

fab·li·au (făb'lē-ō') *n., pl.* **-liaux** (-lē-ō'). **1.** A genre of medieval verse tale, characterized by comic and ribald treatment of themes drawn from life, as for example, Chaucer's "Miller's Tale." **2.** The genre constituted by these tales. [Old French *fabliaux*, plural of *fablel*, diminutive of *fable*, FABLE.]

Fa·bre (fȧ'br'), **Jean Henri.** 1823–1915. French entomologist and man of letters.

fab·ric (făb'rĭk) *n.* **1.** Any material structure consisting of connected parts; a fabrication or framework. **2.** A structure consisting of human relations or of relations between ideas, expressions, emotions, or the like: *"the pattern of her mind, the whole fabric of her nature"* (James Thurber). **3.** A method or style of construction. **4. a.** Any cloth produced by joining fibers as by knitting, weaving, or felting. **b.** The texture or quality of such cloth. [Old French *fabrique*, from Latin *fabrica*, workshop, a trade, from *faber*, workman, artisan. See **dhabh-** in Appendix.*]

fab·ri·cant (făb'rĭ-kənt) *n. Archaic.* A manufacturer.

fab·ri·cate (făb'rĭ-kāt') *tr.v.* **-cated, -cating, -cates. 1.** To prepare, make, or fashion. **2.** To construct by putting together finished parts; assemble. **3.** To devise (a deception): *"The subtle . . . distortions of reality which he is not aware of fabricating"* (Karen Horney). [Middle English *fabricaten*, from Latin *fabricārī* (past participle *fabricātus*), fabricate, build, from *fabrica*, workshop. See **fabric.**] —**fab'ri·ca'tor** (-kā'tər) *n.*

fab·ri·ca·tion (făb'rĭ-kā'shən) *n.* **1. a.** Something, as a deliberately false statement, that is made up or fabricated. **b.** The action of inventing a false statement or of forging a document. **2.** *Rare.* The process of fabricating; manufacture.

Fab·ri·koid (făb'rĭ-koid') *n.* A trademark for a fabric with a waterproof pyroxylin surface.

fab·u·list (făb'yə-lĭst) *n.* **1.** A composer of fables, especially of apologues. **2.** An inventor or teller of falsehoods. [Old French *fabuliste*, from Latin *fābula*, FABLE.]

fab·u·lous (făb'yə-ləs) *adj.* **1.** Of the nature of a fable or myth; legendary. **2.** Told of or celebrated in fables or legends. **3.** Barely credible; astonishing: *the fabulous endurance of a marathon runner.* **4.** *Informal.* Extremely pleasing or successful: *We had a fabulous time at the carnival.* [Middle English, from Latin *fābulōsus*, from *fābula*, FABLE.] —**fab'u·lous·ly** *adv.* —**fab'u·lous·ness** *n.*

fac. 1. facsimile. **2.** *Education.* faculty.

fa·çade (fə-säd') *n.* Also **fa·cade. 1.** *Architecture.* A face of a building; especially, such a face that is given distinguishing treatment: *"Pink classical façades peeled off and showed the mud beneath"* (Graham Greene). **2.** The face or front part of anything; especially, an artificial or false front: *"Of most famous people we know only the imposing façade"* (Edith Hamilton). [French, from Italian *facciata*, from *faccia*, face, from Vulgar Latin *facia* (unattested), FACE.]

face (fās) *n.* **1.** The surface of the front of the head from the top of the forehead to the base of the chin and from ear to ear. **2.** The arrangement or expression of the features of this part of the head; countenance. **3.** An exaggerated facial expression; a grimace. **4.** The outward appearance; aspect; look: *The face of the city has changed.* **5.** Value or standing in the eyes of others; dignity; prestige: *The country feared it would lose face.* **6.** Effrontery; impudence. **7.** The most significant or prominent surface of any object, especially: **a.** The surface presented to view;

façade
Façade of the
Cathedral of Notre Dame,
Paris

ă pat/ā pay/âr care/ä father/b **bib**/ch **church**/d **deed**/ĕ pet/ē be/f **fife**/g **gag**/h **hat**/hw **which**/ĭ pit/ī pie/îr **pier**/j **judge**/k **kick**/l **lid**, needle/m **mum**/n no, sudden/ng **thing**/ŏ pot/ō **toe**/ô **paw**, for/oi **noise**/ou **out**/ŏŏ **took**/ŏŏ **boot**/p **pop**/r **roar**/s **sauce**/sh **ship**, dish/

front: *the face of a building.* **b.** The outer surface: *the face of the earth.* **c.** The upper or marked side; the most meaningful surface: *the face of a clock.* **d.** The side of an instrument or device that is applied: *the face of a golf club.* **8.** *Geometry.* A planar surface bounding a solid. **9.** Any of the surfaces of a rock or crystal. **10.** *Military.* Any of the sides of a formation of men or of a fortified position. **11.** The appearance and geological surface features of an area of land; topography. **12. Typeface** *(see).* —**face to face. 1.** In each other's presence; in direct communication: *We finally spoke, face to face.* **2.** Directly confronting. Used with *with: His illness brought him face to face with death.* —**in the face of. 1.** Despite the opposition of; notwithstanding. **2.** Considering the fact of; in view of. —**on the face of it.** From its appearance alone; apparently. —**show one's face.** To make an appearance. —**to one's face.** Confronting one in the flesh; directly and boldly: *He accused the offender to his face.* —*v.* **faced, facing, faces.** —*tr.* **1.** To turn or be turned in the direction of: *"We all play parts when we face our fellow men"* (H.L. Mencken). **2.** To have the front directly opposite to; front upon: *a window facing the south.* **3. a.** To realize; be cognizant of: *facing facts.* **b.** To confront or deal with boldly or bravely: *"What this generation must do is face its problems"* (John F. Kennedy). **4.** To be certain to encounter; have in store: *The unskilled youth faces a difficult life.* **5.** To cause (a soldier or formation of troops) to change direction sharply by giving a command. **6.** To turn (a playing card) so that the face is up. **7.** To furnish with a surface or cover of a different material: *bronze faced with gold foil.* **8.** *Sewing.* To provide the edge or edges of (a cloth or garment) with finishing or trimming. **9.** To treat or dress the surface of (a material); to smooth. —*intr.* **1.** To be turned or placed with the front toward a specified direction. **2.** To turn the face in a specified direction. —**face down.** To overcome or prevail over by a stare or a resolute manner. —**face off.** To start play in hockey, lacrosse, and other games by releasing the puck or ball between two opposing players. —**face out.** To endure to the end. —**face up to. 1.** To recognize the existence or importance of. **2.** To confront bravely. [Middle English, from Old French, from Vulgar Latin *facia* (unattested), from Latin *faciēs,* form, shape, face, from *facere,* to make, form. See **dhē-¹** in Appendix.*] —**face'a·ble** *adj.* —**face'less** *adj.*

face card. A king, queen, or jack of a deck of playing cards.

face cloth. A **washcloth** *(see).*

face flannel. *British.* A washcloth.

face-hard·en (fās'härd'n) *tr.v.* **-ened, -ening, -ens.** To harden the surface of (a metal).

face lifting. Also **face-lift** (fās'lĭft'). **1.** Plastic surgery for tightening facial tissues and improving the appearance of facial skin. **2.** An extensive restyling or modernizing of an outward appearance: *The old city hall will undergo a face lifting.*

face·plate (fās'plāt') *n.* A disk attached to the mandrel of a lathe to hold flat or irregularly shaped work.

fac·er (fā'sər) *n.* **1.** A person or thing that faces; especially, a device used in smoothing or dressing metal, stone, or other material. **2.** *Chiefly British.* An unexpected blow or defeat.

fac·et (făs'ĭt) *n.* **1.** Any of the flat polished surfaces cut on a gemstone. **2.** A small planar or rounded smooth surface on a bone or tooth. **3.** One of the lenslike divisions of a compound eye, as of an insect. **4.** An aspect; phase: *"The four principal characters are . . . facets of Wordsworth himself"* (Samuel Chew). —See Synonyms at **phase.** [French *facette,* diminutive of *face,* FACE.] —**fac'et·ed, fac'et·ted** *adj.*

fa·cete (fə-sēt') *adj. Archaic.* **1.** Cheerful, facetious, or witty. **2.** *Obsolete.* Characterized by elegance, polish, and grace of manner, bearing, or style. [Latin *facētus,* FACETIOUS.]

fa·ce·ti·ae (fə-sē'shē-ē') *pl.n.* Witty or coarsely humorous writings and sayings; pleasantries. [Latin *facētiae,* plural of *facētia,* a jest, from *facētus,* FACETIOUS.]

fa·ce·tious (fə-sē'shəs) *adj.* Playfully jocular; humorous and flippant: *a facetious remark.* [Old French *facetieux,* from *facetie,* a jest, from Latin *facētia,* from *facētus*†, elegant, fine, facetious.] —**fa·ce'tious·ly** *adv.* —**fa·ce'tious·ness** *n.*

face value. 1. The value printed or written on a bill, bond, coin, or the like. **2.** The apparent value or significance: *He accepted their professed loyalty at face value.*

fa·cial (fā'shəl) *adj.* Of or concerning the face. —*n.* A treatment for the face, usually consisting of a massage and the application of cosmetic creams. —**fa'cial·ly** *adv.*

facial index. The ratio of facial length to facial width multiplied by 100.

-facient. Indicates a bringing about or causing to become something; for example, **absorbefacient.** [From Latin *faciēns* (stem *facient-*), present participle of *facere,* to do. See **dhē-¹** in Appendix.*]

fa·ci·es (fā'shē-ēz) *n., pl.* **facies. 1.** The general aspect or outward appearance, as of a given growth of flora. **2.** *Geology.* **a.** A part differentiated from other parts in a rock by appearance or composition. **b.** A rock distinguished from related or similar rocks. **c.** A stratigraphic body distinguished from others by appearance or composition. [New Latin, from Latin *faciēs,* shape, form, FACE.]

fac·ile (făs'əl, -īl) *adj.* **1.** Done or achieved with little effort or difficulty; easy: *facile tasks.* **2.** Working, acting, or speaking effortlessly; fluent: *a facile speaker.* **3.** Arrived at without due care, effort, or examination; superficial. **4.** Easy and relaxed in manner. **5.** Yielding; compliant. —See Synonyms at **nimble, easy.** [Old French, from Latin *facilis.* See **dhē-¹** in Appendix.*] —**fac'ile·ly** *adv.* —**fac'ile·ness** *n.*

fa·cil·i·tate (fə-sĭl'ə-tāt') *tr.v.* **-tated, -tating, -tates.** To free from difficulties or obstacles; make easier; aid; assist. [French *faciliter,* from Italian *facilitare,* from *facile,* easy, from Latin *facilis,* FACILE.] —**fa·cil'i·ta'tion** *n.*

fa·cil·i·ty (fə-sĭl'ə-tē) *n., pl.* **-ties. 1.** Ease in moving, acting, or doing; aptitude: *"an extreme facility in acquiring new dialects"* (W.H. Hudson). **2.** Ready skill derived from practice or familiarity; fluency: *"the workman's quick facility with his hands"* (Sherwood Anderson). **3.** *Often plural.* The means used to facilitate an action or process; convenience; provision: *the facilities of a library.* **4.** An agreeable, pliable disposition. **5.** *Plural. Informal.* The available toilet arrangements.

fac·ing (fā'sĭng) *n.* **1. a.** A piece of material, often ornamental, sewn to the edge of a dress, coat, or other garment as lining or decoration. **b.** Fabric used for this. **2.** An outer layer or coating of different material applied to a surface for protection or decoration: *a stone wall with wood facing.*

F.A.C.P. Fellow of the American College of Physicians.

F.A.C.S. Fellow of the American College of Surgeons.

fac·sim·i·le (făk-sĭm'ə-lē) *n. Abbr.* **fac., facsim. 1.** An exact copy or reproduction, as of a document. **2. a.** A method of transmitting images or printed matter by electronic means. **b.** An image so transmitted. —*adj.* **1.** Of or used to produce facsimiles. **2.** Exactly reproduced; duplicate. [Latin *fac simile,* make (it) similar : *fac,* imperative of *facere,* to make, do (see **dhē-¹** in Appendix*) + *simile,* neuter of *similis,* SIMILAR.]

fact (făkt) *n.* **1.** Something known with certainty. **2.** Something asserted as certain. **3.** Something that has been objectively verified. **4.** Something having real, demonstrable existence. **5.** *Law.* **a.** An act considered with regard to its legality. Used especially in the phrase *after the fact.* **b.** The aspect of a case at law comprising events determined by evidence as distinguished from interpretation of law: *The jury made a finding of fact.* —**in (point of) fact.** In reality; in truth; actually. [Latin *factum,* a deed, from *factus,* past participle of *facere,* to do. See **dhē-¹** in Appendix.*]

fact-find·ing (făkt'fīn'dĭng) *n.* The discovery or determination of facts or accurate information. —*adj.* Engaged in or designed to ascertain facts: *a Congressional fact-finding committee.* —**fact'-find'er** *n.*

fac·tion (făk'shən) *n.* **1.** A group of persons forming a cohesive, usually contentious, minority within a larger group. **2.** Internal dissension; conflict within an organization or nation: *"And whereas our own beloved country . . . is now afflicted with faction and civil war"* (Lincoln). [Old French, from Latin *factiō,* an acting (together), a making, from *factus,* past participle of *facere,* to do, make. See **dhē-¹** in Appendix.*]

fac·tion·al (făk'shən-əl) *adj.* Of, characterized by, or causing a faction or factions; partisan. —**fac'tion·al·ism'** *n.*

fac·tious (făk'shəs) *adj.* **1.** Produced or characterized by faction. **2.** Creating or promoting faction; divisive: *"The . . . injustice with which a factious spirit has tainted our public administration"* (James Madison). —See Synonyms at **insubordinate.** —**fac'tious·ly** *adv.* —**fac'tious·ness** *n.*

fac·ti·tious (făk-tĭsh'əs) *adj.* **1.** Produced artificially rather than by natural process; contrived: *speculators responsible for the factitious value of some stocks.* **2.** Lacking authenticity or genuineness; sham: *a factitious smile.* [Latin *factīcius,* made by art, from *facere,* to make, do. See **dhē-¹** in Appendix.*] —**fac·ti'tious·ly** *adv.* —**fac·ti'tious·ness** *n.*

fac·ti·tive (făk'tə-tĭv) *adj.* **1.** Of or constituting a transitive verb that in some constructions takes an objective complement to modify its direct object; for example, *They elected him governor.* **2.** Of or being a suffix or other grammatical feature used to form a verb from an adjective or noun to indicate the accomplishment of the state denoted by the adjective or noun; for example, *-en* in *redden, strengthen.* [New Latin *factitivus,* from Latin *factus,* done. See **fact.**] —**fac'ti·tive·ly** *adv.*

fac·tor (făk'tər) *n.* **1. a.** One who acts for someone else; an agent. **b.** A person or firm that accepts accounts receivable as security for short-term loans. **2.** One that actively contributes to an accomplishment, result, or process. **3.** *Mathematics.* One of two or more quantities having a designated product: *2 and 3 are factors of 6.* —*tr.v.* **factored, -toring, -tors.** *Mathematics.* To determine or indicate explicitly the factors of (a polynomial, for example). [Middle English *factour,* from Old French *facteur,* from Latin *factor,* maker, doer, from *factus,* FACT.] —**fac'tor·ship'** *n.*

fac·tor·a·ble (făk'tər-ə-bəl) *adj.* Capable of being expressed as a product of factors. Said especially of mathematical expressions.

fac·tor·age (făk'tər-ĭj) *n.* **1.** The business of a factor; the activity of buying and selling as the agent of another. **2.** The commission or fee paid to a factor.

fac·to·ri·al (făk-tôr'ē-əl, -tōr'ē-əl) *n.* The product of all the positive integers from 1 to a given number. For example, 4 factorial, usually written 4!, is the product $1 \cdot 2 \cdot 3 \cdot 4 = 24$; similarly, $5! = 1 \cdot 2 \cdot 3 \cdot 4 \cdot 5 = 120$. —*adj.* Of or relating to a factor or factorial.

fac·tor·ize (făk'tə-rīz') *tr.v.* **-ized, -izing, -izes.** To factor (a mathematical expression). —**fac'tor·i·za'tion** *n.*

fac·to·ry (făk'tə-rē) *n., pl.* **-ries. 1.** A building or group of buildings in which goods are manufactured; a plant. **2.** A business establishment for commercial agents or factors in a foreign country. [Medieval Latin *factōria,* establishment for factors, from Latin *factor,* FACTOR.]

fac·to·tum (făk-tō'təm) *n.* An employee or assistant who serves in a wide range of capacities. [Medieval Latin *factōtum,* from Latin *fac tōtum,* do everything : *fac,* imperative of *facere,* to do (see **dhē-¹** in Appendix*) + *tōtum,* everything, the whole, from *tōtus,* all (see **teutā-** in Appendix*).]

fac·tu·al (făk′cho͞o-əl) *adj.* **1.** Of the nature of fact; actual; real. **2.** Of or containing facts. —**fac′tu·al·ly** *adv.*

fac·ture (făk′chər) *n.* **1.** The fact, process, or manner of making something. **2.** That which is made.

fac·u·la (făk′yə-lə) *n., pl.* **-lae** (-lē′). Any of various large bright spots or streaks on the sun's **photosphere** *(see)*, most conspicuous at the solar edge or near sunspots. [Latin, diminutive of *fax*† (stem *fac-*), flame, torch.]

fac·ul·ta·tive (făk′əl-tā′tĭv) *adj.* **1.** Of or associated with a mental faculty or faculties. **2.** Capable of occurring or not occurring; contingent. **3.** Granting permission or authority. **4.** *Biology.* Capable of adaptive response to varying environment. In this sense, compare **obligate.**

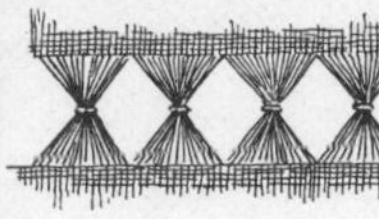

fagoting

fac·ul·ty (făk′əl-tē) *n., pl.* **-ties. 1.** An inherent power or ability: *"Wet grass has a faculty for saturating leather"* (Richard Jefferies). **2.** Any of the powers or capacities possessed by the human mind: *"Her strength lay in her extraordinary faculty for . . . observation"* (J.B. Priestley). **3.** The ability to perform well in a given activity; skill. **4.** *Obsolete.* Occupation; trade. **5.** *Abbr.* **fac.** *Education.* **a.** Any of the divisions or comprehensive branches of learning at a college or university: *the faculty of law.* **b.** The instructors within such a division. **c.** Any body of teachers as distinguished from their students. **6.** All of the members of a learned profession: *the medical faculty.* **7.** Authorization granted by authority; conferred power. —See Synonyms at **ability.** [Middle English *faculte,* from Old French, from Latin *facultās,* power, capability, from Old Latin *facul,* easy. See **dhē-¹** in Appendix.*]

fad (făd) *n.* **1.** A fashion in dress, behavior, or speech that enjoys brief popularity. **2.** The object of this fashion. [Origin obscure.] —**fad′dist** *n.* —**fad′dy** *adj.*

fad·dish (făd′ĭsh) *adj.* **1.** Having the nature of a fad. **2.** Given to adopting fads.

fade (fād) *v.* **faded, fading, fades.** —*intr.* **1.** To lose brightness, loudness, or brilliance gradually; dim. **2.** To lose freshness; wither. **3.** To lose strength or vitality; decline in energy; wane. **4.** To disappear slowly or gradually; die out; vanish. Often used with *out* or *away: All hope of reaching the camp by nightfall soon faded away.* —*tr.* **1.** To cause to fade: *Time has faded her beauty.* **2.** *Slang.* To meet the bet of (an opposing player) in a game of dice. —*n.* A dissolve in motion pictures or television. [Middle English *faden,* from Old French *fader,* from *fade,* faded, vapid, from Vulgar Latin *fatidus* (unattested), probably a blend of Latin *fatuus,* insipid, foolish, FATUOUS, and *vapidus,* VAPID.]

fade in. 1. To appear gradually. **2.** To make (an image or sound) appear gradually. Used of a motion-picture or television image or of a sound.

fade-in (fād′ĭn′) *n.* **1.** The gradual coming or bringing into full visibility of an image in motion pictures or television. **2.** The gradual coming or bringing into audibility of a sound, as in broadcasting.

fade·less (fād′lĭs) *adj.* Not fading or not subject to fading. —**fade′less·ly** *adv.*

fade out. 1. To disappear gradually. **2.** To make (an image or sound) disappear gradually. Used of a motion-picture or television image or of a sound.

fade-out (fād′out′) *n.* The gradual disappearance or loss of audibility of a motion-picture or television image or of a sound.

fad·ing (fā′dĭng) *n.* **1.** A waning; decline: *"The final factor in the fading of the Renaissance was the Counter Reformation"* (Will Durant). **2.** Fluctuation in the strength of received radio signals because of variations in the transmission medium.

fa·do (fä′do͞o) *n., pl.* **-dos.** A plaintive, usually sentimental Portuguese folk song. [Portuguese, fado, "fate," from Latin *fātum,* FATE.]

fae·ces. Variant of **feces.**

fa·e·na (fä-ā′nä) *n.* The final passes performed by the matador preparatory to the killing of the bull. [Spanish, from obsolete Catalan, from Latin *facienda,* "things to be done," neuter plural of the future passive participle of *facere,* to do. See **faculty.**]

Fa·en·za (fä-ĕn′zə; *Italian* fä-ĕn′dzä). A city and ceramic-producing center in northern Italy, 18 miles southwest of Ravenna. Population, 51,000.

fa·er·ie (fā′ə-rē, fâr′ē) *n.* Also **fa·er·y** *pl.* **-ies.** *Archaic.* **1.** A fairy. **2.** The land or realm of the fairies. —*adj.* Also **fa·er·y.** *Archaic.* **1.** Of or like a fairy or fairies. **2.** Enchanted; visionary; fanciful. [Middle English *faierie, fairie,* fairyland, FAIRY.]

Faer·oe Islands (fâr′ō). Also **Far·oe.** *Danish* **Faer·ö·er·ne** (fâr′-û′ər-nə). A group of Danish islands, with a combined area of 540 square miles, in the North Atlantic Ocean between the Shetlands and Iceland. Also called "Faeroes." Population, 35,000. Capital, Thorshavn.

Faer·o·ese. Variant of **Faroese.**

Fae·su·lae. The ancient name for **Fiesole.**

Faf·nir (fäv′nĭr, fäf′-). *Norse Mythology.* The dragon who guarded the treasure of the Nibelungs and was slain by Sigurd.

fag¹ (făg) *n.* **1. a.** Fatiguing or tedious work; drudgery. **b.** A drudge. **2.** *British.* A student at some English public schools who is required to perform menial tasks for a student in a higher class. —*v.* **fagged, fagging, fags.** —*intr.* **1.** To work to exhaustion; become weary from toil. **2.** *British.* To serve as the fag of another student. —*tr.* **1.** To exhaust from long work; to weary; fatigue. Often used with *out: He was fagged out by three hours on the tennis courts.* **2.** *British.* To use (a boy) as a fag. [Origin obscure.]

fag² (făg) *n. Slang.* A cigarette. [Short for FAG END.]

fag³ (făg) *n. Slang.* A male homosexual. [Short for FAGGOT.]

Fa·ga·ras Mountains (fə-gə-räsh′). The highest range of the Transylvanian Alps in southern Rumania. Highest elevation, Negoi (8,361 feet).

fag end. 1. The frayed end of a length of cloth or rope. **2.** An inferior remnant or last part of anything; that which remains of something exhausted of its quality or utility. [From Middle English *fagge*†.]

fag·got¹ (făg′ət) *n. Slang.* A male homosexual. [Origin unknown.]

fag·got². Variant of **fagot.**

Fa·gin (fā′gən) *n.* A man who trains children to steal. [After *Fagin,* an old man in Dickens' *Oliver Twist* who trains children to be pickpockets.]

fag·ot (făg′ət) *n.* Also **fag·got. 1.** A bundle of twigs, sticks, or branches bound together. **2.** A bundle of pieces of iron or steel to be welded or hammered into bars. —*tr.v.* **fagoted, -oting, -ots.** Also **fag·got. 1.** To collect or bind into a fagot or fagots; to bundle. **2.** To decorate with fagoting. [Middle English, from Old French, from Italian *fagotto,* from Vulgar Latin *facus* (unattested), from Greek *phakelos*†.]

fag·ot·ing (făg′ə-tĭng) *n.* Also **fag·got·ing. 1.** A method of decorating cloth by pulling out horizontal threads and tying the remaining vertical threads into hourglass-shaped bunches. **2.** A method of joining hemmed edges by crisscrossing thread over an open seam.

Fahr·en·heit (făr′ən-hīt′; *German* fä′rən-hīt′) *adj. Abbr.* **F** Of or pertaining to a temperature scale that registers the freezing point of water as 32°F and the boiling point as 212°F under standard atmospheric pressure. Fahrenheit temperatures are related to Centigrade temperatures by the equation F = 1.8C + 32. [After Gabriel FAHRENHEIT.]

Fah·ren·heit (fä′rən-hīt′), **Gabriel Daniel.** 1686–1736. German physicist resident in Holland; developed use of mercury in thermometry.

FAI Airport code for Fairbanks, Alaska.

F.A.I.A. Fellow of the American Institute of Architects.

Fa·ial (fə-yäl′). Also **Fa·yal.** An island, 66 square miles in area, in the central Azores.

fa·ience (fī-äns′, fā-; *French* fȧ-yäɴs′) *n.* Also **fa·ïence. 1.** A kind of fine, glazed pottery, usually decorated with colorful glazes. **2.** Moderate to strong greenish blue. See **color.** [French, short for *(vaisselle de) Faïence,* "(vessel of) Faenza."]

fail (fāl) *v.* **failed, failing, fails.** —*intr.* **1.** To prove deficient or lacking; perform ineffectively or inadequately. **2.** To be unsuccessful in attempting to do or become something. **3.** To receive an academic grade below the acceptable minimum. **4.** To prove insufficient in quantity or duration; give out. **5.** To decline in strength or effectiveness; wane; fade away. **6.** To cease functioning properly. **7.** To become bankrupt or insolvent. —*tr.* **1.** To disappoint or prove undependable to: *Our sentries failed us.* **2.** To abandon; forsake: *His strength failed him.* **3.** To omit or neglect. Used with an infinitive: *The defendant failed to appear in court.* **4. a.** To receive an academic grade below the acceptable minimum in (a course, test, or assignment). **b.** To give such a grade of failure to (a student). [Middle English *failen, faillen,* from Old French *faillir,* from Vulgar Latin *fallīre* (unattested), from Latin *fallere*†, to deceive, disappoint, fail.]

fail·ing (fā′lĭng) *n.* **1.** The act of a person or thing that fails; a failure. **2.** A minor fault or weakness; shortcoming; defect. —See Synonyms at **fault.** —*prep.* In the absence of; without: *Failing a rainstorm, the game will be played this afternoon.*

faille (fāl, fīl) *n.* A slightly ribbed, woven fabric of silk, cotton, or rayon. [French, from Old French *faille*†.]

fail-safe (fāl′sāf′) *adj.* **1.** Capable of compensating automatically for a failure. Said of a mechanical device. **2.** Acting to stop a military attack on the occurrence of any of a variety of predetermined conditions. —*n.* A fail-safe mechanism.

fail·ure (fāl′yər) *n.* **1.** The condition or fact of not achieving the desired end or ends: *the failure of an experiment.* **2.** One that fails. **3.** The condition or fact of being insufficient or lacking; a falling short: *the failure of the sugar-cane harvest.* **4.** A cessation of proper functioning or performance: *an electric power failure.* **5.** Nonperformance of what is requested or expected; omission: *failure to report a change of address.* **6.** *Education.* The act or fact of failing to pass a course, test, or assignment. **7.** A decline in strength or effectiveness; a weakening. **8.** The act or fact of becoming bankrupt or insolvent. [Variation of earlier *failer,* from Norman French *failer,* from Old French *faillir,* to FAIL.]

fain (fān) *adv. Archaic.* Preferably; gladly: *"government is an expedient by which men would fain succeed in letting one another alone"* (Thoreau). —*adj. Archaic.* **1.** Ready; willing. **2.** Obliged or required. [Middle English, from *fain,* joyful, happy, Old English *fægen.* See **pek-¹** in Appendix.*]

fai·né·ant (fā′nē-ənt; *French* fĕ-nā-äɴ′) *adj.* Given to doing nothing; idle; lazy. —*n.* An irresponsible idler. [French, folk etymological variant (influenced by *fait,* he does + *néant,* nothing) of Old French *faignant,* idler, present participle of *faindre,* to be idle, FEIGN.]

faint (fānt) *adj.* **fainter, faintest. 1.** Lacking strength or vigor; feeble. **2.** Lacking conviction, boldness, or courage; timid. **3.** Barely perceptible; indistinct; dim: *"Even in Spain the memory of the Crusade was growing faint"* (Garrett Mattingly). **4.** Ready to fall into a faint; suddenly dizzy and weak. —*n.* An abrupt, usually brief loss of consciousness, generally associated with failure of normal blood circulation. —*intr.v.* **fainted, fainting, faints. 1.** To fall into a faint; to swoon. **2.** *Archaic.* To weaken in purpose or spirit; languish. [Middle English *feint, faint,* faint, feigned, from Old French, past participles of *feindre, faindre,* FEIGN.] —**faint′er** *n.* —**faint′ly** *adv.* —**faint′ness** *n.*

faint-heart·ed (fānt′här′tĭd) *adj.* Deficient in conviction or courage; cowardly; timid. —**faint′heart′ed·ly** *adv.* —**faint′-heart′ed·ness** *n.*
faints (fānts) *pl.n.* Also **feints.** The impure spirits produced in the first and last stages of the distillation of liquors. [From FAINT.]
fair[1] (fâr) *adj.* **fairer, fairest. 1.** Visually beautiful or admirable; lovely: *a fair maiden.* **2.** Of light color, as: **a.** Blond: *fair hair.* **b.** Pale or white; not ruddy: *fair skin.* **3.** Clear and sunny; free of clouds or storms: *fair skies.* **4.** Free of blemishes; unstained; clean: *one's fair name.* **5.** Regular and even: *a fair edge.* **6.** Free of obstacles; open: *fair sailing.* **7.** Promising; likely; propitious: *in a fair way to succeed.* **8.** Free of favoritism or bias; impartial: *a fair judge.* **9.** Just to all parties; equitable: *a fair compromise.* **10.** Consistent with rules, logic, or ethics: *a fair tactic.* **11.** Moderately good; mildly satisfying: *a fair job of redecorating.* **12.** Courteous; agreeable: *fair manners.* **13.** Superficially true or good; specious: *They coaxed us with fair words.* **14.** Lawful to hunt or attack: *fair game.* **15.** *Baseball.* Designating or falling into the area of the playing field bounded by the foul lines. —See Synonyms at **average, beautiful.** —*adv.* **1.** In a fair manner; correctly; properly: *playing fair.* **2.** Directly; squarely; straight: *a blow caught fair in the stomach.* —**fair and square.** Just and honest. —*n. Archaic.* **1.** Loveliness; beauty. **2.** A person or thing that is fair; especially, a beautiful or beloved woman. —*v.* **faired, fairing, fairs.** —*tr.* To make (timber, a surface, or a joint) smooth, even, or regular. —*intr. Regional.* To become cloudless or mild: *The weather should fair by the morning.* [Middle English *fair, fager,* Old English *fæger.* See **pek-**[1] in Appendix.*] —**fair′ness** *n.*
Synonyms: *fair, just, equitable, impartial, unprejudiced, unbiased, straightforward, objective, dispassionate.* These adjectives mean showing no evidence of favoritism, self-interest, or the indulgence of one's likes and dislikes. *Fair,* which has the widest range, can imply any of the foregoing senses. *Just* stresses being in accordance with a code of what is legally or ethically right and proper. *Equitable* also implies justice, but less from the standpoint of a rigid code of rules than from a sense of what is in the best interest of all concerned in a given issue. It therefore may imply justice tempered by reason or compromise. *Impartial* emphasizes lack of favoritism in deciding an issue. *Unprejudiced* means without preconceived opinions or judgments, especially those adverse to a person or thing and not soundly based. *Unbiased* implies straightness of judgment or behavior, in the absence of self-interest, prejudice, or emotionalism. *Straightforward* suggests what is frank and honest rather than devious. *Objective* implies detachment that permits a person to observe and judge without undue reference to his own experience and without indulgence of his sympathies. *Dispassionate* means free from coloring by strong personal feelings or emotions.
fair[2] (fâr) *n.* **1.** A gathering held at a specified time and place for the buying and selling of goods; a market. **2.** A regional event, usually held annually, consisting of displays of farm and home products, and various competitions and entertainments: *a state fair.* **3.** A large exhibition presented jointly by a number of nations, each of which maintains a public building containing educational, artistic, and trade exhibits: *a world's fair.* **4.** An event, usually for the benefit of a charity or public institution, including entertainment and the sale of goods; a bazaar: *a church fair.* [Middle English *feire,* from Old French, from Late Latin *fēria,* from Latin *fēriæ,* holidays. See **dhēs-** in Appendix.*]
fair ball. *Baseball.* A batted ball that first strikes the ground or leaves the playing field beyond first or third base within the foul lines, or that is within the foul lines as it bounces past first or third base, or that comes to rest or is touched by a fielder in front of first or third base within the foul lines.
Fair·banks (fâr′băngks). A city in central Alaska, on the Tanana River, some 250 miles north of Anchorage. It is the northern terminus of the Alaska Railroad and the Alaska Highway. Population, 13,000.
Fair·banks (fâr′băngks), **Charles Warren.** 1852–1918. Vice President of the United States under Theodore Roosevelt (1905–09).
Fair·banks (fâr′băngks), **Douglas.** 1883–1939. With his son **Douglas Jr.** (born 1908), American motion-picture actors.
fair catch. *Football.* A catch of a punt on the fly by a defensive player who has signaled that he will not run with the ball and who therefore may not be tackled.
fair copy. A copy of a document made after all corrections and revisions have been completed.
Fair Deal. The principles and legislative program of President Harry S Truman and his liberal supporters. —**Fair Dealer.**
Fair·fax (fâr′făks), **Thomas.** Sixth Baron Fairfax of Cameron. 1692–1782. British colonial proprietor in Virginia.
Fair·field (fâr′fēld). A city and manufacturing center in southwestern Connecticut. Population, 53,000.
fair green. *Golf.* A **fairway** *(see).*
fair·ground (fâr′ground′) *n.* Also **fair·grounds** (-groundz′). An open space of land where fairs, exhibitions, or other public events are held.
fair-haired (fâr′hârd′) *adj.* **1.** Having blond hair. **2.** Favorite; promising: *the fair-haired boy of the neighborhood.*
fair·ing[1] (fâr′ĭng) *n.* An auxiliary structure or the external surface of an aircraft serving to reduce drag. [From FAIR (to make smooth).]
fair·ing[2] (fâr′ĭng) *n. British.* A gift, especially one bought or given at a fair.
fair·ish (fâr′ĭsh) *adj.* Of moderately good size or quality.
Fair Isle. A small island at the southern tip of the Shetland Islands group, noted for its knitting industry.
fair-lead (fâr′lēd′) *n.* Also **fair-lead·er** (-lē′dər). *Nautical.* A device such as a ring or block of wood with a hole in it, through which rigging is passed to hold it in place or prevent it from snagging or chafing.
fair·ly (fâr′lē) *adv.* **1. a.** In a fair or just manner; equitably. **b.** Legitimately; suitably. **2.** Clearly; distinctly. **3.** Actually; completely; fully: *The walls fairly shook with his bellowing.* **4.** Moderately; rather: *a fairly good dinner.* **5.** *Obsolete.* Gently or courteously.
fair-mind·ed (fâr′mīn′dĭd) *adj.* Just and impartial in judgment; unprejudiced. —**fair′-mind′ed·ness** *n.*
Fair·mont (fâr′mŏnt). A city of West Virginia, in the north on the Monongahela. Population, 27,000.
Fair Oaks. A battle site six miles east of Richmond, Virginia, where Union forces under George B. McClellan repulsed the Confederates under Joseph E. Johnston (1862). Also called "Seven Pines."
fair play. Conformance to the established rules or ethics of a sport, business, or other activity.
fair sex. Women collectively.
fair shake. *Slang.* A fair chance.
fair-spo·ken (fâr′spō′kən) *adj.* Civil, courteous, and gentle in speech.
fair-trade (fâr′trād′) *adj.* Of or designating a commercial agreement under which distributors sell products of a given class at no less than a minimum price set by the manufacturer. —*tr.v.* **fair-traded, -trading, -trades.** To sell (a commodity) at a price consistent with a fair-trade agreement.
fair·way (fâr′wā′) *n.* **1.** A stretch of ground free of obstacles to movement. **2.** The part of a golf course covered with short grass and extending from the tee to the putting green. Also called "fair green." **3.** *Nautical.* **a.** A navigable deep-water channel in a river, harbor, or along a coastline. **b.** The usual course taken by vessels through a harbor or coastal waters.
fair-weath·er (fâr′wĕth′ər) *adj.* **1.** Suitable or used only during fair weather. **2.** Present and dependable only in good times; failing in times of trouble: *fair-weather friends.*
Fair·weath·er, Mount (fâr′wĕth′ər). The highest peak (15,300 feet) in the Fairweather Range, on the border between southeastern Alaska and British Columbia.
fair·y (fâr′ē) *n., pl.* **-ies. 1.** A tiny supernatural being in human form, depicted as clever, mischievous, and capable of assisting or harassing humans. **2.** *Slang.* A male homosexual. —*adj.* **1.** Of or associated with fairies. **2.** Resembling a fairy; fanciful, graceful, or delicate. [Middle English *fairie,* from Old French *faerie, faierie,* enchantment, from *fae,* fairy, from Latin *fāta,* the Fates, plural of *fātum,* FATE.]
fair·y·hood (fâr′ē-ho͝od′) *n.* **1.** Fairies collectively. **2.** The condition or nature of fairies.
fair·y·land (fâr′ē-lănd′) *n.* **1.** The imaginary land of the fairies. **2.** Any charming, enchanting place; a wonderland.
fairy lily. The **atamasco lily** *(see).*
fairy ring. A circle of mushrooms in a grassy area, marking the periphery of underground mycelial growth. [The circle is superstitiously believed to be produced by dancing fairies.]
fairy tale. 1. A story about fairies. **2.** A fanciful tale of legendary deeds and romance, usually intended to please children. **3.** A fictitious, highly fanciful story or explanation.
Fai·sal (fī′səl), **Faisal Abdel Aziz al-Saud al-.** Also **Fei·sal, Fei·sul.** Born 1905. King and prime minister of Saudi Arabia (since 1964); deposed his half brother, Ibn Saud.
Fai·sal I (fī′səl). Also **Fei·sal, Fei·sul.** 1885–1933. First king of Iraq (1921–33).
Fai·sal II (fī′səl). Also **Fei·sal, Fei·sul.** 1935–1958. Last king of Iraq (1939–58); assassinated.
fait ac·com·pli (fĕ′tà-kôN-plē′) *pl.* **faits accomplis** (fĕ′tà-kôN-plē′). *French.* An accomplished and presumably irreversible deed or fact. Literally, accomplished fact.
faith (fāth) *n.* **1.** A confident belief in the truth, value, or trustworthiness of a person, idea, or thing. **2.** Belief that does not rest on logical proof or material evidence: *faith in miracles.* **3.** Loyalty to a person or thing; allegiance: *keeping faith with one's supporters.* **4.** Belief and trust in God and in the doctrines expressed in the Scriptures or other sacred works; religious conviction. **5.** A system of religious beliefs: *the Moslem faith.* **6.** Any set of principles or beliefs: *"Realism had been his literary faith from his earliest days"* (Alfred Kazin). —See Synonyms at **trust.** —**bad faith.** Deceit; duplicity; insincerity. —**good faith.** Sincerity; honesty: *promises made in good faith.* —**in faith.** *Archaic.* Indeed; truly. —*interj. Archaic.* In faith; indeed. [Middle English *feith, feth,* from Old French *feid, feit,* from Latin *fidēs.* See **bheidh-** in Appendix.*]
faith cure. A cure of an ailment held to be accomplished through religious faith.
faith·ful (fāth′fəl) *adj.* **1.** Adhering strictly to the person, cause, or idea to which one is bound; dutiful and loyal. **2.** Worthy of trust or credence; consistently reliable: *a faithful guide.* **3.** Consistent with truth or actuality; accurate; exact: *a faithful reproduction.* **4.** *Obsolete.* Having religious faith; believing. —**the faithful. 1.** The practicing members of a religious faith, especially of Christianity or Islam. **2.** The steadfast adherents of any faith or cause. —**faith′ful·ly** *adv.* —**faith′ful·ness** *n.*
Synonyms: *faithful, loyal, true, constant, steadfast, staunch, resolute, devoted, trustworthy.* These adjectives mean firm and unchanging in attachment to a person, cause, or the like. *Faithful* and *loyal* are often interchangeable. *Faithful* in particular suggests long and undeviating attachment; *loyal* can

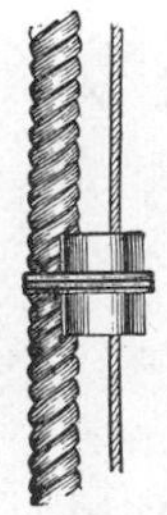
fair-lead

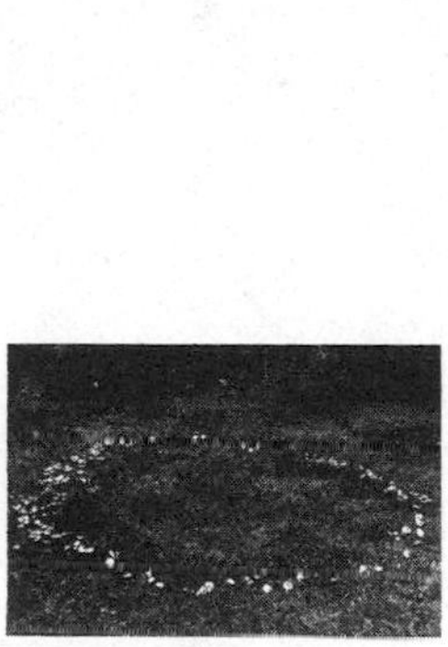
fairy ring

refer to behavior over a long period or in a particular situation, and is the term more often applied to allegiance to a government. *True* suggests steadiness, reliability, and in a closely related sense, genuineness of friendship or the like. *Constant* stresses absence of change and thus lack of fickleness, though it lacks the emotional warmth of the preceding terms. The idea of resistance to change in ties or bonds is intensified by *steadfast* and even more so by *staunch* and *resolute*, which suggest both a strong attachment or allegiance and a readiness to lend support when the object of the allegiance is under attack. *Devoted* implies dedication to a person or cause and consequent lavishing of time or attention. *Trustworthy* refers to one who has established his right to be considered worthy of another's confidence.

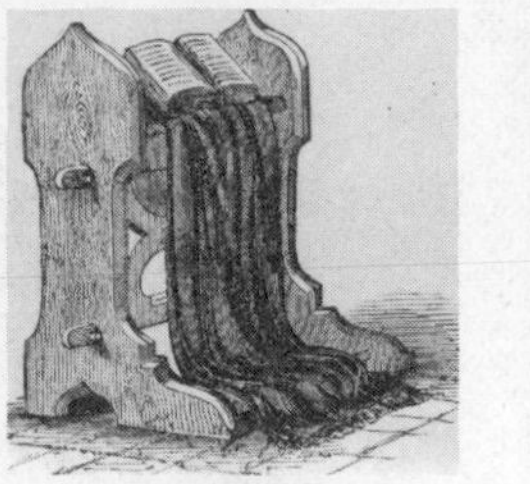

faldstool
Desk for the recitation of the litany

faith healer. One who attempts to effect faith cures.

faith·less (fāth′lĭs) *adj.* **1.** Untrue to duty or obligation; breaking faith; disloyal. **2.** Lacking confidence or trust in a given person or cause. **3. a.** Without religious faith. **b.** Without faith in Christianity; heathen. **4.** Unworthy of faith or trust; unreliable. —**faith′less·ly** *adv.* —**faith′less·ness** *n.*

Synonyms: *faithless, unfaithful, false, disloyal, traitorous, perfidious, inconstant, fickle, undependable.* These adjectives refer to what is unworthy of trust or in violation of it. They vary considerably in specific meaning and application. *Faithless* and *unfaithful* are approximately interchangeable and imply failure to fulfill or honor promises, obligations, or allegiance. *Unfaithful* often has specific reference to failure to respect the vows of marriage. *False* differs from the two preceding terms chiefly in its greater emphasis on actual breach of a promise or pledge, distinguished from a tendency to be untrue. *Disloyal* applies to one who is false to persons or things due allegiance, especially to a nation or superior. *Traitorous* refers most often to disloyalty to a nation. *Perfidious* applies to falseness to any trust or confidence, and stresses vileness of behavior. The remaining terms emphasize lack of reliability without necessarily implying violation of trust. *Inconstant* and *fickle* describe what is susceptible to change and therefore not trustworthy; *fickle* in particular implies capriciousness. *Undependable* refers broadly to that in which trust or reliance cannot be put.

fai·tour (fā′tər) *n. Obsolete.* A deceiver or impostor, especially one feigning illness or posing as a soothsayer. [Middle English, from *faiten*, to deceive, beg under false pretences, from Old French *fait*, past participle of *faire*, to do (probably influenced in sense by *faiture*, sorcery), from Latin *facere*, to do. See **dhē-**[1] in Appendix.*]

Fai·yum. See **El Faiyum.**

Fai·za·bad (fī′zə-băd). A city in east-central Uttar Pradesh, India, a former capital of the Oudh kingdom. Population, 88,000.

Fa·ka·ra·va (fä′kə-rä′və). An atoll and the commercial center of the Tuamotu Archipelago in the South Pacific Ocean.

fake[1] (fāk) *adj.* Having a false or misleading appearance; fraudulent. —*n.* **1.** A person, act, or thing that is not genuine or authentic; a sham; a counterfeit. **2.** *Sports.* A brief feint or aborted change of direction intended to mislead one's opponent or the opposing team. —*v.* **faked, faking, fakes.** —*tr.* **1.** To contrive and present as genuine; to counterfeit. **2.** To simulate; pretend; feign. **3.** To simulate the performance of (a musical passage). —*intr.* **1.** To engage in faking. **2.** *Sports.* To perform a fake. —See Synonyms at **pretend.** [Origin obscure.]

fake[2] (fāk) *n.* One loop or winding of a coiled rope or cable. —*tr.v.* **faked, faking, fakes.** To coil (a rope or cable). [Middle English *faken*†.]

fak·er (fā′kər) *n.* A person who fakes or who produces fakes; swindler. See Synonyms at **impostor.** —**fak′er·y** *n.*

fa·kir (fə-kîr′, fā′kər) *n.* Also **fa·keer** (fə-kîr′). **1.** A Moslem religious mendicant. **2.** A Hindu ascetic or religious mendicant; especially, one who performs feats of magic or endurance. [Arabic *faqīr*, from *faqura*, he was poor.]

Fa·laise (fə-lāz′; *French* fȧ′lĕz′). A town in northwestern France, 21 miles south of Caen, the seat of the Dukes of Normandy and a strategic point in the Normandy campaign in World War II (1944).

Fa·lange (fā′lănj, fə-lănj′; *Spanish* fä-läng′hā) *n.* A fascist organization constituting the official ruling party of Spain after 1939. [Spanish, from *falange*, phalanx, from Latin *phalanx* (stem *phalang-*), PHALANX.] —**Fa·lan′gist** (fə-lăn′jĭst) *n.*

fal·ba·la (făl′bə-lə) *n.* A flounce, frill, or ruffle. [French, from dialectal *ferbelà*†.]

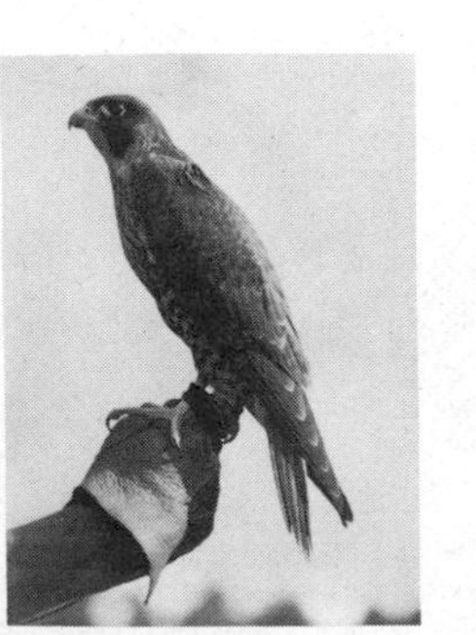

falcon
Falco peregrinus
Peregrine falcon

fal·cate (făl′kāt′) *adj.* Also **fal·ca·ted** (-kā′tĭd). Curved and tapering to a point; sickle-shaped. [Latin *falcātus*, from *falx*† (stem *falc-*), sickle.]

fal·chion (fôl′chən, -shən) *n.* **1.** A short, broad sword with a convex cutting edge and a sharp point, used in medieval times. **2.** *Archaic.* Any sword. [Middle English *fauchoun*, from Old French *fauchon*, from Vulgar Latin *falciō* (unattested), from Latin *falx* (stem *falc-*), sickle. See **falcate.**]

fal·ci·form (făl′sə-fôrm′) *adj.* Curved or sickle-shaped; falcate. [Latin *falx* (stem *falc-*), sickle (see **falcate**) + -FORM.]

fal·con (făl′kən, fôl′-, fô′-) *n.* **1. a.** Any of various birds of prey of the family Falconidae, and especially of the genus *Falco*, having long, pointed, powerful wings adapted for swift flight. **b.** Any of several species of these birds or related birds such as hawks, trained to hunt small game. **2.** A small cannon of the 15th to 17th century. [Middle English *faucoun*, from Old French *faucon*, from Late Latin *falcō*. See **pel-**[2] in Appendix.*]

fal·con·er (făl′kə-nər, fôl′-, fô′-) *n.* **1.** A person who breeds and trains falcons. **2.** One who hunts with falcons.

fal·co·net (făl′kə-nĕt′, fôl′-, fô′-) *n.* **1.** A small or young falcon. **2.** Any of several small falcons of the genus *Microhierax*, chiefly of tropical Asia. [FALCON + -ET.]

fal·con-gen·tle (făl′kən-jĕn′təl, fôl′-, fô′-) *n.* A female falcon, especially a peregrine falcon. [Middle English *faucoun gentil*, from Old French *faucon gentil*, "noble falcon" : *faucon*, FALCON + *gentil*, noble (see **gentle**).]

fal·con·ry (făl′kən-rē, fôl′-, fô′-) *n.* **1.** The sport of hunting with falcons. **2.** The art of training falcons for hunting.

fal·de·ral, fal·de·rol. Variants of **folderol.**

fald·stool (fôld′sto͞ol′) *n.* **1.** A small, usually cushioned stool at which worshipers kneel to pray; especially, one on which the British sovereign kneels at his coronation. **2.** A portable, backless chair or stool used by a bishop when not occupying his throne or when presiding away from his own cathedral. **3.** *Anglican Church.* A desk at which the litany is recited. [Partial translation of Medieval Latin *faldistolium*, folding stool, from Germanic. See **pel-**[3] in Appendix.*]

Fa·lis·can (fə-lĭs′kən) *n.* The Latino-Faliscan language of Falerii, an ancient city of Latium.

Fal·kirk (fôl′kûrk). A city and industrial center in Scotland, 23 miles west of Edinburgh. Population, 38,000.

Falk·land Island Dependencies. The former name for the **British Antarctic Territory.**

Falk·land Islands (fôk′lənd). *Spanish* **Is·las Mal·vi·nas** (ēz′läz mäl-vē′näs). A group of islands in the South Atlantic Ocean off the southeastern coast of Argentina, part of the British Antarctic Territory since 1962, and comprising East Falkland, West Falkland, and some 200 other islands. Population, 2,000. Administrative center, Stanley, on East Falkland.

Falk·ner, William. See **Faulkner.**

fall (fôl) *v.* **fell** (fĕl), **fallen** (fô′lən), **falling, falls.** —*intr.* **1.** To move under the influence of gravity; especially, to drop without restraint. **2.** To drop oneself from an erect to a less erect position: *He stumbled and fell.* **3.** To be severely wounded or to be killed in battle. **4.** To collapse from lack of structural support: *Several buildings fell during the earthquake.* **5.** To come to rest; strike bottom; land: *The aircraft fell in an uninhabited region.* **6.** To hang down: *Her hair fell in ringlets.* **7.** To be cast down; be averted: *Her eyes fell.* **8.** To assume an expression of disappointment: *Her face fell when she heard the report.* **9. a.** To be conquered or seized: *The city fell after a long siege.* **b.** *Slang.* To undergo arrest. **10.** To lose power; be defeated or overthrown: *During periods of crisis, governments may fall.* **11.** To follow a downward direction; to slope: *The plain falls gently toward the coast.* **12.** To undergo a reduction in amount, degree, or value; diminish: *The air pressure is falling.* **13.** To diminish in pitch or volume: *His voice fell to a whisper.* **14.** To decline in rank, status, or importance. **15.** To yield to temptation; to err or sin. **16.** To lose one's chastity. Used especially of a woman. **17.** To pass into a less strong, active, or normal condition: *Suddenly the crowd fell silent.* **18.** To arrive and pervade: *A hush fell on the crowd.* **19.** To occur at a specified time: *Christmas falls on a Tuesday this year.* **20.** To occur at a specified place: *The stress falls on the last syllable.* **21.** To be allotted, by chance or distribution: *The greatest task fell to him.* **22.** To be given, by right or stipulation: *The estate fell to the eldest surviving son.* **23.** To divide naturally. Used with *into: The specimens fall into three categories.* **24.** To be directed by chance: *His gaze fell on a small book in the corner.* **25.** To be uttered as if involuntarily; slip out: *A murmur of impatience fell from his lips.* **26.** To be born. Used chiefly of lambs. —*tr.* To cut down (a tree); fell. —**fall among.** To come by chance into the company of. —**fall away. 1.** To decline; languish; weaken. **2.** To withdraw friendship or support; part company. —**fall back.** To give ground; recede; retreat. —**fall back on** (or **upon**). **1.** To retreat to. **2.** To resort to. —**fall behind. 1.** To lag behind; fail to keep up with. **2.** To be in arrears. —**fall down.** *Informal.* To prove unsuccessful; fail or lag in performance. —**fall flat.** *Informal.* To fail completely to achieve the intended effect. —**fall for.** *Informal.* **1.** To become infatuated with; fall suddenly in love with. **2.** To be tricked or deceived by; be taken in by. —**fall foul** (or **afoul**). **1.** *Nautical.* To collide. Used of vessels. **2.** *Nautical.* To become entangled. Used of rigging. **3.** To quarrel; enter into dispute. **4.** To lose support or approval; come into conflict. —**fall in.** *Military.* To take one's place in a formation; form ranks. —**fall in with. 1.** To come to an agreement. **2.** To meet by chance; join. —**fall off. 1.** To decline; weaken: *Enthusiasm is falling off.* **2.** To decrease; diminish in number. **3.** *Nautical.* To change course to leeward. —**fall on** (or **upon**). To attack suddenly; ambush. —**fall short. 1.** To fail to attain a specified amount, level, or degree. **2.** To prove inadequate or lacking. —**fall through.** To fail; collapse; miscarry. —**fall to. 1.** To begin (a physical activity) energetically. **2.** To shut or move into place by itself. —**fall under. 1.** To occur in the class of; be listed or located within. **2.** To succumb to; come under an influence or power. —*n.* **1.** The act or an instance of falling; a dropping down; free descent. **2.** A sudden drop from a relatively erect to a less erect position: *He took a bad fall.* **3.** That which has fallen: *The field was covered with a fall of hail.* **4. a.** The amount of what has fallen: *a fall of two inches of rain.* **b.** The distance that something falls: *a fall of three stories.* **5.** *Often capital* **F.** Autumn. **6.** *Often plural.* A waterfall; cascade. **7.** A downward movement or slope: *the fall of a river toward its mouth.* **8.** Any of several pendant articles of dress, especially: **a.** A kind of veil hung from a woman's hat and down her back. **b.** An ornamental cascade of lace or trimming attached to a dress, usually at the collar. **c.** A woman's hair piece with long, free-hanging hair. **9. a.** A capture, overthrow, or collapse: *the fall of a government.* **b.** *Slang.*

An arrest: *He took another fall today.* **10.** A reduction in value, amount, or degree. **11.** A decline in status, rank, or importance. **12.** A loss of virtue or moral innocence; a yielding to sin. **13.** *Usually capital* **F.** *Theology.* Adam's sin of disobeying God by eating the forbidden fruit in the Garden of Eden, and the consequent loss of innocence and grace of all his descendants. **14.** *Wrestling.* **a.** The act of throwing or forcing an opponent down on his back. **b.** Any of various maneuvers used for this. **15.** *Nautical.* A break or rise in the level of a deck. **16.** *Plural. Nautical.* The apparatus used to hoist and transfer cargo or lifeboats. **17.** The end of a cable, rope, or chain that is pulled by the power source in hoisting. **18. a.** The birth of an animal; especially, the birth of a lamb. **b.** All of the animals born at one birth; a litter. —See Synonyms at **flock.** [Fall, fell, fallen; Middle English *fallen, fell, fallen,* Old English *feallan, fēol, feallan.* See **phol-** in Appendix.*]

Fall (fôl), **Albert Bacon.** 1861–1944. U.S. Secretary of the Interior (1921–23); central figure in the Teapot Dome scandal.

Fa·lla (fä′lyä), **Manuel de.** 1876–1946. Spanish composer.

fal·la·cious (fə-lā′shəs) *adj.* **1.** Containing or based on a fallacy: *a fallacious syllogism.* **2.** Deceptive in appearance or meaning; misleading: *fallacious evidence.* **3.** Not real or sound; delusive: *fallacious signs of a change in the weather.* —**fal·la′cious·ly** *adv.* —**fal·la′cious·ness** *n.*

fal·la·cy (făl′ə-sē) *n., pl.* **-cies. 1.** An idea or opinion founded on mistaken logic or perception; a false notion: *"This romantic fallacy, that Shakespeare was superhuman"* (Tucker Brooke). **2.** A statement or thesis that is inconsistent with logic or fact and thus renders the conclusion invalid. **3.** The quality of being in error; incorrectness of reasoning or belief. **4.** The quality of being deceptive. [Latin *fallācia,* deceit, trick, from *fallāx* (stem *fallāc-*), deceitful, from *fallere,* to deceive. See **fail.**]

fal·lal (făl-lăl′) *n.* A trifling, showy article of dress; a piece of finery; frippery. Used chiefly in the plural. —*adj. Archaic.* Affected; foppish. [Origin obscure.]

Fallen Timbers. A battle site in northwestern Ohio at which Anthony Wayne defeated the Indians (1794).

fallen woman. A euphemism for a prostitute; a harlot.

fall·fish (fôl′fĭsh′) *n., pl.* **fallfish** or **-fishes.** A small, silvery freshwater fish, *Semotilus corporalis,* of streams and rivers of eastern North America.

fall guy. *Slang.* **1.** One who takes the responsibility or blame, as for another's dereliction or delinquency; a scapegoat. **2.** An easy victim, as of a confidence game.

fal·li·ble (făl′ə-bəl) *adj.* **1.** Capable of erring. **2.** Tending or likely to err. [Middle English, from Medieval Latin *fallibilis,* from Latin *fallere,* to deceive. See **fail.**] —**fal′li·bil′i·ty, fal′li·ble·ness** *n.* —**fal′li·bly** *adv.*

falling band. A wide collar of linen or lace turned down over the shoulders, worn during the 17th century.

fall·ing-out (fôl′ĭng-out′) *n., pl.* **fallings-out** or **falling-outs.** A personal disagreement that has resulted in a broken or more distant relationship; estrangement; breach.

falling sickness. *Pathology.* **Epilepsy** *(see).*

falling star. Any object, such as a meteoroid, rendered visible as a bright streak in the sky by falling and being ignited by atmospheric friction.

fall line. 1. *Geography.* An imaginary line marking a drop in land level or height, formulated by connecting the waterfalls of nearly parallel rivers. **2.** *Usually capital* **F,** *capital* **L.** The line between the **Piedmont** *(see)* and the Atlantic coastal plain where the Appalachians slope sharply. **3.** *Skiing.* The natural line of descent between two points on a slope.

Fal·lo·pi·an tube (fə-lō′pē-ən). Either of a pair of slender ducts that connect the uterus to the region of each of the ovaries in the female reproductive system of humans and higher vertebrates. [First described by Gabriello *Fallopio* (1523–1562), Italian anatomist.]

fall out. 1. *Military.* To leave ranks; withdraw from formation. **2.** To quarrel; become estranged. **3.** To happen; occur.

fall·out (fôl′out′) *n.* **1.** The slow descent of minute particles of radioactive debris in the atmosphere following a nuclear explosion. **2. a.** The particles so descending. **b.** Such particles collectively.

fal·low (făl′ō) *adj.* **1.** Plowed and tilled but left unseeded during a growing season: *a fallow field.* **2. a.** Not pregnant: *a fallow mare.* **b.** Marked by the absence of pregnancy: *After three fallow years, the mare is in foal again.* —**lying fallow.** Going unexercised or unrealized. —*n.* **1.** Land that has been plowed but left unseeded during a growing season. **2.** The process of leaving plowed land unseeded during a growing season. —*tr.v.* **fallowed, -lowing, -lows. 1.** To make (land) fallow by plowing. **2.** To plow (land) by way of preparing it for sowing. [Middle English *falow, falwe,* Old English *fealh*†, arable land.] —**fal′low·ness** *n.*

fallow crop. A crop which tends to nourish soil and is rotated with a more demanding crop to maintain productivity of the soil.

fallow deer. Either of two Eurasian deer, *Dama dama* or *D. mesopotamica,* having a yellowish coat spotted with white in summer, and broad, flattened antlers in the male. [From obsolete *fallow,* reddish-yellow, from Middle English *falwe,* sallow, Old English *fealo.* See **pel-²** in Appendix.*]

Fall River (fôl). An industrial city and former leading textile-manufacturing center in southeastern Massachusetts. Population, 100,000.

Fal·mouth (făl′məth). **1.** A seaport and resort town on the English Channel in southwestern Cornwall, England. Population, 17,000. **2.** A resort town in southeastern Massachusetts; it includes Woods Hole, the site of a major oceanographic institute. Population, 13,000.

false (fôls) *adj.* **falser, falsest. 1.** Contrary to fact or truth; without grounds; incorrect. **2.** Fallacious; specious: *false logic.* **3.** Untruthful. **4.** Without meaning or sincerity; deceiving; sham: *false promises.* **5.** Not keeping faith; treacherous: *a false lover.* **6.** Not real or natural; artificial; synthetic: *false fur.* **7.** Resembling and generally being identified as a similar or related entity. **8.** Resembling but not accurately or properly designated as such. Often used in plant names: *false indigo.* **9.** *Music.* Of incorrect pitch. —See Synonyms at **faithless.** —**play** (a person) **false.** To betray. [Middle English *fals,* from Old French, from Latin *falsus,* past participle of *fallere,* to deceive. See **fail.**] —**false′ly** *adv.* —**false′ness** *n.*

false alarm. 1. A spurious emergency alarm, whether accidental or intentional; especially, a fire alarm where no fire exists. **2.** *Informal.* Any seeming crisis, signal, or warning that is groundless or abortive: *Not yet—it was only a false alarm.*

false arrest. *Law.* An unlawful or unjustifiable arrest.

False Bay (fôls). An inlet of the Atlantic in Cape of Good Hope Province, Republic of South Africa.

false bottom. 1. A partition that seems to be the bottom of a trunk, case, chest, or other receptacle but under which is another compartment. **2.** A base, as of a glass or bowl, which by its shape gives a false idea of the capacity of the vessel.

false colors. 1. The flag, markings, or the like of another country when used for deception, as by pirates on the high seas. **2.** Misleading representation; pretense.

false-heart·ed (fôls′här′tĭd) *adj.* Having a deceitful nature; disloyal; treacherous.

false hellebore. See **hellebore.**

false·hood (fôls′ho͝od′) *n.* **1.** Contradiction to or disparity with truth or fact; that which is groundless or specious; an inaccuracy. **2.** The act of deceiving; perfidy; lying. **3.** An untrue statement; deception; lie.

false imprisonment. *Law.* Unlawful arrest or detention of a person, as enforced without a warrant or with an illegal one.

false indigo. 1. A shrub, *Amorpha fruticosa,* of eastern North America, having compound leaves with numerous leaflets and long clusters of purplish flowers. **2.** A plant, *Baptisia australis,* of the southeastern United States, having compound leaves with three leaflets and deep-blue or purplish flowers.

false keel. A protective strip fixed below a ship's main keel.

false miterwort. The **foamflower** *(see).*

false pretense. 1. *Law.* Calculated misrepresentation of fact for purposes of fraud, as through forged documents. **2.** *Often plural.* Any similar misrepresentation or deception for an ulterior motive.

false rib. Any of the five lower pairs of ribs that do not unite directly with the sternum.

false Solomon's seal. Any of several plants of the genus *Smilacina;* especially, *S. racemosa,* of eastern North America, having a plumelike cluster of small greenish-white flowers.

false step. 1. A slip; stumble. **2.** A social blunder; faux pas.

fal·set·to (fôl-sĕt′ō) *n., pl.* **-tos.** A typically male singing voice when artificially producing tones in an upper register beyond its normal range. —*adj.* Having the quality of falsetto: *a falsetto tone.* —*adv.* In falsetto. [Italian, diminutive of *falso,* false, from Latin *falsus,* FALSE.]

false·work (fôls′wûrk′) *n.* A temporary supporting framework for a structure during construction or demolition.

fals·ies (fôl′sēz) *pl.n. Informal.* Pads or padding worn inside, or as part of, a brassiere to exaggerate the dimensions of the breasts.

fal·si·fy (fôl′sə-fī′) *v.* **-fied, -fying, -fies.** —*tr.* **1.** To state untruthfully; misrepresent. **2.** To alter (a document) in order to deceive. **3.** To counterfeit; forge. —*intr.* To make untrue statements; lie. [Middle English *falsifien,* from Old French *falsifier,* from Medieval Latin *falsificāre* : Latin *falsus,* FALSE + *facere,* to make (see **dhē-¹** in Appendix*).] —**fal′si·fi·ca′tion** *n.* —**fal′si·fi′er** *n.*

fal·si·ty (fôl′sə-tē) *n., pl.* **-ties. 1.** The condition of being false. **2.** Something false; an untruth; a lie or falsehood.

Fal·staff·i·an (fôl-stăf′ē-ən) *adj.* Resembling or characteristic of Falstaff, a fat, merry, ribald, and boastful knight in Shakespeare's *Henry IV:* Parts I and II, and *Merry Wives of Windsor.*

Fal·ster (făl′stər). An island of Denmark, 198 square miles in area, just south of Sjaelland.

falt·boat (fält′bōt′) *n.* A small boat consisting of canvas stretched over a collapsible frame and resembling a kayak. Also called "foldboat." [Partial translation of German *Faltboot,* folding boat, from *falten,* to fold, from Old High German *falden.* See **pel-³** in Appendix.*]

fal·ter (fôl′tər) *intr.v.* **-tered, -tering, -ters. 1.** To waver in confidence; hesitate. **2.** To speak hesitatingly; stammer. **3. a.** To move ineptly or haltingly; stumble: *"her limbs faltered in the grip of ruin"* (Thomas Wolfe). **b.** To operate uncertainly; fail mechanically. —See Synonyms at **hesitate.** —*n.* **1.** An unsteadiness in speech or action. **2.** A faltering sound. [Middle English *falteren*†.] —**fal′ter·ing·ly** *adv.*

fam. 1. familiar. **2.** family.

F.A.M. Free and Accepted Masons.

Fa·ma·gu·sta (fä′mə-go͞o′stə; *Italian* fä′mä-go͞os′tä). The leading port of Cyprus, in the east on the Bay of Famagusta, an inlet of the Mediterranean Sea. Population, 38,000.

fame (fām) *n.* **1.** Great reputation and recognition abroad, usually favorable; public esteem; renown; glory. **2.** *Archaic.* Rumor. —*tr.v.* **famed, faming, fames.** *Archaic.* To make famous by talking of. *"Her foes enough would fame thee in their*

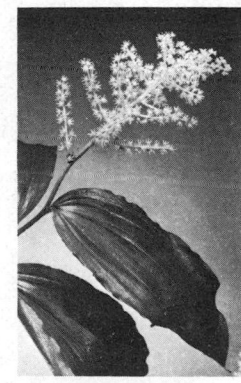

false Solomon's seal
Smilacina racemosa

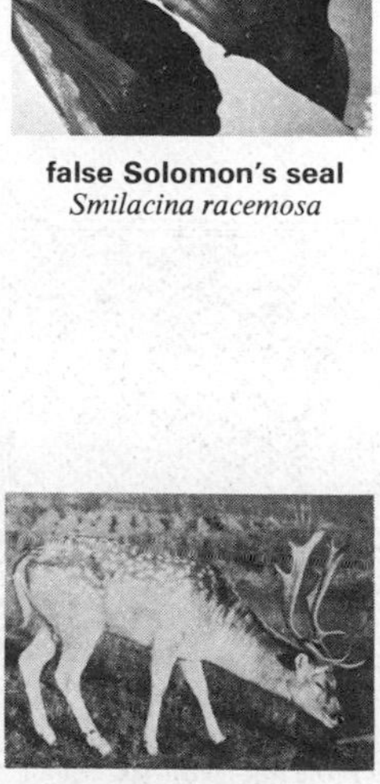

fallow deer
Dama dama

t tight/th thin, path/*th* this, bathe/ŭ cut/ûr urge/v valve/w with/y yes/z zebra, size/zh vision/ə about, item, edible, gallop, circus/ à *Fr.* ami/œ *Fr.* feu, *Ger.* schön/ü *Fr.* tu, *Ger.* über/KH *Ger.* ich, *Scot.* loch/N *Fr.* bon. ***Follows main vocabulary. †Of obscure origin.**

hate." (Jonson). [Middle English, from Old French, from Latin *fāma,* talk, reputation. See **bhā-**² in Appendix.*]

Synonyms: *fame, renown, glory, eminence, repute, notoriety.* These nouns refer to the condition of being very widely known. *Fame* is the broadest in application and consequently the least specific. When not qualified, it usually implies being known favorably. *Renown,* an intensification of *fame,* is always favorably applied and indicative of substantial achievement. *Glory,* an intensification of *renown,* implies an exalted position and generous bestowal of praise and honor. *Eminence* refers to the lofty position of one whose achievement is acknowledged to be foremost in its sphere or among that of the leaders. *Repute* is status or rank, high or low, accorded to one by others; the term, like *eminence,* often suggests critical judgment or evaluation more strongly than widespread popularity. *Notoriety* is the condition of being widely and usually unfavorably known; generally it implies short-lived fame based on something unworthy.

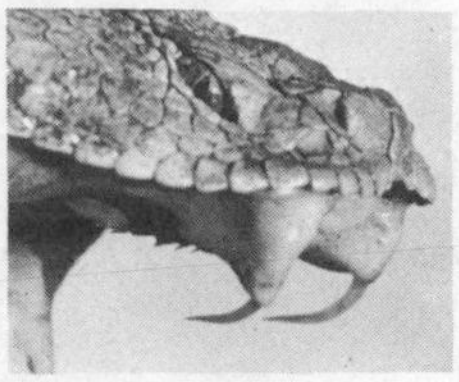

fang
Fangs of a diamondback rattlesnake

famed (fāmd) *adj.* Having great fame; publicly acclaimed; celebrated; famous.

Fa·meuse (fə-myo͞oz′) *n.* A North American variety of apple having red-streaked fruit. Also called "snow apple." [Canadian French, feminine of French *fameux,* from Old French *fameus,* FAMOUS.]

fa·mil·ial (fə-mĭl′yəl) *adj.* **1.** Of or pertaining to a family. **2.** *Genetics.* Passed on in a family; hereditary: *a familial trait.*

fa·mil·iar (fə-mĭl′yər) *adj. Abbr.* **fam. 1.** Of frequent instance or occurrence; often encountered; common: *a familiar sight.* **2.** Having fair knowledge of something; acquainted. Used with *with: familiar with those roads.* **3.** Of established friendship; close; intimate: *be on familiar terms.* **4.** Natural and unstudied; informal: *He lectured in a familiar style.* **5.** Presuming upon acquaintance; taking undue liberties. **6.** *Archaic.* Familial. **7.** Domesticated; tame. Said of animals. —See Synonyms at **common.** —*n.* **1.** A close friend or associate. **2.** An attendant spirit, often taking animal form. **3.** *Roman Catholic Church.* **a.** One who performs domestic service in the household of a bishop. **b.** An officer of the Inquisition whose function it was to apprehend and imprison the accused. [Middle English, familial, from Old French *familier,* from Latin *familiāris,* from *familia,* FAMILY.] —**fa·mil′iar·ly** *adv.*

Synonyms: *familiar, close, intimate, fraternal, confidential, chummy.* These adjectives describe relationships involving persons favorably disposed toward one another. *Familiar* implies a friendly association based on mutual attraction, frequent contact, or common interests. *Close* intensifies the idea of nearness, especially in an emotional sense. *Intimate* suggests extremely strong ties, resulting from affection or understanding, and the sharing of interests, problems, and experiences. *Fraternal* implies a brotherly relationship, and *confidential* stresses trust. *Chummy,* an informal term, suggests sociableness but not necessarily great depth of feeling.

fa·mil·i·ar·i·ty (fə-mĭl′yăr′ə-tē, -ē-ăr′ə-tē) *n., pl.* **-ties. 1.** Substantial or reasonable acquaintance with something; moderate understanding; knowledge. Used with *with.* **2.** Established friendship; candor; intimacy. **3.** Presumption; undue liberty; boldness. **4.** *Plural.* Actions or behavior presuming intimacy, especially sexual advances; liberties.

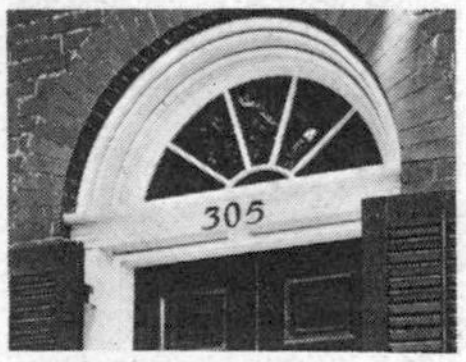

fanlight
Fanlight above a door

fa·mil·iar·ize (fə-mĭl′yə-rīz′) *tr.v.* **-ized, -izing, -izes. 1.** To make generally known, recognized, or familiar; popularize. **2.** To make (oneself or another) acquainted with. —**fa·mil′iar·i·za′tion** *n.* —**fa·mil′iar·iz′er** *n.*

fam·i·ly (făm′ə-lē, făm′lē) *n., pl.* **-lies.** *Abbr.* **fam. 1.** The most instinctive, fundamental social or mating group in man and animal, especially the union of man and woman through marriage and their offspring; parents and their children. **2.** One's spouse and children. **3.** Persons related by blood or marriage; relatives; kinfolk. **4.** Lineage; especially, upper-class lineage. **5.** All the members of a household; those who share one's domestic home. **6. a.** A group of like things; class. **b.** A special or particular world of something; kingdom; fellowship: *the family of man.* **7.** *Biology.* A taxonomic category ranking below an order and above a genus. **8.** *Linguistics.* A language group derived from the same parent language. **9.** A locally independent unit of the Cosa Nostra. —*adj.* Pertaining to family: *a family reunion.* —**in a family way.** *Informal.* Pregnant. [Middle English *familie,* from Latin *familia,* family, household, servants of a household, from *famulus*†, servant.]

family name. 1. A surname. **2.** A first or middle name, often a former surname, given to many members of a family.

family skeleton. A secret cause of shame to a family.

family tree. 1. A genealogical diagram of a family. **2.** The ancestors and descendants collectively of a family.

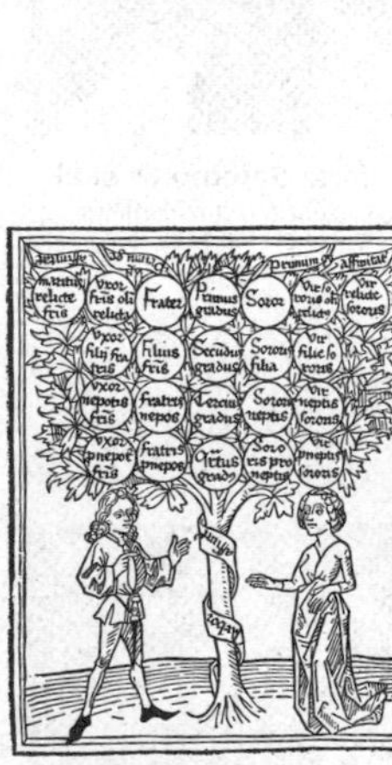

family tree
Fifteenth-century German woodcut showing bride and groom beneath family tree in which relationships are recorded in Latin

fam·ine (făm′ĭn) *n.* **1.** A drastic and wide-reaching shortage of food. **2.** A drastic shortage of anything; dearth. **3.** Severe hunger; starvation. **4.** Extreme appetite, as of a starving person. [Middle English *famine,* from Old French, from Vulgar Latin *famina* (unattested), from Latin *fames*†, hunger.]

fam·ish (făm′ĭsh) *v.* **-ished, -ishing, -ishes.** —*tr. Archaic.* **1.** To cause to endure severe hunger; starve. **2.** To cause to die from hunger; starve to death. —*intr. Archaic.* **1.** To endure severe hunger; starve. **2.** To die from hunger; starve to death. [Middle English *famishen,* probably variant of *famen,* from Old French *afamer,* from Vulgar Latin *affamāre* (unattested) : Latin *ad-,* toward + *fames,* hunger (see **famine**).] —**fam′ish·ment** *n.*

fam·ished (făm′ĭsht) *adj.* Extremely hungry; starving: *"Rip felt famished for want of his breakfast"* (Washington Irving).

fa·mous (fā′məs) *adj.* **1.** Generally recorded in history or currently renowned; publicly acclaimed; celebrated. **2.** *Informal.* First-rate; excellent. **3.** *Archaic.* Infamous; notorious. [Middle English, from Old French *fameus,* from Latin *famōsus,* from *fāma,* FAME.] —**fa′mous·ly** *adv.* —**fa′mous·ness** *n.*

fam·u·lus (făm′yə-ləs) *n., pl.* **-li** (-lī′). An attendant or servant, especially of a medieval magician or scholar. [German *Famulus,* from Latin *famulus,* servant. See **family.**]

fan¹ (făn) *n.* **1.** A hand-waved implement for creating a current of air or a breeze; especially, one in the form of a flat, fixed or collapsible device, usually wedge-shaped or round, and made of a light material such as silk, paper, or fine ivory. **2.** Anything shaped like or resembling a fan, such as an arrangement of seats in an auditorium. **3. a.** An array of thin, rigid blades attached to a central hub. **b.** A machine that rotates one or more such arrays on electrically powered shafts in order to move air, as for cooling or to exhaust an enclosure. **4.** A machine that throws grain and chaff into the air so that the latter will be blown away. **5.** A small rudderlike vane which keeps the sails of a windmill at right angles to the wind. —*v.* **fanned, fanning, fans.** —*tr.* **1.** To cause a current of or move (air) with or as with a fan. **2.** To direct a current of air or a breeze upon, especially in order to cool: *fan one's face.* **3.** To move to action or stir up; activate: *fan resentment.* **4.** To open out (a hand of cards, for example) to a fan shape. **5. a.** To fire (an automatic gun) in a continuous sweep by keeping one's finger on the trigger. **b.** To fire (a nonautomatic gun) rapidly by chopping the hammer with the palm. **6.** To winnow. **7.** *Baseball.* To strike out (a batter). —*intr.* **1.** To spread like a fan. Used with *out.* **2.** *Baseball.* To strike out. [Middle English *fan(ne),* Old English *fann,* from Latin *vannus.* See **wē-** in Appendix.*]

fan² (făn) *n. Informal.* An ardent devotee or admirer, as of a sport, athletic team, or famous person. See Synonyms at **votary.** [Short for FANATIC.]

fa·nat·ic (fə-năt′ĭk) *n.* A person possessed by an excessive and irrational zeal, especially for a religious or political cause. —*adj.* Variant of **fanatical.** [From Latin *fānāticus,* of a temple, inspired by a god, mad, from *fānum,* temple. See **dhēs-** in Appendix.*]

Synonyms: *fanatic, extremist, zealot, enthusiast.* These nouns denote persons who show marked and usually excessive attachment to a cause, faith, activity, or the like. *Fanatic* implies the pursuit of a given interest to lengths that are considered inordinate and even irrational, and often to the exclusion of virtually all other interests. *Extremist* is not strictly limited to the basic idea that relates these terms, but frequently it is applied to one who advocates the advancement of a cause or course of action to limits far beyond those considered wise or proper by the majority, usually by means that are equally excessive. *Zealot* refers to one who is wholeheartedly devoted to a cause or goal and who typically seeks to advance it in a partisan manner. *Enthusiast* now principally implies strong interest in something such as a sport or hobby, and lacks the unfavorable connotations of the other terms.

fa·nat·i·cal (fə-năt′ĭ-kəl) *adj.* Also **fa·nat·ic** (-ĭk). **1.** Possessed or driven by excessive or irrational zeal. **2.** Pertaining to or characteristic of a fanatic. —**fa·nat′i·cal·ly** *adv.*

fa·nat·i·cism (fə-năt′ə-sĭz′əm) *n.* Excessive, irrational zeal; extreme or unscrupulous dedication; monomania.

fa·nat·i·cize (fə-năt′ə-sīz′) *v.* **-cized, -cizing, -cizes.** *Rare.* —*tr.* To make fanatical; incite. —*intr.* To behave as a fanatic.

fan belt. A taut rubber belt that transfers torque from the crankshaft to the shaft of the cooling fan on an engine.

fan·cied (făn′sēd) *adj.* Produced by the fancy; imaginary; unreal: *"the Centaur is the only one of the fancied monsters of antiquity to which any good traits are assigned"* (Thomas Bulfinch).

fan·ci·er (făn′sē-ər) *n.* **1.** A person who has a special enthusiasm for something and who makes a hobby of his interest: *a fancier of antiques.* **2.** A person who breeds plants or animals: *a cat fancier.* **3.** A person given to reverie or whimsy; dreamer.

fan·ci·ful (făn′sĭ-fəl) *adj.* **1.** Created in the fancy; unreal; wishful; dubious: *a fanciful story.* **2.** Showing invention or whimsy in design; imaginative; curious: *a fanciful card.* —See Synonyms at **fantastic.** —**fan′ci·ful·ly** *adv.* —**fan′ci·ful·ness** *n.*

fan·cy (făn′sē) *n., pl.* **-cies. 1.** The light invention or play of the mind through which whims, visions, fantasies, or the like are summoned up; imagination, especially in a conscious or direct sense; caprice: *"Fancy is indeed less than a present palpable reality, but it is greater than remembrance"* (Keats). **2.** An associative image; fantastical invention. **3.** A notion not derived from evidence; an unfounded opinion; delusion. **4.** A capricious idea; vagary; impulse. **5.** *Informal.* Capricious or sudden liking; frivolous inclination. **6.** Taste or preference; critical sensibility. **7.** *Obsolete.* Love. **8.** *Obsolete.* A phantom or wraith. —See Synonyms at **imagination.** —**the fancy.** *Archaic.* The fans or enthusiasts collectively of a sport or entertainment, especially of boxing. —*adj.* **fancier, -ciest. 1.** Appealing to the fancy; decorative; elegant: *a fancy hat.* **2.** Arising in the fancy; illusory; presumptuous or vain: *fancy notions.* **3.** Executed with skill; complex or intricate: *a fancy pass.* **4.** Of superior grade; fine: *fancy preserves and jellies.* **5.** Excessive or exorbitant; inordinate: *a fancy bid.* **6.** Bred for unusual qualities or special points. —*tr.v.* **fancied, -cying, -cies. 1.** To visualize; imagine; picture: *"And she tried to fancy what the flame of a candle looks like after the candle is blown out"* (Lewis Carroll). **2.** To take to or like; be fond of: *"But in open Borstal Institutions they didn't fancy rape cases"* (Brendan Behan). **3.** To suppose; guess; surmise. **4.** To breed for excellence or special points. —See Synonyms at **like.** —*interj.* Used to express surprise. Often used with *that.* [Middle English

fantsy, short for *fantasie,* fancy, FANTASY.] —**fan′ci·ly** *adv.* —**fan′ci·ness** *n.*
fancy dress. A masquerade costume. —**fan′cy-dress′** *adj.*
fan·cy-free (făn′sē-frē′) *adj.* Carefree; without commitment or restriction; unattached.
fan·cy·work (făn′sē-wûrk′) *n.* Any decorative needlework, such as crochet, embroidery, or needlepoint.
fan·dan·go (făn-dăng′gō) *n., pl.* **-gos.** **1.** An animated Spanish or Spanish-American dance in triple time. **2.** A piece of music for such a dance. [Spanish *fandango*†.]
fan·fare (făn′fâr′) *n.* **1.** A loud flourish of trumpets; tantara. **2.** *Informal.* A clamorous or spectacular public display, ceremony, or reaction; a stir. [French (imitative).]
fan·fa·ron (făn′fə-rŏn′) *n. Obsolete.* **1.** A braggart. **2.** A fanfare. [Spanish *fanfarrón* (imitative).]
fan·fa·ron·ade (făn′fər-ə-nād′) *n.* **1.** Any vaunting or blustering manner or behavior. **2.** A fanfare. [French *fanfaronade,* from Spanish *fanfarronada,* from *fanfarrón,* FANFARON.]
fang (făng) *n.* **1.** A long, pointed tooth, especially: **a.** One of the hollow, grooved teeth with which a venomous snake injects its venom. **b.** One of the teeth of a carnivorous animal, with which it seizes and tears its prey. **2.** A similar structure, as a chelicera of a venomous spider. [Middle English *fang,* prey, spoils, Old English *fang,* plunder. See **pag-** in Appendix.*] —**fanged** *adj.*
fan·light (făn′līt′) *n.* **1.** *Architecture.* A half-circle window, often with sash bars arranged like the ribs of a fan. Also called "fan window." **2.** *British.* A transom.
fan mail. Letters, usually of praise, to a public figure from his devotees or admirers.
Fan·ning Island (făn′ĭng). A small island (12 square miles) and cable station in the British colony of the Gilbert and Ellice Islands in the central Pacific Ocean.
fan·ny (făn′ē) *n., pl.* **-nies.** *Slang.* The buttocks. [From FANNY (given name).]
Fan·ny (făn′ē). A feminine given name. [From earlier *Franny,* pet form of FRANCES.]
Fanny May. Nickname (FNMA) of the Federal National Mortgage Association.
fan·on (făn′ən) *n. Ecclesiastical.* **1.** A capelike liturgical garment worn only by the pope when celebrating Solemn High Mass. **2.** Formerly, any of various embroidered cloths, as a maniple, a piece of silk attached to a bishop's crosier, or a cover for the offerings brought by worshipers. [Middle English *fanoun,* from Old French *fanon,* from Frankish *fanon* (unattested). See **pan-** in Appendix.*]
fan palm. Any palm tree having palmate leaves in a fanlike arrangement. Compare **feather palm.**
fan·tail (făn′tāl′) *n.* **1.** One of a breed of domestic pigeons having a rounded, fan-shaped tail. **2.** A goldfish of a breed having a wide, fanlike, double tail fin. **3.** Any of several birds of the genus *Rhipidura,* of eastern Asia and Australia, having a long, fan-shaped tail. **4.** A tail, end, or part having a fanlike shape. **5.** The stern overhang of a ship. —**fan′tailed′** *adj.*
fan-tan (făn′tăn′) *n.* **1.** A Chinese betting game in which the players lay wagers on the number of beans, coins, or other counters that will remain when a hidden pile of them has been divided by four. **2.** A card game in which sevens and their equivalent are played in sequence and the first to discard all his cards is the winner. [Cantonese *fan t'an,* "repeated division" : *fan,* times, division + *t'an,* distribution, division.]
fan·ta·sia (făn-tā′zhə, -zhē-ə, făn′tə-zē′ə) *n. Music.* **1.** A free-form composition, structured according to the composer's fancy. **2.** A medley of familiar themes, with variations and interludes. [Italian, fantasy, from Latin *phantasia,* FANTASY.]
fan·tast (făn′tăst′) *n.* A visionary; dreamer. [German *Fantast, Phantast,* from Medieval Latin *phantasta,* from Greek *phantastēs,* a boaster, one who is ostentatious, from *phantazein,* to make visible. See **fantasy.**]
fan·tas·tic (făn-tăs′tĭk) *adj.* Also **fan·tas·ti·cal** (-tĭ-kəl). **1.** Bizarre in form, conception, or appearance; strange; wondrous; fanciful. **2.** Existing in the fancy; unreal; illusory. **3.** Unrestrainedly fanciful; extravagant: *fantastic hopes.* **4.** Capricious or fitful, as a person or mood. **5.** *Informal.* Wonderful or superb; remarkable; uncanny. —*n. Archaic.* A person who is unrestrainedly fanciful or eccentric in behavior or appearance. [Middle English *fantastik,* from Old French *fantastique,* from Medieval Latin *fantasticus,* from Late Latin *phantasticus,* imaginary, from Greek *phantastikos,* able to produce the appearance of, from *phantazein,* to make visible. See **fantasy.**] —**fan·tas′ti·cal′i·ty, fan·tas′ti·cal·ness** *n.* —**fan·tas′ti·cal·ly** *adv.*
Synonyms: *fantastic, bizarre, grotesque, fanciful, exotic.* These adjectives apply to what is very strange or strikingly unusual. *Fantastic* can mean literally apart from reality, but in this comparison it more often describes what seems to have slight relation to the real world because of its strangeness or extravagance. *Bizarre* stresses oddness of character or appearance that is heightened by striking contrasts and incongruities and that shocks or fascinates. *Grotesque* refers principally to appearance or aspect in which deformity and distortion approach the point of caricature or even absurdity. *Fanciful* suggests a character, nature, or design strongly influenced by imagination, caprice, or whimsy rather than by fact, reality, reason, or experience. *Exotic* means foreign in origin or character and alluring in effect.
fan·ta·sy (făn′tə-sē, -zē) *n., pl.* **-sies.** Also **phan·ta·sy.** **1.** The realm of vivid imagination, reverie, depiction, illusion, and the like; the natural conjurings of mental invention and association; the visionary world; make-believe. **2.** A mental image, especially a disordered and weird image; an illusion; phantasm. **3.** A capricious or whimsical idea or notion; conceit. **4. a.** Literary or dramatic fiction characterized by highly fanciful or supernatural elements. **b.** An example of such fiction. **5.** *Psychology.* An imagined event or condition fulfilling a wish. **6.** *Music.* A fantasia. —See Synonyms at **imagination.** —*tr.v.* **fantasied, -sying, -sies.** To imagine; visualize. [Middle English *fantasie,* fancy, fantasy, from Old French, from Latin *phantasia,* from Greek, appearance, perception, faculty of imagination, from *phantazein,* to make visible, from *phainein,* to show. See **bhā-¹** in Appendix.*]
fan·toc·ci·ni (făn′tə-chē′nē) *pl.n.* **1.** Puppets animated by moving wires; marionettes. **2.** A play with marionettes; puppet show. [Italian, plural of *fantoccino,* diminutive of *fantoccio,* puppet, doll, augmentative of *fante,* child, servant, short for *infante,* from Latin *infāns,* INFANT.]
fan·tom. Variant of **phantom.**
fan vaulting. *Architecture.* An intricate style of traceried vaulting, common in late English Gothic, in which ribs arch out like a fan from a single point such as a capital or corbel.
fan window. *Architecture.* A **fanlight** *(see).*
fan·wort (făn′wûrt′, -wôrt′) *n.* Any of several aquatic plants of the genus *Cabomba,* having finely divided, fanlike, submerged leaves.
FAO Food and Agriculture Organization.
far (fär) *adv.* **farther** (fär′*th*ər) or **further** (fûr′*th*ər), **farthest** (fär′*th*ĭst) or **furthest** (fûr′*th*ĭst).. —See Usage note at **farther.** **1.** To, from, or at considerable distance. **2.** To or at a specific distance, degree, or position: *Just how far are you taking this argument?* **3.** To a considerable degree; much: *"It is a far, far better thing I do"* (Dickens). **4.** Not at all; anything but. Used with *from: He seems far from content.* —**as far as.** To the distance, extent, or degree that: *as far as I know.* —**by far.** To a considerable or evident degree. —**far and away.** Definitely; without a doubt: *He's far and away the better skier.* —**far and wide.** Abroad; everywhere. —**far be it from me.** May I never; I neither hope nor dare: *Far be it from me to have said such a thing.* —**from far.** A distance. —**go far.** **1.** To be successful; accomplish a great deal: *That boy will go far.* **2.** To provide for much or many; last a long time. **3.** To tend strongly; not shrink from. —**in so far** (or **insofar**) **as.** To the degree or extent that; as long as. —**so far.** **1.** Up to the present moment: *So far there's been no word from him.* **2.** To a limited extent: *You can only go so far on 25 cents.* —**so far as.** To the extent that: *so far as I can tell.* —**so far so good.** Free from difficulty up to the present, with difficulties expected. —*adj.* **farther** or **further, farthest** or **furthest.** **1.** At considerable distance: *a far country.* **2.** More distant; opposite: *the far corner.* **3.** Extensive or lengthy: *a far trek.* —See Synonyms at **distant.** [Middle English *fer,* Old English *feor(r),* far, distant, remote. See **per¹** in Appendix.*]
FAR Airport code for Fargo, North Dakota.
fa·rad (făr′əd, -ăd′) *n. Abbr.* **F** A unit of capacitance, equal to the capacitance of a capacitor having a charge of 1 coulomb on each plate and a potential difference of 1 volt between the plates. See **measurement.** [After Michael FARADAY.]
far·a·day (făr′ə-dā′) *n.* The quantity of electricity that is capable of depositing or dissolving 1 gram equivalent weight of a substance in electrolysis, approximately 9.6494×10^4 coulombs. [After Michael FARADAY.]
Fa·ra·day (făr′ə-dā′), **Michael.** 1791–1867. British chemist and physicist.
fa·rad·ic (fə-răd′ĭk) *adj.* Also **far·a·da·ic** (făr′ə-dā′ĭk). Of, pertaining to, or using an intermittent asymmetric alternating electric current produced by an induction coil. [After Michael FARADAY.]
far·a·dism (făr′ə-dĭz′əm) *n.* Faradization.
far·a·di·za·tion (făr′ə-də-zā′shən) *n.* Medical therapy by application of faradic currents.
far·a·dize (făr′ə-dīz′) *tr.v.* **-dized, -dizing, -dizes.** To medically treat (an organ or part) with faradic currents.
Far·al·lon Islands (făr′ə-lŏn′). A group of islets in the Pacific Ocean, about 26 miles west of the Golden Gate, San Francisco, California.
far·an·dole (făr′ən-dōl′; *French* fȧ-räɴ-dôl′) *n.* **1.** A spirited circle dance of Provençal derivation. **2.** The music for this dance. [French, from Provençal *farandoulo*†.]
far·a·way (fär′ə-wā′) *adj.* **1.** Very distant; beyond immediate contact; remote: *faraway lands.* **2.** Bemused or abstracted; dreamy: *a faraway smile.* —See Synonyms at **distant.**
farce (färs) *n.* **1.** A theatrical composition in which broad improbabilities of plot and characterization are used for humorous effect. **2.** Something ludicrous; an empty show; mockery: *"childish family portraits, with their farce of sentiment and smiling lies"* (Thackeray). —*tr.v.* **farced, farcing, farces.** **1.** To intersperse or fill out (one's speech or a play) with jokes or witticisms. **2.** *Obsolete.* To stuff (a bird, for example) for roasting. [Middle English *farse,* stuffing, from Old French *farce,* stuffing, farce, from *farcir,* to stuff, from Latin *farcīre.* See **bhrekw-** in Appendix.*]
far·ceur (fär-sœr′) *n.* Also **farc·er** (fär′sər). **1.** An actor in a farce. **2.** A writer of farces. **3.** A comic; a wag. [French, from Old French, author or actor of farce, from *farce,* FARCE.]
far·ci·cal (fär′sĭ-kəl) *adj.* **1.** Pertaining to farce. **2.** Resembling farce; ludicrous; absurd. —**far′ci·cal′i·ty** (-kăl′ə-tē), **far′ci·cal·ness** *n.* —**far′ci·cal·ly** *adv.*
far·cy (fär′sē) *n. Veterinary Medicine.* Chronic, cutaneous **glanders** *(see).* [Middle English *farsi(n),* from Old French *farcin,* from Late Latin *farcīmen,* farcy, from Latin, sausage, from *farcīre,* to stuff. See **bhrekw-** in Appendix.*]

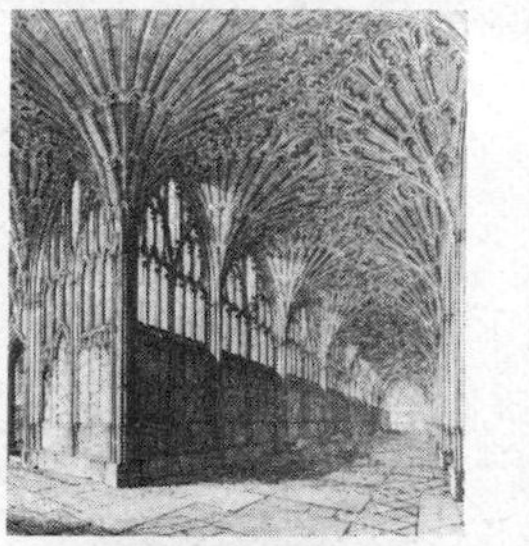
fan vaulting
In the cloister of the cathedral at Gloucester, England

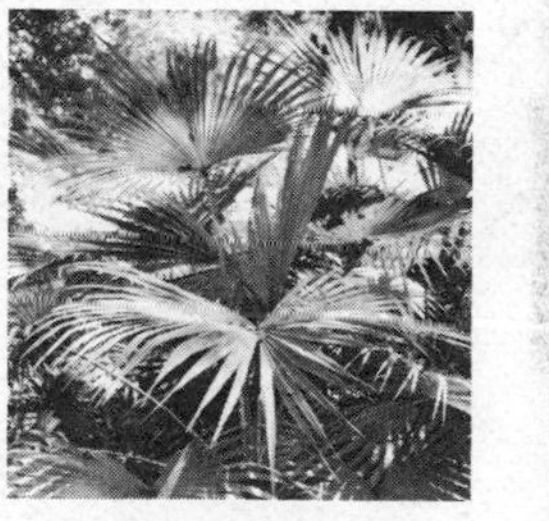
fan palm
Livistona chinensis

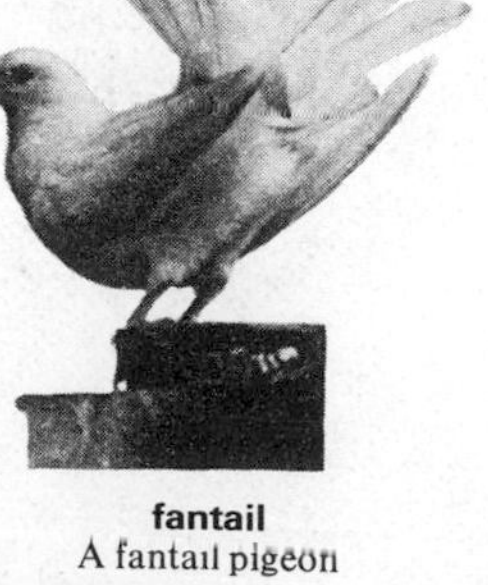
fantail
A fantail pigeon

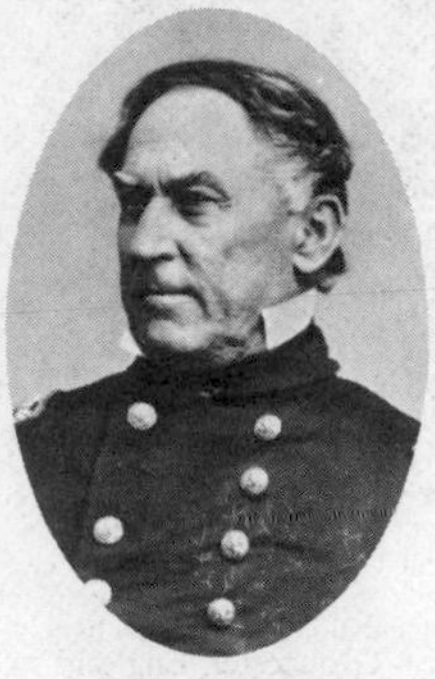

Admiral Farragut

farcy bud. *Veterinary Medicine.* A craterlike ulcer characteristic of farcy.

far·del (fär′dl) *n. Archaic.* A pack; a load; a burden: *"who would fardels bear,/ To grunt and sweat under a weary life?"* (Shakespeare). [Middle English, from Old French, diminutive of *farde,* package, from Vulgar Latin *fardum* (unattested), from Arabic *fardah, farde,* load.]

fare (fâr) *intr.v.* **fared, faring, fares. 1.** To get along: *How did he fare with his project?* **2.** To turn out; go. Used impersonally: *How does it fare with you?* **3.** *Rare.* To be entertained with food and drink. **4.** *Archaic.* To travel; wander. —*n.* **1.** A transportation charge, as for a bus or taxi. **2.** A passenger transported for a fee. **3.** Food and drink; meal; diet: *"I looked in often on the Stroeves and sometimes shared their modest fare"* (Maugham). **4.** *Archaic.* The state or condition of things. [Middle English *faren,* to travel, go, fare, Old English *faran.* See **per-**[2] in Appendix.*] —**far′er** *n.*

Far East. An area held by some to include the countries of China, Japan, and North and South Korea, and the islands belonging to them, and by others to include these and all Asian lands east of Afghanistan.

fare·well (fâr′wĕl′) *interj.* May you fare well; Godspeed; good-by. —*n.* (fâr-wĕl′). **1.** An acknowledgment at parting; a good-by. **2.** A leave-taking; going. —*adj.* (fâr′wĕl′). Pertaining to parting; final: *a farewell party.* [Middle English *fare wel!* : *fare,* go, fare, imperative of *faren,* to FARE + WELL.]

Fare·well, Cape (fâr-wĕl′). A cape at the southernmost tip of Greenland.

far-fetched (fär′fĕcht′) *adj.* Strained or improbable in nature or pertinence: *a far-fetched alibi.*

far-flung (fär′flŭng′) *adj.* **1.** Widely distributed; wide-ranging: *far-flung reporters.* **2.** Remote; distant.

Far·go (fär′gō). The largest city of North Dakota, in the east on the Red River. Population, 47,000.

fa·ri·na (fə-rē′nə) *n.* Fine meal prepared from cereal grain and various other plant products, and often used as a cooked cereal or in puddings. [Latin *farīna,* ground corn, meal, from *far,* a kind of grain. See **bhares-** in Appendix.*]

far·i·na·ceous (făr′ə-nā′shəs) *adj.* **1.** Made from, rich in, or consisting of starch. **2.** Having a mealy or powdery texture. [Late Latin *farīnāceus,* mealy : Latin *farīna,* FARINA + -ACEOUS.]

far·i·nose (făr′ə-nōs′) *adj.* **1.** Similar to or yielding farina. **2.** *Biology.* Covered with mealy dust or powder. [Late Latin *farīnōsus,* mealy, from Latin *farīna,* FARINA.]

far·kle·ber·ry (fär′kəl-bĕr′ē) *n., pl.* **-ries.** A shrub or small tree, *Vaccinium arboreum,* of the southeastern United States, having leathery leaves and hard black berries. [*Farkle-*† + BERRY.]

farm (färm) *n.* **1.** A tract of agricultural land, together with the fields, buildings, animals, and personnel there assembled for the purpose of producing a crop or crops. **2.** Any land or water area devoted to the raising, breeding, or production of a specified type of animal or vegetable life. **3.** *Baseball.* A minor-league club affiliated with a major-league club for the training of recruits and the maintenance of temporarily unneeded players. **4.** A country rest home for alcoholics or psychiatric patients. **5.** *Obsolete.* **a.** The system of leasing out the rights of collecting and retaining taxes in a certain district. **b.** A district so leased. **c.** A rent, tax, or toll so collected. —*v.* **farmed, farming, farms.** —*tr.* **1.** To cultivate or produce a crop on (land). **2.** To receive from a concessioner the rights to operate or supervise and retain profits from (a business or tax district, for example). **3.** To let to a concessionaire the rights to operate or supervise and retain profits from (a business or tax district, for example). Used with *out.* **4.** To offer the services of (a worker) for a fee or rent. **5.** To send (work) from a central point to be done elsewhere. Used with *out: farm out typing.* **6.** *Baseball.* To assign (a player) to a minor-league team. Used with *out.* —*intr.* To engage in farming; be a farmer. —*adj. Baseball.* Of or pertaining to a minor league. [Middle English *ferme,* lease, rent, from Old French, from Medieval Latin *firma,* fixed payment, from Latin *firmāre,* to fortify, fix, confirm, from *firmus,* firm. See **dher-**[2] in Appendix.*]

farm·er (fär′mər) *n.* **1.** One who operates or is employed on a farm. **2.** *Archaic.* One who has paid for and holds a concession on the rights of collecting and retaining taxes.

Far·mer (fär′mər), **Fannie (Merritt).** 1857–1915. American teacher of cooking; author of *Boston Cooking School Cookbook.*

Far·mer (fär′mər), **James Leonard.** Born 1920. American civil-rights leader; national director of CORE (1961–65).

farm·er-gen·er·al (fär′mər-jĕn′ər-əl, -jĕn′rəl) *n., pl.* **farmers-general.** A member of a group privileged to farm certain taxes in prerevolutionary France.

Farm·er-La·bor party (fär′mər-lā′bər). A minor political party, arising from the Farmer's Alliance movement in the Midwest and most active in the 1920's; it merged in 1944 with the Democratic Party.

farm hand. A hired farm laborer.

farm·house (färm′hous′) *n., pl.* **-houses** (hou′zĭz). The farmer's dwelling on a farm.

farm·stead (färm′stĕd′) *n.* A farm, including its land and buildings.

farm·yard (färm′yärd′) *n.* An area surrounded by or adjacent to farm buildings.

far·ne·sol (fär′nə-sōl′, -sŏl′) *n.* A compound, $C_{15}H_{26}O$, extracted from the flowers and essential oils of various plants, and used in perfumery. [New Latin *(Acacia) farnes(iana),* a species of tree having flowers used in perfumery : Odoardo *Farnese,* 17th-century Italian cardinal + -OL.]

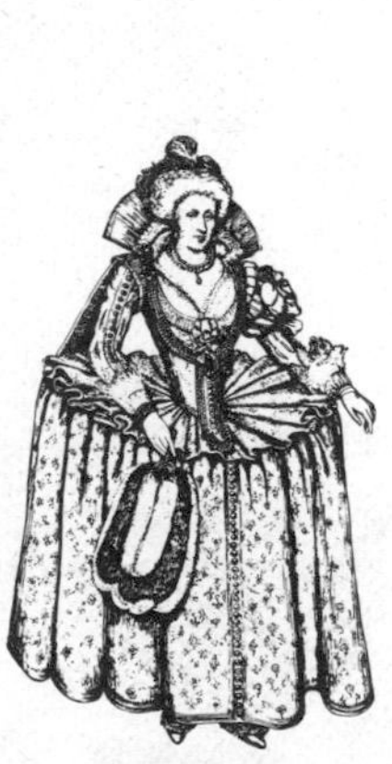

farthingale

Farns·worth (färnz′wûrth), **Philo Taylor.** Born 1906. American inventor and engineer; pioneer in the field of television.

far·o (fâr′ō) *n.* A card game in which the players lay wagers on the top card of the dealer's pack. [Variant of PHARAOH, perhaps because the king of hearts was once supposed to represent the Egyptian pharaoh.]

Far·oe. See **Faeroe Islands.**

Far·o·ese (fâr′ō-ēz′, -ēs′) *n., pl.* **Faroese.** Also **Faer·o·ese. 1.** One of the Germanic people inhabiting the Faeroe Islands. **2.** The North Germanic language spoken by the inhabitants of the Faeroe Islands. —*adj.* Of or pertaining to the Faeroe Islands, the Faroese people, or their language.

far-off (fär′ôf′, -ŏf′) *adj.* Remote in space or time; distant; faraway. See Synonyms at **distant.**

fa·rouche (fȧ-ro͞osh′) *adj. French.* Fiercely sullen or shy; untamed.

Fa·rouk I (fə-ro͞ok′). 1920–1965. King of Egypt (1936–52).

far point. The farthest point at which an object can be seen distinctly by the eye at rest.

Far·quhar (fär′kwər, -kər), **George.** 1678–1707. Irish-born English playwright.

far·ra·go (fə-rā′gō, -rä′gō) *n., pl.* **-goes.** A medley; conglomeration; mixture: *"This is a farrago of absurdity"* (Virginia Woolf). [Latin *farrāgo,* mixed fodder for cattle, from *far* (stem *farr-*), a grain. See **bhares-** in Appendix.*] —**far·rag′i·nous** *adj.*

Far·ra·gut (făr′ə-gət), **David Glasgow.** 1801–1870. American commander of Union naval squadrons in the Civil War.

Far·rar (fə-rär′), **Geraldine.** 1882–1967. American operatic soprano.

far-reach·ing (fär′rē′chĭng) *adj.* Having a wide range, influence, or effect; extending far.

Far·rell (făr′əl), **James T(homas).** Born 1904. American novelist.

far·ri·er (făr′ē-ər) *n. British.* One who shoes horses or treats them medically. [Old French *ferrier,* blacksmith, from Latin *ferrārius,* from *ferrum,* iron. See **ferrum** in Appendix.*]

far·ri·er·y (făr′ē-ə-rē) *n., pl.* **-ies. 1.** The practice of shoeing or treating horses. **2.** A farrier's shop.

far·row[1] (făr′ō) *n.* A litter of pigs. —*v.* **farrowed, -rowing, -rows.** —*tr.* To give birth to (a litter of pigs). —*intr.* To produce a farrow. [Perhaps Middle English *faren* (plural), Old English *fearh,* little pig. See **porko-** in Appendix.*]

far·row[2] (făr′ō) *adj.* Not pregnant; barren. Said of a cow. [Middle English (Scottish dialect) *fer(r)ow,* from Middle Dutch *verwe-* (unattested), cow past the age of bearing. See **per-**[3] in Appendix.*]

Far·rukh·a·bad (fə-ro͞o′kə-băd′, -bäd′). A city in central Uttar Pradesh, India, a Buddhist pilgrimage center. Population, 74,000.

Fars (färz, färs). Ancient name **Per·sis** (pûr′sĭs). A region and former administrative division of southern Iran, along the Persian Gulf.

far·see·ing (fär′sē′ĭng) *adj.* **1.** Prudent; foresighted. **2.** Able to see far; keen-sighted.

far·sight·ed (fär′sī′tĭd) *adj.* **1. a.** Able to see objects better from a distance than from short range. **b.** Hyperopic. See **hyperopia. 2.** Planning prudently for the future; foresighted. —**far′sight′ed·ly** *adv.* —**far′sight′ed·ness** *n.*

fart (färt) *intr.v.* **farted, farting, farts.** *Vulgar.* To expel intestinal gas through the anus; break wind. —*n.* **1.** *Vulgar.* A usually audible anal discharge of intestinal gas. **2.** *Vulgar Slang.* A mean, contemptible person. [Middle English *farten,* Old English *feortan* (unattested). See **perd-** in Appendix.*]

far·ther (fär′thər) *adv.* **1.** To or at a more distant or more remote point in space or time. **2.** In addition. See Usage note. —*adj.* **1.** Remoter; more distant. **2.** Additional. See Usage note. [Middle English *ferther,* variant of *further,* FURTHER.]

Usage: *Farther* and *farthest* are preferably restricted to sentences in which they refer to literal distance, and are preferable to *further* and *furthest* in such examples, though *further* and *furthest* are also possible. In the following example involving physical distance, 80 per cent of the Usage Panel specify *farther* as the preferable choice: *The trip to Newark is farther than I had thought. Further* is usually the choice in all other senses, specifically in figurative usage to indicate additional degree, time, or quantity: *further in debt; a further reason.* In the following example involving such a figurative sense, *further* is the only acceptable choice according to 89 per cent of the Panel: *We must consider this matter further.* Figurative distance is also preferably expressed by *further,* though *farther* is less inappropriate here than in other figurative senses. Thus, *further from the truth* is the form specified by a majority of the Panel, but 33 per cent also accept *farther* in such an example.

far·ther·most (fär′thər-mōst′) *adj.* Farthest.

far·thest (fär′thĭst) *adj.* Most remote or distant. See Usage note at **farther.** —*adv.* To or at the most distant or remote point in space or time. See Usage note at **farther.** [Middle English *ferthest,* from *ferther,* FARTHER.]

far·thing (fär′thĭng) *n. Abbr.* **f. 1.** A former British coin worth one-fourth of a penny. **2.** The sum of one-fourth of a penny. [Middle English *ferthing,* Old English *fēorthing.* See **kwetwer-** in Appendix.*]

far·thin·gale (fär′thĭng-gāl′) *n.* **1.** A hoop or series of hoops extending horizontally from the waist, worn beneath a woman's skirts in the 16th and 17th centuries. **2.** The skirt worn over this device. [Variant of Old French *verdugale, vertugalle,* from Spanish *verdugado,* from *verdugo,* rod, stick, shoot of a tree, from *verde,* green, from Latin *virdis,* from *virēre,* to be green. See **virēre** in Appendix.*]

FAS Foreign Agricultural Service.
f.a.s., F.A.S. free alongside ship.
fasc. fascicle.
fas·ces (făs′ēz′) *pl.n.* A bundle of rods bound together about an ax with the blade projecting, carried before magistrates of ancient Rome as an emblem of authority. [Latin, plural of *fascis,* bundle. See **bhasko-** in Appendix.*]
fas·ci·a (făsh′ē-ə) *n., pl.* **-ciae** (-ē-ē′). **1.** *Anatomy.* A sheet of fibrous tissue beneath the surface of the skin, enveloping the body, enclosing muscles or muscular groups, and separating muscular layers. **2.** A broad and distinct band of color. **3.** *Architecture.* A flat horizontal band or member between moldings; especially, such a member in a classical entablature. [New Latin, from Latin, band, bandage, fillet. See **bhasko-** in Appendix.*] **—fas′ci·al** *adj.*
fas·ci·ate (făsh′ē-āt′) *adj.* Also **fas·ci·at·ed** (-ā′tĭd). **1.** *Botany.* Abnormally flattened or coalesced, as certain stems. **2.** *Zoology.* Marked by broad bands of color, as in certain insects. [New Latin *fasciatus* : FASCI(A) + -ATE.]
fas·ci·a·tion (făsh′ē-ā′shən) *n.* **1.** The act of binding up or fastening, as with bandages or bands. **2.** The manner in which something is bound up or fastened. **3.** *Botany.* An abnormal flattening or coalescence of stems or leaf stalks.
fas·ci·cle (făs′ĭ-kəl) *n.* Also **fas·ci·cule** (-kyo͞ol′) (for sense 2). *Abbr.* **fasc. 1.** A small bundle. **2.** One of the separately published parts or installments of a book. **3.** *Botany.* A bundlelike cluster, as of stems, flowers, or leaves. **4.** *Anatomy.* A **fasciculus** *(see).* [Latin *fasciculus,* diminutive of *fascis,* a bundle. See **bhasko-** in Appendix.*] **—fas′ci·cled** *adj.*
fas·cic·u·lar (fə-sĭk′yə-lər) *adj.* Of, pertaining to, or arranged in a fascicle or fascicles; fasciculate.
fas·cic·u·late (fə-sĭk′yə-lĭt, -lāt′) *adj.* Also **fas·cic·u·lat·ed** (-lā′tĭd). Pertaining to or resembling a fascicle; fascicular. **—fas·cic′u·late·ly** *adv.* **—fas·cic′u·la′tion** *n.*
fas·cic·u·lus (fə-sĭk′yə-ləs) *n.* A bundle of anatomical fibers; especially, a bundle of nerve fibers having common functions and connections. Also called "fascicle." [New Latin, from Latin, FASCICLE.]
fas·ci·nate (făs′ə-nāt′) *tr.v.* **-nated, -nating, -nates. 1.** To be an object of intense interest to; attract irresistibly. **2.** To hold motionless; to spellbind or mesmerize. **3.** *Obsolete.* To bewitch; cast under a spell. [Latin *fascināre,* to enchant, bewitch, from *fascinus,* a bewitching, amulet in the shape of a phallus. See **bhasko-** in Appendix.*]
fas·ci·nat·ing (făs′ə-nā′tĭng) *adj.* Arousing unflagging interest, as by charm or beauty; captivating. **—fas′ci·nat′ing·ly** *adv.*
fas·ci·na·tion (făs′ə-nā′shən) *n.* **1.** The power of fascinating. **2.** The condition of being fascinated. **3.** A fascinating quality.
fas·ci·na·tor (făs′ə-nā′tər) *n.* **1.** One that fascinates. **2.** A woman's head scarf made of net, lace, or the like.
fas·cine (făs-ēn′, fə-sēn′) *n.* A bundle of sticks bound together for use in constructing fortresses, earthworks, or reinforced trenches. [French, from Latin *fascīna,* from *fascis,* bundle. See **bhasko-** in Appendix.*]
fas·cism (făsh′ĭz′əm) *n.* **1.** A philosophy or system of government that advocates or exercises a dictatorship of the extreme right, typically through the merging of state and business leadership, together with an ideology of belligerent nationalism. **2.** *Capital* **F.** The governmental system of Italy under Benito Mussolini from 1922 to 1943. [Italian *fascismo,* from *fascio,* bundle, group, assemblage, from Latin *fascis,* bundle. See **bhasko-** in Appendix.*]
fas·cist (făsh′ĭst) *n.* **1.** A person who advocates or practices fascism. **2.** *Often capital* **F.** A person who belongs to a Fascist organization. [Italian *fascista,* from *fascio,* bundle, group. See **fascism.**] **—fas′cist, fa·scis′tic** (fə-shĭs′tĭk) *adj.*
Fa·scis·ti (fə-shĭs′tē; *Italian* fä-shēs′tē) *pl.n.* The members of the Italian political organization led by Benito Mussolini. [Italian, plural of *fascista,* FASCIST.]
fash·ion (făsh′ən) *n.* **1.** The way in which something is formed; configuration; aspect: *"as he prayed, the fashion of his countenance was altered"* (Luke 9:29). **2.** Kind or variety; sort. **3.** A manner of performing; way: *Do it in this fashion.* **4.** The current style or custom, as in dress or behavior; the mode for the present: *out of fashion.* **5.** Something that is in the current mode. **6.** Fashionable or style-conscious people in general; the social elite. —See Synonyms at **habit, method. —after** (or **in**) **a fashion.** In some way or other; to some extent: *She sings after a fashion.* —*tr.v.* **fashioned, -ioning, -ions. 1. a.** To make into a particular shape or form: *"And wilt thou have me fashion into speech/The love I bear thee"* (Elizabeth Barrett Browning). **b.** To train or influence into a particular state or character. **2.** To make suitable; adapt, as to a purpose or occasion. **3.** *Obsolete* To contrive. [Middle English *facioun,* from Old French *facon,* from Latin *factiō,* "a making," from *factus,* past participle of *facere,* to make, do. See **dhē-¹** in Appendix.*]
Synonyms: *fashion, style, mode, vogue.* These nouns refer to the prevailing or preferred practice in dress, manners, behavior, or the like, at a given time. *Fashion,* the broadest term, can denote custom or practice that prevails among any group of persons. Usually, however, it specifies such practice that follows the conventions of polite society or mass culture. *Style* is sometimes used interchangeably with *fashion,* but *style* can refer to what adheres to standards of elegance, the sense in which *mode* is also used. *Vogue* is applied to what prevails widely and obviously at a given time; often the term suggests enthusiastic acceptance of something for a rather short period.
fash·ion·a·ble (făsh′ən-ə-bəl) *adj.* **1.** Conforming to the current style; in fashion: *"It became fashionable to repair your mistakes by turning your back on them and running"* (Faulkner). **2.** Frequented by or associated with persons of fashion. —*n.* A fashionable person. **—fash′ion·a·ble·ness** *n.* **—fash′ion·a·bly** *adv.*
fash·ioned (făsh′ənd) *adj.* **1.** Formed; shaped. **2.** Having a specified style. Usually used in combination: *new-fashioned.*
fash·ion·mon·ger (făsh′ən-mŭng′gər, -mŏng′gər) *n.* A person concerned with following, spreading, or setting fashions.
fashion plate. 1. An illustration of current styles in dress. **2.** A person who consistently wears the latest fashions.
fast¹ (făst, fäst) *adj.* **faster, fastest. 1.** Acting, moving, or capable of moving quickly; swift; rapid. **2.** Accomplished in relatively little time: *a fast visit.* **3.** Indicating a time somewhat ahead of the actual time: *a fast wristwatch.* **4.** Adapted to or suitable for rapid movement: *a fast turnpike.* **5.** Disposed to flout conventional or moral standards; especially, sexually active: *a fast life.* **6.** Resistant. Often used in combination: *acid-fast.* **7.** Firmly fixed or fastened; not readily moved, removed, or loosened: *"O that I past changing were/Fast in thy Paradise"* (George Herbert). **8.** Fixed firmly in place; secure. **9.** Loyal; constant; firm: *"For twelve days we had been fast companions"* (R.L. Stevenson). **10.** Permanent; resisting fading: *fast dyes.* **11.** Deep; sound: *a fast sleep.* **12.** *Photography.* **a.** Compatible with a high shutter speed: *a fast lens.* **b.** Designed for short exposure; highly sensitive: *fast film.* —*adv.* **1.** Firmly; securely; tightly. **2.** Deeply; soundly: *fast asleep.* **3.** Quickly; rapidly. **4.** In a dissipated, immoderate way: *living fast.* **5.** *Archaic.* Close by; near. [Middle English *fast,* Old English *fæst.* See **past-** in Appendix.*]
Synonyms: *fast, rapid, swift, fleet, speedy, quick, hasty, expeditious, accelerated.* These adjectives refer to rate of activity or movement. All but the last three are so closely related that they are often interchangeable. *Fast* and *rapid* are the most general terms; *fast* is more often applied to a person or thing, and *rapid* to the activity or movement involved: *a fast runner; rapid strides. Swift* suggests smoothness and sureness of movement, and *fleet,* lightness of movement. *Speedy* refers to velocity or, when applied to persons, to hurry or effort to increase progress or conserve time. *Quick* also can refer to velocity; more often it applies to what takes little time or to promptness of response or action in persons. *Hasty* implies hurried action and often lack of care or thought. *Expeditious* combines the senses of rapidity and efficiency as they apply to action. *Accelerated* refers to what is increased, or stepped up, in rate of progress or motion.
fast² (făst, fäst) *intr.v.* **fasted, fasting, fasts.** To abstain from eating all or certain foods, especially as a religious discipline or as a means of protest. —*n.* The act or a period of fasting. [Middle English *fasten,* Old English *fæstan,* to hold fast, to observe, to abstain from food. See **past-** in Appendix.*]
fast day. A day reserved for fasting; especially, a day thus reserved by ecclesiastical authority.
fas·ten (făs′ən, fäs′-) *v.* **-tened, -tening, -tens.** —*tr.* **1.** To attach to something else; join; connect: *fasten the button to the skirt.* **2. a.** To make fast or secure. **b.** To close, as by shutting or fixing firmly in place. **3.** To fix or direct (the gaze, attention, or the like) steadily: *"My eyes fastened themselves upon the old scarlet letter"* (Hawthorne). **4.** To place; attribute: *Don't fasten the blame on him.* —*intr.* **1.** To become attached, fixed, or joined. **2.** To take firm hold; cling fast. Usually used with *on* or *upon.* [Middle English *fastnen,* Old English *fastnian,* to settle, establish, make fast. See **past-** in Appendix.*] **—fas′ten·er** *n.*
fast·en·ing (făs′ə-nĭng, fäs′-) *n.* **1.** The act or a method of making something fast. **2.** Something used to fasten, such as a lock or hook.
fas·tid·i·ous (fă-stĭd′ē-əs, fə-) *adj.* **1.** Careful in all details; exacting; meticulous: *"About her son's clothes she was as fastidious as she was neglectful of her own"* (Andrew Turnbull). **2.** Difficult to please; overcritical. **3.** Easily disgusted; squeamish. —See Synonyms at **meticulous.** [Middle English, disdainful, distasteful, loathsome, from Latin *fastīdiōsus,* from *fastīdium,* a loathing, from *fastus,* disdain. See **bhar-** in Appendix.*] **—fas·tid′i·ous·ly** *adv.* **—fas·tid′i·ous·ness** *n.*
fas·tig·i·ate (fă-stĭj′ē-ĭt, -āt′, fə-) *adj.* Also **fas·tig·i·at·ed** (-ā′tĭd). **1.** Tapering to a point; forming a cone or similar shape. **2.** *Botany.* Erect and almost parallel, as certain branches. [Medieval Latin *fastīgiātus,* high, lofty, from Latin *fastīgium,* top, summit, height. See **bhar-** in Appendix.*]
fast·ness (făst′nĭs, fäst′-) *n.* **1. a.** A fortified place; a stronghold or fortress. **b.** A remote and secret place. **2.** The condition or quality of being fast, especially: **a.** Firmness; security. **b.** Rapidity; swiftness. **c.** Colorfastness.
fat (făt) *n.* **1. a.** The glyceride ester of a **fatty acid** *(see).* **b.** Any of various soft solid or semisolid organic compounds comprising the glyceride esters of fatty acids and associated phosphatides, sterols, alcohols, hydrocarbons, ketones, and related compounds. **c.** A mixture of such compounds occurring widely in organic tissue, especially in the subcutaneous connective tissue of animals and in the seeds, nuts, and fruits of plants. **d.** Loosely, organic tissue containing such substances. **e.** A solidified animal or vegetable oil. See **oil. 2.** Plumpness; obesity. **3.** The best or most desirable part of something. **—chew the fat.** *Slang.* To have a leisurely conversation. —*adj.* **fatter, fattest. 1.** Having much or too much fat or flesh; plump or obese. **2.** Full of fat or oil; oily; greasy. **3.** Abounding in desirable elements: *"Fat pine yields much resin.* **4.** Fertile or productive; rich: *"It was a fine, green, fat landscape"* (R.L. Stevenson). **5.** Having an abundance or amplitude; well-stocked: *a fat larder.* **6.** Yielding profit or plenty; lucrative: *a*

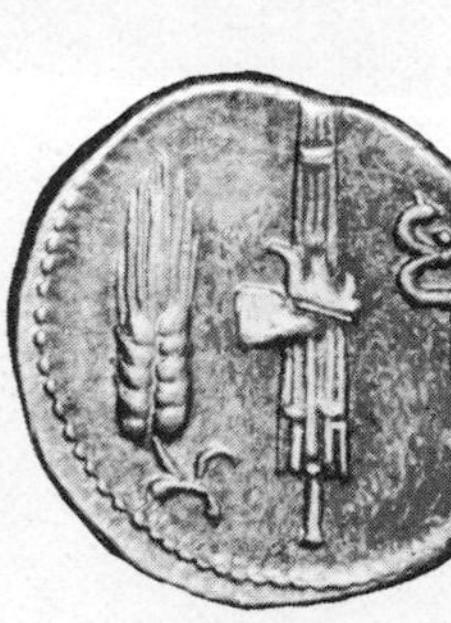

fasces
Shown *(center)* on ancient Roman coin

fat promotion. **7.** Thick; broad; large: *a fat plank.* **8.** *Slang.* Small; meager: *a fat chance.* —*v.* **fatted, fatting, fats.** —*tr.* To make fat. —*intr.* To become fat. [Middle English, from *fat*, plump, Old English *fǣtt.* See **peye-** in Appendix.*] —**fat'ly** *adv.* —**fat'ness** *n.*

Synonyms: *fat, obese, corpulent, fleshy, stout, portly, pudgy, rotund, plump, chubby.* These adjectives mean having an abundance of flesh, often to excess. *Fat* always implies excessive weight and is generally unfavorable in its connotations. *Obese* is employed principally in medical usage with reference to extreme overweight, and *corpulent* is a more general term for the same condition. *Fleshy* implies an abundance of flesh that is not necessarily disfiguring. *Stout* and *portly* are sometimes used as polite terms to describe fatness. *Stout,* in stricter application, suggests a thickset, bulky person, and *portly,* one whose bulk is combined with an imposing bearing. *Pudgy* describes one who is thickset and dumpy. *Rotund* suggests roundness of figure in a squat person. *Plump* is applicable to a pleasing fullness of figure, especially in women. *Chubby* implies abundance of flesh, usually not to excess.

fa·tal (fāt'l) *adj.* **1.** Causing or capable of causing death; mortal. **2.** Causing ruin or destruction; disastrous: *"Such doctrines, if true, would be absolutely fatal to my theory"* (Darwin). **3.** Most decisive; fateful. **4.** Controlling destiny. **5.** *Obsolete.* Destined; inevitable. [Middle English, fated, fatal, from Old French, from Latin *fātālis,* from *fātum,* FATE.]

Synonyms: *fatal, deadly, mortal, lethal.* These adjectives apply to what causes death. *Fatal* describes conditions, circumstances, or events that have produced death or are destined inevitably to cause death or dire consequences: *a fatal illness; a fatal blow. Deadly* applies to persons or things capable of killing or, in figurative usage, of producing severe hardship: *a deadly weapon; a deadly bore. Mortal* can describe a person likely to cause death, as in *a mortal enemy,* or a condition or action that has in fact produced death: *a mortal wound. Lethal* refers to a thing that acts as a sure agent of death and may have been created solely for that purpose: *the lethal chamber.*

fa·tal·ism (fāt'l-ĭz'əm) *n.* **1.** The doctrine that all events are predetermined by fate and therefore unalterable by man. **2.** The acceptance of this doctrine; submission to fate. —**fa'tal·ist** *n.* —**fa'tal·is'tic** *adj.* —**fa'tal·is'ti·cal·ly** *adv.*

fa·tal·i·ty (fā-tăl'ə-tē, fə-) *n., pl.* **-ties. 1.** A death that results from an unexpected occurrence: *fatalities from automobile accidents.* **2.** The ability to cause death or disaster; a lethal quality. **3.** The condition or quality of being governed or determined by fate. **4.** A dictate or determination by fate; a destiny: *"as though there were a fatality and curse on our family"* (Faulkner). **5.** A liability to disaster: *the fatality of his decision.*

fatality rate. Death rate *(see).*

fa·tal·ly (fā'tə-lē) *adv.* **1.** So as to cause death, ruin, or disaster; mortally. **2.** According to the decree of fate; inevitably.

fa·ta mor·ga·na (fä'tə môr-gä'nə). A **mirage** *(see).* [Italian, Morgan le Fay (the mirage was attributed to her witchcraft) : *fata,* fairy, from Latin *fāta,* the Fates, plural of *fātum,* FATE + *Morgana,* from Arabic *margān,* coral, from Greek *margaritēs,* pearl (see **margaritēs** in Appendix*).]

fat·back (făt'băk') *n.* The strip of fat taken from the upper part of a side of pork and usually dried and salt-cured.

fat cat. *Slang.* A wealthy and highly privileged person; especially, a heavy contributor to a political party.

fate (fāt) *n.* **1.** The supposed force, principle, or power that predetermines events. **2.** The inevitable event or events predestined by this force. **3.** A final result or consequence; outcome. **4.** An unfavorable destiny; doom or ruin. [Middle English, from Old French, from Latin *fātum,* from the neuter past participle of *fārī,* to speak. See **bhā-²** in Appendix.*]

fat·ed (fā'tĭd) *adj.* **1.** Governed by fate; predetermined: *his fated lot.* **2.** Condemned to death or destruction; doomed: *the fated city of Troy.*

fate·ful (fāt'fəl) *adj.* **1.** Affecting one's destiny or future: *the fateful final examination.* **2.** Controlled by or as if by fate; predetermined. **3.** Bringing death or disaster; ruinous; fatal. **4.** Portentous; ominous: *a fateful sign.* —**fate'ful·ly** *adv.* —**fate'ful·ness** *n.*

Fates (fāts). *Greek & Roman Mythology.* The three goddesses who govern human destiny. See **Atropos, Clotho,** and **Lachesis.**

fath, fath. fathom.

fat·head (făt'hĕd') *n. Slang.* A stupid person; a dolt.

fa·ther (fä'*th*ər) *n.* **1.** A male parent. **2.** A male who functions in a paternal capacity with regard to another; especially, a man who adopts a child. **3.** Any male ancestor; especially, the founder of a line of descent; a forefather. **4.** A man who creates, founds, or originates something: *"George Stevenson has been called the father of railways"* (Michael Robbins). **5.** *Capital* **F. a.** God. **b.** The first member of the Trinity. **6.** Any elderly or venerable man. Used as a title of respect. **7.** A member of the senate in ancient Rome. **8.** *Sometimes capital* **F.** Any of the authoritative early writers in the Christian Church who formulated doctrines and codified religious observances. **9.** *Abbr.* **Fr.** A priest or other clergyman or dignitary in the Roman Catholic or Anglican churches. Often used as a title of respect with or without the clergyman's name. **10.** *British.* The member holding the longest tenure in a profession, society, or similar organization. —*tr.v.* **fathered, -thering, -thers. 1.** To beget. **2.** To act or serve as a father to. **3.** To create, found, or originate. **4.** To acknowledge as one's work; accept responsibility for. **5. a.** To attribute the paternity, creation, or origin of. Used with *on* or *upon.* **b.** To assign falsely or unjustly; foist. Used with *on* or *upon: You father undue significance upon my words.* [Middle English *fader,* Old English *fæder.* See **pəter** in Appendix.*]

Father Christmas. *British.* Santa Claus.

father confessor. 1. A priest who hears confessions. **2.** Any person in whom one confides.

fa·ther·hood (fä'*th*ər-ho͝od') *n.* The condition of being a father; paternity.

fa·ther-in-law (fä'*th*ər-ĭn-lô') *n., pl.* **fathers-in-law. 1.** The father of one's husband or wife. **2.** *Rare.* A stepfather.

fa·ther·land (fä'*th*ər-lănd') *n.* **1.** A person's native land. **2.** The land of one's forebears.

fa·ther·less (fä'*th*ər-lĭs) *adj.* Having no living or acknowledged father.

fa·ther·ly (fä'*th*ər-lē) *adj.* **1.** Pertaining to, characteristic of, or appropriate to a father. **2.** Showing the tenderness or affection of a father. —*adv.* In a fatherly manner. —**fa'ther·li·ness** *n.*

Father's Day. An annual day of commemoration of fathers and fatherhood observed on the third Sunday in June.

fath·om (făth'əm) *n., pl.* **fathoms** or **fathom.** *Abbr.* **fath, fath., fm.** A unit of length equal to six feet, and used principally in the measurement and specification of marine depths. —*tr.v.* **1.** To determine the depth of; to sound. **2.** To get to the bottom of; penetrate to the meaning of: *"Her simplicity fathomed what clever people falsified"* (Virginia Woolf). [Middle English *fadme,* Old English *fæthm,* a measure of length. See **pet-²** in Appendix.*] —**fath'om·a·ble** *adj.*

Fa·thom·e·ter (fă-*th*ŏm'ə-tər) *n.* A trademark for a sonic depth finder.

fath·om·less (făth'əm-lĭs) *adj.* **1.** Too deep to be fathomed or measured. **2.** Too abstruse or complicated to be understood.

fa·tid·ic (fə-tĭd'ĭk) *adj.* Also **fa·tid·i·cal** (-ĭ-kəl). Pertaining to or characterized by prophecy; prophetic. [Latin *fātidicus* : *fātum,* FATE + *dīcere,* to say (see **deik-** in Appendix*).]

fat·i·ga·ble (făt'ĭ-gə-bəl) *adj.* Subject to weariness; easily tired. [Late Latin *fatīgābilis,* from Latin *fatīgāre,* to FATIGUE.]

fa·tigue (fə-tēg') *n.* **1.** Physical or mental weariness or exhaustion resulting from exertion. **2.** Tiring effort or activity; labor. **3.** *Physiology.* The decreased capacity or complete inability of an organism, organ, or part to function normally because of excessive stimulation or prolonged exertion. **4.** Weakness in metal, wood, or other material resulting from prolonged stress. **5.** *Military.* Manual or menial labor, such as barracks cleaning assigned to soldiers: *a weekend on fatigue.* Also called "fatigue duty." **6.** *Plural. Military.* Clothing designated or permitted for work and field duty. —*v.* **fatigued, -tiguing, -tigues.** —*tr.* **1.** To tire out; exhaust. **2.** To weaken by prolonged stress. —*intr.* To be or become exhausted or tired out. [French, from Old French, from *fatiguer,* to fatigue, from Latin *fatīgāre*†.]

fa·tigued (fə-tēgd') *adj.* Exhausted. See Synonyms at **tired.**

Fat·i·ma (făt'ə-mə, fə-tē'mə). A.D. 606?–632. Daughter of Mohammed.

Fát·i·ma (făt'ə-mə). A village and pilgrimage center in central Portugal.

Fat·i·mid¹ (făt'ə-mĭd). A Moslem dynasty that ruled over northern Africa and parts of Egypt between A.D. 909 and 1171. —**Fat'i·mid, Fat'i·mite'** (-mīt') *adj.*

Fat·i·mid² (făt'ə-mĭd) *n.* A person descended from Fatima, the daughter of Mohammed. —**Fat'i·mid, Fat'i·mite** (-mīt) *adj.*

fat·ling (făt'lĭng) *n.* A young animal, such as a lamb or calf, fattened for slaughter.

Fat·shan. The former name for **Namhoi.**

fat-sol·u·ble (făt'sŏl'yə-bəl) *adj.* Soluble in fats or fat solvents, such as ether. Said of certain vitamins.

fat·ten (făt'n) *v.* **-tened, -tening, -tens.** —*tr.* **1.** To make plump or fat. **2.** To fertilize (land). **3.** To increase the amount or substance of; to swell: *"small politicians prefer as President a man who will bring votes to fatten their base"* (Theodore H. White). —*intr.* To grow fat or fatter. —**fat'ten·er** *n.*

fat·tish (făt'ĭsh) *adj.* Somewhat fat; chubby. —**fat'tish·ness** *n.*

fat·ty (făt'ē) *adj.* **-tier, -tiest. 1. a.** Containing fat. **b.** Containing excessive amounts of fat. **2.** Characteristic of fat; especially, greasy. **3.** Derived from or chemically related to fat. —**fat'ti·ly** *adv.* —**fat'ti·ness** *n.*

fatty acid. Any of a large group of monobasic acids having the general formula $C_nH_{2n+1}COOH$; especially, any of a commercially important subgroup obtained from animals and plants, characteristically saturated or unsaturated aliphatic compounds with an even number of carbon atoms, the most abundant of which contain 16 or 18 carbon atoms and include palmitic, stearic, and oleic acids.

fa·tu·i·ty (fə-to͞o'ə-tē, -tyo͞o'ə-tē) *n., pl.* **-ties. 1.** Stupidity conveyed with an air of pride or self-satisfaction. **2.** A fatuous act, remark, or sentiment. **3.** Futility; vanity. [Old French *fatuite,* from Latin *fatuitās,* from *fatuus,* FATUOUS.]

fat·u·ous (făch'o͞o-əs) *adj.* **1.** Complacently or unconsciously stupid; asinine; inane. **2.** Delusive; self-deceiving: *fatuous hopes.* —See Synonyms at **foolish.** [Latin *fatuus*†, silly, fatuous, absurd.] —**fat'u·ous·ly** *adv.* —**fat'u·ous·ness** *n.*

fat-wit·ted (făt'wĭt'ĭd) *adj.* Thick-headed; stupid; dull.

fau·bourg (fō'bo͝org'; *French* fō-bo͞or') *n.* **1.** A suburb of a city. **2.** A district or quarter within a city. [Middle English *fabour,* from Old French *faubourg,* variant (influenced by *faux,* false) of *forsbo(u)rc,* "(something) outside the city" : *fors,* outside of, from Latin *foris,* out, outside (see **dhwer-** in Appendix*) + *borc,* fortified place, town, from Late Latin *burgus,* from Germanic (see **bhergh-²** in Appendix*).]

fau·cal (fô'kəl) *adj.* Also **fau·cial** (-shəl). **1.** *Anatomy.* Of or relating to the fauces. **2.** *Phonetics.* Produced in or near the fauces. Said of a sound.

ă pat/ā pay/âr care/ä father/b bib/ch church/d deed/ĕ pet/ē be/f fife/g gag/h hat/hw which/ĭ pit/ī pie/îr pier/j judge/k kick/l lid, needle/m mum/n no, sudden/ng thing/ŏ pot/ō toe/ô paw, for/oi noise/ou out/o͝o took/o͞o boot/p pop/r roar/s sauce/sh ship, dish/

fau·ces (fô′sēz) *pl.n.* The space between the mouth and pharynx bounded by the soft palate, the base of the tongue, and the palatine arches. [Latin *faucēs*†, throat.]

fau·cet (fô′sĭt) *n.* A device for drawing a flow of a liquid from a pipe, drum, or other reservoir. [Middle English *faucet,* from Old French *fausset,* plug, from *fausser,* damage, break into, make false, from Late Latin *falsāre,* falsify, from Latin *falsus,* FALSE.]

faugh (fô) *interj.* Used to express contempt, disgust, or dismissal. [Imitative.]

Faulk·ner (fôk′nər), **William Harrison.** Also **Falk·ner.** 1897–1962. American author of novels and short stories.

fault (fôlt) *n.* **1.** Something that prevents perfection, as: **a.** A flaw, blemish, or defect. **b.** A mistake; error. **c.** An offense, transgression, or minor vice. **2.** Responsibility for such a mistake or offense; culpability. **3.** *Geology.* A break in the continuity of a rock formation, caused by a shifting or dislodging of the earth's crust, in which adjacent surfaces are differentially displaced parallel to the plane of fracture. Also called "rift." **4.** *Electricity.* A defect in a circuit or wiring caused by imperfect connections, poor insulation, grounding, or shorting. **5.** *Sports.* A bad service, as in tennis. **6.** *Hunting.* The loss of the scent by a dog or dogs. **7.** *Obsolete.* A lack or deficiency. —See Synonyms at **blame, blemish.** —**at fault. 1.** Deserving of blame; guilty. **2.** Confused and puzzled. **3.** *Hunting.* Unable to recapture the scent of the game. —**find fault.** To seek, find, and complain about faults; to carp. —**in fault.** Deserving of blame; guilty. —**to a fault.** Excessively. —*v.* **faulted, faulting, faults.** —*tr.* **1.** To find a fault in; criticize or blame. See Usage note below. **2.** *Geology.* To produce a fault in; fracture. —*intr.* **1.** To commit a fault or error. **2.** *Geology.* To shift so as to produce a fault. [Middle English *faute,* from Old French, from Vulgar Latin *fallita* (unattested), feminine past participle of Latin *fallere,* to fail, deceive. See **fail.**]

Synonyms: *fault, failing, weakness, frailty, foible, vice.* These nouns denote imperfection or deficiency of character or soundness in persons. *Fault* usually refers to a specific quality or trait that detracts in large or small measure from excellence. *Failing* more often implies a lack that keeps a person from measuring up to a high standard of behavior or performance in general or in specific circumstances. *Weakness* suggests deficiency of moral or intellectual strength. It is closely related to, but stronger than, *frailty,* which implies inability to withstand temptation. Even weaker in imputing censure is *foible,* which refers to a minor fault, shortcoming, or eccentricity that is easily overlooked and may even be endearing. *Vice* can refer to a moral flaw or weakness that inclines one to evil or, in a weaker sense, to any defect of character.

Usage: *Fault,* as a transitive verb equivalent to find a fault in or criticize, is now widely used but still not as well established on a formal level as the equivalents cited. This use was long rare or dialectal in British English; although frequently attested as an Americanism since the mid-19th century, it has been much censured in its more recent vogue. The examples that follow are acceptable to 52 per cent of the Usage Panel: *One cannot fault his performance. To fault him is grossly unfair.*

fault·find·er (fôlt′fīn′dər) *n.* One who seeks out faults; a chronic complainer.

fault·find·ing (fôlt′fīn′dĭng) *n.* Petty criticism; a carping. —*adj.* Disposed to find trivial faults; captious.

fault·less (fôlt′lĭs) *adj.* Without fault; blameless or flawless. —**fault′less·ly** *adv.* —**fault′less·ness** *n.*

fault plane. The plane along which the break or shear of a geological fault occurs.

fault·y (fôl′tē) *adj.* **-ier, -iest. 1.** Containing a fault or faults; imperfect or defective. **2.** *Obsolete.* Deserving of blame; guilty. —**fault′i·ly** *adv.* —**fault′i·ness** *n.*

faun (fôn) *n. Roman Mythology.* One of a group of rural deities represented as having the body of a man and the horns, ears, tail, and sometimes legs of a goat. [Middle English *faun,* from Latin *Faunus,* FAUNUS.]

fau·na (fô′nə) *n., pl.* **-nas** or **-nae** (-nē′). Animals collectively; especially, the animals of a particular region or time. [New Latin, from Latin *Fauna,* sister of Faunus, from *Faunus,* FAUNUS.]

Fau·nus (fô′nəs). *Roman Mythology.* A god of nature and fertility, worshiped by shepherds and farmers, and identified with the Greek Pan. [Latin *Faunus*†.]

Fau·ré (fō-rā′), **Gabriel Urbain.** 1845–1924. French composer.

Faust (foust). *Latin* **Faust·us** (fou′stəs, fô′-). A magician and alchemist, hero of several dramatic works (notably by Marlowe and Goethe), who sells his soul to the devil in exchange for power and worldly experience. [German, after Johann *Faust,* 16th-century magician and astrologer.] —**Faust′i·an** (fou′stē-ən) *adj.*

fau·teuil (fō′tĭl; *French* fō-tœ′y′) *n.* An armchair. [French, from Old French *faudestuel, faldestoel,* folding stool, from Germanic. See **pel-**[3] in Appendix.*]

faux pas (fō pä′) *pl.* **faux pas** (fō päz′; *French* fō pä′). A social blunder; a breach of etiquette. [French, "false step."]

fa·va bean (fä′və). A **broad bean** *(see).* [Italian *fava,* from Latin *faba,* bean (see **bha-bhā-** in Appendix*) + BEAN.]

fa·ve·o·late (fə-vē′ə-lāt′) *adj.* Pitted with cavities or cells; honeycombed. [From New Latin *faveolus,* diminutive of Latin *favus*†, honeycomb.]

fa·vo·ni·an (fə-vō′nē-ən) *adj.* **1.** Of the west wind. **2.** Mild; benign. [Latin *Favōniānus,* from *Favōnius*†, west wind.]

fa·vor (fā′vər) *n.* Also *chiefly British* **fa·vour. 1. a.** A gracious, kind, or friendly attitude. **b.** An act evidencing such an attitude; an act of kindness: *Will you do me a favor?* **c.** *Often plural.* An act requiring sacrifice or special generosity; an indulgence. **2. a.** Friendly regard shown by a group or a superior; partiality. **b.** A state of being held in such regard. **3.** Approval or support; sanction. **4.** Partiality; favoritism. **5.** *Usually plural.* Sexual privileges, as granted by a woman. **6. a.** Something given as a token of love, affection, or remembrance. **b.** A small, decorative gift, such as a paper hat, given to each guest at a party or ball. **7.** Advantage; benefit: *a balance in our favor.* **8.** *Obsolete.* A communication. **9.** *Obsolete.* **a.** Aspect or appearance. **b.** Countenance; visage; face. **c.** One part of the face; a feature. —**in favor of. 1.** In support of; approving. **2.** To the advantage of. **3.** Inscribed or made out to. —*tr.v.* **favored, -voring, -vors.** Also *chiefly British* **fa·vour. 1.** To perform a kindness for; oblige. **2.** To regard with approval; to like. **3.** To be partial to; indulge. **4.** To be or tend to be in support of. **5.** To make easier or more possible; to aid. **6.** To resemble in appearance: *"Annie May favors her father and his people, who were all small and lightly built"* (James Agee). **7.** To treat with care; be gentle with: *The soldier favored his wounded leg.* —See Usage note at **oblige.** [Middle English *favour,* from Old French, from Latin *favor,* from *favēre,* to favor, be favorable. See **ghow-ē-** in Appendix.*] —**fa′vor·er** *n.* —**fa′vor·ing·ly** *adv.*

fa·vor·a·ble (fā′vər-ə-bəl, fāv′rə-) *adj.* **1.** Advantageous; helpful. **2.** Propitious; encouraging. **3.** Manifesting approval; commendatory. **4.** Embodying or conceding that which was desired or requested: *a favorable reply.* **5.** Indulgent or partial. —**fa′vor·a·ble·ness** *n.* —**fa′vor·a·bly** *adv.*

Synonyms: *favorable, propitious, auspicious, benign, conducive.* These adjectives describe what is beneficial or points to a successful outcome. *Favorable* is the widest in application. It can refer to persons, conditions, circumstances, or omens that contribute in some way to the attainment of a goal: *a favorable breeze; a favorable sign. Propitious* applies to persons or things that are favorably disposed toward someone or something or that give concrete assistance. Often it refers to time or circumstances considered as omens of, or contributors to, success: *a political climate propitious to a summit meeting. Auspicious* refers to things that, by their favorable nature, presage good fortune: *an auspicious start for the project. Benign* refers to persons or things favorably disposed toward one or exerting a beneficial influence. *Conducive* applies to things that lead or contribute to an end, usually a desirable result: *a neighborhood program conducive to good will in the community.*

fa·vored (fā′vərd) *adj.* **1.** Treated or thought of with kindness or liking; indulged; privileged. **2.** Having special talents, gifts, or beauty. **3.** Having a physical appearance of a specified kind. Used in combination: *well-favored; ill-favored.*

fa·vor·ite (fā′vər-ĭt, fāv′rĭt) *n.* **1. a.** A person or thing liked or preferred above all others. **b.** A person especially indulged by a superior: *a favorite of the king.* **2.** A contestant or competitor regarded as most likely to win: *the favorite in the fifth race at Belmont.* —*adj.* Liked or preferred above all others; regarded with special favor. [Obsolete French *favorit,* from Italian *favorito,* past participle of *favorire,* to favor, from *favore,* favor, from Latin *favor,* FAVOR.]

favorite son. A man nominated as a Presidential candidate, often merely as an honorary gesture, by the delegates from his own constituency at a national political convention.

fa·vor·it·ism (fā′vər-ə-tĭz′əm, fāv′rə-) *n.* **1.** A display of partiality, especially when unjust, toward a favored person or group. **2.** The state of being held in special favor.

fa·vus (fā′vəs) *n.* A chronic fungous infection of the scalp and nails. [New Latin, from Latin, honeycomb. See **faveolate.**]

Fawkes (fôks), **Guy.** 1570–1606. English Roman Catholic conspirator in the Gunpowder Plot.

fawn[1] (fôn) *intr.v.* **fawned, fawning, fawns. 1.** To exhibit affection, as in the manner of a dog wagging its tail and whining. Used with *on* or *upon.* **2.** To seek favor or attention by flattery and obsequious behavior. [Middle English *faunen,* Old English *fagnian, fægnian,* to rejoice, from *fægen,* FAIN.] —**fawn′er** *n.* —**fawn′ing·ly** *adv.*

fawn[2] (fôn) *n.* **1.** A young deer, especially one less than a year old. **2.** Grayish yellowish brown to light grayish or moderate reddish brown, or moderate yellowish pink. See **color.** [Middle English *foun, fawn,* from Old French *foun, feon,* offspring of an animal, from Vulgar Latin *fētō,* from Latin *fētus,* offspring, a giving birth. See **dhēi-** in Appendix.*]

fawn lily. Any of several North American plants of the genus *Erythronium;* especially, *E. grandiflorum,* of western North America, having nodding yellow flowers. This species is also called "glacier lily," "snow lily."

fay[1] (fā) *v.* **fayed, faying, fays.** —*tr.* To join (beams, for example) closely or tightly. —*intr.* To be fitted or joined tightly. [Middle English *feien,* Old English *fēgan.* See **pag-** in Appendix.*]

fay[2] (fā) *n.* A fairy, sprite, or elf. [Middle English *faie,* one possessing magical powers, from Old French *faie, fae,* from Latin *fāta,* the Fates, plural of *fātum,* FATE.]

fay[3] (fā) *n. Obsolete.* Faith. Used in oaths: *"sirrah, by my fay, it waxes late"* (Shakespeare). [Middle English *fai, fei, feith,* FAITH.]

Fay (fā). Also **Faye.** A feminine given name. [Middle English, either from *fai,* FAY (faith), or from *faie,* FAY (fairy).]

Fa·yal. See **Faial.**

fay·al·ite (fā′ə-līt′, fī-ä′līt′) *n.* A yellowish to black mineral, $FeSiO_4$, of the olivine group. [German *Fayalit* : *Fayal,* German form for FAIAL (where it was first found) + -ITE.]

Fay·ette (fā-ĕt′, fā′ĭt). A village of west-central New York, site

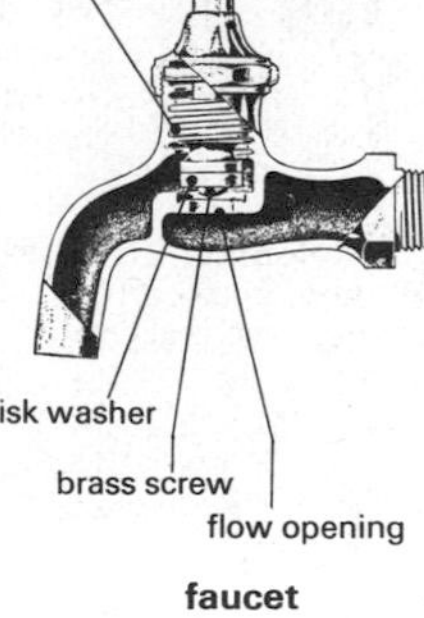
threaded spindle
disk washer
brass screw
flow opening
faucet

of the founding of the Church of Jesus Christ of Latter-day Saints by Joseph Smith.
Fay·ette·ville (fā′ĭt-vĭl). A city of south-central North Carolina, a former capital of the state. Population, 26,000.
faze (fāz) *tr.v.* **fazed, fazing, fazes.** Also **fease, feaze** (fāz). To disrupt the composure of; bother; disconcert; disturb. [Variant of FEEZE.]
fa·zen·da (fə-zĕn′də) *n., pl.* **-das.** In Brazil, a hacienda, estate, or plantation, especially a coffee plantation. [Portuguese, from Latin *facienda,* things to be done, neuter plural gerundive of *facere,* to do. See **dhē-**[1] in Appendix.*]
fb, f.b. fullback.
F.B. freight bill.
F.B.A. Fellow of the British Academy.
FBI, F.B.I. Federal Bureau of Investigation.
fc foot-candle.
f.c. *Printing.* follow copy.
FCA Farm Credit Administration.
fcap., fcp. foolscap.
FCC Federal Communications Commission.
F clef. A bass clef.
F.C.S. Fellow of the Chemical Society.
F.D. 1. Fidei Defensor. 2. fire department.
FDA Food and Drug Administration.
FDIC Federal Deposit Insurance Corporation.
FDR, F.D.R. Franklin Delano Roosevelt.
Fe The symbol for the element iron (Latin *ferrum*).
fe·al·ty (fē′əl-tē) *n., pl.* **-ties.** 1. The obligation of loyalty owed by a vassal to his feudal lord. 2. Faithfulness; allegiance. —See Synonyms at **fidelity.** [Middle English *fealtye, feute,* from Old French *fealte, feau(l)te,* from Latin *fidēlitās,* faithfulness, from *fidēlis,* faithful, from *fidēs,* faith. See **bheidh-** in Appendix.*]
fear (fîr) *n.* 1. A feeling of alarm or disquiet caused by the expectation of danger, pain, disaster, or the like; terror; dread; apprehension. 2. An instance or manifestation of such a feeling. 3. A state or condition of alarm or dread: *The prisoners spent the night in fear.* 4. Extreme reverence or awe, as toward a supreme power. 5. A ground for dread or apprehension; possibility of danger. —**for fear of.** So as to prevent or avoid: *She tiptoed for fear of waking the children.* —**for fear that.** Lest; in case: *He hurried home for fear that he might miss his guests.* —*v.* **feared, fearing, fears.** —*tr.* 1. To be afraid or frightened of. 2. To be anxious or apprehensive about. 3. To be in awe of; revere. 4. To suspect: *I fear you are wrong.* 5. *Archaic.* To feel fear within (oneself). —*intr.* 1. To be afraid, frightened, or terrified. 2. To feel anxious or apprehensive. [Middle English *fer,* Old English *fǣr,* danger, sudden calamity. See **per-**[5] in Appendix.*] —**fear′er** *n.*
Synonyms: *fear, fright, dread, terror, horror, panic, alarm, dismay, consternation, trepidation.* These nouns refer to emotional reaction caused by the presence or imminence of danger, evil, harm, or great misfortune. *Fear* is the most general term. *Fright* is fear suddenly aroused and characterized by great agitation, usually for a short period. *Dread* is strong fear of something thought to be impending, especially of what one is powerless to avoid. *Terror* is violent, paralyzing fear, usually in the presence of great danger. *Horror* is a combination of fear and aversion or repugnance. *Panic* is strong, sudden fear, often groundless and frequently the impetus for mindless action. *Alarm* is fright aroused upon the first realization of danger. *Dismay* is strong apprehension that robs one of courage or power to act effectively. *Consternation* is the state of being confounded, or made confused and helpless. *Trepidation* is apprehension or dread characteristically marked by trembling or hesitancy.
Fear, Cape (fîr). The southern point of Smith Island, off southeastern North Carolina.
fear·ful (fîr′fəl) *adj.* 1. Causing or capable of causing fear; frightening; terrifying. 2. Experiencing fear; frightened. 3. Feeling anxious or apprehensive. 4. Feeling reverence, dread, or awe. 5. Indicating anxiety, fear, or terror. 6. *Informal.* Very bad; dreadful: *a fearful blunder.* —**fear′ful·ly** *adv.* —**fear′ful·ness** *n.*
fear·less (fîr′lĭs) *adj.* Having no fear; unafraid; brave. See Synonyms at **brave.** —**fear′less·ly** *adv.* —**fear′less·ness** *n.*
fear·naught (fîr′nôt′) *n.* Also **fear·nought.** 1. A heavy, thick, often rough woolen material used in making overcoats. 2. A garment made of this cloth.
fear·some (fîr′səm) *adj.* 1. Causing or capable of causing fear; frightening; awesome: *"The Koreans had a fearsome ship with a dragon's mouth that belched gunfire and flaming arrows"* (Oliver Statler). 2. Afraid; frightened; fearful; timid. —**fear′some·ly** *adv.* —**fear′some·ness** *n.*
fea·sance (fē′zəns) *n. Law.* The execution of a condition, obligation, or duty. [Norman French *fesance,* from *faire,* to do, from Latin *facere.* See **dhē-**[1] in Appendix.*]
fease. Variant of **faze.**
fea·si·ble (fē′zə-bəl) *adj.* 1. Capable of being accomplished or brought about; practicable; possible: *a feasible outline for the project.* 2. Capable of being utilized or dealt with successfully; suitable. 3. Logical; likely: *He gave a feasible excuse for his absence.* —See Synonyms at **possible.** [Middle English *faisible, fesable,* from Old French *faisible,* from *faire* (present stem *fais-*), to do, from Latin *facere.* See **dhē-**[1] in Appendix.*] —**fea′si·bil′i·ty, fea′si·ble·ness** *n.* —**fea′si·bly** *adv.*
feast (fēst) *n.* 1. A periodic religious festival in commemoration of an event or in honor of a deity or person. 2. a. A large, elaborately prepared meal, usually for many persons and often with entertainment; a banquet. b. Any large, sumptuous, or delicious meal. 3. Something giving great pleasure or satisfaction: *a feast for the mind.* —*v.* **feasted, feasting, feasts.** —*tr.* 1. To give a feast for; to entertain or feed sumptuously. 2. To provide with pleasure; to delight; gratify: *"Augustus too feasted his eyes on the same plate of fruit"* (Virginia Woolf). —*intr.* 1. To partake of a feast. 2. To experience with gratification or delight. [Middle English *feste,* from Old French, from Latin *fēsta,* neuter plural (taken as feminine singular) of *fēstus,* joyous, festal. See **dhēs-** in Appendix.*] —**feast′er** *n.*
feast·ful (fēst′fəl) *adj.* Lavishly celebrated; festive; joyful.
Feast of Dedication. A Jewish holiday, **Chanukah** *(see).*
Feast of Lanterns. 1. A Chinese festival, held at the first full moon of the new year, at which colored lanterns are displayed. 2. A Japanese festival, **Bon** *(see).*
Feast of Lights. A Jewish holiday, **Chanukah** *(see).*
Feast of Weeks. A Jewish holiday, **Shavuot** *(see).*
feat[1] (fēt) *n.* 1. a. Any act or deed; especially, an act of courage; an exploit. b. Any act of skill, endurance, imagination, or strength; an achievement: *"The ancient Peruvians performed extraordinary feats of water engineering"* (William H. McNeill). 2. *Obsolete.* A specialized skill or craft; technique; knack. [Middle English *fete,* from Old French *fait, fet,* from Latin *factum,* something done, from the neuter past participle of *facere,* to do. See **dhē-**[1] in Appendix.*]
feat[2] (fēt) *adj.* **feater, featest.** *Archaic.* 1. Adroit; dexterous; skillful. 2. Neat; trim. [Middle English *fete,* adroit, skillful, from Old French *fait,* from Latin *factum,* something done. See **feat.**] —**feat′ly** *adv.*
feath·er (fĕth′ər) *n.* 1. One of the light, horny structures forming the plumage of birds, consisting of numerous slender, closely arranged parallel barbs forming a vane on either side of a tapering hollow shaft. 2. *Plural.* Plumage. 3. *Plural.* Clothing; attire. 4. A tuft or fringe of hair, as on the legs or tail of some dogs. 5. Character, kind, or nature: *Birds of a feather flock together.* 6. Something small, trivial, or inconsequential. 7. a. A strip, wedge, or flange, used as a strengthening part. b. A wedge or key that fits into a groove to make a joint. 8. The vane of an arrow, made of real or imitation feathers. 9. A feather-shaped flaw, as in a gem or precious stone. 10. The wake made by a submarine periscope. 11. The act of feathering the blade of an oar in rowing. —**a feather in one's cap.** A distinctive achievement; an act or deed to one's credit. —**in fine** (or **good**) **feather.** In excellent fettle, form, health, or humor: *"The little actress was in fine feather"* (Dreiser). —**in full feather.** 1. Having plenty of money. 2. Completely equipped; elaborately dressed. —*v.* **feathered, -ering, -ers.** —*tr.* 1. To cover, dress, or decorate with or as if with feathers. 2. To fit (an arrow) with a feather; fletch. 3. a. To thin, reduce, or fringe the edge of by cutting, shaving, or wearing away. b. To shorten and taper (hair) by cutting and thinning. 4. To connect with a tongue-and-groove joint. 5. To turn (an oar blade) horizontal to the surface of the water between strokes. 6. *Aviation.* To alter the pitch of (a propeller) so that the blade chords are parallel with the line of flight. —*intr.* 1. To grow feathers or become feathered. 2. To move, spread, or grow in a manner suggestive of feathers. 3. To feather an oar. 4. *Aviation.* To feather a propeller. —**feather one's nest.** To grow wealthy, by making use of property or funds left in one's trust. [Middle English *fether,* Old English *fether.* See **pet-**[1] in Appendix.*] —**feath′er·less** *adj.*
feather bed. A mattress stuffed with feathers or down.
feath·er·bed (fĕth′ər-bĕd′) *intr.v.* **-bedded, -bedding, -beds.** 1. To employ more workers than are actually needed for a given purpose, or to limit their production. 2. To be so employed.
feath·er·bone (fĕth′ər-bōn′) *n.* A lightweight corset bone originally made from the quills of domestic fowl.
feath·er·brain (fĕth′ər-brān′) *n.* A silly, flighty, or empty-headed person. —**feath′er·brained′** *adj.*
feath·ered (fĕth′ərd) *adj.* 1. Having feathers; covered or adorned with feathers. 2. *Aviation.* Having the propeller blade chords parallel to the line of flight.
feath·er·edge (fĕth′ər-ĕj′) *n.* 1. A thin fragile edge; especially, a tapering edge of a board. 2. A **deckle edge** *(see).*
feather grass. Any of various grasses of the genus *Stipa,* having clusters of featherlike spikelets.
feath·er·head (fĕth′ər-hĕd′) *n.* A giddy or lightheaded person; a featherbrain. —**feath′er·head′ed** *adj.*
feather palm. Any palm tree having pinnate leaves forming featherlike fronds. Compare **fan palm.**
feather star. Any of numerous crinoids of the genus *Antedon* and related genera, having a free-moving, stalkless adult stage with branched, feathery arms.
feath·er·stitch (fĕth′ər-stĭch′) *n.* An embroidery stitch that produces a decorative zigzag line. —*v.* **featherstitched, -stitching, -stitches.** —*intr.* To embroider in featherstitch. —*tr.* To embroider (material) in featherstitch.
feath·er-veined (fĕth′ər-vānd′) *adj.* Having veins branching from either side of a midrib. Said of leaves.
feath·er·weight (fĕth′ər-wāt′) *n.* 1. A boxer or wrestler weighing between 118 and 127 pounds. 2. Any person or thing of little weight or size. 3. An insignificant person or thing. 4. The minimum weight that may be carried by a racehorse in a handicap. —*adj.* 1. Of or concerning featherweights: *a featherweight match.* 2. Unimportant; trivial; superficial.
feath·er·y (fĕth′ər-ē) *adj.* 1. Covered with or consisting of feathers. 2. Resembling or suggestive of a feather or feathers, as in form or lightness. —**feath′er·i·ness** *n.*
fea·ture (fē′chər) *n.* 1. The make-up, shape, proportions, form, or outward appearance of something, especially a person.

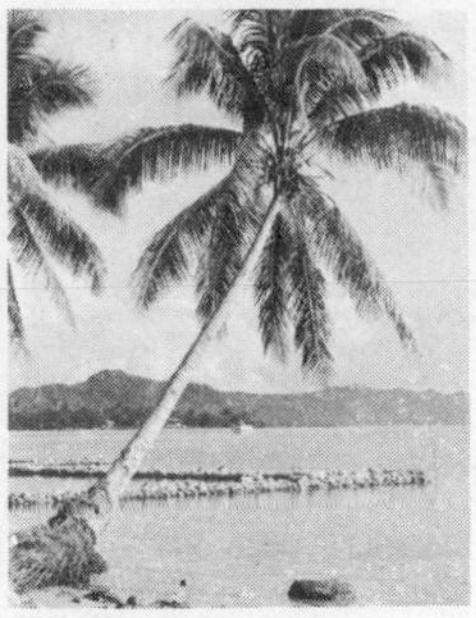

feather palm
Coconut palm

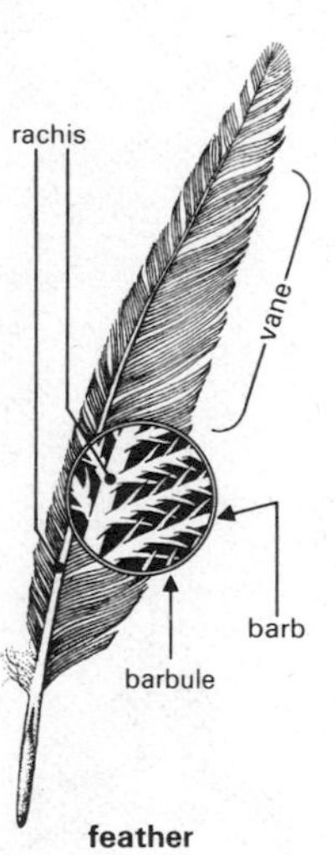
rachis
vane
barb
barbule

feather
With enlarged portion showing structural details

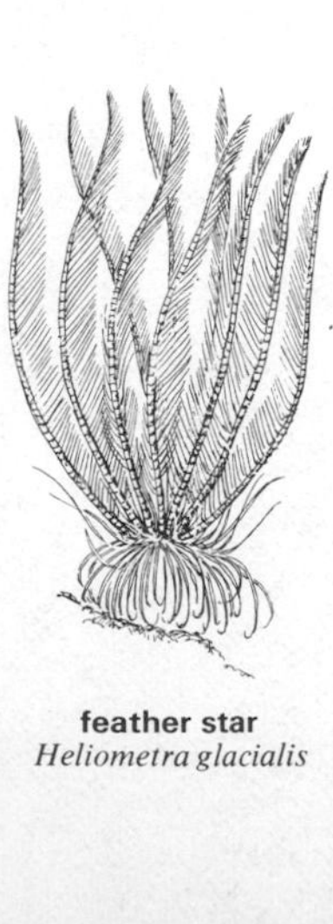

feather star
Heliometra glacialis

2. a. *Plural.* The make-up or appearance of the face or its parts. **b.** Any of the distinct parts of the face, as the nose, mouth, or eyes. **3.** Any prominent or distinctive aspect, quality, or characteristic: *"His lordship's character, of which indecision was one of the strongest features"* (Franklin). **4.** The main presentation at a motion-picture theater. **5.** A prominent or extra article or story in a newspaper or periodical. **6.** Anything advertised as especially attractive or as an inducement, such as a sale item in a store. **7.** *Archaic.* Form; shape; appearance. —*tr.v.* **featured, -turing, -tures. 1.** To give special attention to; make prominent, display, or publicize. **2.** To be a prominent part or characteristic of. **3.** To draw or otherwise portray the features of. **4.** *Informal.* To resemble in facial features; favor. **5.** *Informal.* To imagine, picture mentally, or conceive of. [Middle English *feture,* from Old French *feture, faiture,* form, from Latin *factūra,* a making, formation, from *factus,* past participle of *facere,* to do, make. See **dhē-¹** in Appendix.*]

fea·tured (fē′chərd) *adj.* **1. a.** Given particular attention or publicity; made prominent. **b.** Starring: *a featured actress.* **2.** Having a specified kind of facial features. Often used in combination: *small-featured; sharp-featured.* **3.** Formed or given a particular appearance by facial features.

fea·ture-length (fē′chər-lĕngth′) *adj.* Of normal or full length: *a feature-length film.*

feaze. Variant of **faze.**

Feb. February.

fe·bric·i·ty (fĭ-brĭs′ə-tē) *n.* The condition of having a fever. [Medieval Latin *febricitās,* from Latin *febris,* FEVER.]

feb·ri·fa·cient (fĕb′rə-fā′shənt) *n.* A substance that causes a fever. —*adj.* Causing or producing fever. [Latin *febris,* FEVER + -FACIENT.]

fe·brif·ic (fĭ-brĭf′ĭk) *adj.* **1.** Causing fever. **2.** Having a fever; feverish. [Latin *febris,* FEVER + -FIC.]

feb·ri·fuge (fĕb′rə-fyōōj′) *n.* Any agent that reduces a fever. —*adj.* Fever-reducing. [French *fébrifuge,* from New Latin *febrifugus* : Latin *febris,* FEVER + *fugāre,* to drive away, from *fugere,* to flee (see **bheug-¹** in Appendix*).]

feb·rile (fĕb′rəl, fē′brəl; *chiefly British* fē′brīl′) *adj.* Of, pertaining to, or characterized by fever; feverish. [French *fébrile,* from Latin *febris,* FEVER.]

Feb·ru·ar·y (fĕb′rōō-ĕr′ē, fĕb′yōō-) *n., pl.* **-ies** or **-ys.** *Abbr.* **Feb.** The second month of the year according to the Gregorian calendar. February has 28 days, 29 in leap years. See **calendar.** [Middle English *feveryer,* from Old French *feverier,* from Late Latin *febrārius,* from Latin *februārius,* from *februa,* festival of purification held on February 15, possibly of Sabine origin.]

fec. he (or she) made (or did) it (Latin *fecit*).

fe·cal (fē′kəl) *adj.* Of, pertaining to, or constituting feces.

fe·ces (fē′sēz) *pl.n.* Also **fae·ces.** Waste excreted from the bowels; excrement. [Middle English, from Latin *faex* (stem *faec-*), dregs, probably from Mediterranean.]

Fech·ner (fĕKH′nər), **Gustav Theodor.** 1801–1887. German physicist and experimental psychologist.

feck·less (fĕk′lĭs) *adj.* **1.** Lacking purpose or vitality; feeble; ineffective. **2.** Careless; irresponsible: *"irritated and at times angered by his feckless, childish ways"* (Constantine Fitzgibbon). [Scottish *feck,* efficacy, short for EFFECT + -LESS.] —**feck′less·ly** *adv.* —**feck′less·ness** *n.*

fec·u·lent (fĕk′yə-lənt) *adj.* Full of foul matter, dregs, or sediment; foul; fetid. [Middle English *feculent,* from Latin *faeculentus,* from *faex* (stem *faec-*), FECES.] —**fec′u·lence** *n.*

fe·cund (fē′kənd, fĕk′ənd) *adj.* **1.** Capable of producing offspring or vegetation; fertile; productive; fruitful. **2.** Marked by intellectual productivity. [Middle English *fecound,* from Old French *fecond,* from Latin *fēcundus.* See **dhēi-** in Appendix.*]

fe·cun·date (fē′kən-dāt′, fĕk′ən-) *tr.v.* **-dated, -dating, -dates. 1.** To make fecund or fruitful. **2.** To impregnate; fertilize. [Latin *fēcundāre,* from *fēcundus,* FECUND.]

fe·cun·di·ty (fĭ-kŭn′də-tē) *n.* **1.** The quality or power of producing abundantly; fertility. **2.** The capacity for or power of producing young, especially in abundance; productiveness. **3.** Productive or creative power: *the fecundity of his mind.*

fed. Past tense and past participle of **feed.**

fed. federal; federated; federation.

Fe·da·yee (fĕ-dä′yē) *n., pl.* **-yeen** (-yēn). An Arab commando, operating especially against Israel. [Arabic *fedā′yūn,* commandos, from *fidā′ī,* one who sacrifices himself for his country, from *fidā′,* redemption.]

fed·er·a·cy (fĕd′ər-ə-sē) *n., pl.* **-cies.** *Archaic.* An alliance or confederacy. [Back-formation from CONFEDERACY.]

fed·er·al (fĕd′ər-əl) *adj. Abbr.* **fed. 1.** Of, pertaining to, or designating a form of government in which a union of states recognizes the sovereignty of a central authority while retaining certain residual powers of government. **2.** Of, constituting, or characterized by a form of government in which sovereign power is divided between a central authority and a number of constituent political units. **3.** Of or pertaining to the central government of a federation, as distinct from the governments of its member states: *federal office.* **4.** Favorable to federation; advocating such a union: *His federal leanings were well known.* **5.** Of or pertaining to a league, treaty, or compact, especially between states which have consolidated into a union: *"Our connection had been federal only, and was now dissolved by the commencement of hostilities."* (Jefferson). **6.** *Capital* **F. a.** Of, pertaining to, or designating the central government of the United States. **b.** Of, pertaining to, or characterizing the Federalist Party or Federalism. **c.** Of, pertaining to, or supporting the Federal government during the Civil War; pro-Union. **7.** *Capital* **F.** Pertaining to or characteristic of a style of architecture, furniture, and decoration produced in the United States (1783–1815) and characterized by adaptations of classical forms often combined with typically American motifs. —*n.* **1.** A supporter of federation or federal government. **2.** *Capital* **F. a.** A Federalist. **b.** A supporter of the Union during the Civil War; especially, a Union soldier. [From Latin *foedus* (stem *foeder-*), league, treaty, compact. See **bheidh-** in Appendix.*] —**fed′er·al·ly** *adv.*

Federal Bureau of Investigation. *Abbr.* **FBI, F.B.I.** An agency of the U.S. Justice Department responsible for investigating violations of Federal law.

Federal Capital Territory. The former name for the **Australian Capital Territory.**

Federal Communications Commission. *Abbr.* **FCC** A U.S. government agency responsible for the supervision and regulation of wire, radio, and television communication.

Federal Deposit Insurance Corporation. *Abbr.* **FDIC** An independent U.S. government agency primarily responsible for insuring bank depositors against loss and for preventing unwise banking practices.

Federal District. An area in certain countries that is reserved as the site of the national capital, such as the District of Columbia.

fed·er·al·ism (fĕd′ər-ə-lĭz′əm) *n.* **1. a.** The doctrine or system of federal government. **b.** The advocacy of such a government. **2.** *Capital* **F.** The doctrine of the Federalist Party.

fed·er·al·ist (fĕd′ər-ə-lĭst) *n.* **1.** An advocate of federalism. **2.** *Capital* **F.** A member or supporter of the Federalist Party. —**The Federalist.** A series of 85 articles written by Hamilton, Madison, and Jay during 1787 and 1788, analyzing the proposed Constitution of the United States and urging its ratification. —*adj.* Also **fed·er·al·is·tic** (fĕd′ər-əl-ĭs′tĭk). **1.** Of or pertaining to federalism or its advocates. **2.** *Capital* **F.** Of or pertaining to Federalism or Federalists.

Federalist Party. Also **Federal Party.** *U.S. History.* A political party founded in 1787 that gained prominence in the 1790's under the leadership of Alexander Hamilton during the critical shaping and strengthening of the new government.

fed·er·al·ize (fĕd′ər-ə-līz′) *tr.v.* **-ized, -izing, -izes. 1.** To unite in a federal union. **2.** To subject to the authority of a federal government; put under federal control. —**fed′er·al·i·za′tion** *n.*

Federal Power Commission. *Abbr.* **FPC** A U.S. government agency responsible for the supervision and regulation of hydroelectric power on Federal property, interstate transportation of natural gas, and public utility companies supplying power in interstate commerce.

Federal Reserve System. *Abbr.* **FRS** A U.S. banking system consisting of 12 *Federal Reserve Banks,* each serving member banks in a *Federal Reserve District* and supervised by the *Federal Reserve Board,* appointed by the President.

Federal Trade Commission. *Abbr.* **FTC** A U.S. government agency that supervises and regulates business competition by investigating unfair or harmful trade practices, such as price fixing or misrepresentation in advertising.

fed·er·ate (fĕd′ə-rāt′) *v.* **-ated, -ating, -ates.** —*tr.* To join or bring together in a league, federal union, or similar association. —*intr.* To unite in a federal union. —*adj.* (fĕd′ər-ĭt). United under a central government; federated. [Latin *foederāre,* from *foedus* (stem *foeder-*), league, treaty. See **bheidh-** in Appendix.*]

Federated Ma·lay States (mā′lā, mə-lā′). A former federation of British-protected Malayan states, now part of Malaysia.

fed·er·a·tion (fĕd′ə-rā′shən) *n. Abbr.* **fed. 1.** The act of federating; especially, a joining together of states in a league or federal union. **2.** A league or association formed by federating.

fed·er·a·tive (fĕd′ə-rā′tĭv, fĕd′ər-ə-) *adj.* Forming, belonging to, or of the nature of a federation; federal. —**fed′er·a′tive·ly** *adv.*

fe·do·ra (fĭ-dôr′ə, -dōr′ə) *n.* A soft felt hat with a brim that can be turned up or down and a rather low crown creased lengthwise. [From *Fédora* (1882), play by Victorien Sardou (1831–1908), French playwright.]

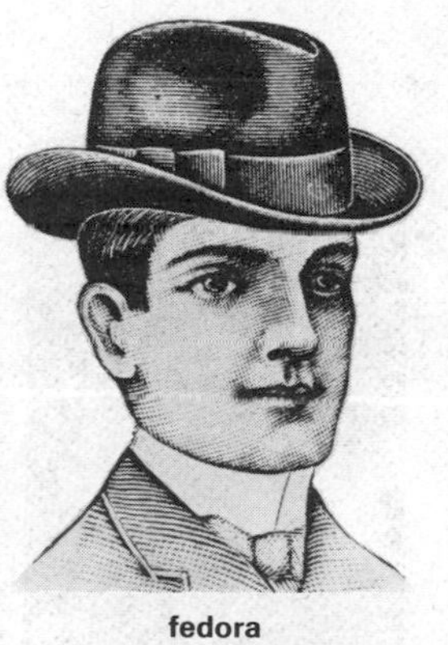

fedora
Wool fedora offered in a 1903 mail-order catalogue

fee (fē) *n.* **1. a.** A charge fixed by an institution or by law: *tuition fees; the fee for a fishing license.* **b.** Any fixed charge. **2.** A payment for professional or special service: *a tax consultant's fee.* **3.** A tip; gratuity. **4.** *Law.* An inherited or heritable estate in land. See **fee simple, fee tail. 5. a.** In feudal law, an estate in land held from a lord on condition of homage and service. In this sense, also called "feud," "fief." **b.** The land so held. —See Synonyms at **price.** —**hold in fee.** To have absolute and legal possession of. —*tr.v.* **feed, feeing, fees.** To give a fee to. [Middle English *fe,* inherited estate, payment, from Old French *fe, fief,* from Frankish *fehu-ōd* (unattested). See **peku-** in Appendix.*]

fee·ble (fē′bəl) *adj.* **-bler, -blest. 1. a.** Lacking strength; weak; especially, frail or infirm: *a feeble old woman.* **b.** Indicating weakness: *a feeble walk.* **2.** Lacking vigor or force; inadequate; ineffective: *a feeble answer.* **3.** Barely discernible; faint; slight: *a feeble cry.* —See Synonyms at **weak.** [Middle English *feble,* from Old French *feble, fieble, fleible,* from Latin *flēbilis,* to be wept over, lamentable, from *flēre,* to weep. See **bhlē-¹** in Appendix.*] —**fee′ble·ness** *n.* —**fee′bly** *adv.*

fee·ble-mind·ed (fē′bəl-mīn′dĭd) *adj.* **1.** Mentally deficient; subnormal in intelligence. **2.** Dull-witted; stupid; foolish. **3.** *Archaic.* Weak-willed. —**fee′ble-mind′ed·ly** *adv.* —**fee′ble-mind′ed·ness** *n.*

feed (fēd) *v.* **fed** (fĕd), **feeding, feeds.** —*tr.* **1. a.** To give food to; supply with nourishment: *feed the children.* **b.** To provide as food or nourishment: *feed fish to a cat.* **2. a.** To serve as food for: *The turkey is large enough to feed a dozen.* **b.** To produce food for: *The valley feeds an entire county.* **3. a.** To supply or

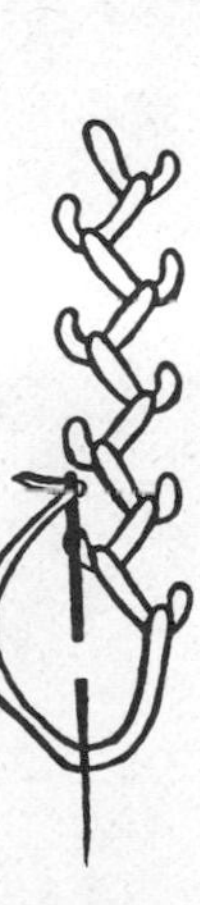

featherstitch

maintain a flow of (a material to be consumed, utilized, or worked upon): *feed ammunition to a gun crew.* **b.** To supply with fuel: *Leaking oil fed the flames.* **4. a.** To minister to; gratify: *The story fed their appetite for the morbid.* **b.** To support or promote: *feed suspicions.* **5.** *Theater.* To supply as a cue: *feed lines to an actor.* **6.** *Sports.* To pass the ball or puck to (a teammate), especially in order to score. —*intr.* To eat. Used chiefly of animals. —**be fed up.** To be out of patience and disgusted. —**feed on** (or **upon**). **1.** To consume as food. **2.** To draw support or satisfaction from: *His ego feeds on flattery.* —*n.* **1. a.** Food for animals or birds; fodder. **b.** The allowance of fodder given at one time. **2.** *Informal.* A meal. **3. a.** Material, or an amount of material, supplied to a machine. **b.** The act of supplying this material. **4. a.** The apparatus that supplies material to a machine. **b.** The aperture through which such material enters a machine. —**off one's feed.** *Slang.* Temporarily without appetite for food, as from an ailment. [Feed, fed, fed; Middle English *feden, fed, fedde,* Old English *fēdan, fēdde, fēdd.* See **pā-** in Appendix.*]

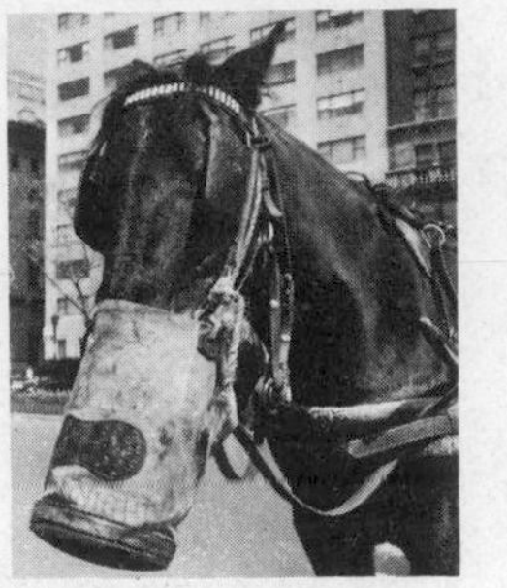

feedbag

feed·back (fēd′băk′) *n.* **1. a.** The return of a portion of the output of any process or system to the input, especially when used to maintain the output within predetermined limits. **b.** The portion of the output so returned. **c.** Control of a system or process by such means: *"When feedback is possible and stable, its advantage . . . is to make performance less dependent on the load."* (Norbert Wiener). **2.** Broadly, any information about the result of a process.

feed·bag (fēd′băg′) *n.* A bag that fits over a horse's muzzle and holds feed. Also called "nosebag."

feed·er (fē′dər) *n.* **1. a.** One that supplies food, especially to animals being fattened for market. **b.** One that ingests food, especially an animal that is being fattened. **2.** One that feeds materials into a machine for further processing. **3.** Anything that contributes to the operation, maintenance, or supply of something else, as: **a.** A tributary. **b.** A feeder line. **4.** *Electricity.* Any of the medium-voltage lines used to distribute electric power from a substation to consumers or smaller substations. —*adj.* Being or functioning as a feeder: *a feeder airline.*

feeder line. A local-service transport system that connects smaller communities with larger transport systems.

feel (fēl) *v.* **felt** (fĕlt), **feeling, feels.** —*tr.* **1. a.** To perceive through the sense of touch. **b.** To perceive as a localized physical sensation: *feel a sharp pain.* **c.** To perceive as a nonlocalized physical sensation: *feel the cold.* **2. a.** To touch. **b.** To examine by touching. **c.** To test carefully; explore with caution: *feel one's way in a new job.* **3. a.** To experience (an emotion): *I felt my interest rising.* **b.** To be aware of; to sense: *She felt his annoyance.* **c.** To suffer from; experience the impact of: *feel the loss of someone.* **d.** To be emotionally perceptive of: *feel a role in a play.* **4.** To believe or consider: *His answer was felt to be evasive.* —*intr.* **1.** To experience sensations of touch. **2.** To give or produce sensation or feeling, especially through the sense of touch: *The sheets felt smooth.* **3. a.** To be conscious of; perceive oneself to be. See Usage note below. **b.** To have or receive a vague overall impression: *I feel that all is well.* **4.** To search or be guided by or as if by the sense of touch. **5.** To have compassion or sympathy. Used with *with* or *for: I feel for him in his troubles.* **6. a.** To be emotionally moved: *feel strongly about the election.* **b.** To be guided by sentiment or emotion: *"We all do no end of feeling and we mistake it for thinking"* (Mark Twain). —**feel like.** *Informal.* To be in the mood for; have a desire for. —**feel (like) oneself.** To sense oneself as being in a normal state of health or spirits. —**feel out.** To try cautiously or indirectly to ascertain the viewpoint of (a person) or the nature of (a situation). —**feel up.** *Vulgar Slang.* To touch or caress the upper thighs, genitals, or posterior of. —**feel up to.** To feel capable of or ready for. —*n.* **1. a.** Perception by touching or feeling: *the feel of a rose petal.* **b.** The act or an instance of touching or feeling: *a feel of this cloth.* **2.** The sense of touch: *rough to the feel.* **3.** The nature, condition, or quality of something perceived: **a.** Chiefly physically: *the feel of a sports car.* **b.** Emotionally or mentally: *get the feel of one's audience.* [Feel, felt, felt; Middle English *felen, felde, feld,* Old English *fēlan, fēlde, fēld.* See **pōl-** in Appendix.*]

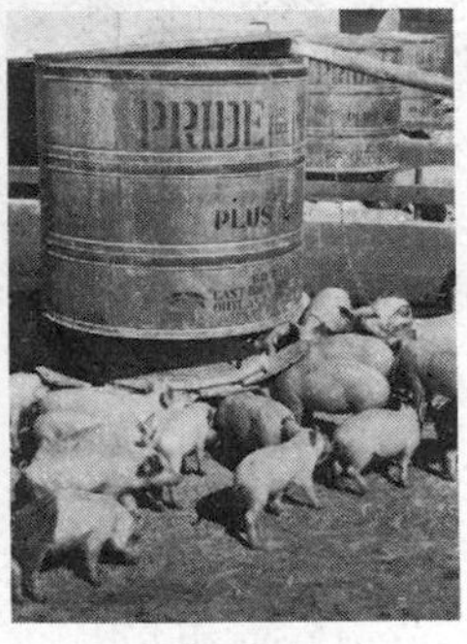

feeder
Pigs at a feeder

Usage: *Feel* (verb) is followed by an adjective when the sense relates to a person's perception of his condition of being: *I was sick last week but now I feel different; today I feel strong.* The adjectives *different* and *strong* describe the subject in such examples. In other senses of *feel,* an adverb is possible in the position following the verb, as, for example, when *feel* means to have an opinion, conviction, or the like: *She feels strongly about equal rights for women. He used to agree with her position, but he feels differently now.* Here *strongly* and *differently* modify the verb with respect to degree and condition. —See also Usage note at **bad.**

feel·er (fē′lər) *n.* **1.** One that feels. **2.** A remark, hint, question, or the like, designed to elicit the attitude or intention of others. **3.** A sensory or tactile organ, such as an antenna, tentacle, or barbel.

feel·ing (fē′lĭng) *n.* **1. a.** The sensation involving perception by touch. **b.** A sensation perceived by touch. **c.** Any physical sensation. **2.** Any affective state of consciousness, such as that resulting from emotions, sentiments, or desires: *a feeling of excitement.* **3.** An awareness; impression: *a feeling that one is being followed.* **4. a.** An emotional state or disposition; emotion: *expressed deep feeling.* **b.** A tender emotion; love; fondness. **5. a.** Refined sensibility, often approaching sentimentality: *a man of feeling.* **b.** *Plural.* Sensitivities: *hurt one's feelings.* **6.** Opinion as distinguished from reason. **7.** An impression produced by a person, place, thing, or event: *The guests gave the feeling of forced gaiety.* **8.** Emotion, or capacity to convey emotion, in a work of art, a performance, or an artist: *"Joyce had a natural feeling for the visual arts"* (Frank Budgen). **9. a.** An appreciative regard. Used with *for: a feeling for propriety.* **b.** A bent; aptitude. Used with *for: a feeling for carpentry.* —See Synonyms at **opinion.** —*adj.* **1. a.** Having the ability to react or feel emotionally; sentient; sensitive. **b.** Easily moved emotionally. **2.** Having sensibility; sympathetic. **3.** Expressive of sensibility; indicating emotion: *a feeling glance.* —**feel′ing·ly** *adv.*

Synonyms: *feeling, emotion, passion.* These nouns refer to nonintellectual, or subjective, human response. *Feeling* and *emotion* are often interchangeable in this sense. *Emotion,* however, is frequently considered the stronger term, especially appropriate to such response marked by excitement or agitation. *Passion,* in its broadest sense, is intense, compelling emotion.

fee simple *pl.* **fees simple.** *Law.* An estate in land of which the inheritor has unqualified ownership and power of disposition.

fee splitting. The practice of paying commissions to colleagues out of the fees received from clients who have been referred by these colleagues.

feet. Plural of **foot.**

fee tail *pl.* **fees tail.** *Law.* An estate in land limited in inheritance to a specified individual, group, or class of heirs.

feeze (fēz, fāz) *n. Regional.* **1.** A heavy impact. **2.** A state of vexation. —*tr.v.* **feezed, feezing, feezes.** **1.** To drive off; put to flight. **2.** To faze. [Middle English *fese,* from *fesen,* to drive off, Old English *fēsian*†.]

feign (fān) *v.* **feigned, feigning, feigns.** —*tr.* **1. a.** To give a false appearance of; pretend; to sham: *jump into bed and feign sleep.* **b.** To represent falsely; pretend to: *feign authorship of a novel.* **2.** To invent; make up; fabricate: *feign an experience.* —*intr.* To pretend; dissemble. —See Synonyms at **pretend.** [Middle English *feinen,* from Old French *faindre, feindre* (present stem *fei(g)n-*), from Latin *fingere,* to form, shape, alter. See **dheigh-** in Appendix.*]

feigned (fānd) *adj.* **1.** Not real; pretended: *"those who, with a feigned modesty, condemn as useless what they write"* (Locke). **2.** Made up; fictitious. —**feign′ed·ly** (fā′nĭd-lē) *adv.*

feint (fānt) *n.* **1.** A misleading movement or feigned attack designed to draw defensive action away from an intended target or objective. **2.** Any pretense intended to mislead; a stratagem. —See Synonyms at **artifice.** —*intr.v.* **feinted, feinting, feints.** To make a feint. [French *feinte,* from Old French, from the past participle of *feindre,* to FEIGN.]

feints. Variant of **faints.**

Fei·sal, Fei·sul. Variants of **Faisal.**

feist (fīst) *n.* Also **fice** (fīs). *Regional.* A small dog of mixed ancestry; mongrel. [Shortening and variation of obsolete *fisting (dog),* from obsolete *fist,* to break wind, from Middle English *fisten,* Old English *fistān* (unattested). See **peis-**[2] in Appendix.*]

feis·ty (fī′stē) *adj.* **-tier, -tiest.** *Regional.* **1.** Touchy; excitable; quarrelsome. **2.** Spirited; frisky. [From FEIST.]

Feke (fēk), **Robert.** 1705?–1750? American portraitist.

Feld·berg (fĕlt′bĕrk). The highest elevation (4,898 feet) in the Black Forest of southwestern West Germany.

feld·spar (fĕld′spär′, fĕl′-) *n.* Also **fel·spar** (fĕl′-). Any of a group of abundant rock-forming minerals occurring principally in igneous, plutonic, and some metamorphic rocks and consisting of silicates of aluminum with potassium, sodium, calcium, and rarely barium. [Partial translation of obsolete German *Feldspath,* "field spar" : *Feld,* field, from Old High German *feld* (see **pelə-**[1] in Appendix*) + *Spath,* spar.]

feld·spath·ic (fĕld-spăth′ĭk, fĕl-) *adj.* Of, relating to, or containing feldspar. [From obsolete German *Feldspath,* feldspar : *Feld,* field (see **feldspar**) + *Spath,* spar, from Middle High German *spāt* (see **sphē-** in Appendix*).]

fe·li·cif·ic (fē′lə-sĭf′ĭk) *adj.* Producing or bringing about happiness. [Latin *fēlīx* (stem *fēlīc-*), favorable, fertile (see **dhēi-** in Appendix*) + -FIC.]

fe·lic·i·tate (fĭ-lĭs′ə-tāt′) *tr.v.* **-tated, -tating, -tates.** **1.** To wish happiness to; congratulate. **2.** *Archaic.* To make happy. —*adj. Obsolete.* Made happy. [Latin *fēlīcitāre,* to make happy, from *fēlīx* (stem *fēlīc-*), happy, FELICIFIC.] —**fe·lic′i·ta′tor** (-tā′tər) *n.*

fe·lic·i·ta·tion (fĭ-lĭs′ə-tā′shən) *n.* Congratulation.

fe·lic·i·tous (fĭ-lĭs′ə-təs) *adj.* **1. a.** Well-chosen; apt; appropriate: *a felicitous comparison.* **b.** Having an appropriate and agreeable manner or style: *a felicitous writer.* **2.** Marked by well-being or good fortune: *a felicitous life.* —See Synonyms at **fit.** —**fe·lic′i·tous·ly** *adv.* —**fe·lic′i·tous·ness** *n.*

fe·lic·i·ty (fĭ-lĭs′ə-tē) *n., pl.* **-ties.** **1. a.** Great happiness; bliss. **b.** An instance of this. **2.** Something that causes or produces happiness. **3. a.** An appropriate and pleasing manner or style: *felicity of speech.* **b.** An instance of this. [Middle English *felicite,* from Old French, from Latin *fēlīcitās,* from *fēlīx* (stem *fēlīc-*), happy, FELICIFIC.]

fe·line (fē′līn′) *adj.* **1.** Of or belonging to the family Felidae, which includes the lions, tigers, jaguars, and wild and domestic cats. **2.** Resembling or suggestive of a cat, as in suppleness, slyness, or stealthiness. —*n.* Also **fe·lid** (fē′lĭd). A feline animal. [Latin *fēlīnus,* from *fēlēs*†, cat.] —**fe′line′ly** *adv.* —**fe′line′ness, fe·lin′i·ty** (fē-lĭn′ə-tē) *n.*

Fe·lix (fē′lĭks). A masculine given name. [Middle English, from Latin, from *fēlīx,* happy. See **dhēi-** in Appendix.*]

fell[1] (fĕl) *tr.v.* **felled, felling, fells.** **1.** To cause to fall; cut or knock down: *fell a tree; fell an opponent.* **2.** To sew or finish (a seam) with the raw edges flattened, turned under, and stitched down. —*n.* **1.** The timber cut down in one season. **2.** A felled seam. [Middle English *fellen*, Old English *fellan*, *fyllan*, strike down, fell. See **phol-** in Appendix.*] **—fell′a·ble** *adj.*

fell[2] (fĕl) *adj.* **1.** Of an inhumanly cruel nature; fierce; unsparing: *fell hordes.* **2.** Able to destroy; lethal: *a fell blow.* **3.** Dire; sinister: *by some fell chance.* **4.** *Scottish.* Sharp and biting: *a fell word.* [Middle English *fel*, from Old French, from Medieval Latin *fellō*, wicked person, FELON.] **—fell′ness** *n.*

fell[3] (fĕl) *n.* The hide of an animal; skin; pelt. [Middle English *fel*, Old English *fell*. See **pel-**[4] in Appendix.*]

fell[4]. Past tense of **fall.**

fel·lah (fĕl′ə, fə-lä′) *n., pl.* **-lahs** or *Arabic* **fellahin** (fĕl′ə-hēn′, fə-lä′hēn′) or **fellaheen.** A peasant or agricultural laborer in Arab countries. [Arabic *fellāḥ*, dialectal variant of *fallāḥ*, from *falaḥa*, to cultivate, till.]

fel·la·ti·o (fə-lā′shē-ō′, fĕ-) *n.* Oral stimulation of the penis. [New Latin, from Latin *fellātus*, past participle of *fellāre*, to suck. See **dhēi-** in Appendix.*]

fell·er (fĕl′ər) *n.* **1.** One that fells. **2.** A sewing machine attachment for felling seams.

fell·mon·ger (fĕl′mŭng′gər, -mŏng′gər) *n. British.* One who prepares hides for making leather.

fel·low (fĕl′ō) *n.* **1. a.** A man or boy. **b.** *Informal.* A boy friend. **2. a.** Anybody in general; any human being. **b.** A person considered to be worthless, unimportant, or of low station. **3.** A comrade; an associate. **4. a.** A person similar to oneself in rank, position, or background; an equal; a peer. **b.** One of a pair; a counterpart; mate. **5.** *Abbr.* **F, F.** A member of a group having common interests, as a member of a learned society. **6.** *Abbr.* **F, F.** A graduate student appointed to a position granting financial aid and providing for further study. **7.** *British.* A member of an incorporated college or university; a trustee. *—adj.* Being of the same kind, group, occupation, society, or locality; having in common certain characteristics or interests: *fellow workers.* [Middle English *felawe*, Old English *fēolaga*, from Old Norse *fēlagi*, partner, fellow, one who lays down money : *fē*, cattle, money (see **peku-** in Appendix*) + *lag*, a laying down (see **legh-** in Appendix*).]

fellow feeling. 1. Sympathetic awareness of others; rapport. **2.** Community of interest.

fellow man *pl.* **fellow men.** Also **fel·low·man** (fĕl′ō-măn′) *pl.* **-men** (mĕn′). **1.** All humanity regarded as united in shared experience. **2.** Any person regarded as related to one through the general human experience.

fellow servant. *Law.* One of a group of employees working together under such circumstances that the employer cannot be expected to protect against or be liable for harm to one employee caused by the negligence of another.

fel·low·ship (fĕl′ō-shĭp′) *n.* **1. a.** The condition of being together or of sharing similar interests or experiences, as do members of a profession, religion, or nationality; companionship. **b.** The companionship of individuals in a congenial atmosphere and on equal terms. **2.** A union of friends or equals sharing similar interests; fraternity; brotherhood. **3.** Friendship; comradeship. **4. a.** A scholarship or grant awarded a graduate student in a college or university. **b.** The state of having been awarded such a scholarship or grant. **c.** A foundation established for the awarding of such a scholarship or grant.

fellow traveler. One who sympathizes with the tenets and programs of an organized group without actually joining it; especially, a supporter of the Communist Party.

fel·ly (fĕl′ē) *n., pl.* **-lies.** Also **fel·loe** (fĕl′ō). **1.** The rim of a wheel supported by spokes. **2.** A section of such a rim. [Middle English *fely*, Old English *felg*, from West Germanic *felgam* (unattested).]

fe·lo de se (fĕl′ō də sā′, sē′) *pl.* **felones de se** (fə-lō′nēz) or **felos de se** (fĕl′ōz). Also **fe·lo-de-se.** *Law.* **1.** The act of suicide. **2.** One who commits suicide. [Medieval Latin, "felon of himself" : *felō*, *fellō*, FELON + *dē*, of + *sē*, ablative of *suī*, himself, oneself, from Latin (see **seu-**[2] in Appendix*).]

fel·on[1] (fĕl′ən) *n.* **1.** *Law.* A person who has committed a felony. **2.** *Archaic.* An evil person. *—adj.* Evil; cruel. [Middle English *feloun*, from Old French *felon*, from Medieval Latin *fellō*, from Vulgar Latin *fellō*† (unattested).]

fel·on[2] (fĕl′ən) *n.* A purulent infection at the distal end of a finger near or around the nail or the bone. [Middle English *feloun*, from Old French, possibly from Latin *fel*, bile, venom. See **ghel-**[2] in Appendix.*]

fe·lo·ni·ous (fə-lō′nē-əs) *adj.* **1.** *Law.* **a.** Of, pertaining to, or concerning a felony. **b.** Characterized by or of the nature of a felony: *felonious intent.* **2.** *Archaic.* Evil; wicked. **—fe·lo′ni·ous·ly** *adv.* **—fe·lo′ni·ous·ness** *n.*

fel·on·ry (fĕl′ən-rē) *n.* Felons collectively.

fel·o·ny (fĕl′ə-nē) *n., pl.* **-nies.** *Law.* **1.** Any of several crimes, such as murder, rape, or burglary, considered more serious than a misdemeanor and punishable by a more stringent sentence. Compare **misdemeanor. 2.** Any of several crimes in early English law that were punishable by forfeiture of land or goods and by possible loss of life or a bodily part.

felony murder. A murder committed during the committing of another felony, such as robbery or arson.

fel·site (fĕl′sīt′) *n.* A fine-grained igneous rock, chiefly feldspar and quartz. [FELS(PAR) + -ITE.] **—fel·sit′ic** (-sĭt′ĭk) *adj.*

fel·spar. Variant of **feldspar.**

felt[1] (fĕlt) *n.* **1.** A fabric of matted, compressed animal fibers, as wool or fur, sometimes mixed with vegetable or synthetic fibers. **2.** Any fabric or material resembling this. **3.** Something made of felt or a similar material. *—adj.* **1.** Made of felt. **2.** Pertaining or similar to felt. *—v.* **felted, felting, felts.** *—tr.* **1.** To make into felt. **2.** To cover with felt. *—intr.* To become like felt; mat together. [Middle English *felt*, Old English *felt*. See **pel-**[6] in Appendix.*]

felt[2]. Past tense and past participle of **feel.**

Felt·ham (fĕl′təm). A former administrative division of London, England, now part of **Hounslow** *(see).*

felt·ing (fĕl′tĭng) *n.* **1.** The practice or process of making felt. **2.** The materials from which felt is made. **3.** Felted fabric.

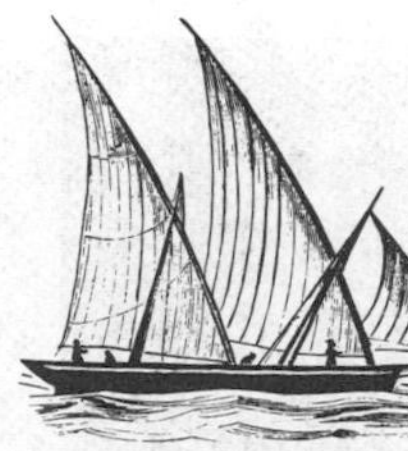

felucca

fe·luc·ca (fə-lōō′kə, -lŭk′ə) *n.* A narrow, swift sailing vessel, chiefly of the Mediterranean, propelled by lateen sails or oars or both. [Italian *feluc(c)a*, from obsolete Spanish *faluca*, from Arabic *fulk*, ship.]

fel·wort (fĕl′wûrt′, -wôrt′) *n.* Any of several plants of the genus *Gentiana* or related genera; especially, *G. amarella*, having small, purplish flowers. [Middle English *feldwort*, Old English *feldwyrt* : *feld*, FIELD + *wyrt*, WORT.]

fem. female; feminine.

fe·male (fē′māl′) *adj. Abbr.* **f, F, f., F., fem. 1.** Of, pertaining to, or designating the sex that produces ova or bears young. **2.** Characteristic of or appropriate to this sex; feminine. **3.** Consisting of members of this sex. **4.** *Botany.* **a.** Pertaining to or designating an organ, such as a pistil or ovary, that functions in producing seeds or spores after fertilization. **b.** Bearing pistils but not stamens: *female flowers.* **5.** *Mechanics.* Indicating or having a part, such as a slot or receptacle, designed to receive a complementary male part, such as a plug or prongs. **6.** *Obsolete.* Effeminate; weak. —See Synonyms at **feminine.** *—n. Abbr.* **f, F, f., F., fem. 1.** A member of the sex that produces ova or bears young. **2.** Anything or anyone female. **3.** A woman or girl, as distinguished from a man or boy. **4.** *Botany.* A plant having only pistillate flowers. [Middle English, variant (influenced by *male*, male) of *femelle*, from Old French, from Latin *fēmella*, diminutive of *fēmina*, woman, female. See **dhēi-** in Appendix.*] **—fe′male′ness** *n.*

female rhyme. A **feminine rhyme** *(see).*

female suffrage. Woman suffrage *(see).*

feme (fĕm) *n.* **1.** *Law.* A wife. **2.** *Obsolete.* A woman. [Norman French, from Latin *fēmina*, woman, FEMALE.]

feme cov·ert (fĕm′ kŭv′ərt). *Law.* A married woman.

feme sole (fĕm′ sōl′). *Law.* A single woman, whether divorced, widowed, or never married.

fem·i·nie (fĕm′ə-nē) *n.* Women collectively; womankind. [Middle English, from Old French, from Latin *fēmina*, woman, FEMALE.]

fem·i·nine (fĕm′ə-nĭn) *adj. Abbr.* **f., F., fem. 1.** Of or belonging to the female sex. Said especially of members of the human species. **2.** Characterized by or possessing qualities generally attributed to a woman; womanly: *feminine tenderness.* **3.** Possessing qualities generally attributed to a woman, although belonging to the male sex: *"an artist of feminine and receptive temperament"* (Havelock Ellis). **4.** Effeminate; womanish. **5.** *Grammar.* Indicating or belonging to the gender of words or grammatical forms that are classified as female: *a feminine noun.* Compare **masculine, neuter.** *—n. Abbr.* **f., F., fem.** *Grammar.* **1.** The feminine gender. **2.** A word or form belonging to that gender. [Middle English, from Old French, from Latin *fēminīnus*, from *fēmina*, FEMALE.] **—fem′i·nine·ly** *adv.* **—fem′i·nine·ness** *n.*

Synonyms: *feminine, female, womanly, womanish, effeminate, ladylike.* These adjectives describe what is of or appropriate to women. *Feminine* and *female* are essentially classifying terms. *Female*, like *male*, merely categorizes by sex: *the female population.* *Feminine* can be used thus narrowly: *the feminine lead in a drama.* Often, as the opposite of "masculine," it refers to things considered characteristic of women: *feminine allure; feminine wiles.* *Womanly* describes things that become a woman: *womanly virtue.* *Womanish* refers to qualities distinctive to women but less admirable, or to such qualities in men with an unfavorable implication: *womanish tears.* *Effeminate* is largely restricted in reference to men or things, and implies lack of manliness or strength: *an effeminate walk.* *Ladylike* is applicable to what befits women of good breeding: *ladylike behavior.*

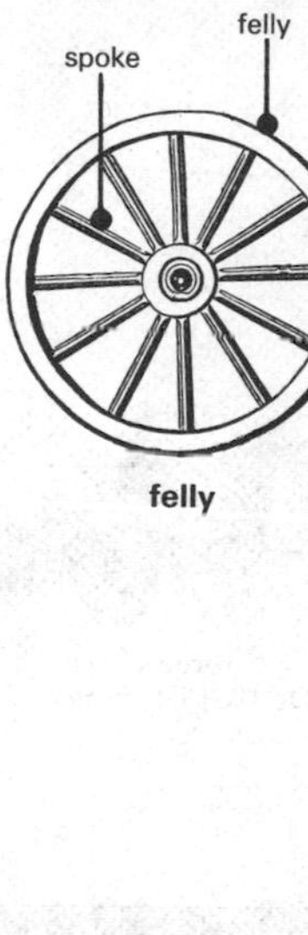

felly

feminine ending. 1. *Prosody.* The termination of a line or verse in an unaccented syllable. **2.** *Grammar.* A final syllable or termination that marks or forms words in the feminine gender. For example, *-ess* is added to *lion* to form *lioness.*

feminine rhyme. *Prosody.* **1.** A rhyme of two syllables in which the second syllable is unstressed; for example, *follow* and *hollow; brightly* and *nightly.* **2.** A rhyme of three syllables in which only the first syllable is stressed; for example, *edible* and *incredible; seventeen* and *Levantine.* Also called "female rhyme." Compare **masculine rhyme.**

fem·i·nin·i·ty (fĕm′ə-nĭn′ə-tē) *n., pl.* **-ties. 1.** The quality or condition of being feminine; womanhood; womanliness. **2.** A female characteristic or trait. **3.** All women; womankind. **4.** Womanishness; effeminacy.

fem·i·nism (fĕm′ə-nĭz′əm) *n.* **1.** A doctrine that advocates or demands for women the same rights granted men, as in political or economic status. **2.** The movement in support of such a doctrine. **—fem′i·nist** *adj.* & *n.* **—fem′i·nis′tic** *adj.*

fem·i·nize (fĕm′ə-nīz′) *v.* **-nized, -nizing, -nizes.** *—tr.* To make feminine. *—intr.* To become feminine. **—fem′i·ni·za′tion** *n.*

femme (fàm). *French.* A woman or wife.

femme fa·tale (fàm fà-tàl′) *pl.* **femmes fatales** (fàm fà-tàl′). *French.* A woman whose seductive charms may lead a man into compromising or dangerous situations.

fem·o·ral (fĕm′ər-əl) *adj.* Of or pertaining to the thigh or the femur. [From Latin *femur* (stem *femor-*), FEMUR.]

femto–. *Symbol* **f** Indicates one-quadrillionth (10^{-15}); for example, **femtometer.** [Danish or Norwegian *femten*, fifteen, from Old Norse *fimmtān*. See **penkwe** in Appendix.*]

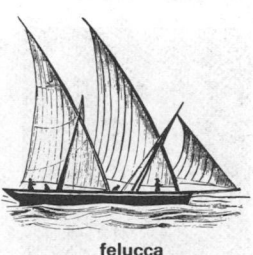

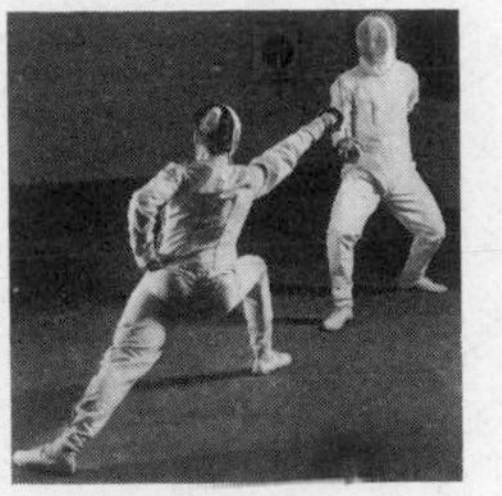
fencing

fem·to·joule (fĕm′tə-jo͞ol, -joul) *n. Abbr.* **fJ** One-quadrillionth (10^{-15}) of a joule.
fem·tom·e·ter (fĕm-tŏm′ə-tər) *n. Abbr.* **fm** One-quadrillionth (10^{-15}) of a meter.
fe·mur (fē′mər) *n., pl.* **-murs** or **femora** (fĕm′ər-ə). **1. a.** The proximal bone of the lower or hind limb in vertebrates, situated between the pelvis and knee in humans. Also called "thighbone." **b.** The thigh. **2.** The usually stout third segment of an insect's leg. [Latin *femur*†, thigh.]
fen¹ (fĕn) *n.* Low, flat, swampy land; a bog; a marsh. [Middle English *fen,* Old English *fenn.* See **pen-** in Appendix.*]
fen² (fĕn) *n., pl.* **fen.** A coin equal to ¹⁄₁₀₀ of the yuan of China. See table of exchange rates at **currency.** [Mandarin Chinese *fen¹.*]
fe·na·gle. Variant of **finagle.**
fence (fĕns) *n.* **1.** A structure serving as an enclosure, barrier, or boundary, usually made of posts, boards, wire, stakes, or rails. **2.** *Archaic.* Something intended as a means of defense; protection. **3.** The art or practice of swordplay; fencing. **4.** Skill in debate and repartee. **5. a.** One who receives and sells stolen goods. **b.** A place where such goods are received and sold. **6.** An attachment on a machine or tool that directs, regulates, and limits its action. **—on the fence.** *Informal.* Undecided as to which of two sides to support; neutral. **—***v.* **fenced, fencing, fences. —***tr.* **1.** To surround or close in by means of a fence. **2.** To separate or close off by means of a fence. **3.** *Archaic.* To defend or ward off. **—***intr.* **1.** To practice or demonstrate the art of fencing. **2.** To engage in the art of skillful conversation or debate. **3.** To avoid giving direct answers; be evasive. **4.** To act as a fence for stolen goods. [Middle English *fens,* short for *defens,* DEFENSE.]
fenc·er (fĕn′sər) *n.* **1.** A person who fences, as with a foil; swordsman. **2.** A person who erects or repairs fences.
fenc·ing (fĕn′sĭng) *n.* **1.** The art, practice, or sport of using a foil, épée, or saber; swordplay. **2.** The art or practice of skillful conversation or debate; repartee. **3.** Material, such as wire, stakes, rails, and the like, used in the construction of fences. **4.** Fences collectively.
fend (fĕnd) *v.* **fended, fending, fends. —***tr. Archaic.* To defend. **—***intr.* To resist. **—fend for oneself.** To provide for oneself; survive without help; manage alone. **—fend off.** To turn aside; deflect; parry. [Middle English *fenden,* shortening of *defenden,* to DEFEND.]
fend·er (fĕn′dər) *n.* **1.** One that fends or wards off. **2. a.** A shaped, usually metallic guard over each wheel of an automotive vehicle. **b.** The portion of the automotive body near each wheel. **3.** A device at the front end of a locomotive or streetcar designed to push aside obstructions. **4.** A metal device placed in front of a fireplace to keep hot coals and debris from falling out; fireguard. **5.** *Nautical.* A device, such as a bundle of rope, a piece of timber, or an automobile tire, used on the side of a vessel or dock to absorb impact or friction.
Fé·ne·lon (fān-lôɴ′), **François de Salignac de la Mothe.** 1651–1715. French Catholic archbishop and author.
fe·nes·tra (fĭ-nĕs′trə) *n., pl.* **-trae** (-trē′). **1.** *Anatomy.* A small opening; especially, either of two apertures in the medial wall of the middle ear. **2.** A windowlike opening. **3.** *Biology.* A transparent spot or marking, as on the wing of an insect. [New Latin, from Latin *fenestra*†, opening in the wall, window.]
fe·nes·trat·ed (fĭ-nĕs′trā′tĭd, fĕn′ə-strā′tĭd) *adj.* Also **fe·nes·trate** (fĭ-nĕs′trāt′, fĕn′ə-strāt′) (especially for sense 2). **1.** Having windows or windowlike openings. **2.** *Biology.* Having fenestrae. [Latin *fenestrātus,* past participle of *fenestrāre,* to provide with windows or openings, from *fenestra,* window, FENESTRA.]
fen·es·tra·tion (fĕn′ə-strā′shən) *n.* **1.** *Architecture.* The design and placement of windows in a building. **2.** An opening in a structure. **3.** *Surgery.* The cutting of an artificial opening from the external auditory canal to the labyrinth of the internal ear to restore normal hearing.

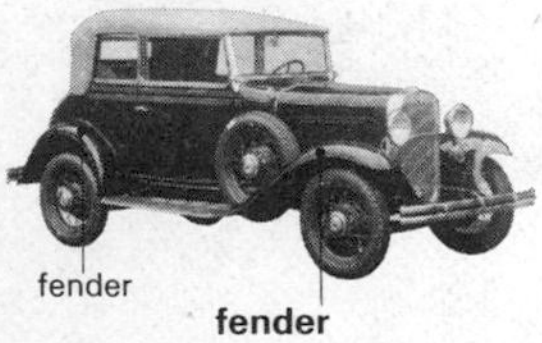

fender
On 1931 Chevrolet

Feng·tien. A former name for **Shenyang.**
Fe·ni·an (fē′nē-ən) *n.* **1. a.** *Plural.* A legendary group of heroic Irish warriors of the second and third centuries A.D. Also called "Fianna." **b.** A member of this group. **2.** A member of a secret organization, founded in New York City in the mid-19th century, whose goal was the overthrow of British rule in Ireland. [Probably from Irish *fēinne,* plural of *fiann,* legendary body of warriors, after *Fiann,* a legendary hero.] **—Fe′ni·an** *adj.* **—Fe′ni·an·ism′** *n.*
fen·nec (fĕn′ĭk) *n.* A small fox, *Fennecus zerda,* of desert regions of northern Africa, having fawn-colored fur and large, pointed ears. [Arabic *fanak, fenek,* fox, small furry animal.]
fen·nel (fĕn′əl) *n.* **1.** A plant, *Foeniculum vulgare,* native to Eurasia, having finely dissected leaves, clusters of small yellow flowers, and aromatic seeds used as flavoring. **2.** The seeds or edible stalks of this plant. **3.** Any of several similar or related plants. [Middle English *fenel,* Old English *fenol, finugle,* from Vulgar Latin *fēnoclum* (unattested), from Latin *fēniculum,* diminutive of *fēnum, faenum,* hay. See **dhēi-** in Appendix.*]
fen·ny (fĕn′ē) *adj.* **1.** Having the nature of a bog; marshy. **2.** Of, pertaining to, or found in fens.
fen·u·greek (fĕn′yo͞o-grēk′) *n.* **1.** A cloverlike Eurasian plant, *Trigonella foenum-graecum,* having white flowers and pungent, aromatic seeds used as flavoring. **2.** The seeds of this plant. [Middle English *fenigrek,* from Old French *fenugrec,* from Latin *fēnugraecum,* from *fēnum graecum,* "Greek hay" (from the use of the dried plant as fodder) : *fēnum,* hay (see **fennel**) + *graecus,* GREEK.]

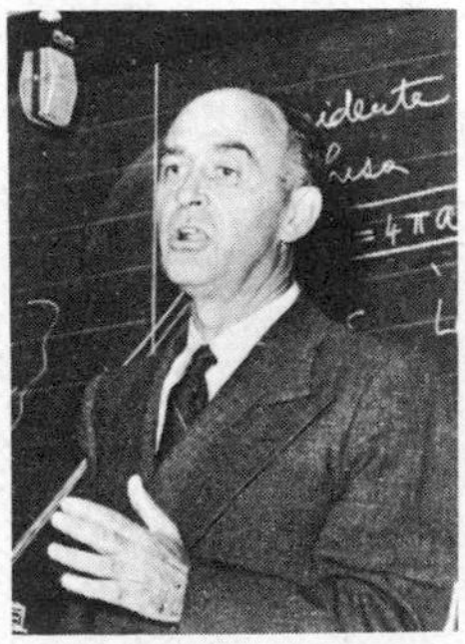
Enrico Fermi
Lecturing in 1949

feoff (fĕf, fēf) *tr.v.* **feoffed, feoffing, feoffs.** To invest with a feudal estate or fee; enfeoff. [Middle English *feoffen, feffen,* from Norman French *feoffer,* from Old French *fieffer,* from *fief,* FIEF.]
feoff·ee (fĕ-fē′, fē-fē′) *n.* A person to whom a feoffment is granted.
feof·fer (fĕf′ər, fē′fər) *n.* Also **feof·for.** A person who grants a feoffment.
feoff·ment (fĕf′mənt, fēf′-) *n.* A grant of lands as a fee.
FEPC Fair Employment Practices Committee.
-fer. Indicates agency, bearing, or production; for example, **aquifer.** [Latin, from *ferre,* to carry, bear. See **bher-¹** in Appendix.*]
fe·ral (fîr′əl, fĕr′-) *adj.* **1.** Existing in a wild or untamed state; especially, having reverted to such a state from domestication. **2.** Of or characteristic of a wild animal; savage. [From Latin *fera,* wild animal, from *ferus,* wild. See **ghwer-** in Appendix.*]
Fer·ber (fûr′bər), **Edna.** 1885–1968. American author.
fer-de-lance (fĕr′də-lăns′, -läns′) *n.* A venomous tropical American snake, *Bothrops atrox,* having brown and grayish markings. [French, iron (head) of a lance : *fer,* iron, from Old French, from Latin *ferrum* (see **ferrum** in Appendix*) + *de,* of, from Latin *dē* + *lance,* spear, lance, from Old French, LANCE.]
Fer·di·nand (fûrd′n-ănd′). A masculine given name. [French, from Germanic. See **nant-** in Appendix.*]
Fer·di·nand I (fûrd′n-ănd′). 1503–1564. King of Bohemia and Hungary (1526–64); Holy Roman Emperor (1558–64).
Fer·di·nand II (fûrd′n-ănd′). 1578–1637. King of Bohemia and Hungary (1617–37); Holy Roman Emperor (1619–37).
Fer·di·nand III (fûrd′n-ănd′). 1608–1657. King of Hungary (1625–57); Holy Roman Emperor (1637–57).
Fer·di·nand V (fûrd′n-ănd′). 1452–1516. Spanish King of Aragon, Castile, Sicily, and Naples; married Isabella of Castile; aided Columbus; organized Inquisition.
fere (fîr) *n. Archaic.* **1.** A companion. **2.** A spouse. [Middle English *fere,* Old English *gefēra.* See **per-²** in Appendix.*]
fer·e·to·ry (fĕr′ə-tôr′ē, -tōr′ē) *n., pl.* **-ries.** **1.** A shrine designed to hold the relics of saints. **2.** An area of a church in which such shrines are kept. [Middle English *fertre, feretory,* from Old French *fiertre,* from Latin *feretrum,* bier, from Greek *pheretron,* from *pherein,* to bear, carry. See **bher-¹** in Appendix.*]
Fer·ga·na (fər-gä′nə). Also **Fer·gha·na.** An irrigated region in the Soviet Union, divided between the Kirghiz S.S.R. and the Uzbek S.S.R.
fe·ri·a (fîr′ē-ə, fĕr′-) *n., pl.* **-as** or **feriae** (fîr′ē-ē′, fĕr′-). *Ecclesiastical.* A day of the week on which no feast is observed. [Spanish, market, fair, from Medieval Latin *fēria,* from Late Latin, day of the week, from Latin *fēriae,* days of rest, holidays, festivals. See **dhēs-** in Appendix.*] **—fe′ri·al** *adj.*
fe·rine (fîr′īn′) *adj.* Untamed; feral. [Latin *ferīnus*†, from *fera,* wild animal. See **feral.**]
Fe·rin·gi (fə-rĭng′gē) *n.* Also **Fe·rin·ghee, Fe·rin·ghi.** A European or Eurasian in India; especially, one of Portuguese ancestry. Usually used disparagingly. [Persian *Farangī,* from Arabic *Faranjī,* from Old French *Franc,* a FRANK.]
fer·i·ty (fĕr′ə-tē) *n.* **1.** The condition of being feral; existence in a wild state. **2.** The condition of being savage; ferocity. [Latin *feritās,* from *ferus,* wild. See **feral.**]
Fer·man·agh (fər-măn′ə). A county occupying 653 square miles in southwestern Northern Ireland. Population, 52,000. County seat, Enniskillen.
Fer·mat (fĕr-mä′), **Pierre de.** 1601–1665. French mathematician.
fer·ma·ta (fĕr-mä′tə) *n. Music.* **1.** The holding or sustaining of a tone, chord, or rest beyond its nominal value. **2.** The sign that indicates such a prolongation. [Italian, pause, stop, from the feminine past participle of *fermare,* to pause, stop, from Latin *firmāre,* to make firm, from *firmus,* firm. See **dher-²** in Appendix.*]
fer·ment (fûr′mĕnt′) *n.* **1.** Anything that causes fermentation, as a yeast, bacterium, mold, or enzyme. **2.** Fermentation. **3.** A state of agitation; unrest; turbulence. **—***v.* (fər-mĕnt′) **fermented, -menting, -ments. —***tr.* **1.** To produce by or as if by fermentation. **2.** To cause to undergo fermentation. **3.** To make turbulent; agitate; excite. **—***intr.* **1.** To undergo fermentation. **2.** To be turbulent; seethe. [Middle English, leaven, yeast, from Old French, from Latin *fermentum.* See **bhreu-²** in Appendix.*] **—fer·ment′a·bil′i·ty** *n.* **—fer·ment′a·ble** *adj.* **—fer·ment′er** *n.*
fer·men·ta·tion (fûr′mĕn-tā′shən) *n.* **1.** Any of a group of chemical reactions induced by living or nonliving ferments that split complex organic compounds into relatively simple substances; especially, the anaerobic conversion of sugar to carbon dioxide and alcohol by yeast. **2.** Unrest; commotion; agitation.
fer·men·ta·tive (fər-mĕn′tə-tĭv) *adj.* **1. a.** Causing fermentation. **b.** Capable of causing or undergoing fermentation. **2.** Pertaining to or of the nature of fermentation.
Fer·mi (fĕr′mē), **Enrico.** 1901–1954. Italian-born American atomic and nuclear physicist; performed experiments leading to the first self-sustaining chain reaction.
fer·mi·on (fûr′mē-ŏn′) *n.* A particle, such as an electron, proton, or neutron, having half-integral spin and obeying statistical rules requiring that not more than one in a set of identical particles may occupy a particular quantum state. Compare **boson.** [After Enrico FERMI.]
fer·mi·um (fûr′mē-əm) *n. Symbol* **Fm** A synthetic transuranic metallic element having known isotopes with masses 252, 253, 255, and 257, and corresponding half-lives of 30 hours, 3 days, 20 hours, and approximately 100 days. Atomic number 100. See **element.** [New Latin, after Enrico FERMI.]

fern (fûrn) *n.* Any of numerous flowerless, seedless vascular plants of the class Filicinae, characteristically having fronds with divided leaflets, and reproducing by means of spores. [Middle English *fern,* Old English *fearn.* See **per-²** in Appendix.*]

Fer·nan·do de No·ro·nha (fĕr-năn′dōō dĭ nō-rō′nyə). A volcanic island of Brazil, seven square miles in area, lying 225 miles northeast of eastern Brazil, and used mainly for military and penal purposes.

Fer·nan·do Po (fər-năn′dō pō′). *Spanish* **Fer·nan·do Po·o** (fĕr-nän′dō pō′ō). An island, 779 square miles in area, in the Gulf of Guinea, part of Equatorial Guinea. Population, 63,000.

fern·er·y (fûr′nə-rē) *n., pl.* **-ies.** 1. A place or container in which ferns are grown. 2. A bed or collection of ferns.

fern seed. The minute spores of ferns, formerly believed to be seeds, and supposed to have the power of making one bearing them invisible.

fern·y (fûr′nē) *adj.* **-ier, -iest.** 1. Abounding in ferns. 2. Of, pertaining to, or characteristic of ferns.

fe·ro·cious (fə-rō′shəs) *adj.* 1. Extremely savage; fierce. 2. Extreme; relentless: *a ferocious blizzard.* —See Synonyms at **cruel.** [From Latin *ferōx* (stem *feroc-*), wild, fierce. See **ghwer-** in Appendix.*] —**fe·ro′cious·ly** *adv.* —**fe·ro′cious·ness** *n.*

fe·roc·i·ty (fə-rŏs′ə-tē) *n., pl.* **-ties.** The condition or quality of being ferocious.

-ferous. Indicates bearing, producing, or ·containing; for example, **crystalliferous, umbelliferous.** [Middle English : -FER + -OUS.]

Fer·ra·ra (fə-rär′ə; *Italian* fär-rä′rä). A city in north-central Italy, 57 miles southwest of Venice. Population, 151,000.

fer·rate (fĕr′āt′) *n.* A ferrite *(see).* [FERR(O)- + -ATE.]

fer·ret¹ (fĕr′ĭt) *n.* 1. A domesticated, usually albino form of the Old World polecat, often trained to hunt rats or rabbits. 2. A related weasellike mammal, *Mustela nigripes,* of central North America, having yellowish fur and dark feet. —*v.* **ferreted, -reting, -rets.** —*tr.* 1. To hunt (rats, for example) with a ferret. 2. To drive out; expel. 3. To uncover and bring to light by searching. Usually used with *out: "piqued by the failure of all his endeavors to ferret out the assassins"* (Poe). —*intr.* 1. To hunt with a ferret or ferrets. 2. To search; investigate intensively. [Middle English *feret, firette,* from Old French *fuiret, furet,* from Vulgar Latin *fūrittus* (unattested), little thief, from Latin *fūr,* thief. See **furtive.**] —**fer′ret·er** *n.* —**fer′ret·y** *adj.*

fer·ret² (fĕr′ĭt) *n.* Also **fer·ret·ing** (-ĭng). A narrow piece of tape used to bind or edge fabric. [Probably from Italian *fioretti,* floss silk, plural of *fioretto,* diminutive of *fiore,* flower, from Latin *flōs* (stem *flōr-*), flower. See **bhel-³** in Appendix.*]

ferri-. *Chemistry.* Indicates iron, especially with a ferric valence; for example, **ferricyanide.** [From Latin *ferrum,* iron. See **ferrum** in Appendix.*]

fer·ri·age (fĕr′ē-ĭj) *n.* 1. The act or business of ferrying. 2. The toll charged for ferrying.

fer·ric (fĕr′ĭk) *adj.* Of, pertaining to, or containing iron; especially, containing iron with valence 3 or with valence higher than in a corresponding ferrous compound. [FERR(O)- + -IC.]

ferric oxide. A dark compound, Fe_2O_3, occurring naturally as hematite ore and rust, and used in pigments, metallurgy, polishing compounds, and magnetic tapes.

fer·ri·cy·an·ic acid (fĕr′ĭ-sī-ăn′ĭk, fĕr′ē-). A reddish-brown solid compound, $H_3[Fe(CN)_6]$.

fer·ri·cy·a·nide (fĕr′ĭ-sī′ə-nīd′, fĕr′ē-) *n.* Any of various salts derived from ferricyanic acid and used in making blue pigments. [FERRI- + CYANIDE.]

fer·rif·er·ous (fə-rĭf′ər-əs, fĕ-) *adj.* Containing or yielding iron: *ferriferous rock.* [FERRI- +-FEROUS.]

Fer·ris wheel (fĕr′ĭs). Also **fer·ris wheel.** A large upright, rotating wheel having suspended cars in which passengers ride for amusement. [Designed for the Chicago World's Fair in 1893 by George W.G. Ferris (1859–1896), American engineer.]

fer·rite (fĕr′īt′) *n.* 1. Any of a group of nonmetallic, ceramiclike, usually ferromagnetic compounds of ferric oxide with other oxides; especially, such a compound with spinel crystalline structure, characterized by extremely high electrical resistivity and used in computer memory elements, permanent magnets, and various solid-state devices. Also called "ferrate." 2. Iron having a body-centered cubic crystalline form, occurring commonly in steel, cast iron, and pig iron below 910°C. [FERR(O)- + -ITE.]

Fer·ro. The former name for **Hierro.**

ferro-, ferr-. Indicates: 1. Iron; for example, **ferromagnetic, ferrite.** 2. Iron in alloy; for example, **ferromanganese.** 3. Iron in its ferrous valence; for example, **ferrocyanide.** [From Latin *ferrum,* iron. See **ferrum** in Appendix.*]

fer·ro·al·loy (fĕr′ō-ăl′oi′, -ə-loi′) *n.* Any of various alloys of iron and one or more other elements, such as manganese or silicon, used as a raw material in the production of steel.

fer·ro·con·crete (fĕr′ō-kŏn′krēt′, -kŏn′krēt′) *n.* Reinforced concrete *(see).*

fer·ro·cy·an·ic acid (fĕr′ō-sī′ăn′ĭk). A solid white compound, $H_4Fe(CN)_6$.

fer·ro·cy·a·nide (fĕr′ō-sī′ə-nīd′) *n.* A salt derived from ferrocyanic acid, the sodium and potassium salts being used in making blue pigments, blueprint paper, and ferricyanide.

fer·ro·e·lec·tric (fĕr′ō-ĭ-lĕk′trĭk) *adj.* Of or pertaining to a crystalline dielectric that can be given a permanent electric polarization by application of an electric field. —*n.* A ferroelectric substance. —**fer′ro·e·lec′tric·i·ty** *n.*

fer·ro·mag·ne·sian (fĕr′ō-măg′nē′shən, -zhən) *adj.* Containing iron and magnesium. Said especially of certain minerals.

fer·ro·mag·net (fĕr′ō-măg′nĭt) *n.* 1. A ferromagnetic substance; broadly, a substance with magnetic properties resembling those of iron. 2. A ferromagnetic magnet.

fer·ro·mag·net·ic (fĕr′ō-măg′nĕt′ĭk) *adj.* Pertaining to or characteristic of substances, such as iron, nickel, cobalt, and various alloys, that exhibit extremely high magnetic permeability, the ability to acquire high magnetization in relatively weak magnetic fields, a characteristic saturation point, and magnetic hysteresis. —**fer′ro·mag′ne·tism′** *n.*

fer·ro·man·ga·nese (fĕr′ō-măng′gə-nēz′, -nēs′) *n.* A ferroalloy of iron and manganese, used in the production of steel.

fer·ro·sil·i·con (fĕr′ō-sĭl′ĭ-kən, -kŏn′) *n.* A ferroalloy of iron and silicon used in the production of carbon steel.

fer·ro·type (fĕr′ə-tīp′) *n.* 1. A positive photograph made directly on an iron plate varnished with a thin sensitized film. Also called "tintype." 2. The process by which such photographs are made. [FERRO- + TYPE.]

fer·rous (fĕr′əs) *adj.* Of, pertaining to, or containing iron, especially with valence 2. [New Latin *ferrosus* : Latin *ferrum,* iron (see **ferrum** in Appendix*) + -OUS.]

ferrous oxide. A black powdery compound, FeO, used in the manufacture of steel, green heat-absorbing glass, and enamels.

ferrous sulfate. A greenish crystalline compound, $FeSO_4 \cdot 7H_2O$, used as a pigment, fertilizer, feed additive, and in sewage and water treatment.

ferrous sulfide. A black to brown sulfide of iron, FeS, used in making hydrogen sulfide.

fer·ru·gi·nous (fə-rōō′jə-nəs, fĕ-) *adj.* 1. Of, containing, or similar to iron. 2. Having the color of iron rust. [Latin *ferrūginus,* from *ferrūgō* (stem *ferrūgin-*), iron rust, from *ferrum,* iron. See **ferrum** in Appendix.*]

fer·rule (fĕr′əl, -ōōl′) *n.* Also **fer·ule.** 1. A metal ring or cap attached to or near the end of a pole, cane, wooden handle, or the like, for reinforcement or to prevent splitting. 2. A bushing used to secure a pipe joint. —*tr.v.* **ferruled, -ruling, -rules.** Also **fer·ule.** To furnish with a ferrule. [Variant (influenced by Latin *ferrum,* iron) of earlier *verrel, virl,* from Middle English *verelle, virol,* from Old French *virelle, virole,* from Latin *viriola,* little bracelet, diminutive of *viriae,* bracelets. See **wei-¹** in Appendix.*]

ferret¹
Mustela nigripes

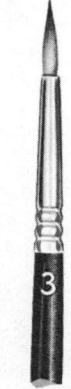

ferrule
Head of
a paintbrush

fer·ry (fĕr′ē) *n., pl.* **-ries.** 1. A commercial service for transporting people, vehicles, goods, or the like, across a body of water. 2. A boat used in such transportation. 3. The place of embarkation of a ferryboat. 4. A franchise or legal right to operate such a service for a fee. 5. The transporting of a vehicle under its own power to its eventual user. Usually used in reference to aircraft. 6. A service for transporting people or goods by aircraft, usually over short distances and on a regular schedule. —*v.* **ferried, -rying, -ries.** —*tr.* 1. To transport (a person or thing) across a body of water. 2. To cross (a body of water) on or as on a ferry. 3. To deliver (a vehicle, especially an aircraft) under its own power to its eventual user. 4. To transport (people or goods) by aircraft. —*intr.* To cross a body of water on or as on a ferry. [Middle English *fery, ferie,* probably from Old Norse *ferja.* See **per-²** in Appendix.*]

fer·ry·boat (fĕr′ē-bōt′) *n.* A boat used to ferry passengers, goods, or the like.

fer·ry·man (fĕr′ē-mən) *n., pl.* **-men** (-mĭn). A person who owns, administers, or operates a ferry.

fer·tile (fûrt′l) *adj.* 1. *Biology.* **a.** Capable of reproducing. **b.** Capable of initiating, sustaining, or supporting reproduction. **c.** Capable of growing and developing; able to mature. 2. *Botany.* Bearing reproductive structures or material such as spores or pollen. 3. Rich in material needed to sustain plant growth: *fertile soil.* 4. Highly or continuously productive; prolific: *a fertile imagination.* [Middle English, from Old French, from Latin *fertilis,* from *ferre,* to bear, carry, produce. See **bher-¹** in Appendix.*] —**fer′tile·ly** *adv.* —**fer′tile·ness** *n.*

Fertile Crescent. A fertile area in the Near East, arching from the Mediterranean coast in the west around the Syrian Desert to Iraq in the east.

fer·til·i·ty (fər-tĭl′ə-tē) *n.* The condition, state, or quality of being fertile.

fer·til·i·za·tion (fûrt′l-ə-zā′shən) *n.* 1. The act or process of initiating biological reproduction. 2. The process in which two gametes unite to form a zygote. 3. The act or process of rendering fertile, especially by use of fertilizer.

fer·til·ize (fûrt′l-īz′) *v.* **-ized, -izing, -izes.** —*tr.* 1. To cause fertilization of (an ovum, for example); especially, to provide with sperm or pollen, thereby causing fertilization. 2. To render fertile, especially by spreading fertilizer. —*intr.* To spread fertilizer. —**fer′til·iz′a·ble** *adj.*

fer·til·iz·er (fûrt′l-ī′zər) *n.* 1. One that fertilizes. 2. Any of a large number of natural and synthetic materials, including manure and nitrogen, phosphorus, and potassium compounds, spread on or worked into soil to increase its fertility.

fer·u·la (fĕr′yə-lə, fĕr′ə-) *n., pl.* **-lae** (-lē′) or **-las.** *Rare.* A flat piece of wood, as a stick; ferule. [New Latin, from Latin, giant fennel. See **ferule.**]

fer·ule¹ (fĕr′əl, -ōōl′) *n.* A baton, cane, or stick used in punishing children. —*tr.v.* **feruled, -uling, -ules.** To punish or discipline with a ferule. [Latin *ferula†,* giant fennel, rod used to punish.]

fer·ule². Variant of **ferrule.**

fer·ven·cy (fûr′vən-sē) *n., pl.* **-cies.** The condition or quality of being fervent.

fer·vent (fûr′vənt) *adj.* 1. Having or showing great emotion or warmth; passionate; ardent. 2. Extremely hot; glowing. [Middle English, from Old French, from Latin *fervēns,* present

ferryboat

Ferris wheel
Photographed at the 1893
Chicago World's Fair

ă pat/ā pay/âr care/ä father/b bib/ch church/d deed/ĕ pet/ē be/f fife/g gag/h hat/hw which/ĭ pit/ī pie/îr pier/j judge/k kick/l lid, needle/m mum/n no, sudden/ng thing/ŏ pot/ō toe/ô paw, for/oi noise/ou out/ōō took/ōō boot/p pop/r roar/s sauce/sh ship, dish/
t tight/th thin, path/*th* this, bathe/ŭ cut/ûr urge/v valve/w with/y yes/z zebra, size/zh vision/ə about, item, edible, gallop, circus/
à Fr. ami/œ Fr. feu, Ger. schön/ü Fr. tu, Ger. über/KH Ger. ich, Scot. loch/N Fr. bon. *Follows main vocabulary. †Of obscure origin.

participle of *fervēre*, to boil, glow. See **bhreu-²** in Appendix.*] —**fer′vent·ly** *adv.* —**fer′vent·ness** *n.*

fer·vid (fûr′vĭd) *adj.* **1.** Intensely fervent or zealous; impassioned. **2.** Extremely hot; burning. —See Synonyms at **eager.** [Latin *fervidus*, glowing, from *fervēre*, to glow, boil. See **bhreu-²** in Appendix.*] —**fer′vid·ly** *adv.* —**fer′vid·ness** *n.*

fer·vor (fûr′vər) *n.* Also *chiefly British* **fer·vour. 1.** Intensity of emotion; fervency; ardor. **2.** Intense heat. —See Synonyms at **passion.** [Middle English *fervour*, from Old French, from Latin *fervor*, a boiling, from *fervēre*, to boil. See **bhreu-²** in Appendix.*]

Fès. See **Fez.**

Fes·cen·nine (fĕs′ə-nīn′, -nēn′) *adj.* Licentious; obscene. [Latin *Fescennīnus*, of the town *Fescennia* in Etruria, noted for licentious festivals and verses.]

fes·cue (fĕs′kyo͞o) *n.* Any of various grasses of the genus *Festuca*, often cultivated as pasturage. [Middle English *festu*, from Old French, from Vulgar Latin *festūcum* (unattested), from Latin *festūca*†, stalk, stem.]

fess (fĕs) *n.* Also **fesse.** *Heraldry.* A wide horizontal band forming the middle section of an escutcheon. [Middle English *fesse*, from Old French, from Latin *fascia*, band, fillet. See **bhasko-** in Appendix.*]

Fess·en·den (fĕs′ən-dən), **William Pitt.** 1806–1869. U.S. Secretary of the Treasury (1864–65).

fess point. *Heraldry.* The center point of an escutcheon.

-fest. Indicates festive gathering or get-together; for example, **gabfest.** [From German *Fest*, feast, festival, from Middle High German *vest*, from Latin *fēstum*, neuter of *fēstus*, joyous, festal. See **dhes-** in Appendix.*]

fes·tal (fĕs′təl) *adj.* Of, pertaining to, or of the nature of a feast or festival; festive; joyous. [Old French, from Latin *fēsta*, FEAST.] —**fes′tal·ly** *adv.*

fes·ter (fĕs′tər) *v.* **-tered, -tering, -ters.** —*intr.* **1.** To generate pus; suppurate. **2.** To form an ulcer. **3.** To decay; rot: *"lilies that fester smell far worse than weeds"* (Shakespeare). **4.** To be or become a source of irritation; rankle. —*tr.* To infect, inflame, or corrupt. —*n.* A small, festering sore or ulcer. [Middle English *festre*, from Old French, from Latin *fistula*, FISTULA.]

fes·ti·na len·te (fĕs-tē′nä lĕn′tā). *Latin.* Make haste slowly.

fes·ti·val (fĕs′tə-vəl) *n.* **1.** An occasion for feasting or celebration; especially, a day or time of religious significance that recurs at regular intervals: *the festival of Chanukah.* **2.** A series of related performances, exhibitions, competitions, or the like; especially, such a series that recurs at regular intervals: *a film festival.* **3.** Conviviality; revelry. —*adj.* Festive. [Middle English, from Old French, from Medieval Latin *fēstivālis*, from *fēstīvus*, FESTIVE.]

fes·tive (fĕs′tĭv) *adj.* **1.** Of, pertaining to, or appropriate to a feast or festival. **2.** Merry; joyous: *a festive occasion.* [Latin *fēstīvus*, from *fēstus*, joyous. See **dhēs-** in Appendix.*] —**fes′tive·ly** *adv.* —**fes′tive·ness** *n.*

fes·tiv·i·ty (fĕs-tĭv′ə-tē) *n., pl.* **-ties. 1.** A joyous feast, holiday, or celebration; festival. **2.** The pleasure, joy, and gaiety of a festival or celebration. **3.** *Plural.* The proceedings or events of a festival; festive activity.

fes·toon (fĕs-to͞on′) *n.* **1.** A string or garland of leaves, flowers, ribbon, or the like, suspended in a loop or curve between two points. **2.** A representation of this, as in sculpture. —*tr.v.* **festooned, -tooning, -toons. 1.** To decorate with or as with a festoon or festoons: *"the aged cobwebs that festoon its dusky beams"* (Hawthorne). **2.** To form or make into a festoon or festoons. **3.** To join together by festoons. [French *feston*, from Italian *festone*, festal ornament, from *fēsta*, feast, festival, from Latin, plural of *fēstus*, joyous, festal. See **dhēs-** in Appendix.*]

fes·toon·er·y (fĕs-to͞o′nə-rē) *n., pl.* **-ies. 1.** An arrangement of or into festoons. **2.** Festoons collectively.

fest·schrift (fĕst′shrĭft′) *n., pl.* **-schriften** (-shrĭf′tən) or **-schrifts.** A volume of learned articles, essays, and the like, contributed by colleagues and admirers as a tribute, especially to a scholar. [German, "festival writings."]

fe·tal (fēt′l) *adj.* Also **foe·tal** (fēt′l). Of, pertaining to, or having the nature of a fetus.

fe·ta·tion (fē-tā′shən) *n.* The development of a fetus; pregnancy. [FET(US) + -ATION.]

fetch¹ (fĕch) *v.* **fetched, fetching, fetches.** —*tr.* **1.** To go after and return with; get; bring. **2.** To cause to come or be drawn forth: *"a great blow . . . which fetched blood"* (Increase Mather). **3. a.** To draw in (breath); inhale. **b.** To bring forth (a sigh, for example). **4.** *Informal.* To bring (a price): *"Our corn will fetch its price in any market in Europe"* (Thomas Paine). **5.** To interest irresistibly; attract. **6.** *Archaic.* To perform or make (a movement, step, or the like). **7.** *Informal.* To strike or deal (a blow). **8.** *Nautical.* To arrive at; come to; reach. —*intr.* **1.** To go after and return with things. **2.** *Hunting.* To retrieve game. Often used as a command to a dog. **3.** *Nautical.* **a.** To hold a course. **b.** To turn about; veer. —See Usage note at **bring.** —**fetch and carry.** To do minor chores or tasks. —**fetch up. 1.** To reach a place and halt there. **2.** To make up (lost time, for example). —*n.* **1.** An act or instance of fetching. **2.** A stratagem or trick. [Middle English *fecchen*, Old English *feccan, fetian.* See **ped-¹** in Appendix.*] —**fetch′er** *n.*

fetch² (fĕch) *n. Chiefly British.* An apparition of a living person; Doppelgänger. [Origin obscure.]

fetch·ing (fĕch′ĭng) *adj. Informal.* Very attractive; charming; captivating. —**fetch′ing·ly** *adv.*

fete (fāt; *French* fĕt) *n.* Also **fête. 1.** A festival or feast. **2.** An elaborate outdoor party or other entertainment, such as a fair or bazaar. **3.** Any elaborate party or dinner. —*tr.v.* **feted, feting, fetes.** Also **fête. 1.** To honor or celebrate with a festival or party. **2.** To pay honor to. [French *fête*, from Old French *feste*, FEAST.]

fête cham·pê·tre (fĕt shäN-pĕ′tr′). *French.* An outdoor dinner, party, or similar entertainment.

fet·e·ri·ta (fĕt′ə-rē′tə) *n.* A variety of sorghum, *Sorghum vulgare caudatum*, grown in warm regions for its grain and as forage. [Arabic (Sudanese dialect).]

fe·ti·cide (fē′tə-sīd′) *n.* The intentional destruction of a human fetus. [FET(US) + -CIDE.] —**fe′ti·ci′dal** *adj.*

fet·id (fĕt′ĭd, fē′tĭd) *adj.* Also **foe·tid** (fē′tĭd). Having an offensive odor; foul-smelling; stinking: *"The ship, full of fetid port air and swarming with mosquitoes, got under way"* (Katherine Anne Porter). [Middle English, from Latin *fētidus, foetidus*, from *fētēre, foetēre*†, to stink.] —**fet′id·ly** *adv.* —**fet′id·ness** *n.*

fet·ish (fĕt′ĭsh, fē′tĭsh) *n.* Also **fet·ich. 1.** A material object believed among primitive cultures to have magical power. **2. a.** An object of fetishism. **b.** Fetishism. **3.** An object of unreasonably excessive attention or reverence: *"Wren's mistress, posing as his wife to satisfy the English fetish of respectability"* (Thomas Pynchon). [French *fétiche*, from Portuguese *feitiço*, charm, sorcery, from Latin *factītius*, made by art, from *facere*, to make, do. See **dhē-¹** in Appendix.*]

fet·ish·ism (fĕt′ĭsh-ĭz′əm, fē′tĭsh-) *n.* Also **fet·ich·ism. 1.** The worship of or belief in fetishes. **2.** Excessive attention to or attachment for something. **3.** Aberrant habitual sexual excitement associated with an inanimate object or a bodily part. —**fet′ish·ist** *n.* —**fet′ish·is′tic** *adj.*

fet·lock (fĕt′lŏk′) *n.* **1. a.** A projection on the lower part of the leg of a horse or related animal, above and behind the hoof. **b.** A tuft of hair on such a projection. **2.** The joint marked by this projection. In this sense, also called "fetlock joint." [Middle English *fitlok*, from Germanic, akin to Middle High German *vizzelach.* See **ped-¹** in Appendix.*]

fe·tor (fē′tər, fē′tôr′) *n.* Also **foe·tor** (fē′tər). An exceptionally offensive odor; strong stench. [Middle English *fetour*, from Latin *fētor, foetor*, from *fētēre, foetēre*, to stink. See **fetid.**]

fet·ter (fĕt′ər) *n.* **1.** A chain or shackle attached to the ankles to restrain movement. **2.** *Usually plural.* Anything that serves to restrict; restraint. —*tr.v.* **fettered, -tering, -ters. 1.** To put fetters on; to shackle. **2.** To restrict the freedom of movement or thought of; confine; impede: *"he strives to free the mind, to fight against the material and moral restrictions which fetter liberty"* (Pierre Brodin). [Middle English *feter*, Old English *feter, fetor.* See **ped-¹** in Appendix.*]

fet·ter·bush (fĕt′ər-bo͝osh′) *n.* **1.** A shrub, *Lyonia lucida*, of the southeastern United States, having evergreen leaves and clusters of white flowers. **2.** Any of several similar, related shrubs, especially one of the genus *Leucothoe.*

fet·tle (fĕt′l) *tr.v.* **-tled, -tling, -tles.** *Metallurgy.* To line (the hearth of a reverberatory furnace) with loose sand or ore preparatory to pouring molten metal. —*n.* **1.** The material used to line a furnace in fettling. **2.** Proper or sound condition; good spirits: *"Mr. Andrews himself, when he got off the train, was in fine fettle"* (Mary McCarthy). [Middle English *fetlen*, to shape, make ready, probably from Old English *fetel*, girdle, belt. See **ped-²** in Appendix.*]

fet·tling (fĕt′lĭng) *n.* The material, such as loose ore and sand, used to line a reverberatory furnace.

fe·tus (fē′təs) *n., pl.* **-tuses.** Also **foe·tus.** The unborn young of a viviparous vertebrate; in humans, the unborn young from the end of the eighth week to the moment of birth as distinguished from the earlier embryo. [Latin *fētus*, pregnancy, fetus, a giving birth. See **dhēi-** in Appendix.*]

feud¹ (fyo͞od) *n.* **1.** A bitter, prolonged hostility between two families, individuals, or clans; vendetta. **2.** A quarrel; strife. [Middle English *fede, feide*, from Old French, from Old High German *fēhida.* See **peig-²** in Appendix.*]

feud² (fyo͞od) *n.* A feudal estate, a **fee** *(see).* [Medieval Latin *feudum*, from Germanic. See **peku-** in Appendix.*]

feud. feudal; feudalism.

feu·dal (fyo͞od′l) *adj. Abbr.* **feud. 1.** Of, pertaining to, or characteristic of feudalism. **2.** Of or pertaining to lands held in fee or to the holding of such lands. [Medieval Latin *feudālis*, from *feudum*, FEUD (estate).] —**feu′dal·ly** *adv.*

feu·dal·ism (fyo͞od′l-ĭz′əm) *n. Abbr.* **feud.** A political and economic system of Europe from the 9th to about the 15th century, based on the relation of lord to vassal as a result of land being held on condition of homage and service. —**feu′dal·ist** *n.* —**feu′dal·is′tic** *adj.*

feu·dal·i·ty (fyo͞o-dăl′ə-tē) *n., pl.* **-ties. 1.** The state or quality of being feudal. **2.** A fee.

feu·dal·ize (fyo͞od′l-īz′) *tr.v.* **-ized, -izing, -izes.** To organize into a feudal system; make feudal. —**feu′dal·i·za′tion** *n.*

feu·da·to·ry (fyo͞o′də-tôr′ē, -tōr′ē) *n., pl.* **-ries. 1.** A person who holds a feudal fee; a vassal. **2.** A feudal fee. —*adj.* **1.** Of, pertaining to, or characteristic of the feudal relationship between vassal and lord. **2.** Owing feudal homage or allegiance. [Medieval Latin *feudātōrius*, from *feudātus*, past participle of *feudāre*, to enfeoff, from *feudum*, FEUD (estate).]

feud·ist¹ (fyo͞o′dĭst) *n.* A person who feuds with another.

feud·ist² (fyo͞o′dĭst) *n.* A person who specializes in feudal law.

Feuil·lant (fœ-yäN′) *n.* A member of a group of constitutional Royalists during the French Revolution, formed in 1791 and forced to disband in August 1792.

feuil·le·ton (fœ′yə-tôN′) *n.* **1.** The part of a French or other European newspaper devoted to light fiction, reviews, and similar articles of general entertainment. **2.** An article appearing in a feuilleton, as an installment of a serialized novel. [French, from *feuillet,* diminutive of *feuille,* leaf, from Old French *fueille, foille,* from Latin *folia,* plural of *folium,* leaf. See **bhel-**[3] in Appendix.*] **—feuil′le·ton·ism′** (fœ′yə-tə-nĭz′əm) *n.* **—feuil′le·ton′ist** *n.*

fe·ver (fē′vər) *n.* **1.** Abnormally high body temperature. **2.** A disease characterized by abnormally high body temperatures. **3.** A condition of heightened activity or excitement; ferment; agitation: *a fever of anticipation.* **4.** A contagious, usually short-lived enthusiasm or eagerness. [Middle English *fever,* Old English *fēfor, fēfer,* from Latin *febris*†.]

fever blister. A **cold sore** *(see).*

fe·ver·few (fē′vər-fyōō′) *n.* An aromatic plant, *Chrysanthemum parthenium,* native to Eurasia, having clusters of buttonlike, white-rayed flowers. [Middle English *feverfu,* from Norman French *fevrefue* (unattested), from Latin *febrifugia* : *febris,* FEVER + *fugāre,* to drive away, from *fugere,* to run away (see **bheug-**[1] in Appendix*).]

fe·ver·ish (fē′vər-ĭsh) *adj.* Also **fe·ver·ous** (-əs). **1. a.** Having a fever, especially a slight fever. **b.** Of, pertaining to, or resembling a fever. **c.** Causing or tending to cause fever. **2.** In an agitated or restless state; intensely emotional or active: *"A feverish energy possessed her and would not let her be still"* (Margaret Mitchell). **—fe′ver·ish·ly** *adv.* **—fe′ver·ish·ness** *n.*

fever therapy. Treatment of disease involving artificially induced fever.

fever tree. Any of several trees, such as certain species of eucalyptus, or *Pinckneya pubens,* of the southeastern United States, having leaves or bark used to allay fever.

fe·ver·weed (fē′vər-wēd′) *n.* Broadly, any of various plants considered to have medicinal properties.

fe·ver·wort (fē′vər-wûrt′, -wôrt′) *n.* Any of several plants considered to have medicinal properties, as the **horse gentian** and **boneset** *(both of which see).*

few (fyōō) *adj.* **fewer, fewest.** Amounting to or consisting of a small number. See Usage note below. *—n.* Singular in form, used with a plural verb. **1.** An indefinitely small number of persons or things; not many: *Bring me a few of your books.* **2.** A limited number of people; the select. Usually preceded by *the: the discerning few.* *—pron.* A small number of persons or things. Used with a plural verb: *"many are called, but few are chosen."* (Matthew 22:14). [Middle English *fewe,* Old English *fēa, fēawe.* See **pōu-** in Appendix.*] **—few′ness** *n.*

Usage: *Fewer,* in contrast to *less,* is the preferred term in most examples involving reference to numbers or units considered individually and therefore capable of being counted or enumerated. *Less* refers to collective quantity or to something abstract: *fewer people, less noise; fewer chances, less opportunity. Less* tends to appear where *fewer* would be preferable. In the following examples, *fewer* alone is acceptable, according to majorities of the Usage Panel: *The industrial trend is in the direction of more machines and fewer people* (*less people* called unacceptable by 77 per cent). *No fewer than ten applicants called* (*less* unacceptable to 67 per cent). *With 40 fewer seats in Parliament, the majority party is proceeding with caution* (*less* unacceptable to 68 per cent). Sentences involving periods of time, sums of money, or measures of distance, weight, or the like usually require *less,* since the sense is collective: *less than three weeks; less than sixty years old; less than $4,000; less than 50 feet.*

fey (fā) *adj.* **1.** *Scottish.* **a.** Fated to die soon. **b.** Full of the sense of approaching death. **2.** Having visionary power; clairvoyant. **3.** Appearing as if under a spell; enchanted; touched. [Middle English *feie,* Old English *fǣge.* See **peig-**[2] in Appendix.*]

Feyn·man (fīn′mən), **Richard Phillips.** Born 1918. American theoretical physicist.

fez (fĕz) *n., pl.* **fezzes.** A man's felt cap in the shape of a truncated cone, usually red with a black tassel hanging from the crown, worn chiefly in the eastern Mediterranean region. [French, from Turkish, from FEZ.]

Fez (fĕz). Also **Fès** (fĕs). A city in north-central Morocco, the religious center of the country and formerly the sultan's northern capital. Population, 235,000.

Fez·zan (fĕ-zăn′). A desert division of Libya, having numerous oases and occupying about 280,000 square miles in the southwestern part of the country.

ff *Music.* fortissimo.

ff. 1. folios. **2.** following.

F.F.A. Future Farmers of America.

F.F.V. First Families of Virginia.

f.g. *Sports.* field goal; field goals.

FHA Federal Housing Administration.

FHLBB Federal Home Loan Bank Board.

f.h.p. friction horsepower.

fi·a·cre (fē-ä′krə) *n.* A small hackney coach. [French, first hired out from Hotel de St. *Fiacre,* Paris.]

fi·an·cé (fē′än-sā′, fē-än′sā′) *n.* A man engaged to be married. [French, past participle of *fiancer,* to betroth, from Old French *fiancier,* from *fier,* to trust, from Vulgar Latin *fīdāre* (unattested), from Latin *fīdere.* See **bheidh-** in Appendix.*]

fi·an·cée (fē′än-sā′, fē-än′sā′) *n.* A woman engaged to be married. [French, feminine of FIANCÉ.]

Fi·an·na (fē′ə-nə) *n.* **Fenian** *(see).*

fi·as·co (fē-ăs′kō) *n., pl.* **-coes** or **-cos.** A complete failure. [French, from Italian *(far) fiasco,* "(to make) a bottle," an unexplained allusion, perhaps from Late Latin *flascō,* FLASK.]

fi·at (fī′ăt′, -ət, fē′ät′) *n.* **1.** An arbitrary order or decree. **2.** Authorization; sanction. [Latin *fiat,* "let it be done," third person singular present subjunctive of *fierī,* to become. See **bheu-** in Appendix.*]

fiat money. Paper money decreed legal tender, not backed by gold or silver, and not necessarily redeemable in coin.

fib (fĭb) *n.* An inconsequential lie. *—intr.v.* **fibbed, fibbing, fibs.** To tell a fib. [Origin obscure.] **—fib′ber** *n.*

fi·ber (fī′bər) *n.* Also *chiefly British* **fi·bre. 1.** Any slender, elongated structure; a filament or strand. **2.** One of the elongated, thick-walled cells that give strength and support to plant tissue. **3.** Any of the filaments constituting the intracellular matrix of connective tissue. **4.** Any of the elongated contractile cells of muscle tissue. **5.** The long threadlike process of a neuron. **6.** A natural or synthetic filament, as of cotton or nylon, capable of being spun into yarn. **7.** Material made of such spun filaments. **8.** The essential substance: *"stirred the deeper fibers of my nature."* (Oscar Wilde). **9.** Internal strength; toughness: *lacking in moral fiber.* [French *fibre,* from Latin *fibra*†.]

fi·ber·board (fī′bər-bôrd′, -bōrd′) *n.* **1.** A building material composed of wood or other plant fibers bonded together and compressed into rigid sheets. **2.** A sheet of this material.

Fi·ber·glas (fī′bər-glăs′, -gläs′) *n.* A trademark for a type of fiber glass.

fiber glass. A composite material consisting of glass fibers in resin. Also called "spun glass."

fiber optics. The optics of light transmission through very fine, flexible glass rods by internal reflection.

fi·bri·form (fī′brə-fôrm′) *adj.* Similar in form or structure to a fiber. [*Fibr(e),* variant of FIBER + -FORM.]

fi·bril (fī′brəl, fĭb′rəl) *n.* Also **fi·bril·la** (fī-brĭl′ə, fĭb′rĭl-ə) *pl.* **-brillae** (-brĭl′ē, fĭb′rĭl-ē). A small, slender fiber, as a root hair. [New Latin *fibrilla,* diminutive of Latin *fibra,* FIBER.] **—fi′bril·lar** (fī′brə-lər, fĭb′rə-), **fi′bril·lar′y** (-lĕr′ē) *adj.*

fib·ril·la·tion (fĭb′rə-lā′shən, fī′brə-) *n.* **1.** The forming of fibers. **2.** Uncoordinated twitching of individual muscular fibers with little or no movement of the muscle as a whole. **3.** Fine, rapid fibrillar movements that replace the normal contraction of the ventricular muscle. In this sense, also called "ventricular fibrillation." [From New Latin *fibrilla,* FIBRIL.]

fi·bril·li·form (fī-brĭl′ə-fôrm′, fĭb-rĭl′-) *adj.* Having the form of a fibril.

fi·bril·lose (fī′brə-lōs′, fĭb′rə-) *adj.* Having or consisting of fibrils.

fi·brin (fī′brĭn) *n.* An elastic, insoluble protein derived from the interaction of fibrinogen with thrombin and forming a fibrous network in the coagulation of blood. [FIBR(O)- + -IN.]

fi·brin·o·gen (fī-brĭn′ə-jən) *n.* A protein in the blood plasma that is converted to fibrin by the action of thrombin in the presence of ionized calcium. [FIBRIN + -GEN.]

fi·bri·nol·y·sin (fī′brə-nŏl′ə-sĭn) *n.* Any enzyme capable of dissolving fibrin. See **plasmin.** [FIBRIN + LYSIN.]

fi·brin·ous (fī′brə-nəs) *adj.* Of, relating to, or having the nature of fibrin.

fibro–, fibr–. Indicates fibrous tissue; for example, **fibrovascular, fibrosis.** [From Latin *fibra,* FIBER.]

fi·broid (fī′broid′) *adj.* Resembling or composed of fibrous tissue. *—n.* A benign neoplasm of smooth muscle, especially in the uterine wall. [FIBR(O)- + -OID.]

fi·bro·in (fī′brō-ĭn) *n.* A white protein that is the essential component of raw silk and spider-web filaments. [French *fibroïne* : FIBRO- + -IN.]

fi·bro·ma (fī-brō′mə) *n., pl.* **-mas** or **-mata** (-mə-tə). A benign neoplasm derived from fibrous tissue. [New Latin : FIBR(O)- + -OMA.] **—fi·brom′a·tous** (fī-brŏm′ə-təs, fī-brō′mə-) *adj.*

fi·bro·sis (fī-brō′sĭs) *n.* The formation of fibrous tissue, as in a reparative or reactive process, in excess of amounts normally present. [New Latin : FIBR(O)- + -OSIS.]

fi·brous (fī′brəs) *adj.* Having, consisting of, or resembling fibers.

fi·bro·vas·cu·lar (fī′brō-văs′kyə-lər) *adj.* Having fibrous tissue and vascular tissue, as in the woody tissue of plants.

fib·u·la (fĭb′yə-lə) *n., pl.* **-lae** (-lē′) or **-las.** The outer and smaller of two bones of the human leg or the hind leg of an animal, between the knee and ankle. [Latin *fībula,* perhaps from the root of *fīgere,* to fix. See **dhīgw-** in Appendix.*]

-fic. Indicates the making, causing, or creating of something; for example, **morbific.** [New Latin *-ficus,* from Latin, from *facere,* to do, make. See **dhē-**[1] in Appendix.*]

FICA Federal Insurance Contributions Act.

fice. Variant of **feist.**

Fich·te (fĭKH′tə), **Johann Gottlieb.** 1762–1814. German philosopher.

Fich·tel·ge·bir·ge (fĭKH′təl-gə-bîr′gə). A mountain region in east-central West Germany, near the East German and Czechoslovak borders. Highest elevation, 3,477 feet.

fi·chu (fĭsh′ōō; *French* fē-shü′) *n.* A woman's triangular scarf of lightweight fabric, worn over the shoulders and crossed or tied in a loose knot at the breast. [French, from the past participle of *ficher,* to fix, attach, from Vulgar Latin *fīgicāre* (unattested), from Latin *fīgere,* to FIX.]

fick·le (fĭk′əl) *adj.* Changeable, especially with regard to affections or attachments; inconstant; capricious. See Synonyms at **faithless.** [Middle English *fikel,* false, treacherous, Old English *ficol.* See **peig-**[2] in Appendix.*] **—fick′le·ness** *n.*

fict. fiction.

fic·tile (fĭk′təl) *adj.* **1.** Moldable; plastic. **2.** Formed of a moldable substance, such as clay or earth. **3.** Of or pertaining to earthenware or pottery. [Latin *fictilis,* from *fictus,* past participle of *fingere,* to touch, form, mold, shape. See **dheigh-** in Appendix.*]

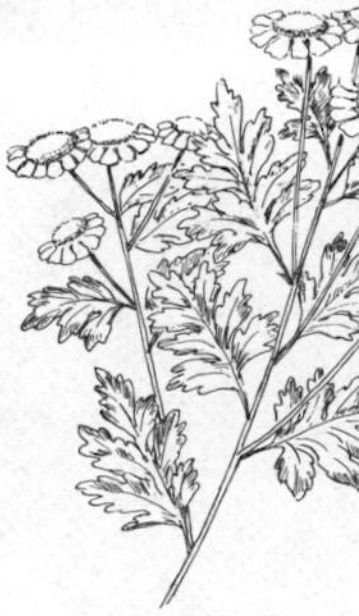

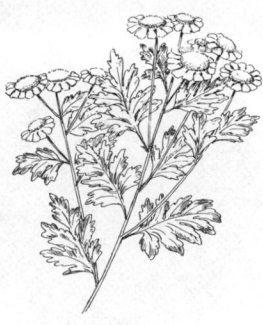

feverfew

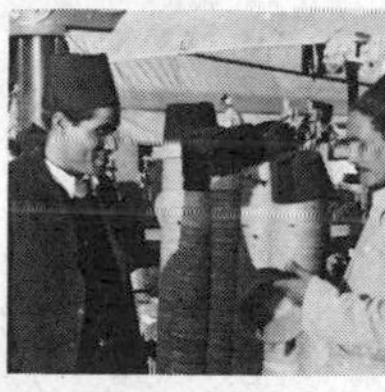

fez
Fez seller in a Cairo street market

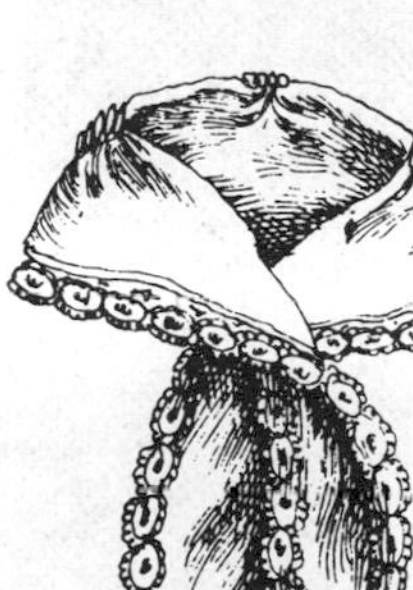

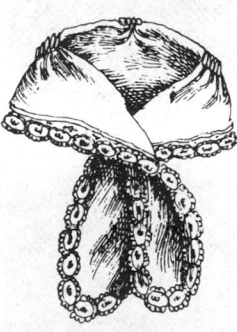

fichu

fic·tion (fĭk′shən) *n.* **1.** An event, statement, or occurrence that has been invented or feigned rather than having actually taken place. **2.** The act of producing such inventions; a feigning. **3.** A lie. **4.** *Abbr.* **fict. a.** A literary work whose content is produced by the imagination and is not necessarily based on fact. **b.** The category of literature comprising works of this kind, including novels, short stories, and plays. **5.** *Law.* Something accepted as fact without any real justification, but merely for the sake of convenience. [Middle English *ficcioun,* invention, from Old French *fiction,* from Latin *fictiō,* a making, fashioning, from *fictus,* past participle of *fingere,* to touch, form, mold. See **dheigh-** in Appendix.*] —**fic′tion·al** *adj.* —**fic′tion·al·ly** *adv.*

fic·ti·tious (fĭk-tĭsh′əs) *adj.* **1.** Of, pertaining to, or characterized by fiction; nonexistent; imaginary; unreal: *a fictitious event.* **2.** Purposefully deceptive; false; untrue: *a fictitious name.* —**fic·ti′tious·ly** *adv.* —**fic·ti′tious·ness** *n.*

fic·tive (fĭk′tĭv) *adj.* **1.** Of or pertaining to the creation of fiction. **2.** Pertaining to or characterized by fiction; fictitious; imaginary. **3.** Feigned; sham. —**fic′tive·ly** *adv.*

fid (fĭd) *n. Nautical.* **1.** A square bar used as a support for a topmast. **2.** A large, tapering pin used to open the strands of a rope prior to splicing. [Origin unknown.]

-fid. Indicates a division or separation into parts or lobes; for example, **pinnatifid.** [Latin *-fidus,* from *findere,* to cleave, split. See **bheid-** in Appendix.*]

fid. fidelity.

fid·dle (fĭd′l) *n.* **1. a.** A **violin** *(see).* **b.** *Informal.* Any member of the violin family, including similarly designed medieval and Oriental instruments. **2.** *Nautical.* A guard rail used on a table during rough weather to prevent things from slipping off. **3.** *Informal.* Nonsensical trifling; stupidity: *"there are things that are more/important beyond all this fiddle"* (Marianne Moore). —**fit as a fiddle.** Of sound body; healthy. —**play second fiddle.** *Informal.* To be subordinate. —*v.* **fiddled, -dling, -dles.** —*intr.* **1.** *Informal.* To play a violin. **2.** To move one's fingers or hands in a nervous, aimless fashion; to fidget. —*tr.* **1.** *Informal.* To play (a tune) on a violin. **2.** To fritter; waste; squander. Used with *away: fiddle time away.* [Middle English *fithele, fidle,* Old English *fithele,* from West German *fithula* (unattested), from Medieval Latin *vītula,* from Latin *vītulārī,* to celebrate a victory, from *Vītula,* goddess of joy and victory, probably of Sabine origin.]

fid·dle-de-dee (fĭd′l-dē-dē′) *interj.* Used to express mild annoyance or impatience. [Nonsensical formation from FIDDLE.]

fid·dle-fad·dle (fĭd′l-făd′l) *interj.* Used to express mild annoyance or impatience. —*intr.v.* **fiddle-faddled, -dling, -dles.** To fritter away one's time; dally. [Reduplication of FIDDLE.] —**fid′dle-fad′dler** *n.*

fid·dle·head (fĭd′l-hĕd′) *n.* **1.** A curved, scroll-like ornamentation at the top of a ship's bow that resembles the neck of a violin. **2.** The coiled young frond of any of various ferns, considered a delicacy when cooked.

fid·dler (fĭd′lər) *n. Informal.* A person who plays the violin.

fiddler crab. Any of various burrowing crabs of the genus *Uca,* of coastal areas, having one of the anterior claws much enlarged in the male. [So called from its large claw which it seems to hold like a fiddle.]

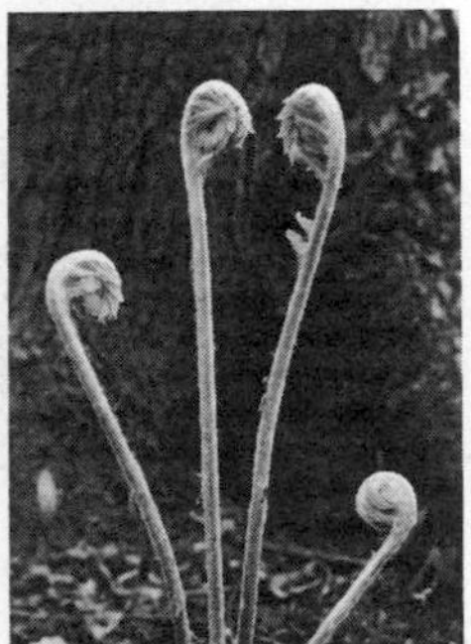

fiddlehead
Fern fiddleheads

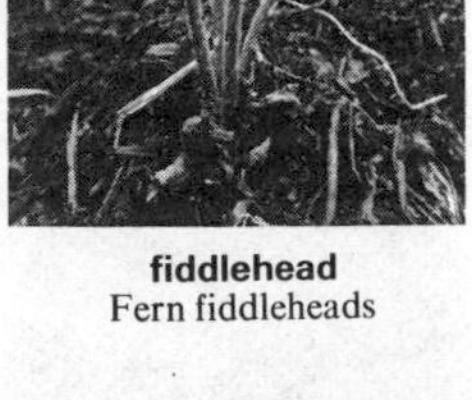

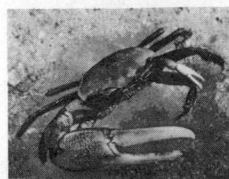

fiddler crab

fid·dle·sticks (fĭd′l-stĭks′) *interj.* Used to express mild annoyance or impatience.

Fi·de·i De·fen·sor (fī′dē-ī′ dĭ-fĕn′sôr′, fē′dā-ē′ dā-fĕn′sōr′) *Abbr.* **F.D.** *Latin.* Defender of the Faith. Used as one of the titles of the British sovereign.

fi·del·i·ty (fī-dĕl′ə-tē, fĭ-) *n., pl.* **-ties. 1.** Faithfulness to obligations, duties, or observances; loyalty. **2.** Correspondence with fact or a given quality, condition, or event; verity; truthfulness; accuracy. **3.** *Abbr.* **fid.** The degree to which an electronic system, such as a radio or phonograph, accurately reproduces at its output the essential characteristics of its input signal. [Middle English *fidelite,* from Old French, from Latin *fidēlitās,* from *fidēlis,* faithful, from *fidēs,* faith. See **bheidh-** in Appendix.*]

Synonyms: *fidelity, allegiance, fealty, loyalty, devotion.* These nouns denote the condition of being faithful. *Fidelity* involves the unfailing fulfillment of one's duties and obligations and the keeping of one's word or vows. In a related, nonpersonal sense it refers to faithfulness to an original, as in the translation of a poem, copy of a painting, or reproduction of sound by means of a recording. *Allegiance* is faithfulness to a government or state to which one is subject, considered as a duty or as what is due in exchange for the rights of citizenship; or the term can denote adherence to any person or thing that has a legitimate claim to one's support. *Fealty,* once applied to the allegiance owed by a tenant or vassal to a feudal lord, now refers in a more general sense to faithfulness to a government, superior, or to persons or things in general. Whereas *allegiance* and *fealty* stress obligation on a rather impersonal level, *loyalty* more often implies a close and voluntary relationship. *Devotion* suggests virtually unlimited support for, or attachment to, a person or thing.

fidg·et (fĭj′ĭt) *v.* **-eted, -eting, -ets.** —*intr.* **1.** To keep some part of one's body in continuous motion, as by shifting one's hands or feet; move nervously or restlessly: *"she . . . began to fidget about the room, tidying everything up more than was necessary"* (R. Prawer Jhabvala). **2.** To play or fuss; fiddle. Used with *with: The lecturer fidgeted with his notes.* —*tr.* To cause (someone) to fidget; make restless or nervous. —*n.* **1.** *Usually plural.* A condition of restlessness. **2.** One who fidgets. [Frequentative of obsolete *fidge,* variant of *fitch, fike,* from Middle English *fiken,* probably from Old Norse *fikjast,* akin to Old English *fācian*†, to try to obtain.]

fidg·et·y (fĭj′ĭt-ē) *adj.* **1.** Habitually fidgeting; nervous; restless. **2.** Unnecessarily fussy. —**fidg′et·i·ness** *n.*

fi·du·cial (fĭ-dōō′shəl, -dyōō′shəl, fī-) *adj.* **1.** Based on or pertaining to faith or trust. **2.** Pertaining or relating to a legal trust; fiduciary. **3.** Regarded or employed as a standard of reference, as in surveying. [Late Latin *fīdūciālis,* from Latin *fīdūcia,* trust, from *fīdere,* to trust. See **bheidh-** in Appendix.*] —**fi·du′cial·ly** *adv.*

fi·du·ci·ar·y (fĭ-dōō′shē-ĕr′ē, fĭ-dyōō′-, fī-) *adj.* **1.** Of, pertaining to, or involving one who holds something in trust for another: *a fiduciary heir; a fiduciary contract.* **2. a.** Of, pertaining to, or denoting a trustee or trusteeship. **b.** Held in trust. **3.** Of, pertaining to, or consisting of fiat money. —*n., pl.* **fiduciaries.** A person who stands in a special relation of trust, confidence, or responsibility in his obligations to others, as a company director or an agent of a principal. [Latin *fīdūciārius,* from *fīdūcia,* trust. See **fiducial.**]

fie (fī) *interj.* Used to express distaste or shock. [Middle English *fi,* from Old French, from Latin *fī,* expression of disgust at a bad smell.]

fief (fēf) *n.* A feudal estate, a **fee** *(see).* [French, from Old French *fie(f),* FEE.]

field (fēld) *n. Abbr.* **fld. 1.** A broad, level, open expanse of land. **2.** A meadow: *a field of buttercups.* **3.** A cultivated expanse of land, especially one devoted to a particular crop. **4.** A portion of land or a geological formation containing a specified natural resource: *an oil field.* **5.** A large, flat surface used by aircraft for landing and taking off; airfield. **6.** An airfield considered with its adjoining buildings; airport. **7.** A background area, as on a flag, painting, or coin: *a blue insignia on a field of red.* **8.** *Heraldry.* The background area of a shield, or one of the divisions of the background. **9.** *Sports.* **a.** A delineated area in which a sports event takes place; ground; stadium. **b.** The portion of a playing field having specific dimensions on which the action of a game takes place: *The spectators were ordered to stay off the field.* **c.** All the contestants or participants in an event. **d.** All the contestants except those specified; all other contestants. **e.** The members of a team engaged in active play. **f.** The body of horsemen following a pack of hounds. **10. a.** An area of human activity or interest: *a field of endeavor.* **b.** A topic, subject, or area of academic interest or specialization. **c.** Profession, employment, or business. **11.** An area or setting of practical activity or application, as distinguished from one of academic study or theoretical research. **12. a.** The scene of a battle. **b.** A battle while it is in progress. **c.** The land, especially when considered topographically, where a battle has been fought; a battlefield. **13.** *Algebra.* A set with two binary operations, designated *addition* and *multiplication,* satisfying the conditions that the set is a commutative group with respect to addition, that the set with the identity of the additive group omitted is a commutative group with respect to multiplication, and that multiplication distributes over addition for all elements in the set. **14.** *Physics.* A region of space characterized by a physical property, such as gravitational or electromagnetic force or fluid pressure, having a determinable value at every point in the region. **15.** *Optics.* The usually circular area in which the image is rendered by the lens system of an optical instrument. —**in the field. 1.** Entered into military operations. **2.** In an operational phase of a marketing program in which the product is made available to the consumer: *It's out of the planning stage and in the field.* —**keep** (or **hold**) **the field.** To continue in one's position against adversity. —**leave the field.** *Informal.* To concede one's interest to another or others. —**play the field.** To indulge in a broad range of interests or possibilities. —**take the field.** To begin or resume activity, as in military operations or in a sport. —*v.* **fielded, fielding, fields.** —*tr.* **1.** *Sports.* **a.** To retrieve (a ball) and perform the required maneuver: *The shortstop fielded the ball and flipped it to the first baseman.* **b.** To place (a team or player) in playing position, or to be able to put (a team) into a contest: *The coach fielded the defensive team.* **2.** To handle adequately and be able to return in kind; cope with: *The senator fielded the question expertly.* —*intr. Sports.* **1.** To retrieve a ball and perform the required maneuver. **2.** To place a team or player in playing position; take the field. —*adj.* **1.** Of, pertaining to, or for a field or fields: *a field hand; field clothes.* **2.** Growing or living in a field or fields. **3.** Of a particular area of work or activity: *field experience.* [Middle English *feld, field,* Old English *feld.* See **pele-**¹ in Appendix.*]

Field (fēld), **Cyrus West.** 1819–1892. American merchant; promoter of transatlantic cable.

Field (fēld), **Eugene.** 1850–1895. American poet and journalist.

Field (fēld), **Marshall.** 1834–1906. American merchant and philanthropist.

field army. *Military.* An administrative and tactical organization composed of a headquarters, certain army troops, service support troops, and a variable number of corps and divisions.

field artillery. *Abbr.* **FA 1.** Artillery, with the exception of antiaircraft artillery, light enough to be mounted for use in the field. **2.** *Capital* **F,** *capital* **A.** A former branch of the U.S. Army.

field battery. A tactical artillery unit usually consisting of four or six field guns.

field cap. *Military.* A fabric cap having a large visor of the same fabric, worn in the field or with **olive drab** *(see).*

field coil. An electric coil used to generate a magnetic field, as in a motor or direct-current generator.

field corn. Any of several varieties of corn used primarily as feed for livestock.

field day. 1. A day spent outdoors in a planned activity such as athletic competition, nature study, or a public demonstration. 2. A festive day, such as one on which a fair is held. 3. *Informal.* An opportunity for expressing or asserting oneself with the fullest pleasure or triumph.

field emission. The emission of electrons from the surface of a conductor, caused by a strong electric field.

field·er (fēl′dər) *n. Sports.* 1. A person who fields a ball. 2. A person who plays a field position, especially an outfielder in baseball.

fielder's choice. *Baseball.* An optional play made by an infielder on a ground ball to put out an advancing base runner, thus allowing the batter to reach first base safely.

field events. The throwing and jumping events of a track meet, as distinguished from the running events. Also called "field sports."

field·fare (fēld′fâr′) *n.* An Old World thrush, *Turdus pilaris,* having gray and brown plumage. [Middle English *feldefare,* probably late Old English *feldefare,* "field-goer" : FIELD + *faran,* to go (see **per-**[2] in Appendix*).]

field glass. A portable binocular instrument used especially outdoors for viewing distant objects. Usually used in the plural.

field goal. 1. *Football.* A score worth three points made, on an ordinary down, by place-kicking or drop-kicking the ball over the crossbar and between the goal posts. 2. *Basketball.* A score worth two points made by throwing the ball through the basket in regulation play.

field gun. A mobile piece of field artillery; fieldpiece.

field hand. A hired laborer or worker on a farm.

field hockey. A form of **hockey** *(see)* played on a turf field.

field hospital. A hospital set up on a temporary basis to serve soldiers in a combat zone.

Field·ing (fēl′dĭng), **Henry.** 1707–1754. English novelist.

field intensity. The effectiveness of a field of force at any point as measured by the force exerted on a unit entity subjected to the field at that point. Also called "field strength."

field magnet. A magnet used to provide a magnetic field in an electrical device such as a generator or motor.

field marshal. *Abbr.* **F.M.** An officer in some European armies, usually ranking just below the commander-in-chief.

field mint. A plant, **corn mint** *(see).*

field mouse. Any of various small mice, as of the genera *Apodemus* or *Microtus,* inhabiting meadows and fields and often causing damage to crops. Also called "meadow mouse."

field music. 1. *Military.* Musicians, such as buglers, drummers, or pipers, who play for marching, ceremonies, or regimental calls. 2. The music that they play.

field officer. *Abbr.* **F.O.** *Military.* An officer, such as a major, lieutenant colonel, or colonel, ranking above a captain and below a brigadier general.

field of force. A region of space throughout which the force produced by a single agent, such as an electric current, is operative. Also called "force field."

field of honor. 1. The scene of a duel involving a matter of personal honor. 2. A battlefield.

field·piece (fēld′pēs′) *n.* A field gun.

Fields (fēldz), **W.C.** Original name, William Claude Dukenfield. 1880–1946. American actor in vaudeville and motion pictures.

fields·man (fēldz′mən) *n., pl.* **-men** (-mĭn). *Cricket.* A fielder.

field sports. Field events *(see).*

field·stone (fēld′stōn′) *n.* A stone naturally occurring in fields, often used as a building material.

field trial. 1. A test for young, untried hunting dogs to determine their competence in pointing and retrieving. 2. *Often plural.* Tests to observe efficiency, durability, or performance, as of a special vehicle or invention.

field trip. A group excursion for the purpose of firsthand observation, as to a museum, woods, or historical place.

field winding. The electrically conducting winding of a field magnet that produces electrical excitation, especially of a motor or generator.

field work. Work done or observations made in the field, as opposed to that done or observed in a laboratory or classroom.

field·work (fēld′wûrk′) *n. Military.* Any temporary fortification erected in the field.

fiend (fēnd) *n.* 1. An evil spirit; demon. 2. *Usually capital* **F.** Satan; the Devil. 3. A diabolically evil or wicked person. 4. *Informal.* **a.** One who is addicted to a given vice: *a dope fiend.* **b.** A person completely absorbed in or obsessed with a given job or pastime: *a crossword-puzzle fiend.* [Middle English *fe(o)nd,* enemy, devil, fiend, Old English *fēond, fīond.* See **pei-** in Appendix.*]

fiend·ish (fēn′dĭsh) *adj.* Pertaining to, similar to, or suggestive of a fiend; diabolical. —**fiend′ish·ly** *adv.* —**fiend′ish·ness** *n.*

fierce (fîrs) *adj.* **fiercer, fiercest.** 1. Having a savage and violent nature; ferocious. 2. Extremely severe or violent; terrible: *"the fierce thunders roar me their music"* (Ezra Pound). 3. Intense or ardent; extreme: *fierce loyalty.* 4. *Informal.* Very difficult or unpleasant: *a fierce exam.* [Middle English *f(i)ers,* from Old French, from Latin *ferus,* wild. See **ghwer-** in Appendix.*] —**fierce′ly** *adv.* —**fierce′ness** *n.*

fi·e·ri fa·ci·as (fī′ə-rī′ fā′shē-əs, fē′ə-rē fä′kē-äs′). *Law.* A writ of execution commanding a sheriff to lay a claim to and seize the goods and chattels of a debtor to fulfill a judgment against him. [Latin, "cause (it) to be done" (words used in such a writ).]

fier·y (fīr′ē, fī′ə-rē) *adj.* **-ier, -iest.** 1. Consisting of or containing fire: *a fiery furnace.* 2. Of, pertaining to, or resembling a fire: *a fiery sunset.* 3. Torridly hot: *a fiery gust of the sirocco.* 4. *Rare.* Flammable. 5. Causing a hot, burning sensation; strong or highly spiced. Said of food or drink: *a fiery curry.* 6. Emitting or appearing to emit sparks; glowing. 7. Easily excited or emotionally volatile; tempestuous: *a fiery temper.* 8. Inflamed. Said of a sore. [Middle English *fiery, firi,* from FIRE.] —**fier′i·ly** *adv.* —**fier′i·ness** *n.*

fiery cross. 1. A burning cross, used by the Ku Klux Klan as a symbol or emblem. 2. Formerly, a wooden cross with charred or bloody ends used by the Scottish clans to summon forth men into battle.

Fie·so·le (fyā′zō-lā). Ancient name **Fae·su·lae** (fē′zo͞o-lē′). A resort northeast of Florence, Italy; site of extensive Etruscan and Roman ruins.

Fie·so·le, Fra Giovanni da. See Fra **Angelico.**

fi·es·ta (fē-ĕs′tə) *n.* 1. A religious feast or holiday; especially, a saint's day celebrated in Spanish-speaking countries. 2. A celebration or festival. [Spanish, from Latin *fēsta,* neuter plural of *fēstus,* joyous, festive. See **dhēs-** in Appendix.*]

fife (fīf) *n.* A musical instrument similar to a flute but higher in range, used primarily to accompany drums in military music. —*v.* **fifed, fifing, fifes.** —*tr.* To play (a tune) on a fife. —*intr.* To play a fife. [German *Pfeife,* from Old High German *pfiffa,* from West Germanic *pīpa* (unattested), from Vulgar Latin *pīpa* (unattested), from Latin *pīpāre,* to chirp. See **pipp-** in Appendix.*]

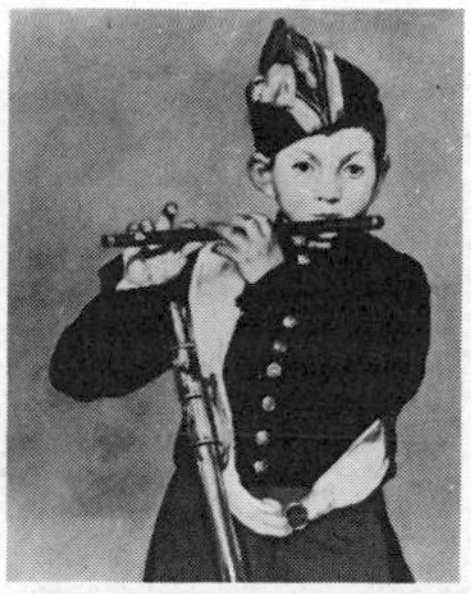

fife
Detail of a painting by Manet of boy playing a fife

fife rail. A rail around the lower part of a ship's mast to which the belaying pins for the rigging are secured.

Fife·shire (fīf′shîr, -shər). Also **Fife** (fīf). A county of Scotland, occupying 505 square miles in the east, north of the Firth of Forth. Population, 380,877. County seat, Cupar.

fif·teen (fĭf-tēn′) *n.* The cardinal number written 15 or in Roman numerals XV. See **number.** [Middle English *fiftene,* Old English *fīftȳne, fīftēne.* See **penkwe** in Appendix.*] —**fif·teen′** *adj.* & *pron.*

fif·teenth (fĭf-tēnth′) *n.* 1. The ordinal number 15 in a series. Also written 15th. 2. One of 15 equal parts. See **number.** —**fif·teenth′** *adj.* & *adv.*

fifth (fĭfth) *n.* 1. The ordinal number five in a series. Also written 5th. 2. One of five equal parts. See **number.** 3. One-fifth of a gallon of liquor; four-fifths of a quart. 4. **a.** A musical interval encompassing five diatonic tones, such as C, D, E, F, and G. **b.** Either of the two tones constituting the extremities of such an interval. **c.** The dominant of a tonality. 5. *Usually capital* **F.** The Fifth Amendment to the Constitution of the United States. Usually preceded by *the.* —**take the Fifth.** To refuse to testify on the grounds that one's testimony might be self-incriminating. [Middle English *fifthe, fifte,* Old English *fīfta.* See **penkwe** in Appendix.*] —**fifth** *adj.* & *pron.*

Fifth Amendment. An amendment to the Constitution of the United States, ratified in 1791, that deals with the rights of accused criminals by providing for due process of law, forbidding double jeopardy, and stating that no person may be forced to testify as a witness against himself.

fifth column. A clandestine subversive organization working within a given country to further an invading enemy's military and political aims. [First applied in 1936 to the Franco supporters and sympathizers in Madrid by General Emilio Mola who was leading four rebel columns of troops against that city.] —**fifth columnist.**

fifth wheel. 1. A wheel or portion of a wheel placed horizontally over the forward axle of a carriage to provide support and stability during turns. 2. An additional wheel carried on a four-wheeled vehicle as a spare. 3. Any extra and unnecessary person or thing.

fif·ti·eth (fĭf′tē-ĭth) *n.* 1. The ordinal number 50 in a series. Also written 50th. 2. One of 50 equal parts. See **number.** —**fif′ti·eth** *adj.* & *adv.*

fif·ty (fĭf′tē) *n.* The cardinal number written 50 or in Roman numerals L. See **number.** [Middle English *fifti,* Old English *fīftig.* See **penkwe** in Appendix.*] —**fif′ty** *adj.* & *pron.*

fif·ty-fif·ty (fĭf′tē-fĭf′tē) *adj. Informal.* Divided or shared in two equal portions: *a fifty-fifty split.* —**fif′ty-fif′ty** *adv.*

fig[1] (fĭg) *n.* 1. Any of several trees or shrubs of the genus *Ficus;* especially, *F. carica,* native to the Mediterranean region, widely cultivated for its edible fruit. 2. The sweet, pear-shaped, many-seeded fruit of this tree. 3. **a.** Any of several plants bearing similar edible fruit. **b.** The fruit of such a plant. 4. A trivial or contemptible amount; a rap; a whit: *"None of them . . would have cared a fig the more for me"* (Hawthorne). [Middle English *fig(e),* from Old French *figue,* from Old Provençal *figa,* from Vulgar Latin *fica* (unattested), from Latin *ficus,* from the same Mediterranean source as Greek *sukon.* See also **syconium.**]

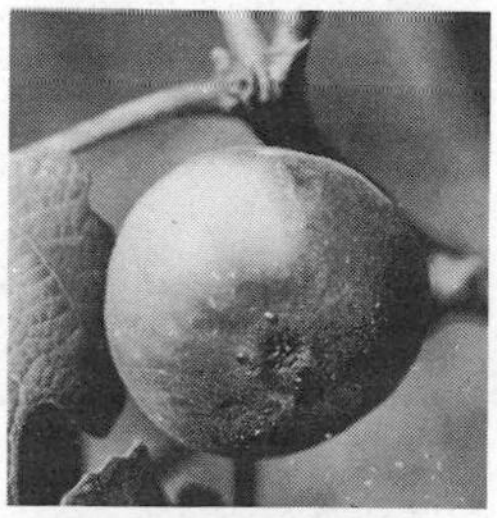

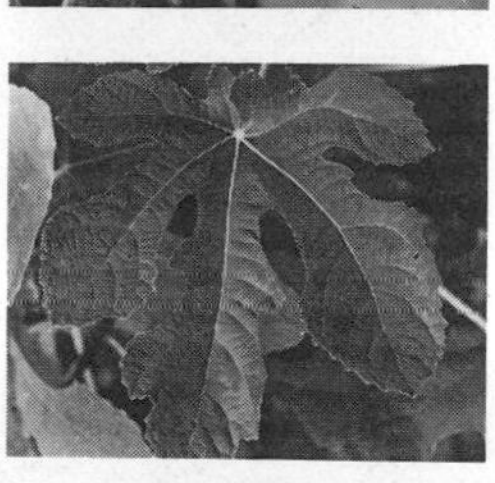

fig[1]
Ficus carica
Above: Fruit
Below: Foliage

fig[2] (fĭg) *tr.v.* **figged, figging, figs.** *Informal.* To dress or furnish with; array; furbish. Used with *up* or *out: all figged out.* —*n. Informal.* 1. Dress; array: *in full fig.* 2. Physical condition; shape: *in poor fig.* [Origin obscure.]

fig[3] (fĭg) *n.* An obscene gesture of contempt made by brandishing a fist with the thumb held between the first and second fingers. [French *(faire la) figue,* to make this gesture, from Italian *fica,* vulva, fig, from Vulgar Latin *fica* (unattested), FIG.]

fig. figurative; figuratively; figure.

fight (fīt) *v.* **fought** (fôt), **fighting, fights.** —*intr.* 1. To participate in combat or battle. 2. To struggle in any way: *fight for the lead in the game.* 3. To quarrel; argue. 4. To stand up against something or assert oneself; be aggressive. —*tr.* 1. To contend with physically or in battle. 2. To box or wrestle against in a ring. 3. To contend with or struggle against in any manner. 4. To try to prevent or undo the development of;

t tight/th thin, path/*th* this, bathe/ŭ cut/ûr urge/v valve/w with/y yes/z zebra, size/zh vision/ə about, item, edible, gallop, circus/ à *Fr.* ami/œ *Fr.* feu, *Ger.* schön/ü *Fr.* tu, *Ger.* über/KH *Ger.* ich, *Scot.* loch/N *Fr.* bon. *Follows main vocabulary. †Of obscure origin.

oppose. **5.** To wage (a battle). **6.** To do battle for; contend for: *"I now resolved that Calais should be fought to the death"* (Winston Churchill). **7.** To make (one's way), as by combat. **8.** To set in combat with another. **—fight it out.** To fight until one side is clearly the victor. **—fight off. 1.** To defend against or drive back (a hostile force). **2.** To struggle to get rid of or avoid: *fight off temptation.* *—n.* **1.** A battle waged between opposing groups; a combat. **2.** A struggle, quarrel, or conflict. **3. a.** A physical conflict between two or more individuals; a brawl. **b.** A boxing or wrestling match; a bout. **4.** The power or inclination to fight; pugnacity. —See Synonyms at **conflict.** [Fight, fought, fought; Middle English *fighten, fa(u)ght, fo(u)ghten,* Old English *feohtan, feaht, fohten.* See **pek-**[2] in Appendix.*]

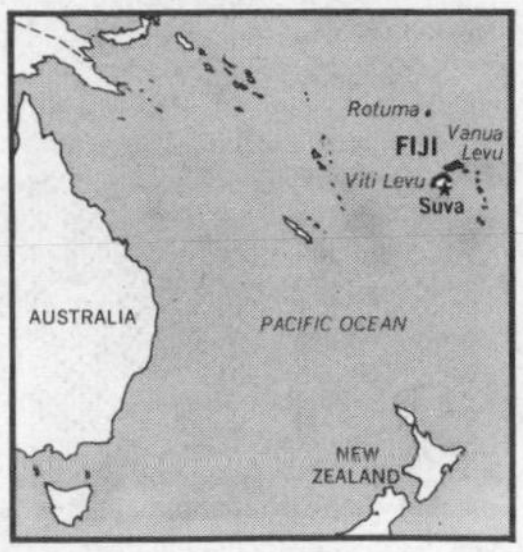

Fiji[1]

fight·er (fī′tər) *n.* **1.** One engaged in fighting; a combatant. **2.** One employed to fight; a pugilist. **3.** A pugnacious, unyielding, or determined person. **4.** *Military.* A fast, maneuverable combat aircraft used to engage enemy aircraft and to escort and defend bombers.

fight·er-bomb·er (fī′tər-bŏm′ər) *n.* An airplane capable of functioning both as a fighter and bomber.

fighter command. A combat group, larger than a wing and smaller than an air force, established by the Army Air Forces during World War II to aid ground forces by detecting and destroying enemy aircraft.

fight·ing (fī′tĭng) *adj.* **1.** Engaged in a fight or battle. **2.** Ready to fight; equipped, prepared, or inclined to oppose. **3.** Constituting extreme provocation: *fighting words.* *—n.* Combat. **—fight′ing·ly** *adv.*

fighting chance. A slight chance to win, following a struggle.

fighting cock. 1. A cock bred for fighting. **2.** *Informal.* A quarrelsome person.

fighting fish. Any of various small freshwater fishes of the genus *Betta,* of tropical Asia; especially, the **Siamese fighting fish** *(see).*

fig leaf. A stylized representation of the leaf of a fig, used especially to conceal the genitalia of male statues.

fig marigold. Any of various plants of the genus *Mesembryanthemum,* native to southern Africa, having thick, fleshy leaves and variously colored flowers.

fig·ment (fĭg′mənt) *n.* **1.** A fabrication of the imagination. **2.** An arbitrary notion. [Middle English, from Latin *figmentum,* a formation, from *fingere,* to mold, fashion. See **dheigh-** in Appendix.*]

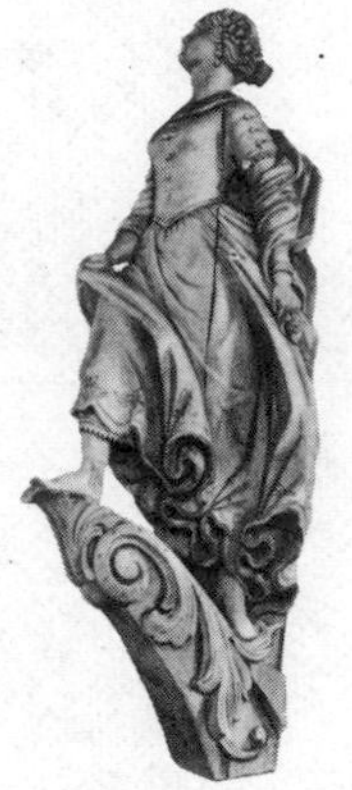

figurehead
Mid-19th-century design

fig·ur·al (fĭg′yər-əl) *adj.* Consisting of or forming a pictorial composition or design of human or animal figures.

fig·u·rant (fĭg′yə-rănt′; *French* fē-gü-räN′) *n.* **1.** A member of a corps de ballet who does not perform solos. **2.** A stage performer without a speaking part; a walk-on. [French, from the present participle of *figurer,* to figure, represent, from Old French, from Latin *figūrāre,* to form, from *figūra,* FIGURE.]

fig·ur·ate (fĭg′yər-ĭt) *adj.* Having a definite or particular shape or form; figured. [Latin *figūrātus,* past participle of *figūrāre,* to shape, from *figūra,* form, FIGURE.]

fig·ur·a·tion (fĭg′yə-rā′shən) *n.* **1.** The act of forming something into a particular shape. **2.** A shape, form, or outline. **3.** The act of representing with figures. **4.** A figurative representation, often symbolic or emblematic. **5.** *Music.* Embellishment; ornamentation.

fig·ur·a·tive (fĭg′yər-ə-tĭv) *adj. Abbr.* **fig. 1. a.** Based on or making use of figures of speech; not literal; metaphorical; rhetorical: *figurative language.* **b.** Containing many figures of speech; ornate. **2.** Represented by a figure or figures; symbolic or emblematic. **3.** Of or relating to representation by means of animal or human figures; figural. **—fig′ur·a·tive·ly** *adv.* **—fig′ur·a·tive·ness** *n.*

fig·ure (fĭg′yər) *n. Abbr.* **fig. 1.** A written symbol representing anything other than a letter; especially, a number. **2.** *Plural.* Mathematical calculation involving the use of such symbols: *He is good at figures.* **3. a.** An amount represented in numbers: *a large figure.* **b.** An estimate: *Can you give me a figure?* **4.** The outline, form, or silhouette of a thing. **5.** The shape or form of a human body, especially as regards weight and proportion: *an hourglass figure.* **6.** An individual, especially a well-known personage. **7.** The impression an individual makes through his behavior or appearance: *He cuts a dashing figure.* **8.** A person, animal, or object that symbolizes something. **9.** A pictorial or sculptural representation, especially of the human body. **10. a.** A diagram. **b.** A design or pattern. **11.** An illustration printed from an engraved plate or block. **12.** A configuration or distinct group of steps in a dance. **13.** *Music.* A brief melodic or harmonic unit often constituting the base for a larger musical phrase or structure. **14.** *Logic.* Any one of the forms that a syllogism can take, depending on the position of the middle term. **15.** *Obsolete.* An illusion; a phantasm. **16.** A **figure of speech** *(see).* —See Synonyms at **form.** *—v.* **figured, -uring, -ures.** *—tr.* **1.** To calculate with numbers; tally or work out mathematically. **2.** To make a likeness of; depict; represent. **3.** To adorn with a design or figures. **4.** *Music.* To indicate the chordal structure of (a bass line of single notes) with a sequence of conventionalized numbers. **5.** *Informal.* **a.** To conclude, believe, or predict: *What do you figure will happen?* **b.** To interpret or see: *I figure him for an impostor.* **c.** To say or think. *—intr.* **1.** To calculate; compute. **2.** To be an element; have mention, pertinence, or importance: *"the Van Winkles who figured so gallantly in the chivalrous days of Peter Stuyvesant"* (Washington Irving). **—figure on** (or **upon**). *Informal.* **1.** To depend on. **2.** To take into consideration; expect. **—figure out.** *Informal.* To solve, decipher, or comprehend. [Middle English, from Old French, from Latin *figūra,* form, shape, figure. See **dheigh-** in Appendix.*]

fig·ured (fĭg′yərd) *adj.* **1.** Shaped or fashioned. **2.** Decorated with a design; patterned: *"My dress is richly figured"* (Amy Lowell). **3.** Represented, as in graphic art or sculpture; depicted.

figured bass. *Music.* A **continuo** *(see).*

figure eight. 1. *Aviation.* The maneuver in which an aircraft flies a path tracing the outline of the number 8. **2.** The maneuver or outline made on ice by skating a continuous path shaped like the number 8. **3.** Any of various forms or representations having the shape of the number 8, such as a knot.

fig·ure·head (fĭg′yər-hĕd′) *n.* **1.** A person given a position of nominal leadership but having no actual authority or responsibility. **2.** *Nautical.* A carved, decorative figure placed on the prow of a ship.

figure of speech. An expression in which words are used, not in their literal sense, but to create a more forceful or dramatic image, as a **metaphor, simile,** or **hyperbole** *(all of which see).*

fig·u·rine (fĭg′yə-rēn′) *n.* A small ornamental figure, as one carved or formed from wood, porcelain, glass, or metal; statuette. [French, from Italian *figurina,* diminutive of *figura,* figure, from Latin *figūra,* FIGURE.]

fig·wort (fĭg′wûrt′, -wôrt′) *n.* Any of various plants of the genus *Scrophularia,* having loose, branching clusters of small greenish or purple flowers. [From FIG (in the obsolete sense of the piles for which this plant was thought to be a cure).]

Fi·ji[1] (fē′jē). A British colony in the southwestern Pacific Ocean, comprising the Fiji Islands, a group of about 250 islands with an area of 7,056 square miles, and Rotuma (18 square miles). Population, 456,000. Capital, Suva, on Viti Levu.

Fi·ji[2] (fē′jē) *n.* **1.** A native of Fiji or the Fiji Islands, being of predominantly Melanesian stock with an admixture of Polynesian. **2.** The Oceanic language of Fiji or the Fiji Islands.

Fi·ji·an (fē′jē-ən) *adj.* Of Fiji or the Fiji Islands, or the people or language of these places. *—n.* **1.** A Fiji. **2.** The language of the Fijis.

fil (fĭl) *n.* A coin equal to 1/1000 of the dinar of Iraq, Jordan, Kuwait, and Southern Yemen. See table of exchange rates at **currency.** [Mistaken as singular of earlier *fils,* from Arabic *fils, fals.*]

fi·la. Plural of **filum.**

fil·a·gree. Variant of **filigree.**

fil·a·ment (fĭl′ə-mənt) *n.* **1.** A fine or thinly spun thread, fiber, wire, or the like. **2.** A slender, threadlike appendage, part, or structure, such as the slender stalk of a stamen on which the anther is borne, or a chainlike series of cells, as in some algae. **3. a.** *Electricity.* A fine wire heated electrically to incandescence in an electric lamp. **b.** *Electronics.* A high-resistance wire or ribbon forming the cathode in some thermionic tubes. [Old French, from Medieval Latin *filamentum,* from Late Latin *filāre,* to wind threads, spin, from Latin *filum,* thread. See **gwhī-** in Appendix.*] **—fil′a·men′tous, fil′a·men′ta·ry** *adj.*

fi·lar (fī′lər) *adj.* **1.** Of or pertaining to a thread or threads. **2.** Having fine threads across the field of view for measuring small distances, as in a microscope or telescope eyepiece. [From Latin *filum,* thread. See **gwhī-** in Appendix.*]

fil·a·ree (fĭl′ə-rē′) *n.* A plant, the **alfilaria** *(see).* [Variant of American Spanish *alfilerillo,* ALFILARIA.]

fi·lar·i·a (fĭ-lâr′ē-ə) *n., pl.* **-iae** (-ē-ē′). Any of various parasitic nematode worms of the superfamily Filarioidea, that infest man and other vertebrates and are often transmitted by biting insects. [New Latin *Filaria* (former genus name), "threadworm," from Latin *filum,* thread. See **gwhī-** in Appendix.*] **—fi·lar′i·al, fi·lar′i·an** *adj.*

fil·a·ri·a·sis (fĭl′ə-rī′ə-sĭs) *n.* Infestation of tissue, especially of the lymph glands, with filariae. [New Latin : FILAR(IA) + -IASIS.]

fil·a·ture (fĭl′ə-chŏŏr′) *n.* **1.** The act or process of spinning, drawing, or twisting into threads. **2.** The act or process of reeling raw silk from cocoons. **3.** A reel used in this process. **4.** An establishment where this process is performed. [French, from Late Latin *filātus,* past participle of *filāre,* to draw out thread, spin. See **filament.**]

fil·bert (fĭl′bərt) *n.* **1.** A Eurasian shrub or tree, *Corylus maxima,* a species of hazel, cultivated for its edible nuts. **2.** The rounded, smooth-shelled nut of this shrub. [Middle English *filbert, philliberd,* from Norman French (*noix de*) *filbert,* "nut of Saint Philibert" (died A.D. 684), Frankish abbot whose feast day on August 22 marks the ripening season of the nut.]

filch (fĭlch) *tr.v.* **filched, filching, filches.** To steal (something) in a furtive manner; pilfer. See Synonyms at **rob.** [Middle English *filchen*†.] **—filch′er** *n.*

file[1] (fīl) *n.* **1.** A receptacle that keeps loose objects, such as papers, cards, or any collection of small items, in useful order. **2.** A collection of objects kept thus: *the accounts-due file.* **3. a.** A line of persons, animals, or things positioned one behind another. **b.** *Military.* A line of soldiers or vehicles so positioned. **4.** *Chess & Checkers.* Any of the rows of squares which run vertically, or between players, on a playing board. **5.** *Obsolete.* A list; roll; catalogue. **—in file.** In line, one behind another, as soldiers, pack animals, or the like. **—on file.** Catalogued or recorded in a file; entered; on hand. *—v.* **filed, filing, files.** *—tr.* **1.** To put or keep (papers or cards, for example) in useful order; to catalogue. **2.** To enter (a legal document, for example) on public record or official record. **3.** To send or submit (copy) to a newspaper or the like; especially, to transmit by wireless. *—intr.* **1.** To march or walk in a line or lines. **2.** To apply: *file for a job.* **3.** To enter one's name in a political contest: *file for Congress.* [Sense 1; Old French *fil,* "thread," wire or string on which documents are strung, from Latin *filum,* thread. See **gwhī-** in Appendix.* Sense 3; Old French *file,* from *filer,* "to draw out thread," march in a line, from Late Latin *filāre,* to spin, from Latin *filum,* thread.] —**fil′er** *n.*

file² (fīl) *n.* **1.** Any of several steel tools with hardened ridged surfaces, used in smoothing, polishing, grinding down, or boring. **2.** *British Slang.* A deceitful, cunning person. —*tr.v.* **filed, filing, files.** To smooth, polish, grind, bore, or remove with or as if with a file. [Middle English *file, fyle,* Old English *fēol, fīl.* See **peig-¹** in Appendix.*] —**fil′er** *n.*

file³ (fīl) *tr.v.* **filed, filing, files.** *Obsolete.* To sully; defile. [Middle English *filen, fulen,* Old English *fȳlan,* to make foul. See **pu-²** in Appendix.*]

file clerk. One who is employed to maintain the files and records of an office.

file·fish (fīl′fĭsh′) *n., pl.* **filefish** or **-fishes.** Any of various chiefly tropical marine fishes of the family Balistidae, related to and resembling the triggerfishes. [From the rough scales of some species.]

fi·let¹ (fĭ-lā′, fĭl′ā′) *n.* A net or lace with a simple pattern of squares. [French, from Old French *filé,* from Old Provençal *filat,* "made of threads," from *fil,* thread, from Latin *filum.* See **gwhī-** in Appendix.*]

fi·let². Variant of **fillet.**

fi·let mi·gnon (fĭ-lā′ mĭn-yŏn′; *French* fē-lĕ′ mē-nyôN′). A small, round, very choice cut of beef from the loin. [French, "small or dainty fillet."]

fil·i·al (fĭl′ē-əl) *adj.* Of, pertaining to, or befitting a son or daughter: *"My filial obedience was natural and easy"* (Gibbon). [Middle English, from Late Latin *filiālis,* from Latin *filius,* son. See **dhēi-** in Appendix.*]

fil·i·ate (fĭl′ē-āt′) *tr.v.* **-ated, -ating, -ates. 1.** To affiliate. **2.** *Law.* To assign paternity to (a bastard child, for example). [Medieval Latin *filiāre,* to acknowledge as a son, from Latin *filius,* son. See **dhēi-** in Appendix.*]

fil·i·a·tion (fĭl′ē-ā′shən) *n.* **1.** The condition or fact of being the child of a certain parent. **2.** A line of descent; derivation; family tree; lineage. **3.** The act or fact of forming a new branch, as of a society or language group; expansion or division. **4.** The branch thus formed; offshoot. **5.** *Law.* The assignment of paternity to someone, as a bastard child.

fil·i·beg (fĭl′ə-bĕg′) *n.* A kilt. [Scottish Gaelic *fèileadhbeag* : *fèileadh*†, fold, kilt + *beag,* small, little, akin to Old Irish *becc,* small, from Common Celtic *biggo-* (unattested).]

fil·i·bus·ter (fĭl′ə-bŭs′tər) *n.* **1.** The use of obstructionist tactics, such as the making of prolonged speeches or the introduction of irrelevant material, for the purpose of delaying legislative action. **2.** An instance of the use of such tactics, especially in the U.S. Senate. **3.** An adventurer who engages in a private military action in a foreign country. —*v.* **filibustered, -tering, -ters.** —*intr.* **1.** To use obstructionist tactics in a legislative body. **2.** To engage in a private military action in a foreign country. —*tr.* To use obstructionist tactics against (a bill, measure, or amendment, for example). [Originally "freebooter," from Spanish *filibustero,* from French *flibustier,* from Dutch *vrijbuiter,* pirate, "one who plunders freely" : *vrij,* free (see **prī-** in Appendix*) + *-buiter,* plunderer, from *buit,* booty, from *buiten,* to plunder, from Middle Dutch *būten,* akin to Middle Low German *būte,* BOOTY.]

fil·i·bus·ter·er (fĭl′ə-bŭs′tər-ər) *n.* One who engages in legislative filibustering.

fil·i·cide (fĭl′ə-sīd′) *n. Rare.* **1.** The act of killing one's child. **2.** One who kills his child. [Latin *filius,* son, or its derivative *filia,* daughter (see **dhēi-** in Appendix*) + -CIDE.]

fil·i·form (fĭl′ə-fôrm′, fī′lə-) *adj.* Resembling or having the form of a thread; threadlike. [Latin *filum,* thread (see **gwhī-** in Appendix*) + -FORM.]

fil·i·gree (fĭl′ə-grē′) *n.* Also **fil·a·gree, fil·la·gree. 1.** Delicate and intricate ornamental work made from gold, silver, or other fine twisted wire. **2.** Any intricate, delicate, or fanciful ornamentation. —*adj.* Resembling or made of filigree. —*tr.v.* **filigreed, -greeing, -grees.** To decorate with or as if with filigree: *"Sun pricked through the live oaks and filigreed his curving driveway"* (Philip Wylie). [Earlier *filigreen,* from French *filigrane,* from Italian *filigrana* : *fili-,* from Latin *filum,* thread (see **gwhī-** in Appendix*) + *grana,* grain, from Latin *grānum* (see **gr̥-no-** in Appendix*).]

fil·ing (fī′lĭng) *n.* A particle or shaving removed by a file. Usually used in the plural.

Fil·i·pi·no (fĭl′ə-pē′nō) *n., pl.* **-nos.** A native, citizen, or inhabitant of the Philippines. —*adj.* Of or pertaining to the Philippines or Filipinos. [Spanish, from *(Islas) Filipinas,* the PHILIPPINE (ISLANDS).]

fill (fĭl) *v.* **filled, filling, fills.** —*tr.* **1.** To put into as much as can be held; load completely; make full. **2.** To stop or plug up (an opening, for example). **3.** To satisfy or meet; fulfill: *fill the requirements.* **4.** To supply or gather together the necessary materials for (a demand or order): *fill a prescription.* **5.** To supply (an empty space) with material, such as writing, an inscription, or an illustration. **6.** To put someone into or elect to (a specific office or position); furnish with a holder or occupant. **7.** To occupy or hold (a specific office or position). **8.** To occupy the whole of; be found throughout; pervade. **9.** To occupy the whole of (the mind or thoughts, for example); consume: *"As I grew older . . . I became more and more filled with a sense of my wretchedness"* (Norman Douglas). **10.** To add a foreign substance or substances to; adulterate: *fill milk.* **11. a.** To cause (a sail) to swell. **b.** To adjust (a yard) so that wind will cause a sail to swell. —**fill (someone) in on.** *Informal.* To provide someone with additional facts, details, or the like. —**fill out. 1.** To complete by insertion or addition; fill in. **2.** To make or become fuller, rounder, broader, or shapelier. —**fill the bill.** *Informal.* To serve or perform adequately; be sufficient. —**fill up.** To make or become full. —*n.* **1.** That which is needed to make full, complete, or satisfied: *eat one's fill.* **2. a.** A built-up piece of land; embankment. **b.** The material, such as earth, gravel, or sand, used for this. —**have one's fill.** To have enough or too much; be thoroughly sated or weary. [Middle English *fillen,* Old English *fyllan.* See **pel-⁸** in Appendix.*]

fil·la·gree. Variant of **filigree.**

fille de joie (fē′y′ də zhwä′). *French.* A prostitute. [French, "daughter of joy."]

filled gold. A relatively inexpensive metal such as brass with a relatively thick surface layer of bonded gold.

filled milk. Skim milk with vegetable oils added to substitute for butter fat.

fill·er (fĭl′ər) *n.* **1.** One who fills. **2.** Something added in order to augment weight or size or to fill space. **3.** A composition, especially a semisolid that hardens on drying, used to fill pores, cracks, or holes in a wood, plaster, or other construction surface prior to finishing. **4.** Tobacco used in a plug or to form the body of a cigar. **5.** A short item used to fill space in a newspaper, magazine, or other publication. **6.** Something, such as a news item, public-service message, or music, used to fill time in a radio, television, or theatrical presentation. **7.** A sheaf of loose papers used to fill a notebook or binder. **8.** A device, such as a funnel, used to fill something. **9.** *Architecture.* Any element, such as a plate, used to fill the space between two supporting members.

fil·lér (fĭl′âr′) *n., pl.* **fillér** or **-lérs.** A coin equal to ¹/₁₀₀ of the forint of Hungary. See table of exchange rates at **currency.** [Hungarian.]

fil·let (fĭl′ĭt; *usually* fĭ-lā′, fĭl′ā′ *for sense 2*) *n.* Also **fi·let** (for sense 2). **1.** A narrow strip of ribbon or similar material. **2. a.** A strip or compact piece of boneless meat or fish. **b.** A boneless strip of meat rolled and tied, as for roasting. **3.** *Architecture.* **a.** A thin, flat molding used as separation between or ornamentation for larger moldings. **b.** A ridge between the indentations of a fluted column. **4. a.** A narrow decorative line impressed upon the cover of a book. **b.** A hand tool or wheel used in making such a line. **5.** *Heraldry.* A narrow horizontal band placed in the lower fourth area of the chief. **6.** *Anatomy.* A loop-shaped band of fibers, such as the lemniscus. —*tr.v.* (fĭl′ĭt; *usually* fĭ-lā′, fĭl′ā′ *for sense 2*), **filleted** (fĭl′ĭt-ĭd; *usually* fĭ-lād′, fĭl′ād′ *for sense 2*), **filleting** (fĭl′ĭt-ĭng; *usually* fĭ-lā′ĭng, fĭl′ā′ĭng *for sense 2*), **fillets** (fĭl′ĭts; *usually* fĭ-lāz′, fĭl′āz′ *for sense 2*). Also **fi·let** (for sense 2). **1.** To bind or decorate with or as with a fillet. **2.** To slice, bone, or make into a fillet or fillets. [Middle English *filet,* from Old French, diminutive of *fil,* thread, from Latin *filum.* See **gwhī-** in Appendix.*]

fill in. 1. To make full of a substance. **2.** To provide or insert; set down: *Fill in the age of your dependents.* **3.** To complete by insertion or addition; fill out. **4.** To act as a substitute; stand in.

fill-in (fĭl′ĭn′) *n.* **1.** One that fills a vacancy, gap, or temporary need. **2.** *Informal.* A summary of necessary or important information; a briefing.

fill·ing (fĭl′ĭng) *n.* **1.** Something used to fill a space, cavity, or container: *a custard filling in a pie; a gold filling in a tooth.* **2.** The horizontal threads that cross the warp in weaving; weft.

filling station. A retail establishment at which vehicles are serviced, especially with gasoline, oil, air, and water. Also called "gas station," "service station."

fil·lip (fĭl′əp) *n.* **1.** A snap or light blow made by pressing a fingertip against the thumb and suddenly releasing it. **2.** A slight goad or incentive; stimulus: *"It is so pleasant to receive a fillip of excitement when suffering from the dull routine"* (Trollope). —*v.* **filliped, -liping, -lips.** —*tr.* **1.** To strike or propel with a fillip. **2.** To excite, arouse, or stimulate. —*intr.* To make a fillip. [Imitative.]

Fill·more (fĭl′môr′, -mōr′), **Millard.** 1800–1874. Thirteenth President of the United States (1850–53).

fil·ly (fĭl′ē) *n., pl.* **-lies. 1.** A female colt; young mare. **2.** *Informal.* A lively and high-spirited girl. [Middle English *filli,* from Old Norse *fylja.* See **pōu-** in Appendix.*]

film (fĭlm) *n.* **1.** A thin skin or membranous coating. **2.** An abnormal, thin, opaque coating on the cornea of the eye. **3.** A haze or mist. **4. a.** Any thin covering or coating. **b.** A thin, generally flexible, transparent sheet, as of plastic or rubber, used in wrapping or packaging. **5.** A thin sheet or strip of flexible cellulose material coated with a photosensitive emulsion, used to make photographic negatives or transparencies. **6. a.** A motion picture. **b.** Motion pictures collectively regarded as an art; the cinema. —*v.* **filmed, filming, films.** —*tr.* **1.** To cover with or as if with a film. **2.** To make a motion picture of or based on. —*intr.* **1.** To become coated or obscured with or as if with a film. **2.** To make a motion picture. [Middle English *film,* Old English *filmen.* See **pel-⁴** in Appendix.*]

film·dom (fĭlm′dəm) *n.* The motion picture industry or those employed in it.

film·go·er (fĭlm′gō′ər) *n.* One who goes to see motion pictures.

film pack. A pack of sheet films that can be exposed in succession and withdrawn from the exposure position for storage at the rear of the pack.

film·strip (fĭlm′strĭp′) *n.* A length of film containing photographs, diagrams, or other graphic matter prepared for still projection.

film·y (fĭl′mē) *adj.* **-ier, -iest. 1.** Resembling or consisting of

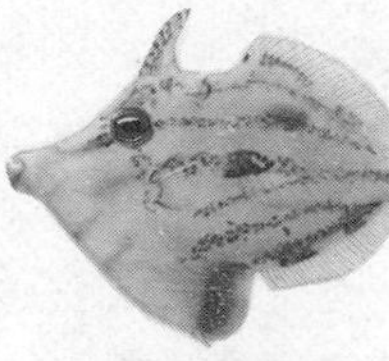

filefish
Monacanthus ciliatus

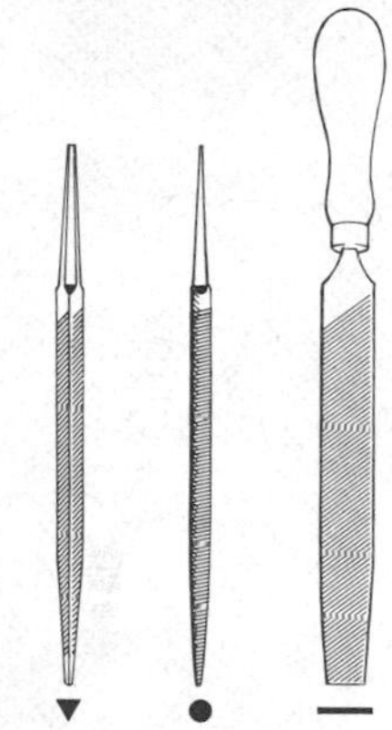

file²
Left to right: Taper file, round file, flat file, with cross sections *(below)*

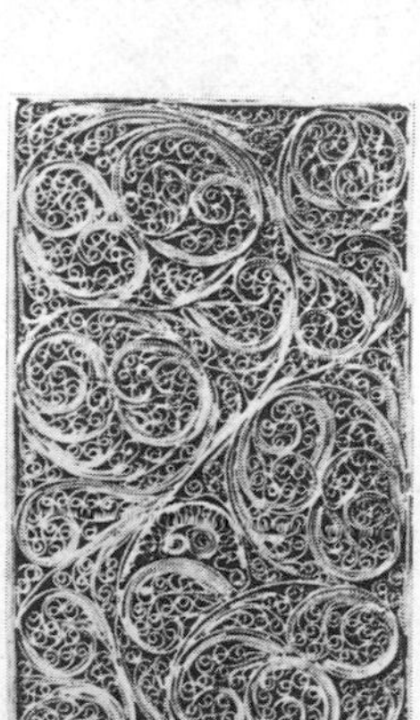

filigree

film; transparent; gauzy. **2.** Covered by or as if by a film; blurred; hazy. **—film′i·ly** *adv.* **—film′i·ness** *n.*

fil·o·plume (fĭl′ə-plo͞om′, fī′lə-) *n.* A hairlike feather having few or no barbs. [Latin *filum*, thread (see **gwhī-** in Appendix*) + PLUME.]

fi·lose (fī′lōs′) *adj.* **1.** Threadlike. **2.** Having or ending in a threadlike part. [From Latin *filum*, thread. See **gwhī-** in Appendix.*]

fils (fēs). *French.* Son. Used with a surname as the equivalent of "Junior": *a novel by Dumas fils.*

fil·ter (fĭl′tər) *n.* **1.** Any porous substance through which a liquid or gas is passed in order to remove constituents such as suspended matter. **2.** A device containing or consisting of such a substance so used. **3.** Any of various electric, electronic, acoustic, or optical devices used to reject signals, vibrations, or radiations of certain frequencies while passing others. *—v.* **filtered, -tering, -ters.** *—tr.* **1.** To pass (a liquid or gas) through a filter. **2.** To remove by passing through a filter. *—intr.* **1.** To pass through or as if through a filter: *"The chapel was flooded by the dull scarlet of light that filtered through the lower blinds"* (Joyce). **2.** To infiltrate. [Middle English *filtre*, a piece of felt (used to strain liquid), from Old French, from Medieval Latin *filtrum*, from Frankish *filtir* (unattested). See **pel-**[6] in Appendix.*] **—fil′ter·er** *n.*

fil·ter·a·ble (fĭl′tər-ə-bəl, fĭl′trə-) *adj.* Also **fil·tra·ble. 1.** Capable of being filtered; especially, capable of being removed by filtering. **2.** Sufficiently minute to pass through a fine filter, thereby maintaining the infectivity of the filtrate. Said of certain viruses and some bacteria. **—fil′ter·a·bil′i·ty** *n.*

filterable virus. A virus sufficiently small to pass through a very fine filter, thereby maintaining the infectivity of the filtrate.

filter bed. A layer of sand or gravel on the bottom of a reservoir or tank used to filter water or sewage.

filter paper. Porous paper suitable for use as a filter.

filth (fĭlth) *n.* **1. a.** Foul or dirty matter. **b.** Refuse. **2.** A dirty or corrupt condition; foulness. **3.** Material or language considered obscene, prurient, or immoral. [Middle English *filth*, *fulth*, Old English *fȳlth*, putrid matter. See **pu-**[2] in Appendix.*]

filth·y (fĭl′thē) *adj.* **-ier, -iest. 1.** Heavily soiled; very dirty. **2.** Obscene; scatological. **3.** Highly objectionable; vile; nasty. —See Synonyms at **dirty. —filth′i·ly** *adv.* **—filth′i·ness** *n.*

fil·trate (fĭl′trāt′) *v.* **-trated, -trating, -trates.** *—tr.* To put through a filter. *—intr.* To go through a filter. *—n.* The portion of the material subjected to filtration that passes through the filter. [Medieval Latin *filtrāre*, from *filtrum*, FILTER.]

fil·tra·tion (fĭl-trā′shən) *n.* The act or process of filtering.

fi·lum (fī′ləm) *n.*, *pl.* **-la** (-lə). Any threadlike anatomical structure; a filament. [Latin *filum*, thread. See **gwhī-** in Appendix.*]

fim·bri·a (fĭm′brē-ə) *n.*, *pl.* **-briae** (-brē-ē′). A fringelike part or structure, as at the opening of an oviduct in mammals. [Late Latin, fiber, fringe, from Latin *fimbriae*†, fibers, threads. See also **fringe.**]

fim·bri·ate (fĭm′brē-ĭt, -āt′) *adj.* Also **fim·bri·at·ed** (-ā′tĭd). Fringed, as the edge of a petal or the opening of a duct. [Late Latin *fimbriātus*, fringed, from FIMBRIA.]

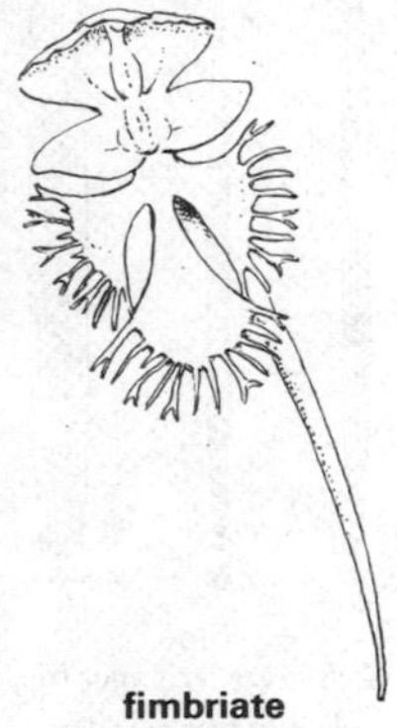

fimbriate
Fimbriate petals of a fringed orchis

fin[1] (fĭn) *n.* **1.** A membranous appendage extending from the body of a fish or other aquatic animal, used for locomotion, steering, or maintaining balance. **2.** Something resembling a fin in shape or function. **3.** *Aviation.* A fixed or movable vane or airfoil used to stabilize an aircraft or missile in flight. **4.** An appendage on a boat, such as a submarine; especially, a **fin keel** *(see).* **5.** A projecting vane used for cooling, as on a radiator or engine cylinder. **6.** An ornamental projection, as on the rear fender of an automobile. *—v.* **finned, finning, fins.** *—tr.* **1.** To equip with fins. **2.** To cut the fins from. *—intr.* To emerge with the fins above water. [Middle English *finne*, Old English *finn*, akin to Middle Low German *finne*†.]

fin[2] (fĭn) *n. Slang.* A five-dollar bill. [Yiddish *finf*, five, from Middle High German *vimf*, from Old High German *funf*, *finf*. See **penkwe** in Appendix.*]

fin. **1.** finance; financial. **2.** finish.

Fin. Finland; Finnish.

fin·a·ble (fī′nə-bəl) *adj.* Also **fine·a·ble.** Liable to a fine or fines.

fi·na·gle (fĭ-nā′gəl) *v.* **-gled, -gling, -gles.** Also **fe·na·gle.** *Informal.* *—tr.* **1.** To achieve by dubious or crafty methods; wangle. **2.** To trick or delude; deceive craftily. *—intr.* To use crafty, deceitful methods. [Origin obscure.] **—fi·na′gler** *n.*

fi·nal (fī′nəl) *adj.* **1.** Forming or occurring at the end; concluding; last. **2.** Pertaining to or constituting the end result of a process or procedure; ultimate: *the final purpose.* **3.** Decisive; conclusive; unalterable: *The judges' decision is final.* —See Synonyms at **last.** *—n.* Something that comes at or forms the end, especially: **a.** The last or one of the last of a series of athletic contests. **b.** The last examination of an academic course. [Middle English, from Old French, from Latin *fīnālis*, from *finis*†, end.]

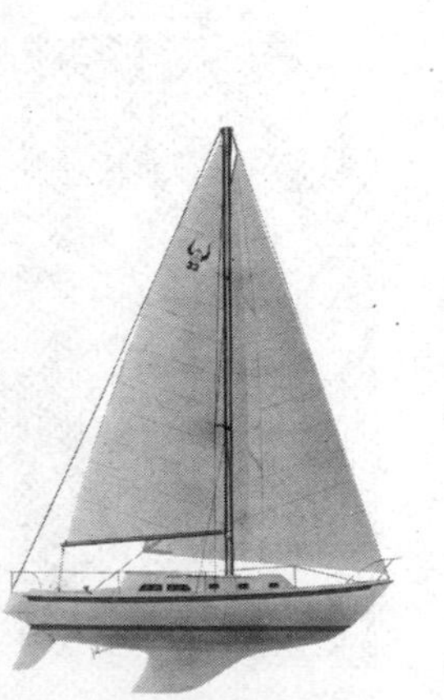

fin keel

fi·na·le (fĭ-năl′ē, -nä′lē) *n.* The concluding part of an entertainment or work, especially a musical composition. [Italian, "final," from Latin *fīnālis*, FINAL.]

fi·nal·ist (fī′nəl-ĭst) *n.* A contestant in the final session of a competition.

fi·nal·i·ty (fī-năl′ə-tē, fĭ-) *n.*, *pl.* **-ties. 1.** The condition or fact of being final; conclusiveness. **2.** A final, conclusive, or decisive act or utterance.

fi·nal·ize (fī′nə-līz′) *tr.v.* **-ized, -izing, -izes.** To put into final form; to complete.

Usage: *Finalize* is closely associated with the language of bureaucracy, in the minds of many careful writers and speakers, and is consequently avoided by them. The example *finalize plans for a class reunion* is termed unacceptable by 90 per cent of the Usage Panel. In most such examples a preferable choice is possible from among *complete, conclude, make final,* and *put in final form.*

fi·nal·ly (fī′nə-lē) *adv.* **1.** At the final point; at the end; last. **2.** Decisively; irrevocably. **3.** After a considerable delay; eventually; at last.

fi·nance (fĭ-năns′, fī′năns′, fī′năns′) *n.* **1.** *Abbr.* **fin. a.** The science of the management of money and other assets. **b.** The disposition of public revenues by a government. **2.** *Plural.* Monetary resources; funds, especially of a government or corporate body. *—v.* **financed, -nancing, -nances.** *—tr.* **1.** To supply the funds or capital for. **2.** To manage the funds of. *—intr.* To manage finances. [Middle English *finaunce*, end, settlement, payment, from Old French *finance*, from *finer*, to end, settle, from *fin*, end, from Latin *finis*. See **final.**]

finance bill. A legislative act designed to raise public revenues.

fi·nan·cial (fĭ-năn′shəl, fī-) *adj. Abbr.* **fin.** Of or pertaining to finances or those who deal with finances. **—fi·nan′cial·ly** *adv.*

Synonyms: *financial, pecuniary, fiscal, monetary.* These adjectives refer in various senses to money. *Financial* is the broadest in application but often has reference to transactions involving money on a large scale. *Pecuniary* is more appropriate to the private, small-scale dealings of individuals. *Fiscal* applies principally to the policies and practices of a branch of government as they relate to money. *Monetary* has special reference to actual money, its coinage and printing, or its circulation.

fin·an·cier (fĭn′ən-sîr′, fī-năn′-, fĭ′năn-) *n.* One who is occupied with or expert in large-scale financial affairs. [French, from Old French, from FINANCE.]

fin·back (fĭn′băk′) *n.* A whale, the **rorqual** *(see).*

finch (fĭnch) *n.* Any of various relatively small birds of the family Fringillidae, such as a goldfinch, bullfinch, cardinal, grosbeak, or canary, having a short, stout bill adapted for cracking seeds. [Middle English *finch*, Old English *finc*. See **sping-** in Appendix.*]

Finch·ley (fĭnch′lē). A former administrative division of London, England, now part of **Barnet** *(see).*

find (fīnd) *v.* **found** (found), **finding, finds.** *—tr.* **1.** To come upon by accident; meet with. **2.** To come upon after a search: *find the cause of the trouble.* **3.** To come upon through experience or study; obtain knowledge or a view of; attain: *found contentment at last.* **4.** To succeed in reaching; arrive at: *The dart found the mark.* **5.** To learn by inquiry or research; determine; ascertain. Sometimes used with *out.* **6.** To consider; regard: *I find her charm irresistible.* **7.** To recover (something lost). **8.** To recover the use of; regain: *He found his voice and replied.* **9.** To declare as a verdict or conclusion. **10.** To furnish; supply. *—intr.* To come to a legal decision or verdict: *The jury found for the defendant.* **—find oneself. 1.** To discover what one truly wishes to be and do in life. **2.** To be aware of one's presence (in a specific condition or place). *—n.* **1.** An act of finding. **2.** That which is found; especially, a rare or valuable discovery. [Find, found, found; Middle English *finden, found, founden*, Old English *findan, fand* (plural *fundon*), *funden*. See **pent-** in Appendix.*]

find·er (fīn′dər) *n.* **1.** One that finds. **2.** *Photography.* A device on a camera that indicates to the photographer what will appear in the field of view of the lens. Also called "view finder." **3.** *Astronomy.* A small telescope attached to the body of a larger one for locating an object to be observed with the larger telescope.

fin de siè·cle (făɴ də syĕk′l′). *French.* Of or characteristic of the last part of the 19th century, especially with reference to its artistic climate of effete sophistication. [French, "end of the century."]

find·ing (fīn′dĭng) *n.* **1.** Something that has been found. **2.** *Often plural.* A conclusion reached after examination or investigation. **3.** *Plural.* The tools and materials used by an artisan or workman.

fine[1] (fīn) *adj.* **finer, finest. 1.** Of superior quality, skill, or appearance; admirable. **2.** Most enjoyable; pleasant. **3.** Free from impurities: *fine copper.* **4.** *Abbr.* **f., F.** Containing pure metal in a specified proportion or amount: *gold 21 carats fine.* **5.** Cut or honed to great sharpness: *a blade with a fine edge.* **6.** Thin; slender: *fine hairs.* **7.** Showing workmanship of great care and delicacy: *fine china.* **8.** Consisting of extremely small particles; not coarse: *fine dust.* **9.** Subtle or precise: *a fine shade of meaning.* **10.** Able to make or detect subtle or precise effects; sensitive: *a fine eye for color.* **11.** Trained to the highest degree of physical efficiency; superbly conditioned: *a fine racehorse.* **12.** Of refined manners; elegant. **13.** Having no clouds; clear; sunny: *a fine day.* **14.** *Informal.* Quite well; in satisfactory health: *I'm fine, and you?* *—adv.* **1.** Finely. **2.** *Informal.* Very well: *doing fine.* *—v.* **fined, fining, fines.** *—tr.* To make finer; refine. *—intr.* To become finer, purer, or cleaner. [Middle English *fin*, from Old French, from Latin *finis*, the end (as in *finis honorum*, the height of honor). See **final.**]

fine[2] (fīn) *n.* **1.** A sum of money imposed as a penalty for an offense. **2.** *Law.* A forfeiture or penalty to be paid to the offended party in a civil action. **3.** *Law.* A fee paid to a feudal lord by his tenant. **4.** *Law.* An amicable settlement of a suit over land ownership. **5.** *Obsolete.* Finish; end; termination. **—in fine. 1.** In conclusion; finally. **2.** In summation; in brief. *—tr.v.* **fined, fining, fines.** To require the payment of a fine from; impose a fine on. [Middle English *fin*, a fine, a payment for completion, an end, from Old French, from Latin *finis*, limit, end. See **final.**]

fi·ne³ (fē'nā) *n. Music.* The end. [Italian, from Latin *fīnis,* end. See final.]

fine·a·ble. Variant of finable.

fine art. *Abbr.* **FA, F.A. 1.** Art produced or intended primarily for beauty alone rather than utility. **2.** Any of such arts, including sculpture, painting, drawing, and often architecture, literature, drama, music, and the dance. Often used in the plural. [Translation of French *beaux arts* (plural).]

fine-cut (fīn'kŭt') *adj.* Finely and evenly shredded, as tobacco.

fine-draw (fīn'drô') *tr.v.* **-drew** (-drōō'), **-drawn** (drôn'), **-drawing, -draws. 1.** To mend or sew (a seam or tear) in such a way that the joint is invisible. **2.** To draw out (wire, for example) to a slender, threadlike state.

fine-drawn (fīn'drôn') *adj.* **1.** Drawn out to a slender, threadlike state, as yarn or wire. **2.** Subtly or precisely fashioned, as an argument or theory. **3.** Delicately formed; suggestive of refinement: *fine-drawn features.*

fine-grained (fīn'grānd') *adj.* Having a fine, smooth, even grain, as leather or wood.

fine·ly (fīn'lē) *adv.* **1.** In a fine manner; excellently; splendidly. **2.** To a fine point; discriminatingly. **3.** In small pieces or parts; minutely: *finely chopped nuts.*

fine·ness (fīn'nĭs) *n.* **1.** The condition or quality of being fine. **2.** The proportion of pure metal, such as gold, in an alloy.

fin·er·y (fī'nə-rē) *n.* Elaborate adornment; fine clothing and accessories. [From FINE (excellent).]

fines herbes (fēn' ûrbz'; *French* fēn' zĕrb'). Finely chopped herbs, such as parsley, chives, tarragon, and thyme, used as a seasoning.

fine-spun (fīn'spŭn') *adj.* **1.** Spun or drawn out to extreme fineness or subtlety; elaborate and delicate. **2.** Developed to excessive fineness; overwrought.

fi·nesse (fĭ-nĕs') *n.* **1.** Artful restraint and delicacy of performance or behavior. **2.** Subtlety or tact in maneuvering; craftiness. **3.** *Bridge.* The playing of a card in a suit in which one holds a nonsequential higher card, either to induce an opponent to play an intermediate card that one's partner can then top, or to win the trick economically. **4.** Any stratagem in which one appears to decline an advantage. —See Synonyms at artifice, tact. —*v.* **finessed, -nessing, -nesses.** —*tr.* **1.** To accomplish by the use of finesse. **2.** To handle with a deceptive or evasive strategy. **3.** To play (a card) as a finesse. —*intr.* **1.** To employ finesse. **2.** To make a finesse in a card game. [Old French, delicacy, fineness, from *fin,* FINE.]

fine-toothed comb (fīn'tōōtht', -tōō*th*d'). A comb with fine teeth. —**go over with a fine-toothed comb.** To examine in exhaustive detail.

Fin·gal's Cave (fĭng'gəlz). A basalt cave, 227 feet long and 117 feet high, on Staffa Island in the Inner Hebrides, Scotland.

fin·ger (fĭng'gər) *n.* **1.** One of the five digits of the hand; especially, one other than the thumb. **2.** The part of a glove designed to cover such a member. **3.** Something resembling a finger, such as a peninsula. **4.** The length or width of a finger. **5.** *Informal.* A quantity of liquor equal to approximately a fingerbreadth. **6.** *Machinery.* Any small projecting machine part. —**burn one's fingers.** To suffer as a result of meddlesome, inquisitive, or incautious behavior. —**have (or put) a finger in the pie.** To be involved, especially meddlesomely, in some matter. —**put one's finger on.** To identify or point out with precision. —**put the finger on.** *Slang.* **1.** To inform on. **2.** To designate as the intended victim or location of a crime. —**twist (or wrap) around one's little finger.** To dominate utterly and effortlessly. —*v.* **fingered, -gering, -gers.** —*tr.* **1.** To touch with the fingers; to handle. **2.** *Music.* To mark (a manuscript) with indications of which fingers are to play the notes. **3.** *Music.* To play (an instrument) by using the fingers in a particular way. **4.** To take; steal; filch. **5.** *Slang.* To inform on. **6.** *Slang.* To designate as an intended victim. —*intr.* **1.** To handle something with the fingers. **2.** To use the fingers, especially in playing an instrument: *That violinist fingers superbly.* **3.** To be played by using the fingers in a particular way: *His clarinet fingers like yours.* [Middle English *finger,* Old English *finger.* See penkwe in Appendix.*] —**fin'ger·er** *n.*

fin·ger·board (fĭng'gər-bôrd', -bōrd') *n.* **1.** A strip of wood on the neck of a stringed instrument against which the strings are pressed in playing. **2.** The keyboard, as of a piano.

finger bowl. A small bowl or basin to hold water for rinsing the fingers at table.

fin·ger·breadth (fĭng'gər-brĕdth', -brĕtth') *n.* The breadth of one finger; approximately ¾ of an inch.

fin·gered (fĭng'gərd) *adj.* Having a finger or fingers, especially of a specific kind or appearance. Often used in compounds: *light-fingered; rosy-fingered.*

fin·ger·ing (fĭng'gər-ĭng) *n.* **1.** The technique used in playing a musical instrument with the fingers. **2.** The indication on a score of which fingers are to be used in playing.

Finger Lakes. A group of elongated glacial lakes in west-central New York State in a resort and truck-farming region.

fin·ger·ling (fĭng'gər-lĭng) *n.* **1.** A young or small fish, as a young salmon or trout. **2.** Any small object or creature.

fin·ger·nail (fĭng'gər-nāl') *n.* A thin, horny, transparent plate covering the dorsal surface of the tip of each finger.

fin·ger·paint (fĭng'gər-pānt') *v.* **-painted, -painting, -paints.** —*intr.* To engage in finger painting. —*tr.* To make by finger painting.

finger painting. 1. The technique of painting by applying color to moistened paper with the fingers. **2.** A painting so made.

finger post. A guidepost in the shape of a pointing hand.

fin·ger·print (fĭng'gər-prĭnt') *n.* An ink impression of the curves formed by the system of ridges on the skin surface of the distal phalanx of a finger; especially, such an impression used as a means of identification. —*tr.v.* **fingerprinted, -printing, -prints.** To take a fingerprint or the fingerprints of.

fin·ger·stall (fĭng'gər-stôl') *n.* A protective covering worn on an injured finger.

finger tip. Also **fin·ger·tip** (fĭng'gər-tĭp'). The extreme end or tip of a finger. —**have at one's finger tips. 1.** To have readily or instantly available. **2.** To have thorough knowledge of.

finger wave. A wave set into dampened hair using only the fingers.

fin·i·al (fĭn'ē-əl) *n. Architecture.* **1.** An ornament fixed to the peak of an arch or arched structure. **2.** Any ornamental terminating part, such as the screw on top of a lampshade. [Middle English *finial,* from adjective, "final," variant of FINAL.]

fin·i·cal (fĭn'ĭ-kəl) *adj.* Fastidious; finicky. [Probably originally university slang, irregularly from FINE (delicate).] —**fin'i·cal·i·ty, fin'i·cal·ness** *n.* —**fin'i·cal·ly** *adv.*

fin·ick·y (fĭn'ĭ-kē) *adj.* Also **fin·nick·y, fin·ick·ing** (fĭn'ĭ-kĭng), **fin·i·kin** (-kĭn). Highly fastidious in tastes or standards; difficult to please; very fussy. [From FINICAL.]

fi·nis (fĭn'ĭs, fī'nĭs) *n.* The end. Formerly used to indicate the end of a book or motion picture. [Middle English, from Latin *fīnis.* See final.]

fin·ish (fĭn'ĭsh) *v.* **-ished, -ishing, -ishes.** —*tr.* **1.** To arrive at or attain the end of: *finish a race.* **2.** To bring to an end; terminate; accomplish: *finish a task.* **3.** To consume all of; use up: *finish a pie.* **4.** To put the final touches on; bring to a desired or required state; perfect: *finish a painting.* **5.** To give (wood or cloth, for example) a desired or particular surface texture. **6.** To complete the education of. **7.** To vanquish; destroy; kill: *finish an enemy.* **8.** To bring about the ruin of: *The stock-market crash finished him.* —*intr.* **1.** To come to a conclusion; to end; stop. **2.** To reach the end of a task, course, or relationship. —See Synonyms at complete. —*n. Abbr.* **fin. 1. a.** The final part or conclusion of something; end: *a close finish in the race.* **b.** The reason for one's ruin; downfall. **2.** Something that completes, concludes, or perfects. **3. a.** The last treatment or coating of a surface. **b.** The surface texture thus produced. **4.** The material used in surfacing or finishing something: *a wax finish.* **5.** Completeness, thoroughness, or smoothness of execution; perfection. **6.** Polish or refinement in speech, manners, and the like. **7.** High-grade lumber used to finish the interior of a building. [Middle English *finishen,* from Old French *fenir, finir* (stems *feniss-, finiss-*), from Latin *fīnīre,* to limit, complete, from *fīnis,* end. See final.] —**fin'ish·er** *n.*

fin·ished (fĭn'ĭsht) *adj.* **1.** Completed; ended. **2.** Skilled; accomplished; perfected. **3.** Smooth and polished, as wood. **4.** Undone; destroyed; ruined.

finishing school. A private school that trains girls in the social graces for life in polite society.

Fin·is·terre, Cape (fĭn'ĭ-stâr'; *Spanish* fē-nēs-tĕr'rĕ). The westernmost point of mainland Spain, on the Atlantic coast of Galicia.

fi·nite (fī'nīt') *adj.* **1. a.** Having boundaries; limited. **b.** Capable of being bounded, enclosed, or encompassed. **2.** Being neither infinite nor infinitesimal. **3.** *Mathematics.* **a.** Bounded in an interval. Said of a quantity defined in an interval. **b.** Incapable of being put into one-to-one correspondence with a part of itself. Said of a set. **c.** Real or complex, as distinguished from ideal. Said of a number. **4.** Existing, persisting, or enduring for a limited time only; impermanent; transient. **5.** *Grammar.* Limited by person, number, tense, and mood; capable of serving as a predicate. Said of verbs. —*n.* Finite entities collectively; the. Preceded by *the.* [Middle English *finit,* from Latin *fīnītus,* past participle of *fīnīre,* to limit, FINISH.] —**fi'nite·ly** *adv.* —**fi'nite·ness** *n.*

fin·i·tude (fĭn'ə-tōōd', -tyōōd', fī'nə-) *n.* The quality or condition of being finite.

fink (fĭngk) *n. Slang.* **1.** A hired strikebreaker. **2.** One who informs against another. **3.** An undesirable person. —*intr.v.* **finked, finking, finks.** *Slang.* **1.** To inform. Used with *on.* **2.** To withhold support or participation. Used with *out: He finked out on me.* [Origin obscure.]

Fink (fĭngk), **Mike.** 1770?–1822. American frontiersman; subject of many legends.

fin keel. A short keel usually made of metal, with ballast on the lower edge, used chiefly on racing yachts.

Fin·land (fĭn'lənd). *Finnish* **Suo·mi** (swô'mē). *Abbr.* **Fin.** A republic, 130,000 square miles in area, of north-central Europe. Population, 4,598,000. Capital, Helsinki.

Fin·land, Gulf of (fĭn'lənd). An arm of the Baltic Sea, extending about 260 miles between Finland and the Soviet Union.

Fin·lay (fĭn'lē). The main tributary of the Peace River, flowing southeast about 210 miles through northern British Columbia, Canada.

Finn (fĭn) *n.* **1.** A native or inhabitant of Finland. Also called "Finlander." **2.** One who speaks Finnish or a Finnic language. [Swedish *Finne* (superseding Old English *Finnas,* Finns), from Germanic *Finnar* (unattested).]

fin·nan had·die (fĭn'ən hăd'ē). Also **fin·nan had·dock** (hăd'ək). Smoked haddock. [Earlier *findon haddock,* from earlier *findhorn haddock,* product of *Findhorn,* fishing port in Scotland (but confused with *Findon,* village in Kincardineshire).]

finned (fĭnd) *adj.* Having a fin, fins, or finlike parts.

Finn·ic (fĭn'ĭk) *adj.* Of or pertaining to Finland or the Finns. —*n.* A branch of Finno-Ugric.

fin·nick·y. Variant of finicky.

finial
Cathedral of Notre Dame, Paris

Finland

fingerprint
Print of a right
index finger

ă pat/ā pay/âr care/ä father/b bib/ch church/d deed/ĕ pet/ē be/f fife/g gag/h hat/hw which/ĭ pit/ī pie/îr pier/j judge/k kick/l lid, needle/m mum/n no, sudden/ng thing/ŏ pot/ō toe/ô paw, for/oi noise/ou out/ōō took/ōō boot/p pop/r roar/s sauce/sh ship, dish/t tight/th thin, path/th this, bathe/ŭ cut/ûr urge/v valve/w with/y yes/z zebra, size/zh vision/ə about, item, edible, gallop, circus/

à *Fr.* ami/œ *Fr.* feu, *Ger.* schön/ü *Fr.* tu, *Ger.* über/KH *Ger.* ich, *Scot.* loch/N *Fr.* bon. *Follows main vocabulary. †Of obscure origin.

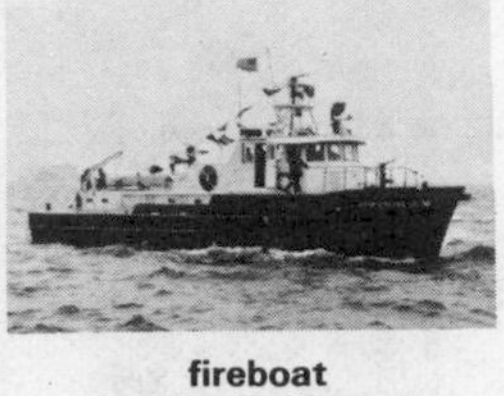

fireboat
The *John H. Glenn, Jr.*,
New York Fire Department

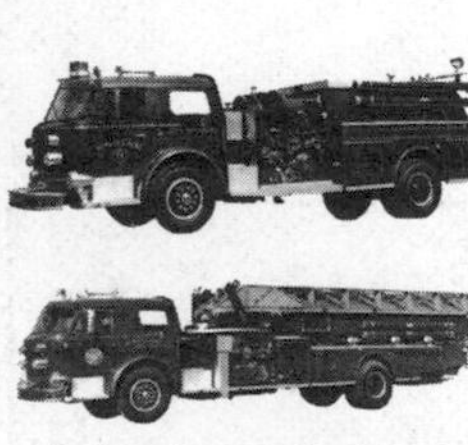

fire engine
Above: A pumper truck
Below: Four-wheel aerial ladder truck

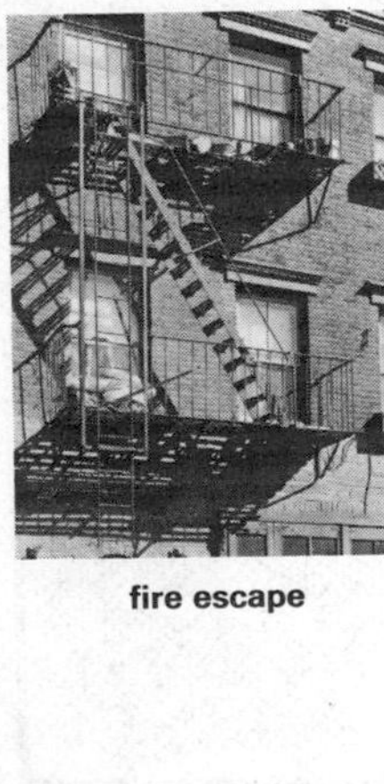

fire escape

Finn·ish (fĭn′ĭsh) *adj. Abbr.* **Fin.** Of or pertaining to Finland, its language, or its people. —*n.* The Uralic language spoken by the Finns.

Fin·no-U·gric (fĭn′ō-o͞o′grĭk, -yo͞o′grĭk) *n.* Also **Fin·no-U·gri·an** (-o͞o′grē-ən, -yo͞o′grē-ən). A subfamily of the Uralic language group, including Magyar and Estonian. —*adj.* **1.** Pertaining to the Finns and the Ugrians. **2.** Pertaining to the language of the Finns and the Ugrians.

fin·ny (fĭn′ē) *adj.* **-nier, -niest. 1.** Having a fin or fins. **2.** Resembling a fin; finlike. **3.** Of, pertaining to, or characteristic of fish.

fi·no·chi·o (fĭ-nō′kē-ō′) *n.* Also **fi·noc·chi·o.** A variety of fennel, *Foeniculum vulgare dulce,* of which the blanched stalks are eaten as a vegetable. [Italian *finocchio,* from Vulgar Latin *fēnuculum* (unattested), fennel, from Latin *fēniculum,* diminutive of *fēnum,* hay. See **dhē-** in Appendix.*]

Fins·bur·y (fĭnz′bə-rē). A former administrative division of London, England, now part of **Islington** *(see).*

Fin·ster·aar·horn (fĭn′stər-är′hôrn′). The highest peak (14,032 feet) in the Bernese Alps of central Switzerland.

fiord. Variant of **fjord.**

Fi·ot (fē-ôt′) *n.* A Bantu language of the lower Congo.

fip·pen·ny bit (fĭp′ə-nē, fĭp′nē). A Spanish coin worth about six cents, circulated in the United States until 1857. [*Fippenny,* dialectal variant of *fivepenny.*]

fip·ple (fĭp′əl) *n.* **1.** A wooden block that forms a flue at the mouth end of certain musical wind instruments. **2.** A similar object in an organ pipe. [Origin unknown.]

fipple flute. A flute with a fipple, as a recorder.

fir (fûr) *n.* **1.** Any of various evergreen trees of the genus *Abies,* having flat needles and erect cones. **2.** Any of several similar or related trees, such as the **Douglas fir** *(see).* **3.** The wood of any of these trees. [Middle English *fir(re),* Old English *fyrh, furh.* See **perkwu-** in Appendix.*]

Fir·dau·si (fĭr-dou′sē). Also **Fir·du·si** (-do͞o′sē). Pen name of Abul Kasim Mansur. A.D. 940?–1020? Persian epic poet.

fire (fīr) *n.* **1.** A rapid, persistent chemical reaction that releases heat and light; especially, the exothermic combination of a combustible substance with oxygen. **2.** Such a reaction distinguished by magnitude, destructive power, or utility: *a forest fire; a cooking fire.* **3.** *Chiefly British.* Fuel; kindling. **4. a.** Intensity, as of feeling; ardor, especially in love or rage: *the fire in a lover's eyes.* **b.** Enthusiasm. **5.** Luminosity or brilliance, as of a cut and polished gemstone. **6.** The result of inspiration; vividness; brilliance: *the fire of his verse.* **7.** An effect of heat; sensation of warmth: *the fire of strong whiskey.* **8.** A torment, trial, or tribulation. **9.** The discharge of firearms; firing. —**between two fires.** Being attacked from two sources or sides simultaneously. —**catch fire. 1.** To become ignited. **2.** To become excited or enthusiastic. —**go through fire (and water).** To experience great danger, tribulation, or torture. —**hang fire. 1.** To fail to fire or to delay firing, as a gun. **2.** To be delayed, as an event or decision. —**on fire. 1.** Ignited; burning; ablaze. **2.** Filled with enthusiasm or excitement. —**open fire. 1.** To commence shooting. **2.** To commence asking questions. —**play with fire.** To take part in a dangerous or risky situation; be foolhardy. —**set fire to** or **set on fire. 1.** To ignite. **2.** To make excited; inflame. —**take fire. 1.** To start burning. **2.** To start to be excited or enthusiastic; respond. —**under fire. 1.** Exposed or subjected to enemy attack. **2.** Exposed or subjected to critical attack or censure. —*v.* **fired, firing, fires.** —*tr.* **1.** To cause to burn; ignite. **2. a.** To add fuel to (something burning). **b.** To maintain or intensify a fire in (a boiler, for example). **3.** To bake in a kiln; *fire a flowerpot.* **4.** To dry or cure by heat: *fire tobacco.* **5.** To arouse the emotions of; make enthusiastic or ardent; stimulate: *He was fired by patriotism.* **6.** To detonate or discharge (a firearm, explosives, or a projectile): *fire a rifle; fire a bullet.* **7.** *Informal.* To project or hurl suddenly and forcefully: *fire a ball at a batter; fire inquiries at a witness.* **8.** *Informal.* To discharge from a position; dismiss: *fire an employee.* —*intr.* **1.** To become ignited; flame up. **2.** To become excited or ardent; feel deeply. **3.** To tend a fire. **4.** To have a specific reaction to being fired in a kiln: *This bowl will fire beautifully.* **5.** To become yellowed, brown, or blotchy before reaching maturity, as grain. **6.** To discharge; go off: *The mortar fired toward the enemy.* **7.** To detonate or shoot a weapon: *He fired at the enemy.* **8.** *Informal.* To project or hurl a missile. —**fire away.** To commence; especially, to commence asking questions. —**fire up. 1.** To start a fire in. **2.** To become excited or emotional. [Middle English *fir, fur, feir, fire,* Old English *fȳr.* See **pūr-** in Appendix.*]

fire alarm. *Abbr.* **f.a. 1.** An announcement of the outbreak of a fire. **2.** A device, as a bell or siren, used in announcing the outbreak of a fire.

fire-and-brim·stone (fīr′ən-brĭm′stōn′) *adj.* **1.** Characteristic or suggestive of hellfire. **2.** Extremely zealous: *a fire-and-brimstone evangelist.* [From *fire and brimstone,* which God often used to destroy sinners. Revelation 20:10.]

fire ant. Any of several ants of the genus *Solenopsis;* especially, *S. geminata* or *S. saevissima,* of the southern United States and tropical America, that build conspicuous mounds and are capable of inflicting a painful sting.

fire·arm (fīr′ärm′) *n.* Any weapon capable of firing a missile, especially a pistol or rifle using an explosive charge as a propellant.

fire·ball (fīr′bôl′) *n.* **1.** Any brilliantly burning sphere. **2.** An exceptionally bright meteor. **3.** A highly luminous, intensely hot, spherical cloud of dust, gas, and vapor generated by a nuclear explosion. **4.** *Slang.* A highly energetic person.

fire beetle. Any of various tropical American click beetles of the genus *Pyrophorus;* especially, *P. noctilucus,* having brightly luminous spots.

fire·bird (fīr′bûrd′) *n.* Broadly, any of various birds having bright scarlet or orange plumage, such as the Baltimore oriole.

fire blight. A destructive disease of apples, pears, and related trees and plants, caused by a bacterium, *Erwinia amylovora.* [From the scorched appearance it produces.]

fire·board (fīr′bôrd′, -bōrd′) *n.* A screen or board used to close off a fireplace when not in use.

fire·boat (fīr′bōt′) *n.* A boat equipped to fight fires along waterfronts and on ships.

fire bomb. An **incendiary bomb** *(see).*

fire·box (fīr′bŏks′) *n.* **1.** A chamber in which fuel is burned, especially the furnace of a steam locomotive. **2.** A box containing a device for sounding a fire alarm.

fire·brand (fīr′brănd′) *n.* **1.** A piece of burning wood. **2.** A person who stirs up trouble or kindles a revolt.

fire·brat (fīr′brăt′) *n.* A small, wingless insect, *Thermobia domestica,* frequenting warm areas of dwellings, and often destructive to paper and other materials.

fire·break (fīr′brāk′) *n.* A strip of cleared or plowed land used to stop the spread of a fire. Also called "fireguard," "fire line."

fire·brick (fīr′brĭk′) *n.* A refractory brick, especially of fire clay, used for lining furnaces, fireboxes, chimneys, or fireplaces.

fire bug. The **harlequin bug** *(see).*

fire·bug (fīr′bŭg′) *n. Informal.* A person who deliberately sets fires to property; a pyromaniac.

fire clay. A type of heat-resistant clay used in the making of firebricks, crucibles, and other objects exposed to high temperatures.

fire company. 1. An organized body of firefighters. Also called "fire brigade." **2.** A business firm that sells fire insurance.

fire control. *Abbr.* **FC** The control of the delivery of gunfire on military targets.

fire·crack·er (fīr′krăk′ər) *n.* A small explosive charge in a cylinder of heavy paper, used to make noise, as at celebrations.

fire-cure (fīr′kyo͝or′) *tr.v.* **-cured, -curing, -cures.** To cure (tobacco) by exposing it to the heat and smoke of a wood fire.

fire·damp (fīr′dămp′) *n.* **1.** A combustible gas, chiefly methane, occurring naturally in coal mines and forming explosive mixtures with air. **2.** The explosive mixture itself.

fire department. *Abbr.* **F.D.** A department, especially of a municipal government, whose purpose is preventing and putting out fires.

fire·dog (fīr′dôg′, -dŏg′) *n.* An **andiron** *(see).*

fire·drake (fīr′drāk′) *n.* A fiery dragon of Germanic mythology. [Middle English *firdrake,* Old English *fȳr-draca* : *fȳr,* FIRE + *draca,* dragon, DRAKE.]

fire drill. A practice exercise in the use of fire-fighting equipment or the exit procedure to be followed in case of a fire.

fire-eat·er (fīr′ē′tər) *n.* **1.** A performer who pretends to swallow fire. **2.** A vigorous or pugnacious person.

fire engine. Any of various large motor vehicles that carry firemen and equipment to a fire, and that support extinguishing operations, as by pumping water or raising telescoping ladders.

fire escape. Any structure or device, as a metal ladder or an outside stairway attached to a building, erected for emergency exit in the event of fire.

fire extinguisher. A portable apparatus containing chemicals that can be discharged in a jet to extinguish a small fire.

fire·fly (fīr′flī′) *n., pl.* **-flies.** Any of various nocturnal beetles of the family Lampyridae, characteristically having luminous abdominal organs that produce a flashing light.

fire·guard (fīr′gärd′) *n.* **1.** A metal screen placed in front of an open fireplace to catch sparks. Also called "fire screen." **2.** A **firebreak** *(see).*

fire·house (fīr′hous′) *n.* A **fire station** *(see).*

firehouse dog. A Dalmatian.

fire hydrant. A **hydrant** *(see).*

fire insurance. Insurance against the damage or loss of property as a result of fire or lightning.

fire irons. The equipment used to tend a fireplace, including tongs, a shovel, and a poker.

Fire Island. A sandbank island and resort off the southern shore of Long Island, New York State.

fire·less cooker (fīr′lĭs). An insulated container which when preheated retains the heat sufficiently to cook food.

fire·light (fīr′līt′) *n.* The light from a fire, as in a fireplace or at a campsite.

fire line. A strip of cleared land, a **firebreak** *(see).*

fire·lock (fīr′lŏk′) *n.* A **flintlock** *(see).*

fire·man (fīr′mən) *n., pl.* **-men** (-mĭn). **1.** A man employed by a fire department to fight fires. **2.** A man who tends fires; a stoker. **3.** *U.S. Navy.* An enlisted man engaged in the operation of the engineering machinery. **4.** *Baseball.* A relief pitcher.

fire-new (fīr′no͞o′, -nyo͞o′) *adj.* Brand-new.

Fi·ren·ze. The Italian name for **Florence.**

fire opal. An opal with brilliant flamelike yellow, orange, and red colors. Also called "girasol."

fire·pan (fīr′păn′) *n.* A metal grate or brazier.

fire pink. A plant, *Silene virginica,* of eastern North America, having red flowers with narrow, notched petals.

fire·place (fīr′plās′) *n.* **1.** An open recess for holding a fire at the base of a chimney; hearth. **2.** A structure, usually of stone or brick, for holding an outdoor fire.

fire·plug (fīr′plŭg′) *n.* A large pipe at which water may be drawn from a water main for use in extinguishing a fire; a hydrant. Also called "plug."

ă pat/ā pay/âr care/ä father/b bib/ch church/d deed/ĕ pet/ē be/f fife/g gag/h hat/hw which/ĭ pit/ī pie/îr pier/j judge/k kick/l lid, needle/m mum/n no, sudden/ng thing/ŏ pot/ō toe/ô paw, for/oi noise/ou out/o͝o took/o͞o boot/p pop/r roar/s sauce/sh ship, dish/

fire·pow·er (fīr′pou′ər) *n.* The capacity, as of a weapon, military unit, or ship, for discharging fire.
fire·proof (fīr′pro͞of′) *adj.* Capable of withstanding or preventing damage by fire. —*tr.v.* **fireproofed, -proofing, -proofs.** To make fireproof.
fir·er (fīr′ər) *n.* **1.** One who kindles, builds, or tends a fire. **2.** A firearm, considered with respect to the speed or technique of its firing. Often used in combination: *rapid-firer.*
fire sale. A sale of commodities damaged by fire.
fire screen. A **fireguard** *(see).*
fire ship. A military vessel loaded with explosives and combustible material and set adrift among enemy ships or fortifications to destroy them.
fire·side (fīr′sīd′) *n.* **1.** The area immediately surrounding a fireplace or hearth. **2.** Home.
fire station. A building for fire equipment and firemen. Also called "firehouse."
fire·stone (fīr′stōn′) *n.* **1.** A flint or pyrites used to strike a fire. **2.** A fire-resistant stone, as certain sandstones, used as a construction material.
fire thorn. Any of various thorny shrubs of the genus *Pyracantha,* native to Asia, and often cultivated for their evergreen foliage and showy reddish or orange berries.
fire tower. A tower in which a lookout for fires is posted.
fire·trap (fīr′trăp′) *n.* A building susceptible to catching fire easily or difficult to escape from in the event of fire.
fire wall. A fireproof wall used as a barrier to prevent the spread of a fire.
fire·wa·ter (fīr′wô′tər, -wŏt′ər) *n. Slang.* Strong liquor, especially whiskey. [Translation of some Algonquian term such as Ojibwa *iškotēwābō.*]
fire·weed (fīr′wēd′) *n.* **1.** A species of willow herb, *Epilobium angustifolium,* having terminal clusters of pinkish-purple flowers. **2.** A weedy North American plant, *Erechtites hieracifolia,* having small white or greenish flowers. Also called "pilewort." **3.** Any of various other plants often appearing as the first vegetation in burned-over areas.
fire·wood (fīr′wo͝od′) *n.* Wood used as fuel.
fire·work (fīr′wûrk′) *n.* **1.** *Usually plural.* Any of various combinations of explosives and combustibles used to generate colored lights, smoke, and noise for amusement. **2.** *Plural.* A display of such devices. **3.** *Plural.* An exciting or spectacular display, as of musical or literary virtuosity.
fir·ing (fīr′ĭng) *n.* **1.** The application of fire or heat, as in the hardening or glazing of ceramics. **2.** The discharging of firearms or cannon. **3.** Fuel for fires.
firing line. **1.** The line of positions from which fire is directed against a target. **2.** The vanguard of an activity or pursuit.
firing pin. The part of the bolt or breech of a firearm that strikes the primer and explodes the charge of the projectile.
firing squad. **1.** A detachment assigned to shoot persons condemned to death. **2.** A detachment of soldiers chosen to fire a salute at a military funeral.
fir·kin (fûr′kĭn) *n.* **1.** A small wooden barrel or keg, used especially for storing butter, cheese, or lard. **2.** Any of several British units of capacity, usually equal to about ¼ of a barrel or nine gallons. [Middle English *ferdekin, ferken,* a cask, one-fourth of a barrel, probably from Middle Dutch *vierdelkijn* (unattested), "little quarter," diminutive of *vierdel,* fourth part : *vierde,* fourth (see **kwetwer-** in Appendix*) + *deel,* part, deal (see **dail-** in Appendix*).]
firm[1] (fûrm) *adj.* **firmer, firmest.** **1.** Unyielding to pressure; solid. **2.** Not easily moved or detached; securely fixed in place. **3.** Indicating determination or resolution. **4.** Constant; steadfast: *a firm ally.* **5.** Fixed formally; definite; final: *a firm bargain.* **6.** Unfluctuating; steady. Said of prices. —*v.* **firmed, firming, firms.** —*tr.* To make firm. —*intr.* To become firm. —*adv.* Resolutely; unwaveringly: *stand firm; hold firm.* [Middle English *ferm,* from Old French *ferme,* from Latin *firmus.* See **dher-**[2] in Appendix.*] —**firm′ly** *adv.* —**firm′ness** *n.*
firm[2] (fûrm) *n.* **1.** A commercial partnership of two or more persons. **2.** The name or designation under which such an establishment transacts business. [Italian *firma,* signature, name of a business establishment or partnership, from *firmare,* to sign, "confirm by signature," from Late Latin *firmāre,* to confirm, from Latin, to strengthen, from *firmus,* FIRM.]
fir·ma·ment (fûr′mə-mənt) *n.* The vault or expanse of the heavens; sky. [Middle English, from Old French, from Late Latin *firmāmentum* (translation of Greek *stereōma,* heavenly vault, translation of Hebrew *rāqī'a*), from Latin, a strengthening, support, from *firmāre,* to make firm, from *firmus,* FIRM.] —**fir′ma·men′tal** (-mĕnt′l) *adj.*
fir·mer chisel (fûr′mər). A chisel or gouge with a thin blade, used manually to shape and finish wood. Also called "firmer." [From French *fermoir,* variant (influenced by *fermer,* to make firm) of Old French *formoir,* from *former,* to form, shape, from Latin *fōrmāre,* from *fōrma,* FORM.]
firn (fĭrn) *n.* Snow that has been partially consolidated by thawing and freezing but not yet converted to glacial ice. [German *Firn,* "last year's (snow)," from (Swiss dialect) *firn,* of last year, from Old High German *firni,* old. See **per**[1] in Appendix.*]
fir·ry (fûr′ē) *adj.* Consisting of or abounding in firs.
first (fûrst) *adj.* **1.** Coming or located before all others. **2.** Occurring or acting prior to all others; earliest. **3.** Ranking above all others in importance or quality; foremost; best. **4.** *Music.* Highest in pitch or foremost in carrying melody: *first soprano; first trumpet.* **5.** Of or pertaining to the transmission gear, or corresponding gear ratio, used to produce the range of lowest drive speeds in an automotive vehicle. —**in the first place.** To begin with. —*adv.* **1.** Before or above all others in time or rank. **2.** For the first time. **3.** Preferably; rather. —*n.* **1.** The ordinal number one in a series. Also written 1st. **2.** The one coming, occurring, or ranking before or above all others. **3.** The beginning; outset: *from the first; at first.* **4.** *Music.* The voice or instrument highest in pitch or foremost in carrying melody. **5.** The transmission gear or corresponding gear ratio used to produce the range of lowest drive speeds in an automotive vehicle. **6.** The winning position in a contest. **7.** *Plural.* The best grade or quality of merchandise. [Middle English *first,* Old English *fyrst.* See **per**[1] in Appendix.*]
Usage: *First* and *last* now usually precede the numeral in collective expressions such as *the first two chapters* and *the last four pages,* with reference to a single book or the like. An alternative and older form, illustrated by *the two first chapters* and *the four last pages,* is used only where low numerals or numbers are involved. Both forms are acceptable, according to the Usage Panel; 51 per cent consider *first two* and *last four* preferable in current writing and speech.
first aid. Emergency treatment administered to injured or sick persons before professional medical care is available.
first base. *Baseball.* **1.** The first of the bases in the infield, counterclockwise from home plate. **2.** The fielding position occupied by the first baseman.
first baseman. *Baseball.* The infielder stationed at or near first base.
first-born (fûrst′bôrn′) *adj.* First in order of birth; born first. —*n.* The first-born child.
first class. **1.** The first, highest, or best group of a specified category. **2.** The most luxurious and most expensive class of accommodations on a train, passenger ship, airplane, or other conveyance. **3.** A class of mail including letters, post cards, and packages sealed against inspection.
first-class (fûrst′klăs′) *adj.* **1.** Indicating the first, highest, or best group of a specified category. **2.** Of the foremost excellence or highest quality; first-rate: *a first-class mind.* —*adv.* **1.** In first-class accommodations. **2.** By first-class mail.
first cousin. See **cousin.**
first-de·gree burn (fûrst′dĭ-grē′). See **burn.**
first floor. **1.** The ground floor of a building. **2.** *Chiefly British.* The floor immediately above the ground floor.
first fruit. Also **first fruits.** **1.** The first product of a season's harvest. **2.** The first result or profit of an undertaking.
first·hand (fûrst′hănd′) *adj.* Received from the original source: *firsthand information.* —*adv.* From the original source; directly. [Originally, *at (the) first hand.*]
First International. See **International.**
first lady. **1.** *Sometimes capital* **F,** *capital* **L.** The wife or hostess of the chief executive of a country, state, or city. **2.** The foremost woman of a specified profession or art: *the first lady of the ballet.*
first lieutenant. See **lieutenant.**
first·ling (fûrst′lĭng) *n.* **1.** The first of a kind or category. **2.** The first-born offspring.
first·ly (fûrst′lē) *adv.* Before all others; in the first place; to begin with.
first mate. A ship's officer ranking immediately below the captain.
first person. **1.** A category of linguistic forms, such as verbs or pronouns, designating the speaker or writer of the sentence in which they appear. **2.** One of these forms; for example, *I, we.* **3.** A discourse or literary style in which the narrator recounts his own experiences and impressions using such forms: *a novel written in the first person.*
first-rate (fûrst′rāt′) *adj.* Foremost in quality or rank. —*adv. Informal.* Excellently; very well.
first sergeant. In the U.S. Army, the highest ranking noncommissioned officer of a company or other military unit.
first water. **1.** The highest degree of quality or purity in diamonds or pearls. **2.** The foremost rank or quality: *a pianist of the first water.* [Probably a translation of Arabic *mā',* water luster.]
First World War. **World War I** *(see).*
firth (fûrth) *n. Chiefly Scottish.* A long, narrow inlet of the sea; fjord. [Middle English *ford, furth,* from Old Norse *fjördhr.* See **per-**[2] in Appendix.*]
Firth of Clyde. See **Clyde.**
Firth of Forth. See **Forth.**
Firth of Tay. See **Tay.**
fisc (fĭsk) *n.* The treasury of a kingdom or state. [Old French, from Latin *fiscus,* woven basket, money basket used by tax collectors, treasury. See **fiscal.**]
fis·cal (fĭs′kəl) *adj.* **1.** Of or pertaining to the treasury or finances of a nation or branch of government. **2.** Of or pertaining to finances in general: *a fiscal agent.* —See Synonyms at **financial.** [Old French, from Latin *fiscālis,* from *fiscus*†, treasury, basket.] —**fis′cal·ly** *adv.*
fiscal year. *Abbr.* **FY** A 12-month period for which an organization plans the use of its funds.
Fisch·er (fĭsh′ər), **Emil Hermann.** 1852–1919. German organic chemist.
Fisch·er (fĭsh′ər), **Hans.** 1881–1945. German chemist.
fish (fĭsh) *n., pl.* **fish** or **fishes.** **1.** Any of numerous cold-blooded aquatic vertebrates of the superclass Pisces, characteristically having fins, gills, and a streamlined body, and including: **a.** Any of the class Osteichthyes, having a bony skeleton. **b.** Any of the class Chondrichthyes, having a cartilaginous skeleton, and including the sharks, rays, and skates. **c.** Any of the class Agnatha, lacking jaws, and including the lampreys and

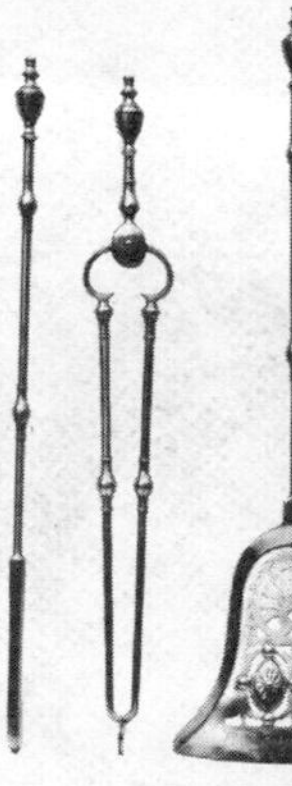

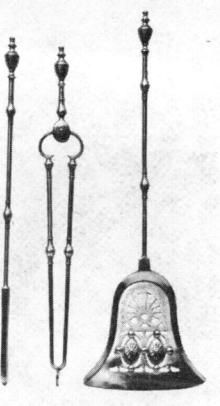

fire irons
Late 18th-century English

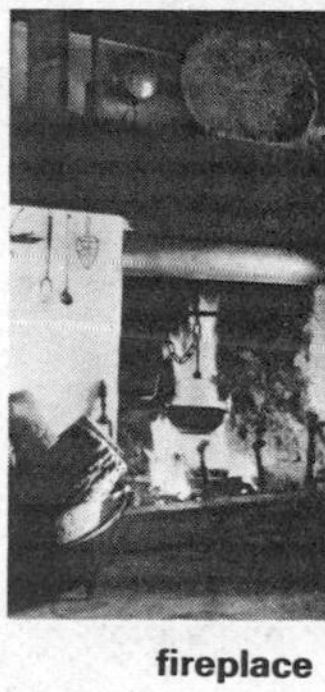

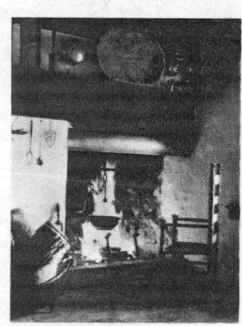

fireplace

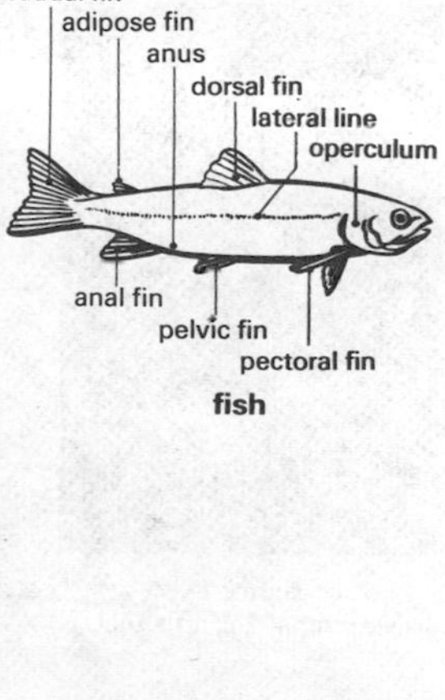
caudal fin
adipose fin
anus
dorsal fin
lateral line
operculum
anal fin
pelvic fin
pectoral fin

fish

hagfishes. **2.** Any of various unrelated aquatic animals, such as a jellyfish, cuttlefish, or crayfish. **3.** *Informal.* A person likened to a fish for lacking some human attribute or advantage: *a cold fish; a poor fish.* —*v.* **fished, fishing, fishes.** —*intr.* **1.** To catch or try to catch fish. **2.** To search or hunt for something in or under water: *fish for sponges.* **3.** To look for something by feeling one's way; grope. **4.** To seek something by circumlocution: *fish for compliments.* —*tr.* **1.** To catch or try to catch fish in. **2.** To catch or pull up in the manner of one who fishes. Used with *out* or *from.* [Middle English *fish, fisk,* Old English *fisc.* See **peisk-** in Appendix.*]

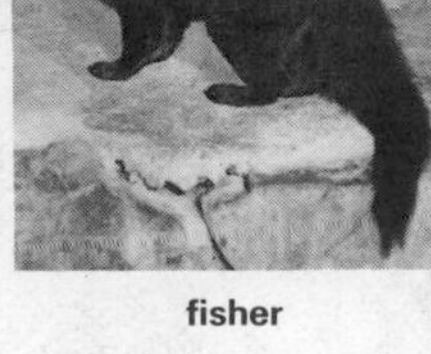
fisher

Fish (fĭsh) *pl.n.* The constellation and sign of the zodiac, **Pisces** *(see).* Usually preceded by *the.*

Fish (fĭsh), **Hamilton.** 1808–1893. U.S. Secretary of State (1869–77).

fish and chips. Fried fillets of fish and French-fried potatoes.

fish·bowl (fĭsh′bōl′) *n.* Also **fish bowl.** **1.** A transparent bowl in which live fish are kept. **2.** Something that can be seen through on all sides or at all points.

fish cake. A fried cake, patty, or ball of chopped fish, often mixed with potato or rice. Also called "fish ball."

fish crow. A crow, *Corvus ossifragus,* of the coast and rivers of the eastern United States.

fish·er (fĭsh′ər) *n.* **1.** One that fishes; a fisherman. **2. a.** A carnivorous mammal, *Martes pennanti,* of northern North America, having thick, dark-brown fur. Also called "pekan." **b.** The fur of this animal.

Fish·er (fĭsh′ər), **Saint John.** 1459–1535. English Roman Catholic bishop and martyr; canonized (1935).

fish·er·man (fĭsh′ər-mən) *n., pl.* **-men** (-mĭn). **1.** One who fishes as an occupation or sport. **2.** A commercial fishing vessel.

fisherman's bend. A knot used to secure the end of a line to a ring or spar, made by two turns with the end passing back under both.

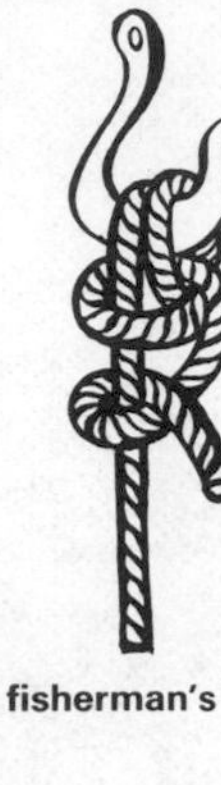
fisherman's bend

fisherman's knot. A knot used to join two lines, made by securing either end to the opposite standing part by an overhand knot. Also called "Englishman's tie."

fish·er·y (fĭsh′ə-rē) *n., pl.* **-ies.** **1.** The industry or occupation of catching, processing, or selling fish, shellfish, or similar aquatic products. **2.** A fishing ground. **3.** A hatchery for fish. **4.** The legal right to fish in specified waters or areas.

Fish·es (fĭsh′ĭz) *pl.n.* The constellation and sign of the zodiac, **Pisces** *(see).* Usually preceded by *the.*

fish·eye (fĭsh′ī′) *n.* A suspicious and unsympathetic stare. Often preceded by *the: give him the fisheye.*

fish flour. A flour made of dried and powdered fish.

fish fry. **1.** A cookout or other meal at which fried fish is the main course. **2.** Fried fish.

fish·gig (fĭsh′gĭg′) *n.* Also **fiz·gig** (fĭz′-). A pronged instrument for spearing fish. [Variant (influenced by FISH) of earlier *fisgig,* from Spanish *fisga*†.]

fish hawk. The **osprey** *(see).*

fish·hook (fĭsh′hŏŏk′) *n.* A barbed metal hook used for catching fish.

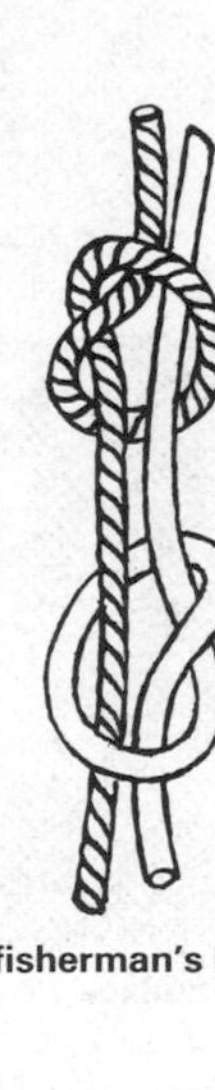
fisherman's knot

fish·ing (fĭsh′ĭng) *n.* **1.** The act or practice of one that fishes. **2.** A place for catching fish; fishery.

fishing rod. A rod of wood, steel, or fiber glass used with a line for catching fish.

fish joint. A joint formed by bolting fishplates to either side of two rails, timbers, or beams.

fish·meal (fĭsh′mēl′) *n.* A nutritive mealy substance produced from fish or fish parts and used as animal feed and fertilizer.

fish·mon·ger (fĭsh′mŭng′gər, -mŏng′gər) *n. Chiefly British.* One who sells fish.

fish·net (fĭsh′nĕt′) *n.* **1.** A net for catching fish. **2.** A meshed openwork fabric resembling netting used for catching fish. —*adj.* Meshed or woven together like a fishing net: *fishnet stockings.*

fish·plate (fĭsh′plāt′) *n.* One of the connecting metal plates bolted along the side of two rails or beams placed end to end, used especially in the laying of railroad track. [Earlier *fish,* a piece of wood used to strengthen a ship's mast, fishplate, probably from Old French *fiche,* peg, nail, joint, from *ficher,* to drive in, fix, from Vulgar Latin *figicāre* (unattested), from Latin *figere,* to fasten, FIX + PLATE.]

fish·pond (fĭsh′pŏnd′) *n.* A small body of clear water abounding in edible fish.

fish·skin disease (fĭsh′skĭn′). A disease, **ichthyosis** *(see).*

fish stick. A piece of fish fillet, breaded, cut in an oblong shape, and baked, broiled, or fried.

fish story. *Informal.* An implausible and boastful story. [From stories of fishermen who exaggerate the size of their catch.]

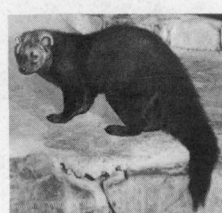

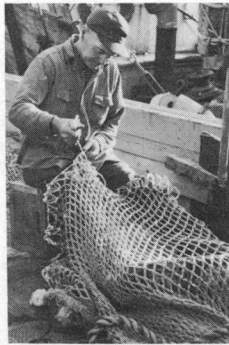

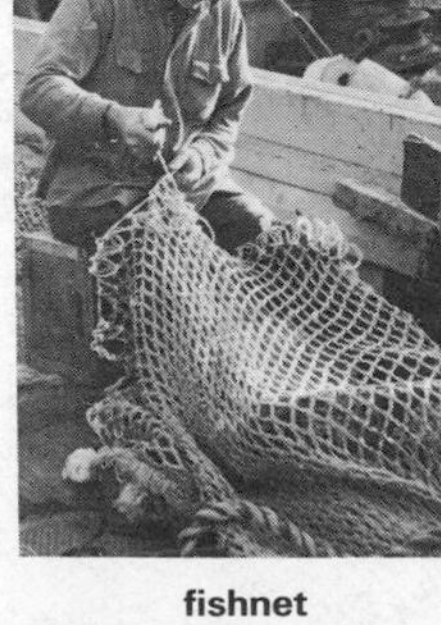
fishnet
Man repairing a fishnet

fish·tail (fĭsh′tāl′) *adj.* Resembling or suggestive of the tail of a fish in shape or movement. —*intr.v.* **fishtailed, -tailing, -tails.** *Slang.* To swing the tail or rear end of an automobile, aircraft, or other vehicle from side to side while moving forward. —*n.* *Slang.* A fishtailing maneuver.

fish·wife (fĭsh′wīf′) *n., pl.* **-wives** (-wīvz′). **1.** A woman who sells fish. **2.** A coarse, abusive woman; termagant; shrew.

fish·y (fĭsh′ē) *adj.* **-ier, -iest.** **1.** Resembling or suggestive of fish, as in taste or odor. **2.** Cold or expressionless: *a fishy stare.* **3.** *Informal.* **a.** Unlikely; questionable. **b.** Inspiring suspicion; dubious. —**fish′i·ly** *adv.* —**fish′i·ness** *n.*

Fisk (fĭsk), **James.** 1834–1872. American railroad magnate and financier.

fissi-. Indicates a split or cleft shape; for example, **fissipalmate.** [From Latin *fissus,* past participle of *findere,* to cleave, split. See **bheid-** in Appendix.*]

fis·sile (fĭs′əl, fĭs′īl′) *adj.* **1.** Capable of being split. **2.** *Physics.* Fissionable, especially by neutrons of all energies. [Latin *fissilis,* from *fissus,* split. See **fissi-**.] —**fis·sil′i·ty** (fĭ-sĭl′ə-tē) *n.*

fis·sion (fĭsh′ən) *n.* **1.** The act or process of splitting into parts. **2.** *Physics.* A nuclear reaction in which an atomic nucleus splits into fragments, usually two fragments of comparable mass, with the evolution of approximately 100 million to several hundred million electron volts of energy. Also called "nuclear fission." Compare **fusion.** **3.** *Biology.* An asexual reproductive process in which a unicellular organism splits into two or more independently maturing daughter cells. [Latin *fissiō,* from *fissus,* past participle of *findere,* to split. See **bheid-** in Appendix.*]

fis·sion·a·ble (fĭsh′ən-ə-bəl) *adj.* Capable of undergoing fission; especially, capable of being induced to undergo nuclear fission by slow neutrons.

fis·si·pal·mate (fĭs′ə-păl′māt′) *adj.* Having lobed or partially webbed, separated toes, as the feet of certain birds.

fis·sip·a·rous (fĭ-sĭp′ər-əs) *adj.* Reproducing by biological fission. [FISSI- + -PAROUS.]

fis·si·ped (fĭs′ə-pĕd′) *adj.* Having the toes separated from one another, as certain carnivorous mammals. —*n.* A carnivorous mammal having such toes. [Late Latin *fissipēs* : FISSI- + -PED.]

fis·sure (fĭsh′ər) *n.* **1.** A narrow crack or cleft, as in a rock face. **2.** The process of separation or division. **3.** A schism; a split. **4.** *Anatomy.* A groove or furrow, as in the liver or brain, that divides an organ into lobes or separates it into areas. —*v.* **fissured, -suring, -sures.** —*tr.* To cause a fissure in; to split. —*intr.* To form fissures; become cleft; crack. [Middle English, fracture, opening, from Old French, from Latin *fissūra,* from *fissus.* See **fission.**]

fist (fĭst) *n.* **1.** The hand closed tightly, with the fingers bent against the palm. **2.** *Informal.* A grasping hand; a clutch: *Don't let him get his fists on this.* **3.** *Informal.* Distinctive handwriting. **4.** A printer's mark, **index** *(see).* —*tr.v.* **fisted, fisting, fists.** **1.** To clench (one's hand) into a fist. **2.** *Nautical.* To grasp or handle: *fisting a slippery anchor chain.* [Middle English *fist, fust,* Old English *fȳst.* See **penkwe** in Appendix.*]

fist·ful (fĭst′fŏŏl′) *n., pl.* **-fuls.** A handful.

fist·ic (fĭs′tĭk) *adj.* Of or pertaining to boxing; pugilistic.

fist·i·cuff (fĭs′tĭ-kŭf′) *n.* **1.** *Rare.* A blow with the fist; a punch. **2.** *Plural.* A fist fight: *The argument came to fisticuffs.* **3.** *Plural.* Boxing. [Earlier *fisty cuff* : *fisty,* from FIST + CUFF (a blow).] —**fist′i·cuff′er** *n.*

fis·tu·la (fĭs′chŏŏ-lə) *n., pl.* **-las** or **-lae** (-lē′). An abnormal duct or passage from an abcess, cavity, or hollow organ to the body surface or to another hollow organ. [Middle English, from Latin *fistula*†, pipe, tube, fistula.]

fis·tu·lous (fĭs′chŏŏ-ləs) *adj.* **1.** Of or resembling a fistula. **2.** Tubular and hollow; reedlike. **3.** Made of or containing tubular parts.

fit[1] (fĭt) *v.* **fitted** or **fit, fitted, fitting, fits.** —*tr.* **1.** To be the proper size and shape for. **2.** To be appropriate or suitable to; be in keeping with. **3.** To adjust; alter. **4.** To adapt; suit. **5.** To render competent or qualified; prepare. **6.** To equip; outfit. Used with *up* or *out.* **7.** To provide a place or time for. Used with *in* or *into.* **8.** To insert or adjust so as to be properly in place. —*intr.* **1.** To conform as to size and shape. **2.** To be appropriate or suitable. **3.** To correspond to or agree with the circumstances of a given situation. Used with *in* or *into.* —*adj.* **fitter, fittest.** **1.** Suited, adapted, or adequate to a given circumstance, end, or design. **2.** Appropriate; proper; fitting. **3.** Physically sound; healthy. —*n.* **1.** Adjustment or alteration to a given pattern or standard. **2.** The manner in which clothing fits. **3.** The degree of precision with which surfaces are adjusted or adapted to each other in a machine or collection of parts. **4.** *Slang.* The needle and other equipment of a narcotics user. [Middle English, probably from the past participle of *fitten*†, to marshal troops, (hence) to arrange.] —**fit′ly** *adv.* —**fit′ness** *n.*

Synonyms: *fit, suitable, meet, proper, appropriate, apt, fitting, happy, felicitous.* These adjectives mean right or correct, in view of the circumstances that exist. Often they are interchangeable. *Fit,* in this sense, refers to what is adapted to certain requirements or capable of measuring up to them: *tools fit for the job; fit for heavy duty. Suitable* also implies ability to meet requirements related to a particular need or to an occasion: *suitable for everyday wear. Meet* applies to what is precisely suitable or suitable in the sense of being morally right or just: *a meet reward. Proper* describes what is harmonious, either by nature or because it observes reason, custom, propriety, or the like: *a proper setting for a monument; the proper form of addressing a clergyman.* What is *appropriate* to a thing or for an occasion especially befits it, and what is *apt* is notably to the point: *appropriate remarks; an apt reply. Fitting* suggests close agreement with a prevailing mood or spirit: *a fitting observance of the holiday. Happy* and *felicitous* are applicable to what seems especially suited to an occasion by its nature or by its timeliness: *a happy turn of phrase; an unplanned but felicitous development.*

fit[2] (fĭt) *n.* **1.** *Medicine.* **a.** An attack of an acute disease. **b.** The sudden appearance of a symptom such as coughing. **c.** A convulsion. **2.** A sudden, violent access of some specified emotion. **3.** A sudden period of vigorous activity. —**by** (or **in**) **fits and starts.** With irregular intervals of action and inaction; intermittently; spasmodically. [Middle English *fit,* hardship, painful experience, Old English *fitt*†, conflict.]

fit[3] (fĭt) *n. Archaic.* A section of a poem or ballad; canto. [Middle English *fit,* Old English *fit(t)*†.]

fitch (fĭch) *n.* The fur of the Old World polecat. [Middle English *fiche,* probably from *ficheux,* FITCHEW.]

ă pat/ā pay/âr care/ä father/b bib/ch church/d deed/ĕ pet/ē be/f fife/g gag/h hat/hw which/ĭ pit/ī pie/îr pier/j judge/k kick/l lid, needle/m mum/n no, sudden/ng thing/ŏ pot/ō toe/ô paw, for/oi noise/ou out/ŏŏ took/ōō boot/p pop/r roar/s sauce/sh ship, dish/

Fitch (fĭch), **John.** 1743–1798. American inventor and naval architect.

Fitch (fĭch), **(William) Clyde.** 1865–1909. American playwright.

fitch·ew (fĭch′o͞o) *n.* Also **fitch·et** (fĭch′ĭt). *Archaic.* The Old World polecat or its fur. [Middle English *ficheux,* from Old French *ficheau,* from Middle Dutch *vitsau*†.]

fit·ful (fĭt′fəl) *adj.* Occurring in or characterized by fits; intermittent; spasmodic; irregular. See Synonyms at **periodic.** —**fit′ful·ly** *adv.* —**fit′ful·ness** *n.*

fit·ter (fĭt′ər) *n.* **1.** One who alters or adjusts garments. **2.** One who installs or adjusts parts of machines or other equipment. **3.** A purveyor of equipment for a specified use or activity.

fit·ting (fĭt′ĭng) *adj.* Suitable; appropriate. See Synonyms at **fit.** —*n.* **1.** A trying-on for fit, as of clothes. **2.** A small, detachable part for a machine or an apparatus. **3.** *Usually plural.* Furnishings or accessories. —**fit′ting·ly** *adv.* —**fit′ting·ness** *n.*

Fitz–. Indicates the son of. Used in surnames. [Middle English, from Norman French *fitz,* variant of Old French *fi(l)z,* son, from Latin *filius.* See **dhēi-** in Appendix.*]

Fitz·Ger·ald (fĭts-jĕr′əld), **Edward.** 1809–1883. English poet and translator.

Fitz·ger·ald (fĭts-jĕr′əld), **F(rancis) Scott (Key).** 1896–1940. American author of novels and short stories.

Fitz·Ger·ald (fĭts-jĕr′əld), **George Francis.** 1851–1901. Irish physicist; hypothesized foreshortening of moving bodies.

five (fīv) *n.* The cardinal number written 5 or in Roman numerals V. See **number.** [Middle English *fif, five,* Old English *fif.* See **penkwe** in Appendix.*] —**five** *adj.* & *pron.*

five-and-ten-cent store (fīv′ən-tĕn′sĕnt′). A variety store selling inexpensive commodities. Also called "five-and-dime," "five-and-ten," "ten-cent store."

Five Civilized Nations. The Cherokee, Chickasaw, Choctaw, Creek, and Seminole, who were forced to leave their own lands in the Southeast for the Indian Territory (eastern Oklahoma) in the 1830's. Also called "Five Civilized Tribes."

five-fin·ger (fīv′fĭng′gər) *n.* Any of several plants having compound leaves with five leaflets, such as the **cinquefoil** *(see).*

five·fold (fīv′fōld′) *adj.* **1.** Consisting of five parts. **2.** Five times greater. —*adv.* By five times.

five iron. A golf club, a **mashie** *(see).*

Five Nations. A confederation of five Iroquoian Indian tribes of the northeastern United States, including the Mohawks, Oneidas, Onondagas, Cayugas, and Senecas.

fiv·er (fī′vər) *n. Informal.* **1.** A five-dollar bill. **2.** *British.* A five-pound note.

fives (fīvz) *n.* Plural in form, used with a singular verb. A British form of handball played on a three-walled court. [Reason for naming obscure.]

Five-Year Plan (fīv′yîr′). A program for national economic development over a five-year period, administered by a socialist government. [Translation of Russian *pyatiletka.*]

fix (fĭks) *v.* **fixed, fixing, fixes.** —*tr.* **1.** To place or fasten securely. **2.** To put into a stable or unalterable form, as: **a.** *Chemistry.* To make a substance nonvolatile or solid. **b.** *Biology.* To convert (nitrogen) into stable, biologically assimilable compounds. **c.** To kill and keep (a specimen) intact for microscopic study. **d.** To prevent discoloration of (a photographic image) by washing or coating with a chemical preservative. **3.** To direct (the gaze, for example) steadily; concentrate. **4.** To establish definitely; specify: *fix a time.* **5.** To ascribe; allot: *fixing the blame.* **6.** To rectify; adjust. **7.** To restore to proper condition or functioning; set right; repair. **8.** To make ready; put together; prepare. **9.** To spay or castrate (an animal). **10.** *Informal.* To take revenge upon; get even with. **11.** To prearrange the outcome of (a contest) by unlawful means. —*intr.* **1.** To become concentrated, directed, or attached. **2.** To become stable or firm; harden. **3.** *Regional.* To make plans or preparations; get ready. —**fix on** (or **upon**). To decide or agree on. —**fix up.** *Informal.* **1.** To set right; repair. **2.** To provide; equip. —*n.* **1.** A difficult or embarrassing position; predicament; dilemma. **2.** The position, as of a ship or aircraft, as determined by observations or radio. **3.** An instance of bribery or collusion. **4.** *Slang.* An intravenous injection of heroin or a related opiate. [Middle English *fixen,* partly from Medieval Latin *fixāre,* to fix, from Latin *figere* (past participle *fixus*), to fasten, partly from Old French *fix,* fixed, from Latin *fixus,* past participle of *figere.* See **dhīgw-** in Appendix.*] —**fix′a·ble** *adj.* —**fix′er** *n.*

fix·ate (fĭk′sāt′) *v.* **-ated, -ating, -ates.** —*tr.* **1.** To make fixed, stable, or stationary. **2.** To focus one's eyes or concentrate one's attention on. **3.** *Psychology.* To attach (oneself) to a person or thing in an immature or neurotic fashion. —*intr.* **1.** To focus or concentrate one's attention. **2.** *Psychology.* **a.** To form a fixation. **b.** To be arrested at an immature stage of psychosexual development.

fix·a·tion (fĭk-sā′shən) *n.* **1.** The act or process of fixing or fixating. **2.** *Psychology.* A strong attachment to a person or thing; especially, such an attachment formed in childhood or infancy and persisting in immature or neurotic behavior.

fix·a·tive (fĭk′sə-tĭv) *adj.* Acting to fix; tending to render permanent, firm, or stable. —*n.* Something that fixes, protects, or preserves, especially: **a.** A liquid preservative applied to art work, such as water-color paintings or charcoal drawings. **b.** A solution used to preserve fresh tissue for microscopic examination. **c.** A liquid mixed with perfume to prevent rapid evaporation.

fixed (fĭkst) *adj.* **1.** Firmly in position; stationary; unmovable. **2.** *Chemistry.* **a.** Nonvolatile: *fixed oils.* **b.** In a stable combined form. **3.** Not subject to change or variation; constant. **4.** Firmly, often dogmatically, held to: *a fixed notion.* **5.** Illegally prearranged as to outcome. —**fix′ed·ly** (fĭk′sĭd-lē) *adv.* —**fix′ed·ness** (-sĭd-nĭs) *n.*

fixed idea. An idea, especially an incorrect idea, held persistently and essentially unmodified by an individual despite contrary evidence or rational refutation.

fixed oil. A nonvolatile oil, especially a fatty oil as distinguished from an essential oil.

fixed star. A star so distant from the earth that its movements can be measured only by precise observations over long periods of time.

fix·ings (fĭk′sĭngz) *pl.n. Informal.* Accessories; trimmings.

fix·i·ty (fĭk′sə-tē) *n., pl.* **-ties. 1.** The quality or condition of being fixed; immutability; stability. **2.** Something that is fixed.

fix·ture (fĭks′chər) *n.* **1.** Something securely fixed in place. **2.** Something attached as a permanent appendage, apparatus, or appliance: *plumbing fixtures.* **3.** *Law.* A chattel bound to realty. **4.** A person or thing long associated with, established in, or restricted to a specified place, position, or function. **5. a.** The action or process of fixing. **b.** The condition of being fixed. [Variant of obsolete *fixure* (influenced by MIXTURE), Late Latin *fixūra,* from Latin *fixus.* See **fix.**]

Fi·zeau (fē-zō′), **Armand Hippolyte Louis.** 1819–1896. French physicist.

fiz·gig¹ (fĭz′gĭg′) *n.* **1.** A frivolous, giddy woman. **2.** A firework that produces a hissing or sputtering sound. [Earlier *fisgigg* : probably obsolete *fise,* breaking wind, fart, probably from Scandinavian (see **peis-²** in Appendix*) + GIG (carriage, original sense "frivolous woman").]

fiz·gig². Variant of **fishgig.**

fizz (fĭz) *intr.v.* **fizzed, fizzing, fizzes.** To make a hissing or bubbling sound. —*n.* **1.** A hissing or bubbling sound. **2.** Effervescence. **3.** An effervescent beverage. [Imitative.]

fiz·zle (fĭz′əl) *intr.v.* **-zled, -zling, -zles. 1.** To make a hissing or sputtering sound. **2.** *Informal.* To fail or die out, especially after a hopeful beginning. Often used with *out.* —*n. Informal.* A failure; fiasco. [Probably frequentative of obsolete *fist,* to break wind. See **feist.**]

fjeld (fyĕld) *n.* A high, barren plateau in the Scandinavian countries. [Danish, from Old Norse *fjall,* mountain. See **pelis-** in Appendix.*]

fjord, fiord (fyôrd, fyōrd) *n.* A long, narrow, often deep inlet from the sea between steep cliffs and slopes, found especially along the coasts of Norway and Alaska. [Norwegian, from Old Norse *fjördhr.* See **per-²** in Appendix.*]

fl fluid.

fL foot-lambert.

FL Florida (with Zip Code).

fl. 1. floor. **2.** florin. **3.** floruit. **4.** fluid. **5.** flute.

Fla. Florida.

flab·ber·gast (flăb′ər-găst′) *tr.v.* **-gasted, -gasting, -gasts.** To confound or overwhelm with astonishment; astound. See Synonyms at **surprise.** [Origin obscure.]

flab·by (flăb′ē) *adj.* **-bier, -biest. 1.** Lacking firmness; loose and yielding to the touch; flaccid: *flabby skin.* **2.** Lacking force or vitality; feeble; ineffectual. [Variant of *flappy,* from FLAP.] —**flab′bi·ly** *adv.* —**flab′bi·ness** *n.*

fla·bel·late (flə-bĕl′ĭt, -āt′) *adj.* Also **fla·bel·li·form** (flə-bĕl′ə-fôrm′). Fan-shaped. [From Latin *flābellum,* fan. See **flabellum.**]

fla·bel·lum (flə-bĕl′əm) *n., pl.* **-bella** (-bĕl′ə). **1.** A fan-shaped anatomical structure. **2.** A fan used in certain religious ceremonies and displayed on certain state occasions. [Latin *flābellum,* small fan, diminutive of *flābrum* (usually in plural *flābra*), gust of wind, from *flāre,* to blow. See **bhlē-²** in Appendix.*]

flac·cid (flăk′sĭd) *adj.* Lacking firmness; soft and limp; flabby: *"His mouth, pink and flaccid, trembled sometimes like the underlip of a cow."* (H.E. Bates). [French *flaccide,* from Latin *flaccidus,* from *flaccus*†, hanging, flabby.] —**flac·cid′i·ty, flac′cid·ness** *n.* —**flac′cid·ly** *adv.*

fla·con (flăk′ən, -ŏn′) *n.* A small stoppered bottle, as for perfume. [French, from Old French *fla(s)con,* FLAGON.]

flag¹ (flăg) *n.* **1.** A piece of cloth or bunting varying in size, color, and design, used as a symbol, standard, signal, or emblem. **2.** In musical notation, the cross stroke added to a note of less than ¼ value, as a single stroke on an eighth note or a double stroke on a sixteenth note. **3.** A ship carrying the flag of an admiral; flagship. **4.** The masthead of a newspaper. **5.** A distinctively shaped or marked tail, as of a dog or deer. —*tr.v.* **flagged, flagging, flags. 1.** To mark with a flag for identification or ornamentation. **2.** To signal or communicate with or as if with a flag. **3.** *Slang.* To take (a suspect) into custody for questioning or arrest. —**flag down.** To attract the attention of and signal to stop; to hail: *flag down a taxi.* [Origin obscure.] —**flag′ger** *n.*

flag² (flăg) *n.* Any of various plants having long bladelike leaves, such as an iris or cattail. [Middle English *flagge*†, rush, reed.]

flag³ (flăg) *intr.v.* **flagged, flagging, flags. 1.** To hang limply; droop. **2.** To become languid; decline in vigor; slacken: *"My spirits flagged. I was even hypochondriac."* (Boswell). **3.** To decline in interest; grow dull. [Origin unknown.]

flag⁴ (flăg) *n.* **1.** A slab of flagstone used for paving. **2.** Flagstone. —*tr.v.* **flagged, flagging, flags.** To pave with flags. [Middle English *flagge,* piece of turf, sod, probably from Old Norse *flaga,* slab of stone. See **plāk-¹** in Appendix.*]

Flag Day. June 14, an annual holiday celebrating the adoption in 1777 of the official U.S. flag.

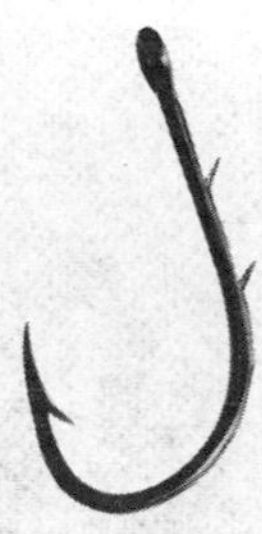

fishhook

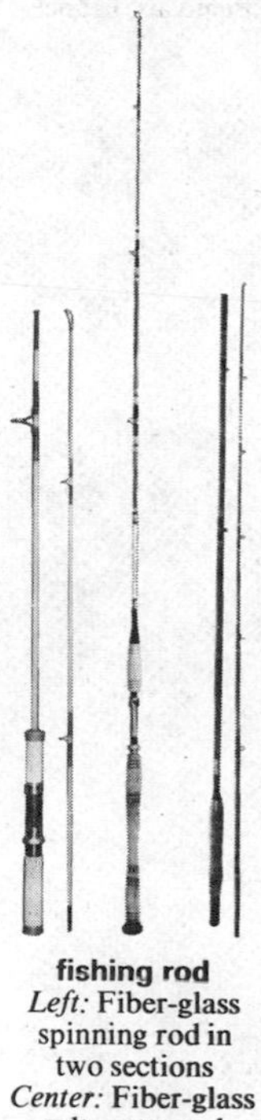

fishing rod
Left: Fiber-glass spinning rod in two sections
Center: Fiber-glass salt-water rod
Right: Fly rod in two sections

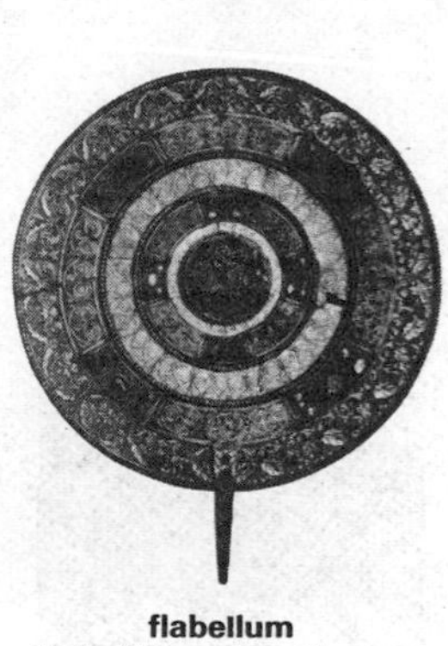

flabellum
Early 13th-century German

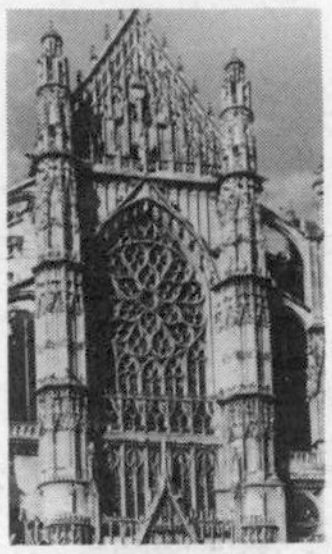
flamboyant
Cathedral at
Beauvais, France

flag·el·lant (flăj'ə-lənt, flə-jĕl'ənt) *n.* **1.** One who whips; especially, one who scourges himself by way of religious discipline or public penance. **2.** One who seeks sexual gratification in beating or being beaten by another person. —*adj.* **1.** Of or pertaining to flagellants. **2.** Whiplike; scathing. [Latin *flagellāns*, present participle of *flagellāre*, to FLAGELLATE.]

flag·el·late (flăj'ə-lāt') *tr.v.* **-lated, -lating, -lates.** To whip or flog; scourge. —*adj.* **1.** Having a flagellum or flagella, as unicellular organisms of the class Flagellata (or Magistophora). **2.** Resembling or having the form of a flagellum; whiplike. —*n.* A flagellate organism. [Latin *flagellāre*, to whip, scourge, from *flagellum*, small whip, diminutive of *flagrum*, whip. See **bhlag-** in Appendix.*]

flag·el·la·tion (flăj'ə-lā'shən) *n.* The act or practice of flagellating; whipping; scourging.

fla·gel·li·form (flə-jĕl'ə fôrm') *adj.* Long, thin, and tapering; whip-shaped: *flagelliform appendages.* [Latin *flagellum*, small whip (see **flagellate**) + -FORM.]

fla·gel·lum (flə-jĕl'əm) *n., pl.* **-gella** (-jĕl'ə). **1.** *Biology.* A long, filamentous process; especially, one of the whiplike extensions of certain cells or unicellular organisms, usually functioning in locomotion. **2.** A whip. [New Latin, from Latin, small whip. See **flagellate.**] —**fla·gel'lar** *adj.*

flag·eo·let (flăj'ə-lĕt', -lā') *n.* A small flutelike instrument having a cylindrical mouthpiece, four finger holes, and two thumb holes. [French, diminutive of Old French *flajol*, from Vulgar Latin *flabeolum* (unattested), flute, from *flāre*, to blow. See **bhlē-**[2] in Appendix.*]

flag·ging[1] (flăg'ĭng) *adj.* **1.** Drooping; languid. **2.** Declining; weakening. —**flag'ging·ly** *adv.*

flag·ging[2] (flăg'ĭng) *n.* A pavement laid with flagstones.

flag·gy (flăg'ē) *adj.* **-gier, -giest.** Abounding in or characteristic of flags or similar reedlike plants.

fla·gi·tious (flə-jĭsh'əs) *adj.* **1.** Guilty of or addicted to extremely brutal or cruel crimes; vicious. **2.** Shockingly evil; infamous; scandalous; heinous: *"that remorseless government persisted in its flagitious project."* (Southey). [Middle English *flagicious*, from Latin *flāgitiōsus*, from *flāgitium*, noisy protest against one's conduct, scandal, shameful act, from *flāgitāre*, to demand fiercely. See **bhlag-** in Appendix.*] —**fla·gi'tious·ly** *adv.* —**fla·gi'tious·ness** *n.*

flag·man (flăg'mən) *n., pl.* **-men** (-mĭn). One who signals with or carries a flag.

flag officer. A naval officer holding the rank of rear admiral, vice admiral, or admiral.

flag of truce. A white flag brought or displayed to an enemy as an invitation to a conference or a signal of surrender.

flag·on (flăg'ən) *n.* **1.** A vessel for holding wine or other liquors, usually made of metal or pottery and having a handle and spout. **2.** The quantity of liquid contained in such a vessel. [Middle English *flagon, flakon*, from Old French *fla(s)con*, from Late Latin *flascō*, bottle, FLASK.]

flag·pole (flăg'pōl') *n.* A pole on which a flag is hoisted; flagstaff.

fla·grant (flā'grənt) *adj.* **1.** Extremely or deliberately conspicuous; notorious; shocking: *a flagrant miscarriage of justice.* **2.** *Obsolete.* Flaming; blazing. —See Synonyms at **outrageous.** [Latin *flagrāns*, present participle of *flagrāre*, to burn, blaze. See **bhel-**[1] in Appendix.*] —**fla'gran·cy, fla'grance** *n.* —**fla'grant·ly** *adv.*

Synonyms: *flagrant, glaring, gross, rank.* These adjectives refer to what is outstandingly bad, evil, erroneous, incapable, or the like. *Flagrant* and *glaring* both stress the conspicuousness of what gives cause for concern or offense. *Glaring* is somewhat more emphatic in suggesting what cannot escape notice, but *flagrant* often makes the stronger implication of wrongdoing as a moral offense rather than as an act of miscalculation or ineptitude. *Gross* and *rank* emphasize extremity or intensity. *Gross* suggests a magnitude of offense or failing that cannot be overlooked or condoned. *Rank*, like *flagrant*, sometimes implies an affront to decency. Often *rank* is used attributively as an intensifying term with the force of absolute or utter: *rank folly.*

fla·gran·te de·lic·to (flə-grăn'tē dĭ-lĭk'tō). Red-handed; in the very act. Used in the phrase *in flagrante (delicto).* [Medieval Latin, "while the crime is blazing."]

flag·ship (flăg'shĭp') *n.* A ship bearing the flag of a fleet or squadron commander.

flag·staff (flăg'stăf', -stäf') *n., pl.* **-staffs** or **-staves** (-stāvz'). A flagpole.

Flag·staff (flăg'stăf', -stäf'). A city and health resort in north-central Arizona. Population, 26,000.

flag·stone (flăg'stōn') *n.* A flat, fine-grained, hard, evenly layered stone split into slabs for use in paving; flag. [FLAG (stone) + STONE.]

flail (flāl) *n.* A manual threshing device, consisting of a long wooden handle or staff and a shorter, free-swinging stick attached to its end. —*v.* **flailed, flailing, flails.** —*tr.* **1.** To thresh using a flail. **2.** To beat, thrash, or strike with or as with a flail. —*intr.* To thresh; wave: *arms flailing.* [Middle English *fleil, flail*, from Old English *flegil* (unattested) and Old French *flaiel*, both from Latin *flagellum*, diminutive of *flagrum*, whip. See **bhlag-** in Appendix.*]

flair (flâr) *n.* **1.** A natural talent or aptitude; bent; knack: *a flair for interior decorating.* **2.** Instinctive discernment; keenness: *"Boswell, with his usual flair, arrived in Florence at a most exciting time."* (Frederick A. Pottle). [French, "sense of smell," from Old French, from *flairer*, to emit an odor, to scent, smell, from Vulgar Latin *flāgrāre* (unattested), from Latin *frāgrāre*, to emit a smell. See **bhrag-** in Appendix.*]

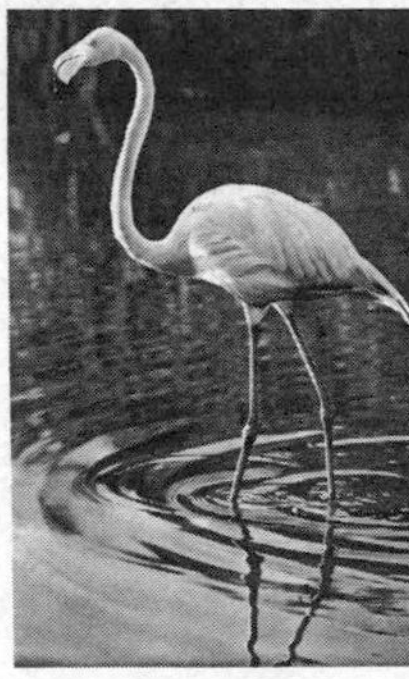
flamingo
Phoenicopterus ruber

flak (flăk) *n.* **1.** Antiaircraft artillery. **2.** The bursting shells fired from such artillery. **3.** *Slang.* Excessive criticism; abuse. [German *Flak*, short for *Fl(ieger)a(bwehr)k(anone)*, "aircraft defense gun."]

flake[1] (flāk) *n.* **1.** A flat, thin piece or layer; chip. **2.** A small exfoliated piece of something; bit. **3.** A small crystalline body of snow. —*v.* **flaked, flaking, flakes.** —*tr.* **1.** To break flakes from; take off in flakes; chip. **2.** To cover, mark, or overlay with or as if with flakes; fleck. —*intr.* To come off in flakes; chip off. —**flake out.** *Slang.* To fall asleep or become unconscious; collapse from fatigue or exhaustion. [Middle English *flake*, from Scandinavian, akin to Norwegian *flak.* See **plāk-**[1] in Appendix.*] —**flak'er** *n.*

flake[2] (flāk) *n.* **1.** A frame or platform for drying fish or produce. **2.** A scaffold lowered over the side of a ship to support workmen or caulkers. [Middle English *fleke*, from Old Norse *fleki, flaki.* See **plāk-**[1] in Appendix.*]

flake white. A pigment made of flakes of white lead.

flak·y (flā'kē) *adj.* **-ier, -iest.** **1.** Made of or resembling flakes. **2.** Forming or tending to form flakes or thin, crisp fragments: *flaky pastry.* —**flak'i·ly** *adv.* —**flak'i·ness** *n.*

flam[1] (flăm) *n. Informal.* **1.** A lie or hoax; deception. **2.** Nonsense; drivel. —*tr.v.* **flammed, flamming, flams.** *Informal.* To deceive or trick. [Short for FLIMFLAM.]

flam[2] (flăm) *n.* A drumbeat produced by two almost simultaneous strokes of which the first is a very rapid grace note. [Perhaps imitative.]

flam·beau (flăm'bō') *n., pl.* **-beaux** (-bōz') or **-beaus.** **1.** A lighted torch. **2.** A large ornamental candlestick. [French, from Old French, from *flambe, flamble*, "small flame," from Latin *flammula*, diminutive of *flamma*, FLAME.]

flam·bée (fläm-bā'; *French* fläN-bā') *adj.* Also **flam·bé.** Served flaming in ignited liquor. Said of food.

Flam·bor·ough Head (flăm'bûr'ə). A chalk peninsula on the coast of Yorkshire, England.

flam·boy·ant (flăm-boi'ənt) *adj.* **1.** Highly elaborate; ornate or overwrought; showy: *a flamboyant manner.* **2.** Richly colored; vivid; resplendent. **3.** *Architecture.* Pertaining to or having waved lines and flamelike forms characteristic of 15th- and 16th-century French Gothic architecture. —See Synonyms at **ornate.** —*n.* A tree, the **royal poinciana** *(see).* [French, from Old French, present participle of *flamboyer, flambeiier*, to blaze, from *flambe, flamble*, small flame. See **flambeau.**] —**flam·boy'ance, flam·boy'an·cy** *n.* —**flam·boy'ant·ly** *adv.*

flame (flām) *n.* **1.** The zone of burning gases and fine suspended matter associated with the combustion of a substance; broadly, a hot, luminous mass of burning gas or vapor. **2.** *Often plural.* The condition of active, blazing combustion: *burst into flames.* **3.** Something flamelike in motion, brilliance, intensity, or shape. **4.** A violent or intense passion; a burning emotion. **5.** *Informal.* A sweetheart. —See Synonyms at **blaze.** —*v.* **flamed, flaming, flames.** —*intr.* **1.** To burn brightly; give off flames or a flame; blaze. Often used with *up.* **2.** To color or flash suddenly: *Her cheeks flamed with embarrassment.* —*tr.* **1.** To burn, ignite, or scorch. **2.** *Obsolete.* To foment; incite; inflame. [Middle English *flaume, flam(m)e*, from Old French *flam(m)e*, from Latin *flamma.* See **bhel-**[1] in Appendix.*]

fla·men (flā'mən) *n., pl.* **-mens** or **flamines** (flăm'ə-nēz'). A priest or servant of a Roman deity. [Middle English *flamin*, a priest in heathen Britain, from Latin *flāmen*, flamen, akin to Sanskrit *Brahmán*, BRAHMA.]

fla·men·co (flə-mĕng'kō) *n.* **1.** A dance style of the Andalusian Gypsies characterized by forceful often improvised rhythms. **2.** The guitar music that usually accompanies this dance style. —*adj.* Of, pertaining to, or intended for such dancing or music: *a flamenco guitar.* [Spanish *flamenco*, Gypsy living in Andalusia, resembling a Gypsy, Flemish, from Middle Dutch *Vlāming*, FLEMING.]

flame·out (flām'out') *n.* Failure of a jet aircraft engine in flight.

flame thrower. A weapon that projects ignited incendiary fuel, such as napalm, in a steady stream.

flam·ing (flā'mĭng) *adj.* **1.** On fire; in flames; ablaze. **2.** Brilliant; splendid; flamelike. **3.** Intense; passionate; ardent. **4.** Arrant; flagrant. —**flam'ing·ly** *adv.*

fla·min·go (flə-mĭng'gō) *n., pl.* **-gos** or **-goes.** **1.** Any of several large, gregarious wading birds of the family Phoenicopteridae, of tropical regions, having reddish or pinkish plumage, long legs, a long, flexible neck, and a bill turned downward at the tip. **2.** Moderate reddish orange. See **color.** [Perhaps Portuguese *flamengo*, from Provençal *flamenc*, probably "fire bird" (from its bright plumage) : *flama*, flame, from Latin *flamma* (see **bhel-**[1] in Appendix*) + *-enc*, from Germanic *-ing*, suffix denoting "belonging to."]

Fla·min·i·an Way (flə-mĭn'ē-ən). A Roman road extending north from Rome to Rimini, built in 220 B.C. [Latin *Flāminiānus*, after Gaius *Flaminius* (died 217 B.C.), Roman general and builder of public works.]

flam·ma·ble (flăm'ə-bəl) *adj.* Easily ignitable and capable of burning with great rapidity; highly combustible; inflammable. [From Latin *flammāre*, to blaze, from *flamma*, FLAME.] —**flam'ma·bil'i·ty** *n.* —**flam'ma·ble** *n.*

Usage: *Flammable* and *inflammable* are alike in meaning and interchangeable in literal usage. One can speak of a *flammable* fluid or of an *inflammable* one. Figuratively, one can refer to an *inflammable* nature or temperament, but not to a *flammable* one. *Flammable* is especially appropriate in technical writing and where the term serves expressly as a warning, since it is less susceptible to confusion than *inflammable*, which is sometimes mistaken for *nonflammable* or *noncombustible*. *Flammable* is as acceptable as *inflammable* in all areas of speech and writing, according to 61 per cent of the Usage Panel, though *inflammable* is more common outside technical contexts.

flam·y (flā′mē) *adj.* **-ier, -iest.** Flamelike; flaming.

flan (flăn, flän) *n.* **1.** A tart with a filling of custard, fruit, or cheese. **2.** A molded custard with a burnt-caramel icing. **3.** A metal disk to be stamped as a coin; a blank. [French, from Old French *fla(o)n*, from Germanic. See **plat-** in Appendix.*]

Flan·ders (flăn′dərz). *Flemish* **Vlaan·de·ren** (vlän′də-rən); *French* **Flan·dre** (fläɴ′dr′). **1.** A region of northwestern Europe, including part of northern France and western Belgium, and bordered by the North Sea. **2.** The area of Belgium comprising the provinces of **East Flanders** and **West Flanders** *(both of which see)*.

flâ·ne·rie (flän-rē′) *n. French.* Aimless idling; dawdling.

flâ·neur (flä-nœr′) *n. French.* An aimless idler; a loafer.

flange (flănj) *n.* A protruding rim, edge, rib, or collar, as on a wheel or a pipe shaft, used to strengthen an object, hold it in place, or attach it to another object. —*tr.v.* **flanged, flanging, flanges.** To furnish with a flange. [Probably variant of earlier *flanch*†.]

flank (flăngk) *n.* **1.** The section of flesh between the last rib and the hip; side. **2.** A cut of meat from this section of an animal. **3.** A side or lateral part: *the flank of a mountain.* **4. a.** The right or left side of a military formation: *attack on both flanks.* **b.** The right or left side of a bastion. —*v.* **flanked, flanking, flanks.** —*tr.* **1.** To protect or guard the flank of. **2.** To menace, attack, or maneuver around the flank of. **3.** To be placed or situated at the flank or side of. —*intr.* **1.** To be at or move along a side. **2.** To be adjacent; border. Used with *on* or *upon.* [Middle English *fla(u)nke*, from Old French *flanc*, from Frankish *hlanca* (unattested), side. See **kleng-** in Appendix.*]

flank·er (flăng′kər) *n.* **1.** One that flanks. **2.** A division of soldiers guarding the flank of a marching column. **3.** A fortification attached to the side or flank of. **4.** A flankerback.

flank·er·back (flăng′kər-băk′) *n. Football.* The halfback of the offensive team stationed just behind the line of scrimmage and to the right of his team's right end.

flan·nel (flăn′əl) *n.* **1.** A soft woven cloth of wool or of a blend of wool and cotton or synthetics. **2.** Canton flannel; flannelette. **3.** *Plural.* Outer clothing, especially trousers, made of flannel. **4.** *Plural.* Underclothing made of flannel. —*tr.v.* **flanneled** or **-nelled, -neling** or **-nelling, -nels. 1.** To rub or polish with flannel. **2.** To wrap in flannel. [Middle English, probably from *flanen*, sackcloth, from Welsh *gwlanen*, "woolen cloth," from *gwlân*, wool. See **wel-⁵** in Appendix.*] —**flan′nel·ly** *adj.*

flannel bush. A shrub or small tree, *Fremontia californica*, of California and northern Mexico, having downy, lobed leaves and showy yellow flowers.

flannel cake. A **pancake** *(see)*.

flan·nel·ette, flan·nel·et (flăn′ə-lĕt′) *n.* A cotton cloth, **Canton flannel** *(see)*.

flan·nel-leaf (flăn′əl-lēf′) *n.* A species of **mullein** *(see)*.

flap (flăp) *v.* **flapped, flapping, flaps.** —*tr.* **1.** To wave (wings or arms) up and down; to beat. **2.** To cause to wave or undulate; agitate. **3.** To hit with something broad and flat; to slap. **4.** *Informal.* To fling down or clap shut. —*intr.* **1.** To wave about while fixed at one edge or corner to something stationary; to flutter. **2.** To wave arms or wings up and down; beat the air. **3.** To fly by beating the air with the wings. —*n.* **1.** A flat appendage or lappet usually intended to double over and protect or cover something, as on an envelope, pocket, or hat. **2.** The action of waving or fluttering; flapping. **3.** The sound of flapping. **4.** A blow given with something flat; a slap. **5.** *Aviation.* A variable control surface on the trailing edge of an aircraft wing, used primarily to increase lift or drag. **6.** *Surgery.* Tissue that has been partially detached and used in plastic surgery to fill an adjacent defect or to cover the cut end of a bone after amputation. **7.** *Slang.* A condition of agitated distress; pother; stew. [Middle English *flappen*. See **plab-** in Appendix.*]

flap·doo·dle (flăp′do͞od′l) *n. Slang.* Foolish talk; balderdash; nonsense. [Origin obscure.]

flap·jack (flăp′jăk′) *n.* A **pancake** *(see)*. [FLAP (to toss) + JACK (name).]

flap·pable (flăp′ə-bəl) *adj. Slang.* Easily excited or upset.

flap·per (flăp′ər) *n.* **1.** One that flaps. **2.** A flipper or similar broad, flexible part. **3.** *Informal.* A young woman, especially one who flaunts her disdain for conventional dress and behavior. Used chiefly during the 1920's.

flare (flâr) *v.* **flared, flaring, flares.** —*intr.* **1.** To flame up with a bright, wavering light; blaze unsteadily. **2.** To burst into intense, short-lived flame. Often used with *up.* **3.** To erupt into emphatic emotion or activity. Often used with *out* or *up.* **4.** To expand outward in shape or configuration, as a skirt, or the lip of a glass or vase. —*tr.* **1.** To cause (something) to flare. **2.** To signal with flares. —*n.* **1.** A brief, wavering blaze of light. **2.** A pyrotechnic device that produces a bright light for signaling, illumination, or identification. **3.** An outbreak, as of emotion or activity. **4.** An expanding contour, as of the lip of a vase. **5.** *Photography.* A lens reflection or the resultant film fogging. —See Synonyms at **blaze.** [Origin unknown.]

flare·back (flâr′băk′) *n.* **1.** A flame produced in the breech of a gun by ignition of residual gases. **2.** A burst of something aimed back at its origin; backfire: *a flareback of publicity.*

flare-up (flâr′ŭp′) *n.* **1.** A sudden outbreak of flame or light. **2.** An outburst or eruption: *a flare-up of anger.* **3.** An intensification of something hitherto mild or dormant: *a flare-up of old antagonisms.*

flash (flăsh) *v.* **flashed, flashing, flashes.** —*intr.* **1.** To occur or emerge suddenly in, or as if in, flame. **2.** To appear or be perceived for an instant only. **3.** To be lighted intermittently; sparkle; scintillate. **4.** To move rapidly. —*tr.* **1. a.** To cause (light) to appear suddenly or in intermittent bursts. **b.** To cause to burst into flame. **c.** To reflect (light). **d.** To reflect light from (a surface). **2.** To expose to a flash or flashes of light. **3.** To signal with light. **4.** To communicate (information) at great speed. **5.** To exhibit (something concealed) briefly. **6.** To display ostentatiously; flaunt. **7.** To fill suddenly with water. **8.** To cover with a thin protective layer. —*n.* **1.** A sudden, brief, intense display of light. **2.** A brief, unexpected, splendid display, as of a quality or mental faculty: *a flash of insight.* **3.** A split second; an instant: *in a flash.* **4.** A brief, important news dispatch or transmission. **5.** *Informal.* The language or cant of thieves, tramps, or underworld figures. **6.** A flashlight. **7. a.** Instantaneous illumination for photography. **b.** Any equipment or device, as a flash bulb, flash gun, or flash lamp, used to produce such illumination. —See Synonyms at **blaze, moment.** —**flash in the pan. 1.** An explosion of the gunpowder in the pan of a flintlock rifle that does not set off the charge. **2.** One that promises great success but fails. —*adj.* **1.** Happening suddenly or very quickly: *a flash flood.* **2.** Pertaining to thieves, confidence men, and underworld figures. [Middle English *flashen*, to splash, burst into flame (imitative).]

Synonyms: *flash, gleam, glance, glint, sparkle, glitter, glisten, shimmer, glimmer, twinkle, spark, scintillate.* These verbs mean to send forth or reflect light. *Flash* refers to a sudden and brilliant but short-lived outburst of light. *Gleam* implies light of moderate brightness, either transient or constant and often appearing against a dark background. *Glance* refers most often to light reflected obliquely. *Glint* refers to emitted or reflected light in flashes. *Sparkle* suggests a rapid succession of flashes of high brilliance, and *glitter* a similar succession of even greater intensity. *Glisten* usually refers to lustrous, reflected light, and *shimmer* to the reflection of soft, undulating light. *Glimmer* is applied to emission or reflection of subdued, fleeting light. *Twinkle* refers to the intermittent emission of soft, wavering light, and *spark* to the production of brief flashes of light or fire. *Scintillate* is applied to what flashes as if throwing off sparks in a continuous stream.

flash back. To interrupt a story in order to portray or recount an incident or scene from the past; cut back.

flash·back (flăsh′băk′) *n.* A reversion to previously depicted events in a film narrative. Also called "cutback."

flash·board (flăsh′bôrd′, -bōrd′) *n.* Boarding that extends above a dam to increase the depth of water held.

flash bulb. A glass bulb filled with finely shredded aluminum or magnesium foil that is ignited by electricity to produce a short-duration high-intensity light flash for taking photographs. Also called "photoflash."

flash burn. A burn resulting from brief exposure to intense radiation.

flash card. One of a set or integrated series of cards used for brief, usually successive, display; especially, such a card used by a teacher in a drill.

flash·er (flăsh′ər) *n.* **1.** One that flashes. **2.** A device that automatically switches an electric lamp off and on, as in a commercial display sign.

flash flood. A sudden, violent flood after a heavy rain.

flash gun. A dry-cell powered photographic apparatus that holds and electrically triggers a flash bulb.

flash·ing (flăsh′ĭng) *n.* **1.** The act of producing a rush of water in a channel. **2.** Sheet metal or weather stripping used to reinforce and weatherproof the joints and angles of a roof.

flash lamp. An electric lamp for producing a high-intensity light of very short duration for use in photography.

flash·light (flăsh′līt′) *n.* **1.** A small, portable lamp consisting of a bulb and dry batteries encased usually in a metal and plastic cylinder. **2.** A brief, brilliant flood of light from a photographic lamp. **3.** A bright, flashing beam or light, as of a beacon or signal lamp.

flash·o·ver (flăsh′ō′vər) *n.* An unintended electric arc, as between two pieces of apparatus.

flash point. The lowest temperature at which the vapor of a combustible liquid can be made to ignite momentarily in air.

flash tube. A gas discharge tube used in an electronic flash to produce a brief, intense pulse of light.

flash unit. 1. An electronic flash system containing both power supply and flash tube in a single compact unit. **2. a.** A flash gun. **b.** A flash gun and reflector.

flash·y (flăsh′ē) *adj.* **-ier, -iest. 1.** Giving a momentary or superficial impression of brilliance. **2.** Cheap and showy; gaudy. —**flash′i·ly** *adv.* —**flash′i·ness** *n.*

flask (flăsk, fläsk) *n.* **1.** A small bottle or other container with a narrow neck and usually a cap, especially: **a.** A container for liquor with a flat, slightly curved shape to fit in a person's pocket. **b.** A container or case for carrying gunpowder or shot. **c.** A vial or round long-necked bottle for laboratory use. **2.** A frame for holding a sand mold in a foundry. [Old French *flasque*, *flaske*, from Late Latin *flascō*, *flasca*, probably from Germanic *flaska-* (unattested).]

flas·ket (flăs′kĭt, fläs′-) *n.* **1.** A long, shallow basket. **2.** *Rare.* A small flask. [Old North French *flasquet*, diminutive of Old French *flasque*, FLASK.]

flat¹ (flăt) *adj.* **flatter, flattest. 1.** Having no curves; of zero curvature. **2.** Extending or lying completely in a plane; planar. **3.** Having a smooth, even, level surface. **4.** Not deep or high; shallow; low: *a flat box.* **5.** Lying prone; prostrate. **6.** Unequivocal; unqualified; absolute; downright: *a flat refusal.* **7.** Fixed;

t tight/th thin, path/*th* this, bathe/ŭ cut/ûr urge/v valve/w with/y yes/z zebra, size/zh vision/ə about, item, edible, gallop, circus/ à *Fr.* ami/œ *Fr.* feu, *Ger.* schön/ü *Fr.* tu, *Ger.* über/KH *Ger.* ich, *Scot.* loch/N *Fr.* bon. ***Follows main vocabulary. †Of obscure origin.**

unvarying: *a flat rate.* **8.** Neither more nor less; to the exact measure: *a flat ten minutes.* **9.** Uninteresting; lackluster; dull; vapid. **10. a.** Lacking zest; flavorless. **b.** Having lost a characteristic effervescence; dead; stale. Said of beverages. **11.** Deflated. Said of a tire. **12.** Commercially inactive; sluggish: *a flat market.* **13.** Unmodulated; monotonous: *a flat voice.* **14.** *Painting.* **a.** Executed with an even thickness of paint; lacking relief. **b.** Lacking variety in tint or shading; uniform. **15.** Mat; not glossy. Said of a paint. **16.** *Music.* **a.** Being below the intended pitch. **b.** Having one or more flats in the key signature. **c.** Being one half step lower than the corresponding natural key: *the key of B flat.* Compare **sharp. 17.** Designating the vowel *a* as pronounced in *bad* or *cat.* **18.** *Grammar.* Designating a word used as a particular part of speech without an inflectional ending or sign. Said especially of: **a.** An adverb without the *-ly* ending, as *quick* in *come quick.* **b.** An infinitive without *to,* as *stop* in *make him stop work.* **19.** Taut. Said of a sail. —See Synonyms at **level.** —*adv.* **1. a.** Horizontally; level with the ground. **b.** Prostrate. **2.** So as to be flat. **3.** Directly; completely: *He went flat against the rules.* **4.** *Music.* Below the intended pitch: *sing flat.* **5.** *Commerce.* Without interest charge. —**fall flat.** To fail: *Our plans fell flat.* —*n.* **1.** A flat surface or part. **2. a.** *Often plural.* A stretch of level ground: *the salt flats.* **b.** Low-lying, partly flooded ground such as tideland. **c.** A shoal. **3.** A shallow frame or box for seeds or seedlings. **4.** Stage scenery on a movable wooden frame. **5.** The palm of the hand. **6.** A flatcar. **7.** A deflated tire. **8.** *Plural.* Women's shoes with flat heels. **9.** *Music.* **a.** A sign (♭) affixed to a note to indicate that it is to be lowered by a half step. **b.** A note that is lowered a half step: *B flat.* In this sense, compare **sharp.** —*v.* **flatted, flatting, flats.** —*tr.* **1.** To make flat; flatten. **2.** *Music.* To lower (a note) a semitone. —*intr. Music.* To sing or play below the proper pitch. [Middle English, from Old Norse *flatr.* See **plat-** in Appendix.*] —**flat′ly** *adv.* —**flat′ness** *n.*

flat[2] (flăt) *n.* **1.** A suite of rooms used as a lodging; an apartment on one floor of a building. **2.** *Archaic.* A story in a house. [Variant (influenced by FLAT) of Scottish *flet,* interior of a house, Middle English *flet,* Old English *flett,* floor, ground, hall. See **plat-** in Appendix.*]

flat-bed press (flăt′bĕd′). A printing press in which the type, locked into a chase, is supported by a flat surface (bed) and the paper is applied to the type either by a flat platen (in older models) or by a cylinder against which the bed moves.

flat·boat (flăt′bōt′) *n.* A boat with a flat bottom and square ends, such as a scow, used for transporting freight on inland waterways; a barge. Also called "flatbottom."

flat·car (flăt′kär′) *n.* A railroad freight car without sides or roof; platform car.

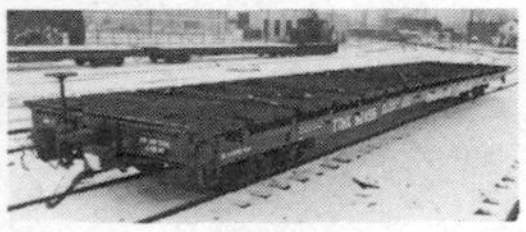
flatcar

flat·fish (flăt′fĭsh′) *n., pl.* **flatfish** or **-fishes.** Any of numerous chiefly marine fishes of the order Pleuronectiformes (or Heterosomata), which includes the flounders, soles, and other fishes having a compressed body in which an early stage of development one eye moves to the same side of the body as the other and the fish swims with its eyeless side downward.

flat foot. A foot with a fallen arch.

flat·foot (flăt′fo͝ot′) *n., pl.* **-feet** (-fēt′) (for sense 1) or **-foots** (for sense 2). **1.** A condition in which the arch of the foot is broken down so that the entire sole makes contact with the ground. **2. a.** *Informal.* A person with flat feet. **b.** *Slang.* A policeman. Used derogatorily. —*intr.v.* **flatfooted, -footing, -foots.** To walk in a flatfooted manner: *"He flatfooted along, twirling his club."* (James T. Farrell).

flat-footed (flăt′fo͝ot′ĭd) *adj.* **1.** Of or afflicted with flatfoot. **2. a.** Steady on the feet. **b.** *Informal.* Without reservation; forthright; uncompromising. **3.** Unprepared; unable to react quickly: *caught him flat-footed.* —**flat′foot′ed·ly** *adv.* —**flat′-foot′ed·ness** *n.*

Flat·head (flăt′hĕd′) *n., pl.* **Flatheads** or **Flathead. 1. a.** One of several tribes of American Indians in the northwestern coast area who practiced or were said to practice head-flattening. **b.** A member of one of these tribes. **2. a.** A Salishan tribe of western Montana. **b.** One of this tribe. **3.** *Small* **f.** *Slang.* An imbecile or fool.

Flathead River. A river rising in southeastern British Columbia and flowing 240 miles to the Clark Fork in northwestern Montana.

flat·i·ron (flăt′ī′ərn) *n.* An externally heated iron for pressing clothes.

flat·ling (flăt′lĭng) *adv.* Also **flat·lings** (-lĭngs). *Archaic.* **1.** At full length; flat. **2.** With the flat of a sword.

flat silver. Table silverware.

flat·ten (flăt′n) *v.* **-tened, -tening, -tens.** —*tr.* **1.** To make flat or flatter. **2.** To knock down; lay low. —*intr.* To become flat or flatter. —**flatten out.** To make or become flat, horizontal, or prostrate. —**flat′ten·er** *n.*

flat·ter[1] (flăt′ər) *v.* **-tered, -tering, -ters.** —*tr.* **1.** To compliment excessively and often insincerely, especially in order to win the favor of; to court; blandish. **2.** To please or gratify; feed the vanity of: *"What really flatters a man is that you think him worth flattering."* (G.B. Shaw). **3. a.** To portray favorably. **b.** To show off becomingly or advantageously. **4.** To persuade (oneself) that something one wants to believe is the case. Used reflexively: *"many flattered themselves that I had turned out a failure"* (John Stuart Mill). —*intr.* **1.** To practice flattery. **2.** To serve to flatter one. [Middle English *flateren,* from Old French *flat(t)er,* "to caress with the hand," smooth, flatter, from Frankish *flat* (unattested), flat, flat part of a person's hand. See **plat-** in Appendix.*] —**flat′ter·er** *n.*

flat·ter[2] (flăt′ər) *n.* **1.** A flat-faced swage or hammer used by blacksmiths. **2.** A die plate for flattening metal into strips, as in the manufacture of watch springs.

flat·ter·ing (flăt′ər-ĭng) *adj.* **1.** Serving to flatter; highly gratifying: *flattering comments.* **2.** Serving to arouse favorable or gratifying attention: *"for men with a well-turned calf, knee breeches can be flattering"* (Duke of Windsor). **3.** Adulatory: *a flattering tongue.* **4.** Representing in an exaggeratedly favorable or attractive manner. Said especially of a pictorial representation: *a flattering likeness.* —**flat′ter·ing·ly** *adv.*

flat·ter·y (flăt′ə-rē) *n., pl.* **-ies. 1.** The act or practice of flattering. **2.** Excessive, false, or sycophantic praise.

Flat·ter·y, Cape (flăt′ə-rē). A headland in northwestern Washington, at the entrance to Juan de Fuca Strait.

flat·tish (flăt′ĭsh) *adj.* Somewhat flat.

flat·top (flăt′tŏp′) *n. Informal.* A U.S. aircraft carrier.

flat·u·lence (flăch′o͞o-ləns) *n.* Also **flat·u·len·cy** (-lən-sē). **1.** The presence of excessive gas in the digestive tract. **2.** Windy, high-flown speech; pomposity.

flat·u·lent (flăch′o͞o-lənt) *adj.* **1. a.** Of or afflicted with flatulence. **b.** Inducing flatulence. **2.** Inflated with self-importance; pompous and pretentious: *flatulent oratory.* [Old French, from New Latin *flatulentus,* from Latin *flātus,* a breaking wind. See **flatus.**] —**flat′u·lent·ly** *adv.*

fla·tus (flā′təs) *n.* Gas generated in the stomach or intestines. [Latin *flātus,* a breaking wind, a blowing, from the past participle of *flāre,* to blow. See **bhlē-**[2] in Appendix.*]

flat·ware (flăt′wâr′) *n.* Tableware that is fairly flat and fashioned usually of a single piece; especially, silver or steel utensils such as knives, forks, and spoons. Compare **hollowware.**

flat·wise (flăt′wīz′) *adv.* Also **flat·ways** (-wāz′). With the flat side down or in contact with a surface.

flat·work (flăt′wûrk′) *n.* Linens and clothes that, in laundering, can be ironed by a mangle rather than by hand.

flat·worm (flăt′wûrm′) *n.* Any worm of the phylum Platyhelminthes; a **platyhelminth** *(see).*

Flau·bert (flō-bâr′), **Gustave.** 1821–1880. French novelist.

flaunt (flônt) *v.* **flaunted, flaunting, flaunts.** —*tr.* **1.** To exhibit ostentatiously; show off: *"Every great hostelry flaunted the flag of some foreign potentate."* (John Dos Passos). **2.** *Nonstandard.* To flout: *"Our English tradition of capitalizing all name-derivatives is so firmly established . . . that it seems a futile gesture to flaunt it"* (Robert A. Hall, Jr.). See Usage note below. —*intr.* **1.** To parade oneself ostentatiously or pertly; show oneself off. **2.** To be gaudily in evidence. **3.** To wave proudly. —See Synonyms at **show.** —*n. Rare.* The action or habit of flaunting. [Origin obscure. Transitive sense 2, folk-etymological substitution for FLOUT.] —**flaunt′er** *n.* —**flaunt′ing·ly** *adv.*

Usage: *Flaunt* in the sense of *flout* (to show contempt or conspicuous disregard for) is rejected by 91 per cent of the Usage Panel. A dissenting member of the Panel observes that it "is in too general usage to be ignored." However, although its appearance in print since the 1930's (especially in the United States) is widely attested, *flaunt* in this sense remains a malapropism in the judgment of most writers and editors.

flaunt·y (flôn′tē) *adj.* **-ier, -iest. 1.** Showy; gaudy. **2.** Inclined to flaunt; ostentatious. —**flaunt′i·ly** *adv.* —**flaunt′i·ness** *n.*

flau·tist (flô′tĭst, flou′-) *n.* A **flutist** *(see).* [Italian *flautista,* from *flauto,* flute, from Old Provençal *flaut,* akin to Old French *flaute,* FLUTE.]

fla·ves·cent (flə-vĕs′ənt) *adj.* Turning yellow; yellowish. [Latin *flāvēscens,* present participle of *flāvēscere,* to turn yellow, inceptive of *flāvēre,* to be yellow, from *flāvus,* yellow. See **bhel-**[1] in Appendix.*]

fla·vin (flā′vən) *n.* **1.** Any of various water-soluble yellow pigments, including riboflavin, found in plant and animal tissue as coenzymes of flavoprotein. **2.** A compound, $C_{10}H_6N_4O_2$, that is the nucleus of various natural yellow pigments. [Latin *flāvus,* yellow (see **bhel-**[1] in Appendix*) + -IN.]

fla·vine (flā′vēn′) *n.* **1.** A brownish-red crystalline powder, $C_{14}H_{15}N_3Cl_2$, used as an antiseptic. **2.** Flavin.

fla·vone (flā′vōn′) *n.* A crystalline compound, $C_{15}H_{10}O_2$, the parent substance of a number of important yellow pigments. [Latin *flāvus,* yellow (see **bhel-**[1] in Appendix*) + -ONE.]

fla·vo·pro·tein (flā′vō-prō′tēn′, -tē-ĭn) *n.* Any of a class of enzymes containing protein-bound flavin and acting as dehydrogenation catalysts in biological reactions. [Latin *flāvus,* yellow (see **bhel-**[1] in Appendix*) + PROTEIN.]

fla·vor (flā′vər) *n.* Also *chiefly British* **fla·vour. 1.** Distinctive taste; savor: *a flavor of smoke in bacon.* **2.** An ineffable quality felt to be characteristic of a given thing: *the flavor of the Orient.* **3.** A seasoning; flavoring. **4.** *Archaic.* Aroma. —*tr.v.* **flavored, -voring, -vors.** Also *chiefly British* **fla·vour.** To give flavor to. [Middle English *flavour,* aroma, variant (influenced by *savour,* SAVOR) of Old French *flaor,* from Vulgar Latin *flātor* (unattested), from Latin *flātus,* blowing, breeze, from the past participle of *flāre,* to blow. See **bhlē-**[2] in Appendix.*] —**fla′vor·er** *n.* —**fla′vor·ous, fla′vor·some** (-səm) *adj.*

fla·vor·ful (flā′vər-fo͝ol) *adj.* Full of flavor; savory; tasty. —**fla′vor·ful·ly** *adv.*

fla·vor·ing (flā′vər-ĭng) *n.* A substance that imparts flavor, as an extract or spice.

fla·vor·less (flā′vər-lĭs) *adj.* Lacking flavor: *"it was a perfectly flavourless Ghost."* (Lewis Carroll).

flaw[1] (flô) *n.* **1.** An imperfection; a blemish or defect. **2.** A defect in a legal document or evidence that renders it invalid. **3.** A small fissure; crack. —See Synonyms at **blemish.** —*v.* **flawed, flawing, flaws.** —*tr.* To make defective; mar. —*intr.* To become defective. [Middle English *flawe, flai,* flake, fragment, from Old Norse *flaga,* slab or layer of stone. See **plāk-**[1] in

Appendix.*] —**flaw'less** *adj.* —**flaw'less·ly** *adv.* —**flaw'less·ness** *n.* —**flaw'y** *adj.*

flaw[2] (flô) *n.* **1.** A brief gust or blast of wind. **2.** A squall; a passing storm. **3.** *Obsolete.* A burst of passion. [Probably from Middle Low German *vlāge* or Middle Dutch *vlāghe*, a push, attack, storm. See **plāk-**[2] in Appendix.*] —**flaw'y** *adj.*

flax (flăks) *n.* **1.** Any of several plants of the genus *Linum;* especially, a widely cultivated species, *L. usitatissimum*, having blue flowers, seeds that yield linseed oil, and slender stems from which a fine, light-colored textile fiber is obtained. **2.** The textile fiber obtained from this plant. **3.** Any of several plants resembling flax. **4.** Grayish yellow. See **color.** [Middle English *flax, flex,* Old English *fleax, flæx.* See **plek-** in Appendix.*]

flax·en (flăk'sən) *adj.* **1.** Made of or resembling flax. **2.** Having the color of flax fiber; pale-yellow.

flax·seed (flăks'sēd') *n.* The seed of flax, the source of linseed oil and of emollient medicinal preparations.

flax·y (flăk'sē) *adj.* **-ier, -iest.** Resembling flax, as in texture.

flay (flā) *tr.v.* **flayed, flaying, flays. 1.** To strip off the skin of. **2.** To strip of money or goods; to plunder; to fleece. **3.** To assail with stinging criticism; excoriate. [Middle English *flen,* Old English *flēan.* See **plēk-** in Appendix.*] —**flay'er** *n.*

F layer. 1. The highest zone of the ionosphere, extending continuously at night from approximately 120 to 250 miles. **2.** Either of two layers into which this zone is divided during the day, especially in summer, usually designated F_1 and F_2, and extending respectively from 90 to 150 miles and from 150 miles upward. Also called "F region," "Appleton layer."

fld. field.

flea (flē) *n.* **1.** Any of various small, wingless, bloodsucking insects of the order Siphonaptera, that have legs adapted for jumping, and are parasitic on warm-blooded animals. **2.** Any of various small crustaceans that resemble or move like fleas. —**a flea in one's ear.** A sharp, stinging rebuke or pointed, annoying hint. [Middle English *fle,* Old English *flēa(h).* See **plou-** in Appendix.*]

flea·bane (flē'bān') *n.* Any of various plants of the genus *Erigeron,* having variously colored, many-rayed, daisylike flowers. [From its supposed ability to drive away fleas.]

flea·bite (flē'bīt') *n.* **1. a.** The bite of a flea. **b.** The little red mark caused by a flea's bite. **2.** A trifling loss, inconvenience, or annoyance.

flea-bit·ten (flē'bĭt'n) *adj.* **1.** Covered with fleas or fleabites. **2.** *Informal.* Shabby; mean; wretched. **3.** Having a pale coat with reddish-brown flecks. Said of horses.

flea market. A shop or open market selling antiques, used household goods, curios, and the like.

flèche (flĕsh) *n.* A slender spire, especially one on a church above the intersection of the nave and transepts. [French, "arrow," from Old French, from Frankish *fliugika* (unattested). See **pleu-** in Appendix.*]

flé·chette (flā-shĕt') *n.* A steel missile or dart dropped from an airplane, used in World War I. [French, from FLÈCHE.]

fleck (flĕk) *n.* **1.** A tiny mark or spot, such as a freckle. **2.** A small bit or flake. **3.** A small patch of color or light. —*tr.v.* **flecked, flecking, flecks.** To spot or streak. [Probably from Middle English *flecked,* spotted, dappled, from Old Norse *flekkōttr,* from *flekkr,* spot, stain. See **plēk-** in Appendix.*]

flec·tion (flĕk'shən) *n.* Also *chiefly British* **flex·ion. 1.** The act or process of bending or flexing. **2.** A bent part; a curve; a bend. **3.** *Grammar.* Inflection. **4.** *Anatomy.* Variant of **flexion.** [Latin *flexiō,* a bending, from *flexus,* past participle of *flectere,* to bend, FLEX.] —**flec'tion·al** *adj.*

fledge (flĕj) *v.* **fledged, fledging, fledges.** —*tr.* **1.** To take care of (a young bird) until it is ready to fly. **2.** To cover with or as if with feathers: *"Far, far around shall those dark-clustered trees/ Fledge the wild-ridged mountains"* (Keats). **3.** To provide with feathers; to feather (an arrow). —*intr.* To grow the plumage necessary for flight. [Probably from obsolete *fledge,* feathered, from Middle English *flegge,* Old English *-flycge.* See **pleu-** in Appendix.*]

fledg·ling (flĕj'lĭng) *n.* Also **fledge·ling. 1.** A young bird that has recently acquired its flight feathers. **2.** One that is young and inexperienced: *"the young republic, fledgling of the nations"* (Ross Lockridge, Jr.).

fledg·y (flĕj'ē) *adj.* **-ier, -iest.** *Rare.* Covered with feathers; feathery.

flee (flē) *v.* **fled** (flĕd), **fleeing, flees.** —*intr.* **1.** To run away, as from trouble or danger. **2.** To withdraw abruptly; rush off: *fled to her bedroom.* **3.** To pass swiftly away; vanish: *"of time fleeing beneath him"* (Faulkner). —*tr.* To run away from; shun. [Middle English *flen, fleon,* Old English *flēon.* (The past tense fled and past participle fled are from Middle English *fledde* and *fledd,* which superseded the strong forms inherited from Old English.) See **pleu-** in Appendix.*] —**fle'er** *n.*

fleece (flēs) *n.* **1.** The coat of wool of a sheep or similar animal. **2.** The yield of wool shorn from a sheep at one time. **3.** Any soft, woolly covering or mass. **4.** Fabric with a soft deep pile. —*tr.v.* **fleeced, fleecing, fleeces. 1.** To shear the fleece from. **2.** To defraud of money or property; to swindle. **3.** To cover with or as if with fleece. [Middle English *flees, fles,* Old English *flēos.* See **pleus-** in Appendix.*] —**fleec'er** *n.*

fleec·y (flē'sē) *adj.* **-ier, -iest.** Of, like, or covered with fleece: *"a thick fleecy sky threatened snow"* (Edith Wharton). —**fleec'i·ly** *adv.* —**fleec'i·ness** *n.*

fleer (flîr) *v.* **fleered, fleering, fleers.** —*tr.* To sneer at; to scoff; scorn. —*intr.* To smirk or laugh in contempt or derision. —*n.* A scoffing or taunting look or gibe. [Middle English *flerien,* to laugh mockingly, jeer, from Scandinavian, akin to Norwegian and Swedish dialectal *flira,* to laugh, Danish dialectal *flire,* to giggle. See **flimflam.**] —**fleer'ing·ly** *adv.*

fleet[1] (flēt) *n.* **1. a.** A number of warships operating together under one command. **b.** The entire navy of a government. **2.** Any group of vehicles, such as taxicabs or fishing boats, owned or operated as a unit. [Middle English *flete,* Old English *flēot,* from *flēotan,* to float. See **pleu-** in Appendix.*]

fleet[2] (flēt) *adj.* **fleeter, fleetest. 1.** Moving swiftly; rapid or nimble. **2.** *Archaic.* Passing swiftly; disappearing. —See Synonyms at **fast.** —*v.* **fleeted, fleeting, fleets.** —*intr.* **1.** To move or pass swiftly. **2.** To glide away; to fade; vanish. **3.** *British Regional.* To float. **4.** *Obsolete.* To flow. —*tr.* **1.** *Archaic.* To pass (time) quickly. **2.** *Nautical.* To alter the position of; to shift. [Probably from Middle English *fleten,* to flow, glide swiftly, Old English *flēotan,* to float, drift. See **pleu-** in Appendix.*] —**fleet'ly** *adv.* —**fleet'ness** *n.*

fleet[3] (flēt) *n. British Regional.* A small inlet or creek. [Middle English *flete,* Old English *flēot.* See **pleu-** in Appendix.*]

Fleet Admiral. A naval officer, the **Admiral of the Fleet** *(see).*

fleet·ing (flē'tĭng) *adj.* Passing quickly; very brief. See Synonyms at **transient.** —**fleet'ing·ly** *adv.* —**fleet'ing·ness** *n.*

Fleet Street. 1. A thoroughfare of central London along which are located many British newspaper publishers. **2.** British journalism. [From *the Fleet,* a creek along which the street originally extended, from Middle English *flete,* FLEET (inlet).]

Flem. Flemish.

Flem·ing (flĕm'ĭng) *n.* **1.** A native of Flanders. **2.** A Belgian who speaks Flemish. Compare **Walloon.** [Middle English, from Old Norse *Flæmingi,* from Middle Dutch *Vlāming,* from *Vlām-,* FLANDERS.]

Flem·ing (flĕm'ĭng), Sir **Alexander.** 1881–1955. British bacteriologist; discovered penicillin.

Flem·ing (flĕm'ĭng), **Ian Lancaster.** 1908–1964. English author of spy stories; creator of James Bond.

Flem·ing (flĕm'ĭng), Sir **John Ambrose.** 1849–1945. British electrical engineer.

Flem·ish (flĕm'ĭsh) *adj. Abbr.* **Flem.** Of or pertaining to Flanders, the Flemings, or their language. —*n. Abbr.* **Flem. 1.** The West Germanic language, related to Dutch, spoken by the Flemings. **2.** The Flemings. Preceded by *the.* [Middle English, from Old Norse *Flæmskr,* from Middle Dutch *Vlāmish,* from *Vlām-,* FLANDERS.]

Flem·ming (flĕm'ĭng), **Walther.** 1843–1915. German physician and biologist.

flense (flĕns) *tr.v.* **flensed, flensing, flenses.** Also **flench** (flĕnch). To strip the blubber or skin from (a whale or seal, for example). [Danish *flense.* See **pele-**[1] in Appendix.*] —**flens'er** *n.*

flesh (flĕsh) *n.* **1.** The soft tissue of the body; especially, skeletal muscle distinguished from bone and viscera. **2.** The meat of animals, as distinguished from the edible tissue of fish or, sometimes, fowl. **3.** The pulpy, usually edible part of a fruit or vegetable. **4.** Excess tissue; fat; avoirdupois. **5.** The surface or skin of the human body. **6. a.** The body as distinguished from the mind or soul. **b.** Man's physical or carnal nature. **c.** Sensual appetites. **7.** Mankind: *"The glory of the Lord shall be revealed, and all flesh shall see it together."* (Isaiah 40:3). **8.** One's family; kin. —**in the flesh. 1.** Alive. **2.** In person. —*v.* **fleshed, fleshing, fleshes.** —*tr.* **1.** To encourage (a hunting dog or falcon) by feeding it flesh; to blood. **2.** To inure to bloodshed. **3.** To fatten (livestock). **4.** To fill out (a structure or framework). **5.** To plunge or thrust (a weapon) into flesh. **6.** To clean (a hide) of adhering flesh. —*intr.* To gain weight; become plump or fleshy. Usually used with *out.* [Middle English *flesh, fleish,* Old English *flǣsc.* See **plēk-** in Appendix.*]

flesh and blood. 1. Human nature or physical existence, together with its weaknesses. **2.** One's blood relatives; kin.

flesh·er (flĕsh'ər) *n.* **1.** A person who fleshes hides. **2.** An instrument for fleshing hides.

flesh fly. Any of various flies of the genus *Sarcophaga,* of which the larvae are parasitic in animal tissue.

flesh·ings (flĕsh'ĭngz) *pl.n.* **1.** Flesh-colored tights. **2.** Bits of flesh removed from a hide in cleaning.

flesh·ly (flĕsh'lē) *adj.* **-lier, -liest. 1.** Of or pertaining to the body; corporeal. **2.** Inclined to or concerned with carnality; sensual; sybaritic. **3.** Not spiritual; worldly. **4.** Tending to plumpness; fleshy. —**flesh'li·ness** *n.*

flesh·pot (flĕsh'pŏt') *n.* **1.** *Archaic.* A pot for cooking flesh or meat. **2.** *Plural.* **a.** Material and physical well-being; sensual gratification. **b.** Places in which such gratification is obtained.

flesh·y (flĕsh'ē) *adj.* **-ier, -iest. 1.** Pertaining to, consisting of, or resembling flesh. **2.** Having much flesh; corpulent; plump. **3.** Not fibrous; firm and pulpy, as fruit or leaves. —See Synonyms at **fat.** —**flesh'i·ness** *n.*

fletch (flĕch) *tr.v.* **fletched, fletching, fletches.** To feather or fledge (an arrow). [Perhaps from FLETCHER.]

fletch·er (flĕch'ər) *n.* One who makes arrows. [Middle English *fleccher,* from Old French *flech(i)er,* from *fleche,* arrow, from Frankish *fliugika* (unattested). See **pleu-** in Appendix.*]

Fletch·er (flĕch'ər), **John.** 1579–1625. English dramatist; collaborated with Francis **Beaumont** *(see).*

Fletch·er·ism (flĕch'ə-rĭz'əm) *n.* The practice of eating small amounts of food by slow and thorough mastication. [After Horace *Fletcher* (1849–1919), American nutritionist.]

Fletsch·horn (flĕch'hôrn'). A peak rising to 13,121 feet in the Lepontine Alps of southern Switzerland.

fleur-de-lis, fleur-de-lys (flûr'də-lē', flŏŏr'-) *n., pl.* **fleurs-de-lis, fleurs-de-lys** (flûr'də-lēz', flŏŏr'-). Also *archaic* **flow·er-de-luce** (flou'ər-də-lōōs') *pl.* **flowers-de-luce. 1.** An iris; especially, a white-flowered form of *Iris germanica.* **2.** A heraldic device

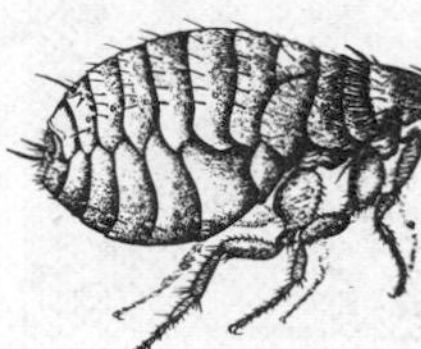

flea
Ctenocephalides canis

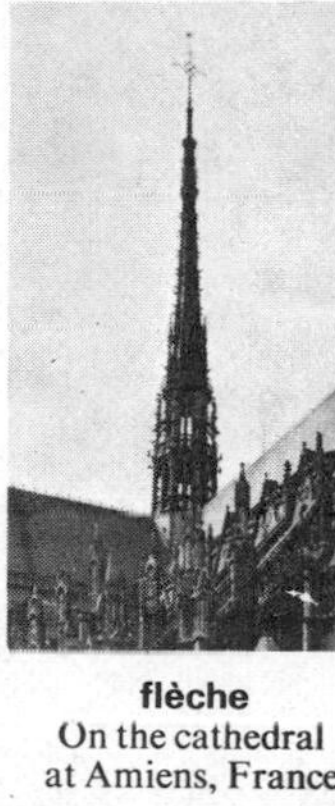

flèche
On the cathedral at Amiens, France

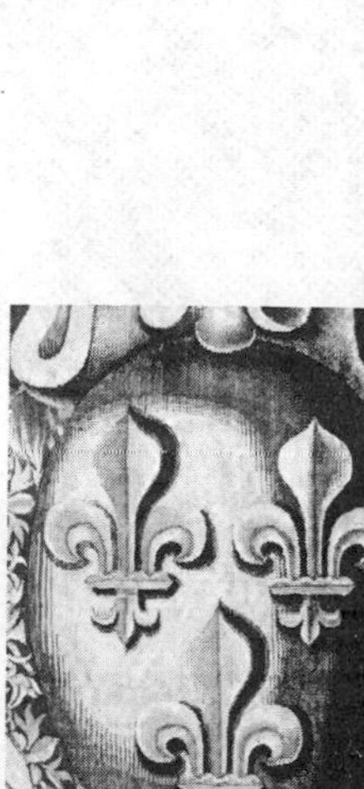

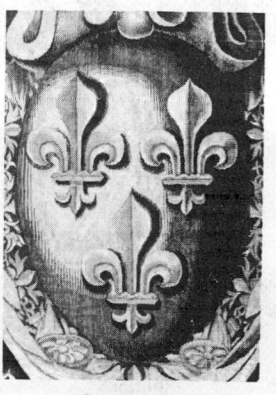

fleur-de-lis

consisting of a stylized three-petaled iris flower, used as the armorial emblem of the kings of France. [Middle English *flour de lice,* from Old French *flor de lis,* lily flower : *flo(u)r,* FLOWER + *de,* of + *lis,* lily, from Latin *līlium,* LILY.]

Fleu·ry (flœ-rē′), **André Hercule de.** 1653–1734. French cardinal and virtual prime minister; tutor of Louis XV.

flew[1]. Past tense of **fly.**

flew[2]. Variant of **flue** (fishing net).

flews (flo͞oz) *pl.n.* The pendulous corners of the upper lip of certain dogs, as a hound. [Origin unknown.]

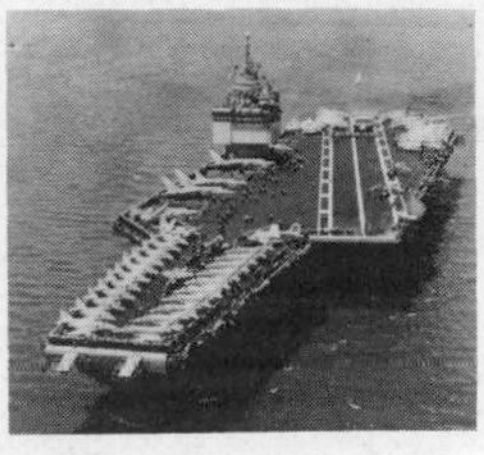

flight deck
U.S.S. *Enterprise*

flex (flěks) *v.* **flexed, flexing, flexes.** *—tr.* **1. a.** To bend (something pliant or elastic). **b.** To bend (a joint). **c.** To bend (a joint) repeatedly. **2.** To contract (a muscle). Compare **extend.** *—intr.* To bend: *"his hands flexed nervously as he spoke"* (Mary McCarthy). *—n. British.* Flexible insulated electric cord. [Latin *flectere*† (past participle *flexus*), to bend.]

flex·i·ble (flěk′sə-bəl) *adj.* Also **flex·ile** (flěk′səl, -sīl′). **1.** Capable of being bent or flexed; pliable. **2.** Susceptible to influence or persuasion; tractable. **3.** Responsive to change; adaptable. **4.** Capable of variation or modification. **—flex′i·bil′i·ty, flex′i·ble·ness** *n.* **—flex′i·bly** *adv.*

Synonyms: *flexible, malleable, ductile, plastic, pliable, pliant, supple, adaptable.* These adjectives are applied to what can readily undergo change or modification. *Flexible* refers to the ability of a thing to be bent, twisted, or turned without breaking, or the ability of persons or things to accommodate to another's wishes, changing conditions, or the like. *Malleable* is applied, literally and figuratively, to capacity for being shaped by or as if by tools. *Ductile* describes the capacity of certain metals to be drawn out or hammered thin, or of certain liquids to be channeled readily. *Plastic* refers to capacity for being molded or modeled after the fashion of plaster or clay. *Pliable* and *pliant* refer to things or materials that can be changed in shape without breaking. Applied to persons, *pliant* indicates readiness to accommodate to change or the wishes of another, and *pliable* may imply tendency to be influenced easily or to be dominated. *Supple* is applied to objects that can bend in many places without damage, or figuratively to what responds readily to change or external influence. *Adaptable* refers to the capacity of persons and things to assume modified form or to change or adjust in other respects in response to new conditions, demands, or circumstances.

flex·ion (flěk′shən) *n.* Also **flec·tion** (for sense 1). **1.** *Anatomy.* **a.** The act of bending. **b.** The condition of being bent. **2.** *Chiefly British.* Variant of **flection.** [Variant of FLECTION.]

flex·or (flěk′sər) *n.* A muscle that acts to flex a joint. [New Latin, from Latin *flexus,* past participle of *flectere,* to FLEX.]

flex·u·ous (flěk′sho͞o-əs) *adj.* Also **flex·u·ose** (-ōs′). Bending or winding alternately from side to side. [Latin *flexuōsus,* from *flexus.* See **flex.**] **—flex′u·ous·ly** *adv.*

flex·ure (flěk′shər) *n.* **1.** A bend, curve, or turn. **2.** A bending or flexing; flexion. **—flex′ur·al** *adj.*

fley (flā) *tr.v.* **fleyed, fleying, fleys.** *Scottish.* To frighten. [Middle English *flayen, fleien,* to put to flight, frighten, Old English *-flȳgan.* See **pleu-** in Appendix.*]

flib·ber·ti·gib·bet (flĭb′ər-tē-jĭb′ĭt) *n.* A silly, scatterbrained, or garrulous person. [Earlier *flibbergib, flipergebet*†.]

flick[1] (flĭk) *n.* **1.** A light, quick blow, jerk, or touch. **2.** The sound accompanying such a movement; a snap. **3.** A light splash, dash, or daub. *—v.* **flicked, flicking, flicks.** *—tr.* **1.** To touch or hit with a light, quick blow. **2.** To cause to move with a light blow; to snap: *"Clay found the overhead-light switch, flicked it on"* (J.D. Salinger). **3.** To remove with a light, quick blow. *—intr.* To twitch or flutter. [Perhaps imitative.]

flick[2] (flĭk) *n. Slang.* A motion picture. [Back-formation from FLICKER.]

flick·er[1] (flĭk′ər) *v.* **-ered, -ering, -ers.** *—intr.* **1.** To move waveringly; flutter. **2.** To give off inconstant, fitful light; burn unsteadily: *"and moth-like stars were flickering out"* (Yeats). **3.** To shine or blaze momentarily, as does lightning. *—tr.* To cause to flicker. *—n.* **1.** A tremor or flutter. **2.** An inconstant or wavering light: *"a flicker like green fire in his eyes"* (J.R.R. Tolkien). **3.** A brief or slight sensation, as of an emotion. **4.** *Slang.* A motion picture; especially, a silent movie. [Middle English *flikeren, flekeren,* to flutter, flicker, Old English *flicorian*†, to flutter, hover.]

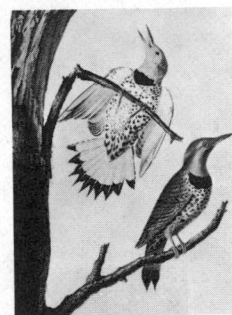

flicker[2]
Colaptes auratus
Painting by
John James Audubon

flick·er[2] (flĭk′ər) *n.* Any of several large North American woodpeckers of the genus *Colaptes,* having a brownish back and a spotted breast. A common species, *C. auratus,* is also called "yellowhammer." [Probably from FLICK (verb).]

flick·er·tail (flĭk′ər-tāl′) *n.* A ground squirrel, *Citellus richardsoni,* of western North America.

flied. Past tense and past participle of **fly** (to hit a fly ball).

fli·er (flī′ər) *n.* Also **fly·er. 1. a.** One that flies. **b.** An airplane pilot; aviator. **2.** A long leap; a bound. **3.** A step in a straight stairway. **4.** *Informal.* A daring financial venture. **5.** *Informal.* A pamphlet or circular for mass distribution.

flight[1] (flīt) *n.* **1. a.** The motion of an object in or through a medium, especially through the earth's atmosphere or through space, that is characterized by lack of contact with any other object, especially with the earth. **b.** An instance of such motion. **c.** The duration of an instance of such motion. **d.** The ability to engage in such motion. **2.** The act or process of flying; locomotion through the air by means of wings. **3.** Any swift passage or movement. **4.** A scheduled airline run or trip, or the plane making it. **5.** A group, especially of birds or aircraft, flying together. **6.** *U.S. Air Force.* A number of aircraft forming a subdivision of a squadron. **7.** An effort that transcends the usual restraints; a soaring: *a flight of far-fetched imagery.* **8.** A series of stairs rising from one landing to another. **9.** *Archery.* A thin, light arrow designed for long-range shooting. Also called "flight arrow." **10.** *Fishing.* A device that whirls the bait rapidly in trolling. —See Synonyms at **flock.** *—intr.v.* **flighted, flighting, flights.** To migrate or fly in flocks. [Middle English *flight,* Old English *flyht.* See **pleu-** in Appendix.*]

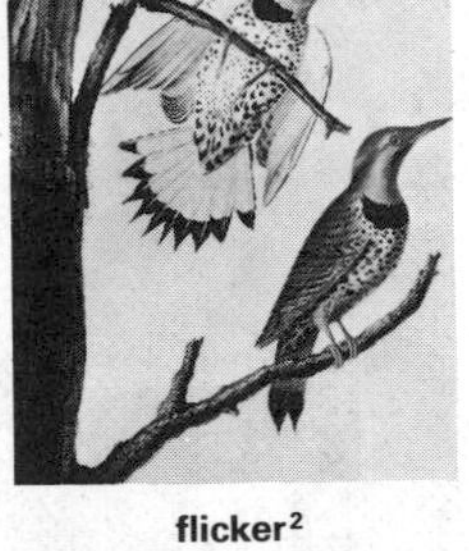

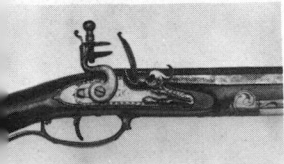

flintlock
Late 18th-century American

flight[2] (flīt) *n.* A running away; an escape: *"our first successful homegrown legend . . . the flight of the dreamer from the shrew"* (Robert Brustein). **—put to flight.** To drive or frighten away; repel; rout. **—take (to) flight.** To run or fly away; withdraw rapidly; flee. [Middle English *flight,* Old English *flyht* (unattested). See **pleu-** in Appendix.*]

flight check. A proficiency check in an airborne aircraft of the pilot, crew members, or a piece of equipment.

flight deck. 1. The upper deck of an aircraft carrier, used as a runway. **2.** An elevated compartment in some aircraft, used by the pilot, copilot, and flight engineer.

flight engineer. The crew member responsible for the mechanical performance of an aircraft flight.

flight feather. One of the comparatively large, stiff feathers of a bird's wing or tail, that are necessary for flight.

flight·y (flī′tē) *adj.* **-ier, -iest. 1.** Given to capricious behavior; fickle or unstable. **2.** Easily excited; skittish. [Originally "swift," from FLIGHT.] **—flight′i·ly** *adv.* **—flight′i·ness** *n.*

flim·flam (flĭm′flăm′) *n. Informal.* **1.** Nonsense; humbug. **2.** A deception; a swindle. *—tr.v.* **flimflammed, -flamming, -flams.** *Informal.* To swindle. [Reduplication of an unknown Scandinavian word akin to Old Norse *flīm,* mockery, Danish dialectal *flire,* to giggle, from Germanic *fli-* (unattested).]

flim·sy (flĭm′zē) *adj.* **-sier, -siest. 1.** Light, thin, and insubstantial. **2.** Lacking solidity or strength: *a flimsy building.* **3.** Lacking plausibility; unconvincing: *a flimsy theory.* *—n., pl.* **flimsies. 1.** Thin paper usually used to make multiple copies. **2.** Something written on such paper. [Origin obscure.] **—flim′si·ly** *adv.* **—flim′si·ness** *n.*

flinch (flĭnch) *intr.v.* **flinched, flinching, flinches. 1.** To betray fear, pain, or surprise with an involuntary gesture such as a start; to wince. **2.** To draw away; retreat. —See Synonyms at **recoil.** *—n.* An act or instance of flinching. [Old French *flenchir, flainchir,* from Germanic. See **kleng-** in Appendix.*] **—flinch′er** *n.* **—flinch′ing·ly** *adv.*

flin·ders (flĭn′dərz) *pl.n.* Bits; fragments; splinters. [Middle English *flenderis,* from Scandinavian, akin to Norwegian *flindra,* splinter. See **splei-** in Appendix.*]

Flin·ders (flĭn′dərz). **1.** The largest (802 square miles) of the Furneaux Islands in Bass Strait. **2.** A river rising in the Eastern Highlands, Australia, and flowing 520 miles northwest to the Gulf of Carpentaria.

Flin·ders (flĭn′dərz), **Matthew.** 1774–1814. British navigator and explorer of the South Pacific.

Flin·ders Ranges (flĭn′dərz). A mountain region of eastern South Australia, extending some 400 miles north from Adelaide.

fling (flĭng) *v.* **flung** (flŭng), **flinging, flings.** *—tr.* **1.** To throw with violence; hurl. **2.** To put or send suddenly or unexpectedly: *The army was flung into battle.* **3.** To throw (oneself) into some activity with abandon and energy. **4.** To throw (an opponent or rider, for example) to the ground. **5.** To toss aside; discard: *fling propriety away.* *—intr.* To move quickly, violently, or impulsively: *"Then he flung outward, feet first, with a swish"* (Robert Frost). —See Synonyms at **throw.** *—n.* **1.** An act of flinging or hurling; a throw. **2.** A brief period of indulging one's impulses; a spree. **3.** A dance in which the arms and legs are flung about; especially, the **Highland fling** *(see).* **4.** *Informal.* A brief trial. [Fling, flung, flung; Middle English *flingen, flung* (more often *flang*), *flungen,* from Scandinavian, akin to Old Norse *flengja,* to flog. See **plāk-**[2] in Appendix.*] **—fling′er** *n.*

flint (flĭnt) *n.* **1.** A very hard, fine-grained quartz that sparks when struck with steel. **2.** A small solid cylinder of a spark-producing alloy, used in lighters to ignite the fuel. **3.** Anything likened to flint in hardness: *a jaw of flint.* [Middle English *flint,* Old English *flint.* See **splei-** in Appendix.*]

Flint (flĭnt). **1.** A city and automobile-manufacturing center in Michigan, 50 miles northwest of Detroit. Population, 197,000. **2.** A river rising in western Georgia and flowing 330 miles generally south to join the Chattahoochee with which it forms the Apalachicola. **3.** See **Flintshire.**

flint corn. A variety of corn, *Zea mays indurata,* having small, hard seeds.

flint glass. A soft, fusible, lustrous, brilliant lead-oxide optical glass with high refraction and low dispersion. Also called "lead glass." Compare **crown glass.**

flint·head (flĭnt′hĕd′) *n.* A bird, the **wood ibis** *(see).*

flint·lock (flĭnt′lŏk′) *n.* **1.** An obsolete gunlock in which a flint embedded in the hammer produces a spark that ignites the charge. **2.** A firearm having such a gunlock. Also called "firelock."

Flint·shire (flĭnt′shĭr, -shər). Also **Flint** (flĭnt). A county occupying 256 square miles in northeastern Wales. Population, 155,000. County seat, Mold.

flint·y (flĭn′tē) *adj.* **-ier, -iest. 1.** Containing or composed of flint. **2.** Unyielding; stony. **—flint′i·ly** *adv.* **—flint′i·ness** *n.*

flip (flĭp) *v.* **flipped, flipping, flips.** *—tr.* **1.** To throw with a brisk motion; to toss. **2.** To toss (a coin, for example) in the air, imparting a spin. **3.** To reverse or overturn quickly and effortlessly. **4.** *Slang.* To overwhelm with delight: *That singing group flips him.* *—intr.* **1.** To strike quickly or lightly, as with a fillip. **2.** To move suddenly or jerkily. **3.** To turn a somersault in the

ă pat/ā pay/âr care/ä father/b bib/ch church/d deed/ĕ pet/ē be/f fife/g gag/h hat/hw which/ĭ pit/ī pie/îr pier/j judge/k kick/l lid, needle/m mum/n no, sudden/ng thing/ŏ pot/ō toe/ô paw, for/oi noise/ou out/o͝o took/o͞o boot/p pop/r roar/s sauce/sh ship, dish/

air. **4.** *Slang.* To have a strong reaction; be overwhelmed: *They flipped when they saw the new car.* —*n.* **1.** An act of flipping, especially: **a.** A fillip or tap. **b.** A quick, jerky movement. **c.** A somersault. **2.** A mixed drink made with any of various alcoholic beverages, often including beaten eggs. —*adj. Informal.* Disrespectful; impertinent: *a flip attitude.* [Origin obscure.]

flip-flop (flĭp′flŏp′) *n.* **1.** *Informal.* The movement or sound of repeated flapping: *the flip-flop of sandals on a tile floor.* **2.** *Informal.* A backward somersault or handspring. **3.** *Informal.* A reversal, as of opinion. **4.** *Electronics.* An electronic circuit having two stable states, either of which can be assumed depending on the input signal, that is used in computers to store a single bit of information. [Reduplication of FLIP.]

flip·pant (flĭp′ənt) *adj.* **1.** Marked by disrespectful levity; pert. **2.** *Archaic.* Talkative; voluble. [Probably FLIP + -ANT.] —**flip′pan·cy** *n.* —**flip′pant·ly** *adv.*

flip·per (flĭp′ər) *n.* **1.** One that flips. **2.** A wide, flat limb, as of a seal, whale, or other aquatic animal, adapted especially for swimming. **3.** A rubber foot covering with a flat, flexible portion that widens as it extends forward from the toes to provide a larger and more efficient propulsion surface than that of the unaided foot, used in swimming. **4.** *Slang.* A hand.

flirt (flûrt) *v.* **flirted, flirting, flirts.** —*intr.* **1.** To amuse oneself in playful amorousness; play lightly or mockingly at courtship. **2.** To deal playfully, triflingly, or coyly; to toy: *The bullfighter flirted with death.* **3.** To move abruptly or jerkily; to dart; to flit. —*tr.* **1.** To toss or flip suddenly; to flick. **2.** To move quickly; jerk or wave briskly. —*n.* **1.** One given to flirting. **2.** An abrupt, jerking movement. [Origin obscure.]

flir·ta·tion (flûr-tā′shən) *n.* **1.** The practice of flirting; coquetry. **2.** A casual or transitory amorous relationship. **3.** Any brief involvement.

flir·ta·tious (flûr-tā′shəs) *adj.* **1.** Given to flirting. **2.** Full of playful allure: *a flirtatious glance.* —**flir·ta′tious·ly** *adv.* —**flir·ta′tious·ness** *n.*

flit (flĭt) *intr.v.* **flitted, flitting, flits.** **1.** To move about rapidly and nimbly; to dart or fly. **2.** To move quickly from one location to another. —*n.* **1.** A fluttering or darting movement. **2.** *Vulgar Slang.* A homosexual male. [Middle English *flitten,* to transport, convey, from Old Norse *flytja,* to convey. See **pleu-** in Appendix.*] —**flit′ter** *n.*

flitch (flĭch) *n.* **1.** A salted and cured side of bacon. **2.** A longitudinal cut from the trunk of a tree. **3.** One of several planks secured together to form a single beam. [Middle English *fliche,* side of animal salted and cured, Old English *flicce.* See **plēk-** in Appendix.*]

flit·ter (flĭt′ər) *intr.v.* **-tered, -tering, -ters.** To flutter. [Frequentative of FLIT.]

flit·ter·mouse (flĭt′ər-mous′) *n., pl.* **-mice** (-mīs′). *Rare.* A bat. [Translation of German *Fledermaus.*]

fliv·ver (flĭv′ər) *n. Slang.* An old or cheap car. [Origin unknown.]

float (flōt) *v.* **floated, floating, floats.** —*intr.* **1. a.** To remain suspended within or on the surface of a fluid without sinking. **b.** To be suspended unsupported in space without falling. **2.** To move from position to position, especially at random; to drift. **3.** To move easily and lightly as if suspended: *"Miss Golightly . . . floated round in their arms light as a scarf"* (Truman Capote). —*tr.* **1.** To cause to remain suspended without sinking or falling. **2.** To flood (land), as for irrigation. **3.** To launch or establish (a business enterprise, for example). **4.** To release (a security) for sale. **5.** To make the surface of (plaster, for example) level or smooth. —*n.* **1.** Something that floats, as: **a.** A raft. **b.** A buoy. **c.** A life preserver. **d.** A cork or other floating object on a fishing line. **e.** A landing platform attached to a wharf and floating on the water. **f.** A pontoon for amphibious aircraft. **g.** A hollow ball attached to a lever to regulate the water level in a tank. **h.** An air-filled or gas-filled organ or sac that enables an organism to remain suspended in water. **2.** A large, flat vehicle bearing an exhibit in a parade. **3.** *Finance.* A sum of money representing checks that are outstanding. **4.** A tool for smoothing the surface of plaster or cement. **5.** A soft drink with ice cream floating in it. [Middle English *floten,* Old English *flotian.* See **pleu-** in Appendix.*]

float·age. Variant of **flotage.**

float·a·tion. Variant of **flotation.**

float·er (flō′tər) *n.* **1.** One that floats. **2.** One who wanders; a drifter. **3.** An employee who is reassigned from job to job or shift to shift within an operation. **4.** One who votes illegally. **5.** An insurance policy that protects movable property that is in transit or that is regularly subject to use in a variety of places, as by being worn on the person.

float·ing (flō′tĭng) *adj.* **1.** Buoyed on or suspended in or as if in a fluid. **2.** Not secured in place; unattached. **3.** Inclined to move about; drifting; errant. **4.** *Finance.* **a.** Available for use; in circulation. Said of capital. **b.** Short-term and usually unfunded. Said of a debt. **5.** Designating an organ of the body that is out of normal position, especially moved downward: *a floating kidney.*

floating dock. A structure that can be submerged to permit the entry and docking of a ship and then raised to lift the ship from the water for repairs. Also called "floating dry dock."

floating heart. Any of several aquatic plants of the genus *Nymphoides;* especially, *N. cordata,* of North America, having floating, heart-shaped leaves and clusters of white flowers.

floating island. A dessert of soft custard with beaten egg whites or whipped cream floating on its surface.

floating rib. One of the four lower ribs that, unlike the other ribs, are not attached at the front.

floc (flŏk) *n.* A flocculent mass as formed in certain serological precipitin tests. [Latin *floccus,* tuft of wool. See **floccose.**]

floc·cose (flŏk′ōs′) *adj.* Having or consisting of dense, woolly tufts. [Late Latin *floccōsus,* from Latin *floccus*†, tuft of wool.]

floc·cu·late (flŏk′yə-lāt′) *v.* **-lated, -lating, -lates.** —*tr.* **1.** To cause (soil) to form lumps or masses. **2.** To cause (clouds) to form fluffy masses. —*intr.* To form lumpy or fluffy masses. [From FLOCCULE.] —**floc′cu·la′tion** *n.*

floc·cule (flŏk′yo͞ol) *n.* Any small, loosely held mass or aggregate of fine particles suspended in or precipitated from a solution. [New Latin FLOCCULUS.]

floc·cu·lent (flŏk′yə-lənt) *adj.* **1.** Having a fluffy or woolly appearance. **2.** Made up of or containing woolly masses. **3.** Flaky, waxy, and woollike, as the secretion covering some insects. [From Late Latin FLOCCULUS.] —**floc′cu·lence** *n.* —**floc′cu·lent·ly** *adv.*

floc·cu·lus (flŏk′yə-ləs) *n., pl.* **-li** (-lī′). **1.** A small, fluffy mass or tuft. **2.** *Anatomy.* Either of two small lobes on the lower posterior border of each lobe of the cerebellum. **3.** *Astronomy.* Any of various masses of gases appearing as bright or dark patches on the sun's surface. [New Latin, from Late Latin, diminutive of Latin *floccus,* tuft of wool. See **floccose.**]

flock[1] (flŏk) *n.* **1.** A group of animals, as birds or sheep, that live, travel, or feed together. **2.** A group of people under the leadership of one person; especially, the members of a church or congregation. **3.** A large crowd or number: *"They had a flock of whiskeys on the strength of the good old times"* (John Dos Passos). —*intr.v.* **flocked, flocking, flocks.** To congregate or travel in a flock or crowd: *"Not all the widows flock to Florida"* (Harry Golden). [Middle English *flok,* Old English *flocc,* from Germanic *flugnaz* (unattested).]

Synonyms: *flock, flight, herd, drove, pack, gang, gaggle, bevy, brood.* These nouns denote a number of animals, birds, or fish considered collectively, and some have human connotations. *Flock* is applied to a congregation of animals of one kind, especially sheep or goats herded by man, and to any congregation of wild or domesticated birds, especially when on the ground. It is also applicable to people who form the membership of a church or to people under someone's care or supervision. *Flight* refers to a flock of birds in flight. *Herd* is used of a number of animals, especially cattle, herded by man; or of such wild animals as antelope, elephants, and zebras; or of whales and seals. Applied to people, it is used disparagingly of a crowd or of the masses, and suggests the gregarious aspect of crowd psychology. *Drove* is used of a herd or flock of cattle, sheep, geese, or the like, that are being moved or driven from one place to another; less often it refers to a crowd of people in movement. *Pack* is applicable to any body of animals, especially wolves, or of birds, especially grouse, and to a body of hounds trained to hunt as a unit. It also refers to a band or gang of persons, especially when engaged in violent or criminal pursuits. *Gang* refers to a herd, especially of buffalo or elk; to a pack of wolves or wild dogs; or to various associations of persons. *Gaggle* denotes a flock of geese or, informally, a company of women. *Bevy* is used of a company of girls, roe deer, larks, or quail. *Brood* is applicable to offspring that are still under the care of a mother, especially the offspring of domestic and game birds or, less formally, of human beings. The following related terms are used as indicated: *cast,* the number of hawks or falcons cast off at one time, usually a pair; *cete,* a company of badgers; *covert,* a flock of coots; *covey,* a family of grouse, partridges, or other game birds; *drift,* a drove or herd, especially of hogs; *exaltation,* a flight of larks; *fall,* a covey of woodcock; *gam,* a herd of whales, or a social congregation of whalers, especially at sea; *kennel,* a number of hounds or dogs housed in one place, or under the same ownership; *kindle,* a brood or litter, especially of kittens; *litter,* the total number of offspring produced at a single birth by a multiparous mammal; *muster,* a flock of peacocks; *nide,* a brood of pheasants; *pod,* a small herd of seals or whales; *pride,* a company of lions; *rout,* a company of people or animals in movement, especially knights or wolves; *school* and *shoal,* a congregation of fish, porpoises, or other aquatic mammals; *shrewdness,* a company of apes; *skein,* a flight of wildfowl; *skulk,* a congregation of vermin, especially foxes, or of thieves; *sloth,* a company of bears; *sord,* a flight of mallards; *sounder,* a herd of wild hogs; *spring,* a flock of teal; *stable,* a number of horses housed in one place, or under the same ownership; *swarm,* a colony of insects, such as ants, bees, or wasps, especially when migrating to a new nest or hive; *troop,* a number of animals, birds, or people, especially when on the move; *warren,* the inhabitants, such as rabbits, of a warren; *watch,* a flock of nightingales; *wisp,* a flock of snipe.

flock[2] (flŏk) *n.* **1.** A tuft, as of fiber or hair. **2.** Waste wool or cotton used for stuffing furniture and mattresses. **3.** An inferior grade of wool added to cloth for extra weight. **4.** Pulverized wool or felt applied to paper, cloth, or metal to produce a texture or pattern. **5.** A floccule. —*tr.v.* **flocked, flocking, flocks.** **1.** To stuff with flock. **2.** To texture or pattern with flock. [Middle English *flok,* probably from Old French *floc,* from Latin *floccus.* See **floccose.**]

Flod·den (flŏd′n). A hill in northern Northumberland, England, near the Scottish border; site of a battle (1513), in which the English defeated the Scots. Also called "Flodden Field."

floe (flō) *n.* **1.** A large, flat mass of ice formed on the surface of a body of water. **2.** A segment separated from such an ice mass. [Probably from Norwegian *flo,* layer, slab, from Old Norse *flō,* stratum, coating. See **plāk-**[1] in Appendix.*]

flog (flŏg, flôg) *v.* **flogged, flogging, flogs.** —*tr.* To beat harshly with a whip or rod. [Perhaps shortened from Latin *flagellāre,*

to whip, from *flagellum*, diminutive of *flagrum*, whip. See **bhlag-** in Appendix.*] —**flog′ger** *n.*

flood (flŭd) *n.* **1.** An overflowing of water onto land that is normally dry; a deluge. **2.** Flood tide. **3.** Any abundant flow or outpouring: *"I had to choke back a flood of reaction"* (H.P. Lovecraft). **4.** *Informal.* A floodlight. —**the Flood.** The universal deluge recorded in the Bible as having occurred during the life of Noah. Genesis 7. —*v.* **flooded, flooding, floods.** —*tr.* **1.** To cover or submerge with a flood; inundate. **2.** To fill with an abundance or an excess: *"the making of the illusions which flood our experience has become the business of America"* (Daniel J. Boorstin). —*intr.* **1.** To become inundated or submerged. **2.** To pour forth; overflow. **3.** *Medicine.* **a.** To have a hemorrhage of the uterus, as after childbirth. **b.** To have an unusually profuse menstrual flow. [Middle English *flod, flud,* Old English *flōd.* See **pleu-** in Appendix.*]

floodgate
Closed floodgate at Lake Okeechobee, Florida

flood·gate (flŭd′gāt′) *n.* **1.** A gate used to control the flow of a body of water. Also called "water gate." **2.** Anything that restrains a flood or outpouring.

flood·light (flŭd′līt′) *n.* **1.** Artificial light in an intensely bright and broad beam. **2.** A unit that produces such a beam. —*tr.v.* **floodlighted** or **-lit** (-lĭt), **-lighting, -lights.** To illuminate with a floodlight.

flood plain. A plain bordering a river, subject to flooding.

flood tide. The incoming or rising tide. Compare **ebb tide.**

floor (flôr, flōr) *n. Abbr.* **fl.** **1.** The surface of a room on which one stands. **2.** The lower or supporting surface of any structure. **3.** The surface of a structure on which vehicles travel. **4.** A bottom or base; lower limit. **5.** The ground or lowermost surface, together with accumulated layers of detritus, as of a forest or ocean. **6.** The lower part of a room, such as a legislative chamber, where business is conducted. **7. a.** The right to address an assembly, as granted under parliamentary procedure. **b.** The body of assembly members: *a motion from the floor.* **8. a.** A story or level of a building. **b.** The occupants of such a story. —*v.* **floored, flooring, floors.** —*tr.* **1.** To provide with a floor. **2.** To knock or press to the floor or ground. **3.** To stun; overwhelm. [Middle English *flor,* Old English *flōr.* See **pele-¹** in Appendix.*] —**floor′er** *n.*

floor·age (flôr′ĭj, flōr′-) *n.* Floor space.

floor·board (flôr′bôrd′, flōr′bōrd′) *n.* One of the boards forming a floor, as at the bottom of a boat.

floor·ing (flôr′ĭng, flōr′-) *n.* **1. a.** Floors collectively. **b.** A floor. **2.** Material, such as lumber or tile, used in making floors.

floor leader. The member of the U.S. Senate or House of Representatives chosen by fellow party members to be in charge of the party's activities on the floor.

floor plan. A scale diagram of a room or building drawn as if seen from above.

floor show. A series of entertainments presented in a nightclub.

floor·walk·er (flôr′wô′kər, flōr′-) *n.* An employee of a department store who supervises sales personnel and assists customers in a designated area of the store.

floo·zy (flo͞o′zē) *n., pl.* **-zies.** Also **floo·zie.** *Slang.* A slovenly or vulgar woman; especially, a cheap prostitute. [Origin unknown.]

flop (flŏp) *v.* **flopped, flopping, flops.** —*intr.* **1.** To fall down heavily and noisily; to plop. **2.** To move about in a clumsy, noisy way; to flap. **3.** *Informal.* To fail utterly. **4.** *Slang.* To go to bed. —*tr.* To cause to fall down suddenly and noisily. —*n.* **1.** The action of flopping. **2.** The sound of flopping; a dull thud. **3.** *Informal.* An utter failure: *"Columbus too thought he was a flop . . . when they sent him back in chains"* (Saul Bellow) [Variant of FLAP.] —**flop′per** *n.*

flop·house (flŏp′hous′) *n., pl.* **-houses** (-hou′zĭz). A cheap hotel for indigent transients.

flop·py (flŏp′ē) *adj.* **-pier, -piest.** Tending to flop; loose and flexible.

Flor. Florida (unofficial).

flo·ra (flôr′ə, flōr′ə) *n., pl.* **-ras** or **florae** (flôr′ē′, flōr′ē′). **1.** Plants collectively; especially, the plants of a particular region or time. **2.** A systematic compilation describing such plants. [From FLORA.]

Flo·ra (flôr′ə, flōr′ə). *Roman Mythology.* The goddess of flowers. [Latin *Flōra,* from *flōs* (stem *flōr-*), flower. See **bhel-³** in Appendix.*]

flo·ral (flôr′əl, flōr′-) *adj.* Of, pertaining to, or suggestive of a flower or flowers. —**flo′ral·ly** *adv.*

flounce¹
Mid-19th-century gown

floral envelope. The perianth of a flower.

Flor·ence¹ (flôr′əns, flŏr′-). A feminine given name. [Latin *Flōrentius,* from *flōrens,* blooming. See **Florence** (city).]

Flor·ence² (flôr′əns, flŏr′-). *Italian* **Fi·ren·ze** (fē-rĕn′tsā). Ancient name **Flo·ren·ti·a** (flō-rĕn′shē-ə). A city and cultural center on the Arno in Tuscany, Italy. Population, 456,000. [French, from Latin *Flōrentia,* "flourishing," from *flōrens,* present participle of *flōrēre,* to bloom, flourish, from *flōs* (stem *flōr-*), flower. See **bhel-³** in Appendix.*]

Flor·en·tine (flôr′ən-tēn′, -tīn′, flŏr′-) *adj.* **1.** Of or pertaining to Florence, Italy. **2.** Of or pertaining to the style of art and architecture that flourished in Renaissance Florence. **3.** *Often small* **f.** Having or characterizing a dull chased or rubbed finish. Said of gold. —*n.* A native or inhabitant of Florence. [Latin *Flōrentīnus,* from *Flōrentia,* FLORENCE (city).]

Flo·res (flôr′əs, flōr′-). **1.** An island of Indonesia, 5,511 square miles in area, separated from Sulawesi to the north by the Flores Sea. Population, 902,000. **2.** The westernmost island of the Azores, with an area of 55 square miles.

flo·res·cence (flô-rĕs′əns, flō-, flə-) *n.* The condition, time, or period of blossoming. [New Latin *florescentia,* from Latin *flōrēscens,* present participle of *flōrēscere,* to begin to bloom, inceptive of *flōrēre,* to bloom, from *flōs* (stem *flōr-*), FLOWER.]

Flo·res Sea (flôr′əs, flōr′-). That part of the Pacific Ocean between the Java and Banda seas, south of Sulawesi.

flo·ret (flôr′ĭt, flōr′-) *n.* A small flower, usually part of a dense cluster; especially, one of the disk or ray flowers of a composite plant, such as a daisy. [Middle English *flouret,* from Old French *florete,* diminutive of *flo(u)r,* FLOWER.]

Flo·rey (flôr′ē, flōr′ē), Sir **Howard Walter.** 1898–1968. British pathologist; helped develop penicillin.

Flo·ri·a·nóp·o·lis (flôr′ē-ə-nŏp′ə-lĭs, flōr′-). The capital of Santa Catarina State, southern Brazil, a seaport on an island just off the coast. Population, 74,000.

flo·ri·at·ed (flôr′ē-ā′tĭd, flōr′-) *adj.* Also **flo·re·at·ed.** Decorated with floral designs; flowery or flowerlike. [From Latin *flōs* (stem *flōr-*), flower. See **bhel-³** in Appendix.*]

flo·ri·bun·da (flôr′ə-bŭn′də, flōr′-) *n.* Any of several hybrid roses bearing numerous single or double flowers. [New Latin, feminine of *floribundus,* blossoming freely, from Latin *flōs* (stem *flōr-*), FLOWER.]

flo·ri·cul·ture (flôr′ə-kŭl′chər, flōr′-) *n.* The cultivation of flowering plants. [Latin *flōs* (stem *flōr-*), FLOWER + CULTURE.]

flor·id (flôr′ĭd, flŏr′-) *adj.* **1.** Flushed with rosy color; ruddy: *"a plump, florid woman of forty-five"* (Lillian Hellman). **2.** Heavily decorated or embellished; flowery: *"their style is clear, masculine, and smooth, but not florid"* (Swift). **3.** *Archaic.* Healthy; blooming. **4.** *Obsolete.* Abounding in or covered with flowers. —See Synonyms at **ornate.** [French *floride,* from Latin *flōridus,* from *flōrēre,* to bloom, from *flōs* (stem *flōr-*), FLOWER.] —**flo·rid′i·ty** (flə-rĭd′ə-tē), **flor′id·ness** *n.* —**flor′id·ly** *adv.*

Flor·i·da (flôr′ə-də, flŏr′-). *Abbr.* **Fla.** The southeasternmost state of the United States, 58,560 square miles in area, much of it forming a peninsula between the Atlantic Ocean and the Gulf of Mexico. It entered the Union in 1845 as the 27th state. Population, 5,805,000. Capital, Tallahassee. See map at **United States of America.** [Spanish, from *(Pascua) Florida,* "(the Feast) of Flowers," the Easter season (during which Ponce de León reached Florida in 1513), from Latin *flōrida,* feminine of *flōridus,* FLORID.]

Flor·i·da, Straits of (flôr′ə-də, flŏr′-). The sea passage between the Florida Keys and Cuba, connecting the Atlantic Ocean with the Gulf of Mexico.

Flor·i·da Keys (flôr′ə-də, flŏr′-). A chain of small islands extending 150 miles southwestward from Miami to Key West.

flo·rif·er·ous (flô-rĭf′ər-əs, flō-) *adj.* Bearing flowers; especially, flowering abundantly. [Latin *flōrifer* : *flōs* (stem *flōr-*), FLOWER + -FEROUS.]

flor·in (flôr′ĭn, flŏr′-) *n. Abbr.* **fl.** **1. a.** A British coin worth two shillings. **b.** The sum of two shillings. **2.** A monetary unit, the **guilder** *(see).* **3. a.** A gold coin first issued at Florence in 1252. **b.** Any of several obsolete European gold coins similar to the Florentine florin. [Middle English *flore(i)n,* from Old French *florin,* from Italian *fiorino,* from *fiore,* flower (the original coins bore the figure of a lily), from Latin *flōs* (stem *flōr-*). See **bhel-³** in Appendix.*]

flo·rist (flôr′ĭst, flōr′-, flŏr′-) *n.* A person whose business is the raising or selling of flowers and ornamental plants. [Latin *flōs* (stem *flōr-*), FLOWER + -IST.]

-florous. Indicates number or kind of flowers; for example, **tubuliflorous.** [Late Latin *-flōrus,* from Latin *flōs* (stem *flōr-*), FLOWER.]

flo·ru·it (flôr′o͞o-ĭt, -yo͞o-ĭt, flōr′-). *Abbr.* **fl.** Flourished. Used to indicate the period of a person's life when accurate birth and death dates are unknown. [Latin, he flourished, from *flōrēre,* to bloom, FLOURISH.]

floss (flôs, flŏs) *n.* **1.** Short fibers or waste silk from the cocoon of a silkworm. **2.** A soft, loosely twisted thread used in embroidery. **3.** Any soft, silky, fibrous substance, such as corn silk. [Possibly from French *floche,* from Old French *flosche*†, down.]

floss·y (flô′sē, flŏs′ē) *adj.* **-ier, -iest.** **1.** Made of or resembling floss; downy; silky. **2.** *Slang.* Ostentatiously stylish; flashy.

flo·tage (flō′tĭj) *n.* Also **float·age.** **1.** Flotation. **2.** Floating objects or material.

flo·ta·tion (flō-tā′shən) *n.* Also **float·a·tion.** **1.** The act or condition of floating or launching. **2.** An act or instance of launching or financing a business venture by selling an issue of stocks or bonds. **3.** Any of several processes in which different materials, notably minerals, are separated by agitation of a pulverized mixture of the materials with water, oil, and chemicals that cause differential wetting of the suspended particles, the unwetted particles being carried by air bubbles to the surface for collection.

flo·til·la (flō-tĭl′ə) *n.* **1. a.** A fleet of small ships. **b.** A small fleet of ships. **c.** Any group resembling a small fleet: *a flotilla of taxis.* **2.** *U.S. Navy.* An organizational unit of two or more squadrons of small warships. [Spanish, diminutive of *flota,* fleet, from Old French *flote,* from Old Norse *floti,* raft, fleet. See **pleu-** in Appendix.*]

flot·sam (flŏt′səm) *n.* **1.** Any wreckage or cargo that remains afloat after a ship has sunk. **2. a.** Any discarded odds and ends. **b.** Unemployed and vagrant people; drifters. [Earlier *flotsen, flotson,* from Norman French *floteson,* from *floter,* to float, from Vulgar Latin *flottāre* (unattested), from Germanic. See **pleu-** in Appendix.*]

flounce¹ (flouns) *n.* A strip of gathered or pleated material secured on its upper edge to another surface, such as a garment or curtain. —*tr.v.* **flounced, flouncing, flounces.** To trim with a flounce or flounces. [Variant of obsolete *frounce,* Middle Eng-

lish *frounce*, a wrinkle, crease, from Old French *fronce*, from *froncis*, to wrinkle, from Frankish *hrunkjan* (unattested). See **sker-³** in Appendix.*]

flounce² (flouns) *intr.v.* **flounced, flouncing, flounces. 1.** To move with exaggerated motions expressive of displeasure or impatience: *She flounced out of the room in a huff.* **2.** To flounder; twist; struggle. —*n.* The act or motion of flouncing. [Origin obscure.]

floun·der¹ (floun′dər) *intr.v.* **-dered, -dering, -ders. 1.** To move clumsily, as to regain balance. **2.** To proceed clumsily and in confusion: *"Major Major floundered . . . from one embarrassing catastrophe to another"* (Joseph Heller). —*n.* The act of floundering. [Probably blend of FOUNDER and BLUNDER (and influenced by FLOUNCE, to move jerkily).]

floun·der² (floun′dər) *n.* Any of various marine flatfishes of the families Bothidae and Pleuronectidae, important as food fishes. [Middle English, from Norman French *floundre*, probably from Scandinavian. See **plat-** in Appendix.*]

flour (flour) *n.* **1.** A soft, fine, powdery substance obtained by grinding and sifting the meal of a grain, especially wheat. **2.** Any similar soft, fine powder. —*tr.v.* **floured, flouring, flours. 1.** To cover or coat with flour. **2.** To make into flour. [Middle English *flour, flur*, finer meal, farina, FLOWER.] —**flour′y** *adj.*

flour·ish (flûr′ĭsh) *v.* **-ished, -ishing, -ishes.** —*intr.* **1.** To grow well or luxuriantly: *Most flowers flourish in full sunlight.* **2.** To fare well; succeed; prosper: *"No village on the railroad failed to flourish"* (John Kenneth Galbraith). **3.** To be in one's prime. **4.** To make bold, sweeping movements; to wave vigorously: *The flag flourished in the wind.* —*tr.* To wield, wave, or exhibit dramatically: *flourish a baton.* —*n.* **1.** An act or instance of waving or brandishing: *"a sword shining when some gentleman made a flourish"* (Eudora Welty). **2.** An embellishment or ornamentation. **3.** A dramatic action or gesture. **4.** A musical fanfare or similar passage. **5.** *Obsolete.* A period or state of thriving or of being in flower. [Middle English *florishen*, from Old French *florir* (stem *floriss-*), to bloom, from Vulgar Latin *flōrīre* (unattested), from Latin *flōrēre*, from *flōs* (stem *flōr-*), flower. See **bhel-³** in Appendix.*] —**flour′ish·er** *n.*

flout (flout) *v.* **flouted, flouting, flouts.** —*tr.* To show contempt for; scoff at; scorn. —*intr.* To be scornful; jeer. —See Usage note at **flaunt.** —*n.* A contemptuous action or remark; an insult. [Probably extended use of Middle English *flouten*, to play the flute, from Old French *flauter*, from *flaute*, FLUTE.] —**flout′er** *n.* —**flout′ing·ly** *adv.*

flow (flō) *v.* **flowed, flowing, flows.** —*intr.* **1.** To move or run freely in the manner characteristic of a fluid. **2.** To circulate, as the blood in the body. **3.** To discharge a stream; pour forth. **4.** To move with a continual shifting of the component particles: *Wheat flowed into the bin.* **5.** To proceed steadily and continuously. **6.** To proceed with ease. **7.** To appear smooth, harmonious, or graceful. **8.** To rise. Used of the tide. **9.** To arise; derive: *Several conclusions flow from this hypothesis.* **10. a.** To abound or be plentiful. **b.** To overflow or flood. **11.** To hang loosely and gracefully: *The cape flowed from his shoulders.* **12.** To undergo plastic deformation without cleavage or breaking. —*tr.* **1.** To release as a flow. **2.** To cause to flow. —*n.* **1. a.** The smooth motion characteristic of fluids. **b.** The act of flowing. **2.** A stream. **3. a.** A continuous output or outpouring; a flood: *a flow of ideas.* **b.** A continuous movement or circulation: *the flow of traffic.* **4.** The amount that flows in a given period of time. **5.** The incoming or rise of the tide. **6.** Continuity and smoothness of appearance. **7.** Menstrual discharge. **8.** The rising of the tide. [Middle English *flouen*, Old English *flōwan*. See **pleu-** in Appendix.*]

flow·age (flō′ĭj) *n.* **1.** The act of flowing or overflowing. **2.** The state of being flooded. **3.** A liquid that flows or overflows. **4.** The gradual plastic deformation of a solid body, as by heat.

flow chart. A schematic representation of a sequence of operations. Also called "flow sheet."

flow·er (flou′ər) *n.* **1. a.** The reproductive structure of a seed-bearing plant, characteristically having specialized male and female organs, as stamens and a pistil, enclosed in an outer envelope of petals and sepals. **b.** Any such structure having showy or colorful parts; a blossom. **2.** Any similar reproductive organ of other plants, as mosses. **3.** A plant cultivated or conspicuous for its blossoms. **4.** That which is produced by any natural process; outgrowth: *"His attitude was simply a flower of his general good-nature"* (Henry James). **5.** The period of highest development; peak. **6.** The highest example or best representative of something: *the flower of our generation.* **7.** An embellishment. **8.** *Usually plural. Chemistry.* A fine powder, produced by condensation or sublimation. —*v.* **flowered, -ering, -ers.** —*intr.* **1.** To produce a flower or flowers; to blossom; bloom. **2.** To develop fully; reach a peak. —*tr.* To decorate with flowers or with a floral pattern. [Middle English *flo(u)r*, from Old French *flo(u)r*, from Latin *flōs* (stem *flōr-*). See **bhel-³** in Appendix.*]

flow·er·age (flou′ər-ĭj) *n.* **1.** Flowers collectively. **2.** The process or state of flowering.

flow·er-de-luce. *Archaic.* Variant of **fleur-de-lis.**

flow·ered (flou′ərd) *adj.* **1.** Having flowers. **2.** Decorated with flowers or a floral pattern: *flowered wallpaper.*

flow·er·et (flou′ər-ĭt) *n.* A small flower. [Middle English *flourette*, from Old French *flo(u)rete*, diminutive of *flo(u)r*, FLOWER.]

flower girl. 1. A girl or woman who sells flowers from a small stand or wagon. **2.** A very young girl who carries flowers in a procession, especially at a wedding.

flowering dogwood. See **dogwood.**

flowering maple. Any of several tropical shrubs of the genus *Abutilon*; especially, *A. hybridum*, having lobed leaves resembling those of the maple and variously colored flowers.

flowering quince. Any of several shrubs of the genus *Chaenomeles*, native to Asia, having spiny branches and red or pink flowers.

flowering wintergreen. A plant, the **fringed polygala** (*see*).

flow·er·pot (flou′ər-pŏt′) *n.* A pot in which plants are grown.

flow·er·y (flou′ə-rē) *adj.* **-ier, -iest. 1.** Abounding in or bedecked with flowers. **2.** Suggestive of flowers: *a flowery perfume.* **3.** Having a floral pattern. **4.** Full of figurative and ornate expressions; highly embellished: *a flowery speech.* —**flow′er·i·ly** *adv.* —**flow′er·i·ness** *n.*

flow·ing (flō′ĭng) *adj.* **1.** Proceeding smoothly and continuously in the manner of a fluid. **2.** Having rhythmic grace of movement. **3.** Having smooth, unbroken lines. **4.** Streaming out or hanging down at full length; hanging loosely. —**flow′ing·ly** *adv.*

flow meter. An apparatus for monitoring, measuring, or recording fluid flow, as of a gaseous fuel.

flown¹ (flōn) *adj. Archaic.* Filled to excess; steeped: *"then wander forth the sons of Belial flown with insolence and wine."* (Milton). [Obsolete past participle of FLOW.]

flown². Past participle of **fly.**

flow sheet. A flow chart (*see*).

Floyd (floid). A masculine given name. [Variant of LLOYD, with substitution of *Fl-* for the Welsh sound *Ll-*.]

flu (flо̄о̄) *n. Informal.* Influenza.

flub·dub (flŭb′dŭb′) *n. Slang.* Pretentious nonsense, especially in argument; bunkum. [Origin unknown.]

fluc·tu·ant (flŭk′chōō-ənt) *adj.* Varying; fluctuating; unstable. [Latin *fluctuāns*, present participle of *fluctuāre*, FLUCTUATE.]

fluc·tu·ate (flŭk′chōō-āt′) *v.* **-ated, -ating, -ates.** —*intr.* **1.** To vary irregularly: *"Prices fluctuated violently from the irregularity of the crops"* (Lesley B. Simpson). **2.** To rise and fall like waves; undulate. —*tr.* To cause to fluctuate. —See Synonyms at **swing.** [Latin *fluctuāre*, from *fluctus*, a flowing, from the past participle of *fluere*, to flow. See **bhleu-** in Appendix.*]

fluc·tu·a·tion (flŭk′chōō-ā′shən) *n.* **1.** Irregular variation. **2.** An instance of such variation. **3.** A result of such variation.

flue¹ (flōо̄) *n.* **1.** A pipe, tube, or channel through which hot air, gas, steam, or smoke may pass, as in a boiler or a chimney. **2. a.** A flue pipe (*see*). **b.** The air passage in such a pipe. [Origin unknown.]

flue² (flōо̄) *n.* The flocculent detritus of textile fabrics, fur, or the like. [Flemish *vluwe*, from French *velu*, velvety, from Old French, shaggy. See **velvet.**]

flue³ (flōо̄) *n.* Also **flew.** One of several kinds of fishing net. [Middle English *flue*, from Middle Dutch *vlūwe*. See **pleu-** in Appendix.*]

flu·ent (flōо̄′ənt) *adj.* **1. a.** Having facility in the use of a language: *a fluent speaker.* **b.** Effortless; flowing; polished: *speak fluent French.* **2.** Flowing smoothly and easily; graceful: *fluent curves.* **3.** Flowing or capable of flowing; fluid; liquid. [Latin *fluēns*, present participle of *fluere*, to flow. See **bhleu-** in Appendix.*] —**flu′en·cy** *n.* —**flu′ent·ly** *adv.*

flue pipe. An organ pipe sounded by means of a current of air striking a lip in the side of the pipe and causing the air within to vibrate. Also called "flue." Compare **reed pipe.**

flue stop. An organ stop controlling a set of flue pipes. Compare **reed stop.**

fluff (flŭf) *n.* **1.** Light down or nap. **2.** Something having a light, soft, or frothy consistency or appearance. **3.** Something of little consequence; froth. **4.** *Informal.* A young woman. **5.** *Informal.* An error or lapse of memory in the reading, recitation, or delivery of lines, as by an actor or announcer. —*v.* **fluffed, fluffing, fluffs.** —*tr.* **1.** To make light and puffy by shaking or patting into a soft, loose mass: *fluff a pillow.* **2.** *Informal.* To misread or forget (one's lines). —*intr.* **1.** To become soft and puffy or feathery. **2.** *Informal.* To forget or botch one's lines. [Probably variant of FLUE (down).]

fluff·y (flŭf′ē) *adj.* **-ier, -iest. 1.** Of, like, or covered with fluff or down. **2.** Light and airy; soft: *fluffy curls.* —**fluff′i·ly** *adv.* —**fluff′i·ness** *n.*

flü·gel·horn (flōо̄′gəl-hôrn′; *German* flü′gəl-hôrn′) *n.* A bugle with valves, similar to the cornet but having a wider bore. [German : *Flügel*, wing, flank (formerly used to summon flanks during a battle), from Middle High German *vlügel* (see **pleu-** in Appendix*) + *Horn*, horn, from Old High German *horn* (see **ker-¹** in Appendix*).]

flu·id (flōо̄′ĭd) *n. Abbr.* **fl, fl.** A substance that exists, or is regarded as existing, as a continuum characterized by low resistance to flow and the tendency to assume the shape of its container. —*adj. Abbr.* **fl, fl. 1.** Characteristic of a fluid; especially, flowing easily. **2.** Used in the measurement of fluids. **3.** Readily deformed; pliable. **4.** Smooth and effortless. **5.** Easily changed or tending to change: *"in these fluid centuries which lie between the end of Roman Britain and the emergence of the new Anglo-Saxon Kingdoms"* (Peter Hunter Blair). **6.** Convertible into cash: *fluid assets.* [Middle English, from Old French *fluide*, from Latin *fluidus*, from *fluere*, to flow. See **bhleu-** in Appendix.*] —**flu·id′i·ty, flu′id·ness** *n.* —**flu′id·ly** *adv.*

fluid dram. One-eighth of a fluid ounce (*see*).

flu·id·ex·tract (flōо̄′ĭd-ĕk′străkt′) *n.* A concentrated alcohol solution of a vegetable drug containing the equivalent of one gram in powdered form of the active principle in each milliliter.

flu·id·ics (flōо̄-ĭd′ĭks) *n.* Plural in form, used with a singular verb. The technology of fluids used as nonmoving, nonelectrical components of control and sensing systems.

fluid ounce. 1. A unit of volume or capacity in the U.S.

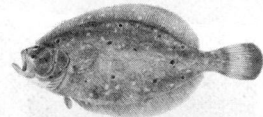

flounder²
Paralichthys dentatus

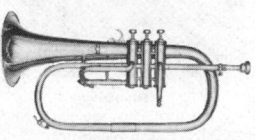

flügelhorn

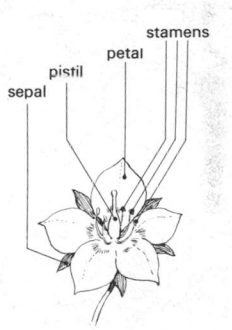

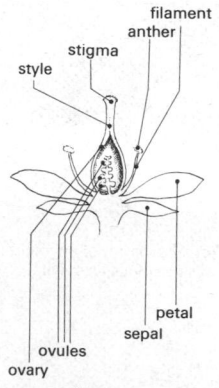

flower
Flower (*above*) and cross section showing details

Customary System, used in liquid measure, equal to 1.804 cubic inches. **2.** A unit of volume or capacity in the British Imperial System, used in liquid and dry measure, equal to 1.734 cubic inches. See **measurement**.

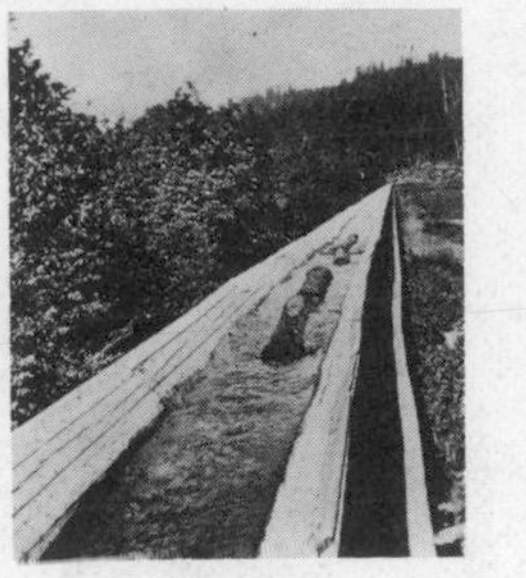

flume
Lumber flume at Spirit Lake, Washington

fluke[1] (flo͝ok) *n., pl.* **fluke** (for sense 1) or **flukes**. **1.** Any of various flatfishes; especially, a flounder of the genus *Paralichthys*. **2.** A flatworm, a **trematode** *(see);* especially, any of various parasitic species. [Middle English *fluke, flok,* Old English *flōc.* See **plāk-**[1] in Appendix.*]

fluke[2] (flo͝ok) *n.* **1.** The triangular blade at the end of either arm of an anchor, designed to catch in the ground. **2.** A barb or barbed head as on an arrow or harpoon. **3.** One of the two horizontally flattened divisions of the tail of a whale or related animal. [Probably from FLUKE (fish or worm, from its shape).]

fluke[3] (flo͝ok) *n.* **1.** An accidentally good or successful stroke in billiards or pool. **2.** Any accidental stroke of good luck. *—v.* **fluked, fluking, flukes.** *—tr.* To get, make, or do by chance. *—intr.* To make a fluke. [Origin obscure.]

fluk·y (flo͞o′kē) *adj.* **-ier, -iest.** Also **fluk·ey. 1.** Resulting from mere chance. **2.** Constantly shifting; uncertain; variable: *a fluky wind.* [From FLUKE (chance shot).]

flume (flo͞om) *n.* **1.** A narrow defile or gorge, usually with a stream flowing through it. **2.** An artificial channel or chute for a stream of water, as for furnishing power or conveying logs. *—tr.v.* **flumed, fluming, flumes. 1.** To divert (water) by means of a flume. **2.** To transport (logs, for example) by the use of a flume. [Earlier, "river," from Middle English *flum,* from Old French, from Latin *flūmen,* from *fluere,* to flow. See **bhleu-** in Appendix.*]

flum·mer·y (flŭm′ə-rē) *n., pl.* **-ies. 1. a.** Any of several soft, light, bland foods, as a custard or blancmange. **b.** Originally, a soft jelly made by straining boiled, slightly fermented oatmeal or flour. **2.** Meaningless flattery; mere nonsense; humbug. [Welsh *llymru*†.]

flum·mox (flŭm′əks) *tr.v.* **-moxed, -moxing, -moxes.** *Slang.* To confuse; perplex. [Origin obscure.]

flung. Past tense and past participle of **fling**.

flunk (flŭngk) *v.* **flunked, flunking, flunks.** *Informal. —intr.* To fail an examination, course, or other school work. *—tr.* **1.** To fail (an examination or course). **2.** To give (someone) a failing grade. **—flunk out.** To be expelled from a school or course because of work that does not meet required standards. *—n.* A failing grade. [Origin uncertain.]

flun·ky (flŭng′kē) *n., pl.* **-kies.** Also **flun·key** *pl.* **-keys.** Often used disparagingly. **1.** A liveried manservant or valet; a lackey. **2.** An obsequious or fawning person; a toady. **3.** A person who does menial or trivial work. [Originally Scottish (dialectal) *flunky*†.] **—flun′ky·ism′** *n.*

flu·or (flo͞o′ôr′, flo͞o′ər) *n.* Fluorite. [New Latin, from Latin, a flowing, fluid (from its use as a flux in smelting), from *fluere,* to flow. See **bhleu-** in Appendix.*]

flu·o·resce (flo͞o-ər-ĕs′, flo͝or-ĕs′) *intr.v.* **-resced, -rescing, -resces.** To undergo, produce, or show fluorescence. [Back-formation from FLUORESCENCE.]

flu·o·res·ce·in (flo͞o-ər-ĕs′ē-ĭn, flo͝or-ĕs′-) *n.* An orange-red compound, $C_{20}H_{12}O_5$, that exhibits intense fluorescence in alkaline solution and is used to dye sea water for spotting or tracing operations. [FLUORESCE + -IN.]

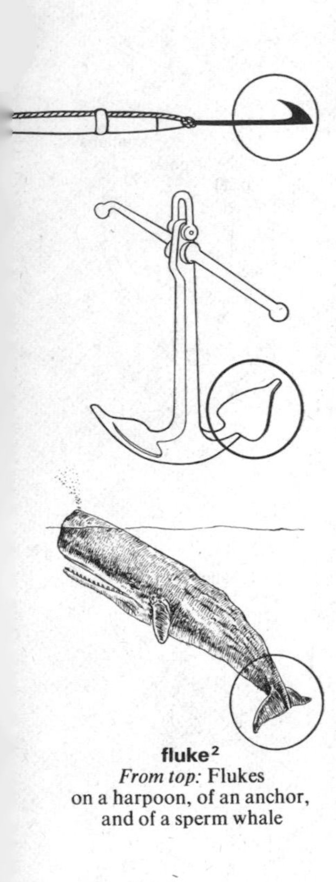

fluke[2]
From top: Flukes on a harpoon, of an anchor, and of a sperm whale

flu·o·res·cence (flo͞o-ər-ĕs′əns, flo͝or-ĕs′-) *n.* **1.** The emission of electromagnetic radiation, especially of visible light, resulting from the absorption of incident radiation and persisting only as long as the stimulating radiation is continued. **2.** The radiation so emitted. [FLUOR + -ESCENCE.]

flu·o·res·cent (flo͞o-ər-ĕs′ənt, flo͝or-ĕs′-) *adj.* Exhibiting or capable of exhibiting fluorescence.

fluorescent lamp. A lamp that produces visible light by fluorescence; especially, a glass tube, the inner wall of which is coated with a material that fluoresces when bombarded with secondary radiation generated by a gaseous discharge within the tube.

flu·o·ri·date (flo͝or′ə-dāt′, flo͞o′ər-ə-) *tr.v.* **-dated, -dating, -dates.** To add a fluorine compound to (a water supply) for the purpose of preventing tooth decay. [Back-formation from *fluoridation* : FLUORID(E) + -ATION.] **—flu′o·ri·da′tion** *n.*

flu·o·ride (flo͞o′ə-rīd′, flo͝or′īd′) *n.* Any binary compound of fluorine with another element. [FLUOR(O)- + -IDE.]

flu·o·rine (flo͞o′ə-rēn′, flo͝or′ēn′, -ĭn) *n. Symbol* **F** A pale-yellow, highly corrosive, highly poisonous, gaseous halogen element, the most electronegative and most reactive of all the elements. It is used in a wide variety of industrially important compounds. Atomic number 9, atomic weight 18.9984, freezing point −219.62°C, boiling point −188.14°C, specific gravity of liquid 1.108, valence 1. See **element**. [French, from New Latin *fluor,* generic name for a group of minerals used as fluxes, FLUOR.]

flu·o·rite (flo͞o′ə-rīt′, flo͝or′īt′) *n.* A generally light-colored green, blue, violet, yellow, brown, or colorless mineral, essentially CaF_2, that is often fluorescent in ultraviolet light. Also, especially in mining, called "fluorspar." [Italian : FLUOR + -ITE.]

fluoro–, fluor–. Indicates: **1.** *Chemistry.* Fluorine in compound; for example, **fluorosis**. **2.** Fluorescence; for example, **fluoroscope**. [From FLUORINE and FLUORESCENCE.]

flu·o·ro·car·bon (flo͞o′ə-rō-kär′bən, flo͝or′ō-) *n.* Any of various inert organic compounds in which fluorine replaces hydrogen, used as aerosol propellants, refrigerants, solvents, lubricants, and in making plastics and resins. [FLUORO- + CARBON.]

flu·o·rom·e·ter (flo͞o-ə-rŏm′ə-tər, flo͞o-rŏm′-) *n.* An instrument for detecting and measuring fluorescence. [FLUORO- + -METER.] **—flu·o·rom′e·try** *n.*

flu·o·ro·scope (flo͝or′ə-skōp′, flo͞o′ər-ə-) *n.* A suitably mounted fluorescent screen on which the contents or internal structure of an optically opaque object, as of the human body, may be continuously viewed as shadows formed by differential transmission of x rays through the object. Also called "radioscope," "roentgenoscope." *—tr.v.* **fluoroscoped, -scoping, -scopes.** To examine the interior of (an object) with a fluoroscope. [FLUORO- + -SCOPE.] **—flu′o·ro·scop′ic** (-skŏp′ĭk) *adj.*

flu·o·ros·co·py (flo͞o-rŏs′kə-pē) *n.* Examination with the use of a fluoroscope.

flu·o·ro·sis (flo͞o-rō′sĭs, flo͞o-ə-rō′-) *n.* An abnormal condition caused by excessive intake of fluorine, characterized chiefly by mottling of the teeth. [New Latin: FLUOR(O)- + -OSIS.]

flu·or·spar (flo͞o′ər-spär′) *n. Mining.* **Fluorite** *(see).* [FLUOR(O)- + SPAR.]

flur·ry (flûr′ē) *n., pl.* **-ries. 1.** A sudden gust of wind. **2.** A light snowfall. **3.** A sudden burst of confusion, excitement, or bustling activity; a stir: *"Perhaps all life was . . . dull and then a heroic flurry at the end."* (Graham Greene). **4.** *Finance.* A short period of active trading on the stock exchange. *—v.* **flurried, -rying, -ries.** *—tr.* To agitate, confuse, or make nervous; fluster. *—intr.* To move or come down in a gust or flurry. [From obsolete *flurr,* to whirl up, scatter, probably an expressive formation on analogy with HURRY.]

flush[1] (flŭsh) *v.* **flushed, flushing, flushes.** *—intr.* **1.** To flow suddenly and abundantly; spread out quickly; flood. **2.** To turn red in the face from fever, embarrassment, or strong emotion; to color; to blush. **3.** To glow, especially with a reddish color. **4. a.** To be cleaned by a rapid, brief gush of water. **b.** To function by means of a flushing mechanism, as a toilet. *—tr.* **1.** To cause to redden or glow. **2.** To excite or elate, as with a feeling of pride or accomplishment: *flushed with victory.* **3.** To wash, empty, or purify with a sudden, rapid flow of water. *—n.* **1.** A brief but copious flow or gushing, as of water. **2.** A blush or glow: *"here and there a flush of red on the lip of a little cloud"* (Willa Cather). **3.** Redness of the skin, as with fever. **4.** A feeling of animation or exhilaration. **5.** A sudden freshness, development, or growth: *"the first flush of ripened beauty"* (H. Rider Haggard). *—adj.* **flusher, flushest. 1.** Having a healthy reddish color; blushing; glowing. **2.** Abundant; plentiful. **3.** Having an abundant supply of money; prosperous; affluent: *"if there was a horse-race, you'd find him flush"* (Mark Twain). **4.** *Rare.* Lively; vigorous; lusty. **5. a.** Having surfaces in the same plane; even; level. **b.** Arranged with adjacent sides, surfaces, or edges close together: *The safe was flush against the wall.* **6.** *Printing.* Having the copy lined up evenly at the margins with no indentations. **7.** *Nautical.* Having a deck that presents an even surface from stem to stern with no deckhouses or other obstructions. **8.** Direct, straightforward, or solid, as a blow. —See Synonyms at **level**. *—adv.* **1.** So as to be even, in one plane, or aligned with a margin. **2.** Squarely; solidly: *The ball hit him flush on the face.* [Probably from FLUSH (to take flight, dart out).]

flush[2] (flŭsh) *n.* A hand in which all the cards are of the same suit, rated above a straight and below a full house in poker or similar games. See **royal flush**. [Probably from Old French *flus, flux,* from Latin *fluxus,* a flow, FLUX.]

flush[3] (flŭsh) *v.* **flushed, flushing, flushes.** *—tr.* To frighten (a game bird, for example) from cover. *—intr.* To dart out or fly from cover; take flight. *—n.* A bird or a flock of birds suddenly taking flight. [Middle English *flusshen,* possibly from (unattested) Old English *flyscan* (imitative).]

Flush·ing (flŭsh′ĭng). An area in Queens, New York City, including Flushing Meadow, site of two New York World's Fairs (1939–40 and 1964–65) and of the headquarters of the United Nations (1946–51).

flus·ter (flŭs′tər) *v.* **-tered, -tering, -ters.** *—tr.* To make nervous or upset by confusing or befuddling. *—intr.* To become nervous or excited, as from confusion or bewilderment. *—n.* A state of agitation, confusion, or excitement; flurry; fuss. [Middle English *flostren,* possibly from Scandinavian, akin to Icelandic *flaustra,* to bustle. See **pleu-** in Appendix.*]

flute (flo͞ot) *n. Abbr.* **fl. 1.** A high-pitched instrument of the woodwind family, tubular in shape and with finger holes and keys on the side and a reedless mouthpiece either at the end, as in the recorder, or on the side, as in the transverse flute. **2.** An organ stop the flue pipe of which produces a flutelike tone. **3.** *Architecture.* One of the long parallel grooves, usually with rounded inner surfaces, incised on the shaft of a column as a decorative motif. **4.** A groove in cloth, as in a pleated ruffle. **5.** Something shaped like a flute. *—v.* **fluted, fluting, flutes.** *—tr.* **1.** To play (a tune) on a flute. **2.** To sing, whistle, or otherwise produce (a flutelike tone). **3.** To make flutes in (a column or piece of cloth, for example). *—intr.* **1.** To play a flute. **2.** To sing or whistle with a flutelike tone. [Middle English *floute, floite,* from Old French *flaute, fleute* (probably imitative); the initial consonant cluster was probably influenced by FLAGEOLET and Latin *flāre,* to blow.]

flut·ed (flo͞o′tĭd) *adj.* **1.** Decorated with parallel grooves, as a column or ruffle. **2.** Having a sound like that of a flute; high-pitched and clear.

flut·er (flo͞o′tər) *n.* **1. a.** One who makes flutings. **b.** A device used in making flutings. **2.** *Rare.* A flutist.

flut·ing (flo͞o′tĭng) *n.* **1.** A decorative motif consisting of a series of long, rounded, parallel grooves, such as those incised in the surface of a column. **2.** The grooves formed by narrow pleats in cloth, as in a ruffle. **3.** The act of incising or making grooves. **4.** The act of playing on a flute or of producing flutelike sounds. **5.** The sound of a flute.

ă pat/ā pay/âr care/ä father/b bib/ch church/d deed/ĕ pet/ē be/f fife/g gag/h hat/hw which/ĭ pit/ī pie/îr pier/j judge/k kick/l lid, needle/m mum/n no, sudden/ng thing/ŏ pot/ō toe/ô paw, for/oi noise/ou out/o͝o took/o͞o boot/p pop/r roar/s sauce/sh ship, dish/

flut·ist (flo͞o′tĭst) *n.* One who plays the flute. Also called "flautist."

flut·ter (flŭt′ər) *v.* **-tered, -tering, -ters.** —*intr.* **1.** To wave or flap lightly and rapidly in an irregular manner: *The curtains fluttered in the breeze.* **2. a.** To fly by a quick, light flapping of the wings. **b.** To flap the wings without flying. **3.** To move or fall in a manner suggestive of tremulous flight: *"Her arms rose, fell, and fluttered with the rhythm of the song"* (Evelyn Waugh). **4.** To vibrate or beat rapidly or erratically: *His heart fluttered wildly.* **5.** To move quickly in a nervous, restless, or excited fashion; flit: *The children fluttered around the birthday cake.* **6.** To be excited, flustered, or nervous. —*tr.* **1.** To cause to flutter; to wave; to flap: *"fluttering her bristly black lashes as swiftly as butterflies' wings"* (Margaret Mitchell). **2.** To make excited or nervous; confuse; fluster. —*n.* **1.** An act of fluttering; a quick flapping. **2.** A condition of nervous excitement or agitation: *"This mystery served to keep Amelia's gentle bosom in a perpetual flutter of excitement"* (Thackeray). **3.** A brief state of excitement, surprise, or bewilderment; a commotion; a flurry. **4.** *Pathology.* Abnormal pulsation, as of the heart. **5.** *Electronics.* A distortion in reproduced sound due to frequency deviations created by faulty recording or reproduction techniques. [Middle English *floteren,* to flutter, be tossed by waves, Old English *floterian.* See **pleu-** in Appendix.*] —**flut′ter·er** *n.* —**flut′ter·y** *adj.*

flutter kick. A swimming kick in which the legs are held horizontally and alternately moved up and down in rapid strokes without bending the knees.

flu·vi·al (flo͞o′vē-əl) *adj.* **1.** Of, pertaining to, or inhabiting a river or stream. **2.** Formed or produced by the action of flowing water. [Middle English, from Latin *fluviālis,* from *fluvius,* river, from *fluere,* to flow. See **bhleu-** in Appendix.*]

flu·vi·o·ma·rine (flo͞o′vē-ō-mə-rēn′) *adj. Geology.* Pertaining to deposits, especially near the mouth of a river, formed by the joint action of the sea and a river. [Latin *fluvius,* river, from *fluere,* to flow (see **bhleu-** in Appendix*) + MARINE.]

flux (flŭks) *n.* **1. a.** A flow or flowing. **b.** A continued flow or flood. **2.** *Physics.* **a.** A flow of matter or energy as a fluid, or regarded as a fluid. **b.** Flux density. **3.** *Medicine.* The discharge of large quantities of fluid material from a bodily surface or cavity. **4.** Change regarded as an abstract influence or condition persisting in time. **5.** *Chemistry & Metallurgy.* A substance that aids, induces, or otherwise actively participates in a flowing, as: **a.** A mineral added to a furnace charge to promote fusing of metals or to prevent the formation of oxides. **b.** A substance applied in soldering and brazing to portions of a surface to be joined, acting on application of heat to prevent oxide formation and to facilitate the flowing of solder. **c.** Any readily fusible glass or enamel used as a base in ceramic work. —*v.* **fluxed, fluxing, fluxes.** —*tr.* **1.** To melt; to fuse. **2.** To apply a flux to. **3.** *Obsolete.* To purge. —*intr.* **1.** To become fluid. **2.** To flow; to stream. [Middle English, from Old French, from Latin *fluxus,* from the past participle of *fluere,* to flow. See **bhleu-** in Appendix.*]

flux density. *Physics.* The quantity of flux per unit area.

flux·ion (flŭk′shən) *n.* **1.** A flowing. **2.** Continual change. **3.** That which flows; a discharge or issue. **4.** *Mathematics Archaic.* **a.** A derivative. **b.** *Plural.* Differential calculus. [Old French, from Latin *fluxiō,* from *fluxus,* FLUX.] —**flux′ion·al, flux′ion·ar′y** *adj.* —**flux′ion·al·ly** *adv.*

fly¹ (flī) *v.* **flew** (flo͞o) or **flied** (for sense 8 only), **flown** (flōn) or **flied** (for sense 8 only), **flying, flies.** —*intr.* **1.** To engage in flight, especially: **a.** To move through the air with the aid of wings. **b.** To travel by air. **c.** To pilot an aircraft. **2.** To glide through the air sustained by winglike parts. **3. a.** To rise in the air or be carried through the air by the wind. **b.** To float or flutter in the air. **4.** To be sent or driven through the air with great speed or force. **5. a.** To rush; to run. **b.** To flee; try to escape. **c.** To hasten; to spring: *He flew to my defense.* **6.** To pass by swiftly, as time or youth. **7.** To be dissipated rapidly; vanish unaccountably, as money. **8.** *Baseball.* To hit a fly ball. **9.** To react explosively; burst: *He flew into a rage.* **10.** To shoot forth: *Sparks flew in all directions from the torch.* —*tr.* **1. a.** To cause to fly, hover, or float in the air. **b.** To keep (a flag) aloft. **2. a.** To pilot (an aircraft). **b.** To dispatch in an aircraft. **c.** To pass over in an aircraft: *fly the ocean.* **3.** To shun; run away from; flee from. —**fly at.** To rush at angrily or excitedly. —**fly blind.** To fly an airplane in bad weather without visibility. —**fly high.** To be in the clouds; be elated. —**fly in the face** (or **teeth**) **of.** To resist or defy openly. —**fly off the handle.** To lose control of one's temper. —**fly on.** *Theater.* To rush on a change of scenery without lowering the curtain. —**fly out.** *Baseball.* To make an out by hitting a fly ball that is caught. —**fly the coop.** *Informal.* To get away; escape. —**fly the kite.** *Finance.* To borrow money or obtain credit using accommodation bills or notes as security. —**let fly.** To emit, send forth, or direct with force or violence. —**make the fur** (or **feathers**) **fly.** To cause a commotion or upset with an insult or by provoking a fight. —*n., pl.* **flies. 1.** An overlapping fold of cloth that hides a zipper, buttons, or other fastening of apparel, as in men's trousers. **2.** A cloth flap that covers an entrance, or forms a roof extension for a tent or wagon. **3.** A flyleaf. **4.** *Baseball.* A fly ball. **5. a.** The span of a flag from the staff to the outer edge. **b.** The outer edge of a flag. **6.** A flywheel, or an analogously functioning mechanism. **7.** *Printing.* A device that carries the printed sheets from the press and places them in a flat pile. **8.** *Plural.* The area directly over the stage of a theater and in back of the proscenium, containing the overhead lights, drop curtains, and equipment for raising and lowering sets. **9.** *British.* A one-horse carriage; a hackney. —**on the fly.** In flight; on the run; in a hurry. [Fly, flew, flown; Middle English *flien, flew, flowen,* Old English *flēogan, flēah* (plural *flugon*), *flogen.* See **pleu-** in Appendix.*]

fly² (flī) *n., pl.* **flies. 1.** Any of numerous winged insects of the order Diptera; especially, one of the family Muscidae, which includes the housefly and the tsetse. **2.** Any of various other flying insects, such as the caddis fly. **3.** A fishing lure simulating a fly. —**fly in the ointment.** Something that detracts from effectiveness; a jarring or negative factor. [Middle English *flie,* Old English *flēoge.* See **pleu-** in Appendix.*]

fly³ (flī) *adj. British Slang.* Alert; clever; sharp. [Probably from FLY (to go swiftly).]

fly agaric. A poisonous mushroom, *Amanita muscaria,* usually having a red or orange cap with white patches. Also called "fly amanita." [From its use as a poison on flypaper.]

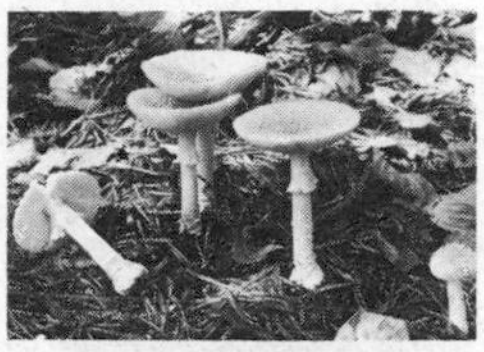

fly agaric

fly·a·way (flī′ə-wā′) *adj.* **1.** Blown by the wind; fluttering or streaming. **2.** Flighty; frivolous; giddy. —*n.* One that is restless, flighty, or elusive.

fly ball. *Baseball.* A ball that is batted in a high arc, usually to the outfield.

fly·blow (flī′blō′) *n.* The egg or larva of a blowfly, usually deposited on food. —*tr.v.* **flyblew** (-blo͞o′), **-blown** (-blōn′), **-blowing, -blows. 1.** To deposit (the eggs of a blowfly) in. **2.** To taint; contaminate.

fly·blown (flī′blōn′) *adj.* **1.** Contaminated with flyblows. **2.** Spoiled; tainted; corrupt.

fly book. A case in which artificial flies for fishing are carried.

fly·boy (flī′boi′) *n. Slang.* A pilot of an aircraft.

fly·by (flī′bī′) *n., pl.* **-bys.** A flight passing close to a specified target or position; especially, a maneuver in which a spacecraft passes sufficiently close to a planet to make relatively detailed observations without landing.

fly-by-night (flī′bī-nīt′) *adj.* **1.** Of unreliable business character. **2.** Dubious and temporary. —*n.* **1.** One who cheats his creditors, as by absconding in the night. **2.** Something of a dubiously transitory nature.

fly·catch·er (flī′kăch′ər) *n.* Any of various birds characterized by the habit of flying suddenly from a perch to catch flying insects; especially, a member of the New World family Tyrannidae or the Old World family Muscicapidae.

fly·er. Variant of **flier.**

fly-fish (flī′fĭsh′) *intr.v.* **-fished, -fishing, -fishes.** To angle using artificial flies for bait.

fly front. A garment front that has a fly concealing the fastenings.

fly gallery. A narrow platform at the side of a theater stage from which a stagehand works the ropes controlling equipment in the flies.

fly·ing (flī′ĭng) *adj.* **1.** Moving through the air with or as if with wings. **2.** Ready to move and act swiftly. **3.** Brief; hurried: *a flying visit.* **4.** Concerned with or used in aviation. **5.** *Nautical.* Not secured by spars or stays. Said of sails. —*n.* **1.** Flight in an aircraft. **2.** The piloting or navigation of an aircraft.

flying boat. A large seaplane that is kept afloat by its hull rather than by pontoons.

flying bomb. A **robot bomb** *(see).*

flying buttress. *Architecture.* A masonry prop that springs from a pier or other support and abuts against another part of the structure to resist thrust. Also called "arc-boutant."

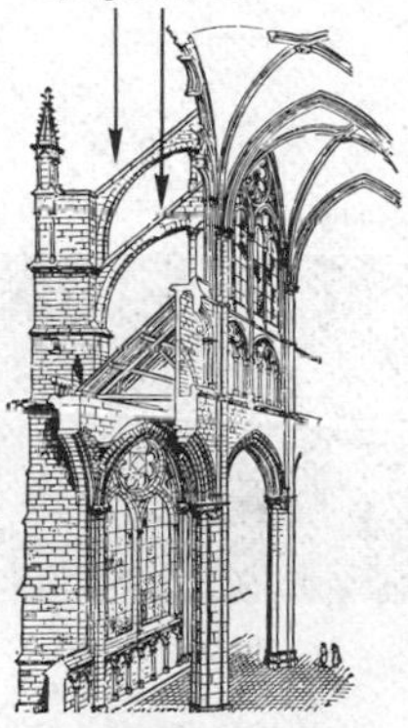

flying buttress

flying circus. 1. A squadron of fighter planes in World War I. **2.** An exhibition of stunt flying.

flying colors. Triumph; victory; success.

Flying Dutchman. 1. A legendary mariner condemned to sail the seas against the wind until Judgment Day. **2.** His spectral ship, said to appear in storms near the Cape of Good Hope.

flying fatigue. **Aeroneurosis** *(see).*

flying field. A field graded for airplane landings and takeoffs.

flying fish. Any of various marine fishes of the family Exocoetidae, having enlarged pectoral or pelvic fins capable of sustaining them in brief, gliding flight over the water.

flying fox. 1. Any of various fruit-eating bats of the genus *Pteropus,* chiefly of tropical Africa, Asia, and Australia, having a foxlike muzzle and ears. **2.** Any of several similar or related mammals.

flying frog. An arboreal frog, *Rhacophorus reinwardtii,* of southeastern Asia, having toes connected by broad webbing, and capable of gliding considerable distances.

flying gurnard. Any of various chiefly tropical marine fishes of the family Dactylopteridae, having winglike, much enlarged pectoral fins.

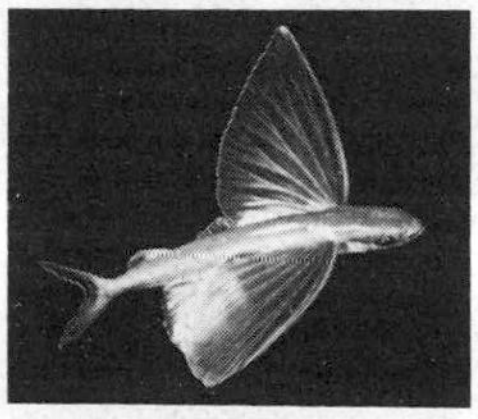

flying fish
Cypselurus californicus

flying jib. *Nautical.* A light sail that extends beyond the jib and is attached to an extension of the jib boom.

flying lemur. Either of two mammals, *Cynocephalus volans* or *C. variegatus,* of tropical Asia, that are sustained in gliding leaps by a wide, fur-covered membrane extending from each side of the body. Also called "gliding lemur," "colugo."

flying lizard. Any of various small tropical Asian lizards of the genus *Draco,* capable of gliding by spreading the winglike membranes on each side of the body. Also called "flying dragon."

flying machine. A machine designed for flight. Used with reference to early experimental types of aircraft.

flying mare. *Wrestling.* A throw in which one grabs the opponent's wrist, turns around quickly, and flips him over one's shoulder onto the ground.

flying phalanger. Any of several small marsupials of the family Phalangeridae; especially, one of the genus *Petaurus,* of Australia, New Guinea, and Tasmania, capable of gliding through

the air sustained by large folds of skin between the forelegs and hind legs.

flying saucer. Any of various unidentified flying objects typically reported and described as luminous disks.

flying squirrel. Any of various squirrels of the genera *Pteromys, Glaucomys,* and related genera, having membranes between the forelegs and hind legs that enable them to glide through the air.

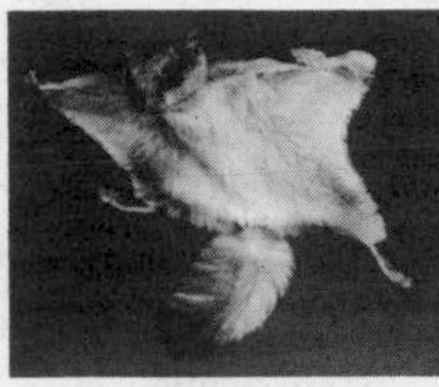

flying squirrel
Glaucomys volans

flying start. **1.** The crossing of the starting line of a race at full speed. **2.** Any quick start.

flying wing. **1.** An airplane in which a single large streamlined wing incorporating the fuselage constitutes the principal portion of the airframe. **2.** In Canadian football, a backfield man who moves to various positions behind the line of scrimmage.

fly·leaf (flī′lēf′) *n., pl.* **-leaves** (-lēvz′). A blank leaf at the beginning or end of a book, between the lining paper and the first or last signature. See **endpaper.**

fly net. A net covering used to keep flies off or out.

fly·o·ver (flī′ō′vər) *n.* **1.** A flight of aircraft at low altitude over a specific location, usually as a military display. **2.** *British.* An overpass on a highway.

fly·pa·per (flī′pā′pər) *n.* Paper coated with a sticky, sometimes poisonous substance, hung from a ceiling or placed on a surface to catch flies.

fly-poi·son (flī′poi′zən) *n.* A poisonous plant, *Amianthium muscaetoxicum,* of the southeastern United States, having narrow basal leaves and a terminal cluster of small white or greenish flowers.

Fly River (flī). The largest river of New Guinea, rising in the central highlands and flowing 650 miles to the Gulf of Papua.

fly·speck (flī′spĕk′) *n.* **1.** A small, dark speck or stain made by the excrement of a fly. **2.** A minute spot. —*tr.v.* **flyspecked, -specking, -specks.** To mark or befoul with flyspecks.

fly swatter. A swatter used to kill flies or other insects.

fly title. A **half title** *(see).*

fly·trap (flī′trăp′) *n.* **1.** A trap for catching flies. **2.** A plant that traps insects, such as the **Venus's-flytrap** *(see).*

fly·weight (flī′wāt′) *n. Boxing.* A boxer of the lightest weight class, weighing 112 pounds or less.

fly·wheel (flī′hwēl′) *n.* A heavy-rimmed rotating wheel used to minimize speed variation in a machine subject to fluctuation in drive and load.

fm frequency modulation.

Fm The symbol for the element fermium.

FM frequency modulation.

fm. **1.** fathom. **2.** from.

F.M. field marshal.

FMB Federal Maritime Board.

FMCS Federal Mediation and Conciliation Service.

fn. footnote.

FNMA Federal National Mortgage Association.

f-num·ber (ĕf′nŭm′bər) *n.* The ratio of focal length to the effective aperture diameter in a lens or lens system. Also called "f-stop."

F.O. field officer.

foal (fōl) *n.* The young offspring of a horse or other equine animal, especially when under a year old. —*v.* **foaled, foaling, foals.** —*tr.* To give birth to (a foal). —*intr.* To give birth to a foal. [Middle English *fole,* Old English *fola.* See **pōu-** in Appendix.*]

flywheel

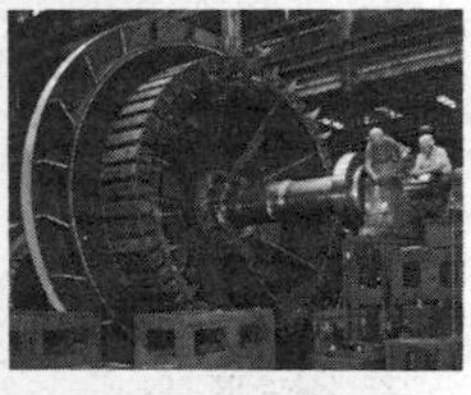

flywheel
A flywheel attached to the rotor of a diesel-driven generator

foam (fōm) *n.* **1.** A mass of gas bubbles in a liquid-film matrix; especially, a light, bubbly, gas and liquid mass formed by agitating a liquid containing certain soaps or detergents. **2. a.** Frothy saliva from the mouth: *"And the foam of his gasping/lay white on the turf"* (Byron). **b.** The frothy sweat of a horse or other equine animal. **3.** *Poetic.* The sea. **4.** Any of various rigid light, bulky, more or less rigid materials used as thermal or mechanical insulators especially in packaging and containers, made by injecting a gas into a material such as polystyrene. —*v.* **foamed, foaming, foams.** —*intr.* To form or come forth in foam; froth. —*tr.* To cause to foam. [Middle English *fom,* saliva, foam, Old English *fām.* See **spoimo-** in Appendix.*] —**foam′ing·ly** *adv.*

foam·flow·er (fōm′flou′ər) *n.* A woodland plant, *Tiarella cordifolia,* of eastern North America, having a narrow cluster of small white flowers. Also called "false miterwort." [From the foamy clusters of white flowers.]

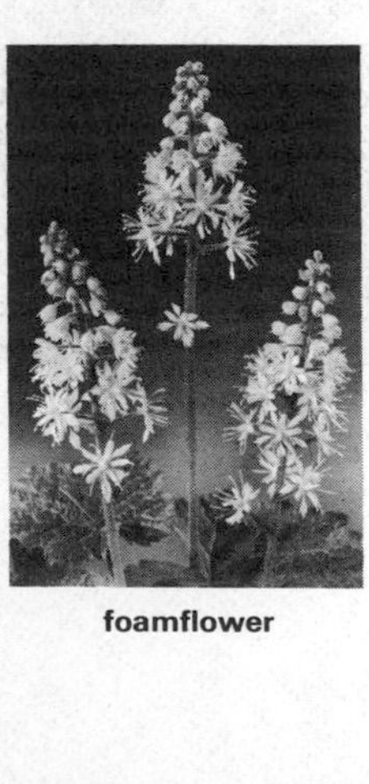

foamflower

foam rubber. A light, firm, spongy rubber, containing several times the volume of air ordinarily found in rubber, made by beating air into latex with subsequent curing, and used as an upholstery material and insulating medium.

foam·y (fō′mē) *adj.* **-ier, -iest.** **1.** Pertaining to or resembling foam. **2.** Consisting of or covered with foam. —**foam′i·ly** *adv.* —**foam′i·ness** *n.*

fob[1] (fŏb) *n.* **1.** A small pocket at the front waistline of a man's trousers or in the front of a vest, used to hold a watch or coins. **2.** A short chain or ribbon attached to a pocket watch and worn hanging in front of the vest or waist. **3.** An ornament or seal attached to the dangling end of a watch chain. [Probably from Germanic, akin to German (dialectal) *Fuppe*†, pocket.]

fob[2] (fŏb) *tr.v.* **fobbed, fobbing, fobs.** **1.** *Archaic.* To deceive; cheat. **2.** To dispose of (goods) by fraud or deception; palm off. Used with *off.* **3.** To put off or appease by deceitful or evasive means. Used with *off.* [Middle English *fobben*†.]

f.o.b., F.O.B. free on board.

fo·cal (fō′kəl) *adj.* **1.** Of or pertaining to a focus. **2.** Placed at or measured from the focus. —**fo′cal·ly** *adv.*

focal infection. An infection localized in a specific part of the body.

fo·cal·ize (fō′kə-līz′) *v.* **-ized, -izing, -izes.** —*tr.* To adjust or bring to a focus. —*intr.* To come or be brought to a focus. —**fo′cal·i·za′tion** *n.*

focal length. *Optics.* The distance of the focal point from the surface of a lens or mirror.

focal point. A point on the axis of symmetry of an optical system, as of a mirror or lens, to which parallel incident rays converge or from which they appear to diverge after passing through the system. Also called "principal focus."

Foch (fôsh, fŏsh), **Ferdinand.** 1851–1929. Marshal of France; commander in chief of Allied armies on the Western front during World War I.

Foc·şa·ni (fôk-shän′, -shä′nē). A town in east-central Rumania; site of the signing of the Rumanian-German truce (1917). Population, 31,000.

fo'c's'le. Variant of **forecastle.**

fo·cus (fō′kəs) *n., pl.* **-cuses** or **-ci** (-sī′). **1.** A point to which something converges or from which something diverges. **2.** *Optics.* **a.** A point in an optical system to which rays converge or from which they appear to diverge; focal point. **b.** Focal length. **c.** The distinctness or clarity with which an optical system renders an image. **d.** Adjustment for distinctness or clarity. **3.** A center of interest or activity. **4.** *Pathology.* The region of a localized bodily infection. **5.** *Geology.* The point of origin of an earthquake. **6.** *Geometry.* A point that together with a directrix determines a conic section. —*v.* **focused** or **focussed, -cusing** or **-cussing, -cuses** or **-cusses.** —*tr.* **1. a.** To produce a clear image of (photographed material, for example) by adjustment of a projection lens or other optical equipment. **b.** To adjust the setting of (a lens, for example) to produce a clear image. **2.** To concentrate on: *"The American black man should be focusing his every effort towards building his own businesses"* (Malcolm X). —*intr.* To converge at a point of focus; be focused. —**in focus.** Sharply or clearly defined; distinct. —**out of focus.** Not distinct; blurred; cloudy. [Latin *focus,* fireplace, hearth (the center of the home). See **fuel.**]

fod·der (fŏd′ər) *n.* **1.** Feed for livestock, often consisting of coarsely chopped stalks and leaves of corn mixed with hay, straw, and other plants. **2. a.** Raw material, as for artistic creation. **b.** Masses of people regarded as raw material for the achievement of a given political or military end: *cannon fodder.* —*tr.v.* **foddered, -dering, -ders.** To feed (animals) with fodder. [Middle English *fodder,* Old English *fōdor.* See **pā-** in Appendix.*]

foe (fō) *n.* **1.** A personal enemy. **2.** An enemy in war. **3.** An adversary; opponent. **4.** Something that serves to oppose, injure, or impede. [Middle English *fo, fa, ifa, ifo,* Old English *gefā,* from *gefāh,* at feud with, hostile. See **peig-**[2] in Appendix.*]

F.O.E. Fraternal Order of Eagles.

foehn (fān; *German* fœn) *n.* Also **föhn.** A warm dry wind coming off the lee slopes of a mountain range. [German *Föhn,* from Old High German *phōnno,* from Vulgar Latin *faōnius* (unattested), from Latin *favōnius,* the west wind. See **favonian.**]

foe·man (fō′mən) *n., pl.* **-men** (-mĭn). A foe in battle; enemy.

foe·tal. Variant of **fetal.**

foe·tid. Variant of **fetid.**

foe·tor. Variant of **fetor.**

foe·tus. Variant of **fetus.**

fog[1] (fôg, fŏg) *n.* **1.** Condensed water vapor in cloudlike masses close to the ground and limiting visibility. **2.** Any mass of floating material, such as dust or smoke, that forms an obscuring haze. **3.** A state of mental confusion or bewilderment. **4.** *Photography.* A dark blur on a developed negative. —*v.* **fogged, fogging, fogs.** —*tr.* **1.** To cover or envelop with fog. **2.** To cause to be clouded or obscured; blur. **3.** To make uncertain or unclear; bewilder. **4.** *Photography.* To obscure or dim (a negative) with a dark blur. —*intr.* **1.** To be covered or enveloped with fog. Often used with *up* or *over: The harbor will fog over by noon.* **2.** To be blurred or obscured. **3.** *Photography.* To be dimmed or obscured with a dark blur. Used of a print or negative. [Possibly a back-formation from earlier *foggy,* murky, moist, boggy, from FOG (rank grass).]

fog[2] (fôg, fŏg) *n.* **1.** A second growth of grass appearing on a field that has been mowed or grazed. **2.** Tall, thick grass left standing after the cutting or grazing season. [Middle English *fogge, fog,* probably from Scandinavian, akin to Norwegian *fogg.* See **pu-**[2] in Appendix.*]

fog bank. An opaque mass of fog sharply defined in contrast to surrounding, clearer air; especially, such a fog occurring at sea or along a coast.

fog·bound (fôg′bound′, fŏg′-) *adj.* **1.** Immobilized by heavy fog. **2.** Clouded or obscured by fog.

fog·bow (fôg′bō′, fŏg′-) *n.* A faint white or yellowish arc-shaped light, similar to a rainbow, often seen opposite the sun in a fog bank. Also called "seadog."

fog·dog (fôg′dôg′, fŏg′dŏg′) *n.* A bright or clear spot in a fog bank.

Fog·gia (fôd′jä). A provincial capital and agricultural center in southern Italy. Population, 128,000.

fog·gy (fô′gē, fŏg′ē) *adj.* **-gier, -giest.** **1.** Full of or surrounded by fog. **2.** Resembling or suggestive of fog. **3.** Clouded; blurred; indistinct. **4.** Bewildered; perplexed. **5.** *Photography.* Obscured or dimmed by a fog or dark blur. —**fog′gi·ly** *adv.* —**fog′gi·ness** *n.*

fog·horn (fôg′hôrn′, fŏg′-) *n.* **1.** A horn used by ships and coastal installations to sound warning signals, typically of long, deep tones, in fog or darkness. **2.** A resounding, insistent voice.

fo·gy (fō′gē) *n., pl.* **-gies.** Also **fo·gey** *pl.* **-geys.** **1.** A person of old-fashioned habits and outmoded attitudes: *an old fogy.*

2. *Military Slang.* An increase in base pay given after a certain number of years of service. [Origin obscure.] —**fo'gy·ish** *adj.* —**fo'gy·ism'** *n.*

föhn. Variant of **foehn.**

foi·ble (foi'bəl) *n.* **1.** A minor weakness or failing of character; a small but persistent personal fault. **2.** The weaker section of a sword blade, from the middle to the tip. In this sense, compare **forte.** —See Synonyms at **fault.** [Obsolete French, from adjective, "feeble," from Old French *feble,* FEEBLE.]

foil[1] (foil) *tr.v.* **foiled, foiling, foils. 1.** To prevent from being successful; thwart. **2.** To obscure or confuse (a trail or scent) so as to evade pursuers. —See Synonyms at **frustrate.** —*n.* **1.** *Archaic.* A foiling; a repulse; setback. **2.** The trail or scent of an animal. [Originally to trample, tread upon, Middle English *foilen,* perhaps from Norman French *fuler* (unattested), variant of Old French *fouler,* to FULL (cloth).]

foil[2] (foil) *n.* **1.** A thin, flexible leaf or sheet of a metal. **2.** A thin layer of bright metal placed under a displayed gem or piece of jewelry to lend it brilliance. **3.** Any person or thing that, by strong contrast, underscores or enhances the distinctive characteristics of another: *"I am resolved my husband shall not be a rival, but a foil to me"* (Charlotte Brontë). **4.** The metal coating applied to the back of a plate of glass to form a mirror. **5.** *Architecture.* A leaflike design or space worked in stone or glass, found especially in Gothic window tracery. —*tr.v.* **foiled, foiling, foils. 1.** To back or cover with a thin, pliant sheet of metal. **2.** To serve as a foil to; set off by contrast. **3.** *Architecture.* To ornament (windows or walls) with foils. [Middle English *foil(le), foile,* thin sheet of metal, leaf, from Old French, from Latin *folium.* See **bhel-[3]** in Appendix.*]

foil[3] (foil) *n.* **1.** A fencing sword with a flat guard for the hand and a thin blade, rectangular in cross section, tipped with a blunt point to prevent injury. **2.** *Plural.* The art of fencing with such swords. [Origin unknown.]

foils·man (foilz'mən) *n., pl.* **-men** (-mĭn). One who fences with a foil; a fencer.

foin (foin) *intr.v.* **foined, foining, foins.** *Archaic.* To thrust with a pointed weapon. —*n. Archaic.* A lunge or thrust with a pointed weapon. [Middle English *foinen,* from *foin,* a thrust, a three-pronged fork for spearing fish, from Old French *foin, foisne,* from Latin *fuscina*†, trident.]

Fo·ism (fō'ĭz'əm) *n.* Chinese Buddhism. [Mandarin Chinese *fo²,* Buddha, from Sanskrit *Buddha,* BUDDHA.] —**Fo'ist** *n.*

foi·son (foi'zən) *n.* **1.** *Archaic.* **a.** A plentiful harvest; good crop. **b.** Abundance; plenty. **2.** *Scottish.* Strength; power; capacity. **3.** *Plural. Obsolete.* Reserves of power; resources. [Middle English *foisoun,* from Old French *foison,* power, abundance, from Vulgar Latin *fusiō* (unattested), from Latin *fūsiō,* an outpouring, effusion, from *fūsus,* past participle of *fundere,* to pour. See **gheu-** in Appendix.*]

foist (foist) *tr.v.* **foisted, foisting, foists. 1.** To pass off as genuine, valuable, or worthy; palm off: *"I can usually tell whether a poet . . . is foisting off on us what he'd like to think is pure invention"* (J.D. Salinger). **2.** To impose (someone or something unwanted) upon another by coercion or trickery. **3.** To insert fraudulently or deceitfully: *He foisted unfair provisions into the contract.* [Original sense, to introduce a palmed die surreptitiously, from Dutch (dialectal) *vuisten,* from *vuist,* fist. See **penkwe** in Appendix.*]

Fo·kine (fō-kēn'), **Michel.** 1880–1942. Russian-born American choreographer.

Fok·ker (fŏk'ər), **Anthony Herman Gerard.** 1890–1939. Dutch-born American airplane designer and manufacturer.

fol. 1. folio. **2.** following.

fold[1] (fōld) *v.* **folded, folding, folds.** —*tr.* **1.** To bend over or double up so that one part lies on another part: *"Neatly he folded his newspaper"* (Carson McCullers). **2.** To make compact by successively bending over parts. Sometimes used with *up.* **3.** To bring from an extended to a closed position: *On alighting, the hawk folded its wings.* **4.** To place together and intertwine: *fold one's arms.* **5.** To bend, clasp, or entwine. **6.** To surround with the arms; enfold; embrace. **7.** To wrap; envelop. **8.** *Cooking.* To mix in (an ingredient) by slowly and gently turning one part over another. Used with *in: When the batter is thick, fold in the beaten egg whites.* —*intr.* **1.** To become folded. **2.** *Informal.* To close for lack of funds; fail financially. **3.** *Informal.* To weaken or collapse from exertion. **4.** *Card Games.* To withdraw from competition during a hand. —*n.* **1.** The act or an instance of folding. **2.** A part or section that has been folded over another. **3.** The space or hollow at the junction of two folded parts. **4.** A hollow or dale in hilly country. **5.** *Geology.* A bend in a stratum of rock. **6.** A coil, as of rope or a snake. **7.** *Anatomy.* A crease apparently formed by folding, as of a membrane. [Middle English *folden, falden,* Old English *faldan, fealdan.* See **pel-[3]** in Appendix.*]

fold[2] (fōld) *n.* **1.** A fenced enclosure for domestic animals, especially sheep. **2.** The sheep enclosed in such a pen. **3.** A flock of sheep. **4.** A church and its members. **5.** Any group of people bound together by common beliefs and aims, or by mutual loyalty. —*tr.v.* **folded, folding, folds.** To place or keep (sheep) in a fold. [Middle English *fold,* Old English *fald, falod,* akin to Middle Low German *valt*†.]

-fold. Indicates: **1.** Division into a specified number of parts; for example, **fivefold. 2.** Multiplication by a specified number; for example, **tenfold.** [Middle English *-fold, -fald,* Old English *-f(e)ald.* See **pel-[3]** in Appendix.*]

fold·boat (fōld'bōt') *n.* A **faltboat** *(see).* [Translation of German *Faltboot.*]

fold·er (fōl'dər) *n.* **1.** One that folds. **2.** A folded sheet of printed matter. **3.** A group of folded, printed sheets, gathered together but not fastened. **4. a.** A sheet of cardboard or thick paper folded in the center and used as a holder for loose paper. **b.** Any folded piece of cardboard or other material used as a container: *a folder of matches.*

fol·de·rol (fŏl'də-rŏl') *n.* Also **fal·de·ral** (făl'də-răl'), **fal·de·rol** (făl'də-rŏl'). **1.** Foolish talk or procedure; nonsense. **2.** A trifle; gewgaw. [From *fol-de-rol* and *fal-deral,* a meaningless refrain in some old songs.]

fold-out (fōld'out') *n. Printing.* A **gatefold** *(see).*

fo·li·a. Plural of **folium.**

fo·li·a·ceous (fō'lē-ā'shəs) *adj.* **1.** Of, relating to, or resembling the leaf of a plant. **2.** Having leaves or leaflike structures. **3.** Consisting of thin laminated layers, as certain rocks. [Latin *foliāceus,* from *folium,* leaf, FOLIUM.]

fo·li·age (fō'lē-ĭj) *n.* **1.** The leaves of growing plants; plant leaves collectively. **2.** An ornamental or artistic representation of leaves, branches, and flowers. [Middle English *foilage,* from Old French *feuillage, foillage,* from *feuille, foille,* leaf, from Latin *folium.* See **bhel-[3]** in Appendix.*] —**fo'li·aged** *adj.*

foliage plant. A plant cultivated chiefly for its ornamental leaves.

fo·li·ar (fō'lē-ər) *adj.* Of or pertaining to a leaf or leaves. [French *foliaire,* from Latin *folium,* leaf, FOLIUM.]

fo·li·ate (fō'lē-ĭt, -āt') *adj.* **1.** Of or pertaining to leaves. **2.** Having a specified number or kind of leaves. Used in combination: *trifoliate, perfoliate.* —*v.* (fō'lē-āt') **foliated, -ating, -ates.** —*tr.* **1.** To hammer or cut (metal) into thin plates, leaf, or foil. **2. a.** To coat (glass) with metal foil. **b.** To furnish or adorn with metal foil. **3.** To separate into thin layers. **4.** To decorate with foliage. **5.** To number the leaves of (a book). In this sense, compare **paginate.** —*intr.* **1.** To produce foliage; put forth leaves. **2.** To split into thin layers. [Latin *foliātus,* bearing leaves, from *folium,* leaf, FOLIUM.]

fo·li·a·tion (fō'lē-ā'shən) *n.* **1.** The state of being in leaf or putting forth leaves. **2.** Decoration with foliage. **3.** *Architecture.* The decoration of an archway, window, or other opening with cusps and foils, as in Gothic tracery. **4. a.** The act or process of foliating metal. **b.** The foliating of glass. **5.** The process of numbering consecutively the leaves of a book. [From Latin *folium,* leaf, FOLIUM.]

fo·lic acid (fō'lĭk). A yellowish-orange compound, $C_{19}H_{19}N_7O_6$, a member of the vitamin-B complex, occurring in green plants, fresh fruit, liver, and yeast, and used medicinally to treat pernicious anemias. Also called "pteroylglutamic acid," "vitamin B_c." [Latin *fol(ium),* leaf, FOLIUM + -IC.]

fo·li·o (fō'lē-ō') *n., pl.* **-os.** *Abbr.* **f., F., fol. 1.** A large sheet of paper, folded once in the middle, making two leaves or four pages of a book or manuscript. **2.** A book or manuscript of the largest common size, usually about 15 inches in height, consisting of such folded sheets. **3.** A leaf of a book numbered only on the front side. **4.** A page number in a book; especially, one assigned to a page during the printing process. **5.** *Bookkeeping.* A page in a ledger, or two facing pages assigned a single number. **6.** *Law.* A specific number of words used as a unit for measuring the length of the text of a document. —*adj.* **1.** Of or pertaining to a folio: *folio pages.* **2.** Presented in the form of a folio: *a folio edition.* —*tr.v.* **folioed, -oing, -os.** To number consecutively the pages of (a book). [Medieval Latin, ablative (used for page references, "at leaf *x*") of Latin *folium,* leaf, FOLIUM.]

fo·li·o·late (fō'lē-ə-lāt') *adj. Botany.* Having or consisting of leaflets. Usually used in combination: *bifoliolate.* [From earlier *foliole,* leaflet, from French, from New Latin *foliolum,* diminutive of Latin *folium,* leaf, FOLIUM.]

fo·li·ose (fō'lē-ōs') *adj.* **1.** Bearing numerous leaves or leaflets; leafy. **2.** Of, pertaining to, or resembling a leaf or leaves. [Latin *foliōsus,* from *folium,* leaf, FOLIUM.]

fo·li·um (fō'lē-əm) *n., pl.* **-lia** (-lē-ə). **1.** *Geology.* A thin layer or stratum occurring especially in metamorphic rock. **2.** *Geometry.* A plane cubic curve having a single loop, a node, and two ends asymptotic to the same line. In this sense, also called "folium of Descartes." [New Latin, from Latin, leaf. See **bhel-[3]** in Appendix.*]

folk (fōk) *n., pl.* **folk** or *informal* **folks. 1.** A people; an ethnic group; a race. **2.** *Usually plural.* People of a specified group or kind: *city folk.* **3.** *Plural. Informal.* The members of one's family or childhood household; one's relatives. **4.** *Plural. Informal.* People in general: *Folks will talk.* —See Synonyms at **nation.** —*adj.* Of, occurring in, or originating among the common people; especially, untutored or unrefined: *"American folk painting cannot be separated from its fine art"* (Harold Rosenberg). [Middle English *folk,* Old English *folc,* the people, nation, tribe, from Germanic *folkam* (unattested).]

folk dance. 1. A traditional dance originating among the common people of a nation or region. **2.** The music accompanying such a dance. **3.** A social gathering at which such dances are performed. —**folk dancing.**

Fol·ke·ting (fōl'kə-tĭng') *n.* Also **Fol·ke·thing.** The unicameral parliament of Denmark. [Danish : *folk,* the people, from Old Norse, from Germanic *folkam* (unattested), FOLK + *ting,* assembly, from Old Norse *thing* (see **tenk-[1]** in Appendix*).]

folk etymology. 1. A change in form of a word or phrase, resulting from an incorrect popular notion of the origin or meaning of the term or from the influence of more familiar terms mistakenly taken to be analogous. **2.** A word or phrase that is a product of this modification, as *sparrowgrass* from *asparagus.* —**folk'-et'y·mo·log'i·cal** *adj.*

folk·lore (fōk'lôr', -lōr') *n.* **1.** The traditional beliefs, practices,

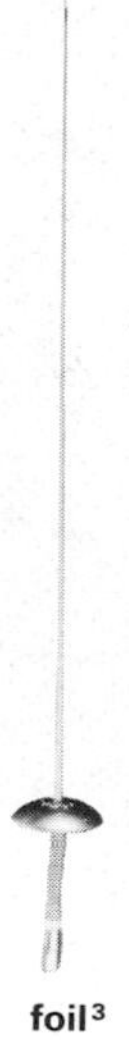

foil[3]

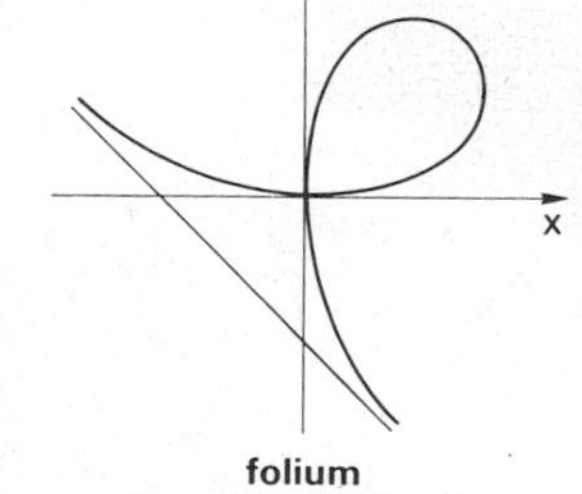

folium
Equation of folium is
$x^3 + y^3 = 3axy$,
where *a* is a constant

legends, and tales of the common, uneducated people, transmitted orally. **2.** The comparative study of folk knowledge and culture. **3.** A body of widely accepted but specious notions about a place, group, or institution: *the folklore of Hollywood.* —**folk′lor′ic** *adj.* —**folk′lor′ist** *n.*

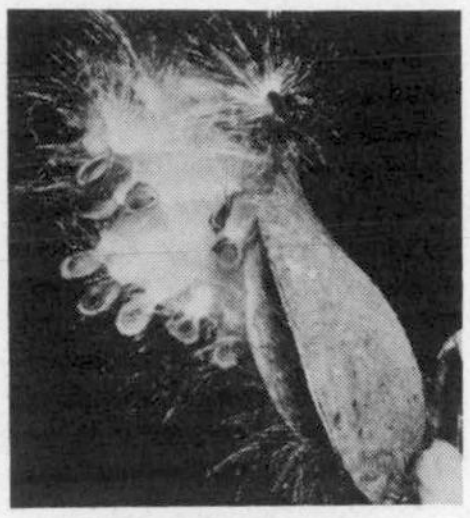

follicle
A milkweed pod

folk·mote (fōk′mōt′) *n.* Also **folk·moot** (-mo͞ot′). A general assembly of the people of a town, district, or shire in medieval England. [Old English *folcmōt* : *folc,* FOLK + *mōt,* meeting, assembly (see **mōd-** in Appendix*).]

folk music. Music originating among the common people of a nation or region and characterized by a tradition of oral transmission and usually anonymous authorship.

folk rock. A variety of popular music that combines elements of rock 'n' roll and folk music, often conveying themes of social protest.

folk singer. A singer of folk songs. —**folk singing.**

folk song. **1.** A song belonging to the folk music of a people or area, characterized chiefly by the directness and simplicity of the feelings expressed and often sung or performed in several versions. **2.** A song of known authorship composed in imitation of such songs.

folk·sy (fōk′sē) *adj.* **-sier, -siest.** *Informal.* **1.** Simple and unpretentious in social behavior; unsophisticated. **2.** Characterized by congeniality and affability. —**folk′si·ness** *n.*

folk·way (fōk′wā′) *n.* A way of thinking or acting adopted unreflectively by the members of a group as part of their shared culture: *"Much prejudice is a matter of blind conformity with prevailing folkways"* (Gordon W. Allport).

fol·li·cle (fŏl′ĭ-kəl) *n.* **1.** *Anatomy.* **a.** An approximately spherical group of cells containing a cavity. **b.** A vascular body in the ovary containing ova. **2.** *Botany.* A single-chambered fruit that splits along only one seam to release its seeds. [Latin *folliculus,* little bag, diminutive of *follis,* bellows. See **bhel-**[2] in Appendix.*]

fol·li·cle-stim·u·lat·ing hormone (fŏl′ĭ-kəl-stĭm′yə-lāt′ĭng). *Abbr.* **FSH** A gonadotropic hormone of the anterior pituitary gland that stimulates the growth of follicles in the ovary and induces spermatogenesis in the testis.

fol·lic·u·lar (fə-lĭk′yə-lər) *adj.* **1.** Relating to, having, or resembling a follicle or follicles. **2.** Affecting or growing out of follicles.

fol·lic·u·late (fə-lĭk′yə-lĭt) *adj.* Also **fol·lic·u·lat·ed** (-lā′tĭd). Having or consisting of a follicle or follicles.

fol·lies (fŏl′ēz) *n.* Plural in form, used with a singular verb. An elaborate, richly costumed theatrical revue consisting of a series of musical or dance skits. [Plural of FOLLY.]

fol·low (fŏl′ō) *v.* **-lowed, -lowing, -lows.** —*tr.* **1.** To come or go after; move behind and in the same direction. **2.** To go after with or as if with the intention of overtaking; pursue: *"The wrong she had done followed her and haunted her dream."* (Katherine Anne Porter). **3.** To come or go with; accompany; attend. **4.** To move along the course of; take (a course or direction): *We followed a path to the shore.* **5.** To accept the guidance or leadership of; have as a model; emulate. **6.** To adhere to the cause or principles of; to advocate: *follow outdated doctrines.* **7.** To be governed by; obey; comply with: *We follow the rules.* **8. a.** To occur after (a designated event) in a temporal sequence. **b.** To occupy or determine a position that is encountered, referred to, or employed after (a designated position) in a specified ordering. **9.** To succeed to the place or position of: *Elizabeth II followed George VI.* **10.** To engage in; work at (a trade or occupation). **11.** To occur or be evident as a consequence of: *Your conclusion does not follow your premise.* **12.** To be attentive to: listen to or watch closely: *I was too sleepy to follow the sermon.* **13.** To grasp the meaning or logic of; keep up with the reasoning of: *Do you follow my argument?* **14.** To inform oneself of the course or progress of: *follow the stock market.* —*intr.* **1.** To come, move, or take place after some other person or thing in order or time. **2.** To occur or be evident as a consequence; to result; ensue: *If you ignore your diet, trouble will follow.* **3.** To grasp the meaning or reasoning of what is said; understand. —**follow out.** To comply with fully; carry out. —**follow suit.** **1.** *Card Games.* To play a card of the same suit as the one led. **2.** To act after another's example. —*n.* **1.** The act or an instance of following. **2.** *Billiards.* A shot in which the cue ball is struck in such a way that it follows the path of the object ball after impact. [Middle English *fol(o)wen,* Old English *folgian* and *fylgan,* from Germanic *fulg-* (unattested).]

Synonyms: *follow, succeed, supplant, ensue, result, supervene.* These verbs mean to come after something or someone. *Follow,* which has the widest application, can refer to coming after in time or order, as a consequence or result, or by the operation of logic. *Succeed* involves coming after in time or order, especially in planned order determined by rank, inheritance, election, or the like. The term commonly is applied to the act of a person who takes the place of another or to a thing that extends continuity. *Supplant* usually refers to decisive, especially abrupt or violent, displacement or ouster. *Ensue* applies to a thing that comes after another in time, often as a consequence or logical development. *Result* refers to an event that is discernibly caused by a prior event or events. *Supervene,* in contrast, refers to the coming after of a thing that has little relation to what has preceded and that is therefore unexpected.

font[1]
Baptismal font in church at Aarhus, Denmark

Usage: *As follows* (not *as follow*) is the established form regardless of the grammatical number of the noun that precedes: *Her reply was as follows. The events scheduled today are as follows.* The example *the events are as follow* is unacceptable to 78 per cent of the Usage Panel. In such constructions the subject of *follows* is generally construed as *it* unexpressed: *as it follows.*

fol·low·er (fŏl′ō-ər) *n.* **1.** One that comes or occurs after another. **2.** A pursuer. **3.** An attendant, servant, or subordinate. **4.** One who subscribes to the teachings or methods of another; an adherent: *"Stalin has always regarded himself as a faithful follower of Lenin."* (John C. Bennett). **5.** A machine element moved by another machine element.

fol·low·ing (fŏl′ō-ĭng) *adj.* **1.** *Abbr.* **f., ff., fol.** Coming next in time or order: *in the following chapter.* **2.** Now to be enumerated: *The following men will report for duty.* —*n.* A group or gathering of admirers, adherents, or disciples: *a lecturer with a large following.* —**the following.** **1.** The ones that are to be mentioned or listed next: *Please buy the following.* **2.** What is now to be said or specified: *Listen closely to the following.*

follow through. **1.** *Sports.* To carry a stroke to natural completion after hitting the ball. **2.** To carry an act or project to completion; pursue fully.

fol·low-through (fŏl′ō-thro͞o′) *n.* **1.** The carrying of a stroke to natural completion after the ball has been hit, as in tennis, golf, or baseball. **2.** The concluding part of a stroke, after the ball has been hit. **3.** The completion of a sequence of acts after the main one.

follow up. **1.** To carry to completion; follow through. **2.** To increase the effectiveness of by repetition or further action.

fol·low-up (fŏl′ō-ŭp′) *n.* **1.** The act or an instance of repeating or adding to previous action, so as to increase effectiveness. **2.** The means, as a letter, procedure, or visit, used to increase or reinforce the effectiveness of previous action. —*adj.* Designed to reinforce previous action: *a follow-up letter.*

fol·ly (fŏl′ē) *n., pl.* **-lies.** **1.** The condition or quality of being foolish; a lack of good sense, understanding, or foresight: *"In place of folly there can be sanity and purpose."* (Norman Cousins). **2. a.** Any act or instance of foolishness. **b.** A costly undertaking having an absurd or ruinous outcome. **3.** *Archaic.* Action or behavior considered immoral or criminal. **4.** *Obsolete.* Evil; wickedness; vice. [Middle English *folie,* from Old French, from *fol,* foolish, from Latin *follis,* bellows. See **fool.**]

Fol·som (fŏl′səm) *adj.* Of or relating to an early North American culture of the Pleistocene period flourishing east of the Rocky Mountains and notable chiefly for the use of leaf-shaped flint implements. [After *Folsom,* New Mexico, where remains were found.]

Fo·mal·haut (fō′məl-hôt′) *n.* The brightest star in the constellation Piscis Austrinus, 24 light-years from earth. [Arabic *fum′l-ḥūt,* "mouth of the fish."]

fo·ment (fō-mĕnt′) *tr.v.* **-mented, -menting, -ments.** **1.** To promote the growth or arousal of; stir up; instigate. **2.** To treat (the skin) by fomentation. —See Synonyms at **incite.** [Middle English *fomenten,* from Old French *fomenter,* from Late Latin *fōmentāre,* from Latin *fōmentum,* warm application, short for *fovementum* (unattested), from *fovēre,* to warm, cherish. See **dhegwh-** in Appendix.*] —**fo·ment′er** *n.*

fo·men·ta·tion (fō′mən-tā′shən) *n.* **1.** The act or an instance of promoting discontent, rebellion, or strife; instigation. **2. a.** A warm, moist, medicinal compress; poultice. **b.** The therapeutic application of warmth and moisture.

fond[1] (fŏnd) *adj.* **fonder, fondest.** **1.** Affectionate; tender: *a fond embrace.* **2.** Having a tender interest or affection. Used with *of: "He was fond of the fine arts, fond of long words, and fond of me"* (Mary McCarthy). **3.** Immoderately or irrationally affectionate; infatuated; doting. **4.** Cherished; dear: *my fondest hopes.* **5.** *Archaic.* Naively credulous or dependent; foolish. [Middle English *fonned,* foolish, probably from *fon†,* a fool.] —**fond′ly** *adv.*

fond[2] (fŏnd) *n.* **1.** The background of a design in lace. **2.** The groundwork; foundation; basis. [French, from Latin *fundus,* bottom. See **bhudh-** in Appendix.*]

fon·dant (fŏn′dənt; *French* fôN-däN′) *n.* **1.** A sweet, creamy sugar paste, eaten as candy or used in icings or as a filling for other candies. **2.** A candy containing fondant. [French, from the present participle of *fondre,* to melt (it melts quickly in the mouth), from Latin *fundere,* to pour, melt. See **gheu-** in Appendix.*]

fon·dle (fŏnd′l) *v.* **-dled, -dling, -dles.** —*tr.* **1.** To handle or stroke with affection; caress lovingly with the hands. **2.** *Obsolete.* To treat with indulgence and solicitude; pamper. —*intr.* To show fondness or affection by caressing. [Back-formation from earlier *fondling* : FOND + -LING.]

fond·ness (fŏnd′nĭs) *n.* **1.** Warm affection; tender liking. **2.** Strong preference; inclination; relish. **3.** *Archaic.* Naive trustfulness; credulity. —See Synonyms at **love.**

fon·due (fŏn-do͞o′; *French* fôN-dü′) *n.* Also **fon·du.** A hot dish made of melted cheese and wine, often with eggs, butter, and milk, and eaten with bread. [French, feminine past participle of *fondre,* to melt. See **fondant.**]

Fond du Lac (fŏn′ də lăk′, dyə lăk′). **1.** During the early period of European settlement in North America, any of various areas adjacent to the Great Lakes. **2.** A city of Wisconsin, in the east at the southern end of Lake Winnebago. Population, 38,000.

Fon·se·ca, Gulf of (fŏn-sā′kä). An inlet of the Pacific Ocean in western Central America, rimmed by El Salvador, Honduras, and Nicaragua.

fons et o·ri·go (fŏnz′ ĕt ō-rī′gō). *Latin.* Source and origin.

font[1] (fŏnt) *n.* **1.** A basin, usually mounted on a stone pedestal, holding baptismal water in a church. **2.** A receptacle for holy water; stoup. **3.** The oil reservoir in an oil-burning lamp. **4.** *Archaic.* A fountain or spring. **5.** Any source of abundance; fount: *The old man is a font of knowledge and sound advice.*

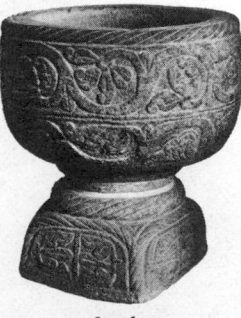

[Middle English *font,* Old English *font, fant,* from Latin *fons* (stem *font-*), spring, fountain. See **dhen-**[1] in Appendix.*] —**font'al** *adj.*

font[2] (fŏnt) *n.* Also *chiefly British* **fount** (fount). *Printing.* A complete set of type of one size and face. [Old French, casting, from *fondre,* to melt, cast. See **fondant.**]

Fon·taine·bleau (fŏn'tən-blō'; *French* fôɴ-tĕn-blō'). A town in France, on the Seine in the Forest of Fontainebleau, about 30 miles south of Paris, site of a former French royal residence. Population, 20,000.

Fon·ta·na (fōn-tä'nä), **Domenico.** 1543–1607. Italian architect.

fon·ta·nel (fŏn'tə-nĕl') *n.* Also **fon·ta·nelle.** Any of the soft membranous intervals between the incompletely ossified cranial bones of fetuses and infants. [Middle English *fontinel,* a hollow, from Old French *fontenele,* diminutive of *fontaine,* FOUNTAIN.]

Foo·chow (fo͞o'chou'; *Chinese* fo͞o'jō'). Also **Fu-chou, Fu·chow.** An industrial center and the capital of Fukien Province, in southern China, on the Min River. Population, 553,000.

food (fo͞od) *n.* **1.** Any material, usually of plant or animal origin, containing or consisting of essential body nutrients, as carbohydrates, fats, proteins, vitamins, or minerals, that is taken in and assimilated by an organism to maintain life and growth. **2.** A specified kind of nourishment: *breakfast food; plant food.* **3.** Nourishment eaten in solid form, as distinguished from liquid nourishment: *good food and wine.* **4.** Anything that nourishes or sustains in a way suggestive of physical nourishment: *"There's sure no passion in the human soul,/But finds its food in music."* (George Lillo). [Middle English *fode,* Old English *fōda.* See **pā-** in Appendix.*]

food poisoning. **1.** Poisoning caused by eating food contaminated by bacteria, especially bacteria of the genus *Staphylococcus,* and characterized, with varying severity, by vomiting, diarrhea, prostration, and sometimes shock. **2.** Poisoning caused by eating foods containing natural toxins.

food·stuff (fo͞od'stŭf') *n.* **1.** Any substance suitable for food; especially, a crude product suitable for food after processing. **2.** Any substance, such as protein or fat, that forms part of a variety of foods.

foo·fa·raw (fo͞o'fə-rô') *n.* **1.** Excessive or flashy ornamentation. **2.** A commotion or disturbance over a trifling matter; a fuss. [Origin unknown.]

fool[1] (fo͞ol) *n.* **1.** One who shows himself, by words or actions, to be deficient in judgment, sense, or understanding; a stupid or thoughtless person: *"Who are a little wise, the best fools be."* (Donne). **2.** One who acts unwisely on a given occasion: *I was a fool to have refused the job.* **3.** Formerly, a member of a royal or noble household who entertained the court with jests, mimicry, and the like; jester; buffoon. **4.** One who has been or can be easily deceived or imposed upon; a dupe: *They made a fool of me.* **5.** *Obsolete.* A feeble-minded person; an idiot. **6.** *Informal.* A person with a talent, fondness, or enthusiasm for a certain activity: *a fool for stamp-collecting.* —*v.* **fooled, fooling, fools.** —*tr.* **1.** To deceive or misinform, especially for amusement or to gain an advantage; to trick; to dupe. **2.** To take unawares; to surprise, especially pleasantly: *We were sure he would fail, but he fooled us.* —*intr.* **1.** To act or speak in jest; to play; to joke; be amusing. **2.** To act, speak, argue, or contend without, but as if with, purposeful or harmful intent: *They thought he might shoot, but he was only fooling.* —**fool around.** *Informal.* To engage in or amuse oneself with useless or trifling activity. —**fool away.** To waste (time or money) foolishly; squander. —**fool with.** To toy or tamper with aimlessly; meddle with. [Middle English *fol(e),* a fool, foolish, from Old French *fol,* from Latin *follis,* "bellows," windbag. See **bhel-**[2] in Appendix.*]

fool[2] (fo͞ol) *n. British.* A dessert made of crushed, stewed fruit, mixed with cream or custard and served cold. [Possibly a specialized use of FOOL.]

fool·er·y (fo͞o'lə-rē) *n., pl.* **-ies. 1.** Foolish behavior or speech; playfulness or facetiousness. **2.** An instance of this; a jest, prank, or trick.

fool·har·dy (fo͞ol'här'dē) *adj.* **-dier, -diest.** Unwisely bold or venturesome; rash. See Synonyms at **reckless.** [Middle English *fol-hardi,* from Old French *folhardi* : *fol,* foolish (see **fool**) + *hardi,* HARDY.] —**fool'har'di·ly** *adv.* —**fool'har'di·ness** *n.*

fool·ish (fo͞o'lĭsh) *adj.* **1.** Lacking good sense or judgment; silly: *foolish remarks.* **2.** Resulting from stupidity or misinformation; ill-advised; unwise: *a foolish decision.* **3.** Devoid of meaning or coherence; ridiculous; inane: *a foolish grin.* **4.** Abashed; embarrassed: *I feel foolish telling you this.* **5.** *Archaic.* Insignificant; worthless: *"We have a trifling foolish banquet"* (Shakespeare). —**fool'ish·ly** *adv.* —**fool'ish·ness** *n.*

Synonyms: *foolish, silly, fatuous, absurd, preposterous, ridiculous, ludicrous.* These adjectives are applied to what is devoid of wisdom or good sense. *Foolish,* the least emphatic and derogatory, usually implies poor judgment in a person or general lack of wisdom or soundness in concepts or entities. *Silly* suggests what lacks point, purpose, or semblance of intellectual content. *Fatuous* intensifies the idea of emptiness or inanity and often also implies, in persons, smugness or lack of awareness of one's stupidity. *Absurd,* together with the remaining terms, implies obvious departure from truth, nature, reason, or common sense. *Preposterous* suggests what is so far from reason or sense that it seems a travesty of them and does not merit consideration. *Ridiculous* refers to what inspires derision and contempt because of its absurdity. *Ludicrous* applies to what causes scornful laughter.

fool·proof (fo͞ol'pro͞of') *adj.* **1.** Designed so as to be proof against human incompetence, error, or misuse: *a foolproof detonator.* **2.** Always effective; completely dependable; infallible: *a foolproof scheme.*

fools·cap (fo͞olz'kăp') *n.* **1.** *Abbr.* **fcp., fcap., fp.** A sheet of writing or printing paper approximately 13x16 inches, becoming 13x8 inches when folded. **2.** A fool's cap. [From the watermark of a fool's cap with bells originally marking this type of paper.]

fool's cap. **1.** A gaily decorated cap, usually with a number of loose peaks tipped with bells, formerly worn by court jesters and clowns. **2.** A dunce cap.

fool's errand. A fruitless errand or undertaking.

fool's gold. **Pyrite** *(see)* or any similar mineral found in gold-colored veins or nuggets, sometimes mistaken for gold.

fool's paradise. A state of delusive contentment or false hope.

fool's-pars·ley (fo͞olz'pär'slē) *n.* A poisonous plant, *Aethusa cynapium,* native to Eurasia, having finely divided leaves, clusters of small white flowers, and an unpleasant odor.

foot (fo͝ot) *n., pl.* **feet** (fēt). **1.** The lower extremity of the vertebrate leg that is in direct contact with the ground in standing or walking. **2.** A structure used for locomotion or attachment in an invertebrate animal, such as the muscular organ extending from the ventral side of a mollusk. **3.** Something resembling or suggestive of a foot in position or function, especially: **a.** The bottom or lowest part of anything standing vertically, or considered in its vertical dimension: *the foot of a mountain; the foot of a page.* **b.** The lower part of the leg on a table or chair. **c.** The end or final section of an order or series; rear: *the foot of a parade.* **d.** The inferior part or rank: *the foot of the class.* **4.** The lower end of an object, or the end opposite the head, as of a bed or table. **5.** The part of a stocking or high-topped boot that encloses the foot. **6.** A manner of moving; a step: *He walks with a light foot.* **7.** Foot soldiers; infantry. **8.** The attachment on a sewing machine that clamps down and guides the cloth. **9.** *Prosody.* A metric unit consisting of a stressed or unstressed syllable or syllables. **10.** *Symbol* ' *Abbr.* **ft** A unit of length in the U.S. Customary and British Imperial systems, equal to ⅓ yard or 12 inches. See **measurement.** See Usage note below. —**on foot.** Walking or standing; not riding. —**put one's best foot forward.** *Informal.* To make a good beginning or favorable first impression. —**put one's foot down.** *Informal.* To assert one's will emphatically; insist on one's way. —**put one's foot in one's mouth.** *Informal.* To make an embarrassing or tactless blunder in speech. —**under foot. 1.** At one's feet; on the ground or floor. **2.** Obstructing free movement; in the way. —*v.* **footed, footing, foots.** —*intr.* **1.** To go on foot; to walk. Often used with the indefinite *it.* **2.** To dance. Often used with the indefinite *it: "We foot it all the night/weaving olden dances"* (Yeats). **3.** To move steadily; proceed. —*tr.* **1.** To go by foot on or through; to pace; tread. **2.** To provide (a stocking, for example) with a foot. **3.** To add (a column of numbers) and write the total at the bottom; to total. Used with *up: Foot up the bill.* **4.** *Informal.* To pay: *Can you foot the monthly rent?* [Foot, feet; Middle English *fot, fet,* Old English *fōt, fēt.* See **ped-**[1] in Appendix.*]

Usage: *Foot* and *feet,* as units of measure, are employed typically in the following: *a four-foot plank; a plank four feet long* (or *four feet in length*); *a man six feet tall; a ledge two feet below.*

foot·age (fo͝ot'ĭj) *n.* **1.** The length or extent of something as expressed in feet. **2.** A portion of motion-picture film; especially, an amount of film depicting a specified event or kind of action: *news footage.* **3.** *Mining.* **a.** Payment computed on the number of feet mined. **b.** The amount of payment thus computed.

foot-and-mouth disease (fo͝ot'ən-mouth'). An acute, highly contagious, degenerative, but usually nonfatal, viral disease of cattle and other cloven-hoofed animals, characterized by fever and the eruption of vesicles around the mouth and hoofs.

foot·ball (fo͝ot'bôl') *n.* **1. a.** A game played with a ball on a rectangular, 100-yard-long field with goal lines and posts at either end. Opposing teams of 11 players seek to gain possession of the ball and advance it in running or passing plays across the opponent's goal line. **b.** The ball used in this game, an inflated ellipsoid made of pigskin or a substitute. **2.** *Chiefly British.* **a. Rugby football** *(see).* **b.** The ball used in Rugby football. **3.** *Chiefly British.* **a. Soccer** *(see).* **b.** The ball used in soccer. **4.** Any problem or issue that is passed about among groups or persons without being settled.

foot·board (fo͝ot'bôrd', -bōrd') *n.* **1.** A board or small raised platform on which to support or rest the feet, as in a carriage. **2.** An upright board across the foot of a bedstead.

foot·boy (fo͝ot'boi') *n.* A youth employed as a servant or page.

foot brake. A brake operated by pressure of the foot on a pedal, as in an automobile or bicycle.

foot·bridge (fo͝ot'brĭj') *n.* A narrow bridge designed to carry only pedestrians.

foot-can·dle (fo͝ot'kănd'l) *n. Abbr.* **fc** *Physics.* The illumination of a surface one foot distant from a source of one candela, equal to one lumen per square foot. Also called "candle-foot."

foot·cloth (fo͝ot'klôth', -klŏth') *n., pl.* **-cloths** (-klôths', -klô*th*z', -klŏths', -klŏ*th*z'). **1.** A richly ornamented cloth draped over the back of a horse and touching the ground. **2.** *Obsolete.* A carpet or rug.

foot·ed (fo͝ot'ĭd) *adj.* **1.** Having a foot or feet. **2.** Having a specified kind or number of feet. Used in combination: *web-footed.*

foot·er (fo͝ot'ər) *n.* **1.** One who goes on foot; a pedestrian. **2.** A person or thing measuring an indicated number of feet in height or length. Used in combination: *a six-footer.*

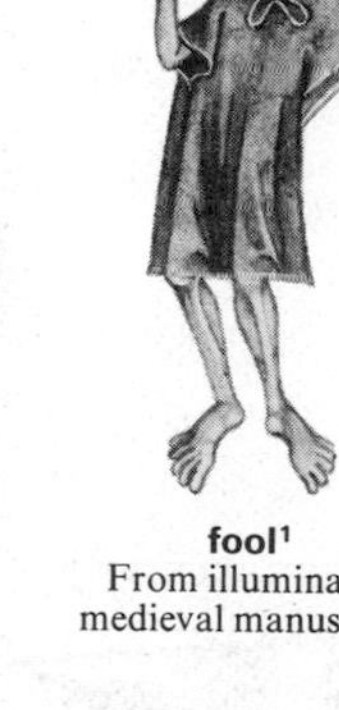

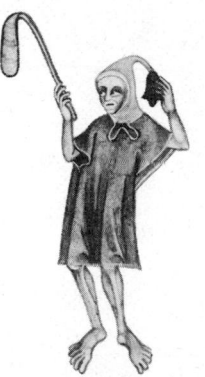

fool[1]
From illuminated medieval manuscript

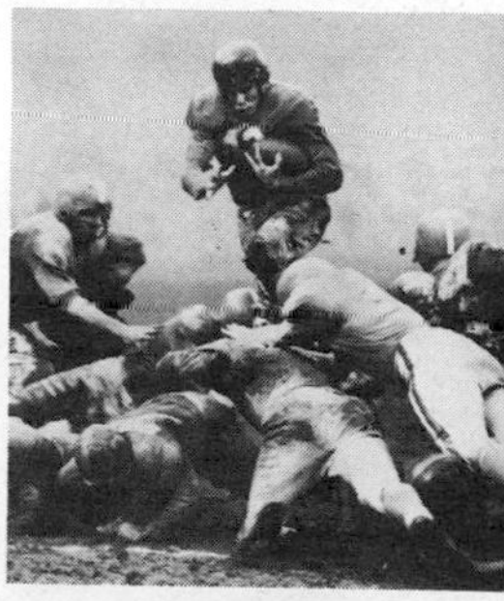

football
Quarterback Charley Conerly of the New York Giants scoring a touchdown at the Polo Grounds, 1950

foot·fall (fŏŏt'fôl') n. 1. A footstep. 2. The sound made by a footstep or footsteps.

foot fault. Tennis. A fault against the server called for failure to keep both feet behind the base line.

foot·gear (fŏŏt'gîr') n. Sturdy footwear, as shoes or boots.

foot·hill (fŏŏt'hĭl') n. A low hill near the base of a mountain or mountain range.

foot·hold (fŏŏt'hōld') n. 1. A place affording support for the foot in climbing or standing. 2. A firm or secure position enabling one to proceed with confidence; especially, a secure military base.

foot·ing (fŏŏt'ĭng) n. 1. A secure placement of the feet in standing or moving. 2. A place on which one can stand or move securely. 3. A surface or the condition of a surface with respect to the ease with which one may walk or run on it: poor footing on the track. 4. Architecture. The supporting base or groundwork of a structure, as for a monument or wall. 5. A basis; foundation: a business begun on a good footing. 6. A basis for social or business transactions with others; a standing: "These gentlemen all associate on a footing of perfect social equality" (Melville). 7. a. The totaling up of a column of figures. b. The sum written at the foot of a column of figures.

foot-lam·bert (fŏŏt'lăm'bərt) n. Abbr. fL Physics. A unit of luminance equal to 1/π candela per square foot.

foot·le (fŏŏt'l) intr.v. -led, -ling, -les. Informal. 1. To fool around or waste time; trifle. Used with around or about: "not used to footling around at the lower levels." (Kim Philby). 2. To talk nonsense. —n. Informal. Foolishness; nonsense; twaddle. [Probably a variant of dialectal footer, probably from French foutre, to copulate with, from Old French, from Latin futuere. See bhau- in Appendix.*]

foot·less (fŏŏt'lĭs) adj. 1. Without feet. 2. Without a firm support or basis. 3. Informal. Without thought, dexterity, or skill; clumsy; inept. —foot'less·ness n.

foot·lights (fŏŏt'līts') pl.n. 1. Lights placed in a row along the front of a stage floor. 2. The theater as a profession; the stage.

foot·ling (fŏŏt'lĭng) adj. Informal. 1. Foolish; trifling; insignificant. 2. Stupid; inept. [Present participle of FOOTLE.]

foot·lock·er (fŏŏt'lŏk'ər) n. A small trunk for storing personal belongings and small items of equipment; especially, one kept by a soldier at the foot of his bunk.

foot·loose (fŏŏt'lōōs') adj. Having no attachments or ties; free to do as one pleases.

foot·man (fŏŏt'mən) n., pl. -men (-mĭn). 1. A male servant employed in the house to wait at table, attend the door, and run various errands. 2. Archaic. A foot soldier; infantryman. 3. Archaic. A pedestrian.

foot·mark (fŏŏt'märk') n. A footprint.

foot·note (fŏŏt'nōt') n. 1. Abbr. fn. A note placed at the bottom of a page of a book or manuscript that comments on or cites a reference for a designated part of the text. 2. Something said or done after the more important work has been completed; an afterthought. —tr.v. footnoted, -noting, -notes. 1. To furnish with footnotes. 2. To add further support or evidence for (a statement or opinion, for example).

foot·pace (fŏŏt'pās') n. 1. A walking pace. 2. A raised platform in a room, as for a lecturer; dais.

foot·pad (fŏŏt'păd') n. Archaic. A highwayman or street robber who goes about on foot. [FOOT + earlier pad, path, probably from Middle Dutch, path (see pent- in Appendix*).]

foot·path (fŏŏt'păth', -päth') n., pl. -paths (-păthz', -päthz', -păths', -päths'). A narrow path for persons on foot; especially, one along the side of a highway.

foot·pound (fŏŏt'pound') n. Abbr. ft-lb A unit of work equal to the work done by a force of one pound acting through a distance of one foot in the direction of the force.

foot·pound·al (fŏŏt'pound'l) n. A unit of work equal to the work done by a force of one poundal acting through a distance of one foot in the direction of the force.

foot·pound-sec·ond (fŏŏt'pound'sĕk'ənd) adj. Abbr. fps Of, pertaining to, or characteristic of a system of units based on the foot, the pound, and the second as the fundamental units of length, weight, and time.

foot·print (fŏŏt'prĭnt') n. An outline or indentation left by a foot on a surface.

foot·rest (fŏŏt'rĕst') n. A low stool, metal bar, or other support on which to rest the feet.

foot·rope (fŏŏt'rōp') n. Nautical. 1. A rope attached to the lower border of a sail. 2. A rope, rigged beneath a yard, for men to stand on during the reefing or furling of sail.

foot·rot (fŏŏt'rŏt') n. A degenerative infection of the feet in certain hoofed animals, especially cattle or sheep, often resulting in loss of the hoof.

foots (fŏŏts) pl.n. The sediment that forms during the refining of oils and other liquids; dregs. [A plural of FOOT.]

foot·sie (fŏŏt'sē) n. Informal. A flirting game in which a couple touch feet or legs, usually in secret, as under a table. —play footsie with. Informal. 1. To carry on a flirtation with, especially in a covert manner. 2. To court favor with or cooperate with deceptively or surreptitiously. [From FOOT.]

foot soldier. A soldier who fights on foot; infantryman.

foot·sore (fŏŏt'sôr', -sōr') adj. Having sore or tired feet from much walking. —foot'sore'ness n.

foot·stalk (fŏŏt'stôk') n. Biology. A supporting stalk, such as a peduncle or pedicel.

foot·stall (fŏŏt'stôl') n. The pedestal or plinth of a pillar.

foot·step (fŏŏt'stĕp') n. 1. A step with the foot. 2. The distance covered by one step: a footstep away. 3. The sound of a foot stepping. 4. A footprint. 5. A step up or down: the footsteps of

a stairway. —follow in one's footsteps. To carry on the work or tradition of a predecessor.

foot·stone (fŏŏt'stōn') n. A marking stone placed at the foot of a grave.

foot·stool (fŏŏt'stōōl') n. A low stool for supporting or resting one's feet.

foot·way (fŏŏt'wā') n. A walk or path for pedestrians.

foot·wear (fŏŏt'wâr') n. Anything worn on the feet, such as shoes or slippers.

foot·work (fŏŏt'wûrk') n. 1. The manner in which the feet are employed, as in boxing, fencing, or tennis. 2. Work done on foot; legwork.

foot·worn (fŏŏt'wôrn', -wōrn') adj. 1. Footsore. 2. Having been worn down by feet, as a path or carpet.

foo yong (fōō' yŭng'). In Chinese cooking, an omelet made with green peppers, bean sprouts, and onion. [Cantonese foo yong tan, corresponding to Mandarin Chinese fu² yung² tan⁴ : fu² yung², hibiscus + tan⁴, egg (from the fancied resemblance between the omelet and the large showy flower).]

fop (fŏp) n. A vain, affected man who is preoccupied with his clothes and manners; a dandy. [Middle English fop, foppe, a fool, perhaps akin to fobben, to cheat, FOB.]

fop·per·y (fŏp'ə-rē) n., pl. -ies. The dress or manner of a fop.

fop·pish (fŏp'ĭsh) adj. Of, pertaining to, or characteristic of a fop; dandified. —fop'pish·ly adv. —fop'pish·ness n.

for (fôr, unstressed fər) prep. 1. Directed or sent to: a letter for me. 2. Directed toward; specializing in: an eye for pretty girls. 3. As a result of; out of: crying for joy. 4. To the extent of: The road is paved for one mile. 5. Through the length of: sit still for an hour. 6. In order to go to: leave for Montana. 7. With an aim or view to: We swim for fun. 8. In order to have or find: look for a bargain. 9. In order to serve in or as: train for the ministry. 10. In the amount of: a bill for three dollars. 11. At the price of: buy a dog for ten dollars. 12. In response to; as requital of: "Eye for eye" (Exodus 21:24). 13. Considering the nature or usual character of: very warm for May. 14. Appropriate or suitable to: a time for dying. 15. At (an appointed time): an appointment for three o'clock. 16. Notwithstanding; despite: For all her experience, she is inefficient. 17. Intended to be used as: Books are for reading. 18. With a desire or longing toward: The puppy whimpered for his supper. 19. So as to obtain: work for a salary. 20. On behalf of: a dinner for the ambassador. 21. In place of: use artificial flowers for real ones. 22. In its effect on: Fresh air is good for you. 23. In favor, defense, or support of: vote for the candidate of one's choice. 24. Accompanying; paired with: one rotten apple for every good one. 25. As against; as measured competitively with: pound for pound. 26. As being: We mistook her for the waitress. 27. In order to retain, conserve, or save: Run for your life! 28. As the duty or task of; up to: It is for the judge to rule. —for to. Archaic. In order to. —conj. Because; since. See Usage notes at because, like, mean (verb). [Middle English for, Old English for (the conjunction develops from Old English phrases such as for thon the, "for the (reason that"). See per¹ in Appendix.*]

for-. Indicates: 1. Exhaustion; for example, forspent. 2. Completely; for example, forgather. [In Old English compounds for- indicates: 1. Incorrectly or wrongly, as in forswear. 2. Destruction, as in fordo. 3. Prohibition, as in forfend. Middle English for-, Old English for-. See per¹ in Appendix.*]

for. 1. foreign. 2. forestry.

fo·ra. Alternate plural of forum.

for·age (fôr'ĭj, fŏr'-) n. 1. Food for domestic animals, such as horses, cows, and sheep; fodder. 2. The act of looking or searching for such food. 3. The act of looking or searching for supplies of any kind. —v. foraged, -aging, -ages. —intr. 1. To search for food or provisions. 2. To make a raid, as for food, supplies, or anything needed or desired. —tr. 1. To wander or rummage through, especially in search of provisions. 2. To raid; to plunder. 3. To provide with fodder; to feed. 4. To secure by searching about. [Middle English, from Old French fo(ur)rage, from feurre, fodder, from Germanic. See pā- in Appendix.*] —for'ag·er n.

forage cap. A military cap with a low, cylindrical crown and a visor worn with undress uniform; kepi.

For·a·ker, Mount (fôr'ĭ-kər, fŏr'-). A peak rising to 17,280 feet in Mount McKinley National Park, south-central Alaska.

fo·ra·men (fə-rā'mən) n., pl. -ramina (-răm'ə-nə) or -mens. An aperture or perforation in a bone or through a membranous anatomical structure. [New Latin, from Latin forāmen, an opening, from forāre, to bore. See bher-² in Appendix.*]

foramen magnum. The large orifice in the base of the skull through which the spinal cord passes and becomes continuous with the medulla oblongata. [New Latin, "large orifice."]

for·a·min·if·er·an (fôr'ə-mĭn'ə-fər-ən, fŏr'-) n. Also **for·am** (fôr'əm, fŏr'-), **for·a·min·i·fer** (fôr'ə-mĭn'ə-fər, fŏr'-). Any of the unicellular microorganisms of the order Foraminifera, characteristically having a calcareous shell with perforations through which numerous pseudopodia protrude. [New Latin Foraminifera : forāmen, opening, FORAMEN + -FER.] —fo·ram'i·nif'er·ous (fə-răm'ə-nĭf'ər-əs), fo·ram'i·nif'er·al adj.

for·as·much as (fôr'əz-mŭch' əz). Inasmuch as; since.

for·ay (fôr'ā') n. 1. A sudden raid or military advance. 2. A venture or initial attempt in some field. —v. forayed, -aying, -ays. —intr. To make a raid. —tr. To make a raid against; to plunder. [Middle English forrai, from forraien, to foray, back-formation from forreour, raider, plunderer, from Old French forrier, from Vulgar Latin fodrārius (unattested), from Germanic. See pā- in Appendix.*]

forb (fôrb) n. Any herbaceous plant other than a grass, espe-

footrope
Sailors using the footrope
in the furling of a sail

ă pat/ā pay/âr care/ä father/b bib/ch church/d deed/ĕ pet/ē be/f fife/g gag/h hat/hw which/ĭ pit/ī pie/îr pier/j judge/k kick/l lid, needle/m mum/n no, sudden/ng thing/ŏ pot/ō toe/ô paw, for/oi noise/ou out/ŏŏ took/ōō boot/p pop/r roar/s sauce/sh ship, dish/

cially one growing in a field or meadow. [Greek *phorbē*, fodder, from *pherbein*†, to feed, graze.]

for·bear[1] (fôr-bâr′) *v.* **-bore** (-bôr′, -bōr′), **-borne** (-bôrn′, -bōrn′), **-bearing, -bears.** —*tr.* **1.** To refrain from; keep oneself from: *forbear replying.* **2.** To desist from; to cease. **3.** *Archaic.* To endure; tolerate. **4.** *Obsolete.* To avoid; shun. —*intr.* **1.** To hold back; refrain. **2.** To be tolerant or patient. [Middle English *forberen*, Old English *forberan*, to bear, endure. See **bher-**[1] in Appendix.*] —**for·bear′er** *n.*

for·bear[2]. Variant of **forebear.**

for·bear·ance (fôr-bâr′əns) *n.* **1.** The act of refraining from something; abstinence. **2.** Tolerance and restraint in the face of provocation; patience. **3.** *Law.* The act of a creditor who refrains from enforcing a debt when it falls due. —See Synonyms at **mercy, patience.**

for·bear·ing (fôr-bâr′ĭng) *adj.* Tolerant; patient.

for·bid (fər-bĭd′, fôr-) *tr.v.* **-bade** (-băd′, -bād′) or **-bad** (-băd′), **-bidden** (-bĭd′n) or **-bid, -bidding, -bids. 1.** To command (someone) not to do something: *I forbid you to go.* **2.** To prohibit; interdict: *Smoking is forbidden.* **3.** To have the effect of preventing; preclude: *"To seek the natural implies a consciousness that forbids all naturalness forever"* (James Russell Lowell). [Middle English *forbidden, forbeden*, Old English *forbēodan.* See **bheudh-** in Appendix.*]

Usage: *Forbid* is often used with an infinitive or a gerund, either of which is capable of expressing the same idea idiomatically: *forbid you to go; forbid your going* (but not *forbid you from going*).

for·bid·dance (fər-bĭd′ns, fôr-) *n.* The act of forbidding or the state of being forbidden.

for·bid·den (fər-bĭd′n, fôr-) *adj.* Not permitted; not allowed; prohibited.

Forbidden City. A walled area in central Peking containing the imperial palaces of the former Chinese Empire. [Translation of (Mandarin) Chinese *chin*[4] *ch'eng*[2].]

forbidden fruit. 1. The fruit produced by the tree of knowledge in the Garden of Eden, forbidden to Adam and Eve. Genesis 2:17. **2.** Anything desirable but forbidden.

for·bid·ding (fər-bĭd′ĭng, fôr-) *adj.* **1.** Tending or threatening to impede progress. **2.** Unfriendly; disagreeable. **3.** Grim; ominous.

force (fôrs, fōrs) *n.* **1.** Capacity to do work or cause physical change; strength; power. **2.** Power made operative against resistance; exertion: *use force in driving a nail.* **3.** The use of such power or exertion. **4.** Intellectual power or vigor, as of a statement. **5.** A capacity for affecting the mind or behavior; efficacy. **6.** Anything or anyone possessing such capacity: *forces of evil.* **7.** A body of persons or other resources organized or available for a certain purpose: *a work force.* **8.** A group organized for military, police, or hostile purposes: *an armed force.* **9.** *Law.* Legal validity; efficacy. **10.** *Symbol* **F** *Physics.* A vector quantity that tends to produce an acceleration of a body in the direction of its application. —See Synonyms at **strength.** —**in force. 1.** In full strength. **2.** In effect; operative: *a rule no longer in force.* —*tr.v.* **forced, forcing, forces. 1.** To compel to perform an action; coerce. **2.** To obtain by the use of force or coercion: *force a confession.* **3.** To produce by effort: *force a tear from one's eye.* **4.** To move (something) against resistance; to push: *force a square peg into a round hole.* **5.** To move, open, or clear by force: *force one's way through a crowd.* **6.** To break down or open by force: *force a lock.* **7.** To rape. **8.** To inflict or impose: *force one's will on someone.* **9.** To place undue strain upon; push beyond normal capacity or use: *force one's voice.* **10.** To cause to grow by artificially accelerating the normal processes: *force flowers in a greenhouse.* **11.** *Baseball.* **a.** To put (a runner) out by tagging the base to which he must advance. Usually used with *out.* **b.** To allow (a run) to be scored or (a runner) to score by walking a batter when the bases are loaded. [Middle English, from Old French, from Vulgar Latin *fortia* (unattested), from Latin *fortis*, strong. See **bhergh-**[2] in Appendix.*] —**force′a·ble** *adj.* —**forc′er** *n.*

Synonyms: *force, compel, coerce, constrain, necessitate, oblige, obligate.* These verbs mean to make a person or thing follow a prescribed or dictated course. *Force* is broadly applicable to any such act and usually implies the exertion of physical strength or the operation of circumstances that permit no alternative to compliance. *Compel*, often interchangeable with *force*, stresses the power or strength of what causes compliance and is especially applicable to an act dictated by a person in authority. *Coerce* invariably implies use of strength or harsh measures in securing compliance. *Constrain* suggests binding one to a course of action, or enforced inaction, by physical or moral means or by the operation of compelling circumstances. *Necessitate* implies the operation of circumstances that create an inescapable need for the course in question. *Oblige* is applicable when compliance is caused by the operation of authority, necessity, or moral or ethical considerations, and *obligate* when compulsion is exerted by terms of a legal contract or promise, or by the dictates of one's conscience or sense of propriety.

forced (fôrst, fōrst) *adj.* **1.** Enforced or imposed; compulsory; involuntary: *forced labor.* **2.** Produced under strain; not spontaneous; unnatural; artificial: *forced laughter.* **3.** Effected in an emergency: *a forced landing.*

forced march. A long march at a rigorously fast pace.

force feed. A system that supplies lubricants under pressure, as to an automobile engine.

force-feed (fôrs′fēd′, fōrs′-) *tr.v.* **-fed** (-fĕd′), **-feeding, -feeds.** To force to ingest food, feed forcibly.

force field. **Field of force** *(see).*

force·ful (fôrs′fəl, fōrs′-) *adj.* Characterized by or full of force; effective; persuasive. See Usage note at **forcible.** —**force′ful·ly** *adv.* —**force′ful·ness** *n.*

force ma·jeure (fôrs mȧ-zhœr′). *French.* An unexpected or uncontrollable event that upsets one's plans or releases one from obligations. Literally, superior force.

force·meat (fôrs′mēt′, fōrs′-) *n.* Finely ground meat or poultry, used in stuffing or as a garnish. [From *force*, variant of FARCE (to stuff).]

force-out (fôrs′out′, fōrs′-) *n. Baseball.* An out made by tagging a base to which a runner must advance.

for·ceps (fôr′səps) *n., pl.* **forceps. 1.** An instrument resembling a pair of pincers or tongs, used for grasping, manipulating, or extracting. **2.** A pincerlike clasping organ at the posterior end of the abdomen in certain insects. [Latin *forceps*, fire tongs, pincers. See **gwher-** in Appendix.*]

force pump. A pump with a solid piston and valves used to raise a liquid or expel it under pressure.

for·ci·ble (fôr′sə-bəl, fōr′-) *adj.* **1.** Effected through the use of force: *a forcible entry.* **2.** Characterized by force; forceful. —**for′ci·ble·ness** *n.* —**for′ci·bly** *adv.*

Usage: *Forcible* and *forceful*, though closely related in meaning, tend to be distinguished in usage. *Forcible* is largely confined to what is accomplished by force: *forcible ejection. Forceful* describes what is characterized by or full of force and therefore effective: *a forceful speaker.*

ford (fôrd, fōrd) *n.* A shallow place in a body of water, such as a river, where a crossing can be made on foot, on horseback, or in a vehicle. —*tr.v.* **forded, fording, fords.** To cross (a body of water) at such a shallow place. [Middle English *ford*, Old English *ford.* See **per-**[2] in Appendix.*] —**ford′a·ble** *adj.*

Ford (fôrd, fōrd), **Henry.** 1863–1947. American automobile designer and manufacturer.

Ford (fôrd, fōrd), **John.** 1586?–1640? English dramatist.

for·do (fôr-do͞o′, fōr-) *tr.v.* **-did** (-dĭd′), **-done** (-dŭn′), **-doing, -does** (-dŭz′). Also **fore·do.** *Archaic.* **1.** To kill. **2.** To bring to ruin. **3.** To exhaust utterly. [Middle English *fordon*, Old English *fordōn* : *for-*, connoting destruction + *dōn*, to DO.]

fore (fôr, fōr) *adj.* Located at or toward the front; anterior. —*n.* **1.** Something at or toward the front. **2.** The front part. **3.** The bow of a ship. —**to the fore.** In, into, or toward a position of prominence: *"money is to the fore now"* (William Dean Howells). —*adv.* Toward or at the bow of a ship; forward. —*prep.* Also **'fore.** *Archaic.* Before. Frequently used in oaths: *Fore God, Sir, you are mistaken!* —*interj. Golf.* Used to warn those ahead that a ball is about to be driven in their direction. [Middle English *fore*, probably from adverb, "beforehand," Old English *for(e).* See **per**[1] in Appendix.*]

fore-. Indicates: **1.** Before in time; for example, **forebode, foresight. 2.** The front or first part; for example, **foredeck, foreskin.** [Middle English *for-, fore-*, Old English *fore-*, from *fore* (adverb), in front, beforehand. See **per**[1] in Appendix.*]

fore and aft. 1. From the bow to the stern of a ship; lengthwise of a ship. **2.** In, at, or toward both ends of a ship.

fore-and-aft (fôr′ən-ăft′, -äft′, fōr′-) *adj.* Parallel with the keel of a ship.

fore-and-aft·er (fôr′ən-ăf′tər, -äf′tər, fōr′-) *n.* A sailing ship, such as a ketch or schooner, carrying a fore-and-aft rig.

fore-and-aft rig. A sailing ship rig with quadrilateral and triangular sails set to the fore-and-aft line and capable of being trimmed to leeward. It seldom carries square sails and is handier to windward than the **square rig** *(see).* —**fore′-and-aft′-rigged′** *adj.*

fore-and-aft sail. A sail set parallel with the keel of a vessel, having the foremost edge or luff attached to the mast with travelers and the upper edge set on a gaff or stay.

fore·arm[1] (fôr-ärm′, fōr-) *tr.v.* **-armed, -arming, -arms.** To prepare or arm in advance of some conflict.

fore·arm[2] (fôr′ärm′, fōr′-) *n.* The part of the arm between the wrist and elbow.

fore·bear (fôr′bâr′, fōr′-) *n.* Also **for·bear.** A forefather; ancestor. [Middle English (Scottish dialect) *forebear* : FORE- + *bear*, "be-er," from *been*, to BE.]

fore·bode (fôr-bōd′, fōr-) *v.* **-boded, -boding, -bodes.** —*tr.* **1.** To indicate the threatening likelihood of; give warning of; portend. **2.** To have a premonition of (a future misfortune). —See Synonyms at **foretell.** [FORE- + BODE.]

fore·bod·ing (fôr-bō′dĭng, fōr-) *n.* **1.** A dark sense of impending evil; premonition. **2.** An evil omen; portent. —See Synonyms at **apprehension.** —*adj.* Ominous. —**fore·bod′ing·ly** *adv.*

fore·brain (fôr′brān′, fōr′-) *n.* The anterior region of the embryonic brain from which the telencephalon and diencephalon develop. Also called "prosencephalon."

fore·cast (fôr′kăst′, -käst′, fōr′-) *v.* **-cast** or **-casted, -casting, -casts.** —*tr.* **1.** To estimate or calculate in advance; especially, to predict (weather conditions) by analysis of meteorological data. **2.** To serve as an advance indication of; foreshadow. —*intr.* To make an estimation or calculation in advance. —See Synonyms at **foretell.** —*n.* **1.** A prediction, as of the weather. **2.** A conjecture concerning the future. [Middle English *forecasten*, to devise beforehand : FORE- + *casten*, to CAST.] —**fore′cast′er** *n.*

fore·cas·tle (fōk′səl, fôr′kăs′əl, -käs′əl, fōr′-) *n.* Also **fo'c's'le** (fōk′səl). **1.** The section of the upper deck of a ship located at the bow, forward of the foremast. **2.** A superstructure at the bow of a merchant ship, where the crew is housed. [Middle English *forecastel* : FORE- + CASTLE.]

fore·close (fôr-klōz′, fōr-) *v.* **-closed, -closing, -closes.** —*tr.* **1.** *Law.* **a.** To deprive (a mortgagor) of the right to redeem

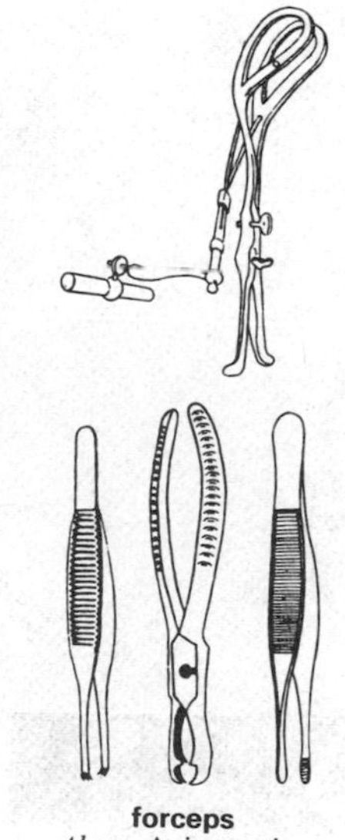

forceps
Above: Axis-traction obstetrical forceps
Below, from left: Mouse-tooth forceps; lion-jaw bone-holding forceps; thumb forceps

t tight/th thin, path/*th* this, bathe/ŭ cut/ûr urge/v valve/w with/y yes/z zebra, size/zh vision/ə about, item, edible, gallop, circus/ à *Fr.* ami/œ *Fr.* feu, *Ger.* schön/ü *Fr.* tu, *Ger.* über/KH *Ger.* ich, *Scot.* loch/N *Fr.* bon. *Follows main vocabulary. †Of obscure origin.

mortgaged property, as when he has failed in his payments. **b.** To bar an equity or right to redeem (a mortgage). **2.** To shut out; to bar. **3.** To settle or resolve beforehand. **4.** To hinder; deter; thwart. —*intr.* To foreclose a mortgage. Often used with *on.* [Middle English *forclosen,* to shut out, preclude, from Old French *forclore* (past participle *forclos*) : *fors-,* outside, from Latin *foris* (see **dhwer-** in Appendix*) + *clore,* to close, from Latin *claudere,* to CLOSE.] —**fore·clos′a·ble** *adj.*

fore·clo·sure (fôr-klō′zhər, fōr-) *n.* The act of foreclosing; especially, a legal proceeding by which a mortgage is foreclosed.

fore·course (fôr′kôrs′, fōr′kōrs′) *n.* A foresail.

fore·court (fôr′kôrt′, fōr′kōrt′) *n.* **1.** A courtyard in front of a building. **2.** The part of a playing court nearest the net or wall, as in tennis or handball.

fore·date (fôr-dāt′, fōr-) *tr.v.* **-dated, -dating, -dates.** To antedate.

fore·deck (fôr′dĕk′; fōr′-) *n.* The forward part of a deck, usually the main deck.

fore·do. Variant of **fordo.**

fore·doom (fôr-dōōm′, fōr-) *tr.v.* **-doomed, -dooming, -dooms.** To doom or condemn beforehand. —*n.* (fôr′dōōm′, fōr′-). *Rare.* A doom or sentence ordained beforehand; predestination.

fore·fa·ther (fôr′fä′*th*ər, fōr′-) *n.* An ancestor. [Middle English *forefader,* from Old Norse *forfadhir : for-,* before (see **per**[1] in Appendix*) + *fadhir,* father (see **pəter** in Appendix*).]

fore·fend. Variant of **forfend.**

fore·fin·ger (fôr′fĭng′gər, fōr′-) *n.* The **index finger** *(see).*

fore·foot (fôr′fŏŏt′, fōr′-) *n., pl.* **-feet** (-fēt′). **1.** One of the front feet of an animal. **2.** *Nautical.* The part of a ship at which the prow joins the keel.

fore·front (fôr′frŭnt′, fōr′-) *n.* **1.** The foremost part or area of something. **2.** The position of most importance, prominence, or responsibility.

fore·gath·er. Variant of **forgather.**

fore·go[1] (fôr-gō′, fōr-) *tr.v.* **-went** (-wĕnt′), **-gone** (-gôn′, -gŏn′), **-going, -goes** (-gōz′). To precede or go before, as in time or place. [Middle English *forgon,* Old English *foregān* : FORE- + GO.] —**fore·go′er** *n.*

fore·go[2]**.** Variant of **forgo.**

fore·go·ing (fôr-gō′ĭng, fōr-, fôr′gō′ĭng, fōr′-) *adj.* Just past; preceding; previously said or written.

fore·gone (fôr′gôn′, -gŏn′, fōr′-) *adj.* Having gone or been completed previously; departed; past. [Past participle of FOREGO.]

foregone conclusion. An end or result regarded as inevitable.

fore·ground (fôr′ground′, fōr′-) *n.* **1.** The part of a view or sight that is nearest to the viewer. **2.** The part of a picture, as a painting or photograph, that is represented as nearest to the viewer. **3.** The most important or prominent position.

fore·gut (fôr′gŭt′, fōr′-) *n.* The anterior part of the embryonic digestive tract from which the pharynx lining, lungs, esophagus, stomach, and small intestine develop.

fore·hand (fôr′hănd′, fōr′-) *adj.* **1.** Made with the hand moving palm forward: *a forehand tennis stroke.* **2.** Foremost; leading. **3.** Taking place beforehand; prior. —*n.* **1.** A forehand stroke, as in tennis. **2.** The part of a horse in front of the rider. **3.** A position of advantage; upper hand.

fore·hand·ed (fôr′hăn′dĭd, fōr′-) *adj.* **1.** Forehand, as in tennis. **2.** Looking or planning ahead. **3.** Having ample financial resources; well-off. —**fore′hand′ed·ness** *n.*

fore·head (fôr′ĭd, fŏr′-, fôr′hĕd′, fōr′-) *n.* The part of the head or face between the eyebrows and the normal hairline. [Middle English *forhed,* Old English *forhēafod* : FORE- + HEAD.]

for·eign (fôr′ĭn, fŏr′-) *adj.* **1.** *Abbr.* **for.** Located away from one's native country: *foreign parts.* **2.** *Abbr.* **for.** Of, characteristic of, or from a country other than one's own: *a foreign custom.* **3.** *Abbr.* **for.** Conducted or involved with other nations or governments; not domestic: *foreign trade.* **4.** Situated in an abnormal or improper place. **5.** Outside of a scope, range, or essential nature; alien: *"I was there in a role foreign to my youth's wildest imaginings"* (John Howard Griffin). **6.** Not germane; extraneous; irrelevant. **7.** *Law.* Subject to the jurisdiction of another political unit. —See Synonyms at **extrinsic.** [Middle English *forein,* from Old French *forein, forain,* from Late Latin *forānus,* from Latin *forās,* out of doors, abroad. See **dhwer-** in Appendix.*] —**for′eign·ness** *n.*

foreign bill. A draft for a sum of money to be paid in another country. Also called "foreign bill of exchange," "foreign draft."

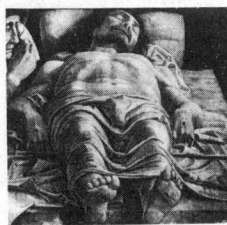

foreshorten
Foreshortened figure of the dead Christ; detail of a painting by Mantegna

for·eign·er (fôr′ə-nər, fōr′-) *n.* A person from a foreign country.

foreign exchange. **1.** The transaction of international monetary business, as between governments or businessmen of different countries. **2.** Negotiable bills drawn in one country to be paid in another country.

Foreign Legion. A former French military unit composed of volunteers of any nationality.

foreign mission. **1.** A group sent to a foreign country for missionary service, as in religion or medicine. **2.** A group sent to a foreign country for diplomatic service.

Foreign Office. *Abbr.* **F.O.** The official name, in several countries, of the department that is in charge of foreign affairs.

fore·judge (fôr-jŭj′, fōr-) *v.* **-judged, -judging, -judges.** Also **forjudge.** —*tr.* To judge beforehand; prejudge. —*intr.* To judge something or someone beforehand.

fore·knowl·edge (fôr-nŏl′ĭj, fōr-) *n.* Knowledge or awareness of something prior to its existence or occurrence; prescience.

fore·la·dy (fôr′lā′dē, fōr′-) *n., pl.* **-dies.** A woman who acts as a foreman.

fore·land (fôr′lənd, -lănd′, fōr′-) *n.* **1.** A projecting land mass; promontory; cape. **2.** Land or territory lying to the fore, as borderland or land at the edge of a body of water.

fore·leg (fôr′lĕg′, fōr′-) *n.* One of the front legs of an animal.

fore·limb (fôr′lĭm′, fōr′-) *n.* An anterior appendage such as a leg, wing, or flipper.

fore·lock[1] (fôr′lŏk′, fōr′-) *n.* A lock of hair that grows or falls on the forehead.

fore·lock[2] (fôr′lŏk′, fōr′-) *n.* A cotter pin; linchpin.

fore·man (fôr′mən, fōr′-) *n., pl.* **-men** (-mĭn). **1.** A man who has charge of a group of workers, as at a factory or ranch. **2.** The chairman and spokesman for a jury. —**fore′man·ship′** *n.*

fore·mast (fôr′məst, -măst′, -mäst′, fōr′-) *n.* The forward mast on any sailing vessel with two or more masts, with the exception of the ketch and the yawl.

fore·milk (fôr′mĭlk′, fōr′-) *n.* **Colostrum** *(see).*

fore·most (fôr′mōst′, fōr′-) *adj.* Ahead of all others, especially in position or rank; paramount. See Synonyms at **chief.** See Usage note below. —*adv.* In the front or first position. [Variant (influenced by FORE-) of Middle English *formest, formost,* Old English *formest,* superlative of *forma,* first. See **per**[1] in Appendix.*]

Usage: *Foremost* (adjective), applied to persons or things to indicate pre-eminent position, is not necessarily restricted to one person or thing in a given reference. An individual can be called *foremost,* to signify undisputed leadership, or the term can be applied to a group of leaders in the sense of being in the front rank. The following example of such usage is acceptable to 76 per cent of the Panel: *Zoltán Kodály was one of the world's foremost composers at the time of his death.*

fore·name (fôr′nām′, fōr′-) *n.* A first name; given name.

fore·named (fôr′nāmd′, fōr′-) *adj.* Named earlier; aforesaid.

fore·noon (fôr′nōōn′, fōr′-, fôr-nōōn′, fōr-) *n.* The period of time between sunrise and noon; daylight morning hours.

fo·ren·sic (fə-rĕn′sĭk) *adj.* **1.** Pertaining to or employed in legal proceedings or argumentation: *forensic medicine.* **2.** Of, pertaining to, or employed in debate or argument; rhetorical. [From Latin *forēnsis,* of a market or forum, public, from *forum,* forum. See **dhwer-** in Appendix.*] —**fo·ren′si·cal·ly** *adv.*

fo·ren·sics (fə-rĕn′sĭks) *n.* Plural in form, used with a singular verb. The study or practice of formal debate; argumentation.

fore·or·dain (fôr′ôr-dān′, fōr′-) *tr.v.* **-dained, -daining, -dains.** To appoint or ordain beforehand; predestine. —**fore′or·dain′ment, fore′or′di·na′tion** *n.*

fore·part (fôr′pärt′, fōr′-) *n.* The first or foremost part.

fore·peak (fôr′pēk′, fōr′-) *n.* The section of the hold of a ship that is within the angle made by the bow.

fore·quar·ter (fôr′kwôr′tər, fōr′-) *n.* **1.** The front section of a side of meat. **2.** *Plural.* The forelegs, shoulders, and adjacent parts of an animal, especially a horse.

fore·reach (fôr-rēch′, fōr-) *v.* **-reached, -reaching, -reaches.** —*tr.* **1.** To get ahead of; pass, especially in a sailing vessel. **2.** To get the advantage over; to best; excel. —*intr.* To move up; gain ground, especially upon a sailing vessel.

fore·run (fôr-rŭn′, fōr-) *tr.v.* **-ran** (-răn′), **-run, -running, -runs.** **1.** To run in advance or in front of. **2.** To be the precursor of; foreshadow. **3.** To forestall; prevent.

fore·run·ner (fôr′rŭn′ər, fōr′-) *n.* **1.** Someone who or something that precedes, as in time; predecessor. **2.** An ancestor; forebear. **3.** Someone who or something that provides advance notice of the coming of others; harbinger; precursor.

fore·said (fôr′sĕd′, fōr′-) *adj.* Previously named or said; aforesaid.

fore·sail (fôr′səl, -sāl′, fōr′-) *n.* *Nautical.* **1.** The principal square sail hung to the foremast of a square-rigged vessel. **2.** The principal triangular sail hung to the mast of a fore-and-aft-rigged vessel. **3.** The triangular sail hung to the forestay of a cutter or sloop. **4.** *Plural.* The sails on the foremast or before the mast.

fore·see (fôr-sē′, fōr-) *tr.v.* **-saw** (-sô′), **-seen** (-sēn′), **-seeing, -sees.** To see or know beforehand; anticipate; envision: *"many families, foreseeing the approach of the distemper, laid up stores of provisions"* (Defoe). See Synonyms at **expect.** —**fore·see′a·ble** *adj.* —**fore·se′er** *n.*

fore·shad·ow (fôr-shăd′ō, fōr-) *tr.v.* **-owed, -owing, -ows.** To present an indication or suggestion of beforehand; to presage.

fore·sheet (fôr′shēt′, fōr′-) *n.* **1.** A rope used in trimming a foresail. **2.** *Plural.* The space near the bow of an open boat.

fore·shore (fôr′shôr′, fōr′shōr′) *n.* **1.** The part of a shore covered at high tide. **2.** The part of a shore between the water and occupied or cultivated land.

fore·short·en (fôr-shôrt′n, fōr-) *tr.v.* **-ened, -ening, -ens.** **1.** To represent the long axis of (an object) by contracting its lines so as to produce an illusion of projection or extension in space. **2.** To shorten beforehand; curtail.

fore·show (fôr-shō′, fōr-) *tr.v.* **-showed, -shown** (-shōn′) or **-showed, -showing, -shows.** To show in advance; prognosticate.

fore·side (fôr′sīd′, fōr′-) *n.* The front or upper side.

fore·sight (fôr′sīt′, fōr′-) *n.* **1.** The act or ability of foreseeing. **2.** The act of looking forward. **3.** Concern or prudence with respect to the future. —**fore′sight′ed** *adj.* —**fore′sight′ed·ly** *adv.* —**fore′sight′ed·ness** *n.*

fore·skin (fôr′skĭn′, fōr′-) *n.* The **prepuce** *(see).*

fore·speak (fôr-spēk′, fōr-) *tr.v.* **-spoken** (-spō′kən), **-speaking, -speaks.** **1.** To speak of in advance; predict. **2.** To arrange for or engage in advance.

fore·spent. Variant of **forspent.**

for·est (fôr′ĭst, fŏr′-) *n.* **1.** A dense growth of trees, together with other plants, covering a large area. **2.** Something that resembles a forest in density, quantity, or profusion: *a forest of skyscrapers.* **3.** *Law.* A defined area of land formerly set aside

ă pat/ā pay/âr care/ä father/b bib/ch church/d deed/ĕ pet/ē be/f fife/g gag/h hat/hw which/ĭ pit/ī pie/îr pier/j judge/k kick/l lid, needle/m mum/n no, sudden/ng thing/ŏ pot/ō toe/ô paw, for/oi noise/ou out/ŏŏ took/ōō boot/p pop/r roar/s sauce/sh ship, dish/

in England as a royal hunting ground. —*tr.v.* **forested, -esting, -ests.** To plant trees on; transform into a forest. [Middle English, from Old French, from Late Latin expression *forestis (silva)*, outside (forest), referring originally to the royal forest or game preserve of Charlemagne, probably from Latin *foris*, outside, outdoors. See **dhwer-** in Appendix.*] —**for'est·al, fo·res'·tial** (fə-rĕs'chəl) *adj.* —**for'es·ta'tion** *n.*

fore·stall (fôr-stôl', fōr-) *tr.v.* **-stalled, -stalling, -stalls. 1.** To prevent, delay, or take precautionary measures against beforehand. **2.** To deal with or think of beforehand; anticipate. **3.** To prevent or hinder normal sales by buying up merchandise, discouraging persons from bringing their goods to market, or encouraging an increase in prices of goods already on the market. Compare **engross.** —See Synonyms at **prevent.** [Middle English *forestallen*, to forestall, obstruct, from *forestal*, the crime of waylaying or ambushing on the highway, Old English *foresteall*, waylaying, interception : *fore-*, in front of + *steall*, position, place (see **stel-**¹ in Appendix*).] —**fore·stall'er** *n.*

fore·stay (fôr'stā', fōr'-) *n.* A stay extending from the head of the foremast to the bowsprit of a ship.

fore·stay·sail (fôr'stā'səl, -sāl', fōr'-) *n.* A triangular sail set on the forestay.

for·est·er (fôr'ĭ-stər, fŏr'-) *n.* **1.** A person trained in forestry. **2.** One that inhabits a forest. **3.** Any of various chiefly tropical moths of the family Agaristidae, many of which are brightly colored.

For·est·er (fôr'ĭ-stər, fŏr'-), **C(ecil) S(cott).** 1899–1966. English novelist.

Forest of Ar·dennes. See **Ardennes.**

for·est·ry (fôr'ĭ-strē, fŏr'-) *n.* **1.** *Abbr.* **for.** The science and art of cultivating, maintaining, and developing forests. **2.** The management of a forest land. **3.** Forest land.

fore·swear. Variant of **forswear.**

fore·taste (fôr'tāst', fōr'-) *n.* An advance taste or realization; anticipation: *a foretaste of doom.* —*tr.v.* **foretasted, -tasting, -tastes.** To have an advance taste of; anticipate.

fore·tell (fôr-tĕl', fōr-) *v.* **-told** (-tōld'), **-telling, -tells.** —*tr.* To tell of or indicate beforehand; prophesy; predict. —*intr.* To tell beforehand. Often used with *of: foretell of impending disaster.* —**fore·tell'er** *n.*

***Synonyms:** foretell, predict, forecast, prophesy, divine, augur, portend, forebode, presage, bode, betoken, foretoken.* These verbs mean to foresee or to give advance word or other indication of what is to come. *Foretell, predict, forecast,* and *prophesy* apply principally to a person's telling of something in advance of its occurrence. *Foretell* is used of any such act. *Predict* and especially *forecast* imply the giving of advance word based on study, observation, or special knowledge. *Prophesy* sometimes refers to such intellectual foretelling, but can also apply to the act of a person considered to be divinely inspired or gifted with extraordinary power of foresight. To *divine* is to foresee, especially what is revealed only to one with remarkable sagacity or insight. To *augur* is to foretell from omens or signs; or the term can apply to a thing that serves as an omen or advance indication of the outcome or issue of something. *Portend* and *forebode* are chiefly used of things that serve as omens or warnings of what is evil, harmful, or unfortunate. *Presage* and *bode* are applied principally to things that give or serve as advance indications of what is to come, and are not necessarily limited to evil or misfortune. *Betoken* and *foretoken* are applicable to things that foreshadow or give advance indication of something in the future, whether favorable or unfavorable.

fore·thought (fôr'thôt', fōr'-) *n.* **1.** Deliberation, consideration, or planning beforehand. **2.** Preparation or thought for the future; anticipation. —**fore'thought'ful** *adj.* —**fore'thought'ful·ly** *adv.* —**fore'thought'ful·ness** *n.*

fore·time (fôr'tīm', fōr'-) *n.* Former time; the past.

fore·to·ken (fôr-tō'kən, fōr-) *tr.v.* **-kened, -kening, -kens.** To foreshow; foreshadow; presage. See Synonyms at **foretell.** —*n.* (fôr'tō'kən, fōr'-). An advance warning.

fore·tooth (fôr'to͞oth', fōr'-) *n., pl.* **-teeth** (-tēth'). An incisor.

fore·top (fôr'təp, fōr'-) *n.* **1.** A platform at the top of a ship's foremast. **2.** A forelock, especially of a horse.

fore·top·gal·lant (fôr'tə-găl'ənt, fōr'-) *adj. Nautical.* Of or relating to the mast directly above the foremast.

fore·top·gal·lant·mast (fôr'tə-găl'ənt-məst', fōr'-) *n.* The mast above the foretopmast.

fore·top·mast (fôr-tŏp'məst, fōr-) *n.* The mast that is above the foretop.

fore·top·sail (fôr-tŏp'səl, fōr-) *n.* The sail hung from the foretopmast.

for·ev·er (fôr-ĕv'ər, fər-) *adv.* **1.** For everlasting time; eternally. **2.** At all times; incessantly.

for·ev·er·more (fôr-ĕv'ər-môr', -mōr', fər-) *adv.* Forever.

for·ev·er·ness (fôr-ĕv'ər-nĭs, fər-) *n.* Eternity.

fore·warn (fôr-wôrn', fōr-) *tr.v.* **-warned, -warning, -warns.** To warn in advance. See Synonyms at **warn.**

fore·went. Past tense of **forego** (to go before).

fore·wing (fôr'wĭng', fōr'-) *n.* One of a pair of anterior wings, as in certain insects.

fore·wom·an (fôr'wo͝om'ən, fōr'-) *n., pl.* **-women** (-wĭm'ĭn). A woman who acts as a foreman.

fore·word (fôr'wûrd', -wərd, fōr'-) *n.* A preface or introductory note, especially at the beginning of a book. [Translation of German *Vorwort.*]

fore·worn. Variant of **forworn.**

fore·yard (fôr'yärd', fōr'-) *n. Nautical.* The lowest yard on a foremast.

For·far (fôr'fər). **1.** Also **For·far·shire** (-shĭr, -shər). A former name for **Angus. 2.** The county seat of Angus, Scotland, 14 miles north of Dundee. Population, 10,000.

for·feit (fôr'fĭt) *n.* **1.** Something surrendered as punishment for a crime, offense, error, or breach of contract; a penalty or fine. **2.** Something placed in escrow and then redeemed after payment of a fine. **3.** A forfeiture. **4.** *Plural.* A game in which forfeits are required. —*adj.* Surrendered or alienated for a crime, offense, error, or breach of contract. —*tr.v.* **forfeited, -feiting, -feits. 1.** To surrender or be forced to surrender as a forfeit. **2.** To subject to forfeiture. [Middle English *forfet*, forfeit, transgression, from Old French *forfet*, from *for(s)faire*, to commit a crime : *fors-*, beyond (here, beyond what is permitted), from Latin *foris*, outside (see **dhwer-** in Appendix*) + *faire*, to do, act, from Latin *facere* (see **dhē-**¹ in Appendix*).] —**for'feit·a·ble** *adj.* —**for'feit·er** *n.*

for·fei·ture (fôr'fĭ-cho͝or') *n.* **1.** The act of surrendering something as a forfeit. **2.** Something that is forfeited.

for·fend (fôr-fĕnd', fōr-) *tr.v.* **-fended, -fending, -fends.** Also **fore·fend. 1.** To keep or ward off; avert. **2.** *Archaic.* To forbid. **3.** To defend or protect. [Middle English *forfenden*, to forbid, prevent : *for-* (connoting prohibition), Old English *for-* + *fenden*, to defend, FEND.]

for·fi·cate (fôr'fĭ-kĭt, -kāt') *adj.* Deeply forked or notched, as the tail of certain birds. [From Latin *forfex* (stem *forfic-*), a pair of scissors. See **bherdh-** in Appendix.*]

for·gath·er (fôr-găth'ər, fōr-) *intr.v.* **-ered, -ering, -ers.** Also **fore·gath·er. 1.** To gather together; assemble. **2.** To have a chance encounter; meet by accident. **3.** To keep company or consort. Used with *with.* [Originally Scottish : FOR- + GATHER.]

for·gave. Past tense of **forgive.**

forge¹

forge¹ (fôrj, fōrj) *n.* **1.** A furnace or hearth where metals are heated or wrought; smithy. **2.** A workshop where pig iron is transformed into wrought iron. —*v.* **forged, forging, forges.** —*tr.* **1.** To form (metal) by heating in a forge and beating or hammering into shape. **2.** To give form or shape to; contrive; devise: *forge a treaty.* **3.** To fashion or reproduce for fraudulent purposes; to counterfeit: *forge a signature.* —*intr.* **1.** To work at a forge or smithy. **2.** To make a forgery or counterfeit. [Middle English, from Old French, from Vulgar Latin *faurga* (unattested), from Latin *fabrica*, smithy, artisan's workshop, from *faber*, smith. See **dhabh-** in Appendix.*] —**forg'er** *n.*

forge² (fôrj, fōrj) *intr.v.* **forged, forging, forges. 1.** To advance gradually but firmly. **2.** To advance with an abrupt increase of speed; shoot ahead. [Perhaps a variant of FORCE, which has been used in the same senses.]

for·ger·y (fôr'jə-rē, fōr'-) *n., pl.* **-ies. 1.** The production of something counterfeit or forged. **2.** Something counterfeit, forged, or fraudulent.

for·get (fər-gĕt', fôr-) *v.* **-got** (-gŏt') or *archaic* **-gat** (-găt'), **-gotten** (-gŏt'n) or **-got, -getting, -gets.** —*tr.* **1.** To be unable to remember or call to mind. **2.** To lack concern for; treat with inattention; neglect: *forget one's family.* **3.** To leave behind unintentionally. **4.** To fail to mention; pass over. **5.** To banish from one's thoughts: *forget a disgrace.* —*intr.* **1.** To cease remembering. **2.** To fail or neglect to become aware at the proper or specified moment: *forget about paying one's taxes.* —**forget oneself.** To lose one's reserve or self-restraint. [Middle English *forgeten*, Old English *forgietan*. See **ghend-** in Appendix.*] —**for·get'ta·ble** *adj.* —**for·get'ter** *n.*

for·get·ful (fər-gĕt'fəl, fôr-) *adj.* **1.** Tending or likely to forget. **2.** Neglectful; thoughtless; careless. —**for·get'ful·ly** *adv.* —**for·get'ful·ness** *n.*

***Synonyms:** forgetful, unmindful, oblivious, abstracted, absent-minded, distracted.* These adjectives refer to failure to remember or to lack of awareness or attentiveness. *Forgetful* usually implies a faulty memory or at least a tendency not to remember. Less often it is used as the equivalent of *unmindful*, which applies principally to one's failure, in a specific instance, to keep in mind what should be remembered, through deliberate oversight, heedlessness, or inattentiveness. *Oblivious* strictly refers to failure to remember or to be aware of something, often because one is preoccupied in another direction; less strictly the term is applied not to failure to remember a specific thing but to general unresponsiveness to, or unawareness of, one's surroundings. The remaining terms stress inattentiveness to immediate surroundings. *Abstracted* implies mental withdrawal as a result of preoccupation elsewhere. *Absent-minded* suggests such preoccupation, often chronic, to the point that one fails to remember or reacts haltingly or ineptly to ordinary demands on attention. *Distracted* implies diversion of attention from matters at hand and, sometimes, resultant confusion or agitation.

for·ge·tive (fôr'jə-tĭv, fōr'-) *adj. Archaic.* Capable of imagining or inventing. [Probably FORGE (verb) + (INVEN)TIVE.]

forget-me-not
Myosotis alpestris

for·get-me-not (fər-gĕt'mē-nŏt', fôr-) *n.* **1.** Any of various low-growing plants of the genus *Myosotis*, having clusters of small blue flowers. **2.** Any of several similar or related plants. [Translation of Old French *ne m'oubliez mie.*]

forg·ing (fôr'jĭng, fōr'-) *n.* **1.** The act or process of one that forges. **2.** Something that is forged.

for·give (fər-gĭv', fôr-) *v.* **-gave** (-gāv'), **-given** (-gĭv'ən), **-giving, -gives.** —*tr.* **1.** To excuse for a fault or offense; to pardon. **2.** To renounce anger or resentment against. **3.** To absolve from payment of. —*intr.* To accord forgiveness. [Middle English *foryeven, forgiven*, Old English *forgiefan* (translation of Medieval Latin *perdōnāre*, to pardon). See **ghabh-** in Appendix.*] —**for·giv'a·ble** *adj.* —**for·giv'er** *n.*

***Synonyms:** forgive, excuse, condone.* These verbs mean to pass over an offense and to free the offender from the consequences of it. To *forgive* is to grant pardon without harboring resentment. To *excuse* is to pass over a mistake or fault, usually a minor one, without demanding punishment or redress. To *condone* is to overlook an offense, usually serious, and thereby give tacit pardon.

for·give·ness (fər-gĭv′nĭs, fôr-) *n.* The act of forgiving; a pardon.

for·go (fôr-gō′) *tr.v.* **-went** (-wĕnt′), **-gone** (-gôn′, -gŏn′), **-going**, **-goes.** Also **fore·go.** To relinquish; abstain from; forsake. See Synonyms at **relinquish.** [Middle English *forgon, forgan,* Old English *forgān,* originally to pass on, pass away : *for-,* connoting exclusion + *gān,* to go (see **ghē-** in Appendix*).] **—for·go′er** *n.*

for·got. Past tense and alternate past participle of **forget.**

for·got·ten. Past participle of **forget.**

fo·rint (fôr′ĭnt) *n.* **1.** The basic monetary unit of Hungary, equal to 100 fillér. See table of exchange rates at **currency. 2.** A coin worth one forint. [Hungarian, from Italian *fiorino,* FLORIN.]

for·judge. Variant of **forejudge.**

fork (fôrk) *n.* **1.** An implement or piece of equipment with two or more prongs used for raising, carrying, piercing, or digging. **2.** A forked utensil for serving or eating food. **3. a.** A bifurcation or separation into two or more branches or parts. **b.** The point at which such a bifurcation or separation occurs: *a fork in a road.* **c.** One of the branches of such a bifurcation or separation: *the right fork.* *—v.* **forked, forking, forks.** *—tr.* **1.** To raise, carry, pitch, or pierce with a fork. **2.** To give the shape of a fork to. **3.** To launch an attack on (two chessmen). *—intr.* **1.** To make a fork; divide into two or more branches. **2.** *Informal.* To hand over; pay. Used with *over, out,* or *up: forked over their savings to buy a color TV.* [Middle English *forke,* Old English *force, forca,* fork (for digging), from Latin *furca†,* two-pronged fork, fork-shaped prop.]

forked (fôrkt, fôr′kĭd) *adj.* **1.** Containing or characterized by a fork: *a forked river.* **2.** Shaped like or similar to a fork: *a forked tail.* **3.** Ambiguous; equivocal; deceitful: *a forked tongue.*

fork·ful (fôrk′fŏŏl) *n., pl.* **forkfuls** or **forksful.** As much as a fork will hold or lift.

fork lift. A small industrial vehicle with a power-operated pronged platform that can be raised and lowered for insertion under a load to be lifted and carried.

For·li (fôr-lē′). A city in eastern Emilia-Romagna, northern Italy. Population, 77,000.

for·lorn (fôr-lôrn′, fər-) *adj.* **1.** Deserted; abandoned. **2.** Suffering extreme want; destitute. **3.** Wretched or pitiful in appearance or condition. **4.** Nearly hopeless; desperate. [Middle English *forloren,* past participle of *forlēsen,* to forfeit, lose, abandon, Old English *forlēosan.* See **leu-¹** in Appendix.*] **—for·lorn′ly** *adv.* **—for·lorn′ness** *n.*

forlorn hope. 1. An advance guard of men sent on a hazardous mission. **2.** A hopeless or arduous undertaking. [Variant by folk etymology of Dutch *verloren hoop,* "lost troop" : *verloren,* past participle of *verliezen,* to lose (see **leu-¹** in Appendix*) + *hoop,* "heap," band, troop (see **keu-²** in Appendix*).]

form (fôrm) *n.* **1.** The contour and structure of something as distinguished from its substance. **2.** The body or outward appearance (of a person or animal) considered separately from the face or head. **3.** The essence of something as distinguished from its matter. **4.** The mode in which a thing exists, acts, or manifests itself; kind; type; variety: *a form of animal life.* **5.** Procedure as determined or governed by regulation or custom. **6.** Manners as governed by etiquette, decorum, or custom. **7.** Performance considered with regard to acknowledged criteria. **8.** Fitness, as of an athlete or animal, with regard to health or training. **9.** A fixed order of words or procedures, as in ceremony or other regulated social situation. **10.** A document with blanks for the insertion of details or information. **11.** Style or manner of presenting ideas or concepts in literary or musical composition or in organized discourse. **12.** The design, structure, or pattern of a work of art. **13.** A model for making a mold. **14.** A copy of the human figure used for modeling clothes. **15.** Linotype that has been assembled and locked up in a chase for printing. **16.** A grade in a British school or in some American private schools: *sixth form.* **17. a.** Linguistic form. **b.** The external aspect of words, with regard to their inflections, pronunciation, or spelling: *verb forms.* **18.** *Chiefly British.* A bench. **19.** The resting place of a hare. *—v.* **formed, forming, forms.** *—tr.* **1.** To give form to; to shape; mold. **2.** To shape or mold into a particular form. **3.** To fashion, train, or develop by instruction or precept: *form the mind.* **4.** To come to have; develop; acquire: *form a habit.* **5.** To constitute or compose an element, part, or characteristic of. **6.** To develop in the mind; conceive: *form an opinion.* **7.** To produce (as a tense) by assuming an inflection: *form the pluperfect.* **8.** To make (a word) by derivation or composition. **9.** To put in order; draw up; arrange. *—intr.* **1.** To become formed or shaped. **2.** To be created; come into being; arise. **3.** To assume a specified form, shape, or pattern. Often used with *up.* [Middle English *forme, fourme,* from Old French, from Latin *fōrma,* form, contour, shape. See **mer-bh-** in Appendix.*]

Synonyms: **form, figure, outline, shape, configuration, contour, profile.** These nouns refer to the distinctive appearance of a thing as determined by its visible lines. *Form,* the least specific, is that which is determined by the thing's overall structure. *Figure* refers usually to identifying form as established by bounding or enclosing lines. *Outline* denotes that which marks the outer limits of a thing and gives it two-dimensional definition. *Shape* implies three-dimensional definition that indicates both outline and bulk or mass. *Configuration,* more definitely than *shape,* implies a pattern comprising an outline together with detailed indication of arrangement of parts within the outline. *Contour* refers to the bounding lines of a three-dimensional, or solid, figure. *Profile* denotes either the outline of the human face in side view or any distinctive outline.

–form. Indicates having the form of; for example, **cuneiform, cruciform.** [New Latin *-formis,* from Latin *-fōrmis,* from *fōrma,* FORM.]

for·mal (fôr′məl) *adj.* **1.** Pertaining to the extrinsic aspect of something as distinguished from its substance or material. **2.** Being or pertaining to the essential form or constitution of something: *a formal principle.* **3.** Following or adhering to accepted forms, conventions, or regulations: *a formal requirement.* **4.** Done in proper or regular form: *a formal reprimand.* **5.** Characterized by strict or meticulous observation of forms. **6.** Stiff or cold; ceremonious: *a formal manner.* **7.** Done for the sake of form only; having the outward appearance but wanting in substance: *a purely formal greeting.* *—n.* **1.** An occasion or ceremony requiring formal attire. **2.** Formal attire. [Middle English, from Old French, from Latin *fōrmālis,* of or for form, from *fōrma,* FORM.] **—for′mal·ly** *adv.*

for·mal·de·hyde (fôr-măl′də-hīd′) *n.* A colorless, gaseous compound, HCHO, used to manufacture melamine and phenolic resins, fertilizers, dyes, embalming fluids, and, in aqueous solution, as a preservative and disinfectant. [German *Formaldehyd* : FORM(IC ACID) + ALDEHYDE.]

For·ma·lin (fôr′mə-lĭn) *n.* A trademark for a 37 per cent by weight aqueous solution of formaldehyde with some methanol.

for·mal·ism (fôr′mə-lĭz′əm) *n.* **1.** Rigorous or excessive adherence to recognized forms. **2.** The mathematical or logical structure of a scientific argument, especially as distinguished from its content. **—for′mal·ist** *n.* **—for′mal·is′tic** *adj.*

for·mal·i·ty (fôr-măl′ə-tē) *n., pl.* **-ties. 1.** The quality or condition of being formal. **2.** Rigorous or ceremonious adherence to established forms, rules, or customs. **3.** An established form, rule, or custom. **4.** Something done for the sake of form, custom, or decorum.

for·mal·ize (fôr′mə-līz′) *tr.v.* **-ized, -izing, -izes. 1.** To give a definite form or shape to. **2.** To render formal. **3.** To give formal endorsement to. **—for′mal·i·za′tion** *n.*

formal logic. The study of the properties of propositions and deductive reasoning by abstraction and analysis of the form rather than the content of propositions under consideration.

for·mant (fôr′mənt) *n.* Any of several frequency regions of relatively great intensity in a sound spectrum, which together determine the characteristic quality of a vowel sound. [German *Formant,* from Latin *fōrmāns,* present participle of *fōrmāre,* to form, from *fōrma,* FORM.]

for·mat (fôr′măt′) *n.* **1.** A plan for the organization and arrangement of a specified production. **2.** The material form or layout of a publication. [French, from German *Format,* from Latin *fōrmātus,* past participle of *fōrmāre,* to form, from *fōrma,* FORM.]

for·mate (fôr′māt′) *n.* A salt or ester of formic acid. [FORM(IC ACID) + -ATE.]

for·ma·tion (fôr-mā′shən) *n.* **1.** The process of forming or producing. **2.** Something that is formed. **3.** The manner or style in which something is formed. **4.** A specified arrangement or deployment, as of troops. **5.** *Geology.* The primary unit of lithostratigraphy, consisting of a succession of strata useful for mapping or description. **—for·ma′tion·al** *adj.*

for·ma·tive (fôr′mə-tĭv) *adj.* **1.** Forming or capable of forming. **2.** Susceptible of transformation by growth and development. **3.** Pertaining to formation, growth, or development: *a formative stage.* **4.** Pertaining to the formation or inflection of words. *—n.* The element of a word that is not contained in the base and that gives the word a suitable form.

form class. A set of linguistic forms whose exact substitutability in a given construction is determined by their common embodiment of one or more morphological or syntactical features.

form·er¹ (fôr′mər) *n.* One that forms.

for·mer² (fôr′mər) *adj.* **1.** Occurring earlier in time; pertaining to a period previous to the one specified. **2.** Coming before in place or order. **3.** The first or first mentioned of two. [Middle English, earlier, from *forme,* first, Old English *forma.* See **per¹** in Appendix.*]

Usage: **Former** is applicable only to the first of two in an enumeration. When reference to the first of three or more is intended, either *first* or *first-named* is possible, but often a repetition of the name of the person or thing involved is an aid to clarity.

for·mer·ly (fôr′mər-lē) *adv.* At a former time; once.

form-fit·ting (fôrm′fĭt′ĭng) *adj.* Closely fitted to the body.

for·mic (fôr′mĭk) *adj.* Of or pertaining to ants. [From Latin *formīca,* ant. See **morwi-** in Appendix.*]

For·mi·ca (fôr-mī′kə) *n.* A trademark for any of various high-pressure laminated plastic sheets of melamine and phenolic materials, used especially for chemical and heat-resistant surfaces.

formic acid. A colorless caustic fuming liquid, HCOOH, used in dyeing and finishing textiles and paper and in the manufacture of fumigants, insecticides, and refrigerants. [From FORMIC (from its natural occurrence in ants).]

for·mi·car·y (fôr′mĭ-kĕr′ē) *n., pl.* **-ies.** A nest of ants; an anthill. [Medieval Latin *formicārium,* from Latin *formīca,* ant. See **morwi-** in Appendix.*]

for·mi·cate (fôr′mĭ-kāt′) *intr.v.* **-cated, -cating, -cates.** To

swarm with or as if with ants. [Latin *formīcāre*, to swarm like ants, from *formīca*, ant. See **formic**.]

for·mi·ca·tion (fôr′mə-kā′shən) *n.* A spontaneous abnormal sensation of ants or other insects running over the skin.

for·mi·da·ble (fôr′mə-də-bəl) *adj.* **1.** Arousing fear, dread, or alarm. **2.** Admirable or awe-inspiring. **3.** Difficult to surmount, defeat, or undertake; awesome. [Middle English, from Old French, from Latin *formīdābilis*, from *formīdāre*, to dread, from *formīdō*, fright, fear. See **mormor-** in Appendix.*] —**for·mi·da·bil′i·ty, for′mi·da·ble·ness** *n.* —**for′mi·da·bly** *adv.*

form·less (fôrm′lĭs) *adj.* Having no specified form; shapeless.

For·mo·sa (fôr-mō′sə). **1.** The former name for **Taiwan**. **2.** A province of Argentina, occupying 28,778 square miles in the northern part of the country. Population, 212,000. **3.** The capital of this province, in the east on the Paraguay River. Population, 17,000. [Portuguese, short for (*Ilha*) *Formosa*, beautiful (island), from *formosa*, beautiful, from Latin *formōsus*, finely formed, beautiful, from *fōrma*, **form**.]

For·mo·sa Strait (fôr-mō′sə). A strait of the Pacific Ocean between Taiwan and China.

for·mu·la (fôr′myə-lə) *n., pl.* **-las** or **-lae** (-lē′). **1.** An established form of words or symbols for use in a ceremony or procedure. **2.** An utterance of conventional notions or beliefs; a hackneyed expression; cliché. **3.** *Chemistry.* **a.** A symbolic representation of the composition, or of the composition and structure, of a chemical compound. **b.** The chemical compound so represented. **4.** A prescription of ingredients in fixed proportion; recipe. **5.** A liquid food prescribed for an infant and containing most required nutrients. **6.** A mathematical statement, especially an equation, of a rule, principle, answer, or other logical relation. [Latin *fōrmula*, diminutive of *fōrma*, **form**.] —**for′mu·la′ic** (fôr′myə-lā′ĭk) *adj.*

for·mu·lar·ize (fôr′myə-lə-rīz′) *tr.v.* **-ized, -izing, -izes.** To formulate. —**for′mu·lar·i·za′tion** *n.*

for·mu·lar·y (fôr′myə-lĕr′ē) *n., pl.* **-ies.** **1.** A book or other collection of formulas. **2.** A statement expressed in formulas. **3.** A formula. **4.** A book containing the names of pharmaceutical substances and listing their uses.

for·mu·late (fôr′myə-lāt′) *tr.v.* **-lated, -lating, -lates.** **1.** To state as a formula. **2.** To express in systematic terms or concepts. **3.** To devise; invent. **4.** To prepare according to a specified formula. —**for′mu·la′tion** *n.* —**for′mu·la′tor** (-lā′tər) *n.*

for·mu·lism (fôr′myə-lĭz′əm) *n.* Adherence to or dependency upon formulas. —**for′mu·lis′tic** *adj.*

for·mu·lize (fôr′myə-līz′) *tr.v.* **-lized, -lizing, -lizes.** To formulate. —**for′mu·li·za′tion** *n.* —**for′mu·liz′er** *n.*

form word. A function word (*see*).

for·myl (fôr′mĭl) *n.* The univalent radical CHO. [FORM(IC ACID) + -YL.]

For·nax (fôr′năks′) *n.* A constellation in the Southern Hemisphere near Sculptor and Eridanus. [Latin *fornāx*, furnace, oven. See **gwher-** in Appendix.*]

for·ni·cate¹ (fôr′nĭ-kĭt, -kāt′) *adj.* Also **for·ni·cat·ed** (-kā′tĭd). Arched or vaulted. [Latin *fornicātus*, from *fornix* (stem *fornic-*), vault, arch. See **gwher-** in Appendix.*]

for·ni·cate² (fôr′nĭ-kāt′) *intr.v.* **-cated, -cating, -cates.** To commit fornication. [Late Latin *fornicārī*, from *fornix* (stem *fornic-*), vault, arch, in the late republican period a vaulted underground dwelling in Rome where poor people and prostitutes lived, hence (especially in early Christian writings) a brothel. See **gwher-** in Appendix.*] —**for′ni·ca′tor** (-kā′tər) *n.*

for·ni·ca·tion (fôr′nĭ-kā′shən) *n.* Sexual intercourse between a man and woman not married to each other.

for·nix (fôr′nĭks) *n., pl.* **-nices** (-nə-sēz′). **1.** *Anatomy.* Either of a pair of bands composed of white fibers beneath the corpus callosum of the brain. **2.** A vaulted space. [New Latin, from Latin, vault, arch. See **fornicate**.]

for·sake (fôr-sāk′, fər-) *tr.v.* **-sook** (-sŏŏk′), **-saken** (-sā′kən), **-saking, -sakes.** **1.** To give up; renounce. **2.** To leave altogether; to desert; abandon. [Forsake, forsook, forsaken; Middle English *forsaken*, *forsok*, *forsaken*, to object to, reject, Old English *forsacan*, *forsōc*, *forsacen*. See **sāg-** in Appendix.*]

for·sooth (fôr-sōōth′, fər-) *adv. Archaic.* In truth; indeed. [Middle English *for soth*, Old English *forsōth* : FOR + SOOTH.]

for·spent (fôr-spĕnt′, fər-) *adj.* Also **fore·spent.** *Archaic.* Worn out with exertion; exhausted. [FOR- + SPENT.]

Forss·mann (fôrs′män′), **Werner Theodor Otto.** Born 1904. German surgeon.

For·ster (fôr′stər), **E(dward) M(organ).** 1879–1969. English novelist.

for·swear (fôr-swâr′) *v.* **-swore** (-swôr′, -swōr′), **-sworn** (-swôrn′, -swōrn′), **-swearing, -swears.** Also **fore·swear.** —*tr.* **1.** To renounce or forsake unalterably. **2.** To disavow or repudiate unalterably. **3.** To perjure. —*intr.* To swear falsely; commit perjury. [Middle English *forsweren*, from Old English *forswerian*, to swear falsely : *for-*, wrongly + *swerian*, to SWEAR.]

for·syth·i·a (fôr-sĭth′ē-ə, fər-) *n.* Any of several shrubs of the genus *Forsythia*, native to Asia, and widely cultivated for their early-blooming yellow flowers. [After William Forsyth (1737–1804), English botanist.]

fort (fôrt, fōrt) *n. Abbr.* **ft.** A fortified place or position stationed with troops; fortification; bastion. [Middle English, from Old French *fort*, from *fort(e)*, strong, from Latin *fortis*. See **bhergh-²** in Appendix.*]

fort. fortification.

For·ta·le·za (fôr′tä-lā′zä). The capital of Ceará State, Brazil, a seaport in the northeastern part of the country. Population, 515,000.

for·ta·lice (fôr′tə-lĭs) *n.* A minor defensive structure or position; a small fort. [Middle English, from Medieval Latin *fortalitia*, from Latin *fortis*, strong. See **bhergh-²** in Appendix.*]

Fort Bay·ard. See **Chanchiang**.

Fort-de-France (fôr-də-fräNs′). The capital of Martinique. Population, 85,000.

Fort Don·el·son National Military Park (dŏn′əl-sən). An area occupying 103 acres in northwestern Tennessee, the site of a Confederate fort captured by General Grant in 1862.

Fort Du·quesne (dōō-kān′). A fur-trading post and French military establishment built in the mid-18th century on the site of present-day Pittsburgh, Pennsylvania. See **Fort Pitt**.

forte¹ (fôrt, fōrt, fôr′tā) *n.* **1.** Something in which a person excels; strong point. **2.** The strong part of a sword blade, between the middle and the hilt. Compare **foible**. [Old French *fort*, from adjective, "strong." See **fort**.]

for·te² (fôr′tā) *adv. Music.* Loudly; forcefully. Used as a direction. —*n. Music.* A note, passage, or chord played forte. —*adj. Abbr.* **f, F** *Music.* Loud; forceful. [Italian, "strongly," from adjective, "strong," from Latin *fortis*. See **bhergh-²** in Appendix.*]

Fort Fred·e·ri·ca National Monument (frĕd′ə-rē′kə, frĕd-rē′-). An area occupying 74 acres on Saint Simon Island, southeastern Georgia, site of an early 18th-century British fort.

Fort George (jôrj). A river rising in west-central Quebec, Canada, and flowing 520 miles westward to James Bay.

forth (fôrth, fōrth) *adv.* **1.** Forward in time, place, or order; on; onward. **2.** Out into view, as from confinement or concealment. **3.** Away from a specified place; abroad. —*prep. Archaic.* Out of; forth from. [Middle English *forth*, Old English *forth*. See **per¹** in Appendix.*]

Forth, Firth of (fôrth; fōrth). An inlet of the North Sea extending about 50 miles into southeastern Scotland.

forth·com·ing (fôrth-kŭm′ĭng, fōrth-) *adj.* **1.** About to appear; approaching; coming: *the forthcoming elections.* **2.** Available when required or as promised: *The money for the new program was forthcoming.* —*n.* An approach or coming forth: *The queen's forthcoming was greeted by cheers from the crowd.*

Fort Hen·ry (hĕn′rē). The site of a fort in northwestern Tennessee, near Fort Donelson National Military Park, that was captured by Union forces in 1862.

forth·right (fôrth′rīt′, fōrth′-) *adj.* Proceeding straight ahead; straightforward; frank; candid: *a forthright appraisal.* —*adv.* **1.** Directly ahead; unhesitatingly; frankly. **2.** *Archaic.* At once; directly; immediately. —**forth′right′ness** *n.*

forth·with (fôrth′wĭth′, -wĭth′, fōrth′-) *adv.* At once; immediately; without delay. See Synonyms at **immediately**.

for·ti·eth (fôr′tē-ĭth) *n.* **1.** The ordinal number 40 in a series. Also written 40th. **2.** One of 40 equal parts. See **number**. —**for′ti·eth** *adj. & adv.*

for·ti·fi·ca·tion (fôr′tə-fĭ-kā′shən) *n. Abbr.* **fort., ft.** **1.** The act, science, or art of fortifying. **2.** Something that serves to defend, strengthen, or fortify; especially, a military defensive work.

fortified wine. A wine, such as sherry, to which alcohol usually in the form of grape brandy has been added.

for·ti·fy (fôr′tə-fī′) *v.* **-fied, -fying, -fies.** —*tr.* **1.** To strengthen and secure (a position) with fortifications. **2.** To add strength to (a structure) by reinforcement; reinforce: *fortify a fence with props.* **3.** To impart physical strength to; invigorate: *The coffee fortified him.* **4.** To give moral or mental strength to; encourage: *He fortified his troubled spirit by praying.* **5.** To corroborate; confirm; support: *The lawyer fortified his allegations with new evidence.* **6.** To strengthen or increase the content of (a substance), as by adding alcohol to wine or vitamins to food: *Milk fortified with vitamin D.* —*intr.* To prepare defensive works; build fortifications. [Middle English *fortifien*, from Old French *fortifier*, from Late Latin *fortificāre*, from Latin *fortis*, strong. See **bhergh-²** in Appendix.*] —**for′ti·fi′a·ble** *adj.* —**for′ti·fi′er** *n.*

for·tis (fôr′tĭs) *adj. Phonetics.* Pronounced with tension and strong articulation. Said of certain consonants such as *f* and *p*. Compare **lenis**. —*n. Phonetics.* A fortis consonant. [New Latin, from Latin *fortis*, strong. See **bhergh-²** in Appendix.*]

for·tis·si·mo (fôr-tĭs′ə-mō′) *adv. Music.* Very loudly. Used as a direction. —*n., pl.* **fortissimos.** *Music.* A note, passage, or chord played loudly. —*adj. Abbr.* **ff** *Music.* Very loud. [Italian, from Latin *fortissimus*, superlative of *fortis*, strong. See **bhergh-²** in Appendix.*]

for·ti·tude (fôr′tə-tōōd′, -tyōōd′) *n.* Strength of mind that allows one to endure pain or adversity with courage: *"There was an infinity of firmest fortitude . . . in the fixed and fearless, forward dedication of that glance"* (Melville). See Synonyms at **courage**. [Middle English, from Old French, from Latin *fortitūdō*, from *fortis*, strong. See **bhergh-²** in Appendix.*]

for·ti·tu·di·nous (fôr′tə-tōōd′n-əs, -tyōōd′n-əs) *adj.* Having or characterized by fortitude; courageous.

Fort Jef·fer·son National Monument (jĕf′ər-sən). An area in the Gulf of Mexico west of southernmost Florida, including the Dry Tortugas of which Garden Key is the site of Fort Jefferson, a massive fortification begun in 1846 and never completed.

Fort Knox (nŏks). A military reservation in northern Kentucky, the site of the U.S. Gold Bullion Depository, established in 1936.

Fort-La·my (fôr′lə-mē′). The capital of the Republic of Chad, on the Shari in the southwest. Population, 45,000.

Fort Lar·a·mie National Monument (lăr′ə-mē). An area occupying about 214 acres in southeastern Wyoming, site of a trading post on the Oregon Trail.

Fort Lau·der·dale (lô′dər-dāl′). A resort city in southern

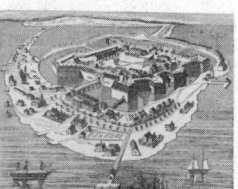

fort
Fort Monroe at the entrance
to Hampton Roads, Virginia,
as it appeared in 1861

Florida, on the Atlantic Ocean, 25 miles north of Miami. Population, 84,000.

Fort Leav·en·worth (lĕv′ən-wûrth′). A fort constructed in 1827 to guard the Santa Fe Trail, now a military reservation and prison in northeastern Kansas.

Fort Ma·tan·zas National Monument (mə-tăn′zəs). An area occupying about 227 acres in northeastern Florida, reserved to protect relics of early Spanish occupation.

Fort Mc·Hen·ry National Monument (mək-hĕn′rē). A fortified area occupying 48 acres in the harbor of Baltimore, Maryland, that was bombarded by the British in 1814, an occasion that inspired Francis Scott Key to write "The Star-Spangled Banner."

Fort Mon·roe (mən-rō′). A fort founded in the 17th century in southeastern Virginia at the entrance to Hampton Roads.

fort·night (fôrt′nīt′, -nĭt) *n.* A period of 14 days and nights; two weeks. [Middle English *fourtenight*, Old English *fēowertiene niht* : FOURTEEN + NIGHT.]

fort·night·ly (fôrt′nīt′lē) *adj.* Happening or appearing once in or every two weeks. —*adv.* Once in two weeks; every fortnight. —*n., pl.* **fortnightlies.** A publication issued every two weeks.

Fort Peck Dam (pĕk). A dam on the Missouri in northeastern Montana, forming Fort Peck Reservoir (383 square miles).

Fort Pierce (pîrs). A city and shipping center of Florida, in the east about 55 miles north of Palm Beach. Population, 25,000.

Fort Pitt (pĭt). The name for Fort Duquesne, following its capture by the British in 1758.

Fort Pu·las·ki National Monument (pə-lăs′kē). An island of over 5,000 acres in the harbor of Savannah, Georgia, site of a fort built in 1829–47, and seized by Union forces in 1862.

FORTRAN (fôr′trăn′) A computer programming language for problems that can be expressed in algebraic terms. [FOR(MULA) + TRAN(SLATION).]

for·tress (fôr′trĭs) *n.* **1.** A fortified place, especially a large and permanent military stronghold, often including a town; a fort. **2.** Any source of refuge or support. —*tr.v.* **fortressed, -tressing, -tresses.** To strengthen or fortify with or as if with a fortress. [Middle English *forteresse*, from Old French, from Vulgar Latin *fortaritia* (unattested), from Latin *fortis*, strong. See **bhergh-²** in Appendix.*]

Fort Smith (smĭth). A city and trading center of Arkansas, in the west on the Arkansas River at the Oklahoma border. Population, 64,000.

Fort Snel·ling (snĕl′ĭng). A fort and the first settlement on the site of Minneapolis, Minnesota, begun in 1820.

Fort Sum·ter National Monument (sŭm′tər). A fort occupying about two acres at the entrance to Charleston harbor, South Carolina, the scene of the first action in the Civil War, when it was taken by Confederate forces (1861).

for·tu·i·tous (fôr-to͞o′ə-təs, fôr-tyo͞o′-) *adj.* Happening by accident or chance; unplanned. See Synonyms at **accidental.** [Latin *fortuitus*, from *forte*, by chance, ablative of *fors*, chance. See **fortune.**] —**for·tu′i·tous·ly** *adv.* —**for·tu′i·tous·ness** *n.*

Usage: *Fortuitous* is often confused with *fortunate.* What is *fortuitous* happens by chance or accident or without plan; *fortunate* and *lucky* are not thus restricted in meaning. What is *fortuitous* can also be *fortunate* or *lucky*, but to employ *fortuitous* in the sense of those terms, without clear indication in the context of the operation of chance or accident, is loose usage. The following example, in which there is no such indication, is termed unacceptable by 85 per cent of the Usage Panel: *The meeting proved fortuitous; I came away with a much better idea of my role.*

for·tu·i·ty (fôr-to͞o′ə-tē, fôr-tyo͞o′-) *n., pl.* **-ties. 1.** An accidental occurrence; chance. **2.** The quality or condition of being fortuitous.

For·tu·na (fôr-to͞o′nə, -tyo͞o′nə). The Roman goddess of fortune. [Latin *Fortūna*, from *fortūna*, FORTUNE.]

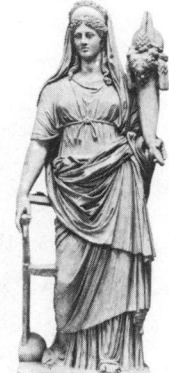

Fortuna
Ancient Roman statue found at Ostia

for·tu·nate (fôr′chə-nĭt) *adj.* **1.** Occurring by good fortune or favorable chance; bringing something good and unforeseen; auspicious. **2.** Receiving unforeseen or unexpected good fortune; lucky. —See Usage note at **fortuitous.**

for·tune (fôr′chən) *n.* **1.** A hypothetical, often personified force or power that favorably or unfavorably governs the events of one's life: *Fortune is on our side.* **2.** The good or bad luck that is to befall someone; destiny; fate: *It is my fortune to be a failure.* **3.** Luck, especially when good; success: *Fortune accompanied his endeavors.* **4. a.** A person's condition or standing in life determined by material possessions or financial wealth. **b.** Extensive amounts of material possessions or money; wealth. **5.** Material or financial success; prosperity. —*v.* **fortuned, -tuning, -tunes.** —*tr. Rare.* To ascribe or give good or bad fortune to. —*intr. Archaic.* To occur by chance; happen. [Middle English, fortune, chance, luck, from Old French, from Latin *fortūna*, chance, fate, (good or bad) luck, from *fors*†, chance, luck.]

fortune cooky. An Oriental cooky made from a thin layer of dough folded and baked around a slip of paper bearing a prediction of fortune or a maxim.

fortune hunter. A person who seeks to become wealthy, especially through marriage.

for·tune·tell·er (fôr′chən-tĕl′ər) *n.* A person who, usually for a fee, will undertake to predict future events in a person's life. —**for′tune·tell′ing** *n.* & *adj.*

Fort Van·cou·ver National Monument (văn-ko͞o′vər). An area occupying 65 acres in southwestern Washington; site of the headquarters of the Hudson's Bay Company and the western terminus of the Oregon Trail.

Fort Wayne (wān). A city and industrial center in northeastern Indiana. Population, 162,000.

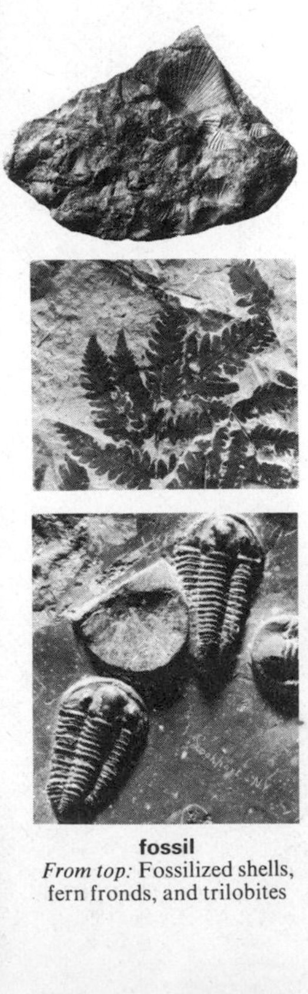

fossil
From top: Fossilized shells, fern fronds, and trilobites

Fort Wil·liam (wĭl′yəm). A city and industrial center in southwestern Ontario, Canada, just south of Port Arthur on the northwestern shore of Lake Superior. Population, 39,000.

Fort Worth (wûrth). An industrial and commercial center near Dallas in northern Texas. Population, 356,000.

for·ty (fôr′tē) *n., pl.* **-ties.** The cardinal number written 40 or in Roman numerals XL. See **number.** [Middle English *fourti*, Old English *fēowertig*. See **kwetwer-** in Appendix.*] —**for′ty** *adj.* & *pron.*

for·ty-five (fôr′tē-fīv′) *n.* **1.** A .45-caliber pistol. **2.** A phonograph record designed to be played at 45 revolutions per minute. Usually written 45. In this sense, also called "forty-five rpm."

for·ty-nin·er (fôr′tē-nī′nər) *n.* One who took part in the 1849 California gold rush.

forty winks. *Informal.* A short nap.

fo·rum (fôr′əm, fōr′-) *n., pl.* **-rums** or **fora** (fôr′ə, fōr′ə). **1.** The public square or marketplace of an ancient Roman city that was the assembly place for judicial and other public activity. **2. a.** Any public meeting place for open discussion. **b.** Any medium for open discussion, as a radio or television program. **3.** A court of law; a tribunal. **4.** *Capital* **F.** The forum in ancient Rome. [Middle English, from Latin, forum, place out-of-doors. See **dhwer-** in Appendix.*]

for·ward (fôr′wərd) *adj.* **1. a.** At, near, or belonging to the front; fore: *the forward part of a train; a forward cabin.* **b.** Located in advance: *the cargo in the ship's forward hole.* **2.** Going, tending, or moving toward a position in front: *a forward thrust of a sword; a forward fall down a flight of stairs.* **3. a.** Ardently inclined; eager; anxious. **b.** Presumptuous; impudent; bold; fresh: *a forward woman.* **4.** Progressive, especially technologically, politically, or economically: *a forward new nation; a forward concept.* **5.** Mentally, physically, socially, or biologically advanced; precocious: *a forward child.* **6.** Prompt; eager: *forward with an offer to work late.* **7.** For the future; completed or made in advance: *My broker does not intend to bid on forward contracts for corn.* —See Synonyms at **shameless, offensive.** —*adv.* Also **for·wards** (-wərdz) (for sense 1). **1.** Toward or tending to the front; frontward: *All volunteers please step forward.* **2.** In or toward the future; at a future time; onward: *I look forward to seeing you.* **3.** Into view or prominence; forth; out: *Come forward out of the shadows so I can see you.* —*n.* *Abbr.* **fwd.** *Sports.* **1.** A player in certain games, such as basketball or soccer, who is part of the front line of offense or defense. **2.** The position itself. —*tr.v.* **forwarded, -warding, -wards. 1.** To send on to a subsequent destination or address. Used especially of mail. **2.** To advance; promote; advocate. **3.** *Bookbinding.* To prepare (a book) for the finisher by supplying with a paper cover. —See Synonyms at **advance.** [Middle English *for(e)ward*, Old English *foreweard* : FORE- + -WARD.]

for·ward·er (fôr′wər-dər) *n.* One that forwards; especially, an agent or agency that facilitates and assures the passage of received goods to their destination.

for·ward·ly (fôr′wərd-lē) *adv.* **1.** At or toward the front; forward. **2.** In a bold or forward manner; presumptuously. **3.** With dispatch or eagerness; promptly.

for·ward·ness (fôr′wərd-nĭs) *n.* **1.** The condition or state of being forward; readiness; zeal; eagerness. **2.** An advanced state of development or progress; precocity. **3.** Overeagerness to promote oneself; audacity; boldness.

forward pass. *Abbr.* **fp, f.p.** *Football.* A pass thrown in the direction of the opponent's goal.

for·went. Past tense of **forgo.**

for·why (fôr-hwī′) *adv. Obsolete.* For what reason; why: *"I will tell you no more at present, guess forwhy."* (Swift). —*conj. Obsolete.* Because; since. [Middle English *forwhy*, Old English *for hwȳ* : FOR + *hwȳ*, instrumental of *hwæt*, WHAT.]

for·worn (fôr-wôrn′, -wōrn′) *adj.* Also **fore·worn.** *Archaic.* Worn-out. [Past participle of obsolete *forwear*, from Middle English *forweren*, to hollow out : *for-*, indicating destruction + *weren*, to WEAR.]

for·zan·do. Variant of **sforzando.**

fos·sa (fŏs′ə) *n., pl.* **fossae** (fŏs′ē′). *Anatomy.* A hollow or depression, as in a bone. [Latin, ditch, trench, from the feminine past participle of *fodere*, to dig. See **bhedh-¹** in Appendix.*]

fosse (fŏs) *n.* Also **foss.** A ditch; especially, a moat around a fortification. [Middle English, from Old French, from Latin *fossa*. See **fossa.**]

fos·sick (fŏs′ĭk) *v.* **-sicked, -sicking, -sicks.** *Chiefly Australian.* —*intr.* **1.** To search for gold, especially by reworking washings or waste piles. **2.** To rummage or search, especially for a possible profit. —*tr.* To search for by or as if by rummaging. [Perhaps variant of British dialectal *fussick*, to bustle about, from FUSS.] —**fos′sick·er** *n.*

fos·sil (fŏs′əl) *n.* **1.** A remnant or trace of an organism of a past geological age, such as a skeleton, footprint, or leaf imprint, embedded in the earth's crust. **2.** One that is outdated or antiquated; especially, a person with outmoded ideas; a fogy. **3.** An obsolete word or word element used only in an idiom, as *fro* in *to and fro.* —*adj.* **1.** Of or pertaining to a fossil or fossils. **2.** Derived from fossils: *Coal is a fossil fuel.* [From Latin *fossilis*, dug up, from *fossus*, past participle of *fodere*, to dig. See **bhedh-¹** in Appendix.*]

fos·sil·if·er·ous (fŏs′ə-lĭf′ər-əs) *adj.* Containing fossils. [FOSSIL + -FEROUS.]

fos·sil·ize (fŏs′ə-līz′) *v.* **-ized, -izing, -izes.** —*tr.* **1.** To convert into a fossil. **2.** To make outmoded, rigid, or fixed; antiquate; to freeze. —*intr.* To become a fossil. —**fos′sil·i·za′tion** *n.*

fos·so·ri·al (fŏ-sôr′ē-əl, -sōr′ē-əl) *adj. Zoology.* Adapted for or used in burrowing or digging. [From Medieval Latin *fossorius,* from Latin *fossus,* past participle of *fodere,* to dig. See **bhedh-**[1] in Appendix.*]

fos·ter (fôs′tər, fŏs′-) *tr.v.* **-tered, -tering, -ters. 1.** To bring up; rear; nurture: *"I grew up/Fostered alike by beauty and fear"* (Wordsworth). **2.** To promote the development or growth of; encourage; cultivate: *"They fostered in him a vigorous expression of his intellectual precocity"* (Erik Erikson). **3.** To nurse; cherish: *foster a secret hope.* —*adj.* Receiving, sharing, or affording parental care and nurture although not related through legal or blood ties: *a foster child.* [Middle English *fostren,* Old English *fōstrian,* to provide with food, nourish, from *fōstor,* food. See **pā-** in Appendix.*] —**fos′ter·age** *n.*

Fos·ter (fôs′tər, fŏs′-), **Stephen (Collins).** 1826–1864. American composer of songs.

Fos·ter (fôs′tər, fŏs′-), **William Z(ebulon).** 1881–1961. American Communist leader; three times Presidential candidate (1924, 1928, and 1932).

fos·ter·ling (fôs′tər-lĭng, fŏs′-) *n.* A foster child.

Foth·er·in·ghay (fŏ*th*′ər-ĭng-gā′, fŏ*th*′rĭng-). A village in Northamptonshire, England, site of Fotheringhay Castle, in which Mary Queen of Scots was imprisoned.

Fou·cault (fōō-kō′), **Jean Bernard Léon.** 1819–1868. French physicist.

Foucault pendulum. A simple pendulum suspended so that the plane of motion is not fixed, set into motion along a meridian, and appearing to turn clockwise in the Northern Hemisphere, or counterclockwise in the Southern Hemisphere, demonstrating the axial rotation of the earth. [Demonstrated by J.B.L. FOUCAULT.]

fou·droy·ant (fōō-droi′ənt; *French* fōō-drwȧ-yäN′) *adj.* Dazzling; stunning. [French, present participle of *foudroyer,* to strike (as with lightning), from Old French *foudroier,* from *foudre,* lightning, from Latin *fulgur,* from *fulgēre,* to shine. See **bhel-**[1] in Appendix.*]

fought. Past tense and past participle of **fight.**

foul (foul) *adj.* **fouler, foulest. 1.** Offensive to the senses; disgusting; revolting. **2.** Having an offensive odor; fetid; rank; smelly. **3.** Spoiled; rotten; putrid. Said especially of food. **4.** Full of dirt or mud; dirty; filthy. **5.** Immoral; wicked; detestable. **6.** Vulgar; obscene; profane: *foul language.* **7.** *Archaic.* Ugly; unattractive. **8.** *Informal.* Terrible; disagreeable; displeasing: *a foul movie.* **9.** Unpleasant; bad; unfavorable. Often said of weather: *a foul day.* **10.** Not according to accepted standards or rules; unfair; dishonorable: *win by foul means.* **11.** *Sports.* Contrary to the rules of a game or sport. **12.** *Baseball.* Outside the foul line, as a ball. **13.** Entangled; twisted: *a foul anchor.* **14.** Clogged or obstructed by something; blocked: *a foul ventilator shaft.* —See Synonyms at **dirty.** —*n.* **1.** Anything that is dirty or foul. **2.** *Abbr.* **f.** *Sports.* An infraction or violation of the rules of play. **3.** *Abbr.* **f.** *Baseball.* A foul ball. **4.** An entanglement or collision. **5.** A clogging or obstructing. —*adv.* In a foul manner. —*v.* **fouled, fouling, fouls.** —*tr.* **1.** To make dirty or foul; to soil; pollute; sully. **2.** To bring into dishonor; to disgrace; besmirch. **3.** To clog or obstruct; to block. **4.** To entangle or catch, as a rope. **5.** To encrust (a ship's hull) with foreign matter, such as barnacles. **6.** *Sports.* To commit a foul against. **7.** *Baseball.* To hit (a ball) outside the foul lines. —*intr.* **1.** To become foul. **2.** *Sports.* To commit a foul. **3.** *Baseball.* To hit a ball outside the foul lines. **4.** To become entangled or twisted: *The anchor fouled on a rock.* **5.** To become clogged or obstructed. —**foul out. 1.** *Baseball.* To make an out by hitting a foul ball that is caught before it touches the ground. **2.** *Sports.* To be put out of play by exceeding the number of permissible fouls. [Middle English *foul,* Old English *fūl.* See **pu-**[2] in Appendix.*] —**foul′ly** *adv.*

fou·lard (fōō-lärd′) *n.* **1.** A lightweight twill or plain-woven fabric of silk, or silk and cotton, usually having a small printed design. **2.** An article of clothing, especially a necktie or scarf, made of this fabric. [French *foulard*†.]

foul ball. *Baseball.* Any batted ball that is not judged a fair ball.

foul line. 1. *Baseball.* Either of two straight lines extending from the rear of home plate to the boundary of the playing field to indicate the area in which a fair ball can be hit. **2.** *Basketball.* A line from which a player makes a foul shot. Also called "free-throw line." **3.** *Sports.* Any boundary limiting the playing area, especially in bowling and tennis.

foul-mouthed (foul′mou*th*d′, -moutht′) *adj.* Using obscene or scurrilous language.

foul·ness (foul′nĭs) *n.* **1.** The state or condition of being foul. **2.** Foul matter; filth; trash; waste. **3.** Obscenity; vulgarity; wickedness.

foul play. Unfair or treacherous action, especially when involving violence.

foul shot. *Basketball.* An unguarded throw to the basket from the foul line, awarded to a fouled player and scored as one point if successful. Also called "free throw."

foul tip. *Baseball.* A pitched ball that is slightly deflected off the bat into the foul zone.

foul up. 1. To make dirty; contaminate. **2.** To entangle, choke, or obstruct. **3.** To cause to blunder because of mistakes or poor judgment. **4.** To blunder; to bungle.

foul-up (foul′ŭp′) *n.* **1.** A condition of confusion caused by poor judgment or mistakes. **2.** Mechanical trouble.

found[1] (found) *v.* **founded, founding, founds.** —*tr.* **1.** To originate or establish (something); create; set up, as a college. **2.** To establish the foundation of; lay a base for. —*intr.* To have a foundation or base. Used with *on* or *upon.* [Middle English *founden,* from Old French *fonder,* from Latin *fundāre,* to lay the foundation for, from *fundus,* bottom. See **bhudh** in Appendix.*] —**found′er** *n.*

found[2] (found) *tr.v.* **founded, founding, founds. 1.** To melt (a material, such as metal) and pour into a mold. **2.** To make (objects) in this fashion; to cast. [Middle English *founden,* from Old French *fondre,* from Latin *fundere,* to pour, melt. See **gheu-** in Appendix.*] —**found′er** *n.*

found[3]. Past tense and past participle of **find.**

foun·da·tion (foun-dā′shən) *n.* **1.** The act of founding or a state of being founded; especially, the establishment of an institution with provisions for future maintenance. **2.** The basis on which a thing stands, is founded, or is supported; an underlying support. **3.** Funds for the perpetual support of an institution, such as a hospital or school; an endowment. **4.** An institution supported by such a fund; an endowed institution. **5.** A foundation garment. **6.** A cosmetic used as a base for facial make-up. —See Synonyms at **base.** —**foun·da′tion·al** *adj.*

foundation garment. A woman's supporting undergarment, such as a corset or girdle.

foun·der (foun′dər) *v.* **-dered, -dering, -ders.** —*intr.* **1.** To become disabled; especially, to go lame. Used of horses. **2.** To fail utterly; collapse or break down; give way. **3.** *Nautical.* To sink below the water. **4.** To cave in; fall in; to sink. Used of ground or buildings. **5.** *Veterinary Medicine.* To be afflicted with founder. Used of horses. —*tr.* To cause to founder. —*n. Veterinary Medicine.* A disease of horses, **laminitis** *(see).* [Middle English *foundren,* to fall to the ground, from Old French *fondrer,* to submerge, from Vulgar Latin *fundorāre* (unattested), from Latin *fundus,* bottom. See **bhudh-** in Appendix.*]

founders' shares. Shares of stock issued to the founders or original subscribers of a public company and often carrying special privileges.

found·ling (found′lĭng) *n.* A child deserted by parents whose identity is not known. [Middle English *foundling,* probably from *founden,* past participle of *finden,* to FIND.]

found object. Any of various objects or materials picked up by chance and incorporated in a work of art. [Translation of French *objet trouvé.*]

foun·dry (foun′drē) *n., pl.* **-dries. 1.** An establishment in which the founding of metals is done. **2. a.** The art or operation of founding. **b.** The castings made by founding.

foundry proof. A proof taken from composed type for a final check before plates are made.

fount[1] (fount) *n.* **1.** A fountain. **2.** Any source. **3.** A reservoir for liquids; especially, an inkwell. [Probably a back-formation from FOUNTAIN.]

fount[2]. *Chiefly British.* Variant of **font** (type).

foun·tain (foun′tən) *n.* **1.** A spring; especially, the source of a stream. **2.** A source; point of origin. **3. a.** An artificially created jet or stream of water. **b.** A device that produces and contains such a jet or stream: *a drinking fountain.* **4.** A reservoir, tank, or chamber containing a supply of something, such as ink or oil, that can be siphoned off as needed. **5.** A **soda fountain** *(see).* [Middle English *fountaine,* spring, from Old French *fontaine,* from Late Latin *fontāna,* from *fontānus,* of a spring, from *fons* (stem *font-*), spring. See **dhen-**[1] in Appendix.*]

foun·tain·head (foun′tən-hĕd′) *n.* **1.** A spring that is the source or head of a stream. **2.** A principal source or origin.

Fountain of Youth. A legendary spring believed to have the power of rejuvenation, sought by Ponce de León and other explorers in Florida and the West Indies.

fountain pen. A pen filled from an external source and containing an ink reservoir that automatically feeds the writing point.

Fou·quet (fōō-kā′), **Jean.** 1416?–1480. French painter.

four (fôr, fōr) *n.* The cardinal number written 4 or in Roman numerals IV. See **number.** [Middle English *four,* Old English *fēower.* See **kwetwer-** in Appendix.*] —**four** *adj. & pron.*

four bits. *Slang.* Fifty cents.

four·chette (fŏŏr-shĕt′) *n.* A narrow, forked strip of material joining the front and back sections of the fingers of gloves. [French, "fork," from Old French *forchete,* diminutive of *forche,* fork, pitchfork, from Latin *furca,* (two-pronged) FORK.]

four-col·or (fôr′kŭl′ər) *adj.* Designating a color printing or photographic process in which three primary colors and black are transferred by four different plates or filters to a surface, reproducing the colors of the subject matter.

four-cy·cle (fôr′sī′kəl, fōr′-) *adj.* Designating an internal-combustion engine that requires four strokes of the piston for a cycle.

four-di·men·sion·al (fôr′dĭ-mĕn′shən-əl, fōr′-) *adj.* Exhibiting or being specified by four dimensions, especially the three spatial dimensions and single temporal dimension of relativity theory.

Four·drin·i·er (fŏŏr-drĭn′ē-ər) *adj.* Designating a papermaking machine used to produce paper in a continuous roll or web. [After Henry (died 1854) and Sealy (died 1847) *Fourdrinier,* English papermakers.]

four-eyed fish (fôr′īd′, fōr′-). Either of two freshwater fishes, *Anableps anableps* or *A. microlepis,* of tropical America, having bulging eyes divided longitudinally, with the upper part adapted for aerial vision, the lower part for underwater vision.

four flush. *Poker.* A five-card hand having four cards in the same suit.

four-flush (fôr′flŭsh′, fōr′-) *intr.v.* **-flushed, -flushing, -flushes. 1.** To bluff in poker with a four-flush hand. **2.** *Slang.* To bluff.

four-flush·er (fôr′flŭsh′ər, fōr′-) *n. Slang.* A person who cannot or does not substantiate his pretensions; bluffer; faker.

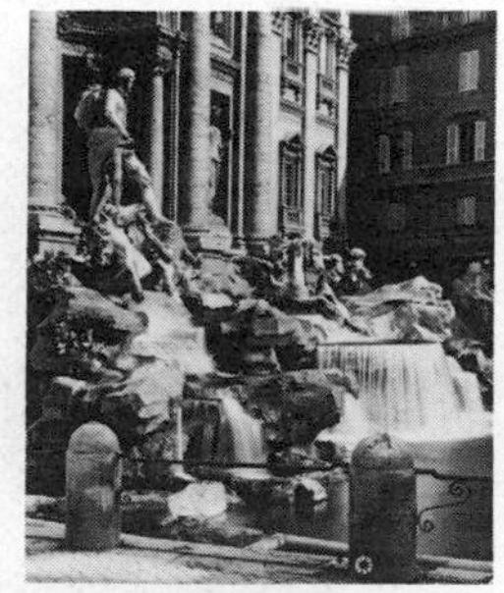

fountain
Fountain of Trevi, Rome, Italy

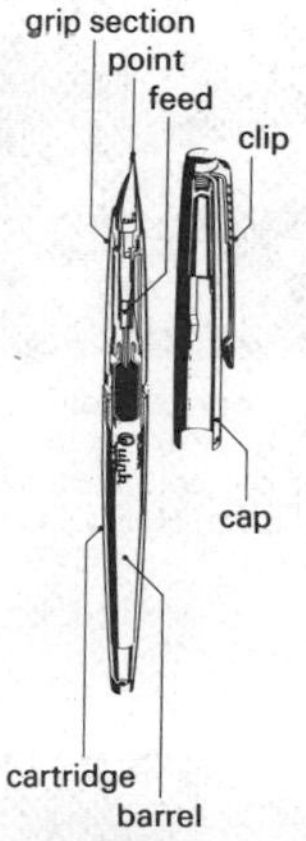
grip section
point
feed
clip
cap
cartridge
barrel

fountain pen

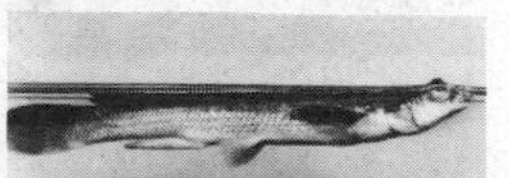

four-eyed fish
Anableps anablops

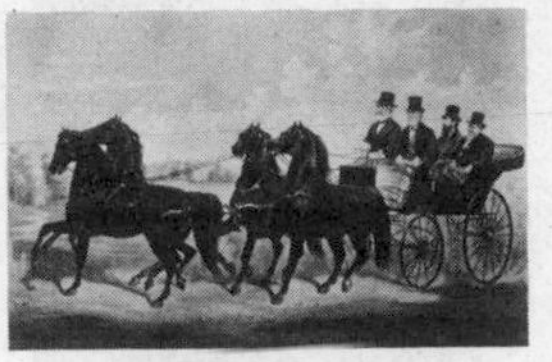

four-in-hand
A four-in-hand and team of stallions shown in an 1875 Currier and Ives print

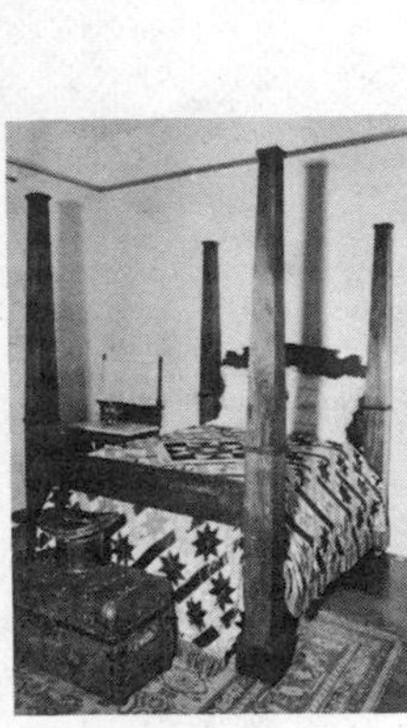

four-poster
Late 18th-century four-poster in Kentucky home of Henry Clay

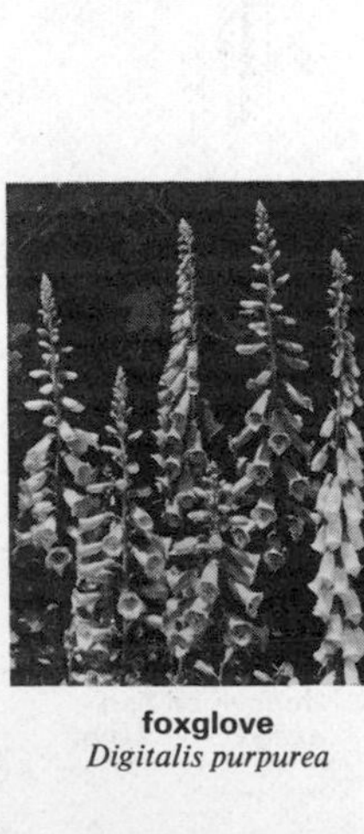

foxglove
Digitalis purpurea

four·fold (fôr′fōld′, fōr′-) *adj.* **1.** Having four units or aspects; quadruple. **2.** Being four times as much or as many as some understood figure. *—adv.* (fôr′fōld′, fōr′-). In quadrupled measure.
four-foot·ed (fôr′fo͝ot′ĭd, fōr′-) *adj.* Having four feet.
Four Forest Cantons, Lake of the. See Lake of **Lucerne.**
Four Freedoms. Basic human freedoms, designated in 1941 by President Franklin D. Roosevelt to be freedom of speech and religion and freedom from want and fear.
four·gon (fo͞or-gôN′) *n., pl.* **-gons** (-gôN′). *French.* A wagon for carrying mainly baggage.
four-hand·ed (fôr′hăn′dĭd, fōr′-) *adj.* **1.** Involving or requiring four players, as some games. **2.** Designed to be played by four hands, as a piano duet. **3.** Having four extremities functioning like hands; quadrumanous.
Four-H Club (fôr′āch′, fōr′-). A youth organization sponsored by the Department of Agriculture and offering instruction in agriculture and home economics. [From its goal of improving head, heart, hands, and health.]
four hundred. Also **Four Hundred.** The wealthiest and most exclusive social set. Preceded by *the.*
Fou·rier (fo͞o-ryā′), **(François Marie) Charles.** 1772–1837. French utopian socialist.
Fou·rier (fo͞o-ryā′), Baron **Jean Baptiste Joseph.** 1768–1830. French physicist and mathematician.
Fou·ri·er·ism (fo͝or′ē-ə-rĭz′əm) *n.* The system for social reform advocated by Charles Fourier in the early 19th century, proposing that society be organized into small self-sustaining communal groups. **—Fou′ri·er·ist, Fou′ri·er·ite′** *n.*
Fourier series. Infinite series of sine and cosine functions, capable if uniformly convergent of approximating a wide variety of mathematical functions. [Devised by J.B.J. FOURIER.]
four-in-hand (fôr′ĭn-hănd′, fōr′-) *n.* **1.** A vehicle drawn by horses driven by one person. **2.** A team of four horses. **3.** A necktie tied in a slipknot with the ends left hanging and overlapping. *—adj.* Designating or having to do with a four-in-hand.
four-leaf clover (fôr′lēf′, fōr′-). Also **four-leaved clover** (-lēvd′). A clover leaf having four leaflets instead of the normal three, considered to be an omen of good luck.
four-let·ter word (fôr′lĕt′ər, fōr′-). Any of several short English words generally regarded as vulgar or obscene.
four-mast·ed (fôr′măs′tĭd, -mäs′tĭd, fōr′-) *adj. Nautical.* Having four masts. **—four′-mast′er** *n.*
four-o'clock (fôr′ə-klŏk′, fōr′-) *n.* Any of several plants of the genus *Mirabilis;* especially, *M. jalapa,* native to tropical America, and widely cultivated for its tubular, variously colored flowers that open in the late afternoon. Also called "marvel-of-Peru."
four·pence (fôr′pəns, fōr′-) *n. British.* **1.** A sum of money equal to four pence, or four British pennies. **2.** Formerly, a small silver coin of this value.
four-post·er (fôr′pō′stər, fōr′-) *n.* A bed having tall corner posts originally intended to support curtains or a canopy.
four·ra·gère (fo͝or′ə-zhâr′) *n.* **1.** An ornamental braided cord usually looped around the left shoulder. **2.** Such a cord awarded to an entire military unit. [French, from the feminine of *fourrager,* of forage, from *fourrage,* forage, from Old French *forage,* FORAGE.]
four·score (fôr′skôr′, fōr′skōr′) *adj.* Four times 20; 80.
four·some (fôr′səm, fōr′-) *n.* **1.** Any group of four persons; especially, two couples each consisting of a man and woman. **2. a.** Any game; especially, a golf match played by four persons, two on each side. **b.** The players in such a game. *—adj.* Consisting of or involving a group of four. [Middle English *four-sum,* from Old English *fēowra sum,* one of four : *fēowra,* genitive of *fēower,* FOUR + *sum,* one, SOME.]
four·square (fôr′skwâr′, fōr′-) *adj.* **1.** Having four equal sides and four right angles; square. **2.** Unyielding; firm. **3.** Forthright; frank. *—n.* (fôr′skwâr′, fōr′-). A square. *—adv.* (fôr′skwâr′, fōr′-). Squarely; forthrightly.
four·teen (fôr-tēn′, fōr-) *n.* The cardinal number written 14 or in Roman numerals XIV. See **number.** [Middle English *fourtene,* Old English *fēowertīene.* See **kwetwer-** in Appendix.*] **—four·teen′** *adj. & pron.*
four·teenth (fôr-tēnth′, fōr-) *n.* **1.** The ordinal number 14 in a series. Also written 14th. **2.** One of 14 equal parts. See **number.** **—four·teenth′** *adj. & adv.*
fourth (fôrth, fōrth) *n.* **1.** The ordinal number four in a series. Also written 4th. **2.** One of four equal parts. See **number.** **3.** *Music.* **a.** In a diatonic scale, a tone four degrees above or below any given tone. **b.** The interval between two such tones. **c.** The harmonic combination of these tones. **d.** In a scale, the subdominant. **—the Fourth.** The Fourth of July. [Middle English *fourthe,* earlier *ferthe, furthe,* Old English *fēortha, fēowertha.* See **kwetwer-** in Appendix.*] **—fourth** *adj. & adv.*
fourth-class (fôrth′klăs′, -kläs′, fōrth′-) *adj.* Designating a class of mail consisting of merchandise or certain printed matter weighing over eight ounces and not sealed against inspection. *—adv.* As or by fourth-class mail.
fourth dimension. Time regarded as a coordinate dimension and required by relativistic geometry, along with three spatial dimensions, to completely specify the location of any event.
fourth estate. The public press; journalism or journalists generally. [Formerly used jocularly to refer to something outside the (three) Estates of the Realm.]
Fourth of July. Independence Day.
four-wheel (fôr′hwēl′, fōr′-) *adj.* **1.** Having four wheels. **2.** Of, pertaining to, or designating an automotive drive mechanism in which all four wheels are connected to the source of driving power.
Fou·ta Djal·lon. See **Futa Jallon.**
fo·ve·a (fō′vē-ə) *n., pl.* **-veae** (-vē-ē′). A shallow cuplike depression or pit in a bone or other organ. [New Latin, from Latin *fovea,* small pit, possibly from Etruscan.] **—fo′ve·al** (-əl), **fo′ve·ate′** (-āt′) *adj.*
fovea cen·tra·lis (sĕn-trā′lĭs). A small depression in the macula lutea of the retina, constituting the area of most distinct vision.
fowl (foul) *n., pl.* **fowl** or **fowls. 1.** Any of various birds of the order Galliformes; especially, the common, widely domesticated chicken, *Gallus gallus.* **2.** Any bird used as food or hunted as game. **3.** The edible flesh of such a bird. **4.** *Archaic.* Any bird. *—intr.v.* **fowled, fowling, fowls.** To hunt, trap, or shoot wild fowl. [Middle English *foul,* Old English *fugol.* See **pleu-** in Appendix.*] **—fowl′er** *n.*
fowl cholera. An acute, infectious, often fatal intestinal disease of domestic poultry and wild birds, caused by a bacterium, *Pasteurella multocida,* and characterized by enteritis, submucous hemorrhage, and vascular congestion.
Fowl·er (fou′lər), **Henry Watson.** 1858–1933. English lexicographer and grammarian.
fowl·ing (fou′lĭng) *n.* The hunting of wild fowl.
fowling net. A net for catching fowl.
fowling piece. A light shotgun for shooting birds and small animals.
fowl pox. A viral infection of poultry and other birds, characterized by wartlike nodules on the skin and cankers in the digestive and upper respiratory tracts.
fox (fŏks) *n.* **1.** Any of various carnivorous mammals of the genus *Vulpes* and related genera, related to the dogs and wolves, and characteristically having upright ears, a pointed snout, and a long, bushy tail. **2.** The fur of a fox. **3.** A crafty, sly, or clever person. **4.** *Archaic.* A sword. **5.** *Nautical.* Small cordage made by twisting together two or more strands of tarred yarn. *—v.* **foxed, foxing, foxes.** *—tr.* **1. a.** To trick or fool by ingenuity or cunning; outwit. **b.** To baffle or confuse. **2.** *Archaic.* To make drunk or intoxicate. **3.** To make (beer) sour by fermenting. **4.** To repair (a shoe) by adding a new upper. *—intr.* **1.** To act slyly or craftily. **2.** To turn sour in fermenting. Used of beer. [Middle English *fox,* Old English *fox.* See **puk-**[2] in Appendix.*]
Fox (fŏks) *n., pl.* **Foxes** or **Fox. 1.** A tribe of Algonquian-speaking Indians mainly of southwestern Wisconsin who merged with the Sauk in 1760. **2.** A member of this tribe.
Fox (fŏks), **Charles James.** 1749–1806. British political leader and orator; supported American colonies and French Revolution.
Fox (fŏks), **George.** 1624–1691. English founder of the Society of Friends.
Foxe (fŏks), **John.** 1516–1587. English author of the *Book of Martyrs.*
Foxe Basin (fŏks). An arm of the Atlantic Ocean between Melville Peninsula and Baffin Island in the Northwest Territories, Canada.
foxed (fŏkst) *adj.* Discolored with yellowish-brown stains, as an old book or print: *"their set of George Eliot was foxed and buckled by the rain"* (John Cheever). [From the resemblance of the stain to the color of a fox.]
fox·fire (fŏks′fīr′) *n.* A phosphorescent glow, especially that produced by certain fungi found on rotting wood. [Middle English *foxfire,* possibly from the silvery quality of certain fox fur.]
fox·glove (fŏks′glŭv′) *n.* **1.** Any of several plants of the genus *Digitalis;* especially, *D. purpurea,* native to Europe, having a long cluster of large, tubular, pinkish-purple flowers, and leaves that are the source of the medicinal drug digitalis. **2.** Any of several similar or related plants. [Middle English *foxes-glove,* Old English *foxes glōfa,* "fox's glove" (the reason for association with the fox is not known) : FOX + *glōf, glōfa,* GLOVE.]
fox grape. A climbing woody vine, *Vitis labrusca,* of the eastern United States, that bears purplish-black fruit and is the source of many cultivated grape varieties.
fox·hole (fŏks′hōl′) *n.* A shallow pit dug by a soldier in combat for immediate individual refuge against enemy fire.
fox·hound (fŏks′hound′) *n.* A dog developed for fox hunting; especially, a short-haired hound of either of two breeds, the *English foxhound* and the *American foxhound.*
fox hunt. The hunting of a fox with hounds; a chase.
fox·ing (fŏk′sĭng) *n.* **1.** A piece of material, such as leather, applied as a trim or reinforcement on the upper of a shoe. **2.** A brownish discoloration of paper or a book.
Fox Islands. A group of islands in the eastern Aleutian Islands, southwestern Alaska, among them Unimak and Unalaska.
Fox River. A river rising in southeastern Wisconsin and flowing 176 miles northeast to Green Bay, forming part of a water route from the Great Lakes to the Mississippi.
fox squirrel. A squirrel, *Sciurus niger,* of the United States, having rusty or grayish fur.
fox·tail (fŏks′tāl′) *n.* **1.** Any of several grasses of the genus *Alopecurus,* having dense, silky or bristly flowering spikes. **2.** Any of several similar or related plants.
foxtail lily. Any of several plants of the genus *Eremurus,* native to Asia, having a tall, spirelike cluster of small, bell-shaped white, yellowish, or pink flowers.
fox terrier. A small dog of a breed originating in England, having a white coat with dark markings, and developed in both wire-haired and smooth-coated varieties.
fox trot. 1. a. A ballroom dance in 2/4 or 4/4 time, composed of a variety of slow and fast steps. **b.** The music for this dance.

ă pat/ā pay/âr care/ä father/b bib/ch church/d deed/ĕ pet/ē be/f fife/g gag/h hat/hw which/ĭ pit/ī pie/îr pier/j judge/k kick/l lid, needle/m mum/n no, sudden/ng thing/ŏ pot/ō toe/ô paw, for/oi noise/ou out/o͝o took/o͞o boot/p pop/r roar/s sauce/sh ship, dish/

2. The slow broken gait of a horse between a trot and a walk. [From the short steps attributed to the comparatively short-legged fox.]

fox-trot (fŏks′trŏt′) *intr.v.* **-trotted, -trotting, -trots.** To dance a fox trot.

fox·y (fŏk′sē) *adj.* **-ier, -iest.** **1.** Suggestive of a fox; sly; cunning; clever. **2.** Having a reddish-brown color. **3.** Discolored as by decay; stained; foxed. **4.** Soured by improper fermentation. Said of beer. **5.** Having the distinctive flavor of some American grapes. Said of wines. —See Synonyms at **sly.** —**fox′i·ly** *adv.* —**fox′i·ness** *n.*

foy (foi) *n. Chiefly Scottish.* A farewell entertainment, feast, drink, or gift, as at the end of a harvest or on the eve of a wedding. [Dialectal Dutch *fooi,* feast given for farm laborers after harvest, from Middle Dutch *foye, voye,* "voyage," feast given at parting, from Old French *voie,* way, journey, from Latin *via.* See **wei-**² in Appendix.*]

foy·er (foi′ər, foi′ā′; *French* fwȧ-yā′) *n.* **1.** The lobby or anteroom of a public building, such as a theater or hotel. **2.** The entrance hall or vestibule of a private dwelling. [French, hearth, home, foyer, from Medieval Latin *focārius,* from Latin *focus,* hearth, fireplace. See **fuel.**]

fp **1.** forward pass. **2.** freezing point.

fp. foolscap.

f.p. forward pass.

FPC Federal Power Commission.

fpm, f.p.m. feet per minute.

FPO fleet post office.

fps foot-pound-second.

f.p.s. **1.** feet per second. **2.** frames per second.

Fr The symbol for the element francium.

fr. **1.** franc. **2.** frequently. **3.** from.

Fr. **1.** father (clergyman). **2.** France; French. **3.** frater. **4.** Frau. **5.** friar. **6.** Friday (unofficial).

f.r. right-hand page (Latin *folio recto*).

Fra (frä) *n.* Brother. The title given to a friar. [Italian, short for *frate,* "brother," from Latin *frāter.* See **bhrāter-** in Appendix.*]

FRA Airport code for Frankfurt am Main, Germany.

fra·cas (frā′kəs; *British* frăk′ä′) *n.* A disorderly uproar; noisy quarrel; row; brawl. [French, from Italian *fracasso,* from *fracassare,* probably a blend of Latin *frangere,* to break (see **bhreg-** in Appendix*), and *quassāre,* to shatter (see **quash**).]

fract·ed (frăk′tĭd) *adj. Obsolete.* Broken. [Latin *fractus.* See **fraction.**]

frac·tion (frăk′shən) *n.* **1.** A small part of something; scant portion: *a fraction of the populace.* **2.** A disconnected piece of something; fragment; scrap; bit. **3.** *Mathematics.* An indicated quotient of two quantities. **4.** *Chemistry.* A component separated by fractionation. [Middle English *fraccioun,* from Late Latin *fractiō,* act of breaking (especially bread), from Latin *fractus,* past participle of *frangere,* to break. See **bhreg-** in Appendix.*]

frac·tion·al (frăk′shən-əl) *adj.* **1.** Of, pertaining to, or constituting a fraction or fractions. **2.** Very small; insignificant; infinitesimal. **3.** Being in fractions or pieces; broken; fragmentary.

fractional currency. **1.** Any currency in a denomination less than the standard monetary unit. **2.** In the United States, a coin worth less than a dollar.

fractional distillation. **1.** Distillation with rectification to obtain the purest possible product. **2.** Distillation in which the product is collected in a series of separate fractions.

frac·tion·ate (frăk′shə-nāt′) *tr.v.* **-ated, -ating, -ates.** To separate (a chemical compound) into components, as by distillation or crystallization. —**frac′tion·a′tion** *n.* —**frac′tion·a′tor** (-shə-nā′tər) *n.*

frac·tion·ize (frăk′shə-nīz′) *v.* **-ized, -izing, -izes.** —*tr.* To divide into fractions. —*intr.* To divide something into fractions. —**frac′tion·i·za′tion** *n.*

frac·tious (frăk′shəs) *adj.* **1.** Inclined to make trouble; unruly: *"when . . . intoxicated he was very fractious"* (Franklin). **2.** Having a peevish nature; cranky; irritable. [From FRACTION, in the sense of "breaking."] —**frac′tious·ly** *adv.* —**frac′tious·ness** *n.*

frac·ture (frăk′chər) *n.* **1. a.** The act or process of breaking. **b.** The condition of being broken. **2.** A break, rupture, or crack, as in bone or cartilage, as: A *comminuted fracture,* a fracture in which the bone is broken into several pieces; a *compound* or *open fracture,* a fracture with an open wound, often with the broken bone exposed; an *impacted fracture,* a fracture in which the broken ends have been forced into each other; a *simple* or *closed fracture,* a fracture with no break in the skin. **3.** *Mineralogy.* **a.** The characteristic manner in which a mineral breaks. **b.** The characteristic appearance of a broken mineral. —*v.* **fractured, -turing, -tures.** —*tr.* To break; to crack. —*intr.* To undergo a fracture. —See Synonyms at **break.** [Middle English, from Old French, from Latin *fractūra,* from *fractus,* broken. See **fraction.**]

frag·ile (frăj′əl, -īl′) *adj.* **1.** Easily broken or damaged; brittle. **2.** Physically weak; frail. **3.** Suggesting fragility; light: *"she put her hand on my arm, a fragile touch careful not to waken"* (Truman Capote). **4.** Tenuous; flimsy: *a fragile claim to fame.* [Old French, from Latin *fragilis,* from *frangere,* to break. See **bhreg-** in Appendix.*] —**frag′ile·ly** *adv.* —**fra·gil′i·ty** (frə-jĭl′ə-tē), **frag′ile·ness** *n.*

Synonyms: *fragile, breakable, frail, delicate, brittle.* These adjectives mean susceptible to being broken or injured. *Fragile* most often describes objects whose lightness or delicacy of material requires that they be handled with great care. *Breakable* refers to what can be broken, but makes a less strong implication of inherent weakness. *Frail,* applicable to persons and things, implies slightness of constitution, build, or structure and consequent lack of durability. *Delicate,* in this comparison, also suggests lack of durability or susceptibility to injury. *Brittle* refers to the hardness and inelasticity of some material that makes it especially subject to fracture or snapping when subjected to pressure.

frag·ment (frăg′mənt) *n.* **1.** A part broken off or detached from a whole. **2.** Something incomplete; an odd bit or piece: *"He notes fragments of conversation on menus, toilet paper, envelopes"* (Anaïs Nin). **3.** An extant part of an unfinished or lost text. —*v.* **fragmented, -menting, -ments.** —*tr.* To break or separate (something) into fragments. —*intr.* To break into pieces. [Middle English, from Latin *fragmentum,* from *frangere,* to break. See **bhreg-** in Appendix.*]

frag·men·tal (frăg-mĕnt′l) *adj.* **1.** Fragmentary. **2.** *Geology.* Consisting of broken material moved from its place of origin.

frag·men·tar·y (frăg′mən-tĕr′ē) *adj.* Consisting of fragments or disconnected parts; broken. —**frag′men·tar′i·ly** *adv.* —**frag′men·tar′i·ness** *n.*

frag·men·ta·tion (frăg′mən-tā′shən, frăg′mĕn-) *n.* **1.** The act or process of breaking into fragments. **2.** The scattering of the fragments of an exploding grenade, bomb, or shell; dispersion. —*adj.* Exploding into lethal fragments of high-velocity metal: *a fragmentation grenade.*

fragmentation bomb. An aerial antipersonnel bomb that scatters shrapnel over a wide area upon explosion.

frag·ment·ed (frăg′mən-tĭd) *adj.* Broken into fragments.

frag·ment·ize (frăg′mən-tīz′) *v.* **-ized, -izing, -izes.** —*tr.* To break (something) into fragments. —*intr.* To fragment.

Fra·go·nard (frȧ-gō-nȧr′), **Jean Honoré.** 1732–1806. French painter.

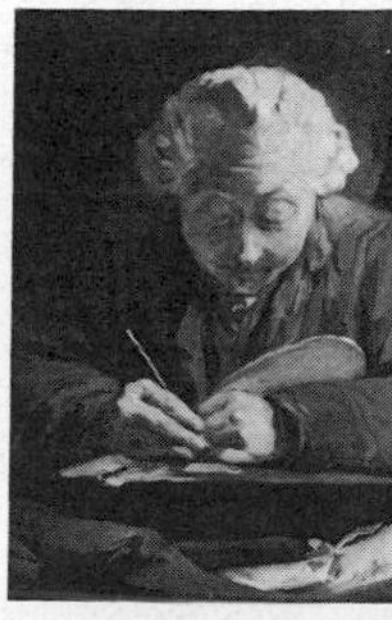
Jean Honoré Fragonard
A self-portrait

fra·grance (frā′grəns) *n.* **1.** The state or quality of being fragrant. **2.** A sweet or pleasant odor; scent. —See Synonyms at **smell.**

fra·grant (frā′grənt) *adj.* Having a pleasant odor; sweet-smelling. [Middle English, from Old French, from Latin *fragrāns,* present participle of *fragrāre,* to emit an odor (good or bad), to reek. See **bhrag-** in Appendix.*]

frail¹ (frāl) *adj.* **frailer, frailest.** **1.** Having a delicate constitution; physically weak; not robust. **2.** Slight; weak; not strong or substantial. **3.** Easily broken or destroyed; vulnerable; fragile; uncertain. **4.** Morally weak; easily led astray or into evil. —See Synonyms at **fragile, weak.** [Middle English *frele, frail,* from Old French *frele, fraile,* from Latin *fragilis,* FRAGILE.] —**frail′ly** *adv.* —**frail′ness** *n.*

frail² (frāl) *n.* **1.** A rush basket for holding fruit, especially dried fruit. **2.** The quantity of fruit, such as raisins or figs, contained in a frail, usually from 50 to 75 pounds. [Middle English *fraiel,* from Old French *fraiel*†.]

frail·ty (frāl′tē) *n., pl.* **-ties.** **1.** The condition or quality of being frail; weakness, especially of resolution. **2.** *Usually plural.* A fault arising from human weakness; failing: *human frailties.* —See Synonyms at **fault.**

fraise (frāz) *n.* **1.** A barrier or defense of pointed, inclined stakes or of barbed wire. **2.** A ruff for the neck worn in the 16th century. [French, "mesentery of a calf or lamb," originally "outer covering," "casing," from Old French *fraiser,* to remove the outer covering (used especially of beans), from Vulgar Latin *frēsāre* (unattested), from Latin *(faba) fresa,* ground (bean), from *frēsus,* past participle of *frendere,* to grind with the teeth. See **ghren-** in Appendix.*]

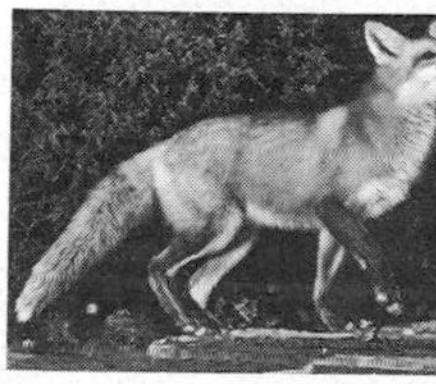
fox
Vulpes fulva
Red fox

frak·tur (fräk-to͝or′) *n.* A style of letter formerly used in German manuscripts and printing. [German *Fraktur,* from Latin *fractūra,* a breaking (from the curlicues which appear to break up the word), FRACTURE.]

fram·be·sia (frăm-bē′zhə) *n. Pathology.* **Yaws** *(see).* [New Latin, from French *framboise,* raspberry (from the appearance of the excrescences), from Old French, variant (influenced by *fraise,* strawberry) of Frankish *brām-besi* (unattested), "brambleberry." See **bhrem-**² in Appendix.*]

fram·boise (fräN-bwäz′) *n.* A French raspberry brandy. [French, "raspberry." See **frambesia.**]

frame (frām) *v.* **framed, framing, frames.** —*tr.* **1.** To construct by putting together the various parts of; to build. **2.** To formulate or conceive; to fashion; design; draw up. **3.** To arrange or adjust for a purpose; to phrase: *The question was framed to draw only one answer.* **4. a.** To put into words; compose: *frame a reply.* **b.** To form (words) silently with the lips. **5.** To provide with a frame; enclose or encircle. **6.** *Slang.* **a.** To rig evidence or events so as to incriminate (a person) falsely. **b.** To fix (a contest) so as to ensure a desired fraudulent outcome: *frame a prize fight.* —*intr.* **1.** *Archaic.* To resort; proceed. **2.** *Obsolete.* To manage or contrive to do something. —*n.* **1.** Something composed of parts fitted and joined together; a structure, such as: **a.** A basic or skeletal structure designed to give shape or support: *the frame of a house.* **b.** An open structure or rim for encasing, holding, or bordering something: *a window frame.* **c.** The human body. **d.** A **cold frame** *(see).* **2.** A machine built upon or utilizing a frame. **3.** The general structure of something; system; order: *the frame of government.* **4.** One of the transverse ribs of a ship's hull from the gunwale to the keel or the bilge, consisting of either a *square frame,* perpendicular to the keel's vertical plane, or a *cant frame,* at an oblique angle to it. **5.** *Billiards.* A rack. **6. a.** A round or period of play in some games, such as bowling or billiards. **b.** *Baseball.* An inning. **7.** A single exposure on a roll of motion picture film. **8.** The

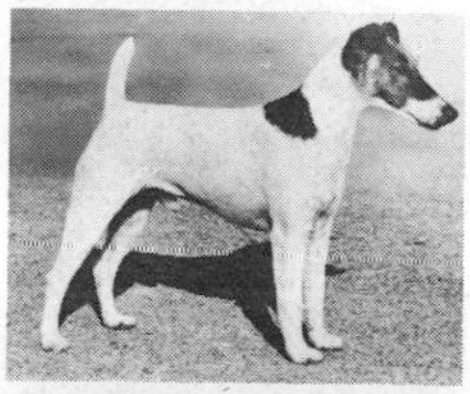
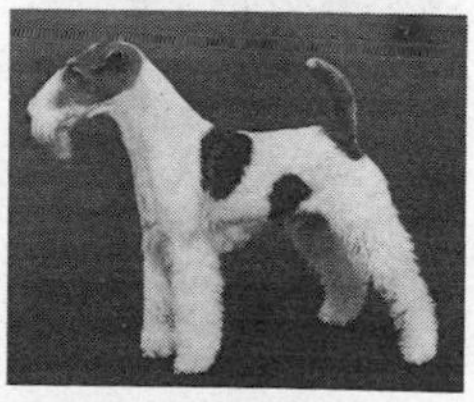
fox terrier
Above: Smooth-coated
Below: Wire-haired

ă tight/th thin, path/*th* this, bathe/ŭ cut/ûr urge/v valve/w with/y yes/z zebra, size/zh vision/ə about, item, edible, gallop, circus/ ȧ *Fr.* ami/œ *Fr.* feu, *Ger.* schön/ü *Fr.* tu, *Ger.* über/KH *Ger.* ich, *Scot.* loch/N *Fr.* bon. ***Follows main vocabulary.** **†Of obscure origin.**

Francisco Franco

total area of a television picture formed by a single traverse of the scanning spot. **9.** *Slang.* A frame-up. **10.** *Obsolete.* Shape; form. [Middle English *framen, framien,* be advantageous, benefit, form, construct, Old English *framian,* to benefit, avail. See **per**[1] in Appendix.*] —**fram′er** *n.*

frame house. A house constructed with a wooden framework, and covered usually with wood siding.

frame of mind. Mental state or attitude; mood.

frame of reference. 1. *Physics.* A set of coordinate axes in terms of which position or movement may be specified, or with reference to which physical laws may be mathematically stated. **2.** A set or system of ideas, as of philosophical or religious doctrine, in terms of which other ideas are interpreted or assigned meaning.

frame-up (frām′ŭp′) *n. Informal.* **1.** A prearranged or fraudulent scheme; a fix. **2.** A conspiracy to throw guilt on an innocent person; a scheme involving falsified charges or evidence.

frame·work (frām′wûrk′) *n.* **1.** A structure for supporting, defining, or enclosing something; especially, skeletal erections and supports used as the basis in something being constructed. **2.** Any outlying erection or work platform that allows access to something being constructed or worked on in some way; a rig; scaffolding. **3.** A basic arrangement, form, or system; a design: "*social structure is a stronger framework for behavior than national feeling.*" (Stanley Kauffman). **4.** The work of making frames or framework.

fram·ing (frā′mĭng) *n.* **1.** The act of one who frames. **2.** The act of providing with a framework. **3.** A frame, framework, or system of frames.

Fra·ming·ham (frā′mĭng-hăm). A city and manufacturing center of Massachusetts, southwest of Boston. Population, 45,000.

franc (frăngk) *n. Abbr.* **f., fr. 1. a.** The basic monetary unit of France, Belgium, Burundi, Cameroun, Central African Republic, Chad, Congo (Brazzaville), Dahomey, Gabon, Guinea, Ivory Coast, Luxembourg, Malagasy Republic, Mali, Mauritania, Niger, Rwanda, Senegal, Switzerland, Togo, Upper Volta, and of various overseas departments and territories of France. It is equal to 100 centimes. See table of exchange rates at **currency. b.** A coin worth one franc. **2.** A monetary unit equal to $\frac{1}{100}$ of the dirham of Morocco. See table of exchange rates at **currency.** [Middle English *frank,* from Old French *franc,* from the Latin legend *Francorum rex,* "king of the Franks," on gold coins struck during the reign of Jean le Bon (1350–64).]

France (frăns, fräns; *French* fräNs). *Abbr.* **Fr.** A republic of western Europe, 212,822 square miles in area, with coastlines on both the Atlantic Ocean and the Mediterranean Sea. Population, 48,700,000. Capital, Paris. [Middle English *Fraunce,* from Old French *France,* from Late Latin *Francia,* country of the Franks, from *Francus,* a FRANK.]

France (frăns, fräns; *French* fräNs), **Anatole.** Pen name of Jacques Anatole Thibault. 1844–1924. French novelist, poet, and critic.

Fran·ces (frăn′sĭs, frän′-). A feminine given name. [Old French *Franceise,* feminine of *Franceis,* FRANCIS.]

Fran·ce·sca, Piero della. See Piero della Francesca.

Fran·ce·sca da Ri·mi·ni (frän-chĕs′kə dä rĭm′ə-nē, frän-). Died 1285? Italian noblewoman; immortalized by Dante in the *Inferno.*

Franche-Com·té (fräNsh-kôN-tā′). A former region of eastern France, the object of invasion and conquest by several states until its cession to France by Spain (1678), after which it held provincial status until 1790.

fran·chise (frăn′chīz′) *n.* **1.** A privilege or right granted a person or a group by a government, state, or sovereign, especially: **a.** The constitutional or statutory right to vote; suffrage. **b.** The official establishment of a corporation's existence. **c.** The grant of certain rights and powers to a corporation. **d.** Formerly, legal immunity from certain burdens, servitude, or other restrictions. **2.** Authorization granted by a manufacturer to a distributor or dealer to sell his products. **3.** The territory or limits within which some privilege, right, or immunity may be exercised. **4.** The deductible feature of an insurance policy. —See Synonyms at **right.** —*tr.v.* **franchised, -chising, -chises.** To endow with a franchise; enfranchise. [Middle English *fraunchise,* freedom, privilege, from Old French *franchise,* from *franc* (feminine *franche*), free, FRANK.]

Fran·cis (frăn′sĭs, frän′-). A masculine given name. [Old French *Franceis,* from Medieval Latin *Franciscus,* a Frenchman, from Late Latin *Francia,* FRANCE.]

Fran·cis I (frăn′sĭs, frän′-). 1494–1547. King of France (1515–47).

Fran·cis II (frăn′sĭs, frän′-). 1768–1835. Last Holy Roman Emperor (1792–1806); abdicated; as Francis I, emperor of Austria (1804–35).

Fran·cis·can (frăn-sĭs′kən) *n.* A member of a religious mendicant order founded by Saint Francis of Assisi in 1209 and now divided into three independent branches. Often called "Gray Friar." —*adj.* Of or pertaining to Saint Francis of Assisi or to the order founded by him.

Fran·cis Jo·seph (frăn′sĭs, frän′-; jō′zəf, -səf). *German* **Franz Jo·sef** (fränts′ yō′zĕf). 1830–1916. Emperor of Austria (1848–1916) and king of Hungary (1867–1916).

Fran·cis of As·si·si (frăn′sĭs, frän′-; ə-sē′zē), **Saint.** 1182?–1226. Italian monk; founder of the Franciscan order.

Fran·cis of Sales (frăn′sĭs, frän′-; sälz), **Saint.** 1567–1622. French bishop and devotional author.

Fran·cis Xa·vi·er, Saint. See Saint Francis Xavier.

francolin
Francolinus clappertoni

fran·ci·um (frăn′sē-əm) *n. Symbol* **Fr** An extremely unstable radioactive metallic element, having approximately 19 isotopes, the most stable of which is Fr 223 with a half-life of 21 minutes. Atomic number 87, valence 1. See **element.** [New Latin, from FRANCE.]

Franck (frängk), **César Auguste.** 1822–1890. Belgian-born French composer.

Franck (frängk), **James.** 1882–1964. German-born American atomic physicist.

Fran·co (fräng′kō, frăng′-), **Francisco.** Born 1892. Chief of the Spanish state (since 1939).

Franco–. Indicates French; for example, **Francophile.** [From Medieval Latin *Francus,* a Frenchman, from Late Latin, a FRANK.]

fran·co·lin (frăng′kə-lĭn) *n.* Any of various Old World birds of the genus *Francolinus,* related to and resembling the quails and partridges. [French, from Italian *francolino*†.]

Fran·co·ni·a (frăng-kō′nē-ə, -kōn′yə). *German* **Fran·ken** (fräng′-kən). A former duchy of southern Germany, founded in the ninth century A.D., and now constituting three administrative districts of Bavaria.

Fran·co·phile (frăng′kə-fīl′) *n.* Also **Fran·co·phil** (-fĭl′). An admirer of France, its people, and its customs. —*adj.* Given to or expressing such admiration. [FRANCO- + -PHILE.]

Fran·co·phone (frăng′kə-fōn′) *adj.* French-speaking. —*n.* A French-speaking person. [FRANCO- + -PHONE.]

Fran·co-Prus·sian War (frăng′kō-prŭsh′ən). The war of 1870–71 between Prussia and France.

fran·gi·ble (frăn′jə-bəl) *adj.* Easily broken; breakable. [Middle English, from Old French, from Medieval Latin *frangibilis,* from Latin *frangere,* to break. See **bhreg-** in Appendix.*] —**fran′gi·bil′i·ty, fran′gi·ble·ness** *n.*

fran·gi·pan·i (frăn′jə-păn′ē, -pä′nē) *n.* Also **fran·gi·pane** (frăn′-jə-pān′). **1.** Any of various tropical American shrubs of the genus *Plumeria,* having milky juice and showy, fragrant, variously colored flowers. **2.** A perfume derived from or similar in scent to these flowers. **3.** A creamy pastry filling flavored with almonds. [French *frangipane,* from (*gants de*) *frangipane,* (gloves with) frangipani, after the Marquis *Frangipani* of Rome, who invented a perfume for scenting gloves in the 16th century.]

Fran·glais (fräN-glĕ′) *n. Slang.* French as used with numerous borrowings from English. [Blend of French *Français,* French, and *Anglais,* English.]

frank (frăngk) *adj.* **franker, frankest. 1.** Open and sincere in expression; straightforward. **2.** Clearly manifest; undisguised; evident: *frank enjoyment.* **3.** *Rare.* Liberal in giving; generous. **4.** *Obsolete.* Free; open. —*tr.v.* **franked, franking, franks. 1. a.** To put an official mark (on a piece of mail) so that it can be sent and delivered free of postage, through special official privilege. **b.** To send (mail) free of charge. **2.** To place a stamp or mark (on a piece of mail) to show the payment of postage. **3.** *Rare.* To enable (a person) to come and go easily; allow to go free of charge. —*n.* **1. a.** A mark or signature placed on a piece of mail to indicate the right to send it free of postage. **b.** The right to send mail free. **2.** A franked piece of mail. [Middle English, free, generous, from Old French *franc,* free, from Medieval Latin *francus,* from Late Latin *Francus,* FRANK (in Frankish Gaul full freedom was the right only of the conquering people or those under their protection).]

Synonyms: *frank, candid, outspoken, straightforward, open, ingenuous.* These adjectives mean disposed to reveal one's thoughts honestly and without reserve. *Frank* implies forthrightness of expression, sometimes to the point of bluntness. *Candid* stresses sincerity and honesty in the sense of refusing to evade issues or to distort one's true thought. *Outspoken* usually implies boldness of speech. *Straightforward* implies directness of manner and expression. *Open* suggests freedom from all trace of secretiveness, dissembling, or reserve in manner or countenance. *Ingenuous* likewise implies freedom from disguise or deceit, but can also suggest artlessness in the sense of naiveté.

Frank[1] (frăngk). A masculine given name. [Partly a pet form of FRANCIS and partly from Old French *Franc,* a FRANK.]

Frank[2] (frăngk) *n.* A member of one of the Germanic tribes of the Rhine region in the early Christian era; especially, one of the Salian Franks who conquered Gaul about 500 A.D. and established an extensive empire which reached its greatest power in the ninth century. [Middle English *Franc,* from Old English *Franca,* and Old French *Franc,* from Late Latin *Francus,* from Germanic. See **frankon-** in Appendix.*]

Fran·ken. The German name for Franconia.

Frank·en·stein monster (frăng′kən-stīn). Also **Frank·en·stein's monster** (-stīnz′). **1.** Any agency or creation that slips from the control of and ultimately destroys its creator. **2.** A monster having the appearance of a man; specifically, the monster created by the protagonist of Mary W. Shelley's novel *Frankenstein* (1818), which brought about the ruin of its creator. Also called "Frankenstein."

Frank·fort (frăngk′fərt). The capital of Kentucky, on the Kentucky River in the north-central part of the state. Population, 18,000.

Frank·furt am Main (frăngk′foŏrt′ äm mīn′). *English* **Frank·fort on the Main** (frăngk′fərt; män′). A river port and industrial center on the Main in Hesse, West Germany. Population, 692,000.

Frank·furt an der O·der (frăngk′foŏrt′ än dər ō′dər). *English* **Frank·fort on the O·der** (frăngk′fərt). A city and manufacturing center of East Germany, on the Oder, 50 miles east of Berlin. Population, 58,000.

frank·furt·er (frăngk′fər-tər) *n.* Also **frank·fort·er, frank·furt**

(frăngk′fərt), **frank·fort.** A smoked sausage of beef or beef and pork made in long, reddish links. [From FRANKFURT (AM MAIN).]

frank·in·cense (frăngk′ĭn-sĕns′) *n.* An aromatic gum resin obtained from African and Asian trees of the genus *Boswellia,* and used chiefly as incense. Also called "olibanum." [Middle English *frank encens,* from Old French *franc encens* : *franc,* free, superior, FRANK + *encens,* INCENSE.]

Frank·ish (frăng′kĭsh) *adj.* Of or pertaining to the Franks or their language. —*n.* The West Germanic language of the Franks.

Frank·land (frăngk′lənd), Sir **Edward.** 1825–1899. British chemist; worked on water pollution and chemical valence.

frank·lin (frăngk′lĭn) *n.* In England during the late medieval period, a freeholder of nonnoble birth but with extensive property; a country gentleman. [Middle English *frankelein,* from Medieval Latin *francālānus,* from *francālis,* (feudal estate) held without dues, from *francus,* free, FRANK.]

Frank·lin (frăngk′lĭn). **1.** The northernmost district of the Northwest Territories, Canada, with an area of 549,253 square miles and comprising Baffin Island, other Arctic islands, and Boothia and Melville peninsulas. Population, 23,000. **2.** A state formed in 1784 of three counties of North Carolina, restored to North Carolina in 1788, and now constituting part of eastern Tennessee.

Frank·lin (frăngk′lĭn), **Benjamin.** 1706–1790. American statesman, author, and scientist.

Frank·lin (frăngk′lĭn), Sir **John.** 1786–1847. British explorer of the Arctic.

frank·lin·ite (frăngk′lə-nīt′) *n.* A black, slightly magnetic mineral of zinc, iron, and manganese, that is a valuable source of zinc. [Found in *Franklin,* New Jersey.]

Franklin stove. A cast-iron stove shaped like a fireplace but employing metal baffles to increase its heating efficiency, invented by Benjamin Franklin.

frank·ly (frăngk′lē) *adv.* **1.** In a frank manner; openly; candidly. **2.** Speaking honestly; in truth: *Frankly, I don't care.*

frank·ness (frăngk′nĭs) *n.* Openness and directness of speech; straightforwardness; candor. See Synonyms at **truth.**

frank·pledge (frăngk′plĕj′) *n.* **1.** In old English law, a system in which units or tithings composed of ten households were formed, in each of which members were held responsible for one another's conduct. **2.** A member of such a group, bound in pledge for his neighbors. **3.** The tithing itself. [Middle English *fraunkiplegge,* from Norman French *frauncplege,* intended as a translation of Old English *frithborh* (unattested), "peace pledge," with *frith,* peace, misapprehended as meaning free : *franc,* FRANK + Old French *plege,* PLEDGE.]

Franks Peak (frăngks). The highest peak (13,140 feet) of the Absaroka Range of the Rocky Mountains in northwestern Wyoming.

fran·tic (frăn′tĭk) *adj.* **1.** Emotionally distraught, as from fear, pain, worry, or passion; desperate or exasperated; frenzied. **2.** *Archaic.* Mad; insane. [Middle English *frantik, frenetik,* FRENETIC.] —**fran′ti·cal·ly, fran′tic·ly** *adv.* —**fran′tic·ness** *n.*

Franz Jo·sef. See **Francis Joseph.**

Franz Jo·sef Land (frănts′ jō′səf lănd, jō′səf lănd′; *German* fränts′ yō′zĕf länt′). *Russian* **Zem·lya Fran·tsa Io·si·fa** (zĭm-lyä′ frän′tsə yô′sĭ-fə). An archipelago in the Arctic Ocean comprising about 85 islands with a combined area of some 8,000 square miles, and claimed by the Soviet Union in 1928. Also called "Fridtjof Nansen Land."

frap (frăp) *tr.v.* **frapped, frapping, fraps.** *Nautical.* **1.** To make secure by lashing: *frap a sail.* **2.** To tighten; take up the slack of. [Middle English *frapen,* to strike, from Old French *fraper,* possibly from Frankish *hrappan*† (unattested).]

frap·pé (fră-pā′, frăp) *n.* **1.** A frozen, fruit-flavored mixture similar to sherbet and served as a dessert or appetizer. **2.** A beverage, usually a liqueur, poured over shaved ice. **3.** A milk shake containing ice cream. [French, from the past participle of *frapper,* "to strike," chill, from Old French *fraper,* to strike. See **frap.**]

Fra·sca·ti (frä-skä′tē). A town in Italy about ten miles southeast of Rome; the site of the ruins of the villa of Cicero and other Roman structures.

Frasch (fräsh), **Herman.** 1851–1914. German-born American geological chemist.

Fra·ser (frā′zər). A river in British Columbia, Canada, rising in the Rocky Mountains and flowing 850 miles south and then west to the Strait of Georgia, south of Vancouver.

Fra·ser (frā′zər), **Simon.** 1776?–1862. American-born explorer and fur trader in western Canada.

frat (frăt) *n. Informal.* A college fraternity.

fra·ter (frā′tər) *n. Abbr.* **Fr.** A brother, as in a religious order or a fraternity. [Medieval Latin *frāter,* from Latin. See **bhrāter-** in Appendix.*]

fra·ter·nal (frə-tûr′nəl) *adj.* **1. a.** Of or pertaining to brothers. **b.** Brotherly. **2.** Pertaining to or constituting a fraternity. **3.** *Biology.* Of or pertaining to a twin or twins developed from separately fertilized ova. In this sense, compare **identical.** —See Synonyms at **familiar.** [Middle English, from Medieval Latin *frāternālis,* from Latin *frāternus,* from *frāter,* FRATER.] —**fra·ter′nal·ism′** *n.* —**fra·ter′nal·ly** *adv.*

fra·ter·ni·ty (frə-tûr′nə-tē) *n., pl.* **-ties. 1.** A body of men, such as a religious order or a guild, associated for some common purpose or interest. **2.** A group of men linked together by similar backgrounds, predilections, or occupations: *the fraternity of bird watchers.* **3.** A chiefly social organization of male college students, usually designated by Greek letters. Compare **sorority. 4.** The relationship of a brother or brothers; brotherhood. **5.** Brotherliness. —See Synonyms at **circle.** [Middle English *fraternite,* from Old French, from Latin *frāternitās,* from *frāternus,* FRATERNAL.]

frat·er·nize (frăt′ər-nīz′) *intr.v.* **-nized, -nizing, -nizes. 1.** To associate with others in a brotherly or congenial way. **2.** To mix intimately with the people of an enemy or conquered country, often in violation of military law. [French *fraterniser,* from Medieval Latin *frāternizāre,* from Latin *frāternus,* FRATERNAL.] —**frat′er·ni·za′tion** *n.* —**frat′er·niz′er** *n.*

frat·ri·cide (frăt′rə-sīd′) *n.* **1.** The killing of one's brother or sister. **2.** One who has killed one's brother or sister. [Middle English (sense 2 only), from Old French (both senses), from Latin *frātricīda* (the person) and *frātricīdium* (the act) : *frāter,* FRATER + -CIDE.] —**frat′ri·ci′dal** *adj.*

Frau (frou) *n., pl.* **Frauen** (frou′ən). *Abbr.* **Fr. 1.** A married woman in a German-speaking country or district. Used as a title corresponding to *Mrs.* **2.** *Slang.* **a.** One's wife. **b.** A housewife. [German *Frau,* from Middle High German *vrouwe,* from Old High German *frouwa.* See **per**[1] in Appendix.*]

fraud (frôd) *n.* **1.** A deception deliberately practiced in order to secure unfair or unlawful gain. **2.** A piece of trickery; a swindle. **3. a.** One who defrauds; a cheat. **b.** One who assumes a false pose; an impostor; a sham. [Middle English *fraude,* from Old French, from Latin *fraus*† (stem *fraud-*).]

fraud·u·lent (frô′jə-lənt) *adj.* **1.** Engaging in fraud; deceitful. **2.** Characterized by, constituting, or gained by fraud: *a fraudulent contract.* [Middle English, from Old French, from Latin *fraudulentus,* from *fraus,* FRAUD.] —**fraud′u·lence** *n.* —**fraud′u·lent·ly** *adv.*

Frau·en·burg (frou′ən-bŏŏrk′). *Polish* **From·bork** (frôm′bôrk). A town of former East Prussia, now in northern Poland; the home (1512–43) and burial place of Copernicus.

fraught (frôt) *adj.* **1.** Attended; accompanied: *an occasion fraught with peril.* **2.** Laden; freighted: "*A work so full with various learning fraught*" (Dryden). —*n. Obsolete.* Freight; cargo. [Middle English, past participle of *fraughten,* to load a ship, from Middle Dutch *vrachten,* from *vracht,* freight. See **eik-** in Appendix.*]

Fräu·lein (froi′līn′, frou′-) *n., pl.* **Fräulein.** *Abbr.* **Frl. 1.** An unmarried girl or woman in a German-speaking country or district. Used as a title corresponding to *Miss.* **2.** *Chiefly British.* A German governess. [German, from Middle High German *vrouwet,* diminutive of *vrouwe,* wife, FRAU.]

Fraun·ho·fer (froun′hō′fər), **Joseph von.** 1787–1826. German physicist and astronomer.

Fraunhofer lines. A set of several hundred dark lines appearing against the bright background of the continuous solar spectrum, produced by absorption of light by the cooler gases in the sun's outer atmosphere at frequencies corresponding to the atomic transition frequencies of these gases. [After J. FRAUNHOFER.]

frax·i·nel·la (frăk′sə-nĕl′ə) *n.* The **gas plant** *(see).* [New Latin, diminutive from Latin *fraxinus,* ash (from the resemblance of its leaves to those of the ash). See **bherəg-** in Appendix.*]

fray[1] (frā) *n.* **1.** A fight; a scuffle; a brawl. **2.** A heated dispute or contest. —*v.* **frayed, fraying, frays.** *Obsolete.* —*tr.* **1.** To alarm; frighten. **2.** To drive away. —*intr.* To fight. [Middle English, fright, commotion, conflict, from *fraien,* to frighten, short for *afraien, affraien,* from Old French *affreer,* to AFFRAY.]

fray[2] (frā) *v.* **frayed, fraying, frays.** —*tr.* **1.** To unravel, wear away, or tatter (the edges of fabric, for example) by rubbing. **2.** To strain; chafe: *nerves frayed by noise.* —*intr.* To become tattered, unraveled, or threadbare along the edges. —*n.* A raveled, ragged, or threadbare spot caused by friction. [Middle English *fraien,* from Old French *fraier,* from Latin *fricāre,* to rub. See **bhrēi-** in Appendix.*]

Fra·zer (frā′zər), Sir **James George.** 1854–1941. British anthropologist; author of *The Golden Bough.*

fraz·zle (frăz′əl) *v.* **-zled, -zling, -zles.** *Informal.* —*tr.* **1.** To fray; chafe. **2.** To wear out the nerves of. —*intr.* To become frazzled or worn out. —*n.* **1.** A frayed or tattered condition. **2.** A condition of nervous exhaustion. [Probably a blend of FRAY (wear) and dialectal *fazzle,* to fray, from Middle English *faselen,* from *fasel,* fringe, frayed edge, diminutive of *fas,* fringe, Old English *fæs,* from Germanic *fas-* (unattested).]

F.R.B. Federal Reserve Board.

F.R.C.P. Fellow of the Royal College of Physicians.

F.R.C.S. Fellow of the Royal College of Surgeons.

freak[1] (frēk) *n.* **1.** A thing or an occurrence that is very unusual or irregular. **2.** An abnormally formed organism; especially, a person or animal regarded as a curiosity or a monstrosity. **3.** A sudden capricious turn of the mind; whim; vagary: "*The freaks of the psyche can no more be explained than the Devil.*" (Maurice Collis). **4.** *Archaic.* A prank: "*the children of the settlement . . . scaring one another with freaks of imitative witchcraft.*" (Hawthorne). —See Synonyms at **caprice.** [Origin obscure.]

freak[2] (frēk) *n.* A fleck or streak of color. —*tr.v.* **freaked, freaking, freaks.** To speckle or streak with color: "*The white pink, and the pansy freaked with jet*" (Milton). [Originally *freaked,* probably formed by Milton, probably variant (influenced by STREAK) of obsolete *freckt,* from FRECKLE.]

freak·ish (frē′kĭsh) *adj.* **1.** Unusual; outlandish; abnormal. **2.** Pertaining to or characteristic of a freak. **3.** Capricious. —**freak′ish·ly** *adv.* —**freak′ish·ness** *n.*

freak·y (frē′kē) *adj.* **-ier, -iest.** Freakish. —**freak′i·ly** *adv.* —**freak′i·ness** *n.*

freck·le (frĕk′əl) *n.* A small precipitation of pigment in the skin, often brought out by the sun. —*v.* **freckled, -ling, -les.** —*tr.* To

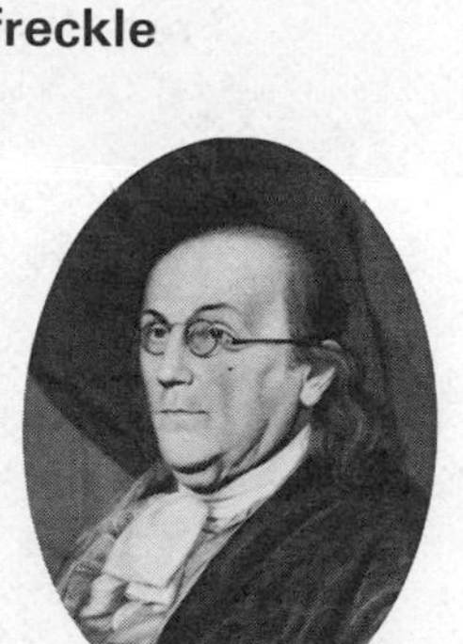

Benjamin Franklin
Contemporary portrait by
Charles Willson Peale

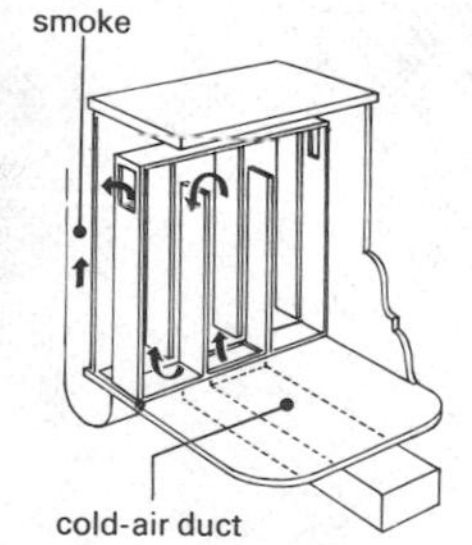

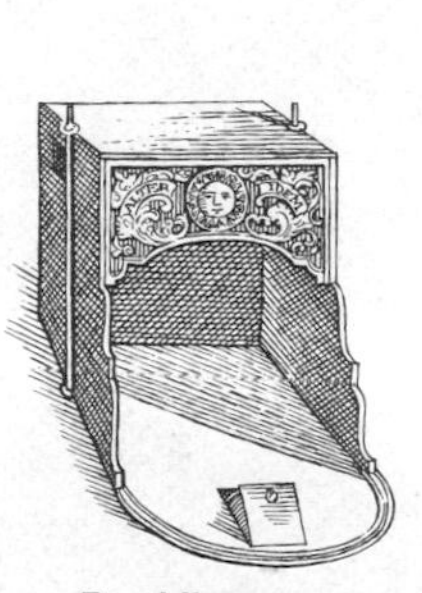

Franklin stove
Above: Diagram
Below: Franklin's design

dot with freckles or spots of color. —*intr.* To become dotted with freckles. [Middle English *frakles* (plural), variant of *fraknes*, from Old Norse *freknur* (plural). See **sphereg-** in Appendix.*] —**freck′ly** *adj.*

Fred·er·i·ca (frĕ-drē′kə). A feminine given name. [French *Frédérica*, feminine of *Frédéric*, FREDERICK.]

Fred·er·ick (frĕd′rĭk). A masculine given name. [French *Frédéric*, from German *Friedrich*, from Old High German *Fridurīh*, "peaceful ruler." See **prī-** in Appendix.*]

Fred·er·ick I (frĕd′rĭk). Called "Barbarossa." 1123?–1190. Holy Roman Emperor (1152–90); king of Germany (1152–90); king of Italy (1155–90).

Fred·er·ick II[1] (frĕd′rĭk). 1194–1250. Holy Roman Emperor (1215–50); king of Sicily (as Frederick I, 1198–1250); attempted to found Mediterranean empire.

Fred·er·ick II[2] (frĕd′rĭk). Called "the Great." 1712–1786. King of Prussia (1740–86); patron of artists and philosophers.

Fred·er·ick IX (frĕd′rĭk). Born 1899. King of Denmark (since 1947).

Fred·er·icks·burg (frĕd′rĭks-bûrg′). A city in northeastern Virginia; the site of the Civil War battle (1862) in which Lee's Confederate forces repulsed the Union forces under Burnside. Population, 14,000.

Fred·er·ick Wil·liam (frĕd′rĭk wĭl′yəm). 1620–1688. Elector of Brandenburg (1640–88).

Fred·er·ic·ton (frĕd′rĭk-tən). The capital of New Brunswick, Canada, in the southwestern part of the province. Population, 20,000.

Fred·er·iks·berg (frĕd′rĭks-bûrg′; *Danish* frĕth′ə-rĕks-bĕrk′). A city of Denmark, on Sjaelland, just east of Copenhagen, of which it is the principal suburb. Population, 114,000.

free (frē) *adj.* **freer, freest. 1.** At liberty; not bound or constrained. **2.** Discharged from arrest or detention. **3.** Not under obligation or necessity. **4. a.** Politically independent. Said of a country or nation. **b.** Governed by consent and possessing civil liberties: *a free society.* **c.** Immune to arbitrary interference by government or others: *a free press.* **5. a.** Not affected or restricted by a given condition or circumstance. Used with *from* or *of: free from need; free of avarice.* **b.** Not subject to a given condition; exempt. Often used in combination: *duty-free; graft-free.* **6.** Not subject to external restraint: *"Comment is free but facts are sacred."* (Charles Prestwich Scott). **7.** Not literal: *a free translation.* **8. a.** Costing nothing; gratuitous: *a free pass.* **b.** Publicly supported: *free education.* **c.** Not paying the usual fee: *a free patient.* **9. a.** Unoccupied; available for use: *a free shelf.* **b.** Unobstructed; clear: *a free lane.* **10.** Guileless; frank: *"The Moor is of a free and open nature."* (Shakespeare). **11.** Taking undue liberties; forward. **12.** Liberal or lavish: *free with his money.* **13.** Uninhibited; racy: *much free talking and jesting at the party.* **14.** Uncommitted; independent. **15.** *Chemistry & Physics.* **a.** Unconstrained; unconfined: *free expansion.* **b.** Not fixed in position; capable of relatively unrestricted motion: *a free electron.* **c.** Not chemically bound in a molecule: *free oxygen.* **d.** Involving no collisions or interactions: *a free path.* **e.** Empty: *a free space.* **f.** Unoccupied: *a free level.* **16.** *Nautical.* Favorable. Said of a wind. **17.** *Phonetics.* Designating a vowel in an open syllable, unchecked by a consonant; for example, *o* in *go* is a free vowel. —*adv.* **1.** In a free manner; freely. **2.** Without charge. —**make free with.** To take liberties with. —**run free.** *Nautical.* To sail with the wind aft. —**sail free.** *Nautical.* To sail with the wind more than six points off dead ahead and the sails and boom let out. —*tr.v.* **freed, freeing, frees. 1.** To set at liberty. **2.** To rid or release. Used with *of* or *from: a people freed from fear.* **3.** To disengage; untangle: *free a rope.* [Middle English *fre(e)*, Old English *frēo*. See **prī-** in Appendix.*] —**free′ly** *adv.* —**free′ness** *n.*

free alongside ship. *Abbr.* **f.a.s., F.A.S.** Delivered to the pier at no extra charge. Said of cargo going by sea. Also "free alongside vessel."

free and clear. Not mortgaged or otherwise encumbered.

free association. 1. A spontaneous, logically unconstrained association of ideas and feelings. **2.** A psychoanalytic technique in which a patient's articulation of such associations is encouraged in order to elicit repressed thoughts and emotions.

free·board (frē′bôrd′, -bōrd′) *n. Nautical.* **1.** The distance between the water line and the uppermost full deck. **2.** The distance between the ground and the undercarriage of an automobile.

freeboard deck. The uppermost deck that is officially considered completely watertight.

free·boot (frē′bōōt′) *intr.v.* **-booted, -booting, -boots.** To act as a freebooter; to plunder.

free·boot·er (frē′bōō′tər) *n.* A person who pillages and plunders; especially, a pirate; buccaneer. [Partial translation of Dutch *vrijbuiter*, from *vrijbuit*, free booty : *vrij*, free + *buit*, booty, from *buiten*, to plunder, from Middle Dutch *būten*, from Middle Low German, to exchange, from *būte*, exchange (see **booty**).]

free·born (frē′bôrn′) *adj.* **1.** Born as a free man. **2.** Pertaining to or befitting a person born free.

free capital. 1. Capital available for investment. **2.** Capital not earmarked for a specific use.

free city. 1. A sovereign city-state, such as those established in Germany and Italy in the Middle Ages. **2.** A city governed as an autonomous political unit under international auspices.

free coinage. Coinage by a government mint of any specified bullion brought to it by a person, with or without charge.

free companion. A mercenary of the Middle Ages.

free company. A company of free companions.

freed·man (frĕd′mən) *n., pl.* **-men** (-mĭn). A man who has been freed from bondage; an emancipated slave.

free·dom (frē′dəm) *n.* **1.** The condition of being free of restraints. **2.** Liberty of the person from slavery, oppression, or incarceration. **3. a.** Political independence. **b.** Possession of civil rights; immunity from the arbitrary exercise of authority. **4.** Exemption from unpleasant or onerous conditions. Used with *from: "the poorer man's leisure demonstrated his freedom from long hours of hard work"* (Rueul Denney). **5.** The capacity to exercise choice; free will: *"The only freedom which deserves the name, is that of pursuing our own good in our own way."* (John Stuart Mill). **6.** Facility, as of motion. **7.** Originality of style or conception. **8.** Frankness. **9. a.** Boldness; impertinence. **b.** An instance of improper boldness; a liberty. **10.** Unrestricted use or access. **11.** The right of enjoying all of the privileges of membership or citizenship: *the freedom of the city.* [Middle English *fredom*, Old English *frēodōm* : *frēo*, FREE + -DOM.]

Synonyms: *freedom, liberty, license.* These nouns refer to the power to act, speak, or think without the imposition of restraint. *Freedom* is the most general term and preferable when total absence of restraint or lack of restraint in general is meant. *Liberty* applies especially to individual rights defined by law, and thus suggests absence of specific restrictions. However, *freedom* is sometimes also used in the narrower sense associated with individual rights. *License* in one sense denotes abuse of freedom; in another it refers to exemption from prevailing rules, granted in special cases.

freedom of the seas. *International Law.* **1.** The doctrine that ships of any nation may travel through international waters unhampered. **2.** The right of neutral shipping in wartime to trade at will except where blockades are established.

free electron. An electron that is not bound to an atom; especially, an electron in a conductor that is available to move in a current.

free energy. 1. A thermodynamic quantity that is the difference between the internal energy and the product of the absolute temperature and entropy of a system. Also called "Helmholtz free energy." **2.** A thermodynamic quantity that is the difference between the enthalpy and the product of the absolute temperature and entropy of a system. In this sense, also called "Gibbs free energy."

free enterprise. The freedom of private businesses to operate competitively for profit, with minimal government regulation.

free fall. 1. The fall of a body within the atmosphere without a drag-producing device such as a parachute. **2.** The unconstrained motion of a body in a gravitational field.

free flight. Flight, as of an aircraft or spacecraft, after termination of powered flight.

free-for-all (frē′fər-ôl′) *n.* A brawl, argument, or competition in which one and all take part.

free form. *Linguistics.* A morpheme capable of standing alone and retaining meaning. Compare **bound form.**

free-form (frē′fôrm′) *adj.* Designating a usually flowing asymmetrical shape or outline free of formal conventions.

free gold. Gold maintained by the U.S. Treasury in excess of the amount required to redeem gold certificates.

free hand. Full liberty to do or decide as one sees fit.

free-hand (frē′hănd′) *adj.* Drawn by hand without the aid of tracing or drafting devices: *a freehand sketch.* —*adv.* By hand, without mechanical aids.

free-hand·ed (frē′hăn′dĭd) *adj.* Openhanded; generous; unstinting. —**free′hand′ed·ly** *adv.* —**free′hand′ed·ness** *n.*

free-heart·ed (frē′här′tĭd) *adj.* Unreserved; open; generous; liberal. —**free′heart′ed·ly** *adv.* —**free′heart′ed·ness** *n.*

free·hold (frē′hōld′) *n.* **1.** *Law.* **a.** An estate held in fee or for life. **b.** The tenure by which such an estate is held. **2.** A tenure of an office or a dignity for life. —*adj.* Of the nature of a freehold. [Middle English *frehold* (translation of Norman French *fraunc tenement*, "free or frank holding") : FREE + HOLD.] —**free′hold′er** *n.*

free lance. 1. A person, especially a writer or an artist, who sells his services to employers without a long-term commitment to any one of them. Also called "free-lancer." **2.** One who remains uncommitted to a party and proceeds as an independent. **3.** A medieval mercenary; a free companion.

free-lance (frē′lăns′, -läns′) *v.* **-lanced, -lancing, -lances.** —*intr.* To work as a free lance. —*tr.* To produce and sell as a free lance. —*adj.* Pertaining to or produced by a free lance.

free-liv·ing (frē′lĭv′ĭng) *adj.* **1.** Given to self-indulgence. **2.** *Biology.* Living or moving independently; not part of a parasitic or symbiotic relationship.

free·load (frē′lōd′) *intr.v.* **-loaded, -loading, -loads.** *Slang.* To act as a freeloader; to sponge.

free·load·er (frē′lō′dər) *n. Slang.* One who lives habitually on the charity, generosity, or hospitality of others.

free love. Belief in or practice of sexual relations without marriage and without formal obligations.

free·man (frē′mən) *n., pl.* **-men** (-mĭn). **1.** A person not in slavery or serfdom. **2.** One who possesses the rights or privileges of a citizen.

free·mar·tin (frē′märt′n) *n.* A sterile or otherwise sexually deficient female calf born as the twin of a bull calf. [Origin unknown.]

free·ma·son (frē′mā′sən) *n.* **1.** A member of a guild of skilled, itinerant masons of the Middle Ages. **2.** *Capital* F. A member of the Free and Accepted Masons, an international secret fraternity. In this sense, also called "Mason."

free·ma·son·ry (frē′mā′sən-rē) *n.* **1.** Tacit fellowship and sympathy among a number of people. **2.** *Capital* **F.** **a.** The institutions, precepts, and rites of the Freemasons. **b.** The Freemasons. In this sense, also called "Masonry."

free on board. *Abbr.* **f.o.b., F.O.B.** Delivered on board or into a carrier without charge.

free port. **1.** A port open on equal terms to all commercial vessels. **2.** An area in which imported goods can be held or processed before re-export, free of customs duties.

fre·er[1] (frē′ər) *n.* One who frees.

fre·er[2]. Comparative of **free.**

free radical. An atom or group of atoms having at least one unpaired electron.

free·si·a (frē′zhē-ə, -zhə, -zē-ə) *n.* Any of several plants of the genus *Freesia,* native to southern Africa, having one-sided clusters of fragrant, variously colored flowers. [New Latin, after Friedrich H.T. *Freese* (died 1876), German physician.]

free silver. The free coinage of silver, especially at a fixed ratio to gold.

free soil. U.S. territory in which slavery was prohibited.

free-soil (frē′soil′) *adj.* **1.** Prohibiting slavery: *free-soil states.* **2.** Opposing the extension of slavery prior to the Civil War. **3.** *Capital* **F,** *capital* **S.** Pertaining to or designating a U.S. political party founded in 1848 to oppose the extension of slavery into U.S. Territories and the admission of slave states into the Union.

free-spo·ken (frē′spō′kən) *adj.* Candid in expression; outspoken; frank. **—free′-spo′ken·ness** *n.*

fre·est. Superlative of **free.**

free·stand·ing (frē′stăn′dĭng) *adj.* Standing independently; free of support or attachment.

Free State. **1.** A state prohibiting slavery, prior to the Civil War. **2.** The Irish Free State.

free·stone (frē′stōn′) *n.* **1.** A stone, such as sandstone or limestone, soft enough to be cut easily without shattering or splitting. **2.** A fruit, especially a peach, having a stone that does not adhere to the pulp. In this sense, compare **clingstone.** *—adj.* Having a stone that does not adhere to the pulp.

free-swim·ming (frē′swĭm′ĭng) *adj. Zoology.* Able to swim freely; not sessile or attached: *the free-swimming larva of the oyster.* **—free′-swim′mer** *n.*

free·think·er (frē′thĭng′kər) *n.* One who has rejected authority and dogma, especially in his religious thinking, in favor of rational inquiry and speculation. **—free′think′ing** *adj.* & *n.*

free thought. Freethinking; unorthodox thought.

free throw. *Basketball.* A **foul shot** *(see).*

free-throw line (frē′thrō′). *Basketball.* The **foul line** *(see).*

Free·town (frē′toun′). A seaport and the capital of Sierra Leone, in the west on the Atlantic Ocean. Population, 128,000.

free trade. Trade between nations or states without protective customs tariffs.

free verse. Verse that does not follow a conventional metrical or stanzaic pattern and has either an irregular rhyme or no rhyme. [Translation of French *vers libre.*]

free·way (frē′wā′) *n.* **1.** A highway having several lanes and no intersections or stoplights; expressway. **2.** A highway without tolls.

free wheel. **1.** An automotive transmission device that allows the drive shaft to continue turning when its speed is greater than that of the engine shaft. **2.** A device in the rear-wheel hub of a bicycle that permits the wheel to turn without pedal action, as in coasting. **—free′-wheel′** *adj.*

free·wheel·ing (frē′hwē′lĭng) *n.* A free-wheel mechanism. *—adj.* **1.** Pertaining to or equipped with free wheel. **2.** *Informal.* **a.** Free of restraints or rules in organization, methods, or procedure. **b.** Heedless; carefree.

free will. **1.** The power or discretion to choose; free choice. **2.** The belief that man's choices ultimately are or can be voluntary, and not determined by external causes. [Translation of Late Latin *liberum arbitrium.*]

free·will (frē′wĭl′) *adj.* Done of one's own accord; voluntary.

freeze (frēz) *v.* **froze** (frōz), **frozen** (frō′zən), **freezing, freezes.** *—intr.* **1. a.** To pass from the liquid to the solid state by loss of heat. **b.** To acquire a surface of ice from cold. Often used with *over.* **2.** To become inoperative due to frost or the formation of ice: *The pipes froze.* **3.** To become stiff from cold, as laundry or the ground. **4.** To turn rigid and inflexible; solidify: *"the legitimate defense of the new soon froze into dogma."* (Wayne C. Booth). **5. a.** To be at that degree of temperature at which ice forms. Used impersonally: *It may freeze tonight.* **b.** To be uncomfortably cold. Used impersonally: *It's freezing in here.* **6.** To be harmed, ruined, or killed by cold or frost: *The crops froze.* **7.** To feel the cold acutely: *I'm freezing.* **8.** To become fixed, stuck, or attached by or as if by frost: *The bolt had frozen in place.* **9.** To become paralyzed from fear, horror, or shyness. **10.** To become icily silent in manner. Often used with *up: She froze up at the rebuke.* *—tr.* **1. a.** To convert into ice. **b.** To cause ice to form upon. **c.** To cause to congeal or stiffen from extreme cold. **2.** To preserve by subjecting to freezing temperatures. **3.** To damage, kill, or make inoperative by cold or by the formation of ice. **4. a.** To make very cold; to chill. **b.** To chill with an icy or formal manner. **5.** To make rigid and inflexible: *"they freeze the English language to death"* (Kenneth Koch). **6.** To fix (prices or wages) at a given or current level. **7.** To prohibit further manufacture or use of. **8.** To prevent or restrict the exchange, liquidation, or granting of by law: *The banks have agreed to freeze investment loans.* **9.** *Surgery.* To anesthetize by freezing. **—freeze in one's tracks.** To stop short and remain motionless, as with fear. **—freeze onto.** *Slang.* To seize and hold tenaciously. **—freeze out.** *Informal.* To shut out or bar, as from a business or a social group, by boycotting, snubbing, or cold treatment. *—n.* **1. a.** An act of freezing. **b.** The state of being frozen. **2.** *Informal.* A refrigerator. **3.** A spell of cold weather; frost. [Freeze, froze, frozen; Middle English *fresen, frose, frosen,* variant (influenced by present tense) of *froren,* Old English *frēosan, frēas, froren.* See **preus-** in Appendix.*]

freeze-dry (frēz′drī′) *tr.v.* **-dried, -drying, -dries.** To preserve by freeze-drying.

freeze-dry·ing (frēz′drī′ĭng) *n.* Preservation, as of foodstuffs, by rapid freezing and drying in a high vacuum.

freez·er (frē′zər) *n.* One that freezes; especially, a thermally insulated cabinet or room that maintains a subfreezing temperature for the rapid freezing and storing of perishable food.

freeze-up (frēz′ŭp′) *n. Informal.* The freezing over of lakes and rivers.

freezing point. *Abbr.* **fp** **1.** The temperature at which a liquid of specified composition solidifies under a specified pressure. **2.** The temperature at which the liquid and solid phases of a substance of specified composition are in equilibrium at atmospheric pressure.

free zone. An area at a port or city where goods may be received and held without the payment of duty.

F region. A region of the ionosphere, the **F layer** *(see).*

Frei·burg (frī′bo͝ork′). **1.** Also **Frei·burg im Breis·gau** (ĭm brīs′gou′). A manufacturing and tourist center of West Germany, in the southwest near the Black Forest. Population, 150,000. **2.** The German name for **Fribourg.**

freight (frāt) *n. Abbr.* **frt.** **1. a.** Goods carried by a vessel or vehicle; lading. **b.** Goods transported as cargo by a commercial carrier, as distinguished from baggage, mail, and express. **2.** A charge or burden. **3.** The commercial transportation of goods. **4.** The charge for transporting goods by cargo carrier. **5.** A railway train carrying goods only. *—tr.v.* **freighted, freighting, freights.** **1.** To convey commercially as cargo. **2.** To load with goods to be transported. **3.** To load; charge; impregnate. [Middle English *fraught, freight,* from Middle Dutch *vrecht, vracht,* cargo, fee for a transport vessel. See **eik-** in Appendix.*]

freight·age (frā′tĭj) *n.* **1.** The commercial transportation of goods. **2.** The charge for such transportation. **3.** Cargo.

freight car. A railway car designed for carrying freight.

freight·er (frā′tər) *n.* **1.** A vehicle, especially a ship, for carrying freight. **2.** A shipper of cargo.

freight train. A railroad train made up of freight cars.

Fre·man·tle (frē-mănt′l). The principal seaport of Western Australia, on the Indian Ocean about 10 miles southwest of Perth. Population, 24,000.

frem·i·tus (frĕm′ə-təs) *n., pl.* **fremitus.** *Pathology.* A palpable vibration, as felt by the hand placed on the chest during coughing or speaking. [Latin, noise, roar, from the past participle of *fremere,* to roar. See **bhrem-**[1] in Appendix.*]

Fré·mont (frē′mŏnt), **John Charles.** 1813–1890. American military leader in the Mexican War; explorer of the Far West; Presidential candidate (1856).

french (frĕnch) *tr.v.* **frenched, frenching, frenches.** Also **French.** **1.** To cut into thin strips before cooking. **2.** To trim fat or bone from (a chop, for example). [This method was originally a French one.]

French (frĕnch) *adj. Abbr.* **F., Fr.** Of, pertaining to, or characteristic of France or its people, language, or culture. *—n. Abbr.* **F., Fr.** **1.** The Romance language spoken by the people of France, western Switzerland, and southern Belgium, and in various former French possessions. **2.** The people of France. Preceded by *the.* Used with a plural verb. [Middle English *french,* Old English *frencisc.* See **frankon-** in Appendix.*]

French (frĕnch), **Daniel Chester.** 1850–1931. American sculptor.

French Academy. *French* **A·ca·dé·mie Fran·çaise** (ȧ-kȧ-dā-mē′ fräN-sĕz′). An association of 40 scholars, writers, and intellectual leaders founded in 1635 to maintain the purity of the French language and establish standards of correct usage.

French and Indian War. A war (1754–63) fought in North America between England and France, who had the support of Indian allies.

French bread. Bread made with water, flour, and yeast and baked in long, slim, crusty loaves.

French Broad River. A river flowing 204 miles from western North Carolina to the Tennessee River at Knoxville, Tennessee.

French bulldog. A small compact dog of a breed developed in France from toy English bulldogs and native breeds.

French-Ca·na·di·an (frĕnch′kə-nā′dē-ən) *n.* Also **French Canadian.** **1.** A Canadian of French descent. **2.** *Rare.* The French language as spoken in Canada. **—French′-Ca·na′di·an** *adj.*

French chalk. Chalk made of a soft, white variety of talc, used by tailors for marking fabrics, and by dry cleaners for removing grease spots.

French chop. A rib chop with the meat and fat trimmed from the end of the rib.

French Community. An association of the Republic of France with six former French colonies, now the independent states of Chad, Central African Republic, Republic of Congo (Brazzaville), Gabon, Malagasy, and Senegal.

French cuff. A wide cuff that is folded back and fastened with a cuff link.

French curve. A flat drafting instrument, usually of celluloid, with curved edges and scroll-shaped cutouts, used as a guide in connecting a set of individual points with a smooth curve.

French door. A door of light construction with glass panes often extending the full length, and usually hung in pairs.

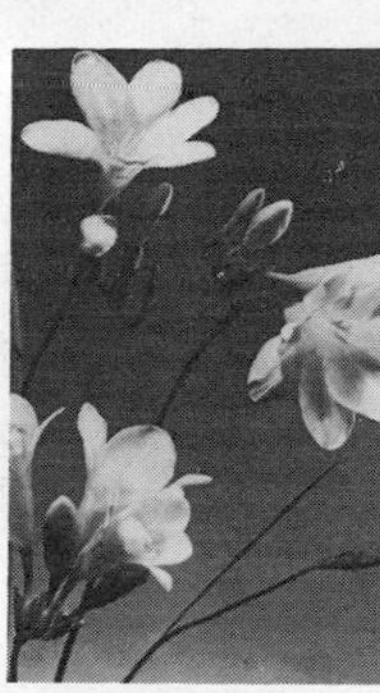

freesia
Freesia hybrida

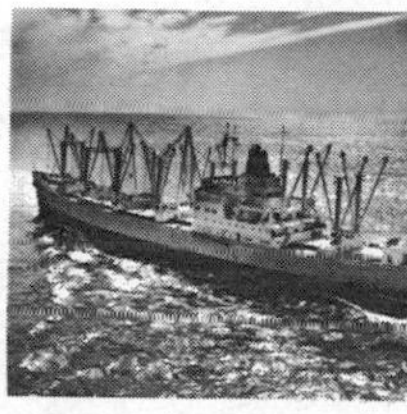

freighter

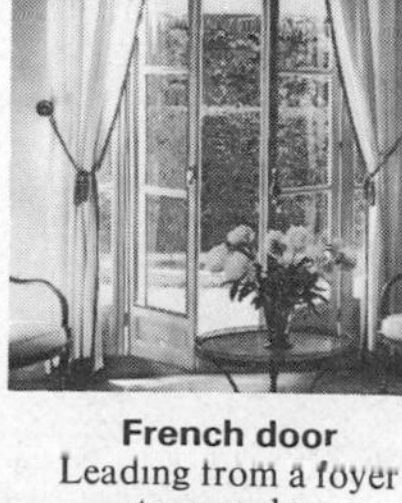

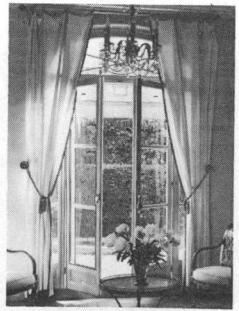

French door
Leading from a foyer to a garden

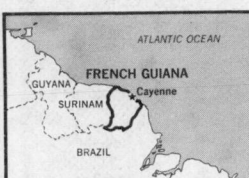

French Guiana

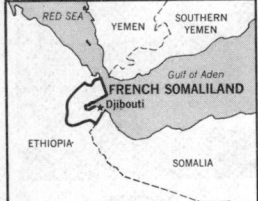

French Somaliland

French dressing. A seasoned oil and vinegar salad dressing.

French Equatorial Af·ri·ca (ăf′rĭ-kə). A former administrative unit in western and north-central Africa, created by France in 1910 and comprising Gabon, Middle Congo, Ubangi-Shari, and Chad until its dissolution in 1958.

French fries. Thin strips of potatoes fried in deep fat.

French fry. To fry (potato strips, onion rings, or the like) in deep fat.

French Gui·an·a (gē-ăn′ə, -ä′nə). *French* **Guy·ane Fran·çaise** (gwē-yàn′ frän-sĕz′). An Overseas Department of France, occupying 35,135 square miles in northern South America between Surinam and Brazil. Population, 34,000. Capital, Cayenne.

French Guin·ea. The former name for **Guinea.**

French harp. *Informal.* A mouth organ; harmonica.

French heel. A curved moderately high heel used on women's shoes.

French horn. A valved brass wind instrument with a circular shape, tapering from a narrow mouthpiece to a flaring bell at the other end, and producing a mellow tone.

French ice cream. An ice cream rich in egg yolks and cream.

French·i·fy (frĕn′chə-fī′) *v.* **-fied, -fying, -fies.** —*tr.* To give a French character or quality to. —*intr.* To assume French ways or characteristics.

French In·di·a (ĭn′dē-ə). A former Overseas Territory of France in India, including the settlements of Chandernagore, Pondicherry (the capital), and Yanaon on the east coast, and Mahé on the west, with a combined area of 193 square miles. The territory was returned to India (1949–54).

French In·do·chi·na. The former name for **Indochina.**

French kiss. *Slang.* A kiss in which the tongue enters the partner's mouth.

French knot. A decorative stitch made by looping the thread two or more times around the needle which is then inserted into the fabric.

French leave. An informal, unannounced, or abrupt departure. [From the 18th-century French custom of leaving without bidding good-by to the host or hostess.]

French·man (frĕnch′mən) *n., pl.* **-men** (-mĭn). **1.** A native or citizen of France. **2.** A French ship.

French marigold. A widely cultivated plant, *Tagetes patula,* native to Mexico, having divided leaves and yellow flowers with reddish markings.

French Mo·roc·co (mə-rŏk′ō). A former French protectorate established over most of the area of present-day Morocco in 1912, and now part of the Kingdom of Morocco.

French mulberry. A species of **beautyberry** (*see*).

French North Af·ri·ca (ăf′rĭ-kə). A term formerly used to designate Algeria, French Morocco, and Tunisia collectively.

French omelet. An omelet prepared in a slant-sided pan, consisting of lightly beaten eggs stirred gently until set, and often having any of a variety of fillings.

French pastry. Any of a wide variety of rich and elaborate pastries prepared in individual portions.

French Pol·y·ne·sia (pŏl′ə-nē′zhə, -shə). Formerly **French Settlements in O·ce·an·i·a** (ō′shē-ăn′ē-ə), **French O·ce·an·i·a.** An Overseas Territory of France in the South Pacific Ocean, including the Society, Tubuai, Rapa, Tuamotu, and Marquesas islands. Population, 85,000. Capital, Papeete, on Tahiti.

French Revolution. A revolt in France against the monarchy and aristocracy lasting from 1789 to 1799, when Napoleon gained control.

French seam. A seam stitched first on the right side and then turned in and stitched on the wrong side so that the raw edges are enclosed in the seam.

French Shore. A section of the northern and western coasts of Newfoundland, where the French fishing industry held the right to engage in specified activities from 1713 to 1904.

French So·ma·li·land (sō-mä′lē-lănd′). An Overseas Territory of France, occupying 8,996 square miles in eastern Africa on the Gulf of Aden. Population, 81,000. Capital, Djibouti.

French Southern and Antarctic Lands. A French Overseas Territory, created in 1955 as an administrative unit of territories claimed by France in the southern Indian Ocean.

French telephone. A telephone with the receiver and transmitter contained in a single hand piece; handset.

French toast. Sliced bread soaked in a milk and egg batter and lightly fried.

French To·go·land (tō′gō-lănd′). A former United Nations Trust Territory in western Africa, administered by France (1946–60). See **Togoland**, Republic of **Togo.**

French Union. An association established under the constitution of the Fourth French Republic in 1946, consisting of the Republic and its overseas departments and territories, and replaced by the French Community in 1958.

French West Af·ri·ca (ăf′rĭ-kə). A former group of eight French Overseas Territories in western Africa, now the independent states of Dahomey, Ivory Coast, Mauritania, Niger, Senegal, Upper Volta, Guinea, and Mali.

French West In·dies (ĭn′dēz). Unofficially, the French Overseas Departments of Guadeloupe and Martinique, in the Caribbean.

French window. **1.** A window similar to a French door and usually hung in pairs. **2.** A casement window.

French·y (frĕn′chē) *adj.* **-ier, -iest.** *Informal.* Displaying French characteristics. —*n., pl.* **Frenchies.** *Slang.* A Frenchman.

Fre·neau (frə-nō′, frĕ-), **Philip (Morin).** 1752–1832. American poet.

fre·net·ic (frə-nĕt′ĭk) *adj.* Also **fre·net·i·cal** (-ĭ-kəl), **phre·net·ic,**

phre·net·i·cal. Frantic; frenzied. —*n.* Also **phre·net·ic.** A frenzied person. [Middle English *frenetik,* frenzied, insane, from Old French *frenetique,* from Latin *phrenēticus,* from Greek *phrenitikos,* from *phrenitis,* brain disease, insanity, from *phrēn,* mind. See **gwhren-** in Appendix.*] —**fre·net′i·cal·ly** *adv.*

fre·num (frē′nəm) *n., pl.* **-nums** or **-na** (-nə). A membranous structure that restrains the movement of or supports a part, as the fold under the tongue. [Latin *frēnum,* bridle. See **ghren-** in Appendix.*]

fren·zied (frĕn′zēd) *adj.* Affected with or filled with frenzy; frantic. —**fren′zied·ly** *adv.*

fren·zy (frĕn′zē) *n., pl.* **-zies.** Also **phren·sy.** **1.** A seizure of violent agitation or wild excitement, often accompanied by manic activity. **2.** Temporary madness or delirium: *"I struggled with the frenzy, though I felt it must tear me in pieces."* (Mary Renault). **3.** An extravagant idea; mania; craze. Used with *for: "man had a frenzy for getting away from any control"* (D.H. Lawrence). —*tr.v.* **frenzied, -zying, -zies.** Also **phren·sy.** To drive into a frenzy. [Middle English *frenesie,* from Old French, from Medieval Latin *phrenēsia,* from Latin *phrenēsis,* from *phrēn,* mind, from Greek. See **gwhren-** in Appendix.*]

Fre·on (frē′ŏn′) *n.* A trademark for any of various nonflammable, nontoxic gaseous or liquid fluorocarbons that are used mainly as working fluids in refrigeration and air conditioning and as aerosol propellants.

freq. 1. frequentative. **2.** frequently.

fre·quence (frē′kwəns) *n.* Frequency. [Middle English, crowd, crowded state, from Old French, from Latin *frequentia,* FREQUENCY.]

fre·quen·cy (frē′kwən-sē) *n., pl.* **-cies.** **1.** *Mathematics & Physics.* The number of times a specified phenomenon occurs within a specified interval, as: **a.** The number of repetitions of a complete sequence of values of a periodic function per unit variation of an independent variable. **b.** The number of complete cycles of a periodic process occurring per unit time. **c.** The number of repetitions per unit time of a complete waveform, as of an electric current. **2.** *Statistics.* **a.** The number of measurements in an interval of a frequency distribution. **b.** The ratio of the number of times an event occurs in a series of trials of a chance experiment to the number of trials of the experiment performed. Also called "relative frequency." **3.** The property or condition of occurring repeatedly in short intervals. [Latin *frequentia,* crowd, from *frequēns,* FREQUENT.]

frequency band. A band of frequencies. See **band.**

frequency curve. A graphic approximation of the frequency polygon of a statistical distribution, usually a smooth curve with the property that its abscissa is never negative, and such that the area under the curve cut off by a class is the approximate fraction of the total frequency contained in that class.

frequency distribution. A set of intervals, usually adjacent and of equal width, into which the range of a statistical **distribution** (*see*) is divided, each associated with a **frequency** (*see*) indicating the number of measurements in that interval.

frequency modulation. *Abbr.* **FM, fm** *Electronics.* The encoding of a carrier wave by variation of its frequency in accordance with an input signal. Compare **amplitude modulation.**

frequency polygon. A graphic representation of a frequency distribution consisting of a set of points each obtained by plotting class frequency as ordinate and class mark as abscissa, together with line segments joining points of adjacent classes.

fre·quent (frē′kwənt) *adj.* Occurring or appearing quite often or at close intervals: *frequent errors of judgment; frequent service stations on the freeway.* —*tr.v.* (frē-kwĕnt′, frē′kwənt) **frequented, -quenting, -quents.** To pay frequent visits to; be in or at often. [Middle English, profuse, ample, from Old French, from Latin *frequēns,* full, frequent. See **bhrekw-** in Appendix.*] —**fre·quent′er** *n.* —**fre′quent·ness** *n.*

fre·quen·ta·tion (frē′kwĕn-tā′shən, frē′kwən-) *n.* The act or practice of frequenting a place.

fre·quen·ta·tive (frē-kwĕn′tə-tĭv) *adj. Abbr.* **freq.** *Grammar.* Expressing or denoting repeated action. —*n. Abbr.* **freq.** A frequentative verb, such as *flicker* or *hobble.*

fre·quent·ly (frē′kwənt-lē) *adv. Abbr.* **fr., freq.** At frequent intervals; often.

fres·co (frĕs′kō) *n., pl.* **-coes** or **-cos.** **1.** The art of painting by pressing earth colors dissolved in water into fresh plaster. **2.** A painting executed on plaster. —*tr.v.* **frescoed, -coing, -coes.** To paint on fresh plaster. [Italian, from phrases such as (*in*) *fresco,* (on the) fresh (plaster), from West Germanic *friskaz* (unattested), FRESH.] —**fres′co·er, fres′co·ist** *n.*

Fres·co·bal·di (frĕs′kō-bäl′dē), **Girolamo.** 1583–1643. Italian composer and organist.

fresh (frĕsh) *adj.* **fresher, freshest. 1.** New to one's experience; not encountered before. **2.** Novel; different; original: *a fresh slant.* **3.** Recently made, produced, or harvested; not stale, spoiled, or withered: *fresh bread.* **4.** Not preserved, as by canning, smoking, or freezing: *fresh vegetables.* **5.** Not saline or salty: *fresh water.* **6.** Not yet used or soiled; clean: *a fresh sheet of paper.* **7.** Additional; new: *a fresh start.* **8.** Bright and clear; not dull or faded: *a fresh color; a fresh memory.* **9.** Having the glowing, unspoiled appearance of youth. **10.** Untried; inexperienced: *fresh recruits.* **11.** Having just arrived; straight: *fresh from Paris.* **12. a.** Revived or reinvigorated; refreshed. **b.** Charged with energy; frisky. **13.** Revivifying; cool and invigorating: *fresh morning air.* **14.** Fairly strong; brisk: *a fresh wind.* **15.** Having recently calved and therefore with milk: *"I also tended seventeen yaks and cows and milked them when they were fresh."* (Anna Louise Strong). **16.** *Informal.* Bold and saucy; impudent. —*adv.* Recently; newly. Usually used in combination: *fresh-baked bread.* **—fresh out.** *Informal.* Having just run out: *fresh out of sugar.* —*n.* **1.** The early and fresh part: *the fresh of the day.* **2.** A freshet. [Middle English, from Old French *freis* (feminine *fresche*), from West Germanic *friskaz* (unattested).] **—fresh'ly** *adv.* **—fresh'ness** *n.*

fresh breeze. A wind whose speed is 19 to 24 miles per hour.

fresh·en (frĕsh'ən) *v.* **-ened, -ening, -ens.** —*intr.* **1.** To become fresh. Often used with *up.* **2.** To make oneself clean and fresh. Used with *up: freshen up after a day's work.* **3.** To become brisk; increase in strength. Used of a wind. **4.** To lose saltiness. **5.** To calve and therefore produce milk. —*tr.* To impart a fresh quality to; make fresh. **—fresh'en·er** *n.*

fresh·et (frĕsh'ĭt) *n.* **1.** A sudden overflow of a stream resulting from a heavy rain or a thaw. **2.** A stream of fresh water that empties into a body of salt water. [FRESH + -ET.]

fresh gale. A wind whose speed is 39 to 46 miles per hour.

fresh·man (frĕsh'mən) *n., pl.* **-men** (-mĭn). **1.** A student in the first-year class of a high school, college, or university. **2.** Any beginner; a novice.

fresh·wa·ter (frĕsh'wô'tər, -wŏt'ər) *adj.* **1.** Of, pertaining to, living in, or consisting of fresh water. **2.** Situated away from the sea; inland. **3. a.** Unaccustomed to the seas: *a freshwater sailor.* **b.** New to the job; inexperienced.

Fres·nel (frā-nĕl'), **Augustin Jean.** 1788–1827. French physicist; experimented with diffraction of light.

Fres·no (frĕz'nō). A city and commercial center in the San Joaquin Valley of central California. Population, 134,000.

fret¹ (frĕt) *v.* **fretted, fretting, frets.** —*tr.* **1.** To cause to be uneasy; distress; vex. **2. a.** To gnaw or wear away. **b.** To produce a hole or worn spot in; chafe; corrode. **3.** To form (a passage or channel) by erosion. **4.** To disturb the surface of (water or a stream); agitate. —*intr.* **1.** To be vexed or troubled; to worry. **2.** To be worn or eaten away; become corroded. **3.** To move agitatedly; be ruffled. **4.** To gnaw with the teeth in the manner of a rodent. —*n.* **1.** An act or instance of fretting. **2.** A hole, worn spot, or path made by abrasion or erosion. **3.** Irritation; annoyance; worry. [Middle English *freten,* to devour, irritate, Old English *fretan.* See **ed-** in Appendix.*]

fret² (frĕt) *n.* One of several ridges, usually of metal, set across the fingerboard of a guitar or other stringed instrument. —*tr.v.* **fretted, fretting, frets.** To provide with frets. [Origin uncertain.]

fret³ (frĕt) *n.* **1.** An ornamental design contained within a band or border, consisting of repeated, symmetrical, and often geometrical figures. **2.** Such an ornamental design made in relief, often with numerous small openings. **3.** A headdress worn by women of the Middle Ages, consisting of interlaced wire. —*tr.v.* **fretted, fretting, frets.** To provide with a fret or frets. [Middle English, from Old French *frete*†, trellis, embossed work.]

fret·ful (frĕt'fəl) *adj.* Inclined to fret; peevish; plaintive. Also "fretsome." **—fret'ful·ly** *adv.* **—fret'ful·ness** *n.*

fret saw. A long, narrow-bladed saw having fine teeth, used in producing ornamental work in thin wood or metal.

fret·work (frĕt'wûrk') *n.* **1.** Ornamental work consisting of three-dimensional frets; geometric openwork. **2.** Such ornamental work represented two-dimensionally by chiaroscuro.

Froud (froid), **Sigmund.** 1856–1939. Austrian physician and neurologist; founder of psychoanalysis.

Freu·di·an (froi'dē-ən) *adj.* Pertaining to or in accordance with the psychoanalytic theories of Sigmund Freud. —*n.* **1.** One who actively applies the psychoanalytic methods or theories of Freud in conducting psychotherapy. **2.** One who studies or applies the psychoanalytic theories of Freud for interpretation or explanation, as in historical or literary criticism.

Frey (frā). Also **Freyr** (frār). *Norse Mythology.* The god who dispenses peace, good weather, prosperity, and bountiful crops.

Frey·a (frā'ə). Also **Frey·ja.** *Norse Mythology.* The sister of Frey and the goddess of love and beauty.

Fri. Friday.

fri·a·ble (frī'ə-bəl) *adj.* Readily crumbled; brittle. [French, from Latin *friābilis,* crumbling, from *friāre,* to crumble. See **bhrēi-** in Appendix.*] **—fri'a·bil'i·ty, fri'a·ble·ness** *n.*

fri·ar (frī'ər) *n. Abbr.* **Fr.** A member of a Roman Catholic order, usually mendicant, such as the Dominicans or Franciscans. [Middle English *frere,* from Old French, from Latin *frāter* (stem *frātr-*), brother. See **bhrāter-** in Appendix.*]

fri·ar·bird (frī'ər-bûrd') *n.* Any of various birds of the genus *Philemon,* of Australia and adjacent regions, having a partly naked head. Also called "leatherhead." [From its bare head.]

friar's lantern. **Ignis fatuus** *(see).*

fri·ar·y (frī'ə-rē) *n., pl.* **-ies.** A monastery of friars.

frib·ble (frĭb'əl) *v.* **-bled, -bling, -bles.** —*tr.* To waste (time, for example). —*intr.* To waste time; trifle. —*n.* **1.** A frivolity; trifle. **2.** A frivolous person. [Origin unknown.] **—frib'bler** *n.*

Fri·bourg (frē-bo͝or'). *German* **Frei·burg** (frī'bo͝ork'). A city and religious and cultural center in western Switzerland, 17 miles southwest of Bern. Population, 30,000.

fric·an·deau (frĭk'ən-dō') *n., pl.* **-deaux** (-dōz'). A cut of veal, usually rump or shoulder, that has been larded and braised or roasted with vegetables. [French, from *fricasser,* to FRICASSEE.]

fric·as·see (frĭk'ə-sē') *n.* Poultry or meat cut into pieces, stewed, and served with a thick gravy. —*tr.v.* **fricasseed, -seeing, -sees.** To prepare as a fricassee. [French *fricassée,* from the feminine past participle of *fricasser*†, to fry.]

fric·a·tive (frĭk'ə-tĭv) *adj. Phonetics.* Produced by the forcing of breath through a constricted passage, as are such consonantal sounds as (f) and (v), (s) and (z), (sh) and (zh), (th) and (*th*). —*n. Phonetics.* A fricative consonant. Also called "spirant." [From Latin *fricāre,* to rub. See **bhrēi-** in Appendix.*]

Frick (frĭk), **Henry Clay.** 1849–1919. American steel manufacturer and philanthropist.

fric·tion (frĭk'shən) *n.* **1.** The rubbing of one object or surface against another. **2.** A conflict, as of dissimilar ideas, persons, or interests obliged to coexist; a clashing. **3.** *Physics.* A force tangential to the common boundary of two bodies in contact that resists the motion or tendency to motion of one relative to the other. [Old French, from Latin *frictiō,* from *frictus,* past participle of *fricāre,* to rub. See **bhrēi-** in Appendix.*] **—fric'tion·al** *adj.* **—fric'tion·al·ly** *adv.*

fret³

friction clutch. A clutch in which axial pressure with resultant friction between the clutch faces, rather than the interlocking of mated parts, transmits torque.

friction drive. An automotive transmission system in which motion is transmitted from one part to another by the surface friction of rolling contact rather than by toothed gears.

friction match. A match that ignites when struck on an abrasive surface.

friction tape. A sturdy moisture-resistant adhesive tape, used chiefly to insulate electrical conductors.

Fri·day (frī'dē, -dā') *n. Abbr.* **Fri.** The sixth day of the week. [Middle English *fridai,* Old English *frigedæg.* See **prī-** in Appendix.*]

fridge (frĭj) *n. Informal.* A refrigerator.

Fridt·jof Nan·sen Land. See **Franz Josef Land.**

fried cake. A small pastry fried in deep fat, as a doughnut.

friend (frĕnd) *n.* **1.** A person whom one knows, likes, and trusts. **2.** Any associate or acquaintance. Often used as a form of address. **3.** A favored companion; boy friend or girl friend. **4.** One with whom one is allied in a struggle or cause; a comrade. **5.** One who supports, sympathizes with, or patronizes a group, cause, or movement. **6.** *Capital* **F.** A member of the Society of Friends; a Quaker. **—be friends with.** To be a friend of. **—make friends with.** To enter into friendship with. —*tr.v.* **friended, friending, friends.** *Archaic.* To befriend. [Middle English *frend,* Old English *frēond.* See **prī-** in Appendix.*]

friend·less (frĕnd'lĭs) *adj.* Without friends.

friend·ly (frĕnd'lē) *adj.* **-lier, -liest.** **1.** Of, pertaining to, or befitting a friend. **2.** Favorably disposed; not antagonistic. **3.** Warm; comforting. **4.** On terms of friendship. —*adv.* Also **friend·li·ly** (frĕnd'lə-lē). In the manner of a friend; amicably. —*n., pl.* **friendlies.** One fighting on or favorable to one's own side. **—friend'li·ness** *n.*

Friendly Islands. See **Tonga.**

friend·ship (frĕnd'shĭp') *n.* **1.** The condition or relation of being friends. **2.** Friendly feeling toward another; friendliness.

fri·er. Variant of **fryer.**

Fri·ern Bar·net (frī'ərn bär'nĭt). A former administrative division of London, England, now part of **Barnet** *(see).*

Frie·sian. Variant of **Frisian.**

Fries·land (frēz'lənd, -lănd', frēs'-; *Dutch* frēs'länt'). A province of the Netherlands, 1,248 square miles in area, in the north with coastlines on the IJsselmeer and Waddenzee. Population, 496,000. Capital, Leeuwarden.

Sigmund Freud

frieze¹ (frēz) *n. Architecture.* **1.** A plain or decorated horizontal part of an entablature between the architrave and cornice. **2.** Any decorative horizontal band, as along the upper part of a wall in a room. [French *frise,* from Old French, from Medieval Latin *frisium, frigium,* fringe, embroidered cloth, from Latin *Phrygium,* of Phrygia, a place noted for its embroidery.]

frieze² (frēz) *n.* A coarse, shaggy woolen cloth with an uncut nap. Also called "frisé." [Middle English *frise,* from Old French, from Middle Dutch *vriese,* perhaps from *Vriese,* from Latin *Frīsiī,* FRISIAN.]

frig (frĭg) *v.* **frigged, frigging, frigs.** *Vulgar Slang.* —*tr.* **1.** To have sexual intercourse with. **2.** *Chiefly British.* To masturbate. —*intr.* **1.** To have sexual intercourse. **2.** *Chiefly British.* To masturbate. [Possibly related to Old English *frīgan*†, to love.]

frig·ate (frĭg'ĭt) *n.* **1.** A high-speed, medium-sized sailing war vessel of the 17th, 18th, and 19th centuries. **2.** A U.S. warship of approximately 5,000 to 7,000 tons, intermediate between a cruiser and destroyer, used primarily for escort duty. **3.** *Archaic.* Any fast, light vessel, as a sailboat. [French *frégate,* from Italian *fregata*†.]

friarbird
Philemon corniculatus

frigate bird. Any of various tropical sea birds of the genus *Fregata,* having long, powerful wings and dark plumage, and characteristically snatching food from other birds in flight. Also called "man-o'-war bird."

Frigg (frĭg). Also **Frig·ga** (frĭg'ə). *Norse Mythology.* The wife of Odin and goddess of the heavens. [Old Norse. See **prī-** in Appendix.*]

fright (frīt) *n.* **1.** Sudden, intense fear, as of something immediately threatening; alarm. **2.** *Informal.* Something extremely unsightly, alarming, or strange. —See Synonyms at **fear.** —*tr.v.* **frighted, frighting, frights.** *Archaic.* To frighten. [Middle English *fright,* Old English *fryhto, fyrhto,* from Germanic *furht-* (unattested), afraid.]

fright·en (frīt'n) *tr.v.* **-ened, -ening, -ens.** **1.** To make suddenly afraid; alarm or startle. **2.** To drive or force by arousing fear. Used with *away, into, off,* or *out: He was frightened into confessing.* [From FRIGHT.] **—fright'en·er** *n.*

Synonyms: *frighten, scare, alarm, terrify, terrorize, startle, panic.* These verbs mean to cause a person to experience fear. *Frighten* and *scare* are the most general and applicable to a wide range of such experience. *Alarm* implies the sudden onset of fear or apprehension caused by awareness of danger. *Terrify*

frigate bird
Fregata minor

implies overwhelming, often paralyzing fear. *Terrorize* implies fear that intimidates, sometimes as a means of deliberate coercion. *Startle* suggests fear that shocks momentarily and may cause involuntary movement. *Panic* implies incapacitating terror and consequent loss of self-control and rationality.

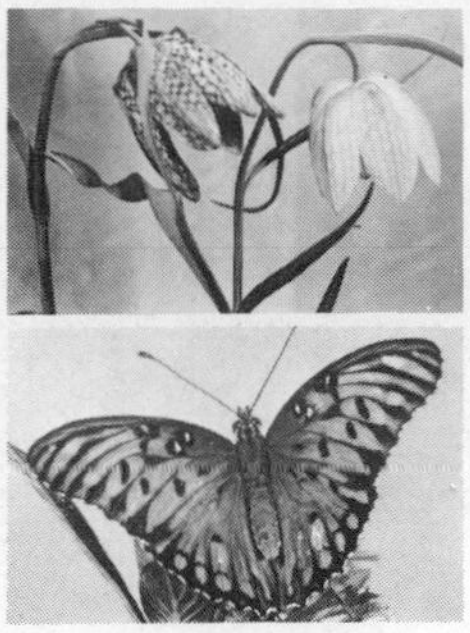

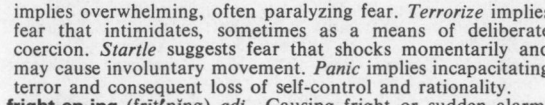

fritillary
Above: Fritillaria meleagris
Below: Agraulis vanillae

fright·en·ing (frīt′nĭng) *adj.* Causing fright or sudden alarm. —**fright′en·ing·ly** *adv.*

fright·ful (frīt′fəl) *adj.* **1.** Causing disgust or shock; horrifying. **2.** Causing fright; terrifying. **3.** *Informal.* **a.** Excessive; extreme: *a frightful liar.* **b.** Disagreeable; distressing: *frightful weather.* —**fright′ful·ly** *adv.* —**fright′ful·ness** *n.*

frig·id (frĭj′ĭd) *adj.* **1.** Extremely cold. **2.** Lacking warmth of feeling; stiff and formal in manner. **3.** Abnormally lacking sexual desire. Said chiefly of women. In this sense, compare **impotent.** [Latin *frīgidus,* from *frīgēre,* to be cold, from *frīgus,* cold. See **srīg-** in Appendix.*] —**fri·gid′i·ty** (frĭ-jĭd′ə-tē), **frig′id·ness** *n.* —**frig′id·ly** *adv.*

Frig·id·aire (frĭj′ə-dâr′) *n.* A trademark for a refrigerator. [FRIGID + AIR.]

Frigid Zone. The area within the Arctic Circle or that within the Antarctic Circle.

frig·o·rif·ic (frĭg′ə-rĭf′ĭk) *adj.* Also **frig·o·rif·i·cal** (-ĭ-kəl). Causing coldness; chilling. [Latin *frīgorificus* : *frīgus* (stem *frīgor-*), FRIGID + -FIC.]

fri·jol (frē-hōl′) *n., pl.* **frijoles** (-hō′lēz; *Spanish* frē-hō′lās). Also **fri·jole.** *Southwestern U.S.* A bean cultivated and used for food. [Spanish, variant of *fresol,* from Latin *phaseolus,* diminutive of *phasēlus,* kidney bean, from Greek *phasēlos*†.]

frill (frĭl) *n.* **1.** A ruffled, gathered, or pleated border or projection, such as a fabric edge used to trim clothing or a curled paper strip for decorating the bone of a piece of meat. **2.** *Zoology.* A ruff of hair or feathers or a similar membranous projection about the neck of an animal or bird. **3.** *Photography.* A wrinkling of the edge of a film. **4.** *Informal.* Anything superfluous, pretentious, and artificial; frippery. —*v.* **frilled, frilling, frills.** —*tr.* **1.** To make into a ruffle or frill. **2.** To add a ruffle or frill to. —*intr. Photography.* To become wrinkled along the edge. [Origin uncertain.]

frilled lizard. An Australian lizard, *Chlamydosaurus kingi,* having a broad, contractile membrane extending from the neck and throat.

fril·ly (frĭl′ē) *adj.* **-lier, -liest. 1.** Decorated with or having a frill or frills. **2.** Similar to or suggesting a frill or frills. **3.** *Informal.* Superfluously ornamental.

Friml (frĭm′əl), **(Charles) Rudolf.** Born 1881. Bohemian-born American composer of operettas.

fringe (frĭnj) *n.* **1.** A decorative border or edging of hanging threads, cords, or strips, often attached to a separate band. **2.** Anything placed or growing along an edge. **3.** A marginal or peripheral part; an edge: *the fringes of the crowd.* **4.** Those members of a group or political party holding extreme views. **5.** *Optics.* Any of the light or dark bands produced by the diffraction or interference of light. —*tr.v.* **fringed, fringing, fringes. 1.** To decorate with a fringe. **2.** To grow or occur along the edge of; to border: *"deep and sullen pools fringed with tall rushes"* (H. Rider Haggard). [Middle English *frenge,* from Old French, from Vulgar Latin *frimbia* (unattested), from Late Latin *fimbria.* See **fimbria.**]

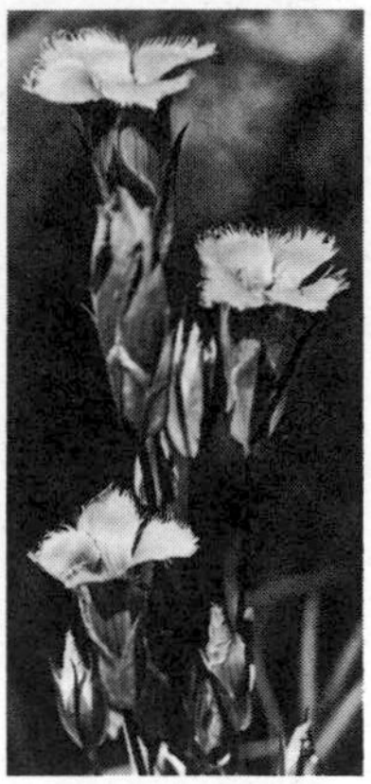

fringed gentian

fringe benefit. An employment benefit given in addition to one's wages or salary.

fringed gentian. A plant, *Gentiana crinita,* of eastern North America, having blue, tubular flowers with fringed petals.

fringed orchis. Any of various orchids of the genus *Habenaria,* having variously colored flowers with a fringed lip.

fringed polygala. A plant, *Polygala paucifolia,* of eastern North America, having fringed, reddish-purple flowers. Also called "flowering wintergreen," "gaywings."

fringe of consciousness. The components of awareness of a complex experience that are at any instant outside the focus of attention.

fringe tree. A shrub or small tree, *Chionanthus virginicus,* of the southeastern United States, having drooping clusters of white flowers and dark-blue fruit.

frin·gil·lid (frĭn-jĭl′ĭd) *adj.* Also **frin·gil·line** (-īn′, -ĭn). Of or belonging to the family Fringillidae, which includes relatively small birds, such as the finches, sparrows, and buntings. —*n.* A member of the Fringillidae. [New Latin *Fringillidae* : *Fringilla* (type genus), from Latin *fringilla*†, finch + -ID.]

fring·y (frĭn′jē) *adj.* **-ier, -iest. 1.** Like a fringe. **2.** Decorated with a fringe or fringes.

frip·per·y (frĭp′ə-rē) *n., pl.* **-ies. 1.** Pretentious finery; excessively ornamented dress. **2.** Pretentious elegance; ostentation. **3.** Trivia. [French *friperie,* from Old French *freperie,* from *frepe, felpe,* frill, from Medieval Latin *faluppa*†, fiber.]

Fris. Frisian.

Fris·co (frĭs′kō). *Informal.* San Francisco, California.

fri·sé (frē-zā′) *n.* A fabric, **frieze** *(see).* [French, from the past participle of *friser,* to curl, FRIZZ.]

fri·sette. Variant of **frizette.**

fri·seur (frē-zœr′) *n. French.* A hairdresser; coiffeur.

Fri·sian (frĭzh′ən, frē′zhən) *adj.* Also **Frie·sian** (frē′zhən). *Abbr.* **Fris., Frs.** Of the Frisian Islands or Friesland. —*n.* Also **Frie·sian.** *Abbr.* **Fris., Frs. 1.** A native or inhabitant of the Frisian Islands or Friesland. **2.** The Germanic language spoken by the Frisian people. [From Latin *Frīsiī,* the Frisians.]

Frisian Islands. A chain of islands in the North Sea, divided into groups belonging to the Netherlands, West Germany, and Denmark.

frisk (frĭsk) *v.* **frisked, frisking, frisks.** —*intr.* To move about briskly and playfully, as a puppy; to gambol; frolic. —*tr.* **1.** To move in a brisk, playful manner. **2.** To search (a person) for something concealed, especially weapons, by passing the hands quickly over clothes or through pockets. —*n.* **1.** An energetic, playful movement; a gambol; caper. **2.** An act of frisking, as for concealed weapons. [From obsolete *frisk,* lively, from Old French *frisque,* from Common Germanic *friskaz* (unattested), FRESH.] —**frisk′er** *n.*

fris·ket (frĭs′kĭt) *n.* **1.** A light frame with a windowed sheet of parchment that protects areas of the paper not to be printed in a hand printing press. **2.** A mask used in illustrating, photography, or photoengraving. [French *frisquette*†.]

frisk·y (frĭs′kē) *adj.* **-ier, -iest.** Energetic, lively, and playful: *"Their quiet ponies were almost frisky, sniffing and moving restlessly"* (J.R.R. Tolkien). [From obsolete *frisk,* lively. See **frisk.**] —**frisk′i·ly** *adv.* —**frisk′i·ness** *n.*

frit (frĭt) *n.* **1.** The fused or partially fused materials used in making glass. **2.** A vitreous substance used in making porcelain or glazes. —*tr.v.* **fritted, fritting, frits.** To make into frit. [Italian *fritta,* from the feminine past participle of *friggere,* to fry, from Latin *frīgere,* to FRY.]

frit fly (frĭt). Any of several small flies of the family Chloropidae (or Oscinidae); especially, *Oscinella frit,* having larvae that are destructive to cereal plants. [Origin obscure.]

frith (frĭth) *n. Scottish.* An estuary. [Variant of FIRTH.]

frit·il·lar·y (frĭt′l-ĕr′ē) *n., pl.* **-ies. 1.** Any of various bulbous plants of the genus *Fritillaria,* having nodding, variously colored, often spotted or checkered flowers. **2.** Any of various butterflies of the family Nymphalidae, and especially of the genera *Speyeria* and *Boloria,* having brownish wings marked with black or silvery spots. [New Latin *Fritillaria,* from Latin *fritillus*†, dice box, a reference to the checkered markings.]

frit·ter¹ (frĭt′ər) *tr.v.* **-tered, -tering, -ters. 1.** To reduce or squander little by little: *"Our life is frittered away by detail."* (Thoreau). **2.** *Rare.* To break, tear, or cut into bits; to shred. [Probably altered from obsolete *fritter,* to break in pieces, perhaps related to Middle High German *vetze,* rags. See **ped-²** in Appendix.*]

frit·ter² (frĭt′ər) *n.* A small cake made of batter, often containing fruit, vegetables, or fish, sautéed or fried in deep fat. [Middle English *friture,* from Old French, from Vulgar Latin *frictūra* (unattested), from Latin *frīctus,* past participle of *frīgere,* to FRY.]

Fri·u·li (frē-ōō′lē, frē′ə-lē). A historic region and former duchy of northeastern Italy, part of which now extends into Yugoslavia. [Latin *Forojulium,* from *Forum Julii,* "Forum of Julius," supposedly founded by Julius Caesar.]

Fri·u·li·an (frē-ōō′lē-ən) *n.* **1.** One of a people inhabiting Friuli in northeastern Italy. **2.** The Rhaeto-Romanic dialect spoken by these people.

friv·ol (frĭv′əl) *intr.v.* **-oled** or **-olled, -oling** or **-olling, -ols.** *Informal.* To behave frivolously. [Back-formation from FRIVOLOUS.] —**friv′ol·er** *n.*

fri·vol·i·ty (frĭ-vŏl′ə-tē) *n., pl.* **-ties. 1.** The condition or quality of being frivolous. **2.** A frivolous act or thing.

friv·o·lous (frĭv′ə-ləs) *adj.* **1.** Unworthy of serious attention; insignificant; trivial: *"the new middle class found literature frivolous"* (Leslie Fiedler). **2.** Marked by flippancy; silly or gay. —See Synonyms at **playful.** [Middle English, from Latin *frivolus*†.] —**friv′o·lous·ly** *adv.* —**friv′o·lous·ness** *n.*

fri·zette (frĭ-zĕt′) *n.* Also **fri·sette.** A curled fringe of hair, usually worn on the forehead by a woman. [French *frisette,* "little curl," from *friser,* to curl, FRIZZ.]

frizz¹ (frĭz) *v.* **frizzed, frizzing, frizzes.** Also **friz.** —*tr.* To form (nap or hair, for example) into small, tight curls or tufts. —*intr.* To be formed into small, tight curls or tufts. —*n.* **1.** The condition of being frizzed. **2.** A tight curl of hair or fabric. [French *friser,* to curl, to shrivel up (as when fried), perhaps from *frire* (stem *fris-*), to fry, from Old French, to FRY.] —**friz′zer** *n.*

frizz² (frĭz) *v.* **frizzed, frizzing, frizzes.** Also **friz.** —*tr.* To fry or burn with a sizzling noise. —*intr.* To be fried or burned with a sizzling noise. [Perhaps from FRIZZLE (to fry).]

friz·zle¹ (frĭz′əl) *v.* **-zled, -zling, -zles.** —*tr.* **1.** To fry until crisp and curled: *frizzled the bacon.* **2.** To scorch or sear with heat. —*intr.* To fry or sear with a sizzling noise. [Perhaps blend of FRY and SIZZLE.]

friz·zle² (frĭz′əl) *v.* **-zled, -zling, -zles.** —*tr.* To frizz (hair). —*intr.* To form tight curls. —*n.* A small, tight curl. [Origin obscure.]

friz·zly (frĭz′lē) *adj.* **-zlier, -zliest.** Tightly curled.

friz·zy (frĭz′ē) *adj.* **-zier, -ziest.** Tightly curled; frizzly. —**friz′zi·ly** *adv.* —**friz′zi·ness** *n.*

Frl. Fräulein.

fro (frō) *adv.* Away; back. Used in the phrase *to and fro.* —*prep. Scottish.* From. [Middle English *fra, fro,* adverb and preposition, from Old Norse *frā.* See **per¹** in Appendix.*]

Fro·bish·er (frō′bĭ-shər), Sir **Martin.** 1535?–1594. English navigator and explorer of Arctic waters.

Fro·bish·er Bay (frō′bĭ-shər). An inlet of the Atlantic extending about 150 miles into southeastern Baffin Island, Canada.

frock (frŏk) *n.* **1.** A long, loose outer garment, such as that worn by artists and craftsmen; a smock. **2.** A woolen garment formerly worn by sailors; jersey. **3.** A frock coat. **4.** A robe worn by monks, friars, and other clerics; habit. **5.** The state of being a priest or clergyman. **6.** A woman's dress. —*tr.v.* **frocked, frocking, frocks. 1.** To clothe in a frock. **2.** To invest with clerical office. [Middle English *frok,* from Old French *froc,* from Germanic *hrok-* (unattested).]

frock coat. A man's dress overcoat with knee-length skirts, worn chiefly in the 19th century.

froe (frō) n. Also **frow.** A cleaving tool having a heavy blade set at right angles to the handle. [Origin uncertain.]

Froe·bel (frœ′bəl), **Friedrich Wilhelm August.** 1782–1852. German educator; founded the kindergarten system.

frog (frôg, frŏg) n. 1. Any of numerous tailless, chiefly aquatic amphibians of the order Salientia, and especially of the family Ranidae, characteristically having a smooth, moist skin, webbed feet, and long hind legs adapted for leaping. 2. A wedge-shaped, horny prominence in the sole of a horse's hoof. 3. A loop fastened to a belt to hold a tool or weapon. 4. An ornamental looped braid or cord with a button or knot for fastening the front of a garment. 5. A device on intersecting railroad tracks that permits wheels to cross the junction. 6. A spiked or perforated object placed in a container and used to support stems in a decorative floral arrangement. 7. Informal. Hoarseness in the throat. 8. Slang. A Frenchman. Used disparagingly. [Middle English frogge, Old English frogga. See preu- in Appendix.*]

frog-eye (frôg′ī′, frŏg′-) n. A plant disease caused by fungi and characterized by rounded spots on the leaves.

frog·fish (frôg′fĭsh′, frŏg′-) n., pl. **frogfish** or **-fishes.** Any of various anglerfishes of the family Antennariidae, of tropical and temperate seas, characteristically covered with fleshy or filamentous processes.

frog·gy (frô′gē, frŏg′ē) adj. **-gier, -giest.** 1. Of, resembling, or characteristic of a frog. 2. Full of frogs.

frog·hop·per (frôg′hŏp′ər, frŏg′-) n. The **spittlebug** (see).

frog kick. A swimming kick in which the legs are drawn up close beneath one, then thrust outward and together vigorously.

frog·man (frôg′măn′, -mən, frŏg′-) n., pl. **-men** (-měn′, -mĭn). A swimmer provided with breathing apparatus and other equipment to execute underwater, especially military, maneuvers.

frog·mouth (frôg′mouth′, frŏg′-) n. Any of various brown or gray nocturnal birds of the genera Podargus and Batrachostomus, of southeastern Asia and Australia, having a wide mouth and a hooked bill.

frog spit. Also **frog spittle.** 1. An insect secretion, **cuckoo spit** (see). 2. A foamlike aggregation of small aquatic plants, such as green algae, on the surface of a pond.

Frois·sart (frwä-sär′, froi′särt′), **Jean.** 1333?–1400? French historian.

frol·ic (frŏl′ĭk) n. 1. Gaiety; merriment. 2. A gay, carefree time. 3. A prank, trick, or antic. —intr.v. **frolicked, -icking, -ics.** 1. To behave playfully and uninhibitedly; to romp. 2. To engage in merrymaking, joking, or teasing. —adj. Archaic. Merry; frisky; prankish. [Dutch vrolijk, from Middle Dutch vrolijc : vro, gay, happy (see preu- in Appendix*) + -lijc, -ly (see lĭk- in Appendix*).] —**frol′ick·er** n.

frol·ic·some (frŏl′ĭk-səm) adj. Full of high-spirited fun; frisky; playful.

from (frŭm, frŏm) prep. Abbr. **fm., fr.** 1. Beginning at a specified place or time: walked home from the station; from six o'clock on. 2. With a specified time or point as the first of two limits: from age four to age eight. 3. With a person, place, or thing as the source, cause, or instrument: a note from the teacher. 4. Out of: take a book from the shelf. 5. Out of the jurisdiction, control, or possession of: escape from the gallows. 6. So as not to be engaged in: keep someone from making a mistake. 7. Measured by reference to: far away from home. 8. As opposed to: know right from wrong. 9. Because of: faint from hunger. —See Usage notes at **different, off.** [Middle English from, fram, Old English from, fram. See per¹ in Appendix.*]

From·bork. The Polish name for **Frauenburg.**

fro·men·ty. Variant of **frumenty.**

Fromm (frŏm), **Erich.** Born 1900. German-born American psychoanalyst.

frond (frŏnd) n. 1. The usually compound leaf of a fern. 2. A large compound leaf of certain other plants, such as a palm. 3. A leaflike thallus, as of a seaweed or lichen. [Latin frons† (stem frond-), branch, leaf.] —**frond′ed** adj.

Fronde (frŏnd, frŏnd; French frônd) n. The French political party that opposed Cardinal Mazarin and the court during the minority of Louis XIV in the mid-17th century. [French, "sling" (a derogatory comparison to schoolboys who use slings only behind a teacher's back), from Old French, from Vulgar Latin fundula (unattested), from Latin funda, probably akin to Greek sphendonē†.]

fron·des·cent (frŏn-děs′ənt) adj. Bearing, resembling, or having a profusion of leaves or fronds; leafy. [Latin frondescens, present participle of frondescere, to become leafy, from frondēre, to put forth leaves, from frons (stem frond-), leaf, FROND.] —**fron·des′cence** n.

fron·dose (frŏn′dōs′) adj. 1. Bearing fronds. 2. Resembling a frond or fronds; frondlike. [Latin frondōsus : frōns (stem frond-), FROND + -OSE.] —**fron′dose′ly** adv.

front (frŭnt) n. 1. The forward part or surface, as of a building. 2. The area, location, or position directly before or ahead: Meet me in front of the fountain. 3. The position of leadership or superiority; forefront. 4. The first part; beginning; opening. 5. The forehead, especially of an animal or bird. 6. Archaic. The entire face; countenance. 7. Demeanor or bearing, when faced with a particular situation: maintain a brave front. 8. An outward or feigned aspect; a false appearance or manner. 9. Land bordering a lake, river, or street: a house on the lake front. 10. A promenade along the water; boardwalk. 11. A hotel bellboy or page who is first or most available. 12. A detachable part of a man's dress shirt covering the chest;

dickey. 13. Military. a. The most forward line of a military combat force. b. The area of contact between opposing combat forces; battlefront. 14. Meteorology. The interface between air masses at different temperatures. 15. A group or movement uniting various individuals or organizations for the achievement of a common purpose; a coalition. 16. A nominal leader lacking in real authority; figurehead. 17. An apparently respectable person, group, or business under whose cover secret or illegal activities are carried on. —adj. 1. Of, pertaining to, aimed at, or located in the front. 2. Phonetics. Produced with the front of the tongue in a forward position. Said of vowel sounds. —v. **fronted, fronting, fronts.** —tr. 1. To face; look out upon. 2. To meet in opposition; confront. 3. To provide a front for. 4. To serve as a front for. —intr. To have a front; to face. Usually used with on: Her property fronts on the highway. [Middle English, from Old French, from Latin frōns† (stem front-), front, forehead.]

front. frontispiece.

front·age (frŭn′tĭj) n. 1. The front part of a piece of property, as a lot or building. 2. The dimensions of such a part. 3. The land between a building and the street. 4. The direction in which something faces. 5. Land adjacent to something such as a building, street, or body of water.

fron·tal¹ (frŭnt′l) adj. 1. Of, pertaining to, or situated at the front. 2. Of or pertaining to the forehead. —**fron′tal·ly** adv.

fron·tal² (frŭnt′l) n. 1. An ornamental, detachable drapery covering the front of an altar. 2. The façade of a building. [Middle English frontel, from Medieval Latin frontellum, from Latin frōns (stem front-), FRONT.]

frontal bone. A cranial bone consisting of a vertical portion corresponding to the forehead and an orbital or horizontal portion that enters into the formation of the roofs of the orbital and nasal cavities.

frontal lobe. The largest part of the anterior portion of the cerebral cortex.

frontal lobotomy. Surgery. A prefrontal lobotomy.

Fron·te·nac (frŏn′tə-năk′; French frônt-năk′), **Comte de.** Title of Louis de Buade. 1620–1698. French colonial governor of Canada (1672–82 and 1689–98).

fron·tier (frŭn-tîr′) n. 1. An international border, or the area along it. 2. A region just beyond or at the edge of a settled area. 3. Any undeveloped area or field, as of scientific research. —See Synonyms at **boundary.** —adj. Of, pertaining to, or situated at a frontier. [Middle English frountier, from Old French frontiere, from front, FRONT.]

fron·tiers·man (frŭn-tîrz′mən) n., pl. **-men** (-mĭn). A man who lives on the frontier.

fron·tis·piece (frŭn′tĭs-pēs′) n. 1. Abbr. **front.** An illustration that faces or immediately precedes the title page of a book, book section, or magazine. 2. Archaic. A title page. 3. Architecture. A façade; especially, an ornamental façade. 4. Architecture. A small ornamental pediment, as on top of a door or window. [Variant (influenced by PIECE) of earlier frontispice, from Old French, from Late Latin frontispicium, "examination of the front," building exterior : Latin frōns (stem front-), FRONT + specere, to look at (see spek- in Appendix*).]

front·let (frŭnt′lĭt) n. 1. An ornament or band worn on the forehead, as a phylactery. 2. The forehead of an animal or bird, especially when distinctively marked. 3. Ecclesiastical. The ornamental border of a frontal. [Middle English, from Old French frontelet, diminutive of frontel, from Latin frontāle, from frōns (stem front-), FRONT.]

front matter. The material, as the preface, frontispiece, and title page, preceding the text in a book. Compare **end matter.**

front office. The executive or policy-making officers of an organization.

fron·to·gen·e·sis (frŭn′tō-jĕn′ə-sĭs) n. Development or intensification of a meteorological front. [New Latin : FRONT + -GENESIS.]

fron·tol·y·sis (frŭn-tŏl′ə-sĭs) n. The disintegration of a meteorological front. [New Latin : FRONT + -LYSIS.]

front-page (frŭnt′pāj′) adj. Receiving or worthy of coverage on the front page of a newspaper; sensational.

Front Range. The eastern range of the Rocky Mountains, extending about 300 miles in Wyoming and Colorado. Highest elevation, Grays Peak (14,274 feet).

front·ward (frŭnt′wərd) adv. Also **front·wards** (-wərdz). Toward the front.

frore (frôr, frōr) adj. Archaic. Extremely cold; frosty. [Middle English froren, Old English froren, past participle of frēosan, to FREEZE.]

frosh (frŏsh) n., pl. **frosh.** Informal. A freshman, as at a college. [Shortened variant of FRESHMAN.]

frost (frôst, frŏst) n. 1. A deposit or covering of minute ice crystals formed from frozen water vapor. 2. The atmospheric conditions when the temperature is below the freezing point of water. 3. The process of freezing. 4. A cold or icy manner; haughtiness. 5. Informal. Something given a cold reception; fiasco; failure. —v. **frosted, frosting, frosts.** —tr. 1. To cover with frost. 2. To damage or kill by frost. 3. To cover (glass or metal) with a roughened or speckled decorative surface. 4. To cover or decorate with icing, as a cake. —intr. To become covered with or as if with frost. [Middle English frost, Old English frost, forst. See preus- in Appendix.*]

Frost (frôst, frŏst), **Robert (Lee).** 1875–1963. American poet.

frost·bite (frôst′bīt′, frŏst′-) n. Local tissue destruction resulting from freezing. —tr.v. **frostbit** (-bĭt′), **-bitten** (-bĭt′n), **-biting, -bites.** To injure or damage by freezing.

frost·ed (frôs′tĭd, frŏs′-) adj. 1. Covered by frost. 2. Frostbit-

frock coat

parietal
sphenoid
zygomatic
nasal

frontal bone

ten. **3.** Covered or decorated with icing. **4.** Decorated with a frostlike surface, as metal or glass. —*n.* A milk shake containing ice cream and flavoring.

frost·ing (frôs′tĭng, frŏs′-) *n.* **1.** Icing. **2.** A roughened or speckled surface imparted to glass or metal.

frost line. The limit to which frost penetrates the earth.

frost·weed (frôst′wēd′, frŏst′-) *n.* A plant, the **rockrose** *(see).* [From the ice crystals which form on it at the first frost.]

frost·work (frôst′wûrk′, frŏst′-) *n.* **1.** The intricate patterns produced by frost, as on a windowpane. **2.** Similar ornamental patterns produced artificially, as on metal or glass.

frost·y (frôs′tē, frŏs′-) *adj.* **-ier, -iest. 1.** Producing or characterized by frost; freezing. **2.** Covered with or as if with frost. **3.** Silvery white; hoary. **4.** Cold in manner; haughty; distant. —**frost′i·ly** *adv.* —**frost′i·ness** *n.*

froth (frôth, frŏth) *n.* **1.** A mass of bubbles in or on a liquid; foam. **2.** A salivary foam released as a result of disease or exhaustion. **3.** Anything unsubstantial; triviality; ephemera. —*v.* **frothed, frothing, froths.** —*tr.* **1.** To exude or expel in the form of foam. **2.** To cover with foam. **3.** To cause to foam. —*intr.* To exude or expel froth; to foam. [Middle English, from Old Norse *frodha,* from Germanic *frudh-* (unattested).]

froth·y (frô′thē, frŏth′ē) *adj.* **-ier, -iest. 1.** Made of, covered with, or resembling froth; foamy. **2.** Playfully frivolous in character or content. —**froth′i·ly** *adv.* —**froth′i·ness** *n.*

frou-frou (fro͞o′fro͞o) *n.* **1.** A rustling sound, as of silk. **2.** Fussy or showy dress or ornamentation. [French (imitative).]

frow. Variant of **froe.**

fro·ward (frō′wərd, frō′ərd) *adj.* Stubbornly contrary and disobedient; obstinate. [Middle English *froward* : FRO + -WARD.] —**fro′ward·ly** *adv.* —**fro′ward·ness** *n.*

Fro·ward, Cape (frō′wərd, frō′ərd). The southernmost point of the South American mainland, in southern Chile on the Strait of Magellan.

frown (froun) *v.* **frowned, frowning, frowns.** —*intr.* **1.** To wrinkle the brow, as in thought or displeasure. **2.** To regard with disapproval or distaste. Used with *on* or *upon: "The English frown on the use of tea bags"* (Craig Claiborne). —*tr.* **1.** To express (disapproval or distaste, for example) by wrinkling the brow. **2.** To achieve a specified result by or as if by a wrinkling of the brow: *frown objections away.* —*n.* A wrinkling of the brow in thought or displeasure; a scowl. [Middle English *frounen,* from Old French *froigner,* from Celtic, akin to Welsh *ffroen*†, nose.] —**frown′er** *n.* —**frown′ing·ly** *adv.*

frowst·y (frou′stē) *adj.* **-ier, -iest.** *Chiefly British.* Having a stale smell; musty. [Perhaps a variant of FROWZY.]

frow·zy (frou′zē) *adj.* **-zier, -ziest.** Also **frou·zy, frow·sy. 1.** Unkempt in appearance; slovenly; shabby. **2.** Having an unpleasant smell; musty. —See Synonyms at **sloppy.** [Origin unknown.] —**frow′zi·ness** *n.*

froze. Past tense of **freeze.**

fro·zen (frō′zən). Past participle of **freeze.** —*adj.* **1.** Made into, covered with, or surrounded by ice. **2.** Very cold. **3.** Preserved by freezing. **4.** Rendered immobile. **5.** Expressive of cold unfriendliness or disdain: *a frozen stare.* **6. a.** Kept at an arbitrary level. Said of wages, profits, or the like. **b.** Incapable of being withdrawn, sold, or liquidated. Said of investments, assets, or the like.

FRS Federal Reserve System.

Frs. Frisian.

F.R.S. Fellow of the Royal Society.

frt. freight.

fruc·tif·er·ous (frŭk-tĭf′ər-əs, fro͝ok-) *adj.* Bearing fruit. [From Latin *frūctifer* : *frūctus,* FRUIT + -FEROUS.]

fruc·ti·fi·ca·tion (frŭk′tə-fĭ-kā′shən, fro͝ok′-) *n.* **1.** The producing of fruit. **2.** A seed-bearing or spore-bearing structure.

fruc·ti·fy (frŭk′tə-fī′, fro͝ok′-) *v.* **-fied, -fying, -fies.** —*tr.* To cause to produce fruit; make fruitful or productive. —*intr.* To bear fruit. [Middle English *fructifien,* from Old French *fructifier,* from Latin *frūctificāre* : *frūctus,* FRUIT + *facere,* to make, do (see **dhē-**[1] in Appendix*).]

fruc·tose (frŭk′tōs′, fro͝ok′-) *n.* A very sweet sugar, $C_6H_{12}O_6$, occurring in many fruits and honey and used as a preservative for foodstuffs and as an intravenous nutrient. Also called "fruit sugar," "levulose." [Latin *frūctus,* FRUIT + -OSE.]

fruc·tu·ous (frŭk′cho͞o-əs, fro͝ok′-) *adj.* Fruitful; productive. [Middle English, from Old French, from Latin *frūctuōsus,* from *frūctus,* FRUIT.]

frug (fro͞og) *n.* A dance performed with free thrusting movements of the arms, head, and torso and minimal footwork. [Origin uncertain.]

fru·gal (fro͞o′gəl) *adj.* **1.** Avoiding unnecessary expenditure of money; thrifty. **2.** Costing little; inexpensive. —See Synonyms at **sparing.** [Latin *frūgālis,* back-formation from *frūgālior,* comparative of *frūgī,* useful, worthy, dative of *frūx* (stem *frūg-*), fruit. See **bhrūg-** in Appendix.*] —**fru·gal′i·ty** (fro͞o-găl′ə-tē), **fru′gal·ness** *n.* —**fru′gal·ly** *adv.*

fru·giv·o·rous (fro͞o-jĭv′ər-əs) *adj.* Feeding on fruit; fruit-eating. [Latin *frūx* (stem *frūg-*), fruit (see **bhrūg-** in Appendix*) + -VOROUS.]

fruit (fro͞ot) *n., pl.* **fruit** or **fruits. 1.** The ripened ovary or ovaries of a seed-bearing plant, together with accessory parts, containing the seeds and occurring in a wide variety of forms. **2. a.** An edible, usually sweet and fleshy form of such a structure. **b.** A part or amount of such a plant product, served as food. **3.** The fertile, often spore-bearing structure of a plant that does not bear seeds. **4.** A plant crop or product. **5.** Result; issue; outcome: *the fruit of their labor.* **6.** Offspring; progeny. **7.** *Slang.* A male homosexual. —*v.* **fruited, fruiting, fruits.** —*intr.* To produce fruit. —*tr.* To cause to produce fruit. [Middle English, from Old French, from Latin *frūctus,* enjoyment, use, produce, fruit, from the past participle of *fruī,* to enjoy, to eat fruit. See **bhrūg-** in Appendix.*]

fruit·age (fro͞o′tĭj) *n.* **1.** The process, time, or condition of bearing fruit. **2.** Fruit collectively. **3.** A result or effect.

fruit bat. Any of various fruit-eating bats of the family Pteropodidae, of tropical and subtropical regions of the Old World.

fruit·cake (fro͞ot′kāk′) *n.* A heavy, spiced cake containing citron, nuts, raisins, and preserved fruits.

fruit cup. A mixture of fresh or preserved fruits cut into pieces and served as an appetizer or dessert.

fruit·er (fro͞o′tər) *n.* Also **fruit·er·er** (-tər-ər) for sense 2. **1.** A tree that produces fruit. **2.** One who grows or sells fruit. **3.** A ship that transports fruit.

fruit fly. 1. Any of various small flies of the family Drosophilidae, having larvae that feed on ripening or fermenting fruit; especially, a common species, *Drosophila melanogaster.* Also called "pomace fly." **2.** Any of various flies of the family Tripetidae (or Tephritidae), having larvae that hatch in and damage plant tissue.

fruit·ful (fro͞ot′fəl) *adj.* **1.** Producing fruit. **2.** Producing in abundance; prolific. **3.** Conducive to productivity; causing to bear in abundance: *a fruitful climate.* **4.** Producing results; profitable. —**fruit′ful·ly** *adv.* —**fruit′ful·ness** *n.*

fruiting body. A specialized spore-producing structure, especially of a fungus.

fru·i·tion (fro͞o-ĭsh′ən) *n.* **1.** Enjoyment derived from use or possession; pleasure. **2. a.** The condition of bearing fruit. **b.** The achievement of something desired or worked for; accomplishment; realization: *"The hours we spend with happy prospects in view are more pleasing than those crowned with fruition."* (Goldsmith). [Middle English *fruicioun,* from Old French *fruition,* from Late Latin *fruitiō,* from *fruī,* to enjoy, eat fruit. See **bhrūg-** in Appendix.*]

fruit·less (fro͞ot′lĭs) *adj.* **1.** Producing no fruit. **2.** Having negligible or no results; unproductive: *"In these fruitless searches he spent ten months"* (Samuel Johnson). —**fruit′less·ly** *adv.* —**fruit′less·ness** *n.*

fruit salad. 1. A salad containing fruit. **2.** *Slang.* Ribbons and decorations worn on the breast of a military uniform.

fruit sugar. Fructose *(see).*

fruit·y (fro͞o′tē) *adj.* **-ier, -iest. 1.** Of, containing, or relating to fruit. **2.** Tasting and smelling richly of fruit. **3.** Exuding sentiment or unctuousness. **4.** *Slang.* **a.** Homosexual. **b.** Crazy; odd. —**fruit′i·ness** *n.*

fru·men·ta·ceous (fro͞o′mən-tā′shəs) *adj.* Resembling or consisting of grain, especially wheat. [Late Latin *frūmentāceus* : Latin *frūmentum,* grain, perhaps from *fruī,* to enjoy, eat fruit (see **bhrūg-** in Appendix*) + -ACEOUS.]

fru·men·ty (fro͞o′mən-tē) *n.* Also **fur·men·ty** (fûr′-), **fro·men·ty** (frō′-). *British.* Hulled wheat boiled in milk and flavored with sugar and spices. [Middle English *frumente,* from Old French *frumentee,* from *frument,* grain, from Latin *frūmentum.* See **frumentaceous.**]

frump (frŭmp) *n.* **1.** A dull, plain, unfashionably dressed girl or woman. **2.** A colorless, primly sedate person. [Perhaps short for dialectal *frumple,* to wrinkle, from Middle English *fromplen,* from Middle Dutch *verrompelen* : *ver-,* for- (see **per**[1] in Appendix*) + *rompelen,* to RUMPLE.] —**frump′ish, frump′y** *adj.* —**frump′ish·ly, frump′i·ly** *adv.* —**frump′ish·ness, frump′i·ness** *n.*

Frun·ze (fro͞on′zə). Formerly **Pish·pek** (pĭsh-pĕk′). The capital of the Kirghiz S.S.R., in the north near the Kazakh border. Population, 340,000.

frus·trate (frŭs′trāt′) *tr.v.* **-trated, -trating, -trates. 1. a.** To prevent from accomplishing a purpose or fulfilling a desire; thwart. **b.** To cause feelings of discouragement or bafflement in. **2.** To prevent the accomplishment or development of; nullify. —*adj.* *Archaic.* Baffled or thwarted. [Middle English *frustraten,* from Latin *frūstrāre* (past participle *frūstrātus*), to disappoint, frustrate, from *frūstrā*†, in error, uselessly.] —**frus′trat′er** *n.*

Synonyms: *frustrate, thwart, foil, balk.* These verbs mean to prevent the attainment or fulfillment of a goal or purpose. They are often interchangeable. *Frustrate* suggests defeating in the sense of nullifying another's accomplishment or making it ineffective. *Thwart* makes a stronger implication of direct opposition to another. *Foil* implies defeating either by direct confrontation or by outwitting, confounding, or disconcerting. *Balk* implies the placing of barriers or hindrances in another's course.

frus·tra·tion (frŭs-trā′shən) *n.* **1.** The condition or an instance of being frustrated. **2.** One that frustrates.

frus·tule (frŭs′cho͞ol, -tyo͞ol) *n.* The hard, siliceous shell of a diatom. [French, from Latin *frustulum,* diminutive of *frustum,* piece. See **bhreus-**[2] in Appendix.*]

frus·tum (frŭs′təm) *n., pl.* **-tums** or **-ta** (-tə). A part of a solid, such as a cone or pyramid, between two parallel planes cutting the solid, especially the section between the base and a plane parallel to it. [Latin, piece, piece cut off. See **bhreus-**[2] in Appendix.*]

fru·tes·cent (fro͞o-tĕs′ənt) *adj.* Pertaining to, resembling, or assuming the form of a shrub; shrubby. [Latin *frutex,* bush (see **fruticose**) + -ESCENT.] —**fru·tes′cence** *n.*

fru·ti·cose (fro͞o′tĭ-kōs′) *adj.* Shrublike, especially in form. [Latin *fruticōsus,* from *frutex*† (stem *frutic-*), shrub, bush.]

fry[1] (frī) *v.* **fried, frying, fries.** —*tr.* To cook over direct heat in hot oil or fat. —*intr.* **1.** To be cooked over direct heat in hot oil or fat. **2.** *Slang.* To undergo execution in an electric chair. —*n., pl.* **fries. 1.** A dish of any fried food. **2.** A social gathering

featuring fried food: *a fish fry.* [Middle English *frien,* from Old French *frire,* from Latin *frigere.* See **bher-**[4] in Appendix.*]
fry[2] (frī) *n., pl.* **fry. 1.** A small fish, especially a young, recently hatched fish. **2.** The similar young of certain other animals. **3.** Individuals; persons: *Plan to invite the young fry to a party.* [Middle English, young offspring, perhaps from Norman French *frie,* from Old French *freier,* to spawn, to rub, from Latin *fricāre,* to rub. See **bhrēi-** in Appendix.*]
Fry (frī), **Christopher.** Born 1907. English playwright.
fry·er (frī′ər) *n.* Also **fri·er. 1.** One that fries. **2.** A small, young chicken suitable for frying.
frying pan. A shallow, long-handled pan used for frying food.
FS Forest Service.
FSA Federal Security Agency.
FSD Airport code for Sioux Falls, South Dakota.
FSH follicle-stimulating hormone.
f-stop (ĕf′stŏp′) *n.* **1.** A camera lens aperture setting calibrated to a corresponding f-number. **2.** An **f-number** *(see).* [F(OCAL LENGTH) stop.]
f-sys·tem (ĕf′sĭs′təm) *n.* A method of indicating the relative aperture of a camera lens based on the f-number.
ft foot.
ft. fort; fortification.
F.T.A. Future Teachers of America.
FTC Federal Trade Commission.
ft-lb foot-pound.
fub·sy (fŭb′zē) *adj.* **-sier, -siest.** *British Regional.* Somewhat fat and squat. [From obsolete *fubs*†, a chubby person.]
Fu·chien. See **Fukien.**
Fu·chou, Fu·chow. See **Foochow.**
fuch·sia (fyo͞o′shə) *n.* **1.** Any of various chiefly tropical shrubs of the genus *Fuchsia,* widely cultivated for their showy, drooping, purplish, reddish, or white flowers. **2.** The **California fuchsia** *(see).* **3.** Strong, vivid purplish red. See **color.** [New Latin, after Leonhard *Fuchs* (1501–1566), German botanist.]
fuch·sin (fyo͞ok′sĭn, -sēn′) *n.* Also **fuch·sine** (-sĭn, -sēn′). A dark-green synthetic aniline dyestuff, the hydrochloride of rosaniline, used to make a purple-red dye employed in coloring textiles and leather and as a bacterial stain. Also called "magenta." [FUCHS(IA) + -IN.]
fuck (fŭk) *v.* **fucked, fucking, fucks.** —*tr.* **1.** *Vulgar.* To have sexual intercourse with. **2.** *Vulgar Slang.* To deal with in an aggressive, unjust, or spiteful manner. **3.** *Vulgar Slang.* To mishandle; bungle. Usually used with *up.* —*intr.* **1.** *Vulgar.* To engage in sexual intercourse. **2.** *Vulgar Slang.* To meddle; interfere. Used with *with.* —*n.* **1.** *Vulgar.* An act or instance of sexual intercourse. **2.** *Vulgar Slang.* A partner in sexual intercourse. [Middle English *fucken*; a Germanic verb originally meaning "to strike, move quickly, penetrate" (akin to or perhaps borrowed from Middle Dutch *fokken,* to strike, copulate with); details uncertain owing to lack of early attestations. See **peig-** in Appendix.*]
fuck·ing (fŭk′ĭng) *adj. Vulgar Slang.* Damned. Used as an intensive. —*adv. Vulgar Slang.* Very. Used as an intensive.
fu·coid (fyo͞o′koid′) *adj.* Of or belonging to the order Fucales, which includes brown algae such as gulfweed, rockweed, and similar seaweeds. —*n.* **1.** A member of the Fucales. **2.** A fossilized cast or impression of or resembling a seaweed. [Perhaps FUC(US) + -OID.]
fu·cus (fyo͞o′kəs) *n.* Any of various brown algae of the genus *Fucus,* which includes many of the rockweeds. [New Latin *Fucus,* from Latin *fūcus,* red dye, orchil, from Greek *phukos.* See **phyco-.**]
fud·dle (fŭd′l) *v.* **-dled, -dling, -dles.** —*tr.* To muddle with or as if with liquor; intoxicate. —*intr.* To drink; tipple. —*n.* A state of intoxication or confusion. [Origin unknown.]
fud·dy-dud·dy (fŭd′ē-dŭd′ē) *n., pl.* **-dies.** One who is old-fashioned and fussy. [Origin uncertain.]
fudge (fŭj) *n.* **1.** A soft rich candy made of sugar, butter, and flavoring. **2.** Nonsense; humbug. **3.** *Printing.* A small section of newspaper copy inserted after the plate or type is on the printing press. —*interj.* Used to express disbelief, disappointment, or annoyance. —*v.* **fudged, fudging, fudges.** —*tr.* To fake or falsify. —*intr.* To act in a dishonest or indecisive manner; to fake. [Probably variant of archaic *fadge*†.]
Fue·gi·an (fwā′jē-ən) *adj.* Of or relating to Tierra del Fuego, its inhabitants, or its culture. —*n.* An inhabitant of Tierra del Fuego.
fueh·rer. Variant of **führer.**
fu·el (fyo͞o′əl) *n.* **1.** Anything consumed to produce energy, especially: **a.** A material such as wood, coal, gas, or oil burned to produce heat. **b.** Fissionable material used in a nuclear reactor. **c.** Nutritive material metabolized by a living organism. **2.** Anything that maintains or heightens an activity or an emotion. —*v.* **fueled** or **-elled, -eling** or **-elling, -els.** —*tr.* To provide with fuel. —*intr.* To take in fuel. [Middle English *feuel,* from Old French *fouaille,* from Vulgar Latin *focālia* (unattested), from *focus*†, fire, hearth.] —**fu′el·er** *n.*
fuel cell. An electrochemical cell in which the energy of a reaction between a fuel such as liquid hydrogen and an oxidant such as liquid oxygen is converted directly and continuously into the energy of direct electric current.
fuel injection. Any of several methods or mechanical systems by which a fuel is vaporized and sprayed into the cylinders of a diesel or other internal-combustion engine and ignited spontaneously by the heat of air compressed within the cylinders rather than by spark plugs.
fuel oil. Any liquid or liquefiable petroleum product with a flash point above 100°F that is used to generate heat or power.

Fuer·te·ven·tu·ra (fwĕr′tā-vĕn-to͞o′rä). The second-largest (666 square miles) of the Canary Islands and the nearest to the northwestern coast of Africa.
fu·ga·cious (fyo͞o-gā′shəs) *adj.* **1.** Passing away quickly; evanescent. **2.** *Botany.* Withering or dropping off early: *fugacious petals.* [From Latin *fugāx* (stem *fugāc-*), swift, fleeting, from *fugere,* to flee. See **bheug-**[1] in Appendix.*] —**fu·ga′cious·ly** *adv.* —**fu·ga′cious·ness, fu·gac′i·ty** (fyo͞o-găs′ə-tē) *n.*
-fuge. Indicates an expulsion or driving away; for example, **vermifuge.** [From Latin *fugāre,* to put to flight, expel, from *fuga,* flight. See **bheug-**[1] in Appendix.*]
fu·gi·o (fyo͞o′jē-ō′) *n.* A copper coin issued in 1787 as the first coinage authorized by the U.S. Congress. [Latin, "I flee" (the inscription *fugio* appears on the coin), from *fugere,* to flee. See **bheug-**[1] in Appendix.*]
fu·gi·tive (fyo͞o′jə-tĭv) *adj.* **1.** Running or having run away; fleeing, as from justice, the law, or the like. **2. a.** Passing quickly; fleeting: *fugitive hours.* **b.** Difficult to comprehend or retain; elusive. **c.** Given to change or disappearance; perishable. **3.** Tending to wander; vagabond. **4.** Having to do with topics of temporary interest; ephemeral. —See Synonyms at **transient.** —*n.* **1.** One who flees; a runaway; refugee. **2.** Anything fleeting or ephemeral. [Middle English *fugitif,* from Old French, from Latin *fugitīvus,* from adjective, "fleeing," from *fugitus,* past participle of *fugere,* to flee. See **bheug-**[1] in Appendix.*] —**fu′gi·tive·ly** *adv.* —**fu′gi·tive·ness** *n.*
fu·gle (fyo͞o′gəl) *intr.v.* **-gled, -gling, -gles.** *Archaic.* **1.** To act as a fugleman. **2.** To make signals. [Back-formation from FUGLEMAN.]
fu·gle·man (fyo͞o′gəl-mən) *n., pl.* **-men** (-mĭn). **1.** *Archaic.* A soldier who serves as a guide and model for his company. **2.** A leader; especially, a political leader. [German *Flügelmann,* soldier, "man on the wing" : *Flügel,* wing, from Middle High German *vlügel* (see **pleu-** in Appendix*) + *Mann,* man, from Old High German *man* (see **man-**[1] in Appendix*).]
fugue (fyo͞og) *n.* **1.** A polyphonic musical style or form in which a theme or themes stated sequentially and in imitation are developed contrapuntally. **2.** A pathological amnesiac condition during which the patient is apparently conscious of his actions but on return to normal has no recollection of them. [French *fugue,* or Italian *fuga,* flight, from Latin, flight. See **bheug-**[1] in Appendix.*] —**fu′gal** (fyo͞o′gəl) *adj.* —**fu′gal·ly** *adv.*
füh·rer (fyo͝or′ər; *German* fü′rər) *n.* Also **fueh·rer. 1.** A leader; especially, one exercising the powers of a tyrant. **2.** *Capital* **F.** The title of Adolf Hitler as the leader of the German Nazis. [German *Führer,* from Middle High German *vüerer,* bearer, from *vüeren,* to lead, bear, from Old High German *fuoren,* to lead. See **per-**[2] in Appendix.*]
Fu·ji (fo͞o′jē). Also **Fu·ji·san** (fo͞o′jē-sän′), **Fu·ji·ya·ma** (fo͞o′jē-yä′mə). The highest peak (12,389 feet) in Japan, an extinct volcanic cone on south-central Honshu.
Fu·kien (fo͞o′kyĕn′). Also **Fu·chien. 1.** A province of China, occupying 45,000 square miles in the southeastern part of the country. Population, 14,650,000. Capital, Foochow. **2.** Any of the Chinese dialects spoken in Fukien Province, Taiwan, and eastern Kwangtung.
Fu·ku·o·ka (fo͞o′ko͞o-ō′kə). A city and seaport of Japan, in northern Kyushu. Population, 718,000.
Fu·ku·shi·ma (fo͞o′ko͞o-shē′mə). A city and textile-manufacturing center of Japan, in northeastern Honshu. Population, 149,000.
-ful. Indicates: **1.** Fullness or abundance; for example, **playful. 2.** Having the characteristics; for example, **masterful. 3.** Tendency or ability; for example, **useful. 4.** The amount or number that will fill; for example, **armful.** [Middle English *-ful,* Old English *-ful, -full,* from *full,* FULL.]
Usage: The plurals of nouns that end in *-ful* are most often indicated, especially in writing, by the addition of the letter *s: glassfuls; spoonfuls; tablespoonfuls; teaspoonfuls.*
Fu·la (fo͞o′lə) *n., pl.* **Fula** or **-las.** Also **Fu·lah.** A mostly Moslem people of northwestern and central Africa, of mixed Hamitic and Negroid stock.
Fu·la·ni (fo͞o′lä-nē, fo͞o-lä′nē) *n., pl.* **Fulani** or **-nis. 1.** One of the Fula. **2.** The language of the Fula.
Ful·bright (fo͝ol′brīt′), **J(ames) William.** Born 1905. American educator and political leader; chairman, Senate Foreign Relations Committee (since 1959).
ful·crum (fo͝ol′krəm, fŭl′-) *n., pl.* **-crums** or **-cra** (-krə). **1.** The point or support on which a lever turns. **2.** A position, element, or agency through, around, or by means of which vital powers are exercised: *"This is where the fulcrum of our fears lies"* (Jacob Bronowski). [Latin, bedpost, support, from *fulcīre,* to prop up, support. See **bhelg-** in Appendix.*]
ful·fill (fo͝ol-fĭl′) *tr.v.* **-filled, -filling, -fills.** Also **ful·fil, -filled, -filling, -fils. 1.** To bring into actuality; to effect. **2.** To carry out (an order or duty, for example). **3.** To measure up to; satisfy. **4.** To go to the end of (a period of time); finish or complete. —See Synonyms at **perform.** [Middle English *fulfillen,* Old English *fullfyllan,* to fill full : FULL + *fyllan,* to FILL.] —**ful·fill′er** *n.* —**ful·fill′ment** *n.*
ful·gent (fŭl′jənt, fo͝ol′-) *adj.* Shining brilliantly. [Middle English, from Latin *fulgēns,* present participle of *fulgēre,* to flash, shine. See **bhel-**[1] in Appendix.*] —**ful′gent·ly** *adv.*
ful·gu·rant (fŭl′gyər-ənt, fo͝ol′-) *adj.* Flashing like lightning. [Latin *fulgurāns,* present participle of *fulgurāre,* to FULGURATE.]
ful·gu·rate (fŭl′gyə-rāt′, fo͝ol′-) *intr.v.* **-rated, -rating, -rates.** To give off or seem to give off flashes of lightning. [Latin *fulgurare,* to flash, glow like lightning, from *fulgur,* lightning, from *fulgēre,* to flash, shine. See **bhel-**[1] in Appendix.*]

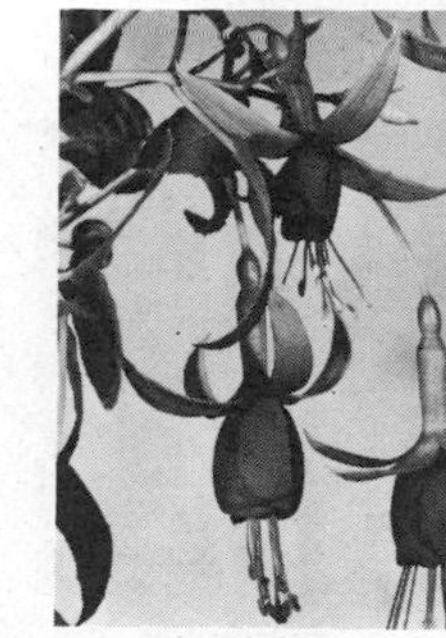

fuchsia
Fuchsia hybrida

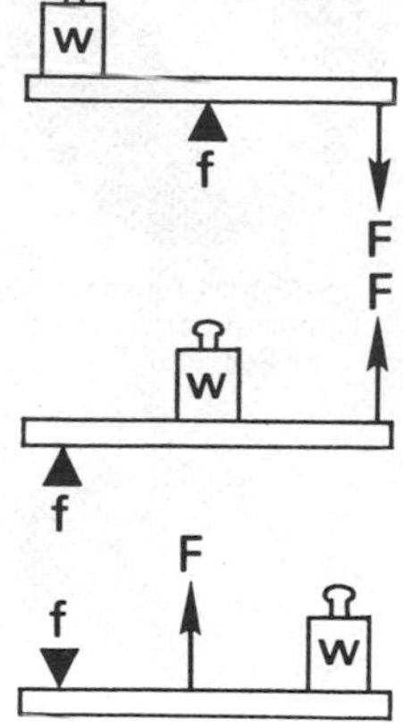

fulcrum
Black triangles represent the fulcrums of three basic levers

t tight/th thin, path/*th* this, bathe/ŭ cut/ûr urge/v valve/w with/y yes/z zebra, size/zh vision/ə about, item, edible, gallop, circus/ à *Fr.* ami/œ *Fr.* feu, *Ger.* schön/ü *Fr.* tu, *Ger.* über/KH *Ger.* ich, *Scot.* loch/N *Fr.* bon. ***Follows main vocabulary. †Of obscure origin.**

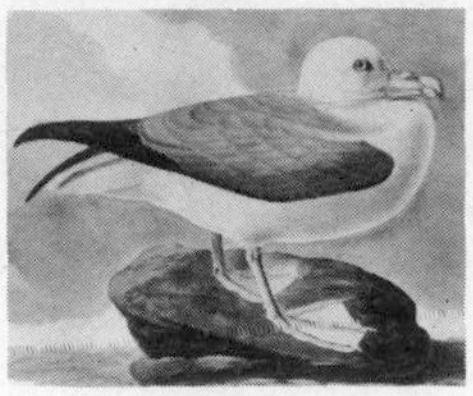

fulmar
Fulmarus glacialis
Painting by
John James Audubon

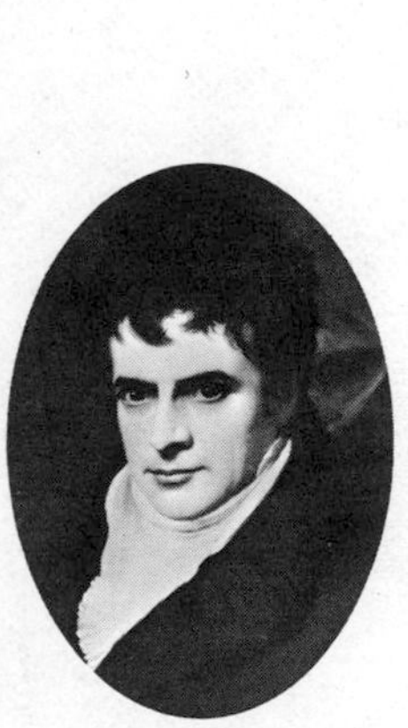

Robert Fulton
Contemporary portrait
by Benjamin West

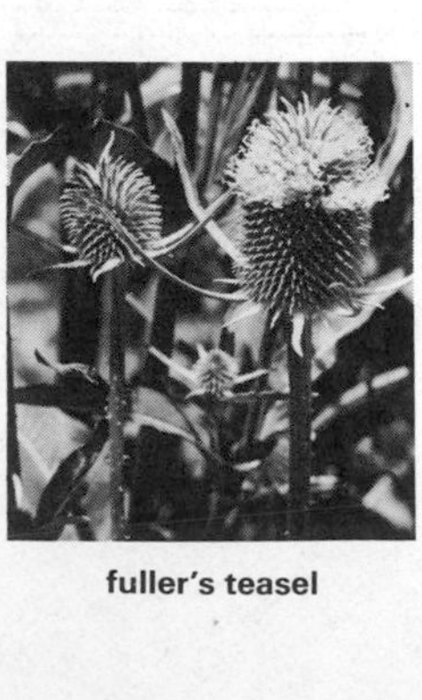

fuller's teasel

ful·gu·ra·tion (fŭl′gyə-rā′shən, fo͝ol′-) *n.* **1.** The act of flashing like lightning or flashing with light. **2.** The destruction of tissue with electric current.

ful·gu·rite (fŭl′gyə-rīt′, fo͝ol′-) *n.* A tubular body of glassy rock produced by lightning striking exposed surfaces. [Latin *fulgur*, lightning (see **fulgurate**) + -ITE.]

ful·gu·rous (fŭl′gyər-əs, fo͝ol′-) *adj.* **1.** Emitting flashes of lightning. **2.** Appearing or acting like lightning. [From Latin *fulgur*, lightning. See **fulgurate.**]

Ful·ham (fo͝ol′əm). A former administrative division of London, England, now part of **Hammersmith** *(see).*

fu·lig·i·nous (fyo͞o-lĭj′ə-nəs) *adj.* **1.** Sooty. **2.** Colored by or as if by soot. [Late Latin *fūlīginōsus*, from Latin *fūlīgō* (stem *fūlīgin-*), soot. See **dheu-¹** in Appendix.*] —**fu·lig′i·nous·ly** *adv.*

full¹ (fo͝ol) *adj.* **fuller, fullest. 1.** Containing all that is normal or possible; filled: *a full pail.* **2.** Not deficient or partial; complete: *full view of the stage.* **3.** Of maximum or highest degree or development: *at full speed.* **4.** Having a great deal or many of; abounding in. Used with *of: "History is full of the errors of states and princes"* (Franklin). **5.** Totally qualified or unanimously accepted: *a full member.* **6.** Charged or engrossed with. Used with *of: full of dread.* **7. a.** Rounded in shape; shapely: *a full figure.* **b.** Of ample cut; of generous proportions; wide: *full draperies.* **8.** Satiated, especially with food or drink; abundantly fed. **9. a.** Having depth and body; rich: *a full color.* **b.** Resonant: *in full voice.* **10.** Full-bodied. Said of wines. **11.** Thoroughly documented and presented; detailed: *a full report.* **12.** Having the observable surface completely illuminated. Said of the moon. **13.** At the flood; high. Said of the tide. —*adv.* **1.** To a complete extent; entirely. Often used in combination: *full-grown.* **2.** Exactly; directly: *full in the path of the moon.* **3.** Quite; equally: *full wicked as I am.* —**full well.** Very well: *I know full well how you feel.* —*v.* **fulled, fulling, fulls.** —*tr.* To make (a garment) full, as by pleating or gathering. —*intr.* To become full. Used of the moon. —*n. Rare.* The maximum or complete size, amount, or development. —**at the full.** At the state or period of fullness. —**in full. 1.** To, for, or with the entire amount. **2.** Completely; with nothing left out. —**to the full.** To the utmost extent; completely. [Middle English *full(l)*, Old English *full.* See **pel-⁸** in Appendix.*]

full² (fo͝ol) *v.* **fulled, fulling, fulls.** —*tr.* To increase the weight and bulk of (cloth) by shrinking and beating or pressing. —*intr.* To become heavier and more compact. Used of cloth. [Middle English *fullen*, from Old French *fouler*, from Vulgar Latin *fullāre* (unattested), from Latin *fullō*†, a fuller.]

full-au·to·mat·ic (fo͝ol′ô′tə-măt′ĭk) *adj.* **Automatic** *(see).*

full·back (fo͝ol′băk′) *n. Abbr.* **fb, f.b. 1. a.** *Football.* A backfield player whose position is behind the quarterback and halfbacks and who performs offensive blocking and line plunges and defensive linebacking. **b.** A similar player in field hockey, soccer, and rugby. **2.** The position played by a fullback.

full blood. 1. Relationship established through having the same set of parents. **2.** A person or animal of unmixed race or breed; a purebred.

full-blood·ed (fo͝ol′blŭd′ĭd) *adj.* Also **full-blood** (fo͝ol′blŭd′) (for sense 1). **1. a.** Of unmixed ancestry; purebred. **b.** Related through having the same parents. **2. a.** Not pale or anemic. **b.** Vigorous and virile.

full-blown (fo͝ol′blōn′) *adj.* **1.** In full blossom; fully open: *a full-blown tulip.* **2.** Fully developed or matured: *a full-blown beauty.*

full-bod·ied (fo͝ol′bŏd′ēd) *adj.* Having richness and intensity of flavor. Said of wines.

full brother. See **brother.**

full cousin. See **cousin.**

full dress. The attire appropriate for formal or ceremonial events.

full-dress (fo͝ol′drĕs′) *adj.* **1.** Requiring or consisting of full dress; formal: *a full-dress banquet.* **2.** Characterized by exhaustive thoroughness; complete: *a full-dress investigation.*

full·er¹ (fo͝ol′ər) *n.* A person who fulls cloth. [Middle English *fullere*, Old English *fullere*, from Latin *fullō.* See **full** (verb).]

full·er² (fo͝ol′ər) *n.* **1.** A hammer used by a blacksmith for grooving or spreading iron. **2.** A groove made with this tool. [Perhaps from the name *Fuller.*]

Ful·ler (fo͝ol′ər), **George.** 1822–1884. American painter.

Ful·ler (fo͝ol′ər), **R(ichard) Buckminster.** Born 1895. American architect and inventor.

Ful·ler (fo͝ol′ər), **(Sarah) Margaret.** 1810–1850. American editor and feminist leader.

Ful·ler·board (fo͝ol′ər-bôrd′, -bōrd′) *n.* A trademark for a heavy pressed cardboard used as a protective material, especially for insulating, in electrical apparatus. [Perhaps from the name *Fuller.*]

fuller's earth. A highly absorbent claylike substance used predominantly in fulling woolen cloth, in talcum powders, as a filter, and as a catalyst.

fuller's teasel. A European plant, *Dipsacus fullonum*, having bristly flower heads used by fullers to raise the nap on cloth.

Ful·ler·ton (fo͝ol′ər-tən). An industrial city of California, in the southwest near Long Beach. Population, 56,000.

full-fash·ioned (fo͝ol′făsh′ənd) *adj.* Knitted in a shape that conforms closely to body lines.

full-fledged (fo͝ol′flĕjd′) *adj.* **1.** Having fully developed adult plumage. **2.** Having reached full development; mature. **3.** Having full status or rank: *a full-fledged lawyer.*

full gainer. A forward dive in which one executes a full back somersault before entering the water.

full house. *Poker.* A hand containing three of a kind and a pair.

full-length (fo͝ol′lĕngkth′, -lĕngth′) *adj.* **1.** Showing or fitted to the entire length of something: *a full-length mirror.* **2.** Of a normal or standard length; unabridged: *a full-length novel.*

full moon. 1. The phase of the moon when it is visible as a fully illuminated disk. **2.** The period of the month when this occurs.

full-mouthed (fo͝ol′mouthd′, -moutht′) *adj.* **1.** Having a complete set of teeth. Said of cattle and other livestock. **2.** Uttered loudly or noisily: *a full-mouthed oath.*

full nelson. A wrestling hold in which both hands are first thrust under the opponent's arms from behind and then pressed against the back of his neck. Compare **half nelson.**

full·ness (fo͝ol′nĭs) *n.* Also **ful·ness.** The quality or state of being full. —**fullness of time.** The proper, appointed time.

full rhyme. A **perfect rhyme** *(see).*

full-scale (fo͝ol′skāl′) *adj.* **1.** Of the actual or full size; not reduced: *a full-scale model.* **2.** Employing all resources; not limited or partial: *a full-scale antiwar campaign.*

full sister. See **sister.**

full stop. A period indicating the end of a sentence.

ful·ly (fo͝ol′ē) *adv.* **1.** Totally or completely. **2.** Adequately; sufficiently. **3.** At a conservative estimate; at least.

ful·mar (fo͝ol′mər, -mär′) *n.* **1.** A gull-like bird, *Fulmarus glacialis*, of Arctic regions, having smoky gray plumage. **2.** Any of several similar, related birds. [Perhaps from Old Norse *fūlmār*, "foul gull" (probably referring to its smell) : *fūll*, foul (see **pu-²** in Appendix*) + *mār*, gull, from Germanic *maiwa-* (unattested), gull, MEW.]

ful·mi·nant (fŭl′mə-nənt, fo͝ol′-) *adj.* **1.** Fulminating. **2.** *Pathology.* Occurring suddenly, rapidly, and with great intensity. Said of pain. [Latin *fulmināns*, present participle of *fulmināre*, to strike with lightning, FULMINATE.]

ful·mi·nate (fŭl′mə-nāt′, fo͝ol′-) *v.* **-nated, -nating, -nates.** —*intr.* **1.** To issue a thunderous verbal attack or denunciation; inveigh: *fulminate against political chicanery.* **2.** To explode or detonate with sudden violence. —*tr.* **1.** To thunder out or issue (a decree or denunciation, for example). **2.** To cause to explode. —*n.* An explosive salt of fulminic acid; especially, **fulminate of mercury** *(see).* [Middle English *fulminaten*, from Medieval Latin *fulmināre* (past participle *fulminātus*), to censure ecclesiastically, from Latin, to strike with lightning, from *fulmen* (stem *fulmin-*), lightning. See **bhel-¹** in Appendix.*] —**ful′mi·na′tor** (-nā′tər) *n.* —**ful′mi·na·to′ry** (-nə-tôr′ē, -tōr′ē) *adj.*

fulminate of mercury. A gray crystalline powder, $Hg(CNO)_2$, that explodes when dry under the slightest friction or shock and is used as a high explosive. Also called "fulminate."

ful·mi·na·tion (fŭl′mə-nā′shən, fo͝ol′-) *n.* **1.** The act of fulminating. **2.** A thunderous denunciation or censure. **3.** A violent explosion.

ful·mine (fŭl′mĭn, fo͝ol′-) *v.* **-mined, -mining, -mines.** *Rare.* —*tr.* To fulminate. —*intr.* To fulminate. [Old French *fulminer*, from Latin *fulmināre*, FULMINATE.]

ful·min·ic acid (fŭl-mĭn′ĭk, fo͝ol-). An unstable acid, HONC, that forms highly explosive salts. [From Latin *fulmen* (stem *fulmin-*), lightning. See **fulminate.**]

ful·some (fo͝ol′səm) *adj.* **1.** Offensively excessive or insincere. **2.** Offensive to the senses; loathsome; disgusting. [Middle English *fulsom*, abundant : FULL + -SOME.] —**ful′some·ly** *adv.* —**ful′some·ness** *n.*

Usage: *Fulsome* is often misapplied, especially in *fulsome praise*, by those who think that the term is equivalent merely to *full* and *abundant.* In modern usage *full* and *abundant* are obsolete as senses of *fulsome*, which now combines the idea of fullness or abundance with that of excess or insincerity.

Ful·ton (fo͝ol′tən), **Robert.** 1765–1815. American engineer and inventor; designed and built early steamboats.

fu·mar·ic acid (fyo͞o-măr′ĭk). An acid, $C_4H_4O_4$, found in various plants and produced synthetically, used mainly in resins, paints, and varnishes. [From New Latin *Fumaria*, genus of fumitory, from Late Latin *fūmāria*, fumitory, from Latin *fūmus*, smoke. See **dheu-¹** in Appendix.*]

fu·ma·role (fyo͞o′mə-rōl′) *n.* A hole in a volcanic area from which hot smoke and gases arise. [Italian *fumarola*, from Late Latin *fūmāriolum*, smoke hole, from Latin *fūmārium*, smoke chamber, from *fūmus*, smoke. See **dheu-¹** in Appendix.*]

fu·ma·to·ri·um (fyo͞o′mə-tôr′ē-əm, -tōr′ē-əm) *n., pl.* **-ums** or **-toria** (-tôr′ē-ə, -tōr′ē-ə). An airtight fumigation chamber in which chemical vapors are used to destroy insects and fungi on plants. [New Latin, from Latin *fūmātus*, past participle of *fūmāre*, to smoke, from *fūmus*, smoke. See **dheu-¹** in Appendix.*]

fu·ma·to·ry (fyo͞o′mə-tôr′ē, -tōr′ē) *adj.* Of or pertaining to smoke or fumigating. —*n., pl.* **fumatories.** A fumatorium. [New Latin *fumatorius*, from FUMATORIUM.]

fum·ble (fŭm′bəl) *v.* **-bled, -bling, -bles.** —*intr.* **1.** To touch or handle nervously or idly: *fumble with a necktie.* **2.** To grope awkwardly to find or to accomplish: *fumble for a key.* **3.** To proceed awkwardly and uncertainly; blunder: *fumble through a speech.* **4. a.** *Baseball.* To mishandle a ground ball. **b.** *Football.* To drop a ball that is in play. —*tr.* **1.** To touch or handle clumsily or idly. **2.** To make a botch of; bungle. **3.** To feel or make (one's way) awkwardly. **4. a.** *Baseball.* To mishandle (a ground ball). **b.** *Football.* To drop (the ball while in play). —*n.* **1. a.** The act of fumbling. **b.** An instance of fumbling. **2.** *Sports.* A ball that has been fumbled. [Perhaps from Scandinavian, akin to Norwegian or Swedish *fumla*†.] —**fum′bler** *n.*

fume (fyo͞om) *n.* **1.** An exhalation of smoke, vapor, or gas; especially, an irritating or disagreeable exhalation. **2.** A strong or acrid odor. **3.** A state of irritation or anger: *"The conscious fume and fret of resolutions and clenched teeth"* (C.S. Lewis).

—*v.* **fumed, fuming, fumes.** —*tr.* **1.** To subject to or treat with fumes. **2.** To give off in or as if in fumes. —*intr.* **1.** To emit fumes. **2.** To rise or dissipate in vapor. **3.** To feel or show agitation or anger. [Middle English, from Old French *fum,* from Latin *fūmus,* smoke, steam. See **dheu-**¹ in Appendix.*]

fu·mi·gate (fyo͞o′mĭ-gāt′) *v.* **-gated, -gating, -gates.** —*tr.* To subject to smoke or fumes, usually in order to exterminate vermin or insects. —*intr.* To employ smoke or fumes in order to exterminate. [Latin *fūmigāre* : *fūmus,* smoke, FUME + *agere,* to make, do (see **ag-** in Appendix*).] —**fu′mi·ga′tion** *n.* —**fu′mi·ga′tor** (-gā′tər) *n.*

fu·mi·to·ry (fyo͞o′mə-tôr′ē, -tōr′ē) *n., pl.* **-ries. 1.** A climbing plant, *Fumaria officinalis,* native to Europe, having finely divided leaves and spurred purplish flowers. **2.** Any of several similar or related plants. [Middle English *fumetere,* from Old French *fumeterre,* from Medieval Latin *fūmus terrae,* "smoke of the earth" (its growth resembles a cloud of smoke over the ground) : Latin *fūmus,* smoke, FUME + *terrae,* genitive of *terra,* earth (see **ters-** in Appendix*).]

fum·y (fyo͞o′mē) *adj.* **-ier, -iest.** Pertaining to, full of, or producing fumes.

fun (fŭn) *n.* **1.** A source of enjoyment or pleasure; amusing diversion: *Clowns are fun.* **2.** Enjoyment; pleasure; amusement: *have fun at the beach.* **3.** Excited, noisy activity or altercation. —**for** (or **in**) **fun.** As a joke; playfully. —**like fun.** *Slang.* Absolutely not; of course not. —**make fun of.** To ridicule. —*intr.v.* **funned, funning, funs.** To behave playfully; joke. —*adj. Informal.* Providing fun; amusing: *a fun group of people.* [Perhaps from obsolete *fun,* to trick, from Middle English *fonnen,* to make fun of, from *fon, fonne,* a fool. See **fond.**]

Fu·na·fu·ti (fo͞o′nə-fo͞o′tē). An atoll and the seat of government of the Ellice Islands, in the southwestern Pacific Ocean.

fu·nam·bu·list (fyo͞o-năm′byə-lĭst) *n.* One who performs on a tightrope or a slack rope. [Probably from Latin *fūnambulus,* rope dancer : *fūnis*†, rope + *ambulāre,* to walk around (see **al-**² in Appendix*).] —**fu·nam′bu·lism′** *n.*

Fun·chal (fo͞on-shäl′). **1.** The administrative district of Portugal consisting of the Madeira Islands. Population, 287,000. **2.** The capital of this district, a seaport and resort on the island of Madeira. Population, 43,000.

func·tion (fŭngk′shən) *n.* **1.** The natural or proper action for which a person, office, mechanism, or organ is fitted or employed. **2. a.** Assigned duty or activity: *His functions include collecting interoffice mail.* **b.** Specific occupation or role: *in his function as attorney.* **3.** An official ceremony or elaborate social occasion. **4.** Something closely related to another thing and dependent upon it for its existence, value, or significance. **5.** *Grammar.* The role or position of a linguistic element in a construction. **6.** *Mathematics.* **a.** A variable so related to another that for each value assumed by one there is a value determined for the other. **b.** A rule of correspondence between two sets such that there is a unique element in one set assigned to each element in the other. —*intr.v.* **functioned, -tioning, -tions.** To have or perform a function; to serve. [Latin *functiō,* activity, performance, from *functus,* past participle of *fungī,* to perform. See **bheug-**² in Appendix.*] —**func′tion·less** *adj.*

func·tion·al (fŭngk′shən-əl) *adj.* **1.** Of or pertaining to a function or functions. **2. a.** Designed for or adapted to a particular need or activity: *functional clothing for infants.* **b.** Stressing the function of something over extraneous embellishment: *functional architecture.* **3.** Capable of performing; operative. **4.** *Pathology.* Pertaining to a disease having no apparent physiological or structural cause. **5.** *Mathematics.* Of, relating to, or indicating a function or functions. —**func′tion·al·ly** *adv.*

func·tion·al·ism (fŭngk′shən-ə-lĭz′əm) *n.* **1.** The doctrine or the application of the doctrine that the function of an object should determine its design and materials. **2.** Any doctrine or its application stressing purpose, practicality, and utility.

functional shift. *Linguistics.* A shift in the syntactic function of a word without a change in its form, as when a noun serves as a verb.

func·tion·ar·y (fŭngk′shə-nĕr′ē) *n., pl.* **-ies.** A person who holds an office or a trust; an official.

function word. *Linguistics.* A word used to show a grammatical relationship in a sentence or phrase, such as a preposition, conjunction, or auxiliary verb. Also called "form word."

fund (fŭnd) *n.* **1.** A source of supply; a stock: *a fund of good will.* **2. a.** A sum of money or other resources set aside for a specific purpose: *orphans' fund.* **b.** *Plural.* Available money; ready cash. **3.** *Plural. British.* The permanent national debt, considered as securities. Preceded by *the.* **4.** An organization established to administer a fund. —*tr.v.* **funded, funding, funds. 1.** To provide money for paying off the interest or principal of (a debt). **2.** To convert (a debt) into a long-term or floating debt with fixed interest payments. **3.** To place in a fund or accumulate. **4.** To furnish a fund for: *fund cancer research; fund a space program.* [Blend of French *fond,* bottom, and *fonds,* stock, both from Latin *fundus,* bottom, landed property. See **bhudh-** in Appendix.*]

fun·da·ment (fŭn′də-mənt) *n.* **1. a.** The buttocks. **b.** The anus. **2.** The natural features of a land surface unaltered by human beings. **3.** A foundation. **4.** A theoretical basis; underlying principle: *"all neighbor states . . . must revise . . . their policy fundaments"* (C.L. Sulzberger). [Middle English *foundement,* foundation, lower part, from Old French *fondement,* from Latin *fundāmentum,* from *fundāre,* to lay the bottom for, from *fundus,* bottom. See **bhudh-** in Appendix.*]

fun·da·men·tal (fŭn′də-mĕnt′l) *adj.* **1. a.** Having to do with the foundation; elemental; basic. **b.** Major; central, key: *of fundamental importance.* **2.** Having to do with the origin; generative; primary. **3.** *Physics.* **a.** Of or pertaining to the component of lowest frequency of a periodic wave or quantity. **b.** Of or pertaining to the lowest possible frequency of a vibrating element or system. **4.** *Music.* Having the root in the bass: *a fundamental chord.* —*n.* **1.** Something that is an elemental part of a system, as a principle or law; an essential. **2.** *Physics.* The lowest frequency of a periodically varying quantity or of a vibrating system. —**fun′da·men′tal·ly** *adv.*

fun·da·men·tal·ism (fŭn′də-mĕnt′l-ĭz′əm) *n.* **1.** Belief in the Bible as factual historical record and incontrovertible prophecy, including such doctrines as the Genesis, the Virgin Birth, the Second Advent, and Armageddon. **2. a.** *Often capital* **F.** A movement among U.S. Protestants of the 19th century based upon this belief. **b.** Adherence to this belief. —**fun′da·men′tal·ist** *n.* & *adj.* —**fun′da·men′tal·ist′ic** *adj.*

fundamental particle. *Physics.* An **elementary particle** *(see).*

fun·dus (fŭn′dəs) *n., pl.* **-di** (-dī′). *Anatomy.* The inner basal surface of an organ farthest away from the opening, as in the eye or uterus. [New Latin, from Latin, bottom. See **bhudh-** in Appendix.*]

Fun·dy, Bay of (fŭn′dē). An inlet of the Atlantic Ocean, extending about 100 miles between Maine and New Brunswick on the north and Nova Scotia on the south, and famous for its tides of up to 70 feet.

Fü·nen. The German name for **Fyn.**

fu·ner·al (fyo͞o′nər-əl) *n.* **1.** The ceremonies held in connection with the burial or cremation of the dead. **2.** A party accompanying a body to the grave; funeral procession. —*adj.* Of or relating to a funeral. [Middle English *funerelles,* rites for a dead person, from Old French *funerailles,* from Medieval Latin *fūnerālia,* from Late Latin, neuter plural of *fūnerālis,* funereal, from Latin *fūnus*† (stem *fūner-*), funeral, death.]

fu·ner·ar·y (fyo͞o′nə-rĕr′ē) *adj.* Of or suitable for a funeral or burial. [From Latin *fūnerārius,* from *fūnus* (stem *fūner-*), FUNERAL.]

fu·ne·re·al (fyo͞o-nîr′ē-əl) *adj.* **1.** Of or suitable for a funeral: *a funereal wreath.* **2.** Mournful. [From Latin *fūnereus,* from *fūnus* (stem *fūner-*), FUNERAL.] —**fu·ne′re·al·ly** *adv.*

Fünf·kir·chen. The German name for **Pécs.**

fun·gal (fŭng′gəl) *adj.* Of or pertaining to a fungus; fungous.

fun·gi. Plural of **fungus.**

fun·gi·ble (fŭn′jə-bəl) *adj. Law.* Being of such a nature or kind that one unit or part may be exchanged or substituted for another equivalent unit or part in the discharging of an obligation. —*n.* Something fungible, as money or grain. [Medieval Latin *fungibilis,* serving a function, from *fungī,* to perform. See **bheug-**² in Appendix.*]

fun·gi·cide (fŭn′jə-sīd′, fŭng′gə-) *n.* A substance that destroys or inhibits the growth of fungi. [FUNG(US) + -CIDE.] —**fun′gi·ci′dal** *adj.*

fun·gi·form (fŭn′jə-fôrm′, fŭng′gə-) *adj.* Shaped like a mushroom. [FUNG(US) + -FORM.]

fun·go (fŭng′gō) *n., pl.* **-goes.** *Baseball.* A practice fly ball hit to a fielder with a specially designed bat. [Origin unknown.]

fun·goid (fŭng′goid′) *adj.* Of or resembling a fungus; funguslike. [FUNG(US) + -OID.]

fun·gous (fŭng′gəs) *adj.* **1.** Of, pertaining to, resembling, or characteristic of a fungus. **2.** Caused by a fungus. [Middle English, from Latin *fungōsus,* from *fungus,* FUNGUS.]

fun·gus (fŭng′gəs) *n., pl.* **fungi** (fŭn′jī′) or **-guses.** Any of numerous plants of the division or subkingdom Thallophyta, lacking chlorophyll, ranging in form from a single cell to a body mass of branched filamentous hyphae that often produce specialized fruiting bodies, and including the yeasts, molds, smuts, and mushrooms. [Latin, perhaps from Greek *sp(h)ongos,* SPONGE.]

fu·nic·u·lar (fyo͞o-nĭk′yə-lər, fə-) *adj.* **1.** Of, pertaining to, or resembling a rope or cord. **2.** Operated or moved by a cable. **3.** Of, pertaining to, or constituting a funiculus. —*n.* A cable railway on a steep incline; especially, such a railway with simultaneously ascending and descending cars counterbalancing one another. Also called "funicular railway."

fu·nic·u·lus (fyo͞o-nĭk′yə-ləs, fə-) *n., pl.* **-li** (-lī′). Also **fu·ni·cle** (fyo͞o′nĭ-kəl). **1.** *Anatomy.* A slender cordlike strand or band, especially: **a.** A bundle of nerve fibers in the nerve trunk. **b.** The umbilical cord. **2.** *Botany.* A stalk connecting an ovule or seed with the placenta. [New Latin, from Latin *fūniculus,* diminutive of *fūnis,* rope. See **funambulist.**]

funk (fŭngk) *n. Chiefly British.* **1. a.** A state of cowardly fright; panic. **b.** A state of extreme depression. **2.** A cowardly, fearful person. —*v.* **funked, funking, funks.** *Chiefly British.* —*tr.* **1.** To try to avoid out of fright; shrink from. **2.** To frighten. —*intr.* To shrink in fright; cower. [Perhaps from obsolete Flemish *fonck*†, a blow.]

Funk (fŭngk), **Casimir.** 1884–1967. Polish-born American biochemist; studied and first named vitamins.

fun·nel (fŭn′əl) *n.* **1.** A conical utensil with a small hole or narrow tube at the apex used to channel a substance into a small-mouthed container. **2.** Something having such a conical form. **3.** A shaft, flue, or stack for the passage of smoke; especially, the smokestack of a ship or locomotive. —*v.* **funneled, -neling, -nels.** Also *chiefly British* **-nelled, -nelling.** —*intr.* **1.** To assume the shape of a funnel. **2.** To move through or as if through a funnel: *Tourists funnel slowly through customs.* —*tr.* To cause to funnel. [Middle English *fonel,* from Provençal *fonilh,* from Latin *infundibulum,* from *infundere,* to pour in : *in-,* in + *fundere,* to pour (see **gheu-** in Appendix*).]

funnel

fun·ny (fŭn′ē) *adj.* **-nier, -niest. 1.** Causing laughter or amuse-

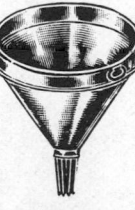

t tight/th thin, path/*th* this, bathe/ŭ cut/ûr urge/v valve/w with/y yes/z zebra, size/zh vision/ə about, item, edible, gallop, circus/ à *Fr.* ami/œ *Fr.* feu, *Ger.* schön/ü *Fr.* tu, *Ger.* über/KH *Ger.* ich, *Scot.* loch/N *Fr.* bon. ***Follows main vocabulary. †Of obscure origin.**

ment; mirthful. **2.** Strange; odd; curious. —*n., pl.* **funnies.** *Informal.* **1.** A joke or witticism. **2.** *Plural.* Comic strips. [From FUN.] —**fun'ni·ly** *adv.* —**fun'ni·ness** *n.*

funny bone. *Informal.* **1.** The point near the elbow where a nerve may be pressed against bone to produce a tingling sensation. **2.** A sense of humor.

funny paper. A newspaper section or supplement containing comic strips.

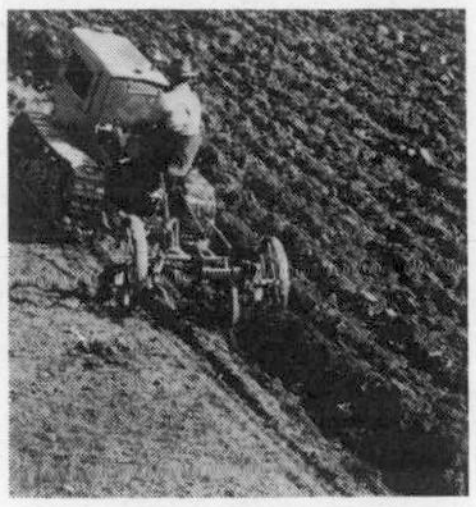

furrow

fur (fûr) *n.* **1.** The thick coat of soft hair covering the body of any of various animals, such as a fox, beaver, or cat. **2. a.** A dressed animal pelt, or part of one, used in the making of garments, trimmings, or decoration. **b.** Such pelts collectively. **3.** Any garment made of or lined with such pelts. **4.** Any coating of furlike material. —**make the fur fly.** *Slang.* To cause or engage in a dispute or brawl. —*adj.* Made of or lined with fur. —*tr.v.* **furred, furring, furs. 1.** To cover or line with fur. **2.** To provide fur garments for. **3.** To cover with a furlike deposit: *intestinal disorders that fur the tongue.* **4.** To line (a wall or floor) with furring. [Middle English *furre,* from *furren,* to line with fur, from Old French *forrer,* from *forre,* lining, from Germanic. See **pōi-**[2] in Appendix.*]

fur. furlong.

fu·ran (fyŏŏr'ăn', fyŏŏ-răn') *n.* Also **fur·fur·an** (fûr'fə-răn'). A colorless, volatile, liquid hydrocarbon, C_4H_4O, derived from the dehydration of certain carbohydrates, used in the synthesis of organic compounds, especially nylon. [FUR(FURAL) + -AN.]

fur·be·low (fûr'bə-lō') *n.* **1.** A ruffle or flounce on a garment. **2.** Any small piece of showy ornamentation. —*tr.v.* **furbelowed, -lowing, -lows.** To decorate with furbelows. [Variant of FALBALA.]

fur·bish (fûr'bĭsh) *tr.v.* **-bished, -bishing, -bishes. 1.** To brighten by cleaning or rubbing; burnish. **2.** To restore to attractive or serviceable condition; renovate. [Middle English *furbishen,* from Old French *fo(u)rbir* (stem *fo(u)rbiss-*), from Germanic. See **prep-** in Appendix.*] —**fur'bish·er** *n.*

fur·cate (fûr'kāt') *intr.v.* **-cated, -cating, -cates.** To divide into branches; to fork. —*adj.* Forked. [Late Latin *furcātus,* from Latin *furca,* FORK.]

fur·cu·la (fûr'kyə-lə) *n., pl.* **-lae** (-lē'). Also **fur·cu·lum** (fûr'kyə-ləm) *pl.* **-la** (-lə). A forked process or bone; especially, the wishbone of a bird. [New Latin, from Latin, diminutive of *furca,* FORK.]

fur·fur (fûr'fər) *n., pl.* **-fures** (-fyə-rēz'). An epidermal scale, as in dandruff. Sometimes used in the plural. [Latin *furfur*†, bran, scales.]

fur·fur·a·ceous (fûr'fyə-rā'shəs) *adj.* **1.** Made of or covered with scaly particles, as dandruff. **2.** Pertaining to or resembling bran. [Late Latin *furfurāceus* : FURFUR + -ACEOUS.]

fur·fur·al (fûr'fə-răl', fûr'fyə-) *n.* A colorless mobile liquid, C_4H_3OCHO, used as a solvent for nitrocellulose and in the manufacture of dyes and plastics. [FURFUR + AL(DEHYDE).]

Fu·ries (fyŏŏr'ēz). *Greek & Roman Mythology.* The three terrible, winged goddesses with serpentine hair, Alecto, Megaera, and Tisiphone, who pursue and punish doers of unavenged crimes. [Latin *Furiae,* plural of *furia,* FURY.]

fu·ri·o·so (fyŏŏr'ē-ō'sō) *adv. Music.* In a tempestuous and headlong manner. Used as a direction. —*adj.* Played furioso. [Italian, from Latin *furiōsus,* FURIOUS.]

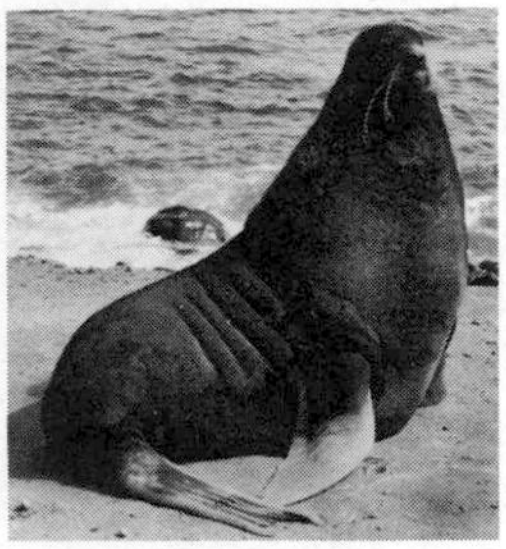

fur seal
Callorhinus ursinus

fu·ri·ous (fyŏŏr'ē-əs) *adj.* **1.** Full of or characterized by extreme anger; raging. **2.** Suggestive of extreme anger in action or appearance; fierce. [Middle English, from Old French *furieus,* from Latin *furiōsus,* from *furia,* FURY.] —**fu'ri·ous·ly** *adv.* —**fu'ri·ous·ness** *n.*

furl (fûrl) *v.* **furled, furling, furls.** —*tr.* To roll up and secure (a flag or sail) to a pole, yard, or mast. —*intr.* **1.** To be rolled up. **2.** To disappear as if furled: *the clouds furled away.* —*n.* **1.** The act of furling. **2.** A single roll or rolled section of something furled. [Old French *ferler, ferlier* : *fer(m),* firm, from Latin *firmus,* FIRM + *lier,* to bind, from Latin *ligāre* (see **leig-**[1] in Appendix*).]

fur·long (fûr'lông', -lŏng') *n. Abbr.* **fur.** A unit for measuring distance, equal to ⅛ mile or 220 yards. [Middle English *furlong,* Old English *furlang* : *furh,* FURROW + *lang,* LONG. Originally the length of the furrow made on a square field of 10 acres.]

fur·lough (fûr'lō) *n.* A leave of absence; vacation, especially: **a.** A leave of absence from duty granted to enlisted personnel of the armed services, usually covering a period longer than a weekend. Now officially called "leave" in the U.S. Armed Forces. **b.** The length of such a leave of absence. **c.** The papers certifying permission for such a leave of absence. —*tr.v.* **furloughed, -loughing, -loughs.** To grant a furlough to. [Dutch *verlof,* leave, permission, from Middle Dutch. See **leubh-** in Appendix.*]

fur·men·ty. Variant of **frumenty.**

furn. furnished.

fur·nace (fûr'nĭs) *n.* **1.** An enclosure in which energy in a nonthermal form is converted to heat; especially, such an enclosure in which heat is generated by the combustion of a suitable fuel. **2.** Any intensely hot, enclosed place. **3.** A severe test or trial. [Middle English *furna(i)s,* from Old French *fornais,* from Latin *fornāx* (stem *fornāc-*). See **gwher-** in Appendix.*]

Fur·neaux Islands (fûr'nō). A group of islands in Bass Strait off the northeastern coast of Tasmania, Australia.

fur·nish (fûr'nĭsh) *tr.v.* **-nished, -nishing, -nishes. 1.** To equip with what is needed; especially, to provide furniture for. **2.** To supply; give: *"The story of Orpheus has furnished Pope with an illustration"* (Thomas Bulfinch). [Middle English *furnisshen,* from Old French *furnir* (stem *furniss-*), *fornir,* from Common Romance *fornir* (unattested), to supply, from Germanic. See **per**[1] in Appendix.*] —**fur'nish·er** *n.*

Synonyms: *furnish, equip, outfit, accouter.* These verbs mean to provide with what is necessary for use or operation. *Furnish* refers primarily to the provision of basic necessities. *Equip,* a narrower term, usually implies provision of more specialized items for a particular need or particular service: *equip a car with snow tires. Outfit* suggests comprehensive provision of necessary items for a larger purpose, as for an expedition or the pursuit of a line of work. *Accouter* refers most often to provisioning for military service or something comparable.

fur·nish·ing (fûr'nĭsh-ĭng) *n.* **1.** Any piece of equipment necessary or useful for comfort or convenience. **2.** *Plural.* The furniture, appliances, and other movable articles in a home or office. **3.** *Plural.* Wearing apparel and accessories.

fur·ni·ture (fûr'nə-chər) *n.* **1.** The movable articles in a room or establishment that render it fit for living or working. **2.** The necessary equipment, as for a factory, ship, a saddle horse, or draft animal. **3.** *Printing.* Blank strips of wood or metal, placed between and around type on a page to hold it in place. [Old French *fourniture,* from *fournir, furnir,* to FURNISH.]

fu·ror (fyŏŏr'ôr', -ōr') *n.* Also *chiefly British* **fu·rore** (for sense 4). **1.** Violent anger; frenzy. **2.** A state of intense excitement or ecstasy. **3.** A general commotion; public disorder or uproar. **4.** A fashion adopted enthusiastically by the public; fad. [Latin, from *furere,* to rage. See **fury.**]

furred (fûrd) *adj.* **1.** Bearing fur. **2.** Made, covered, or trimmed with fur. **3.** Wearing fur garments. **4.** Covered with a furlike deposit, as the tongue. **5.** Provided with furring, as a wall, ceiling, or floor.

fur·ri·er (fûr'ē-ər) *n.* One whose occupation is the dressing, designing, selling, or repairing of furs. [Middle English *furrer,* from Old French *forreor,* from *forrer,* to line with fur. See **fur.**]

fur·ri·er·y (fûr'ē-ər-ē) *n., pl.* **-ies. 1.** Fur garments and trimmings collectively. **2.** The business of a furrier.

fur·ring (fûr'ĭng) *n.* **1. a.** A trimming or lining made of fur. **b.** Fur trimmings and linings, collectively. **2.** A furlike coating, as on the tongue. **3. a.** The act of preparing a wall, ceiling, or floor with strips of wood or metal to provide a level surface or air space above which a new surface will be applied. **b.** Strips of material used for this.

fur·row (fûr'ō) *n.* **1.** A long, narrow, shallow trench made in the ground by a plow or other implement. **2.** Any rut, groove, or narrow depression similar to this. **3.** A deep wrinkle in the skin, as on the forehead. —*v.* **furrowed, -rowing, -rows.** —*tr.* **1.** To make furrows in; to plow. **2.** To form deep wrinkles in. —*intr.* To become furrowed or deeply wrinkled. [Middle English *for(o)we, furgh,* Old English *furh.* See **perk-**[3] in Appendix.*]

fur·ry (fûr'ē) *adj.* **-rier, -riest. 1.** Consisting of or decorated with fur. **2.** Covered with fur or a furlike coating. **3.** Resembling fur in thickness or softness. —**fur'ri·ness** *n.*

fur seal. Any of several eared seals of the genera *Callorhinus* or *Arctocephalus,* having thick, soft underfur that is valued commercially.

fur·ther (fûr'*th*ər) *adj.* **1.** More distant in time or degree. **2.** Additional. **3.** More distant in space. See Usage note at **farther.** —*adv.* **1.** To a greater extent; more. **2.** In addition; furthermore; also. **3.** At or to a more distant point in space or time. See Usage note at **farther.** —*tr.v.* **furthered, -thering, -thers.** To help the progress of; to forward; advance. See Synonyms at **advance.** [Middle English *further,* Old English *furthor.* See **per**[1] in Appendix.*] —**fur'ther·er** *n.*

fur·ther·ance (fûr'*th*ər-əns) *n.* **1.** The act of furthering, advancing, or helping forward. **2.** One that furthers or assists.

fur·ther·more (fûr'*th*ər-môr', -mōr') *adv.* Moreover; in addition. See Synonyms at **also.**

fur·ther·most (fûr'*th*ər-mōst') *adj.* Most distant or remote.

fur·thest (fûr'*th*ĭst) *adj.* **1.** Most distant in time or degree. **2.** Most distant in space. See Usage note at **farther.** —*adv.* **1.** To the greatest extent or degree. **2.** At or to the most distant point in space or time. See Usage note at **farther.** [Middle English, from FURTHER.]

fur·tive (fûr'tĭv) *adj.* **1.** Characterized by stealth; surreptitious. **2.** Expressive of hidden motives or purposes; shifty. —See Synonyms at **secret.** [French *furtif,* from Old French, from Latin *furtīvus,* from *furtum,* theft, from *fūr*†, thief.] —**fur'tive·ly** *adv.* —**fur'tive·ness** *n.*

fu·run·cle (fyŏŏr'ŭng'kəl) *n. Pathology.* A **boil** *(see).* [Latin *fūrunculus,* petty thief, vine knob that "steals" the sap from the main branches, boil, diminutive of *fūr,* thief. See **furtive.**] —**fu·run'cu·lar** (fyŏŏ-rŭng'kyə-lər) *adj.*

fu·ry (fyŏŏr'ē) *n., pl.* **-ries. 1.** Violent anger; rage. **2.** An outburst of violent rage. **3.** Violent, uncontrolled action; turbulence. **4.** One given to fits of violent anger, especially a woman. —See Synonyms at **anger.** [Middle English *furie,* from Old French, from Latin *furia,* from *furere*†, to rage.]

furze (fûrz) *n.* A spiny shrub, **gorse** *(see).* [Middle English *furse, firse,* Old English *fyrs.* See **pūro-** in Appendix.*]

fu·sain (fyŏŏ-zān', fyōō'zān') *n.* **1.** Fine charcoal in stick form, made from the wood of a spindle tree. **2.** A sketch or drawing made with this. [French, from Vulgar Latin *fūsāgō* (unattested), spindle (formerly made from the wood of the spindle tree), from Latin *fūsus,* spindle. See **fuse.**]

Fu·san. The Japanese name for **Pusan.**

fuse[1] (fyōōz) *n.* **1.** A length of readily combustible material that is lighted at one end to carry a flame to and detonate an explosive at the other. **2.** Variant of **fuze.** [Italian *fuso,* from Latin *fūsus*†, spindle.]

fuse[2] (fyōōz) *v.* **fused, fusing, fuses.** —*tr.* **1.** To liquefy or

ă pat/ā pay/âr care/ä father/b bib/ch church/d deed/ĕ pet/ē be/f fife/g gag/h hat/hw which/ĭ pit/ī pie/îr pier/j judge/k kick/l lid, needle/m mum/n no, sudden/ng thing/ŏ pot/ō toe/ô paw, for/oi noise/ou out/ŏŏ took/ōō boot/p pop/r roar/s sauce/sh ship, dish/

reduce to a plastic state by heating; melt. **2.** To mix together by or as if by melting; to blend. —*intr.* **1.** To become liquefied from heat. **2.** To become mixed or united by or as if by melting together: *"There was no separation between joy and sorrow: they fused into one"* (Henry Miller). —*n.* A device containing an element that protects an electric circuit by melting when overloaded, thereby opening the circuit. —See Synonyms at **melt, mix.** [Latin *fundere* (past participle *fūsus*), to pour, melt. See **gheu-** in Appendix.*]

fu·see (fyōō-zē′) *n.* Also **fu·zee. 1.** A friction match with a large head capable of burning in a wind. **2.** A colored flare used as a railway warning signal. **3.** A grooved, cone-shaped pulley in old-style clocks, used to equalize the force of the mainspring by maintaining a differential winding and unwinding of the cord or chain from the spring container. **4.** A fuse for detonating explosives. [French *fusée,* spindle-shaped figure, from Old French *fusee,* from *fus,* spindle, from Latin *fūsus.* See **fuse.**]

fu·se·lage (fyōō′sə-läzh′, fyōō′zə-) *n.* The central body of an airplane that accommodates passengers, cargo, and crew, and to which the wings and tail assembly are attached. [French, from *fuseler,* to shape like a spindle, from *fuseau,* spindle, from Old French *fusel,* spindle, diminutive of *fus,* spindle, from Latin *fūsus.* See **fuse.**]

fu·sel oil (fyōō′zəl). A clear, colorless, poisonous, liquid mixture of amyl alcohols, obtained as a by-product of the fermentation of starch-containing and sugar-containing plant materials, and used as a solvent for fats, oils, resins, and waxes, and in the manufacture of explosives and pure amyl alcohols. [From German *Fusel*†, bad liquor.]

Fu·shun (fōō′shōōn′). A city and coal-mining center of China, 28 miles east of Shenyang, Manchuria. Population, 985,000.

fu·si·bil·i·ty (fyōō′zə-bĭl′ə-tē) *n.* The quality, state, or degree of being fusible.

fu·si·ble (fyōō′zə-bəl) *adj.* Capable of being fused or melted by heating. —**fu′si·ble·ness** *n.*

fusible metal. A metal alloy having a melting point below 300°F, used as solder and for safety plugs and fuses. Also called "fusible alloy."

fu·si·form (fyōō′zə-fôrm′) *adj.* Tapering at each end; spindle-shaped. [Latin *fūsus,* spindle (see **fuse**) + -FORM.]

fu·sil[1] (fyōō′zəl) *n.* A light, flintlock musket. [French, musket, from Old French *fuisil,* fusil, steel for a tinderbox, from Vulgar Latin *focile* (unattested), from Latin *focus,* fireplace. See **fuel.**]

fu·sil[2]. Variant of **fusile.**

fu·sile (fyōō′zəl, -zīl′) *adj.* Also **fu·sil** (-zəl). **1.** Formed by melting or casting. **2.** Capable of being fused. [Latin *fūsilis,* from *fūsus,* past participle of *fundere,* to melt, pour. See **gheu-** in Appendix.*]

fu·si·lier (fyōō′zə-lîr′) *n.* Also **fu·si·leer. 1.** A soldier armed with a fusil. **2.** *Capital* **F.** *Plural.* Soldiers belonging to certain British army regiments. Used in the names of regiments: *Royal Welch Fusiliers.* [French, from FUSIL.]

fu·sil·lade (fyōō′sə-lād′, -läd′, fyōō′zə-) *n.* **1.** A discharge of many firearms, simultaneously or in rapid succession. **2.** Any rapid outburst or barrage: *a fusillade of insults.* —*tr.v.* **fusilladed, -lading, -lades.** To attack or shoot down with a fusillade. [French, from *fusiller,* to shoot, from FUSIL.]

fu·sion (fyōō′zhən) *n.* **1.** The act or procedure of liquefying or melting together by heat. **2.** The liquid or melted state induced by heat. **3.** A union resulting from fusing. **4.** The merging of different elements into a union: *"the fusion of two words, black and power, had further divided blacks and antagonized whites"* (Paul Goodman). **5.** *Physics.* A nuclear reaction in which nuclei combine to form more massive nuclei with the simultaneous release of energy. In this sense, also called "nuclear fusion." Compare **fission.** [Latin *fūsiō,* from *fūsus,* past participle of *fundere,* to pour, melt. See **gheu-** in Appendix.*]

fusion bomb. An atomic bomb that derives its energy output principally from fusion reactions among light nuclei; especially, a **hydrogen bomb** *(see).*

fu·sion·ism (fyōō′zhə-nĭz′əm) *n.* The theory, practice, or advocacy of forming coalitions of political groups or factions. —**fu′sion·ist** *n.*

fuss (fŭs) *n.* **1.** Needlessly nervous or useless activity; commotion; bustle. **2. a.** A state of excessive and unwarranted concern over an unimportant matter; needless worry. **b.** Objection; protest. **3.** A quarrel. —*v.* **fussed, fussing, fusses.** —*intr.* **1.** To trouble or worry over trifles. **2.** To be excessively careful or solicitous. —*tr. Informal.* To disturb or vex (someone) with unimportant matters. [Origin unknown.] —**fuss′er** *n.*

fuss-budg·et (fŭs′bŭj′ĭt) *n.* A person who fusses over trifles.

fuss·y (fŭs′ē) *adj.* **-ier, -iest. 1.** Given to fussing; easily upset: *"The bridegroom, fussy as a poodle, pops his eyes"* (Kenneth Tynan). **2.** Insistent upon petty matters or details; fastidious. **3.** Calling for or requiring great attention to trivial details; meticulous. **4.** Full of superfluous details or trimmings; ornate: *"It can indeed be fussy, filling with ornament what should be empty space"* (H.D.F. Kitto). —**fuss′i·ly** *adv.* —**fuss′i·ness** *n.*

fus·ta·nel·la (fŭs′tə-nĕl′ə, fōō′stə-) *n.* A short stiff skirt of white cloth worn by men in modern Greece. [Italian, from Modern Greek *phoustanella,* diminutive of *phoustani,* from Italian *fustagno,* coarse cloth, from Medieval Latin *fustāneus,* FUSTIAN.]

fus·tian (fŭs′chən) *n.* **1. a.** *Obsolete.* A coarse, sturdy cloth made of cotton and flax. **b.** Any of several thick, twilled cotton fabrics with a short nap, such as corduroy. **2.** Pretentious speech or writing; pompous language: *"Yossarian was unmoved by the fustian charade of the burial ceremony"* (Joseph Heller). —See Synonyms at **bombast.** —*adj.* **1.** Made of fustian. **2.** Pompous; ranting; bombastic. [Middle English, from Old French *fustai(g)ne,* from Medieval Latin *fustāneus,* cloth, perhaps of *Fostat,* suburb of Cairo.]

fus·tic (fŭs′tĭk) *n.* **1.** A small tropical American tree, *Chlorophora tinctoria,* having wood yielding a yellow dyestuff. **2.** The yellow wood of this tree or similar trees. **3.** The dyestuff obtained from such wood. [Middle English *fustik,* from Old French *fustoc,* from Arabic *fustuq,* from Greek *pistakē,* PISTACHIO.]

fus·ti·gate (fŭs′tə-gāt′) *tr.v.* **-gated, -gating, -gates.** To beat with a club; to cudgel. [Late Latin *fūstigāre* : Latin *fūstis*†, club + *agere,* to do (see **ag-** in Appendix*).] —**fus′ti·ga′tion** *n.* —**fus′ti·ga′tor** (-gā′tər) *n.*

fus·ty (fŭs′tē) *adj.* **-tier, -tiest. 1.** Smelling of mildew or decay; musty; moldy. **2.** Old-fashioned; antique; spent. [Middle English, from Old French *fuste,* barrel, stale odor of a barrel, from *fust,* barrel, tree trunk, club, from Latin *fūstis,* club. See **fustigate.**] —**fus′ti·ly** *adv.* —**fus′ti·ness** *n.*

fut. *Grammar.* future.

Fu·ta Jal·lon (fōō′tə jə-lōn′). Also **Fou·ta Djal·lon.** A mountainous area in northwestern Guinea, the source of the Niger, Gambia, and Senegal rivers.

fu·thark (fōō′thärk′) *n.* Also **fu·tharc, fu·thorc** (-thôrk′), **fu·thork.** The runic alphabet. [From the first six letters of the alphabet: *f, u, th* (thorn), *a* or *o, r, k.*]

fu·tile (fyōōt′l, fyōō′tīl′) *adj.* **1.** Having no useful result; ineffectual; useless; vain. **2.** Unproductive; frivolous; idle: *futile talk.* [Latin *futtilis, fūtilis,* untrustworthy, useless. See **gheu-** in Appendix.*] —**fu′tile·ly** *adv.* —**fu′tile·ness** *n.*

fu·til·i·tar·i·an (fyōō-tĭl′ə-târ′ē-ən) *adj.* Holding or based on the view that human endeavor is futile. —*n.* One who holds such a view. [Blend of FUTILE and UTILITARIAN.]

fu·til·i·ty (fyōō-tĭl′ə-tē) *n., pl.* **-ties. 1.** The quality of being futile; uselessness; ineffectiveness. **2.** Lack of importance or purpose. **3.** Anything that is futile.

fut·tock (fŭt′ək) *n. Nautical.* One of the curved timbers that form a rib in the frame of a wooden ship. [Middle English *fottek,* perhaps variant of *fothok* (unattested) : FOOT + HOOK.]

futtock plate. *Nautical.* One of the iron plates attached to the top of a mast to hold the ends of the futtock shrouds.

futtock shroud. *Nautical.* One of the iron rods extending from the futtock plate, used to brace the base of a mast.

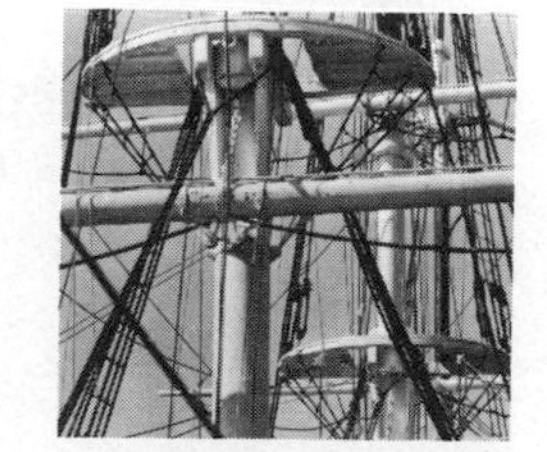

futtock shroud
Futtock shroud extending from futtock plate to the band fitted around the mast directly below the yardarm

fu·ture (fyōō′chər) *n.* **1.** The indefinite period of time yet to be; time that is to come. **2.** That which will happen in time to come. **3.** The prospective or foreseen condition of a person or thing: *a man's future.* **4.** Prospects of advancement; chances of success: *a business with no future.* **5.** *Usually plural.* Commodities or stocks bought or sold upon agreement of delivery in time to come. **6.** *Abbr.* **fut.** *Grammar.* **a.** The future tense. **b.** A verb in the future tense. —*adj.* That is to be or come in the future. [Middle English, from Old French *futur,* from Latin *futūrus.* See **bheu-** in Appendix.*]

future life. An existence posited for human beings after death.

future perfect. *Grammar.* **1.** A verb tense expressing action completed by a specified time in the future. This tense is formed in English by combining *will have* or *shall have* with a past participle; for example, *They will have counted all the votes by midnight.* **2.** A verb in this tense.

future tense. A verb tense used to express action in the future.

fu·tur·ism (fyōō′chə-rĭz′əm) *n.* An artistic movement originating in Italy in about 1910 and marked by an attempt to depict vividly the energetic and dynamic quality of contemporary life influenced by the motion and force of modern machinery. —**fu′tur·ist** *n.* & *adj.* —**fu′tur·is′tic** (-chə-rĭs′tĭk) *adj.*

fu·tu·ri·ty (fyōō-tōōr′ə-tē, fyōō-tyōōr′-, fyoo-chōōr′-) *n., pl.* **-ties. 1.** The future. **2.** The condition or quality of being in or of the future. **3.** A future event or possibility. **4.** A futurity race.

futurity race. A race, especially a horse race, for which entries are made well in advance, as at birth.

futurity stakes. 1. The stakes awarded to the winner or winners in a futurity race. **2.** A futurity race.

fuze (fyōōz) *n.* Also **fuse.** A mechanical or electrical mechanism used to detonate an explosive charge or device such as a bomb or grenade. [Variant of FUSE (detonator).]

fu·zee. Variant of **fusee.**

fuzz[1] (fŭz) *n.* A mass of fine, light particles, fibers, or hairs; down: *the fuzz on a peach.* —*tr.v.* **fuzzed, fuzzing, fuzzes.** To cover with fuzz. [Perhaps back-formation from FUZZY.]

fuzz[2] (fŭz) *n. Slang.* The police; policemen collectively. [Origin obscure.]

fuzz·y (fŭz′ē) *adj.* **-ier, -iest. 1.** Covered with fuzz. **2.** Of or resembling fuzz. **3.** Not sharply delineated or focused; indistinct; blurred. **4.** Not clearly reasoned or expressed; confused. [Perhaps from Low German *fussig,* spongy. See **pu-**[2] in Appendix.*] —**fuzz′i·ly** *adv.* —**fuzz′i·ness** *n.*

f.v. on the back of the page (Latin *folio verso*).

FWA Federal Works Agency.

fwd. *Sports.* forward.

-fy. Indicates a making or forming into; for example, **reify, nitrify.** [Middle English *-fien,* from Old French *-fier,* from Latin *-ficāre,* from *-ficus,* -FIC.]

FY fiscal year.

fyke (fīk) *n.* A long, bag-shaped net held open by hoops, used for catching fish. [Dutch *fuik,* from Middle Dutch *fūke*†.]

fyl·fot (fĭl′fŏt′) *n.* An ornamental figure identified with the swastika. [Middle English, device for filling the foot of a painted window : *fillen,* to FILL + FOOT.]

Fyn (fün). *German* **Fü·nen** (fü′nən). The second-largest island of Denmark, lying between Jutland and Sjaelland.

F.Z.S. Fellow of the Zoological Society.

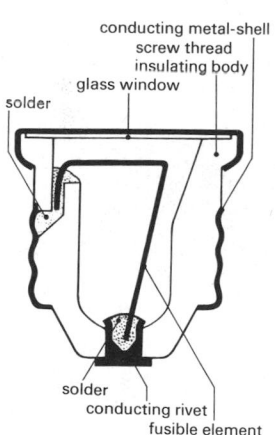

conducting metal-shell
screw thread
insulating body
glass window
solder
solder
conducting rivet
fusible element

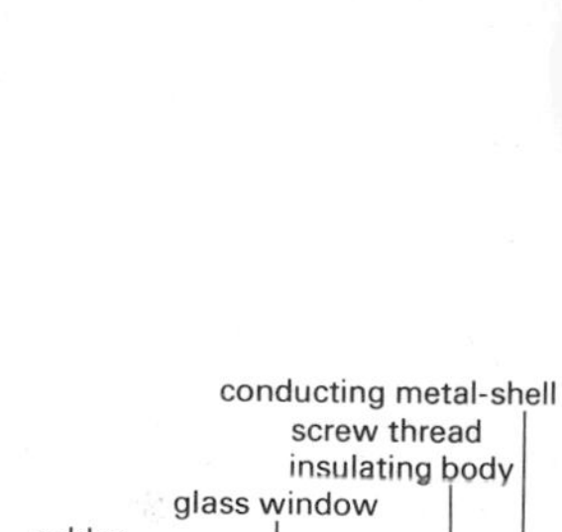
end-sealing washer
fixed end cap
removable end cap
case
conducting blade
replaceable link

fuse[2]
Above: Plug fuse
Below: Cartridge fuse

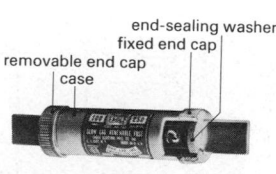

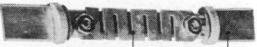

Gg

gable

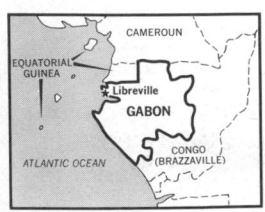

Gabon

Around 1000 B.C. the Phoenicians and other Semites of Syria and Palestine began to use a graphic sign in the forms (1,2). They gave it the name gīmel, meaning "camel," and used it for the consonant g. After 900 B.C. the Greeks borrowed the sign from the Phoenicians (3,4) and later developed other forms reversing the orientation (5,6,7). They also changed its name to gamma, but used it with the same consonantal value. The Greek form (5) passed via Etruscan to the Roman alphabet (8). The Romans used the sign originally for both the sound g (writing Caius for Gaius) and for the sound k. In the course of time they developed a graphic differentiation for the two sounds, by adding a small horizontal bar for the sound g, while leaving the sign unchanged for the sound c (see C). The Roman Monumental Capital (10) is the prototype of our modern capital, printed (13) and written (14). The written Roman form (9) developed into the late Roman and medieval Uncial (11) and Cursive (12), which are the bases of our modern small letter, printed (15) and written (16).

g, G (jē) *n., pl.* **g's** or *rare* **gs, G's** or **Gs.** **1.** The seventh letter of the modern English alphabet. See **alphabet. 2.** Any of the speech sounds represented by this letter.

g, G, g., G. *Note:* As an abbreviation or symbol, *g* may be a small or a capital letter, with or without a period. Established forms or those generally preferred precede the definition. When no form is given, all four forms are in general use in that sense. **1. g** acceleration of gravity. **2. G** *Physics.* gauss. **3. g.** gender. **4. g.** genitive. **5. G** giga-. **6. g., G.** gourde. **7. g** gram. **8. G** *Physics.* gravitation constant. **9. g.** guide. **10. g., G.** guilder. **11. g., G.** guinea (money). **12. g., G.** gulf (ocean area). **13.** The seventh in a series. **14. G** *Music.* **a.** The fifth tone in the scale of C major, or the seventh tone in the relative minor scale. **b.** The key or a scale in which G is the tonic. **c.** A written or printed note representing this tone. **d.** A string, key, or pipe tuned to the pitch of this tone. **15. G** *Slang.* grand (one thousand dollars).

G-1, G-2, G-3, G-4. *Military.* Each of the four sections of a **general staff** *(see).* They are personnel (G-1), intelligence (G-2), training and operations (G-3), and supplies (G-4).

Ga The symbol for the element gallium.

GA 1. general assembly. **2.** Georgia (with Zip Code).

Ga. Georgia.

G.A. 1. general assembly. **2.** general average.

gab (găb) *intr.v.* **gabbed, gabbing, gabs.** *Informal.* To talk easily or excessively about trivial matters; to chatter. —*n.* Chatter; prattle. —**gift of gab.** A talent for speaking easily or well. [Perhaps from Scottish *gab*, mouthful, lump, mouth, variant of GOB (lump).] —**gab′ber** *n.*

gab·ar·dine (găb′ər-dēn′, găb′ər-dēn′) *n.* **1.** A worsted cotton, wool, or rayon twill, used in making dresses, suits, and coats. **2.** A gaberdine. [Variant of GABERDINE.]

gab·bart (găb′ərt) *n.* Also **gab·bard** (-ərd). *Scottish.* A flat-bottomed barge used to load and unload cargo offshore or to transport goods on inland waterways. [Modification of Old French *gab(b)arre*, from Old Provençal *gabarra*, probably from Late Latin *carabus*, a small, rawhide-covered boat, from Greek *karabos*, horned beetle, crayfish, light ship. See **caravel.**]

gab·ble (găb′əl) *v.* **-bled, -bling, -bles.** —*intr.* **1.** To speak rapidly or incoherently; jabber. **2.** To make rapid, repeated cackling noises, as a goose or duck. —*tr.* To utter quickly or unintelligibly. —*n.* **1.** Rapid, incoherent, or meaningless speech. **2.** A jumble of cackling noises or meaningless utterances. [Middle Dutch *gabbelen* (imitative).]

gab·bro (găb′rō) *n., pl.* **-bros. 1.** A usually coarse-grained igneous rock composed chiefly of calcic plagioclase and pyroxene, sometimes with other minerals. Also called "norite." **2.** Any dark, coarse-grained igneous rock. [Italian, from Latin *glaber*, smooth, bald. See **ghel-²** in Appendix.*]

gab·by (găb′ē) *adj.* **-bier, -biest.** *Informal.* Tending to talk excessively.

ga·belle (gə-běl′) *n.* The salt tax imposed in France prior to 1790. [Middle English, from Old French, from Old Italian *gabella*, from Arabic *qabāla*, tribute, "receipt," from *qabala*, he received.]

gab·er·dine (găb′ər-dēn′, găb′ər-dēn′) *n.* **1.** A long, coarse garment, such as a cloak or frock, worn during the Middle Ages, especially by Jews. **2.** *British.* A loose smock worn by laborers. **3.** Gabardine. [Earlier *gawbardine*, from Old French *gauvardine, gallevardine*, "pilgrim's frock," from Middle High German *wallevart*, pilgrimage : *wallen*, to roam, from Old High German *wallōn* (see **wel-³** in Appendix*) + *vart*, journey, way, from Old High German, from *faran*, to go (see **per-²** in Appendix*).]

Ga·be·ro·nes (găb′ə-rō′nĭs). The capital of Botswana, in the southeast near the South African border. Population, 5,000.

Ga·bès (gä′běs). A seaport of Tunisia, in the southeast on the Gulf of Gabès. Population, 24,000.

Ga·bès, Gulf of (gä′běs). Ancient name **Syr·tis Mi·nor** (sûr′tĭs mī′nər). An inlet of the Mediterranean, extending about 60 miles into southeastern Tunisia.

gab·fest (găb′fěst′) *n. Slang.* A small informal gathering for the exchange of news and gossip. [GAB (chatter) + -FEST.]

ga·bi·on (gā′bē-ən) *n.* **1.** A cylindrical wicker basket filled with earth and stones, formerly used in building fortifications. **2.** A similar cylinder, often of metal, used in constructing dams, foundations, and the like. [Old French *gabion*, from Old Italian *gabbione*, augmentative of *gabbia*, cage, from Latin *cavea*, a hollow, enclosure, from *cavus*, hollow. See **keu-³** in Appendix.*]

ga·bi·on·ade (gā′bē-ə-nād′) *n.* Also **ga·bi·on·nade.** A fortification or defensive embankment or wall built with gabions. [French *gabionnade*, from Old Italian *gabbionata*, from *gabbione*, GABION.]

ga·ble (gā′bəl) *n. Architecture.* **1.** The triangular wall section at the ends of a pitched roof, bounded by the two roof slopes and the ridge pole. **2.** That end of a building having a gable in the roof section. **3.** Any triangular architectural section, usually ornamental, as over a door or window. [Middle English *gable, gabyl*, from Old French *gable*, probably from Old Norse *gafl*. See **ghebhel-** in Appendix.*] —**ga′bled** *adj.*

gable roof. A pitched roof that ends in a gable.

Ga·bon (gà-bôN′). A republic of east-central Africa, 103,317 square miles in area; formerly an overseas territory of French Equatorial Africa. Population, 462,000. Capital, Libreville.

Ga·bri·el¹ (gā′brē-əl). A masculine given name. [Hebrew *Gabhrī′ēl*, "man of God" : *gabher*, man + *Ēl*, God.]

Ga·bri·el² (gā′brē-əl). An archangel who acts as the messenger of God in the Bible.

Ga·bro·vo (gä′brô-vô). A city of central Bulgaria, situated in the Balkan Mountains; an industrial and manufacturing center. Population, 38,000.

gad¹ (găd) *intr.v.* **gadded, gadding, gads.** To roam about or ramble restlessly or excitedly; rove. Used with *about* or *around.* See Synonyms at **wander.** —*n.* The action of gadding. Used only in the phrase *on the gad.* [Middle English *gadden*, probably back-formation from *gadeling*, companion, (hence) wanderer, Old English *gædeling*. See **ghedh-** in Appendix.*] —**gad′der** *n.*

gad² (găd) *n.* **1.** *Mining.* A spike or other pointed tool for working or breaking rock or ore. **2.** A goad, as for prodding cattle to make them move. **3.** *Western U.S.* A spur. —*tr.v.* **gadded, gadding, gads. 1.** *Mining.* To break up (rock or ore, for example) with a gad. **2.** To goad (cattle). **3.** *Western U.S.* To spur. [Middle English *gad(de),* from Old Norse *gaddr,* rod, goad, spike. See **ghasto-** in Appendix.*]

Gad[1] (găd). A son of Zilpah and Jacob. Genesis 30:11. [Hebrew *Gādh,* from *gādh,* fortune.]

Gad[2] (găd) *n.* The tribe of Israel descended from Gad.

Gad[3] (găd). Euphemism for God.

gad·a·bout (găd′ə-bout′) *n.* One who gads; especially, one who goes about seeking gossip or excitement. —*adj.* Given to gadding.

Gad·a·ra (găd′ər-ə). An ancient city of Palestine, six miles southeast of the Sea of Galilee; a member of the Decapolis.

gad·fly (găd′flī′) *n., pl.* **-flies. 1.** Any of various flies, especially of the family Tabanidae, that bite or annoy livestock and other animals. **2.** One that acts as a constructively provocative stimulus. **3.** One habitually engaged in provocative criticism of existing institutions, typically as an individual citizen. [GAD (goad, sting) + FLY.]

gadg·et (găj′ĭt) *n. Informal.* A small specialized mechanical device; a contrivance. See Synonyms at **tool.** [Possibly from French *gâchette,* catch (of a lock), from Old French *gâche,* lock, from Frankish *gaspia*†, buckle.]

gadg·e·teer (găj′ə-tîr′) *n. Informal.* A person who designs, builds, or delights in the use of gadgets.

gadg·et·ry (găj′ə-trē) *n.* **1.** Gadgets collectively. **2.** The designing or constructing of gadgets.

Ga·dhel·ic. Variant of **Goidelic.**

ga·doid (gā′doid′) *adj.* Also **ga·did** (gā′dĭd). Of or belonging to the family Gadidae, which includes fishes such as the cod and the hake. —*n.* A member of the Gadidae. [New Latin *Gadus* (genus name), from Greek *gados*†, kind of fish + -OID.]

gad·o·lin·i·um (găd′l-ĭn′ē-əm) *n. Symbol* **Gd** A silvery-white, malleable, ductile, metallic rare-earth element obtained from monazite and bastnaesite. It has the highest neutron-absorption cross section known and is useful in improving high-temperature characteristics of iron, chromium, and related metallic alloys. Atomic number 64, atomic weight 157.25, melting point 1,312°C, boiling point approximately 3,000°C, specific gravity from 7.8 to 7.896, valence 3. See **element.** [New Latin, named in honor of Johann *Gadolin* (1760–1852), Finnish chemist.]

ga·droon (gə-dro͞on′) *n.* Also **go·droon. 1.** *Architecture.* A band of convex molding ornamentally carved with beading or reeding. **2.** Any ornamental band, especially as used in silverwork, embellished with fluting, reeding, beading, or other continuous pattern. [French *godron,* from Old French *goderon,* perhaps diminutive of *godet,* drinking cup, from Middle Dutch *codde*†, cylindrical piece of wood.]

Gads·den (gădz′dən). A city and industrial center of northeast-central Alabama. Population, 58,000.

Gads·den (gădz′dən), **James.** 1788–1858. American diplomat, Indian commissioner, and railroad promoter.

Gads·den Purchase (gădz′dən). An area of land, comprising 29,640 square miles of modern Arizona and New Mexico south of the Gila River, acquired from Mexico in 1853.

gad·wall (găd′wôl′) *n.* A widely distributed duck, *Anas strepera,* having grayish or brown plumage. [Origin unknown.]

Gae·a (jē′ə). Also **Gai·a** (gā′ə), **Ge** (jē, gē). *Greek Mythology.* The goddess of the earth, who bore and married Uranus and became the mother of the Titans, the Furies, and the Cyclopes. [Greek *Gaia,* personification of *gaia, ge,* earth. See **gē** in Appendix.*]

Gae·dhel·ic. Variant of **Goidelic.**

Gae·kwar (gī′kwär) *n.* The hereditary title of the ruling princes of Baroda, a city of southeastern Gujarat State, India. [Marathi *Gaekvād,* "Protector of Cows" : Sanskrit *gauh,* ox, cow (see **gwou-** in Appendix*) + *-vād,* "watcher," from *veda,* I have seen, I know (see **weid-** in Appendix*).]

Gael (gāl) *n.* **1.** A Gaelic-speaking Celt of Scotland, Ireland, or the Isle of Man. **2.** A Scottish Highlander. [Scottish Gaelic *Gaidheal,* probably from Old Irish *goidel,* a Celt, from Old Welsh *Gwyddel,* Irishman, probably from *gwydd,* wild. See **widhu-** in Appendix.*]

Gael·ic (gā′lĭk) *adj. Abbr.* **Gael.** Of or relating to the Gaels or their languages. —*n. Abbr.* **Gael. 1.** The Goidelic family of the Celtic languages. **2.** One of the languages of the Gaels; Irish, Manx, or the language of the Scottish Highlanders. [Scottish Gaelic *Gaidhealach,* of the Gaels, and *Gaidhlig,* the Gaelic language, from *Gaidheal,* GAEL.]

Ga·e·ta (gä-â′tä). A resort city of west-central Italy, 45 miles northwest of Naples, on the Gulf of Gaeta. Population, 21,000.

gaff (găf) *n.* **1.** An iron hook attached to a pole and used to land and maneuver large fish. **2.** *Nautical.* A spar used to extend the top edge of a fore-and-aft sail. **3.** A metal spur attached to the leg of a gamecock during a cockfight. **4.** *Slang.* Harshness of treatment; abuse. —*tr.v.* **gaffed, gaffing, gaffs. 1.** To hook or land (a fish) using a gaff. **2.** To equip (a gamecock) with a gaff. **3.** *Slang.* **a.** To take in; trick; cheat. **b.** To alter or fix (dice, for example) in order to cheat. [Middle English *gaffe,* from Old French, from Old Provençal *gaf*†.]

gaffe (găf; *French* gȧf) *n.* A clumsy social error; a faux pas: *"The excursion had in his eyes been a monstrous gaffe, a breach of sensibility and good taste"* (Mary McCarthy). [French, from *gaffer,* to hook, hence in seaman's slang, to blunder, from *gaffe,* hook, GAFF.]

gaf·fer (găf′ər) *n. Regional.* An old man or rustic. [Contraction of GODFATHER.]

gaff rig. *Nautical.* A rig with a fore-and-aft sail that has its upper edge supported by a gaff. —**gaff′-rigged′** *adj.*

gaff-top·sail (găf′tŏp′səl, -sāl′) *n. Nautical.* A light, triangular or quadrilateral sail set over a gaff.

Gaf·sa (găf′sə). Ancient name **Cap·sa** (kăp′sə). A city, mining center, and oasis of west-central Tunisia. Population, 24,000.

gag (găg) *n.* **1.** Something forced into or put over the mouth to prevent the utterance of sound. **2.** Any obstacle to or censoring of free speech. **3.** A device placed in the mouth to keep it open, as in dentistry or surgery. **4.** *Informal.* **a.** A practical joke; a hoax. **b.** A comic effect or remark; a joke. —See Synonyms at **joke.** —**pull a gag.** *Informal.* To play a trick or practical joke. —*v.* **gagged, gagging, gags.** —*tr.* **1.** To prevent from uttering any sounds by using a gag. **2.** To repress or censor (free speech). **3.** To keep (the mouth) open by using a gag. **4.** To block off or stop up (a pipe or valve, for example). **5.** To cause to choke or retch. —*intr.* **1.** To choke; to retch from nausea: *"the smell of smashed perfume bottles made me gag"* (Truman Capote). **2.** *Informal.* To make jokes or quips. [Middle English *gaggen,* to suffocate (probably imitative).]

ga·ga (gä′gä′) *adj. Slang.* Senseless; crazy. [French, from *gaga,* foolish old man (imitative of stammering).]

Ga·ga·rin (gä-gä′rĭn), **Yuri Alekseyevitch.** 1934–1968. Soviet cosmonaut; first man to orbit the earth in space (1961).

gage[1] (gāj) *n.* **1.** Something deposited or given as security against an obligation; a pledge. **2.** Something, such as a glove, offered or thrown down as a pledge or challenge to fight. **3.** Any test or challenge. —*tr.v.* **gaged, gaging, gages.** *Archaic.* **1.** To pledge as security. **2.** To offer as a stake in a bet; to wager. [Middle English, from Old French, from Frankish *wadi* (unattested). See **wadh-** in Appendix.*]

gage[2] (gāj) *n.* Any of several varieties of plum, such as the greengage. [Introduced into England from France by Sir William *Gage* (1777–1864), English botanist.]

gage[3] (gāj) *n. Slang.* **Marijuana** *(see).* [Originally any cheap liquor or tobacco, Middle English *gage,* quart pot, perhaps "pot holding enough liquor to pledge one with," from *gage,* GAGE (pledge).]

gage[4]. Variant of **gauge.**

Gage (gāj), **Thomas.** 1721–1787. British general and colonial governor of Massachusetts (1774–75).

gag·er Variant of **gauger.**

gag·ger (găg′ər) *n.* **1.** One that gags. **2.** A piece of iron used to keep the core in position in a foundry mold.

gag·gle (găg′əl) *intr.v.* **-gled, -gling, -gles.** To make gabbling sounds; to cackle. —*n.* **1.** A flock of geese. **2.** A gabbling or cackling sound: *"There was a gaggle of sound from the henhouse beyond the hedge"* (John Cheever). —See Synonyms at **flock.** [Middle English *gagelen*†.]

gag·man (găg′măn′) *n., pl.* **-men** (-mĕn′). A person who writes jokes or comedy routines for plays, films, or performers.

gag rule. A rule, as in a legislative body, limiting discussion or debate on a given issue. Also called "gag law."

gahn·ite (gä′nīt′) *n.* A dark-green to brown or black mineral, $ZnAl_2O_4$. [German *Gahnit,* after Johan G. *Gahn* (1745–1818), Swedish chemist.]

Gai·a. Variant of **Gaea.**

gai·e·ty (gā′ə-tē) *n., pl.* **-ties.** Also **gay·e·ty. 1.** A state of being gay or merry; cheerfulness. **2.** Activity brought about by or inspiring joyousness; festivity; merriment. **3.** Gay color or showiness, as of dress; finery. [French *gaieté,* from Old French *gai,* GAY.]

Gail (gāl). A feminine given name. [Short form of ABIGAIL.]

Gail·lard Cut (gĭl-yärd′). An eight-mile excavation through a hill in the Canal Zone, Panama, occupied by the southeastern section of the Panama Canal. [After David Du Bose *Gaillard* (1859–1913), American army engineer, who supervised the project.]

gail·lar·di·a (gā-lär′dē-ə) *n.* Any of several plants of the genus *Gaillardia,* of western North America, having yellow or reddish rayed flowers. Also called "blanketflower." [New Latin *Gaillardia,* after *Gaillard* de Marentonneau, 18th-century French botanist.]

gai·ly (gā′lē) *adv.* Also **gay·ly. 1.** In a joyful, cheerful, or happy manner; merrily. **2.** With brightness; colorfully; showily: *gaily dressed.*

gain[1] (gān) *v.* **gained, gaining, gains.** —*tr.* **1.** To become the owner of; acquire; obtain; get. **2.** To acquire in competition; win. **3.** To secure as a profit or through labor; earn. **4.** To build up an increase of, as weight, impetus, or time. **5.** To come to; arrive at; reach. —*intr.* **1.** To become better or more; to benefit; to advance or progress. **2.** To come nearer; get closer. Used with *on* or *upon.* **3.** To increase a lead. Used with *on, upon,* or *over.* —See Synonyms at **reach.** —*n.* **1.** Something earned, won, or otherwise acquired; a profit; an advantage; increase. **2.** The act of acquiring something; attainment. **3.** *Electronics.* **a.** An increase in signal power. **b.** The ratio of output to input, as of output power to input power in an antenna or of output voltage to input voltage in an amplifier. [Old French *gaaignier, gaigner,* from Germanic. See **wei-**[2] in Appendix.*]

gain[2] (gān) *n.* A notch or mortise cut into a board to receive another part. —*tr.v.* **gained, gaining, gains. 1.** To cut out such a mortise or notch. **2.** To join by or fit into such a mortise or notch. [Origin unknown.]

gain·er (gā′nər) *n.* **1.** One that gains. **2.** A dive in which the diver leaves the board facing forward, does a back somersault, and enters the water feet first.

gain·ful (gān′fəl) *adj.* Earning a profit; profitable; lucrative. —**gain′ful·ly** *adv.* —**gain′ful·ness** *n.*

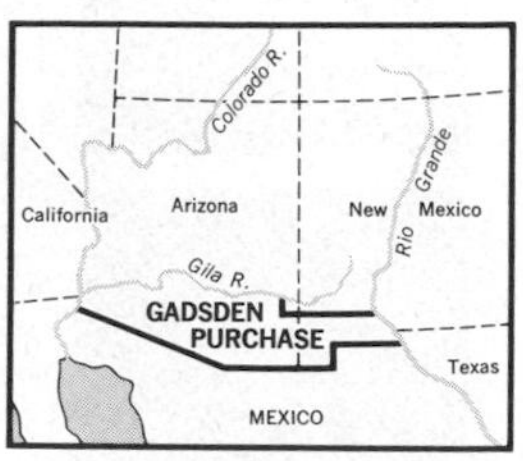

Gadsden Purchase

gadwall

gaff

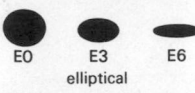

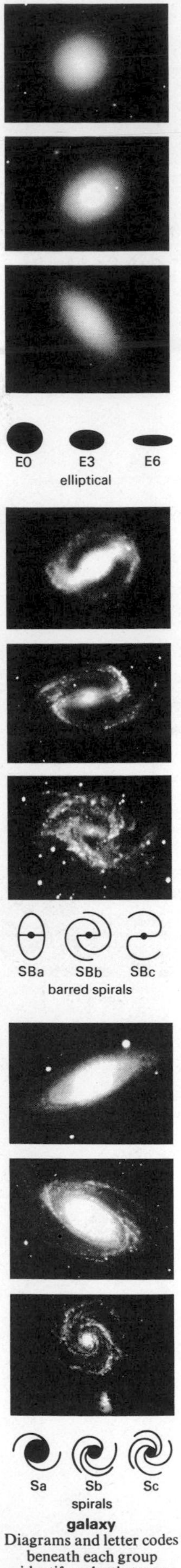

EO   E3   E6
elliptical

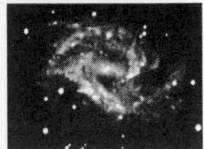

SBa   SBb   SBc
barred spirals

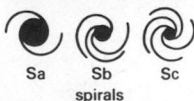

Sa   Sb   Sc
spirals
galaxy
Diagrams and letter codes
beneath each group
identify galactic types

gain·less (gān′lĭs) adj. Earning no profits; profitless. —**gain′·less·ness** n.

gain·ly (gān′lē) adj. **-lier, -liest.** Rare. Not ungainly; graceful; handsome. [Middle English geinli, from gein, direct, suitable, convenient, Old English gēn, from Old Norse gegn, against, direct. See gagina in Appendix.*] —**gain′li·ness** n.

gain·say (gān-sā′) tr.v. **-said** (-sĕd′), **-saying, -says. 1.** To declare false; deny. **2.** To be contrary to; oppose; contradict. —See Synonyms at **deny.** [Middle English gaynsayen, "to say against" : gayn-, against, Old English gegn- (see gagina in Appendix*) + SAY.] —**gain·say′er** n.

Gains·bor·ough (gānz′bûr′ō, -bər-ə), **Thomas.** 1727–1788. English painter.

'gainst (gĕnst; chiefly British gānst) prep. Also **gainst.** Poetic. Against.

gait (gāt) n. **1.** A way of moving on foot; a particular fashion of walking, running, or the like: "that indescribable gait of the long-distance tramp the world over" (Kipling). **2.** Any of the ways a horse may move by lifting the feet in different order or rhythm, as a canter, trot, or walk. —tr.v. **gaited, gaiting, gaits.** To teach a certain gait or gaits to (a horse). [Middle English gate, gait, way, passage, from Old Norse gata, path, street. See ghē- in Appendix.*]

gait·ed (gā′tĭd) adj. Having a specified gait or number of gaits. Usually used in combination: fast-gaited; a three-gaited mare.

gai·ter (gā′tər) n. **1.** A leather or heavy cloth covering for the legs extending from the knee to the instep; a legging. **2.** A smaller covering worn over a shoe and extending from the ankle to the instep; a spat. **3.** An ankle-high shoe with elastic sides and no laces or buckles. **4.** An overshoe having a cloth top. [French guêtre, from Old French guestre, guietre, probably from Frankish wrist (unattested), instep. See wer-³ in Appendix.*]

Gait·skell (gāt′skəl), **Hugh Todd Naylor.** 1906–1963. British Labour Party leader.

gal (găl) n. Informal. A girl.

gal. gallon.

Gal. Galatians (New Testament).

ga·la (gā′lə, găl′ə, gä′lə) n. A festive occasion or celebration; festival. —**in gala.** Festively attired. —adj. Characterized by or suitable to celebration; festive: "The frenzy on hundreds of stages all over Paris reflected the gala life around them" (Roger Shattuck). [Italian, from Spanish, from Old French gale, pleasure, merrymaking, from galer, to make merry, live a gay life, from Gallo-Roman walare (unattested), from Frankish wala (unattested), well. See wel-² in Appendix.*]

ga·lac·tic (gə-lăk′tĭk) adj. **1.** Of or pertaining to a galaxy or galaxies. **2.** Sometimes capital G. Of, pertaining to, occurring, or originating in the Milky Way. [Late Latin galacticus, milky, from Greek galaktikos, from gala (stem galakt-), milk. See melg- in Appendix.*]

galactic equator. The great circle of the celestial sphere that lies in the plane bisecting the band of the Milky Way, inclined at an angle of approximately 62 degrees to the celestial equator.

galactic nebula. A nebula lying within the Milky Way.

galactic noise. Radio-frequency radiation originating within the Milky Way.

galacto-, galact-. Indicates milk or milky; for example, galactopoiesis, galactose. [From Greek gala (stem galakt-), milk. See melg- in Appendix.*]

ga·lac·to·poi·e·sis (gə-lăk′tə-poi-ē′sĭs) n. The secretion and continued production of milk. [GALACTO- + -POIESIS.] —**ga·lac′to·poi·et′ic** (-ĕt′ĭk) adj.

ga·lac·tose (gə-lăk′tōs′) n. A simple sugar, $C_6H_{12}O_6$, commonly occurring in lactose (see). [GALACT(O)- + -OSE.]

gal·a·go (găl′ə-gō′, gə-lā′-) n., pl. **-gos.** Any of several small African primates of the genera Galago and Euoticus, having dense, woolly fur, large, round eyes, prominent ears, and a long tail. Also called "bush baby." [New Latin Galago, perhaps from an African word goigkh, monkey.]

Gal·a·had¹ (găl′ə-hăd′). Arthurian Legend. The purest of the knights of the Round Table who alone succeeded in the quest for the Holy Grail.

Gal·a·had² (găl′ə-hăd′) n. Any man considered to be noble, pure, or chivalrous. [After GALAHAD.]

ga·lan·gal (gə-lăng′gəl) n. **1.** A plant, Alpinia officinarum, of eastern Asia, having pungent, aromatic roots used medicinally and as seasoning. **2.** The dried roots of this plant. [Originally a variant of GALINGALE.]

gal·an·tine (găl′ən-tēn′) n. A dish of boned, stuffed meat or fish, cooked and served cold coated with aspic or its own jelly. [Middle English galauntyne, a sauce for fish and poultry, from Old French galantine, galatine, from Medieval Latin galatīna, gelatina, probably from Latin gelāre, to freeze. See gel-³ in Appendix.*]

ga·lan·ty show (gə-lăn′tē). A shadow play performed by casting the shadows of miniature figures on a screen or wall. [Perhaps from Italian galanti, plural of galante, a gallant, from Old French galant (from the stories of gallantry portrayed in the show). See gallant.]

Ga·lá·pa·gos Islands (gə-lä′pə-gəs, gə-lăp′ə-). Officially, Archipiélago de Colón. An island group, 2,966 square miles in area, forming a province of Ecuador and situated in the Pacific 650 miles west of the mainland. Population, 2,400.

Gal·a·ta (găl′ə-tə). The chief commercial district and a port of Istanbul, Turkey.

gal·a·te·a (găl′ə-tē′ə) n. A durable cotton fabric, often striped, used in making clothing. [Originally used for children's sailor suits, after the Galatea, 19th-century British warship.]

Gal·a·te·a (găl′ə-tē′ə). Greek Mythology. An ivory statue of a maiden, brought to life by Aphrodite in answer to the pleas of the sculptor, Pygmalion, who had fallen in love with his creation.

Ga·la·ţi (gä-läts′, -lä′tsē). Also **Ga·latz** (gä′läts). A port city of eastern Rumania on the lower Danube. Population, 112,000.

Ga·la·tia (gə-lā′shə, -shē-ə). An ancient country forming part of north-central Asia Minor. Chief city, Ancyra (modern Ankara, Turkey).

Ga·la·tian (gə-lā′shən) adj. Of or pertaining to ancient Galatia or its people. —n. A native or inhabitant of ancient Galatia.

Ga·la·tians (gə-lā′shənz) n. Full name, Epistle to the Galatians. Abbr. **Gal.** A book of the New Testament consisting of an Epistle written to the Christians of Galatia by the apostle Paul in about A.D. 58.

gal·a·vant. Variant of **gallivant.**

ga·lax (gā′lăks′) n. A plant, Galax aphylla, of the southeastern United States, having glossy, evergreen leaves and a cluster of small white flowers. Also called "beetleweed." [New Latin Galax, probably from Greek galaxias, the Milky Way, GALAXY (from its white flowers).]

gal·ax·y (găl′ək-sē) n., pl. **-ies. 1.** Astronomy. **a.** Any of numerous large-scale aggregates of stars, gas, and dust, having one of a group of more or less definite overall structures, containing an average of 100 billion (10^{11}) solar masses, and ranging in diameter from 1,500 to 300,000 light-years. **b.** Usually capital G. The galaxy of which the earth's sun is a part, the **Milky Way** (see). Usually preceded by the. **2.** An assembly of brilliant, beautiful, or distinguished persons or things. [Middle English galaxie, the Milky Way, from Old French, from Latin galaxiās, from Greek galaxias (kuklos), "milky (circle)," from gala, milk. See melg- in Appendix.*]

gal·ba·num (găl′bə-nəm) n. A bitter, aromatic gum resin extracted from an Asiatic plant, Ferula galbaniflua, or any of several related plants, and used in incense and medicinally as a counterirritant. [Middle English, from Latin, from Greek khalbanē, from Hebrew ḥelbᵊnāh.]

gale¹ (gāl) n. **1. a.** A very strong wind. **b.** Meteorology. A wind having a speed between 32 and 63 miles per hour. **2.** Poetic. A breeze. **3.** A forceful outburst, as of hilarity. —See Synonyms at **wind.** [Probably short for gale wind, "bad wind," perhaps from Norwegian galen, bad, probably from Old Norse galinn, bewitched, enchanted, from gala, to sing, enchant, bewitch. See ghel-¹ in Appendix.*]

gale² (gāl) n. See **sweet gale.** [Middle English gale, gayl, Old English gagel, akin to Middle Dutch gaghel†.]

ga·le·a (gā′lē-ə) n., pl. **-leae** (-lē-ē′). Biology. A helmet-shaped part, such as the upper petal of certain plants or part of the maxilla of an insect. [Latin, leather helmet, originally "cap made of weasel skin," from Greek galeē, weasel. See geli- in Appendix.*]

ga·le·ate (gā′lē-āt′) adj. Also **ga·le·at·ed** (-ā′tĭd). **1.** Biology. Having a galea. **2.** Helmet-shaped. [Latin galeātus, from galea, GALEA.]

ga·le·i·form (gā′lē-ə-fôrm′, gə-lē′-) adj. Helmet-shaped. [French galéiforme : Latin galea, GALEA + -FORM.]

Ga·len (gā′lən). Latin name, Claudius Galenus. A.D. 130?–201? Greek anatomist, physiologist, and physician.

ga·le·na (gə-lē′nə) n. A gray mineral, essentially PbS, the principal ore of lead. [Latin galēna†, lead ore.]

Ga·len·ism (gā′lə-nĭz′əm) n. The medical theories or practices advanced by the Greek physician Galen. —**Ga·len′ic** (gə-lĕn′ĭk, -lē′nĭk), **Ga·len′i·cal** adj.

Ga·le·ras Volcano (gä-lā′räs). An active volcano, 14,000 feet high, in the southwestern Colombian Andes.

Ga·li·bi (gä-lē′bē) n., pl. **Galibi** or **-bis. 1.** A member of the Carib people of French Guiana. **2.** The language of these people. [Carib galibi, "strong man," akin to Cariban caribe, brave, CARIB.]

Ga·li·cia (gə-lĭsh′ē-ə, -lĭsh′ə). **1.** Polish **Ha·licz** (hä′lĕch); Russian **Ga·li·tsi·ya** (gə-lē′tsĭ-yə). A region of southeastern Poland and the northwestern Ukrainian S.S.R., 30,645 square miles in area, including the cities of Kraków and Lvov. **2.** Ancient name **Gal·lae·ci·a** (gə-lē′shē-ə). A region and ancient kingdom, 11,256 square miles in area, of northwestern Spain.

Ga·li·cian (gə-lĭsh′ən) adj. **1.** Of or pertaining to Spanish Galicia, its people, or their language. **2.** Of or pertaining to Polish Galicia or its people. —n. **1.** A native or inhabitant of Spanish Galicia. **2.** The Portuguese dialect spoken in Spanish Galicia. **3.** A native or inhabitant of Polish Galicia.

Gal·i·le·an¹ (găl′ə-lē′ən) adj. Also **Gal·i·lae·an.** Of or pertaining to Galilee or its people. —n. **1.** A native or inhabitant of Galilee. **2.** A Christian. —**the Galilean.** Jesus.

Gal·i·le·an² (găl′ə-lē′ən) adj. Of, pertaining to, or in accordance with the work of Galileo.

gal·i·lee (găl′ə-lē′) n. A small chapel or porch at the western end of some medieval English churches. Also called "galilee porch." [Middle English galile, from Old French galilee, from Medieval Latin galilaea, from Latin Galilaea, GALILEE.]

Gal·i·lee (găl′ə-lē′). A hilly region of northern Palestine. [Latin Galilaea, from Greek Galilaia, from Hebrew hagālîl, "the district," shortening of gᵊlîl hagōyim, "district (of) nations" : gᵊlîl, from gālîl, district + ha, the + gōyim, plural of goy, nation, people (see goy).]

Gal·i·lee, Sea of (găl′ə-lē′). Old Testament **Sea of Chin·ne·reth** (kĭn′ə-rĕth′); New Testament **Lake of Gen·nes·ar·et** (gə-nĕs′ə-rĕt′). A freshwater lake, 64 square miles in area, bordered by Israel, Syria, and Jordan, lying at 696 feet below sea level. Also called "Lake Tiberias."

ă pat/ā pay/âr care/ä father/b bib/ch church/d deed/ĕ pet/ē be/f fife/g gag/h hat/hw which/ĭ pit/ī pie/îr pier/j judge/k kick/l lid, needle/m mum/n no, sudden/ng thing/ŏ pot/ō toe/ô paw, for/oi noise/ou out/ŏŏ took/ōō boot/p pop/r roar/s sauce/sh ship, dish/

Gal·i·le·o (găl′ə-lā′ō). Full name, Galileo Galilei. 1564–1642. Italian scientist and philosopher; performed fundamental observations, experiments, and mathematical analysis in astronomy and physics.

gal·i·ma·ti·as (găl′ə-mā′shē-əs, -măt′ē-əs) *n.* Nonsensical talk; gibberish. [French, perhaps originally students' jargon : Latin *gallus,* "cock," student who takes part in a discussion (see **gal-**[2] in Appendix*) + Greek *-mathia,* knowledge, from *manthanein,* to learn (see **mendh-** in Appendix*).]

gal·in·gale (găl′ĭn-gāl′) *n.* Any of various sedges of the genus *Cyperus;* especially, *C. longus,* of Europe, having rough-edged leaves, reddish spikelets, and aromatic roots. [Middle English *galengal, galingale,* from Old French *galingal,* Arabic *khalanjān* or Persian *khūlanjān,* from Chinese *kao*[1]*liang*[2]*chiang*[1] : *kao*[1]*-liang*[2], an area in Kwangtung Province + *chiang*[1], ginger.]

gal·i·ot (găl′ē-ət) *n.* Also **gal·li·ot.** **1.** A light, swift galley propelled by sails and oars, formerly used on the Mediterranean. **2.** A light, single-masted, flat-bottomed Dutch merchant ship or seagoing barge. [Middle English *galiot,* a light galley, and Middle Dutch *galiōte,* merchant ship, both from Old French *galiote,* from Medieval Latin *galiota,* diminutive of *galea,* GALLEY.]

Ga·li·tsi·ya. The Russian name for Polish **Galicia.**

gall[1] (gôl) *n.* **1. a.** Liver **bile** *(see).* **b.** The **gallbladder** *(see).* **2.** Rancor; bitterness. **3.** Something bitter to endure. **4.** Impudence; effrontery: *He had the gall to try to borrow money.* —See Synonyms at **temerity.** [Middle English *gall(e),* Old English *gealla.* See **ghel-**[2] in Appendix.*]

gall[2] (gôl) *n.* **1.** A skin sore caused by friction and abrasion: *a saddle gall.* **2. a.** Exasperation; irritation; vexation. **b.** The cause of such vexation. —*v.* **galled, galling, galls.** —*tr.* **1.** To make (the skin) sore by abrasion; chafe; excoriate. **2.** To damage or break the surface of by or as if by friction or abrasion; abrade: *the bark of saplings galled by improper staking.* **3.** To exasperate; vex. —*intr.* To become irritated, chafed, or sore. [Middle English *galle,* from Old English *gealla,* sore place, from Latin *galla,* gallnut. See **gall** (of a plant).]

gall[3] (gôl) *n.* An abnormal swelling of plant tissue, caused by insects, microorganisms, or external injury. [Middle English *galle,* from Old French, from Latin *galla*†.]

Gal·la (găl′ə) *n., pl.* **Galla** or **-las. 1.** A member of a pastoral Hamitic people of southern Ethiopia and the Somali Republic. **2.** The language of this people, belonging to the Ethiopian or Cushitic group of the Afro-Asiatic languages. —*adj.* Of or pertaining to this people or their language. [Perhaps from Arabic *ghalīẓ,* rough.]

Gal·lae·ci·a. The ancient name for Spanish **Galicia.**

gal·lant (găl′ənt *for senses 1, 2, 3;* gə-lănt′, -länt′, găl′ənt *for sense 4*) *adj.* **1.** Showy and gay in appearance, dress, or bearing; dashing: *a gallant feathered hat.* **2.** Stately; majestic; noble: *"On my word, master, this is a gallant trout"* (Walton). **3.** High-spirited and courageous; daring; valorous: *gallant soldiers.* **4. a.** Attentive to women; chivalrous; courteous. **b.** Flirtatious. —See Synonyms at **brave.** —*n.* (gə-lănt′, -länt′, găl′ənt). **1.** A fashionable young man. **2. a.** A man courteously attentive to women. **b.** A woman's lover; paramour. —*v.* (gə-lănt′, -länt′) **gallanted, -lanting, -lants.** —*tr.* To woo, attend, or escort (a lady); pay court to. —*intr.* To play the gallant. [Middle English *galaunt,* from Old French *galant,* gorgeous, showy, brave, from the present participle of *galer,* to live a gay life, rejoice, from Gallo-Roman *walāre* (unattested), from Frankish *wala* (unattested), well. See **wel-**[2] in Appendix.*] —**gal′lant·ly** *adv.*

gal·lant·ry (găl′ən-trē) *n., pl.* **-ries. 1.** Nobility of spirit or action; courage. **2.** Chivalrous attention toward women; courtliness; courteousness: *"the air of faintly mocking gallantry with which he habitually treated mother"* (Louis Auchincloss). **3.** An act or instance of gallantry in speech or behavior. **4.** *Archaic.* A bold or colorful display or appearance.

Gal·la·tin (găl′ə-tən), **(Abraham Alphonse) Albert.** 1761–1849. Swiss-born American financier and political leader; Secretary of the Treasury (1801–14).

Gal·la·tin Range (găl′ə-tən). A section of the Rocky Mountains, extending 45 miles in northwestern Wyoming and southwestern Montana. Highest elevation, Electric Peak (11,155 feet).

gall·blad·der (gôl′blăd′ər) *n.* Also **gall bladder.** A small, pear-shaped, muscular sac located under the right lobe of the liver, in which bile secreted by the liver is stored.

Galle (gäl, găl). Formerly **Point de Galle** (point′ də gäl′, găl′). A port city and trade center on the southeastern coast of Ceylon. Population, 65,000.

gal·le·ass (găl′ē-ăs′, -əs) *n.* Also **gal·li·ass. 1.** A large, heavily armed, three-masted Mediterranean galley of the 16th and 17th centuries. **2.** A small Baltic sailing coaster. [Old French *galeasse,* from Old Italian *galeaza,* augmentative of *galea,* galley, from Medieval Latin, GALLEY.]

gal·le·on (găl′ē-ən) *n.* A large three-masted sailing ship generally having two or more decks, used during the 15th and 16th centuries by Spain and other countries as a merchantman or warship. [Spanish *galeon,* from Old French *galion,* from *galie,* GALLEY.]

gal·ler·y (găl′ə-rē) *n., pl.* **-ies. 1.** A roofed promenade, especially one extending along the wall of a building and supported by arches on the outer side. **2. a.** Any similar enclosed narrow passageway, as a hall or corridor. **b.** Any place or establishment generally resembling such a corridor in length, and used for a specified purpose: *a shooting gallery.* **3.** *Regional.* A porch; veranda. **4. a.** An upper floor projecting over the rear part of the main floor of a theater, and usually providing cheaper seats than those in the orchestra. **b.** The seats in such a section. **c.** The audience occupying these seats. **d.** Any similar upper floor in a large building, as in a church. **5. a.** Any large audience or group of spectators, as in a stadium, grandstand, or legislative assembly. **b.** The general public when considered as exemplifying a lack of artistic discrimination or sophistication. **6. a.** A building or hall in which sculpture, paintings, photographs, or other artistic work is displayed. **b.** A collection of sculpture, paintings, photographs, or other artistic work. **c.** An institution that sells works of art, especially by auction. **7.** A building where any objects are sold at auction. **8.** An underground tunnel or other passageway, as one dug for military or mining purposes. **9.** *Nautical.* A platform or balcony at the stern or quarters of certain early sailing ships. **10.** A decorative upright trimming or molding along the edge of a table top, tray, or shelf. —**play to the gallery. 1.** To perform a play, scene, or role in a manner calculated to please the less sophisticated members of an audience who, in former times, were mainly congregated in the gallery. **2.** To try to gain the favor or applause of the general public, especially by crude or obvious means. [Middle English *galerie,* from Old French, portico, from Italian *galleria,* from Medieval Latin *galeria,* perhaps variant of *galilaea,* porch of a church, GALILEE.]

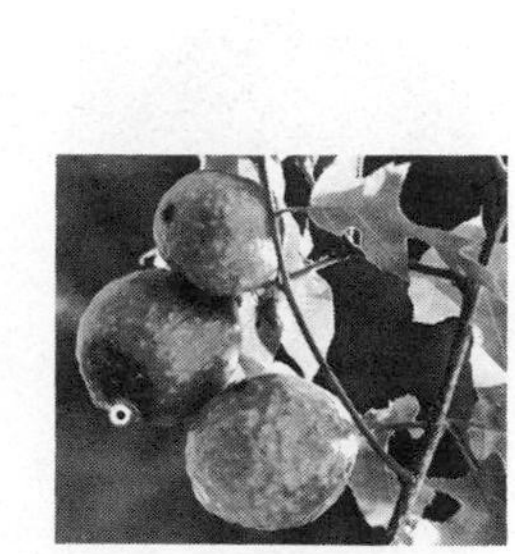

gall[3]
Insect galls on oak twig

gal·ley (găl′ē) *n., pl.* **-leys. 1.** A large medieval ship of shallow draft, propelled by sails and oars, and used as a merchantman or warship in the Mediterranean. **2.** An ancient seagoing vessel propelled by oars. **3.** A large rowboat formerly used in England. **4.** The kitchen of a ship or airliner. **5.** *Printing.* **a.** A long tray, usually of metal, used for holding composed type. **b.** A **galley proof** *(see).* **c.** A rough unit of measurement, approximately 22 inches, used for type composition. [Middle English *galeie, galy,* from Old French *galie, galee,* from Medieval Latin *galea,* from Medieval Greek *galea*†.]

galley proof. *Printing.* A printer's proof taken from composed type before page composition to allow for the detection and correction of errors. Also called "galley."

galley slave. 1. A slave or convict forced to man an oar of a galley. **2.** A person forced to perform tedious or menial tasks; a drudge.

galley west. *Informal.* Out of shape; out of commission. Used in the phrase *to knock galley west.* [Perhaps alteration of dialectal *collywest,* askew, probably from a personal name.]

gall·fly (gôl′flī′) *n., pl.* **-flies.** Any of various small insects of the family Cecidomyiidae that deposit their eggs on plant stems or in the bark of trees, causing the formation of galls in which their larvae grow. Also called "gall gnat," "gall midge."

Gal·li·a. The Latin name for **Gaul.**

gal·liard (găl′yərd) *adj. Archaic.* Spirited; lively; gay. —*n.* **1.** A spirited dance popular in France in the 16th and 17th centuries. **2.** The triple time music for this dance. [Middle English *galiard, gaillard,* valiant, lively, from Old French *gaillard,* from Gallo-Roman *galia* (unattested), strength, power. See **gal-**[3] in Appendix.*]

gal·li·ass. Variant of **galleass.**

Gal·lic (găl′ĭk) *adj.* Of or pertaining to ancient Gaul or to modern France; French. [Latin *Gallicus,* Gaulish, from *Galli,* Gauls. See **Volcae** in Appendix.*]

gal·lic acid (găl′ĭk). A colorless crystalline compound, $C_7H_6O_5 \cdot H_2O$, derived from tannin and used in photography, as a tanning agent, and in ink and paper manufacture.

Gal·li·can (găl′ĭ-kən) *adj.* **1.** Pertaining to or characteristic of Gallicanism. **2.** Gallic. —*n.* A supporter of Gallicanism. [Middle English, from Old French, from Medieval Latin *Gallicānus,* French, from Latin, Gaulish, from *Gallicus,* GALLIC.]

Gal·li·can·ism (găl′ĭ-kə-nĭz′əm) *n.* A movement originating among the French Roman Catholic clergy, favoring the restriction of papal control and the achievement by each nation of individual administrative autonomy. Compare **Ultramontanism.**

Gal·li·cism (găl′ĭ-sĭz′əm) *n.* **1.** A French phrase or idiom appearing in another language. **2.** A characteristic French trait.

Gal·li·cize (găl′ĭ-sīz′) *v.* **-cized, -cizing, -cizes.** —*intr.* To become like the French in form, pronunciation, character, or custom. —*tr.* To make French in any of these ways.

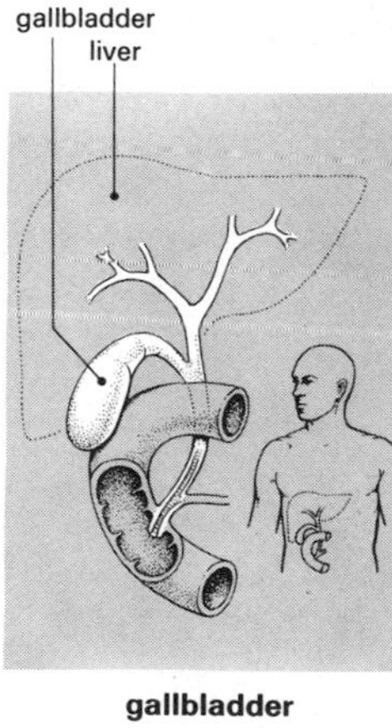

gallbladder

gal·li·gas·kins (găl′ĭ-găs′kĭnz) *pl.n.* Also **gal·ly·gas·kins. 1.** Full length, loosely fitting hose or breeches worn in the 16th and 17th centuries. **2.** Any loose breeches. **3.** *Regional.* Leggings. [Earlier *gallogascaine, garragascoyne,* perhaps from Old French *garguesque, greguesque,* from Old Italian *grechesca,* "Grecian breeches," from the feminine of *grechesco,* Grecian, from *greco,* Greek, from Latin *Graecus,* GREEK.]

gal·li·mau·fry (găl′ə-mô′frē) *n., pl.* **-fries. 1.** A hash made from leftovers. **2.** A jumble; hodgepodge. [French *galimafrée,* from Old French *calimafree* : probably *galer,* to live a gay life (see **gallant**) + Picard *mafrer,* to eat voraciously, from Middle Dutch *maffelen*†.]

gal·li·na·ceous (găl′ə-nā′shəs) *adj.* Of, belonging to, or characteristic of the order Galliformes, which includes the common domestic fowl as well as the pheasants, turkeys, and grouse. [Latin *gallīnāceus,* of poultry, from *gallīna,* hen, feminine of *gallus,* cock. See **gal-**[2] in Appendix.*]

Ga·lli·nas Point (gä-yē′näs). *Spanish* **Pun·ta Ga·lli·nas** (po͞on′tä). A cape in north-central Colombia, the northernmost point of South America.

gall·ing (gô′lĭng) *adj.* Causing acute irritation, exasperation, or discomfort. —**gal′ling·ly** *adv.*

gal·li·nip·per (găl′ə-nĭp′ər) *n.* A large mosquito or similar insect capable of inflicting a painful bite. [Origin unknown.]

gal·li·nule (găl′ə-no͞ol′, -nyo͞ol′) *n.* Any of various wading birds of the genera *Gallinula, Porphyrio,* or *Porphyrula,* frequenting

John Galsworthy

swampy regions and characteristically having dark, iridescent plumage. [New Latin *Gallīnula,* from Latin *gallīnula,* chicken, diminutive of *gallina,* hen. See **gallinaceous.**]

gal·li·ot. Variant of **galiot.**

Gal·lip·o·li (gə-lĭp′ə-lē). *Turkish* **Ge·li·bo·lu** (gĕl′ə-bə-lōō′). A peninsula of European Turkey extending 63 miles between the Dardanelles and the Gulf of Saros.

gal·li·pot (găl′ə-pŏt′) *n.* A small, glazed earthenware jar formerly used by druggists for medicaments. [Middle English *galy pott* : probably GALLEY + POT (originally imported from the Mediterranean by galleys).]

gal·li·um (găl′ē-əm) *n. Symbol* **Ga** A rare metallic element that is liquid near room temperature, expands on solidifying, and is found as a trace element in coal, bauxite, and other minerals. It is used in semiconductor technology and as a component of various low-melting alloys. Atomic number 31, atomic weight 69.72, melting point 29.78°C, boiling point 2,403°C, specific gravity 5.907 (20°C), valences 2, 3. See **element.** [New Latin, from Latin *gallus,* cock (playful translation of the name of its discoverer, *Lecoq* de Boisbaudran, 1838–1912, French chemist). See **gallinaceous.**]

gallium arsenide. A dark-gray crystalline compound, GaAs, used in transistors, solar cells, and semiconducting lasers.

gal·li·vant (găl′ə-vănt′, găl′ə-vănt′) *intr.v.* **-vanted, -vanting, -vants.** **1.** To roam about aimlessly or frivolously; traipse; to gad. **2.** To consort frivolously with members of the opposite sex; to flirt. —See Synonyms at **wander.** [Perhaps alteration of GALLANT (form influenced by LEVANT).]

gal·li·wasp (găl′ə-wŏsp′, -wôsp′) *n.* Also **gal·ly·wasp.** Any of several long-bodied lizards of the genera *Diploglossus* or *Celestus,* of Central America and the West Indies. [Origin unknown.]

gall midge. A gallfly *(see).*

gall·nut (gôl′nŭt′) *n.* A plant gall having a rounded form suggestive of a nut.

Gallo–. Indicates Gaul or France; for example, **Gallo-Roman, Gallomania.** [From Latin *Gallus,* a Gaul. See **Volcae** in Appendix.*]

gal·lo·glass. Variant of **gallowglass.**

Gal·lo·ma·ni·a (găl′ə-mā′nē-ə) *n.* A strong predilection for anything French. [French *gallomanie* : GALLO- + -MANIA.]

gal·lon (găl′ən) *n. Abbr.* **gal. 1. a.** A unit of volume or capacity in the U.S. Customary System, used in liquid measure, equal to 4 quarts or 231 cubic inches. **b.** A unit of volume in the British Imperial System, used in liquid and dry measure, equal to 277.420 cubic inches. See **measurement. 2.** A container with such capacity. [Middle English *gallun, gallon,* from Old North French, from Medieval Latin *gallēta,* jug, measure for wine, perhaps from Celtic.]

gal·lon·age (găl′ə-nĭj) *n.* The amount of something measured in gallons.

gal·loon (gə-lōōn′) *n.* A narrow band or braid used as trimming, and commonly made of lace, metallic thread, or embroidery. [French *galon,* from Old French *galonner,* to decorate with ribbons, perhaps from Frankish *wŏlon,* to tie up with cord. See **wel-³** in Appendix.*]

gal·loot. Variant of **galoot.**

gal·lop (găl′əp) *n.* **1. a.** A natural three-beat gait of a horse, faster than a canter and slower than a run. **b.** A rapid, running motion of other quadrupeds. **2.** A ride taken at the gallop. —*v.* **galloped, -loping, -lops.** —*tr.* **1.** To cause to gallop. **2.** To transport at or as if at a gallop: *gallop the guns to the rear.* —*intr.* **1.** To ride a horse at a gallop. **2.** To move or progress rapidly. [Middle English *galopen,* from Old French *galoper,* variant of Old North French *waloper,* from Frankish *walahlaupan* (unattested), "to run well" : *wala* (unattested), well (see **wel-²** in Appendix*) + *hlaupan* (unattested), to jump, run (see **klou-** in Appendix*).] —**gal′lop·er** *n.*

gal·lo·pade. Variant of **galop.**

gal·lop·ing (găl′ə-pĭng) *adj.* **1.** Of or resembling a gallop, especially in rhythm or rapidity. **2.** Developing at an accelerated rate and leading to death. Said of certain diseases, principally in nontechnical contexts.

Gal·lo-Ro·man (găl′ō-rō′mən) *n.* **1.** A native or inhabitant of Roman Gaul. **2.** The Vulgar Latin spoken by the Romanized inhabitants of Gaul. —**Gal′lo-Ro′man** *adj.*

Gal·lo-Ro·mance (găl′ō-rō-măns′) *n.* The Romance language that developed out of Vulgar Latin in what is now France. —**Gal′lo-Ro·mance′** *adj.*

Gal·lo·way (găl′ə-wā). A district in southwestern Scotland comprising Wigtownshire and Kirkcudbrightshire counties. [Medieval Latin *Gallovidia,* from Irish Gaelic *Gallgaedheal,* "foreign Gaels" : *gall,* foreigner (see **Volcae** in Appendix*) + *Gaedheal,* variant of Scottish Gaelic *Gaidheal,* GAEL.] —**Gal·we′gian** *adj.* & *n.*

gal·low·glass (găl′ō-glăs′, -gläs′) *n.* Also **gal·lo·glass.** Formerly, an armed retainer or mercenary in the service of an Irish chieftain. [Irish Gaelic *galloglach,* "foreign youth" : *gall,* foreigner (see **Volcae** in Appendix*) + *oglach,* youth : *og,* young, from Old Irish *ōac* (see **yeu-²** in Appendix*) + *-lach,* abstract suffix.]

gal·lows (găl′ōz) *n., pl.* **gallowses** or **gallows. 1.** A device usually consisting of two upright beams supporting a crossbeam from which a noose is suspended, and used for execution by hanging. Also called "gallowstree." **2.** Any similar structure used for supporting or suspending. **3.** Execution on a gallows or by hanging. **4.** A gallows bird. [Middle English *galwes, galawis,* plural of *galwe,* gallows, cross, from Old English *gealga.* See **ghalgh-** in Appendix.*]

gallows bird. *Informal.* One who deserves to be hanged.

gall·stone (gôl′stōn′) *n.* A small, hard, pathological concretion, chiefly of cholesterol crystals, formed in the gallbladder or in a bile duct.

Gal·lup (găl′əp), **George Horace.** Born 1901. American statistician, and founder of the American Institute of Public Opinion.

gal·lus·es (găl′ə-sĭz) *pl.n. Informal.* Suspenders for trousers. [Plural of *gallus,* variant of GALLOWS (obsolete sense "suspenders").]

gall wasp. Any of various wasps of the family Cynipidae, that produce distinctively shaped galls on oaks and other plants.

gal·ly·gas·kins. Variant of **galligaskins.**

gal·ly·wasp. Variant of **galliwasp.**

ga·loot (gə-lōōt′) *n.* Also **gal·loot.** *Slang.* A clumsy, uncouth, or sloppily dressed person. [Origin unknown.]

gal·op (găl′əp) *n.* Also **gal·o·pade** (-ə-pād′), **gal·lo·pade. 1.** A lively dance in duple rhythm, popular in the 19th century. **2.** The music for this dance. [French, gallop, from Old French *galoper,* to GALLOP.]

ga·lore (gə-lôr′, -lōr′) *adj. Informal.* In great numbers; in abundance. Used after the noun it modifies: *dresses galore; opportunities galore.* [Irish Gaelic *go leór* : *go,* to, from Old Irish *co, cu†* + *leór,* sufficiency, enough, from Old Irish *lour* (see **lāu-** in Appendix*).]

ga·losh (gə-lŏsh′) *n.* Also **ga·loshe, go·losh. 1.** *Usually plural.* A waterproof overshoe. **2.** *Obsolete.* A sturdy heavy-soled boot or shoe. [Middle English *galoche,* from Old French, probably from Late Latin *gallicula,* diminutive of Latin *gallica (solea),* "Gaulish (sandal)," from the feminine of *gallicus,* Gaulish, Gaelic, from *Galli,* Gauls. See **Volcae** in Appendix.*]

Gals·wor·thy (gôlz′wûr′thē), **John.** 1867–1933. English novelist and playwright.

Gal·ton (gôl′tən), **Sir Francis.** 1822–1911. British meteorologist, statistician, and biologist.

galv. galvanized.

Gal·va·ni (găl-vä′nē), **Luigi.** 1737–1798. Italian physiologist; devised theory of production of electricity in animals.

gal·van·ic (găl-văn′ĭk) *adj.* **1.** Of or pertaining to direct-current electricity, especially when produced chemically. **2.** Having the effect of or produced as if by an electric shock. [French *galvanique,* from *galvanisme,* GALVANISM.] —**gal·van′i·cal·ly** *adv.*

galvanic cell. *Electricity.* A primary cell *(see).*

galvanic couple. *Electricity.* A voltaic couple *(see).*

gal·va·nism (găl′və-nĭz′əm) *n.* Direct-current electricity, especially when produced chemically. Also called "voltaism." [French *galvanisme,* from Italian *galvanismo,* first described by Luigi GALVANI.]

gal·va·nize (găl′və-nīz′) *tr.v.* **-nized, -nizing, -nizes. 1.** To stimulate or shock with an electric current. **2.** To arouse to awareness or action; to spur; startle: *"A blast in my ear, like the voice of fifty trombones, galvanized me into full consciousness."* (Erskine Childers). **3.** To coat (iron or steel) with rust-resistant zinc, by spraying, immersion, or electrolytic deposition. —**gal′va·ni·za′tion** *n.* —**gal′va·niz′er** *n.*

galvanized iron. Iron coated with zinc to prevent rust.

gal·va·nom·e·ter (găl′və-nŏm′ə-tər) *n.* A device for detecting or measuring small electric currents by means of mechanical effects produced by the current to be measured. [GALVAN(ISM) + -METER.] —**gal′va·no·met′ric** (-nō-mĕt′rĭk, găl-văn′ō-), **gal′va·no·met′ri·cal** *adj.* —**gal′va·nom′e·try** *n.*

gal·va·no·scope (găl′və-nə-skōp′, găl-văn′ə-) *n.* A galvanometer used to detect the presence and direction of electric currents by the deflection of a magnetic needle. [GALVAN(ISM) + -SCOPE.] —**gal′va·no·scop′ic** (găl′və-nə-skŏp′ĭk, găl-văn′ə-) *adj.* —**gal′va·nos′co·py** (găl′və-nŏs′kə-pē) *n.*

Gal·ves·ton (găl′və-stən). A port city in southeastern Texas on the northwestern tip of Galveston Island, an island at the entrance to Galveston Bay. Population, 67,000.

Gal·ves·ton Bay (găl′vəs-tən). An inlet of the Gulf of Mexico in southeastern Texas, 20 miles southeast of Houston.

Galveston plan. A form of municipal government, a commission plan *(see).*

Gal·way (gôl′wā). A county, 2,293 square miles in area, of west-central Ireland. Population, 150,000.

Gal·way Bay (gôl′wā). An inlet of the Atlantic in west-central Ireland.

gal·yak (găl′yăk′) *n.* Also **gal·yac.** A flat, glossy fur made from the pelt of a stillborn lamb or kid. [Russian dialectal *galyak,* perhaps from Russian *golyĭ,* bald, naked. See **gal-¹** in Appendix.*]

gam¹ (găm) *n.* **1.** A school or herd of whales. **2.** A social visit or friendly conversation, especially between whalers at sea. —See Synonyms at **flock.** —*v.* **gammed, gamming, gams.** —*intr.* To come together socially; to visit, especially while at sea. —*tr.* **1.** To visit with. **2.** To spend (time) in visiting. [Perhaps short for GAMMON (deceptive talk).]

gam² (găm) *n. Slang.* A person's leg; especially, a shapely female leg. [Probably from obsolete *gamb,* leg of an animal, from Old North French *gambe,* Late Latin *gamba,* hook, leg, from Greek *kampē,* a bend. See **kamp-** in Appendix.]

Ga·ma (găm′ə; *Portuguese* gä′mə), **Vasco da.** 1469?–1524. Portuguese explorer and colonial administrator; first to reach India by sea (1498).

gam·ba·do¹ (găm-bā′dō) *n., pl.* **-does** or **-dos.** Also **gam·bade** (-bād′). **1.** A low leap of a horse in which all four feet are off the ground. **2.** A leaping or gamboling movement; an antic; a flourish. [Spanish *gambada,* from Italian *gambata,* GAMBOL.]

gam·ba·do² (găm-bā′dō) *n., pl.* **-does** or **-dos. 1.** Either of a pair of protective leather gaiters attached to a saddle. **2.** A rider's legging or gaiter. [From Italian *gamba,* leg (perhaps influenced by BASTINADO). See **gambol.**]

gam·be·son (găm′bə-sən) *n.* A sleeveless garment of leather or quilted material worn under armor in the Middle Ages. [Middle English *gambisoun,* from Old French *gambe(i)son,* from *gambais, wambais,* probably from Frankish *wamba* (unattested), belly, from Common Germanic *wambō* (unattested), WOMB.]

Gam·bi·a (găm′bē-ə). **1.** A republic and former British colony of western Africa, 4,033 square miles in area, bordered on the north, east, and south by the Republic of Senegal and on the west by the Atlantic. Population, 330,000. Capital, Bathurst. **2.** A river of western Africa, rising in northern Guinea and flowing 460 miles west to the Atlantic at Bathurst.

gam·bir (găm′bîr) *n.* Also **gam·bier.** A resinous, astringent extract obtained from a woody vine, *Uncaria gambier,* of south-central Asia, used medicinally and in tanning and dyeing. [Malay *gambir.*]

gam·bit (găm′bĭt) *n.* **1.** *Chess.* An opening move in which one or more pieces are sacrificed in order to gain a favorable position. **2.** An opening remark or stratagem. See Usage note below. [Earlier *gamet,* from Italian *gambetto,* "a tripping up," from *gamba,* leg. See **gambol.**]

Usage: *Gambit,* apart from its use in chess, is often applied to any opening procedural move, especially one that furthers strategy or promotes discussion: *As negotiations with the union began, the employers' gambit was a presentation of economic forecasts that showed declining demand for new automobiles. Gambit* is acceptably employed here, according to 63 per cent of the Usage Panel. The minority contend that even in extended usage, the term necessarily involves the sense of initial sacrifice or concession made to gain advantage, as it does in chess. The example cited, like most others employing *gambit* in this sense, is less strict in interpretation.

gam·ble (găm′bəl) *v.* **-bled, -bling, -bles.** —*intr.* **1. a.** To bet money on the outcome of a game, contest, or other event. **b.** To play a game of chance for money or other stakes. **2.** To take a risk in the hope of gaining an advantage; speculate. —*tr.* **1.** To put up in gambling; to wager. **2.** To expose to hazard; to risk. —*n.* **1.** A bet, wager, or other gambling venture. **2.** An act or undertaking of uncertain outcome; a risk. [Probably from earlier *gamel,* from *gamner,* gambler, from *gamene,* to gamble, Middle English *gamenen,* Old English *gamenian,* to sport, play, from *gamen,* amusement. See **game.**] —**gam′bler** (-blər) *n.*

gam·boge (găm-bōj′, -bo͞ozh′) *n.* **1.** A brownish or orange resin obtained from any of several trees of the genus *Garcinia,* of south-central Asia, and yielding a golden-yellow pigment. Also "cambogia." **2.** Strong yellow. See **color.** [New Latin *gambogium, cambugium,* obtained from CAMBODIA.] —**gam·boge′** *adj.*

gam·bol (găm′bəl) *intr.v.* **-boled** or **-bolled, -boling** or **-bolling, -bols.** To leap about playfully; to frolic; skip. —*n.* A skipping or frolicking about. [Earlier *gamba(u)de,* from Old French *gambade,* from Italian *gambata,* from *gamba,* leg, from Late Latin, hoof, leg, from Greek *kampē,* bend. See **kamp-** in Appendix.*]

gam·brel (găm′brəl) *n.* **1.** The hock of a horse or other animal. **2.** A wooden or metal frame used by butchers for hanging carcasses by the legs. [Old North French *gamberel,* diminutive of *gambier,* gambrel, from *gambe,* leg, from Late Latin *gamba,* hoof, leg. See **gambol.**]

gambrel roof. A ridged roof having two slopes on each side, the lower slope having the steeper pitch.

game¹ (gām) *n.* **1.** A way of amusing oneself; a pastime; diversion. **2.** *Mathematics.* A set of rules completely specifying a competition, including the permissible actions of and information available to each participant, the probabilities with which chance events may occur, the criteria for termination of the competition, and the distribution of payoffs. **3.** A sport or other competitive activity governed by specific rules: *the game of tennis.* **4.** A single instance of such an activity: *We lost the first game.* **5. a.** The total number of points required to win a game: *One hundred points is game in bridge.* **b.** The score accumulated at any given time in a game: *At half time, the game was 14 to 12.* **6.** The equipment needed for playing certain games: *pack the children's games in the car.* **7.** A particular style or manner of playing a game: *His bridge game is only adequate.* **8.** A calculated action or approach; a scheme; plan: *You'll never see through his game.* **9. a.** Wild animals, birds, or fish hunted for food or sport. **b.** The flesh of game, eaten as food. **10. a.** Anything hunted or fit to be hunted; quarry; prey. **b.** An object of ridicule, teasing, or scorn: *They made game of him.* **11.** *Informal.* A vocation or business, especially a competitive one: *the publishing game.* —*v.* **gamed, gaming, games.** —*tr. Archaic.* To waste or lose by gambling. —*intr.* To play for money or other stakes. —*adj.* **gamer, gamest. 1.** Of or pertaining to wild game. **2.** Plucky and unyielding in manner; resolute; brave. **3.** *Informal.* Ready and willing: *Are you game for a swim?* —See Synonyms at **brave.** [Middle English *game(n),* Old English *gamen,* amusement, sport, from Common Germanic *gam-* (unattested), to enjoy.]

game² (gām) *adj.* **gamer, gamest.** Lame: *"to jump with his game leg foremost might mean to collapse under the impact of arrival"* (Aldous Huxley). [Perhaps from French *gambi*†, crooked.]

game·cock (gām′kŏk′) *n.* A rooster trained for cockfighting.

game fowl. 1. A bird sought after as game. **2.** Any of several breeds of domestic fowl raised especially for cockfighting.

game·keep·er (gām′kē′pər) *n.* A person employed to protect and maintain wildlife, especially on an estate or game preserve.

gam·e·lan (găm′ə-lăn′) *n.* A type of orchestra common to Southeast Asia, consisting mainly of tuned metal or wooden chimes and other percussion instruments.

game laws. Regulations for the protection of game animals, including birds and fish, that define the hunting season for each species and place restrictions on the method of capture and on the number of animals that may be taken.

game·ly (gām′lē) *adv.* With pluck; courageously.

game·ness (gām′nĭs) *n.* Courage; pluck.

games·man·ship (gāmz′mən-shĭp′) *n.* The method or art of winning a game or contest by means of unsportsmanlike behavior or other conduct which does not actually break the rules.

game·some (gām′səm) *adj.* Frolicsome; playful; merry. —**game′some·ly** *adv.* —**game′some·ness** *n.*

game·ster (gām′stər) *n.* A habitual gambler.

gam·e·tan·gi·um (găm′ə-tăn′jē-əm) *n., pl.* **-gia** (-jē-ə). *Botany.* An organ or cell in which gametes are produced, especially in primitive plant forms. [GAMET(O)- + Greek *angeion,* diminutive of *angos,* vessel (see **angiology**).] —**gam′e·tan′gi·al** *adj.*

gam·ete (găm′ēt, gə-mēt′) *n.* A germ cell possessing the haploid number of chromosomes; especially, a mature sperm or egg, capable of participating in fertilization. See **fertilization.** [New Latin *gameta,* from Greek *gametē,* wife, and *gametēs,* husband, both from *gamos,* marriage. See **gemə-** in Appendix.*]

game theory. The mathematical analysis of abstract models of strategic competition with the determination of best strategy as a goal, having applications in linear programming, statistical decision making, operations research, and military and economic planning. Also called "theory of games." See **game.**

gameto–. Indicates gamete; for example, **gametophyte, gametophore.** [From New Latin *gameta,* GAMETE.]

ga·me·to·cyte (gə-mē′tə-sīt′) *n.* A cell from which gametes are developed by division; a spermatocyte or an oocyte. [GAMETO- + -CYTE.]

ga·me·to·gen·e·sis (găm′ə-tō-jĕn′ə-sĭs) *n.* Also **gam·e·tog·e·ny** (găm′ə-tŏj′ə-nē). The production of gametes. [GAMETO- + -GENESIS.] —**ga′me·to·gen′ic, gam′e·tog′e·nous** (-tŏj′ə-nəs) *adj.*

ga·me·to·phore (gə-mē′tə-fôr′, -fōr′) *n. Botany.* A structure, as in mosses, on which gametangia are borne. [GAMETO- + -PHORE.] —**ga·me′to·phor′ic** (-fôr′ĭk, -fŏr′ĭk) *adj.*

ga·me·to·phyte (gə-mē′tə-fīt′) *n. Botany.* The generation or form that reproduces sexually in a plant characterized by alternation of generations. [GAMETO- + -PHYTE.] —**gam′e·to·phyt′ic** (găm′ə-tə-fĭt′ĭk) *adj.*

gam·ic (găm′ĭk) *adj.* Of or requiring fertilization in reproduction; sexual. [From Greek *gamos,* marriage. See **gamete.**]

gam·i·ly (gā′mə-lē) *adv.* In a gamy manner; gamely.

gam·in (găm′ĭn; *French* gȧ-măɴ′) *n.* A boy who roams about the streets; street urchin; waif. [French, perhaps from German *Gammel,* loud rejoicing, (hence) ungainly young man, good-for-nothing, from Old High German *gaman,* amusement, game, from Common Germanic *gam-* (unattested), to enjoy. See **game.**]

ga·mine (gă-mēn′; *French* gȧ-mēn′) *n.* **1.** A girl who roams about the streets; tomboy. **2.** A girl or woman having elfin appeal. [French, feminine of GAMIN.]

gam·ing (gā′mĭng) *n.* The playing of games of chance; gambling.

gam·ma (găm′ə) *n.* **1.** The third letter in the Greek alphabet, written γ. Transliterated in English as *g,* or as *n* before *g, k,* or *kh.* See **alphabet. 2.** A gamma ray. [Greek *gamma,* from Semitic, akin to Hebrew *gimel,* probably "camel."]

gam·ma·di·on (gə-mā′dē-ən) *n.* A cross composed of four capital Greek gammas, especially so as to form a swastika; fylfot. [Medieval Greek, from Greek GAMMA.]

gamma globulin. Any of several globulin fractions of blood serum that are closely associated with immune bodies and used to treat measles, poliomyelitis, infectious hepatitis, and other infectious diseases.

gamma ray. 1. Electromagnetic radiation emitted by radioactive decay and having energies in a range overlapping that of the highest energy x rays, extending up to several hundred thousand electron volts. **2.** Any electromagnetic radiation with energy greater than several hundred thousand electron volts. **3.** A **ray** *(see)* of such radiation.

gam·mer (găm′ər) *n. Regional.* An elderly woman. [Probably contraction of GODMOTHER or GRANDMOTHER.]

gam·mon¹ (găm′ən) *n.* A victory in backgammon occurring before the loser has removed a single man. —*tr.v.* **gammoned, -moning, -mons.** To defeat in backgammon by scoring a gammon. [Probably from Middle English *gamen,* GAME.]

gam·mon² (găm′ən) *n. British Informal.* Misleading or nonsensical talk; blather. —*v.* **gammoned, -moning, -mons.** *British Informal.* —*tr.* To mislead by deceptive talk. —*intr.* To talk gammon. [Perhaps from thieves' slang expressions *to give gammon, to keep in gammon,* to talk to and divert the attention of (someone) while another thief is robbing him, perhaps slang use of GAMMON (backgammon term).] —**gam′mon·er** *n.*

gam·mon³ (găm′ən) *n.* **1.** A ham that has been cured or smoked. **2.** The lower or bottom part of a side of bacon. [Old North French *gambon,* from *gambe,* leg, from Late Latin *gamba,* hoof, leg, from Greek *kampē,* a bend. See **kamp-** in Appendix.*]

gam·mon⁴ (găm′ən) *tr.v.* **-moned, -moning, -mons.** *Nautical.* To fasten (a bowsprit) to the stem of a ship. [Perhaps from GAMMON (cured ham, hence, "the tying up of a ham").]

gamo–. Indicates: **1.** Sexual union; for example, **gamogenesis. 2.** Union or fusion; for example, **gamopetalous.** [From Greek *gamos,* marriage. See **gemə-** in Appendix.*]

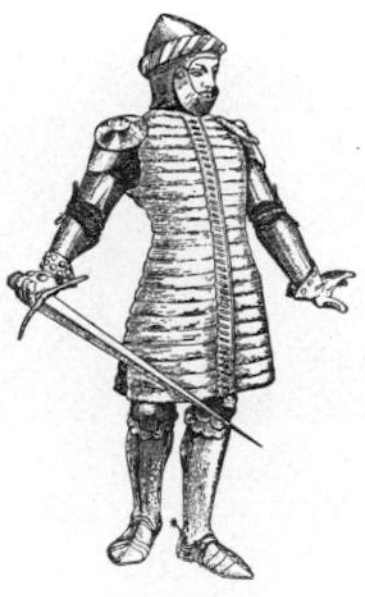

gambeson

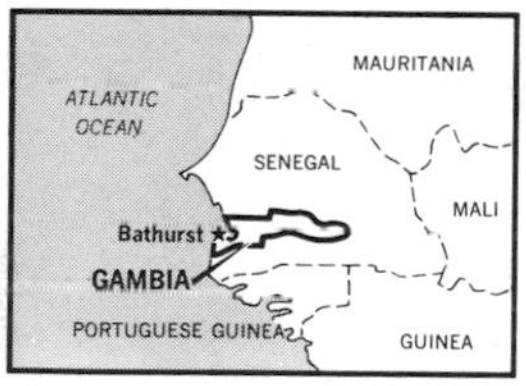

Gambia

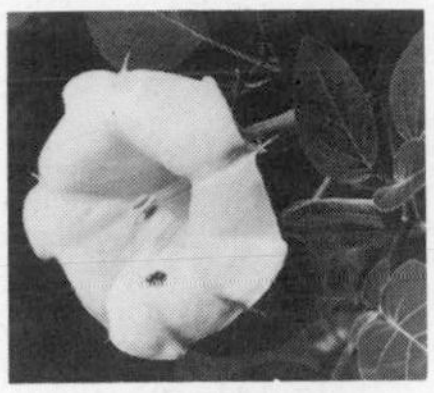
gamopetalous
Gamopetalous flower

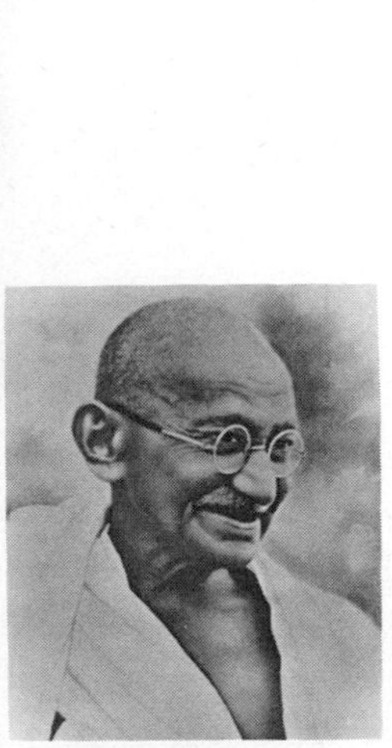
Mahatma Gandhi

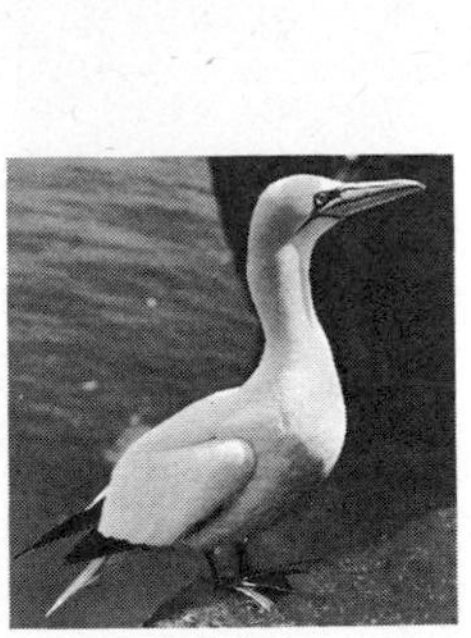
gannet
Morus bassanus

gam·o·gen·e·sis (găm′ə-jĕn′ə-sĭs) *n.* Sexual reproduction. [GAMO- + -GENESIS.] —**gam′o·ge·net′ic** (găm′ə-jə-nĕt′ĭk) *adj.* —**gam′o·ge·net′i·cal·ly** *adv.*
gam·o·pet·al·ous (găm′ə-pĕt′l-əs) *adj. Botany.* Having or characterizing a corolla with the petals fused or partially fused. Also "sympetalous." [New Latin *gamopetalus* : GAMO- + PETALOUS.]
gam·o·phyl·lous (găm′ə-fĭl′əs) *adj. Botany.* Having or designating united leaves or leaflike parts. [GAMO- + -PHYLLOUS.]
gam·o·sep·al·ous (găm′ə-sĕp′ə-ləs) *adj. Botany.* Having the sepals united or partly united. [GAMO- + -SEPALOUS.]
-gamous. Indicates marriage or sexual union; for example, **cleistogamous, dichogamous.** [From Greek *gamos,* marriage. See **geme-** in Appendix.*]
Ga·mow (gă′mou′), **George.** 1904–1968. Russian-born American nuclear physicist.
gamp (gămp) *n. Chiefly British.* A large, baggy umbrella. Used humorously. [After Mrs. Sarah *Gamp,* nurse in Charles Dickens' *Martin Chuzzlewit,* who owns such an umbrella.]
gam·ut (găm′ət) *n.* **1.** The complete range of anything; extent: *"He traverses the gamut of lovers' feelings everywhere."* (Edith Hamilton). **2.** The entire series of recognized musical notes. [Middle English, contracted from Medieval Latin *gamma ut* : *gamma,* note one tone lower than the first note in Guido d'Arezzo's scale, from Greek letter GAMMA + *ut* (now *do*), lowest note in Guido's scale. (The notes of the scale are named after syllables in a Latin hymn to Saint John: *Ut* queant laxis *re*sonāre fibris *Mi*ra gestorum *fa*muli tuorum, *Sol*ve polluti *la*bii reatum, *S*ancte *I*ohannes.)]
gam·y (gā′mē) *adj.* **-ier, -iest. 1.** Having the flavor or odor of game; especially, the flavor of game that has been hung too long. **2.** Showing an unyielding spirit; plucky; hardy: *a gamy little mare.* —**gam′i·ness** *n.*
-gamy. Indicates marriage or sexual union; for example, **allogamy.** [Greek *-gamia,* from *gamos,* marriage. See **geme-** in Appendix.*]
Ga·na. See **Ghana.**
Gand. The French name for **Ghent.**
Gan·dak (gŭn′dŭk). A river rising in southern Nepal and flowing 420 miles southwest and southeast into the Ganges in northern Bihar, Republic of India.
gan·der (găn′dər) *n.* **1.** A male goose. **2.** *Informal.* A simpleton; halfwit. **3.** *Slang.* A quick look; a glance. Used chiefly in the phrase *take a gander.* [Middle English *gander,* Old English *gandra, ganra.* See **ghans-** in Appendix.*]
Gan·der (găn′dər). A town in east-central Newfoundland, the site of an air base and of a major transatlantic airport. Population, 6,000.
Gan·dhi (gän′dē, găn′-), **Indira Nehru.** Born 1917. Prime minister of India (since 1966); daughter of Jawaharlal Nehru.
Gan·dhi (gän′dē, găn′-), **Mohandas Karamchand.** Called "Mahatma." 1869–1948. Hindu nationalist and spiritual leader; assassinated.
gan·dy dancer (găn′dē). *Slang.* **1.** A railroad worker. **2.** An itinerant laborer. [From the rhythmic movements of the railroad laborer working with tools produced by the now defunct *Gandy* Manufacturing Company in Chicago.]
Gan·dzha. The former name for **Kirovabad.**
ga·nef (gä′nəf) *n.* Also **go·nif, ga·nof.** *Yiddish.* A thief, scoundrel, or rascal. [Yiddish *ganef, gannef,* from Hebrew *gannābh,* from *gānabh,* he stole.]
gang[1] (găng) *n.* **1.** A group of people, usually young, who associate regularly on a social basis. **2.** A group of criminals or hoodlums who band together for mutual protection and profit. **3.** A group of laborers organized together on one job or under one foreman: *a railroad gang.* **4.** A set, especially of matched tools: *a gang of chisels.* **5. a.** A pack of wolves or wild dogs. **b.** A herd, especially of buffalo or elk. —See Synonyms at **flock.** —*v.* **ganged, ganging, gangs.** —*intr.* To band together as a group or gang. —*tr.* **1.** To group together into a gang. **2.** *Informal.* To attack as a gang. —**gang up on.** *Informal.* To harass or attack as a group. [Originally "a going," "journey," "way," Middle English *gang,* Old English *gang.* See **ghengh-** in Appendix.*]
gang[2]. Variant of **gangue.**
gang·bus·ter (găng′bŭs′tər) *n. Slang.* A law officer who fights to break up organized criminal groups.
gang·er (găng′ər) *n. Chiefly British.* A gang foreman.
Gan·ges (găn′jēz). *Hindi* **Gan·ga** (gŭng′gä). A river in northern India and East Pakistan, sacred to Hindus, flowing 1,560 miles generally southeast from the Himalayas to its wide delta and the Bay of Bengal.
gang hook. A multiple fishhook consisting of two or more hooks joined shank to shank. [From GANG (set of tools).]
gan·gli·at·ed (găng′glē-ā′tĭd) *adj.* Also **gan·gli·ate** (-ĭt, -āt′), **gan·gli·on·at·ed** (-ə-nā′tĭd). Having ganglia.
gan·gling (găng′glĭng) *adj.* Also **gang·ly** (-glē), **-lier, -liest.** Tall, thin, and ungraceful; awkwardly built; lanky; rangy: *"that gangly, craning look a kid's head has"* (Robert Penn Warren). [Irregularly from dialectal *gang,* to go, straggle, Middle English *gangen.* See **gangrel.**]
gan·gli·on (găng′glē-ən) *n., pl.* **-glia** (-glē-ə) or **-ons. 1.** *Anatomy.* A group of nerve cells, such as one located outside the brain or spinal cord, in vertebrates. **2.** Any center of power, activity, or energy. **3.** *Pathology.* A cystic lesion resembling a tumor, occurring in a tendon sheath or joint capsule. [Greek *ganglion,* cystlike tumor, hence nerve bundle, ganglion. See **gel-**[1] in Appendix.*] —**gan′gli·on′ic** (-ŏn′ĭk) *adj.*
gang·plank (găng′plăngk′) *n.* A board or ramp used as a movable footway between a ship and a pier. [GANG (in obsolete sense "passage") + PLANK.]
gang·plow (găng′plou′) *n.* A plow equipped with several blades that make parallel furrows. [GANG (set of tools) + PLOW.]
gan·grel (găng′grəl, -rəl) *n. Scottish.* A vagabond; drifter. [Middle English, from *gangen,* to go, Old English *gangan.* See **ghengh-** in Appendix.*]
gan·grene (găng′grēn′, găng-grēn′) *n.* Death and decay of tissue in a part of the body, usually a limb, due to failure of blood supply, injury, or disease. Compare **necrobiosis.** —*v.* **gangrened, -grening, -grenes.** —*tr.* To affect with gangrene. —*intr.* To become affected with gangrene. [Old French *gangrine,* from Latin *gangraena,* from Greek *gangraina.* See **gras-** in Appendix.*] —**gan′gre·nous** (-grə-nəs) *adj.*
gang·ster (găng′stər) *n.* A member of an organized group of criminals; racketeer. [GANG + -STER.]
Gang·tok (gŭng′tŏk). The capital of Sikkim, in the south-central part of the protectorate, 28 miles northeast of Darjeeling, India. Population, 7,000.
gangue (găng) *n.* Also **gang.** The worthless rock or other material in which valuable minerals are found. [French, from German *Gang,* course, lode, vein, from Old High German, a going. See **ghengh-** in Appendix.*]
gang·way (găng′wā′) *n.* **1.** A passageway, as through a crowd or an obstructed area. Often used as an interjection. **2.** *Nautical.* **a.** A passage along either side of a ship's upper deck. **b.** A gangplank. **c.** An opening in the bulwark of a ship through which passengers may board. **3.** *British.* **a.** The aisle that divides the front and rear seating sections of the House of Commons. **b.** Any aisle between seating sections, as in a theater. **4.** *Mining.* The main level of a mine. [GANG (in obsolete sense "passage") + WAY.]
gan·is·ter (găn′ĭ-stər) *n.* Also **gan·nis·ter. 1.** A silicon-rich sedimentary rock used for refractory furnace linings. **2.** A mixture of fire clay and ground quartz, used to line furnaces. [Origin unknown.]
gan·net (găn′ĭt) *n.* Any of several large sea birds of the family Sulidae; especially, *Morus bassanus,* of northern coastal regions, having white plumage with black wing tips. [Middle English *ganat, ganett,* Old English *ganot.* See **ghans-** in Appendix.*]
Gan·nett Peak (găn′ĕt, -ĭt). The highest mountain (13,785 feet) in Wyoming, part of the Wind River Range in the center of the state.
ga·nof. Variant of **ganef.**
gan·oid (găn′oid′) *adj.* Of, pertaining to, or characteristic of certain bony fishes, such as the sturgeon and the gar, having armorlike scales consisting of bony plates covered with layers of dentine and enamel. —*n.* A ganoid fish. [New Latin *Ganoidei* (former designation), from French *ganoïde,* having a shiny surface : Greek *ganos,* brightness, joy, from *ganusthai,* to rejoice (see **gāu-** in Appendix*) + -OID.]
gant·let[1] (gônt′lĭt, gänt′-) *n.* Also **gaunt·let.** A section of overlapping but independent railroad track where two sets of tracks are overlapped to afford passage at a narrow place without switching. See Usage note at **gauntlet.** —*tr.v.* **gantleted, -leting, -lets.** Also **gaunt·let.** To overlap (railroad tracks) of form a gantlet. [Alteration (influenced by GAUNTLET) of earlier *gant(e)lope,* from Swedish *gatlopp,* from Old Swedish *gatulop,* "passageway" : *gata,* road, way, from Germanic *gatwōn* (unattested) + *lop,* course, from Middle Low German *lōp* (see **klou-** in Appendix*).]
gant·let[2]. **1.** Variant of **gauntlet** (glove). **2.** Variant of **gauntlet** (ordeal).
gant·line (gănt′līn′) *n.* A rope passed through a single block at the top of a mast or stackpole and used for hoisting. [Perhaps alteration of *girtline* : GIRT (girdle) + LINE.]
gan·try (găn′trē) *n., pl.* **-tries.** Also **gaun·try. 1.** A support for a barrel lying on its side. **2.** A bridgelike frame over which a traveling crane moves. **3.** A similar spanning frame supporting a group of railway signals over several tracks. **4.** *Aerospace.* A massive vertical frame structure used in assembling or servicing rockets. [Probably from Old North French *gantier,* variant of Old French *chantier,* from Latin *canthērius,* rafter, from Greek *kanthēlios*†, pack ass.]
Gan·y·mede[1] (găn′ə-mēd′). *Greek Mythology.* A Trojan boy of great beauty whom Zeus carried away to be cupbearer to the gods.
Gan·y·mede[2] (găn′ə-mēd′) *n.* A young waiter or bar attendant. Used humorously. [After GANYMEDE.]
Gan·y·mede[3] (găn′ə-mēd′) *n. Astronomy.* The fourth moon of Jupiter, one of the largest planetary satellites in the solar system. [After GANYMEDE.]
GAO General Accounting Office.
gaol. *Chiefly British.* Variant of **jail.**
gap (găp) *n.* **1.** An opening, as in a partition or wall; a fissure; cleft. **2.** A break or pass through mountains. **3.** A suspension of continuity; interval; hiatus: *a gap in his report.* **4.** A conspicuous difference; disparity: *a gap between expenses and receipts.* **5.** *Electricity.* A space traversed by an electric spark; spark gap. —*tr.v.* **gapped, gapping, gaps.** To make an opening or gap in. [Middle English *gap(pe),* from Old Norse *gap,* chasm. See **ghēi-** in Appendix.*]
gape (gāp, găp) *intr.v.* **gaped, gaping, gapes. 1.** To open the mouth wide; to yawn. **2.** To stare wonderingly, as with the mouth open. **3.** To become widely open or separated: *The curtains gaped when the wind blew.* —See Synonyms at **gaze.** —*n.* **1.** An act or instance of gaping. **2.** A large opening. **3.** *Zoology.* The width of the space between the open jaws or mandibles of a vertebrate. **4.** *Plural.* A disease of birds, especially

young domesticated chickens and turkeys, caused by gapeworms and resulting in obstructed breathing. Used with a singular verb. **—the gapes.** A fit of yawning: *"another hour of music was to give pleasure or the gapes, as real or affected taste for it prevailed"* (Jane Austen). [Middle English *gapen,* Old Norse *gapa,* to open the mouth. See **ghēi-** in Appendix.*] **—gap′er** *n.*

gape·worm (gāp′wûrm′) *n.* Any of several nematode worms of the genus *Syngamus;* especially, *S. trachea,* infecting the trachea of certain birds and causing gapes.

gap·ing (gā′pĭng) *adj.* Deep and wide open; cavernous: *a gaping wound.* **—gap′ing·ly** *adv.*

gap·y (gā′pē) *adj.* Afflicted with the gapes, as a bird.

gar[1] (gär) *n.* **1.** Any of several ganoid fishes of the genus *Lepisosteus,* of fresh and brackish waters of North and Central America, having an elongated body and a long snout. **2.** A similar or related fish, such as the needlefish. Also called "garfish," "garpike." [Short for GARFISH.]

gar[2] (gär) *tr.v.* **garred, garring, gars.** *Chiefly Scottish.* To cause or compel. [Middle English *gere,* from Old Norse *gera,* to make, do. See **garwian** in Appendix.*]

GAR, G.A.R. Grand Army of the Republic.

ga·rage (gə-räzh′, -räj′; *British* găr′ĭj, -äzh) *n.* **1.** A building or wing of a building, as of a house, in which to park a car or cars. **2.** A commercial establishment where cars are repaired and serviced. *—tr.v.* **garaged, -raging, -rages.** To put in or bring to a garage. [French, from *garer,* to dock (ships), store in a garage, from Old French, to warn, protect, guard, from Frankish *warōn* (unattested). See **wer-**[5] in Appendix.*]

garb (gärb) *n.* Clothing; especially, the distinctive attire of one's occupation or station: *sailors' garb.* *—tr.v.* **garbed, garbing, garbs.** To cover with or as if with clothing; to dress; array. [Obsolete French *garbe,* graceful appearance, from Italian *garbo,* grace, elegance of dress, from Germanic. See **garwian** in Appendix.*]

gar·bage (gär′bĭj) *n.* **1. a.** Food wastes, as from a kitchen. **b.** Refuse. **2.** Trash; rubbish: *rhetorical garbage.* [Middle English *garbage,* offal of an animal, probably from Norman French *garbage* (unattested), possibly from Italian dialectal *garbužo,* from Old Italian *garbuglio,* mess, GARBOIL.]

gar·ban·zo (gär-băn′zō) *n., pl.* **-zos.** A plant, the **chickpea** *(see),* or its edible seed. [Spanish *garbanzo,* alteration (influenced by *garroba,* carob) of Old Spanish *arvanço,* from Germanic, akin to Old High German *araweiz,* pea, Latin *ervum,* bitter vetch, probably of Asiatic origin.]

gar·ble (gär′bəl) *tr.v.* **-bled, -bling, -bles.** **1.** To distort or scramble (an account or message) so as to be unintelligible. **2.** To sort out; sift; cull. *—n.* The act or an instance of garbling. [Middle English *garbelen,* to sift, select, from Italian *garbellare,* from Arabic *gharbala,* from *ghirbāl,* sieve, from Late Latin *crībellāre,* to sift, from *crībellum,* diminutive of *crībrum,* sieve. See **skeri-** in Appendix.*] **—gar′bler** *n.*

Gar·bo (gär′bō), **Greta.** Original surname, Gustaffson. Born 1905. Swedish-born American motion-picture actress.

gar·board (gär′bôrd′, -bōrd′) *n. Nautical.* The first range or strake of planks laid next to the ship's keel. [Obsolete Dutch *gaarboord* : perhaps *garen,* to gather, contraction of Middle Dutch *gaderen* (see **ghedh-** in Appendix*) + Dutch *boord,* border, ship's side, from Middle Dutch *bort,* board (see **bherdh-** in Appendix*).]

gar·boil (gär′boil′) *n. Archaic.* Confusion; uproar. [Old French *garbouil(le),* from Old Italian *garbuglio,* reduplicative formation (with *gar-* for *bar-*) from Latin *bullīre,* to boil, bubble. See **beu-**[1] in Appendix.*]

Gar·ci·a Lor·ca. See **Lorca.**

gar·çon (gär-sôN′) *n., pl.* **-çons** (-sôN′). *French.* A waiter. Literally, boy.

Gar·da, Lake (gär′dä). *Italian* **La·go di Gar·da** (lä′gō dē gär′dä). The largest lake of Italy (143 square miles), situated in the north 65 miles east of Milan.

gar·dant. Variant of **guardant.**

gar·den (gärd′n) *n.* **1.** A plot of land used for the cultivation of flowers, vegetables, or fruit. **2.** *Often plural.* Grounds adorned with flowers, shrubs, and trees for public enjoyment. **3.** A yard; lawn. **4.** A fertile, well-cultivated region. *—v.* **gardened, -dening, -dens.** *—tr.* **1.** To cultivate (a plot of ground) as a garden. **2.** To furnish with a garden or gardens. *—intr.* To work as a gardener. *—adj.* **1.** Of, pertaining to, intended for, or found in a garden. **2.** Surrounded by gardens; provided with open areas and greenery: *garden apartments.* **3.** Ordinary; usual: *the common garden variety.* [Middle English *gardyn,* from Old North French *gardin,* from Vulgar Latin *(hortus) gardīnus* (unattested), "enclosed (garden)," from *gardo* (unattested), fence, enclosure, from Frankish *gardo* (unattested). See **gher-**[2] in Appendix.*]

gar·den·er (gärd′nər, gärd′n-ər) *n.* A person who works in or tends a garden for pleasure or profit.

Garden Grove. A city of southwestern California near Anaheim. Population, 84,000.

garden heliotrope. A widely cultivated species of valerian, *Valeriana officinalis,* having clusters of small purplish, pink, or white flowers.

gar·de·ni·a (gär-dēn′yə, -dē′nē-ə) *n.* **1.** Any of various shrubs and trees of the genus *Gardenia;* especially, *G. jasminoides,* native to China, having glossy, evergreen leaves and large, fragrant, usually white flowers. This species is also called "Cape jasmine." **2.** The flower of this shrub. [New Latin *Gardinia,* after Dr. Alexander Garden (1731–1790), Scottish naturalist and vice president of the Royal Society.]

gar·den·ing (gärd′nĭng, gärd′n-ĭng) *n.* The work or occupation of tending a garden or cultivating plants.

Garden of Eden. **Eden** *(see).*

Garden State. The nickname for New Jersey.

garde·robe (gärd′rōb′) *n. Archaic.* **1. a.** A chamber for storing clothes; wardrobe. **b.** The contents of a wardrobe. **2.** Any private chamber. [Middle English, from Old French : *garder,* guarder, to GUARD + *robe,* ROBE.]

Gar·eth (găr′ĭth). A nephew of King Arthur and one of the Knights of the Round Table.

Gar·field (gär′fēld′), **James Abram.** 1831–1881. Twentieth President of the United States (1881); assassinated.

gar·fish (gär′fĭsh′) *n., pl.* **garfish** or **-fishes.** A fish, the **gar** *(see).* [Middle English *garfyssh,* probably "spear fish" : *gare, gore,* spear, Old English *gār* (see **ghaiso-** in Appendix*) + *fish,* FISH.]

gar·ga·ney (gär′gə-nē) *n., pl.* **-neys.** An Old World duck, *Anas querquedula,* having the head conspicuously striped with white in the male. [Italian dialectal *gargenei* (imitative).]

Gar·gan·tu·a (gär-găn′cho͞o-ə). A giant king noted for his enormous physical and intellectual appetites, the hero of Rabelais' satire *Gargantua and Pantagruel.*

gar·gan·tu·an (gär-găn′cho͞o-ən) *adj.* Also **Gar·gan·tu·an.** Of immense size or volume; gigantic; colossal; huge. See Synonyms at **enormous.**

gar·get (gär′gĭt) *n.* Mastitis of domestic animals, especially cattle. [Perhaps specialized use of Middle English *garget, gargat,* throat; from Old French *garguette, gargate,* from Old Provençal *gargata,* probably from Latin *gurges,* throat. See **gwerə-**[2] in Appendix.*]

gar·gle (gär′gəl) *v.* **-gled, -gling, -gles.** *—intr.* **1.** To force exhaled air through a liquid held in the back of the mouth, with the head tilted back, in order to cleanse or medicate the mouth or throat. **2.** To produce the sound of gargling when speaking or singing. *—tr.* **1.** To rinse or medicate (the mouth or throat) by gargling. **2.** To circulate or apply (a solution or medicine) by gargling. **3.** To utter with a gargling sound. *—n.* **1.** A medicated solution for gargling. **2.** A gargling sound. [Old French *gargouiller,* from *gargouille, garoule,* throat, GARGOYLE.]

gar·goyle (gär′goil′) *n.* **1.** A roof spout carved to represent a grotesque human or animal figure, and projected from a gutter to carry rainwater clear of the wall. **2.** Any grotesque ornamental figure or projection. [Middle English *gargoyl,* from Old French *gargouille, gargoul,* "throat," from Latin *gurguliō,* windpipe. See **gwerə-**[2] in Appendix.*]

gar·i·bal·di (găr′ə-bôl′dē) *n.* A loose high-necked blouse styled after the red shirts of Garibaldi and his soldiers, fashionable among women in the mid-19th century.

Gar·i·bal·di (găr′ə-bôl′dē; *Italian* gä′rē-bäl′dē), **Giuseppe.** 1807–1882. Italian general and nationalist leader.

gar·ish (gâr′ĭsh) *adj.* **1. a.** Marred by strident color or excessive ornamentation; gaudy; tawdry. **b.** Loud and flashy: *garish make-up.* **2.** Glaring; dazzling: *"Hide me from Day's garish eye"* (Milton). [Formerly also *gaurish,* perhaps from obsolete *gaur,* to stare, Middle English *gauren*†.] **—gar′ish·ly** *adv.* **—gar′ish·ness** *n.*

gar·land (gär′lənd) *n.* **1.** A wreath, circlet, or festoon of flowers, leaves, or other material worn as a crown or collar, or hung as an ornament. **2.** A wreath worked in metal for ornamentation or as a heraldic device. **3.** Something resembling a garland: *"The coated moss hung in blue and shining garlands over the trees"* (Eudora Welty). **4.** *Nautical.* A ring or collar of rope or wire used to hoist spars or prevent rubbing or fraying. **5.** An anthology, as of ballads or poems. *—tr.v.* **garlanded, -landing, -lands.** **1.** To embellish or deck with a garland. **2.** To form into a garland. [Middle English *gerlond, garland,* from Old French *gerlande, garlande,* "ornament made with gold threads," from Frankish *wiara, weara* (unattested), wire, thread. See **wei-**[1] in Appendix.*]

gar·lic (gär′lĭk) *n.* **1.** A plant, *Allium sativum,* related to the onion, having a bulb with a strong, distinctive odor and flavor. **2.** The bulb of this plant, divisible into separate cloves, and used as a seasoning. [Middle English *garlec, garly,* Old English *gārlēac,* "spear leek" (from its spear-shaped leaves) : *gār,* spear (see **ghaiso-** in Appendix*) + *lēac,* leek (see **leug-**[1] in Appendix*).]

gar·lick·y (gär′lĭk-ē) *adj.* Containing, tasting of, or redolent of garlic, especially too much garlic.

garlic mustard. A weedy plant, *Alliaria officinalis,* native to Europe, having small white flowers and an odor of garlic.

gar·ment (gär′mənt) *n.* **1.** Any article of clothing, especially of outer clothing such as a coat or dress. **2.** *Plural.* Clothes; apparel. *—tr.v.* **garmented, -menting, -ments.** To clothe; to dress. [Middle English *gar(ne)ment,* from Old French *garnement,* "equipment," from *g(u)arnir,* to furnish, equip. See **wer-**[5] in Appendix.*]

Gar·mo Peak (gär′mō). The highest elevation (24,590 feet) in the U.S.S.R., part of the Pamirs in Tadzhik S.S.R.

gar·ner (gär′nər) *tr.v.* **-nered, -nering, -ners.** **1.** To gather and store in or as if in a granary. **2.** To amass; acquire. *—n.* A granary. [Middle English *gerner, garner,* granary, from Old French *gernier, grenier,* from Latin *grānārium,* from *grānum,* grain. See **gr̥no-** in Appendix.*]

Gar·ner (gär′nər), **John Nance.** 1868–1967. Vice President of the United States under Franklin D. Roosevelt (1933–41).

gar·net[1] (gär′nĭt) *n.* **1.** Any of several common, widespread silicate minerals, occurring in two internally isomorphic series, generally crystallized, often imbedded in igneous and metamorphic rocks, colored red, brown, black, green, yellow, or white, and used both as gemstones and as abrasives. **2.** Dark to very dark red. See **color.** [Middle English *gernet, granate,* from Old

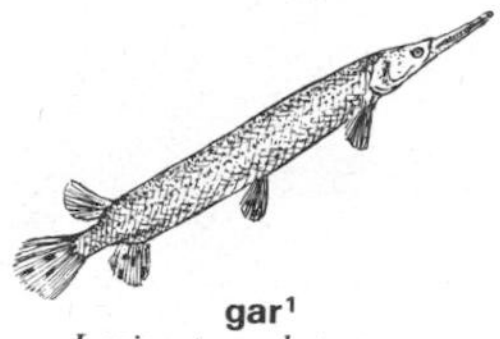

gar[1]
Lepisosteus platostomus

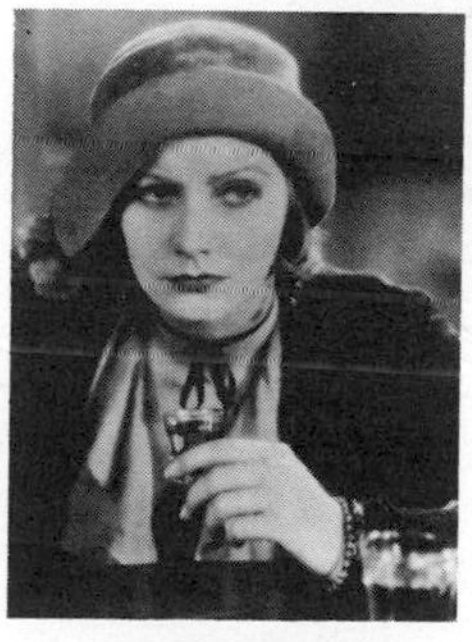

Greta Garbo
In the 1930 film
Anna Christie

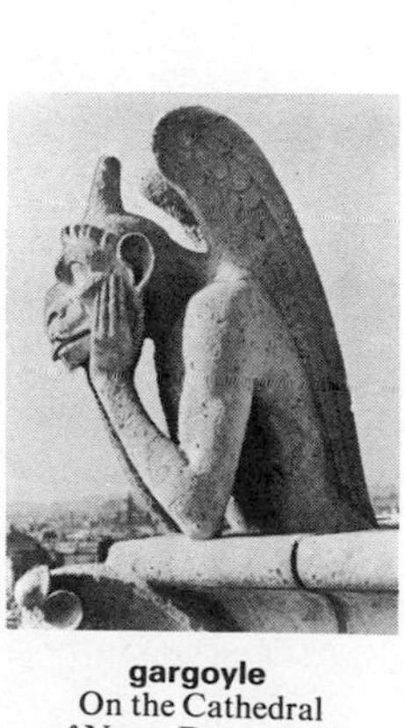

gargoyle
On the Cathedral
of Notre Dame, Paris

t tight/th thin, path/*th* this, bathe/ŭ cut/ûr urge/v valve/w with/y yes/z zebra, size/zh vision/ə about, item, edible, gallop, circus/ à *Fr.* ami/œ *Fr.* feu, *Ger.* schön/ü *Fr.* tu, *Ger.* über/KH *Ger.* ich, *Scot.* loch/N *Fr.* bon. ***Follows main vocabulary.** †**Of obscure origin.**

French *grenat*, dark red, garnet, pomegranate-colored, from *pome grenate*, POMEGRANATE.]

gar·net² (gär′nĭt) *n. Nautical.* A tackle for hoisting light cargo. [Middle English *garnett*, probably from Middle Dutch *garnaat*, *karnaat†.*]

gar·ni·er·ite (gär′nē-ə-rīt′) *n.* An earthy, apple-green mineral, (Ni,Mg)₆(OH)₆Si₄O₁₁·H₂O, an important nickel ore. [Discovered by Jules *Garnier* (died 1904), French geologist.]

gar·nish (gär′nĭsh) *tr.v.* **-nished, -nishing, -nishes. 1. a.** To furnish with beautifying details; adorn; embellish: *"garnished with silver studs."* **b.** To provide (food) with a garnish. **2.** *Law.* To garnishee. —*n.* **1. a.** Ornamentation; embellishment. **b.** An embellishment, usually savory, for a dish of food or a drink, such as a sprig of parsley or a slice of lemon. **2.** *Slang.* An unwarranted fee, as one extorted from a new prisoner by a jailer [Middle English *garnysshen*, to equip, adorn, from Old French *guarnir, garnir* (present stem *garniss-*), from Germanic. See **wer-⁵** in Appendix.*]

gar·nish·ee (gär′nĭ-shē′) *n. Law.* **1.** A debtor against whom a plaintiff has instituted process of garnishment. **2.** A third party who has been warned that money or property in his control, but due or belonging to the defendant, has been attached. —*tr.v.* **garnisheed, -eeing, -ees.** *Law.* **1.** To attach (a debtor's pay, for example) by garnishment. **2.** To serve with a garnishment.

gar·nish·ment (gär′nĭsh-mənt) *n.* **1.** *Law.* **a.** A legal proceeding whereby money or property due or belonging to a debtor but in the possession of another is applied to the payment of the debt to the plaintiff. **b.** A court order directing a third party who owes the defendant money, or holds property belonging to him, to withhold such money or property, and to appear in court to answer inquiries. Also called "trustee process." **2.** Ornamentation; embellishment.

gar·ni·ture (gär′nĭ-chər) *n.* Something that garnishes or decorates; embellishment. [Old French *garniture, garneture*, from *garnir*, to GARNISH.]

Ga·ronne (gà-rôn′). Ancient name **Ga·rum·na** (gə-rŭm′nə). A river of southwestern France, rising in the Spanish Pyrenees and flowing 355 miles northwest to unite with the Dordogne and form the Gironde estuary.

gar·pike (gär′pīk′) *n.* **1.** A fish, the gar *(see).* **2.** A marine fish, *Belone belone*, of European waters, having green bones.

gar·ret (gär′ĭt) *n.* A room on the top floor of a house, typically immediately under a pitched roof; an attic; a loft. [Middle English *garet(te)*, turret, watchtower, from Old French *garite*, from *g(u)arir*, to defend, protect, from Germanic. See **wer-⁵** in Appendix.*]

gar·ret·eer (gär′ə-tîr′) *n.* A person who lives in a garret, especially a struggling artist.

Gar·rick (gär′ĭk), **David.** 1717–1779. British actor and theater manager.

gar·ri·son (gär′ĭ-sən) *n.* **1.** A military post, especially one permanently established. **2.** The troops stationed at such a post. —*tr.v.* **garrisoned, -soning, -sons. 1.** To assign (troops) to a military post. **2.** To supply (a post) with troops. **3.** To occupy as or convert into a garrison. [Middle English *gariso(u)n*, protection, fortress, from Old French *garison*, from *g(u)arir*, to protect, from Germanic. See **wer-⁵** in Appendix.*]

Gar·ri·son (gär′ĭ-sən), **William Lloyd.** 1805–1879. American abolitionist editor and lecturer.

garrison cap. A soft cloth cap without a visor, worn as a dress headgear chiefly by Army and Air Force personnel. Also called "overseas cap."

Garrison finish. A finish in which the winner comes from behind at the last moment. [After Edward H. *Garrison* (1868–1930), American jockey who was well known for his knack of winning by such finishes.]

Gar·ri·son Reservoir (gär′ĭ-sən). A reservoir 140 miles long in western North Dakota, formed in the Missouri River by the Garrison Dam.

gar·rote, gar·rotte (gə-rŏt′, -rōt′) *n.* **1. a.** A former Spanish method of execution by strangulation or by breaking the neck with an iron collar screwed tight with a knoblike device. **b.** A collar used for this. **2.** Strangulation, especially in order to rob. —*tr.v.* **garroted** or **garrotted, -roting** or **-rotting, -rotes** or **rottes. 1.** To execute by garrote. **2.** To strangle or throttle in order to rob. [Spanish, cudgel, probably from Old French *garrot*, earlier *guaroc*, club, turning rod, from *garokier†*, to bend down, strangle.] —**gar·rot′er** *n.*

gar·ru·li·ty (gə-rōō′lə-tē) *n.* Talkativeness; chattiness: *"Its style is relaxed to the point of garrulity"* (Dwight Macdonald).

gar·ru·lous (gär′ə-ləs, -yə-ləs) *adj.* **1.** Habitually talkative; loquacious. **2.** Wordy; prolix. —See Synonyms at **talkative.** [Latin *garrulus*, from *garrire*, to chatter. See **gar-** in Appendix.*] —**gar′ru·lous·ly** *adv.* —**gar′ru·lous·ness** *n.*

gar·ter (gär′tər) *n.* **1. a.** An elasticized band worn around the leg to support hose. **b.** A suspender strap with a fastener attached to a girdle or belt for supporting hose. **c.** An elasticized band worn around the arm to keep the sleeve pushed up. **2. a.** *Capital* G. The badge of the Order of the Garter, England's highest order of knighthood. **b.** The order itself. **c.** Membership in this order. —*tr.v.* **gartered, -tering, -ters. 1.** To fasten and hold with a garter. **2.** To put a garter upon. [Middle English *garter, garder*, from Old North French *gartier*, from *garet*, bend of the knee, from Gaulish *garr-* (unattested), leg.]

garter belt. An undergarment for women consisting of an adjustable belt with garters for the support of hose.

garter snake. Any of various nonvenomous North American snakes of the genus *Thamnophis*, having longitudinal stripes.

garth (gärth) *n.* **1.** A grassy quadrangle surrounded by cloisters.

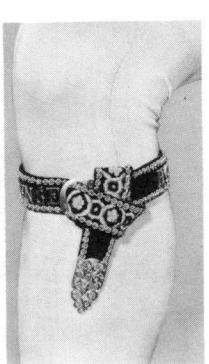
garter
Order of the Garter

2. *Archaic.* A yard, garden, or paddock. [Middle English, from Old Norse *gardhr*, yard. See **gher-²** in Appendix.*]

Ga·rum·na. The ancient name for the **Garonne.**

Gar·vey (gär′vē), **Marcus (Moziah) Aurelius.** 1887–1940. Jamaican Negro leader active in United States (1916–25); advocated racial separation and emigration of American Negroes to Africa; deported.

Gar·y (gär′ē). A city and steel-manufacturing center of northwestern Indiana on Lake Michigan. Population, 178,000.

gas (găs) *n., pl.* **gases** or **gasses. 1. a.** The state of matter distinguished from the solid and liquid states by very low density and viscosity, relatively great expansion and contraction with changes in pressure and temperature, the ability to diffuse readily, and the spontaneous tendency to become distributed uniformly throughout any container. **b.** A substance in this state. **c.** A substance in this state at room temperature and atmospheric pressure. **2.** A gaseous fuel such as **natural gas** *(see).* **3. a.** Gasoline. **b.** The speed control of a gasoline engine: *step on the gas.* **4.** A gaseous asphyxiant, irritant, or poison. **5.** A gaseous anesthetic. **6.** *Slang.* Idle or boastful talk. **7.** *Slang.* Something providing great fun and excitement. —*v.* **gassed, gassing, gases** or **gasses.** —*tr.* **1.** To supply with gas or gasoline. **2.** To treat chemically with gas. **3.** To poison with gas, as in war. —*intr.* **1.** To give off gas. **2.** *Slang.* To talk excessively. **3.** *Informal.* To supply one's car with gas. Used with *up.* [Dutch *gas*, an occult principle supposed to be present in all bodies, coined (by J.B. van Helmont, 1577–1644, Belgian chemist) from Greek *khaos*, chasm, chaos. See **gheu-** in Appendix.*]

gas·bag (găs′băg′) *n.* **1.** An expansible bag for holding gas. **2.** *Slang.* One given to flatulent talk.

gas black. **Channel black** *(see).*

gas burner. 1. A nozzle or jet on a fitting through which combustible gas is released to burn. **2.** A stove that burns gas.

gas chamber. A sealed enclosure in which prisoners are executed by a poisonous gas.

gas chromatography. Chromatography in which the substance to be analyzed is vaporized and diffused along with a carrier gas through a liquid or solid adsorbent for differential adsorption.

Gas·coigne (găs′koin′), **George.** 1525?–1577. English poet, dramatist, and essayist.

gas·con (găs′kən) *n.* A boastful person; braggart. [French, from Old French *gascon*, GASCON (from the traditional garrulity of the Gascons).]

Gas·con (găs′kən) *n.* **1.** A native of Gascony. **2.** The French dialect of the Gascons. —*adj.* Of or pertaining to Gascony or the Gascons.

gas·con·ade (găs′kə-nād′) *n.* Boastfulness; bravado; swagger. —*intr.v.* **gasconaded, -ading, -ades.** To boast or swagger. —**gas′con·ad′er** *n.*

Gas·co·ny (găs′kə-nē). French **Gas·cogne** (gàs-kôn′y′). A region and former province of southwestern France.

gas·e·lier (găs′ə-lîr′) *n.* Also **gas·o·lier.** A chandelier having tubular branches with gas jets. [GAS + (CHAND)ELIER.]

gas·e·ous (găs′ē-əs, -yəs, găsh′əs) *adj.* **1.** Of, pertaining to, or existing as a gas. **2.** Lacking concreteness; tenuous.

gas fitter. A workman who installs or repairs gas pipes, fixtures, or appliances.

gas gangrene. Gangrene occurring in a wound infected with bacteria of the genus *Clostridium*, especially with *C. welchi* or *C. oedematiens*, and characterized by the presence of gas in the affected tissue and constitutional septic symptoms.

gash (găsh) *tr.v.* **gashed, gashing, gashes.** To make a long, deep cut in; slash deeply. —*n.* **1.** A long, deep cut. **2.** A deep flesh wound. [Earlier *garsh, garse*, Middle English *garsen*, to cut, slash, from Old North French *garser*, probably from Late Latin *charaxāre*, from Greek *kharassein*, to carve, cut. See **gher-⁵** in Appendix.*]

Gash·er·brum I (gŭ′shər-brōōm′). A peak rising to 26,470 feet in the Karakoram range of northern Kashmir. Also called "Hidden Peak."

Gash·er·brum II (gŭ′shər-brōōm′). A peak of the Karakoram range of northern Kashmir, rising to 26,630 feet just northwest of Gasherbrum I.

gas·hold·er (găs′hōl′dər) *n.* A storage container for fuel gas, especially a large, telescoping, cylindrical tank.

gas·house (găs′hous′) *n.* A gasworks.

gas·i·form (găs′ə-fôrm′) *adj.* In the form of gas; gaseous.

gas·i·fy (găs′ə-fī′) *v.* **-fied, -fying, -fies.** —*tr.* To convert into gas. —*intr.* To become gas. —**gas′i·fi′a·ble** *adj.* —**gas′i·fi·ca′tion** *n.*

gas jet. 1. A gas burner. **2.** The flame of burning gas from a gas burner.

gas·ket (găs′kĭt) *n.* **1.** *Machinery.* Any of a wide variety of seals or packings used between matched machine parts or around pipe joints to prevent the escape of a gas or fluid. **2.** *Nautical.* A cord or canvas strap used to secure a furled sail to a yard boom or gaff. —**blow a gasket.** *Slang.* To explode with anger. [French *garcette*, "little girl," rope, diminutive of *garce*, girl, from *gars*, boy, probably from Frankish *wrakjō* (unattested), "one pursued, an exile." See **wreg-** in Appendix.*]

gas·kin (găs′kĭn) *n.* **1.** The part of the hind leg of a horse or related animal between the stifle and the hock. **2.** *Plural. Obsolete.* Galligaskins. [Probably shortened from GALLIGASKINS.]

gas·light (găs′līt′) *n.* Also **gas light. 1.** Light produced by burning illuminating gas. **2.** A gas burner or lamp.

gas log. A gas heater designed to look like a log for use in a fireplace.

gas main. A major pipeline or conduit conveying gas to smaller pipes for distribution to consumers.
gas·man (găs′măn′) *n., pl.* **-men** (-mĕn′). **1.** A person employed to read gas meters for the billing of consumers. **2.** A gas fitter.
gas mantle. The **Welsbach burner** *(see).*
gas mask. A respirator covering the face and having a chemical air filter to protect against poisonous gases.
gas·o·lier. Variant of **gaselier.**
gas·o·line (găs′ə-lēn′, găs′ə-lēn′) *n.* A volatile mixture of flammable liquid hydrocarbons derived chiefly from crude petroleum and used principally as a fuel for internal-combustion engines, and as a solvent, illuminant, and thinner. [GAS + -OL + -INE.]
gas·om·e·ter (găs-ŏm′ə-tər) *n.* **1.** An apparatus for measuring gases. **2.** A gasholder. [French *gazomètre* : *gaz,* from GAS + -METER.]
gasp (găsp, gäsp) *v.* **gasped, gasping, gasps.** *—intr.* **1.** To draw in or catch the breath sharply, as from shock. **2.** To breathe convulsively or laboriously. *—tr.* To utter between gasps. Often used with *out.* *—n.* **1.** A short convulsive intake or catching of the breath. **2.** Something said while gasping. **—at the last gasp.** At the final extremity; at the moment of death. [Middle English *ga(y)spen,* from Old Norse *geispa.* See **ghēi-** in Appendix.*]
Gas·par. See **Caspar.**
Gas·pé Peninsula (găs-pā′). A peninsula comprising 11,390 square miles of southeastern Quebec Province, Canada, between Chaleur Bay and the mouth of the St. Lawrence River.
gasp·er (găs′pər, gäs′-) *n. British Slang.* A cigarette. [From GASP.]
gas plant. A plant, *Dictamnus albus,* native to Eurasia, having aromatic foliage and white flowers, and emitting a vapor capable of being ignited. Also called "burning bush," "dittany," "fraxinella."
gas·ser (găs′ər) *n.* **1.** A well or drilling that yields natural gas. **2.** *Slang.* Something unusually entertaining.
gas station. A **filling station** *(see).*
gas·sy (găs′ē) *adj.* **-sier, -siest. 1.** Containing, full of, or resembling gas. **2.** *Slang.* Bombastic; boastful; windy.
gast (găst) *tr.v.* **gasted, gasting, gasts.** *Obsolete.* To scare. [Middle English *gasten,* Old English *gæstan.* See **gheis-** in Appendix.*]
gas·ter·o·pod. *Rare.* Variant of **gastropod.**
gas·tight (găs′tīt′) *adj.* Not permitting the escape or entry of gas.
gas·trec·to·my (găs-trĕk′tə-mē) *n., pl.* **-mies.** Surgical excision of part or all of the stomach. [GASTR(O)- + -ECTOMY.]
gas·tric (găs′trĭk) *adj.* Of or pertaining to the stomach. [French *gastrique,* from New Latin *gastricus,* from Greek *gastēr,* belly, womb. See **gras-** in Appendix.*]
gastric juice. The colorless, watery, acidic digestive fluid secreted by the stomach glands and containing hydrochloric acid, pepsin, rennin, and mucin.
gas·trin (găs′trən) *n.* A secretion of the gastric mucosa that stimulates production of gastric juice. [GASTR(O)- + -IN.]
gas·tri·tis (găs-trī′tĭs) *n.* Chronic or acute inflammation of the stomach. [New Latin : GASTR(O)- + -ITIS.]
gastro–, gastr–. Indicates stomach; for example, **gastroscope, gastritis.** [From Greek *gastēr* (stem *gastr-*), belly, womb. See **gras-** in Appendix.*]
gas·tro·en·ter·i·tis (găs′trō-ĕn′tə-rī′tĭs) *n.* Inflammation of the mucous membrane of the stomach and intestine.
gas·tro·en·ter·ol·o·gy (găs′trō-ĕn′tə-rŏl′ə-jē) *n.* The medical study and specialty of the stomach and the intestines. **—gas′tro·en·ter′ic** (-ĕn-tĕr′ĭk) *adj.* **—gas′tro·en′ter·ol′o·gist** *n.*
gas·tro·en·ter·os·to·my (găs′trō-ĕn′tə-rŏs′tə-mē) *n., pl.* **-mies.** The surgical formation of a passage between the stomach and the small intestine.
gas·tro·in·tes·ti·nal (găs′trō-ĭn-tĕs′tə-nəl) *adj.* Of or pertaining to the stomach and intestines; gastroenteric.
gas·tro·lith (găs′trə-lĭth′) *n.* A pathological small stony mass formed in the stomach; a gastric calculus. [GASTRO- + -LITH.]
gas·trol·o·gy (găs-trŏl′ə-jē) *n.* The medical study of the stomach and its diseases. [Greek *Gastrologia,* title of poem by the fourth-century B.C. Greek poet Archestratos about luxurious food : GASTRO- + -LOGY.] **—gas·trol′o·gist** *n.*
gas·tro·nome (găs′trə-nōm′) *n.* Also **gas·tron·o·mer** (găs-trŏn′ə-mər), **gas·tron·o·mist** (-mĭst). A connoisseur of good food and drink; a gourmet. [From GASTRONOMY.]
gas·tro·nom·ic (găs′trə-nŏm′ĭk) *adj.* Also **gas·tro·nom·i·cal** (-ĭ-kəl). Of or pertaining to gastronomes or gastronomy. **—gas′tro·nom′i·cal·ly** *adv.*
gas·tron·o·my (găs-trŏn′ə-mē) *n.* **1.** The art or science of good eating. **2.** Cooking, as of a particular region or country. [French *gastronomie,* from Greek *gastronomia* (subtitle of the Greek poem *Gastrologia,* GASTROLOGY) : GASTRO- + -NOMY.]
gas·tro·pod (găs′trə-pŏd′) *n.* Also *rare* **gas·ter·o·pod** (-tər-ə-pŏd′). Any mollusk of the class Gastropoda, such as a snail, slug, cowry, or limpet, characteristically having a single, usually coiled shell and a ventral muscular mass serving as an organ of locomotion. *—adj.* Of or belonging to the Gastropoda. [New Latin *Gastropoda,* "belly-footed creatures" (from their ventral disks used as feet) : GASTRO- + -POD.] **—gas·trop′o·dan** (găs-trŏp′ə-dən), **gas·trop′o·dous** (-dəs) *adj.*
gas·tro·scope (găs′trə-skōp′) *n.* An instrument used for examining the interior of the stomach. [GASTRO- + -SCOPE.] **—gas′tro·scop′ic** (-skŏp′ĭk) *adj.* **—gas·tros′co·pist** (-trŏs′kə-pĭst) *n.* **—gas·tros′co·py** (-trŏs′kə-pē) *n.*
gas·tros·to·my (găs-trŏs′tə-mē) *n., pl.* **-mies.** The surgical construction of a permanent opening from the external surface of the body into the stomach, usually for inserting a feeding tube. [GASTRO- + -STOMY.]
gas·trot·o·my (găs-trŏt′ə-mē) *n., pl.* **-mies.** *Surgery.* An incision into the stomach. [GASTRO- + -TOMY.]
gas·tro·vas·cu·lar (găs′trō-văs′kyə-lər) *adj.* Having both a digestive and circulatory function.
gas·tru·la (găs′trōō-lə) *n., pl.* **-las** or **-lae** (-lē′). An embryo at the stage following the blastula and consisting of ectoderm, endoderm, and archenteron. [New Latin, "small stomach" (from its shape), diminutive of Greek *gastēr,* belly, womb. See **gras-** in Appendix.*] **—gas′tru·lar** *adj.*
gas·tru·late (găs′trōō-lāt′) *intr.v.* **-lated, -lating, -lates.** To form or become a gastrula. **—gas′tru·la′tion** *n.*
gas turbine. An air-breathing internal-combustion engine consisting essentially of an air compressor, a combustion chamber, and a turbine wheel, used especially for propulsion rather than fixed power generation.
gas·works (găs′wûrks′) *n.* Plural in form, usually used with a singular verb. A factory where gas for heating and lighting is produced.
gat[1] (găt) *n.* A narrow passage extending inland from a shore; a channel. [Probably from Dutch *gat,* "opening," from Middle Dutch, from Germanic *gatam* (unattested). See **gate[1]**.]
gat[2] (găt) *n. Slang.* A pistol. [Short for GAT(LING GUN).]
gat[3]. *Archaic.* Past tense of **get.**
gate[1] (gāt) *n.* **1.** A structure that may be swung, drawn, or lowered to block an entrance or passageway. **2. a.** An opening in a wall or fence for entrance or exit. **b.** The structure surrounding such an opening, as the monumental or fortified entrance to a palace. **3.** Something that gives access: *the gate to fortune.* **4.** A device for controlling the passage of water or gas through a dam or conduit. **5.** The total admission receipts or attendance at a public spectacle. **6.** *Metallurgy.* The channel through which molten metal flows into the shaped cavity of a mold. **7.** *Electronics.* **a.** A circuit extensively used in computers that has an output dependent on some function of its input. **b.** Such a circuit having an output when any or all of a designated set of inputs are received within a specified time interval. In this sense, also called "coincidence gate." **—get the gate.** *Slang.* To be dismissed or ejected. **—give the gate to.** *Slang.* To dismiss or eject. *—tr.v.* **gated, gating, gates.** *British.* To punish (a student) by confining within the college gates after a certain hour. [Middle English *gat, g(e)ate,* Old English *geat,* from Common Germanic *gatam* (unattested).]
gate[2] (gāt) *n.* **1.** *Archaic.* A path or road; way. **2.** *Regional.* A particular way of acting or doing; a manner. [Middle English, from Old Norse *gata,* path, passage. See **ghe-** in Appendix.*]
gate·crash·er (gāt′krăsh′ər) *n. Slang.* A person who gains admittance without being invited or enters without paying admission.
gate·fold (gāt′fōld′) *n.* A folded insert in a book or other publication whose full size exceeds that of the regular page. Also called "fold-out."
gate·keep·er (gāt′kē′pər) *n.* A person in charge of a gate. Also called "gateman."
gate-leg table (gāt′lĕg′). A drop-leaf table with movable legs arranged in pairs.

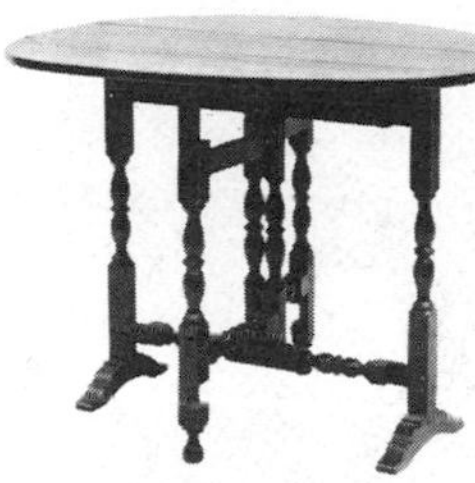

gate-leg table
Early 18th-century
New England

gate·post (gāt′pōst′) *n.* An upright post on which a gate is hung or against which a gate is closed.
Gates (gāts), **Horatio.** 1728?–1806. American Revolutionary general.
Gates·head (gāts′hĕd). A city and industrial center of northern England, in Durham County on the Tyne. Population, 102,000.
gate·way (gāt′wā′) *n.* **1.** A structure, such as an arch, framing an entrance or passage that may be closed by a gate. **2.** Something that serves as an entrance or means of access: *a gateway to success.*
gath·er (găth′ər) *v.* **-ered, -ering, -ers.** *—tr.* **1.** To cause to come together; convene. **2. a.** To accumulate gradually; amass. **b.** To harvest or pick: *gather flowers.* **c.** To gain or increase by degrees: *gather velocity.* **3. a.** To collect into one place; assemble. **b.** *Bookbinding.* To arrange (signatures) in sequence. **4.** To pull (cloth) along a thread so as to create small folds or puckers. **5.** To draw (a garment, for example) about or closer to something. **6.** To conclude or apprehend; infer: *I gather that a decision has not been reached.* **7. a.** To summon up; muster: *gather courage.* **b.** To collect (one's wits or powers). Often used with *together.* **8.** To attract or be a center of attraction for. *—intr.* **1.** To come together or assemble. **2.** To accumulate. **3.** To grow or increase by degrees. **4.** To come to a head, as a boil; to fester. *—n.* **1. a.** An act or instance of gathering. **b.** The quantity gathered. **2.** *Usually plural.* A small tuck or pucker in cloth. [Middle English *gad(e)ren,* Old English *gad(e)rian,* to put together, come together. See **ghedh-** in Appendix.*] **—gath′er·er** *n.*

Synonyms: *gather, collect, assemble, congregate, accumulate, amass, marshal, rally.* These verbs mean to bring together or come together in a group or mass. *Gather,* in both transitive and intransitive use, is the most general term and therefore the most widely applicable. *Collect* is sometimes interchangeable with *gather.* Frequently, in transitive usage, *collect* refers to the careful selection of like or related things which become part of an organized whole: *collect antiques; collect stamps.* Intransitively, *collect* suggests the gradual coming together, or steady increase, of things or persons. *Assemble* in all of its senses implies that the persons or things involved have a definite and usually close relationship. With respect to persons, the term suggests convening out of common interest or purpose; with respect to

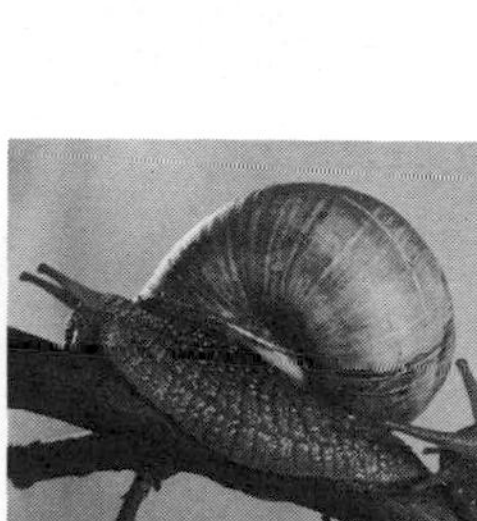

gastropod
Helix pomatia

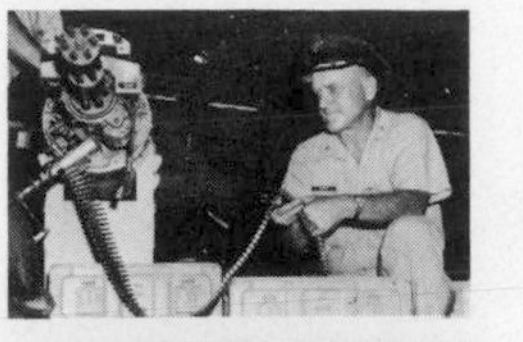

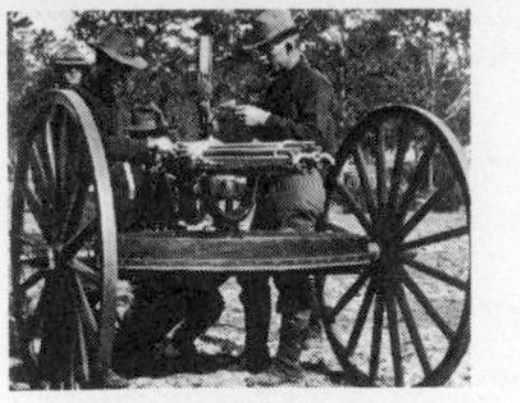

Gatling gun
Above: Modern
Below: Nineteenth-century

things, *assemble* implies fitting together component parts of a structure or machine. *Congregate* refers chiefly to the coming together of a large number of persons or animals, usually for a specific purpose. *Accumulate* is applied to the gradual increase of like or related things over an extended period. *Amass* refers to the collection or accumulation of things, especially valuable ones, to form an imposing quantity. *Marshal* implies the assembling and ordering of persons, things, or intangibles, such as thoughts or facts, so as to have them readily available for anticipated use. *Rally,* in this comparison, implies the gathering together of persons united in a common cause.

gath·er·ing (găth′ər-ĭng) *n.* **1.** Something gathered; collection; accumulation. **2.** An assembly of persons; a meeting. **3.** A gather in cloth. **4.** A suppurated swelling; a boil or abscess.

Ga·ti·neau (găt′n-ō′; *French* gȧ-tē-nō′). A river rising in southwestern Quebec, Canada, and flowing 240 miles south to the Ottawa River.

Gat·ling gun (găt′lĭng). A machine gun having a cluster of barrels fired as the cluster is turned. [Designed by Richard J. *Gatling* (1818–1903), American inventor.]

GATT General Agreement on Tariffs and Trade.

Ga·tun (gä-to͞on′). A lake occupying 164 square miles in the northern Canal Zone, Panama, formed by the Gatun Dam.

gauche (gōsh) *adj.* Awkward of manner; lacking social grace; tactless; clumsy. See Synonyms at **awkward**. [French, "left," originally "bent," "askew," from Old French *gauchir,* to turn aside, detour, probably altered from earlier *guenchir,* from Frankish *wenkjan* (unattested). See **weng-** in Appendix.*] —**gauche′ly** *adv.* —**gauche′ness** *n.*

gau·che·rie (gō′shə-rē′) *n.* **1.** An awkward or tactless action, manner, or expression. **2.** Tactlessness; awkwardness. [French, from *gauche,* left, GAUCHE.]

Gau·cho (gou′chō) *n., pl.* **-chos.** A cowboy of the South American pampas. [American Spanish, probably from Quechua *wáhcha,* poor person, vagabond.]

gaud (gôd) *n.* Something gaudy or showy. [Middle English *gaude, gawde,* jest, plaything, toy, from Old French *gaudir,* to rejoice, from Latin *gaudēre,* to delight in. See **gāu-** in Appendix.*]

gaud·er·y (gô′də-rē) *n., pl.* **-ies.** Showy things; finery.

gaud·y[1] (gô′dē) *adj.* **-ier, -iest.** Characterized by tasteless or showy colors; garish. See Synonyms at **ornate.** [From GAUD.]

gaud·y[2] (gô′dē) *n., pl.* **-ies.** *British.* A feast; especially, an annual university dinner. [Latin *gaudium,* joy, from *gaudēre,* to rejoice. See **gāu-** in Appendix.*]

gauf·fer. Variant of **goffer.**

gauge (gāj) *n.* Also **gage. 1. a.** A standard or scale of measurement. **b.** A standard dimension, quantity, or capacity. **2.** An instrument for measuring or testing. **3.** A means of estimating or evaluating; a test: *a gauge of character.* **4.** The position of a vessel in relation to another vessel and the wind. **5. a.** The distance between the two rails of a railroad. **b.** The distance between two wheels on an axle. **6.** The diameter of a shotgun barrel as determined by the number of lead balls in a pound that exactly fit the barrel. **7.** The amount of plaster of Paris mixed with common plaster to speed its setting. **8.** Thickness or diameter, as of sheet metal or wire. **9.** The fineness of knitted cloth as determined by the number of loops per 1$\frac{1}{2}$ inches. —*tr.v.* **gauged, gauging, gauges. 1.** To measure precisely. **2.** To determine the capacity, volume, or contents of. **3.** To evaluate or judge: *gauge ability.* **4.** To adapt to a specified measurement. **5.** To mix (plaster) in specific proportions. **6.** To chip or rub (bricks or stones) to size. [Middle English, from Old North French, from Frankish *galga* (unattested), cross, perch, windlass. See **ghalgh-** in Appendix.*]

gaug·er (gā′jər) *n.* Also **gag·er. 1.** One that gauges. **2.** *Chiefly British.* A revenue officer who inspects bulk goods subject to duty.

Gau·guin (gō-găN′), **(Eugène Henri) Paul.** 1848–1903. French painter.

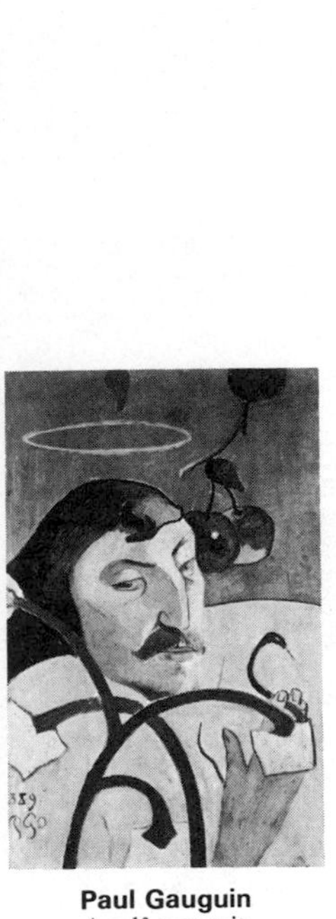

Paul Gauguin
A self-portrait

Gaul[1] (gôl). *Latin* **Gal·li·a** (găl′ē-ə). The name given in antiquity to the region in Europe south and west of the Rhine, west of the Alps, and north of the Pyrenees, comprising approximately the territory of modern France and Belgium. [French *Gaule,* from Latin *Gallia,* from *Galli,* the Gauls. See **Volcae** in Appendix.*]

Gaul[2] (gôl) *n.* **1.** A Celt of ancient Gaul. **2.** A Frenchman.

Gaul·ish (gô′lĭsh) *n.* The Celtic language of ancient Gaul.

Gaull·ism (gō′lĭz′əm, gô′-) *n.* **1.** The political movement supporting Charles de Gaulle as leader of the French government in exile during World War II. **2.** The body of political theory and practice characterizing General de Gaulle's exercise of the presidency in France after 1958. —**Gaull′ist** *adj.*

gaum (gôm) *tr.v.* **gaumed, gauming, gaums.** *Regional.* To smudge or smear. [Dialectal variant of GUM (verb).]

gaun. Present participle of **gae.**

gaunt (gônt) *adj.* **gaunter, gauntest. 1.** Thin and bony; angular; lank. **2.** Emaciated and haggard; drawn. **3.** Bleak and desolate; barren. —See Synonyms at **lean.** [Middle English *gawnt, gaunt,* slim, lean, probably from Scandinavian, akin to Norwegian dialectal *gand*†, thin stick, lanky person.] —**gaunt′ly** *adv.* —**gaunt′ness** *n.*

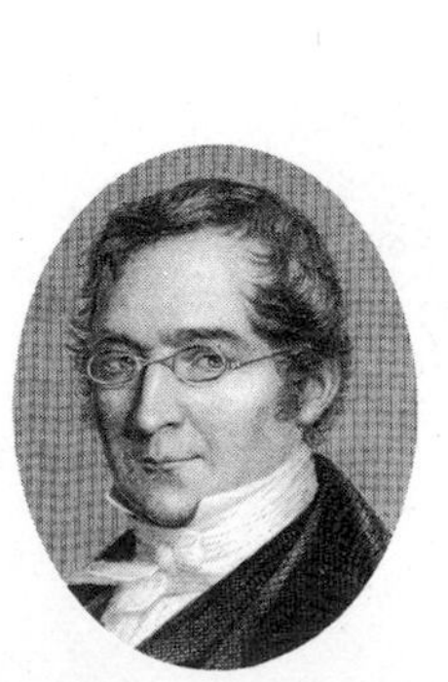

Joseph Louis Gay-Lussac

gaunt·let[1] (gônt′lĭt, gänt′-) *n.* Also **gant·let. 1.** A protective glove worn with medieval armor. **2.** A protective glove with a flaring cuff used in manual labor. **3.** A challenge: *fling down the gauntlet.* [Middle English *gaunt(e)let,* from Old French *gantelet,* diminutive of *gant,* glove, from Frankish *want*† (unattested), mitten.]

gaunt·let[2] (gônt′lĭt, gänt′-) *n.* Also **gant·let. 1.** Two lines of men facing each other and armed with sticks or other weapons with which they beat a person forced to run between them. **2.** A severe trial; an ordeal. [Earlier *gantlope.* See **gantlet** (railroad track).]

Usage: In the expression *run the gauntlet,* this spelling alternates with *gantlet. Gantlet* is the more common spelling in earlier American usage, and is still considered preferable by some authorities and mandatory by others, but *gauntlet* is acceptable in this expression to 77 per cent of the Usage Panel. *Gauntlet* is the term used in *fling* (or *throw*) *down the gauntlet,* to issue a challenge, and *take up the gauntlet,* to accept a challenge. *Run the gauntlet* (or *gantlet*) is sometimes confused with *run the gamut,* to cover an entire range.

gaunt·let[3]. Variant of **gantlet** (railroad track).

gaun·try. Variant of **gantry.**

gaur (gour) *n.* A large, dark-coated bovine mammal, *Bos gaurus,* of hilly areas of southeastern Asia. [Hindi *gaur,* from Sanskrit *gaura.* See **gwou-** in Appendix.*]

gauss (gous) *n. Abbr.* **G** The centimeter-gram-second electromagnetic unit of magnetic flux density, equal to one maxwell per square centimeter. See **measurement.** [After Karl F. GAUSS.]

Gauss (gous), **Karl Friedrich.** 1777–1855. German mathematician, astronomer, and physicist.

Gauss·i·an distribution (gou′sē-ən). **Normal distribution** *(see).*

Gau·ta·ma (gô′tə-mə, gou′-). See **Buddha.**

Gau·tier (gō-tyā′), **Théophile.** 1811–1872. French poet and critic.

gauze (gôz) *n.* **1. a.** A thin, transparent fabric with a loose open weave, used for curtains or clothing. **b.** A cotton surgical dressing. **c.** A thin plastic or metal woven mesh. **2.** A mist or haze. [Earlier *gais,* from Old French *gaze,* probably after GAZA, where it was supposed to be made.] —**gauz′i·ly** *adv.* —**gauz′i·ness** *n.* —**gauz′y** *adj.*

ga·vage (gə-väzh′) *n.* The introduction of usually nutritive material into the stomach by means of a tube. [French, from *gaver,* to force down the throat, stuff, from Picard, from Old Latin *gaba*† (unattested), throat.]

gave. Past tense of **give.**

gav·el[1] (găv′əl) *n.* **1.** The mallet or hammer used by a presiding officer or auctioneer to signal for attention or order. **2.** A maul used by masons in fitting stones. [Origin unknown.]

gav·el[2] (găv′əl) *n.* Tribute or rent in ancient and medieval England. [Middle English *gavel,* Old English *gafol,* tribute. See **ghabh-** in Appendix.*]

gav·el·kind (găv′əl-kīnd′) *n.* An English system of land tenure from Anglo-Saxon times to 1926 that provided for the equal division of an intestate's estate among all the sons or other heirs. [Middle English *gavelkynde,* Old English *gafolgecynd* (unattested), "tenure by payment of rent" : *gafol,* GAVEL (rent) + *cynd, gecynd,* KIND.]

ga·vi·al (gā′vē-əl) *n.* A large reptile, *Gavialis gangeticus,* of southern Asia, related to and resembling the crocodiles, and having a long, slender snout. [French, from Hindi *ghaṛiyāl*†.]

Gav·in (găv′ən). A masculine given name. [Middle English, from Old French *Gauvain,* perhaps from Welsh *Gwalchmai* : *gwalch*†, hawk + *Mei,* May, from Latin *Maius,* MAY (month).]

ga·votte (gə-vŏt′) *n.* **1.** A French peasant dance resembling the minuet. **2.** Music for this dance in moderately quick $\frac{4}{4}$ time. [French, from Provençal *gavoto,* from *Gavot,* "mountaineer," "rustic," inhabitant of the Alps (where the dance originated), from *gava,* crop of a bird, frill, goiter, from Old Latin *gaba* (unattested), throat. See **gavage.**]

GAW guaranteed annual wage.

Ga·wain (gä′wĭn, gô′-). Also **Ga·waine.** A nephew of King Arthur and a knight of the Round Table.

gawk (gôk) *n.* An awkward, loutish person; oaf. —*intr.v.* **gawked, gawking, gawks.** *Informal.* To stare like a gawk; gape stupidly. [Perhaps alteration of obsolete *gaw,* to stare, gape, Middle English *gawen,* from Old Norse *gā,* to heed. See **ghow-ē-** in Appendix.*]

gawk·y (gô′kē) *adj.* **-ier, -iest.** Awkward; clumsy. —**gawk′i·ly** *adv.* —**gawk′i·ness** *n.*

gay (gā) *adj.* **gayer, gayest. 1.** Showing or characterized by exuberance or mirthful excitement. **2.** Bright or lively, especially in color. **3.** Full of or given to social or other pleasures. **4.** Dissolute; licentious. **5.** *Slang.* Homosexual. [Middle English *gay, gai,* from Old French *gai,* from Old Provençal, probably from Gothic *gaheis* (unattested), akin to Old High German *gāhi*†, sudden, impetuous.] —**gay′ness** *n.*

Gay (gā), **John.** 1685–1732. English poet and playwright.

Ga·ya (gə-yä′). A city and Hindu pilgrimage center of central Bihar, in northeastern India. Population, 157,000.

ga·yal (gə-yäl′) *n.* A domesticated bovine mammal, *Bos frontalis,* of India and Burma, having thick, pointed horns, a dark coat, and a tufted tail. [Bengali *gayāl,* probably from Sanskrit *gauḥ,* cow. See **gwou-** in Appendix.*]

gay·e·ty. Variant of **gaiety.**

Gay-Lus·sac (gā-lü-săk′), **Joseph Louis.** 1778–1850. French chemist and physicist.

Gay-Lussac's law. Charles's law *(see).*

gay·ly. Variant of **gaily.**

gay·wings (gā′wĭngz′) *n.* Plural in form, used with a singular or plural verb. A plant, the **fringed polygala** *(see).* [From the winglike sepals on its flowers.]

gaz. gazette; gazetteer.

Ga·za (gä′zə). *Arabic* **Ghaz·ze** (găz′ē). A city in the Gaza Strip near the Mediterranean. Population, 38,000.

ga·za·bo (gə-zā′bō) *n., pl.* **-bos** or **-boes.** *Slang.* A fellow; guy. [Origin unknown.]

Ga·za Strip (gä′zə). An area of 135 square miles in southern Palestine near the Mediterranean; occupied by Israel in 1967. Population, 204,000.

gaze (gāz) *intr.v.* **gazed, gazing, gazes.** To look intently or with fixed attention; to stare. —*n.* A steady, fixed look. [Middle English *gazen,* probably from Scandinavian, akin to Swedish dialectal *gasa*†.] —**gaz′er** *n.*

Synonyms: gaze, stare, gape, glare, peer, ogle. These verbs mean to look long and fixedly. *Gaze* usually refers to prolonged and studied looking, often indicative of wonder, fascination, awe, or admiration. *Stare* stresses fixity of one's look and usually indicates marked curiosity, boldness, or insolence of manner. Both *gaze* and *stare* also can refer to a prolonged, vacant look. *Gape* suggests a prolonged, open-mouthed look reflecting amazement, awe, or stupidity. To *glare* is to fix another with a hard, hostile look, and to *peer* is to look narrowly and searchingly and seemingly with difficulty. To *ogle* is to stare impertinently in a way that indicates improper interest.

ga·ze·bo (gə-zē′bō, -zā′bō) *n., pl.* **-bos** or **-boes.** A pavilion or belvedere. [Probably mock Latin formation from GAZE (with Latin future suffix *-ēbō,* as in *vidēbō,* I shall see).]

gaze·hound (gāz′hound′) *n.* A dog that hunts its prey by sight rather than scent.

ga·zelle (gə-zĕl′) *n.* Any of various hoofed mammals of the genus *Gazella* and related genera, of Africa and Asia, characteristically having a slender neck, and ringed, lyrate horns. [French, from Old French, probably from Spanish *gacela,* from Arabic *ghazāl.*]

ga·zette (gə-zĕt′) *n. Abbr.* **gaz. 1.** A newspaper. **2.** An official journal. **3.** *British.* An announcement or report in an official journal. —*tr.v.* **gazetted, -zetting, -zettes.** *British.* To announce or publish in a gazette. [French, from Italian *gazetta,* from Venetian *gazeta (de la novita),* (newspaper sold for) a small copper coin, from *gazeta,* a small copper coin, probably diminutive of *gaz(z)a,* magpie, from Latin *gaia,* from *gaius,* jay (perhaps imitative).]

gaz·et·teer (găz′ə-tîr′) *n. Abbr.* **gaz. 1.** A geographical dictionary or index. **2.** *Archaic.* A person who writes for a gazette or newspaper; a journalist.

Ga·zi·an·tep (gä′zē-än-tĕp′). Formerly **Ain·tab** (īn-täb′). A city in southern Asian Turkey north of Aleppo, Syria. Population, 124,000.

G.B. Great Britain.

GCA *Aviation.* ground control approach.

g.c.d. greatest common divisor.

g.c.f. greatest common factor.

GCI *Aviation.* ground control intercept.

G clef. The **treble clef** *(see).*

GCM Good Conduct Medal.

G.c.t. Greenwich civil time.

Gd The symbol for the element gadolinium.

G.D. grand duchess; grand duchy; grand duke.

Gdańsk (gə-dänsk). *German* **Dan·zig** (dän′tsĭk). A port city in northern Poland on the Gulf of Danzig. Population, 310,000.

gde. gourde.

gds. goods.

Gdy·nia (gə-dĭn′yə). *German* **Gding·en** (gə-dĭng′ən). The chief port city of Poland, on the Gulf of Danzig ten miles northwest of Gdańsk. Population, 159,000.

Ge. Variant of **Gaea.**

Ge The symbol for the element germanium.

ge·an·ti·cline (jē-ăn′tĭ-klīn′) *n.* A large upward fold of the earth's crust. [Greek *gē,* earth (see **gē** in Appendix*) + ANTICLINE.] —**ge·an′ti·cli′nal** *adj.*

gear (gîr) *n.* **1. a.** A toothed wheel, cylinder, or other machine element that meshes with another toothed element to transmit motion or to change speed or direction. **b.** A complete assembly that performs a specific function in a larger machine. **c.** A transmission configuration for a specific ratio of engine to axle torque in a motor vehicle. **2.** Equipment, such as tools, clothing, or the like, required for a particular activity or purpose; paraphernalia. **3.** The harness for a horse. **4.** The rigging of a ship. **5.** A sailor's personal effects. —*v.* **geared, gearing, gears.** —*tr.* **1. a.** To provide with gears. **b.** To connect by gears. **c.** To put into gear. **2.** To adjust or adapt. **3.** To provide with gear. —*intr.* **1.** To be or become in gear. **2.** To adjust so as to fit or blend. [Middle English *gere,* from Old Norse *gervi,* equipment, gear. See **garwian** in Appendix.*]

gear·box (gîr′bŏks′) *n.* An automotive transmission.

gear·ing (gîr′ĭng) *n.* **1.** A system of gears and associated elements by which motion is transferred within a machine. **2.** The act or technique of providing with gears.

gear·shift (gîr′shĭft′) *n.* A mechanism for changing from one gear to another in a transmission.

gear train. A system of interconnected gears.

gear·wheel (gîr′hwēl′) *n.* Also **gear wheel.** A wheel with a toothed rim.

Ge·ba (gā′bə). The principal river of Portuguese Guinea, rising in the Republic of Guinea and flowing 200 miles generally southwest through Bissau to the Atlantic.

geck·o (gĕk′ō) *n., pl.* **-os** or **-oes.** Any of various usually small lizards of the family Gekkonidae, of warm regions, having toes with adhesive pads that enable them to climb on vertical surfaces. [Malay *ge'kok* (imitative of its cry).]

Ge·diz (gĕ-dēz′). Ancient name **Her·mus** (hûr′məs). A river rising in east-central Asian Turkey and flowing 200 miles west into the Gulf of Izmir. Also called "Sarabat."

gee[1] (jē) *n.* The letter *g.*

gee[2] (jē) *interj.* Used to express a command, as to a horse or ox, to turn to the right or to go forward. Compare **haw.** —*intr.v.* **geed, geeing, gees.** To turn to the right.

gee[3] (jē) *interj.* Also **jee.** Used as a mild expletive or exclamation of surprise. [Euphemistic shortening of JESUS.]

gee[4] (jē) *n.* The gravitational acceleration at the earth's surface. [From the symbol "g" for gravitational acceleration.]

gee[5] (jē) *intr.v.* **geed, geeing, gees.** *Informal.* To fit or go with; agree with. [Origin unknown.]

gee[6] (jē) *n. Slang.* A thousand dollars. [Short for GRAND.]

geek (gēk) *n. Slang.* A carnival performer whose act usually consists of biting the head off a live chicken or snake. [Perhaps from dialectal *geck, geek,* fool, from Middle Low German *geck*†.]

Gee·long (jĭ-lông′). A manufacturing city and port in south-central Victoria, Australia, 50 miles southwest of Melbourne. Population, 96,000.

Geel·vink Bay (KHāl′vĭngk). An inlet, 250 miles wide at its mouth, of the western Pacific in northern West Irian, Indonesia.

gee·pound (jē′pound′) *n.* A unit of mass, the **slug** *(see).* [GEE (gravitational acceleration) + POUND (weight).]

geese. Plural of **goose.**

Ge·ez (gē-ĕz′) *n.* **Ethiopic** *(see).*

gee·zer (gē′zər) *n. Slang.* An eccentric old man. [Probably dialectal pronunciation of *guiser,* one in disguise, masquerader, Middle English *giser,* from *gisen,* to disguise, masquerade, from *gise, guise,* GUISE (manner, disguise).]

ge·fil·te fish (gĕ-fĭl′tə). Also **ge·füll·te fish.** Chopped fish mixed with crumbs, eggs, and seasonings, cooked in a broth and usually served chilled in the form of balls or oval-shaped cakes. [Yiddish, "filled fish."]

ge·gen·schein (gā′gən-shīn′) *n.* A faint, glowing spot in the sky, exactly opposite the position of the sun. Also called "counterglow." [German *Gegenschein,* "opposite light" : *gegen,* against, opposite, from Old High German *gegin, gagan* (see **gagina** in Appendix*) + *Schein,* light, shine, from *scheinen,* to shine, from Old High German *scīnan* (see **skī-** in Appendix*).]

Ge·hen·na (gĭ-hĕn′ə) *n.* **1.** A place or state of torment or suffering. **2.** Hell. [Late Latin, from Greek *Geenna,* from Hebrew *Gē' Hinnōm,* Valley of Hinnom, a ravine outside ancient Jerusalem where refuse was dumped, (hence figuratively) hell.]

Gei·ger counter (gī′gər). *Abbr.* **GM counter.** An instrument consisting of a Geiger tube and associated electronic equipment, used to detect, measure, and record nuclear emanations, cosmic rays, and artificially produced subatomic particles. Also called "Geiger-Müller counter." [After Hans *Geiger* (1882–1945), German physicist.]

Geiger tube. *Abbr.* **GM tube.** A gas-filled tube containing coaxial cylindrical electrodes between which a potential difference slightly below the breakdown voltage is maintained, so that production of a pair of ions in the gas by passage of a charged particle or by ionizing radiation causes a breakdown throughout the volume of the tube. Also called "Geiger-Müller tube." [After Hans *Geiger.* See **Geiger counter.**]

gei·sha (gā′shə, gē′-) *n., pl.* **geisha** or **-shas.** A Japanese girl trained to provide entertainment, such as singing, dancing, or amusing talk, especially for men. [Japanese, "artist" : *gei,* art, from Ancient Chinese *ngi* (Mandarin *yi*[4]) + *sha,* person, from Ancient Chinese *che* (Mandarin *chê*[3]).]

gel (jĕl) *n.* A colloid in which the disperse phase has combined with the continuous phase to produce a semisolid material, such as a jelly. [Short for GELATIN.]

gel·a·ble (jĕl′ə-bəl) *adj.* Capable of gelling.

ge·la·da (jə-lä′də, jĕl′ə-) *n.* A baboon, *Theropithecus gelada,* of Ethiopia, having a dark coat with a bare reddish area on the chest, and a mane covering the shoulders. Also called "gelada baboon." [Perhaps from Arabic *qilādah,* mane.]

ge·län·de·sprung (gə-lĕn′də-shprŏŏng′) *n.* A jump in skiing made from a crouching position with the use of both poles. [German : *Gelände,* level land, from *Land,* land, from Old High German *lant* (see **lendh-**[2] in Appendix*) + *Sprung,* a jump, from *gesprungen,* past participle of *springan,* to jump, from Old High German (see **spergh-** in Appendix*).]

gel·a·tin (jĕl′ə-tən) *n.* Also **gel·a·tine. 1.** A colorless or slightly yellow, transparent, brittle protein formed by boiling the specially prepared skin, bones, and connective tissue of animals, and used in foods, drugs, and photographic film. **2.** Any of various similar substances. **3.** A jelly made with gelatin, popular as a dessert or salad base. **4.** A thin, transparent, colored membrane, used in theatrical lighting. [French *gélatine,* from Italian *gelatina,* diminutive of *gelata,* jelly, from Vulgar Latin *gelāta* (unattested), from Latin, feminine past participle of *gelāre,* to freeze, congeal. See **gel-**[3] in Appendix.*]

ge·lat·i·nize (jə-lăt′n-īz′) *v.* **-nized, -nizing, -nizes.** —*tr.* **1.** To convert to gelatin or jelly. **2.** To coat with gelatin. —*intr.* To become gelatinous. —**ge·lat′i·ni·za′tion** *n.*

ge·lat·i·nous (jə-lăt′n-əs) *adj.* **1.** Thick and viscous; resembling a gelatin gel. **2.** Of, pertaining to, containing, or similar to gelatin. —**ge·lat′i·nous·ly** *adv.* —**ge·lat′i·nous·ness** *n.*

ge·la·tion (jĕ-lā′shən) *n.* **1.** Solidification by cooling or freezing. **2.** The process of forming a gel. [Latin *gelātiō,* from *gelāre,* to freeze, congeal. See **gel-**[3] in Appendix.*]

geld[1] (gĕld) *tr.v.* **gelded** or **gelt** (gĕlt), **gelding, gelds.** To castrate (a horse, for example). [Middle English *gelden,* from Old Norse *gelda.* See **ghel-**[3] in Appendix.*]

geld[2] (gĕld) *n.* A tax paid to the crown by English landholders under Anglo-Saxon and Norman kings. [Medieval Latin (Domesday Book) *geldum,* from Old English *g(i)eld,* payment, tribute. See **ghelt-** in Appendix.*]

Gel·der·land (gĕl′dər-lănd′, *Dutch* KHĕl′dər-länt′). Also **Guel-**

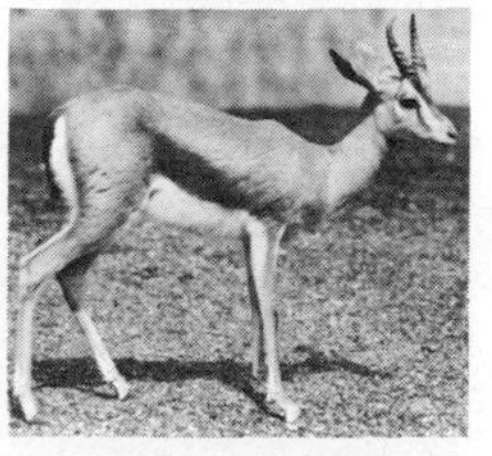

gazelle
Gazella dorcas

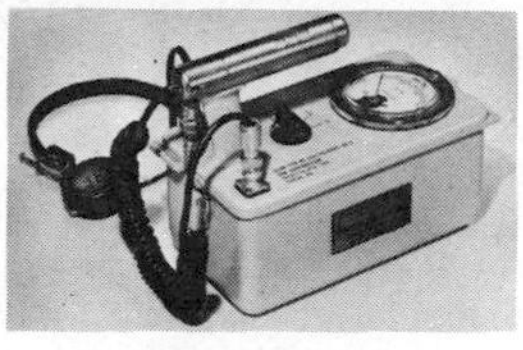

Geiger counter

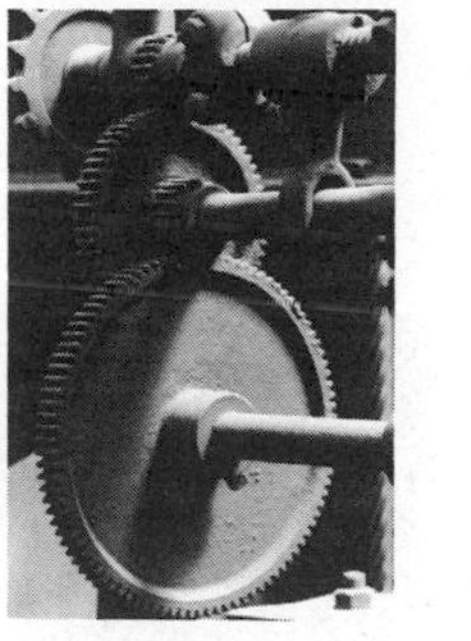

gear
Gear train in an elevator mechanism

t tight/th thin, path/*th* this, bathe/ŭ cut/ûr urge/v valve/w with/y yes/z zebra, size/zh vision/ə about, item, edible, gallop, circus/ à *Fr.* ami/œ *Fr.* feu, *Ger.* schön/ü *Fr.* tu, *Ger.* über/KH *Ger.* ich, *Scot.* loch/N *Fr.* bon. ***Follows main vocabulary.** †**Of obscure origin.**

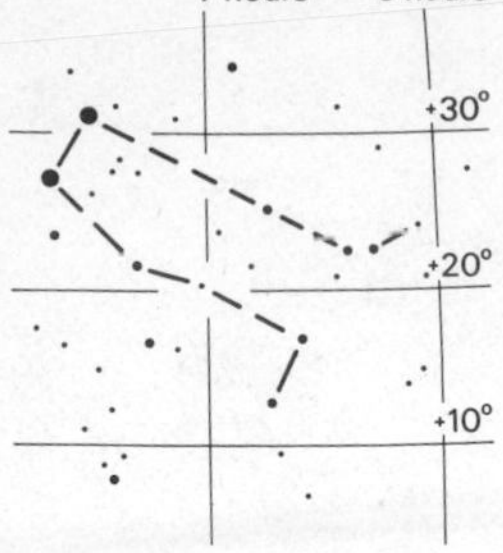
7 hours
6 hours
+30°
+20°
+10°
Gemini

der·land, Guel·ders (-dərz). A province, 1,965 square miles in area, of the east-central Netherlands. Population, 1,274,000. Capital, Arnhem.

geld·ing (gĕl′dĭng) *n.* A castrated animal; especially, a male horse. [Middle English, from Old Norse *geldingr*, from *gelda*, GELD (to castrate).]

Ge·li·bo·lu. The Turkish name for **Gallipoli.**

gel·id (jĕl′ĭd) *adj.* Very cold; icy. [Latin *gelidus*, from *gelū*, cold, frost. See **gel-³** in Appendix.*] **—ge·lid′i·ty** (jə-lĭd′ə-tē), **gel′id·ness** *n.* **—gel′id·ly** *adv.*

Gel·sen·kir·chen (gĕl′zən-kĭr′KHən). A city and industrial center in North Rhine-Westphalia, West Germany, 15 miles west of Dortmund. Population, 381,000.

gelt¹ (gĕlt) *n. Slang.* Money. [Yiddish *gelt* and German *Geld*, from Old High German *gelt*, recompense, reward. See **ghelt-** in Appendix.*]

gelt². Alternate past tense and past participle of **geld.**

gem (jĕm) *n.* **1.** A precious or semiprecious stone, especially one that has been cut and polished. **2. a.** Something that is valued for its beauty or perfection. **b.** A beloved or highly prized person: *a gem of a servant.* **3.** A kind of muffin. **—*tr.v.*** **gemmed, gemming, gems.** To adorn with or as if with gems. [Middle English *gemme*, from Old French, from Latin *gemma*, bud, precious stone. See **gembh-** in Appendix.*]

Ge·ma·ra (gə-mär′ə, -môr′ə) *n.* The second part of the Talmud, consisting primarily of commentary on the Mishnah. [Aramaic *gəmārā*, completion, from *gəmār*, to complete.] **—Ge·ma′ric** *adj.* **—Ge·ma′rist** *n.*

gem·i·nate (jĕm′ə-nāt′) *v.* **-nated, -nating, -nates.** **—*tr.*** To arrange in pairs or to double. **—*intr.*** To occur in pairs. **—*adj.*** (jĕm′ə-nĭt, -nāt′). Forming a pair; doubled. [Latin *gemināre*, from *geminus*, twin. See **Gemini.**] **—gem′i·nate′ly** *adv.* **—gem′i·na′tion** *n.*

Gem·i·ni (jĕm′ə-nī′, -nē′) *n.* **1.** *Astronomy.* A constellation in the Northern Hemisphere containing the stars Castor and Pollux. **2.** The third sign of the **zodiac** *(see).* Also called the "Twins." [Latin, plural of *geminus*, twin. See **yem-** in Appendix.*]

gem·ma (jĕm′ə) *n., pl.* **gemmae** (jĕm′ē′). An asexual reproductive structure, as in liverworts or the hydra, consisting of a cell or group of cells capable of developing into a new individual; a bud. [Latin, bud, precious stone. See **gembh-** in Appendix.*] **—gem·ma′ceous** (jĕ-mā′shəs) *adj.*

gem·mate (jĕm′āt′) *adj.* Having or reproducing by gemmae. **—*intr.v.*** **gemmated, -mating, -mates.** To produce gemmae or reproduce by means of gemmae. [Latin *gemmāre*, to bud, from *gemma*, bud, GEMMA.] **—gem·ma′tion** (jĕ-mā′shən) *n.*

gem·mip·a·rous (jĕ-mĭp′ər-əs) *adj.* Reproducing by buds or gemmae. [New Latin *gemmiparus* : Latin *gemma*, bud, GEMMA + -PAROUS.]

gem·mu·la·tion (jĕm′yə-lā′shən) *n.* Production of or reproduction by gemmules.

gem·mule (jĕm′yōōl) *n.* **1.** A small gemma or similar structure; especially, a reproductive structure in some sponges that remains dormant through the winter and later develops into a new individual. **2.** A hypothetical particle of heredity postulated in the theory of **pangenesis** *(see).* [French, from Latin *gemmula*, diminutive of *gemma*, GEMMA.]

gem·my (jĕm′ē) *adj.* **1.** Full of or set with gems. **2.** Like a gem; glittering.

gem·ol·o·gy, gem·mol·o·gy (jĕ-mŏl′ə-jē) *n.* The study of gems. **—gem′o·log′i·cal** (jĕm′ə-lŏj′ĭ-kəl) *adj.* **—gem·ol′o·gist** *n.*

ge·mot (gə-mōt′) *n.* Also **ge·mote.** A public meeting or local judicial assembly in England prior to the Norman Conquest. [Old English *gemōt* : *ge-*, perfective prefix + *mōt*, assembly, council (see **mōd-** in Appendix*).]

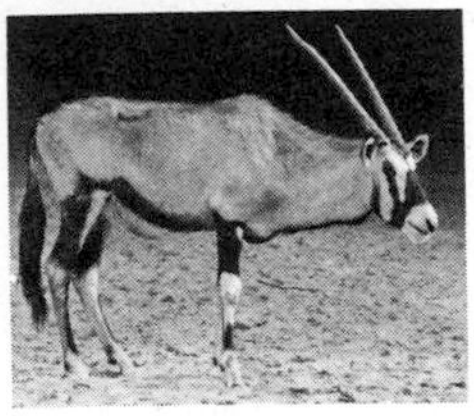
gemsbok

gems·bok (gĕmz′bŏk′) *n.* An antelope, *Oryx gazella*, of arid regions of southern Africa, having long, sharp, straight horns. [Afrikaans, from Dutch *gemsbok*, "male chamois," from German *Gemsbock* : *Gemse*, chamois, from Old High German *gamiza* (unattested), from Late Latin *camox* (see **chamois**) + *Bock*, he-goat, buck, from Old High German *boc* (see **bhugo-** in Appendix*).]

gem·stone (jĕm′stōn′) *n.* A precious or semiprecious stone that may be used as a jewel when cut and polished.

ge·müt·lich (gə-müt′lĭKH) *adj. German.* Having a feeling of warmth or congeniality; cheerful; friendly; cozy.

-gen, -gene. Indicates: **1.** That which produces; producing; for example, **oxygen.** **2.** Something produced; for example, **antigen, phosgene.** [French *-gène*, from Greek *-genēs*, born. See **gene-** in Appendix.*]

gen. **1.** gender. **2.** general; generally. **3.** generator. **4.** generic. **5.** genitive. **6.** genus.

Gen. **1.** general (military rank). **2.** Genesis (Old Testament).

gen·darme (zhän′därm′; *French* zhäN-dȧrm′) *n., pl.* **-darmes** (-därmz′; *French* -dȧrm′). **1.** A member of a French national police organization constituting a branch of the armed forces with responsibilities for internal defense, frontier and customs guard, highway patrol, and general law enforcement in rural districts. **2.** A cavalryman belonging to any of various successively organized units under royal authority in France from the 15th century until 1789. **3.** *Informal.* A French policeman. **4.** *Slang.* Any policeman. [French, from *gens d'armes*, "men of arms" : Old French *gens*, people, from Latin *gēns*, race, people, sex (see **gene-** in Appendix*) + *de*, of + *armes*, ARMS.]

gen·darm·e·rie (zhän-där′mə-rē; *French* zhäN-dȧr′mə-rē) *n.* Also **gen·dar·me·ry** (for sense 2). **1.** A French military police organization having general responsibility for public security and law enforcement within the frontiers of the national territory. **2.** A French royal cavalry corps, as variously organized at different times between the 15th century and 1789. [French, from GENDARME.]

gen·der (jĕn′dər) *n. Abbr.* **g., gen.** **1.** *Grammar.* **a.** Any set of two or more categories, such as masculine, feminine, and neuter, into which words are divided according to sex, animation, psychological associations, or some other characteristic, and that determine agreement with or the selection of modifiers, referents, or grammatical forms. **b.** One category of such a set. See also **common gender, grammatical gender, natural gender.** **c.** The classification of a word or grammatical form in such a category. **d.** The distinguishing form or forms used. **2.** Classification of sex; sex. **3.** *Obsolete.* Kind; type; genre. **—*tr.v.*** **gendered, -dering, -ders.** *Archaic.* To engender. [Middle English *gendre*, from Old French *gen(d)re*, kind, sort, from Latin *genus* (stem *gener-*), race, kind. See **gene-** in Appendix.*]

gene (jēn) *n.* A functional hereditary unit that occupies a fixed location on a chromosome, has a specific influence on phenotype, and is capable of mutation to various allelic forms. [German *Gen*, short for *Pangen* : PAN- + -GEN.]

-gene. Variant of **-gen.**

ge·ne·al·o·gy (jē′nē-ăl′ə-jē, -ŏl′ə-jē, jĕn′ē-) *n., pl.* **-gies.** *Abbr.* **geneal.** **1.** A record or table of the descent of a family, group, or person from an ancestor or ancestors. **2.** Direct descent from an ancestor; lineage; pedigree. **3.** The study or investigation of ancestry and family histories. [Middle English *genealogie*, from Old French, from Late Latin *genealogia*, from Greek : *genea*, race, generation (see **gene-** in Appendix*) + -LOGY.] **—ge′ne·a·log′i·cal** (-ə-lŏj′ĭ-kəl) *adj.* **—ge′ne·a·log′i·cal·ly** *adv.* **—ge′ne·al′o·gist** *n.*

gen·e·ra. Plural of **genus.**

gen·er·a·ble (jĕn′ər-ə-bəl) *adj.* Capable of being generated. [Middle English *generabill*, from Latin *generābilis*, from *generāre*, GENERATE.]

gen·er·al (jĕn′ər-əl) *adj. Abbr.* **gen., genl.** **1.** Relating to, concerned with, or applicable to the whole, or every member of a class or category: *a program to improve general welfare.* **2.** Widespread; prevalent: *a general discontent.* **3.** Being usually the case; true or applicable in most instances but not all: *the general correctness of his decisions.* **4. a.** Not limited in scope, area, or application; not restricted: *a general rule to follow.* **b.** Not limited to one class of things; diversified; miscellaneous: *general studies; general merchandise.* **5.** Involving only the main or more obvious features of something; lacking detail or precision: *a general grasp of a subject.* **6.** Highest or superior in rank; chief within a particular sphere: *the general manager.* **—*n.*** **1.** *Abbr.* **Gen.** **a.** An officer in the U.S. Army, Air Force, or Marine Corps holding a rank above colonel; especially, an officer of the second-highest rank in the U.S. Army or Air Force and the highest rank in the Marine Corps. **b.** In England, Canada, and some other countries, a military officer holding a rank just below field marshal. **2.** Something, such as a condition, principle, or fact, that embraces or is applicable to the whole. **3.** *Archaic.* The public: *" 'twas caviare to the general"* (Shakespeare). **—in general.** Generally. [Middle English, from Old French, from Latin *generālis*, belonging to a kind or species, relating to all, from *genus* (stem *gener-*), birth, race, kind. See **gene-** in Appendix.*] **—gen′er·al·ness** *n.*

general anesthetic. An anesthetic that anesthetizes the entire body and induces unconsciousness. Compare **local anesthetic.**

general assembly. *Abbr.* **GA, G.A.** **1.** A legislative body; especially, a U.S. state legislature. **2.** *Capital* **G**, *capital* **A.** The principal deliberative body of the United Nations in which each member nation is represented and has one vote. **3.** The supreme governing body of some religious denominations.

General Court. **1.** A Colonial legislative body with judicial powers. **2.** The state legislature of Massachusetts and New Hampshire.

general court-martial. A court-martial consisting of at least five officers for trying major offenses.

gen·er·al·cy (jĕn′ər-əl-sē) *n., pl.* **-cies.** The rank, appointment, authority, or tenure of a general.

general delivery. **1.** A department of a post office which holds mail for addressees until it is called for. **2.** Mail sent to this department.

general election. An election involving most or all constituencies of a state or nation in the choice of candidates.

gen·er·al·is·si·mo (jĕn′ər-ə-lĭs′ə-mō′) *n., pl.* **-mos.** The commander in chief of all the armed forces in certain countries, or, occasionally, of the armed forces of allied countries in a joint campaign. [Italian, superlative of *generale*, general, from Latin *generālis*, belonging to a kind, GENERAL.]

gen·er·al·i·ty (jĕn′ə-răl′ə-tē) *n., pl.* **-ties.** **1.** The condition or quality of being general. **2.** An observation or principle having general application; a generalization. **3.** A statement or idea that is imprecise or vague. **4.** The greater portion or number; the majority.

gen·er·al·i·za·tion (jĕn′ər-ə-lə-zā′shən) *n.* **1.** An act or instance of generalizing. **2.** A general principle, statement or idea.

gen·er·al·ize (jĕn′ər-ə-līz′) *v.* **-ized, -izing, -izes.** **—*tr.*** **1. a.** To reduce to a general form, class, or law. **b.** To render indefinite or unspecific. **2. a.** To infer from many particulars. **b.** To draw inferences or a general conclusion from. **3. a.** To make generally or universally applicable. **b.** To popularize. **—*intr.*** **1. a.** To form a concept inductively. **b.** To form general notions or conclusions. **2.** To speak or think in generalities; speak vaguely. **3.** *Medicine.* To spread through the body. Said of a usually localized disease.

gen·er·al·ized (jĕn′ər-ə-līzd′) *adj.* Not well-adapted to a specific

ă pat/ā pay/âr care/ä father/b bib/ch church/d deed/ĕ pet/ē be/f fife/g gag/h hat/hw which/ĭ pit/ī pie/îr pier/j judge/k kick/l lid, needle/m mum/n no, sudden/ng thing/ŏ pot/ō toe/ô paw, for/oi noise/ou out/ŏŏ took/ōō boot/p pop/r roar/s sauce/sh ship, dish/

environment or function; undifferentiated: *"the undeveloped eye is too slow and too generalized to foresee and to isolate the most illuminating moment"* (James Agee).
gen·er·al·ly (jĕn′ər-ə-lē) *adv. Abbr.* **gen. 1.** For the most part; widely: *generally known.* **2.** As a rule; usually; ordinarily. **3.** In disregard of particular instances and details; not specifically: *generally speaking.*
general officer. *Military.* Any officer ranking above colonel.
General of the Air Force. *Military.* A general having the highest rank in the U.S. Air Force and having an insignia of five stars.
General of the Army. A general having the highest rank in the U.S. Army and having an insignia of five stars.
general paresis. A brain disease of syphilitic origin, characterized by mental deterioration, speech disturbances, and progressive muscular weakness.
gen·er·al-pur·pose (jĕn′ər-əl-pûr′pəs) *adj.* Having more than one use.
general relativity. The geometric theory of gravitation developed by Albert Einstein, incorporating and extending the special theory of relativity to accelerated frames of reference, and introducing the principle that gravitational and inertial forces are equivalent. Also called "general theory of relativity." Compare **special relativity.**
general semantics. A doctrine proposed by Alfred Korzybski (1879–1950) that presents a method of improving human behavior through a more critical use of words and symbols.
gen·er·al·ship (jĕn′ər-əl-shĭp′) *n.* **1.** The rank, office, or tenure of a general. **2.** Leadership or skill in the conduct of a war. **3.** Any skillful management or leadership.
general staff. *Abbr.* **GS, G.S.** *Military.* A group of officers who are charged with assisting the commander of a division or higher unit in planning and supervising operations.
gen·er·ate (jĕn′ə-rāt′) *tr.v.* **-ated, -ating, -ates. 1.** To bring into existence; cause to be; produce: *"A painter may indulge in any liberty providing he generates the lyricism of forms."* (Wallace Fowlie). **2.** To engender (offspring); beget. **3.** To form (a geometric figure) by describing a curve or surface. [Latin *generāre,* from *genus* (stem *gener-*), birth, race, kind. See **gene-** in Appendix.*] —**gen′er·a′tive** (-ə-rā′tĭv, -ə-rə-tĭv) *adj.*
gen·er·a·tion (jĕn′ə-rā′shən) *n.* **1.** The act or process of generating; especially, origination, production, or procreation. **2.** Offspring having a common parent or parents and constituting a single stage of descent. **3.** A class of objects derived from a preceding class: *the new generation of miniature computers.* **4. a.** A group of contemporaneous individuals. **b.** A group of individuals regarded as having a common, more or less contemporaneous cultural or social attribute. **5.** The average time interval between the birth of parents and the birth of their offspring.
generative transformational grammar. *Linguistics.* A system of rules intended to produce all the well-formed sentences of a language when applied to its lexicon; specifically, such a system whose syntactic component is generated successively by rules for the construction of phrases containing a semantic component (deep structure) and by rules for the production of a phonological component (surface structure) by transforming one grammatical structure into another that is semantically equivalent.
gen·er·a·tor (jĕn′ə-rā′tər) *n. Abbr.* **gen. 1.** One that generates. **2.** A machine that converts mechanical energy into electrical energy. **3.** An apparatus that generates vapor or gas. **4.** A generatrix.
gen·er·a·trix (jĕn′ə-rā′trĭks) *n., pl.* **generatrices** (jĕn′ər-ə-trī′sēz). A geometric element that generates a geometric figure; especially, a straight line that generates a surface by moving in a specified fashion.
ge·ner·ic (jĭ-nĕr′ĭk) *adj. Abbr.* **gen. 1.** Relating to or descriptive of an entire group or class; general. **2.** *Biology.* Of or relating to a genus. **3.** Commonly available; not protected by trademark; nonproprietary. Said of drugs. [French *générique,* from Latin *genus* (stem *gener-*), race, species, kind. See **gene-** in Appendix.*] —**ge·ner′i·cal·ly** *adv.*
gen·er·os·i·ty (jĕn′ə-rŏs′ə-tē) *n., pl.* **-ties. 1.** The quality of being generous; liberality or willingness in giving; unselfishness; munificence. **2.** Nobility of thought or behavior; magnanimity. **3.** Amplitude; abundance. **4.** A generous act.
gen·er·ous (jĕn′ər-əs) *adj.* **1.** Willingness to give or share; munificent; unselfish: *"Therefore be generous among friends with kisses"* (George Barker). **2.** Lacking pettiness or meanness in thought or behavior; magnanimous. **3.** Characterized by abundance; bountiful; ample: *"her frame was generous, but her figure could pass as good"* (Doris Lessing). **4.** Rich-flavored, as wine. **5.** *Obsolete.* Of noble lineage. [Old French *genereux,* from Latin *generōsus,* of noble birth, excellent, magnanimous, from *genus* (stem *gener-*), birth, race, kind. See **gene-** in Appendix.*] —**gen′er·ous·ly** *adv.* —**gen′er·ous·ness** *n.*
Gen·e·see (jĕn′ə-sē′). A river rising in the Alleghenies in northern Pennsylvania and flowing 158 miles generally north through New York State to Lake Ontario at Rochester.
gen·e·sis (jĕn′ə-sĭs) *n., pl.* **-ses** (-sēz′). The coming into being of anything; origin; creation. [Latin, from Greek, generation, birth, origin. See **gene-** in Appendix.*]
Gen·e·sis (jĕn′ə-sĭs) *n. Abbr.* **Gen.** The first book of the Old Testament, recounting the creation of the world and the establishment and early history of Israel.
-genesis. Indicates generation; for example, **biogenesis, paragenesis.** [New Latin, from Latin *genesis,* birth, GENESIS.]
gen·et¹ (jə-nĕt′) *n.* Any of several Old World carnivorous mammals of the genus *Genetta,* having grayish or yellowish fur with dark spots, and a long, ringed tail. [Middle English *genete,* from Old French, from Arabic *jarnayt.*]
gen·et². Variant of **jennet.**
Ge·nêt (zhə-nĕ′), **Edmond Charles Edouard.** 1763–1834. First minister from France to the United States (1792–94).
Ge·nêt (zhə-nĕ′), **Jean.** Born 1910. French novelist, poet, and playwright.
ge·net·ic (jə-nĕt′ĭk) *adj.* Also **ge·net·i·cal** (-ĭ-kəl). **1.** Of or relating to the origin or development of something. **2. a.** Of or pertaining to genetics. **b.** Affecting or affected by genes. [From GENESIS.] —**ge·net′i·cal·ly** *adv.*
ge·net·i·cist (jə-nĕt′ə-sĭst) *n.* One who specializes in genetics.
ge·net·ics (jə-nĕt′ĭks) *n.* Plural in form used with a singular or plural verb. **1.** The biology of heredity; especially, the study of mechanisms of hereditary transmission and variation of organismal characteristics. Used with a singular verb. **2.** The genetic constitution of an individual, group, or class. Used with a plural verb.
Ge·ne·va (jə-nē′və). *French* **Ge·nève** (zhə-nĕv′); *German* **Genf** (gĕnf). A city of Switzerland, in the southwest on the Lake of Geneva and bisected by the Rhône. Population, 174,000.
Ge·ne·va, Lake of (jə-nē′və). A lake occupying 225 square miles of southwestern Switzerland with its southern shore in eastern France and traversed from east to southwest by the Rhône. Also called "Lake Leman."
Geneva bands. Two strips of white cloth hanging from the collar of some clerical or academic robes. [Originally worn by Calvinist clergymen in Geneva.]
Geneva Convention. An agreement first formulated at an international convention held in Geneva, Switzerland, in 1864, establishing rules for the wartime treatment of prisoners and the sick or wounded.
Geneva cross. A red Greek or St. George's cross on a white ground, used as a symbol by the Red Cross and as a sign of neutrality.
Geneva gown. A loose black academic or clerical gown with wide sleeves. [Originally worn by Calvinist clergymen in Geneva.]
Ge·ne·van (jə-nē′vən) *adj.* Also **Gen·e·vese** (jĕn′ə-vēz′, -vēs′). **1.** Of or relating to Geneva, Switzerland. **2.** Of or relating to Geneva during the time of Calvin; Calvinist. —*n.* Also **Gen·e·vese. 1.** A native or inhabitant of Geneva, Switzerland. **2.** A follower of Calvin; a Calvinist.
Gen·ghis Khan (jĕn′gĭz kän′, jĕng′gĭs, gĕng′gĭs). Also **Jen·ghis, Jen·ghiz, Jin·ghis.** Original name, Temujin or Temuchin. 1162?–1227. Mongol conqueror.
gen·ial¹ (jēn′yəl, jē′nē-əl) *adj.* **1.** Having a pleasant or friendly disposition or manner; cordial; kindly. **2.** Conducive to life or growth; giving warmth; mild: *"the genial sunshine . . . saturating his miserable body with its warmth"* (Jack London). **3.** *Rare.* Characteristic of or relating to genius. **4.** *Obsolete.* Of or relating to marriage; nuptial. [Latin *geniālis,* of generation or birth, nuptial, hence festive, joyous, from *genius,* deity of generation and birth. See **gene-** in Appendix.*] —**gen′ial·ly** *adv.* —**gen′ial·ness** *n.*
ge·ni·al² (jə-nī′əl) *n.* Of or pertaining to the chin. [From Greek *geneion,* chin, from *genus,* jaw. See **genu-²** in Appendix.*]
ge·ni·al·i·ty (jē′nē-ăl′ə-tē) *n.* The quality of being genial; friendliness; cordiality.
gen·ic (jĕn′ĭk) *adj.* Of, relating to, produced by, or being a gene or genes; genetic.
-genic. Indicates generation or production; for example, **antigenic.** [From -GEN.]
ge·nic·u·late (jə-nĭk′yə-lāt′, -lĭt) *adj.* Also **ge·nic·u·lat·ed** (-lā′tĭd). **1.** Bent at an abrupt angle like that of a bent knee. **2.** Jointed so as to be capable of bending at an abrupt angle. [Latin *geniculātus,* with bent knee, curved, from *geniculum,* diminutive of *genu,* knee. See **genu-¹** in Appendix.*] —**ge·nic′u·late′ly** *adv.* —**ge·nic′u·la′tion** *n.*
ge·nie (jē′nē) *n.* **1.** A supernatural creature who does one's bidding. **2.** Variant of **jinni.** [Sense 1, from French *génie,* spirit, from Latin *genius,* guardian spirit, GENIUS.]
ge·ni·i. Alternate plural of **genius.**
gen·ip (jĕn′əp) *n.* **1.** A tropical American tree, *Melicocca bijuga,* having small greenish-white flowers and small yellow fruit. **2.** The sweet, edible fruit of this tree. **3.** The **genipap** *(see).* [Spanish *genipa,* from French, from Guarani.]
gen·i·pap (jĕn′ə-păp′) *n.* **1.** An evergreen tree, *Genipa americana,* of the West Indies, having yellowish-white flowers and edible fruit. **2.** The reddish-brown fruit of this tree. Also called "genip," "marmalade box." [Portuguese *genipapo,* from Tupi.]
genit. genitive.
gen·i·tal (jĕn′ə-təl) *adj.* **1.** Of or relating to biological reproduction. **2.** Of or pertaining to the genitals. [Middle English *genytal,* from Old French *genital,* from Latin *genitālis,* from *gignere* (past participle *genitus*), to beget, produce. See **gene-** in Appendix.*]
gen·i·ta·li·a (jĕn′ə-tā′lē-ə, -tāl′yə) *pl.n.* The reproductive organs, especially the external sex organs. [Latin *genitālia (membra),* genital (members), neuter plural of *genitālis,* GENITAL.]
gen·i·tals (jĕn′ə-təlz) *pl.n.* Genitalia.
gen·i·ti·val (jĕn′ə-tī′vəl) *adj. Grammar.* Of, relating to, or in the genitive case. —**gen′i·ti′val·ly** *adv.*
gen·i·tive (jĕn′ə-tĭv) *adj. Abbr.* **g., gen., genit.** *Grammar.* **1.** Of, pertaining to, or designating a case that expresses possession, measurement, or source. **2.** Of or pertaining to an affix or a construction, such as a prepositional phrase, characteristic of

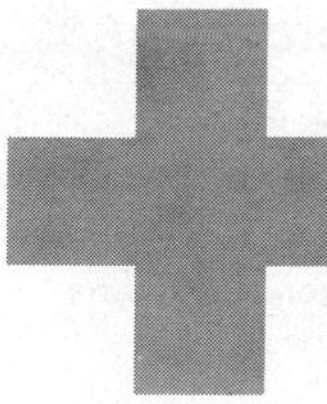
Geneva cross

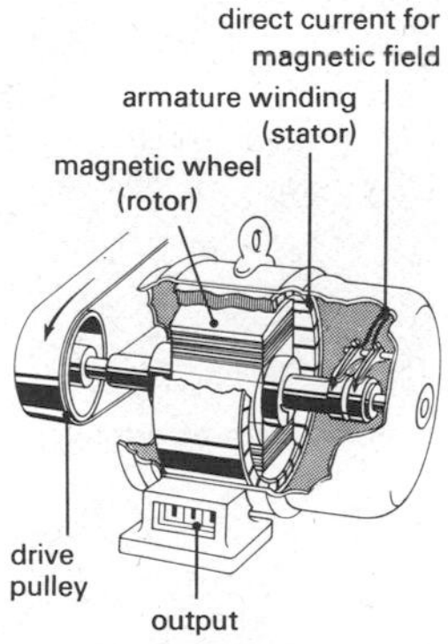
direct current for magnetic field
armature winding (stator)
magnetic wheel (rotor)
drive pulley
output
generator

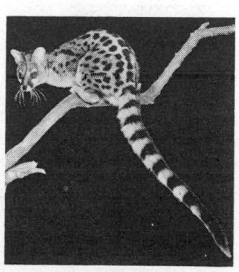

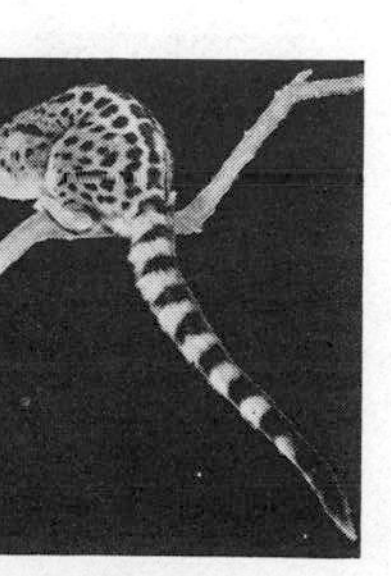
genet¹
Genetta genetta

this case. —*n. Abbr.* **g., gen., genit.** *Grammar.* **1.** The genitive case. **2.** A genitive form or construction. [Middle English *genitif (case),* from Latin *(casus) genitīvus,* "case of production or origin" (translation of Greek *genikē ptōsis,* "case of race"), from *gignere* (past participle *genitus*), to beget, produce. See **gene-** in Appendix.*]

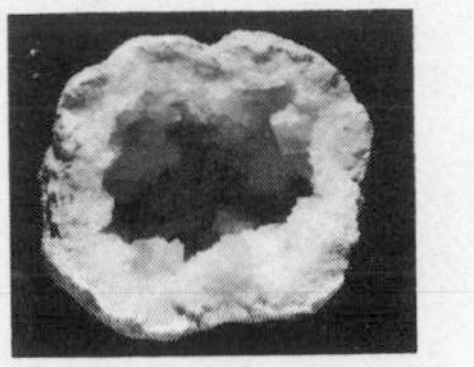
geode

gen·i·tor (jĕn'ə-tər) *n.* **1.** One who begets or creates. **2.** *Anthropology.* A natural father as distinguished from the socially responsible foster father in certain cultures. [Middle English *genytur,* from Latin *genitor,* from *gignere* (past participle *genitus*), to beget. See **gene-** in Appendix.*]

gen·i·to·u·ri·nar·y (jĕn'ə-tō-yŏŏr'ə-nĕr'ē) *adj. Abbr.* **GU, G.U.** Of or pertaining to the genital and urinary organs or their functions. [GENIT(AL) + URINARY.]

gen·ius (jēn'yəs) *n., pl.* **-iuses** or **genii** (jē'nē-ī') (for senses 4, 6). **1. a.** Exceptional or transcendent intellectual and creative power: *"True genius rearranges old material in a way never seen . . . before"* (John Hersey). **b.** One who possesses such power. **2. a.** A natural talent or inclination. Used with *to* or *for: She has a genius for acting.* **b.** One who has such a talent or inclination: *He is a genius at diplomacy.* **3.** The prevailing spirit or character, as of a place, person, time, or group: *the genius of the Elizabethan poets.* **4.** *Roman Mythology.* **a.** A tutelary deity or guardian spirit allotted to a person from birth. **b.** Any guiding spirit of a person or place. **5.** A person who has great influence over another. **6.** *Moslem Mythology.* A jinni or demon. [Latin *genius,* deity of generation and birth, guardian spirit. See **gene-** in Appendix.*]

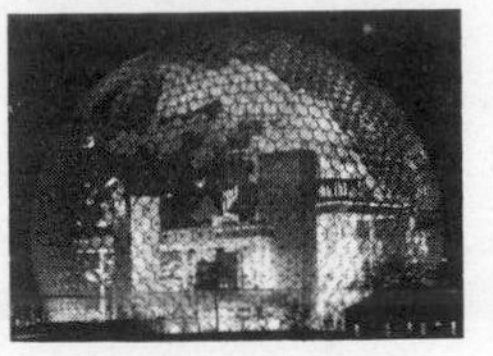
geodesic dome

ge·ni·us lo·ci (jē'nē-əs lō'sē). *Latin.* **1.** A guardian deity of a particular locality. **2.** The distinctive atmosphere or particular character of a place.

genl. general.

Gen·nes·a·ret, Lake of (jə-nĕs'ə-rĕt). The New Testament name for the Sea of Galilee.

Gen·o·a (jĕn'ō-ə). *Italian* **Ge·no·va** (jĕ'nō-vä). A city and port of northwestern Italy on the Ligurian Sea. Population, 784,000.

gen·o·cide (jĕn'ə-sīd') *n.* The systematic, planned annihilation of a racial, political, or cultural group. [Greek *genos,* race (see **gene-** in Appendix*) + -CIDE.] —**gen'o·ci'dal** (-sīd'l) *adj.*

Gen·o·ese (jĕn'ō-ēz', -ēs') *adj.* Of or relating to Genoa, Italy. —*n., pl.* **Genoese.** A native or inhabitant of Genoa, Italy.

ge·nome (jē'nōm') *n.* Also **ge·nom.** *Biology.* A complete haploid set of chromosomes. [German *Genom* : *Gen,* GENE + (CHROMOS)OME.]

gen·o·type (jĕn'ə-tīp') *n.* **1.** The genetic constitution of an organism, especially as distinguished from its physical appearance. Compare **phenotype. 2.** A group or class of organisms having the same genetic constitution. **3.** The type species of a genus. [Greek *genos,* race (see **gene-** in Appendix*) + TYPE.] —**gen'o·typ'ic** (-tĭp'ĭk), **gen'o·typ'i·cal** *adj.* —**gen'o·typ'i·cal·ly** *adv.* —**gen'o·ty·pic'i·ty** (-tī-pĭs'ĭ-tē) *n.*

-genous. Indicates: **1.** Generating or producing; for example, **androgenous. 2.** Generated by, produced by, or arising from; for example, **endogenous.** [From -GEN.]

gen·re (zhän'rə) *n.* **1.** Type; class; variety. **2. a.** A category of art distinguished by a definite style, form, or content; especially, a style of painting concerned with depicting scenes and subjects of common everyday life. **b.** A distinctive class or category of literary composition. —*adj.* Of or relating to genre. [French, kind, from Old French *gen(d)re,* from Latin *genus* (stem *gener-*), race, kind. See **gene-** in Appendix.*]

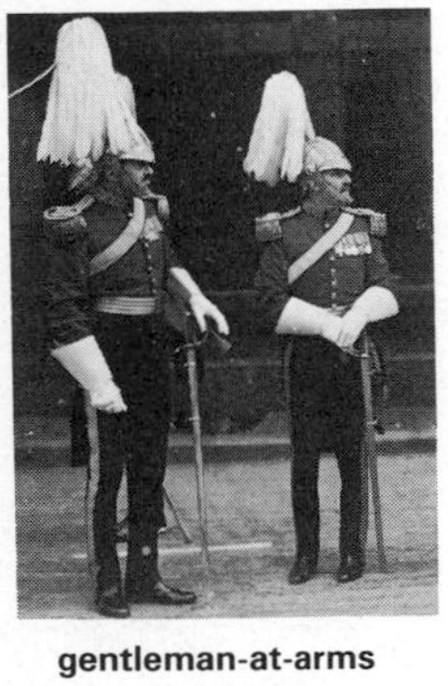
gentleman-at-arms

gen·ro (gĕn'rō) *n., pl.* **-ros. 1.** In Japan, a group of elder statesmen, formerly advisers to the emperor. **2.** One of these elder statesmen. [Japanese *genrō,* from Ancient Chinese *nguan lao* (Mandarin *yüan[2] lao[3]*) : *nguan,* first, principal + *lao,* old, elder.]

gens (jĕnz) *n., pl.* **gentes** (jĕn'tēz'). **1.** The patrilinear clan forming the basic unit of the Roman tribe and having originally a common name, land, cult, and burial ground. **2.** *Anthropology.* An exogamous patrilineal clan. [Latin *gēns,* clan. See **gene-** in Appendix.*]

Gen·san. The Japanese name for **Wonsan.**

gent[1] (jĕnt) *adj. Obsolete.* **1.** Noble; highborn. **2.** Graceful or neat; elegant. [Middle English, from Old French, from Latin *genitus,* born, well-born, past participle of *gignere,* to beget. See **gene-** in Appendix.*]

gent[2] (jĕnt) *n. Informal.* A man; fellow. [Shortened from GENTLEMAN.]

Gent. The Flemish name for **Ghent.**

gen·teel (jĕn-tēl') *adj.* **1.** Refined in manner; well-bred; polite. **2.** Free from vulgarity or rudeness. **3.** Fashionable; elegant: *"It was a genteel old-fashioned house, very quiet and orderly"* (Dickens). **4. a.** Striving to convey a manner or appearance of refinement and respectability. **b.** Marked by affected and somewhat prudish refinement. —See Synonyms at **polite.** [Old French *gentil,* GENTLE.] —**gen·teel'ly** *adv.* —**gen·teel'ness** *n.*

gen·teel·ism (jĕn-tēl'ĭz'əm) *n.* A word or expression thought by its user to be genteel.

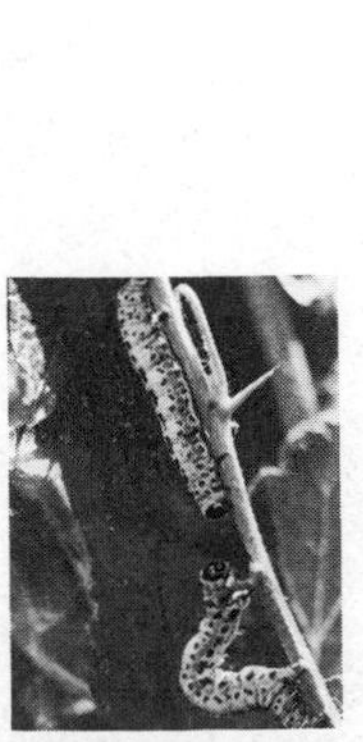
geometrid

gen·tian (jĕn'shən) *n.* **1.** Any of numerous plants of the genus *Gentiana,* characteristically having showy blue flowers. **2.** The dried rhizome and roots of a yellow-flowered European gentian, *G. lutea,* sometimes used as a tonic. [Middle English *gencian,* from Old French *genciane,* from Latin *gentiāna,* probably after *Gentius,* king of Illyria (second century B.C.), supposed discoverer of the medicinal properties of the plant.]

gentian violet. A purple dye used chiefly as a biological stain and bactericide.

gen·tile (jĕn'tīl, -tīl) *adj.* **1.** Of or pertaining to the gens or to the tribal society based on it. **2.** Of or relating to Gentiles. **3.** *Grammar.* Of or pertaining to a noun or adjective designating a nation, place, or people: *"American" and "Italian" are gentile nouns.* —*n.* **1.** A member of a gens. **2.** A gentile noun or adjective. [Latin *gentīlis,* from *gēns,* clan, GENS.]

Gen·tile (jĕn'tīl) *n.* **1.** Anyone who is not of the Jewish faith or is of a non-Jewish nation. **2.** A Christian as distinguished from a Jew. **3.** A pagan or heathen. **4.** Among Mormons, a person who is not a Mormon. —*adj.* Of or relating to a Gentile. [Middle English *gentil, gentyle,* from Late Latin *gentīles,* pagans, heathens, from *gentīlis,* pagan, from Latin, of the same clan, from *gēns,* clan, GENS.]

Gen·ti·le da Fa·bri·a·no (jān-tē'lā dä fä-brē-ä'nō). 1370?–1427. Italian painter of the Umbrian school.

gen·ti·lesse (jĕn'tə-lĕs') *n. Archaic.* Refinement; courtesy; good breeding. [Middle English, from Old French, from *gentil,* GENTLE.]

gen·til·i·ty (jĕn-tĭl'ə-tē) *n.* **1.** The condition of being genteel. **2.** Gentle birth. **3.** Persons of gentle birth or refinement collectively; the gentry. —See Synonyms at **culture.** [Middle English *gentilete,* from Old French, from Latin *gentīlitās,* clanship, from *gentīlis,* belonging to a clan, GENTLE.]

gen·tle (jĕnt'l) *adj.* **-tler, -tlest. 1.** Considerate or kindly in disposition; amiable; patient: *a gentle mother.* **2.** Not harsh, severe, or violent; mild; soft: *a gentle scolding.* **3.** Easily managed or handled; docile; tame: *a gentle horse.* **4.** Gradual; not steep or sudden: *a gentle incline.* **5.** Moderate. **6.** Of good family; well-born. **7.** *Archaic.* Noble; chivalrous: *a gentle knight.* —*n.* **1.** *Archaic.* One of gentle birth or station. **2.** The larva of a bluebottle fly. —*tr.v.* **gentled, -tling, -tles. 1.** To make gentle; pacify; mollify. **2.** To tame or break (a horse). **3.** *Obsolete.* To raise to the status of a noble. [Middle English *gentil,* wellborn, noble, graceful, from Old French, from Latin *gentīlis,* of the same clan, of noble birth, from *gēns,* clan. See **gene-** in Appendix.*] —**gen'tle·ness** *n.* —**gen'tly** *adv.*

gen·tle·folk (jĕnt'l-fōk') *pl.n.* Also **gen·tle·folks** (-fōks'). Persons of good family and breeding.

gen·tle·man (jĕnt'l-mən) *n., pl.* **-men** (-mĭn). **1.** A man of gentle or noble birth or superior social position. **2.** A polite, gracious, or considerate man with high standards of propriety or correct behavior. **3. a.** Any man. **b.** *Plural.* A form of address for a group of men. Used both in speech and writing. **4.** A manservant; a valet. **5.** *British.* Formerly, a man higher than a yeoman in social position. [GENTLE + MAN (after French *gentilhomme*).] —**gen'tle·man·ly** *adj.*

gen·tle·man-at-arms (jĕnt'l-mən-ət-ärmz') *n., pl.* **gentlemen-at-arms** (-mĭn-ət-ärmz'). Any of a military corps of 40 gentlemen who attend the British sovereign as a ceremonial guard on state occasions.

gentleman farmer *pl.* **gentlemen farmers.** A man who farms chiefly for pleasure rather than income or whose means permit him to be an absentee proprietor of his farming interests.

gentleman's agreement. An agreement guaranteed only by the honor of the participants.

gentleman's gentleman. A manservant; valet.

gentle sex. Women collectively.

gen·tle·wom·an (jĕnt'l-wŏŏm'ən) *n., pl.* **-women** (-wĭm'ĭn). **1.** A woman of gentle or noble birth or superior social position. **2.** A polite, gracious, or considerate woman. **3.** A woman acting as a personal attendant to a lady of rank.

Gen·too (jĕn-tōō') *n., pl.* **-toos.** *Archaic.* A Hindu. [Portuguese *gentio,* "a pagan," from Late Latin *gentīlis,* pagan, GENTILE.]

gen·try (jĕn'trē) *n.* **1.** People of gentle birth, good breeding, or high social position. **2.** The upper middle classes in England. **3.** People of a particular class or group. [Middle English *gentri(se),* gentle birth, from Old French *genterise, gentelise,* from *gentil,* GENTLE.]

gen·u·flect (jĕn'yə-flĕkt') *intr.v.* **-flected, -flecting, -flects. 1.** To bend the knee in a kneeling or half-kneeling position, as in worship. **2.** To exhibit a deferential or obsequious attitude or manner. [Late Latin *genuflectere* : Latin *genu,* knee (see **genu-[1]** in Appendix*) + *flectere,* to bend (see **flex**).]

gen·u·flec·tion (jĕn'yə-flĕk'shən) *n.* Also *chiefly British* **gen·u·flex·ion.** The act of kneeling briefly by bending one knee, as in worship or obeisance.

gen·u·ine (jĕn'yōō-ĭn) *adj.* **1.** Actually possessing or produced by the alleged or apparent attribute, character, or source; not artificial or fake; real; authentic: *genuine sorrow; genuine leather.* **2.** Not spurious or counterfeit; authentic. **3.** Free from hypocrisy or dishonesty; sincere; frank: *"She found behind his too incessant flattery a genuine affection for his mates"* (Sinclair Lewis). **4.** Being of pure or original stock: *a genuine Hawaiian.* —See Synonyms at **real.** [Latin *genuīnus,* perhaps originally "placed on the knees" (from the ancient custom that a father acknowledges a child by placing him or her on his knees), from *genu,* knee. See **genu-[1]** in Appendix.*]

ge·nus (jē'nəs) *n., pl.* **genera** (jĕn'ər-ə). *Abbr.* **gen. 1.** *Biology.* A taxonomic category ranking below a family and above a species, used in taxonomic nomenclature, either alone or followed by a Latin adjective or epithet, to form the name of a species. **2.** *Logic.* A class of objects divided into subordinate species having certain common attributes. **3.** Any class, group, or kind with common attributes: *"His temperament, formed by a modern genus of solitude"* (Wallace Fowlie). [Latin *genus,* birth, race, kind. See **gene-** in Appendix.*]

-geny. Indicates manner of origin or development; for example, **ontogeny.** [Greek *-geneia,* from *-genēs,* born. See **gene-** in Appendix.*]

geo–. Indicates the earth; for example, **geotropism, geology.** [Greek *geō-,* from *gē,* earth. See **gē** in Appendix.*]

ge·o·cen·tric (jē′ō-sĕn′trĭk) *adj.* **1.** Pertaining to, measured from, or observed from the center of the earth. **2.** Having the earth as a center. —**ge′o·cen′tri·cal·ly** *adv.*

ge·o·chem·is·try (jē′ō-kĕm′ĭ-strē) *n.* The chemistry of the composition and alterations of the earth's crust. —**ge′o·chem′i·cal** *adj.* —**ge′o·chem′ist** *n.*

ge·o·chro·nol·o·gy (jē′ō-krə-nŏl′ə-jē) *n.* The chronology of the earth's history as determined by geological events.

ge·ode (jē′ōd′) *n.* A small, hollow, usually spheroidal rock with crystals lining the inside wall. [Latin *geōdēs*, from Greek, earthlike : *gē*, earth (see **gē** in Appendix*) + -ODE (resembling).]

ge·o·des·ic (jē′ə-dĕs′ĭk) *adj.* **1.** *Mathematics.* Of or pertaining to the geometry of geodesics. **2.** Geodetic. —*n. Mathematics.* In three-dimensional Euclidean space, a curve whose principal normal at any point is the normal to the surface on which the curve occurs; the shortest line between two points on any mathematically derived surface.

geodesic dome. A domed or vaulted structure of lightweight straight elements that form interlocking polygons.

ge·od·e·sy (jē-ŏd′ə-sē) *n.* The geological science of the size and shape of the earth. [French *geodesie*, from New Latin *geodaesia*, from Greek *geōdaisia*, "division of the earth" : GEO + *daiesthai*, to divide (see **dā-** in Appendix*).] —**ge·od′e·sist** *n.*

ge·o·det·ic (jē′ə-dĕt′ĭk) *adj.* **1.** Of or pertaining to geodesy. **2.** Geodesic. —**ge′o·det′i·cal·ly** *adv.*

geo·duck (gōō′ē-dŭk′) *n.* Also **gwe·duc.** A very large, edible clam, *Panope generosa*, of the Pacific coast of northwestern North America. [Chinook jargon *go-duck.*]

Geof·frey. Variant of **Jeffrey.**

Geof·frey of Mon·mouth (jĕf′rē; mŏn′məth). 1100?-1154. Welsh bishop and historian; collector of Arthurian legends.

geog. geographer; geographic; geography.

ge·og·no·sy (jē-ŏg′nə-sē) *n.* The scientific study of the organization and structure of the earth and its materials. [GEO- + Greek *-gnosia*, knowledge, -GNOSIS.]

ge·o·graph·ic (jē′ə-grăf′ĭk) *adj.* Also **ge·o·graph·i·cal** (-ĭ-kəl). *Abbr.* **geog. 1.** Pertaining to geography. **2.** Concerning topography of a specific region. —**ge′o·graph′i·cal·ly** *adv.*

geographic mile. A nautical mile.

ge·og·ra·phy (jē-ŏg′rə-fē) *n., pl.* **-phies.** *Abbr.* **geog. 1.** The study of the earth and its features and of the distribution on the earth of life, including human life and the effects of human activity. **2.** The geographic characteristics of any area. **3.** A book on geography. **4.** An ordered arrangement of constituent elements. [Latin *geōgraphia*, from Greek : GEO- + -GRAPHY.] —**ge·og′ra·pher** *n.*

ge·oid (jē′oid′) *n.* The hypothetical surface of the earth that coincides everywhere with mean sea level. [German *Geoid*, from Greek *geoidēs*, earthlike : GE(O)- + -OID.]

geol. geologic; geologist; geology.

ge·ol·o·gize (jē-ŏl′ə-jīz′) *intr.v.* **-gized, -gizing, -gizes.** To study geology or make geological investigations.

ge·ol·o·gy (jē-ŏl′ə-jē) *n., pl.* **-gies.** *Abbr.* **geol. 1.** The scientific study of the origin, history, and structure of the earth. **2.** The structure of a specific region of the earth's surface: *the geology of the Hudson River valley.* [New Latin *geologia* : GEO- + -LOGY.] —**ge′o·log′ic** (jē′ə-lŏj′ĭk), **ge′o·log′i·cal** *adj.* —**ge′o·log′i·cal·ly** *adv.* —**ge·ol′o·gist, ge·ol′o·ger** *n.*

geom. geometric; geometry.

geomagnetic equator. The great circle on the earth's surface formed by the intersection of a plane passing through the earth's center perpendicular to the axis connecting the north and south magnetic poles. It is the geometric rationalization of the empirically defined **magnetic equator** *(see).*

ge·o·mag·ne·tism (jē′ō-măg′nə-tĭz′əm) *n.* **1.** The magnetism of the earth. **2.** The study of the earth's magnetic field. —**ge′o·mag·net′ic** (-nĕt′ĭk) *adj.* —**ge′o·mag·net′i·cal·ly** *adv.*

ge·o·man·cy (jē′ə-măn′sē) *n.* Divination by means of lines and figures. [Middle English, from Old French *geomancie*, from Medieval Latin *geōmantia*, from Late Greek *geōmanteia*, divination from signs obtained from the earth : GEO- + -MANCY.] —**ge′o·man′cer** *n.* —**ge′o·man′tic** *adj.*

ge·o·met·ric (jē′ə-mĕt′rĭk) *adj.* Also **ge·o·met·ri·cal** (-rĭk-əl). *Abbr.* **geom. 1.** Of or pertaining to geometry, its methods and principles. **2.** Using simple geometrical forms in design and decoration. —**ge′o·met′ri·cal·ly** *adv.*

geometric mean. The *n*th root, usually the positive *n*th root, of a product of *n* factors.

geometric progression. A sequence of terms, such as 1, 3, 9, 27, 81, each of which is a constant multiple of the immediately preceding term.

ge·om·e·trid (jē-ŏm′ə-trĭd) *n.* Any of various moths of the family Geometridae, having caterpillars that move by looping the body in alternate contractions and expansions and are commonly called "measuring worms" or "inchworms." —*adj.* Of or belonging to the Geometridae. [New Latin *Geometridae*, "land measurers" (from the movement of the caterpillars), from Latin *geōmetrēs*, geometrician, from Greek, from *geōmetrein*, to measure land. See **geometry.**]

ge·om·e·trize (jē-ŏm′ə-trīz′) *intr.v.* **-trized, -trizing, -trizes. 1.** To study geometry. **2.** To apply the methods of geometry.

ge·om·e·try (jē-ŏm′ə-trē) *n., pl.* **-tries.** *Abbr.* **geom. 1. a.** The mathematics of the properties, measurement, and relationships of points, lines, angles, surfaces, and solids. **b.** A system of geometry: *Euclidean geometry.* **c.** A geometry restricted to a class of problems or objects: *solid geometry.* **2.** Configuration; arrangement. **3.** A surface shape. **4.** Any physical arrangement suggesting geometric forms or lines. [Middle English, from Old French *geometrie*, from Latin *geōmetria*, from Greek, from *geōmetrein*, to measure land : GEO- + *metrein*, to measure, from *metron*, measure (see **mē-²** in Appendix*).] —**ge·om′e·tri′cian** (jē-ŏm′ə-trĭsh′ən, jē′ə-mə-), **ge·om′e·ter** *n.*

ge·o·mor·phic (jē′ə-môr′fĭk) *adj.* Of, relating to, or resembling the earth, its shape, or surface configuration. [GEO- + -MORPHIC.]

ge·o·mor·phol·o·gy (jē′ō-môr-fŏl′ə-jē) *n.* The geological study of the configuration and evolution of land forms. Also called "morphology." —**ge′o·mor′pho·log′ic** (-fə-lŏj′ĭk), **ge′o·mor′pho·log′i·cal** *adj.* —**ge′o·mor′pho·log′i·cal·ly** *adv.*

ge·oph·a·gy (jē-ŏf′ə-jē) *n.* The practice of eating earthy substances, such as clay. [GEO- + -PHAGY.] —**ge·oph′a·gism′** *n.* —**ge·oph′a·gist** *n.*

ge·o·phys·ics (jē′ō-fĭz′ĭks) *n.* Plural in form, used with a singular verb. The physics of geological phenomena, including fields such as meteorology, oceanography, geodesy, and seismology.

GEOLOGIC TIME SCALE

ERA	PERIOD	EPOCH	YEARS BEFORE THE PRESENT
Cenozoic	Quarternary	Holocene (Recent)	11,000
		Pleistocene (Glacial)	500,000 to 2,000,000
	Tertiary	Pliocene	13,000,000
		Miocene	25,000,000
		Oligocene	36,000,000
		Eocene	58,000,000
		Paleocene	63,000,000
Mesozoic	Cretaceous		135,000,000
	Jurassic		180,000,000
	Triassic		230,000,000
Paleozoic	Permian		280,000,000
	Carboniferous	Pennsylvanian (Upper Carboniferous)	310,000,000
		Mississippian (Lower Carboniferous)	345,000,000
	Devonian		405,000,000
	Silurian		425,000,000
	Ordovician		500,000,000
	Cambrian		600,000,000
Precambrian			

ă pat/ā pay/âr care/ä father/b bib/ch church/d deed/ĕ pet/ē be/f fife/g gag/h hat/hw which/ĭ pit/ī pie/îr pier/j judge/k kick/l lid, needle/m mum/n no, sudden/ng thing/ŏ pot/ō toe/ô paw, for/oi noise/ou out/ŏŏ took/ōō boot/p pop/r roar/s sauce/sh ship, dish/t tight/th thin, path/*th* this, bathe/ŭ cut/ûr urge/v valve/w with/y yes/z zebra, size/zh vision/ə about, item, edible, gallop, circus/à *Fr.* ami/œ *Fr.* feu, *Ger.* schön/ü *Fr.* tu, *Ger.* über/KH *Ger.* ich, *Scot.* loch/N *Fr.* bon. *Follows main vocabulary. †Of obscure origin.

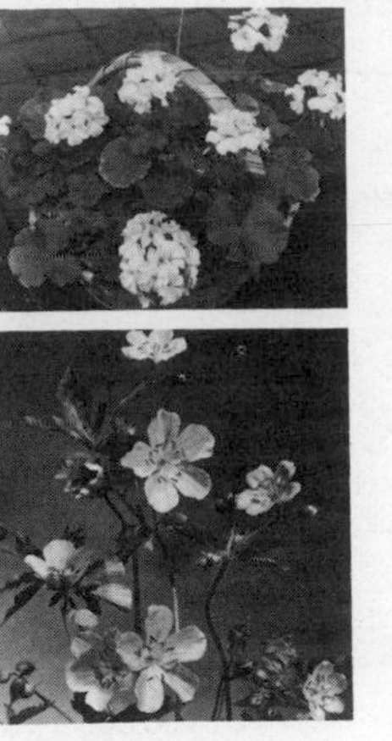

geranium
Above: Pelargonium domesticum
Below: Geranium maculatum

ge·o·phyte (jē′ə-fīt′) *n. Botany.* A perennial plant propagated by underground buds. [GEO- + -PHYTE.]

ge·o·pol·i·tics (jē′ō-pŏl′ə-tĭks) *n.* Plural in form, used with a singular verb. **1.** The study of the relationship between politics and geography. **2.** A Nazi doctrine of expansion that concentrated on the reallocation of geographic, economical, and political boundaries. —**ge′o·po·lit′i·cal** (-pə-lĭt′ĭ-kəl) *adj.*

ge·o·pon·ic (jē′ə-pŏn′ĭk) *adj.* **1.** Of or relating to agriculture or farming. **2.** Rustic; bucolic. [Greek *geōponikos,* from *geōponia,* tillage, from *geōponein,* to till land : GEO- + *ponein,* to toil, labor (see **spen-** in Appendix*).]

ge·o·pon·ics (jē′ə-pŏn′ĭks) *n.* Plural in form, used with a singular verb. The study or science of agriculture.

Geor·die (jôr′dē) *n. Scottish.* A guinea. [Diminutive of GEORGE (from the image of Saint George formerly stamped on it).]

George[1] (jôrj). A masculine given name. [Middle English, from Old French *George(s),* from Late Latin *Geōrgius,* from Greek *Geōrgios,* from *geōrgos,* farmer. See **georgic.**]

George[2] (jôrj). A river rising in northern Quebec, Canada, on the Labrador boundary, and flowing 365 miles northwest to Ungava Bay.

George[3] (jôrj) *n.* A jeweled figure of Saint George killing the dragon, used as an insignia of the Knights of the Garter.

George[4] (jôrj) *n.* An English coin during the reign of Henry VIII, imprinted with a figure of Saint George.

George I (jôrj). 1660–1727. King of Great Britain and Ireland (1714–27); elector of Hanover (1698–1727).

George II (jôrj). 1683–1760. King of Great Britain and Ireland (1727–60); elector of Hanover (1727–60); son of George I.

George III (jôrj). 1738–1820. King of Great Britain and Ireland (1760–1820); king of Hanover (1815–20); grandson of George II; lost American colonies.

George IV (jôrj). 1762–1830. King of Great Britain and Ireland and king of Hanover (1820–30); son of George III.

George V (jôrj). 1865–1936. King of Great Britain and Northern Ireland and Emperor of India (1910–36); son of Edward VII.

George VI (jôrj). 1895–1952. King of Great Britain and Northern Ireland (1936–52); Emperor of India (1936–48); son of George V; brother of Edward VIII; father of Elizabeth II.

George, David Lloyd. See **Lloyd George.**

George (jôrj), **Henry.** 1839–1897. American economist.

George, Lake (jôrj). **1.** A lake about 11 miles long, formed by a widening of the St. Johns River in northeastern Florida. **2.** A lake extending 33 miles in the Adirondack foothills of northeastern New York State.

George (jôrj), **Saint.** Christian martyr of the early fourth century A.D.; patron saint of England (from the 14th century).

Ge·or·ge (gē-ôr′gə), **Stefan.** 1868–1933. German poet.

George Town. The former name for **Penang.**

George·town (jôrj′toun). **1.** The capital and chief seaport of Guyana, in the north at the mouth of the Demerara River. Population, 78,000. **2.** A section of western Washington, D.C. **3.** The capital of the Caymans, on Grand Cayman Island. Population, 3,000.

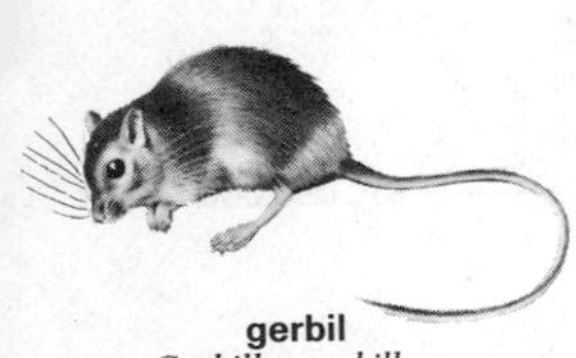

gerbil
Gerbillus gerbillus

Geor·gette crepe (jôr-jĕt′). A sheer, strong silk or silklike fabric with a dull, creped surface, used for dresses, blouses, or trimming. Also called "georgette." [Originally a trademark, after Madame *Georgette* de la Plante, a French modiste.]

George Washington Birthplace National Monument. An area comprising 394 acres of northeastern Virginia, the site of the house where George Washington was born.

Geor·gia (jôr′jə). **1.** *Abbr.* **Ga.** A Southern Atlantic state of the United States, one of the original 13 states, 58,876 square miles in area. Population, 4,357,000. Capital, Atlanta. See map at **United States of America.** **2.** *Russian* **Gru·zi·ya** (grōō′zyĭ-yə). An ancient and medieval kingdom coextensive with the present-day Georgian S.S.R. **3.** The Georgian S.S.R.

Geor·gia, Strait of (jôr′jə). A channel 150 miles long bordered on the west by Vancouver Island, on the east and northeast by the mainland of British Columbia, and on the southeast by Washington State.

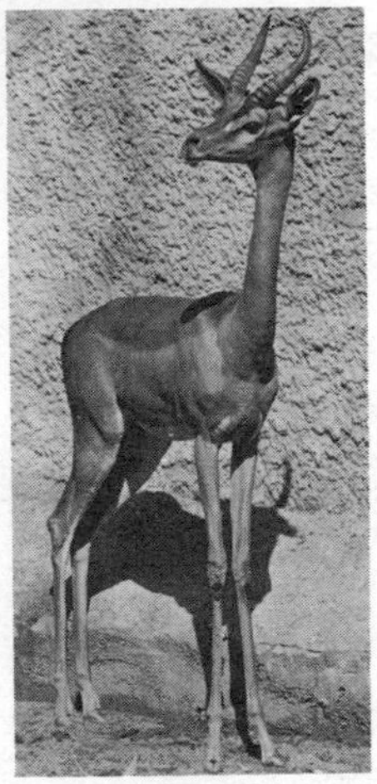

gerenuk

Geor·gian (jôr′jən) *adj.* **1.** Of, pertaining to, or characteristic of the reigns of the four Georges who ruled Great Britain from 1714 to 1830. **2.** Pertaining to the U.S. state of Georgia or to its inhabitants. **3.** Pertaining to the Georgian S.S.R, or to its people or their language. —*n.* **1.** A native or inhabitant of the state of Georgia. **2.** A native or inhabitant of the Georgian S.S.R. **3.** The language of Caucasian Georgia. **4.** A person belonging to or whose style is imitative of the period of the first four Georges of England.

Georgian Bay. An inlet of Lake Huron 125 miles long, in southeastern Ontario, Canada.

Georgian Soviet Socialist Republic. A constituent republic, 26,875 square miles in area, of the U.S.S.R., south of the Caucasus Mountains and bordered on the west by the Black Sea. Population, 4,271,000. Capital, Tiflis.

geor·gic (jôr′jĭk) *adj.* Also **geor·gi·cal** (-jĭ-kəl). Of or pertaining to agriculture or rural life. —*n.* **1.** *Capital* **G.** *Plural.* A poem by Virgil in four books, concerning agriculture and country life. **2.** Any poem concerning farming or rural life; a bucolic. [Latin *Georgica,* from Greek *geōrgika,* cultivated lands, from neuter plural of *geōrgikos,* agricultural, from *geōrgos,* farmer, "(one) tilling the soil" : GEO- + *ergon,* work (see **werg-**[1] in Appendix*).]

ge·o·stroph·ic (jē′ō-strŏf′ĭk) *adj.* Of or pertaining to force caused by the earth's rotation. [GEO- + Greek *strophē,* a turning, STROPHE.]

ge·o·syn·cline (jē′ō-sĭn′klīn′) *n.* An extensive, usually linear depression in the earth's crust in which a succession of sedimentary strata have accumulated. [GEO- + SYNCLINE.]

ge·o·tax·is (jē′ō-tăk′sĭs) *n. Biology.* The movement of an organism in response to the forces of gravity. —**ge′o·tac′tic** (-tăk′tĭk) *adj.* —**ge′o·tac′ti·cal·ly** *adv.*

ge·o·tec·ton·ic (jē′ō-tĕk-tŏn′ĭk) *adj.* Of or relating to the shape, structure, and arrangement of the rock masses constituting the earth's crust.

ge·o·ther·mal (jē′ō-thûr′məl) *adj.* Also **ge·o·ther·mic** (-mĭk). Pertaining to the internal heat of the earth.

ge·ot·ro·pism (jē-ŏt′rə-pĭz′əm) *n. Biology.* The response of a living organism to gravity, as the downward growth of plant roots. [GEO- + -TROPISM.] —**ge′o·trop′ic** (jē′ō-trŏp′ĭk) *adj.* —**ge′o·trop′i·cal·ly** *adv.*

ger. gerund.

Ger. German; Germany.

Ge·ra (gā′rə). A city of East Germany, in the south-central part of the country. Population, 103,000.

ge·rah (gē′rə) *n.* A Hebrew coin and unit of weight; $1/20$ of a shekel. [Hebrew *gērāh,* "bean."]

Ge·raint (jə-rānt′). In Arthurian legend, a knight of the Round Table and husband of Enid.

Ger·ald (jĕr′əld). A masculine given name. [Middle English, from Old French *Giraut,* from Old High German *Gēr(w)ald,* "spear wielder" : *gēr,* spear (see **ghaiso-** in Appendix*) + *waldan,* to rule (see **wal-** in Appendix*).]

Ger·al·dine (jĕr′əl-dēn′). A feminine given name. [Feminine of GERALD.]

ge·ra·ni·al (jĭ-rā′nē-əl) *n.* A perfume and flavoring ingredient, **citral** *(see).* [GERANI(UM) + -AL (aldehyde).]

ge·ra·ni·ol (jĭ-rā′nē-ôl′, -ōl′) *n.* A fragrant pale-yellow liquid, $C_{10}H_{18}O$, derived chiefly from the oils of geranium and citronella, and used in cosmetics and flavorings. [GERANI(UM) + -OL (alcohol).]

ge·ra·ni·um (jĭ-rā′nē-əm) *n.* **1.** Any of various plants of the genus *Geranium,* having divided leaves and pink or purplish flowers. Also called "cranesbill." **2.** Any of various plants of the genus *Pelargonium,* native chiefly to southern Africa; especially, *P. domesticum,* widely cultivated for its rounded, often variegated leaves and showy clusters of red, pink, or white flowers. **3.** Strong to vivid red. See **color.** [Latin, from Greek *geranion,* "small crane" (because the fruit resembles a crane's bill), from *geranos,* crane. See **ger-**[4] in Appendix.*]

Ge·rard (jĭ-rärd′). A masculine given name. [Middle English, from Old French *Girart, Gerart,* from Old High German *Gērhart,* "strong with the spear" : *gēr,* spear (see **ghaiso-** in Appendix*) + *hart,* hard, hardy (see **kar-**[1] in Appendix*).]

ger·bil (jûr′bĭl) *n.* Any of various small, mouselike rodents of the genus *Gerbillus* and related genera, of arid regions of Africa and Asia Minor, having long hind legs and a long tail. [French *gerbille,* from New Latin *Gerbillus,* diminutive of *gerboa, jerboa,* JERBOA.]

ge·rent (jîr′ənt) *n. Rare.* A ruler or manager; overseer. [Latin *gerēns,* present participle of *gerere,* to carry, conduct, govern. See **gerere** in Appendix.*]

ge·re·nuk (gĕr′ə-nŏŏk′) *n.* An African gazelle, *Litocranius walleri,* having long legs, a long, slender neck, and backward curving horns in the male. [Somali *garanug.*]

ger·fal·con. Variant of **gyrfalcon.**

ger·i·at·ric (jĕr′ē-ăt′rĭk) *adj.* **1.** Of or pertaining to geriatrics. **2.** Of or pertaining to the aged or their characteristic afflictions: *geriatric problems.* —*n.* An aged person viewed as an object of geriatrics or geriatric care: *"the tea-and-toast geriatric . . . too enfeebled to shop for food and cook"* (New York Times). [Greek *gēras,* old age (see **ger-**[2] in Appendix*) + -IATRIC.]

ger·i·at·rics (jĕr′ē-ăt′rĭks) *n.* Plural in form, used with a singular verb. The medical study of the physiology and pathology of old age. —**ger′i·a·tri′cian** (-ə-trĭsh′ən), **ger′i·at′rist** (jĕr′ē-ăt′rĭst, jĭ-rī′ə-trĭst) *n.*

Gé·ri·cault (zhā-rē-kō′), **Jean Louis André Théodore.** 1791–1824. French painter.

Ger·la·chov·ka (gĕr′lə-kôf′kə). The highest (8,737 feet) of the Carpathian Mountains, situated in eastern Czechoslovakia.

germ (jûrm) *n.* **1.** *Biology.* A small organic structure or cell from which a new organism may develop. **2.** Something that may serve as the basis of further growth or development: *the germ of a program.* **3.** *Medicine.* A microorganism; especially, a pathogen. [French *germe,* from Latin *germen,* offshoot, sprout, fetus. See **gene-** in Appendix.*]

Synonyms: *germ, microbe, bacteria, bacillus, virus.* These nouns denote minute organisms or agents, invisible to the unaided human eye, some of which are related to the production of disease. They are not interchangeable in careful usage except as indicated. *Germ* and *microbe* are nonscientific terms for such microorganisms; in popular usage they usually refer to disease-producing bodies. *Bacteria* (plural of *bacterium*) is the scientific term for a large group of microorganisms, only some of which produce disease. Many others are active in processes beneficial or not harmful to human, animal, and plant life. *Bacillus* is the scientific designation for a specific class of bacteria that includes some disease-producing microorganisms; only in loose popular usage is the term employed as the equivalent of any bacterium or any pathogenic bacterium. *Virus* is the technical term for any of a group of extremely small infective agents capable of producing certain diseases in human, animal, and plant life.

ger·man[1] (jûr′mən) *n.* **1.** A cotillion. **2.** A party for dancing a cotillion. [Short for *German cotillion.*]

ger·man² (jûr′mən) *adj.* **1.** Having the same parents, or having the same grandparents on one side. Obsolete except as the second element in combinations: *cousin-german.* **2.** Related; germane. [Middle English *germa(i)n,* from Old French *germain,* from Latin *germānus,* "from the same race," from *germen,* offshoot, fetus. See **gene-** in Appendix.*]

Ger·man (jûr′mən) *adj. Abbr.* **Ger.** Of, pertaining to, or characteristic of Germany, its people, or their language. —*n. Abbr.* **Ger. 1. a.** A native or citizen of Germany. **b.** A person of German descent. **2.** The West Germanic language spoken in Germany, Austria, and part of Switzerland. [Middle English *Germanes,* Teutons, Germans, from Latin *Germānus,* German, perhaps from Celtic, akin to Old Irish *gair*†, neighbor.]

German Baptist Brethren. A sect of German-American Baptists, the **Dunkers** *(see).*

German cockroach. The **Croton bug** *(see).*

German Democratic Republic. See **Germany.**

ger·man·der (jər-măn′dər) *n.* Any of various usually aromatic plants of the genus *Teucrium,* having purplish or reddish flowers. [Middle English *germandre,* from Old French *germandree,* from Medieval Latin *germandra,* alteration of *gama(n)drea,* from Latin *chamadreos,* from Greek *khamaidrus,* "ground oak" : *khamai,* on the ground (see **dhghem-** in Appendix*) + *drus,* oak (see **deru-** in Appendix*).]

ger·mane (jər-mān′) *adj.* Having a significant bearing upon a point at hand; related; pertinent. Usually used with *to.* See Synonyms at **relevant.** [Middle English *germa(i)n,* having the same parents, GERMAN.]

German East Af·ri·ca (ăf′rĭ-kə). A former German protectorate in eastern Africa (1885–1922).

German Federal Republic. See **Germany.**

Ger·man·ic (jûr-măn′ĭk) *adj.* **1. a.** Characteristic of Germany, any of the German people, or their culture. **b.** Of or pertaining to Teutons. **c.** Of or pertaining to people who speak a Germanic language. **2.** Of, pertaining to, or constituting the Germanic languages. —*n.* **1.** A branch of the Indo-European language family, divided into North Germanic, West Germanic, and East Germanic. **2.** Proto-Germanic.

Ger·man·ism (jûr′mə-nĭz′əm) *n.* **1.** An attitude, custom, or the like that seems characteristically German. **2.** A German idiom or phrasing appearing in another language. **3.** Esteem for Germany and emulation of German ways.

ger·ma·ni·um (jər-mā′nē-əm) *n. Symbol* **Ge** A brittle, crystalline, gray-white metalloid element, widely used as a semiconductor, as an alloying agent and catalyst, and in certain optical glasses. Atomic number 32, atomic weight 72.59, melting point 937.4°C, boiling point 2,830°C, specific gravity 5.323 (25°C), valences 2, 4. [New Latin, from Latin *Germānia,* Germany, from Latin *Germānus,* GERMAN.]

Ger·man·ize (jûr′mə-nīz′) *v.* **-ized, -izing, -izes.** —*tr.* **1.** To give a German quality to; make German. **2.** *Archaic.* To translate into German. —*intr.* To adopt German customs or attitudes. —**Ger′man·i·za′tion** *n.* —**Ger′man·iz′er** *n.*

German measles. A mild, contagious, eruptive disease caused by a virus spread in droplet sprays from the nose and throat and capable of causing congenital defects in infants born to mothers infected during the first three months of pregnancy. Also called "rubella," "rubeola."

German New Gui·nea (gĭn′ē). A former German colony including northeastern New Guinea and the Bismarck Archipelago, under Australian administration since 1914.

Ger·man·o·phile (jər-măn′ə-fīl′) *n.* One who loves Germany and German things. [Latin *Germānus,* GERMAN + -PHILE.]

Ger·man·o·phobe (jər-măn′ə-fōb′) *n.* One who hates or has an obsessive fear of Germany and German things. [Latin *Germānus,* GERMAN + -PHOBE.]

German shepherd. A large dog of a breed developed in Germany, having a dense brownish or black coat, and often trained to assist the police and the blind. Also called "police dog," and in Great Britain "Alsatian."

German silver. Formerly, an alloy, **nickel silver** *(see).*

German Southwest Af·ri·ca (ăf′rĭ-kə). A former German colony, now South-West Africa, mandated to South Africa in 1919.

Ger·ma·ny (jûr′mə-nē). *German* **Deutsch·land** (doich′länt′). *Abbr.* **Ger.** A former state of central Europe bordered in the north by the North and Baltic seas and divided in 1949 into the **German Democratic Republic** (East Germany), 41,535 square miles in area (population 17,136,000; capital, East Berlin); and the **German Federal Republic** (West Germany), 95,914 square miles in area (population, 57,974,000; capital, Bonn).

germ cell. A cell having reproduction as its principal function; especially, an egg or sperm cell.

ger·mi·cide (jûr′mə-sīd′) *n.* Any agent that kills germs. [GERM + -CIDE.] —**ger′mi·ci′dal** (-sīd′l) *adj.*

ger·mi·nal (jûr′mə-nəl) *adj.* **1.** Of, pertaining to, or having the nature of a germ cell. **2.** Of, in, or pertaining to the earliest stage of development. [French, from Latin *germen* (stem *germin-*), offshoot, GERM.]

germinal disc. A disklike region from which the embryo begins to develop in certain ova. Also called "blastodisc."

germinal vesicle. *Embryology.* The nucleus of an oocyte.

ger·mi·nant (jûr′mə-nənt) *adj.* Germinating; sprouting.

ger·mi·nate (jûr′mə-nāt′) *v.* **-nated, -nating, -nates.** —*intr.* To begin to grow; sprout. —*tr.* To cause to sprout. [Latin *germināre,* to sprout, from *germen* (stem *germin-*), sprout, GERM.] —**ger′mi·na·ble** (-nə-bəl), **ger′mi·na′tive** *adj.* —**ger′mi·na′tion** *n.* —**ger′mi·na′tor** (-nā′tər) *n.*

Ger·mis·ton (jûr′mĭ-stən). A city and gold-refining center of South Africa, in southern Transvaal nine miles east of Johannesburg. Population, 148,000.

germ layer. Any of three cellular layers, the ectoderm, endoderm, or mesoderm, into which most animal embryos differentiate.

germ plasm. 1. The cytoplasm of a germ cell. **2.** Germ cells collectively. **3.** Hereditary material; genes.

germ theory. The doctrine that infectious diseases are caused by the activity of microorganisms within the body.

Ge·ro·na (jə-rō′nə). A city of northeastern Spain, in Catalonia, 50 miles northeast of Barcelona. Population, 28,000.

Ge·ron·i·mo (jə-rŏn′ə-mō′). 1829–1909. American Indian leader; chief of the Apaches; campaigned against whites (1885–86).

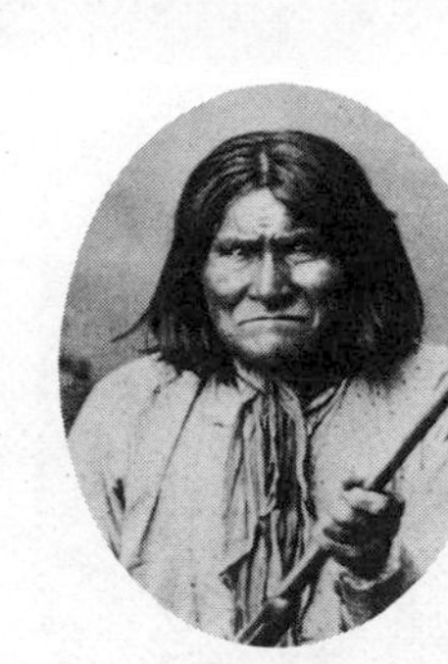

Geronimo

geronto-, geront-. Indicates old people or old age; for example, **gerontology.** [French *géronto-,* from Greek *gerōn* (stem *geront-*), old man. See **ger-²** in Appendix.*]

ger·on·toc·ra·cy (jĕr′ən-tŏk′rə-sē) *n., pl.* **-cies. 1.** Government based on rule by the elders. **2.** A governing group of elders. [French *gérontocratie* : GERONTO- + -CRACY.] —**ge·ron′to·crat′ic** (jə-rŏn′tō-krăt′ĭk) *adj.*

ger·on·tol·o·gy (jer′ən-tŏl′ə-jē) *n.* The scientific study of the physiological and pathological phenomena associated with aging. [GERONTO- + -LOGY.] —**ger′on·to·log′i·cal** (jə-rŏnt′l-ŏj′ĭ-kəl) *adj.* —**ger′on·tol′o·gist** *n.*

Ger·ry (gĕr′ē), **Elbridge.** 1744–1814. Vice President of the United States under James Madison (1813–14); died in office.

ger·ry·man·der (jĕr′ē-măn′dər, gĕr′-) *v.* **-dered, -dering, -ders.** —*intr.* To divide a state, county, or city into voting districts to give unfair advantage to one party in elections. —*tr.* **1.** To divide (a voting area) in this manner. **2.** To machinate or alter to one's own advantage. —*n.* An act, process, or instance of gerrymandering. [Elbridge GERRY + (SALA)MANDER, from the shape of an election district formed (1812) in Massachusetts while Gerry was governor.]

Gersh·win (gûrsh′wĭn), **George.** 1898–1937. American composer.

Ger·trude (gûr′trōōd′). A feminine given name. [French, from German, from Old High German *Gērdrūd.* See **ghaiso-** in Appendix.*]

ger·und (jĕr′ənd) *n. Abbr.* **ger. 1.** In Latin, a verbal form that can be used as a noun in all singular cases except the nominative, while conveying the meaning of the verb; for example, in the phrase *modus vivendi* (a manner of living), *vivendi* is a gerund, formed from the verb *vivere,* to live. **2.** In English, the verbal form ending in *-ing* when used as a noun, while conveying the meaning of the verb; for example, in the sentences *Cooking is an art* and *I don't like cooking, cooking* is a gerund formed from the verb *cook.* **3.** The analogous grammatical form in some other languages. —See Usage note at **participle.** [Late Latin *gerundium,* from Latin *gerundum, gerendum,* acting, carrying, gerund of *gerere,* to carry, act. See **gerere** in Appendix.*] —**ge·run′di·al** (jə-rŭn′dē-əl) *adj.*

ge·run·dive (jə-rŭn′dĭv) *n.* **1.** In Latin, a verbal adjective with the construction of a future passive participle, suggesting fitness or propriety, necessity, or imminence; for example, in the sentence *Legibus parendum est* ("The laws must be obeyed" or "The laws are to be obeyed"), *parendum* is a gerundive. **2.** The analogous grammatical form or construction in some other languages. —*adj.* **1.** Pertaining to or like a gerundive. **2.** Pertaining to or like a gerund. [Middle English *gerundif,* from Late Latin *gerundīvus,* from *gerundium,* GERUND.]

Ge·ry·on (jîr′ē-ən, gĕr′-). *Greek Mythology.* A winged monster with three heads or three bodies who was robbed of his herd and slain by Hercules.

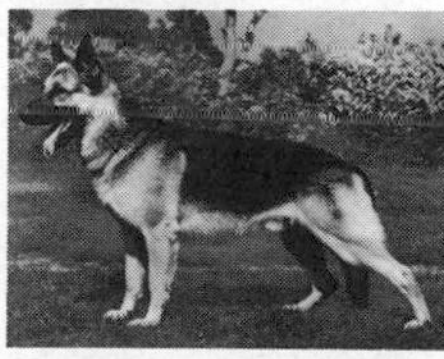

German shepherd

Ge·sell (gə-zĕl′), **Arnold Lucius.** 1880–1961. American psychologist and pediatrician.

Ges·ner (gĕs′nər), **Konrad von.** 1516–1565. Swiss naturalist and encyclopedist.

ges·so (jĕs′ō) *n.* **1.** A preparation of plaster of Paris and glue used as a base for low relief or as a surface for painting. **2.** A surface of this preparation. [Italian, gypsum, chalk, from Latin *gypsum,* GYPSUM.]

gest, geste¹ (jĕst) *n. Archaic.* **1.** A feat or exploit; notable deed. **2. a.** A verse romance or tale. **b.** A prose romance. [Middle English *geste, jeste,* from Old French, from Latin *gesta,* actions, exploits, from *gestus,* past participle of *gerere,* to act, carry. See **gerere** in Appendix.*]

gest, geste² (jĕst) *n. Archaic.* **1.** Mien or bearing. **2.** A gesture. [Old French *geste,* from Latin *gestus.* See **gesture.**]

ge·stalt, Ge·stalt (gə-shtält′, -shtôlt′) *n., pl.* **-stalts** or **-stalten** (-shtält′n, -shtôlt′n). A unified physical, psychological, or symbolic configuration having properties that cannot be derived from its parts. [German *Gestalt,* form, shape, from Middle High German *gestalt,* from *ungestalt,* deformity, from Old High German *ungistalt,* ugly : *un-,* not + *gistalt,* past participle of *stellen,* to set, place (see **stel-¹** in Appendix*).]

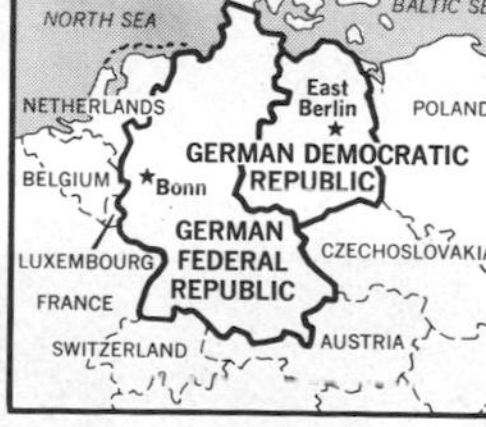

Germany

gestalt psychology. Also **Gestalt psychology.** A psychological school or doctrine holding that psychological phenomena are irreducible gestalts.

Ge·sta·po (gə-stä′pō; *German* gə-shtä′pō) *n.* The German internal security police as organized under the Nazi regime. [German, short for *Ge(heime) Sta(ats)po(lizei),* "secret state police."]

Ges·ta Ro·ma·no·rum (jĕs′tə rō′mə-nôr′əm, -nōr′əm). An anthology of popular tales in Latin, collected in England at the turn of the 14th century, and used as a historical source by Chaucer and Shakespeare. [Latin, deeds of the Romans.]

ges·tate (jĕs′tāt′) *tr.v.* **-tated, -tating, -tates. 1.** To carry (un-

born young) within the uterus for a period following conception. **2.** To conceive and develop (a plan or idea, for example) in the mind. [Back-formation from GESTATION.]

ges·ta·tion (jĕ-stā′shən) *n.* **1.** The period of carrying developing offspring in the uterus after conception; pregnancy. **2.** The development or duration of development of a plan or idea in the mind. [Latin *gestātiō*, from *gestāre*, frequentative of *gerere* (past participle *gestus*), to carry, bear. See **gerere** in Appendix.*] —**ges′ta·to′ry** (jĕs′tə-tôr′ē, -tōr′ē) *adj.*

ges·tic (jĕs′tĭk) *adj.* Pertaining to movement of the body, especially in dancing. [From GEST (bearing).]

ges·tic·u·late (jĕ-stĭk′yə-lāt′) *v.* **-lated, -lating, -lates.** —*intr.* To make deliberate and vigorous motions or gestures, especially as an expression complementing or substituting for speech. —*tr.* To say or express by gestures. [Latin *gesticulārī*, from *gesticulus*, diminutive of *gestus*, action, GEST.] —**ges·tic′u·la′tive** *adj.* —**ges·tic′u·la′tor** (-lā′tər) *n.*

ges·tic·u·la·tion (jĕ-stĭk′yə-lā′shən) *n.* **1.** The act of gesticulating. **2.** A deliberate and vigorous motion or gesture: *"above all things avoid any peculiar gesticulations of the body"* (Lord Chatham). —**ges·tic′u·la·to′ry** (-lə-tôr′ē, -tōr′ē) *adj.*

ges·ture (jĕs′chər) *n.* **1.** A motion of the limbs or body made to express or help express thought or to emphasize speech. **2.** The act of moving the limbs or body as an expression of thought or emphasis. **3.** Any act or expression made as a sign, often formal, of intention or attitude; especially, a sign of friendship or good intentions. —*v.* **gestured, -turing, -tures.** —*intr.* To make gestures. —*tr.* To show, express, or direct by gestures. [Medieval Latin *gestūra*, bearing, carriage, from Latin *gestus*, past participle of *gerere*, to carry, act. See **gerere** in Appendix.*] —**ges′tur·er** *n.*

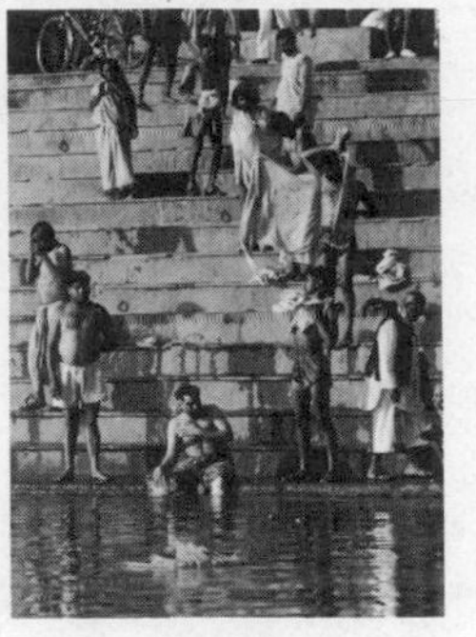

ghat
Bathing ghat leading to the Jumna River in Old Delhi, India

Ge·sund·heit (gə-zŏŏnt′hīt′) *interj. German.* Used to wish good health to a person who has just sneezed.

get (gĕt; gĭt *for intransitive sense 5*) *v.* **got** (gŏt) or *archaic* **gat** (găt), **got** or **gotten** (gŏt′n), **getting, gets.** —*tr.* **1.** To obtain or acquire. **2.** To procure; gain; secure. **3.** To go after; fetch; retrieve; reach. **4.** To reach or make contact with by or as if by radio or telephone. **5.** To earn; gain: *get a reward.* **6.** To receive or come into possession of: *get a present.* **7.** To buy. **8.** To incur: *get a tongue-lashing.* **9.** *Informal.* To meet with; suffer: *He got a few knocks, but he'll recover.* **10.** To catch; contract: *They all got chicken pox at once.* **11.** To have or reach by calculation: *If you add them, you'll get 1,000.* **12.** To have obtained or received and now have. Used only in the form of the present perfect, and generally equivalent to *have: I've got a large collection of books.* **13.** To possess or gain understanding or mastery of by study: *I must get this by heart.* **14.** To understand; comprehend: *Do you get his point?* **15.** *Informal.* To register or catch, as by eye or ear: *I'm sorry, I didn't get your name.* **16.** To beget. **17.** To prepare or make ready: *get dinner.* **18.** To cause to become or to be in a specific condition: *He can get the hook loose.* **19.** To cause to move, come, or go: *Get that dog out of here!* **20.** To bring or take: *I'll get him in here, and you can talk to him.* **21.** To induce or persuade; prevail upon; cause: *I'll get my friend to show you his house.* **22.** To overpower; destroy: *Frost got our tomato crop.* **23.** To capture or catch: *The police got him.* **24.** *Slang.* To cause harm to; especially, to reciprocate by causing harm: *I'll get you for that remark.* **25.** *Informal.* To strike or hit; affect: *That blow got him on the chin.* **26. a.** *Baseball.* To put out: *The catcher got him sliding in to home plate.* **b.** *Football.* To tackle; touch. **27.** *Slang.* To puzzle: *Her attitude gets me.* **28.** *Slang.* To elicit a strong, usually negative reaction in: *Noisy eaters really get me.* **29.** To catch (a scheduled train or plane, for example). **30.** To have the obligation; be constrained. Used only in the form of the present perfect, and equivalent to *must: I have got to go.* —*intr.* **1.** To become or grow. Used as a copula or linking verb, subordinating its own meaning to the stronger meaning of a predicate complement: *I got well again.* **2.** To arrive: *When will we get to New York?* **3.** To betake oneself: *Get out!* **4.** *Informal.* To start: *Get going!* **5.** *Regional & Informal.* To be off; depart: *Now get!* **6.** To work for gain or profit; make money: *He spends all his time getting and spending.* —**get about** (or **around**). **1.** To move around: *He gets about by himself now.* **2.** *Informal.* To be active in a social circuit; go to many social events. **3.** To spread or travel. Used of a rumor or news. —**get across. 1.** To make understandable or clear: *Am I getting this across to you?* **2.** To be clear or understandable: *It's not getting across to him.* **3.** To communicate one's meaning or personality, as to an audience. —**get ahead.** To be successful; attain prosperity. —**get ahead of.** To pass or surpass; outstrip. —**get along. 1.** To be mutually congenial; be at harmony. **2.** To manage or fare with reasonable success: *He hasn't much money, but he gets along.* **3.** To make progress; to advance; improve. **4.** To advance in years. **5.** To move along; to leave. —**get around. 1.** To get about. **2.** To avoid doing or encountering; circumvent. **3.** *Informal.* To convince or gain the favor of by flattering or cajoling. —**get around to.** To consider or deal with after a postponement. —**get at. 1.** To determine; ascertain; uncover: *I'm trying to get at his point.* **2.** To reach; find a way to: *It's under the desk and I can't get at it.* **3.** To lead up to or arrive at, as a conclusion or meaning: *Do you understand what I'm getting at?* **4.** To attend to; apply oneself to. **5.** *Informal.* To influence, especially by bribery. —**get away with.** *Informal.* To be successful in avoiding retribution or the discovery of something done. —**get back. 1.** To return to or take up again: *Let's get back to work.* **2.** To regain. —**get back at.** *Informal.* To retaliate or have revenge against: *He swears he'll get back at him.* —**get by. 1.** To pass within range of, especially without drawing unfavorable attention: *His past record got by the judge altogether.* **2.** To manage; survive; fare: *It will be a hard year, but we'll get by.* —**get down to.** To concentrate on; give full attention to: *Let's get down to the real problems.* —**get in. 1.** To enter or be allowed to enter: *Can we get in?* **2.** To arrive: *What time does the train get in?* **3.** To inject, as into a conversation: *He gets in a great many references to himself.* **4.** To receive: *The store got in a new shipment.* **5.** *Slang.* To gain the favor of. Used with *with: He will get in with that teacher.* **6.** To become involved in or part of. Used with *with: She wants to get in with a different crowd.* —**get it. 1.** To comprehend; understand. **2.** *Informal.* To be punished or scolded. —**get nowhere.** To make no progress; have no success. —**get off. 1.** To get down from or out of. **2.** To leave; depart. **3.** To write and send, as a letter. **4.** *Informal.* To say or make, as a joke; especially, to say at the appropriate moment. **5.** To escape, as punishment or labor: *He got off scot-free.* **6.** To remove something. **7.** To intercede for and lessen the punishment of (a person). —**get on. 1.** To climb up onto or into; enter. **2.** To get along. **3.** To advance. Used of time or aging: *It's getting on toward noon. He's getting on in years.* —**get out of. 1.** To derive or draw: *He gets out of it what he can.* **2.** To avoid or get around. **3.** To move out of (range, sight, or earshot of, for example). **4.** To escape. —**get over. 1.** To get across. **2.** To recover from (a sorrow or illness, for example). —**get there.** *Informal.* To attain one's goal. —**get through. 1.** To finish or complete. **2.** To undergo and survive: *I wonder if that tree will get through the winter.* —**get through to. 1.** To make contact with. **2.** To make understandable or apparent to. —**get to. 1.** To have the opportunity of or be able to: *I hope I get to go.* **2.** To reach: *We never got to that point.* **3.** *Informal.* To happen to start; begin: *Then we got to remembering good times.* **4.** To make contact with or communicate with: *Your message is getting to me.* —**get with.** *Slang.* To become up to date with: *You have to get with the new styles.* —*n.* **1.** The act of begetting. **2.** Progeny; offspring. **3.** *Tennis.* A return on a shot that seems impossible to reach. [Get, got, got or gotten; Middle English *getten, gat, getten*, from Old Norse *geta, gat, getinn*. See **ghend-** in Appendix.*] —**get′a·ble, get′ta·ble** *adj.* —**get′ter** *n.*

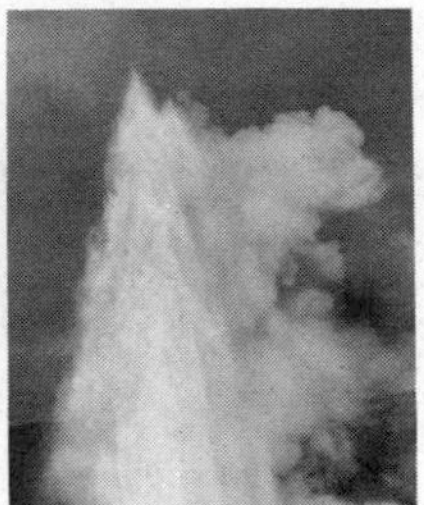

geyser
Old Faithful, Yellowstone National Park

get away. 1. To escape. **2.** To leave; depart. **3.** To go away, as on a vacation. **4.** To start off in a race.

get·a·way (gĕt′ə-wā′) *n.* **1.** The act or instance of escaping. **2.** The start, as of a race; takeoff. —*adj.* Used for escape: *a getaway car.*

geth·sem·a·ne (gĕth-sĕm′ə-nē) *n.* Any instance or place of great suffering.

Geth·sem·a·ne (gĕth-sĕm′ə-nē). The garden outside Jerusalem that was the scene of the agony and arrest of Jesus. Matthew 26:36–57.

get out. 1. To go out or away; to leave. **2.** To become public, as news. **3.** To publish, as a newspaper.

get-out (gĕt′out′) *n. Informal.* An escape or means of avoiding difficulty: *A feigned headache was her get-out.* —**all get-out.** *Informal.* Used as a generalized superlative in comparisons: *cold as all get-out; hot as all get-out.*

get·ter (gĕt′ər) *n.* **1.** One that gets. **2.** A material added in small amounts during a chemical or metallurgical process to absorb impurities. —*v.* **gettered, -tering, -ters.** —*tr.* To remove impurities from (a metal, for example) with a getter. —*intr.* To use a getter, as in removing impurities from a substance.

get together. 1. To come together; assemble, especially socially: *Let's get together for a drink.* **2.** To collect or assemble; put together: *I'll get a few things together and we can go.* **3.** To come to accord; synchronize; agree: *We must get together on our understanding of this.*

get-to·geth·er (gĕt′tə-gĕth′ər) *n. Informal.* A small party.

Get·tys·burg (gĕt′ĭz-bûrg). A town in southern Pennsylvania, the site of the Gettysburg National Military Park (2,463 acres), of a national cemetery, and of a battle victory won by Meade's Union forces over Lee's Confederate forces in the Civil War (1863). Population, 8,000.

get up. 1. To arise, as from bed or a stooping or prone position. **2.** To climb up. **3.** To create; devise; invent. **4.** *Informal.* To dress or make up elaborately.

get-up (gĕt′ŭp′) *n.* **1.** An outfit or costume, especially one remarkable or bizarre in some way. **2.** The arrangement and production style, as of a magazine or book. **3.** Energy and ambition; drive; initiative. In this sense, also "get-up-and-go."

GeV *Physics.* Giga (10^9) electron volts. See **BeV.**

gew·gaw (gyōō′gô′) *n.* A decorative trinket; bauble. —*adj.* Decorative and showy, but valueless. [Origin unknown.]

gey·ser (gī′zər *for sense 1;* gē′zər *for sense 2*) *n.* **1.** A natural hot spring that intermittently ejects a column of water and steam into the air. **2.** *British.* A gas-operated hot-water heater. [Icelandic *Geysir*, "gusher," the name of a hot spring in Iceland, from *geysa*, to gush, from Old Norse. See **gheu-** in Appendix.*]

gey·ser·ite (gī′zə-rīt′) *n.* An opaline siliceous deposit formed around natural hot springs.

Ge·zi·ra (jə-zîr′ə). *Arabic* **El Je·zi·ra** (ăl jă-zē′rŏ). A fertile region of east-central Sudan situated between the Blue Nile and White Nile rivers.

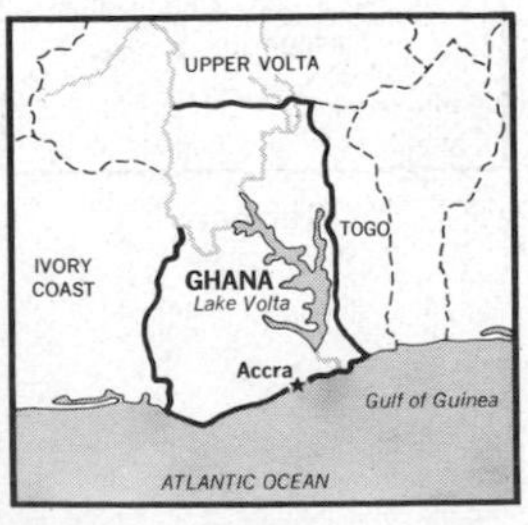

Ghana

Gha·na (gä′nə). **1.** An independent republic and member of the Commonwealth of Nations, occupying 91,844 square miles in western Africa, on the northern shore of the Gulf of Guinea. It was formed in 1957 of the British Gold Coast colony, along with the protectorates of Ashanti and the Northern Territories, and the trusteeship of British Togoland. Population, 7,600,000. Capital, Accra. **2.** Also **Ga·na.** A medieval African kingdom in the western Sudan. —**Gha·na′ian, Gha′ni·an** *adj.* & *n.*

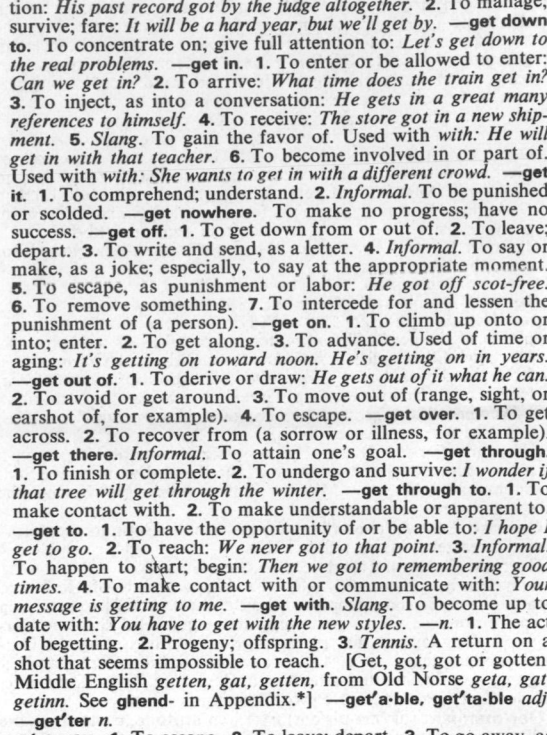

ghast·ly (găst′lē, gäst′-) *adj.* **-lier, -liest. 1.** Terrifying; dreadful. **2.** Having a deathlike pallor: *"amid the dim and ghastly glare of a snowy night"* (Washington Irving). **3.** Extremely unpleasant or bad: *"in the most abominable passage of his ghastly little book"* (Conor Cruise O'Brien). *—adv.* **1.** Dreadfully; horribly. **2.** With a ghostlike pallor. [Middle English *gastlich,* Old English *gāstlīc,* spiritual, ghostly, ghastly, from *gāst,* soul, ghost. See **gheis-** in Appendix.*] **—ghast′li·ness** *n.*

Synonyms: *ghastly, grim, gruesome, grisly, macabre, lurid.* These adjectives describe what is extremely forbidding in aspect. *Ghastly* implies having an appearance that suggests death or otherwise inspires shock or horror. *Grim* refers to what repels because of its stern or fierce aspect or its harsh, relentless nature. *Gruesome* and *grisly* describe what horrifies or revolts because of its crudity or utter inhumanity. *Macabre* implies an aspect that suggests or represents death in a bizarre or grotesque way rather than in naturalistic terms. *Lurid* sometimes describes physical appearance that suggests death or destruction, but more often refers to what shocks because of the vividness of its sensationalism or unsavoriness.

ghat (gôt, gät) *n.* Also **ghaut.** *Anglo-Indian.* **1.** A mountain pass. **2.** A mountain chain. **3.** A flight of steps down to the bank of a river. [Hindi *ghāt,* from Sanskrit *ghaṭṭa,* perhaps from *ghṛṣṭa,* rubbed. See **gher-⁵** in Appendix.*]

Ghats (gôts, gäts). Two mountain ranges of southern India, the Eastern Ghats extending 500 miles along the Bay of Bengal coast (highest elevation, Dodabetta, 8,640 feet), and the Western Ghats extending 800 miles along the Arabian Sea coast (highest elevation, Anai Mudi, 8,841 feet).

Gha·zal, Bahr el. See **Bahr el Ghazal.**

gha·zi (gä′zē) *n., pl.* **-zies.** A Moslem warrior who has fought successfully against infidels. Often used as a title of honor. [Arabic *ghāzī,* participle of *ghazā,* he made war.]

Ghaz·ni (gäz′nē). A city and commercial center of east-central Afghanistan, the capital of a former Moslem kingdom comprising the territory between the Tigris and the Ganges. Population, 25,000.

Ghaz·ze. The Arabic name for **Gaza.**

ghee (gē) *n.* Clarified butter from the butterfat of buffalo or other milk. It is used especially in India and neighboring countries. [Hindi *ghī,* from Sanskrit *ghṛta,* present participle of *ghṛ*†, to sprinkle.]

Ghent (gĕnt). *Flemish* **Gent** (gĕnt); *French* **Gand** (gäɴ). The capital of East Flanders, northwest-central Belgium; a commercial and manufacturing center and river port. Population, 158,000.

ghe·rao (gĕ-rou′) *n.* In India, a coercive tactic adopted during labor disputes whereby workers surround an employer and detain him on his own premises until he agrees to their demands: *"Recently, the technique of the gherao has been spreading to state-owned enterprises"* (New York Times). *—tr.v.* **gheraoed, -raoing, -raoes.** To coerce (an employer) by using this technique. [Bengali, to surround, from Indic *gher-* (unattested), causative of *ghir-* (unattested), "to go around," from Dravidian.]

gher·kin (gûr′kĭn) *n.* **1.** A tropical American vine, *Cucumis anguria,* bearing prickly, edible fruit. **2.** The fruit of this vine. **3.** A small cucumber, especially one used for pickling. [Dutch *agurk(je),* from Low German *agurke,* from Lithuanian *agurkas,* from Polish *ogorek, ogurek,* from Late Greek *angourion,* probably from Greek *agouros,* youth, "unripe," from *aōros* : *a-,* not + *ōros,* time (see **yēro-** in Appendix*).]

ghet·to (gĕt′ō) *n., pl.* **-tos** or **-toes. 1.** A section or quarter in a European city to which Jews are or were restricted. **2.** A slum section of an American city occupied predominantly by members of a minority group who live there because of social or economic pressure: *"A ghetto can be improved in one way only: out of existence."* (James Baldwin). [Italian *ghetto*†.]

Ghib·el·line (gĭb′ə-lĭn, -lēn′) *n.* A member of the aristocratic political faction who fought during the Middle Ages for German imperial control of Italy, in opposition to the Guelphs, who favored papal control. Compare **Guelph.** [Italian *Ghibellino,* from Middle High German *Waiblingen,* name of a Hohenstaufen estate.]

Ghi·ber·ti (gē-bĕr′tē), **Lorenzo.** 1378–1455. Florentine sculptor and painter.

ghil·lie (gĭl′ē) *n., pl.* **-lies.** Also **gil·lie.** A low-cut sports shoe with fringed laces. [Scottish Gaelic *gille,* boy, servant, GILLIE.]

Ghir·lan·da·jo (gĭr′län-dä′yō), **Domenico.** Also **Ghir·lan·da·io.** 1449–1494. Florentine painter.

ghost (gōst) *n.* **1.** The spirit or shade of a dead person, supposed to haunt living persons or former habitats; specter; phantom; wraith. **2.** *Archaic.* The animus or soul, as opposed to the body. **3.** A returning or haunting memory or image. **4.** A slight trace or vestige of something; a hint; semblance: *a ghost of a smile; a ghost of a chance.* **5.** A faint, false, sometimes secondary, photographic or television image. **6.** *Printing.* A variation or unevenness of color intensity on a surface intended to be solidly tinted, as the result of irregular distribution of ink. **7.** *Obsolete.* The Holy Ghost. **8.** *Informal.* A **ghostwriter** *(see).* **9.** A nonexistent publication listed in bibliographies. **—give up the ghost.** To die. *—v.* **ghosted, ghosting, ghosts.** *—intr. Informal.* To work as a ghostwriter. *—tr.* **1.** To haunt. **2.** *Informal.* To write (something) as a ghostwriter. [Middle English *gost, gast,* Old English *gāst.* See **gheis-** in Appendix.*]

ghost crab. Any of several light-colored burrowing crabs of the genus *Ocypoda,* frequenting the tide line along sandy shores.

ghost dance. Either of two religious dances practiced chiefly by certain North American Indians of the southwestern United States and California during the latter half of the 19th century to invoke a return of their former condition.

ghost·ly (gōst′lē) *adj.* **-lier, -liest. 1.** Pertaining to or resembling a ghost, wraith, or apparition; spectral. **2.** Pertaining to the spirit or to religion; spiritual: *"it would cure you of all evils ghostly and bodily"* (Sterne). **—ghost′li·ness** *n.*

ghost town. A town, especially a boom town of the West, that has been completely abandoned.

ghost word. A word that has come into a language through the perpetuation of a misreading of a manuscript, a typographical error, or a misunderstanding. For example, in *Ye Olde Sweete Shoppe, Ye* is a ghost word, the *y* having been a misreading of the runic letter thorn.

ghost·write (gōst′rīt′) *v.* **-wrote** (-rōt′), **-written** (-rĭt′n), **-writing, -writes.** *—intr.* To work as a ghostwriter. *—tr.* To write (something) as a ghostwriter.

ghost·writ·er (gōst′rī′tər) *n.* A person who writes for and gives credit of authorship to another person, who hires him to do so. Also informally called "ghost."

ghoul (go͞ol) *n.* **1.** An evil spirit or demon in Moslem folklore supposed to plunder graves and feed on corpses. **2.** A grave robber. **3.** One who delights in the revolting or loathsome. [Arabic *ghūl,* from *ghāla,* he took suddenly.] **—ghoul′ish** *adj.* **—ghoul′ish·ly** *adv.* **—ghoul′ish·ness** *n.*

GHQ general headquarters.

ghyll. Variant of **gill** (ravine or brook).

gi gill (liquid measure).

GI (jē′ī′) *n., pl.* **GIs** or **GI's.** An enlisted man in or veteran of any of the U.S. armed forces. *—adj.* **1.** Pertaining to or characteristic of a GI. **2.** In conformity to or accordance with U.S. military regulations or procedures. **3.** Issued by an official U.S. military supply department. [Originally abbreviation for *galvanized iron,* army clerks' term for items such as trash cans, but later taken to be abbreviation for *general issue* or *government issue,* and extended to include all articles issued and finally soldiers themselves.]

GI 1. general issue. **2.** Government Issue.

G.I. Government Issue.

Gia·co·met·ti (jä′kō-mĕt′tē), **Alberto.** 1901–1966. Swiss sculptor and painter.

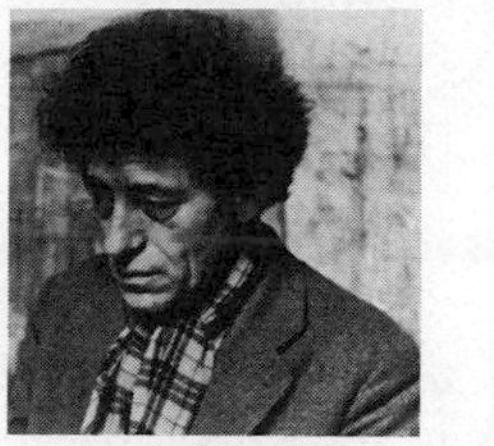

Alberto Giacometti

gi·ant (jī′ənt) *n.* **1.** A person or thing of extraordinary size or importance: *He is a giant in his field.* **2.** *Greek Mythology.* One of a race of manlike beings of enormous strength and stature who warred with the Olympians, by whom they were finally destroyed. **3.** Any similar being in folklore or myth. *—adj.* Of immense size; gigantic; huge. [Middle English *geant,* from Old French, from Vulgar Latin *gangante* (unattested), from Latin *gigās* (stem *gigant-*), from Greek *gigas*†.]

giant anteater. See **anteater.**

giant chinquapin. See **chinquapin.**

gi·ant·ess (jī′ən-tĭs) *n.* A female giant.

gi·ant·ism (jī′ən-tĭz′əm) *n.* **1.** The condition of being a giant. **2.** *Pathology.* **Gigantism** *(see).*

giant panda. See **panda.**

Giant's Causeway. A headland on the northern coast of Antrim, Northern Ireland, a formation of eroded basalt pillars.

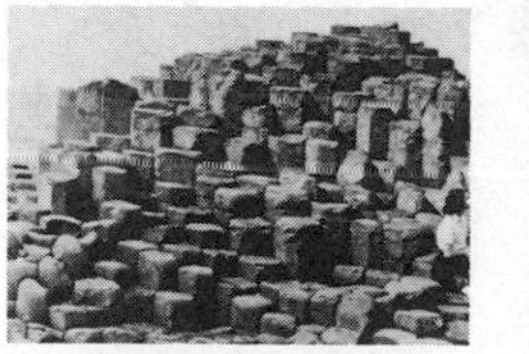

Giant's Causeway

giant sequoia. A very tall evergreen tree, *Sequoia gigantea,* of mountainous regions of southern California, having a massive trunk and light-colored, reddish wood. Also called "big tree." Compare **redwood.**

giant star. Any of a class of highly luminous, exceptionally massive stars.

giaour (jour) *n. Islam.* A nonbeliever; especially, a Christian. [Turkish *giaur,* infidel, from Persian *gaur,* variant of *gābr*†, fire worshiper.]

Gi·auque (jē-ōk′), **William Francis.** Born 1895. American physical chemist; studied thermodynamics.

gib (gĭb) *n.* A plain or notched, often wedge-shaped, piece of wood or metal designed to hold parts of a machine or structure in place or to provide a bearing surface, usually adjusted by a screw or key. [Origin uncertain.]

Gib. Gibraltar.

Gi·ba·ra Bay (hē-vä′rä). An inlet of the Atlantic on the north-ern coast of Oriente Province, eastern Cuba; the site of the first landing by Columbus in the New World (1492).

gib·ber (jĭb′ər, gĭb′-) *intr.v.* **-bered, -bering, -bers.** To prattle and chatter unintelligibly. *—n.* Senseless talk or prate; gibberish. [Imitative.]

gib·ber·el·lic acid (jĭb′ə-rĕl′ĭk). A substance, $C_{19}H_{22}O_6$, produced from a fungus, *Gibberella fujikuroi,* and used to promote the growth of plants, especially seedlings. [From GIBBEREL-LIN.]

gib·ber·el·lin (jĭb′ə-rĕl′ən) *n.* Any of several substances of plant origin, such as gibberellic acid, used to promote stem growth of plants. [From New Latin *Gibberella,* diminutive of Latin *gibber,* hunchbacked, akin to Latin *gibbus,* hump. See **gibbous.**]

gib·ber·ish (jĭb′ər-ĭsh, gĭb′-) *n.* Nonsensical, rapid talk; prattle: *"even madmen manage to convey unwelcome truths in lonely gibberish"* (W.H. Auden).

gib·bet (jĭb′ĭt) *n.* **1.** A gallows. **2.** An upright post with a crosspiece, forming a T-shaped structure from which executed criminals were hung for public viewing. *—tr.v.* **gibbeted** or **-betted, -beting** or **-betting, -bets. 1.** To execute by hanging. **2.** To hang on a gibbet for public viewing. **3.** To expose to infamy or public ridicule. [Middle English *gibet,* from Old French, diminutive of *gibe,* staff, club, possibly from Frankish *gibb-*† (unattested), forked stick.]

gib·bon (gĭb′ən) *n.* Any of several arboreal apes of the genera *Hylobates* or *Symphalangus,* of tropical Asia, having a slender

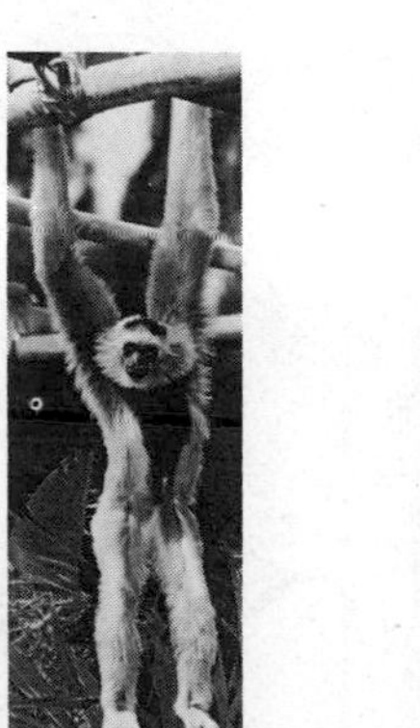

gibbon
Hylobates lar

body and long arms. [French, perhaps from a native word in India.]

Gib·bon (gĭb′ən), **Edward.** 1737–1794. English historian; author of *Decline and Fall of the Roman Empire.*

gib·bos·i·ty (gĭ-bŏs′ə-tē) *n., pl.* **-ties.** **1.** The condition of being gibbous. **2.** A rounded hump or protuberance; a swelling.

gib·bous (gĭb′əs) *adj.* **1.** Rounded; convex; protuberant. **2.** More than half but less than fully illuminated. Said of the moon or a planet: *"the gibbous moon, its light reflecting whitely"* (John Barth). **3.** Hunchbacked. [Middle English, from Late Latin *gebbōsus,* humpbacked, from *gibbus,* hump (expressive).] —**gib′bous·ly** *adv.* —**gib′bous·ness** *n.*

Gibbs (gĭbz), **Josiah Willard.** 1790–1861. American mathematician and physicist; formulated theoretical foundation of physical chemistry, developed vector analysis, and performed optical and thermodynamic research.

gibe (jīb) *v.* **gibed, gibing, gibes.** Also **jibe.** —*intr.* To make heckling or mocking remarks. —*tr.* To reproach by taunting; scoff. —See Synonyms at **ridicule.** —*n.* Also **jibe.** A derisive remark; a taunt. [Possibly from Old French *giber*†, to handle roughly.] —**gib′er** *n.* —**gib′ing·ly** *adv.*

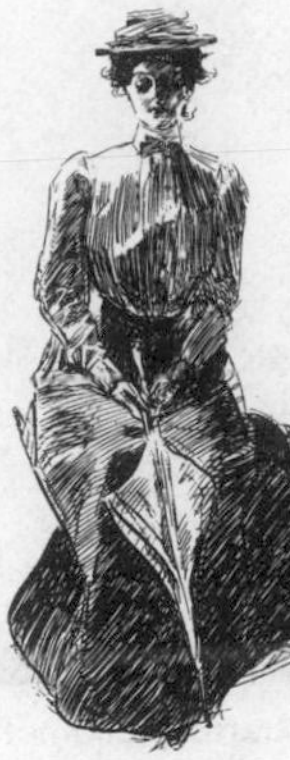
Gibson girl

Gib·e·on (gĭb′ē-ən). Modern name **El Jib** (ĕl jēb′). A village of ancient Palestine, six miles northwest of Jerusalem, the home of a people allied with Joshua.

Gib·e·on·ite (gĭb′ē-ə-nīt′) *n.* One of the inhabitants of Gibeon, condemned by Joshua to serve as manual laborers for the Israelites. Joshua 9.

gib·let (jĭb′lĭt) *n.* The heart, liver, or gizzard of a fowl. Usually used in the plural for these organs as a kind of meat. [Middle English *gibelet,* from Old French, probably variant of *giberet* (unattested), diminutive of *gibier,* hunting, game, from Frankish *gabaiti* (unattested), hunting with falcons. See **bheid-** in Appendix.*]

Gib·ral·tar (jĭ-brôl′tər). *Abbr.* **Gib.** A British crown colony occupying about two square miles on the Rock of Gibraltar, and comprising a town, seaport, and fortress dominating the Strait of Gibraltar. Population, 25,000.

Gib·ral·tar, Rock of (jĭ-brôl′tər). Ancient name **Cal·pe** (kăl′pē). A peninsula on the south-central coast of Spain; highest elevation, 1,396 feet. Also called "The Rock."

Gib·ral·tar, Strait of (jĭ-brôl′tər). Formerly **The Straits.** A waterway 8 to 27 miles wide extending for 36 miles between Spain and northern Africa, and connecting the Mediterranean Sea with the Atlantic Ocean.

Gib·ran (jŏŏb-rän′), **Kahlil.** 1883–1931. Syrian poet and painter; author of *The Prophet;* resident in America after 1910.

Gib·son (gĭb′sən) *n.* A dry martini having a small pickled onion in place of an olive or a twist of lemon peel. [From the surname *Gibson.*]

Gib·son (gĭb′sən), **Charles Dana.** 1867–1944. American illustrator.

Gib·son Desert (gĭb′sən). The central section of the desert of Western Australia, lying between the Great Sandy Desert on the north and the Victoria Desert on the south.

Gibson girl. The American girl of the 1890's as idealized in sketches by Charles Dana Gibson and typically dressed in a tailored shirtwaist with leg-of-mutton sleeves, and a long skirt.

gid (gĭd) *n.* A disease of sheep caused by the presence of the larva of a tapeworm, *Taenia caenurus,* in the brain, and resulting in a staggering gait. Also called "sturdy." [Back-formation from GIDDY.]

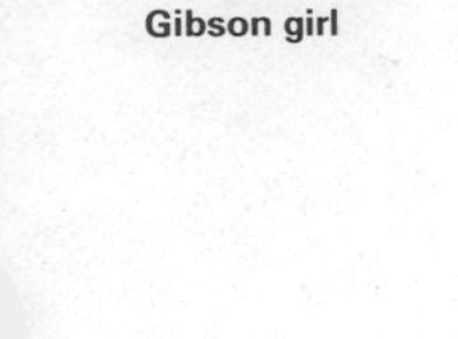
Gila monster

gid·dy (gĭd′ē) *adj.* **-dier, -diest.** **1. a.** Having a reeling, lightheaded sensation; dizzy. **b.** Causing or capable of causing dizziness: *a giddy climb to the topmast.* **2.** Frivolous and lighthearted; flighty: *giddy young girls.* —*v.* **giddied, -dying, -dies.** —*intr.* To become giddy. —*tr.* To make giddy. [Middle English *gidy,* mad, foolish, Old English *gydig,* possessed by a god, insane. See **gheu(ə)-** in Appendix.*] —**gid′di·ly** *adv.* —**gid′di·ness** *n.*

Gide (zhēd), **André.** 1869–1951. French novelist, dramatist, poet, essayist, diarist, and critic.

Gid·e·on (gĭd′ē-ən). A judge of Israel; conqueror of the Midianites. Judges 6–8. [Hebrew *Gidh'ōn,* "hewer," "feller," from *gādha,* he cut down.]

gie (gē). *Scottish.* Give.

gift (gĭft) *n.* **1.** Something that is bestowed voluntarily and without compensation; a present. **2.** The act, right, or power of giving: *Your request is not in my gift.* **3.** A talent, endowment, aptitude, or bent. —*tr.v.* **gifted, gifting, gifts.** **1.** *Informal.* To present with a gift. See Usage note. **2.** *Chiefly British.* To bestow as a gift. **3.** To endow with; invest. [Middle English *gift, yift,* from Old Norse *gipt, gift.* See **ghabh-** in Appendix.*]

Usage: The recent use of *gift* as a transitive verb, though not incorrect, has not established itself on a formal level. The following representative example involving the active voice is termed unacceptable by 94 per cent of the Usage Panel: *He gifted each of his nephews.*

gift·ed (gĭf′tĭd) *adj.* **1.** Endowed with natural ability, talent, or other assets: *a gifted child.* **2.** Revealing talent: *a gifted rendition of an aria.* —**gift′ed·ly** *adv.* —**gift′ed·ness** *n.*

gift of tongues. An ecstatic utterance that is partly or wholly unintelligible to hearers, especially as practiced liturgically in certain Christian congregations. Also called "glossolalia." [By allusion to the Pentecostal miracle whereby the Apostles "were all filled with the Holy Ghost, and began to speak with other tongues, as the Spirit gave them utterance." Acts 2:4.]

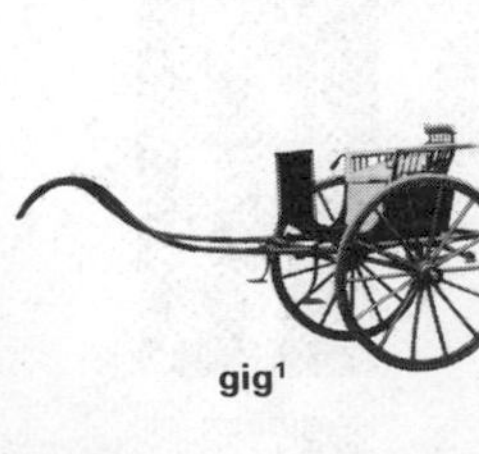
gig[1]

Gi·fu (gē′fōō′). A city and manufacturing center of central Honshu Island, Japan. Population, 353,000.

gig[1] (gĭg) *n.* **1.** A light, two-wheeled carriage drawn by one horse. **2. a.** A long, light ship's boat having oars, sails, or a motor, and usually reserved for use by the ship's captain. **b.** A fast, light rowboat. —*intr.v.* **gigged, gigging, gigs.** To ride in a gig. [Middle English *gigg*†, giddy girl, something that whirls.]

gig[2] (gĭg) *n.* **1.** An arrangement of barbless hooks that is dragged through a school of fish to hook them in the bodies. **2.** A pronged spear for fishing. —*v.* **gigged, gigging, gigs.** —*tr.* **1.** To catch with a gig. **2.** *Regional.* To goad; prod. —*intr.* To fish with a gig. [Short for FISHGIG.]

gig[3] (gĭg) *n. Slang.* **1.** An official report of an infraction of rules, as in the army or a school. **2.** A demerit assigned as a punishment. —*tr.v.* **gigged, gigging, gigs.** *Slang.* **1.** To give a demerit to. **2.** To punish with a demerit. [Origin unknown.]

gig[4] (gĭg) *n. Slang.* A job; especially an engagement or booking for musicians.

giga-. *Symbol* **G** Indicates one billion (10^9); for example, *gigavolt,* or one billion volts. [From Greek *gigas,* GIANT.]

gi·gan·tesque (jī′găn′tĕsk′) *adj.* Pertaining to or suitable for a giant; huge; enormous. [French, from Italian *gigantesco,* from Greek *gigas* (stem *gigant-*), GIANT.]

gi·gan·tic (jī-găn′tĭk) *adj.* **1.** Pertaining to or suitable for a giant. **2. a.** Exceedingly large of its kind: *a gigantic toadstool.* **b.** Very large or extensive: *a gigantic radio network.* —See Synonyms at **enormous.** [From Latin *gigās* (stem *gigant-*), GIANT.] —**gi·gan′ti·cal·ly** *adv.*

gi·gan·tism (jī-găn′tĭz′əm) *n.* **1.** Excessive growth of the body or any of its parts as a result of oversecretion of the pituitary growth hormone. Also called "giantism." **2.** Abnormal size.

gi·gan·tom·a·chy (jī′găn-tŏm′ə-kē) *n.* Also **gi·gan·to·ma·chi·a** (jī-găn′tō-mā′kē-ə). **1.** *Greek Mythology.* The war of the giants against Zeus and the other Olympian gods. **2.** Any battle between gigantic powers. [Greek *gigantomakhia* : *gigas* (stem *gigant-*), GIANT + -MACHY.]

gig·gle (gĭg′əl) *intr.v.* **-gled, -gling, -gles.** To laugh with repeated short, high-pitched, convulsive sounds, as when nervous or when attempting to suppress mirth. —*n.* A high-pitched, spasmodic laugh. [Imitative.] —**gig′gler** *n.* —**gig′gling·ly** *adv.*

gig·gly (gĭg′lē) *adj.* **-glier, -gliest.** Inclined to giggle.

gig·o·lo (jĭg′ə-lō′, zhĭg′-) *n., pl.* **-los.** A young man who is kept as a lover by a woman. [French, from *gigolette,* dance-hall pickup, from *giguer,* to dance, from *gigue,* leg, fiddle, from Old French, from Old High German *giga*†.]

gig·ot (jĭg′ət) *n.* **1.** A leg of mutton, lamb, or veal for cooking. **2.** A leg-of-mutton sleeve. [Old French, diminutive of *gigue,* leg, fiddle. See **gigolo.**]

gigue (zhēg) *n.* **1.** A dance, the **jig** *(see).* **2.** *Music.* A lively dance form in 6/8, 9/8, or 12/8 time, often forming the final movement of a suite. [French, from English JIG.]

GI Joe. *Informal.* An enlisted man in the U.S. Army, especially during World War II.

Gi·jón (hē-hôn′). A city, manufacturing center, and port on the Bay of Biscay, northwest-central Spain. Population, 134,000.

Gi·la Cliff Dwellings National Monument (hē′lə). A park with Pueblo cliff dwellings occupying 160 acres in southwestern New Mexico.

Gi·la monster (hē′lə). A venomous lizard, *Heloderma suspectum,* of the southwestern United States and northern Mexico, having a stout body covered with black and pinkish or yellowish scales.

Gi·la River (hē′lə). A river rising in southwestern New Mexico and flowing 630 miles generally west across southern Arizona to the Colorado.

gil·bert (gĭl′bərt) *n.* The centimeter-gram-second electromagnetic unit of magnetomotive force, equal to $10/4\pi$ ampere-turn. See **measurement.** [After William GILBERT.]

Gil·bert (gĭl′bərt). A masculine given name. [Middle English, from Old French, from Old High German *Gīselberht* : *gīsal,* pledge, from Celtic, akin to Old Irish *giall*† + *berht,* bright (see **bhereg-** in Appendix*).]

Gil·bert (gĭl′bərt), **Cass.** 1859–1934. American architect.

Gil·bert (gĭl′bərt), Sir **Humphrey.** 1539?–1583. English navigator; established colony at St. John's, Newfoundland (1583).

Gil·bert (gĭl′bərt), **William.** 1540–1603. English physicist and court physician; hypothesized that the earth is a magnet.

Gil·bert (gĭl′bərt), Sir **William S(chwenck).** 1836–1911. English playwright; collaborated with Arthur Sullivan on 14 comic operas.

Gil·bert and El·lice Islands (gĭl′bərt; ĕl′ĭs). A British colony comprising 16 atolls, occupying 375 square miles in the central Pacific Ocean. Population, 50,000. Capital, Tarawa.

Gil·bert Islands (gĭl′bərt). Part of the Gilbert and Ellice Islands, 144 square miles in area; occupied by Japan (1941–43), recaptured by the United States, and used as a base for operations in the Marshall Islands. Population, 38,000.

Gil·bo·a, Mount (gĭl-bō′ə). A mountain rising to 1,696 feet in northeastern Israel on the Jordanian border; the site of King Saul's final defeat and suicide.

gild[1] (gĭld) *tr.v.* **gilded** or **gilt** (gĭlt), **gilding, gilds.** **1.** To cover with or as if with a thin layer of gold: *"The lanterns gilded the leaves of the trees"* (Flannery O'Connor). **2.** To give an often deceptively attractive or improved appearance to; gloss or gloss over. **3.** *Archaic.* To smear with blood. —**gild the lily.** To adorn unnecessarily something already beautiful. [Middle English *gilden,* Old English *gyldan.* See **ghel-**[2] in Appendix.*]

gild[2]. Variant of **guild.**

gild·er[1] (gĭl′dər) *n.* A person whose work is gilding.

gild·er[2]. Variant of **guilder.**

gild·hall. Variant of **guildhall.**

gild·ing (gĭl′dĭng) *n.* **1.** The art or process of applying gilt to a

ă pat/ā pay/âr care/ä father/b bib/ch church/d deed/ĕ pet/ē be/f fife/g gag/h hat/hw which/ĭ pit/ī pie/îr pier/j judge/k kick/l lid, needle/m mum/n no, sudden/ng thing/ŏ pot/ō toe/ô paw, for/oi noise/ou out/ŏŏ took/ōō boot/p pop/r roar/s sauce/sh ship, dish/

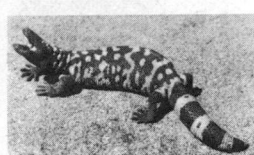

surface. **2.** Gold leaf or a paint containing or simulating gold; gilt. **3.** Something employed to give a superficially attractive appearance.

Gil·e·ad (gĭl′ē-əd, -ăd′). A mountainous region of Jordan, situated east of the Jordan River between the Sea of Galilee and the Dead Sea. Highest elevation, Mount Gilead (3,597 feet).

gill¹ (gĭl) *n.* **1.** *Zoology.* The respiratory organ of fishes, larval amphibians, and numerous aquatic invertebrates. **2.** *Usually plural.* The wattle of a bird. **3.** *Usually plural. Informal.* The area around the chin and neck: *green around the gills.* **4.** *Botany.* One of the thin, platelike structures on the underside of the cap of a mushroom or similar fungus. *—tr.v.* **gilled, gilling, gills. 1.** To catch (fish) in a gill net. **2.** To gut or clean (fish). [Middle English *gille,* probably from Old Norse *gil* (unattested). See **ghelunā** in Appendix.*]

gill² (jĭl) *n. Abbr.* **gi 1.** A unit of volume or capacity in the U.S. Customary System, used in liquid measure, equal to 4 fluid ounces (¼ pint) or 7.216 cubic inches. **2.** A unit of volume or capacity in the British Imperial System, used in dry and liquid measure, equal to 5 fluid ounces (¼ pint) or 8.670 cubic inches. See **measurement.** [Middle English *gille,* from Old French *gille, gelle,* from Late Latin *gillo*†, water pot.]

gill³ (gĭl) *n.* Also **ghyll.** *British.* **1.** A ravine. **2.** A narrow stream. [Middle English *gille,* from Old Norse *gil.* See **ghei-** in Appendix.*]

gill⁴ (jĭl) *n.* Also **jill, Gill.** Girl; sweetheart: *Every Jack must have his gill.* [From the feminine name *Gill,* short for *Gillian, Jillian,* Anglicized form of JULIANA.]

gill fungus (gĭl). Any fleshy fungus having a cap with gills on the underside.

gil·lie (gĭl′ē) *n.* Also **gil·ly** *pl.* **-lies. 1.** *Scottish.* A professional guide and servant for sportsmen, especially in fishing and deer-stalking. **2.** Variant of **ghillie.** [Scottish Gaelic *gille,* boy, servant, akin to Irish *giolla*†.]

gill net (gĭl). A fishnet set vertically in the water so that fish swimming into it are entangled by the gills in its mesh.

gill-o·ver-the-ground (gĭl′ō-vər-*th*ə-ground′) *n.* A plant, the **ground ivy** *(see).*

gill slit (gĭl). One of several narrow external openings connecting with the pharynx, present in all vertebrates during embryonic development, and characteristic of sharks and related fishes.

gil·ly·flow·er (gĭl′ē-flou′ər) *n.* Also **gil·li·flow·er. 1.** The carnation or a similar plant of the genus *Dianthus.* **2.** Any of several other plants having fragrant flowers, such as the stock or wallflower. [Alteration (influenced by FLOWER) of Middle English *gilofre, gelofer,* from Old French *girofre, girofle,* from Medieval Latin *caryophylum,* clove, from Greek *karuophullon* : *karuon,* nut (see **kar-¹** in Appendix*) + *phullon,* leaf (see **bhel-³** in Appendix*).]

Gil·son·ite (gĭl′sə-nīt′) *n.* A natural black bitumen found in Utah and Colorado, used in the manufacture of acid, alkali, and waterproof coatings. Also called "uintaite." [Trademark, after its discoverer, S.H. *Gilson,* of Salt Lake City, Utah.]

gilt¹ (gĭlt). Alternate past tense and past participle of **gild.** *—adj.* **1.** Gilded. **2.** Having the appearance of gold. *—n. Abbr.* **gt. 1.** A thin layer of gold or something simulating it that is applied in gilding. **2.** Shining brilliance; glitter.

gilt² (gĭlt) *n.* A young sow that has not farrowed. [Middle English *gilt,* young sow, from Old Norse *gylta,* sow. See **ghel-²** in Appendix.*]

gilt-edged (gĭlt′ĕjd′) *adj.* Also **gilt-edge** (-ĕj′). **1.** Having gilded edges, as the pages of a book. **2.** Of the highest quality or value: *gilt-edged securities.*

gim·bals (jĭm′bəlz, gĭm′-) *pl.n.* A device consisting of two rings mounted on axes at right angles to each other so that an object such as a ship's compass will remain suspended in a horizontal plane between them regardless of the motion of the ship. [Plural of *gimbal,* from Old French *gemel,* GIMMAL.]

gim·crack (jĭm′krăk′) *n.* A cheap and showy object of little or no use; gewgaw; knickknack. *—adj.* Cheap and shoddy; flimsy. [Middle English *gibecrake*†, ornament, gimcrack.] **—gim′crack′er·y** *n.*

gim·el (gĭm′əl) *n.* The third letter of the Hebrew alphabet. See **alphabet.** [Hebrew *gīmel,* "camel" (from the ancient form of the letter), akin to *gāmāl,* CAMEL.]

gim·let (gĭm′lĭt) *n.* **1.** A small hand tool for boring holes, having a spiraled shank, a screw tip, and a cross handle. **2.** A cocktail made with vodka or gin and lime juice, garnished with a slice of lime. *—tr.v.* **gimleted, -leting, -lets.** To penetrate with or as if with a gimlet; puncture; pierce. *—adj.* Piercing; penetrating: *gimlet eyes.* [Middle English, from Old French *guimbelet,* probably from Middle Dutch *wimmelkijn,* diminutive of *wimmel,* auger. See **weip-** in Appendix.*]

gim·mal (gĭm′əl) *n.* A ring made of two narrower rings interlocked. [Earlier *gemel,* from Old French, from Latin *gemelus,* diminutive of *geminus,* twin. See **yem-** in Appendix.*]

gim·mick (gĭm′ĭk) *n. Slang.* **1.** A device employed, often illegally, to cheat, deceive, or trick, especially: **a.** A mechanism for the secret control of a gambling wheel or other apparatus. **b.** A device used by a magician. **2.** A stratagem employed to promote a project: *an advertising gimmick.* **3.** An undesirable feature concealed or played down in the promotion of a project; a catch; snag. **4.** A trivial or unnecessary innovation, as a gadget, added to enhance appeal. **5.** A small object whose name eludes one. *—tr.v.* **gimmicked, -micking, -micks.** To add gimmicks to; clutter with gadgets or catchy details. Often used with *up: gimmick up a dress.* [Origin unknown.] **—gim′mick·y** *adj.*

gimp¹ (gĭmp) *n.* A narrow braid or cord of fabric, sometimes stiffened, used to trim or pipe clothes, curtains, or upholstered furniture. Also called "guimpe," "guipure." *—tr.v.* **gimped, gimping, gimps.** To trim or edge with gimp. [French *guimpe,* from Old French *guimple, wimple,* from Old High German *wimpal.* See **weip-** in Appendix.*]

gimp² (gĭmp) *n. Slang.* **1.** A limp or limping gait. **2.** A person who limps; a cripple. *—intr.v.* **gimped, gimping, gimps.** *Slang.* To limp. [Origin unknown.] **—gimp′y** *adj.*

gimp³ (gĭmp) *n.* Spirit; pep. [Origin unknown.]

gin¹ (jĭn) *n.* **1.** A strong alcoholic beverage made by distilling rye or other grains with juniper berries. **2.** A similar liquor flavored with some other aromatic substance, as aniseed. [Shortened from Dutch *jenever,* from Middle Dutch *geniver, genever,* juniper, from Old French *geneivre,* from Latin *jūniperus,* JUNIPER.]

gin² (jĭn) *n.* **1.** Any of several machines or devices, as: **a.** A machine for hoisting or moving heavy objects. **b.** A pile driver. **c.** A snare or trap for game. **d.** A pump operated by a windmill. **2.** A **cotton gin** *(see).* *—tr.v.* **ginned, ginning, gins. 1.** To remove the seeds from (cotton) with a gin. **2.** To trap in a gin. [Middle English *gin,* short for *engin,* ENGINE.]

gin³ (jĭn) *n.* A card game, **gin rummy** *(see).*

gin·ger (jĭn′jər) *n.* **1.** A plant, *Zingiber officinale,* of tropical Asia, having yellowish-green flowers and a pungent, aromatic rootstock. **2.** The rootstock of this plant, often dried and powdered and used as flavoring, or, in sugared form, as a sweetmeat. **3.** Any of various other plants of the family Zingiberaceae, having variously colored, often fragrant flowers. **4.** The **wild ginger** *(see).* **5.** Strong brown. See **color. 6.** *Informal.* Liveliness; vigor; pep. *—tr.v.* **gingered, -gering, -gers. 1.** To spice with ginger. **2.** *Informal.* To make more lively. Often used with *up: She gingered up the party.* [Middle English *gingivere,* from Old English *gingifer* and Old French *gingivre, gingembre,* from Medieval Latin *gingiber, gingiver,* from Latin *zinziberi,* from Greek *ziggiberis,* from Prakrit *singabēra,* from Sanskrit *śṛṅgaveram* : *śṛṅga-,* horn (see **ker-¹** in Appendix*) + *vera-*†, body (so called from its shape).]

ginger ale. An effervescent soft drink flavored with ginger.

ginger beer. A nonalcoholic drink popular in England, similar to ginger ale but flavored with fermented ginger.

gin·ger·bread (jĭn′jər-brĕd′) *n.* **1. a.** A dark molasses cake flavored with ginger. **b.** A soft molasses and ginger cooky cut in various shapes, sometimes elaborately decorated with colored frosting and, formerly, with gilt. **2. a.** Any elaborate ornamentation. **b.** Any superfluous or tasteless embellishment, especially in architecture. [Middle English *gingebred,* preserved ginger, alteration (influenced by *bred,* BREAD) of Old French *gingebras,* from Medieval Latin *gingibrātum,* from *gingiber,* GINGER.]

gingerbread palm. A tree, the **doom palm** *(see).*

gin·ger·ly (jĭn′jər-lē) *adv.* **1.** With great care or delicacy. **2.** Cautiously; carefully; timidly. *—adj.* Cautious; careful; timid. [Earliest sense "daintily," possibly from Old French *gensor, genzor,* comparative of *gent,* pretty, of noble birth, from Latin *genitus,* past participle of *gignere,* to bring forth. See **gene-** in Appendix.*] **—gin′ger·li·ness** *n.*

gin·ger·snap (jĭn′jər-snăp′) *n.* A flat, brittle cooky spiced with ginger and sweetened with molasses.

gin·ger·y (jĭn′jə-rē) *adj.* **1.** Having the spicy flavor of ginger. **2.** Sharp and pungent; biting: *a gingery remark.* **3.** Strong brown. See **color.**

ging·ham (gĭng′əm) *n.* A yarn-dyed cotton fabric woven in stripes, checks, plaids, or solid colors. [Dutch *gingang,* from Malay *ginggang, gĕnggang,* "interspace."]

gin·gi·va (jĭn-jī′və, jĭn′jə-) *n. Anatomy.* The **gum** *(see).*

gin·gi·val (jĭn-jī′vəl, jĭn′jə-) *adj.* **1.** Of or having to do with the gums. **2.** *Linguistics.* Alveolar. [From Latin *gingīva*†, gum.]

gin·gi·vi·tis (jĭn′jə-vī′tĭs) *n.* Inflammation of the gums. [New Latin : Latin *gingīva,* gum (see **gingival**) + -ITIS.]

gink (gĭngk) *n. Slang.* A man or boy, especially one considered odd in some way. [Origin unknown.]

gink·go (gĭng′kō) *n., pl.* **-goes.** Also **ging·ko.** A tree, *Ginkgo biloba,* native to China, having fan-shaped leaves and fleshy, yellowish fruit, and often used as an ornamental street tree. Also called "maidenhair tree." [Japanese *ginkyō,* from ancient Chinese *ngien hang* (Mandarin *yin² hsing⁴*), "silver apricot" : *ngien,* silver + *hang,* apricot.]

gin mill. *Slang.* A saloon.

gin rummy. A variety of rummy for two or more persons in which a person may win by matching all his cards or may end the game by melding when his unmatched cards add up to ten points or less. Also called "gin." [GIN (alcohol) + RUMMY, suggested by a play on RUM (alcohol).]

gin·seng (jĭn′sĕng′) *n.* **1.** Any of several plants of the genus *Panax;* especially, *P. schinseng,* of eastern Asia, or *P. quinquefolium,* of North America, having small greenish flowers and a forked root believed to have medicinal properties. **2.** The root of either of these plants. [Mandarin Chinese *jen² shen¹* : *jen²,* man (because the forked root resembles a human being with limbs) + *shen¹,* ginseng.]

Gior·gio·ne (jôr-jō′nā), **Il.** Original name, Giorgio Barbarelli. 1478?–1511. Venetian painter.

Giot·to (jŏt′tō). In full, Giotto di Bondone. 1276?–1337? Florentine painter, architect, and sculptor.

gip. Variant of **gyp.**

Gip·sy. Variant of **Gypsy.**

gi·raffe (jĭ-răf′, -räf′) *n.* An African ruminant mammal, *Giraffa camelopardis,* having a very long neck and legs, a tan coat with

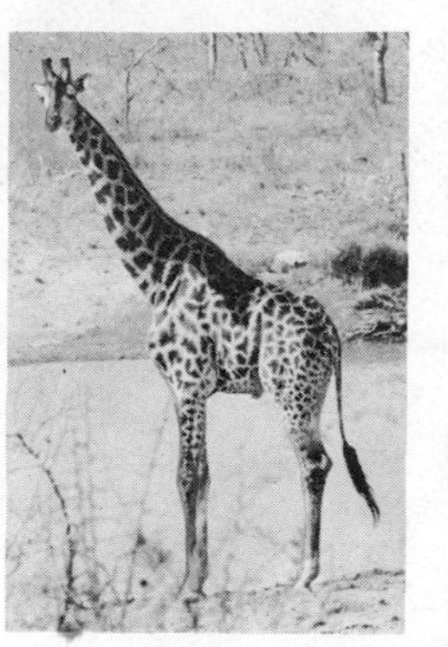

giraffe

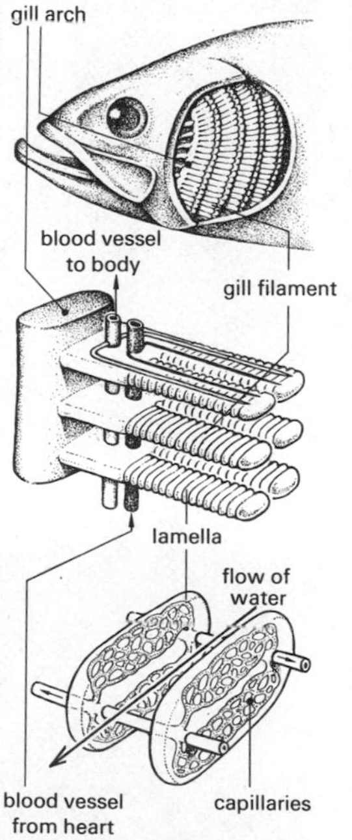
gill arch
blood vessel to body
gill filament
lamella
flow of water
blood vessel from heart
capillaries

gill¹
Gill of a fish with operculum removed and enlarged portions showing structural details

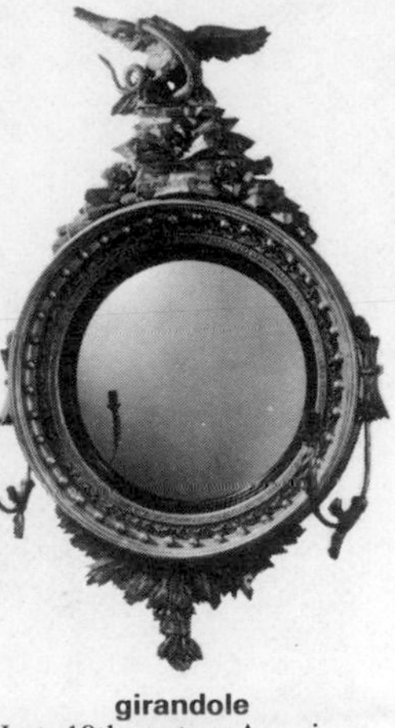

girandole
Late 18th-century American

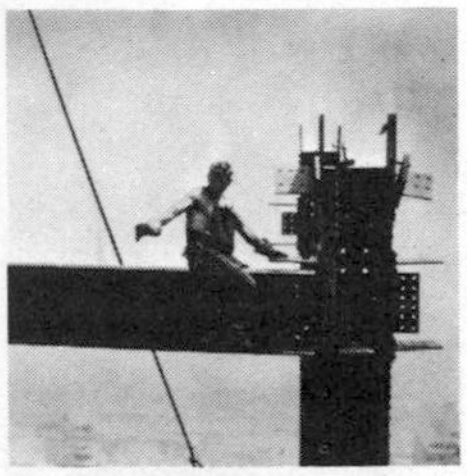

girder
Placing a girder during construction of the Empire State Building, New York City, 1931

brown blotches, and short horns. [Italian *giraffa,* from Arabic *zirāfah,* probably of African origin.]
gir·an·dole (jĭr′ən-dōl′) *n.* **1. a.** A composition or structure in radiating form or arrangement; a rotating display, as of fireworks. **b.** A branched candleholder, sometimes backed by a mirror. **2.** A piece of jewelry, such as an earring, having a large stone surrounded by several small drops. [French *girandole,* from Italian *girandola,* from *girare,* to turn, from Latin *gȳrāre,* to GYRATE.]
gir·a·sol (jĭr′ə-sôl′, -sōl′, -sŏl′) *n.* Also **gir·o·sol.** A **fire opal** *(see).* —*adj.* Opalescent. [Italian *girasole* : *girare,* to turn (see **girandole**) + *sole,* sun, from Latin *sōl* (see **sawel-** in Appendix*).]
Gi·rau·doux (zhē-rō-do͞o′), **Jean.** 1882–1944. French playwright and novelist.
gird[1] (gûrd) *tr.v.* **girded** or **girt** (gûrt), **girding, girds. 1. a.** To encircle with a belt or band. **b.** To fasten or secure with a belt, cord, or the like. **c.** To surround: *an island girded by water.* **2. a.** To equip: *gird with the sword of knighthood.* **b.** To endow with some attribute: *girded with righteousness.* **3.** To prepare (oneself) for action. [Middle English *girden,* Old English *gyrdan.* See **gher-**[2] in Appendix.*]
gird[2] (gûrd) *v.* **girded, girding, girds.** —*tr. Obsolete.* To jeer at; mock. —*intr.* To make taunting remarks; jeer. —*n. Obsolete.* A sarcastic remark. [Middle English *girden*†, to strike, cut, charge.] —**gird′er** *n.*
gird·er (gûr′dər) *n.* A horizontal beam, as of steel or wood, used as a main support for a vertical load.
gir·dle (gûrd′l) *n.* **1. a.** A belt, sash, or the like, worn at the waist. **b.** A band or structure that encircles like a belt. **2.** An elasticized, flexible undergarment worn over the waist and hips. **3.** A band made around the trunk of a tree by the removal of a strip of bark. **4.** The edge of a cut gem held by the setting. **5.** *Anatomy.* The pelvic or pectoral arch. —*tr.v.* **girdled, -dling, -dles. 1.** To encircle with or as if with a belt. **2.** To put on a girdle. **3.** To remove a band of bark completely from the circumference of (a tree), usually to kill it. [Middle English *girdel,* Old English *gyrdel.* See **gher-**[2] in Appendix.*]
gird·ler (gûrd′lər) *n.* **1.** One that girdles. **2.** One who makes girdles. **3.** Any of various insects that chew circular bands around twigs or stems in preparing nesting sites.
girl (gûrl) *n.* **1.** One who has not yet attained womanhood. **2.** A female child. **3.** A single young woman of marriageable age. **4.** *Informal.* Any woman. **5.** A daughter. **6.** A sweetheart. **7.** A female servant. [Middle English *girle, gerle, gurle*†.]
girl Friday. *Informal.* A female employee, especially one having a great variety of responsibilities. [By humorous analogy with MAN FRIDAY.]
Girl Guide. A member of the Girl Guides, a British youth organization founded in 1910.
girl·hood (gûrl′ho͝od′) *n.* **1.** The state or time of being a girl. **2.** Girls collectively.
girl·ish (gûr′lĭsh) *adj.* Pertaining to, characteristic of, or suitable for a girl or girls.
Girl Scout. A member of the Girl Scouts, a youth organization founded in the United States in 1912 on the plan of the Girl Guides.
Gi·ronde[1] (jĭ-rŏnd′; *French* zhē-rôNd′). An estuary on the Bay of Biscay in southwestern France, formed by the confluence of the Garonne and the Dordogne and extending generally northwest for 45 miles.
Gi·ronde[2] (jĭ-rŏnd′; *French* zhē-rôNd′) *n.* A moderate republican political party of revolutionary France (1791–93). [After *Gironde,* a department in southwestern France, because the leaders of the party were deputies of that department.] —**Gi·ron′dist** *adj.* & *n.*
gir·o·sol. Variant of **girasol.**
girt[1] (gûrt) *v.* **girted, girting, girts.** —*tr.* **1.** To gird. **2.** To measure the girth of. —*intr.* To measure in girth. [Variant of GIRD.]
girt[2]. Alternate past tense and past participle of **gird** (to encircle).
girth (gûrth) *n.* **1.** The distance around something; circumference. **2.** The size of something; bulk. **3.** A strap encircling an animal's body to secure a load or saddle upon its back; a cinch. —*tr.v.* **girthed, girthing, girths. 1.** To measure the circumference of. **2.** To encircle. **3.** To secure with a girth. [Middle English *gerth,* from Old Norse *gyǫrdh,* girdle. See **gher-**[2] in Appendix.*]
gi·sarme (gĭ-zärm′) *n.* A halberd with a long shaft and a two-sided blade, carried by medieval foot soldiers. [Middle English, from Old French *g(u)isarme,* from Old High German *getisarn* : *getan*†, to weed + *īsarn,* iron, from Common Germanic *īsarna-* (unattested), IRON.]
gis·mo (gĭz′mō) *n., pl.* **-mos.** Also **giz·mo.** *Slang.* A mechanical device or part the name of which is forgotten or not yet designated. [Origin unknown.]
gist (jĭst) *n.* **1.** The central idea of some matter, such as an argument or a speech; essence. **2.** *Law.* The grounds for action in a suit. [From Old French *(cest action) gist,* (this action) lies, from *gesir,* to lie, from Latin *jacēre,* from *jacere,* to throw. See **yē-** in Appendix.*]
Giu·lio Ro·ma·no (jo͞o′lyō rō-mä′nō). 1499–1546. Italian painter and architect of the Roman school.
give (gĭv) *v.* **gave** (gāv), **given** (gĭv′ən), **giving, gives.** —*tr.* **1. a.** To make a present of; bestow: *He gave her flowers for her birthday.* **b.** To deliver in exchange or in recompense; pay or sell. Used with *for: He will give five dollars for the book.* **c.** To put temporarily at the disposal of; entrust to: *give them the cottage for a week.* **d.** To place in the hands of: *Give me the scissors.* **2. a.** To convey or offer for conveyance: *Give him my best wishes.* **b.** To bestow; confer: *give authority.* **c.** To impart: *give order to chaos.* **d.** To grant: *give permission.* **e.** To bestow upon: *give him your confidence.* **3.** To contribute; furnish; donate: *give one's time.* **4. a.** To be a source of; afford: *His remark gave offense.* **b.** To expose or subject one to: *She gave him the measles.* **c.** To prompt: *It gives one pause.* **5.** To produce; bring forth: *This cow gives three gallons of milk per day.* **6.** To provide (something required or expected): *give one's name and address.* **7.** To administer: *give a spanking.* **8. a.** To accord; concede: *give the benefit of the doubt to.* **b.** To allow: *give odds of five to one.* **c.** To relinquish; yield: *give ground.* **d.** To yield sexually. **9.** To emit or issue: *give a sigh.* **10. a.** To allot; assign: *give her five minutes to finish.* **b.** To designate; cite: *give a departure date.* **11.** To award: *give first prize to.* **12.** To ascribe; attribute: *give him the blame.* **13.** To grant as a supposition; acknowledge: *Given their superiority, we can't expect to win.* **14. a.** To stage: *give a dinner party.* **b.** To proffer: *give a toast.* **c.** To manifest: *give promise of brilliance.* **d.** To perform for an audience: *give a play.* **e.** To execute: *give a bow.* **15.** To submit for consideration or acceptance; tender: *give an opinion.* **16.** To allow or lead: *She gave me to think she loved me.* **17.** To devote: *give oneself to one's work.* **18.** To sacrifice: *give a son to the war.* —*intr.* **1.** To make gifts or donations: *give generously to charity.* **2.** To be unable to hold up; yield: *give under pressure.* **3.** To afford a view of or access to; open: *The French doors give onto a terrace.* —**give a good account of (oneself).** To behave or perform creditably. —**give a wide berth to.** To steer clear of; avoid. —**give back.** To return. —**give birth (to). 1.** To bear offspring. **2.** To produce. —**give cause.** To furnish grounds or reason; justify. —**give forth. 1.** To report; circulate. **2.** To emit. —**give in. 1.** To cease opposition; concede. **2.** To hand in; submit: *give in a report.* —**give it to.** *Informal.* To scold or thrash soundly. —**give off.** To discharge; send forth; emit. —**give out. 1.** To let (something) be known; to broadcast. **2.** To distribute. **3.** To break down; fail. —**give over. 1.** To hand over; relinquish the care of. **2.** To abandon; quit. —**give rise to.** To cause; occasion. —**give up. 1.** To surrender: *give yourself up.* **2.** To stop: *give up smoking.* **3.** To relinquish: *give up hope.* **4.** To abandon hope for: *give her up as lost.* —**give way. 1. a.** To withdraw; retreat. **b.** To make room for: *give way to an oncoming car.* **2.** To collapse; break: *The ladder gave way.* **3.** To abandon oneself: *give way to hysteria.* —*n. Informal.* Resilient springiness: *The mattress has lots of give.* [Give, gave, given; Middle English *given, gaf, given,* Old English *giefan, geaf, giefen.* See **ghabh-** in Appendix.*]
give and take. To exchange on equal or even terms.
give-and-take (gĭv′ən-tāk′) *n.* **1.** The practice of compromise. **2.** Lively exchange of ideas or conversation.
give away. 1. To make a gift of. **2.** To observe ceremonially the transfer of a bride from her family to her husband. **3.** To reveal or make known, often accidentally.
give·a·way (gĭv′ə-wā′) *n. Informal.* **1.** Something given away at no charge. **2.** Something that betrays or exposes, often accidentally. —*adj. Informal.* Characterized by the awarding of prizes. Said of a television or radio program.
giv·en (gĭv′ən) *adj.* **1. a.** Specified: *a given date.* **b.** Issued on a specified date. Said of legal documents. **2.** Accepted as a fact; acknowledged. **3.** Habitually inclined. Used with *to: given to shyness.* **4.** Bestowed; presented.
given name. A name given to a person at birth or at baptism.
Gi·za (gē′zə). Also **Gi·zeh, El Gi·zeh** (ĕl). A city of northeastern Egypt on the west bank of the Nile, three miles southwest of Cairo, near the site of the Great Pyramids and the Sphinx. Population, 276,000.
giz·mo. Variant of **gismo.**
giz·zard (gĭz′ərd) *n.* **1.** An enlargement of the alimentary canal in birds, often having dense muscular walls and containing fine grit eaten to aid in the digestion of seeds. **2.** A similar digestive organ of certain invertebrates, such as the earthworm. **3.** *Informal.* The stomach. [Middle English *giser,* from Old French *giser, gezier,* from Vulgar Latin *gicerium* (unattested), from Latin *gigeria,* cooked entrails of poultry, possibly from Persian *jigar.* See **yekwr̥** in Appendix.*]
Gk. Greek.
gl. gloss.
GLA Airport code for Glasgow, Scotland.
gla·bel·la (glə-bĕl′ə) *n., pl.* **-bellae** (-bĕl′ē′). The smooth area between the eyebrows just above the nose. [New Latin, from Latin *glabellus,* hairless, from *glaber,* hairless, bald, GLABROUS.]
gla·brous (glā′brəs) *adj. Biology.* Having no hairs or pubescence; smooth. [Latin *glaber,* hairless, bald. See **ghel-**[2] in Appendix.*]
gla·cé (glă-sā′) *adj.* **1.** Having a glazed, glossy surface. **2.** Coated with a sugar glaze; candied. —*tr.v.* **glacéed, -céing, -cés. 1.** To glaze. **2.** To candy. [French, past participle of *glacer,* to ice, glaze, from *glace,* ice, from Latin *glaciēs.* See **glacier.**]
gla·cial (glā′shəl) *adj.* **1.** Of, pertaining to, or derived from a glacier. **2.** *Often capital* **G.** Characterized or dominated by the existence of glaciers. Said especially of the Pleistocene. **3.** Extremely cold. **4.** Having the appearance of ice. [Latin *glaciālis,* icy, from *glaciēs,* ice. See **glacier.**] —**gla′cial·ly** *adv.*
glacial acetic acid. **Acetic acid** *(see)* that is at least 99.8 per cent pure.
glacial epoch. 1. Any of several periods during the Pleistocene epoch up to 1,000,000 years ago, when much of the earth's surface was covered by glaciers. **2.** The Pleistocene epoch.
gla·cial·ist (glā′shə-lĭst) *n.* One who studies glaciers.
gla·ci·ate (glā′shē-āt′) *tr.v.* **-ated, -ating, -ates. 1.** To subject to

glacial action. **2.** *Rare.* To freeze. [Latin *glaciāre,* to freeze, from *glaciēs,* ice. See **glacier.**] **—gla'ci·a'tion** *n.*

gla·cier (glā'shər) *n.* A huge mass of laterally limited, moving ice originating from compacted snow. [French, from *glace,* ice, from Latin *glaciēs.* See **gel-**[3] in Appendix.*]

Glacier Bay National Monument. An area of mountains and glaciers comprising 3,590 square miles of southeastern Alaska on the British Columbia border.

glacier lily. The **fawn lily** *(see).*

Glacier National Park. A park comprising 1,560 square miles of northwestern Montana and including numerous lakes and small glaciers.

gla·ci·ol·o·gy (glā'sē-ŏl'ə-jē) *n.* The scientific study of glaciers. [GLACIER + -LOGY.] **—gla'ci·o·log'ic** (-ə-lŏj'ĭk), **gla'ci·o·log'i·cal** *adj.* **—gla'ci·ol'o·gist** *n.*

gla·cis (glā'sĭs, glăs'ĭs, glă-sē') *n.* **1.** A gentle slope; an incline: *"The foam . . . mounts in an instant to the ridge of the sand glacis."* (R.L. Stevenson). **2.** A slope extended in front of a fortification in such a way that it can be swept by the defenders' fire. [French, from Old French *glacier,* to slide, from *glace,* ice, from Latin *glaciēs.* See **gel-**[3] in Appendix.*]

Glack·ens (glăk'ənz), **William James.** 1870–1938. American painter and illustrator.

glad (glăd) *adj.* **gladder, gladdest. 1.** Experiencing or exhibiting joy and pleasure. **2.** Providing joy and pleasure: *a glad occasion.* **3.** Pleased; willing: *glad to help.* **4.** *Archaic.* Of a cheerful disposition. **—***v.* **gladded, gladding, glads.** *Obsolete.* **—***tr.* To gladden. **—***intr.* To gladden. [Middle English *glad,* joyful, happy, shining, Old English *glæd.* See **ghel-**[2] in Appendix.*] **—glad'ly** *adv.* **—glad'ness** *n.*

Synonyms: *glad, happy, cheerful, lighthearted, joyful, joyous.* These adjectives mean in good spirits. *Glad* often has reference to the strong feeling that results from gratification of a wish or from satisfaction with immediate circumstances. *Happy,* a more general term, can describe almost any condition of good spirits, temporary or sustained. *Cheerful* suggests good spirits made obvious by an outgoing nature, and *lighthearted* makes more explicit the absence of care. *Joyful* and *joyous,* the strongest of these terms, suggest extremely high spirits or a strong sense of fulfillment or satisfaction.

Glad·beck (glät'bĕk'). A city and coal-mining center of North Rhine-Westphalia, West Germany, 22 miles northwest of Dortmund. Population, 84,000.

glad·den (glăd'n) *v.* **-dened, -dening, -dens. —***tr.* To make glad. **—***intr. Archaic.* To become glad.

glade (glād) *n.* An open space in a forest. [Perhaps from GLAD (obsolete sense "shining").]

glad eye. *Slang.* A leer. Usually used with *give: He gave her the glad eye.*

glad hand. *Informal.* **1. a.** A hearty and friendly handshake. **b.** A hearty welcome or greeting. **2.** An effusive, typically insincere and offensively familiar greeting.

glad-hand (glăd'hănd') *v.* **-handed, -handing, -hands.** *Informal.* **—***tr.* To extend a glad hand to. **—***intr.* To extend a glad hand. **—glad'-hand'er** *n.*

glad·i·ate (glăd'ē-āt', -ĭt, glā'dē-) *adj.* Sword-shaped, as a leaf. [New Latin *gladiatus,* from Latin *gladius,* sword. See **gladiator.**]

glad·i·a·tor (glăd'ē-ā'tər) *n.* **1.** A professional combatant, slave, captive, or condemned prisoner trained to entertain the public by engaging in mortal combat in the ancient Roman arena. **2.** A controversialist or disputant, especially one chosen to represent his faction or party in a public debate. **3.** A prize fighter. [Middle English, from Latin *gladiātor,* from *gladius,* sword. See **kel-**[2] in Appendix.*] **—glad'i·a·to'ri·al** (-ə-tôr'ē-əl, -tōr'ē-əl) *adj.*

glad·i·o·lus (glăd'ē-ō'ləs) *n., pl.* **-li** (-lī', -lē') or **-luses.** Also **glad·i·o·la** (-lə) (for sense 1). **1.** Any of various plants of the genus *Gladiolus,* native to tropical regions but widely cultivated elsewhere, having sword-shaped leaves and a spike of showy, variously colored flowers. **2.** *Anatomy.* The large middle section of the sternum. [Latin, diminutive of *gladius,* sword. See **gladiator.**]

glad rags. *Informal.* One's best or most elegant clothes.

glad·some (glăd'səm) *adj.* **1.** Glad; joyful. **2.** Causing gladness. **—glad'some·ly** *adv.* **—glad'some·ness** *n.*

Glad·stone (glăd'stōn', -stən) *n.* **1.** A light four-wheeled convertible carriage with two interior seats and places outside for a driver and footman. **2.** A Gladstone bag. [After W.E. GLADSTONE.]

Glad·stone (glăd'stōn', -stən), **William Ewart.** 1809–1898. British statesman; four times prime minister (1868–94).

Gladstone bag. A piece of light hand luggage consisting of two hinged compartments. [After W.E. GLADSTONE.]

Glad·ys (glăd'ĭs). A feminine given name. [Welsh *Gwladys,* perhaps from Latin *Claudia,* feminine of *Claudius,* name of two Roman gentes.]

Glag·o·lit·ic (glăg'ə-lĭt'ĭk) *adj.* Also **Glag·o·lith·ic** (-lĭth'ĭk). Belonging to or written in an alphabet attributed to Saint Cyril, formerly used in the writing of various Slavic languages but now limited to the Catholic liturgical books used by some communities along the Dalmatian coast. Compare **Cyrillic alphabet.** [New Latin *glagoliticus,* from Serbo-Croatian *glagolica,* the Glagolitic alphabet, from *glagól,* word, akin to Old Church Slavonic *glagolŭ,* word. See **gal-**[2] in Appendix.*]

glair (glâr) *n.* Also **glaire. 1.** Raw egg white used in sizing or glazing. **2.** A size or glaze made of egg white. **—***tr.v.* **glaired, glairing, glairs.** To apply glair to. [Middle English *glaire,* from Old French, from Vulgar Latin *clāria ovi* (unattested), white of egg, from *clārus,* clear. See **kel-**[3] in Appendix.*]

glair·y (glâr'ē) *adj.* **-ier, -iest.** Also **glair·e·ous** (glâr'ē-əs). **1.** Like glair. **2.** Coated with glair. **—glair'i·ness** *n.*

glaive (glāv) *n. Archaic & Poetic.* A sword; especially, a broadsword. [Middle English *glaive,* from Old French, from Latin *gladius,* sword. See **kel-**[2] in Appendix.*]

Glå·ma. The Swedish name for the **Glomma.**

Gla·mor·gan·shire (glə-môr'gən-shĭr, -shər). Also **Gla·mor·gan** (glə-môr'gən). A county, 813 square miles in area, of southeastern Wales; a mining and manufacturing district. Population, 1,244,000. County seat, Cardiff.

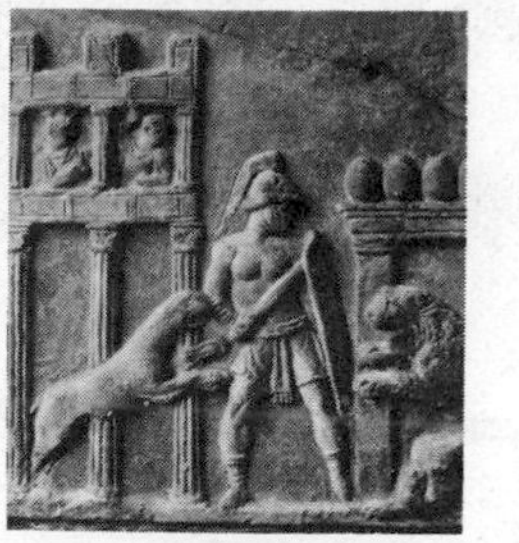

gladiator
Terra-cotta low relief

glam·or·ize (glăm'ə-rīz') *tr.v.* **-ized, -izing, -izes.** Also **glam·our·ize. 1.** To make glamorous or add glamour to. **2.** To treat or portray in a romantic manner; romanticize, idealize, or glorify. **—glam'or·i·za'tion** *n.* **—glam'or·iz'er** *n.*

glam·or·ous (glăm'ər-əs) *adj.* Also **glam·our·ous.** Characterized by glamour. **—glam'or·ous·ly** *adv.* **—glam'or·ous·ness** *n.*

glam·our (glăm'ər) *n.* Also **glam·or. 1.** Compelling charm, romance, and excitement; especially, such qualities when delusively alluring. **2.** *Archaic.* Magic; enchantment; a magic spell. [Scottish variant of GRAMMAR (because learning was associated with magic).]

glance[1] (glăns, gläns) *v.* **glanced, glancing, glances. —***intr.* **1.** To strike a surface at such an angle as to be deflected: *A pebble glanced off the windshield.* **2.** To direct the gaze briefly: *glance at the menu.* **3.** To shine briefly; glint. **4.** To refer to or touch upon briefly. **—***tr.* **1.** To strike (a surface) at an angle; graze: *The baseball glanced the fence.* **2.** To cause to strike a surface at an angle: *glance a stone over the stream.* —See Synonyms at **flash. —***n.* **1.** An oblique movement following impact; deflection. **2.** A brief or cursory look. **3.** A quick flash of light; a gleam. [Alteration of Middle English *glacen* (influenced by *glenten,* to shine, GLINT), from Old French *glacier,* to slide, from *glace,* ice, from Latin *glaciēs.* See **gel-**[3] in Appendix.*]

glance[2] (glăns, gläns) *n.* Any of various minerals that have a brilliant luster: *silver glance.* [German *Glanz,* from Old High German *glanz,* bright. See **ghel-**[2] in Appendix.*]

gland (glănd) *n. Anatomy.* **1.** An organ that extracts specific substances from the blood and concentrates or alters them for subsequent secretion. **2.** Any of various nonsecretory or excretory organs that resemble such organs. **3.** *Botany.* An organ or structure that secretes a substance. **4.** *Machinery.* A sliding part that is designed to hold something in place. [French *glande,* from Old French, glandular swelling, acorn, from Latin *glāns* (stem *gland-*), acorn. See **gwel-**[3] in Appendix.*]

glan·ders (glăn'dərz) *n.* A contagious, often chronic, sometimes fatal disease of horses and other animals, caused by a bacillus, *Actinobacillus mallei,* and characterized by a nasal discharge and ulcers in the lungs, respiratory tract, and skin. [Old French *glandres,* plural of *glandre,* glandular swelling, from Latin *glandula,* diminutive of *glāns* (stem *gland-*), acorn. See **gland.**] **—glan'der·ous** *adj.*

glan·du·lar (glăn'jə-lər) *adj.* **1.** Of, pertaining to, affecting, or resembling a gland or its secretion. **2.** Functioning as a gland. **3.** Having glands. **4. a.** Resulting from abnormal gland function. **b.** *Nonstandard.* Afflicted with a gland disorder. **5.** Innate; instinctive: *a glandular hatred of flabbiness.* [French *glandulaire,* from *glandule,* small gland, from Latin *glandula,* glandular swelling. See **glanders.**]

glandular fever. *Pathology.* **Infectious mononucleosis** *(see).*

glans (glănz) *n., pl.* **glandes** (glăn'dēz). *Anatomy.* **1.** The glans penis. **2.** The glans clitoridis. [Latin *glāns,* "acorn" (from its shape). See **gwel-**[3] in Appendix.*]

glans cli·tor·i·dis (klī-tôr'ə-dĭs, klĭ-). The small mass of erectile tissue at the tip of the clitoris.

glans penis. The head or tip of the penis.

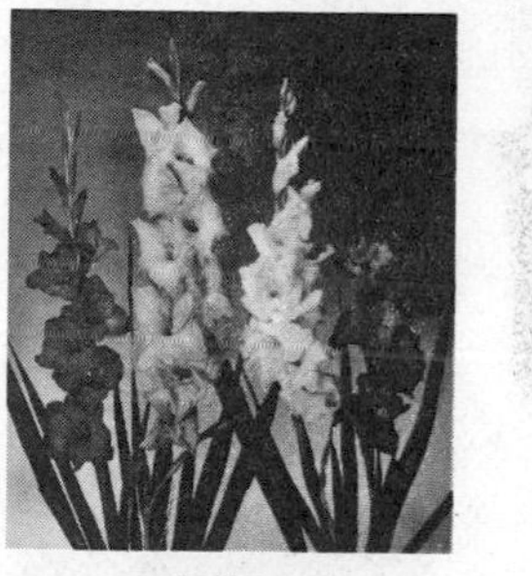

gladiolus
Gladiolus hortulanus

glare[1] (glâr) *v.* **glared, glaring, glares. —***intr.* **1.** To stare fixedly and angrily. **2.** To shine intensely and blindingly; dazzle. **3.** To be conspicuous; stand out obtrusively. **—***tr.* To express (an emotion) by staring fixedly and angrily. —See Synonyms at **gaze. —***n.* **1.** A fixed, angry stare. **2.** An intense and blinding light. **3.** *Rare.* Showy brilliance; gaudiness: *the pomp and glare of rhetoric.* —See Synonyms at **blaze.** [Middle English *glaren,* probably from Middle Low German, to gleam. See **ghel-**[2] in Appendix.*]

glare[2] (glâr) *n.* A sheet or surface of ice. [Probably from GLARE (shine).]

glar·ing (glâr'ĭng) *adj.* **1.** Staring fixedly and angrily. **2.** Shining intensely and blindingly. **3.** Ostentatious; gaudy; garish. **4.** Painfully conspicuous; egregious. —See Synonyms at **flagrant. —glar'ing·ly** *adv.*

glar·y (glâr'ē) *adj.* **-ier, -iest.** Dazzlingly bright.

Gla·ser (glā'zər), **Donald Arthur.** Born 1926. American nuclear physicist; invented the bubble chamber.

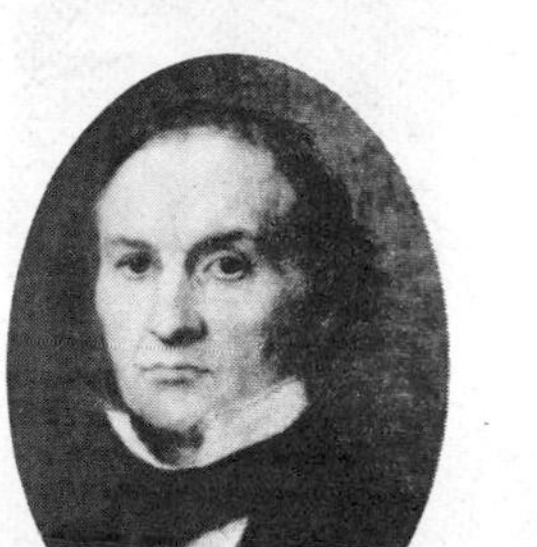

William Ewart Gladstone
Contemporary portrait by George Frederick Watts

Glas·gow (glăs'gō, -kō, gläs'-). The largest city of Scotland, a shipbuilding and manufacturing center located in the southwest on the Clyde. Population, 1,796,000.

glass (glăs, gläs) *n.* **1.** Any of a large class of materials with highly variable mechanical and optical properties that solidify from the molten state without crystallization, that are typically based on silicon dioxide, boric oxide, aluminum oxide, or phosphorus pentoxide, that are generally transparent or translucent, and are regarded physically as supercooled liquids rather than true solids. **2.** Objects made of glass collectively; glassware. **3.** Something made of glass, especially: **a.** A drinking vessel. **b.** A mirror. **c.** A barometer. **d.** A windowpane. **4. a.** *Usually plural.* Any device containing a lens or lenses and used as an aid to vision. **b.** *Plural.* **Eyeglasses** *(see).* **5.** The quantity contained by a drinking vessel; glassful. **—***adj.* Of,

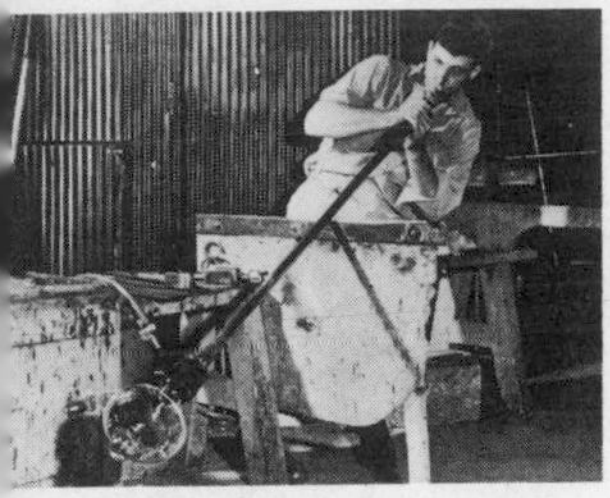
glass blowing

pertaining to, or made of glass. —*v.* **glassed, glassing, glasses.** —*tr.* **1.** To place within glass or a glass container. **2.** To provide with glass or glass parts. **3.** To make like glass; to glaze. **4.** *Poetic.* **a.** To see reflected, as in a mirror. **b.** To mirror; reflect. —*intr.* To become like glass. [Middle English *glas,* Old English *glæs.* See **ghel-²** in Appendix.*]
glass blower. One engaged in glass blowing.
glass blowing. The art or process of shaping an object from molten glass by blowing air into it through a tube.
glass eel. An eel in its transparent, postlarval stage.
glass·ful (glăs′fo͝ol′, gläs′-) *n., pl.* **-fuls.** The quantity contained in a glass.
glass harmonica. A musical instrument consisting of a set of graduated glass bowls that produce tones when a moistened finger is passed over their rims. Also called "musical glasses."
glass·house (glăs′hous′, glas′-) *n.* **1.** A glassworks. **2.** *Chiefly British.* A greenhouse.
glass·ine (glă-sēn′) *n.* A nearly transparent, resilient, glazed paper resistant to the passage of air and grease.
glass·mak·er (glăs′mā′kər, gläs′-) *n.* One who makes glass. —**glass′mak′ing** *n.*
glass·man (glăs′mən, gläs′-) *n., pl.* **-men** (-mĭn). **1.** One who sells glass. **2.** A glassmaker.
glass snake. Any of several slender, limbless, snakelike lizards of the genus *Ophisaurus,* having a tail that breaks or snaps off readily. [From the brittleness of its tail.]
glass·ware (glăs′wâr′, gläs′-) *n.* Objects, especially vessels, made of glass.
glass wool. Fine-spun fibers of glass used for insulation, air filters, and the like.
glass·work (glăs′wûrk′, gläs′-) *n.* **1. a.** The manufacture of glassware or glass. **b.** The cutting and fitting of glass panes; glaziery. **2.** Glassware. **3.** *Plural.* An establishment where glass is manufactured. Used with a singular verb.
glass·wort (glăs′wûrt′, -wôrt′, gläs′-) *n.* Any of various plants of the genus *Salicornia,* growing in salt marshes and having fleshy stems and rudimentary, scalelike leaves. Also called "samphire." [Formerly used in making glass.]
glass·y (glăs′ē, gläs′ē) *adj.* **-ier, -iest. 1.** Resembling or characterizing glass. **2.** Lifeless; expressionless: *"the face changing to a demon's face with a fixed glassy grin"* (Katherine Anne Porter). —**glass′i·ly** *adv.* —**glass′i·ness** *n.*
Glas·ton·bury (glăs′tən-bĕr′ē). A town of central Somerset, England, where, according to tradition, Saint Joseph of Arimathea founded the first Christian church in England.
Glat·zer Neis·se (glät′sər nī′sə). *Polish* **Ny·sa Klodz·ka** (nī′sə klôts′kä). A river rising in southwest Poland and flowing approximately 120 miles northeast to join the Oder.
Glau·ber (glou′bər), **Johann Rudolf.** 1604–1668. German chemist and physician.
Glauber's salts. Also **Glauber's salt.** A hydrated sodium sulfate, $Na_2SO_4 \cdot 10H_2O$, used in paper and glass manufacturing and as a cathartic. [Invented by J.R. GLAUBER.]
glau·co·ma (glô-kō′mə, glou-) *n.* A disease of the eye characterized by high intraocular pressure, damaged optic disk, hardening of the eyeball, and partial or complete loss of vision. [Latin *glaucōma,* cataract, from Greek *glaukōma,* from *glaukos,* GLAUCOUS.] —**glau·co′ma·tous** *adj.*
glau·co·nite (glô′kə-nīt′) *n.* A hydrous silicate of potassium, iron, aluminum, or magnesium, $K_2(Mg,Fe)_2Al_6(Si_4O_{10})_3(OH)_{12}$, found in greensand, and used as a water softener and fertilizer. [Greek *glaukon,* neuter of *glaukos,* GLAUCOUS + -ITE.] —**glau′co·nit′ic** (glô′kə-nĭt′ĭk) *adj.*
glau·cous (glô′kəs) *adj. Botany.* Grayish green or bluish green, as are many leaves due to a fine, whitish, powdery coating. [Latin *glaucus,* from Greek *glaukos*†, gleaming, bluish green or gray.]
glaze (glāz) *n.* **1.** A thin, smooth, shiny coating. **2.** A thin, glassy coating of ice. **3. a.** A coating of colored, opaque, or transparent material applied to ceramics before firing. **b.** A coating applied to food, as of syrup. **c.** A transparent coating applied to the surface of a painting to modify the color tones. **4.** A glassy film, as over the eyes. —*v.* **glazed, glazing, glazes.** —*tr.* **1.** To fit or furnish with glass, as a window. **2.** To apply a glaze to. **3.** To give a smooth, lustrous surface to. —*intr.* **1.** To be or become glazed. **2.** To form a glaze. [Middle English *glāsen,* to provide with glass or a glassy surface, from *glas,* GLASS.] —**glaz′er** *n.*
gla·zier (glā′zhər) *n.* One who cuts and fits window glass. [Middle English *glasier,* from *glas,* GLASS.]
gla·zier·y (glā′zhə-rē) *n.* Glasswork.
glaz·ing (glā′zĭng) *n.* **1. a.** Glaziery. **b.** Glass set or made to be set in frames. **2. a.** A glaze. **b.** The process of applying a glaze.
gld. guilder.
gleam (glēm) *n.* **1.** A fleeting beam or flash of light. **2.** A steady but subdued shining; a glow. **3.** A brief or dim manifestation or indication: *a gleam of intelligence.* —*intr.v.* **gleamed, gleaming, gleams. 1.** To emit a gleam; to flash or glow: *"It shone with gold and gleamed with ivory"* (Edith Hamilton). **2.** To be manifested or indicated briefly or faintly. —See Synonyms at **flash.** [Middle English *gleem, glem.* Old English *glǣm.* See **ghel-²** in Appendix.*]
glean (glēn) *v.* **gleaned, gleaning, gleans.** —*intr.* To gather grain left behind by reapers. —*tr.* **1.** To gather (grain) left behind by reapers. **2.** To collect (knowledge or information, for example) bit by bit: *"records from which historians glean their knowledge"* (Kemp Malone). [Middle English *glenen,* from Old French *glener,* from Late Latin *glennāre,* from Celtic *glend-no-* (unattested).]

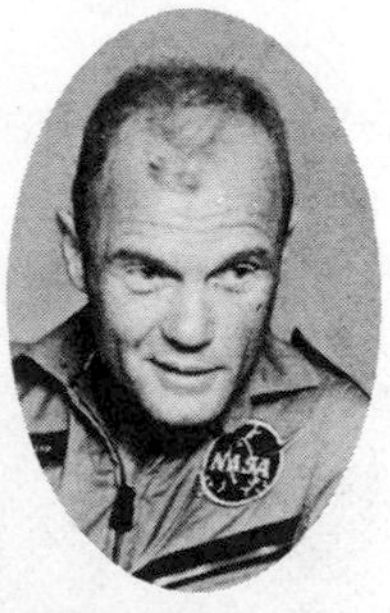
John H. Glenn, Jr.

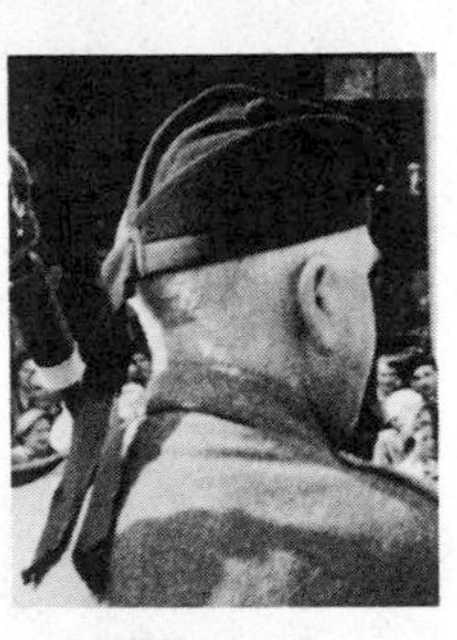
Glengarry

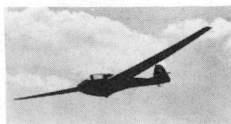

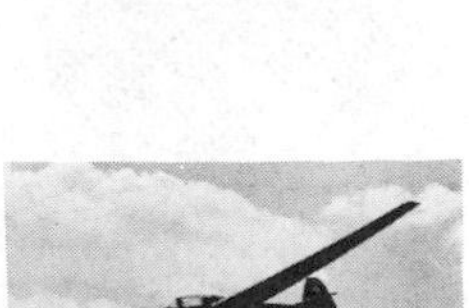
glider

gle·ba (glē′bə) *n., pl.* **-bae** (-bē′). *Botany.* The inner, spore-bearing mass of a puffball. [New Latin, from Latin *glēba, glǣba,* clod, GLEBE.]
glebe (glēb) *n.* **1.** *British.* A plot of land granted to a clergyman as part of his benefice during his tenure of office. **2.** *Poetic.* The soil or earth, regarded as the source of vegetation; land. [Latin *glēba, glǣba,* clod. See **gel-¹** in Appendix.*]
glede (glēd) *n. British Regional.* A predatory bird, the kite, *Milvus milvus.* [Middle English *glede,* Old English *glida.* See **ghel-²** in Appendix.*]
glee (glē) *n.* **1.** Merriment; joy. **2.** An unaccompanied part song scored for three or more male voices that was popular in the 18th century. —See Synonyms at **mirth.** [Middle English *glē,* Old English *glēo,* merriment, play, music. See **ghel-²** in Appendix.*]
glee club. A group of singers who perform usually short pieces of choral music.
gleed (glēd) *n. British Regional.* A glowing coal; an ember. [Middle English *glede, gleed,* Old English *glēd.* See **ghel-²** in Appendix.*]
glee·ful (glē′fəl) *adj.* Full of glee; merry. —**glee′ful·ly** *adv.* —**glee′ful·ness** *n.*
glee·man (glē′mən) *n., pl.* **-men** (-mĭn). *Archaic.* A medieval itinerant singer; minstrel. [Middle English *gleeman,* Old English *glēoman* : *glēo,* GLEE + *mann,* MAN.]
glee·some (glē′səm) *adj. Archaic.* Gleeful.
gleet (glēt) *n.* **1.** Chronic inflammation of the urethra, characterized by mucopurulent discharge. **2.** The discharge characterizing this condition. [Middle English *glet,* slime, mucus, from Old French *glete,* from Latin *glittus,* sticky. See **gel-¹** in Appendix.*] —**gleet′y** *adj.*
gleg (glĕg) *adj. Scottish.* Alert and quick to respond. [Middle English *gleg,* clear-sighted, from Old Norse *glöggr.* See **ghel-²** in Appendix.*]
Glei·witz. The German name for **Gliwice.**
glen (glĕn) *n. Chiefly Scottish.* A valley. [Middle English *glen,* from Scottish Gaelic *gle(a)nn,* from Old Irish *glend*†.]
Glen Al·byn. See **Great Glen of Scotland.**
Glen·coe (glĕn-kō′). A valley in northern Argyll, Scotland; the site of the MacDonalds' massacre by the Campbells and by English troops (1692).
Glen·dale (glĕn′dāl′). A city in southwestern California, six miles north of Los Angeles. Population, 119,000.
Glen·gar·ry (glĕn-găr′ē) *n., pl.* **-ries.** A woolen cap originating in Scotland that is creased lengthwise and often has short ribbons at the back.
Glen More. See **Great Glen of Scotland.**
Glenn (glĕn), **John H(erschel), Jr.** Born 1921. American astronaut; first American to orbit the earth in space (1962).
gley (glā) *n.* A sticky, bluish-gray soil layer formed under the influence of excessive moisture. [Russian *gleĭ,* clay. See **gel-¹** in Appendix.*]
gli·a·din (glī′ə-dĭn) *n.* Any of several simple proteins derived from rye or wheat gluten. [Italian *gliadina,* from Medieval Greek *glia, gloia,* glue. See **gel-¹** in Appendix.*]
glib (glĭb) *adj.* **glibber, glibbest. 1. a.** Performed with ease and informality. **b.** Superficial; insincere. **2.** Easy and fluent in speech and writing. —See Synonyms at **talkative.** [Probably from Low German *glibbrig,* from Middle Low German *glibberich,* slippery. See **ghel-²** in Appendix.*] —**glib′ly** *adv.* —**glib′ness** *n.*
glide (glīd) *v.* **glided, gliding, glides.** —*intr.* **1.** To move in a smooth, effortless manner. **2.** To occur or pass imperceptibly. **3.** *Aviation.* To descend slowly without engine power. **4.** *Music.* To blend one tone into the next; to slur. **5.** *Phonetics.* To articulate a glide. —*tr.* To cause to glide. —See Synonyms at **slide.** —*n.* **1.** A smooth effortless movement. **2.** *Aviation.* A powerless descent in an airplane. **3.** *Music.* A slur. **4.** *Phonetics.* **a.** The transitional sound produced by passing from the articulatory position of one speech sound to that of another. **b.** A **semivowel** *(see).* [Middle English *gliden,* Old English *glīdan.* See **ghel-²** in Appendix.*]
glid·er (glī′dər) *n.* **1.** One that glides. **2.** *Aviation.* A light, engineless aircraft with lift surfaces, especially extended wings, designed for long periods of gliding after launch from a towing vehicle. **3.** A swinging couch suspended from a vertical frame. **4.** A device that aids gliding.
gliding lemur. The **flying lemur** *(see).*
glim (glĭm) *n. Archaic Slang.* **1.** A source of light, such as a candle. **2.** An eye. [Perhaps shortened from GLIMMER.]
glim·mer (glĭm′ər) *n.* **1.** A dim or intermittent light; a flicker. **2.** A faint manifestation or indication; a glimpse. —*intr.v.* **glimmered, -mering, -mers. 1.** To emit a dim or intermittent light. **2.** To appear or be indicated faintly. —See Synonyms at **flash.** [Middle English *glimeren,* probably from Scandinavian, akin to Swedish *glimra.* See **ghel-²** in Appendix.*]
glimpse (glĭmps) *n.* **1.** A brief, incomplete view or look. **2.** *Archaic.* A brief flash of light. —*v.* **glimpsed, glimpsing, glimpses.** —*tr.* To obtain a brief, incomplete view of. —*intr.* To obtain a brief, incomplete view. Used with *at.* [Middle English *glimsen, glymsen,* from Germanic, akin to Middle High German *glimsen,* to gleam. See **ghel-²** in Appendix.*]
Glin·ka (glĭng′kə; *Russian* glĕn′kä), **Mikhail Ivanovich** 1803–1857. Russian composer.
glint (glĭnt) *n.* **1.** A momentary flash of light; a sparkle. **2.** A faint or fleeting manifestation; a trace. **3.** *Archaic.* A glance. —*v.* **glinted, glinting, glints.** —*intr.* **1.** To gleam or flash. **2.** *Archaic.* To move abruptly; to dart. —*tr.* To cause to gleam or flash. —See Synonyms at **flash.** [Middle English *glinten,*

ă pat/ā pay/âr care/ä father/b bib/ch church/d deed/ĕ pet/ē be/f fife/g gag/h hat/hw which/ĭ pit/ī pie/îr pier/j judge/k kick/l lid, needle/m mum/n no, sudden/ng thing/ŏ pot/ō toe/ô paw, for/oi noise/ou out/o͝o took/o͞o boot/p pop/r roar/s sauce/sh ship, dish/

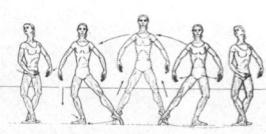

glenten, to shine, move quickly, from Scandinavian, akin to Swedish dialectal *glänta, glinta,* to shine. See **ghel-**[2] in Appendix.*]

glis·sade (glĭ-säd′, -sād′) *n.* **1.** A gliding ballet step. **2.** A controlled slide, in either a standing or a sitting position, used in descending a steep icy or snowy incline. —*intr.v.* **glissaded, -sading, -sades.** To perform a glissade. [French, from Old French, sliding motion, from *glisser,* to slide, from *glier,* to glide, from Frankish *glīdan* (unattested). See **ghel-**[2] in Appendix.*]

glis·san·do (glĭ-sän′dō) *n., pl.* **-di** (-dē) or **-dos.** *Music.* A blending of one tone into the next in a scalelike passage. [Probably pseudo-Italian formation from GLISSADE.]

glis·ten (glĭs′ən) *intr.v.* **-tened, -tening, -tens.** To shine by reflection; reflect lustrously. See Synonyms at **flash.** —*n.* A shine or sparkle. [Middle English *glistnen,* Old English *glisnian.* See **ghel-**[2] in Appendix.*]

glis·ter (glĭs′tər) *intr.v.* **-tered, -tering, -ters.** *Poetic.* To glisten. —*n. Poetic.* Glitter; brilliance. [Middle English *glistren,* probably from Middle Dutch *glisteren.* See **ghel-**[2] in Appendix.*]

glit·ter (glĭt′ər) *n.* **1.** A sparkling light or brightness. **2. a.** Brilliant attractiveness. **b.** Showy splendor. **3.** Small pieces of highly reflective decorative material. —*intr.v.* **glittered, -tering, -ters. 1.** To sparkle brilliantly; glisten. **2.** To be brilliantly attractive or colorful. —See Synonyms at **flash.** [Middle English *gliteren,* from Old Norse *glitra.* See **ghel-**[2] in Appendix.*] —**glit′ter·ing·ly** *adv.* —**glit′ter·y** *adj.*

Gli·wi·ce (glə-vē′tsĕ). *German* **Glei·witz** (glī′vĭts). A city and manufacturing center of southwestern Poland, in former Prussian Silesia. Population, 146,000.

gloam·ing (glō′mĭng) *n.* Also *archaic* **gloam** (glōm). *Poetic.* Twilight. [Middle English *gloming* (Scottish dialect), Old English *glōmung,* from *glōm,* dusk. See **ghel-**[2] in Appendix.*]

gloat (glōt) *intr.v.* **gloated, gloating, gloats.** To regard with great, excessive, or malicious pleasure or satisfaction. Often used with *over: gloat over one's golf score.* [Perhaps from Scandinavian, akin to Old Norse *glotta,* to smile scornfully. See **ghel-**[2] in Appendix.*]

glob (glŏb) *n.* **1.** A small drop of something; globule. **2.** A rounded, usually large, lump or mass of something: *a glob of mashed potatoes.* [Middle English *globbe,* large mass, from Latin *globus,* GLOBE.]

glob·al (glō′bəl) *adj.* **1.** Having the shape of a globe; spherical. **2.** Of, relating to, or involving the entire earth; worldwide: *a global disarmament treaty.* **3.** Comprehensive; entire; total. —**glob′al·ly** *adv.*

glo·bate (glō′bāt′) *adj.* Also **glo·bat·ed** (-bā′tĭd). Having the shape of a globe; globular. [Latin *globātus,* past participle of *globāre,* to form into a globe, from *globus,* GLOBE.]

globe (glōb) *n.* **1.** Any body having the shape of a sphere; especially, a representation of the earth or heavens in the form of a hollow ball. **2. a.** The earth itself. Usually used with *the.* **b.** Any planet. **3.** Any object resembling a globe; especially, a rounded container, such as a fishbowl or a protective or decorative covering for a light bulb. **4.** A sphere emblematic of sovereignty; an orb. —*v.* **globed, globing, globes.** —*intr.* To assume the shape of a globe. —*tr.* To form into a globe. [Middle English, from Old French, from Latin *globus.* See **gel-**[1] in Appendix.*]

globe amaranth. A tropical Old World plant, *Gomphrena globosa,* cultivated for its variously colored flowers that retain their colors when dried.

globe artichoke. See **artichoke.**

globe·fish (glōb′fĭsh′) *n., pl.* **globefish** or **-fishes.** Any of various fishes, such as the **ocean sunfish** *(see),* having or capable of assuming a globular shape.

globe·flow·er (glōb′flou′ər) *n.* Any of several plants of the genus *Trollius,* having globe-shaped, usually yellow flowers.

globe·trot·ter (glōb′trŏt′ər) *n.* One who travels often and widely, especially for sightseeing. —**globe′trot′ting** *n.* & *adj.*

glo·bin (glō′bən) *n.* A simple protein obtained from hemoglobin. [Latin *globus,* GLOBE + -IN.]

glo·boid (glō′boid′) *adj.* Having a globelike shape; spheroid. —*n.* A globe-shaped object; a spheroid. [GLOB(E) + -OID.]

glo·bose (glō′bōs′) *adj.* Also **glo·bous** (-bəs). Spherical; globular. [Latin *globōsus,* from *globus,* GLOBE.] —**glo′bose′ly** *adv.* —**glo′bose′ness, glo·bos′i·ty** (-bŏs′ə-tē) *n.*

glob·u·lar (glŏb′yə-lər) *adj.* **1.** Having the shape of a globe or globule; spherical. **2.** Consisting of globules. **3.** Worldwide; global. —**glob′u·lar·ly** *adv.* —**glob′u·lar·ness** *n.*

glob·ule (glŏb′yōōl) *n.* A small, often minute, spherical mass; especially, a small drop of liquid. [Latin *globulus,* diminutive of *globus,* GLOBE.]

glob·u·lif·er·ous (glŏb′yə-lĭf′ər-əs) *adj.* Composed of or producing globules. [GLOBUL(E) + -FEROUS.]

glob·u·lin (glŏb′yə-lən) *n.* Any of a class of simple proteins that are found extensively in blood, milk, muscle, and plant seeds, are insoluble in pure water, soluble in dilute salt solution, and coagulable by heat. [GLOBUL(E) + -IN.]

glo·chid·i·um (glō-kĭd′ē-əm) *n., pl.* **-ia** (-ē-ə). Also **glo·chid** (glō′kĭd) (for sense 2). **1.** *Zoology.* A parasitic larva of certain freshwater mussels of the family Unionidae, having hooks for attaching to a host fish. **2.** *Botany.* One of the barbed hairs or bristles on certain plants, such as the prickly pear. [New Latin, from Greek *glōkhis,* barb of an arrow. See **glōgh-** in Appendix.*] —**glo·chid′i·ate** (-ĭt, -āt′) *adj.*

glock·en·spiel (glŏk′ən-spēl′, -shpēl′) *n.* A percussion musical instrument having a series of metal bars tuned to the chromatic scale and played with two light hammers. [German *Glockenspiel,* "play of bells" : *Glocke,* bell, from Old High German *glocka* (imitative) + *Spiel,* play (see **spiel**).]

glogg (glŏg) *n.* Also **glögg** (glœg). A hot punch made of red wine, brandy, and sherry flavored with almonds, raisins, and orange peel, originally made in Sweden for serving during the Christmas holiday season.

glom·er·ate (glŏm′ə-rĭt, -rāt′) *adj.* Formed into a compact, rounded mass; tightly clustered; conglomerate. [Latin *glomerātus,* past participle of *glomerāre,* to make into a ball, from *glomus* (stem *glomer-*), ball. See **gel-**[1] in Appendix.*]

glom·er·ule (glŏm′ə-rōōl′) *n.* **1.** *Botany.* A compact cluster of flowers. **2.** *Anatomy.* A glomerulus. [New Latin *glomerulus,* from Latin *glomus* (stem *glomer-*), ball. See **gel-**[1] in Appendix.*] —**glo·mer′u·late′** (glō-mĕr′yə-lāt′) *adj.*

glo·mer·u·lus (glō-mĕr′yə-ləs) *n., pl.* **-li** (-lī′). **1.** A tuft of capillaries situated at the origin of a vertebrate kidney. **2.** The twisted secretory portion of a sweat gland. [New Latin, GLOMERULE.]

Glom·ma (glôm′ə). Also **Glå·ma.** A river of eastern Norway flowing 375 miles generally south into the Skagerrak.

gloom (glōōm) *n.* **1.** Partial or total darkness; dimness. **2.** A partially or totally dark place, area, or location. **3. a.** An appearance or atmosphere of melancholy or depression. **b.** A state of melancholy or depression; dejection; despondency. —*v.* **gloomed, glooming, glooms.** —*intr.* **1.** To be or become dark, shaded, or obscure. **2.** To appear despondent, sad, or mournful. —*tr.* **1.** To make dark, shaded, or obscure. **2.** To make despondent; sadden. [Middle English *gloum(b)en*†, to look glum, become dark.]

gloom·y (glōō′mē) *adj.* **-ier, -iest. 1.** Dismal, dark, or dreary. **2.** Showing or filled with gloom: *"Their gloomy faces took away his appetite"* (Edith Hamilton). **3. a.** Causing or producing gloom or dejection; depressing: *gloomy news.* **b.** Marked by hopelessness; pessimistic: *gloomy predictions.* —See Synonyms at **glum.** —**gloom′i·ly** *adv.* —**gloom′i·ness** *n.*

glo·ri·a (glôr′ē-ə, glōr′-) *n.* **1.** A halo, aureole, or nimbus. **2.** A lightweight fabric chiefly of silk, wool, or cotton, used for umbrellas and dresses. [Late Latin *glōria,* from Latin, GLORY.]

Glo·ri·a (glôr′ē-ə, glōr′-) *n.* **1.** Any of the Christian doxologies beginning with the word *Gloria.* **2.** The music to which one of these is set. [Middle English, from Latin *glōria,* GLORY.]

Gloria in ex·cel·sis De·o (ĭn ĕk-sĕl′sĭs dā′ō, dē′ō). A Latin doxology forming part of the Ordinary of the Mass, beginning with the words *Gloria in excelsis Deo.* Also called the "greater doxology." [Late Latin, "Glory to God in the highest."]

Gloria Pa·tri (păt′rē, pä′trē). A Latin doxology beginning with the words *Gloria Patri.* Also called the "lesser doxology." [Late Latin, "Glory to the Father."]

glo·ri·fi·ca·tion (glôr′ə-fĭ-kā′shən, glōr′-) *n.* **1.** The act of glorifying or the state of being glorified. **2.** *Informal.* An enhanced or glorified version of something.

glo·ri·fy (glôr′ə-fī′, glōr′-) *tr.v.* **-fied, -fying, -fies. 1.** To invest with glory or radiance; to secure honor, worship, or praise for. **2.** To bestow glory, honor, or praise upon; extol. **3.** To cause to be or seem more glorious or excellent than is actually the case. **4.** To give glory to, especially through worship. [Middle English *glorifien,* from Old French *glorifier,* from Late Latin *glōrificāre* : Latin *glōria,* GLORY + -FY.] —**glo′ri·fi′er** *n.*

glo·ri·ole (glôr′ē-ōl′, glōr′-) *n.* A halo, aureole, or nimbus; gloria. [French, from Latin *glōriola,* diminutive of *glōria,* GLORY.]

glo·ri·ous (glôr′ē-əs, glōr′-) *adj.* **1.** Having or deserving glory; famous; illustrious. **2.** Conferring or advancing glory: *a glorious achievement.* **3.** Characterized by great beauty and splendor; magnificent; resplendent. **4.** *Informal.* Very pleasant; delightful; wonderful. —**glo′ri·ous·ly** *adv.* —**glo′ri·ous·ness** *n.*

Glorious Revolution. The period in English history (1688–89) during which King James II was deposed and William and Mary of Holland were invited to assume the throne. Also called "Bloodless Revolution."

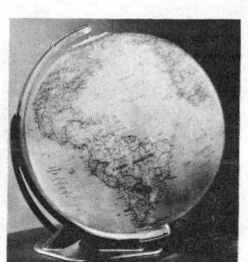

glo·ry (glôr′ē, glōr′ē) *n., pl.* **-ries. 1.** Exalted honor, praise, or distinction accorded by common consent; renown: *"For what is glory but the praise of fame"* (Milton). **2.** Something that brings honor or renown: *the glory of her position as president of the club.* **3.** A highly praiseworthy asset: *Her hair is her crowning glory.* **4.** Adoration, praise, and thanksgiving offered in worship: *We sing Thy glory.* **5.** Majestic beauty and splendor; resplendence: *"And the glory of the Lord shall be revealed."* (Isaiah 40:5). **6.** The splendor and bliss of heaven; a state of perfect happiness. **7.** A height of achievement, enjoyment, or prosperity. **8.** A halo, nimbus, or aureole. —See Synonyms at **fame.** —*intr.v.* **gloried, -rying, -ries. 1.** To rejoice triumphantly; exult. Used with *in.* **2.** *Obsolete.* To brag; boast. Used with *in.* [Middle English *glorie,* from Old French, from Latin *glōria*†, glory.]

glo·ry-of-the-snow (glôr′ē-əv-*th*ə-snō′, glōr′-) *n.* A small bulbous plant, *Chionodoxa luciliae,* native to Asia Minor, cultivated for its early-blooming blue flowers.

Glos. Gloucestershire.

gloss[1] (glôs, glŏs) *n. Abbr.* **gl. 1.** A surface shininess or luster. **2.** A deceptive or superficially attractive appearance. —*v.* **glossed, glossing, glosses.** —*tr.* **1.** To give a bright sheen or luster to. **2.** To make attractive or acceptable by deception or superficial discussion. Used with *over: He glossed over the war news.* —*intr.* To become shiny or lustrous. [Probably from Scandinavian, akin to Icelandic *glossi,* spark. See **ghel-**[2] in Appendix.*]

gloss[2] (glôs, glŏs) *n. Abbr.* **gl. 1.** A brief explanatory note or translation of a difficult or technical expression usually inserted

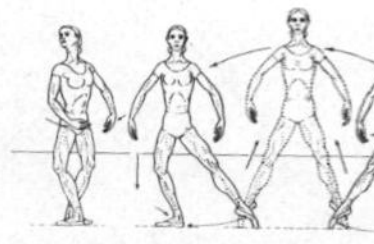

glissade

globe

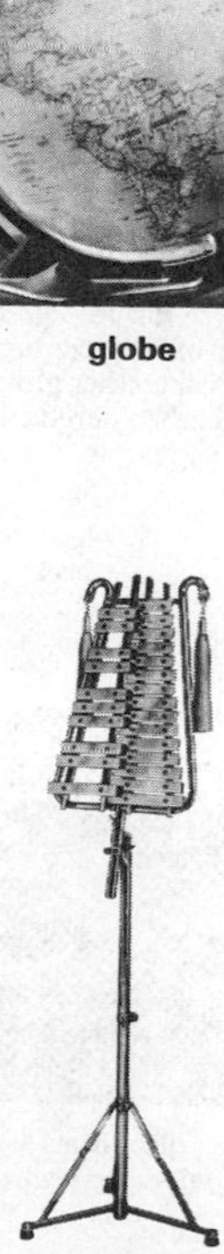

glockenspiel

in the margin or between lines of a text or manuscript. **2.** An expanded version of such notes; a glossary. **3.** A purposefully misleading interpretation or explanation. **4.** An extensive commentary, often accompanying a text or publication. —*v.* **glossed, glossing, glosses.** —*tr.* **1.** To provide (a text) with glosses. **2.** To give a false interpretation to. Often used with *over.* —*intr.* To make glosses. [Middle English *glose,* from Old French, from Medieval Latin *glōsa,* from Latin *glōssa,* word that needs explanation, from Greek *glōssa,* tongue, language. See **glōgh-** in Appendix.*] —**gloss'er** *n.*

gloss. glossary.

glos·sal (glôs'əl, glŏs'-) *adj.* Of or pertaining to the tongue. [From Greek *glōssa,* tongue. See **gloss** (explanation).]

glos·sa·ry (glôs'ə-rē, glŏs'-) *n., pl.* **-ries.** *Abbr.* **gloss.** A collection of glosses, such as a vocabulary of specialized terms with accompanying definitions. [Latin *glossārium,* from *glōssa,* GLOSS (explanation).] —**glos·sar'i·al** (glô-sâr'ē-əl, glŏ-) *adj.* —**glos·sar'i·al·ly** *adv.* —**glos'sa·rist** *n.*

glos·sog·ra·phy (glô-sŏg'rə-fē, glŏ-) *n.* The writing and compilation of glosses or glossaries. [Greek *glōssa,* tongue, language, GLOSS (explanation) + -GRAPHY.] —**glos·sog'ra·pher** *n.*

glos·so·la·li·a (glôs'ō-lā'lē-ə, glŏs'-) *n.* **1.** Fabricated nonmeaningful speech, especially as associated with certain schizophrenic syndromes. **2.** The **gift of tongues** *(see).* [New Latin *glossolalia,* from (New Testament) Greek *glōssais lalein,* "to speak with tongues" : *glossa,* tongue (see **glōgh-** in Appendix*) + *lalein,* to talk, babble (see **la-** in Appendix*).]

glos·sol·o·gy (glô-sŏl'ə-jē, glŏ-) *n. Obsolete.* Linguistics. [Greek *glōssa,* tongue, language, GLOSS (explanation) + -LOGY.] —**glos·sol'o·gist** *n.*

gloss·y (glôs'ē, glŏs'ē) *adj.* **-ier, -iest. 1.** Having a smooth, shiny, lustrous surface. **2.** Superficially attractive; specious. —*n., pl.* **glossies.** *Photography.* A print on smooth, shiny paper. Also called "glossy print." —**gloss'i·ly** *adv.* —**gloss'i·ness** *n.*

glost (glôst, glŏst) *n.* **1.** A lead glaze used for pottery. **2.** Glazed pottery. [Variation of GLOSS (sheen).]

glot·tal (glŏt'l) *adj.* **1.** Of or relating to the glottis. **2.** *Phonetics* Articulated in the glottis. [From GLOTTIS.]

glottal stop. *Phonetics.* A speech sound produced by a momentary complete closure of the glottis, followed by an explosive release.

glot·tis (glŏt'ĭs) *n., pl.* **-tises** or **glottides** (glŏt'ə-dēz') **1.** The space between the vocal cords at the upper part of the larynx. **2.** The vocal structures of the larynx. [New Latin, from Greek *glōttis,* from *glōtta, glōssa,* tongue, language. See **glōgh-** in Appendix.*]

Glouces·ter (glôs'tər, glŏs'-). **1.** Also **Glouces·ter·shire** (-shîr, -shər). *Abbr.* **Glos.** A county of south-central England, 1,257 square miles in area. Population, 1,034,000. **2.** The county seat of this county. Population, 72,000. **3.** A city, resort center, and fishing port of Massachusetts, 27 miles northeast of Boston. Population, 26,000.

glove (glŭv) *n.* **1. a.** A fitted covering for the hand, usually made of leather, wool, or cloth, having a separate sheath for each finger and the thumb. **b.** A gauntlet. **2. a.** *Baseball.* An oversized padded leather covering for the hand, used in catching balls; especially, one with more finger sheathes than the catcher's or first baseman's mitt. **b.** A **boxing glove** *(see).* —**hand in glove.** In a close or harmonious relationship. —*tr.v.* **gloved, gloving, gloves. 1.** To furnish with gloves. **2.** To cover with or as if with a glove. [Middle English *glove,* Old English *glōf.* See **lep-**[2] in Appendix.*]

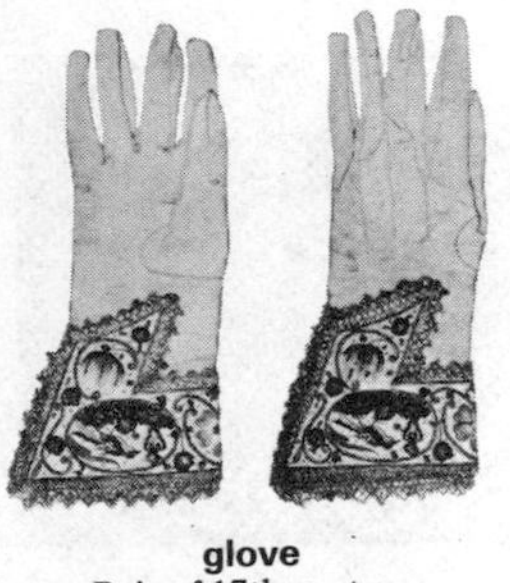

glove
Pair of 17th-century English leather gloves with embroidered cuffs

glove compartment. A small storage container in the dashboard of an automobile.

glov·er (glŭv'ər) *n.* One who makes or sells gloves.

glow (glō) *intr.v.* **glowed, glowing, glows. 1.** To shine brightly and steadily, especially without a flame: *"a red bed of embers glowing in the furnace"* (Richard Wright). **2.** To have a bright, warm color, usually reddish. **3. a.** To have a healthful, ruddy coloration. **b.** To flush; to blush. **4.** To be exuberant or radiant, as with pride. —*n.* **1.** A light produced by a body heated to luminosity; incandescence. **2.** Brilliance or warmth of color, especially redness: *"the evening glow of the city streets when the sun has gone behind the tallest houses"* (Sean O'Faolain). **3.** A sensation of physical warmth. **4.** A warm feeling of passion or emotion; ardor. —See Synonyms at **blaze.** [Middle English *glowen,* Old English *glōwan.* See **ghel-**[2] in Appendix.*]

glow·er (glou'ər) *intr.v.* **-ered, -ering, -ers.** To look or stare angrily or sullenly; to frown. —*n.* An angry, sullen, or threatening stare. [Middle English *glo(u)ren,* to shine, stare, probably from Scandinavian, akin to Norwegian dialectal *glora.* See **ghel-**[2] in Appendix.*] —**glow'er·ing·ly** *adv.*

glow·ing (glō'ĭng) *adj.* **1.** Incandescent; luminous. **2.** Characterized by rich, warm coloration; especially, having a ruddy, healthy complexion. **3.** Ardently enthusiastic or favorable.

glow plug. A small heating element in a diesel engine cylinder used to facilitate starting.

glow·worm (glō'wûrm') *n.* A firefly; especially, the luminous larva or wingless, grublike female of a firefly.

glox·in·i·a (glŏk-sĭn'ē-ə) *n.* Any of several tropical South American plants of the genus *Sinningia;* especially, *S. speciosa,* cultivated as a house plant for its showy, variously colored flowers. [New Latin, after Benjamin Peter *Gloxin,* 18th-century German botanist and physician.]

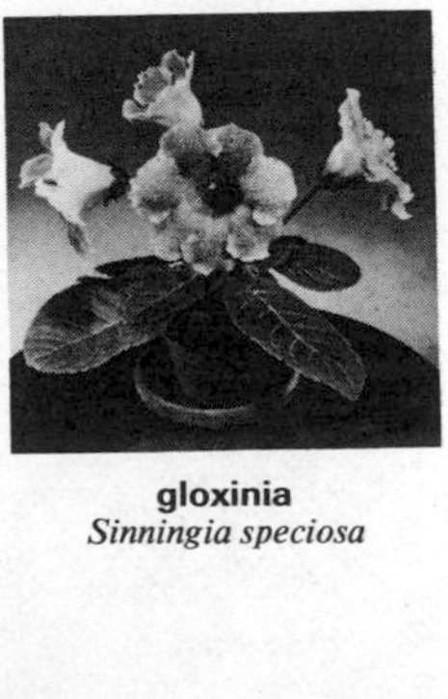

gloxinia
Sinningia speciosa

gloze (glōz) *v.* **glozed, glozing, glozes.** —*tr.* To minimize or underplay; to gloss. Used with *over.* —*intr. Archaic.* To use flattery or cajolery. [Middle English *glosen,* to gloss, falsify, flatter, from Old French *glosser,* from *glose,* GLOSS (explanation).]

Gluck (glŏŏk), **Christoph Willibald.** 1714–1787. German composer of operas.

glu·cose (glōō'kōs') *n.* **1.** A sugar, **dextrose** *(see).* **2.** A colorless to yellowish syrupy mixture of dextrose, maltose, and dextrins with about 20 per cent water, used in confectionery, alcoholic fermentation, tanning, and treating tobacco. [French, from Greek *gleukos,* sweet new wine, must. See **dlku-** in Appendix.*]

glu·co·side (glōō'kə-sīd') *n.* A **glycoside** *(see),* the sugar component of which is glucose. —**glu'co·sid'ic** (-sĭd'ĭk) *adj.*

glue (glōō) *n.* **1.** An adhesive substance or solution; a viscous substance used to join or bond. **2.** An adhesive obtained by boiling animal **collagen** *(see)* and drying the residue. In this sense, also called "animal glue." —*tr.v.* **glued, gluing, glues.** To stick or fasten together with or as if with glue. [Middle English *gleu,* glue, birdlime, gum, from Old French *glu,* from Late Latin *glūs* (stem *glūt-*), from Latin *glūten.* See **gel-**[1] in Appendix.*]

glum (glŭm) *adj.* **glummer, glummest. 1.** In low spirits; dejected. **2.** Gloomy; dismal. [From Middle English *glomen, gloumen,* to look sullen, GLOOM.] —**glum'ly** *adv.* —**glum'ness** *n.*

Synonyms: *glum, gloomy, morose, dour, saturnine.* These adjectives mean having a cheerless or repugnant aspect or disposition. *Glum* implies dejection and silence, and more often than the other terms refers to a mood or temporary condition rather than to a person's characteristic state. *Gloomy* differs little except in being more applicable to a person given to somberness or depression by nature. *Morose* implies sourness of temper and a tendency to be uncommunicative. *Dour* especially suggests a grim or humorless exterior and sometimes an unyielding nature. *Saturnine* suggests severity of aspect, extreme gravity of nature, and often a tendency to be bitter or sardonic.

glu·ma·ceous (glōō-mā'shəs) *adj.* Having or resembling a glume or glumes.

glume (glōōm) *n. Botany.* A chaffy basal bract on the spikelet of a grass. [New Latin *gluma,* from Latin *glūma,* husk. See **gleubh-** in Appendix.*]

glut (glŭt) *v.* **glutted, glutting, gluts.** —*tr.* **1.** To fill beyond capacity; satiate. **2.** To flood (a market) with an excess of goods so that supply exceeds demand. —*intr.* To eat excessively. —See Synonyms at **satiate.** —*n.* **1.** An oversupply. **2.** The act or process of glutting. [Middle English *glotten, glouten,* probably from Old French *gloutir,* to swallow, from Latin *gluttīre.* See **gwel-**[5] in Appendix.*]

glu·tam·ic acid (glōō-tăm'ĭk) *n.* An amino acid present in all complete proteins, found widely in plant and animal tissue, and having a salt, sodium glutamate, that is used as a flavor-intensifying seasoning. [GLUT(EN) + AM(IDE) + -IC.]

glu·ta·mine (glōō'tə-mēn', -mĭn) *n.* A white crystalline amino acid, $C_5H_{10}N_2O_3$, occurring in plant and animal tissue and produced commercially for use in medicine and biochemical research. [GLUT(EN) + AMINE.]

glu·ten (glōōt'n) *n.* A mixture of plant proteins occurring in cereal grains, chiefly corn and wheat, and used as an adhesive and as a flour substitute. [Latin *glūten,* glue. See **gel-**[1] in Appendix.*] —**glu'te·nous** *adj.*

gluten bread. Bread made from flour with a high gluten content and low starch content.

glu·te·us (glōō'tē-əs, glōō-tē'-) *n., pl.* **-tei** (-tē-ī', -tē'ī'). Any of three large muscles of the buttocks: **a.** *gluteus maximus,* which extends the thigh; **b.** *gluteus medius,* which rotates and abducts the thigh; **c.** *gluteus minimus,* which abducts the thigh. [New Latin, from Greek *gloutos,* buttock. See **gel-**[1] in Appendix.*] —**glu'te·al** *adj.*

glu·ti·nous (glōōt'n-əs) *adj.* Resembling or of the nature of glue; sticky; adhesive. [Latin *glūtinōsus,* from *glūten,* glue. See **gel-**[1] in Appendix.*] —**glu'ti·nous·ly** *adv.* —**glu'ti·nous·ness, glu'ti·nos'i·ty** (-ŏs'ə-tē) *n.*

glut·ton[1] (glŭt'n) *n.* **1.** One that eats or consumes immoderately. **2.** One that has inordinate capacity to receive or withstand something: *a glutton for punishment.* [Middle English *glotoun,* from Old French *gluton, gloton,* from Latin *gluttō.* See **gwel-**[5] in Appendix.*] —**glut'ton·ous** *adj.* —**glut'ton·ous·ly** *adv.*

glut·ton[2] (glŭt'n) *n.* A mammal, the **wolverine** *(see).* [From GLUTTON (eater), translation of German *Vielfrass,* "great eater."]

glut·ton·y (glŭt'n-ē) *n.* Excess in eating or drinking.

glyc·er·ic acid (glĭ-sĕr'ĭk, glĭs'ər-). A syrupy, colorless compound, $C_3H_6O_4$. [From GLYCERIN.]

glyc·er·ide (glĭs'ə-rīd') *n.* An ester of glycerol and fatty acids. [GLYCER(IN) + -IDE.]

glyc·er·in (glĭs'ər-ĭn) *n.* Glycerol. [French, from Greek *glukeros,* sweet. See **dlku-** in Appendix.*]

glyc·er·ol (glĭs'ə-rōl', -rôl', -rŏl') *n.* A syrupy, sweet, colorless or yellowish liquid, $C_3H_8O_3$, obtained from fats and oils as a by-product of the manufacture of soaps and fatty acids, and used as a solvent, antifreeze and antifrost fluid, plasticizer, and sweetener, and in the manufacture of dynamite, cosmetics, liquid soaps, inks, and lubricants. [GLYCER(IN) + -OL.]

glyc·er·yl (glĭs'ər-əl) *n.* The trivalent glycerol radical CH_2CHCH_2. [GLYCER(IN) + -YL.]

gly·cin (glī'sĭn) *n.* Also **gly·cine** (-sēn', -sĭn). A poisonous compound, $C_8H_9NO_3$, used as a photographic developer. [From GLYCINE.]

gly·cine (glī'sēn', -sən) *n.* **1.** A white, very sweet crystalline amino acid, $C_2H_5NO_2$, the principal amino acid occurring in sugar cane, derived by alkaline hydrolysis of gelatin, and used in biochemical research and medicine. **2.** Variant of **glycin.** [GLYC(O)- + -INE.]

glyco-, glyc-. Indicates: **1.** Sugar; for example, **glycine. 2.** Glycogen; for example, **glycogenesis.** [From Greek *glukus,* sweet. See **dlku-** in Appendix.*]

gly·co·gen (glī′kə-jən) *n.* A white, sweet-tasting powder, $(C_6H_{10}O_5)_n$, occurring as the chief animal storage carbohydrate, primarily in the liver. Also called "animal starch," "liver starch." [GLYCO- + -GEN.] —**gly′co·gen′ic** *adj.*

gly·co·gen·e·sis (glī′kə-jĕn′ə-sĭs) *n.* **1.** The formation of glycogen. **2.** The formation of sugar from glycogen. [GLYCO- + -GENESIS.]

gly·col (glī′kôl′, -kōl′, -kŏl′) *n.* **1. Ethylene glycol** *(see).* **2.** Any of various dihydric alcohols. [GLYC(O)- + -OL.]

gly·col·ic acid (glī-kŏl′ĭk). A colorless, crystalline compound, $C_2H_4O_3$, found in sugar beets, cane sugar, and unripe grapes, and used in leather dyeing and tanning, in pharmaceuticals, pesticides, adhesives, and plasticizers.

gly·con·ic (glī-kŏn′ĭk) *n.* Also **Gly·con·ic. 1.** A verse line much used by Catullus and Horace, consisting typically of a spondee, a dactyl, and an amphimacer. **2.** *Often plural.* A poem or verses having this rhythmic structure. —*adj.* Also **Gly·con·ic.** Consisting of or characterized by this meter.

gly·co·pro·tein (glī′kō-prō′tēn′, -tē-ĭn) *n.* Any of several conjugated proteins that contain carbohydrates as prosthetic groups.

gly·co·side (glī′kə-sīd′) *n.* Any of a group of organic compounds, occurring abundantly in plants, that produce sugars and related substances on hydrolysis. [*Glycose,* variant of GLUCOSE + -IDE.] —**gly′co·sid′ic** (-sĭd′ĭk) *adj.*

gly·co·su·ri·a (glī′kə-so͝or′ē-ə) *n.* The excretion of abnormal quantities of sugar in the urine. [*Glycose,* variant of GLUCOSE + -URIA.] —**gly′co·su′ric** *adj.*

gly·ox·a·line (glī-ŏk′sə-lən) *n.* A chemical compound, **imidazole** *(see).* [GLY(COL) + OXAL(IC ACID) + -INE.]

glyph (glĭf) *n.* **1.** *Architecture.* A vertical groove, especially in a Doric column or frieze. **2.** A symbolic figure, either engraved or incised; hieroglyph. [Greek *gluphē,* carving, from *gluphein,* to carve. See **gleubh-** in Appendix.*] —**glyph′ic** *adj.*

glyp·tic (glĭp′tĭk) *adj.* Of or relating to engraving or carving, especially on precious stones. [Greek *gluptikos,* from *gluptēs,* carver, from *gluphein,* to carve. See **glyph.**] —**glyp′tics** *n.*

glyp·to·graph (glĭp′tə-grăf′, -gräf′) *n.* An engraved inscription on a precious stone. [Greek *gluptos,* carved, from *gluphein,* to carve (see **glyph**) + -GRAPH.]

glyp·tog·ra·phy (glĭp-tŏg′rə-fē) *n.* The art or process of carving or engraving on precious stones. —**glyp·tog′ra·pher** *n.* —**glyp′-to·graph′ic** (-tə-grăf′ĭk), **glyp′to·graph′i·cal** *adj.*

gm gram.

G.M. 1. general manager. **2.** grand master.

G-man (jē′măn′) *n., pl.* **-men** (-mĕn′). An agent of the Federal Bureau of Investigation. [G(OVERNMENT) MAN.]

G.m.a.t. Greenwich mean astronomical time.

GM counter. Geiger counter.

G.m.t. Greenwich mean time.

GM tube. Geiger tube.

gnar (när) *intr.v.* **gnarred, gnarring, gnars.** Also **gnarr.** To snarl; growl. [Imitative.]

gnarl¹ (närl) *intr.v.* **gnarled, gnarling, gnarls.** To snarl; growl. [Frequentative of GNAR.]

gnarl² (närl) *n.* A protruding knot on a tree. —*tr.v.* **gnarled, gnarling, gnarls.** To make knotted; cause to be deformed; to twist. See Synonyms at **distort.** [Back-formation from GNARLED.]

gnarled (närld) *adj.* **1.** Having gnarls; knotty or misshapen: *gnarled branches.* **2.** Crabbed in temperament. **3.** Rugged in appearance. [Probably variant of KNURLED.]

gnash (năsh) *v.* **gnashed, gnashing, gnashes.** —*tr.* **1.** To grind or strike (the teeth) together. **2.** To bite by grinding the teeth. —*intr.* To grind the teeth together. —*n.* The grinding together of the teeth, or an action resembling this. [Middle English *gnasten, gnaisten,* probably from Scandinavian, akin to Old Norse *gnast(r)an,* gnashing (probably imitative).]

gnat (năt) *n.* Any of numerous small, winged insects, especially one that bites. [Middle English *gnat,* Old English *gnæt.* See **ghen-** in Appendix.*]

gnat·catch·er (năt′kăch′ər) *n.* Any of several small New World birds of the genus *Polioptila,* having grayish and white plumage and a long tail.

gnath·ic (năth′ĭk) *adj.* Of or relating to the jaw. [From Greek *gnathos,* jaw. See **genu-²** in Appendix.*]

gna·thite (nā′thīt′) *n.* A jaw or jawlike appendage of an insect or other arthropod. [Greek *gnathos,* jaw (see **gnathic**) + -ITE.]

-gnathous. Indicates the jaw; for example, **prognathous.** [New Latin *-gnathus,* from Greek *gnathos,* jaw. See **genu-²** in Appendix.*]

gnaw (nô) *v.* **gnawed, gnawed** or **gnawn** (nôn), **gnawing, gnaws.** —*tr.* **1.** To bite, chew on, or erode with the teeth. **2.** To produce by gnawing: *gnaw a hole.* **3.** To erode or diminish gradually as if by gnawing. **4.** To afflict or irritate. —*intr.* **1.** To bite or chew persistently. **2.** To cause erosion or gradual diminishment. **3.** To cause pain or distress. [Middle English *gnawen,* Old English *gnagan.* See **ghen-** in Appendix.*] —**gnaw′er** *n.* —**gnaw′ing·ly** *adv.*

gneiss (nīs) *n.* A banded or foliated metamorphic rock, usually of the same composition as granite, in which the minerals are arranged in layers. [German *Gneis,* perhaps from Middle High German *gneiste,* spark (because of its sheen), from Old High German *gneisto.* See **gnag-** in Appendix.*] —**gneiss′ic** (nī′sĭk), **gneiss′oid′** (nī′soid′), **gneiss′ose′** (nī′sōs′) *adj.*

gnoc·chi (nyôk′ē) *pl.n.* Dumplings made of flour, semolina, or potatoes, boiled or baked and served with grated Parmesan cheese or with various sauces. [Italian, plural of *gnocco, nocchio,* "knot (of a tree)," "lump," from Germanic. See **gen-** in Appendix.*]

gnome¹ (nōm) *n.* **1.** One of a fabled race of dwarflike creatures who live underground and guard treasure hoards. **2.** A shriveled old man. [French, from New Latin *gnomus*† (coined by Paracelsus).] —**gnom′ish** *adj.*

gnome² (nōm) *n.* A pithy saying that expresses a general truth or fundamental principle; a maxim; an aphorism. [Greek *gnōmē,* intelligence, judgment, maxim, from *gignōskein,* to know. See **gnō-** in Appendix.*]

gno·mic (nō′mĭk) *adj.* Of or of the nature of gnomes; aphoristic: *gnomic poetry.*

gno·mon (nō′mŏn) *n.* **1.** An object, such as the style of a sundial, that projects a shadow used as an indicator. **2.** *Geometry.* The figure that remains after a parallelogram has been removed from a similar but larger parallelogram with which it has a common corner. [Latin *gnōmōn,* from Greek, one who knows, indicator, interpreter, from *gignōskein,* to know. See **gnō-** in Appendix.*] —**gno·mon′ic** (nō-mŏn′ĭk), **gno·mon′i·cal** *adj.*

gno·sis (nō′sĭs) *n.* Intuitive apprehension of spiritual truths, an esoteric form of knowledge sought by the Gnostics. [Greek *gnōsis,* knowledge, from *gignōskein,* to know. See **gnō-** in Appendix.*]

-gnosis. *Medicine.* Indicates knowledge or recognition; for example, **psychognosis.** [Latin, from Greek *-gnōsia,* from *gnōsis,* knowledge, GNOSIS.]

gnos·tic (nŏs′tĭk) *adj.* Of, relating to, or possessing intellectual or spiritual knowledge.

Gnos·ti·cism (nŏs′tĭ-sĭz′əm) *n.* The doctrines of certain early Christian sects that valued inquiry into spiritual truth above faith, thought salvation attainable only by the few whose faith enabled them to transcend matter, and viewed Christ as noncorporeal. —**Gnos′tic** *adj.* & *n.*

GNP gross national product.

gnu (no͞o, nyo͞o) *n.* Either of two large African antelopes, *Connochaetes gnou* or *C. taurinus,* having a drooping beard, a long, tufted tail, and curved horns in both sexes. Also called "wildebeest." [From Kaffir *nqu.*]

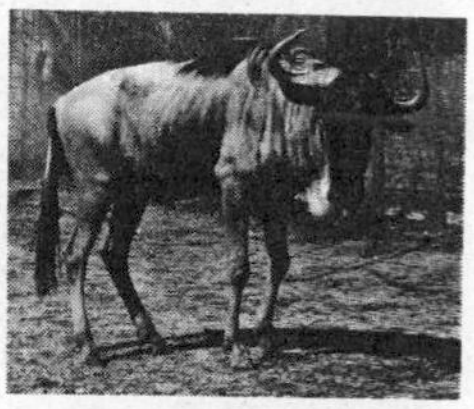

gnu
Connochaetes taurinus

go¹ (gō) *v.* **went** (wĕnt), **gone** (gôn, gŏn), **going, goes.** —*intr.* **1.** To move along; proceed. **2.** To move to a particular place. **3.** To move from a particular place; depart. **4.** To start to move away; begin to move. **5.** To get out of sight; move out of someone's presence: *Go away!* **6.** To move: *The car won't go.* **7.** To proceed to the performance of an activity: *went to eat.* **8.** Used in the form *be going* with the sense of *will* to indicate indefinite future intent or expectation: *He is going to learn to fly.* **9.** To engage in an activity. Followed by a present participle: *go riding.* **10.** To function; operate. **11.** To make a specified sound: *The glass went crack.* **12.** To belong in a definite place or position. **13.** To extend from one place or thing to another. **14.** To spread. **15.** To pass or be given into someone's possession. **16.** To be allotted: *money to go for food.* **17.** To serve; to help: *It goes to show he was wrong.* **18.** To be compatible; harmonize: *The rug goes well with this room.* **19.** To proceed in a particular form or sequence: *Is this the way the song goes?* **20.** To die. **21.** To come apart; cave in. **22.** To fail, as hearing or vision. **23.** To be consumed or used up. **24.** To lose effect; disappear. **25.** To be given up or abolished: *Unnecessary expenditures must go.* **26.** To pass, as time or youth. **27.** To pass in a transaction; be sold or auctioned off. **28.** To enter into a specified condition; become: *go insane.* **29.** To be or continue to be in a specified condition: *go unchallenged.* **30.** To fare. **31.** To be thought of; be judged: *As cats go, this one is well-behaved.* **32.** To pursue a course: *go too far; go to a lot of trouble.* **33.** To act, especially under guidance or on advice: *go on someone's word.* **34.** To hold out; endure. —*tr.* **1.** To proceed along; follow: *go the same way.* **2.** To withstand; endure: *went the distance.* **3.** To wager; bid: *He went five dollars on a bet.* **4.** To furnish: *go bail for a client.* **5.** To take part to the extent of: *go fifty-fifty on a deal.* —**go about. 1.** To busy oneself with. **2.** To move around. **3.** To change direction in a sailing vessel; to tack. —**go against.** To be or act in opposition to. —**go along.** To be in agreement; cooperate. Usually used with *with.* —**go at. 1.** To attack verbally or physically. **2.** To work at diligently or energetically. —**go back on.** To back down on; repudiate. —**go for. 1.** To try to obtain. **2.** *Informal.* To enjoy or appreciate. **3.** To be sold for. **4.** To pass as; be thought of as. **5.** To attack. —**go in for.** *Informal.* To enjoy participating in. —**go into. 1.** To investigate; inquire about. **2.** To take up or turn to as an occupation, study, or pastime. —**go off. 1.** To happen in a specified manner: *went off according to plan.* **2.** To be fired or shot; explode. —**go one better.** To surpass or outdo by one degree. —**go over. 1.** To check or examine. **2.** To be received: *a speech that went over well.* —**go through. 1.** To search or examine thoroughly. **2.** To suffer; undergo; experience. **3.** To use up entirely. **4.** To gain acceptance; be voted for, as a plan or law. —**to go.** To be consumed off the premises. Said of restaurant food. —*n., pl.* **goes.** *Informal.* **1.** A try; venture. **2.** A bargain; agreement; deal: *no go.* **3.** An action or instance of going or occurring. **4.** A turn, as in a game. **5.** Energy; vitality. —**from the word go.** *Informal.* From the very beginning. —**on the go.** *Informal.* Perpetually busy; active. —*adj. Informal.* Prepared to go into action: *All planes are go.* [Go, gone; Middle English *gon, gōn(e),* Old English *gān, gegān.* See **ghē-** in Appendix.* Went; Middle English *wente,* past tense of *wenden,* to turn, WEND.]

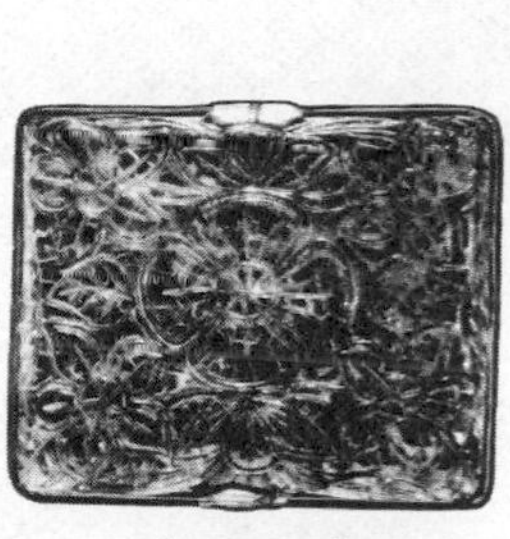

glyptograph
The Schletter emerald, weighing over 87 carats

go² (gō) *n.* A Japanese game for two, played with pebblelike counters on a board divided into 361 squares.

GO general order.

go·a (gō'ə) *n.* A gazelle, *Procapra picticaudata*, of eastern Asia, the male of which has backward-curving horns. [Tibetan *dgoba.*]

Go·a (gō'ə). **1.** A district, 1,348 square miles in area, on the western coast of India, formerly under Portuguese rule. Population, 627,000. **2.** Also **No·va Go·a** (nō'və). The capital of this district under Portuguese rule.

goad (gōd) *n.* **1.** A long stick with a pointed end used for prodding animals. **2.** That which prods or urges; a stimulus or irritating incentive. —*tr.v.* **goaded, goading, goads.** To prod with or as if with a goad; give impetus to; incite. [Middle English *gode,* Old English *gād.* See ghei-¹ in Appendix.*]

go·a·head (gō'ə-hĕd') *n. Informal.* Permission to proceed.

goal (gōl) *n.* **1.** The purpose toward which an endeavor is directed; an end; objective. **2.** The finish line of a race. **3.** *Sports.* **a.** A specified structure or area into or over which players endeavor to advance a ball or puck. **b.** The score awarded for such an act. —See Synonyms at **intention.** [Middle English *gol,* boundary, limit, probably from Old English *gǣl*† (unattested), obstacle.]

goal·keep·er (gōl'kē'pər) *n.* A player assigned to protect the goal in various sports. Also called "goalie," "goaltender."

goal post. One of a pair of posts joined with a crossbar and set at each end of a football or soccer field, forming the goal.

Go·a powder (gō'ə). Araroba *(see).*

goat (gōt) *n.* **1.** Any of various horned, bearded ruminant mammals of the genus *Capra,* originally of mountainous regions of the Old World; especially, one of the domesticated forms of *C. hircus.* **2.** *Capital* G. *Astronomy.* The constellation and sign of the zodiac, **Capricornus** *(see).* Usually preceded by *the.* **3.** A lecherous man. **4.** A scapegoat. —**get one's goat.** *Informal.* To make someone angry or annoyed. [Middle English *gote,* Old English *gāt.* See ghaido- in Appendix.*] —**goat'ish** *adj.*

goat antelope. Any of various ruminant mammals, such as the mountain goat or the chamois, having characteristics of both goats and antelopes.

goat·ee (gō-tē') *n.* A small chin beard trimmed into a point, and resembling that of a goat. [From GOAT + -EE.]

goat·fish (gōt'fish') *n., pl.* **goatfish** or **-fishes.** Any of various brightly colored fishes of the family Mullidae, of warm seas, having two sensory barbels on the chin. Also called "surmullet."

Goat Island. An island in the Niagara River in New York State, between the American Falls and the Canadian Falls.

goats·beard (gōts'bird') *n.* Also **goat's-beard.** **1.** A plant, *Tragopogon pratensis,* native to Europe, having grasslike leaves and yellow, dandelionlike flowers. **2.** A tall plant, *Aruncus dioicus,* having compound leaves and branching clusters of small white flowers.

goat·skin (gōt'skĭn') *n.* **1.** The skin of a goat. **2.** A container, as for wine, made from such a skin.

goat's-rue (gōts'rōō') *n.* **1.** A North American plant, *Tephrosia virginiana,* having yellow and pink flowers. **2.** A Eurasian plant, *Galega officinalis,* cultivated for its showy, variously colored flowers.

goat·suck·er (gōt'sŭk'ər) *n.* Any of various chiefly nocturnal birds of the family Caprimulgidae, which includes the nighthawk and the whippoorwill. [The bird was thought to suck goat's milk.]

gob¹ (gŏb) *n.* **1.** A small piece or lump. **2.** *Plural. Informal.* A large quantity, as of money. [Middle English *gobbe,* lump, mass, from Old French *gobe,* mouthful, lump, from *gober,* to swallow, gulp, from Gallo-Roman *gobb-* (unattested), from Celtic *gobbo-* (unattested), mouth, beak, GOB.]

gob² (gŏb) *n. Slang.* The mouth. [Scottish and Irish Gaelic *gob,* beak, mouth, from Celtic *gobbo-* (unattested).]

gob³ (gŏb) *n. Slang.* A sailor. [Origin unknown.]

gob·bet (gŏb'ĭt) *n.* A piece or chunk, especially of raw meat. [Middle English *gobet,* from Old French, diminutive of *gobe,* GOB (lump).]

gob·ble¹ (gŏb'əl) *v.* **-bled, -bling, -bles.** —*tr.* **1.** To devour in large, greedy gulps. **2.** To snatch greedily; to grab. —*intr.* To eat greedily or rapidly. [Frequentative of Middle English *gobben,* to drink greedily, probably from *gobbe,* lump, GOB.]

gob·ble² (gŏb'əl) *intr.v.* **-bled, -bling, -bles.** To make the guttural, chortling sound of a male turkey. —*n.* This sound. [Imitative.]

gob·ble·dy·gook (gŏb'əl-dē-gōōk') *n.* Also **gob·ble·de·gook.** Unclear, often verbose, usually bureaucratic jargon. [From GOBBLE (to sound like a turkey), influenced by GOOK.]

gob·bler (gŏb'lər) *n.* A male turkey.

Gob·e·lin (gŏb'ə-lĭn, gŏb'ə-; *French* gō-blăN') *n.* A tapestry of a kind woven at the Gobelin works in Paris, noted for rich pictorial design. —**Gob'e·lin** *adj.*

go-be·tween (gō'bĭ-twēn') *n.* One who acts as an intermediary in a transaction.

Go·bi Desert (gō'bē). *Chinese* **Han-hai** (hän'hī'). A desert region occupying 500,000 square miles in east-central Asia, mostly in the Mongolian People's Republic.

gob·let (gŏb'lĭt) *n.* **1.** A drinking glass or similar vessel with a stem and base. **2.** *Archaic.* A drinking bowl without handles. [Middle English *gobelet,* from Old French, diminutive of *gobel,* cup, from Gallo-Roman *gobb-* (unattested), from Celtic *gobbo-* (unattested), mouth, beak, GOB.]

gob·lin (gŏb'lĭn) *n.* **1.** A grotesque, elfin creature of folklore, thought to work mischief or evil. **2.** A haunting ghost. [Mid-

dle English *gobelin,* from Old French, from Middle High German *kobolt,* goblin. See ku- in Appendix.*]

go·by (gō'bē) *n., pl.* **-bies** or **goby.** Any of numerous usually small freshwater and marine fishes of the family Gobiidae, having the pelvic fins united to form a sucking disk. [Latin *gōbius,* variant of *cōbius,* from Greek *kōbios*†.]

go-by (gō'bī') *n. Informal.* An intentional slight; snub.

go-cart (gō'kärt') *n.* **1.** A small wagon for children to ride in, drive, or pull. **2.** A small frame on casters designed to help support a child learning to walk. **3.** A handcart.

god (gŏd) *n.* **1.** A being of supernatural powers or attributes, believed in and worshiped by a people; especially, a male deity thought to control some part of nature or reality or to personify some force or activity. **2.** An image of a deity; idol. **3.** One that is worshiped or idealized as a god. **4.** A man godlike in aspect or power. [Middle English *god,* Old English *god.* See gheu(ə)- in Appendix.*]

God (gŏd) *n.* **1.** A being conceived as the perfect, omnipotent, omniscient originator and ruler of the universe, the principal object of faith and worship in monotheistic religions. **2.** The force, effect, or a manifestation or aspect of this being. **3.** The single supreme agency postulated in some philosophical systems to explain the phenomena of the world, having a nature variously conceived in such terms as prime mover, an immanent vital force, or infinity. **4.** *Christian Science.* "Infinite Mind; Spirit; Soul; Principle; Life; Truth; Love." (Mary Baker Eddy). —*interj.* Used as an oath.

Go·da·va·ri (gō-dä'və-rē). A river rising in the Western Ghats of central India and flowing 900 miles generally southeast to the Bay of Bengal.

God-aw·ful (gŏd'ô'fəl) *adj. Slang.* Extremely trying; atrocious.

god·child (gŏd'chīld') *n., pl.* **-children** (-chĭl'drĭn). One for whom another serves as sponsor at baptism.

God damn. Also **god-damn** (gŏd'dăm'). Used as a profane oath, once a strong one invoking God's curse, now a general exclamation.

god·damned (gŏd'dămd') *adj.* Damned. Used as an intensive. —*adv. Slang.* Extremely; very.

God·dard (gŏd'ərd), **Robert Hutchings.** 1882–1945. American physicist; performed pioneering rocketry studies; first to build and launch a liquid-fueled rocket.

god·daugh·ter (gŏd'dô'tər) *n.* A female godchild.

god·dess (gŏd'ĭs) *n.* **1.** A female deity. **2.** A woman of great beauty or grace. **3.** A woman adored as a deity.

Gö·del (gœd'l), **Kurt.** Born 1906. Austrian-born American mathematician and logician.

Gödel's proof. A mathematical proof that under a specified consistency condition, any sufficiently strong formal axiomatic system must contain a proposition such that neither it nor its negation is provable and that any consistency proof for the system must use ideas and methods beyond those of the system itself. [Formulated by Kurt GÖDEL.]

Go·des·berg (gō'dəs-bĕrk'). Also **Bad Go·des·berg** (bät). A city and manufacturing center in North Rhine-Westphalia, West Germany, on the Rhine four miles south of Bonn. Population, 65,119.

go-dev·il (gō'dĕv'əl) *n.* **1.** A logging sled. **2.** A railway handcar. **3.** A jointed tool for cleaning an oil pipeline and disengaging obstructions. **4.** An iron dart dropped into an oil well to explode a charge of dynamite.

Go·dey (gō'dē), **Louis Antoine.** 1804–1878. American publisher of *Godey's Lady's Book.*

god·fa·ther (gŏd'fä'thər) *n.* A man who sponsors a child at its baptism.

god·for·sak·en (gŏd'fər-sā'kən) *adj.* Also **God·for·sak·en.** Appearing as if deprived of God's blessing, as: **1.** Desperate; depraved. **2.** Desolate; cheerless; forlorn.

God·frey (gŏd'frē) *n.* A masculine given name. [Middle English, from Norman French, from Old High German *Godafrid,* "peace of god" : *got,* god (see gheu(ə)- in Appendix*) + *fridu,* peace (see prī- in Appendix*).]

god·head (gŏd'hĕd') *n.* **1.** Divinity; godhood. **2.** *Capital* G. God, or the essential and divine nature of God, regarded abstractly. Preceded by *the.* [Middle English *godhede* : GOD + *-hede,* variant of *-hode,* -HOOD.]

god·hood (gŏd'hōōd') *n.* The quality or state of being a god; divinity. [Middle English *godhode,* Old English *godhād* : GOD + -HOOD.]

god·less (gŏd'lĭs) *adj.* **1.** Recognizing or worshiping no god. **2.** Irreverent; wicked. —**god'less·ly** *adv.* —**god'less·ness** *n.*

god·like (gŏd'līk') *adj.* Resembling or of the nature of a god or God. —**god'like'ness** *n.*

god·ling (gŏd'lĭng) *n.* A minor god.

god·ly (gŏd'lē) *adj.* **-lier, -liest.** **1.** Having great reverence for God; pious. **2.** Divine. —**god'li·ness** *n.*

god·moth·er (gŏd'mŭth'ər) *n.* A woman who sponsors a child at its baptism.

Go·dol·phin (gō-dŏl'fĭn), **Sidney.** First Earl of Godolphin. 1645–1712. English statesman.

god·par·ent (gŏd'pâr'ənt) *n.* A godfather or godmother.

go·droon. Variant of **gadroon.**

God's acre. A churchyard or burial ground. [Translation of German *Gottesacker,* God's field.]

god·send (gŏd'sĕnd') *n.* An unexpected boon or stroke of luck; windfall. [Middle English *goddes sand,* God's message : GOD + *sand,* message, Old English *sand,* message, messenger (see sent- in Appendix*).]

god·son (gŏd'sŭn') *n.* A male godchild.

God·speed (gŏd'spēd') *n.* Success or good fortune. Used in the

goat
Capra hircus
Angora goat

Gobelin
Detail from a 17th-century Gobelin tapestry

expression *wish (someone) Godspeed.* [From the phrase *God speed,* may God prosper (someone).]

Godt·haab (gôt′hôp′). The capital of Greenland, on the southwestern coast of the island. Population, 1,400.

Go·du·nov (gə-də-nôf′), **Boris Fedorovich.** 1552–1605. Czar of Russia (1598–1605).

God·ward (gŏd′wərd) *adv.* Also **God·wards** (-wərdz). Toward God. —*adj.* Directed toward God.

God·win Aus·ten (gŏd′wĭn ô′stĭn). The second-highest mountain in the world (28,250 feet), in the Karakoram Range of northern Kashmir. Also called "Dapsang," "K2."

god·wit (gŏd′wĭt′) *n.* Any of various wading birds of the genus *Limosa,* having a long, slender, slightly upturned bill. [Origin unknown.]

Goeb·bels (gœb′əls), **Joseph Paul.** 1897–1945. German Nazi propaganda minister.

Goep·pert-May·er (gĕp′ərt-mā′ər), **Marie.** Born 1906. German-born American nuclear physicist.

Goe·ring. See Göring.

Goe·thals (gō′thəlz), **George Washington.** 1858–1928. American army officer; chief engineer in construction of Panama Canal.

Goe·the (gœ′tə), **Johann Wolfgang von.** 1749–1832. German poet and dramatist.

goe·thite (gō′thīt′, gā′tīt′) *n.* A brown mineral, essentially HFeO₂, used as an iron ore. [Named in honor of Johann W. von GOETHE.]

gof·fer (gŏf′ər, gôf′-) *tr.v.* **-fered, -fering, -fers.** Also **gauf·fer.** To press ridges or narrow pleats into (a frill, for example); to flute; crimp. —*n.* Also **gauf·fer.** **1.** An iron used for goffering. **2.** Ridged or pleated ornamentation produced by goffering. [French *gaufrer,* to crimp lace, from Old French *gaufre,* honeycomb, waffle, from Middle Low German *wāfel.* See **webh-** in Appendix.*]

Gog and Ma·gog (gŏg′ ən mā′gŏg′). In Biblical prophecy, the heathen nations to be led by Satan in a war against the Kingdom of God. Revelation 20:7–8.

go-get·ter (gō′gĕt′ər) *n. Informal.* An enterprising, hustling person.

gog·gle (gŏg′əl) *v.* **-gled, -gling, -gles.** —*intr.* **1.** To stare with wide and bulging eyes. **2.** To roll or bulge. Used of the eyes. —*tr.* To roll or bulge (the eyes). —*n.* **1.** A stare or leer. **2.** *Plural.* A pair of large, usually tinted spectacles with shielding sidepieces worn as a protection against wind, dust, or glare. [Middle English *gog(e)len,* to roll the eyes, perhaps from *gog-,* root expressive of up and down movement.] —**gog′gly** *adj.*

gog·gle-eyed (gŏg′əl-īd′) *adj.* Having prominent or rolling eyes.

Gogh. See van Gogh.

go-go (gō′gō′) *adj.* Also **go·go.** *Informal.* Lively in the manner of active modern youth. [From À GO-GO.]

go-go girl. A girl who dances solo, often on a platform, in a discothèque or cabaret. Also called "go-go dancer."

Go·gol (gō′gəl), **Nikolai Vasilievich.** 1809–1852. Russian novelist and dramatist.

Gog·ra (gŏg′rə). A river rising in southwestern Tibet and flowing 570 miles south through the Himalayas, then southeast to the Ganges on the Bihar border.

Goi·â·ni·a (goi-ân′ē-ə). The capital of Goiás State, Brazil, in the south, southeast of Brasília. Population, 133,000.

Goi·ás (goi-äs′). A state of central Brazil, 240,333 square miles in area, and containing the Federal District and Brasília. Population, 2,452,000. Capital, Goiânia.

Goi·del·ic, Goi·dhel·ic (goi-dĕl′ĭk) *n.* Also **Ga·dhel·ic, Gae·dhel·ic** (gə-dĕl′ĭk, -dē′lĭk). A group of Celtic languages comprising Irish Gaelic, Scottish Gaelic, and Manx. —*adj.* Also **Ga·dhel·ic, Gae·dhel·ic** (gə-dĕl′ĭk, -dē′lĭk). **1.** Of or pertaining to the Gaels. **2.** Of, pertaining to, or characteristic of Goidelic. [From Old Irish *Goidel,* Gael, Celt, from Old Welsh *gwyddel,* from *gwydd,* wild. See **widhu-** in Appendix.*]

go·ing (gō′ĭng) *n.* **1. a.** Departure. **b.** Demise. **2.** The condition underfoot as it affects one's headway in walking or riding. **3.** *Informal.* Progress or existence considered with regard to the conditions to be coped with. —**a going over. 1.** An examination; a quick inspection. **2.** A rehearsal. **3.** A castigation. —**goings on.** *Informal.* Proceedings or behavior, especially when regarded with disapproval. —*adj.* **1.** Working; running: *in going order.* **2.** In full operation; flourishing: *a going business.* **3.** Current; prevailing: *The going rates are low.* **4.** Available; to be found: *the best products going.*

goi·ter (goi′tər) *n.* Also **goi·tre.** A chronic, noncancerous enlargement of the thyroid gland, visible as a swelling at the front of the neck, occurring without hyperthyroidism, and associated with iodine deficiency. Also called "struma." See also **exophthalmic goiter.** [French *goitre,* from Provençal *goitron,* from Vulgar Latin *gutturōnem* (unattested), from Latin *guttur†,* throat.] —**goi′trous** (-trəs) *adj.*

Gök·cha. The Turkish name for Lake Sevan.

Gol·con·da¹ (gŏl-kŏn′də). A ruined city of western Andhra Pradesh, Republic of India, the capital (1512–1687) of a former Moslem kingdom.

Gol·con·da² (gŏl-kŏn′də) *n.* A source of great riches, as a mine. [After GOLCONDA.]

gold (gōld) *n.* **1.** *Symbol* **Au** A soft, yellow, corrosion-resistant element, the most malleable and ductile metal, occurring in veins and alluvial deposits, and recovered by mining or by panning or sluicing. It is a good thermal and electrical conductor, is generally alloyed to increase its strength, and is used as an international monetary standard, in jewelry, for decora-

tion, and as a plated coating on a wide variety of electrical and mechanical components. Atomic number 79, atomic weight 196.967, melting point 1,063.0°C, boiling point 2,966.0°C, specific gravity 19.32, valences 1, 3. See **element.** **2. a.** Coinage made of gold. **b.** A gold standard. **3.** Money; riches. **4.** Light olive-brown to dark yellow, or moderate, strong, to vivid yellow. See **color. 5.** Something regarded as having great value or goodness: *a heart of gold.* —*adj.* **1.** Pertaining to or containing gold. **2.** Having the color of gold. **3.** Redeemable or secured by gold: *gold certificate.* [Middle English *gold,* Old English *gold.* See **ghel-²** in Appendix.*]

gold basis. A gold standard as a basis for determining prices.

gold·beat·er's skin (gōld′bē′tərz). Treated animal membrane used to separate sheets of gold being hammered into gold leaf.

gold·beat·ing (gōld′bē′tĭng) *n.* The act, art, or process of beating sheets of gold into gold leaf. —**gold′beat′er** *n.*

Gold·berg (gōld′bûrg), **Arthur Joseph.** Born 1908. American jurist and diplomat.

Gold·berg (gōld′bûrg), **Rube.** Original name, Ruben L. Goldberg. Born 1883. American cartoonist and sculptor, creator of extremely intricate diagrams of contraptions designed to effect relatively simple results.

Gold·ber·ger (gōld′bûr′gər), **Joseph.** 1874–1929. Austrian-born American physician; discovered cure for pellagra.

gold brick. 1. A bar of gilded cheap metal that appears to be, or is passed off as, genuine gold. **2.** A fraudulent and worthless substitute.

gold-brick (gōld′brĭk′) *n.* Also **gold·brick·er** (-ər). *Slang.* A person, especially a soldier, who avoids assigned duties or work; shirker. —*v.* **goldbricked, -bricking, -bricks.** *Slang.* —*intr.* To shirk one's assigned duties or responsibilities. —*tr.* To cheat; to swindle.

gold bug. A North American beetle, *Metriona bicolor,* having a metallic luster.

gold certificate. A monetary note formerly issued to the public by the U.S. Treasury and redeemable in gold but now issued to Federal Reserve Banks to certify conformity with their legal reserve requirements.

Gold Coast. 1. A coast on the Gulf of Guinea in western Africa along the southern shore of the Republic of Ghana, bordering the Ivory Coast on the west. **2.** A former British colony in the southern Gold Coast region, since 1957 part of the Republic of Ghana.

gold digger. 1. *Slang.* A woman who seeks gifts and expensive pleasures from men. **2.** One that digs for gold.

gold dust. Gold in powder form, such as that found in placer digging.

gold·en (gōl′dən) *adj.* **1.** Made of or containing gold. **2. a.** Having the color of gold or a yellow color suggestive of gold. **b.** Lustrous; radiant; resplendent: *the golden sun.* **c.** Suggestive of gold, as in richness or splendor: *a golden voice.* **3.** Of the greatest value or importance; precious. **4.** Marked by peace, prosperity, and often creativeness. **5.** Very favorable or advantageous; excellent: *a golden opportunity.* **6.** Having a promising future; seemingly assured of success. —**gold′en·ly** *adv.* —**gold′en·ness** *n.*

golden age. 1. *Greek & Roman Mythology.* The first age of the world, an untroubled and prosperous era during which man lived in ideal happiness. **2.** A period when a nation or some wide field of endeavor reaches its height.

golden Alexanders. A plant, *Zizia aurea,* of eastern North America, having clusters of small yellow flowers.

golden anniversary. A 50th anniversary, symbolized by gold.

golden aster. Any of various North American plants of the genus *Chrysopsis,* having yellow, rayed flowers.

golden bantam. A variety of corn having large, bright-yellow kernels on a relatively small ear.

golden bough. Mistletoe.

golden calf. 1. A golden image of a sacrificial calf fashioned by Aaron and worshiped by the Israelites. Exodus 32. **2.** Money as an object of worship; mammon.

golden chain. A shrub, the laburnum *(see).*

golden club. An aquatic plant, *Orontium aquaticum,* of the eastern United States, having small golden-yellow flowers covering a clublike spadix.

golden eagle. An eagle, *Aquila chrysaetos,* of mountainous areas of the Northern Hemisphere, having dark plumage with yellowish feathers on the head and neck.

gol·den·eye (gōl′dən-ī′) *n.* Either of two ducks, *Bucephala clangula* or *B. islandica,* of northern regions, having a short black bill, a rounded head, and black and white plumage. [From their golden-yellow eyes.]

Golden Fleece. *Greek Mythology.* The fleece of the golden ram, stolen by Jason and the Argonauts from the king of Colchis with Medea's aid.

Golden Gate. A strait in west-central California two miles wide and five miles long connecting the Pacific Ocean and San Francisco Bay.

golden glow. A tall plant, *Rudbeckia laciniata hortensis,* cultivated for its yellow, many-rayed, double flowers.

Golden Horde. The Mongol army that swept over eastern Europe in the 13th century and established a suzerain in Russia. [Translation of Tatar *altun ordū,* from the color of the tent of their commander, Batu Khan.]

Golden Horn. *Turkish* **Ha·liç** (hä-lēch′). An inlet of the Bosporus in European Turkey forming the harbor of Istanbul.

golden mean. The course between extremes; moderation.

golden pheasant. A pheasant, *Chrysolophus pictus,* of China and Tibet, having a long tail and brilliantly colored plumage.

godwit
Limosa fedoa

Johann Wolfgang von Goethe
Contemporary portrait low relief by David d'Angers

Golden Gate
Aerial view of the entrance spanned by the Golden Gate Bridge

goldenrod
Solidago canadensis

goldfish

goldfinch
Above: Spinus tristis
Below: Carduelis carduelis

gondola

gold·en·rod (gōl′dən-rŏd′) *n.* Any of numerous chiefly North American plants of the genus *Solidago,* having clusters of small yellow flowers that bloom in late summer or fall.

golden rule. The maxim or teaching that one should behave toward others as one would have others behave toward oneself. Matthew 7:12.

gold·en·seal (gōl′dən-sēl′) *n.* A woodland plant, *Hydrastis canadensis,* of eastern North America, having small greenish-white flowers and a yellow root formerly used medicinally.

golden section. *Fine Arts.* A ratio between the two dimensions of a plane figure or the two divisions of a line such that the smaller is to the larger as the larger is to the sum of the two, roughly a ratio of three to five.

Golden State. The nickname for California.

golden wedding. The 50th anniversary of a marriage.

gold-ex·change standard (gōld′ĭks-chānj′). A monetary system in which a country maintains its currency at par with the currency of another country on the gold standard.

gold-filled (gōld′fĭld′) *adj.* Made of a hard base metal with an outer layer of gold.

gold·finch (gōld′fĭnch′) *n.* **1.** Any of several small New World birds of the genus *Spinus;* especially, *S. tristis,* of which the male has yellow plumage with a black forehead, wings, and tail. **2.** A small Old World bird, *Carduelis carduelis,* having brownish plumage with red, yellow, and black markings.

gold·fish (gōld′fĭsh′) *n., pl.* **goldfish** or **-fishes.** A freshwater fish, *Carassius auratus,* native to eastern Asia, characteristically having brassy or reddish coloring, and bred in many ornamental forms as an aquarium fish.

gold foil. Gold rolled or beaten into thin sheets thicker than gold leaf.

gold·i·locks (gōl′dē-lŏks′) *n.* A European plant, *Linosyrus vulgaris,* having narrow leaves and clusters of small yellow flowers. [Obsolete *goldy,* golden, from GOLD + LOCK(s).]

Gold·ing (gōl′dĭng), **William Gerald.** Born 1911. English novelist.

gold leaf. Gold beaten into extremely thin sheets, used for gilding.

Gold·man (gōld′mən), **Emma.** 1869–1940. Russian-born American anarchist.

gold mine. 1. A mine yielding gold ore. **2.** *Informal.* A source of great wealth or profit.

gold-of-pleas·ure (gōld′əv-plĕzh′ər) *n.* A plant, *Camelina sativa,* native to the Old World, having small yellow flowers and seeds rich in oil.

Gol·do·ni (gōl-dō′nē), **Carlo.** 1707–1793. Italian author; creator of modern Italian comedy.

gold point. The point in foreign-exchange rates at which it is no more expensive to import or export gold bullion in settling international accounts than to buy or sell bills of exchange.

gold reserve. The reserve of gold bullion held by a government or central bank to redeem its notes.

gold rush. A rush of migrants to an area where gold has been discovered, as to California in 1849.

gold·smith (gōld′smĭth′) *n.* **1.** An artisan who fashions objects of gold. **2.** A tradesman who deals in gold articles.

Gold·smith (gōld′smĭth′), **Oliver.** 1728–1774. English poet, dramatist, and novelist.

goldsmith beetle. Either of two scarabaeid beetles, *Cotalpa lanigera* or *Cetonia aurata,* having metallic greenish-yellow coloring.

gold standard. A monetary standard under which the basic unit of currency is equal in value to and exchangeable for a specified amount of gold.

gold·stone (gōld′stōn′) *n.* An **aventurine** *(see)* with gold-colored inclusions.

gold·thread (gōld′thrĕd′) *n.* A low-growing woodland plant, *Coptis trifolia,* having white flowers and slender yellow roots. Also called "cankerroot."

Gold·wa·ter (gōld′wô′tər, -wŏt′ər), **Barry Morris.** Born 1909. U.S. senator (1953–64 and since 1969); Republican Presidential candidate (1964).

Gold·wyn (gōld′wĭn), **Samuel.** Original surname, Goldfish. Born 1882. Polish-born American motion-picture producer.

go·lem (gō′lĕm, -ləm) *n.* In Jewish folklore, an artificially created human being endowed with life by supernatural means.

golf (gŏlf, gôlf, gŏf, gôf) *n.* A game played on a large outdoor obstacle course having a series of nine or eighteen holes spaced far apart, the object being to propel a small ball with the use of a club into each hole with as few strokes as possible. *—intr.v.* **golfed, golfing, golfs.** To play golf. [Middle English *golf†* (Scottish dialect).] **—golf′er** *n.*

golf club. 1. One of a set of clubs having a slender shaft and a head of wood or iron, used in golf. **2.** An organization of golfers.

golf course. A large tract of land laid out for golf. Also called "golf links."

Gol·gi (gŏl′jē), **Camillo.** 1844–1926. Italian histologist.

Golgi apparatus. A network of fibrils, granules, and membranous structures present in living cells and believed to function in the formation of secretions within the cell. Also called "Golgi body," "Golgi complex." [After Camillo GOLGI.]

gol·go·tha (gŏl′gə-thə) *n.* **1.** A place of burial. **2.** A place or occasion of suffering or agony. [From GOLGOTHA.]

Gol·go·tha (gŏl′gə-thə). The hill of Calvary, where Jesus was crucified. [Late Latin, from Greek, from Aramaic *gulgūltha,* skull (from the shape of the hill).]

gol·iard (gōl′yərd) *n.* One of a class of wandering students in medieval Europe, to whom a life of conviviality, license, and the making of ribald and satirical Latin songs is traditionally ascribed. [Middle English *goliard,* from Old French, glutton, trickster, from *gole,* throat, from Latin *gula,* gullet. See **gwel-⁵** in Appendix.*]

gol·iar·dic (gōl-yär′dĭk) *adj.* **1.** Of or relating to the type of satirical verse written by the goliards. **2.** Ribald or satirical in the manner of the goliards.

Go·li·ath (gə-lī′əth). The giant Philistine warrior who was slain by David with a stone and sling. I Samuel 17:4–51.

gol·li·wog, gol·li·wogg (gŏl′ē-wŏg′) *n.* **1.** A black male doll of grotesque appearance. **2.** A grotesque person; boogieman. [Originally the name of a doll designed by Florence Upton (died 1922) for a series of children's books by Bertha Upton (died 1912); possibly after POLLIWOG.]

gol·ly (gŏl′ē) *interj.* Used to express mild surprise or wonder. [Euphemism for GOD.]

go·losh. Variant of galosh.

Gom·berg (gŏm′bûrg), **Moses.** 1866–1947. Russian-born American chemist; discovered free radicals.

gom·bo. Variant of gumbo.

gom·broon (gŏm-brōōn′) *n.* A kind of Persian pottery. [After *Gombroon,* town in Iran.]

Go·mel (gō′məl, gô′-). A city and trade center of the southeastern Byelorussian S.S.R. Population, 199,000.

Go·me·ra (gō-mā′rä). An island, 114 square miles in area, of the Canary group, 22 miles west of Tenerife Island. Population, 28,000.

Go·mor·rah (gə-môr′ə, -mŏr′ə). A city of ancient Palestine near Sodom *(see).*

Gom·pers (gŏm′pərz), **Samuel.** 1850–1924. British-born American labor leader.

gom·pho·sis (gŏm-fō′sĭs) *n.* An immovable peg and rigid socket articulation, as of a tooth and its bony socket. [New Latin, from Greek *gomphōsis,* from *gomphoun,* to fasten with bolts, from *gomphos,* bolt. See **gembh-** in Appendix.*]

Go·mul·ka (gō-mōōl′kə, -mŭl′kə), **Wladyslaw.** Born 1905. First secretary of the Communist Party in Poland (since 1956).

-gon. Indicates a figure having a designated number of angles; for example, **nonagon.** [Greek *-gōnon,* from *-gōnos,* -angled, from *gōnia,* angle. See **genu-¹** in Appendix.*]

go·nad (gō′năd′, gŏn′ăd′) *n.* The organ that produces gametes; a testis or ovary. [New Latin, from Greek *gonos;* offspring, procreation, genitals. See **genə-** in Appendix.*] **—go·nad′al, go·nad′ic** *adj.*

gon·a·do·trop·ic (gŏn′ə-dō-trŏp′ĭk) *adj.* Also **gon·a·do·troph·ic** (-trŏf′ĭk). Acting on or stimulating the gonads, as a hormone. [GONAD + -TROPIC.]

gon·a·do·tro·pin (gŏn′ə-dō-trō′pĭn) *n.* Also **gon·a·do·tro·phin** (-trō′fĭn). A gonadotropic substance.

Go·na·ïves (gō′nä-ēv′). A city and port of western Haiti on the northeastern shore of the Gulf of Gonaïves, the site of the proclamation of Haiti's independence (1804). Population, 15,000.

Go·na·ïves, Gulf of (gō′nä-ēv′). The principal gulf of Haiti, attaining a width of 75 miles on the western coast of the island of Hispaniola.

Gon·court (gôN-kōōr′), **Edmond Louis Antoine de.** 1822–1896. French novelist and historian; collaborated with his brother Jules Alfred Huot de Goncourt (1830–1870).

Gond (gŏnd) *n.* One of a people of Dravidian stock of central India.

Gon·dar (gŏn′där). The capital of northwestern Ethiopia, on Lake Tana; the capital of Ethiopia from the 17th to the 19th century. Population, 25,000.

Gon·di (gŏn′dē) *n.* The Dravidian language of the Gonds.

gon·do·la (gŏn′dl-ə, gŏn-dō′lə) *n.* **1.** A narrow, lightweight barge having ends that curve up into a point and often a small cabin in the middle, propelled with a single oar from the stern, used on the canals of Venice. **2.** A flat-bottomed river boat. **3.** A gondola car. **4.** A basket, enclosure, or instrument sling suspended from and carried aloft by a balloon. [Italian (Venetian dialect), *gondola†,* roll, rock.]

gondola car. An open, shallow freight car.

gon·do·lier (gŏn′dl-îr′) *n.* The boatman of a gondola.

Gond·wa·na·land (gŏnd-wä′nə-lănd′). A hypothetical continent of the Mesozoic era thought by geologists to have linked land masses that later separated to form parts of South America, Africa, India, and Australia.

gone (gôn, gŏn). Past participle of go. *—adj.* **1.** Past; bygone. **2.** Advanced beyond hope or recall. **3.** Dying or dead. **4.** Ruined; lost: *a gone cause.* **5.** Carried away; absorbed. **6.** Used up; exhausted. **7.** *Slang.* Very exciting; great. **8.** *Slang.* Infatuated: *gone on the girl.* [Past participle of GO.]

gon·er (gôn′ər, gŏn′-) *n. Slang.* One who is ruined or doomed. [From GONE.]

gon·fa·lon (gŏn′fə-lən) *n.* A banner suspended from a crosspiece, especially as a standard in an ecclesiastical procession or as the ensign of a medieval Italian republic. [Italian *gonfalone,* standard, from Germanic. See **gwhen-¹** in Appendix.*]

gon·fa·lon·ier (gŏn′fə-lə-nîr′) *n.* **1.** The bearer of a gonfalon. **2.** The chief magistrate in any of several medieval Italian republics.

gong (gŏng, gông) *n.* **1.** A rimmed metal disk that produces a loud, sonorous tone when struck with a padded mallet. **2.** A usually saucer-shaped bell that is struck with a mechanically operated hammer. [Malay *gōng* (imitative).]

Gon·gor·ism (gŏng′gə-rĭz′əm) *n.* A florid, cluttered literary style. [Popularized by Luis de Góngora y Argote (1561–1627), Spanish poet.] **—Gon′go·ris′tic** (gŏng′gə-rĭs′tĭk) *adj.*

go·nid·i·um (gō-nĭd′ē-əm) *n., pl.* **-ia** (-ē-ə). **1.** An asexually produced reproductive cell that separates from the parent body, as in certain colonial microorganisms. **2.** An algal cell in the thallus of a lichen. [New Latin : GON(O)- + Greek *-idion,* diminutive suffix.]

go·nif. Variant of **ganef.**

go·ni·om·e·ter (gō′nē-ŏm′ə-tər) *n.* **1.** An optical instrument for measuring crystal angles. **2.** A radio receiver and directional antenna used as a system to determine the angular direction of incoming radio signals. [Greek *gōnia,* angle (see **genu-**[1] in Appendix*) + -METER.] —**go′ni·o·met′ric** (-nē-ō-mĕt′rĭk), **go′ni·o·met′ri·cal** *adj.*

go·ni·om·e·try (gō′nē-ŏm′ə-trē) *n.* The science of measuring angles. [Greek *gōnia,* angle (see **genu-**[1] in Appendix*) + -METRY.]

go·ni·on (gō′nē-ŏn′) *n.* The point of the angle on either side of the lower jaw. [New Latin, from Greek *gōnia,* angle. See **genu-**[1] in Appendix.*]

-gonium. Indicates a reproductive cell or seed; for example, **oogonium.** [From New Latin *gonium,* seed, cell, from Greek *gonos,* seed, procreation. See **gono-.**]

gono-, gon-. Indicates sexual, reproductive, or procreative; for example, **gonococcus, gonidium.** [New Latin *gono-,* from Greek, from *gonos,* offspring, seed, procreation. See **gena-** in Appendix.*]

gon·o·coc·cus (gŏn′ə-kŏk′əs) *n., pl.* **-cocci** (-kŏk′sī′). A bacterium, *Neisseria gonorrhoeae,* that causes gonorrhea. [New Latin : GONO- + -COCCUS.]

gon·o·phore (gŏn′ə-fôr′, -fōr′) *n.* A structure bearing or consisting of a reproductive organ or part, such as a reproductive cell or bud in a hydroid colony. [GONO- + -PHORE.] —**gon′o·phor′ic** (-fôr′ĭk, -fŏr′ĭk), **go·noph′o·rous** (gə-nŏf′ər-əs) *adj.*

gon·o·pore (gŏn′ə-pôr′, -pōr′) *n.* A reproductive aperture or pore.

gon·or·rhe·a (gŏn′ə-rē′ə) *n.* An infectious disease of the genitourinary tract, rectum, and cervix, caused by the gonococcus, transmitted chiefly by sexual intercourse, and characterized by acute purulent urethritis with dysuria. [Late Latin *gonorrhoea,* from Greek *gonorrhoia* : GONO- + -RRHEA.] —**gon′or·rhe′al, gon′or·rhe′ic** *adj.*

-gony. Indicates the production of; for example, **sporogony.** [Latin *-gonia,* from Greek, from *-goneia,* generation, from *gonos,* offspring, seed. See **gena-** in Appendix.*]

goo (gōō) *n. Informal.* **1.** A sticky wet substance. **2.** Sentimental drivel. [Possibly short for BURGOO.]

goo·ber (gōō′bər) *n. Regional.* A **peanut** *(see).* [Angolese *nguba.*]

good (gŏŏd) *adj.* **better** (bĕt′ər), **best** (bĕst). **1.** Having positive or desirable qualities; not bad or poor. **2.** Serving the end desired; suitable; serviceable: *a good outdoor paint.* **3. a.** Not spoiled or ruined; able to be used: *The milk is still good.* **b.** In excellent condition; whole; sound: *a good tooth.* **4. a.** Superior to the average: *a good student.* **b.** Designating the U.S. Government grade of meat higher than *standard* and lower than *choice.* **5. a.** Of high quality: *good books.* **b.** Discriminating: *good taste.* **6.** Used or suitable for special or formal occasions: *good clothes.* **7.** Beneficial; salutary: *a good night's rest.* **8.** Competent; skilled: *a good machinist.* **9.** Complete; thorough: *a good workout.* **10. a.** Safe; sure: *a good investment.* **b.** Valid or sound: *a good reason.* **c.** Genuine; real: *a good dollar bill.* **11. a.** Ample; substantial; considerable: *a good income.* **b.** Bountiful: *a good table.* **12.** Full: *a good mile from here.* **13. a.** Pleasant; enjoyable: *having a good time at the party.* **b.** Propitious; favorable: *good weather; a good omen.* **14. a.** Of moral excellence; virtuous; upright: *a good man.* **b.** Benevolent; cheerful; kind: *a good soul.* **c.** Loyal; staunch: *a good Republican.* **15. a.** Well-behaved; obedient: *a good child.* **b.** Socially correct; proper: *good manners.* —**as good as.** Practically; virtually; nearly: *as good as new.* —**good and.** *Informal.* Very; entirely: *good and tired.* —**good for. 1.** Able to serve or continue performing for a specified period of time: *good for another year.* **2.** Able to be counted upon for producing: *good for a laugh.* **3.** Worth in exchange: *a coupon good for two passes.* —**make good. 1.** To fulfill a promise, commitment, or the like; make valid. **2.** To compensate for or replace. **3.** To prove; verify. **4.** *Informal.* To succeed; do well. —**no good.** *Informal.* **1.** Worthless. **2.** Futile; useless: *It's no good trying to coax him.* —*n.* **1. a.** That which is good. **b.** The good, valuable, or useful part or aspect: *get the good out of something.* **2.** Welfare; benefit; well-being: *for the common good.* **3.** Goodness; virtue; merit: *There is much good in him.* —**come to no good.** To come to a bad end; prove worthless. —**for good.** For all time to come; permanently; forever: *She came home to stay for good.* —**to the good.** To one's benefit; for the best. —*adv. Informal.* Well. See Usage note below. [Middle English *god, gode,* Old English *gōd.* See **ghedh-** in Appendix.*]

Usage: *Good* occurs frequently after linking verbs such as *be, feel, seem, smell, sound,* and *taste: The news sounds good.* In such usage, acceptable on all levels, *good* is an adjective that qualifies the subject of the verb. Except in distinctly informal usage, *good* does not function as an adverb by qualifying verbs directly; instead, *well* is used: *He dances well* (not *good*). This is true also when the subject is a thing rather than a person, though *good* often occurs adverbially, and informally, in such examples. The following sentences illustrate *well* employed adverbially in this way: *My watch always runs well after it is cleaned. When things are going well, one seldom hears such complaints.* In the first, considered as an example in writing, *good* is termed unacceptable as a replacement for *well* by the entire Usage Panel; in the second, *good* is unacceptable to 86 per cent. In the same sentences, considered as examples in speech apart from dialogue or other deliberately informal usage, *good* is unacceptable to 73 per cent of the Panel. Many of the members consider *going good* closer to standard usage than *good* employed adverbially with other verbs, including *run.*

good book. Also **Good Book.** The Bible. Often preceded by *the.*

good-by, good-bye (gŏŏd′bī′) *interj.* Used to express farewell. —*n., pl.* **good-bys** or **good-byes.** An expression of farewell. [Contraction of *God be with you.*]

good fellow. A genial, companionable person.

good-fel·low·ship (gŏŏd′fĕl′ō-shĭp′) *n.* Pleasant sociability; comradeship.

good-for-noth·ing (gŏŏd′fər-nŭth′ĭng) *n.* A person of little worth or usefulness. —*adj.* Having little worth; useless.

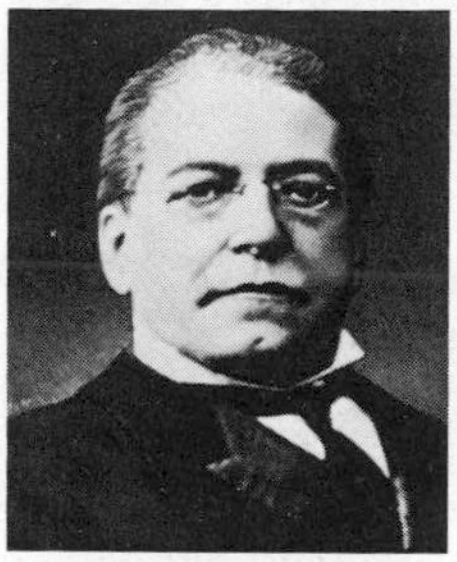

Samuel Gompers

Good Friday. The Friday before Easter, observed by Christians in commemoration of the Crucifixion of Jesus.

good·heart·ed (gŏŏd′här′tĭd) *adj.* Kind and generous. —**good′heart′ed·ly** *adv.* —**good′heart′ed·ness** *n.*

Good Hope, Cape of. A promontory on the southwestern coast of Cape of Good Hope Province, Republic of South Africa, 30 miles south of Cape Town.

good-hu·mored (gŏŏd′hyōō′mərd) *adj.* Cheerful; amiable. —**good′hu′mored·ly** *adv.* —**good′-hu′mored·ness** *n.*

good·ish (gŏŏd′ĭsh) *adj.* **1.** Somewhat good. **2.** Somewhat large or big; goodly.

good-look·ing (gŏŏd′lŏŏk′ĭng) *adj.* Of a pleasing appearance; attractive; handsome.

good looks. Attractive appearance; handsomeness.

good·ly (gŏŏd′lē) *adj.* **-lier, -liest. 1.** Of pleasing appearance; comely. **2.** Somewhat large; considerable: *a goodly sum.* —**good′li·ness** *n.*

good·man (gŏŏd′mən) *n., pl.* **-men** (-mĭn). *Archaic.* **1. a.** The male head of a household; master. **b.** A husband. **2.** A courteous title of address for a man not of gentle birth.

good nature. Cheerful, obliging disposition.

good-na·tured (gŏŏd′nā′chərd) *adj.* Having an easygoing, cheerful disposition. See Synonyms at **amiable.** —**good′-na′tured·ly** *adv.* —**good′-na′tured·ness** *n.*

Good Neighbor Policy. A policy for promoting friendly economic and political relations between the United States and Latin America, first espoused by President Franklin D. Roosevelt in 1933.

good·ness (gŏŏd′nĭs) *n.* **1.** The state or quality of being good; excellence; merit; worth. **2.** Virtuousness; moral rectitude. **3.** Kindness; benevolence; generosity. **4.** The good part of something; essence; strength. **5.** A euphemism for **God** in such phrases as *Thank goodness!* and used interjectionally to express surprise.

goods (gŏŏdz) *pl.n. Abbr.* **gds. 1.** Merchandise; wares. **2.** Portable personal property. **3.** Fabric; material. Used with a singular or plural verb. **4.** *British.* Freight. —**deliver the goods.** *Slang.* To produce what is expected; carry out a promise. —**get** (or **have**) **the goods on.** *Slang.* To obtain or have incriminating information or material against. [Plural of GOOD.]

Good Samaritan. 1. In a New Testament parable, the only passer-by to aid a man who had been beaten and robbed. Luke 10:30–37. **2.** A compassionate person who unselfishly helps another or others.

Good Shepherd. A name for Jesus. John 10:11–12.

good-sized (gŏŏd′sīzd′) *adj.* Of a fairly large size.

good speed. A farewell wish for a traveler's good fortune or success; Godspeed.

good-tem·pered (gŏŏd′tĕm′pərd) *adj.* Having an even or mild temper; not easily irritated. —**good′-tem′pered·ly** *adv.* —**good′-tem′pered·ness** *n.*

good·wife (gŏŏd′wīf′) *n., pl.* **-wives** (-wīvz′). *Archaic.* **1.** The female head of a household; mistress. **2.** A courteous title of address for a woman not of gentle birth.

good will. Also **good·will** (gŏŏd′wĭl′). **1.** An attitude of kindness or friendliness; benevolence. **2.** Cheerful acquiescence or willingness. **3.** The good relationship of a business enterprise with its customers, reckoned as an intangible asset.

Good·win Sands (gŏŏd′wĭn). A ten-mile stretch of shoals in the Strait of Dover, five miles off the eastern coast of Kent, England.

good·y[1] (gŏŏd′ē) *n., pl.* **-ies.** *Informal.* **1.** Something attractive or delectable; especially, something sweet to eat. **2.** A goody-goody. —*adj. Informal.* Goody-goody. —*interj.* Used to express childish delight.

good·y[2] (gŏŏd′ē) *n., pl.* **-ies.** *Archaic.* A polite title usually applied to a married woman of humble rank. Often used with a surname. [Short for GOODWIFE.]

Good·year (gŏŏd′yîr′), **Charles.** 1800–1860. American inventor of vulcanized rubber.

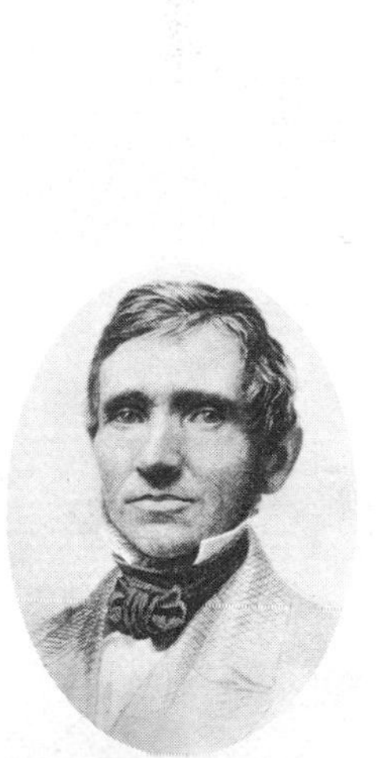

Charles Goodyear

good·y-good·y (gŏŏd′ē-gŏŏd′ē) *adj.* Affectedly sweet, or good; cloyingly sanctimonious. —*n., pl.* **goody-goodies.** One who is affectedly good or virtuous.

goo·ey (gōō′ē) *adj.* **-ier, -iest.** *Informal.* Viscous; sticky. [From GOO.]

goof (gōōf) *n. Slang.* **1.** An incompetent, foolish, or stupid person. **2.** A careless mistake; slip. —*v.* **goofed, goofing, goofs.** *Slang.* —*intr.* **1.** To make a silly mistake; blunder. **2.** To waste or kill time. Often used with *off.* —*tr.* To spoil; bungle. Often used with *up.* [Possibly variant of obsolete *goff,* dope, from Old French *goffe,* awkward, from Italian *goffo*†.]

goof·y (gōō′fē) *adj.* **-ier, -iest.** *Slang.* Silly; ridiculous: *a goofy hat.* —**goof′i·ly** *adv.* —**goof′i·ness** *n.*

goo·gol (gōō′gôl′) *n* The number 10 raised to the power 100

(10^{100}); the number 1 followed by 100 zeros. [Coined by Edward Kasner (1878–1955), American mathematician.]

goo·gol·plex (go͞o′gŏl-plĕks′) *n.* The number 10 raised to the power googol; the number 1 followed by 10^{100} zeros. [GOOGOL + (DU)PLEX.]

gook (go͝ok, go͞ok) *n. Slang.* **1.** A dirty, sludgy, or slimy substance. **2.** An Oriental. An offensive term used derogatorily. [Perhaps from Scottish *gowk*, simpleton, from Middle English *gowke*, cuckoo, from Old Norse *gaukr*, from Common Germanic *gaukaz* (unattested).]

goon (go͞on) *n.* **1.** *Informal.* A thug hired to commit acts of intimidation or violence. **2.** *Slang.* A stupid or oafish person. [From dialectal *gooney*, *gony*†, fool; popularized by the comic-strip character Alice the *Goon*, created by E.C. Segar (1894–1938).]

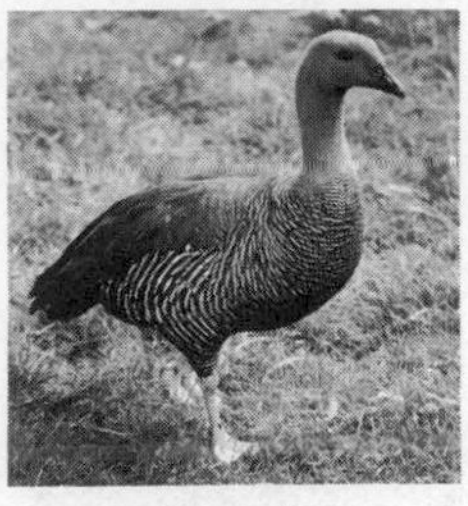

goose[1]
Chloephaga picta
A female of the species

goo·ney bird (go͞o′nē). *Slang.* An albatross; especially, *Diomedea nigripes*, common on islands of the Pacific. [From dialectal *gooney*, fool. See **goon**.]

goop (go͞op) *n. Slang.* An ill-mannered person. [Coined by Gelett Burgess (1866–1951), American humorist.]

goos·an·der (go͞os-ăn′dər) *n. British.* A bird, the common merganser, *Mergus merganser.* [Probably GOOS(E) + Old Norse *önd* (stem *andar-*), duck (see **anet-** in Appendix*).]

goose[1] (go͞os) *n., pl.* **geese** (gēs) or **gooses** (for sense 5). **1.** Any of various wild or domesticated water birds of the family Anatidae, and especially of the genera *Anser* and *Branta*, characteristically having a shorter neck than that of a swan and a shorter, more pointed bill than that of a duck. **2.** The female of such a bird, as distinguished from a gander. **3.** The flesh of such a bird, used as food. **4.** *Informal.* A silly person; a simpleton. **5.** A tailor's pressing iron with a long curved handle. **—cook one's goose.** *Informal.* To ruin one's chances. [Goose, geese; Middle English *goos*, *gees*, Old English *gōs*, *gēs*. See **ghans-** in Appendix.*]

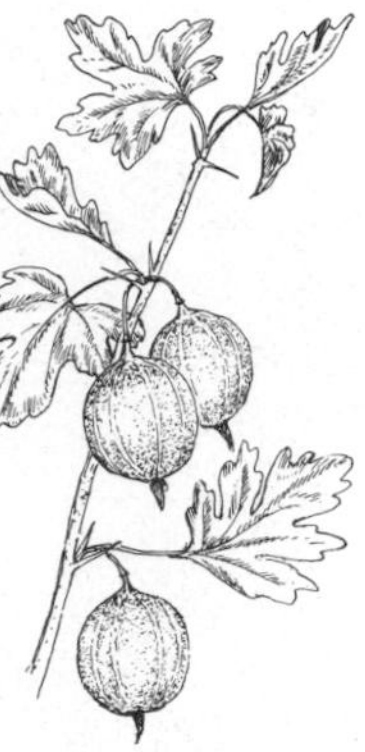

gooseberry
Ribes grossularia

goose[2] (go͞os) *tr.v.* **goosed, goosing, gooses.** *Slang.* To poke (a person) between the buttocks. **—***n., pl.* **gooses.** *Slang.* An unforewarned jab in the backside. [Possibly after GOOSE, from the supposed resemblance of an upturned thumb to an outstretched goose's neck.]

goose·ber·ry (go͞os′bĕr′ē, -bə-rē, go͞oz′-) *n., pl.* **-ries. 1.** A spiny shrub, *Ribes grossularia*, native to Eurasia, having lobed leaves, greenish flowers, and edible greenish berries. **2.** The fruit of this plant. **3.** Any of several plants bearing fruit similar to the gooseberry, such as the **Cape gooseberry** *(see).* [Perhaps GOOSE + BERRY.]

goose egg. *Slang.* Zero, especially when written as a numeral to indicate that no points have been scored.

goose·fish (go͞os′fĭsh′) *n., pl.* **goosefish** or **-fishes.** Any of several anglerfishes of the genus *Lophius*, such as *L. americanus*, of North American Atlantic waters. Also called "monkfish."

goose flesh. Momentary roughness of skin caused by erection of the papillae in response to cold or fear. Also called "goose bumps," "goose pimples."

goose·foot (go͞os′fo͝ot′) *n., pl.* **-foots.** Any of various usually weedy plants of the genus *Chenopodium*, having small greenish flowers. [From the shape of its leaves.]

goose grass. A plant, **cleavers** *(see).*

goose·herd (go͞os′hûrd′) *n.* One who tends a flock of geese.

goose·neck (go͞os′nĕk′) *n.* A slender, curved object or part, such as the flexible shaft of a type of desk lamp.

goose step. A military parade step done by swinging the legs sharply from the hips and keeping the knees locked.

goose-step (go͞os′stĕp′) *intr.v.* **-stepped, -stepping, -steps.** To execute or march in a goose step.

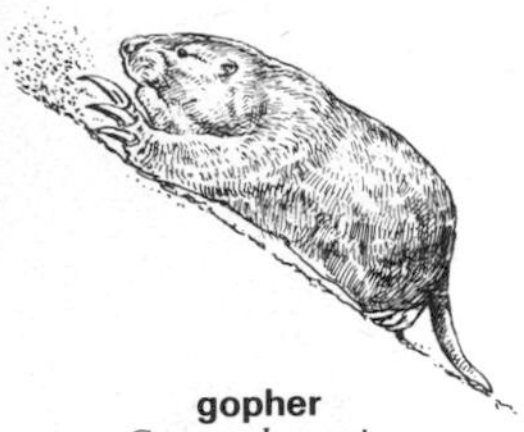

gopher
Geomys bursarius

goos·y (go͞o′sē) *adj.* **-ier, -iest.** Also **goos·ey. 1.** Pertaining to or resembling a goose. **2.** Foolish; scatterbrained. **3.** Causing or affected with goose flesh.

G.O.P. Grand Old Party.

go·pher (gō′fər) *n.* **1.** Any of various short-tailed, burrowing mammals of the family Geomyidae, of North America, having fur-lined external cheek pouches. Also called "pocket gopher." **2.** A **ground squirrel** *(see)*, especially one of the genus *Citellus.* **3.** Any of several burrowing tortoises of the genus *Gopherus;* especially, *G. polyphemus*, of the southeastern United States. Also called "gopher tortoise." [Shortening of earlier *magopher*†.]

gopher snake. A **bull snake** *(see).*

Gopher State. A nickname for Minnesota.

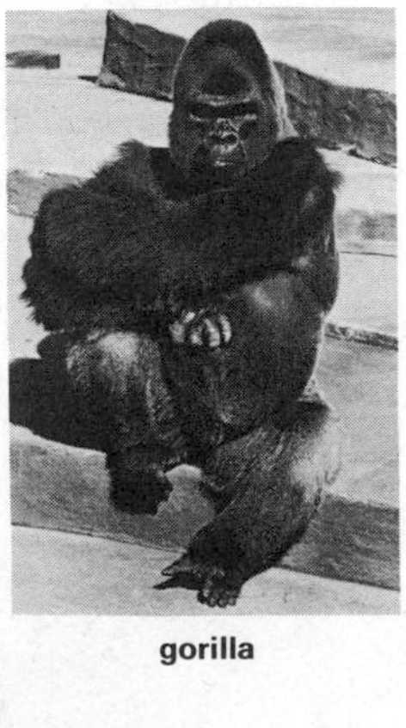

gorilla

go·pher·wood (gō′fər-wo͝od′) *n.* Also **gopher wood** (for sense 1). **1.** An unidentified wood, probably a kind of cypress, used in the construction of Noah's ark. Genesis 6:14. **2.** A tree, the **yellowwood** *(see).* [Hebrew *gōpher.*]

Go·rakh·pur (gōr′ək-po͝or′, gôr′-). A city of eastern Uttar Pradesh, Republic of India. Population, 196,000.

go·ral (gôr′əl, gōr′-) *n.* Either of two goatlike antelopes, *Naemorhedus goral* or *N. cranbrooki*, of mountainous regions of eastern Asia, having short, ridged, backward-curving horns in both sexes. [Hindi *gūral*, *goral*, possibly from Sanskrit *gaura*, gaur. See **gwou-** in Appendix.*]

Gor·di·an knot (gôr′dē-ən). **1.** An intricate knot tied by King Gordius of Phrygia and cut by Alexander the Great with his sword after hearing an oracle promise that whoever could undo it would be the next ruler of Asia. **2.** An exceedingly complicated problem or deadlock. **—cut the Gordian knot.** To solve a problem by resorting to prompt and bold measures.

Gor·don (gôrd′n), **Charles George.** 1833–1885. British general in China, Africa, and India.

Gordon setter. A hunting dog of a breed originating in Scotland, having a silky black and tan coat.

gore[1] (gôr) *tr.v.* **gored, goring, gores.** To pierce or stab with a horn or tusk. [Middle English *gōren*, to pierce, from *gore*, spear, Old English *gār*. See **ghaiso-** in Appendix.*]

gore[2] (gôr) *n.* **1.** A triangular or tapering piece of cloth used as a part of a garment, such as a skirt, or in an umbrella, sail, or the like. **2.** A small triangular piece of land. **—***tr.v.* **gored, goring, gores. 1.** To make or provide with a gore or gores. **2.** To cut into a gore. [Middle English *gore*, Old English *gāra*, triangular piece of land. See **ghaiso-** in Appendix.*]

gore[3] (gôr) *n.* Blood, especially coagulated blood from a wound. [Middle English *gore*, Old English *gor*†, dung, dirt.]

Gor·gas (gôr′gəs), **William Crawford.** 1854–1920. American army surgeon.

gorge (gôrj) *n.* **1.** A deep, narrow passage with precipitous rocky sides, enclosed between mountains. **2.** A narrow entrance or passageway from the rear into the bastion or other outwork of a fortification. **3.** The throat; gullet. **4.** An instance of gluttonous eating; a gorging. **5.** A mass obstructing a narrow passage: *The shipping lane was blocked by an ice gorge.* **—make one's gorge rise.** To make one feel violent anger or strong revulsion. **—***v.* **gorged, gorging, gorges. —***tr.* **1.** To stuff; satiate; glut. Usually used reflexively. **2.** To devour greedily. **—***intr.* To eat gluttonously. —See Synonyms at **satiate.** [Middle English, throat, from Old French, throat, from Vulgar Latin *gurga* (unattested), variant of Latin *gurges*, whirlpool, throat. See **gwerə-**[2] in Appendix.*] **—gorg′er** *n.*

gor·geous (gôr′jəs) *adj.* **1.** Dazzlingly brilliant; resplendent; magnificent. **2.** Strikingly beautiful or attractive. **3.** *Informal.* Wonderful; delightful. [Middle English *gorgeouse*, showy, splendid, from Old French *gorgias*, stylish, fine, elegant, possibly from *Gorgias* (circa 483–376 B.C.), Greek sophist and rhetorical stylist.] **—gor′geous·ly** *adv.* **—gor′geous·ness** *n.*

gor·ger·in (gôr′jər-ən) *n. Architecture.* The necking of a column.

gor·get (gôr′jĭt) *n.* **1.** A piece of armor protecting the throat. **2.** An ornamental collar. **3.** The scarflike part of a wimple covering the neck and shoulders. **4.** A band or patch of distinctive color on the throat, especially of a bird. [Middle English, from Old French, diminutive of *gorge*, throat, GORGE.]

Gor·gon (gôr′gən) *n.* **1.** *Greek Mythology.* Any of the three sisters Stheno, Euryale, and the mortal Medusa who had snakes for hair, and eyes which, if looked into, turned the beholder into stone. **2.** *Small* **g.** A repulsively ugly or terrifying woman. [Middle English, from Latin *Gorgō*, from Greek, from *gorgos*†, terrible.] **—Gor·go′ni·an** (-gō′nē-ən) *adj.*

gor·go·nei·on (gôr′gə-nē′ən) *n., pl.* **-neia** (-nē′ə). A representation of a Gorgon's head, especially one of Medusa. [Greek, from the neuter of *gorgoneios*, of a Gorgon, from *Gorgō*, GORGON.]

gor·go·ni·an (gôr-gō′nē-ən) *n.* Any of various corals of the order Gorgonacea, having a flexible, often branching skeleton of horny material. **—***adj.* Of or belonging to the Gorgonacea. [From Latin *Gorgonia*, coral, from *Gorgō*, GORGON.]

gor·gon·ize (gôr′gə-nīz′) *tr.v.* **-ized, -izing, -izes.** To have a paralyzing effect upon; petrify, as with fear. [From GORGON.]

Gor·gon·zo·la (gôr′gən-zō′lə) *n.* A pungent, blue-veined, cream-colored Italian cheese made of pressed cow's milk. [First made at *Gorgonzola*, village near Milan, Italy.]

go·ril·la (gə-rĭl′ə) *n.* **1.** A large anthropoid ape, *Gorilla gorilla*, of forests of equatorial Africa, having a stocky body and coarse, dark hair. **2.** A brutish or thuglike man. [New Latin, from Greek *Gorillai*†, name of African tribe of hairy men.]

Gö·ring (gœ′rĭng), **Hermann.** Also **Goe·ring.** 1893–1946. German field marshal and Nazi politician.

Go·ri·zia (gō-rē′tsyä). A city and tourist center of northeastern Italy on the Yugoslav border. Population, 42,000.

Gor·ki (gôr′kē), **Maxim.** Pen name of Aleksei Peshkov. 1868–1936. Russian author of novels, plays, and essays.

Gor·kiy (gôr′kē). Also **Gor·ki, Gor·ky.** Formerly **Nizh·ni Nov·go·rod** (nĭzh′nē nôv′gə-rŏd′). The fourth-largest city of the U.S.S.R., a major industrial and manufacturing center on the southern bank of the Volga in the west-central Russian S.F.S.R. Population, 1,042,000.

Gör·litz (gûr′lĭts). A city and manufacturing center of southeastern East Germany on the western bank of the Neisse, 55 miles east of Dresden. Population, 96,000.

Gor·lov·ka (gər-lôf′kə). A city and industrial center of the east-central Ukrainian S.S.R., 25 miles north of Donetsk. Population, 309,000.

gor·mand. Variant of **gourmand.**

gor·mand·ize (gôr′mən-dīz′) *v.* **-ized, -izing, -izes. —***intr.* To eat gluttonously; to gorge. **—***tr.* To devour (food) gluttonously; to gorge. **—***n. Rare.* Variant of **gourmandise.** [From GOURMANDISE (obsolete sense "gluttony").] **—gor′mand·iz′er** *n.*

Gor·no-Al·tay Autonomous Region (gôr′nō-ăl-tī′). Also **Gor·no-Al·tai.** An administrative division, 35,740 square miles in area, of the south-central Russian S.F.S.R. Population, 169,000. Capital, Gorno Altaysk.

Gor·no-Ba·dakh·shan Autonomous Region (gôr′nō-bä′däk-shän′). An administrative division, 24,590 square miles in area, of the southeastern Tadzhik S.S.R. Population, 86,000. Capital, Khorog.

gorse (gôrs) *n.* Any of several spiny, thickset shrubs of the genus *Ulex;* especially, *U. europeaus*, native to Europe, having fragrant yellow flowers. Also called "furze," "whin." [Middle English *gorst*, *gors*, Old English *gorst*, *gors*. See **ghers-** in Appendix.*]

go·ry (gôr′ē, gōr′ē) *adj.* **-rier, -riest. 1.** Covered or stained with gore; bloody; bloodstained. **2.** Characterized by a great effusion of blood: *a gory battle.* **3.** Full of or characterized by bloodshed, slaughter, or acts of violence: *a gory narrative.* —**gor'i·ly** *adv.* —**gor'i·ness** *n*

gosh (gŏsh) *interj.* Used to express mild surprise or delight. [Euphemistic variant of GOD.]

gos·hawk (gŏs'hôk') *n.* **1.** A large hawk, *Accipiter gentilis,* having broad, rounded wings and gray or brownish plumage. **2.** Any of several similar or related hawks. [Middle English *goshawke,* Old English *gōshafoc* : *gōs,* GOOSE + *hafoc,* HAWK.]

Go·shen (gō'shən). A region of ancient Egypt on the eastern delta of the Nile, inhabited by the Israelites from the time of Joseph until the Exodus.

gos·ling (gŏz'lĭng) *n.* **1.** A young goose. **2.** An inexperienced young person. [Middle English, earlier *gesling,* from Old Norse *gæslingr.* See **ghans-** in Appendix.*]

gos·pel (gŏs'pəl) *n.* **1.** *Sometimes capital* **G.** The teachings of Jesus and the Apostles. **2. a.** *Capital* **G.** One of the first four books of the New Testament, describing the life, death, and resurrection of Jesus Christ. **b.** A similar narrative. **3.** *Often capital* **G.** A lection from any of these books included as part of a religious service. **4.** A teaching or doctrine of a religious teacher. **5.** Something accepted as unquestionably true. [Middle English *gospel,* Old English *godspell,* "good news" (translation of Late Latin *evangelium,* EVANGEL) : *gōd,* GOOD + *spel,* news (see **spel-³** in Appendix*).]

gos·pel·er (gŏs'pə-lər) *n.* Also *chiefly British* **gos·pel·ler.** **1.** One who teaches or professes faith in a gospel. **2.** A person who reads or sings the Gospel as part of a church service. [Middle English *gospeler,* Old English *godspellere,* from *godspellian,* to teach the gospel, from *godspell,* GOSPEL.]

gos·po·din (gŏs'pə-dēn') *n., pl.* **-da** (-dä'). A courteous form of address used in the Soviet Union as a title for non-Russians. [Russian, "master," "lord." See **ghos-ti-** in Appendix.*]

gos·sa·mer (gŏs'ə-mər) *n.* **1.** A fine film of cobwebs often seen floating in the air or caught on bushes or grass. **2.** A soft, sheer, gauzy fabric. **3.** Anything delicate, light, or insubstantial. —*adj.* Also **gos·sa·mer·y** (-mə-rē). Light, thin, and delicate. [Middle English *gossomer, gosesomer* : perhaps *goos, gos,* GOOSE + *somer,* SUMMER (from its appearance in the Indian summer when geese are in season).]

gos·sip (gŏs'əp) *n.* Also **gos·sip·er** (gŏs'ə-pər) (for sense 2). **1.** Trifling, often groundless rumor, usually of a personal, sensational, or intimate nature; idle talk. **2.** A person who habitually engages in such talk. **3.** Trivial, chatty talk or writing. **4.** *Archaic.* A close friend or companion. **5.** *Archaic.* A godparent. —*intr.v.* **gossiped, -siping, -sips.** To engage in or spread gossip. See Synonyms at **speak.** [Middle English *godsib,* godparent, godchild, close friend, Old English *godsibb* : *god,* GOD + *sibb,* kinsman (see **seu-²** in Appendix*).] —**gos'sip·er** *n.*

gos·sip·mong·er (gŏs'ĭp-mŭng'gər, -mŏng'gər) *n.* A person who relates gossip.

gos·sip·ry (gŏs'əp-rē) *n.* **1.** The act or practice of gossiping. **2.** Gossips collectively.

gos·sip·y (gŏs'ə-pē) *adj.* Full of or inclined to gossip.

gos·soon (gŏ-sōōn') *n. Irish.* A boy; especially, a servant boy. [French *garçon,* GARÇON.]

got. Past tense and past participle of **get.**

Gö·ta Canal (yœ'tä, -tə). A waterway of southern Sweden extending for a total length of 360 miles and linking Göteborg on the west with Stockholm on the east.

Gö·te·borg (yœ'tə-bôr'y'). Also **Goth·en·burg** (gŏt'n-bûrg', gŏth'-). The second-largest city of Sweden, a major seaport and shipbuilding center located in the southwest on the Göta Canal. Population, 414,000.

Goth (gŏth) *n.* **1.** A member of the Germanic people that originally settled between the Elbe and Vistula rivers and that invaded the Roman Empire in the early centuries of the Christian era. See **Ostrogoth, Visigoth.** **2.** An uncultured, uncivilized, or rude person; a barbarian. [Middle English *Gothes,* Goths, from Late Latin *Gothī* (singular *Gothus*), from Gothic *Gutans*† (unattested), tribal name.]

Goth. Gothic.

Go·tha (gō'tä). A city in southwestern East Germany, 15 miles west of Erfurt. Population, 56,000.

Goth·am (gŏth'əm). **1.** A village of southern Nottinghamshire, England, whose inhabitants are reputed by legend to have feigned stupidity in order to prevent King John from establishing a residence there. **2.** New York City. Used as a nickname. —**Goth'am·ite'** *n.*

Goth·ic (gŏth'ĭk) *adj. Abbr.* **Goth.** **1. a.** Of or pertaining to the Goths or their language. **b.** Germanic; Teutonic. **2.** Of or pertaining to the Middle Ages; medieval. **3. a.** Of or pertaining to an architectural style prevalent in western Europe from the 12th through the 15th century, and characterized by pointed arches, rib vaulting, and flying buttresses. **b.** Of or pertaining to painting, sculpture, or other art forms prevalent in northern Europe from the 12th through the 15th century. **c.** Of or relating to an architectural style derived from medieval Gothic. **4.** *Sometimes small* **g.** Of or pertaining to a literary style of fiction prevalent in the late 18th and early 19th centuries which emphasized the grotesque, mysterious, and desolate: *a Gothic novel.* **5.** *Sometimes small* **g.** Barbarous; uncivilized; primitive; crude. —*n. Abbr.* **Goth.** **1.** The extinct East Germanic language of the Goths. **2.** Gothic art or architecture. **3.** *Often small* **g.** *Printing.* **a.** A typeface, **black letter** *(see).* **b.** A typeface, **sans serif** *(see).* —**Goth'i·cal·ly** *adv.*

Gothic arch. *Architecture.* A pointed arch, especially one with a jointed apex.

Gothic hand. A style of handwriting, **court hand** *(see).*

Goth·i·cism (gŏth'ĭ-sĭz'əm) *n.* **1.** Use of, imitation of, or an instance of Gothic style, as in architecture, art, or literature. **2.** A barbarous or crude manner or style.

Goth·i·cize (gŏth'ĭ-sīz') *tr.v.* **-cized, -cizing, -cizes.** To make Gothic.

Got·land (gŏt'lənd; *Swedish* gôt'länd'). Formerly **Gott·land, Goth·land.** An island constituting a county of Sweden, 1,225 square miles in area, in the Baltic Sea off the southeastern coast. Population, 54,000.

got·ten. Past participle of **get.**

Göt·tin·gen (gœt'ĭng-ən). A city and manufacturing center of southern Lower Saxony, West Germany. Population, 80,000.

Götz von Ber·lich·ing·en. See **Berlichingen.**

gouache (gwŏsh, gōō-äsh') *n.* **1.** A method of painting using opaque water colors mixed with a preparation of gum. **2.** An opaque pigment prepared in such a way. **3.** A painting executed with such pigments. [French, from Italian *guazzo,* "puddle," from Latin *aquātiō,* watering, from *aquārī,* to bring water to, from *aqua,* water. See **akwā-** in Appendix.*]

Gou·da¹ (gou'də, gōō'-; *Dutch* hou'də). A city of the western Netherlands, famous for its cheese market. Population, 44,000.

Gou·da² (gou'də, gōō'-) *n.* A mild, close-textured, pale-yellow cheese made from whole or partially skimmed milk and often covered with a protective coating of red wax. Also called "Gouda cheese." [Originally made in GOUDA.]

gouge (gouj) *n.* **1.** A chisel with a rounded, troughlike blade. **2.** A scooping or digging action, as with a gouge. **3.** A groove, hole, or indentation scooped with or as if with a gouge: *"With his heel he kicked shallow gouges in the gritty soil"* (Irvin S. Cobb). **4.** *Informal.* A large amount exacted or extorted. —*tr.v.* **gouged, gouging, gouges.** **1.** To cut or scoop out with or as if with a gouge: *"He began to gouge a small pattern in the sand with his cane"* (Vladimir Nabokov). **2.** To force out: *gouged out his eyes.* **3.** To exact exorbitantly or extort from. **4.** *Slang.* To swindle. [Middle English *gouge,* from Old French, from Late Latin *gubia,* from Celtic, akin to Old Irish *gulban*†.] —**goug'er** *n.*

gou·lash (gōō'läsh, -lăsh) *n.* A stew of beef or veal and vegetables, seasoned mainly with paprika. Also called "Hungarian goulash." [Hungarian *gulyás (hus),* "herdsman's meat," from *gulya,* herd.]

Gould (gōōld), **Jay.** Original given name, Jason. 1836–1892. American financier and railroad speculator.

Gou·nod (gōō-nō'), **Charles François.** 1818–1893. French composer.

gou·ra·mi (gōō-rä'mē, gōōr'ə-mē) *n., pl.* **-mis.** Any of various freshwater fishes of the family Anabantidae, of southeastern Asia, many species of which are brightly colored and popular in home aquariums. [Malay *gurami.*]

gourd (gôrd, gōrd, gōōrd) *n.* **1.** Any of several vines of the family Cucurbitaceae, related to the pumpkin, squash, and cucumber, and bearing fruits with a hard rind. **2.** The fruit of such a vine, as a calabash, often of irregular and unusual shape. **3.** The dried and hollowed-out shell of one of these fruits, used as a drinking vessel or utensil. [Middle English *gourde,* from Old French, from Latin *cucurbita,* probably of Mediterranean origin.]

gourde (gōōrd) *n. Abbr.* **g., G., gde.** **1.** The basic monetary unit of Haiti, equal to 100 centimes. See table of exchange rates at **currency.** **2.** A coin worth one gourde. [French, feminine of *gourd,* heavy, from Latin *gurdus*†, heavy, dull, stupid.]

gour·mand (gōōr'mənd; *French* gōōr-mäN') *n.* Also **gor·mand.** A person who delights in eating well and heartily. [Middle English *gourmaunt,* glutton, from Old French *gourmand, gourmant*†.]

gour·mand·ise (gōōr'mən-dēz') *n.* Also *rare* **gor·mand·ize** (gôr'-). A taste and relish for good food: *"You could see the gourmandise shining on his rosy lips"* (Glenway Wescott). [Middle English *gromandise,* gluttony, from Old French *gourmandise,* from *gourmand,* glutton, GOURMAND.]

gour·met (gōōr-mā'; *French* gōōr-mĕ') *n.* A connoisseur of fine food and drink; an epicure. [French (influenced in sense by *gourmand*), from Old French *gromet, gourmet*†, wine merchant's servant.]

Gour·mont (gōōr-môN'), **Remy de.** 1858–1915. French symbolist poet, critic, and novelist.

gout (gout) *n.* **1.** *Pathology.* A disturbance of the uric-acid metabolism occurring predominantly in males, characterized by arthritic attacks, capable of becoming chronic and producing deformity, and precipitated by minor trauma, as by ill-fitting shoes, by excessive consumption of food or alcohol, by surgical procedures, infection, or certain drugs. **2.** A large blob or clot: *"and makes it bleed great gouts of blood"* (Oscar Wilde). [Middle English *goute,* from Old French, "drop" (from the belief that gout was caused by drops of morbid humors), from Latin *gutta*†, drop.]

gout·y (gou'tē) *adj.* **-ier, -iest.** **1.** Of, relating to, or resembling gout. **2.** Suffering from or showing the effects of gout. —**gout'i·ness** *n.*

gov. **1.** government. **2.** governor.

Gov. governor.

gov·ern (gŭv'ərn) *v.* **-erned, -erning, -erns.** —*tr.* **1.** To control the actions or behavior of; guide; direct. **2.** To make and administer public policy for (a political unit); exercise sovereign authority in. **3.** To control the speed or magnitude of; regulate: *a valve governing fuel intake.* **4.** To keep under control; restrain. **5.** To decide; determine: *Chance usually governs the outcome of the game.* **6.** *Grammar.* **a.** To require (a noun or verb) to be in a particular case or mood. **b.** To require the use of (a certain case or mood). —*intr.* **1.** To exercise political authority. **2.** To

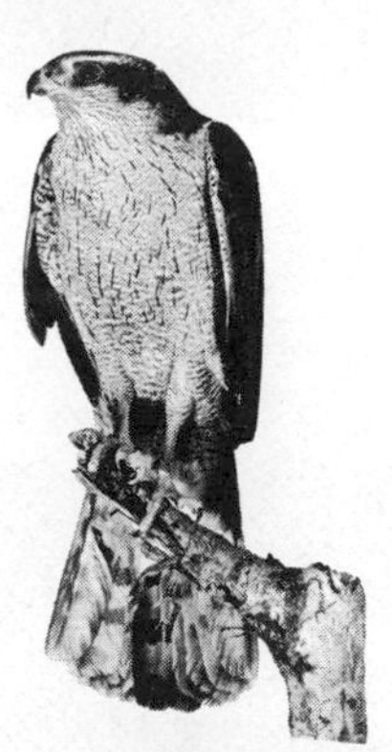

goshawk
Accipiter gentilis

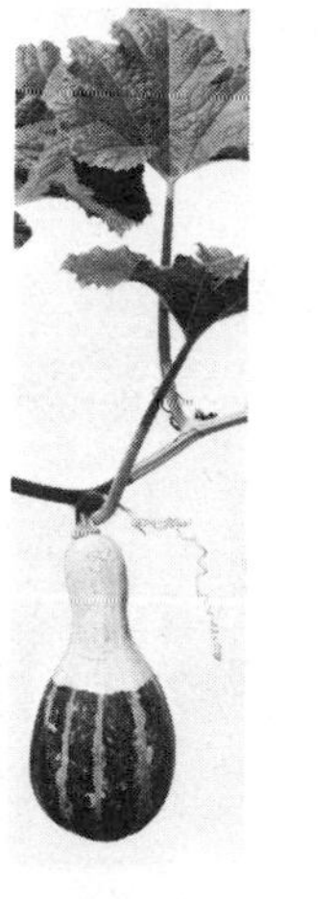

gourd
Lagenaria siceraria

have or exercise a predominating influence. [Middle English *governen*, from Old French *governer*, from Latin *gubernāre*, to direct, steer, from Greek *kubernan*†. See also **cybernetics**.] —**gov'ern·a·ble** *adj.*

gov·ern·ance (gŭv'ər-nəns) *n.* **1.** The act, process, or power of governing; government. **2.** The state of being governed.

gov·ern·ess (gŭv'ər-nĭs) *n.* **1.** A woman employed to educate and train the children of a private household. **2.** A female governor.

gov·ern·ment (gŭv'ərn-mənt) *n. Abbr.* **gov., govt. 1.** The act or process of governing; especially, the administration of public policy in a political unit; political jurisdiction. **2.** The office, function, or authority of one who governs or a governing body. **3.** A system or policy by which a political unit is governed. **4.** Political science. **5.** A governing body or organization. **6.** An area within a single rule; a political unit. —**gov'ern·ment'al** (-mĕnt'l) *adj.* —**gov'ern·men'tal·ly** *adv.*

Usage: *Government,* as the subject of a sentence or clause, takes a singular verb in American usage: *The government is determined to enforce the agreement.* In British usage, *government,* in its political sense of a group of officials, is more often construed as a plural collective: *The government are determined to follow this course.*

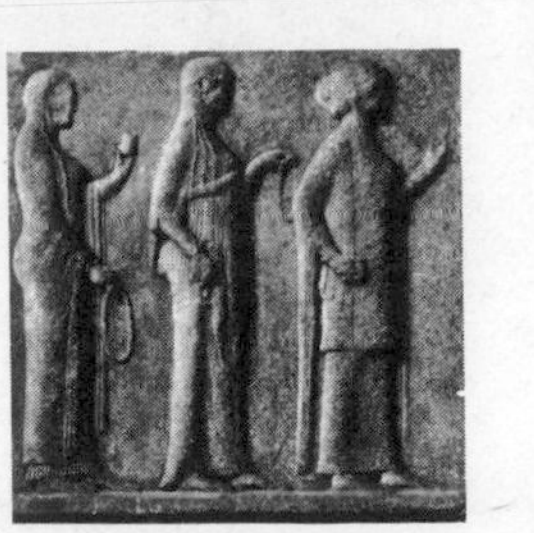

Graces
Ancient Greek low relief

Government House. The official residence of a governor, especially of a British colony.

Government Issue. *Abbr.* **GI, G.I.** Anything issued by the government or a government agency, as U.S. Army equipment.

gov·er·nor (gŭv'ər-nər) *n. Abbr.* **gov., Gov. 1.** A person who governs, especially: **a.** The chief executive of a state in the United States. **b.** An official appointed to govern a colony or territory. **2.** The manager or administrative head of an organization, business, or institution. **3.** A military commandant. **4.** *British Informal.* Mister; sir. Used in direct address. **5.** *Machinery.* A feedback device on a machine or engine used to provide automatic control, as of speed, pressure, or temperature. [Middle English *governour*, from Old French *governeor*, from Latin *gubernātor*, from *gubernāre*, GOVERN.]

governor general *pl.* **governors general.** Also *chiefly British* **gov·er·nor-gen·er·al** (gŭv'ər-nər-jĕn'ər-əl) *pl.* **governors-general** or **governor-generals.** *Abbr.* **Gov. Gen. 1.** *Often capital* **G**, *capital* **G**. The highest-ranking representative of the Crown in a British colony or dominion. **2.** A governor of a large territory who has other, subordinate governors under his jurisdiction. —**gov'er·nor-gen'er·al·ship'** *n.*

gov·er·nor·ship (gŭv'ər-nər-shĭp') *n.* The office, term, or jurisdiction of a governor.

Governors Island. An island of New York State occupying 173 acres in New York Bay, the site of a U.S. Coast Guard base.

Gov. Gen. governor general.

govt. government.

gow·an (gou'ən) *n. Scottish.* A yellow or white wildflower, especially the Old World daisy. [Middle English *gollan*, probably from Scandinavian, akin to Old Norse *gullinn*, golden. See **ghel-**[2] in Appendix.*]

gowk (gôk) *n. Scottish.* **1.** A cuckoo. **2.** A stupid person; a fool. [Middle English *gowke*, from Old Norse *gaukr*, a cuckoo, from Germanic *gaukaz* (imitative).]

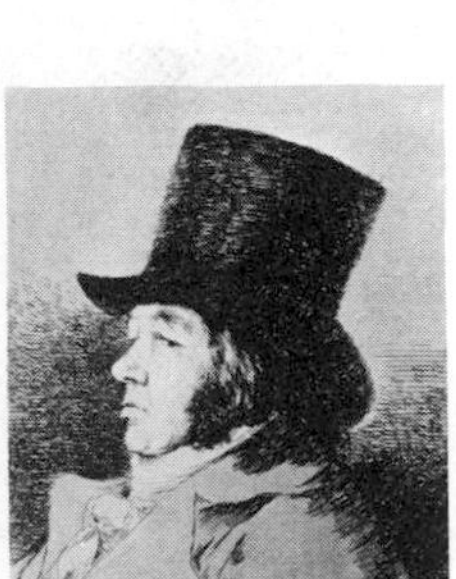

Goya
Self-portrait

gown (goun) *n.* **1.** A long, loose, flowing garment, as a robe or nightgown. **2.** A long, usually formal woman's dress. **3.** A distinctive outer robe worn on ceremonial occasions, as by scholars or clergymen. **4.** *Rare.* The university faculty and student body, as distinguished from townspeople: *town and gown.* —*tr.v.* **gowned, gowning, gowns.** To dress in or invest with a gown. [Middle English *goune*, from Old French, from Late Latin *gunna*†, robe, fur.]

gowns·man (gounz'mən) *n., pl.* **-men** (-mĭn). One who wears a distinctive gown as a mark of his profession or office.

goy (goi) *n., pl.* **goyim** (goi'ĭm) or **goys.** A person who is not a Jew; a Gentile. Often used disparagingly. [Yiddish, from Hebrew *gōy*, people.] —**goy'ish** *adj.*

Go·ya (gō'yä), **Francisco José de.** Full name, Francisco José de Goya y Lucientes. 1746–1828. Spanish artist.

G.P. general practitioner.

g.p.m. gallons per minute.

GPO 1. general post office. **2.** Government Printing Office.

g.p.s. gallons per second.

GPU, G.P.U. Government Political Administration (Russian *Gosudarstvennoyje Politicheskoyje Upravlenie*), a former administrative branch of the Soviet government functioning as a successor organization to the **Cheka** *(see)* and corresponding in broad outline to the later **KGB** *(see).*

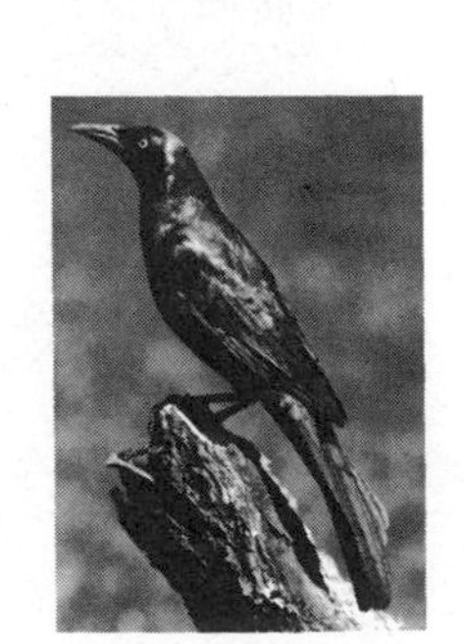

grackle
Quiscalus quiscula

GQ general quarters.

gr. 1. grade. **2.** gross. **3.** group.

Gr. Greece; Greek.

Graaf·i·an follicle (grä'fē-ən). *Anatomy.* Any of the follicles in the mammalian ovary, containing a maturing ovum. [After Regnier de *Graaf* (1641–1673), Dutch anatomist.]

grab[1] (grăb) *v.* **grabbed, grabbing, grabs.** —*tr.* **1.** To take or grasp suddenly; snatch; seize. **2.** To capture or restrain; arrest. **3.** To obtain or appropriate unscrupulously or forcibly. **4.** To take hurriedly: *He grabbed a bite to eat.* —*intr.* To make a snatch: *He grabbed for the gun.* —*n.* **1.** The act of grabbing; a sudden seizure. **2.** Anything grabbed. **3.** A mechanical device for gripping an object. —**up for grabs.** *Informal.* Available for anyone to take. [Middle Dutch and Middle Low German *grabben*. See **ghrebh-**[1] in Appendix.*] —**grab'ber** *n.*

grab[2] (grăb) *n.* An Oriental coastal vessel with two or three masts. [Arabic *ghurāb*, raven, swift galley.]

grab bag. 1. A container filled with articles, such as party gifts, to be drawn sight unseen. **2.** Any miscellaneous collection of often valuable items.

grab·ble (grăb'əl) *intr.v.* **-bled, -bling, -bles. 1.** To feel around with the hands; grope. **2.** To fall down; sprawl. [Dutch *grabbelen*, frequentative of Middle Dutch *grabben*, GRAB (to seize).]

gra·ben (grä'bən) *n.* A usually elongated depression of the earth's crust between two parallel faults. [German *Graben*, trench, from Old High German *grabo*, from *graban*, to dig. See **ghrebh-**[2] in Appendix.*]

grab rope. A rope for steadying oneself, as on a gangplank or an open deck.

Grac·chus (grăk'əs). Roman family of statesmen, including **Gaius Sempronius** (153–121 B.C.) and his brother, **Tiberius Sempronius** (163–133 B.C.), who are known as "the Gracchi."

grace (grās) *n.* **1.** Seemingly effortless beauty or charm of movement, form, or proportion. **2.** A characteristic or quality pleasing for its charm or refinement. **3.** Skill at avoiding the inept or clumsy course; a sense of fitness or propriety. **4. a.** A disposition to be generous or helpful; good will. **b.** Mercy; clemency. **5.** A favor rendered by one who need not do so; indulgence. **6.** Temporary immunity from penalties granted after a deadline has been passed: *a period of grace before a new law is enforced.* **7.** *Theology.* **a.** Divine love and protection bestowed freely upon mankind. **b.** The state of being protected or sanctified by the favor of God. **c.** An excellence or power granted by God; an unmerited gift from God. **8.** A short prayer of blessing or thanksgiving said before or after a meal. **9.** Used with *his, her,* or *your* as a title of courtesy for a duke, duchess, or archbishop. **10.** A musical embellishment, such as an appoggiatura. —**in the good** (or **bad**) **graces of.** In (or out) of favor with. —**with good** (or **bad**) **grace.** In a willing (or grudging) manner. —*tr.v.* **graced, gracing, graces. 1.** To honor or favor. **2.** To give beauty, elegance, or charm to. **3.** *Music.* To embellish with grace notes. [Middle English, from Old French, from Latin *grātia*, pleasure, favor, thanks, from *grātus*, favorable, pleasing. See **gwerə-**[1] in Appendix.*]

grace cup. 1. A cup used at the end of a meal, usually after grace, for the final toast. **2.** The final toast.

grace·ful (grās'fəl) *adj.* Showing grace of movement, form, or proportion. —**grace'ful·ly** *adv.* —**grace'ful·ness** *n.*

grace·less (grās'lĭs) *adj.* **1.** Lacking grace; clumsy: *"They studied the graceless adolescent body and found it good"* (Hannah Green). **2.** Having no sense of propriety or decency. —**grace'less·ly** *adv.* —**grace'less·ness** *n.*

grace note. 1. A musical note, especially an appoggiatura, added as an embellishment. **2.** Any decorative flourish.

Grac·es (grā'sĭz) *pl.n. Greek Mythology.* Three sister goddesses, Aglaia, Euphrosyne, and Thalia, who dispense charm and beauty. Also called the "Three Graces."

grac·ile (grăs'ĭl) *adj.* **1.** Gracefully slender. **2.** Graceful. [Latin *gracilis*†, slim, slender.] —**gra·cil'i·ty** (grə-sĭl'ə-tē) *n.*

gra·ci·o·so (grä'shē-ō'sō; *Spanish* grä-thyō'sō) *n., pl.* **-sos. 1.** A clown or buffoon in Spanish comedies. **2.** *Obsolete.* A court favorite. [Spanish, "amusing (person)," clown, from Latin *grātiōsus*, GRACIOUS.]

gra·cious (grā'shəs) *adj.* **1.** Characterized by kindness and warm courtesy. **2.** Merciful; compassionate. **3.** Condescendingly courteous; indulgent. **4.** Leisurely; elegant: *a gracious dinner.* **5.** *Obsolete.* Fortunate; prosperous. —See Synonyms at **kind.** —*interj.* Used to express surprise or mild emotion. [Middle English, from Old French, from Latin *grātiōsus*, favorable, pleasing, from Latin *grātia*, GRACE.] —**gra'cious·ly** *adv.* —**gra'cious·ness** *n.*

grack·le (grăk'əl) *n.* **1.** Any of several New World blackbirds of the family Icteridae, and especially of the genera *Quiscalus* or *Cassidix*, having iridescent blackish plumage. Sometimes called "crow blackbird." **2.** Any of several Asian mynas of the genus *Gracula.* [New Latin *Gracula*, from Latin *grāculus*, jackdaw. See **ger-**[4] in Appendix.*]

grad (grăd) *n. Informal.* A graduate of a school or college.

grad. graduate; graduated.

gra·date (grā'dāt') *v.* **-dated, -dating, -dates.** —*intr.* To pass imperceptibly from one degree, shade, or tone to another. —*tr.* **1.** To cause to pass imperceptibly from one degree, shade, or tone to another. **2.** To arrange according to or in grades. [Back-formation from GRADATION.]

gra·da·tion (grā-dā'shən) *n.* **1.** A series of gradual, successive stages; a systematic progression. **2.** A degree or stage in such a progression. **3.** Advancement by successive stages, tones, or shades, as from one color to another. **4.** The act of gradating or arranging in grades. **5.** *Linguistics.* An **ablaut** *(see).* [Latin *gradātiō*, from *gradus*, step, GRADE.] —**gra·da'tion·al** *adj.* —**gra·da'tion·al·ly** *adv.*

grade (grād) *n. Abbr.* **gr. 1.** A stage or degree in a process. **2.** A position in a scale of size or quality, as of eggs or beef. **3.** A group of persons or things all falling in the same specified limits; a class. **4. a.** A class at an elementary school, or the pupils in it. **b.** *Plural.* Elementary school. Preceded by *the.* **5.** A mark indicating a student's level of accomplishment. **6.** A military, naval, or civil-service rank. **7.** The degree of inclination of a slope, road, or other surface. **8.** A slope or gradual inclination, especially of a road or railroad track. **9.** A domestic animal produced by crossbreeding one of purebred stock with one of ordinary stock. —**at grade. 1.** On the same level. **2.** At the same degree of inclination. —**make the grade. 1.** To reach the highest point of an inclination. **2.** *Informal.* To succeed; reach a goal. **3.** *Informal.* To meet a standard. —**up to grade.** Equal to a standard. —*v.* **graded, grading, grades.** —*tr.* **1.** To arrange in steps or degrees; to rank; sort. **2.** To arrange in a series or according to a scale. **3. a.** To determine the quality of (academic work, for example); evaluate. **b.** To give a grade to (a student, for example). **4.** To level or smooth to a desired or horizontal gradient. **5.** To gradate. **6.** To improve the quality of (livestock) by crossbreeding with purebred stock. Often used with *up.* —*intr.* **1.** To hold a certain rank or position. **2.** To change or progress gradually. [French, from Latin *gradus,* step. See **ghredh-** in Appendix.*]

-grade. Indicates progression or movement; for example, **plantigrade, retrograde.** [French, from Latin *-gradus,* stepping, going, from *gradī,* to step, go. See **ghredh-** in Appendix.*]

grade crossing. An intersection of roads, railroad tracks, or a road and a railroad track at the same level. Also *British* "level crossing."

grade school. An **elementary school** *(see).*

gra·di·ent (grā′dē-ənt) *n.* **1.** A rate of inclination; slope. **2.** An ascending or descending part; an incline. **3.** *Physics.* The maximum rate at which a variable physical quantity changes in value per unit change in position. **4.** *Mathematics.* A vector having coordinate components that are the partial derivatives of a function with respect to its variables. [Perhaps from GRADE.]

gra·din (grā′dĭn; *French* grȧ-dăN) *n.* Also **gra·dine** (grə-dēn′). One of a series of steps or tiered seats, as in an amphitheater. [French, from Italian *gradino,* diminutive of *grado,* step, from Latin *gradus,* step, GRADE.]

grad·u·al (grăj′o͞o-əl) *adj.* **1.** Occurring in small stages or degrees or by even, continuous change. **2.** Moderate and regular: *gradual slope.* —*n. Roman Catholic Church.* **1.** A book containing the choral portions of the Mass. **2.** The antiphon sung between the Epistle and the Gospel of the Mass. [Middle English, from Medieval Latin *graduālis,* step by step, from Latin *gradus,* step, GRADE.] —**grad′u·al·ly** *adv.* —**grad′u·al·ness** *n.*

grad·u·al·ism (grăj′o͞o-ə-lĭz′əm) *n.* The belief in or policy of advancing toward a goal by gradual, often slow stages. —**grad′u·al·ist** *n.* & *adj.* —**grad′u·al·is′tic** *adj.*

grad·u·ate (grăj′o͞o-āt′) *v.* **-ated, -ating, -ates.** —*intr.* **1.** To be granted an academic degree or diploma. **2.** To change gradually, or by degrees. —*tr.* **1.** To grant a diploma or degree to. See Usage note below. **2.** To arrange or divide into categories, steps, or grades. **3.** To divide into marked intervals, especially for use in measurement. —*n.* (grăj′o͞o-ĭt). *Abbr.* **grad. 1.** One who has received an academic degree or diploma. **2.** A graduated container, such as a beaker or flask. —*adj.* (grăj′o͞o-ĭt). **1.** Possessing an academic degree or diploma. **2.** Of, for, or relating to studies beyond a bachelor's degree: *graduate courses.* [Middle English *graduaten,* from Medieval Latin *graduāre,* from Latin *gradus,* degree, step, GRADE.] —**grad′u·a′tor** (-ā′tər) *n.*

Usage: Either *graduated* or *was graduated* is possible in sentences such as *She graduated* (or *was graduated*) *from college. Graduated* is now more common. Although *was graduated* is considered an affectation by some, it is an equally acceptable alternative in such examples, according to 77 per cent of the Usage Panel. *From* is necessary in either case. *She graduated college* is termed unacceptable by 93 per cent of the Panel.

graduate school. A school of a university that offers studies beyond the bachelor's degree.

graduate student. A student at a graduate school, especially one matriculated in a specific department and studying for a specific degree.

grad·u·a·tion (grăj′o͞o-ā′shən) *n.* **1.** The conferring or receipt of an academic degree or diploma marking completion of studies. **2.** A ceremony at which degrees or diplomas are conferred; commencement. **3. a.** A division or interval on a graduated scale. **b.** A mark indicating the boundary of such an interval. **4.** An arrangement in or division into stages or degrees.

gra·dus (grā′dəs) *n., pl.* **-duses.** A dictionary of prosody used as an aid in writing Latin or Greek poetry. [Short for *Gradus ad Parnassus,* "step to Parnassus," from Latin *gradus,* step, GRADE.]

Grae·ae (grē′ē′) *pl.n.* Also **Grai·ae.** *Greek Mythology.* Three female sea deities, who, with only one eye and one tooth among them, guarded their sisters, the Gorgons.

Grae·cism. Variant of **Grecism.**

Grae·cize. Variant of **Grecize.**

Grae·co-Ro·man. Variant of **Greco-Roman.**

Graf (gräf) *n., pl.* **Grafen** (gräf′ən). *Feminine* **Gräf·in** (grĕf′ĕn′) *pl.* **-inen** (-ĕn′ən). A count. Used as a title of German, Austrian, or Swedish nobility corresponding to the English earl. [German, from Old High German *grāvo.* See **gravo-** in Appendix.*]

graf·fi·to (grə-fē′tō) *n., pl.* **-ti** (-tē). **1.** A crude drawing or inscription scratched on stone, plaster, or some other hard surface. **2.** *Usually plural.* Any scrawling written or drawn so as to be seen by the public, as on a wall or lavatory door. [Italian, diminutive of *graffio,* a scratching, from *graffiare,* to scratch, perhaps from *grafio,* a pencil, stylus, from Latin *graphium,* from Greek *graphion,* from *graphein,* to write. See **gerebh-** in Appendix.*]

graft[1] (grăft, gräft) *v.* **grafted, grafting, grafts.** —*tr.* **1.** *Horticulture.* **a.** To unite (a shoot or bud) with a growing plant by insertion or placing in close contact. **b.** To join (a plant or plants) by such union. **2.** *Surgery.* To transplant or implant (tissue, for example) into a bodily part to compensate for a defect. —*intr.* **1.** To make a graft. **2.** To be or become grafted. —*n.* **1.** *Horticulture.* **a.** A detached shoot or bud united or to be united with a growing plant. **b.** The union or point of union of a detached shoot or bud with a growing plant by insertion or attachment. **c.** A plant produced by such union. **2.** *Surgery.* **a.** Material, especially tissue or an organ, surgically attached to or inserted into a bodily part to compensate for a defect. **b.** The procedure of implanting or transplanting such material. **c.** The configuration or condition resulting from such a procedure. [Middle English *grafte, graff,* from Old French *grafe, grefe,* pencil, shoot for grafting (from its pencillike shape), from Latin *graphium.* See **graffito.**] —**graft′er** *n.*

graft[2] (grăft, gräft) *n.* **1.** The unscrupulous use of one's position to derive profit or advantages; extortion. **2.** Money or an advantage gained or yielded under such circumstances. —*v.* **grafted, grafting, grafts.** —*tr.* To gain by graft. —*intr.* To practice graft. [Perhaps extended use of GRAFT (insertion, hence "additional activity").] —**graft′er** *n.*

graft·age (grăf′tĭj, gräf′-) *n.* The process of making a graft or grafts.

gra·ham (grā′əm) *adj.* Made from or consisting of whole-wheat flour. [After Sylvester *Graham* (1794–1851), American vegetarian who urged dietary reform.]

Gra·ham (grā′əm), **Martha.** Born 1894? American choreographer and pioneer in modern dance.

Gra·ham (grā′əm), **Thomas.** 1805–1869. Scottish chemist; studied diffusion of gases.

Gra·ham (grā′əm), **William Franklin ("Billy").** Born 1918. American evangelist.

graham cracker. A slightly sweet, usually rectangular cracker, made of whole-wheat flour.

Gra·ham Island (grā′əm). An island, 2,485 square miles in area, off the northwestern coast of British Columbia, Canada; the largest of the Queen Charlotte group.

Gra·ham Land (grā′əm). See **Antarctic Peninsula.**

Grai·ae. Variant of **Graeae.**

Gra·ian Alps (grā′ən, grī′-). The northern arc of the western Alps on the French-Italian border. Highest elevation, Gran Paradiso (13,324 feet).

grail (grāl) *n.* Also **Grail. 1.** The cup or chalice in medieval legend used by Christ at the Last Supper and subsequently the object of many chivalrous quests. Also called "Holy Grail." **2.** The object of a prolonged endeavor. [Middle English *graal,* from Old French, from Medieval Latin *gradālis*†, dish.]

grain (grān) *n.* **1.** A small, hard seed or fruit, especially that produced by a cereal grass such as wheat, barley, rice, or oats. **2.** The seeds of such plants collectively, especially after having been harvested. **3.** Cereal grasses collectively: *a field of grain.* **4.** A relatively small discrete particulate or crystalline mass: *a grain of sand.* **5.** *Aerospace.* A mass of solid propellant formed from a number of smaller pieces. **6.** The very smallest amount; a tiny quantity: *a grain of truth.* **7.** A unit of weight in the U.S. Customary System, an avoirdupois unit equal to 0.002285 ounce or 0.036 dram. See **measurement. 8.** The arrangement, direction, or pattern of the fibrous tissue in wood. **9.** The side of a hide or piece of leather from which the hair or fur is removed. **10.** The pattern or markings on this side of leather. **11.** The pattern produced, as in stone, by the arrangement of particulate constituents. **12.** The relative size of the particles composing a substance or pattern: *a coarse grain.* **13.** Any painted, stamped, or printed design that imitates the pattern found in wood, leather, or stone. **14.** The direction or texture of fibers in a woven fabric. **15.** A state of fine crystallization. **16.** Temperament; nature; character. **17.** *Archaic.* Color; tint; hue. **18.** *Obsolete.* **a.** Cochineal or kermes. **b.** Red dye made from cochineal or kermes. **c.** Any fast dye. —**against one's** (or **the**) **grain.** In contradiction to one's natural disposition or character. —**with a grain of salt.** With reservations; skeptically. —*v.* **grained, graining, grains.** —*tr.* **1.** To form or cause to form into grains; granulate; crystallize. **2.** To paint, stamp, or print with a design imitating the grain of wood, leather, or stone. **3.** To give a granular or rough texture to. **4.** To remove the hair or fur from (hides) in preparation for tanning. —*intr.* To form grains. [Middle English, from Old French, from Latin *grānum,* seed. See **grə-no-** in Appendix.*] —**grain′er** *n.*

grain alcohol. Alcohol *(see).*

Grain Coast. The coast of Liberia, bordering on the Gulf of Guinea.

grain elevator. A building equipped with mechanical lifting devices, used for storing grain.

grains (grānz) *n.* Plural in form, usually used with a singular verb. An iron harpoon with two or more barbed prongs used for spearing fish. [Middle English *grein,* fork, from Old Norse *grein*†, branch, twig.]

grains of paradise. 1. The pungent, aromatic seeds of a tropical African plant, *Aframomum melegueta,* used medicinally. **2.** The seeds of **cardamom** *(see).*

grain·y (grā′nē) *adj.* **-ier, -iest. 1.** Made of or resembling grain; granular. **2.** Resembling the grain of wood.

gram[1] (grăm) *n.* Also *chiefly British* **gramme.** *Abbr.* **g** A metric unit of mass and weight, equal to one-thousandth (10^{-3}) of a kilogram. See **measurement.** [French *gramme,* from Late Latin *gramma,* a small unit, from Greek, letter. See **gerebh-** in Appendix.*]

gram[2] (grăm) *n.* **1.** Any of several plants, such as a bean, *Phaseolus mungo,* or the chickpea, bearing seeds widely used as food in tropical Asia. **2.** The seeds of such a plant. [Obsolete Portuguese, from Latin *grānum,* seed, GRAIN.]

-gram[1]. Indicates something written or drawn; for example, **diagram, telegram.** [Latin *-gramma,* something written, from Greek, *-gramma, -grammos,* respectively from *gramma,* letter and *grammē,* line. See **gerebh-** in Appendix.*]

-gram[2]. Indicates a gram, as used in the metric system; for example, **kilogram.** [From GRAM (unit).]

gram. grammar.

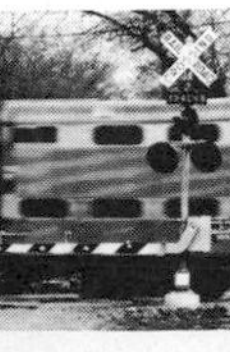

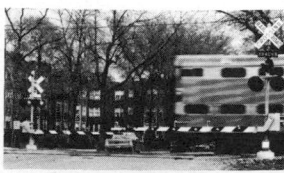

grade crossing
Signal installation at grade crossing of highway and railroad

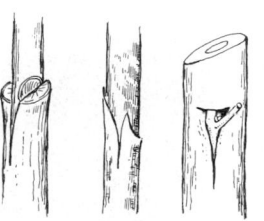

graft[1]
Left: Cleft graft
Center: Whip graft
Right: Bud graft

gra·ma (grä′mə) *n.* Any of various grasses of the genus *Bouteloua*, of western North America and South America, forming dense tufts or mats, and often used as pasturage. Also called "grama grass." [Spanish *grama*, from Latin *grāmina*, plural of *grāmen*, grass. See **gras-** in Appendix.*]

gram·a·rye (grăm′ə-rē) *n.* Occult learning; magic; necromancy: "*It took a long time to separate grammar from astrology and magic, grammar from gramarye.*" (James Sledd). [Middle English *gramarie*, from Old French *gramaire*, GRAMMAR.]

gram-at·om (grăm′ăt′əm) *n.* The mass in grams of an element numerically equal to the atomic weight.

gram calorie. A **calorie** (*see*).

gra·mer·cy (grə-mûr′sē, grăm′ər-sē) *interj. Archaic.* Used to express surprise or gratitude. [Middle English *gramercye*, *grand mercy*, great thanks, from Old French *grand merci* : *grand*, GRAND + *merci*, thanks, MERCY.]

gram·i·cid·in (grăm′ə-sĭd′n) *n.* An antibiotic produced by a bacterium, *Bacillus brevis*, and used against most Gram-positive pathogenic bacteria. [GRAM-(POSITIVE) + -CID(E) + -IN.]

gra·min·e·ous (grə-mĭn′ē-əs) *adj.* 1. Of, pertaining to, or characteristic of grasses. 2. Of or belonging to the family Gramineae, which includes the grasses. [From Latin *grāmineus*, grassy, from *grāmen* (stem *grāmin-*), grass. See **gras-** in Appendix.*]

gram·i·niv·or·ous (grăm′ə-nĭv′ər-əs) *adj.* Feeding on grasses, grain, or seeds. [Latin *grāmen* (stem *grāmin-*), grass (see **gramineous**) + -VOROUS.]

gram·mar (grăm′ər) *n. Abbr.* **gram.** 1. The study of language as a systematically composed body of words that exhibit discernible regularity of structure (morphology) and arrangement into sentences (syntax), sometimes including such aspects of language as the pronunciation of words (phonology), the meanings of words (semantics), and the history of words (etymology). 2. **a.** The phenomena with which this study deals, as exhibited by a specific language at a specific time. **b.** The system of rules implicit in a language, viewed as a mechanism for generating all sentences possible in that language. 3. A normative or prescriptive system of rules setting forth the current standard of usage for pedagogical or reference purposes. 4. Writing or speech judged with regard to the rules or practice of grammar: *bad grammar.* 5. A book containing the morphologic, syntactic, and semantic rules for a specific language: "*We find queer statements in our school grammars because their authors know little about the English language.*" (George O. Curme). 6. The basic principles of any area of knowledge: *the grammar of music.* 7. A book dealing with such principles. [Middle English *gramere*, from Old French *gramaire*, from Latin *grammatica*, from Greek *grammatikē (tekhnē)*, "(art) of the letters," from *grammatikos*, pertaining to letters, from *gramma*, letter. See **gerebh-** in Appendix.*]

grammar school. 1. An **elementary school** (*see*). 2. *British.* A secondary or preparatory school. 3. A school stressing the study of classical languages.

gram·mat·i·cal (grə-măt′ĭ-kəl) *adj.* 1. Of or relating to grammar. 2. Conforming to the rules of grammar. [Late Latin *grammaticālis*, from Latin *grammaticus*, from Greek *grammatikos*, pertaining to letters. See **grammar**.] —**gram·mat′i·cal·ly** *adv.*

grammatical gender. The gender assigned to a word in the grammar of a language, as distinct from natural gender or sex. Compare **common gender**, **natural gender**.

Gram·mat·i·cus. See Aelfric.

gram·ma·tol·o·gy (grăm-ə-tŏl′ə-jē) *n.* The study and science of systems of graphic script. —**gram′ma·to·log′ic** (-tə-lŏj′ĭk), **gram′ma·to·log′i·cal** *adj.* —**gram·ma·tol′o·gist** *n.*

gramme. *Chiefly British.* Variant of **gram** (metric unit).

gram-mo·lec·u·lar weight (grăm′mə-lĕk′yə-lər). *Chemistry.* A **mole** (*see*).

gram mol·e·cule. *Chemistry.* A mole (*see*).

Gram-neg·a·tive (grăm′nĕg′ə-tĭv) *adj.* Of, pertaining to, or being a microorganism that does not retain the purple dye used in Gram's method.

gram·o·phone (grăm′ə-fōn′) *n.* A record player; phonograph. [Originally a trademark from earlier *graphophone*, inversion of PHONOGRAPH.]

Gram·pi·ans, The (grăm′pē-ənz). A mountain range of central Scotland, dividing The Highlands from The Lowlands. Highest elevation, Ben Nevis (4,406 feet).

Gram-pos·i·tive (grăm′pŏz′ə-tĭv) *adj.* Of, pertaining to, or being a microorganism that retains the purple dye used in Gram's method.

gram·pus (grăm′pəs) *n.* 1. A marine mammal, *Grampus griseus*, related to and resembling the dolphins but lacking a beaklike snout. 2. Any of several similar cetaceans, such as the **killer whale** (*see*). [Middle English *graspeis*, from Old French *graspois*, *craspois* : *cras*, fat, from Latin *crassus* (see **crass**) + *pois*, fish, from Latin *piscis* (see **peisk-** in Appendix*).]

Gram's method (grămz). A differential staining technique using the retention or lack of retention of a purple dye to classify bacteria. [After Hans Christian Joachim Gram (1855–1938), Danish physician.]

Gra·na·da (grə-nä′də; *Spanish* grä-nä′thä). 1. An ancient Moorish kingdom in southern Spain. 2. A city and manufacturing center of southern Spain in the Sierra Nevada southeast of Córdoba, the former capital of Moorish Granada. Population, 150,000. 3. The oldest city of Nicaragua, on the northwestern shore of Lake Nicaragua. Population, 29,000.

gran·a·dil·la (grăn′ə-dĭl′ə) *n.* 1. Any of various tropical American passionflowers; especially, *Passiflora quadrangularis*, bearing edible fruit. 2. The egg-shaped, fleshy fruit of such a plant. [Spanish, diminutive of *granada*, pomegranate, from Vulgar Latin *grānāta* (unattested), from Latin *grānātum*, seedy, from *grānum*, GRAIN.]

gran·a·ry (grăn′ə-rē, grā′nə-) *n., pl.* **-ries.** 1. A building for storing threshed grain. 2. A region yielding a copious quantity of grain. [Latin *grānārium* : *grānum*, GRAIN + -ARY.]

Gran Ca·na·ria. The Spanish name for **Grand Canary**.

Gran Cha·co. See Chaco.

grand (grănd) *adj.* **grander**, **grandest.** 1. Large and impressive in size, scope, or extent. 2. Magnificent; splendid. 3. Rich and sumptuous: *grand furnishings.* 4. Having higher rank than others of the same category: *grand duke.* 5. The most important; principal; main: *grand ballroom.* 6. Illustrious; outstanding: *a grand assemblage.* 7. **a.** Pretentious. **b.** Calculated to impress: *a grand manner.* 8. Dignified and admirable: *a grand old man.* 9. Stately; regal. 10. Lofty; noble: *a grand purpose.* 11. *Music.* **a.** Written for a large ensemble. **b.** Complete in form; containing all the movements. 12. Inclusive; complete: *grand total.* —*n.* 1. A **grand piano** (*see*). 2. *Abbr.* **G** *Slang.* A thousand dollars. [French, from Old French, from Latin *grandis†*, grand, full-grown.] —**grand′ly** *adv.* —**grand′ness** *n.*

Synonyms: *grand, magnificent, imposing, stately, majestic, august, grandiose.* These adjectives mean extremely impressive in some respect. Both *grand* and *magnificent* apply to what is on a large or otherwise impressive scale, physically or aesthetically. *Grand* also can imply dignity, sweep, or eminence, and *magnificent* suggests sumptuousness and excellence of quality. *Imposing* describes what is impressive with respect to size, bearing, power, or general excellence. *Stately* refers principally to dignified and lofty appearance or manner. *Majestic* is applicable to appearance, bearing, manner, or artistic quality, and suggests dignity, nobility, or grandeur. *August* describes persons or things that inspire reverence or awe because of exalted rank or character or because of impressive aspect. *Grandiose* refers principally to things that are on an exceedingly large scale, often with the implication of false pretension to greatness or of affectation or pompousness on the part of their creators.

gran·dam (grăn′dăm′, -dəm) *n.* Also **gran·dame** (-dām′, -dəm). 1. A grandmother. 2. An old woman. [Middle English *graundam*, from Norman French *graund dame* : Old French *grand*, GRAND + *dame*, mother, DAME.]

Grand Army of the Republic. *Abbr.* **GAR, G.A.R.** A society, founded in 1866, of Civil War veterans who served in the Union forces.

grand·aunt (grănd′ănt′, -änt′) *n.* A sister of one's grandparent. Also called "great-aunt."

Grand Ba·ha·ma (bə-hä′mə, -hā′mə). An island of the Bahama group, 430 square miles in area, situated in the Atlantic 60 miles east of West Palm Beach, Florida. Population, 8,000.

Grand Bal·lon (grän bà-lôn′). The highest mountain (4,672 feet) in the Vosges range of eastern France.

Grand Banks. Also **Grand Bank.** A shoal and fishing area in the Atlantic off the southern and eastern coasts of Newfoundland, 200 miles wide and extending 500 miles from west to east.

Grand Bas·sam (bà-säm′). A port and the former capital of the Ivory Coast, located in the southeast on the Gulf of Guinea. Population, 12,000.

Grand Canal. 1. An inland waterway of northeastern China extending 1,000 miles from Tientsin to Hangchow. 2. The principal waterway of Venice, Italy.

Grand Ca·nar·y (kə-nâr′ē). *Spanish* **Gran Ca·na·ria** (gräng′ kä-nä′ryä). The principal island of the Canary group, 592 square miles in area. Population, 226,000.

Grand Canyon. A gorge formed by the Colorado River in northwestern Arizona, extending 217 miles westward from the mouth of the Little Colorado to Lake Mead, with a width of from 4 to 18 miles and a maximum depth of 1 mile.

Grand Canyon National Monument. The inner gorge of the Grand Canyon, occupying an area of 306 square miles.

Grand Canyon National Park. An area of 1,008 square miles in northwestern Arizona including most of the Grand Canyon and adjacent areas.

Grand Canyon of the Arkansas. See Royal Gorge.

Grand Canyon of the Snake. See Hells Canyon.

Grand Canyon State. The nickname for Arizona.

Grand Cay·man. See Caymans.

grand·child (grănd′chīld′) *n., pl.* **-children** (-chĭl′drən). A child of one's son or daughter.

Grande Co·more. The French name for **Great Comoro**.

Grand Cou·lee Dam (kōō′lē). A dam on the Columbia River in northeast-central Washington.

grand·dad (grăn′dăd′) *n.* Also **grand·dad·dy** (grăn′dăd′ē) *pl.* **-dies.** *Informal.* Grandfather.

grand·daugh·ter (grăn′dô′tər) *n.* The daughter of one's son or daughter.

grand duchess. *Abbr.* **G.D.** 1. The wife or widow of a grand duke. 2. A woman who is sovereign of a grand duchy. 3. The daughter of a czar or of one of his male descendants.

grand duchy. *Abbr.* **G.D.** A territory ruled by a grand duke or a grand duchess.

grand duke. *Abbr.* **G.D.** 1. A nobleman who is below a king in rank and is sovereign of a grand duchy. 2. A son or grandson of a czar.

Grande, Ri·o. See Rio Grande.

gran·dee (grăn-dē′) *n.* 1. A nobleman of the highest rank in Spain or Portugal. 2. A person of eminence or high rank. [Spanish and Portuguese *grande*, "great (one)," from Latin *grandis*, GRAND.]

gramophone
The instrument invented by Emile Berliner in the 1880's

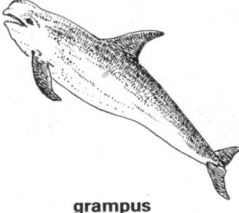

grampus
Grampus griseus

Grande Sou·fri·ère (gränd soo-fryâr′). A volcano constituting the highest elevation (4,869 feet) of Guadeloupe and of the Lesser Antilles, located in southern Basse-Terre. Also called "La Soufrière."

Grande-Terre (gränd-târ′). An island of the French West Indies constituting the eastern section of Guadeloupe.

gran·deur (grăn′jər, -joŏr) n. Greatness; splendor: "*The world is charged with the grandeur of God.*" (Gerard Manley Hopkins). [Middle English, from Old French, from *grand*, GRAND.]

Grand Falls. A waterfall, 200 feet wide and 316 feet high, of western Labrador on the Hamilton River.

grand·fa·ther (grănd′fä′thər) n. 1. The father of one's mother or father. 2. A forefather; ancestor.

grandfather clause. A clause in the constitutions of several Southern states prior to 1915, exempting from poll taxes and property and literacy requirements lineal descendants of persons who were registered voters before 1867.

grandfather clock. Also **grandfather's clock.** A pendulum clock enclosed in a tall, narrow cabinet.

grand·fa·ther·ly (grănd′fä′thər-lē) adj. 1. Characteristic of or befitting a grandfather. 2. Having the qualities of a grandfather; kindly; indulgent; benevolent.

Grand Forks. A city of east-central North Dakota on the Red River. Population, 34,000.

gran·dil·o·quence (grăn-dĭl′ə-kwəns) n. Pompous or bombastic speech or expression. [From Latin *grandiloquus*, speaking loftily : *grandis*, GRAND + *loquī*, to speak (see **tolkw-** in Appendix*).] —**gran·dil′o·quent** adj. —**gran·dil′o·quent·ly** adv.

gran·di·ose (grăn′dē-ōs′, grăn′dē-ōs′) adj. 1. Characterized by greatness of scope or intent; grand. 2. Characterized by feigned or affected grandeur; pompous. —See Synonyms at **grand**. [French, from Italian *grandioso*, from *grande*, great, grand, from Latin *grandis*, GRAND.] —**gran′di·ose′ly** adv. —**gran′di·os′i·ty** (-ŏs′ə-tē), **gran′di·ose′ness** n.

gran·di·o·so (grăn′dē-ō′sō) adv. *Music.* In a grand and noble style. Used as a direction. —adj. *Music.* Expansive in style. [Italian, GRANDIOSE.]

Grand Island. A city and railroad center of southeast-central Nebraska. Population, 26,000.

grand jury. A jury of 12 to 23 persons convened in private session to evaluate accusations against persons charged with crime and to determine whether the evidence warrants a bill of indictment. Compare **petit jury.**

Grand La·ma (grănd′ lä′mə). The **Dalai Lama** (see).

grand larceny. The theft of property of a value exceeding the amount constituting **petit larceny** (see).

grand·ma (grănd′mä′, grăn′mä′, grăm′mä′, grăm′ə) n. Also **grand·ma·ma** (grănd′mə-mä′, -mä′mə). *Informal.* Grandmother.

grand mal (grăn mäl′). A form of epilepsy characterized by severe seizures involving spasms and loss of conscious·ness. Compare **petit mal.** [French, "great illness" : GRAND + *mal*, illness, from Old French, bad, ill, from Latin *malus* (see **mel-⁵** in Appendix*).]

Grand·ma Mo·ses (mō′zĭz, -zĭs). In full, Anna Mary Robertson Moses. 1860–1961. American painter.

grand·moth·er (grănd′mŭth′ər) n. 1. The mother of one's father or mother. 2. A female ancestor.

grand·moth·er·ly (grănd′mŭth′ər-lē) adj. 1. Characteristic of or befitting a grandmother. 2. Having the qualities of a grandmother; overprotective; solicitous.

grand·neph·ew (grănd′nĕf′yoo, -nĕv′yoo, grăn′-) n. A son of one's nephew or niece.

grand·niece (grănd′nēs′, grăn′-) n. A daughter of one's nephew or niece.

Grand Old Party. Abbr. **G.O.P.** The Republican Party.

grand opera. A serious or melodramatic drama having the entire text set to music.

grand·pa (grănd′pä′, grăm′pä′, grăm′pə) n. Also **grand·pa·pa** (grănd′pə-pä′, -pä′pə). *Informal.* Grandfather.

grand·par·ent (grănd′pâr′ənt, grăn′-) n. A parent of one's mother or father; a grandmother or grandfather.

grand piano. A piano having the strings strung in a horizontal harp-shaped frame supported usually on three legs and ranging in size from the baby grand to the concert grand.

Grand Prix (grän prē′, grän prē′) pl. **Grands Prix** or **Grand Prixes** (prēz′, prē′). Any of several competitive international road races for sports cars of specific engine size over an exacting and usually risky course. [French, from *Grand Prix de Paris*, "Great Prize of Paris" (originally established for an international horse race).]

Grand Rapids (răp′ĭdz). A furniture-manufacturing center of southwest-central Michigan. Population, 177,000.

Grand River. 1. A river rising in southwest-central Iowa and flowing 300 miles southeast across northwestern Missouri to the Missouri River. 2. A river rising in southwestern Michigan and flowing 260 miles north and west into Lake Michigan.

grand sherif. A **sherif** (see).

grand·sire (grănd′sir′, -sər) n. *Archaic.* 1. A grandfather. 2. A male ancestor; forefather. 3. An old man.

grand slam. *Card Games.* See **slam.**

grand·son (grănd′sŭn′, grăn′-) n. The son of one's son or daughter.

grand·stand (grănd′stănd′, grăn′-) n. 1. A roofed stand for spectators at a stadium or racetrack. 2. The spectators seated in such a stand. —intr.v. **grandstand, -standing, -stands.** To perform ostentatiously so as to win the applause or approbation of an audience. —**grand′stand′er** n.

grandstand play. A sports play or other action performed in an ostentatious manner to impress onlookers.

Grand Te·ton (tē′tŏn′, tēt′n). The highest elevation (13,766 feet) of the Teton Range, in northwestern Wyoming.

Grand Teton National Park. A park occupying 465 square miles in northwestern Wyoming and including Grand Teton mountain.

grand tour. 1. An extended tour of continental Europe formerly considered a finishing course in the education of young men of the English upper class. 2. A comprehensive tour or survey.

grand·un·cle (grănd′ŭng′kəl) n. The uncle of one's father or mother. Also called "great-uncle."

grange (grānj) n. 1. *Capital* **G. a.** The Patrons of Husbandry, an association of farmers founded in the United States in 1867. **b.** One of its branch lodges. 2. *British.* A farm; especially, the residence and attached farm buildings of a gentleman farmer. 3. A feudal farm building used for storing grain paid as tithes. 4. *Archaic.* A granary. [Middle English, from Old French, from Medieval Latin *grānica*, from Latin *grānum*, GRAIN.]

Grange·mouth (grānj′məth, -mouth). A town, port, and ship-building center of southeastern Stirling, Scotland, on the Firth of Forth. Population, 20,000.

grang·er (grān′jər) n. A member of a grange.

grang·er·ize (grān′jə-rīz′) tr.v. **-ized, -izing, -izes.** 1. To illustrate (a book) with drawings, prints, or engravings taken from other books. 2. To mutilate (a book) by clipping out its illustrative material for such use. [After J. *Granger* (1723–1776), English biographer who published (1769) his *Biographical History of England* to be thus illustrated.] —**grang′er·ism′, grang′er·i·za′tion** n. —**grang′er·iz′er** n.

grani-. Indicates grain; for example, **granivorous, graniform.** [Latin *grāni-*, from *grānum*, GRAIN.]

gra·nif·er·ous (grə-nĭf′ər-əs) adj. Bearing grain. [From Latin *grānifer* : GRANI- + -FER.]

gran·i·form (grăn′ə-fôrm′) adj. Resembling a grain in form. [GRANI- + -FORM.]

gran·ite (grăn′ĭt) n. 1. A common, coarse-grained, light-colored, hard igneous rock consisting chiefly of quartz, orthoclase or microcline, and mica, used in monuments and for building. 2. Unyielding endurance; steadfastness; firmness. [Italian *granito*, "grained," from the past participle of *granire*, to impart a grained surface to, from *grano*, grain, from Latin *grānum*, GRAIN.] —**gra·nit′ic** (grə-nĭt′ĭk), **gran′it·oid′** adj.

granite paper. A paper containing a low proportion of colored mottling fibers.

Granite Peak. The highest elevation (12,850 feet) of Montana, in the south-central section of the state.

Granite State. A nickname for New Hampshire.

gran·ite·ware (grăn′ĭt-wâr′) n. 1. Enameled iron utensils. 2. Earthenware with a speckled glaze resembling granite.

gra·niv·o·rous (grə-nĭv′ər-əs) adj. Feeding on grain and seeds. [GRANI- + -VOROUS.]

gran·ny, gran·nie (grăn′ē) n., pl. **-nies.** 1. *Informal.* A grandmother. 2. An old woman. 3. A fussy person. 4. *Southern U.S.* A midwife. [Shortened from GRANDMOTHER.]

granny knot. Also **granny's knot.** A knot like a square knot but with the second tie crossed incorrectly. [Originally a sailor's term regarding such a knot as tied by a woman or landman.]

grano-. Indicates: 1. Of or like granite; for example, **granolith.** 2. Granular; for example, **granophyre.** [German, from *Granit*, granite, from Italian *granito*, GRANITE.]

gran·o·lith (grăn′ə-lĭth′) n. A paving stone of crushed granite and cement. [GRANO- + -LITH.] —**gran′o·lith′ic** adj.

gran·o·phyre (grăn′ə-fīr′) n. A fine-grained granite porphyry having a groundmass with irregular intergrowths of quartz and feldspar. [German *Granophyr* : GRANO- + *Porphyr*, porphyry, from Medieval Latin *porphyrium*, PORPHYRY.] —**gran′o·phyr′ic** (-fîr′ĭk) adj.

Gran Pa·ra·di·so (grän′ pä-rä-dē′zō). The highest elevation (13,324 feet) of the Graian Range in northwest Italy.

Gran Qui·vi·ra National Monument (grän′ kĭ-vîr′ə). An area of 451 acres in central New Mexico.

grant (grănt, gränt) tr.v. **granted, granting, grants.** 1. To allow to have; consent to the fulfillment of: *grant a wish.* 2. To permit or accord, as a favor or privilege: *grant a kiss.* 3. **a.** To bestow; confer: *grant aid.* **b.** To transfer (property) by a deed. 4. To concede; acknowledge. —n. 1. The act of granting. 2. Something granted. 3. *Law.* A transfer of property by deed. 4. One of several tracts of land in New Hampshire, Maine, and Vermont originally granted to an individual or group. [Middle English *graunten*, from Old French gr(e)anter, creanter, to insure, guarantee, from Vulgar Latin *crēdentāre* (unattested), from Latin *crēdēns*, present participle of *crēdere*, to believe, trust. See **kerd-¹** in Appendix.*] —**grant′a·ble** adj. —**grant′er** n.

Synonyms: *grant, vouchsafe, concede.* These verbs refer to giving. *Grant* usually implies that the giver is in a favored position with respect to the receiver, sometimes in a position of authority, and that he acts out of justice, mercy, or generosity. *Vouchsafe* emphasizes more strongly the giver's superior position and suggests that he acts from generosity or courtesy, often condescendingly. *Concede* usually implies giving reluctantly in response to a strong claim. In another related sense, *grant* and *concede* mean to admit something to be true. *Grant* refers to voluntary admission, and *concede* to a more reluctant act. *Grant* often suggests that one does not insist on establishment of proof before yielding; *concede* usually implies that one yields to an adversary's superior claim.

Grant (grănt), **Ulysses S(impson).** Originally, Hiram Ulysses. 1822–1885. Eighteenth President of the United States.

grant·ee (grăn-tē′, grän′-) n. *Law.* One to whom a grant is made.

granny knot

Ulysses S. Grant

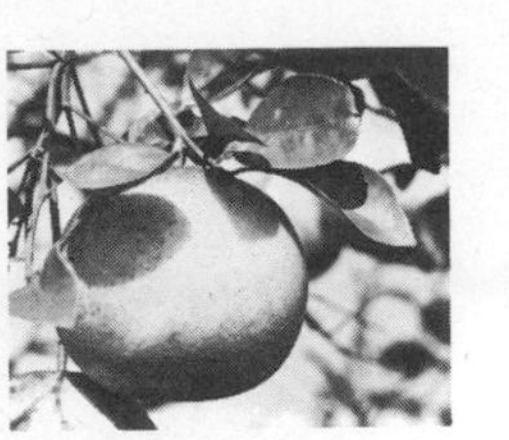

grapefruit

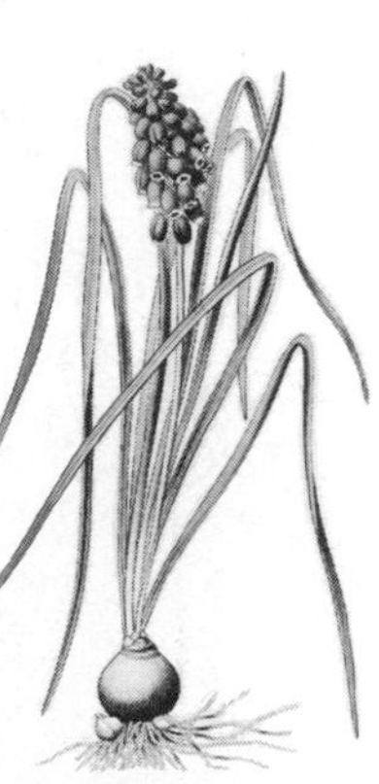

grape hyacinth
Muscari atlanticum

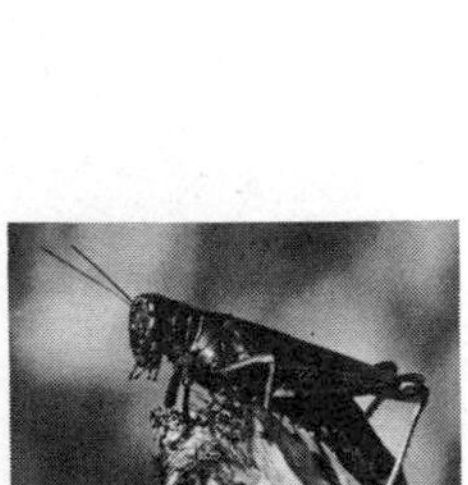

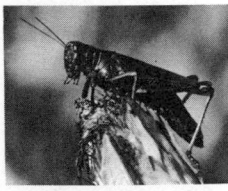

grasshopper
Melanoplus differentialis

gran·tor (grăn′tər, grăn′-) *n. Law.* One who makes a grant.

gran·u·lar (grăn′yə-lər) *adj.* **1.** Composed of or appearing to be composed of granules or grains. **2.** Grainy. —**gran′u·lar′i·ty** *n.* —**gran′u·lar·ly** *adv.*

gran·u·late (grăn′yə-lāt′) *v.* **-lated, -lating, -lates.** —*tr.* **1.** To form into grains or granules. **2.** To make rough and grainy. —*intr.* To become granular or grainy. —**gran′u·la′tive** *adj.* —**gran′u·la′tor** (-lā′tər), **gran′u·la′ter** *n.*

gran·u·la·tion (grăn′yə-lā′shən) *n.* **1. a.** The act or process of granulating. **b.** The condition or appearance of being granulated. **2.** *Physiology.* **a.** The formation of small, fleshy, beadlike protuberances on the surface of a wound while healing. **b.** One of these protuberances.

gran·ule (grăn′yo͞ol) *n.* **1.** A small grain or pellet; a particle. **2.** *Astronomy.* Any of the smallest transient, brilliant markings visible in the photosphere of the sun. [Late Latin *grānulum,* diminutive of *grānum,* GRAIN.]

gran·u·lite (grăn′yə-līt′) *n.* A granular metamorphic rock often banded in appearance and composed chiefly of feldspar, quartz, and garnet. [GRANUL(E) + -ITE.] —**gran′u·lit′ic** (-lĭt′ĭk) *adj.*

gran·u·lo·ma (grăn′yə-lō′mə) *n., pl.* **-mas** or **-mata** (-mə-tə). One of numerous granulated nodules of inflamed tissue, usually occurring with ulcerated infections. [New Latin : GRANUL(E) + -OMA.] —**gran′u·lom′a·tous** (-lŏm′ə-təs) *adj.*

gran·u·lose (grăn′yə-lōs′) *adj.* Having a surface covered with granules. [GRANUL(E) + -OSE.]

grape (grāp) *n.* **1.** Any of numerous woody vines of the genus *Vitis,* bearing clusters of edible fruit, and widely cultivated in many species and varieties. **2.** The fleshy, smooth-skinned, purple, red, or green fruit of such a vine, eaten raw or dried, and widely used in winemaking. **3.** Dark violet to dark grayish purple. See **color. 4.** Grapeshot. [Middle English, from Old French, bunch of grapes, hook, from Germanic. See **ger-³** in Appendix.*]

grape fern. Any of various ferns of the genus *Botrychium,* having a fertile frond bearing small, grapelike clusters of spore cases. One species, *B. lunaria,* is also called "moonwort."

grape·fruit (grāp′fro͞ot′) *n.* **1.** An evergreen tropical or semitropical tree, *Citrus paradisi,* cultivated for its edible fruit. **2.** The large, round fruit of this tree, having a yellow rind and juicy, somewhat acid pulp. Sometimes called "pomelo." [So called because the fruit grows in clusters.]

grape hyacinth. Any of various plants of the genus *Muscari,* native to Eurasia, having narrow leaves and dense terminal clusters of rounded, usually blue flowers.

grap·er·y (grā′pə-rē) *n., pl.* **-ies.** A building or enclosed area where grapes are grown.

grape·shot (grāp′shŏt′) *n.* A cluster of small iron balls formerly used as a cannon charge. [From its resemblance to a cluster of grapes.]

grape·stone (grāp′stōn′) *n.* A seed of a grape.

grape sugar. Dextrose *(see).*

grape·vine (grāp′vīn′) *n.* **1.** A vine on which grapes grow. **2.** An informal, often secret means of transmitting information, gossip, or rumor from person to person. **3.** A secret information source. [Senses 2 and 3, from Civil War popular expression *a dispatch by grapevine telegraph,* rumor transmitted by irregular means rather than by regular telegraphic lines.]

graph (grăf, gräf) *n.* **1.** A drawing that exhibits a relationship, often functional, between two sets of numbers as a set of points having coordinates determined by the relationship. **2.** Any pictorial device, as a pie chart or bar graph, used to display numerical relationships. Also called "chart." **3.** A representation of a quantity, as of a complex number, by a geometric object such as a point in a plane. —*tr.v.* **graphed, graphing, graphs. 1.** To represent by a graph. **2.** To plot (a function) on a graph. [Short for *graphic formula.*]

-graph. Indicates: **1.** An apparatus that writes or records; for example, **telegraph, seismograph. 2.** Something drawn or written; for example, **lithograph, monograph.** [French *-graphe,* from Latin *-graphum,* from Greek *-graphon,* neuter of *-graphos,* written, from *graphein,* to write. See **gerebh-** in Appendix.*]

graph·eme (grăf′ēm′) *n.* **1.** A letter of an alphabet. **2.** The sum of letters and letter combinations that represent a single phoneme. [Greek *graphēma,* letter, from *graphein,* to write. See **-graph.**] —**gra·phe′mic** *adj.* —**gra·phe′mi·cal·ly** *adv.*

-grapher. Indicates: **1.** A person who writes about a specific subject; for example, **geographer. 2.** One who employs a specific means to write, draw, or record; for example, **stenographer.** [From Late Latin *-graphus,* from Greek *-graphos,* from *graphein,* to write. See **gerebh-** in Appendix.*]

graph·ic (grăf′ĭk) *adj.* Also **graph·i·cal** (-ĭ-kəl). **1.** Of or pertaining to written or pictorial representation. **2.** Of, pertaining to, or represented by or as if by a graph. **3.** Described in vivid detail; clearly outlined or set forth: *a graphic account.* **4.** Of or pertaining to the graphic arts. **5.** Of or pertaining to graphics. **6.** *Geology.* Having crystals resembling printed characters. [Latin *graphicus,* from Greek *graphikos,* from *graphē,* a writing, from *graphein,* to write. See **gerebh-** in Appendix.*] —**graph′i·cal·ly** *adv.* —**graph′ic·ness** *n.*

graphic arts. 1. Any of the fine or applied visual arts that involves the application of lines and strokes to a two-dimensional surface. **2.** The reproductions made from blocks, plates, or type, such as engravings, etchings, woodcuts, and lithographs.

graph·ics (grăf′ĭks) *n.* Plural in form, used with a singular or plural verb. **1.** The making of drawings in accordance with the rules of mathematics, as in engineering or architecture. **2.** Calculations, as of structural stress, from such drawings.

graph·ite (grăf′īt′) *n.* The soft, steel-gray to black, hexagonally crystallized allotrope of carbon, used in lead pencils, lubricants, paints and coatings, and various fabricated forms including molds, bricks, electrodes, crucibles, and rocket nozzles. [German *Graphit* : Greek *graphein,* to write (see **gerebh-** in Appendix*) + -ITE.] —**gra·phit′ic** (-fĭt′ĭk) *adj.*

graph·i·tize (grăf′ə-tīz′) *tr.v.* **-tized, -tizing, -tizes. 1.** To convert into graphite by a heating process. **2.** To coat or impregnate with graphite. —**graph′i·ti·za′tion** *n.*

graph·ol·o·gy (gră-fŏl′ə-jē) *n.* The study of handwriting, especially when employed as a means of analyzing the character of the writer. [Greek *graphē,* a writing (see **graphic**) + -LOGY.] —**graph′o·log′i·cal** (grăf′ə-lŏj′ĭ-kəl) *adj.* —**graph·ol′o·gist** *n.*

graph paper. Paper ruled into small squares of equal size for use in drawing charts, graphs, or diagrams.

-graphy. Indicates: **1.** A process or method of writing or other graphic representation; for example, **cacography, planography. 2.** A descriptive science of a specific subject or field; for example, **oceanography.** [Latin *-graphia,* from Greek, from *graphein,* to write. See **gerebh-** in Appendix.*]

grap·nel (grăp′nəl) *n.* A small anchor with three or more flukes. Also called "grappling." [Middle English *grapenel,* from Norman French *grapenel* (unattested), diminutive of Old French *grapon,* anchor, hook, from Germanic. See **ger-³** in Appendix.*]

grap·pa (grä′pə; *Italian* gräp′pä) *n.* An Italian brandy distilled from the residue of pressed wine. [Italian, "grape stalk," from Germanic. See **ger-³** in Appendix.*]

grap·ple (grăp′əl) *n.* **1. a.** An iron shaft with claws at one end for grasping and holding; especially, one for drawing and holding an enemy ship alongside. Also called "grappling," "grappling hook," "grappling iron." **b.** A grapnel. **2.** The act of grappling. **3. a.** A contest in which the participants attempt to clutch or grip each other. **b.** A grasp or grip in such a contest. —*v.* **grappled, -pling, -ples.** —*tr.* **1.** To seize and hold with a grapple. **2.** To seize firmly with the hands. —*intr.* **1.** To hold on to something with or as if with a grapple. **2.** To use a grapple, as for dragging. **3.** To struggle, as in wrestling: *grapple with one's conscience.* **4.** To attempt to cope: *grapple with the political realities of our time.* [Middle English *grapel,* from Old French *grapil,* from Old Provençal, diminutive of *grapa,* hook. See **ger-³** in Appendix.*] —**grap′pler** *n.*

grap·to·lite (grăp′tə-līt′) *n.* Any of numerous extinct colonial marine animals chiefly of the orders Dendroidea and Graptoloidea, of the Cambrian to the Mississippian periods. [Greek *graptos,* written, painted, from *graphein,* to write (see **graphic**) + -LITE (so called from the fossilized impressions resembling markings on slate).]

grap·y (grā′pē) *adj.* **-ier, -iest.** Of, like, or suggestive of grapes.

Gras·mere (grăs′mîr, gräs′-). A lakeside village of western Westmoreland, England; site of residences occupied by De Quincey, Coleridge, and Wordsworth, and of Wordsworth's tomb.

grasp (grăsp, gräsp) *v.* **grasped, grasping, grasps.** —*tr.* **1.** To take hold of or seize firmly with or as if with the hand. **2.** To hold firmly with or as if with the hand; to clutch; clasp. **3.** To take hold of intellectually; comprehend: *"It is this distinction between freedom and license that many parents cannot grasp"* (A.S. Neill). —See Synonyms at **keep, apprehend.** —*intr.* **1.** To make a motion of seizing, snatching, or clutching. **2.** To show eager and prompt willingness or acceptance. Used with *at.* —*n.* **1.** The act of grasping. **2.** A firm hold or grip. **3.** The ability or power to seize or attain; reach: *The presidency was within his grasp.* **4.** Understanding; comprehension: *"only a vague intuitive grasp of the meaning of greatness in literature"* (Gilbert Highet). [Middle English *graspen,* Old English *grapsan* (unattested). See **ghrebh-¹** in Appendix.*]

grasp·ing (grăs′pĭng, gräs′-) *adj.* Eager for gain; greedy; avaricious. —**grasp′ing·ly** *adv.* —**grasp′ing·ness** *n.*

grass (grăs, gräs) *n.* **1. a.** Any of numerous plants of the family Gramineae, characteristically having narrow leaves, hollow, jointed stems, and spikes or clusters of membranous flowers borne in smaller spikelets. **b.** Such plants collectively. **2.** Any of various plants having slender leaves like those of the true grasses. **3.** An expanse of ground covered with grass or similar plants, such as a meadow or lawn. **4.** Grazing land; pasture. **5.** *Slang.* **Marijuana** *(see).* —*v.* **grassed, grassing, grasses.** —*tr.* **1.** To cover with grass; grow grass on. **2.** To feed (livestock) with grass. —*intr.* **1.** To become covered with grass. **2.** To graze. [Middle English *gras,* Old English *græs.* See **ghrē-** in Appendix.*]

grass green. Moderate yellow-green to moderate, strong or dark yellowish-green. See **color.** —**grass′-green′** *adj.*

grass·hop·per (grăs′hŏp′ər, gräs′-) *n.* **1.** Any of numerous insects of the families Locustidae (or Acrididae) and Tettigoniidae, often destructive to plants and characteristically having long hind legs adapted for jumping. **2.** A cocktail consisting of crème de menthe, crème de cacao, and cream.

grass·land (grăs′lănd′, gräs′-) *n.* An area, such as a prairie or meadow, of grass or grasslike vegetation.

grass-of-Par·nas·sus (grăs′əv-pär-năs′əs, gräs′-) *n.* Any of various plants of the genus *Parnassia,* having stalked basal leaves and a stem bearing a single white or yellowish flower.

grass pink. An orchid, *Calopogon pulchellus,* of marshy areas of eastern North America, having a single narrow leaf and a cluster of pinkish flowers.

grass·roots (grăs′ro͞ots′, -ro͝ots′, gräs′-) *pl.n.* Often used with a singular verb. **1.** People removed or somewhat isolated from a major political center. **2.** The groundwork or source of something; basis; origin. —*adj.* **1.** Originating in or emerging from people at a distance from a major political center: *a grassroots candidate.* **2.** Fundamental; basic.

grass snake. Any of several greenish snakes; especially, *Natrix natrix,* of Europe, or *Opheodrys vernalis,* of eastern North America.

grass snipe. A bird, the **pectoral sandpiper** *(see).*

grass tree. Any of several woody-stemmed Australian plants of the genus *Xanthorrhoea,* having stiff, grasslike leaves and a spike of small white flowers.

grass widow. 1. A woman who is divorced or separated from her husband. **2.** A woman whose husband is temporarily absent. **3.** An abandoned mistress. **4.** The mother of an illegitimate child. [Earliest sense "an unwed mother," probably with an allusion to a bed of straw or grass as a symbol of illicit conduct.]

grass·y (grăs′ē, gräs′ē) *adj.* **-ier, -iest. 1.** Covered with or abounding in grass. **2.** Resembling or suggestive of grass, as in color or odor.

grate¹ (grāt) *v.* **grated, grating, grates.** —*tr.* **1.** To reduce to fragments, shreds, or powder by rubbing against an abrasive surface: *grate cabbage.* **2.** To cause to make a harsh grinding or rasping sound through friction: *grate one's teeth.* **3.** To irritate or annoy persistently. **4.** *Archaic.* To rub or wear away. —*intr.* **1.** To make a harsh rasping sound by or as if by scraping or grinding. **2.** To cause irritation or annoyance. Used with *on: grate on one's nerves.* —*n.* A harsh, rasping sound made by scraping or rubbing: *the grate of a key in a lock.* [Middle English *graten,* from Old French *grater,* to scrape, from Germanic. See **grat-** in Appendix.*]

grate² (grāt) *n.* **1.** A framework of parallel or latticed bars for blocking an opening; a grill: *a grate over a storm sewer.* **2.** Such a framework of metal, used to hold the fuel in a stove, furnace, or fireplace. **3.** A fireplace. **4.** A perforated iron plate or screen for sieving and grading crushed ore. —*tr.v.* **grated, grating, grates.** To equip with a grate. [Middle English, from Old French, grille, from Vulgar Latin *grata* (unattested), variant of Latin *crātis,* frame, wicker basket. See **kert-** in Appendix.*]

grate·ful (grāt′fəl) *adj.* **1.** Appreciative of benefits received; thankful. **2.** Expressing gratitude. **3.** Affording pleasure or comfort; agreeable; satisfying: *"he left his home to enjoy the grateful air"* (Ronald Firbank). [From obsolete *grate,* agreeable, thankful, from Latin *grātus,* pleasing, favorable. See **gwerə-¹** in Appendix.*] —**grate′ful·ly** *adv.* —**grate′ful·ness** *n.*

grat·er (grā′tər) *n.* **1.** One that grates. **2.** An implement with rough or sharp-edged slits and perforations on which to shred or grate foods.

Gra·ti·an (grā′shē-ən, -shən). A.D. 359–383. Roman emperor (A.D. 375–383); ruled jointly with **Theodosius I** *(see).*

grat·i·fi·ca·tion (grăt′ə-fĭ-kā′shən) *n.* **1.** The act of gratifying. **2.** The condition of being gratified; satisfaction; pleasure. **3.** An instance or cause of gratification. **4.** *Archaic.* A reward; gratuity; bonus.

grat·i·fy (grăt′ə-fī′) *tr.v.* **-fied, -fying, -fies. 1.** To please or satisfy: *His achievement gratified his father.* **2.** To indulge; to humor: *"I shall perhaps not a little gratify my own vanity."* (Franklin). **3.** *Archaic.* To requite; to reward. [Middle English *gratifien,* to favor, from Old French, from Latin *grātificārī,* to reward, do favor to, from *grātus,* favorable, pleasurable. See **gwerə-¹** in Appendix.*] —**grat′i·fi′er** *n.*

gra·tin (grät′n, grăt′n; *French* grȧ-tăN′) *n.* A crust consisting of browned crumbs and butter, often with grated cheese. [French, from Old French, from *grater,* to GRATE (scrape).]

grat·ing¹ (grā′tĭng) *adj.* **1.** Rasping or scraping in sound. **2.** Nerve-racking; irritating. —**grat′ing·ly** *adv.*

grat·ing² (grā′tĭng) *n.* **1.** A grill or network of bars set in a window or door or used as a partition; lattice; grate. **2.** *Physics.* **Diffraction grating** *(see).*

gra·tis (grā′tĭs, grăt′ĭs) *adv.* Freely; for nothing; without charge. —*adj.* Free; gratuitous. [Middle English, from Latin *grātis,* reduced form of *grātiīs,* without reward, out of favor, from *grātia,* favor, from *grātus,* favorable. See **gratify.**]

grat·i·tude (grăt′ə-to͞od′, -tyo͞od′) *n.* An appreciative awareness and thankfulness, as for kindness shown or something received. [Middle English, from Old French, from Medieval Latin *grātitūdō,* from *grātus,* favorable. See **gratify.**]

gra·tu·i·tous (grə-to͞o′ə-təs, -tyo͞o′ə-təs) *adj.* **1.** Given or granted without return or recompense; unearned. **2.** Given or received without cost or obligation; free; gratis. **3.** Unnecessary or unwarranted; unjustified: *gratuitous criticism.* [Latin *grātuītus,* given as a favor, from *grātus,* favorable, pleasing. See **gratify.**] —**gra·tu′i·tous·ly** *adv.* —**gra·tu′i·tous·ness** *n.*

gra·tu·i·ty (grə-to͞o′ə-tē, -tyo͞o′ə-tē) *n., pl.* **-ties.** A material favor or gift, usually in the form of money, given in return for service; a tip. See Synonyms at **bonus.** [Old French *gratuite,* from Medieval Latin *grātuitās,* present, gift, from Latin *grātuītus,* given free, GRATUITOUS.]

grat·u·lant (grăch′o͝o-lənt) *adj.* Congratulatory.

grat·u·late (grăch′o͝o-lāt′) *tr.v.* **-lated, -lating, -lates.** *Archaic.* **1.** To greet with pleasure; welcome. **2.** To congratulate. [Latin *grātulārī,* to greet, salute, from *grātus,* pleasing, GRATEFUL.] —**grat′u·la′tion** *n.* —**grat′u·la·to′ry** (-lə-tôr′ē, -tōr′ē) *adj.*

grau·pel (grou′pəl) *n.* Precipitation consisting of pellets of snow. Also called "snow pellets," "soft hail." [German *Graupel,* diminutive of *Graupe,* hulled grain, groats, probably from Serbo-Croatian *krupa.* See **kreup-** in Appendix.*]

gra·va·men (grə-vā′mən) *n., pl.* **-vamina** (-văm′ə-nə). *Law.* **1. a.** The part of a charge or accusation that weighs most substantially against the accused. **b.** The essential part of a complaint. **2.** A grievance. [Late Latin *gravamen,* from Latin *grāvāre,* to weigh down, burden, from *gravis,* heavy, GRAVE.]

grave¹ (grāv) *n.* **1.** An excavation for the interment of a corpse; burial place. **2.** Any place of burial or final disposition: *The sea was his grave.* **3.** The sign or marker of a burial place. **4.** The receptacle or resting place of anything dead in a figurative sense: *"She was dry and sandy with working in the graves of deceased languages"* (Dickens). **5.** Death or extinction. [Middle English *grave,* Old English *græf.* See **ghrebh-²** in Appendix.*]

grave² (grāv; *also* gräv *for sense 6*) *adj.* **graver, gravest. 1.** Extremely serious; important; weighty: *a grave decision in a time of crisis.* **2.** Fraught with danger; critical: *a grave wound.* **3.** Grievous; dire: *a grave sin.* **4.** Dignified in conduct; sedate: *a grave procession.* **5.** Somber; dark. Said of colors. **6.** *Linguistics.* **a.** Written with or modified by the mark `, as the *è* in *Sèvres.* **b.** Articulated toward the back of the oral cavity. —See Synonyms at **serious.** —*n.* (grāv, gräv). The grave accent, `, indicating a pronounced *e* for the sake of meter in the usually nonsyllabic ending *-ed* in English poetry. [Old French, from Latin *gravis,* heavy, weighty. See **gwer-²** in Appendix.*] —**grave′ly** *adv.* —**grave′ness** *n.*

grave³ (grāv) *tr.v.* **graved, graven** (grā′vən), **graving, graves. 1.** To sculpt or carve; engrave: *"I wish I could grave my sonnets on an ivory tablet."* (Oscar Wilde) **2.** To stamp or impress deeply; fix permanently, as words or ideas. [Grave, graven; Middle English *graven, graven,* Old English *grafan, grafen.* See **ghrebh-²** in Appendix.*]

grave⁴ (grāv) *tr.v.* **graved, graving, graves.** To clean (the bottom of a wooden ship) by removing barnacles and other accretions, and coating with pitch. [Middle English *graven,* probably from Old French *greve, grave,* sand, GRAVEL.]

gra·ve⁵ (grä′vā) *adv. Music.* Slowly and solemnly. Used as a direction to the performer. —*adj.* Slow and solemn. [Italian, from Latin *gravis,* heavy, weighty, GRAVE.]

grave·clothes (grāv′klōz′ -klōthz) *pl.n.* The clothes or shroud in which a body is interred.

grave·dig·ger (grāv′dĭg′ər) *n.* A person whose occupation is digging graves.

grav·el (grăv′əl) *n.* **1.** Any unconsolidated mixture of rock fragments or pebbles. **2.** *Pathology.* The sandlike granular material of urinary calculi. —*tr.v.* **graveled** or **-velled, -veling** or **-velling, -vels. 1.** To apply a surface of gravel: *gravel a driveway.* **2.** To confuse; perplex: *His inconsistencies gravel the reader.* **3.** *Informal.* To irritate. [Middle English, from Old French *gravele, gravelle,* diminutive of *grave, greve,* gravel, sand, pebbly shore, from Celtic. See **ghrēu-** in Appendix.*]

grav·el-blind (grăv′əl-blīnd′) *adj.* Having minimal vision; purblind. [GRAVEL + BLIND (formed after SANDBLIND).]

graven image. An idol or fetish carved in wood or stone.

grav·er (grā′vər) *n.* **1.** A person who carves or engraves; stonecarver. **2.** An engraver's cutting tool; burin.

grave robber. A person who plunders valuables from tombs or graves or who steals corpses, as for illicit dissection.

Graves (grāvz; *French* gräv) *n.* A dry, usually white wine produced near Bordeaux, southwestern France. [After LES GRAVES.]

Graves, Les (lā grȧv). A grape-producing and wine-manufacturing region in the Garonne valley of southwestern France.

Graves (grāvz), **Robert (Ranke).** Born 1895. English poet, novelist, and critic.

Graves' disease (grāvz). *Pathology.* **Exophthalmic goiter** *(see).* [After Robert James *Graves* (1796–1853), Irish physician.]

Graves·end (grāvz′ĕnd′). A town, port, and shipbuilding center of northwestern Kent, England, on the Thames estuary. Population, 54,000.

grave·stone (grāv′stōn′) *n.* A stone placed over a grave as a marker; tombstone.

grave·yard (grāv′yärd′) *n.* An area set aside as a burial ground; cemetery.

graveyard shift. 1. A work shift that runs during the early morning hours, as from midnight to 8:00 A.M. **2.** The workers on such a shift.

grav·id (grăv′ĭd) *adj.* **1.** Pregnant. **2.** Full of ripe eggs or distended by such fullness: *a fish gravid with roe.* [Latin *gravidus,* pregnant, from *gravis,* heavy. See **gwer-²** in Appendix.*] —**gra·vid′i·ty** (grə-vĭd′ə-tē), **grav′id·ness** *n.* —**grav′id·ly** *adv.*

gra·vim·e·ter (grə-vĭm′ə-tər) *n.* Any instrument used to determine specific gravity. [French *gravimètre* : Latin *gravis,* heavy, GRAVE + -METER.]

grav·i·met·ric (grăv′ə-mĕt′rĭk) *adj.* Also **grav·i·met·ric·al** (-rĭ-kəl). Of or pertaining to measurement by weight. [Latin *gravis,* heavy, GRAVE + METRIC.] —**grav′i·met′ri·cal·ly** *adv.* —**gra·vim′e·try** (grə-vĭm′ə-trē) *n.*

graving dock. A dry dock where ships are repaired and their hulks are cleaned.

grav·i·tate (grăv′ə-tāt′) *intr.v.* **-tated, -tating, -tates. 1.** To move in response to the force of gravity. **2.** To move downward; sink; settle. **3.** To be attracted by or as if by an irresistible force. Used with *to* or *toward: "My excuse must be that all Celts gravitate towards each other."* (Oscar Wilde). [New Latin *gravitare,* from Latin *gravitās,* GRAVITY.] —**grav′i·tat′er** *n.*

grav·i·ta·tion (grăv′ə-tā′shən) *n.* **1.** *Physics.* **a.** The natural phenomenon of attraction between massive bodies. **b.** The degree of such attraction; broadly, gravity. **c.** *Rare.* The action or process of moving under the influence of this attraction. **2.** Any movement toward a source of attraction: *the gravitation of the middle classes to the suburbs.* —**grav′i·ta′tion·al, grav′i·ta′tive** *adj.* —**grav′i·ta′tion·al·ly** *adv.*

grav·i·ton (grăv′ə-tŏn′) *n.* A particle postulated to be the quantum of gravitational interaction, and presumed to have

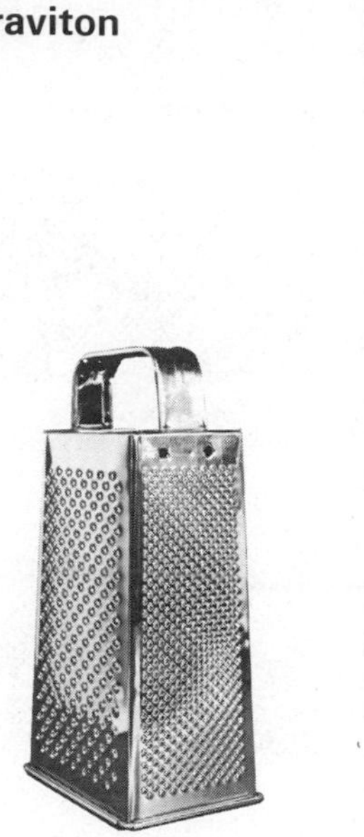

grater

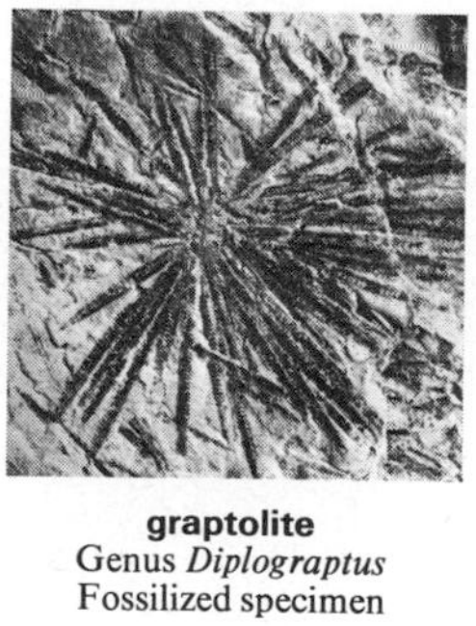

graptolite
Genus *Diplograptus*
Fossilized specimen

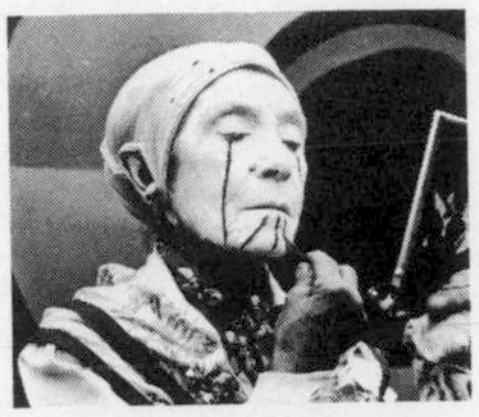

grease paint
Clown applying grease paint

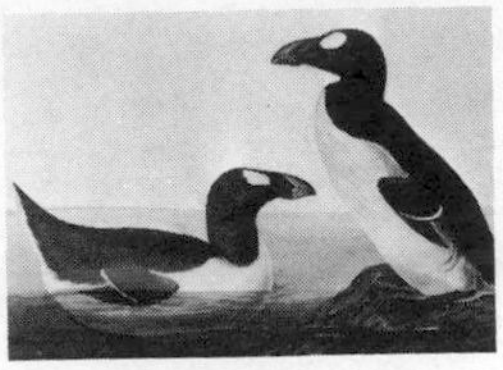

great auk
Painting by
John James Audubon

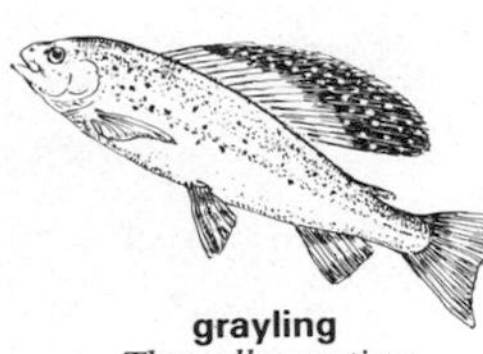

grayling
Thymallus arcticus

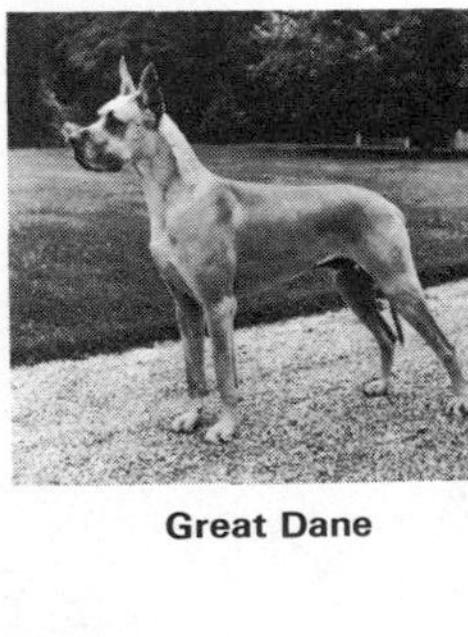

Great Dane

zero electric charge, zero rest mass, and spin 2. [GRAVIT(ATION) + -ON.]

grav·i·ty (grăv′ə-tē) *n.* **1.** *Physics.* **a.** The force of gravitation, being, for any two sufficiently massive bodies, directly proportional to the product of their masses and inversely proportional to the square of the distance between them; especially, the attractive central gravitational force exerted by a celestial body such as the earth. **b.** Loosely, gravitation. **c.** *Rare.* Weight. **2.** Grave consequence; seriousness; importance: *the gravity of their problem.* **3.** Solemnity or dignity of manner: *"With stern and austere gravity he persevered in his task"* (Scott). [Old French *gravite,* from Latin *gravitās,* from *gravis,* heavy, serious, GRAVE.]

gra·vure (grə-vyŏŏr′) *n.* **1.** A method of printing with etched plates or cylinders; intaglio printing; especially, a tonal reproduction process using photomechanically prepared plates or cylinders to reproduce photographs on newsprint; photogravure. **2.** A plate or reproduction produced by gravure or used in the process. [French, from *graver,* to engrave, dig into, from Old French, from Frankish *graban* (unattested). See **ghrebh-²** in Appendix.*]

gra·vy (grā′vē) *n., pl.* **-vies. 1. a.** The juices that drip from cooking meat. **b.** A sauce made by thickening and seasoning these juices. **2.** *Slang.* Money or profit easily or unexpectedly gained; especially, money in excess of that required for necessities. [Middle English *gravey,* from Old French *grave,* misreading of *grane,* perhaps "(dish) seasoned with grains," from *grain,* spice, GRAIN.]

gravy boat. An elongated dish or pitcher for serving gravy.

gravy train. *Slang.* An occupation or job that requires little effort while yielding considerable profit.

gray (grā) *adj.* Also **grey. 1.** Of or pertaining to an achromatic color of any lightness between the extremes of black and white. **2. a.** Dull or dark, as from lack of light: *a gray, rainy afternoon.* **b.** Lacking in cheer; gloomy. **3. a.** Having gray hair; hoary: *"Shoot if you must this old gray head"* (Whittier). **b.** Old; venerable; ancient. **4.** Intermediate in character or position. —*n.* Also **grey. 1.** An achromatic color of any lightness between the extremes of black and white. See **color. 2.** An object or animal of this color. **3.** *Sometimes capital* **G. a.** A member of the Confederate Army in the Civil War. **b.** The Confederate Army itself. Compare **blue.** [Middle English *gray,* Old English *græg.* See **gher-⁴** in Appendix.*]

Gray (grā), **Asa.** 1810–1888. American botanist.

Gray (grā), **Thomas.** 1716–1771. English poet.

gray·beard (grā′bîrd′) *n.* An old man.

gray·fish (grā′fĭsh′) *n., pl.* **grayfish** or **-fishes.** A **dogfish** *(see).*

Gray Friar. A **Franciscan** *(see).*

gray hen. Variant of **greyhen.**

gray·hound. *Rare.* Variant of **greyhound.**

gray·ish (grā′ĭsh) *adj.* Having a perceptible quality of grayness. See **color.**

gray lag goose. A gray goose, *Anser anser,* of marshy areas of the Old World. Also called "graylag," "greylag." [From its migrating later than other geese.]

gray·ling (grā′lĭng) *n., pl.* **grayling** (for sense 1) or **-lings. 1.** Any of several freshwater food fishes of the genus *Thymallus,* of the Northern Hemisphere, having a small mouth and a large dorsal fin. **2.** Any of several grayish or brownish butterflies of the family Satyridae, such as the European species *Eumenis semele.*

gray matter. 1. *Anatomy.* The brownish-gray nerve tissue of the brain and spinal cord, composed of nerve cells and fibers and some supportive tissue. Compare **white matter. 2.** *Informal.* Brains; intellect.

gray mullet. A fish, the **mullet** *(see).*

Gray's Inn (grāz). One of the four legal societies forming the Inns of Court in England.

Grays Peak (grāz). The highest elevation (14,274 feet) of the Front Range in central Colorado.

gray squirrel. A common squirrel, *Sciurus carolinensis,* of eastern North America, having gray or blackish fur and a very bushy tail.

gray·wacke (grā′wăk′, -wăk′ə) *n.* Any of various shale-containing dark-gray sandstones. [Translation of German *Grauwacke* : *grau,* gray + *Wacke,* boulder, from Old High German *wacko, waggo* (see **wegh-** in Appendix*).]

gray whale. A whalebone whale, *Eschrichtius glaucus,* of Pacific waters, having grayish coloring with white blotches.

gray wolf. The **timber wolf** *(see).*

Graz (gräts). The capital of Styria, Austria, on the Mur 87 miles southwest of Vienna. Population, 237,000.

graze¹ (grāz) *v.* **grazed, grazing, grazes.** —*intr.* To feed on growing grasses and herbage. —*tr.* **1.** To feed on (herbage) in a field or on pasture land. **2.** To feed on the herbage of (land). **3.** To put (livestock) out to feed. **4.** To afford sufficient herbage for: *This field will graze 30 head of cattle.* **5.** To tend (feeding livestock) in a pasture. [Middle English *grasen,* to feed on grass, Old English *grasian,* from *græs,* GRASS.] —**graz′er** *n.*

graze² (grāz) *v.* **grazed, grazing, grazes.** —*tr.* **1.** To touch lightly in passing; to skim; brush. **2.** To scrape or scratch slightly; abrade. —*intr.* To scrape or touch something lightly in passing. —*n.* **1.** A brushing or scraping along a surface. **2.** A scratch or abrasion resulting from such contact. [Perhaps from GRAZE (to feed).] —**graz′ing·ly** *adv.*

gra·zier (grā′zhər) *n.* A person who grazes cattle.

graz·ing (grā′zĭng) *n.* Land used for feeding; pasturage.

gra·zio·so (grä-tsyō′sō) *adv. Music.* Gracefully; smoothly. Used as a direction. —*adj. Music.* Graceful in style. [Italian, from Latin *grātiōsus,* GRACIOUS.]

grease (grēs) *n.* **1.** Animal fat when melted or soft. **2.** Any thick oil or viscous lubricant. **3. a.** The oily substance present in raw wool; suint. **b.** Raw wool that has not been cleansed of this. In this sense, also called "grease wool." —*tr.v.* **greased, greasing, greases.** To coat, smear, lubricate, or soil with grease or lard. —**grease the palm** (or **hand**) **of.** *Slang.* To bribe. [Middle English *grese,* from Old French *graisse,* from Vulgar Latin *crassia* (unattested), from Latin *crassus,* fat. See **crass.**]

grease monkey. *Slang.* A mechanic who lubricates machinery; especially, a garage attendant.

grease paint. Theatrical make-up. Also called "paint."

grease·wood (grēs′wŏŏd′) *n.* **1.** A spiny shrub, *Sarcobatus vermiculatus,* of western North America, having small alternate leaves, white stems, and small greenish flowers. **2.** Any of various similar or related plants, as the **creosote bush** *(see).*

greas·y (grē′sē, -zē) *adj.* **-ier, -iest. 1.** Coated or soiled with grease. **2.** Containing grease, especially too much grease. **3.** Suggestive of or resembling something greased; slick; unctuous: *a greasy character.* —**greas′i·ly** *adv.* —**greas′i·ness** *n.*

great (grāt) *adj.* **greater, greatest.** *Abbr.* **gt. 1.** Extremely large; bulky; big. **2.** Larger than others of the same kind: *the great auk.* **3.** Large in quantity or number: *A great throng awaited him.* **4.** Of considerable duration; extensive in time or distance. **5.** Remarkable or outstanding in magnitude, degree, or extent: *a great crisis.* **6.** Significant; important; meaningful: *A great work of art.* **7.** Chief or principal: *the great house on the estate.* **8.** Superior in quality or character; noble; excellent: *"For he was great, ere fortune made him so"* (Dryden). **9.** Powerful; influential: *"Seek to be good, but aim not to be great."* (George Lyttelton). **10.** Eminent; distinguished: *a great leader.* **11.** Grand; aristocratic. **12.** *Archaic.* Pregnant. Used with *with: great with child.* **13.** *Informal.* Enthusiastic: *a great boxing fan.* **14.** *Informal.* Skillful: *He is great at algebra.* **15.** *Informal.* First-rate; very good: *a great book.* **16.** *Archaic.* Capital. Said of letters: *a great A.* **17.** *Genealogy.* Being one generation removed from the relative specified. Used in combination: *a great-grandfather.* —See Synonyms at **large.** —*n.* One that is great: *Many of the nation's greats were there.* —*adv. Informal.* Very well. [Middle English *grete,* Old English *grēat,* thick, coarse. See **ghrēu-** in Appendix.*] —**great′ness** *n.*

Great Appalachian Valley. A chain of lowlands of the Appalachian Mountains, extending from Canada in the northeast to Alabama in the south. Also called "Great Valley."

great auk. A large, flightless sea bird, *Pinguinus impennis,* formerly common on northern Atlantic coasts but extinct since the middle of the 19th century.

great-aunt (grāt′ănt′, -änt′) *n.* A **grandaunt** *(see).*

Great Australian Bight. A bay of the Indian Ocean attaining a width of 600 miles on the southern coast of Australia.

Great Barrier Reef. The largest coral formation in the world, extending 1,250 miles off the eastern coast of Queensland, Australia.

Great Basin. A region of interior drainage, 210,000 square miles in area, comprising most of Nevada as well as portions of Utah, California, Idaho, Wyoming, and Oregon.

Great Bear. *Astronomy.* A constellation, **Ursa Major** *(see).*

Great Bear Lake. A lake occupying about 12,000 square miles of north-central Mackenzie District, Northwest Territories, Canada.

Great Brit·ain (brĭt′n). *Abbr.* **G.B.** An island off the western coast of Europe, occupying 88,745 square miles and comprising England, Scotland, and Wales. Population, 52,608,000. Also called "Britain."

great circle. A circle that is the intersection of the surface of a sphere with a plane passing through the center of the sphere.

great·coat (grāt′kōt′) *n.* A heavy overcoat.

Great Com·o·ro (kŏm′ə-rō′). *French* **Grande Co·more** (gräɴd kô-môr′). The largest of the Comoro Islands (442 square miles), in the northern Mozambique Channel of the Indian Ocean. Population, 89,000.

Great Dane. A large and powerful dog of a breed developed in Germany, having a smooth, short coat and a narrow head.

Great Divide. 1. See **Continental Divide. 2.** See **Rocky Mountains.**

Great Dividing Range. See **Eastern Highlands.**

great·en (grāt′n) *v.* **-ened, -ening, -ens.** *Archaic.* —*tr.* To make great or greater; enlarge. —*intr.* To become great or greater.

great·er (grā′tər) *adj.* Also **Great·er.** Designating a city and its populous suburbs: *Greater Los Angeles.*

Greater An·til·les (ăn-tĭl′ēz). An island group forming part of the West Indies and including Cuba, Jamaica, Hispaniola, and Puerto Rico.

greater doxology. The **Gloria in excelsis Deo** *(see).*

Greater Lon·don. See **London.**

Greater New York. See **New York.**

greater panda. See **panda.**

Great Falls¹. A city and industrial center on the Missouri in west-central Montana. Population, 55,000.

Great Falls². A waterfall 35 feet high in the Potomac River 15 miles northwest of Washington, D.C., on the Virginia-Maryland boundary.

Great Glen of Scotland. A fault valley of Scotland extending 60 miles from Moray Firth in the northeast to an inlet of the Atlantic Ocean in the southwest. Also called "Glen More," "Glen Albyn."

great-grand·child (grāt′grănd′chīld′) *n., pl.* **-children** (-chĭl′drən). Any of the children of a grandchild.

great-grand·daugh·ter (grāt′grăn′dô′tər, -grănd′dô′tər) *n.* Any daughter of a grandchild.

great-grand·fa·ther (grāt′grănd′fä′thər) *n.* The father of any grandparent.

great-grand·moth·er (grāt′grănd′mŭth′ər) *n.* The mother of any grandparent.

great-grand·par·ent (grāt′grănd′pâr′ənt) *n.* Either of the parents of any grandparent.

great-grand·son (grāt′grănd′sŭn′) *n.* Any of the sons of a grandchild.

great gross. A dozen gross.

great·heart·ed (grāt′här′tĭd) *adj.* **1.** Noble or courageous in spirit; stouthearted. **2.** Great in generosity; unselfish; magnanimous. —**great′heart′ed·ly** *adv.* —**great′heart′ed·ness** *n.*

great horned owl. A large North American owl, *Bubo virginianus,* having brownish plumage and prominent ear tufts.

Great Indian Desert. See Thar Desert.

Great Kar·roo (kə-rōō′). An arid plateau region of south-central Cape Province, Republic of South Africa. Also called "Central Karroo."

Great Khing·an Mountains. See Khingan Mountains.

Great Lakes. The largest group of freshwater lakes in the world, occupying an area of 94,710 square miles in central North America on either side of the U.S.-Canadian boundary and including lakes Superior, Huron, Erie, Ontario, and Michigan.

great laurel. A shrub, a species of rosebay *(see).*

great·ly (grāt′lē) *adv.* **1.** In a style or manner befitting greatness; nobly. **2.** To a great degree; very much; exceedingly.

Great Mogul. The title of the ruler of the Mogul Empire.

great-neph·ew (grāt′nĕf′yōō, -nĕv′yōō) *n.* A grandnephew.

great-niece (grāt′nēs′) *n.* A grandniece.

Great Ouse. See Ouse.

Great Plains. A region of valley and plateau land in central North America, extending from the Central Plains in the United States and the Laurentian Highlands in Canada to the eastern base of the Rocky Mountains.

great primer. *Printing.* A size of type, 18-point.

Great Pyrenees. A large, heavy-boned dog of an ancient breed, having a thick white coat.

Great Rift Valley. A massive depression in southwestern Asia and eastern Africa, extending from the valley of the Jordan south to Mozambique.

Great Russian. **1.** A member of the Russian-speaking people inhabiting the central and northeastern U.S.S.R. **2.** The Russian language.

Great Salt Lake. A highly saline lake occupying 2,360 square miles of northern Utah in the Great Basin of the United States. Also called "Salt Lake."

Great Salt Lake Desert. A flat, arid region of northwestern Utah extending westward and southward from the Great Salt Lake.

Great Sanhedrin. The Sanhedrin *(see).*

Great Schism. The division in the Roman Catholic Church from 1378 to 1417, when rival popes ruled at Rome and Avignon.

great seal. Also **Great Seal.** The principal seal of a government or state, with which official documents are stamped.

Great Slave Lake. A lake occupying 11,172 square miles of southern Mackenzie District, Northwest Territories, Canada.

Great Smoky Mountains. A range forming part of the Appalachians and extending along the North Carolina-Tennessee boundary; the site of the 720-square-mile Great Smoky Mountains National Park. Also called "Smoky Mountains." Highest elevation, Clingmans Dome (6,642 feet).

Great Spirit. The principal deity in the religion of many North American Indian tribes.

Great St. Ber·nard Pass. See St. Bernard Pass.

great-un·cle (grāt′ŭng′kəl) *n.* A granduncle *(see).*

Great Valley. See Great Appalachian Valley.

Great Wall of Chi·na (chī′nə). A defensive wall, over 1,500 miles long, in northern China, extending from Kansu in the west to the Yellow Sea in the east, constructed between 246 and 209 B.C., and defining the historical boundary between China and Mongolia.

Great War. World War I *(see).*

Great Yar·mouth (yär′məth). Also **Yar·mouth.** A city of southeastern Norfolk, England, located on the North Sea, 110 miles northeast of London. Population, 53,000.

greave (grēv) *n.* Leg armor worn below the knee. Usually used in the plural. [Middle English, from Old French, "shin," perhaps from *greve,* line where the hair is parted, from *graver,* to part the hair, dig, from Frankish *graban* (unattested). See **ghrebh-²** in Appendix.*]

greaves (grēvz) *pl.n.* The unmelted residue left after animal fat or tallow has been rendered; cracklings. [Low German *greven.* See **ghrebh-²** in Appendix.*]

grebe (grēb) *n.* Any of various diving birds of the family Podicipedidae, having lobed, fleshy membranes along each toe and a pointed bill. [French *grebe†.*]

Gre·cian (grē′shən) *adj.* Greek. —*n.* **1.** A native of Greece. **2.** One skilled in the Greek language or literature. [From Latin *Graecia,* Greece, from *Graecus,* GREEK.]

Grecian bend. A posture in which the upper torso is thrust forward and the pelvis and buttocks backward, assumed by women of fashion in the late 19th century and often emphasized by wearing a bustle.

Gre·cism (grē′sĭz′əm) *n.* Also **Grae·cism.** **1.** The style or spirit of Greek culture, art, or thought. **2.** Anything done in imitation of such style or spirit. **3.** An idiom of the Greek language.

Gre·cize (grē′sīz′) *v.* -cized, -cizing, -cizes. Also **Grae·cize.** —*tr.*

To provide with or convert into a Greek form or style; Hellenize. —*intr.* To follow or adopt Greek culture, art, or thought. [French *gréciser,* from Latin *Graecizāre,* from Greek *Graikizein,* to speak Greek, from *Graikos,* GREEK.]

Gre·co (grĕk′ō, grā′kō), **El.** Original name, Kyriakos Theotokopoulos. 1548?-1614? Spanish painter born in Crete.

Gre·co-Ro·man (grĕ′kō-rō′mən, grĕk′ō-) *adj.* Also **Grae·co-Ro·man.** Of, relating to, or pertaining to both Greece and Rome: *Greco-Roman mythology.* [*Greco-,* from Latin *Graecus,* GREEK.]

gree¹ (grē) *n.* Scottish. **1.** Superiority or victory. **2.** The prize or reward for victory. [Middle English, rank, from Old French *gre,* from Latin *gradus,* GRADE.]

gree² (grē) *n.* Obsolete. Good will; favor. [Middle English, from Old French *gre,* from Late Latin *grātum,* from Latin *grātus,* pleasing, thankful. See **gwere-¹** in Appendix.*]

Greece (grēs). *Greek* **Hel·las** (hĕl′əs). *Modern Greek* **El·las** (ĕ-läs′). *Abbr.* **Gr.** A kingdom, 50,147 square miles in area, of southeastern Europe in the southern Balkan Peninsula. Population, 8,550,000. Capital, Athens. [Latin *Graecia,* from *Graecus,* GREEK.]

greed (grēd) *n.* A rapacious desire for more than one needs or deserves, as of food, wealth, or power; avarice. [Back-formation from GREEDY.]

greed·y (grē′dē) *adj.* -ier, -iest. **1.** Excessively desirous of acquiring or possessing something, especially in quantity; covetous; avaricious. **2.** Wanting to eat or drink more than one can reasonably consume; gluttonous; voracious. [Middle English *gredy,* Old English *grǣdig.* See **gher-⁶** in Appendix.*] —**greed′i·ly** *adv.* —**greed′i·ness** *n.*

gree-gree. Variant of grigri.

Greek (grēk) *n. Abbr.* **Gk., Gr. 1.** The language of the Hellenes, constituting the Hellenic group of Indo-European, chronologically divided into **Proto-Greek, Ancient Greek** with the **Koine, Late Greek, Medieval Greek,** and **Modern Greek** *(all of which see).* **Note:** Any of these, and any of their numerous subdivisions, may correctly be referred to simply as *Greek* when the context is not ambiguous. Most frequently, however, *Greek* is used to mean *Ancient Greek* or *Classical Greek,* as in the etymologies of this Dictionary. **2.** An indigenous inhabitant of Greece, or a descendant of such. **3.** *Informal.* Something unintelligible. Used chiefly in the expression *It's Greek to me.* **4.** *Slang.* A member of a fraternity or sorority having a name composed of Greek letters. —*adj.* **1.** *Abbr.* **Gk., Gr.** Of, pertaining to, or designating Greece, the Hellenes, their language, or their culture. **2.** Of, pertaining to, or designating the Greek Orthodox Church. [Middle English *Grek,* Old English *Grēcas, Crēcas* (plural), from Germanic *Krēkaz* (unattested), from Latin *Graecus* (singular), from Greek *Graikos,* the name of a tribe of Epirus, probably from Illyrian.]

Greek Catholic. **1.** A member of the Eastern Orthodox Church. **2.** A member of a Uniat Church.

Greek Church. **1.** The Eastern Church *(see).* **2.** The Eastern Orthodox Church *(see).*

Greek cross. A cross formed by two bars of equal length crossing at the middle at right angles to each other.

Greek fire. An incendiary composition used by the Byzantine Greeks to set fire to enemy ships.

Gree·ley (grē′lē), **Horace.** 1811-1872. American journalist and political leader.

Gree·ly (grē′lē), **Adolphus Washington.** 1844-1935. American army officer and explorer of the Arctic.

green (grēn) *n.* **1.** Any of a group of colors that may vary in lightness and saturation, whose hue is that of the emerald, or somewhat less yellow than that of growing grass; the hue of that portion of the spectrum lying between yellow and blue; one of the additive or light primaries; one of the psychological primary hues, evoked in the normal observer by radiant energy having a wavelength of approximately 530 nanometers. See **color, primary color. 2.** Something green in color. **3.** *Plural.* Green growth or foliage, especially: **a.** The branches and leaves of green plants used for decoration: *Christmas greens.* **b.** Leafy plants or plant parts eaten as vegetables: *turnip greens.* **4.** A grassy lawn, plot, or similar area; especially, a **putting green** *(see).* —*adj.* **1.** Of the color green. **2.** Abounding in or covered with green growth or foliage. **3.** Made with green or leafy vegetables: *a green salad.* **4.** Mild or temperate in climate. **5.** Fresh; youthful; vigorous. **6.** Not mature or ripe; young: *green persimmons.* **7.** Pale and sickly in appearance; wan. **8.** Not yet fully processed, as: **a.** Not aged: *green wood.* **b.** Not cured or tanned: *green pelts.* **9.** Lacking training, conditioning, or experience; undisciplined; unschooled. **10.** Easily duped or deceived; gullible. —*v.* greened, greening, greens. —*tr.* To make green. —*intr.* To become green. [Middle English *grene,* Old English *grēne.* See **ghrē-** in Appendix.*] —**green′ly** *adv.* —**green′ness** *n.*

Green (grēn), **William.** 1873-1952. American labor leader; president of the American Federation of Labor (1924-52).

green algae. Any of the numerous algae of the division Chlorophyta, which includes spirogyra, sea lettuce, and others having pronounced green coloring.

green·back (grēn′băk′) *n.* A legal-tender note of U.S. currency.

Greenback Party. A former U.S. political party, organized in 1874, that advocated the use of inconvertible paper money. —**Green′back′er** *n.*

Green Bay. **1.** An inlet of Lake Michigan, 120 miles long, extending into northeast Wisconsin. **2.** A city and port of Wisconsin, at the southern end of this bay. Population, 63,000.

green bean. The string bean *(see).*

Greece

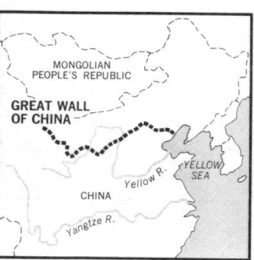

Great Wall of China

green dragon

green·belt (grēn′bĕlt′) *n.* A belt of recreational parks, farmland, or uncultivated land surrounding a community.
green·bri·er (grēn′brī′ər) *n.* A plant, the **catbrier** *(see)*.
green corn. Young, tender ears of sweet corn.
green dragon. A plant, *Arisaema dracontium,* of eastern North America, having divided leaves and minute flowers at the base of a long, slender spadix projecting from a narrow green spathe. Also called "dragonroot."
Greene (grēn), **Nathanael.** 1742–1786. American Revolutionary general.
Greene (grēn), **Robert.** 1560–1592. English poet and dramatist.
green·er·y (grē′nə-rē) *n., pl.* **-ies.** **1. a.** Green foliage; verdure. **b.** Such foliage used for decoration. **2.** A place where plants are grown.
green-eyed (grēn′īd′) *adj.* **1.** Having green eyes. **2.** Jealous.
green·finch (grēn′fĭnch′) *n.* A Eurasian bird, *Carduelis chloris* (or *Chloris chloris*), having green and yellow plumage.
green·fly (grēn′flī′) *n., pl.* **-flies.** Any of several greenish insects, especially an aphid.
green·gage (grēn′gāj′) *n.* A variety of plum having yellowish-green skin and sweet flesh. [GREEN + GAGE (plum).]
green·gro·cer (grēn′grō′sər) *n. Chiefly British.* A retailer of fresh fruit and vegetables. —**green′gro′cer·y** *n.*
green·head (grēn′hĕd′) *n.* A male mallard duck.
green·heart (grēn′härt′) *n.* **1.** A tropical American tree, *Ocotea rodioei* (or *Nectandra rodioei*), having dark, greenish, durable wood. **2.** Any of various similar or related trees. **3.** The wood of such a tree.
green·horn (grēn′hôrn′) *n.* **1.** An inexperienced or immature person. **2.** A recent immigrant or arrival. **3.** A gullible person. [Originally, a young animal with immature horns.]
green·house (grēn′hous′) *n.* **1.** A usually glass-enclosed structure used for cultivating plants that require controlled temperature and humidity. **2.** *Slang.* A part of an aircraft covered with a clear plastic bubble or shell.
greenhouse effect. The sequence of phenomena comprising the absorption of solar radiation by the earth, its conversion and re-emission in the infrared, and the absorption of this radiation, especially in the wavelength region from 5 to 17 microns, by atmospheric ozone, water vapor, and carbon dioxide, preventing its dissipation into space and resulting in a steady, gradual rise in the temperature of the atmosphere.
green·ing (grē′nĭng) *n.* Any of several varieties of apple having green-skinned fruit and used chiefly in cooking.
green·ish (grē′nĭsh) *adj.* Somewhat green.
Green·land (grēn′lənd, -lănd′). *Danish* **Grøn·land** (grœn′län′). An island, 842,800 square miles in area, located in the North Atlantic off the northeastern coast of Canada and constituting an integral part of the kingdom of Denmark. Population, 36,000. Capital, Godthaab.
Green·land Sea (grēn′lənd, -lănd′). The southern section of the Arctic Ocean, off the eastern coast of Greenland and north of the Norwegian Sea.
Greenland spar. A mineral, **cryolite** *(see).*
green·let (grēn′lĭt) *n.* Any of various greenish birds of the genus *Hylophilus,* of Central and South America, related to the vireos.
green light. **1.** The green-colored light that signals traffic to proceed. **2.** Permission to proceed.
green·ling (grēn′lĭng) *n.* Any of various food fishes of the family Hexagrammidae, of the northern Pacific. [GREEN + -LING.]
green manure. A growing crop, such as a clover or grass, that is plowed under the soil to improve fertility.
green monkey. Any of several African monkeys of the genus *Cercopithecus;* especially, *C. aethiops sabaeus,* having yellowish-gray fur with a greenish tinge.
Green Mountain Boy. **1.** A Vermont soldier under the command of Ethan Allen in the Revolutionary War. **2.** A male native or resident of Vermont.
Green Mountains. A section of the Appalachians, extending from Canada through Vermont to Massachusetts. Highest elevation, Mount Mansfield (4,393 feet).
Green Mountain State. A nickname for Vermont.
Green·ock (grē′nək, grĭn′ək, grĕn′-). A city, port, and shipbuilding center of northwestern Renfrewshire, Scotland, on the Firth of Clyde. Population, 74,000.
green·ock·ite (grēn′ə-kīt′) *n.* A yellow to brown or red mineral, essentially CdS, used as a cadmium ore. [After Charles Cathcart, Lord *Greenock* (died 1859), English soldier.]
green pepper. The unripened green fruit of various pepper plants, such as the **bell pepper** *(see).*
green plover. A bird, the **lapwing** *(see).*
Green River. **1.** A river rising in southwestern Wyoming and flowing 730 miles south, then east, then southwest to the Colorado in southeast-central Utah. **2.** A river rising in central Kentucky and flowing 360 miles west, then generally northwest to join the Ohio at Evansville, Indiana.
green·room (grēn′rōōm′, -rōōm′) *n.* A waiting room or lounge in a theater or concert hall for the use of performers when off-stage. [From its being typically painted green.]
green·sand (grēn′sănd′) *n.* A sand or sediment given a dark greenish color by grains of glauconite.
Greens·bo·ro (grēnz′bûr′ō). A manufacturing and industrial city of north-central North Carolina. Population, 120,000.
green·shank (grēn′shăngk′) *n.* An Old World wading bird, *Tringa nebularia,* having greenish legs and a long bill.
green·sick·ness (grēn′sĭk′nĭs) *n. Pathology.* **Chlorosis** *(see).* —**green′sick′** *adj*

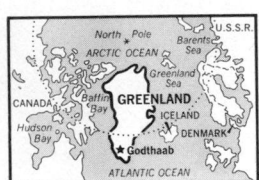

Greenland

green snake. Any of several nonvenomous North American snakes of the genus *Opheodrys,* having a slender yellow-green body.
green soap. A translucent, yellowish-green soft or liquid soap made chiefly from vegetable oils, potassium hydroxide, oleic acid, glycerin, and purified water, used medicinally as a stimulant in chronic skin disorders.
green·stone (grēn′stōn′) *n.* Any of various altered basic igneous rocks colored green by chlorite, hornblende, and epidote.
green·sward (grēn′swôrd′) *n.* Turf on which the grass is green.
green tea. Tea made from leaves that are not fermented before being dried. Compare **black tea.**
green thumb. The ability to foster the growth and health of plants.
green turtle. A large marine turtle, *Chelonia mydas,* having greenish flesh esteemed as food.
Green·ville (grēn′vĭl). **1.** A city and textile-manufacturing center of northwestern South Carolina. Population, 66,000. **2.** A city and cotton-growing center of western Mississippi, on the Mississippi River. Population, 42,000.
green·weed (grēn′wēd′) *n.* See **dyer's greenweed.**
Green·wich (grĭn′ĭj, -ĭch, grĕn′- *for sense 1;* grĕn′ĭch, grĕn′wĭch, grĭn′- *for sense 2*). **1.** A borough of London, England, comprising the former administrative divisions of Greenwich and Woolwich. Population, 230,000. **2.** A residential city in southwestern Connecticut. Population, 54,000.
Green·wich time (grĭn′ĭj, -ĭch, grĕn′-). Mean solar time for the meridian at Greenwich, England, used as a basis for calculating time throughout most of the world. Also called "Greenwich mean time."
Green·wich Village (grĕn′ĭch). A section of Manhattan, New York City, long famous as a community of artists, bohemians, and nonconformists.
green·wood (grēn′wōōd′) *n.* A wood or forest when the foliage is green.
greet (grēt) *tr.v.* **greeted, greeting, greets.** **1.** To address in a friendly and respectful way; to welcome or salute. **2.** To receive with a specified reaction: *greet a joke with laughter.* **3.** To present itself to; be perceived by: *A din greeted our ears.* [Middle English *greten,* Old English *grētan.* See **gher-³** in Appendix.*]
greet·ing (grē′tĭng) *n.* A gesture or word of welcome or salutation.
greg·a·rine (grĕg′ə-rĭn′, -rĭn) *n.* Any of various sporozoan protozoans of the order Gregarinida, that are parasitic within invertebrates such as arthropods and annelids. —*adj.* Of or belonging to the Gregarinida. [New Latin *Gregarina* (genus name), from Latin *gregārius,* GREGARIOUS.]
gre·gar·i·ous (grĭ-gâr′ē-əs) *adj.* **1.** Tending to move in or form a group with others of the same kind, as a herd, pack, or flock. **2.** Seeking and enjoying the company of others of one's kind; sociable. **3.** *Botany.* Growing in groups that are close together but not densely clustered or matted. [From Latin *gregārius,* belonging to a flock, from *grex* (stem *greg-*), herd, flock. See **ger-¹** in Appendix.*] —**gre·gar′i·ous·ly** *adv.* —**gre·gar′i·ousness** *n.*
Gre·go·ri·an (grĭ-gôr′ē-ən, grĭ-gōr′-) *adj.* Pertaining to, associated with, or introduced by Pope Gregory I or Pope Gregory XIII.
Gregorian calendar. The calendar now in use throughout most of the world, sponsored by Pope Gregory XII. See **calendar.**
Gregorian chant. The monodic liturgical plainsong of the Roman Catholic Church, systematized during the papacy of Gregory I. Also called "plainsong."
Greg·o·ry (grĕg′ə-rē) *n.* A masculine given name. [Middle English, from Latin *Grēgorius,* from Greek *Grēgorios,* from *grēgorein,* to be awake, watch, from *grēgoros,* watchful, from *egeirein,* to awaken. See **ger-⁵** in Appendix.*]
Greg·o·ry I (grĕg′ə-rē), **Saint.** Called "the Great." A.D. 540?–604. Pope (590–604); a leader in Christianizing Europe.
Greg·o·ry VII (grĕg′ə-rē), **Saint.** Original name, Hildebrand. 1020?–1085. Pope (1073–85); extended temporal power of the papacy.
Greg·o·ry XIII (grĕg′ə-rē). Original name, Ugo Buoncompagni. 1502–1585. Pope (1572–85); promoted education.
Greg·o·ry (grĕg′ə-rē), **Lady (Isabella) Augusta (Persse).** 1852–1932. Irish playwright; a founder and director of the Abbey Theater.
grei·sen (grī′zən) *n.* A granitic rock composed chiefly of quartz and mica. [German *Greisen, Greissen,* from *greissen†,* to split.]
grem·lin (grĕm′lən) *n.* **1.** An imaginary gnomelike creature to whom mechanical problems in military aircraft were frequently attributed during World War II. **2.** Any mischief-maker. [Origin uncertain.]
Gre·na·da (grə-nā′də). An island, 120 square miles in area, the southernmost of the Windward group of the West Indies; with its adjacent island dependencies, the southern Grenadines, it constitutes a member of the West Indies Associated States. Population, 92,000. Capital, St. George's.
gre·nade (grə-nād′) *n.* **1.** A missile containing priming and bursting charges, designed to be thrown by hand or fired from a launcher-equipped rifle. **2.** A glass container filled with a volatile chemical or a liquid that is dispersed when the glass is thrown and smashed. [French, from Old French *pome grenate,* POMEGRANATE (from its shape).]
gren·a·dier (grĕn′ə-dîr′) *n.* **1. a.** A member of the British Grenadier Guards, the first regiment of the royal household infantry. **b.** A soldier formerly bearing grenades. **2.** Any of various fishes of the family Macrouridae, chiefly of the deep ocean, having a

long tapering tail and lacking a tail fin. In this sense, also called "rat-tail." [French, "grenade thrower," from *grenade,* GRENADE.]

gren·a·dine (grĕn′ə-dēn′, grĕn′ə-dēn′) *n.* **1.** A thick, sweet syrup made from pomegranates or red currants and used as flavoring, especially in beverages. **2.** A thin, openwork fabric of silk, cotton, or a synthetic. [French, from Old French *pome grenate,* POMEGRANATE.]

Gren·a·dines (grĕn′ə-dēnz′, grĕn′ə-dēnz). An island chain in the central Windward group of the West Indies, situated between Grenada and St. Vincent.

Gre·no·ble (grə-nō′bəl; *French* grə-nô′bl′). A city and manufacturing center of southeast-central France. Population, 156,000.

Gresh·am's law (grĕsh′əmz). *Economics.* The theory that if two kinds of money in circulation have the same denominational value but different intrinsic values, the money with higher intrinsic value (called *good*) will be hoarded and eventually driven out of circulation by the money with lesser intrinsic value (called *bad*). [Expounded by Sir Thomas *Gresham* (1519?–1579), English financier.]

gres·so·ri·al (grĕ-sôr′ē-əl, grĕ-sōr′-) *adj. Zoology.* Adapted for walking or having legs adapted for walking. [New Latin *gressorius,* from *gressor,* one that walks, from Latin *gradī* (past participle *gressus*), to step, go. See **ghredh-** in Appendix.*]

Gre·ta (grĕt′ə, grē′tə). A feminine given name. [German, short for *Margarete,* Margaret, from Latin *Margarita,* MARGARET.]

Gretch·en (grĕch′ən; *German* grāt′shən). A feminine given name. [German, shortened diminutive of *Margarete,* Margaret. See **Greta.**]

Gret·na Green (grĕt′nə). A village of southern Dumfriesshire, Scotland, near the English border; noted as a place where marriages were performed for eloping couples.

grew. Past tense of **grow.**

grew·some. Variant of **gruesome.**

grey. Variant of **gray.**

Grey (grā), **Charles.** Second Earl Grey. 1764–1845. Prime Minister of Great Britain (1830–34); political and social reformer.

Grey (grā), Lady **Jane.** 1537–1554. Queen of England (July 9–19, 1553); great-granddaughter of Henry VII; succeeded Edward VI; imprisoned and executed.

grey·hen (grā′hĕn′) *n.* Also **gray hen.** The female of the **black grouse** *(see).*

grey·hound (grā′hound′) *n.* Also *rare* **gray·hound.** A large, slender dog of an ancient breed, having a smooth coat, a narrow head, and long legs, and capable of running swiftly. [Middle English *grehound,* Old English *grīghund.* See **gher-⁴** in Appendix.*]

grey·lag (grā′lăg′) *n.* The **gray lag goose** *(see).*

Grey·lock, Mount (grā′lŏk′). The highest mountain (3,491 feet) in the Berkshire Hills, northwest-central Massachusetts.

Grey (grā), **Zane.** 1875–1939. American author.

GRG Airport code for Georgetown, Guyana.

grib·ble (grĭb′əl) *n.* Any of several small, wood-boring marine crustaceans of the genus *Limnoria;* especially, *L. lignorum,* often damaging underwater wooden structures. [Possibly a diminutive of GRUB.]

grid (grĭd) *n.* **1.** A framework of parallel or crisscrossed bars; gridiron. **2.** A pattern of horizontal and vertical lines forming squares of uniform size on a map, chart, or aerial photograph, used as a reference for locating points. **3.** A football field. **4.** *Electricity.* **a.** An interconnected system of electric cables and power stations that distributes electricity over a large area. **b.** A corrugated or perforated conducting plate in a storage battery. **c.** A network or coil of fine wires located between the plate and the filament in an electron tube. [Short for GRIDIRON.]

grid·dle (grĭd′l) *n.* A flat pan or other flat metal surface used for cooking by dry heat. —*tr.v.* **griddled, -dling, -dles.** To cook on a griddle. [Middle English *gredil,* from Old French, from Vulgar Latin *crāticulum,* small grid, from Latin *crāticula,* diminutive of *crātis,* wickerwork. See **kert-** in Appendix.*]

grid·dle·cake (grĭd′l-kāk′) *n.* A **pancake** *(see).*

grid·i·ron (grĭd′ī′ərn) *n.* **1.** A flat framework of parallel metal bars used for broiling meat or fish. **2.** Any framework or network suggestive of a gridiron. **3.** A football field. **4.** A metal structure high above the stage of a theater, from which ropes or cables are strung to scenery and lights. [Middle English *gredire,* perhaps variant (influenced by *iren,* IRON) of *gredile, gredil,* GRIDDLE.]

grief (grēf) *n.* **1.** Intense mental anguish; deep remorse, acute sorrow, or the like. **2.** A source of deep remorse or acute sorrow. **3.** *Obsolete.* A grievance. —See Synonyms at **regret.** —**come to grief.** To meet with disaster; fail. [Middle English *gref,* from Old French *grief, gref,* from *grever,* GRIEVE.]

Grieg (grēg; *Norwegian* grĭg), **Edvard Hagerup.** 1843–1907. Norwegian composer.

griev·ance (grē′vəns) *n.* **1. a.** An actual or supposed circumstance regarded as just cause for protest. **b.** A complaint or protestation based on such a circumstance. **2.** Indignation or resentment stemming from a feeling of having been wronged. **3.** *Obsolete.* **a.** The act of inflicting hardship or harm. **b.** The cause of harm or hardship. —See Synonyms at **injustice.** [Middle English *grievaunce,* from Old French *grevance,* from *grever,* GRIEVE.]

grieve (grēv) *v.* **grieved, grieving, grieves.** —*tr.* **1.** To cause to be sorrowful or anguished; to distress. **2.** *Archaic.* To hurt or harm. —*intr.* To be sorrowful; to lament; mourn. [Middle English *greven,* from Old French *grever,* from Latin *gravāre,* to oppress, weigh upon, from *gravis,* heavy, weighty. See **gwer-²** in Appendix.*] —**griev′ing·ly** *adv.*

griev·ous (grē′vəs) *adj.* **1. a.** Causing grief, pain, or anguish. **b.** Expressing grief; mourning. **2.** Serious or dire; grave. —**griev′ous·ly** *adv.* —**griev′ous·ness** *n.*

grif·fin (grĭf′ən) *n.* Also **grif·fon, gry·phon.** *Greek Mythology.* A fabulous beast with the head and wings of an eagle and the body of a lion. [Middle English *griffon,* from Old French *grifoun,* from Late Latin *grȳphus,* from Latin, from Greek *grups,* possibly from Hebrew *kərūbh,* CHERUB.]

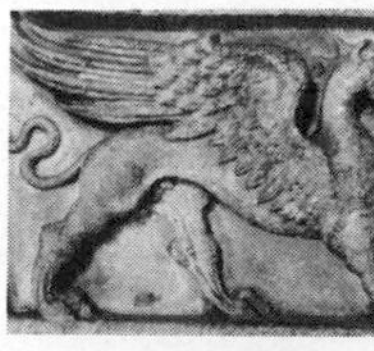

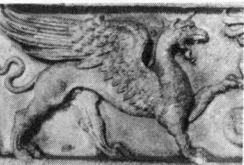

griffin
Detail from
a Hellenistic capital

Grif·fith (grĭf′ĭth), **D(avid Lewelyn) W(ark).** 1875–1948. American director and producer of motion pictures.

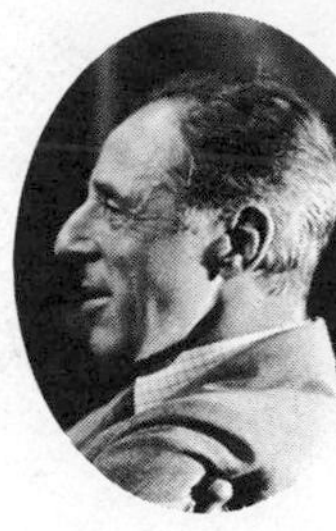

D. W. Griffith

grif·fon (grĭf′ən) *n.* **1.** Any of several breeds of dog having a wiry coat; especially, a small dog of a breed originating in Belgium, having a short, bearded muzzle. **2.** Variant of **griffin.** [From *griffon,* variant of GRIFFIN.]

grift (grĭft) *n. Slang.* **1.** Money made dishonestly, as by a swindle. **2.** A swindle or confidence game. —*intr.v.* **grifted, grifting, grifts.** *Slang.* To practice swindling or cheating. [Variant of GRAFT (money).] —**grift′er** *n.*

grig (grĭg) *n. Archaic.* A lively, bright person. [From *merry grig,* possibly alteration of *merry crick,* from CRICKET.]

Gri·gnard (grē-nyär′), **Victor.** 1871–1934. French chemist; worked on catalytic reactions.

gri·gri (grē′grē) *n.* Also **gree·gree, gris·gris.** An African Negro charm, fetish, or amulet. [Of African origin.]

grill (grĭl) *v.* **grilled, grilling, grills.** —*tr.* **1.** To broil on a gridiron. **2.** To torture as if by broiling. **3.** *Informal.* To question relentlessly; cross-examine. **4.** To mark or emboss with a gridiron. —*intr.* To undergo broiling. —*n.* **1.** A cooking utensil containing parallel thin metal bars; gridiron. **2.** Food cooked by broiling or grilling. **3.** A **grillroom** *(see).* **4.** A series of marks grilled or embossed on a surface. **5.** Variant of **grille.** [French *griller,* from *gril, grille,* a grating, gridiron, from Old French *grille, grail,* from Vulgar Latin *grāticula* (unattested), variant of Latin *crāticula.* See **griddle.**]

gril·lage (grĭl′ĭj) *n.* A network or frame of crossed timbers serving as a foundation, usually on treacherous soil. [French, from *grille,* grating, GRILL.]

grille (grĭl) *n.* Also **grill.** **1.** A metal grating used as a screen, divider, barrier, or decorative element, as in a window or gateway. **2.** A square opening at the back of the hazard side of a tennis court. [French, grating, GRILL.]

grilled (grĭld) *adj.* **1.** Broiled on a grill. **2.** Having a grille.

grill·room (grĭl′ro͞om′, -ro͝om′) *n.* A restaurant or room in a restaurant where grilled foods are served. Also called "grill."

grilse (grĭls) *n., pl.* **grilse.** A young salmon on its first return from the sea to fresh or brackish waters. [Middle English *grilles,* variant of *girsil,* possibly from Old French *grisel,* gray. See **grizzle.**]

grim (grĭm) *adj.* **grimmer, grimmest.** **1.** Unrelenting; rigid; stern. **2.** Uninviting or unnerving in aspect; forbidding; terrible: *"undoubtedly the grimmest part of him was his iron claw"* (J.M. Barrie). **3.** Ghastly; sinister: *"he made a grim jest at the horrifying nature of his wound"* (Reginald Pound). **4.** Ferocious; savage. —See Synonyms at **ghastly.** [Middle English *grim,* Old English *grim,* fierce, severe. See **ghrem-** in Appendix.*] —**grim′ly** *adv.* —**grim′ness** *n.*

gri·mace (grĭ-mās′, grĭm′ĭs) *n.* A sharp contortion of the face expressive of pain, contempt, or disgust. —*intr.v.* **grimaced, -macing, -maces.** To contort the facial features. [French, from Old French, *grimas(se), grimuche,* from Frankish *grīma* (unattested), mask. See **ghrem-** in Appendix.*]

gri·mal·kin (grĭ-măl′kən, grĭ-môl′-) *n.* **1.** A cat; especially, an old female cat. **2.** A shrewish old woman. [Variant of *graymalkin* : GRAY + dialectal *malkin,* lewd woman, hussy, Middle English *Malkyn,* feminine name, probably diminutive of *Mald,* pet form for MATILDA.]

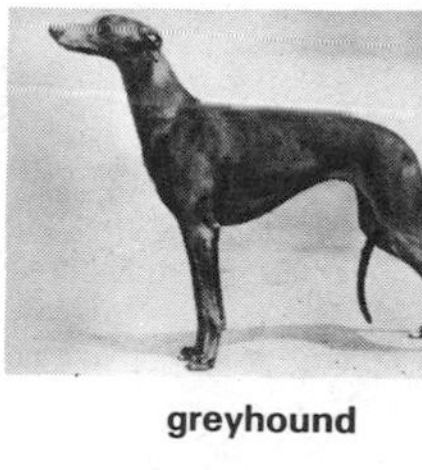

greyhound

grime (grīm) *n.* Black dirt or soot; especially, such dirt clinging to or ingrained in a surface. —*tr.v.* **grimed, griming, grimes.** To cover with dirt; begrime. [Middle English *grim(e),* from Middle Dutch *grīme.* See **ghrēi-** in Appendix.*]

Grim·ké (grĭm′kē), **Sarah Moore.** 1792–1873. With her sister **Angelina Emily** (1805–1879), American feminist and abolitionist leader.

Grimm (grĭm), **Jakob.** 1785–1863. With his brother **Wilhelm** (1786–1859), German philologist and folklorist.

Grimm's Law. A formula describing the regular changes undergone by Indo-European stop consonants represented in Germanic. Essentially, it states that Indo-European *p, t,* and *k* become Germanic *f, th,* and *h;* Indo-European *b, d,* and *g* become Germanic *p, t,* and *k;* and Indo-European *bh, dh,* and *gh* become Germanic *b, d,* and *g.* [Formulated by Jakob GRIMM.]

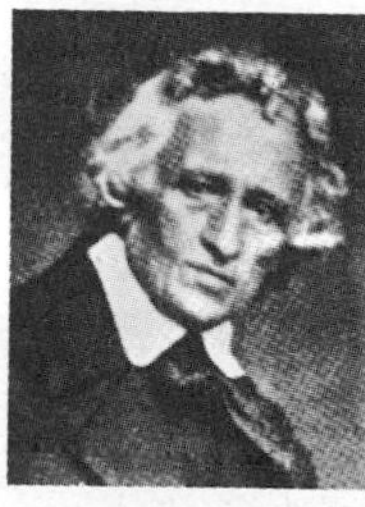

Jakob Grimm

Grims·by (grĭmz′bē). A city and fishing port of northeast-central Lincolnshire, England, on the Humber. Population, 95,000.

grim·y (grī′mē) *adj.* **-ier, -iest.** Covered or ingrained with grime. See Synonyms at **dirty.** —**grim′i·ly** *adv.* —**grim′i·ness** *n.*

grin (grĭn) *v.* **grinned, grinning, grins.** —*intr.* To draw back the lips and bare the teeth, especially in a wide smile. —*tr.* To express with a grin. —*n.* **1.** The act of grinning. **2.** The expression of the face produced by grinning. —See Synonyms at **smile.** [Middle English *grinnen,* Old English *grennian,* to grimace (in pleasure or displeasure), akin to *grānian,* to GROAN.] —**grin′ner** *n.* —**grin′ning·ly** *adv.*

grind (grīnd) *v.* **ground** (ground), **grinding, grinds.** —*tr.* **1. a.** To

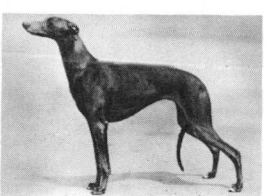

crush, pulverize, or powder with friction, especially by rubbing between two hard surfaces: *grind wheat into flour.* **b.** To shape, sharpen, or refine with friction: *grind a lens.* **2.** To rub (two surfaces) together; gnash: *grind the teeth.* **3.** To bear down on harshly; crush. **4. a.** To operate by turning a crank. **b.** To produce by turning a crank. **5.** To produce mechanically or without inspiration. Used with *out:* *"The production line grinds out a uniform product"* (Dwight Macdonald). **6.** To instill or teach by persistent repetition. Used with *into: grind the truth into their heads.* —*intr.* **1.** To perform the operation of grinding something. **2.** To be ground. **3.** To move with noisy friction; to grate. **4.** *Informal.* To devote oneself to study or work. **5.** *Slang.* To rotate the pelvis in the manner of a stripteaser. —*n.* **1.** The act of grinding. **2.** A crunching or grinding noise. **3.** A specific grade or degree of pulverization, as of coffee beans: *drip grind.* **4.** *Informal.* **a.** A laborious task, routine, or study. **b.** One who works or studies excessively. **5.** *Slang.* A single erotic rotation of the pelvis. —*adj.* Devoted to grinding out a product or entertainment, usually on a lengthy, uninterrupted schedule: *a grind theater on 42nd Street.* [Grind, ground, ground; Middle English *grinden, grond, ygrounden;* Old English *grindan, grond* (plural *grundon*), *gegrunden.* See **ghren-** in Appendix.*] —**grind'ing·ly** *adv.*

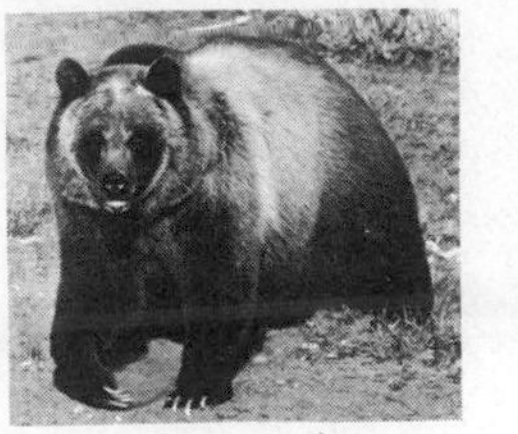

grizzly bear

grind·er (grīn'dər) *n.* **1.** One that grinds; especially, a person who sharpens cutting edges. **2.** A molar. **3.** *Plural. Informal.* The teeth. **4.** *Slang.* A sandwich, the **hero** *(see).*

grind·stone (grīnd'stōn') *n.* **1.** A stone disk turned on an axle for grinding, polishing, or sharpening tools. **2.** A millstone. —**keep** (or **have**) **one's nose to the grindstone.** To work diligently and continuously.

grin·go (grĭng'gō) *n., pl.* **-gos.** In Latin America, a foreigner; especially, an American or Englishman. Used contemptuously. [Spanish *gringo*†, unknown tongue, gibberish.]

grip[1] (grĭp) *n.* **1.** A tight hold; a firm grasp. **2.** The pressure or strength of such a grasp. **3.** A manner of grasping and holding. **4.** A prescribed manner of clasping hands, used by members of a fraternal society. **5.** Mastery; command; understanding: *a good grip on French grammar.* **6.** A spasm or seizure, as of pain. **7. a.** A mechanical device that grasps and holds. **b.** A part designed to be grasped and held; a handle. **8.** A suitcase or valise. **9. a.** A stagehand who helps in shifting scenery. **b.** A member of a film production crew who adjusts sets and props and sometimes assists the cameraman. —**come to grips. 1.** To fight in hand-to-hand combat. **2.** To deal actively and conclusively, as with a problem. —*v.* **gripped, gripping, grips.** —*tr.* To secure and maintain a tight hold on; seize firmly; to capture: *"His helpless condition . . . gripped my sympathies"* (James Weldon Johnson). —*intr.* To hold securely. [Middle English *grip,* partly Old English *gripa,* grasp, and partly Old English *gripa,* handful. See **ghreib-** in Appendix.*] —**grip'ping·ly** *adv.*

grip[2]. Variant of **grippe.**

gripe (grīp) *v.* **griped, griping, gripes.** —*tr.* **1.** To cause sharp pain in the bowels of. **2.** *Informal.* To irritate; annoy. **3.** To grasp; seize. **4.** *Archaic.* To oppress or afflict. —*intr.* **1.** *Informal.* To complain naggingly or petulantly; to grumble. **2.** To have sharp pains in the bowels. —*n.* **1.** *Informal.* A complaint. **2.** *Plural.* Sharp, repeated pains in the bowels. **3.** A grip; grasp: *"the ineluctable gripe in which mortality clutches the highest and purest of earthly mould"* (Hawthorne). **4.** A handle. [Middle English *gripen,* Old English *grīpan.* See **ghreib-** in Appendix.*]

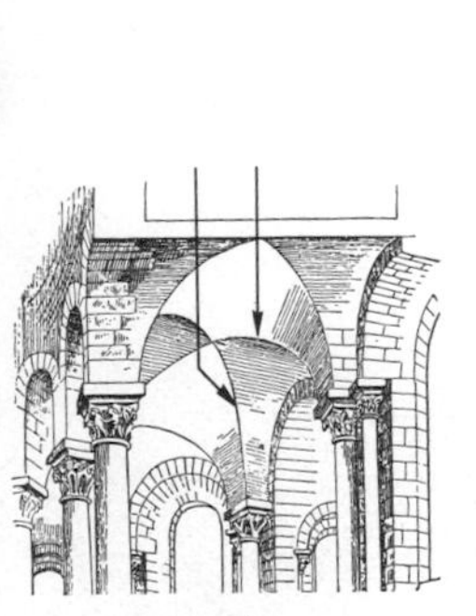

groin
Groins in early 12th-century vaulting

grippe (grĭp) *n.* Also **grip.** *Pathology.* **Influenza** *(see).* [French, from *gripper,* to seize, from Old French, from Frankish *grīpan* (unattested). See **ghreib-** in Appendix.*] —**grip'py** *adj.*

grip·sack (grĭp'săk') *n.* A small suitcase. [GRIP + SACK.]

Gris (grēs), **Juan.** 1887–1927. Spanish cubist painter in France.

gri·saille (grĭ-zāl'; *French* grē-zä'y') *n.* **1.** A style of monochromatic painting in shades of gray. **2.** A painting or design in this style. [French, from *gris,* gray, from Old French, from Frankish *gris* (unattested). See **gher-**[4] in Appendix.*]

gris·e·ous (grĭs'ē-əs, grĭz'-) *adj.* Grayish; mottled or grizzled with gray. [Medieval Latin *griseus,* from Germanic. See **gher-**[4] in Appendix.*]

gri·sette (grĭ-zĕt') *n.* A French working girl. [French, an inexpensive gray fabric for dresses, a woman wearing such a dress, from *gris,* gray. See **grisaille.**]

gris-gris. Variant of **grigri.**

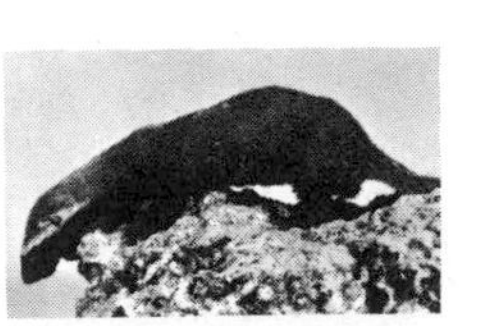

grison

gris·ly (grĭz'lē) *adj.* **-lier, -liest.** Horrifying; repugnant; gruesome. See Synonyms at **ghastly.** [Middle English *grisly,* Old English *grislīc.* See **ghrēi-** in Appendix.*]

Gris-Nez, Cape (grē-nā'). A promontory of northern France, extending into the Strait of Dover.

gri·son (grī'sən, grĭz'ən) *n.* Either of two carnivorous mammals, *Grison vittatus* or *G. cuja,* of Central and South America, having grizzled fur, a slender body, and short legs. [French, from Old French, gray animal, from *gris,* gray. See **grisaille.**]

grist (grĭst) *n.* **1.** Grain or a quantity of grain for grinding. **2.** Ground grain. —**grist for** (or **to**) **one's mill.** Something that can be turned to one's advantage. [Middle English *grist,* Old English *grīst.* See **ghren-** in Appendix.*]

gris·tle (grĭs'əl) *n.* **Cartilage** *(see),* especially when present in meat. [Middle English *gristil,* Old English *gristle,* from Germanic *gristil-* (unattested).]

gris·tly (grĭs'lē) *adj.* **-tlier, -tliest. 1.** Composed of or containing gristle. **2.** Resembling gristle. —**gris'tli·ness** *n.*

grist·mill (grĭst'mĭl') *n.* A mill for grinding grain.

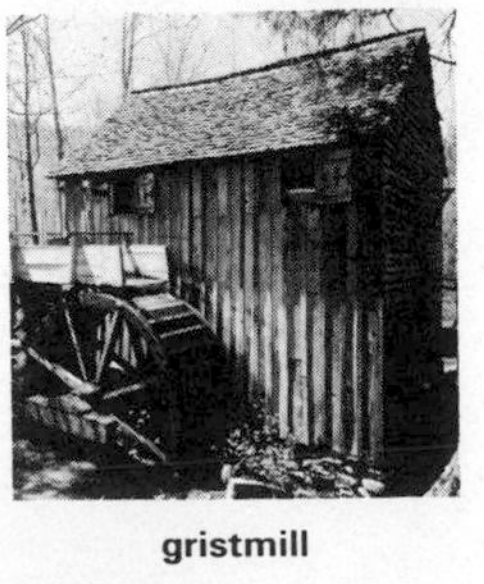

gristmill

grit (grĭt) *n.* **1.** Minute rough granules, as of sand or stone. **2.** The texture or structure of stone to be used in grinding. **3.** A coarse hard sandstone, used for making grindstones and millstones. **4.** *Informal.* Indomitable spirit; pluck. —*v.* **gritted, gritting, grits.** —*tr.* **1.** To clamp (the teeth) together. **2.** To cover or treat with grit. —*intr.* To make a grinding noise. [Middle English *grete,* Old English *grēot.* See **ghrēu-** in Appendix.*]

grith (grĭth) *n.* **1.** Protection or sanctuary provided persons by Old English law in certain circumstances, as when in a church or traveling on the king's highway. **2.** *Archaic.* Quarter given in battle. [Middle English *grith,* Old English *grith,* from Old Norse *gridh*†.]

grits (grĭts) *pl.n.* Coarsely ground grain, especially corn. [From Middle English *gryt,* bran, Old English *grytt.* See **ghrēu-** in Appendix.*]

grit·ty (grĭt'ē) *adj.* **-tier, -tiest. 1.** Containing or resembling grit. **2.** Showing resolution and fortitude; plucky. —See Synonyms at **brave.** —**grit'ti·ness** *n.*

gri·vet (grĭv'ĭt) *n.* A long-tailed African monkey, *Cercopithecus aethiops,* having a greenish-gray coat. [French *grivet*†.]

griz·zle (grĭz'əl) *v.* **-zled, -zling, -zles.** —*tr.* To make gray. —*intr.* To become gray. —*n.* **1.** *Archaic.* Gray hair. **2. a.** The color of a roan. **b.** A roan. —*adj.* **1.** Gray. **2.** Roan. [Middle English *grisel,* gray, from Old French, diminutive of *gris,* gray, from Frankish *gris* (unattested). See **gher-**[4] in Appendix.*]

griz·zly (grĭz'lē) *adj.* **-zlier, -zliest.** Grayish or flecked with gray. —*n., pl.* **grizzlies.** A grizzly bear.

grizzly bear. The grayish form of the brown bear, *Ursus arctos,* of northwestern North America, often considered a separate species, *U. horribilis.*

gro. gross.

groan (grōn) *v.* **groaned, groaning, groans.** —*intr.* **1.** To voice a deep, wordless, prolonged sound expressive of pain, grief, annoyance, or disapproval. **2.** To produce a similar sound expressive of stress or strain: *"I stretched out . . . hearing the springs groan beneath me"* (Ralph Ellison). **3.** To suffer oppression or strain. —*tr.* To utter or convey with groaning. —*n.* The sound made in groaning; a moan or creak. [Middle English *gronen,* Old English *grānian,* akin to *grennian,* to GRIN.] —**groan'ing·ly** *adv.*

groat (grōt) *n.* A British silver fourpence piece used from the 14th to the 17th century. [Middle English *grote,* from Middle Dutch *groot.* See **ghrēu-** in Appendix.*]

groats (grōts) *pl.n.* Hulled, usually crushed grain, especially oats. [Middle English *grotes,* Old English *grotan.* See **ghrēu-** in Appendix.*]

gro·cer (grō'sər) *n.* A storekeeper who sells foodstuffs and sundry household supplies. [Middle English, from Old French *grossier,* wholesale dealer, from Medieval Latin *grossārius,* from Latin *grossus,* thick, GROSS.]

gro·cer·y (grō'sə-rē) *n., pl.* **-ies. 1.** A store selling foodstuffs and household supplies. **2.** The occupation of a grocer. **3.** *Plural.* Commodities sold by a grocer.

grog (grŏg) *n.* Alcoholic liquor; especially, rum diluted with water. [After Admiral Edward Vernon (1684–1757), nicknamed Old Grog because of his habit of wearing a GROGRAM coat. He ordered that diluted rum be served to his sailors.]

grog·gy (grŏg'ē) *adj.* **-gier, -giest.** Unsteady and dazed; shaky. [From GROG.] —**grog'gi·ly** *adv.* —**grog'gi·ness** *n.*

grog·ram (grŏg'rəm) *n.* **1.** A coarse, often stiffened fabric of silk, mohair, or wool, or a blend of these. **2.** A garment of this fabric. [Alteration of GROSGRAIN.]

groin (groin) *n.* **1. a.** *Anatomy.* The crease at the junction of the thigh with the trunk, together with the adjacent region. **b.** The external genital organs. **2.** *Architecture.* The curved edge at the junction of two intersecting vaults. —*tr.v.* **groined, groining, groins.** To provide or build with groins. [Earlier *gryne,* Middle English *grynde,* perhaps from Old English *grynde,* abyss, depression, from Germanic *grundja-* (unattested), from Common Germanic *grunduz* (unattested), GROUND.]

Gro·lier de Ser·vières (grô-lyā' də sĕr-vyâr'), **Jean.** 1479–1565. French bibliophile and statesman.

grom·met (grŏm'ĭt) *n.* **1.** A reinforced eyelet in cloth, leather, or the like, through which a fastener may be passed. **2.** *Nautical.* A rope or metal ring used for securing the edge of a sail. Also called "grummet." [Obsolete French *grom(m)ette, gourmette,* bridle ring, from Old French *gourmel,* perhaps from Frankish *worm* (unattested), worm. See **wer-**[3] in Appendix.*]

grom·well (grŏm'wəl) *n.* **1.** Any of several plants of the genus *Lithospermum,* having small yellow or white flowers. **2.** Any of several similar or related plants. [Middle English *gromil,* from Old French, perhaps from Vulgar Latin *gruīnum milium* (unattested), "crane's millet" : Latin *gruīnus,* of a crane, from *grūs,* crane (see **ger-**[4] in Appendix*) + *milium,* MILLET.]

Gro·my·ko (grō-mē'kō; *Russian* grə-mĭ'kô), **Andrei Andrevich.** Born 1909. Soviet diplomat.

Gro·ning·en (grō'nĭng-ən). **1.** A province, 867 square miles in area, of the northeastern Netherlands. Population, 475,000. **2.** The capital of this province. Population, 140,000.

Grøn·land. The Danish name for **Greenland.**

groom (groom) *n.* **1.** A man or boy employed to take care of horses. **2.** A bridegroom. **3.** One of several officers in an English royal household. **4.** *Archaic.* **a.** A man. **b.** A manservant. —*tr.v.* **groomed, grooming, grooms. 1.** To make neat and trim; polish. **2.** To clean and brush (an animal). **3.** To train, as for a specific position: *groom a candidate for Congress.* [As "bridegroom," shortening of BRIDEGROOM; as "man," "servant," Middle English *grom*†.]

Usage: *Groom* (noun), as a substitute for *bridegroom,* is appropriate to all but the most formal contexts. It is acceptable on all other levels in writing and speech, according to 90 per cent of the Usage Panel.

grooms·man (gro͝omz′mən, gro͝omz′-) *n., pl.* **-men** (-mĭn). The best man or an usher at a wedding.

Groote Ey·landt (gro͞ot′ ī′lənd). An island of Australia, oc cupying 950 square miles in the western Gulf of Carpentaria.

groove (gro͞ov) *n.* **1.** A long, narrow furrow or channel. **2. a.** A situation or activity to which one is especially well suited; niche. **b.** A settled, humdrum routine; rut. —*tr.v.* **grooved, grooving, grooves.** To cut a groove in. [Middle English *grofe,* from Middle Dutch *groeve,* ditch. See **ghrebh-²** in Appendix.*]

groov·y (gro͞o′vē) *adj.* **-ier, -iest.** *Slang.* Pleasing; deeply satisfying. [From slang expression *in the groove,* exciting, satisfying.]

grope (grōp) *v.* **groped, groping, gropes.** —*intr.* **1.** To reach about uncertainly; feel one's way. **2.** To search blindly or uncertainly: *grope for an answer.* —*tr.* To make (one's way) by groping. —*n.* The act of groping. [Middle English *gropen,* Old English *grāpian.* See **ghreib-** in Appendix.*] —**grop′ing·ly** *adv.*

Gro·pi·us (grō′pē-əs; *German* grō′pē-o͞os′), **Walter.** Born 1883. German-born American architect; founder of the Bauhaus school.

gros·beak (grōs′bēk′) *n.* Any of various finches of the genera *Hesperiphona, Pinicola,* and related genera, having a thick, rounded bill. [Partial translation of French *grosbec* : Old French *gros,* thick, GROSS + *bec,* beak.]

gro·schen (grō′shən) *n., pl.* **groschen.** A coin equal to 1/100 of the schilling of Austria. See table of exchange rates at **currency.** [German *Groschen,* from Middle High German *gros(se), grosche,* from Czech *grosh,* from Medieval Latin *(denārius) grossus,* "thick (penny)," from Latin *grossus,* thick, GROSS.]

gros·grain (grō′grān′) *n.* **1.** A heavy silk or rayon fabric with narrow horizontal ribs. **2.** A ribbon made of this. [French *gros grain,* "coarse grain" : Old French *gros,* thick, GROSS + GRAIN.]

gros point (grō). **1.** A large needlepoint stitch, covering two vertical and two horizontal threads. **2.** Work done in this stitch. [French, "large point."]

gross (grōs) *adj.* **grosser, grossest. 1. a.** Exclusive of deductions; total; entire: *gross profits.* **b.** Unmitigated in any way; utter. **2.** Glaringly obvious; flagrant: *gross injustice.* **3. a.** Coarse; vulgar; obscene. **b.** Lacking sensitivity or discernment; unrefined. **c.** Carnal; sensual. **4. a.** Overweight; corpulent. **b.** Dense; profuse. **c.** Impenetrable; thick. **5.** *Pathology.* Visible to the naked eye: *a gross lesion.* —See Synonyms at **coarse, flagrant.** —*n., pl.* **grosses** (for sense 1) or **gross** (for sense 2). **1.** The entire body or amount; a total. **2.** *Abbr.* **gr., gro. a.** Twelve dozen, used as a unit of measurement. **b.** A group of 144 or 12 dozen items. —**in the gross. 1.** Taken as a whole; in bulk. **2.** Wholesale. —*tr.v.* **grossed, grossing, grosses.** To earn as a total income or profit before deductions. [Middle English, from Old French *gros,* thick, large, from Latin *grossus.* See **gwres-** in Appendix.*] —**gross′ly** *adv.* —**gross′ness** *n.*

Gross·glock·ner (grōs′glŏk′nər). The highest elevation (12,461 feet) in Austria, located in the southwest and forming part of the Hohe Tauern range.

gross national product. *Abbr.* **GNP** The total market value of all the goods and services produced by a nation during a specified period. Compare **national income.**

gros·su·lar·ite (grŏs′yə-lə-rīt′) *n.* A light-green, pink, gray, or brown garnet with composition $Ca_3Al_2(SiO_4)_3$, found alone or as a constituent part of the common garnet. [German *Grossularit,* "gooseberry stone" (from the color of certain kinds of garnet), from New Latin *Grossularia,* former genus of gooseberry, from Old French *groiselle, grosele,* gooseberry, from Middle Dutch *croesel,* "curly berry" (from its beard), diminutive of *kroes,* curled. See **ger-³** in Appendix.*]

Gros Ventre (grō′ vänt′). A river rising in northwest-central Wyoming and flowing 100 miles generally west to the Snake River.

grosz (grôsh) *n., pl.* **groszy** (grôsh′ē). A coin equal to 1/100 of the zloty of Poland. See table of exchange rates at **currency.** [Polish, from Czech *grosh.* See **groschen.**]

Grosz (grōs), **George.** 1893–1959. German-born American artist.

gro·tesque (grō-tĕsk′) *adj.* **1.** Characterized by ludicrous or incongruous distortion. **2.** Extravagant; outlandish; bizarre. **3.** *Fine Arts.* Of or designating the grotesque or a work executed in this style. —See Synonyms at **fantastic.** —*n.* **1.** A strange and incongruous medley, as of things or events. **2.** Anything thought to resemble the grotesque style in art. **3.** *Fine Arts.* **a.** An artistic and decorative style developed in 16th-century Italy, characterized by incongruous combinations of monstrous or natural forms. **b.** A work of art executed in this style. [Earlier *crotescque,* from Old French *crotesque, grotesque,* from Old Italian *(pittura) grottesca,* "grottolike (painting)," from *grottesco,* of a grotto, from *grotta,* GROTTO.] —**gro·tesque′ly** *adv.* —**gro·tesque′ness** *n.*

gro·tes·que·ry (grō-tĕs′kə-rē) *n., pl.* **-ries.** Also **gro·tes·que·rie. 1.** The state of being grotesque; grotesqueness. **2.** Something grotesque.

Gro·ti·us (grō′shē-əs), **Hugo.** Original name, Huig de Groot. 1583–1645. Dutch jurist and statesman; codifier of international law.

grot·to (grŏt′ō) *n., pl.* **-toes** or **-tos. 1.** A small cave or cavern. **2.** An artificial structure or excavation made to resemble a cave or cavern. —See Synonyms at **hole.** [Italian *grotta, grotto,* from Old Italian, from Vulgar Latin *grupta* (unattested), variant of Latin *crypta,* vault, CRYPT.]

grouch (grouch) *intr.v.* **grouched, grouching, grouches.** To grumble or sulk. —*n.* **1.** A grumbling or sulky mood. **2.** A complaint; grudge. **3.** A habitually complaining or irritable person. [Middle English *grutchen,* to GRUDGE.]

grouch·y (grou′chē) *adj.* **-ier, -iest.** Inclined to grumbling and complaint; ill-humored; peevish; grumpy. —**grouch′i·ly** *adv.* —**grouch′i·ness** *n.*

ground¹ (ground) *n.* **1. a.** The solid surface of the earth. **b.** The floor of a body of water, especially the sea. **2.** Soil; earth: *level the ground for a lawn.* **3.** *Often plural.* An area of land designated for a particular purpose: *burial grounds.* **4.** *Plural.* The land surrounding or forming part of a house or other building: *The embassy has beautiful grounds.* **5.** *Often plural.* The foundation for an argument, belief, or action; basis; premise. **6.** *Usually plural.* The underlying condition prompting some action; a cause; a reason. Used with *for: grounds for suspicion; a ground for divorce.* **7.** An area of reference; subject. **8.** A surrounding area; background. **9.** The preparatory coat of paint on which a picture is to be painted. **10.** *Plural.* The sediment at the bottom of a liquid, especially coffee. **11.** *Music.* A **ground bass** *(see).* **12.** *Electricity.* **a.** The position or portion of an electric circuit that is at zero potential with respect to the earth. **b.** A conducting connection to such a position or to the earth. **c.** A large conducting body, such as the earth, used as a return for electric currents and as an arbitrary zero of potential. —See Synonyms at **base.** —**break ground. 1.** To cut or dig into the soil, as in plowing or excavating. **2.** To start in on an undertaking. **3.** *Nautical.* To free or raise from the bottom, as a ship's anchor. —**cover ground. 1.** To move about or travel, especially over a considerable distance. **2.** To make headway in some work; accomplish a great deal. —**from the ground up.** Leaving out nothing; completely; thoroughly. —**gain ground. 1.** To make progress. **2.** To gain favor or popularity. —**give ground.** To give way; yield an advantage. —**hold** (or **stand**) **one's ground.** To maintain one's position; not yield or retreat. —**on home ground.** In a familiar area or on a familiar subject. —**run into the ground.** To overdo to the point of being tedious. —**shift one's ground.** To take another position or approach, as in argumentation. —*adj.* **1.** Of, on, or near the ground. **2.** Flourishing in or on the ground. —*v.* **grounded, grounding, grounds.** —*tr.* **1.** To place or set on the ground. **2.** To provide a basis for (an argument, theory, or the like); substantiate; justify. **3.** To supply with basic and essential information; instruct in fundamentals; to school. **4.** To prevent (an aircraft or pilot) from flying. **5.** *Electricity.* To connect (an electric circuit) to a ground. **6.** *Nautical.* To run (a vessel) aground. **7.** To cover (a canvas or other surface) with a preparatory coat of paint. —*intr.* **1.** To hit or reach the ground. **2.** *Baseball.* To hit a ground ball. **3.** *Nautical.* To run aground. [Middle English *ground,* Old English *grund,* from Common Germanic *grunduz* (unattested).]

ground². Past tense and past participle of **grind.**

ground ball. *Baseball.* A batted ball that hits the ground before being caught by a fielder. Also called "grounder."

ground bass. A short musical bass passage or motif that is continually repeated under the changing harmonies and melodies of the upper range. Also called "ground."

ground beetle. Any of numerous chiefly black or brown beetles of the family Carabidae, that often crawl under stones, logs, or debris.

ground cherry. Any of various chiefly New World plants of the genus *Physalis,* having round, fleshy fruit enclosed in a papery, bladderlike husk.

ground cloth. A **ground sheet** *(see).*

ground cover. Low-growing plants that form a dense, extensive growth and tend to prevent soil erosion.

ground crew. A team of mechanics and technicians who maintain and service aircraft on the ground.

ground floor. The floor of a building at or nearly at ground level. —**get in on the ground floor.** To work with a project or business from its inception.

ground glass. Glass that has been subjected to grinding or etching to diffuse light. —**ground′-glass′** *adj.*

ground hemlock. A low-growing yew, *Taxus canadensis,* of northeastern North America.

ground hog. A rodent, the **woodchuck** *(see).*

ground-hog day (ground′hôg′, -hŏg′). February 2, traditionally the point that indicates an early or late spring. [Supposedly the day when the ground hog emerges from hibernation, and hurries back to his burrow if it is sunny and he sees his own shadow, presaging prolonged winter weather.]

ground ivy. A creeping or trailing aromatic plant, *Glechoma hederacea,* native to Eurasia, having rounded, scalloped leaves and small purplish flowers. Also called "gill-over-the-ground."

ground·less (ground′lĭs) *adj.* Having no ground or foundation; unsubstantiated: *groundless optimism.* —**ground′less·ly** *adv.* —**ground′less·ness** *n.*

ground·ling (ground′lĭng) *n.* **1. a.** A plant or animal living on or close to the ground. **b.** A fish that lives at the bottom of the water. **2.** A person with uncultivated tastes. **3.** A spectator in the cheaper part of a theater.

ground loop. A sharp, uncontrollable turn of an aircraft in taxiing, landing, or taking off.

ground·mass (ground′măs′) *n.* The fine-grained crystalline base of porphyritic rock, in which phenocrysts are embedded.

ground·nut (ground′nŭt′) *n.* **1.** A climbing vine, *Apios tuberosa,* of eastern North America, having compound leaves, clusters of fragrant brownish flowers, and small, edible tubers. **2.** Any of several other plants having underground tubers or nutlike parts. **3.** The tuber or nutlike part of such a plant. **4.** *Chiefly British.* The **peanut** *(see).*

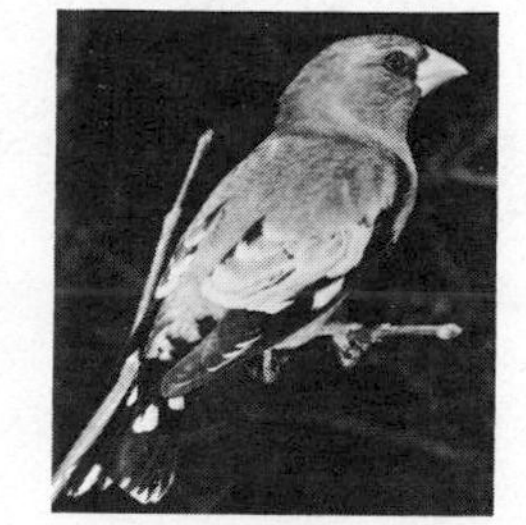

grosbeak
Hesperiphona vespertina

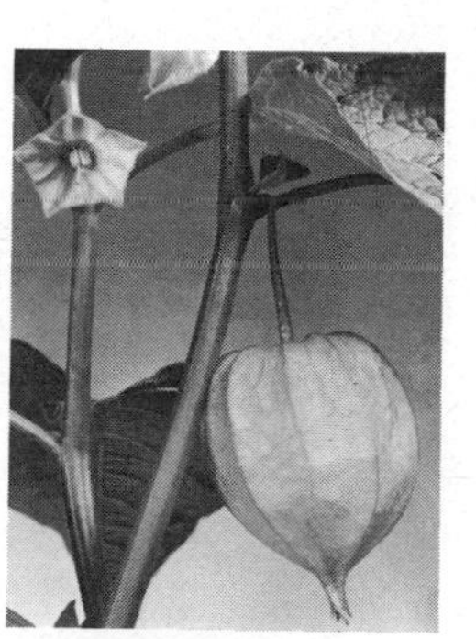

ground cherry
Physalis alkekengi

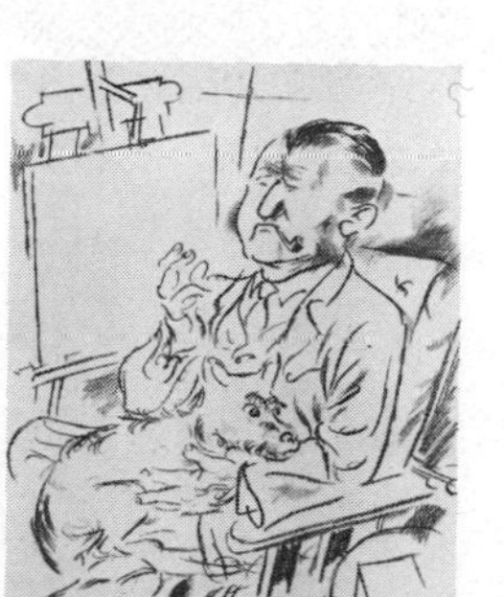

George Grosz
Self-portrait

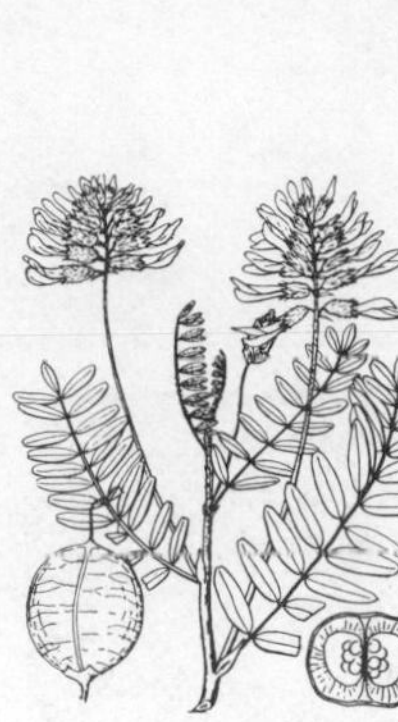
ground plum

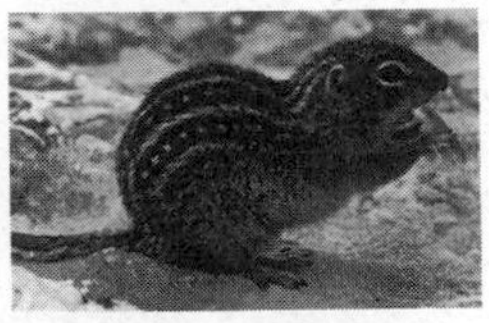
ground squirrel
Citellus tridecemlineatus

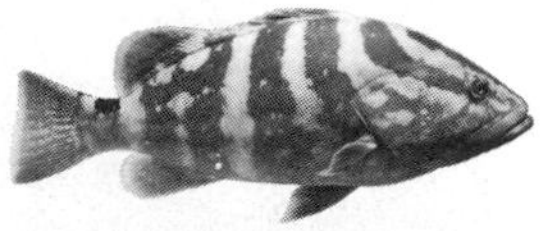
grouper
Epinephelus striatus

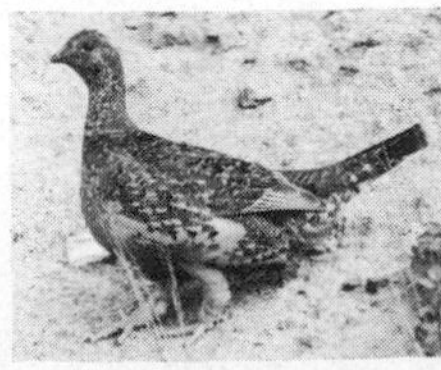
grouse¹
Canachites canadensis

ground pine. **1.** A **club moss** *(see);* especially, *Lycopodium obscurum,* or any similar species. **2.** A low-growing plant, *Ajuga chamaepitys,* native to the Old World, having narrow leaves, yellow flowers, and a resinous odor.
ground pink. A plant, the **moss pink** *(see).*
ground plan. **1.** A plan of a floor of a building as if seen from overhead. **2.** A preliminary or basic plan.
ground plum. **1.** A plant, *Astragalus crassicarpus,* of the central and western United States, having compound leaves, purple or white flowers, and green, plumlike, edible fruit. **2.** The fruit of this plant.
ground rent. *Chiefly British.* Rent paid for land to be used chiefly for building.
ground robin. A bird, the **towhee** *(see).*
ground rule. Any rule of procedure modified or amended to fit a particular situation or event: *ground rules for international negotiation.*
ground·sel¹ (ground′səl) *n.* Any of various plants of the genus *Senecio,* having rayed, usually yellow flowers. [Middle English *groundeswele,* Old English *grundeswylige,* variant (influenced by *grund,* GROUND) of *gundæswelgæ,* "pus-absorber" (from its use to reduce abscesses) : *gund,* pus (see **ghendh-** in Appendix*) + *swelgan,* to swallow (see **swel-¹** in Appendix*).]
ground·sel². Variant of **groundsill.**
groundsel tree. A shrub, *Baccharis halimifolia,* of coastal areas of the eastern United States, having white, plumelike fruiting clusters.
ground sheet. **1.** A waterproof cover used to protect an area of ground, such as a baseball field. **2.** A waterproof sheet placed under camp bedding as a protection against damp. Also called "ground cloth."
ground·sill (ground′sĭl′) *n.* Also **ground·sel.** The horizontal timber nearest the ground in the frame of a building. Also called "ground plate."
ground speed. Also **ground·speed** (ground′spēd′). *Aviation.* The speed of an airborne aircraft computed in terms of the ground distance traversed in a given period of time.
ground squirrel. Any of various rodents of the genus *Citellus* (or *Spermophilus*) and related genera, related to and resembling the chipmunks. Also called "gopher."
ground state. *Physics.* The stationary state of least energy in a physical system.
ground swell. **1.** An undulation of the ocean with deep rolling waves, often caused by a distant storm or earthquake. **2.** An unexpected, sudden gathering of force, as of public opinion.
ground water. Water beneath the earth's surface between saturated soil and rock that supplies wells and springs.
ground wave. A radio wave that travels along the earth's surface.
ground·work (ground′wûrk′) *n.* A foundation; basis; preliminary work. See Synonyms at **base.**
group (gro͞op) *n. Abbr.* **gr.** **1.** An assemblage of persons or objects; aggregation: *a group of dinner guests; a group of Chinese porcelains.* **2.** Two or more figures that make up a unit or a design, as in sculpture or painting. **3.** A number of individuals or things considered together because of certain similarities. **4.** *Linguistics.* A subdivision of a linguistic family, less inclusive than a branch. **5.** A military unit consisting of two or more battalions and a headquarters. **6.** *U.S. Air Force.* A unit of two or more squadrons, smaller than a wing. **7.** Any class or collection of related objects or entities, as: **a.** Two or more atoms behaving or regarded as behaving as a single chemical unit. **b.** A vertical column in the periodic table of elements. **c.** A geological stratigraphic unit, especially a unit consisting of two or more formations. **8.** *Mathematics.* A set together with a binary operation under which the set is closed and associative, and for which the set contains an identity element and an inverse for every element in the set. —*v.* **grouped, grouping, groups.** —*tr.* To place or arrange in a group or groups. —*intr.* To form or be part of a group. [French *groupe,* from Italian *gruppo,* "knot," from Germanic. See **ger-³** in Appendix.*]
Usage: *Group,* as a collective noun, can be construed as singular or plural in determining the number of the verb it governs. A singular verb occurs when the persons or things in question are considered as one or as acting as one, or when they are related by membership in a class or category. A plural verb is possible when *group* refers to persons thought of as acting individually. The grammatical number of related pronouns and pronominal adjectives in turn agrees with that of the verb: *The group* (of persons) *is determined to retain its identity despite the merger. The group* (of persons) *were divided in their sympathies. This group* (of plants) *shows variation in coloring.*
group·er (gro͞o′pər) *n., pl.* **groupers** or **grouper.** Any of various often large fishes of the genera *Epinephelus, Mycteroperca,* and related genera, of warm seas. [Portuguese *garoupa,* probably from a native South American name.]
group·ing (gro͞o′pĭng) *n.* **1.** The act or process of arranging in groups. **2.** A collection of objects arranged in a group: *a well-planned grouping of lithographs.*
group insurance. Insurance covering members of a group under a single contract or under individual contracts, usually at reduced cost.
group·oid (gro͞o′poid′) *n. Algebra.* A nonempty set G together with a binary operation that associates with every pair of elements x, y in G a third element z in G denoted by xy or $x \cdot y$.
grouse¹ (grous) *n., pl.* **grouse.** Any of various plump birds of the family Tetraonidae, chiefly of the Northern Hemisphere, having mottled brown or grayish plumage. [Origin uncertain.]
grouse² (grous) *intr.v.* **groused, grousing, grouses.** *Informal.* To complain; to carp; to grumble. —*n.* A cause for complaint; grievance. [Origin unknown.] —**grous′er** *n.*
grout (grout) *n.* **1. a.** A thin mortar used to fill cracks and crevices between masonry. **b.** A finishing plaster. **2.** *Usually plural. Chiefly British.* Sediment; lees. **3. a.** *Plural.* Groats. **b.** Whole meal porridge. —*tr.v.* **grouted, grouting, grouts.** To fill or finish with grout. Often used with *in: grout in brickwork.* [Middle English *grout,* Old English *grūt.* See **ghrēu-** in Appendix.*] —**grout′er** *n.*
grove (grōv) *n.* A small wood or stand of trees lacking dense undergrowth. [Middle English *grove,* Old English *grāf*†.]
Grove (grōv), Sir **George.** 1820–1900. British musicologist and civil engineer.
grov·el (grŭv′əl, grŏv′-) *intr.v.* **-eled, -eling, -els.** Also *chiefly British* **-elled, -elling.** **1.** To humble oneself in a servile or demeaning manner; to cringe. **2.** To lie or creep in a prostrate position, often as a token of subservience or humility. **3.** To give oneself over to base pleasures. [Back-formation from obsolete *groveling,* prone, from Middle English *grufinge,* in prostrate position, from phrase *on grufe,* on the face, from Old Norse *ā grūfu* : *ā,* on + *grūfa*†, proneness.] —**grov′el·er** *n.* —**grov′el·ing·ly** *adv.*
Groves (grōvz), **Leslie Richard.** Born 1896. American army officer; military head of atomic-bomb project (1942–48).
grow (grō) *v.* **grew** (gro͞o), **grown** (grōn), **growing, grows.** —*intr.* **1.** To increase naturally in size by the addition of material through assimilation or accretion. **2. a.** To expand; to gain: *The business grew under new management.* **b.** To increase in amount or degree; become extended or intensified: *Her anxiety grew.* **3.** To develop and reach maturity. **4.** To be capable of growth; thrive; flourish: *plants that will grow in deep shade.* **5.** To become attached by or as if by the process of growth. **6.** To follow as a result of; originate. Usually used with *out: Their love grew out of friendship.* **7.** To develop by a gradual process or by degrees; become: *grow angry; grow cold; grow rich.* **8.** To come into existence; spring up: *Friendship grew between the two men.* —*tr.* **1.** To cause to grow; cultivate; raise: *grow tulips.* **2.** To let grow: *grow a beard.* **3.** To cover with a growth: *a path grown with moss.* —See Synonyms at **increase.** —**grow on** (or **upon**). To become more pleasurable, acceptable, or essential to: *a style that grows on one.* —**grow out of.** **1.** To outgrow. **2.** To result or develop from. —**grow up.** **1.** To reach maturity; become an adult. **2.** To come into being; develop. [Grow, grew, grown; Middle English *growen, grewe, growen,* Old English *grōwan, grēow, grōwen.* See **ghrē-** in Appendix.*]
growing pains. **1.** Pains in the limbs and joints of children, often mistakenly attributed to rapid growth. **2.** Problems arising in the initial stages of an enterprise.
growl (groul) *v.* **growled, growling, growls.** —*intr.* **1.** To utter a deep, guttural sound, as certain animals. **2.** To make a sound suggestive of this: *The wind growled.* **3.** To speak in an angry or surly manner: *"He growled out a blessing, which sounded gruffly as a curse"* (Thackeray). —*tr.* To utter by growling: *growl orders.* —*n.* **1.** The low, guttural, menacing sound made by a dog or other animal, usually in anger. **2.** A sound like this. **3.** A gruff, surly utterance. [Perhaps imitative.]
growl·er (grou′lər) *n.* **1.** One that growls. **2.** A small iceberg or floe ice. **3.** *Electricity.* An electromagnetic device with two poles, used for magnetizing, demagnetizing, and finding short-circuited coils.
grown (grōn). Past participle of **grow.** —*adj.* **1.** Having full growth; mature; adult. **2.** Produced or cultivated in a certain way or place. Used in combination: *home-grown vegetables.*
grown-up (grōn′ŭp′) *adj.* Characteristic of or suitable for an adult.
grown-up (grōn′ŭp′) *n.* An adult.
growth (grōth) *n.* **1. a.** The process of growing. **b.** A stage in the process of growing; size. **c.** Full development; maturity. **2.** Development from a lower or simpler to a higher or more complex form; evolution. **3.** An increase, as in size, number, value, or strength; extension or expansion: *population growth.* **4.** Something that grows or has grown: *a new growth of grass.* **5.** Broadly, an abnormal tissue formation. **6.** The result of growth; production; cultivation.
growth company. A company whose rate of growth exceeds that of the average in its field or the overall rate of economic growth.
Groz·ny (grôz′nē). A city and petroleum-producing center of the southwestern Russian S.F.S.R., 300 miles northwest of Baku. Population, 314,000.
grub (grŭb) *v.* **grubbed, grubbing, grubs.** —*tr.* **1.** To clear of roots and stumps by digging. **2.** To dig up by the roots. Often used with *up* or *out.* **3.** *Slang.* To provide with food. **4.** *Slang.* To obtain by importunity: *grub a cigarette.* —*intr.* **1.** To dig in the earth; dig underground. **2. a.** To search laboriously; rummage. **b.** To toil arduously; to drudge: *grub for a living.* **3.** *Slang.* To eat. —*n.* **1.** The thick, wormlike larva of certain beetles and other insects. Sometimes called "grubworm." **2.** A drudge. **3.** *Slang.* Food. [Middle English *grubben,* Old English *grybban* (unattested). See **ghrebh-²** in Appendix.*]
grub·ber (grŭb′ər) *n.* **1.** A person who grubs: *"The archaeologist is the last grubber among things mortal"* (Loren Eiseley). **2.** A **grub hoe** *(see).*
grub·by (grŭb′ē) *adj.* **-bier, -biest.** **1.** Dirty; unkempt. **2.** Infested with grubs. **3.** Contemptible; beggarly. —**grub′bi·ly** *adv.* —**grub′bi·ness** *n.*
grub hoe. A heavy hoe for grubbing up roots. Also called "grubbing hoe," "grubber."
grub·stake (grŭb′stāk′) *n.* Supplies or funds advanced to a

ă pat/ā pay/âr care/ä father/b bib/ch church/d deed/ĕ pet/ē be/f fife/g gag/h hat/hw which/ĭ pit/ī pie/îr pier/j judge/k kick/l lid, needle/m mum/n no, sudden/ng thing/ŏ pot/ō toe/ô paw, for/oi noise/ou out/o͝o took/o͞o boot/p pop/r roar/s sauce/sh ship, dish/

mining prospector or a person starting a business, in return for a promised share of the profits. —*tr.v.* **grubstaked, -staking, -stakes.** To supply with a grubstake. [GRUB (food) + STAKE (bet).] —**grub′stak′er** *n.*

Grub Street (grŭb). The world of impoverished writers and literary hacks. [From *Grub Street,* London, now Milton Street, formerly inhabited by such writers.]

grub·street (grŭb′strēt′) *adj.* Turned out by hacks; poor; inferior: *a shelf of grubstreet novels.*

grudge (grŭj) *tr.v.* **grudged, grudging, grudges.** To be reluctant to give or admit: *"His nature grudged thinking, for it crippled his speed in action"* (T.E. Lawrence). —*n.* **1.** A deep-seated feeling of resentment or rancor provoked by some incident or situation. **2.** The provocation causing such a feeling. [Middle English *gruggen,* variant of *grutchen,* from Old French *grouchier, groncier,* probably from Middle High German *grunzen,* to grunt, from Old High German *grunnizōn.* See **gru-** in Appendix.*] —**grudg′er** *n.* —**grudg′ing·ly** *adv.*

gru·el (grōō′əl) *n.* **1.** A thin, watery porridge. **2.** *Chiefly British.* Severe punishment. —*tr.v.* **grueled, -eling, -els.** Also *chiefly British* **-elled, -elling. 1.** To exhaust and disable. **2.** To punish. [Middle English *grewel,* from Old French *gruel,* diminutive of *gru,* groats, oatmeal, from Frankish *grūt* (unattested). See **ghrēu-** in Appendix.*]

gru·el·ing (grōō′ə-lĭng) *adj.* Demanding and exhausting.

grue·some (grōō′səm) *adj.* Also **grew·some.** Causing horror and repugnance; frightful and shocking: *"The place was not so gruesome as last night, but oh, how utterly mean-looking when the sunshine streamed in"* (Bram Stoker). See Synonyms at **ghastly.** [From obsolete *grue,* to shiver, Middle English *gruen,* probably from Middle Dutch *grūwen.* See **ghrēu-** in Appendix.*] —**grue′some·ly** *adv.* —**grue′some·ness** *n.*

gruff (grŭf) *adj.* **gruffer, gruffest.** Brusque and stern in manner, voice, or appearance; harsh. [Dutch *grof,* from Middle Dutch. See **kreup-** in Appendix.*] —**gruff′ly** *adv.* —**gruff′ness** *n.*

Synonyms: *gruff, brusque, blunt, bluff, curt, crusty.* These adjectives mean abrupt and sometimes markedly impolite in manner or speech. *Gruff* implies roughness of manner and often a forbidding aspect and harsh speech, but does not necessarily suggest intentional rudeness. *Brusque* emphasizes abruptness of manner and often lack of civility. *Blunt* stresses utter frankness and usually a disconcerting directness of speech. *Bluff* refers to unpolished, unceremonious manner but usually implies good nature. *Curt* refers to shortness of speech and usually implies calculated rudeness. *Crusty* emphasizes exterior qualities such as forbidding countenance and rough manner, but does not necessarily imply meanness.

grum (grŭm) *adj.* **grummer, grummest.** Morose; sullen; glum. [Perhaps blend of GRIM and GLUM.]

grum·ble (grŭm′bəl) *v.* **-bled, -bling, -bles.** —*intr.* **1.** To mumble in discontent: *"The governed will always find something to grumble about"* (Crane Brinton). **2.** To rumble or growl. —*tr.* To express in a grumbling, discontented manner. —*n.* **1.** A grumbling utterance. **2.** A rumble. [Frequentative of Middle English *grummen,* to grumble, perhaps from Middle Dutch *grommen.* See **ghrem-** in Appendix.*] —**grum′bler** *n.* —**grum′bling·ly** *adv.* —**grum′bly** *adj.*

grum·met (grŭm′ĭt) *n.* A **grommet** *(see).*

gru·mous (grōō′məs) *adj.* Also **gru·mose** (-mōs′). *Botany.* Formed of or consisting of clustered grains, as certain roots. [From Latin *grūmus*†, little heap of earth.]

grump (grŭmp) *n.* **1.** *Plural.* A fit of ill temper. **2.** A cranky, complaining person. [Probably akin to GRUMBLE.]

grump·y (grŭm′pē) *adj.* **-ier, -iest.** Fretful and peevish; irritable; cranky. [From dialectal *grump,* ill-tempered, perhaps imitative of noises associated with ill temper.] —**grump′i·ly** *adv.* —**grump′i·ness** *n.*

Grü·ne·wald (grü′nə-vält′), **Matthias.** 1480?–1528? German painter.

grun·ion (grŭn′yən) *n.* A small fish, *Leuresthes tenuis,* of coastal waters of California and Mexico, that spawns along beaches during high spring tides at the time of the full moon. [Perhaps from Spanish *gruñón,* grumbler, from *gruñir,* to grumble, grunt, from Latin *grunnire.* See **gru-** in Appendix.*]

grunt (grŭnt) *v.* **grunted, grunting, grunts.** —*intr.* **1.** To utter a deep, guttural sound, as does a hog. **2.** To utter a similar sound, as in disgust, annoyance, indifference, strain, or effort: *"One of the old men grunted approval and smiled a toothless smile"* (Ivan Gold). —*tr.* To utter or express with a grunt. —*n.* **1.** A deep, guttural sound. **2.** Any of various chiefly tropical marine fishes of the genus *Haemulon* and related genera, that produce grunting sounds. [Middle English *grunten,* Old English *grunnettan,* probably frequentative of *grunnian.* See **gru-** in Appendix.*] —**grunt′ing·ly** *adv.*

Grus (grŭs) *n.* A constellation in the Southern Hemisphere near Indus and Phoenix. [New Latin, from Latin *grūs,* crane. See **ger-**[4] in Appendix.*]

Gru·yère (grōō-yâr′, grē-; *French* grü-yâr′) *n.* A pale-yellow, firm-textured cheese, with or without holes, made from whole milk. Also called "Gruyère cheese." [Originally made in *Gruyère,* a district in Switzerland.]

Gru·zi·ya. The Russian name for **Georgia.**

gr. wt. gross weight.

gry·phon. Variant of **griffin.**

GS, G.S. general staff.

GSA General Services Administration.

G.S.A. Girl Scouts of America.

GSC general staff corps.

GSO general staff officer.

G-string (jē′strĭng′) *n.* **1.** A narrow loincloth supported by a waistband; a breechcloth. **2.** A similar often decorative garment worn especially by stripteasers. **3.** A string tuned to G on a musical instrument.

G-suit (jē′sōōt′) *n.* A flight garment designed to counteract the effects of high acceleration by exerting pressure on parts of the body below the chest. [*G,* short for GRAVITY.]

GSW Airport code for Fort Worth, Texas.

gt. 1. gilt. **2.** great. **3.** *Medicine.* gutta.

G.T.C. good till canceled.

gtd. guaranteed.

GTS gas turbine ship.

GU 1. genitourinary. **2.** Guam (with Zip Code).

G.U. genitourinary.

GUA Airport code for Guatemala City, Guatemala.

gua·ca·mo·le (gwä′kə-mō′lē) *n.* Also **gua·cha·mo·le. 1.** Any of a variety of Mexican or South American salads featuring avocado. **2.** A spread of mashed avocado, tomato pulp, mayonnaise, and seasoning. [Mexican Spanish, from Nahuatl *ahuacamolli,* "avocado sauce" : *ahuacatl,* AVOCADO + *molli,* sauce.]

gua·cha·ro (gwä′chä-rō′) *n., pl.* **-ros.** A nocturnal bird, *Steatornis caripensis,* of tropical America, the young having a layer of fat that yields an oil used in cooking and for lighting. Also called "oilbird." [Spanish *guácharo,* from *guacho,* orphan, little bird, from Quechua *wáhcha,* diminutive of *wah,* strange.]

gua·co (gwä′kō) *n., pl.* **-cos.** Any of several tropical American plants used as an antidote against snakebite; especially, *Mikania guaco* or *Aristolochia serpentina.* [American Spanish, from a native word in South America.]

Gua·da·la·ja·ra (gwŏd′l-ə-här′ə; *Spanish* gwä′thä-lä-hä′rä). **1.** The capital of Jalisco, west-central Mexico, the center of a mining, industrial, and agricultural area. Population, 978,000. **2.** A city of central Spain, 35 miles northeast of Madrid, near the site of a Loyalist victory over Italian forces (1937) in the Spanish Civil War. Population, 20,000.

Gua·dal·ca·nal (gwŏd′l-kə-năl′). An island, 2,509 square miles in area, in the southeastern Solomon group of the western Pacific; occupied by Japanese forces in July 1942, and recaptured by the Allies in February 1943, after a series of major battles.

Gua·dal·qui·vir (gwŏd′l-kwĭv′ər; *Spanish* gwä′thäl-kē-vĭr′). A river rising in southern Spain and flowing 374 miles west and southwest to the Gulf of Cádiz.

Gua·da·lu·pe Hi·dal·go (gwä′thä-lōō′pā ē-thäl′gō). A former city in central Mexico, now constituting part of Gustavo A. Madero City.

Gua·da·lu·pe Mountains (gwŏd′l-ōōp′, gwŏd′l-ōō′pē, gôd′-). *Spanish* **Sier·ra de Gua·da·lu·pe** (syĕr′rä thā gwä′thä-lōō′pä). A range in southern New Mexico and western Texas. Highest elevation, Guadalupe Peak (8,751 feet) in western Texas; also the highest elevation of this state.

Gua·da·lu·pe River (gwŏd′l-ōōp′, gwŏd′l-ōō′pē, gôd′-). A river rising in southeastern Texas and flowing 300 miles southeast to the San Antonio River.

Gua·dar·ra·ma, Sier·ra de. See **Sierra de Guadarrama.**

Gua·de·loupe (gwŏd′l-ōōp′, gôd′-; *French* gwȧd-lōōp′). Two islands in the West Indies, Basse-Terre (or Guadeloupe proper) and Grande-Terre, and their adjacent island dependencies, occupying 687 square miles and constituting an Overseas Department of France. Population, 295,000. Administrative center, Basse-Terre.

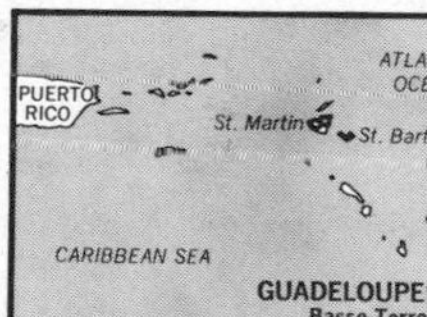

Guadeloupe

Gua·di·a·na (gwä′dē-ä′nə, -ăn′ə; *Spanish* gwä-thyä′nä; *Portuguese* gwä′dē-ä′nä). A river rising in south-central Spain and flowing 510 miles west, then south, to form sections of the Spanish-Portuguese border and empty into the Gulf of Cádiz.

guai·a·col (gwī′ə-kôl′, -kōl′) *n.* A yellowish, oily, aromatic liquid, $C_7H_8O_2$, used chiefly as an expectorant and a local anesthetic. [GUAIAC(UM) + -OL.]

guai·a·cum (gwī′ə-kəm) *n.* Also **guai·ac** (-ăk′) (for sense 3). **1.** A tree of the genus *Guaiacum;* a lignum vitae. **2.** The wood of such a tree. **3.** A greenish-brown resin obtained from the lignum vitae, and used medicinally and in varnishes. [New Latin, from Spanish *guayacan,* from Taino.]

Guam (gwŏm). The largest (216 square miles) of the Mariana Islands in the western Pacific; a U.S. possession seized by the Japanese (1941) and retaken by the United States (1944) in World War II. Population, 72,000. Capital, Agana.

guan (gwän) *n.* Any of several birds of the genus *Penelope* and related genera, of the jungles of tropical America, related to and resembling the curassows. [American Spanish, from a native name in South America.]

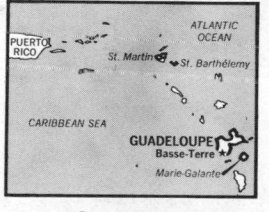

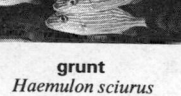

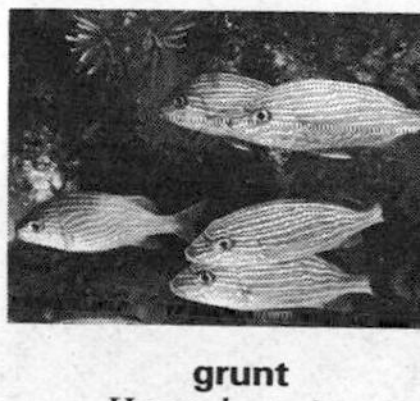
grunt
Haemulon sciurus

Gua·na·ba·ra (gwä′nə-vär′ə). A state of southeast-central Brazil, 451 square miles in area. Population, 3,857,000. Capital, Rio de Janeiro.

Gua·na·ba·ra Bay (gwä′nə-vär′ə). An inlet of the Atlantic in southeastern Guanabara, Brazil, with Rio de Janeiro on its southwestern shore.

gua·na·co (gwə-nä′kō) *n., pl.* **-cos.** A brownish South American mammal, *Lama guanicoe,* related to and resembling the domesticated llama. [Spanish, from Quechua *huanaco.*]

Gua·na·jua·to (gwä′nä-hwä′tō). **1.** A state of central Mexico, 11,804 square miles in area. Population, 1,735,000. **2.** The capital of this state, 170 miles northwest of Mexico City. Population, 28,000.

gua·ni·dine (gwä′nə-dēn′) *n.* A strong crystalline base, CH_5N_3, found in plant and animal tissues and used for organic syntheses. [GUAN(INE) + -ID(E) + -INE.]

gua·nine (gwä′nēn′) *n.* A purine, $C_5H_5N_5O$, that is a constituent

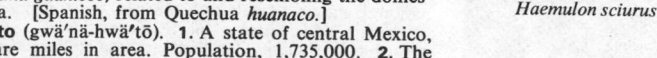

t tight/th thin, path/*th* this, bathe/ŭ cut/ûr urge/v valve/w with/y yes/z zebra, size/zh vision/ə about, item, edible, gallop, circus/ à *Fr.* ami/œ *Fr.* feu, *Ger.* schön/ü *Fr.* tu, *Ger.* über/KH *Ger.* ich, *Scot.* loch/N *Fr.* bon. ***Follows main vocabulary. †Of obscure origin.**

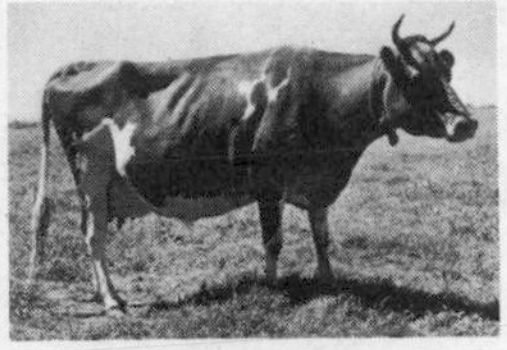

Guernsey[2]

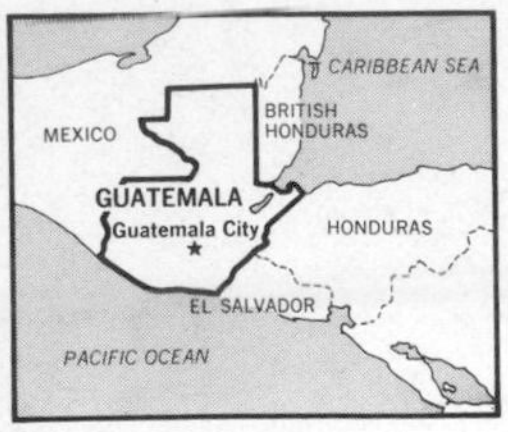

Guatemala

of both ribonucleic and deoxyribonucleic acids. [From GUANO, in which it is found.]

gua·no (gwä′nō) *n.* **1.** A substance composed chiefly of the dung of sea birds or bats, accumulated along certain coastal areas or in caves, and used as fertilizer. **2.** A similar substance, as one made from waste products of canneries. [Spanish, from Quechua *huanu*, dung.]

Guan·tá·na·mo (gwän-tä′nə-mō′). A city in an agricultural region of southeastern Cuba. Population, 87,000.

Guan·tá·na·mo Bay (gwän-tä′nə-mō′). An inlet of the Caribbean in southeastern Cuba, eight miles south of Guantánamo; the site of a U.S. naval base.

Gua·po·ré (gwä-pô-rā′). **1.** A river of central South America, rising in western Mato Grosso, Brazil, and flowing 750 miles northwest to form part of the Brazil-Bolivia boundary on its course and then join the Mamoré. Also called "Iténez." **2.** The former name for **Rondônia.**

guar. guaranteed.

gua·ra·ni (gwär′ə-nē′) *n., pl.* **guarani** or **-nis.** **1.** The basic monetary unit of Paraguay, equal to 100 centimos. See table of exchange rates at **currency.** **2.** A note worth one guarani. [Spanish *guaraní*, GUARANI.]

Gua·ra·ni (gwär′ə-nē′) *n., pl.* **-nis** or **Guarani.** **1.** A Tupi-Guaranian group of South American Indians of Paraguay, Bolivia, and southern Brazil. **2.** A member of one of these tribes. **3.** The Tupian language spoken by these tribes. [Spanish *guaraní*, a native tribal name.]

guar·an·tee (găr′ən-tē′) *n.* **1.** A guarantor. **2.** A guaranty. **3.** An agreement by which one person assures another of the enjoyment or possession of something. **4.** Something given or held as security. —*tr.v.* **guaranteed, -teeing, -tees.** **1.** To assume responsibility for the debt, default, or miscarriage of; vouch for. **2.** To assume responsibility for the quality or execution of. **3.** To undertake to accomplish or secure something: *He guaranteed to free the captives.* **4.** To furnish security for. **5.** To express or declare with conviction. [Earlier *garante*, perhaps from Spanish, warrant, from Frankish *wārjan* (unattested), to vouch for the truth of. See **wer-**[5] in Appendix.*]

guar·an·tor (găr′ən-tər, -tôr′) *n.* **1.** One that makes or gives a guarantee. **2.** One that makes or gives a guaranty.

guar·an·ty (găr′ən-tē) *n., pl.* **-ties.** **1.** An agreement by which one person assumes the responsibility of assuring payment or fulfillment of another's debts or obligations. **2.** That which guarantees something: *His record is a guaranty of his honesty.* **3.** Anything held or provided as security for the execution, completion, or existence of something. **4.** The act of providing such security. **5.** A guarantor. —*tr.v.* **guarantied, -tying, -ties.** To guarantee. [Old French *garantie*, from *garant*, warrant, from Frankish *wārjan* (unattested), to vouch for the truth of, GUARANTEE.]

guard (gärd) *v.* **guarded, guarding, guards.** —*tr.* **1.** To protect from harm; watch over; defend. **2.** To watch over to prevent escape, violence, or indiscretion; keep in check. **3.** To keep watch at (a door or gate, for example) to supervise entries and exits. **4.** To supply with proper controls and checks; safeguard. **5.** To furnish (a device or object) with a protective piece. **6.** *Archaic.* To escort. —*intr.* To take precautions; secure. Used with *against*: *guard against infection.* —See Synonyms at **defend.** —*n.* **1.** One that guards, keeps watch over, or protects. **2.** An individual or a group that stands watch or acts as a sentinel. **3.** One who supervises prisoners. **4.** A body of persons who form an escort or perform drill exhibitions on ceremonial occasions: *an honor guard.* **5.** *British.* A railway employee in charge of a train. **6.** *Football.* **a.** One of the two players on either side of the center. **b.** The position played by either player. **7.** *Basketball.* Either of the two players who initiate plays from the center of the court. **8.** A defensive position or stance in certain sports such as boxing or fencing. **9.** The act, condition, or duty of guarding: *"Have you had quiet guard?"* (Shakespeare). **10.** Something that gives protection; a safeguard; defense: *a guard against tooth decay.* **11.** Any device or apparatus that prevents injury, damage, or loss. **12.** An attachment or covering put on a machine to protect the operator. **13.** A chain or band used to help safeguard a thing, as a watch or bracelet, from loss. **14.** A ring used to prevent a more valuable ring from sliding off the finger. **15.** The portion of the hilt of a sword or of the handle of a knife or fork that protects the hand. **16.** The metal apparatus that encircles and guards the trigger of a firearm. —**mount guard.** To go on duty, as a sentinel. —**off (one's) guard.** Unprepared; not alert. —**on (one's) guard.** Alert and watchful; cautious. —**stand guard.** **1.** To act as a sentinel. **2.** To keep watch over. —*adj.* Of, relating to, or acting as a guard: *guard duty.* [As verb, Middle English *garden*, from Old French *garder*, *guarder*, from Germanic. See **wer-**[4] in Appendix.* As noun, Middle English, from Old French *garde*, from *garder*, to guard.] —**guard′er** *n.*

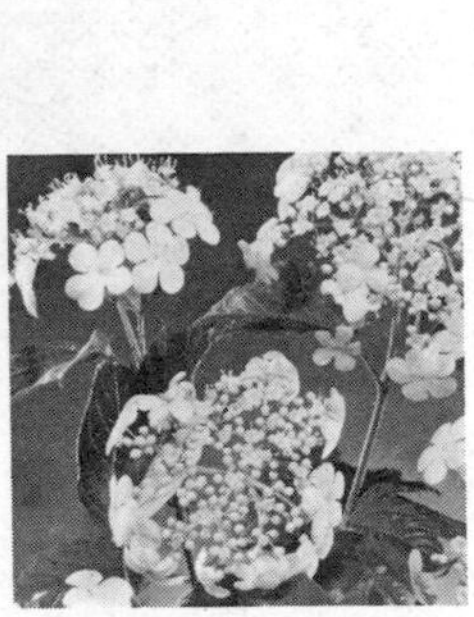

guelder rose

Guar·da·fui, Cape (gwär′də-fwē′). *Arabic* **Ras As·sir** (räs′ ä-sîr′). A promontory of northeastern Somalia, extending into the Indian Ocean at the southern entrance to the Gulf of Aden.

guar·dant (gär′dənt) *adj.* Also **gar·dant.** *Heraldry.* Indicating an animal shown in full face, turned toward the viewer. [Old French *gardant*, present participle of *garder*, to GUARD.]

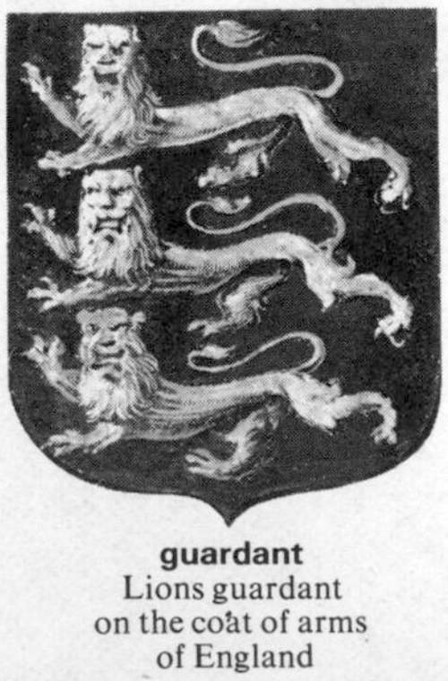

guardant
Lions guardant on the coat of arms of England

guard cell. *Botany.* One of the paired epidermal cells that control the opening and closing of a stoma in plant tissue.

guard·ed (gär′dĭd) *adj.* **1.** Kept safe; protected; defended. **2.** Held in check; watched over; supervised. **3.** Cautious; restrained; prudent: *guarded words.*

guard hair. Any of the coarse hairs covering the underfur of certain mammals.

guard·house (gärd′hous′) *n.* **1.** A building that accommodates a military guard. **2.** A military detention house for personnel guilty of minor offenses.

guard·i·an (gär′dē-ən) *n.* **1.** One who guards, protects, or defends. **2.** *Law.* A person who is legally responsible for the care and management of the person or property of one who is considered by law to be incompetent to manage his own affairs, as a child during its minority. **3.** A superior in a Franciscan convent. [Middle English *gardein*, from Norman French, variant of Old French *gardien*, from *garder*, to GUARD.] —**guard′i·an·ship′** *n.*

guard·rail (gärd′rāl′) *n.* **1.** A protective rail. **2.** An inner rail placed along the main rail of a railroad track at curves and crossings to prevent a train from jumping the tracks.

guard·room (gärd′ro͞om′, -ro͝om′) *n.* **1.** A room used by guards on duty. **2.** A room in which prisoners are confined.

guards·man (gärdz′mən) *n., pl.* **-men** (-mĭn). **1.** One who acts as a guard. **2. a.** A member of the U.S. National Guard. **b.** *British.* A soldier in a regiment of household guards.

Guá·ri·co (gwär′ĭ-kō′). A river of Venezuela, rising near Valencia and flowing 300 miles east and south to join the Apure.

Guar·nie·ri (gwär-nyâr′ē), **Andrea.** Also **Guar·ne·ri** (-nâr′ē). 1626–1698. With his sons **Giuseppe** (1666–1739) and **Pietro** (1655–1728), Italian violinmakers.

Guar·ne·ri·us (gwär-nâr′ē-əs, -nîr′ē-əs) *n.* One of the violins of superlative tone made by members of the Guarnieri family in the 17th and 18th centuries.

Gua·te·ma·la (gwä′tə-mä′lə). *Abbr.* **Guat.** **1.** A republic occupying 42,042 square miles in northern Central America, with coastlines on the Pacific Ocean and the Caribbean Sea. Population, 4,343,000. **2.** Also **Gua·te·ma·la City.** The capital of this republic, located in the south-central part of the country. Population, 573,000. —**Gua′te·ma′lan** *adj.* & *n.*

gua·va (gwä′və) *n.* **1.** Any of various tropical American shrubs and trees of the genus *Psidium*; especially, *P. guajava*, having white flowers and edible fruit. **2.** The fruit of this tree, having a yellow rind and pink flesh, and used for jellies and preserves. [Spanish *guava*, *guayaba*, of South American Indian origin.]

Gua·via·re (gwä-vyä′rā). A river of central and eastern Colombia, rising in the Andes and flowing 650 miles generally east to the Orinoco at the Colombia-Venezuela boundary.

Gua·ya·na. The Spanish name for **Guiana.**

Gua·ya·quil (gwī′ə-kēl′). Officially, Santiago de Guayaquil. The largest city and a seaport of Ecuador, located on the Guayas River. Population, 506,000.

Gua·ya·quil, Gulf of (gwī′ə-kēl′). An inlet of the Pacific in southwestern Ecuador, 45 miles south of Guayaquil.

Gua·yas (gwī′əs). A river of west-central Ecuador, rising in the Andes and flowing 100 miles southwest into the Gulf of Guayaquil.

gua·yu·le (gwī-o͞o′lē) *n.* A woody plant or shrub, *Parthenium argentatum*, of the southwestern United States and Mexico, having sap sometimes used as a source of rubber. [American Spanish, from Nahuatl *cuauhuli* : *cuahuitl*, tree + *uli*, gum.]

gu·ber·na·to·ri·al (go͞o′bər-nə-tôr′ē-əl, -tōr′ē-əl, gyo͞o′-) *adj.* Of or relating to a governor. [From Late Latin *gubernātōrius*, from Latin *gubernātor*, GOVERNOR.]

gu·ber·ni·ya (go͞o-bĕr′nē-ə) *n.* **1.** An administrative subdivision of a soviet in the Soviet Union. **2.** An administrative division equivalent to a province in Russia prior to 1917. [Russian, province, perhaps from Polish *gubernja*, from Latin *gubernāre*, GOVERN.]

guck (gŭk, go͝ok) *n. Slang.* A messy substance, such as sludge.

gudg·eon[1] (gŭj′ən) *n.* **1.** A small Eurasian freshwater fish, *Gobio gobio.* **2.** Any of various similar fishes. **3.** An enticement; a bait. **4.** *Slang.* Someone who is easily duped; a gullible person. —*tr.v.* **gudgeoned, -eoning, -eons.** *Slang.* To dupe; to cheat. [Middle English *gojoun*, from Old French *goujon*, from Latin *gōbiō*, *gōbius*, GOBY.]

gudg·eon[2] (gŭj′ən) *n.* **1.** A metal pivot or journal at the end of a shaft or axle, around which a wheel or other device turns. **2.** The socket of a hinge into which the pin fits. **3.** *Nautical.* The socket for the pintle of a rudder. **4.** A metal pin that joins two pieces of stone. [Middle English *gudyon*, from Old French *goujon*, diminutive of *gouge*, GOUGE (chisel).]

gudgeon pin. A **wrist pin** *(see).*

Gud·run (go͝od′ro͞on′). Also **Guth·run** (go͝oth′-), **Kud·run** (ko͝od′-). **1.** The Danish heroine of the 13th-century German epic *Gudrun Lied.* **2.** The daughter of the king of the Nibelungs and wife of Sigurd in the *Volsunga Saga.*

Guel·der·land. See **Gelderland.**

guel·der rose (gĕl′dər). A shrub, *Viburnum opulus*, native to Eurasia, having clusters of white flowers and small red fruit. Also called "cranberry tree." [Originally grown in GELDERLAND.]

Guel·ders. See **Gelderland.**

Guelph[1] (gwĕlf). A city and manufacturing center of southeastern Ontario, Canada. Population, 40,000.

Guelph[2] (gwĕlf) *n.* Also **Guelf.** **1.** A member of a strong faction in medieval Italy that supported the power of the pope and the city-states in a struggle against the German emperors and the Ghibellines. **2.** A member of a German ducal family established in the ninth century A.D. —**Guelph′ism′** *n.*

Guen·e·vere. Variant of **Guinevere.**

gue·non (gə-nōn′; *French* gə-nôN′) *n.* Any of various African monkeys of the genus *Cercopithecus*, having long hind legs and a long tail. [French *guenon*†.]

guer·don (gûrd′n) *n. Poetic.* A reward; requital. —*tr.v.* **guerdoned, -doning, -dons.** *Poetic.* To reward. [Middle English, from Old French, from Medieval Latin *widerdōnum*, alteration (influenced by Latin *dōnum*, gift) of Old High German *widarlōn* : *widar*, again (see **wi-** in Appendix*) + *lōn*, reward, payment (see **lāu-** in Appendix*).]

Gue·rick·e (gä′rĭ-kə), **Otto von.** 1602–1686. German physicist; studied air pressure and friction.

Guer·ni·ca (gwâr′nĭ-kə; *Spanish* gĕr-nē′kä). Also **Guer·ni·ca y Lu·no** (gĕr-nē′kä ē lo͞o′nō). A town in north-central Spain, 12 miles northeast of Bilbao; destroyed during the Spanish Civil War by German and Italian aircraft in the first mass bombing of an urban community (1937). Population, 5,000.

guern·sey (gûrn′zē) *n., pl.* **-seys.** A snug knitted wool shirt often worn by seamen. [First worn by seamen on the island of GUERNSEY.]

Guern·sey¹ (gûrn′zē). An island of the Channel group, occupying 25 square miles in the southwest-central English Channel, and constituting with its adjacent island dependencies a bailiwick of England. Population, 45,000. Capital, St. Peter Port.

Guern·sey² (gûrn′zē) *n., pl.* **-seys.** One of a breed of brown and white dairy cattle originally developed on the Isle of Guernsey.

Guer·re·ro (gə-râr′ō; *Spanish* gĕr-rĕ′rō). A state, 24,885 square miles in area, of southwestern Mexico. Population, 1,187,000. Capital, Chilpancingo.

guer·ril·la, gue·ril·la (gə-rĭl′ə) *n.* **1.** A member of the military forces of a patriotic or revolutionary movement that seeks to immobilize and isolate the superior forces of an occupying enemy, strategically by means of the political mobilization of the local peasant population and tactically by means of sudden acts of harassment executed by small bands recruited in part from the able-bodied section of this population. **2.** *Archaic.* A war fought in accordance with these tactics. —*adj.* Of or relating to guerrillas or their methods of fighting: *guerrilla warfare.* [Spanish *guerrilla*, diminutive of *guerra*, war, from Germanic. See **wers-** in Appendix.*]

guess (gĕs) *v.* **guessed, guessing, guesses.** —*tr.* **1. a.** To predict (a result or event) without sufficient information. **b.** To assume, presume, or assert (a fact) without sufficient information. **2.** To estimate correctly. **3.** To suppose; to judge. —*intr.* **1.** To make a conjecture. Often used with *at: We only guessed at his motives.* **2.** To make a correct guess. —See Synonyms at **conjecture.** —*n.* **1.** An act or instance of guessing. **2.** A conjecture arrived at by guessing. [Middle English *gessen*, probably from Scandinavian, akin to Old Swedish and Danish *gisse*. See **ghend-** in Appendix.*] —**guess′er** *n.*

guess·work (gĕs′wûrk′) *n.* **1.** The process of making guesses. **2.** An instance of inference by guessing.

guest (gĕst) *n.* **1.** A recipient of hospitality at the home or table of another. **2.** One to whom some entertainment or service is extended gratuitously by an establishment. **3.** A visitor such as a foreign dignitary to whom the hospitality of an institution, municipality, or government has been extended. **4.** The patron of a restaurant, hotel, boarding-house, or the like. **5.** A contestant, performer, or other person featured as a visiting participant in a program. **6.** *Zoology.* A commensal organism; especially, an insect that lives in the nest or burrow of another species. —*v.* **guested, guesting, guests.** *Rare.* —*tr.* To entertain as one's guest. —*intr.* To be a guest. [Middle English *gest*, from Old Norse *gestr*. See **ghos-ti-** in Appendix.*]

guest rope. *Nautical.* **1.** An extra line used with the towline to steady a ship being towed. **2.** A rope dropped over the side of a ship for steadying or securing a smaller boat coming alongside. Also called "guess rope."

guff (gŭf) *n. Slang.* Foolish talk; nonsense. [Perhaps imitative.]

guf·faw (gə-fô′) *n.* A hearty or coarse burst of laughter. —*intr.v.* **guffawed, -fawing, -faws.** To laugh explosively. [Imitative.]

Gug·gen·heim (go͝og′ən-hīm′), **Daniel.** 1856–1930. American industrialist and philanthropist.

Gui·an·a (gē-ăn′ə, -ä′nə). *Spanish* **Gua·ya·na** (gwä-yä′nä). A region of northeastern South America bordered by the Orinoco, Negro, and Amazon rivers and the Atlantic Ocean, and including southeastern Venezuela, part of northern Brazil, and French Guiana, Surinam, and Guyana.

Gui·an·a Highlands (gē-ăn′ə, -ä′nə). A region of mountainous tableland extending from southern and southeastern Venezuela into Guyana and part of northern Brazil.

gui·dance (gīd′ns) *n.* **1.** An act or instance of guiding. **2.** Counseling as on vocational, educational, or marital problems. **3.** Any of various processes or techniques by which missiles carrying sensing or information-processing equipment are guided in flight.

guide (gīd) *n. Abbr.* **g. 1.** One who shows the way by leading, directing, or advising, usually by reason of his greater experience with the course to be pursued. **2.** A person employed to guide a tour, group, or the like. **3. a.** Any sign or mark that serves to direct. **b.** An example, model, or criterion of accuracy to be followed. **4. a.** A guidebook. **b.** A book or manual that serves to instruct or to direct one's thinking. **5.** Any device, such as a ruler, line, ring, tab, or bar, that acts as an indicator or that regulates the motion of one's hand, a tool, or a machine part. **6.** A soldier stationed at the right or left of a column to control the alignment of the marchers, show the direction, or mark the point of pivot. —*v.* **guided, guiding, guides.** —*tr.* **1.** To show the way to; to conduct; lead; direct. **2.** To direct the course of; to steer: *guide a plank through a saw.* **3.** To manage the affairs of; govern. **4.** To influence the conduct or opinions of; be a criterion for or motive of. —*intr.* To serve as a guide. [Middle English *g(u)ide*, from Old French, from Old Provençal *guida*, from *guidar*, to show the way, from Frankish *wītan* (unattested). See **weid-** in Appendix.*] —**guid′a·ble** *adj.* —**guid′er** *n.*

guide·board (gīd′bôrd′, -bōrd′) *n.* A sign on a guidepost giving directions to travelers, as at a crossroads.

guide·book (gīd′bo͝ok′) *n.* A handbook of information for travelers, tourists, or students.

guide·line (gīd′līn′) *n.* **1.** A mark used to orient lettering, a drawing, or the like. **2.** A statement of policy by a person or group having authority over an activity.

guided missile. Any missile capable of being guided while it is in flight. Also called "robot bomb." Compare **ballistic missile.**

guide·post (gīd′pōst′) *n.* **1.** A post with a directional sign placed at an intersection or fork in a road. **2.** One that gives direction.

guide rope. A rope fastened to another rope that is lifting a load, to guide the rope and steady the load.

guide·word (gīd′wûrd′) *n. Printing.* A catchword.

Gui·do d'A·rez·zo (gwē′dō dä-rāt′tsō). A.D. 995?–1050? Benedictine monk and musical theorist.

gui·don (gī′dŏn′, gīd′n) *n. Military.* **1.** A small flag or pennant, often with a forked end, carried as a standard by a regiment or other military unit. **2.** The soldier bearing this standard. [French, from Italian *guidone*, from *guida*, guide, from Old Provençal. See **guide.**]

Gui·enne (gē-ĕn′). *French* **Guy·enne** (gwē-yĕn′). A region and former province of southwest-central France, with its capital in Bordeaux.

guild (gĭld) *n.* Also **gild. 1.** An association or corporation of persons of the same trade, pursuits, or interests formed for their mutual aid and protection, the maintenance of standards, or the furtherance of some purpose; especially, in medieval times, a society of merchants or artisans. **2.** *Ecology.* One of four groups of plants having a characteristic mode of existence that involves some dependence upon other plant life: the lianas, epiphytes, saprophytes, and parasites. [Middle English *gilde*, from Old Norse *gildi*, payment, fraternity, contribution. See **ghelt-** in Appendix.*]

guil·der (gĭl′dər) *n.* Also **gild·er.** *Abbr.* **G., g., gld. 1.** The basic monetary unit of the Netherlands, Surinam, and the Netherlands Antilles, equal to 100 cents. See table of exchange rates at **currency. 2.** A coin worth one guilder. Also called "gulden," "florin." [Alteration of Dutch *gulden*, GULDEN.]

Guild·ford (gĭl′fərd). The county seat of Surrey, England, located in the southwest, 28 miles southwest of London. Population, 54,000.

guild·hall (gĭld′hôl′) *n.* **1.** The meeting hall of a guild. **2. a.** A town hall. **b.** *Capital* **G.** The meeting hall of the Corporation of the City of London.

guilds·man (gĭldz′mən) *n., pl.* **-men** (-mĭn). A member of a guild.

guild socialism. A type of socialism formerly advocated in England in which industry would be owned by the state but managed by a council of workers.

guile (gīl) *n.* **1.** Insidious, treacherous cunning; craftiness; dissimulation. **2.** *Obsolete.* A trick; stratagem. —See Synonyms at **artifice.** —*tr.v.* **guiled, guiling, guiles.** *Archaic.* To beguile; deceive. [Middle English *gile*, from Old French *guile*, from Germanic, akin to Old English *wigle*, divination, sorcery. See **weik-²** in Appendix.*]

guile·ful (gīl′fəl) *adj.* Full of guile; artfully deceitful; crafty; treacherous. See Synonyms at **sly.** —**guile′ful·ly** *adv.* —**guile′ful·ness** *n.*

guile·less (gīl′lĭs) *adj.* Free of guile; simple; artless. See Synonyms at **naive.** —**guile′less·ly** *adv.* —**guile′less·ness** *n.*

Guil·laume (gē-yōm′), **Charles Édouard.** 1861–1938. Swiss-born French physicist; worked on weights and measures.

guil·le·mot (gĭl′ə-mŏt′) *n.* **1.** Any of several small sea birds of the genus *Cepphus*, of northern regions, having black plumage with white markings. **2.** *British.* A related bird, the murre. [French, diminutive of *Guillaume*, WILLIAM.]

guil·loche (gĭ-lōsh′, gē-yōsh′) *n. Architecture.* An ornamental border formed of two or more bands interlaced in such a way as to repeat a design. [French *guillochis*, from *guillocher*, to decorate with guilloche, perhaps from Italian *ghiocciare*, dialectal variant of *gocciare*, to drip, trickle, from *goccia*, drop, from Latin *gutta*. See **gout.**]

guil·lo·tine (gĭl′ə-tēn′, gē′ə-) *n.* **1. a.** A machine employing a heavy blade that falls freely between upright guides to behead a condemned prisoner. **b.** Any of various other machines used for execution by beheading. **c.** Execution by such a machine. **2.** Any of various more or less similar cutting instruments, as a surgical device used to remove tonsils. **3.** *British.* A method of cutting off debate on a bill in Parliament by fixing beforehand a time for voting. —*tr.v.* (gĭl′ə-tēn′) **guillotined, -tining, -tines.** To behead with a guillotine. [After Joseph Ignace *Guillotin* (1738–1814), French doctor who proposed its use.]

guilt (gĭlt) *n.* **1.** The fact of being responsible for an offense or wrongdoing. **2.** *Law.* **a.** Culpability for a crime or lesser breach of regulations. **b.** The disposition to break the law. **3.** *Rare.* Guilty behavior. **4.** Remorseful awareness of having done something wrong. —See Synonyms at **blame.** [Middle English *gult, gilt*, Old English *gylt*†.]

guilt·less (gĭlt′lĭs) *adj.* **1.** Free from guilt; blameless; innocent. **2.** Without knowledge or experience of (something). —**guilt′less·ly** *adv.* —**guilt′less·ness** *n.*

guilt·y (gĭl′tē) *adj.* **-ier, -iest. 1.** Responsible for or chargeable with some reprehensible act. Often used with *of: guilty of cheating.* **2.** *Law.* Having committed a crime: *plead guilty.* **3.** At fault; delinquent; culpable: *the guilty party.* **4.** Laden

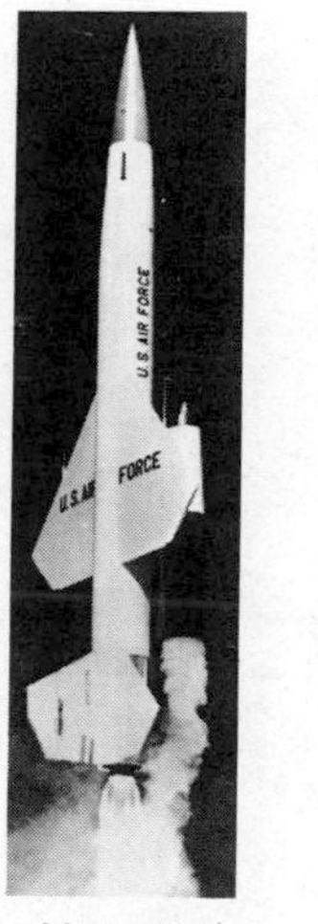

guided missile
A U.S. Air Force guided interceptor missile

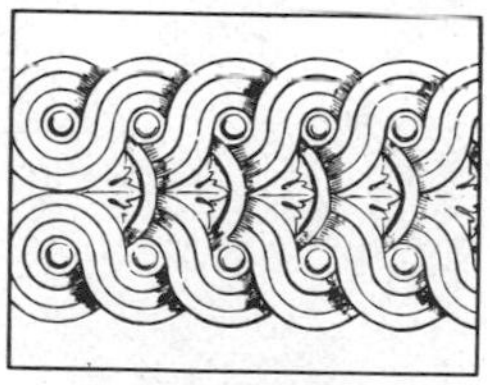

guilloche

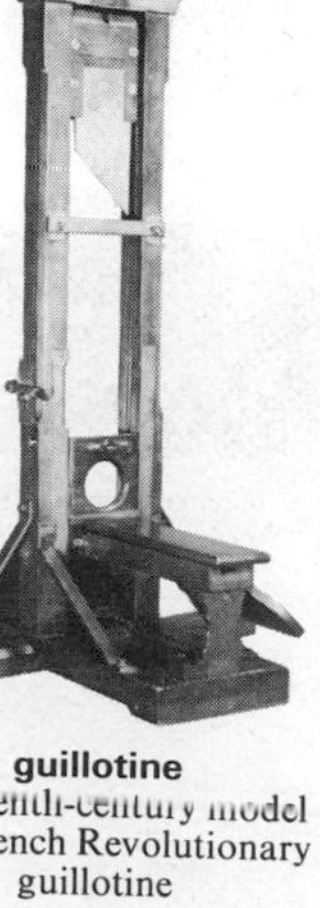

guillotine
Nineteenth-century model of a French Revolutionary guillotine

with, prompted by, or showing a sense of guilt: *a guilty conscience.* —**guilt′i·ly** *adv.* —**guilt′i·ness** *n.*
guimpe (gĭmp, gămp) *n.* **1.** A short, sleeved blouse worn with a jumper. **2.** A yoke insert for a low-necked dress. **3.** A starched cloth covering the neck and shoulders as part of a nun's habit. **4.** A trimming, **gimp** *(see).*
Guin. Guinea.
guin·ea (gĭn′ē) *n.* **1.** *Abbr.* **G., g. a.** A former British gold coin worth one pound and one shilling. **b.** The sum of one pound and one shilling. **2.** *Slang.* An Italian or a person of Italian parentage. A derogatory and offensive term. [Originally made of gold from the *Guinea* coast of Africa.]

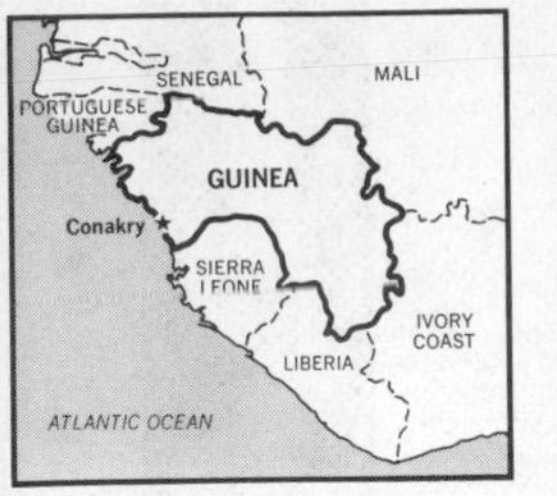

Guinea

Guin·ea, Gulf of (gĭn′ē). An inlet of the Atlantic on the coast of west-central Africa extending eastward to include the bights of Benin and Biafra.
Guin·ea, Republic of (gĭn′ē). Formerly **French Guin·ea.** *Abbr.* **Guin.** A country occupying 95,000 square miles in west-central Africa, with a coast on the Atlantic; a former French territory independent since 1958. Population, 3,420,000. Capital, Conakry.
Guin·ea Current (gĭn′ē). A warm ocean current in the Atlantic, flowing eastward off the western coast of Africa and through the Gulf of Guinea.
guinea fowl. Any of several pheasantlike birds of the family Numididae, native to Africa; especially, a widely domesticated species, *Numida meleagris,* having blackish plumage marked with many small white spots. Also called "guinea hen." [From the *Guinea* coast of Africa.]
guinea hen. 1. A female guinea fowl. **2.** The guinea fowl.
guinea pig. 1. Any of various South American burrowing rodents of the genus *Cavia,* having variously colored hair and no visible tail, and widely domesticated as pets and as experimental animals. **2.** Any person who is used as a subject for experimentation. [Probably from a confusion of GUIANA with the *Guinea* coast of Africa.]
guinea worm. A long, threadlike nematode worm, *Dracunculus medinensis,* of tropical Asia and Africa, that is a subcutaneous parasite of man and other animals. [Probably from the *Guinea* coast of Africa.]
Guin·e·vere (gwĭn′ə-vîr′). Also **Guen·e·vere** (gwĕn′-). In Arthurian legend, the wife of King Arthur and the mistress of Lancelot. [Welsh *Gwenhwyvar,* perhaps "white phantom" : *gwyn,* white (see **weid-** in Appendix*) + *-hwyvar*†, phantom.]
gui·pure (gĭ-pyŏŏr′; *French* gē-pür′) *n.* **1.** A kind of coarse, large-patterned lace without a net ground. **2.** A trimming, **gimp** *(see).* [French, from Old French, from *guiper,* to cover with silk, wool, and the like, from Frankish *wīpan.* See **weip-** in Appendix.*]
guise (gīz) *n.* **1.** Outward appearance; aspect. **2.** False appearance; pretense. **3.** Mode of dress; garb: *in the guise of a beggar.* **4.** *Obsolete.* Custom; habit. —*v.* **guised, guising, guises.** —*tr. Archaic.* To costume. —*intr. Chiefly British Informal.* To go in disguise; to masquerade. [Middle English, fashion, manner, from Old French, from Germanic. See **weid-** in Appendix.*]
gui·tar (gĭ-tär′) *n.* A musical instrument similar to the lute, having a large flat-backed sound box generally in the shape of a violin, a long fretted neck, and usually six strings, played by strumming or plucking. [French *guitare,* from Old French, from Spanish *guitarra,* from Arabic *qītār,* from Greek *kithara,* lyre. See **cithara.**] —**gui·tar′ist** *n.*
gui·tar·fish (gĭ-tär′fĭsh′) *n., pl.* **guitarfish** or **-fishes.** Any of several marine fishes of the family Rhinobatidae, related to the skates and rays, and having a guitar-shaped body.

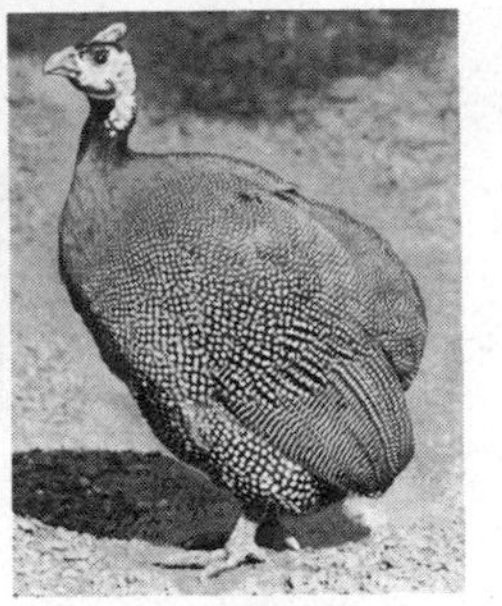
guinea fowl
Numida meleagris

Gu·ja·rat (gŏŏj′ə-rät′). Also **Gu·je·rat, Gu·ze·rat** (gŏŏz′ə-). **1.** A region of western India. **2.** A state, 72,245 square miles in area, of the west-central Republic of India. Population, 20,633,000. Capital, Ahmadabad.
Gu·ja·ra·ti (gŏŏj′ə-rä′tē) *n., pl.* **Gujarati. 1.** The Indic language spoken in Gujarat. **2.** A native or inhabitant of Gujarat or speaker of Gujarati.
Gu·ja·rat States (gŏŏj′ə-rät′). A group of former princely states occupying 7,493 square miles in west-central India; now part of Gujarat State.
Guj·ran·wa·la (gŏŏj′rən-wä′lə). A city and industrial center of northeast-central West Pakistan. Population, 196,000.
gul (gōōl) *n.* A motif in oriental carpets, typically a stylized compact device that is repeated at regular intervals in the central field. [Persian *gul*†, rose, flower.]
gu·lar (gōō′lər, gyōō′-) *adj.* Of, pertaining to, or located on the throat. [From Latin *gula,* throat. See **gwel-**[5] in Appendix.*]
gulch (gŭlch) *n.* A small shallow canyon with smoothly inclined slopes and steep sides; a small ravine. [Origin obscure.]
gul·den (gōōl′dən) *n., pl.* **guldens** or **gulden.** A monetary unit, the **guilder** *(see).* [Dutch *gulden (florijn),* golden (florin), from Middle Dutch. See **ghel-**[2] in Appendix.*]
Gü·lek Bo·gaz (gü-lĕk′ bō-gäz′). Ancient name **Ci·li·cian Gates** (sə-lĭsh′ən). A mountain pass over a section of the Taurus Range in southern Turkey.

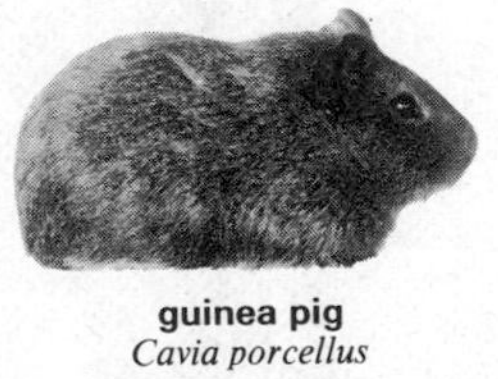
guinea pig
Cavia porcellus

gules (gyōōlz) *n. Heraldry.* The color red, indicated on a blazon by engraved vertical lines. [Middle English *goules,* from Old French *go(u)les,* red, red fur neckpiece, from the plural of *gole,* throat, from Latin *gula,* throat. See **gwel-**[5] in Appendix.*]
gulf (gŭlf) *n.* **1.** *Abbr.* **G., g.** A large area of a sea or ocean partially enclosed by land; especially, a long landlocked portion of sea opening through a strait. **2.** A deep, wide chasm; abyss. **3.** A separating distance; wide gap: *"the gulf between the Victorian sensibility and our own"* (Babette Deutsch). **4.** A whirlpool; an eddy. —*tr.v.* **gulfed, gulfing, gulfs.** To swallow; engulf. [Middle English *golf, goulf,* from Old French *golfe,* from Old Italian *golfo,* from Vulgar Latin *colp(h)us* (unattested), from Greek *kolpos, kolphos,* bosom, fold, bay. See **kwelp-**[1] in Appendix.*]
Gulf Intracoastal Waterway. An inland waterway comprising bays, canals, and rivers and extending along the coast from northwestern Florida to Brownsville, Texas.
Gulf·port (gŭlf′pôrt′, -pōrt′). A city and port of south-central Mississippi, on the Mississippi Sound. Population, 30,000.
Gulf States. The five southern states of the United States with coastlines on the Gulf of Mexico; Florida, Alabama, Mississippi, Louisiana, and Texas.
Gulf Stream. A warm ocean current of the North Atlantic, issuing from the Gulf of Mexico and flowing east through the Straits of Florida, then northeast along the southeastern coast of the United States, then east to the North Atlantic Current.
gulf·weed (gŭlf′wēd′) *n.* Any of several brownish seaweeds of the genus *Sargassum,* of tropical Atlantic waters, having rounded air bladders, and often forming dense, floating masses. Also called "sargasso," "sargasso weed." [It is found in the Gulf of Mexico.]
gull[1] (gŭl) *n.* Any of various chiefly coastal aquatic birds of the subfamily Larinae, having long wings, webbed feet, and usually gray and white plumage. [Middle English *gull,* probably from Welsh *gwylan,* from Celtic *voilenno-* (unattested).]
gull[2] (gŭl) *n.* A gullible person; dupe; simpleton. —*tr.v.* **gulled, gulling, gulls.** To deceive; cheat; dupe. [Probably from dialectal *gull,* unfledged bird, Middle English *golle, gulle,* probably from *gul,* yellow, pale, from Old Norse *gulr.* See **ghel-**[2] in Appendix.*]
Gul·lah (gŭl′ə) *n.* **1.** One of a group of Negroes inhabiting the Sea Islands and coastal area of South Carolina, Georgia, and northern Florida. **2.** The English-African language or patois spoken by these people.
gul·let (gŭl′ĭt) *n.* **1.** *Anatomy.* The esophagus. **2.** The throat. **3.** A gully or ravine, especially one that serves as a water channel. **4.** A cut in the earth preliminary to mining or excavating. [Middle English *golet,* from Old French *goulet,* diminutive of *gole, goule,* throat, from Latin *gula.* See **gwel-**[5] in Appendix.*]
gul·li·ble (gŭl′ə-bəl) *adj.* Able to be gulled; easily deceived or duped; credulous. [From GULL (dupe).] —**gul′li·bil′i·ty** *n.* —**gul′li·bly** *adv.*
Gul·li·ver (gŭl′ə-vər), **Lemuel.** In Jonathan Swift's satire *Gulliver's Travels* (1726), the Englishman who travels to the imaginary lands of Lilliput, Brobdingnag, Laputa, and the land of the Houyhnhnms.
gul·ly[1] (gŭl′ē) *n., pl.* **-lies.** A deep ditch or channel cut in the earth by running water, usually after a downpour. —*tr.v.* **gullied, -lying, -lies.** To wear a gully in. [Alteration of GULLET.]
gul·ly[2] (gŭl′ē) *n., pl.* **-lies.** *Chiefly Scottish.* A large knife. [Short for *gully knife* : *gully,* probably alteration of GULLET + KNIFE.]
gulp (gŭlp) *v.* **gulped, gulping, gulps.** —*tr.* **1.** To swallow greedily or rapidly in large amounts. Usually used with *down: gulp down coffee.* **2.** To stifle by or as if by swallowing. —*intr.* **1.** To choke or gasp; swallow air, as in nervousness. **2.** To swallow food or drink in gulps. **3.** To make a noise in the throat when swallowing. —*n.* **1.** The act of gulping. **2.** A large mouthful. **3.** A convulsive attempt to swallow; catching of air in the throat. [Middle English *gulpen,* from Middle Dutch *gulpen* (imitative).] —**gulp′er** *n.* —**gulp′ing·ly** *adv.*
gum[1] (gŭm) *n.* **1. a.** Any of various viscous substances that are exuded by certain plants and trees and that dry into water-soluble, noncrystalline, brittle solids. **b.** A similar plant exudate, such as a resin. **2.** A product, such as rubber, made from a plant exudate for use in industry, the arts, or the like. **3.** *Plural. Regional.* Rubber overshoes. **4. a.** Any of various trees, such as one of the genera *Eucalyptus, Liquidambar,* or *Nyssa,* that are a source of gum. Also called "gum tree." **b.** The wood of such a tree. Also called "gumwood." **5.** A hollowed log of a gum tree made into a trough or barrel. **6.** Chewing gum. —*v.* **gummed, gumming, gums.** —*tr.* To cover, smear, seal, fill, or fix in place with gum. —*intr.* **1.** To exude or form gum. **2.** To become sticky or clogged with gum or something similar. —**gum up. 1.** To become clogged, as with gum. **2.** *Slang.* To ruin; bungle; spoil: *gum up the works.* [Middle English *gumme, gomme,* from Old French *gomme,* from Vulgar Latin *gumma* (unattested), from Latin *gummi, cummi,* from Greek *kommi,* from Egyptian *kemai.*]
gum[2] (gŭm) *n.* The firm connective tissue that is covered by mucous membrane and that envelops the alveolar arches of the jaw and surrounds the bases of the teeth. Also called "gingiva." [Middle English *gome,* Old English *gōma,* palate, jaw. See **ghĕu-** in Appendix.*]
GUM Airport code for Guam.
gum ammoniac. A gum resin, **ammoniac** *(see).*
gum arabic. A gum exuded by various African trees of the genus *Acacia,* especially *A. senegal,* and used in the preparation of pills and emulsions, the manufacture of mucilage and candies, and in general as a thickener and colloidal stabilizer. Also called "acacia."
gum benjamin. A gum resin, **benzoin** *(see).*
gum benzoin. A gum resin, **benzoin** *(see).*
gum·bo (gŭm′bō) *n., pl.* **-bos.** Also **gom·bo. 1.** The mucilaginous pods of okra. **2.** A soup or stew thickened with okra. **3.** A fine silty soil, common in the southern and western United States, that forms an unusually sticky mud when wet. **4.** *Often capital* **G.** A patois spoken by some Negroes and Creoles in

ă pat/ā pay/âr care/ä father/b bib/ch church/d deed/ĕ pet/ē be/f fife/g gag/h hat/hw which/ĭ pit/ī pie/îr pier/j judge/k kick/l lid, needle/m mum/n no, sudden/ng thing/ŏ pot/ō toe/ô paw, for/oi noise/ou out/ŏŏ took/ōō boot/p pop/r roar/s sauce/sh ship, dish/

Louisiana and the French West Indies. [Louisiana French *gombo*, from Bantu.]

gum·boil (gŭm′boil′) *n*. A small boil or abscess on the gum.

gum·bo·lim·bo (gŭm′bō-lĭm′bō) *n*., *pl*. **-bos**. An aromatic tree, *Bursera simaruba*, of Florida and the West Indies, having compound leaves and small white flowers. [Possibly GUMBO + -limbo, birdlime (from its resin), from Bantu.]

gum·drop (gŭm′drŏp′) *n*. A small candy made of sweetened, colored, and flavored gum arabic or gelatin, and coated with coarse granulated sugar.

gum·ma (gŭm′ə) *n*., *pl*. **-mas** or **gummata** (gŭm′ə-tə). A small, rubbery tumor formed in an advanced stage of syphilis. [New Latin, from Latin *gummi*, GUM.] **—gum′ma·tous** *adj*.

gum·mo·sis (gŭ-mō′sĭs) *n*. The pathological formation of patches of gum on certain plants, such as sugar cane and certain fruit trees, resulting from attack by insects, microorganisms, or adverse weather conditions. [New Latin : Latin *gummi*, GUM + -OSIS.]

gum·mous (gŭm′əs) *adj*. Also **gum·mose** (-ōs′). **1**. Gumlike; gummatous. **2**. Gummy.

gum·my (gŭm′ē) *adj*. **-mier**, **-miest**. **1**. Consisting of or containing gum. **2**. Suffused with or yielding gum. **3**. Sticky; viscid. **4**. Coated with gum or something gumlike.

gum plant. Any of several North American plants of the genus *Grindelia*; especially, *G. squarosa*, having sticky leaves and bracts and yellow, rayed flowers. Also called "gumweed," "rosinweed."

gump·tion (gŭmp′shən) *n*. *Informal*. **1**. Shrewdness: "*Did you really have the gumption to suspect me just because I brought you up to this bare part of the heath?*" (G.K. Chesterton). **2**. Boldness of enterprise; initiative. [Origin unknown.]

gum resin. A mixture of gum and resin that exudes from some plants or trees.

gum·shoe (gŭm′shōō′) *n*. **1**. A rubber shoe or overshoe. **2**. A sneaker. **3**. *Slang*. A detective. **—intr.v. gumshoed, -shoeing, -shoes**. *Slang*. To investigate stealthily; to pry.

Gum·ti (gōōm′tē). A river rising in northeastern Uttar Pradesh, Republic of India, and flowing 500 miles southeast to the Ganges.

gum tree. A tree, the **gum** *(see)*.

gum·wood (gŭm′wŏŏd′) *n*. The wood of a gum tree. See **gum**.

gun (gŭn) *n*. **1**. A weapon consisting essentially of a metal tube from which a projectile is fired at high velocity into a flat trajectory. **2**. A cannon, as distinguished from a small firearm. **3**. A portable firearm. **4**. A device that shoots a projectile. **5**. A discharge of a gun as a signal or salute. **6**. One who carries or uses a gun, as a member of a shooting party or a gunfighter. **7**. A mechanism controlling the flow of fuel to an engine; a throttle. **—big gun**. *Informal*. **1**. An eminent or influential person: " 'The stage,' he went on, 'is all right if you can be one of the big guns' " (Dreiser). **2**. An officer of high rank. **—jump the gun**. To begin a race before the starting signal. **—stick to one's guns**. To hold fast to an opinion or appointed course of action. **—v. gunned, gunning, guns. —tr. 1**. To fire upon; shoot. **2**. To open the throttle of so as to accelerate: *gun an engine*. **—intr**. To hunt or shoot with a gun. **—gun for**. **1**. To seek to catch, overcome, or destroy. **2**. To seek with tenacity: *gun for high office*. [Middle English *gunne, gonne*, probably from *Gunne*, pet form of feminine name *Gunhild* (sometimes applied to a war engine), from Old Norse *Gunnhildr* : *gunnr*, war (see gwhen-¹ in Appendix*) + *hildr*, war.]

gun·boat (gŭn′bōt′) *n*. A small armed vessel.

gun carriage. A frame or structure upon which a gun is mounted for firing or maneuvering.

gun·cot·ton (gŭn′kŏt′n) *n*. An explosive, **nitrocellulose** *(see)*.

gun dog. A dog trained to assist hunters, as in flushing or retrieving game.

gun·fight (gŭn′fīt′) *n*. Also **gun·fight·ing** (-ĭng). A duel or battle with firearms. **—gun′fight′er** *n*.

gun·fire (gŭn′fīr′) *n*. The firing of guns.

gun·flint (gŭn′flĭnt′) *n*. The piece of flint used to strike the igniting spark in a flintlock.

gung ho (gŭng′ hō′). *Slang*. **1**. Unswervingly dedicated and loyal. **2**. Foolishly enthusiastic. [Pidgin English : probably Mandarin Chinese *kung¹*, work + *ho²*, together.]

gunk (gŭngk) *n*. *Informal*. A filthy, slimy, or greasy substance. [Perhaps expressive.]

gun·lock (gŭn′lŏk′) *n*. A device for igniting the charge of a firearm.

gun·man (gŭn′mən) *n*., *pl*. **-men** (-mĭn). **1. a**. A hired gunfighter. **b**. A desperado; an outlaw. **c**. A professional killer. **2**. *Archaic*. An American Indian warrior armed with a gun.

gun metal. **1**. An alloy of copper with ten per cent tin. **2**. Metal used for guns. **—gun′met′al** *adj*.

gun·met·al (gŭn′mĕt′l) *n*. Dark gray. See **color**. **—gun′met′al** *adj*.

gun moll. *Slang*. The girl friend or female accomplice of a gunman.

Gun·nar (gōōn′är′). *Norse Mythology*. The husband of Brynhild, the brother-in-law of Sigurd, and the brother of Gudrun. Identified with Gunther.

gun·nel¹ (gŭn′əl) *n*. Any of various long, eellike fishes of the family Pholidae, of northern seas. [Origin unknown.]

gun·nel². Variant of **gunwale**.

gun·ner (gŭn′ər) *n*. **1**. A soldier, sailor, or airman who aims or fires a gun. **2**. One who hunts with a gun. **3**. *U.S. Navy*. A warrant officer having charge of ordnance.

gun·ner·y (gŭn′ə-rē) *n*. **1**. The art and science of constructing and operating guns. **2**. The use of guns.

Gun·ni·son (gŭn′ĭ-sən). A river rising in west-central Colorado and flowing 180 miles west and northwest to the Colorado.

gun·ny (gŭn′ē) *n*. **1**. A coarse fabric made of jute or hemp. **2**. Burlap. [Hindi *gōnī*, from Sanskrit *goṇī*, sack, probably from Dravidian.]

gunny sack. A sack made of burlap or gunny.

gun·pow·der (gŭn′pou′dər) *n*. Any of various explosive powders used to propel projectiles from guns; especially, a black explosive mixture of potassium nitrate, charcoal, and sulfur.

Gunpowder Plot. See **Guy Fawkes Day**.

gunpowder tea. A type of green tea of which the leaves are rolled into pellets.

gun·room (gŭn′rōōm′, -rŏŏm′) *n*. The quarters of midshipmen and junior officers on a British warship.

gun·run·ner (gŭn′rŭn′ər) *n*. One that smuggles firearms and ammunition. **—gun′run′ning** *n*. & *adj*.

gun·shot (gŭn′shŏt′) *n*. **1**. Shot fired from a gun. **2**. The range of a gun: *within gunshot*.

gun·shy (gŭn′shī′) *adj*. Afraid of gunfire. Said especially of gun dogs.

gun·sling·er (gŭn′slĭng′ər) *n*. A gunfighter; gunman. **—gun′sling′ing** *n*. & *adj*.

gun·smith (gŭn′smĭth′) *n*. One who makes or repairs firearms.

gun·stock (gŭn′stŏk′) *n*. A **stock** *(see)*.

Gun·ter's chain (gŭn′tərz). *Measurement*. A **chain** *(see)*. [After Edmund *Gunter* (1581-1626), English mathematician.]

Gun·ther (gŏŏn′tər). In the *Nibelungenlied*, a king of Burgundy, the husband of Brunhild, and brother of Kriemhild. Identified with Gunnar.

Gun·tur (gŏŏn-tŏŏr′). A city and trading center of east-central Andhra Pradesh, Republic of India. Population, 208,000.

gun·wale (gŭn′əl) *n*. Also **gun·nel**. The upper edge of a ship's side. [Middle English *gonnewale* : GUN + WALE (so called because it served formerly as a prop for the ship's guns).]

gup·py (gŭp′ē) *n*., *pl*. **-pies**. A small, brightly colored freshwater fish, *Poecilia reticulata* (or *Lebistes reticulatus*), of northern South America and adjacent islands of the West Indies, that is popular in home aquariums. [Introduced into England by R.J.L. *Guppy* of Trinidad.]

Gur (gŏŏr) *n*. A group of languages of the Niger-Congo family spoken chiefly in Ghana and Upper Volta.

Gur·gan (gŏŏr-gän′). A river rising in northeast-central Iran and flowing 150 miles west to the Caspian Sea.

gur·gi·ta·tion (gûr′jə-tā′shən) *n*. A whirling motion; ebullition. [From Late Latin *gurgitāre*, to engulf, from Latin *gurges* (stem *gurgit-*), whirlpool, gulf. See gwerə-² in Appendix.*]

gur·gle (gûr′gəl) *v*. **-gled**, **-gling**, **-gles**. **—intr. 1**. To flow in a broken, uneven current making intermittent low sounds. **2**. To make such sounds. **—tr**. To express or pronounce with a gurgling sound. **—n**. The act or sound of gurgling. [Probably from Vulgar Latin *gurgulāre*, from Latin *gurguliō*, gullet. See gwerə-² in Appendix.*] **—gur′gling·ly** *adv*.

Gur·kha (gŏŏr′kə) *n*. **1**. A member of a Rajput ethnic group predominant in Nepal. **2**. A soldier from Nepal serving in the British or Indian armies.

gur·nard (gûr′nərd) *n*., *pl*. **gurnard** or **gurnards**. **1**. Any of various marine fishes of the family Triglidae, and especially of the Old World genus *Trigla*, having large, fanlike pectoral fins. **2**. A similar fish, the **flying gurnard** *(see)*. [Middle English, from Old French *gornart*, from Latin *grundīre, grunnīre*, to grunt (because it grunts when caught). See gru- in Appendix.*]

gur·ry (gûr′ē) *n*. Fish offal. [Origin unknown.]

gu·ru (gōō-rōō′, gōō′rōō′) *n*. **1**. *Often capital* G. *Hinduism*. A spiritual teacher. **2**. *Informal*. A charismatic leader or guide. [Hindi *gurū*, "the venerable one," from Sanskrit *guruh*, heavy, venerable. See gwer-² in Appendix.*]

gush (gŭsh) *v*. **gushed**, **gushing**, **gushes**. **—intr. 1**. To flow forth suddenly and violently. **2**. To issue or emanate abundantly. **3**. To make an excessively demonstrative display of sentiment or enthusiasm. **—tr**. To emit abundantly. **—n. 1**. A sudden, violent, or copious outflow: *a gush of tears*. **2**. Mawkish sentiment. [Middle English *guschen, gosshen*, perhaps from Scandinavian, akin to Icelandic *gusa*. See gheu- in Appendix.*]

gush·er (gŭsh′ər) *n*. **1**. One that gushes. **2**. A gas or oil well with an abundant natural flow.

gush·y (gŭsh′ē) *adj*. **-ier**, **-iest**. Characterized by excessive displays of sentiment or enthusiasm.

gus·set (gŭs′ĭt) *n*. A triangular insert, as in a garment, for strengthening or enlarging. [Middle English, from Old French *gousset*, armpit, piece of armor under the armpit, diminutive of *gousse†*, pod.]

gust¹ (gŭst) *n*. **1**. A violent, abrupt rush of wind. **2**. An abrupt outburst of emotion, as of rage. **—See Synonyms at wind**. [From Old Norse *gustr*. See gheu- in Appendix.*] **—gust′i·ly** *adv*. **—gust′i·ness** *n*. **—gust′y** *adj*.

gust² (gŭst) *n*. **1**. *Archaic*. Relish; gusto. **2**. *Obsolete*. Personal taste or inclination; liking. [Middle English *guste*, taste, from Latin *gustus*. See **gusto**.]

gus·ta·tion (gŭs-tā′shən) *n*. The act or faculty of tasting; taste. [Latin *gustātiō*, from *gustāre*, to taste, from *gustus*, taste. See **gusto**.]

gus·ta·tive (gŭs′tə-tĭv) *adj*. Gustatory.

gus·ta·to·ry (gŭs′tə-tôr′ē, -tōr′ē) *adj*. Of or pertaining to the sense of taste.

Gus·ta·vo A. Ma·de·ro (gōōs-tä′vō ä mä-thā′rō). A city of central Mexico north of Mexico City, incorporating the former city of Guadalupe Hidalgo. Population, 60,000.

Gus·ta·vus II (gŭ-stā′vəs). Known as Gustavus Adolphus. 1594-1632. King of Sweden (1611-32).

gull¹
Larus argentatus
Herring gull

guppy
A male of the species

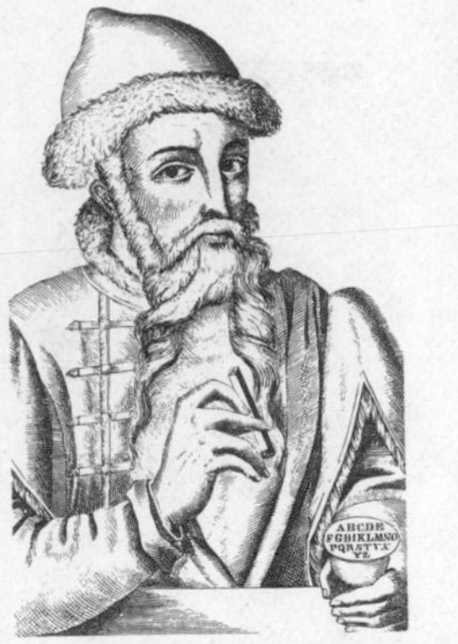

Johann Gutenberg

Gus·ta·vus VI (gu-stā′vəs). Also **Gus·tav** (gŭs′täv). Born 1882. King of Sweden (since 1950).

gus·to (gŭs′tō) *n.* **1.** Fondness; taste; liking. **2.** Vigorous enjoyment; relish; zest. **3.** *Archaic.* Artistic style: *grand gusto.* [Italian, from Latin *gustus,* taste. See **geus-** in Appendix.*]

gut (gŭt) *n.* **1.** The alimentary canal or a portion thereof; especially, the intestine or stomach. **2.** *Plural.* The bowels; entrails; viscera. **3.** *Plural.* The essential contents of something: *"These hunks of metal are the guts of an atomic bomb."* (Stewart Alsop and Ralph Lapp). **4.** The intestines of some animals used as strings for musical instruments or as surgical sutures. **5.** *Plural. Slang.* Courage; fortitude. **6.** A narrow passage or channel. **7.** Fibrous material taken from the silk gland of a silkworm before it spins a cocoon, used for fishing tackle. —*tr.v.* **gutted, gutting, guts. 1.** To remove the intestines or entrails of; eviscerate; disembowel. **2.** To destroy the contents or interior of: *gut a house.* [Middle English *gut,* Old English *guttas* (plural). See **gheu-** in Appendix.*]

Gu·ten·berg (go͞ot′n-bûrg′; *German* go͞o′tən-bĕrk′), **Johann.** 1400?–1468? German inventor of movable type.

Guth·rie (gŭth′rē), **Woodrow Wilson ("Woody").** 1912–1967. American composer and folk singer.

Guth·run. Variant of **Gudrun.**

gut·less (gŭt′lĭs) *adj.* Lacking fortitude, courage, or vigor. —**gut′less·ness** *n.*

gut·ta (gŭt′ə) *n., pl.* **guttae** (gŭt′ē′). **1.** *Architecture.* One of a group of small, droplike ornaments on a Doric entablature. **2.** *Abbr.* **gt.** *Medicine.* A drop. [Latin, drop. See **gout.**]

gut·ta-per·cha (gŭt′ə-pûr′chə) *n.* **1.** Any of several tropical trees of the genera *Palaquium* and *Payena,* having sap in the form of milky latex. **2.** A rubbery substance derived from the latex of these trees, used as electrical insulation and for waterproofing. [Malay *gĕtah percha* : *gĕtah,* sap + *percha,* strip of cloth.]

gut·tate (gŭt′āt′) *adj.* Also **gut·tat·ed** (-ā′tĭd). **1.** In the form of drops or having drops. **2.** Spotted as if by drops. [Latin *guttatus,* from *gutta,* drop. See **gout.**]

gut·ter (gŭt′ər) *n.* **1.** A channel for draining off water at the edge of a street or road. **2.** A pipe or trough for draining off water under the border of a roof. **3.** A furrow or groove formed by running water. **4.** The trough on either side of a bowling alley. **5.** *Printing.* The white space between the facing pages of a book. **6.** The lowest social class of a city: *language of the gutter.* —*v.* **guttered, -tering, -ters.** —*tr.* To form gutters or furrows in. —*intr.* **1.** To flow in channels or rivulets. **2.** To melt away through the channel formed by a burning wick. Said of candles. **3.** To burn with a low flame; flicker. [Middle English *guter, goter,* sewer, trough, drain, from Norman French *gotere,* from Old French *gotiere,* from Vulgar Latin *guttāria* (unattested), from Latin *gutta,* drop. See **gout.**]

gut·ter·snipe (gŭt′ər-snīp′) *n.* A street urchin.

gut·tur·al (gŭt′ər-əl) *adj.* **1.** Of or pertaining to the throat. **2.** Produced in the throat. **3.** *Phonetics.* Velar. —*n.* A sound produced in or near the throat, a **velar** *(see).* [Old French, from Latin *guttur,* throat. See **goiter.**] —**gut′tur·al·ism′, gut′tur·al′i·ty, gut′tur·al·ness** *n.* —**gut′tur·al·ly** *adv.*

gut·tur·al·ize (gŭt′ər-ə-līz′) *tr.v.* **-ized, -izing, -izes.** *Phonetics.* To velarize. —**gut′tur·al·i·za′tion** *n.*

gut·ty (gŭt′ē) *adj.* **-tier, -tiest.** Vivid; bold; stark.

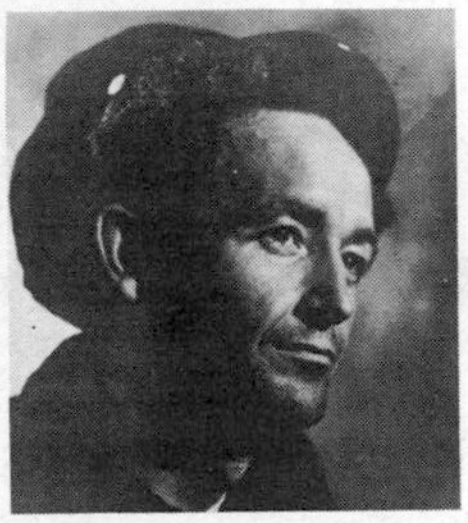

"Woody" Guthrie

guy[1] (gī) *n.* A rope, cord, or cable used for steadying, guiding, or holding something. —*tr.v.* **guyed, guying, guys.** To fasten, guide, or hold with a guy. [Probably from Low German, akin to Dutch *gei*†, brail.]

guy[2] (gī) *n.* **1.** *Informal.* A man; fellow. **2.** *British.* One who is odd or grotesque in appearance or dress. **3.** An effigy of Guy Fawkes, formerly paraded through the streets of English towns and burned on Guy Fawkes Day. —*tr.v.* **guyed, guying, guys.** To make fun of; mock.

Guy (gī). A masculine given name. [Middle English, from Old French *Wido, Guido,* from Common Germanic *Wido* (unattested).]

Guy·a·na (gī-ăn′ə). Formerly **British Gui·a·na** (gē-ăn′ə, -ä′nə). A republic, 89,480 square miles in area, of northeast-central South America; a former British colony independent since 1966. Population, 628,000. Capital, Georgetown.

Guy·ane Fran·çaise. The French name for **French Guiana.**

Guy·enne. The French name for **Guienne.**

Guy Fawkes Day (gī′ fôks′). A British celebration in commemoration of the Gunpowder Plot (November 5, 1605), an attempt led by Guy Fawkes (1570–1606) to assassinate the king and assembled parliament in retaliation for increasing repression of Roman Catholics in England.

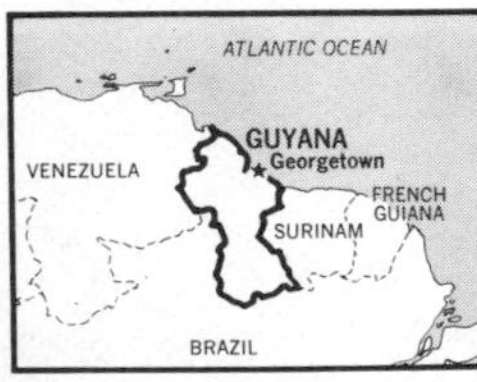

Guyana

Gu·ze·rat. See **Gujarat.**

guz·zle (gŭz′əl) *tr.v.* **-zled, -zling, -zles.** To drink greedily or inordinately: *"The way those men drank, gluttonized and guzzled was disgusting"* (Frank Harris). [Possibly from Old French *gosiller,* from *gosier*†, throat.] —**guz′zler** *n.*

GVA Airport code for Geneva, Switzerland.

Gwa·li·or (gwä′lē-ôr′). **1.** A former princely state occupying 26,367 square miles in the north-central Republic of India. **2.** A city of north-central Madhya Pradesh, Republic of India. Population, 320,000.

gwe·duc. Variant of **geoduck.**

Gwyn (gwĭn), **Nell.** Original name, Eleanor Gwynne. 1650?–1687. English actress; mistress of Charles II.

gybe. Variant of **jibe** (to swing).

gym (jĭm) *n. Informal.* **1.** A gymnasium. **2.** Gymnastics. **3.** A frame supporting structures used in outdoor play.

gym. gymnasium; gymnastics.

gym·kha·na (jĭm-kä′nə) *n. Chiefly British.* A display of athletic or equestrian contests. [Blend of GYM(NASIUM) + Hindi *(gend)-khānā,* "(ball) house," racket court, from *khāna,* house, from Persian *khāna*†.]

gym·na·si·um (jĭm-nā′zē-əm *for sense 1;* gĭm-nä′zē-o͞om′ *for sense 2*) *n., pl.* **-ums** or **-sia** (-zē-ə). *Abbr.* **gym. 1.** A room or building equipped for gymnastics and sports. **2.** An academic high school in various central European countries, especially Germany. [Latin, *gymnasium,* school, from Greek *gumnasion,* from *gumnazein,* "to train naked," practice gymnastics, from *gumnos,* naked. See **nogw-** in Appendix.*]

gym·nast (jĭm′năst′) *n.* One skilled in gymnastic exercises. [Greek *gumnastēs,* from *gumnazein,* to practice gymnastics. See **gymnasium.**]

gym·nas·tic (jĭm-năs′tĭk) *adj.* Pertaining to gymnastics. —**gym·nas′ti·cal·ly** *adv.*

gym·nas·tics (jĭm-năs′tĭks) *pl.n. Abbr.* **gym.** Body-building exercises, especially those performed with special apparatus in a gymnasium.

gym·nos·o·phist (jĭm-nŏs′ə-fĭst′) *n.* One of an ancient sect of Hindu ascetics, as reported in classical antiquity. [French *gymnosophiste,* from Latin *gymnosophistae* (plural), from Greek *gumnosophistai* : *gumnos,* naked (see **gymnasium**) + *sophistēs,* SOPHIST.]

gym·no·sperm (jĭm′nə-spûrm′) *n.* Any plant of the class Gymnospermae, which includes the coniferous trees and other plants having seeds not enclosed within an ovary. [New Latin *Gymnospermae* : Greek *gumnos,* naked (see **gymnasium**) + -SPERM.] —**gym′no·sperm′ous** *adj.*

gyn. gynecological; gynecology.

gy·nae·ce·um (jĭn′ə-sē′əm, jī′nə- *for sense 1;* jī-nē′sē-əm, jī- *for sense 2*) *n., pl.* **-cea** (-sē′ə *for sense 1;* -sē-ə *for sense 2*). Also **gy·nae·ci·um** *pl.* **-cia** (-sē-ə). **1.** The women's quarters in an ancient Greek or Roman household. **2.** Variant of **gynoecium.** [Latin, from Greek *gunaikeion,* from *gunaikeios,* of women, from *gunē* (stem *gunaik-*), woman. See **gwen-** in Appendix.*]

gy·nan·dro·morph (jī-năn′drə-môrf′, jī-, gī-) *n.* An individual having male and female characteristics. [GYN(O)- + ANDRO- + -MORPH.] —**gy·nan′dro·mor′phic, gy·nan′dro·mor′phous** *adj.* —**gy·nan′dro·mor′phism′, gy·nan′dro·mor′phy** *n.*

gy·nan·drous (jĭ-năn′drəs, jī-, gī-) *n.* **1.** *Botany.* Having the stamens and pistil united to form a column. **2.** Characterized by gynandry; hermaphroditic. [Greek *gunandros,* of questionable sex : GYN(O)- + -ANDROUS.]

gy·nan·dry (jĭ-năn′drē, jī-, gī-) *n.* The condition of a female having external genital organs resembling those of the male; hermaphroditism. [New Latin *gynandria,* from Greek *gunandros,* GYNANDROUS.]

gy·nar·chy (jĭn′är′kē, jī′när′-, gī′-) *n., pl.* **-chies.** Government by women. [GYN(O)- + -ARCHY.] —**gy·nar′chic** *adj.*

gy·ne·coc·ra·cy (jĭn′ə-kŏk′rə-sē, jī′nə-, gī′-) *n., pl.* **-cies.** Government by women. [Greek *gunaikokratia* : *gunē* (stem *gunaik-*), woman (see **gwen-** in Appendix*) + -CRACY.]

gynecol. gynecological; gynecology.

gy·ne·col·o·gy (gī′nə-kŏl′ə-jē, jī′-, jĭn′ə-) *n. Abbr.* **gyn., gynecol.** The medical science of disease, reproductive physiology, and endocrinology in females. [Greek *gunē* (stem *gunaik-*), woman (see **gynecocracy**) + -LOGY.] —**gy′ne·co·log′i·cal** (-kə-lŏj′ĭ-kəl), **gy′ne·co·log′ic** (-kə-lŏj′ĭk) *adj.* —**gy′ne·col′o·gist** *n.*

gyno–, gyn–. Indicates: **1.** Woman or female; for example, **gynarchy, gynandromorph. 2.** Female reproductive organ; for example, **gynophore.** [Greek *guno-,* from *gunē,* woman. See **gwen-** in Appendix.*]

gy·noe·ci·um (jĭ-nē′sē-əm, jī-) *n., pl.* **-cia** (-sē-ə). Also **gy·nae·ce·um, gy·ne·ci·um.** *Botany.* The female reproductive organs of a flower; the pistil or pistils collectively. [New Latin, alteration of GYNAECEUM.]

gy·no·phore (jĭn′ə-fôr′, -fōr′, jī′nə-, gī′-) *n. Botany.* The stalk of a pistil. [GYNO- + -PHORE.] —**gy′no·phor′ic** (jĭn′ə-fôr′ĭk, -fŏr′ĭk, jī′nə-, gī′-) *adj.*

–gynous. Indicates: **1.** Women or females; for example, **monogynous. 2.** Female organs such as pistils; for example, **perigynous.** [New Latin *-gynus,* having pistils, from Greek *-gunos,* having a wife or wives, from *gunē,* woman. See **gwen-** in Appendix.*]

–gyny. Indicates: **1.** The condition of having women or females; for example, **monogyny. 2.** The condition of having female organs or pistils; for example, **epigyny.** [From Greek *gunē,* woman. See **gwen-** in Appendix.*]

Győr (dyûr). *German* **Raab** (räp). An industrial city and railroad center of northwestern Hungary. Population, 74,000.

gyp (jĭp) *tr.v.* **gypped, gypping, gyps.** Also **gip.** *Informal.* To swindle, cheat, or defraud. —*n.* **1.** The act or an instance of cheating; a swindle. **2.** One who cheats; a swindler. [Probably short for GYPSY.] —**gyp′per** *n.*

gyp joint. *Slang.* A store or other public establishment that makes a practice of defrauding its clientele.

gyp·soph·i·la (jĭp-sŏf′ə-lə) *n.* Any of various plants of the genus *Gypsophila,* having small white or pink flowers, and including the baby's-breath. [New Latin *Gypsophila* : Latin *gypsum,* GYPSUM + -PHILA.]

gyp·sum (jĭp′səm) *n.* A white mineral, $CaSO_4 \cdot 2H_2O$, used in the manufacture of plaster of Paris, gypsum plaster and plasterboard, Portland cement, wallboards, and fertilizers. [Latin, from Greek *gupsos,* from Semitic, akin to Hebrew *gephes,* plaster.] —**gyp′se·ous** (-sē-əs), **gyp·sif′er·ous** (-sĭf′ər-əs) *adj.*

gypsum plaster. A plaster, the principal constituent of which is gypsum.

ă pat/ā pay/âr care/ä father/b bib/ch church/d deed/ĕ pet/ē be/f fife/g gag/h hat/hw which/ĭ pit/ī pie/îr pier/j judge/k kick/l lid, needle/m mum/n no, sudden/ng thing/ŏ pot/ō toe/ô paw, for/oi noise/ou out/o͝o took/o͞o boot/p pop/r roar/s sauce/sh ship, dish/

Gyp·sy (jĭp′sē) *n., pl.* **-sies.** Also **Gip·sy. 1.** One of a nomadic Caucasoid people originally migrating from the border region between Iran and India to Europe in the 14th or 15th century and now living principally in Europe and the United States. **2.** The Indic language spoken by this people; Romany. **3.** *Often small* g. One that resembles a Gypsy in appearance or behavior. —*adj.* Also **Gip·sy.** Pertaining to or resembling Gypsies. [Shortening of EGYPTIAN, because they were believed to have come from Egypt.]

gypsy moth. A moth, *Porthetria dispar*, native to the Old World, having hairy caterpillars that feed on foliage and are very destructive to trees.

gy·ral (jī′rəl) *adj.* **1.** Moving in a circular or spiral path; gyratory. **2.** Pertaining to a gyrus. —**gy′ral·ly** *adv.*

gy·rate (jī′rāt′) *intr.v.* **-rated, -rating, -rates. 1.** To revolve on or around a center or axis. **2.** To circle or spiral. —See Synonyms at **turn.** —*adj. Biology.* In rings; coiled. [Latin *gȳrāre,* from *gȳrus,* circle, from Greek *guros,* GYRE.] —**gy·ra′tion** *n.* —**gy′ra·tor** (-rā′tər) *n.* —**gy′ra·tor′y** (-rə-tôr′ē, -tōr′ē) *adj.*

gyre (jīr) *n.* **1.** A ring or circle; vortex; spiral. **2.** A circular or spiral motion. [Latin *gyrus,* from Greek *guros,* circle. See **gêu-** in Appendix.*]

gy·rene (jī′rēn′) *n. Slang.* A marine. [Perhaps alteration (influenced by GYRE) of MARINE.]

gyr·fal·con (jûr′făl′kən, -fôl′kən, -fô′kən) *n.* Also **ger·fal·con.** A large falcon, *Falco rusticolus,* of northern regions, having various color phases ranging from black to white. [Middle English *gerfaucoun,* from Old French *gerfaucon,* from Old Norse *geirfalki.* See **pel-²** in Appendix.*]

gy·ro (jī′rō) *n., pl.* **-ros.** A gyroscope (*see*).

gyro-. Indicates: **1.** Gyrating; for example, **gyroplane. 2.** Spiral; for example, **gyroscope. 3.** Gyroscope; for example, **gyrocompass.** [Latin, from Greek *guro-,* from *guros,* circle. See **gêu-** in Appendix.*]

gy·ro·com·pass (jī′rō-kŭm′pəs, -kŏm′pəs) *n.* A navigational device in which the interaction of a gyroscope's angular momentum with the force produced by the earth's rotation is used to maintain a north-south orientation of the gyroscopic spin axis, thereby providing a stable directional reference.

gy·ro·mag·net·ic (jī′rō-măg-nĕt′ĭk) *adj.* Of, pertaining to, or resulting from the magnetic properties of a spinning, electrically charged particle.

gyromagnetic ratio. The ratio of the magnetic moment to the intrinsic angular momentum of a spinning particle.

gyro pilot. An automatic pilot incorporating a gyroscope to initiate corrections to aircraft control surfaces and thus maintain a preset course and altitude.

gy·ro·plane (jī′rə-plān′) *n.* An aircraft such as a helicopter or autogyro that is equipped with wings that rotate about an approximately vertical axis. [GYRO- + PLANE.]

gy·ro·scope (jī′rə-skōp′) *n.* **1.** A device consisting essentially of a spinning mass, typically a disk or wheel, the spin axis of which turns between two low-friction supports and maintains its angular orientation with respect to inertial coordinates when not subjected to external torques. **2.** Broadly, any spinning mass. Also called "gyro." [French : GYRO- + -SCOPE.] —**gy′ro·scop′ic** (-skŏp′ĭk) *adj.* —**gy′ro·scop′i·cal·ly** *adv.*

gy·ro·sta·bi·liz·er (jī′rō-stā′bə-lī′zər) *n.* A device having a heavy gyroscope whose axis spins in a vertical plane to reduce the side-to-side rolling of a ship or airplane.

gy·ro·stat (jī′rə-stăt′) *n.* A gyrostabilizer. [GYRO- + -STAT.] —**gy′ro·stat′ic** *adj.* —**gy′ro·stat′i·cal·ly** *adv.*

gy·rus (jī′rəs) *n., pl.* **-ri** (-rī′). Any of the prominent, rounded, elevated convolutions at the surfaces of the cerebral hemispheres. [New Latin, from Latin, circle, GYRE.]

gyve (jīv) *n. Archaic.* A shackle or fetter, especially for the leg. Usually used in the plural. —*tr.v.* **gyved, gyving, gyves.** To shackle or fetter. [Middle English *gyve†.*]

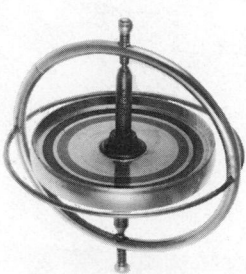

gyroscope

---

t **tight**/th **thin,** path/*th* **this,** bathe/ŭ **cut**/ûr **urge**/v **valve**/w **with**/y **yes**/z **zebra,** size/zh **vision**/ə **about,** item, edible, gallop, circus/ à *Fr.* **ami**/œ *Fr.* **feu,** *Ger.* **schön**/ü *Fr.* **tu,** *Ger.* **über**/KH *Ger.* **ich,** *Scot.* **loch**/N *Fr.* **bon.** ***Follows main vocabulary.** †**Of obscure origin.**

gyrfalcon
Painting by
John James Audubon

Hh

| 1 | 2 | 3 | 4 | 5 | 6 | 7 | 8 | 9 | 10 | 11 | 12 | 13 |
| Phoenician | | Greek | | Roman | | | Medieval | | | Modern | | |

Around 1000 B.C. the Phoenicians and other Semites of Syria and Palestine began to use a graphic sign in the forms (1,2). They gave it the name ḥēth, and used it for a laryngeal consonant ḥ, which is not found in English or in any other Indo-European language. After 900 B.C. the Greeks borrowed the sign from the Phoenicians, first using the form (3), later eliminating the upper and lower horizontal bars (4). They also changed its name to ēta, and since they had no use in their language for the Semitic sound ḥ, they used the sign at first for their consonant h. (In later Greek the sign acquired the value of a long ē, in distinction from the sign called epsilon, reserved for the short e.) The Greek forms passed via Etruscan to the Roman alphabet (5,6), retaining the consonantal value h. The Roman Monumental Capital (7) is the prototype of our modern capital, printed (10) and written (11). The written Roman form (6) developed into the late Roman and medieval Uncial (8) and Cursive (9), in which the horizontal bar and the upper part of the right vertical line were replaced by a single curved line. These are the bases of our modern small letter, printed (12) and written (13).

h, H (āch) *n., pl.* **h's** or *rare* **hs, H's** or **Hs. 1.** The eighth letter of the modern English alphabet. See **alphabet. 2.** Any of the speech sounds represented by this letter.

h, H, h., H. *Note:* As an abbreviation or symbol, *h* may be a small or a capital letter, with or without a period. Established forms or those generally preferred precede the definition. When no form is given, all four forms are in general use in that sense. **1. H** *Physics.* Hamiltonian. **2. h.**, **H.** harbor. **3. h.**, **H.** hard; hardness. **4. h** hecto-. **5. h.**, **H.** height. **6. H** henry. **7. h.**, **H.** high (gear). **8. h, h.** hit. **9. h.**, **H.** *Music.* horn. **10. h** hour. **11. h.** hundred. **12. h.**, **H.** husband. **13. H** The symbol for the element hydrogen. **14. h** The symbol for Planck's constant. **15.** The eighth in a series.

ha (hä) *interj.* Also **hah.** Used to express surprise, wonder, triumph, puzzlement, or pique. [Middle English *ha.*]

ha hectare.

h.a. this year (Latin *hoc anno*).

Haar·lem (här′ləm). The capital of North Holland, the Netherlands; a tulip-growing center in the southwest-central part of the province. Population, 168,000.

Hab. Habakkuk (Old Testament).

Ha·bak·kuk¹ (hə-băk′ək, hăb′ə-kŭk′). Also **Ha·bac·uc.** Hebrew prophet of the late seventh century B.C.

Ha·bak·kuk² (hə-băk′ək, hăb′ə-kŭk′) *n. Abbr.* **Hab.** A book of prophecies by Habakkuk in the Old Testament.

ha·ba·ne·ra (ä-bä-nä′rä) *n.* **1.** A slow Cuban dance. **2.** The music for this dance, in duple time, with a repetitive rhythmic pattern of a dotted eighth and sixteenth note pair followed by a pair of eighth notes. [Spanish *(danza) habenera,* "Havanan (dance)," from feminine of *habenero,* HABANERO.]

Ha·ba·ne·ro (ä-bä-nä′rō) *n.* A native or inhabitant of Havana. [Spanish, from *La Habana,* HAVANA.]

Hab·ba·ni·ya, Lake (hə-băn′ē-ə, -ē-yə). A salt lake occupying 54 square miles on the western bank of the Euphrates River, central Iraq.

hab. corp. habeas corpus.

hab·da·lah (häv′dä-lä′) *n.* Also **Hab·da·lah.** A Jewish religious ceremony observed at the close of a Sabbath or holy day. [Hebrew *habdālāh,* separation.]

ha·be·as cor·pus (hā′bē-əs kôr′pəs). *Abbr.* **hab. corp.** *Law.* One of a variety of writs that may be issued to bring a party before a court or judge, having as its function the release of a party from unlawful restraint. [Middle English, from Medieval Latin *habeās corpus,* "you shall have the body" (the first words of such a writ) : Latin *habeās,* second person singular present subjunctive of *habēre,* to have (see **ghabh-** in Appendix*) + *corpus,* body, CORPUS.]

Ha·ber (hä′bər), **Fritz.** 1868–1934. German industrial chemist; awarded Nobel Prize in chemistry (1918).

hab·er·dash·er (hăb′ər-dăsh′ər) *n.* **1.** A dealer in men's furnishings such as hats, shirts, and socks. **2.** *British.* A dealer in sewing notions and small wares. [Middle English *haberdasher,* from Norman French *haberdasser, hapertasser* (both unattested), from *hapertas†,* fabric, cloth.]

hab·er·dash·er·y (hăb′ər-dăsh′ə-rē) *n., pl.* **-ies. 1.** The goods and wares of a haberdasher. **2.** A haberdasher's shop.

hab·er·geon (hăb′ər-jən) *n.* Also **hau·ber·geon. 1.** A short, sleeveless coat of mail. **2.** A hauberk. [Middle English, from Old French *haubergeon,* from *hauberc,* HAUBERK.]

hab·ile (hăb′ïl) *adj. Rare.* Adroit; handy. [French, from Old French, from Latin *habilis,* able, easily handled, from *habēre,* to hold, have. See **ghabh-** in Appendix.*]

ha·bil·i·ment (hə-bĭl′ə-mənt) *n.* **1.** *Plural.* **a.** The dress or garb associated with an office or occasion: *"shrouded from head to foot in the habiliments of the grave"* (Poe). **b.** Clothes. **2.** *Rare.* Outfit; attire. [Old French *(h)abillement,* from *habiller,* to make fit, fit out, perhaps from *habile,* HABILE.]

ha·bil·i·tate (hə-bĭl′ə-tāt′) *v.* **-tated, -tating, -tates.** —*tr.* **1.** To supply with the means; especially, to back (a mining operation) with working capital. **2.** *Rare.* To clothe. **3.** *Obsolete.* To capacitate; qualify. —*intr.* To qualify oneself for an office, especially as a teacher in a German university. [Late Latin *habilitāre,* to qualify, from Latin *habilitās,* ability, from *habilis,* HABILE.] —**ha·bil′i·ta′tion** *n.*

hab·it (hăb′ĭt) *n.* **1. a.** A constant, often unconscious inclination to perform some act, acquired through its frequent repetition. **b.** An established trend of the mind or character. **2.** *Often plural.* Customary manner or practice: *a man of ascetic habits.* **3.** An addiction. **4.** *Rare.* Physical constitution. **5.** Characteristic appearance, form, or manner of growth, especially of a plant. **6. a.** A distinctive dress or costume, especially of a religious order. **b.** A riding habit. —*tr.v.* **habited, -iting, -its. 1.** To clothe; dress. **2.** *Archaic.* To habituate. **3.** *Archaic.* To inhabit. [Middle English *(h)abit,* from Old French, from Latin *habitus,* from the past participle of *habēre,* to hold, have. See **ghabh-** in Appendix.*]

Synonyms: *habit, practice, custom, usage, use, wont, habitude, fashion.* These nouns refer to patterns of behavior set by continual repetition. *Habit* applies to any activity so well established that it occurs without thought on the part of an individual. *Practice* denotes any chosen pattern of individual or group behavior. *Custom* is either individual or group behavior, especially as established by long practice and accepted conventions. *Usage* refers to customary practice that has become an accepted standard for a group, and thus regulates individual behavior. *Use* and *wont* are terms for customary and distinctive practice of an individual or a group. *Habitude* refers to an individual's habitual inclination to follow a set course; unlike *habit,* it applies to a disposition to behave in a certain way, rather than to a specific act. *Fashion* implies behavior based on prevailing customs of a group or, in a contrasting sense, on individual tendencies: *in his own characteristic fashion.*

hab·it·a·ble (hăb′ə-tə-bəl) *adj.* Suitable to live in; inhabitable. [Middle English *abitable,* from Old French *(h)abitable,* from Latin *habitābilis,* from *habitāre,* to inhabit, reside, to have frequently, from *habēre* (past participle *habitus*), to have, hold. See

---

ă pat/ā pay/âr care/ä father/b bib/ch church/d deed/ĕ pet/ē be/f fife/g gag/h hat/hw which/ĭ pit/ī pie/îr pier/j judge/k kick/l lid/
needle/m mum/n no, sudden/ng thing/ŏ pot/ō toe/ô paw, for/oi noise/ou out/ŏŏ took/ōō boot/p pop/r roar/s sauce/sh ship, dish/

ghabh- in Appendix.*] —**hab′i·ta·bil′i·ty, hab′i·ta·ble·ness** *n.* —**hab′it·a·bly** *adv.*

hab·i·tant (hăb′ə-tənt; *French* à-bē-täɴ′ *for sense 2*) *n.* Also **ha·bi·tan** (*French* à-bē-täɴ′) (for sense 2). **1.** An inhabitant. **2.** An inhabitant of French descent in Canada or Louisiana belonging to the small farmer class. [Old French, from the present participle of *habiter,* to inhabit, from Latin *habitāre.* See **habitable.**]

hab·i·tat (hăb′ə-tăt′) *n.* **1.** The area or type of environment in which an organism or biological population normally lives or occurs. **2.** The place where a person or thing is most likely to be found. [Latin, it dwells (the first word in Latin descriptions of plant and animal species in old natural histories), third person singular present indicative of *habitāre,* to inhabit. See **habitable.**]

hab·i·ta·tion (hăb′ə-tā′shən) *n.* **1.** The act of inhabiting. **2.** The state of being inhabited. **3. a.** Natural environment or locality. **b.** Place of abode: *"his habitation is a flimsy affair of canes and thatch"* (Lesley B. Simpson). [Middle English *habitacioun,* from Old French *habitation,* from Latin *habitātiō,* from *habitātus,* past participle of *habitāre,* to inhabit. See **habitable.**]

hab·it·ed (hăb′ə-tĭd) *adj.* **1. a.** Dressed. **b.** Attired in a habit. **2.** *Archaic.* Inhabited.

hab·it-form·ing (hăb′ĭt-fôr′mĭng) *adj.* **1.** Leading to physiological addiction: *a habit-forming drug.* **2.** Tending to become habitual.

ha·bit·u·al (hə-bĭch′o͞o-əl) *adj.* **1. a.** Of the nature of a habit; done constantly or repeatedly. **b.** By habit: *a habitual smoker.* **2.** Customary; constant; inveterate: *habitual rudeness.* **3.** Established by long use; usual: *his habitual place.* —See Synonyms at **usual.** —**ha·bit′u·al·ly** *adv.* —**ha·bit′u·al·ness** *n.*

ha·bit·u·ate (hə-bĭch′o͞o-āt′) *tr.v.* **-ated, -ating, -ates.** To accustom by frequent repetition or prolonged exposure. [Late Latin *habituāre,* from Latin *habitus,* HABIT.] —**ha·bit′u·a′tion** *n.*

hab·i·tude (hăb′ə-to͞od′, -tyo͞od′) *n.* A customary behavior or manner; propensity. See Synonyms at **habit.** [Middle English *(h)abitude,* from Old French *habitude,* from Latin *habitūdo,* condition, habit, from *habitus,* HABIT.]

ha·bit·u·é (hə-bĭch′o͞o-ā′, hə-bĭch′o͞o-ā′; *French* à-bē-tü-ā′) *n.* A frequenter of a particular club, restaurant, or other place of entertainment. See Synonyms at **votary.** [French, from the past participle of *habituer,* to frequent, from Late Latin *habituāre,* HABITUATE.]

hab·i·tus (hăb′ə-təs) *n., pl.* **habitus.** Physical and constitutional characteristics, especially as related to susceptibility to a disease. [New Latin, from Latin, appearance, HABIT.]

Habs·burg. See **Hapsburg.**

ha·chure (hă-sho͝or′, hăsh′o͝or) *n.* One of the short lines used to shade or to indicate slopes on maps and also their degree and direction. —*tr.v.* (hă-sho͝or′) **hachured, -churing, -chures.** To make hatching on (a map). [French, from *hacher,* engrave lines on, chop up. See **hash.**]

ha·ci·en·da (hä′sē-ĕn′də; *Spanish* ä-syĕn′dä) *n.* **1.** In Spanish-speaking countries or areas influenced by Spain, a large estate; a plantation or large ranch. **2.** The house of the owner of the hacienda; especially in the southwestern United States, a low sprawling house with a projecting roof and wide porches. [Spanish, domestic work, landed property, from Latin *facienda,* things to be done, neuter plural gerundive of *facere,* to do. See **dhē-**[1] in Appendix.*]

hack[1] (hăk) *v.* **hacked, hacking, hacks.** —*tr.* **1.** To cut with irregular and heavy blows or in a random manner; to chip, notch, chop off, or chop up roughly with a pick, knife, ax, or other tool. **2.** To break up (earth) into clods or ridges. **3.** To strike the arm or kick the shin of (an opponent) in field sports. **4.** To mangle (a narrative) by cutting. —*intr.* **1.** To chop or chip away at something. **2.** To cough in short, dry-throated spasms. —*n.* **1.** A rough irregular cut or notch made by hacking. **2.** A tool used for chopping or breaking up something, as a hoe or mattock. **3. a.** A kick or chopping blow. **b.** A wound from this. **4.** A rough, dry cough. [Middle English *hacken,* Old English *(tō)haccian,* to cut to pieces. See **keg-** in Appendix.*] —**hack′er** *n.*

hack[2] (hăk) *n.* **1.** A horse used for riding or driving; a hackney. **2.** A broken-down horse for hire; a jade. **3. a.** A political hireling. **b.** One who hires himself out to do routine writing. **4.** A carriage or hackney for hire. **5.** *Informal.* A taxicab. **6.** *Slang.* A prison guard. —*v.* **hacked, hacking, hacks.** —*tr.* **1.** To let out for hire. **2.** To employ as a hack. **3.** *Informal.* To write as a hack. **4.** To make banal or hackneyed with indiscriminate use. —*intr.* **1.** *Informal.* To work as a hack, especially as a taxicab driver or as a writer. **2.** To ride on horseback along the path at a leisurely jog. —*adj.* **1.** For, by, or designating a hack. **2.** Banal; routine; commercial. [Short for HACKNEY.]

hack[3] (hăk) *n.* **1.** A drying frame or rack, as for cheese, fish, or bricks. **2.** A row of unfired bricks laid out to dry. **3.** A feeding rack, especially for hawks. —*tr.v.* **hacked, hacking, hacks. 1.** To set out on a rack to dry. **2.** To keep (hawks) at partial liberty. [From (influenced by dialectal *heck,* frame used in textile manufacture) HATCH (door).]

hack·a·more (hăk′ə-môr′, -mōr′) *n.* A rope or rawhide halter with a wide band that can be lowered over a horse's eyes, used in breaking horses to a bridle. [Corruption of Spanish *jaquima,* headstall of a halter, from Old Spanish *xaquima,* from Arabic *shakīmah,* bit of a bridle, restraint.]

hack·ber·ry (hăk′bĕr′ē) *n., pl.* **-ries. 1.** Any of various trees or shrubs of the genus *Celtis,* having inconspicuous flowers and berrylike, often edible fruit. **2.** The fruit of a hackberry. **3.** The soft, yellowish wood of a hackberry. Also called "sugarberry." [Variant of earlier *hagberry* : *hag-,* from Scandinavian, akin to Old Norse *heggr,* hackberry (see **kagh-** in Appendix*) + BERRY.]

hack·but (hăk′bŭt′) *n.* Also **hag·but** (hăg′-). A **harquebus** *(see).* [Old French *haguebute, hacquebute,* from Middle Dutch *hakebusse,* HARQUEBUS.] —**hack′bu·teer′** (hăk′bə-tîr′), **hack′but·ter** (hăk′bŭt′ər) *n.*

Hack·en·sack (hăk′ən-săk). **1.** A river rising in southeastern New York and flowing 45 miles south through northeastern New Jersey to Newark Bay. **2.** A city and manufacturing center of northeastern New Jersey, on this river. Population, 31,000.

hack·ie (hăk′ē) *n. Slang.* A taxicab driver.

hack·le[1] (hăk′əl) *n.* **1.** One of the long, slender, often glossy feathers on the neck of a bird, especially a male domestic fowl. **2.** *Plural.* The erectile hairs at the back of the neck, especially of a dog or similar animal. **3. a.** A tuft of cock feathers trimming an artificial fishing fly. **b.** A **hackle fly** *(see).* —**get one's hackles up.** To be ready to fight. —**make the hackles rise. 1.** To put in a fighting mood. **2.** To cause a dog to bristle belligerently. —*tr.v.* **hackled, -ling, -les.** To trim (a fly) with a hackle. [Middle English *hakell, hekele, hechele,* HATCHEL.]

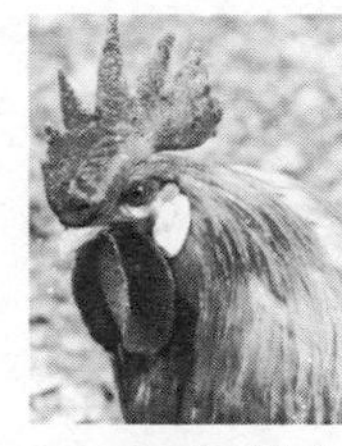

hackle[1]
Hackles of a
Rhode Island Red

hack·le[2] (hăk′əl) *v.* **-led, -ling, -les.** *Rare.* —*tr.* To chop roughly; mangle by hacking. —*intr.* To hack. [Frequentative of HACK (cut).]

hackle fly. An artificial fishing fly trimmed with hackles and usually without wings. Also called "hackle."

hack·ly (hăk′lē) *adj.* Nicked or notched; jagged; rough. [From HACKLE (to hack).]

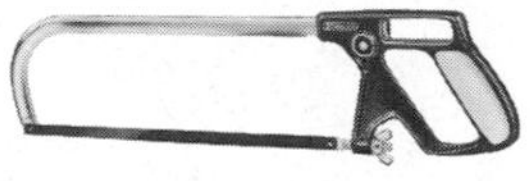

hacksaw

hack·man (hăk′mən) *n., pl.* **-men** (-mĭn). The driver of a hack or hired carriage.

hack·ma·tack (hăk′mə-tăk′) *n.* A tree, the **tamarack** *(see).* [From Algonquian, akin to Abnaki *akemantak,* snowshoe wood.]

hack·ney (hăk′nē) *n., pl.* **-neys. 1.** *Often capital* **H.** A horse of a breed developed in England, having a gait characterized by pronounced flexion of the knee. **2.** A horse suited for routine riding or driving. **3.** A coach or carriage for hire. —*tr.v.* **hackneyed, -neying, -neys. 1.** To overuse and cause to become banal and trite; cheapen. **2.** To hire out; let. —*adj.* **1.** Banal; trite. **2.** Hired. [Middle English *hakeney,* probably from *Hakenei,* HACKNEY (former administrative division) where such horses were raised.]

Hack·ney (hăk′nē). A borough of London, England, comprising the former administrative divisions of Hackney, Stoke Newington, and Shoreditch. Population, 257,000.

hack·neyed (hăk′nēd) *adj.* Overused and thus cheapened; trite; banal. See Synonyms at **trite.**

hack·saw (hăk′sô′) *n.* Also **hack saw.** A saw consisting of a tough, fine-toothed blade stretched taut in a frame, used for cutting metal.

had. Past tense and past participle of **have.**

Had·ding·ton (hăd′ĭng-tən). **1.** Also **Had·ding·ton·shire** (-shîr, -shər). The former name for **East Lothian. 2.** The county seat of East Lothian, southeastern Scotland. Population, 6,000.

had·dock (hăd′ək) *n., pl.* **haddock** or **-docks.** A food fish, *Melanogrammus aeglefinus,* of northern Atlantic waters, related to and resembling the cod. [Middle English *haddok,* from Norman French *hadoc,* variant of Old French *(h)adot*†.]

hade (hād) *n.* The angle of inclination from the vertical of a vein, fault, or lode. —*intr.v.* **haded, hading, hades.** To incline from the vertical. Used of a vein, fault, or lode. [Origin unknown.]

ha·des (hā′dēz) *n.* Also **Ha·des.** Hell. [From HADES.]

Ha·des[1] (hā′dēz). *Greek Mythology.* The god of the nether world and dispenser of earthly riches; a brother of Zeus and husband of Persephone; identified with the Roman god Pluto.

Ha·des[2] (hā′dēz). *Greek Mythology.* The nether-world kingdom of Hades, the abode of the shades of the dead. [Greek *Haidēs.* See **weid-** in Appendix.*]

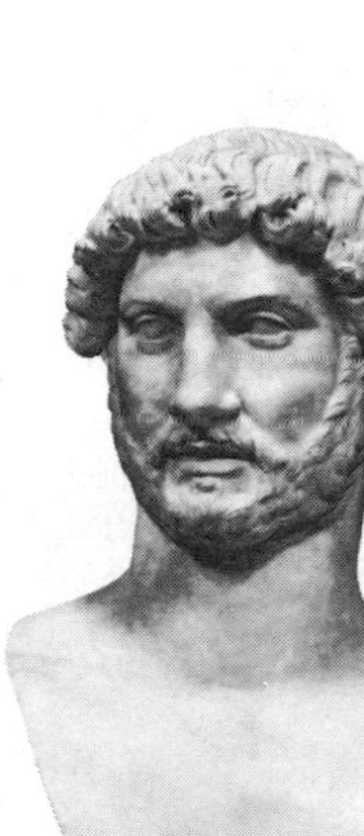

Hadrian

Ha·dhra·maut (hä′drä-mout′, -môt′). Also **Ha·dra·maut.** A coastal region occupying 58,000 square miles of South Arabia, on the Arabian Sea.

hadj (hăj) *n.* Also **haj, hajj.** A pilgrimage to Mecca made during Ramadan as an objective of the religious life of a Moslem. [Arabic *ḥajj,* pilgrimage, from *ḥajja,* he went on a pilgrimage.]

hadj·i (hăj′ē) *n., pl.* **-is.** Also **haj·i, haj·ji. 1. a.** A Moslem who has made a pilgrimage to Mecca. **b.** A title of address used before the name of a Moslem who has made this pilgrimage. **2.** A Christian of the Near East or Orient who has visited the Holy Sepulcher in Jerusalem. [Arabic *ḥājjī,* from *ḥajj,* HADJ.]

had·n't (hăd′ənt). Contraction of *had not.*

Ha·dri·an (hā′drē-ən). Latin name, Publius Aelius Hadrianus. A.D. 76–138. Roman emperor (117–138); nephew of Trajan.

Hadrian's Wall (hā′drē-ənz). A fortified wall in northern England, extending from Solway Firth to the Tyne River; constructed A.D. 120–123.

Had·ru·me·tum. The ancient name for **Sousse.**

hadst. *Archaic.* Past tense and past participle of **have.**

hae (hā, hă) *tr.v.* **haed, haen** (hān, hăn), **haeing, haes.** *Scottish.* To have.

Haeck·el (hĕk′əl), **Ernst Heinrich.** 1834–1919. German biologist and natural philosopher.

Hae·ju (hī′jo͞o). *Japanese* **Kai·shu** (kī′sho͞o). A city and port of southwestern North Korea, on the Yellow Sea. Population, 82,000.

hae·res. Variant of **heres.**

haet (hāt) *n. Scottish.* A minute amount; whit; jot. [Contraction of *hae it!,* take it!]

ha·fiz (hä′fĭz) *n.* **1.** A Moslem who has memorized the Koran,

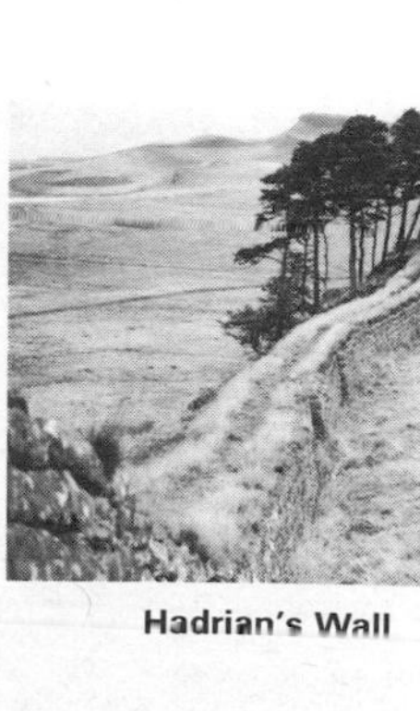

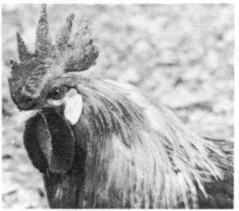

Hadrian's Wall

t tight/th thin, path/*th* this, bathe/ŭ cut/ûr urge/v valve/w with/y yes/z zebra, size/zh vision/ə about, item, edible, gallop, circus/
à *Fr.* ami/œ *Fr.* feu, *Ger.* schön/ü *Fr.* tu, *Ger.* über/KH *Ger.* ich, *Scot.* loch/ɴ *Fr.* bon. *Follows main vocabulary. †Of obscure origin.

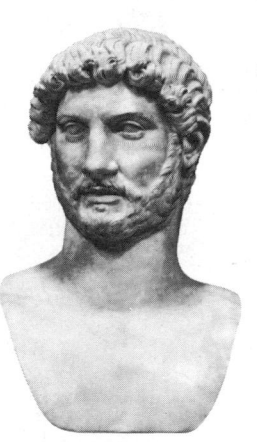

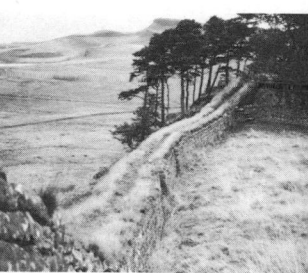

2. A title of respect used with the name of a Moslem who has accomplished this memorization. [Persian, from Arabic *hāfiz*, guard, watch, one who knows the Koran by heart, from *hafiza*, watch, protect, memorize.]

haf·ni·um (hăf′nē-əm) *n. Symbol* **Hf** A brilliant, silvery, metallic element separated from ores of zirconium and used in nuclear reactor control rods, as a getter for oxygen and nitrogen, and in the manufacture of tungsten filaments. Atomic number 72, atomic weight 178.49, melting point 2,150°C, boiling point 5,400°C, specific gravity 13.29, valence 4. [New Latin, from *Hafnia*, Latin name for Copenhagen, Denmark.]

haft (hăft, häft) *n.* A handle or hilt; especially, a handle of a bladed instrument, such as a sword, knife, or sickle. —*tr.v.* **hafted, hafting, hafts.** To fit or equip with a hilt or handle; to set into a handle. [Middle English *haft*, Old English *hæft*. See **kap-** in Appendix.*]

haf·ta·rah. Variant of **haphtarah.**

Ha·fun (hä-fōōn′). A promontory on the northeastern coast of Somalia.

hag[1] (hăg) *n.* **1.** An ugly, frightful old woman; a termagant; crone. **2.** A witch; sorceress. **3.** *Obsolete.* A female demon. **4.** A **hagfish** *(see).* [Middle English *hagge*, probably short for Old English *hægtesse*, witch. See **kagh-** in Appendix.*]

hag[2] (hăg) *n. Scottish & British Regional.* **1.** A boggy area; marsh; quagmire. **2.** A spot in boggy land that is distinguished from the surrounding area by being either softer or more solid. **3.** A cutting in a peat bog. [Middle English *hag*, gap, chasm, probably from Old Norse *högg*, gap, cutting blow. See **kau-**[2] in Appendix.*]

Hag. Haggai (Old Testament).

Ha·gar (hā′gər). The concubine of Abraham, mother of his bastard son Ishmael, and handmaiden to his wife Sarah, who, through jealousy for her own son Isaac, turned Hagar and Ishmael out of Abraham's household. Genesis 16–19.

hag·born (hăg′bôrn′) *adj.* Born of a witch or hag.

hag·but. Variant of **hackbut.**

Ha·gen[1] (hä′gən). In the *Nibelungenlied*, the murderer of Siegfried.

Ha·gen[2] (hä′gən). A city and steel-manufacturing center of central North Rhine-Westphalia, West Germany. Population, 199,000.

Ha·gers·town (hā′gərz-toun). A city and manufacturing center of northwestern Maryland. Population, 37,000.

hag·fish (hăg′fĭsh′) *n., pl.* **hagfish** or **-fishes.** Any of various primitive, eel-shaped marine fishes of the family Myxinidae, having a jawless sucking mouth with rasping teeth with which they bore into and feed on other fishes. Also called "hag."

Hag·ga·dah (hə-gä′də, -gô′də) *n., pl.* **-doth** (-dōt, -dōth). Also **Hag·ga·da.** **1.** Traditional Jewish literature; especially, the nonlegal part of the Talmud. Compare **Halakah.** **2.** The book containing the story of the Exodus and the ritual of the Seder, read at the Passover Seder. [Hebrew *haggādāh*, narration, telling, from *hagged*, narrate, tell, from the Semitic root *ngd*, to rise, to become conspicuous.] —**hag·gad′ic** (-găd′ĭk, -gä′dĭk, -gô′dĭk) *adj.*

hag·ga·dist (hə-gä′dĭst) *n.* **1.** A haggadic writer. **2.** A student of haggadic literature. —**hag′ga·dis′tic** (hăg′ə-dĭs′tĭk) *adj.*

Hag·ga·i[1] (hăg′ē-ī′, hăg′ī′). A Hebrew prophet of the sixth century B.C.

Hag·ga·i[2] (hăg′ē-ī′, hăg′ī′) *n. Abbr.* **Hag.** A book of the Old Testament attributed to Haggai.

hag·gard (hăg′ərd) *adj.* **1. a.** Appearing worn and exhausted from or as if from suffering or deprivation; emaciated; gaunt: *"he looked as haggard as an actor by daylight"* (Henry James). **b.** Wild and unruly; uncontrolled. **2.** Wild and intractable. Said of a hawk used in falconry. —*n.* An adult hawk captured for training. [Old French *hagard*, untamed hawk, wild hawk, perhaps from Germanic. See **kagh-** in Appendix.*] —**hag′gard·ly** *adv.* —**hag′gard·ness** *n.*

Synonyms: *haggard, wasted, worn, careworn.* These adjectives mean showing the effects of anxiety, disease, hunger, or fatigue. *Haggard* refers particularly to facial appearance and implies thinness, tiredness, and often the expression of one seemingly distraught or harried. *Wasted* stresses emaciation, or marked loss of flesh, with consequent frailness or enfeeblement; the term is most often associated with illness or extreme physical hardship. *Worn* can refer to emaciation or to the effects of overwork or worry. *Careworn* is applicable to one whose physical appearance reveals the effects of worry, anxiety, or burdensome responsibility.

hag·gis (hăg′ĭs) *n.* A Scottish dish consisting of a mixture of the minced heart, lungs, and liver of a sheep or calf mixed with suet, onions, oatmeal, and seasonings, and boiled in the stomach of the animal. [Middle English *hageset*.]

hag·gish (hăg′ĭsh) *adj.* Of or characteristic of a hag; haglike. —**hag′gish·ly** *adv.* —**hag′gish·ness** *n.*

hag·gle (hăg′əl) *v.* **-gled, -gling, -gles.** —*intr.* **1.** To bargain, as over the price of something; dicker: *"he preferred to be overcharged than to haggle"* (Maugham). **2.** To argue in an attempt to come to terms. —*tr.* **1.** To cut in a crude, unskillful manner; to hack; mangle. **2.** *Archaic.* To harass or worry by wrangling. —See Synonyms at **argue.** —*n.* An instance of haggling. [Frequentative of dialectal *hag*, to cut, from Middle English *haggen*, from Old Norse *höggva*. See **kau-**[2] in Appendix.*] —**hag′gler** *n.*

hag·i·ar·chy (hăg′ē-är′kē, hā′jē-) *n., pl.* **-chies.** Also **hag·i·oc·ra·cy** (hăg′ē-ŏk′rə-sē) (for sense 1). **1.** Government by holy men, such as saints. **2.** A hierarchy of saints. [HAGI(O)- + -ARCHY.]

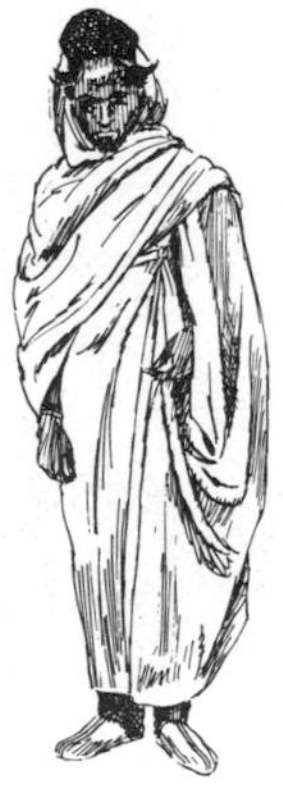

haik

hagio-, hagi-. Indicates: **1.** A saint or body of saints; for example, **hagiology, hagiarchy.** **2.** A sacred or holy place; for example, **hagioscope.** [Late Latin, from Greek, from *hagios*, holy. See **yag-** in Appendix.*]

Hag·i·og·ra·pha (hăg′ē-ŏg′rə-fə, hā′jē-) *n.* Plural in form, used with a singular or plural verb. The third of the three ancient Jewish divisions of the Old Testament, containing those books not in the Law (Torah) or the Prophets, and comprising usually the Psalms, Proverbs, Job, the Song of Solomon, Ruth, Lamentations, Ecclesiastes, Esther, Daniel, Ezra, Nehemiah, and Chronicles. Also called "Writings." [Late Latin, from Greek, "sacred writings" : *hagio-*, sacred + *-grapha*, writings, plural of *-graphos*, -GRAPH.]

hag·i·og·ra·phy (hăg′ē-ŏg′rə-fē, hā′jē-) *n., pl.* **-phies.** **1.** Biography of saints. **2.** Any idealizing or worshipful biography. [HAGIO- + -GRAPHY.] —**hag′i·og′raph·er** *n.* —**hag′i·o·graph′ic** (-ə-grăf′ĭk), **hag′i·o·graph′i·cal** *adj.*

hag·i·ol·o·gy (hăg′ē-ŏl′ə-jē, hā′jē-) *n., pl.* **-gies.** **1.** Literature dealing with the lives of saints. **2.** A history of sacred writings. **3.** An authoritative list of saints. [HAGIO- + -LOGY.] —**hag′i·o·log′ic** (-ə-lŏj′ĭk), **hag′i·o·log′i·cal** *adj.* —**hag′i·ol′o·gist** *n.*

hag·i·o·scope (hăg′ē-ə-skōp′, hā′jē-) *n.* A small opening provided in an interior wall of a church to enable those in the transept to have a view of the main altar. [HAGIO- + -SCOPE.] —**hag′i·o·scop′ic** (-skŏp′ĭk) *adj.*

hag·rid·den (hăg′rĭd′n) *adj.* **1.** Harassed or pursued by or as if by a witch. **2.** Tormented or harassed, as by nightmares or unreasoning fears: *"a man hagridden by the future—haunted by visions of an imminent heaven or hell upon earth"* (C.S. Lewis).

Hague, The (hāg). *Dutch* **'s Gra·ven·ha·ge** (sKHrä′vən-hä′KHə). The de facto capital of the Netherlands, a port in western South Holland on the North Sea. Population, 602,000.

Hague Tribunal. Officially, the Permanent Court of Arbitration. A tribunal established at The Hague in 1899 for the peaceful settlement of international disputes.

hah. Variant of **ha.**

ha-ha[1] (hä′hä′) *n.* A sound made in imitation of laughter. —*interj.* Also **haw-haw** (hô′hô′). Used to express amusement or scorn. [Middle English *ha ha*, Old English *ha ha*.]

ha-ha[2] (hä′hä′) *n.* Also **haw-haw** (hô′hô′). A moat, walled ditch, or hedge sunk in the ground to serve as a fence without impairing the view or scenic appeal; sunken fence. [French *haha*, from *haha!*, interjection used to express surprise, presumably because the fence is an unexpected obstacle.]

Hahn (hän), **Otto.** 1879–1968. German physical chemist; worked on atomic fission.

Hah·ne·mann (hä′nə-mən), **Christian Friedrich Samuel.** 1755–1843. German physician; founder of homeopathic medicine.

Hai·da (hī′də) *n., pl.* **Haida** or **-das.** **1.** Any of the Haidan-speaking North American Indian tribes inhabiting the Queen Charlotte Islands, British Columbia, and Prince of Wales Island, Alaska. **2.** A member of these tribes. **3.** The language of these tribes, the sole survivor of the Haida family of languages. **4.** A family of the Na-Dene phylum. —**Hai′dan** *adj.*

Hai·dar·a·bad. See **Hyderabad.**

Hai·fa (hī′fə). A city and port of Israel, located in the northwest on the Bay of Acre. Population, 195,000.

haik (hīk, hāk) *n.* A large piece of cotton, silk, or wool cloth, draped over the head and about the body, worn as an outer garment by Arabs. [Arabic *ḥā′ik*, from *ḥāka*, to weave.]

hai·ku (hī′kōō) *n., pl.* **haiku.** A Japanese lyric poem of a fixed, 17-syllable form that often simply points to a thing or pairing of things in nature that has moved the poet. [Japanese : *hai*, from Ancient Chinese *b′ai* (Mandarin *p′ai*[2]), amusement + *ku*, from Ancient Chinese *kiu* (Mandarin *chü*[4]), sentence, verse.]

hail[1] (hāl) *n.* **1. a.** Precipitation in the form of pellets of ice and hard snow. **b.** A hailstone. **c.** *Archaic.* A hailstorm. **2.** Something that falls with the force and quantity of a shower of hail: *a hail of criticism.* —*v.* **hailed, hailing, hails.** —*intr.* **1.** To precipitate. **2.** To fall like hail. —*tr.* To pour down or forth: *hail oaths at someone.* [Middle English *hail, hagel*, Old English *hagol*. See **kaghlo-** in Appendix.*]

hail[2] (hāl) *v.* **hailed, hailing, hails.** —*tr.* **1. a.** To salute or greet; to welcome. **b.** To greet or acclaim enthusiastically. **c.** To designate by tribute: *They hailed him their leader.* **2.** To call out to in order to catch the attention of: *hail a cab.* —*intr.* To signal or call to a passing ship as a greeting or an identification of oneself. —**hail from.** To come or originate from: *He hails from Tampa.* —*n.* **1.** The act of hailing. **2.** A shout made to greet or catch the attention of someone. **3.** Hailing distance. —*interj.* Used to express a greeting or tribute. [Middle English *hailen, haeilen*, from *(wæs)haeil*, "(be) healthy," hail, from Old Norse *heill*, whole, healthy. See **kailo-** in Appendix.*] —**hail′er** *n.*

Hai·lar (hī′lär′). A river rising in northwestern Manchuria and flowing 240 miles west to the Argun.

Hai·le Se·las·sie (hī′lē sə-lăs′ē, sə-lä′sē). Title of Ras Taffari Makonnen. Born 1891. Emperor of Ethiopia since 1930; forced into exile as a result of Italian conquest (1936–41).

hail-fel·low (hāl′fĕl′ō) *adj.* Heartily friendly and congenial. Also "hail-fellow-well-met." —*n.* Also **hail fellow.** A boon companion; congenial comrade. Also called "hail fellow well met." [From the archaic greetings *Hail, fellow!* and *Hail, fellow! well met!*]

Hail Mary. The **Ave Maria** *(see).*

hail·stone (hāl′stōn′) *n.* A hard pellet of snow and ice.

hail·storm (hāl′stôrm′) *n.* A storm with hail.

Hai·nan (hī′nän′). **1.** An island occupying 13,000 square miles

ă pat/ā pay/âr care/ä father/b bib/ch church/d deed/ĕ pet/ē be/f fife/g gag/h hat/hw which/ĭ pit/ī pie/îr pier/j judge/k kick/l lid, needle/m mum/n no, sudden/ng thing/ŏ pot/ō toe/ô paw, for/oi noise/ou out/ŏŏ took/ōō boot/p pop/r roar/s sauce/sh ship, dish/

in the South China Sea and forming part of Kwangtung, China. **2.** A strait between this island and the South China Sea linking the Luichow Peninsula with the Gulf of Tonkin.

Hai·naut (ĕ'nō'). *Flemish* **He·ne·gou·wen** (hā'nə-gou'wən). A province, 1,436 square miles in area, of southwestern Belgium. Population, 1,249,000. Capital, Mons.

hain't (hānt). *Regional Nonstandard.* Contraction of *have not* or *has not.* [Influenced by AIN'T.]

Hai·phong (hī'fŏng'). A city and port of North Vietnam, 60 miles east of Hanoi, near the Gulf of Tonkin. Population, 182,000.

hair (hâr) *n.* **1. a.** One of the cylindrical often pigmented filaments characteristically growing from the epidermis of a mammal. **b.** A growth of such filaments, as that forming the coat of an animal or covering the scalp of a human being. **2.** Any similar filamentous projection or bristle, such as a seta of an arthropod or an epidermal process of a plant. **3.** Fabric made from the hair of certain animals: *a coat of camel's hair.* **4.** A minute distance or narrow margin: *win by a hair.* **5.** A precise or exact degree. **—get in one's hair.** To upset or annoy one. **—let one's hair down.** To drop one's reserve or inhibitions. **—split hairs.** To make petty and fine distinctions. **—turn a hair.** To reveal discomfiture. Used in negative constructions: *accepted the challenge without turning a hair.* —*adj.* **1.** Made of or with hair. **2.** For the hair: *a hair dryer.* [Middle English *haire, hare,* Old English *hǣr,* from Germanic *hēram* (unattested).] **—haired** (hârd) *adj.*

hair·ball (hâr'bôl') *n.* A small mass of hair swallowed by an animal, often causing indigestion or convulsions.

hair·breadth (hâr'brĕdth') *adj.* Extremely close: *a hairbreadth escape.* —*n.* Variant of **hairsbreadth.**

hair·brush (hâr'brŭsh') *n.* A brush for grooming the hair.

hair·cloth (hâr'klôth', -klŏth') *n.* A wiry fabric having usually a cotton or linen warp with a horsehair filler, used for upholstering and for stiffening and interlining garments.

hair·cut (hâr'kŭt') *n.* **1.** A cutting of the hair. **2.** The style in which hair is cut.

hair·do (hâr'do͞o') *n., pl.* **-dos. 1.** The style in which a woman's hair is arranged. **2.** The hair so arranged; coiffure.

hair·dress·er (hâr'drĕs'ər) *n.* A person who cuts or arranges women's hair.

hair·dress·ing (hâr'drĕs'ĭng) *n.* **1.** The occupation of a hairdresser. **2.** The act of dressing or arranging the hair. **3.** A cosmetic or medicinal preparation for dressing the hair.

hair·less (hâr'lĭs) *adj.* Having little or no hair.

hair·line (hâr'līn') *n.* **1.** The outline of the growth of hair on the head, especially across the front. **2.** A very slender line. **3.** *Printing.* **a.** A very fine line on a typeface. **b.** A style of type using such lines. **4. a.** A textile design having thin, threadlike stripes. **b.** A fabric, usually a worsted, with such stripes. **—hair'line'** *adj.*

hair piece. A covering or bunch of human or artificial hair used to cover baldness or give shape to a coiffure.

hair·pin (hâr'pĭn') *n.* A thin, cylindrical strip of metal, tortoiseshell, or other material bent in a long U shape, used by women to secure a hairdo or a headdress. —*adj.* Doubled back in a deep U: *a hairpin curve in the road.*

hair-rais·er (hâr'rā'zər) *n.* Something that causes wild excitement, terror, or thrills: *The ride in that sports car was a real hair-raiser.*

hair-rais·ing (hâr'rā'zĭng) *adj.* Horrifying; terrifying.

hairs·breadth, hair's-breadth (hârz'brĕdth') *n.* Also **hair·breadth** (hâr'brĕdth'). A small space or distance; narrow margin: *win by a hairsbreadth.*

hair seal. Any of various seals of the family Phocidae, having a stiff, hairlike coat in the adult and ears visible only as small indentations.

hair shirt. A coarse haircloth garment worn next to the skin by religious ascetics to mortify the flesh.

hair space. *Printing.* The narrowest of the metal spaces used for separating words or letters.

hair·split·ting (hâr'splĭt'ĭng) *n.* The making of unreasonably fine distinctions; quibbling. —*adj.* Concerned with subtle but petty distinctions. **—hair'split'ter** *n.*

hair·spring (hâr'sprĭng') *n.* A fine coiled spring that regulates the movement of the balance wheel in a watch or clock.

hair·streak (hâr'strēk') *n.* Any of numerous butterflies of the subfamily Theclinae, having transverse streaks on the underwings and fine, hairlike projections on the hind wings.

hair stroke. A very fine line in writing or printing, as a serif.

hair style. The design of a coiffure. **—hair stylist.**

hair trigger. A gun trigger adjusted to respond to a very slight pressure.

hair-trig·ger (hâr'trĭg'ər) *adj.* Responding to the slightest provocation: *a hair-trigger temper.*

hair·worm (hâr'wûrm') *n.* **1.** Any of various slender, parasitic nematode worms of the genus *Trichostrongylus,* that infest the stomach and small intestine of cattle, sheep, and related animals. **2.** A **horsehair worm** *(see).*

hair·y (hâr'ē) *adj.* **-ier, -iest. 1.** Covered with hair or hairlike projections; hirsute: *a hairy arm.* **2.** Of or like hair: *a hairy coat.* **3.** *Slang.* **a.** Fraught with difficulties; hazardous: *a hairy escape.* **b.** Outstanding; awesome. **—hair'i·ness** *n.*

Hai·ti (hā'tē). **1.** Also **Hay·ti.** *French* **Ha·ï·ti** (à-ē-tē'). A republic of the West Indies, 10,700 square miles in area, occupying the western third of Hispaniola. Population, 4,660,000. Capital, Port-au-Prince. **2.** The former name for **Hispaniola.**

Hai·ti·an (hā'shən, -tē-ən) *adj.* Also **Hay·ti·an.** Of or pertaining to Haiti, its people, or its dialect. —*n.* **1.** A native or inhabitant of Haiti. **2.** The French patois spoken by most Haitians. Also called "Haitian Creole."

haj, hajj. Variants of **hadj.**

haj·i, haj·ji. Variants of **hadji.**

hake (hāk) *n., pl.* **hake** or **hakes.** Any of various marine food fishes of the genera *Merluccius* and *Urophycis,* related to and resembling the cod. [Middle English *hake,* possibly from Old Norse *haki,* hook (from the shape of its underjaw). See **keg-** in Appendix.*]

Ha·ken·kreuz (hä'kən-kroits') *n.* The swastika used as a symbol of Nazi Germany or of anti-Semitism. [German, "hooked cross."]

ha·kim¹ (hä'kēm) *n.* Also **ha·keem.** A Moslem physician. [Arabic *ḥakīm,* wise, learned, philosopher, from *ḥakama,* to be wise, exercise authority.]

ha·kim² (hä'kēm) *n. pl.* **hakim** or **-kims.** A Moslem ruler, provincial governor, or judge. [Arabic *ḥākim,* governor, from *ḥakama,* to exercise authority.]

Hak·luyt (hăk'lo͞ot'), **Richard.** 1552?–1616. English geographer; compiler of voyages (1588–1600).

Ha·ko·da·te (hä'kō-dä'tē). A city and port of southwestern Hokkaido, Japan, on Tsugaru Strait. Population, 251,000.

Ha·la·kah (hä'lä-KHä') *n., pl.* **-koth** (-KHōt', -KHōth') or **-kahs.** Also **Hal·la·cha** *pl.* **-choth** or **-chas.** *Judaism.* The legal part of Talmudic literature, an interpretation of the laws of the Scriptures. Compare **Haggadah.** [Mishnaic Hebrew *halākhāh,* rule, tradition, from *hālakh,* go.] **—Ha·lak'ic** (hə-lăk'ĭk) *adj.*

ha·la·kist (hä'lə-kĭst, hə-lä'kĭst) *n.* Also **ha·la·chist.** A Hebrew judge or scholar who has written parts of the Halakah.

ha·la·tion (hā-lā'shən) *n.* **1.** A blurring or spreading of light around bright objects or areas on a photographic negative or print. **2.** A ring of light appearing around a bright object on a television screen. [HAL(O) + -ATION.]

ha·la·vah. Variant of **halvah.**

hal·berd (hăl'bərd) *n.* Also **hal·bert** (-bərt). A weapon of the 15th and 16th centuries having an axlike blade and a steel spike mounted on the end of a long shaft. [Middle English *halberd,* from Old French *hallebarde,* from Middle High German *helmbarde,* "handle ax" : *helm,* handle (see **kelp-** in Appendix*) + *barte,* ax, hatchet, from Old High German *barta* (see **bhardhā** in Appendix*).]

hal·ber·dier (hăl'bər-dîr') *n.* A soldier, attendant, or guard armed with a halberd.

hal·cy·on (hăl'sē-ən) *n.* **1.** A fabled bird, identified with the kingfisher, that was supposed to have had the power to calm the wind and the waves during the winter solstice while it nested on the sea. **2.** *Poetic.* A kingfisher. —*adj.* **1.** Calm and peaceful; tranquil. **2.** Prosperous; golden: *halcyon years.* —See Synonyms at **calm.** [Middle English *alceon,* from Latin *(h)alcyon,* from Greek *(h)alkuōn*†, a mythical bird, perhaps the kingfisher.]

halcyon days. 1. Days of fine weather occurring near the winter solstice, especially the seven days before and the seven after, attributed by legend to the magical powers of the halcyon. **2.** A period of peace and tranquillity.

Hal·cy·o·ne. Variant of **Alcyone.**

Hal·dane (hôl'dān'), **J(ohn) B(urdon) S(anderson).** 1892–1964. British geneticist.

hale¹ (hāl) *adj.* **haler, halest.** Sound in health; not infirm; vigorous; robust. See Synonyms at **healthy, strong.** [Middle English *hal(e),* Old English *hāl.* See **kailo-** in Appendix.*] **—hale'ness** *n.*

hale² (hāl) *tr.v.* **haled, haling, hales. 1.** To compel to go; to force: *hale a man into court.* **2.** *Archaic.* To pull, drag, draw, or hoist: *"The rope that haled the buckets from the well."* (Tennyson). [Middle English *halen,* from Norman French *haler,* from Old Norse *hala,* from Middle Low German *halen,* to pull. See **kel-³** in Appendix.*]

Hale (hāl), **Edward Everett.** 1822–1909. American Unitarian minister and author.

Hale (hāl), **George Ellery.** 1868–1938. American astronomer.

Hale (hāl), **Nathan.** 1755–1776. American army officer; hanged by the British for spying.

Ha·le·a·ka·la (hä'lā-ä-kä-lä'). A mountain rising to 10,032 feet in Haleakala National Park on eastern Maui Island, Hawaii, a dormant volcano containing the largest crater in the world.

ha·ler (hä'lər, -lĕr) *n., pl.* **-lers** or **-leru** (-lə-ro͞o'). A monetary unit equal to $^1/_{100}$ of the koruna of Czechoslovakia. See table of exchange rates at **currency.** [Czech, from Middle High German *haller,* an early German silver coin, from *Hall,* town in Swabia, Germany, where they were once minted.]

Hales (hālz), **Stephen.** 1677–1761. British botanist and physiologist.

half (hăf, häf) *n., pl.* **halves** (hăvz, hävz). **1. a.** One of two equal parts that together constitute a whole. **b.** A part of something approximately equal to the remainder. **2.** *Informal.* A fifty-cent piece. **3. a.** In some sports, one of the two playing periods into which a game is divided. **b.** The turn of one baseball team at bat. **4.** *Football.* A halfback. **5.** A golf score equal to the opponent's score on a hole or a round. **6.** *Chiefly British.* A school term; semester. **7.** Half an hour. Used in expressing time: *a half past one.* **—better half.** *Informal.* One's spouse; especially, one's wife. **—by half.** By a considerable extent; very much. **—by halves. 1.** Partially; imperfectly: *"If you injure your neighbor, better not do it by halves"* (G.B. Shaw). **2.** Reluctantly; unenthusiastically. **—in half.** Into halves. **—not the half of.** Only a fraction or a small part of. —*adj.* **1.** Being a half. **2.** Being approximately a half. **3.** Partial; incomplete. **4.** Having only one parent in common with another person. —*adv.* **1.** To the extent of exactly or nearly 50 per cent: *a half-*

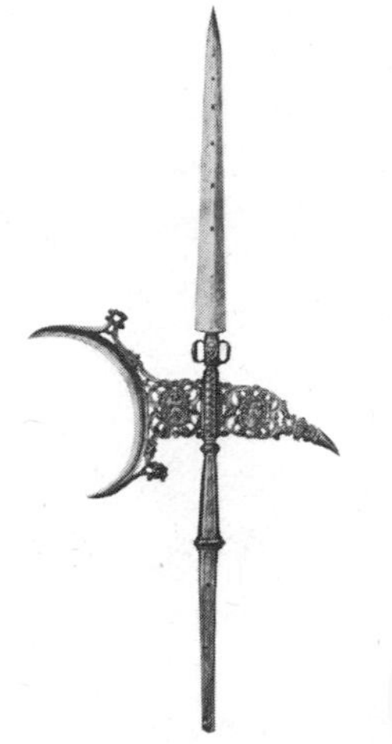

halberd
Sixteenth-century ceremonial halberd

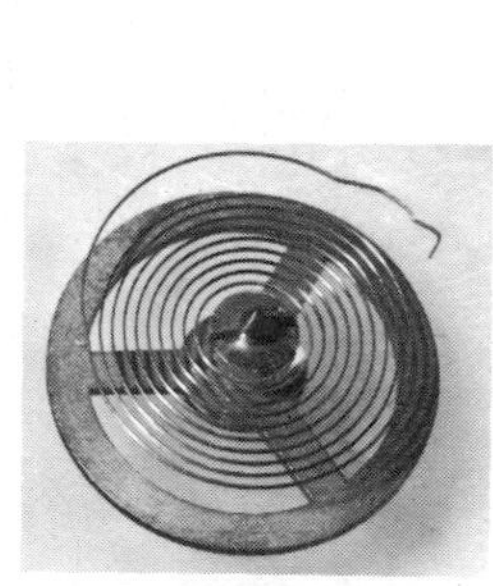

hairspring

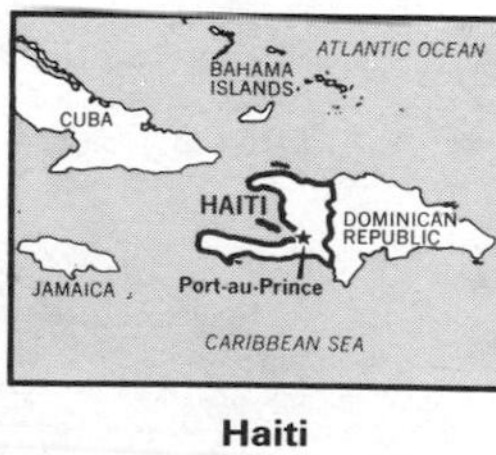

Haiti

empty tank. **2.** Not completely or sufficiently; partly: *only half-prepared.* **—go halves.** To share equally. [Middle English *half,* Old English *healf.* See **skel-**[1] in Appendix.*]

half-a-crown. Variant of **half-crown.**

half-and-half (hăf′ənd-hăf′, häf′ənd-häf′) *adj.* Being half one thing and half another. *—adv.* In equal portions. *—n.* **1.** A mixture of two things in equal portions; especially, a mixture of equal parts of milk and cream. **2.** *British.* A blend of malt liquors, especially porter and ale.

half-assed (hăf′ăst′, häf′äst′) *adj. Vulgar Slang.* **1.** Without full experience, knowledge, or ability. **2.** Without complete or proper plans, organization, or efficiency.

half·back (hăf′băk′, häf′-) *n. Abbr.* **hb, hb. 1.** *Football.* One of the two players positioned near the flanks behind the line of scrimmage. **2.** One of several players in various sports stationed behind the forward line. **3.** The position played by a halfback.

half-baked (hăf′bākt′, häf′-) *adj.* **1.** Only partly baked; not cooked through. **2.** *Informal.* Not sufficiently thought out; ill-conceived; foolish: *a half-baked scheme.* **3.** *Informal.* Lacking good judgment or common sense: *a half-baked visionary.*

half·beak (hăf′bēk′, häf′-) *n.* Any of various marine and fresh-water fishes of the family Hemiramphidae, related to the flying fishes, and having the lower jaw extended beyond the upper jaw.

half binding. A bookbinding in which the back and often the corners of the volume are bound in a material differing from the rest of the cover: *a half binding of leather.*

half blood. Also **half-blood** (hăf′blŭd′, häf′-). **1.** The relationship existing between persons having only one parent in common. **2.** A person existing in such a relationship. **3.** A half-breed. **4.** A half-blooded domestic animal.

half-blood·ed (hăf′blŭd′ĭd, häf′-) *adj.* **1.** Having only one parent in common. **2.** Having parents of different ethnic types. **3.** Having one parent of pedigreed stock and the other of unknown or mixed ancestry. Said of animals.

half boot. A low boot extending just above the ankle.

half-bound (hăf′bound′, häf′-) *adj.* Having a half binding. Said of a book.

half-bred (hăf′brĕd′, häf′-) *adj.* Having only one parent that is purebred; half-blooded.

half-breed (hăf′brēd′, häf′-) *n.* A person having parents of different ethnic types; especially, the offspring of a Caucasian and an American Indian. *—adj.* Half-blooded; hybrid.

half brother. A brother related through one parent only.

half-caste (hăf′kăst′, häf′käst′) *n.* A person of mixed racial descent; especially, a Eurasian. *—adj.* Of mixed racial descent.

half cock. The position of the hammer of a firearm when it is raised halfway and locked by a catch so that the trigger cannot be pulled.

half-cocked (hăf′kŏkt′, häf′-) *adj.* **1.** At the position of half cock. **2.** *Informal.* Inadequately prepared or conceived; not fully thought out. *—adv. Informal.* Prematurely; hastily; carelessly: *fall halfcocked into an argument.*

half-crown (hăf′kroun′, häf′-) *n.* Also **half-a-crown** (-ə-kroun′). **1.** A British coin worth two shillings and sixpence. **2.** The sum of two shillings and sixpence.

half dime. An obsolete five-cent silver coin minted in the United States between 1792 and 1873.

half dollar. A U.S. silver coin worth 50 cents.

half eagle. An obsolete U.S. gold coin worth five dollars, last issued in 1929.

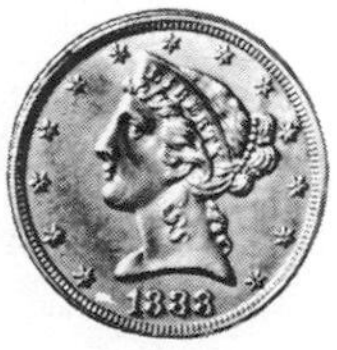

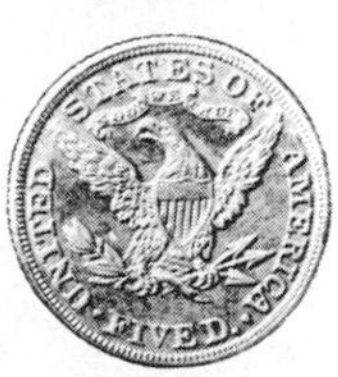

half eagle
Above: Obverse
Below: Reverse

half gainer. A dive in which the diver springs from the board facing forward, rotates backward in the air in a half backward somersault, and enters the water headfirst, facing the board.

half-heart·ed (hăf′här′tĭd, häf′-) *adj.* Done with or possessing little interest or enthusiasm; uninspired: *a halfhearted attempt at painting.* **—half′heart′ed·ly** *adv.* **—half′heart′ed·ness** *n.*

half hitch. A hitch made by looping a rope or strap around an object, and then back around itself, bringing the end of the rope through the loop.

half-hour (hăf′our′, häf′-) *n.* **1.** A period of 30 minutes. **2.** The point that marks the first 30 minutes of a given hour. *—adj.* **1.** Lasting 30 minutes. **2.** Occurring on or indicating the half-hour: *a half-hour chime.* **—half′-hour′ly** *adj.* & *adv.*

half-in·te·gral (hăf′ĭn′tə-grəl, häf′-) *adj.* Having an integer as a numerator and 2 as a denominator. Said of a fraction.

half-length (hăf′lĕngth′, häf′-) *n.* A portrait that shows only the upper half and hands of a person. *—adj.* **1.** Of or denoting such a portrait. **2.** Of half the full length.

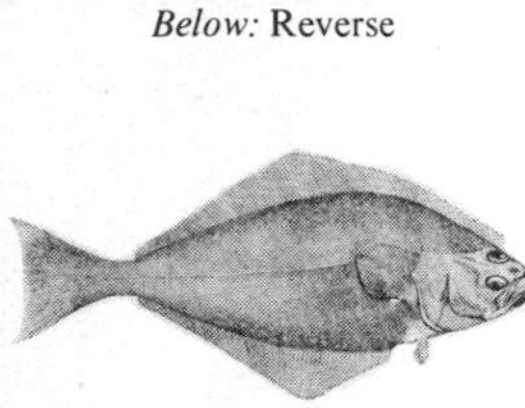

halibut
Hippoglossus hippoglossus

half-life (hăf′līf′, häf′-) *n., pl.* **-lives** (-līvz′). **1.** *Physics.* The time required for half the nuclei in a sample of a specific isotopic species to undergo **radioactive decay** *(see).* **2.** *Biology.* **a.** The time required by living tissue, an organ, or an organism to eliminate by biological processes half the quantity of a substance taken in. Also called "biological half-life." **b.** The time required for the radioactivity of material taken in by a living organism to be reduced to half its initial value by a combination of biological elimination processes and radioactive decay. Also called "effective half-life."

half-light (hăf′līt′, häf′-) *n.* The soft, subdued light found at dusk or dawn or in dimly lit interiors.

half-line (hăf′līn′, häf′-) *n.* A straight line extending in just one direction from a given point.

half-mast (hăf′măst′, häf′mäst′) *n.* The position about halfway up a mast or pole at which a flag is flown as a symbol of mourning for the dead or as a signal of distress. Also called "half-staff." *—tr.v.* **half-masted, -masting, -masts.** To place (a flag) at this position.

half-moon (hăf′mo͞on′, häf′-) *n.* **1.** The moon when only half its disk is illuminated. **2.** Something shaped like a crescent, as the lunula of the fingernail. *—adj.* (hăf′mo͞on′, häf′-). Shaped like a half-moon.

half nelson. A wrestling hold in which one arm is passed under the opponent's arm from behind to the back of his neck. Compare **full nelson.**

half note. *Music.* A note having one half the value of a whole note.

half·pen·ny (hā′pə-nē, hāp′nē) *n., pl.* **-nies** (for sense 1); **half-pence** (hā′pəns) (for sense 2). **1.** A British coin worth 1/2 of a penny. **2.** The sum of 1/2 of a penny.

half pint. *Slang.* A small person or animal.

half-plane (hăf′plān′, häf′-) *n.* The part of a plane lying to one side of a line in the plane.

half relief. Sculptural relief composed of modeled forms that project approximately halfway from the background. Also called "demirelief," "mezzo-relievo."

half-rigged saddle (hăf′rĭgd′, häf′-). A saddle with the seat partially covered with leather.

half sister. A sister related through one parent only.

half-slip (hăf′slĭp′, häf′-) *n.* A woman's underskirt that extends from the waist to the hem of the outer garment.

half sole. A shoe sole extending from the shank to the toe.

half-sole (hăf′sōl′, häf′-) *tr.v.* **-soled, -soling, -soles.** To fit or repair with a half sole.

half sovereign. An obsolete gold coin of Britain worth ten shillings.

half-staff (hăf′stăf′, häf′stäf′) *n.* A **half-mast** *(see).*

half step. 1. *Music.* A **semitone** *(see).* **2.** A marching step of 15 inches at quick time and 18 at double time.

half tide. 1. The condition of the tide at a time halfway between high tide and low tide. **2.** The period during which this condition exists.

half-tim·bered (hăf′tĭm′bərd, häf′-) *adj.* Also **half-tim·ber** (-bər). *Architecture.* Having a wooden framework with plaster, brick, stone, or other masonry filling the spaces.

half time. The intermission between halves in a game such as football or basketball.

half title. 1. The title of a book printed at the top of the first page of the text or on a full page preceding the main title page. Also called "fly title." **2.** The title of a section of a book, consisting of only one line and printed on the leaf preceding the text of that section.

half tone. *Music.* A **semitone** *(see).*

half·tone (hăf′tōn′, häf′-) *n.* **1.** *Art.* A tone or value halfway between a highlight and a dark shadow. **2.** *Photoengraving.* **a.** A picture in which the gradations of light are obtained by the relative darkness and density of tiny dots produced by photographing the subject through a fine screen. **b.** The technique or process that produces such pictures. **c.** The metal plate obtained by such a process. **d.** A picture made from such a plate. *—adj.* Relating to, used in, or made by halftone.

half-track (hăf′trăk′, häf′-) *n.* A military motor vehicle, often lightly armored, with caterpillar treads in place of wheels. **—half′-track′, half′-tracked′** *adj.*

half-truth (hăf′tro͞oth′, häf′-) *n.* A statement, especially one intended to deceive, that omits some of the facts necessary for a truthful description or account.

half volley. A stroke in tennis, cricket, or similar games in which the ball is hit immediately after it bounces off the ground.

half·way (hăf′wā′, häf′-) *adj.* **1.** Midway between two points or conditions; in the middle. **2.** Reaching or including only half or a portion; partial: *halfway measures.* **—half′way′** *adv.*

half-wit (hăf′wĭt′, häf′-) *n.* **1.** A mentally retarded person. **2.** A stupid, foolish, or frivolous person; simpleton. **—half′-wit′ted** *adj.* **—half′-wit′ted·ly** *adv.* **—half′-wit′ted·ness** *n.*

hal·i·but (hăl′ə-bət, hŏl′-) *n., pl.* **halibut** or **-buts.** Any of several large, edible flatfishes of the genus *Hippoglossus* and related genera, of northern Atlantic or Pacific waters. [Middle English *halybutte* : *hali, holi,* HOLY (it was eaten on holy days) + *butte,* flatfish, from Middle Dutch (see **bhau-** in Appendix*).]

Ha·liç. The Turkish name for the **Golden Horn.**

Hal·i·car·nas·sus (hăl′ə-kär-năs′əs). An ancient Greek city of southwestern Asia Minor on the Aegean Sea; site of the famed tomb of Mausolus, the Mausoleum.

Ha·licz. The Polish name for **Galicia.**

hal·ide (hăl′īd′, -ĭd, hā′līd′, -lĭd) *n.* A binary chemical compound of a halogen with a more electropositive element or group. [HAL(O)- + -IDE.]

hal·i·dom (hăl′ə-dəm) *n. Obsolete.* **1.** Holiness; sanctity. **2.** A holy relic. **3.** A sanctuary. [Middle English *halidom,* Old English *hāligdōm* : *hālig,* HOLY + -DOM.]

Hal·i·fax (hăl′ə-făks). **1.** The capital and largest city of Nova Scotia, Canada; an Atlantic port on the southern coast. Population, 93,000. **2.** A city of southwest-central Yorkshire, England. Population, 95,000.

hal·ite (hăl′īt′, hā′līt′) *n.* **Rock salt** *(see).* [New Latin *halites* : HAL(O)- + -ITE.]

hal·i·to·sis (hăl′ə-tō′sĭs) *n.* Stale or foul-smelling breath. [New Latin : Latin *hālitus,* breath, from *hālāre*†, to breathe + -OSIS.]

hall (hôl) *n.* **1.** A corridor or passageway in a house, hotel, or other building. **2.** A large entrance room or vestibule in a building; a lobby. **3. a.** A building for public gatherings or entertainments, as concerts, lectures, or plays. **b.** The large room in which such events are held. **4.** A building used for the meetings, entertainments, or living quarters of a fraternity or other social or religious organization. **5. a.** A building belonging to a school, college, or university, or a large room in such a building, that provides classroom, dormitory, or dining facilities. **b.** The group of students occupying such a building. **c.** *British.* A meal served in such a building. **6.** The main house on a landed estate; especially, the house of a nobleman. **7. a.** The house or castle of a medieval king, chieftain, or nobleman. **b.** The large principal room in such a house or castle, used for dining, entertaining, and sleeping. [Middle English *hal(le),* Old English *h(e)all.* See **kel-**[4] in Appendix.*]

Hall (hôl), Sir **James.** 1761–1832. Scottish geologist and paleontologist.

hal·lah. Variant of **challah.**

Hal·le (hä′lə). Also **Hal·le an der Saa·le** (ăn dər zä′lə). A city and industrial center of East Germany, 31 miles northwest of Leipzig. Population, 278,000.

Hall effect. The generation of an electric potential perpendicular to both an electric current flowing along a thin conducting material and an external magnetic field applied at right angles to the current upon application of the magnetic field. [Discovered by Edwin Herbert *Hall* (1855–1938), American physicist.]

hal·lel (hä-lāl′, hä′lĕl′) *n.* A chant of praise consisting of Psalms 113 through 118, used during Passover and on certain other Jewish holidays. [Hebrew *hallēl,* song of praise, praise, from *hallēl,* to praise.]

hal·le·lu·jah (hăl′ə-lo͞o′yə) *interj.* Used to express praise or joy. —*n.* **1.** The exclamation of "hallelujah." **2.** A musical composition expressing praise and based on the word *hallelujah.* [Hebrew *hallelūyāh,* praise the Lord : *hallelū,* plural imperative of *hallēl,* to praise + *yāh,* short for YAHWEH.]

Hal·ler (hä′lər), **Albrecht von.** 1708–1777. Swiss physiologist, botanist, and poet.

Hal·ley (hăl′ē), **Edmund.** 1656–1742. British astronomer, mathematician, and inventor.

Halley's comet. A comet with a period of approximately 76 years, the first for which a return was successfully predicted. It last appeared in 1910. [After Edmund HALLEY, who predicted its return after observing it in 1682.]

hal·liard. Variant of **halyard.**

hall·mark (hôl′märk′) *n.* **1.** A mark used in England to stamp gold and silver articles that meet established standards of purity. **2.** Any mark indicating quality or excellence. **3.** Any conspicuous indication of the character or quality of something: *"The sense of guilt is the hallmark of civilized humanity"* (Theodor Reik). —*tr.v.* **hallmarked, -marking, -marks.** To mark with a hallmark. [From Goldsmith's *Hall,* London, where gold and silver articles were appraised and stamped.]

hall of fame. Also **Hall of Fame. 1.** A room or building housing memorial items, such as busts, plaques, or the like, honoring illustrious persons. **2.** A group of persons judged outstanding in a sport, profession, or other category.

hal·loo (hə-lo͞o′) *interj.* Also **hal·loa** (hə-lō′). **1.** Used to gain someone's attention. **2.** Used to urge on hounds in a hunt. —*n.* Also **hal·loa.** A shout or call of "halloo." —*v.* **hallooed, -looing, -loos.** Also **hal·loa, -loaed, -loaing, -loas.** —*intr.* To shout "halloo"; call out. —*tr.* **1.** To urge on or pursue by calling "halloo" or shouting. **2.** To call out to. **3.** To shout or yell. [Perhaps variant of earlier *hallow,* to shout so as to incite hounds, from Middle English *halowen,* from Old French *halloer* (imitative).]

hal·low (hăl′ō) *tr.v.* **-lowed, -lowing, -lows. 1.** To make or set apart as holy; sanctify; consecrate. **2.** To honor as being holy; revere; adore. [Middle English *halowen,* Old English *hālgian.* See **kailo-** in Appendix.*]

hal·lowed (hăl′ōd) *adj.* **1.** Made or set apart as being holy; sanctified; consecrated. **2.** Highly venerated; unassailable; sacrosanct.

Hal·low·een (hăl′ō-ēn′) *n.* Also **Hal·low·e'en.** The eve of All Saints' Day, falling on October 31 and celebrated by children who go in costume from door to door begging treats or playing pranks. [Short for *All Hallow E'en.*]

Hal·low·mas (hăl′ō-məs, -măs) *n.* Also **Hal·low·mass.** *Archaic.* The feast of All Saints' Day or Allhallowmas on November 1. [Short for ALLHALLOWMAS.]

Hall process. The electrolytic reduction process by means of which aluminum metal is recovered from aluminum oxide. [Invented by Charles Martin *Hall* (1864–1914), American chemist.]

Hall·statt (hôl′stät; *German* häl′shtät′) *adj.* Of or pertaining to a dominant Iron Age culture of central and western Europe, probably chiefly Celtic, that flourished from the ninth century B.C. to the fifth. [After the type-site at *Hallstatt,* Austria.]

hall tree. A **clothes tree** *(see).*

hal·lu·ci·nate (hə-lo͞o′sə-nāt′) *v.* **-nated, -nating, -nates.** —*intr.* To undergo hallucination. —*tr.* To cause to have hallucinations. [Latin *hallūcinārī, alūcinārī,* to wander in mind, from Greek *aluein,* to wander, be distraught. See **alu-** in Appendix.*]

hal·lu·ci·na·tion (hə-lo͞o′sə-nā′shən) *n.* **1.** False perception with a characteristically compelling sense of the reality of objects or events perceived in the absence of relevant and adequate stimuli. **2.** The complex of material so perceived. **3.** Any false or mistaken idea; delusion.

hal·lu·ci·na·to·ry (hə-lo͞o′sə-nə-tôr′ē, -tōr′ē) *adj.* **1.** Characterizing or characterized by hallucination. **2.** Inducing hallucination.

hal·lu·cin·o·gen (hə-lo͞o′sə-nə-jən) *n.* A drug, such as mescaline, that induces hallucination. [HALLUCIN(ATION) + -GEN.] —**hal·lu′cin·o·gen′ic** *adj.*

hal·lu·ci·no·sis (hə-lo͞o′sə-nō′sĭs) *n.* Any abnormal condition or mental state characterized by hallucination. [New Latin : HALLUCIN(ATION) + -OSIS.]

hal·lux (hăl′əks) *n., pl.* **halluces** (hăl′yə-sēz′). **1.** The inner or first digit on the hind foot of a mammal; in man, the big toe. **2.** The homologous, often backward directed toe of a bird. [New Latin, from Latin *hallux, (h)allus*†, big toe.]

hall·way (hôl′wā′) *n.* **1.** A corridor, passageway, or hall in a house or building. **2.** An entrance hall; foyer; vestibule.

halm. Variant of **haulm.**

Hal·ma·he·ra (häl-mä-hā′rä). *Dutch* **Djai·lo·lo** (jī-lō′lō). The largest island, 6,870 square miles in area, of the Molucca group, northwest-central Indonesia. Population, 97,000.

Halm·stad (hälm′städ). A city, port, and industrial center of southwestern Sweden on the Kattegat. Population, 40,000.

ha·lo (hā′lō) *n., pl.* **-los** or **-loes. 1.** A luminous ring or disk of light surrounding the heads or bodies of sacred figures, as of saints in religious paintings; a nimbus. **2.** The aura of majesty or glory surrounding a person, thing, or event regarded with reverence, awe, or sentiment. **3.** A circular band of colored light around a light source, as around the sun or moon, caused by the refraction and reflection of light by ice particles suspended in the intervening atmosphere. —*v.* **haloed, -loing, -los** or **-loes.** —*tr.* To adorn or invest with a halo. —*intr.* To form a halo. [Medieval Latin *halō,* from Latin *halōs,* from Greek *halōs*†, threshing floor, halo, disk of the sun or moon.]

halo-, hal-. Indicates salt or the sea; for example, **halophyte, halite.** [French, from Greek, from *hals,* salt, sea. See **sal-**[1] in Appendix.*]

ha·lo·bi·ont (hăl′ō-bī′ŏnt′) *n.* An organism that lives or grows in a saline environment. [HALO- + BIONT.]

hal·o·gen (hăl′ə-jən) *n.* Any of a group of five chemically related nonmetallic elements that includes fluorine, chlorine, bromine, iodine, and astatine. [Swedish : HALO- + -GEN.] —**ha·log′e·nous** (hə-lŏj′ə-nəs) *adj.*

hal·o·gen·ate (hăl′ə-jə-nāt′) *tr.v.* **-nated, -nating, -nates.** To treat or cause to combine with a halogen. —**hal′o·gen·a′tion** *n.*

hal·o·phyte (hăl′ə-fīt′) *n.* A plant that grows in saline soil. [HALO- + -PHYTE.] —**hal′o·phyt′ic** (-fĭt′ĭk) *adj.*

Hals (häls), **Frans.** 1580?–1666. Dutch painter.

Hal·sey (hôl′zē), **William Frederick ("Bull").** 1882–1959. American Admiral of the Fleet; commander of U.S. Pacific fleet in World War II.

Häl·sing·borg (hĕl′sĭng-bôr′y′). A city and port of southwestern Sweden, opposite Helsingør, Denmark, on the Öresund. Population, 78,000.

Hal·sted (hôl′stəd), **William Stewart.** 1852–1922. American surgeon; developed use of cocaine in anesthesiology.

halt[1] (hôlt) *n.* A suspension of movement or progress, particularly of marching; a temporary stop; a pause. —**call a halt to.** To put a stop to; end. —*v.* **halted, halting, halts.** —*tr.* To cause to stop; arrest. —*intr.* To stop; pause. [German *Halt,* from Middle High German *halt,* from the imperative of *halten,* to stop, hold, from Old High German *haltan.* See **kel-**[5] in Appendix.*]

halt[2] (hôlt) *intr.v.* **halted, halting, halts. 1.** To be defective or to proceed poorly, as in the development of an argument in logic or in the rhythmical structure of a verse. **2.** To proceed or act with uncertainty or indecision; waver. **3.** To limp or hobble, as a cripple. —*n. Archaic.* The act of limping; lameness. —*adj. Archaic.* Having a limp; lame; crippled. [Middle English *halten,* to be lame, Old English *healtian.* See **kel-**[2] in Appendix.*]

hal·ter[1] (hôl′tər) *n.* **1.** A device made of rope or leather straps that fits around the head or neck of an animal, particularly a horse or cow, and can be used to lead or secure it. **2.** A rope with a noose used for execution by hanging. **3.** Death or execution by hanging. **4.** A bodice for women which ties behind the neck and across the back, leaving the arms, shoulders, and back bare. —*tr.v.* **haltered, -tering, -ters. 1.** To put a halter on; control with a halter. **2.** To hang (someone). [Middle English *halter,* Old English *haelftre.* See **kelp-** in Appendix.*]

hal·ter[2] (hôl′tər, hăl′-) *n., pl.* **halteres** (hôl-tîr′ēz, hăl-). Either of the small, clublike balancing organs that are the rudimentary hind wings of dipterous insects such as flies or mosquitoes. Also called "balancer." [New Latin, from Latin *haltēr,* leaden weights used in leaping exercises, from Greek, from *hallesthai,* to jump. See **sel-**[4] in Appendix.*]

halt·ing (hôl′tĭng) *adj.* **1.** Limping; lame. **2.** Imperfect; defective: *a halting verse.* **3.** Hesitant or wavering: *a halting voice.*

hal·vah (häl-vä′, häl′vä) *n.* Also **ha·la·vah** (hä′lə-vä′), **hal·va.** A confection of Turkish origin consisting of crushed sesame seeds in a binder of honey. [Yiddish *halva,* from Rumanian, from Turkish *helve,* from Arabic *ḥalwā.*]

halve (hăv, häv) *v.* **halved, halving, halves.** —*tr.* **1.** To separate or divide into two equal portions or parts. **2.** To lessen or reduce by half; remove half of. **3.** *Informal.* To share equally; divide up. **4.** *Carpentry.* To attach (two pieces of wood) by cutting off half of each at the joint so they will fit together smoothly. **5.** *Golf.* To play (a game or hole) using the same number of strokes as one's opponent. —*intr.* To divide into or form two equal parts. [Middle English *halven, halfen,* from *half,* HALF.]

halves. Plural of **half.**

hal·yard (hăl′yərd) *n.* Also **hal·liard.** A rope used to raise or lower a sail, flag, or yard. [Variant (influenced by YARD) of Middle English *halier,* from *halen,* to pull, HALE.]

Ha·lys. The ancient name for **Kizil-Irmak.**

ham (hăm) *n.* **1.** The thigh of the hind leg of certain animals, especially a hog. **2.** The meat of this part of a hog, often pre-

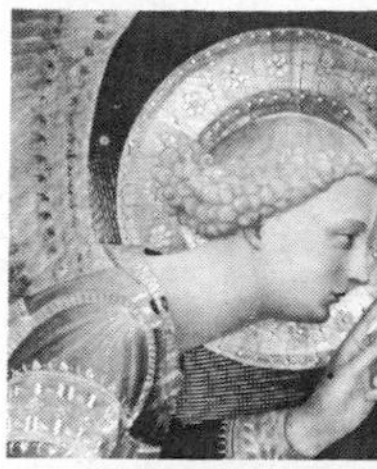

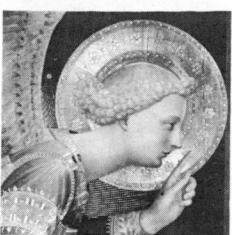

halo
Detail of painting by Fra Angelico

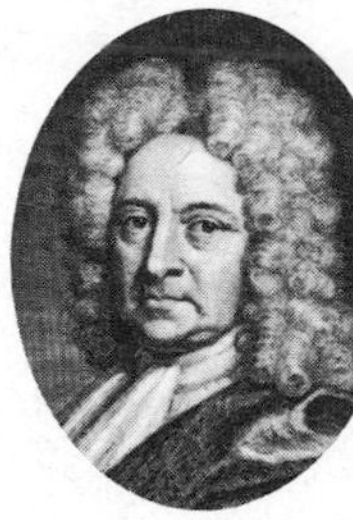

Edmund Halley

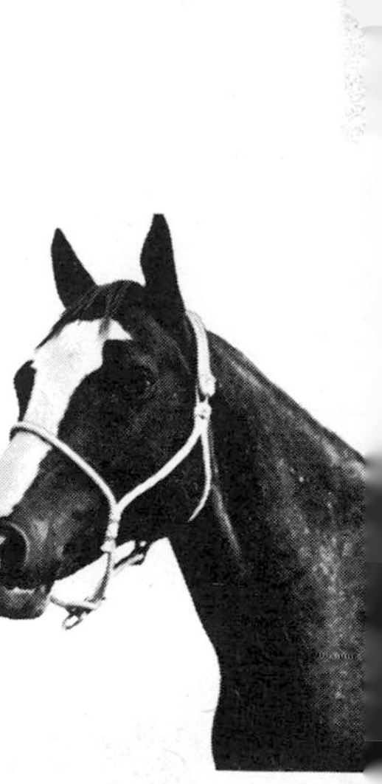

halter[1]

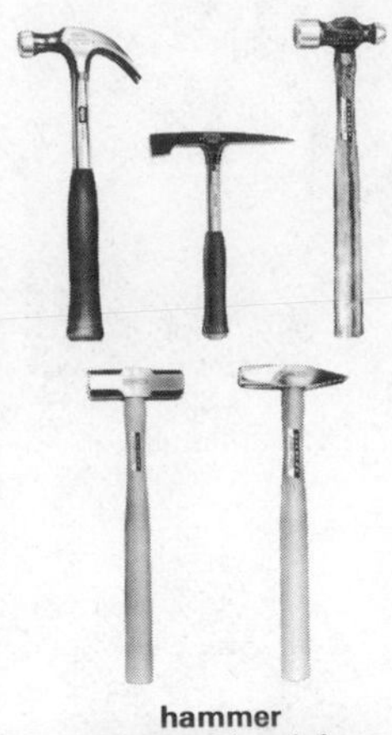

hammer
Top row, from left:
Standard claw hammer, bricklayer's hammer, ball-peen hammer
Bottom row, from left:
Double-faced hammer, riveting hammer

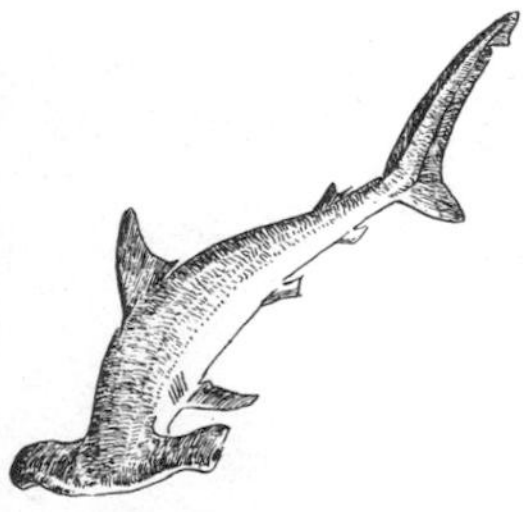

hammerhead
Sphyrna zygaena

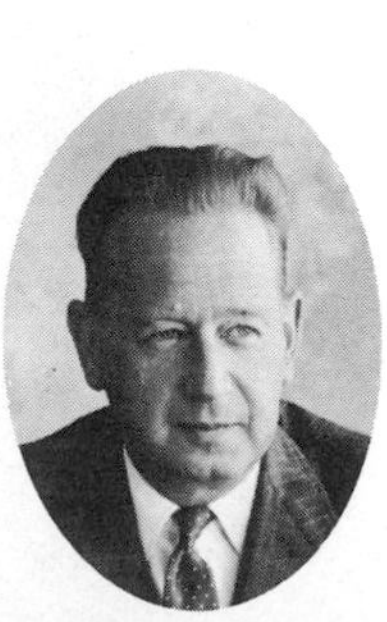

Dag Hammarskjöld

served by smoking or drying. **3.** The back of the knee. **4.** The back of the thigh. **5.** *Plural.* The buttocks. **6.** *Slang.* **a.** An actor who overacts or a performer who exaggerates too much. **b.** Any person who, liking attention or acclaim, makes himself ridiculous or obnoxious. **7.** *Informal.* A licensed amateur radio operator. —*v.* **hammed, hamming, hams.** —*intr.* To overact. —*tr.* To exaggerate or overdo (a role, line, or the like). [Middle English *ham(me),* Old English *ham(m).* See **konemo-** in Appendix.*]

Ham (hăm). The second of the three sons of Noah and in some traditions considered the ancestor of the Egyptians. Genesis 5:32.

HAM Airport code for Hamburg, West Germany.

Ha·ma (hä′mä). Biblical name **Ha·math** (hā′măth). A city and agricultural center of west-central Syria on the Orontes River. Population, 126,000.

Ha·ma·dan (hä′mä-dän′). Ancient name **Ec·bat·a·na** (ĕk-băt′ə-nə). A commercial center of western Iran. Population, 115,000.

ham·a·dry·ad (hăm′ə-drī′əd) *n., pl.* **-ads** or **-ades** (-ə-dēz′). **1.** *Greek & Roman Mythology.* A wood nymph living only as long as the tree of which she is the spirit and in which she lives. **2.** A snake, the **king cobra** *(see).* [Latin *Hamādryas* (stem *Hamādryad-*), from Greek *Hamadruas,* "one together with a tree" : *hama,* together with (see **sem-¹** in Appendix*) + *druas,* dryad, from *drus,* tree (see **deru-** in Appendix*).]

ha·ma·dry·as (hăm′ə-drī′əs) *n.* A baboon, *Comopithecus hamadryas,* of northern Africa and Arabia, the adult male of which has a heavy mane. [New Latin, from Latin, HAMADRYAD.]

ha·mal (hə-mäl′, -môl′) *n.* Also **ha·maul, ham·mal.** A porter or bearer in certain Moslem countries. [Arabic *ḥammāl,* porter, from *ḥamala,* to carry.]

Ha·ma·mat·su (hä-mä-mät′so͞o). An industrial center of south-central Honshu, Japan. Population, 368,000.

Ha·man (hā′mən). A chief minister of the Persian king Ahasuerus, who was hanged from his own gallows when his plot against the Jews was revealed by Esther. Esther 8:7.

ha·mate (hā′māt′) *adj.* Hooked at the tip. [Latin *hāmātus,* from *hāmus,* hook. See **hamulus.**]

Ham·ble·to·ni·an (hăm′bəl-tō′nē-ən) *n.* One of a strain of American trotting horses descended from the stallion, Hambletonian (1849–1876).

Ham·born. See **Duisburg.**

Ham·burg (hăm′bûrg). A port of north-central West Germany on the Elbe; since 1948 a state of the German Federal Republic. Population, 1,851,000.

ham·burg·er (hăm′bûr′gər) *n.* Also **ham·burg** (-bûrg′). **1.** Ground or chopped meat, usually beef. **2.** A patty of such meat, cooked by frying, grilling, broiling, or baking. **3.** A sandwich made with such a patty, usually in a roll or bun. [Short for *Hamburger steak,* from HAMBURG.]

hame (hām) *n.* One of the two curved wooden or metal pieces of a harness which fit around the neck of a draft animal and to which the traces are attached. [Middle English, probably from Middle Dutch. See **kei-¹** in Appendix.*]

Ham·e·lin (hăm′lən, -ə-lən). *German* **Ha·meln** (hä′məln). A city and river port of southwest-central Lower Saxony, West Germany, on the Weser. Population, 50,000.

Ham·hung (häm′ho͝ong′). A city and agricultural center of east-central North Korea. Population, 112,000.

Ham·il·ton (hăm′əl-tən). **1.** A city, port, and manufacturing center of southeastern Ontario, Canada, on Lake Ontario 40 miles west of Toronto. Population, 274,000. **2.** The capital of Bermuda, a port on Bermuda Island. Population, 2,800. **3.** A city and industrial center of southwestern Ohio. Population, 72,000. **4.** A city and mining and industrial center of south-central Scotland. Population, 44,000. **5.** A river rising in south-central Labrador, Canada, and flowing 600 miles north, then southeast, then northeast to Lake Melville.

Ham·il·ton (hăm′əl-tən), **Alexander.** 1755–1804. American lawyer and Revolutionary statesman; first U.S. Secretary of the Treasury (1789–95).

Ham·il·to·ni·an (hăm′əl-tō′nĭ-ən) *n. Symbol* **H** *Physics.* A mathematical function that can be used systematically and with great generality to generate the equations of motion of a dynamic system, equal for many such systems to the sum of the kinetic and potential energies of the system expressed in terms of the system's coordinates and momenta treated as independent variables. [Formulated by William Rowan *Hamilton* (1805–1865), Irish mathematician.]

Ham·ite (hăm′īt′) *n.* **1.** One said to be descended from Ham. **2.** A member of a group of related peoples inhabiting northern and northeastern Africa, including the Berbers and the descendants of the ancient Egyptians.

Ha·mit·ic (hă-mĭt′ĭk) *adj.* Of or relating to Ham, the Hamites, or the language of the Hamites. —*n.* A group of North African languages related to Semitic, including the Berber dialects, ancient Egyptian and its descendant, Coptic, and the Cushitic dialects spoken in Ethiopia.

Ham·i·to-Se·mit·ic (hăm′ə-tō-sə-mĭt′ĭk) *n.* **Afro-Asiatic** *(see).* [From HAMITIC + SEMITIC.]

ham·let (hăm′lĭt) *n.* A small village. [Middle English, from Old French *hamelet,* diminutive of *hamel,* diminutive of *ham,* from Germanic. See **kei-¹** in Appendix.*]

Ham·let (hăm′lĭt). The hero of Shakespeare's tragedy *Hamlet.*

Ham·lin (hăm′lən), **Hannibal.** 1809–1891. Vice President of the United States under Abraham Lincoln (1861–65).

ham·mal. Variant of **hamal.**

Ham·mar·skjöld (häm′är-shœld′), **Dag Hjalmar Agne Carl.** 1905–1961. Swedish diplomat and man of letters; secretary-general of the United Nations (1953–61).

ham·mer (hăm′ər) *n.* **1.** A hand tool used to exert an impulsive force by striking; especially, such a tool consisting of a handle with a perpendicularly attached head of a relatively heavy, rigid material, such as iron or hard rubber, used to drive nails or shape construction materials. **2.** Any tool or device of analogous function or action, as: **a.** The part of a gunlock that hits the primer or firing pin or explodes the percussion cap causing the gun to go off. **b.** One of the padded wooden pieces of a piano that strike the strings. **c.** Any part of an apparatus that strikes a gong or bell, as in a clock. **d.** An exhaust-controlling lever in an internal-combustion machine. **3.** *Anatomy.* A bone, the **malleus** *(see).* **4.** *Sports.* A metal ball weighing 16 pounds and having a long wire or wooden handle by which it is thrown in track-and-field competition. **5.** A small mallet used by auctioneers. —**go (or come) under the hammer.** To be put up for auction. —**hammer and tongs.** With tremendous energy or effort; vigorously. —*v.* **hammered, -mering, -mers.** —*tr.* **1.** To hit once or repeatedly with or as if with a hammer; to strike; pound. **2.** To beat into a shape or flatten with a hammer. Often used with *out: The mechanic hammered out the dents in the fender.* **3.** To put together, fasten, or seal, particularly with nails, by hammering. **4.** To force upon by constant repetition. —*intr.* **1.** To deal repeated blows with or as if with a hammer; to pound; pummel: *"wind hammered at us violently in gusts"* (Thor Heyerdahl). **2.** To beat in the manner of a hammer: *His pulse hammered.* **3.** *Informal.* To work diligently; keep at something continuously. Often used with *away: He hammered away at his homework.* [Middle English *hamer,* Old English *hamor.* See **ak-** in Appendix.*] —**ham′mer·er** *n.*

hammer and sickle. An emblem of the Communist movement, consisting of a crossed hammer and sickle signifying the alliance of workers and peasants.

ham·mered (hăm′ərd) *adj.* Created, shaped, or worked by hand with a metalworker's hammer or other tools and often showing the marks of these tools: *hammered gold.*

Ham·mer·fest (häm′ər-fĕst′). A town, port, and fishing center of northern Norway, on an island in the Arctic Ocean; the northernmost town of Europe. Population, 6,000.

ham·mer·head (hăm′ər-hĕd′) *n.* **1.** The head of a hammer. **2.** Any of several large, predatory sharks of the genus *Sphyrna,* having the sides of the head elongated into large, fleshy extensions with the eyes at the ends. **3.** A bird, *Scopus umbretta,* of Africa and southwestern Asia, having brown plumage, a large, bladelike bill, and a long, backward-pointing crest. In this sense, also called "hammerkop."

hammer lock. A wrestling hold in which the opponent's arm is pulled behind his back and twisted upward.

ham·mer·smith (hăm′ər-smĭth′) *n.* One who works metals by hand with a hammer.

Ham·mer·smith (hăm′ər-smĭth′). A borough of London, England, comprising the former administrative divisions of Hammersmith and Fulham. Population, 222,000.

Ham·mer·stein (hăm′ər-stīn′), **Oscar.** 1895–1960. American librettist and songwriter.

ham·mer·toe (hăm′ər-tō′) *n. Pathology.* A toe, usually the second, that is congenitally bent downward.

ham·mock¹ (hăm′ək) *n.* A hanging, easily swung cot or lounge of canvas or netting suspended between two trees or other supports. [Spanish *hamaca,* from Taino.]

ham·mock². Variant of **hummock.**

Ham·mond (hăm′ənd). A city and industrial center of northwestern Indiana, near Chicago. Population, 112,000.

Ham·mu·ra·bi (hä′mo͝o-rä′bē, hăm′ə-). Babylonian king and lawgiver of the 18th century B.C.

ham·per¹ (hăm′pər) *tr.v.* **-pered, -pering, -pers.** To prevent the free movement, action, or progress of; impede. See Synonyms at **hinder.** —*n. Nautical.* Necessary but encumbering equipment on a ship. [Middle English *hamperen*†.]

ham·per² (hăm′pər) *n.* A large basket, usually with a cover. [Middle English *hampere,* variant of *hanaper,* HANAPER.]

Hamp·shire¹ (hămp′shĭr, -shər). Also **Hants** (hănts). Officially, Southampton. A county, 1,503 square miles in area, of southern England. Population, 1,436,000. County seat, Winchester.

Hamp·shire² (hămp′shĭr, -shər) *n.* **1.** A large sheep of a breed originating in England. **2.** A pig of a breed developed in the United States, having a black body with a white, beltlike band. [From HAMPSHIRE.]

Hamp·stead (hămp′stĕd′, -stĭd). A former administrative division of London, England, now part of **Camden** *(see).*

Hamp·ton (hămp′tən). A port and fishing center of southeastern Virginia, on Hampton Roads. Population, 89,000.

Hampton Roads. A channel of southeastern Virginia, connecting the James and Elizabeth rivers with Chesapeake Bay.

ham·shack·le (hăm′shăk′əl) *tr.v.* **-led, -ling, -les. 1.** To hobble (an animal) by tying a rope or strap between one of the legs and the head. **2.** To hold back; hinder. [Perhaps from HAMPER (verb) + SHACKLE.]

ham·ster (hăm′stər) *n.* Any of several Eurasian rodents of the family Cricetidae; especially, *Mesocricetus auratus,* having large cheek pouches and a short tail, popular as a pet and used in laboratory research. [German *Hamster,* from Old High German *hamustro,* from Slavic, akin to Old Slavic *chomĕstorŭ*†.]

ham·string (hăm′strĭng′) *n.* **1.** Either of two tendons at the rear hollow of the human knee. **2.** The large sinew in the back of the hock of a quadruped. —*tr.v.* **hamstrung** (-strŭng′), **-stringing, -strings. 1.** To cut the hamstring of (an animal or person) and thereby cripple. **2.** To destroy or hinder the efficiency of (somebody or something); to frustrate. [HAM (thigh) + STRING.]

Ham·tramck (hăm-trăm′ĭk). An automobile-manufacturing center of southeastern Michigan, lying within the city limits of Detroit. Population, 34,000.

ham·u·lus (hăm′yə-ləs) *n.*, *pl.* **-li** (-lī′). A small hooklike projection or process, as at the end of a bone. [New Latin, from Latin *hāmulus*, little hook, diminutive of *hāmus*†, hook.]

ham·za (hăm′zə) *n.* Also **ham·zah**. A sign in Arabic orthography used to represent the sound of a glottal stop, transliterated in English as an apostrophe. [Arabic *hamza*, compression (of the windpipe), from *hamaza*, to press on, spur, goad.]

Han¹ (hän) *n.* **1.** A Chinese dynasty (206 B.C.–A.D. 221) noted for the unification and expansion of the national territory and for the promotion of literature and the arts. **2.** The Chinese as distinguished from other ethnic groups in China such as the Manchus and the Mongols. *—adj.* Of or pertaining to the Han dynasty or the Chinese.

Han² (hän). **1.** *Chinese* **Han Kiang** (hän′ jyäng′), **Han Chiang.** A river of southern China, rising on the Fukien-Kiangsi boundary and flowing 210 miles south to the South China Sea. **2.** *Chinese* **Han Shui** (hän′ shwē′). A river of southeast-central China, rising in Shensi and flowing 750 miles southeast through Hupei to the Yangtze at Hankow. **3.** *Korean* **Han-gang** (hän′gäng′); *Japanese* **Kan-ko** (kän′kō′). A river of central South Korea, rising 100 miles east of Seoul and flowing 292 miles southwest, then northwest, to the Yellow Sea.

han·a·per (hăn′ə-pər) *n.* A wicker container or hamper used for storing documents. [Middle English *hanaper*, from Old French *hanapier*, case for holding goblets, from *hanap*, goblet, akin to Old English *hnæpp*, bowl, from Germanic *hnapp* (unattested).]

hance (hăns) *n.* **1.** *Architecture.* **a.** The half arch that joins a lintel to a jamb. **b.** A **haunch** *(see)*. **2.** *Nautical.* A curved rise or contour on a ship, as of the bulwarks. [Obsolete *ha(u)nce*, lintel, from *ha(u)nce*, to raise, from Middle English *hauncen*, probably short for *enhauncen*, to ENHANCE.]

Han Cities. See **Wuhan.**

Han·cock (hăn′kŏk′), **John.** 1737–1793. American statesman; first signer of Declaration of Independence; first governor of state of Massachusetts (1780–85); again governor (1787–93).

hand (hănd) *n. Abbr.* **hd. 1.** The terminal part of the human arm below the wrist, consisting of the palm, four fingers, and an opposable thumb, used for grasping and holding. **2.** A homologous or similar part in other animals. **3.** A unit of length equal to four inches, used especially to specify the height of a horse. **4.** Something suggesting the shape or function of the human hand. **5. a.** Any of the rotating pointers used as indexes on the face of a mechanical clock. **b.** A pointer on any of various similar instruments, such as on gauges or meters; a needle. **6.** A printer's mark, **index** *(see)*. **7.** Lateral direction indicated according to the way in which one is facing: *at my right hand.* **8.** A style or individual sample of writing; handwriting; penmanship. **9.** A round of applause to signify approval; a clapping. **10.** Physical assistance; a help: *Give me a hand with these trunks.* **11.** *Card Games.* **a.** The cards held by a given player at any time: *a winning hand.* **b.** The number of cards dealt each player; a deal. **c.** A player or participant: *a fourth hand for bridge.* **d.** A portion or section of a game during which all the cards dealt out are played: *a hand of poker.* **12.** A person who performs manual labor: *a factory hand.* **13.** A person who is part of a group or crew. **14.** Any participant in an activity. **15.** A person regarded in terms of a specialized skill or trait. **16.** The immediacy of a source of information; degree of reliability: *at first hand.* **17. a.** *Usually plural.* Possession, ownership, or keeping: *The books should be in her hands by noon.* **b.** *Often plural.* Power; jurisdiction; care: *in good hands.* **c.** Doing or involvement; participation: *"In all this was evident the hand of the counterrevolutionaries."* (John Reed). **d.** An influence or effect; a share: *your professor's hand in your decision.* **18.** Permission or a promise, especially: **a.** A pledge to wed. **b.** A business agreement sealed by a clasp or handshake; word: *You have my hand on that.* **19.** Evidence of craftsmanship or artistic skill. **20.** A manner or way of performing something; emphasis; an approach: *a light hand with make-up.* **—at hand. 1.** Close by; near; easily accessible. **2.** Soon in time; imminent. **—at the hand (or hands) of.** Performed by someone or through the agency of someone. **—bite the hand that feeds one.** To repay kindness with malice. **—by hand.** Performed by using the hands as opposed to mechanical means; individually: *sorted by hand.* **—by one's own hand.** By one's own act or agency: *die by one's own hand.* **—come to hand. 1.** To become apparent; come to pass. **2.** To be received; arrive. **—eat out of another's hand.** To be governed or ruled by the wishes of another. **—force one's hand.** To force one to act prematurely or unwillingly in a given situation. **—from hand to hand.** From one person successively to another person. **—hand and foot. 1.** So as to prevent movement or escape: *tied up hand and foot.* **2.** With absolute fidelity; in every way: *She served her master hand and foot.* **—hand in (or and) glove.** On intimate terms or in close association. **—hand in hand. 1.** Holding each other's hand. **2.** In cooperation; jointly. **—hand over fist.** *Slang.* At a tremendous rate: *making money hand over fist.* **—hands down.** With no trouble; easily. **—Hands off.** Do not touch. Keep away. **—Hands up.** Raise your hands in the air. Used as a command, usually by an armed person, to another to offer no resistance. **—have a hand in.** To be a participant in or contributor to: *a hand in getting scholarships for needy boys.* **—have one's hands full.** To be unable to take on more duties or responsibilities; be fully occupied. **—in hand. 1.** Under control. **2.** Presently accessible. **3.** In preparation. **—join hands. 1.** To become business partners. **2.** To wed. **—lay hands on. 1.** To seize or come into possession of, especially with intent to injure or destroy. **2.** To assault, either hostilely or sexually. **3.** To bless, ordain, or consecrate by touching. **—off one's hands.** Out of one's jurisdiction, responsibility, or care. **—on hand.** Available. **—on (or upon) one's hands.** In one's possession, often as an imposed responsibility or burden. **—on (the) one hand.** As one point of view or side of an issue; in one respect. **—on the other hand.** As another, or opposite, point of view; from another standpoint. **—out of hand. 1.** Out of control. **2.** At once; immediately. **3.** Over and done with; finished; completed. **4.** Uncalled for or improper; indiscreet. **—show one's hand.** To reveal something previously hidden, such as a plan, intentions, or the like. **—take in hand. 1.** To put under control or care. **2.** To deal with; treat. **3.** To strive; try; attempt. **—throw up one's hands.** To give up in hopelessness; concede. **—tip one's hand.** To reveal something unwittingly. **—to hand. 1.** Nearby. **2.** In one's possession. **—turn (or put) one's hand to.** To take up as an activity; work at. **—with a heavy hand. 1.** In a clumsy or awkward manner. **2.** With great severity or emphasis. **—with a high hand.** In a presumptuous or cavalier fashion; overbearingly. **—with clean hands.** Not involved in crime or corruption; guiltless; innocent. *—adj.* **1.** Of or pertaining to the hand. **2.** Made to be transported in one's hand: *hand luggage.* **3.** Performed or operated by hand; manual. **4.** Created by hand. *—tr.v.* **handed, handing, hands. 1.** To give or pass with or as if with the hands; transmit; to present: *Hand me your keys.* **2.** To aid, direct, or conduct with the hands: *The usher handed the patron to her seat.* **3.** *Nautical.* To roll up and secure (a sail); furl. **—hand down. 1.** To bequeath as an inheritance to one's heirs; hand on. **2.** To release or pronounce a court decision or verdict. **—hand in.** To turn in; submit: *hand in term papers.* **—hand it to.** *Slang.* To give credit to. **—hand on. 1.** To give to a successor; turn over. **2.** To hand down. **—hand over.** To release into the possession of another; relinquish. [Middle English *hand*, Old English *hand, hond*, from Germanic *handuz* (unattested).]

Hand (hănd), **Learned.** 1872–1961. American jurist; Federal judge (1909–51).

hand·bag (hănd′băg′) *n.* **1.** A woman's bag for carrying articles such as money, keys, and cosmetics; pocketbook. **2.** A piece of small hand luggage.

hand·ball (hănd′bôl′) *n.* **1.** A wall game, similar in scoring to volleyball, played by two or more players batting a ball against the wall with their hands, usually with a special glove. **2.** The small rubber ball used in this game.

hand·bar·row (hănd′băr′ō) *n.* A flat framework or litter having carrying poles at each end.

hand·bill (hănd′bĭl′) *n.* A printed sheet or pamphlet distributed by hand; leaflet; notice or advertisement.

hand·book (hănd′bo͝ok′) *n. Abbr.* **hdbk. 1.** A manual or small reference book providing specific information or instruction about a subject, activity, place, or the like; guide; directory. **2. a.** A book in which off-track bets are recorded. **b.** A place where off-track bets are taken.

hand·breadth (hănd′brĕdth′) *n.* Also **hand's-breadth** (hăndz′-), **hand's breadth.** A linear measurement approximating the width of the palm of the hand, from 2½ to 4 inches, but most often taken to be 4 inches.

hand·car (hănd′kär′) *n.* A small open railroad car used to transport workers over short distances, propelled by a hand pump or a small motor.

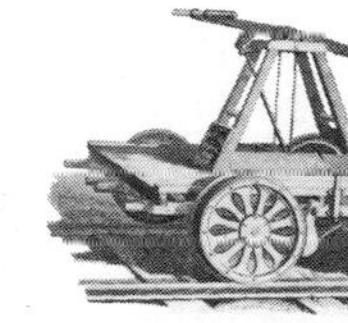

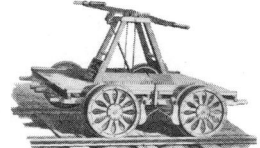

handcar
U.S. handcar used in the 1880's

hand·cart (hănd′kärt′) *n.* A small, usually two-wheeled, cart pulled or pushed by hand.

hand·clasp (hănd′klăsp′, -kläsp′) *n.* The act of clasping the hand of another person, especially to show warmth or friendship.

hand·cuff (hănd′kŭf′) *n.* A restraining device consisting of a pair of strong, connected hoops which can be tightened and locked about the wrists and used on one or both arms of a prisoner in custody; manacle. Usually used in the plural. Also called "cuff." *—tr.v.* **handcuffed, -cuffing, -cuffs.** To restrain with handcuffs.

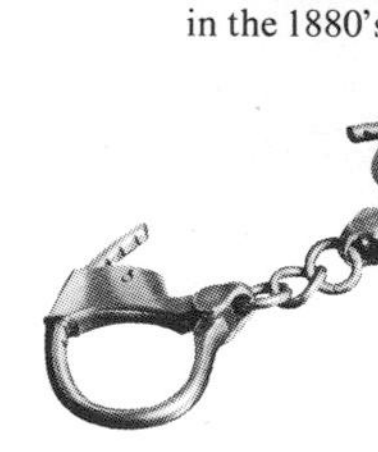

handcuff

hand·ed (hăn′dĭd) *adj.* **1.** Of or pertaining to dexterity or preference as regards a hand or hands. Used in combination: *one-handed; left-handed.* **2.** Pertaining to a specified number of people. Used in combination: *a four-handed card game.*

Han·del (hănd′l), **George Frederick.** German name, Georg Friedrich Händel. 1685–1759. German-born British composer.

hand·fast (hănd′făst′, -fäst′) *n. Archaic.* **1.** A secure grasp or grip. **2.** A handclasp used to signify a pledge, as a contract or a marriage. *—tr.v.* **handfasted, -fasting, -fasts.** *Archaic.* **1.** To grip securely with the hand. **2.** To betroth or marry by joining the hands.

hand·ful (hănd′fo͝ol′) *n., pl.* **-fuls. 1.** The quantity or number that can be held in the hand. **2.** A small but undefined quantity or number: *a handful of requests.* **3.** *Informal.* A person or thing too difficult to control or handle easily.

hand glass. 1. A small magnifying glass held in the hand. **2.** A mirror with a handle. **3.** A time glass used in timing the running out of a line used with a nautical log.

hand grenade. A small grenade to be thrown by hand.

hand·grip (hănd′grĭp′) *n.* **1.** A grip by the hand or hands. **2.** Something suited to or facilitating a grip by the hand, as a handle or indentation. **3.** *Plural.* Hand-to-hand combat.

hand·gun (hănd′gŭn′) *n.* A firearm that can be used with one hand; a pistol.

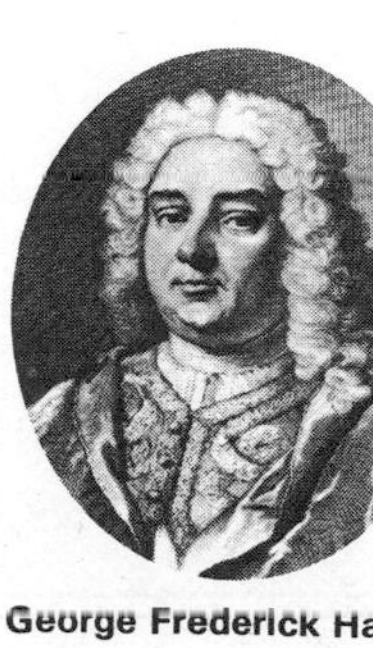

George Frederick Handel

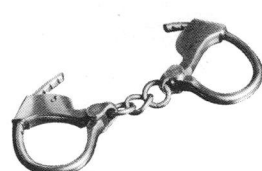

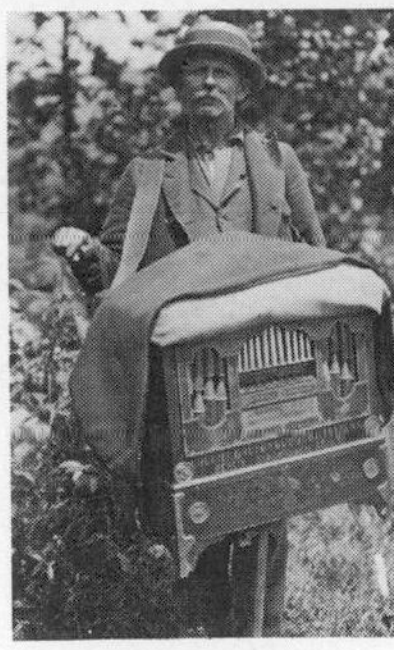

hand organ

hand·hold (hănd′hōld′) *n.* **1.** A grip by the hand or hands. **2.** Something that one can hold by the hand or hands for support, such as a branch or indentation on a rock surface.

hand·i·cap (hăn′dē-kăp′) *n.* **1.** A race or contest in which advantages or compensations are given different contestants, according to their varied abilities or experience, to equalize the chances of winning. **2.** Such an advantage or penalty. **3. a.** A deficiency, especially an anatomical, physiological, or mental deficiency, that prevents or restricts normal achievement. **b.** Any disadvantage or disability. **4.** A hindrance: *"he was always a child and that was a handicap to his worldly development"* (Sherwood Anderson). *—tr.v.* **handicapped, -capping, -caps. 1.** To assign a handicap or handicaps to (a contestant). **2.** To constitute a hindrance; impede. [From earlier *hand in cap*, originally a lottery game in which players held forfeits in a cap.] **—hand′i·cap′per** *n.*

hand·i·capped (hăn′dē-kăpt′) *adj.* **1.** Disabled or crippled. **2.** Mentally deficient. **3.** Having or being under a handicap. Said of a contestant. *—n.* Handicapped persons collectively. Used with *the: employ the handicapped.*

hand·i·craft (hăn′dē-krăft′, -kräft′) *n.* **1.** Skill and facility with the hands; workmanship. **2.** A trade, craft, or occupation requiring skilled use of the hands, as basketry. **3.** The work produced by hand, such as sewing. [Middle English *handie-craft*, variant of *handcraft* : HAND + CRAFT.]

hand·i·crafts·man (hăn′dē-krăfts′mən, -kräfts′mən) *n., pl.* **-men** (-mĭn). A person skilled in handicraft; a craftsman.

hand·i·ly (hăn′dĭ-lē) *adv.* **1.** In a handy or easy manner; dexterously. **2.** Conveniently.

hand·i·ness (hăn′dē-nĭs) *n.* **1.** The quality of being handy; facility; expertise. **2.** The quality of being easy to use; convenience.

hand·i·work (hăn′dē-wûrk′) *n.* **1.** Work performed by hand or the objects produced by hand. **2.** That which is accomplished by a single person's efforts. **3.** The results of a person's actions. [Middle English *handiwork*, Old English *handgeweorc* : HAND + *geweorc*, work : *ge-*, collective prefix (see **kom** in Appendix*) + *weorc*, WORK.]

hand·ker·chief (hăng′kər-chĭf) *n. Abbr.* **hdkf. 1.** A small square of cotton, linen, or silk, carried by a person for use in wiping the nose, mouth, or the like. **2.** A slightly larger piece of cloth worn as a decorative article; kerchief; scarf. [HAND + KERCHIEF.]

hand-knit (hănd′nĭt′) *adj.* Also **hand-knit·ted** (-nĭt′ĭd). Knit by hand. *—n.* Also **hand-knit·ting** (-nĭt′ĭng). **1.** The act of knitting by hand. **2.** An article or articles knit by hand.

hand-laun·der (hănd′lôn′dər, -län′dər) *tr.v.* **-dered, -dering, -ders.** To launder (clothing or fabrics) by hand or with special attention, as distinguished from automatically by machine.

han·dle (hăn′dl) *v.* **-dled, -dling, -dles.** *—tr.* **1.** To touch, lift, or turn with the hands. **2.** To operate with the hands; manipulate. **3.** To specialize in or have responsibility for; deal with or in; to conduct: *handle corporation law.* **4.** To promote, execute, or dispose of: *handle an investment.* **5.** To manage, administer to, or represent: *handle a boxer.* **6.** To behave or act toward; to treat. **7.** To confront or cope with, especially: **a.** To control or command: *handle a crowd.* **b.** To meet or solve: *handle a problem.* *—intr.* To respond or react to control or manipulation; function under operation. —See Synonyms at **conduct.** *—n.* **1.** That by which a tool, object, door, or the like is held or manipulated with the hand. **2.** An opportunity that may serve as an advantage for someone; a means; an opening. **3.** *Slang.* A person's name. **—fly off the handle.** *Informal.* To fly into a rage. [Middle English *handelen*, Old English *handlian.* See **kend-** in Appendix.*]

***Synonyms:** handle, manipulate, wield, ply.* These verbs mean to use, operate, or manage things or, less often, persons. *Handle* can refer to management or control of tools, implements, persons, or nonphysical things such as problems and situations. In every case, unless it is qualified by an adverb, the term suggests competence in gaining an end or objective. *Manipulate* connotes skillful or artful management of physical things, such as tools or instruments, or of persons or personal affairs, in which case it often implies use of improper influence or fraud in gaining an end. *Wield* implies that one has full command of what is used, principally tools and implements, weapons, means of expression such as the pen, or intangibles such as authority and influence. The term likewise suggests that the means are used effectively. *Ply* refers principally to use of tools and to the regular and diligent pursuit of a given trade.

han·dle·bar (hăn′dl-bär′) *n.* **1.** A curved metal steering bar, as on a bicycle. Often used in the plural. **2.** A long, curved mustache. In this sense, also called "handlebar mustache."

han·dler (hănd′lər) *n.* **1.** One that handles. **2.** *Sports.* **a.** A person who trains or exhibits an animal, such as a dog. **b.** A person who acts as the trainer or second of a boxer.

han·dling (hănd′lĭng) *n.* **1.** A touching, feeling, or manipulating with the hands. **2.** The way in which a matter is taken care of or treated; management; execution.

hand·made (hănd′mād′) *adj.* Made or prepared by hand rather than by machine.

hand·maid (hănd′mād′) *n.* A female servant or attendant; personal maid.

hand·maid·en (hănd′mād′n) *n.* **1.** A handmaid. **2.** That which serves as an aid.

hand-me-down (hănd′mē-doun′) *adj.* **1.** Handed down to one person after being used and discarded by another; secondhand. **2.** Of inferior quality; shabby. *—n.* Something passed on from one person to another.

hand-off (hănd′ôf′, -ŏf′) *n.* A football play in which one player hands the ball to another.

hand organ. A barrel organ operated by turning a crank.

hand out. To distribute or offer (merchandise, gifts, or tracts, for examples); disseminate; proffer.

hand·out (hănd′out′) *n.* **1.** Food, clothing, or money donated to a beggar or destitute person. **2.** A folder or leaflet circulated free of charge. **3.** A prepared news or publicity release.

hand-pick (hănd′pĭk′) *tr.v.* **-picked, -picking, -picks. 1.** To gather or pick by hand. **2.** To select carefully. **3.** To select personally for a specified position or task. **—hand′-picked′** *adj.*

hand·rail (hănd′rāl′) *n.* A narrow rail to be grasped with the hand for support.

hand·sel (hănd′səl) *n.* Also **han·sel** (hăn′-). *Chiefly British.* A gift to express good wishes at the beginning of a new year or enterprise. *—tr.v.* **handseled** or **-selled, -seling** or **-selling, -sels.** *Chiefly British.* To give a handsel to. [Middle English *hanselle*, from Old Norse *handsal*, a giving of the hand : *hand*, hand, from Germanic *handuz* (unattested), HAND + *sal*, a giving, payment (see **sel-**[3] in Appendix*).]

hand·set (hănd′sĕt′) *n.* A portable telephone transmitter and receiver module.

hand·shake (hănd′shāk′) *n.* The grasping of right hands by two people as a gesture of greeting, leave-taking, congratulation, agreement, or the like.

hand·some (hăn′səm) *adj.* **1.** Pleasing and dignified in form or appearance. **2.** Generous or copious; liberal: *a handsome reward.* **3.** Proficient or dexterous. **4.** Marked by or requiring great skill or accomplishment: *a handsome piece of work.* **5.** Appropriate or fitting; compatible. —See Synonyms at **beautiful.** [Middle English *handsom*, easy to handle, handy : HAND + -SOME.] **—hand′some·ly** *adv.* **—hand′some·ness** *n.*

hand·spike (hănd′spīk′) *n.* A heavy bar used as a lever.

hand·spring (hănd′sprĭng′) *n.* A gymnastic feat in which the body is flipped completely forward or backward from an upright position, landing first on the hands, then on the feet.

hand·stand (hănd′stănd′) *n.* The act of balancing on the hands with one's feet in the air.

hand-to-hand (hănd′tə-hănd′) *adj.* At close quarters.

hand-to-mouth (hănd′tə-mouth′) *adj.* Characterized by a sparse and day-to-day economy.

hand·work (hănd′wûrk′) *n.* Manual labor as distinguished from machine labor.

hand·writ·ing (hănd′rī′tĭng) *n.* **1.** Writing done with the hand. **2.** The writing characteristic of a particular hand or person.

hand·y (hăn′dē) *adj.* **-ier, -iest. 1.** Manually adroit. **2.** Readily accessible. **3.** Easy to use or handle. —See Synonyms at **dexterous.** [From HAND.]

hand·y·man (hăn′dē-măn′) *n., pl.* **-men** (-mĕn′). Also **handy man.** One who does odd jobs or various small tasks.

hang (hăng) *v.* **hung** (hŭng) or **hanged** (see Usage note below), **hanging, hangs.** *—tr.* **1.** To fasten from above with no support from below; suspend. **2.** To suspend or fasten so as to allow free movement at or about the point of suspension. **3.** To execute by suspending by the neck. **4.** To fix or attach at an appropriate angle: *hang a scythe to its handle.* **5.** To alter the hem of (a garment) so as to fall evenly at a specified height. **6.** To furnish, decorate, or appoint by suspending objects around or about: *hang a room with curtains.* **7.** To hold or incline downward; let droop: *hang one's head in sorrow.* **8.** To attach to a wall: *hang wallpaper.* **9.** To deadlock (a jury) by failing to render a unanimous verdict. *—intr.* **1.** To be attached from above with no support from below. **2.** To suffer death by hanging. **3.** To remain suspended or poised over a place or object; hover. **4.** To attach oneself as an impediment or dependent; cling. **5.** To incline downward; to droop. **6.** To depend. **7.** To maintain close contact; pay strict attention: *hang on every word.* **8.** To remain unresolved or uncertain: *hang in the balance.* **9.** To fit the body in loose lines. **10.** To be unwilling or unable to depart; linger; tarry. **—hang around.** *Informal.* **1.** To spend time in idleness; loiter. **2.** To keep company; to consort. **—hang back. 1.** To lag. **2.** To be averse; hold back. **—hang fire. 1.** To be temporarily delayed in exploding. **2.** To delay. **—hang off.** To hold or hang back; be averse. **—hang on. 1.** To cling to something. **2.** To continue persistently or resolutely; persevere. **3.** To keep a telephone connection open; hold the line. **—hang one on. 1.** *Informal.* To strike (a person). **2.** *Slang.* To become drunk. **—hang together. 1.** To stand united; stick together. **2.** To constitute a coherent totality. *—n.* **1.** The way in which something hangs. **2.** A downward inclination or slope. **3.** *Informal.* The proper method for doing, using, or handling something: *get the hang of it.* **4.** A suspension of motion; slackening. **—give** (or **care**) **a hang.** To be concerned or anxious. [Hang, hung, hung; partly Middle English *hon, hong, hongen*, Old English *hōn* (transitive verb), to hang, suspend, *heng, hangen;* partly Middle English *hangen, hong, hanged*, Old English *hangian* (transitive and intransitive verb), to hang, be hung, suspend, *hangode, hanged;* partly Middle English *hingen*, from Old Norse *hanga* (transitive verb), to cause to hang. See **konk-** in Appendix.*]

Usage: *Hanged* is preferable to *hung* as the past tense and past participle when the verb is used in the sense of capital punishment: *Frontier courts hanged many a prisoner after just such a summary trial. Only a few citizens objected to seeing such men hanged.* In the first example *hung* is acceptable, as an alternative to *hanged*, to only 31 per cent of the Usage Panel; in the second, *hung* is acceptable to 34 per cent. In other senses of the verb, *hung* is the customary form as past tense and past participle.

Han-gang. The Korean name for the **Han.**

han·gar (hăng′ər) *n.* A shed or shelter; especially, a structure for housing aircraft. [French, from Old French, probably from Medieval Latin *angarium*†, shed for shoeing horses.]

hang·bird (hăng′bûrd′) *n.* A bird, such as an oriole, that builds a hanging nest. Also called "hangnest."

Hang·chow (hăng′chou′; *Chinese* häng′jō′). The capital of Chekiang, China, a port located in the northeast on Hangchow Bay. Population, 794,000.

Hang·chow Bay (hăng′chou′; *Chinese* häng′jō′). An inlet of the East China Sea in northeastern Chekiang, China.

hang·dog (hăng′dôg′, -dŏg′) *adj.* **1.** Shamefaced or guilty. **2.** Downcast; intimidated. —*n.* A sneak.

hang·er (hăng′ər) *n.* **1.** One that hangs. **2.** A contrivance to which something hangs or by which something is hung. **3.** A device around which a garment is draped for hanging from a hook or rod. **4.** A loop or strap by which something is hung. **5.** A bracket on an automobile's spring shackle designed to hold it to the chassis. **6.** A decorative strip of cloth hung on a garment or wall.

hang·er-on (hăng′ər-ŏn′, -ôn′) *n., pl.* **hangers-on** (hăng′ərz-). A sycophant; parasite.

hang·ing (hăng′ĭng) *n.* **1.** An execution on a gallows. **2.** Something hung, as: **a.** Drapery. **b.** Wallpaper. **3.** A descending slope or inclination. —*adj.* **1.** Situated on a sharp declivity. **2.** Projecting downward; overhanging. **3.** Suited for holding something that hangs. **4. a.** Susceptible to or meriting death by hanging: *a hanging crime.* **b.** Disposed to inflict the sentence of death by hanging: *a hanging judge.*

hanging indention. The indention of every line in a paragraph except the first.

hang·man (hăng′mən) *n., pl.* **-men** (-mĭn). One employed to execute condemned prisoners by hanging.

hang·nail (hăng′nāl′) *n.* A small piece of dead skin at the side or the base of a fingernail that is partly detached from the rest of the skin. [By folk-etymology from AGNAIL.]

hang out. 1. To project downward. **2.** *Slang.* To hang around. **3.** To suspend for public display: *hang out one's shingle.*

hang·out (hăng′out′) *n.* A frequently visited place.

hang·o·ver (hăng′ō′vər) *n.* **1.** Unpleasant physical effects following the heavy use of alcohol. **2.** A letdown or deflation, as after a period of excitement or elation. **3.** A vestige; holdover: *hangovers from prewar legislation.*

hang up. 1. To suspend on a hook or hanger. **2.** To replace (a telephone receiver) on its cradle. **3.** To retard, impede, or interrupt: *hang up a project.* **4.** To halt the movement or action of. **5.** To end a telephone conversation. **6.** To become halted or snagged.

hang-up (hăng′ŭp′) *n. Informal.* **1. a.** A source of irritation or inhibition. **b.** An inhibition or fixation. **2.** An obstacle; inconvenience.

Han-hai. The Chinese name for the **Gobi Desert.**

hank (hăngk) *n.* **1.** A coil or loop. **2.** A ring on a stay attached to the head of a jib or staysail. **3.** A looped bundle, as of yarn. [Middle English, from Scandinavian, akin to Old Norse *hŏnk*†, hank, skein.]

Han·ka. See Lake **Khanka.**

han·ker (hăng′kər) *intr.v.* **-kered, -kering, -kers.** To have a longing; crave. See Synonyms at **yearn.** [From dialectal *hank,* probably from Dutch (dialectal) *hankeren.* See **konk-** in Appendix.*] —**hank′er·er** *n.*

Han Kiang. A Chinese name for the **Han.**

Han·kow (hăng′kou′; *Chinese* häng′jō′). A former city of southeastern Hupei, China; now part of **Wuhan** (*see*).

han·ky-pan·ky (hăng′kē-păng′kē) *n. Slang.* **1.** Devious or mischievous activity. **2.** Foolish talk or action. [Coined on analogy with HOCUS-POCUS.]

Han·nah (hăn′ə). A feminine given name. [Hebrew *Hannāh,* "graciousness," from the stem of *ḥānah,* be gracious.]

Han·ni·bal (hăn′ə-bəl). 247–183 B.C. Carthaginian general.

Ha·noi (hä-noi′, hă-). The capital of North Vietnam; an industrial center on the Red River in the northeast. Population, 415,000.

Han·o·ver¹ (hăn′ō′vər). *German* **Han·no·ver** (hä-nō′vər). The capital of Lower Saxony, West Germany; a commercial and industrial center located on the Leine, 60 miles southeast of Bremen. Population, 571,000.

Han·o·ver² (hăn′ō′vər). **1.** An electoral house of Germany (1692–1815). **2.** A royal family of England (1714–1901).

Han·o·ve·ri·an (hăn′ō-vîr′ē-ən) *adj.* Of or pertaining to the city of Hanover, the electoral house, or the royal family of Hanover.

Han·sard (hăn′sərd) *n. British & Canadian.* The official report of the proceedings and debates of Parliament. [After its first printer Luke *Hansard* (1752–1828).]

hanse (hăns) *n.* **1.** A medieval merchant guild or trade association. **2.** *Capital* **H.** A town belonging to the Hanseatic League. Also called "Hanse town." **3.** *Capital* **H.** *Rare.* The Hanseatic League. [Middle English *hans,* from Old French *hanse,* from Middle Low German *hanse,* from Old High German *hansa,* troop, company, from Germanic *khansō* (unattested).] —**han′se·at·ic** (hăn′sē-ăt′ĭk) *adj.*

Hanseatic League. A protective and commercial association of free towns in northern Germany and neighboring areas, formally organized in 1358 and dissolved in the 17th century.

han·sel. Variant of **handsel.**

Han·sen's disease (hăn′sənz). **Leprosy** (*see*). [After the Norwegian physician A.G.H. *Hansen* (1841–1912), who discovered the bacillus that causes leprosy.]

Han Shui. The Chinese name for the **Han.**

han·som (hăn′səm) *n.* A two-wheeled covered carriage with the driver's seat above and behind. [After its designer, English architect Joseph A. *Hansom* (1803–1882).]

Hants. See Hampshire (county).

Ha·nuk·kah, Ha·nu·kah. Variants of **Chanukah.**

han·u·man (hä′nŏŏ-mən) *n., pl.* **-mans.** A monkey, *Presbytis entellus,* of southern Asia, having bristly hairs on the crown and the sides of the face. [Sanskrit *hanumant,* "having jaws," from *hanu,* jaw. See **genu-²** in Appendix.*]

Han·yang (hän′yäng′). A former city of southeastern Hupei, China, now part of **Wuhan** (*see*).

hap (hăp) *n. Archaic.* **1.** Fortune; chance. **2.** A happening; an occurrence. —*intr.v.* **happed, happing, haps.** *Archaic.* To happen. [Middle English, from Old Norse *happ,* good luck, chance. See **kob-** in Appendix.*]

ha·pax le·go·me·non (hă′păks′ lə-gŏm′ə-nŏn′) *pl.* **hapax legomena** (-ə-nə). *Greek.* A word or form that occurs only once in the recorded corpus of a given language. Often shortened to "hapax." [Greek, "a thing said only once."]

hap·haz·ard (hăp-hăz′ərd) *adj.* Dependent upon or characterized by mere chance. See Synonyms at **chance.** —*n.* Mere chance; fortuity. —*adv.* Casually; by chance. [HAP + HAZARD.] —**hap·haz′ard·ly** *adv.* —**hap·haz′ard·ness** *n.*

haph·ta·rah (häf′tä-rä′, -tôr′ə) *n., pl.* **-taroth** (-tä-rōt′, -tôr′ōt, -ōth′, -ōs′). Also **haf·ta·rah.** A reading selected from the Prophets, read in the synagogue service on the Sabbath following each lesson from the Torah. [Mishnaic Hebrew *haphṭārah,* "conclusion," from *haphṭēr,* conclude, discard, dismiss, from Hebrew *pāṭar,* separated, discharged.]

hap·less (hăp′lĭs) *adj.* Luckless; unfortunate.

hap·lite. Variant of **aplite.**

hap·loid (hăp′loid′) *adj. Genetics.* Having the number of chromosomes present in the normal germ cell, equal to half the number in the normal somatic cell. Compare **diploid.** —*n.* A haploid individual. [Greek *haploeidēs,* single : *haplo(u)s,* single, simple : *ha-,* one (see **sem-¹** in Appendix*) + *-plo(u)s,* -fold (see **pel-⁸** in Appendix*) + -OID.]

hap·loi·dy (hăp′loi-dē) *n. Genetics.* The state or condition of being haploid.

hap·lol·o·gy (hăp-lŏl′ə-jē) *n.* The shortening of a word by contraction of a sound or syllable in its pronunciation. [Greek *haplos,* single, simple (see **haploid**) + -LOGY.]

hap·lo·sis (hăp-lō′sĭs) *n. Genetics.* Reduction of the diploid number of chromosomes by one half to the haploid number by meiosis. [New Latin : Greek *haplos,* single, simple (see **haploid**) + -OSIS.]

hap·ly (hăp′lē) *adv. Archaic.* By chance or accident; perhaps.

hap·pen (hăp′ən) *intr.v.* **-pened, -pening, -pens. 1.** To come to pass; come into being; take place. **2.** To take place or come about by chance. **3.** To come upon something by chance. **4.** To appear by chance; turn up. [Middle English *happenen,* from *hap,* HAP.]

Synonyms: happen, occur, chance, befall, betide, supervene. These verbs mean to come about. *Happen* and *occur,* the most common, are frequently interchangeable in this sense. *Happen* often implies coming about by accident; *occur* is applicable both to what is accidental and to what comes about through obvious cause. In sentences in which *occur* might be misconstrued in the sense of come to mind, only *happen* is possible: *Nothing of the sort happened to her.* When the desired sense is to be met with or appear, only *occur* is possible: *Violence occurs often in his later plays. An epidemic of this kind seldom occurs now. Chance* stresses lack of apparent cause or plan. *Befall* and *betide* generally apply to what comes about beyond human control, and especially to misfortune. *Supervene* refers to coming about as an additional development, often an unexpected one.

hap·pen·ing (hăp′ə-nĭng) *n.* **1.** An event. **2.** An improvised spectacle or performance. —See Synonyms at **occurrence.**

hap·pen·stance (hăp′ən-stăns′) *n.* Also **hap·pen·chance** (-chăns′, -chäns′). A chance circumstance. [HAPPEN + (CIRCUM)STANCE.]

hap·py (hăp′ē) *adj.* **-pier, -piest. 1.** Characterized by luck or good fortune; prosperous. **2.** Having or demonstrating pleasure or satisfaction; gratified. **3.** Well-adapted; appropriate; felicitous: *a happy turn of phrase.* **4.** Characterized by a spontaneous or obsessive inclination to use something. Used in combination: *trigger-happy.* —See Synonyms at **fit, glad.** [Middle English, from HAP.] —**hap′pi·ly** *adv.* —**hap′pi·ness** *n.*

hap·py-go-luck·y (hăp′ē-gō-lŭk′ē) *adj.* Taking things easily; trusting to luck; carefree.

Haps·burg (hăps′bûrg′). Also *German* **Habs·burg** (häps′bŏŏrk′). **1.** A princely German family furnishing sovereigns to Austria (1278–1918) and to Spain (1516–1700). **2.** A member of this family.

hap·ten (hăp′tĕn′) *n.* Also **hap·tene** (-tēn′). An antigen that is incomplete and cannot by itself cause antibody formation but can neutralize specific antibodies in an artificial environment outside the body. [German *Hapten* : Greek *haptein,* to fasten (see **synapse**) + -ENE.]

HAR Airport code for Harrisburg, Pennsylvania.

ha·ra·ki·ri (här′ə-kîr′ē) *n.* Ritual suicide by disembowelment as formerly practiced by the Japanese upper classes. Also called "seppuku." [Japanese *harakiri.*]

ha·rangue (hə-răng′) *n.* **1.** A long, pompous speech; especially, one delivered before a gathering. **2.** A speech characterized by strong feeling or vehement expression; tirade. —*v.* **harangued, -ranguing, -rangued.** —*tr.* To deliver a harangue to. —*intr.* To deliver a harangue. [Middle English *arang,* from Old French *arenge, harangue,* from Medieval Latin *harenga,* perhaps from Germanic. See **koro-** in Appendix.*] —**ha·rangu′er** *n.*

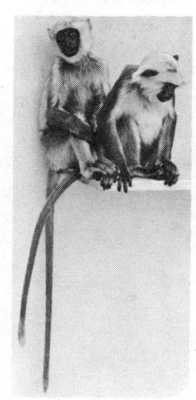

hanuman

hansom

Warren G. Harding

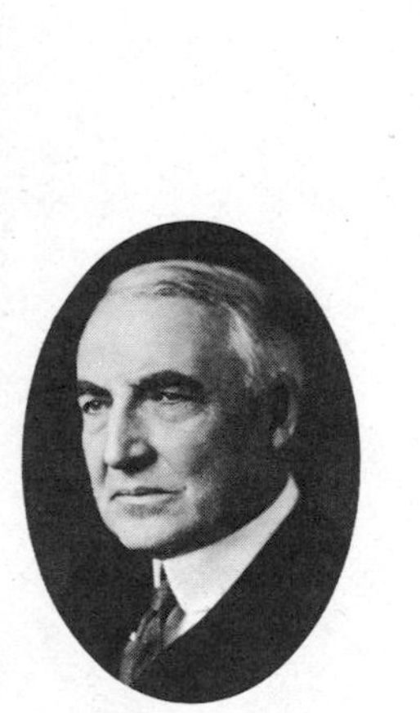

Thomas Hardy

Ha·rar (hä′rər). **1.** The largest province of Ethiopia, occupying 156,000 square miles in the southeast. Population, 3,199,000. **2.** The capital of this province, located in the center. Population, 41,000.

har·ass (hăr′əs, hə-răs′) *tr.v.* **-assed, -assing, -asses. 1.** To disturb or irritate persistently. **2.** To wear out; exhaust. **3.** To enervate (an enemy) by repeated attacks or raids. [French *harasser,* from Old French *harer,* to set a dog on, from *hare,* cry used to set a dog on, perhaps from Old High German *harên,* to call. See **kar-**[2] in Appendix.*] **—har′ass·er** *n.* **—har′ass·ment** *n.*

Synonyms: *harass, hound, badger, pester, plague, bait, torment.* These verbs are closely related when they mean to trouble or disturb persons. *Harass* implies systematic persecution by besetting with annoyances, threats, or demands. *Hound* suggests unrelentingly pursuing or dunning in order to gain a desired end. *Badger* refers to persistent nagging or teasing, *pester* to the inflicting of a succession of petty annoyances or distractions, and *plague* to the inflicting of worry, vexation, or other mental tribulation over an extended period. *Bait* implies deliberate persecution by taunting, insulting, or heckling. *Torment,* the most general of these terms, is applicable to any action that inflicts distress, vexation, or the like.

Har·at. See **Herat.**

Har·bin (här′bən). *Chinese* **Pin·kiang** (bĭn′gyäng′). The capital of Heilungkiang, Manchuria; a port located in the southwest on the Sungari. Population, 1,595,000.

har·bin·ger (här′bən-jər) *n.* A forerunner: *"in a few minutes would appear the train's harbinger . . . a puff of white smoke"* (Vladimir Nabokov). *—tr.v.* **harbingered, -gering, -gers.** To signal the approach of; presage. [Middle English *harbergere,* from Old French, from *herbergier,* to provide lodging for, from *herberge,* lodging, from Old Saxon *heriberga,* lodging. See **koro-** in Appendix.*]

har·bing·er-of-spring (här′bən-jər-əv-sprĭng′) *n.* A small plant, *Erigenia bulbosa,* of eastern North America, having compound small white flowers that bloom in early spring.

har·bor (här′bər) *n.* Also *chiefly British* **har·bour.** *Abbr.* **h., H. 1.** A sheltered part of a body of water deep enough to provide anchorage for ships; a port. **2.** Any protected place; a shelter; a refuge. *—tr.v.* **harbored, -boring, -bors.** Also *chiefly British* **harbour. 1.** To give shelter to; protect; keep. **2.** To entertain or nourish a thought or feeling about. [Middle English *herberge, herber,* late Old English *herebeorg.* See **koro-** in Appendix.*] **—har′bor·er** *n.*

har·bor·age (här′bər-ĭj) *n.* **1.** Shelter and anchorage for ships. **2.** Shelter; refuge. **3.** A place of shelter.

har·bor·mas·ter (här′bər-măs′tər, -mäs′tər) *n.* An officer who oversees and enforces the regulations of a harbor.

harbor seal. A hair seal, *Phoca vitulina,* having a spotted coat, of coastal waters of the Northern Hemisphere.

hard (härd) *adj.* **harder, hardest.** *Abbr.* **h., H. 1.** Resistant to pressure; not readily penetrated; firm; rigid; unyielding. **2.** Physically toughened; rugged: *"Hard as the palm of ploughman"* (Shakespeare). **3.** Mentally toughened; strong-minded. **4.** Rigorous; stringent; demanding. **5.** Stern; austere; callous; cold. **6.** Stubborn; intractable; obstinate. **7.** Intense; forceful; keen. **8.** Sharp; probing; penetrating. **9.** Assiduous; diligent; energetic: *a hard worker.* **10.** Difficult to accomplish, finish, or continue; strenuous; arduous. **11.** Difficult to understand, express, or convey; abstruse; knotty. **12.** Intricate; tight. **13.** Difficult to endure. **14.** Cruel; oppressive; unjust. **15.** Bitter; rancorous; harsh. **16.** Suggesting hardness or coldness. **17.** Metallic, as opposed to paper. Said of money: *hard money.* **18. a.** Backed by bullion rather than by credit. Said of money. **b.** Readily exchangeable; in currency rather than a promissory note. Said of money. **19.** Unchangeable; real: *hard facts.* **20.** Durable; lasting: *hard merchandise.* **21.** Having a cloth, cardboard, or leather binding. Said of books, and usually used in combination: *hard-bound.* **22.** Having alcoholic or high alcoholic content; intoxicating. **23.** Containing dissolved substances, as salts, that interfere with the lathering action of soap. Said of water. **24.** *Phonetics.* **a.** Pronounced as a stop, as the *c* in *cake* and the *g* in *log.* **b.** Voiceless. Said of consonants. **c.** Not palatalized. Said of consonants in Slavic languages. **25.** *Physics.* Of relatively high energy; penetrating: *hard x rays.* **26.** *Agriculture.* High in gluten content: *hard wheat.* **—be hard on. 1.** To be unpleasant and difficult for. **2.** To deal with severely; be harsh with. **—hard and fast. 1.** Defined, fixed, and invariable: *hard and fast rules.* **2.** Secure in port. Said of a ship. **—hard of hearing.** Deaf to some degree. **—hard up.** In need; poor. *—adv.* **1.** Energetically; vigorously: *drink hard.* **2.** Intently; earnestly; persistently: *think hard.* **3.** With difficulty; strenuously. **4.** With reluctance; resistantly: *die hard.* **5.** Close; near. Used with *by* or *upon.* **6.** Firmly; securely. **7.** Toward or into a solid condition: *The cement will set hard within a day.* **8.** *Nautical.* Completely; fully: *hard alee.* **—be hard put.** To have a good deal of difficulty in doing. **—go hard with.** To cause pain or distress; to gall: *This news will go hard with him.* *—n.* **1.** *British Slang.* Hard labor. **2.** *Vulgar Slang.* An erection of the penis. [Middle English *hard,* Old English *hard, heard.* See **kar-**[1] in Appendix.*]

Synonyms: *hard, difficult, arduous, intricate, troublesome.* These adjectives are closely related when they mean requiring great physical or mental effort. *Hard* and *difficult,* the most general terms, are interchangeable in many examples, but *difficult* is often the more appropriate where a challenge requiring special skills or ingenuity is involved. *Arduous* refers to what involves burdensome labor or persistent effort, especially physical. *Intricate* describes what is difficult because its complexity makes great mental demands. *Troublesome* implies demands that cause vexation, worry, or anxiety.

Har·dang·er Fjord (här-däng′ər fyôrd′, fyōrd′). An inlet of the North Sea, extending 80 miles into southwestern Norway.

hard·back (härd′băk′) *adj.* Bound in cloth, cardboard, or leather rather than paper. Said of books. Also "hard-bound." *—n.* A hardback book.

hard-bit·ten (härd′bĭt′n) *adj.* Obdurate; stubborn; toughened.

hard-boiled (härd′boild′) *adj.* **1.** Cooked by boiling to a solid consistency. Said of eggs. **2.** *Informal.* Callous; unfeeling.

hard cash. Available money; cash.

hard cider. Fermented cider.

hard coal. Anthracite *(see).*

hard core. The durable and resistant central part of a given entity; especially, the most intractable or die-hard nucleus of a specified group or organization: *the hard core of the separatist movement.*

hard-core (härd′kôr′) *adj.* Also **hard·core. 1.** Stubbornly resistant or inveterate: *the hard-core criminal element.* **2.** Held to constitute an intractable social problem: *hard-core poverty cases.*

hard·en (härd′n) *v.* **-ened, -ening, -ens.** *—tr.* **1.** To make firm or firmer; make solid or hard. **2.** To toughen mentally or physically; make rugged; inure; set. **3.** To make unfeeling or cold in spirit; make unyielding emotionally: *"To love love and not its meaning hardens the heart in monstrous ways"* (Archibald MacLeish). **4.** To make sharp, as in outline; set; fix. *—intr.* **1.** To become hard or hardened; set; fix; firm; freeze. **2.** *Economics.* **a.** To rise. Used of prices. **b.** To become stable. **3.** To become inured: *"But poor boys either harden early or are destroyed"* (T.H. White).

Har·den (härd′n), Sir **Arthur.** 1865–1940. British biochemist; studied fermentation.

hard·en·er (härd′n-ər) *n.* **1.** One that hardens. **2.** A substance added to varnish or paint to give a harder surface or finish.

hard·en·ing (härd′n-ĭng) *n.* **1.** The act or process of becoming hard or harder. **2.** Something that hardens, such as a substance added to iron to yield steel.

hard-fea·tured (härd′fē′chərd) *adj.* Having sharp or harsh features: *"A tall . . . man with a hard-featured countenance"* (Smollett). Also *archaic* "hard-favored."

hard-fist·ed (härd′fĭs′tĭd) *adj.* Tight-fisted; stingy; niggardly.

hard·hack (härd′hăk′) *n.* A woody plant, *Spiraea tomentosa,* of eastern North America, having leaves with rusty down on the undersides and spirelike clusters of small, rose-pink flowers. Also called "steeplebush." [HARD + HACK (cut).]

hard-hand·ed (härd′hăn′dĭd) *adj.* **1.** Having hands calloused or hardened by work. **2.** Heavy-handed; oppressive; tyrannical.

hard hat. A lightweight protective helmet, usually of metal or reinforced plastic, worn by construction workers or baseball players.

hard-hat (härd′hăt′) *n. Informal.* A construction worker. Also called "hard-hatter." *—adj.* Pertaining to construction work or demolition.

hard·head (härd′hĕd′) *n., pl.* **-heads** or **hardhead** (for sense 3). **1.** A shrewd and tough person. **2.** A stubborn, unmovable person. **3.** Any of several fishes having a bony head; especially, a freshwater fish, *Mylopharodon conocephalus,* of the western United States, or a common croaker, *Micropogon undulatus,* of Atlantic waters.

hard·head·ed (härd′hĕd′ĭd) *adj.* **1.** Stubborn; willful. **2.** Realistic: *"he was too hardheaded to be a thorough sentimentalist"* (George Sherburn). **—hard′head′ed·ly** *adv.* **—hard′head′ed·ness** *n.*

hard·heart·ed (härd′här′tĭd) *adj.* Hardened in feeling; cold; pitiless. **—hard′heart′ed·ly** *adv.* **—hard′heart′ed·ness** *n.*

har·di·hood (här′dē-ho͝od′) *n.* Boldness and daring; audacity: *"the soul and spirit of New England hardihood, comprehending all perils, and encountering all"* (Hawthorne). [HARDY + -HOOD.]

har·di·ly (härd′l-ē) *adv.* In a hardy manner; boldly.

Har·din (härd′n), **John Wesley.** 1853–1895. American outlaw in Texas and Kansas.

har·di·ness (här′dē-nĭs) *n.* **1.** Vigor; robustness; strength. **2.** Hardihood; daring.

Har·ding (här′dĭng), **Warren Gamaliel.** 1865–1923. Twenty-ninth U.S. President (1921–23); died in office.

hard labor. Compulsory physical labor coincident with a prison term imposed as a legal punishment for a crime.

hard landing. The landing, by impact, of a spacecraft lacking devices, such as retrorockets, to slow it down.

hard liquor. Distilled liquor.

hard·ly (härd′lē) *adv.* **1.** Barely; scarcely; just. **2.** To almost no degree; almost not. **3.** Probably not or almost surely not: *"Easily was a man made an infidel, but hardly might he be converted to another faith"* (T.E. Lawrence). **4.** Harshly. **5.** *Obsolete.* Strenuously or violently. [Middle English *hardli,* boldly, hardily, Old English *h(e)ardlice* : HARD + -LY.]

Synonyms: *hardly, scarcely, barely.* These adverbs are frequently interchangeable as they refer to sufficiency in quantity, capacity, or ability. *Hardly* and *scarcely* imply either scant sufficiency or, less often, possible insufficiency: *hardly enough; scarcely sufficient to go around; hardly able to see; scarcely large enough to be visible.* In both senses *scarcely* is the stronger term. *Barely* usually suggests no doubt as to sufficiency, but implies a narrowness of margin that leaves nothing, or virtually nothing, to spare: *barely enough; barely on time; barely able to hear.*

Usage: *Hardly* has the force of a negative; therefore it is not used with another negative: *I could hardly see* (not *couldn't hardly*). *He accepted it with hardly an acknowledgment* (not *with-*

ă pat/ā pay/âr care/ä father/b bib/ch church/d deed/ĕ pet/ē be/f fife/g gag/h hat/hw which/ĭ pit/ī pie/îr pier/j judge/k kick/l lid, needle/m mum/n no, sudden/ng thing/ŏ pot/ō toe/ô paw, for/oi noise/ou out/o͝o took/o͞o boot/p pop/r roar/s sauce/sh ship, dish/

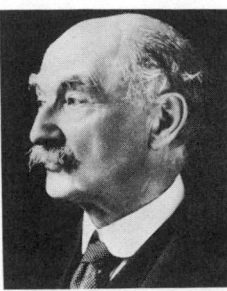

out hardly). *Hardly* is idiomatically followed by clauses introduced by *when*, or, less often, *before*, but not by *than* or *until*: *We were hardly seated when* (or *before*) *the fire broke out. Hardly had he arrived when* (or *before*) *the message came.*

hard maple. A tree, the **sugar maple** *(see)*, or its wood.

hard·ness (härd′nĭs) *n. Abbr.* **h., H. 1.** The quality or condition of being hard. **2.** *Mineralogy.* The relative resistance of a mineral to scratching, as measured by the **Mohs scale** *(see)*. **3.** The relative resistance of a metal to denting, scratching, or bending.

hard-on (härd′ŏn) *n., pl.* **-ons.** *Vulgar Slang.* An erection of the penis.

hard palate. The relatively hard, bony anterior portion of the **palate** *(see)*.

hard·pan (härd′păn′) *n.* **1.** A layer of hard subsoil or clay. **2.** Hard, unbroken ground. **3.** A foundation; bedrock.

hard rubber. A relatively inelastic rubber made with 30 to 50 per cent sulfur and usually some lime or magnesia as a filler.

hards (härdz) *n.* Plural in form, used with a singular verb. The coarse refuse of flax or similar fiber. [Middle English *herdes, hurdes,* Old English *heordan* (plural). See **kes-** in Appendix.*]

hard sauce. A creamy sauce of butter and sugar with rum, brandy, or vanilla flavoring, served chilled with puddings, gingerbread, or fruitcakes.

hard·scrab·ble (härd′skrăb′əl) *adj.* Earning a bare subsistence, as on the land; marginal: *the sharecropper's hardscrabble life.* —*n.* Barren or marginal farmland. [HARD + SCRABBLE.]

hard sell. *Informal.* Aggressive, high-pressure selling or promotion.

hard·set (härd′sĕt′) *adj.* **1.** In a difficult or ticklish position. **2.** Rigid; fixed. **3.** Obstinate.

hard·shell (härd′shĕl′) *adj.* Also **hard-shelled** (-shĕld′). **1.** Having a thick, heavy, or hardened shell. **2.** Unyieldingly orthodox; uncompromising; confirmed. —*n.* A hard-shell clam or crab.

hard-shell clam. The **quahog** *(see)*.

hard-shell crab. A marine crab with a fully hardened shell; especially, the edible species, *Callinectes sapidus,* of eastern North America, in this stage.

hard·ship (härd′shĭp′) *n.* **1.** Extreme privation; adversity; suffering. **2.** A source or cause of privation or difficulty.

hard-spun (härd′spŭn′) *adj.* Twisted tightly in spinning, often to the point of curling and looping. Said of yarn.

hard·stand (härd′stănd′) *n.* A hard-surfaced area, usually adjacent to an airstrip, for parking planes or ground vehicles.

hard·tack (härd′tăk′) *n.* A hard biscuit or bread made only with flour and water; sea bread; sea biscuit. Also called "pilot bread," "ship biscuit." [HARD + TACK (food).]

hard·top (härd′tŏp′) *n.* An automobile designed to look like a convertible, but having a rigidly fixed, hard top. Also called "hardtop convertible." —*adj.* Having a hard top.

Har·dwar (hŭr′dwär). A city and Hindu pilgrimage center of northern Uttar Pradesh, Republic of India. Population, 59,000.

hard·ware (härd′wâr′) *n.* **1.** Metal goods and utensils such as locks, tools, and cutlery. **2.** *Technology.* **a.** A computer and the associated physical equipment directly involved in the performance of communications or data-processing functions. **b.** Broadly, machines and other physical equipment directly involved in performing an industrial, technological, or military function. **3.** *Informal.* Weapons; especially, military weapons. **4.** *Informal & Regional.* A pistol or pistols; a six-gun.

hard water. Water containing dissolved salts of calcium and magnesium; especially, water containing more than 85.5 parts per million of calcium carbonate. Compare **soft water.**

hard·wood (härd′wo͝od′) *n.* **1.** The wood of a broad-leaved flowering tree, as distinguished from that of a conifer. **2.** A broad-leaved flowering tree. Compare **softwood.**

har·dy¹ (här′dē) *adj.* **-dier, -diest. 1.** Stalwart and rugged; strong: *"a rude and hardy race, that lived mostly out of doors"* (Thoreau). **2.** Courageous; intrepid; stouthearted. **3.** Brazenly daring; audacious; hotheaded. **4.** Capable of surviving unfavorable conditions such as cold weather or lack of moisture. Said chiefly of cultivated plants. —See Synonyms at **healthy.** [Middle English *hardy, hardi,* from Old French *hardi,* from the past participle of *hardir,* to become bold, make hard, from Germanic. See **kar-¹** in Appendix.*]

har·dy² (här′dē) *n., pl.* **-dies.** A square-shanked chisel or fuller that fits into a square hole in an anvil. [Probably from HARD.]

Har·dy (här′dē), **Thomas.** 1840–1928. English novelist and poet.

hardy hole. The square hole in an anvil for inserting a hardy.

hare (hâr) *n.* Any of various mammals of the family Leporidae, and especially of the genus *Lepus,* related to and resembling the rabbits but characteristically having longer ears, large hind feet, and long legs adapted for jumping. [Middle English *hare,* Old English *hara.* See **kas-** in Appendix.*]

hare and hounds. A game in which one group of players leaves a trail of paper scraps for a pursuing group to follow.

hare·bell (hâr′bĕl′) *n.* A plant, *Campanula rotundifolia,* having slender stems and leaves and bell-shaped blue flowers. Also called "bluebell." [Middle English *harebelle* : HARE (perhaps because it grows in places frequented by hares) + BELL.]

hare·brained (hâr′brānd′) *adj.* Giddy; flighty: *"Harebrained schemes were aired for averting this terrible outcome"* (A.J.P. Taylor).

hare·lip (hâr′lĭp′) *n.* A congenital fissure or pair of fissures in the upper lip. —**hare′lipped′** *adj.*

har·em (hâr′əm, hăr′-) *n.* Also **ha·reem** (hä-rēm′). **1.** A house or a section of a house reserved for women members of a Moslem household; gynaeceum. **2.** The women occupying a harem; the wives, concubines, female relatives, and servants of a Moslem household. [Arabic *ḥarīm,* sacred, forbidden place, from *ḥarama,* he prohibited.]

Har·gei·sa (här-gā′sə). Also **Har·ghes·sa** (här-gĕs′ə). A city of northwestern Somalia; the capital of former British Somaliland. Population, 30,000.

Har·greaves (här′grēvz′), **James.** Died 1778. British inventor of the spinning jenny.

Ha·ri·a·na (hăr′ē-ä′nə). A state of the Republic of India, occupying 16,984 square miles in the northwest, formed by the division of Punjab into the two smaller states of Hariana and Punjab in 1966. Population, 7,600,000. Capital, Chandigarh.

har·i·cot (hăr′ĭ-kō′) *n.* **1.** The edible pod or seed of any of several beans, especially the string bean. **2.** A highly seasoned mutton or lamb stew with vegetables. [French, perhaps from Aztec *ayacotl* or Nahuatl *ayecotli.*]

Ha·ri·ri (hä-rē′rē), **Abu Muhammad al-.** 1054–1122. Arab scholar and poet.

Ha·ri Rud (hăr′ē ro͞od′). Also **He·ri Rud** (hĕr′ē). Ancient name **Ar·i·us** (âr′ē-əs, ə-rī′əs). A river of Afghanistan, Iran, and the Turkmen S.S.R., rising in northwestern Afghanistan and flowing 700 miles west to form part of the Iran-Afghanistan boundary and then north to the Kara Kum desert.

hark (härk) *intr.v.* **harked, harking, harks.** To listen attentively; hearken: *"The youth lies awake . . . and harks to the musical rain"* (Walt Whitman). —**hark back.** To return to a previous point, as in a narrative. [Middle English *herk(i)en,* Old English *heorcian* (unattested). See **keu-¹** in Appendix.*]

hark·en. Variant of **hearken.**

harl (härl) *n.* Filaments or fibers, as of hemp or flax. [Middle English *herle,* fiber, probably from Middle Low German *herle, harle*†.]

Har·lem (här′ləm). **1.** A river channel in New York City separating the northern end of Manhattan Island from the Bronx. **2.** A section of New York City bordering on this river channel and on the East River.

har·le·quin (här′lə-kwən, -kən) *n.* **1.** *Capital* **H.** A conventional buffoon of the commedia dell'arte, traditionally presented in a mask and parti-colored tights. **2.** A clown; buffoon. **3.** A small duck, *Histrionicus histrionicus,* having a short bill and distinctively patterned plumage. In this sense, also called "harlequin duck." —*adj.* **1.** Bright; parti-colored; spangled; suggesting the dress of Harlequin. **2.** Having frames that flare in an upward slant, suggesting the slits of Harlequin's mask. Said of eyeglasses. [Variant (influenced by obsolete French *harlequin*) of earlier *Harlicken, Harlaken,* from Old French *Herlequin, Hellequin,* leader of a troop of demon horsemen riding at night, probably from Old English *Herla cyning,* King *Herla,* a mythical figure who has been identified with Woden.]

har·le·quin·ade (här′lə-kwə-nād′) *n.* **1.** A comedy or pantomime in which Harlequin is the main attraction. **2.** A succession of farcical clownings. **3.** A fantastic procedure: *"Every trick of thought and every harlequinade of phrase"* (Poe).

harlequin bug. A flat-bodied, brightly colored insect, *Murgantia histrionica,* that has a fetid odor, and is destructive to cabbage and other plants. Also called "calicoback," "fire bug."

Har·ley Street (här′lē). A street of central London, England, notably occupied by the offices of prominent members of the medical profession.

har·lot (här′lət) *n.* A woman of ill repute, especially a whore or prostitute. [Middle English *harlot, herlot,* vagabond, itinerate jester, male servant, prostitute, from Old French *(h)arlot, herlot*†, young fellow, vagabond.] —**har′lot·ry** (här′lə-trē) *n.*

harm (härm) *n.* **1.** Injury or damage. **2.** Wrong; evil. —**in harm's way.** In danger; in a risky position. —**out of harm's reach (way).** Out of danger; in a safe place. —*tr.v.* **harmed, harming, harms.** To damage; injure; impair. See Synonyms at **injure.** [Middle English *harm,* Old English *hearm.* See **kormo-** in Appendix.*]

har·mat·tan (här′mə-tăn′, här-măt′n) *n.* A dry, dusty wind that blows from the Sahara and along the northwestern coast of Africa. [Twi *haramata,* probably from Arabic *ḥarām,* a forbidden or accursed thing, from the stem of *ḥarama,* forbid, akin to *ḥaruma,* to be forbidden. See **harem.**]

harm·ful (härm′fəl) *adj.* Capable of harming or causing harm; damaging; injurious. —**harm′ful·ly** *adv.* —**harm′ful·ness** *n.*

harm·less (härm′lĭs) *adj.* Not harmful; not capable of harming; inoffensive. —**harm′less·ly** *adv.* —**harm′less·ness** *n.*

har·mon·ic (här-mŏn′ĭk) *adj.* **1. a.** Of or pertaining to musical harmony as distinguished from melody or rhythm. **b.** Of or pertaining to harmonics. **2.** Characterized by harmony; concordant. —*n. Acoustics.* **1.** A tone in the harmonic series of overtones produced by a fundamental tone. Also called "overtone," "partial," "partial tone." **2.** Such a tone produced on a stringed instrument by lightly touching an open or stopped vibrating string at a given fraction of its length so that both segments vibrate. [Latin *harmonicus,* from Greek *harmonikos,* from *harmonia,* HARMONY.] —**har·mon′i·cal·ly** *adv.*

har·mon·i·ca (här-mŏn′ĭ-kə) *n.* **1.** A small, rectangular musical instrument consisting of a row of free reeds set back in air holes, played by exhaling or inhaling. Also called "mouth organ." **2.** A musical instrument consisting of a series of glass bowls of varying sizes played by rubbing the finger along the wet rims. **3.** A musical instrument consisting of tuned strips of metal or glass fixed to a frame and struck with a hammer. [Variant (influenced by HARMONIC) of earlier *armonica,* from Italian, from *armonico,* harmonious, from Latin *harmonicus,* HARMONIC.]

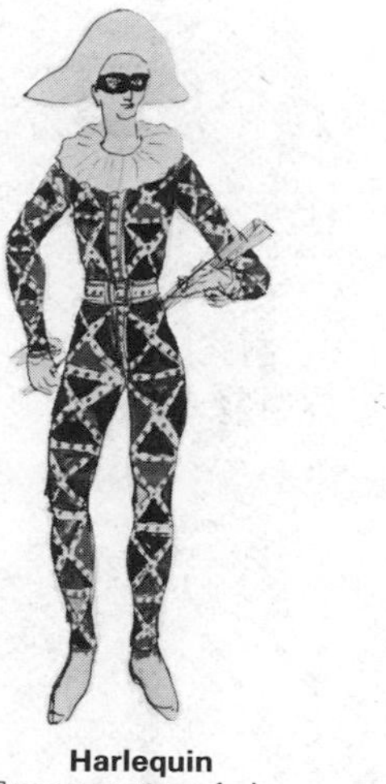

Harlequin
From a costume design
by Rouben Ter-Arutunian

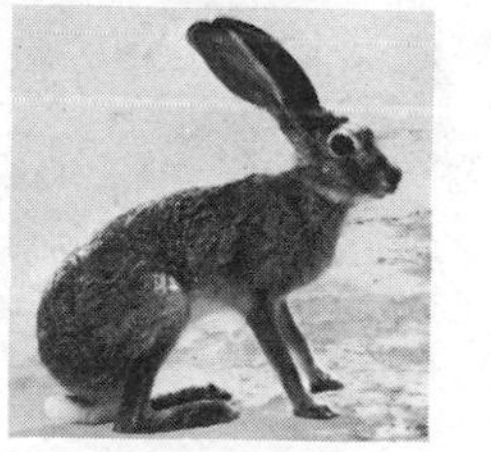

hare

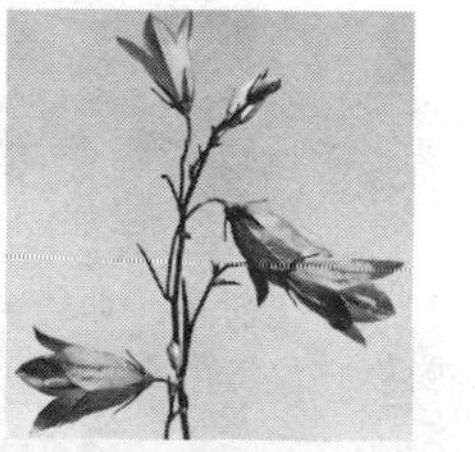

harebell

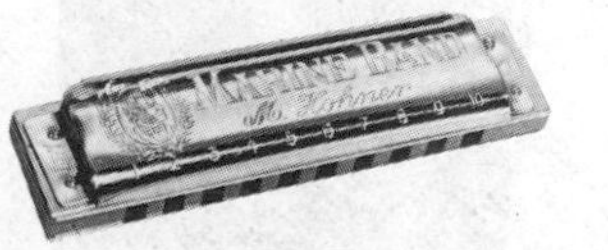

harmonica

t tight/th thin, path/*th* this, bathe/ŭ cut/ûr urge/v valve/w with/y yes/z zebra, size/zh vision/ə about, item, edible, gallop, circus/ à *Fr.* ami/œ *Fr.* feu, *Ger.* schön/ü *Fr.* tu, *Ger.* über/KH *Ger.* ich, *Scot.* loch/N *Fr.* bon. ***Follows main vocabulary. †Of obscure origin.**

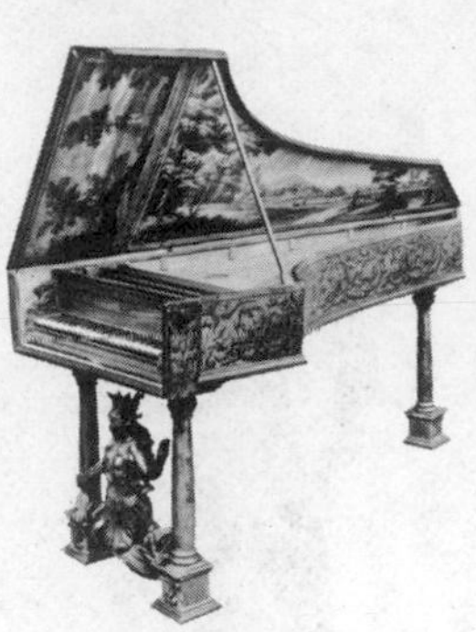
harpsichord
Eighteenth-century Italian

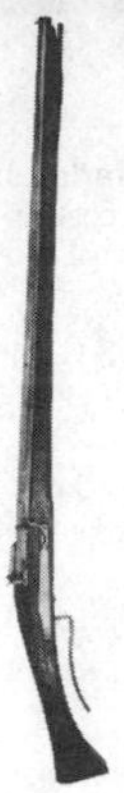
harquebus

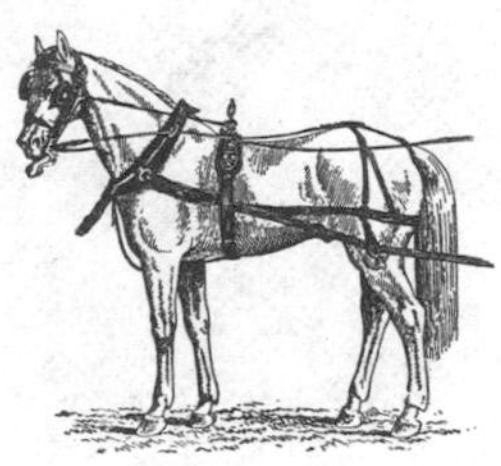
harness

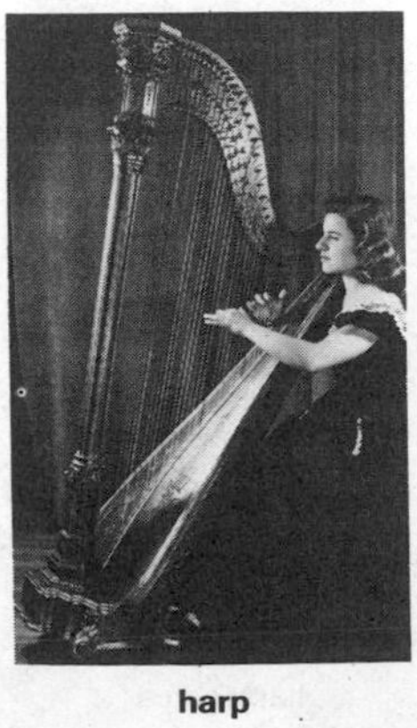
harp

harmonic analysis. The representation of mathematical functions by means of linear operations such as summation or integration on characteristic sets of functions; especially, such representation by Fourier series.
harmonic mean. The reciprocal of the arithmetic mean of the reciprocals of a specified set of numbers.
harmonic progression. A sequence of quantities the reciprocals of which form an arithmetic progression; for example, $1, \frac{1}{3}, \frac{1}{5}, \frac{1}{7}, \ldots$
har·mon·ics (här-mŏn′ĭks) *n.* Plural in form, used with a singular verb. The theory or study of the physical properties and characteristics of musical sound.
harmonic series. **1.** *Mathematics.* A series whose terms are in harmonic progression; for example, $1 + \frac{1}{3} + \frac{1}{5} + \frac{1}{7} + \ldots$. **2.** *Acoustics.* A series of tones consisting of a fundamental tone and the overtones produced by it, whose frequencies are consecutive integral multiples of the frequency of the fundamental.
har·mo·ni·ous (här-mō′nē-əs) *adj.* **1.** Exhibiting accord in feeling or action; sympathetic: *a harmonious relationship.* **2.** Having component elements pleasingly or appropriately combined: *a harmonious structure.* **3.** Characterized by harmony of sound; concordant. —**har·mo′ni·ous·ly** *adv.* —**har·mo′ni·ous·ness** *n.*
har·mo·nist (här′mə-nĭst) *n.* **1.** A student who collates and seeks to harmonize the discrepancies in parallel passages of Scripture, especially of the Gospels. **2. a.** One skilled in musical harmony. **b.** *Poetic.* A maker of harmonious music: *"The Ocean is a mighty harmonist"* (Wordsworth). **3.** One of a school of ancient Greek musical theorists whose principles were based on the subjective effects of tones rather than on the mathematical relations. **4.** One who brings into consonance or accord; harmonizer.
har·mo·nis·tic (här′mə-nĭs′tĭk) *adj.* **1.** Of or relating to a harmony. **2.** Of or relating to the harmonizing of parallel passages in Scripture. —**har′mo·nis′ti·cal·ly** *adv.*
har·mo·ni·um (här-mō′nē-əm) *n.* An organlike keyboard instrument that produces tones with free metal reeds actuated by air forced from a bellows. [French, from *harmonie,* harmony, from Old French *armonie,* HARMONY.]
har·mo·nize (här′mə-nīz′) *v.* **-nized, -nizing, -nizes.** —*tr.* **1.** To bring into agreement or harmony; make harmonious: *"Some realisms can be harmonized with some notions of poetic purity"* (Wayne C. Booth). **2.** To provide harmony for (a melody). —*intr.* **1.** To be in agreement; be harmonious. **2.** To sing or play in harmony. —See Synonyms at **agree.**
har·mo·ny (här′mə-nē) *n., pl.* **-nies.** **1.** Agreement in feeling, approach, action, disposition, or the like; sympathy; accord. **2.** The pleasing interaction or appropriate combination of the elements in a whole. **3.** *Music.* **a.** The study of the structure, progression, and relation of chords. **b.** The simultaneous combination of notes in a chord. **c.** The structure of a musical work or passage as considered from the point of view of its chordal characteristics and relationships. **4.** *Archaic.* Pleasing sounds; music. **5.** A collation of parallel passages from the Gospels, with a commentary demonstrating their consonance and explaining their discrepancies. —See Synonyms at **proportion.** [Middle English *armonie,* from Old French *(h)armonie,* from Latin *harmonia,* from Greek, agreement, harmony, means of joining, from *harmos,* joint. See **ar-** in Appendix.*]
har·ness (här′nĭs) *n.* **1.** The gear or tackle other than a yoke used by a draft animal to pull a vehicle or implement. **2.** Anything resembling a harness, such as the arrangement of straps used to hold a parachute to the body. **3.** A device that raises and lowers the warp threads on a loom. **4.** *Archaic.* Armor for a man or a horse. —**in harness.** On duty. —*tr.v.* **harnessed, -nessing, -nesses.** **1.** To put a harness on (a draft animal). **2.** To bring under control and direct the force of: *If he can harness his energy, he will accomplish a great deal.* **3.** *Archaic.* To fit with armor; arm or equip for battle. [Middle English *harness, harnais,* baggage, equipment, trappings of a horse, from Old French *harneis,* military equipment, from Old Norse *hernest* (unattested), provisions for an army : *herr,* army (see **koro-** in Appendix*) + *nest,* provisions (see **nes-**[1] in Appendix*).] —**har′ness·er** *n.*
harnessed antelope. Any of several African antelopes with markings resembling the straps of a harness, such as the **bushbuck** *(see).*
harness hitch. A type of knot forming a fixed loop in the bight of a rope.
harness race. A horse race between pacers or trotters harnessed to sulkies.
Har·ney Peak (här′nē). The highest elevation (7,242 feet) of the Black Hills, southwestern South Dakota.
Har·old (hăr′əld). A masculine given name. [Middle English *Harold,* from Scandinavian, akin to Old Norse *Haraldr.* See **koro-** in Appendix.*]
harp (härp) *n.* **1.** A musical instrument consisting of an upright, open, triangular frame with 46 strings of graded lengths which are played by plucking with the fingers. **2.** Something similar to a harp. —*v.* **harped, harping, harps.** —*intr.* To play a harp. —*tr. Archaic.* To give expression to. —**harp on** (or **upon**). To talk or write about to an excessive and tedious degree; dwell upon. [Middle English *harp(e),* Old English *hearpe,* from Germanic *harpōn-* (unattested).] —**harp′er** *n.*
Har·pers Ferry (här′pərz). A town of northeastern West Virginia; site of John Brown's rebellion (1859). Population, 572.
har·pins (här′pĭnz) *pl.n.* Also **har·pings.** Extensions of the ribbands of a ship under construction. [Perhaps from HARP.]
harp·ist (här′pĭst) *n.* A person who plays the harp.
har·poon (här-po͞on′) *n.* A spearlike weapon having a barbed head with toggle action that is hurled by hand or shot from a gun, and is used in hunting whales and large fish. —*tr.v.* **harpooned, -pooning, -poons.** To strike, kill, or capture with or as if with a harpoon: *"The Master harpooned a breakfast-roll."* (O.W. Holmes). [French *harpon,* from *harpe,* clamp, dog's claw, from Latin *harpē, harpa,* sickle, from Greek *harpē.* See **serp-**[1] in Appendix.*] —**har·poon′er, har′poon·eer′** (här′po͞o-nîr′) *n.*
harpoon gun. A small cannonlike apparatus used to fire harpoons.
harp·si·chord (härp′sĭ-kôrd′, -kōrd′) *n.* A keyboard instrument in which the strings are sounded by means of quill or leather plectrums rather than hammers. [Obsolete French *harpechorde,* from Italian *arpicordo* : *arpi,* harp, from Late Latin *harpa,* from Germanic *harpōn-* (unattested), HARP + *corda,* string, from Latin *chorda,* from Greek *khordē* (see **gher-**[1] in Appendix*).]
har·py (här′pē) *n., pl.* **-pies.** **1.** A predatory person. **2.** A shrewish woman. [From HARPY.]
Har·py (här′pē) *n., pl.* **-pies.** *Greek Mythology.* One of several loathsome, voracious monsters, having a woman's head and trunk and a bird's tail, wings, and talons. [French *harpie,* from Latin *harpȳia,* from Greek *harpuiai*†, "snatchers."]
har·que·bus (här′kə-bəs, -kwĭ-bŭs′) *n.* A heavy, portable, matchlock gun invented during the 15th century. Also called "hackbut." [Old French *(h)arquebuse,* from Middle Dutch *hakebusse* : *hake,* hook (see **keg-** in Appendix*) + *busse,* box, gun, from Late Latin *buxis,* BOX.]
har·ri·dan (hăr′ə-dən) *n.* A vicious, scolding old woman; vixen. [Possibly variant of French *haridelle*†, worn-out horse.]
har·ri·er[1] (hăr′ē-ər) *n.* **1.** One that harries. **2.** Any of various slender, narrow-winged hawks of the genus *Circus,* that prey on small animals.
har·ri·er[2] (hăr′ē-ər) *n.* **1.** One of a breed of small hounds originally used in hunting hares. **2.** A cross-country runner. [From HARE.]
Har·ri·et (hăr′ē-ət, hâr′-). A feminine given name. [From French *Henriette,* HENRIETTA.]
Har·rin·gay (hăr′ĭng-gā′). A borough of London, England, comprising the former administrative divisions of Hornsey, Tottenham, and Wood Green. Population, 259,000.
Har·ris. See **Lewis with Harris.**
Har·ris (hăr′ĭs, hâr′-), **Joel Chandler.** 1848–1908. American author; creator of Uncle Remus.
Har·ris (hăr′ĭs, hâr′-), **Townsend.** 1804–1878. American diplomat; first U.S. consul general to Japan (1855–61).
Har·ris·burg (hăr′ĭs-bûrg, hâr′-). The capital of Pennsylvania, a manufacturing center located on the Susquehanna in the southeastern part of the state. Population, 80,000.
Har·ri·son (hăr′ĭ-sən), **Benjamin**[1]. 1726?–1791. American Revolutionary leader; signer of the Declaration of Independence; father of William Henry Harrison.
Har·ri·son (hăr′ĭ-sən), **Benjamin**[2]. 1833–1901. Twenty-third President of the United States (1889–93); grandson of William Henry Harrison.
Har·ri·son (hăr′ĭ-sən), **William Henry.** 1773–1841. Ninth President of the United States (1841); died in office.
Har·row (hăr′ō). Formerly **Har·row-on-the-Hill.** A borough of London, England. Population, 210,000.
har·row[1] (hăr′ō) *n.* A farm instrument consisting of a heavy frame with teeth or upright disks, used to break up and even off plowed ground. —*tr.v.* **harrowed, -rowing, -rows.** **1.** To break up and level (soil or land) with a harrow. **2.** To inflict great distress or torment on the mind of; to torment. [Middle English *harwe*†.]
har·row[2] (hăr′ō) *tr.v.* **-rowed, -rowing, -rows.** **1.** To plunder; spoil; rob. Used in the phrase *harrow hell* (as said of Jesus after his death). **2.** To despoil; harry: *"They long racked and harrowed the people"* (Sir William Jones). [Middle English *harwen,* variant of *harien,* to HARRY.]
har·row·ing[1] (hăr′ō-ĭng) *adj.* Extremely distressing: *"It is a harrowing experience to watch anyone die"* (Duke of Windsor).
har·row·ing[2] (hăr′ō-ĭng) *n.* An action of plundering or spoiling. Used in the phrase *harrowing of hell* (as said of Jesus' rescue, following his crucifixion, of the souls of the righteous held captive in hell since the generation of Adam).
har·ry (hăr′ē) *tr.v.* **-ried, -rying, -ries.** **1.** To raid, as in a war; to sack; to pillage. **2.** To disturb or annoy by constant attacks; harass. [Middle English *harien, herien,* Old English *hergian.* See **koro-** in Appendix.*]
Har·ry (hăr′ē). A masculine given name. [Old French *Henri,* HENRY.]
harsh (härsh) *adj.* **1.** Producing an unpleasant sensory response; irritating. **2.** Extremely severe or exacting; stern. —See Synonyms at **burdensome, rough.** [Middle English *harsk*†.] —**harsh′ly** *adv.* —**harsh′ness** *n.*
harsh·en (här′shən) *v.* **-ened, -ening, -ens.** —*tr.* To make harsh. —*intr.* To become harsh.
hars·let. Variant of **haslet.**
hart (härt) *n., pl.* **harts** or **hart.** A male deer; especially, a male red deer over five years old. [Middle English *hert,* Old English *heor(o)t.* See **ker-**[1] in Appendix.*]
Hart (härt), **Lorenz.** 1895–1943. American lyricist; collaborated with Richard Rodgers.
Hart (härt), **Moss.** 1904–1961. American playwright and theatrical director.
har·tal (här-täl′) *n.* A halting of work and business in India; a strike or boycott. [Hindi *harṭāl,* from *haṭṭāl,* "locking of shops" : *hāṭ,* shop, from Sanskrit *haṭṭa,* shop, perhaps from

haṭika, gold, from *hari,* yellow (see **ghel-**[2] in Appendix*) + *tālā,* lock bolt, from Sanskrit *tālā, tāḍā,* latch, probably from Dravidian.]

Harte (härt), **(Francis) Bret(t).** 1836–1902. American author of short stories and verse.

har·te·beest (här′tə-bēst′, härt′bēst′) *n.* Also **hart·beest** (härt′-). Either of two African antelopes, *Alcelaphus buselaphus* or *A. lichtensteini,* having a brownish coat and ridged, outward-curving horns. [Obsolete Afrikaans, from Dutch *hartebeest, hertebeest,* deer : *hert, hart,* deer, hart, from Middle Dutch *hert* (see **ker-**[1] in Appendix*) + *beest,* beast, from Middle Dutch, from Old French *beste,* BEAST.]

Hart·ford (härt′fərd). The capital of Connecticut, a commercial and industrial center located on the Connecticut River in the central part of the state. Population, 162,000.

hart's-tongue (härts′tŭng′) *n.* An evergreen fern, *Phyllitis scolopendrium,* having narrow, undivided fronds. [So called from the shape of its fronds.]

har·um-scar·um (hâr′əm-skâr′əm) *adj.* Lacking a sense of responsibility; rash; reckless. —*adv.* With abandon; recklessly. —*n. Informal.* **1.** One who acts recklessly. **2.** Reckless behavior. [Perhaps from HARE + SCARE.]

Ha·run al-Ra·shid (hä-rōōn′ ăl-rä-shēd′). A.D. 764?–809. Caliph of Baghdad (A.D. 786–809).

Ha·ru·no·bu (här′ōō-nō′bōō), **Suzuki.** 1725?–1770. Japanese painter and graphic artist.

ha·rus·pex (hə-rŭs′pĕks′, hăr′əs-) *n., pl.* **haruspices** (hə-rŭs′pə-sēz′). Also **a·rus·pex** (ə-rŭs′-). A Roman priest who practiced divination by the inspection of the entrails of animals. [Latin. See **gher-**[1] in Appendix.*]

Har·vard (här′vərd), **John.** 1607–1638. English clergyman in America; benefactor of Harvard University.

Har·vard, Mount (här′vərd). A peak rising to 14,414 feet in the Sawatch Range of central Colorado.

har·vest (här′vĭst) *n.* **1.** The act or process of gathering a crop. **2.** The crop thus gathered. **3.** The amount or measure of the crop thus gathered. **4.** The time or season of such a gathering. **5.** The result or consequence of any action. —*v.* **harvested, -vesting, -vests.** —*tr.* **1.** To gather (a crop). **2.** To gather a crop from (a field or orchard, for example). **3.** To receive (the benefits or consequences of an action). —*intr.* To gather a crop. —*adj.* Of or relating to a harvest: *a harvest lunch.* [Middle English *hervest,* autumn, Old English *hærfest.* See **kerp-** in Appendix.*]

harvest bug. An insect, the **chigger** *(see).*

har·vest·er (här′vĭ-stər) *n.* A reaper.

harvest fly. Any of several cicadas of the genus *Tibicen,* that produce a shrill sound heard late in summer.

harvest home. 1. The completion of the harvest. **2. a.** The time of completing the harvest. **b.** A festival held at this time. **c.** A song sung at this time.

har·vest·man (här′vĭst-mən) *n., pl.* **-men** (-mĭn). **1.** One who harvests. **2.** An arachnid, the **daddy longlegs** *(see).*

harvest mite. An insect, the **chigger** *(see).*

harvest moon. The full moon that occurs nearest the autumnal equinox.

Har·vey (här′vē). A masculine given name. [Middle English, probably from Breton *Haerveu*†, "bitter."]

Har·vey (här′vē), **William.** 1578–1657. English physician and anatomist; discovered blood circulation.

Har·wich (hăr′ĭj, -ĭch). A city and port of northeastern Essex, England, on the North Sea. Population, 14,000.

Harz Mountains (härts). A mountain range of central Germany between the Weser and the Elbe. Highest elevation, Brocken (3,747 feet).

has (hăz). Third person singular present indicative of **have.**

Ha·sa (hä′sä′). Also **El Ha·sa** (ĕl häs′ə). The largest province and the principal oil-producing region of Saudi Arabia, occupying 22,500 square miles in the northeast on the Persian Gulf. Population, 2,250,000. Capital, Hofuf.

has-been (hăz′bĭn′) *n. Informal.* One that is no longer famous, popular, successful, or useful.

ha·sen·pfef·fer (hä′sən-fĕf′ər) *n.* A highly seasoned stew of marinated rabbit meat, often served with sour cream. [German *Hasenpfeffer* : *Hase,* rabbit, from Middle High German, from Old High German *haso* (see **kas-** in Appendix*) + *Pfeffer,* from Old High German *pfeffar,* from Latin *piper,* PEPPER.]

hash[1] (hăsh) *n.* **1.** A main dish of chopped meat, potatoes, and sometimes vegetables, usually browned and baked. **2.** A jumble, hodgepodge, or mess. **3.** A reworking or restatement of material already familiar. —**make a hash of. 1.** To make a mess of; to botch. **2.** To defeat soundly. —**settle one's hash.** To silence or subdue. —*tr.v.* **hashed, hashing, hashes. 1.** To chop into pieces; to mince. **2.** *Informal.* To make a mess of; to mangle. **3.** *Informal.* To discuss carefully; to review. Often used with *over: hash over future plans.* [French *hachis,* from *hacher,* to chop up, from Old French *hachier,* from *hache,* ax, HATCHET.]

hash[2] (hăsh) *n. Informal.* **Hashish** *(see).*

hash house. *Slang.* A cheap restaurant.

hash·ish (hăsh′ēsh′, -ĭsh) *n.* Also **hash·eesh** (hä′shēsh′). A purified extract prepared from the dried flowers of the hemp plant, smoked or chewed in the Orient as a mild narcotic. Also informally "hash." [Arabic *ḥashīsh,* hemp, dried grass.]

hash mark. *Military Slang.* A service stripe on the sleeve of an enlisted man's uniform.

Has·i·dim. Variant of **Chassidim.**

has·let (hăs′lĭt, hāz′-) *n.* Also **hars·let** (härs′-). The heart, liver, and other edible viscera of an animal; especially, hog viscera. [Middle English *hastelet, hastlet,* from Old French *hastelet,* diminutive of *haste,* spit, roast meat, perhaps from Latin *hasta,* spear. See **ghasto-** in Appendix.*]

Has·mo·ne·ans (hăz′mə-nē′ənz). Also **Has·mo·nae·ans.** Original name of the **Maccabees** *(see).*

has·n't (hăz′ənt). Contraction of *has not.*

hasp (hăsp, häsp) *n.* A metal fastener having a hinged, slotted part that fits over a staple and may be secured by a pin, bolt, or padlock. —*tr.v.* **hasped, hasping, hasps.** To fasten or lock with a hasp. [Middle English *hasp,* Old English *hæsp(e), hæpse,* fastening, hinge, from Germanic *hasp-* (unattested).]

Has·sam (hăs′əm), **Childe.** 1859–1935. American impressionist painter and graphic artist.

Has·san II (hă-săn′). Born 1929. King of Morocco (since 1961).

Has·selt (häs′əlt). The capital of Limburg Province, Belgium, a coal-mining center located in the west. Population, 37,000.

Has·si·dim. Variant of **Chassidim.**

has·sle (hăs′əl) *n. Informal.* **1.** An argument or fight. **2.** Trouble; bother. —*intr.v.* **hassled, -sling, -sles.** *Informal.* To argue or fight. [Perhaps blend of HAGGLE + TUSSLE.]

has·sock (hăs′ək) *n.* **1.** A thick cushion used as a footstool or for kneeling. **2.** A dense clump of grass. [Middle English *hassok,* Old English *hassuc*†, clump of matted vegetation.]

hast (hăst). *Archaic.* Second person singular present indicative of **have.** Used with *thou.*

has·tate (hăs′tāt′) *adj.* Shaped like the head of an arrow or spear: *a hastate leaf.* [New Latin *hastatus,* from Latin *hasta,* spear. See **ghasto-** in Appendix.*]

haste (hāst) *n.* **1.** Swiftness; rapidity. **2.** Eagerness or necessity to move swiftly; urgency. **3.** Careless or headlong hurrying; precipitateness. —**make haste.** To move or act swiftly; to hurry. —*v.* **hasted, hasting, hastes.** *Poetic.* —*intr.* To hasten. —*tr.* To cause to hurry; hasten. [Middle English, from Old French, from West Germanic *haisti-* (unattested), from Germanic *haifsti-* (unattested).]

has·ten (hā′sən) *v.* **-tened, -tening, -tens.** —*intr.* To move swiftly. —*tr.* To cause to move swiftly; hurry. —See Synonyms at **speed.**

Has·tings (hā′stĭngz). **1.** A city of southern Nebraska. Population, 21,000. **2.** A city and resort center of southeastern East Sussex, England, on the Strait of Dover, near the scene of the Saxon defeat by a Norman army under William the Conqueror (1066). Population, 67,000.

hast·y (hā′stē) *adj.* **-ier, -iest. 1.** Characterized by speed; swift; rapid. **2.** Done or made too quickly to be accurate or wise; rash: *a hasty decision.* **3.** Thoughtless or inconsiderate. **4.** Easily angered; irritable. —See Synonyms at **fast, impetuous.** —**hast′i·ly** *adv.* —**hast′i·ness** *n.*

hasty pudding. 1. Cornmeal mush. **2.** *British.* A porridge of flour or oatmeal boiled with seasonings in water or milk.

hat (hăt) *n.* **1.** A covering for the head; especially, one having a shaped crown and brim. **2. a.** The red four-cornered hat worn by a cardinal of the Roman Catholic Church. **b.** The office of cardinal. —**pass the hat.** To take up a monetary collection. —**take one's hat off to.** To respect, admire, or congratulate. —**talk through one's hat. 1.** To talk nonsense. **2.** To bluff. —**throw** (or **toss**) **one's hat into the ring.** To enter a race or contest; especially, to run for office. —**under one's hat.** Confidential; secret. —*tr.v.* **hatted, hatting, hats.** To supply or cover with a hat. [Middle English *hat,* Old English *hæt(t).* See **kadh-** in Appendix.*]

hat·band (hăt′bănd′) *n.* **1.** A band of ribbon or cloth worn on a hat just above the brim. **2.** A similar band of black cloth, worn to denote mourning.

hat·box (hăt′bŏks′) *n.* A round box or case for a hat.

hatch[1] (hăch) *n.* **1. a.** An opening in the deck of a ship leading to the hold. **b.** The cover for such an opening. **c.** A hatchway. **d.** A ship's compartment. **2.** Any small door or opening, as in a roof or floor. **3. a.** A Dutch door. **b.** The lower half of a Dutch door. **4.** A floodgate. —**down the hatch.** *Slang.* Drink up. Used as a toast. [Middle English *hacche, hecche,* Old English *hæc(c),* hatch, wicket, from Germanic *khak-* (unattested).]

hatch[2] (hăch) *v.* **hatched, hatching, hatches.** —*intr.* To emerge from or break out of the egg. —*tr.* **1.** To produce (young) from an egg. **2.** To cause (an egg or eggs) to produce young. **3.** To originate or formulate. —*n.* **1.** The act or an instance of hatching. **2.** The young hatched at one time; a brood. [Middle English *hacchen,* Old English *hæccan* (unattested).] —**hatch′er** *n.*

hatch[3] (hăch) *tr.v.* **hatched, hatching, hatches.** To shade by drawing or etching fine parallel or crossed lines on. —*n.* Such a line. [Middle English *hachen,* from Old French *hach(i)er,* from *hache,* ax. See **hatchet.**]

hatch·er·y (hăch′ə-rē) *n., pl.* **-ies.** A place where eggs, especially those of fish or domestic fowl, are hatched.

hatch·et (hăch′ĭt) *n.* **1.** A small, short-handled ax, for use in one hand. **2.** A tomahawk. —**bury the hatchet.** To stop fighting; make peace. —**dig up the hatchet.** To begin fighting; declare war. [Middle English *hachet, hatchet,* small ax, from Old French *hachette,* diminutive of *hache,* ax, from Germanic. See **skep-** in Appendix.*]

hatchet face. A long, gaunt face with sharp features.

hatch·ing (hăch′ĭng) *n.* **1.** The fine lines used in graphic arts to show shading. **2.** The process of decorating with such lines.

hatch·ment (hăch′mənt) *n. Heraldry.* A panel bearing the coat of arms of a dead person. [Earlier *(h)achement, achiment,* perhaps short for ACHIEVEMENT.]

hatch·way (hăch′wā′) *n.* **1. a.** An opening in the deck of a ship

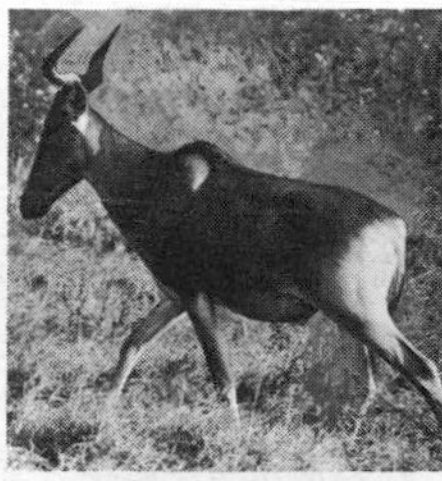

hartebeest
Alcelaphus buselaphus

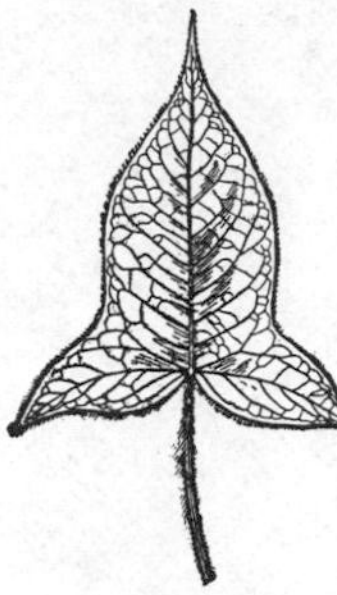

hastate
Hastate leaf

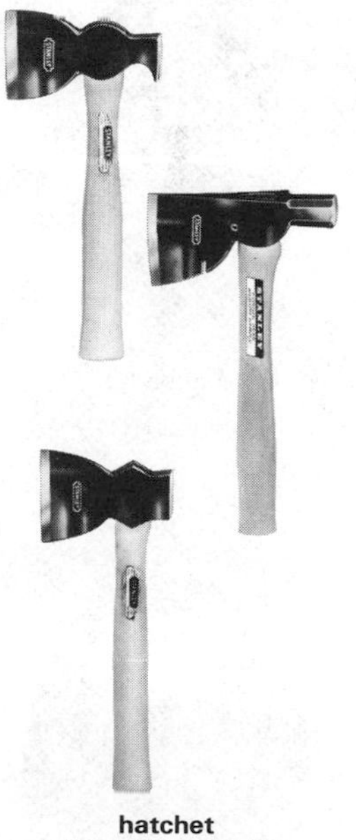

hatchet
Above: Claw hatchet
Center: Half hatchet
Below: Broad hatchet

t tight/th thin, path/*th* this, bathe/ŭ cut/ûr urge/v valve/w with/y yes/z zebra, size/zh vision/ə about, item, edible, gallop, circus/
à *Fr.* ami/œ *Fr.* feu, *Ger.* schön/ü *Fr.* tu, *Ger.* über/KH *Ger.* ich, *Scot.* loch/N *Fr.* bon. ***Follows main vocabulary.** †**Of obscure origin.**

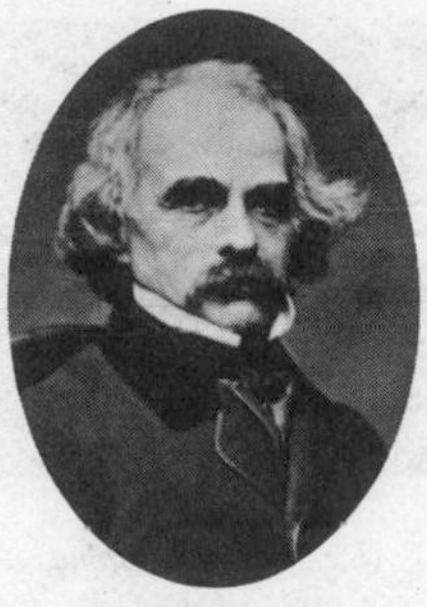

Nathaniel Hawthorne
Photograph by
Mathew Brady

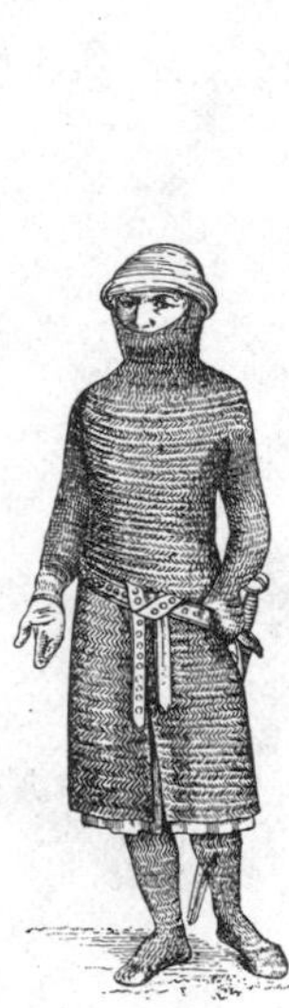

hauberk

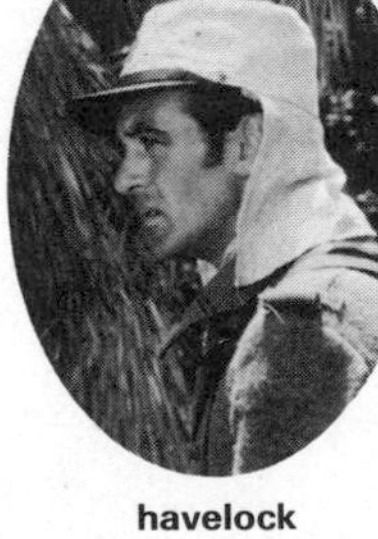

havelock

leading to a hold, compartment, or lower deck. **b.** A ladder or stairway within such an opening. **2. a.** Any similar opening, as in a roof or floor. **b.** Any similar ladder or stairway.

hate (hāt) *v.* **hated, hating, hates.** —*tr.* **1.** To loathe; detest. **2.** To dislike; wish to shun. —*intr.* To feel hatred. —*n.* **1.** Strong dislike; animosity; hatred. **2.** An object of detestation or hatred: *a pet hate.* [Middle English *haten,* Old English *hatian.* See **kād-** in Appendix.*] —**hat'er** *n.*

hate·ful (hāt'fəl) *adj.* **1.** Inspiring hatred; detestable; despicable. **2.** *Rare.* Feeling or expressing hatred; malevolent. —**hate'ful·ly** *adv.* —**hate'ful·ness** *n.*

Synonyms: *hateful, detestable, odious, obnoxious, offensive, repellent.* These adjectives, closely related and often interchangeable, describe what causes strong dislike or distaste. *Hateful* refers to what stirs hatred, enmity, or animosity, and *detestable* to what arouses intense hatred or scorn. *Odious* suggests being the object of one's disgust or aversion. *Obnoxious* is applied to what causes irritation, resentment, or even stronger feeling, and often has reference to rude or insulting behavior. *Offensive* has wide application to what offends or stirs displeasure, and is the least forceful of these terms unless qualified by an adverb. *Repellent* implies having a character or nature that drives people away or causes the possessor to be shunned.

hath (hăth). *Archaic.* Third person singular present indicative of **have.**

Hath·a·way (hăth'ə-wā'), **Anne.** 1557?–1623. Wife of William Shakespeare.

Hath·or (hăth'ôr'). The ancient Egyptian goddess of heaven and beauty, represented as having a cow's head. [Greek *Hathōr,* from Egyptian *ḥt-ḥr.*]

Ha·thor·ic (hə-thôr'ĭk, -thŏr'ĭk) *adj.* **1.** Of or pertaining to the goddess Hathor. **2.** *Architecture.* Designating a column with a head of Hathor as its capital.

ha·tred (hā'trĭd) *n.* Violent dislike or animosity; abhorrence. [Middle English *hatred, hatereden* : *hate, hete,* hate, Old English *hete* (see **kād-** in Appendix*) + *-reden,* Old English *rǣden,* condition (see **ar-** in Appendix*).]

Hat·shep·sut (hăt-shĕp'so͞ot'). Also **Hat·shep·set** (-sĕt'). Queen of Egypt of the 18th dynasty (1490?–1469? B.C.).

hat·ter (hăt'ər) *n.* One whose occupation is the manufacture, selling, or repair of hats.

Hat·ter·as (hăt'ər-əs). An island off the coast of eastern North Carolina, between Pamlico Sound and the Atlantic.

Hat·ter·as, Cape (hăt'ər-əs). A promontory on Hatteras Island, off the coast of North Carolina between Pamlico Sound and the Atlantic Ocean.

hat trick. 1. *British. Cricket.* Three wickets taken by a bowler in three consecutive balls. **2.** Three consecutive wins, hits, or goals in any sport. [The feat was once rewarded by the gift of a hat.]

hau·ber·geon. Variant of **habergeon.**

hau·berk (hô'bûrk) *n.* A long tunic made of chain mail. [Middle English *hauberk,* from Old French *hauberc,* from Germanic. See **kwel-**[1] in Appendix.*]

haugh (häKH, häf) *n. Scottish.* A low-lying meadow, part of a river valley. [Middle English (Scottish) *holch, hawch,* Old English *healh,* corner of land. See **kel-**[4] in Appendix.*]

haugh·ty (hô'tē) *adj.* **-tier, -tiest.** Proud and vain to the point of arrogance; scornful and self-satisfied. See Synonyms at **proud.** [From archaic *haught,* haughty, from Middle English *haute,* from Old French *haut,* "high," from Latin *altus,* high. See **al-**[3] in Appendix.*] —**haugh'ti·ly** *adv.* —**haugh'ti·ness** *n.*

haul (hôl) *v.* **hauled, hauling, hauls.** —*tr.* **1.** To pull or drag forcibly; to tug. **2.** To transport, as with a truck or wagon; to cart. **3.** To change the course of (a ship); especially, to sail (a ship) closer into the wind. —*intr.* **1.** To pull; to tug. **2.** To provide transportation; to cart. **3. a.** To change compass bearing in a clockwise direction. Used of the wind. **b.** To change one's mind. **4. a.** To sail, as on a certain course. **b.** To change the course of a ship. —**haul off. 1.** To move back; to retreat. **2.** To steer a ship away from an object. **3.** To pull the arm back in order to deliver a blow. —**haul up. 1.** To halt; to stop. **2.** To sail close to the direction of the wind. **3.** To transport forcibly. —*n.* **1.** The act of pulling or dragging. **2.** The act of transporting or carting. **3.** A distance; especially, the distance over which something is pulled or transported. **4.** Something that is pulled or transported; a load. **5.** Everything collected or acquired by a single effort; the take: *a haul of fish.* [Middle English *halen,* to pull, draw, from Old French *haler,* from Germanic. See **kel-**[3] in Appendix.*]

haul·age (hô'lĭj) *n.* **1.** The act or process of hauling. **2.** The force required to haul something. **3.** The charge made for hauling something.

haulm (hôm) *n.* Also **halm.** *Chiefly British.* The stems of peas, beans, potatoes, or grasses, used for litter or for thatching. [Middle English *halm,* Old English *h(e)alm,* straw, stem. See **kolem-** in Appendix.*]

haunch (hônch, hänch) *n.* **1.** The hip, buttock, and upper thigh in man and animals. **2.** The loin and leg of an animal as used for food: *a haunch of venison.* **3.** *Architecture.* Either of the sides of an arch, curving down from the apex to an impost. In this sense, also called "hance." [Middle English *ha(u)nche,* from Old French *hanche,* from Germanic *hanka* (unattested).]

haunt (hônt, hänt) *v.* **haunted, haunting, haunts.** —*tr.* **1.** To visit or appear to in the form of a ghost or other supernatural being. **2.** To visit often; to frequent. **3.** To recur to continually; obsess: *"the riddle continued to haunt me"* (Haakon Chevalier). **4.** To linger or remain in profusion; pervade. —*intr.* To recur or visit often; especially, to visit as a ghost or other supernatural being. —*n.* (hônt, hänt; *also* hänt *for sense 2*). **1.** A place much frequented. **2.** *Regional.* A ghost or other supernatural being. [Middle English *haunten,* from Old French *hanter,* perhaps from Germanic. See **kei-**[1] in Appendix.*]

haunt·ed (hôn'tĭd) *adj.* **1.** Supposedly frequented by ghosts or other spectral beings: *a haunted house.* **2.** Obsessed by a constantly recurring memory or thought.

haunt·ing (hôn'tĭng) *adj.* Continually recurring to the mind; unforgettable. —**haunt'ing·ly** *adv.*

Haupt·mann (houpt'män'), **Gerhart.** 1862–1946. German dramatist, novelist, and poet.

Hau·ra·ki Gulf (hou-răk'ē, -rä'kē). An inlet of the South Pacific on the northern coast of North Island, New Zealand.

Hau·sa (hou'sə, -zə) *n., pl.* **Hausa.** Also **Haus·sa. 1.** One of a Negroid people of the Sudan and northern Nigeria. **2.** Their language, used widely as a trade language in Africa.

haus·frau (hous'frou') *n.* A housewife. [German *Hausfrau.*]

Hauss·mann (ōs-män'), Baron **Georges Eugène.** 1809–1891. French public official; directed reconstruction of Paris.

haus·tel·lum (hô-stĕl'əm) *n., pl.* **haustella** (hô-stĕl'ə). A mouth part prolonged into a proboscis and adapted as a sucking organ, as in many insects. [New Latin, from Latin *haustus,* past participle of *haurīre,* to draw, draw up. See **aus-** in Appendix.*] —**haus·tel'late** (-stĕl'ĭt, hô'stə-lāt') *adj.*

haus·to·ri·um (hô-stôr'ē-əm, hô-stōr'-) *n., pl.* **haustoria** (hô-stôr'ē-ə, hô-stōr'-). *Botany.* A specialized branch of hyphae, or a similar structure, by which parasitic plants such as fungi obtain food from a host plant. [New Latin, from Latin *haustus,* past participle of *haurīre,* to draw, draw up. See **aus-** in Appendix.*]

haut·boy (hō'boi', ō'boi') *n., pl.* **-boys.** Also **haut·bois** *pl.* **hautbois.** An oboe. [French *hautbois,* "high wood" (from its pitch) : *haut,* high, from Latin *altus* (see **al-**[3] in Appendix*) + *bois,* wood, from Germanic (see **busk-** in Appendix*).]

haute é·cole (ō-tĕ-kôl'). The art, techniques, or practice of expert horsemanship. [French, "high school."]

hau·teur (hō-tûr'; *French* ō-tœr') *n.* Haughtiness in bearing and attitude; arrogance. [French, from *haut,* high, pious, from Old French. See **hautboy.**]

Haute-Vol·ta. The French name for **Upper Volta.**

Ha·van·a (hə-văn'ə). *Spanish* **La Ha·ba·na** (lä ä-vä'nä). **1.** A province, 3,174 square miles in area, of western Cuba. Population, 1,594,000. **2.** The capital of this province and of Cuba. Population, 800,000.

have (hăv) *v.* **had** (hăd) or *archaic* **hadst** (hădst), **having, has** (hăs). Present tense, first person, **have;** second person, **have** (also *archaic* **hast**); third person singular **has** (also *archaic* **hath**); third person plural **have.** Used as an auxiliary verb before a past participle to form the past, present, and future perfect tenses, indicating completed or virtually completed action: *We had left before dawn. They have done it. I shall have finished by then.* —*tr.* **1.** To be in possession of, as one's property; own. **2.** To be related or in a particular relationship to: *have three children.* **3.** To be in a relationship to (as specified by an infinitive following the object): *have time to play.* **4.** To hold in one's mind; entertain: *have doubts.* **5.** To hold by law or entitlement. **6.** To bribe or buy off. **7.** To engage the attention of; captivate. **8.** To win a victory over; to down: *He has you on that point.* **9.** To cheat, deceive, or trick. **10.** To possess sexually. **11.** To keep or put in a specified place or position; arrange: *have the carpet in the hall.* **12.** To accept or take: *I'll have the gray jacket.* **13.** To partake of; consume, as by eating or drinking. **14.** To be made of, consist of, or contain. **15.** To be characterized by; possess, as a physical quality: *have gray hair.* **16.** To feel, as an emotion: *have great love for.* **17.** To exercise or bring into play: *have mercy.* **18.** To allow; permit: *have the children out after dark.* **19.** To order or compel to: *have him go home.* **20.** To perform; execute: *have the next dance.* **21.** To carry out or stage: *have a party.* **22.** To be the subject of: *have a large funeral.* **23.** To experience; undergo; spend, as time: *have a good summer.* **24.** To suffer from, as a physical disability. **25.** To give birth to; to bear. **26.** *Archaic.* To know or understand: *have Latin and Greek.* **27.** To be scheduled for: *have an appointment at noon.* **28.** To be able to use; be in command of: *have the necessary technique.* **29.** To associate with, as friend, employee, or the like. **30.** To receive as a guest. **31.** To infer or state: *have on good authority.* —**had better.** Ought to: *You had better go now.* —**had just as well.** Might as well. —**had rather** (or **sooner**). Would prefer to: *had rather make love than war.* —**have at.** To attack. —**have done with.** To be through with; finish. —**have had it.** *Informal.* To be physically and mentally exhausted. —**have on. 1.** To be wearing. **2.** *Informal.* To be scheduled for. —**have to do with.** To be concerned or associated with. —**let (someone) have it.** *Informal.* To attack (someone). —*n.* One of a class enjoying material comforts, as opposed to a have-not. Used chiefly in the plural. [Have, had, had, has; Middle English *haven* or *habben, hadde, had, has,* Old English *habban, hæfde, (ge)hæfd, hæbbe.* See **kap-** in Appendix.*]

Ha·vel (hä'fəl). A river of East Germany, rising in the north and flowing 225 miles southwest, then west, to the Elbe.

have·lock (hăv'lŏk', -lək) *n.* A cloth covering for a cap, having a flap to protect the back of the neck. [After Sir Henry *Havelock* (died 1857), British general in India.]

ha·ven (hā'vən) *n.* **1.** A harbor or anchorage; a port. **2.** A place of refuge; sanctuary. —See Synonyms at **shelter.** —*tr.v.* **ha·vened, -vening, -vens.** *Rare.* To put into a haven. [Middle English *haven,* Old English *hæfen.* See **kap-** in Appendix.*]

have-not (hăv'nŏt') *n.* One having little or no property or material comforts. Used chiefly in the plural.

have·n't (hăv'ənt). Contraction of *have not.*

Hav·er·ford (hăv′ər-fərd). A residential city of southeastern Pennsylvania, near Philadelphia. Population, 54,000.

Hav·er·ing (hăv′ər-ĭng). A borough of London, England, comprising the former administrative divisions of Hornchurch and Romford. Population, 243,000.

hav·er·sack (hăv′ər-săk′) *n.* A one-strapped canvas bag worn over a shoulder to transport supplies on a hike or march. [French *havresac,* from German *Habersack,* haversack, originally bag for oats : *Haber,* oats, from Old High German *habaro,* from Germanic *hafur* (unattested) + *Sack,* bag, sack, from Old High German *sac,* from Latin *saccus,* SACK.]

hav·oc (hăv′ək) *n.* Destruction, as caused by a natural calamity or war; devastation. —**cry havoc.** *Archaic.* To signal an army to begin collecting spoils or pillaging. —**play havoc with.** To destroy or ruin. —*v.* **havocked, -ocking, -ocs.** *Rare.* —*tr.* To destroy or pillage. —*intr.* To lay waste. [Middle English *havok,* from Norman French, variant of Old French *havot*†, plunder, cry used to begin plunder, from Germanic.]

Ha·vre, Le. See **Le Havre.**

haw[1] (hô) *n.* A vocalized pause in speech. —*intr.v.* **hawed, hawing, haws.** To pause in speaking. Chiefly used in the phrase *hem and haw.* [Imitative.]

haw[2] (hô) *n.* **1.** The fruit of a hawthorn. **2.** A hawthorn or similar tree or shrub. [Middle English *haw(e),* Old English *haga,* hawthorn, hedge. See **kagh-** in Appendix.*]

haw[3] (hô) *n.* The nictitating membrane, especially of a domesticated animal. [Origin unknown.]

haw[4] (hô) *interj.* Used to command an animal to turn left. Compare **gee.** —*v.* **hawed, hawing, haws.** —*tr.* To cause to turn left. —*intr.* To turn left. [Origin unknown.]

Ha·wai·i (hə-wä′ē, -wä′yə). **1.** Also **Ha·wai·ian Islands** (-wä′yən). Formerly **Sand·wich Islands** (sănd′wĭch). A state of the United States, admitted to the Union in 1959; an island group, 6,424 square miles in area, located in the central Pacific. Population, 711,000. Capital, Honolulu. See map at **United States of America.** **2.** The largest island of this group, occupying 4,020 square miles in the southeast. Population, 61,000. [Hawaiian *Hawai'i,* akin to Marquesan *Havaiki,* legendary homeland of the Polynesians.]

Ha·wai·ian (hə-wä′yən) *n.* **1.** A native or resident of Hawaii. **2.** The Polynesian language spoken by the inhabitants of Hawaii. —*adj.* Of or relating to Hawaii.

haw·finch (hô′fĭnch′) *n.* **1.** An Old World bird, *Coccothraustes coccothraustes,* having a thick bill, brown, white, and black plumage, and a short tail. **2.** Any of various similar or related birds. [HAW (fruit) + FINCH.]

haw-haw[1]. Variant of **ha-ha** (laughter).

haw-haw[2]. Variant of **ha-ha** (a fence).

hawk[1] (hôk) *n.* **1.** Any of various birds of prey of the order Falconiformes, and especially of the genera *Accipiter* and *Buteo,* characteristically having a short, hooked bill and strong claws adapted for seizing. See **falcon.** **2.** Any of various similar birds. **3.** A ruthless person who preys on others; a shark. **4.** *Informal.* One who favors a militaristic version of his country's foreign policy. In this sense, compare **dove.** —*intr.v.* **hawked, hawking, hawks.** **1.** To hunt with trained hawks. **2.** To swoop and strike in the manner of a hawk. [Middle English *hauk,* Old English *h(e)afoc.* See **kap-** in Appendix.*]

hawk[2] (hôk) *v.* **hawked, hawking, hawks.** —*intr.* To peddle; especially, to peddle wares by crying them in the streets. —*tr.* To cry (wares) in the streets; peddle. [Back-formation from HAWKER.]

hawk[3] (hôk) *v.* **hawked, hawking, hawks.** —*intr.* To clear or attempt to clear the throat by coughing up phlegm. —*tr.* To clear the throat of (phlegm). —*n.* An audible effort to clear the throat by expelling phlegm. [Imitative.]

hawk[4] (hôk) *n.* A small board with a handle on the underside, used to hold a mason's mortar or plaster. [Origin uncertain.]

haw·ker (hô′kər) *n.* A peddler, typically one who solicits business by calling at private houses. [Probably from Low German *höker,* from Middle Low German *hōker,* from *hōken,* to peddle, to bend. See **keu-**[2] in Appendix.*]

hawk-eyed (hôk′īd′) *adj.* Having very sharp eyesight.

Haw·kins (hô′kĭnz), Sir **John.** 1532–1595. English naval commander.

hawk moth. Any of various moths of the family Sphingidae, having a large body, long, narrow forewings, and characteristically feeding while in flight on nectar from flowers. Also called "sphinx moth," "hummingbird moth."

hawk's-beard (hôks′bîrd′) *n.* Any of various plants of the genus *Crepis,* related to and resembling the dandelion. [Named for its large bristly pappus.]

hawks·bill (hôks′bĭl′) *n.* A tropical sea turtle, *Eretmochelys imbricata,* valued as a source of tortoiseshell.

hawk·weed (hôk′wēd′) *n.* Any of various often hairy plants of the genus *Hieracium,* having yellow or orange dandelionlike flowers.

hawse (hôz) *n. Nautical.* **1.** The part of a ship where the hawseholes are located. **2.** *Plural.* The hawseholes. **3.** The space between the bows of an anchored ship and her anchors. **4.** The arrangement of a ship's anchor cables when both starboard and port anchors are secured. [Middle English *halse,* from Old Norse *hals,* neck, ship's bow. See **kwel-**[1] in Appendix.*]

hawse·hole (hôz′hōl′) *n. Nautical.* An opening in the bow of a ship through which a cable or hawser is passed.

haw·ser (hô′zər) *n. Nautical.* A cable or rope used in mooring or towing a ship. [Middle English *hauceour, hawser,* from Norman French *hauceour,* from Old French *haucier,* to lift, hoist, from Vulgar Latin *altiāre* (unattested), from Latin *altus,* high. See **al-**[3] in Appendix.*]

haw·thorn (hô′thôrn′) *n.* Any of various thorny trees or shrubs of the genus *Crataegus,* having white or pinkish flowers and reddish fruit. [Middle English *haw(e)thorn,* Old English *hagathorn* : *haga,* HAW (fruit) + THORN.]

Haw·thorne (hô′thôrn′), **Nathaniel.** 1804–1864. American author of novels and short stories.

hay[1] (hā) *n.* **1.** Grass or other plants such as clover or alfalfa, cut and dried for fodder. **2.** *Slang.* A trifling amount of money. Used only in negative phrases, especially in *that ain't hay.* —**hit the hay.** *Slang.* To go to bed. —*v.* **hayed, haying, hays.** —*intr.* To convert grass and herbage into hay. —*tr.* **1.** To make (grass) into hay. **2.** To feed with hay. [Middle English *hei, hay,* Old English *hieg.* See **kau-**[2] in Appendix.*]

hay[2] (hā) *n.* A country-dance with interweaving movements. [Old French *haye*†.]

Hay (hā). A river rising in northeastern British Columbia, Canada, and flowing 350 miles east, then north through Alberta, to the Great Slave Lake.

Hay (hā), **John Milton.** 1838–1905. American statesman and author; private secretary to Lincoln during the Civil War; Secretary of State (1898–1905).

Ha·ya·stan. The Armenian name for **Armenia.**

hay·cock (hā′kŏk′) *n. Chiefly British.* A conical mound of hay in a field.

Hay·dn (hīd′n), **Franz Joseph.** 1732–1809. Austrian composer.

Hayes (hāz). A river rising in eastern Manitoba, Canada, and flowing 300 miles northeast to Hudson Bay.

Hayes (hāz), **Rutherford B(irchard).** 1822–1893. Nineteenth President of the United States (1877–81).

Hayes and Har·ling·ton (hāz′; här′lĭng-tən). A former administrative division of London, England, now part of **Hillingdon** *(see).*

Hayes Peninsula (hāz). A peninsula of northwestern Greenland, projecting 100 miles into Baffin Bay.

hay fever. An acute allergic condition of the mucous membranes of the upper respiratory tract and the eyes, characterized by a running nose and sneezing, conjunctivitis, and headaches, and caused by an abnormal sensitivity to certain airborne pollens, especially of the ragweed and related plants.

hay·fork (hā′fôrk′) *n.* **1.** A hand tool for pitching hay. **2.** A machine-operated fork for moving hay.

hay·loft (hā′lôft′, -lŏft′) *n.* A loft for storing hay.

hay·mak·er (hā′mā′kər) *n.* **1.** One who makes grass into hay. **2.** *Slang.* A powerful blow with the fist.

Hay·mar·ket (hā′mär′kĭt). A street of London, England, located between Piccadilly Circus and Pall Mall, the site of many theaters.

hay·mow (hā′mou′) *n.* **1.** A hayloft. **2.** The hay stored in a hayloft. **3.** *Archaic.* A haystack.

Haynes (hānz), **Elwood.** 1857–1925. American inventor; designed and constructed early automobile (1893).

hay·rack (hā′răk′) *n.* **1.** A rack from which livestock eat hay. **2. a.** A rack fitted to a wagon for carrying hay. **b.** A wagon so fitted.

hay·seed (hā′sēd′) *n.* **1.** Grass seed shaken out of hay. **2.** Pieces of chaff or straw that fall from hay. **3.** *Slang.* A country bumpkin.

hay·stack (hā′stăk′) *n.* A large stack of hay for winter storage in the open. Now often built of baled hay.

Hay·ti. See **Haiti.**

Hay·ti·an. Variant of **Haitian.**

hay·ward (hā′wôrd′) *n.* An officer formerly charged with the repair of cattle fences and the retention of cattle in the town common. [Middle English *hayward, heiward* : *heie,* hedge, fence, Old English *hege* (see **kagh-** in Appendix*) + WARD.]

Hay·ward (hā′wərd). A city of west-central California, five miles east of San Francisco Bay. Population, 73,000.

hay·wire (hā′wīr′) *n.* Wire used in baling hay. —*adj. Informal.* **1.** Put together in a makeshift way. **2.** Not functioning properly; broken. **3.** Mentally confused or erratic; crazy. —**go haywire.** **1.** To break down and function improperly. **2.** To break down mentally and act erratically. [Baling wire is often used for makeshift repairs.]

haz·ard (hăz′ərd) *n.* **1.** A chance or accident. **2.** A danger; peril; risk: *"It is the hazard . . . of a revolution, that retards . . . progress"* (Thomas Paine). **3.** *Obsolete.* A gamble or bet; a stake. **4.** A dice game resembling craps. **5. a.** Any of the openings in a court-tennis court through which the ball may be hit for points. **b.** That side of the court into which the ball is served. Also called "hazard side." **6.** A sandtrap or other obstacle on a golf course. —See Synonyms at **danger.** —*tr.v.* **hazarded, -arding, -ards.** **1.** To imperil; jeopardize. **2.** To run the risk of; expose oneself to. **3.** To venture (something); to dare: *hazard a guess.* [Middle English *hasard, hazard,* from Old French *hasard,* from Spanish *azar,* unlucky throw of the dice, accident, from Arabic *yásara,* he played at dice.]

haz·ard·ous (hăz′ər-dəs) *adj.* **1.** Marked by danger; perilous. **2.** Depending on chance; risky.

haze[1] (hāz) *n.* **1. a.** Atmospheric moisture, dust, smoke, and vapor suspended to form a partially opaque condition. **b.** The atmospheric condition so formed. **2.** A vague or confused state of mind. —*intr.v.* **hazed, hazing, hazes.** To become misty or hazy; to blur. [Back-formation from HAZY.]

haze[2] (hāz) *tr.v.* **hazed, hazing, hazes.** **1.** *Nautical.* To persecute or harass with meaningless, difficult, or humiliating tasks. **2.** To initiate (as into a college fraternity) by exacting humil-

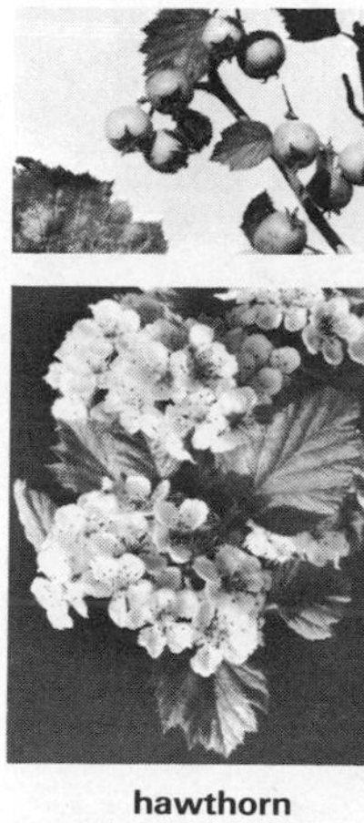

hawthorn
Crataegus mollis
Above: Fruit
Below: Flowers

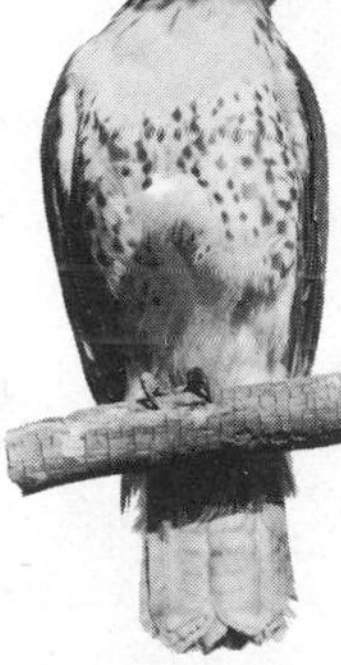

hawk[1]
Buteo jamaicensis

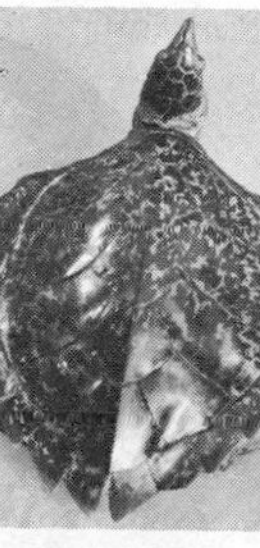

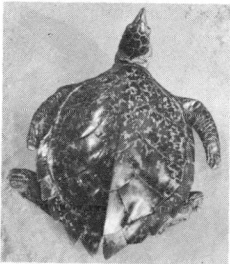

hawksbill

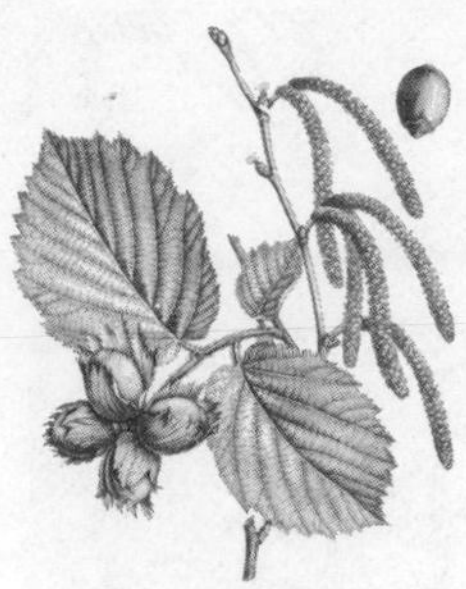

hazel
Corylus avellana
Above: Nut

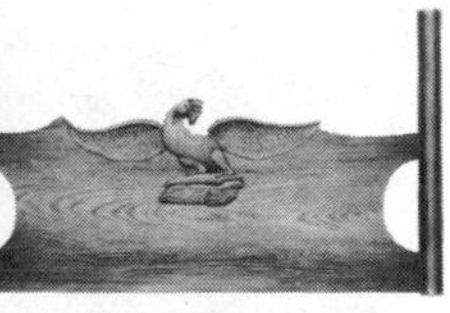

headboard
Early 19th-century American

iating performances from or playing rough practical jokes upon. **3.** *Regional.* To drive (cattle or horses) with saddle horses. [Origin uncertain.] —**haz′er** *n.*

ha·zel (hā′zəl) *n.* **1.** Any of various shrubs or small trees of the genus *Corylus;* especially, *C. avellana,* of Europe, or *C. americana,* of North America, bearing edible nuts enclosed in a leafy husk. **2.** The nut of such a tree or shrub, having a smooth brown shell. Also called "hazelnut." See **filbert.** **3.** Light to strong brown or yellowish brown. See **color.** [Middle English *hasel,* Old English *hæsel.* See **koselo-** in Appendix.*] —**ha′zel** *adj.*

ha·zel·nut (hā′zəl-nŭt′) *n.* The hard-shelled, edible nut of a hazel.

Haz·litt (hăz′lĭt), **William.** 1778–1830. English essayist.

haz·y (hā′zē) *adj.* **-ier, -iest.** **1.** Marked by the presence of haze; misty. **2.** Not clearly defined; vague; confused. [Origin unknown.] —**haz′i·ly** *adv.* —**haz′i·ness** *n.*

haz·zan. Variant of **chazan.**

hb halfback.

Hb hemoglobin.

hb. halfback.

H-bomb (āch′bŏm′) *n.* A **hydrogen bomb** *(see).*

H.C. **1.** Holy Communion. **2.** House of Commons.

h.c.f. highest common factor.

hd. **1.** hand. **2.** head.

hdbk. handbook.

hdkf. handkerchief.

hdqrs. headquarters.

he[1] (hē) *pron.* The third person singular pronoun in the nominative case, masculine gender. **1.** Used to represent the male person, animal, or other being last mentioned or implied. **2.** Used to represent any person whose sex is not specified: *Everyone knows he is mortal.* —*n.* **1.** A male animal or person: *Is the cat a he?* **2.** Often used in combination: *a he-cat.* [Middle English *he,* Old English *hē,* he. See **ko-** in Appendix.*]

he[2] (hā) *n.* The fifth letter of the Hebrew alphabet. See **alphabet.** [Hebrew *hē,* possibly "lattice window."]

He The symbol for the element helium.

HE high explosive.

H.E. **1.** His Eminence. **2.** His Excellency.

head (hĕd) *n., pl.* **heads** or **head** (for sense 10b). *Abbr.* **hd.** **1. a.** The upper or anterior vertebrate extremity, containing the brain or the principal ganglia, and the eyes, ears, nose, mouth, and jaws. **b.** The analogous part of an invertebrate. **2.** The seat of the faculty of reason; intelligence, intellect, or mind. **3. a.** A mental facility or aptitude: *a head for mathematics.* **b.** Capacity for strong drink. Used usually with such adjectives as *weak* or *strong.* **4. a.** Poise; wits; self-control: *Keep your head in a crisis.* **b.** Freedom of choice or of action: *Give him his head.* **5.** *Slang.* One who is a frequent user of drugs. **6.** Any portrait or representation of a head. **7.** *Often plural.* The obverse side of a coin. Used with a singular verb. **8.** *Informal.* A headache. **9.** The hair on the human head. **10. a.** Each individual within a group: *count heads.* **b.** A single animal within a herd: *20 head of cattle.* **11. a.** One who occupies the foremost position; leader, chief, or director: *head of the committee.* **b.** The foremost or leading position: *at the head of the parade.* **12.** A headwater. **13. a.** The difference in depth of a liquid at two given points. **b.** The measure of pressure at the lower point expressed in terms of this difference. **c.** Pressure. Said of a liquid or vapor: *a head of steam.* **14.** The foam on an effervescent liquid. **15.** The breaking point or tip of a suppurating abscess, boil, or pimple. **16.** A turning point; crisis: *bring matters to a head.* **17. a.** A projection, weight, or fixture at one end of an elongated object: *the head of a pin.* **b.** The working end of a tool or implement: *the head of a hammer.* **c.** The part of an explosive device that carries the explosive; warhead. **18.** An attachment to or part of a machine that holds or contains the operative device: *the recording head of a tape recorder.* **19.** A rounded, compact mass of leaves, or sometimes flower buds, as of cabbage, lettuce, or cauliflower. **20.** *Botany.* A dense, compact cluster of flowers, as of composite plants or clover. **21.** The upper end or extremity of something: **a.** The top of a door or window frame. **b.** The end opposite to an entrance: *the head of the bay.* **c.** The end associated with a real or figurative head: *head of the table.* **22.** The end of an object whose two ends are interchangeable, as a drum. **23.** *Nautical.* **a.** The forepart of a vessel. **b.** The latrine of a vessel. **c.** The top part or upper edge of a sail. **24.** A passage or gallery in a mine. **25.** A promontory, cape, or cliff rising above a body of water. **26. a.** The top of a book or of a page. **b.** *Informal.* A headline or heading. **c.** A distinct topic or category. **27.** Headway; progress. **28.** *Grammar.* A word in an endocentric construction that determines the syntactical character of the construction; for example, in the construction *a lazy young boy, boy* determines that the whole construction functions as a noun. —**(down) by the head.** With the bow lying lower in the water than the stern. —**come to a head.** **1.** To suppurate, as an abscess. **2.** To reach a critical point. —**go to one's head.** **1.** To make one lightheaded or drunk. **2.** To increase one's pride or conceit. —**head and shoulders above.** Far superior to. —**head over heels.** **1.** Rolling, as in a somersault: *head over heels down the hill.* **2.** To the point of abandon: *head over heels in love.* —**keep one's head above water.** To keep out of trouble, such as debt or poverty. —**on** (or **upon**) **one's head.** Within one's responsibility: *"My deeds upon my head!"* (Shakespeare). —**one's head off.** *Informal.* Immoderately; inordinately; to extreme: *He snored his head off.* —**out of** (or **off**) **one's head.** **1.** Out of one's mind; insane. **2.** Delirious. —**over one's head.** **1.** Beyond one's ability to understand or deal with: *a subject that is over her head.* **2.** To one higher in command: *go over the sergeant's head.* —**put** (or **lay**) **heads together.** To combine forces or abilities. —**turn one's head.** To make one conceited. —*adj.* **1.** Foremost in importance: *the head librarian.* **2.** Placed at the top or front: *the head name on the list.* **3.** Coming from ahead or the front: *head winds.* —*v.* **headed, heading, heads.** —*tr.* **1.** To be director or chief of; to command: *head the committee.* See Usage note below. **2.** To assume or be placed in the first or foremost position of: *head the line of march.* **3.** To aim or direct: *head the horse for home.* **4.** To remove the top of (a plant or tree). **5.** *Soccer.* To drive (the ball) by hitting it with the head. —**head (someone or something) off.** To block the progress of and force to change direction; to intercept. —*intr.* **1.** To proceed or set out: *head for town.* **2.** To form a head, as lettuce or cabbage. **3.** To originate; to rise. Used of a stream or river. [Middle English *heved, he(f)d,* Old English *hēafod.* See **kaput** in Appendix.*]

Usage: *Head,* as a transitive verb meaning to be director or chief of, is both more economical than *head up* and more appropriate to a formal level: *head a committee to study tax revision.* The alternative *head up,* for *head,* is termed unacceptable in the preceding example by 85 per cent of the Usage Panel.

head·ache (hĕd′āk′) *n.* **1.** A pain in the head. **2.** *Informal.* Something that annoys or bothers. —**head′ach′y** (-ā′kē) *adj.*

head·band (hĕd′bănd′) *n.* **1.** A fillet or band worn around the head. **2.** An ornamental strip at the top of a page or beginning of a chapter or paragraph. **3.** A cloth band attached to the top of the spine of a book.

head·board (hĕd′bôrd′, -bōrd′) *n.* A board, panel, or the like, that stands at the head, as of a bed.

head·cheese (hĕd′chēz′) *n.* A jellied loaf or sausage containing chopped and boiled parts of the feet, head, and sometimes the tongue and heart of an animal, usually a hog.

head cold. **Coryza** *(see).*

head·dress (hĕd′drĕs′) *n.* **1.** Anything worn on the head, as a covering or ornament. **2.** A hairdo; coiffure.

head·ed (hĕd′ĭd) *adj.* **1.** Growing or grown into a head. **2.** Having a head or heading.

head·er (hĕd′ər) *n.* **1.** One that fits a head on an object. **2.** One that removes a head from an object; especially, a machine that reaps the heads of grain and passes them into a wagon or receptacle. **3.** A pipe that serves as a central connection for two or more smaller pipes. **4.** A wooden beam in a floor or roof placed between two long beams and supporting the ends of one or more tailpieces. **5.** A brick laid across rather than parallel with the wall. **6.** *Informal.* A headlong dive or fall.

head·first (hĕd′fûrst′) *adv.* Also **head·fore·most** (hĕd′fôr′mōst′, -məst, hĕd′fōr′-). **1.** With the head leading; headlong: *go headfirst down the stairs.* **2.** Impetuously; brashly.

head gate. **1.** A control gate upstream of a lock or canal. **2.** A floodgate controlling the flow of water in a ditch, sluice, race, or the like.

head·gear (hĕd′gîr′) *n.* **1.** A covering, such as a hat or helmet, for the head. **2.** The part of a harness that fits about a horse's head. **3.** The rigging for hauling or lifting located at the head of a mine shaft. **4.** *Nautical.* The rigging on the forward sails.

head-hunt·ing (hĕd′hŭn′tĭng) *n.* **1.** The taking of human heads as trophies, practiced for religious purposes in some primitive societies. **2.** *Slang.* The process of eliminating political enemies. **3.** *Slang.* The procurement of executive personnel. —**head′-hunt′er** *n.*

head·ing (hĕd′ĭng) *n.* **1.** A word or words at the head of a chapter, paragraph, letter, or the like. **2.** *Navigation.* The course or direction of movement of a ship or aircraft. **3.** *Mining.* **a.** A gallery or drift. **b.** The end of a gallery or drift.

head·land (hĕd′lənd, -lănd′) *n.* **1.** A point of land, usually high and with a sheer drop, extending out into a body of water; promontory. **2.** The unplowed land at the end of a plowed furrow.

head·less (hĕd′lĭs) *adj.* **1. a.** Formed without a head. **b.** Decapitated. **2.** Without a leader or director. **3.** Witless; foolish.

head·light (hĕd′līt′) *n.* A lamp mounted on the front of a vehicle.

head·line (hĕd′līn′) *n.* **1.** The title or caption of a newspaper article, set in large type, the size denoting the importance of the article. **2.** A line at the head of a page giving the title, author, page number, or the like. —*v.* **headlined, -lining, -lines.** —*tr.* **1.** To supply (an article or page) with a headline. **2. a.** To present as a headliner: *The Palace Theater headlines a magician.* **b.** To serve as the headliner of: *He headlines the bill.*

head·lin·er (hĕd′lī′nər) *n.* A performer who receives prominent billing; a star.

head·lock (hĕd′lŏk′) *n.* A wrestling hold in which the head of one wrestler is locked under the arm of the other.

head·long (hĕd′lông′, -lŏng′) *adv.* **1.** With the head leading; headfirst. **2.** Impetuously; rashly. **3.** At breakneck speed or with uncontrolled force. —*adj.* (hĕd′lông′, -lŏng′). **1.** Headfirst; done with the head leading: *a headlong dive.* **2.** Impetuous; rash. **3.** Uncontrollably forceful or fast. **4.** *Rare.* Steep; sheer. —See Synonyms at **impetuous.** [Middle English *hedlong,* variant of *hedling* : *hed,* HEAD + -LING.]

head·mas·ter (hĕd′măs′tər, -mäs′tər) *n.* Also **head master.** A male school principal, usually of a private school.

head·mis·tress (hĕd′mĭs′trĭs) *n.* Also **head mistress.** A woman who is principal of a school, usually a private girls' school.

head money. **1.** A poll tax. **2.** A reward paid for the capture and delivery of a fugitive; bounty.

head·most (hĕd′mōst′, -məst) *adj.* Leading; foremost.

head-on (hĕd′ŏn′, -ôn′) *adj.* **1.** Facing forward; frontal.

2. With the front end exposed and receiving the impact: *a head-on collision.* **3.** Direct and uncompromising: *a head-on denunciation.* **—head′-on′** *adv.*
head·phone (hĕd′fōn′) *n.* A receiver, as for a telephone, radio, or phonograph, held to the ear by a headband.
head·piece (hĕd′pēs′) *n.* **1.** A helmet, hat, or other headgear. **2.** A set of headphones; headset. **3.** A **headstall** *(see).* **4.** *Printing.* An ornamental design at the top of a page.
head pin. *Bowling* A **kingpin** *(see).*
head·quar·ter (hĕd′kwôr′tər) *v.* **-tered, -tering, -ters.** *—intr. Informal.* To establish headquarters. *—tr. Informal.* To provide with a headquarters. See Usage note. [Back-formation from HEADQUARTERS.]
Usage: *Headquarter,* though concise, has not established itself well on a formal level in either intransitive or transitive usage. Both of the following examples are disapproved by large majorities of the Usage Panel: *The European correspondent will headquarter in Paris* (unacceptable to 92 per cent). *The magazine has headquartered him in a building that houses many foreign journalists* (unacceptable to 90 per cent).
head·quar·ters (hĕd′kwôr′tərz) *pl.n.* Sometimes used with a singular verb. *Abbr.* **hdqrs., h.q., HQ, H.Q. 1.** The offices of a commander, as of a military unit, from which official orders are issued. **2.** Any center of operations: *Father makes the den his headquarters.*
head·race (hĕd′rās′) *n.* A watercourse that feeds water into a mill, water wheel, or turbine.
head·rest (hĕd′rĕst′) *n.* A support for the head, as at the back of a chair.
head·sail (hĕd′səl) *n. Nautical.* Any sail, such as a jib, set forward of a foremast.
head·set (hĕd′sĕt′) *n.* A pair of headphones.
head·ship (hĕd′shĭp′) *n.* The position or office of the head or leader; primacy; command.
head shrinker. *Slang.* A psychiatrist.
heads·man (hĕdz′mən) *n., pl.* **-men** (-mĭn). A public executioner who beheads condemned prisoners.
head·spring (hĕd′sprĭng′) *n.* A fountainhead; source.
head·stall (hĕd′stôl′) *n.* The section of a bridle that fits over the horse's head. Also called "headpiece."
head start. A start before other contestants in a race, or any analogous advantage.
head·stock (hĕd′stŏk′) *n.* A nonmoving part of a machine or powered tool that supports a revolving part, such as the spindle of a lathe.
head·stone (hĕd′stōn′) *n.* Also **head stone** (for sense 2). **1.** A memorial stone set at the head of a grave. **2.** A keystone.
head·strong (hĕd′strông′, -strŏng′) *adj.* **1.** Inclined to insist on having one's own way; willful; obstinate. **2.** Resulting from willfulness or obstinacy. —See Synonyms at **obstinate, unruly.**
head·wait·er (hĕd′wā′tər) *n.* A waiter in charge of the other waiters in a restaurant, who often seats guests and generally serves as host. Also called "maître d'hôtel."
head·wa·ters (hĕd′wô′tərz, -wŏt′ərz) *pl.n.* The waters from which a river rises. Also called "headstreams."
head·way (hĕd′wā′) *n.* **1.** Movement forward; advance. **2.** Progress; achievement. **3.** *Architecture.* The clear vertical space beneath a ceiling or archway; clearance. **4.** The distance in time or space between two vehicles traveling the same route.
head wind. A wind blowing directly against the course of a plane or ship.
head·work (hĕd′wûrk′) *n.* **1.** Mental activity or work. **2.** Ornamentation of the keystone of an arch. **—head′work′er** *n.*
head·y (hĕd′ē) *adj.* **-ier, -iest. 1.** Tending to upset the balance of the senses or mental faculties; intoxicating. **2.** Headstrong; obstinate. **—head′i·ly** *adv.* **—head′i·ness** *n.*
heal (hēl) *v.* **healed, healing, heals.** *—tr.* **1.** To restore to health; cure. **2.** To set right; amend: *healed the rift between us.* **3.** To rid of sin, anxiety, or the like; restore. *—intr.* To become whole and sound; return to health. [Middle English *helen,* Old English *hǣlen.* See **kailo-** in Appendix.*] **—heal′a·ble** *adj.*
heal-all (hēl′ôl′) *n.* A plant, the **self-heal** *(see).*
heal·er (hē′lər) *n.* **1.** One that heals; especially, a physician. **2.** A person who essays cures by spiritual, magical, or other nonmedical means.
health (hĕlth) *n.* **1.** The state of an organism with respect to functioning, disease, and abnormality at any given time. **2.** The state of an organism functioning normally without disease or abnormality. **3.** Optimal functioning with freedom from disease and abnormality. **4.** Broadly, any state of optimal functioning, well being, or progress. **5.** A wish for someone's good health, expressed as a toast. [Middle English *helthe,* Old English *hǣlth.* See **kailo-** in Appendix.*]
health·ful (hĕlth′fəl) *adj.* **1.** Conducive to good health; salutary. **2.** *Rare.* Healthy. **—health′ful·ly** *adv.* **—health′ful·ness** *n.*
health·y (hĕl′thē) *adj.* **-ier, -iest. 1.** Possessing good health. **2.** Conducive to good health; healthful: *healthy air.* **3.** Indicative of a rational or constructive frame of mind; sound: *a healthy attitude.* **4.** Sizable; considerable: *a healthy portion.* **—health′i·ly** *adv.* **—health′i·ness** *n.*
Synonyms: *healthy, sound, wholesome, hale, robust, well, hardy, vigorous, well-preserved.* These adjectives are compared in the sense of being in good physical or mental condition. *Healthy* stresses the absence of disease and often implies energetic activity. *Sound* emphasizes freedom from imperfection or impairment of function. *Wholesome* suggests appealing healthiness and moral fitness. *Hale* stresses absence of infirmity, especially in elderly persons. *Robust* emphasizes physical strength and ruggedness. *Well* merely specifies absence of sickness. *Hardy* is applicable to one capable of withstanding physical hardship, and *vigorous* to one whose energy and activity are indicative of a sound mind and body. *Well-preserved* refers to lack of outward evidence of bodily deterioration.
heap (hēp) *n.* **1.** A group of things haphazardly gathered or in disorder; a pile. **2.** *Often plural. Informal.* A great deal; lots. **3.** *Slang.* An old or run-down car; rattletrap. *—v.* **heaped, heaping, heaps.** *—tr.* **1.** To put or throw in a heap; pile up. **2.** To fill to overflowing: *heap a plate with vegetables.* **3.** To bestow (praise, for example) in abundance; to lavish. *—intr.* To rise in a heap; pile up. Used with *up.* [Middle English *heap, hep(e),* Old English *hēap.* See **keu-²** in Appendix.*]
heap·ing (hē′pĭng) *adj.* Piled high; full to overflowing.
hear (hîr) *v.* **heard** (hûrd), **hearing, hears.** *—tr.* **1.** To perceive (sound) by the ear. **2.** To listen to attentively. **3.** To learn by the speech of others; be told. **4.** To listen to in an official, professional, or formal capacity: *The fourth witness was heard in the afternoon.* **5.** To attend (a concert, for example). **6.** To listen to with favor; give consideration to: *Lord, hear my plea.* *—intr.* **1.** To be capable of perceiving sound. **2.** To receive communication in some form. Used with *from.* **3.** To be informed; learn: *I heard about your accident.* **—not hear of.** To forbid mention or consideration of: *I won't hear of your going!* [Middle English *heren,* Old English *hīeran.* See **keu-¹** in Appendix.*] **—hear′er** *n.*
hear·ing (hîr′ĭng) *n.* **1.** The sense by which sound is perceived; the capacity to hear. **2.** The range of audibility; earshot. **3.** An opportunity to be heard. **4.** *Law.* **a.** A preliminary examination of an accused person. **b.** The trial of an equity case. **5.** A session, as of an investigatory committee, at which testimony is taken from witnesses.
hearing aid. A small portable electronic apparatus that amplifies sound and is worn to compensate for poor hearing.
heark·en (här′kən) *v.* **-ened, -ening, -ens.** Also **hark·en.** *—intr. Poetic.* To listen attentively; give heed. *—tr. Archaic.* To listen to; hear. [Middle English *herk(n)en,* Old English *he(o)rcnian,* from *he(o)rcian,* to hark, hear. See **keu-¹** in Appendix.*]
hear·say (hîr′sā′) *n.* **1.** Information heard from another. **2.** *Law.* Evidence based on the reports of others rather than on a witness' own knowledge, and therefore generally not admissible as testimony. In this sense, also called "hearsay evidence."
hearse (hûrs) *n.* **1.** A vehicle for conveying a dead person to a church or cemetery. **2.** A triangular candelabrum used at Tenebrae during Holy Week in the Roman Catholic Church. **3.** A framelike structure over a coffin or tomb on which to hang epitaphs. [Middle English *herse,* harrow-shaped triangular frame for holding candles and placed over the bier at the funeral service, from Old French, from Latin *hirpex* (stem *hirpic-*), harrow, rake, probably from Oscan (Samnite) *hirpus,* wolf (alluding to its teeth).]
Hearst (hûrst), **William Randolph.** 1863–1951. American publisher of newspapers and magazines.
heart (härt) *n.* **1. a.** *Anatomy.* The hollow, muscular organ in vertebrates that pumps blood received from the veins into the arteries, thereby supplying the entire circulatory system. **b.** A similarly functioning structure in invertebrates. **2.** The approximate location of this organ in or on the body; breast; bosom. **3.** The heart thought of as the vital center of one's being, emotions, and sensibilities; the seat or repository of emotions. **4. a.** Emotional constitution, disposition, or mood: *a heavy heart; a change of heart.* **b.** Capacity for sympathy or generosity; compassion: *He has no heart.* **c.** Love; affection: *The child won his heart.* **5.** Inner strength or character; fortitude: *men of heart.* **6.** A person esteemed as lovable, loyal, or courageous: *a dear heart.* **7. a.** The central or innermost part: *the heart of the financial district; the heart of a rose.* **b.** The basis or essence: *the heart of the problem.* **8.** A conventionalized two-lobed representation of the heart, usually colored red. **9. a.** A playing card bearing a red, heart-shaped symbol. **b.** *Plural.* The suit of cards designated by this symbol. **10.** *Plural.* A card game in which the object is either to avoid hearts when taking tricks or to take all the hearts. Used with a singular verb. **—after one's own heart.** Meeting one's personal preferences or desires. **—at heart.** Essentially; fundamentally. **—break one's heart.** To cause one disappointment, sorrow, or grief. **—by heart.** By memory or rote. **—do one's heart good.** To lift one's spirits; make one happy. **—from (the bottom of) one's heart.** With deepest feeling or appreciation; most earnestly. **—Have a heart.** Have compassion. Don't be cruel. **—have one's heart in one's mouth.** To be anxious or apprehensive to an extreme. **—have one's heart in the right place.** To mean well; have good intentions. **—have the heart.** To have the will equal to an unpleasant responsibility or task: *Nobody had the heart to be hard on the boy.* **—heart and soul.** With all one's being. **—lose heart.** To become discouraged and despondent. **—lose one's heart to.** To fall in love with. **—near to one's heart.** Important to one. **—set one's heart at rest.** To relieve one of anxiety; reassure. **—set one's heart on.** To want above all else. **—take to heart. 1.** To take seriously and be affected by. **2.** To be troubled by. **—to one's heart's content.** To one's entire satisfaction, without limitation. **—wear one's heart on one's sleeve.** To show one's feelings clearly by one's behavior. **—with all one's heart. 1.** With great willingness or pleasure. **2.** With the deepest feeling or devotion. *—tr.v.* **hearted, hearting, hearts.** *Rare.* To encourage; hearten. [Middle English *he(o)rt, hart,* Old English *heorte.* See **kerd-¹** in Appendix.*]
heart·ache (härt′āk′) *n.* Emotional anguish; deep sorrow. See Synonyms at **regret.**
heart attack. 1. The condition or an instance of **heart failure**

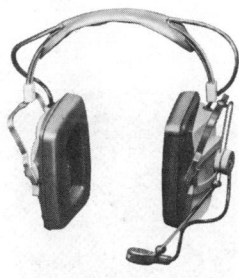

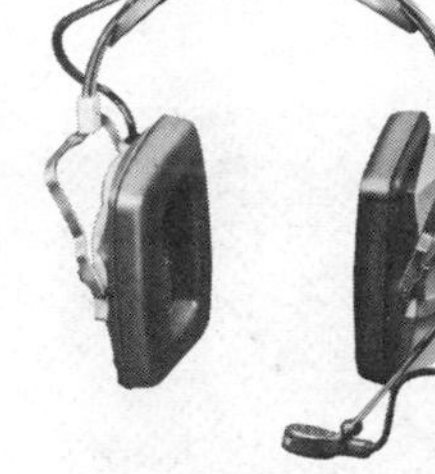
headset

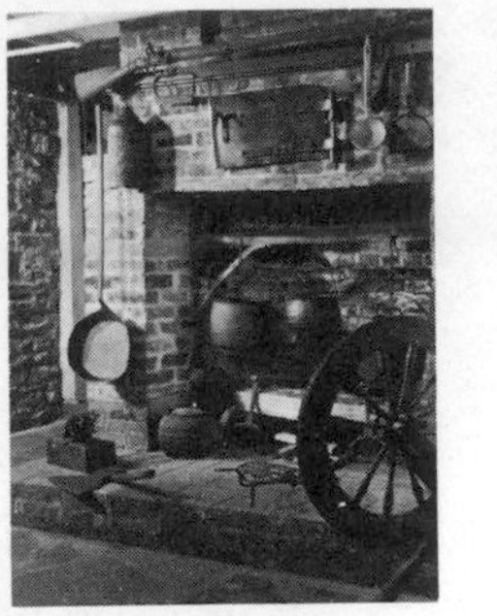

hearth
In mid-18th-century home, New York State

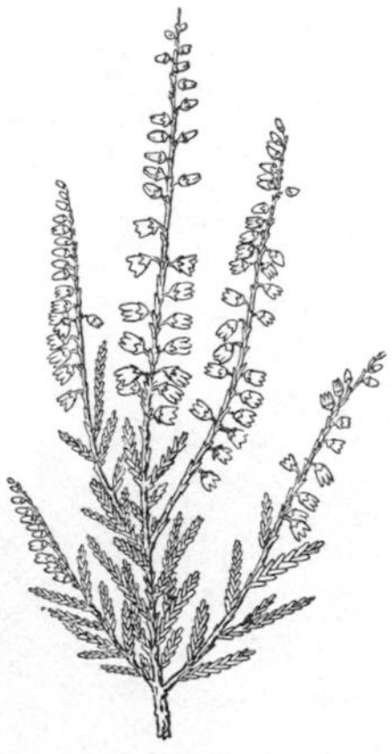

heather
Calluna vulgaris

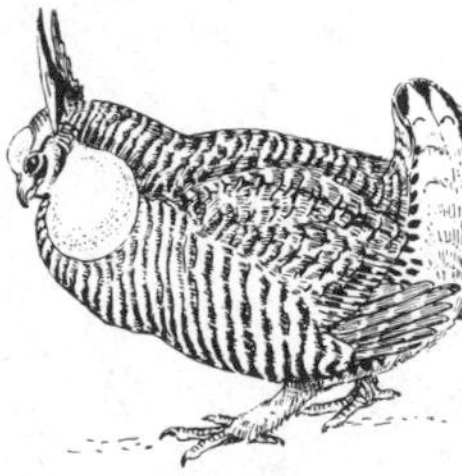

heath hen

(see). **2.** Any seizure of abnormal heart functioning, as a **coronary thrombosis** *(see).*

heart·beat (härt′bēt′) *n.* A single complete pulsation of the heart.

heart block. Reduction or complete lack of coordination in the beating of the atria and ventricles of the heart.

heart·break (härt′brāk′) *n.* Intense sorrow or grief; crushing disappointment.

heart·break·ing (härt′brā′kĭng) *adj.* Causing heartbreak; acutely saddening or pitiful. —**heart′break′ing·ly** *adv.*

heart·bro·ken (härt′brō′kən) *adj.* Suffering from crushing grief or despair; having a broken heart. —**heart′bro′ken·ly** *adv.* —**heart′bro′ken·ness** *n.*

heart·burn (härt′bûrn′) *n.* A burning sensation in the stomach and esophagus, often accompanied by the eructation of small quantities of a highly acid fluid, caused by excess acidity of stomach fluids; pyrosis. Also called "cardialgia."

heart disease. Any organic or functional abnormality of the heart.

heart·ed (här′tĭd) *adj.* Having a specified kind of heart. Used in combination: *lighthearted; false-hearted.*

heart·en (härt′n) *tr.v.* **-ened, -ening, -ens.** To give strength or hope to; encourage; cheer.

heart failure. The partial mechanical failure of the heart as a pump, resulting in congestion in the tissues, shortness and wheezing of breath, pitting edema, and enlarged and tender liver.

heart·felt (härt′fĕlt′) *adj.* Deeply or sincerely felt; earnest: *"The soul's calm sunshine, and the heartfelt joy"* (Pope). See Synonyms at **sincere.**

hearth (härth) *n.* **1.** The floor of a fireplace, usually extending into a room and paved with brick, flagstone, or the like. **2.** The fireside; home; family life. **3.** *Metallurgy.* **a.** The lowest part of a blast furnace or cupola, from which the molten metal flows. **b.** The bottom of a reverberatory furnace where ore is exposed to the flame. **4.** The fireplace or brazier used by a blacksmith. [Middle English *herth,* Old English *heorth.* See **ker-⁴** in Appendix.*]

hearth money. An ecclesiastical tax, **Peter's pence** *(see).*

hearth·stone (härth′stōn′) *n.* **1.** Stone used in the construction of a hearth. **2.** The fireside; home. **3.** A soft stone or powder used for scouring and whitening a hearth, steps, or the like.

heart·i·ly (här′tĭl-ē) *adv.* **1.** In a hearty manner. **2.** Enthusiastically; warmly. **3.** Thoroughly; completely: *"wishing heartily that all the delegates and alternates were dead"* (T.H. White). **4.** With great appetite or enjoyment: *eat heartily.*

heart·land (härt′lănd′) *n.* A central region; especially, one held in geopolitical theory to be strategically, economically, or militarily vital to the nation controlling it.

heart·less (härt′lĭs) *adj.* **1.** Without compassion; pitiless; cruel. **2.** Without enthusiasm; spiritless. **3.** Not heartfelt; without warmth. —**heart′less·ly** *adv.* —**heart′less·ness** *n.*

heart-rend·ing (härt′rĕn′dĭng) *adj.* Inciting anguish or deep sympathy; acutely moving.

hearts·ease (härts′ēz′) *n.* Also **heart's-ease. 1.** Peace of mind. **2.** A plant, *Viola tricolor,* native to Eurasia, having small, spurred, variously colored flowers. Also called "Johnny-jump-up," "wild pansy." [Middle English *herts ease* : *herts,* genitive of *hert,* HEART + EASE.]

heart·sick (härt′sĭk′) *adj.* Sick at heart; profoundly disappointed; despondent. —**heart′sick′ness** *n.*

heart-strick·en (härt′strĭk′ən) *adj.* Also **heart-struck** (-strŭk′). Overwhelmed with grief, dismay, or remorse.

heart·strings (härt′strĭngz′) *pl.n.* **1.** The deepest feelings or affections. Often used facetiously: *a performance geared to tug at the heartstrings.* **2.** In notions of anatomy held before the 17th century, sinews and tendons bracing and sustaining the heart.

heart-to-heart (härt′tə-härt′) *adj.* Personal and candid; frank.

heart·wood (härt′wo͝od′) *n.* The older, inactive, central wood of a tree or woody plant, usually darker and harder than the sapwood. Sometimes called "duramen."

heart·worm (härt′wûrm′) *n.* A nematode worm, *Dirofilaria immitis,* parasitic in the heart and bloodstream of dogs and other mammals.

heart·y (här′tē) *adj.* **-ier, -iest. 1.** Expressed with warmth of feeling; exuberant and unrestrained: *a hearty welcome.* **2.** Complete or thorough; unequivocal: *hearty support.* **3.** Vigorous; robust. **4. a.** Enjoying or requiring much food: *a hearty appetite.* **b.** Providing abundant nourishment; substantial: *a hearty bowl of soup.* —See Synonyms at **sincere.** —*n., pl.* **hearties.** A good fellow; comrade; especially, a sailor.

heat (hēt) *n.* **1.** A form of energy associated with the motion of atoms or molecules in solids and capable of being transmitted through solid and fluid media by conduction, through fluid media by convection, and through empty space by radiation. **2.** The perceptible, sensible, or measurable effect of such energy so transmitted; especially, a physiological sensation of being hot. **3.** An intense or pathological manifestation of such a perception or sensation; excessive warmth. **4.** The condition of being warm or hot. **5.** Intensity, as of color, appearance, emotion, or effect. **6.** A period or condition of sexual excitement, **estrus** *(see).* **7.** One of a series of efforts or attempts. **8.** *Sports.* **a.** A single course in a race or competition made up of several. **b.** A preliminary race to determine finalists. **9.** *Slang.* Pressure, as from police pursuing criminals. —*v.* **heated, heating, heats.** —*tr.* **1.** To make warm or hot. **2.** To excite the feelings of; inflame. —*intr.* **1.** To become warm or hot. **2.** To become excited emotionally or intellectually. [Middle English *he(e)te,* Old English *hǣtu.* See **kai-** in Appendix.*]

heat capacity. The amount of heat required to raise the temperature of a body by one degree, either at constant pressure or at constant volume and without inducing chemical changes or change of phase.

heat engine. An engine that converts heat to mechanical energy.

heat·er (hē′tər) *n.* **1.** An apparatus that heats or provides heat. **2.** Someone who heats something or tends a heating apparatus. **3.** *Slang.* A pistol.

heat exchanger. A device used to transfer heat from a fluid flowing on one side of a barrier to a fluid or fluids flowing on the other.

heat exhaustion. A reaction to excessive heat, marked by prostration, weakness, and collapse, resulting from dehydration. Also called "heat prostration." Compare **heat stroke.**

heath (hēth) *n.* **1.** Any of various usually low-growing shrubs of the genus *Erica* and related genera, native to the Old World, having small, evergreen leaves and small, urn-shaped pink or purplish flowers. Many species are also called "heather." **2.** An extensive tract of open, uncultivated land covered with such shrubs or similar plants; a moor. [Middle English *he(e)th, heath,* Old English *hǣth.* See **kaito-** in Appendix.*]

hea·then (hē′*th*ən) *n., pl.* **heathens** or **heathen. 1. a.** One who adheres to the religion of a tribe or nation that does not acknowledge the God of Judaism, Christianity, or Islam. **b.** Such persons collectively; the unconverted. **2. a.** One who is regarded as irreligious, uncivilized, or unenlightened. **b.** Such persons collectively. [Middle English *hethen,* Old English *hǣthen.* See **kaito-** in Appendix.*] —**hea′then** *adj.* —**hea′then·dom** (hē′*th*ən-dəm), **hea′then·ism′, hea′then·ry** *n.*

hea·then·ish (hē′*th*ə-nĭsh) *adj.* **1.** Of or having to do with the heathen. **2.** Uncouth or barbarous in the manner ascribed to the heathen. —**hea′then·ish·ly** *adv.* —**hea′then·ish·ness** *n.*

hea·then·ize (hē′*th*ə-nīz′) *tr.v.* **-ized, -izing, -izes.** To make heathen; barbarize.

heath·er (hĕ*th*′ər) *n.* **1.** A low-growing shrub, *Calluna vulgaris,* native to Eurasia, growing in dense masses and having small evergreen leaves and clusters of small, urn-shaped, pinkish-purple flowers. Also called "ling." **2.** Any of several similar, related plants of the genus *Erica* or other genera; heath. **3.** Grayish purple to purplish red. See **color.** [Middle English (Scottish) *hadder,* probably from *he(e)th, heath,* HEATH.] —**heath′er** *adj.*

heath·er·y (hĕ*th*′ə-rē) *adj.* **1.** Of or like heather. **2.** Covered with heather: *heathery hills.*

heath hen. A form of the prairie chicken, *Tympanuchus cupido,* that became extinct in eastern North America during the first part of the 20th century.

heat lightning. Intermittent flashes of light across the horizon on a hot summer evening, unaccompanied by thunder and thought to be cloud reflections of distant lightning.

heat of fusion. The quantity of heat required to melt a unit mass of a solid at a specified temperature.

heat of vaporization. The amount of heat required to convert a unit liquid mass at a specified temperature into vapor.

heat prostration. Heat exhaustion *(see).*

heat pump. An engine that transfers heat from a relatively low-temperature reservoir to one at a higher temperature.

heat rash. *Pathology.* **Miliaria** *(see).*

heat shield. A barrier that prevents the heating of a space by absorbing, reflecting, or dissipating external heat; especially, a protective structure on a spacecraft or missile that dissipates heat on atmospheric re-entry by melting and vaporizing.

heat sink. 1. An environment having a much greater heat capacity and at a lower temperature than an object with which it is in thermal contact. **2.** Any device by means of which heat is absorbed or stored in or removed from a thermal system.

heat stroke. A severe illness caused by exposure to excessively high temperatures, and characterized by severe headache, high fever with a dry, hot skin, tachycardia, and in serious cases, collapse and coma. Compare **heat exhaustion.**

heaume (hōm) *n.* A medieval helmet worn over an inner cap of mail or steel. [Old French *heaume, helme,* helmet, from Frankish *helm* (unattested). See **kel-⁴** in Appendix.*]

heave (hēv) *v.* **heaved** or *chiefly nautical* **hove** (hōv), **heaving, heaves.** —*tr.* **1.** To raise or lift with strenuous effort; hoist. **2. a.** To throw with great effort (a heavy object, for example); hurl: *heave the shot-put.* **b.** To throw. **3.** To breathe or emit painfully or unhappily: *heaved a sigh.* **4.** *Nautical.* **a.** To raise (an anchor or net, for example). **b.** To pull on or haul (a rope or cable, for example). —*intr.* **1.** To rise up or swell, especially from turbulence; to bulge; billow. **2.** *Informal.* To vomit. **3.** *Nautical.* **a.** To come to be in a specified position. Used of ships: *She hove alongside.* **b.** To pull on or haul a rope, cable, or the like: *heave around on the anchor.* **c.** To push or pull, on a capstan bar or the like. —See Synonyms at **lift, throw.** —**heave ho!** *Nautical.* Used to express a command to give a hard push or pull together. —**heave into sight** (or **view**). *Nautical.* To rise or seemingly rise into view, as a ship. —**heave to. 1.** *Nautical.* **a.** To turn a sailing ship so that its bow heads into the wind, as by way of meeting a storm. **b.** To turn an engine-powered vessel in a similar situation so that its bow heads into the seas while proceeding at low speed. **c.** To come to a stop. **2.** *Informal.* To stop and turn around. —*n.* **1.** The act or strain of heaving. **2.** *Informal.* A throw, especially considered in terms of distance: *a heave of 63 feet.* [Heave, hove, hove; Middle English *hebben* or *heven, hove, hove,* Old English *hebban, hōf, hafen.* See **kap-** in Appendix.*]

heav·en (hĕv′ən) *n.* **1.** *Often plural.* The sky or universe as seen from the earth; firmament. **2.** The abode of God, the angels, and the souls of those who are granted salvation. **3. a.** *Capital* **H.** The divine Providence: *May Heaven help you.* **b.** *Often plural.* A euphemism for God, used in exclamations: *Oh, for heaven's sake! Good heavens!* **4.** *Plural.* The celestial powers; the gods: *The heavens favored the young ruler.* **5. a.** Supreme happiness; a state of bliss. **b.** A thing or place which is wonderful or enchantingly perfect; a sheer delight: *The lake was heaven.* **—in seventh heaven.** Supremely happy. **—move heaven and earth.** To do everything possible to bring something about. [Middle English *heven, hefen,* Old English *heofon, hefen.* See **kamer-** in Appendix.*]

heav·en·ly (hĕv′ən-lē) *adj.* **1.** Sublime; enchanting; lovely. **2.** Of or having to do with the firmament; celestial. **3.** Of or pertaining to the abode of God. **—heav′en·li·ness** *n.*

heav·en·ward (hĕv′ən-wərd) *adv.* Also **heav·en·wards** (-wərdz). Toward heaven. **—heav′en·ward** *adj.*

heav·er (hē′vər) *n.* **1.** One that lifts or heaves. **2.** *Nautical.* A short bar used as a lever for twisting rope.

heaves (hēvz) *n.* Plural in form, used with a singular or plural verb. **1.** A pulmonary disease of horses, characterized by coughing and other serious respiratory irregularities, and noticeable especially after exercise or in cold weather. Also called "broken wind." **2.** *Slang.* A seizure of vomiting. Usually preceded by *the.*

heav·i·er-than-air (hĕv′ē-ər-thən-âr′) *adj.* Being an aircraft that is heavier than the air it displaces.

heav·i·ness (hĕv′ē-nĭs) *n.* The state or quality of being heavy.

Heav·i·side layer (hĕv′ĭ-sīd′). A component of the earth's atmosphere, the **E layer** *(see).* [After Oliver *Heaviside* (died 1925), English physicist.]

heav·y (hĕv′ē) *adj.* **-ier, -iest. 1.** Having relatively great weight: *a heavy load.* **2.** Having relatively high density: *a heavy metal.* **3. a.** Large in number, yield, output, or the like; voluminous or populous; substantial: *heavy rainfall; a heavy turnout.* **b.** Intense or sustained: *heavy activity.* **4. a.** Dense or thick: *heavy fog.* **b.** Having considerable thickness, body, or strength. Said of materials and garments: *a heavy coat.* **5. a.** Concerted or powerful; severe: *a heavy punch.* **b.** In turmoil; rough; violent: *heavy seas.* **6. a.** Indulging to a great or habitual degree; chronic: *a heavy drinker.* **b.** Involved or participating on a large scale; prodigious; generous: *a heavy investor.* **7. a.** Of great import or seriousness; grave: *heavy matters of state.* **b.** Sad or painful: *heavy news.* **8. a.** Hard to do or accomplish; arduous. **b.** Not easily borne; oppressive: *heavy taxes.* **9. a.** Copious: *a heavy breakfast.* **b.** Not easily or quickly digested: *an unusually heavy fruitcake.* **10.** Having large or marked physical features; coarse. **11.** Weighed with concern or sadness; despondent: *a heavy heart.* **12.** Ponderous. **13.** Lumbering; clumsy. **14.** Strong and pervasive; pungent: *a heavy odor.* **15. a.** Weighed down, as from being full; laden: *trees heavy with plums.* **b.** Showing weariness; listless: *heavy eyes.* **16.** Involving large-scale manufacturing, as of machinery or armaments: *heavy industry.* **17.** *Archaic.* Gravid; pregnant. **18.** *Theater.* **a.** Of or pertaining to a serious dramatic role. **b.** Of or pertaining to the role of a villain. **19.** *Physics.* **a.** Designating an isotope with a mass greater than that of others found in the same element. **b.** Designating an atomic particle having a mass between that of pi mesons and protons. **20.** Bearing heavy arms or armor: *heavy cavalry.* **21.** *Slang.* Ingenious or profound. *—adv.* Heavily. **—hang heavy.** To pass slowly or tediously: *the time hanging heavy on his hands.* *—n., pl.* **heavies. 1.** A villain in a story or play. **2.** *Informal.* A scoundrel; villain. **3. a.** A serious or tragic role in a play. **b.** An actor playing such a role. [Middle English *hevi,* Old English *hefig.* See **kap-** in Appendix.*] **—heav′i·ly** *adv.*

Synonyms: *heavy, weighty, hefty, massive, ponderous, cumbersome, unwieldy.* These adjectives are applied to persons or things with respect to weight, size, or shape, especially as these qualities affect their movement or management. Some also have related figurative application. *Heavy,* in careful usage, refers to great weight or high density. Figuratively, *heavy* applies to what is burdensome or oppressive to the spirit. *Weighty* literally denotes having great weight, without reference to an implied comparison; figuratively, it describes what is very serious or important. *Hefty* refers principally, and less formally, to heaviness or browniness of physique. *Massive* describes what is imposing in size or bulk and in solidity and strength. *Ponderous* refers to what has great mass and weight, and usually implies heaviness of movement. Figuratively, *ponderous* describes what is complicated, involved, or lacking in grace or lightness of spirit. *Cumbersome* stresses difficulty of movement or operation caused by heaviness or bulkiness. *Unwieldy* refers less to sheer weight than to peculiarity of construction that causes a thing to be unmanageable or clumsy in operation.

heav·y-dut·y (hĕv′ē-do͞o′tē, -dyo͞o′tē) *adj.* Made for hard use or wear.

heav·y-foot·ed (hĕv′ē-fo͝ot′ĭd) *adj.* Having a heavy, lumbering gait.

heav·y-hand·ed (hĕv′ē-hăn′dĭd) *adj.* **1.** Clumsy. **2.** Tactless. **3.** Oppressive; harsh.

heav·y-heart·ed (hĕv′ē-här′tĭd) *adj.* Melancholy; sad; depressed. **—heav′y-heart′ed·ly** *adv.* **—heav′y-heart′ed·ness** *n.*

heavy hydrogen. An isotope of hydrogen with mass number greater than 1, **deuterium** *(see).*

heav·y-lad·en (hĕv′ē-lād′n) *adj.* **1.** Laden with a heavy load. **2.** Burdened with cares; troubled.

heav·y·set (hĕv′ē-sĕt′) *adj.* Having a heavy, compact build.

heavy spar. A mineral, **barite** *(see).*

heavy water. Any of several isotopic varieties of water, especially **deuterium oxide** *(see),* consisting chiefly or exclusively of molecules containing hydrogen with mass number greater than 1, and used as a moderator in certain nuclear reactors.

heav·y·weight (hĕv′ē-wāt′) *n.* **1.** One of above average weight. **2.** One that competes in the heaviest class; specifically, a boxer weighing more than 175 pounds. **3.** *Informal.* A person of great importance or influence.

Heb. 1. Hebrew. **2.** Hebrews (New Testament).

heb·do·mad (hĕb′də-măd′) *n.* **1.** A group of seven. **2.** A period of seven days; a week. [Latin *hebdomas* (stem *hebdomad-*), the number seven, seven days, from Greek, from *hepta,* seven. See **septm̥** in Appendix.*]

heb·dom·a·dal (hĕb-dŏm′ə-dəl) *adj.* Also **heb·dom·a·dar·y** (-dĕr′ē). Weekly. **—heb·dom′a·dal·ly** *adv.*

He·be (hē′bē). *Greek Mythology.* The goddess of youth and spring. [Greek *Hēbē,* personification of *hēbē,* youth, youthful vigor. See **yēgwā** in Appendix.*]

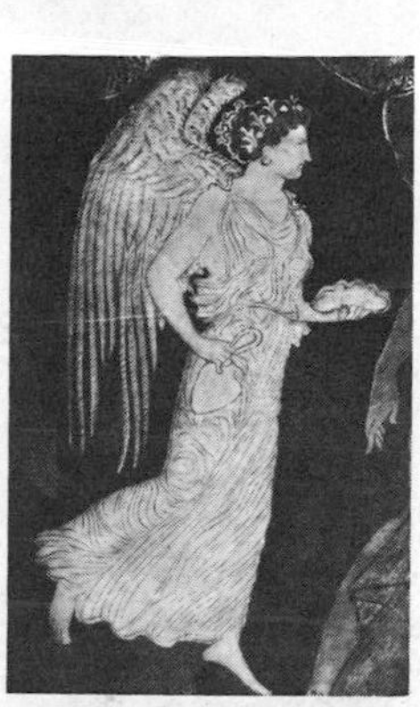

Hebe
Detail from ancient Greek vase painting

he·be·phre·ni·a (hē′bə-frē′nē-ə) *n.* A schizophrenia characterized by foolish mannerisms, delusions, hallucinations, and regressive behavior. [Greek *hēbē,* youth (see **yēgwā** in Appendix*) + -PHRENIA.] **—he′be·phren′ic** (-frĕn′ĭk) *adj.*

heb·e·tate (hĕb′ə-tāt′) *v.* **-tated, -tating, -tates.** *—tr.* To make blunt or dull. *—intr.* To become blunt or dull. [Latin *hebetāre,* from *hebes*† (stem *hebet-*), blunt, dull.] **—heb′e·ta′tion** *n.* **—heb′e·ta′tive** *adj.*

heb·e·tude (hĕb′ə-to͞od′, -tyo͞od′) *n.* Dullness of mind; mental lethargy. [Late Latin *hebetūdo* : Latin *hebes* (stem *hebet-*), blunt, dull (see **hebetate**) + -TUDE.] **—heb′e·tu′di·nous** *adj.*

Hebr. Hebrew.

He·bra·ic (hĭ-brā′ĭk) *adj.* Also **He·bra·i·cal** (-ĭ-kəl). Of, pertaining to, or characteristic of the Hebrews or their language or culture. [Middle English *Ebrayke,* from Late Latin *Hebraicus,* from Greek *Hebraikos,* from *Hebraios,* HEBREW.] **—He·bra′i·cal·ly** *adv.*

He·bra·ism (hē′brā-ĭz′əm, hē′brə-) *n.* **1.** A manner or custom characteristic of the Hebrews; especially, a Hebrew expression or idiom. **2.** The culture, spirit, or character of the Hebrew people. **3.** Judaism. [From HEBRAIC.]

He·bra·ist (hē′brā′ĭst) *n.* A Hebrew scholar. **—He′bra·is′tic, He′bra·is′ti·cal** *adj.* **—He′bra·is′ti·cal·ly** *adv.*

He·bra·ize (hē′brā-īz′) *v.* **-ized, -izing, -izes.** *—tr.* To make Hebraic in form or idiom. *—intr.* To use or adopt Hebraisms.

He·brew (hē′bro͞o) *n. Abbr.* **Heb., Hebr. 1.** A member of the Semitic people claiming descent from Abraham, Isaac, and Jacob; an Israelite. **2. a.** The Semitic language of the ancient Hebrews, used in most of the Old Testament. **b.** Any of various later forms of this language, especially the form now spoken by the people of Israel. *—adj.* Of or having to do with the Hebrews. [Middle English *Ebreu, Hebrewe,* from Old French *Ebreu,* from Latin *Hebraeus,* Hebraic, from Greek *Hebraios,* from Aramaic *'ibhray, 'ebhray,* from Hebrew *'ibhrī,* "he who came from across (the river)," from *'ēbher,* region across, from *ābhar,* pass across or over.]

Hebrew calendar. The lunisolar calendar used by the Jews. See **calendar.**

He·brews (hē′bro͞oz) *n.* Plural in form, used with a singular verb. *Abbr.* **Heb.** A book of the New Testament; the Epistle to the Hebrews.

Hebrew Scriptures. The Pentateuch, the Prophets, and the Hagiographa, forming the covenant between God and the Jewish people that is the foundation and Bible of Judaism, while constituting for Christians the **Old Testament** *(see).*

Heb·ri·des (hĕb′rə-dēz). An island group occupying 3,000 square miles in the Atlantic off the western coast of Scotland and divided into the Inner Hebrides and the Outer Hebrides. Population, 49,000. Also called "Western Islands."

He·bron (hē′brən). *Arabic* **El Kha·lil** (ăl KHä-lēl′). A city of western Jordan, south of Jerusalem. Population, 38,000.

Hec·a·te (hĕk′ə-tē). Also **Hek·a·te.** *Greek Mythology.* An ancient fertility goddess who later became identified with Persephone as queen of Hades and protectress of witches.

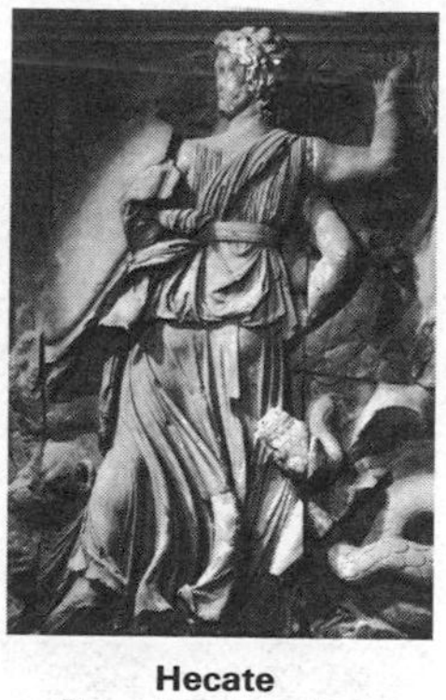

Hecate
From frieze on altar of Zeus at Pergamum

Hec·a·te Strait (hĕk′ə-tē). An inlet of the Pacific separating the Queen Charlotte Islands from the western coast of British Columbia, Canada.

hec·a·tomb (hĕk′ə-tōm′, -to͞om′) *n.* **1.** In ancient Greece, a large-scale public offering to the gods, originally of 100 oxen. **2.** Any large-scale sacrifice. [Latin *hecatombē,* from Greek *hekatombē* : *hekaton,* hundred (see **dekm̥** in Appendix*) + *-bē,* from *bous,* ox (see **gwou-** in Appendix*).]

heck (hĕk). Euphemism for **hell.**

heck·le (hĕk′əl) *tr.v.* **-led, -ling, -les. 1.** To harass (a speaker or performer) persistently, as with questions, gibes, or objections. **2.** To comb (flax or hemp) with a hatchel. **3.** Variant of **hatchel.** [Middle English *hekelen,* to comb flax, from *hekell, hechele,* flaxcomb, hatchel, Old English *hæcel* (unattested). See **keg-** in Appendix.*] **—heck′ler** *n.*

hec·tare (hĕk′târ′) *n. Abbr.* **ha** A metric unit of area equal to 100 ares or 2.471 acres. [French : HECT(O)- + ARE.]

hec·tic (hĕk′tĭk) *adj.* **1.** Characterized by feverish activity, confusion, or haste: *"There was nothing feverish or hectic about his vigor"* (Erik Erikson). See Usage note below. **2.** Of, relating to, or having an undulating fever, as in diseases such as tuberculosis or septicemia. **3.** Consumptive; feverish. **4.** Flushed. [Middle English *etik,* from Old French *etique,* from Late Latin *hecticus,* from Greek *hektikos,* formed by habit, consumptive, hectic, from *hexis,* condition, habit, from *ekhein,* to have, hold, be in a certain condition. See **segh-** in Appendix.*]

Usage: *Hectic* is well established in its general sense related to

feverish activity, confusion, or haste. In earlier usage, that sense was sometimes deprecated as a loose extension of the term's meaning in medicine. It is acceptable on all levels now, however, according to 92 per cent of the Usage Panel.

hecto–, hect–. *Symbol* **h** Indicates 100; for example, **hectocotylus, hectare.** [French, from Greek *hekaton,* hundred. See **dekm̥** in Appendix.*]

hec·to·cot·y·lus (hĕk′tō-kŏt′l-əs) *n., pl.* **-li** (-lī′). A modified arm of the male of certain cephalopods, such as the octopus, containing sperm and functioning as a reproductive organ. Also called "hectocotylus arm," "hectocotylized arm." [New Latin *Hectocotylus,* name given by G. L. Cuvier to the detached arm which he thought was a parasitic worm : HECTO- + Greek *kotulē,* cup, hollow object (see **cotyledon**).]

hec·to·gram (hĕk′tə-grăm′) *n.* Also **hec·to·gramme.** *Abbr.* **hg** A metric unit of mass equal to 100 grams or 3.527 avoirdupois ounces. [French *hectogramme* : HECTO- + GRAM.]

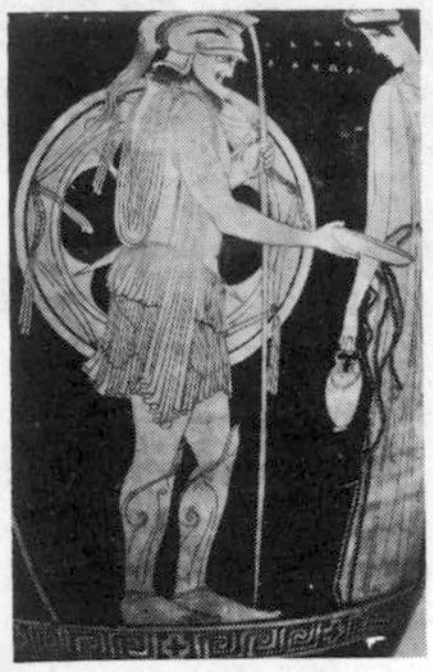

Hector
Fifth-century B.C.
Greek vase painting

hec·to·graph (hĕk′tə-grăf′, -gräf′) *n.* A machine using a glycerin-coated layer of gelatin to make copies of typed or written material. Also called "copygraph." —*tr.v.* **hectographed, -graphing, -graphs.** To copy by means of a hectograph. [German *Hektograph* : HECTO- + -GRAPH.] —**hec′to·graph′ic** *adj.* —**hec′to·graph′i·cal·ly** *adv.*

hec·to·li·ter (hĕk′tə-lē′tər) *n.* Also **hec·to·li·tre.** *Abbr.* **hl** **1.** A metric unit of capacity or volume, used in liquid measure, equal to 100 liters or 1.056 liquid quarts. **2.** A metric unit of capacity or volume, used in dry measure, equal to 100 liters or 0.908 dry quart. See **measurement.** [French *hectolitre* : HECTO- + LITER.]

hec·to·me·ter (hĕk′tə-mē′tər) *n.* Also **hec·to·me·tre.** *Abbr.* **hm** A metric unit of length equal to 100 meters or 328 feet. [French *hectomètre* : HECTO- + METER.]

hec·tor (hĕk′tər) *v.* **-tored, -toring, -tors.** —*tr.* To intimidate or dominate in a blustering way. —*intr.* To behave like a bully; to swagger. —*n.* A bully. [After HECTOR.]

Hec·tor (hĕk′tər). A Trojan prince killed by Achilles in Homer's *Iliad.* [Greek *Hektōr.* See **segh-** in Appendix.*]

Hec·u·ba (hĕk′yo͝o-bə). The wife of Priam in Homer's *Iliad.*

he'd (hēd). **1.** Contraction of *he had.* **2.** Contraction of *he would.*

hed·dle (hĕd′l) *n.* One of a set of parallel cords or wires in a loom used to separate and guide the warp threads and make a path for the shuttle. [Probably altered from Middle English *helde,* heddle, Old English *hefeld.* See **kap-** in Appendix.*]

hedge (hĕj) *n.* **1.** A row of closely planted shrubs or low-growing trees forming a fence or boundary. **2.** A means of protection or defense, especially against financial loss. **3.** A noncommittal, ambiguous statement. —*v.* **hedged, hedging, hedges.** —*tr.* **1.** To enclose or bound with or as if with hedges. **2.** To restrict; hem in; confine. Often used with *in.* **3.** To counterbalance (a bet, for example) with other transactions, so as to limit the risk of loss. —*intr.* **1.** To plant or cultivate hedges. **2.** To take compensatory measures against possible loss. **3.** To avoid committing oneself, as by making cautious or ambiguous statements. [Middle English *hegge,* Old English *hecg.* See **kagh-** in Appendix.*] —**hedg′er** *n.* —**hedg′y** *adj.*

hedge·hog (hĕj′hôg′, -hŏg′) *n.* **1.** Any of several small Old World mammals of the family Erinaceidae, and especially of the genus *Erinaceus,* having the back covered with dense, erectile spines, and characteristically rolling into a ball for protection. **2.** Any of several similar spiny animals. [From its piglike snout and its habit of frequenting hedges.]

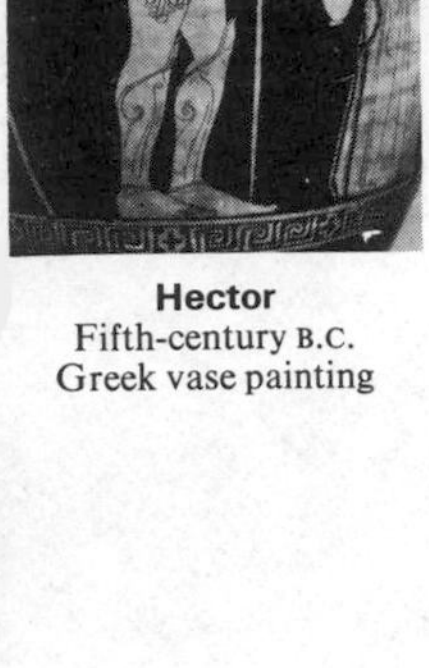

hedgehog
Erinaceus europaeus

hedge·hop (hĕj′hŏp′) *intr.v.* **-hopped, -hopping, -hops.** To fly an airplane close to the ground, rising above objects as they appear, as in spraying crops. —**hedge′hop′per** *n.*

hedge hyssop. Any of various plants of the genus *Gratiola,* growing in damp places and having small yellow or whitish flowers.

hedge parson. *British.* One of a former class of illiterate, itinerant priests. Also called "hedge priest."

hedge·row (hĕj′rō′) *n.* A row of bushes, shrubs, or trees forming a hedge.

He·djaz. See **Hejaz.**

he·don·ic (hĭ-dŏn′ĭk) *adj.* **1.** Of, pertaining to, or marked by pleasure. **2.** Of hedonism or hedonics. [Greek *hēdonikos,* from *hēdonē,* pleasure. See **swād-** in Appendix.*]

he·don·ics (hĭ-dŏn′ĭks) *n.* Plural in form, used with a singular verb. **1.** *Psychology.* The study of pleasant and unpleasant sensations. **2.** *Philosophy.* A branch of ethics that deals with the relation of pleasure to duty.

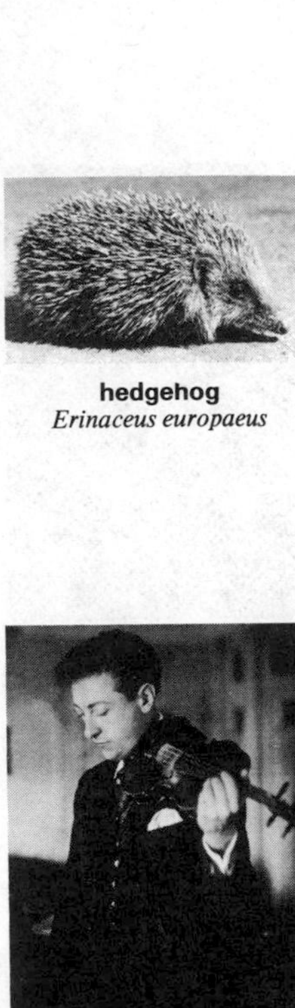

Jascha Heifetz

he·don·ism (hēd′n-ĭz′əm) *n.* **1.** Pursuit of or devotion to pleasure. **2.** The ethical doctrine that only that which is pleasant or has pleasant consequences is intrinsically good. **3.** *Psychology.* The doctrine that behavior is motivated by the desire for pleasure and the avoidance of pain. [Greek *hēdonē,* pleasure (see **hedonic**) + -ISM.]

he·don·ist (hēd′n-ĭst) *n.* One who holds that pleasure is the chief good. —**he′don·is′tic** *adj.* —**he′don·is′ti·cal·ly** *adv.*

–hedral. Indicates surfaces or faces of a given number; for example, **dihedral.** [From -HEDRON.]

–hedron. Indicates a geometric figure having a given number of faces or surfaces; for example, **pentahedron.** [Greek *-edron,* from *hedra,* base, seat. See **sed-¹** in Appendix.*]

hee·bie-jee·bies (hē′bē-jē′bēz) *pl.n. Slang.* A feeling of uneasiness or nervousness; the jitters. [Coined by Billy De Beck (1890–1942), American cartoonist, in his comic strip *Barney Google.*]

heed (hēd) *v.* **heeded, heeding, heeds.** —*tr.* To pay attention to; listen to and consider: *"he did not heed my gibes, and chattered on"* (Sean O'Faolain). —*intr.* To pay attention. —*n.* Close attention or consideration. [Middle English *heden,* Old English *hēdan.* See **kadh-** in Appendix.*]

heed·ful (hēd′fəl) *adj.* Paying close attention; taking heed; mindful. —**heed′ful·ly** *adv.* —**heed′ful·ness** *n.*

heed·less (hēd′lĭs) *adj.* Paying little or no attention; not taking heed; unmindful. See Synonyms at **careless, impetuous.** —**heed′less·ly** *adv.* —**heed′less·ness** *n.*

hee·haw (hē′hô′) *n.* **1.** The braying sound made by a donkey. **2.** A noisy laugh; a guffaw. —*intr.v.* **heehawed, -hawing, -haws.** **1.** To bray. **2.** To laugh noisily; to guffaw. [Imitative.]

heel¹ (hēl) *n.* **1.** The rounded posterior portion of the human foot under and behind the ankle. **2.** The corresponding part of the hind foot of other vertebrates. **3.** A similar anatomical part, such as the fleshy rounded base of the human palm or the hind toe of a bird. **4.** That part of footwear, such as a sock, shoe, or stocking, that covers the heel. **5.** The built-up portion of a shoe or boot, supporting the heel. **6.** One of the crusty ends of a loaf of bread. **7.** A lower, rearward surface, as of the head of a golf club. **8.** *Nautical.* **a.** The lower end of a mast. **b.** The after end of a ship's keel. **9.** *Horticulture.* The basal end of a cutting, tuber, or other plant part used in propagation. **10.** *Slang.* A callous or dishonorable man; cad. —**at heel.** Close behind. —**down at the heels.** **1.** Having one's shoe heels worn down. **2.** Shabby; run-down. —**lay by the heels.** To put in fetters or shackles; imprison or confine: *"If the king blames me for 't, I'll lay ye all/By the heels."* (Shakespeare). —**on** (or **upon**) **the heels of.** **1.** Directly behind. **2.** Immediately following. —**take to one's heels.** To flee; run away. —**to heel.** **1.** Close behind; at one's heel. **2.** Under discipline or control. —*v.* **heeled, heeling, heels.** —*tr.* **1.** To furnish with a heel or heels. **2.** *Slang.* To furnish (a person) with something, especially money or firearms. **3.** To arm (a gamecock) with spurs. **4.** To follow upon the heels of; follow closely behind. —*intr.* **1.** To follow at one's heels. **2.** To perform a dance step or movement with the heels. [Middle English *heel, he(e)le,* Old English *hēla.* See **kenk-³** in Appendix.*] —**heel′less** *adj.*

heel² (hēl) *v.* **heeled, heeling, heels.** —*intr.* To tip to one side; to tilt; to list. Used especially of ships. —*tr.* To cause (a ship) to list. —*n.* A tilting or inclining to one side; a cant; a list. [Probably altered from earlier *heeld,* Middle English *he(e)lden,* Old English *hieldan.* See **kel-⁶** in Appendix.*]

heel-and-toe (hēl′ən-tō′) *adj.* Characterized by a stride in which the heel of one foot touches ground before the toe of the other foot is lifted, as in walking races.

heel bone. The **calcaneus** *(see).*

heeled (hēld) *adj.* **1.** Having or fitted with heels. **2.** *Slang.* **a.** Provided with money. **b.** Armed, especially with a firearm.

heel·er (hē′lər) *n.* **1.** One who heels shoes. **2.** *Informal.* A **ward heeler** *(see).*

heel·piece (hēl′pēs′) *n.* A piece made for or serving as the heel of a shoe or stocking.

heel·post (hēl′pōst′) *n.* The post to which a door or gate is hinged.

heel·tap (hēl′tăp′) *n.* **1.** A layer of material added to the heel of a shoe; a lift. **2.** A small amount of liquor remaining in a container or drinking vessel.

heft (hĕft) *n. Informal.* Weight; heaviness; bulk. —*v.* **hefted, hefting, hefts.** —*tr.* **1.** To determine or estimate the weight of by lifting. **2.** To hoist up; to heave. —*intr.* To weigh. [From HEAVE (by analogy with such pairs as CLEAVE, CLEFT).]

heft·y (hĕf′tē) *adj.* **-ier, -iest.** **1.** Weighty; heavy. **2.** Large and powerful; bulky; muscular. —See Synonyms at **heavy.**

He·gel (hā′gəl), **Georg Wilhelm Friedrich.** 1770–1831. German philosopher.

He·ge·li·an·ism (hā-gā′lē-ə-nĭz′əm) *n.* The philosophy of Hegel; especially, Hegel's doctrine of the phenomenology of the spirit, or the becoming of knowledge, which attempts by dialectical method to make scientific the final truths of religion. —**He·ge′li·an** *adj.* & *n.*

he·gem·o·ny (hĭ-jĕm′ə-nē, hĕj′ə-mō′nē) *n., pl.* **-nies.** Predominance; especially, preponderant influence of one state over others. [Greek *hēgemonia,* authority, rule, from *hēgemōn,* leader, from *hēgeisthai,* to lead. See **sāg-** in Appendix.*] —**heg′e·mon′ic** (-mŏn′ĭk) *adj.*

He·gi·ra (hĭ-jī′rə, hĕj′ər-ə) *n.* Also **He·ji·ra.** **1.** The flight of Mohammed from Mecca to Medina in A.D. 622. **2.** The Moslem era, which is reckoned from this date. **3.** *Small* **h.** Any flight, as from danger. [Arabic *(al)hijrah,* emigration, abandonment of Mecca, flight, departure, from *hajara,* to leave, depart.]

he·gu·men (hĭ-gyo͞o′mĕn) *n.* Also **he·gu·me·nos** (-mĕ-nŏs). The head of a religious community in the Greek Orthodox Church. [Late Latin *hēgūmenus,* from Late Greek *hēgoumenos,* from Greek, leader, from *hēgeisthai,* to lead. See **sāg-** in Appendix.*]

Hei·del·berg (hīd′l-bûrg; *German* hī′dəl-bĕrk). A city and manufacturing center of northwestern Baden-Württemberg, West Germany, on the Neckar. Population, 127,000.

Heidelberg man. An extinct, early member of the human species, a form of *Homo erectus,* known primarily from a fossil jawbone found near Heidelberg, West Germany, in 1907.

heif·er (hĕf′ər) *n.* A young cow, especially one that has not yet given birth to a calf. [Middle English *heyfre, hayfre,* Old English *hēahfore,* young ox. See **per-³** in Appendix.*]

Hei·fetz (hī′fĭts), **Jascha.** Born 1901. Russian-born American violinist.

heigh (hā, hī) *interj. Archaic.* Used to express encouragement or to call attention.

heigh-ho (hī′hō′, hā′-) *interj.* Used to express fatigue, melancholy, mild surprise, or disappointment.

ă pat/ā pay/âr care/ä father/b bib/ch church/d deed/ĕ pet/ē be/f fife/g gag/h hat/hw which/ĭ pit/ī pie/îr pier/j judge/k kick/l lid, needle/m mum/n no, sudden/ng thing/ŏ pot/ō toe/ô paw, for/oi noise/ou out/o͝o took/o͞o boot/p pop/r roar/s sauce/sh ship, dish/

height (hīt) *n.* Also *obsolete* **heighth, highth** (hītth, hīth). *Abbr.* **h., H., hgt., ht** **1.** The highest or uppermost point; summit; apex. **2. a.** The highest or most advanced degree; zenith. **b.** The point of highest intensity; climax: *the height of a storm.* **3. a.** The distance from the base to the top of something. **b.** The elevation of something above a given level; altitude. **4. a.** The condition or attribute of being sufficiently or relatively high or tall. **b.** Stature, especially of the human body. **5. a.** An eminence, as a hill or mountain. **b.** A high point, position, or degree: *"To attain / the highth and depth of thy Eternal wayes."* (Milton). **6.** *Obsolete.* High rank, estate, or degree: *"Such by crying down all heighth, raise themselves up higher than ever."* (William Penn). **7. a.** *Archaic.* Loftiness of mind. **b.** *Obsolete.* Arrogance; hauteur: *"he returned me a very resolute answer, and full of height."* (Cromwell). [Middle English *he(i)ghth,* Old English *hēhthu, hiehthu.* See **keu-²** in Appendix.*]

Synonyms: *height, elevation, stature.* These nouns refer to vertical measurement relative to a perpendicular plane or base. *Height* is the general term, implying distance from the bottom to the top of a thing or from a plane, such as the earth's surface, to the point of farthest ascent. *Elevation* usually refers to vertical distance above a base or plane, such as sea level. *Stature* is applied principally to the height of the human body.

height·en (hīt'n) *v.* **-ened, -ening, -ens.** —*tr.* **1.** To increase the quantity or degree of; intensify. **2.** To make high or higher; to raise. —*intr.* **1.** To rise in degree or quantity; intensify. **2.** To become high or higher; to be raised. —**height'en·er** *n.*

height-to-pa·per (hīt'tə-pā'pər) *n. Printing.* The height of type from foot to face, standardized at 0.9186 inch.

heil (hīl) *interj.* Hail! Used as a greeting. [German, from Middle High German, "healthy," from Old High German, whole, healthy. See **kailo-** in Appendix.*]

Heil·bronn (hīl'brŏn). A city and industrial center of north-central Baden-Württemberg, West Germany, on the Neckar. Population, 89,000.

Hei·lung·kiang (hā'lo͝ong'jyäng'). A province, 178,996 square miles in area, of northeastern China. Population, 14,860,000. Capital, Harbin.

Hei·ne (hī'nə), **Heinrich.** 1797–1856. German poet and critic.

hei·nie (hī'nē) *n. Slang.* The buttocks. [Variant of dialectal *hinder,* from HINDER (behind).]

hei·nous (hā'nəs) *adj.* Grossly wicked or reprehensible; abominable; odious; vile: *"It would have been a heinous breach of loyalty to his lord had Gawain made love to his lord's wife"* (Alan M. Markman). [Middle English *heynous,* hateful, from Old French *haïneus,* from *haïne,* hate, from *haïr,* to hate, from Frankish *hatjan* (unattested). See **kād-** in Appendix.*] —**hei'nous·ly** *adv.* —**hei'nous·ness** *n.*

heir (âr) *n.* **1.** *Law.* A person who inherits or is entitled by law or by the terms of a will to inherit the estate of another. **2.** A person who succeeds or is in line to succeed to a hereditary rank, title, or office. **3.** One who receives or is expected to receive a heritage, as of ideas, from a predecessor. [Middle English *(h)eir, (h)air,* from Old French *(h)eir,* from Latin *hērēs.* See **ghē-** in Appendix.*]

heir apparent *pl.* **heirs apparent.** *Law.* An heir whose right to inheritance is indefeasible by law, provided he survives his ancestor.

heir·dom (âr'dəm) *n.* **1.** Succession by right of blood; heirship. **2.** An inheritance.

heir·ess (âr'ĭs) *n.* A female heir, especially one who inherits great wealth.

heir·loom (âr'lo͞om') *n.* **1.** A valued possession passed down in a family through succeeding generations. **2.** *Law.* An article of personal property included in an inherited estate. [Middle English *heir lome* : HEIR + *lome,* utensil, tool, LOOM.]

heir presumptive *pl.* **heirs presumptive.** *Law.* An heir whose claim can be defeated by the birth of a closer relative before the death of the ancestor.

heir·ship (âr'shĭp') *n.* **1.** The condition of being an heir. **2.** The right to inheritance; heirdom.

Hei·sen·berg (hī'zən-bĕrk'), **Werner.** Born 1901. German atomic physicist.

heist (hīst) *tr.v.* **heisted, heisting, heists.** *Slang.* To rob; steal. —*n. Slang.* A robbery; burglary. [Dialectal variant of HOIST.]

He·jaz (hĕ-jăz'). Also **He·djaz.** A viceroyalty of western Saudi Arabia, occupying 150,000 square miles on the Red Sea. Population, 2,000,000. Capital, Mecca.

He·ji·ra. Variant of **Hegira.**

Hek·a·te. Variant of **Hecate.**

Hek·la (hĕk'lə). An active volcano rising to 4,747 feet in southwestern Iceland.

Hel¹ (hĕl). *Norse Mythology.* The daughter of Loki and the goddess of death. [Old Norse *Hel.* See **kel-⁴** in Appendix.*]

Hel² (hĕl). *Norse Mythology.* The underworld for the dead not killed in battle. [After HEL.]

HEL Airport code for Helsinki, Finland.

held. Past tense and past participle of **hold.**

Hel·en (hĕl'ən). A feminine given name. [Old French *Helene,* from Latin *Helena,* from Greek *Helenē,* originally goddess of light, from *helenē,* "the bright one." See **swel-²** in Appendix.*]

Hel·e·na (hĕl'ə-nə). The capital of Montana, located in the west-central part of the state. Population, 20,000.

Helen of Troy. *Greek Mythology.* The daughter of Zeus and Leda and wife of Menelaus. Her abduction by Paris caused the Trojan War.

Hel·go·land (hĕl'gō-lănd'; *German* hĕl'gə-länt'). Also **Hel·i·go·land** (hĕl'ə-gō-lănd'). A small island, one-quarter square mile in area, in the North Sea off the western coast of Schleswig-Holstein, West Germany, near the scene of a British naval victory in World War I (1914).

he·li·a·cal (hĭ-lī'ə-kəl) *adj.* Of or pertaining to the sun; especially, rising and setting with the sun. [From Late Latin *hēliacus,* from Greek *hēliakos,* from *hēlios,* the sun. See **sāwel-** in Appendix.*]

hel·i·cal (hĕl'ĭ-kəl) *adj.* **1.** Having the shape of a helix. **2.** Having a shape approximating that of a helix. [From Greek *helix* (stem *helik-*), HELIX.] —**hel'i·cal·ly** *adv.*

he·lic·i·ty (hē-lĭs'ə-tē, hĕl-ĭs'-) *n. Physics.* The component of the spin of a particle along its direction of motion. [Greek *helix* (stem *helik-*), HELIX + -ITY.]

hel·i·coid (hĕl'ĭ-koid') *adj.* Arranged in or having the approximate shape of a flattened spiral. —*n. Geometry.* A surface generated by a plane curve or a twisted curve that is rotated about a linear axis and at the same time is translated in the direction of the axis so that the two rates have a constant ratio. [Greek *helikoeidēs* : HELIX + -OID (shaped).]

hel·i·con (hĕl'ĭ-kŏn', -kən) *n.* A large circular brass tuba that fits around the player's shoulder. [Perhaps from Greek *helix* (stem *helik-*), HELIX.]

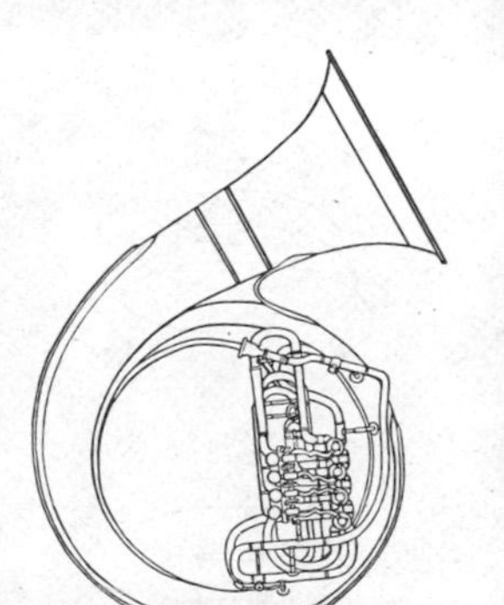

helicon

Hel·i·con (hĕl'ĭ-kŏn', -kən). A mountain rising to 5,738 feet in southwestern Boeotia, Greece; the home of the Muses in Greek mythology. [Greek *Helikōn,* "willow mountain," from *helikē,* willow, "winding," from *helix,* HELIX.]

hel·i·cop·ter (hĕl'ĭ-kŏp'tər) *n.* An aircraft that derives its lift from blades that rotate about an approximately vertical central axis. [French *hélicoptère,* "spiral wing" : Greek *helix* (stem *helik-*), HELIX + -PTER.]

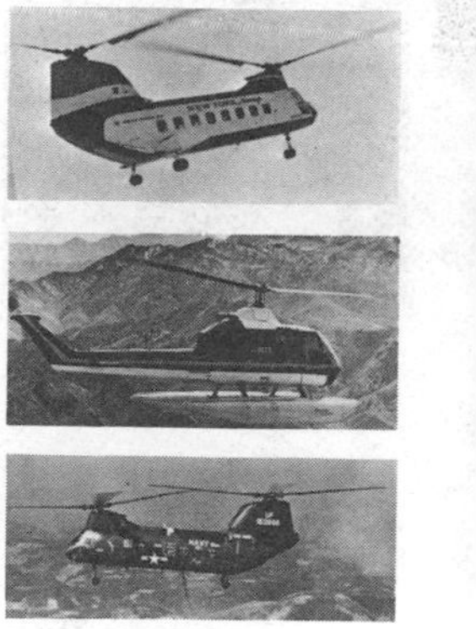

helicopter
From top to bottom:
Shuttle helicopter, executive helicopter, cargo helicopter

helio–. Indicates the sun or of or by the sun; for example, **heliograph, heliotrope.** [From Greek *hēlios,* the sun. See **sāwel-** in Appendix.*]

he·li·o·cen·tric (hē'lē-ō-sĕn'trĭk) *adj.* Also **he·li·o·cen·tri·cal** (-trĭ-kəl). **1.** Referred or relative to the sun. **2.** Having the sun as a center. —**he'li·o·cen·tric'i·ty** (-sĕn-trĭs'ə-tē) *n.*

He·li·o·gab·a·lus (hē'lē-ə-găb'ə-ləs) *n.* Also **El·a·gab·a·lus** (ĕl'ə-, ē'lə-). One likened to the Roman emperor Heliogabalus or Elagabalus, as in capricious profligacy or extravagance: *"Had I been a Sardanapulus, or a Heliogabalus, I think that . . . the great travel over the mountains had tamed me."* (Jeremy Taylor). [After *Heliogabalus,* adopted name of the emperor Varius Avitus Bassianus (A.D. 204–222); blend of Greek *hēlios,* sun (see **sāwel-** in Appendix*) and *Elagabalus,* latinized form of *Elagabal,* a Syrian sun god with whom the emperor identified himself.]

he·li·o·gram (hē'lē-ə-grăm') *n.* A message sent by heliograph. [HELIO- + -GRAM.]

he·li·o·graph (hē'lē-ə-grăf', -gräf') *n.* **1.** An apparatus once used to photograph the sun. **2.** A signaling apparatus that reflects sunlight with a movable mirror to flash coded messages. —*v.* **heliographed, -graphing, -graphs.** —*tr.* To transmit (messages) by heliograph. —*intr.* To signal by heliograph. [HELIO- + -GRAPH.] —**he'li·og'raph·er** (-ŏg'rə-fər) *n.* —**he'li·o·graph'ic** *adj.* —**he'li·og'raph·y** *n.*

he·li·o·gra·vure (hē'lē-ō-grə-vyo͝or') *n. Printing.* Photogravure.

he·li·om·e·ter (hē'lē-ŏm'ə-tər) *n.* A telescope equipped to measure small angular distances between celestial bodies. [French *héliomètre* : HELIO- + -METER.] —**he'li·o·met'ric** (-ə-mĕt'rĭk), **he'li·o·met'ri·cal** *adj.* —**he'li·om'e·try** *n.*

He·li·op·o·lis (hē'lē-ŏp'ə-lĭs). **1.** An ancient city of northern Egypt, in the Nile Delta region near Cairo. **2.** The ancient name for **Baalbek. 3.** *Arabic* **Masr-el-Ge·dI·da** (măs'ər-ĕl-jə-dē'də). A northeastern suburb of Cairo. Population, 125,000.

He·li·os (hē'lē-ŏs'). *Greek Mythology.* The sun god, son of Hyperion, depicted as driving his chariot across the sky from east to west daily. [Greek *Hēlios,* from *hēlios,* the sun. See **sāwel-** in Appendix.*]

he·li·o·stat (hē'lē-ə-stăt') *n.* An instrument in which a mirror is automatically moved so that it reflects sunlight in a constant direction. [New Latin *heliostata* : HELIO- + -STAT.]

he·li·o·tax·is (hē'lē-ə-tăk'sĭs) *n. Biology.* The movement of an organism in response to the light of the sun. [New Latin : HELIO- + -TAXIS.]

he·li·o·ther·a·py (hē'lē-ə-thĕr'ə-pē) *n.* Medical therapy involving exposure to sunlight.

he·li·o·trope (hē'lē-ə-trōp') *n.* **1.** Any of several plants of the genus *Heliotropium;* especially, *H. arborescens,* native to South America, having small, fragrant, purplish flowers. **2.** The **garden heliotrope** *(see).* **3.** Any of various plants that turn toward the sun. **4. Bloodstone** *(see).* **5.** Moderate, light, or brilliant violet to moderate or deep reddish purple. See **color.** —*adj.* Being heliotrope in color. [New Latin *Heliotropium,* from Latin *hēliotropium,* from Greek *hēliotropion,* sundial, bloodstone, heliotrope : HELIO- + *tropos,* a turning (see **trope**).]

he·li·o·trop·ic (hē'lē-ə-trŏp'ĭk, -trō'pĭk) *adj.* Pertaining to, characterized, or affected by heliotropism. [HELIO- + -TROPIC.] —**he'li·o·trop'i·cal·ly** *adv.*

hel·i·o·trop·in (hē'lē-ə-trō'pĭn, -ŏt'rə-pĭn') *n. Chemistry.* **Piperonal** *(see).* [New Latin *Heliotropium,* HELIOTROPE + -IN.]

he·li·ot·ro·pism (hē'lē-ŏt'rə-pĭz'əm) *n. Biology.* Growth or movement of an organism toward or away from the light of the sun. [HELIO- + -TROPISM.]

he·li·o·type (hē'lē-ə-tīp') *n.* Also **he·li·o·typ·y** (-tī'pē) (for sense 2). *Printing.* **1.** A photomechanically produced plate for pictures or type made by exposing a gelatin film under a negative, hardening it with chrome alum, and printing directly from it. **2.** The process of producing such a plate. —*tr.v.* **heliotyped, -typing, -types.** To produce a heliotype of. —**he'li·o·typ'ic** (-tĭp'ĭk) *adj.*

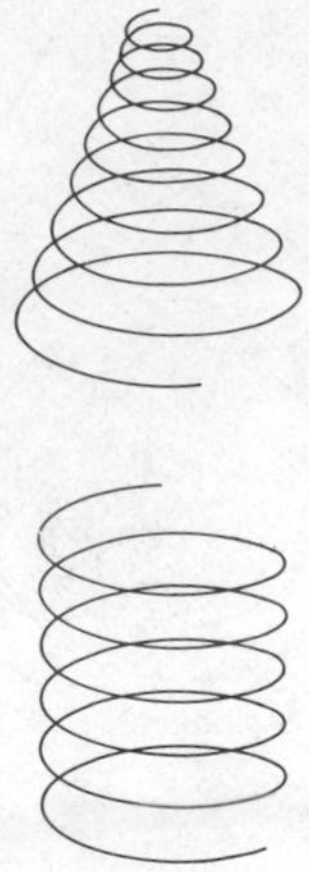

helix
Above: Conical helix
Below: Cylindrical helix

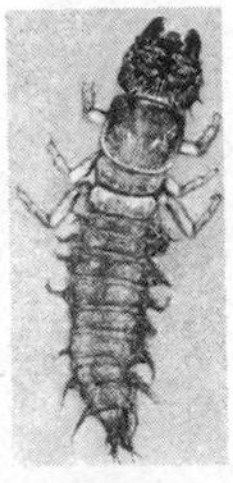

hellgrammite

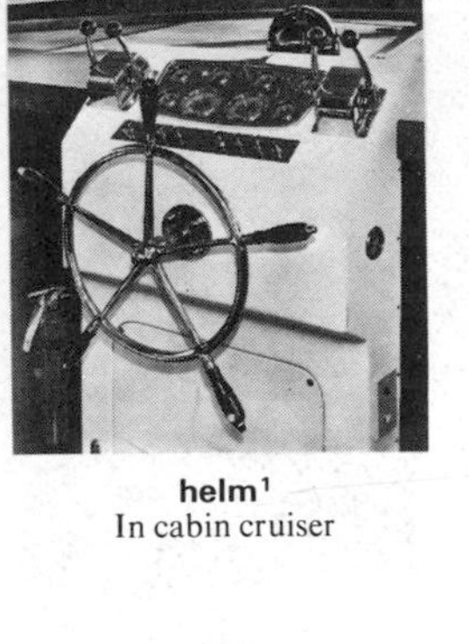

helm[1]
In cabin cruiser

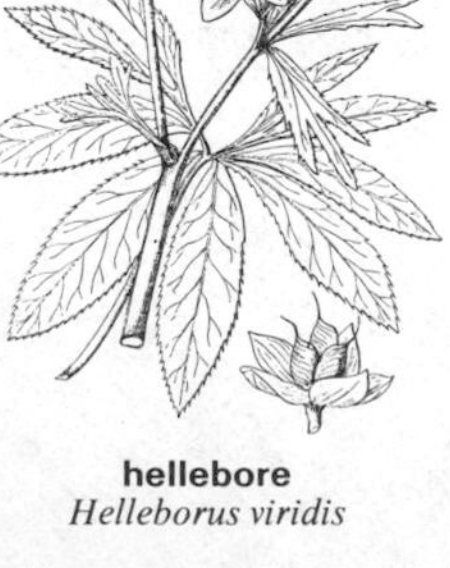

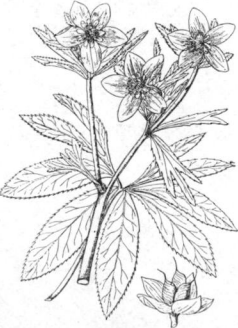

hellebore
Helleborus viridis

he·li·o·zo·an (hē′lē-ə-zō′ən) *n.* Any of various aquatic protozoans of the order Heliozoa, having numerous stiff, radiating pseudopodia. [New Latin *Heliozoa* : HELIO- + -ZOAN.]

hel·i·port (hĕl′ə-pôrt′, -pōrt′) *n.* An airport for helicopters. [HELI(COPTER) + -PORT.]

he·li·um (hē′lē-əm) *n. Symbol* **He** A colorless, odorless, tasteless, inert gaseous element used to inflate and so provide lift for balloons, as an inert component of various artificial atmospheres, in gaseous laser media, and as a superfluid in the form of helium II for extensive cryogenic research. Atomic number 2, atomic weight 4.0026, boiling point −268.6°C, liquid density at boiling point 7.62 pounds per cubic foot. [New Latin, from Greek *hēlios,* the sun (the element was first discovered in an examination of the solar spectrum). See **sāwel-** in Appendix.*]

helium I. *Symbol* **He** I Liquid helium existing as a normal fluid between the superfluid transition point of approximately 2.178°K at 1 atmosphere pressure and its boiling point of 4.2°K.

helium II. *Symbol* **He** II Liquid helium existing as a superfluid below the transition point of approximately 2.178°K at 1 atmosphere and having extremely low viscosity and extremely high thermal conductivity.

he·lix (hē′lĭks) *n., pl.* **-lixes** or **helices** (hĕl′ə-sēz′, hē′lə-). **1.** *Geometry.* A three-dimensional curve that lies on a cylinder or cone and cuts the elements at a constant angle. **2.** Any spiral form or structure. **3.** *Anatomy.* The folded rim of skin and cartilage around the outer ear. **4.** *Architecture.* A volute on a Corinthian or Ionic capital. [Latin, from Greek, spiral, spiral object. See **wel-**[3] in Appendix.*]

hell (hĕl) *n.* **1.** The abode of the dead; the underworld where departed souls were believed to dwell; specifically, in the Hebrew Scriptures, Sheol, and in Greco-Roman tradition, Hades. **2.** The abode of condemned souls and devils; the place or state of torture and punishment for the wicked after death, presided over by Satan. **3.** The infernal powers of evil and darkness. **4.** A place or state of great iniquity, misery, discord, or destruction. **5. a.** Torment; anguish. **b.** Something that causes agony. **6.** *Capital* **H.** *Christian Science.* Mortal belief; sin or error. **7.** *Archaic.* A gambling house. **8. a.** A tailor's receptacle for discarded material. **b.** A hellbox. **—a** (or **one**) **hell of a.** *Informal.* Unusually (bad, good, hard, easy, or the like): *"It's a charming town, with a hell of a hotel . . . the worst hotel in Australia."* (Mark Twain). **—be hell for.** To be fanatically concerned about or insistent upon: *He's hell for punctuality.* **—be hell on.** *Informal.* **1.** To be very painful or unpleasant for. **2.** To be very rough or damaging to. **—catch** (or **get**) **hell.** *Slang.* To receive harsh punishment or scolding for. **—give (someone) hell.** *Informal.* **1.** To upbraid sharply. **2.** To inflict harm upon: *"We have met the enemy and given them hell."* (O.W. Norton). **—hell and (or) high water.** *Informal.* Troubles or difficulties of whatever magnitude: *We're staying, come hell or high water.* **—hell to pay.** *Informal.* Bad trouble to be faced: *If he's late, there'll be hell to pay.* **—like hell.** *Informal.* **1. a.** Violently; excessively: *He was swearing like hell.* **b.** To the utmost possible capacity or extent: *drive like hell.* **2.** Most assuredly not; never. Used for emphasis in rejecting a possibility. **—play hell with.** *Slang.* To wreak havoc with. **—raise hell.** *Slang.* To cause a disturbance, trouble, or uproar: *"Kansas had better stop raising corn and begin raising hell."* (Mary Elizabeth Lease). **—to hell and gone.** *Informal.* Extremely or inaccessibly far away: *The line parted and the boat was carried to hell and gone.* **—what the hell.** *Informal.* Used to express indifference or resignation. **—***intr. v.* **helled, helling, hells.** *Informal.* **1.** To carouse or behave riotously. Used chiefly with *around: out all night helling around.* **2.** To drive at high speed: *A jeep came helling down to the pier.* **—***interj. Slang.* Used to express acute anger, disgust, or impatience. [Middle English *hel(l),* Old English *hel(l).* See **kel-**[4] in Appendix.*]

he'll (hēl). **1.** Contraction of *he will.* **2.** Contraction of *he shall.*

Hel·lad·ic (hĕ-lăd′ĭk) *adj.* Of or pertaining to the Bronze Age culture on the mainland of Greece prior to 1100 B.C. [Latin *Helladicus,* from Greek *Helladikos,* from *Hellas* (stem *Hellad-*), HELLAS.]

Hel·las. The Greek name for **Greece.** [Greek, from *Hellēn*†, eponymous ancestor of the Greeks.]

hell·bend·er (hĕl′bĕn′dər) *n.* A large aquatic salamander, *Cryptobranchus alleganiensis,* of eastern and central North America.

hell-bent (hĕl′bĕnt′) *adj.* Impetuously or recklessly bent on doing, reaching, or achieving something. Used with *on* or *for.* **—***adv.* Recklessly and determinedly.

hell·box (hĕl′bŏks′) *n.* A printer's receptacle for broken or discarded type.

hell·cat (hĕl′kăt′) *n.* **1.** A furious and evil woman; vixen; witch. **2.** A fiendish person.

hell·div·er (hĕl′dī′vər) *n. Informal.* A New World grebe, *Podilymbus podiceps.*

Hel·le (hĕl′ē). *Greek Mythology.* The daughter of a Greek king who, while fleeing with her brother from their stepmother, drowned in the Hellespont, thereafter named for her.

hel·le·bore (hĕl′ə-bôr′, -bōr′) *n.* **1.** Any of various plants of the genus *Helleborus,* native to Eurasia, most species of which are poisonous. See **Christmas rose. 2.** Any of various plants of the genus *Veratrum;* especially, *V. viride,* of North America, having large leaves and greenish flowers, and yielding a toxic alkaloid used medicinally. In this sense, also called "false hellebore," "Indian poke." [Middle English *ellebre,* from Old French, from Latin *elleborous,* from Greek *(h)elleboros,* perhaps "eaten by fawns" : *(h)ellos,* fawn (see **el-**[2] in Appendix*) + *-boros,* eaten, from *bibrōskein,* to eat, devour (see **gwerə-**[2] in Appendix*).]

hel·le·bor·in (hĕl′ə-bôr′ən, -bōr′ən, hə-lĕb′ər-ən) *n.* A poisonous compound, $C_{28}H_{36}O_6$, extracted from a species of hellebore, *Helleborus viridis.* [HELLEBOR(E) + -IN.]

Hel·lene (hĕl′ēn′) *n.* Also **Hel·le·ni·an** (hĕ-lē′nē-ən). A Greek. [From Greek *Hellēn.* See **Hellas.**]

Hel·len·ic (hĕ-lĕn′ĭk) *adj.* Of or relating to the ancient Greeks or their language. **—***n.* The Greek language in both its early and modern forms; Greek.

Hel·le·nism (hĕl′ə-nĭz′əm) *n.* **1.** An idiom, custom, or the like peculiar to the Greeks. **2.** The civilization and culture of ancient Greece. **3.** The adoption of Greek ideas, style, or culture. **4.** Greek nationalism.

Hel·le·nist (hĕl′ə-nĭst) *n.* **1.** One in classical times who adopted the Greek language and culture, particularly a Jew of the Diaspora. **2.** A devotee or student of Greek civilization, language, or literature.

Hel·le·nis·tic (hĕl′ə-nĭs′tĭk) *adj.* Also **Hel·le·nis·ti·cal** (-tĭ-kəl). **1.** Relating to the Hellenists. **2.** Of or relating to Greek history and culture from the time of Alexander the Great into the first century B.C. **3.** Pertaining to or in the style of the Greek art or architecture of this period.

Hel·le·nize (hĕl′ə-nīz′) *v.* **-nized, -nizing, -nizes. —***intr.* To adopt Greek ways and speech; become Greek. **—***tr.* To make Greek; Grecize. **—Hel′le·ni·za′tion** *n.* **—Hel′le·niz′er** *n.*

hel·ler[1] (hĕl′ər) *n., pl.* **heller.** One of several coins of small denomination formerly used in Austria and Germany. [German *Heller,* from Middle High German *heller, haller,* HALER.]

hel·ler[2] (hĕl′ər) *n. Regional.* A person who behaves recklessly or wildly. [From HELL.]

Hel·les, Cape (hĕl′əs). A promontory in Turkey at the southern extremity of the Gallipoli Peninsula.

Hel·les·pont. The ancient name for the **Dardanelles.**

hell·fire (hĕl′fīr′) *n.* The fires, torment, or punishment of hell: *"The combined threat of hellfire and ugliness is too much for her"* (Katherine Griffith McDonald). **—***adj.* Preaching or zealously believing in the torments of hell: *an old-time hellfire preacher.*

hell-fired (hĕl′fīrd′) *adj. Regional & Informal.* Extremely; very: *She is so hell-fired inquisitive.*

hell-for-leath·er (hĕl′fər-lĕth′ər) *adv. Informal.* At breakneck speed: *"The journey back he made along the coast road, traveling hell-for-leather."* (Idival Jones). **—***adj.* Characterized by audacious speed, power, and resolution.

Hell Gate. A narrow channel of the East River, New York City, between Manhattan and Long Island.

hell·gram·mite (hĕl′grə-mīt′) *n.* The large, brownish, aquatic larva of the dobson fly, often used as fishing bait. Sometimes called "dobson." [Origin unknown.]

hell·hole (hĕl′hōl′) *n.* **1.** A hellish place, especially one of extreme wretchedness and squalor. **2.** A place characterized as hellish by reason of riotousness or lewdness supposedly prevailing there. **3.** *Obsolete.* The pit of hell.

hell·hound (hĕl′hound′) *n.* **1.** A hound of hell; especially, Cerberus, watchdog of Hades. **2.** A devilish person; fiend.

hel·lion (hĕl′yən) *n. Informal.* A mischievous, unrestrainable person, especially a young person or child. [Probably altered from dialectal *hallion*†, scurvy person.]

hell·ish (hĕl′ĭsh) *adj.* **1.** Of or relating to hell. **2.** *Informal.* Like or worthy of hell; fiendish; devilish. **—hell′ish·ly** *adv.* **—hell′ish·ness** *n.*

hel·lo (hĕ-lō′, hə-) *interj.* Also **hul·lo** (hə-). **1.** An informal expression used to greet another, answer the telephone, or summon attention. **2.** Used to express surprise. **—***n., pl.* **hel·loes.** Also **hul·lo.** A calling or greeting of "hello." **—***v.* **helloed, -loing, -loes.** Also **hul·lo. —***tr.* To say or call "hello" to. **—***intr.* To call "hello." [Variant of earlier *holla,* stop!, probably from French *holà.* See **holler.**]

Hells Canyon. A gorge of the Snake River extending for 125 miles on the Idaho-Oregon boundary and attaining a maximum depth of 7,900 feet. Also called "Grand Canyon of the Snake."

helm[1] (hĕlm) *n.* **1.** *Nautical.* The tiller or wheel or the whole steering gear of a ship. **2.** A position of leadership or control. **—***tr.v.* **helmed, helming, helms.** To take the helm of; steer; to guide. [Middle English *helme,* Old English *helma.* See **kelp-** in Appendix.*]

helm[2] (hĕlm) *n. Archaic.* A helmet. **—***tr.v.* **helmed, helming, helms.** To cover or furnish with a helmet. [Middle English *helm(e), healm,* Old English *helm.* See **kel-**[4] in Appendix.*]

Hel·mand (hĕl′mənd). Also **Hil·mand** (hĭl′-). A river of Afghanistan, rising 35 miles west of Kabul and flowing 700 miles generally southwest to the Iranian border.

hel·met (hĕl′mĭt) *n.* **1.** A piece of ancient, medieval, or modern armor, usually of metal, designed to protect the head. **2. a.** A head covering of hard material, such as leather, metal, or plastic, worn by policemen, firemen, cyclists, and others to protect the head. **b.** The headgear with a glass mask worn by deep-sea divers. **c.** A pith helmet; topi. **d.** Any hat having the shape of a helmet. **3.** *Botany.* The hood-shaped sepal or corolla of some flowers. **—***tr.v.* **helmeted, -meting, -mets.** To provide with or don a helmet. [Middle English, from Old French, diminutive of *helme, heaume,* helmet, from Frankish *helm* (unattested). See **kel-**[4] in Appendix.*] **—hel′met·ed** *adj.*

Helm·holtz (hĕlm′hōlts′), Baron **Hermann Ludwig Ferdinand von.** 1821–1894. German physician, physicist, mathematician, and philosopher.

hel·minth (hĕl′mĭnth′) *n.* A worm; especially, a parasitic intestinal nematode or trematode worm. [Greek *helmi(n)s* (stem *helminth-*), parasitic worm. See **wel-**[3] in Appendix.*]

ă pat/ā pay/âr care/ä father/b bib/ch church/d deed/ĕ pet/ē be/f fife/g gag/h hat/hw which/ĭ pit/ī pie/îr pier/j judge/k kick/l lid, needle/m mum/n no, sudden/ng thing/ŏ pot/ō toe/ô paw, for/oi noise/ou out/o͝o took/o͞o boot/p pop/r roar/s sauce/sh ship, dish/

hel·min·thi·a·sis (hĕl'mĭn-thī'ə-sĭs) *n.* A disease, worms. See **worm**. [New Latin : HELMINTH + -IASIS.]

hel·min·thic (hĕl-mĭn'thĭk) *adj.* **1.** Of or pertaining to worms, especially parasitic intestinal worms. **2.** Tending to expel worms; anthelmintic. —*n.* A vermifuge or anthelmintic.

hel·min·thol·o·gy (hĕl'mĭn-thŏl'ə-jē) *n.* The scientific study of worms, especially parasitic worms. [HELMINTH + -LOGY.] —**hel'min·thol'o·gist** *n.*

Hel·mont (hĕl'mŏnt'), **Jan Baptista van.** 1577?–1644? Flemish alchemist and physician; experimented with gases.

helms·man (hĕlmz'mən) *n.*, *pl.* **-men** (-mĭn). One who steers a ship.

Hé·lo·ise (ā-lō-ēz'). 1101?–1164? The beloved of Abelard.

hel·ot (hĕl'ət, hē'lət) *n.* **1.** *Capital H.* One of a class of serfs in ancient Sparta, neither a slave nor a free citizen. **2.** A serf; bondsman. [Latin *Hēlōtes*, serfs, helots, from Greek *Heilōtes*, plural of *Heilōs†.*]

hel·ot·ism (hĕl'ə-tĭz'əm, hē'lə-) *n.* A system under which a nominally free social class or religious, national, or racial minority is permanently oppressed and degraded: *"Lamenting over the helotism of Ireland"* (Blackwood's Magazine).

hel·ot·ry (hĕl'ə-trē, hē'lə-) *n.* **1.** The condition of serfdom. **2.** The Helots as a class.

help (hĕlp) *v.* **helped** or *archaic* **holp** (hōlp), **helped** or *archaic* **holpen** (hōl'pən), **helping, helps.** —*tr.* **1. a.** To give assistance to; to aid: *I helped her find the book.* **b.** To give a hand to assist (another in some action). Used elliptically with a preposition or an adverb: *He helped her into her coat.* **2.** To contribute to in some way; to further; promote. **3.** To give relief to (those in difficulty or distress); succor. **4.** To alleviate or cure. **5.** To improve; benefit. **6.** To be able to prevent, change, or rectify. Used with *can* or *cannot: I cannot help her laziness.* See Usage note below. **7.** To refrain from; avoid. Used with *can* or *cannot: He cannot help laughing.* See Usage note below. **8.** To wait on; serve in a shop or at a table. —*intr.* To be of use or service; give assistance; aid. —See Synonyms at **improve.** —**cannot help but.** To be compelled to; unable to avoid or resist: *He cannot help but do what they ask.* See Usage note below. —**help oneself to. 1.** To serve oneself. **2.** To take (something) without asking permission. —**help out.** To help with a problem or difficulty. —**so help me God.** An oath used in solemn affirmation of what one has declared. —*n.* **1. a.** The act of helping. **b.** Aid; assistance. **2.** Relief; remedy. **3.** Succor. **4. a.** One that helps. **b.** The assistance given or services rendered. **5. a.** A person employed to assist; especially, a farm worker or a domestic servant. **b.** Such employees collectively. **6.** *Rare.* A helping. [Middle English *helpen*, Old English *helpan.* See **kelb-** in Appendix.*] —**help'er** *n.*

Synonyms: help, aid, assist, succor. These verbs mean to contribute to the fulfillment of a need or to the achievement of a purpose or end. *Help* and *aid*, the most general, are frequently interchangeable, though *help* sometimes conveys a stronger suggestion of effectual action. *Assist* usually implies making a secondary contribution or acting as a subordinate. *Succor* refers to going to the relief of one in want or distress.

Usage: The construction *cannot help but* is a less formal variant of *cannot help* plus gerund and of *cannot but* plus infinitive without *to.* All three express substantially the same idea: *One cannot help but admire his courage. One cannot help admiring his courage. One cannot but admire his courage.* All three forms are well established, but the last two are frequently preferred in formal writing and speech. The first example, employing *cannot help but,* is acceptable on the formal level to only 42 per cent of the Usage Panel.

help·ful (hĕlp'fəl) *adj.* Providing help; useful; beneficial. —**help'ful·ly** *adv.* —**help'ful·ness** *n.*

help·ing (hĕl'pĭng) *n.* A portion of food for one person.

help·less (hĕlp'lĭs) *adj.* **1.** Unable to manage by oneself; defenseless; dependent. **2.** Lacking power or strength; impotent; ineffectual. **3.** Without help. **4.** Unable to be remedied. —**help'less·ly** *adv.* —**help'less·ness** *n.*

help·mate (hĕlp'māt') *n.* A helper or helpful companion, particularly a spouse. [HELP + MATE (influenced by HELPMEET).]

help·meet (hĕlp'mēt') *n.* A helpmate. [From *I will make an help meet for him* (Genesis 2:18, 20), "I will make a help suitable for him" : HELP + MEET (suitable).]

Hel·sing·ør. The Danish name for **Elsinore.**

Hel·sin·ki (hĕl'sĭng'kē). *Swedish* **Hel·sing·fors** (hĕl'sĭng-fôrs', -fôsh'). The capital of Finland, a Baltic port in the south on the Gulf of Finland. Population, 470,000.

hel·ter-skel·ter (hĕl'tər-skĕl'tər) *adv.* **1.** In disorderly haste; pell-mell. **2.** In confusion. **3.** Haphazardly. —*adj.* **1.** Carelessly hurried and confused. **2.** Haphazard. —*n.* Chaos; confusion. [Origin uncertain.]

helve (hĕlv) *n.* A handle of a wagon or tool, such as an ax, chisel, or hammer. —*tr.v.* **helved, helving, helves.** To put a handle on. [Middle English *helve, hilf,* Old English *hielf(e).* See **kelp-** in Appendix.*]

Hel·ve·tia. The Latin name for **Switzerland.**

Hel·ve·tian (hĕl-vē'shən) *adj.* **1.** Of or relating to the Helvetii. **2.** Swiss. —*n.* **1.** One of the Helvetii. **2.** A Swiss. [From Latin *Helvētius,* of the Helvetii, from *Helvētiī,* HELVETII.]

Hel·vet·ic (hĕl-vĕt'ĭk) *adj.* Helvetian; Swiss. —*n.* A Swiss Protestant; Zwinglian.

Hel·ve·ti·i (hĕl-vē'shē-ī') *pl.n.* A Celtic people inhabiting Helvetia during the time of Julius Caesar.

hem¹ (hĕm) *n.* **1.** An edge or border of a piece of cloth; especially, a finished edge for a garment, curtain, or the like, made by folding the selvage or raw edge under and stitching it down.

2. The height or level of the hem of a skirt or dress. Also called "hemline." —*tr.v.* **hemmed, hemming, hems. 1.** To fold back and stitch down the edge of. **2.** To encircle and confine; enclose; shut in. Used with *in, about,* or *around: hemmed in by mountains.* [Middle English *hem(m),* Old English *hem(m).* See **kem-²** in Appendix.*] —**hem'mer** *n.*

hem² (hĕm) *n.* A short cough or clearing of the throat made to gain attention, warn, fill a pause in speech, hide embarrassment, or the like. Often used as an interjection. —*intr.v.* **hemmed, hemming, hems. 1.** To utter this sound. **2.** To hesitate in speaking. —**hem and haw.** To be hesitant and indecisive; be noncommittal. [Imitative.]

hema-. Variant of **hemo-.**

he·ma·cy·tom·e·ter (hē'mə-sī-tŏm'ə-tər, hĕm'ə-) *n.* An instrument for estimating the number of blood cells in a measured volume of blood. Also called "erythrocytometer." [HEMA- + CYTO- + -METER.]

he·mag·glu·tin·ate (hē'mə-glōōt'n-āt', hĕm'ə-) *tr.v.* **-ated, -ating, -ates.** To cause agglutination of red blood cells. [HEM(O)- + AGGLUTINATE.]

he·mag·glu·ti·na·tion (hē'mə-glōōt'n-ā'shən, hĕm'ə-) *n.* The agglutination of red blood cells by hemagglutinin.

he·mag·glu·ti·nin (hē'mə-glōōt'n-ən, hĕm'ə-) *n.* An antibody that causes agglutination of red blood cells containing or coated with the corresponding antigen. [HEMO- + AGGLUTININ.]

he·ma·gogue (hē'mə-gôg', -gŏg', hĕm'ə-) *n.* Also **he·ma·gog.** An agent that promotes the flow of blood, especially in menstruation. [HEM(O)- + -AGOG(UE).]

he·mal (hē'məl) *adj.* **1.** Of or pertaining to the blood or blood vessels. **2.** Relating to or located on or in the side of the body that contains the heart. [HEM(O)- + -AL.]

he-man (hē'măn') *n.*, *pl.* **-men** (-mĕn'). *Informal.* A strong, muscular, virile man.

he·ma·te·in (hē'mə-tē'ən, hĕm'ə-) *n.* A dark-purple crystalline compound, $C_{16}H_{12}O_6$, used as an indicator and as a biological stain. [HEMAT(O)- + -ein, variant of -IN.]

he·mat·ic (hĭ-măt'ĭk) *adj.* Of, pertaining to, resembling, containing, or acting on blood. —*n. Medicine.* A remedy for anemia or other blood diseases. [Greek *haimatikos,* from *haima* (stem *haimat-*), blood. See **hemo-.**]

hem·a·tin (hĕm'ə-tən, hē'mə-) *n.* A blue to blackish-brown powder, $C_{34}H_{32}N_4O_4 \cdot FeOH$, that is the hydroxide of heme, containing ferric iron. [HEMAT(O)- + -IN.]

hem·a·tin·ic (hĕm'ə-tĭn'ĭk, hē'mə-) *adj.* Acting to improve the blood. —*n.* A hematinic drug. [HEMATIN + -IC.]

hem·a·tite (hĕm'ə-tīt', hē'mə-) *n.* A blackish-red to brick-red mineral, essentially Fe_2O_3, the chief ore of iron. [Latin *haematitēs,* from Greek *(lithos) haimatitēs,* "bloodlike (stone)," red iron ore, from *haima* (stem *haimat-*), blood. See **hemo-.**]

hemato-, hemat-. Indicates blood; for example, **hematology, hematin.** [Greek *haimato-,* from *haima* (stem *haimat-*), blood.]

hem·a·to·blast (hĕm'ə-tō-blăst', hē'mə-) *n.* **1.** A platelet of the blood. **2.** An immature blood cell. [HEMATO- + -BLAST.] —**hem'a·to·blas'tic** *adj.*

hem·a·to·cele (hĕm'ə-tō-sēl', hē'mə-) *n.* A hemorrhage contained within a membranous cavity. [HEMATO- + -CELE.]

hem·a·to·crit (hĕm'ə-tō-krĭt', hē'mə-) *n.* A centrifuge used to separate the cellular and other particulate matter of blood from the plasma. [HEMATO- + Greek *kritēs,* judge, from *krinein,* to separate, decide, judge (see **skeri-** in Appendix*).]

hem·a·to·gen·e·sis (hĕm'ə-tō-jĕn'ə-sĭs, hē'mə-) *n.* **Hematopoiesis** *(see).* [HEMATO- + -GENESIS.] —**hem'a·to·gen'ic, hem'a·to·ge·net'ic** (-jə-nĕt'ĭk) *adj.*

he·ma·tog·e·nous (hē'mə-tŏj'ə-nəs, hĕm'ə-) *adj.* **1.** Producing blood. **2.** Originating in the blood. [HEMATO- + -GENOUS.]

he·ma·toid (hē'mə-toid', hĕm'ə-) *adj.* **1.** Bloody. **2.** Like blood. [Greek **haimatoeidēs** : HEMAT(O)- + -OID.]

he·ma·tol·o·gy (hē'mə-tŏl'ə-jē, hĕm'ə-) *n.* Also **he·ma·to·lo·gi·a** (-tə-lō'jē-ə). The science encompassing the generation, anatomy, physiology, pathology, and therapeutics of blood. [HEMATO- + -LOGY.] —**he'ma·to·log'i·cal** (-tə-lŏj'ĭ-kəl) *adj.* —**he'ma·to·log'i·cal·ly** *adv.* —**he'ma·tol'o·gist** *n.*

he·ma·tol·y·sis (hē'mə-tŏl'ə-sĭs, hĕm'ə-) *n. Biology.* **Hemolysis** *(see).* [New Latin : HEMATO- + -LYSIS.]

he·ma·to·ma (hē'mə-tō'mə, hĕm'ə-) *n.*, *pl.* **-mas** or **-mata** (-mə-tə). *Pathology.* A localized swelling filled with blood. [New Latin : HEMAT(O)- + -OMA.]

hem·a·to·poi·e·sis (hē'mə-tō-poi-ē'sĭs, hĕm'ə-) *n.* The formation of blood in the body. Also called "hematogenesis," "hemopoiesis." [New Latin : HEMATO- + -POIESIS.] —**hem'a·to·poi·et'ic** (-ĕt'ĭk) *adj.*

he·ma·to·sis (hē'mə-tō'sĭs, hĕm'ə-) *n.* Oxygenation of venous blood in the lungs. [HEMAT(O)- + -OSIS.]

hem·a·tox·y·lin (hĕm'ə-tŏk'sə-lən, hē'mə-) *n.* A yellow or red crystalline compound, $C_{16}H_{14}O_6 \cdot 3H_2O$, the coloring principle of logwood, used in dyes, inks, and stains. [New Latin *Haematoxyl(on)* (plant genus) : *haemato-,* variant of HEMATO- + XYL(O)- + -IN.]

hem·a·to·zo·on (hĕm'ə-tə-zo'ŏn', hē'mə-) *n.*, *pl.* **-zoa** (-zō'ə). A parasitic protozoan or similar organism that lives in the blood. [New Latin : HEMATO- + -ZOON.]

hem·a·tu·ri·a (hĕm'ə-tyŏŏr'ē-ə, -tyŏr'ē-ə, hē'mə-) *n.* A condition in which there is blood or red blood cells in the urine. [New Latin : HEMAT(O)- + -URIA.]

heme (hēm) *n.* The nonprotein, ferrous-iron-containing component of hemoglobin, having composition $C_{34}H_{32}FeN_4O_4$. [From HEMATIN.]

hem·el·y·tron (hĕ-mĕl'ə-trŏn') *n.*, *pl.* **-tra** (-trə). Also **hem·i·el·y·tron** (hĕm'ē-ĕl'ə-trŏn'). An insect forewing that is thickened

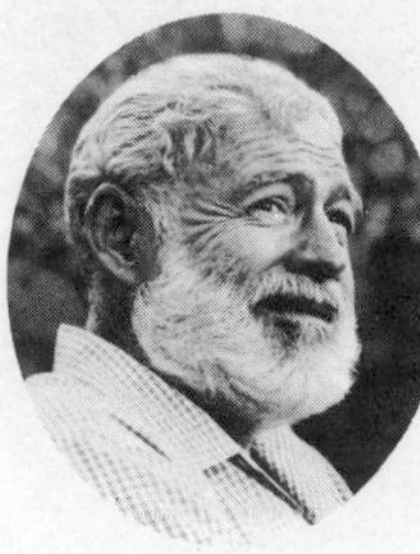
Ernest Hemingway

at the base and membranous at the apex, characteristic of the true bugs. [HEM(I)- + ELYTRON.]
hem·er·a·lo·pi·a (hĕm′ər-ə-lō′pē-ə) *n.* A visual defect manifested as the inability to see as clearly in bright light as in dim light. Also called "day blindness." Compare **nyctalopia.** [New Latin, from Greek *hēmeralōps,* "day blind" : *hēmera,* day (see **amer-** in Appendix*) + *alaos*†, blind + -OPIA.]
hemi–, hem–. Indicates half; for example, **hemichordate, hemelytron.** [Latin *hēmi-,* from Greek. See **sēmi-** in Appendix.*]
–hemia. Variant of **-emia.**
hem·i·al·gi·a (hĕm′ē-ăl′jē-ə) *n.* Pain affecting one entire half of the body. [New Latin : HEMI- + -ALGIA.]
he·mic (hē′mĭk, hĕm′ĭk) *adj.* Of blood. [HEM(O)- + -IC.]
hem·i·cel·lu·lose (hĕm′ĭ-sĕl′yə-lōs′) *n.* Any of several polysaccharides that are more complex than a sugar and less complex than cellulose, derived from plants and produced commercially from corn grain hulls.
hem·i·chor·date (hĕm′ĭ-kôr′dāt′) *n.* Any of various wormlike marine animals of the phylum or subphylum Hemichordata, having a primitive notochord and gill slits. —*adj.* Of or belonging to the Hemichordata. [New Latin *Hemichordata* : HEMI- + CHORDATE.]
hem·i·cy·cle (hĕm′ĭ-sī′kəl) *n.* A semicircular structure or arrangement. [French *hémicycle,* from Latin *hēmicyclium,* from Greek *hēmikuklion* : HEMI- + *kuklos,* circle, CYCLE.]
hem·i·dem·i·sem·i·qua·ver (hĕm′ē-dĕm′ē-sĕm′ē-kwā′vər) *n. Music. Chiefly British.* A **sixty-fourth note** *(see).* [HEMI- + DEMISEMIQUAVER.]
hem·i·he·dral (hĕm′ĭ-hē′drəl) *adj.* Exhibiting only half the faces required for complete symmetry. Said of a crystal. [HEMI- + -HEDR(ON) + -AL.]
hem·i·hy·drate (hĕm′ĭ-hī′drāt′) *n.* A hydrate in which the molecular ratio of water molecules to anhydrous compound is 1:2. [HEMI- + HYDRATE.] —**hem′i·hy′drat′ed** *adj.*
hem·i·mor·phic (hĕm′ĭ-môr′fĭk) *adj.* Asymmetric at the axial ends. [HEMI- + -MORPHIC.]
hem·i·mor·phite (hĕm′ĭ-môr′fīt′) *n. Mineralogy.* **Calamine** *(see).* [HEMIMORPH(IC) + -ITE.]
he·min (hē′mən) *n.* A brown or blue crystalline compound, $C_{34}H_{32}N_4O_4FeCl$, that is the chloride of heme and is used in identifying blood stains. [HEM(O)- + -IN.]
Hem·ing·way (hĕm′ĭng-wā′), **Ernest (Miller).** 1899–1961. American novelist.
hem·i·par·a·site (hĕm′ĭ-păr′ə-sīt′) *n.* An organism that is partially parasitic. Also called "semiparasite."
hem·i·ple·gi·a (hĕm′ĭ-plē′jē-ə) *n.* Paralysis of one side of the body only. [New Latin, from Middle Greek *hēmiplēgia* : HEMI- + -PLEGIA.] —**hem′i·ple′gic** (-plē′jĭk, -plĕj′ĭk) *adj.*

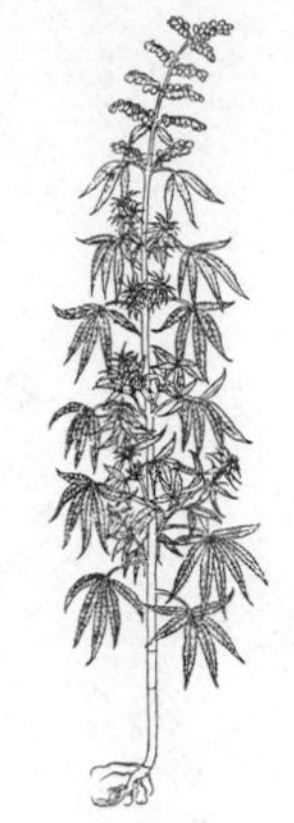
hemp
Cannabis sativa

he·mip·ter·an (hĭ-mĭp′tər-ən) *n.* Also **he·mip·ter·on** (-tə-rŏn′). A hemipterous insect. —*adj.* Of or belonging to the Hemiptera; hemipterous. [From New Latin *Hemiptera* : HEMI- + -PTER.]
he·mip·ter·ous (hĭ-mĭp′tər-əs) *adj.* Of or belonging to the Hemiptera, a large group of insects that includes the true bugs of the order Heteroptera and their allies of the order Homoptera. [New Latin *Hemiptera* : HEMI- + -PTER + -OUS.]
hem·i·sphere (hĕm′ə-sfîr′) *n.* **1. a.** A half of a sphere bounded by a great circle. **b.** A half of a symmetric, approximately spherical object as divided by a plane of symmetry: *cerebral hemisphere.* **2.** Either half of the celestial sphere, as divided by the ecliptic, the celestial equator, or the horizon. **3.** Either the northern or southern half of the earth as divided by the equator, or the eastern or western half as divided by a meridian. [Middle English *(h)emisper(i)e,* from Latin *hēmisphaerium,* from Greek *hēmisphairion* : HEMI- + *sphairion,* diminutive of *sphaira,* SPHERE.] —**hem′i·spher′ic** (-sfîr′ĭk, -sfĕr′ĭk), **hem′i·spher′i·cal** *adj.* —**hem′i·spher′i·cal·ly** *adv.*

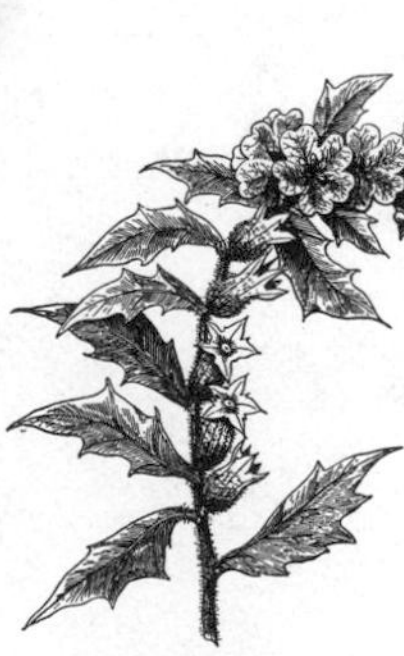
henbane

hem·i·stich (hĕm′ĭ-stĭk′) *n. Prosody.* **1.** Half a line of verse, especially when separated rhythmically from the rest of the line by a caesura. **2.** An incomplete or imperfect line of verse. [Latin *hēmistichium,* from Greek *hēmistikhion* : HEMI- + *stikhos,* line (see **steigh-** in Appendix*).]
hem·line (hĕm′līn′) *n.* A **hem** *(see).*
hem·lock (hĕm′lŏk′) *n.* **1. a.** Any of various evergreen trees of the genus *Tsuga,* of North America and eastern Asia, having short, flat needles and small cones. **b.** The wood of such a tree, used as a source of lumber, wood pulp, and tannic acid. **2. a.** Any of several poisonous plants of the genera *Conium* and *Cicuta,* such as the **poison hemlock** and the **water hemlock** *(both of which see).* **b.** A poison obtained from the poison hemlock. [Middle English *hemlok,* Old English *hemlic, hymlic*†.]

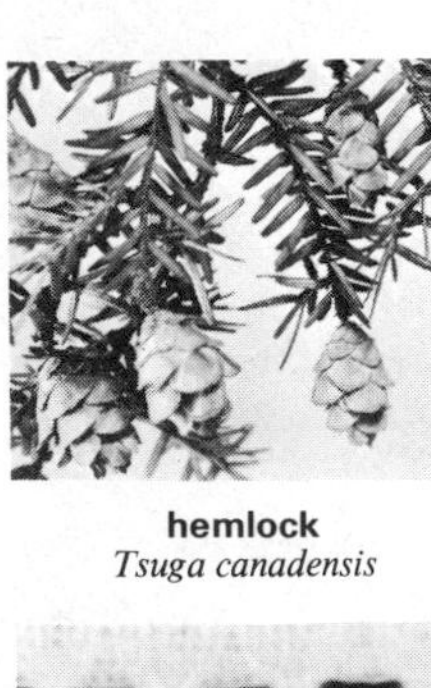
hemlock
Tsuga canadensis

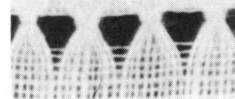

hemo–, hema–, hem–. Indicates blood; for example, **hemocyte, hemacytometer, hemin.** [From Greek *haima*†, blood.]
he·mo·cy·a·nin (hē′mō-sī′ə-nən, hĕm′ə-) *n.* A bluish, oxygen-bearing, copper-containing substance similar to hemoglobin, present in the blood of certain insects, crustaceans, and other invertebrates. [HEMO- + CYAN(O)- + -IN.]
he·mo·cyte (hē′mə-sīt′, hĕm′ə-) *n.* A cell or similar formation in the blood. [HEMO- + -CYTE.]
he·mo·flag·el·late (hē′mə-flăj′ə-lāt′, -lĭt, hĕm′ə-) *n.* A flagellate protozoan, such as a trypanosome, that is parasitic in the blood.

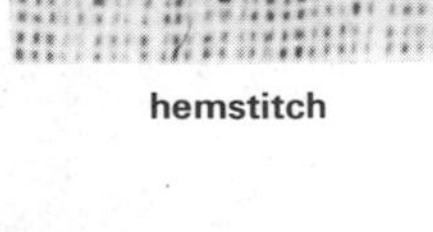
hemstitch

he·mo·glo·bin (hē′mə-glō′bən, hĕm′ə-) *n. Abbr.* **Hb** The oxygen-bearing, iron-containing conjugated protein in vertebrate red blood cells, consisting of about 6 per cent heme and 94 per cent globin, and having as a typical formula $(C_{738}H_{1166}FeN_{203}O_{208}S_2)_4$. [Shortening of earlier *hematoglobulin* : HEMATO- + GLOBULIN.]
he·mo·leu·ko·cyte (hē′mə-lo͞o′kə-sīt′, hĕm′ə-) *n.* A white blood cell; leukocyte.
he·mo·ly·sin (hē′mə-lī′sən, hĕm′ə-, hĭ-mŏl′ə-sən) *n.* An agent or substance that initiates lysis of red blood cells, thereby liberating hemoglobin. [HEMO- + LYSIN.]
he·mol·y·sis (hĭ-mŏl′ə-sĭs) *n.* The lysis of red blood cells. Also called "hematolysis." [New Latin : HEM(O)- + -LYSIS.] —**he′mo·lyt′ic** (hē′mə-lĭt′ĭk) *adj.*
he·mo·phil·i·a (hē′mə-fĭl′ē-ə, hĕm′ə-) *n.* A hereditary plasma-coagulation disorder, principally affecting males but transmitted by females, and characterized by excessive, sometimes spontaneous, bleeding. [New Latin : HEMO- + -PHILIA.]
he·mo·phil·i·ac (hē′mə-fĭl′ē-ăk′, hĕm′ə-) *n.* A person who suffers from hemophilia. Also called "bleeder."
he·mo·phil·ic (hē′mə-fĭl′ĭk, hĕm′ə-) *adj.* **1.** Pertaining to hemophilia. **2.** Growing well in blood, or in a culture containing blood, as certain bacteria.
he·mo·pho·bi·a (hē′mə-fō′bē-ə, hĕm′ə-) *n.* A morbid fear of blood. [New Latin : HEMO- + -PHOBIA.] —**he′mo·pho′bic** *adj.*
he·mo·poi·e·sis (hē′mə-poi-ē′sĭs, hĕm′ə-) *n. Physiology.* **Hematopoiesis** *(see).* [New Latin : HEMO- + -POIESIS.]
he·mop·ty·sis (hĭ-mŏp′tə-sĭs) *n.* The spitting up of blood from the lungs or bronchial tubes. [New Latin : HEMO- + Greek *ptusis,* a spitting, from *ptuein,* to spit (see **spyeu-** in Appendix*).]
hem·or·rhage (hĕm′ə-rĭj) *n.* Bleeding; especially, copious discharge of blood from the vessels. —*intr.v.* **hemorrhaged, -rhaging, -rhages.** To bleed copiously in or as if in a hemorrhage. [Earlier *hemeragie,* from Old French *hemorragie,* from Latin *haemorrhagia,* from Greek *haimorrhagia* : HEMO- + -RRHAGIA.] —**hem′or·rhag′ic** (-răj′ĭk) *adj.*
hem·or·rhoid (hĕm′ə-roid′) *n.* **1.** An itching or painful mass of dilated veins in swollen anal tissue. **2.** *Plural.* The pathological condition in which such swollen masses occur. In this sense, also called "piles." [Middle English *emeroudis,* from Old French *emeroyde, hemorrhoides,* from Latin *haemorrhoida,* from Greek *haimorrhois* (accusative *haimorrhoida*), liable to discharge blood, from *haimorrhoos,* flowing with blood : HEMO- + *-rrhoos,* flowing, discharging, from *rhein,* to flow (see **sreu-** in Appendix*).]
hem·or·rhoid·al (hĕm′ə-roid′l) *adj.* **1.** Of or pertaining to hemorrhoids. **2.** *Anatomy.* Supplying the region of the rectum and anus. Said of certain arteries.
hem·or·rhoid·ec·to·my (hĕm′ə-roi-dĕk′tə-mē) *n., pl.* **-mies.** The removal of hemorrhoids by surgery. [HEMORRHOID + -ECTOMY.]
he·mo·sta·sis (hē′mə-stā′sĭs, hĕm′ə-, hĭ-mŏs′tə-) *n.* Also **he·mo·sta·sia** (-zhə, -zhē-ə, -zē-ə). The stopping of a flow or circulation of blood. [New Latin, from Greek *haimostasis* : HEMO- + -STASIS.]
he·mo·stat (hē′mə-stăt′) *n.* **1.** Any agent, as a chemical, that stops bleeding. **2.** A clamplike instrument used in surgery to reduce or prevent bleeding. [HEMO- + -STAT.]
he·mo·stat·ic (hē′mə-stăt′ĭk) *adj.* Acting to stop the flow of blood. —*n.* A hemostatic agent. [Late Greek *haimostatikos* : HEMO- + STATIC.]
hemp (hĕmp) *n.* **1.** A tall plant, *Cannabis sativa,* native to Asia, having stems that yield a coarse fiber used in cordage, and small greenish flowers. Also called "Indian hemp," "marijuana," "bhang." **2.** The fiber of this plant. **3.** A narcotic, such as hashish, derived from this plant. **4. a.** Any of various similar or related plants, especially one yielding a fiber similar to that of *Cannabis sativa.* **b.** The fiber of such a plant. [Middle English *hemp(e),* Old English *hænep, henep.* See **kannabis** in Appendix.*]
hemp agrimony. A Eurasian plant, *Eupatorium cannabinum,* having clusters of small reddish-purple flowers.
hemp·en (hĕm′pən) *adj.* Made of or resembling hemp.
hemp nettle. Any of various plants of the genus *Galeopsis;* especially, *G. tetrahit,* native to Eurasia, having bristly stems and white or reddish flowers.
hemp tree. The **chaste tree** *(see).*
hemp·weed (hĕmp′wēd′) *n.* See **climbing hempweed.**
hem·stitch (hĕm′stĭch′) *n.* Also **hem·stitch·ing** (-ĭng). **1.** A decorative stitch usually bordering a hem, as on a handkerchief, made by drawing out several parallel threads and catching together the cross threads in uniform groups, thus creating an open design. **2.** Needlework using this stitch. —*tr.v.* **hemstitched, -stitching, -stitches.** To ornament or embroider with this stitch. —**hem′stitch′er** *n.*
hen (hĕn) *n.* **1.** A female bird; especially, the adult female of the domestic fowl. **2.** The female of certain aquatic animals, such as an octopus or a lobster. **3.** *Slang.* A woman, especially a fussy old woman. [Middle English *hen,* Old English *hen(n).* See **kan-** in Appendix.*]
hen-and-chick·ens (hĕn′ən-chĭk′ənz) *n., pl.* **hens-and-chickens** (hĕnz′-). Any of several plants having many runners or offshoots; especially, the **houseleek** *(see).*
hen·bane (hĕn′bān′) *n.* A poisonous plant, *Hyoscyamus niger,* native to the Mediterranean region, having an unpleasant odor, clammy leaves, and funnel-shaped greenish-yellow flowers, and yielding a juice used medicinally.
hen·bit (hĕn′bĭt′) *n.* A plant, *Lamium amplexicaule,* native to Europe, having toothed leaves and small white or purplish-red flowers. [HEN + BIT (morsel).]
hence (hĕns) *adv.* **1. a.** For this reason; as a result; therefore: *handmade and hence expensive.* **b.** From this source: *She grew up in the Sudan; hence her interest in Nubian art.* **2. a.** From this time; from now: *A year hence he will have forgotten.* **b.** *Rare.* Henceforth: *Hence I'll trust no one.* **3. a.** Forth from this place;

ă pat/ā pay/âr care/ä father/b bib/ch church/d deed/ĕ pet/ē be/f fife/g gag/h hat/hw which/ĭ pit/ī pie/îr pier/j judge/k kick/l lid, needle/m mum/n no, sudden/ng thing/ŏ pot/ō toe/ô paw, for/oi noise/ou out/o͝o took/o͞o boot/p pop/r roar/s sauce/sh ship, dish/

away from here. Usually used imperatively: *Get thee hence!*
b. *Rare.* Distant: *an inn two miles hence.* **c.** *Rare.* From this life:
depart hence. **—from hence.** *Archaic.* From this place. **—interj.**
Archaic. Go; get out: *"Hence, loathed Melancholy"* (Milton).
—hence with! Away with! [Middle English *hennes,* extended
form of *henne,* hence, Old English *heonane,* from here, away.
See **ko-** in Appendix.*]

hence·forth (hĕns'fôrth') *adv.* Also **hence·for·ward** (hĕns'-
fôr'wərd). From this time forth; from now on.

hench·man (hĕnch'mən) *n., pl.* **-men** (-mĭn). **1. a.** A loyal and
trusted follower or subordinate. **b.** A person who supports a
political figure chiefly out of self-seeking interests. **2.** A
member of a criminal gang. **3.** *Obsolete.* A page of honor to a
prince or other person of high rank. [Middle English *hengest-
man, henxl st)man,* probably groom, squire : *hengest,* horse,
stallion, Old English *hengest,* from Germanic *hangista-* (unattested) + **MAN**.]

hen·coop (hĕn'kōōp', -kŏōp') *n.* A coop or cage for poultry.

hen·dec·a·syl·lab·ic (hĕn-dĕk'ə-sĭ-lăb'ĭk) *adj.* Containing 11
syllables. **—n.** Also **hen·dec·a·syl·la·ble** (hĕn-dĕk'ə-sĭl'ə-bəl). A
verse of 11 syllables. [From Latin *hendecasyllabus,* a hendeca-
syllable : Greek *hendeka,* eleven : *hen,* neuter of *heis,* one (see
sem-¹ in Appendix*) + *deka,* ten (see **dekm̥** in Appendix*) +
sullabē, **SYLLABLE**.]

hen·di·a·dys (hĕn-dī'ə-dəs) *n.* A figure of speech in which two
connotative words connected by a conjunction are used to express a single complex notion that would normally be expressed
by an adjective and a substantive. [Medieval Latin, from
Greek *hen dia duoin,* one by means of two : *hen,* neuter of *heis,*
one (see **sem-¹** in Appendix*) + *dia,* through (see **dia-**) + *duoin,*
genitive of *duō,* two (see **dwō** in Appendix*).]

Hen·dricks (hĕn'drĭks), **Thomas Andrews.** 1819–1885. Vice
President of the United States under Grover Cleveland (1885);
died in office.

He·ne·gou·wen. The Flemish name for **Hainaut.**

hen·e·quen (hĕn'ə-kwən) *n.* Also **hen·e·quin.** **1.** A tropical
American plant, *Agave fourcroydes,* having large, thick leaves
that yield a coarse reddish fiber used in making rope and twine.
2. The fiber obtained from this plant. [Spanish *henequén,*
jeniquén, perhaps from Taino.]

Heng·e·lo (hĕng'ə-lō'). A city of the eastern Netherlands.
Population, 58,000.

Heng·yang (hĕng'yäng'). A city of southeast-central Hunan,
China. Population, 240,000.

Hen·ley (hĕn'lē). Also **Hen·ley-on-Thames** (-ŏn-tĕmz'). A town
of southern Oxford, England, on the Thames; site of an annual
crew regatta. Population, 9,000.

Hen·lo·pen, Cape (hĕn-lō'pən). A promontory of southeast-
central Delaware, at the southern entrance to Delaware Bay.

hen·na (hĕn'ə) *n.* **1.** A tree or shrub, *Lawsonia inermis,* of Asia
and northern Africa, having fragrant white or reddish flowers.
2. A reddish dyestuff obtained from the leaves of this plant,
used as a cosmetic dye and for coloring leather. **3.** Moderate or
strong reddish brown to strong brown. See **color.** *—tr.v.* **hen·
naed, -naing, -nas.** To dye or rinse (hair) with henna. [Arabic
ḥinnā'.] **—hen'na** *adj.*

Honno·pin (ĕn-păn'), **Louis.** 1640–1701? Flemish-born Roman
Catholic friar and explorer of Canada and the upper Mississippi
area.

hen·ner·y (hĕn'ə-rē) *n., pl.* **-ies.** **1.** A poultry farm. **2.** A pen for
domestic fowl.

hen·o·the·ism (hĕn'ə-thē'ĭz'əm) *n.* Belief in one god without
denying the existence of others. [German *Henotheismus* :
Greek *heno-,* from *hen,* neuter of *heis,* one (see **sem-¹** in
Appendix*) + **THEISM**.] **—hen'o·the'ist** *n.* **—hen'o·the·is'tic**
adj.

hen·peck (hĕn'pĕk') *tr.v.* **-pecked, -pecking, -pecks.** *Informal.* To
dominate or harass (one's husband) with persistent nagging.
[Back-formation from **HEN-PECKED**.]

hen·pecked (hĕn'pĕkt') *adj.* Also **hen·pecked.** *Informal.* Dominated or persistently harassed by a wife: *"After all, the hen-
pecked husband with his shrewish wife is a comic figure of long
standing"* (Philip Reaves). [By allusion to the plucking of
some of the rooster's feathers by his hens.]

Hen·ri·et·ta (hĕn'rē-ĕt'ə). A feminine given name. [Latinized
form of French *Henriette,* feminine diminutive of *Henri,*
HENRY.]

hen·ry (hĕn'rē) *n., pl.* **-ries** or **-rys.** *Abbr.* **H** The unit of inductance in which an induced electromotive force of one volt is
produced when the current is varied at the rate of one ampere
per second. [After Joseph **HENRY**.]

Hen·ry (hĕn'rē). A masculine given name. [Middle English,
from Old French *Henri,* from Late Latin *Henricus,* from Old
High German *Heimerich,* "ruler of the house" : *heim,* house,
home (see **kei-¹** in Appendix*) + *rīhhi,* rule (see **reg-¹** in
Appendix*).]

Hen·ry I (hĕn'rē). 1068–1135. King of England (1100–35);
youngest son of William the Conqueror.

Hen·ry II (hĕn'rē). 1133–1189. King of England (1154–89); first
of Plantagenet line; married Eleanor of Aquitaine; father of
Richard I and John.

Hen·ry III¹ (hĕn'rē). 1207–1272. King of England (1216–72);
father of Edward I.

Hen·ry III² (hĕn'rē). 1551–1589. King of France (1574–89); last
of Valois line; with his mother Catherine de Médicis, plotted
the Saint Bartholomew's Day Massacre (1572).

Hen·ry IV¹ (hĕn'rē). 1050–1106. Holy Roman Emperor and
King of Germany (1056–1106); excommunicated by Pope
Gregory VII.

Hen·ry IV² (hĕn'rē). 1367–1413. Surname, Bolingbroke. King
of England (1399–1413); first of House of Lancaster; defeated
Richard II.

Hen·ry IV³ (hĕn'rē). Known as Henry of Navarre. 1553–1610.
King of France (1589–1610); first of Bourbon line; leader of
Huguenots; assassinated.

Hen·ry V (hĕn'rē). 1387–1422. King of England (1413–22);
defeated French at Battle of Agincourt (1415); married Catherine of Valois; son of Henry IV and father of Henry VI.

Hen·ry VI (hĕn'rē). 1421–1471. King of England (1422–61;
1470–71); last of House of Lancaster; son of Henry V; succeeded by Edward IV.

Hen·ry VII (hĕn'rē). Known as Henry Tudor. 1457–1509. King
of England (1485–1509); first of House of Tudor; defeated
Richard III; father of Henry VIII.

Hen·ry VIII (hĕn'rē). 1491–1547. King of England (1509–47);
married six times; created Church of England; father of Edward
VI, Mary I, and Elizabeth I.

Hen·ry, Cape (hĕn'rē). A promontory of southeastern Virginia,
at the southern entrance to Chesapeake Bay.

Hen·ry (hĕn'rē), **Joseph.** 1797–1878. American physicist; performed extensive fundamental studies of electromagnetic phenomena.

Hen·ry, O. See William Sydney **Porter.**

Hen·ry (hĕn'rē), **Patrick.** 1736–1799. American Revolutionary
leader and orator.

Hen·ry the Navigator (hĕn'rē). Portuguese name, Dom Hen-
rique o Navegador. 1394–1460. Prince of Portugal; established
school of navigation and astronomical observatory.

Hens·lowe (hĕnz'lō), **Philip.** Died 1616. English theater manager and diarist.

hent (hĕnt) *tr.v.* **hented, henting, hents.** *Obsolete.* To take hold
of; seize; grasp. [Middle English *henten,* Old English *hentan,*
to pursue, attack, from Germanic *hantjan* (unattested), from
hanthatjan (unattested).]

hep. Variant of **hip** (aware).

hep·a·rin (hĕp'ər-ən) *n.* A complex organic acid found especially in lung and liver tissue and having the ability in certain
circumstances to prevent the clotting of blood. [New Latin
hepar, liver, from Late Latin *hēpar,* from Greek (see **yekwr̥** in
Appendix*) + **-IN**.]

he·pat·ic (hĭ-păt'ĭk) *adj.* **1.** Of or resembling the liver. **2.** Acting on or occurring in the liver. **3.** Liver colored. **4.** Of or belonging to the Hepaticae, a class of mosslike plants that includes the liverworts. **—n.** **1.** A drug used in liver diseases.
2. A plant of the class Hepaticae, a **liverwort** (*see*). [Middle
English *epatik,* from Latin *hēpaticus,* of liver, from Greek
hēpatikos, from *hēpar* (stem *hēpat-*), liver. See **yekwr̥** in Appendix.*]

he·pat·i·ca (hĭ-păt'ĭ-kə) *n.* Any of several woodland plants of
the genus *Hepatica;* especially, *H. americana,* of eastern North
America, having three-lobed leaves and white or lavender
flowers. Also called "liverleaf," "liverwort." [New Latin *Hepatica,* from Medieval Latin *hēpatica,* liverwort, from Latin,
feminine of *hēpaticus,* **HEPATIC**.]

hep·a·ti·tis (hĕp'ə-tī'tĭs) *n.* Inflammation of the liver, caused by
infectious or toxic agents, characterized by jaundice, and usually accompanied by fever and other systemic manifestations.
[New Latin : Greek *hēpar* (stem *hēpat-*), liver (see **yekwr̥** in
Appendix*) + **-ITIS**.]

hep·a·to·gen·ic (hĕp'ə-tō-jĕn'ĭk) *adj.* Also **hep·a·tog·e·nous**
(-tŏj'ə-nəs). Produced by or originating in the liver. [Greek
hēpar (stem *hēpat-*), liver (see **yekwr̥** in Appendix*) + **-GENIC**.]

hep·cat (hĕp'kăt') *n. Slang.* A performer or devotee of swing
and jazz during the 1940's.

He·phaes·tus (hĭ-fĕs'təs). The Greek god of fire and metalworking; identified with the Roman god Vulcan.

Hep·ple·white (hĕp'əl-hwīt') *adj.* Designating an English style
of furniture of the late 18th century, noted for its light, graceful
lines, its use of concave curves, and the shield or heart backs of
its chairs. [After George *Hepplewhite* (died 1786), English
cabinetmaker.]

hepta-, hept-. Indicates seven; for example, **heptahedron,
heptane.** [From Greek *hepta,* seven. See **septm̥** in Appendix.*]

hep·tad (hĕp'tăd') *n.* A group or series of seven. [Greek
heptas (stem *heptad-*), the number seven, period of seven years,
from *hepta,* seven. See **septm̥** in Appendix.*]

hep·ta·gon (hĕp'tə-gŏn') *n.* A seven-sided polygon. [Greek
heptagonos, having seven angles : **HEPTA-** + **-GON**.] **—hep·tag'-
o·nal** (-tăg'ə-nəl) *adj.*

hep·ta·he·dron (hĕp'tə-hē'drən) *n.* A polyhedron with seven
faces. [**HEPTA-** + **-HEDRON**.] **—hep'ta·he'dral** (-drəl) *adj.*

hep·tam·e·ter (hĕp-tăm'ə-tər) *n. Prosody.* **1.** A metrical unit
consisting of seven feet. **2.** A line of verse written in such
meter. [**HEPTA-** + **-METER**.]

hep·tane (hĕp'tān') *n.* A volatile, colorless, highly flammable
liquid hydrocarbon, $CH_3(CH_2)_5CH_3$, obtained in the fractional
distillation of petroleum, and used as a standard in determining
octane ratings, as an anesthetic, and as a solvent. [**HEPT(A)-**
(from the number of carbon atoms it possesses) + **-ANE**.]

hep·tar·chy (hĕp'tär'kē) *n., pl.* **-chies.** **1. a.** Government by
seven persons. **b.** A state so governed. **2.** *Often capital* **H.** The
informal confederation of the Anglo-Saxon kingdoms from the
fifth to the ninth century, consisting of Kent, Sussex, Wessex,
Essex, Northumbria, East Anglia, and Mercia. [**HEPT(A)-** +
-ARCHY.]

hep·ta·stich (hĕp'tə-stĭk') *n.* A stanza or strophe consisting of
seven lines. [**HEPTA-** + **STICH**.]

Hep·ta·teuch (hĕp'tə-tōōk', tyōōk') *n.* The first seven books of

hepatica
Hepatica americana

Hepplewhite
Hepplewhite side chair

the Old Testament. [Greek *heptateukhos (biblos),* "(book) in seven volumes" : HEPTA- + *teukhos,* tool, case holding writing material, volume (see **dheugh-** in Appendix*).]

her (hûr; *unstressed* hər, ər). The possessive form of the pronoun *she.* **1.** Used attributively to indicate possession, agency, or reception of an action by the feminine person or entity spoken of: *her purse; pursuing her tasks; suffered her first rebuff.* **2.** Used traditionally of certain objects and institutions such as ships and nations. **3.** Applied in a certain informal style to things not usually personified: *The engine's all right, so start her up.* [Middle English *hire, her(e),* Old English *hire.* See **ko-** in Appendix.*]

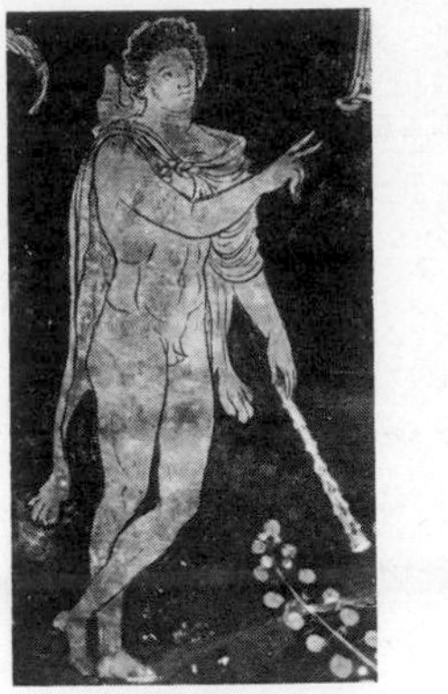
Hercules[1]
Fourth-century B.C.
Greek vase painting

her. heraldry.

He·ra (hîr′ə). Also **He·re** (hîr′ē). *Greek Mythology.* The sister and wife of Zeus; identified by the Romans with Juno.

Her·a·cle·a (hĕr′ə-klē′ə). An ancient city of southern Italy; site of a battle in which an army under Pyrrhus of Epirus defeated Roman forces (280 B.C.).

Her·a·cle·op·o·lis (hĕr′ə-klē-ŏp′ə-lĭs). An ancient city of north-east-central Egypt; the capital of the Middle Kingdom from 2445–2160 B.C.

Her·a·cles, Her·a·kles. Variants of **Hercules.**

Her·a·clid (hĕr′ə-klĭd) *n., pl.* **Heraclidae** (hĕr′ə-klī′dē). A descendant of Hercules; specifically, a Spartan nobleman who claimed such descent. —**Her′a·cli′dan** (hĕr′ə-klīd′n) *adj.*

Her·a·cli·tus (hĕr′ə-klī′təs). Greek philosopher of the sixth century B.C.

He·rak·li·on. The Greek name for **Candia.**

her·ald (hĕr′əld) *n.* **1. a.** A person who proclaims important news; a crier or messenger. **b.** A state messenger; envoy. **2.** A person or thing that announces or gives indication of something to come; harbinger; precursor. **3.** *British.* An official whose specialty is heraldry. **4. a.** An official formerly charged with making royal proclamations and with bearing messages of state between sovereigns. **b.** An official who formerly made proclamations and conveyed challenges at a tournament. —*tr.v.* **heralded, -alding, -alds.** To proclaim; announce; usher in: *"the cocks that herald dawn all night"* (Malcolm Lowry). [Middle English *herau(l)d,* from Old French *herau(l)t,* from Germanic. See **koro-** in Appendix.*]

he·ral·dic (hə-răl′dĭk) *adj.* Of or pertaining to heralds or heraldry. —**he·ral′di·cal·ly** *adv.*

her·ald·ry (hĕr′əl-drē) *n., pl.* **-ries.** **1.** *Abbr.* **her. a.** The profession of devising, granting, and blazoning arms, of tracing pedigrees, and of ruling on questions of precedence, as exercised by an officer of arms. **b.** A branch of knowledge constituted by the history and description in proper terms of armorial bearings and their accessories; armory. **2.** Armorial ensigns or similar insignia. **3.** Pomp and ceremony, especially as attended with armorial trappings; pageantry: *the heraldry of a royal progress.* —**her′ald·ist** *n.*

Heralds' College. A royal corporation instituted in England during the 15th century to handle matters of heraldry. Also called "College of Arms," "College of Heralds."

Her·at (hə-rät′). Also **Har·at.** A city of northwestern Afghanistan. Population, 62,000.

herb (ûrb, hûrb) *n.* **1.** A plant that has a fleshy stem as distinguished from the woody tissue of shrubs and trees, and that generally dies back at the end of each growing season. **2.** Any of various often aromatic plants used especially in medicine or as seasoning. See Note at **plant.** [Middle English *(h)erbe,* from Old French, from Latin *herba*†.]

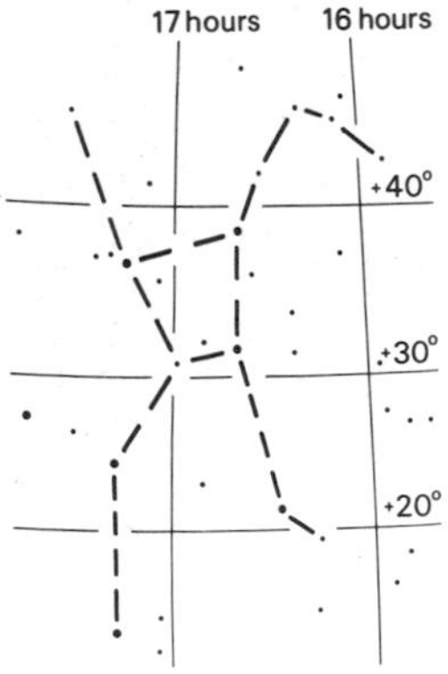

Hercules[2]

her·ba·ceous (hûr-bā′shəs) *adj.* **1.** Pertaining to or characteristic of an herb as distinguished from a woody plant. **2.** Green and leaflike in appearance or texture. [Latin *herbāceus* : *herba,* HERB + -ACEOUS.]

herb·age (ûr′bĭj, hûr′-) *n.* **1.** Herbaceous plant growth, especially grass or similar vegetation used for pasturage. **2.** The fleshy, often edible parts of plants. [Middle English *(h)erbage,* from Old French, from *(h)erbe,* HERB.]

herb·al (hûr′bəl, ûr′-) *adj.* Of, relating to, or containing herbs. —*n.* A book about plants and herbs, especially those that are useful to man.

herb·al·ist (hûr′bə-lĭst, ûr′-) *n.* One who grows, collects, or specializes in the use of herbs, especially medicinal herbs.

her·bar·i·um (hûr-bâr′ē-əm) *n., pl.* **-ums** or **-ia** (-ē-ə). **1.** A collection of dried plants mounted and labeled for use in scientific study. **2.** A place or institution where such a collection is kept. [Late Latin *herbārium,* from Latin *herba,* HERB.] —**her·bar′i·al** *adj.*

herb bennet. A hairy Eurasian plant, *Geum urbanum,* having small yellow flowers and an astringent root formerly used medicinally. [Middle English *herb beneit,* from Old French *herbe beneite* (or *benoite*), from Medieval Latin *herba benedicta,* "blessed herb" (from its medicinal properties) : Latin *herba,* HERB + *benedicta,* feminine past participle of *benedīcere,* to bless (see **benediction**).]

Her·bert (hûr′bərt). A masculine given name. [Middle English, from Medieval Latin *Herbertus,* from Old High German *Heriberht,* "bright army" : *heri, hari,* army (see **koro-** in Appendix*) + *beraht,* bright (see **bhereg-** in Appendix*).]

Her·bert (hûr′bərt), **George.** 1593–1633. English poet.

Her·bert (hûr′bərt), **Victor.** 1859–1924. Irish-born American composer of light operas.

her·bi·cide (hûr′bĭ-sīd′) *n.* A substance used to destroy plants, especially weeds. [HERB + -CIDE.] —**her′bi·ci′dal** *adj.*

her·bi·vore (hûr′bə-vôr′, -vōr′) *n.* A herbivorous animal. [New Latin *Herbivora* (former designation of herbivores), from the neuter plural of *herbivorus,* HERBIVOROUS.]

her·biv·o·rous (hûr-bĭv′ər-əs) *adj.* Feeding on plants; plant-eating. [New Latin *herbivorus* : HERB + -VOROUS.]

Her·block. Pen name of Herbert Lawrence **Block** *(see).*

herb-of-grace (ûrb′əv-grās′, hûrb′-) *n., pl.* **herbs-of-grace.** *Archaic.* A plant, **rue** *(see).* [Probably from the association of rue (the plant) with rue (repentance).]

herb Par·is (păr′ĭs). A European plant, *Paris quadrifolia,* having a whorl of four leaves and a solitary yellow or greenish flower. [Probably Medieval Latin *herba paris,* "herb of a pair" (perhaps a reference to the two pairs of leaves on the whorl) : Latin *herba,* HERB + *paris,* genitive of *par,* equal (see **pera-** in Appendix*).]

herb Robert. A low-growing plant, *Geranium robertianum,* having divided leaves and small reddish-purple flowers. [Middle English *herbe Robert,* from Medieval Latin *herba Roberti,* "herb of Robert," variously supposed to be named after *Robert* Duke of Normandy, Saint *Robert* (died 1067), French divine, or Saint *Rupert,* seventh-century Bavarian ecclesiastic.]

Her·ce·go·vi·na. The Serbo-Croatian name for **Herzegovina.**

Her·cu·la·ne·um (hûr′kyə-lā′nē-əm). An ancient city of southwest-central Italy near Naples; destroyed with Pompeii by a volcanic eruption of Mount Vesuvius (A.D. 79).

her·cu·le·an (hûr′kyə-lē′ən, -kyōō′lē-ən) *adj.* **1.** Tremendously difficult or demanding: *herculean labors.* **2.** *Often capital* **H.** Resembling Hercules in size, power, or courage: *Herculean strength.* **3.** *Capital* **H.** Of or relating to Hercules.

Her·cu·les[1] (hûr′kyə-lēz′). Also **Her·a·cles** (hĕr′ə-klēz′), **Her·a·kles.** *Greek & Roman Mythology.* The son of Zeus and Alcmene, a hero of extraordinary strength and courage who won immortality by performing the 12 labors demanded by Hera.

Her·cu·les[2] (hûr′kyə-lēz′) *n.* **1.** *Sometimes small* **h.** A man of prodigious size and strength. **2.** *Astronomy.* A constellation in the Northern Hemisphere near Lyra and Corona Borealis, that contains the star Ras Algheti and the globular cluster M13. [After HERCULES.]

Her·cu·les′-club (hûr′kyə-lēz-klŭb′) *n.* **1.** A tree or shrub, *Aralia spinosa,* of the southeastern United States, having prickly compound leaves and large clusters of small white flowers. Also called "devil's walking stick," and sometimes "angelica tree." **2.** A spiny tree, *Zanthoxylum clava-herculis,* of the southeastern United States, having clusters of small, greenish-yellow flowers. [From the spiny club of HERCULES.]

herd (hûrd) *n.* **1. a.** A group of cattle or other domestic animals of a single kind kept together for a specific use. **b.** A number of wild animals of one species that remain together as a group: *a herd of elephants.* **2.** A number of people grouped together by some common factor: *a herd of stranded passengers.* —See Synonyms at **flock.** —**the herd.** The multitude of common people regarded as a mass of cattle: *"It is the luxurious and dissipated who set the fashions which the herd so diligently follow."* (Thoreau). —*v.* **herded, herding, herds.** —*intr.* **1.** To congregate in a herd. **2.** *Rare.* To keep company; to associate. —*tr.* **1.** To gather, keep, or drive (animals) in a herd. **2.** To place in a group. **3.** To tend (sheep or cattle). [Middle English *herd(e),* Old English *heord.* See **kerdh-** in Appendix.*]

herd·er (hûr′dər) *n.* **1.** A person who tends or drives a herd. **2.** A person who owns or breeds livestock. In this sense, also called "herdsman."

her·dic (hûr′dĭk) *n.* A small horse-drawn cab having two wheels, side seats, and an entrance at the back. [Invented by Peter *Herdic* (1824–1888), American carriage-maker.]

here (hîr) *adv.* **1.** At or in this place: *Stop here.* **2.** At this time; now: *I will call here for a vote.* **3.** At or on this point, detail, or item: *There is great disagreement here.* **4.** In the present life or condition. **5.** To this place; hither: *Come here.* **6. a.** Used for emphasis after a demonstrative pronoun: *Which word? This one here.* **b.** Used for emphasis after a noun modified by a demonstrative pronoun: *this word here.* **c.** *Nonstandard.* Used for emphasis between a demonstrative pronoun and a noun: *this here word.* See Usage note below. —*interj.* An exclamation used as a response to a roll call, as a command to an animal, or as a rebuke or admonishment to a child. [Middle English *her(e),* Old English *hēr.* See **ko-** in Appendix.*]

Usage: *Here* (adverb), meaning *in this place,* is placed after the noun, not before it, in constructions introduced by the demonstrative *this: this girl here* (not *this here girl*). Constructions introduced by *here is* and *here are* are similar to those beginning *there is* and *there are* with respect to determining the number of the verb. See also Usage note at **there.**

He·re. Variant of **Hera.**

here·a·bout (hîr′ə-bout′) *adv.* Also **here·a·bouts** (-bouts′). In this general vicinity; around here.

here·af·ter (hîr-ăf′tər, -äf′tər) *adv.* **1.** Immediately following this in time, order, or place; after this. **2.** In a world to come; in the afterlife: *win salvation hereafter.* —*n.* The world to come; life after death: *belief in a hereafter.*

here·at (hîr-ăt′) *adv.* **1.** Upon this event; at this time. **2.** Because of this; at this.

here·by (hîr-bī′) *adv.* By virtue of this act, decree, bulletin, or document; by this means.

He·re·dia (ā-rā′*th*yä, ā-rā-dyä′), **José Maria de.** 1842–1905. French poet and translator.

her·e·dit·a·ment (hĕr′ə-dĭt′ə-mənt) *n. Law.* Any kind of property that can be inherited. [Medieval Latin *hērēditāmentum,* from Late Latin *hērēditāre,* to inherit, from Latin *hērēs* (stem *hērēd-*), heir. See **ghē-** in Appendix.*]

he·red·i·tar·y (hə-rĕd′ə-tĕr′ē) *adj.* **1.** *Law.* **a.** Descending from an ancestor to a legal heir; passing down by inheritance.

ă pat/ā pay/âr care/ä father/b bib/ch church/d deed/ĕ pet/ē be/f fife/g gag/h hat/hw which/ĭ pit/ī pie/îr pier/j judge/k kick/l lid, needle/m mum/n no, sudden/ng thing/ŏ pot/ō toe/ô paw, for/oi noise/ou out/ŏŏ took/ōō boot/p pop/r roar/s sauce/sh ship, dish/

b. Having title or possession through inheritance. 2. Genetically transmitted or transmissible. 3. a. Appearing in or characteristic of successive generations. b. Derived from or fostered by one's ancestors: *a hereditary prejudice.* 4. Ancestral; traditional. 5. Of or relating to heredity or inheritance. —See Synonyms at **innate**. [Latin *hērēditārius,* from *hērēditās,* HEREDITY.] —**he·red'i·tar'i·ly** *adv.* —**he·red'i·tar'i·ness** *n.*

he·red·i·tist (hə-rĕd'ə-tĭst) *n.* One who supports the theory that heredity rather than environment determines personality.

he·red·i·ty (hə-rĕd'ə-tē) *n., pl.* **-ties.** 1. The genetic transmission of characteristics from parents to offspring. 2. The totality of characteristics and associated potentialities so transmitted to an individual organism. In this sense, compare **environment**. [Old French *heredite,* from Latin *hērēditās,* inheritance, from *hērēs* (stem *hērēd-*), heir. See **ghē-** in Appendix.*]

Her·e·ford¹ (hĕr'ə-fərd). 1. Also **Her·e·ford·shire** (-shîr, -shər). *Abbr.* **Heref.** A county occupying 842 square miles in south-west-central England. Population, 136,000. 2. The county seat of this county, located in the west. Population, 44,000.

Her·e·ford² (hĕr'ə-fərd, hûr'fərd) *n.* Any of a breed of beef cattle developed in Herefordshire, England, having a reddish coat with white markings.

here·in (hîr-ĭn') *adv.* In or into this.

here·in·af·ter (hîr'ĭn-ăf'tər, -äf'tər) *adv.* In a following part of this document, statement, or book; after this.

here·in·be·fore (hîr'ĭn-bĭ-fôr', -fōr') *adv.* In a preceding part of this text, speech, or book; before this.

here·in·to (hîr-ĭn'to͞o) *adv.* Into this matter, circumstance, situation, or place; into this.

here·of (hîr-ŭv', -ŏv') *adv.* Pertaining to or concerning this.

here·on (hîr-ŏn', -ôn') *adv.* Hereupon.

he·res (hā'rās') *n., pl.* **heredes** (hā-rā'dēz'). Also **hae·res** (hī'rās'). *Law.* An heir. [Latin *hērēs.* See **ghē-** in Appendix.*]

he·re·si·arch (hə-rē'zē-ärk', hĕr'ə-sē-) *n.* The founder or chief proponent of a heresy. [Late Latin *haeresiarcha,* from Late Greek *hairesiarkhēs* : Greek *hairesis,* sect (see **heresy**) + -ARCH.]

her·e·sy (hĕr'ə-sē) *n., pl.* **-sies.** 1. a. An opinion or doctrine at variance with established religious beliefs; especially, dissention from or denial of Roman Catholic dogma by a professed believer or baptized church member. b. Adherence to such dissenting opinion or belief. 2. a. A controversial or unorthodox opinion or doctrine in politics, philosophy, science, or other fields. b. Adherence to such unorthodox opinion. [Middle English *(h)eresie,* from Old French, from Late Latin *haeresis,* from Late Greek *hairesis,* from Greek, "a taking," school of thought, faction, from *hairein*†, to take, grasp, choose.]

her·e·tic (hĕr'ə-tĭk) *n.* A person who holds controversial opinions in any area; especially, one who publicly dissents from the officially accepted dogma of the Roman Catholic Church. [Middle English *(h)eretik,* from Old French *(h)eretique,* from Late Latin *haereticus,* from Greek *hairetikos,* able to choose, factious, from *hairetos,* from *hairein,* to take, choose. See **heresy**.]

he·ret·i·cal (hə-rĕt'ĭ-kəl) *adj.* 1. Of or pertaining to heresy or heretics. 2. Characterized by, revealing, or approaching departure from established beliefs or standards: *"The once heretical view that the moon shows geological activity is now taken for granted."* (Nature Magazine). —**he·ret'i·cal·ly** *adv.*

here·to (hîr-to͞o') *adv.* To this place, document, matter, or proposition; to this: *Attached hereto is my voucher.*

here·to·fore (hîr'tə-fôr', -fōr') *adv.* Up to the present time; before this; previously. [Middle English : HERE + *tofore, toforn,* before, Old English *tōforan* : TO + *foran,* before, from *fore,* FORE (in front).]

here·un·to (hîr-ŭn'to͞o) *adv.* Hereto.

here·up·on (hîr'ə-pŏn', -pôn') *adv.* Following instantly upon this; immediately after this; at this.

here·with (hîr-wĭth', -wĭth') *adv.* 1. Along with this. 2. By this means; hereby.

her·i·ot (hĕr'ē-ət) *n. Feudal Law.* A service rendered to a lord on the death of a tenant, consisting originally of the return of military equipment of which the tenant had had the usufruct, subsequently of the deceased tenant's best single beast or other possession, and latterly of a money payment, now surviving in some manorial tenancies in England. [Middle English *heriet, heriot,* Old English *heregeatwe,* military equipment, "army-trappings" : *here,* army (see **koro-** in Appendix*) + *geatwa,* equipment, trappings (see **taw-** in Appendix*).]

He·ri Rud. See **Hari Rud.**

her·i·ta·ble (hĕr'ə-tə-bəl) *adj.* 1. Capable of being inherited; hereditary. 2. Capable of inheriting or of taking by inheritance. [Middle English *heretable,* from Old French *heritable,* from *heriter,* to inherit. See **heritage**.]

her·i·tage (hĕr'ə-tĭj) *n.* 1. Property that is or can be inherited; inheritance. 2. Something other than property passed down from preceding generations; legacy; tradition. 3. The status or lot acquired by a person through birth; birthright: *a heritage of affluence and position.* [Middle English *(h)eritage,* from Old French, from *heriter,* to inherit, from Late Latin *hērēditāre,* from Latin *hērēs* (stem *hērēd-*), heir. See **ghē-** in Appendix.*]

her·i·tor (hĕr'ə-tər) *n.* An inheritor. [Middle English *heriter,* from Norman French, variant of Old French *heritier,* from Latin *hērēditārius,* HEREDITARY.]

her·i·tress (hĕr'ə-trĭs) *n.* A female inheritor.

herl (hûrl) *n.* 1. The barb of a feather used in trimming an artificial fly for angling. 2. A fishing fly made with this. [Middle English *herle,* probably from Middle Low German *herle, harle*†.]

her·ma (hûr'mə) *n., pl.* **-mae** (-mē', -mī') or **-mai** (-mī'). Also **herm** (hûrm). A statue consisting of the head of the Greek god Hermes mounted on a square stone post. [Latin, from Greek *hermēs,* from *Hermēs,* HERMES.]

Her·man (hûr'mən). A masculine given name. [Middle English, from Norman French, from Old High German *Hariman,* "man of the army" : *hari, heri,* army (see **koro-** in Appendix*) + *man,* man (see **man-¹** in Appendix*).]

Her·mann·stadt. The German name for **Sibiu.**

her·maph·ro·dite (hər-măf'rə-dīt') *n.* 1. One having the sex organs and many of the secondary sex characteristics of both male and female. 2. *Biology.* An organism, such as an earthworm or a monoclinous plant, having male and female reproductive organs in the same individual. 3. Anything comprised of a combination of diverse or contradictory elements. [Middle English *hermofrodite,* from Latin *hermaphrodītus,* from Greek *hermaphroditos,* after *Hermaphroditos,* HERMAPHRODITUS.] —**her·maph'ro·dit'ic** (-dĭt'ĭk) *adj.* —**her·maph'ro·dit'i·cal·ly** *adv.*

hermaphrodite brig. A two-masted vessel having a square-rigged foremast and a schooner-rigged mainmast. [It combines the characteristics of a brig and a schooner.]

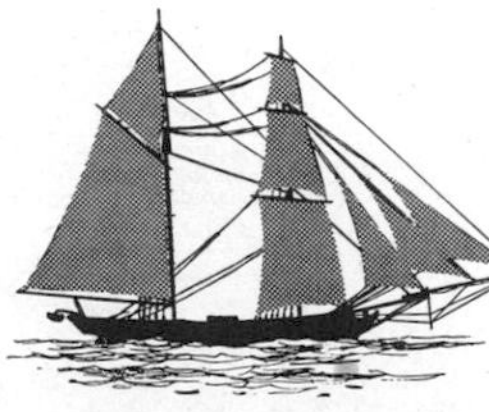

hermaphrodite brig

hermaphrodite rig. A **jackass rig** *(see).*

her·maph·ro·dit·ism (hər-măf'rə-dī'tĭz'əm) *n.* Also **her·maph·rod·ism** (-rə-dĭz'əm). The condition of being a hermaphrodite.

Her·maph·ro·di·tus (hər-măf'rō-dī'təs). *Greek Mythology.* The son of Hermes and Aphrodite, who became united in one body with the nymph Salmacis. [Greek *Hermaphroditos* : HERM(ES) + APHRODITE.]

her·me·neu·tic (hûr'mə-no͞o'tĭk, -nyo͞o'tĭk) *adj.* Also **her·me·neu·ti·cal** (-tĭ-kəl). Interpretive; explanatory. [Greek *hermēneutikos.* See **hermeneutics**.] —**her'me·neu'ti·cal·ly** *adv.*

her·me·neu·tics (hûr'mə-no͞o'tĭks, -nyo͞o'tĭks) *n.* Plural in form, used with a singular verb. The science and methodology of interpretation, especially of Scriptural text. [New Latin *hermeneutica,* from Greek *hermēneutikē (tekhnē),* (art) of interpretation, from the feminine of *hermēneutikos,* of interpretation, from *hermēneutēs,* interpreter, from *hermēneuein,* to interpret, from *hermēneus*†, interpreter.]

Her·mes (hûr'mēz'). *Greek Mythology.* The god of commerce, invention, cunning, and theft, who also served as messenger and herald for the other gods, as patron of travelers and rogues, and as the conductor of the dead to Hades; identified with the Roman god Mercury. [Greek *Hermēs*†.]

Her·mes Tris·me·gis·tus (hûr'mēz' trĭs'mə-jĭs'təs). The Greek name for the Egyptian god Thoth, the supposed author of works on alchemy, astrology, and magic. [Latin, from Greek *Hermēs trismegistos,* "Hermes the thrice greatest."]

her·met·ic (hər-mĕt'ĭk) *adj.* Also **her·met·i·cal** (-ĭ-kəl). 1. a. Completely sealed; especially, sealed against the escape or entry of air. b. Impervious to outside interference or influence; insulated; cloistered: *retreated to the hermetic confines of his room.* 2. *Capital* **H.** Of or relating to Hermes Trismegistus or to the works ascribed to him. 3. Having to do with the occult sciences, especially alchemy; magical. [New Latin *hermeticus,* from Latin *Hermes* (stem *Hermet-*) *Trismegistus,* HERMES TRISMEGISTUS. He is said to have invented a magic seal to make vessels airtight.] —**her·met'i·cal·ly** *adv.*

her·mit (hûr'mĭt) *n.* 1. A person who has withdrawn from society and lives a solitary existence; recluse. 2. A spiced cooky made with molasses, raisins, and nuts. [Middle English *(h)ermite,* from Old French, from Late Latin *erēmīta,* from Greek *erēmitēs,* "(one) of the desert," from *erēmia,* desert, solitude, from *erēmos,* deserted, solitary. See **erə-²** in Appendix.*] —**her·mit'ic, her·mit'i·cal** *adj.* —**her·mit'i·cal·ly** *adv.*

her·mit·age (hûr'mə-tĭj) *n.* 1. a. The habitation of a hermit or group of hermits. b. A monastery or abbey. 2. A place where one can live in seclusion; a retreat; hideaway. 3. The condition or way of life of a hermit.

Her·mi·tage (hûr'mə-tĭj) *n.* A rich, full-bodied, usually red wine produced in southeastern France. [From Tain-l'*Ermitage,* commune in Drôme, France.]

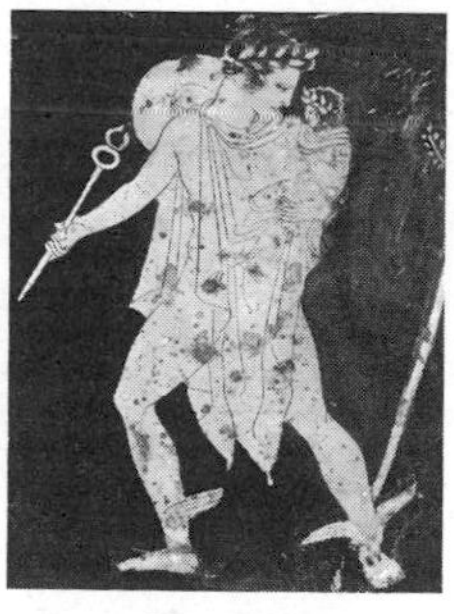

Hermes
Detail of painting on ancient Greek bowl, showing Hermes with the infant Dionysus

hermit crab. Any of various crustaceans of the section Anomura within the order Decapoda, having a soft, unarmored abdomen, and occupying and carrying about the empty shell of a snail or other univalve mollusk.

hermit thrush. A North American bird, *Hylocichla guttata,* having brownish plumage, a spotted breast, and a distinctive, melodious song.

Her·mon, Mount (hûr'mən). The highest elevation (9,232 feet) of the Anti-Lebanon range, on the Syria-Lebanon boundary.

Her·mo·si·llo (ĕr'mō-sē'yō). The capital of Sonora, Mexico, located in the west-central part of the state. Population, 132,000.

Her·mou·po·lis (hər-mo͞o'pə-lĭs). The capital and largest city of the Cyclades on Syros Island, Greece. Population, 21,000.

Her·mus. The ancient name for **Gediz.**

hern (hûrn) *n. Archaic & Regional.* A heron. [Variant of HERON.]

Her·ne (hĕr'nə). A city and industrial center of central North Rhine-Westphalia, West Germany. Population, 111,000.

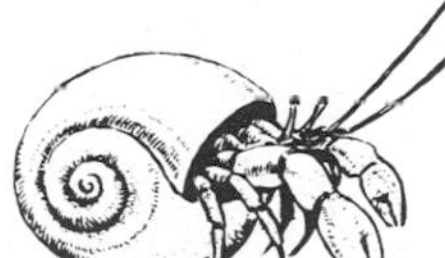

hermit crab

her·ni·a (hûr'nē-ə) *n., pl.* **-as** or **-niae** (-nē-ē'). The protrusion of an organ, organic part, or any bodily structure through the wall that normally contains it. Also called "rupture." [Middle English *hernia, hirnia,* from Latin *hernia.* See **gher-¹** in Appendix.*] —**her'ni·al** *adj.*

her·ni·ate (hûr'nē-āt') *intr.v.* **-ated, -ating, -ates.** To protrude through an abnormal bodily opening. [HERNI(A) + -ATE.] —**her'ni·a'tion** *n.*

he·ro (hîr'ō) *n., pl.* **-roes.** 1. In mythology and legend, a man, often born of one mortal and one divine parent, who is endowed with great courage and strength, celebrated for his bold exploits, and favored by the gods. **2.** Any man noted for feats of courage or nobility of purpose; especially, one who has risked or sacrificed his life: *heroes of forgotten wars.* **3.** A person prominent in some event, field, period, or cause by reason of his special achievements or contributions: *the heroes of medicine.* **4.** The principal male character in a novel, poem, or dramatic presentation. **5.** *Informal.* Any male regarded as a potential lover or protector. **6.** *Slang.* A sandwich of heroic size made with a small loaf of crusty bread split lengthwise, containing lettuce, condiments, and a variety of meats and cheeses. In this sense, also called "grinder," "hero sandwich," "hoagie," "sub," "submarine." [Back-formation from Middle English *heroes* (plural), from Latin *hērōs* (plural *hērōes*), a hero, from Greek *hērōs* (plural *hērōes*). See **ser-¹** in Appendix.*]

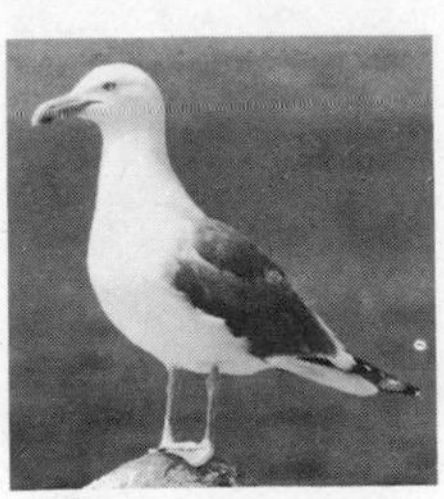

herring gull

He·ro (hîr′ō). *Greek Mythology.* A priestess of Aphrodite beloved by Leander, who nightly swam the Hellespont to visit her; upon finding him drowned, Hero drowned herself.

Her·od (hĕr′əd). Called "the Great." 73?–4 B.C. King of Judea 37–4 B.C.; convert to Judaism.

Her·od An·ti·pas (hĕr′əd ăn′tĭ-păs′). Son of Herod the Great; tetrarch of Galilee (4 B.C.–A.D. 40); examined Jesus at the request of Pilate.

He·ro·di·as (hĭ-rō′dē-əs). Niece and second wife of Herod Antipas; mother of Salome.

He·rod·o·tus (hĭ-rŏd′ə-təs). Called "Father of History." Greek historian of the fifth century B.C.

he·ro·ic (hĭ-rō′ĭk) *adj.* Also **he·ro·i·cal** (-ĭ-kəl). **1.** Of, relating to, or resembling the heroes of the classical age. **2.** Having or displaying the qualities of a hero; courageous; noble: *heroic deeds.* **3.** Calling for heroism; involving risk; gallant: *a heroic rescue.* **4. a.** Impressive in size or scope; grand; grandiose: *a heroic undertaking.* **b.** *Fine Arts.* Of a size somewhat larger than life: *heroic sculpture.* **5.** High-flown; ostentatious: *heroic language.* —*n.* **1.** A heroic verse or poem. **2.** *Plural.* Melodramatic behavior or language: *"We trust the House . . . will come up with answers without all the political heroics."* (Atlanta Constitution). —**he·ro′i·cal·ly** *adv.* —**he·ro′i·cal·ness** *n.*

heroic age. The period in a nation's history, especially that of ancient Greece and Rome, when its legendary heroes are supposed to have lived.

heroic couplet. A verse unit consisting of two rhymed lines in iambic pentameter.

heroic play. A type of Restoration tragedy written in rhymed couplets and generally characterized by extravagant declamatory rhetoric.

heroic quatrain. An iambic pentameter quatrain rhymed *abab.*

heroic verse. One of several verse forms suitable for and traditionally used in epic and dramatic poetry; typically, the dactylic hexameter in Greek and Latin, and the iambic pentameter in English. Also called "heroic meter."

her·o·in (hĕr′ō-ən) *n.* A white, odorless, bitter crystalline compound, $C_{17}H_{17}NO(C_2H_3O_2)_2$, that is derived from morphine and is a highly addictive narcotic. Also called "diacetylmorphine." [From a trademark.]

her·o·ine (hĕr′ō-ĭn) *n.* **1.** The female counterpart of a hero. **2.** The principal female character in a novel, poem, or dramatic presentation. [Latin *hērōīna,* Greek *hērōinē,* feminine of *hērōs,* HERO.]

her·o·ism (hĕr′ō-ĭz′əm) *n.* **1.** The condition or quality of being a hero. **2.** Heroic characteristics or conduct; courage; gallantry.

he·ron (hĕr′ən) *n.* Any of various wading birds of the family Ardeidae, having a long neck, long legs, and a long, pointed bill. [Middle English *he(i)roun, hern(e),* from Old French *hairon,* from Frankish *haigro* (unattested). See **ker-²** in Appendix.*]

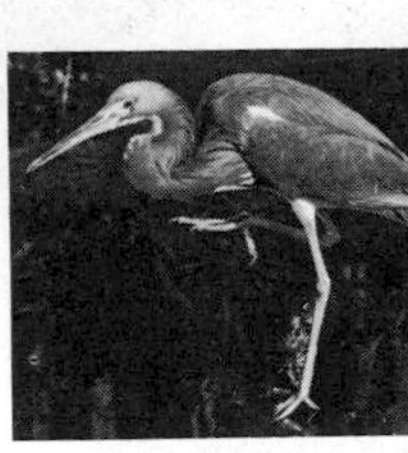

heron
Hydranassa tricolor

her·on·ry (hĕr′ən-rē) *n., pl.* **-ries.** A place frequented by herons.

He·roph·i·lus (hĭ-rŏf′ə-ləs). Greek anatomist and surgeon at Alexandria in the third century B.C.

hero worship. Profound or excessive admiration for popular heroes or for other persons revered as ideals.

he·ro-wor·ship (hîr′ō-wûr′shĭp) *tr.v.* **-shiped** or **-shipped, -shiping** or **-shipping, -ships. 1.** To revere as an ideal. **2.** To adulate. —**he′ro-wor′ship·er** *n.*

herp. herpetology.

her·pes (hûr′pēz′) *n.* Any of several viral diseases causing eruptions of the skin or mucous membrane; especially, herpes simplex or herpes zoster. [Latin *herpēs,* from Greek, shingles, "a creeping," from *herpein,* to creep. See **serp-²** in Appendix.*] —**her·pet′ic** (-pĕt′ĭk) *adj.*

herpes la·bi·al·is (lā′bē-ăl′ĭs). *Pathology.* A **cold sore** *(see).* [New Latin, "herpes of the lip."]

herpes sim·plex (sĭm′plĕks′). A viral infection with blistering of the lips, external nares, glans, prepuce, or vulva. [New Latin, "simple herpes."]

herpes zos·ter (zŏs′tər, zōs′-). A viral infection with eruption of vesicles along a nerve path on one side of the body, often accompanied or followed by severe neuralgia. Also called "shingles." [New Latin, "girdle herpes."]

herpetol. herpetology.

her·pe·tol·o·gist (hûr′pə-tŏl′ə-jĭst) *n.* A zoologist specializing in the study of reptiles and amphibians.

her·pe·tol·o·gy (hûr′pə-tŏl′ə-jē) *n. Abbr.* **herp., herpetol.** The scientific study of reptiles and amphibians as a branch of zoology. [Greek *herpeton,* "creeping thing," reptile, from *herpetos,* creeping, from *herpein,* to creep (see **serp-²** in Appendix*) + -LOGY.] —**her′pe·to·log′ic** (-tə-lŏj′ĭk), **her′pe·to·log′i·cal** *adj.* —**her′pe·to·log′i·cal·ly** *adv.*

Herr (hĕr) *n., pl.* **Herren** (hĕr′ən). *Abbr.* **Hr. 1.** A title of courtesy prefixed to the name or professional title of a German, equivalent to the English *Mister,* or *Sir,* according to the rank of the person. **2.** Lord. Applied to God the Father or Christ. [German, "Lord."]

Her·ren·volk (hĕr′ən-fôlk′) *n., pl.* **-völker** (-fœl′kər). A people assertedly endowed with the right to dominate and exploit other supposedly inferior peoples; especially, the German nation viewed as such a master race in the ideology of German imperialism (about 1890–1945). [German, "master race."]

Her·rick (hĕr′ĭk), **Robert.** 1591–1674. English Cavalier poet.

her·ring (hĕr′ĭng) *n., pl.* **herring** or **-rings.** Any of various fishes of the family Clupeidae; especially, a commercially important food fish, *Clupea harengus,* of Atlantic and Pacific waters. [Middle English *hering, heirreng,* Old English *hæring,* from West Germanic *hēringaz* (unattested).]

her·ring·bone (hĕr′ĭng-bōn′) *n.* **1.** A pattern consisting of rows of short, slanted parallel lines, with the direction of the slant alternating row by row, used in masonry, parquetry, embroidery, and weaving. **2.** A twilled fabric woven in this pattern. **3.** *Skiing.* A method of climbing a slope with the skis pointed outward, thus making tracks in a herringbone pattern. —*adj.* **1.** Having this pattern: *a herringbone brick sidewalk.* **2.** Made of herringbone-patterned cloth: *a herringbone suit.* —*v.* **herringboned, -boning, -bones.** —*tr.* To arrange or decorate with a herringbone pattern. —*intr.* **1.** To produce this pattern. **2.** *Skiing.* To ascend a slope by executing a herringbone. [From its resemblance to the skeletal structure of a herring.]

herring gull. A common, widely distributed gull, *Larus argentatus,* having gray and white plumage with black wing tips. [From its habit of preying on herrings.]

hers (hûrz). Possessive pronoun, absolute form of *her.* **1.** Belonging to her; her own. Used predicatively: *The brown boots are hers.* **2.** The one or ones belonging to her. Used substantively: *If you can't find your hat, take hers.* —**of hers.** Belonging or pertaining to her: *a friend of hers.* [Middle English *hirs, hires,* a double possessive from *hire,* HER.]

Her·schel (hûr′shəl; *German* hĕr′shəl), Sir **William.** Original name, Friedrich Wilhelm. 1738–1822. German-born English astronomer; worked with his sister, **Caroline Lucretia** (1750–1848), and his son, Sir **John Frederick William** (1792–1871).

her·self (hûr-sĕlf′) *pron.* A specialized form of the third person singular feminine pronoun. It is used: **1.** As a reflexive pronoun, forming the direct or indirect object of a verb or the object of a preposition: *She hurt herself.* **2.** For emphasis, after *she: She herself wasn't certain.* **3.** As an emphasizing substitute for *her* in a compound object: *The burden fell upon her sister and herself.* **4.** In an absolute construction: *In debt herself, she could offer no financial help.* **5.** As an indication of her real, normal, or healthy condition or identity: *She isn't herself today.*

Her·shey (hûr′shē), **Lewis Blaine.** Born 1893. American general; director of Selective Service (since 1941).

Herst·mon·ceux (hûrst′mən-sōō′). Also **Hurst·mon·ceux.** A village of southeastern Sussex, England; site of the Royal Observatory and the British meteorological station.

Hert·ford (här′fərd, härt′-). **1.** Also **Hert·ford·shire** (-shîr, -shər), **Herts** (härts, hûrts). *Abbr.* **Herts.** A county, 632 square miles in area, of southeast-central England. Population, 848,000. **2.** The county seat of this county, located in the west. Population, 18,000.

hertz (hûrts) *n. Symbol* **Hz** A unit of frequency equal to one cycle per second. [After Heinrich HERTZ.]

Hertz (hĕrts), **Gustav.** Born 1887. German atomic physicist.

Hertz (hĕrts), **Heinrich Rudolf.** 1857–1894. German physicist; worked on electromagnetic phenomena.

Hertz·i·an wave (hĕrt′sē-ən, hûrt′-). The former name for a **radio wave** *(see).* [After Heinrich HERTZ.]

Hertz·sprung-Rus·sell diagram (hĕrts′sprŭng-rŭs′əl). A graph of the logarithms of the luminosities of stars plotted against the logarithms of their surface temperatures. See **main sequence.** [Developed by Ejnar *Hertzsprung* (born 1873), Danish astronomer, and Henry N. *Russell* (1877–1957), American astronomer.]

Her·ze·go·vi·na (hûr′tsə-gō-vē′nə). *Serbo-Croatian* **Her·ce·go·vi·na** (hĕr′tsĕ-gō′vē-nä). A region, 3,531 square miles in area, of west-central Yugoslavia; now included in the federated republic of **Bosnia and Herzegovina** *(see).*

Her·zl (hĕr′tsəl), **Theodor.** 1860–1904. Hungarian-born Austrian man of letters; founder of Zionism.

he's (hēz). **1.** Contraction of *he is.* **2.** Contraction of *he has.*

Hesh·van (hĕsh-vän′, hĕsh′văn′, -vən) *n.* Also **Hesh·wan.** The second month on the Hebrew calendar. Also called "Marcheshvan." See **calendar.** [Hebrew *ḥeshwān,* short for *marḥeshwān.*]

He·si·od (hē′sē-əd, hĕs′ē-). Greek poet of the eighth century B.C. —**He′si·od′ic** (-ŏd′ĭk) *adj.*

hes·i·tan·cy (hĕz′ə-tən-sē) *n., pl.* **-cies. 1.** The state or quality of being hesitant; indecision. **2.** An instance of hesitating.

hes·i·tant (hĕz′ə-tənt) *adj.* Inclined or tending to hesitate. —**hes′i·tant·ly** *adv.*

hes·i·tate (hĕz′ə-tāt′) *intr.v.* **-tated, -tating, -tates. 1. a.** To be slow to act or decide; hold back in uncertainty; waver. **b.** To be reluctant, especially out of propriety, or concern or respect for others; have qualms about; demur: *"do you think she will hesitate to sacrifice you?"* (Shaw). **2.** To pause briefly as in uncertainty: *hesitate on the way upstairs.* **3.** To speak haltingly; falter. [Latin *haesitāre,* to stick fast, be undecided, hesitate, frequentative of *haerēre* (past participle *haesum*), to hold or hang fast, stick. See **ghais-** in Appendix.*] —**hes′i·tat′er** *n.* —**hes′i·tat′ing·ly** *adv.*

Synonyms: *hesitate, vacillate, waver, falter.* These verbs mean to express uncertainty or indecision. *Hesitate* implies inaction caused by uncertainty about what to do or say. *Vacillate* implies prolonged inaction during which one weighs alternative and usually conflicting courses without making a decisive choice. *Waver* suggests either inability to act, resulting from indecision, or tentative and ineffectual action once a choice has been made. *Falter* refers to acting indecisively or ineffectually and implies retreat from a course decided on or inability to carry it out.

hes·i·ta·tion (hĕz′ə-tā′shən) *n.* **1.** The act or an instance of hesitating. **2.** The state of being hesitant. **3.** A pause or faltering in speech. —**hes′i·ta′tive** *adj.* —**hes′i·ta′tive·ly** *adv.*

Hes·pe·ri·a (hĕ-spîr′ē-ə). The Western Land. A poetic name applied by the Greeks to Italy and by the Romans to Spain or regions beyond. [Latin, from Greek, from *hesperos, hesperios,* of evening, western, from *hesperos,* evening. See **wespero-** in Appendix.*]

Hes·pe·ri·an (hĕ-spîr′ē-ən) *adj. Poetic.* **1.** Of or pertaining to Hesperia or the west. **2.** Of or relating to the Hesperides.

Hes·per·i·des (hĕ-spĕr′ə-dēz′) *pl.n. Greek Mythology.* **1.** The nymphs, daughters of Hesperus, who together with a dragon watched over the garden of the golden apples in the Isles of the Blest. **2.** The garden of the golden apples. Used with a singular verb. **3.** The Isles of the Blest, situated at the western end of the earth. [Latin *Hesperidēs,* from Greek *Hesperides,* plural of *Hesperis,* "western," daughter of the west, from *hesperos, hesperios,* of evening, western. See **Hesperia.**] —**Hes′per·id′i·an** (-pə-rĭd′ē-ən), **Hes′per·id′e·an** *adj.*

hes·per·i·din (hĕs-pĕr′ə-dən). A white or colorless crystalline compound, C28H34O15, occurring in citrus fruit. [HESPERID(IUM) + -IN.]

hes·per·id·i·um (hĕs′pə-rĭd′ē-əm) *n., pl.* **-ia** (-ē-ə). *Botany.* A form of berry having a thickened, leathery rind and juicy pulp divided into segments, as an orange, lemon, or other citrus fruit. [New Latin, after the golden apples in the garden of HESPERIDES.]

Hess (hĕs), **Victor Franz.** 1883–1964. Austrian-born American physicist; studied cosmic rays.

Hess (hĕs), **(Walter Richard) Rudolf.** Born 1894. German Nazi leader; sentenced to life imprisonment (1946).

Hesse (hĕs). German **Hes·sen** (hĕs′ən). A state, 8,150 square miles in area, of central West Germany. Population, 4,494,000. Capital, Wiesbaden.

Hesse-Cas·sel (hĕs′kăs′əl). German **Hes·sen-Kas·sel** (hĕs′ən-käs′əl). A former German administrative division included in Hesse since 1945.

Hesse-Darm·stadt (hĕs′därm′stät). German **Hes·sen-Darm·stadt** (hĕs′ən-därm′shtät). A former German grand duchy, included in Hesse since 1945.

Hesse-Nas·sau (hĕs′năs′ô). German **Hes·sen-Nas·sau** (hĕs′ən-näs′ou′). A former German province, included in Hesse since 1945.

Hes·sian (hĕsh′ən) *n.* **1.** An inhabitant of Hesse. **2.** A Hessian mercenary in the British army in America during the Revolutionary War. **3.** Any mercenary. —*adj.* Of or relating to Hesse or its people.

Hessian boots. High, tasseled men's boots introduced into England by Hessians in the 19th century.

Hessian fly. A small fly, *Mayetiola destructor,* having larvae that infest and destroy wheat and other grain plants. [Supposed to have been brought to America by the Hessian troops during the Revolutionary War.]

hes·son·ite. Variant of **essonite.**

hest (hĕst) *n. Archaic.* Command; behest. [Middle English *heste,* variant of *hes,* command, Old English *hǣs.* See **kei-³** in Appendix.*]

Hes·ti·a (hĕs′tē-ə). *Greek Mythology.* The goddess of the hearth, daughter of Cronus and Rhea.

Hes·ton and I·sle·worth (hĕs′tən; ī′zəl-wûrth′). A former administrative division of London, England, now part of **Hounslow** *(see).*

he·tae·ra (hĭ-tîr′ə) *n., pl.* **-ras** or **-taerae** (-tîr′ē′). Also **he·tai·ra** (-tîr′ə) *pl.* **-ras** or **-tairai** (-tîr′ī′). **1.** In ancient Greece, a courtesan or concubine; especially, one of a special class of cultivated female companions. **2.** An adventuress. [Greek *hetaira,* feminine of *hetairos,* companion. See **seu-²** in Appendix.*]

he·tae·rism (hĭ-tîr′ĭz′əm) *n.* Also **he·tai·rism** (-tîr′ĭz′əm). **1.** Concubinage. **2.** The practice of communal marriage, supposed to have been characteristic of primitive societies.

hetero-, heter-. Indicates other, another, or different; for example, **heterogamy, heterosexual.** [From Greek *heteros,* other. See **sem-¹** in Appendix.*]

het·er·o·cer·cal (hĕt′ə-rō-sûr′kəl) *adj.* Pertaining to, designating, or characterized by a tail fin having two unequal lobes, with the vertebral column extending into the upper, usually larger lobe, as in sharks. [HETERO- + Greek *kerkos,* tail (see **ker-²** in Appendix*) + -AL.]

het·er·o·chro·mat·ic (hĕt′ə-rō-krə-măt′ĭk) *adj.* **1.** Of or pertaining to different colors; varicolored. **2.** Consisting of different wavelengths of light. **3.** Of or pertaining to heterochromatin. —**het′er·o·chro′ma·tism′** (-krō′mə-tĭz′əm) *n.*

het·er·o·chro·ma·tin (hĕt′ə-rō-krō′mə-tən) *n.* Chromosomal material exhibiting maximal staining in the nuclear meiotic interphase and lacking specific genetic activity.

het·er·o·chro·mo·some (hĕt′ə-rō-krō′mə-sōm′) *n.* A chromosome composed primarily of heterochromatin.

het·er·o·cy·clic (hĕt′ə-rō-sī′klĭk, -sĭk′lĭk) *adj. Chemistry.* Containing more than one kind of atom joined in a ring.

het·er·o·dox (hĕt′ə-rə-dŏks′) *adj.* **1.** Not in agreement with accepted beliefs; especially, departing from church doctrine or

dogma. Compare **orthodox. 2.** Holding unorthodox opinions. [Late Latin *heterodoxus,* from Greek *heterodoxos,* differing in opinion : HETERO- + *doxa,* opinion, notion, from *dokein,* to expect, think (see **dek-¹** in Appendix*).]

het·er·o·dox·y (hĕt′ər-ə-dŏk′sē) *n., pl.* **-ies. 1.** The condition or quality of being heterodox. **2.** A heterodox opinion or doctrine.

het·er·o·dyne (hĕt′ər-ə-dīn′) *adj.* Having alternating currents of two different frequencies that are combined to generate a current that has sum and difference frequencies, either of which may be used in radio or television receivers by proper tuning or filtering. —*tr.v.* **heterodyned, -dyning, -dynes.** To combine (a radio-frequency wave) with a locally generated wave of different frequency in order to produce a new frequency equal to the sum or difference of the two. [HETERO- + DYNE.]

het·er·oe·cious (hĕt′ə-rē′shəs) *adj.* Spending alternate stages of a life cycle on different, unrelated hosts. Said of parasites such as rusts and tapeworms. [HETERO- + Greek *oikia,* house (see **weik-¹** in Appendix*) + -OUS.] —**het′er·oe′cism′** (-sĭz′əm) *n.*

het·er·o·gam·ete (hĕt′ə-rō-găm′ēt′, -gə-mēt′) *n.* Either of two conjugating gametes such as the small, motile male spermatozoon and the larger, nonmotile female ovum, that differ in size, form, or behavior.

het·er·o·ga·met·ic (hĕt′ə-rō-gə-mĕt′ĭk) *adj.* Having a dissimilar pair of sex chromosomes, as in human males, or one unpaired sex chromosome, as in some male insects.

het·er·og·a·mous (hĕt′ə-rŏg′ə-məs) *adj.* **1.** *Biology.* Characterized by the fusion of unlike gametes in the reproductive process. **2.** *Botany.* Bearing flowers of different kinds, especially both male and female flowers. [HETERO- + -GAMOUS.]

het·er·og·a·my (hĕt′ə-rŏg′ə-mē) *n.* **1.** Alternation of generations, one sexual, the other parthenogenetic, as in some aphids. **2.** A state in which uniting gametes are dissimilar in structure and size as well as in function. [HETERO- + -GAMY.] —**het′er·o·gam′ic** (-rō-găm′ĭk) *adj.*

het·er·o·ge·ne·i·ty (hĕt′ə-rō-jə-nē′ə-tē) *n.* The quality or state of being heterogeneous; nonuniformity; dissimilarity.

het·er·o·ge·ne·ous (hĕt′ər-ə-jē′nē-əs, -jēn′yəs) *adj.* Also **het·er·og·e·nous** (hĕt′ə-rŏj′ə-nəs) (for sense 1). **1.** Consisting of or involving parts that are unlike or without interrelation; having dissimilar elements; not homogeneous: *a heterogeneous collection.* **2.** Completely different; incongruous. —See Synonyms at **miscellaneous.** [Medieval Latin *heterogeneus,* from Greek *heterogenēs* : HETERO- + *genos,* kind, sex (see **gene-** in Appendix*).] —**het′er·o·ge′ne·ous·ly** *adv.* —**het′er·o·ge′ne·ous·ness** *n.*

het·er·o·gen·e·sis (hĕt′ə-rō-jĕn′ə-sĭs) *n.* **Metagenesis** *(see).* —**het′er·o·ge·net′ic** (-jə-nĕt′ĭk) *adj.*

het·er·og·e·nous¹ (hĕt′ə-rŏj′ə-nəs) *adj.* Also **het·er·o·gen·ic** (-ə-rō-jĕn′ĭk). Originating outside the body. [HETERO- + -GENOUS.] —**het′er·og′en·y** *n.*

het·er·og·e·nous². Variant of **heterogeneous.**

het·er·og·o·nous (hĕt′ə-rŏg′ə-nəs) *adj.* Characterized by the alternation of sexual and asexual generations. [HETERO- + -GON(Y) + -OUS.] —**het′er·og′o·ny** *n.*

het·er·og·ra·phy (hĕt′ə-rŏg′rə-fē) *n., pl.* **-phies.** *Rare.* **1.** Spelling that is inconsistent, as the spelling of modern English: "*All climates alike groan under heterography.*" (De Quincey). **2.** Spelling that departs from conventional usage. [HETERO- + -GRAPHY.]

het·er·og·y·nous (hĕt′ə-rŏj′ə-nəs) *adj.* Having two types of females, one able to reproduce sexually, the other infertile, as in ants. [HETERO- + -GYNOUS.]

het·er·o·lec·i·thal (hĕt′ə-rō-lĕs′ə-thəl) *adj.* Having nonhomogeneous nutrient distribution in an ovum. [HETERO- + Greek *lekithos,* yolk (see **lecithin**) + -AL.]

het·er·ol·o·gous (hĕt′ə-rŏl′ə-gəs) *adj.* **1.** Derived from a different species: *a heterologous graft.* **2.** Of or pertaining to cytologic or histological elements not normally occurring in a designated part of the body. [HETERO- + Greek *logos,* word (see -logy) + -OUS.]

het·er·ol·o·gy (hĕt′ə-rŏl′ə-jē) *n.* Lack of correspondence between bodily parts, as in structure, arrangement, or development, arising from differences in origin. [HETERO- + -LOGY.]

het·er·ol·y·sis (hĕt′ə-rŏl′ə-sĭs) *n., pl.* **-ses** (-sēz′). **1.** *Biology.* Dissolution of cells or protein components in one species by lytic agents of another. **2.** *Chemistry.* An organic reaction in which the breaking of bonds leads to the formation of ion pairs. [New Latin : HETERO- + -LYSIS.] —**het′er·o·lyt′ic** (-rō-lĭt′ĭk) *adj.*

het·er·om·er·ous (hĕt′ə-rŏm′ər-əs) *adj. Biology.* Having unequal or differing parts within the same structure or similar structures. [HETERO- + -MEROUS.]

het·er·o·mor·phic (hĕt′ə-rō-môr′fĭk) *adj.* **1.** Having different forms at different periods of the life cycle. **2.** Heteromorphous. [HETERO- + -MORPHIC.] —**het′er·o·mor′phism′** *n.*

het·er·o·mor·phous (hĕt′ə-rō-môr′fəs) *adj.* Having an irregular or atypical form or forms, as in stages of insect metamorphosis. [HETERO- + -MORPHOUS.]

het·er·on·o·mous (hĕt′ə-rŏn′ə-məs) *adj.* **1.** Subject to external or foreign laws or domination; not autonomous. **2.** Differing in development or manner of specialization, as the dissimilar segments of certain arthropods. [HETERO- + Greek *nomos,* law (see **nem-²** in Appendix*) + -OUS.] —**het′er·on′o·mous·ly** *adv.*

het·er·o·nym (hĕt′ər-ə-nĭm′) *n.* One of two or more words that have identical spelling but different meanings and pronunciations; for example, *row* (a line) and *row* (a fight). [Back-formation from HETERONYMOUS.]

het·er·on·y·mous (hĕt′ə-rŏn′ə-məs) *adj.* **1.** Pertaining to or of the nature of a heteronym. **2.** Being different names or terms

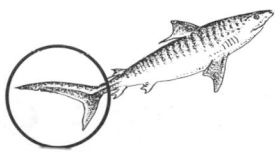

heterocercal
Heterocercal tail fin
of tiger shark

t tight/th thin, path/th this, bathe/ŭ cut/ûr urge/v valve/w with/y yes/z zebra, size/zh vision/ə about, item, edible, gallop, circus/

but having correspondence or interrelationship; for example, *master* and *mistress*. [Late Greek *heterōnumos* : HETERO- + Greek *onoma*, name (see **nomen-** in Appendix*).]

Het·er·o·ou·si·an (hĕt'ə-rō-ōō'sē-ən, -ou'sē-ən) *n.* Also **Het·er·ou·si·an** (hĕt'ə-rōō'-, hĕt'ə-rou'-). A Christian holding that the substance and nature of God the Father and God the Son are different; an Arian. Compare **Homoiousian, Homoousian.** —*adj.* Designating or pertaining to the Heteroousians or their beliefs. [From Late Greek *hetero(o)usios*, of different substance : HETERO- + Greek *ousia*, substance, essence, from *ōn* (stem *ous-*), present participle of *einai*, to be (see **es-** in Appendix*).]

het·er·o·phyl·lous (hĕt'ə-rō-fĭl'əs) *adj. Botany.* Having unlike leaves on one plant. [HETERO- + -PHYLLOUS.] —**het'er·o·phyl'ly** *n.*

het·er·o·phyte (hĕt'ər-ə-fīt') *n.* A plant, such as a parasite or saprophyte, that obtains its nourishment from living or dead organic sources. [HETERO- + -PHYTE.]

het·er·o·plas·ty (hĕt'ər-ə-plăs'tē) *n., pl.* **-ties.** The surgical grafting of tissue obtained from another person or from a lower animal. [HETERO- + -PLASTY.]

het·er·o·pla·sy (hĕt'ər-ō-plā'sē, -plăs'ē) *n.* Also **het·er·o·pla·sia** (-plā'zhə). *Biology. Obsolete.* Abnormal formation of tissue. [HETERO- + -PLASY.]

het·er·op·ter·ous (hĕt'ə-rŏp'tər-əs) *adj.* Of or belonging to the insect order Heteroptera, which includes the true bugs, characterized by forewings and hind wings that differ from one another. [New Latin *Heteroptera* : HETERO- + -PTEROUS.]

het·er·o·sex·u·al (hĕt'ə-rō-sĕk'shōō-əl) *adj.* 1. Characterized by attraction to the opposite sex. 2. Of or pertaining to different sexes. —*n.* A heterosexual person. —**het'er·o·sex'u·al'i·ty** *n.*

het·er·o·sis (hĕt'ə-rō'sĭs) *n.* Increased vigor or other superior qualities arising from the crossbreeding of genetically different plants or animals. Also called "hybrid vigor." [New Latin, from Greek *heter(oi)ōsis*, alteration, transformation, from *heteroioun*, to alter, from *heteroios*, different in kind, from *heteros*, one of two, the other. See **sem-**[1] in Appendix*.]

het·er·os·po·rous (hĕt'ə-rŏs'pər-əs, -ər-ə-spôr'əs, -spōr'əs) *adj. Botany.* Producing microspores and megaspores. [HETERO- + -SPOROUS.] —**het'er·os'po·ry** *n.*

het·er·o·tax·is (hĕt'ə-rō-tăk'sĭs) *n.* Also **het·er·o·tax·y** (hĕt'ər-ə-tăk'sē), **het·er·o·tax·i·a** (hĕt'ə-rō-tăk'sē-ə). Abnormal structural arrangement. [HETERO- + -TAXIS.] —**het'er·o·tac'tic** (-tăk'tĭk), **het'er·o·tac'tous** *adj.*

het·er·o·thal·lic (hĕt'ə-rō-thăl'ĭk) *adj.* Producing male gametangia in one structure or plant and female gametangia in a different structure or plant, as in some algae and fungi. [HETERO- + Greek *thallos*, young shoot, THALLUS.]

het·er·o·troph·ic (hĕt'ər-ə-trŏf'ĭk, -trō'fĭk) *adj.* Obtaining nourishment from organic substances, as do all animals and some plants. [HETERO- + -TROPHIC.] —**het'er·o·troph'i·cal·ly** *adv.* —**het'er·ot'ro·phy** (-ə-rŏt'rə-fē) *n.*

het·er·o·typ·ic (hĕt'ə-rō-tĭp'ĭk) *adj.* 1. *Biology.* Relating to or designating the first reduction division of meiosis. 2. Of a different type or form. [HETERO- + TYPIC(AL).]

het·er·o·zy·go·sis (hĕt'ə-rō-zĭ-gō'sĭs) *n.* 1. Derivation from or union between genetically different gametes. 2. The condition of being a heterozygote.

het·er·o·zy·gote (hĕt'ə-rō-zī'gōt') *n.* A zygote that has inherited different alleles at one or more loci. —**het'er·o·zy'gous** *adj.*

heth (KHĕt, KHĕth, KHĕs) *n.* Also **cheth.** The eighth letter in the Hebrew alphabet. See **alphabet.** [Hebrew *hēth.*]

heu·land·ite (hyōō'lən-dīt') *n.* A white, red, or yellow zeolite mineral with composition (Ca,Na,K)$_6$Al$_{10}$(Al,Si) Si$_{29}$O$_{80}$· 25H$_2$O. [After Henry *Heuland*, 19th-century English mineral collector.]

heu·ris·tic (hyōō-rĭs'tĭk) *adj.* 1. Helping to discover or learn; guiding or furthering investigation: *"the historian discovers the past by the judicious use of such a heuristic device as the 'ideal type'"* (Karl J. Weintraub). 2. Designating the educational method in which the student is allowed or encouraged to learn independently through his own investigation. [From Greek *heuriskein*, to discover, find. See **wer-**[11] in Appendix*.]

He·ve·li·us (hā-vā'lē-ŏōs), **Johan.** 1611–1687. German astronomer; mapped the moon and studied comets.

He·ve·sy (hĕ've̊-shē), **Georg von.** 1885–1966. Hungarian-born Danish chemist; worked on radioisotope indicators.

hew (hyōō) *v.* **hewed, hewn** (hyōōn) or **hewed, hewing, hews.** —*tr.* 1. a. To make or shape with an ax, knife, or other cutting tool. Often used with *out: hew out a small canoe.* b. To create a fissure, channel, or the like by natural means, as by lightning or dripping water. 2. To cut down with an ax; to fell. Used with *down: hew down an oak.* 3. To strike or cut; cleave; chop: *hewed in pieces.* —*intr.* 1. To cut by repeated blows of an ax, sword, or the like. 2. To adhere or conform; to keep; hold: *hew to the line.* [Hew, hewn; Middle English *hewen, hewen,* Old English *hēawan, hēawen.* See **kau-**[2] in Appendix*.]

HEW Department of Health, Education, and Welfare.

hex[1] (hĕks) *n.* 1. An evil spell; a curse. 2. A bad influence on or dominating control over someone or something. 3. A person who has such an influence or control; nemesis. —*tr.v.* **hexed, hexing, hexes.** 1. To work evil on; bewitch. 2. To wish or bring bad luck to, especially through superstitious means. [Pennsylvania Dutch, from German *Hexe*, witch, from Middle High German *hecse, häxe*, probably from Old High German *hagazussa, hagzissa.* See **kagh-** in Appendix*.]

hex[2] (hĕks) *adj.* Hexagonal. Said of hardware.

hex. hexagon; hexagonal.

hexa-, hex-. Indicates six; for example, **hexagram, hexane.** [Greek, from *hex*, six. See **sweks** in Appendix*.]

hex·a·chlo·ro·eth·ane (hĕk'sə-klôr'ō-ĕth'ān', hĕk'sə-klōr'-) *n.* Also **hex·a·chlor·eth·ane** (-klō'rĕth'ān', -klō'rĕth'ān'). A colorless crystalline compound, Cl$_3$CCCl$_3$, that is used as a camphor substitute and in pyrotechnics, explosives, and veterinary medicine. [HEXA- + CHLOR(O)- + ETHANE.]

hex·a·chlo·ro·phene (hĕk'sə-klôr'ə-fēn', -klōr'ə-fēn') *n.* An almost odorless white powder, (C$_6$HCl$_3$OH)$_2$CH$_2$, used as a bactericidal agent in soaps, cosmetics, and skin medications. [HEXA- + CHLORO- + PHEN(OL).]

hex·a·chord (hĕk'sə-kôrd') *n.* In medieval music, a diatonic sequence of tones, having a semitone in the middle and the others whole tones. [HEXA- + -CHORD.]

hex·ad (hĕk'săd') *n.* A group or series of six. [Late Latin *hexas* (stem *hexad-*), the number six, from Greek, from *hex*, six. See **sweks** in Appendix*.] —**hex·ad'ic** *adj.*

hex·a·gon (hĕk'sə-gŏn') *n. Abbr.* **hex.** A polygon having six sides. [Late Latin *hexagōnum*, from Greek *hexagōnon*, from *hexagōnos*, six-angled : HEXA- + -GON.]

hex·ag·o·nal (hĕk-săg'ə-nəl) *adj. Abbr.* **hex.** 1. Having six sides. 2. Containing or shaped like a hexagon. 3. *Mineralogy.* Having three equal axes intersecting at 60 degrees in one plane, and one axis of variable length that is at right angles to the others. —**hex·ag'o·nal·ly** *adv.*

hex·a·gram (hĕk'sə-grăm') *n.* 1. A six-pointed star, formed by extending each of the sides of a regular hexagon into equilateral triangles. See **Magen David.** 2. Any figure of six lines or sides. [HEXA- + -GRAM.]

hex·a·he·dron (hĕk'sə-hē'drən) *n., pl.* **-drons** or **-dra** (-drə). A polyhedron with six faces. [Greek *hexaedron*, from *hexaedros*, six-sided : HEXA- + -HEDRON.] —**hex'a·he'dral** *adj.*

hex·am·er·ous (hĕk-săm'ər-əs) *adj.* 1. Having six similar parts or divisions. 2. *Botany.* Having flower parts, such as petals, sepals, and stamens, in sets of six. Also written *6-merous.* [HEXA- + -MEROUS.] —**hex·am'er·ism'** *n.*

hex·am·e·ter (hĕk-săm'ə-tər) *n.* A dactylic line consisting of five dactyls and a trochee or spondee. [Latin, from Greek *hexametron*, from *hexametros*, having six metrical feet : HEXA- + -METER.] —**hex'a·met'ric** (-sə-mĕt'rĭk), **hex'a·met'ri·cal** *adj.*

hex·a·meth·yl·ene·tet·ra·mine (hĕk'sə-mĕth'ə-lēn'tĕt'rə-mēn') *n. Chemistry.* Methenamine *(see).* [HEXA- + METHYLENE + TETR(A)- + -AMINE.]

hex·ane (hĕk'sān') *n.* A colorless, flammable liquid, CH$_3$-(CH$_2$)$_4$CH$_3$, derived from the fractional distillation of petroleum and used as a solvent and as the working fluid in low-temperature thermometers. [HEX(A)- + -ANE.]

hex·a·pod (hĕk'sə-pŏd') *n.* Any member of the class Insecta (or Hexapoda); an insect. —*adj.* Also **hex·ap·o·dous** (hĕk-săp'ə-dəs). 1. Of or belonging to the Hexapoda. 2. Having six legs or feet. [Noun; from New Latin *Hexapoda* : HEXA- + -POD. Sense 2; Greek *hexapous* (stem *hexapod-*) : HEXA- + -POD.]

Hex·a·teuch (hĕk'sə-tōōk', -tyōōk') *n.* The first six books of the Old Testament. [HEXA- + Greek *teukhos*, tool, case holding writing material, roll of papyrus, volume (see **dheugh-** in Appendix*).]

hex·o·san (hĕk'sə-săn') *n.* Any of several polysaccharides that form a hexose on hydrolysis. [HEXOS(E) + -AN.]

hex·ose (hĕk'sōs') *n.* Any of various simple sugars that have six carbon atoms per molecule. [HEX(A)- + -OSE.]

hex·yl (hĕk'səl) *n.* The hydrocarbon radical C$_6$H$_{13}$, having a valence of 1. [HEX(A)- + -YL.]

hex·yl·re·sor·ci·nol (hĕk'səl-rə-zôr'sə-nôl', -nōl') *n.* A yellowish-white crystalline phenol, C$_{12}$H$_{18}$O$_2$, used as an antiseptic and anthelmintic.

hey (hā) *interj.* 1. Used to express surprise, appreciation, wonder, or the like: *Hey, that's nice!* 2. Used to attract attention: *Hey, you!* [Middle English *hei, hay.*]

hey·day (hā'dā') *n.* The period of greatest popularity, success, fashion, power, or the like; prime: *"Those tough Negroes' heyday had been before the big 1931 Seabury Investigation"* (Malcolm X). [Earlier *heyda*, probably an extension of HEY.]

Heywood (hā'wŏŏd'), **Thomas.** 1574–1641. English playwright and actor.

Hez·e·ki·ah (hĕz'ĭ-kī'ə). Also **Ez·e·chi·as** (ĕz'ĭ-kī'əs), **Ez·e·ki·as.** 740?–692? B.C. King of Judah (720?–692? B.C.). [Hebrew *hizqiyyāh(ū)*, "the Lord has strengthened" : *hizeq*, he strengthened + *yāh*, God, short for YAHWEH.]

hf high frequency.

Hf The symbol for the element hafnium.

hfs hyperfine structure.

hg hectogram.

Hg The symbol for the element mercury (Latin *hydrargyrum*).

HG, H.G. High German.

hgt. height.

H.H. 1. His (or Her) Highness. 2. His Holiness.

hhd hogshead.

HHFA Housing and Home Finance Agency.

H-hour (āch'our') *n. Military.* Zero hour *(see).* [H, abbreviation for HOUR.]

hi (hī) *interj.* 1. *Informal.* Used to express greeting. 2. *British.* Used expressively to call attention. [Middle English *hy.*]

HI Hawaii with Zip Code.

H.I. Hawaiian Islands.

Hi·a·le·ah (hī'ə-lē'ə). A city of southeastern Florida, five miles northwest of Miami. Population, 67,000.

hi·a·tus (hī-ā'təs) *n., pl.* **hiatuses** or **hiatus.** 1. A gap or missing section; lacuna. 2. Any loss or interruption in time or continuity; break: *"we are likely to be disconcerted by ... hiatuses of*

hexagram

ă pat/ā pay/âr care/ä father/b bib/ch church/d deed/ĕ pet/ē be/f fife/g gag/h hat/hw which/ĭ pit/ī pie/îr pier/j judge/k kick/l lid, needle/m mum/n no, sudden/ng thing/ŏ pot/ō toe/ô paw, for/oi noise/ou out/ŏŏ took/ōō boot/p pop/r roar/s sauce/sh ship, dish/

thought" (Edmund Wilson). **3.** The immediate sequence of two vowel sounds, each of which constitutes a separate syllable. **4.** *Anatomy.* A separation, aperture, or fissure. [Latin *hiātus,* a gaping, gap, from the past participle of *hiāre,* to gape. See **ghēi-** in Appendix.*]

Hi·a·wath·a (hī'ə-wŏth'ə, -wô'thə, hē'ə-) *n.* **1.** The Indian hero of Longfellow's long narrative poem *The Song of Hiawatha* (1855). **2.** A 16th-century Mohawk chief who is credited with the organization of the Five Nations.

hi·ba·chi (hĭ-bä'chē) *n., pl.* **-chis.** A portable charcoal-burning brazier with a grill, often used for cooking at table. [Japanese : *hi,* fire + *bachi,* bowl.]

hi·ber·nac·u·lum (hī'bər-năk'yə-ləm) *n., pl.* **-la** (-lə). Also **hi·ber·na·cle** (-năk'əl) (for sense 2). *Biology.* **1.** A case, covering, or structure in which an organism remains dormant for the winter. **2.** The shelter of a hibernating animal. [Latin *hībernāculum,* winter residence, from *hībernus,* winter. See **ghei-**[2] in Appendix.*]

hi·ber·nal (hī-bûr'nəl) *adj.* Of or pertaining to winter. [Latin *hībernālis,* from *hībernus,* winter. See **ghei-**[2] in Appendix.*]

hi·ber·nate (hī'bər-nāt') *intr.v.* **-nated, -nating, -nates.** To pass the winter in a dormant or torpid state. [Latin *hībernāre,* from *hībernus,* winter. See **ghei-**[2] in Appendix.*] **—hi'ber·na'tor** (-nā'tər) *n.*

hi·ber·na·tion (hī'bər-nā'shən) *n.* **1.** The action of hibernating. **2.** The state of torpidity or inactivity in which some organisms pass the winter. Compare **aestivation.** **3.** Any state or period of inactivity likened to that of a wintering animal: "*Stirring suddenly from long hibernation I knew myself once more a poet*" (Robert Graves).

Hi·ber·ni·a (hī-bûr'nē-ə). The Latin name for Ireland. [Latin, variant (influenced by *hībernus,* winter) of *I(u)verna, Juberna,* from Greek *Iernē.* See **Iveriū** in Appendix.*] **—Hi·ber'ni·an** *adj.* **—Hi·ber'ni·an·ism'** *n.*

hi·bis·cus (hī-bĭs'kəs) *n.* Any of various chiefly tropical plants, shrubs, or trees of the genus *Hibiscus,* having large, showy, variously colored flowers. [New Latin *Hibiscus,* Latin, from Greek *hibiskos*†, marshmallow.]

hic·cup (hĭk'ŭp) *n.* Also **hic·cough** (hĭk'ŭp). **1.** A spasm of the diaphragm resulting in a sudden, abortive inhalation that is stopped by a spasmodic glottal closure. **2.** *Plural.* An attack of hiccups. *—intr.v.* **hiccupped, -cupping, -cups.** Also **hic·cough, -coughed, -coughing, -coughs. 1.** To make a sound resembling that of a hiccup. **2.** To have an attack of hiccups. [Earlier *hicket, hickop* (imitative).]

hick (hĭk) *n. Informal.* A gullible, provincial person; yokel. *—adj.* Rural. Used disparagingly. [From *Hick,* pet form of RICHARD.]

hick·ey (hĭk'ē) *n., pl.* **-eys.** *Informal.* **1.** Any device or contrivance; a gadget. **2.** A pimple or visible birthmark. **3.** *Slang.* A reddish mark on the skin caused by kissing. **4.** A pipe-bending apparatus. **5.** A usually threaded electrical fitting to connect a fixture to an outlet box. [Origin unknown.]

Hick·ok (hĭk'ŏk'), **James Butler.** Known as Wild Bill Hickok. 1837–1876. U.S. frontier marshal.

hick·o·ry (hĭk'ə-rē) *n., pl.* **-ries. 1.** Any of several chiefly North American deciduous trees of the genus *Carya,* having smooth or shaggy bark, compound leaves, and hard, smooth nuts with an edible kernel. **2.** The hard, tough, heavy wood of any of these trees. **3.** A walking stick or switch made from such wood. [Shortening of earlier *pohickery,* from Virginian native name *pawcohiccora,* food prepared from crushed hickory nuts.]

Hicks·ville (hĭks'vĭl'). A city of western Long Island, New York State. Population, 50,000.

Hic·po·chee, Lake (hĭk-pō'chē). A lake of south-central Florida; a link in the Cross-Florida Waterway.

hi·dal·go (hĭ-dăl'gō; *Spanish* ē-thäl'gō) *n., pl.* **-gos.** A member of the minor nobility in Spain. [Spanish, from Old Spanish *hijo dalgo,* "son of something (that is to say, property)" : *hijo,* son, from Latin *fīlius* (see **dhēi-** in Appendix*) + *de,* of + *algo,* something, from Latin *aliquid* : *alius,* some, other (see **al-**[1] in Appendix*) + *quid,* what, something (see **kwo-** in Appendix*).]

Hi·dal·go (hĭ-dăl'gō; *Spanish* ē-thäl'gō). A state, 8,058 square miles in area, of central Mexico. Population, 995,000. Capital, Pachuca.

hid·den·ite (hĭd'n-īt') *n.* A transparent emerald-green variety of spodumene, used as a gemstone. [Discovered by William E. Hidden (1853–1918), American mineralogist.]

Hidden Peak. See **Gasherbrum I.**

hide[1] (hīd) *v.* **hid** (hĭd), **hidden** (hĭd'n) or **hid, hiding, hides.** *—tr.* **1.** To put or keep out of sight; secrete. **2.** To prevent the disclosure or recognition of; conceal. **3.** To cut off from sight; cover up. **4.** To avert (one's gaze) in shame or grief. *—intr.* **1.** To keep oneself out of sight. **2.** To seek refuge. [Hide, hid, hidden or hid; Middle English *hiden, hid, hidden* (formed by analogy with RIDE, RIDDEN) or *hidd,* Old English *hȳdan, hȳdde, hȳdd.* See **skeu-** in Appendix.*] **—hid'er** *n.*

Synonyms: *hide, conceal, secrete, cache, screen, bury, cloak.* These verbs mean to keep from the sight or knowledge of others. *Hide* and *conceal* refer both to putting physical things out of sight and to withholding information or disguising one's feelings or thoughts. *Conceal* often implies deliberate intent to keep from sight or knowledge, whereas *hide* also can refer to natural phenomena: *The thief hid* (or *concealed*) *the stolen money. Night hides the city's ugliness. Secrete, cache, screen,* and *bury* refer chiefly to removing physical objects from sight. *Secrete* and *cache* involve concealment in a place unknown to others, and *cache* also implies storing protectively for later use. To *screen* is to shield or block from view by interposing another object, and to *bury* is to cover. *Cloak* usually refers to concealing thoughts, plans, or the like by secrecy or by masking or disguising them.

hide[2] (hīd) *n.* The skin of an animal; especially, the comparatively thick, tough skin or pelt of a large animal. *—tr.v.* **hided, hiding, hides.** To beat the hide of; flog. [Middle English *hyde, hide,* Old English *hȳd.* See **skeu-** in Appendix.*]

hide[3] (hīd) *n.* Old English measure of land, usually the amount held adequate for one free family and its dependents. [Middle English *hide, hyde,* Old English *hīgid, hīd.* See **kei-**[1] in Appendix.*]

hide-and-seek (hīd'n-sēk') *n.* **1.** A children's game in which one player tries to find and catch others who are hiding. **2.** Any game or action involving evasion.

hide·a·way (hīd'ə-wā') *n.* **1.** A place of concealment; hide-out. **2.** A secluded or isolated place.

hide·bound (hīd'bound') *adj.* **1.** Having abnormally dry, stiff skin that adheres closely to the underlying flesh. Said of domestic animals such as cattle. **2.** Having the bark so contracted and unyielding as to hinder growth. Said of trees. **3.** Unduly adhering to one's own opinions or prejudices; narrow-minded.

hid·e·ous (hĭd'ē-əs) *adj.* **1.** Physically repulsive; revolting; ugly. **2.** Repugnant to the moral sense; despicable; odious. [Middle English *hidous,* from Old French *hidous, hideus,* from *hi(s)de,* fear, horror, perhaps from Latin *hispidus,* rough, shaggy. See **ghers-** in Appendix.*] **—hid'e·ous·ly** *adj.* **—hid'e·ous·ness** *n.*

hide-out (hīd'out') *n.* A place of shelter or concealment.

hi·dro·sis (hĭ-drō'sĭs) *n.* Perspiration, especially in excessive or abnormal amounts. [New Latin, from Greek *hidrōsis,* sweating, from *hidrōs,* sweat. See **sweid-**[2] in Appendix.*] **—hi·drot'ic** (-drŏt'ĭk) *adj.*

hie (hī) *intr.v.* **hied, hieing** or **hying, hies.** To go quickly; hasten; hurry. [Middle English *hien, hyghen,* Old English *hīgian,* to strive, exert oneself, hurry. See **kīgh-** in Appendix.*]

hi·e·mal (hī'ə-məl) *adj.* Of or pertaining to winter. [Latin *hiemālis,* from *hiems,* winter. See **ghei-**[2] in Appendix.*]

hi·er·arch (hī'ə-rärk', hī'rärk') *n.* **1.** One who occupies a position of authority in an ecclesiastical hierarchy. **2.** One who occupies a high position in a hierarchy. [Old French *hierarche,* from Medieval Latin *hierarcha,* from Greek *hierarkhēs,* president of sacred rites, high priest : HIER(O)- + -ARCH.]

hi·er·ar·chism (hī'ə-rär-kĭz'əm, hī'rär-) *n.* Hierarchical practice or principles. **—hi'er·ar'chist** *n.*

hi·er·ar·chy (hī'ə-rär'kē, hī'rär'-) *n., pl.* **-chies. 1. a.** A body of persons organized or classified according to rank, capacity, or authority. **b.** A body of entities arranged in a graded series. **2.** Ecclesiastical rule or authority. **3.** A body of clergy organized into successive ranks or grades. [Middle English *ierarchie,* from Old French, from Medieval Latin *(h)ierarchia,* rule of a priest, from Greek *hierarkhia,* from *hierarkhēs,* HIERARCH.] **—hi'er·ar'chi·cal, hi'er·ar'chic** *adj.* **—hi'er·ar'chi·cal·ly** *adv.*

hi·er·at·ic (hī'ə-răt'ĭk, hī-răt'-) *adj.* Also **hi·er·at·i·cal** (-ĭ-kəl) (for sense 1). **1.** Of or associated with sacred persons or offices; sacerdotal: *a hieratic gesture.* **2.** Constituting or pertaining to a simplified cursive style of Egyptian hieroglyphics that was developed and chiefly used by the priestly class. Compare **demotic.** [Latin *hieraticus,* from Greek *hieratikos,* from *hieratos* (unattested), from *hierasthai,* to be a priest, from *hiereus,* priest, from *hieros,* sacred, supernatural. See **eis-**[1] in Appendix.*] **—hi'er·at'i·cal·ly** *adv.*

hiero–. Indicates sacred or holy; for example, **hierocracy, hierogram.** [Greek, from *hieros,* holy, sacred, supernatural. See **eis-**[1] in Appendix.*]

hi·er·oc·ra·cy (hī'ə-rŏk'rə-sē) *n., pl.* **-cies.** Government by the clergy; ecclesiastical rule : "*Vermont will emerge next, because least . . . under the yoke of hierocracy.*" (Jefferson). [HIERO- + -CRACY.] **—hi'er·o·crat'ic** (-ər-ə-krăt'ĭk), **hi'er·o·crat'i·cal** *adj.*

hi·er·o·dule (hī'ər-ə-dōōl', -dyōōl') *n.* A temple slave in the service of a specified deity. Used especially with reference to the ritual prostitution at the temple of Aphrodite in Corinth. [Late Latin *hierodūlus,* from Greek *hierodoulos* : HIERO- + *doulos*†, slave.]

hi·er·o·glyph·ic (hī'ər-ə-glĭf'ĭk, hī'rə-) *adj.* Also **hi·er·o·glyph·i·cal** (-ĭ-kəl). **1.** Written in or pertaining to a system of writing used in ancient Egypt, in which figures or objects are used to represent words or sounds. **2.** Written with hieroglyphic pictures or symbols. **3.** Hard to read; illegible; undecipherable. *—n.* Also **hi·er·o·glyph** (hī'ər-ə-glĭf', hī'rə-). **1.** A picture or symbol used in hieroglyphic writing. **2.** *Plural.* Hieroglyphic writing. **3.** A picture or symbol with a hidden meaning; emblem. **4.** *Plural.* Illegible or undecipherable writing. [Old French *hieroglyphique,* from Late Latin *hieroglyphicus,* from Greek *hierogluphikos,* written in hieroglyphics : HIERO- (originally used in Egyptian sacred writings) + *gluphē,* carving, engraving, from *gluphein,* to carve (see **gleubh-** in Appendix*).] **—hi'er·o·glyph'i·cal·ly** *adv.* **—hi'er·o·glyph'ist** *n.*

hi·er·o·gram (hī'ər-ə-grăm', hī'rə-) *n.* A sacred symbol. [HIERO- + -GRAM.]

hi·er·ol·o·gy (hī'ə-rŏl'ə-jē) *n., pl.* **-gies.** The sacred literature of a given people. [HIERO- + -LOGY.]

hi·er·o·phant (hī'ər-ə-fănt', hī'rə-, hī-ĕr'ə-) *n.* **1.** An expounder of Eleusinian mysteries. **2.** An interpreter of sacred mysteries or arcane knowledge: "*What did even the hierophants of science know of . . . evil?*" (Malcolm Lowry). [Late Latin *hierophanta, hierophantēs,* from Greek *hierophantēs,* interpreter of sacred mysteries : HIERO- + *phainein,* to reveal, show (see **bhā-**[1] in Appendix*).] **—hi'er·o·phan'tic** *adj.*

Hi·er·o·sol·y·ma. The ancient name for **Jerusalem.**

hibachi

hibiscus
Hibiscus rosa-sinensis

Wild Bill Hickok

hieroglyphic
Inscription from Theban tomb of about 650 B.C.

Hier·ro (yĕr′rō). Formerly **Fer·ro** (fĕr′rō). The smallest island (107 square miles) of the Canary group, Spain.

hi·fa·lu·tin. Variant of **highfalutin.**

hi-fi (hī′fī′) n. **1.** High fidelity (see). **2.** An electronic system for reproducing high-fidelity sound from radio, records, or magnetic tape. [HI(GH) FI(DELITY).]

Hig·gin·son (hĭg′ən-sən), **Thomas Wentworth Storrow.** 1823–1911. American clergyman and author.

hig·gle (hĭg′əl) intr.v. **-gled, -gling, -gles.** To haggle. [Variant of HAGGLE.]

hig·gle·dy-pig·gle·dy (hĭg′əl-dē-pĭg′əl-dē) adv. In utter disorder or confusion. —n. A jumble. —adj. Topsy-turvy; jumbled. [Rhyming and jingling formation probably based on PIG (presumably from the manner in which pigs huddle together).]

high (hī) adj. **higher, highest. 1.** Extending or projecting upward; tall; elevated. **2.** Having a specified elevation: ten feet high. **3.** Being at or near its peak or culmination: high noon. **4.** Beginning to decompose, as meat; excessively gamy. **5.** Far removed in time; remote: high antiquity. **6.** Piercing in tone or sound: a high note. **7.** Situated far from the equator: a high latitude. **8.** Of great moment or importance. **a.** Pre-eminent in rank or standing: the high priest. **b.** Serious; weighty; grave: high treason. **9.** Lofty or exalted in quality, character, or style: "the glorious language and high metaphors of St. Paul" (Walton). **10. a.** Of great quantity, magnitude, or degree: a high temperature. **b.** Of great force or violence: high winds. **11.** Costly or expensive; dear: high prices. **12.** Showing pride, arrogance, or disdain. **13.** In a state of excitement or euphoria; elated: high spirits. **14.** Slang. Intoxicated by alcohol or a narcotic. **15.** At an advanced stage of development or complexity. **16.** Phonetics. Pronounced with part of the tongue close to the palate: a high vowel. —n. **1.** A high place or region. **2.** Abbr. h., H. The transmission gear of an automotive vehicle producing maximum speed. **3.** A center of high atmospheric pressure; anticyclone. **4.** Slang. Intoxication or euphoria induced by a stimulant or narcotic. —high and dry. **1.** Helpless; destitute. **2.** Out of water. Said of ships. —high and low. Here and there; all around; everywhere. —high and mighty. Arrogant; domineering; disdainful. [Middle English hei, high, Old English hēah. See keu-² in Appendix.*] —high′ly adv.

Synonyms: high, tall, lofty, towering, elevated. These adjectives mean standing out or otherwise distinguished because of height. High and tall, the most general terms, are sometimes interchangeable. In general high refers to what rises a considerable distance from a base or is situated at a level well above another level considered as a base: a high mountain; a high ceiling; a high shelf. Tall describes what rises to a considerable extent; it often refers to living things and to what has great height in relation to breadth or in comparison with like things: a tall man; tall trees; a tall building. Lofty describes what is imposingly or inspiringly high. Towering suggests height that causes awe or makes something stand out conspicuously. Elevated stresses height in relation to immediate surroundings; it refers principally to being raised or situated above a normal level or above the average level of an area.

High At·las (ăt′ləs). A mountain range of central Morocco; part of the **Atlas Mountains** (see).

high·ball (hī′bôl′) n. **1.** A beverage consisting of alcoholic liquor and water or a carbonated liquid served in a tall glass. **2.** A railroad signal indicating full speed ahead. —intr.v. **highballed, -balling, -balls.** To move ahead at full speed.

high·bind·er (hī′bīn′dər) n. **1.** A member of a Chinese-American secret society of paid assassins and blackmailers. **2.** A corrupt politician. [From the High-binders, a New York City gang (circa 1806).]

high-born (hī′bôrn′) adj. Of noble birth.

high·boy (hī′boi′) n. A tall chest of drawers divided into two sections and supported on four legs. Also British "tallboy."

high-bred (hī′brĕd′) adj. Of superior breed or stock; highborn.

high·brow (hī′brou′) n. Informal. One who has or affects superior learning or culture. Compare **middlebrow, lowbrow.** —high′brow′, high′browed′ adj.

high-bush cranberry (hī′bŏosh′). A North American shrub, Viburnum trilobum, having broad clusters of white flowers and scarlet fruit. Also called "cranberry bush."

high·chair (hī′châr′) n. A baby's feeding chair, usually with a detachable tray and mounted on tall legs.

High-Church (hī′chûrch′) adj. Pertaining to the most orthodox branch of the Anglican Church which emphasizes the sacerdotal, sacramental, and liturgical Catholic elements of orthodox Christianity. Compare **Broad-Church, Low-Church.** —High′-Church′man n.

high-class (hī′klăs′, -kläs′) adj. First-class.

high day. A holy day; feast day.

higher criticism. Critical study of Biblical texts with regard to questions of their character, composition, editing, and collection. Compare **lower criticism.**

high·er-up (hī′ər-ŭp′) n. Informal. One who has a higher rank, position, or status.

high explosive. Abbr. **HE** A powerful, fast-acting explosive.

high-fa·lu·tin, hi·fa·lu·tin (hī′fə-lōōt′n) adj. Also **high-fa·lu·ting** (-lōōt′n, -lōō′tĭng). Informal. Pompous or pretentious. [HIGH + falutin, perhaps variant of fluting, present participle of the verb FLUTE.] —high′fa·lu′tin n.

high fidelity. The electronic reproduction of sound, especially from broadcast, recorded, or taped sources, with minimal distortion. Also called "hi-fi." —high′-fi·del′i·ty adj.

high-fli·er (hī′flī′ər) n. Also **high-fly·er. 1.** One that flies high. **2.** An improvident undertaking.

highboy
Mid-18th century

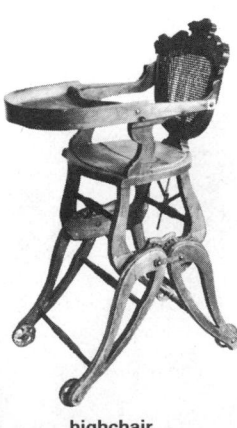

highchair
Nineteenth-century American

high-flown (hī′flōn′) adj. **1.** Lofty; exalted. **2.** Pretentious; inflated.

high-fly·ing (hī′flī′ĭng) adj. **1.** That flies high. **2.** Lofty in form or ambitions.

high frequency. Abbr. **hf** A radio frequency (see) in the range between 3 and 30 megacycles per second.

High German. 1. Abbr. **HG, H.G.** German as indigenously spoken and written in southern Germany. See **Low German, Old High German, Middle High German. 2.** German. [Translation of German Hochdeutsch.]

high-grade (hī′grād′) adj. Of superior quality.

high-hand·ed (hī′hăn′dĭd) adj. In an arrogant or arbitrary manner. —high′hand′ed·ly adv. —high′hand′ed·ness n.

high-hat (hī′hăt′) n. Slang. One thought likely to wear a high hat; a snob. —tr.v. (hī′hăt′) **high-hatted, -hatting, -hats.** To be condescending or supercilious toward. —high′-hat′ adj.

high·jack. Variant of **hijack.**

high jinks. Mischievous merriment; lively sport.

high jump. 1. A jump for height made over an adjustable horizontal bar in a field contest. **2.** Such a contest.

high-keyed (hī′kēd′) adj. **1.** Having a high pitch; shrill. **2.** Excitable; nervous; high-strung. **3.** Bright in color; intense.

high·land (hī′lənd) n. **1.** Elevated land. **2.** Plural. A mountainous or hilly region or part of a country. —adj. **1.** Of, relating to, or characteristic of such a region. **2.** Capital **H.** Of or relating to The Highlands.

high·land·er (hī′lən-dər) n. **1.** One who lives in a highland area. **2.** Capital **H.** An inhabitant of The Highlands.

Highland fling. A folk dance of The Highlands.

High·lands, The (hī′ləndz). A mountainous region of northern and western Scotland, north of and including the Grampians.

Highlands of the Hud·son (hŭd′sən). A hilly region of southeastern New York State, on either side of the Hudson River. Highest elevation, 1,340 feet.

high life. 1. A fashionable or luxurious style of living. **2.** A modern ballroom dance of West African origin, consisting of variations of the one-step made to a decisive beat.

high·light (hī′līt′) n. **1.** In painting or photography, a brilliantly lighted area of the subject appearing as a luminous spot. **2.** An outstanding event or detail. —tr.v. **highlighted, -lighting, -lights. 1.** To give prominence to, as with illumination. **2.** To add highlights to, as in painting. **3.** To be the highlight of.

High Mass. Roman Catholic Church. A sung Mass celebrated by a priest or prelate, assisted by a deacon and a subdeacon, and following the complete ritual with the use of music and incense.

high-mind·ed (hī′mīn′dĭd) adj. **1.** Characterized by morally lofty ideals or conduct; magnanimous. **2.** Archaic. Disdainfully proud; arrogant; haughty. —high′mind′ed·ly adv. —high′mind′ed·ness n.

high muckamuck. Slang. A muckamuck (see). [Chinook jargon hiu muckamuck, "plenty to eat."]

high·ness (hī′nĭs) n. **1.** Tallness; height. **2.** Greatness, as of degree or amount. **3.** Capital **H.** A title of honor for royalty. Used with His, Her, Your, or Their: Their Highnesses the King and Queen.

high-oc·tane (hī′ŏk′tān′) adj. Having a high octane number.

high-pitched (hī′pĭcht′) adj. **1. a.** Having a high pitch to the ear. **b.** Tuned high. **2.** Lofty; exalted. **3.** Steeply sloped.

high place. In early Semitic religions, a place of worship on top of a hill.

High Point. A city of north-central North Carolina. Population, 62,000.

high-pres·sure (hī′prĕsh′ər) adj. **1.** Of or pertaining to pressures higher than normal; especially, higher than atmospheric pressure. **2.** Informal. Using aggressive and persistent persuasion in selling. —tr.v. **high-pressured, -suring, -sures.** Informal. To convince or influence by using such methods of persuasion.

high relief. A sculptural relief in which the modeled forms project from the background by at least half their depth. Also called "alto-relievo." [Translation of French haut-relief.]

high-rise (hī′rīz′) adj. Designating a tall building with many stories or levels reached by elevators.

high-road (hī′rōd′) n. **1.** Chiefly British. A main road; highway. **2.** A simple, direct, or sure path: the highroad to happiness.

high school. Abbr. **h.s., H.S. 1.** A secondary school that includes grades 9 through 12. **2.** A secondary school that includes junior and senior high school, consisting of grades 7 through 12. —high′-school′ adj.

high seas. The open waters of an ocean or sea beyond the limits of national territorial jurisdiction.

high sign. Informal. A gesture or other discreet signal given as a secret warning that it is time to leave, or the like.

high-sound·ing (hī′soun′dĭng) adj. Impressively ostentatious; pompous.

high-spir·it·ed (hī′spîr′ə-tĭd) adj. **1.** Having a proud or unbroken spirit; brave. **2.** Vivacious.

high-strung (hī′strŭng′) adj. Tending to be acutely nervous and sensitive.

hight (hīt) adj. Archaic. Named; called. [Middle English highten, hihten, from hehte, hight, past tense of hoten, to call, be called, Old English hātan (past tense heht). See kei-³ in Appendix.*]

high-tail (hī′tāl′) intr.v. **-tailed, -tailing, -tails.** Slang. To take off or go in a great hurry; especially, to escape. —hightail it. To rush; hurry. [A reference to some animals who, when startled, raise their tails and flee.]

High Ta·tra. See **Tatra Mountains.**

high tea. British. A substantial meal that typically includes tea, a hot course, and bread and butter, served in the late afternoon or early evening.

high-ten·sion (hī′tĕn′shən) *adj.* Having a high voltage.

high-test (hī′tĕst′) *adj.* **1.** Meeting the most exacting requirements. **2.** Of or pertaining to highly volatile, high-octane gasoline.

high tide. **1.** The tide at its full, when the water reaches its highest level. **2.** The time at which this occurs. **3.** A point of culmination; an acme.

high time. **1.** A time almost too late; about time; fully time. **2.** *Informal.* A good time.

high-toned (hī′tōnd′) *adj.* **1.** Intellectually superior: *a high-toned lecture.* **2.** Socially superior: *a high-toned finishing school.* **3.** *Informal.* Having pretensions to elegance or slickness: *a high-toned woman.*

high treason. Treason against one's state or sovereign.

high·ty-tigh·ty. Variant of **hoity-toity.**

high-up (hī′ŭp′) *adj. Informal.* Of high position or status. —*n. Informal.* A person who has a high rank or position.

high water. *Abbr.* **H.W.** **1.** High tide. **2.** The state of a body of water that has reached its highest level.

high-wa·ter mark (hī′wô′tər, -wŏt′ər). **1.** A mark indicating the highest level reached by a body of water. **2.** The highest point of achievement; apex.

high·way (hī′wā′) *n.* **1.** A main public road connecting towns and cities. **2.** Any main route, on land, over water, or in the air.

high·way·man (hī′wā′mən) *n., pl.* **-men** (-mĭn). A robber who holds up travelers on a highway.

H.I.H. His (or Her) Imperial Highness.

Hii·u·maa (hē′ōō-mä). An island of the Estonian S.S.R., occupying 371 square miles in the Baltic Sea.

hi·jack (hī′jăk′) *tr.v.* **-jacked, -jacking, -jacks.** Also **high·jack.** *Informal.* **1.** To rob (a vehicle, such as a truck, train, or armored car) by stopping it in transit. **2.** To steal (goods) from a vehicle by stopping it in transit. **3.** To forcibly seize or commandeer (a moving vehicle, such as an aircraft, ship, or car). **4.** To steal from (a person). **5.** To force or coerce (someone). [Origin uncertain.] —**hi′jack′er** *n.*

hike (hīk) *v.* **hiked, hiking, hikes.** —*intr.* **1. a.** To go on an extended walk, particularly for pleasure. **b.** To go on an extended march, especially over rough terrain; to tramp. **2.** To go up, as prices. Often used with *up: The cost of living has hiked up again.* **3.** To be raised, caught up, or uneven. Usually used with *up: Her coat is hiked up in back.* —*tr.* **1.** To increase or raise in amount. Usually used with *up.* **2.** To pull, move, or raise with a sudden motion; to hitch. Usually used with *up: He hiked up his pants.* —*n.* **1.** A walk or march. **2.** A rise, as in prices. [Origin uncertain.] —**hik′er** *n.*

hi·lar·i·ous (hĭ-lâr′ē-əs, hī-) *adj.* Boisterously funny, gay, or merry. [From Latin *hilarus, hilaris.* See **hilarity.**] —**hi·lar′i·ous·ly** *adv.* —**hi·lar′i·ous·ness** *n.*

hi·lar·i·ty (hĭ-lăr′ə-tē, hī-) *n.* Boisterous merriment. See Synonyms at **mirth.** [Old French *hilarite,* from Latin *hilaritās,* from *hilaris, hilarus,* cheerful, from Greek *hilaros.* See **sel-**[2] in Appendix.*]

Hil·a·ry (hĭl′ə-rē). A masculine or feminine given name. [Middle English *Hillarius,* from Late Latin *Hilarius* (Saint Hilary of Poitiers, died A.D. 368), from Latin *hilaris,* cheerful, merry. See **hilarity.**]

Hil·bert (hĭl′bərt), **David.** 1862–1943. German mathematician.

Hil·da (hĭl′də). A feminine given name. [Middle English *Hilde,* Old English *Hild.* See **kel-**[2] in Appendix.*]

Hil·des·heim (hĭl′dəs-hīm). A city and manufacturing center of southeast-central Lower Saxony, West Germany. Population, 96,000.

hill (hĭl) *n.* **1.** A well-defined, naturally elevated area of land smaller than a mountain. **2.** *Plural.* **a.** A range or group of such elevations. **b.** *Informal.* Any remote rural area located in such elevated areas. **3.** A heap, pile, or mound, such as that formed by a living organism. Often used in combination: *anthill.* **4. a.** A mound of earth piled around and over a plant or plants. **b.** A plant or plants thus covered. **5.** An incline, especially in a road; slope. —*tr.v.* **hilled, hilling, hills.** **1.** To form into a hill, pile, or heap. **2.** To cover (a plant or plants) with a mound of soil. [Middle English *hill,* Old English *hyll.* See **kel-**[8] in Appendix.*] —**hill′er** *n.*

Hill (hĭl), **Archibald Vivian.** Born 1886. British biochemist; worked on muscle energy.

Hill (hĭl), **James Jerome.** 1838–1916. American transportation magnate; promoter of Great Northern Railway.

Hil·lar·y (hĭl′ə-rē), Sir **Edmund.** Born 1919. New Zealand-born British explorer and mountaineer; with Sherpa guide, Tenzing Norkay, first to reach summit of Mount Everest (1953).

hill·bil·ly (hĭl′bĭl′ē) *n., pl.* **-lies.** *Informal.* A person from a rural mountainous area, especially of the southeastern United States. Usually used disparagingly. —*adj.* Of or characteristic of the culture of such an area: *hillbilly music.* [HILL + *Billy,* pet form of WILLIAM.]

Hill·ing·don (hĭl′ĭng-dən). A borough of London, England, comprising the former administrative divisions of Hayes and Harlington, Ruislip and Northwood, Yiewsley, West Drayton, and Uxbridge. Population, 228,000.

hill·ock (hĭl′ək) *n.* A small hill. [Middle English *hilloc* : HILL + -OCK.] —**hill′ock·y** *adj.*

hill·side (hĭl′sīd′) *n.* The side or slope of a hill.

hill·top (hĭl′tŏp′) *n.* The crest or top of a hill.

hill·y (hĭl′ē) *adj.* **-ier, -iest.** **1.** Having many hills. **2.** Similar to or characteristic of a hill or hills. —**hill′i·ness** *n.*

Hil·mand. See **Helmand.**

Hi·lo (hē′lō). The largest city of Hawaii Island, Hawaii, located on the east-central coast. Population, 26,000.

hilt (hĭlt) *n.* The handle of a weapon or tool, particularly of a sword or dagger. —**to the hilt.** Completely. —*tr.v.* **hilted, hilting, hilts.** To provide with a hilt. [Middle English *hilt,* Old English *hilt,* from Germanic *hilt-* (unattested).]

hi·lum (hī′ləm) *n., pl.* **-la** (-lə). Also **hi·lus** (-ləs) (for sense 2) *pl.* **-li** (-lī′). **1.** *Botany.* **a.** The scarlike mark on a seed, such as a bean, formed at the point where it was joined to the stalk connecting it to the placenta. **b.** The nucleus of a starch grain. **2.** *Anatomy.* Any small openings or notches through which ducts, nerves, or vessels enter or leave an organ. [New Latin, from Latin *hīlum*†, trifle.]

Hil·ver·sum (hĭl′vər-səm). A city of the Netherlands, located in southeastern North Holland. Population, 99,000.

him (hĭm) *pron.* The objective case of the third person pronoun *he.* It is used: **1.** As the direct object of a verb: *They assisted him.* **2.** As the indirect object of a verb: *They offered him a ride.* **3.** As the object of a preposition: *This letter is addressed to him.* **4.** After *than* or *as* in comparisons in which the first term is in the objective case: *The judges praised her more than him.* **5.** *Informal.* In place of the reflexive pronoun *himself,* as the indirect object of a verb: *He went to buy him a car.* **6.** In various elliptical, absolute, or interjectional phrases in which it is neither subject nor object: *Him and his sweet talk!* [Middle English *him,* Old English *him.* See **ko-** in Appendix.*]

H.I.M. His (or Her) Imperial Majesty.

Hi·ma·chal Pra·desh (hĭ-mä′chəl prə-dāsh′). A Union Territory occupying 10,600 square miles in two areas of the northern Republic of India. Population, 1,351,000. Capital, Simla.

Hi·ma·la·yas (hĭm′ə-lā′əz, hĭ-mäl′yəz). A mountain range of south-central Asia, extending 1,500 miles through northwestern Pakistan, Kashmir, northern India, southern Tibet, Nepal, Sikkim, and Bhutan. Highest elevation, Mount Everest (29,028 feet). Also called "Himalaya Mountains."

hi·mat·i·on (hĭ-măt′ē-ŏn′) *n., pl.* **-ia** (-ē-ə). A long loose outer garment worn by men and women in ancient Greece. [Greek, diminutive of *hima* (stem *himat-*), garment, from *hennunai,* to clothe. See **wes-**[4] in Appendix.*]

Hi·me·ji (hē′mĕ′jē′). A city and industrial center of southwest-central Honshu, Japan. Population, 360,000.

Himm·ler (hĭm′lər), **Heinrich.** 1900–1945. German Nazi leader; chief of the Gestapo (1936–45).

him·self (hĭm-sĕlf′) *pron.* A specialized form of the third person singular masculine pronoun. It is used: **1.** As a reflexive pronoun, forming the direct or indirect object of a verb or the object of a preposition: *He hurt himself.* **2.** For emphasis, after *he: He himself wasn't certain.* **3.** As an emphasizing substitute for *him* in a compound object: *The burden fell entirely upon his brother and himself.* **4.** In an absolute construction: *In debt himself, he could offer no financial assistance.* **5.** As an indication of his real, normal, or healthy condition or identity: *He hasn't been himself lately.* [Middle English *himself,* Old English *him selfum* : HIM + *selfum,* dative of *self,* SELF.]

Him·yar·ite (hĭm′yə-rīt′) *n.* **1.** A member of an ancient tribe of southwestern Arabia. **2.** An Arabic dialect, closely related to Ethiopian, spoken by these people. —*adj.* Of, relating to, or characteristic of these people, their language, or their culture. [After *Himyar,* legendary ancient king in Yemen.] —**Him′yar·it′ic** (-yə-rĭt′ĭk) *adj.*

Hi·na·ya·na (hē′nə-yä′nə) *n.* A small, conservative branch of Buddhism following the Pali scriptures and the nontheistic ideal of self-purification to nirvana. Compare **Mahayana.** [Sanskrit *hīnayāna,* "lesser action or vehicle."] —**Hi′na·ya′nist** *n.* —**Hi′na·ya·nis′tic** *adj.*

hind[1] (hīnd) *adj.* Also **hind·er** (hīn′dər). Located at or forming the back or rear; posterior: *hind legs.* [Middle English *hint,* perhaps from Old English *hinder,* behind, or *hindan,* from behind. See **ko-** in Appendix.*]

hind[2] (hīnd) *n.* **1.** A female red deer. **2.** Any of several fishes of the genus *Epinephelus,* of Atlantic waters, related to and resembling the groupers. [Middle English *hinde,* Old English *hind.* See **kem-**[1] in Appendix.*]

hind·brain (hīnd′brān′) *n.* The **rhombencephalon** *(see).*

Hin·de·mith (hĭn′də-mĭth; *German* hĭn′də-mĭt), **Paul.** 1895–1963. German composer.

Hin·den·burg. The German name for **Zabrze.**

Hin·den·burg (hĭn′dən-bûrg′; *German* hĭn′dən-bŏŏrk′), **Paul von.** 1847–1934. German general; president (1925–34).

hin·der[1] (hĭn′dər) *v.* **-dered, -dering, -ders.** —*tr.* **1.** To hold back; be in the way of; hamper; delay. **2.** To obstruct or delay the progress of; prevent; to stop. —*intr.* To be an obstacle or encumbrance. [Middle English *hindren,* Old English *hindrian.* See **ko-** in Appendix.*] —**hin′der·er** *n.*

Synonyms: *hinder, hamper, impede, retard, encumber, obstruct, block, dam, bar, balk.* These verbs mean to slow or prevent progress, movement, or other desired action. *Hinder* and *hamper* are applied to any restraining influence, physical or otherwise, intentional or accidental. *Impede* usually implies slowing by making movement difficult. To *retard* is to delay or hold back, and to *encumber* is to weigh down or burden, physically or figuratively. *Obstruct* implies interference that brings progress to a virtual halt or prevents a desired action. *Block* refers to preventing progress, passage, or other action, and *dam* to restraining the progress or release of something, such as water or emotion, by interposing a barrier. To *bar* is to prevent entry or exit or to rule out a course of action, and to *balk* is to frustrate a course by putting obstacles in one's path.

hin·der[2]. Variant of **hind.**

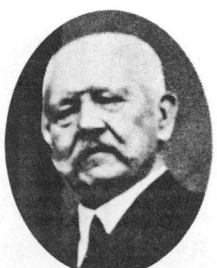

Paul von Hindenburg

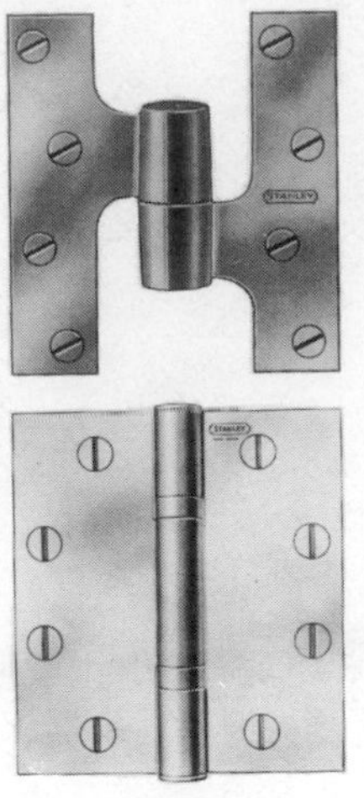
hinge
Metal hinges

hip roof

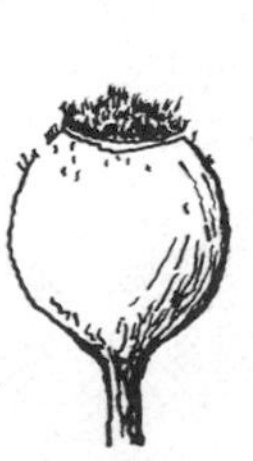
hip³

hind·gut (hīnd′gŭt′) *n.* The posterior portion of the embryonic alimentary canal.

Hin·di (hĭn′dē) *n.* **1.** A group of vernacular Indic dialects spoken in northern India. **2.** A literary language based upon these dialects, usually written in the Devanagari alphabet. **3.** A member of a cultural group of northern India speaking a Hindi dialect. [Hindi *Hindi,* from *Hind,* India, from Persian, from Old Persian *Hindu,* the river Indus. See **India.**] —**Hin′di** *adj.*

hind·most (hīnd′mōst′) *adj.* Also **hin·der·most** (hīn′dər-). Farthest to the rear; most remote; last.

hind·quar·ter (hīnd′kwôr′tər) *n.* **1.** The posterior portion of a side of beef, lamb, veal, or mutton, including a hind leg and one or two ribs. **2.** *Usually plural.* The posterior part of a quadruped, adjacent to the hind legs; the rump.

hin·drance (hĭn′drəns) *n.* **1.** The act of hindering; an obstruction. **2.** One that hinders; an impediment. —See Synonyms at **obstacle.** [Middle English *hind(e)raunce,* from *hindren,* to HINDER.]

hind·sight (hīnd′sīt′) *n.* **1.** The rear sight of a firearm. **2.** Perception of events after they have occurred.

Hin·du (hĭn′do͞o) *n.* Also *archaic* **Hin·doo. 1.** A native of India, especially northern India. **2.** A believer in Hinduism. —*adj.* Also *archaic* **Hin·doo. 1.** Of or pertaining to the Hindus and their culture. **2.** Of or pertaining to Hinduism. [Urdu, from Persian *Hindū,* from *Hind,* India. See **Hindi.**]

Hindu calendar. The lunisolar calendar of the Hindus. See **calendar.**

Hin·du·ism (hĭn′do͞o-ĭz′əm) *n.* Also *archaic* **Hin·doo·ism.** A diverse body of religion, philosophy, and cultural practice native to and predominant in India, characterized broadly by beliefs in reincarnation and a supreme being of many forms and natures, by the view that opposing theories are aspects of one eternal truth, and by a desire for liberation from earthly evils.

Hindu Kush (ko͝osh). Ancient name **Cau·ca·sus In·di·cus** (kô′kə-səs ĭn′dĭ-kəs). A mountain range of central Asia, extending 500 miles from central Afghanistan to the Pakistan boundary. Highest elevation, Tirich Mir (25,263 feet).

Hin·du·stan (hĭn′do͞o-stăn′, -stän′). Also **Hin·do·stan** (hĭn′dō-). **1.** The part of northern India where Indic languages prevail, roughly the Ganges plain from the Punjab to Assam. **2.** The Indian subcontinent.

Hin·du·sta·ni (hĭn′do͞o-stä′nē, -stăn′ē) *n.* **1.** A subdivision of the Indic branch of languages, including Urdu, Hindi, and other languages of northern India. **2.** A native of Hindustan. —*adj.* Of or pertaining to Hindustani or Hindustan.

Hines (hīnz), **Earl ("Fatha").** Born 1905. American jazz pianist and conductor.

hinge (hĭnj) *n.* **1.** A jointed or flexible device permitting turning or pivoting of a part, such as a door, lid, or flap, on a stationary frame. **2.** A similar structure or part, such as that enabling the valves of a bivalve mollusk to open and close. **3.** A small folded paper rectangle gummed on one side, used to fasten stamps, photographs, or the like in an album. **4.** A point or circumstance upon which subsequent events depend. —*v.* **hinged, hinging, hinges.** —*tr.* To attach by or equip with a hinge or hinges. —*intr.* **1.** To turn or hang, as on a hinge. **2.** To depend; be contingent. Usually used with *on* or *upon.* [Middle English *he(e)ng.* See **konk-** in Appendix.*]

hin·ny¹ (hĭn′ē) *n., pl.* **-nies.** The hybrid offspring of a male horse and a female ass. Compare **mule.** [From Latin *hinnus,* variant (influenced by *hinnīre,* to HINNY) of Greek *innos, ginnos*†.]

hin·ny² (hĭn′ē) *intr.v.* **-nied, -nying, -nies.** *Rare.* To whinny; neigh. [Earlier *henny,* from Old French *hennir,* from Latin *hinnīre* (imitative).]

Hin·shel·wood (hĭn′chəl-wo͝od′), Sir **Cyril Norman.** 1897–1967. British chemist; worked on mechanisms of chemical reaction.

hint (hĭnt) *n.* **1.** A subtle suggestion or slight indication; an intimation. **2.** A statement or gesture conveying veiled information; clue. **3.** A barely perceptible amount: *gin with a hint of vermouth.* **4.** *Obsolete.* An occasion; opportunity. —*v.* **hinted, hinting, hints.** —*tr.* To make known by a hint; intimate. —*intr.* To give a hint or hints. Often used with *at: He hinted at the true purpose of his visit.* —See Synonyms at **suggest.** [Origin obscure.] —**hint′er** *n.*

hin·ter·land (hĭn′tər-lănd′) *n.* **1.** The land directly adjacent to and inland from a coast. **2.** A region served by a port city and its facilities. **3.** A region remote from urban areas; back country. [German *Hinterland* : *hinter,* behind, rear, from Old High German *hintar* (see **ko-** in Appendix*) + *Land,* land, from Old High German *lant* (see **lendh-²** in Appendix*).]

Hin·ton (hĭn′tən), Sir **Christopher.** Born 1901. British nuclear engineer; director of first atomic power station.

hip¹ (hĭp) *n.* **1.** The laterally projecting prominence of the pelvis or pelvic region from the waist to the thigh. **2.** A homologous posterior part in quadrupeds. **3.** The hip joint. **4.** *Architecture.* The external angle formed by the meeting of two adjacent, sloping sides of a roof. —**on the hip.** In an unfavorable or disadvantageous position. [Middle English *hip, hupe,* Old English *hype.* See **keu-²** in Appendix.*]

hip² (hĭp) *adj.* **hipper, hippest.** Also **hep** (hĕp). *Slang.* **1.** Aware of or in accordance with advanced tastes and attitudes. **2.** Cognizant; wise: *hip to the plan.* [Variant of earlier *hep*†.]

hip³ (hĭp) *n.* The fleshy, berrylike, often brightly colored seed receptacle of a rose. [Middle English *hepe, hipe,* Old English *hēope.* See **keub-** in Appendix.*]

hip⁴ (hĭp) *interj.* Used as a cheer or a signal for a cheer: *Hip, hip, hurrah!* [Origin uncertain.]

hip·bone (hĭp′bōn′) *n.* The **innominate bone** *(see).*

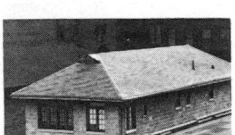

hip joint. The joint between the innominate bone and the femur.

hip·parch (hĭp′ärk′) *n.* An ancient Greek cavalry commander. [Greek *hipparkhos,* "horse leader" : *hippos,* horse (see **ekwo-** in Appendix*) + -ARCH.]

Hip·par·chus (hĭ-pär′kəs). Greek astronomer who flourished in the late second century B.C.

hipped¹ (hĭpt) *adj.* **1.** Having hips of a specified kind. Used in combination: *swivel-hipped, broad-hipped.* **2.** Having the hip dislocated. **3.** *Architecture.* Having a hip or hips. Said of roofs.

hipped² (hĭpt) *adj.* Also **hip·pish** (hĭp′ĭsh). *British.* Melancholy; sad; depressed. [Shortened variant of HYPOCHONDRIAC.]

hip·pie (hĭp′ē) *n.* Also **hip·py** *pl.* **-pies.** A member of a loosely knit, nonconformist group generally characterized by emphasis on universal love, withdrawal from conventional society, and a general rejection of its mores, especially regarding dress, personal appearance, and living habits. —*adj.* Also **hip·py.** Of, relating to, or characteristic of such people. [From HIP (aware).]

hip·po (hĭp′ō) *n., pl.* **-pos.** *Informal.* A hippopotamus.

Hip·po (hĭp′ō). Also **Hip·po Re·gi·us** (rē′jē-əs). An ancient Numidian city in Algeria.

hip·po·cam·pus (hĭp′ə-kăm′pəs) *n., pl.* **-pi** (-pī′, -pē′). **1.** *Greek & Roman Mythology.* A sea horse having the forelegs of a horse and the tail of a fish or dolphin. **2.** *Anatomy.* One of two ridges along each lateral ventricle of the brain. [Late Latin, from Greek *hippokampos* : *hippos,* horse (see **hipparch**) + *kampos*†, sea monster.]

hip·po·cras (hĭp′ə-krăs′) *n.* A cordial made from wine and flavored with spices, formerly used as a medicine. [Middle English *ypocras,* from Old French, from Medieval Latin *(vinum) Hippocraticum,* (wine) of Hippocrates (it was strained through a filter called Hippocrates' bag).]

Hip·poc·ra·tes (hĭ-pŏk′rə-tēz′). 460?–377? B.C. Greek physician.

Hip·po·crat·ic oath (hĭp′ə-krăt′ĭk). An oath of ethical professional behavior sworn by new physicians, attributed to Hippocrates.

Hip·po·crene (hĭp′ə-krēn′, hĭp′ə-krē′nē). *Greek Mythology.* A fountain on Mount Helicon, Greece, held sacred to the Muses and regarded as a source of poetic inspiration. [Latin *Hippocrēnē,* from Greek *Hippokrēnē* : *hippos,* horse (see **hipparch**) (supposedly created by a stroke of Pegasus' hoof) + *krēnē*†, fountain.]

hip·po·drome (hĭp′ə-drōm′) *n.* **1.** An open-air stadium with an oval course for horse and chariot races in ancient Greece and Rome. **2.** An arena for horse shows. [Old French, from Latin *hippodromus,* from Greek *hippodromos* : *hippos,* horse (see **hipparch**) + -DROME.]

hip·po·griff (hĭp′ə-grĭf′) *n.* Also **hip·po·gryph.** A mythological monster having the wings, claws, and head of a griffin and the body and hindquarters of a horse. [French *hippogriffe,* from Italian *ippogrifo* : *ippo-,* horse, from Latin *hippos,* from Greek (see **hipparch**) + *grifo,* griffin, from Late Latin *grȳphus,* GRIFFIN.]

Hip·pol·y·ta (hĭ-pŏl′ə-tə). *Greek Mythology.* A queen of the Amazons slain by Hercules in completion of his labors.

Hip·pol·y·tus (hĭ-pŏl′ə-təs). *Greek Mythology.* A son of Theseus who spurned the advances of his stepmother, Phaedra, and was killed by Poseidon.

hip·po·pot·a·mus (hĭp′ə-pŏt′ə-məs) *n., pl.* **-muses** or **-mi** (-mī′). **1.** A large, chiefly aquatic African mammal, *Hippopotamus amphibius,* having dark, thick, almost hairless skin, short legs, and a broad, wide-mouthed muzzle. Also called "river horse." **2.** A similar but smaller animal, *Choeropsis liberiensis.* [Latin, from Late Greek *hippopotamos,* from Greek *hippos ho potamios,* "horse of the river" : *hippos,* horse (see **ekwo-** in Appendix*) + *potamos,* river (see **pet-¹** in Appendix*).]

Hip·po Re·gi·us. See **Hippo.**

hip·py¹ (hĭp′ē) *adj.* Having broad or prominent hips.

hip·py². Variant of **hippie.**

hip roof. A roof having sloping edges and sides.

hip·ster (hĭp′stər) *n. Slang.* One who is aware of or in accordance with advanced tastes and attitudes. [HIP + -STER.]

hi·ra·ga·na (hîr′ə-gä′nə) *n.* One of two sets of Japanese syllabaries of the kana system, having a cursive form. Also called "kana." See **katakana.** [Japanese, "flat kana."]

hir·cine (hûr′sĭn, -sīn′) *adj.* Of or characteristic of a goat, especially in strong odor or lustfulness. [Latin *hircīnus,* from *hircus*†, he-goat.]

hire (hīr) *tr.v.* **hired, hiring, hires. 1.** To engage the services of (a person) for a fee; to employ. **2.** To engage the temporary use of (something) for a fee; to rent: *hire a car for the day.* **3.** To grant the services or allow the use of for remuneration; to rent out. Often used with *out: I hire out my country home for the summer.* —**hire out.** To grant one's services in exchange for compensation: *He hires out as a field hand when work is slow on his farm.* —*n.* **1.** The payment for services or use of something. **2.** The act of hiring. **3.** The condition or fact of being hired. —**for hire.** Available for use or services in exchange for compensation. [Middle English *hiren,* Old English *hȳr(i)an,* from Germanic (Low German area) *khūrjan* (unattested), from *khūrjō* (unattested), payment.] —**hir′a·ble, hire′a·ble** *adj.* —**hir′er** *n.*

hire·ling (hīr′lĭng) *n.* One who offers his service solely for compensation; especially, a person willing to perform odious or offensive tasks for a fee; a mercenary. —*adj.* Of, pertaining to, or characteristic of a hireling.

Hi·ro·hi·to (hîr′ō-hē′tō). Born 1901. Emperor of Japan (since 1926).

ă pat/ā pay/âr care/ä father/b bib/ch church/d deed/ĕ pet/ē be/f fife/g gag/h hat/hw which/ĭ pit/ī pie/îr pier/j judge/k kick/l lid, needle/m mum/n no, sudden/ng thing/ŏ pot/ō toe/ô paw, for/oi noise/ou out/o͝o took/o͞o boot/p pop/r roar/s sauce/sh ship, dish/

Hi·ro·shi·ge (hîr'ō-shē'gē), **Ando.** 1797–1858. Japanese woodblock print artist.

Hi·ro·shi·ma (hîr'ə-shē'mə, hĭ-rō'shĭ-mə). A city and port of southwestern Honshu, Japan; destroyed by the first atomic bomb employed in warfare (August 6, 1945). Population, 485,000.

hir·sute (hûr'so͞ot', hûr'so͞ot') *adj.* **1.** Covered or coated with hair; hairy. **2.** Of, pertaining to, or consisting of hair. [Latin *hirsūtus.* See **ghers-** in Appendix.*] —**hir'sute'ness** *n.*

hir·u·din (hîr'ə-dən, -yə-dən) *n.* A substance extracted from the salivary glands of leeches and used as an anticoagulant. [Originally a trademark, from New Latin *hirudo,* a leech, from Latin *hirūdo*†.]

hi·run·dine (hĭ-rŭn'dĭn, -dīn') *adj.* Of, pertaining to, or characteristic of a swallow. [Latin *hirundo*†, a swallow + -INE.]

his (hĭz). The possessive form of the pronoun *he.* Used to indicate possession, agency, or reception of an action by the masculine being or person spoken of: **1.** Used attributively: *his wallet; pursuing his tasks; suffered his first rebuff.* **2.** Used absolutely: **a.** As a predicate adjective: *The brown boots are his.* **b.** As a substantive: *If you can't find your hat, take his.* —**of his.** Belonging or pertaining to him: *a friend of his.* [Middle English *his,* Old English *his.* See **ko-** in Appendix.*]

his'n (hĭz'ən) *pron.* Also **hisn.** *Nonstandard.* His. [Middle English *hysene,* variant (influenced by *mīn, thīn*) of HIS.]

His·pa·ni·a. An ancient name for the **Iberian Peninsula.**

His·pan·ic (hĭ-spăn'ĭk) *adj.* **1.** Of or pertaining to Spain and its language, people, and culture. **2.** Having cultural origins in Iberia. [Latin *Hispānicus,* from *Hispānia,* SPAIN.]

His·pa·nio·la (hĭs'pən-yō'lə). *Spanish* **Es·pa·ño·la** (ĕs'pä-nyō'lä). Formerly **Hai·ti** (hā'tē; *French* à-ē-tē'). An island of the West Indies, 30,000 square miles in area; occupied in the west by the Republic of Haiti and in the center and east by the Dominican Republic.

his·pid (hĭs'pĭd) *adj.* Covered with stiff or rough hairs; bristly: *hispid stems.* [Latin *hispidus.* See **ghers-** in Appendix.*]

hiss (hĭs) *n.* **1.** A sharp, sibilant sound similar to a sustained *s.* **2.** An expression of disapproval, contempt, or dissatisfaction by making this sound. —*v.* **hissed, hissing, hisses.** —*intr.* **1.** To make a hiss. **2.** To direct hisses at in disapproval. —*tr.* **1.** To utter (words or sounds) with a hissing sound. **2.** To express disapproval, derision, or hatred for by hissing. [Middle English *hissen* (imitative).] —**hiss'er** *n.*

Hiss (hĭs), **Alger.** Born 1904. American lawyer and State Department official; convicted of perjury (1950) as a result of espionage charges made by Whittaker **Chambers** *(see).*

hiss·ing (hĭs'ĭng) *n.* The act or instance of producing a hiss.

hist. historian; historical; history.

his·tam·i·nase (hĭ-stăm'ə-nās', -nāz', hĭs'tə-mə-) *n.* An enzyme that occurs in the digestive system and converts histidine to histamine. [HISTAMIN(E) + -ASE.]

his·ta·mine (hĭs'tə-mēn', -mĭn) *n.* A white crystalline compound, $C_5H_9N_3$, found in plant and animal tissue, formed from histidine by the action of putrefactive bacteria. It is a stimulant of gastric secretion, and is used medicinally as a vasodilator. [HIST(O)- + -AMINE.] —**his'ta·min'ic** (-mĭn'ĭk) *adj.*

his·ti·dine (hĭs'tə-dēn', -dĭn) *n.* A colorless, crystalline amino acid, $C_6H_9N_3O_2$, used as a feed additive and dietary supplement. [HIST(O)- + -ID(E) + -INE.]

histo-, hist-. Indicates bodily tissue; for example, **histamine, histolysis.** [From Greek *histos,* web, beam, mast. See **stā-** in Appendix.*]

his·to·chem·is·try (hĭs'tō-kĕm'ĭ-strē) *n.* The chemistry of cells and tissues. —**his'to·chem'i·cal** *adj.*

his·to·gen·e·sis (hĭs'tə-jĕn'ə-sĭs) *n.* The formation and development of bodily tissues. [New Latin : HISTO- + -GENESIS.] —**his'to·ge·net'ic** (-tō-jə-nĕt'ĭk), **his'to·gen'ic** *adj.* —**his'to·ge·net'i·cal·ly, his'to·gen'i·cal·ly** *adv.*

his·to·gram (hĭs'tə-grăm') *n. Statistics.* A graphic representation of a frequency distribution in which the widths of contiguous vertical bars are proportional to the class widths of the variable and the heights of the bars are proportional to the class frequencies. [HISTO(RY) + -GRAM.]

his·tol·o·gy (hĭ-stŏl'ə-jē) *n.* **1.** The anatomical study of the microscopic structure of animal and plant tissues. **2.** The microscopic structure of tissue. [French *histologie* : HISTO- + -LOGY.] —**his'to·log'i·cal** (hĭs'tə-lŏj'ĭ-kəl) *adj.* —**his'to·log'i·cal·ly** *adv.* —**his·tol'o·gist** *n.*

his·tol·y·sis (hĭ-stŏl'ə-sĭs) *n.* The breakdown and disintegration of organic tissue. [New Latin : HISTO- + -LYSIS.] —**his'to·lyt'ic** (hĭs'tə-lĭt'ĭk) *adj.* —**his'to·lyt'i·cal·ly** *adv.*

his·tone (hĭs'tōn') *n.* Any of several simple water-soluble proteins, found especially in glandular tissues, that can release on hydrolysis a high proportion of basic amino acids. [HIST(O)- + -ONE.]

his·to·pa·thol·o·gy (hĭs'tō-pə-thŏl'ə-jē) *n.* The pathology of changes in diseased tissue. —**his'to·path'o·log'i·cal** (-păth'ə-lŏj'ĭ-kəl) *adj.*

his·to·phys·i·ol·o·gy (hĭs'tō-fĭz'ē-ŏl'ə-jē) *n.* The physiology of the microscopic functioning of bodily tissues. —**his'to·phys'i·o·log'i·cal** (-ē-ə-lŏj'ĭ-kəl) *adj.*

his·to·ri·an (hĭ-stôr'ē-ən, hĭ-stŏr'-) *n. Abbr.* **hist. 1.** A writer or student of history. **2.** A person who makes a record of proceedings: *the historian of the drama club.* [Old French *historien,* from Latin *historia,* HISTORY.]

his·tor·ic (hĭ-stôr'ĭk, hĭ-stŏr'-) *adj.* **1.** Having importance in or influence on history; famous; renowned. **2.** Historical.

Usage: *Historic* and *historical* are differentiated in usage, though their senses overlap. *Historic* is largely restricted to what is important in or contributes to history: *historic first voyage in outer space; historic meeting of Stanley and Livingstone. Historical* refers more broadly to what is concerned with history: *historical pageant; historical novel* (as distinguished from *a historic novel,* a history-making work).

his·tor·i·cal (hĭ-stôr'ĭ-kəl, hĭ-stŏr'-) *adj. Abbr.* **hist. 1.** Of, relating to, or of the nature of history as opposed to fiction or legend. **2.** Based on or concerned with events in history. **3.** Having considerable importance or influence in history; historic. **4.** *Linguistics.* Diachronic. —See Usage note at **historic.** —**his·tor'i·cal·ly** *adv.* —**his·tor'i·cal·ness** *n.*

historical linguistics. The study of language development chronologically with emphasis on evolutionary development. Compare **descriptive linguistics.**

historical method. A method of analysis or exposition whereby a subject is considered in its origin and subsequent historical development.

historical present. The present tense used in the narration of events set in the past.

historical school. A school of theorists, as in law or economics, stressing the influence of historical conditions.

his·tor·i·cism (hĭ-stôr'ə-sĭz'əm, hĭ-stŏr'-) *n.* **1.** The belief that processes are at work in history that man can do little to alter. **2.** The theory that the historian must avoid all value judgments in his study of past periods or former cultures. **3.** Veneration of the past or of tradition. —**his·tor'i·cist** *adj.* & *n.*

his·to·ric·i·ty (hĭs'tə-rĭs'ə-tē) *n.* Historical authenticity.

his·to·ri·og·ra·pher (hĭ-stôr'ē-ŏg'rə-fər, hĭ-stŏr'-) *n.* **1.** One trained in or practicing historiography. **2.** A historian; especially, one designated by a group or public institution.

his·to·ri·og·ra·phy (hĭ-stôr'ē-ŏg'rə-fē, hĭ-stŏr'-) *n.* **1.** The principles or methodology of historical study. **2.** The writing of history. **3.** Historical literature. [Old French *historiographie,* from Greek *historiographia* : HISTORY + -GRAPHY.]

his·to·ry (hĭs'tə-rē) *n., pl.* **-ries. 1.** *Abbr.* **hist.** A narrative of events; a story; chronicle. **2.** A chronological record of events, as of the life or development of a people, country, or institution. **3.** *Abbr.* **hist.** The branch of knowledge that records and analyzes past events. **4.** The events forming the subject matter of history. **5.** An interesting past: *a house with a history.* **6.** That which is not of current concern: *My youth is now history.* **7.** A drama based on historical events. **8.** A record of a patient's medical background. [Latin *historia,* from Greek, inquiry, observation, from *histōr,* learned man. See **weid-** in Appendix.*]

his·tri·on·ic (hĭs'trē-ŏn'ĭk) *adj.* Also **his·tri·on·i·cal** (-ĭ-kəl). **1.** Of or pertaining to actors or acting. **2.** Overemotional or dramatic; theatrical; affected. [Late Latin *histriōnicus,* theatrical, from *histriō*†, actor.] —**his'tri·on'i·cal·ly** *adv.*

his·tri·on·ics (hĭs'trē-ŏn'ĭks) *pl.n.* **1.** Theatrical arts. Used with a singular verb. **2.** Exaggerated emotional behavior calculated for effect. Used with a plural verb.

hit (hĭt) *v.* **hit, hitting, hits.** —*tr.* **1.** To come in contact with forcefully; to strike. **2.** To cause to make sudden and forceful contact; to knock; to bump: *hit her hand against the wall.* **3.** To deal a blow to. **4.** To strike with a missile: *He fired and hit the target.* **5.** To reach and affect adversely: *hit hard by the depression.* **6.** To come upon; arrive at. **7.** To accord with; appeal to; suit: *The idea hit his fancy.* **8.** To propel with a blow. **9.** *Baseball.* To succeed in getting (a base hit): *hit a triple.* **10.** *Informal.* To set out on: *hit the road.* **11.** *Informal.* To request or obtain money from: *The vagrant hit me for a dime.* **12.** *Informal.* To resort to excessively: *hitting the bottle.* —*intr.* **1.** To strike or deal a blow. **2.** To come in contact; to bump. **3.** To attack. **4.** To achieve or find something desired or sought. Used with *on* or *upon.* **5.** *Baseball.* To bat. —**hit it off.** To get along well together. —**hit off.** To mimic or imitate. —*n.* **1.** A collision or impact. **2.** A successfully executed shot, blow, thrust, or throw. **3.** A successful or popular venture: *a Broadway hit.* **4.** A bit of luck. **5.** An apt or effective jest, remark, or witticism. **6.** *Abbr.* **h, h.** *Baseball.* A base hit. [Hit (infinitive, past tense, and past participle); Middle English *hitten, hitte, hit,* from Old Norse *hitta*†, to hit.]

hit-and-run (hĭt'n-rŭn') *adj.* **1.** Designating or involving the driver of a motor vehicle who drives on after striking a pedestrian or another vehicle. **2.** *Baseball.* Pertaining to or designating a play in which a man on base runs with the pitch, and the batter attempts to hit the ball.

hitch (hĭch) *v.* **hitched, hitching, hitches.** —*tr.* **1.** To fasten or catch temporarily with a loop, hook, or noose; to tie. **2.** To connect or attach, as to a vehicle. Often used with *up.* **3.** *Informal.* To join in marriage. **4.** To raise by pulling or jerking. Often used with *up: hitch up one's trousers.* **5.** *Informal.* To hitchhike (a ride). —*intr.* **1.** To move haltingly; to limp; to hobble. **2.** To become entangled, snarled, or fastened. **3.** *Slang.* To be united in marriage: *get hitched.* **4.** *Informal.* To hitchhike. —*n.* **1.** Any of various knots, such as a **harness hitch** or **half hitch** *(both of which see).* **2.** A short jerking motion; tug. **3.** A hobble or limp. **4.** An impediment or delay: *a hitch in our plans for the party.* **5.** A term of military service. [Middle English *hytchen*†, to move or lift with a jerk.]

hitch·hike (hĭch'hīk') *v.* **-hiked, -hiking, -hikes.** —*intr.* To travel by soliciting free rides along a road. —*tr.* To solicit or get (a free ride) along a road. —**hitch'hik'er** *n.*

hitching post. A post for temporarily tying up a horse or other animal.

hith·er (hĭth'ər) *adv.* To or toward this place: *come hither.* —*adj.* Located toward this side; nearer. [Middle English *hither,* Old English *hider.* See **ko-** in Appendix.*]

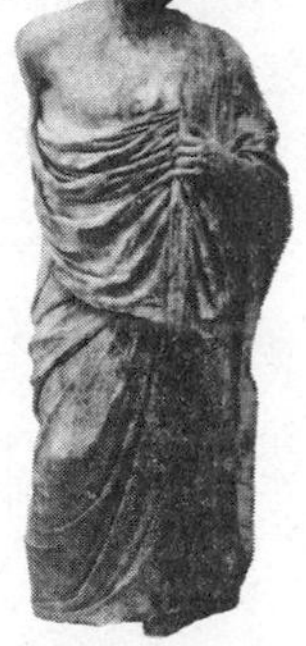

Hippocrates

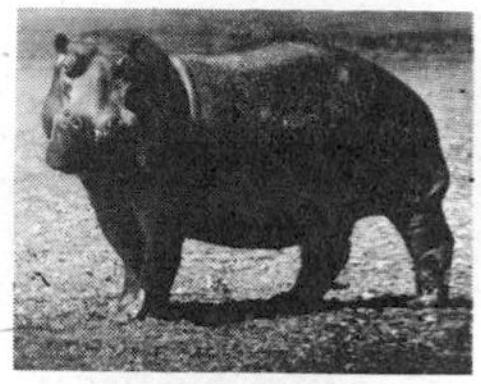

hippopotamus
Hippopotamus amphibius

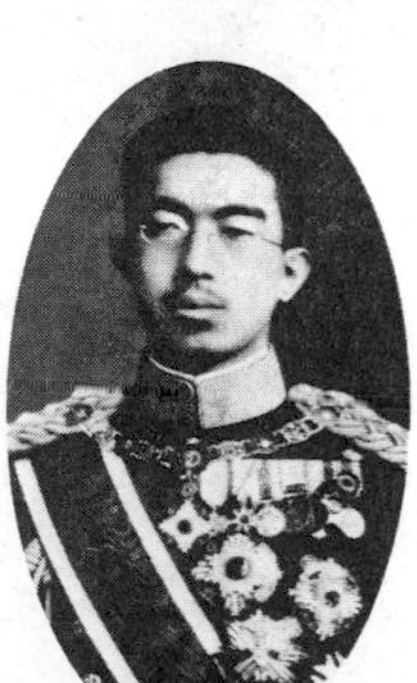

Hirohito
Photographed in 1932

t tight/th thin, path/*th* this, bathe/ŭ cut/ûr urge/v valve/w with/y yes/z zebra, size/zh vision/ə about, item, edible, gallop, circus/ à *Fr.* ami/œ *Fr.* feu, *Ger.* schön/ü *Fr.* tu, *Ger.* über/KH *Ger.* ich, *Scot.* loch/N *Fr.* bon. ***Follows main vocabulary. †Of obscure origin.**

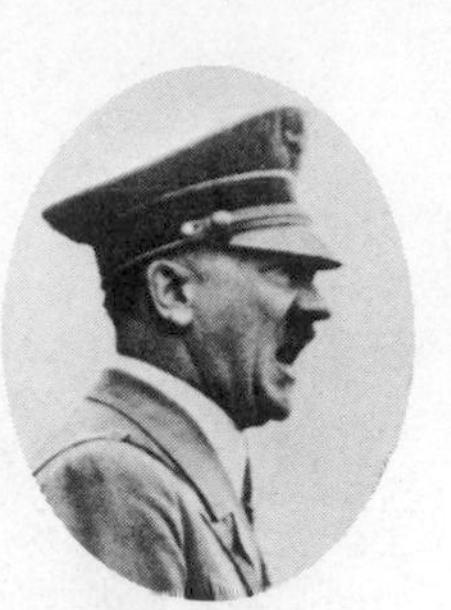
Adolf Hitler

hither and thither. In or toward one place and another. Also "hither and yon."
hith·er·most (hĭth′ər-mōst′) *adj.* Nearest this place or direction.
hith·er·to (hĭth′ər-to͞o′) *adv.* **1.** Until this time; up to now. **2.** *Archaic.* To this place; thus far.
hith·er·ward (hĭth′ər-wərd) *adv.* Also **hith·er·wards** (-wərdz). Hither.
Hit·ler (hĭt′lər), **Adolf.** 1889–1945. Austrian-born Nazi leader; assumed title of "Führer" (1934) as dictator of German Reich.
hit-or-miss (hĭt′ər-mĭs′) *adj.* Lacking accuracy; random; haphazard; careless.
hit·ter (hĭt′ər) *n.* **1.** One who hits or strikes something. **2.** *Baseball.* A batter.
Hit·tite (hĭt′īt′) *n.* **1.** A member of an ancient people living in Asia Minor and northern Syria about 2000–1200 B.C. **2.** An extinct Indo-European language spoken by these people. —*adj.* Of or pertaining to the Hittites, their culture, or their language. [Hebrew *Hittī,* from Hittite *Hatti.*]
Hi·va O·a (hē′və ō′ə). Also **Hi·va·o·a.** An island, 154 square miles in area, of the southeastern Marquesas group, French Polynesia.
hive (hīv) *n.* **1.** A natural or artificial structure for housing bees, especially honeybees. **2.** A colony of bees living in a hive. **3.** A place swarming with active people. —*v.* **hived, hiving, hives.** —*tr.* **1.** To collect (bees) into a hive. **2.** To store (honey) in a hive. **3.** To store up; accumulate. —*intr.* **1.** To enter a hive. **2.** To live with many others in close association. [Middle English *hive,* Old English *hӯf.* See **keu-**[2] in Appendix.*]
hives (hīvz) *n. Pathology.* **Urticaria** *(see).* [Origin uncertain.]
Hjäl·ma·ren (yĕl′mə-rœn′). A lake occupying 190 square miles in southern Sweden.
HKG Airport code for Hong Kong.
hl hectoliter.
H.L. House of Lords.
HLN Airport code for Helena, Montana.
hm hectometer.
H.M. His (or Her) Majesty.
H.M.S. His (or Her) Majesty's Ship.
HNL Airport code for Honolulu, Hawaii.
ho (hō) *interj.* Used to express surprise or joy or to attract attention to something sighted or to urge onward: *Land ho! Westward ho!* [Middle English, partly from Old Norse *hō!* and partly from Old French *ho!,* halt!]
Ho The symbol for the element holmium.
ho. house.
hoa·gie (hō′gē) *n. Slang.* A sandwich, the **hero** *(see).* [Origin unknown.]
hoar (hôr, hōr) *adj.* Hoary. —*n.* **1.** Hoariness. **2.** A hoary surface or coating. **3.** **Hoarfrost** *(see).* [Middle English *ho(o)r,* Old English *hār.* See **kei-**[2] in Appendix.*]
hoard (hôrd, hōrd) *n.* A hidden or stored fund or supply guarded for future use; cache; treasure. —*v.* **hoarded, hoarding, hoards.** —*intr.* To gather or accumulate a hoard. —*tr.* To accumulate or gather by saving or hiding. [Middle English *hord,* Old English *hord.* See **skeu-** in Appendix.*] —**hoard′er** *n.*

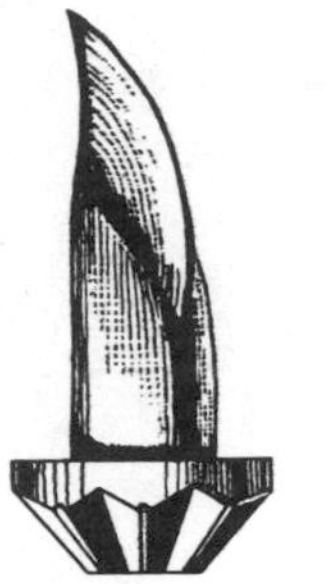
hobnail

hoard·ing[1] (hôr′dĭng, hōr′-) *n.* **1.** The act of gathering and saving a hoard. **2.** A hoard.
hoard·ing[2] (hôr′dĭng, hōr′-) *n. British.* **1.** A temporary wooden fence around a building or structure under construction or repair. **2.** A billboard. [From earlier *hoard,* a fence, from earlier *hourd,* from Norman French *hurdis,* from Old French *hourd,* scaffold, from Germanic. See **kert-** in Appendix.*]
hoar·frost (hôr′frôst′, -frŏst′, hōr′-) *n.* Frozen dew that forms a white coating on a surface. Also called "hoar," "white frost."
hoar·hound. Variant of **horehound.**
hoarse (hôrs, hōrs) *adj.* **1.** Low and grating in sound; husky; croaking. **2.** Having a husky, grating voice. [Middle English *hors,* from Old Norse *hārs* (unattested), variant of *hās,* from Germanic *hai(r)sa-* (unattested).]
hoars·en (hôr′sən, hōr′-) *v.* **-ened, -ening, -ens.** —*tr.* To cause to be hoarse. —*intr.* To become hoarse.
hoar·y (hôr′ē, hōr′ē) *adj.* **-ier, -iest.** **1.** Gray or white with or as if with age. **2.** Covered with grayish hair or pubescence: *hoary leaves.* **3.** Very old; ancient. —**hoar′i·ness** *n.*
ho·at·zin (hō-ăt′sĭn, wät′-) *n.* Also **ho·act·zin** (hō-ăk′tsĭn, wäk′-). A brownish, crested bird, *Opisthocomus hoazin,* of tropical South America, having claws on the first and second digits of the wings in the young. [American Spanish, from Nahuatl *uatzin,* pheasant.]

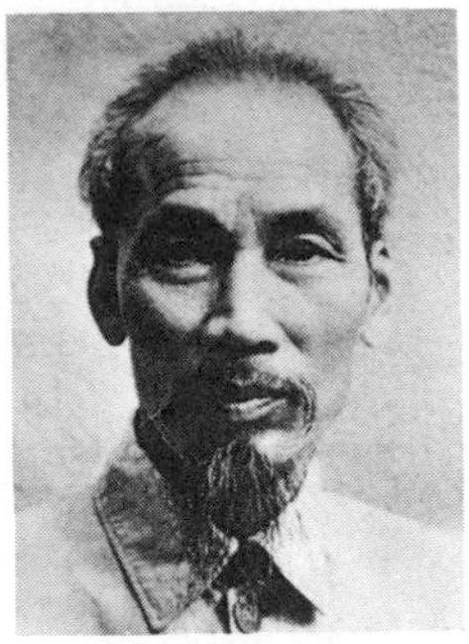
Ho Chi Minh

hoax (hōks) *n.* An act intended to deceive or trick, either as a practical joke or as a serious fraud. —*tr.v.* **hoaxed, hoaxing, hoaxes.** To deceive or cheat by using a hoax. [Perhaps shortened variant of HOCUS.] —**hoax′er** *n.*
hob[1] (hŏb) *n.* A shelf or projection at the back or side of the inside of a fireplace, for keeping things warm. [Origin unknown.]
hob[2] (hŏb) *n.* A hobgoblin, sprite, or elf. —**play** (or **raise**) **hob.** To make mischief or trouble. Often used with *with.* [Middle English *hob,* from *Hobbe,* pet form of ROBERT or ROBIN.]
Ho·bart (hō′bərt, -bärt). The capital of Tasmania, Australia; a port located in the southeast. Population, 119,000.
Ho·bart (hō′bərt, -bärt), **Garret Augustus.** 1844–1899. Vice President of the United States under William McKinley (1897–99); died in office.
Hobbes (hŏbz), **Thomas.** 1588–1679. English philosopher.
Hobb·ism (hŏb′ĭz′əm) *n.* A theory promulgated by Thomas Hobbes, advocating powerful, especially monarchical, government as the only means of adequately controlling the problems created by competing individual interests.
hob·ble (hŏb′əl) *v.* **-bled, -bling, -bles.** Also **hop·ple** (hŏp′əl). —*intr.* **1.** To walk or move awkwardly or with difficulty; to limp. **2.** To proceed haltingly or unsteadily. —*tr.* **1.** To put a hobble on (an animal). **2.** To cause to limp. **3.** To hamper the action or progress of; restrain; impede. —*n.* Also **hop·ple.** **1.** An awkward, clumsy, or irregular walk or gait. **2.** A device, such as a rope or strap, used to hobble an animal. **3.** *Archaic.* An unfortunate or awkward situation. [Middle English *hoblen,* of Low German origin, akin to Middle Dutch *hobbelen*†, to roll.] —**hob′bler** *n.*
hob·ble·bush (hŏb′əl-bo͝osh′) *n.* A shrub, *Viburnum alnifolium,* of northeastern North America, having flat clusters of white flowers with the marginal flowers larger than the others. [From HOBBLE (in the obsolete sense of hindrance, from the hindrance caused by its drooping branches).]
hob·ble·de·hoy (hŏb′əl-dē-hoi′) *n., pl.* **-hoys.** A gawky adolescent boy. [Origin uncertain.]
hobble skirt. A type of long skirt, popular between 1910 and 1914, that was so narrow below the knees that it restricted normal stride.
hob·by[1] (hŏb′ē) *n., pl.* **-bies.** **1.** An occupation, activity, or interest, as stamp-collecting or gardening, engaged in primarily for pleasure; a pastime. **2.** *Regional.* A little horse; a nag. **3.** A hobbyhorse. —**ride a hobby.** Devote oneself to a hobby. [Middle English *hoby,* a hobbyhorse, something one pursues, perhaps from *Hobbin,* pet form of ROBIN.] —**hob′by·ist** *n.*
hob·by[2] (hŏb′ē) *n., pl.* **-bies.** Any of several small falcons of the genus *Falco;* especially, an Old World species, *F. subbuteo,* formerly used for hawking. [Middle English *hoby,* from Old French *hobe, hobel,* from *hobeler,* to skirmish, probably from Middle Dutch *hobbelen,* to roll. See **hobble.**]
hob·by·horse (hŏb′ē-hôrs′) *n.* **1.** A child's toy consisting of a long stick with an imitation horse's head on one end. **2.** A rocking horse. **3. a.** A figure of a horse worn around the waist of a mummer pretending to ride a horse. **b.** A person wearing such a costume. **4.** A favorite topic or hobby.
hob·gob·lin (hŏb′gŏb′lən) *n.* **1.** A goblin variously represented as being mischievous or as ugly and evil. **2.** A bugbear. [HOB (elf) + GOBLIN.]
hob·nail (hŏb′nāl′) *n.* A short nail with a thick head used to protect the soles of shoes or boots. [HOB (projection, archaic sense peg) + NAIL.]
hob·nob (hŏb′nŏb′) *intr.v.* **-nobbed, -nobbing, -nobs.** To associate familiarly. Used with *with: He hobnobs with some of your brother's old friends.* [Originally *hob or nob,* (drink) to one another, from earlier *hab or nab,* hit or miss : perhaps Middle English *habbe,* present subjunctive of *habben,* to HAVE + *nabbe,* present subjunctive of *nabben,* not to have : *ne,* not, Old English *ne* (see **ne** in Appendix*) + *habben,* to HAVE.]
ho·bo (hō′bō) *n., pl.* **-boes** or **-bos.** **1.** A tramp; vagrant. **2.** A migratory, usually unskilled worker. [Origin unknown.] —**ho′bo·ism′** *n.*
Ho·bo·ken (hō′bō′kən). A city of northeastern New Jersey, on the Hudson River. Population, 48,000.
Hob·son-Job·son (hŏb′sən-jŏb′sən) *n.* Folk-etymological alteration of a borrowed word. An example of Hobson-Jobson is the word **compound**[2] which is from Malay *kampong.* [Anglo-Indian, coinage, itself a Hobson-Jobson alteration (influenced by *Hobson* and *Jobson,* English surnames) of Arabic *yā Ḥasan, yā Ḥusayn!* O Hasan, O Husain! (ritual cry of mourning for Hasan and Husain, Mohammed's grandsons who were killed in battle).]
Hob·son's choice (hŏb′sənz). An apparent freedom of choice with no real alternative. [After Thomas *Hobson* (died 1631), English liveryman, who required his customers to take the next available horse rather than give them a choice.]
Ho Chi Minh (hō′ chē′ mĭn′). Original name, Nguyen That Tan. Born 1890? President of Vietnam (1945–54) and of North Vietnam (since 1954).
hock[1] (hŏk) *n.* **1.** The tarsal joint of the hind leg of a digitigrade quadruped, such as a horse, corresponding to the human ankle. **2.** A similar joint in the leg of a domestic fowl. —*tr.v.* **hocked, hocking, hocks.** To disable by cutting the tendons of the hock; hamstring. [Middle English *hoch,* Old English *hōh,* heel. See **kenk-**[3] in Appendix.*]
hock[2] (hŏk) *n. Chiefly British.* White Rhine wine. [Short for obsolete *hockamore,* from German *Hochheimer (Wein),* wine of *Hochheim,* West Germany.]
hock[3] (hŏk) *tr.v.* **hocked, hocking, hocks.** *Informal.* To pawn. —*n. Informal.* The state of being pawned. —**in hock.** *Informal.* **1.** Being in pawn. **2.** Being held in jail. **3.** In debt. [From Dutch *hok*†, prison.]
hock·ey (hŏk′ē) *n.* **1.** A game played on ice in which two opposing teams of skaters, using curved sticks, try to drive a flat disk, or puck, into the opponents' goal. Also called "ice hockey." **2.** A similar game played on foot, using a ball rather than a puck. In this sense, also called "field hockey." [Origin uncertain.]
hockey stick. A stick with one curved end, used in hockey.
hock·shop (hŏk′shŏp′) *n. Informal.* A pawnshop.
ho·cus (hō′kəs) *tr.v.* **-cused** or **-cussed, -cusing** or **-cussing, -cuses** or **-cusses.** **1.** To fool or deceive; to hoax; to cheat. **2.** To adulterate. **3.** To infuse (food or drink) with a drug. [Short for HOCUS-POCUS.]
ho·cus-po·cus (hō′kəs-pō′kəs) *n.* **1.** Nonsense words or phrases used as a formula by conjurers. **2.** A trick performed by a magician or juggler; sleight of hand. **3.** The skill or power of a magician. **4.** Any deception or chicanery. —*v.* **hocus-pocused** or **-cussed, -cusing** or **-cussing, -cuses** or **-cusses.** —*tr.*

ă pat/ā pay/âr care/ä father/b bib/ch church/d deed/ĕ pet/ē be/f fife/g gag/h hat/hw which/ĭ pit/ī pie/îr pier/j judge/k kick/l lid, needle/m mum/n no, sudden/ng thing/ŏ pot/ō toe/ô paw, for/oi noise/ou out/o͝o took/o͞o boot/p pop/r roar/s sauce/sh ship, dish/

To deceive; to fool; to cheat. —*intr.* To be deceptive.

hod (hŏd) *n.* **1.** A trough carried over the shoulder for transporting loads, such as bricks or mortar. **2.** A coal scuttle. [Perhaps variant of earlier dialectal *hot,* from Old French *hotte*†.]

Ho·dei·da (hō-dā′də, -dī′də). Also **Ho·dei·dah, Hu·dai·da** (hŏŏ-dā′də, -dī′də). A city and port of west-central Yemen on the Red Sea. Population, 40,000.

hodge·podge (hŏj′pŏj′) *n.* A mixture of dissimilar ingredients; hotchpotch. [Variant of HOTCHPOTCH.]

Hodg·kin (hŏj′kĭn), **Alan Lloyd.** Born 1914. British biophysicist.

Hodg·kin (hŏj′kĭn), **Dorothy Mary Crowfoot.** Born 1910. British chemist.

Hodg·kin's disease (hŏj′kĭnz). A usually chronic, progressive, ultimately fatal disease of unknown etiology, marked by inflammatory enlargement of the lymph nodes, spleen, and often of the liver and kidneys, and occurring approximately twice as often in adult males as females. [First described by Thomas *Hodgkin* (1798–1866), English physician.]

hoe (hō) *n.* A tool with a flat blade attached approximately at right angles to a long handle, used for weeding, cultivating, and gardening. —*v.* **hoed, hoeing, hoes.** —*tr.* To weed, cultivate, or dig up with a hoe. —*intr.* To work with a hoe. [Middle English *howe,* from Old French *houe,* from Frankish *hauwa* (unattested). See **kau-**[2] in Appendix.*] —**ho′er** *n.*

hoe·cake (hō′kāk′) *n.* A thin cake made of cornmeal. [It is sometimes baked on the blade of a hoe.]

hoe-down (hō′doun′) *n.* **1.** A boisterous dance; especially, a square dance. **2.** The music for a hoe-down. **3.** A party at which hoe-downs are danced. [HOE + DOWN.]

Hoek van Hol·land. The Dutch name for **Hook of Holland.**

Ho·fei (hŭ′fā′). Formerly **Lu·chow** (lōō′jō′). A city of central Anhwei, China. Population, 360,000.

Hoff·man (hŏf′mən), **Malvina.** 1887–1966. American sculptor.

Hof·mann (hŏf′män′), **Hans.** 1880–1966. German-born American artist.

Hof·stadt·er (hŏf′stăd′ər), **Robert.** Born 1915. American nuclear physicist.

Ho·fuf (hŏŏ-fōōf′). The capital of Hasa, Saudi Arabia, in the southeastern part of the province. Population, 83,000.

hog (hôg, hŏg) *n.* Also **hogg** (for sense 4). **1.** Any of various mammals of the family Suidae, which includes the domesticated pig as well as wild species, such as the boar and the wart hog. **2.** A domesticated pig, especially one weighing over 120 pounds. **3.** A self-indulgent, gluttonous, or vulgar person. **4.** *British.* A young sheep before its second shearing. —**whole hog.** Without reservation or constraint. Usually in the phrase *go (the) whole hog.* —*v.* **hogged, hogging, hogs.** —*tr.* **1.** To take more than one's share of. **2.** To cause (the back) to arch like that of a hog. **3.** To shorten (a horse's mane). —*intr.* To arch upward in the middle. Used of a ship's keel. [Middle English *hogge,* Old English *hogg,* from Celtic. See **su-**[1] in Appendix.*]

ho·gan (hō′gôn′, -gən) *n.* An earth-covered Navaho dwelling. [Navaho *hogan.*]

Ho·garth (hō′gärth′), **William.** 1697–1764. British painter and engraver.

hog·back (hôg′băk′, hŏg′-) *n.* A sharp ridge with steeply sloping sides, produced by the erosion of the broken edges of highly tilted strata. [From a fancied resemblance to a hog's back.]

hog cholera. A highly infectious, often fatal, viral disease of swine, characterized by fever, loss of appetite, diarrhea, and exhaustion.

hog·fish (hôg′fĭsh′, hŏg′-) *n., pl.* **hogfish** or **-fishes. 1.** A colorful fish, *Lachnolaimus maximus,* of warm Atlantic waters, having a long snout in the adult male. **2.** Any of several similar or related fishes, such as the **pigfish** *(see).*

Hog·gar Mountains. See **Ahaggar Mountains.**

hog·gish (hôg′ĭsh, hŏg′-) *adj.* **1.** Coarsely self-indulgent or gluttonous. **2.** Filthy. —**hog′gish·ly** *adv.* —**hog′gish·ness** *n.*

Hog·ma·nay (hŏg′mə-nā′) *n. Chiefly Scottish.* New Year's Eve, when children traditionally go from house to house asking for presents. [Origin obscure.]

hog·nosed skunk (hôg′nōzd′, hŏg′-). Any of several New World skunks of the genus *Conepatus,* ranging from the southwestern United States to southern South America, having the back broadly streaked with white and a pointed snout.

hog·nose snake (hôg′nōz′, hŏg′-). Any of several thick-bodied, nonvenomous North American snakes of the genus *Heterodon,* having an upturned snout. Also called "puff adder."

hog peanut. A twining North American vine, *Amphicarpa bracteata,* having clusters of pinkish or white flowers and bearing curving pods as well as basal or underground fleshy, one-seeded fruit.

hogs·head (hôgz′hĕd′, hŏgz′-) *n. Abbr.* **hhd 1.** Any of various units of volume or capacity ranging from 62.5 to 140 gallons; especially, a unit of capacity used in liquid measure in the United States, equal to 63 gallons. **2.** A large barrel or cask with such capacity. [The reason for naming is obscure.]

hog-tie (hôg′tī′, hŏg′-) *tr.v.* **-tied, -tying** or **-tieing, -ties.** Also **hog·tie. 1.** To tie together the legs of. **2.** To impede or disrupt in movement or action.

hog·wash (hôg′wŏsh′, -wôsh′, hŏg′-) *n.* **1.** Garbage fed to hogs; swill. **2.** Worthless, false, or ridiculous speech or writing.

hog·weed (hôg′wēd′, hŏg′-) *n.* Any of various coarse, weedy plants.

hog wild. *Slang.* Crazy with excitement; berserk.

Ho·hen·lin·den (hō′ən-lĭn′dən). A village of southeastern Bavaria, West Germany, 20 miles east of Munich; site of a major French victory over Austrian forces (1800).

Ho·hen·lo·he (hō′ən-lō′ə). A German princely family; ruled from the 12th to the 19th century.

Ho·hen·stau·fen (hō′ən-shtou′fən). A German princely family, including rulers of Sicily and the Holy Roman Empire in the 12th and 13th centuries.

Ho·hen·zol·lern[1] (hō′ən-tsôl′ərn). A German royal family, including rulers of Brandenburg, Prussia, and Germany from 1415 to 1918.

Ho·hen·zol·lern[2] (hō′ən-tsôl′ərn). A former province of Prussia, in modern Baden-Württemberg, West Germany.

Ho·he Tau·ern (hō′ə tou′ərn). A mountain range of southwest-central Austria, between Carinthia and Tirol. Highest elevation, Grossglockner (12,461 feet).

hoicks. Variant of **yoicks.**

hoi·den. Variant of **hoyden.**

Hoi·how (hoi′hou′). A city and port of northeastern Hainan Island, China. Population, 402,000.

hoi pol·loi (hoi′ pə-loi′). The common people viewed from a position of social or intellectual advantage or privilege. [Greek *hoi polloi,* the many, the masses : *hoi,* plural of *ho,* the (see **so-** in Appendix*) + *polloi,* plural of *polus,* many (see **pel-**[8] in Appendix*).]

hoist (hoist) *tr.v.* **hoisted, hoisting, hoists.** To raise or haul up, particularly with the help of a mechanical apparatus. See Synonyms at **lift.** —*n.* **1.** An apparatus for lifting heavy or cumbersome objects. **2.** The act of hoisting; a pull; lift. **3.** *Nautical.* **a.** The height or vertical dimension of a flag or of any square sail other than a course. **b.** A group of flags raised together as a signal. [Variant of dialectal *hoise,* from earlier *heise,* akin to Dutch *hijsen,* Low German *hissen*†.] —**hoist′er** *n.*

hoi·ty-toi·ty (hoi′tē-toi′tē) *adj.* Also **high·ty-tigh·ty** (hī′tē-tī′tē). **1.** Arrogant; pompous; pretentious. **2.** Lightheaded; flighty. **3.** Tending to take offense easily; peevish; touchy. —*n., pl.* **hoity-toities.** Also **high·ty-tigh·ty. 1.** Pretentiousness; arrogance. **2.** Giddiness. [Reduplication of *hoity,* from dialectal *hoit*†, to romp.]

Hok·kai·do (hŏ-kī′dō; *Japanese* hôk′kī′dō′). Formerly **Ye·zo** (yĕ′zō′). The second-largest island of Japan, 29,600 square miles in area, situated north of Honshu.

ho·kum (hō′kəm) *n.* **1.** That which may seem convincing or impressive but is untrue or insincere; nonsense; fakery. **2.** A stock technique for eliciting a desired response from an audience. [Perhaps from HOCUS-POCUS.]

Ho·ku·sai (hō′kōō′sī′), **Katsushika.** 1760–1849. Japanese color print-maker.

Hol·arc·tic (hŏl-ärk′tĭk, -är′tĭk, hōl-) *adj.* Of or designating the zoogeographic region that includes the northern areas of the earth and is divided into Nearctic and Palearctic regions. [HOL(O)- + ARCTIC.]

Hol·bein (hōl′bīn′; *German* hôl′bīn′), **Hans.** Called "the Younger." 1497?–1543. German painter; resident in England (from 1536).

Hol·born (hō′bərn, hōl′-). A former administrative division of London, England, now part of **Camden** *(see).*

hold[1] (hōld) *v.* **held** (hĕld), **hold** or *archaic* **holden** (hōl′dən), **holding, holds.** —*tr.* **1.** To have and keep in possession, as in the hands, arms, or teeth; to grasp; clasp. **2.** To support; keep up; bear: *This nail is too small to hold that mirror.* **3.** To maintain in a certain position or relationship; keep: *held his assailant at arm's length.* **4.** To contain; be filled by: *The jar holds one pint.* **5.** To keep in one's possession; own. **6.** To have or maintain for use; wield. **7.** To maintain control over; restrain: *The dam held the flood waters.* **8.** To retain the attention or interest of. **9.** To defend from attack; preserve. **10.** To detain; delay; stall: *Try to hold him until the police arrive.* **11.** To have the position of; occupy: *He holds the office of governor.* **12.** *Law.* **a.** To be the legal possessor of. **b.** To bind by a contract. **c.** To adjudge or decree. **13.** To cause to keep; bind; obligate: *They held him to his promise.* **14.** To keep in one's mind or heart; to harbor. **15. a.** To believe; regard. **b.** To assert; affirm. **16.** To cause to take place; put on: *The race was held in Florida.* **17.** To assemble; convene: *Court was held in the morning.* —*intr.* **1.** To maintain a grasp, clutch, or grip. **2.** To maintain a desired or accustomed position or condition. **3.** To adhere closely; keep: *They held to a southwesterly course.* **4.** To stand up under stress, pressure, or opposition; to last. **5.** To be valid, applicable, or true: *His theory holds.* —See Synonyms at **contain.** —**hold down. 1.** To keep in check; restrain; suppress. **2.** To work at and keep a job. —**hold for.** To include or apply to: *The same holds for you.* —**hold forth. 1.** To talk at length; lecture; rant. **2.** To propose; suggest. —**hold in. 1.** To keep back; curb; restrain. **2.** To control, check, or hide an impulse or emotion. —**hold off. 1.** To keep apart, far away, or at some distance. **2.** To stop or delay doing something: *Hold off for a minute.* —**hold on. 1.** To maintain one's grip; cling. **2.** To keep at; continue. **3.** To stop or wait for someone or something. —**hold one's own. 1.** To maintain one's ground or position; not falter. **2.** To keep at an adequate or average level; be good enough. —**hold out for.** To insist upon or wait for, accepting no compromises. —**hold to.** To keep true or steadfast to; remain loyal or faithful to. —**hold water.** To stand up under examination; be believable, valid, or tenable. —**hold with. 1.** To agree with. **2.** To be on the side of; support. **3.** To approve of; subscribe to. —*n.* **1.** The act or a means of grasping; a grip; clasp. **2.** A means of obtaining, retaining, or controlling something. **3.** Something held onto, as for support. **4.** A container; receptacle. **5.** A device that grips something so as to keep it in place.

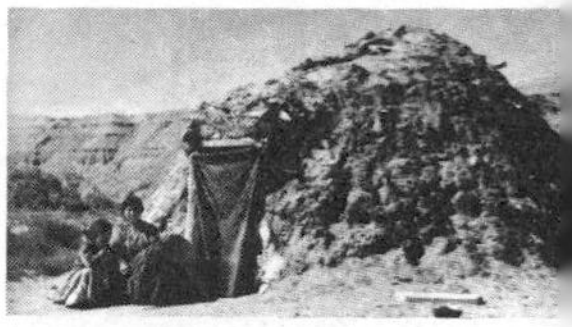
hogan

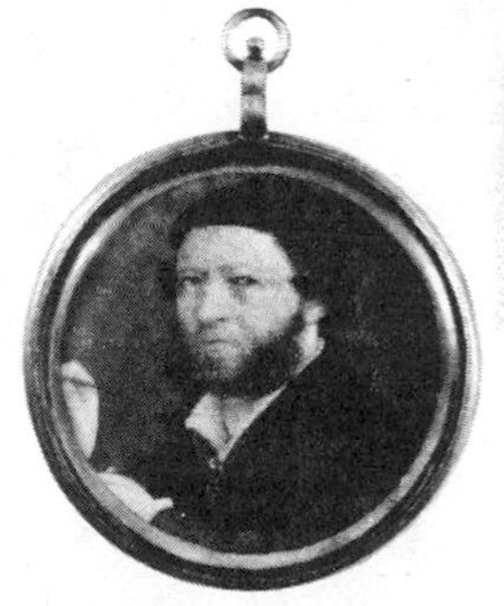
Hans Holbein

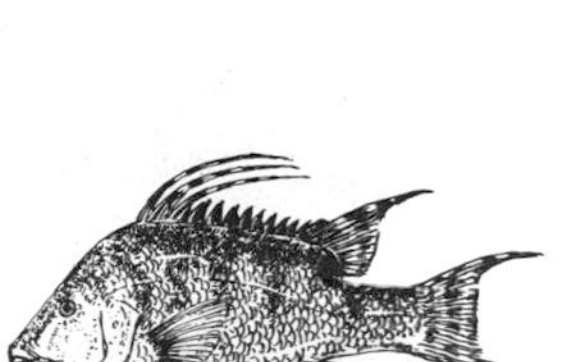
hogfish
Lachnolaimus maximus

6. A strong influence or power. 7. A prison cell. 8. *Archaic.* A fortified place; stronghold. 9. *Music.* a. The sustaining of a note longer than its indicated time value. b. The symbol designating this pause; a fermata. 10. A temporary halt, as in a countdown. [Hold, held, held, holden; Middle English *holden, heold, haldan, holden,* Old English *healdan, hēold, healden.* See **kel-**[5] in Appendix.*]

hold[2] (hōld) *n. Nautical.* The interior of a ship below decks where cargo is stored. [Variant (influenced by HOLD) of Middle English *hole,* HOLE.]

hold·all (hōld′ôl′) *n.* A case or bag for carrying miscellaneous items, as when traveling; a carryall.

hold back. 1. To curb; restrain. 2. To refrain. 3. To save for future use; keep apart or aside; retain.

hold·back (hōld′băk′) *n.* A strap or iron between the shaft and the harness on a drawn wagon, allowing the horse to stop or back up.

hold·en. *Archaic.* Past participle of **hold.**

hold·er (hōl′dər) *n.* 1. A person who holds something. 2. A device for holding something. 3. a. One who possesses something; an owner. Often used in combination: *landholder.* b. One who occupies or controls something; a keeper; defender: *holders of the fort.* 4. *Law.* One who legally possesses and is entitled to the payment of a check, bill, or promissory note.

hold·fast (hōld′făst′, -fäst′) *n.* 1. Any of various devices used to fasten something securely. 2. *Biology.* An organ or structure of attachment; especially, the basal, rootlike formation by which certain seaweeds or other algae are attached to a surface.

hold·ing (hōl′dĭng) *n.* 1. Land rented or leased from another. 2. *Often plural.* Legally possessed property, such as land, capital, or stocks. 3. An illegal hampering of an opponent's movement with the arms or hands, usually by a defensive player in some sports.

holding company. A company controlling partial or complete interest in other companies.

hold out. 1. To present; offer. 2. To last; stand up; endure. 3. To refuse to surrender or give up; continue resisting. 4. To refuse to give or divulge something expected or deserved.

hold·out (hōld′out′) *n. Informal.* A person who withholds or delays cooperation or agreement.

hold over. 1. To postpone taking action or making a decision on. 2. To keep longer than expected. 3. To use as a threat or for blackmail.

hold·o·ver (hōld′ō′vər) *n.* 1. Someone or something left or kept from an earlier time; a carry-over. 2. An officeholder kept in his position after his term is over. 3. An entertainer or entertainment kept beyond the original engagement.

hold up. 1. To prevent from falling; to support. 2. To present for exhibit; to show. 3. To last; stand up; endure. 4. To stop or interrupt; to delay. 5. To rob.

hold·up (hōld′ŭp′) *n.* 1. A suspension of activity; delay; interruption. 2. A robbery; especially, an armed robbery.

hole (hōl) *n.* 1. A cavity in a solid. 2. An opening or perforation through something; a gap; aperture: *a hole in the clouds.* 3. a. A deep place in water. b. A small, deep pond. c. A small bay; cove. 4. An animal's hollowed-out habitation, such as a burrow: *a gopher hole.* 5. An ugly, squalid, or depressing dwelling. 6. A deep or isolated place of confinement; a dungeon. 7. A fault or flaw; an error: *the holes in his argument.* 8. A bad situation from which it seems difficult to extract oneself; a predicament; bind. 9. *Golf.* a. The small pit lined with a cup into which the ball must be hit. b. One of the 9 or 18 divisions of a golf course, from tee to cup. 10. *Electronics.* A vacant electron energy state that is manifested as a charge defect in a crystalline solid, the defect behaving as a positive charge carrier with charge magnitude equal to that of the electron. **—hole in one.** *Golf.* The driving of the ball from the tee into the hole in only one stroke. **—hole in the wall.** A small, confining, or out-of-the-way place. **—in the hole.** *Informal.* In debt. —*v.* **holed, holing, holes.** —*tr.* 1. To put a hole or holes in; to puncture; perforate. 2. To put, propel, or drive into a hole. —*intr.* To make a hole or holes. **—hole up.** 1. To hibernate in, or as if in, a hole. 2. To hide out or shut oneself up: *The bandits holed up in the mountains.* [Middle English *hol(e),* hole, ship's hold, Old English *hol,* hollow place. See **kel-**[4] in Appendix.*] **—hole′y** *adj.*

Synonyms: *hole, hollow, cavity, excavation, cave, grotto, pit, pocket, crater.* These nouns refer to unfilled space in an otherwise solid body. *Hole* is applicable to any opening in or through such an object. *Hollow* denotes either an unfilled area in a solid body or a surface depression in such a body; examples of the second sense are valleys and ravines. *Cavity* refers to any unfilled space in a solid object, and *excavation* to a man-made cavity. A *cave* is a hollow, or empty chamber, in the earth, and a *grotto* is a cave or an artificially created area made to resemble a cave. A *pit* is a cavity or hole in the earth, often one that descends to a considerable depth from an opening on the surface. *Pocket* is applied principally to a cavity in the earth that contains water or a mineral deposit or to any cavity in a solid body that contains foreign matter. *Crater* refers to a bowl-shaped surface depression found naturally around the mouth of a volcano or geyser or created in warfare by the action of bombs or land mines.

hol·i·day (hŏl′ə-dā′) *n.* 1. A day on which custom or the law dictates a halting of general business activity to commemorate or celebrate a particular event. 2. A religious feast day; a holy day. 3. A day free from work which one may spend at leisure; a day off. 4. *Often plural. Chiefly British.* A period of time during which one is free from work; a vacation. —*adj.* Of, suitable for, or characteristic of a holiday: *a holiday mood.* —*intr.v.* **holidayed, -daying, -days.** *Chiefly British.* To pass a holiday or vacation: *holidaying in the Bahamas.* [Middle English *holiday,* Old English *hāligdæg* : *hālig,* HOLY + *dæg,* DAY.]

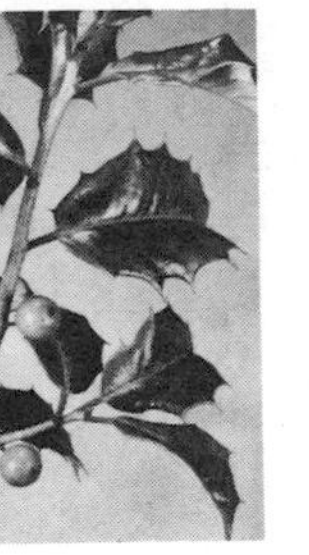

holly
Ilex opaca

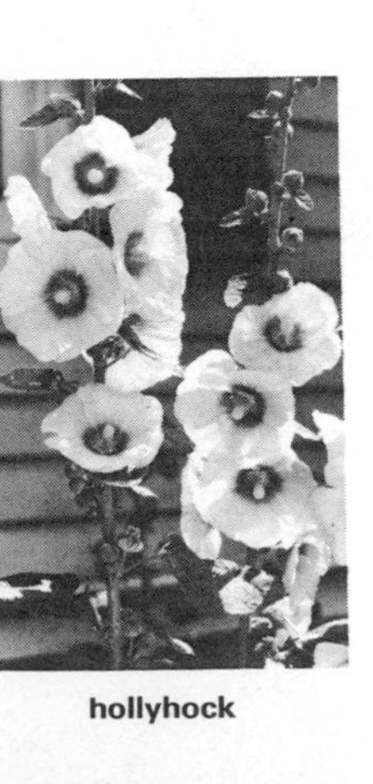

hollyhock

Hol·i·day (hŏl′ə-dā′), **Eleanor ("Billie").** Called "Lady Day." 1915–1959. American jazz singer.

ho·li·er-than-thou (hō′lē-ər-*thən-thou*′) *adj.* Showing an attitude of superior virtue; self-righteously pious.

ho·li·ness (hō′lē-nĭs) *n.* 1. The state or quality of being holy; sanctity. 2. *Capital* **H.** A title of address used for various high ecclesiastical dignitaries and especially for the pope. Preceded by *His* or *Your.*

Hol·ins·hed (hŏl′ĭnz-hĕd′, -ĭn-shĕd′), **Raphael.** Also **Hol·lings·head** (hŏl′ĭngz-hĕd′). Died 1580? English chronicler.

hol·land (hŏl′ənd) *n.* A fabric of linen or cotton, often glazed, and used for children's clothing, window shades, and upholstery. [Originally manufactured in HOLLAND.]

Hol·land. The **Netherlands** *(see).*

Hol·land (hŏl′ənd), **John Philip.** 1840–1914. Irish-born American inventor and designer of submarines.

Hol·land, Parts of (hŏl′ənd). An administrative county occupying 420 square miles in southeastern Lincolnshire, England. Population, 105,000. County seat, Boston.

hol·lan·daise sauce (hŏl′ən-dāz′, hŏl′ən-dāz′). A creamy sauce of butter, egg yolks, and lemon or vinegar, used with seafood and vegetables such as asparagus and broccoli. [Translation of French *sauce Hollandaise,* Dutch sauce, from *Hollandaise,* feminine of *Hollandais,* Dutch, from *Hollande,* Holland.]

Hol·land·er (hŏl′ən-dər) *n.* An inhabitant or native of the Netherlands; a Dutchman.

hol·ler (hŏl′ər) *v.* **-lered, -lering, -lers.** —*intr.* To yell or shout; cry out; call. —*tr.* To yell or shout (an utterance). —*n.* A yell or shout; call. [From French *holà,* stop : *ho,* HO + *là,* there.]

hol·low (hŏl′ō) *adj.* 1. Having a cavity, gap, or space within; not solid: *a hollow wall.* 2. Being deeply indented or concave; having depth or inclines; depressed: *"I am old with wandering/Through hollow lands and hilly lands"* (Yeats). 3. Deeply recessed; sunken; fallen: *hollow cheeks.* 4. Without substance or character; empty; superficial: *a hollow person.* 5. Without validity; shallow; specious: *hollow arguments.* 6. Having a reverberating, sepulchral sound; booming; echoing: *hollow footsteps.* **—a hollow leg.** An insatiable capacity for drink or food. —*n.* 1. A cavity, gap, or space within something: *the hollow behind a wall.* 2. An indented or concave surface or area; a shallow pocket: *the hollow of one's hand.* 3. A valley or depression. Often used in place names: *Sleepy Hollow.* 4. A void; vacuum; emptiness: *a hollow in one's life.* —See Synonyms at **hole.** —*v.* **hollowed, -lowing, -lows.** —*tr.* 1. To make hollow. Used with *out: hollow out a pumpkin.* 2. To scoop or form by making concave. Used with *out: hollow out a nest in the sand.* —*intr.* To become hollow. [Middle English *hol(e)we,* from *holh,* hole, Old English *holh,* hole, hollow place. See **kel-**[4] in Appendix.*] **—hol′low·ly** *adv.* **—hol′low·ness** *n.*

hol·low·ware (hŏl′ō-wâr′) *n.* Serving pieces, especially of silver, such as bowls, pitchers, and the like. Compare **flatware.**

hol·ly (hŏl′ē) *n., pl.* **-lies.** 1. a. Any of numerous trees or shrubs of the genus *Ilex,* such as *I. opaca,* of the eastern United States, or *I. aquifolium,* of the Old World, often having bright-red berries and glossy, evergreen leaves with spiny margins. b. Branches or leaves of such a tree or shrub, traditionally used for Christmas decoration. 2. Any of various similar or related plants. [Middle English *holi(n),* Old English *holen.* See **kel-**[9] in Appendix.*]

hol·ly·hock (hŏl′ē-hŏk′) *n.* A tall plant, *Althaea rosea,* native to China and widely cultivated for its showy spike of large, variously colored flowers. [Middle English *holihoc* : *holi,* HOLY + *hoc,* a mallow, Old English *hoc*†.]

Hol·ly·wood[1] (hŏl′ē-wo͝od′). A district of Los Angeles, California; center of the American motion-picture industry. Population, 100,000.

Hol·ly·wood[2] (hŏl′ē-wo͝od′) *n.* The U.S. motion-picture industry or the somewhat meretriciously glamorous atmosphere often attributed to it.

holm (hōm, hōlm) *n. Chiefly British.* 1. An island in a river. 2. Low land near a stream. [Middle English *holm,* from Old Norse *holmr,* islet, meadow. See **kel-**[8] in Appendix.*]

Holmes (hōmz, hōlmz), **Oliver Wendell**[1]. 1809–1894. American author of verse, essays, and novels.

Holmes (hōmz, hōlmz), **Oliver Wendell**[2]. 1841–1935. Associate Justice of the U.S. Supreme Court (1902–32); son of O.W. Holmes.

hol·mic (hōl′mĭk) *adj.* Pertaining to holmium in its trivalent state.

hol·mi·um (hōl′mē-əm) *n. Symbol* **Ho** A relatively soft, malleable, stable rare-earth element occurring in gadolinite, monazite, and other rare-earth minerals. Atomic number 67, atomic weight 164.930, melting point 1,461°C, boiling point 2,600°C, specific gravity 8.803, valence 3. See **element.** [From New Latin *holmia,* Latinized form of Stock*holm,* Sweden.]

holm oak (hōm, hōlm). A tree, *Quercus ilex,* native to the Mediterranean region, having prickly evergreen leaves. Also called "holly oak," "ilex." [From Middle English, variant of *holin,* HOLLY.]

holo-, hol-. Indicates whole or a whole, or entirely; for example, **Holarctic, holoblastic.** [From Greek *holos,* whole, entire. See **sol-** in Appendix.*]

hol·o·blas·tic (hŏl′ō-blăs′tĭk, hō′lō-) *adj.* Exhibiting cleavage in which the entire egg separates into individual blastomeres. Compare **meroblastic.** [HOLO- + -BLASTIC.]

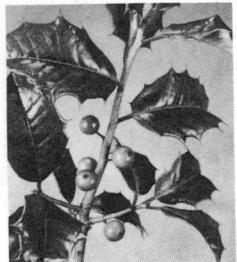

hol·o·caust (hŏl′ə-kôst′, hō′lə-) *n.* **1.** *Rare.* A sacrificial offering that is consumed entirely by flames; burnt offering. **2.** Great or total destruction by fire; a conflagration. **3.** Any widespread destruction. —See Synonyms at **disaster.** [Middle English, from Old French *holocauste,* from Latin *holocaustum,* from Greek *holokauston,* from *holokaustos,* burnt whole : *holo-,* whole + *kaustos,* variant of *kautos,* burnt, from *kaein,* to burn (see **kēu-** in Appendix*).] —**hol′o·caus′tal, hol′o·caus′tic** *adj.*

Hol·o·cene (hŏl′ə-sēn′, hō′lə-) *adj. Geology.* Of, belonging to, or designating the geologic time, rock series, or sedimentary deposits of the more recent of the two epochs of the Quaternary period, extending from the end of the Pleistocene to the present. See **geology.** —*n. Geology.* The Holocene epoch or system of deposits. Preceded by *the.* [HOLO- + -CENE.]

hol·o·crine (hŏl′ə-krĭn, -krēn′, -krīn′, hō′lə-) *adj.* Pertaining to a gland whose secretion is formed by the degeneration of the gland's cells, as sebaceous glands. Compare **merocrine.** [HOLO- + Greek *krinein,* to separate, divide (see **skeri-** in Appendix*).]

Hol·o·fer·nes (hŏl′ə-fûr′nēz). In the Apocrypha, an Assyrian general of Nebuchadnezzar's army killed by Judith.

hol·o·gram (hŏl′ə-grăm′, hō′lə-) *n.* **1.** The pattern produced on a photosensitive medium that has been exposed by holography and then photographically developed. **2.** The photosensitive medium so exposed and so developed. Also called "holograph." [HOLO- + -GRAM.]

hol·o·graph[1] (hŏl′ə-grăf′, -gräf′, hō′lə-) *n.* **1.** A document written wholly in the handwriting of the person whose signature it bears. **2.** A **hologram** *(see).* [From Late Latin *holographus,* entirely written by the signer, from Greek *holographos,* written in full : *holo-,* whole + -GRAPH.] —**hol′o·graph′ic, hol′o·graph′i·cal** *adj.* —**hol′o·graph′i·cal·ly** *adv.*

ho·lo·graph[2] (hŏl′ə-grăf′, -gräf′, hō′lə-) *tr.v.* **-graphed, -graphing, -graphs.** **1.** To produce an image of (a physical object) by holography. **2.** To form a hologram of (a physical object). [HOLO- + -GRAPH.] —**hol′o·graph′ic, hol′o·graph′i·cal** *adj.* —**hol′o·graph′i·cal·ly** *adv.*

ho·log·raph·y (hō-lŏg′rə-fē, hə-) *n.* The technique of producing images by wavefront reconstruction, especially by using lasers to record on a photographic plate the diffraction pattern from which a three-dimensional image can be projected. [HOLO- + -GRAPHY.]

hol·o·he·dral (hŏl′ō-hē′drəl, hō′lō-) *adj.* Having as many planes as required for complete symmetry in a given crystal system. [HOLO- + -HEDRAL.]

hol·o·phras·tic (hŏl′ō-frăs′tĭk, hō′lō-) *adj. Linguistics.* **Polysynthetic** *(see).* [HOLO- + Greek *phrastikos,* indicative, expressive, from *phrazein,* to show (see **phrazein** in Appendix*).]

hol·o·thu·ri·an (hŏl′ō-thŏŏr′ē-ən, hō′lō-) *n.* Any of various echinoderms of the class Holothuroidea, which includes the sea cucumbers. —*adj.* Of or belonging to the class Holothuroidea. [From New Latin *Holothuria* (genus), from Latin *holothūria,* water polyp, from Greek *holothourion*†.]

hol·o·type (hŏl′ə-tīp′, hō′lə-) *n.* The single specimen used as the basis of the original published description of a taxonomic species and later designated as the type specimen. [HOLO- + TYPE.] —**hol′o·typ′ic** (hŏl′ō-tĭp′ĭk, hō′lō-) *adj.*

hol·o·zo·ic (hŏl′ō-zō′ĭk, hō′lō-) *adj.* Obtaining nourishment by the ingestion of organic material, as do animals. [HOLO- + -ZOIC.]

holp. *Archaic.* Past tense of **help.**

holp·en. *Archaic.* Past participle of **help.**

Hol·stein[1] (hōl′stīn; *German* hôl′shtīn). A former duchy of Denmark, annexed by Prussia in 1866, and now part of Schleswig-Holstein, West Germany.

Hol·stein[2] (hōl′stīn) *n.* Any of a breed of large black and white dairy cattle originally developed in Friesland. Also called "Holstein-Friesian." [Later raised in HOLSTEIN.]

hol·ster (hōl′stər) *n.* A leather case shaped to hold a pistol. [Dutch. See **kel-**[4] in Appendix.*] —**hol′stered** *adj.*

Hol·ston (hōl′stən). A river rising in northeastern Tennessee and flowing 115 miles southwest to join the French Broad River and form the Tennessee.

holt (hōlt) *n. Archaic.* **1.** A wood or grove; copse. Often used in surnames and place names. **2.** A wooded hill. [Middle English *holt,* wood, Old English *holt.* See **kel-**[2] in Appendix.*]

ho·ly (hō′lē) *adj.* **-lier, -liest.** **1.** Belonging to, derived from, or associated with a divine power; sacred. **2.** Worthy of worship or high esteem; revered: *a holy book.* **3.** Living according to a religious or spiritual system: *a holy man.* **4.** Specified or set apart for a religious purpose: *a holy hour.* **5.** Solemnly undertaken; sacrosanct: *a holy pledge.* **6. a.** Formally associated with or pertaining to an established or organized religion. **b.** Religious in theme, depiction, or subject: *holy paintings.* [Middle English *holy, holi, hali,* Old English *hālig.* See **kailo-** in Appendix.*] —**ho′li·ly** *adv.* —**ho′li·ness** *n.*

Holy Ark. The cabinet in a synagogue in which the scrolls of the Torah are kept.

Holy Bible. The Bible.

Holy Communion. *Abbr.* **H.C.** The **Eucharist** *(see).*

Holy Cross, Mount of the. A peak rising to 13,996 feet in the Sawatch mountains of west-central Colorado, and having near its summit deep snow-filled crevices in the shape of a cross.

holy day. Also **ho·ly·day** (hō′lē-dā′). A day specified for religious observance.

Holy Father. One of the titles of the pope.

Holy Ghost. The third person of the Christian Trinity. Also called "Holy Spirit."

Holy Grail. The **Grail** *(see).*

Holy Land. See **Palestine.**

Holy Office. Official name, Congregation of the Holy Office. A congregation of the Roman Catholic Church that deals with such matters as the protection of the faith and morals.

holy of holies. **1.** The innermost shrine of a Jewish tabernacle and temple. **2.** Any place held to be especially sacrosanct.

Hol·yoke (hōl′yōk). A city of southwest-central Massachusetts. Population, 53,000.

holy orders. *Ecclesiastical.* **1.** The sacrament or rite of ordination; the ceremony of admission into the priesthood or ministry. **2.** The rank of an ordained Christian minister; clerical status. **3.** The principal orders of the clergy in Christian churches: **a.** *Roman Catholic Church.* The priests, deacons, and subdeacons, comprising the major orders. See **minor orders.** **b.** *Eastern Orthodox Church.* The bishops, priests, deacons, subdeacons, and readers. **c.** *Anglican Church.* The bishops, priests, and deacons.

Holy Roller. A member of any of various religious sects in which spiritual fervor is expressed by shouts and violent bodily movements. Considered a derogatory term.

Holy Roman Empire. *Abbr.* **H.R.E.** An empire, consisting largely of Germanic states in central and western Europe, established in A.D. 962 with the crowning of Otto I by the pope, and ending with the renunciation by Francis II in 1806.

holy rood. **1.** A cross or crucifix; especially, one placed over a rood screen. **2.** *Capital* **H,** *capital* **R.** The cross upon which Jesus was crucified.

Holy Saturday. The Saturday before Easter.

Holy Scripture. The Old and New Testaments of the Bible. Also called "Holy Writ," "Scripture," "Scriptures."

Holy See. *Roman Catholic Church.* **1.** The See of Rome; the office or jurisdiction of the pope. **2.** The court of the pope.

Holy Sepulcher. The tomb of Jesus outside Jerusalem, regarded as a Christian shrine.

Holy Spirit. The **Holy Ghost** *(see).*

ho·ly·stone (hō′lē-stōn′) *n.* A piece of soft sandstone used for scouring the wooden decks of a ship. —*tr.v.* **holystoned, -stoning, -stones.** To scrub or scour with a holystone. [From its use while in a kneeling position.]

Holy Synod. The administrative or governing body of any of the Eastern Orthodox churches.

Holy Thursday. **1.** *Roman Catholic Church.* **Maundy Thursday** *(see).* **2.** *Anglican Church.* **Ascension Day** *(see).*

holy water. Water blessed by a priest.

Holy Week. The week before Easter.

hom·age (hŏm′ĭj, ŏm′-) *n.* **1.** Ceremonial acknowledgment under feudal law by a vassal or tenant of allegiance to his lord: *"the loyalty of the vassal was symbolized by the annual act of homage"* (O.R. Gurney). **2.** Honor or respect publicly expressed to a person or idea: *"With the exception of peace, no social ideal receives more homage than education"* (Bernard Wright). —See Synonyms at **honor.** [Middle English, acknowledgment of a man's allegiance, from Old French, from Medieval Latin *hominātīcum,* from Latin *homō* (stem *homin-*), man. See **dhghem-** in Appendix.*]

hom·bre[1] (ŏm′brā, -brē) *n. Western Slang.* A man; fellow. [Spanish, from Latin *homō.* See **dhghem-** in Appendix.*]

hom·bre[2]. Variant of **ombre.**

Hom·burg (hŏm′bûrg′) *n.* Also **hom·burg.** A man's felt hat having a soft, dented crown and a shallow, slightly rolled brim. [First manufactured in *Homburg,* town near Wiesbaden, West Germany.]

home (hōm) *n.* **1.** A place where one lives; residence; habitation. **2.** The physical structure or portion thereof within which one lives, as a house or apartment. **3.** One's close family and one's self; a person's most personal relationships and possessions: *house and home.* **4.** An environment or haven of shelter, of happiness and love. **5.** Any valued place, original habitation, or emotional attachment regarded as a refuge or place of origin. **6.** The place where one was born or spent his early childhood, as a town, state, or country. **7.** The native habitat of a plant, animal, or the like. **8.** The place where something is discovered, founded, developed, or promoted; traditional centrum; source: *"And this is good old Boston, / The home of the bean and the cod"* (John C. Bossidy). **9.** A headquarters or base of operations from which activities are coordinated; home base. **10.** A goal or place of safety toward which players of a game, such as baseball, backgammon, or tag, progress; home base. **11.** An institution where people are cared for: *a nursing home.* —*adj.* **1.** Of or pertaining to a home, especially to one's household or house: *home furnishings.* **2.** Of or pertaining to one's country, place of birth, or nation, rather than to that which is foreign; domestic. **3.** Of or pertaining to a base of operations or headquarters; central: *a home office.* **4.** Going straight to the point; reaching its mark directly and accurately: *a home parry.* **5.** Taking place in the city where a team is franchised; hosted: *a home game.* —*adv.* **1.** At, to, or toward the direction of home. **2.** To the point at which something is directed; on target: *The arrow struck home.* **3.** To the center or heart of something; deeply. **4.** *Nautical.* Toward a vessel. —**at home.** **1.** In one's own house, locale, city or country; not away or absent. **2.** Held in one's house, as a party. **3.** Available to receive visitors: *at home Thursdays.* **4.** At ease; unconstrained; comfortable: *Make yourself at home.* **5.** Having facility in a field or skill; feeling an easy competence and familiarity: *at home in French.* —*v.* **homed, homing, homes.** —*intr.* **1.** To go or return home. **2.** To be guided to a target automatically, as by inertial guidance or heat sensing. —*tr.* To guide (a missile or aircraft) to a target automatically. [Middle English *hom(e),* Old English *hām.* See **kei-**[1] in Appendix.*]

Holstein[2]

Oliver Wendell Holmes[2]

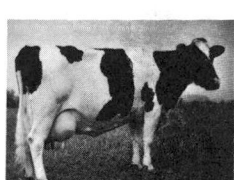

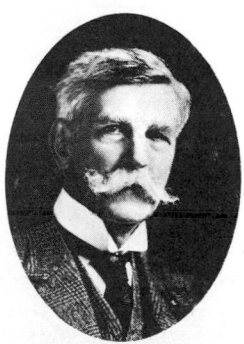

home base. 1. *Baseball.* The **plate** *(see).* 2. A base of operations; headquarters; home. 3. An objective toward which players of a game, such as baseball or backgammon, progress; home.
home·bod·y (hōm′bŏd′ē) *n. pl.* **-ies.** One who likes to stay or work at home; a domestic person.
home·bred (hōm′brĕd′) *adj.* 1. Raised, bred, or reared at home; domestic. 2. Not cultivated or sophisticated; rough.
home-brew (hōm′brōō′) *n.* An alcoholic beverage, especially beer, that is made at home. **—home′-brewed′** *adj.*
home·com·ing (hōm′kŭm′ĭng) *n.* 1. A coming to or returning home; an inaugurating or a welcoming back. 2. In colleges and universities, an annual event for visiting alumni.
home economics. The science and art of home management, including household budgets, purchase of food and clothing, child care, cooking, nutrition, and the like.
home front. The civilian population of a country at war.
home guard. A volunteer force formed to protect and defend a homeland or country while the regular army is fighting in the field; militia.
home·land (hōm′lănd′) *n.* 1. The land of one's allegiance. 2. The place of origin of a people.
home·less (hōm′lĭs) *adj.* Having no home or haven; orphaned.
home·ly (hōm′lē) *adj.* **-lier, -liest.** 1. Of a nature associated with or suited to the home; domestic; familiar; homey: *homely virtues.* 2. Of a simple or unpretentious nature; uncomplicated; plain: *"There is a sort of homely truth and naturalness in some books"* (Thoreau). 3. Lacking elegance or refinement; crude: *"the homeliest tasks get beautified if loving hands do them"* (Louisa May Alcott). 4. Not attractive or good-looking; ugly. Said usually of persons. **—home′li·ness** *n.*
home·made (hōm′mād′) *adj.* 1. Made or prepared in the home: *homemade pie.* 2. Made or assembled by oneself; not bought: *a homemade dress.* 3. Crudely or simply made: *a homemade bomb.*
home·mak·er (hōm′mā′kər) *n.* A person who manages a household; especially, a housewife.
homeo–, homoio–. Indicates like or similar; for example, **homeostasis, homeotherm, homoiotherm.** [Latin *homoeo-*, from Greek *homoio-*, from *homoios*, similar, from *homos*, same. See **sem-**[1] in Appendix.*]
Home Office. A department of the government of Great Britain corresponding to the U.S. Department of the Interior.
ho·me·o·mor·phism (hō′mē-ō-môr′fĭz′əm, hŏm′ē-) *n.* 1. *Chemistry.* A close similarity in the crystal forms of unlike chemical compounds. 2. *Mathematics.* A one-to-one correspondence between the points of two geometric figures that is continuous in both directions. [Greek *homoiomorph(os)*, of similar form : HOMEO- + -MORPH(OUS) + -ISM.] **—ho′me·o·mor′phous** *adj.*
ho·me·op·a·thy (hō′mē-ŏp′ə-thē, hŏm′ē-) *n.* A system of medical treatment based on the use of minute quantities of remedies that in massive doses produce effects similar to those of the disease being treated. Compare **allopathy.** [German *Homöopathie* : HOMEO- + -PATHY.] **—ho′me·o·path′** (hō′mē-ə-păth′, -päth′, hŏm′ē-), **ho′me·op′a·thist** *n.* **—ho′me·o·path′ic** (-ō-păth′ĭk) *adj.* **—ho′me·o·path′i·cal·ly** *adv.*
ho·me·o·sta·sis (hō′mē-ō-stā′sĭs, hŏm′ē-) *n.* A state of physiological equilibrium produced by a balance of functions and of chemical composition within an organism. [New Latin : HOMEO- + -STASIS.] **—ho′me·o·stat′ic** (-stăt′ĭk) *adj.*
ho·me·o·therm. Variant of **homoiotherm.**
home plate. *Baseball.* The **plate** *(see).*
hom·er[1] (hō′mər) *n.* 1. *Baseball.* A home run. 2. A homing pigeon. [From HOME.]
ho·mer[2] (hō′mər) *n.* An ancient Hebrew measure of capacity containing 10 ephahs (about 10 or 11 bushels) in dry measure, or 10 baths (about 100 gallons) in liquid measure. Also called "kor." [Hebrew *ḥomer.*]
Ho·mer (hō′mər). Greek epic poet traditionally believed to have been author of the *Iliad* and the *Odyssey.* [Latin *Homērus*, from Greek *Homēros*†.]
Ho·mer (hō′mər), **Winslow.** 1836–1910. American marine and genre painter.

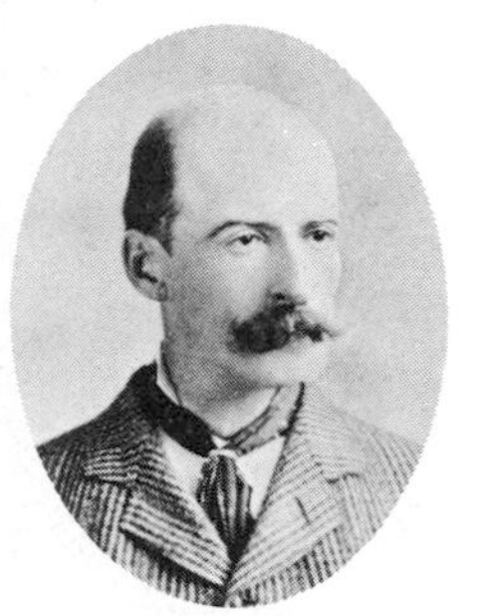
Winslow Homer

Ho·mer·ic (hō-mĕr′ĭk) *adj.* Also **Ho·me·ri·an** (-mîr′ē-ən), **Ho·mer·i·cal** (-mĕr′ĭ-kəl). 1. Of, pertaining to, or characteristic of the poet Homer, his works, or the legends and age of which he wrote. 2. Heroic in proportion, degree, or character: *Homeric laughter.* **—Ho·mer′i·cal·ly** *adv.*
home·room (hōm′rōōm′, -rŏŏm′) *n.* A school classroom to which a group of pupils of the same grade are required to report before morning and afternoon classes.
home rule. *Abbr.* **H.R.** The principle or practice of self-government in domestic matters in a dependent country or province.
home ruler. One who favors home rule.
home run. *Abbr.* **h.r.** *Baseball.* A hit that allows the batter to make a complete circuit of the diamond and score a run.
home·sick (hōm′sĭk′) *adj.* Acutely affected by separation from one's family and home; longing for home. **—home′sick′ness** *n.*
home·spun (hōm′spŭn′) *adj.* 1. Spun or woven in the home. 2. a. Made of a homespun fabric. b. Homemade. 3. Simple and homely in character; unpretentious. *—n.* 1. A plain coarse woolen cloth made of homespun yarn. 2. A similar sturdy fabric made on a power loom.
home·stead (hōm′stĕd′) *n.* 1. A house, especially a farmhouse, with adjoining buildings and land. 2. *Law.* Property designated by a householder as his home and protected by law from forced sale to meet debts. 3. Land claimed by a settler or a squatter, especially under the Homestead Act. 4. The place where one's home is. *—v.* **homesteaded, -steading, -steads.** *—intr.* To settle and farm land, especially under the Homestead Act. *—tr.* To claim and settle (land) as a homestead. **—home′stead′er** *n.*

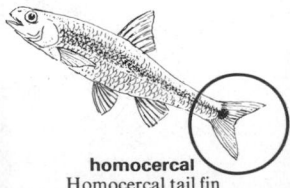

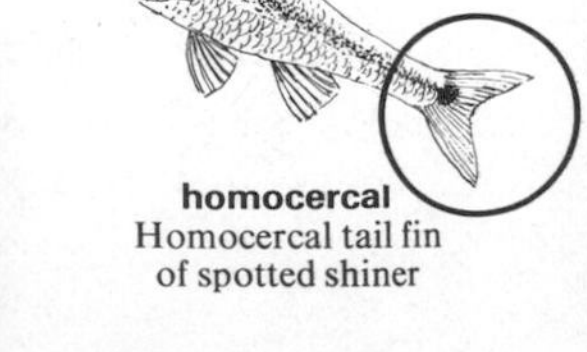
homocercal
Homocercal tail fin of spotted shiner

Homestead Act. An act passed by Congress in 1862 promising ownership of a 160-acre tract of public land to a head of a family after he had cleared and improved the land and lived on it for five years.
homestead law. Any of several laws passed in most states exempting a householder's homestead from attachment or forced sale to meet general debts.
Homestead National Monument. An area of 163 acres in southeastern Nebraska; site of first homestead entered under the Homestead Act.
home·stretch (hōm′strĕch′) *n.* 1. The portion of a racetrack from the last turn to the finish line. 2. The final stages of an undertaking.
home·ward (hōm′wərd) *adv.* Also **home·wards** (-wərdz). Toward home. *—adj.* Directed toward home.
home·work (hōm′wûrk′) *n.* 1. Work, such as schoolwork, office work, or piecework, that is to be done at home. 2. Any work of a preparatory or preliminary nature.
home·y (hō′mē) *adj.* **-ier, -iest.** Also **hom·y.** *Informal.* Having a feeling of home; homelike. **—hom′ey·ness** *n.*
hom·i·ci·dal (hŏm′ə-sīd′l, hō′mə-) *adj.* 1. Of or pertaining to homicide. 2. Tending to homicide. **—hom′i·ci′dal·ly** *adv.*
hom·i·cide (hŏm′ə-sīd′, hō′mə-) *n.* 1. The killing of one person by another. Compare **murder.** 2. A person who kills another person. [Middle English, from Old French, from Latin *homicīda*, killer, and *homicīdium*, killing : *homō*, man (see **dhghem-** in Appendix*) + *-cīda*, *-cīdium*, -CIDE (killer and killing).]
hom·i·let·ic (hŏm′ə-lĕt′ĭk) *adj.* Also **hom·i·let·i·cal** (-ĭ-kəl). 1. Pertaining to or of the nature of a homily. 2. Pertaining to homiletics. **—hom′i·let′i·cal·ly** *adv.*
hom·i·let·ics (hŏm′ə-lĕt′ĭks) *n.* Plural in form, used with a singular verb. The art of preaching as a subject of theological study. [Greek *homilētikē*, art of conversing, from *homilētikos*, social, affable, from *homilētos*, conversation, from *homilein*, to consort with, from *homilos*, crowd. See **homily.**]
hom·i·ly (hŏm′ə-lē) *n., pl.* **-lies.** 1. A sermon, especially one intended to edify a congregation on some practical matter. 2. A tedious moralizing lecture or admonition. [Learned respelling of Middle English *omelie*, from Old French, from Late Latin *homīlia*, from Greek *homilia*, discourse, intercourse, association, from *homilos*, crowd : *homou*, together (see **sem-**[1] in Appendix*) + *ilē*†, crowd.] **—hom′i·list** *n.*
hom·ing (hō′mĭng) *adj.* 1. Having the faculty of returning home or impelling one to return home, especially from a distance: *"for the homing instinct survives even when the home is a park bench"* (O. Henry). 2. Assisting in guiding a craft home: *a homing guidance system.*
homing pigeon. A domestic pigeon, such as one used for racing or for carrying messages, trained to return to its home roost.
hom·i·nid (hŏm′ə-nĭd) *n.* A primate of the family Hominidae, of which modern man, *Homo sapiens*, is the only extant species. *—adj.* Of the Hominidae. [New Latin *Hominidae* : *Homo* (stem *homin-*), HOMO + -ID.]
hom·i·noid (hŏm′ə-noid′) *adj.* 1. Of or belonging to the superfamily Hominoidea, which includes the apes and man. 2. Resembling a human being; manlike. *—n.* A member of the Hominoidea. [New Latin *Hominoidea* : *Homo* (stem *homin-*), HOMO + *-oidea*, from -OID.]
hom·i·ny (hŏm′ə-nē) *n.* Hulled and dried kernels of corn, prepared as food by boiling. [Perhaps of Algonquian origin.]
hominy grits. Hominy ground into a coarse white meal.
ho·mo[1] (hō′mō) *n.* Any member of the genus *Homo*, which includes the extinct and extant species of man. [New Latin *Homo*, from Latin *homō*, man. See **dhghem-** in Appendix.*]
ho·mo[2] (hō′mō) *n., pl.* **-mos.** *Slang.* A homosexual.
homo–. Indicates same or like; for example, **homogamous, homograph.** [Latin, from Greek, from *homos*, same. See **sem-**[1] in Appendix.*]
Usage: Words beginning with the prefix *homo-* are often construed (by folk etymology) as being derived from Latin *homo* meaning man. For example, *homocentric* may be felt to be synonymous with *anthropocentric.* This is an error. There is no connection between Greek *homos*, same, and Latin *homo*, man. If analogous words were to be formed on Latin *homo*, the form would be either *homi-*, as in *homicide*, or *homini-*, as in *hominid.*
ho·mo·cen·tric (hō′mō-sĕn′trĭk, hŏm′ō-) *adj.* Having the same center. [New Latin *homocentricus*, from Greek *homokentros* : *homo-*, same + *kentron*, CENTER.]
ho·mo·cer·cal (hō′mō-sûr′kəl, hŏm′ō-) *adj.* Pertaining to, designating, or characterized by a tail fin having two symmetrical lobes extending from the end of the vertebral column, as in most bony fishes. [HOMO- + *-cercal*, from Greek *kerkos*, tail (see **ker-**[2] in Appendix*).]
ho·mo·chro·mat·ic (hō′mō-krə-măt′ĭk, hŏm′ō-) *adj.* Of or characterized by one color; monochromatic. **—ho′mo·chro′ma·tism′** (-mə-krō′mə-tĭz′əm) *n.*
ho·mo·e·rot·i·cism (hō′mō-ĭ-rŏt′ĭ-sĭz′əm, hŏm′ō-) *n.* Also **ho·mo·er·o·tism** (-ĕr′ə-tĭz′əm). Sexual attraction for one's own sex; homosexuality. **—ho′mo·e·rot′ic** (-ĭ-rŏt′ĭk) *adj.*
ho·mog·a·mous (hō-mŏg′ə-məs) *adj. Botany.* 1. Having flowers that are sexually alike in the same plant or inflorescence. 2. Having stamens and pistils that mature simultaneously. [HOMO- + -GAMOUS.]
ho·mo·ge·ne·i·ty (hō′mō-jĭ-nē′ə-tē, hŏm′ō-) *n.* The state or quality of being homogeneous. See Synonyms at **unity.**
ho·mo·ge·ne·ous (hō′mə-jē′nē-əs, -jēn′yəs, hŏm′ə-) *adj.* 1. Like

ă pat/ā pay/âr care/ä father/b bib/ch church/d deed/ĕ pet/ē be/f fife/g gag/h hat/hw which/ĭ pit/ī pie/îr pier/j judge/k kick/l lid, needle/m mum/n no, sudden/ng thing/ŏ pot/ō toe/ô paw, for/oi noise/ou out/ŏŏ took/ōō boot/p pop/r roar/s sauce/sh ship, dish/

in nature or kind; similar; congruous. **2.** Uniform in structure or composition throughout. **3.** *Mathematics.* Consisting of terms of the same degree or elements of the same dimension. [Medieval Latin *homogeneus,* from Greek *homogenēs* : *homo-,* same + *-genēs,* born (see -GEN) + -OUS.] —**ho′mo·ge′ne·ous·ly** *adv.* —**ho′mo·ge′ne·ous·ness** *n.*

ho·mog·en·ize (hō-mŏj′ə-nīz′, hə-) *tr.v.* **-ized, -izing, -izes. 1.** To make homogeneous. **2. a.** To reduce to particles and disperse throughout a fluid. **b.** To make uniform in consistency; especially, to render (milk) uniform in consistency by emulsifying the fat content. [From HOMOGENEOUS.] —**ho·mog′en·i·za′tion** *n.* —**ho·mog′en·iz′er** *n.*

ho·mog·e·nous (hō-mŏj′ə-nəs, hə-) *adj.* **1.** *Biology.* Of or exhibiting homogeny. **2.** Homogeneous. [Medieval Latin *homogen(e)us,* HOMOGENEOUS.]

ho·mog·e·ny (hō-mŏj′ə-nē, hə-) *n. Biology.* Correspondence between organs or parts, possibly of dissimilar function, related by common descent. [Greek *homogeneia,* from *homogenēs,* HOMOGENEOUS.]

ho·mo·graft (hō′mə-grăft′, -gräft′, hŏm′ə-) *n.* A graft of tissue obtained from a member of the same species as the individual receiving it.

hom·o·graph (hŏm′ə-grăf′, -gräf′, hō′mə-) *n.* A word that is spelled the same as another word but differs in meaning and origin and may differ in pronunciation and syllabication. [HOMO- + -GRAPH.] —**hom′o·graph′ic** *adj.*

homoio-. Variant of **homeo-.**

ho·moi·o·therm (hō-moi′ə-thûrm′) *n.* Also **ho·me·o·therm** (hō-mē′ō-). A homoiothermous organism, such as a bird or mammal. [HOMOIO- + -THERM.]

ho·moi·o·ther·mous (hō-moi′ō-thûr′məs) *adj.* Also **ho·moi·o·ther·mal** (-məl), **ho·me·o·ther·mous** (hō′mē-ō-thûr′məs). Maintaining a relatively constant and warm body temperature that is independent of environmental temperature; warm-blooded. Compare **poikilothermous.**

Ho·moi·ou·si·an (hō′moi-ōō′sē-ən, -ou′sē-ən) *n.* A member of an Arian party in the fourth century that held that Jesus the Son and God the Father were of similar but not of the same substance. Compare **Heteroousian, Homoousian.** [From Greek *homoiousios,* of similar substance : HOMOIO- + *ousia,* substance, from *ōn* (stem *ous-*), present participle of *einai,* to be (see **es-** in Appendix*).]

ho·mol·o·gate (hō-mŏl′ə-gāt′, hə-) *tr.v.* **-gated, -gating, -gates.** *Chiefly Scottish.* To ratify; assent to; approve. [Medieval Latin *homologāre,* from Greek *homologein,* concur, agree, from *homologos,* HOMOLOGOUS.]

ho·mo·log·i·cal (hō′mə-lŏj′ĭ-kəl, hŏm′ə-) *adj.* Also **ho·mo·log·ic** (-lŏj′ĭk). Homologous. —**ho′mo·log′i·cal·ly** *adv.*

ho·mol·o·gize (hō-mŏl′ə-jīz′, hə-) *tr.v.* **-gized, -gizing, -gizes. 1.** To make homologous. **2.** To show to be homologous. —**ho·mol′o·giz′er** *n.*

ho·mol·o·gous (hō-mŏl′ə-gəs, hə-) *adj.* **1.** Corresponding or similar in position, value, structure, or function. **2.** *Biology.* Corresponding in structure and evolutionary origin, as the flippers of a seal and the arms of a human being. Compare **analogous. 3.** *Genetics.* Having the same linear sequence of genes as another chromosome. **4.** *Chemistry.* Belonging to or being a series of organic compounds, each successive member of which differs from the preceding member by a constant increment, especially by an added CH₂ group. [Greek *homologos,* agreeing : *homo-,* same + *logos,* word, proportion, from *legein,* to speak (see **leg-** in Appendix*).]

hom·o·lo·graph·ic (hŏm′ə-lō-grăf′ĭk) *adj.* Maintaining the ratio of parts. [Irregularly from Greek *homalos,* even, level (see **sem-1** in Appendix*) + GRAPHIC.]

homolographic projection. An equal-area projection reproducing the same area ratios as exist on the earth's surface.

hom·o·logue (hŏm′ə-lôg′, -lŏg′) *n.* Also **hom·o·log.** Something homologous; a homologous organ or part.

ho·mol·o·gy (hō-mŏl′ə-jē, hə-) *n., pl.* **-gies. 1.** The quality or condition of being homologous. **2.** A homologous relationship or correspondence. **3.** *Mathematics.* A topological classification of configurations into distinct types that imposes an algebraic structure or hierarchy on families of geometric figures. [Greek *homologia,* agreement, from *homologos,* HOMOLOGOUS.]

ho·mol·o·sine projection (hō-mŏl′ə-sīn′). An equal-area map of the earth's surface laid out on the basis of sinusoidal curves, with the interruptions over ocean areas so that the continents may appear with minimal distortion. [Irregularly from Greek *homalos,* even, flat (see **sem-1** in Appendix*) + -INE.]

ho·mo·mor·phism (hō′mō-môr′fĭz′əm, hŏm′ō-) *n.* Similarity of external form, appearance, or size. [HOMO- + MORPH(O)- + -ISM.] —**ho′mo·mor′phic, ho′mo·mor′phous** *adj.*

hom·o·nym (hŏm′ə-nĭm′, hō′mə-) *n.* **1.** One of two or more words that have the same sound and often the same spelling but differ in meaning. Compare **homophone. 2. a.** A word that is used to designate several different things. **b.** A namesake. **3.** *Biology.* One or more identical but conflicting taxonomic designations independently proposed for members of different categories. [Latin *homōnymum,* from Greek *homōnumon,* from *homōnumos,* HOMONYMOUS.] —**hom′o·nym′ic** *adj.*

ho·mon·y·mous (hō-mŏn′ə-məs, hə-) *adj.* **1.** Having the same name. **2.** Of the nature of a homonym; homonymic. [Latin *homōnymus,* from Greek *homōnumos* : HOMO- + *onuma,* name (see **nomen-** in Appendix*).] —**ho·mon′y·mous·ly** *adv.*

ho·mon·y·my (hō-mŏn′ə-mē, hə-) *n.* The quality or condition of being homonymous.

Ho·mo·ou·si·an (hō′mō-ōō′sē-ən, -ou′sē-ən, hŏm′ō-) *n.* Also **Ho·mou·si·an** (hō-mōō′sē-ən, hō-mou′-). A Christian supporting the Council of Nicaea's Trinitarian definition of Jesus the Son of God as consubstantial with God the Father. Compare **Heteroousian, Homoiousian.** [Late Latin *homousiānus,* from *homousius,* consubstantial, from Greek *homoousios,* of identical substance : HOMO- + *ousia,* being (see **Homoiousian**).]

hom·o·phone (hŏm′ə-fōn′, hō′mə-) *n.* A word having the same sound as another word but differing from it in spelling, origin, and meaning; for example, English *sum* and *some* are homophones. Compare **homonym.** [HOMO- + -PHONE.]

ho·mo·phon·ic (hŏm′ə-fŏn′ĭk, hō′mə-) *adj.* **1.** Having the same sound. **2.** *Music.* Having or characterized by a single melodic line with accompaniment. [From Greek *homophōnos,* having the same sound : HOMO- + *phōnē,* sound (see -PHONE).]

ho·moph·o·ny (hō-mŏf′ə-nē, hə-) *n.* **1.** The quality or condition of being homophonic. **2.** Homophonic music. Compare **polyphony, monophony.**

ho·mo·phy·ly (hō′mə-fī′lē, hŏm′ə-, hō-mŏf′ə-lē, hə-) *n.* Resemblance arising from common ancestry. [HOMO- + Greek *phulē,* tribe, PHYLE.] —**ho′mo·phyl′ic** (hō′mə-fīl′ĭk, hŏm′ə-) *adj.*

ho·mo·plas·tic (hō′mō-plăs′tĭk, hŏm′ō-) *adj.* **1.** Of, pertaining to, or exhibiting homoplasy. **2.** Of, pertaining to, or derived from a different individual of the same species: *a homoplastic graft.* [HOMO- + -PLASTIC.] —**ho′mo·plas′ti·cal·ly** *adv.*

ho·mo·pla·sy (hō′mə-plā′sē, -plăs′ē, hŏm′ə-) *n.* Superficial structural similarity arising from **convergence** (*see*). [HOMO- + -PLASY.]

ho·mop·ter·an (hō-mŏp′tər-ən, hə-) *n.* A homopterous insect. —*adj.* Of or belonging to the order Homoptera; homopterous. [New Latin *Homoptera* : HOMO- + -PTER.]

ho·mop·ter·ous (hō-mŏp′tər-əs, hə-) *adj.* Of or belonging to the order Homoptera, which includes insects such as the cicadas, aphids, and scale insects. [New Latin *Homoptera* : HOMO- + -PTEROUS.]

hom·or·gan·ic (hŏm′ôr-găn′ĭk, hō′môr-) *adj. Phonetics.* Designating two or more speech sounds, such as the alveolar consonants *t, d,* and *n,* formed in the same area or with the same organs of articulation. [HOM(O)- + ORGANIC.]

Ho·mo sa·pi·ens (hō′mō sā′pē-ĕnz′, -ənz). **1.** The taxonomic designation for modern man, the only extant species of the genus *Homo.* Usually written in italics. **2.** Man as a thinking creature as distinguished from other organisms. [New Latin : HOMO + Latin *sapiēns,* SAPIENT.]

ho·mo·sex·u·al (hō′mə-sĕk′shōō-əl, hŏm′ə-) *adj.* Pertaining to, characteristic of, or exhibiting homosexuality. —*n.* A homosexual person.

ho·mo·sex·u·al·i·ty (hō′mə-sĕk′shōō-ăl′ə-tē, hŏm′ə-) *n.* **1.** Sexual desire for others of one's own sex. **2.** Sexual activity with another of the same sex.

ho·mos·po·rous (hō-mŏs′pər-əs, hō′mə-spôr′əs, -spōr′əs, hŏm′ə-) *adj. Botany.* Producing spores of one kind only. [HOMO- + -SPOROUS.] —**ho·mos′po·ry** *n.*

ho·mo·tax·is (hō′mō-tăk′sĭs, hŏm′ō-) *n.* Similarity of arrangement and fossils in noncontemporaneous or widely separated geologic deposits. [New Latin : HOMO- + -TAXIS.] —**ho′mo·tax′ic** (-tăk′sĭk), **ho′mo·tax′i·al** *adj.*

ho·mo·thal·lic (hō′mō-thăl′ĭk, hŏm′ō-) *adj. Botany.* Having male and female reproductive structures in the same thallus, as in some fungi and algae.

Ho·mou·si·an. Variant of **Homoousian.**

ho·mo·zy·go·sis (hō′mō-zī-gō′sĭs, hŏm′ō-) *n.* The union of genetically identical gametes, resulting in the formation of a homozygote. [New Latin : HOMO- + ZYGOSIS.] —**ho′mo·zy·got′ic** (-gŏt′ĭk) *adj.*

ho·mo·zy·gote (hō′mō-zī′gōt′, hŏm′ō-) *n.* A zygote derived from the union of genetically identical gametes. [HOMO- + ZYGOTE.]

ho·mo·zy·gous (hō′mō-zī′gəs, hŏm′ə-) *adj.* Having identical alleles at corresponding chromosomal loci. [HOMO- + -ZYGOUS.] —**ho′mo·zy′gous·ly** *adv.*

Homs (hôms). Also **Hums** (hōōms). Ancient name **Em·e·sa** (ĕm′ə-sə). A city and silk-manufacturing center of west-central Syria on the Orontes. Population, 175,000.

ho·mun·cu·lus (hō-mŭng′kyə-ləs) *n., pl.* **-li** (-lī′). A diminutive man; pygmy; manikin. [Latin, diminutive of *homō,* man. See **dhghem-** in Appendix*.]

hom·y. Variant of **homey.**

hon. honorary.

Hon. 1. Honorable (title). **2.** honorary.

ho·nan (hō′năn′) *n.* Also **Ho·nan.** A pongee fabric of even color made originally from silk produced by the silkworms of Honan.

Ho·nan (hō′năn′). A province, 64,479 square miles in area, of east-central China. Population, 48,670,000. Capital, Kaifeng.

Ho·nan·fu. The former name for **Loyang.**

Hond. Honduras.

hon·da (hŏn′də) *n.* A knotted, spliced, or metal eye at one end of a lariat, through which the other end is passed to make a running noose. [Spanish, sling, from Latin *funda.* See **Fronde.**]

Hon·do. See **Honshu.**

Hon·du·ran (hŏn-dŏŏr′ən, -dyŏŏr′ən) *adj.* Of or pertaining to Honduras or its people. —*n.* A citizen of Honduras.

Hon·du·ras (hŏn-dŏŏr′əs, -dyŏŏr′əs) *n. Abbr.* **Hond.** A republic, 43,277 square miles in area, of northeastern Central America. Population, 2,315,000. Capital, Tegucigalpa.

Hon·du·ras, British. See **British Honduras.**

Hon·du·ras, Gulf of (hŏn-dŏŏr′əs, -dyŏŏr′əs). An inlet of the Caribbean, on the coasts of British Honduras, Honduras, and Guatemala.

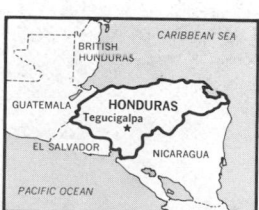

Honduras

ă pat/ā pay/âr care/ä father/b bib/ch church/d deed/ĕ pet/ē be/f fife/g gag/h hat/hw which/ĭ pit/ī pie/îr pier/j judge/k kick/l lid, needle/m mum/n no, sudden/ng thing/ŏ pot/ō toe/ô paw, for/oi noise/ou out/ōō took/ōō boot/p pop/r roar/s sauce/sh ship, dish/t tight/th thin, path/th this, bathe/ŭ cut/ûr urge/v valve/w with/y yes/z zebra, size/zh vision/ə about, item, edible, gallop, circus/ à *Fr.* ami/œ *Fr.* feu, *Ger.* schön/ü *Fr.* tu, *Ger.* über/KH *Ger.* ich, *Scot.* loch/N *Fr.* bon. *Follows main vocabulary. †Of obscure origin.

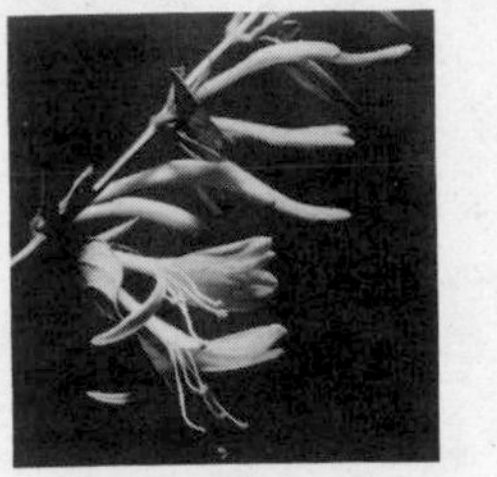

honeysuckle
Lonicera japonica

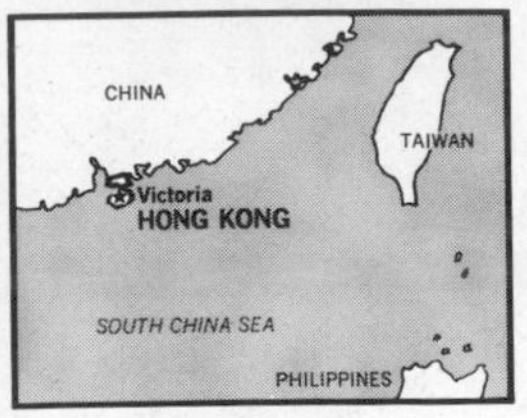

Hong Kong

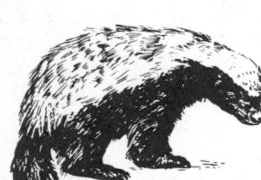

honey badger

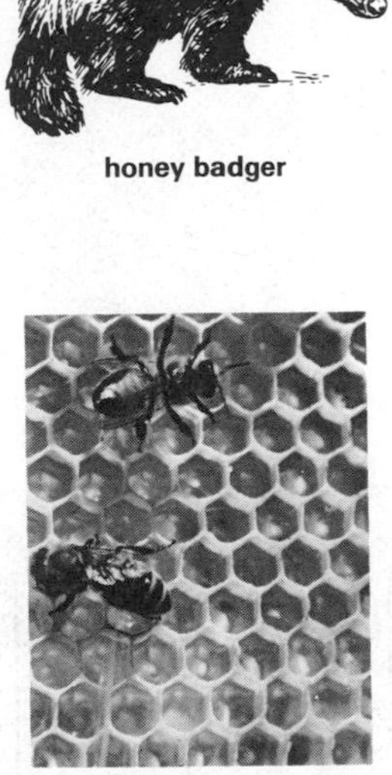

honeycomb

hone[1] (hōn) *n.* **1.** A fine-grained whetstone for giving a keen edge to razors and tools. **2.** A tool with a rotating abrasive tip for enlarging holes to precise dimensions. *—tr.v.* **honed, honing, hones.** To sharpen on or as if on a hone; give an edge to. [Middle English *hone,* Old English *hān,* stone. See **kē-** in Appendix.*]

hone[2] (hōn) *intr.v.* **honed, honing, hones.** *Informal.* **1.** To whine or moan. **2.** To hanker; yearn. Often used with *for* or *after.* [Old French *hoigner*†.]

Ho·neg·ger (hŏn′ĭ-gər; *French* ô-nĕ-gâr′), **Arthur.** 1892–1955. French-born Swiss composer of oratorios and symphonies.

hon·est (ŏn′ĭst) *adj.* **1.** Not lying, cheating, stealing, or taking unfair advantage; honorable; truthful; trustworthy. **2. a.** Not characterized by deception or fraud; genuine. **b.** Not calculated or constructed to defraud: *honest dice.* **3.** Equitable; fair: *honest wages for an honest day's work.* **4. a.** Having or manifesting integrity and truth; not false: *honest reporting.* **b.** Sincere; frank; blunt: *"A good honest and painful sermon"* (Pepys). **5. a.** Of guileless or ingenuous appearance; open: *"Flushed with purple grace/He shows his honest face."* (Dryden). **b.** Unfeigned; undisguised: *honest pleasure.* **6. a.** Of good repute; respectable; decent. **b.** Unpretentious; unaffected: *honest country folk.* **7.** *Archaic.* Free from moral stain; virtuous; chaste. Usually said of women. **—honest to goodness. 1.** Absolutely genuine. **2.** Used to express surprise, affirmation, and the like. [Middle English, from Old French *honeste,* from Latin *honestus,* honorable, from *honōs,* HONOR.]

hon·est·ly (ŏn′ĭst-lē) *adv.* **1.** In an honest manner. **2.** Genuinely: *"the American of today is much more honestly English . . . than the so-called standard English of England"* (Mencken). **3.** Really; truly. Used as an intensifier: *I honestly don't know.*

hon·es·ty (ŏn′ĭ-stē) *n.* **1.** The capacity or condition of being honest; integrity; trustworthiness. **2.** Truthfulness; sincerity: *in all honesty.* **3.** *Archaic.* Chastity. **4.** A plant, *Lunaria annua,* native to Eurasia, cultivated for its fragrant purplish flowers and round, flat, papery, silver-white seed pods. In this sense, also called "moonwort," "satinpod."

Synonyms: *honesty, veracity, honor, integrity, probity.* These nouns denote qualities closely associated with moral excellence. *Honesty* implies truthfulness, fairness in dealing, and absence of fraud, deceit, and dissembling. *Veracity* is truthfulness in expression. *Honor* implies close adherence to a strict moral or ethical code. *Integrity* is moral soundness, especially as it is revealed in dealings that test steadfastness to truth, purpose, responsibility, or trust. *Probity* is proven integrity.

hone·wort (hōn′wûrt′, -wôrt′) *n.* Any of several plants of the genus *Cryptotaenia;* especially, *C. canadensis,* of eastern North America, having clusters of small whitish flowers. [*Hone-* (meaning and origin unknown) + WORT.]

hon·ey (hŭn′ē) *n., pl.* **-eys. 1.** A sweet, yellowish or brownish, viscid fluid produced by various bees from the nectar of flowers and used as food. **2.** A similar substance made by certain other insects. **3.** A sweet substance, such as the nectar of flowers. **4.** Sweetness. **5.** *Informal.* Sweet one; dear. Used as a term of endearment. **6.** *Slang.* Something remarkably fine. Often used with *of a.* *—tr.v.* **honeyed** or **-ied, -eying, -eys. 1.** To sweeten with or as if with honey. **2.** To cajole with sweet talk. *—adj.* Of or resembling honey. [Middle English *hony,* Old English *hunig.* See **kenəko-** in Appendix.*]

honey ant. Any of various ants, such as one of the genus *Myrmecocystus,* that collect and store honeydew in the distensible abdomens of specialized workers.

honey badger. A carnivorous mammal, *Mellivora capensis,* of Africa and Asia, having short legs and a thick coat that is dark below and whitish on the top of the head and back. Also called "ratel."

honey bear. A mammal, the **kinkajou** *(see).*

hon·ey·bee (hŭn′ē-bē′) *n.* Any of several social bees of the genus *Apis* that produce honey; especially, *A. mellifera,* widely domesticated as a source of honey and beeswax.

hon·ey·comb (hŭn′ē-kōm′) *n.* **1.** A structure of hexagonal, thin-walled cells constructed from beeswax by honeybees to hold honey and eggs. **2.** Something suggesting this in structure or pattern. *—tr.v.* **honeycombed, -combing, -combs. 1.** To fill with holes; to riddle: *His story was honeycombed with lies.* **2.** To form in or cover with a honeycomb pattern.

hon·ey·creep·er (hŭn′ē-krē′pər) *n.* **1.** Any of various small, often brightly colored tropical American birds of the subfamily Dacninae, having a curved bill adapted for sucking nectar from flowers. **2.** Any of several similar birds of the family Drepanididae, of Hawaii.

hon·ey·dew (hŭn′ē-dōō′, -dyōō′) *n.* **1.** A sweet, sticky substance excreted by various insects, especially aphids, on the leaves of plants. **2.** Any similar sweet exudate on the leaves of plants. **3.** A honeydew melon.

honeydew melon. A melon, a variety of *Cucumis melo,* having a smooth, whitish rind and green flesh.

hon·ey·eat·er (hŭn′ē-ē′tər) *n.* Any of various birds of the family Meliphagidae, of Australia and adjacent regions, having a long, extensible tongue adapted for sucking nectar from flowers.

hon·eyed (hŭn′ēd) *adj.* Also **hon·ied. 1.** Containing, full of, or sweetened with honey. **2.** Ingratiating; sugary: *honeyed words.* **3.** Sweet; dulcet: *a honeyed voice.*

honey guide. Any of various tropical Old World birds of the family Indicatoridae, some species of which lead animals or people to the nests of wild honeybees, where they eat the wax that remains after the honey has been removed.

honey locust. 1. A thorny tree, *Gleditsia triacanthos,* of eastern North America, having compound leaves, greenish flowers, and long pods. **2.** A similar tree, the **mesquite** *(see).*

hon·ey·moon (hŭn′ē-mōōn′) *n.* **1.** A holiday or trip taken by a newly married couple. **2.** The early harmonious period in any joint undertaking. *—intr.v.* **honeymooned, -mooning, -moons.** To spend a honeymoon. [HONEY + MOON (month), the first month of marriage being thought of as the sweetest.]

hon·ey·suck·le (hŭn′ē-sŭk′əl) *n.* **1.** Any of various shrubs or vines of the genus *Lonicera,* having tubular, often very fragrant yellowish, white, or pink flowers. **2.** Any of various similar or related plants. [Middle English *honysoukel,* variant of *honysouke,* Old English *hunigsūce* : *hunig,* HONEY + *sūcan,* to SUCK.]

hong (hŏng, hông) *n.* **1.** In China, a factory or warehouse. **2.** A foreign trading house in China. [Cantonese *hong,* corresponding to Mandarin Chinese *hang*[2], profession, business establishment.]

Hong Kong (hŏng′ kŏng′, hông′ kông′). Also **Hong·kong. 1.** A British Crown Colony, occupying 391 square miles on the coast of Kwangtung, China, and including Hong Kong Island, Kowloon Peninsula, and the New Territories. Population, 3,982,000. Capital, Victoria. **2.** An island, 32 square miles in area, constituting part of this Crown Colony south of Kowloon Peninsula.

Ho·ni·a·ra (hō′nē-är′ə). The capital of the British Solomons, on the northwestern coast of Guadalcanal. Population, 6,400.

honk (hôngk, hŏngk) *n.* **1.** The raucous, resonant sound characteristically uttered by a wild goose. **2.** A similar sound, such as that made by an automobile horn. *—v.* **honked, honking, honks.** *—intr.* To emit a honk. *—tr.* To cause (a horn) to produce a honk. [Imitative.] **—honk′er** *n.*

hon·ky, hon·kie (hông′kē, hŏng′kē) *n., pl.* **-kies.** *Slang.* A white man. An offensive term used derogatorily. [Origin obscure.]

hon·ky-tonk (hông′kē-tôngk′, hŏng′kē-tŏngk′) *n. Slang.* A cheap, noisy saloon or dance hall. *—adj.* Designating a type of ragtime usually played on a tinny old piano. [Origin unknown.]

Hon·o·lu·lu (hŏn′ə-lōō′lōō). The capital and largest city of Hawaii, a port on the southern coast of Oahu. Population, 294,000.

hon·or (ŏn′ər) *n.* Also *chiefly British* **hon·our. 1.** Esteem; respect; reverence: *the honor shown to him.* **2. a.** Reputation; good name. **b.** Credit: *It was to his honor that he refused the award.* **3. a.** Glory; fame; distinction. **b.** A mark, token, or gesture of respect or distinction: *the place of honor at the table.* **c.** A decoration, as the Navy Cross. **d.** A title conferred for achievement, as a knighthood. **4.** Nobility of mind; probity; integrity. **5.** High rank. **6. a.** The dignity accorded to position: *He is awed by the honor of his office.* **b.** One that imparts distinction by association: *He is an honor to our organization.* **7.** Great privilege: *I have the honor to present the governor.* **8.** *Capital* **H.** A title of address often accorded to mayors and judges. Preceded by *Your, His,* or *Her.* **9. a.** A code of principally male dignity, integrity, and pride, maintained in some societies, as in feudal Europe, by force of arms. **b.** Personal integrity maintained without legal or other obligation. **c.** A woman's chastity; a reputation for chastity. **10.** *Plural.* Courtesies offered to guests. **11.** *Plural.* **a.** Special recognition for unusual academic achievement: *graduate with honors.* **b.** A program of individual advanced study for exceptional students: *Four students are in honors this year.* **12.** *Golf.* The right of being first at the tee. **13.** *Plural. Card Games.* The four or five highest cards in trump or in all suits. —See Synonyms at **honesty. —do the honors.** To perform the social courtesies required of a host. **—on** (or **upon**) **one's honor.** With one's good name as a pledge. *—tr.v.* **honored, -oring, -ors.** Also *chiefly British* **hon·our. 1. a.** To esteem; hold in respect. **b.** To show respect for. **2.** To confer distinction upon: *The ambassador honored us with his presence.* **3.** To accept or pay as valid (a credit card or check, for example). [Middle English *hono(u)r,* from Old French *honor,* from Latin *honor, honōs*† (stem *honōr-*).] **—hon′or·er** *n.*

Synonyms: *honor, homage, reverence, veneration, deference.* These nouns refer to the feeling or expression of admiration, respect, or esteem. *Honor,* the most general term, is applicable both to the feeling and to the expression. *Homage* is an expression of high regard, often a ceremonial tribute that conveys allegiance or professional respect. *Reverence* is a feeling of deep respect and devotion. *Veneration* is both the feeling and worshipful expression of respect, love, and awe, especially for one whose wisdom, dignity, sacredness, rank, or age merits such attention. *Deference* is respect or courteous regard for one which takes the form of yielding to his judgment or wishes.

Ho·no·ra (ŏn′ər-ə, ŏ-nôr′ə, ŏ-nōr′ə). A feminine given name. [Middle English *Honora, Annora,* from Norman French *Honour,* probably from Latin *honor,* HONOR.]

hon·or·a·ble (ŏn′ər-ə-bəl) *adj.* **1.** Deserving or winning honor and respect; creditable: *an honorable deed.* **2.** Bestowing honor; bringing distinction or recognition: *honorable mention.* **3.** Possessing and characterized by honor: *"for Brutus is an honorable man"* (Shakespeare). **4.** Consistent with honor or good name: *the only honorable course.* **5.** Distinguished; illustrious: *an honorable gathering.* **6.** Attended by marks of recognition and honor; doing honor: *an honorable burial.* **7.** *Capital* **H.** *Abbr.* **Hon. a.** Used with *the* as a title of respect for certain high officials. **b.** *British.* Used with *the* as a courtesy title of the children of barons and viscounts and the younger sons of earls. **—hon′or·a·ble·ness** *n.* **—hon′or·a·bly** *adv.*

honorable mention. A citation to one who has performed well in a competition but has not been awarded a prize.

hon·o·rar·i·um (ŏn′ə-râr′ē-əm) *n., pl.* **-ums** or **-ia** (-ē-ə). A payment given to a professional person for services for which fees are not legally or traditionally required. [Latin *honōrārium*, from *honōrārius*, HONORARY.]

hon·or·ar·y (ŏn′ə-rĕr′ē) *adj. Abbr.* **hon., Hon. 1.** Held, given, or bestowed as a mark of honor; especially, conferred as an honor without the usual adjuncts: *an honorary degree.* **2. a.** Holding an office or title given as an honor, without payment: *the honorary secretary of the association.* **b.** Voluntary. **3.** Relying upon honor; not legally enforceable. Said of a duty or obligation. [Latin *honōrārius*, from *honōrāre*, to honor, from *honor*, HONOR.]

hon·or·if·ic (ŏn′ə-rĭf′ĭk) *adj.* Conferring or showing respect or honor. —*n.* A title, phrase, or grammatical form conveying respect, used especially when addressing a social superior. [Latin *honōrificus* : *honor*, HONOR + -FIC.] —**hon′or·if′i·cal·ly** *adv.*

honors of war. Certain courtesies granted a surrendering foe, as the privilege of marching out bearing arms and colors.

hon·our. *Chiefly British.* Variant of **honor.**

Hon·shu (hŏn′shōō). Also **Hon·do** (hŏn′dō). The largest island of Japan (88,000 square miles), located between the Sea of Japan and the Pacific.

hooch (hōōch) *n.* Also **hootch.** *Slang.* Alcoholic liquor; especially, inferior or bootleg liquor. [Short for Alaskan *Hoochinoo*, a tribe that made a kind of distilled liquor.]

hood[1] (hŏŏd) *n.* **1.** A loose pliable covering for the head and neck, either attached to a robe or jacket or separate. **2.** An ornamental draping of cloth hung from the shoulders of an academic or ecclesiastical robe. **3.** A sack used to cover a falcon's head to keep it quiet. **4.** Something resembling a hood in shape or function, as: **a.** A metal cover or cowl for a hearth or stove. **b.** A carriage top. **c.** The hinged metal lid over an automobile engine. **d.** An expanded part, crest, or marking on or near the head of an animal. —*tr.v.* **hooded, hooding, hoods.** To supply or cover with a hood. [Middle English *ho(o)d*, Old English *hōd*. See **kadh-** in Appendix.*]

hood[2] (hŏŏd) *n. Slang.* **1.** A hoodlum; thug. **2.** A tough-looking youth. [Short for HOODLUM.]

-hood. Indicates: **1.** The state, condition, or quality of being; for example, **manhood. 2.** All the members of a grouping of a specified nature; for example, **neighborhood.** [Middle English *-hod(e)*, Old English *-hād*. See **skai-** in Appendix.*]

Hood (hŏŏd), **John Bell.** 1831–1879. American commander of Confederate troops in the Civil War.

Hood, Mount (hŏŏd). A volcanic peak, 11,245 feet high, of the Cascade Range in northwestern Oregon.

Hood, Robin. See **Robin Hood.**

Hood (hŏŏd), **Thomas.** 1799–1845. English poet and editor.

hood·ed (hŏŏd′ĭd) *adj.* **1.** Covered with or having a hood. **2.** Shaped like a hood, cowl, or similar covering. **3.** *Zoology.* Having a crest, coloration, or skin formation suggesting a hood.

hooded merganser. A North American duck, *Mergus cucullatus* (or *Lophodytes cucullatus*), having a narrow, hooked bill and a fanlike black and white crest in the male.

hooded seal. A seal, *Cystophora cristata*, of northern seas, having a grayish, spotted coat and an inflatable hoodlike or bladderlike pouch in the region of the nose. Also called "bladdernose."

hood·lum (hŏŏd′ləm, hōōd′-) *n.* **1.** A gangster; thug. **2.** A tough, destructive youth. [Origin unknown.]

hoo·doo (hōō′dōō) *n., pl.* **-doos. 1.** Voodoo. **2. a.** Bad luck. **b.** One that brings bad luck. —*tr.v.* **hoodooed, -dooing, -doos.** To bring bad luck to. [Perhaps variant of VOODOO.] —**hoo′doo·ism′** *n.*

hood·wink (hŏŏd′wĭngk′) *tr.v.* **-winked, -winking, -winks. 1.** To deceive; trick; take in. **2.** *Archaic.* To blindfold. **3.** *Obsolete.* To conceal. —See Synonyms at **deceive.** [HOOD + WINK.]

hoo·ey (hōō′ē) *n. Slang.* Nonsense. [Origin unknown.]

hoof (hŏŏf, hōōf) *n., pl.* **hoofs** or **hooves** (hōōvz, hŏŏvz). **1.** The horny sheath covering the toes or lower part of the foot of a mammal of the orders Perissodactyla and Artiodactyla, such as a horse, ox, or deer. **2.** The foot of such an animal, especially a horse. **3.** *Slang.* The human foot. —**on the hoof.** Alive; not yet butchered. Said especially of cattle. —*v.* **hoofed, hoofing, hoofs.** —*tr.* **1.** To trample with the hoofs. **2.** *Informal.* To walk. —*intr. Slang.* **1.** To dance. **2.** To go on foot; walk. Often used with *it: Let's hoof it instead of taking a cab.* [Middle English *hoof*, Old English *hōf*. See **kapho-** in Appendix.*]

hoof·bound (hŏŏf′bound′, hōōf′-) *adj.* Afflicted with drying and contraction of the hoof, resulting in lameness. Said of a horse.

hoofed (hŏŏft, hōōft) *adj.* Having hoofs; ungulate.

hoof·er (hŏŏf′ər, hōō′fər) *n. Slang.* A professional dancer; especially, a tap dancer.

Hoogh·ly (hōōg′lē). Also **Hug·li.** A branch of the Ganges, rising in West Bengal, Republic of India, and flowing 160 miles south to the Bay of Bengal.

hook (hŏŏk) *n.* **1.** A curved or sharply bent device, usually of metal, used to catch, drag, suspend, or fasten something. **2.** A fishhook. **3.** A catch; snag. **4.** Anything shaped like a hook, as: **a.** A curved or barbed plant or animal part. **b.** A short angled or curved line on a letter. **c.** *Surfing.* The lip of a breaking wave. **d.** A sickle. **5.** The fixed part of a door hinge; the pin. **6.** *Baseball.* A curve. **7.** *Boxing.* A short swinging blow delivered with a crooked arm. **8.** *Golf.* A stroke which sends the ball to the left of the player. —**by hook or (by) crook.** By whatever means possible, fair or unfair. —**get the hook.** *Slang.* To be dismissed or thrown out. —**hook, line, and sinker.** *Slang.* Without reservation; entirely; completely. —**off the hook. 1.** *Slang.* Freed as from blame or a vexatious obligation. **2.** Left off the cradle. Said of a telephone receiver. —**on one's own hook.** *Informal.* By one's own efforts; on one's own account. —*v.* **hooked, hooking, hooks.** —*tr.* **1. a.** To get hold of or catch with or as if with a hook. **b.** *Informal.* To snare. **c.** *Informal.* To please and make a fan of. **d.** *Slang.* To become addicted. **e.** *Slang.* To steal; snatch. **2.** To fasten by means of a hook. **3.** To pierce or gore as if with a hook. **4.** To make (a rug) by looping yarn through canvas with a type of crochet hook. **5.** *Baseball.* To pitch (a ball) with a curve. **6.** *Boxing.* To hit with a hook. **7.** *Golf.* To curve (a ball) to one's left. —*intr.* **1.** To bend like a hook. **2.** To fasten by means of a hook or a hook and eye. —**hook it.** *Slang.* To make a getaway; to escape. [Middle English *ho(o)k*, Old English *hōc*. See **keg-** in Appendix.*]

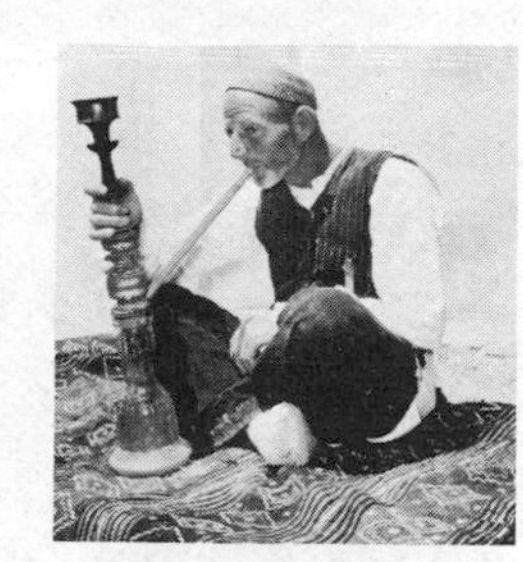
hookah

hook·ah (hŏŏk′ə) *n.* An Eastern smoking pipe designed with a long tube passing through an urn of water which cools the smoke as it is drawn through. Also called "hubble-bubble," "water pipe." [Urdu, from Arabic *ḥuqqah*, bottle of water through which tobacco smoke is drawn.]

hook and eye. A clothes fastener consisting of a small blunt metal hook with a corresponding loop.

hook-and-lad·der truck (hŏŏk′ən-lăd′ər). A fire engine equipped with extension ladders and hooked poles.

Hooke (hŏŏk), **Robert.** 1635–1703. English philosopher, physicist, chemist, and inventor.

hooked (hŏŏkt) *adj.* **1.** Bent or angled like a hook. **2.** Having a hook or hooks. **3.** Made by hooking yarn. **4.** *Slang.* **a.** Addicted to a narcotic. **b.** Entrapped by some custom or thing. —**hook′ed·ness** (hŏŏk′ĭd-nĭs) *n.*

hook·er[1] (hŏŏk′ər) *n.* **1.** A single-masted fishing smack used off Ireland. **2.** Any old worn-out or clumsy ship. Often used as a term of affection. [Dutch *hoeker*, from *hoek*, hook, fishhook (as in *hoekboot*, hookboat), from Middle Dutch *hoec*. See **keg-** in Appendix.*]

hook·er[2] (hŏŏk′ər) *n.* **1.** One that hooks. **2.** *Slang.* A neat shot of liquor, especially of whiskey. **3.** *Slang.* A prostitute.

Hook·er (hŏŏk′ər), **Thomas.** 1586?–1647. English Puritan clergyman; one of the founders of the city of Hartford, Connecticut (1636).

hook·nose (hŏŏk′nōz′) *n.* An aquiline nose. —**hook′nosed′** *adj.*

Hook of Hol·land (hŏŏk; hŏl′ənd). *Dutch* **Hoek van Hol·land** (hōōk′ vän hôl′änt). A cape and harbor on the southwestern coast of South Holland, the Netherlands.

hook up. 1. To assemble or wire (a mechanism). **2.** To connect a mechanism and a source of power. Often used with *to.* **3.** *Slang.* **a.** To form a tie or connection. Often used with *with.* **b.** To marry. Often used with *with.* **4.** To fasten together with a hook or hooks.

hook·up (hŏŏk′ŭp′) *n.* **1.** A system of electric circuits and electrically powered equipment designed to operate together. **2.** Any configuration of mechanical parts or devices acting as an integrated unit. **3.** A plan or schematic drawing of such a system or such a configuration. **4.** *Informal.* A connection, often between unlikely associates or factors.

hook·worm (hŏŏk′wûrm′) *n.* Any of numerous small, parasitic nematode worms of the family Ancylostomatidae, having hooked mouth parts with which they fasten themselves to the intestinal walls of various hosts, including man, causing the disease ancylostomiasis.

hookworm disease. Ancylostomiasis *(see).*

hook·y[1] (hŏŏk′ē) *adj.* **-ier, -iest.** Resembling a hook; hookshaped.

hook·y[2] (hŏŏk′ē) *n. Informal.* Absence without leave; truancy. Used in the phrase *play hooky.* [Perhaps from HOOK (to escape).]

hoo·li·gan (hōō′lĭ-gən) *n. Informal.* A young ruffian; hoodlum. [Origin obscure.] —**hoo′li·gan·ism′** *n.*

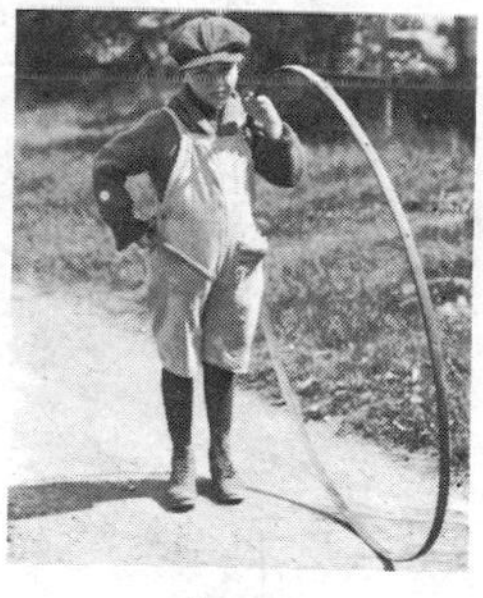
hoop

hoop (hōōp, hŏŏp) *n.* **1.** A circular band of metal or wood put around a cask or barrel to bind the staves together. **2.** A large wooden, plastic, or metal ring used as a plaything. **3.** One of the lightweight circular supports for a **hoop skirt** *(see).* **4.** A circular, ringlike earring. **5.** One of a pair of circular wooden or metal frames used to hold material taut for embroidery or similar needlework. **6.** A croquet wicket. —*tr.v.* **hooped, hooping, hoops. 1.** To hold together or support with or as if with a hoop or hoops. **2.** To encircle. [Middle English *hoop*, Old English *hōp*, from Germanic *hōpaz* (unattested).]

hoop·er (hōō′pər, hŏŏp′ər) *n.* A **cooper** *(see).*

hoop·la (hōōp′lä′, hŏŏp′-) *n. Slang.* **1.** Boisterous jovial commotion or excitement. **2.** Talk intended to mislead or confuse. [French *houp-là*†.]

hoo·poe (hōō′pōō, -pō) *n.* An Old World bird, *Upupa epops*, having distinctively patterned plumage, a fanlike crest, and a slender, downward-curving bill. [Variant of obsolete *hoop*, from Old French *huppe*, from Latin *upupa* (imitative).]

hoop-pet·ti·coat narcissus (hōōp′pĕt′ĭ-kōt′, hŏŏp′-). The **petticoat narcissus** *(see).*

hoop skirt. A long full skirt belled out with a series of connected hoops.

hoop snake. Any of several snakes, such as the **mud snake** *(see)*, that supposedly grasp the tail in the mouth and move with a rolling, hooplike motion.

hoo·ray. Variant of **hurrah.**

Hoo·sac Mountains (hōō′sək). A section of the Green Range, in western Massachusetts. Highest elevation, Spruce Hill (2,588 feet).

hoose·gow (hōōs′gou′) *n. Slang.* A jail. [Spanish *juzgado*, courtroom, from the past participle of *juzgar*, to judge, from Latin *jūdicāre*, to JUDGE.]

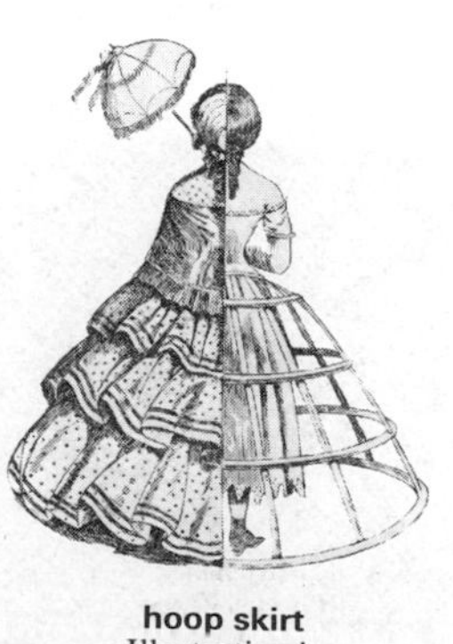
hoop skirt
Illustration in *Punch*, August 1856

t tight/th thin, path/*th* this, bathe/ŭ cut/ûr urge/v valve/w with/y yes/z zebra, size/zh vision/ə about, item, edible, gallop, circus/
à *Fr.* ami/œ *Fr.* feu, *Ger.* schön/ü *Fr.* tu, *Ger.* über/KH *Ger.* ich, *Scot.* loch/N *Fr.* bon. ***Follows main vocabulary.** †**Of obscure origin.**

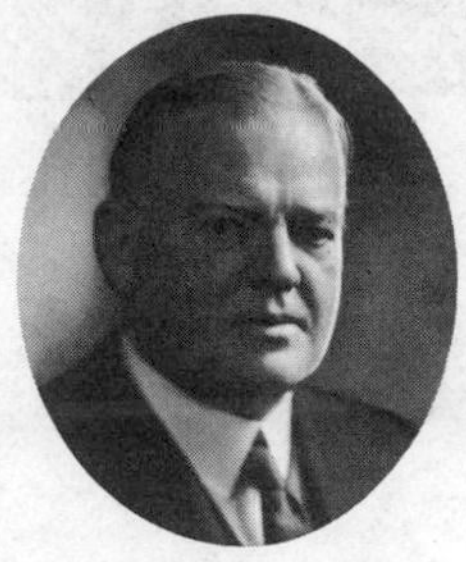

Herbert Hoover

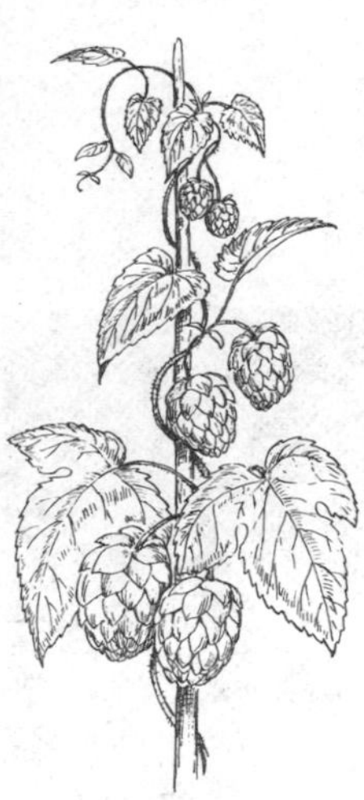

hop²
Humulus lupulus

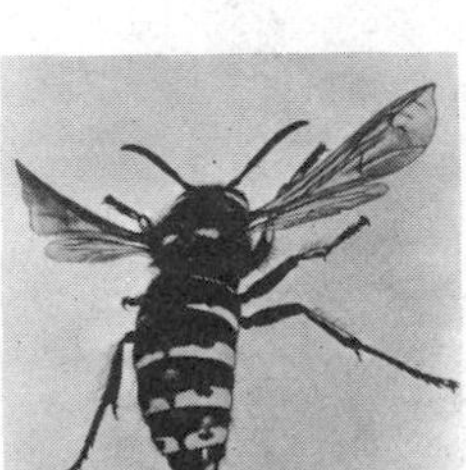

hornet
Genus *Vespa*

Hoo·sier (ho͞o′zhər) *n.* A nickname for a native or resident of Indiana. [Origin uncertain.]

Hoosier State. The nickname for Indiana.

hoot¹ (ho͞ot) *v.* **hooted, hooting, hoots.** —*intr.* **1.** To utter the characteristic cry of an owl. **2.** To make a loud derisive or contemptuous cry. **3.** To make or cause to make a hollow raucous sound like the cry of an owl. —*tr.* **1.** To shout down or drive off with jeering cries. Used with *down, off, out,* or *away: hoot a speaker off a platform.* **2.** To express or convey by hooting: *hoot one's disgust.* —*n.* **1. a.** The characteristic cry of an owl. **b.** A sound suggesting an owl's cry; especially, the sound of an automobile horn. **2.** An inarticulate cry of contempt or derision. **3.** A whit; jot. —**give a hoot.** To care the least bit. Usually used in the negative: *I don't give a hoot.* [Middle English *h(o)uten* (imitative).]

hoot² (ho͞ot, o͞ot) *interj.* Also **hoots** (ho͞ots, o͞ots). *Chiefly Scottish.* Used to express annoyance or objection. [Origin unknown.]

hootch. Variant of **hooch.**

hoot·chy-koot·chy (ho͞o′chē-ko͞o′chē) *n., pl.* **-chies.** Also **hoot·chie-koot·chie.** A deliberately sensual form of belly dance, typically performed as part of a carnival. [Origin uncertain.]

hoot·en·an·ny (ho͞ot′n-ăn′ē) *n., pl.* **-nies.** Also **hoot·nan·ny** (-năn′ē). **1.** A gathering of folk singers, typically with participation by the audience. **2.** *Informal.* An unidentified or unidentifiable gadget. [Origin uncertain.]

hoot·er (ho͞o′tər) *n. Chiefly British.* An automobile horn or similar noise-making device.

hoot owl. Any of various owls having a hooting cry.

Hoo·ver (ho͞o′vər), **Herbert Clark.** 1874–1964. Thirty-first President of the United States (1929–33).

Hoo·ver (ho͞o′vər), **J(ohn) Edgar.** Born 1895. Director of the Federal Bureau of Investigation (since 1924).

Hoo·ver Dam (ho͞o′vər). Formerly **Boulder Dam.** A dam rising to 726 feet in the Colorado River on the Arizona-Nevada boundary and forming Lake Mead.

Hoo·ver·ville (ho͞o′vər-vĭl′) *n.* A jerrybuilt camp erected usually on the edge of a town to house the jobless during the depression of the 1930's. [(Herbert) HOOVER + *-ville,* from their prevalence during his administration.]

hooves. Alternate plural of **hoof.**

hop¹ (hŏp) *v.* **hopped, hopping, hops.** —*intr.* **1.** To move with light bounding skips or leaps, using one foot or both or all four feet. **2.** To jump in one spot, especially on one foot. **3.** To limp. **4.** To make a quick trip, especially by air. **5.** *Informal.* To leave. —*tr.* **1.** To skip or fly over. **2.** To jump aboard: *hop a freight.* —**hop it.** *British Slang.* To go away; clear out. —**hop off.** *Slang.* To take off, as an aircraft. —*n.* **1.** A light springy jump or leap, especially on one foot. **2.** *Informal.* **a.** A type of dance step. **b.** A dance. **3.** A distance easily traversed by a few paces. **4.** A short airplane trip. **5.** A ride; lift. —**hop, skip, and (a) jump.** A short distance. [Middle English *hoppen,* Old English *hoppian.* See **keu-²** in Appendix.*]

hop² (hŏp) *n.* **1.** Any of several twining vines of the genus *Humulus;* especially, *H. lupulus,* having lobed leaves and green, conelike flowers. **2.** *Plural.* The dried, ripe flowers of this plant, containing a bitter, aromatic oil and used in brewing beer. —*v.* **hopped, hopping, hops.** —*tr.* To flavor with hops. —*intr.* To gather hops. —**hop up.** *Slang.* **1.** To increase the power or energy of. **2.** To stimulate with a narcotic. [Middle English *hoppe,* from Middle Dutch. See **skeup-** in Appendix.*]

hop·cal·ite (hŏp′kə-līt′) *n.* A granular mixture of the oxides of copper, cobalt, manganese, and silver, used in gas masks to convert carbon monoxide to carbon dioxide. [*(Johns) Hop(kins University + University of) Cal(ifornia)* + -ITE.]

hop clover. A clover, *Trifolium agrarium,* or one of a similar, closely related species, native to Eurasia, having small yellow flower heads that resemble hops when withered.

hope (hōp) *v.* **hoped, hoping, hopes.** —*intr.* **1.** To entertain a wish for something with some expectation. **2.** To be confident; trust. —*tr.* To look forward to with confidence of fulfillment; expect with desire. —See Synonyms at **expect.** —**hope against hope.** To persist in hoping for something against the odds. —*n.* **1.** A wish or desire supported by some confidence of its fulfillment. **2.** A ground for expectation or trust. **3.** That which is desired or anticipated. **4.** That in which one places one's confidence. **5.** Expectation; confidence. [Middle English *hopen,* Old English *hopian,* akin to Old Frisian *hopia*†.]

hope chest. A chest used by a young woman for the gradual collection of fine linens, silver, and other small household items in anticipation of marriage.

hope·ful (hōp′fəl) *adj.* **1.** Having or manifesting hope. **2.** Inspiring hope; promising. —*n.* A person who aspires to success or who shows promise of succeeding. —**hope′ful·ness** *n.*

hope·ful·ly (hōp′fə-lē) *adv.* **1.** With hope; in a hopeful manner. **2.** It is to be hoped; let us hope. See Usage note.

Usage: *Hopefully,* as used to mean it is to be hoped or let us hope, is still not accepted by a substantial number of authorities on grammar and usage. The following example of *hopefully* in this sense is acceptable to only 44 per cent of the Usage Panel: *Hopefully, we shall complete our work in June.*

Ho·pei (hō′pā′; *Chinese* hŭ′bā′). Formerly **Chih·li** (chē′lē′; *Chinese* jĭr′lē′). A province, 78,242 square miles in area, of northeastern China. Population, 44,720,000. Capital, Tientsin.

hope·less (hōp′lĭs) *adj.* **1.** Having no hope; despairing. **2.** Offering no hope; bleak. **3.** Incurable. **4.** Insoluble; discouraging; impossible. —**hope′less·ly** *adv.* —**hope′less·ness** *n.*

hop·head (hŏp′hĕd′) *n. Slang.* A habitual user of euphoriant drugs. [From obsolete slang *hop,* opium, probably from HOP (plant).]

hop hornbeam. Any of several trees of the genus *Ostrya;* especially, *O. virginiana,* of eastern North America, having fruit resembling hops. Also called "ironwood."

Ho·pi (hō′pē) *n., pl.* **Hopi** or **-pis. 1.** A tribe of Uto-Aztecan-speaking North American Indians now inhabiting a reservation in northeastern Arizona. Also called "Moki," "Moqui." **2.** A member of this tribe. **3.** The language of these people. [Hopi *hópi,* peaceful.]

Hop·kins (hŏp′kĭnz), Sir **Frederick Gowland.** 1861–1947. British biochemist; performed pioneer research on vitamins.

Hop·kins (hŏp′kĭnz), **Gerard Manley.** 1844–1889. English poet.

Hop·kins (hŏp′kĭnz), **Mark.** 1813–1878. American financier; builder of Central Pacific and Southern Pacific railroads.

Hop·kin·son (hŏp′kĭn-sən), **Francis.** 1737–1791. American Revolutionary leader and writer.

hop·lite (hŏp′līt′) *n.* A heavily armed foot soldier of ancient Greece. [French, from Greek *hoplitēs,* from *hoplon*†, weapon.] —**hop·lit′ic** (-lĭt′ĭk) *adj.*

hop-o'-my-thumb (hŏp′ə-mī-thŭm′) *n.* A tiny person; a dwarf. [From the imperative phrase *hop on my thumb,* used to indicate a person so small as to be able to hop on one's thumb.]

hopped-up (hŏpt′ŭp′) *adj. Slang.* **1.** Stimulated by or as if by narcotics; excited. **2.** Given higher power; supercharged. Said of an engine. [From *hop up,* to impregnate with narcotics, from obsolete slang *hop,* opium, from HOP (plant).]

hop·per (hŏp′ər) *n.* **1.** One that hops; especially, a hopping insect. **2. a.** A large funnel in which materials, such as grain or fuel, are stored in readiness for dispensation and use. **b.** Any receptacle in which something is held in readiness prior to usage or consideration: *the legislative hopper.*

Hop·per (hŏp′ər), **Edward.** 1882–1967. American painter.

hop·ple. Variant of **hobble.**

hop·sack·ing (hŏp′săk′ĭng) *n.* Also **hop·sack** (-săk′). A loosely woven, coarse fabric of cotton or wool used in clothing. [Used by hop growers for bags.]

hop·scotch (hŏp′skŏch′) *n.* A children's game in which players toss an object into succeeding sections of a figure on the ground, then hop through the figure and back on one foot as they retrieve the object. [HOP + SCOTCH (vine).]

Hor, Mount (hôr, hōr). *Arabic* **Je·bel Ha·run** (jă′băl′ hä-ro͞on′). A mountain rising to 4,383 feet in south-central Jordan, the traditional death and burial place of Aaron. Numbers 20: 22–29.

hor. horizontal.

ho·ra (hôr′ə, hōr′ə) *n.* Also **ho·rah. 1.** A traditional round dance of Rumania and Israel. **2.** The music to which this dance is performed. [Modern Hebrew *hōrāh,* from Rumanian *horă,* from Turkish *hora.*]

Hor·ace (hôr′ĭs, hŏr′-). Latin name, Quintus Horatius Flaccus. 65–8 B.C. Latin poet.

ho·ral (hôr′əl, hōr′-) *adj.* **1.** Of or pertaining to an hour or hours. **2.** Hourly. [Late Latin *hōrālis,* from Latin *hōra,* HOUR.]

ho·ra·ry (hôr′ə-rē, hōr′-) *adj.* **1.** Relating to or indicating an hour or the hours. **2.** Occurring once an hour. **3.** Lasting one hour. [From Medieval Latin *hōrārius,* from Latin *hōra,* HOUR.]

Ho·ra·tian (hə-rā′shən) *adj.* Of, relating to, or characteristic of the poet Horace, as in formal rigor, succinctness, or elegance.

Horatian ode. An ode in which a fixed strophic pattern is followed. [After HORACE.]

Ho·ra·tius Co·cles (hə-rā′shəs kō′klēz′). A Roman folk hero of the sixth century B.C. who held off an army of Etruscans at a bridge on the Tiber.

horde (hôrd, hōrd) *n.* **1.** A throng or swarm, as of people, animals, or insects. **2.** A nomadic Mongol tribe. **3.** Any nomadic group. —*intr.v.* **horded, hording, hordes.** To form or live in a horde. [Old French, from German *Horde,* from Polish *horda,* from Turkish *ordū,* camp. See also **Urdu.**]

Ho·reb (hôr′ĕb′, hōr′-). A mountain generally identified in the Old Testament with Mount **Sinai** *(see).*

hore·hound (hôr′hound′, hōr′-) *n.* Also **hoar·hound. 1.** An aromatic plant, *Marrubium vulgare,* native to Eurasia, having leaves covered with whitish pubescence and yielding a bitter extract used as flavoring and as a cough remedy. **2.** A candy or preparation flavored with this extract. **3.** Any of several similar or related plants, such as the **black horehound** *(see).* [Middle English *horhoune,* Old English *hārhūne* : *hār,* HOAR + *hūne*†, horehound.]

ho·ri·zon (hə-rī′zən) *n.* **1.** The apparent intersection of the earth and sky as seen by an observer. Also called "apparent horizon," "visible horizon." **2.** *Astronomy.* **a.** The circular intersection of a plane tangent to the earth at the observer's station with the celestial sphere. Also called "sensible horizon." **b.** The intersection with the celestial sphere of a plane through the center of the earth and perpendicular to the line connecting the zenith and the nadir. Also called "rational horizon." **c.** The great circle of the celestial sphere at the intersection of the sensible and rational horizons at infinity, its plane passing through the center of the earth. Also called "celestial horizon." **3.** The range of an individual's knowledge, experience, observation, or interest. **4.** *Geology.* **a.** A specific position in a stratigraphic column, as the location of one or more fossils, that serves to identify the stratum with a particular period. **b.** A specific layer of soil in a cross section of land. [Middle English *orizon(te),* from Old French, from Late Latin *horizōn,* from Greek *horizōn,* from the present participle of *horizein,* to divide, separate, from *horos*†, boundary, limit.]

ă pat/ā pay/âr care/ä father/b bib/ch church/d deed/ĕ pet/ē be/f fife/g gag/h hat/hw which/ĭ pit/ī pie/îr pier/j judge/k kick/l lid, needle/m mum/n no, sudden/ng thing/ŏ pot/ō toe/ô paw, for/oi noise/ou out/o͝o took/o͞o boot/p pop/r roar/s sauce/sh ship, dish/

hor·i·zon·tal (hôr'ə-zŏnt'l, hŏr'-) *adj. Abbr.* **hor. 1.** Of, relating to, or near the horizon. **2.** Parallel to or in the plane of the horizon. Compare **vertical. 3.** Occupying or restricted to the same level in a hierarchy: *a horizontal study of verbal ability.* **4.** Flat. —*n. Abbr.* **hor.** Anything, as a line, plane, or object, that is horizontal or assumed to be parallel with the horizon. [From Late Latin *horīzōn* (stem *horīzont-*), HORIZON.] —**hor'i·zon'tal·ly** *adv.*

horizontal union. A **craft union** *(see).*

hor·mone (hôr'mōn') *n.* A substance formed by one organ and conveyed, as by the blood stream, to another, which it stimulates to function by means of its chemical activity. [Greek *hormōn,* from the present participle of *horman,* to urge on, from *hormē*†, impulse, onrush.] —**hor'mo'nal, hor·mon'ic** (-mŏn'ĭk) *adj.*

Hor·muz (hôr'mŭz', hôr-mōōz'). Also **Or·muz** (ôr'-, ôr-). **1.** An island, 17 square miles in area, off the southeastern coast of Iran in the Strait of Hormuz. **2.** A strait linking the Persian Gulf with the Gulf of Oman.

horn (hôrn) *n.* **1.** One of the hard, usually permanent structures projecting from the head of certain mammals, such as cattle, sheep, goats, or antelopes, consisting of a bony core covered with a sheath of keratinous material. **2.** A similar hard protuberance, such as an antler or a projection on the head of a giraffe or rhinoceros. **3.** A projecting structure or growth suggestive of a horn. **4. a.** The hard, smooth, keratinous material forming the outer covering of the horns of cattle or related animals. **b.** A substance resembling this. **5. a.** A container made from a horn: *a powder horn.* **b.** The amount held by such a container. **6.** *Archaic.* A symbol or source of strength. **7.** *Archaic.* A symbol of the cuckold. **8.** Anything having the shape of a horn, especially: **a.** A cornucopia. **b.** Either of the ends of a new moon. **c.** The point of an anvil. **d.** The pommel of a saddle. **e.** An ear trumpet. **f.** A device for projecting sound waves, as in a loud-speaker. **g.** A hollow, metallic, electromagnetic transmission antenna with a characteristically rectangular cross section. Also called "horn antenna." **9.** *Abbr.* **h., H.** *Music.* **a.** A wind instrument made of an animal horn. **b.** A wind instrument made of brass. **c.** A French horn. **d.** *Informal.* A trumpet. **10.** A signaling device, usually electrical, that produces a sound similar to that of a sounded animal horn: *a fog horn.* **11.** *Aviation.* Any short lever attached to a cable, line, or rod that operates a control surface on an aircraft. —**blow** (or **toot**) **one's own horn.** To promote one's own interest; brag. —**on the horns of a dilemma.** Forced to choose between equally undesirable alternatives. —**pull** (or **draw** or **haul**) **in one's horn. 1.** To control one's emotions; restrain oneself. **2.** To take back a previous statement; recant. —*tr.v.* **horned, horning, horns. 1.** To provide with a horn or horns. **2.** To form into a horn. **3.** To gore or wound with a horn. **4.** *Archaic.* To cuckold. —**horn in.** *Slang.* To join without being invited; intrude. —*adj.* Made of horn. [Middle English *horn,* Old English *horn.* See **ker-¹** in Appendix.*]

Horn, Cape. A headland on an island of Tierra del Fuego, Chile; the southernmost point of South America.

horn·beam (hôrn'bēm') *n.* **1.** Any of various trees of the genus *Carpinus,* having smooth, grayish bark and hard, whitish wood. **2.** The wood of such a tree. Also called "ironwood." [From its tough, close-grained wood.]

horn·bill (hôrn'bĭl') *n.* Any of various tropical Old World birds of the family Bucerotidae, having a very large bill, often surmounted by an enlarged protuberance at the base.

horn·blende (hôrn'blĕnd') *n.* A common, green or bluish-green to black amphibole mineral, $CaNa(Mg,Fe)_4(Al,Fe,Ti)_3Si_6O_{22}(O,OH)_2$, formed in the late stages of cooling in igneous rock. [German *Hornblende* : *Horn,* horn, from Old High German *horn* (see **ker-¹** in Appendix*) + *Blende,* BLENDE.]

horn·book (hôrn'bŏŏk') *n.* **1.** An early primer consisting of a single page protected by a transparent sheet of horn, formerly used in teaching children to read. **2.** A rudimentary text.

Horn·church (hôrn'chûrch'). A former administrative division of London, England, now part of **Havering** *(see).*

horned (hôrnd) *adj.* **1.** Having a horn or horns. **2.** Having hornlike projections such as ear tufts: *a horned owl.* **3.** *Archaic.* Cuckolded.

horned toad. Any of several lizards of the genus *Phrynosoma,* of western North America and Central America, having hornlike projections on the head, a flattened, spiny body, and a short tail. Also called "horned lizard."

horned viper. A venomous African snake, *Cerastes cornutus,* having a hornlike projection above each eye. Also called "sand viper."

hor·net (hôr'nĭt) *n.* Any of various large stinging wasps, chiefly of the genera *Vespa* and *Vespula,* characteristically building a large papery nest. [Middle English *hernet,* Old English *hyrnet.* See **ker-¹** in Appendix.*]

Hor·ney (hôr'nī', hōr'-), **Karen (Danielsen).** 1885–1952. German-born American psychiatrist and author.

hor·ni·to (hôr-nē'tō) *n., pl.* **-tos.** *Geology.* A low mound of volcanic origin, sometimes emitting smoke or vapor. [Spanish, diminutive of *horno,* oven, from Latin *furnus.* See **gwher-** in Appendix.*]

horn-mad (hôrn'măd') *adj.* Extremely angry; furious; enraged. [Originally "enraged enough to horn someone."] —**horn'-mad'ness** *n.*

horn of plenty. A cornucopia.

horn·pipe (hôrn'pīp') *n.* **1.** An obsolete musical instrument with a single reed, finger holes, and a bell and mouthpiece made of horn. **2.** A spirited dance, usually performed by one person and originally accompanied by a hornpipe. **3.** The music accompanying such a dance.

horn·pout (hôrn'pout') *n.* A freshwater catfish, *Ictalurus nebulosus* (or *Ameiurus nebulosus*), native to eastern North America, having a large head with barbels. Also called "horned pout."

Horn·sey (hôrn'zē). A former administrative division of London, England, now part of **Harringay** *(see).*

horn·swog·gle (hôrn'swŏg'əl) *tr.v.* **-gled, -gling, -gles.** *Regional Slang.* To deceive; bamboozle. [Origin unknown.]

horn·tail (hôrn'tāl') *n.* Any of various sawflies of the family Siricidae, the female of which has a long, stout ovipositor.

horn·worm (hôrn'wûrm') *n.* The larva of the hawk moth, having a hornlike posterior segment.

horn·wort (hôrn'wûrt', -wôrt') *n.* Any of several aquatic plants of the genus *Ceratophyllum,* forming submerged branching masses in quiet water.

horn·y (hôr'nē) *adj.* **-ier, -iest. 1.** Having horns or similar projections. **2.** Made of horn. **3.** Resembling horn in hardness. **4.** *Slang.* Sexually aroused. —**horn'i·ness** *n.*

hor·o·loge (hôr'ə-lōj', hŏr'-) *n.* A timepiece. [Middle English *horologe, orloge,* from Old French *orloge,* from Latin *hōrologium,* from Greek *hōrologion,* from *hōrologos,* "hour-teller" : *hōra,* HOUR + *legein,* to speak (see **leg-** in Appendix*).]

ho·rol·o·ger (hô-rŏl'ə-jər, hō-) *n.* Also **ho·rol·o·gist** (-jĭst). One who practices or is skilled in horology.

hor·o·log·ic (hôr'ə-lŏj'ĭk, hŏr'-) *adj.* Also **hor·o·log·i·cal** (-ĭ-kəl). Of or relating to horology.

Hor·o·lo·gi·um (hôr'ə-lō'jē-əm, hŏr'-) *n.* A constellation in the Southern Hemisphere near Hydrus, Eridanus, and Reticulum. [Latin *hōrologium,* HOROLOGE.]

ho·rol·o·gy (hô-rŏl'ə-jē, hō-) *n.* **1.** The science of measuring time. **2.** The art of making timepieces. [Middle English *horologie,* from Latin *hōrologium,* HOROLOGE.]

hor·o·scope (hôr'ə-skōp', hŏr'-) *n. Astrology.* **1.** The aspect of the planets and stars at a given moment, such as the moment of a person's birth. **2.** A diagram of the signs of the zodiac based on such an aspect. **3.** A forecast of a person's future based on such a diagram. [Old French, from Latin *hōroscopus,* from Greek *hōroskopos,* astrologer : *hōra,* HOUR + *skopos,* observer (see **spek-** in Appendix*).]

ho·ros·co·py (hô-rŏs'kə-pē, hō-) *n., pl.* **-pies. 1.** The casting and reading of horoscopes. **2.** The configuration of the heavens at a given moment, as at a birth; a horoscope.

Ho·ro·witz (hôr'ə-wĭts', hŏr'-), **Vladimir.** Born 1904. Russian-born American pianist.

hor·ren·dous (hô-rĕn'dəs, hō-) *adj.* Hideous; dreadful. [From Latin *horrendus,* from the gerundive of *horrēre,* to tremble. See **horror.**] —**hor·ren'dous·ly** *adv.*

hor·rent (hôr'ənt, hŏr'-) *adj.* **1.** *Poetic.* Bristling. **2.** *Rare.* Terrified; shuddering. [Latin *horrēns,* present participle of *horrēre,* to tremble. See **horror.**]

hor·ri·ble (hôr'ə-bəl, hŏr'-) *adj.* **1.** Causing horror; dreadful: *"War is beyond all words horrible"* (Winston Churchill). **2.** Unpleasant; disagreeable; offensive. [Middle English, from Old French, from Latin *horribilis,* from *horrēre,* to tremble. See **horror.**] —**hor'ri·ble·ness** *n.* —**hor'ri·bly** *adv.*

hor·rid (hôr'ĭd, hŏr'-) *adj.* **1.** Causing horror. **2.** Unpleasant; offensive. **3.** *Archaic.* Bristling; rough: *"horrid with fern and intricate with thorn"* (Dryden). [Latin *horridus,* from *horrēre,* to tremble. See **horror.**] —**hor'rid·ly** *adv.* —**hor'rid·ness** *n.*

hor·rif·ic (hô-rĭf'ĭk, hŏ-) *adj.* Causing horror; terrifying. [Old French *horrifique,* from Latin *horrificus* : *horrēre,* to tremble (see **horror**) + -FIC.]

hor·ri·fy (hôr'ə-fī', hŏr'-) *tr.v.* **-fied, -fying, -fies. 1.** To cause to feel horror. **2.** To cause unpleasant surprise; to shock. —See Synonyms at **dismay.** [Latin *horrificāre,* from *horrificus,* HORRIFIC.] —**hor'ri·fi·ca'tion** *n.*

hor·rip·i·la·tion (hô-rĭp'ə-lā'shən, hŏ-) *n.* The bristling of the body hair, as from fear or cold; goose flesh. [Late Latin *horripilātiō,* from Latin *horripilātus,* past participle of *horripilāre,* to bristle with hairs : *horrēre,* to bristle (see **horror**) + *pilus,* hair (see **pilo-** in Appendix*).]

hor·ror (hôr'ər, hŏr'-) *n.* **1.** An intense and painful feeling of repugnance and fear; terror. **2.** Intense dislike; abhorrence; loathing. **3.** One who causes horror. **4.** An aspect or quality that causes horror. **5.** *Informal.* Something unpleasant. **6.** *Plural. Slang.* **a.** Intense, nervous depression or anxiety: *a bad case of the horrors.* **b.** Delirium tremens. **7.** *Obsolete.* A bristling or shuddering condition. —See Synonyms at **fear.** [Middle English *(h)orrour,* from Old French, from Latin *horror,* from *horrēre,* to tremble, bristle, be in horror. See **ghers-** in Appendix.*]

hors de com·bat (ôr də kôN-bä'). *French.* Out of action; sidelined or disabled.

hors d'oeuvre (ôr dûrv'; *French* ôr dœ'vr') *pl.* **hors d'oeuvres** (ôr dûrvz') or **hors d'oeuvre.** An appetizer or canapé served with cocktails or before a meal. [French, outside of the ordinary meal, side dish, "outside of work" : *hors,* outside, from Latin *foris* (see **dhwer-** in Appendix*) + *de,* of + *oeuvre,* work, from Latin *opera,* from *opus* (stem *oper-*), work, OPUS.]

horse (hôrs) *n.* **1.** A large hoofed mammal, *Equus caballus,* having a short-haired coat, a long mane, and a long tail, and domesticated since ancient times for riding and to pull vehicles or carry loads. **2.** An adult male horse. **3.** Any of various other equine mammals, such as the wild Asian species, *E. przewalskii,* or certain extinct forms related ancestrally to the modern horse. **4.** Mounted soldiers; cavalry: *a squadron of horse.* **5.** A supportive frame or device, usually having four legs. **6.** A gymnastic device having four legs and an upholstered body used for

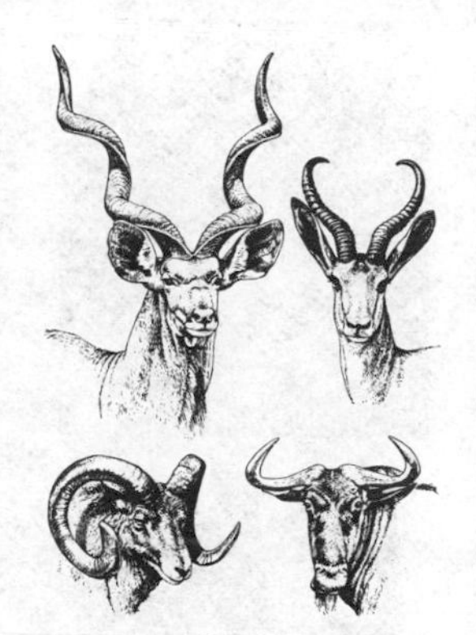

horn
Above: Horns of the kudu *(left)* and the springbok
Below: Horns of the mouflon *(left)* and the gnu

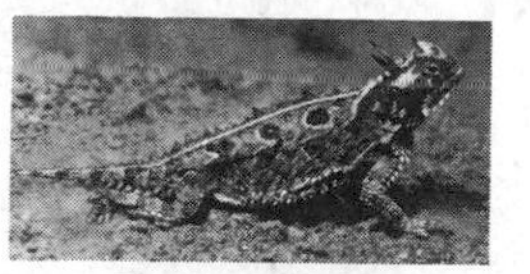

horned toad
Phrynosoma cornutum

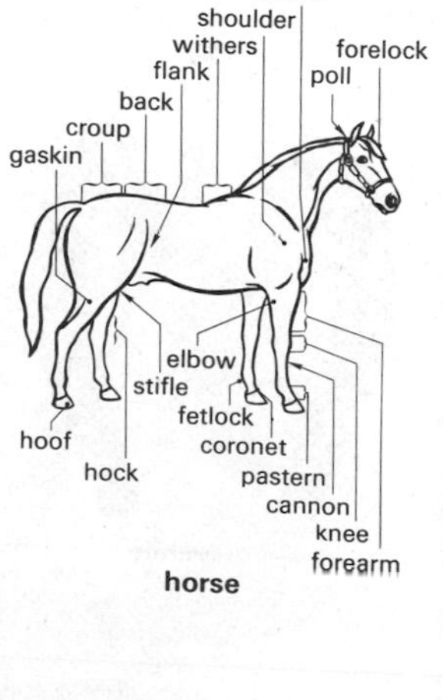

horse

t tight/th thin, path/*th* this, bathe/ŭ cut/ûr urge/v valve/w with/y yes/z zebra, size/zh vision/ə about, item, edible, gallop, circus/ à *Fr.* ami/œ *Fr.* feu, *Ger.* schön/ü *Fr.* tu, *Ger.* über/KH *Ger.* ich, *Scot.* loch/N *Fr.* bon. *Follows main vocabulary. †Of obscure origin.

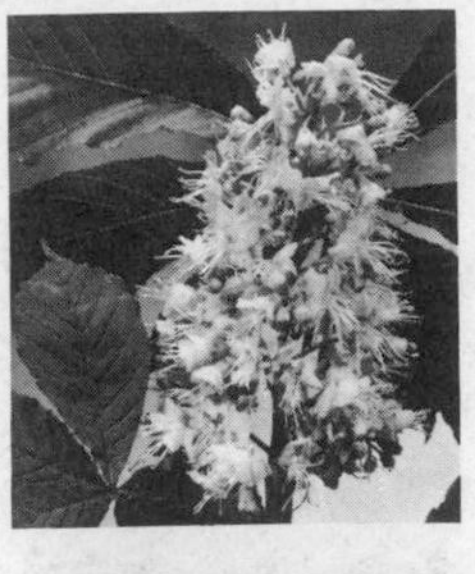

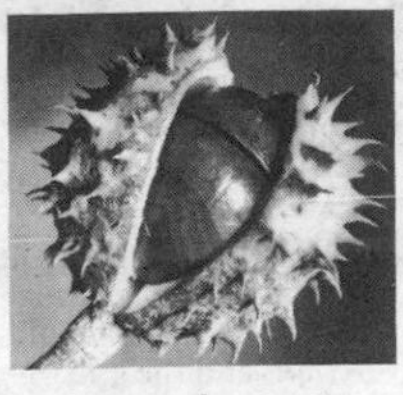

horse chestnut
Aesculus hippocastanum
Above: Flower cluster
Below: Open bur

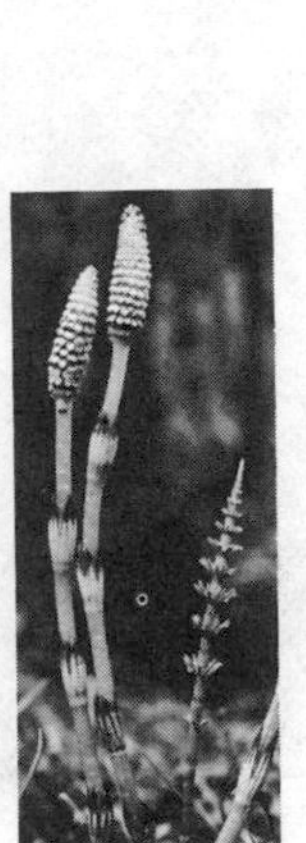

horsetail
Equisetum arvense

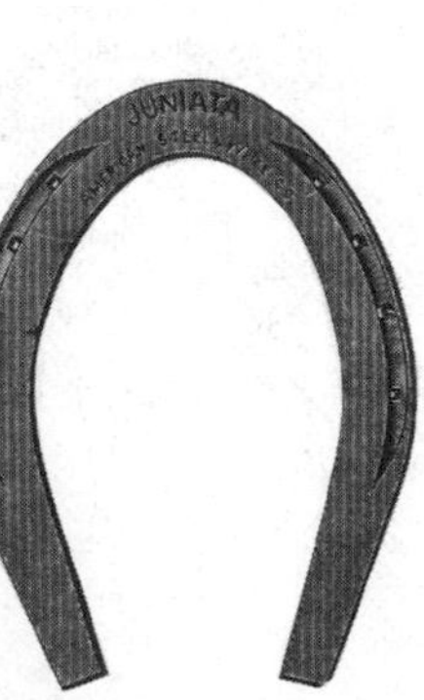

horseshoe

vaulting and other exercises. **7.** *Slang.* Heroin. **8.** *Informal.* Something larger or cruder than the average. **9.** *Often plural.* Horsepower. **10.** *Geology.* **a.** A block of rock interrupting a vein and containing no minerals. **b.** A large block of displaced rock that is caught along a fault. —**a horse of another** (or **a different**) **color.** Another matter entirely; something else. —**be** (or **get**) **on one's high horse.** To be or become disdainful, superior, or conceited. —**hold one's horses.** To check or rein one's eagerness; restrain oneself. —**the horse's mouth.** Any source of information regarded as original or unimpeachable. —**to horse!** Used to express a command or the intention to mount one's horse. —*v.* **horsed, horsing, horses.** —*tr.* **1.** To provide with or place upon a horse. **2.** To haul or hoist energetically: *horse in a bluefish.* **3.** To subject to horseplay. —*intr.* **1.** To mount or ride upon a horse. **2.** *Informal.* To indulge in horseplay. Usually used with *around.* **3.** To be in heat. Said of mares. —*adj.* **1.** Of or pertaining to a horse. **2.** Mounted on a horse or horses. **3.** Drawn or operated by a horse or horses. **4.** Larger and cruder than its fellows. [Middle English *hors,* Old English *hors,* from Germanic *hors-* (unattested).]

horse·back (hôrs′băk′) *n.* **1.** The back of a horse. **2.** A low natural ridge; a hogback. —*adv.* On the back of a horse.

horse balm. A plant, *Collinsonia canadensis,* of eastern North America, having clusters of yellow, lemon-scented flowers. Also called "richweed."

horse bean. The **broad bean** *(see).*

horse·car (hôrs′kär′) *n.* **1.** A streetcar drawn by horses. **2.** A car equipped to transport horses.

horse chestnut. **1.** Any of several trees of the genus *Aesculus;* especially, *A. hippocastanum,* native to Eurasia, having palmate leaves, erect clusters of white flowers tinged with red, and brown, shiny nuts enclosed in a spiny bur. **2.** The nut of such a tree. [Formerly used in treating ailments of horses.]

horse·flesh (hôrs′flĕsh′) *n.* **1.** The flesh of a horse; especially, edible horse meat. **2.** Horses collectively; especially, riding or racing horses.

horse·fly (hôrs′flī′) *n., pl.* **-flies.** Also **horse fly.** Any of numerous large flies of the family Tabanidae, the females of which suck the blood of various mammals.

horse gentian. Any of various plants of the genus *Triosteum,* having small purplish-brown flowers and leathery orange-yellow fruit. Also called "feverwort."

Horse Guards. The cavalry brigade of the household troops of the British royal family, especially the Royal Horse Guards.

horse·hair (hôrs′hâr′) *n.* **1.** The hair of a horse, especially from the mane or tail. **2.** Cloth made of horsehair, used chiefly in upholstery. —*adj.* **1.** Made of horsehair. **2.** Covered or stuffed with horsehair.

horsehair worm. Any of various slender aquatic worms of the phylum Nematomorpha, the larvae of which are parasitic within insects. Also called "hairworm." [These hairlike worms were once thought to have formed from horsehairs that dropped into drinking troughs.]

horse·hide (hôrs′hīd′) *n.* **1. a.** The hide of a horse. **b.** Leather made from this hide. **2.** *Informal.* A baseball.

horse latitudes. Either of two belts of latitudes located over the oceans at about 30 to 35 degrees north and south, having high barometric pressure, calms, and light, changeable winds.

horse·laugh (hôrs′lăf′, -läf′) *n.* A loud, coarse, often mocking laugh; a guffaw.

horse·leech (hôrs′lēch′) *n.* **1.** Any of several large leeches of the genus *Haemopis.* **2.** *Archaic.* A veterinarian; horse doctor.

horseless carriage. An automobile. Used jocosely.

horse mackerel. **1.** Any of several marine fishes of the genus *Trachurus.* **2.** Any of several tunas or related fishes.

horse·man (hôrs′mən) *n., pl.* **-men** (-mĭn). **1. a.** A man who rides a horse. **b.** A cavalryman. **c.** One skilled at horsemanship. **2.** One who breeds and raises horses.

horse·man·ship (hôrs′mən-shĭp′) *n.* The art of equitation.

horse marine. **1. a.** A marine assigned to the cavalry. **b.** A cavalryman assigned to a ship. **2.** A misfit.

horse·mint (hôrs′mĭnt′) *n.* Any of several coarse, aromatic plants, such as *Monarda punctata* or *Mentha longifolia.*

horse nettle. A prickly-stemmed plant, *Solanum carolinense,* of eastern and central North America, having purplish or white star-shaped flowers and yellowish berries.

horse opera. A film or other theatrical work about the U.S. West. Used in disparaging jest.

horse pistol. A large pistol formerly carried by horsemen.

horse·play (hôrs′plā′) *n.* Rowdy, prankish play.

horse·pow·er (hôrs′pou′ər) *n. Abbr.* **hp** **1.** A unit of power in the U.S. Customary System, equal to 745.7 watts or 33,000 foot-pounds per minute. See **measurement.** **2.** The power exerted by a horse in pulling.

horse·rad·ish (hôrs′răd′ĭsh) *n.* **1.** A coarse plant, *Armoracia rusticana* (or *A. lapathifolia*), native to Eurasia, having a thick, whitish, pungent root. **2.** The shredded or grated root of this plant, often combined with vinegar or other ingredients, and used as a condiment.

horse sense. *Informal.* Common sense.

horse·shit (hôrs′shĭt′) *n.* **1.** *Vulgar.* Excrement of a horse. **2.** *Vulgar Slang.* Nonessential or insincere talk or action; nonsense.

horse·shoe (hôrs′shōō′, hôrsh′-) *n.* **1.** A narrow U-shaped iron plate fitted and nailed to a horse's hoof. **2.** Something having a similar shape. **3.** *Plural.* A game in which players try to toss horseshoes around a stake. Used with a singular verb. —*tr.v.* **horseshoed, -shoeing, -shoes.** To shoe (a horse).

horseshoe crab. Any of various marine arthropods of the class Merostomata; especially, *Limulus polyphemus* (or *Xiphosura polyphemus*), of eastern North America, having a large, rounded body and a stiff, pointed tail. Also called "king crab."

Horseshoe Falls. Canadian Falls *(see).*

horse's neck. A nonalcoholic drink consisting usually of ginger ale over ice with various fruit garnishes. [Perhaps from the shape of a lemon peel.]

horse·tail (hôrs′tāl′) *n.* Any of various nonflowering plants of the genus *Equisetum,* having a jointed, hollow stem and narrow, sometimes much reduced leaves.

horse trade. A transaction characterized by shrewd and vigorous bargaining.

horse·weed (hôrs′wēd′) *n.* A weedy North American plant, *Erigeron canadensis,* having narrow leaves and numerous small white or greenish flowers. Also called "butterweed."

horse·whip (hôrs′hwĭp′) *n.* A whip used to control a horse. —*tr.v.* **horsewhipped, -whipping, -whips.** To flog with a horsewhip.

horse·wom·an (hôrs′wŏŏm′ən) *n., pl.* **-women** (-wĭm′ĭn). **1. a.** A woman who rides a horse. **b.** A woman skilled at horsemanship. **2.** A woman who breeds and raises horses.

horst (hôrst) *n.* A massive block of the earth's crust that lies between two faults and is higher than the surrounding land. [German *Horst,* from Old High German *hurst,* thicket. See **kert-** in Appendix.*]

hors·y (hôr′sē) *adj.* **-ier, -iest.** Also **hors·ey.** **1. a.** Of, pertaining to, or characteristic of a horse. **b.** Suggestive of a horse in appearance or actions; coarse or oversized. **2.** Devoted to horses and horsemanship: *the horsy crowd.*

hort. horticultural; horticulture.

hor·ta·tive (hôr′tə-tĭv) *adj.* Giving exhortation; advisory. [Late Latin *hortātīvus,* from Latin *hortātus,* past participle of *hortārī,* to exhort. See **gher-**[6] in Appendix.*] —**hor′ta·tive·ly** *adv.*

hor·ta·to·ry (hôr′tə-tôr′ē, -tōr′ē) *adj.* Characterized by or expressing exhortation; exhortatory. [Late Latin *hortātōrius,* from *hortātus.* See **hortative.**]

hor·ti·cul·ture (hôr′tə-kŭl′chər) *n. Abbr.* **hort.** **1.** The science or art of cultivating plants, especially for ornamental use. **2.** The cultivation of a garden. [Latin *hortus,* garden (see **gher-**[2] in Appendix*) + (AGRI)CULTURE.] —**hor′ti·cul′tur·al** *adj.* —**hor′ti·cul′tur·al·ly** *adv.* —**hor′ti·cul′tur·ist** *n.*

hor·tus sic·cus (hôr′təs sĭk′əs). *Latin.* A collection of dried plants; herbarium. Literally, "dry garden."

Ho·rus (hôr′əs, hōr′-). The ancient Egyptian god of the sun, represented as having the head of a hawk.

Hos. Hosea (Old Testament).

ho·san·na (hō-zăn′ə) *interj.* Used to express praise or adoration to God or the Messiah. —*n.* **1.** A cry of "hosanna." **2.** Any shout of fervent and worshipful praise. [Middle English *osanna,* from Late Latin *(h)ōsanna,* from Greek, from Hebrew *hosha'nā,* "save us!"]

hose (hōz) *n., pl.* **hose** or *archaic* **hosen** (hō′zən) (for senses 1, 2); **hoses** (for sense 3). **1. a.** Stockings. **b.** Socks. **2. a.** A man's garment covering legs and hips and fastening to a doublet by points; tights. **b.** Short full breeches meeting the stockings at the knees. **3.** A flexible tube for conveying liquids or gases under pressure. —*tr.v.* **hosed, hosing, hoses.** To water, drench, or wash with a hose. [Middle English *hose,* a stocking, Old English *hosa,* leg covering. See **skeu-** in Appendix.*]

Ho·se·a[1] (hō-zē′ə, -zā′ə). Hebrew Minor Prophet of the eighth century B.C.

Ho·se·a[2] (hō-zē′ə, -zā′ə) *n. Abbr.* **Hos.** A prophetic book of the Old Testament, attributed to Hosea.

ho·sier (hō′zhər) *n.* A maker of or dealer in hose and knitted underclothing. [Middle English *hosyer,* from *hose,* HOSE.]

ho·sier·y (hō′zhə-rē) *n.* **1. a.** Stockings and socks; hose. **b.** *British.* Stockings, socks, and underclothing. **2.** The business of a hosier.

hosp. hospital.

hos·pice (hŏs′pĭs) *n.* A shelter or lodging for travelers, children, or the destitute, often maintained by a monastic order. [French, from Old French, from Latin *hospitium,* hospitality, from *hospes* (stem *hospit-*), HOST (receiver of guests).]

hos·pi·ta·ble (hŏs′pə-tə-bəl, hŏs-pĭt′ə-bəl) *adj.* **1. a.** Welcoming guests with warmth and generosity. **b.** Fond of entertaining. **c.** Well-disposed toward strangers. **2.** Having an open and charitable mind; receptive. [New Latin *hospitabilis,* from Latin *hospitārī,* to be hospitable to, from *hospes* (stem *hospit-*), HOST (receiver of guests).] —**hos′pi·ta·bly** *adv.*

hos·pi·tal (hŏs′pə-təl) *n. Abbr.* **hosp.** **1.** An institution providing medical or surgical care and treatment for the sick and the injured. **2.** A similar place for animals. **3.** *Archaic.* A home, often charitable, for old people, the infirm, or foundlings. **4.** A repair shop for specified items: *a doll hospital.* [Middle English, hospice, from Old French, from Medieval Latin *hospitāle,* from Latin *hospitālis,* of a guest, from *hospes* (stem *hospit-*), HOST.]

Hos·pi·tal·er (hŏs′pə-tə-lər) *n.* Also **Hos·pi·tal·ler.** **1.** A member of a military religious order founded among European crusaders in 12th-century Palestine. **2.** A member of any of several religious orders dedicated to the care of hospital patients. [Middle English *Hospitalier,* from Old French, from Medieval Latin *hospitāle,* hospice. See **hospital.**]

Hos·pi·ta·let (ōs-pē′tä-lĕt′). A southwestern suburb of Barcelona, Spain. Population, 123,000.

hos·pi·tal·i·ty (hŏs′pə-tăl′ə-tē) *n., pl.* **-ties.** **1.** The act or practice of or a tendency toward being hospitable. **2.** An instance of being hospitable. [Middle English *hospitalite,* from Old French, from Latin *hospitālitās,* from *hospitālis,* of a guest. See **hospital.**]

hos·pi·tal·i·za·tion (hŏs′pə-tə-lə-zā′shən, -lī-zā′shən) *n.* **1. a.** The state or act of being hospitalized. **b.** The length of time spent by a patient in a hospital. **2.** A form of insurance that completely or partially covers a patient's hospital expenses.

hos·pi·tal·ize (hŏs′pə-tə-līz′) *tr.v.* **-ized, -izing, -izes.** To put (a patient) into a hospital.

host¹ (hōst) *n.* **1.** One who entertains guests in a social or business capacity. **2.** *Biology.* An organism that harbors and provides nourishment for a parasite. —*tr.v.* **hosted, hosting, hosts. 1.** *Informal.* To serve as host for (a party, reception, or the like). See Usage note below. **2.** *Obsolete.* To receive or entertain (a guest): *"Such was that hag, unmeet to host such guests."* (Spenser). [Middle English *(h)oste,* from Old French, host, guest, from Latin *hospes* (stem *hospit-*), guest, host, stranger. See **ghos-ti-** in Appendix.*]

Usage: *Host,* as a verb, has not won wide acceptance on a serious level. The following examples are termed unacceptable by 82 per cent of the Usage Panel: *The Cleveland chapter will host this year's convention; a television series hosted by the mayor.*

host² (hōst) *n.* **1.** An army. **2.** A great number: *"a host of golden daffodils"* (Wordsworth). —See Synonyms at **multitude.** [Middle English, from Old French, from Late Latin *hostis,* from Latin, stranger, enemy. See **ghos-ti-** in Appendix.*]

host³ (hōst) *n.* Also **Host.** *Ecclesiastical.* The consecrated bread or wafer of the Eucharist. [Middle English *oste,* from Old French *oiste,* from Latin *hostia*†, sacrifice, victim.]

hos·tage (hŏs′tĭj) *n.* **1.** A person held as a security for the fulfillment of certain terms. **2.** The state of being so held. [Middle English *(h)ostage,* from Old French, either from *oste, hoste,* guest, HOST, or from Vulgar Latin *obsidāticum* (unattested), from Late Latin *obsidātus,* hostage (sense 2), from Latin *obses* (stem *obsid-*), a hostage : *ob-,* in the way of, in front of + *sedēre,* to sit (see **sed-¹** in Appendix*).]

hos·tel (hŏs′təl) *n.* **1.** A supervised, inexpensive lodging for youthful travelers. Also called "youth hostel." **2.** *Archaic.* An inn. [Middle English *(h)ostel,* from Old French, from Medieval Latin *hospitāle,* hospice. See **hospital.**]

hos·tel·er (hŏs′təl-ər) *n.* **1.** *Archaic.* An innkeeper. **2.** A traveling youth who stops at hostels.

hos·tel·ry (hŏs′təl-rē) *n., pl.* **-ries.** An inn.

host·ess (hōs′tĭs) *n.* **1.** A woman who acts as a host. **2.** A woman whose occupation is greeting and serving patrons, as in a restaurant or dance hall.

hos·tile (hŏs′təl; *chiefly British* hŏs′tīl′) *adj.* **1.** Of or pertaining to an enemy. **2.** Feeling or showing enmity; antagonistic. **3.** Not hospitable. —*n.* One that is hostile; especially, a member of one of the North American Indian tribes who resisted internment on reservations (1860–1900). [Old French, from Latin *hostīlis,* from *hostis,* HOST (enemy).] —**hos′tile·ly** *adv.*

hos·til·i·ty (hŏ-stĭl′ə-tē) *n., pl.* **-ties. 1.** The state of being hostile; antagonism; enmity. **2. a.** A hostile act or incident. **b.** *Plural.* Overt warfare. —See Synonyms at **enmity.**

hos·tler (hŏs′lər) *n.* Also **os·tler** (ŏs′lər). **1.** A person who takes charge of horses, as at an inn; a stableman. **2.** A worker who services a large vehicle or engine, such as a locomotive. [Middle English *host(e)ler,* from Old French *(h)ostelier,* from *(h)ostel,* HOSTEL.]

hot (hŏt) *adj.* **hotter, hottest. 1. a.** Possessing great heat. **b.** Yielding much heat. **c.** Being at a high temperature. **2.** Warmer than is normal or desirable: *a hot forehead.* **3.** Highly spiced: *hot mustard.* **4. a.** Charged or as if charged with electricity: *a hot wire.* **b.** Radioactive. **5.** Explosive, fiery, or dangerous: *a hot dispute.* **6.** *Slang.* Sexually aroused or arousing. **7.** *Slang.* **a.** Recently stolen: *hot goods.* **b.** Wanted for criminal activity. **8.** Close to success or achievement: *hot on the trail.* **9.** *Slang.* Moving or capable of moving with speed; fast. **10.** *Informal.* **a.** New; fresh: *hot off the press.* **b.** Currently popular: *a hot sales item.* **11.** *Slang.* **a.** Good or impressive. **b.** Ridiculous; incredible: *That's a hot one!* **12.** *Slang.* **a.** Performing with unusual skill. **b.** Lucky. **13.** *Slang.* Producing exciting emotional and physical reactions by means of strong rhythms and inspired improvisation. Said of jazz. —**hot under the collar.** *Informal.* Angry. —**in hot water.** *Informal.* In trouble. —**make it hot for.** *Informal.* To make things uncomfortable or dangerous for. [Middle English *hot,* Old English *hāt.* See **kai-** in Appendix.*]

hot air. *Slang.* Empty talk; boastful nonsense.

hot·bed (hŏt′bĕd′) *n.* **1.** A glass-covered bed of soil heated with fermenting manure or by electricity, used for the germination of seeds or for protecting tender plants. **2.** An environment conducive to rapid, excessively vigorous growth, especially of something bad: *a hotbed of intrigue.*

hot-blood·ed (hŏt′blŭd′ĭd) *adj.* **1.** Easily excited or angered. **2.** Passionate. **3.** Rash or reckless. —**hot′blood′ed·ness** *n.*

hot·box (hŏt′bŏks′) *n.* An overheated axle or journal box, as on a railway car or locomotive, caused by excessive friction.

hot cake. A pancake. —**sell** (or **go**) **like hot cakes.** To be in great demand.

hotch (hŏch) *v.* **hotched, hotching, hotches.** *Scottish.* —*tr.* To wiggle or waggle. —*intr.* To fidget. [Perhaps from Old French *hocher, hochier,* perhaps from Frankish *hottisōn*† (unattested).]

hotch·pot (hŏch′pŏt′) *n. Law.* The gathering together of properties to secure an equal division of the total for distribution among the heirs of an intestate parent. [Middle English *hochepot,* from Old French : *hocher, hochier,* HOTCH + *pot,* pot, from (unattested) Vulgar Latin *pottus* (see **pott-** in Appendix*).]

hotch·potch (hŏch′pŏch′) *n.* **1.** A hodgepodge. **2.** *Law.* A hotchpot. [Variant of HOTCHPOT.]

hot cross bun. A sweet bun made with raisins and having a cross of frosting on top, traditionally eaten during Lent.

hot dog. 1. A hot frankfurter, usually served in a long soft roll. **2.** *Informal.* Used to express satisfaction or enthusiasm. [Perhaps from its fancied resemblance to a dachshund.]

ho·tel (hō-tĕl′) *n.* A public house that provides lodging and usually board and other services. [French *hôtel,* from Old French *hostel,* HOSTEL.]

hot flash. A transient vasomotor symptom of menopause that involves the whole body in a flash of heat.

hot flush. A vasomotor symptom of menopause that involves the face, neck, and upper part of the chest in a sensation of heat, often followed by profuse sweating.

hot·foot¹ (hŏt′fo͝ot′) *intr.v.* **-footed, -footing, -foots.** To go in haste. Used with *it.* —*adv.* In haste.

hot·foot² (hŏt′fo͝ot′) *n., pl.* **hotfoots.** The clandestine insertion and ignition of a match in the side of someone's shoe.

hot·head (hŏt′hĕd′) *n.* One who is hotheaded.

hot·head·ed (hŏt′hĕd′ĭd) *adj.* **1.** Having a fiery temper. **2.** Impetuous; rash. —**hot′head′ed·ly** *adv.* —**hot′head′ed·ness** *n.*

hot·house (hŏt′hous′) *n., pl.* **-houses** (-hou′zĭz). A heated greenhouse or conservatory for plants requiring an even, relatively warm temperature. —*adj.* **1.** Grown in a hothouse. **2.** Like or characteristic of a plant grown in a hothouse; delicate; sensitive.

hot pants. *Vulgar Slang.* Anxious sexual desire.

hot pepper. 1. The pungent fruit of any of several varieties of *Capsicum frutescens.* **2.** A condiment made from such fruit.

hot plate. 1. An electrically heated plate or tray for cooking or keeping food warm. **2.** A table-top cooking stove having one or two burners.

hot-press (hŏt′prĕs′) *tr.v.* **-pressed, -pressing, -presses.** To subject (paper or cloth) to heat and pressure in order to extract oil. —*n.* (hŏt′prĕs′). A machine for hot-pressing.

hot rod. Also **hot·rod** (hŏt′rŏd′), **hot-rod.** *Slang.* An automobile rebuilt or remodeled for increased speed and acceleration. —**hot rodder.**

hot seat. *Slang.* The electric chair.

hot·shot (hŏt′shŏt′) *n.* **1.** *Slang.* An ostentatiously skillful person. **2.** A nonstop freight train.

hot spring. A natural spring discharging water that is above body temperature, or over 98°F.

Hot Springs. A city and resort center of west-central Arkansas within Hot Springs National Park (1.6 square miles). Population, 28,000.

hot·spur (hŏt′spûr′) *n.* A fiery or impetuous person; hothead.

Hot·ten·tot (hŏt′n-tŏt′) *n., pl.* **Hottentot** or **-tots. 1. a.** A people of southern Africa held to be related to the Bantu and Bushmen. **b.** A member of this people. **2.** The language of the Hottentot. [Afrikaans.]

Hottentot fig. A plant, *Mesembryanthemum edule,* native to South Africa, having three-sided leaves, showy yellow flowers, and edible, fleshy fruit.

hot toddy. A beverage, a **toddy** *(see).*

hot-wa·ter heat (hŏt′wô′tər, -wŏt′ər). The heating of buildings with water over 170°F but not over 212°F, circulated through a system of pipes and radiators. Compare **steam heating.**

HOU Airport code for Houston, Texas.

hou·dah. Variant of **howdah.**

Hou·dan (ho͞o′dăn′) *n.* A domesticated fowl of a breed developed in France, having black and white plumage and a V-shaped comb. [French, developed in the village of *Houdan,* France.]

hound¹ (hound) *n.* **1.** A dog of any of various breeds used for hunting, characteristically having drooping ears, a short coat, and a deep, resonant voice. **2.** Any dog. **3.** A contemptible person; scoundrel. **4.** An enthusiast or addict: *a coffee hound.* —**follow** (or **ride to**) **the hounds.** To take part in a fox hunt. —*tr.v.* **hounded, hounding, hounds. 1. a.** To pursue relentlessly and tenaciously. **b.** To nag. **2.** To incite to give chase to; urge on. —See Synonyms at **harass.** [Middle English *h(o)und,* Old English *hund.* See **kwon-** in Appendix.*]

hound² (hound) *n.* **1.** Either of two projections at the side of a masthead that supports the trestletrees of large vessels or the rigging of smaller ones. **2.** Either of a pair of horizontal braces for reinforcing the running gear of a vehicle. [Middle English *hune, hownde,* probably from Old Norse *hūnn,* knob, knob at the top of a masthead. See **keu-³** in Appendix.*]

hound's-tongue (houndz′tŭng′) *n.* Any of several plants of the genus *Cynoglossum;* especially *C. officinale,* native to Eurasia, having hairy leaves, small reddish-purple flowers, and prickly, clinging fruit. [From the shape of its leaves.]

hound's-tooth check (houndz′to͞oth′). A small checkered textile design.

Houns·low (hounz′lō). A borough of London, England, comprising the former administrative divisions of Brentford and Chiswick, of Heston and Isleworth, and of Feltham. Population, 209,000.

hour (our) *n. Abbr.* **h, hr 1.** The 24th part of a day. **2. a.** One of the points on a timepiece marking off 12 or 24 successive intervals of 60 minutes, from midnight to noon and noon to midnight, or from midnight to midnight. **b.** The time of day indicated by a 12-hour clock. **c.** *Plural.* The time of day determined on a 24-hour basis: *1700 hours.* **3. a.** A customary time:

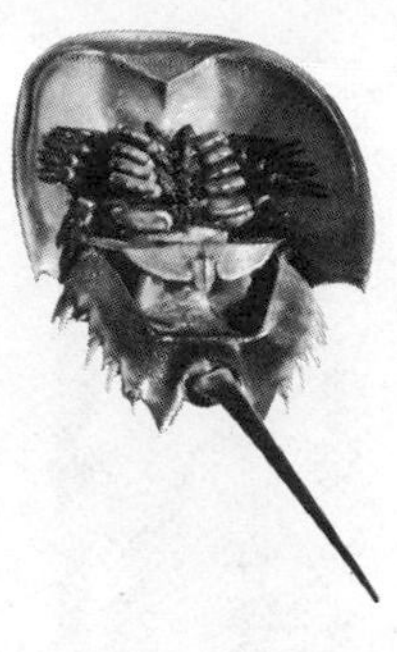

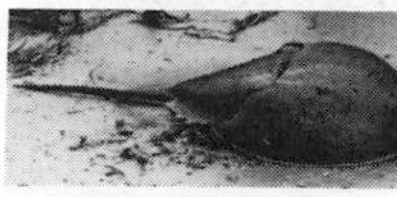

horseshoe crab
Limulus polyphemus
Above: Ventral view

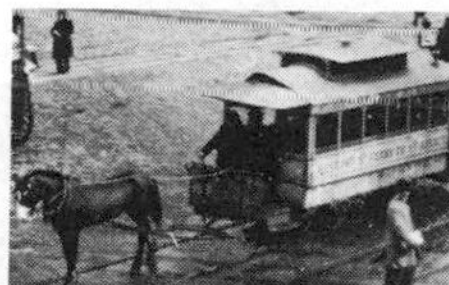

horsecar

t tight/th thin, path/*th* this, bathe/ŭ cut/ûr urge/v valve/w with/y yes/z zebra, size/zh vision/ə about, item, edible, gallop, circus/ à *Fr.* ami/œ *Fr.* feu, *Ger.* schön/ü *Fr.* tu, *Ger.* über/KH *Ger.* ich, *Scot.* loch/N *Fr.* bon. ***Follows main vocabulary.** †**Of obscure origin.**

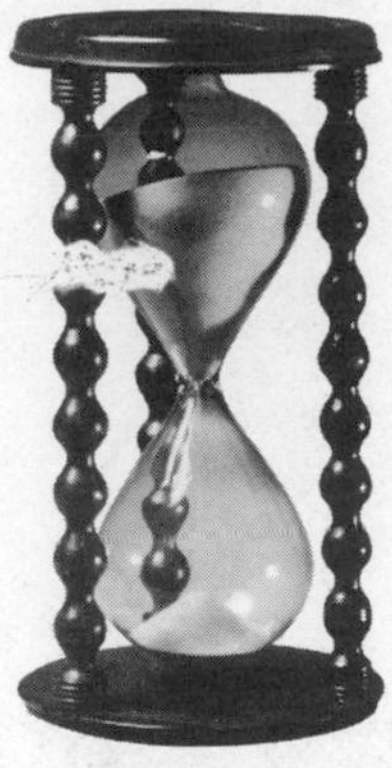

hourglass

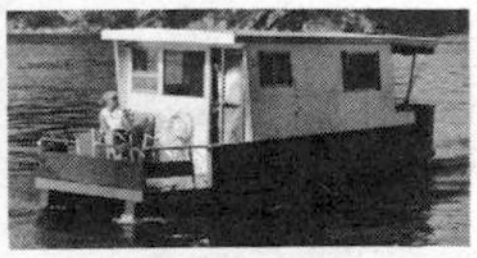

houseboat

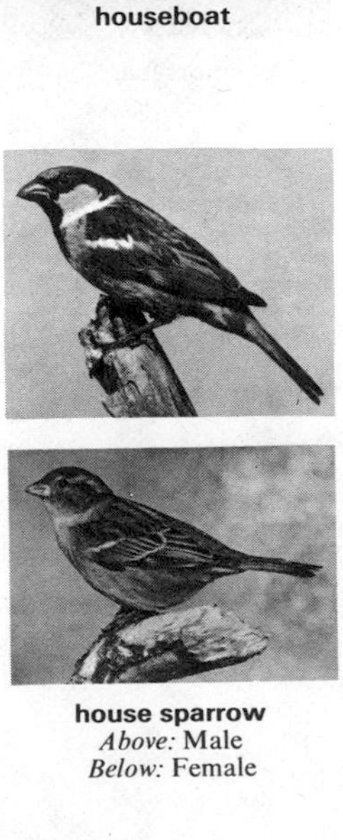

house sparrow
Above: Male
Below: Female

dinner hour. **b.** *Plural.* A specified time: *bank hours.* **4. a.** The work that can be accomplished in an hour. **b.** The distance that can be traveled in an hour. **5. a.** A session; séance. **b.** A time for daily liturgical devotion, as the canonical hours. [Middle English *hour, (o)ure,* from Old French *(h)ore,* from Latin *hōra,* from Greek, time, season. See **yēro-** in Appendix.*]

hour angle. The angle measured westward along the celestial equator from the celestial meridian of the observer to the hour circle passing through a celestial body.

hour circle. A great circle passing through the poles of the celestial sphere and intersecting the celestial equator at right angles.

hour·glass (our′glăs′, -gläs′) *n.* An instrument for measuring time consisting of two glass chambers with a narrow connecting channel, and containing sand or mercury requiring exactly one hour to trickle from one chamber to the other.

hour hand. The indicator on a timepiece that points to the hour.

hou·ri (ho͝or′ē, hour′ē) *n., pl.* **-ris. 1.** A voluptuous woman. **2.** One of the beautiful virgins of the Koranic paradise. [French, from Persian *hūrī,* from Arabic *hūr,* plural of *haurā′,* dark-eyed woman.]

hour·ly (our′lē) *adj.* **1. a.** Every hour. **b.** Frequent; continual. **2.** By the hour as a unit: *hourly pay.* —*adv.* **1.** At or during every hour. **2.** Frequently; continually.

Hou·sa·ton·ic (ho͞o′sə-tŏn′ĭk). A river rising in western Massachusetts and flowing 148 miles south through western Connecticut to Long Island Sound.

house (hous) *n., pl.* **houses** (hou′zĭz). *Abbr.* **ho. 1. a.** A structure serving as a dwelling for one or several families. **b.** A place of abode; residence. **c.** Something that serves as an abode. **2.** A building used for shelter or storage. Often used in combination: *a warehouse.* **3.** A building having a specified function or making available a specified thing. Often used in combination: *a schoolhouse.* **4.** A dwelling for a religious community or for students. **5.** A household. **6.** *Often capital* **H.** A family line, including ancestors and descendants; especially, a noble family: *House of Orange.* **7.** A commercial firm: *banking house.* **8.** The management of a business establishment. **9. a.** A theater: *movie house.* **b.** A theater audience. **10. a.** A hotel or bar; public house: *a drink on the house.* **b.** *Slang.* A brothel. **11. a.** A legislative or deliberative assembly. **b.** The hall where such an assembly meets. **c.** A quorum of an assembly. **12.** *Astrology.* **a.** One of the 12 parts into which the heavens are divided. **b.** The sign of the zodiac indicating the seat or station of a planet in the heavens. Also called "mansion." **13.** *Obsolete.* A square on a chessboard. —*v.* (houz) **housed, housing, houses.** —*tr.* **1.** To provide with a house; furnish living quarters to: *The cottage housed ten boys.* **2.** To lodge. **3.** To cover with or as with a roof; to shelter. **4.** To store. **5.** To contain; to harbor. —*intr.* To lodge; dwell. [Middle English *h(o)us, house,* Old English *hūs,* from Germanic *hūsam* (unattested).]

House (hous), **Edward Mandell.** Called "Colonel House." 1858–1938. American diplomat; adviser and confidant of Woodrow Wilson.

house arrest. Confinement to one's domicile by administrative or judicial order.

house·boat (hous′bōt′) *n.* A barge equipped for use as a domicile or cruiser.

house·break·ing (hous′brā′kĭng) *n.* The unlawful breaking into another's domicile for the purpose of committing a felony. —**house′break′er** *n.*

house·bro·ken (hous′brō′kən) *adj.* Trained to live indoors. Said of a pet animal.

house·carl (hous′kärl′) *n.* A member of the bodyguard or household troops of a Danish or early English king or noble.

house·coat (hous′kōt′) *n.* A woman's garment usually having a long skirt, worn for lounging at home.

house·fly (hous′flī′) *n., pl.* **-flies.** A common, widely distributed fly, *Musca domestica,* that frequents human dwellings, breeds in moist or decaying organic matter, and is a transmitter of a wide variety of diseases.

house·hold (hous′hōld′) *n.* A domestic establishment including the members of a family and others living under the same roof. [Middle English *household* : *hous,* HOUSE + *hold,* possession, property, Old English *heald,* from *healdan,* to HOLD.] —**house′hold′** *adj.*

household arts. Home economics.

house·hold·er (hous′hōl′dər) *n.* One who occupies a house or apartment as his own dwelling.

household word. A commonly used word, phrase, or name.

house·keep·er (hous′kē′pər) *n.* One who has charge of domestic tasks in a household. —**house′keep′ing** *n.*

hou·sel (hou′zəl) *n. Archaic.* The Eucharist. —*tr.v.* **houseled, -seling, -sels.** *Archaic.* To administer the Eucharist to. [Middle English *housel,* Old English *hūsl.* See **kwen-** in Appendix.*]

house·leek (hous′lēk′) *n.* Any of various plants of the genus *Sempervivum,* native to the Old World; especially, *S. tectorum,* having a basal rosette of fleshy leaves and a branching cluster of pinkish or purplish flowers. Also called "hen-and-chickens," "old-man-and-woman."

house·line (hous′līn′) *n. Nautical.* A small line formed of three strands, used for seizings. [From its use in housing larger ropes.]

house·maid (hous′mād′) *n.* A woman employed to do housework.

housemaid's knee. A chronic, inflammatory swelling of the bursa of the knee anterior to the kneecap, caused by prolonged labor on the knees.

house martin. An Old World bird, *Delichon urbica,* having blue-black plumage with white markings and a forked tail.

house·mas·ter (hous′măs′tər, -mäs′tər) *n.* A teacher in charge of a residence hall of a boys' school.

house·moth·er (hous′mŭth′ər) *n.* A woman employed as supervisor or housekeeper of a young people's residence hall or dormitory.

House of Burgesses. The lower house of the legislature of colonial Virginia.

House of Commons. *Abbr.* **H.C. 1.** The lower house of Parliament in the United Kingdom, having the main legislative powers and an elected membership. **2.** The lower house of the Canadian parliament.

house of correction. An institution housing persons convicted of minor criminal offenses.

House of Delegates. The lower house of the state legislature of Maryland, Virginia, and West Virginia.

House of Lords. *Abbr.* **H.L.** The upper house of Parliament in the United Kingdom, a nonelective chamber having limited powers.

House of Representatives. *Abbr.* **H.R.** The lower branch of the U.S. Congress and of most state legislatures.

house organ. A periodical published by a business establishment for its employees or clients.

house party. A party at which guests stay overnight or for several days in a private home or other residence.

house physician. 1. A resident physician in a hospital. **2.** A physician employed by a hotel or other establishment.

house·rais·ing (hous′rā′zĭng) *n.* The collective construction of a house or its framework by a group of neighbors.

house·room (hous′ro͞om′, -ro͝om′) *n.* A room for lodging or storage in a house.

house snake. The **milk snake** *(see).*

house sparrow. A small bird, *Passer domesticus,* native to the Old World but widely naturalized elsewhere, having brown and gray plumage, and a black throat in the male. Also called "English sparrow."

house·top (hous′tŏp′) *n.* The cover of a house; roof.

house·warm·ing (hous′wôr′mĭng) *n.* A party to celebrate the occupancy of a new home.

house·wife (hous′wīf′ *for sense 1;* hŭz′ĭf *for sense 2*) *n., pl.* **-wives** (-wīvz′) (for sense 1); **housewifes** (hŭz′ĭfs) or **housewives** (hŭz′ĭvz) (for sense 2). **1.** A married woman who supervises the affairs of a household. **2.** *Chiefly British.* A pocket container for sewing equipment.

house·wife·ly (hous′wīf′lē) *adj.* Of, pertaining to, or suited to a housewife; domestic. —**house′wife′li·ness** *n.*

house·wif·er·y (hous′wī′fə-rē, -wīf′rē) *n.* The function or duties of a housewife; housekeeping.

house·work (hous′wûrk′) *n.* The tasks performed in housekeeping, as cleaning or cooking. —**house′work′er** *n.*

hous·ing¹ (hou′zĭng) *n.* **1.** Buildings or other shelters in which people live. **2.** A place to live; a dwelling. **3. a.** Something that covers, protects, or guards. **b.** A frame, bracket, or box for holding or protecting a mechanical part: *a wheel housing.* **c.** An enclosing frame in which a shaft revolves. **4.** A hole, groove, or slot in a piece of wood for the insertion of another piece. **5.** A niche for a statue. **6.** The part of a mast that is below deck or of a bowsprit that is inside the hull.

hous·ing² (hou′zĭng) *n.* **1.** An ornamental or protective covering for a saddle. **2.** *Usually plural.* Trappings. [Middle English, from *house,* covering, from Old French *houce,* from Medieval Latin *hultia,* from Germanic. See **kel-⁴** in Appendix.*]

Hous·man (hous′mən), **A(lfred) E(dward).** 1859–1936. English poet.

Hous·say (o͞o-sī′), **Bernardo Alberto.** Born 1887. Argentine physiologist.

Hous·ton (hyo͞o′stən). The largest city of Texas, a port located about 20 miles northwest of Galveston Bay. Population, 938,000.

Hous·ton (hyo͞o′stən), **Sam(uel).** 1793–1863. American general and political leader; president of the Republic of Texas (1836–38 and 1841–44).

hove. *Chiefly Nautical.* Past tense and past participle of **heave.**

hov·el (hŭv′əl, hŏv′-) *n.* **1.** A small, miserable dwelling. **2.** An open, low shed. [Middle English *hovel*†.]

hov·er (hŭv′ər, hŏv′-) *intr.v.* **-ered, -ering, -ers. 1.** To fly, soar, or float as if suspended: *gulls hovering over the waves.* **2.** To remain or linger in close proximity; move back and forth in or near a place. **3.** To be in a state of uncertainty; waver; vacillate: *hover between skepticism and belief.* —*n.* **1.** The condition of hovering. **2.** An act or instance of hovering. [Middle English *hoveren,* frequentative of *hoven*†, to hover, linger.] —**hov′er·er** *n.* —**hov′er·ing·ly** *adv.*

hov·er·craft (hŭv′ər-krăft′, -kräft′, hŏv′-) *n.* A motorized vehicle capable of low-level flight over land or water on a cushion of air formed by the action of downward-directed fans.

how¹ (hou) *adv.* **1.** In what manner or way; by what means: *He showed us how to work the machine.* **2.** In what state or condition: *How do I look in this jacket?* **3.** To what extent, amount, or degree: *How do you like that?* **4.** For what effect or purpose; why: *I can't see how he bought such an expensive car.* **5.** At what cost; for what price: *How are these shirts sold on sale?* **6.** With what meaning: *How should I interpret this?* **7.** By what name: *How is he called?* **8.** What. Usually used in requesting that something said be repeated: *How is that again?* —**how about?** What is your feeling or thought regarding? —**how come?** Why? —**how so?** Why is it so? —*conj.* **1.** In what way or manner: *not concerned how it is accomplished.* **2.** Of the manner

or style in which: *Be careful how you address the ambassador.*
3. The way or manner in which: *told us how he had made the trip.* —*n.* A manner or method of doing or performing: *learn the how of a procedure.* [Middle English *hou, how,* Old English *hū.* See kwo- in Appendix.*]

how² (hou) *interj.* Used to express greeting in presumed imitation of American Indian speech. [From Sioux, akin to Dakota *háo,* and Omaha *hau.*]

How·ard (hou′ərd), **Catherine.** 1520?–1542. Queen of England (1540–42); fifth wife of Henry VIII; beheaded.

How·ard (hou′ərd), **Henry.** See Earl of **Surrey.**

how·be·it (hou-bē′ĭt) *adv. Archaic.* Be that as it may; nevertheless. —*conj. Obsolete.* Although.

how·dah (hou′də) *n.* Also **hou·dah.** A seat, usually fitted with a canopy and railing, placed on the back of an elephant or camel. [Urdu, from Persian *haudah,* from Arabic *haudaj,* burden carried by a camel or elephant.]

how do you do. Used in greeting a person as an equivalent of the address "hello."

how-do-you-do (hou′də-yə-dōō′) *n.* Also **how-d′ye-do** (hou′-dyə-dōō′, hou′dē-). *Informal.* A difficult or embarrassing predicament. Usually used with *pretty, fine,* or *nice.*

how·dy (hou′dē) *interj. Regional.* Used to express greeting. [Shortening of *how-de-do.*]

Howe (hou), **Elias.** 1819–1867. American inventor of the sewing machine (1846).

Howe (hou), **Julia Ward.** 1819–1910. American feminist, pacifist, and author of "The Battle Hymn of the Republic".

Howe (hou), Sir **William.** Fifth Viscount Howe. 1729–1814. British commander in chief in America (1775–78).

how·e′er (hou-âr′). *Poetic.* Contraction of *however.*

How·ells (hou′əlz), **William Dean.** 1837–1920. American author and editor.

how·ev·er (hou-ĕv′ər) *adv.* **1.** By whatever manner or means: *However you come, come early.* **2.** To whatever degree or extent: *"I never am bored, however familiar the scene."* (Theodore Roethke). —*conj.* **1.** Nevertheless; yet: *The tickets are expensive; however, we will go.* **2.** *Archaic.* Although; notwithstanding that. —See Synonyms at **but.**

Usage: However is redundant in combination with *but.* One or the other should be used to express the sense of the following: *He had an invitation but didn't go. He had an invitation; however, he didn't go.* The two-word form *how ever* is sometimes used as an emphatic variant of *how* in interrogative sentences expressing surprise or perplexity: *How ever did he manage?*

how·it·zer (hou′ĭt-sər) *n.* A cannon with a barrel longer than a mortar that delivers shells with medium velocities, either by a low or, more usually, by a high trajectory against targets that cannot be reached by flat trajectories. [Dutch *houwitser,* from German *Haubitze,* earlier *haufenitz,* from Czech *houfnice,* catapult : *houf,* troop, crowd (see keu-² in Appendix*) + *nice,* feminine noun suffix.]

howl (houl) *v.* **howled, howling, howls.** —*intr.* **1.** To utter or emit a long, mournful, plaintive sound characteristic of wolves or dogs. **2.** To cry or wail loudly and uncontrollably in pain, sorrow, or anger. **3.** *Slang.* **a.** To laugh uproariously. **b.** To go on a carousal or spree. —*tr.* **1.** To express or utter with a howl or howls. **2.** To effect, drive, or force by or as if by howling. —*n.* **1.** The sound of one that howls. **2.** *Slang.* Something uproariously funny or absurd. [Middle English *houlen, howlen,* perhaps from Middle Dutch *hūlen.* See ul- in Appendix.*]

howl·er (hou′lər) *n.* **1.** One that howls. **2.** Any of several monkeys of the genus *Alouatta,* of tropical America, having a long, prehensile tail and a loud, howling call. **3.** *Informal.* An amusing or ridiculous blunder.

how·let (hou′lĭt) *n. Archaic.* An owl or owlet. [Middle English *howlat,* diminutive of *(h)owle,* OWL.]

howl·ing (hou′lĭng) *adj.* **1.** Characterized by or uttering howls. **2.** *Slang.* Very great; tremendous: *a howling success.*

How·rah (hou′rə). A city and industrial center of southeastern West Bengal, Republic of India, on the Hooghly near Calcutta. Population, 539,000.

how·so·ev·er (hou′sō-ĕv′ər) *adv.* **1.** To whatever degree or extent. **2.** By whatever means.

hoy¹ (hoi) *n., pl.* **hoys.** **1.** A small sloop-rigged coasting ship formerly used for transporting passengers or as a tender to a larger vessel. **2.** A heavy barge used for freight. [Middle English, from Middle Dutch *hoei, hoede†.*]

hoy² (hoi) *interj.* Used to attract attention or to drive or direct animals. [Middle English (expressive).]

hoy·den (hoid′n) *n.* Also **hoi·den.** A high-spirited, often impudent girl or woman. —*adj.* Also **hoi·den.** High-spirited; boisterous. [Originally, a rude youth, probably from Middle Dutch *heiden,* "heathen." See kaito- in Appendix.*]

Hoyle (hoil) *n.* A reference book of rules for card games and other indoor games originally compiled by Sir Edmund Hoyle (died 1769), English writer on games. —**according to Hoyle.** **1.** Adhering to the prescribed rules and regulations of play. **2.** In a sportsmanlike or honorable manner; fairly.

hp horsepower.

HQ, h.q., H.Q. headquarters.

hr hour.

Hr. Herr.

h.r. home run.

H.R. **1.** home rule. **2.** House of Representatives.

H.R.E. Holy Roman Emperor; Holy Roman Empire.

H.R.H. His (or Her) Royal Highness.

Hrolf. See **Rollo.**

hrs hours.

howdah

Hr·vat·ska. The Serbo-Croatian name for **Croatia.**

h.s., H.S. high school.

H.S.H. His (or Her) Serene Highness.

Hsiang. See **Siang.**

Hsien·yang. The ancient name for **Sian.**

Hsin·chu (shĭn′chōō′). A city and port of northwestern Taiwan. Population, 125,000.

Hsin·king. The former name for **Ch′angchun.**

H.S.M. His (or Her) Serene Majesty.

Hsüan T′ung (shüän′ tōong′). Known as Henry Pu-yi. 1906–1967. Last emperor of China (1908–12); puppet emperor of Manchukuo (1935–45); postwar convert to communism.

ht height.

Hts. heights (in place names).

Hual·la·ga (wä-yä′gä). A river rising in the Andes mountains of west-central Peru and flowing 700 miles generally north to the Marañon.

Huam·bo. The former name for **Nova Lisboa.**

Huang Hai. The Chinese name for the **Yellow Sea.**

Huang Ho. The Chinese name for the **Yellow River.**

hua·ra·che (wə-rä′chĕ, -chä, hōō-) *n.* Also **hua·ra·cho** (-chō). A flat-heeled sandal with an upper of woven leather strips. [Mexican Spanish *guarache, huarache†.*]

Huas·ca·rán (wäs′kä-rän′). An extinct volcano in the Cordillera Occidental; the highest elevation (22,205 feet) in Peru.

hub (hŭb) *n.* **1.** The center portion of a wheel, fan, or propeller. **2.** A center of activity or interest; focal point. [Probably a variant of HOB (a projection).]

hub·ba-hub·ba (hŭb′ə-hŭb′ə) *interj.* Used especially during World War II to express enthusiastic approval, as for an attractive girl or woman. [Origin uncertain.]

Hub·ble (hŭb′əl), **Edwin Powell.** 1889–1953. American astronomer.

hub·ble-bub·ble (hŭb′əl-bŭb′əl) *n.* **1.** A noisy commotion or uproar; hubbub. **2.** A water pipe, the **hookah** (*see*). [Reduplication of BUBBLE.]

Hubble′s constant. The ratio of the speed at which a distant galaxy is receding from the earth to its distance from the earth, approximately equal to 100 kilometers per second per million parsecs. [After E.P. HUBBLE.]

hub·bub (hŭb′ŭb′) *n.* **1.** A confused babble of loud sounds and voices; din; uproar. **2.** Confusion; upheaval; tumult. —See Synonyms at **noise.** [Irish *hooboobbes,* akin to Old Irish *abu!,* a war cry, from Old Irish *buide,* "victory," from Celtic *bod-io-* (unattested).]

Hub·li (hōōb′lē). A city and textile center of northwestern Mysore, Republic of India. Population, 185,000.

hu·bris (hyōō′brĭs) *n.* Overbearing pride or presumption; arrogance. [Greek *hubris,* insolence, outrage. See ud- in Appendix.*]

huck·a·back (hŭk′ə-băk′) *n.* A coarse absorbent cotton or linen fabric used especially for toweling. Also called "huck." [Origin unknown.]

huck·le (hŭk′əl) *n. Rare.* The hip or haunch. [Diminutive of earlier *huck,* hip, haunch, from Middle English *huck-, huke-,* perhaps from Germanic, akin to Middle Low German *hūken,* to sit bent. See keu-² in Appendix.*]

huck·le·ber·ry (hŭk′əl-bĕr′ē) *n., pl.* **-ries.** **1.** Any of various New World shrubs of the genus *Gaylussacia,* related to the blueberries and bearing edible fruit. **2.** The glossy, blackish, many-seeded berry of such a bush. [Probably variant of dialectal *hurtleberry,* WHORTLEBERRY.]

huck·ster (hŭk′stər) *n.* **1.** A person who sells wares in the street; peddler; hawker. **2.** A person who promotes a commercial product on radio or television. **3.** *Slang.* A writer of advertising copy, as for radio or television. —*v.* **huckstered, -stering, -sters.** —*tr.* **1.** To sell; peddle. **2.** To promote or sell on radio or television. **3.** To haggle over; bargain in. —*intr.* To haggle. [Middle English *huccstere,* perhaps from Middle Dutch *hokester.* See keu-² in Appendix.*]

HUD, H.U.D. Housing and Urban Development.

Hu·dai·da. See **Hodeida.**

Hud·ders·field (hŭd′ərz-fēld′). A textile center of southwestern West Riding, Yorkshire, England. Population, 132,000.

hud·dle (hŭd′əl) *n.* **1.** A densely packed group or crowd, as of people or animals. **2.** A confused array; jumble. **3.** *Football.* A brief gathering for signals behind the line of scrimmage before a play. **4.** A small private conference. —*v.* **huddled, -dling, -dles.** —*intr.* **1.** To crowd together, as from cold or fear; nestle; snuggle. **2.** To draw oneself together; curl or hunch up; crouch. **3.** *Football.* To gather in a huddle. **4.** To gather for conference or consultation; to meet. —*tr.* **1.** To crowd together. **2.** To draw (oneself) together; hunch; crouch. **3.** *British.* To arrange, do, or make hastily or carelessly; throw together. [Origin uncertain.]

Hu·di·bras·tic (hyōō′də-brăs′tĭk) *adj.* In the mock-heroic style of Samuel Butler′s satire *Hudibras* (1663–78). [From *Hudibras,* by analogy with such words as *bombastic, fantastic, periphrastic.*]

Hud·son (hŭd′sən), **Henry.** Died 1611. English navigator and explorer of Arctic waters.

Hud·son (hŭd′sən), **William Henry.** 1841–1922. English naturalist and author.

Hud·son Bay (hŭd′sən). An inland sea occupying 472,000 square miles in east-central Canada.

Hud·son River (hŭd′sən). A river rising in the Adirondacks of eastern New York State, flowing 315 miles generally south to its mouth at New York City, and forming part of the New York-New Jersey boundary at the end of its course.

howitzer

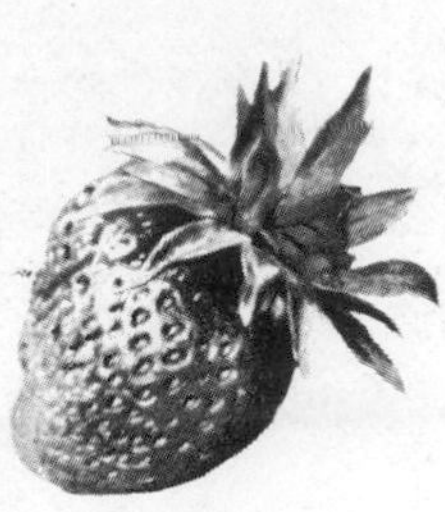

hull
Strawberry hull

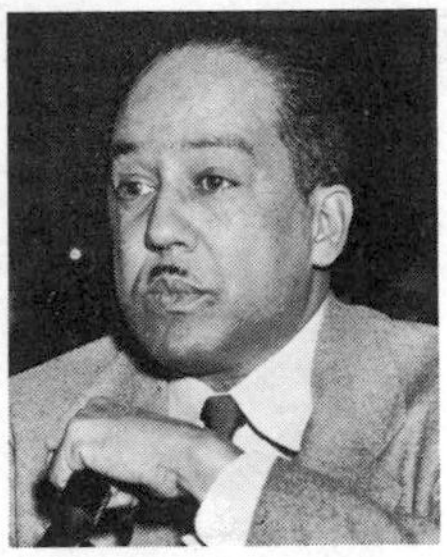

Langston Hughes

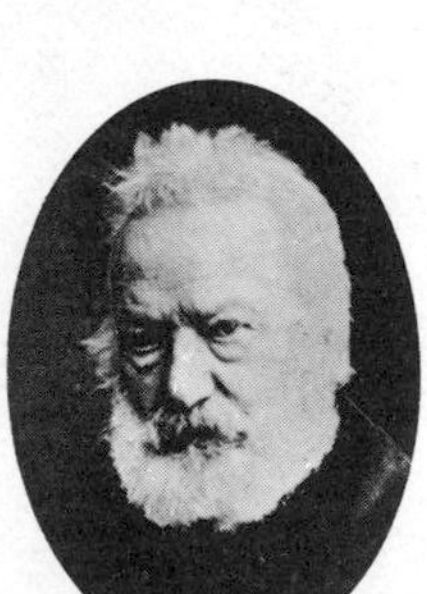

Victor Hugo

Hud·son's Bay Company (hŭd′sənz). A British joint-stock company chartered in 1670 to participate in fur trading with the North American Indians in competition with the French in the St. Lawrence River area.

Hudson seal. Muskrat fur that is dyed, plucked, and sheared in imitation of seal.

Hud·son Strait (hŭd′sən). A strait extending 450 miles between southern Baffin Island and northern Quebec, Canada, and connecting Hudson Bay with the Atlantic.

hue¹ (hyo͞o) *n.* **1.** The dimension of color that is referred to a scale of perceptions ranging from red through yellow, green, and blue, and (circularly) back to red. See **color**. **2.** A particular gradation of color; tint; shade. **3.** Color: *all the hues of the rainbow.* **4.** Character; aspect: *the weird hue of the deserted house.* [Middle English *hewe*, complexion, appearance, Old English *hēo, hīw*, appearance, form, color, beauty. See **kei-²** in Appendix.*]

hue² (hyo͞o) *n.* A loud outcry. **—hue and cry. 1. a.** The pursuit of a felon announced by loud shouts to alert others then legally obliged to aid in the chase. **b.** The loud shout used to arouse the pursuers. **2.** Any public clamor or stir, as of protest or demand: *"a recent hue and cry for wider teaching of English"* (L.M. Kable). [Middle English *hew, heu*, from Old French *heu, hu*, an outcry, from *huer*, to cry out, shout (imitative).]

Hue (hwā, hyo͞o-ā′). *French* **Hué** (ü-ā′). A city and port of northeastern South Vietnam. Population, 106,000.

hued (hyo͞od) *adj.* Having a given hue, aspect, or character. Used in combination: *rosy-hued dawn.*

Huel·va (hwĕl′vä). A city, mining center, and Atlantic port of southwestern Spain, on the Gulf of Cádiz. Population, 82,000.

Huer·ta (hwĕr′tä), **Victoriano.** 1854–1916. Mexican revolutionist; provisional president (1913–14); exiled.

huff (hŭf) *n.* A fit of anger or annoyance; pique. **—***v.* **huffed, huffing, huffs.** **—***intr.* **1.** To puff; blow. **2.** To speak or act with noisy, empty threats; bluster. **3.** To act or react indignantly; take offense. **—***tr.* **1.** To puff or blow up; inflate. **2.** *Archaic.* To treat with insolence; bully; tease. **3.** To put in a huff; to anger; annoy. [Imitative of the sound of puffing.]

huff·ish (hŭf′ĭsh) *adj.* **1.** Peevish; sulky; irritable. **2.** *Obsolete.* Arrogant; contemptuous; insolent. **—huff′ish·ly** *adv.* **—huff′ish·ness** *n.*

huff·y (hŭf′ē) *adj.* **-ier, -iest. 1.** Easily offended; sensitive; touchy. **2.** Irritated or annoyed; indignant. **3.** Arrogant; disdainful; haughty. **—huff′i·ly** *adv.* **—huff′i·ness** *n.*

hug (hŭg) *v.* **hugged, hugging, hugs.** **—***tr.* **1.** To clasp or hold closely, especially in one's arms; embrace or enfold, as in affection. **2.** To ascribe steadfastly to (a belief or opinion, for example); cherish. **3.** To keep, remain, or be situated close to: *"The old footpath . . . winds inland here, hugging a gentler slope"* (Oliver Statler). **—***intr.* To embrace or be in physical contact with; lie closely together; snuggle. **—***n.* An affectionate or crushing embrace. [From Scandinavian, akin to Old Norse *hugga*, to comfort, console, from Germanic *hugjan* (unattested).] **—hug′ger** *n.*

huge (hyo͞oj) *adj.* Of exceedingly great size, extent, or quantity; tremendous. See Synonyms at **enormous.** [Middle English *huge, hoge*, shortened from Old French *ahuge, ahoge*†.] **—huge′ly** *adv.* **—huge′ness** *n.*

huge·ous (hyo͞o′jəs) *adj. Informal.* Huge. Used chiefly for humorous effect. **—huge′ous·ly** *adv.* **—huge′ous·ness** *n.*

hug·ger-mug·ger, hug·ger-mug·ger (hŭg′ər-mŭg′ər) *n.* **1.** Disorder; confusion; muddle. **2.** Concealment; secrecy. **—***adj.* **1.** Disordered; jumbled: *"worry out her financial problems in her own hugger-mugger way"* (Samuel Butler). **2.** Secret; surreptitious; clandestine: *huggermugger political deals.* **—***v.* **huggermuggered, -gering, -gers.** **—***tr.* To keep concealed or secret. **—***intr.* To act in a surreptitious manner. [Origin uncertain.]

Hug·gins (hŭg′ĭnz), **Charles Brenton.** Born 1901. Canadian-born American surgeon.

Hugh (hyo͞o). A masculine given name. [Middle English *Hew, How*, from Old North French *Hugues, Hugon*, from Germanic *hug-* (unattested), akin to *hugjan* (unattested), to HUG.]

Hugh Ca·pet (hyo͞o kā′pĭt, kăp′ĭt). *French* **Hugues Ca·pet** (üg kȧ-pĕ′). A.D. 940?–996. King of France (A.D. 987–996), first of Capetian line.

Hughes (hyo͞oz), **Charles Evans.** 1862–1948. American jurist and diplomat; Chief Justice of the United States (1930–41).

Hughes (hyo͞oz), **(James) Langston.** 1902–1967. American novelist and poet.

Hug·li. See **Hooghly.**

hug-me-tight (hŭg′mē-tīt′) *n.* A woman's close-fitting, usually knitted jacket, with or without sleeves.

Hu·go (hyo͞o′gō; *French* ü-gō′), **Victor Marie.** 1802–1885. French author of novels, plays, and poetry; leader of romantic movement.

Hu·gue·not (hyo͞o′gə-nŏt′) *n.* A French Protestant of the 16th and 17th centuries. [French *huguenot*, alteration (influenced by gate of Roi-*Hugon* where the Protestants of Tours assembled at night) of earlier (Genevan) French *eyguenot*, referring to those who opposed annexation by the Duke of Savoy, from Swiss German *Eidgenosse(n)*, confederate(s), from Middle High German *eitgenōz* : *eit*, oath, from Old High German *eid* (see **oito-** in Appendix*) + *genōz*, companion, from Old High German *ginōz* (see **neud-** in Appendix*).] **—Hu′gue·not′ic** *adj.* **—Hu′gue·not′ism′** *n.*

huh (hŭ) *interj.* Used as an interrogative or to express surprise, contempt, or indifference.

Hu·he·hot (ho͞o′hā′hōt′). The capital of the Inner Mongolian Autonomous Region, located in the south. Also called "Kweisui." Population, 320,000.

Hui·la (wē′lä). A volcano rising to 18,700 feet in the Cordillera Central of western Colombia.

hu·la (ho͞o′lə) *n.* Also **hu·la-hu·la** (ho͞o′lə-ho͞o′lə). **1.** A Polynesian ethnic dance performed by men or women alone or together and characterized by undulating movements of the hips, arms, and hands, pantomiming a story. **2.** The music for this dance, composed typically of rhythmic drumbeats and chants. [Hawaiian.]

Hu·la, Lake (ho͞o′lə). Also **Hu·le.** An expansion of the headwaters of the Jordan, occupying 5.5 square miles in northeastern Israel near the Syrian border. Also called "Waters of Merom."

hulk (hŭlk) *n.* **1.** A heavy, unwieldy ship. **2. a.** The hull of an old, unseaworthy, or wrecked ship. **b.** An old or unseaworthy ship used as a prison or warehouse. **3. a.** A clumsy, awkward, or overweight person. **b.** A clumsy or bulky object. **—***intr.v.* **hulked, hulking, hulks. 1.** To loom or rise in a towering or impressive fashion: *The truck hulked out of the fog in front of our car.* **2.** *British Regional.* To move about clumsily; clump; slouch. [Middle English *hulke*, Old English *hulc*, ship, from Medieval Latin *hulcus*, from Greek *holkas*, "ship that is towed," merchant vessel, from *helkein*, to pull, tow. See **selk-** in Appendix.*]

hulk·ing (hŭl′kĭng) *adj.* Also **hulk·y** (hŭl′kē). Unwieldy, clumsy, or bulky; towering: *a hulking lumberjack.*

hull (hŭl) *n.* **1. a.** The enlarged calyx of a strawberry or similar fruit, usually green and easily detached. **b.** The dry outer covering of a fruit, seed, or nut; husk. **2.** *Nautical.* The main body of a ship, exclusive of masts, sails, yards, and rigging. **3.** *Aviation.* The fuselage of a flying boat. **4.** *Aerospace.* The outer casing of a rocket, guided missile, or spaceship. **—***tr.v.* To remove the hull or hulls of (fruit or seeds). [Middle English *hull, hole*, husk, Old English *hulu*. See **kel-⁴** in Appendix.*]

Hull (hŭl). **1.** Also **King·ston-up·on-Hull** (kĭng′stən-ə-pŏn-). A city and port of southeastern East Riding, Yorkshire, England, on the Humber. Population, 300,000. **2.** A city of southwest-central Quebec, Canada, on the Ottawa River near Ottawa, Ontario. Population, 57,000.

Hull (hŭl), **Cordell.** 1871–1955. American diplomat and political leader; Secretary of State (1933–44).

Hull (hŭl), **Isaac.** 1773–1843. American naval officer; commander of the *Constitution* in the War of 1812.

hul·la·ba·loo (hŭl′ə-bə-lo͞o′) *n., pl.* **-loos.** Also **hul·la·bal·loo.** A great noise or excitement; an uproar. See Synonyms at **noise.** [Earlier *hollo-ballo*, akin to the interjection HALLOO.]

hul·lo. Variant of **hello.**

Hu·lun Nor (ho͞o′lo͞on′ nôr′). The largest lake (35 miles long, 5 miles wide) of Manchuria, located in the northwestern Inner Mongolian Autonomous Region.

hum (hŭm) *v.* **hummed, humming, hums.** **—***intr.* **1.** To utter a continuous low droning sound like that of the speech sound (m) when prolonged. **2. a.** To emit the continuous droning sound of an insect on the wing, or a similar sound. **b.** To move with such a sound. **3. a.** To give out a low, continuous drone blended of many sounds: *The avenue hummed with traffic.* **b.** To be full of activity. **4.** To sing a tune without opening the lips or forming words. **—***tr.* To sing without opening the lips or saying words. **—***n.* **1.** The noise produced by humming; a murmur; drone. **2.** The act of humming. **—***interj.* **1.** Uttered as a pause in speech or to indicate thought. **2.** Used to express surprise or displeasure. [Middle English *hummen*, akin to Middle High German *hummen* (imitative).] **—hum′mer** *n.*

hu·man (hyo͞o′mən) *adj.* **1.** Of, relating to, or characteristic of man or mankind: *the course of human events.* **2.** Having or manifesting the form, nature, or qualities characteristic of man. **3. a.** Pertaining to or being a man as distinguished from a lower animal; intellectually and morally superior. **b.** Pertaining to or being a man as distinguished from a divine entity or infinite intelligence; mortal; earthly. **4.** Made up of people: *They formed a human bridge across the river.* **—***n.* A human being; a person. See Usage note. [Middle English *humain(e), humayn(e)*, from Old French *humain* (feminine *humaine*), from Latin *hūmānus.* See **dhghem-** in Appendix.*] **—hu′man·ness** *n.*

Usage: *Human* (noun) is acceptable on all levels and in contexts not limited to the scientific or technical, according to 72 per cent of the Usage Panel: *air not fit for humans to breathe.* In somewhat earlier usage, *human being* was often recommended as the better choice on a formal level, though *human* has a long history as a noun.

human being. A member of the genus *Homo*, and especially of the species *Homo sapiens.* See Usage note at **human.**

hu·mane (hyo͞o-mān′) *adj.* **1.** Having the good qualities of human beings, as kindness, mercy, or compassion: *a humane judge.* **2.** Tending to evoke or promote these qualities; refining; civilizing: *a humane education.* [Middle English *humaine*, HUMAN.] **—hu·mane′ly** *adv.* **—hu·mane′ness** *n.*

human engineering. 1. The industrial management of labor. **2.** The technology of efficient use of machines by human beings.

hu·man·ism (hyo͞o′mə-nĭz′əm) *n.* **1.** The condition or quality of being human. **2.** A philosophy or attitude that is concerned with human beings, their achievements and interests, rather than with the abstract beings and problems of theology. **3.** The study of the humanities; polite or cultured learning. **4.** *Often capital* **H.** A cultural and intellectual movement which occurred during the Renaissance following the rediscovery of the literature, art, and civilization of ancient Greece and Rome, and which stimulated a renewed interest in man and his capabilities.

ă pat/ā pay/âr care/ä father/b bib/ch church/d deed/ĕ pet/ē be/f fife/g gag/h hat/hw which/ĭ pit/ī pie/îr pier/j judge/k kick/l lid, needle/m mum/n no, sudden/ng thing/ŏ pot/ō toe/ô paw, for/oi noise/ou out/o͝o took/o͞o boot/p pop/r roar/s sauce/sh ship, dish/

hu·man·ist (hyōō′mə-nĭst) *n.* **1.** One who studies the humanities; especially, a student of classical learning. **2.** One who is concerned with the study and welfare of human beings. **3.** *Often capital* **H.** A Renaissance student or follower of Humanism. —*adj.* Also **hu·man·is·tic** (hyōō′mə-nĭs′tĭk). Of or relating to humanism or the humanities. —**hu′man·is′ti·cal·ly** *adv.*

hu·man·i·tar·i·an (hyōō-măn′ə-târ′ē-ən) *adj.* **1.** Concerned with the needs of mankind and the alleviation of human suffering. **2.** Of or relating to theological or ethical humanitarianism. —*n.* One devoted to the promotion of human welfare and the advancement of social reforms; a philanthropist.

hu·man·i·tar·i·an·ism (hyōō-măn′ə-târ′ē-ə-nĭz′əm) *n.* **1.** The ideas, principles, or methods of humanitarians; charity; philanthropy. **2.** *Ethics.* **a.** The belief that man's sole moral obligation is to work for the improved welfare of humanity. **b.** The belief that the nature of man may reach perfection through his own efforts without divine aid. **3.** *Theology.* The belief or doctrine that Jesus was mortal rather than divine.

hu·man·i·ty (hyōō-măn′ə-tē) *n., pl.* **-ties. 1.** Human beings collectively; the human race; mankind. **2.** The condition, quality, or fact of being human; human nature; humanness. **3.** The quality of being humane; benevolence; kindness; mercy. **4.** A humane quality or action. **5.** *Plural.* **a.** The study of the classical languages and literature of Greece and Rome. **b.** Those branches of knowledge concerned with man and his culture, as philosophy, literature, and the fine arts, as distinguished from the sciences. [Middle English *humanite,* from Old French, from Latin *hūmānitās,* from *hūmānus,* HUMAN.]

hu·man·ize (hyōō′mə-nīz′) *v.* **-ized, -izing, -izes.** —*tr.* **1.** To make human; cause to have human characteristics or attributes. **2.** To make humane; cause to be kind, benevolent, or gentle. —*intr.* **1.** To become human. **2.** To become humane. —**hu′man·i·za′tion** *n.* —**hu′man·iz′er** *n.*

hu·man·kind (hyōō′mən-kīnd′) *n.* The human race; mankind.

hu·man·ly (hyōō′mən-lē) *adv.* **1.** In a human way. **2.** By human means, capabilities, or powers. **3.** According to human experience or knowledge.

hu·man·oid (hyōō′mə-noid′) *adj.* Resembling a human being in appearance. —*n.* A synthetic man, an **android** *(see).*

Hum·ber (hŭm′bər). The estuary of the Ouse and Trent rivers, rising between Yorkshire and Lincolnshire, England, and flowing 40 miles generally east to the North Sea.

hum·ble (hŭm′bəl) *adj.* **-bler, -blest. 1.** Having or showing feelings of humility rather than of pride; aware of one's shortcomings; modest; meek. **2.** Showing deferential respect. **3.** Lacking high station; lowly; unpretentious: *"a set of low fellows of the humblest extraction"* (G.G. Coulton). —*tr.v.* **humbled, -bling, -bles. 1.** To curtail or destroy the pride of; humiliate. **2.** To give a lower condition or station to; abase. —See Synonyms at **degrade.** [Middle English *(h)umble,* from Old French *(h)umble,* from Latin *humilis,* low, lowly, base, from *humus,* ground, soil. See **dhghem-** in Appendix.*] —**hum′ble·ness** *n.* —**hum′bler** *n.* —**hum′bly** *adv.*

Synonyms: *humble, meek, lowly, modest, reserved, retiring, self-conscious.* These adjectives refer primarily to demeanor or behavior. *Humble* stresses lack of pride, pretense, or assertiveness. *Meek* describes one who is patient, undemonstrative, and submissive or timid. *Lowly* implies both humility and meekness. *Modest* suggests lack of vanity or forwardness. One who is *reserved* is by temperament restrained and not readily communicative, and one who is *retiring* is shy and given to diverting attention from himself. *Self-conscious* implies embarrassment, often from a sense of inadequacy. *Humble* and *lowly* also can refer to low rank or station, and *modest* to what is unassuming or unpretentious.

hum·ble·bee (hŭm′bəl-bē′) *n.* A bumblebee. [Middle English *humbylbee,* perhaps from Middle Low German *hummelbē* : *hummel,* bumblebee (see **kem-**[3] in Appendix*) + *bē,* bee (see **bhei-**[1] in Appendix*).]

humble pie. A pie made from the edible organs of a deer. —**eat humble pie.** To be made to apologize for or admit one's faults; to be humiliated. [*Humble,* from earlier *humbles,* edible organs of an animal, variant of *umbles,* from Middle English, variant of *noumbles,* from Old French *nombles,* plural of *nomble,* pork loin, piece of a deer's thigh, from Latin *lumbulus,* diminutive of *lumbus,* LOIN.]

Hum·boldt (hŭm′bōlt). **1.** A river rising in north-central Nevada and flowing 290 miles west and southwest to Rye Patch reservoir. **2.** A bay of the Pacific Ocean in northwestern California.

Hum·boldt (hŭm′bōlt; *German* hōōm′bōlt), Baron **(Friedrich Heinrich) Alexander von.** 1769–1859. German naturalist, statesman, and explorer of South America and Asia.

Hum·boldt Current (hŭm′bōlt). A cold ocean current of the South Pacific, flowing north along the northern coast of Chile and Peru to southern Ecuador.

hum·bug (hŭm′bŭg′) *n.* **1.** Something intended to deceive; a hoax; imposture. **2.** One who tries to trick or deceive others; an impostor; charlatan. **3.** Nonsense; rubbish. —See Synonyms at **impostor.** —*v.* **humbugged, -bugging, -bugs.** —*tr.* To deceive; to trick; to cheat. —*intr.* To practice trickery. [Origin unknown.] —**hum′bug′ger** *n.* —**hum′bug′ger·y** *n.*

hum·ding·er (hŭm′dĭng′ər) *n. Slang.* Someone or something extraordinary or superior: a marvel. [Perhaps from *hummer,* one who hums.]

hum·drum (hŭm′drŭm′) *adj.* Without change, variety, or excitement; monotonous; ordinary. See Synonyms at **boring.** —*n.* Something or someone dull or unexciting. [Originally also *humtrum,* probably reduplication of HUM.]

Hume (hyōōm), **David.** 1711–1766. Scottish philosopher and historian.

hu·mec·tant (hyōō-mĕk′tənt) *n.* A moistening agent. —*adj.* Promoting moisture retention. [From Latin *hūmectāns,* present participle of *(h)ūmectāre,* to moisten, from *(h)ūmectus,* moist, from *(h)ūmēre,* to be moist. See **wegw-** in Appendix.*]

hu·mer·al (hyōō′mər-əl) *adj.* **1.** Pertaining to or located in the region of the humerus or the shoulder. **2.** Pertaining to or being a body part analogous to the humerus. —**hu′mer·al** *n.*

humeral veil. *Roman Catholic Church.* A silk veil covering the shoulders that is worn at a High Mass by a subdeacon or priest.

hu·mer·us (hyōō′mər-əs) *n., pl.* **-meri** (-mə-rī′). The long bone of the upper part of the arm, extending from the shoulder to the elbow. [New Latin, from Latin *umerus, humerus,* upper arm, shoulder. See **omeso-** in Appendix.*]

hu·mic (hyōō′mĭk) *adj.* Of, pertaining to, or derived from humus.

hu·mid (hyōō′mĭd) *adj.* Containing a high amount of water or water vapor. Said especially of air. See Synonyms at **wet.** [Old French *humide,* from Latin *(h)ūmidus,* from *(h)ūmēre,* to be moist. See **wegw-** in Appendix.*] —**hu′mid·ly** *adv.*

hu·mid·i·fi·er (hyōō-mĭd′ə-fī′ər) *n.* An apparatus for increasing the humidity in a room, greenhouse, or other enclosure.

hu·mid·i·fy (hyōō-mĭd′ə-fī′) *tr.v.* **-fied, -fying, -fies.** To make more humid; especially, to increase the amount of water vapor in (the air). —**hu·mid′i·fi·ca′tion** *n.*

hu·mid·i·stat (hyōō-mĭd′ĭ-stăt′) *n.* An instrument designed to indicate or control the relative humidity of the air. [HUMID-I(TY) + -STAT.]

hu·mid·i·ty (hyōō-mĭd′ə-tē) *n.* Dampness, especially of the air. See **relative humidity.** [Middle English *humidite,* from Old French, from Latin *hūmiditās,* from *hūmidus,* HUMID.]

hu·mi·dor (hyōō′mə-dôr′) *n.* A case for the storage of cigars and other tobacco products, containing a device for keeping the humidity level constant. [From HUMID.]

hu·mil·i·ate (hyōō-mĭl′ē-āt′) *tr.v.* **-ated, -ating, -ates. 1.** To lower the pride, dignity, or status of; to humble or disgrace; degrade. **2.** To subject to humiliation; mortify. —See Synonyms at **degrade.** [Late Latin *humiliāre,* from *humilis,* HUMBLE.] —**hu·mil′i·a·to′ry** (hyōō-mĭl′ē-ə-tôr′ē, -tōr′ē) *adj.*

hu·mil·i·a·tion (hyōō-mĭl′ē-ā′shən) *n.* **1.** The act of humiliating; degradation. **2.** The state or condition of being humiliated; disgrace; shame. **3.** Religious mortification: *"Humiliation is the beginning of sanctification."* (Donne).

hu·mil·i·ty (hyōō-mĭl′ə-tē) *n., pl.* **-ties. 1.** The quality or condition of being humble; lack of pride; modesty. **2.** *Usually plural.* An act of modesty, submission, or self-abasement. [Middle English *humilite,* from Old French *humilite,* from Latin *humilitās,* from *humilis,* HUMBLE.]

hum·ming·bird (hŭm′ĭng-bûrd′) *n.* Any of numerous chiefly tropical New World birds of the family Trochilidae, usually very small in size, and having a long, slender bill, wings capable of beating very rapidly, and often brilliantly colored plumage. [From the humming sound produced by the rapidly vibrating wings.]

hummingbird moth. A **hawk moth** *(see).* [From its resemblance to a hummingbird when hovering over and feeding from flowers.]

hum·mock (hŭm′ək) *n.* Also **ham·mock** (hăm′-). **1.** A low mound or ridge of earth; knoll. **2.** A tract of forested land elevated above the level of an adjacent marsh. **3.** A ridge or hill of ice in an ice field. [Origin obscure.] —**hum′mock·y** *adj.*

hu·mor (hyōō′mər) *n.* Also *British* **hu·mour. 1.** The quality of being laughable or comical; funniness: *He saw the humor of the situation.* **2.** Something designed to induce laughter or amusement. **3.** The ability to perceive, enjoy, or express what is comical or funny: *a sense of humor.* **4.** In medieval physiology, one of the four fluids of the body, blood, phlegm, choler, and black bile, the dominance of which was thought to determine the character and general health of a man. Accordingly, one's disposition might be **sanguine, phlegmatic, choleric,** or **melancholy** *(all of which see).* **5.** A state of mind; mood; spirit: *in a bad humor.* **6.** Disposition; character; personality; temper: *a girl of most sullen humor.* **7. a.** A sudden, unanticipated whim. **b.** Capricious or peculiar behavior or action. **8.** *Physiology.* **a.** Any clear or hyaline body fluid, such as blood, lymph, or bile. **b. Aqueous humor** *(see).* —See Synonyms at **mood, wit.** —**out of humor.** In a bad mood; irritable; grouchy. —*tr.v.* **humored, -moring, -mors. 1.** To comply with the wishes or ideas of (another); go along with; indulge. **2.** To adapt or accommodate oneself to: *"I don't intend to humor your silliness"* (Tennessee Williams). —See Synonyms at **pamper.** [Middle English *(h)umour,* fluid from an animal or plant, one of the four principal body fluids that affected mental disposition, from Norman French, from Latin *(h)ūmor,* liquid, fluid. See **wegw-** in Appendix.*]

hu·mor·al (hyōō′mər-əl) *adj.* Pertaining to or arising from any of the bodily humors.

hu·mor·esque (hyōō′mə-rĕsk′) *n.* A whimsical or playful musical composition. [German *Humoreske,* from *Humor,* humor, from English HUMOR.]

hu·mor·ist (hyōō′mər-ĭst) *n.* **1.** A person with a sharp sense of humor. **2.** A performer or writer of comedy.

hu·mor·less (hyōō′mər-lĭs) *adj.* **1.** Devoid of a sense of humor. **2.** Said or done with high seriousness: *"She winked at me, but it was humorless; a wink of warning"* (Truman Capote). —**hu′mor·less·ly** *adv.* —**hu′mor·less·ness** *n.*

hu·mor·ous (hyōō′mər-əs) *adj.* **1.** Having or characterized by humor; funny; laughable; comical: *a humorous sight.* **2.** Em-

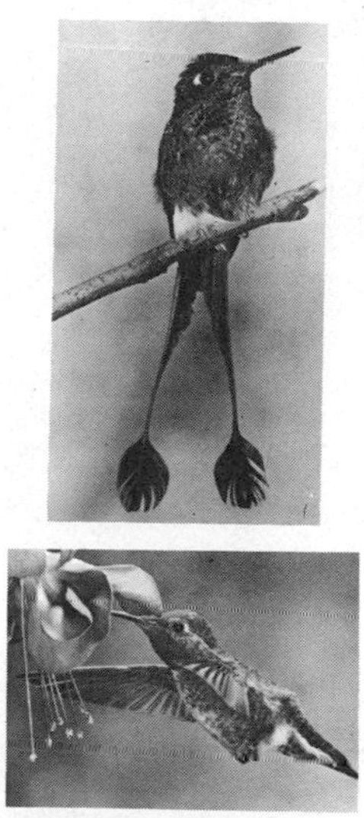

hummingbird
Above: Loddigesia mirabilis
Below: Calypte anna

t tight/th thin, path/*th* this, bathe/ŭ cut/ûr urge/v valve/w with/y yes/z zebra, size/zh vision/ə about, item, edible, gallop, circus/ à *Fr.* ami/œ *Fr.* feu, *Ger.* schön/ü *Fr.* tu, *Ger.* über/KH *Ger.* ich, *Scot.* loch/N *Fr.* bon. ***Follows main vocabulary.** †**Of obscure origin.**

ploying or expressing humor; comic; witty; droll: *a humorous comedian.* 3. *Archaic.* Capricious. 4. *Obsolete.* Damp; moist. —**hu′mor·ous·ly** *adv.* —**hu′mor·ous·ness** *n.*

hump (hŭmp) *n.* 1. A rounded mass or protuberance, such as the fleshy structure on the back of a camel or over the shoulders of some cattle. 2. A deformity of the back, due in human beings to an abnormal curvature of the spine. 3. A low mound of earth; hummock. 4. *British Slang.* A feeling of depression; an emotional slump. 5. *Capital* **H.** The Himalayas regarded as a barrier to air transportation in World War II. —**over the hump.** 1. Past the worst or most difficult part of something. 2. More than halfway through. —*v.* **humped, humping, humps.** —*tr.* 1. To make into a hump; to arch; round. 2. *Slang.* To exert (oneself). 3. *Vulgar Slang.* To copulate with. —*intr.* 1. To bend or arch so as to become a hump. 2. *Slang.* To exert oneself. 3. *Vulgar Slang.* To copulate. [Shortened from earlier *humpback(ed),* possibly a blend of earlier *crumpbacked* and HUNCHBACK(ED).]

hump·back (hŭmp′băk′) *n.* 1. An individual afflicted with an abnormally curved or humped back; hunchback. 2. A pathological condition, **kyphosis** *(see).* 3. An abnormally curved or humped back. 4. A whalebone whale, *Megaptera novaeangliae,* having a rounded back and long, knobby flippers. —**hump′-backed′** *adj.*

humped (hŭmpt) *adj.* 1. Having a hump: *humped cattle.* 2. Formed into a hump.

humph (hŭmf) *interj.* Used to express doubt, displeasure, or contempt.

Hum·phrey (hŭm′frē), **Hubert Horatio.** Born 1911. Vice President of the United States under Lyndon B. Johnson (1965–69).

Humph·reys Peak (hŭm′frēz). A mountain rising to 12,655 feet in the San Francisco Peaks of north-central Arizona; the highest point in the state.

Hump·ty Dump·ty (hŭmp′tē dŭmp′tē). An egg-shaped character in a nursery rhyme who fell off a wall and shattered irrecoverably.

hump·y (hŭm′pē) *adj.* **-ier, -iest.** 1. Covered with or containing humps. 2. Resembling a hump.

Hums. See **Homs.**

hu·mus (hyōō′məs) *n.* A brown or black organic substance consisting of partially or wholly decayed vegetable matter that provides nutrients for plants and increases the ability of soil to retain water. [Latin *humus,* earth, ground, soil. See **dhghem-** in Appendix.*]

Hun (hŭn) *n.* 1. One of a fierce barbaric race of Asiatic nomads who, led by Attila, ravaged Europe in the fourth and fifth centuries A.D. 2. Any savage, uncivilized, or destructive person. 3. *Slang.* A German soldier. Used derogatorily. [Old English *Hūne* and *Hūnas* (both plural), from Late Latin *Hūnī,* from Turki *Hun-yü.*]

Hun. Hungarian; Hungary.

Hu·nan (hōō′nän′). A province, 105,467 square miles in area, of southeast-central China. Population, 36,220,000. Capital, Changsha.

hunch (hŭnch) *n.* 1. An intuitive feeling or guess about something; premonition: *"Trust my hunches and my instincts."* (Ray Bradbury). 2. A hump. 3. A lump or chunk. —*v.* **hunched, hunching, hunches.** —*tr.* 1. To bend, arch, or draw up into a hump: *hunched his shoulders against the wind.* 2. To push or shove forward jerkily. —*intr.* 1. To draw oneself up closely into a crouched or cramped posture: *The scared child hunched in a corner.* 2. To proceed jerkily; thrust oneself forward; lunge. [Origin unknown.]

hunch·back (hŭnch′băk′) *n.* 1. An individual afflicted with an abnormally curved or hunched back; humpback. 2. A pathological condition, **kyphosis** *(see).* 3. An abnormally curved or hunched back. —**hunch′backed′** *adj.*

hun·dred (hŭn′drĭd) *n., pl.* **-dreds** or **hundred.** *Abbr.* **h.** 1. The cardinal number written 100 or in Roman numerals C. See **number.** 2. A currency note worth 100 dollars. 3. The number in the third position left of the decimal point in an Arabic numeral. 4. *Plural.* The numbers between 100 and 999: *The dress was valued in the hundreds.* 5. An administrative division of some English and American counties. [Middle English *hundred,* Old English *hundred, hund.* See **dekm̥** in Appendix.*] —**hun′dred** *adj. & pron.*

hun·dredth (hŭn′drĭdth) *n.* 1. The ordinal number 100 in a series. Also written 100th. 2. One of 100 equal parts. See **number.** —**hun′dredth** *adj. & adv.*

hun·dred·weight (hŭn′drĭd-wāt′) *n., pl.* **hundredweight** or **-weights.** *Abbr.* **cwt.** 1. A unit of weight in the U.S. Customary System equal to 100 pounds. Also called "short hundredweight." 2. A unit of weight in the British Imperial System equal to 112 pounds. Also called "quintal."

Hundred Years' War. A series of wars between England and France lasting from 1337 until 1453, during which England lost all her French possessions except Calais.

hung (hŭng). Past tense and past participle of **hang.** See Usage note at **hang.** —*adj. Slang.* Hung over.

Hung. Hungarian; Hungary.

Hun·gar·i·an (hŭng-gâr′ē-ən) *adj. Abbr.* **Hun., Hung.** Of or relating to Hungary, its people, language, or culture. —*n.* 1. A citizen or native of Hungary; especially, a Magyar. 2. The Finno-Ugric language spoken in Hungary; Magyar.

Hungarian goulash. Goulash *(see).*

Hun·ga·ry (hŭng′gə-rē). *Hungarian* **Mag·yar·or·szág** (mô′dyôr-ōr′säg). Officially, Hungarian People's Republic. *Abbr.* **Hun., Hung.** A republic occupying 35,902 square miles in central Europe. Population, 10,123,000. Capital, Budapest. [Medieval Latin *Hungaria,* from *(H)ungarī, U(n)grī,* name of the people, from Old Russian *Ugre.* See **Ugrian.**]

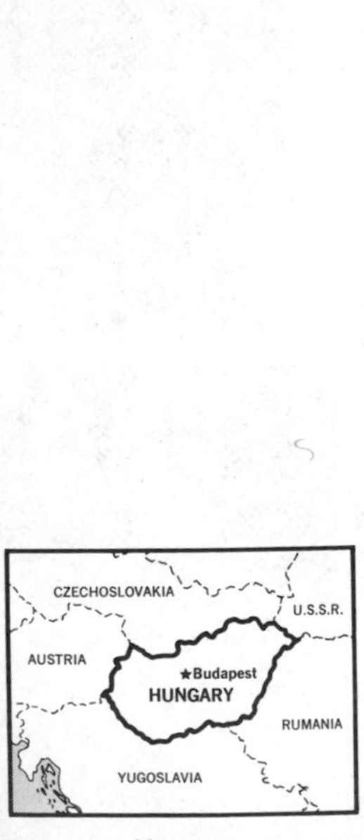

Hungary

hun·ger (hŭng′gər) *n.* 1. A strong desire for food. 2. a. The weakness, debilitation, or pain caused by a prolonged lack of food; starvation. b. Mild discomfort or an uneasy sensation caused by a lack of food. 3. A strong desire or craving for anything: *a hunger for affection.* —*v.* **hungered, -gering, -gers.** —*intr.* 1. To have a need or desire for food. 2. To have a strong desire or craving for anything. Used with *after* or *for: Reduced to poverty, he hungered for his old life.* —*tr.* To cause to experience hunger; make hungry: *The thought of food hungered him even more.* —See Synonyms at **yearn.** [Middle English *hunger,* Old English *hungor, hungur.* See **kenk-**[2] in Appendix.*]

hunger strike. A refusal to eat or a voluntary fast undertaken as a method of protest.

Hung·nam (hŭng′näm′). *Japanese* **Ko·nan** (kō′nän′). A city and port of central North Korea, on the Sea of Japan. Population, 144,000.

hung over. Suffering from a hangover.

hun·gry (hŭng′grē) *adj.* **-grier, -griest.** 1. Experiencing weakness, pain, or other discomfort from lack of food. 2. Desiring or craving food. 3. Strongly desiring or craving anything: *hungry for recognition.* 4. Characterized by or expressing hunger, greed, or craving: *"a stranger with hungry eyes, a man to be pitied"* (Bernard Malamud). 5. Lacking richness or fertility: *hungry soil.* [Middle English *hungri,* Old English *hungri(g),* from *hungor,* HUNGER.] —**hun′gri·ly** *adv.* —**hun′gri·ness** *n.*

Hung·shui (hōōng′shwā′). A river of south-central China, rising on the Kweichow-Yunnan boundary and flowing 900 miles south and east to unite with the Yü and form the Si Kiang.

Hung·tze (hōōng′dzŭ′). A lake of eastern China, extending 65 miles along the Kiangsu-Anhwei boundary.

hunk (hŭngk) *n.* 1. *Informal.* A large piece; a chunk. 2. *Slang.* A sexually appealing man or woman. [Probably akin to West Flemish *hunke*†, hunk of food.]

hun·ker (hŭng′kər) *intr.v.* **-kered, -kering, -kers.** To squat close to the ground with the body leaning slightly forward, the weight resting on the calves. [Probably from Scandinavian, akin to Old Norse *hokra,* to crouch. See **keu-**[2] in Appendix.*]

hun·kers (hŭng′kərz) *pl.n. Regional.* The haunches. —**on one's hunkers.** Squatting; hunkering.

hunks (hŭngks) *n., pl.* **hunks.** 1. An irritable or disagreeable old person; a grouch. 2. A stingy, covetous man; a miser. [Origin unknown.]

hunk·y (hŭng′kē) *n., pl.* **-ies.** *Slang.* A **bohunk** *(see).*

hun·ky-do·ry (hŭng′kē-dôr′ē, -dōr′ē) *adj. Slang.* Perfectly all right; quite satisfactory; fine. [From obsolete *hunk,* goal, from Dutch *honk,* from Middle Dutch *honc,* hiding place, akin to West Frisian *honcke*†.]

Hun·nish (hŭn′ĭsh) *adj.* 1. Of or pertaining to the Huns. 2. Of or pertaining to the language of the Huns. 3. *Sometimes small* **h.** Barbarous. —*n.* The language of the Huns, variously classified as Turkic or Mongolian. —**Hun′nish·ness** *n.*

hunt (hŭnt) *v.* **hunted, hunting, hunts.** —*tr.* 1. a. To pursue (game or other wild animals) for food or sport. b. To seek out; search for. 2. To search through (an area), as for game or prey. 3. To make use of (hounds or horses, for example) in pursuing game. 4. To drive out forcibly; chase away, especially by harassing. 5. To harass persistently; persecute. —*intr.* 1. To pursue game or other animals in order to capture or kill them. 2. To conduct a diligent search; seek. 3. *Aerospace.* a. To yaw back and forth about a flight path, as if seeking a new direction or another angle of attack. Used of aircraft, rockets, and space vehicles. b. To rotate up and down or back and forth without being deflected by the pilot. Used of a control surface or a rocket motor in gimbals. 4. a. To oscillate about a selected value. Used of a control system. b. To swing back and forth or to oscillate. Used of an indicator on a display or instrument panel. —**hunt down.** 1. To pursue and capture. 2. To search for and locate. —**hunt up.** 1. To search for; to seek. 2. To find after searching. —*n.* 1. The act or sport of hunting game; the chase. 2. a. A hunting expedition or outing. b. Those taking part in a hunt with horses and hounds. 3. A diligent search or pursuit. [Middle English *hunten,* Old English *huntian,* from Germanic *huntjan* (unattested), akin to *hanthatjan* (unattested), to HENT.]

hunt and peck. A crude method of typewriting by searching out each individual letter and striking it with an index finger.

Hunt (hŭnt), **(James Henry) Leigh.** 1784–1859. English poet and essayist.

Hun·te (hōōn′tə). A river rising in southwest-central Lower Saxony, West Germany, and flowing 117 miles northwest, then northeast, to the Weser near Bremen.

hunt·er (hŭn′tər) *n.* 1. One that hunts; especially, a person who hunts game for food or sport, or who captures wild animals. 2. A dog bred or trained for use in hunting. 3. A horse bred or trained for use in hunting, typically a fast, strong jumper.

Hun·ter (hŭn′tər). A river rising in northeast-central New South Wales, Australia, and flowing 300 miles south, then east, to the South Pacific at Newcastle.

hunter's moon. The full moon following the harvest moon.

hunt·ing (hŭn′tĭng) *n.* 1. The sport or activity of pursuing game. 2. *Electricity.* The periodic variation in speed of a synchronous motor with respect to the current.

Hun·ting·don (hŭn′tĭng-dən). Also **Hunts** (hŭnts). A former administrative county of England, now included in **Huntingdon and Peterborough** *(see).*

ă pat/ā pay/âr care/ä father/b bib/ch church/d deed/ĕ pet/ē be/f fife/g gag/h hat/hw which/ĭ pit/ī pie/îr pier/j judge/k kick/l lid, needle/m mum/n no, sudden/ng thing/ŏ pot/ō toe/ô paw, for/oi noise/ou out/ŏŏ took/ōō boot/p pop/r roar/s sauce/sh ship, dish/

Hun·ting·don and Pe·ter·bor·ough (hŭn′tĭng-dən; pē′tər-bûr′ō; pē′tər-bər-ə). A county, 100 square miles in area, of east-central England. Population, 183,710. County seat, Huntingdon-Godmanchester.

hunting leopard. The **cheetah** (*see*).

hunting pink. *Chiefly British.* **1.** The scarlet coat worn by fox-hunting men. **2.** The color of such coats.

Hunt·ing·ton (hŭn′tĭng-tən). A city and commercial and mining center of western West Virginia, on the Ohio River. Population, 84,000.

Hunt·ing·ton (hŭn′tĭng-tən), **Collis Potter.** 1821–1900. American transportation executive; a builder of Central Pacific and Southern Pacific railroads.

Hunt·ing·ton Park (hŭn′tĭng-tən). An industrial suburb of Los Angeles, California. Population, 30,000.

hunting watch. A watch with a hinged metal cover protecting the crystal.

hunt·ress (hŭn′trĭs) *n.* **1.** A woman or female that hunts. **2.** *Rare.* A mare used for hunting.

hunts·man (hŭnts′mən) *n., pl.* **-men** (-mĭn). **1.** A person who hunts; a hunter. **2.** One who manages a pack of foxhounds, harriers, beagles, or the like, and handles them in the hunting field.

Hunts·ville (hŭnts′vĭl). A city of northern Alabama; site of a NASA space-flight center. Population, 72,000.

Hu·on Gulf (hyōō′ŏn′). An inlet of the Solomon Sea, on the eastern coast of New Guinea.

Hu·pei (hōō′pā′; *Chinese* hōō′bĕ′). Also **Hu·peh.** A province, 72,375 square miles in area, of east-central China. Population, 30,790,000. Capital, Wuhan.

hur·dle (hûr′dl) *n.* **1.** A light, portable barrier used in obstacle races, usually consisting of two uprights between which a horizontal bar may be hung at varying heights. **2.** *Often plural.* A race for horses or men in which such barriers must be jumped. **3.** Any obstacle or problem that must be overcome. **4.** *Chiefly British.* A portable section of fencing made of intertwined branches or wattle and used chiefly for folding sheep. **5.** *British.* A frame or sledge formerly used to carry condemned persons to their executions. —*v.* **hurdled, -dling, -dles.** —*tr.* **1.** To jump or leap over (a barrier) in or as if in a race. **2.** To make or surround with hurdles. **3.** To overcome or successfully deal with (an obstacle or problem). —*intr.* To jump over barriers in or as if in a race. [Middle English *hurdel, hirdle,* Old English *hyrdel.* See **kert-** in Appendix.*] —**hur′dler** *n.*

hur·dy-gur·dy (hûr′dē-gûr′dē) *n., pl.* **-dies.** **1.** A medieval instrument shaped like a lute, played by street musicians with a crank that causes a resin-covered wheel to scrape across the strings. **2.** *Informal.* Any musical instrument played by turning a crank, such as a barrel organ. [Probably imitative.]

hurl (hûrl) *v.* **hurled, hurling, hurls.** —*tr.* **1.** To throw with great force; to fling; pitch. **2.** To move or impel vigorously; to thrust. **3.** To throw down; to overthrow. **4.** To exclaim vehemently. —*intr.* To move with great speed, force, or violence; to hurtle. —See Synonyms at **throw.** —*n.* The act of hurling; a forceful pitch or throw. [Middle English *h(o)urlen†,* to be driven with great force, throw, rush on.] —**hurl′er** *n.*

hurl·ing (hûr′lĭng) *n.* An Irish game resembling lacrosse but played with a broad-bladed, netless stick. [From the gerund of HURL.]

hur·ly-bur·ly (hûr′lē-bûr′lē) *n., pl.* **-lies.** Turbulence; commotion; disorder. Also called "hurly." —*adj.* Full of noise or commotion. [Earlier *hurling and burling,* reduplication of *hurling,* tumult, from Middle English, gerund of HURL.]

Hu·ron (hyōōr′ən, -ŏn′) *n., pl.* **Huron** or **-rons.** **1.** A confederation of four tribes of Iroquoian-speaking North American Indians formerly inhabiting the region east of Lake Huron and the St. Lawrence Valley. **2.** A member of any of these tribes. **3.** The Iroquoian language spoken among these tribes. [French, "one who has disheveled hair," boor, from *hure,* disheveled head, from Old French *hure†.*] —**Hu′ron** *adj.*

Hu·ron, Lake (hyōōr′ən, -ŏn′). The second-largest (23,010 square miles) of the Great Lakes, lying between eastern Michigan and southern Ontario, Canada.

hur·rah (hŏō-rä′, -rô′) *interj.* Also **hoo·ray** (-rā′), **hur·ray** (-rā′). Used as an exclamation of pleasure, approval, elation, or victory. —*n.* A shout of "hurrah." —*v.* **hurrahed, -rahing, -rahs.** Also **hoo·ray, hur·ray.** —*tr.* To applaud, cheer, or approve by shouting "hurrah." —*intr.* To shout "hurrah." [Variant of HUZZA.]

hur·ri·cane (hûr′ə-kān′) *n.* A severe tropical cyclone with winds exceeding 75 miles per hour, originating in the tropical regions of the Atlantic Ocean or Caribbean Sea, traveling north, northwest, or northeast from its point of origin, and usually involving heavy rains. See Synonyms at **wind.** [Earlier *furacano, haurachana,* from Spanish *huracan* and Portuguese *furacão,* both from Carib *huracan, furacan.*]

hurricane deck. The upper deck on a passenger steamship of inland waterways.

hurricane lamp. A lamp consisting of a candle or electric bulb covered by a glass chimney.

hur·ried (hûr′ēd) *adj.* **1.** Obliged to move or act rapidly; rushed. **2.** Done in great haste: *a hurried tour.* —**hur′ried·ly** *adv.* —**hur′ried·ness** *n.*

hur·ry (hûr′ē) *v.* **-ried, -rying, -ries.** —*intr.* To move with haste or speed quickly. —*tr.* **1.** To cause to move or act rapidly; hasten: *hurry the children.* **2.** To cause to move or act too quickly, to rush: *hurried into marriage.* **3.** To hasten to completion; expedite. —See Synonyms at **speed.** —*n., pl.* **hurries. 1.** The act of hurrying; hastened progress. **2.** The need or wish

to hurry; a condition of urgency: *Are you in a hurry to leave?* [Probably imitative.]

hur·ry-scur·ry (hûr′ē-skûr′ē) *intr.v.* **-ried, -rying, -ries.** Also **hur·ry-skur·ry.** To move or act with undue hurry and confusion. —*n., pl.* **hurry-scurries.** Also **hur·ry-skur·ry.** Confused haste; agitation; bustle. [Reduplication of HURRY.] —**hur′ry-scur′ry** *adj. & adv.*

Hurst·mon·ceux. See **Herstmonceux.**

hurt (hûrt) *v.* **hurt, hurting, hurts.** —*tr.* **1.** To cause physical damage or pain to; to make suffer; to injure; wound. **2.** To cause to suffer mental or emotional anguish; to distress or offend. **3.** To damage; to harm; impair: *hurt his chances.* —*intr.* **1.** To have a feeling of pain or discomfort: *His leg hurts.* **2.** To cause pain, hardship, or damage: *The tax bill hurts.* —See Synonyms at **injure.** —*n.* **1.** Something that hurts; a pain, injury, or wound. **2.** Mental suffering; anguish. **3.** A wrong; damage; harm. [Middle English *hurten, hirten,* to strike, harm, from Old French *hurter,* from Gallo-Roman *hūrtare†* (unattested).] —**hurt′er** *n.*

hurt·ful (hûrt′fəl) *adj.* Causing hurt or injury; painful; damaging. —**hurt′ful·ly** *adv.* —**hurt′ful·ness** *n.*

hur·tle (hûr′tl) *v.* **-tled, -tling, -tles.** —*intr.* **1.** To move with or as if with great speed and a rushing or crashing noise: *"To come to the river/The brook/hurtles through rainy/woods"* (Denise Levertov). **2.** To collide violently; to crash. —*tr.* **1.** To throw or send forcibly or violently; hurl. [Middle English *hurtlen,* dash one thing against another, collide, frequentative of *hurten,* to strike, HURT.]

hurt·less (hûrt′lĭs) *adj. Archaic.* **1.** Harmless. **2.** Having no injury; unhurt.

Hus, Jan. See **John Huss.**

Hu·sain, Hu·sayn. See **Hussein I.**

hus·band (hŭz′bənd) *n.* **1.** *Abbr.* **h., H.** A man joined to a woman in marriage; a woman's spouse. **2.** *Archaic.* A manager or steward, as of a household or wine cellar. **3.** A prudent and thrifty manager, as of money or expenses. —*tr.v.* **husbanded, -banding, -bands. 1.** To spend or use economically; to budget; to conserve: *husband one's energy.* **2.** *Rare.* To marry. **3.** *Archaic.* To find a husband for. [Middle English *housbonde, hus(e)bonde,* husband, husbandman, Old English *hūsbonda,* master of a household, husband, from Old Norse *hūsbōndi : hūs,* house, from Germanic *hūsam* (unattested), HOUSE + *bōndi,* earlier *bōandi, būandi,* present participle of *bōa, būa,* to dwell (see **bheu-** in Appendix*).]

hus·band·man (hŭz′bənd-mən) *n., pl.* **-men** (-mĭn). One whose occupation is husbandry; a farmer. [Middle English *housbondeman : housbonde,* husbandman, HUSBAND + MAN.]

hus·band·ry (hŭz′bən-drē) *n.* **1. a.** The cultivation of plants or the raising of livestock; farming; agriculture. **b.** The application of scientific principles to a branch of farming, especially animal breeding. **2.** The careful management of resources; conservation. [Middle English *housbondrie : housbonde,* husbandman, HUSBAND + -(E)RY.]

Hu·sein. See **Hussein I.**

Hu·sein ibn-A·li (hōō-sĭn′ ĭb′ən-ă-lē′, hōō-sān′). 1856–1931. First king of the Hejaz (1916–24).

hush (hŭsh) *v.* **hushed, hushing, hushes.** —*tr.* **1.** To cause to be silent; to quiet. **2.** To quell or still; to calm; soothe. **3.** To withhold mention of; suppress; conceal. —*intr.* To be or become silent or still. —*n.* A silence; stillness; quiet. —*adj. Archaic.* Silent; quiet. [Back-formation from earlier *husht* (interjection), from Middle English *huissht.*]

hush-hush (hŭsh′hŭsh′) *adj. Informal.* Secret; confidential; unpublicized.

Hu Shih (hōō′ shœ′). 1891–1962. Nationalist Chinese philosopher, linguist, and diplomat.

hush money. *Informal.* A bribe or payment made to keep something secret.

hush-pup·py (hŭsh′pŭp′ē) *n., pl.* **-pies.** A fried cornmeal fritter, commonly eaten in the South. [It is occasionally used as food for dogs.]

husk (hŭsk) *n.* **1.** The membranous or green outer envelope of many fruits and seeds, as of an ear of corn or a nut. **2.** The shell or outer covering of anything, especially when worthless. —*tr.v.* **husked, husking, husks.** To remove the husk or husks from. [Middle English *husk(e),* probably from Middle Dutch *hūskijn,* of *hūs,* house, from Germanic *hūsam* (unattested), HOUSE.] —**husk′er** *n.*

husking bee. A cornhusking (*see*).

husk·y¹ (hŭs′kē) *adj.* **-ier, -iest. 1.** Hoarse, as from overuse or emotion: *"I listen to her voice which is dark, heavy, husky."* (Anaïs Nin). **2.** Like or resembling a husk. **3.** Full of or containing husks. [Originally, "dry as a husk."] —**husk′i·ly** *adv.* —**husk′i·ness** *n.*

husk·y² (hŭs′kē) *adj.* **-ier, -iest.** *Informal.* Rugged and strong; burly. —*n., pl.* **huskies.** A husky person. [From HUSKY (hoarse).] —**husk′i·ness** *n.*

hus·ky³ (hŭs′kē) *n., pl.* **-kies. 1.** *Sometimes capital* **H.** A dog of a breed developed in Siberia for pulling sleds, having a dense, furry, variously colored coat. Also called "Siberian husky." **2.** A dog of any of several similar breeds of Arctic origin. [Probably a shortened variant of ESKIMO.]

Huss (hŭs), **John.** *Czech* **Jan Hus** (yän′ hōōs′). 1369?–1415. Bohemian religious reformer; tried as heretic and burned at the stake.

hus·sar (hŏō-zär′) *n.* **1.** A horseman of the Hungarian light cavalry that was organized during the 15th century. **2.** A member of a light cavalry regiment having dress uniforms of ultimately Hungarian style, typically with much frogging.

hurdy-gurdy
Eighteenth-century
French painting

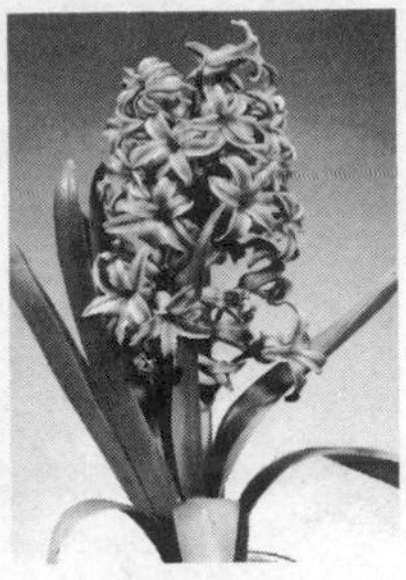

hyacinth
Hyacinthus orientalis

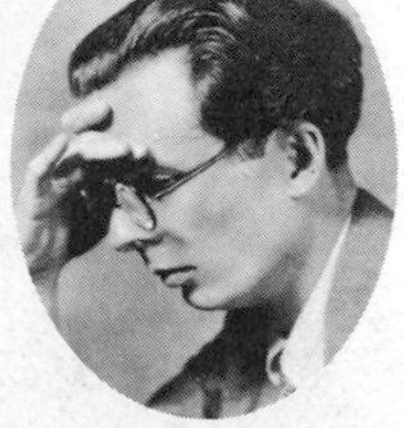

Aldous Huxley

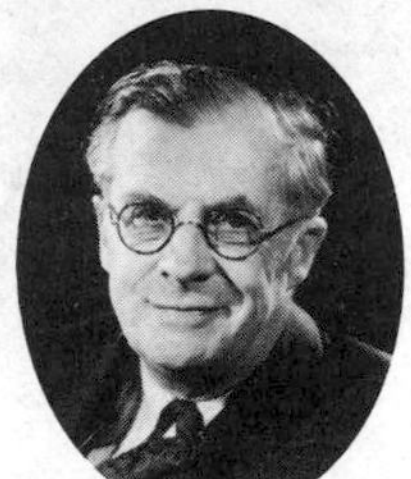

Sir Julian Huxley

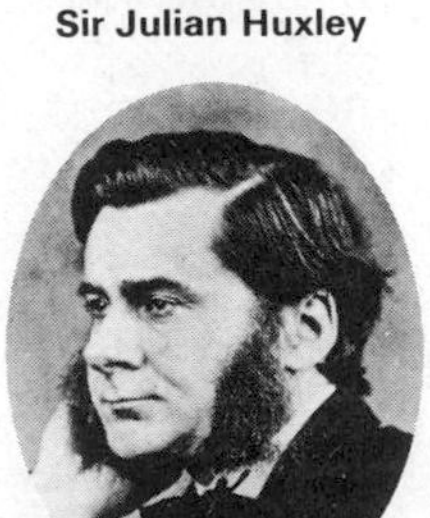

Thomas Huxley

[Hungarian *huszár,* "freebooter," hussar, from Old Serbian *husar, gusar,* from Old Italian *corsaro,* CORSAIR.]

Hus·sein I (ho͝o-sīn′, -sān′). Also **Hu·sain, Hu·sayn, Hu·sein.** Born 1935. King of Jordan (since 1953).

Hus·serl (ho͝os′ərl), **Edmund.** 1859–1938. German philosopher; founder of phenomenology.

Huss·ite (hŭs′īt′, ho͞os′-) *n.* A follower of John Huss. *—adj.* Of or pertaining to John Huss or his religious theories. **—Huss′-it′ism′** (-ĭt′ĭz′əm) *n.*

hus·sy (hŭz′ē, hŭs′ē) *n., pl.* **-sies. 1.** A saucy or flippant girl. **2.** A strumpet; trollop. [Variant of HOUSEWIFE.]

hust·ings (hŭs′tĭngz) *n.* Plural in form, usually used with a singular verb. **1.** *British.* A court formerly held in some English cities, and still held infrequently in London. **2.** *British.* **a.** A platform on which candidates for Parliament formerly stood to address the electors. **b.** The proceedings at a parliamentary election. **3.** Any place where political speeches are made. **4.** Any act or instance of political campaigning. [From Middle English *husting,* an assembly, Old English *hūsting,* from Old Norse *husthing,* "house assembly" : *hūs,* house, from Germanic *hūsam* (unattested), HOUSE + *thing,* assembly (see **tenk-**¹ in Appendix*).]

hus·tle (hŭs′əl) *v.* **-tled, -tling, -tles.** *—tr.* **1.** To jostle or shove roughly. **2.** To usher hurriedly or urgently: *hustle the prisoner onto a plane.* **3.** *Informal.* To speed up; hurry along; dispatch: *He hustled the discussion to a conclusion and left.* **4.** *Slang.* **a.** To obtain (money) in questionable ways: *He hustles a living somehow.* **b.** To sell by high-pressure means. **5.** *Slang.* To induce (someone) to gamble in a game set up against him. *—intr.* **1.** To jostle and push. **2.** *Informal.* To work busily and quickly. **3.** *Slang.* To make money by questionable means. **4.** *Slang.* To solicit customers for or as a prostitute. *—n.* **1.** The act of hustling; a jostling; a pushing. **2.** *Informal.* Activity; business; industry. [Originally to shake back and forth, from Middle Dutch *husselen,* frequentative of *hutsen,* to shake, from (unattested) Germanic *khut-* (probably imitative).] **—hus′tler** *n.*

hut (hŭt) *n.* **1.** A makeshift or crude dwelling or shelter; a shed; shack. **2.** *Military.* A temporary structure for sheltering troops or arms. *—v.* **hutted, hutting, huts.** *—tr.* To shelter or store in a hut. *—intr.* To live or take shelter in a hut. [Old French *hutte,* from Middle High German *hütte,* or Old High German *hutt(e)a.* See **skeu-** in Appendix.*]

hutch (hŭch) *n.* **1.** A box, pen, or coop for small animals, especially rabbits. **2.** A cupboard having drawers for storage and usually open shelves above. **3.** A chest or bin for storage. **4.** A hut. *—tr.v.* **hutched, hutching, hutches.** To store in or as if in a hutch. [Middle English *huche,* chest, from Old French *huche, huge,* from Medieval Latin *hutica*†.]

Hutch·ins (hŭch′ĭnz), **Robert Maynard.** Born 1899. American educator.

Hutch·in·son (hŭch′ĭn-sən), **Anne.** 1591–1643. English religious reformer in America; banished from Massachusetts Bay Colony (1637) to Rhode Island.

Hutch·in·son (hŭch′ĭn-sən), **Thomas.** 1711–1780. British Colonial administrator in America; governor of Massachusetts (1771–74).

hut·ment (hŭt′mənt) *n.* An encampment of huts; especially, a military camp.

Hux·ley (hŭk′slē), **Aldous Leonard.** 1894–1963. English novelist and critic; resident in America; brother of J.S. Huxley and grandson of T.H. Huxley.

Hux·ley (hŭk′slē), Sir **Julian Sorell.** Born 1887. British biologist and author; brother of A.L. Huxley and grandson of T.H. Huxley.

Hux·ley (hŭk′slē), **Thomas Henry.** 1825–1895. British biologist and advocate of Darwinism; grandfather of A.L. Huxley and J.S. Huxley.

Huy·gens (hī′gənz; *Dutch* hœ′gəns), **Christian.** 1629–1695. Dutch physicist and astronomer.

Huygens' principle. *Physics.* The principle that any point on a wavefront may be regarded as the source of a secondary wave and that the position of the wavefront at any time is determined by the envelope at that time of the secondary waves arising from a previous wavefront. [After Christian HUYGENS.]

huz·za (hə-zä′) *n.* Also **huz·zah.** *Archaic.* A shout of encouragement or triumph; a cheer. *—interj.* Also **huz·zah.** *Archaic.* Used to express joy, encouragement, appreciation, or the like. *—v.* **huzzaed, huzzaing, huzzas.** Also **huz·zah.** *—intr.* To shout "huzza"; cheer. *—tr.* To cheer or encourage with shouts of huzza. [Origin unknown.]

H.W. high water.

Hwai (hwī). A river of east-central China, rising on the Hunan-Hopei boundary and flowing 600 miles northeast to Lake Hungtze.

Hwai·nan (hwī′nän′). Formerly **Show·hsien** (shō′shyĕn′). A city of north-central Anhwei, China. Population, 287,000.

Hwai·ning. The former name for **Anking.**

Hwang Ho. The Chinese name for the **Yellow River.**

Hwang·poo (hwäng′po͞o′). Formerly **Whang·poo.** A river rising in southern Kiangsu, China, and flowing 60 miles northeast and north past Shanghai to the Yangtze.

hy·a·cinth (hī′ə-sĭnth) *n.* **1.** Any of several bulbous plants of the genus *Hyacinthus,* native to the Mediterranean region, having narrow leaves and a terminal cluster of variously colored, usually very fragrant flowers; especially, the widely cultivated species *H. orientalis.* **2.** Any of several similar or related plants. **3.** A plant, perhaps a lily, gladiolus, or iris, that, according to Greek mythology, sprang from the blood of the slain Hyacinthus. **4.** Deep purplish blue to vivid violet. See **color. 5.** A reddish or cinnamon-colored variety of transparent zircon, used as a gemstone. Also called "jacinth." **6.** A blue semiprecious stone known in antiquity, possibly aquamarine. [Latin *hyacinthus,* from Greek *huakinthos,* wild hyacinth (connected by folk etymology with HYACINTHUS), of Mediterranean origin.] **—hy′-a·cin′thine** (-sĭn′thĭn, -thīn) *adj.*

hyacinth bean. A twining vine, *Dolichos lablab,* of the Old World tropics, having purple or white flowers and edible pods and seeds.

Hy·a·cin·thus (hī′ə-sĭn′thəs). *Greek Mythology.* A beautiful youth loved but accidentally killed by Apollo, from whose blood Apollo caused the hyacinth to grow.

Hy·a·des (hī′ə-dēz′) *pl.n.* Also **Hy·ads** (-ădz). **1.** *Greek Mythology.* The five daughters of Atlas and sisters of the Pleiades, placed by Zeus in the heavens. **2.** *Astronomy.* An asterism of five stars in the constellation Taurus, supposed by ancient astronomers to indicate rain when they rose with the sun.

hy·ae·na. Variant of **hyena.**

hy·a·lin (hī′ə-lĭn) *n.* Also **hy·a·line** (-lĭn, -līn′). **1.** *Physiology.* The uniform matrix of hyaline cartilage. **2.** *Pathology.* A transparent substance occurring in certain degenerative skin conditions. [Greek *hualos,* glass (see **hyaline**) + -IN.]

hy·a·line (hī′ə-lĭn, -līn′) *adj.* Resembling glass; glassy; translucent or transparent. *—n.* **1.** A glassy or transparent appearance. **2.** Something having such an appearance, as a calm lake. **3.** Variant of **hyalin.** [Late Latin *hyalinus,* from Greek *hualinos,* of crystal or glass, from *hualos, huelos*†, crystalline stone, glass.]

hyaline cartilage. Cartilage that has a glassy, translucent appearance and a bluish color, which in the adult is composed of cells in a seemingly homogeneous, translucent matrix, as in joints, and which in the fetus forms most of the skeleton.

hy·a·lite (hī′ə-līt′) *n.* A clear, colorless opal. [German *Hyalit,* from Greek *hualos,* glass, crystal. See **hyaline.**]

hy·a·loid (hī′ə-loid′) *adj.* Glassy or transparent in appearance; hyaline. [Greek *hualoeidēs* : *hualos,* glass (see **hyaline**) + -OID.]

hy·a·lo·plasm (hī′ə-lō-plăz′əm) *n.* The clear, fluid portion of cytoplasm, as distinguished from included granular and netlike components. [German *Hyaloplasma* : Greek *hualos,* crystal (see **hyaline**) + PLASM.]

Hy·att (hī′ət), **John Wesley.** 1837–1920. American inventor.

hy·brid (hī′brĭd) *n. Abbr.* **hyb. 1.** *Genetics.* The offspring of genetically dissimilar parents or stock; especially, the offspring produced by breeding plants or animals of different varieties, species, or races. **2.** Something of mixed origin or composition. **3.** A word whose elements are derived from different languages. [Latin *hybrida, hibrida*†, hybrid, mongrel.] **—hy′brid** *adj.* **—hy′brid·ism′** *n.* **—hy·brid′i·ty** *n.*

hy·brid·ize (hī′brĭ-dīz′) *v.* **-ized, -izing, -izes.** *—tr.* To cause to produce hybrids; crossbreed. *—intr.* To produce hybrids. **—hy′brid·i·za′tion** *n.* **—hy′brid·iz′er** *n.*

hybrid vigor. Heterosis *(see).*

hy·da·tid (hī′də-tĭd) *n.* **1.** A cyst formed as a result of infestation by a tapeworm, *Echinococcus granulosus,* in a larval stage. Also called "hydatid cyst." **2.** The encysted larva of *E. granulosus.* Also called "hydatid cyst." [Greek *hudatis* (stem *hudatid-*), watery vesicle, hydatid, from *hudōr* (stem *hudat-*), water. See **wed-**¹ in Appendix.*] **—hy′da·tid** *adj.*

Hyde. See **Jekyll and Hyde.**

Hyde, Edward. See First Earl of **Clarendon.**

Hyde Park (hīd). **1.** A public park occupying 361 acres in central London, England. **2.** A village of southeastern New York, on the Hudson River; birthplace of President Franklin D. Roosevelt. Population, 2,000.

Hy·der·a·bad (hī′dər-ə-băd′, -bäd′). Also **Hai·dar·a·bad. 1.** A former state of India, incorporated in 1956 into the states of Andhra Pradesh, Bombay, and Mysore. **2.** The capital of Andhra Pradesh, Republic of India, located in the northwestern part of the state. Population, 1,293,000. **3.** A city and handicraft center of southern West Pakistan. Population, 435,000.

hy·dra¹ (hī′drə) *n., pl.* **-dras** or **-drae** (-drē′). Any of various small, freshwater polyps of the genus *Hydra* and related genera, having a naked, cylindrical body and an oral opening surrounded by tentacles. [New Latin *Hydra,* HYDRA (so called because polyps may reproduce themselves from parts cut off).]

hy·dra² (hī′drə) *n.* A multifarious source of destruction that cannot be eradicated by a single attempt. [After HYDRA.]

Hy·dra¹ (hī′drə). *Greek Mythology.* A many-headed monster, which, growing back two heads for each one cut off, was finally slain by Hercules who cauterized each neck after severing its head. [Middle English *Ydre,* from Old French, from Latin *Hydra,* from Greek *Hudra,* from *hudra,* water serpent. See **wed-**¹ in Appendix.*]

Hy·dra² (hī′drə) *n.* A constellation in the equatorial region of the southern sky near Cancer, Libra, and Centaurus. Also called the "Snake." [After HYDRA.]

hy·dran·ge·a (hī-drān′jē-ə, -jə) *n.* Any of various shrubs or trees of the genus *Hydrangea,* having large, flat-topped or rounded clusters of white, pink, or blue flowers. [New Latin, "water vessel" (from the cuplike shape of the seed pod) : HYDR(O)- + Greek *angos,* vessel, pitcher (see **angiology**).]

hy·drant (hī′drənt) *n.* An outlet from a water main consisting of an upright pipe with one or more nozzles or spouts. Also called "fire hydrant." [HYDR(O)- + -ANT.]

hy·dranth (hī′drănth′) *n.* The oral opening and tentacles of a feeding polyp in a hydroid colony. [HYDR(O)- + Greek *anthos,* blossom, flower (see **andh-** in Appendix*).]

hy·drar·gy·rism (hī-drär′jə-rĭz′əm) *n.* **Mercurialism** *(see).*

ă pat/ā pay/âr care/ä father/b bib/ch church/d deed/ĕ pet/ē be/f fife/g gag/h hat/hw which/ĭ pit/ī pie/îr pier/j judge/k kick/l lid, needle/m mum/n no, sudden/ng thing/ŏ pot/ō toe/ô paw, for/oi noise/ou out/o͝o took/o͞o boot/p pop/r roar/s sauce/sh ship, dish/

[From New Latin *hydrargyrum,* from Latin *hydrargyrus,* from Greek *hudrarguros,* "silver water" : HYDR(O)- + *aguros,* silver (see **arg-** in Appendix*).]

hy·dras·tine (hī-drăs′tēn′, -tĭn) *n.* A poisonous white alkaloid, $C_{21}H_{21}NO_6$, obtained from the root of the goldenseal, *Hydrastis canadensis,* and used locally to treat catarrhal inflammation of mucous membranes. [From New Latin *Hydrastis* (plant genus), probably from HYDR(O)-.]

hy·drate (hī′drāt′) *n.* A compound containing water combined in a definite ratio, the water being retained or regarded as being retained in its molecular state. —*v.* **hydrated, -drating, -drates.** —*tr.* To combine with water; especially, to form a hydrate. —*intr.* To become a hydrate. [HYDR(O)- + -ATE.] —**hy·dra′tion** *n.* —**hy′dra′tor** (-drā′tər) *n.*

hy·drat·ed (hī′drā′tĭd) *adj.* Chemically combined with water; especially, existing in the form of a hydrate.

hy·drau·lic (hī-drô′lĭk) *adj.* **1.** Of, involving, moved, or operated by a fluid, especially water, under pressure. **2.** Setting and hardening under water, as Portland cement. **3.** Of or pertaining to hydraulics. [Latin *hydraulicus,* from Greek *hudraulis,* a water organ invented by Ctesibius in the second century B.C. : HYDRO- + *aulos,* tube, pipe (see **aulo-** in Appendix*).] —**hy·drau′li·cal·ly** *adv.*

hydraulic brake. A brake in which the braking force is transmitted to the braking surface by a compressed fluid.

hydraulic cement. A cement capable of solidifying under water. See **Portland cement.**

hydraulic press. A machine in which a large force is exerted on the larger of two pistons in a pair of hydraulically coupled cylinders by means of a relatively small force applied to the smaller piston.

hydraulic ram. **1.** A water pump in which the downward flow of naturally running water is intermittently halted by a valve so that the flow is forced upward through an open pipe into a reservoir. **2.** The large output piston of a hydraulic press.

hy·drau·lics (hī-drô′lĭks) *n.* Plural in form, used with a singular verb. The physical science and technology of the static and dynamic behavior of fluids.

hy·dra·zine (hī′drə-zēn′, -zĭn) *n.* A colorless, fuming, corrosive, hygroscopic liquid, H_2NNH_2, used in jet and rocket fuels. [HYDR(O)- + AZ(O)- + -INE.]

hy·dric (hī′drĭk) *adj.* **1.** Of, containing, or pertaining to hydrogen. **2.** Pertaining to, characterized by, or requiring considerable moisture. [HYDR(O)- + -IC.]

hy·dride (hī′drīd′) *n.* A compound of hydrogen with another, more electropositive element or group. [HYDR(O)- + -IDE.]

hy·dri·od·ic acid (hī′drē-ŏd′ĭk). A clear, colorless or pale-yellow aqueous solution of hydrogen iodide, HI, that is a strong acid and reducing agent. [HYDR(O)- + -IODIC ACID.]

hydro–, hydr–. Indicates: **1.** Water; for example, **hydrous, hydroelectric.** **2.** Liquid; for example, **hydrometallurgy, hydrostatic.** **3.** Composed of or combined with hydrogen; for example, **hydrochloride, hydrosulfide.** **4.** Hydroid; for example, **hydrozoan.** [From Greek *hudōr,* water. See **wed-**[1] in Appendix.*]

hy·dro·bro·mic acid (hī′drə-brō′mĭk). A clear, colorless or faintly yellow, highly acidic and corrosive aqueous solution of hydrogen bromide, HBr, used in the manufacture of bromides.

hy·dro·car·bon (hī′drə-kär′bən) *n.* Any of numerous organic compounds, such as benzene and methane, that contain only carbon and hydrogen.

hy·dro·cele (hī′drə-sēl′) *n.* A pathological accumulation of serous fluid in a bodily cavity, especially in the testes. [Latin *hydrocēlē,* from Greek *hudrokēlē* : HYDRO- + -CELE.]

hy·dro·ceph·a·lus (hī′drō-sĕf′ə-ləs) *n.* Also **hy·dro·ceph·a·ly** (-lē). A usually congenital condition in which an abnormal accumulation of fluid in the cerebral ventricles causes enlargement of the skull and compression of the brain. [Late Latin, from Greek *hudrokephalon* : HYDRO- + *kephalē,* head (see **ghebhel-** in Appendix*).] —**hy′dro·ce·phal′ic** (-sə-făl′ĭk), **hy′dro·ceph′a·loid′, hy′dro·ceph′a·lous** *adj.*

hy·dro·chlo·ric acid (hī′drə-klôr′ĭk, -klōr′ĭk). A clear, colorless, fuming, poisonous, highly acidic, aqueous solution of hydrogen chloride, HCl, used in petroleum production, as a chemical intermediate, in ore reduction, food processing, pickling, and metal cleaning.

hy·dro·chlo·ride (hī′drə-klôr′īd′, -klōr′īd′) *n.* A compound resulting or regarded as resulting from the reaction of hydrochloric acid with an organic base.

hy·dro·cor·al (hī′drə-kôr′əl, -kŏr′əl) *n.* Any of various colonial marine hydrozoans of the order Hydrocorallinae, having a limestone skeleton and thus resembling the true corals.

hy·dro·cor·ti·sone (hī′drō-kôr′tə-sōn′, -zōn′) *n.* A bitter, crystalline hormone, $C_2H_{30}O_5$, derived from the adrenal cortex, and having activity and medical uses similar to those of **cortisone** *(see).*

hy·dro·cy·an·ic acid (hī′drō-sī-ăn′ĭk). A colorless, volatile, extremely toxic, flammable, aqueous solution of hydrogen cyanide, HCN, used in the manufacture of dyes, fumigants, and plastics. Also called "prussic acid," "hydrogen cyanide."

hy·dro·dy·nam·ic (hī′drō-dī-năm′ĭk) *adj.* **1.** Of or pertaining to hydrodynamics. **2.** Of, pertaining to, or operated by the force of liquid in motion. —**hy′dro·dy·nam′i·cal** *adj.* —**hy′dro·dy·nam′i·cal·ly** *adv.*

hy·dro·dy·nam·ics (hī′drō-dī-năm′ĭks) *n.* Plural in form, used with a singular verb. The dynamics of fluids, especially incompressible fluids, in motion.

hy·dro·e·lec·tric (hī′drō-ĭ-lĕk′trĭk) *adj.* **1.** Generating electricity by conversion of the energy of running water. **2.** Using or involving electricity so generated. —**hy′dro·e·lec′tric′i·ty** (-ĭ-lĕk′-trĭs′ə-tē) *n.*

hy·dro·flu·or·ic acid (hī′drō-flōō-ôr′ĭk, -ŏr′ĭk, -flŏŏr′ĭk). A colorless, fuming, corrosive, dangerously poisonous aqueous solution of hydrogen fluoride, HF, used to etch or polish glass, pickle certain metals, and clean masonry.

hy·dro·foil (hī′drə-foil′) *n.* **1.** One of a set of blades attached to the hull of a boat and aligned in the water at a small angle to the horizontal so that when the boat is in motion the fluid striking each blade's underside creates a high-pressure region below the blade, low pressure above it, and a resultant lift that raises the craft out of the water for efficient high-speed operation. **2.** A boat equipped with hydrofoils. In this sense, also called "hydroplane." [HYDRO- + FOIL.]

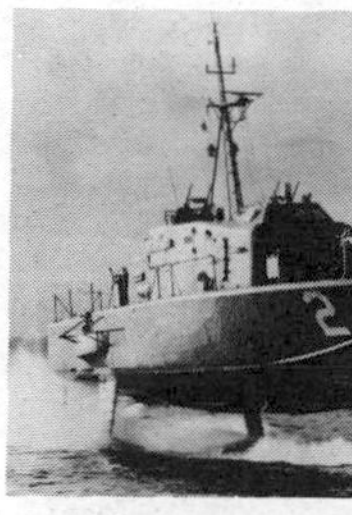

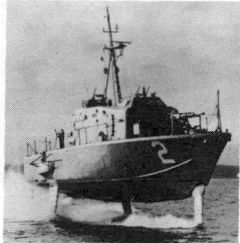

hydrofoil
Water-jet propelled hydrofoil gunboat

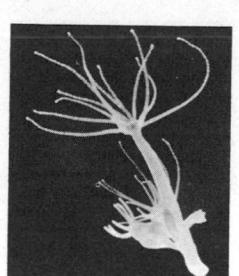

hy·dro·gen (hī′drə-jən) *n. Symbol* **H** A colorless, highly flammable gaseous element, the lightest of all gases and the most abundant element in the universe, used in the production of synthetic ammonia and methanol, in petroleum refining, hydrogenation of organic materials, as a reducing atmosphere, in oxyhydrogen torches, and in rocket fuels. Atomic number 1, atomic weight 1.00797, melting point −259.14°C, boiling point −252.5°C, density 0.08988 gram per liter, valence 1. [French *hydrogène,* "water generating" (it forms water when oxidized) : HYDRO- + -GEN.] —**hy·drog′e·nous** (-drŏj′ə-nəs) *adj.*

hy·dro·gen·ate (hī′drə-jə-nāt′, hī-drŏj′ə-) *tr.v.* **-ated, -ating, -ates.** To combine with or subject to the action of hydrogen; especially, to combine (an unsaturated compound) with hydrogen. —**hy′dro·gen·a′tion** *n.* —**hy′dro·gen·a′tor** (-jə-nā′tər) *n.*

hydrogen bomb. An explosive weapon of great destructive power derived from the fusion of nuclei of various hydrogen isotopes in the formation of helium nuclei. Also called "H-bomb," "fusion bomb."

hydrogen bond. An essentially ionic chemical bond between a strongly electronegative atom and a hydrogen atom already bonded to another strongly electronegative atom.

hydrogen bromide. An irritating colorless gas, HBr, used in the manufacture of barbiturates and synthetic hormones.

hydrogen chloride. A colorless, fuming, corrosive, suffocating gas, HCl, used in the manufacture of plastics.

hydrogen fluoride. A colorless, fuming, mobile, corrosive liquid, or a highly soluble corrosive gas, HF, used in the manufacture of hydrofluoric acid, as a reagent, catalyst, and fluorinating agent, and in the refining of uranium and the preparation of many fluorine compounds.

hydrogen iodide. A corrosive, colorless, suffocating gas, HI, used to manufacture hydriodic acid.

hydrogen ion. The positively charged ion of hydrogen, H^+, formed by removal of the electron from atomic hydrogen.

hy·dro·gen·ol·y·sis (hī′drō-jĭ-nŏl′ĭ sĭs) *n.* The breaking of a chemical bond in an organic molecule with the simultaneous addition of a hydrogen atom to each of the resulting molecular fragments. [HYDROGEN + -LYSIS.]

hydrogen peroxide. A colorless, heavy, strongly oxidizing liquid, H_2O_2, an essentially unstable compound, capable of reacting explosively with combustibles, and used principally in aqueous solution as an antiseptic, bleaching agent, oxidizing agent, and laboratory reagent.

hydrogen sulfide. A colorless, flammable, poisonous compound, H_2S, having a characteristic rotten-egg odor, and used as a precipitator, purifier, and reagent.

hy·drog·ra·phy (hī-drŏg′rə-fē) *n., pl.* **-phies.** **1.** The scientific description and analysis of the physical conditions, boundaries, flow, and related characteristics of oceans, lakes, rivers, and other surface waters. **2.** The mapping of such bodies of water. **3.** A book on this subject. [Old French *hydrographie* : HYDRO- + -GRAPHY.] —**hy·drog′ra·pher** *n.* —**hy′dro·graph′ic** (hī′drə-grăf′ĭk) *adj.* —**hy′dro·graph′i·cal·ly** *adv.*

hy·droid (hī′droid′) *n.* **1.** Any of numerous characteristically colonial hydrozoan coelenterates having a polyp rather than a medusoid form as the dominant stage of the life cycle. **2.** The asexual polyp in the life cycle of any hydrozoan. —*adj.* Of, pertaining to, or characteristic of a hydroid. [HYDR(A) (genus name) + -OID.]

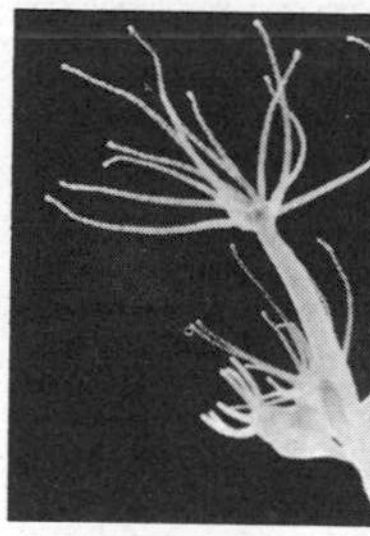

hydra[1]
Hydra with buds

hy·dro·ki·net·ic (hī′drō-kĭ-nĕt′ĭk) *adj.* Also **hy·dro·ki·net·i·cal** (-ĭ-kəl). **1.** Of or pertaining to hydrokinetics. **2.** Of or pertaining to the kinetic energy and motion of fluids.

hy·dro·ki·net·ics (hī′drō-kĭ-nĕt′ĭks, -kī-nĕt′ĭks) *n.* Plural in form, used with a singular verb. The kinetics of fluids, especially incompressible fluids, in motion.

hy·drol·o·gy (hī-drŏl′ə-jē) *n.* The scientific study of the properties, distribution, and effects of water on the earth's surface, in the soil and underlying rocks, and in the atmosphere. [New Latin *hydrologia* : HYDRO- + -LOGY.] —**hy′dro·log′ic** (hī′drə-lŏj′ĭk), **hy′dro·log′i·cal** *adj.* —**hy′dro·log′i·cal·ly** *adv.* —**hy·drol′o·gist** *n.*

hy·drol·y·sate (hī-drŏl′ə-sāt′) *n.* A product of hydrolysis. [HYDROLYS(IS) + -ATE.]

hy·drol·y·sis (hī-drŏl′ə-sĭs) *n.* Decomposition of a chemical compound by reaction with water, such as the dissociation of a dissolved salt or the catalytic conversion of glucose to starch. [HYDRO- + -LYSIS.] —**hy′dro·ly′tic** (hī′drə-lĭt′ĭk) *adj.* —**hy′dro·lyte′** (hī′drə-līt′) *n.*

hy·dro·lyze (hī′drə-līz′) *v.* **-lyzed, -lyzing, -lyzes.** —*tr.* To subject to hydrolysis. —*intr.* To undergo hydrolysis. [From HYDROLYSIS.] —**hy′dro·liz′a·ble** *adj.* —**hy′dro·ly·za′tion** *n.*

hy·dro·man·cy (hī′drə-măn′sē) *n.* Divination by water. [Middle English *ydromancy,* from Old French *hydromancie,* from Latin *hydromantīa,* from Greek *hydromanteia* (unattested) : HYDRO- + -MANCY.] —**hy′dro·manc′er** *n.* —**hy′dro·man′tic** *adj.*

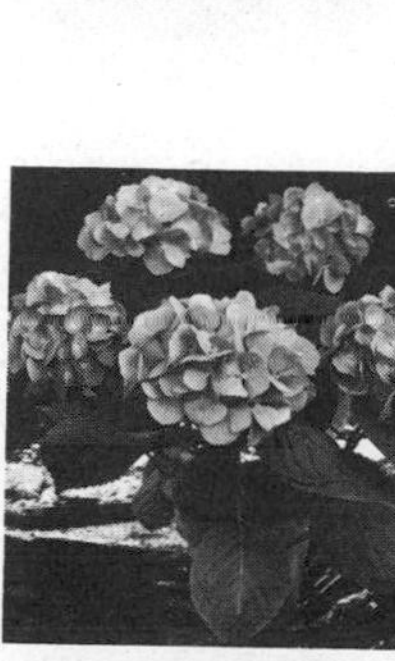

hydrangea
Hydrangea macrophylla

t tight/th thin, path/*th* this, bathe/u cut/ûr urge/v valve/w with/y yes/z zebra, size/zh vision/ə about, item, edible, gallop, circus/
à *Fr.* ami/œ *Fr.* feu, *Ger.* schön/ü *Fr.* tu, *Ger.* über/KH *Ger.* ich, *Scot.* loch/N *Fr.* bon. ***Follows main vocabulary.** †**Of obscure origin.**

hy·dro·me·du·sa (hī′drō-mə-dōō′sə, -dyōō′sə) *n., pl.* **-sas** or **-sae** (-sē′). *Rare.* A hydrozoan in its medusoid stage.

hy·dro·mel (hī′drə-měl′) *n.* A liquor composed of honey and water that, after fermentation, is called mead. [Middle English *ydromel*, from Old French, from Late Latin *hydromel*, from Latin *hydromeli*, from Greek *hudromeli* : HYDRO- + *meli*, honey (see melit- in Appendix*).]

hy·dro·met·al·lur·gy (hī′drō-mĕt′l-ûr′jē) *n.* The separation of metal from ores and ore concentrates by chemical reactions in aqueous solution, such as leaching, extraction, and precipitation. —**hy′dro·met′al·lur′gi·cal** *adj.*

hy·dro·me·te·or (hī′drō-mē′tē-ər) *n.* A precipitation body, such as rain, snow, sleet, or hail, derived from the condensation of water in the atmosphere.

hy·dro·me·te·or·ol·o·gy (hī′drō-mē′tē-ə-rŏl′ə-jē) *n.* The meteorology of the occurrence, motion, and changes of state of atmospheric water.

hy·drom·e·ter (hī-drŏm′ə-tər) *n.* An instrument used to determine specific gravity; especially, a sealed, graduated tube, weighted at one end, that sinks in a fluid to a depth used as a measure of the fluid's specific gravity. [HYDRO- + METER.] —**hy′dro·met′ric** (hī′drə-mĕt′rĭk), **hy′dro·met′ri·cal** *adj.* —**hy′dro·met′ri·cal·ly** *adv.* —**hy·drom′e·try** *n.*

hy·dro·ni·um (hī-drō′nē-əm) *n.* A hydrated hydrogen ion, H_3O^+. Also called "hydronium ion." [HYDR(O)- + (AMM)O-NIUM.]

hy·drop·a·thy (hī-drŏp′ə-thē) *n.* The therapeutic use of water. [HYDRO- + -PATHY.] —**hy′dro·path′ic** (hī′drə-păth′ĭk), **hy′dro·path′i·cal** *adj.* —**hy·drop′a·thist, hy′dro·path′** *n.*

hy·dro·phane (hī′drə-fān′) *n.* An opal that is almost opaque when dry, but transparent when wet. [HYDRO- + -PHANE.] —**hy·droph′a·nous** (hī-drŏf′ə-nəs) *adj.*

hy·dro·phil·ic (hī′drə-fĭl′ĭk) *adj.* Having an affinity for, absorbing, wetting smoothly with, tending to combine with, or capable of dissolving in water. [From New Latin *hydrophilus*, HYDROPHILOUS.] —**hy′dro·phile′** (hī′drə-fīl′) *n.*

hy·droph·i·lous (hī-drŏf′ə-ləs) *adj. Botany.* Growing or thriving in water. [New Latin *hydrophilus* : HYDRO- + -PHILOUS.] —**hy·droph′i·ly** *n.*

hy·dro·pho·bi·a (hī′drə-fō′bē-ə) *n.* 1. Fear of water. 2. *Pathology.* Rabies *(see).* [Late Latin, from Greek *hudrophobia* : HYDRO- + -PHOBIA.]

hy·dro·phob·ic (hī′drə-fō′bĭk, -fŏb′ĭk) *adj.* 1. Antagonistic to, shedding, tending not to combine with, or incapable of dissolving in water. 2. Of or exhibiting hydrophobia.

hy·dro·phone (hī′drə-fōn′) *n.* An electrical instrument for detecting or monitoring sound under water. [HYDRO- + -PHONE.]

hy·dro·phyte (hī′drə-fīt′) *n.* A plant that grows in and is adapted to an aquatic or very wet environment. Compare **mesophyte, xerophyte.** [HYDRO- + -PHYTE.] —**hy′dro·phyt′ic** (-fĭt′ĭk) *adj.*

hy·dro·plane (hī′drə-plān′) *n.* 1. A seaplane. 2. A motorboat designed so that the prow and much of the hull lift out of the water and skim the surface at high speeds. 3. A hydrofoil *(see).* 4. A horizontal rudder on a submarine. —*intr.v.* **hydroplaned, -planing, -planes.** 1. To drive or ride in a hydroplane. 2. To skim along on the surface of the water.

hy·dro·pon·ics (hī′drə-pŏn′ĭks) *n.* Plural in form, used with a singular verb. The cultivation of plants in water containing dissolved inorganic nutrients, rather than in soil. Sometimes called "aquiculture." [HYDRO- + (GEO)PONICS.] —**hy′dro·pon′ic** *adj.* —**hy′dro·pon′i·cal·ly** *adv.*

hy·dro·qui·none (hī′drō-kwĭ-nōn′, -kwĭn′ōn′) *n.* Also **hy·dro·qui·nol** (-kwĭn′ōl′, -ōl′). A white, crystalline compound, $C_6H_4(OH)_2$, used as a photographic developer, antioxidant, stabilizer, and reagent.

hy·dro·scope (hī′drə-skōp′) *n.* An optical device used for viewing objects much below the surface of water. [HYDRO- + -SCOPE.] —**hy′dro·scop′ic** (-skŏp′ĭk) *adj.*

hy·dro·sol (hī′drə-sŏl′, -sōl′) *n.* A sol with water as the dispersing medium. [HYDRO- + SOL(UTION).]

hy·dro·sphere (hī′drə-sfîr′) *n.* The waters of the earth distinguished from the lithosphere and the atmosphere.

hy·dro·stat·ic (hī′drə-stăt′ĭk) *adj.* Also **hy·dro·stat·i·cal** (-ĭ-kəl). Of or pertaining to hydrostatics. —**hy′dro·stat′i·cal·ly** *adv.*

hy·dro·stat·ics (hī′drə-stăt′ĭks) *n.* Plural in form, used with a singular verb. The statics of fluids, especially incompressible fluids.

hy·dro·sul·fate (hī′drə-sŭl′fāt′) *n.* Also **hy·dro·sul·phate.** A salt formed by the union of sulfuric acid with an alkaloid or other organic base.

hy·dro·sul·fide (hī′drə-sŭl′fīd′) *n.* A chemical compound derived from hydrogen sulfide by replacement of one of the hydrogen atoms with a basic radical or base.

hy·dro·sul·fite (hī′drə-sŭl′fīt′) *n.* 1. A salt of hyposulfurous acid. 2. A bleaching agent, **sodium hydrosulfite** *(see).*

hy·dro·sul·fu·rous acid (hī′drō-sŭl-fyŏŏr′əs, -sŭl′fər-əs). Hyposulfurous acid *(see).*

hy·dro·tax·is (hī′drō-tăk′sĭs) *n. Biology.* Movement of an organism in response to moisture. [New Latin : HYDRO- + -TAXIS.] —**hy′dro·tac′tic** (-tăk′tĭk) *adj.*

hy·dro·ther·a·peu·tics (hī′drō-thĕr′ə-pyōō′tĭks) *n.* Plural in form, used with a singular verb. Hydrotherapy. —**hy′dro·ther′a·peu′tic** *adj.*

hy·dro·ther·a·py (hī′drō-thĕr′ə-pē) *n., pl.* **-pies.** The medical use of water in the treatment of certain diseases.

hy·dro·ther·mal (hī′drō-thûr′məl) *adj.* 1. Of or relating to hot water. 2. *Geology.* a. Of or relating to hot magmatic emanations that are rich in water. b. Of or relating to the rocks, ore

deposits, and springs produced by such emanations. —**hy′dro·ther′mal·ly** *adv.*

hy·dro·tho·rax (hī′drō-thôr′ăks′, -thōr′ăks′) *n.* The presence of serous fluid from the blood in one or both pleural cavities, often associated with cardiac failure.

hy·drot·ro·pism (hī-drŏt′rə-pĭz′əm) *n. Biology.* Growth or movement of an organism in response to water. [HYDRO- + -TROPISM.] —**hy′dro·trop′ic** (hī′drə-trŏp′ĭk) *adj.* —**hy′dro·trop′i·cal·ly** *adv.*

hy·drous (hī′drəs) *adj.* Containing water, especially that of crystallization or hydration. [HYDR(O)- + -OUS.]

hy·drox·ide (hī-drŏk′sīd′) *n.* A chemical compound consisting of an element or radical containing a hydroxyl group. [HYDR(O)- + OXIDE.]

hydroxide ion. The ion OH^-, characteristic of basic hydroxides. Also called "hydroxyl ion."

hy·drox·y (hī-drŏk′sē) *adj.* Containing the hydroxyl group: *a hydroxy acid.* [From HYDROXYL.]

hy·drox·yl (hī-drŏk′sĭl) *n.* The univalent radical or group, OH, characteristic of bases, certain acids, phenols, alcohols, carboxylic and sulfonic acids, and amphoteric compounds. [HYDR(O)- + OX(YGEN) + -YL.]

hy·drox·yl·a·mine (hī-drŏk′sĭl-ə-mēn′, -ăm′ən) *n.* A colorless, crystalline compound, NH_2OH, explosive when heated above 130°C, that is used as a reducing agent and in organic synthesis.

hy·dro·zo·an (hī′drə-zō′ən) *n.* Any of numerous coelenterates of the class Hydrozoa, which includes the hydroids, hydrocorals, and siphonophores. —*adj.* Of, pertaining to, or belonging to the class Hydrozoa. [New Latin *Hydrozoa* : HYDRO- + -ZOAN.] —**hy′dro·zo′an** *adj.*

Hy·drus (hī′drəs) *n.* A constellation in the Southern Hemisphere near Tucana and Mensa. [Latin, "water serpent," from Greek *hudros.* See wed-¹ in Appendix.*]

hy·e·na (hī-ē′nə) *n.* Also **hy·ae·na.** Any of several carnivorous mammals of the genera *Hyaena* or *Crocuta* of Africa and Asia, having powerful jaws, relatively short hind limbs, and coarse hair. [Middle English *hyene*, from Latin *hyaena*, from Greek *huaina*, from *hus*, swine. See su-¹ in Appendix.*]

Hy·ères (ē-âr′). French **Hyères** (yâr′). A city and resort center on the southeastern coast of France. Population, 18,000.

hy·e·tal (hī′ə-təl) *adj.* Of or relating to rain. [From Greek *huetos*, rain, a heavy shower. See seu-⁴ in Appendix.*]

Hy·ge·ia (hī-jē′ə). *Greek Mythology.* The goddess of health. [Greek *Hugieia*, from *hugieia*, health, from *hugiēs*, healthy. See gwei- in Appendix.*]

hy·giene (hī′jēn′) *n.* The science of health and the prevention of disease. Also *rare* "hygienics." [French *hygiène*, earlier *hygiaine*, from New Latin *hygieina*, from Greek *hugieinē*, feminine of *hugieinos*, healthful, from *hugiēs*, healthy. See gwei- in Appendix.*] —**hy·gien′ist** (-jěn′ĭst) *n.*

hy·gi·en·ic (hī′jē-ěn′ĭk) *adj.* 1. Of or pertaining to hygiene. 2. Tending to promote or preserve health. 3. Sanitary. —**hy′gi·en′i·cal·ly** *adv.*

hygro–. Indicates wet, moist, or moisture; for example, **hygrograph.** [From Greek *hugros*, wet, moist. See wegw- in Appendix.*]

hy·gro·graph (hī′grə-grăf′, -gräf′) *n.* An automatic hygrometer that records variations in atmospheric humidity. [HYGRO- + -GRAPH.]

hy·grom·e·ter (hī-grŏm′ə-tər) *n.* Any of several instruments that measure atmospheric humidity. [HYGRO- + -METER.] —**hy′gro·met′ric** (hī′grə-mĕt′rĭk) *adj.* —**hy·grom′e·try** *n.*

hy·gro·scope (hī′grə-skōp′) *n.* An instrument that measures changes in atmospheric moisture. [HYGRO- + -SCOPE.]

hy·gro·scop·ic (hī′grə-skŏp′ĭk) *adj.* Readily absorbing moisture, as from the atmosphere. [HYGROSCOP(E) + -IC.] —**hy′gro·scop′i·cal·ly** *adv.* —**hy′gro·sco·pic′i·ty** (-skō-pĭs′ə-tē) *n.*

hy·lo·zo·ism (hī′lə-zō′ĭz′əm) *n.* The philosophical doctrine that life is a property or derivative of matter, that life and matter are inseparable, or that matter possesses a spiritual component. [Greek *hulē*, wood (see hulē in Appendix*) + ZO(O)- + -ISM.] —**hy′lo·zo′ic** *adj.* —**hy′lo·zo′ist** *n.*

hy·men (hī′mən) *n.* A membranous fold of tissue partly or completely occluding the vaginal external orifice. [Latin *hymēn*, from Greek *humēn*, membrane. See syū- in Appendix.*] —**hy′men·al** *adj.*

Hy·men (hī′mən). *Greek Mythology.* The god of marriage. [Latin, from Greek *Humēn*†.]

hy·me·ne·al (hī′mə-nē′əl) *adj.* Of or pertaining to a wedding or marriage. —*n.* A wedding song or poem. [From Latin *hymenaeus*, from Greek *humēnaios*, bridal song, wedding, from *Humēn*, HYMEN.]

hy·me·ni·um (hī-mē′nē-əm) *n., pl.* **-nia** (-nē-ə) or **-ums.** The spore-bearing layer of the fruiting body of certain fungi, containing asci or basidia. [New Latin, from HYMEN.]

hy·men·op·ter·an (hī′mə-nŏp′tər-ən) *n.* Also **hy·men·op·ter·on** (-ŏn). Any insect of the order Hymenoptera, characteristically having two pairs of membranous wings and including the bees, wasps, ants, and others. —*adj.* Also **hy·men·op·ter·ous** (-tər-əs). Of or belonging to the Hymenoptera. [New Latin *Hymenoptera*, from Greek *humenopteros*, "membrane-wing" : *humēn*, membrane, HYMEN + -PTEROUS.]

Hy·met·tus (hī-mĕt′əs). *Greek* **Hy·met·tos** (ē-mē-tôs′), **I·mit·tos** (ē-mē-tôs′). A mountain ridge rising to 3,367 feet in east-central Greece, near Athens.

hymn (hĭm) *n.* 1. A song of praise or thanksgiving to God. 2. Any song of praise or joy; paean. —*v.* **hymned, hymning, hymns.** —*tr.* To praise, glorify, or worship in a hymn. 2. To express in a hymn. —*intr.* To sing hymns. [Middle English

hyena
Crocuta crocuta

hydroplane

ymne, imne, from Old French *ymne,* from Latin *hymnus,* from Greek *humnos*†, hymn, ode of praise of gods or heroes.]

hym·nal (hĭm′nəl) *n.* A book or collection of church hymns. Also called "hymnbook." —*adj.* Of or pertaining to a hymn or hymns. [Middle English *hymnale,* from Medieval Latin *hymnāle,* from Latin *hymnus,* HYMN.]

hym·nist (hĭm′nĭst) *n.* Also **hym·no·dist** (-nə-dĭst). A composer of hymns.

hym·no·dy (hĭm′nə-dē) *n., pl.* **-dies. 1.** The singing of hymns. **2.** The composing of hymns. **3.** The study of the history of hymns. **4.** The hymns of a particular period or church. [From Medieval Latin *hymnōdia,* from Greek *humnōidia* : *humnos,* HYMN + *ōidē,* song (see **wed-**[2] in Appendix*).]

hym·nol·o·gy (hĭm-nŏl′ə-jē) *n.* Hymnody. [Greek *humnologia,* "hymn-singing" : *humnōs,* HYMN + -LOGY.] —**hym′no·log′ic** (hĭm′nə-lŏj′ĭk), **hym′no·log′i·cal** *adj.* —**hym·nol′o·gist** *n.*

hy·oid bone (hī′oid′). A U-shaped bone between the mandible and the larynx at the base of the tongue. Also called "hyoid." [French *hyoïde,* from New Latin *hyoides,* from Greek *huoeides,* "in the form of an upsilon" : *hu,* name of the letter upsilon + -OID.] —**hy′oid′, hy·oid′e·an** *adj.*

hy·os·cine (hī′ə-sēn′) *n.* A drug, **scopolamine** *(see).* [German *Hyoscin,* from New Latin *Hyoscyamus,* genus of henbane from which it is obtained, from Greek *huoskuamus* : *huos,* genitive of *hus,* pig (see **su-**[1] in Appendix*) + *kuamos*†, bean.]

hy·os·cy·a·mine (hī′ə-sī′ə-mēn′) *n.* A poisonous, white, crystalline alkaloid, $C_{17}H_{23}NO_3$, isometric with atropine, and used as an antispasmodic, analgesic, and sedative. [From New Latin *Hyoscyamus.* See **hyoscine.**]

hyp. 1. hypotenuse. **2.** hypothesis.

hyp·a·bys·sal (hĭp′ə-bĭs′əl, hī′pə-) *adj.* Solidifying chiefly as a minor intrusion, especially as a dike or sill, before reaching the earth's surface. Said of rocks. [HYP(O)- + ABYSSAL.]

hy·pae·thral (hī-pē′thrəl) *adj.* Open to the sky; roofless: *an ancient hypaethral temple.* [From Latin *hypaethrus,* from Greek *hupaithros* : *hupo-,* beneath + *aithēr,* sky (see **aidh-** in Appendix*).]

hy·pan·thi·um (hĭ-păn′thē-əm, hī-) *n., pl.* **-thia** (-thē-ə). The modified, often enlarged floral receptacle of various plants, having a cup-shaped or tubular form. [New Latin : HYP(O)- + ANTH(O)- + -IUM.] —**hy·pan′thi·al** *adj.*

hyper-. Indicates: **1.** Over, above, or in great amount; for example, **hypercritical. 2.** In abnormal excess; for example, **hyperacid.** [From Greek *huper,* over, above, beyond, exceeding. See **uper** in Appendix.*]

hy·per·ac·id (hī′pər-ăs′ĭd) *adj.* Containing excessive acid; excessively acidic. —**hy′per·ac·id′i·ty** (-ə-sĭd′ə-tē) *n.*

hy·per·ac·tive (hī′pər-ăk′tĭv) *adj.* Excessively or abnormally active.

hy·per·ae·mi·a. Variant of **hyperemia.**

hy·per·aes·the·sia. Variant of **hyperesthesia.**

hy·per·bar·ic (hī′pər-băr′ĭk) *adj.* Of, pertaining to, producing, operating, or occurring at pressures higher than normal atmospheric pressure: *a hyperbaric chamber; hyperbaric therapy.* [HYPER- + BAR(O)- + -IC.]

hy·per·bo·la (hī-pûr′bə-lə) *n. Geometry.* A plane curve having two branches, formed by: **a.** A conic section intersecting both halves of a right circular cone. **b.** The locus of points related to two given points such that the difference in the distances of each point from the two given points is a constant. [New Latin, from Greek *huperbolē,* "a throwing beyond," excess (when a hyperbola is formed from a conic section, the angle made by the base of the cone and the intersecting plane is greater than the angle formed by a parabola), from *huperballein,* "to throw beyond," exceed : *huper-,* beyond + *ballein,* to throw (see **gwel-**[1] in Appendix*).]

hy·per·bo·le (hī-pûr′bə-lē) *n.* An exaggeration or extravagant statement used as a figure of speech; for example, *I could sleep for a year. This book weighs a ton.* [Earlier *yperbole,* from Latin *hyperbolē,* from Greek *huperbolē,* excess. See **hyperbola.**]

hy·per·bol·ic (hī′pər-bŏl′ĭk) *adj.* Also **hy·per·bol·i·cal** (-ĭ-kəl). **1.** Of, pertaining to, or employing hyperbole. **2.** *Mathematics.* **a.** Of, pertaining to, or having the form of a hyperbola. **b.** Based on or having a metric that is a hyperbola: *hyperbolic geometry.* **c.** Of or pertaining to a hyperbolic function: *hyperbolic cosine.* —**hy′per·bol′i·cal·ly** *adv.*

hyperbolic function. Any of a set of six functions related, for a real variable *z,* to the hyperbola in a manner analogous to the relationship of the trigonometric functions to a circle, including: **a.** *Symbol* **sinh** The *hyperbolic sine,* defined by the equation $\sinh z = \frac{1}{2}(e^z - e^{-z})$. **b.** *Symbol* **cosh** The *hyperbolic cosine,* defined by the equation $\cosh z = \frac{1}{2}(e^z + e^{-z})$. **c.** *Symbol* **tanh** The *hyperbolic tangent,* defined by the equation $\tanh z = \sinh z/\cosh z$. **d.** *Symbol* **coth** The *hyperbolic cotangent,* defined by the equation $\coth z = \cosh z/\sinh z$. **e.** *Symbol* **sech** The *hyperbolic secant,* defined by the equation $\text{sech}\, z = 1/\cosh z$. **f.** *Symbol* **csch** The *hyperbolic cosecant,* defined by the equation $\text{csch}\, z = 1/\sinh z$.

hyperbolic paraboloid. *Geometry.* A surface of which all sections parallel to one coordinate plane are hyperbolas and all sections parallel to another coordinate plane are parabolas.

hy·per·bo·lism (hī-pûr′bə-lĭz′əm) *n.* **1.** The use of hyperbole. **2.** A hyperbole.

hy·per·bo·lize (hī-pûr′bə-līz′) *v.* **-lized, -lizing, -lizes.** —*intr.* To use hyperbole; exaggerate. —*tr.* To express with hyperbole; exaggerate.

hy·per·bo·loid (hī-pûr′bə-loid′) *n. Geometry.* Either of two quadric surfaces having a finite center with certain plane sections that are hyperbolas and others that are ellipses or circles.

hy·per·bo·re·an (hī′pər-bôr′ē-ən, -bōr′ē-ən, -bə-rē′ən) *adj.* **1.** Of or pertaining to the far north; arctic. **2.** Very cold; frigid. [From Latin *Hyperborei,* HYPERBOREAN.]

Hy·per·bo·re·an (hī′pər-bôr′ē-ən, -bōr′ē-ən, -bə-rē′ən) *n. Greek Mythology.* One of a people known to the ancient Greeks from the earliest times, living in an unidentified country in the far north, and renowned as pious and divinely favored adherents of the cult of Apollo. —*adj.* Of or pertaining to the Hyperboreans. [From Latin *Hyperborei,* from Greek *Huperboreoi* (plural) : *huper-,* beyond, extreme + *boreios,* northern, from *Boreas,* "north wind," north (see **gwer-**[1] in Appendix*).]

hy·per·cat·a·lex·is (hī′pər-kăt′l-ĕk′sĭs) *n. Prosody.* The addition of one or more syllables in excess of the normal number in a verse or metrical line. Also called "hypermeter." [New Latin : HYPER- + *catalexis,* omission in the last foot of a line, from Greek *katalēxis,* from *katalēgein,* to leave off (see **catalectic**).] —**hy′per·cat′a·lec′tic** (-kăt′l-ĕk′tĭk) *adj.*

hy·per·charge (hī′pər-chärj′) *n. Symbol* **Y** *Physics.* A quantum number numerically equal to twice the average electric charge of a particle multiplet or, equivalently, to the sum of the strangeness and the baryon number.

hy·per·cho·les·ter·o·le·mi·a (hī′pər-kə-lĕs′tər-ō-lē′mē-ə) *n.* Also **hy·per·cho·les·ter·e·mi·a** (-tə-rē′mē-ə). The presence of abnormally large quantities of cholesterol in the blood.

hy·per·cor·rec·tion (hī′pər-kə-rĕk′shən) *n. Linguistics.* A change in a speech habit on the basis of an incorrect analogy; for example, after being criticized for saying *Who am I speaking to?* a person incorrectly substitutes *whom* for *who* in: *He is the one whom I think is most likely to succeed.*

hy·per·crit·ic (hī′pər-krĭt′ĭk) *n.* A person who is excessively critical.

hy·per·crit·i·cal (hī′pər-krĭt′ĭ-kəl) *adj.* Overcritical; captious. —**hy′per·crit′i·cal·ly** *adv.* —**hy′per·crit′i·cism′** (-krĭt′ə-sĭz′əm) *n.*

hy·per·e·mi·a (hī′pər-ē′mē-ə) *n.* Also **hy·per·ae·mi·a.** The presence of an abnormally large blood supply. [New Latin : HYPER- + -EMIA.]

hy·per·es·the·sia (hī′pər-ĕs-thē′zhə, -zhē-ə) *n.* Also **hy·per·aes·the·sia.** Abnormal sensitivity of the senses. [New Latin : HYPER- + ESTHESIA.] —**hy′per·es·thet′ic** (-ĕs-thĕt′ĭk) *adj.*

hy·per·eu·tec·tic (hī′pər-yōō-tĕk′tĭk) *adj. Chemistry.* Having the minor component present in a larger amount than in the eutectic composition of the same components.

hy·per·ex·ten·sion (hī′pər-ĭk-stĕn′shən) *n.* Extension of a bodily limb beyond normal limits.

hy·per·fine structure (hī′pər-fīn′). *Abbr.* **hfs** *Physics.* The splitting of a spectral line into two or more components as a result of the spin or magnetic moment of the atomic nucleus.

hy·per·gly·ce·mi·a (hī′pər-glī-sē′mē-ə) *n.* The presence of an abnormally high concentration of glucose in the blood. —**hy′per·gly·ce′mic** *adj.*

hy·per·gol·ic (hī′pər-gŏl′ĭk) *adj.* Igniting spontaneously on contact of its components. Said of a rocket fuel. [From German *Hypergol* : HYP(ER)- + Greek *ergon,* work (see **werg-**[1] in Appendix*) + -OL(E).]

hy·per·in·su·lin·ism (hī′pər-ĭn′sə-lə-nĭz′əm) *n.* The presence of abnormally great quantities of insulin in the blood, resulting in hypoglycemia.

Hy·pe·ri·on (hī-pîr′ē-ən). *Greek Mythology.* A Titan, the son of Gaea and Uranus, and father of Helios, the sun god.

hy·per·ir·ri·ta·bil·i·ty (hī′pər-ĭr′ə-tə-bĭl′ə-tē) *n.* Excessive sensitivity to irritation. —**hy′per·ir′ri·ta·ble** *adj.*

hy·per·ker·a·to·sis (hī′pər-kĕr′ə-tō′sĭs) *n.* Hypertrophy of the horny layer of the skin. [New Latin : HYPER- + Greek *keras* (stem *kerat-*), horn (see **keratin**) + -OSIS.] —**hy′per·ker′a·tot′ic** (-tŏt′ĭk) *adj.*

hy·per·ki·ne·sia (hī′pər-kĭ-nē′zhə, -zhē-ə) *n.* Also **hy·per·ki·ne·sis** (-sĭs). Pathologically excessive motion. [New Latin : HYPER- + Greek *kinēsis,* movement, from *kinein,* to move (see **kei-**[3] in Appendix*).] —**hy′per·ki·net′ic** (-nĕt′ĭk) *adj.*

hy·per·me·ter (hī-pûr′mə-tər) *n. Prosody.* **Hypercatalexis** *(see).* —**hy′per·met′ric** (hī′pər-mĕt′rĭk), **hy′per·met′ri·cal** *adj.*

hy·per·me·tro·pi·a (hī′pər-mə-trō′pē-ə) *n. Pathology.* **Hyperopia** *(see).* [New Latin, from Greek *hupermetros,* beyond measure, excessive : *huper-,* beyond, excessive + *metron,* measure (see **mē-**[2] in Appendix*) + -OPIA.] —**hy′per·me·trop′ic** (-trŏp′ĭk), **hy′per·me·trop′i·cal** *adj.* —**hy′per·met′ro·py** (-mĕt′rə-pē) *n.*

hy·perm·ne·sia (hī′pərm-nē′zhə, -zhē-ə) *n.* Unusually exact or vivid memory. [New Latin : HYPER- + (A)MNESIA.]

hy·per·on (hī′pə-rŏn′) *n. Physics.* A subatomic particle with mass greater than the nucleon, decaying into a nucleon or another hyperon and lighter particles, and having $2I + 1$ charge states, where I is the isospin of the particle multiplet. See **particle.** [HYPER- + -ON.]

hy·per·o·pi·a (hī′pər-ō′pē-ə) *n.* A pathological condition of the eye in which parallel rays are focused behind the retina because of a refractive error, or because of flattening of the globe of the eye, so that vision is better for distant than near objects. Also called "hypermetropia," "farsightedness," "long-sightedness." [New Latin : HYPER- + -OPIA.] —**hy′per·ope′** *n.* —**hy′per·op′ic** (-ŏp′ĭk) *adj.*

hy·per·os·to·sis (hī′pər-ŏ-stō′sĭs) *n.* Excessive or abnormal thickening or growth of bone tissue. [New Latin : HYPER- + OST(EO)- + -OSIS.] —**hy′per·os·tot′ic** (-ŏ-stŏt′ĭk) *adj.*

hy·per·pi·tu·i·ta·rism (hī′pər-pĭ-tōō′ə-tə-rĭz′əm, -tyōō′ə-tə-rĭz′əm) *n.* Pathologically excessive production of anterior pituitary hormones, especially growth hormones, resulting in acromegaly or gigantism. —**hy′per·pi·tu′i·tar′y** *adj.*

hy·per·pla·sia (hī′pər-plā′zhə, -zhē-ə) *n.* A nontumorous increase in the number of cells in an organ or tissue with con-

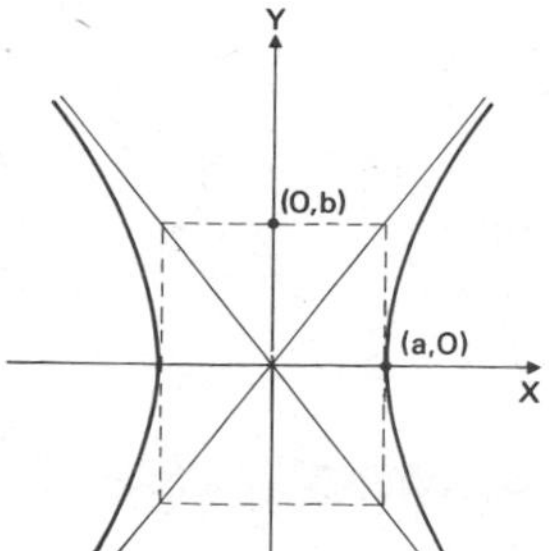

hyperbola
The equation of the hyperbola shown is
$$\frac{x^2}{a^2} - \frac{y^2}{b^2} = 1$$

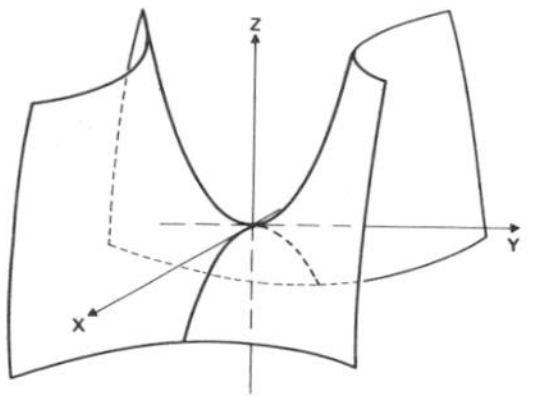

hyperbolic paraboloid

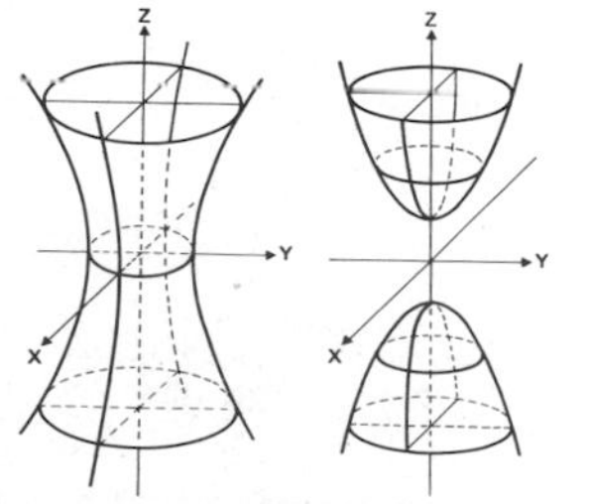

hyperboloid

sequent enlargement of the affected part. [New Latin : HYPER- + -PLASIA.] —**hy′per·plas′tic** (-plăs′tĭk) *adj.*

hy·per·ploid (hī′pər-ploid′) *adj. Genetics.* Having a chromosome number in excess of, but not an exact multiple of, the normal diploid number. [HYPER- + -PLOID.] —**hy′per·ploid′y** *n.*

hy·perp·ne·a (hī′pərp-nē′ə, hī′pər-) *n.* Abnormally deep and rapid breathing. [New Latin : HYPER- + Greek *pnoia,* breath, from *pnein,* to breathe (see **pneu-** in Appendix*).]

hy·per·py·rex·i·a (hī′pər-pī-rĕk′sē-ə) *n.* Abnormally high fever; hyperthermia. [New Latin : HYPER- + PYREXIA.] —**hy′per·py·rex′i·al, hy′per·py·ret′ic** (-rĕt′ĭk) *adj.*

hy·per·sen·si·tive (hī′pər-sĕn′sə-tĭv) *adj.* Abnormally sensitive. —**hy′per·sen′si·tive·ness, hy′per·sen′si·tiv′i·ty** *n.*

hy·per·son·ic (hī′pər-sŏn′ĭk) *adj.* Of, pertaining to, or relating to speed equal to or exceeding five times the speed of sound. —**hy′per·son′ics** *n.*

hy·per·sthene (hī′pərs-thēn′) *n.* A green, brown, or black, splintery, cleavable, pyroxene mineral, essentially $(Fe,Mg)_2Si_2O_6$. [French *hypersthène* : HYPER- + Greek *sthenos,* strength (see **asthenia**).] —**hy′per·sthen′ic** (-thĕn′ĭk) *adj.*

hy·per·ten·sion (hī′pər-tĕn′shən) *n.* **1.** Abnormally high arterial blood pressure. **2.** A state of high emotional tension. —**hy′per·ten′sive** *adj.* & *n.*

hy·per·ther·mi·a (hī′pər-thûr′mē-ə) *n.* Unusually high fever; hyperpyrexia. [New Latin : HYPER- + THERM(O)- + -IA.] —**hy′per·therm′al** *adj.*

hy·per·thy·roid (hī′pər-thī′roid′) *adj.* Pertaining to or afflicted with hyperthyroidism. —*n.* A person afflicted with hyperthyroidism.

hy·per·thy·roid·ism (hī′pər-thī′roi-dĭz′əm) *n.* Pathologically excessive production of thyroid hormones.

hy·per·to·ni·a (hī′pər-tō′nē-ə) *n.* Also **hy·per·to·ni·ci·ty** (-tō-nĭs′ə-tē). The state of being hypertonic. [HYPER- + -TONIA.]

hy·per·ton·ic (hī′pər-tŏn′ĭk) *adj.* **1.** *Pathology.* Having extreme muscular or arterial tension. **2.** *Chemistry.* Having the higher osmotic pressure of two solutions.

hy·per·tro·phy (hī-pûr′trə-fē) *n.* Also **hy·per·tro·phi·a** (hī′pər-trō-fē′ə). *Pathology.* A nontumorous increase in the size of an organ or part as a result of the enlargement, without increase in number, of constituent cells. —*v.* **hypertrophied, -phying, -phies.** —*tr.* To cause to grow abnormally large. —*intr.* To grow abnormally large. [HYPER- + -TROPHY.] —**hy′per·troph′ic** (-trŏf′ĭk) *adj.*

hy·per·ven·ti·la·tion (hī′pər-vĕnt′l-ā′shən) *n.* Abnormally fast or deep respiration in which excessive quantities of air are taken in, causing buzzing in the ears, tingling of extremities, and sometimes fainting.

hy·per·vi·ta·min·o·sis (hī′pər-vī′tə-mə-nō′sĭs) *n.* Any of various abnormal conditions in which the physiological effect of a vitamin is produced to a pathological degree by excessive use of the vitamin.

hy·pes·the·si·a. Variant of **hypoesthesia.**

hy·pha (hī′fə) *n., pl.* **-phae** (-fē). Any of the threadlike filaments forming the mycelium of a fungus. [New Latin, from Greek *huphē,* web. See **webh-** in Appendix.*] —**hy′phal** *adj.*

hy·phen (hī′fən) *n.* A punctuation mark (-) used to connect the parts of a compound word or between syllables, especially of a word divided at the end of a line. —*tr.v.* **hyphened, -phening, -phens.** To hyphenate. [Late Latin, from Late Greek *huphen,* a sign written below two consecutive letters to show that they belong to the same word, from Greek, in the same word : *hupo-,* under + *hen,* neuter of *heis,* one (see **sem-**[1] in Appendix*).]

hy·phen·ate (hī′fə-nāt′) *tr.v.* **-ated, -ating, -ates.** To divide or connect (syllables or word elements) with a hyphen. —**hy′phen·a′tion** *n.*

hy·phen·at·ed (hī′fə-nā′tĭd) *adj. Informal.* Of foreign birth or mixed national origin: *German-Americans and other hyphenated Americans.*

hy·phen·ize (hī′fə-nīz′) *tr.v.* **-ized, -izing, -izes.** To hyphenate. —**hy′phen·i·za′tion** *n.*

hyp·na·gog·ic (hĭp′nə-gŏj′ĭk) *adj.* Also **hyp·no·gog·ic.** **1.** Inducing sleep. **2.** Of or pertaining to the state of drowsiness preceding sleep. [French *hypnagogique* : HYPN(O)- + Greek *agōgos,* leading, from *agein,* to lead (see **ag-** in Appendix*).]

hypno–, hypn–. Indicates: **1.** Sleep; for example, **hypnopompic. 2.** Hypnosis; for example, **hypnoanalysis, hypnoid.** [From Greek *hupnos,* sleep. See **swep-**[1] in Appendix.*]

hyp·no·a·nal·y·sis (hĭp′nō-ə-năl′ə-sĭs) *n.* A psychoanalytic technique in which hypnosis is used to elicit unconscious material from a patient.

hyp·no·gen·e·sis (hĭp′nō-jĕn′ə-sĭs) *n.* The process of inducing or entering a hypnotic state. —**hyp′no·ge·net′ic** (-jə-nĕt′ĭk) *adj.* —**hyp′no·ge·net′i·cal·ly** *adv.*

hyp·noid (hĭp′noid′) *adj.* Also **hyp·noid·al** (hĭp-noid′l). Of or resembling hypnosis or sleep. [HYPN(O)- + -OID.]

hyp·no·pho·bi·a (hĭp′nə-fō′bē-ə) *n.* Abnormal fear of sleep. [New Latin: HYPNO- + -PHOBIA.] —**hyp′no·pho′bic** *adj.*

hyp·no·pom·pic (hĭp′nə-pŏm′pĭk) *adj.* Of or pertaining to the partially conscious state preceding complete awakening. [HYPNO- + Greek *pompē,* a sending off, procession, POMP + -IC.]

Hyp·nos (hĭp′nŏs). Also **Hyp·nus** (hĭp′nəs). *Greek Mythology.* The god of sleep. [Greek. See **swep-**[1] in Appendix.*]

hyp·no·sis (hĭp-nō′sĭs) *n., pl.* **-ses** (-sēz′). **1.** An artificially induced sleeplike condition in which an individual is extremely responsive to suggestions made by the hypnotist. **2.** Hypnotism. **3.** Any sleeplike condition. [New Latin : Greek *hupnos,* sleep (see **swep-**[1] in Appendix*) + -OSIS.]

hyp·no·ther·a·py (hĭp′nō-thĕr′ə-pē) *n.* Therapy based on or using hypnosis.

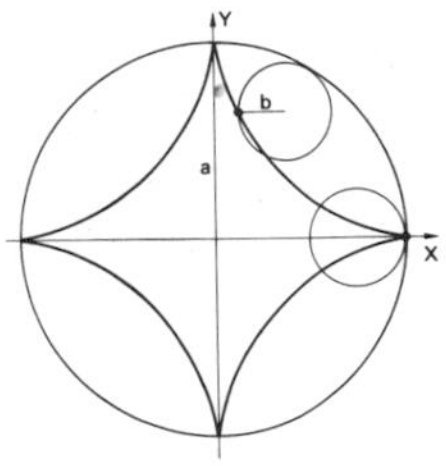

hypocycloid
A hypocycloid of four cusps; $a = 4b$

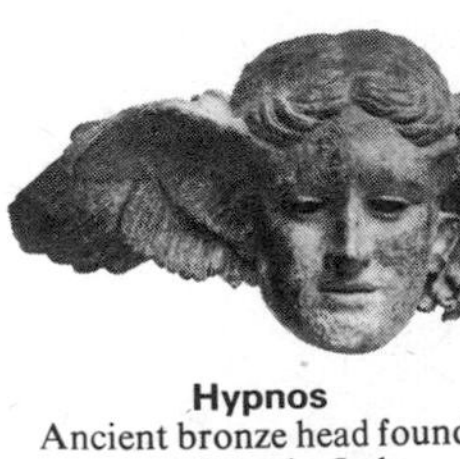

Hypnos
Ancient bronze head found near Perugia, Italy

hyp·not·ic (hĭp-nŏt′ĭk) *adj.* **1. a.** Of, involving, or inducing hypnosis. **b.** Being or resembling hypnosis. **c.** Of, pertaining to, or practicing hypnotism. **2.** Inducing sleep; soporific. —*n.* **1. a.** A person who is hypnotized. **b.** A person who can be hypnotized. **2. a.** An agent that causes sleep; a soporific. **b.** An agent used to produce a hypnotic state. [French *hypnotique,* from Late Latin *hypnōticus,* from Greek *hupnōtikos,* sleepy, from *hupnoun,* to put to sleep, from *hupnos,* sleep. See **swep-**[1] in Appendix.*] —**hyp·not′i·cal·ly** *adv.*

hyp·no·tism (hĭp′nə-tĭz′əm) *n.* **1.** The theory or practice of inducing hypnosis. **2.** An act of inducing hypnosis.

hyp·no·tist (hĭp′nə-tĭst) *n.* A person who induces hypnosis.

hyp·no·tize (hĭp′nə-tīz′) *tr.v.* **-tized, -tizing, -tizes. 1.** To put in a state of hypnosis. **2.** To fascinate; to entrance. —**hyp′no·tiz′a·ble** *adj.* —**hyp′no·ti·za′tion** *n.* —**hyp′no·tiz′er** *n.*

hy·po[1] (hī′pō) *n. Chemistry.* **Sodium thiosulfate** *(see).* [Short for HYPOSULFITE.]

hy·po[2] (hī′pō) *n., pl.* **-pos.** *Informal.* A hypodermic syringe or injection.

hypo–, hyp–. Indicates: **1.** Below or beneath; for example, **hypodermic. 2.** At a lower point; for example, **hypogenous. 3.** Abnormally low; for example, **hypoglycemia. 4.** Deficient; for example, **hypoxia. 5.** Partial or incomplete; for example, **hypoesthesia.** [Greek *hupo-,* from *hupo,* under, from under, beneath. See **upo** in Appendix.*]

hy·po·a·cid·i·ty (hī′pō-ə-sĭd′ə-tē) *n.* **1.** *Chemistry.* Slight acidity. **2.** *Medicine.* Below normal acidity.

hy·po·bar·ic (hī′pə-băr′ĭk) *adj.* Below normal pressure. [HYPO- + BAR(O)- + -IC.] —**hy′po·bar′ism′** *n.*

hy·po·blast (hī′pə-blăst′) *n. Embryology.* **Endoblast** *(see).* [HYPO- + -BLAST.] —**hy′po·blas′tic** *adj.*

hy·po·caust (hī′pə-kôst′, hĭp′ə-) *n.* In ancient Rome, a space under the floor where heat from a furnace was accumulated to heat a room or a bath. [Latin *hypocaustum,* from Greek *hupokauston,* from *hupokaiein,* to burn underneath : *hupo-,* under + *kaiein,* to burn (see **kēu-** in Appendix*).]

hy·po·cen·ter (hī′pō-sĕn′tər) *n.* The surface position directly beneath the center of a nuclear explosion.

hy·po·chlo·rite (hī′pə-klôr′īt′, -klōr′īt′) *n.* A salt or ester of hypochlorous acid.

hy·po·chlo·rous acid (hī′pə-klôr′əs, -klōr′əs). A weak, unstable acid, HOCl, occurring only in solution and used as a bleach, oxidizer, deodorant, and disinfectant.

hy·po·chon·dri·a (hī′pə-kŏn′drē-ə) *n.* The persistent neurotic conviction that one is or is likely to become ill, often involving experiences of real pain, when illness is neither actually present nor likely. Also called "hypochondriasis." [Originally a region of the abdomen (formerly held to be the seat of melancholy), from Late Latin, from Greek *hupokhondria,* plural of *hupokhondrion,* belly, abdomen, from *hupokhondrios,* under the cartilage of the breastbone : *hupo-,* under + *khondros,* cartilage (see **ghren-** in Appendix*).]

hy·po·chon·dri·ac (hī′pə-kŏn′drē-ăk′) *n.* A person afflicted with hypochondria. —*adj.* **1.** Pertaining to or afflicted with hypochondria. **2.** *Anatomy.* Pertaining to or located in the hypochondrium. —**hy′po·chon·dri′a·cal** (-kən-drī′ə-kəl) *adj.* —**hy′po·chon·dri′a·cal·ly** *adv.*

hy·po·chon·dri·um (hī′pə-kŏn′drē-əm) *n., pl.* **-dria** (-drē-ə). The upper lateral region of the abdomen, below the lowest ribs. [New Latin, from Greek *hupokhondrion,* abdomen. See **hypochondria.**]

hy·poc·o·rism (hī-pŏk′ə-rĭz′əm, hī-) *n.* **1.** A name of endearment or a pet name. **2.** The use of such names. **3.** A euphemism. [Late Latin *hypocorisma,* from Greek *hupokorisma,* from *hupokorizesthai,* to call by endearing names : *hupo-,* below, beneath + *korizesthai,* to caress, from *koros,* boy, and *korē,* girl (see **ker-**[3] in Appendix*).] —**hy′po·co·ris′tic** (hī′pō-kə-rĭs′tĭk), **hy′po·co·ris′ti·cal** (-tĭ-kəl) *adj.* —**hy′po·co·ris′ti·cal·ly** *adv.*

hy·po·cot·yl (hī′pə-kŏt′l) *n. Botany.* The part of the axis of a plant embryo or seedling plant that is below the cotyledons. [HYPO- + COTYL(EDON).]

hy·poc·ri·sy (hĭ-pŏk′rə-sē) *n., pl.* **-sies. 1.** The feigning of beliefs, feelings, or virtues that one does not hold or possess; insincerity. **2.** An instance of such falseness. [Middle English *ipocrisie, ypocrisy,* from Old French *ypocrisie,* from Late Latin *hypocrisis,* from Greek *hupokrisis,* playing of a part on the stage, from *hupokrinein,* to separate gradually, to answer, answer one's fellow actor, play a part : *hupo-,* under + *krinein,* to separate (see **skeri-** in Appendix*).]

hyp·o·crite (hĭp′ə-krĭt′) *n.* A person given to hypocrisy. [Middle English *ipocrite, ypocrite,* from Old French *ypocrite,* from Late Latin *hypocrita,* from Greek *hupocritēs,* actor, hypocrite, from *hupokrinein,* to play a part. See **hypocrisy.**] —**hyp′o·crit′i·cal** *adj.* —**hyp′o·crit′i·cal·ly** *adv.*

hy·po·cy·cloid (hī′pō-sī′kloid′) *n. Geometry.* The plane locus of a point fixed on a circle that rolls on the inside circumference of a fixed circle.

hy·po·der·mal (hī′pə-dûr′məl) *adj.* **1.** Of or pertaining to the hypodermis. **2.** Lying below the epidermis.

hy·po·der·mic (hī′pə-dûr′mĭk) *adj.* **1.** Of or pertaining to the layer just beneath the epidermis. **2.** Pertaining to the hypodermis. **3.** Injected beneath the skin. —*n.* **1.** A hypodermic injection. **2.** A hypodermic needle or syringe. [HYPO- + DERM(ATO)- + -IC.] —**hy′po·der′mi·cal·ly** *adv.*

hypodermic injection. A subcutaneous, intramuscular, or intravenous injection by means of a hypodermic syringe and needle.

hypodermic needle. 1. A hollow needle used with a hypodermic syringe. **2.** A hypodermic syringe complete with needle.

ă pat/ā pay/âr care/ä father/b bib/ch church/d deed/ĕ pet/ē be/f fife/g gag/h hat/hw which/ĭ pit/ī pie/îr pier/j judge/k kick/l lid, needle/m mum/n no, sudden/ng thing/ŏ pot/ō toe/ô paw, for/oi noise/ou out/ŏŏ took/ōō boot/p pop/r roar/s sauce/sh ship, dish/

hypodermic syringe. A syringe fitted with a hypodermic needle for hypodermic injections.

hy·po·der·mis (hī′pə-dûr′mĭs) *n.* Also **hy·po·derm** (hī′pə-dûrm′). **1.** *Zoology.* An epidermal layer of cells that secretes an overlying chitinous cuticle, as in arthropods. **2.** *Botany.* A layer of cells lying immediately below the epidermis. [New Latin : HYPO- + *dermis*, DERMA (skin).]

hy·po·es·the·sia (hī′pō-ĕs-thē′zhə, -zhē-ə) *n.* Also **hy·pes·the·sia** (hī′pēs-). *Pathology.* Partial loss of sensation; diminished sensibility. [New Latin : HYPO- + (AN)ESTHESIA.]

hy·po·eu·tec·tic (hī′pō-yo͞o-tĕk′tĭk) *adj. Chemistry.* Having the minor component present in a smaller amount than in the eutectic composition of the same components.

hy·po·gas·tri·um (hī′pō-găs′trē-əm) *n.* The lowest of the three median regions of the abdomen. [New Latin, from Greek *hupogastrion* : HYPO- + GASTR(O)- + -IUM.] —**hy′po·gas′tric** *adj.*

hy·po·ge·al (hī′pə-jē′əl) *adj.* Also **hy·po·ge·an** (-ən), **hy·po·ge·ous** (-əs). **1.** Located under the earth's surface; underground. **2.** *Botany.* Designating or characterized by cotyledons that remain below the surface of the ground. [From Late Latin *hypogēus*, from Greek *hupogaios* : HYPO- + *gē*, *gaia*, earth (see **gē** in Appendix*).]

hyp·o·gene (hĭp′ə-jēn′) *adj.* Formed or situated below the earth's surface. Said of rocks. [HYPO- + (EPI)GENE.]

hy·pog·e·nous (hī-pŏj′ə-nəs) *adj. Botany.* Developing or growing on a lower surface, as fungi on leaves. [HYPO- + -GENOUS.]

hyp·o·ge·um (hĭp′ə-jē′əm, hī′pə-) *n., pl.* **-gea** (-jē′ə). **1.** A subterranean chamber of an ancient building. **2.** An ancient subterranean burial chamber, such as a catacomb. [Latin *hypogēum*, from Greek *hupogaion*, from *hupogaios*, HYPOGEAL.]

hy·po·glos·sal (hī′pə-glŏs′əl) *adj.* **1.** Located under the tongue. **2.** *Anatomy.* Of or pertaining to the hypoglossal nerve. —*n.* The hypoglossal nerve. [From New Latin *hypoglossus*, hypoglossal nerve : HYPO- + Greek *glōssa*, tongue (see **glōgh-** in Appendix*).]

hypoglossal nerve. A motor nerve attached to the medulla oblongata and innervating the muscles of the tongue.

hy·po·gly·ce·mi·a (hī′pō-glī-sē′mē-ə) *n.* An abnormally low level of sugar in the blood. —**hy′po·gly·ce′mic** *adj.*

hy·pog·y·nous (hī-pŏj′ə-nəs) *adj. Botany.* Having or characterizing floral parts or organs that are below and not in contact with the ovary. [HYPO- + -GYNOUS.] —**hy·pog′y·ny** *n.*

hy·po·ma·ni·a (hī′pə-mā′nē-ə, -mān′yə) *n.* A mild state of mania involving slightly abnormal elation and overactivity. —**hy′po·ma′nic** (-mā′nĭk, -măn′ĭk) *adj.*

hy·po·nas·ty (hī′pə-năs′tē) *n.* An upward bending of leaves or other plant parts, resulting from growth of the lower side. [German *Hyponastie* : HYPO- + -NASTY.] —**hy′po·nas′tic** *adj.*

hy·po·phos·phite (hī′pə-fŏs′fīt′) *n.* A salt of hypophosphorous acid.

hy·po·phos·pho·rous acid (hī′pə-fŏs′fər-əs). A clear, colorless or slightly yellow liquid, H_3PO_2, used in the preparation of hypophosphites.

hy·poph·y·sis (hī-pŏf′ə-sĭs) *n., pl.* **-ses** (-sēz′). *Anatomy.* The **pituitary gland** *(see)*. [New Latin, outgrowth, from Greek *hupophusis*, attachment underneath, growth, from *hupophuein*, to grow up under : *hupo-*, under + *phuein*, to bring forth, grow (see **bheu-** in Appendix*).] —**hy′po·phys′e·al** (hī′pə-fĭz′ē-əl, hī-pŏf′ə-sē′əl) *adj.*

hy·po·pi·tu·i·ta·rism (hī′pō-pĭ-to͞o′ə-tə-rĭz′əm, hī′pō-pĭ-tyo͞o′-) *n.* Deficient or diminished production of pituitary hormones. —**hy′po·pi·tu′i·tar′y** (-tĕr′ē) *adj.*

hy·po·pla·sia (hī′pə-plā′zhə, -zhē-ə) *n. Pathology.* Incomplete or arrested development of an organ or part. [New Latin : HYPO- + -PLASIA.] —**hy′po·plas′tic** (-plăs′tĭk) *adj.*

hy·po·ploid (hī′pə-ploid′) *adj. Genetics.* Having a chromosome number less by only a few chromosomes than the normal diploid number. [HYPO- + -PLOID.] —**hy′po·ploid′y** *n.*

hy·po·pne·a (hī′pə-nē′ə) *n.* Abnormally slow and shallow breathing. [New Latin : HYPO- + Greek *pnoē*, breathing, from *pnein*, to breathe (see **pneu-** in Appendix*).]

hy·po·sen·si·tiv·i·ty (hī′pō-sĕn′sə-tĭv′ə-tē) *n.* Also **hy·po·sen·si·tive·ness** (-sĕn′sə-tĭv-nĭs). Less than normal sensitivity. —**hy′po·sen′si·tive** *adj.*

hy·po·sen·si·tize (hī′pō-sĕn′sə-tīz′) *tr.v.* **-tized, -tizing, -tizes.** To make less sensitive; desensitize. —**hy′po·sen′si·ti·za′tion** *n.*

hy·pos·ta·sis (hī-pŏs′tə-sĭs) *n., pl.* **-ses** (-sēz′). **1.** *Philosophy.* **a.** Something that underlies something else; substance; foundation. **b.** The essence or principle of something. **2.** *Theology.* **a.** *Obsolete.* The nature or essence of the Trinity. **b.** Any of the persons of the Trinity. **c.** The essential person of Christ in which his human and divine natures are united. **3.** A hypothetical or conceptual entity. **4. a.** A settling of solid particles in a fluid. **b.** Something that settles to the bottom of a fluid; a sediment. **5.** *Genetics.* A condition in which the action of one gene conceals or suppresses the action of another gene that is not its allele but that affects the same organ, part, or state of the body. [Late Latin, substance, from Greek *hupostasis*, "a standing under," origin, substance, existence : *hupo-*, under + *stasis*, a standing (see **stā-** in Appendix*).] —**hy′po·stat′ic** (hī′pə-stăt′ĭk), **hy′po·stat′i·cal** *adj.* —**hy′po·stat′i·cal·ly** *adv.*

hypostatic union. *Theology.* The union of Christ's human and divine natures in one hypostasis or person. [From Greek *hupostatikos*, of substance, from *hupostatos*, standing under, from *huphistasthai*, to stand under : *hupo-*, under + *histasthai*, middle voice of *histanai*, to cause to stand (see **stā-** in Appendix*).]

hy·pos·ta·tize (hī-pŏs′tə-tīz′) *tr.v.* **-tized, -tizing, -tizes. 1.** To symbolize (a concept) in a concrete form. **2.** To ascribe material existence to. [From Greek *hupostatos*, standing under. See **hypostatic union.**] —**hy·pos′ta·ti·za′tion** *n.*

hy·po·sthe·ni·a (hī′pəs-thē′nē-ə) *n.* Abnormal lack of strength; weakness. [New Latin : HYPO- + Greek *sthenos*, strength (see **asthenia**).] —**hy′po·sthe′nic** (-thĕn′ĭk) *adj.*

hyp·o·style (hĭp′ə-stīl′, hī′pə-) *n.* A building having a roof or ceiling supported by rows of columns, as in ancient Egyptian architecture. [From Greek *hupostulos*, resting upon pillars set underneath : *hupo-*, under + *stulos*, pillar (see **stā-** in Appendix*).] —**hyp′o·style′** *adj.*

hy·po·sul·fite (hī′pə-sŭl′fīt′) *n.* **Sodium thiosulfate** *(see)*.

hy·po·sul·fu·rous acid (hī′pō-sŭl-fyo͝or′əs, -pə-sŭl′fər-əs). An unstable acid, $H_2S_2O_4$, known only in aqueous solution, and used as a bleaching and reducing agent. Also called "hydrosulfurous acid."

hy·po·tax·is (hī′pə-tăk′sĭs) *n.* The dependent or subordinate construction or relationship of clauses with connectives; for example, *I shall despair if you don't come.* Compare **parataxis.** [Greek *hupotaxis*, subjection, submission, from *hupotassein*, to arrange under : *hupo-*, under + *tattein*, to arrange (see **tāg-** in Appendix*).] —**hy′po·tac′tic** (-tăk′tĭk) *adj.*

hy·pot·e·nuse (hī-pŏt′n-o͞os′, -yo͞os′) *n.* Also **hy·poth·e·nuse** (hī-pŏth′ən-). *Abbr.* **hyp.** The side of a right triangle opposite the right angle. [Latin *hypotēnūsa*, from Greek *hupoteinousa*, line subtending the right angle, hypotenuse, from *hupoteinein*, to stretch under : *hupo-*, under + *teinein*, to stretch (see **ten-** in Appendix*).]

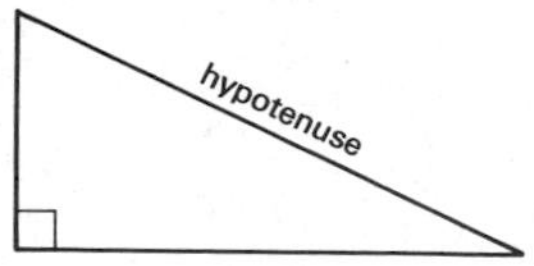

hypotenuse

hypoth. hypothesis.

hy·po·thal·a·mus (hī′pō-thăl′ə-məs) *n.* The part of the brain that lies below the thalamus, forming the major portion of the ventral region of the diencephalon, and that functions to regulate bodily temperature, certain metabolic processes, and other autonomic activities. —**hy′po·tha·lam′ic** (-thə-lăm′ĭk) *adj.*

hy·poth·ec (hī-pŏth′ĭk) *n. Law.* A security granted a creditor on the property of a debtor without transfer of possession or title. [French *hypothèque*, from Late Latin *hypothēca*, pledge, mortgage, from Greek *hupothēkē*, from *hupotithenai*, "to place under," put down as a deposit : *hupo-*, under + *tithenai*, to place (see **dhē-**[1] in Appendix*).]

hy·poth·e·cate (hī-pŏth′ĭ-kāt′) *tr.v.* **-cated, -cating, -cates.** To pledge (property) as security to a creditor without transfer of title or possession; to mortgage. [Medieval Latin *hypothēcāre*, from Late Latin *hypothēca*, HYPOTHEC.] —**hy·poth′e·ca′tion** *n.* —**hy·poth′e·ca′tor** (-kā′tər) *n.*

hy·po·ther·mal (hī′pō-thûr′məl) *adj. Geology.* Of, pertaining to, or being high-temperature deposits derived from magmatic emanations forced under pressure into place in pre-existing rock openings. [HYPO- + THERMAL.]

hy·poth·e·sis (hī-pŏth′ə-sĭs) *n., pl.* **-ses** (-sēz′). *Abbr.* **hyp., hypoth. 1.** An assertion subject to verification or proof, as: **a.** A proposition stated as a basis for argument or reasoning. **b.** A premise from which a conclusion is drawn. **c.** A conjecture that accounts, within a theory or ideational framework, for a set of facts and that can be used as a basis for further investigation. **2.** An assumption used as the basis for action. [Late Latin, from Greek *hupothesis*, proposal, suggestion, supposition, from *hupotithenai*, "to place under," propose, suppose : *hupo-*, under + *tithenai*, to place (see **dhē-**[1] in Appendix*).]

hy·poth·e·size (hī-pŏth′ə-sīz′) *v.* **-sized, -sizing, -sizes.** —*tr.* To assert as a hypothesis. —*intr.* To form a hypothesis.

hy·po·thet·i·cal (hī′pə-thĕt′ĭ-kəl) *adj.* Also **hy·po·thet·ic** (-thĕt′ĭk). **1.** Of or based on a hypothesis. **2. a.** Suppositional; conjectural; uncertain. **b.** Conditional; contingent. [From Late Latin *hypotheticus*, from Greek *hupothetikos*, from *hupothesis*, HYPOTHESIS.] —**hy′po·thet′i·cal·ly** *adv.*

hypothetical imperative. In the philosophy of Immanuel Kant, an imperative of conduct arising from expediency or necessity rather than from moral law. Compare **categorical imperative.**

hy·po·thy·roid (hī′pō-thī′roid′) *adj.* Affected by or manifesting hypothyroidism. —*n.* A person affected by hypothyroidism.

hy·po·thy·roid·ism (hī′pō-thī′roi-dĭz′əm) *n.* **1.** Insufficient production of thyroid hormones. **2.** A pathological condition resulting from severe thyroid insufficiency; especially, **myxedema** or **cretinism** *(see)*. Also called "hypothyrea," "hypothyroidea." [HYPO- + THYROID + -ISM.]

hy·po·ton·ic (hī′pə-tŏn′ĭk) *adj.* **1.** *Pathology.* Having less than normal tone or tension. **2.** *Chemistry.* Having the lower osmotic pressure of two fluids. [HYPO- + TONIC.] —**hy′po·to·nic′i·ty** (-tə-nĭs′ə-tē) *n.*

hy·pot·ro·phy (hī-pŏt′rə-fē) *n.* Less than normal growth. [HYPO- + -TROPHY.] —**hy′po·tro′phic** (hī′pə-trō′fĭk, -trŏf′ĭk) *adj.*

hy·po·xan·thine (hī′pō-zăn′thēn′, -thĭn) *n.* A white powder, $C_5H_4N_4O$, that is an intermediate in the metabolism of animal purines. [HYPO- + XANTHINE.]

hy·pox·i·a (hī-pŏk′sē-ə) *n.* Deficiency in the amount of oxygen reaching bodily tissues. [New Latin : HYP(O)- + OX(Y)- + -IA.]

hypso-. Indicates height; for example, **hypsometry.** [From Greek *hupsos*, height, summit. See **upo** in Appendix.*]

hyp·sog·ra·phy (hĭp-sŏg′rə-fē) *n.* **1.** The scientific study of the earth's topological configuration above sea level, especially the measurement and mapping of land elevations. **2.** A representation or description of such features, as on a map or in an atlas. **3.** Hypsometry. [HYPSO- + -GRAPHY.] —**hyp′so·graph′ic** (hĭp′sə-grăf′ĭk), **hyp′so·graph′i·cal** *adj.*

hyp·som·e·ter (hĭp-sŏm′ə-tər) *n.* An instrument using the altitude-pressure dependence of boiling points to determine land elevations. [HYPSO- + -METER.]

hyp·som·e·try (hĭp-sŏm′ə-trē) *n.* The measurement of elevation relative to sea level. [HYPSO- + -METRY.] —hyp′so·met′ric (hĭp′sə-mĕt′rĭk), hyp′so·met′ri·cal adj. —hyp′so·met′ri·cal·ly adv. —hyp·som′e·trist n.

hy·rax (hī′răks′) n., pl. **-raxes** or **-races** (-rə-sēz′). Any of several herbivorous mammals of the family Procaviidae within the order Hyraoidea, of Africa and adjacent Asia, resembling woodchucks or similar rodents, but more closely related to the hoofed mammals. Also called "dassie," and, especially in the Old Testament, "cony." [New Latin, from Greek hurax†, shrew mouse.]

Hyr·ca·ni·a (hûr-kā′nē-ə). A province of the ancient Persian empire, on the southeastern shore of the Caspian Sea.

hy·son (hī′sən) n. A type of Chinese green tea, the leaves of which are twisted or curled. [Cantonese hei ch'on, corresponding to Mandarin Chinese hsi¹ ch'un¹, "bright spring" (so called because the tea leaves are picked in early spring).]

hys·sop (hĭs′əp) n. **1.** A woody plant, Hyssopus officinalis, native to Asia, having spikes of small blue flowers and aromatic leaves used in perfumery and as a condiment. **2.** Any of several similar or related plants. **3.** An unidentified plant mentioned in the Bible as the source of twigs used for sprinkling in certain Hebraic purificatory rites. Exodus 12:22. [Middle English ysop, from Old English hysope and Old French ysope, both from Latin hyssōpus, from Greek hussōpos, from Semitic, akin to Hebrew 'ēzōbh.]

hys·ter·ec·to·my (hĭs′tə-rĕk′tə-mē) n., pl. **-mies.** Total or partial surgical removal of the uterus. [HYSTER(O)- + -ECTOMY.]

hys·ter·e·sis (hĭs′tə-rē′sĭs) n., pl. **-ses** (-sēz′). Physics. The failure of a property that has been changed by an external agent to return to its original value when the cause of the change is removed. See **magnetic hysteresis.** [New Latin, from Greek husterēsis, a shortcoming, from husterein, to be behind, come later, from husteros, later, behind. See **ud-** in Appendix.*] —hys′ter·et′ic (-rĕt′ĭk) adj.

hys·ter·i·a (hĭ-stĕr′ē-ə) n. **1.** A neurosis characterized by conversion symptoms, a calm mental attitude, and episodes of hallucination, somnambulism, amnesia, and other mental aberrations. **2.** Excessive or uncontrollable fear or other strong emotion. [New Latin, from Latin hystericus, HYSTERIC.]

hys·ter·ic (hĭ-stĕr′ĭk) n. A person suffering from hysteria. —adj. Hysterical. [Latin hystericus, from Greek husterikos, suffering in the womb (hysteria was once thought to be caused by uterine disturbances), from hustera, womb. See **udero-** in Appendix.*]

hys·ter·i·cal (hĭ-stĕr′ĭ-kəl) adj. **1.** Of, characterized by, or arising from hysteria. **2.** Having or prone to having hysterics. —**hys·ter′i·cal·ly** adv.

hys·ter·ics (hĭ-stĕr′ĭks) n. Plural in form, usually used with a singular verb. **1.** A fit of uncontrollable laughing and crying. **2.** An attack of hysteria.

hystero-, hyster-. Indicates: **1.** Womb or uterus; for example, **hysterectomy. 2.** Hysteria; for example, **hysterogenic.** [From Greek hustera, womb. See **udero-** in Appendix.*]

hys·ter·o·gen·ic (hĭs′tə-rō-jĕn′ĭk) adj. Causing hysteria. [HYSTERO- + -GENIC.]

hys·ter·oid (hĭs′tə-roid′) adj. Also **hys·ter·oid·al** (hĭs′tə-roid′l). Resembling hysteria. [HYSTER(O)- + -OID.]

hys·ter·on prot·er·on (hĭs′tə-rŏn′ prŏt′ə-rŏn′). **1.** A figure of speech in which the natural or rational order of its terms is reversed; for example, bred and born instead of born and bred. **2.** Logic. The fallacy of assuming as a premise a proposition following something yet to be proved. [Late Latin, from Greek husteron proteron, "latter first" : husteron, neuter of husteros, latter (see **ud-** in Appendix*) + proteron, neuter of proteros, first, former (see **per¹** in Appendix*).]

hys·ter·ot·o·my (hĭs′tə-rŏt′ə-mē) n., pl. **-mies.** Surgery. Incision of the uterus. [New Latin hysterotomia : HYSTERO- + -TOMY.]

Hz hertz.

ă pat/ā pay/âr care/ä father/b bib/ch church/d deed/ĕ pet/ē be/f fife/g gag/h hat/hw which/ĭ pit/ī pie/îr pier/j judge/k kick/l lid, needle/m mum/n no, sudden/ng thing/ŏ pot/ō toe/ô paw, for/oi noise/ou out/ŏŏ took/ōō boot/p pop/r roar/s sauce/sh ship, dish/

hyrax
Procavia capensis

Ii

Around 1000 B.C. the Phoenicians and other Semites of Syria and Palestine began to use a graphic sign in the forms (1,2). They gave it the name yōdh, meaning "hand," and used it for a semiconsonant y, as in English boy, boys. After 900 B.C. the Greeks borrowed the sign from the Phoenicians, using at first various angular versions (3,4,5), and then a simplified form (6). They also changed its name to iōta and made it stand for their vowel i. The Greek form (6) passed unchanged via Etruscan to the Roman alphabet (7,8), and thence to our modern capital, printed (11) and written (12). The written Roman form (7) passed into late Roman and medieval Uncial (9) and Cursive (10), without essential modification until the dot was added in late medieval times to avoid confusion with similarly shaped letters; it was retained in our modern small letter, printed (13) and written (14).

i, I (ī) *n., pl.* **i's. I's** or **Is. 1.** The ninth letter of the modern English alphabet. See **alphabet. 2.** Any of the speech sounds represented by this letter.

i, I, i., I. *Note:* As an abbreviation or symbol, *i* may be a small or a capital letter, with or without a period. Established forms or those generally preferred precede the definition. When no form is given, all four forms are in general use in that sense. **1. i, I** *Electricity.* current. **2. i** *Mathematics.* imaginary unit. **3. i.** interest. **4. i.** intransitive. **5. I** The symbol for the element iodine. **6. i., I.** island; isle. **7. I** isospin. **8. i, I** The Roman numeral for one. **9.** The ninth in a series.

I (ī) *pron.* The first person singular pronoun in the nominative case. Used to represent the speaker or writer; also sometimes used in a conditional construction depending on the elliptically understood clause *if I were you,* to express advice or indirect injunction: *I wouldn't go out without a coat today.* See Usage note at **me.** —*n., pl.* **I's.** The self; the ego. [Middle English *i, ich,* Old English *ic.* See **eg** in Appendix.*]

Usage: The use of *I* in the objective case, typically as the second of a pair of pronouns linked by a copula (as in *between you and I*), is nonstandard, although it tends to occur frequently in speech; in the 17th century it was very common at every level of usage, including the most formal.

i–. Variant of **y-.**

–ia¹. Used to form: **1.** Names of diseases and disorders; for example, **alexia, diphtheria. 2.** Names of plants; for example, **poinsettia, begonia. 3.** Names of alkaloids; for example, **morphia. 4.** Names of areas and countries; for example, **Manchuria.** [New Latin, from Latin and Greek, suffix of feminine abstract nouns.]

–ia². Used to form: **1.** Collective nouns; for example, **trivia, genitalia. 2.** Names of things relating or belonging to; for example, **pedodontia.** [New Latin, from Latin, neuter plural of *-ius,* and from Greek, neuter plural of *-ios.*]

IA Iowa (with Zip Code).

Ia. Iowa (unofficial).

i.a. in absentia.

IAD Airport code for Dulles International Airport, Washington, D.C.

IADB Inter-American Defense Board.

IAEA International Atomic Energy Agency.

–ial. Indicates of, pertaining to, or characterized by; for example, **managerial, residential.** [Middle English, from Old French *-ial, -iel,* from Latin *-iālis : -i-,* stem + *-ālis,* -AL.]

i·amb (ī′ămb′) *n. Prosody.* A metrical foot consisting of a short syllable followed by a long (in quantitative verse), or an unstressed syllable followed by a stressed (in accentual verse). Also called "iambic." There are four iambs in the following line:

"I-am′bics march′ from short′ to long′" (Coleridge). [French *iambe,* from Latin *iambus,* IAMBUS.]

i·am·bic (ī-ăm′bĭk) *adj.* **1.** Consisting of iambs or characterized by their predominance: *iambic pentameter.* **2.** Employing this rhythm, especially in the various genres associated with its use: *the iambic poets of antiquity.* —*n. Prosody.* **1.** An iamb *(see).* **2.** *Usually plural.* A verse, stanza, or poem written in iambs: *the lethal iambics of Archilochus.* [Latin *iambicus,* from Greek *iambikos,* from *iambos,* IAMBUS.]

i·am·bus (ī-ăm′bəs) *n., pl.* **-buses** or **-bi** (-bī′). An iamb. [Latin, from Greek *iambos†.*]

–ian¹. Indicates: **1.** Of or belonging to; for example, **Bostonian. 2.** Characteristic of or resembling; for example, **Johnsonian.** [Old French *-ien,* from Latin *-iānus : -i-,* stem + *-ānus,* -AN.]

–ian². Indicates: **1.** Admirer or follower of; for example, **Chaucerian. 2.** One skilled in or a specialist; for example, **pediatrician, logistician. 3.** One belonging to a certain period of time or place; for example, **Edwardian.** [From -IAN.]

–iana. Variant of -ana (a collection).

IAS *Aviation.* indicated air speed.

Ia·și (yäsh, yä′shē) Also **Jas·sy** (yä′sē). A city and commercial center of northeastern Rumania. Population, 127,000.

–iasis. Indicates a pathological condition; for example, **teniasis.** [New Latin, from Greek, suffix of action.]

i·at·ric (ī-ăt′rĭk) *adj.* Also **i·at·ri·cal** (-rĭ-kəl). *Rare.* Pertaining to medicine or physicians; medical. [Greek *iatrikos,* from *iatros,* physician, healer, from *iasthai†,* to heal, cure.]

–iatric. Indicates pertaining to a specific kind of medical treatment; for example, **geriatric.** [From IATRIC.]

–iatrics. Indicates medical treatment; for example, **pediatrics.** [From IATRIC.]

i·at·ro·gen·ic (ī-ăt′rə-jĕn′ĭk) *adj.* Induced in a patient by a physician's words or actions. Said especially of imagined illnesses. [Greek *iatros,* physician (see **iatric**) + -GENIC.]

–iatry. Indicates medical treatment; for example, **psychiatry.** [French *-iatrie,* from New Latin *-iatria,* from Greek *iatreia,* the art of healing, from *iatros,* physician. See **iatric.**]

ib. ibidem.

I·ba·dan (ē-bä′dän). The second-largest city of Nigeria, located in the southwest. Population, 627,000.

I·ba·gué (ē′vä-gā′). A city of west-central Colombia. Population, 160,000.

I-beam (ī′bēm′) *n.* A steel beam or girder with a cross section formed like the capital letter I.

I·be·ri·a (ī-bîr′ē-ə). **1.** The ancient name for the region roughly corresponding to the modern Georgian S.S.R. **2.** An ancient name for the **Iberian Peninsula.**

I·be·ri·an (ī-bîr′ē-ən) *adj.* **1. a.** Of or pertaining to the ancient ethnological group or groups that inhabited the Iberian Peninsula. **b.** Of or pertaining to the language or culture of these groups. **2.** Of or pertaining to the Iberian Peninsula. **3.** Of or pertaining to ancient Iberia in the Caucasus, to its inhabitants, their language, or their culture. —*n.* **1. a.** A member of the ancient Caucasoid people that inhabited the Iberian Peninsula. **b.** The language of this people. **2.** An inhabitant of the Iberian Peninsula. **3.** An inhabitant of ancient Iberia in the Caucasus.

Iberian Peninsula. Ancient names **His·pa·ni·a** (hĭ-spā′nē-ə, -spăn′yə, -spā′nē-ə), **I·be·ri·a** (ī-bîr′ē-ə). The region of southwestern Europe separated from France by the Pyrenees and consisting of Spain and Portugal.

I·ber·us. The ancient name for the **Ebro.**

i·bex (ī′bĕks) *n.* Any of several wild goats of the genus *Capra,* of mountainous regions of the Old World; especially, *C. ibex,*

ibex
Capra ibex

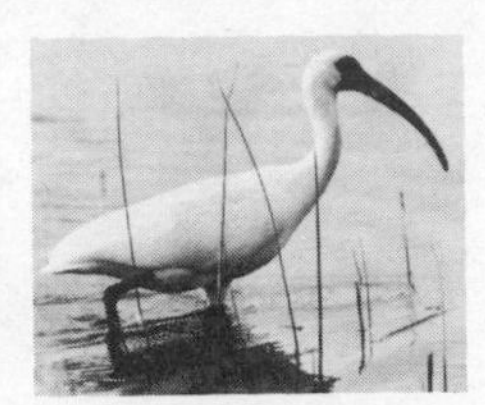
ibis
Eudocimus albus

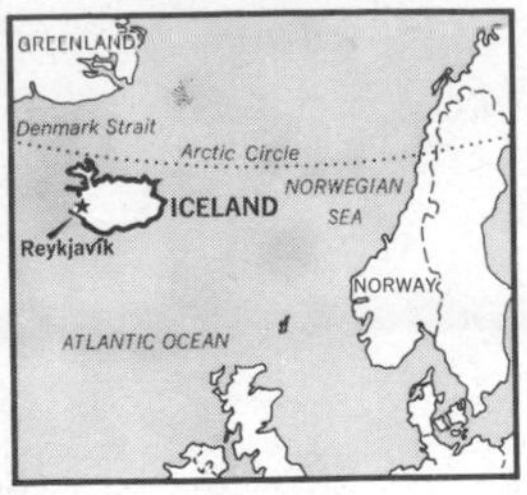

Iceland

having long, ridged, backward-curving horns. [Latin, perhaps of Alpine origin.]

I·bib·i·o (ĭ-bĭb′ē-ō) *n., pl.* **Ibibio** or **-os.** **1.** A people of southeastern Nigeria. **2.** A member of the Ibibio. **3.** The Niger-Congo language of this people.

ibid. ibidem.

i·bi·dem (ĭb′ə-dĕm′, ĭ-bī′dəm) *adv. Latin. Abbr.* **ib., ibid.** In the same place. Used in footnotes and bibliographies to refer to the book, chapter, article, or page cited just before.

i·bis (ī′bĭs) *n.* **1.** Any of various long-billed wading birds of the family Threskiornithidae. **2.** The **wood ibis** *(see).* [Latin *ībis,* from Greek *ibis,* from Egyptian *hīb.*]

I·bi·za (ē-vē′thä). Also **I·vi·za.** An island, 221 square miles in area, of the Balearic group, Spain, located in the western Mediterranean, 90 miles east of Valencia. Population, 35,000.

–ible. Variant of **-able.**

Ib·lis. Variant of **Eblis.**

ibn-Khal·dun (ĭb′ən-KHăl-do͞on′), **Abd al-Rahman.** 1332–1406. Arab historian.

ibn-Rushd. The Arabic name for **Averroës.**

ibn Sa·ud. See **Saud.**

ibn-Si·na. The Arabic name for **Avicenna.**

I·bo (ē′bō) *n., pl.* **Ibo** or **Ibos.** **1.** A member of one of various Negroid tribes of Nigeria. **2.** The Sudanese-Guinean language spoken by these people.

Ib·sen (ĭb′sən), **Henrik.** 1828–1906. Norwegian dramatist.

–ic. **1.** Used to form adjectives meaning of, pertaining to, or characteristic of; for example, **seismic, Gaelic, mythic.** **2.** *Chemistry.* Having or taking a valence higher than in corresponding -ous compounds; for example, **ferric.** Compare **-ous.** [Middle English *-ic, -ik,* from Latin *-icus.*]

ICA International Cooperation Administration.

ICAO International Civil Aviation Organization.

I·car·i·a. See **Ikaria.**

I·car·i·an Sea (ĭ-kâr′ĭ-ən). The ancient name for the part of the Aegean Sea along the coast of Asia Minor.

Ic·a·rus[1] (ĭk′ər-əs). *Greek Mythology.* The son of Daedalus, who, in escaping from Crete on artificial wings made for him by his father, flew so close to the sun that the wax with which his wings were fastened melted, so that he fell into the Aegean Sea.

Ic·a·rus[2] (ĭk′ər-əs) *n. Astronomy.* The asteroid that passes closest to the sun. [After ICARUS.]

ICBM intercontinental ballistic missile.

ICC **1.** Indian Claims Commission. **2.** Interstate Commerce Commission.

ice (īs) *n.* **1.** Water frozen solid. **2.** A surface, layer, or mass of frozen water. **3.** Anything resembling frozen water. **4.** A dessert consisting of sweetened and flavored crushed ice, distinguished from a similar dessert made with milk or cream. **5.** Cake frosting; icing. **6.** *Slang.* A diamond or diamonds. **7.** The playing field in ice hockey; rink. **—break the ice.** **1.** To relax a tense or unduly formal atmosphere or social situation. **2.** To make a start; begin something. **—cut no ice.** *Informal.* To have no influence or effect. **—on ice.** **1.** In a refrigerator or cooler. **2.** *Informal.* **a.** In reserve or readiness. **b.** Put aside; shelved; postponed. **c.** Held incommunicado. **3.** Certain to be won. Said of games or a hand of cards. **—on thin ice.** In a risky situation; on uncertain ground. *—v.* **iced, icing, ices.** *—tr.* **1.** To coat or slick with ice. **2.** To cause to become ice; freeze. **3.** To chill by setting in or as if in ice. **4.** To cover or decorate (a cake) with a sugar coating. **5.** *Slang.* To remove any question of victory, as in a game; decide; clinch. **6.** *Ice Hockey.* **a.** To shoot (the puck) far out of defensive territory. **b.** To put or field (a hockey team) on the ice. *—intr.* To turn into, or become coated with, ice; freeze. Often used with *over* or *up.* [Middle English *is,* Old English *īs.* See **eis-**[2] in Appendix.*]

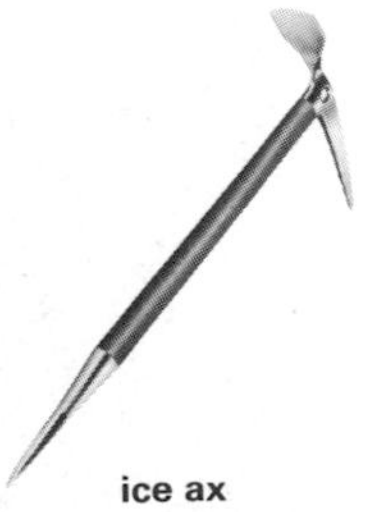
ice ax

Ice. Iceland; Icelandic.

ice age. **1.** Any of a series of cold periods marked by extensive glaciation alternating with periods of relative warmth, together constituting the Pleistocene or glacial epoch. **2.** *Capital* **I,** *capital* **A.** The Pleistocene or glacial epoch.

ice ax. An ax used by mountaineers for cutting steps in ice.

ice bag. A small waterproof bag used as an **ice pack** *(see).*

ice·berg (īs′bûrg′) *n.* **1.** A massive floating body of ice broken away from a glacier. Also called "berg." **2.** *Informal.* One who appears to be cold or aloof. [Probably partial translation of Danish and Norwegian *isberg* : *is,* ice + *berg,* mountain, from Old Norse (see **bhergh-**[2] in Appendix*).]

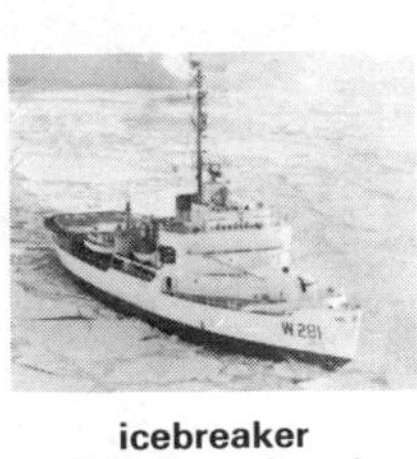
icebreaker
U.S. Coast Guard icebreaker *Westwind*

ice·blink (īs′blĭngk′) *n.* **1.** A yellowish glare in the sky over an ice field. Also called "blink." **2.** A coastal ice cliff.

ice·boat (īs′bōt′) *n.* **1.** A boatlike vehicle set on runners that sails on ice. **2.** An icebreaker.

ice·bound (īs′bound′) *adj.* **1.** Locked in by ice, as a ship. **2.** Jammed or covered over by ice, as a harbor or waterway.

ice·box (īs′bŏks′) *n.* **1.** An insulated chest or box in which ice is put to cool and preserve food. **2.** A refrigerator.

ice·break·er (īs′brā′kər) *n.* **1.** A sturdy ship built for breaking a passage through icebound waters. **2.** A protective pier or dock apron used as a buffer against floating ice.

ice cap. An extensive perennial cover of ice and snow.

ice cream. A smooth, sweet, cold food prepared from a frozen mixture of milk products, usually containing 10 to 14 per cent butterfat and an average of 10.5 per cent nonfat milk solids, approximately 15 per cent cane or beet sugar, flavoring, and sometimes small amounts of colloidal materials and emulsifiers.

ice-cream cone (īs′krēm′). **1.** A conical wafer used to hold a scoop of ice cream. **2.** This wafer with the ice cream in it.

ice-cream soda (īs′krēm′). A refreshment consisting of ice cream scoops in a mixture of soda water and flavoring syrup.

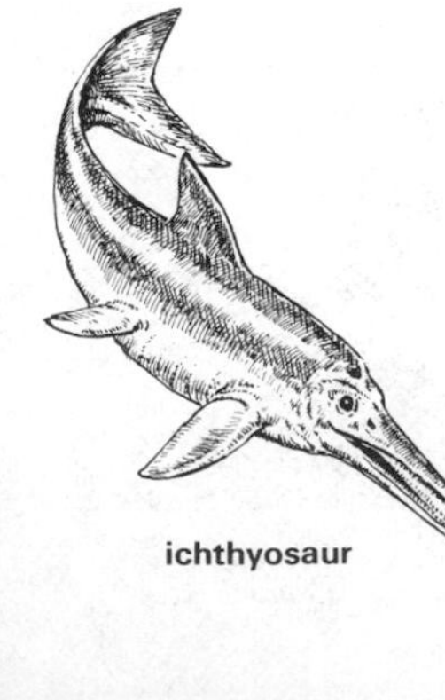
ichthyosaur

iced (īst) *adj.* **1.** Covered over with ice. **2.** Chilled with ice. **3.** Decorated or coated with icing.

ice·fall (īs′fôl′) *n.* **1.** The face or sheer side of a glacier, resembling a frozen waterfall. **2.** An avalanche of ice.

ice field. A large, level expanse of floating ice; an ice floe.

ice floe. A flat expanse of floating ice, smaller than an ice field.

ice fog. **Pogonip** *(see).*

ice foot. A belt or ledge of ice that forms along the shoreline in Arctic regions.

ice hockey. A game, **hockey** *(see).*

Icel. Iceland; Icelandic.

Ice·land (īs′lənd). *Icelandic* **Īs·land** (ēs′länt). *Abbr.* **Ice., Icel.** An island republic, 39,709 square miles in area, in the North Atlantic. Population, 200,000. Capital, Reykjavík.

Ice·land·er (īs′lən-dər) *n.* A native or inhabitant of Iceland.

Ice·land·ic (īs-lăn′dĭk) *adj. Abbr.* **Ice., Icel.** Of or pertaining to Iceland, its inhabitants, their language, or culture. *—n.* The North Germanic language spoken in Iceland, specifically: **a.** This language as spoken since the 16th century. **b.** Old Icelandic.

Iceland moss. A brittle, grayish-brown, edible lichen, *Cetraria islandica,* of northern regions.

Iceland spar. A doubly refracting transparent calcite, especially from Iceland, used in optical instruments.

ice milk. A smooth, sweet, cold food prepared from a frozen mixture of milk products, usually containing 3 to 6 per cent butterfat, 11 to 14 per cent nonfat milk solids, and 12 to 15 per cent sugar.

ice needle. Any of the thin ice crystals that float high in the atmosphere in certain conditions of clear, cold weather.

ice pack. **1.** A floating mass of compacted ice fragments. **2.** A **pack** *(see).*

ice pick. A pointed awl for chipping or breaking ice.

ice plant. A plant, *Mesembryanthemum crystallinum,* native to southern Africa, having fleshy leaves and stems covered with glistening encrustations, and white or pink flowers.

ice point. The temperature at which pure water and ice are in equilibrium in a mixture at one atmosphere of pressure.

ice skate. **1.** A metal runner or blade that is fitted to the sole of a shoe for skating on ice. **2.** A shoe or light boot with such a runner permanently fixed to it.

ice-skate (īs′skāt′) *intr.v.* **-skated, -skating, -skates.** To skate on ice. **—ice′skat·er** *n.*

ice water. **1. a.** Very cold drinking water. **b.** Such water containing ice. **2.** Melted ice.

ICFTU International Confederation of Free Trade Unions.

ich (ĭk) *n.* A contagious disease of tropical aquarium fishes, caused by a protozoan, *Ichthyophthirius multifiliis,* and characterized by small white pustules on the body. [From New Latin *Ichthyophthirius,* "fish louse" : ICHTHYO- + *Phthirius,* louse, from Greek *phtheir,* louse (see **gzwher-** in Appendix*).]

ich·neu·mon (ĭk-no͞o′mən, -nyo͞o′mən) *n.* A mongoose of the genus *Herpestes;* especially, *H. ichneumon,* of Africa. [Latin, from Greek *ikhneumōn,* "tracker," a weasel that hunts out crocodile eggs, from *ikhneuein,* to track, from *ikhnos*†, track.]

ichneumon fly. Any of various wasplike insects of the family Ichneumonidae, having larvae that are parasitic on the larvae of other insects. Also called "ichneumon wasp."

ich·nite (ĭk′nīt′) *n.* A fossilized footprint. [Greek *ikhnos,* footstep, track (see **ichneumon**) + -ITE.]

i·chor (ī′kôr′, ī′kər) *n.* **1.** *Greek Mythology.* The rarefied fluid said to run in the veins of the gods. **2.** A fluid likened to blood. **3.** *Pathology.* A watery, acrid discharge from a wound or ulcer. [Greek *ikhōr*†.] **—i′chor·ous** (ī′kər-əs) *adj.*

ich·thy·ic (ĭk′thē-ĭk) *adj.* Of, pertaining to, or characteristic of fishes. [From Greek *ikhthus,* fish. See **ichthyo-.**]

ichthyo–, ichthy–. Indicates fish; for example, **ichthyology, ichthyornis.** [Latin, from Greek *ikhthuo-,* from *ikhthus,* fish. See **gzhū-** in Appendix.*]

ich·thy·oid (ĭk′thē-oid′) *adj.* Also **ich·thy·oid·al** (ĭk′thē-oid′l). Characteristic of or resembling a fish. *—n.* A fish or fishlike vertebrate. [Greek *ikhthuoeidēs* : ICHTHY(O)- + -OID.]

ich·thy·ol·o·gy (ĭk′thē-ŏl′ə-jē) *n.* Zoology specializing in the study of fishes. [ICHTHYO- + -LOGY.] **—ich′thy·o·log′ic** (-ə-lŏj′ĭk), **ich′thy·o·log′i·cal** *adj.* **—ich′thy·ol′o·gist** *n.*

ich·thy·oph·a·gous (ĭk′thē-ŏf′ə-gəs) *adj.* Feeding on fish; fish-eating. [Greek *ikhthuophagos* : ICHTHYO- + -PHAGOUS.]

ich·thy·or·nis (ĭk′thē-ôr′nĭs) *n.* Any of various extinct, toothed, fish-eating birds of the genus *Ichthyornis,* that existed during the Cretaceous period. [New Latin "fish bird" : ICHTHY(O)- + Greek *ornis,* bird (see **er-**[2] in Appendix*).]

ich·thy·o·saur (ĭk′thē-ə-sôr′) *n.* Also **ich·thy·o·saur·us** (ĭk′thē-ə-sôr′əs). Any of various extinct fishlike marine reptiles of the order Ichthyosauria, of the Triassic to the Cretaceous periods. [New Latin *Ichthyosaurus* : ICHTHYO- + -SAUR.]

ich·thy·o·sis (ĭk′thē-ō′sĭs) *n.* A congenital skin disease, characterized by dry, thickened, scaly skin. Also called "fishskin disease." [New Latin : ICHTHY(O)- + -OSIS.]

–ician. Used to form nouns meaning a person who practices or is a specialist in a given field; for example, **mortician.**

i·ci·cle (ī′sĭ-kəl) *n.* A tapering spike of ice formed by the freezing of dripping or falling water. [Middle English *isikel* : *is,* ICE + *ikel,* icicle, Old English *gicel* (see **yeg-** in Appendix*).]

i·ci·ly (ī′sĭ-lē) *adv.* In an icy or chilling manner.

i·ci·ness (ī′sē-nĭs) *n.* The condition or quality of being icy.

ic·ing (ī′sĭng) *n.* **1.** A sweet glaze made of sugar, butter, water, egg whites or milk, and often flavored and cooked, used to cover or decorate cakes, cookies, and other baked goods. **2.** *Ice Hockey.* The intentional shooting of the puck far out of defensive territory, as by a team with a man in the penalty box; not permitted when construed as stalling.

ICJ International Court of Justice.

Ick·nield Way (ĭk′nēld′). A prehistoric road in Britain that ran northeast on high ground from Salisbury Plain to the Wash.

i·con (ī′kŏn′) *n.* Also **i·kon, ei·kon** (for sense 2). **1. a.** An image; representation. **b.** A simile or symbol. **2.** A representation or picture of a sacred Christian personage, itself regarded as sacred, especially in the tradition of the Eastern Churches. [Latin *īcōn,* from Greek *eikōn,* likeness, image. See **weik-³** in Appendix.*]

i·con·ic (ī-kŏn′ĭk) *adj.* **1.** Pertaining to or having the character of an icon. **2.** Having a conventional formularized style. Said of certain memorial statues and busts, such as the ancient portrait statues of victorious athletes.

icono–. Indicates likeness, image; for example, **iconolatry.** [Greek *eikono-,* from *eikōn,* image, ICON.]

i·con·o·clasm (ī-kŏn′ə-klăz′əm) *n.* **1.** The action or doctrine of destroying sacred images. **2.** The attacking or overthrow of established or venerated institutions, practices, or attitudes. [From ICONOCLAST.]

i·con·o·clast (ī-kŏn′ə-klăst′) *n.* **1.** A destroyer of sacred images, specifically: **a.** Any of the opponents of the use and veneration of icons in the Eastern Churches during the eighth and ninth centuries A.D. **b.** A Protestant in the 16th and 17th centuries who opposed the veneration of sacred images and traditions. **2.** One who attacks and seeks to overthrow traditional or popular ideas or institutions. [Medieval Latin *īconoclastēs,* from Medieval Greek *eikonoklastēs,* "image breaker" : ICONO- + -CLAST.] —**i·con′o·clas′tic** (-klăs′tĭk) *adj.*

i·co·nog·ra·phy (ī′kə-nŏg′rə-fē) *n., pl.* **-phies. 1. a.** Pictorial illustration of a given subject. **b.** The collected representations illustrating a subject. **2. a.** A given set of symbolic forms bearing the meaning of a stylized work of art. **b.** The conventions defining them and governing their interrelationship. [Greek *eikonographia,* description, sketch, "drawing of images" : ICONO- + -GRAPHY.] —**i·con′o·graph′ic** (ī-kŏn′ə-grăf′ĭk), **i·con′o·graph′i·cal** *adj.*

i·co·nol·a·try (ī′kə-nŏl′ə-trē) *n.* The worship of images or icons. [ICONO- + -LATRY.] —**i′co·nol′a·ter** *n.*

i·co·nol·o·gy (ī′kə-nŏl′ə-jē) *n., pl.* **-gies.** The branch of art history dealing with the description, analysis, and interpretations of icons or iconic representations. [French *iconologie* : ICONO- + -LOGY.] —**i·con′o·log′i·cal** (ī-kŏn′ə-lŏj′ĭ-kəl) *adj.*

i·con·o·scope (ī-kŏn′ə-skōp′) *n.* A television-camera tube equipped for rapid scanning of an information-storing, photoactive mosaic. [Originally a trademark : ICONO- + -SCOPE.]

i·co·nos·ta·sis (ī′kə-nŏs′tə-sĭs) *n., pl.* **-ses** (-sēz′). The screen dividing the sanctuary from the main body of an Eastern Orthodox church. [From Late Greek *eikonostasion,* shrine, "place where images stand" : ICONO- + Greek *stasis,* a standing (see **stā-** in Appendix*).]

i·co·sa·he·dron (ī-kō′sə-hē′drən) *n., pl.* **-dra** (-drə) or **-drons.** A polyhedron having 20 faces. [Greek *eikosaedron* : *eikosi,* twenty (see **wīkm̥tī** in Appendix*) + -HEDRON.]

–ics. Indicates: **1.** The science or art of; for example, **graphics, poetics.** Used with a singular verb. **2.** The act, practices, or activities of; for example, **hysterics, athletics.** Used with a plural verb. [From -IC, originally used to render the Greek plural noun ending *-ika,* as in *mathēmatika,* MATHEMATICS.]

ic·ter·ic (ĭk-tĕr′ĭk) *adj.* **1.** Pertaining to or having jaundice. **2.** Used to treat jaundice. —*n.* A remedy for jaundice.

ic·ter·us (ĭk′tər-əs) *n. Pathology.* **Jaundice** *(see).* [New Latin, from Greek *ikteros*†, jaundice.]

ic·tus (ĭk′təs) *n., pl.* **-tuses** or **ictus.** *Pathology.* A sudden attack; a fit; stroke. [Latin, blow, stroke, from the past participle of *īcere*†, to strike.]

i·cy (ī′sē) *adj.* **icier, iciest. 1.** Containing or covered with ice; frozen; slippery: *an icy road.* **2.** Resembling ice; cold, slippery, or raw: *icy fingers.* **3.** Bitterly cold; freezing: *an icy day.* **4.** Chilling in manner; frigid: *an icy smile.*

id (ĭd) *n. Psychoanalysis.* The division of the psyche associated with instinctual impulses and demands for immediate satisfaction of primitive needs. [New Latin (translation of German *es,* it), from Latin, it, neuter of *is,* he. See **i-** in Appendix.*]

I'd (īd). **1.** Contraction of *I had.* **2.** Contraction of *I would.* **3.** Contraction of *I should.*

–id. Indicates: **1.** *Astronomy.* A meteor or comet that appears to originate in a particular constellation; for example, **Geminid. 2.** *Zoology.* A member of a family; for example, **hominid. 3.** *Chemistry.* Variant of **-ide.** [Partly from New Latin -IDAE and partly from French *-ide,* from Latin *-is* (stem *-id-*), feminine patronymic suffix.]

ID Idaho (with Zip Code).

id. idem.

Id. Idaho (unofficial).

i.d. inside diameter.

I.D. 1. identification. **2.** intelligence department.

I·da (ī′də). A feminine given name. [Middle English *Ida,* from Medieval Latin, from Old High German, perhaps related to Old North French *idh*†, work, labor.]

IDA International Development Association.

I·da, Mount (ī′də). *Greek* **I·dhi** (ē′thē). The highest mountain (8,058 feet) of Crete, located in the central part of the island.

–idae. Indicates taxonomic names of families in zoology; for example, Hominidae, the family that includes man. See **hominid.**

I·da·ho (ī′də-hō). A Northwestern state of the United States, 83,557 square miles in area; admitted to the Union in 1890. Population, 692,000. Capital, Boise. See map at **United States of America.**

I·da·ho Falls (ī′də-hō). A city and food-shipping center of southeast-central Idaho. Population, 33,000.

I·da Mountains (ī′də). *Turkish* **Kaz·da·gi** (käs′dä-ī′). A range of northwestern Turkey, near the site of ancient Troy. Highest elevation, Mount Gargarus (5,810 feet).

–ide, –id. Used to form the names of chemical compounds; for example, **chloride.** [German *-id,* from French *-ide* (first used in *oxide,* OXIDE), from *acide,* ACID.]

i·de·a (ī-dē′ə) *n.* **1.** That which exists in the mind, potentially or actually, as a product of mental activity, such as thought or knowledge; a thought; conception: *many good ideas.* **2.** An opinion, conviction, or principle: *Upon what do you base your political ideas?* **3.** A plan, scheme, or method. **4.** The gist of a specific action or situation; significance. **5.** A notion; fancy. **6.** *Obsolete.* A mental image of something remembered. **7.** *Music.* A theme or motif. **8.** *Philosophy.* **a.** In the philosophy of Plato, an archetype of which a corresponding being in phenomenal reality is an imperfect replica. **b.** In the philosophy of Kant, a concept of reason that is transcendent but nonempirical. **c.** In the philosophy of Hegel, absolute truth; the complete and ultimate product of reason. [Latin, from Greek, form, model, class, notion. See **weid-** in Appendix.*]

Synonyms: *idea, thought, notion, conception, concept.* These nouns refer to what is formed or represented consciously in the mind. *Idea* has the widest range and refers to the product of all such mental function. *Thought* is applied to what is distinctively intellectual and thus produced by contemplation and reasoning distinguished from mere perceiving, feeling, or willing. *Notion,* in contrast, refers to what is formed tentatively or without great consideration, and may have little basis in fact or actual experience. *Conception* and *concept* are applied to mental formulations on a broad scale and in some detail: *the artist's conception of hell. Concept,* in addition, can mean such a representation formed by generalizing from particulars.

i·de·al (ī-dē′əl, ī-dēl′) *n.* **1.** A conception of something in its absolute perfection. **2.** One regarded as a standard or model of perfection. **3.** An ultimate object of endeavor; a goal. **4.** An honorable or worthy principle or aim. **5.** That which exists only in the mind. —*adj.* **1.** Conforming to an ultimate form of perfection or excellence. **2.** Considered the best of its kind. **3.** Completely or highly satisfactory. **4.** Existing only in the mind; visionary; imaginary. **5.** Of, pertaining to, or consisting of ideas or mental images. **6.** *Philosophy.* **a.** Existing as an archetype or pattern, especially as a Platonic idea. **b.** Of or pertaining to idealism. [French *idéal,* from Late Latin *ideālis,* from Latin *idea,* model, IDEA.]

Synonyms: *ideal, model, exemplar, standard, prototype, archetype.* These nouns refer to things or, less often, to persons that serve as the basis of direction or guidance in work or behavior. An *ideal* is a goal of perfection in the form of a person or thing, sometimes imaginary. A *model* is a pattern or a person who serves as a pattern in the creation of something; in a related sense the term refers to a person or thing worthy of imitation. The latter sense approaches that of *exemplar,* a person or thing that serves as an ideal example by reason of being either very worthy or truly representative of a type, admirable or otherwise. A *standard* is an established criterion or recognized level of excellence used as a measure of achievement. *Prototype* and *archetype* both denote original models of things subsequently reproduced. What develops from a *prototype* may represent significant modifications from the original. An *archetype,* in contrast, is usually construed as an ideal form that establishes an unchanging pattern for all things of its kind.

i·de·al·ism (ī-dē′ə-lĭz′əm) *n.* **1.** The action of envisioning things in an ideal form. **2.** Pursuit of one's ideals. **3.** An idealizing treatment of a subject in literature or art. **4.** The theory that the object of external perception, in itself or as perceived, consists of ideas. In this sense, compare **materialism, realism.**

i·de·al·ist (ī-dē′ə-lĭst) *n.* **1.** One whose conduct is influenced by idealism. **2.** One who is unrealistic and impractical; a visionary. **3.** An artist or writer whose work is imbued with idealism. **4.** An adherent of any system of philosophical idealism.

i·de·al·is·tic (ī-dē′ə-lĭs′tĭk) *adj.* Pertaining to or having the nature of an idealist or idealism. —**i·de′al·is′ti·cal·ly** *adv.*

i·de·al·i·ty (ī′dē-ăl′ə-tē) *n., pl.* **-ties. 1.** The state or quality of being ideal. **2.** Existence in idea only.

i·de·al·ize (ī-dē′ə-līz′) *v.* **-ized, -izing, -izes.** —*tr.* **1.** To regard as ideal; hold in high esteem. **2.** To make or envision as ideal. —*intr.* **1.** To render something as an ideal. **2.** To conceive an ideal or ideals. —**i·de′al·i·za′tion** *n.* —**i·de′al·iz′er** *n.*

i·de·al·ly (ī-dē′ə-lē) *adv.* **1.** In conformity with an ideal; perfectly. **2.** In theory or imagination; theoretically.

i·de·ate (ī-dē′āt′) *v.* **-ated, -ating, -ates.** —*tr.* To form an idea of; imagine; conceive. —*intr.* To conceive mental images; think. [From IDEA.] —**i′de·a′tion** *n.* —**i′de·a′tion·al** *adj.*

i·dée fixe (ē-dā fēks′) *pl.* **idées fixes** (ē-dā fēks′). *French.* A fixed idea; obsession.

i·dem (ī′dĕm′). *Abbr.* **id.** Used to indicate a reference previously mentioned. [Latin *īdem* (masculine), *idem* (neuter), the same, from *id,* it, neuter of *is,* he. See **i-** in Appendix.*]

i·den·tic (ī-dĕn′tĭk) *adj.* **1.** Designating diplomatic action or language in which two or more governments agree to use the same forms in their relations with other governments. **2.** *Archaic.* Identical. [Medieval Latin *identicus,* IDENTICAL.]

i·den·ti·cal (ī-dĕn′tĭ-kəl) *adj.* **1.** Being the same. **2.** Being exactly equal. **3.** *Biology.* Developed from the same ovum. In this sense, compare **fraternal.** —See Synonyms at **same.** [Medieval

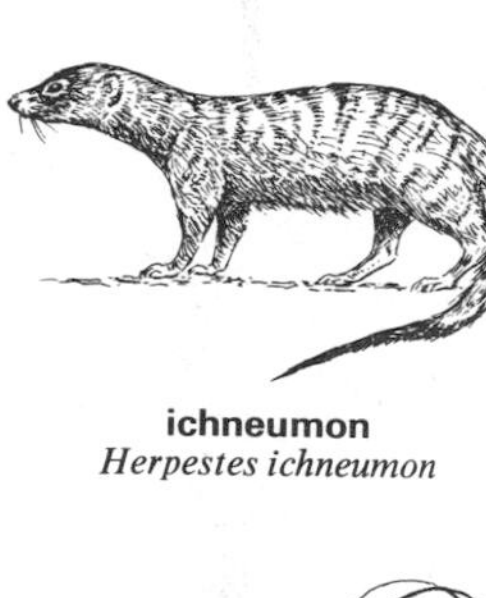

ichneumon
Herpestes ichneumon

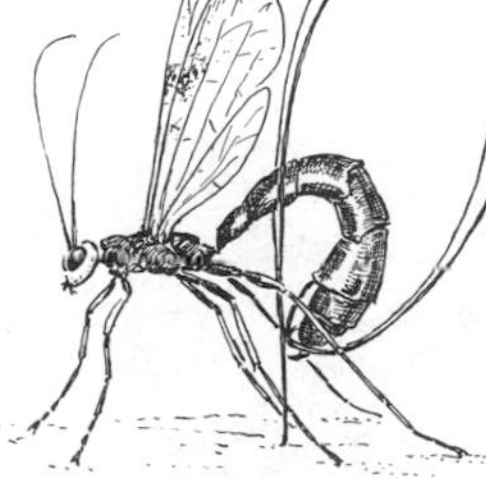

ichneumon fly
Megarhyssa atrata

Latin *identicus,* from Late Latin *identitās,* IDENTITY.] —**i·den′ti·cal·ly** *adv.* —**i·den′ti·cal·ness** *n.*

identical rhyme. See **rime riche.**

identical twin. Either of a pair of twins developed from a single fertilized ovum, having identical genetic constitutions and pronounced mutual resemblance.

i·den·ti·fi·ca·tion (ī-dĕn′tə-fĭ-kā′shən) *n.* **1.** The act of identifying. **2.** The state of being identified. **3.** *Abbr.* **I.D.** Proof of one's identity, as a document. **4.** *Psychology.* **a.** An individual's recognition of a personal or group identity. **b.** The transferral of response to an object considered identical to another.

i·den·ti·fy (ī-dĕn′tə-fī′) *v.* **-fied, -fying, -fies.** —*tr.* **1. a.** To establish the identity of. **b.** To ascertain the origin, nature, or definitive characteristics of: *His accent was difficult to identify.* **2.** To determine the taxonomic classification of. **3.** To consider as identical; equate. **4.** To associate with. **5.** *Psychology.* To associate or affiliate (oneself) closely with a person or group. —*intr.* To establish an identification with another or others. [Medieval Latin *identificāre* : Late Latin *identitās,* IDENTITY + -FY.] —**i·den′ti·fi′a·ble** *adj.* —**i·den′ti·fi′er** *n.*

Usage: *Identify* is well established in the sense, popularized by psychology, of associating oneself closely with a person or group or with the aims of a political or social movement: *He identified himself with the hero of a new novel.* The word is acceptably used in that sense on all levels, according to 93 per cent of the Usage Panel. The preceding example is also acceptable with *himself* omitted, according to 57 per cent of the members. The minority of the Panel takes the position that the reflexive pronouns must be expressed in such constructions.

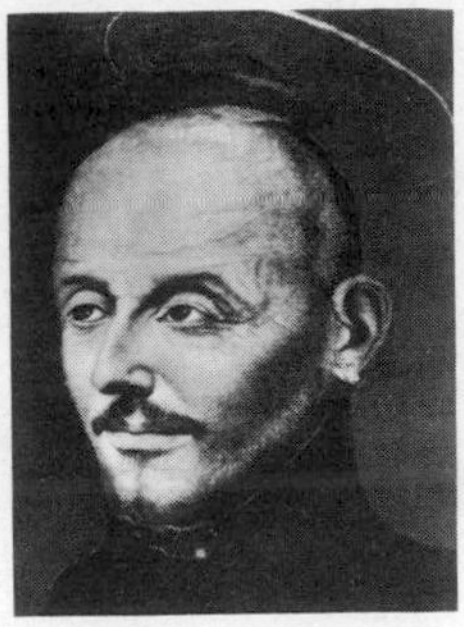

Saint Ignatius Loyola

i·den·ti·ty (ī-dĕn′tə-tē) *n., pl.* **-ties. 1.** The collective aspect of the set of characteristics by which a thing is definitively recognizable or known. **2.** The set of behavioral or personal characteristics by which an individual is recognizable as a member of a group. **3.** The quality or condition of being exactly the same as something else. **4.** The quality or condition of being or remaining the same. **5.** The personality of an individual regarded as a persisting entity. **6.** *Mathematics.* **a.** An equality satisfied by all values of the variables for which the expressions involved in the equality are defined. **b.** A **unity** *(see).* [Late Latin *identitās,* from Latin *idem,* the same, IDEM.]

ideo–. Indicates idea; for example, **ideogram.** [French *idéo-,* from Greek *idea,* form, notion. See **weid-** in Appendix.*]

id·e·o·gram (ĭd′ē-ə-grăm′, ī′dē-) *n.* Also **id·e·o·graph** (-grăf′, -gräf′). **1.** A character or symbol representing an idea or thing without expressing a particular word or phrase for it, as the characters in Chinese. **2.** A graphic symbol; for example, &, $, %, @. [IDEO- + -GRAM.]

ideogram
Chinese characters

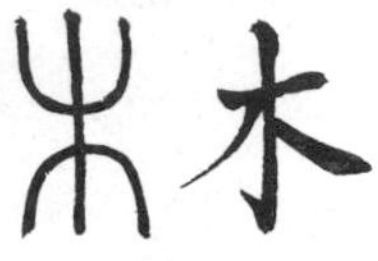

tree

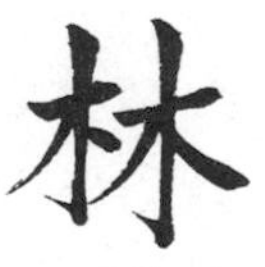

grove, forest

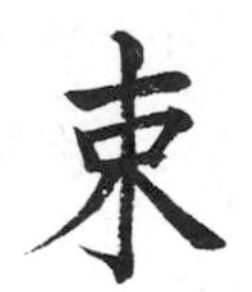

faggot, bundle; hence, to bind

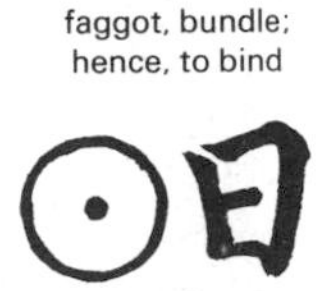

the sun

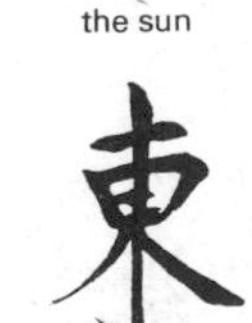

the sun seen in the trees; hence, east

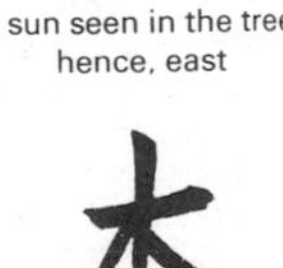

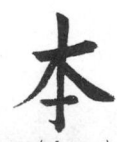

root (of a tree); hence, origin

id·e·og·ra·phy (ĭd′ē-ŏg′rə-fē, ī′dē-) *n.* **1.** The representation of ideas by graphic symbols. **2.** The use of ideograms to express ideas. [IDEO- + -GRAPHY.] —**id′e·o·graph′ic** *adj.*

i·de·ol·o·gist (ī′dē-ŏl′ə-jĭst, ĭd′ē-) *n.* **1.** An advocate or adherent of a given ideology. **2.** *Archaic.* A visionary; theorist.

i·de·o·logue (ī′dē-ə-lŏg, ĭd′ē-) *n.* An advocate of a given ideology; especially, one of its official exponents. [French *idéologue,* back-formation from *idéologie,* IDEOLOGY.]

i·de·ol·o·gy (ī′dē-ŏl′ə-jē, ĭd′ē-) *n., pl.* **-gies.** The body of ideas reflecting the social needs and aspirations of an individual, group, class, or culture. [French *idéologie* : IDEO- + -LOGY.]

i·de·o·mo·tor (ī′dē-ə-mō′tər, ĭd′ē-) *adj.* Of or being a motor response to an ideational rather than a sensory stimulus.

ides (īds) *n.* Plural in form, used with a singular verb. In the ancient Roman calendar, the 15th day of March, May, July, or October or the 13th day of the other months. [Middle English *idus, ides,* from Old French *ides,* from Latin *īdūs*†.]

id est (ĭd ĕst′). *Abbr.* **i.e.** *Latin.* That is.

Id·fu (ĭd′fo͞o). Also **Ed·fu** (ĕd′-). A city of Egypt on the Nile; site of the ancient temple of Horus. Population, 25,000.

I·dhi. The Greek name for Mount **Ida.**

idio–. Indicates individuality, peculiarity, isolation, or spontaneity; for example, **idiolect.** [Greek, from *idios*†, personal, peculiar, separate.]

id·i·o·cy (ĭd′ē-ə-sē) *n., pl.* **-cies. 1.** *Psychology.* A condition of subnormal intellectual development or ability, characterized by intelligence in the lowest measurable range. **2.** Extreme folly or stupidity. **3.** A foolish or stupid utterance or deed.

id·i·o·lect (ĭd′ē-ə-lĕkt′) *n.* The speech of an individual, considered as a linguistic pattern unique among speakers of his language or dialect. [IDIO- + (DIA)LECT.] —**id′i·o·lect′al, id′i·o·lect′ic** *adj.*

id·i·om (ĭd′ē-əm) *n.* **1.** A speech form that is peculiar to itself within the usage of a given language. **2.** The specific grammatical, syntactical, and structural character of a given language. **3.** A regional speech or dialect. **4.** A specialized vocabulary used by a group of people; jargon: *legal idiom.* **5.** A style of artistic expression characteristic of a given individual, school, period, or medium. [Old French *idiome,* from Late Latin *idiōma,* from Greek, peculiarity, idiom, peculiar phraseology, from *idiousthai,* to make one's own, from *idios,* own, personal. See **idio-**.]

id·i·o·mat·ic (ĭd′ē-ə-măt′ĭk) *adj.* **1.** Peculiar to or characteristic of a given language. **2.** Resembling or having the nature of an idiom. **3.** Using many idioms. —**id′i·o·mat′i·cal·ly** *adv.*

id·i·o·mor·phic (ĭd′ē-ə-môr′fĭk) *adj.* Having the characteristic shape. Said of well-crystallized minerals. [From Greek *idiomorphos,* having one's own form : IDIO- + -MORPHOUS.]

id·i·op·a·thy (ĭd′ē-ŏp′ə-thē) *n. Medicine.* **1.** A disease of unknown origin or cause; a primary disease. **2.** A disease for which no cause is known. [Greek *idiopathia,* disease having its own origin : IDIO- + -PATHY.] —**id′i·o·path′ic** (-ō-păth′ĭk) *adj.*

id·i·o·plasm (ĭd′ē-ə-plăz′əm) *n.* A hypothetical structural unit of germ plasm. [IDIO- + -PLASM.] —**id′i·o·plas′mic, id′i·o·plas·mat′ic** (-ō-plăz-măt′ĭk) *adj.*

id·i·o·syn·cra·sy (ĭd′ē-ō-sĭng′krə-sē) *n., pl.* **-sies. 1.** A structural or behavioral characteristic peculiar to an individual or group. **2.** A physiological or temperamental peculiarity. **3.** Hypersensitivity to a drug. —See Synonyms at **eccentricity.** [Greek *idiosunkrasia* : IDIO- + *sunkrasis,* a mingling, mixture, temperament : *syn-,* together + *krasis,* mixture, CRASIS.] —**id′i·o·syn·crat′ic** (-sĭn-krăt′ĭk) *adj.* —**id′i·o·syn·crat′i·cal·ly** *adv.*

id·i·ot (ĭd′ē-ət) *n.* **1.** *Psychology.* A mentally deficient person, having intelligence in the lowest measurable range, being unable to guard against common dangers, and incapable of learning connected speech. **2.** An imbecile; blockhead. [Middle English, from Old French *idiote,* from Latin *idiōta,* ignorant person, from Greek *idiōtēs,* private person, plebeian, layman, ignorant person, from *idios,* peculiar, private. See **idio-**.]

id·i·ot·ic (ĭd′ē-ŏt′ĭk) *adj.* Exhibiting idiocy. —**id′i·ot′i·cal·ly** *adv.*

–idium. Used to indicate a small structure or form; for example, **nephridium.** [New Latin, from Greek *-idion.*]

i·dle (īd′l) *adj.* **idler, idlest. 1.** Not employed; inactive: *an idle man.* **2.** Avoiding employment; lazy; shiftless. **3.** Lacking foundation in fact; useless and worthless. —See Synonyms at **inactive.** —*v.* **idled, idling, idles.** —*intr.* **1.** To pass time without working or in avoiding work. **2.** To move lazily and without purpose. **3.** To run at a slow speed or out of gear. Used of a motor or a machine. —*tr.* **1.** To pass (time) without working or in avoiding work; to waste. Often used with *away: idle the afternoon away.* **2.** To cause to be unemployed or inactive. See Usage note below. **3.** To cause (a motor or machine) to idle. See Usage note below. [Middle English *idel,* idle, void, empty, Old English *īdel,* from West Germanic *īdal* (unattested).] —**i′dle·ness** *n.* —**i′dly** *adv.*

Usage: *Idle,* as a transitive verb meaning to cause a person or thing to be inactive or unemployed, has been popularized by modern journalism but occurs on all levels. It is acceptably used in the following examples, according to 62 per cent of the Usage Panel: *The dock strike has idled many crews and their ships. An outbreak of influenza has closed most of the schools and idled many teachers. Made idle,* for *idled,* would be more likely to occur in such sentences on a formal level.

idle pulley. A pulley on a shaft that rests on or presses against a drive belt to guide it or take up slack. Also called "idler pulley."

i·dler (īd′lər) *n.* **1.** One that idles. **2.** An idle wheel or idle pulley. **3.** A sailor exempt from night watch. **4.** An empty flatcar.

idle wheel. 1. A gear, wheel, or roller interposed between two similar parts to convey motion from one to the other without change in speed or direction of motion. **2.** An idle pulley.

id·o·crase (ĭd′ō-krās′, ī′dō-) *n.* A green, brown, yellow, or blue mineral, essentially $Ca_{10}Al_4(Mg,Fe)_2Si_9O_{34}(OH)_4$. Also called "vesuvianite," "vesuvian." [French : Greek *eidos,* form, shape (see **weid-** in Appendix*) + *krasis,* mixture (see **kere-** in Appendix*).]

i·dol (īd′l) *n.* **1.** An image used as an object of worship. **2.** One that is adored. **3.** *Archaic.* Something visible but without substance. [Middle English *idol, idel,* from Old French *idole, idele,* from Late Latin *īdōlum,* from Greek *eidōlon,* image, form, apparition, from *eidos,* form. See **weid-** in Appendix.*]

i·dol·a·ter (ī-dŏl′ə-tər) *n.* **1.** One who worships idols or an idol. **2.** One who blindly admires or adores another. [Middle English *idolatrer,* from Old French *idolatre,* from Late Latin *īdōlolatrēs,* from Greek *eidōlolatreia* : *eidōlon,* IDOL + *-latrēs,* worshiper (see **lēi-**¹ in Appendix*).]

i·dol·a·trize (ī-dŏl′ə-trīz′) *tr.v.* **-trized, -trizing, -trizes.** To make an idol of. See Synonyms at **revere.**

i·dol·a·trous (ī-dŏl′ə-trəs) *adj.* **1.** Given to idolatry. **2.** Constituting idolatry. —**i·dol′a·trous·ly** *adv.* —**i·dol′a·trous·ness** *n.*

i·dol·a·try (ī-dŏl′ə-trē) *n., pl.* **-tries. 1.** The worship of idols. **2.** Blind admiration of or devotion to something or someone. [Middle English *idolatrie,* from Old French, from Medieval Latin *īdōlatria,* from Late Latin *īdōlolatria,* from Greek *eidōlolatreia* : *eidōlon,* IDOL + *-latreia,* -LATRY.]

i·dol·ism (īd′l-ĭz′əm) *n.* **1.** Idolatry. **2.** A fallacy.

i·dol·ize (īd′l-īz′) *tr.v.* **-ized, -izing, -izes. 1.** To regard with blind admiration or devotion. **2.** To worship as an idol. —See Synonyms at **revere.** —**i′dol·i·za′tion** *n.* —**i′dol·iz′er** *n.*

Id·u·mae·a, Id·u·me·a. See **Edom.**

I·dun. Variant of **Ithunn.**

i·dyll (īd′l) *n.* Also **i·dyl. 1.** A short poem describing a picturesque episode or scene of rustic life. **2.** A scene or event of rural simplicity, fit to be the subject of such a work. [Latin *idyllium,* from Greek *eidullion,* diminutive of *eidos,* form, picture. See **weid-** in Appendix.*]

i·dyl·lic (ī-dĭl′ĭk) *adj.* **1.** Of, pertaining to, or having the nature of an idyll. **2.** Having a natural charm and picturesqueness. —**i·dyl′li·cal·ly** *adv.*

i·dyl·list (īd′l-ĭst) *n.* A writer of idylls.

–ie. Variant of **-y.**

i.e. id est.

if (ĭf) *conj.* **1.** Used to introduce a subjunctive clause, meaning: **a.** In the event that: *If I were to go, I would be late.* **b.** Granting that: *Even if that's true, what should we do?* **c.** On condition that: *She will sing only if she is paid.* **2.** Used to introduce a negative conditional clause, meaning although possibly or even though: *a handsome if useless trinket.* **3.** Used to introduce an indirect question, meaning whether: *Ask if he will come.* **4.** Used to introduce an exclamatory clause, indicating: **a.** A wish: *If she had only come earlier!* **b.** Surprise, anger, or a

ă pat/ā pay/âr care/ä father/b bib/ch church/d deed/ĕ pet/ē be/f fife/g gag/h hat/hw which/ĭ pit/ī pie/îr pier/j judge/k kick/l lid, needle/m mum/n no, sudden/ng thing/ŏ pot/ō toe/ô paw, for/oi noise/ou out/o͝o took/o͞o boot/p pop/r roar/s sauce/sh ship, dish/

similar emotion: *If she ever does that again!* —*n.* A possibility, condition, or stipulation. [Middle English *(y)if,* Old English *gif.* See i- in Appendix.*]
IF intermediate frequency.
i.f. intermediate frequency.
IFC International Finance Corporation.
IFF identification, friend or foe.
if·fy (ĭf′ē) *adj. Informal.* Characterized by doubt, uncertainty, or chance. [From IF.]
If·ni (ēf′nē). An overseas province of Spain, occupying 580 square miles on the southwestern coast of Morocco. Population, 51,517. Capital, Sidi Ifni.
I formation. An alignment of the offensive team in football in which the quarterback, fullback, and running back line up in single file behind the center.
IG, I.G. inspector general.
ig·loo (ĭg′lo͞o) *n., pl.* **-loos.** Also **ig·lu.** An Eskimo house, sometimes built of blocks of ice or hard snow. [Eskimo *iglu, igdlu,* house.]
Ign. ignition.
Ig·na·tius (ĭg-nā′shəs, -shē-əs), **Saint.** Bishop of Antioch; martyred at Rome in the second century A.D.
Ig·na·tius Loy·o·la (ĭg-nā′shəs loi-ō′lə), **Saint.** 1491–1556. Spanish soldier and ecclesiastic; founder of the Society of Jesus (1534).
ig·ne·ous (ĭg′nē-əs) *adj.* **1.** Of, relating to, or characteristic of fire. **2.** *Geology.* **a.** Formed by solidification from a molten or partially molten state. Said of rocks. **b.** Of or pertaining to rock so formed. In this sense, also "pyrogenic." [Latin *igneus,* from *ignis,* fire. See **egnis** in Appendix.*]
ig·nis fat·u·us (ĭg′nĭs făch′o͞o-əs) *pl.* **ignes fatui** (ĭg′nēz′ făch′o͞o-ī′). **1.** A phosphorescent light that hovers or flits over swampy ground at night, possibly caused by spontaneous combustion of gases emitted by rotting organic matter. Also called "friar's lantern," "will-o'-the-wisp." **2.** Something that misleads or deludes; a deception. [Medieval Latin, "foolish fire."]
ig·nite (ĭg-nīt′) *v.* **-nited, -niting, -nites.** —*tr.* **1. a.** To cause to burn. **b.** To set fire to. **2.** To arouse or kindle. —*intr.* To begin to burn; catch fire. [Latin *ignīre,* to set on fire, from *ignis,* fire. See **egnis** in Appendix.*] —**ig·nit′a·ble, ig·nit′i·ble** *adj.* —**ig·nit′er, ig·ni′tor** (-nī′tər) *n.*
ig·ni·tion (ĭg-nĭsh′ən) *n.* **1.** The raising of a substance to its **ignition point** *(see),* as by electric current, friction, or mechanical shock. **2.** *Abbr.* **Ign. a.** An electrical system, typically powered by a battery or magneto, that provides the spark to ignite the fuel mixture in an internal-combustion engine. **b.** A switch that activates this system.
ignition point. The minimum temperature at which a substance will continue to burn without additional application of external heat. Also called "kindling point."
ig·ni·tron (ĭg-nī′trŏn′, ĭg′nə-) *n.* A single-anode, mercury-vapor rectifier in which current passes as an arc between the anode and a mercury-pool cathode, used in power rectification. [Latin *ignis,* fire (see **ignite**) + -TRON.]
ig·no·ble (ĭg-nō′bəl) *adj.* **1.** Not having a noble character or purpose; dishonorable. **2.** Not of the nobility; common. —See Synonyms at **mean** (base). [Latin *ignōbilis* : *in-,* not + *nōbilis,* NOBLE.] —**ig′no·bil′i·ty, ig·no′ble·ness** *n.* —**ig·no′bly** *adv.*
ig·no·min·i·ous (ĭg′nō-mĭn′ē-əs) *adj.* **1.** Characterized by shame or disgrace. **2.** Deserving disgrace or shame; despicable. **3.** Degrading; debasing. —**ig′no·min′i·ous·ly** *adv.* —**ig′no·min′i·ous·ness** *n.*
ig·no·min·y (ĭg′nə-mĭn′ē, -mə-nē) *n., pl.* **-ies. 1.** Dishonor; infamy. **2.** That which causes dishonor; a disgraceful act or conduct. —See Synonyms at **disgrace.** [Latin *ignōminia* : *in-,* not + *nōmen,* name, reputation (see **nomen-** in Appendix*).]
ig·no·ra·mus (ĭg′nə-rā′məs) *n.* An ignorant person. [New Latin, from Latin, "we do not know," from *ignōrāre,* to be ignorant, IGNORE.]
ig·no·rance (ĭg′nər-əns) *n.* The condition of being ignorant; lack of knowledge.
ig·no·rant (ĭg′nər-ənt) *adj.* **1.** Without education or knowledge. **2.** Exhibiting lack of education or knowledge. **3.** Unaware or uninformed. [Middle English *ignoraunt,* from Old French *ignorant,* from Latin *ignōrāns,* present participle of *ignōrāre,* to be ignorant, IGNORE.] —**ig′no·rant·ly** *adv.*
Synonyms: *ignorant, uneducated, untaught, unlearned, untutored, unlettered, illiterate.* These adjectives mean lacking in knowledge or education. *Ignorant* can refer to a person's low level of knowledge in general or, in a narrower sense, to his being uninformed or unaware of a specific thing. *Uneducated, untaught, unlearned,* and *untutored* imply lack of schooling. *Unlettered* describes one deficient in book learning or in the ability to read and write. *Illiterate* refers most often to inability to meet an established minimum level of achievement in reading and writing.
ig·nore (ĭg-nôr′, -nōr′) *tr.v.* **-nored, -noring, -nores.** To refuse to pay attention to; disregard. See Synonyms at **refuse.** [French *ignorer,* from Latin *ignōrāre,* not to know, disregard. See **gnō-** in Appendix.*] —**ig·nor′a·ble** *adj.* —**ig·nor′er** *n.*
I·go·rot (ĭg′ə-rōt′, ē′gə-) *n., pl.* **Igorot** or **-rots.** Also **I·gor·ro·te** (ē′gôr-rō′tā). **1.** A member of any of several related tribes of mountainous northern Luzon, Philippines. **2.** The Malayo-Polynesian language of these people.
I·gua·çú (ē-gwä-so͞o′). Also **I·guas·sú.** *Spanish* **I·gua·zú. 1.** A river rising in southern Brazil and flowing 380 miles west to the Paraná on the Argentina border. **2.** A waterfall on this river, extending 2.5 miles and dropping 210 feet, near the Argentina-Brazil border.
i·gua·na (ĭ-gwä′nə) *n.* Any of various large tropical American lizards of the family Iguanidae, often having spiny projections along the back. [Spanish, from Arawak *iwana.*]
i·guan·o·don (ĭ-gwä′nə-dŏn′) *n.* Any of various large dinosaurs of the genus *Iguanodon,* of the Jurassic and Cretaceous periods. [New Latin *Iguanodon* : IGUAN(A) + -ODON.]
IGY International Geophysical Year.
ih·ram (ē-räm′) *n.* **1.** The sacred dress of Moslem pilgrims, consisting of two lengths of white cotton. **2.** The sacred state in which the pilgrim exists while wearing this dress. [Arabic *iḥrām,* "prohibition," from *ḥarama,* he prohibited. See **harem.**]
IHS A graphic symbol for Jesus. [From ΙΗΣΟΥΣ or IHSOUS, Jesus (in Greek capitals).]
Ijs·sel (ī′səl). *Dutch* **IJs·sel.** A river of the eastern Netherlands, rising at the northern mouth of the Rhine and flowing 70 miles north to the Ijsselmeer.
Ijs·sel·meer (ī′səl-mâr′). *Dutch* **IJs·sel·meer** (-mār′). A lake, 465 square miles in area, of the northwestern Netherlands, formed by the diking of the Zuyder Zee.
I·ka·ri·a (ē′kä-rē′ä). Also **I·car·i·a** (ĭ-kâr′ē-ə). An island of Greece, 99 square miles in area. Population, 11,000.
I·ke·da (ĭ-kā′də; *Japanese* ē′kĕ′dä′), **Hayato.** 1899–1965. Premier of Japan (1960–64).
Ikh·na·ton. See **Akhenaton.**
i·kon. Variant of **icon.**
IL Illinois (with Zip Code).
ILA International Longshoremen's Association.
i·lang-i·lang. Variant of **ylang-ylang.**
-ile. Used to indicate relationship with, similarity to, or capability of; for example, **audile.** [Middle English, from Old French, from Latin *-ilis.*]
il·e·ac (ĭl′ē-ăk′) *adj.* **1.** Of or pertaining to ileus. **2.** Of or pertaining to the ileum; ileal.
Île de France. The former name for **Mauritius.**
Île-de-France (ēl-də-fräɴs′). A region and former province of north-central France. Principal city, Paris.
Île du Dia·ble. The French name for **Devil's Island.**
il·e·i·tis (ĭl′ē-ī′tĭs) *n.* Inflammation of the ileum. [New Latin : ILE(UM) + -ITIS.]
Îles Co·mores. The French name for the **Comoro Islands.**
il·e·um (ĭl′ē-əm) *n., pl.* **-ea** (-ē-ə). The portion of the small intestine extending from the jejunum to the cecum. [New Latin, from Latin *īlium, īleum*†, groin, flank.] —**il′e·al** *adj.*
il·e·us (ĭl′ē-əs) *n.* Intestinal obstruction causing colic, vomiting, and toxemia. [Latin *īleus,* from Greek *(e)ileos,* "a twisting," from *eilein, illein,* to roll, wind. See **wel-**[3] in Appendix.*]
i·lex (ī′lĕks′) *n.* **1.** Any of various trees or shrubs of the genus *Ilex;* a holly. **2.** The **holm oak** *(see).* [Latin *īlex,* holm oak, of Mediterranean origin.]
Il·ford (ĭl′fərd). A former administrative division of London, England, now part of **Redbridge** *(see).*
I.L.G.W.U. International Ladies' Garment Workers' Union.
I·lhas do Ca·bo Ver·de. The Portuguese name for **Cape Verde Islands.**
I·li (ē′lē′). A river rising in the Sinkiang-Uigur Autonomous Region of China and flowing 800 miles west and northwest to Lake Balkhash in the Kazakh S.S.R.
Il·i·ad (ĭl′ē-əd) *n.* A Greek epic poem attributed to Homer, recounting the siege of Troy.
Il·i·am·na (ĭl′ē-ăm′nə). **1.** The largest lake of Alaska, 75 miles long and 10 to 25 miles wide, located in the southwest. **2.** A volcano rising to 10,085 feet on the northern shore of this lake.
Il·i·ci. The ancient name for **Elche.**
il·i·um (ĭl′ē-əm) *n., pl.* **-ia** (-ē-ə). The uppermost and widest of three bones comprising one of the lateral halves of the pelvis. [New Latin, from Latin *īlium, īleum,* groin, flank. See **ileum.**]
Il·i·um. The Latin name for **Troy.**
ilk[1] (ĭlk) *n.* Type or kind. See Synonyms at **type.** —*pron. Scottish.* The same. Used following a name in the phrase *of that ilk* to indicate that the one named resides in an area bearing the same name: *Duncan of that ilk.* [Middle English *ilke, ilk,* Old English *ilca,* same. See i- in Appendix.*]
Usage: *Ilk* has long been used as the equivalent of *type* or *kind,* sometimes facetiously and sometimes disparagingly. Though this sense has long been disputed as well, it is recognized by a majority of the Usage Panel. The following example is acceptable to 65 per cent of the Panel: *Men of that ilk cannot be expected to behave otherwise.*
ilk[2]. Variant of **ilka.**
il·ka (ĭl′kə) *adj.* Also **ilk** (ĭlk). *Scottish.* Each; every. [Middle English *ilka(n),* each one : *ilk, ech,* EACH + *a,* A.]
ill (ĭl) *adj.* **worse, worst. 1.** Not healthy; sick. **2.** Not normal; unsound. **3.** Resulting in suffering; distressing. **4.** Having evil intentions; hostile. **5.** Boding evil; unpropitious. **6.** Not up to recognized standards of excellence or conduct. **7.** Harmful; cruel. —See Synonyms at **sick.** —**ill at ease.** Nervous and uncomfortable. —*adv.* **worse, worst. 1.** In an ill manner; not well. **2.** Scarcely or with difficulty. ***Note:*** The adverb *ill* combines with many adjectives, usually derived from the participles of verbs, to form attributive modifiers before nouns: *an ill-regulated life; an ill-deserving woman.* In such use, the elements are joined with a hyphen. However, when *ill* modifies a predicate adjective, the two words are written separately: *His life was ill regulated. The woman is ill deserving.* —*n.* **1.** Evil; wrongdoing; sin. **2.** Disaster or harm. [Middle English *ill(e),* from Old Norse *illr*†, bad.]
I'll (īl). **1.** Contraction of *I will.* **2.** Contraction of *I shall.*
ill. illustrated; illustration; illustrator.
Ill. Illinois.

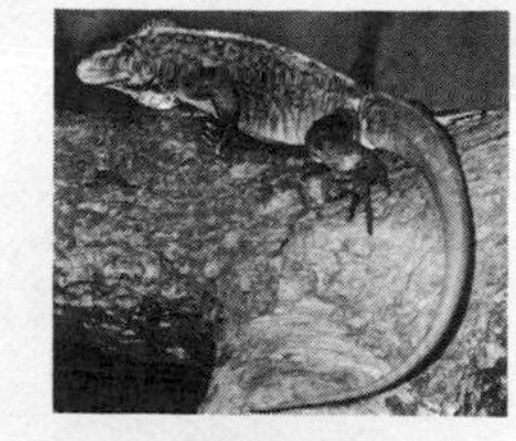
iguana
Cyclura rileyi

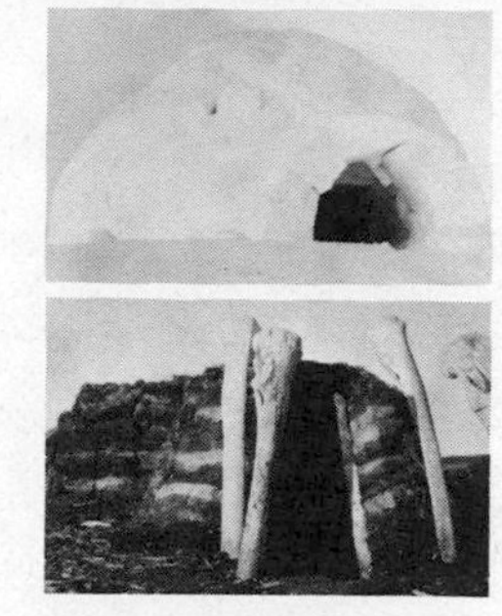
igloo
Above: Constructed of snow
Below: Constructed of sod with whale ribs at entrance

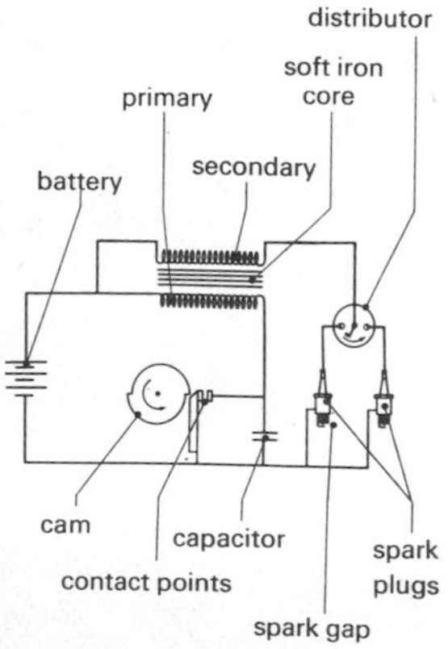

ignition
Common automobile ignition

ill-ad·vised (ĭl′əd-vīzd′) *adj.* Done without wise counsel or careful deliberation. —**ill′-ad·vis′ed·ly** *adv.*
I·llam·pu (ē-yäm′po͞o). A peak of Mount Sorata, rising to 21,276 feet in the Cordillera Oriental of western Bolivia.
il·la·tion (ĭ-lā′shən) *n.* **1.** The act of inferring or drawing conclusions. **2.** A drawn conclusion; deduction. [Late Latin *illātiō*, from Latin, "a carrying in," deduction, from *illātus* (past participle of *inferre*, to bring in) : *in-*, in + *-lātus*, "carried" (see **tel-**[1] in Appendix*).]
il·la·tive (ĭl′ə-tĭv, ĭ-lā′-) *adj.* **1.** Of, pertaining to, or of the nature of an illation. **2.** Expressing or preceding an inference. Said of a word.
ill-bod·ing (ĭl′bō′dĭng) *adj.* Portending evil; inauspicious.
ill-bred (ĭl′brĕd′) *adj.* **1.** Badly brought up; ill-mannered; impolite. **2.** Not thoroughbred.
il·le·gal (ĭ-lē′gəl) *adj.* **1.** Prohibited by law. **2.** Prohibited by official rules. —**il·le′gal·ly** *adv.*
il·le·gal·i·ty (ĭl′ē-găl′ə-tē) *n., pl.* **-ties. 1.** The state or quality of being illegal. **2.** An illegal act.
il·leg·i·ble (ĭ-lĕj′ə-bəl) *adj.* Not legible or decipherable. —**il·leg′i·bil′i·ty, il·leg′i·ble·ness** *n.* —**il·leg′i·bly** *adv.*
il·le·git·i·ma·cy (ĭl′ĭ-jĭt′ə-mə-sē) *n.* The condition or state of being illegitimate; specifically, bastardy.
il·le·git·i·mate (ĭl′ĭ-jĭt′ə-mĭt) *adj.* **1.** Against the law; illegal. **2.** Born out of wedlock; bastard. **3.** Not in correct grammatical usage. **4.** Incorrectly deduced. —**il′le·git′i·mate·ly** *adv.*
ill-fat·ed (ĭl′fā′tĭd) *adj.* **1.** Destined for misfortune; doomed. **2.** Marked by or causing misfortune; unlucky.
ill-fa·vored (ĭl′fā′vərd) *adj.* **1.** Having an ugly or unattractive face. **2.** Objectionable; offensive.
ill-got·ten (ĭl′gŏt′n) *adj.* Obtained in an evil manner or by dishonest means.
ill humor. An irritable state of mind; surliness.
ill-hu·mored (ĭl′hyo͞o′mərd) *adj.* Irritable and surly. —**ill′-hu′mored·ly** *adv.* —**ill′-hu′mored·ness** *n.*
il·lib·er·al (ĭ-lĭb′ər-əl) *adj.* **1.** Narrow-minded; bigoted. **2.** *Archaic.* Ungenerous, mean, or stingy. **3.** *Archaic.* **a.** Lacking liberal culture. **b.** Ill-bred; ungentlemanly; vulgar. [Latin *illīberālis* : *in-*, not + *līberālis*, LIBERAL.] —**il·lib′er·al′i·ty, il·lib′er·al·ness** *n.* —**il·lib′er·al·ly** *adv.*
il·lic·it (ĭ-lĭs′ĭt) *adj.* Not sanctioned by custom or law; illegal; unlawful. [Latin *illicitus*, not allowed : *in-*, not + *licitus*, allowed, LICIT.] —**il·lic′it·ly** *adv.* —**il·lic′it·ness** *n.*
I·lli·ma·ni (ē′yē-mä′nē). An Andean peak in western Bolivia, rising to 21,185 feet, southeast of La Paz.
il·lim·it·a·ble (ĭ-lĭm′ĭ-tə-bəl) *adj.* Incapable of being limited or circumscribed; limitless. See Synonyms at **infinite.** —**il·lim′it·a·bil′i·ty, il·lim′it·a·ble·ness** *n.* —**il·lim′it·a·bly** *adv.*
Il·li·noi·an (ĭl′ə-noi′ən) *adj.* Of or pertaining to the third glacial stage in North America. [From ILLINOIS (state).]
Il·li·nois[1] (ĭl′ə-noi′, -noiz′) *n., pl.* **Illinois. 1.** A confederacy of Algonquian-speaking Indian tribes that inhabited Illinois and parts of Iowa, Wisconsin, and Missouri. **2.** A member of this confederacy or one of the member tribes. **3.** The Algonquian language of the Illinois and Miami peoples. [French, from Algonquian, akin to Miami *alānia*, man, Shawnee *hilenawe*.]
Il·li·nois[2] (ĭl′ə-noi′, -noiz′). **1.** *Abbr.* **Ill.** A Midwestern state of the United States, 56,400 square miles in area; admitted to the Union in 1818. Population, 10,644,000. Capital, Springfield. See map at **United States of America. 2.** A river rising in northeastern Illinois and flowing 273 miles southwest to the Mississippi. [From ILLINOIS (tribes).] —**Il′li·nois′an** *adj.* & *n.*
illit. illiterate.
il·lit·er·a·cy (ĭ-lĭt′ər-ə-sē) *n., pl.* **-cies. 1.** The quality or condition of being unable to read and write. **2.** An error caused by or thought characteristic of this condition.
il·lit·er·ate (ĭ-lĭt′ər-ĭt) *adj. Abbr.* **illit. 1.** Unable to read and write. **2. a.** Marked by inferiority to an expected standard of familiarity with language and literature. **b.** Violating prescribed standards of speech or writing. **3.** Ignorant of the fundamentals of a given art or branch of knowledge: *musically illiterate.* —See Synonyms at **ignorant.** —*n. Abbr.* **illit.** One who is illiterate. [Latin *illiterātus* : *in-*, not + *literātus*, LITERATE.] —**il·lit′er·ate·ly** *adv.* —**il·lit′er·ate·ness** *n.*
ill-look·ing (ĭl′lo͝ok′ĭng) *adj. Archaic.* Of an evil or ugly appearance.
ill-man·nered (ĭl′măn′ərd) *adj.* Lacking or indicating a lack of good manners; impolite; rude. —**ill′-man′nered·ly** *adv.*
ill nature. A disagreeable, irritable, or malevolent disposition.
ill-na·tured (ĭl′nā′chərd) *adj.* Disagreeable; surly. —**ill′-na′tured·ly** *adv.* —**ill′-na′tured·ness** *n.*
ill·ness (ĭl′nĭs) *n.* **1. a.** Sickness of body or mind. **b.** A sickness. **2.** *Obsolete.* Evil; wickedness.
il·log·ic (ĭ-lŏj′ĭk) *n.* The lack of logic.
il·log·i·cal (ĭ-lŏj′ĭ-kəl) *adj.* **1.** Contradicting or disregarding the principles of logic. **2.** Without logic; senseless. —**il·log′i·cal′i·ty, il·log′i·cal·ness** *n.* —**il·log′i·cal·ly** *adv.*
ill-o·mened (ĭl′ō′mənd) *adj.* Marked by bad omens.
ill-sort·ed (ĭl′sôrt′əd) *adj.* Badly matched.
ill-starred (ĭl′stärd′) *adj.* Ill-fated; unlucky.
ill-tem·pered (ĭl′tĕm′pərd) *adj.* **1.** Having a bad temper; irritable. **2.** *Archaic.* Out of sorts; unwell. —**ill′-tem′pered·ly** *adv.* —**ill′-tem′pered·ness** *n.*
ill-timed (ĭl′tīmd′) *adj.* Done or occurring at an inappropriate time; untimely.
ill-treat (ĭl′trēt′) *tr.v.* **-treated, -treating, -treats.** To maltreat. See Synonyms at **abuse.** —**ill′-treat′ment** *n.*
il·lume (ĭ-lo͞om′) *tr.v.* **-lumed, -luming, -lumes.** *Poetic.* To illuminate. [Shortened from ILLUMINE.]
il·lu·min·ance (ĭ-lo͞o′mə-nəns) *n. Physics.* **Illumination** *(see).*
il·lu·mi·nant (ĭ-lo͞o′mə-nənt) *n.* Something that gives off light.
il·lu·mi·nate (ĭ-lo͞o′mə-nāt′) *v.* **-nated, -nating, -nates.** —*tr.* **1.** To provide with light; turn or focus light upon. **2.** To decorate or hang with lights. **3.** To make understandable; clarify. **4.** To enable to understand; enlighten. **5.** To endow with fame or splendor; celebrate. **6.** To adorn (a text, page, or initial letter) with ornamental designs, miniatures, or lettering in brilliant colors or precious metals. —*intr.* To become lighted; glow. —*n.* (ĭ-lo͞o′mə-nĭt). One who has or professes to have an unusual degree of enlightenment. [Latin *illūmināre* : *in-*, in + *lūmināre*, to light up, from *lūmen*, light (see **leuk-** in Appendix*).]
Il·lu·mi·na·ten (ē-lo͞o′mē-nä′tən) *pl.n. German.* The members of a secret society of freethinkers and republicans that flourished in Germany during the late 18th century. Also called "Illuminati."
il·lu·mi·na·ti (ĭ-lo͞o′mə-nä′tē) *pl.n.* **1.** Persons claiming to be unusually enlightened with regard to some subject. **2.** *Capital* **I. a.** The **Illuminaten** *(see).* **b.** Persons regarded as atheists, libertines, or radical republicans during the 18th century (such as the French Encyclopedists, the Freemasons, or the freethinkers): *"The doctrines of the Illuminati and principles of Jacobinism"* (George Washington). **3.** *Capital* **I.** The members of a heretical sect of 16th-century Spain, who claimed special religious enlightenment. [Latin *illūmināti*, "enlightened ones," plural of *illūminātus*, past participle of *illūmināre*, ILLUMINATE.]
il·lu·mi·na·tion (ĭ-lo͞o′mə-nā′shən) *n.* **1.** The act of illuminating. **2.** The state of being illuminated. **3.** A light source. **4.** Light or lights used as decoration. **5.** Spiritual or intellectual enlightenment. **6.** Clarification; elucidation. **7. a.** The art or act of decorating a text, page, or initial letter with ornamental designs, miniatures, or lettering. **b.** An example of this art. **8.** *Physics.* The luminous flux per unit area at any point on a surface exposed to incident light. Also called "illuminance."
il·lu·mi·na·tive (ĭ-lo͞o′mə-nā′tĭv) *adj.* Causing or able to cause illumination.
il·lu·mi·na·tor (ĭ-lo͞o′mə-nā′tər) *n.* **1.** One that illuminates. **2.** A device for producing, concentrating, or reflecting light. **3.** A person who illuminates manuscripts or the like.
il·lu·mine (ĭ-lo͞o′mĭn) *v.* **-mined, -mining, -mines.** —*tr.* To illuminate; give light to. —*intr.* To be or become illuminated. [Middle English *illuminen*, from Latin *illūmināre*, to ILLUMINATE.] —**il·lu′mi·na·ble** *adj.*
il·lu·mi·nism (ĭ-lo͞o′mə-nĭz′əm) *n.* **1.** Belief in or proclamation of a special personal enlightenment. **2.** *Capital* **I.** The ideas and principles of various groups of illuminati. [ILLUMIN(ATI) + -ISM.] —**il·lu′mi·nist** *n.*
illus. illustrated; illustration; illustrator.
ill-use (ĭl′yo͞oz′) *tr.v.* **-used, -using, -uses.** To maltreat. —*n.* (ĭl′yo͞os′). Also **ill-us·age** (-yo͞o′sĭj). Bad or unjust treatment.
il·lu·sion (ĭ-lo͞o′zhən) *n.* **1. a.** An erroneous perception of reality. **b.** An erroneous concept or belief; loosely, a delusion. **2.** The state or condition of being deceived by such perceptions or beliefs. **3.** Something that causes an erroneous belief or perception. **4.** *Art.* Illusionism. **5.** A fine transparent cloth, used for dresses or trimmings. —See Usage note at **delusion.** [Middle English *illusioun*, from Old French *illusion*, from Late Latin *illūsiō*, from Latin, a mocking, jeering, from *illūdere* (past participle *illūsus*), to mock, jeer at : *in-*, against + *lūdere*, to play, from *lūdus*, game (see **leid-** in Appendix*).] —**il·lu′sion·al, il·lu′sion·ar′y** *adj.*
il·lu·sion·ism (ĭ-lo͞o′zhə-nĭz′əm) *n.* **1.** The doctrine that the material world is an immaterial product of the senses. **2.** Use of illusionary techniques and devices in art or decoration. —**il·lu′sion·is′tic** *adj.*
il·lu·sion·ist (ĭ-lo͞o′zhə-nĭst) *n.* **1.** An adherent of the doctrine of illusionism. **2.** A conjuror or ventriloquist. **3.** An artist whose work is marked by illusionism.
il·lu·sive (ĭ-lo͞o′sĭv) *adj.* Of, pertaining to, or of the nature of an illusion; lacking reality; illusory. [From ILLUSION.] —**il·lu′sive·ly** *adv.* —**il·lu′sive·ness** *n.*
il·lu·so·ry (ĭ-lo͞o′sə-rē, -zə-rē) *adj.* Tending to deceive; of the nature of an illusion; illusive.
il·lus·trate (ĭl′ə-strāt′, ĭ-lŭs′trāt′) *v.* **-trated, -trating, -trates.** —*tr.* **1. a.** To clarify by use of examples, comparisons, or the like. **b.** To clarify by serving as an example, comparison, or the like. **2.** To provide (a publication) with explanatory or decorative pictures, photographs, diagrams, or the like. **4.** *Obsolete.* To illuminate. —*intr.* To present a clarification, example, or explanation. [Latin *illūstrāre* : *in-*, in + *lūstrāre*, to make bright, enlighten (see **leuk-** in Appendix*).] —**il′lus·tra′tor** (ĭl′ə-strā′tər) *n.*
il·lus·tra·tion (ĭl′ə-strā′shən) *n. Abbr.* **ill., illus. 1. a.** The action of clarifying or explaining. **b.** The state of being clarified or explained. **2.** Material used to clarify or explain. **3.** Visual matter used to clarify or to decorate a text. **4.** *Obsolete.* Illumination. —See Synonyms at **example.**
il·lus·tra·tive (ĭ-lŭs′trə-tĭv, ĭl′ə-strā′tĭv) *adj.* Acting as an illustration. —**il·lus′tra·tive·ly** *adv.*
il·lus·tri·ous (ĭ-lŭs′trē-əs) *adj.* Renowned; famous; celebrated. [Latin *illūstris*, shining, clear, probably back-formation from *illūstrāre*, ILLUSTRATE.] —**il·lus′tri·ous·ly** *adv.* —**il·lus′tri·ous·ness** *n.*
il·lu·vi·a·tion (ĭ-lo͞o′vē-ā′shən) *n.* The deposition in an underlying soil layer of colloids, soluble salts, and mineral particles leached out of an overlying soil layer. [IN- (in) + (AL)LUVI(UM) + -ATION.] —**il·lu′vi·al** *adj.*
ill will. Unfriendly feeling; hostility; enmity.

ă pat/ā pay/âr care/ä father/b bib/ch church/d deed/ĕ pet/ē be/f fife/g gag/h hat/hw which/ĭ pit/ī pie/îr pier/j judge/k kick/l lid, needle/m mum/n no, sudden/ng thing/ŏ pot/ō toe/ô paw, for/oi noise/ou out/o͝o took/o͞o boot/p pop/r roar/s sauce/sh ship, dish/

il·ly (ĭl′lē) *adv.* Badly; ill: *"Beauty is jealous, and illy bears the presence of a rival."* (Jefferson).

Il·lyr·i·a (ĭ-lĭr′ē-ə). An ancient country of southern Europe, on the Adriatic.

Il·lyr·i·an (ĭ-lĭr′ē-ən) *n.* **1.** One of a people inhabiting Illyria. **2.** The Indo-European language of the Illyrians. *—adj.* Of, pertaining to, or characteristic of the Illyrians or their language.

Il·men, Lake (ĭl′mən). A lake occupying 425-850 square miles, depending on the season, in the northwestern Russian S.F.S.R.

il·men·ite (ĭl′mə-nīt′) *n.* A lustrous black-to-brownish titanium ore, essentially $FeTiO_3$. [German *Ilmenit;* first found in *Ilmen,* range in the Ural Mountains.]

ILO International Labor Organization.

I·lo·ca·no (ē′lō-kä′nō) *n., pl.* **Ilocano** or **-nos.** Also **I·lo·ka·no. 1.** One of a people inhabiting northwestern Luzon, Philippines. **2.** The Austronesian language of these people. *—adj.* Of, pertaining to, or characteristic of the Ilocano or their language. [Spanish, from *iloko,* native name in the Philippines.]

I·lo·rin (ē′lôr-ēn′, ĭ-lôr′ēn). A city of Nigeria, in the southwestern part of the Northern Region. Population, 209,000.

I.L.P. *British.* Independent Labour Party.

ILS *Aviation.* instrument landing system.

I'm (īm). Contraction of *I am.*

im·age (ĭm′ĭj) *n.* **1.** A reproduction of the appearance of someone or something; especially, a sculptured likeness. **2.** An optically formed duplicate, counterpart, or other representative reproduction of an object; especially, an optical reproduction of an object formed by a lens or mirror. **3.** One that closely resembles another; a double: *He is the image of his uncle.* **4. a.** The concept of someone or something that is held by the public. **b.** The character projected by someone or something to the public. **5.** A personification of something specified: *He is the image of health.* **6.** A mental picture of something not real or present. **7.** A representation to the mind by speech or writing. **8.** *Obsolete.* An apparition. *—tr.v.* **imaged, -aging, -ages. 1.** To make or produce a likeness of; copy or portray. **2.** To mirror or reflect. **3.** To symbolize or typify. **4.** To picture mentally; imagine or recall. **5.** To describe; especially, to describe so as to call up a mental picture of. [Middle English, from Old French, from Latin *imāgō,* related to *imitārī,* IMITATE.]

image orthicon. An **orthicon** *(see).*

im·age·ry (ĭm′ĭj-rē) *n., pl.* **-ries. 1.** Mental pictures or images. **2. a.** The employment of figures of speech or vivid descriptions in writing or speaking to produce mental images. **b.** Any metaphoric representation, as in music, art, or motion pictures. **3. a.** Representative images, particularly statues or icons. **b.** The art of making such images. [Middle English *imagerie,* from Old French, from *image,* IMAGE.]

im·ag·i·na·ble (ĭ-măj′ə-nə-bəl) *adj.* Capable of being conceived of by the imagination. **—im·ag′i·na·bly** *adv.*

im·ag·i·nal (ĭ-măj′ə-nəl, ĭ-mā′gə-) *adj.* Of or relating to an insect imago. [From New Latin *imago* (stem *imagin-*), IMAGO.]

im·ag·i·nar·y (ĭ-măj′ə-nĕr′ē) *adj.* **1.** Having existence only in the imagination; unreal. **2.** *Mathematics.* **a.** Of, pertaining to, or being the coefficient of the imaginary unit in a complex number. **b.** Of, pertaining to, involving, or being an imaginary number. **c.** Involving only a complex number of which the real part is zero. In this sense, also "pure imaginary." *—n., pl.* **imaginaries.** *Mathematics.* An imaginary number. **—im·ag′i·nar′i·ly** *adv.* **—im·ag′i·nar′i·ness** *n.*

imaginary number. A **complex number** *(see)* in which the real part is zero and the coefficient of the imaginary unit is not zero.

imaginary unit. *Symbol* **i** The positive square root of −1.

im·ag·i·na·tion (ĭ-măj′ə-nā′shən) *n.* **1. a.** The formation of a mental image or concept of that which is not real or present. **b.** A mental image or idea. **2.** The ability or tendency to form such mental images or concepts. **3.** The ability to deal creatively with reality. **4.** *Archaic.* **a.** An unrealistic idea or notion; a fancy. **b.** A plan or scheme. **—im·ag′i·na′tion·al** *adj.*

Synonyms: *imagination, fancy, fantasy.* These nouns refer to the power of the mind to form images of things not present to the senses or within the actual experience of the person involved. *Imagination* is broadly applicable to all such functions. *Fancy* suggests mental invention that is capricious, whimsical, or playful, and characteristically well removed from reality. *Fantasy* is applied principally to the product of imagination given free rein, especially to elaborate mental representation having little similarity to the real world.

im·ag·i·na·tive (ĭ-măj′ə-nə-tĭv, -nā′tĭv) *adj.* **1.** Having a strong imagination, especially creative imagination. **2.** Tending to indulge in the fanciful or in make-believe. **3.** Created by, indicative of, or characterized by imagination or creativity. **—im·ag′i·na·tive·ly** *adv.* **—im·ag′i·na·tive·ness** *n.*

im·ag·ine (ĭ-măj′ən) *v.* **-ined, -ining, -ines.** *—tr.* **1.** To form a mental picture or image of; create in the mind. **2.** To think; to conjecture. *—intr.* **1.** To employ the imagination. **2.** To make a guess; to conjecture. [Middle English *imaginen,* from Old French *imaginer,* from Latin *imāginārī,* to picture to oneself, from *imāgō,* IMAGE.] **—im·ag′in·er** *n.*

im·a·gism (ĭm′ə-jĭz′əm) *n.* A literary movement, launched early in the 20th century in revolt against romanticism, to promote free verse and precise imagery. **—im′a·gist** *n.* **—im′a·gis′tic** *adj.*

i·ma·go (ĭ-mā′gō) *n., pl.* **-goes** or **imagines** (ĭ-măj′ə-nēz′). **1.** An insect in its sexually mature adult stage after metamorphosis. **2.** *Psychoanalysis.* An often idealized image of a person, usually a parent, formed in childhood and persisting into adulthood. [New Latin, from Latin *imāgō,* IMAGE.]

i·mam (ĭ-mäm′) *n.* Also **i·maum** (ĭ-mäm′, ĭ-môm′). **1.** A prayer leader of Islam. **2.** A Moslem scholar; especially, an authority on Islamic law. **3.** *Capital* **I. a.** A title accorded to Mohammed and his four immediate successors. **b.** One of the leaders regarded by the Shiites as successors of Mohammed. **c.** Any of various religious and temporal leaders claiming descent from Mohammed. [Arabic *imām,* leader, from *amma,* he led.]

i·mam·ate (ĭ-mä′māt′) *n.* **1.** The office of an Imam. **2.** A country governed by an Imam.

i·ma·ret (ĭ-mä′rĕt) *n.* An inn or hostel for pilgrims in Turkey. [Turkish, from Arabic *imārah,* hospice, "cultivated land," from *amara,* he built.]

im·bal·ance (ĭm-băl′əns) *n.* A lack of balance.

im·be·cile (ĭm′bə-sĭl, -səl) *n.* **1.** A feeble-minded person. **2.** A dolt. *—adj.* Also **im·be·cil·ic** (ĭm′bə-sĭl′ĭk). **1.** Deficient in mental ability. **2.** Stupid. [Old French *imbecille,* from Latin *imbēcillus,* "without support," feeble : *in-,* not + *bacillum,* diminutive of *baculum,* staff, rod (see **bak-** in Appendix*).] **—im′be·cile·ly** *adv.* **—im′be·cil′i·ty** *n.*

im·bed. Variant of **embed.**

im·bibe (ĭm-bīb′) *v.* **-bibed, -bibing, -bibes.** *—tr.* **1.** To drink. **2.** To absorb or take in as if by drinking: *"the whole body . . . imbibes delight through every pore"* (Thoreau). **3.** To receive and absorb into the mind: *"Gladstone had . . . imbibed a strong prejudice against Americans"* (Philip Magnus). **4.** *Obsolete.* To permeate; saturate. *—intr.* To drink. [Middle English *enbiben,* to absorb, from Old French *embiber,* from Latin *imbibere,* to drink in : *in-,* in + *bibere,* to drink (see **pōi-**[1] in Appendix*).] **—im·bib′er** *n.* **—im′bi·bi′tion** (-bĭ-bĭsh′ən) *n.*

im·bri·cate (ĭm′brĭ-kāt′) *adj.* **1.** Having the edges overlapping in a regular arrangement, as tiles on a roof, the scales of a fish, or bracts or sepals of a plant. **2.** Covered or ornamented with a pattern or design of overlapping parts or edges. *—v.* **imbricated, -cating, -cates.** *—tr.* To overlap in a regular pattern. *—intr.* To be arranged with regular overlapping edges. [Latin *imbricātus,* past participle of *imbricāre,* to cover with roof tiles, from *imbrex* (stem *imbric-*), roof tile, from *imber* (stem *imbr-*), rain. See **ombhro-** in Appendix.*]

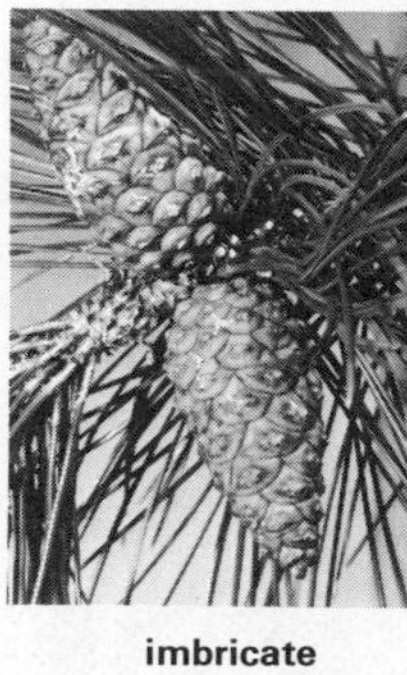

imbricate
Imbricate scales of pine cone

im·bri·ca·tion (ĭm′brĭ-kā′shən) *n.* **1.** A regular overlapping of edges. **2.** A pattern or design having such overlapping.

im·bro·glio (ĭm-brōl′yō) *n., pl.* **-glios. 1.** A confused or difficult situation; predicament; entanglement. **2.** A confused heap; a tangle. [Italian *imbroglio* : probably *in-,* in, from Latin + *broglio,* grove, bush, from Old French *breuil,* from Late Latin *brogilus,* from Gaulish *brogilos* (unattested), from *brogos, broga*†, field.]

Im·bros (ĭm′brəs). *Turkish* **İm·roz** (ĭm-rôz′). An island of Turkey, occupying 108 square miles in the Aegean, off the southwestern coast of the Gallipoli Peninsula.

im·brue (ĭm-brōō′) *tr.v.* **-brued, -bruing, -brues.** Also **em·brue** (ĕm-). To stain or saturate. [Middle English *enbrewen, enbrowen,* from Old French *embruer, embrouer,* to soak : *en-,* in + *breu,* broth, from Germanic (see **bhreu-**[2] in Appendix*).]

im·brute (ĭm-brōōt′) *v.* **-bruted, -bruting, -brutes.** *—tr.* To cause to become brutal. *—intr.* To become brutal.

im·bue (ĭm-byōō′) *tr.v.* **-bued, -buing, -bues. 1.** To make thoroughly wet; saturate, as with stain or dye. **2.** To inspire, permeate, or pervade: *"His work is imbued with the evolutionary spirit"* (Bernard Wright). [Latin *imbuere,* to moisten, stain. See **ombhro-** in Appendix.*]

IMF International Monetary Fund.

im·id·az·ole (ĭm′ĭd-ăz′ōl′, -ə-zōl′) *n.* Any of a group of heterocyclic compounds, especially the white crystalline base, $C_3H_4N_2$. Also called "glyoxaline." [IMID(E) + AZOLE.]

im·ide (ĭm′īd′, -ĭd) *n.* A compound derived from ammonia containing the divalent NH group combined with two acid radicals. [Alteration of AMIDE.]

i·mine (ĭ-mēn′, ĭm′ĭn) *n.* A compound derived from ammonia containing the divalent NH group combined with alkyl or other nonacid radicals. [Alteration of AMINE.]

im·i·tate (ĭm′ə-tāt′) *tr.v.* **-tated, -tating, -tates. 1.** To model oneself after the behavior or actions of. **2. a.** To copy the appearance, mannerisms, or speech of. **b.** To copy the literary, artistic, or musical style of. **3.** To copy; reproduce. **4.** To resemble. [Latin *imitārī*†.] **—im′i·ta′tor** (-tā′tər) *n.*

Synonyms: *imitate, copy, mimic, ape, parody, simulate.* These verbs mean to follow something or someone taken as a model. To *imitate* is to act like another person or to follow a pattern or style set by another. To *copy* is to duplicate an original as precisely as possible. To *mimic* is to copy another person's actions, speech, or mannerisms closely, either seriously or with intent to ridicule. To *ape* is to ridicule by mimicry or to follow another's lead slavishly. To *parody* is either to make fun of another's style by imitating it with comic effect or to attempt a serious imitation and fail. To *simulate* is to feign, or assume the appearance of something falsely, by imitating its identifying signs or characteristics.

im·i·ta·tion (ĭm′ə-tā′shən) *n.* **1.** An act of imitating. **2.** Something derived or copied from an original. **3.** *Music.* The repetition of a phrase or sequence often with variations in key, rhythm, and voice. **—im′i·ta′tion·al** *adj.*

im·i·ta·tive (ĭm′ə-tā′tĭv) *adj.* **1.** Of or involving imitation. **2.** Not original; derivative; copied. **3.** Tending to imitate. **4.** Onomatopoeic. **—im′i·ta′tive·ly** *adv.* **—im′i·ta′tive·ness** *n.*

I·mit·tos. The Greek name for **Hymettus.**

im·mac·u·la·cy (ĭ-măk′yə-lə-sē) *n.* The quality or condition of being immaculate; immaculateness.

im·mac·u·late (ĭ-măk′yə-lĭt) *adj.* **1.** Free from stain or blemish; spotless; pure. **2.** Free from fault or error. **3.** Impeccably clean. 4. Having no markings. [Middle English *immaculat*, from Latin *immaculātus* : *in-*, not + *maculātus*, past participle of *maculāre*, to stain, blemish, from *macula*, spot (see **macula** in Appendix*).] —**im·mac′u·late·ly** *adv.* —**im·mac′u·late·ness** *n.*

Immaculate Conception. The Roman Catholic doctrine that the Virgin Mary was conceived in her mother's womb free from all stain of original sin. Compare **virgin birth.**

im·ma·nent (ĭm′ə-nənt) *adj.* 1. Existing or remaining within; inherent. 2. Restricted entirely to the mind; subjective. Compare **transeunt.** [Late Latin *immanēns*, present participle of *immanēre*, to remain in : Latin *in-*, in + *manēre*, to remain (see **men-³** in Appendix*).] —**im′ma·nent·ly** *adv.*

im·ma·te·ri·al (ĭm′ə-tîr′ē-əl) *adj.* 1. Having no material body or form. 2. Of no importance or relevance; inconsequential. —**im′ma·te′ri·al·ly** *adv.* —**im′ma·te′ri·al·ness** *n.*

im·ma·te·ri·al·ism (ĭm′ə-tîr′ē-ə-lĭz′əm) *n.* A metaphysical doctrine asserting the nonexistence of corporeal reality. —**im′ma·te′ri·al·ist** *n.*

im·ma·te·ri·al·i·ty (ĭm′ə-tîr′ē-ăl′ə-tē) *n., pl.* **-ties.** 1. The state or quality of being immaterial. 2. Something immaterial.

im·ma·te·ri·al·ize (ĭm′ə-tîr′ē-ə-līz′) *tr.v.* **-ized, -izing, -izes.** To render immaterial.

im·ma·ture (ĭm′ə-tyŏŏr′, -tŏŏr′, -chŏŏr′) *adj.* 1. Not fully grown or developed; unripe. 2. Behaving with less than normal maturity. [Latin *immātūrus* : *in-*, not + *mātūrus*, MATURE.] —**im′ma·ture′ly** *adv.* —**im′ma·tur′i·ty, im′ma·ture′ness** *n.*

im·meas·ur·a·ble (ĭ-mĕzh′ər-ə-bəl) *adj.* 1. Incapable of being measured. 2. Vast; limitless. —**im·meas′ur·a·bil′i·ty, im·meas′ur·a·ble·ness** *n.* —**im·meas′ur·a·bly** *adv.*

im·me·di·a·cy (ĭ-mē′dē-ə-sē) *n., pl.* **-cies.** 1. The condition or quality of being immediate; directness. 2. Something immediate. 3. Immediate or direct perception; intuitiveness.

im·me·di·ate (ĭ-mē′dē-ĭt) *adj.* 1. Acting or occurring without mediation or interposition; direct: *immediate implementation.* 2. Directly apprehended or perceived: *immediate awareness.* 3. Next in line or relation: *the immediate successor.* 4. Occurring without delay: *an immediate response.* 5. Of or near the present time: *the immediate future.* 6. Close at hand; near: *the immediate vicinity.* [Late Latin *immediātus* : Latin *in-*, not + *mediātus*, past participle of *mediāre*, to be in the middle, MEDIATE.] —**im·me′di·ate·ness** *n.*

im·me·di·ate·ly (ĭ-mē′dē-ĭt-lē) *adv.* 1. Without intermediary; directly. 2. Without delay. —*conj.* As soon as; directly.

Synonyms: *immediately, instantly, forthwith, directly, promptly, presently.* These adverbs mean with little or no delay. They are arranged in approximate order of intensity. *Immediately* and *instantly* imply no delay whatever, as between request and response. *Forthwith, directly,* and *promptly* all stress readiness of response but with a brief interval prior to fulfillment of the action involved. *Presently* has the mere force of soon.

im·med·i·ca·ble (ĭ-mĕd′ĭ-kə-bəl) *adj.* Incurable.

Im·mel·mann turn (ĭm′əl-mən, -män′). A maneuver in which an airplane first completes half a loop then half a roll in order to simultaneously gain altitude and change direction in flight. [After the German aviator Max *Immelmann* (1890–1916).]

im·me·mo·ri·al (ĭm′ə-môr′ē-əl, -mōr′ē-əl) *adj.* Reaching beyond the limits of memory, tradition, or recorded history. [Medieval Latin *immemoriālis* : Latin *in-*, not + *memoriālis*, memorial, from *memoria*, MEMORY.] —**im′me·mo′ri·al·ly** *adv.*

im·mense (ĭ-mĕns′) *adj.* 1. Extremely large; huge. 2. Boundless. 3. *Informal.* Surpassingly good; excellent. —See Synonyms at **enormous.** [Old French, from Latin *immēnsus*, immeasurable : *in-*, not + *mēnsus*, past participle of *mētīrī*, to measure (see **mē-²** in Appendix*).] —**im·mense′ly** *adv.* —**im·mense′ness** *n.*

im·men·si·ty (ĭ-mĕn′sə-tē) *n., pl.* **-ties.** 1. The quality or state of being immense. 2. Something immense.

im·men·sur·a·ble (ĭ-mĕn′shər-ə-bəl) *adj.* Immeasurable.

im·merge (ĭ-mûrj′) *v.* **-merged, -merging, -merges.** —*tr.* To immerse. —*intr.* To submerge or disappear in or as if in a liquid. [Latin *immergere*, IMMERSE.] —**im·mer′gence** *n.*

im·merse (ĭ-mûrs′) *tr.v.* **-mersed, -mersing, -merses.** 1. To cover completely in a liquid; submerge. 2. To baptize by submerging in water. 3. To involve profoundly; absorb. [Latin *immergere* (past participle *immersus*), to dip in : *in-*, in + *mergere*, to dip (see **mezg-¹** in Appendix*).]

im·mer·sion (ĭ-mûr′zhən, -shən) *n.* 1. An act of immersing. 2. The condition of being immersed. 3. Baptism performed by totally submerging a person in water. 4. The obscuring of a celestial body by another or by the shadow of another.

im·mesh. Variant of **enmesh.**

im·mi·grant (ĭm′ĭ-grənt) *n.* 1. One who leaves a country to settle permanently in another. 2. An organism that appears where it was formerly unknown. —**im′mi·grant** *adj.*

im·mi·grate (ĭm′ĭ-grāt′) *v.* **-grated, -grating, -grates.** —*intr.* To enter and settle in a country or region to which one is not a native. —*tr.* To send or introduce as immigrants. —See Usage note at **migrate.** [Latin *immigrāre*, to remove into, go in : *in-*, in + *migrāre*, to remove, MIGRATE.] —**im′mi·gra′tion** *n.*

im·mi·nence (ĭm′ə-nəns) *n.* Also **im·mi·nen·cy** (-nən-sē) *pl.* **-cies.** 1. The quality or condition of being imminent. 2. Something imminent.

im·mi·nent (ĭm′ə-nənt) *adj.* About to occur; impending. [Latin *imminēns*, present participle of *imminēre*, to project over or toward, threaten : *in-*, toward + *-minēre*, to project (see **men-²** in Appendix*).] —**im′mi·nent·ly** *adv.*

im·min·gle (ĭ-mĭng′gəl) *v.* **-gled, -gling, -gles.** —*intr.* To intermingle; blend. —*tr.* To blend.

im·mis·ci·ble (ĭ-mĭs′ə-bəl) *adj.* Incapable of mixing or blending. —**im·mis′ci·bil′i·ty** *n.* —**im·mis′ci·bly** *adv.*

im·mit·i·ga·ble (ĭ-mĭt′ĭ-gə-bəl) *adj.* Incapable of being mitigated. —**im·mit′i·ga·bly** *adv.*

im·mix (ĭ-mĭks′) *tr.v.* **-mixed, -mixing, -mixes.** To commingle; blend. [Back-formation from Middle English *immixte*, mixed in, from Latin *immixtus*, past participle of *immiscēre*, to mix in : *in-*, in + *miscēre*, to mix (see **meik-** in Appendix*).] —**im·mix′ture** *n.*

im·mo·bile (ĭ-mō′bəl, -bēl′) *adj.* 1. a. Unable to move. b. Incapable of being moved. 2. Not moving. [Middle English *inmobile*, from Latin *immōbilis* : *in-*, not + *mōbilis*, MOBILE.] —**im′mo·bil′i·ty** *n.*

im·mo·bi·lize (ĭ-mō′bə-līz′) *tr.v.* **-lized, -lizing, -lizes.** 1. To render immobile. 2. To impede movement or use of: *immobilize troops.* 3. a. To withdraw (specie) from circulation and reserve as security for other money. b. To convert (floating capital) into fixed capital. —**im·mo′bi·li·za′tion** *n.* —**im·mo′bi·liz′er** *n.*

im·mod·er·ate (ĭ-mŏd′ər-ĭt) *adj.* Not moderate; extreme. See Synonyms at **excessive.** [Middle English *immoderat*, from Latin *immoderātus* : *in-*, not + *moderātus*, MODERATE.] —**im·mod′er·ate·ly** *adv.* —**im·mod′er·ate·ness, im·mod′er·a′tion** *n.*

im·mod·est (ĭ-mŏd′ĭst) *adj.* 1. Lacking modesty. 2. Morally offensive. 3. Arrogant. [Latin *immodestus* : *in-*, not + *modestus*, MODEST.] —**im·mod′est·ly** *adv.* —**im·mod′es·ty** *n.*

im·mo·late (ĭm′ə-lāt′) *tr.v.* **-lated, -lating, -lates.** 1. To kill as a sacrifice. 2. To destroy or renounce for the sake of something else. [Latin *immolāre*, to sacrifice, originally "to sprinkle with sacrificial meal" : *in-*, on + *mola*, meal (see **mela-** in Appendix*).] —**im′mo·la′tion** *n.* —**im′mo·la′tor** (-lā′tər) *n.*

im·mor·al (ĭ-môr′əl, ĭ-mŏr′-) *adj.* 1. Contrary to established morality. 2. Morally dissolute. —**im′mor·al′i·ty** (ĭm′ô-răl′ə-tē, ĭm′ə-) *n.* —**im·mor′al·ly** *adv.*

im·mor·tal (ĭ-môrt′l) *adj.* 1. Not subject to death. 2. Having eternal fame; imperishable. 3. Of or pertaining to immortality. —*n.* 1. One not subject to death. 2. One whose fame is enduring. 3. *Plural.* The gods of ancient Greece and Rome. [Middle English, from Latin *immortālis* : *in-*, not + *mortālis*, MORTAL.] —**im·mor′tal·ly** *adv.*

im·mor·tal·i·ty (ĭm′ôr-tăl′ə-tē) *n.* 1. The quality or condition of being immortal. 2. Endless life. 3. Enduring fame.

im·mor·tal·ize (ĭ-môrt′l-īz′) *tr.v.* **-ized, -izing, -izes.** To make immortal.

im·mor·telle (ĭm′ôr-tĕl′) *n.* A plant with flowers that retain their color when dried. [French, from the feminine of *immortel*, immortal, from Latin *immortālis*, IMMORTAL.]

im·mo·tile (ĭ-mōt′l) *adj.* Not motile. —**im′mo·til′i·ty** *n.*

im·mov·a·ble (ĭ-mōō′və-bəl) *adj.* 1. a. Incapable of being moved. b. Incapable of movement. 2. Not capable of alteration. 3. Unyielding in principle, purpose, or adherence; steadfast. 4. Showing no sign of emotional stress; unimpressionable. 5. *Law.* Not liable to be removed: *immovable property.* —*n.* 1. One that is incapable of movement. 2. Immovable property. —**im·mov′a·ble·ness, im·mov′a·bil′i·ty** *n.* —**im·mov′a·bly** *adv.*

im·mune (ĭ-myōōn′) *adj.* 1. a. Exempt. b. Not affected or responsive. 2. *Medicine.* Having immunity. [Latin *immūnis.* See **mei-¹** in Appendix.*] —**im·mune′** *n.*

im·mu·ni·ty (ĭ-myōō′nə-tē) *n., pl.* **-ties.** 1. The quality or condition of being immune. 2. An inherited, acquired, or induced condition to a specific pathogen.

im·mu·nize (ĭm′yə-nīz′) *tr.v.* **-nized, -nizing, -nizes.** To render immune. —**im′mu·ni·za′tion** *n.*

immuno–. Indicates immune or immunity; for example, **immunogenetics, immunogenic.** [From IMMUNE.]

im·mu·no·chem·is·try (ĭm′yə-nō-kĕm′ĭ-strē) *n.* The chemistry of immunologic phenomena, as of antigen stimulation of tissue or of antigen-antibody reactions.

im·mu·no·ge·net·ics (ĭm′yə-nō-jə-nĕt′ĭks) *n.* Plural in form, used with a singular verb. The study of the interrelation between immunity to disease and genetic make-up.

im·mu·no·gen·ic (ĭm′yə-nō-jĕn′ĭk) *adj.* Producing immunity.

im·mu·nol·o·gy (ĭm′yə-nŏl′ə-jē) *n.* The medical study of immunity. [IMMUNO- + -LOGY.] —**im′mu·no·log′ic** (-nə-lŏj′ĭk), **im′mu·no·log′i·cal** *adj.* —**im′mu·no·log′i·cal·ly** *adv.*

im·mu·no·sup·pres·sive (ĭm′yə-nō-sə-prĕs′ĭv) *adj.* Tending to suppress a natural immune response of an organism to an antigen: *an immunosuppressive drug.*

im·mure (ĭ-myŏŏr′) *tr.v.* **-mured, -muring, -mures.** 1. To confine within walls; imprison. 2. To build into a wall; entomb in a wall. [Medieval Latin *immūrāre* : Latin *in-*, in + *mūrus*, wall (see **mei-³** in Appendix*).] —**im·mure′ment** *n.*

im·mu·ta·ble (ĭ-myōō′tə-bəl) *adj.* Not mutable; not susceptible to change. [Middle English, from Latin *immūtābilis* : *in-*, not + *mūtābilis*, MUTABLE.] —**im·mu′ta·bil′i·ty, im·mu′ta·ble·ness** *n.* —**im·mu′ta·bly** *adv.*

imp (ĭmp) *n.* 1. A mischievous child. 2. A small demon. 3. *Archaic.* A descendant. 4. *Archaic.* A graft. —*tr.v.* **imped, imping, imps.** 1. *Falconry.* To graft (new feathers) onto the wing of a bird to repair damage or to increase flying capacity. 2. *Archaic.* To furnish with wings. 3. *Archaic.* To eke out. [Middle English *impe*, scion, offspring, child, Old English *impa*, young shoot, sapling, from *impian*, to graft on, from Common Romance *impotare* (unattested), from Medieval Latin *impotus*, graft, from Greek *emphutos*, implanted, from *emphuein*, to implant : *en-*, in + *phuein*, plant (see **bheu-** in Appendix*).]

imp. 1. imperative. 2. imperfect. 3. imperial. 4. import; imported; importer. 5. important. 6. imprimatur.

im·pact (ĭm′păkt′) *n.* 1. The striking of one body against another; a collision. 2. The effect of one thing upon another.

—*tr.v.* (ĭm-păkt′) **impacted, -pacting, -pacts.** To pack firmly together. [From Latin *impactus,* past participle of *impingere,* to dash or strike against, IMPINGE.] —**im·pac′tion** *n.*

im·pact·ed (ĭm-păk′tĭd) *adj.* **1.** Wedged together at the broken ends. Said of a fractured bone. **2. a.** Placed in the alveolus in a manner prohibiting eruption into a normal position. Said of a tooth. **b.** Driven upward into the alveolar process or surrounding tissue. Said of a tooth.

im·pair (ĭm-pâr′) *tr.v.* **-paired, -pairing, -pairs.** To diminish in strength, value, quantity, or quality. See Synonyms at **injure.** [Middle English *empairen,* from Old French *empeirer,* from Vulgar Latin *impējōrāre* (unattested), to make worse : *in-* (intensive) + Late Latin *pējōrāre,* to make or become worse, from Latin *pējor,* worse (see **ped-**[1] in Appendix*).] —**im·pair′ment** *n.*

im·pa·la (ĭm-pä′lə) *n.* An African antelope, *Aepyceros melampus,* having a reddish coat, and ridged, curved horns in the male. [Zulu.]

im·pale (ĭm-pāl′) *tr.v.* **-paled, -paling, -pales.** Also **em·pale** (ĕm-). **1. a.** To pierce with a sharp stake or point. **b.** To torture or kill by impaling. **2.** To render helpless as if by impaling. [Medieval Latin *impālāre* : Latin *in-,* in + *pālus,* stake, pole (see **pag-** in Appendix*).] —**im·pale′ment** *n.* —**im·pal′er** *n.*

im·pal·pa·ble (ĭm-păl′pə-bəl) *adj.* **1.** Not perceptible to the touch; intangible. **2.** Not easily perceived or grasped by the mind. —**im·pal′pa·bil′i·ty** *n.* —**im·pal′pa·bly** *adv.*

im·pan·el (ĭm-păn′əl) *tr.v.* **-eled, -eling, -els.** Also *chiefly British* **-elled, -elling.** Also **em·pan·el** (ĕm-). To enroll (a jury) upon a panel or list. —**im·pan′el·ment** *n.*

im·par·i·ty (ĭm-păr′ə-tē) *n., pl.* **-ties.** Inequality; disparity; dissimilarity. [Late Latin *impāritās,* from Latin *impār,* not equal : *in-,* not + *pār,* equal (see **perə-** in Appendix*).]

im·park (ĭm-pärk′) *tr.v.* **-parked, -parking, -parks. 1.** To confine (deer, for example) in a park. **2.** To enclose (land) for a park. —**im′par·ka′tion** *n.*

im·part (ĭm-pärt′) *tr.v.* **-parted, -parting, -parts. 1.** To grant a share of; bestow. **2.** To make known; disclose. —See Synonyms at **reveal.** [Latin *impartīre,* to cause to share in, share with : *in-,* in + *partīre,* to share, divide, from *pars* (stem *part-*), part, share (see **perə-** in Appendix*).]

im·par·tial (ĭm-pär′shəl) *adj.* Not partial; unprejudiced. See Synonyms at **fair.** —**im′par·ti·al′i·ty** (-shē-ăl′ə-tē), **im·par′tial·ness** *n.* —**im·par′tial·ly** *adv.*

im·part·i·ble (ĭm-pär′tə-bəl) *adj.* Not partible; indivisible. [Late Latin *impartibilis* : Latin *in-,* not + *partībilis,* PARTIBLE.] —**im·part′i·bil′i·ty** *n.* —**im·part′i·bly** *adv.*

im·pass·a·ble (ĭm-păs′ə-bəl) *adj.* Impossible to traverse. —**im·pass′a·bil′i·ty, im·pass′a·ble·ness** *n.* —**im·pass′a·bly** *adv.*

im·passe (ĭm′păs′) *n.* **1.** A road or passage having no exit; dead end; cul-de-sac. **2.** A dilemma. [French : Old French *in-,* not, in- + *passer,* to PASS.]

im·pas·si·ble (ĭm-păs′ə-bəl) *adj.* **1.** Not subject to suffering or pain. **2.** Impassive. [Middle English, from Old French, from Late Latin *impassibilis* : *in-,* not + *passibilis,* PASSIBLE.] —**im·pas′si·bil′i·ty, im·pas′si·ble·ness** *n.* —**im·pas′si·bly** *adv.*

im·pas·sion (ĭm-păsh′ən) *tr.v.* **-sioned, -sioning, -sions.** To arouse the passions of. [Italian *impassionare* : *in-,* in, from Latin + *passione,* passion, from Late Latin *passiō,* PASSION.]

im·pas·sioned (ĭm-păsh′ənd) *adj.* Filled with passion; ardent.

im·pas·sive (ĭm-păs′ĭv) *adj.* **1.** Devoid of or not subject to emotion; apathetic. **2.** Revealing no emotion; expressionless. **3.** Incapable of physical sensation. **4.** Motionless; still. [IN- (not) + Latin *passīvus,* capable of feeling, PASSIVE.] —**im·pas′sive·ly** *adv.* —**im·pas′sive·ness, im′pas·siv′i·ty** *n.*

im·paste (ĭm-pāst′) *tr.v.* **-pasted, -pasting, -pastes. 1.** To make into a paste. **2.** To apply pigment thickly to. [Italian *impastare* : *in-,* in, from Latin + *pasta,* paste, from Late Latin, PASTE.]

im·pas·to (ĭm-păs′tō, -päs′tō) *n.* The application of thick layers of pigment. [Italian, from *impastare,* IMPASTE.]

im·pa·tience (ĭm-pā′shəns) *n.* **1.** The inability to wait patiently. **2.** The inability to endure irritation. **3.** Restive eagerness, desire, or anticipation. [Middle English *impacience,* from Old French *impatience,* from Latin *impatientia,* from *impatiēns,* not patient : *in-,* not + *patiēns,* PATIENT.] —**im·pa′tient** *adj.* —**im·pa′tient·ly** *adv.*

im·pa·tiens (ĭm-pā′shəns, -shənz, -shē-ənz) *n.* Any plant of the genus *Impatiens,* which includes the jewelweed. [New Latin *Impatiens,* from Latin *impatiēns,* IMPATIENT (so called because the ripe pods burst open when touched).]

im·peach (ĭm-pēch′) *tr.v.* **-peached, -peaching, -peaches. 1.** To charge with malfeasance in office before a proper tribunal. **2.** To challenge or discredit; attack; degrade. [Middle English *empeachen,* to impede, accuse, from Old French *empe(s)cher,* impede, from Late Latin *impedicāre,* to entangle, put in fetters : Latin *in-,* in + *pedica,* fetter (see **ped-**[1] in Appendix*).] —**im·peach′a·ble** *adj.* —**im·peach′er** *n.* —**im·peach′ment** *n.*

im·pearl (ĭm-pûrl′) *tr.v.* **-pearled, -pearling, -pearls. 1.** To form into pearls. **2.** To adorn with or as if with pearls.

im·pec·ca·ble (ĭm-pĕk′ə-bəl) *adj.* **1.** Without flaw; faultless. **2.** Not capable of sin or wrongdoing. [Latin *impeccābilis,* not liable to sin : *in-,* not + *peccāre,* to sin (see **ped-**[1] in Appendix*).] —**im·pec′ca·bil′i·ty** *n.* —**im·pec′ca·bly** *adv.*

im·pe·cu·ni·ous (ĭm′pĭ-kyo͞o′nē-əs) *adj.* Lacking money; penniless. [IN- (not) + obsolete *pecunious,* rich, Middle English *pecunyous,* from Latin *pecūniōsus,* from *pecūnia,* money (see **peku-** in Appendix*).] —**im′pe·cu′ni·ous·ly** *adv.* —**im′pe·cu′ni·ous·ness, im′pe·cu′ni·os′i·ty** (-ŏs′ə-tē) *n.*

im·pe·dance (ĭm-pē′dəns) *n. Symbol* **Z** A measure of the total opposition to current flow in an alternating-current circuit, equal to the ratio of the rms electromotive force in the circuit to the rms current produced by it, and usually represented in complex notation as $Z = R + iX$, where R is the ohmic resistance and X is the reactance. [From IMPEDE.]

impedance matching. The use of electric circuits, transmission lines, and other devices to make the impedance of a load equal to the internal impedance of the source of power, thereby making possible the most efficient transfer of power.

im·pede (ĭm-pēd′) *tr.v.* **-peded, -peding, -pedes.** To obstruct the way of; block. See Synonyms at **hinder.** [Latin *impedīre,* to entangle, fetter. See **ped-**[1] in Appendix.*] —**im·ped′er** *n.*

im·ped·i·ment (ĭm-pĕd′ə-mənt) *n.* **1.** A hindrance; an obstruction. **2.** Something that impedes, especially: **a.** An organic defect preventing clear articulation: *a speech impediment.* **b.** *Law.* Something that obstructs the making of a legal contract. —See Synonyms at **obstacle.** [Latin *impedīmentum,* from *impedīre,* IMPEDE.] —**im·ped′i·men′tal** (-mĕnt′l), **im·ped′i·men′tar·y** *adj.*

im·ped·i·men·ta (ĭm-pĕd′ə-mĕn′tə) *pl.n.* Objects, as provisions or baggage, that impede or encumber. [Latin *impedīmenta,* plural of *impedīmentum,* IMPEDIMENT.]

im·pel (ĭm-pĕl′) *tr.v.* **-pelled, -pelling, -pels. 1.** To urge to action through moral pressure; compel; constrain. **2.** To drive forward; propel. [Latin *impellere,* to drive on or against : *in-,* against + *pellere,* to drive (see **pel-**[6] in Appendix*).]

im·pel·lent (ĭm-pĕl′ənt) *adj.* Impelling. —*n.* One that impels.

im·pel·ler (ĭm-pĕl′ər) *n.* **1.** One that impels. **2.** *Mechanics.* **a.** A rotor or rotor blade. **b.** A rotating device used to force a gas in a given direction under pressure.

im·pend (ĭm-pĕnd′) *intr.v.* **-pended, -pending, -pends. 1.** To hang or hover menacingly. **2.** To be about to take place. **3.** *Archaic.* To overhang. [Latin *impendēre* : *in-,* against + *pendēre,* to hang (see **spen-** in Appendix*).]

im·pen·dent (ĭm-pĕn′dənt) *adj.* Impending.

im·pend·ing (ĭm-pĕn′dĭng) *adj.* Likely or due to happen soon; imminent.

im·pen·e·tra·bil·i·ty (ĭm-pĕn′ə-trə-bĭl′ə-tē) *n.* **1.** The quality or condition of being impenetrable. **2.** The inability of two bodies to occupy the same space at the same time.

im·pen·e·tra·ble (ĭm-pĕn′ə-trə-bəl) *adj.* **1.** Not capable of being penetrated or entered. **2.** Incomprehensible; inscrutable; unfathomable. **3.** Impervious to argument or sentiment. [Middle English *impenetrabel,* from Old French *impenetrable,* from Latin *impenetrābilis* : *in-,* not + *penetrābilis,* PENETRABLE.] —**im·pen′e·tra·ble·ness** *n.* —**im·pen′e·tra·bly** *adv.*

im·pen·i·tent (ĭm-pĕn′ə-tənt) *adj.* Not penitent; unrepentant. [Late Latin *impaenitēns* : Latin *in-,* not + *paenitēns,* PENITENT.] —**im·pen′i·tence** *n.* —**im·pen′i·tent** *n.* —**im·pen′i·tent·ly** *adv.*

im·per·a·tive (ĭm-pĕr′ə-tĭv) *adj. Abbr.* **imp. 1.** Expressing a command or plea; peremptory. **2.** Having the power or authority to command or control. **3.** *Grammar.* Of, pertaining to, or constituting the mood that expresses a command or request. **4.** Obligatory; mandatory. —See Synonyms at **urgent.** —*n. Abbr.* **imp. 1.** *Grammar.* **a.** The imperative mood. **b.** A verb form of the imperative mood. **2. a.** A command; an order. **b.** An obligation. [Late Latin *imperātīvus,* from Latin *imperāre,* "to prepare against (an occasion)," hence to command : *in-,* against + *parāre,* to prepare (see **per-**[4] in Appendix*).] —**im·per′a·tive·ly** *adv.* —**im·per′a·tive·ness** *n.*

im·pe·ra·tor (ĭm′pĕ-rä′tôr′, -tōr′, -rā′tər) *n.* **1.** A supreme commander in ancient Rome. **2.** An emperor. [Latin *imperātor,* EMPEROR.]

im·per·cep·ti·ble (ĭm′pər-sĕp′tə-bəl) *adj.* **1.** Not perceptible. **2.** Barely perceptible. —**im′per·cep′ti·bil′i·ty, im′per·cep′ti·ble·ness** *n.* —**im′per·cep′ti·bly** *adv.*

im·per·cep·tive (ĭm′pər-sĕp′tĭv) *adj.* Not perceptive; lacking perception. —**im′per·cep·tiv′i·ty, im′per·cep′tive·ness** *n.*

im·per·fect (ĭm-pûr′fĭkt) *adj. Abbr.* **imp., imperf. 1.** Not perfect. **2.** Of or being the tense of a verb that shows, usually in the past, an action or condition as incomplete, continuous, or coincident with another action. **3.** Having either stamens or a pistil only: *imperfect flowers.* **4.** Not legally enforceable. —*n. Abbr.* **imp., imperf. 1.** The imperfect tense. **2.** A verb in this tense. [Middle English *imperfit,* from Old French *imparfait,* from Latin *imperfectus* : *in-,* not + *perfectus,* PERFECT.] —**im·per′fect·ly** *adv.* —**im·per′fect·ness** *n.*

im·per·fec·tion (ĭm′pər-fĕk′shən) *n.* **1.** The quality or condition of being imperfect. **2.** Something imperfect; a defect; flaw. —See Synonyms at **blemish.**

im·per·fec·tive (ĭm′pər-fĕk′tĭv) *adj.* Denoting a verb aspect or form that expresses action without regard to its beginning or completion. Compare **perfective.**

im·per·fo·rate (ĭm-pûr′fər-ĭt) *adj.* **1.** Not perforated; having no opening. **2.** Not perforated into perforated rows. Said of stamps and sheets of stamps. —*n.* An imperforate stamp.

im·pe·ri·al[1] (ĭm-pîr′ē-əl) *adj. Abbr.* **imp. 1.** Of or pertaining to an empire or emperor. **2.** Designating a nation or government having sovereign rights over colonies or dependencies. **3. a.** *Obsolete.* Having supreme authority; sovereign. **b.** Regal; majestic. **4.** Outstanding in size or quality. **5.** Of or relating to the British Imperial System of weights and measures. See **measurement.** —*n.* **1.** *Capital* **I.** A supporter or a soldier of the Holy Roman Empire. **2.** An emperor or empress. **3.** The top of a carriage. **4.** Something outstanding in size or quality. **5.** A variable size of paper, usually 23 by 33 inches in America. [Middle English *emperial, imperial,* from Old French, from Late Latin *imperiālis,* from Latin *imperium,* command, EMPIRE.] —**im·pe′ri·al·ly** *adv.*

im·pe·ri·al[2] (ĭm-pîr′ē-əl) *n.* A pointed beard grown from the

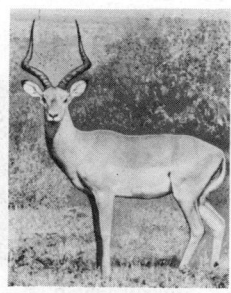

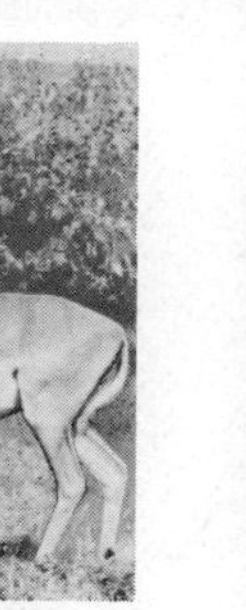
impala

lower lip and chin. [French *impériale,* IMPERIAL (after Napoleon III).]

im·pe·ri·al·ism (ĭm-pîr′ē-ə-lĭz′əm) *n.* **1.** The policy of extending a nation's authority by territorial acquisition or by the establishment of economic and political hegemony over other nations. **2.** The system, policies, or practices of an imperial government. —**im·pe′ri·al·ist** *n.* & *adj.* —**im·pe′ri·al·is′tic** *adj.* —**im·pe′ri·al·is′ti·cal·ly** *adv.*

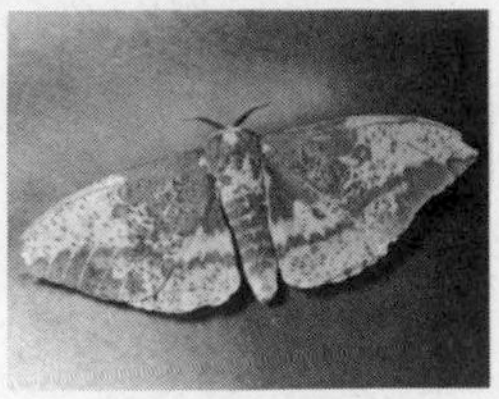

imperial moth

imperial moth. A large New World moth, *Eacles imperialis,* having yellow wings with purplish or brownish markings.

Imperial Valley. A valley in southeastern California and northeastern Baja California, Mexico.

im·per·il (ĭm-pĕr′əl) *tr.v.* **-iled** or **-illed, -iling** or **-illing, -ils.** To put in peril; endanger. —**im·per′il·ment** *n.*

im·pe·ri·ous (ĭm-pîr′ē-əs) *adj.* **1.** Domineering; overbearing. **2.** *Obsolete.* Regal; imperial. **3.** Urgent; pressing. —See Synonyms at **dictatorial.** [Latin *imperiōsus,* from *imperium,* IMPERIUM.] —**im·pe′ri·ous·ly** *adv.* —**im·pe′ri·ous·ness** *n.*

im·per·ish·a·ble (ĭm-pĕr′ĭ-shə-bəl) *adj.* Not perishable. —**im·per′ish·a·bil′i·ty, im·per′ish·a·ble·ness** *n.* —**im·per′ish·a·bly** *adv.*

im·pe·ri·um (ĭm-pîr′ē-əm) *n., pl.* **-peria** (-pîr′ē-ə). **1.** Absolute rule; supreme power. **2.** A sphere of power or dominion; an empire. **3.** *Law.* The right or power to employ the force of a state to enforce the law. [Latin, EMPIRE.]

im·per·ma·nent (ĭm-pûr′mə-nənt) *adj.* Not permanent; not lasting or durable. —**im·per′ma·nence, im·per′ma·nen·cy** *n.*

im·per·me·a·ble (ĭm-pûr′mē-ə-bəl) *adj.* Not permeable. [Late Latin *impermeābilis* : *in-,* not + *permeābilis,* PERMEABLE.] —**im·per′me·a·ble·ness** *n.* —**im·per′me·a·bly** *adv.*

im·per·mis·si·ble (ĭm′pər-mĭs′ə-bəl) *adj.* Not permissible. —**im′per·mis′si·bil′i·ty** *n.* —**im′per·mis′si·bly** *adv.*

im·per·son·al (ĭm-pûr′sə-nəl) *adj.* **1.** *Grammar.* **a.** Denoting a verb that expresses the action of an unspecified agent and is used in the third person singular with no defined subject (as *meseems*) or a purely nominal subject (as *snowed* in *it snowed*). **b.** Indefinite. Said of pronouns. **2. a.** Not personal; not related or connected to a person or persons: *impersonal possessions.* **b.** Exhibiting no emotion or personality. —**im·per′son·al′i·ty** *n.* —**im·per′son·al·ly** *adv.*

im·per·son·al·ize (ĭm-pûr′sə-nə-līz′) *tr.v.* **-ized, -izing, -izes.** To make impersonal.

im·per·son·ate (ĭm-pûr′sə-nāt′) *tr.v.* **-ated, -ating, -ates. 1.** To act the character or part of. **2.** *Archaic.* To embody; personify. [IN- (in) + PERSON + -ATE.] —**im·per′son·ate** (-nĭt) *adj.* —**im·per′son·a′tion** *n.* —**im·per′son·a′tor** (-sə-nā′tər) *n.*

im·per·ti·nence (ĭm-pûrt′n-əns) *n.* Also **im·per·ti·nen·cy** (-ən-sē) *pl.* **-cies. 1.** The quality or condition of being impertinent, as: **a.** Insolence. **b.** Irrelevance. **2.** An impertinent act, person, statement, or the like.

im·per·ti·nent (ĭm-pûrt′n-ənt) *adj.* **1.** Impudent; presumptuous; rude. **2.** Not pertinent; irrelevant. [Middle English, irrelevant, from Old French, from Late Latin *impertinēns* : Latin *in-,* not + *pertinēns,* PERTINENT.] —**im·per′ti·nent·ly** *adv.*

im·per·turb·a·ble (ĭm′pər-tûr′bə-bəl) *adj.* Not capable of being perturbed. See Synonyms at **cool.** —**im′per·turb′a·bil′i·ty, im′per·turb′a·ble·ness** *n.* —**im′per·turb′a·bly** *adv.*

im·per·vi·ous (ĭm-pûr′vē-əs) *adj.* **1.** Incapable of being penetrated. **2.** Incapable of being affected. [Latin *impervius* : *in-,* not + *pervius,* PERVIOUS.] —**im·per′vi·ous·ly** *adv.* —**im·per′vi·ous·ness** *n.*

im·pe·ti·go (ĭm′pə-tī′gō, -tē′gō) *n.* A contagious skin disease characterized by superficial pustules that burst and form characteristic thick yellow crusts. [Latin *impetīgō,* "an attack," from *impetere,* to assail, attack. See **impetus.**]

im·pe·trate (ĭm′pə-trāt′) *tr.v.* **-trated, -trating, -trates. 1.** To obtain by entreaty or petition. **2.** To beseech. [Latin *impetrāre,* to accomplish : *in-* (intensive) + *patrāre,* to father, achieve, accomplish, from *pater,* father (see **peter-** in Appendix*).] —**im′pe·tra′tion** *n.* —**im′pe·tra′tor** (-trā′tər) *n.*

im·pet·u·os·i·ty (ĭm-pĕch′o͞o-ŏs′ə-tē) *n., pl.* **-ties.** Also **im·pet·u·ous·ness** (-əs-nĭs). **1.** The quality or condition of being impetuous. **2.** An impetuous act. —See Synonyms at **temerity.**

im·pet·u·ous (ĭm-pĕch′o͞o-əs) *adj.* **1.** Characterized by sudden energy, emotion, or the like; impulsive; brash. **2.** Having great impetus; rushing with violence: *impetuous, heaving waves.* [Middle English, from Old French *impetueux,* from Latin *impetuōsus,* from *impetus,* IMPETUS.] —**im·pet′u·ous·ly** *adv.*

Synonyms: *impetuous, heedless, hasty, headlong, sudden.* These adjectives describe persons and their actions and decisions when marked by abruptness or lack of deliberation. *Impetuous* suggests impulsiveness, impatience, or lack of thoughtfulness. *Heedless* implies carelessness or lack of a sense of responsibility or proper regard for the consequences of action. *Hasty* and *headlong* both stress hurried action, and the latter especially implies recklessness. *Sudden* is applied to action or to personal attributes, such as moods, that make themselves apparent abruptly or unexpectedly.

im·pe·tus (ĭm′pə-təs) *n., pl.* **-tuses. 1. a.** An impelling force; impulse. **b.** Something that incites; a stimulus. **2.** Loosely, the force or energy associated with a moving body. [Latin, attack, from *impetere,* to assail, attack : *in-,* against + *petere,* to go toward, seek, attack (see **pet-**[1] in Appendix*).]

Imp·hal (ĭmp′hŭl). The capital of Manipur, Republic of India, in the central part of the territory. Population, 100,000.

im·pi·e·ty (ĭm-pī′ə-tē) *n., pl.* **-ties. 1.** The quality or state of being impious. **2.** An impious act. **3.** Undutifulness.

im·pinge (ĭm-pĭnj′) *intr.v.* **-pinged, -pinging, -pinges. 1.** To collide; strike; dash. Used with *on, upon,* or *against.* **2.** To encroach; trespass. Used with *on* or *upon.* [Latin *impingere,* to push against : *in-,* against + *pangere,* to fasten, drive in (see **pag-** in Appendix*).] —**im·pinge′ment** *n.* —**im·ping′er** *n.*

im·pi·ous (ĭm′pē-əs, ĭm-pī′-) *adj.* **1.** Not pious; lacking reverence; profane. **2.** Lacking due respect. [Latin *impius* : *in-,* not + *pius,* PIOUS.] —**im′pi·ous·ly** *adv.* —**im′pi·ous·ness** *n.*

imp·ish (ĭm′pĭsh) *adj.* Of or befitting an imp; mischievous. See Synonyms at **playful.** —**imp′ish·ly** *adv.* —**imp′ish·ness** *n.*

im·pla·ca·ble (ĭm-plā′kə-bəl, -plăk′ə-bəl) *adj.* **1.** Not placable; incapable of appeasement; inexorable. **2.** Unalterable; inflexible. [Latin *implācābilis* : *in-,* not + *plācābilis,* PLACABLE.] —**im·pla′ca·bil′i·ty, im·pla′ca·ble·ness** *n.* —**im·pla′ca·bly** *adv.*

im·plant (ĭm-plănt′, -plänt′) *tr.v.* **-planted, -planting, -plants. 1.** To entrench or set in firmly, as in the ground; infix. **2.** To establish decisively, as in the mind or consciousness; instill; ingrain. **3.** *Medicine.* To insert or embed surgically, as in grafting. —*n.* (ĭm′plănt′, -plänt′). Something implanted; especially, surgically implanted tissue.

im·plan·ta·tion (ĭm′plăn-tā′shən) *n.* **1.** An act or instance of implanting. **2.** The condition of being implanted. **3.** An implanted object. **4.** The attachment and embedding of the fertilized ovum in the uterine wall.

im·plau·si·ble (ĭm-plô′zə-bəl) *adj.* Not plausible. —**im·plau′si·bil′i·ty, im·plau′si·ble·ness** *n.* —**im·plau′si·bly** *adv.*

im·plead (ĭm-plēd′) *tr.v.* **-pleaded, -pleading, -pleads.** To sue in a court of law. [Middle English *impleden,* from Old French *empleid(i)er* : *en-* (intensive) + *pleid(i)er,* PLEAD.]

im·ple·ment (ĭm′plə-mənt) *n.* **1.** A tool, utensil, or instrument. **2.** An article used to outfit or equip. **3.** A means or vehicle employed to achieve a given end; an agent. —See Synonyms at **tool.** —*tr.v.* **implemented, -menting, -ments. 1.** To provide a definite plan or procedure to ensure the fulfillment of; carry into effect. **2.** To supply with implements. [Middle English, from Late Latin *implēmentum,* a filling up, supplement, from Latin *implēre,* to fill up, fulfill : *in-* (intensive) + *plēre,* to fill (see **pel-**[8] in Appendix*).] —**im′ple·men·ta′tion** *n.*

im·pli·cate (ĭm′plĭ-kāt′) *tr.v.* **-cated, -cating, -cates. 1.** To involve intimately or incriminatingly. **2.** To imply. **3.** *Archaic.* To interweave or entangle; entwine. [Latin *implicāre* : *in-,* in + *plicāre,* to fold (see **plek-** in Appendix*).]

im·pli·ca·tion (ĭm′plĭ-kā′shən) *n.* **1.** The act of implicating or the condition of being implicated. **2.** The act of implying or the condition of being implied. **3.** That which is implied, especially: **a.** An indirect indication. **b.** An inference.

im·pli·ca·tive (ĭm′plĭ-kā′tĭv) *adj.* Also **im·pli·ca·to·ry** (-kə-tôr′ē, -tōr′ē). Having a tendency to implicate. —**im′pli·ca′tive·ly** *adv.*

im·plic·it (ĭm-plĭs′ĭt) *adj.* **1.** Implied or understood although not directly expressed: *His anger was implicit.* **2.** Inherent or contained in the nature of something although not directly expressed. Used with *in: Suspicion is implicit in such a tone of voice.* **3.** Having no doubts or reservations; unquestioning: *Her trust in him was implicit.* [Latin *implicitus,* earlier *implicātus,* involved, entangled, from the past participle of *implicāre,* to involve, IMPLICATE.] —**im·plic′it·ly** *adv.* —**im·plic′it·ness** *n.*

im·plied (ĭm-plīd′) *adj.* Suggested, involved, or understood although not clearly or openly expressed.

im·plode (ĭm-plōd′) *v.* **-ploded, -ploding, -plodes.** —*intr.* To undergo implosion. —*tr. Phonetics.* To pronounce by implosion. [IN- (in) + (EX)PLODE.]

im·plore (ĭm-plôr′, -plōr′) *v.* **-plored, -ploring, -plores.** —*tr.* **1.** To appeal to in supplication; entreat; beseech: *I implore you to have mercy on the defendant.* **2.** To plead or beg for urgently: *I implore your mercy.* —*intr.* To make earnest appeal. —See Synonyms at **beg.** [Latin *implōrāre,* to invoke with tears : *in-,* in + *plōrāre,* to weep, lament (perhaps imitative).] —**im′plo·ra′tion** *n.* —**im·plor′er** *n.* —**im·plor′ing·ly** *adv.*

im·plo·sion (ĭm-plō′zhən) *n.* **1.** A more or less violent collapse inward, as of a highly evacuated glass vessel. **2.** *Phonetics.* The stopping of the breath in the formation of a stop consonant. Compare **plosion.** [IN- (in) + (EX)PLOSION.]

im·plo·sive (ĭm-plō′sĭv) *adj. Phonetics.* Pronounced by implosion. —*n. Phonetics.* A consonant pronounced by implosion.

im·ply (ĭm-plī′) *tr.v.* **-plied, -plying, -plies. 1.** To involve or suggest by logical necessity; entail: *His aims imply a good deal of energy.* **2.** To say or express indirectly; to hint; suggest: *His tone implied a malicious purpose.* **3.** *Obsolete.* To entangle. —See Synonyms at **suggest.** —See Usage note at **infer.** [Middle English *implien, emplien,* from Old French *emplier,* from Latin *implicāre,* infold, involve, IMPLICATE.]

im·po·lite (ĭm′pə-līt′) *adj.* Discourteous; unmannerly; not polite. [Latin *impolītus,* unpolished : *in-,* not + *polītus,* polished, POLITE.] —**im′po·lite′ly** *adv.* —**im′po·lite′ness** *n.*

im·pol·i·tic (ĭm-pŏl′ə-tĭk) *adj.* Not wise or expedient; not politic. —**im·pol′i·tic·ly** *adv.* —**im·pol′i·tic·ness** *n.*

im·pon·der·a·ble (ĭm-pŏn′dər-ə-bəl) *adj.* Incapable of being weighed or measured with preciseness. —**im·pon′der·a·ble·ness** *n.* —**im·pon′der·a·bly** *adv.*

im·pone (ĭm-pōn′) *tr.v.* **-poned, -poning, -pones.** *Obsolete.* To wager or stake. [Latin *impōnere,* to place on : *in-,* on + *pōnere,* to place (see **apo-** in Appendix*).]

im·port (ĭm-pôrt′, -pōrt′, ĭm′pôrt′, -pōrt′) *v.* **-ported, -porting, -ports.** —*tr.* **1.** To bring or carry in from an outside source; especially, to bring in (goods) from a foreign country for trade or sale. **2.** To mean; signify. **3.** To imply. **4.** *Archaic.* To have meaning for. —*intr.* To be significant. —See Synonyms at **mean** (convey sense). —*n.* (ĭm′pôrt′, -pōrt′). **1.** *Abbr.* **imp.** Something imported. **2.** The occupation of importing. **3.** Meaning; signification. **4.** Importance; significance: *"Here man's import is small/Beside the turbine, his rewards are slight"* (Howard Baker). —See Synonyms at **importance, meaning.**

[Middle English *importen*, from Latin *importāre*, to carry in : *in-*, in + *portāre*, to carry (see **per-**[2] in Appendix*).] —**im·port'a·bil'i·ty** *n.* —**im·port'a·ble** *adj.* —**im·port'er** *n.*

im·por·tance (ĭm-pôr'təns) *n.* **1.** The condition or quality of being important; significance; consequence. **2.** Personal status; standing. **3.** *Obsolete.* An important matter. **4.** *Obsolete.* Meaning; import. **5.** *Obsolete.* Importunity.

Synonyms: *importance, consequence, moment, significance, import, weight.* These nouns refer to the quality of a thing that makes it influential or worthy of note, esteem, or the like. *Importance,* the most general term, usually can be substituted for any of the others, although it lacks their special implications. *Consequence* is especially applicable to persons or things of notable rank or position and to things that are important with respect to what follows them as an outcome or development. *Moment* implies importance or consequence that is readily apparent. *Significance* and *import* refer to the quality of a thing, often not readily apparent, that gives the thing special meaning or value. *Weight* is frequently used when a personal evaluation or judgment of importance is suggested.

im·por·tant (ĭm-pôr'tənt) *adj. Abbr.* **imp. 1.** Carrying a great deal of weight or value; significant; noteworthy. **2.** Suggesting or having an air of great weight or moment; authoritative. **3.** *Obsolete.* Importunate. [Old French, from Old Italian *importante*, from Medieval Latin *importāns*, present participle of *importāre*, to mean, be significant, from Latin, to carry in, IMPORT.] —**im·por'tant·ly** *adv.*

Usage: *Important,* rather than the adverb *importantly,* is prescribed by most grammarians in the following typical construction: *His research has helped to verify several medical theories; more important, it suggests a whole new field of inquiry. More important* is thus construed as an elliptical rendering of *what is more important,* with *important* (adjective) modifying *is.* Though *importantly* is not defensible grammatically, it often appears in such sentences. It is an acceptable alternative to *important* in the preceding example, according to 50 per cent of the Usage Panel.

im·por·ta·tion (ĭm'pôr-tā'shən, ĭm'pōr-) *n.* **1.** The act, occupation, or business of importing. **2.** Something imported; an import.

im·por·tu·nate (ĭm-pôr'cho͝o-nĭt) *adj.* Stubbornly or unreasonably persistent in request or demand. —**im·por'tu·nate·ly** *adv.* —**im·por'tu·nate·ness** *n.*

im·por·tune (ĭm'pôr-to͞on', -tyo͞on', ĭm-pôr'chən) *tr.v.* **-tuned, -tuning, -tunes. 1.** To beset with repeated and insistent requests. **2.** *Obsolete.* To ask for insistently and repeatedly. **3.** *Obsolete.* To annoy; vex. —See Synonyms at **beg.** —*adj.* Importunate. [Medieval Latin *importūnārī*, to be troublesome, from Latin *importūnus*, "without a port," difficult of access, unfit, unsuitable : *in-*, not + *portus*, port, harbor (see **per-**[2] in Appendix*).] —**im'por·tune'ly** *adv.* —**im'por·tun'er** *n.*

im·por·tu·ni·ty (ĭm'pôr-to͞o'nə-tē, -tyo͞o'nə-tē) *n., pl.* **-ties. 1. a.** The act of importuning. **b.** The state or quality of being importunate. **2.** *Plural.* Insistent demands or requests.

im·pose (ĭm-pōz') *v.* **-posed, -posing, -poses.** —*tr.* **1.** To establish or apply as compulsory; to levy: *The amount of duties imposed now constitutes a protective tariff.* **2.** To apply or make prevail by or as if by authority. **3.** To obtrude or force (oneself, for example) upon another or others. **4.** *Printing.* To arrange (type or plates) on an imposing stone. **5.** To pass off (something) on others: *He imposed a fraud on his company.* —*intr.* To take unfair advantage of something or someone. Used with *on* or *upon.* [Old French *imposer*, from Latin *impōnere* (past participle *impositus*), to put on : *in-*, on + *pōnere*, to put, place (see **apo-** in Appendix*).] —**im·pos'er** *n.*

im·pos·ing (ĭm-pō'zĭng) *adj.* Impressive or awesome. See Synonyms at **grand.**

imposing stone. *Printing.* A stone or metal slab on which material to be printed is arranged. Also called "imposing table."

im·po·si·tion (ĭm'pə-zĭsh'ən) *n.* **1.** The act of imposing. **2.** Something imposed, as a tax, undue burden, or fraud. **3.** *Printing.* The arrangement of printed matter to form a sequence of pages.

im·pos·si·bil·i·ty (ĭm-pŏs'ə-bĭl'ə-tē) *n., pl.* **-ties. 1.** The condition or quality of being impossible. **2.** Something impossible.

im·pos·si·ble (ĭm-pŏs'ə-bəl) *adj.* **1.** Not capable of existing or happening. **2.** Having little likelihood of happening or being accomplished. **3.** Unacceptable. **4.** Not capable of being dealt with or tolerated. [Middle English, from Old French, from Latin *impossibilis* : *in-*, not + *possibilis*, POSSIBLE.] —**im·pos'si·bly** *adv.*

im·post[1] (ĭm'pōst') *n.* **1.** Something imposed or levied, as a tax or duty. **2.** The weight a horse must carry in a handicap race. [Old French, from Medieval Latin *impositum*, from Latin *impositus*, past participle of *impōnere*, IMPOSE.]

im·post[2] (ĭm'pōst') *n. Architecture.* The uppermost part of a column or pillar supporting an arch. [French *imposte*, from Italian *imposta*, from Latin, feminine past participle of *impōnere*, IMPOSE.]

im·pos·tor (ĭm-pŏs'tər) *n.* A person who deceives under an assumed identity. [Old French *imposteur*, from Late Latin *impos(i)tor*, from Latin *impōnere* (past participle *impositus*), IMPOSE.]

Synonyms: *impostor, quack, faker, humbug, mountebank, charlatan.* These nouns denote persons who pretend to be other than what they are or who otherwise practice deception for gain. An *impostor* assumes the identity of another for the purpose of deceiving. A *quack* usually practices medicine without being properly qualified. *Faker,* informal, refers broadly to one who perpetrates fraud. A *humbug* is a self-important or self-deluded cheat who misrepresents himself. A *mountebank* is either a dealer in quack medicines or any flamboyant, unscrupulous dealer or promoter. A *charlatan* makes false claim to skill or knowledge, using a deceitful display to hide his deficiency.

im·pos·ture (ĭm-pŏs'chər) *n.* Deception or fraud; especially, assumption of a false identity. [Late Latin *impostura*, from Latin *impos(i)tus*, past participle of *impōnere*, IMPOSE.]

im·po·tence (ĭm'pə-təns) *n.* Also **im·po·ten·cy** (-tən-sē). The quality or condition of being impotent.

im·po·tent (ĭm'pə-tənt) *adj.* **1.** Lacking physical strength or vigor; weak. **2.** Powerless; ineffectual. **3.** Incapable of sexual intercourse. Said of males. Compare **frigid. 4.** *Obsolete.* Lacking self-restraint. —See Synonyms at **sterile.** [Middle English, from Old French, from Latin *impotēns* : *in-*, not + *potēns*, POTENT.] —**im'po·tent·ly** *adv.*

im·pound (ĭm-pound') *tr.v.* **-pounded, -pounding, -pounds. 1.** To confine in or as if in a pound. **2.** To seize and retain in legal custody. **3.** To accumulate (water) in a reservoir. —**im·pound'age, im·pound'ment** *n.* —**im·pound'er** *n.*

im·pov·er·ish (ĭm-pŏv'ər-ĭsh) *tr.v.* **-ished, -ishing, -ishes. 1.** To diminish or exhaust the wealth of; reduce to poverty. **2.** To deprive of natural richness or strength. —See Synonyms at **deplete.** [Middle English *enpoverisen*, from Old French *empovrir* (present stem *empovriss-*), to make poor : *en-* (causative) + *povre*, POOR.] —**im·pov'er·ish·ment** *n.*

im·prac·ti·ca·ble (ĭm-prăk'tĭ-kə-bəl) *adj.* **1.** Not capable of being done or carried out. **2.** Unfit for passage, as a road. **3.** *Archaic.* Unmanageable; intractable. —**im·prac'ti·ca·ble·ness** *n.* —**im·prac'ti·ca·bly** *adv.*

im·prac·ti·cal (ĭm-prăk'tĭ-kəl) *adj.* **1.** Unwise to implement or maintain in practice. **2.** Incapable of dealing efficiently with practical matters, especially financial matters. **3.** Not a part of experience, fact, or practice; hypothetical; theoretical. **4.** Impracticable. —**im·prac'ti·cal'i·ty, im·prac'ti·cal·ness** *n.*

im·pre·cate (ĭm'prə-kāt') *tr.v.* **-cated, -cating, -cates.** To invoke (evil or a curse) upon. [Latin *imprecārī* : *in-*, on + *precārī*, to pray, entreat, ask (see **perk-**[2] in Appendix*).] —**im'pre·ca'tor** (-kā'tər) *n.* —**im'pre·ca·to'ry** (-kə-tôr'ē, -tōr'ē) *adj.*

im·pre·ca·tion (ĭm'prə-kā'shən) *n.* **1.** The act of imprecating. **2.** A curse.

im·pre·cise (ĭm'prĭ-sīs') *adj.* Not precise. —**im'pre·cise'ly** *adv.* —**im'pre·ci'sion** (-sĭzh'ən) *n.*

im·preg·na·ble[1] (ĭm-prĕg'nə-bəl) *adj.* **1.** Able to resist capture or entry by force: *an impregnable castle.* **2.** Unable to be shaken or criticized, as an argument or conviction. [Middle English *imprenable*, from Old French : *in-*, not + *prenable*, PREGNABLE.]

im·preg·na·ble[2] (ĭm-prĕg'nə-bəl) *adj.* Able to be impregnated. [From IMPREGNATE.]

im·preg·nate (ĭm-prĕg'nāt') *tr.v.* **-nated, -nating, -nates. 1.** To make pregnant; inseminate. **2.** To fertilize (an ovum, for example). **3.** To fill throughout or saturate. **4.** To permeate or imbue. —*adj.* Impregnated; made pregnant. [Late Latin *impraegnāre* : Latin *in-*, in + *praegnās*, PREGNANT.] —**im'preg·na'tion** *n.* —**im·preg'na'tor** (-tər) *n.*

im·pre·sa (ĭm-prā'zə) *n.* An emblem or device with a motto. [French *impresse*, from Italian *impresa*, undertaking, emblem. See **impresario.**]

im·pre·sa·ri·o (ĭm'prə-sär'ē-ō', -sâr'ē-ō') *n., pl.* **-rios** or **-sari** (-sär'ē). **1.** One who sponsors or produces entertainment; especially, the director of an opera company. **2.** A manager; producer. [Italian, undertaker, manager, from *impresa*, undertaking, chivalric deed, emblem, from the feminine of *impreso*, past participle of *imprendere*, to undertake, from Vulgar Latin *imprendere* (unattested). See **emprise.**]

im·pre·scrip·ti·ble (ĭm'prĭ-skrĭp'tə-bəl) *adj.* Immune from prescription; inalienable. —**im'pre·scrip'ti·bly** *adv.*

im·press[1] (ĭm-prĕs') *tr.v.* **-pressed** or *archaic* **-prest** (-prĕst'), **-pressing, -presses. 1.** To produce or apply with pressure. **2.** To mark or stamp with or as if with pressure. **3.** To produce a vivid perception or image of. **4.** To affect or influence deeply or forcibly. **5.** To transmit a force or motion to. —See Synonyms at **affect.** —*n.* (ĭm'prĕs'). **1.** The act of impressing. **2.** A mark or pattern produced by impressing. **3.** A stamp or seal meant to be impressed. [Middle English *impressen*, from Latin *imprimere* (past participle *impressus*) : *in-*, in + *premere*, to press (see **per-**[6] in Appendix*).]

im·press[2] (ĭm-prĕs') *tr.v.* **-pressed, -pressing, -presses. 1.** To compel (a person) to serve in a military force. **2.** To confiscate (property). —*n.* Impressment. [IN- (intensive) + PRESS (to force into service).]

im·press·i·ble (ĭm-prĕs'ə-bəl) *adj.* Susceptible to being impressed. —**im·press'i·bly** *adv.*

im·pres·sion (ĭm-prĕsh'ən) *n.* **1.** The act or process of impressing. **2.** The effect, mark, or imprint made on a surface by pressure. **3.** An effect, image, or feeling retained as a consequence of experience. **4.** A vague notion, remembrance, or belief. **5.** *Printing.* **a.** All the copies of a publication printed at one time from the same set of type. **b.** A single copy of this printing. **6.** *Dentistry.* An imprint of the teeth and surrounding tissue in material such as wax or plaster, used as a mold in making dentures or inlays. —See Synonyms at **opinion.**

im·pres·sion·a·ble (ĭm-prĕsh'ən-ə-bəl) *adj.* Readily influenced; suggestible. —**im·pres'sion·a·bil'i·ty, im·pres'sion·a·ble·ness** *n.*

im·pres·sion·ism (ĭm-prĕsh'ə-nĭz'əm) *n.* **1.** A theory or style of painting originating and developed in France during the 1870's, characterized chiefly by concentration on the general impres-

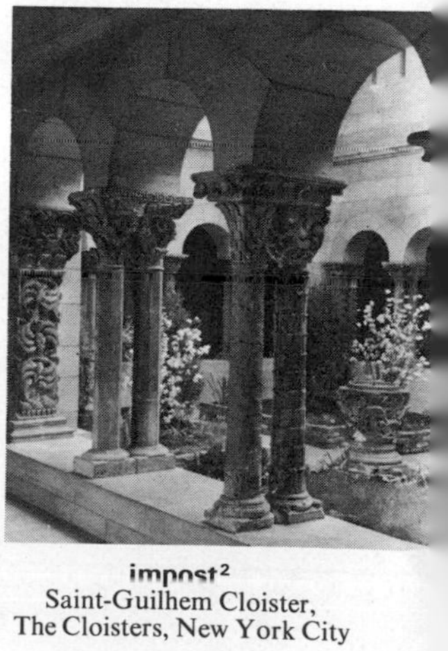

impost[2]
Saint-Guilhem Cloister,
The Cloisters, New York City

sion produced by a scene or object and by the use of unmixed primary colors and small strokes to simulate actual reflected light. **2.** A literary style characterized generally by the use of details and mental associations to evoke subjective and sensory impressions rather than the re-creation of objective reality. **3.** A musical style of the late 19th and early 20th centuries, using lush and somewhat vague harmony and rhythm to evoke suggestions of mood, place, and natural phenomena. —**im·pres′sion·ist** *n.* & *adj.* —**im·pres′sion·is′tic** *adj.*

im·pres·sive (ĭm-prĕs′ĭv) *adj.* Commanding attention; making strong impressions; awesome or stirring. —**im·pres′sive·ly** *adv.* —**im·pres′sive·ness** *n.*

im·press·ment (ĭm-prĕs′mənt) *n.* The act or policy of impressing men or property for public service or use.

im·pres·sure (ĭm-prĕsh′ər) *n. Archaic.* Impression.

im·prest[1] (ĭm-prĕst′) *n.* An advance or loan of government or public funds toward the performance of some service for the government. [Probably from Italian *imprestare,* to make a loan to : *in-,* toward, from Latin + *prestare,* to lend, from Latin *praestāre,* to pay, give, from *praestō,* at hand (see **presto**).]

im·prest[2]. *Archaic.* Past tense and past participle of **impress**.

im·pri·ma·tur (ĭm′prə-mā′tər, -mä′tər) *n.* **1.** *Abbr.* **imp.** Official approval or license to print or publish, especially under conditions of censorship. **2.** Official sanction; authorization. [New Latin, let it be printed, from Latin *imprimere,* to print, IMPRESS.]

im·pri·mis (ĭm-prī′mĭs) *adv.* In the first place. [Middle English, from Latin *in prīmis,* among the first (things) : *in,* in + *prīmīs,* ablative plural of *prīmus,* first (see **per**[1] in Appendix*).]

im·print (ĭm-prĭnt′) *tr.v.* **-printed, -printing, -prints.** **1.** To produce or impress (a mark or pattern) on a surface. **2.** To stamp or produce a mark on. **3.** To establish firmly or impress, as on the mind or memory. —*n.* (ĭm′prĭnt′). **1.** A mark or pattern produced by imprinting. **2.** A distinguishing manifestation: *the imprint of defeat.* **3. a.** The publisher's name, often with the date, address, and edition of a publication, printed at the bottom of a title page. **b.** The printer's name placed usually on the copyright page. [Middle English *imprenten,* from Old French *empreinter,* from *empreinte,* impression, from *empreindre,* to print, from Latin *imprimere,* to IMPRESS.]

im·pris·on (ĭm-prĭz′ən) *tr.v.* To put in or as if in prison. [Middle English *inprisonen, emprisonen,* from Old French *emprisoner* : *en-* (causative) + *prison,* PRISON.] —**im·pris′on·ment** *n.*

im·prob·a·bil·i·ty (ĭm-prŏb′ə-bĭl′ə-tē, ĭm′prŏb-) *n., pl.* **-ties.** **1.** The quality or condition of being improbable. **2.** Something improbable.

im·prob·a·ble (ĭm-prŏb′ə-bəl) *adj.* Not probable; doubtful or unlikely. [Latin *improbābilis* : *in-,* not + *probābilis,* PROBABLE.] —**im·prob′a·ble·ness** *n.* —**im·prob′a·bly** *adv.*

im·pro·bi·ty (ĭm-prō′bə-tē) *n.* Lack of probity; dishonesty. [Latin *improbitās,* from *improbus,* dishonest : *in-,* not + *probus,* honest, good (see **per**[1] in Appendix*).]

im·promp·tu (ĭm-prŏmp′to͞o, -tyo͞o) *adj.* Not rehearsed; extempore. See Synonyms at **extemporaneous**. —*adv.* Without rehearsal or preparation; spontaneously. —*n.* Something made or done impromptu, as a musical composition or remark. [French, from Latin *in promptū,* in readiness, at hand : *in,* in + *promptū,* ablative of *promptus,* ready, PROMPT.]

im·prop·er (ĭm-prŏp′ər) *adj.* **1.** Not suited to circumstances or intention. **2.** Not in keeping with conventional mores; indecorous. **3.** Not consistent with fact or rule; incorrect. **4.** Irregular or abnormal. [Old French *impropre,* from Latin *improprius* : *in-,* not + *proprius,* one's own, PROPER.] —**im·prop′er·ly** *adv.* —**im·prop′er·ness** *n.*

Synonyms: *improper, unbecoming, unseemly, indelicate, indecent, indecorous.* These adjectives mean in violation of accepted standards of what is right or proper. *Improper* can apply to any act or statement contrary to such standards, but often refers to unethical conduct, violation of etiquette, or morally offensive behavior. *Unbecoming* suggests what is beneath the standard implied by one's character or position. What is *unseemly* or *indelicate* violates good taste; *indelicate* suggests immodesty, coarseness, or tactlessness. *Indecent* refers to what is offensive or harmful morally. *Indecorous,* the weakest of these terms, implies violation of the manners of polite society.

improper fraction. A fraction in which the numerator is larger than or equal to the denominator.

improper integral. An integral having at least one nonfinite limit or having an integrand that becomes infinite between the limits of integration.

im·pro·pri·e·ty (ĭm′prə-prī′ə-tē) *n., pl.* **-ties.** **1.** The quality or condition of being improper. **2.** An improper act. **3.** An improper or unacceptable usage in speech or writing.

im·prove (ĭm-pro͞ov′) *v.* **-proved, -proving, -proves.** —*tr.* **1.** To advance to a better state or quality; make better. **2.** To increase the productivity or value of (land). —*intr.* **1.** To become or get better. **2.** To make beneficial additions or changes: *improve on the translation.* [Norman French *emprouer,* to turn to profit : Old French *en-* (causative) + *prou,* profit, from Late Latin *prōde,* advantageous (see **proud**).]

Synonyms: *improve, better, help, ameliorate, enhance.* These verbs mean to make more attractive or desirable in some respect. *Improve,* the most general term, refers to an act of raising in quality or value or of relieving an undesirable situation. *Better* is often interchangeable with *improve* in the preceding senses; used reflexively, *better* implies worldly gain: *better himself by changing jobs. Help* usually implies limited relief or change for the better: *medicine that helped her. Ameliorate* refers to improving or bettering conditions that cry out for change. *Enhance,* in contrast, suggests adding to something already attractive or worthy and thus increasing its value.

im·prove·ment (ĭm-pro͞ov′mənt) *n.* **1.** The act or procedure of improving. **2.** The state of being improved. **3.** A change or addition that improves.

im·prov·i·dent (ĭm-prŏv′ə-dənt) *adj.* **1.** Not providing for the future; thriftless. **2.** Rash; incautious. —**im·prov′i·dence** *n.* —**im·prov′i·dent·ly** *adv.*

im·pro·vi·sa·tion (ĭm-prŏv′ə-zā′shən, ĭm′prə-və-) *n.* **1.** The act of improvising. **2.** Something improvised.

im·prov·i·sa·tor (ĭm-prŏv′ə-zā′tər) *n.* One who improvises.

im·pro·vi·sa·to·ry (ĭm′prə-vī′zə-tôr′ē, -tōr′ē) *adj.* Also **im·prov·i·sa·to·ri·al** (ĭm-prŏv′ə-zə-tôr′ē-əl, -tōr′ē-əl). **1.** Of or pertaining to improvisation. **2.** Of or pertaining to an improviser.

im·pro·vise (ĭm′prə-vīz′) *v.* **-vised, -vising, -vises.** —*tr.* **1.** To invent, compose, or recite without preparation. **2.** To make or provide from available materials. —*intr.* To invent, compose, recite, or execute something offhand. [French *improviser,* from Italian *improvvisare,* from *improvviso,* unforeseen, impromptu, from Latin *imprōvīsus,* : *in-,* not + *prōvīsus,* past participle of *prōvidere,* to foresee, PROVIDE.] —**im′pro·vis′er** *n.*

im·pru·dence (ĭm-pro͞o′dəns) *n.* **1.** The quality of being imprudent. **2.** An imprudent act.

im·pru·dent (ĭm-pro͞o′dənt) *adj.* Not prudent; unwise or injudicious; rash. [Middle English, from Latin *imprūdēns* : *in-,* not + *prūdēns,* PRUDENT.]

im·pu·dence (ĭm′pyə-dəns) *n.* Also **im·pu·den·cy** (-dən-sē). **1.** The quality of being impudent. **2.** Impudent behavior.

im·pu·dent (ĭm′pyə-dənt) *adj.* **1.** Impertinent; rude; disrespectful. **2.** *Obsolete.* Immodest. —See Synonyms at **shameless**. [Middle English, from Latin *impudēns* : *in-,* not + *pudēns,* present participle of *pudēre,* to be ashamed (see **speud-** in Appendix*).] —**im′pu·dent·ly** *adv.*

im·pu·dic·i·ty (ĭm′pyo͞o-dĭs′ə-tē) *n.* Immodesty; shamelessness. [Old French *impudicite,* from Latin *impudicus,* immodest : *in-,* not + *pudicus,* modest, from *pudēre,* to be ashamed (see **impudent**).]

im·pugn (ĭm-pyo͞on′) *tr.v.* **-pugned, -pugning, -pugns.** To oppose or attack as false; criticize; refute. [Middle English *impugnen,* from Old French *impugner,* from Latin *impugnāre,* to fight against : *in-,* against + *pugnāre,* to fight (see **peuk-** in Appendix*).] —**im·pugn′a·ble** *adj.* —**im·pugn′er** *n.*

im·pu·is·sance (ĭm-pyo͞o′ə-səns, ĭm-pwĭs′əns) *n.* Lack of power or effectiveness; weakness; impotence. —**im·pu′is·sant** *adj.*

im·pulse (ĭm′pŭls′) *n.* **1.** An impelling force or the motion it produces; a thrust; a push; momentum; impetus. **2.** A sudden inclination or urge; a desire; whim: *an impulse to speak up.* **3.** A motivating propensity; a drive; an instinct: *"Respect for the liberty of others is not a natural impulse in most men"* (Bertrand Russell). **4.** General tendency or spirit; current: *"The Romantic impulse led in Germany to a technical recasting of the novel form"* (Leslie Fiedler). **5.** *Physics.* The product of the average value of a force with the time during which it acts, equal in general to the change in momentum produced by the force in this time interval. **6.** *Physiology.* An instance of the transmission of energy from one neuron to another. [Latin *impulsus,* from the past participle of *impellere,* IMPEL.]

im·pul·sion (ĭm-pŭl′shən) *n.* **1.** The act of impelling or the condition of being impelled. **2.** An impelling force; a thrust. **3.** Motion produced by an impelling force; momentum. **4.** An urging; compulsion: *"I do not move . . . unless it be under the impulsion of a third party"* (Samuel Beckett).

im·pul·sive (ĭm-pŭl′sĭv) *adj.* **1.** Inclined to act on impulse rather than thought. **2.** Produced as a result of impulse; precipitate; uncalculated: *an impulsive act.* **3.** Having force or power to impel or incite; forceful. **4.** *Physics.* Acting within brief time intervals. Said especially of a force. —See Synonyms at **spontaneous**. —**im·pul′sive·ly** *adv.* —**im·pul′sive·ness** *n.*

im·pu·ni·ty (ĭm-pyo͞o′nə-tē) *n., pl.* **-ties.** **1.** Exemption from punishment or penalty. **2.** Immunity or preservation from recrimination, regret, or the like; escape from what is probable, certain, or just: *"No nation is permitted to live in ignorance with impunity"* (Jefferson). [Latin *impūnitās,* from *impūnis,* not punished : *in-,* not + *poena,* penalty, pain, from Greek *poina, poinē,* expiation, punishment (see **kwei-**[1] in Appendix*).]

im·pure (ĭm-pyo͝or′) *adj.* **1.** Not pure or clean; contaminated. **2.** Not purified by religious rite; defiled. **3.** Immoral or obscene; unchaste. **4.** Mixed with another substance; alloyed; adulterated. **5.** Being a composite of more than one color, or mixed with black or white. Said of color. **6.** Deriving from more than one source, style, or convention; bastardized. Said of the arts. **7.** Not proper or consistent in grammar, vocabulary, idiom, or the like. Said opprobriously of usage that is felt to be nonstandard. —**im·pure′ly** *adv.* —**im·pure′ness** *n.*

im·pu·ri·ty (ĭm-pyo͝or′ə-tē) *n., pl.* **-ties.** **1.** The quality or condition of being impure, especially: **a.** Contamination or pollution. **b.** Lack of consistency or homogeneity; adulteration. **c.** A state of immorality; sin. **2.** Something that renders something else impure; a contaminant. **3.** Something said or expressed that is objectionable or sinful; profanity.

im·put·a·ble (ĭm-pyo͞o′tə-bəl) *adj.* Capable of being ascribed or imputed; attributable. —**im·put′a·bly** *adv.*

im·pu·ta·tion (ĭm′pyo͞o-tā′shən) *n.* **1.** The act of imputing. **2.** Something imputed or ascribed.

im·pu·ta·tive (ĭm-pyo͞o′tə-tĭv) *adj.* **1.** By imputation; inferred. **2.** Characterized by imputation. —**im·pu′ta·tive·ly** *adv.*

im·pute (ĭm-pyo͞ot′) *tr.v.* **-puted, -puting, -putes.** **1.** To ascribe (a crime or fault) to another. **2.** To attribute to a cause or source. **3.** To attribute (wickedness or merit) to a person as transmitted

ă pat/ā pay/âr care/ä father/b bib/ch church/d deed/ĕ pet/ē be/f fife/g gag/h hat/hw which/ĭ pit/ī pie/îr pier/j judge/k kick/l lid, needle/m mum/n no, sudden/ng thing/ŏ pot/ō toe/ô paw, for/oi noise/ou out/o͝o took/o͞o boot/p pop/r roar/s sauce/sh ship, dish/

by another. —See Synonyms at **attribute**. [Middle English *inputen*, from Old French *imputer*, from Latin *imputāre*, to bring into the reckoning : *in-*, in, into, + *putāre*, to reckon, compute, consider (see **peuə-**[2] in Appendix).]

Im·roz. The Turkish name for **Imbros**.

in (ĭn) *prep.* **1. a.** Within the confines of; inside. **b.** Within the area covered by: *playing in the mud.* **2.** On or affecting some part of: *He was hit in the head.* **3.** As a part, aspect, or property of. **4.** During the course of or before the expiration of: *ready in a few minutes.* **5.** At the position or business of: *put in command.* **6.** After the pattern or form of: *going around in circles.* **7.** To or at the condition or situation of; into: *in trouble.* **8.** As an expression of; out of: *said in anger.* **9.** During or as part of the act or process of: *in hot pursuit.* **10.** With the attribute of: *in silence.* **11. a.** By means of: *paid in cash.* **b.** Made with or through the medium of; using: *a text written in French.* **12.** Within the category or class of: *the latest thing in fashion.* **13.** With reference to; as regards: *in my opinion; equal in speed.* —**in that.** Inasmuch as; since. —*adv.* **1.** To or toward the inside: *He stepped in.* **2.** To or toward a center or goal by converging: *The group closed in.* **3.** Into a given place or position: *Let her in.* **4.** Indoors: *time to go in.* **5.** Into a given activity together: *joined in and sang.* **6.** Inward: *caved in.* —**all in.** *Informal.* Fatigued to exhaustion. —**in for.** Guaranteed or about to get or have something unpleasant: *He's in for a big surprise.* —**have it in for.** *Informal.* To have a grudge against. —*adj.* **1.** Fashionable; popular; prestigious. **2.** Exclusive or private; appealing to a clique: *a member of the in crowd.* **3.** Available or at home: *He wasn't in.* **4.** For coming or going in; entering. **5.** Having power; incumbent. —*n.* **1.** *Often plural.* Those in power or having the advantage. **2.** *Informal.* A means of access or favor. —**ins and outs. 1.** The twists and turns, as of a roadway. **2.** The intricacies of an activity or process. [Middle English *in*, Old English *in, inn.* See **en** in Appendix.*]

Usage: *In* (preposition) primarily indicates position, location, or condition: *She was in the kitchen. He was in a bad mood. Into* indicates direction or movement to an interior location or, figuratively, change of condition: *She went into the house. He flew into a rage. In* is often also possible in such examples as *went in the house* or *flew in a rage*, but conveys the desired sense less forcefully and less clearly. The two-word form *in to* is used in constructions, such as the following, in which *in* is an adverb: *They went in to supper. You may go in to see her now.*

in–[1]. Indicates not, lacking, or without; for example, **inaction**. See Usage notes at **un-**, **non-**. [Middle English, from Old French, from Latin. See **ne** in Appendix.* In borrowed, and sometimes Modern English, compounds, *in-* becomes *i-* before *g*, *il-* before *l*, *im-* before *b, m, p*, and *ir-* before *r*.]

in–[2]. Indicates: **1.** In, into, within, or inward; for example, **incretion, intubation. 2.** Intensive action; for example, **impress, implant, inosculate. 3.** Causative function (with basic meaning "to cause to become," "to put in"); for example, **intenerate, impound, imperil.** [Middle English, from Old French, from Latin, from *in*, in, within. See **en** in Appendix.* In borrowed Latin compounds, *in-* indicates (in addition to the above senses): 1. On, upon, as in **inunction**. 2. Toward, to, as in **irradiate, imminent.** 3. Against, as in **impugn, infest.** *In-* becomes *il-* before *l*, *im-* before *b, m, p*, and *ir-* before *r.*]

–in. Also **-ein** (for sense 1). Indicates: **1.** A neutral chemical compound, such as glyceride or protein, as distinguished from an alkaloid or basic substance; for example, **globulin, phthalein. 2.** Enzyme; for example, **pancreatin. 3.** Names of drugs and other pharmaceutical products; for example, **penicillin, aspirin. 4.** Variant of **-ine** (chemical suffix). [French *-ine*, from Latin *-ina*, feminine of *-īnus*, belonging to. See **-ine**.]

in inch.

In The symbol for the element indium.

IN Indiana (with Zip Code).

in. inch.

in·a·bil·i·ty (ĭn′ə-bĭl′ə-tē) *n.* Lack of ability or means.

in ab·sen·ti·a (ĭn ăb-sĕn′shē-ə, -shə) *Latin. Abbr.* **i.a.** In absence; while or although not present.

in·ac·ces·si·ble (ĭn′ăk-sĕs′ə-bəl) *adj.* Not accessible; unapproachable. —**in′ac·ces′si·bly** *adv.*

in·ac·cu·ra·cy (ĭn-ăk′yər-ə-sē) *n., pl.* **-cies. 1.** The quality or condition of being inaccurate. **2.** An error.

in·ac·cu·rate (ĭn-ăk′yər-ĭt) *adj.* **1.** Not accurate. **2.** Mistaken or incorrect. —**in·ac′cu·rate·ly** *adv.* —**in·ac′cu·rate·ness** *n.*

in·ac·tion (ĭn-ăk′shən) *n.* Lack or absence of action.

in·ac·ti·vate (ĭn-ăk′tə-vāt′) *tr.v.* **-vated, -vating, -vates.** To render inactive. —**in·ac′ti·va′tion** *n.*

in·ac·tive (ĭn-ăk′tĭv) *adj.* **1.** Not active or not tending to be active. **2. a.** Being out of use. **b.** Retired from duty or service. **3. a.** *Chemistry.* Not readily participating in chemical reactions. **b.** *Biology.* Having no significant effect on or interaction with living organisms. **c.** *Medicine.* Quiescent. Said especially of a disease. **d.** *Physics.* Displaying little or no radioactivity. **4.** Not functioning or operating. —**in·ac′tive·ly** *adv.* —**in·ac′tive·ness, in′ac·tiv′i·ty** *n.*

Synonyms: *inactive, idle, inert, passive, dormant, torpid, supine.* These adjectives mean not involved in, or disposed to, activity. *Inactive* merely indicates absence of activity in a person or thing. *Idle* refers to inactivity of persons, whether through unemployment, choice, laziness, or any other cause. *Inert* describes things powerless to move themselves, to resist motion impressed on them, or to produce a desired effect. Applied to persons, *inert* implies lethargy or unreceptiveness, especially of mind or spirit. *Passive* is applied to persons and things that are acted upon by external force or provocation but do not themselves react positively, as by resisting or showing emotion. *Dormant* refers principally to things in a state of suspended activity, such as volcanoes long inactive but not extinct. *Torpid* suggests the inactivity of a hibernating animal. *Supine* implies abjectness in persons, made manifest by lack of will or stamina, especially in situations that test courage or resolution.

in·ad·e·qua·cy (ĭn-ăd′ĭ-kwə-sē) *n., pl.* **-cies. 1.** The quality or condition of being inadequate. **2.** A failing or lack; defect.

in·ad·e·quate (ĭn-ăd′ĭ-kwĭt) *adj.* **1.** Not adequate; insufficient. **2.** Not able; incapable. —**in·ad′e·quate·ly** *adv.*

in·ad·mis·si·ble (ĭn′əd-mĭs′ə-bəl) *adj.* Not admissible. —**in′ad·mis′si·bil′i·ty** *n.* —**in′ad·mis′si·bly** *adv.*

in·ad·ver·tence (ĭn′əd-vûr′təns) *n.* Also **in·ad·ver·ten·cy** (-tən-sē) *pl.* **-cies. 1.** The quality of being inadvertent. **2.** An instance of being inadvertent; a mistake; oversight. [Medieval Latin *inadvertentia* : Latin *in-*, not + *advertēns*, present participle of *advertere*, to ADVERT.]

in·ad·ver·tent (ĭn′əd-vûr′tənt) *adj.* **1.** Not duly attentive. **2.** Accidental; unintentional. —See Synonyms at **careless.** [Back-formation from INADVERTENCE.] —**in′ad·ver′tent·ly** *adv.*

in·ad·vis·a·ble (ĭn′əd-vī′zə-bəl) *adj.* Inexpedient; unwise; not recommended. —**in′ad·vis′a·bil′i·ty** *n.*

in ae·ter·num (ĭn ē-tûr′nəm) *Latin.* Forever; to eternity.

in·al·ien·a·ble (ĭn-āl′yə-nə-bəl) *adj.* Not to be transferred to another; not alienable. —**in·al′ien·a·bly** *adv.*

in·al·ter·a·ble (ĭn-ôl′tər-ə-bəl) *adj.* Not alterable; unchangeable. —**in·al′ter·a·bil′i·ty** *n.* —**in·al′ter·a·bly** *adv.*

in·am·o·ra·ta (ĭn-ăm′ə-rä′tə, ĭn′ăm-) *n., pl.* **-tas.** A woman with whom one is in love. [Italian, from feminine of *inamorato*, past participle of *inam(m)orare*, to inspire love in, enamor : *in-*, in, into + *amore*, love, from Latin *amor*, love, from *amāre*, to love (see **amma** in Appendix*).]

in·am·o·ra·to (ĭn-ăm′ə-rä′tō, ĭn′ăm-) *n., pl.* **-tos.** A male lover; suitor. [Italian, from the past participle of *inam(m)orare*, enamor. See **inamorata**.]

in-and-in (ĭn′ən-ĭn′) *adv.* Repeatedly within the same or closely related stocks: *to breed pigs in-and-in.* —**in′-and-in′** *adj.*

in·ane (ĭn-ān′) *adj.* Lacking sense or substance; empty: *an inane comment.* —*n. Rare.* Empty space; the void. Used as a borrowing from philosophical Latin. [Latin *inānis*†, empty, vain.] —**in·ane′ly** *adv.*

in·an·i·mate (ĭn-ăn′ə-mĭt) *adj.* **1.** Not animate; not having the qualities associated with active, living organisms. **2.** Not exhibiting life; appearing lifeless or dead. **3.** Not animated or energetic; listless; spiritless. —See Synonyms at **dead.** —**in·an′i·mate·ly** *adv.* —**in·an′i·mate·ness** *n.*

in·a·ni·tion (ĭn′ə-nĭsh′ən) *n.* **1.** Exhaustion, as from lack of nourishment. **2.** The condition or quality of being empty. [Middle English *in-anisioun*, from Late Latin *inānītiō*, from *inānire*, to make empty, from *inānis*, empty, INANE.]

in·an·i·ty (ĭn-ăn′ə-tē) *n., pl.* **-ties. 1.** The condition or quality of being inane. **2.** Something fatuous or absurd: *"his mind was steeled against the inanities she uttered"* (Henry James).

in·ap·peas·a·ble (ĭn′ə-pē′zə-bəl) *adj.* Incapable of being appeased.

in·ap·pe·tence (ĭn-ăp′ə-təns) *n.* Also **in·ap·pe·ten·cy.** Lack of appetite. [IN- (without) + APPETENCE.] —**in·ap′pe·tent** *adj.*

in·ap·pli·ca·ble (ĭn-ăp′lĭ-kə-bəl) *adj.* Not applicable. —**in·ap′pli·ca·bil′i·ty** *n.* —**in·ap′pli·ca·bly** *adv.*

in·ap·po·site (ĭn-ăp′ə-zĭt) *adj.* Not pertinent; unsuitable. —**in·ap′po·site·ly** *adv.*

in·ap·pre·ci·a·ble (ĭn′ə-prē′shē-ə-bəl) *adj.* Not appreciable; insignificant; negligible. —**in′ap·pre′ci·a·bly** *adv.*

in·ap·pre·ci·a·tive (ĭn′ə-prē′shə-tĭv, -shē-ā′tĭv) *adj.* Feeling or showing no appreciation; unappreciative. —**in′ap·pre′ci·a·tive·ly** *adv.* —**in′ap·pre′ci·a·tive·ness** *n.*

in·ap·proach·a·ble (ĭn′ə-prō′chə-bəl) *adj.* Not approachable. —**in′ap·proach′a·bil′i·ty** *n.* —**in′ap·proach′a·bly** *adv.*

in·ap·pro·pri·ate (ĭn′ə-prō′prē-ĭt) *adj.* Not appropriate. —**in′ap·pro′pri·ate·ly** *adv.* —**in′ap·pro′pri·ate·ness** *n.*

in·ap·ti·tude (ĭn-ăp′tə-to͞od′, -tyo͞od′) *n.* **1.** Inappropriateness. **2.** Lack of skill; ineptitude.

in·arch (ĭn-ärch′) *tr.v.* **-arched, -arching, -arches.** To graft by joining branches or stems that have not been removed from the growing plants of the parent stock. [IN + ARCH.]

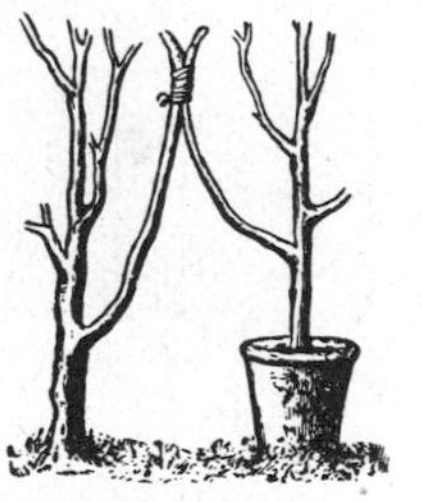

inarch
Graft made by inarching

in·ar·tic·u·la·cy (ĭn′är-tĭk′yə-lə-sē) *n.* Inarticulateness: *"were it not for their inarticulacy, many of them would not be there"* (Kennedy Fraser).

in·ar·tic·u·late (ĭn′är-tĭk′yə-lĭt) *adj.* **1.** Uttered without the use of normal words or syllables; incomprehensible as speech or language: *"a cry . . . that . . . sank down into an inarticulate whine"* (Jack London). **2.** Unable to speak; speechless: *inarticulate with astonishment.* **3.** Unable to speak with clarity or eloquence. **4.** Unexpressed: *inarticulate sorrow.* **5.** *Biology.* Not having joints or segments. —**in′ar·tic′u·late·ly** *adv.* —**in′ar·tic′u·late·ness** *n.*

in·as·much as (ĭn′əz-mŭch′). **1.** Because of the fact that; since. **2.** To the extent that; insofar as. —See Usage note at **because.**

in·at·ten·tion (ĭn′ə-tĕn′shən) *n.* Lack of attention, notice, or regard; heedlessness; neglect.

in·at·ten·tive (ĭn′ə-tĕn′tĭv) *adj.* Showing a lack of attention; negligent. —**in′at·ten′tive·ly** *adv.* —**in′at·ten′tive·ness** *n.*

in·au·di·ble (ĭn-ô′də-bəl) *adj.* Incapable of being heard; not audible. —**in·au′di·bly** *adv.*

in·au·gu·ral (ĭn-ô′gyər-əl) *adj.* Of, relating to, or characteristic of an inauguration. —*n.* A speech made by a President of the United States at his inauguration.

in·au·gu·rate (ĭn-ô′gyə-rāt′) *tr.v.* **-rated, -rating, -rates. 1.** To induct into office by a formal ceremony. **2.** To begin or start

t tight/th thin, path/*th* this, bathe/ŭ cut/ûr urge/v valve/w with/y yes/z zebra, size/zh vision/ə about, item, edible, gallop, circus/
à *Fr.* ami/œ *Fr.* feu, *Ger.* schön/ü *Fr.* tu, *Ger.* über/KH *Ger.* ich, *Scot.* loch/N *Fr.* bon. ***Follows main vocabulary. †Of obscure origin.**

officially. **3.** To open or begin use of formally with a ceremony; dedicate. —See Synonyms at **begin.** [Latin *inaugurāre,* to take omens from the flight of birds, to consecrate, install : *in,* in + *augurāre,* to augur, from *augur,* soothsayer (see **aug-**[1] in Appendix*).] —**in·au′gu·ra′tor** (-rā′tər) *n.*

in·au·gu·ra·tion (ĭn-ô′gyə-rā′shən) *n.* **1.** A formal beginning or introduction. **2.** Formal introduction to an office.

in·aus·pi·cious (ĭn′ô-spĭsh′əs) *adj.* Not auspicious; ill-omened. —**in′aus·pi′cious·ly** *adv.* —**in′aus·pi′cious·ness** *n.*

inbd. inboard.

in between. Between two things, limits, or the like.

in-be·tween (ĭn′bĭ-twēn′) *adj.* Intermediate. —*n.* An intermediate or intermediary: *conservatives, radicals, and in-betweens.*

in·board (ĭn′bôrd′, -bōrd′) *adj. Abbr.* **inbd. 1.** *Nautical.* Within the hull or toward the center of a ship. **2.** *Aviation.* Relatively close to the fuselage of an aircraft: *the inboard engines.* **3.** Toward the center of a machine. —*n.* A motor attached to the inside of the hull of a boat. [IN + BOARD.] —**in′board′** *adv.*

in·born (ĭn′bôrn′) *adj.* **1.** Possessed by an organism at birth. **2.** Inherited or hereditary. —See Synonyms at **innate.**

in·bound (ĭn′bound′) *adj.* Homeward bound or incoming.

in·breathe (ĭn′brēth′, ĭn-brēth′) *tr.v.* **-breathed, -breathing, -breathes. 1.** To breathe (something) into: *"So true and delicate a spirit is inbreathed into the old forms"* (J.A. Symonds). **2.** To inspire.

in·bred (ĭn′brĕd′) *adj.* **1.** Produced by inbreeding. **2.** Innate; deep-seated. —See Synonyms at **innate.**

in·breed (ĭn′brēd′, ĭn-brēd′) *tr.v.* **-bred,** (-brĕd′), **-breeding, -breeds. 1.** To produce by the continued breeding of closely related individuals. **2.** To breed or develop within; engender.

in·burst (ĭn′bûrst′) *n.* **1.** The act or process of bursting in, into, or within. **2.** That which bursts in.

inc. 1. income. **2.** incorporated. **3.** increase.

Inc. incorporated.

In·ca (ĭng′kə) *n., pl.* **Inca** or **-cas. 1.** An Indian of the group of Quechuan peoples who ruled Peru before the Spanish conquest. **2.** A king or other member of the royal family of this group of peoples. [Spanish, from Quechua *inka,* king, prince.]

in·cage. Variant of **encage.**

in·cal·cu·la·ble (ĭn-kăl′kyə-lə-bəl) *adj.* **1.** Not calculable; indeterminate. **2.** Incapable of being foreseen; unpredictable; uncertain: *"The motions of her mind were as incalculable as the flit of a bird"* (Edith Wharton). —**in·cal′cu·la·bil′i·ty, in·cal′cu·la·ble·ness** *n.* —**in·cal′cu·la·bly** *adv.*

in cam·er·a (ĭn kăm′ər-ə). **1.** In secret, private, or closed session. **2.** *Law.* In private with a judge rather than in open court; in the chambers of a judge. [Latin, "in the chamber."]

In·can (ĭng′kən) *adj.* Also **In·ca·ic** (-kā′ĭk). Of or relating to the Incas, their civilization, or their language. —*n.* **1.** An Inca. **2.** The language spoken by the Incas; Quechua.

in·can·desce (ĭn′kən-dĕs′) *v.* **-desced, -descing, -desces.** —*intr.* To become incandescent. —*tr.* To cause to become incandescent. [Latin *incandēscere,* to become white with heat, glow : *in-* (intensive) + *candēscere,* to become white, glow, from *candēre,* to be white, shine (see **kand-** in Appendix*).]

in·can·des·cence (ĭn′kən-dĕs′əns) *n.* **1.** The emission of visible light by a hot object. **2.** The light emitted by an incandescent object. **3.** A high degree of emotion, intensity, brilliance, or the like: *"the bishop's wrath reached incandescence"* (Lesley B. Simpson). —See Synonyms at **blaze.**

in·can·des·cent (ĭn′kən-dĕs′ənt) *adj.* **1.** Emitting visible light as a result of being heated. **2.** Shining brilliantly; very bright. —See Synonyms at **bright.** —**in′can·des′cent·ly** *adv.*

incandescent lamp. An electric lamp in which a filament is heated to incandescence by an electric current.

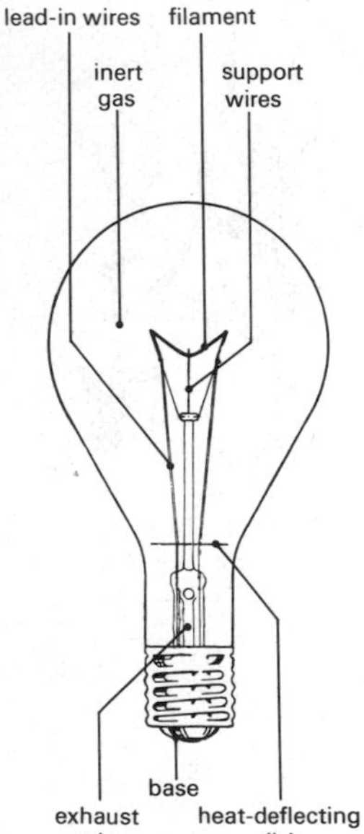
lead-in wires
filament
inert gas
support wires
base
exhaust tube
heat-deflecting disk
incandescent lamp

in·can·ta·tion (ĭn′kăn-tā′shən) *n.* **1.** Ritual recitation of verbal charms or spells to produce a magical effect. **2. a.** The formulaic words, phrases, or sounds used in this manner. **b.** *Often plural.* Conventionalized words and slogans used and repeated in a manner likened to the utterance of spells, as by the spokesmen of an ideology: *the pious incantations of the administration.* **3.** The casting of spells. [Middle English *incantacioun,* from Old French *incantation,* from Late Latin *incantātiō,* enchantment, spell, from Latin *incantāre,* ENCHANT.] —**in·can′ta·to′ry** (-tə-tôr′ē, -tōr′ē) *adj.*

in·ca·pa·ble (ĭn-kā′pə-bəl) *adj.* **1.** Not capable; lacking the requisite ability or power. **2.** *Law.* Lacking legal qualifications or requirements; ineligible. —**incapable of. 1.** Lacking the ability or power to: *incapable of singing.* **2.** Lacking the capacity for. **3.** *Law.* Not legally eligible for. —**in·ca′pa·bil′i·ty, in·ca′pa·ble·ness** *n.* —**in·ca′pa·bly** *adv.*

in·ca·pac·i·tate (ĭn′kə-păs′ə-tāt′) *tr.v.* **-tated, -tating, -tates. 1.** To deprive of strength or ability. **2.** To make legally ineligible; disqualify. —**in′ca·pac′i·ta′tion** *n.*

in·ca·pac·i·ty (ĭn′kə-păs′ə-tē) *n., pl.* **-ties. 1.** Lack of strength or ability; disability; helplessness. **2.** *Law.* That which renders legally ineligible; a disqualification.

in·cap·su·late. Variant of **encapsulate.**

in·car·cer·ate (ĭn-kär′sə-rāt′) *tr.v.* **-ated, -ating, -ates. 1.** To put in jail. **2.** To shut in; confine. [Latin *incarcerāre* : *in-,* in + *carcer,* prison, enclosed place (see **carcer** in Appendix*).] —**in·car′cer·a′tion** *n.* —**in·car′cer·a′tor** (-sə-rā′tər) *n.*

in·car·na·dine (ĭn-kär′nə-dīn′, -dēn′, -dĭn) *adj.* **1.** Flesh-colored. **2.** Blood-red. —*n.* A color resembling flesh or blood. —*tr.v.* **incarnadined, -dining, -dines.** To make the color of blood or flesh. [Old French *incarnadin,* from Old Italian *incarnadino, incarnatino,* from *incarnato,* flesh-colored, from Late Latin *incarnāre,* INCARNATE.]

in·car·nate (ĭn-kär′nĭt) *adj.* **1. a.** Invested with bodily nature and form. **b.** Personified: *wisdom incarnate.* **2.** Incarnadine. —*tr.v.* (ĭn-kär′nāt′) **incarnated, -nating, -nates. 1.** To give bodily, especially human, form to. **2.** To embody or personify. **3.** To actualize; realize. [Late Latin *incarnāre,* to make flesh : Latin *in-* (causative) + *carō* (stem *carn-*), flesh (see **sker-**[1] in Appendix*).]

in·car·na·tion (ĭn′kär-nā′shən) *n.* **1.** A manifestation or the act of making manifest in bodily form. **2.** *Capital* **I.** *Theology.* The embodiment of God in the human form of Jesus. **3.** Any bodily manifestation of a supernatural being. **4.** One held to personify a given abstract quality or idea.

in·case. Variant of **encase.**

in·cen·di·ar·y (ĭn-sĕn′dē-ĕr′ē) *adj.* **1. a.** Causing or capable of causing fire. **b.** Producing intensely hot fire as a military weapon. **c.** Of or involving arson. **2.** Tending to inflame; inflammatory. [Latin *incendiārius,* from *incendium,* burning, fire, from *incendere,* to set on fire. See **incense** (to enrage).] —**in·cen′di·a·rism′** (-ə-rĭz′əm) *n.*

incendiary bomb. A bomb used to start a fire. Also called "fire bomb."

in·cense[1] (ĭn-sĕns′) *tr.v.* **-censed, -censing, -censes.** To cause to be angry; infuriate; enrage. [Middle English *encensen,* from Old French *incenser,* from Latin *incendere* (past participle *incensus*), to set on fire, enrage. See **kand-** in Appendix.*]

in·cense[2] (ĭn′sĕns′) *n.* **1.** An aromatic substance, as a gum or wood, that burns with a pleasant odor. **2.** The smoke or odor produced by the burning of such a substance. **3.** Any pleasant smell. **4.** Adulation; praise; admiration. —*tr.v.* **incensed, -censing, -censes. 1.** To perfume with incense. **2.** To burn incense to, as by way of a ritual offering. [Middle English *insens, encens,* from Old French *encens,* from Late Latin *incensum,* neuter past participle of Latin *incendere,* to set on fire. See **incense** (to enrage).]

in·cen·tive (ĭn-sĕn′tĭv) *n.* Something inciting to action or effort, as the fear of punishment or the expectation of reward. —*adj.* Inciting; motivating. [Middle English, from Latin *incentīvum,* from the neuter of *incentīvus,* that sets the tune, inciting, from *incinere* (past participle *incentus*), to sing, sound : *in-* (intensive) + *canere,* to sing (see **kan-** in Appendix*).]

in·cep·tion (ĭn-sĕp′shən) *n.* The beginning of something. See Synonyms at **origin.** [Latin *inceptiō,* from *incipere,* to take in hand, begin : *in-,* in + *capere,* to take (see **kap-** in Appendix*).]

in·cep·tive (ĭn-sĕp′tĭv) *adj.* **1.** Incipient; beginning. **2.** *Grammar.* Expressing an action, state, or occurrence in its initial phase: *an inceptive verb suffix.* —*n.* An inceptive verb. —**in·cep′tive·ly** *adv.*

in·cer·ti·tude (ĭn-sûr′tə-to͞od′, -tyo͞od′) *n.* **1.** Uncertainty. **2.** Absence of confidence; doubt. **3.** Insecurity or instability. [Old French, from Late Latin *incertitūdō* : *in-,* not + *certitūdō,* CERTITUDE.]

in·ces·sant (ĭn-sĕs′ənt) *adj.* Continuing without respite or interruption; unceasing. See Synonyms at **continual.** [Late Latin *incessāns* : *in-,* not + *cessāns,* present participle of *cessāre,* CEASE.] —**in·ces′sant·ly** *adv.*

in·cest (ĭn′sĕst′) *n.* **1.** Sexual union between persons who are so closely related that their marriage is illegal or forbidden by custom. **2.** The statutory crime committed by such closely related persons who marry, cohabit, or copulate illegally. [Middle English, from Latin *incestus,* "unchaste," "impure" : *in-,* not + *castus,* CHASTE.]

in·ces·tu·ous (ĭn-sĕs′cho͞o-əs) *adj.* **1.** Of or involving incest. **2.** Having committed incest. **3.** Resulting from incest. —**in·ces′tu·ous·ly** *adv.* —**in·ces′tu·ous·ness** *n.*

inch[1] (ĭnch) *n. Abbr.* **in, in.** A unit of length in the U.S. Customary and British Imperial systems, equal to $\frac{1}{12}$ of a foot. See **measurement.** [Middle English *inch(e),* Old English *ince, ynce,* from Latin *uncia,* twelfth part, inch, ounce, from *ūnus,* one. See **oino-** in Appendix.*]

inch[2] (ĭnch) *n. Scottish.* A small island. [Middle English *inch, ynche,* from Scottish Gaelic *innis,* akin to Old Irish *inis*†.]

inch·meal (ĭnch′mēl′) *adv.* Gradually; little by little. [INCH + (PIECE)MEAL.]

in·cho·ate (ĭn-kō′ĭt) *adj.* **1.** In an initial or early stage; just beginning; incipient. **2.** Immature; imperfect. [Latin *inchoātus,* past participle of *inchoāre, incohāre,* to begin, originally "to harness" : *in-,* in + *cohum,* strap fastening the plow beam to the yoke (see **kagh-** in Appendix*).] —**in·cho′ate·ly** *adv.* —**in·cho′ate·ness** *n.*

in·cho·a·tion (ĭn′kō-ā′shən) *n.* A beginning; start; origin.

in·cho·a·tive (ĭn-kō′ə-tĭv) *adj. Grammar.* **Inceptive** *(see).*

In·chon (ĭn′chŏn′). Also **Che·mul·po** (chĕ′mo͝ol′pō′). A port of northwestern South Korea. Population, 430,000.

inch·worm (ĭnch′wûrm′) *n.* A **measuring worm** *(see).*

in·ci·dence (ĭn′sə-dəns) *n.* **1.** An act, instance, or manner of occurring or affecting; occurrence. **2.** The extent or frequency of the occurrence of something. **3.** *Physics.* The arrival of incident radiation or of an incident projectile at a surface.

in·ci·dent (ĭn′sə-dənt) *n.* **1.** A definite, distinct occurrence; an event. **2.** An event that is subordinate to another. **3.** Something contingent upon or related to something else. **4.** A relatively minor occurrence or event that precipitates a public crisis. —See Synonyms at **occurrence.** —*adj.* **1.** Tending to arise or occur as a minor concomitant. Used with *to: "There is a professional melancholy . . . incident to the occupation of a tailor"* (Lamb). **2.** Related to or dependent on another thing. **3.** *Law.* Contingent upon or related to something else. **4.** *Physics.* Falling upon; striking: *incident radiation.* [Middle English, from Old French, from Latin *incidēns,* present participle of *incidere,* to fall upon, happen to : *in-,* on + *cadere,* to fall (see **kad-** in Appendix*).]

in·ci·den·tal (ĭn′sə-dĕnt′l) *adj.* Occurring as a fortuitous or minor concomitant: *incidental expenses.* See Synonyms at **accidental.** —**incidental to.** Attending or liable to attend: *"the chores incidental to the business of living"* (Haakon Chevalier). —**incidental upon.** Following upon incidentally. —*n. Usually plural.* A minor concomitant circumstance, event, expense, or the like.

in·ci·den·tal·ly (ĭn′sə-dĕnt′l-ē) *adv.* **1.** Casually; by chance. **2.** Parenthetically.

in·cin·er·ate (ĭn-sĭn′ə-rāt′) *v.* **-ated, -ating, -ates.** —*tr.* To consume by burning. —*intr.* To burn or burn up. [Medieval Latin *incinerāre* : Latin *in-,* in, into + *cinis* (stem *ciner-*), ashes (see **keni-** in Appendix*).] —**in·cin′er·a′tion** *n.*

in·cin·er·a·tor (ĭn-sĭn′ə-rā′tər) *n.* One that incinerates; especially, a furnace or other apparatus for burning waste.

in·cip·i·ent (ĭn-sĭp′ē-ənt) *adj.* In an initial or early stage; just beginning to exist or appear: *"that incipient smile which is apt to accompany agreeable recollections"* (George Eliot). [Latin *incipiēns,* beginning, present participle of *incipere,* to take in hand, begin : *in-,* in + *capere,* to take (see **kap-** in Appendix*).] —**in·cip′i·en·cy, in·cip′i·ence** *n.* —**in·cip′i·ent·ly** *adv.*

in·ci·pit (ĭn′sĭ-pĭt′). *Latin.* It begins.

in·cise (ĭn-sīz′) *tr.v.* **-cised, -cising, -cises. 1.** To cut into or mark with a sharp instrument. **2.** To cut (designs or writing, for example) into a surface; engrave; carve. [Old French *inciser,* from Latin *incīdere* (past participle *incīsus*) : *in-,* into, in + *caedere,* to cut (see **skhai-** in Appendix*).]

in·cised (ĭn-sīzd′) *adj.* **1.** Cut into; engraved; carved. **2.** Made with or as if with a sharp instrument. **3.** Deeply notched: *the incised margin of a leaf.*

in·ci·sion (ĭn-sĭzh′ən) *n.* **1.** The act of incising. **2. a.** A surgical cut into soft tissue. **b.** The scar resulting from such a cut. **3.** A notch, as in the edge of a leaf. **4.** Incisiveness.

in·ci·sive (ĭn-sī′sĭv) *adj.* **1.** Cutting; penetrating. **2.** Trenchant. [Medieval Latin *incīsīvus,* from Latin *incīsus,* past participle of *incīdere,* INCISE.] —**in·ci′sive·ly** *adv.* —**in·ci′sive·ness** *n.*

Synonyms: *incisive, trenchant, biting, cutting, crisp, clear-cut.* These adjectives are synonymous when they refer to thought or expression marked by keenness and forcefulness. *Incisive* and *trenchant* are applicable both to sharp mental perception and to its expression. They suggest the ability of the mind to penetrate to the heart of a subject and the power to express the thought thus formed clearly, usually succinctly, and very forcefully. *Biting* and *cutting* apply to expression capable of penetrating or making a sharp impression on another person, as through sarcasm. *Crisp,* in this comparison, refers to a style of expression that is clear, concise, and invigorating. *Clear-cut* specifies distinctness of outline and thus sharpness of definition of what is formed in the mind and then expressed.

in·ci·sor (ĭn-sī′zər) *n.* A tooth adapted for cutting, located at the apex of the dental arch.

in·ci·ta·tion (ĭn′sī′tā′shən) *n.* **1.** An act or instance of inciting; provocation; stimulation. **2.** Something that incites; incentive.

in·cite (ĭn-sīt′) *tr.v.* **-cited, -citing, -cites.** To provoke to action, stir up, or urge on. See Synonyms at **provoke.** [Old French *inciter,* from Latin *incitāre,* to urge, set in violent motion : *in-* (intensive) + *citāre,* frequentative of *ciēre, cīre,* to set in violent motion, rouse, provoke (see **kei-**[3] in Appendix*).] —**in·cite′ment** *n.* —**in·cit′er** *n.*

Synonyms: *incite, instigate, foment, abet.* These verbs mean to stir a group of persons to action or to give support to such action. *Incite* primarily is applied to arousing the will and spirit to act, as by forceful oratory. *Instigate* refers to conceiving a plan of action, often one involving drastic change, and making it operative. *Foment* usually refers to the systematic arousing of feelings of discord, rebellion, or the like, which produce violent action. *Abet* implies either active aid or tacit approval of actions, especially acts in violation of what is right or proper.

incl. including; inclusive.

in·clasp. Variant of **enclasp.**

in·clem·ent (ĭn-klĕm′ənt) *adj.* **1.** Stormy. **2.** Severe or unmerciful. [Latin *inclēmēns* : *in-,* not + *clēmēns,* CLEMENT.] —**in·clem′en·cy** *n.* —**in·clem′ent·ly** *adv.*

in·clin·a·ble (ĭn-klī′nə-bəl) *adj.* **1.** Favorably disposed; amenable. **2.** *Archaic.* Disposed or inclined to do something.

in·cli·na·tion (ĭn′klə-nā′shən) *n.* **1.** An attitude or disposition toward something. **2.** A trend or general tendency toward a particular aspect, condition, or character. **3.** Something for which one has a preference or leaning: *"I shall indulge the inclination so natural in old men, to be talking of themselves"* (Franklin). **4.** The act of inclining. **5.** The state of being inclined. **6.** A deviation from a definite direction, especially from a horizontal or vertical. **7.** The degree of deviation from a horizontal or vertical. —See Synonyms at **opinion, tendency.**

in·cline (ĭn-klīn′) *v.* **-clined, -clining, -clines.** —*intr.* **1.** To deviate from a horizontal or vertical; to lean; to slant; to slope. **2.** To have or express a mental tendency; be disposed. **3.** To tend toward a particular state or condition. **4.** To lower or bend the head or body as in a nod or bow. —*tr.* **1.** To cause to lean, slant, or slope; place at an inclination. **2.** To influence (someone or something) to have a certain preference, leaning, or disposition; dispose. **3.** To bend or lower in a nod or bow. —**incline one's ear.** To listen sympathetically; take notice of; heed. —*n.* An inclined surface; a slope or gradient. [Middle English *inclinen, enclinen,* from Old French *encliner,* from Latin *inclīnāre* : *in-,* toward + *-clīnāre,* to bend, lean (see **klei-** in Appendix*).] —**in·clin′er** *n.*

in·clined (ĭn-klīnd′) *adj.* **1.** Having a preference, disposition, or tendency; disposed. **2.** Sloping, slanting, or leaning.

inclined plane. A plane inclined to the horizontal, a simple machine used to raise or lower a load by rolling or sliding.

in·cli·nom·e·ter (ĭn′klə-nŏm′ə-tər) *n.* **1.** An instrument used to determine **magnetic dip** *(see).* **2.** An instrument for showing the attitude of an airplane or ship relative to the horizontal. Also called "dip needle." **3.** *Machinery.* A **clinometer** *(see).*

in·close. Variant of **enclose.**

in·clude (ĭn-klo͞od′) *tr.v.* **-cluded, -cluding, -cludes. 1.** To have as a part or member; be made up of, at least in part; contain. **2.** To contain as a minor or secondary element; imply. **3.** To cause to be a part of something; consider with or put into a group, class, or total. [Middle English *includen,* from Latin *inclūdere,* to shut in : *in-,* in + *claudere,* to close (see **klēu-** in Appendix*).] —**in·clud′a·ble, in·clud′i·ble** *adj.*

Synonyms: *include, comprise, comprehend, embrace, involve.* These verbs mean to take in or contain one or more things as part of something larger. *Include* and *comprise* both take as their objects things or persons that are constituent parts. *Comprise* usually implies that all of the components are stated: *The track meet comprises 15 events* (that is, consists of or is composed of). *Include* can be so used, but, like the remaining terms, more often implies an incomplete listing: *The meet includes among its high points a return match between leading sprinters. Comprehend* and *embrace* usually refer to the taking in of intangibles as part of a broader subject: *Law and order comprehend much more than exercise of police power. A person's tastes in reading need not embrace every subject fashionable at the moment. Involve* usually suggests the relationship of a thing that is a logical consequence or required condition of something more inclusive: *A heavy scholastic schedule involves extra effort.*

in·clud·ed (ĭn-klo͞o′dĭd) *adj.* **1.** *Botany.* Not protruding beyond a surrounding part, as stamens that do not project from a corolla. **2.** *Geometry.* Formed by and between two intersecting straight lines: *an included angle.*

in·clu·sion (ĭn-klo͞o′zhən) *n.* **1.** The act of including or the state of being included. **2.** Something included. **3.** *Mineralogy.* Any solid, liquid, or gaseous foreign body enclosed in a mineral or rock. **4.** *Biology.* Any nonliving mass in cytoplasm. [Latin *inclūsiō,* from *inclūdere* (past participle *inclūsus*), to INCLUDE.]

inclusion body. An abnormal structure in a cell nucleus or cytoplasm having characteristic staining properties and associated especially with the presence of filterable viruses.

in·clu·sive (ĭn-klo͞o′sĭv) *adj. Abbr.* **incl. 1.** Taking everything into account; including everything; comprehensive. **2.** Including the specified extremes or limits as well as the area between them. —**in·clu′sive·ly** *adv.* —**in·clu′sive·ness** *n.*

in·co·er·ci·ble (ĭn′kō-ûr′sə-bəl) *adj.* Not subject to coercion.

incog. incognito.

in·cog·i·tant (ĭn-kŏj′ə-tənt) *adj. Rare.* Thoughtless; unthinking; inconsiderate. [Latin *incōgitāns* : *in-,* not + *cōgitāns,* present participle of *cōgitāre,* to think about, COGITATE.]

in·cog·ni·ta (ĭn-kŏg′nə-tə, ĭn′kŏg′ne′tə) *adv.* Incognito. Used only of a woman. —*n.* A woman who is incognito.

in·cog·ni·to (ĭn-kŏg′nə-tō′, ĭn′kŏg′nē′tō) *adv. Abbr.* **incog.** In a nonofficial capacity or under a name or title intended to elude public notice. —*n. Abbr.* **incog. 1.** One who is incognito. **2.** The anonymity assumed by one who is incognito: *"His incognito . . . was not meant to hide a personality but a fact"* (Conrad). [Italian, from Latin *incognitus,* unknown : *in-,* not + *cognitus,* past participle of *cognōscere,* to know (see **cognition**).] —**in·cog′ni·to′** *adj.*

in·cog·ni·zant (ĭn′kŏg′nə-zənt) *adj.* Lacking knowledge or awareness of something; unaware.

in·co·her·ence (ĭn′kō-hîr′əns) *n.* Also **in·co·her·en·cy** (-ən-sē) *pl.* **-cies. 1.** The condition or quality of being incoherent. **2.** Something incoherent.

in·co·her·ent (ĭn′kō-hîr′ənt) *adj.* **1.** Not coherent; disordered; unconnected; inharmonious. **2.** Unable to think or express one's thoughts in a clear or orderly manner: *incoherent with grief.* —**in′co·her′ent·ly** *adv.* —**in′co·her′ent·ness** *n.*

in·com·bus·ti·ble (ĭn′kəm-bŭs′tə-bəl) *adj.* Incapable of burning. —*n.* An incombustible object or material. [Middle English, from Medieval Latin *incombustibilis* : Latin *in-,* not + *combūrere* (past participle *combustus*), to burn up (see **combust**).] —**in′com·bus′ti·bil′i·ty** *n.* —**in′com·bus′ti·bly** *adv.*

in·come (ĭn′kŭm′) *n. Abbr.* **inc. 1.** The amount of money or its equivalent received during a period of time in exchange for labor or services, from the sale of goods or property, or as profit from financial investments. **2.** *Archaic.* An influx. [Middle English, a coming in, entry: IN + *comen,* COME.]

in·com·er (ĭn′kŭm′ər) *n.* One that comes in.

income tax. A graduated tax levied on annual income.

in·com·ing (ĭn′kŭm′ĭng) *adj.* **1.** Coming in; entering. **2.** About to come in; next in succession: *the incoming president.* —*n.* **1.** The act of coming in; an entrance; arrival. **2.** *Usually plural.* Income; revenue.

in·com·men·su·ra·ble (ĭn′kə-mĕn′shər-ə-bəl, -sər-ə-bəl) *adj.* **1.** Having no common quality upon which to make a comparison; incapable of being measured or judged comparatively. **2.** *Mathematics.* Having no common measure. —*n.* Something that is incommensurable. —**in′com·men′su·ra·bil′i·ty** *n.* —**in′com·men′su·ra·bly** *adv.*

in·com·men·su·rate (ĭn′kə-mĕn′shər-ĭt, -sər-ĭt) *adj.* **1. a.** Not commensurate; unequal; disproportionate: *a reward incommensurate with his efforts.* **b.** Inadequate. **2.** Incommensurable. —**in′com·men′su·rate·ly** *adv.* —**in′com·men′su·rate·ness** *n.*

in·com·mode (ĭn′kə-mōd′) *tr.v.* **-moded, -moding, -modes.** To cause to be inconvenienced; disturb. [French *incommoder,* from Old French, from Latin *incommodāre,* from *incommodus,* inconvenient : *in-,* not + *commodus,* convenient (see **commode**).]

in·com·mo·di·ous (ĭn′kə-mō′dē-əs) *adj.* Inconvenient or uncomfortable, as by not affording sufficient space: *"It was very small, very dark, very ugly, very incommodious."* (Dickens). —**in′com·mo′di·ous·ly** *adv.* —**in′com·mo′di·ous·ness** *n.*

in·com·mod·i·ty (ĭn′kə-mŏd′ə-tē) *n., pl.* **-ties.** **1.** Inconvenience; discomfort. **2.** Something that is inconvenient.

in·com·mu·ni·ca·ble (ĭn′kə-myōō′nĭ-kə-bəl) *adj.* **1.** Not communicable. **2.** *Rare.* Incommunicative. —**in′com·mu′ni·ca·bil′i·ty** *n.* —**in′com·mu′ni·ca·bly** *adv.*

in·com·mu·ni·ca·do (ĭn′kə-myōō′nĭ-kä′dō) *adj.* Without the means or right of communicating with others, as one held in solitary confinement. [Spanish, past participle of *incomunicar,* to deny communication : *in-,* not, from Latin + *comunicar,* to communicate, from Latin *commūnicāre,* COMMUNICATE.] —**in′com·mu′ni·ca′do** *adv.*

in·com·mu·ni·ca·tive (ĭn′kə-myōō′nĭ-kā′tĭv, -kə-tĭv) *adj.* Not communicative; uncommunicative. —**in′com·mu′ni·ca′tive·ly** *adv.* —**in′com·mu′ni·ca′tive·ness** *n.*

in·com·mut·a·ble (ĭn′kə-myōō′tə-bəl) *adj.* **1.** Incapable of being exchanged. **2.** Not changeable; unalterable. —**in′com·mut′a·bil′i·ty, in′com·mut′a·ble·ness** *n.* —**in′com·mut′a·bly** *adv.*

in·com·pa·ra·ble (ĭn-kŏm′pər-ə-bəl) *adj.* **1.** Incapable of being compared; incommensurable. **2.** Above all comparisons; beyond equal; unsurpassed; matchless. —**in·com′pa·ra·bil′i·ty, in·com′pa·ra·ble·ness** *n.* —**in·com′pa·ra·bly** *adv.*

in·com·pat·i·bil·i·ty (ĭn′kəm-păt′ə-bĭl′ə-tē) *n., pl.* **-ties.** **1.** The state or quality of being incompatible; lack of harmony or consistency; disagreement; incongruity. **2.** *Plural.* Mutually exclusive or antagonistic qualities or things.

in·com·pat·i·ble (ĭn′kəm-păt′ə-bəl) *adj.* **1.** Not compatible; inharmonious; antagonistic. **2.** Incapable of being held simultaneously by one person, as offices, ranks, or the like. **3.** *Logic.* Incapable of being simultaneously true; mutually exclusive. —See Synonyms at **inconsistent.** —*n.* Incompatible elements, persons, objects, or the like. Usually used in the plural. [Medieval Latin *incompatibilis* : *in-,* not + *compatibilis,* COMPATIBLE.] —**in′com·pat′i·ble·ness** *n.* —**in′com·pat′i·bly** *adv.*

in·com·pe·tent (ĭn-kŏm′pə-tənt) *adj.* Not competent. —*n.* An incompetent person. —**in·com′pe·tence, in·com′pe·ten·cy** *n.* —**in·com′pe·tent·ly** *adv.*

in·com·plete (ĭn′kəm-plēt′) *adj.* **1.** Not complete. **2.** *Football.* Not caught, or not caught in bounds, by a receiver. Said of a forward pass. —**in′com·plete′ly** *adv.* —**in′com·plete′ness, in′com·ple′tion** *n.*

in·com·pli·ant (ĭn′kəm-plī′ənt) *adj.* Not compliant; unyielding. —**in′com·pli′ance, in′com·pli′an·cy** *n.* —**in′com·pli′ant·ly** *adv.*

in·com·pre·hen·si·ble (ĭn′kŏm-prĭ-hĕn′sə-bəl, ĭn-kŏm′-) *adj.* **1.** Incapable of being understood or comprehended, as: **a.** Unintelligible. **b.** Unknowable; unfathomable. **2.** *Archaic.* Without limits; boundless. —**in′com·pre·hen′si·bil′i·ty, in′com·pre·hen′si·ble·ness** *n.* —**in′com·pre·hen′si·bly** *adv.*

in·com·pre·hen·sion (ĭn′kŏm-prĭ-hĕn′shən, ĭn-kŏm′-) *n.* Lack of comprehension or understanding.

in·com·pre·hen·sive (ĭn′kŏm-prĭ-hĕn′sĭv, ĭn-kŏm′-) *adj.* Not comprehensive or all-inclusive; limited in range or scope. —**in′com·pre·hen′sive·ly** *adv.* —**in′com·pre·hen′sive·ness** *n.*

in·com·press·i·ble (ĭn′kəm-prĕs′ə-bəl) *adj.* Incapable of being compressed. —**in′com·press′i·bil′i·ty** *n.*

in·com·put·a·ble (ĭn′kəm-pyōō′tə-bəl) *adj.* Incapable of being computed or calculated. —**in′com·put′a·bil′i·ty** *n.*

in·con·ceiv·a·ble (ĭn′kən-sē′və-bəl) *adj.* Incapable of being conceived or thought of; unbelievable. —**in′con·ceiv′a·bil′i·ty, in′con·ceiv′a·ble·ness** *n.* —**in′con·ceiv′a·bly** *adv.*

in·con·clu·sive (ĭn′kən-klōō′sĭv) *adj.* Not conclusive. —**in′con·clu′sive·ly** *adv.* —**in′con·clu′sive·ness** *n.*

in·con·den·sa·ble (ĭn′kən-dĕn′sə-bəl) *adj.* Also **in·con·den·si·ble.** Incapable of being condensed. —**in′con·den′sa·bil′i·ty** *n.*

in·con·dite (ĭn-kŏn′dĭt, -dīt′) *adj. Rare.* Badly constructed; crude. [Latin *inconditus* : *in-,* not + *conditus,* past participle of *condere,* to put together. See **dhē-¹** in Appendix.*] —**in·con′dite·ly** *adv.*

in·con·form·i·ty (ĭn′kən-fôr′mə-tē) *n.* Resistance to or lack of conformity; nonconformity.

in·con·gru·ent (ĭn-kŏng′grōō-ənt) *adj.* **1.** Not congruent. **2.** Incongruous. —**in·con′gru·ence** *n.* —**in·con′gru·ent·ly** *adv.*

in·con·gru·i·ty (ĭn′kŏng-grōō′ə-tē, ĭn′kən-) *n., pl.* **-ties.** **1.** Lack of congruence. **2.** The state or quality of being incongruous. **3.** That which is incongruous.

in·con·gru·ous (ĭn-kŏng′grōō-əs) *adj.* **1.** Not corresponding; inharmonious; disagreeing; incompatible: *a plan incongruous with good sense.* **2.** Made up of disparate, inconsistent, or discordant parts or qualities: *an incongruous group of people.* **3.** Not consistent with what is correct, proper, or logical; unsuitable; inappropriate: *an incongruous remark.* —See Synonyms at **inconsistent.** [Latin *incongruus* : *in-,* not + *congruus,* CONGRUOUS.] —**in·con′gru·ous·ly** *adv.* —**in·con′gru·ous·ness** *n.*

in·con·se·quent (ĭn-kŏn′sə-kwənt) *adj.* **1.** Not obtained as a result. **2.** Not derived from the premises or obtained by logic or reason; irrelevant. **3.** Proceeding without logical sequence; haphazard. **4.** Out of character with the nature or style of something. **5.** Unimportant; insignificant. [Late Latin *inconsequēns* : Latin *in-,* not + *consequēns,* CONSEQUENT.] —**in·con′se·quence** *n.* —**in·con′se·quent·ly** *adv.*

in·con·se·quen·tial (ĭn-kŏn′sə-kwĕn′shəl) *adj.* **1.** Without consequence; lacking importance; petty. **2.** Inconsequent. —*n.* A triviality. —**in·con′se·quen′ti·al′i·ty, in′con·se·quen′tial·ness** *n.* —**in·con′se·quen′tial·ly** *adv.*

in·con·sid·er·a·ble (ĭn′kən-sĭd′ər-ə-bəl) *adj.* Too small or unimportant to merit attention or consideration; trivial. —**in′con·sid′er·a·ble·ness** *n.* —**in′con·sid′er·a·bly** *adv.*

in·con·sid·er·ate (ĭn′kən-sĭd′ər-ĭt) *adj.* Not considerate. [Latin *inconsīderātus* : *in-,* not + *consīderātus,* CONSIDERATE.] —**in′con·sid′er·ate·ly** *adv.* —**in′con·sid′er·ate·ness, in′con·sid·er·a′tion** *n.*

in·con·sis·ten·cy (ĭn′kən-sĭs′tən-sē) *n., pl.* **-cies.** Also **in·con·sis·tence** (-təns) (for sense 1). **1.** The state or quality of being inconsistent; lack of consistency or uniformity; incongruity. **2.** Something that is inconsistent.

in·con·sis·tent (ĭn′kən-sĭs′tənt) *adj.* Not consistent, especially: **a.** Erratic. **b.** Incongruous. **c.** Contradictory. **d.** Illogical. —**in′con·sis′tent·ly** *adv.*

Synonyms: *inconsistent, incongruous, incompatible, discordant, uncongenial.* These adjectives mean in marked disagreement. *Inconsistent* describes what reveals lack of uniformity in overall purpose, design, procedure, or content. Human thought or behavior is *inconsistent* when a succession of individual acts reveals basic disagreement or contradiction; two or more accounts of a single occurrence are *inconsistent* when they differ in important details. *Incongruous* implies disagreement that shows up noticeably or even glaringly. The term is frequently applied to human behavior or speech at odds with a person's character or temperament, or improper under the circumstances, and to things that reveal lack of harmony in design or that clash with surroundings. *Incompatible* refers to what is unsuited to coexistence, to persons of differing temperaments, and to things that have fundamental differences or contradictions. *Discordant* implies a relationship of persons or things marked by clash of temperaments, opinions, or principles. *Uncongenial* suggests a less stridently unharmonious relationship involving persons or persons and their environments.

in·con·sol·a·ble (ĭn′kən-sō′lə-bəl) *adj.* Incapable of being consoled or solaced; despondent. —**in′con·sol′a·bil′i·ty, in′con·sol′a·ble·ness** *n.* —**in′con·sol′a·bly** *adv.*

in·con·so·nant (ĭn-kŏn′sə-nənt) *adj.* Lacking harmony, agreement, or compatibility; discordant. —**in·con′so·nance** *n.* —**in·con′so·nant·ly** *adv.*

in·con·spic·u·ous (ĭn′kən-spĭk′yōō-əs) *adj.* Not readily noticeable. —**in′con·spic′u·ous·ly** *adv.* —**in′con·spic′u·ous·ness** *n.*

in·con·stan·cy (ĭn-kŏn′stən-sē) *n., pl.* **-cies.** **1.** Fickleness; faithlessness. **2.** Unreliability; instability. **3.** An act or instance of being inconstant.

in·con·stant (ĭn-kŏn′stənt) *adj.* **1.** Not constant. **2.** Fickle. —See Synonyms at **faithless.** —**in·con′stant·ly** *adv.*

in·con·sum·a·ble (ĭn′kən-sōō′mə-bəl) *adj.* Incapable of being consumed. —**in′con·sum′a·bly** *adv.*

in·con·test·a·ble (ĭn′kən-tĕs′tə-bəl) *adj.* Incapable of being contested; unquestionable. —**in′con·test′a·bil′i·ty, in′con·test′a·ble·ness** *n.* —**in′con·test′a·bly** *adv.*

in·con·ti·nence (ĭn-kŏn′tə-nəns) *n.* The quality or condition of being incontinent; lack of continence.

in·con·ti·nent (ĭn-kŏn′tə-nənt) *adj.* **1.** Not continent; unrestrained; uncontrolled. **2.** Incapable of holding back, containing, or retaining. Usually used with *of: incontinent of anger.* **3.** Incapable of controlling the excretory functions. [Middle English, from Old French, from Latin *incontinēns,* unrestrained : *in-,* not + *continēns,* restrained, CONTINENT.] —**in·con′ti·nent·ly** *adv.*

in·con·trol·la·ble (ĭn′kən-trō′lə-bəl) *adj.* Not controllable; uncontrollable.

in·con·tro·vert·i·ble (ĭn′kŏn-trə-vûr′tə-bəl) *adj.* Indisputable; unquestionable. —**in′con·tro·vert′i·bil′i·ty, in′con·tro·vert′i·ble·ness** *n.* —**in′con·tro·vert′i·bly** *adv.*

in·con·ven·ience (ĭn′kən-vēn′yəns) *n.* Also **in·con·ven·ien·cy** (-yən-sē) *pl.* **-cies.** **1.** The state or quality of being inconvenient; lack of ease or comfort; trouble; difficulty. **2.** Something that causes difficulty, trouble, or discomfort; an inconvenient thing. —*tr.v.* **inconvenienced, -iencing, -iences.** To cause inconvenience for; to discomfort; to trouble; to bother.

in·con·ven·ient (ĭn′kən-vēn′yənt) *adj.* Not convenient, especially: **a.** Not accessible or handy. **b.** Difficult or awkward to perform. [Middle English, from Old French, from Latin *inconveniēns* : *in-,* not + *conveniēns,* CONVENIENT.] —**in′con·ven′ient·ly** *adv.*

in·con·vert·i·ble (ĭn′kən-vûr′tə-bəl) *adj.* Incapable of being converted, changed, or exchanged; especially, designating paper currency not redeemable for specie. —**in′con·vert′i·bil′i·ty, in′con·vert′i·ble·ness** *n.* —**in′con·vert′i·bly** *adv.*

in·con·vin·ci·ble (ĭn′kən-vĭn′sə-bəl) *adj.* Incapable of being convinced.

in·co·or·di·nate (ĭn′kō-ôrd′n-ĭt, -āt′) *adj.* **1.** Not of the same order. **2.** Uncoordinated. —**in′co·or′di·nate·ly** *adv.*

in·co·or·di·na·tion (ĭn′kō-ôrd′n-ā′shən) *n.* **1.** Lack of coordination. **2.** The inability to exercise normal voluntary control of relatively complex muscular movement.

in·cor·po·rate¹ (ĭn-kôr′pə-rāt′) *v.* **-rated, -rating, -rates.** —*tr.* **1.** To unite with or blend indistinguishably into something already in existence. **2.** To admit as a member to a corporation or similar organization. **3.** To cause to merge or combine together into a united whole. **4.** To cause to form into a legal corporation. **5.** To give substance or material form to; embody; substantiate. —*intr.* **1.** To become united or combined into an organized body. **2.** To form a legal corporation. —*adj.* (ĭn-kôr′pər-ĭt). **1.** Combined into one united body; merged. **2.** Formed into a legal corporation. [Middle English *incorpo-*

raten, from Late Latin *incorporāre,* to form into a body : Latin *in-* (intensive) + *corporāre,* to form into a body (see **corporate**).] —**in·cor′po·ra′tion** *n.* —**in·cor′po·ra′tive** *adj.* —**in·cor′po·ra′tor** (-rā′tər) *n.*

in·cor·po·rate² (ĭn-kôr′pər-ĭt) *adj. Rare.* Incorporeal. [Late Latin *incorporātus,* not in the body, spiritual : Latin *in-,* not + *corporātus,* embodied, CORPORATE.]

in·cor·po·rat·ed (ĭn-kôr′pə-rā′tĭd) *adj.* **1.** United into one body; combined. **2.** *Abbr.* **Inc., inc.** Organized and maintained as a legal business corporation.

in·cor·po·ra·ting (ĭn-kôr′pə-rā′tĭng) *adj.* **Polysynthetic** *(see).*

in·cor·po·re·al (ĭn′kôr-pôr′ē-əl, -pōr′ē-əl) *adj.* **1.** Lacking material form or substance. **2.** Spiritual. **3.** *Law.* Lacking material substance but existing in the eyes of the law; intangible, as a right or patent. [Latin *incorporeus* : *in-,* not + *corporeus,* CORPOREAL.] —**in′cor·po′re·al·ly** *adv.*

in·cor·po·re·i·ty (ĭn′kôr′pə-rē′ə-tē) *n.* Immateriality. [From Latin *incorporeus,* INCORPOREAL.]

in·cor·rect (ĭn′kə-rĕkt′) *adj.* Not correct, especially: **a.** Erroneous. **b.** Improper; inappropriate. —**in′cor·rect′ly** *adv.* —**in′cor·rect′ness** *n.*

in·cor·ri·gi·ble (ĭn-kôr′ə-jə-bəl, ĭn-kŏr′-) *adj.* **1.** Incapable of being corrected or reformed: *"Even the most incorrigible maverick has to be born somewhere."* (James Baldwin). **2.** Firmly rooted; impossible to eliminate; ineradicable: *incorrigible innocence.* —*n.* A person or animal that will not be tamed or corrected. [Middle English, from Late Latin *incorrigibilis* : Latin *in-,* not + *corrigere,* to CORRECT.] —**in·cor′ri·gi·bil′i·ty, in·cor′ri·gi·ble·ness** *n.* —**in·cor′ri·gi·bly** *adv.*

in·cor·rupt (ĭn′kə-rŭpt′) *adj. Rare.* **1.** Not corrupt or immoral. **2.** Not decayed; unspoiled. [Middle English, from Latin *incorruptus* : *in-,* not + *corruptus,* CORRUPT.] —**in′cor·rupt′ly** *adv.* —**in′cor·rupt′ness** *n.*

in·cor·rupt·i·ble (ĭn′kə-rŭp′tə-bəl) *adj.* Incapable of being corrupted morally; not subject to corruption or decay. —**in′cor·rupt′i·bil′i·ty** *n.* —**in′cor·rupt′i·bly** *adv.*

in·crease (ĭn-krēs′) *v.* **-creased, -creasing, -creases.** —*intr.* **1.** To become greater or larger. **2.** To multiply; reproduce. —*tr.* To make greater or larger. —*n.* (ĭn′krēs′). *Abbr.* **inc., incr. 1.** The act of increasing; enlargement; multiplication. **2.** The amount of such increase; increment: *a tax increase of ten per cent.* [Middle English *encresen,* from Old French *encreistre* (present stem *encreiss-*), from Latin *incrēscere,* to grow in or on : *in-,* in + *crēscere,* to grow (see **ker-³** in Appendix*).] —**in·creas′a·ble** *adj.* —**in·creas′er** *n.* —**in·creas′ing·ly** *adv.*

Synonyms: increase, magnify, enlarge, expand, extend, augment, grow. These verbs mean to become greater or to make greater. They vary considerably with respect to areas of application. *Increase* has a broad range, since it pertains to greatness in quantity, physical dimensions, rate, as of productivity, degree, or intensity. *Magnify* refers principally to making larger physically, in appearance or actuality, or figuratively by exaggeration. *Enlarge* refers to increase in size, extent, capacity, or scope, and *expand* to increase in size, volume, or range. To *extend* is to lengthen in space or time or to broaden, figuratively, in range of application. To *augment* is to add to something so as to increase it in amount or degree. To *grow* is to increase in size, amount, strength, scope, or influence, usually by progressive stages.

in·cre·ate (ĭn′krē-āt′, ĭn-krē′ĭt) *adj.* Existing without having been created, as divine beings. —**in′cre·ate′ly** *adv.*

in·cred·i·bil·i·ty (ĭn-krĕd′ə-bĭl′ə-tē) *n., pl.* **-ties. 1.** The condition or quality of being incredible. **2.** Something incredible.

in·cred·i·ble (ĭn-krĕd′ə-bəl) *adj.* Unbelievable. [Middle English, from Latin *incrēdibilis* : *in-,* not + *crēdibilis,* CREDIBLE.] —**in·cred′i·ble·ness** *n.* —**in·cred′i·bly** *adv.*

in·cre·du·li·ty (ĭn′krə-dōō′lə-tē, -dyōō′lə-tē) *n.* Also **in·cred·u·lous·ness** (ĭn-krĕj′ə-ləs-nĭs). Disbelief.

in·cred·u·lous (ĭn-krĕj′ə-ləs) *adj.* **1.** Disbelieving; skeptical. **2.** Expressing disbelief: *an incredulous stare.* [Latin *incrēdulus* : *in-,* not + *crēdulus,* CREDULOUS.] —**in·cred′u·lous·ly** *adv.*

in·cre·ment (ĭn′krə-mənt) *n.* **1.** An increase in number, size, or extent; growth; enlargement. **2.** Something added or gained. **3.** A small increase in quantity. **4.** *Mathematics.* A small positive or negative change in a variable. [Middle English, from Latin *incrēmentum,* from *incrēscere,* to INCREASE.] —**in′cre·men′tal** (-mĕnt′l) *adj.*

in·cres·cent (ĭn-krĕs′ənt) *adj.* Waxing. Said of the moon. [Latin *incrēscēns,* present participle of *incrēscere,* to INCREASE.]

in·cre·tion (ĭn-krē′shən) *n.* **1.** The process of internal secretion characteristic of endocrine glands. **2.** The product of such secretion; a hormone. [IN- (in) + (SE)CRETION.]

in·crim·i·nate (ĭn-krĭm′ə-nāt′) *tr.v.* **-nated, -nating, -nates.** To charge with or involve in a crime or other wrongful act. [Late Latin *incrīmināre* : Latin *in-,* in + *crīmen,* CRIME.] —**in·crim′i·na′tion** *n.* —**in·crim′i·na·to′ry** (-nə-tôr′ē, -tōr′ē) *adj.*

in·crust. Variant of **encrust.**

in·cu·bate (ĭn′kyə-bāt′, ĭng′-) *v.* **-bated, -bating, -bates.** —*tr.* **1.** To warm (eggs), as by bodily heat, so as to promote embryonic development and the hatching of young; to brood. **2.** To maintain (a bacterial culture, for example) at optimum environmental conditions for development. **3.** To cause to develop; foment. —*intr.* **1.** To brood eggs. **2.** To develop and hatch. Used of eggs. **3.** To undergo incubation. [Latin *incubāre,* to hatch, lie down upon : *in-,* on + *cubāre,* to lie down (see **keu-²** in Appendix*).] —**in′cu·ba′tive** *adj.*

in·cu·ba·tion (ĭn′kyə-bā′shən, ĭng′-) *n.* **1.** The act of incubating or the state of being incubated. **2.** *Medicine.* The development of an infection from the time of its entry into or initiation within an organism up to the time of the first appearance of signs or symptoms. —**in′cu·ba′tion·al** *adj.*

in·cu·ba·tor (ĭn′kyə-bā′tər, ĭng′-) *n.* One that incubates, especially: **a.** A cabinet in which a uniform temperature can be maintained, used in growing bacterial cultures. **b.** An apparatus for maintaining an infant, especially a premature infant, in an environment of controlled temperature, humidity, and oxygen.

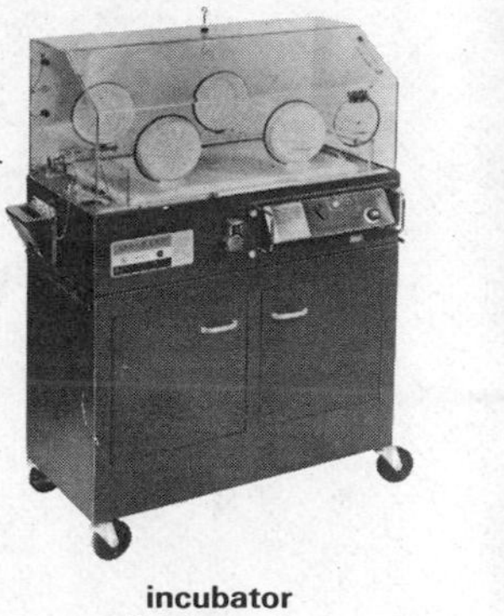

incubator
Incubator for
an infant

in·cu·bus (ĭn′kyə-bəs, ĭng′-) *n., pl.* **-buses** or **-bi** (-bī′). **1.** An evil spirit believed to descend upon and have sexual intercourse with sleeping women. Compare **succubus. 2.** A nightmare. **3.** Something oppressively or nightmarishly burdensome. [Middle English, from Late Latin, from Latin *incubāre,* to lie down upon, INCUBATE.]

in·cu·des. Plural of **incus.**

in·cul·cate (ĭn-kŭl′kāt′) *tr.v.* **-cated, -cating, -cates.** To teach or impress by forceful urging or frequent repetition; instill: *inculcate a code of ethics.* [Latin *inculcāre,* to trample in, impress upon : *in-,* in + *calcāre,* to trample, from *calx* (stem *calc-*), heel (see **calk**).] —**in·cul′ca′tion** *n.* —**in·cul′ca′tor** (-kā′tər) *n.*

in·cul·pa·ble (ĭn-kŭl′pə-bəl) *adj.* Not culpable; free from guilt; blameless.

in·cul·pate (ĭn-kŭl′pāt′) *tr.v.* **-pated, -pating, -pates.** To incriminate. [Late Latin *inculpāre* : *in-,* on + *culpāre,* to blame, from Latin *culpa,* fault, CULPA.] —**in·cul′pa′tion** *n.* —**in·cul′pa·to′ry** (-pə-tôr′ē, -tōr′ē) *adj.*

in·cult (ĭn-kŭlt′) *adj.* **1.** Not cultured; uncultivated. **2.** *Archaic.* Not tilled or cultivated. [Latin *incultus,* uncultivated : *in-,* not + *cultus,* past participle of *colere,* to till (see **kwel-¹** in Appendix*).]

in·cum·ben·cy (ĭn-kŭm′bən-sē) *n., pl.* **-cies. 1.** The condition or quality of being incumbent. **2.** Something that is incumbent. **3.** The holding and administering of an office or ecclesiastical benefice. **4.** The term of such a benefice or office.

in·cum·bent (ĭn-kŭm′bənt) *adj.* **1.** Lying, leaning, or resting upon something else. **2.** Imposed as an obligation or duty; required; obligatory. **3.** Holding a specified office or ecclesiastical benefice. —*n.* A person who holds an office or ecclesiastical benefice. [Middle English, from Latin *incumbēns,* present participle of *incumbere,* to lean upon : *in-,* on + *cumbere,* to lean, recline (see **keu-²** in Appendix*).] —**in·cum′bent·ly** *adv.*

in·cu·nab·u·lum (ĭn′kyōō-năb′yə-ləm) *n., pl.* **-la** (-lə). **1.** A book printed from movable type before 1501. **2.** An artifact of an early period. [From Latin *incūnābula* (plural), swaddling clothes, cradle, infancy : *in-,* in + *cūnābula,* infancy, origin, cradle, from *cūnae,* cradle (see **kei-¹** in Appendix*).] —**in′cu·nab′u·lar** *adj.*

in·cur (ĭn-kûr′) *tr.v.* **-curred, -curring, -curs. 1.** To meet with; run into. **2.** To become liable or subject to as a result of one's own actions; bring upon oneself. [Latin *incurrere,* to run into, come upon : *in-,* in + *currere,* to run (see **kers-²** in Appendix*).]

in·cur·a·ble (ĭn-kyŏŏr′ə-bəl) *adj.* **1.** Not curable. Said of a disease. **2.** Broadly, not susceptible to modification. —**in·cur′a·bil′i·ty, in·cur′a·ble·ness** *n.* —**in·cur′a·bly** *adv.*

in·cu·ri·ous (ĭn-kyŏŏr′ē-əs) *adj.* **1.** Not curious; uninterested. **2.** Not arousing interest; lacking novelty. —See Synonyms at **indifferent.** [Latin *incūriōsus,* indifferent : *in-,* not + *cūriōsus,* CURIOUS.] —**in′cu′ri·os′i·ty** (-ŏs′ə-tē), **in·cu′ri·ous·ness** *n.* —**in·cu′ri·ous·ly** *adv.*

in·cur·rent (ĭn-kûr′ənt) *adj.* Affording passage to an inflowing current. [Latin *incurrēns,* present participle of *incurrere,* to run into, INCUR.]

in·cur·sion (ĭn-kûr′zhən, -shən) *n.* **1.** A sudden attack on or invasion of hostile territory; a raid. **2.** A running or entering into. [Middle English, from Old French, from Latin *incursiō,* from *incurrere* (past participle *incursus*), to run into, attack, INCUR.]

in·cur·vate (ĭn-kûr′vāt′) *tr.v.* **-vated, -vating, -vates.** To bend (something) into an inward curve. —*adj.* (ĭn-kûr′vāt′, -vĭt). Curved, especially inward. [Latin *incurvāre* : *in-,* in + *curvāre,* to bend, from *curvus,* CURVE.] —**in′cur·va′tion** *n.* —**in·cur′va·ture′** (-chŏŏr′) *n.*

in·curve (ĭn-kûrv′) *v.* **-curved, -curving, -curves.** —*intr.* To bend into an inward curve. —*tr.* To incurvate. —*n.* (ĭn′kûrv). An inward curve. [Latin *incurvāre,* INCURVATE.]

in·cus (ĭng′kəs) *n., pl.* **incudes** (ĭn-kyōō′dēz). An anvil-shaped bone in the mammalian middle ear. Also called "anvil." [Latin *incūs,* anvil, from *incūdere* (past participle *incūsus*), to forge with a hammer, beat in : *in-,* in + *cūdere,* to strike, stamp (see **kau-²** in Appendix*).]

in·cuse (ĭn-kyōōz′, -kyōōs′) *adj.* Hammered, stamped, or pressed in. Said of a design or feature of a design on a coin. —*n.* A design impressed in such a manner. [Latin *incūsus,* past participle of *incūdere,* to beat or stamp in. See **incus.**]

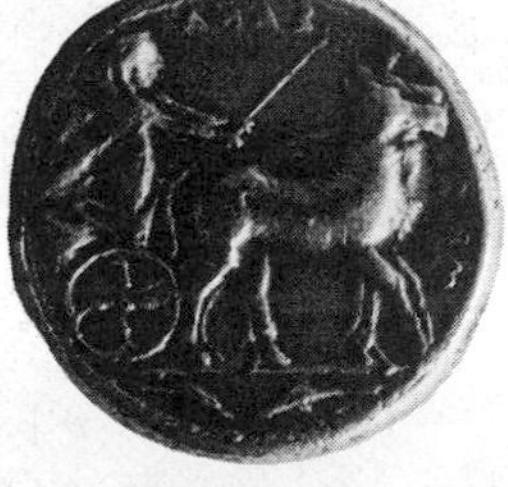

incuse
Fifth-century B.C.
coin of Messana (Messina)

Ind (ĭnd) *n.* **1.** *Archaic.* India. **2.** *Obsolete.* The Indies.

IND Airport code for Indianapolis, Indiana.

ind. 1. independence; independent. **2.** index. **3.** indigo. **4.** industrial; industry.

Ind. 1. India. **2.** Indian. **3.** Indiana. **4.** Indies.

in·da·ba (ĭn-dä′bə) *n.* A conference of indigenous tribes in southern Africa. [Zulu *in-daba,* business, affair.]

in·da·mine (ĭn′də-mēn′, -mĭn) *n.* Any of a group of organic bases that form unstable bluish or greenish salts used as dyes. [IND(IGO) + AMINE.]

in·debt·ed (ĭn-dĕt′ĭd) *adj.* Morally, socially, or legally obligated to another to repay something; beholden. [Middle English *endetted,* from Old French *endette,* from the past participle of *endetter,* to involve in debt, oblige : *en-,* in + *dette,* DEBT.]

in·debt·ed·ness (ĭn-dĕt′ĭd-nĭs) *n.* **1.** The state of being indebted. **2.** Something owed to another.

in·de·cen·cy (ĭn-dē′sən-sē) *n., pl.* **-cies. 1.** The state or quality of being indecent. **2.** Something that is indecent.

in·de·cent (ĭn-dē′sənt) *adj.* **1.** Offensive to good taste; unseemly. **2.** Offensive to public moral values; immodest: *indecent exposure.* —See Synonyms at **improper.** —**in·de′cent·ly** *adv.*

in·de·ci·pher·a·ble (ĭn′dĭ-sī′fər-ə-bəl) *adj.* Incapable of being deciphered. —**in′de·ci′pher·a·bil′i·ty, in′de·ci′pher·a·ble·ness** *n.*

in·de·ci·sion (ĭn′dĭ-sĭzh′ən) *n.* Irresolution.

in·de·ci·sive (ĭn′dĭ-sī′sĭv) *adj.* **1.** Not decisive; inconclusive. **2.** Prone to or characterized by indecision; vacillating; hesitant. **3.** Not clearly defined; indefinite. —**in′de·ci′sive·ly** *adv.* —**in′de·ci′sive·ness** *n.*

in·de·clin·a·ble (ĭn′dĭ-klī′nə-bəl) *adj.* Having no set of grammatical inflections; not declinable.

in·de·com·pos·a·ble (ĭn′dē-kəm-pō′zə-bəl) *adj.* Not capable of being split into component parts.

in·dec·o·rous (ĭn-dĕk′ər-əs) *adj.* Lacking propriety or good taste; unseemly. See Synonyms at **improper.** —**in·dec′o·rous·ly** *adv.* —**in·dec′o·rous·ness** *n.*

in·de·cor·um (ĭn′dĭ-kôr′əm, -kōr′əm) *n.* **1.** Lack of decorum; lack of propriety or good taste. **2.** An instance of indecorous behavior or action.

in·deed (ĭn-dēd′) *adv.* **1.** Without a doubt; certainly; truly. **2.** In fact; in reality. **3.** Admittedly; unquestionably. —*interj.* Used to express surprise, skepticism, or irony. [Middle English *in dede,* in reality : *in,* IN + *dede,* DEED.]

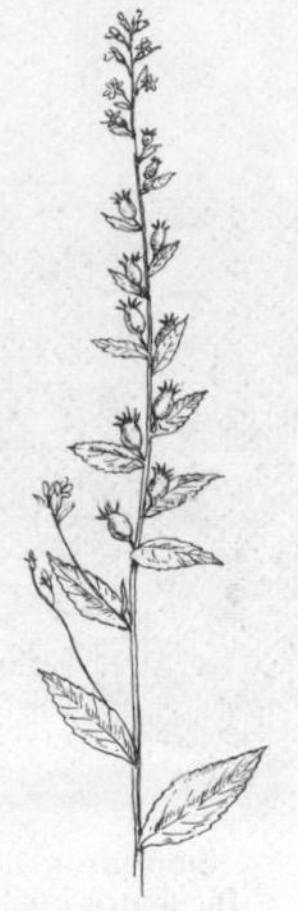

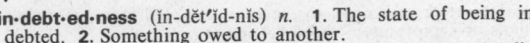

Indian tobacco

indef. indefinite.

in·de·fat·i·ga·ble (ĭn′dĭ-făt′ə-gə-bəl) *adj.* Untiring; tireless. [Latin *indēfatigābilis* : *in-,* not + *dēfatigāre,* to tire out : *de-* (intensive) + *fatigāre,* to FATIGUE.] —**in′de·fat′i·ga·bil′i·ty, in′de·fat′i·ga·ble·ness** *n.* —**in′de·fat′i·ga·bly** *adv.*

in·de·fea·si·ble (ĭn′dĭ-fē′zə-bəl) *adj.* Not capable of being annulled or made void. —**in′de·fea′si·bil′i·ty** *n.* —**in′de·fea′si·bly** *adv.*

in·de·fec·ti·ble (ĭn′dĭ-fĕk′tə-bəl) *adj.* **1.** Having the ability to resist defect or failure; permanent; lasting. **2.** Without flaw or defect; perfect. —**in′de·fec′ti·bil′i·ty** *n.* —**in′de·fec′ti·bly** *adv.*

in·de·fen·si·ble (ĭn′dĭ-fĕn′sə-bəl) *adj.* Not capable of being defended, especially: **a.** Inexcusable. **b.** Invalid; untenable. **c.** Vulnerable to attack. —**in′de·fen′si·bil′i·ty, in′de·fen′si·ble·ness** *n.* —**in′de·fen′si·bly** *adv.*

in·de·fin·a·ble (ĭn′dĭ-fī′nə-bəl) *adj.* Not capable of being defined, described, or analyzed. —*n.* One that is unable to be defined. —**in′de·fin′a·ble·ness** *n.* —**in′de·fin′a·bly** *adv.*

in·def·i·nite (ĭn-dĕf′ə-nĭt) *adj. Abbr.* **indef.** Not definite, especially: **a.** Unclear; vague. **b.** Lacking precise limits. **c.** Uncertain; undecided. [Latin *indēfīnītus* : *in-,* not + *dēfīnītus,* DEFINITE.] —**in·def′i·nite·ly** *adv.* —**in·def′i·nite·ness** *n.*

indefinite article. *Grammar.* An article, as English *a* or *an,* that does not fix or immediately fix the identity of the noun modified. Compare **definite article.**

indefinite integral. *Mathematics.* The set of all functions of which a given function is the derivative, usually represented by $\int f(x)dx + C$, where $\int f(x)dx$ is any member of the set and C is an arbitrary constant.

indefinite pronoun. *Grammar.* A pronoun, as English *any* or *some,* that does not specify the identity of its object.

in·de·his·cent (ĭn′dĭ-hĭs′ənt) *adj.* Not splitting open at maturity: *indehiscent fruit.* Compare **dehiscent.** —**in′de·his′cence** *n.*

in·del·i·ble (ĭn-dĕl′ə-bəl) *adj.* **1.** Incapable of being removed, erased, or washed away; permanent; enduring. **2.** Making a mark not easily erased or washed away: *an indelible laundry pencil.* [Latin *indēlēbilis* : *in-,* not + *dēlēbilis,* that can be obliterated, from *dēlēre,* to obliterate, DELETE.] —**in·del′i·bil′i·ty, in·del′i·ble·ness** *n.* —**in·del′i·bly** *adv.*

in·del·i·ca·cy (ĭn-dĕl′ĭ-kə-sē) *n., pl.* **-cies. 1.** The quality or condition of being indelicate. **2.** An instance of indelicate speech or behavior; a crudity.

in·del·i·cate (ĭn-dĕl′ĭ-kĭt) *adj.* **1. a.** Offensive to propriety. **b.** Coarse; tasteless. **2.** Tactless. —See Synonyms at **coarse, improper.** —**in·del′i·cate·ly** *adv.* —**in·del′i·cate·ness** *n.*

in·dem·ni·fi·ca·tion (ĭn-dĕm′nə-fĭ-kā′shən) *n.* **1.** The act of indemnifying or the condition of being indemnified. **2.** Something that indemnifies.

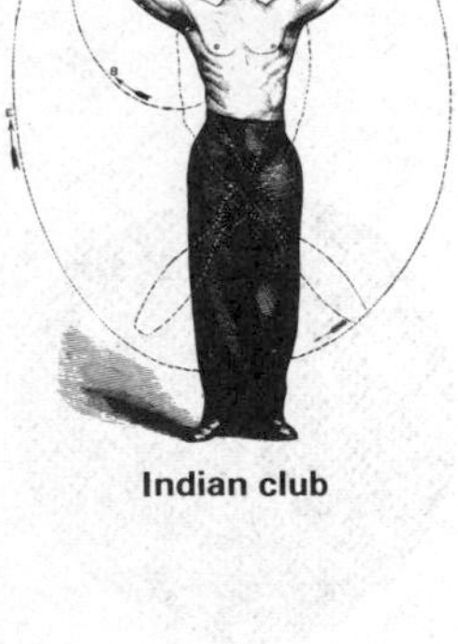

Indian club

in·dem·ni·fy (ĭn-dĕm′nə-fī′) *tr.v.* **-fied, -fying, -fies. 1.** To protect against possible damage, legal suit, or bodily injury; insure. **2.** To make compensation to for incurred damage or hurt. [Latin *indemnis,* uninjured (see **indemnity**) + -FY.] —**in·dem′ni·fi′er** *n.*

in·dem·ni·ty (ĭn-dĕm′nə-tē) *n., pl.* **-ties. 1.** Insurance or other security against possible damage, loss, or hurt. **2.** A legal exemption from liability for damages. **3.** Compensation for damage, loss, or hurt incurred; indemnification. —See Synonyms at **reparation.** [Middle English *indempnyte,* from Old French *indemnite,* from Late Latin *indemnitās,* from Latin *indemnis,* unhurt, uninjured : *in-,* not + *damnum,* hurt, harm (see **dap-** in Appendix*).]

in·de·mon·stra·ble (ĭn′dĭ-mŏn′strə-bəl) *adj.* Incapable of being proved or demonstrated. —**in′de·mon′stra·ble·ness, in′de·mon′stra·bil′i·ty** *n.* —**in′de·mon′stra·bly** *adv.*

in·dene (ĭn′dēn′) *n.* A colorless organic liquid, C_9H_8, obtained from coal tar and used in preparing synthetic resins. [German *Inden* : *Indol,* IND(OLE) + -ENE.]

in·dent¹ (ĭn-dĕnt′) *v.* **-dented, -denting, -dents.** —*tr.* **1.** To cut or tear (a document with two or more copies) along an irregular line so that the parts can later be matched for establishing authenticity. **2.** To draw up (a deed or other document) in duplicate or triplicate. **3.** To notch or serrate the edge of; make jagged. **4. a.** To make notches, grooves, or holes in (wood, for example) for the purpose of mortising. **b.** To fit or join together by or as if by mortising. **5.** To set in from the margin (the first line of a paragraph, for example). **6.** *Chiefly British.* To order (goods) by purchase order or official requisition. —*intr.* **1.** To form an indentation. **2.** *Chiefly British.* To draw up or order an indent for something. —*n.* (ĭn-dĕnt′, ĭn′dĕnt′). **1.** An indenture. **2.** A U.S. certificate issued at the close of the Revolutionary War for interest due on the public debt. **3.** *Chiefly British.* An official requisition or purchase order for goods. **4.** An indention. [Middle English *indenten, endenten,* to make a toothlike incision into, from Old French *endenter* : *en-,* in + *dent,* tooth, from Latin *dēns* (see **dent-** in Appendix*).] —**in·dent′er, in·den′tor** (-tər) *n.*

in·dent² (ĭn-dĕnt′) *tr.v.* **-dented, -denting, -dents. 1.** To push in or press down upon so as to form a dent or impression. **2.** To make a dent in. —*n.* An indentation.

in·den·ta·tion (ĭn′dĕn′tā′shən) *n.* **1.** The act of indenting or the condition of being indented. **2.** A notch or jagged cut in an edge. **3.** A deep recess in a border, coastline, or other boundary. **4.** The blank space between a margin and the beginning of an indented line.

in·den·tion (ĭn-dĕn′shən) *n.* **1.** The act of indenting or the condition of being indented. **2.** The blank space between a margin and the beginning of an indented line. **3.** *Archaic.* An indentation or dent.

in·den·ture (ĭn-dĕn′chər) *n.* **1.** A document in duplicate having indented edges. **2.** *Law.* A deed or contract executed between two or more parties. **3.** *Usually plural.* A contract binding one party into the service of another for a specified term. **4.** An official or authenticated inventory, list, or voucher. **5.** Indentation. —*tr.v.* **indentured, -turing, -tures. 1.** To bind by indenture. **2.** *Archaic.* To form an indentation in. [Middle English *indenture, endenture,* from Old French *endenture,* from *endenter,* INDENT.]

in·de·pend·ence (ĭn′dĭ-pĕn′dəns) *n. Abbr.* **ind. 1.** The state or quality of being independent. **2.** *Archaic.* Sufficient income for self-support; competence.

In·de·pend·ence (ĭn′dĭ-pĕn′dəns). A residential suburb of Kansas City, Missouri; home of President Harry S Truman. Population, 62,000.

Independence Day. July 4, a U.S. legal holiday celebrating the anniversary of the adoption of the Declaration of Independence in 1776.

in·de·pend·en·cy (ĭn′dĭ-pĕn′dən-sē) *n., pl.* **-cies. 1.** Independence. **2.** An independent territory or state. **3.** *Capital* **I.** The Independent movement in England.

in·de·pend·ent (ĭn′dĭ-pĕn′dənt) *adj. Abbr.* **ind. 1.** Politically autonomous; self-governing. **2.** Free from the influence, guidance, or control of another or others; self-reliant. **3.** Not contingent. **4.** Affiliated with or loyal to no one political party or organization: *the independent vote.* **5.** Not dependent on or affiliated with a larger or controlling group, system, or the like; separate: *an independent food store; independent results.* **6.** Financially self-sufficient; self-supporting. **7.** Not having to work for a living; wealthy in one's own right; having a competence. **8.** Constituting a competence: *independent means.* **9.** *Mathematics.* **a.** Not dependent on other variables: *independent variable.* **b.** Of or pertaining to a system of equations, no one of which is necessarily satisfied by a set of values of the independent variables that satisfy all the others. **c.** Of, pertaining to, describing, or being an outcome of a trial of a chance experiment the probability of which does not depend on the outcome of any other trial of the chance experiment. —*n. Abbr.* **ind.** One that is independent; especially, a voter who does not pledge allegiance to any one political party.

In·de·pend·ent (ĭn′dĭ-pĕn′dənt) *n.* **1.** A member of a movement in England in the 17th century advocating the political and religious independence of individual congregations. **2.** *British.* A Congregationalist. —**In′de·pen′dent** *adj.*

independent clause. *Grammar.* A clause containing a subject, a verb, and sometimes an object and modifiers, capable of standing alone as a complete sentence.

in·de·scrib·a·ble (ĭn′dĭ-skrī′bə-bəl) *adj.* **1.** Incapable of description; undefinable. **2.** Beyond description. —**in′de·scrib′a·bil′i·ty, in′de·scrib′a·ble·ness** *n.* —**in′de·scrib′a·bly** *adv.*

in·de·struc·ti·ble (ĭn′dĭ-strŭk′tə-bəl) *adj.* Not capable of being destroyed; unbreakable. —**in′de·struc′ti·bil′i·ty, in′de·struc′ti·ble·ness** *n.* —**in′de·struc′ti·bly** *adv.*

in·de·ter·mi·na·ble (ĭn′dĭ-tûr′mə-nə-bəl) *adj.* **1.** Not capable of being fixed or measured; not ascertainable. **2.** Incapable of being finally settled or decided. —**in′de·ter′mi·na·bly** *adv.*

in·de·ter·mi·na·cy (ĭn′dĭ-tûr′mə-nə-sē) *n.* The state or quality of being indeterminate. [From INDETERMINATE.]

in·de·ter·mi·nate (ĭn′dĭ-tûr′mə-nĭt) *adj.* **1. a.** Not precisely or quantitatively determined. **b.** Incapable of being so determined. **c.** Lacking clarity or precision. **d.** Not capable of clear interpretation; inconclusive; ambiguous. **e.** Not known in advance. **2.** *Botany.* Not terminating in a flower and continuing to grow at the apex: *an indeterminate inflorescence.* [Middle English *indeterminat,* from Late Latin *indēterminātus* : Latin *in-,* not + *dēterminātus,* DETERMINATE.] —**in′de·ter′mi·nate·ly** *adv.* —**in′de·ter′mi·nate·ness, in′de·ter′mi·na′tion** (-nā′shən) *n.*

in·de·ter·min·ism (ĭn′dĭ-tûr′mə-nĭz′əm) *n.* The philosophical doctrine that in some circumstances volition occurs independent of physiological and psychological antecedents. —**in′de·ter′min·ist** *n. & adj.* —**in′de·ter′min·is′tic** *adj.*

in·dex (ĭn′dĕks′) *n., pl.* **-dexes** or **-dices** (-də-sēz′). **1.** Anything

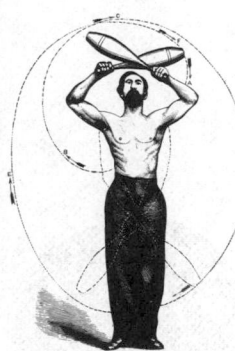

that serves to guide, point out, or otherwise facilitate reference, as: **a.** *Abbr.* **ind.** An alphabetized listing of names, places, and subjects included in a printed work that gives for each item the page on which it may be found. **b.** A series of notches cut into the edge of a book for easy access to chapters or other divisions. **c.** Any table, file, or catalogue. **2.** Anything that reveals or indicates; a sign; token: *"Her face . . . was a fair index to her disposition."* (Samuel Butler). **3.** A character (☞) used in printing to call attention to a particular paragraph or section. Also called "fist," "hand." **4.** Something that serves as an indicator or pointer, as in a scientific instrument. **5.** *Mathematics.* **a.** A number or symbol, often written as a subscript or superscript to a mathematical expression, that indicates an operation to be performed on, an ordering relation involving, or a use of the associated expression. **b.** A number derived from a formula used to characterize a set of data: *cost-of-living index.* —*tr.v.* **indexed, -dexing, -dexes. 1.** To furnish with an index. **2.** To enter (an item) in an index. **3.** To indicate or signal. [Latin *index* (plural *indicēs*), forefinger, indicator. See **deik-** in Appendix.*]

index finger. The finger next to the thumb. Also called "forefinger."

In·dex Li·bro·rum Pro·hib·i·to·rum (ĭn′dĕks′ lī-brôr′əm prō-hĭb′ə-tôr′əm, lī-brōr′əm prō-hĭb′ə-tōr′əm). A list formerly published by Church authority for Roman Catholics, restricting or forbidding the reading of certain books. Also shortened to "Index." [New Latin, "index of prohibited books."]

index number. A number indicating change in magnitude, as of price, wage, employment, or production shifts, relative to the magnitude at some specified point usually taken as 100.

index of refraction. The ratio of the speed of light in a vacuum to the speed of light in a medium under consideration.

In·di·a (ĭn′dē-ə). *Hindi* **Bha·rat** (bŭ′rŭt). *Abbr.* **Ind. 1.** A subcontinent of southern Asia comprising the Republic of India, Nepal, Bhutan, Sikkim, and both divisions of Pakistan. **2.** Officially, Republic of India. A republic occupying 1,196,995 square miles in southern Asia. Population, 476,278,000. Capital, New Delhi. [Latin *India,* from Greek, from *Indos,* the river Indus, from Old Persian *Hindu,* from Sanskrit *Sindhuḥ,* from *sindhuḥ*†, river.]

India ink. 1. A black pigment made from lampblack mixed with a binding agent and molded into cakes or sticks. **2.** A liquid ink made from this. Also called "Chinese ink." [Formerly thought to be a product of India.]

In·di·a·man (ĭn′dē-ə-mən) *n., pl.* **-men** (-mĭn). A large merchant ship formerly used on trade routes to India.

In·di·an (ĭn′dē-ən) *n. Abbr.* **Ind. 1.** A native or inhabitant of India or of the East Indies. **2.** A member of any of the aboriginal peoples of North America, South America, or the West Indies. **3.** Loosely, any of the languages spoken by the American Indians. **4.** A constellation, **Indus** *(see).* —*adj.* **1.** Of or pertaining to India or the East Indies, their culture, or their people. **2.** Of or pertaining to the aboriginal people of North America, South America, or the West Indies.

In·di·an·a (ĭn′dē-ăn′ə). *Abbr.* **Ind.** A Midwestern state of the United States, 36,291 square miles in area; entered the Union in 1816. Population, 4,885,000. Capital, Indianapolis. See map at **United States of America.** —**In′di·an′i·an** *n. & adj.*

In·di·an·a Dunes National Lakeshore (ĭn′dē-ăn′ə). A conservation and recreation area occupying 8,720 acres along the shore of Lake Michigan in northern Indiana.

Indian almond. A tree, *Terminalia catappa,* of tropical Asia, having fruit with edible seeds. Also called "myrobalan."

In·di·an·ap·o·lis (ĭn′dē-ə-năp′ə-lĭs). The capital and largest city of Indiana, located in the central part of the state. Population, 476,000.

Indian bean. A tree, the **catalpa** *(see).*

Indian bread. Any of various plants, such as the breadroot, having edible parts used by American Indians for food.

Indian cholera. A disease, **cholera** *(see).*

Indian club. A bottle-shaped wooden club swung in the hand for gymnastic exercise.

Indian corn. See **corn.**

Indian currant. A plant, the **coralberry** *(see),* or its fruit.

Indian Desert. See **Thar Desert.**

Indian file. Single file *(see).*

Indian giver. *Informal.* One who gives something as a gift to another and then takes or demands it back.

Indian hemp. A plant, **hemp** *(see).*

Indian licorice. A plant, the **rosary pea** *(see).*

Indian meal. Cornmeal *(see).*

Indian Ocean. An ocean, 28,350,000 square miles in area, bounded by Asia, Antarctica, Africa, and Australia.

Indian paintbrush. Any of various plants of the genus *Castilleja,* having spikes of flowers surrounded by showy, brightly colored bracts. Also called "painted cup."

Indian physic. A plant, **bowman's root** *(see).*

Indian pipe. A waxy white or sometimes pinkish saprophytic woodland plant, *Monotropa uniflora,* having scalelike leaves and a solitary, nodding flower.

Indian poke. A species of **hellebore** *(see).*

Indian pudding. A pudding made of cornmeal and milk and sweetened with molasses.

Indian red. An iron oxide used as a paint and cosmetic pigment.

Indian River. A lagoon extending 120 miles along the coast of east-central Florida.

Indian States. The 560 semi-independent states of India that were formerly under British protection. All except Kashmir were incorporated into either Pakistan or the Republic of India (1947–49).

Indian summer. 1. A period of mild weather, occurring in late autumn or early winter. **2.** A pleasant, tranquil, or flourishing period occurring during the end of a condition or period.

Indian Territory. A former territory occupying 31,000 square miles in the south-central United States, now part of Oklahoma.

Indian tobacco. A poisonous North American plant, *Lobelia inflata,* having light-blue flowers and rounded seed pods.

Indian turnip. 1. A plant, the **jack-in-the-pulpit** *(see).* **2.** The acrid tuber of this plant.

India paper. 1. A thin, uncoated, delicate paper made of vegetable fiber, used especially for taking impressions of engravings. **2. Bible paper** *(see).*

India rubber. A **rubber** *(see).*

In·dic (ĭn′dĭk) *adj.* **1.** Of or pertaining to India, its people, or their culture. **2.** Of, pertaining to, or constituting the Indic languages. —*n.* A branch of the Indo-European languages that comprises Sanskrit and its modern descendants, Pali, Prakrit, and Dard.

indic. 1. *Grammar.* indicative. **2.** indicator.

in·di·cant (ĭn′dĭ-kənt) *n.* Something that serves to indicate. [Latin *indicāns,* present participle of *indicāre,* INDICATE.]

in·di·cate (ĭn′dĭ-kāt′) *tr.v.* **-cated, -cating, -cates. 1. a.** To demonstrate or point out with precision: *indicate a route.* **b.** To state or exhibit in complete detail. **2.** To serve as a sign, symptom, or token of; signify: *"The cracking and booming of the ice indicate a change of temperature."* (Thoreau). **3.** To suggest or demonstrate the necessity, expedience, or advisability of: *The symptoms indicate immediate surgery.* **4.** To state, disclose, or express briefly. [Latin *indicāre,* to show, from *index,* forefinger, indicator, INDEX.] —**in′di·ca·to′ry** (-kə-tôr′ē, -tōr′ē) *adj.*

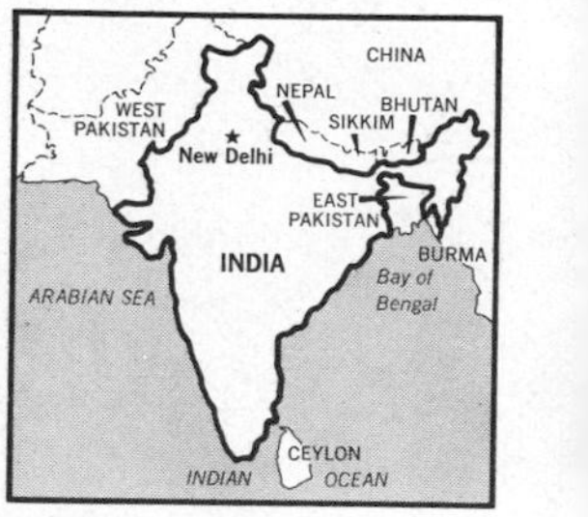

India

in·di·ca·tion (ĭn′dĭ-kā′shən) *n.* **1.** The action of indicating. **2. a.** Something that indicates; a sign, token, or symptom. **b.** Something indicated as necessary or expedient. **3.** The degree indicated by a measuring instrument. —See Synonyms at **sign.**

in·dic·a·tive (ĭn-dĭk′ə-tĭv) *adj.* **1.** Serving to point out or indicate. **2.** *Abbr.* **indic.** *Grammar.* Pertaining to or designating a verb mood used to indicate that the denoted act or condition is an objective fact. Compare **subjunctive.** —*n. Abbr.* **indic.** *Grammar.* **1.** The indicative mood. **2.** A verb in this mood. —**in·dic′a·tive·ly** *adv.*

in·di·ca·tor (ĭn′dĭ-kā′tər) *n. Abbr.* **indic. 1.** One that indicates, as a pointer or index. **2.** Any of various meters, gauges, or other instruments that are used to monitor the operation or condition of an engine, furnace, electrical network, reservoir, or other physical system. **3.** The needle, dial, or other registering device on such an instrument. **4.** *Chemistry.* Any of various substances, such as litmus or phenolphthalein, that indicate the presence, absence, or concentration of a substance, or the degree of reaction between two or more substances, by means of a characteristic change, especially in color.

in·di·ces. Alternate plural of **index.**

in·di·ci·a (ĭn-dĭsh′ē-ə, -dĭsh′ə) *pl.n.* **1.** Identifying marks or indications; signs. **2.** Markings on bulk mailings used as a substitute for stamps or cancellations. [Latin, plural of *indicium,* sign, from *indicāre,* INDICATE.]

in·dict (ĭn-dīt′) *tr.v.* **-dicted, -dicting, -dicts. 1.** To accuse of a crime or other offense; charge. **2.** *Law.* To make a formal accusation or indictment against by the findings of a jury, especially a grand jury. [Alteration (influenced by obsolete *indict,* to proclaim) of Middle English *enditen,* to accuse, from Norman French *enditer,* to dictate, INDITE.] —**in·dict′a·ble** *adj.* —**in·dict·ee′** (-dī-tē′) *n.* —**in·dict′er, in·dic′tor** (-dī′tər) *n.*

in·dic·tion (ĭn-dĭk′shən) *n.* A 15-year cycle used as a chronological unit in ancient Rome and incorporated in some medieval systems. [Middle English *indiccioun,* from Late Latin *indictiō,* "proclamation" (of Diocletian fixing a 15-year assessment of property tax), from *indīcere,* to proclaim, INDITE.]

in·dict·ment (ĭn-dīt′mənt) *n.* **1.** The act of indicting or the state of being indicted. **2.** *Law.* A written statement charging a party with the commission of a crime, drawn up by the prosecuting attorney and found and presented by the grand jury.

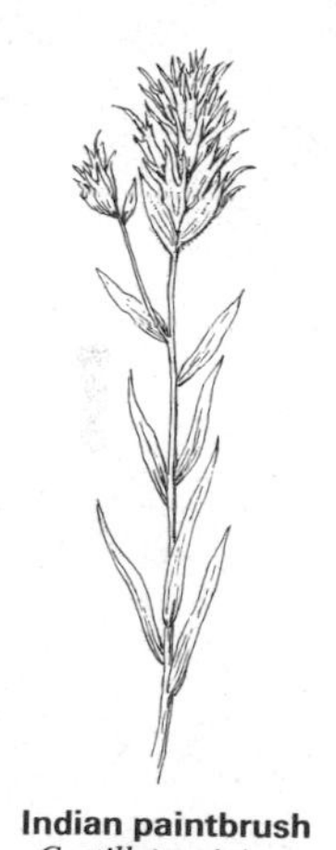
Indian paintbrush
Castilleja miniata

In·dies. See **East Indies, West Indies.**

in·dif·fer·ence (ĭn-dĭf′ər-əns) *n.* Also *archaic* **in·dif·fer·en·cy** (-ən-sē). **1.** The state or quality of being indifferent. **2.** Lack of interest or concern. **3.** Lack of importance; insignificance.

in·dif·fer·ent (ĭn-dĭf′ər-ənt) *adj.* **1.** Characterized by a lack of partiality or bias. **2.** Not mattering one way or the other; of no great importance; insignificant. **3.** Having no marked feeling for one way or the other; not liking or disliking. **4.** Having no particular interest in or concern for; apathetic. **5.** Being neither too much nor too little; moderate. **6.** Being neither good nor bad; mediocre. **7.** Being neither right nor wrong. **8.** Not active or involved; neutral. **9.** Not required, obligatory, or essential, as an observance. **10.** *Biology.* Undifferentiated, as cells or tissue. —See Synonyms at **average, careless.** [Middle English, from Old French, from Latin *indifferēns* : *in-,* not + *differēns,* DIFFERENT.] —**in·dif′fer·ent·ly** *adv.*

Synonyms: *indifferent, unconcerned, apathetic, incurious, detached, disinterested.* These adjectives mean marked by absence of interest or of self-interest. *Indifferent* and *unconcerned* can imply nothing beyond that, but sometimes they suggest that a person has a tendency to be aloof or unfeeling when a display of interest would be in order. *Apathetic* implies listlessness and lack of concern where interest would be expected or proper. *Incurious* stresses absence of intellectual interest or curiosity.

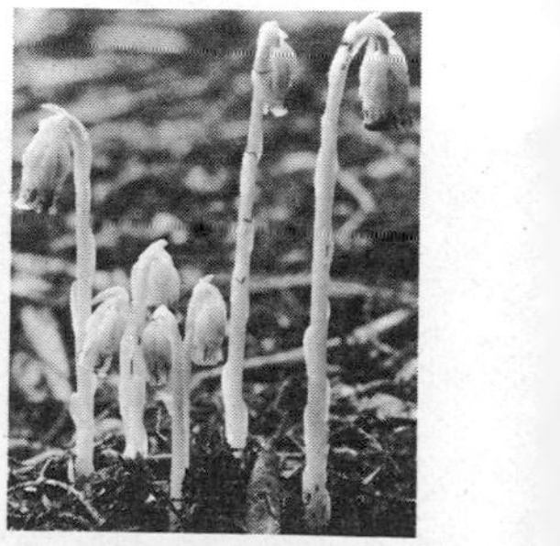
Indian pipe

t tight/th thin, path/*th* this, bathe/ŭ cut/ûr urge/v valve/w with/y yes/z zebra, size/zh vision/ə about, item, edible, gallop, circus/ à *Fr.* ami/œ *Fr.* feu, *Ger.* schön/ü *Fr.* tu, *Ger.* über/KH *Ger.* ich, *Scot.* loch/N *Fr.* bon. ***Follows main vocabulary.** **†Of obscure origin.**

Detached suggests absence of close involvement with the matter at hand, together with a striving for an objective, impersonal point of view, but not lack of interest. *Disinterested* implies impartiality and freedom from self-interest or desire for gain rather than lack of concern.

in·dif·fer·ent·ism (ĭn-dĭf′ər-ən-tĭz′əm) *n.* The belief that religions are all of like validity. —**in·dif′fer·ent·ist** *n.*

in·di·gen (ĭn′də-jən, -jĕn′) *n.* Also **in·di·gene** (-jēn′). One that is native or indigenous to an area. [Latin *indigena*, native. See **gene-** in Appendix.*]

in·di·gence (ĭn′də-jəns) *n.* Want or neediness.

in·dig·e·nous (ĭn-dĭj′ə-nəs) *adj.* **1.** Occurring or living naturally in an area; not introduced; native. **2.** Intrinsic; innate. —See Synonyms at **native.** [From Latin *indigena*, native. See **indigen.**] —**in·dig′e·nous·ly** *adv.* —**in·dig′e·nous·ness** *n.*

in·di·gent (ĭn′də-jənt) *adj.* **1.** Lacking the means of subsistence; impoverished; needy. **2.** *Archaic.* Lacking or deficient in something specified. Usually used with *of.* —See Synonyms at **poor.** —*n.* A destitute or needy person. [Middle English, from Old French, from Latin *indigēns*, present participle of *indigēre*, to lack : *indi-*, strengthened form of *in-*, in + *egēre*, to lack, want (see **eg-** in Appendix*).] —**in′di·gent·ly** *adv.*

in·di·gest·ed (ĭn′dī-jĕs′tĭd, ĭn′dĭ-) *adj. Archaic.* **1. a.** Not carefully thought over or considered. **b.** Shapeless or chaotic. **2.** Not digested.

in·di·gest·i·ble (ĭn′dī-jĕs′tə-bəl, ĭn′dĭ-) *adj.* Difficult or impossible to digest. —**in′di·gest′i·bil′i·ty** *n.* —**in′di·gest′i·bly** *adv.*

in·di·ges·tion (ĭn′dī-jĕs′chən, ĭn′dĭ-) *n.* **1.** The inability to digest food. **2.** Discomfort or illness resulting from this.

In·di·gir·ka (ĭn′dĭ-gîr′kə). A river rising in the east-central Yakut A.S.S.R. and flowing 1,113 miles north to the East Siberian Sea.

in·dign (ĭn-dīn′) *adj. Obsolete.* **1.** Unworthy. **2.** Shameful; disgraceful. [Middle English *indigne*, from Old French, from Latin *indignus* : *in-*, not + *dignus*, worthy (see **dek-**[1] in Appendix*).]

in·dig·nant (ĭn-dĭg′nənt) *adj.* Characterized by or filled with indignation. [Latin *indignāns*, present participle of *indignārī*, to regard as unworthy, from *indignus*, unworthy, INDIGN.] —**in·dig′nant·ly** *adv.*

in·dig·na·tion (ĭn′dĭg-nā′shən) *n.* Anger aroused by something unjust, mean, or unworthy. See Synonyms at **anger.** [Middle English *indignacioun*, from Latin *indignātiō*, from *indignārī*, to regard as unworthy. See **indignant.**]

in·dig·ni·ty (ĭn-dĭg′nə-tē) *n., pl.* **-ties. 1. a.** Humiliating, degrading, or abusive treatment of an individual. **b.** An offense to dignity; affront. **2.** *Obsolete.* The want of dignity or honor. [Latin *indignitās*, from *indignus*, unworthy, INDIGN.]

in·di·go (ĭn′dĭ-gō′) *n., pl.* **-gos** or **-goes. 1.** Any of various plants of the genus *Indigofera*, some of which yield a blue dyestuff. **2.** Any of several similar or related plants. **3.** A blue dye obtained from indigo or other plants or produced synthetically. **4.** *Abbr.* **ind.** Dark blue to grayish purplish blue. See **color.** [Earlier *indico*, from Spanish, from Latin *indicum*, from Greek *indikon (pharmakon)*, "Indian (dye)," from *Indikos*, Indian, from *India*, INDIA.]

indigo bunting. A small bird, *Passerina cyanea*, of North and Central America, the male of which has deep-blue plumage.

in·di·goid (ĭn′dĭ-goid′) *adj.* Of or relating to those dyes that produce indigo blue. —*n.* Such a dye.

indigo snake. A nonvenomous bluish-black snake, *Drymarchon corais*, of the southern United States and northern Mexico.

in·dig·o·tin (ĭn-dĭg′ə-tən, ĭn′də-gō′-) *n.* A dark-blue, crystalline compound, $C_{16}H_{10}N_2O_2$, the principal coloring matter of indigo. [INDIGO + -IN.]

in·di·rect (ĭn′dĭ-rĕkt′, -dī-rĕkt′) *adj.* **1.** Not taking a direct course; roundabout. **2.** Not descending in a straight line of succession. Said of an inheritance or title. **3. a.** Not straight to the point; circumlocutory. **b.** Evasive; devious. **4.** Not directly planned for; secondary: *indirect benefits.* **5.** Relating to or characteristic of indirect discourse. In this sense, also "oblique." —**in·di·rect′ly** *adv.* —**in·di·rect′ness** *n.*

Synonyms: *indirect, circuitous, roundabout.* These adjectives mean not leading directly to a destination. *Indirect* refers to any deviation from the shortest route between starting point and destination. *Circuitous* and *roundabout* are stronger in their suggestion of time-consuming deviation from a straight path; *circuitous* implies a twisting or winding course, and *roundabout* one that circles or winds. Figuratively, the terms are applied to procedure or discourse that is not straightforward. In this sense they can imply an effort to deceive or evade.

indirect discourse. Discourse reporting the words of another with consequent changes of person and tense to conform the reported statement to the sentence in which it is included.

in·di·rec·tion (ĭn′dĭ-rĕk′shən, ĭn′dī-) *n.* **1.** The quality or state of being indirect. **2.** Aimlessness. **3.** Lack of straightforwardness. **4.** Deviousness.

indirect lighting. Illumination by reflected or diffused light.

indirect object. A grammatical object indirectly affected by the action of a verb; for example, *me* in *Sing me a song* and *the turtle* in *He feeds the turtle lettuce* are indirect objects.

indirect tax. A tax demanded of persons who ultimately pass on the burden of the tax to others; especially, a tax on manufactured or imported goods passed on to the consumer in the form of higher prices.

in·dis·creet (ĭn′dĭs-krēt′) *adj.* Lacking discretion; injudicious; imprudent. —**in′dis·creet′ly** *adv.* —**in′dis·creet′ness** *n.*

in·dis·crete (ĭn′dĭs-krēt′) *adj.* Not divided or divisible into separate parts; unified.

in·dis·cre·tion (ĭn′dĭs-krĕsh′ən) *n.* **1.** Lack of discretion. **2.** An indiscreet act or remark.

in·dis·crim·i·nate (ĭn′dĭs-krĭm′ə-nĭt) *adj.* **1.** Wanting in discrimination: *indiscriminate admiration of power.* **2.** Random; haphazard. **3.** Confused; motley. **4.** Not properly restricted or restrained; promiscuous. —**in′dis·crim′i·nate·ly** *adv.* —**in′dis·crim′i·nate·ness** *n.*

in·dis·crim·i·na·tion (ĭn′dĭs-krĭm′ə-nā′shən) *n.* The condition or quality of being indiscriminate. —**in′dis·crim′i·na′tive** *adj.*

in·dis·pen·sa·ble (ĭn′dĭs-pĕn′sə-bəl) *adj.* **1.** Incapable of being dispensed with; essential; required. **2.** Incapable of being set aside or escaped; inevitable. —See Synonyms at **necessary.** —*n.* An indispensable person or thing. —**in′dis·pen′sa·bil′i·ty, in′dis·pen′sa·ble·ness** *n.* —**in′dis·pen′sa·bly** *adv.*

in·dis·pose (ĭn′dĭs-pōz′) *tr.v.* **-posed, -posing, -poses. 1.** To make averse; disincline. **2.** To render unfit; disqualify. **3.** *Archaic.* To cause to be or feel ill; sicken.

in·dis·posed (ĭn′dĭs-pōzd′) *adj.* **1.** Mildly ill. **2.** Disinclined; unwilling. —See Synonyms at **sick.**

in·dis·po·si·tion (ĭn′dĭs-pə-zĭsh′ən) *n.* **1.** Disinclination; unwillingness. **2.** A minor ailment.

in·dis·put·a·ble (ĭn′dĭs-pyōō′tə-bəl) *adj.* Beyond doubt; undeniable. —**in′dis·put′a·ble·ness** *n.* —**in′dis·put′a·bly** *adv.*

in·dis·sol·u·ble (ĭn′dĭ-sŏl′yə-bəl) *adj.* **1.** Impossible to break or undo; binding: *an indissoluble contract.* **2.** Incapable of being dissolved, disintegrated, or decomposed. —**in′dis·sol′u·bil′i·ty, in′dis·sol′u·ble·ness** *n.* —**in′dis·sol′u·bly** *adv.*

in·dis·tinct (ĭn′dĭs-tĭngkt′) *adj.* **1.** Not clearly delineated. **2.** Faint; dim. —**in′dis·tinct′ly** *adv.* —**in′dis·tinct′ness** *n.*

in·dis·tinc·tive (ĭn′dĭs-tĭngk′tĭv) *adj.* **1.** Lacking distinctive qualities; not distinctive. **2.** Undiscriminating. —**in′dis·tinc′tive·ly** *adv.* —**in′dis·tinc′tive·ness** *n.*

in·dis·tin·guish·a·ble (ĭn′dĭs-tĭng′gwĭ-shə-bəl) *adj.* Not distinguishable, especially: **a.** Not readily perceptible. **b.** Without distinctive qualities. —**in′dis·tin′guish·a·ble·ness, in′dis·tin′guish·a·bil′i·ty** *n.* —**in′dis·tin′guish·a·bly** *adv.*

in·dite (ĭn-dīt′) *tr.v.* **-dited, -diting, -dites. 1.** To write; compose. **2.** To set down in writing. **3.** *Obsolete.* To dictate. [Middle English *enditen*, to compose, write down, from Norman French *enditer*, from Vulgar Latin *indictāre* (unattested), frequentative of Latin *indīcere* (past participle *indictus*), to proclaim : *in-*, toward + *dīcere*, to pronounce (see **deik-** in Appendix*).] —**in·dite′ment** *n.* —**in·dit′er** *n.*

in·di·um (ĭn′dē-əm) *n. Symbol* **In** A soft, malleable, silvery-white metallic element found primarily in ores of zinc and tin, used as a plating over silver in making mirrors, in plating aircraft bearings, and in compounds for making transistors. Atomic number 49, atomic weight 114.82, melting point 156.61°C, boiling point 2,000°C, specific gravity 7.31, valences 1, 2, 3. See **element.** [New Latin, from Latin *indicum*, INDIGO (from the indigo-blue color of its spectrum).]

in·di·vi·du·al (ĭn′də-vĭj′ōō-əl) *adj.* **1. a.** Of or relating to a single human being. **b.** By or for one person: *an individual portion.* **2.** Existing as a distinct entity; single; separate. **3.** Distinguished by particular attributes; distinctive: *"There was nothing individual about him except a deep scar . . . across his right cheek"* (Rebecca West). **4.** Indivisible as an entity; inseparable. —See Synonyms at **characteristic, single.** —*n.* **1. a.** A single human being considered separately from his group or from society. **b.** A single organism as distinguished from a group or colony. **2.** An independent, strong-willed person. **3.** A particular person. [Middle English *indyvyduall*, separate, indivisible, from Medieval Latin *indīviduālis*, from Latin *indīviduus*, indivisible : *in-*, not + *dīviduus*, divisible, from *dīvidere*, to DIVIDE.] —**in′di·vi′du·al·ly** *adv.*

Usage: *Individual* (noun), in the sense of a person, is most fitting in examples in which a single human being is distinguished from a group or mass, by contrast or stress on individuality: *the individual's right to dissent from a majority view; an individual to the core.* In modern usage, *individual* has less acceptance when it is employed to indicate eccentricity or disparagement: *She was an odd but fascinating individual* (acceptable to 55 per cent of the Usage Panel). *He could be a disagreeable individual* (acceptable to 47 per cent). It has still less acceptance when it has no meaning that the word *person* would not convey more appropriately: *Two individuals sought to influence the witness' testimony* (acceptable to only 38 per cent of the Panel).

in·di·vid·u·al·ism (ĭn′də-vĭj′ōō-ə-lĭz′əm) *n.* **1.** Individuality. **2.** The assertion of one's uniqueness. **3.** *Economics.* **a.** The theory that a citizen should have freedom in his economic pursuits and should succeed by his own initiative. **b.** The practice of this: *rugged individualism.* **4.** The doctrine that the interests of the individual should take precedence over the interests of the state or social group.

in·di·vid·u·al·ist (ĭn′də-vĭj′ōō-ə-lĭst) *n.* **1.** One who asserts his individuality by his independence of thought and action. **2.** One who advocates individualism. —**in′di·vid′u·al·ist, in′di·vid′u·al·is′tic** *adj.* —**in′di·vid′u·al·is′ti·cal·ly** *adv.*

in·di·vid·u·al·i·ty (ĭn′də-vĭj′ōō-ăl′ə-tē) *n., pl.* **-ties. 1.** The quality of being individual; distinctness. **2.** The aggregate of distinguishing attributes of a person or thing. **3.** A single, distinct entity. **4.** *Archaic.* Indivisibility.

in·di·vid·u·al·ize (ĭn′dĭ-vĭj′ōō-ə-līz′) *tr.v.* **-ized, -izing, -izes. 1.** To give individuality to. **2.** To consider individually; specify; particularize. **3.** To modify to suit a particular individual. —**in′di·vid′u·al·i·za′tion** *n.*

in·di·vid·u·ate (ĭn′də-vĭj′ōō-āt′) *tr.v.* **-ated, -ating, -ates. 1.** To individualize. **2.** To form into a separate and distinct entity.

in·di·vid·u·a·tion (ĭn′də-vĭj′ōō-ā′shən) *n.* **1.** The act or process of individuating; specifically, the process by which social individuals become differentiated one from the other. **2.** The condition of being individuated; individuality.

in·di·vis·i·ble (ĭn′də-vĭz′ə-bəl) *adj.* **1.** Incapable of being divided. **2.** *Mathematics.* Incapable of being divided exactly. —**in′di·vis′i·ble·ness, in′di·vis′i·bil′i·ty** *n.* —**in′di·vis′i·bly** *adv.*

Indo–. Indicates India or East Indian; for example, **Indochina.**

In·do-Ar·y·an (ĭn′dō-âr′ē-ən) *adj.* **1.** Belonging to or characteristic of any of the Indo-European-speaking peoples of the Indian subcontinent. **2.** Indo-Iranian. —*n.* **1.** One of the Indo-Aryan peoples. **2.** An Indo-Iranian.

In·do·chi·na (ĭn′dō-chī′nə). **1.** Formerly **French In·do·chi·na.** The former French colonies and protectorates of Cochin China, Annam, Tonkin, Laos, and Cambodia. **2.** The southeastern peninsula of Asia, including North Vietnam, South Vietnam, Laos, Cambodia, Thailand, Burma, and the Malay Peninsula. —**In′do·chi′nese′** *adj.* & *n.*

in·doc·ile (ĭn-dŏs′əl) *adj.* Difficult to control or instruct; not docile. —**in′do·cil′i·ty** *n.*

in·doc·tri·nate (ĭn-dŏk′trə-nāt′) *tr.v.* **-nated, -nating, -nates. 1.** To instruct in a body of doctrine. **2.** To teach to accept a system of thought uncritically. —**in·doc′tri·na′tion** *n.*

In·do-Eu·ro·pe·an (ĭn′dō-yŏŏr′ə-pē′ən) *adj.* **1.** Belonging to or constituting a family of languages that includes the Germanic, Celtic, Italic, Baltic, Slavic, Greek, Armenian, Hittite, Tocharian, Iranian, and Indic groups. **2.** Belonging to or constituting Proto-Indo-European. **3.** Of, relating to, or characteristic of cultural traits appearing to be common to or widely distributed among peoples who speak Indo-European languages, and presumed to be inherited from the original speakers of Proto-Indo-European. —*n.* **1.** The Indo-European family of languages. **2.** Proto-Indo-European. **3.** A member of any of the peoples who speak Indo-European languages. **4.** A member of the presumed prehistoric people who spoke Proto-Indo-European. ***Note:*** The Appendix of this Dictionary contains a description of Proto-Indo-European and a lexicon of the Indo-European roots that are ancestral to the English words in this Dictionary. [Named from the geographical extremities of the distribution of the languages : INDO- + EUROPEAN.]

In·do-Eu·ro·pe·an·ist (ĭn′dō-yŏŏr′ə-pē′ə-nĭst) *n.* A historical linguist specializing in the study of Indo-European.

In·do-Ger·man·ic (ĭn′dō-jər-măn′ĭk) *adj. Obsolete.* Indo-European. —*n. Obsolete.* Indo-European. [Translation of German *indogermanisch.*]

In·do-Hit·tite (ĭn′dō-hĭt′īt′) *n.* Indo-European together with Hittite. Used by those who do not consider Hittite to be itself within the Indo-European family proper.

In·do-I·ra·ni·an (ĭn′dō-ĭ-rā′nē-ən, -ī-rā′nē-ən) *adj.* Belonging to or constituting the branch of Indo-European made up of the Indic and the Iranian language groups. —*n.* The Indo-Iranian branch of Indo-European.

in·dole (ĭn′dōl′) *n.* A white crystalline compound, C_8H_7N, obtained from coal tar and used in perfumery, medicine, and as a flavoring. [IND(IGO) + -OLE.]

in·do·lent (ĭn′də-lənt) *adj.* **1.** Disinclined to work; habitually lazy. **2.** *Pathology.* Causing little or no pain: *an indolent tumor.* [Late Latin *indolēns,* painless : Latin *in-,* not + *dolēns,* present participle of *dolēre,* to give pain, feel pain (see **del-³** in Appendix*).] —**in′do·lence** *n.*

in·dom·i·ta·ble (ĭn-dŏm′ə-tə-bəl) *adj.* Incapable of being overcome, subdued, or vanquished; unconquerable. [Late Latin *indomitābilis,* untamable : Latin *in-,* not + *domitāre,* frequentative of *domāre* (past participle *domitus*), to tame (see **deme-²** in Appendix*).] —**in·dom′i·ta·bly** *adv.*

In·do·ne·sia (ĭn′də-nē′zhə, -shə). **1.** Officially, Republic of Indonesia. Formerly **Neth·er·lands East In·dies** (nĕth′ər-ləndz; ĭn′dēz), **Dutch East In·dies.** A republic of southeastern Asia, 735,268 square miles in area, comprising the islands of Sumatra, Java, Sulawesi, and the Moluccas, as well as numerous other islands, and Indonesian Timor, West Irian on New Guinea, and Kalimantan on Borneo. Population, 102,200,000. Capital, Djakarta on Java. **2.** Loosely, the Malay Archipelago.

In·do·ne·sian (ĭn′də-nē′zhən, -shən) *n.* **1.** A native or inhabitant of the Republic of Indonesia. **2.** A member of a hypothetical non-Malay race of Indonesia, Malaysia, and the Philippines, having both Mongoloid and Polynesian characteristics. **3.** A group of dialects derived chiefly from Malay and constituting the national language of the Republic of Indonesia. —*adj.* Of or pertaining to Indonesia, its people, or their language.

Indonesian Ti·mor (tē′môr′, tī-môr′). Formerly **Neth·er·lands Ti·mor** (nĕth′ər-ləndz). The western part of the island of Timor in the Malay Archipelago, a possession of Indonesia occupying 5,765 square miles. Population, 703,000. Capital, Kupang.

in·door (ĭn′dôr′, -dōr′) *adj.* **1.** Of, pertaining to, or situated in the interior of a house or other building: *an indoor pool.* **2.** Carried on within doors: *an indoor life; an indoor party.* [Short for earlier *within-door* : WITHIN + DOOR.]

in·doors (ĭn-dôrz′, -dōrz′) *adv.* In or into a house or other building. [Short for earlier *withindoors* : WITHIN + DOORS.]

In·do-Pa·cif·ic (ĭn′dō-pə-sĭf′ĭk). A region including intertropical Asia and the western Pacific. —**In′do-Pa·cif′ic** *adj.*

In·dore (ĭn-dôr′, -dōr′). **1.** A former princely state of central India, incorporated in 1956 into Madhya Pradesh. **2.** A city and textile-manufacturing center of western Madhya Pradesh, Republic of India. Population, 423,000.

in·dorse. Variant of **endorse.**

In·dra (ĭn′drə). *Hinduism.* A principal Vedic deity associated with rain and thunder. [Sanskrit *Indraḥ*†.]

in·draft (ĭn′drăft′, -dräft′) *n.* **1.** A pulling or drawing inward. **2.** An inward flow or current: *an indraft of cold air.*

in·drawn (ĭn′drôn′) *adj.* **1.** Drawn in. **2.** Introspective.

in·dri (ĭn′drē) *n., pl.* **-dris.** A large lemur, *Indri indri,* of Madagascar, having silky fur and a short tail. [From Malagasay *indry!* look! (mistakenly assumed by the French naturalist Pierre Sonnerat to be the animal's name).]

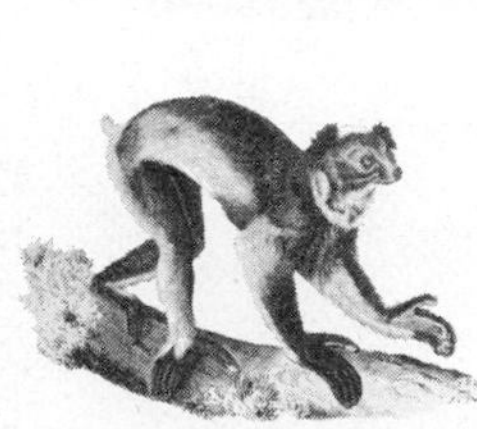
indri

in·du·bi·ta·ble (ĭn-dōō′bə-tə-bəl, ĭn-dyōō′-) *adj.* Too apparent to be doubted; unquestionable. —**in·du′bi·ta·bly** *adv.*

in·duce (ĭn-dōōs′, -dyōōs′) *tr.v.* **-duced, -ducing, -duces. 1.** To lead or move by influence or persuasion; to prevail upon: *finally induced him to give up smoking.* **2.** To stimulate the occurrence of; cause: *induce childbirth.* **3.** To infer by inductive reasoning. **4.** *Physics.* To produce (an electric current or magnetic effect) by induction. —See Synonyms at **persuade.** [Middle English *inducen,* from Latin *indūcere* : *in-,* in + *dūcere,* to lead (see **deuk-** in Appendix*).] —**in·duc′er** *n.* —**in·duc′i·ble** *adj.*

in·duce·ment (ĭn-dōōs′mənt, ĭn-dyōōs′-) *n.* **1.** The act or process of inducing: *the inducement of sleep.* **2.** That which induces; an incentive; motive. **3.** An introductory or background statement explaining the main allegations in a legal proceeding.

in·duct (ĭn-dŭkt′) *tr.v.* **-ducted, -ducting, -ducts. 1. a.** To place ceremoniously or formally in an office or benefice; install. **b.** To admit as a member of; to initiate. **c.** To call into military service. **2.** *Physics.* To induce. [Middle English *inducten,* from Medieval Latin *indūcere* (past participle *inductus*), from Latin, to lead in, INDUCE.] —**in′duc·tee′** *n.*

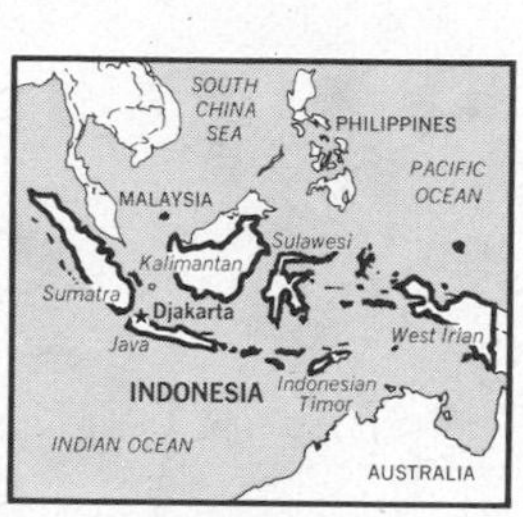

Indonesia

in·duc·tance (ĭn-dŭk′təns) *n.* A circuit element, typically a conducting coil, in which electromotive force is generated by electromagnetic induction.

in·duc·tion (ĭn-dŭk′shən) *n.* **1.** The act of inducting or of being inducted. **2.** *Electricity.* **a.** The generation of electromotive force in a closed circuit by a varying magnetic flux through the circuit. Also called "electromagnetic induction." **b.** The charging of an isolated conducting object by momentarily grounding it while a charged body is nearby. Also called "electrostatic induction." **3. a.** *Logic.* A principle of reasoning to a conclusion about all the members of a class from examination of only a few members of the class; broadly, reasoning from the particular to the general. Compare **deduction. b.** *Mathematics.* A deductive method of proof in which verification of a proposition consists of proving the first case and the case immediately following an arbitrary case for which the proposition is assumed to be correct. **4.** The act of inducing. **5.** A preface or preamble.

induction coil. A transformer, often used in automotive ignition systems, in which an interrupted, low-voltage direct current in the primary is converted into an intermittent, high-voltage current in the secondary.

in·duc·tive (ĭn-dŭk′tĭv) *adj.* **1.** Of or utilizing induction: *inductive method.* **2.** *Electricity.* Of or arising from inductance: *inductive reactance.* **3.** Causing or influencing; inducing. **4.** Introductory. —**in·duc′tive·ly** *adv.* —**in·duc′tive·ness** *n.*

in·duc·tor (ĭn-dŭk′tər) *n.* **1.** A person who inducts, as into office. **2.** *Electricity.* A device that functions by or introduces inductance into a circuit.

in·due. Variant of **endue.**

in·dulge (ĭn-dŭlj′) *v.* **-dulged, -dulging, -dulges.** —*tr.* **1.** To yield to the desires and whims of (oneself or another), especially to an excessive degree; humor; pamper. **2.** To gratify or yield to: *indulge a craving for chocolate.* **3.** To grant an ecclesiastical indulgence or dispensation to. —*intr.* To allow oneself some special pleasure; indulge oneself. Used with *in: indulge in an afternoon nap.* —See Synonyms at **pamper.** [Latin *indulgēre*†, to be forbearing, grant as a favor.] —**in·dulg′er** *n.*

in·dul·gence (ĭn-dŭl′jəns) *n.* **1.** The act of indulging or the state of being indulgent. **2.** Something indulged in: *Sports cars are an expensive indulgence.* **3. a.** Something granted as a favor or privilege. **b.** Permission to extend the time of payment or performance, as in business. **4.** Liberal or lenient treatment; tolerance: *the government's indulgence of the new nation's political vagaries.* **5.** *Roman Catholic Church.* The remission of temporal punishment due for a sin after the guilt has been forgiven. **6.** *English History.* A royal dispensation during the reigns of Charles II and James II granting special religious freedom to the Nonconformists and the Roman Catholics. —*tr.v.* **indulgenced, -gencing, -gences.** *Roman Catholic Church.* To grant an indulgence to.

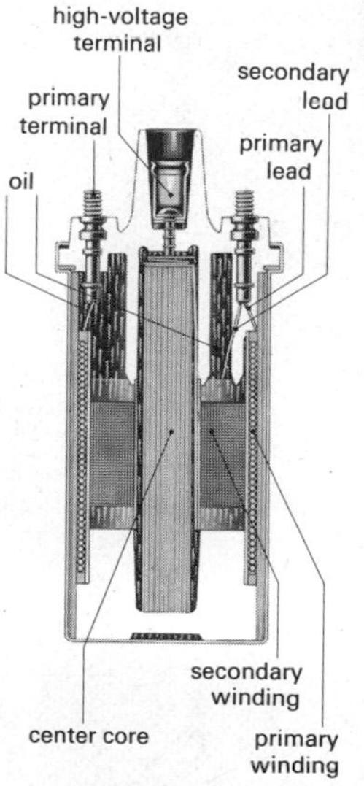

induction coil

in·dul·gent (ĭn-dŭl′jənt) *adj.* Showing, characterized by, or given to indulgence; lenient: *an indulgent employer.* See Synonyms at **thoughtful.** —**in·dul′gent·ly** *adv.*

in·dult (ĭn-dŭlt′) *n.* A temporary privilege granted a person in the Roman Catholic Church. [Middle English, from Medieval Latin *indultum,* from Latin *indultus,* past participle of *indulgēre,* INDULGE.]

in·du·pli·cate (ĭn-dōō′plĭ-kĭt, ĭn-dyōō′-) *adj. Botany.* Having the edges folded or turned inward. [IN- (in, inward) + Latin *duplicātus,* doubled up, DUPLICATE.]

in·du·rate (ĭn′dōō-rāt′, ĭn′dyōō-) *v.* **-rated, -rating, -rates.** —*tr.* **1.** To make hard; harden. **2.** To make callous. —*intr.* **1.** To harden. **2.** To become obdurate. —*adj.* (ĭn′dōō-rĭt, ĭn′dyōō-). Hardened; obstinate; unfeeling. [Latin *indūrāre,* to harden : *in-* (intensive) + *dūrāre,* to harden, from *dūrus,* hard (see **deru-** in Appendix*).] —**in′du·ra′tion** *n.* —**in′du·ra′tive** *adj.*

In·dus¹ (ĭn′dəs). A river rising in southwestern Tibet and flowing 1,900 miles northwest through Tibet, then southwest through Pakistan to the Arabian Sea.

In·dus² (ĭn′dəs) *n.* A constellation in the Southern Hemisphere near Tucana and Pavo. Also called the "Indian."

t tight/th thin, path/*th* this, bathe/ŭ cut/ûr urge/v valve/w with/y yes/z zebra, size/zh vision/ə about, item, edible, gallop, circus/ à *Fr.* ami/œ *Fr.* feu, *Ger.* schön/ü *Fr.* tu, *Ger.* über/KH *Ger.* ich, *Scot.* loch/N *Fr.* bon. ***Follows main vocabulary.** †**Of obscure origin.**

in·du·si·um (ĭn-dōō′zē-əm, -zhē-əm, ĭn-dyōō′-) *n.*, *pl.* **-sia** (-zē-ə, -zhē-ə). An enclosing membrane, as that covering the sorus of a fern. [Latin, tunic, from Greek *endusis*, from *enduein*, to sink or slip into, put on : *en-*, in + *duein*, to sink (see **adytum**).]

in·dus·tri·al (ĭn-dŭs′trē-əl) *adj.* *Abbr.* **ind.** **1.** Of, pertaining to, or derived from industry: *an industrial exhibition.* **2.** Having highly developed industries: *an industrial nation.* **3.** Employed, required, or used in industry: *industrial supplies.* —*n.* **1.** A person employed in industry. **2.** An industrial firm. **3.** *Plural.* Stocks or bonds issued by an industrial enterprise.

industrial arts. A subject of study in schools aimed at developing the manual and technical skills required in industry.

in·dus·tri·al·ism (ĭn-dŭs′trē-ə-lĭz′əm) *n.* An economic system in which industries are dominant. —**in·dus′tri·al·ist** *n.*

in·dus·tri·al·ize (ĭn-dŭs′trē-ə-līz′) *v.* **-ized, -izing, izes.** —*tr.* **1.** To develop industry in. **2.** To organize as an industry. —*intr.* To become industrial. —**in·dus′tri·al·i·za′tion** *n.*

industrial revolution. **1.** Social and economic changes brought about when extensive mechanization of production systems results in a shift from home manufacturing to large-scale factory production. **2.** *Capital* I, *capital* R. A period of such change beginning in the middle of the 18th century in England.

industrial union. A labor union to which all the workers of a particular industry can belong regardless of their trade. Compare **craft union.**

Industrial Workers of the World. *Abbr.* **IWW, I.W.W.** An international industrial labor organization founded in Chicago in 1905 and in existence until the early 1920's.

in·dus·tri·ous (ĭn-dŭs′trē-əs) *adj.* **1.** Diligently active; assiduous in work or study. **2.** *Obsolete.* Skillful; clever. —See Synonyms at **busy.** [From Latin *industriōsus*, from *industria*, skill, **INDUSTRY.**] —**in·dus′tri·ous·ly** *adv.* —**in·dus′tri·ous·ness** *n.*

in·dus·try (ĭn′də-strē) *n.*, *pl.* **-tries.** *Abbr.* **ind.** **1.** The commercial production and sale of goods and services. **2.** A specific branch of manufacture and trade: *the textile industry.* **3.** Industrial management as distinguished from labor. **4.** Diligence; assiduity. —See Synonyms at **business.** [Middle English *industrie*, skill, diligence, from Old French, from Latin *industria.* See **ster-²** in Appendix.*]

in·dwell (ĭn-dwĕl′) *v.* **-dwelt** (-dwĕlt′), **-dwelling, -dwells.** —*intr.* To abide as a divine inner spirit, force, or principle. Usually used with *in.* —*tr.* To abide within as a divine spirit, force, or principle. —**in′dwell′er** *n.*

-ine¹. Indicates of, pertaining to, or belonging to; for example, **Ursuline, Sistine.** [Middle English *-ine, -in*, from Old French *-in*, from Latin *-īnus, -inus*, from Greek *-inos.*]

-ine², -in. Indicates halogens; for example, **chlorine, fluorine.** [Middle English *-ine, -in*, from Old French *-ine*, from Latin *-īna*, feminine of *-īnus*, **-INE** (pertaining to).]

-ine³. Indicates made of or resembling; for example, **opaline, petaline.** [Middle English *-ine*, **-INE** (pertaining to).]

in·e·bri·ant (ĭn-ē′brē-ənt) *adj.* Intoxicating. —*n.* An intoxicant.

in·e·bri·ate (ĭn-ē′brē-āt′) *tr.v.* **-ated, -ating, -ates.** **1.** To make drunk; intoxicate. **2.** To exhilarate or stupefy with or as if with alcohol. —*adj.* (ĭn-ē′brē-ĭt). Intoxicated. —*n.* (ĭn-ē′brē-ĭt). An intoxicated person; especially, a drunkard. [Latin *inēbriāre* : *in-* (intensive) + *ēbriāre*, to intoxicate, from *ēbrius*, drunk (see **egw-** in Appendix*).] —**in·e′bri·a′tion** *n.*

in·e·bri·at·ed (ĭn-ē′brē-ā′tĭd) *adj.* Exhilarated or confused by or as if by alcohol; intoxicated; drunk.

in·e·bri·e·ty (ĭn′ĭ-brī′ə-tē) *n.* Drunkenness; intoxication.

in·ed·i·ble (ĭn-ĕd′ə-bəl) *adj.* Not suitable for food; not edible.

in·ed·it·ed (ĭn-ĕd′ĭ-tĭd) *adj.* **1.** Not edited. **2.** Not published.

in·ef·fa·ble (ĭn-ĕf′ə-bəl) *adj.* **1.** Beyond expression; indescribable or unspeakable: *ineffable delight.* **2.** Not to be uttered; taboo: *the ineffable name of the Deity.* [Middle English, from Old French, from Latin *ineffābilis* : *in-*, not + *effābilis*, **EFFABLE.**] —**in·ef′fa·bil′i·ty, in·ef′fa·ble·ness** *n.* —**in·ef′fa·bly** *adv.*

in·ef·face·a·ble (ĭn′ĭ-fā′sə-bəl) *adj.* Not effaceable; indelible. —**in′ef·face′a·bil′i·ty** *n.* —**in′ef·face′a·bly** *adv.*

in·ef·fec·tive (ĭn′ĭ-fĕk′tĭv) *adj.* **1.** Not effective; ineffectual. **2.** Incompetent. —**in′ef·fec′tive·ly** *adv.* —**in′ef·fec′tive·ness** *n.*

in·ef·fec·tu·al (ĭn′ĭ-fĕk′chōō-əl) *adj.* **1.** Not effectual; vain. **2.** Powerless; impotent: *an ineffectual king.* —**in′ef·fec′tu·al′i·ty, in′ef·fec′tu·al·ness** *n.* —**in′ef·fec′tu·al·ly** *adv.*

in·ef·fi·ca·cious (ĭn′ĕf-ĭ-kā′shəs) *adj.* Not producing a desired effect or result; ineffective. —**in′ef·fi·ca′cious·ly** *adv.*

in·ef·fi·ca·cy (ĭn-ĕf′ĭ-kə-sē) *n.* The state or quality of being inefficacious.

in·ef·fi·cien·cy (ĭn′ĭ-fĭsh′ən-sē) *n.* The quality, condition, or fact of being inefficient.

in·ef·fi·cient (ĭn′ĭ-fĭsh′ənt) *adj.* **1.** Not efficient. **2.** Wanting in ability; incompetent. **3.** Wasteful of time, energy, or materials. **4.** Not producing the intended result. —**in′ef·fi′cient·ly** *adv.*

in·e·las·tic (ĭn′ĭ-lăs′tĭk) *adj.* Not elastic; unyielding; unadaptable. See Synonyms at **stiff.** —**in′e·las·tic′i·ty** (-lă-stĭs′ə-tē) *n.*

in·el·e·gant (ĭn-ĕl′ə-gənt) *adj.* **1.** Lacking elegance. **2.** Coarse; vulgar. [Old French, from Latin *inēlegāns* : *in-*, not + *ēlegāns*, **ELEGANT.**] —**in·el′e·gant·ly** *adv.* —**in·el′e·gance** *n.*

in·el·i·gi·ble (ĭn-ĕl′ə-jə-bəl) *adj.* **1.** Not qualified for some office or position. **2.** Not worthy of being chosen. —*n.* A person who is not eligible. —**in·el′i·gi·bil′i·ty** *n.* —**in·el′i·gi·bly** *adv.*

in·el·o·quent (ĭn-ĕl′ə-kwənt) *adj.* Not eloquent; not fluent or vivid in expression. —**in·el′o·quence** *n.* —**in·el′o·quent·ly** *adv.*

in·e·luc·ta·ble (ĭn′ĭ-lŭk′tə-bəl) *adj.* Not to be avoided or overcome; inevitable. [Latin *inēluctābilis* : *in-*, not + *ēluctārī*, to struggle out : *ex-*, out + *luctārī*, to struggle (see **leug-¹** in Appendix*).] —**in′e·luc′ta·bil′i·ty** *n.* —**in′e·luc′ta·bly** *adv.*

in·ept (ĭn-ĕpt′) *adj.* **1.** Not apt or fitting; unsuitable; inappropriate: *an inept comparison.* **2.** Not sensible; foolish: *an inept argument.* **3. a.** Awkward; clumsy: *an inept carpenter.* **b.** Incompetent. —See Synonyms at **awkward.** [Latin *ineptus* : *in-*, not + *aptus*, **APT.**] —**in·ept′ly** *adv.* —**in·ept′ness** *n.*

in·ep·ti·tude (ĭn-ĕp′tə-tōōd′, -tyōōd′) *n.* **1.** The quality of being inept. **2.** An inept act or remark.

in·e·qual·i·ty (ĭn′ĭ-kwŏl′ə-tē) *n.*, *pl.* **-ties. 1.** The condition of being unequal. **2.** Social or economic disparity. **3.** Unevenness; lack of smoothness or regularity. **4.** Variability; changeability. **5.** An instance of being unequal. **6.** *Mathematics.* An algebraic statement that a quantity is greater than another quantity or that it is less than another quantity.

in·eq·ui·ta·ble (ĭn-ĕk′wə-tə-bəl) *adj.* Not equitable; unfair; unjust. —**in·eq′ui·ta·bly** *adv.*

in·eq·ui·ty (ĭn-ĕk′wə-tē) *n.*, *pl.* **-ties. 1.** Lack of equity; injustice; unfairness. **2.** An instance of injustice or unfairness.

in·e·rad·i·ca·ble (ĭn′ĭ-răd′ĭ-kə-bəl) *adj.* That cannot be uprooted, eradicated, or erased. —**in′e·rad′i·ca·bly** *adv.*

in·er·rant (ĭn-ĕr′ənt, ĭn-ûr′-) *adj.* Making no errors; unerring. —**in·er′ran·cy** *n.*

in·ert (ĭn-ûrt′) *adj.* **1.** Unable to move or act. **2.** Resisting motion or action. **3.** *Chemistry.* **a.** Exhibiting no chemical activity; totally unreactive. **b.** Exhibiting chemical activity under special or extreme conditions only. —See Synonyms at **inactive.** [Latin *iners* (stem *inert-*), inactive, unskilled : *in-*, not + *ars*, skill, **ART.**] —**in·ert′ly** *adv.* —**in·ert′ness** *n.*

in·er·tia (ĭn-ûr′shə) *n.* **1.** *Physics.* The tendency of a body to resist acceleration; the tendency of a body at rest to remain at rest or of a body in motion to stay in motion in a straight line unless disturbed by an external force. **2.** Resistance to motion, action, or change. [New Latin, from Latin, lack of skill, idleness, from *iners*, **INERT.**]

in·er·tial (ĭn-ûr′shəl) *adj.* **1.** Of or pertaining to inertia. **2.** Arising from or depending upon the effects of inertia. **3.** Referred to an inertial frame of reference.

inertial frame. Any frame of reference relative to which the Newtonian law of motion, that a mass *m* subjected to a force *F* moves in accordance with the equation $F = ma$, where *a* is the acceleration, is valid. Also called "Newtonian frame."

inertial guidance. Guidance in which gyroscopic and accelerometer data are used by a computer to maintain a predetermined course.

in·es·cap·able (ĭn′ə-skā′pə-bəl) *adj.* That cannot be escaped; unavoidable; inevitable. —**in′es·cap′a·bly** *adv.*

in·es·sen·tial (ĭn′ə-sĕn′shəl) *adj.* **1.** Not essential; unessential. **2.** Without essence. —*n.* Something inessential. —**in′es·sen′ti·al′i·ty** *n.*

in·es·ti·ma·ble (ĭn-ĕs′tə-mə-bəl) *adj.* **1.** Incapable of being estimated or computed; indeterminable: *inestimable damage.* **2.** Of incalculable value. —**in·es′ti·ma·bly** *adv.*

in·ev·i·ta·ble (ĭn-ĕv′ə-tə-bəl) *adj.* Incapable of being avoided or prevented. —**in·ev′i·ta·bil′i·ty** *n.* —**in·ev′i·ta·bly** *adv.*

in·ex·act (ĭn′ĭg-zăkt′) *adj.* Not exact; not quite accurate or precise. —**in′ex·act′ly** *adv.* —**in′ex·act′ness** *n.*

in·ex·ac·ti·tude (ĭn′ĭg-zăk′tə-tōōd′, -tyōōd′) *n.* Lack of exactitude; inexactness.

in·ex·cus·a·ble (ĭn′ĭk-skyōō′zə-bəl) *adj.* Not excusable; unpardonable. —**in′ex·cus′a·ble·ness** *n.* —**in′ex·cus′a·bly** *adv.*

in·ex·haust·i·ble (ĭn′ĭg-zô′stə-bəl) *adj.* **1.** Incapable of being exhausted. **2.** Unfailing; tireless; indefatigable. —**in′ex·haust′i·bil′i·ty, in′ex·haust′i·ble·ness** *n.* —**in′ex·haust′i·bly** *adv.*

in·ex·is·tent (ĭn′ĭg-zĭs′tənt) *adj.* Not existent; nonexistent. —**in′ex·ist′ence, in′ex·ist′en·cy** *n.*

in·ex·o·ra·ble (ĭn-ĕk′sər-ə-bəl) *adj.* Not capable of being persuaded by entreaty; unyielding: *"and more inexorable far/Than empty tigers or the roaring sea."* (Shakespeare). See Synonyms at **inflexible.** —**in′ex·o·ra·ble·ness** *n.* —**in·ex′o·ra·bly** *adv.*

in·ex·pe·di·ent (ĭn′ĭk-spē′dē-ənt) *adj.* Not expedient; inadvisable. —**in′ex·pe′di·ence, in′ex·pe′di·en·cy** *n.* —**in′ex·pe′di·ent·ly** *adv.*

in·ex·pen·sive (ĭn′ĭk-spĕn′sĭv) *adj.* Not expensive; low-priced; cheap. —**in′ex·pen′sive·ly** *adv.* —**in′ex·pen′sive·ness** *n.*

in·ex·pe·ri·ence (ĭn′ĭk-spîr′ē-əns) *n.* Lack of experience.

in·ex·pe·ri·enced (ĭn′ĭk-spîr′ē-ənst) *adj.* Lacking experience and the knowledge gained from experience.

in·ex·pert (ĭn-ĕk′spûrt′) *adj.* Not expert; unskilled. —**in·ex′pert·ly** *adv.* —**in·ex′pert·ness** *n.*

in·ex·pi·a·ble (ĭn-ĕk′spē-ə-bəl) *adj.* **1.** Not capable of being expiated or atoned for: *inexpiable crimes.* **2.** *Obsolete.* Implacable; unrelenting: *inexpiable vengeance.* —**in·ex′pi·a·bly** *adv.*

in·ex·plain·a·ble (ĭn′ĭk-splā′nə-bəl) *adj.* Not explainable; inexplicable. —**in′ex·plain′a·bly** *adv.*

in·ex·pli·ca·ble (ĭn-ĕk′splĭ-kə-bəl, ĭn′ĭk-splĭk′ə-bəl) *adj.* Not explicable; not possible to explain. —**in·ex′pli·ca·bil′i·ty, in·ex′pli·ca·ble·ness** *n.* —**in·ex′pli·ca·bly** *adv.*

in·ex·plic·it (ĭn′ĭk-splĭs′ĭt) *adj.* Not explicit; indefinite.

in·ex·press·i·ble (ĭn′ĭk-sprĕs′ə-bəl) *adj.* Not capable of being expressed; indescribable: *inexpressible joy.* —**in′ex·press′i·bil′i·ty, in′ex·press′i·ble·ness** *n.* —**in′ex·press′i·bly** *adv.*

in·ex·pug·na·ble (ĭn′ĭk-spŭg′nə-bəl, ĭn′ĭk-) *adj.* Not expugnable; impregnable. —**in′ex·pug′na·bly** *adv.*

in·ex·ten·si·ble (ĭn′ĭk-stĕn′sə-bəl) *adj.* Not extensible.

in ex·ten·so (ĭn ĕk-stĕn′sō, ĭk-). *Latin.* At full length: *His article was published in extenso.*

in·ex·tin·guish·a·ble (ĭn′ĭk-stĭng′gwĭ-shə-bəl) *adj.* Not capable of being extinguished. —**in′ex·tin′guish·a·bly** *adv.*

in·ex·tir·pa·ble (ĭn′ĭk-stûr′pə-bəl) *adj.* Incapable of being extirpated; impossible to exterminate.

ă pat/ā pay/âr care/ä father/b bib/ch church/d deed/ĕ pet/ē be/f fife/g gag/h hat/hw which/ĭ pit/ī pie/îr pier/j judge/k kick/l lid, needle/m mum/n no, sudden/ng thing/ŏ pot/ō toe/ô paw, for/oi noise/ou out/ōō took/ōō boot/p pop/r roar/s sauce/sh ship, dish/

in·ex·tre·mis (ĭn ĕk-strē'mĭs, ĭk-). At the point of death. [Latin, "in the last (straits)."]

in·ex·tri·ca·ble (ĭn-ĕk'strĭ-kə-bəl) adj. 1. a. Incapable of being disentangled or untied. b. Too intricate or complicated to solve. 2. a. Firmly resisting one's attempts at escape or resolution: an inextricable quandary. b. Incapable of being freed: The screws were rusted in and quite inextricable. —in·ex'tri·ca·bil'i·ty, in·ex'tri·ca·ble·ness n. —in·ex'tri·ca·bly adv.

inf. 1. infantry. **2.** inferior. **3.** infinitive. **4.** influence. **5.** information.

Inf. infantry.

in·fal·li·ble (ĭn-făl'ə-bəl) adj. 1. Incapable of erring; dependable: an infallible source of information. 2. Incapable of failing: an infallible antidote. 3. Incapable of error in expounding doctrine on faith or morals. Said especially of the pope speaking ex cathedra. —n. An infallible person or thing. [French, from Medieval Latin infallibilis : in-, not + fallibilis, FALLIBLE.] —in·fal'li·bil'i·ty, in·fal'li·ble·ness n. —in·fal'li·bly adv.

in·fa·mous (ĭn'fə-məs) adj. 1. Having an exceedingly bad reputation; notorious; detestable. 2. Causing or deserving infamy; loathsome; grossly shocking: an infamous deed. 3. Law. Of, pertaining to, or constituting a crime involving moral turpitude, as treason or felony. —See Synonyms at outrageous, mean (base). [Middle English, from Medieval Latin infamosus, from Latin infāmis : in-, not + fāma, FAME.] —in'fa·mous·ly adv. —in'fa·mous·ness n.

in·fa·my (ĭn'fə-mē) n., pl. -mies. 1. Evil fame or reputation. 2. The condition of being infamous. 3. An infamous act. 4. Law. The loss of various civil rights consequent upon conviction for an infamous offense. —See Synonyms at disgrace. [Middle English infamye, from Old French infamie, infame, from Latin infāmia, from infāmis, INFAMOUS.]

in·fan·cy (ĭn'fən-sē) n., pl. -cies. 1. The state or period of being an infant. 2. The earliest years or stage of something: television in its infancy. 3. Law. The state or period of being a minor.

in·fant (ĭn'fənt) n. 1. A child in the earliest period of its life; a baby. 2. Law. One under the legal age of majority; a minor. —adj. 1. Of or being in infancy. 2. Intended for infants or very young children. 3. Young and growing: an infant enterprise. [Middle English enfaunt, from Old French enfant, from Latin infāns, "(one) unable to speak" : in-, not + fāns, present participle of fāri, to speak (see bhā-2 in Appendix*).]

in·fan·ta (ĭn-făn'tə) n. 1. A daughter of a Spanish or Portuguese king. 2. The wife of an infante. [Spanish, feminine of infante, INFANTE.]

in·fan·te (ĭn-făn'tā) n. Any son of a Spanish or Portuguese king other than the heir to the throne. [Spanish and Portuguese, "infant," from Latin infāns, INFANT.]

in·fan·ti·cide (ĭn-făn'tĭ-sīd') n. 1. The killing of an infant. 2. A person who kills an infant. [Late Latin infanticidium (killing) and infanticida (killer) : Latin infāns, INFANT + -cidium, -cida, -CIDE.]

in·fan·tile (ĭn'fən-tīl', -tĭl) adj. 1. Of or relating to infants or infancy. 2. Lacking maturity, sophistication, or reasonableness. [French, from infantilis, from infāns, INFANT.]

infantile autism. Psychology. Autism (see).

infantile paralysis. Pathology. Poliomyelitis (see).

in·fan·til·ism (ĭn'fən-tə-lĭz'əm) n. A state of arrested development in an adult, characterized by a retention of infantile mentality accompanied by stunted growth and sexual immaturity.

in·fan·try (ĭn'fən-trē) n., pl. -tries. Abbr. Inf., inf. The branch of an army made up of units trained to fight on foot. [French infanterie, from Italian infanteria, from infante, youth, foot soldier, from Latin infāns, INFANT.] —in'fan·try·man n.

in·farct (ĭn-färkt') n. A necrotic area of tissue resulting from failure of local blood supply. [New Latin infarctus, from Latin infarctus, infartus, past participle of infarcīre, to stuff in, cram : in-, in + farcīre, to stuff (see bhrekw- in Appendix*).]

in·fat·u·ate (ĭn-făch'ōō-āt') tr.v. -ated, -ating, -ates. 1. To cause to behave foolishly. 2. To inspire with foolish and unreasoning passion or attraction. —adj. (ĭn-făch'ōō-it, -āt') Infatuated. [Latin infatuāre : in- (causative) + fatuus, FATUOUS.]

in·fat·u·at·ed (ĭn-făch'ōō-ā'tĭd) adj. Possessed by an unreasoning passion or attraction. —in·fat'u·at'ed·ly adv.

in·fat·u·a·tion (ĭn-făch'ōō-ā'shən) n. 1. The state or an instance of being infatuated. 2. An object of extravagant, short-lived passion. —See Synonyms at love.

in·fea·si·ble (ĭn-fē'zə-bəl) adj. Not feasible; impracticable.

in·fect (ĭn-fĕkt') tr.v. -fected, -fecting, -fects. 1. To contaminate with pathogenic microorganisms. 2. To communicate a disease to (another person). 3. To invade and produce infection in. 4. To corrupt. 5. To affect as if by contagion: "His fear infected me, and . . . I followed as fast as I could" (W.H. Hudson). [Middle English infecten, from Latin inficere (past participle infectus), to work in, dye, taint : in-, in + facere, to do (see dhē-1 in Appendix*).]

in·fec·tion (ĭn-fĕk'shən) n. 1. Invasion by pathogenic microorganisms of a bodily part in which conditions are favorable for growth, production of toxins, and subsequent injury to tissue. 2. An instance of such invasion. 3. The pathological state resulting from such invasion. 4. An agent or contaminated substance responsible for such invasion. 5. An infectious disease. 6. Persuasion or corruption by argument or example.

in·fec·tious (ĭn-fĕk'shəs) adj. 1. Capable of causing infection. 2. Capable of being transmitted by infection without actual contact. Said of a disease. 3. Caused by a microorganism. Said of a disease. 4. Tending to spread easily or catch on: an infectious chuckle. —in·fec'tious·ly adv. —in·fec'tious·ness n.

infectious enterohepatitis. Blackhead (see).

infectious mononucleosis. An acute, contagious, febrile disease, mononucleosis (see). Also called "glandular fever."

in·fec·tive (ĭn-fĕk'tĭv) adj. Capable of producing infection; infectious. —in·fec'tive·ness, in·fec·tiv'i·ty n.

in·fe·lic·i·tous (ĭn'fə-lĭs'ə-təs) adj. 1. Not happy; unfortunate; sad. 2. Inappropriate; inopportune. —in'fe·lic'i·tous·ly adv.

in·fe·lic·i·ty (ĭn'fə-lĭs'ə-tē) n., pl. -ties. 1. The quality or condition of being infelicitous. 2. Something inappropriate or unpleasing. [Middle English infelicite, from Latin infēlicitās, from infēlix, unhappy : in-, not + fēlix, happy (see dhēi- in Appendix*).]

in·fer (ĭn-fûr') v. -ferred, -ferring, -fers. —tr. 1. To conclude from evidence; deduce. See Usage note below. 2. To have as a logical consequence. —intr. To draw inferences. —See Synonyms at conjecture. [Old French inferer, from Latin inferre, to bring in, introduce, deduce : in-, in + ferre, to bear (see bher-1 in Appendix*).] —in·fer'a·ble adj. —in·fer'a·bly adv.

Usage: Infer and imply, in their most frequently used senses, are carefully distinguished in modern usage. To imply is to state indirectly, hint, or intimate: The report implies that we were to blame. To infer is to draw a conclusion or make a deduction based on facts or indications: Reading the report led him to infer that we were to blame. In these senses the words are not interchangeable. Although infer sometimes appears in examples such as the first, it is not acceptable there, according to 92 per cent of the Usage Panel.

in·fer·ence (ĭn'fər-əns) n. 1. The act or process of inferring. 2. Something inferred; a conclusion based on a premise.

in·fer·en·tial (ĭn'fə-rĕn'shəl) adj. Derived or capable of being derived from inference. —in'fer·en'tial·ly adv.

in·fe·ri·or (ĭn-fîr'ē-ər) adj. Abbr. inf. 1. Situated under or beneath. 2. Low or lower in order, degree, or rank. 3. Low or lower in quality, status, or estimation. 4. Botany. Located below the perianth and other floral parts. Said of an ovary. 5. Printing. Set below the normal line. Said of type. —n. 1. A person of lesser rank or status than others. 2. Printing. An inferior character. —See Usage note at superior. [Middle English, from Latin inferior, comparative of inferus, low. See ndher- in Appendix*.] —in·fe'ri·or'i·ty (-ôr'ə-tē, -ŏr'ə-tē) n.

inferiority complex. A persistent sense of inadequacy or tendency to self-diminishment.

in·fer·nal (ĭn-fûr'nəl) adj. 1. Of or relating to the world of the dead in classical mythology. 2. Of or relating to hell. 3. Abominable; damnable. [Middle English, from Old French, from Late Latin infernālis, from infernus, hell, from Latin, lower. See ndher- in Appendix*.] —in·fer'nal·ly adv.

infernal machine. An explosive device maliciously designed to harm or destroy.

in·fer·no (ĭn-fûr'nō) n., pl. -nos. 1. Hell. 2. Any place likened to hell. [Italian, hell, from Late Latin infernus. See infernal.]

in·fer·tile (ĭn-fûrt'l) adj. Not fertile; unproductive; barren. See Synonyms at sterile. —in·fer·til'i·ty (ĭn'fər-tĭl'ə-tē) n.

in·fest (ĭn-fĕst') tr.v. -fested, -festing, -fests. To inhabit or overrun in large numbers so as to be harmful or unpleasant. [Middle English infesten, to attack, molest, trouble, from Old French infester, from Latin infestāre, from infestus, hostile. See dhers- in Appendix*.] —in·fest'er n.

in·fes·ta·tion (ĭn'fĕ-stā'shən) n. 1. The act or process of infesting. 2. The condition of being infested.

in·fi·del (ĭn'fə-dəl, -dĕl') n. 1. One who has no religious beliefs. 2. One who is an unbeliever with respect to some religion, especially Christianity or Islam. —adj. 1. Of or relating to unbelievers. 2. Having no religious beliefs. 3. Not believing in a particular religion, especially Christianity. [Middle English infydel, from Old French infidel, from Latin infidēlis, unfaithful : in-, not + fidēs, faith (see bheidh- in Appendix*).]

in·fi·del·i·ty (ĭn'fə-dĕl'ə-tē) n., pl. -ties. 1. Lack of religious faith, especially in Christianity or Islam. 2. Lack of fidelity or loyalty; unfaithfulness. 3. A disloyal act; a breach of allegiance or duty. 4. Adultery.

in·field (ĭn'fēld') n. 1. A field located near a farmhouse. 2. Baseball. a. The area of a baseball field enclosed by the foul lines and the arc of the outfield grass just beyond the bases. b. The defensive positions of first base, second base, third base, and shortstop. Compare outfield.

in·field·er (ĭn'fēl'dər) n. Baseball. A player who plays in the infield.

in·fil·trate (ĭn-fĭl'trāt', ĭn'fĭl-) v. -trated, -trating, -trates. —tr. 1. To pass (a liquid or gas) into something through its interstices. 2. To permeate with a liquid or gas passed through interstices. 3. To pass (troops, for example) surreptitiously into enemy-held territory. 4. To take up positions in (a political party, for example) surreptitiously. —intr. To gain entrance gradually or surreptitiously. —n. A substance that accumulates gradually in bodily tissues. [IN- (in) + FILTRATE.]

in·fil·tra·tion (ĭn'fĭl-trā'shən) n. 1. The act or process of infiltrating. 2. The state of being infiltrated. 3. Something that infiltrates. —in·fil'tra·tive (-trə-tĭv) adj.

infin. infinitive.

in·fi·nite (ĭn'fə-nĭt) adj. 1. Having no boundaries or limits. 2. Immeasurably or uncountably large. 3. Mathematics. a. Existing beyond or being greater than any arbitrarily large value. b. Unlimited in spatial extent. c. Of or pertaining to a set capable of being put into one-to-one correspondence with a proper subset of itself. 4. Continuing endlessly in time. —n. Something infinite. —the Infinite (Being). God. [Middle English infinit, from Old French, from Latin infīnitus : in-, not + fīnitus, FINITE.] —in'fi·nite·ly adv. —in'fi·nite·ness n.

Synonyms: infinite, limitless, illimitable, boundless, measure-

less, eternal, innumerable, numberless, countless. These adjectives are applicable to what does not have known limits or boundaries. *Infinite,* the most inclusive, refers to what has no limits with respect to quantity, extent, time, or degree and is therefore indeterminate. In usage it is applied most often to what is large beyond measure. *Limitless, illimitable, boundless,* and *measureless* refer principally to what has no known limits in extent, size, or quantity, physical or figurative: *the limitless reaches of outer space; boundless opportunity. Eternal* indicates the absence of limits in time; it applies to what has no known beginning and presumably no end, and is thus everlasting. *Innumerable, numberless,* and *countless* refer to quantity beyond reckoning.

in·fin·i·tes·i·mal (ĭn′fə-nə-tĕs′ə-məl) *adj.* **1.** Immeasurably or incalculably minute. **2.** *Mathematics.* Capable of having values arbitrarily close to zero. —*n.* **1.** An infinitesimal amount or quantity. **2.** *Mathematics.* A function having values arbitrarily close to zero. [From New Latin *infinitesimus* : Latin *infīnītus,* INFINITE + *-esimus,* ordinal suffix.] —**in′fin·i·tes′i·mal·ly** *adv.*

infinitesimal calculus. Differential and integral calculus.

in·fin·i·ti·val (ĭn′fĭ-nə-tī′vəl) *adj.* Relating to the infinitive.

in·fin·i·tive (ĭn-fĭn′ə-tĭv) *n. Abbr.* **inf., infin.** A verb form that is not inflected to indicate person, number, or tense, and is used in English: **1.** To serve as a substantive while retaining some verbal aspects, such as connection with an object and modification by adverbs. Preceded by *to: To go willingly is to show strength.* **2.** To participate in verb phrases: *He wished to go.* With certain verbs used without *to: He may go.* —See Usage note at **split infinitive.** —*adj.* Of, relating to, or using the infinitive. [Late Latin *infīnītivus,* "unlimited" (because it has no definite numbers or persons), from Latin *infīnītus,* INFINITE.]

in·fin·i·tude (ĭn-fĭn′ə-to͞od′, -tyo͞od′) *n.* **1.** The state or quality of being infinite. **2.** An infinite quantity, number, or extent.

in·fin·i·ty (ĭn-fĭn′ə-tē) *n., pl.* **-ties. 1.** The quality or condition of being infinite. **2.** Unbounded space, time, or quantity. **3.** An indefinitely large number. **4.** *Mathematics.* The limit that a function f is said to approach at $x = a$ when for x close to a, $f(x)$ is larger than any preassigned number.

in·firm (ĭn-fûrm′) *adj.* **1.** Weak in body, especially from old age; feeble. **2.** Lacking moral firmness; irresolute. **3.** *Rare.* Legally insecure. —See Synonyms at **weak.** [Middle English *infirme,* from Latin *infirmus* : *in-,* not + *firmus,* FIRM.] —**in·firm′ly** *adv.*

in·fir·ma·ry (ĭn-fûr′mə-rē) *n., pl.* **-ries.** A place for the care of the sick or injured; especially, a small hospital or dispensary. [Medieval Latin *infirmāria,* from Latin *infirmus,* INFIRM.]

in·fir·mi·ty (ĭn-fûr′mə-tē) *n., pl.* **-ties. 1.** Lack of power; disability. **2.** Bodily debilitation; frailty. **3.** Moral weakness.

in·fix (ĭn-fĭks′) *tr.v.* **-fixed, -fixing, -fixes. 1.** To fix into another. **2.** To fix in the mind; inculcate; instill. **3.** *Grammar.* To insert (a morphological element) as an infix. —*n.* (ĭn′fĭks′). An inflectional or derivational element inserted into the body of a word, as the infix *-n-* is added to the Old Latin verb root *frag-,* "break," to form the imperfective *frang-,* "is breaking." [Latin *infigere* (past participle *infixus*) : *in-,* in + *figere,* to FIX.]

infl. influence; influenced.

in·flame (ĭn-flām′) *v.* **-flamed, -flaming, -flames.** —*tr.* **1.** To set on fire; kindle. **2.** To arouse to strong emotion. **3.** To intensify intolerably: *"inflamed to madness an already savage nature"* (Robert Graves). **4.** To produce inflammation in. —*intr.* **1.** To catch fire. **2.** To become excited or aroused. **3.** To be affected by inflammation. [Middle English *inflamen,* from Old French *enflammer,* from Latin *inflammāre* : *in-* (intensive) + *flammāre,* to set on fire, from *flamma,* FLAME.]

in·flam·ma·ble (ĭn-flăm′ə-bəl) *adj.* **1.** Tending to ignite easily and burn rapidly; flammable. **2.** Quickly or easily aroused to strong emotion; passionate. —See Usage note at **flammable.** —*n.* Something flammable. [French, from Medieval Latin *inflammābilis,* from Latin *inflammāre,* to INFLAME.] —**in·flam′ma·bly** *adv.*

in·flam·ma·tion (ĭn′flə-mā′shən) *n.* **1.** The act of inflaming or the state of being inflamed. **2.** Localized heat, redness, swelling, and pain as a result of irritation, injury, or infection.

in·flam·ma·to·ry (ĭn-flăm′ə-tôr′ē, -tōr′ē) *adj.* **1.** Arousing strong emotion. **2.** Characterized or caused by inflammation.

in·flate (ĭn-flāt′) *v.* **-flated, -flating, -flates.** —*tr.* **1.** To fill and swell with a gas. **2.** To cause to increase unduly: *Success inflated his ego.* **3.** *Economics.* To raise or expand abnormally, as prices, wages, or circulating currency. —*intr.* To become inflated; swell; expand. [Latin *inflāre,* to blow into : *in-,* in + *flāre,* to blow (see **bhlē-** in Appendix*).]

in·flat·ed (ĭn-flā′tĭd) *adj.* **1.** Distended or expanded by or as if by gas or air. **2.** Unduly increased or puffed up: *"Louis XIV of inflated memory"* (Mark Twain). **3.** Increased or raised to abnormal economic levels: *inflated wages.* **4.** Resulting from inflation. **5.** Hollow and enlarged: *an inflated calyx.*

in·fla·tion (ĭn-flā′shən) *n.* **1.** The act of inflating or the state of being inflated. **2.** *Economics.* An abnormal increase in available currency and credit beyond the proportion of available goods, resulting in a sharp and continuing rise in price levels. In this sense, compare **deflation.** —**in·fla′tion·ar′y** (-shə-nĕr′ē) *adj.*

in·fla·tion·ist (ĭn-flā′shə-nĭst) *n.* One who advocates inflation. —**in·fla′tion·ism′** *n.*

in·flect (ĭn-flĕkt′) *v.* **-flected, -flecting, -flects.** —*tr.* **1.** To turn from a course or alignment; to bend. **2.** To alter (the voice) in tone or pitch; modulate. **3.** *Grammar.* To alter (a word) as by conjugating or declining. —*intr. Grammar.* To be modified by inflection. [Middle English *inflecten,* from Latin *inflectere,* to bend, warp, change : *in-* (intensive) + *flectere,* to bend (see **flex**).] —**in·flec′tive** *adj.* —**in·flec′tor** (-flĕk′tər) *n.*

in·flec·tion (ĭn-flĕk′shən) *n.* Also *chiefly British* **in·flex·ion. 1.** The act of inflecting or a state of being inflected. **2.** An alteration in pitch or tone of the voice. **3.** *Grammar.* **a.** An alteration of the form of a word to indicate different grammatical and syntactical relations, such as the declension of nouns, adjectives, and pronouns or the conjugation of verbs. **b.** An element added to a word to denote a grammatical function, as the *s* in *apples* indicating the plural form or the *'s* in *girl's* indicating possessive case. **c.** An inflected form of a word. —**in·flec′tion·al** *adj.* —**in·flec′tion·al·ly** *adv.*

in·flexed (ĭn-flĕkst′) *adj.* Bent or curved inward or downward, as petals or sepals. [From Latin *inflexus,* past participle of *inflectere,* to bend, INFLECT.]

in·flex·i·ble (ĭn-flĕk′sə-bəl) *adj.* **1.** Not flexible; stiff; rigid. **2.** Incapable of being changed; unalterable: *inflexible standards.* **3.** Obstinate; unyielding. —See Synonyms at **stiff.** —**in·flex′i·bil′i·ty, in·flex′i·ble·ness** *n.* —**in·flex′i·bly** *adv.*

Synonyms: *inflexible, inexorable, adamant, obdurate.* These adjectives mean not capable of being swayed or diverted from a course. *Inflexible* is applicable to things not capable of change or to persons whose conduct is governed by principles that do not permit alteration of a course. *Inexorable* implies lack of sensitivity to persuasion or entreaty. The term describes things, such as fate or law, that are inevitable in operation and uncompromising in effect. *Adamant* refers to personal conduct and implies adherence to a determined course, despite pleas to the contrary. *Obdurate* adds to *adamant* the implication of hard-heartedness.

in·flict (ĭn-flĭkt′) *tr.v.* **-flicted, -flicting, -flicts. 1.** To cause or carry out by physical assault or other aggressive action. **2.** To impose: *"malignant Nature, who reserves the right to inflict upon her children the most terrifying jests"* (Thornton Wilder). **3.** To afflict. [Latin *inflīgere* (past participle *inflictus*) : *in-,* on + *flīgere,* to strike (see **bhlīg-** in Appendix*).] —**in·flict′er, in·flic′tor** (-flĭk′tər) *n.* —**in·flic′tive** *adj.*

in·flic·tion (ĭn-flĭk′shən) *n.* **1.** The act or process of inflicting. **2.** Something inflicted, as blows or punishment.

in·flo·res·cence (ĭn′flə-rĕs′əns) *n.* **1.** *Botany.* A characteristic arrangement of flowers on a stalk or in a cluster. **2.** A flowering. [New Latin *inflorescentia,* from Late Latin *inflōrēscere,* to begin to flower : Latin *in-* (intensive) + *flōrēscere,* to begin to flower (see **florescence**).]

in·flow (ĭn′flō′) *n.* **1.** The act or process of flowing in or into. **2.** Something that flows in or into.

in·flu·ence (ĭn′flo͞o-əns) *n. Abbr.* **inf., infl. 1.** A power indirectly or intangibly affecting a person or a course of events. **2.** Power to sway or affect based on prestige, wealth, ability, or position. **3.** A person or thing exercising such power. **4.** An effect or change produced by such power. **5.** *Astrology.* **a.** An occult ethereal fluid flowing from the stars to affect the fate of men. **b.** The occult power emanating from the stars. —*tr.v.* **influenced, -encing, -ences. 1.** To have power over; affect. **2.** To cause a change in the character, thought, or action of. —See Synonyms at **affect.** [Middle English, from Old French, from Medieval Latin *influentia,* "a flowing in," from Latin *influēns,* present participle of *influere,* to flow in : *in-,* in + *fluere,* to flow (see **bhleu-** in Appendix*).] —**in′flu·enc·er** *n.*

in·flu·ent (ĭn′flo͞o-ənt) *adj.* Flowing in or into. —*n.* Something that flows in or into; especially, a tributary. [Middle English, from Latin *influēns,* flowing in. See **influence.**]

in·flu·en·tial (ĭn′flo͞o-ĕn′shəl) *adj.* Having or exercising influence. —**in′flu·en′tial·ly** *adv.*

in·flu·en·za (ĭn′flo͞o-ĕn′zə) *n.* An acute infectious viral disease characterized by inflammation of the respiratory tract, fever, muscular pain, and irritation in the intestinal tract. Also called "grippe." [Italian, influence, hence "intangible visitation," epidemic (specifically the European epidemic of influenza of 1743), from Medieval Latin *influentia,* INFLUENCE.]

in·flux (ĭn′flŭks′) *n.* **1.** A flowing in of substance. **2.** An incursion of individuals or entities: *"The swinging doors of the church were shoved to admit influxes of worshipers."* (James T. Farrell). **3.** The mouth of a river or stream. [Late Latin *influxus,* from Latin, past participle of *influere,* to flow in. See **influence.**]

in·fold (ĭn-fōld′) *tr.v.* **-folded, -folding, -folds. 1.** To fold inward. **2.** Variant of **enfold.** —**in·fold′er** *n.* —**in·fold′ment** *n.*

in·form (ĭn-fôrm′) *v.* **-formed, -forming, -forms.** —*tr.* **1.** To give form or character to; be the formative principle of. **2.** To animate or inspire with a particular quality or character; imbue. **3.** *Rare.* To form or shape (the mind or character) by teaching or training. **4.** To impart information to. —*intr.* To disclose or give often incriminating information. [Middle English *enfourmen,* from Old French *enfourmer,* from Latin *informāre,* to give form to, form an idea of : *in-* (intensive) + *formāre,* to form, from *forma,* FORM.] —**in·form′er** *n.*

in·for·mal (ĭn-fôr′məl) *adj.* **1.** Not performed or made according to prescribed regulations or forms; unofficial; irregular: *an informal truce.* **2.** Completed or performed without ceremony or formality. **3.** Of, for, or pertaining to ordinary everyday use; casual; relaxed: *informal clothes.* **4.** Belonging to the usage of natural spoken language but considered inappropriate in certain cultural contexts, as in the standard written prose of ceremonial and official communications. —**in·for′mal·ly** *adv.*

in·for·mal·i·ty (ĭn′fôr-măl′ə-tē) *n., pl.* **-ties. 1.** The state or quality of being informal. **2.** An informal act.

in·form·ant (ĭn-fôr′mənt) *n.* **1.** One who discloses information; an informer. **2.** A speaker of a particular language or dialect used as a source of evidence by a linguistic researcher.

in·for·ma·tion (ĭn′fər-mā′shən) *n. Abbr.* **inf. 1.** The act of informing or the condition of being informed; communication of

ă pat/ā pay/âr care/ä father/b bib/ch church/d deed/ĕ pet/ē be/f fife/g gag/h hat/hw which/ĭ pit/ī pie/îr pier/j judge/k kick/l lid, needle/m mum/n no, sudden/ng thing/ŏ pot/ō toe/ô paw, for/oi noise/ou out/o͝o took/o͞o boot/p pop/r roar/s sauce/sh ship, dish/

knowledge. **2.** Knowledge derived from study, experience, or instruction. **3.** Knowledge of a specific event or situation; news; word. **4.** A service or facility for supplying facts or news. **5.** *Law.* An accusation of a crime made by a public officer rather than by indictment by a grand jury. **6.** A nonaccidental signal used as an input to a computer or communications system. **7.** A numerical measure of the uncertainty of an experimental outcome. —See Synonyms at **knowledge.** —**in'for·ma'tion·al** *adj.*

information theory. The theory of the probability of transmission of messages with specified accuracy when the bits of information constituting the messages are subject, with certain probabilities, to transmission failure, distortion, and accidental additions.

in·form·a·tive (ĭn-fôr'mə-tĭv) *adj.* Also **in·form·a·to·ry** (-tôr'ē, -tōr'ē). Providing or disclosing information; instructive.

in·formed (ĭn-fôrmd') *adj.* Knowledgeable; educated.

in·form·er (ĭn-fôr'mər) *n.* **1.** An informant. **2.** One who informs against others, especially to authorities, often for compensation.

infra–. Indicates: **1.** Below, beneath, inferior to; for example, **infrared. 2.** After, later; for example, **infralapsarianism.** [Latin *infrā,* below, beneath. See **ndher-** in Appendix.*]

in·fract (ĭn-frăkt') *tr.v.* **-fracted, -fracting, -fracts.** To break (a legal or legalistic rule or right); infringe; violate. [Latin *infringere* (past participle *infractus*), to destroy, INFRINGE.] —**in·frac'tor** (-frăk'tər) *n.*

in·frac·tion (ĭn-frăk'shən) *n.* The act of breaching or violating; infringement; violation. See Synonyms at **breach.**

in·fra dig (ĭn'frə dĭg'). Beneath one's dignity. [Latin *infrā dignitātem.*]

in·fra·lap·sar·i·an·ism (ĭn'frə-lăp-sâr'ē-ə-nĭz'əm) *n.* The predestinarian doctrine that God allowed the fall of man and elected some from the fallen to be saved by a redeemer. Also called "sublapsarianism." [From INFRA- + Latin *lapsus,* to fall, LAPSE.] —**in'fra·lap·sar'i·an** *n.* & *adj.*

in·fran·gi·ble (ĭn-frăn'jə-bəl) *adj.* **1.** Unbreakable. **2.** Inviolable. [Old French, from Late Latin *infrangibilis* : Latin *in-,* not + *frangere,* to break (see **bhreg-** in Appendix*).] —**in·fran'gi·bil'i·ty** *n.* —**in·fran'gi·bly** *adv.*

in·fra·red (ĭn'frə-rĕd') *adj.* **1.** Of, pertaining to, or being electromagnetic radiation having wavelengths greater than those of visible light and shorter than those of microwaves. **2.** Generating, using, or sensitive to such radiation. [INFRA- + RED.]

in·fra·son·ic (ĭn'frə-sŏn'ĭk) *adj.* **1.** Generating or using waves or vibrations with frequencies below that of audible sound. **2. Subsonic** *(see).*

in·fre·quent (ĭn-frē'kwənt) *adj.* **1.** Not frequent; rare. **2.** Not steady; irregular; occasional: *an infrequent guest.* —**in·fre'quence, in·fre'quen·cy** *n.* —**in·fre'quent·ly** *adv.*

in·fringe (ĭn-frĭnj') *v.* **-fringed, -fringing, -fringes.** —*tr.* To break or ignore the terms or obligations of (an oath, agreement, law, or the like); to disregard; violate. —*intr.* To go beyond the boundaries or limits of; trespass; encroach. Used with *on* or *upon.* [Latin *infringere* : *in-* (intensive) + *frangere,* to break (see **bhreg-** in Appendix*).] —**in·fring'er** *n.*

in·fringe·ment (ĭn-frĭnj'mənt) *n.* **1.** A violation, as of a law, regulation, or agreement; a breach. **2.** An encroachment, as of a right or privilege. —See Synonyms at **breach.**

in·fun·dib·u·li·form (ĭn'fən-dĭb'yə-lə-fôrm') *adj.* Funnel-shaped.

in·fun·dib·u·lum (ĭn'fən-dĭb'yə-ləm) *n., pl.* **-la** (-lə). Any of various funnel-shaped bodily passages or parts. [Latin, funnel, from *infundere,* to pour in, INFUSE.] —**in'fun·dib'u·lar, in'fun·dib'u·late'** (-lāt', -lĭt) *adj.*

in·fu·ri·ate (ĭn-fyŏŏr'ē-āt') *tr.v.* **-ated, -ating, -ates.** To make furious; enrage; anger. —*adj.* (ĭn-fyŏŏr'ē-ĭt'). *Archaic.* Furious; angry. [Medieval Latin *infuriāre,* to enrage : Latin *in-* (intensive) + *furiāre,* to enrage, from *furia,* FURY.] —**in·fu'ri·at'ing·ly** *adv.*

in·fuse (ĭn-fyōōz') *tr.v.* **-fused, -fusing, -fuses. 1.** To put in or introduce into by or as if by pouring. Used with *into.* **2.** To fill; imbue. **3.** To instill; inculcate. **4.** To steep or soak without boiling, in order to extract soluble elements or active principles. [Middle English *infusen,* from Old French *infuser,* from Latin *infundere* (past participle *infūsus*), to pour in : *in-,* in + *fundere,* to pour (see **gheu-** in Appendix*).] —**in·fus'er** *n.*

in·fus·i·ble¹ (ĭn-fyōō'zə-bəl) *adj.* Incapable of being fused or melted; resistant to heat. —**in·fus'i·bil'i·ty, in·fus'i·ble·ness** *n.*

in·fus·i·ble² (ĭn-fyōō'zə-bəl) *adj.* Capable of being infused. —**in·fus'i·bil'i·ty, in·fus'i·ble·ness** *n.*

in·fu·sion (ĭn-fyōō'zhən) *n.* **1.** The act or process of infusing. **2.** An admixture. **3.** The liquid product obtained by infusing. **4.** The introduction of a solution into a vein.

in·fu·sion·ism (ĭn-fyōō'zhə-nĭz'əm) *n. Theology.* The Christian doctrine that a pre-existing soul of divine origin is infused into the body at conception or birth. Compare **creationism.** —**in·fu'sion·ist** *n.*

in·fu·so·ri·al (ĭn'fyōō-sôr'ē-əl, -sōr'ē-əl) *adj.* **1.** Of or pertaining to infusorians. **2.** Containing or consisting of infusorians.

in·fu·so·ri·an (ĭn'fyōō-sôr'ē-ən, -sōr'ē-ən) *n.* Any of numerous microscopic organisms, especially of the phylum Protozoa or the order Rotifera, occurring in stagnant water or in infusions containing organic material. —*adj.* Of or pertaining to such organisms. [New Latin *Infusoria,* "found in infusions," from Latin *infundere* (past participle *infūsus*), to INFUSE.]

–ing¹. Used to form: **1.** The present participle of verbs; for example, **going, seeing, hoping. 2.** Participial adjectives; for example, the **living** screen, **crippling** diseases. **3.** Adjectives resembling participial adjectives but not derived from verbs; for example, **swashbuckling.** [Middle English *-inge, -ing,* variants of *-end, -ind,* Old English *-ende,* related to Latin *-āns,* -ANT.]

–ing². Used to form nouns from verbs, nouns, and occasionally other parts of speech. Indicates: **1.** The act, process, or art of performing an action designated by a root verb; for example, **dancing, thinking. 2.** The thing or substance that accomplishes such an action; for example, **coating, wadding. 3.** Something necessary for the performance of such an action; for example, **living, mooring. 4.** The result of such an action; for example, **peeling, grooming, opening, drawing. 5.** Belonging to, connected with, or having the character of the noun root; for example, **legging, boarding. 6.** An action upon or involving the noun root; for example, **sounding, berrying.** [Middle English *-ing,* Old English *-ung, -ing.*]

–ing³. Used to form nouns from other nouns or proper nouns. Indicates the possession of a certain quality or nature; for example, **wilding.** [Middle English *-ing,* Old English *-ing, -ung,* of, belonging to, descended from.]

in·gen·ious (ĭn-jēn'yəs) *adj.* **1.** Owing to or displaying ingenuity. **2.** Having or arising from an inventive or cunning mind; clever: *"fear . . . is not barren of ingenious suggestions"* (Conrad). **3.** *Obsolete.* Having genius; brilliant. —See Synonyms at **clever.** [French *ingénieux,* from Latin *ingeniōsus,* from *ingenium,* inborn talent, skill. See **gena-** in Appendix.*] —**in·gen'ious·ly** *adv.* —**in·gen'ious·ness** *n.*

in·gé·nue (ăn'zhə-nōō', -nyōō'; *French* ăN-zhā-nü') *n.* **1.** An artless, innocent girl or young woman. **2.** An actress playing an ingénue. [French, feminine of *ingénu,* guileless, artless, from Latin *ingenuus,* INGENUOUS.]

in·ge·nu·i·ty (ĭn'jə-nōō'ə-tē, -nyōō'ə-tē) *n., pl.* **-ties. 1.** Inventive skill or imagination; cleverness. **2.** The state of being ingeniously contrived. **3.** *Usually plural.* An ingenious or imaginative device. **4.** *Archaic.* Ingenuousness. [Latin *ingenuitās,* frankness, innocence (but influenced in meaning by INGENIOUS), from *ingenuus,* INGENUOUS.]

in·gen·u·ous (ĭn-jĕn'yōō-əs) *adj.* **1.** Without sophistication or worldliness; artless; innocent. **2.** Open or honest; frank; candid. —See Synonyms at **frank, naive.** [Latin *ingenuus,* native, free-born, noble, honest, frank. See **gena-** in Appendix.*] —**in·gen'u·ous·ly** *adv.* —**in·gen'u·ous·ness** *n.*

In·ger·soll (ĭng'gər-sôl', -səl), **Robert Green.** 1833–1899. American political leader, orator, and agnostic.

in·gest (ĭn-jĕst') *tr.v.* **-gested, -gesting, -gests.** To take (food, for example) in by or as if by swallowing. [Latin *ingerere* (past participle *ingestus*), to carry in : *in-,* in + *gerere,* to bear, carry (see **gerere** in Appendix*).] —**in·ges'tion** *n.* —**in·ges'tive** *adj.*

in·ges·ta (ĭn-jĕs'tə) *pl.n.* Ingested matter, especially food. [New Latin, from Latin, neuter plural of *ingestus,* past participle of *ingerere,* INGEST.]

In·gle·wood (ĭng'gəl-wŏŏd). A southwestern suburb of Los Angeles, California. Population, 63,000.

in·glo·ri·ous (ĭn-glôr'ē-əs, ĭn-glōr'-) *adj.* Ignominious; dishonorable. [From Latin *inglōrius* : *in-,* not + *glōria,* GLORY.] —**in·glo'ri·ous·ly** *adv.* —**in·glo'ri·ous·ness** *n.*

in·go·ing (ĭn'gō'ĭng) *adj.* **1.** Entering; new or succeeding: *the ingoing mayor.* **2.** Going in.

in·got (ĭng'gət) *n.* **1.** A mass of metal shaped for convenience in storage or transportation. **2.** A casting mold for metal. [Middle English *ingot,* mass of metal, "something poured into (the mold)" : *in,* IN + Old English *goten,* past participle of *geotan,* to pour, cast in metal (see **gheu-** in Appendix*).]

in·graft. Variant of **engraft.**

in·grain (ĭn-grān') *tr.v.* **-grained, -graining, -grains. 1.** To impress indelibly on the mind or nature; to fix; infuse. **2.** *Archaic.* To dye or stain into the fiber of. —*adj.* **1.** Deeply rooted; instilled. **2.** Dyed in the yarn before weaving or knitting. **3.** Made of fiber or yarn dyed before weaving. Said especially of rugs. —*n.* **1.** Yarn or fiber dyed before manufacture. **2.** Any article made of ingrained yarns, as carpets. [IN- (in) + GRAIN (dye).]

in·grained (ĭn-grānd') *adj.* **1.** Deeply infused; imbued; deep-seated: *ingrained faults.* **2.** Complete; utter: *an ingrained cad.*

in·grate (ĭn'grāt') *n.* An ungrateful person. [Middle English *ingrat,* from Latin *ingrātus,* ungrateful : *in-,* not + *grātus,* pleasing, thankful (see **gwera-¹** in Appendix*).]

in·gra·ti·ate (ĭn-grā'shē-āt') *tr.v.* **-ated, -ating, -ates.** To bring (oneself) purposely into the good graces or favor of another. [IN- (in) + Latin *grātia,* GRACE.] —**in·gra'ti·at'ing·ly** *adv.* —**in·gra'ti·a'tion** *n.* —**in·gra'ti·a·to'ry** (-shē-ə-tôr'ē, -tōr'ē) *adj.*

in·grat·i·tude (ĭn-grăt'ə-tōōd', -tyōōd') *n.* Lack of gratitude; ungratefulness. [Middle English, from Old French, from Medieval Latin *ingrātitūdō* : *in-,* not + *grātitūdō,* GRATITUDE.]

in·gre·di·ent (ĭn-grē'dē-ənt) *n.* **1.** Something added or required to form a mixture or compound: *ingredients for onion soup.* **2.** A component or constituent. [Middle English, "something that enters into a mixture," from Latin *ingrediēns,* present participle of *ingredī,* to enter into. See **ingress.**]

In·gres (ăN'gr'), **Jean Auguste Dominique.** 1780–1867. French classicist painter.

in·gress (ĭn'grĕs') *n.* Also **in·gres·sion** (ĭn-grĕsh'ən). **1.** A going in or entering. **2.** The right or permission to enter. **3.** A means or place of entering. [Middle English *ingresse,* from Latin *ingressus,* from the past participle of *ingredī,* to enter into : *in-,* in, into + *gradī,* to step (see **ghredh-** in Appendix*).]

in·gres·sive (ĭn-grĕs'ĭv) *adj.* Of or pertaining to ingress. —**in·gres'sive** *n.* —**in·gres'sive·ness** *n.*

in-group (ĭn'grōōp') *n.* A group united by common beliefs, attitudes, and interests characteristically excluding outsiders.

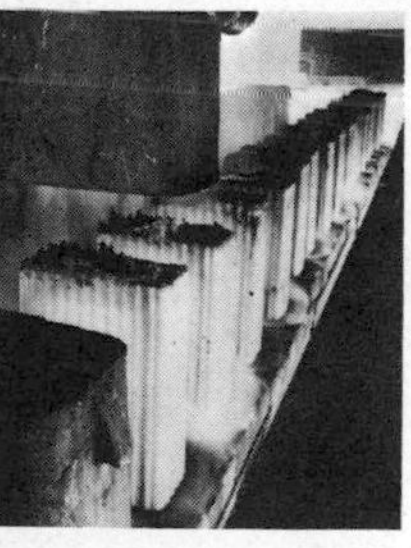

ingot
Steel ingots being stripped of their molds

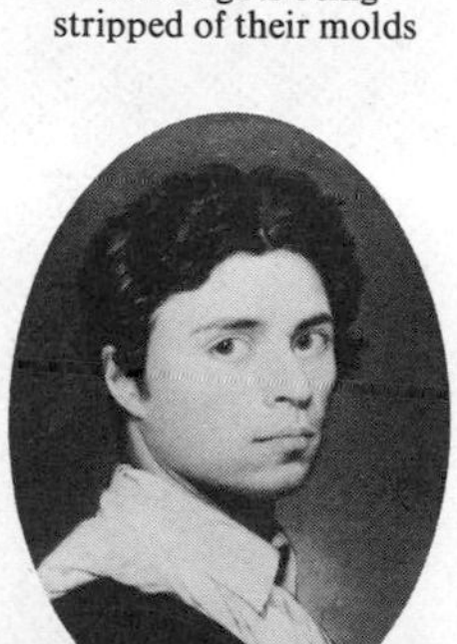

Ingres
Self-portrait at age 24

t tight/th thin, path/*th* this, bathe/ŭ cut/ûr urge/v valve/w with/y yes/z zebra, size/zh vision/ə about, item, edible, gallop, circus/ à *Fr.* ami/œ *Fr.* feu, *Ger.* schön/ü *Fr.* tu, *Ger.* über/KH *Ger.* ich, *Scot.* loch/N *Fr.* bon. *Follows main vocabulary. †Of obscure origin.

in·grow·ing (ĭn′grō′ĭng) *adj.* Growing inward or into something.
in·grown (ĭn′grōn′) *adj.* **1.** Grown abnormally into the flesh: *an ingrown toenail.* **2.** Grown within; innate: *an ingrown habit.*
in·growth (ĭn′grōth′) *n.* **1.** The act of growing inward. **2.** Something that grows inward or within.
in·gui·nal (ĭng′gwə-nəl) *adj.* Of, relating to, or located in the groin. [Latin *inguinālis,* from *inguen* (stem *inguin-*), groin. See **engw-** in Appendix.*]
in·gulf. Variant of **engulf.**
in·gur·gi·tate (ĭn-gûr′jə-tāt′) *tr.v.* **-tated, -tating, -tates.** To swallow greedily or in excessive amounts; to swill; gorge. [Latin *ingurgitāre* : *in-,* in + *gurges* (stem *gurgit-*), whirlpool, abyss (see **gwerə-²** in Appendix*).] —**in·gur′gi·ta′tion** *n.*
in·hab·it (ĭn-hăb′ĭt) *v.* **-ited, -iting, -its.** —*tr.* To reside in. —*intr. Archaic.* To dwell. [Middle English *enhabiten,* from Old French *enhabiter,* from Latin *inhabitāre* : *in-,* in + *habitāre,* to dwell, frequentative of *habēre* (past participle *habitus*), to have, possess (see **ghabh-** in Appendix*).] —**in·hab′it·a·bil′i·ty** *n.* —**in·hab′i·ta·ble** *adj.* —**in·hab′i·ta′tion** *n.* —**in·hab′it·er** *n.*
in·hab·i·tan·cy (ĭn-hăb′ə-tən-sē) *n., pl.* **-cies.** The act of inhabiting or the state of being inhabited; occupancy.
in·hab·i·tant (ĭn-hăb′ə-tənt) *n.* A permanent resident.
in·hab·it·ed (ĭn-hăb′ə-tĭd) *adj.* Having inhabitants; populated.
in·ha·lant (ĭn-hā′lənt) *adj.* Used in or for inhaling. —*n.* Something that is inhaled, as a medicine.
in·ha·la·tion (ĭn′hə-lā′shən) *n.* The act or instance of inhaling.
in·ha·la·tor (ĭn′hə-lā′tər) *n.* A device that produces a vapor to ease breathing or to medicate by inspiration.
in·hale (ĭn-hāl′) *v.* **-haled, -haling, -hales.** —*tr.* To draw in by breathing. —*intr.* To breathe in. [Latin *inhālāre* : *in-,* in + *hālāre,* to breathe (see **halitosis.**)]
in·hal·er (ĭn-hā′lər) *n.* **1.** One that inhales. **2.** An inhalator. **3.** A respirator.
in·har·mon·ic (ĭn′här-mŏn′ĭk) *adj.* Also **in·har·mon·i·cal** (-ĭ-kəl). Not harmonic; discordant. Said of sounds.
in·har·mo·ni·ous (ĭn′här-mō′nē-əs) *adj.* **1.** Not in harmony; discordant. Said of sounds. **2.** Not in accord or agreement. —**in′har·mo′ni·ous·ly** *adv.* —**in′har·mo′ni·ous·ness** *n.*
in·haul (ĭn-hôl′) *n.* Also **in·haul·er** (-hô′lər). *Nautical.* A rope used to draw in a ship's sail.
in·here (ĭn-hîr′) *intr.v.* **-hered, -hering, -heres.** To be inherent or innate. [Latin *inhaerēre* : *in-,* in + *haerēre,* to stick, remain fixed (see **ghais-** in Appendix*).] —**in·her′ence** (-hîr′əns, -hĕr′əns), **in·her′en·cy** *n.*
in·her·ent (ĭn-hîr′ənt, -hĕr′ənt) *adj.* Existing as an essential constituent or characteristic; intrinsic. [Latin *inhaerēns,* present participle of *inhaerēre,* INHERE.] —**in·her′ent·ly** *adv.*
in·her·it (ĭn-hĕr′ĭt) *v.* **-ited, -iting, -its.** —*tr.* **1.** To come into possession of; possess. **2.** To receive (property) from an ancestor or another person by legal succession or will. **3.** *Biology.* To receive (a character or characteristic) genetically from an ancestor. —*intr.* To succeed as an heir; take possession of an inheritance. [Middle English *enheriten,* from Old French *enheriter,* from Late Latin *inhērēditāre* : *in-* (intensive) + *hērēditāre,* to inherit, from *hērēs* (stem *hērēd-*), heir (see **ghē-** in Appendix*).] —**in·her′i·tor** (-ə-tər) *n.* —**in·her′i·trix** (-ə-trĭks) *n.*
in·her·it·a·ble (ĭn-hĕr′ə-tə-bəl) *adj.* **1.** Capable of inheriting; having the right to inherit. **2.** Capable of being inherited.
in·her·i·tance (ĭn-hĕr′ə-təns) *n.* **1.** The act of inheriting. **2.** That which is inherited or to be inherited; legacy; bequest. **3.** Anything regarded as a heritage: *the cultural inheritance of Rome.* **4.** *Biology.* **a.** The process of genetic transmission of characters or characteristics. **b.** The configuration of characters or characteristics so inherited.
inheritance tax. A tax on inherited property. Also called "death tax."
in·hib·it (ĭn-hĭb′ĭt) *tr.v.* **-ited, -iting, -its.** **1.** To restrain or hold back; prevent. **2.** To prohibit; forbid. —See Synonyms at **restrain.** [Middle English *inhibiten,* from Latin *inhibēre* (past participle *inhibitus*), to restrain, hold in : *in-,* in + *habēre,* to have, hold (see **ghabh-** in Appendix*).] —**in·hib′it·a·ble** *adj.* —**in·hib′it·er** *n.* —**in·hib′i·tive, in·hib′i·to′ry** (-tôr′ē, -tōr′ē) *adj.*
in·hi·bi·tion (ĭn′hĭ-bĭsh′ən, ĭn′ĭ-) *n.* **1.** The act of inhibiting or the state of being inhibited. **2. a.** *Psychology.* Restraint of a behavioral process or the condition inducing such restraint. **b.** *Psychoanalysis.* The process by which the superego prevents conscious expression of an instinct.
in·hib·i·tor (ĭn-hĭb′ə-tər) *n.* **1.** A substance used to retard or halt an undesirable reaction such as rusting. **2.** One that inhibits; an inhibiter.
in·hos·pi·ta·ble (ĭn-hŏs′pĭ-tə-bəl, ĭn′hŏ-spĭt′ə-bəl) *adj.* **1.** Displaying no hospitality; unfriendly. **2.** Not affording shelter or sustenance; barren. —**in·hos′pi·ta·ble·ness** *n.* —**in·hos′pi·ta·bly** *adv.* —**in·hos′pi·tal′i·ty** (-tăl′ə-tē) *n.*
in·hu·man (ĭn-hyo͞o′mən) *adj.* **1.** Not human. **2.** Not possessing desirable human qualities; lacking kindness or pity; barbarous; brutal. **3.** Not of ordinary human form; monstrous. —See Synonyms at **cruel.** [Latin *inhūmānus* : *in-,* not + *hūmānus,* HUMAN.] —**in·hu′man·ly** *adv.* —**in·hu′man·ness** *n.*
in·hu·mane (ĭn′hyo͞o-mān′) *adj.* Not humane; lacking in pity or compassion. —**in·hu·mane′ly** *adv.*
in·hu·man·i·ty (ĭn′hyo͞o-măn′ə-tē) *n., pl.* **-ties.** **1.** Lack of pity or compassion. **2.** An inhuman or cruel act.
in·hu·ma·tion (ĭn′hyo͞o-mā′shən) *n.* Burial; interment.
in·hume (ĭn-hyo͞om′) *tr.v.* **-humed, -huming, -humes.** To place in a grave; bury; inter. [Latin *inhumāre* : *in-,* in + *humus,* earth, ground (see **dhghem-** in Appendix*).] —**in·hum′er** *n.*
in·im·i·cal (ĭn-ĭm′ĭ-kəl) *adj.* **1.** Not conducive; harmful; adverse: *habits inimical to good health.* **2.** Unfriendly; hostile; antagonistic: *"a voice apparently cold and inimical"* (Arnold Bennett). [Late Latin *inimīcālis,* from Latin *inimīcus,* enemy : *in-,* not + *amīcus,* friend (see **amma** in Appendix*).]
in·im·i·ta·ble (ĭn-ĭm′ĭ-tə-bəl) *adj.* Defying imitation; matchless; unique. —**in·im′i·ta·bil′i·ty** *n.* —**in·im′i·ta·bly** *adv.*
in·iq·ui·tous (ĭ-nĭk′wə-təs) *adj.* Of the nature of iniquity; wicked; sinful. —**in·iq′ui·tous·ly** *adv.* —**in·iq′ui·tous·ness** *n.*
in·iq·ui·ty (ĭ-nĭk′wə-tē) *n., pl.* **-ties.** **1.** Moral turpitude or sin; wickedness: *"the human mind, since the Fall, was nothing but a sink of iniquity"* (Fielding). **2.** A grossly immoral act; a sin. [Middle English *iniquite,* from Old French, from Latin *iniquitās,* from *inīquus,* unjust : *in-,* not + *aequus,* just, EQUAL.]
in·i·tial (ĭ-nĭsh′əl) *adj. Abbr.* **init.** **1.** Occurring at the very beginning; incipient. **2.** Denoting the first letter or letters of a word. —*n. Abbr.* **init.** **1.** *Often plural.* The first letter or letters of a person's name or names, used as a shortened signature or for identification. **2.** The first letter of a word. **3.** A large, often highly decorated letter set at the beginning of a chapter, verse, paragraph, or the like of a book. —*tr.v.* **initialed, -tialing, -tials.** Also *chiefly British* **-tialled, -tialling.** To mark or sign with one's own initial or initials. [Latin *initiālis,* from *initium,* beginning. See **ei-¹** in Appendix.*] —**in·i′tial·ly** *adv.*
in·i·ti·ate (ĭ-nĭsh′ē-āt′) *tr.v.* **-ated, -ating, -ates.** **1.** To begin or originate. **2.** To introduce (a person) to a new field, interest, skill, or the like; instruct; guide. **3.** To admit into membership, as with ceremonies or ritual. —See Synonyms at **begin.** —*adj.* (ĭ-nĭsh′ē-ĭt) Initiated. —*n.* (ĭ-nĭsh′ē-ĭt) **1.** One who has been initiated. **2.** A novice; beginner. [Latin *initiāre,* from *initium,* beginning. See **initial.**] —**in·i′ti·a′tor** (-ā′tər) *n.*
in·i·ti·a·tion (ĭ-nĭsh′ē-ā′shən) *n.* **1.** An initiating or being initiated; a rudimentary exposure; instruction. **2.** A ceremony, ritual, test, or period of instruction with which a new member is admitted to an organization or office or to knowledge.
in·i·ti·a·tive (ĭ-nĭsh′ē-ə-tĭv, -ē′ā-tĭv, -nĭsh′ə-tĭv) *n.* **1.** The power, ability, or instinct to begin or to follow through with a plan or task; enterprise and determination. **2.** The first step or action; opening move; active role: *take the initiative.* **3.** *Government.* **a.** The power or right to introduce a new legislative measure. **b.** The right and procedure by which citizens can propose a law by petition and ensure its submission to the electorate. —**on one's own initiative.** Spontaneously or on one's own; self-motivated; without instruction or coercion. —*adj.* **1.** Of or pertaining to initiation. **2.** Used to initiate; initiatory. —**in·i′ti·a·tive·ly** *adv.*
in·i·ti·a·to·ry (ĭ-nĭsh′ē-ə-tôr′ē, -tōr′ē) *adj.* **1.** Introductory; initial. **2.** Used to initiate; initiative.
inj. injection.
in·ject (ĭn-jĕkt′) *tr.v.* **-jected, -jecting, -jects.** **1. a.** To force or drive (a fluid) into. **b.** *Medicine.* To introduce (a fluid) into the skin, subcutaneous tissue, muscle, blood vessels, or a bodily cavity. **2.** To introduce (a comment or new element) into conversation or consideration: *inject a note of humor into the negotiations.* **3.** To place into an orbit, trajectory, or stream. [Latin *inicere, injicere* (past participle *injectus*), to throw or put in : *in-,* in + *jacere,* to throw (see **yē-** in Appendix*).] —**in·jec′tor** (-jĕk′tər) *n.*
in·jec·tion (ĭn-jĕk′shən) *n. Abbr.* **inj.** **1.** The act of injecting. **2.** A fluid that is injected. **3.** Broadly, anything injected.
in·ju·di·cious (ĭn′jo͞o-dĭsh′əs) *adj.* Lacking judgment or discretion. —**in′ju·di′cious·ly** *adv.* —**in′ju·di′cious·ness** *n.*
In·jun (ĭn′jən) *n. Nonstandard.* An American Indian. [Facetious respelling of INDIAN.]
in·junc·tion (ĭn-jŭngk′shən) *n.* **1.** The act of enjoining. **2.** That which is enjoined; a command, directive, or order. **3.** *Law.* A court order enjoining or prohibiting a party from a specific course of action. [Late Latin *injunctiō,* from Latin *injungere* (past participle *injunctus*), to enjoin : *in-,* in + *jungere,* to join (see **yeug-** in Appendix*).] —**in·junc′tive** *adj.*
in·jure (ĭn′jər) *tr.v.* **-jured, -juring, -jures.** **1.** To cause harm or damage to; hurt. **2.** To commit an injustice or offense against; wound; wrong. [Back-formation from INJURY.] —**in′jur·er** *n.*
Synonyms: *injure, harm, hurt, damage, impair, mar, spoil, wound.* These verbs refer to acts causing loss in some respect. *Injure* has the widest range. With respect to persons, it can refer to acts that adversely affect health, appearance, feelings, or reputation or that do injustice according to law. Applied to things, it implies an act that lowers value. *Harm* and *hurt* refer principally to what causes physical or mental distress to living things or diminishes the worth of inanimate objects. *Damage* usually implies injury to reputation or status or injury that decreases the value of property. *Impair* refers to what diminishes the quality of health or the strength or utility of things. *Mar* applies principally to acts that injure things, either physically by disfiguring or figuratively by depriving them of highest quality. *Spoil* refers both to destroying the usefulness or value of things and to causing harm to human character or personality through overindulgence. *Wound* refers to causing either physical injury to persons or animals or mental distress to persons.
in·ju·ri·ous (ĭn-jo͝or′ē-əs) *adj.* **1.** Harmful or damaging; deleterious. **2.** Slanderous; libelous.
in·ju·ry (ĭn′jə-rē) *n., pl.* **-ries.** **1.** Damage of or to a person, property, reputation, or thing. **2.** A specific damage or wound: *a leg injury.* **3.** Injustice. **4.** *Law.* Any wrong or damage done to another person or to his property, reputation, or rights when caused by the wrongful act of another. **5.** *Obsolete.* An insult. —See Synonyms at **injustice.** [Middle English *injurie,* from Norman French, from Latin *injūria,* injustice, wrong, from

injūrius, unjust, wrongful : *in-,* not + *jūs* (stem *jūr-*), right, law (see **yewo-**[1] in Appendix*).]

in·jus·tice (ĭn-jŭs′tĭs) *n.* **1.** The fact, practice, or quality of being unjust; lack of justice. **2.** A specific unjust act; a wrong. [Middle English, from Old French, from Latin *injūstitia,* from *injūstus,* unjust : *in-,* not + *jūstus,* JUST.]

Synonyms: *injustice, injury, wrong, grievance.* These nouns denote acts or conditions that cause persons to suffer hardship or loss undeservedly. *Injustice* refers to violation of a person's rights. *Injury* is damage or hurt, suffered through violation of one's rights, for which he can seek legal redress. *Wrong,* in a legal sense, refers to what violates the rights of an individual or adversely affects the public welfare. In the general sense, *wrong* is an intensification of *injustice. Grievance* refers to an act or condition, regarded as a wrong, that gives rise to a complaint.

ink (ĭngk) *n.* **1.** A pigmented liquid or paste used especially for writing or printing. **2.** A dark liquid secreted by cuttlefish and other cephalopods. [Middle English *enke,* from Old French *enke, enque,* from Late Latin *encaustum,* from Greek *enkauston,* purple ink, from *enkaiein,* to burn in, brand, paint in encaustic. See **encaustic.**]

ink·ber·ry (ĭngk′bĕr′ē) *n., pl.* **-ries. 1.** A shrub, *Ilex glabra,* of eastern North America, having black, berrylike fruit. **2. Pokeweed** *(see).* **3.** The fruit of either of these plants.

ink·blot (ĭngk′blŏt′) *n.* **1.** A blotted pattern of spilled ink. **2.** Such a pattern used in the Rorschach test.

ink·horn[1] (ĭngk′hôrn′) *n.* A small container made of horn or similar material, formerly used to hold writing ink.

ink·horn[2] (ĭngk′hôrn′) *adj.* Pedantic; recondite.

ink·ling (ĭngk′lĭng) *n.* **1.** A hint or intimation. **2.** A vague idea or notion. [From Middle English *inklet*†, to mutter.]

ink·stand (ĭngk′stănd′) *n.* **1.** A tray or rack for bottles of ink, pens, and other writing implements. **2.** An inkwell.

Ink·ster (ĭngk′stər). A western suburb of Detroit, Michigan. Population, 36,000.

ink·well (ĭngk′wĕl′) *n.* A small ink reservoir into which a pen is dipped for filling.

ink·y (ĭng′kē) *adj.* **-ier, -iest. 1.** Of or containing ink. **2.** Dark or murky. **3.** Stained or smeared with ink. **—ink′i·ness** *n.*

inky cap. Any of various mushrooms of the genus *Coprinus,* having gills that dissolve into a dark liquid on maturing.

in·lace. Variant of **enlace.**

in·laid (ĭn′lād′, ĭn-lād′) *adj.* **1.** Set into a surface in a decorative pattern. **2.** Decorated with a pattern set into a surface.

in·land (ĭn′lənd) *adj.* **1.** Of, pertaining to, or located in the interior part of a land mass. **2.** Operating or applying within the borders of a country, region, or state; domestic: *inland tariffs.* —*adv.* In, toward, or into the interior of a land mass. —*n.* The interior of a country, region, or state. **—in′land·er** *n.*

Inland Empire. An agricultural region of the northwestern United States between the Cascade Range and the Rocky Mountains, comprising portions of eastern Washington, northeastern Oregon, northern Idaho, and western Montana.

Inland Passage. See **Inside Passage.**

Inland Sea. *Japanese* **Se·to Nai·kai** (sĕ′tō nī′kī). An inlet of the Pacific in southeastern Japan, extending 240 miles between Honshu on the north and Shikoku and Kyushu on the south.

in-law (ĭn′lô′) *n.* Any relative by marriage. [From -IN-LAW.]

-in-law. Indicates parental, filial, or fraternal relation through marriage; for example, **father-in-law.**

in·lay (ĭn-lā′, ĭn′lā′) *tr.v.* **-laid, -laying, -lays. 1.** To set (pieces of wood, ivory, or the like) into a surface, usually at the same level, to form a design. **2.** To decorate (a surface) with wood, ivory, or the like; to parquet. **3.** To insert (a page or photograph, for example) within a mat in a book. —*n.* (ĭn′lā′). **1.** An article, material, or substance that has been inlaid. **2.** A design, pattern, or decoration made by inlaying. **3.** *Dentistry.* A solid filling of gold, plastic, porcelain, or the like, fitted to a cavity in a tooth and cemented in place. **—in·lay′er** *n.*

in·let (ĭn′lĕt, -lĭt) *n.* **1.** A relatively narrow channel or pocket of water. **2.** A stream or bay leading inland, as from the ocean; an estuary. **3.** A narrow passage of water between two islands. **4.** An entry or drainage passage, as to a culvert. **5.** Something that is inserted, let in, or inlaid.

in·li·er (ĭn′lī′ər) *n.* An older rock formation completely surrounded by newer strata.

in lo·co pa·ren·tis (ĭn lō′kō pə-rĕn′tĭs). *Latin.* In the position or place of a parent: *"I stood towards him in loco parentis; because he was as a child to me."* (Thackeray).

in·ly (ĭn′lē) *adv. Poetic.* Inwardly.

in·mate (ĭn′māt′) *n.* **1.** A resident in a building or dwelling. **2.** A person confined to an institution such as a prison, hospital, or asylum. [Perhaps INN (influenced by IN) + MATE.]

in me·di·as res (ĭn mā′dē-äs′ rās′; ĭn mē′dē-əs rēz′). *Latin.* Into the middle of things. Used chiefly of the classical literary or dramatic device whereby an author starts his narrative by plunging his audience into the middle of an objective sequence of events. [Taken from the passage *"in medias res . . . audi torem rapit,"* "(the poet) plunges his hearer into the middle of things" (Horace, *Ars Poetica*).]

in me·mo·ri·am (ĭn mə-môr′ē-əm, mə-mōr′-). *Latin.* In memory of; as a memorial to. Used in epitaphs.

in·most (ĭn′mōst′) *adj.* Innermost.

inn (ĭn) *n.* **1.** A public lodging house serving food and drink to travelers; hotel; motel; hostel. **2.** A tavern or restaurant. **3.** *British.* Formerly, a residence hall for students. [Middle English *inn,* Old English *inn.* See **en** in Appendix.*]

Inn (ĭn). A river rising in Switzerland and flowing 320 miles through Austria and Bavaria to the Danube.

in·nards (ĭn′ərdz) *pl.n. Informal.* **1.** Internal bodily organs; viscera. **2.** Any inner parts. [Variant of INWARDS.]

in·nate (ĭ-nāt′, ĭn′āt′) *adj.* **1.** Possessed at birth; inborn. **2.** Possessed as an essential characteristic; inherent: *"these savages have an innate sense of delicacy"* (Melville). **3.** Of or produced by thought as distinguished from experience. [Middle English *innat,* from Latin *innātus,* past participle of *innāscī,* to be born in : *in-,* in + *nāscī,* to be born (see **gene-** in Appendix*).] **—in·nate′ly** *adv.* **—in·nate′ness** *n.*

Synonyms: *innate, inborn, inbred, congenital, hereditary.* These adjectives mean belonging by nature or from birth rather than through acquisition at a later time. *Innate, inborn,* and *inbred* are often used interchangeably with reference to persons. *Inborn* is strongest in implying possession of something from birth. What is *inbred* is either present from birth or developed through one's earliest training or associations, and what is *innate* seems essential to the nature or make-up of the person or thing in question. *Congenital* is applied principally to physical characteristics, especially to defects acquired during fetal development. *Hereditary* refers to what is genetically transmitted, or the term can describe what is handed down by right of inheritance.

in·ner (ĭn′ər) *adj.* **1.** Located further inside: *an inner room.* **2.** Occurring within: *inner action.* **3.** Less apparent or superficial: *the inner meaning of a poem.* **4.** Pertaining to the soul or mind: *"Beethoven's manuscript looks like a bloody record of a tremendous inner battle"* (Leonard Bernstein). **5.** More exclusive, private, or important: *the inner circles of government.* [Middle English *inner,* Old English *innera, innra.* See **en** in Appendix.*] **—in′ner·ly** *adv.* **—in′ner·ness** *n.*

Inner Heb·ri·des. See **Hebrides.**

Inner Mon·go·li·a (mŏng-gō′lē-ə). Officially, Inner Mongolian Autonomous Region. An administrative division, 326,285 square miles in area, of northern China. Population, 9,200,000. Capital, Huhehot.

in·ner·most (ĭn′ər-mōst′) *adj.* **1.** Situated or occurring farthest within. **2.** Most intimate: *innermost feelings.*

inner product. *Mathematics.* **Scalar product** *(see).*

Inner Temple. 1. One of the four legal societies forming the Inns of Court. **2.** The building housing this society.

inner tube. An inflatable tube used inside some tires.

in·ner·vate (ĭ-nûr′vāt′, ĭn′ər-) *tr.v.* **-vated, -vating, -vates. 1.** To supply (a bodily part) with nerves. **2.** To stimulate (a nerve or bodily part). [IN- + NERVE + -ATE.] **—in·ner′va′tion** *n.*

in·nerve (ĭ-nûrv′) *tr.v.* **-nerved, -nerving, -nerves.** To give nervous energy to; stimulate. [IN- (causative) + NERVE.]

In·ness (ĭn′ĭs), **George.** 1825–1894. American painter.

in·ning (ĭn′ĭng) *n.* **1.** *Baseball.* One of nine divisions or periods of a regulation game, in which each team has a turn at bat as limited by three outs. **2.** *Plural. Cricket.* The division or period of a game during which one team is at bat. Used with a singular verb. **3.** *Often plural.* Any period of opportunity and action: *He will get his innings soon.* **4.** *Archaic.* The reclamation of flooded or marshy land. [From IN.]

inn·keep·er (ĭn′kē′pər) *n.* One who owns or manages an inn.

in·no·cence (ĭn′ə-səns) *n.* **1.** The state, quality, or virtue of being innocent: *"Innocence doth like a rose/Bloom on every maiden's cheek"* (Blake). **2.** A plant, **bluets** *(see).*

in·no·cent (ĭn′ə-sənt) *adj.* **1.** Uncorrupted by evil, malice, or wrongdoing; sinless; untainted; pure: *as innocent of evil as a child.* **2. a.** Not guilty of a specific crime; legally blameless: *found innocent of all charges.* **b.** Not responsible for or guilty of something wrong or unethical; not to be accused: *innocent of negligence.* **3.** Not dangerous or harmful; not serious; innocuous: *an innocent prank.* **4.** Not experienced or worldly; lacking maturity; credulous; naive: *innocent tourists.* **5.** Not exposed to or familiar with; devoid of; without. Used with *of: "Our uncle, innocent of books,/Was rich in love of fields and brooks"* (Whittier). **6.** Betraying or suggesting no deception or guile; simple; artless: *an innocent smile.* —See Synonyms at **naive.** —See Usage note at **plead.** —*n.* **1.** A person who is free or relatively free of evil or sin; one who is pure or uncorrupted. **2.** A simple, guileless, inexperienced, or unsophisticated person; one who is vulnerable or credulous: *"an embattled innocent in matters of love"* (Herbert Gold). **3.** A very young child. [Middle English, from Old French, from Latin *innocēns* : *in-,* not + *nocēns,* present participle of *nocēre,* to harm, hurt (see **nek-**[1] in Appendix*).] **—in′no·cent·ly** *adv.*

In·no·cent III (ĭn′ə-sənt). 1161–1216. Pope (1198–1216); increased papal power and instituted Fourth Crusade.

in·noc·u·ous (ĭ-nŏk′yo͞o-əs) *adj.* **1.** Having no adverse effect; harmless; innocent. **2.** Lacking significance or impact; banal: *an innocuous speech.* [From Latin *innocuus* : *in-,* not + *nocuus,* harmful, from *nocēre,* to harm (see **nek-**[1] in Appendix*).] **—in·noc′u·ous·ly** *adv.* **—in·noc′u·ous·ness** *n.*

in·nom·i·nate (ĭ-nŏm′ə-nĭt) *adj.* **1.** Having no specific name. **2.** Anonymous. [Late Latin *innōminātus* : Latin *in-,* not + *nōminātus,* past participle of *nōmināre,* to name, NOMINATE.]

innominate bone. *Anatomy.* The **hipbone** *(see).*

in·no·vate (ĭn′ə-vāt′) *v.* **-vated, -vating, -vates.** —*tr.* To begin or introduce (something new). —*intr.* To begin or introduce something new; be creative. [Latin *innovāre,* to renew : *in-* (intensive) + *novāre,* to make new, renew, from *novus,* new (see **newo-** in Appendix*).] **—in′no·va′tive** *adj.* **—in′no·va′tor** (-vā′tər) *n.*

in·no·va·tion (ĭn′ə-vā′shən) *n.* **1.** The act of innovating. **2.** That which is newly introduced; a change. **—in′no·va′tion·al** *adj.*

Inns·bruck (ĭnz′bro͝ok′; *German* ĭns′bro͝ok′). The capital of Tyrol, a resort center of western Austria, on the Inn River. Population, 101,000.

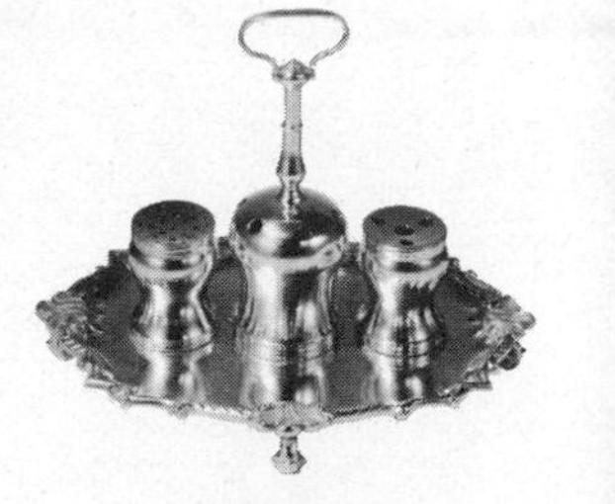

inkstand
Silver inkstand used by the signers of the Declaration of Independence

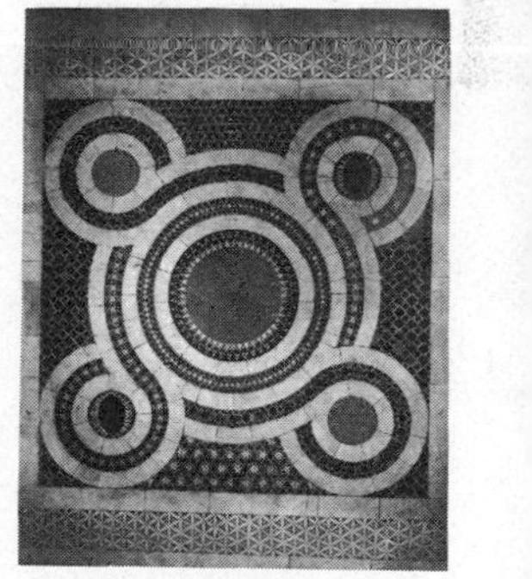

inlay

Inns of Court. 1. The four legal societies in England founded about the beginning of the 14th century, consisting of Gray's Inn, Lincoln's Inn, the Inner Temple, and the Middle Temple, which have the exclusive right to confer the degree of barrister on law students. 2. The buildings housing these societies.

in·nu·en·do (ĭn'yōō-ĕn'dō) n., pl. -does. 1. An indirect, oblique, or subtle implication in expression, usually derogatory in nature; a hint. 2. Law. a. A plaintiff's interpretation, in a libel suit, of allegedly libelous or slanderous material. b. Any explanation of a word or charge. [Latin innuendō, by hinting, from innuendum, gerund of innuere, to nod, to signal to : in, toward + -nuere, to nod (see neu-² in Appendix*).]

In·nu·it (ĭn'yōō-ĭt) n., pl. -its or Innuit. 1. An Eskimo of North America and Greenland as distinguished from one of Asia and the Aleutian Islands. 2. The language of these Eskimos. [Eskimo innuit, "people," plural of innuk, person.]

in·nu·mer·a·ble (ĭ-nōō'mər-ə-bəl, ĭ-nyōō'-) adj. Also in·nu·mer·ous (-mər-əs). Too many to be counted or numbered. See Synonyms at infinite. —in·nu'mer·a·ble·ness n. —in·nu'mer·a·bly adv.

in·nu·tri·tion (ĭn'nōō-trĭsh'ən, ĭn'nyōō-, ĭn'yōō-) n. Lack of nutrition; poor nourishment. —in'nu·tri'tious adj.

in·ob·serv·ance (ĭn'əb-zûr'vəns) n. 1. Lack of heed or attention; disregard. 2. Nonobservance, as of a law or custom. —in'ob·serv'ant adj.

in·ob·tru·sive (ĭn'əb-trōō'sĭv) adj. Not noticeable; unobtrusive.

in·oc·u·la·ble (ĭ-nŏk'yə-lə-bəl) adj. 1. Transmissible by inoculation. 2. Susceptible to a disease transmitted by inoculation. [From INOCULATE.] —in·oc'u·la·bil'i·ty n.

in·oc·u·late (ĭ-nŏk'yə-lāt') v. -lated, -lating, -lates. —tr. 1. To communicate a disease to by transferring its virus or other causative agent into. 2. To introduce the virus of a disease or other antigenic material into (subcutaneous tissue, a blood vessel, or an abraded or absorbing surface) in order to immunize, cure, or experiment. 3. To implant microorganisms or infectious material into (a culture medium). [Middle English inoculaten, from Latin inoculāre, to engraft : in-, in + oculus, eye, bud (see okw- in Appendix*).]

in·oc·u·la·tion (ĭ-nŏk'yə-lā'shən) n. 1. The act, process, or an instance of inoculating. 2. Inoculum.

in·oc·u·lum (ĭ-nŏk'yə-ləm) n. The material used in an inoculation. Also called "inoculant."

in·o·dor·ous (ĭn-ō'də-rəs) adj. Having no odor.

in·of·fen·sive (ĭn'ə-fĕn'sĭv) adj. Giving no offense; harmless; unobjectionable. —in'of·fen'sive·ly adv.

in·of·fi·cious (ĭn'ə-fĭsh'əs) adj. Law. Contrary to natural affection or moral duty. Said of a will in which the testator disinherits his rightful heirs without sufficient reason. [Latin inofficiōsus : in-, not + officiōsus, dutiful, OFFICIOUS.] —in'of·fi'cious·ly adv.

I·nö·nü (ē-nœ'nü), **İsmet.** Original name, Paşa. Born 1884. Prime minister of Turkey (1923–37); president (1938–50); premier (1961–65).

in·op·er·a·ble (ĭn-ŏp'ər-ə-bəl) adj. 1. Not operable. 2. Not susceptible to surgery. —in·op'er·a·bly adv.

in·op·er·a·tive (ĭn-ŏp'ər-ə-tĭv) adj. Not working or functioning.

in·op·por·tune (ĭn-ŏp'ər-tōōn', -tyōōn') adj. Not opportune; ill-timed. —in·op'por·tune'ly adv. —in·op'por·tune'ness n.

in·or·di·nate (ĭn-ôrd'n-ĭt) adj. 1. Exceeding reasonable limits; immoderate; unrestrained. 2. Not regulated; disorderly. —See Synonyms at excessive. [Middle English inordinat, from Latin inordinātus : in-, not + ōrdinātus, past participle of ōrdināre, to set in order, from ōrdō (stem ōrdin-), order (see ar- in Appendix*).] —in·or'di·na·cy, in·or'di·nate·ness n. —in·or'di·nate·ly adv.

in·or·gan·ic (ĭn'ôr-găn'ĭk) adj. Abbr. inorg. 1. a. Involving neither organic life nor the products of organic life. b. Not composed of organic matter; especially, mineral. 2. Of or relating to the chemistry of compounds not usually classified as organic (see). 3. Not arising in normal growth; artificial. 4. Lacking system or structure. —in'or·gan'i·cal·ly adv.

in·os·cu·late (ĭn-ŏs'kyə-lāt') v. -lated, -lating, -lates. —tr. 1. To unite (blood vessels, nerve fibers, or ducts) by small openings. 2. To make continuous; blend. —intr. 1. To open into one another. 2. To unite so as to be continuous; blend. [IN- + Latin ōsculāre, to provide with an opening, from ōsculum, little mouth, opening, diminutive of ōs, mouth (see ōs- in Appendix*).] —in·os'cu·la'tion n.

in·o·si·tol (ĭn-ō'sə-tōl', -tôl', -tŏl') n. Any of nine isomeric alcohols, $C_6H_6(OH)_6$, especially one found in plant and animal tissue and classified as a member of the vitamin B complex. Also called "muscle sugar." [Greek is (genitive inos), tendon, sinew, muscle (see wei-¹ in Appendix* + -IT(E) + -OL.]

in·pa·tient (ĭn'pā'shənt) n. A patient living in a hospital.

in per·so·nam (ĭn pər-sō'nəm). Law. Against a person. Said of a proceeding. [Latin.]

in pet·to (ĭn pĕt'tō). Secretly; privately. Said of appointments of cardinals by the pope undisclosed in consistory. [Italian, "in the breast."]

in·phase (ĭn'fāz') adj. Electricity. Having the same phase.

in pos·se (ĭn pŏs'ē). Latin. Possible but not actual; potential. Literally, in possibility.

in pro·pri·a per·so·na (ĭn prō'prē-ə pûr-sō'nə). Latin. In one's own person; in one's self.

in·put (ĭn'pŏŏt') n. 1. Anything put into a system or expended in its operation to achieve a result or output, especially: a. Energy, work, or power used to drive a machine. b. Current, electromotive force, or power supplied to an electric circuit, network, or device. c. Information put into a communications system for transmission or into a data-processing system for processing. d. The entirety of basic resources, including materials, equipment, and funds, required to complete a project. 2. A position, terminal, or station at which any such input enters a system.

in·quest (ĭn'kwĕst') n. 1. A judicial inquiry of some matter, usually before a jury. 2. A jury making such an inquiry. 3. An investigation. [Middle English enquest, from Old French enqueste, from Vulgar Latin inquesta (unattested), from the feminine past participle of inquaerere (unattested), INQUIRE.]

in·qui·e·tude (ĭn-kwī'ə-tōōd', -tyōōd') n. 1. Restlessness. 2. Uneasiness; disquietude. [Middle English, from Old French, from Late Latin inquiētūdō, from Latin inquiētus, restless : in-, not + quiētus, QUIET.]

in·qui·line (ĭn'kwə-lĭn', -lĭn) n. An animal that characteristically lives commensally in the burrow or dwelling place of an animal of another kind. —adj. Being or living as an inquiline. [Latin inquilīnus, tenant, dweller. See kwel-¹ in Appendix.*] —in'qui·lin·ism' (-lə-nĭz'əm), in'qui·lin'i·ty (-lĭn'ə-tē) n. —in'qui·lin'ous (-lī'nəs) adj.

in·quire (ĭn-kwīr') v. -quired, -quiring, -quires. Also en·quire. —intr. 1. a. To put a question. b. To request information. Used with about or after: inquire after another's health. 2. To make an inquiry; look into; investigate. Used with into. —tr. 1. To ask about. 2. To ask: "I am free to inquire what a work of art means to me" (Bernard Berenson). —See Synonyms at ask. [Middle English enquiren, enqueren, from Old French enquerrer, from Vulgar Latin inquaerere (unattested), variant of Latin inquīrere : in- (intensive) + quaerere, to seek, ask (see quaerere in Appendix*).] —in·quir'er n. —in·quir'ing·ly adv.

in·quir·y (ĭn'kwĭr'ē, ĭn'kwə-rē) n., pl. -ies. 1. The act of inquiring. 2. A question; query. 3. A close examination of some matter in a quest for information or truth.

in·qui·si·tion (ĭn'kwə-zĭsh'ən) n. 1. The act of inquiring into a matter; an investigation. 2. a. An inquest. b. The verdict of a judicial inquiry. 3. Capital I. A former tribunal in the Roman Catholic Church directed at the suppression of heresy. 4. Any inquisitorial scrutiny. [Middle English inquisicioun, from Old French inquisition, from Latin inquisitiō, from inquīrere (past participle inquisītus), INQUIRE.] —in'qui·si'tion·al adj.

in·quis·i·tive (ĭn-kwĭz'ə-tĭv) adj. 1. Unduly curious and inquiring; prying. 2. Eager to learn. —See Synonyms at curious. —in·quis'i·tive·ly adv. —in·quis'i·tive·ness n.

in·quis·i·tor (ĭn-kwĭz'ə-tər) n. 1. One who inquires; a questioner. 2. One who investigates officially. 3. A member of the Inquisition.

in·quis·i·to·ri·al (ĭn-kwĭz'ə-tôr'ē-əl, -tōr'ē-əl) adj. 1. Pertaining to or having the function of an inquisitor. 2. Law. a. Pertaining to a trial in which one party acts as both prosecutor and judge. b. Pertaining to a criminal proceeding conducted in secrecy. 3. Resembling or characteristic of an inquisitor. 4. Offensively prying. —in·quis'i·to'ri·al·ly adv.

in re (ĭn rē'). Law. In the matter or case of; in regard to. See Usage note at re (preposition). [Latin.]

in rem (ĭn rĕm'). Law. Against a thing, as a property, status, or right. [Latin.]

I.N.R.I. Jesus of Nazareth, King of the Jews (Latin Iesus Nazarenus Rex Iudaeorum).

in·road (ĭn'rōd') n. 1. A hostile invasion; raid; incursion. 2. An encroachment; intrusion. [IN + ROAD (obsolete sense "raid").]

in·rush (ĭn'rŭsh') n. A sudden rushing in; an irruption; influx.

INS International News Service.

ins. 1. inspector. 2. insulated; insulation. 3. insurance.

in·sal·i·vate (ĭn-săl'ə-vāt') tr.v. -vated, -vating, -vates. To mix (food) with saliva in chewing. —in·sal'i·va'tion n.

in·sa·lu·bri·ous (ĭn'sə-lōō'brē-əs) adj. Not salubrious.

in·sane (ĭn-sān') adj. 1. Of, exhibiting, or afflicted with insanity. 2. Characteristic of, used by, or for the insane. 3. Very foolish; rash; wild. [Latin insānus : in-, not + sānus, SANE.] —in·sane'ly adv. —in·sane'ness n.

in·san·i·tar·y (ĭn-săn'ə-tĕr'ē) adj. Not sanitary.

in·san·i·ty (ĭn-săn'ə-tē) n., pl. -ties. 1. Persistent mental disorder or derangement. 2. a. Civil Law. Unsoundness of mind sufficient, in the judgment of a court, to render a person unfit to maintain a contractual or other legal relationship or to warrant commitment to a mental hospital. b. Criminal Law. In most jurisdictions, a degree of mental malfunctioning sufficient to prevent the accused from knowing right from wrong, as to the act he is charged with, or to render him unaware of the nature of the act when committing it. 3. a. Extreme foolishness; total folly. b. Something foolish.

Synonyms: insanity, lunacy, madness, mania, dementia. These nouns denote conditions of mental disability. *Insanity* is a pronounced and usually prolonged condition of mental disorder that legally renders a person not responsible for his actions. *Lunacy* is sometimes used interchangeably with *insanity*, or it can denote derangement relieved intermittently by periods of clear-mindedness. *Madness*, a more general term, often stresses the violent side of mental illness. *Mania* refers principally to the excited phase of manic-depressive psychosis. *Dementia* implies mental deterioration brought on by organic disorders.

in·sa·tia·ble (ĭn-sā'shə-bəl, -shē-ə-bəl) adj. Incapable of being satiated. [Middle English insaciable, from Old French, from Latin insatiābilis : in-, not + satiāre, to SATIATE.] —in·sa'tia·bil'i·ty, in·sa'tia·ble·ness n. —in·sa'tia·bly adv.

in·sa·ti·ate (ĭn-sā'shē-ĭt) adj. Not satisfied; never satisfied; insatiable. —in·sa'ti·ate·ly adv. —in·sa'ti·ate·ness n.

in·scribe (ĭn-skrīb') tr.v. -scribed, -scribing, -scribes. 1. To write, print, carve, or engrave (words or letters) on or in a paper, stone, wood, or other surface. **2.** To mark or engrave (a surface) with words or letters. **3.** To enter (a name) on a list or in a register. **4.** To dedicate (a book or photograph, for example) to another. **5.** *Geometry.* To enclose (a polygon or polyhedron) within a closed configuration of lines, curves, or surfaces so that every vertex of the enclosed figure is incident on the enclosing configuration. [Latin *inscrībere* : *in-*, in + *scrībere,* to write (see **skeri-** in Appendix*).] —**in·scrib′er** *n.*

in·scrip·tion (ĭn-skrĭp′shən) *n.* **1.** The act or instance of inscribing. **2.** That which is inscribed, such as the wording on a coin or medal, an epitaph, or a dedication of a book or work of art. **3.** An enrollment or registration of names. [Middle English *inscripcioun,* from Latin *inscriptiō,* a writing in or upon, from *inscrībere* (past participle *inscriptus*), INSCRIBE.] —**in·scrip′tion·al, in·scrip′tive** *adj.* —**in·scrip′tive·ly** *adv.*

in·scru·ta·ble (ĭn-skro͞o′tə-bəl) *adj.* Not able to be fathomed or understood; impenetrable; enigmatic: *"people who prefer to stand at the bar have, universally, an inscrutable look"* (Thomas Pynchon). See Synonyms at **mysterious.** —**in·scru′ta·bil′i·ty, in·scru′ta·ble·ness** *n.* —**in·scru′ta·bly** *adv.*

in·sect (ĭn′sĕkt′) *n.* **1.** Any of numerous usually small invertebrate animals of the class Insecta (or Hexapoda), having an adult stage characterized by three pairs of legs, a segmented body with three major divisions, and usually two pairs of wings. **2.** Loosely, any of various similar invertebrate animals such as a spider, centipede, or tick. **3.** One who is small or contemptible. [Latin *insectum (animale),* "segmented (animal)" (translation of Greek *entomon;* see **entomo-**), from *insectus,* past participle of *insecāre,* to cut into : *in-*, in + *secāre,* to cut (see **sek-** in Appendix*).]

in·sec·tar·i·um (ĭn′sĕk-târ′ē-əm) *n., pl.* **-ums** or **-ia** (-ē-ə). Also **in·sec·tar·y** (ĭn′sĕk-tĕr′ē) *pl.* **-ies.** A place in which living insects are kept or bred.

in·sec·ti·cide (ĭn-sĕk′tə-sīd′) *n.* An agent used to kill insects. —**in·sec′ti·ci′dal** (-sīd′l) *adj.*

in·sec·ti·vore (ĭn-sĕk′tə-vôr′, -vōr′) *n.* **1.** Any of various mammals of the order Insectivora, characteristically feeding on insects, and including the shrews, moles, and hedgehogs. **2.** An organism that feeds on insects. [New Latin *Insectivora* (order) : Latin *insectum,* INSECT + *-vorus,* -VOROUS.]

in·sec·tiv·o·rous (ĭn′sĕk-tĭv′ər-əs) *adj.* **1.** Feeding on insects. **2.** *Botany.* Capable of trapping and absorbing insects, as the pitcher plant or Venus's-flytrap. [INSECT + -VOROUS.]

in·se·cure (ĭn′sĭ-kyo͝or′) *adj.* **1.** Not secure or safe; inadequately guarded or protected. **2.** Unsure; unstable; shaky. **3.** Apprehensive or lacking self-confidence. —**in′se·cure′ly** *adv.* —**in′se·cu′ri·ty, in′se·cure′ness** *n.*

in·sem·i·nate (ĭn-sĕm′ə-nāt′) *tr.v.* **-nated, -nating, -nates.** **1. a.** To sow seed in. **b.** To introduce semen into the uterus of. **2.** To sow ideas in. [Latin *insēmināre* : *in-*, in + *sēmināre,* to plant, from *sēmen* (stem *sēmin-*), seed, SEMEN.] —**in·sem′i·na′tion** *n.* —**in·sem′i·na′tor** (-nā′tər) *n.*

in·sen·sate (ĭn-sĕn′sāt′, -sĭt) *adj.* **1. a.** Lacking sensation; inanimate. **b.** Unconscious. **2.** Lacking sensibility; inhuman; unfeeling. **3.** Lacking sense; foolish. —**in·sen′sate′ly** *adv.*

in·sen·si·ble (ĭn-sĕn′sə-bəl) *adj.* **1.** Imperceptible; inappreciable: *an insensible change.* **2.** Deprived of the power of feeling; unconscious: *"Sir Henry lay insensible where he had fallen."* (Arthur Conan Doyle). **3. a.** Unsusceptible to or unaffected by: *insensible to the cold.* **b.** Unheeding; incognizant; unmindful: *I am not insensible of your concern.* **c.** Unfeeling; indifferent; callous. **4.** *Rare.* Lacking intelligence; irrational. —**in·sen′si·bil′i·ty** *n.* —**in·sen′si·bly** *adv.*

in·sen·si·tive (ĭn-sĕn′sə-tĭv) *adj.* **1.** Not sensitive; lacking sensitivity. **2.** Unfeeling. —**in·sen′si·tiv′i·ty, in·sen′si·tive·ness** *n.* —**in·sen′si·tive·ly** *adv.*

in·sen·ti·ent (ĭn-sĕn′shənt) *adj.* Without sensation or consciousness; inanimate. —**in·sen′ti·ence** *n.*

in·sep·a·ra·ble (ĭn-sĕp′ər-ə-bəl) *adj. Abbr.* **insep.** Incapable of being separated. —**in·sep′a·ra·bil′i·ty, in·sep′a·ra·ble·ness** *n.* —**in·sep′a·ra·bly** *adv.*

in·sert (ĭn-sûrt′) *tr.v.* **-serted, -serting, -serts.** **1.** To put or set into, between, or among another or other things. **2.** To introduce into the body or text of something; interpolate. **3.** To place into an orbit, trajectory, or stream. —*n.* (ĭn′sûrt′). Something inserted or intended for insertion, such as a paragraph, a map, an extra leaf, or a circular inserted in an article or a book. [Latin *inserere* (past participle *insertus*) : *in-*, in + *serere,* to sow, plant (see **sē-¹** in Appendix*).] —**in·sert′er** *n.*

in·sert·ed (ĭn-sûr′tĭd) *adj.* Joined to another part, as stamens to a corolla.

in·ser·tion (ĭn-sûr′shən) *n.* **1.** The act of inserting. **2.** Something inserted. **3.** A point or mode of attachment. **4.** A strip of lace, embroidery, or other trim to be inserted in a garment, tablecloth, or the like. —**in·ser′tion·al** *adj.*

in·ses·so·ri·al (ĭn′sə-sôr′ē-əl, -sōr′ē-əl) *adj. Rare.* Perching or adapted for perching. [From Late Latin *insessor,* "one that perches," from Latin *insidēre* (past participle *insessus*), to sit upon : *in-*, on + *sedēre,* to sit (see **sed-¹** in Appendix*).]

in·set (ĭn-sĕt′) *tr.v.* **-set, -setting, -sets.** To insert; set in. —*n.* (ĭn′sĕt′). **1.** Something set in, as: **a.** A small map or illustration set within a larger one. **b.** A leaf or group of pages inserted in a publication. **c.** A piece of material set into a dress as trim. **2. a.** An inflow, as of water. **b.** A channel.

in·shore (ĭn′shôr′, -shōr′) *adj.* **1.** Close to the shore. **2.** Coming toward the shore. —*adv.* Toward the shore.

in·shrine. Variant of **enshrine.**

in·side (ĭn-sīd′, ĭn′sīd′) *n.* **1.** The inner or interior part. **2.** An inner side or surface. **3.** The middle part; the part away from the edge. **4.** *Plural. Informal.* **a.** The inner organs; entrails. **b.** The inner parts or workings. **5.** *Slang.* Confidential information; tip. —**inside out.** With the inner surface turned out; reversed. —**on the inside.** In a position of confidence or influence. —*adj.* **1.** Inner; interior. **2.** For the interior. **3.** Pertaining to or coming from those in authority: *the inside office.* **4.** *Baseball.* Passing too near the body of the batter. Said of a pitch. —*adv.* (ĭn-sīd′). Into or in the interior; within. —*prep.* (ĭn′sīd′). **1.** Within: *inside an hour.* **2.** Into: *to go inside the house.* —**inside of.** Within the boundaries of; inside.

Usage: *Inside* (preposition) is capable of functioning without a succeeding *of.* Especially in writing, *inside* is preferably used without *of* to indicate position or location: *Stay inside the house.* *Inside of* is used informally for *within* in references to time or distance: *inside of an hour; inside of a mile.*

Inside Passage. A protected navigation route extending 950 miles off the coasts of Alaska and British Columbia, Canada, through the islands of the Alexander Archipelago. Also called "Inland Passage."

in·sid·er (ĭn-sī′dər) *n.* **1.** An accepted member of a clique. **2.** One who has the ear of those in charge.

inside track. **1.** In a curved race track, the path next to the inner rail. **2.** An advantageous spot in a competition.

in·sid·i·ous (ĭn-sĭd′ē-əs) *adj.* **1.** Working or spreading harmfully in a subtle or stealthy manner. **2.** Intended to entrap; wily; treacherous: *"a tedious argument of insidious intent"* (T.S. Eliot). **3.** Sly; beguiling: *"I was now a woman/Insidious, subtle, versed in the world and rich."* (Edgar Lee Masters). **4.** Lying in wait. [Latin *insidiōsus,* "lying in wait for," from *insidiae,* ambush, from *insidēre,* to sit in or on, lie in wait for. See **insessorial.**] —**in·sid′i·ous·ly** *adv.* —**in·sid′i·ous·ness** *n.*

in·sight (ĭn′sīt′) *n.* **1.** The capacity to discern the true nature of a situation; penetration. **2.** An elucidating glimpse.

in·sig·ni·a (ĭn-sĭg′nē-ə) *n., pl.* **insignia** or **-as.** Also **in·sig·ne** (-nē). See Usage note below. **1.** A badge of office, rank, membership, or nationality; emblem. **2.** A distinguishing sign: *the insignia of success.* [Latin, plural of *insigne,* sign, mark, from *insignis,* distinguished, marked : *in-*, in + *signum,* SIGN.]

Usage: *Insignia* is acceptably used as a singular, according to 73 per cent of the Usage Panel. The plural *insignias,* a newer coinage, is acceptable to 56 per cent of the Panel.

in·sig·nif·i·cance (ĭn′sĭg-nĭf′ĭ-kəns) *n.* The quality or state of being insignificant.

in·sig·nif·i·can·cy (ĭn′sĭg-nĭf′ĭ-kən-sē) *n., pl.* **-cies.** **1.** Insignificance. **2.** Something insignificant.

in·sig·nif·i·cant (ĭn′sĭg-nĭf′ĭ-kənt) *adj.* **1. a.** Not significant. **b.** Trivial. **2.** Small. **3.** Meaningless. —**in′sig·nif′i·cant·ly** *adv.*

in·sin·cere (ĭn′sĭn-sîr′) *adj.* Not sincere; hypocritical. —**in′sin·cere′ly** *adv.* —**in·sin·cer′i·ty** (-sĕr′ə-tē) *n.*

in·sin·u·ate (ĭn-sĭn′yo͞o-āt′) *v.* **-ated, -ating, -ates.** —*tr.* **1. a.** To introduce gradually and insidiously. **b.** To edge or worm (oneself) by subtle and artful means: *"she insinuated herself into the company of those who were celebrated for their conversation"* (Thornton Wilder). **2.** To convey with oblique hints and allusions; hint covertly. —*intr.* To make insinuations. —See Synonyms at **suggest.** [Latin *insinuāre,* to wind one's way into : *in-*, in + *sinuāre,* to curve, from *sinus,* curve, SINUS.] —**in·sin′u·a′tive** *adj.* —**in·sin′u·a′tor** (-ā′tər) *n.*

in·sin·u·at·ing (ĭn-sĭn′yo͞o-ā′tĭng) *adj.* **1.** Provoking gradual doubt or suspicion; suggestive: *insinuating remarks.* **2.** Ingratiating: *a silky insinuating voice.* —**in·sin′u·at′ing·ly** *adv.*

in·sin·u·a·tion (ĭn-sĭn′yo͞o-ā′shən) *n.* **1.** The act or practice of insinuating. **2.** An artfully indirect suggestion.

in·sip·id (ĭn-sĭp′ĭd) *adj.* **1.** Lacking flavor or zest; unpalatable. **2.** Lacking excitement or interest; unstimulating; vapid: *"I have no taste of those insipid dry discourses"* (Congreve). [Late Latin *insipidus* : Latin *in-*, not + *sapidus,* SAPID.] —**in′si·pid′i·ty** (ĭn′sĭ-pĭd′ə-tē), **in·sip′id·ness** *n.* —**in·sip′id·ly** *adv.*

in·sip·i·ence (ĭn-sĭp′ē-əns) *n. Archaic.* Lack of wisdom. [Middle English, from Old French, from Latin *insipientia,* from *insipiēns,* unwise : *in-*, not + *sapiēns,* wise, SAPIENT.]

in·sist (ĭn-sĭst′) *v.* **-sisted, -sisting, -sists.** —*intr.* To keep resolutely to or emphasize an assertion, demand, or course. Usually used with *on* or *upon.* —*tr.* To assert or demand vehemently and persistently: *We insist that you accept these gifts.* [Latin *insistere,* to stand on, persist : *in-*, on + *sistere,* to cause to stand, stand firm (see **stā-** in Appendix*).] —**in·sis′tence, in·sis′ten·cy** *n.*

in·sis·tent (ĭn-sĭs′tənt) *adj.* **1.** Persistent; pertinacious. **2.** Demanding notice: *insistent hunger.* —**in·sis′tent·ly** *adv.*

in si·tu (ĭn sī′to͞o, sĭt′o͞o). *Latin.* In (its original) place.

in·snare. Variant of **ensnare.**

in·so·bri·e·ty (ĭn′sə-brī′ə-tē) *n.* Lack of sobriety; intemperance.

in·so·far (ĭn′sō-fär′) *adv.* To such an extent. Used with *as: "The scientist loves both the truth he discovers and himself insofar as he discovers it."* (Paul Tillich).

in·so·late (ĭn′sō-lāt′) *tr.v.* **-lated, -lating, -lates.** To expose to sunlight, as for bleaching. [Latin *insōlāre* : *in-*, in + *sōl,* sun (see **sāwel-** in Appendix*).]

in·so·la·tion (ĭn′sō-lā′shən) *n.* **1. a.** Exposure to sunlight. **b.** Therapeutic exposure to sunlight. **2. Sunstroke** *(see).* **3. a.** The solar radiation incident on the earth or another planet. **b.** The rate of delivery of such radiation per unit area surface.

in·sole (ĭn′sōl′) *n.* **1.** The inner sole of a shoe or boot. **2.** An extra strip of material put inside a shoe for comfort or protection.

in·so·lence (ĭn′sə-ləns) *n.* **1.** The quality of being insolent. **2.** An instance of insolent behavior.

in·so·lent (ĭn′sə-lənt) *adj.* **1.** Presumptuous and insulting in

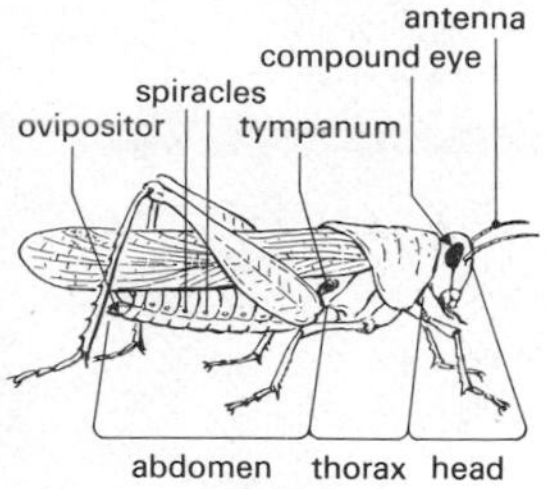
antenna
compound eye
spiracles
ovipositor
tympanum
abdomen
thorax
head

insect
Grasshopper

manner or speech; arrogant. 2. Audaciously impudent; impertinent. [Middle English, from Latin *insolēns*, perhaps originally "unusual," "quaint" : *in-*, not + *solēns*, present participle of *solēre*, to use (see **obsolete**).] —**in'so·lent·ly** *adv.*

in·sol·u·ble (ĭn-sŏl'yə-bəl) *adj.* 1. Incapable of being dissolved. 2. Not able to be solved or explained. [Learned respelling of Middle English *insolible*, from Latin *insolūbilis* : *in-*, not + *solvere*, to SOLVE.] —**in·sol'u·bil'i·ty**, **in·sol'u·ble·ness** *n.* —**in·sol'u·bly** *adv.*

in·solv·a·ble (ĭn-sŏl'və-bəl) *adj.* Incapable of being solved.

in·sol·ven·cy (ĭn-sŏl'vən-sē) *n.* The state or condition of being insolvent.

in·sol·vent (ĭn-sŏl'vənt) *adj.* 1. Unable to meet debts or discharge liabilities; bankrupt. 2. Pertaining to insolvency or bankrupt persons. —*n.* One who is insolvent.

in·som·ni·a (ĭn-sŏm'nē-ə) *n.* Chronic inability to sleep. [Latin, from *insomnis*, sleepless : *in-*, not + *somnus*, sleep (see **swep-**[1] in Appendix*).] —**in·som'ni·ous** *adj.*

in·som·ni·ac (ĭn-sŏm'nē-ăk') *n.* A person with insomnia.

in·so·much (ĭn'sō-mŭch') *adv.* 1. To such extent or degree. Used with *as* or *that*. 2. Since; inasmuch. Used with *as*. [Middle English *in so muche*, translation of Old French *en tant (que)*.]

in·sou·ci·ance (ĭn-sōō'sē-əns) *n.* Lack of concern; indifference.

in·sou·ci·ant (ĭn-sōō'sē-ənt) *adj.* Blithely indifferent; carefree. [French : *in-*, not + *souciant*, present participle of *soucier*, to trouble, upset (reflexively, "to care"), from Latin *sollicitāre*, to agitate, vex (see **solicit**).] —**in·sou'ci·ant·ly** *adv.*

in·soul. Variant of **ensoul.**

insp. inspected; inspector.

in·spect (ĭn-spĕkt') *tr.v.* **-spected, -specting, -spects.** 1. To examine carefully and critically, especially for flaws. 2. To review or examine officially. [Latin *inspectāre*, frequentative of *inspicere* (past participle *inspectus*), to look into : *in-*, in + *specere*, to look (see **spek-** in Appendix*) or from Latin *inspectāre*, from *inspicere* (past participle *inspectus*).]

in·spec·tion (ĭn-spĕk'shən) *n.* 1. The act of inspecting. 2. Official examination or review. —**in·spec'tion·al** *adj.*

in·spec·tive (ĭn-spĕk'tĭv) *adj.* Given to inspecting; searching; watchful: *an inspective glance.*

in·spec·tor (ĭn-spĕk'tər) *n. Abbr.* **ins., insp.** 1. A person, especially an official, who inspects. 2. A police officer of the rank next below superintendent. —**in·spec'to·ral, in'spec·to'ri·al** (-tôr'ē-əl, -tōr'ē-əl) *adj.* —**in·spec'tor·ship'** *n.*

in·spec·tor·ate (ĭn-spĕk'tər-ĭt) *n.* 1. The office or duties of an inspector. 2. A staff of inspectors. 3. An inspector's district.

inspector general *pl.* **inspectors general.** *Abbr.* **IG, I.G.** An officer having general investigative powers within a civil, military, or other organization.

in·sphere. Variant of **ensphere.**

in·spi·ra·tion (ĭn'spə-rā'shən) *n.* 1. Stimulation of the faculties to a high level of feeling or activity. 2. The condition of being so stimulated. 3. An agency, such as a person or a work of art, that moves the intellect or emotions. 4. Something that is inspired, as an idea or action. 5. *Theology.* Divine guidance or influence exerted directly upon the mind and soul of man. 6. The act of breathing in; inhalation.

in·spi·ra·tion·al (ĭn'spə-rā'shən-əl) *adj.* 1. Of or pertaining to inspiration. 2. Providing, or intended to convey, inspiration. 3. Resulting from inspiration. —**in'spi·ra'tion·al·ly** *adv.*

in·spi·ra·tor (ĭn'spə-rā'tər) *n.* 1. An inhaler. 2. A respirator.

in·spir·a·to·ry (ĭn-spīr'ə-tôr'ē, -tōr'ē) *adj.* Pertaining to or used for the drawing in of air.

in·spire (ĭn-spīr') *v.* **-spired, -spiring, -spires.** —*tr.* 1. To animate the mind or emotions of. 2. To stimulate to an indicated feeling or action. 3. To elicit; create: *a woman capable of inspiring love.* 4. a. To affect, guide, or arouse by divine influence. b. To communicate by divine influence. 5. To inhale (air). 6. *Archaic.* a. To breathe upon. b. To breathe life into. —*intr.* 1. To rouse latent energies, ideals, or reverence. 2. To inhale. [Middle English *inspiren*, from Old French *inspirer*, from Latin *inspīrāre*, to breathe into : *in-*, into + *spīrāre*, to breathe (see **spirāre** in Appendix*).] —**in·spir'er** *n.*

in·spir·it (ĭn-spĭr'ĭt) *tr.v.* **-ited, -iting, -its.** To instill courage or life into; animate; enliven. [IN- (causative) + SPIRIT.]

in·spis·sate (ĭn-spĭs'āt', ĭn'spĭ-sāt') *v.* **-sated, -sating, -sates.** —*tr.* To cause to thicken, as by boiling or evaporation; condense. —*intr.* To thicken. [Late Latin *inspissāre* : Latin *in-* (intensive) + *spissāre*, to thicken, from *spissus*†, thick.] —**in'spis·sa'tion** *n.* —**in·spis'sa'tor** (ĭn-spĭs'ā'tər) *n.*

inst. 1. instant. 2. institute; institution. 3. instrument.

Inst. institute; institution.

in·sta·bil·i·ty (ĭn'stə-bĭl'ə-tē) *n., pl.* **-ties.** Lack of stability.

in·stall (ĭn-stôl') *tr.v.* **-stalled, -stalling, -stalls.** Also **in·stal, -stalled, -stalling, -stals.** 1. To set in position and connect or adjust for use. 2. To put in an office, rank, or position. 3. To settle in a place or condition indicated; establish. Used reflexively. [Old French *installer*, from Medieval Latin *installāre* : *in-* (causative) + *stallum*, place, stall (see **stel-**[1] in Appendix*).] —**in·stall'er** *n.*

in·stal·la·tion (ĭn'stə-lā'shən) *n.* 1. The act of installing or the state of being installed. 2. A system of machinery or other apparatus set up for use. 3. A military base or camp.

in·stall·ment[1] (ĭn-stôl'mənt) *n.* Also **in·stal·ment.** 1. One of several successive payments in settlement of a debt. 2. A portion of anything issued at intervals. 3. A chapter or part of a work presented serially. [Variant of earlier *estallment*, from Norman French *estalement*, from *estaler*, to fix (as payments), from *estal*, place, fixed position, from Old High German *stal*, place, stall. See **stel-**[1] in Appendix.*]

in·stall·ment[2] (ĭn-stôl'mənt) *n.* Also **in·stal·ment.** Installation.

installment plan. A credit system by which payment for merchandise is made in installments over a fixed period of time.

in·stance (ĭn'stəns) *n.* 1. A case or example: *"It may be thought an instance of vanity that I pretend at all to write my life"* (Hume). 2. A legal proceeding or process; suit. 3. A step in proceeding: *In this instance I choose to remain silent.* 4. a. Prompting; request: *He called at the instance of his wife.* b. *Archaic.* Urgent solicitation. 5. *Obsolete.* An impelling motive. —See Synonyms at **example.** —*tr.v.* **instanced, -stancing, -stances.** 1. To offer as an example; cite. 2. To demonstrate or show by being an example of; exemplify. [Middle English *instaunce*, from Old French *instance*, from Latin *instantia*, presence, perseverence, urgency, from *instāns*, INSTANT.]

in·stan·cy (ĭn'stən-sē) *n.* 1. Urgency. 2. Immediateness; instantaneousness.

in·stant (ĭn'stənt) *n. Abbr.* **inst.** 1. A very brief time; a moment. 2. A particular point in time: *the instant he arrives.* —See Synonyms at **moment.** —*adj. Abbr.* **inst.** 1. Immediate: *instant attention.* 2. Imperative; urgent: *an instant need.* 3. *Archaic.* a. Present; now under consideration. b. Of the current month. Compare **proximo.** 4. Prepared for rapid completion with minimal effort. —*adv. Poetic.* Instantly. [Middle English, urgent, immediate, from Old French, from Latin *instāns*, present participle of *instāre*, to stand upon, be present, persist : *in-*, upon + *stāre*, to stand (see **stā-** in Appendix*).]

in·stan·ta·ne·ous (ĭn'stən-tā'nē-əs) *adj.* 1. Occurring or completed without perceptible delay. 2. Occurring at a specific instant. [Medieval Latin *instantāneus*, from Latin *instāns*, urgent, INSTANT.] —**in'stan·ta'ne·ous·ly** *adv.* —**in'stan·ta'ne·ous·ness** *n.*

in·stan·ter (ĭn-stăn'tər) *adv.* Instantly. [Medieval Latin, from Latin, urgently, from *instāns*, urgent, INSTANT.]

in·stant·ly (ĭn'stənt-lē) *adv.* 1. At once. 2. *Archaic.* Urgently. —See Synonyms at **immediately.** —*conj.* As soon as.

in·star[1] (ĭn-stär') *tr.v.* **-starred, -starring, -stars.** To stud with or as if with stars. [IN- (causative) + STAR.]

in·star[2] (ĭn'stär) *n.* 1. An insect or other arthropod between molts, as during metamorphosis. 2. This stage of development. [New Latin, from Latin *instar*†, image, form.]

in·state (ĭn-stāt') *tr.v.* **-stated, -stating, -states.** To put in office; install. [IN- (causative) + STATE (rank).]

in·stau·ra·tion (ĭn'stô-rā'shən) *n. Archaic.* 1. Renovation; restoration. 2. Institution; establishment. [Latin *instaurātiō*, from *instaurāre*, to restore. See **stā-** in Appendix.*]

in·stead (ĭn-stĕd') *adv.* In the place of that previously mentioned; as an alternative or substitute: *Planning to drive, he walked instead.* —**instead of.** In lieu of; rather than: *"Instead of eating monkeys/They are eating Christians"* (T.S. Eliot). [Middle English *in sted (of)* : IN + STEAD.]

in·step (ĭn'stĕp') *n.* 1. The arched medial portion of the human foot. 2. The part of a shoe or stocking covering the instep. [Probably IN + STEP.]

in·sti·gate (ĭn'stĭ-gāt') *tr.v.* **-gated, -gating, -gates.** 1. To urge on; to goad. 2. To foment; stir up. —See Synonyms at **incite.** [Latin *instīgāre* : *in-* (intensive) + *stīgāre*, to spur on (see **steig-** in Appendix*).] —**in'sti·ga'tion** *n.* —**in'sti·ga'tive** *adj.* —**in'sti·ga'tor** (-gā'tər) *n.*

in·still (ĭn-stĭl') *tr.v.* **-stilled, -stilling, -stills.** Also *chiefly British* **in·stil, -stilled, -stilling, -stils.** 1. To introduce by gradual, persistent efforts; implant: *"morality . . . may be instilled into their minds"* (Jefferson). 2. To pour in drop by drop. [Latin *instillāre*, to drip in : *in-*, in + *stillāre*, to drip, from *stilla*†, drop.] —**in'stil·la'tion** (ĭn'stə-lā'shən) *n.* —**in·still'er** *n.* —**in·still'ment, in·stil'ment** *n.*

in·stinct (ĭn'stĭngkt') *n.* 1. a. The innate aspect of behavior that is unlearned, complex, and normally adaptive. b. A powerful motivation or impulse. 2. An innate aptitude. —*adj.* (ĭn-stĭngkt'). 1. *Obsolete.* Impelled from within. 2. Imbued. [Middle English, from Latin *instinctus*, instigation, from the past participle of *instinguere*, to instigate, urge on : *in-*, on + *stinguere*, to prick, incite (see **steig-** in Appendix*).]

in·stinc·tive (ĭn-stĭngk'tĭv) *adj.* 1. Of or pertaining to instinct. 2. Arising from instinct. 3. Deep-seated; inveterate. —See Synonyms at **spontaneous.** —**in·stinc'tive·ly** *adv.*

in·sti·tute (ĭn'stə-tōōt', -tyōōt') *tr.v.* **-tuted, -tuting, -tutes.** 1. a. To establish, organize, and set in operation. b. To initiate; begin. 2. To establish or invest in a position. —*n.* 1. *Obsolete.* The act of instituting. 2. Something instituted; especially, an authoritative rule or precedent. 3. *Abbr.* **inst., Inst.** An organization founded to promote some cause. 4. *Abbr.* **inst., Inst.** a. An educational institution. b. The building or buildings of such an institution. 5. A short, intensive workshop or seminar on one specific subject. 6. *Plural.* A digest of the principles or rudiments of some subject; especially, a legal abstract. [Middle English *instituten*, from Latin *instituere*, to establish, ordain : *in-*, in + *statuere*, to set up, from *stāre* (past participle *status*), to stand (see **stā-** in Appendix*).]

in·sti·tu·tion (ĭn'stə-tōō'shən, -tyōō'shən) *n. Abbr.* **inst., Inst.** 1. The act of instituting. 2. a. A relationship or behavioral pattern of importance in the life of a community or society. b. *Informal.* An ever-present feature; a fixture. 3. An established organization; especially, one dedicated to public service, as a university. 4. The building or buildings housing such an organization. 5. A place of confinement, as a mental asylum. —**in'sti·tu'tion·al** *adj.*

in·sti·tu·tion·al·ism (ĭn'stə-tōō'shən-ə-lĭz'əm, ĭn'stə-tyōō'-) *n.* 1. Belief in established forms; especially, belief in organized religion. 2. a. The system of civic or philanthropic institutions.

b. Institutional maintenance of those incapable of self-maintenance. —**in′sti·tu′tion·al·ist** *n.*
in·sti·tu·tion·al·ize (ĭn′stə-to͞o′shən-ə-līz′, ĭn′stə-tyo͞o′-) *tr.v.* **-ized, -izing, -izes. 1.** To make into or treat as an institution. **2.** To confine (a person) in an institution. —**in′sti·tu′tion·al·i·za′tion** *n.*
in·sti·tu·tive (ĭn′stə-to͞o′tĭv, -tyo͞o′tĭv) *adj.* **1.** Concerned with the establishing of something; tending to institute. **2.** Sanctioned by usage or law; established. —**in′sti·tu′tive·ly** *adv.*
in·sti·tu·tor (ĭn′stə-to͞o′tər, -tyo͞o′tər) *n.* **1.** One who institutes; founder. **2.** A bishop or his substitute who institutes a clergyman into a parish or church of the U.S. Episcopal Church.
instr. 1. instruction; instructor. **2.** instrument.
in·stroke (ĭn′strōk′) *n.* An inward stroke; especially, a piston stroke moving away from the crankshaft. Compare **outstroke.**
in·struct (ĭn-strŭkt′) *tr.v.* **-structed, -structing, -structs. 1.** To furnish with knowledge; teach; educate. **2.** To give orders to; to direct. —See Synonyms at **command, teach.** [Middle English *instructen,* from Latin *instruere* (past participle *instructus*), to build, prepare, instruct : *in-,* in + *struere,* to build (see **ster-**[2] in Appendix*).]
in·struc·tion (ĭn-strŭk′shən) *n. Abbr.* **instr. 1.** The act, practice, or profession of instructing; education. **2. a.** Imparted knowledge. **b.** An imparted or acquired item of knowledge; a lesson. **3.** *Plural.* Directions; orders. —**in·struc′tion·al** *adj.*
in·struc·tive (ĭn-strŭk′tĭv) *adj.* Conveying knowledge or information. —**in·struc′tive·ly** *adv.* —**in·struc′tive·ness** *n.*
in·struc·tor (ĭn-strŭk′tər) *n. Abbr.* **instr. 1.** One who instructs; a teacher. **2. a.** An academic rank below an assistant professor. **b.** One who holds such a rank. —**in·struc′tor·ship′** *n.*
in·stru·ment (ĭn′strə-mənt) *n. Abbr.* **inst., instr. 1.** A means by which something is done; agency. **2.** One used to accomplish some purpose. **3.** A mechanical implement. **4.** A device for recording or measuring; especially, such a device functioning as part of a control system. **5.** A device for producing music. **6.** A legal document. —See Synonyms at **tool.** —*tr.v.* **instrumented, -menting, -ments. 1.** To provide or equip with instruments. **2.** To address a legal document to. [Middle English, from Latin *instrūmentum,* implement, equipment, tool, from *instruere,* to prepare, equip, INSTRUCT.]
in·stru·men·tal (ĭn′strə-mĕnt′l) *adj.* **1.** Serving as an instrument; helpful. **2.** Of, pertaining to, or accomplished with an instrument or tool. **3.** Performed on or written for a musical instrument or instruments. **4.** *Grammar.* Of or designating a case in Russian, Sanskrit, and certain other languages used typically to express means, agency, or accompaniment. —*n.* **1.** The instrumental case. **2.** A word in this case. —**in′stru·men′tal·ly** *adv.*
in·stru·men·tal·ism (ĭn′strə-mĕnt′l-ĭz′əm) *n.* A pragmatic theory that ideas are instruments that function as guides of action, their validity being determined by the success of the action.
in·stru·men·tal·ist (ĭn-strə-mĕnt′l-ĭst) *n.* **1.** One who plays a musical instrument. **2.** A student of instrumentalism.
in·stru·men·tal·i·ty (ĭn′strə-mĕn-tăl′ə-tē) *n., pl.* **-ties. 1.** The quality or circumstance of being instrumental. **2.** Agency; means.
in·stru·men·ta·tion (ĭn′strə-mĕn-tā′shən) *n.* **1.** The application or use of instruments in the performance of some work. **2. a.** The study and practice of arranging music for instruments. **b.** The arrangement or orchestration resulting from such a practice. **3.** The study, development, and manufacture of instruments, as for scientific use. **4.** Instrumentality.
instrument panel. A mounted array of instruments used to monitor performance. Also called "instrument board."
in·sub·or·di·nate (ĭn′sə-bôrd′n-ĭt) *adj.* **1.** Not submissive to authority. **2.** Not in a subordinate position. —**in′sub·or′di·na′tion** (-ā′shən) *n.* —**in′sub·or′di·nate·ly** *adv.*
Synonyms: *insubordinate, rebellious, mutinous, factious, seditious.* These adjectives are applied to persons or their actions and mean in opposition to, and usually in defiance of, established authority. *Insubordinate* implies failure to recognize or accept the authority of a superior. *Rebellious* implies open defiance of authority to which one is subject. *Mutinous,* a still stronger term, pertains to uprising against lawful authority, especially that of a naval or military command. *Factious* describes what promotes divisiveness, dissension, or disunity within a group or organization. *Seditious* applies principally to the stirring up of resistance against a government.
in·sub·stan·tial (ĭn′səb-stăn′shəl) *adj.* **1.** Lacking substance; imaginary. **2.** Not firm; unsubstantial. —**in′sub·stan′ti·al′i·ty** (-shē-ăl′ə-tē) *n.*
in·suf·fer·a·ble (ĭn-sŭf′ər-ə-bəl) *adj.* Not endurable; intolerable. —**in·suf′fer·a·ble·ness** *n.* —**in·suf′fer·a·bly** *adv.*
in·suf·fi·cien·cy (ĭn′sə-fĭsh′ən-sē) *n., pl.* **-cies. 1.** The quality or state of being insufficient. **2.** Something insufficient.
in·suf·fi·cient (ĭn′sə-fĭsh′ənt) *adj.* Not sufficient; inadequate. —**in′suf·fi′cient·ly** *adv.*
in·suf·flate (ĭn-sŭf′lāt′, ĭn′sə-flāt′) *tr.v.* **-flated, -flating, -flates. 1.** To blow or breathe into or upon. **2.** To treat medically by blowing a powder, gas, or vapor into a bodily cavity. [Late Latin *insufflāre* : Latin *in-,* on, into + *sufflāre,* to blow (see **soufflé**).] —**in·suf′fla′tor** (-sŭf′lā′tər) *n.*
in·suf·fla·tion (ĭn′sə-flā′shən) *n.* **1.** The act or an instance of insufflating. **2.** *Ecclesiastical.* A ritual breathing upon baptismal water or upon one being baptized.
in·su·lar (ĭn′sə-lər, ĭns′yə-) *adj.* **1.** Of or constituting an island. **2. a.** Characteristic or suggestive of the isolated life of an island. **b.** Circumscribed and detached in outlook and experience. **3.** *Anatomy.* Designating isolated tissue or an island of tissue. [Late Latin *insulāris,* from Latin *insula,* island, ISLE.] —**in′su·lar·ism′, in′su·lar′i·ty** (ĭn′sə-lăr′ə-tē, ĭns′yə-) *n.* —**in′su·lar·ly** *adv.*
insular sclerosis. Multiple sclerosis *(see).*
in·su·late (ĭn′sə-lāt′, ĭns′yə-) *tr.v.* **-lated, -lating, -lates. 1.** To detach; isolate. **2.** *Physics.* To prevent the passage of heat or electricity or sound into or out of (a body or region), especially by interposition of an appropriate insulator. [Originally "to convert into an island," from Latin *insula,* island, ISLE.]
in·su·la·tion (ĭn′sə-lā′shən, ĭns′yə-) *n.* **1.** The act of insulating. **2.** *Abbr.* **ins.** Material used in insulating.
in·su·la·tor (ĭn′sə-lā′tər, ĭns′yə-) *n.* **1.** A material that insulates. **2.** A device that insulates.
in·su·lin (ĭn′sə-lən, ĭns′yə-) *n.* **1.** A polypeptide hormone secreted by the islands of Langerhans and functioning to regulate carbohydrate metabolism by controlling blood glucose levels. **2.** A preparation derived from the pancreas of the pig or the ox for use in the medical treatment of diabetes. [From Latin *insula,* island.]
in·sult (ĭn-sŭlt′) *v.* **-sulted, -sulting, -sults.** —*tr.* **1. a.** To speak to or treat in a callous or contemptuous way. **b.** To reveal a disdainful estimate of. **2.** *Obsolete.* To make an attack upon; to assault. —*intr. Obsolete.* To behave arrogantly. —See Synonyms at **offend.** —*n.* (ĭn′sŭlt′). **1.** An offensive action or remark. **2.** *Medicine.* An injury, irritation, or trauma. [Old French *insulter,* to triumph over, behave arrogantly, from Latin *insultāre,* to leap on, jump over : *in-,* on, upon + *saltāre,* frequentative of *salīre,* to jump (see **sel-**[4] in Appendix*).]
in·su·per·a·ble (ĭn-so͞o′pər-ə-bəl) *adj.* Incapable of being overcome; insurmountable: *an insuperable barrier.* —**in·su′per·a·bil′i·ty, in·su′per·a·ble·ness** *n.* —**in·su′per·a·bly** *adv.*
in·sup·port·a·ble (ĭn′sə-pôr′tə-bəl, -pōr′tə-bəl) *adj.* **1.** Unbearable; intolerable. **2.** Lacking grounds or defense; unjustifiable.
in·sup·press·i·ble (ĭn′sə-prĕs′ə-bəl) *adj.* Irrepressible.
in·sur·ance (ĭn-sho͝or′əns) *n. Abbr.* **ins., insur. 1. a.** The act, business, or system of insuring persons or property. **b.** The state of being insured. **c.** The means of being insured. **2.** A contract binding a company to indemnify an insured party against specified loss in return for premiums paid. **3.** The sum or coverage so insured. **4.** The periodical premium paid for this indemnification. **5.** A protective measure or device.
in·sur·ant (ĭn-sho͝or′ənt) *n.* One who is insured.
in·sure (ĭn-sho͝or′) *v.* **-sured, -suring, -sures.** Also **en·sure** (ĕn-) (for senses 2, 3). —*tr.* **1.** To cover with insurance. **2.** To make sure or certain; to guarantee. **3.** To make safe or secure. Used with *from* or *against.* —*intr.* To buy or sell insurance. —See Usage note at **assure.** [Middle English *insuren, ensuren,* to guarantee, from Norman French *enseurer,* perhaps variant of Old French *ass(e)urer,* ASSURE.] —**in·sur′a·bil′i·ty** *n.* —**in·sur′a·ble** *adj.*
in·sured (ĭn-sho͝ord′) *n.* One covered by insurance.
in·sur·er (ĭn-sho͝or′ər) *n.* One that insures; an underwriter.
in·sur·gence (ĭn-sûr′jəns) *n.* Uprising; revolt.
in·sur·gen·cy (ĭn-sûr′jən-sē) *n.* **1.** The quality or circumstance of being insurgent. **2.** Insurgence.
in·sur·gent (ĭn-sûr′jənt) *adj.* Rising in nonbelligerent revolt against civil authority or a government in power. —*n.* One who revolts against authority; especially, a member of a political party who rebels against its leadership. [Latin *insurgēns,* present participle of *insurgere,* to rise up : *in-* (intensive) + *surgere,* to rise, SURGE.]
in·sur·mount·a·ble (ĭn′sər-moun′tə-bəl) *adj.* Incapable of being surmounted; insuperable. —**in′sur·mount′a·bly** *adv.*
in·sur·rec·tion (ĭn′sə-rĕk′shən) *n.* An act or instance of open revolt against civil authority or a constituted government. See Synonyms at **rebellion.** [Middle English *insurrecioun,* from Old French *insurrection,* from Latin *insurrectiō,* from *insurgere* (past participle *insurrectus*), to rise up. See **insurgent.**] —**in′sur·rec′tion·al** *adj.* —**in′sur·rec′tion·ar′y** *adj.* & *n.* —**in′sur·rec′tion·ism′** *n.* —**in′sur·rec′tion·ist** *n.*
in·sus·cep·ti·ble (ĭn′sə-sĕp′tə-bəl) *adj.* Not susceptible.
in·swathe. Variant of **enswathe.**
int. 1. interest. **2.** interior. **3.** interval. **4.** international.
in·tact (ĭn-tăkt′) *adj.* **1.** Not impaired in any way. **2.** Having all parts; whole. [Middle English *intacte,* untouched, from Latin *intactus* : *in-,* not + *tactus,* past participle of *tangere,* to touch (see **tag-** in Appendix*).] —**in·tact′ness** *n.*
in·ta·glio (ĭn-tăl′yō; *Italian* ĭn-tä′lyō) *n., pl.* **-glios** or **-tagli** (-tăl′yē; *Italian* -tä′lyē). **1. a.** A figure or design incised beneath the surface of hard metal or stone. **b.** The art or process of carving a design in this manner. **2.** A gemstone carved in intaglio. Compare **cameo. 3.** Printing done with a plate bearing an image in intaglio. **4.** A die incised to produce a design in relief. [Italian, from *intagliare,* to engrave : *in-,* in, from Latin + *tagliare,* to cut, from (unattested) Vulgar Latin *tālliāre* (see **tailor**).]
in·take (ĭn′tāk′) *n.* **1.** An opening by which a fluid is admitted into a container or conduit. **2. a.** The act of taking in. **b.** That which is taken in; especially, energy taken in.
in·tan·gi·ble (ĭn-tăn′jə-bəl) *adj.* Incapable of being perceived, precisely defined, or identified; elusive. —*n.* Something intangible; especially, an asset that cannot be perceived by the senses. —**in·tan′gi·bil′i·ty, in·tan′gi·ble·ness** *n.* —**in·tan′gi·bly** *adv.*
in·tar·si·a (ĭn-tär′sē-ə) *n.* **1.** A mosaic worked in wood. **2.** The art or practice of making such mosaics. [Perhaps IN(LAY) + *tarsia,* an inlaid mosaic, from Arabic *tarṣī.*]
in·te·ger (ĭn′tə-jər) *n.* **1.** Any member of the set of positive whole numbers (1, 2, 3, . . .), negative whole numbers (−1,

−2, −3, . . .), and zero (0). **2.** Any intact unit or entity. [Latin, whole, complete, perfect, virtuous. See **tag-** in Appendix.]

in·te·gra·ble (ĭn′tə-grə-bəl) *adj.* Capable of being integrated.

in·te·gral (ĭn′tə-grəl) *adj.* **1.** Essential for completion; necessary to the whole; constituent. **2.** Whole; entire; intact. **3.** *Mathematics.* **a.** Expressed or expressible as or in terms of integers. **b.** Expressed as or involving integrals. —*n.* **1.** A complete unit; a whole. **2.** *Mathematics.* **a.** A **definite integral** *(see).* **b.** An **indefinite integral** *(see).* [Middle English, from Late Latin *integrālis,* making up a whole, from Latin *integer,* whole. See **integer.**] —**in′te·gral′i·ty** *n.* —**in′te·gral·ly** *adv.*

integral calculus. The mathematical study of integration, the properties of integrals, and their applications.

integral domain. A commutative ring with unity having no proper divisors of zero, that is, having no nonzero elements *a, b* such that $a \cdot b = 0$, where 0 is the additive identity.

in·te·grand (ĭn′tə-grănd′) *n.* A function or equation to be integrated. [Latin *integrandus,* gerundive of *integrāre,* INTEGRATE.]

in·te·grant (ĭn′tə-grənt) *adj.* Integral. [Latin *integrāns,* present participle of *integrāre,* INTEGRATE.]

in·te·grate (ĭn′tə-grāt′) *v.* **-grated, -grating, -grates.** —*tr.* **1.** To make into a whole by bringing all parts together; unify. **2.** To join with something else; to unite. **3.** To open to people of all races or ethnic groups without restriction; desegregate. **4.** *Mathematics.* **a.** To calculate the integral of. **b.** To perform integration upon. **5.** To bring about the integration of (personality traits). —*intr.* To become integrated or undergo integration. [Latin *integrāre,* to make complete, from *integer,* whole. See **integer.**] —**in′te·gra′tive** *adj.*

in·te·gra·tion (ĭn′tə-grā′shən) *n.* **1. a.** An act or the process of integrating. **b.** The state of becoming integrated. **c.** Desegregation. **2.** The organization of organic, psychological, or social traits and tendencies of a personality into a harmonious whole.

in·te·gra·tor (ĭn′tə-grā′tər) *n.* **1.** One that integrates. **2.** An instrument for mechanically calculating definite integrals.

in·teg·ri·ty (ĭn-tĕg′rə-tē) *n.* **1.** Rigid adherence to a code of behavior; probity. **2.** The state of being unimpaired; soundness. **3.** Completeness; unity. —See Synonyms at **honesty.** [Middle English *integrite,* from Old French, from Latin *integritās,* completeness, purity, from *integer,* whole. See **integer.**]

in·teg·u·ment (ĭn-tĕg′yo͞o-mənt) *n.* An outer covering or coat, such as the skin of an animal, the coat of a seed, or the membrane enclosing an organ. [Latin *integumentum,* from *integere,* to cover : *in-,* on + *tegere,* to cover (see **steg-**[1] in Appendix*).] —**in·teg′u·men′ta·ry** *adj.*

in·tel·lect (ĭn′tə-lĕkt′) *n.* **1. a.** The ability to learn and reason as distinguished from the ability to feel or will; capacity for knowledge and understanding. **b.** The ability to think abstractly or profoundly. **3. a.** A person of great intellectual ability. **b.** The intellectual members of a group. —See Synonyms at **mind.** [Middle English, from Old French, from Latin *intellectus,* perception, comprehension, from the past participle of *intellegere,* to perceive, choose between. See **intelligent.**]

in·tel·lec·tion (ĭn′tə-lĕk′shən) *n.* **1.** The act or process of exercising the intellect; mental activity. **2.** A thought or idea. [Middle English *intelleccioun,* understanding, from Latin *intellectiō,* from *intellectus,* INTELLECT.]

in·tel·lec·tive (ĭn′tə-lĕk′tĭv) *adj.* Of, pertaining to, or generated by the intellect. —**in′tel·lec′tive·ly** *adv.*

in·tel·lec·tu·al (ĭn′tə-lĕk′cho͞o-əl) *adj.* **1. a.** Of or pertaining to the intellect. **b.** Rational rather than emotional. **2.** Appealing to or engaging the intellect. **3. a.** Having superior intelligence. **b.** Given to exercise of the intellect. —See Synonyms at **intelligent.** —*n.* An intellectual person. —**in′tel·lec′tu·al·ly** *adv.*

in·tel·lec·tu·al·ism (ĭn′tə-lĕk′cho͞o-ə-lĭz′əm) *n.* **1.** The exercise or application of the intellect. **2.** Devotion to exercise or development of the intellect. **3.** The doctrine that knowledge is the product of pure reason; rationalism. —**in′tel·lec′tu·al·ist** *n.* —**in′tel·lec′tu·al·is′tic** *adj.*

in·tel·lec·tu·al·ize (ĭn′tə-lĕk′cho͞o-ə-līz′) *tr.v.* **-ized, -izing, -izes. 1.** To make rational. **2.** To avoid emotional insight into (an emotional problem) by performing an intellectual analysis. —**in′tel·lec′tu·al·i·za′tion** *n.*

in·tel·li·gence (ĭn-tĕl′ə-jəns) *n.* **1. a.** The capacity to acquire and apply knowledge. **b.** The faculty of thought and reason. **c.** Superior powers of mind. **2. a.** *Rare.* An intelligent being. **b.** *Often capital* **I.** An incorporeal being that personifies the mind; especially, an angel. **c.** *Capital* **I.** *Christian Science.* "The primal and eternal quality of . . . God" (Mary Baker Eddy). **3.** Received information; news. **4. a.** Secret information; especially, such information about an enemy. **b.** The work of gathering such information. **c.** An agency, staff, or office employed in such work. —See Synonyms at **mind.**

intelligence quotient. *Abbr.* **IQ, I.Q.** The ratio of tested mental age to chronological age, usually expressed as a quotient multiplied by 100.

in·tel·li·genc·er (ĭn-tĕl′ə-jən-sər) *n. Archaic.* **1.** One who conveys news; an informant. **2.** A secret agent, informer, or spy.

intelligence test. A standardized test used to establish an intelligence level rating by measuring an individual's ability to form concepts, solve problems, acquire information, reason, and perform other intellectual operations.

in·tel·li·gent (ĭn-tĕl′ə-jənt) *adj.* **1.** Having intelligence. **2.** Having a high degree of intelligence; mentally acute. **3.** Showing intelligence; perceptive and sound. **4.** Guided or motivated by the intellect; rational. [Latin *intelligēns,* present participle of *intellegere, intelligere,* to perceive, choose between : *inter-,* between + *legere,* to gather, choose (see **leg-** in Appendix*).] —**in·tel′li·gen′tial** (ĭn-tĕl′ə-jĕn′shəl) *adj.* —**in·tel′li·gent·ly** *adv.*

Synonyms: *intelligent, bright, brilliant, knowing, quick-witted, smart, intellectual.* These adjectives are applied to persons and their behavior when they give evidence of mental keenness. *Intelligent* usually implies the ability to cope with demands created by novel situations and new problems, to apply what is learned from experience, and to use the power of reasoning and inference effectively as a guide to behavior. *Bright,* sometimes used interchangeably with *intelligent,* implies mental acuteness in general, and *brilliant* suggests the same quality, especially when it is displayed impressively. *Knowing* implies discernment and shrewdness, and *quick-witted,* alertness and adroitness of mental function. *Smart* is often a general term implying mental keenness; more specifically it can refer to practical knowledge, ability to learn quickly, or to sharpness or shrewdness, sometimes considered unfavorably. *Intellectual* activities stress the working of the intellect, and *intellectual* persons are those who show mental capacity well beyond the ordinary.

in·tel·li·gent·si·a (ĭn-tĕl′ə-jĕnt′sē-ə, -gĕnt′sē-ə) *n.* The intellectual class within a society. [Russian *intelligentsiya,* from Polish *inteligiencja,* from Latin *intelligentia,* intelligence, from *intelligēns,* INTELLIGENT.]

in·tel·li·gi·ble (ĭn-tĕl′ə-jə-bəl) *adj.* **1.** Comprehensible. **2.** Capable of being apprehended by the intellect alone. [Middle English, from Latin *intelligibilis,* from *intelligere,* to perceive. See **intelligent.**] —**in·tel′li·gi·bil′i·ty** *n.* —**in·tel′li·gi·bly** *adv.*

in·tem·per·ance (ĭn-tĕm′pər-əns) *n.* Lack of temperance, as in the indulgence of an appetite or passion.

in·tem·per·ate (ĭn-tĕm′pər-ĭt) *adj.* Not temperate or moderate. —**in·tem′per·ate·ly** *adv.* —**in·tem′per·ate·ness** *n.*

in·tend (ĭn-tĕnd′) *v.* **-tended, -tending, -tends.** —*tr.* **1.** To have in mind; to plan. **2.** To design for a specific purpose or destine to a particular use. **3.** To signify; to mean. —*intr.* To have in mind some purpose or design. [Middle English *entenden,* from Old French *entendre,* from Latin *intendere,* to stretch toward, direct one's mind to : *in,* toward + *tendere,* to stretch, tend (see **ten-** in Appendix*).]

Usage: *Intend* is often followed by a clause introduced by *that* and with a subjunctive form of verb: *I intended that he call her* (but not *I intended for him to call her*).

in·ten·dance (ĭn-tĕn′dəns) *n.* **1.** The function of an intendant; management; superintendence. **2.** An intendancy.

in·ten·dan·cy (ĭn-tĕn′dən-sē) *n., pl.* **-cies. 1.** The position or function of an intendant. **2.** Intendants collectively. **3.** The district supervised by an intendant, as in Latin America.

in·ten·dant (ĭn-tĕn′dənt) *n.* **1.** A provincial or colonial administrative official serving a French, Spanish, or Portuguese monarch. **2.** A district administrator in some countries of Latin America. [French, from Old French, "director," administrator, from Latin *intendēns,* present participle of *intendere,* to direct one's mind to, INTEND.]

in·tend·ed (ĭn-tĕn′dĭd) *adj.* **1.** Planned; intentional. **2.** Prospective; future. —*n. Informal.* A person's prospective spouse.

in·tend·ment (ĭn-tĕnd′mənt) *n.* The true meaning or intention of something as fixed by law.

in·ten·er·ate (ĭn-tĕn′ə-rāt′) *tr.v.* **-ated, -ating, -ates.** *Rare.* To make tender; soften. [IN- (causative) + Latin *tener,* TENDER + -ATE.] —**in·ten′er·a′tion** *n.*

in·tense (ĭn-tĕns′) *adj.* **1.** Of great intensity. **2.** Extreme in degree, strength, or size. **3.** Involving or showing strain. **4. a.** Deeply felt; profound. **b.** Tending to feel deeply. [Middle English, from Old French, from Latin *intensus,* stretched tight, from the past participle of *intendere,* to stretch toward, INTEND.] —**in·tense′ly** *adv.* —**in·tense′ness** *n.*

in·ten·si·fi·er (ĭn-tĕn′sə-fī′ər) *n.* **1.** One that intensifies. **2.** An intensive.

in·ten·si·fy (ĭn-tĕn′sə-fī′) *v.* **-fied, -fying, -fies.** —*tr.* **1.** To make intense or more intense. **2.** To increase the contrast of (a photographic image). —*intr.* To become intense or more intense. [INTENSE + -FY.] —**in·ten′si·fi·ca′tion** *n.*

in·ten·sion (ĭn-tĕn′shən) *n.* **1.** *Logic.* The properties connoted by a term. Compare **extension. 2.** *Rare.* Intensity. [Latin *intensiō,* from *intensus,* INTENSE.]

in·ten·si·ty (ĭn-tĕn′sə-tē) *n., pl.* **-ties. 1.** Exceptionally great concentration, power, or force. **2.** *Physics.* **a.** The measure of effectiveness of a force field given by the force per unit test element. **b.** The energy transferred by a wave per unit time across a unit area perpendicular to the direction of propagation.

in·ten·sive (ĭn-tĕn′sĭv) *adj.* **1.** Of, pertaining to, or characterized by intensity. **2.** Relating to or being a linguistic intensive. **3.** Concentrated and exhaustive: *intensive care.* **4.** Constituting or relating to a method of land cultivation calling for large-scale employment of capital and labor. **5.** *Physics.* Having the same value for any subdivision of a thermodynamic system. Said of pressure, for example. —*n.* A linguistic element that increases the semantic effect of a word or phrase but has itself little or no independent semantic content, as Latin *com-* in *complēre,* to fill up (see etymology at **complete**).

in·tent (ĭn-tĕnt′) *n.* **1.** That which is intended; aim; purpose. **2.** The state of mind operative at the time of an action. **3. a.** Meaning; purport. **b.** Connotation. —See Synonyms at **intention.** —*adj.* **1.** Firmly fixed; concentrated. **2.** Having the attention applied; engrossed. **3.** Having the mind fastened upon some purpose. [Middle English *entent,* from Old French, from Latin *intentus,* a stretching out, from the alternative past participle of *intendere,* to stretch toward, INTEND.]

in·ten·tion (ĭn-tĕn′shən) *n.* **1.** A plan of action; a design. **2. a.** An aim that guides action; an object. **b.** *Plural.* Purpose in regard to marriage: *honorable intentions.* **3.** The general connotation or concept of something; what something is meant to convey. **4.** *Medicine.* The course or manner of healing of a surgical wound. **5.** *Archaic.* The import; meaning. **6.** *Archaic.* Intentness. [Middle English *entencioun,* from Old French *entention,* from Latin *intentiō,* "a stretching out," from *intendere,* to stretch toward, INTEND.]

   Synonyms: *intention, intent, purpose, object, goal, end, aim, objective.* These nouns refer to what one hopes to achieve or attain. *Intention* signifies a course of action that one proposes to follow. *Intent,* often a legal term, more strongly implies a fixed course pursued deliberately, and *purpose* adds to this the idea of resolution or determination to carry out what one proposes. *Object* and *goal* are sometimes interchangeable in referring to the proposed attainment. *Object,* however, often implies something clearcut and attainable by practical means, and *goal* something more idealistic or remote. *End* suggests an ultimate attainment, viewed from long range, and *aim,* the direction one's efforts take in pursuit of the end. *Objective* refers to an end or goal with the implication that it can be reached.

in·ten·tion·al (ĭn-tĕn′shə-nəl) *adj.* **1.** Done deliberately; intended: *an intentional slight.* **2.** Having to do with logical intention or connotation. —See Synonyms at **voluntary.** —**in·ten′tion·al′i·ty** (ĭn-tĕn′shə-năl′ə-tē) *n.* —**in·ten′tion·al·ly** *adv.*

in·ter (ĭn-tûr′) *tr.v.* **-terred, -terring, -ters.** To place in a grave; bury. [Middle English *enteren,* from Old French *enterrer,* from Vulgar Latin *interrāre* (unattested) : Latin *in,* in + *terra,* earth, ground (see **ters-** in Appendix*).]

inter– Indicates: **1.** Between or among; for example, **intercollegiate, international. 2.** Mutually or together; for example, **interact, intermingle. Note:** Many compounds other than those entered here may be formed with *inter-.* In forming compounds, *inter-* is normally joined with the following element without space or hyphen: *interregnum.* However, if the second element begins with a capital letter, it is separated with a hyphen: *inter-American.* Note that in Latin phrases used in English, the Latin preposition remains a separate word: *inter alia.* [Middle English *inter-, entre-,* from Old French, from Latin *inter-,* from *inter,* between, among. See **en** in Appendix.* In borrowed Latin compounds, *inter-* indicates: **1.** Between, among, as in **inter-regnum. 2.** Mutually, each other, as in **intersect. 3.** At intervals, as in **intermit. 4.** Preventively, destructively, as in **interdict, internecine.**]

inter. intermediate.

in·ter·act (ĭn′tər-ăkt′) *intr.v.* **-acted, -acting, -acts.** To act on each other. —**in′ter·ac′tion** *n.* —**in′ter·ac′tive** *adj.*

in·ter a·li·a (ĭn′tər ā′lē-ə). *Latin.* Among other things.

in·ter a·li·os (ĭn′tər ā′lē-ōs′). *Latin.* Among other persons.

in·ter·brain (ĭn′tər-brān′) *n.* The diencephalon.

in·ter·breed (ĭn′tər-brēd′) *v.* **-bred** (-brĕd′), **-breeding, -breeds.** —*intr.* **1.** To breed with another kind or species; crossbreed; hybridize. **2.** To breed within a narrow range or with closely related types or individuals; inbreed. —*tr.* To cause to interbreed.

in·ter·ca·lar·y (ĭn-tûr′kə-lĕr′ē) *adj.* **1.** Added to the calendar to make the calendar year correspond to the solar year. Said of a day or a month. **2.** Having such a day or month added. Said of a year. **3.** Interpolated. [Latin *intercalārius,* from *intercalāre,* to INTERCALATE.]

in·ter·ca·late (ĭn-tûr′kə-lāt′) *tr.v.* **-lated, -lating, -lates. 1.** To add (a day or month) to a calendar. **2.** To insert, interpose, or interpolate. [Latin *intercalāre,* to proclaim the insertion of a day : *inter-,* among, between + *calāre,* to call (see **kel-³** in Appendix*).] —**in·ter′ca·la′tion** *n.* —**in·ter′ca·la′tive** *adj.*

in·ter·cede (ĭn′tər-sēd′) *intr.v.* **-ceded, -ceding, -cedes. 1.** To plead on another's behalf. **2.** To act as mediator in a dispute. [Latin *intercēdere,* to come between : *inter-,* between + *cēdere,* to go (see **ked-¹** in Appendix*).] —**in′ter·ced′er** *n.*

in·ter·cel·lu·lar (ĭn′tər-sĕl′yə-lər) *adj.* Among or between cells.

in·ter·cept (ĭn′tər-sĕpt′) *tr.v.* **-cepted, -cepting, -cepts. 1.** To stop, deflect, or interrupt the progress or intended course of. **2.** *Obsolete.* **a.** To cut off from access or communication. **b.** To prevent. **3.** To intersect. **4.** *Mathematics.* To cut off or bound a part of (a line, plane, surface, or solid). —*n.* (ĭn′tər-sĕpt′) *Mathematics.* The distance from the origin of coordinates along a coordinate axis to the point at which a line, curve, or surface intersects the axis. [Latin *intercipere* (past participle *interceptus*), to intercept, seize in transit : *inter,* preventively + *capere,* to take, seize (see **kap-** in Appendix*).] —**in′ter·cep′tive** *adj.*

in·ter·cep·tor (ĭn′tər-sĕp′tər) *n.* Also **in·ter·cep·ter. 1.** One that intercepts. **2.** A fast-climbing, highly maneuverable fighter plane designed to intercept enemy aircraft.

in·ter·ces·sion (ĭn′tər-sĕsh′ən) *n.* **1.** Entreaty in favor of another. **2.** Mediation in a dispute. [Old French, from Latin *intercessiō,* from *intercēdere* (past participle *intercessus*), INTERCEDE.] —**in′ter·ces′sion·al** *adj.* —**in′ter·ces′sor** (-sĕs′ər) *n.* —**in′ter·ces′so·ry** *adj.*

in·ter·change (ĭn′tər-chānj′) *v.* **-changed, -changing, -changes.** —*tr.* **1.** To switch each of (two things) into the place of the other. **2.** To give and receive mutually; to exchange. **3.** To cause to succeed each other; to alternate. —*intr.* **1.** To change places with each other. **2.** To succeed each other; to alternate. —*n.* (ĭn′tər-chānj′). **1.** The act or process or an instance of interchanging, especially: **a.** A switch of places. **b.** An exchange. **2.** Alternation. **3.** A highway intersection designed to permit traffic to move freely from one road to another. [Middle English *entrechaungen,* from Old French *entrechangier* : INTER- + *changier,* to CHANGE.] —**in′ter·chang′er** *n.*

in·ter·change·a·ble (ĭn′tər-chān′jə-bəl) *adj.* Capable of mutual interchange; admitting transposition. —**in′ter·change′a·bil′i·ty, in′ter·change′a·ble·ness** *n.* —**in′ter·change′a·bly** *adv.*

in·ter·col·le·giate (ĭn′tər-kə-lē′jĭt, -jē-ĭt) *adj.* Involving or representing two or more colleges.

in·ter·co·lum·ni·a·tion (ĭn′tər-kə-lŭm′nē-ā′shən) *n.* **1.** The open spaces between the columns in a colonnade. **2.** The system whereby they are spaced.

in·ter·com (ĭn′tər-kŏm′) *n.* An intercommunication system, as between two rooms. [Short for INTERCOMMUNICATION.]

in·ter·com·mu·ni·cate (ĭn′tər-kə-myōō′nə-kāt′) *intr.v.* **-cated, -cating, -cates. 1.** To communicate with each other. **2.** To be connected or adjoined, as rooms. —**in′ter·com·mu′ni·ca′tion** *n.* —**in′ter·com·mu′ni·ca′tive** *adj.*

in·ter·con·nect (ĭn′tər-kə-nĕkt′) *v.* **-nected, -necting, -nects.** —*intr.* To be connected one to the other. —*tr.* To connect (one thing with another). —**in′ter·con·nec′tion** *n.*

in·ter·con·ti·nen·tal (ĭn′tər-kŏn′tə-nĕnt′l) *adj.* **1.** Extending from one continent to another: *intercontinental flight.* **2.** Waged between continents: *intercontinental warfare.* **3.** Capable of flight from one continent to another: *intercontinental ballistic missile.*

in·ter·con·ver·sion (ĭn′tər-kən-vûr′zhən, -shən) *n.* Mutual conversion. —**in′ter·con·vert′i·ble** *adj.*

in·ter·cos·tal (ĭn′tər-kŏst′l) *adj.* Located or occurring between the ribs. [New Latin *intercostalis* : Latin *inter-,* between + *costa,* rib (see **kost-** in Appendix*).]

in·ter·course (ĭn′tər-kôrs′, -kōrs′) *n.* **1.** Interchange between persons or groups; communication. **2.** Coitus. [Middle English *intercurse,* from Old French *entrecours,* from Latin *intercursus,* past participle of *intercurrere,* to run between : *inter-,* between + *currere,* to run (see **kers-²** in Appendix*).]

in·ter·crop (ĭn′tər-krŏp′) *v.* **-cropped, -cropping, -crops.** —*intr.* To grow a secondary crop between the rows of a principal crop. —*tr.* To plant such a crop on. —*n.* A secondary crop grown between the rows of a principal crop.

in·ter·cur·rent (ĭn′tər-kûr′ənt) *adj.* **1.** Occurring as an interruption in a process. **2.** *Pathology.* Occurring during the course of an existing disease. [Latin *intercurrēns,* present participle of *intercurrere,* to run between. See **intercourse.**]

in·ter·den·tal (ĭn′tər-dĕnt′l) *adj.* **1.** Located between the teeth. **2.** *Phonetics.* Pronounced with the tip of the tongue protruding between the teeth, as (*th*) in *that* or (th) in *thumb.* —*n.* *Phonetics.* A consonant pronounced in this manner.

in·ter·dict (ĭn′tər-dĭkt′) *tr.v.* **-dicted, -dicting, -dicts. 1.** To prohibit or place under an ecclesiastical or legal sanction. **2.** To cut or destroy (an enemy line of communication) by firepower so as to halt an enemy's advance. —*n.* **1.** A prohibition by court order. **2.** A Roman Catholic ecclesiastical censure whereby an offending person or district is excluded from participation in most sacraments and from Christian burial. [Learned respelling of Middle English *entrediten,* to announce ecclesiastical censure, from Old French *entredire* (past participle *entredit*), from Latin *interdīcere,* to forbid : *inter-,* preventively + *dīcere,* to say (see **deik-** in Appendix*).] —**in′ter·dic′tive, in′ter·dic′to·ry** *adj.* —**in′ter·dic′tive·ly** *adv.* —**in′ter·dic′tor** (-dĭk′tər) *n.*

in·ter·dic·tion (ĭn′tər-dĭk′shən) *n.* **1.** The act of interdicting. **2.** The state of being interdicted. **3.** An interdict.

in·ter·est (ĭn′trĭst, -tər-ĭst) *n.* **1. a.** A feeling of curiosity, fascination, or absorption. **b.** The cause of any such feeling. **c.** The quality or aspect of something that enables it to cause any such feeling. **2.** *Often plural.* Advantage; self-interest. **3. a.** A right, claim, or legal share in something. **b.** *Usually plural.* Something in which such a right, claim, or share is held. **c.** Involvement with or participation in something. **4. a.** *Abbr.* **i., int.** A charge for a financial loan, usually a percentage of the amount loaned. **b.** An excess or bonus beyond what is expected or due: *She returned his ardor with interest.* **5.** *Usually plural.* A group of persons sharing an interest in an enterprise, industry, or segment of society. —**in the interest** (or **interests**) **of.** For the benefit of; in behalf of. —*tr.v.* **interested, -esting, -ests. 1.** To arouse the curiosity or hold the attention of. **2.** To cause to become involved or concerned with. **3.** *Obsolete.* To concern or affect. [Middle English, variant (influenced by Old French *interest,* damage) of *interesse,* concern, share, from Norman French, substantive use of Latin *interesse,* "to be in between," to matter, be of concern : *inter-,* between + *esse,* to be (see **es-** in Appendix*).]

in·ter·est·ed (ĭn′trĭ-stĭd, -tər-ĭ-stĭd, -tə-rĕs′tĭd) *adj.* **1.** Having or showing curiosity, fascination, or concern. **2.** Possessing a right, claim, or share. **3.** Desirous of personal gain; self-seeking. —**in′ter·est·ed·ly** *adv.* —**in′ter·est·ed·ness** *n.*

in·ter·est·ing (ĭn′trĭ-stĭng, -tər-ĭ-stĭng, -tə-rĕs′tĭng) *adj.* Arousing or holding attention; absorbing. —**in′ter·est·ing·ly** *adv.*

in·ter·face (ĭn′tər-fās′) *n.* A surface forming a common boundary between adjacent regions. —**in′ter·fa′cial** (-fā′shəl) *adj.*

in·ter·fere (ĭn′tər-fîr′) *intr.v.* **-fered, -fering, -feres. 1.** To be a hindrance or obstacle; impede. **2.** *Football.* To impede illegally the catching of a pass. **3.** To intervene or intrude in the affairs of others; meddle. **4.** To strike one hoof against the opposite hoof or leg while moving. Used of a horse. **5.** *Physics.* To produce interference with (another wave). **6.** *Electronics.* To inhibit or prevent clear reception of (broadcast signals). [Old French (*s'*)*entreferir,* to strike each other : INTER- + *ferir,* to strike, from Latin *ferīre* (see **bher-²** in Appendix*).] —**in′ter·fer′er** *n.* —**in′ter·fer′ing·ly** *adv.*

   Synonyms: *interfere, meddle, tamper.* These verbs are compared in the sense of concerning oneself in the affairs of other persons. *Interfere* and *meddle* are sometimes interchangeable.

Meddle is the stronger in implying unwanted, unwarranted, or unnecessary intrusion. It is somewhat weaker than *interfere* in implying action that seriously hampers, hinders, or frustrates. *Tamper* refers to intervention in the form of making unauthorized alterations or changes, especially ones that corrupt.

in·ter·fer·ence (ĭn′tər-fîr′əns) *n.* **1.** The act, process, or an instance of interfering. **2.** *Football.* **a.** The tackling or blocking of defensive tacklers to protect the ball carrier. **b.** The players protecting the ball carrier in such a manner. **c.** The illegal obstruction of the receiving of a pass. **4.** *Law.* Application for a patent on an invention entirely or partially covered in an already existing or pending patent. **5.** *Physics.* The phenomenon of two or more waves of the same frequency combining to form a wave in which the disturbance at any point is the algebraic or vector sum of the disturbances due to the interfering waves at that point. **6.** *Electronics.* **a.** The inhibition or prevention of clear reception of broadcast signals. **b.** The distorted portion of a received signal. —**in′ter·fer·en′tial** *adj.*

in·ter·fe·rom·e·ter (ĭn′tər-fə-rŏm′ə-tər) *n.* Any of several optical, acoustical, or radio-frequency instruments that use interference phenomena between a reference wave and an experimental wave, or between two parts of an experimental wave, to determine wavelengths, wave velocities, distances, and directions. [INTERFER(E) + -METER.]

in·ter·fer·on (ĭn′tər-fîr′ŏn) *n.* A cellular protein produced in response to, and acting to prevent replication of, an infectious viral form within an infected cell. [INTERFER(E) + -ON.]

in·ter·fer·tile (ĭn′tər-fûrt′l) *adj.* Having the ability to interbreed.

in·ter·ga·lac·tic (ĭn′tər-gə-lăk′tĭk) *adj.* Between galaxies.

in·ter·gla·cial (ĭn′tər-glā′shəl) *adj.* Between glacial epochs.

in·ter·grade (ĭn′tər-grād′) *intr.v.* **-graded, -grading, -grades.** To merge or grow into each other in a series of stages, forms, or types. —*n.* (ĭn′tər-grād′). A transitional step, grade, or form. —**in′ter·gra·da′tion** *n.* —**in′ter·gra′di·ent** (ĭn′tər-grā′dē-ənt) *adj.*

in·ter·im (ĭn′tər-ĭm) *n.* An interval of time between one event, process, or period and another. —*adj.* Belonging to or taking place during an interim; temporary. [Latin, in the meantime, from *inter*, at intervals, among. See **en** in Appendix.*]

in·te·ri·or (ĭn-tîr′ē-ər) *adj. Abbr.* **int. 1.** Of, relating to, or located in the inside; inner. **2.** Of or relating to one's mental or spiritual being. **3.** Situated away from a coast or border; inland. —*n. Abbr.* **int. 1.** The internal portion or area of something; the inside. **2.** One's mental or spiritual being. **3.** A representation of the inside of a building or room, as in a painting. **4.** The inland part of a given political or geographical entity. [Latin, comparative of *inter*, in, within. See **en** in Appendix.*] —**in·te′ri·or′i·ty** (ĭn-tîr′ē-ôr′ə-tē, -ŏr′ə-tē) *n.* —**in·te′ri·or·ly** *adv.*

interior angle. 1. a. Any of four angles formed between two straight lines cut by a transversal. **b.** A vertex angle measured wholly within a polygon. **2.** The angle formed inside a polygon by two adjacent sides.

interior decorator. One who plans and executes the layout and decoration of an architectural interior. Also called "interior designer." —**interior decoration.**

interj. interjection.

in·ter·ject (ĭn′tər-jĕkt′) *tr.v.* **-jected, -jecting, -jects.** To interpose parenthetically or by way of an interruption. [Latin *interjicere* (past participle *interjectus*), to throw between : *inter-*, between + *jacere*, to throw (see **yē-** in Appendix.*).] —**in′ter·jec′tor** (-jĕk′tər) *n.* —**in′ter·jec′to·ry** (-tôr′ē, -tōr′ē) *adj.*

in·ter·jec·tion (ĭn′tər-jĕk′shən) *n.* **1.** An exclamation; ejaculation. **2.** *Abbr.* **interj. a.** A part of speech consisting of exclamatory words capable of standing alone; for example, *oh!* **b.** A word, phrase, or other sound used exclamatorily and capable of standing alone; for example, *Heavens!* —**in′ter·jec′tion·al** *adj.* —**in′ter·jec′tion·al·ly** *adv.*

in·ter·lace (ĭn′tər-lās′) *v.* **-laced, -lacing, -laces.** —*tr.* **1.** To connect together by or as if by weaving; interweave. **2.** To intersperse. —*intr.* To intertwine. —**in′ter·lace′ment** *n.*

In·ter·la·ken (ĭn′tər-lä′kən, ĭn′tər-lä′kən). A town and resort center of west-central Switzerland. Population, 5,000.

in·ter·lam·i·nate (ĭn′tər-lăm′ə-nāt′) *tr.v.* **-nated, -nating, -nates. 1.** To insert between layers. **2.** To arrange in alternating layers. —**in′ter·lam′i·nar** *adj.* —**in′ter·lam′i·na′tion** *n.*

in·ter·lard (ĭn′tər-lärd′) *tr.v.* **-larded, -larding, -lards. 1.** To insert something foreign into; intersperse. **2.** To be interspersed through; occur in repeatedly. [Old French *entrelarder*, to alternate layers of fat and lean : INTER- + *larder*, to insert fat, cover with lard, from *lard*, LARD.]

in·ter·leaf (ĭn′tər-lēf′) *n., pl.* **-leaves** (-lēvz′). A blank leaf inserted between the regular pages of a book.

in·ter·leave (ĭn′tər-lēv′) *tr.v.* **-leaved, -leaving, -leaves.** To provide with an interleaf or interleaves.

in·ter·line¹ (ĭn′tər-līn′) *tr.v.* **-lined, -lining, -lines.** Also **in·ter·lin·e·ate** (-lĭn′ē-āt′), **-ated, -ating, -ates. 1.** To insert (writing) between printed or written lines. **2.** To insert words between the lines of (a text). —**in′ter·lin′e·a′tion** (-lĭn′ē-ā′shən) *n.*

in·ter·line² (ĭn′tər-līn′) *tr.v.* **-lined, -lining, -lines.** To fit (a garment) with an interlining.

in·ter·lin·e·ar (ĭn′tər-lĭn′ē-ər) *adj.* **1.** Inserted between the lines of a text. **2.** Written or printed with different languages or versions in alternating lines.

in·ter·lin·ing (ĭn′tər-lī′nĭng) *n.* An extra lining between the outer fabric and the regular lining of a garment.

in·ter·lock (ĭn′tər-lŏk′) *intr.v.* **-locked, -locking, -locks.** To unite firmly or join closely, as by hooking or dovetailing.

in·ter·lo·cu·tion (ĭn′tər-lō-kyōō′shən) *n. Rare.* Speech between two or more persons; conversation. [Latin *interlocūtiō*, from

interloquī (past participle *interlocūtus*), to speak between : *inter-*, between + *loquī*, to speak (see **tolkw-** in Appendix.*).]

in·ter·loc·u·tor (ĭn′tər-lŏk′yə-tər) *n.* **1. a.** Someone who takes part in a conversation. **b.** A partner in this dialogue. **2.** The performer in a minstrel show who is placed midway between the end men and engages in banter with them.

in·ter·loc·u·to·ry (ĭn′tər-lŏk′yə-tôr′ē, -tōr′ē) *n.* A temporary decree made during the course of a suit, divorce trial, or the like. —*adj.* Of or relating to such a decree.

in·ter·lope (ĭn′tər-lōp′) *intr.v.* **-loped, -loping, -lopes. 1.** To violate the legally established trading rights of others. **2.** To interfere in the affairs of others; intrude; meddle. —See Synonyms at **intrude.** [Back-formation from *interloper* : INTER- + Dutch *loper*, running, from Middle Dutch, from *loopen*, to run (see **klou-** in Appendix.*).] —**in′ter·lo′per** *n.*

in·ter·lude (ĭn′tər-lōōd′) *n.* **1.** An intervening episode, feature, or period of time. **2. a.** A short farcical entertainment performed between the acts of a medieval mystery or morality play. **b.** A 16th-century genre of comedy derived from this. **c.** An entertainment between the acts of a play. **3.** A short musical piece inserted between the parts of a longer composition. [Middle English *enterlude*, from Medieval Latin *interlūdium*, performance between acts : Latin *inter-*, between + *lūdus*, play (see **leid-** in Appendix.*).]

in·ter·lu·nar (ĭn′tər-lōō′nər) *adj.* Of or relating to the period between the old and new moon when the moon is not visible.

in·ter·mar·ry (ĭn′tər-măr′ē) *intr.v.* **-ried, -rying, -ries. 1.** To marry a member of another group. **2.** To be bound together by the marriages of members. **3.** To marry within one's family, tribe, or clan. —**in′ter·mar′riage** *n.*

in·ter·med·dle (ĭn′tər-mĕd′l) *intr.v.* **-dled, -dling, -dles.** To interfere in the affairs of others; meddle. [Middle English *entermedlen*, from Old French *entremedler, entremesler* : INTER- + *mesler, medler*, to mix, MEDDLE.] —**in′ter·med′dler** *n.*

in·ter·me·di·a·cy (ĭn′tər-mē′dē-ə-sē) *n.* The state of being intermediate.

in·ter·me·di·ar·y (ĭn′tər-mē′dē-ĕr′ē) *n., pl.* **-ies. 1.** One who acts as a mediator. **2.** One that acts as an agent between persons or things; a means. **3.** An intermediate state or stage. —*adj.* **1.** Acting as a mediator. **2.** In between; intermediate.

in·ter·me·di·ate (ĭn′tər-mē′dē-ĭt) *adj. Abbr.* **inter.** Lying or occurring between two extremes; in between; in the middle. —*n. Abbr.* **inter. 1.** One that is intermediate. **2.** An intermediary. **3.** *Chemistry.* A substance formed as a necessary stage in the manufacture of a desired end-product. —*intr.v.* (ĭn′tər-mē′dē-āt′) **intermediated, -ating, -ates.** To act as an intermediary; mediate. [Medieval Latin *intermediātus*, from Latin *intermedius* : *inter-*, between + *medius*, middle (see **medhyo-** in Appendix.*).] —**in′ter·me′di·ate·ly** *adv.* —**in′ter·me′di·ate·ness** *n.* —**in′ter·me′di·a′tion** *n.* —**in′ter·me′di·a′tor** (-ā′tər) *n.*

in·ter·ment (ĭn-tûr′mənt) *n.* The act or ritual of interring.

in·ter·mez·zo (ĭn′tər-mĕt′sō, -mĕd′zō) *n., pl.* **-zos** or **-zi** (-sē, -zē). **1.** A brief entr'acte. **2. a.** A short movement separating the major sections of a symphonic work. **b.** An independent instrumental composition having the character of such a movement. [Italian, from Latin *intermedius*, INTERMEDIATE.]

in·ter·mi·na·ble (ĭn-tûr′mə-nə-bəl) *adj.* Tiresomely protracted; endless. See Synonyms at **continual.** —**in·ter′mi·na·bly** *adv.*

in·ter·min·gle (ĭn′tər-mĭng′gəl) *v.* **-gled, -gling, -gles.** —*tr.* To mix or mingle. —*intr.* To mix with one another.

in·ter·mis·sion (ĭn′tər-mĭsh′ən) *n.* **1. a.** The act of intermitting. **b.** The state of being intermitted. **2.** A respite or recess. **3.** The period between the acts of a theatrical performance. [Latin *intermissiō*, from *intermittere* (past participle *intermissus*), INTERMIT.]

in·ter·mit (ĭn′tər-mĭt′) *v.* **-mitted, -mitting, -mits.** —*intr.* To suspend activity temporarily or repeatedly. —*tr.* To cause to suspend activity temporarily or repeatedly; interrupt. [Latin *intermittere*, to interrupt at intervals : *inter-*, at intervals + *mittere*, to send, let go (see **smeit-** in Appendix.*).] —**in′ter·mit′tence** *n.*

in·ter·mit·tent (ĭn′tər-mĭt′ənt) *adj.* Stopping and starting at intervals. See Synonyms at **periodic.** —**in′ter·mit′tent·ly** *adv.*

intermittent current. A periodically interrupted unidirectional electric current.

in·ter·mix (ĭn′tər-mĭks′) *v.* **-mixed, -mixing, -mixes.** —*tr.* To mix together. —*intr.* To be or become mixed together. [Back-formation from earlier *intermixt*, intermixed, from Latin *intermixtus*, past participle of *intermiscēre*, to mix together : *inter-*, mutually + *miscēre*, to mix (see **meik-** in Appendix.*).]

in·ter·mix·ture (ĭn′tər-mĭks′chər) *n.* **1.** The act or process of intermixing. **2.** The state or condition of being intermixed. **3.** Something composed of various ingredients; a mixture. **4.** Something added to a mixture; an admixture.

in·tern (ĭn′tûrn′) *n.* Also **in·terne. 1.** An advanced student or recent graduate undergoing supervised practical training. **2.** One who is interned; an internee. —*v.* **interned, -terning, -terns.** —*intr.* (ĭn′tûrn′). To train or serve as an intern. —*tr.* (ĭn-tûrn′). To detain or confine, especially in wartime. —*adj.* (ĭn-tûrn′). *Archaic.* Internal. [French *interne*, inmate, resident assistant physician, from Old French, internal, from Latin *internus*, INTERNAL.] —**in′tern·ship′** *n.*

in·ter·nal (ĭn-tûr′nəl) *adj.* **1.** Of, relating to, or located within the limits or surface of something; inner; interior. **2.** Emanating from or dependent on the nature of something; intrinsic; inherent. **3.** Located, acting, or effective within the body. **4.** Of or relating to the domestic affairs of a country. [New Latin *internalis*, from Latin *internus*, from *inter*, in, within. See **en** in Appendix.*] —**in′ter·nal′i·ty** *n.* —**in·ter′nal·ly** *adv.*

in·ter·nal-com·bus·tion engine (ĭn-tûr′nəl-kəm-bŭs′chən). An engine, such as an automotive gasoline piston engine or a diesel, in which fuel is burned within the engine proper rather than in an external furnace as in a steam engine.

internal ear. The portion of the ear that includes the semi-circular canals, the vestibule, and the cochlea. See **ear.**

internal medicine. The medical study and treatment of non-surgical constitutional diseases in adults.

internal revenue. Governmental income from taxes levied within the country.

internal rhyme. Rhyme in which a rhyming syllable occupies any position other than the beginning or the end of the line of which it is a unit.

internal secretion. A secretion of an endocrine gland discharged directly into the blood.

in·ter·na·tion·al (ĭn′tər-năsh′ən-əl) adj. Abbr. **int., intl.** Of, relating to, or involving two or more nations or nationalities: an international incident. —**in′ter·na′tion·al·ly** adv.

In·ter·na·tion·al (ĭn′tər-năsh′ən-əl) n. **1.** Any of several socialist organizations of international scope formed during the late 19th and early 20th centuries, especially: **a.** The First International (International Workingmen's Association), organized in 1864 by Marx and Engels to associate the trade unions of all nations. **b.** The Second International (Socialist International), an association formed (1889) to promote the unity of socialist parties in various countries. **c.** The Third International (Communist International), organized (1919) by the Bolsheviks to coordinate the activities of communist movements throughout the world. Also called "Comintern." **2.** The **Internationale** (see). —adj. Of or relating to an International.

international candle. A candle (see).

International Court of Justice. Abbr. **ICJ** The main judicial body of the United Nations founded in 1945. Also called "World Court."

International Date Line. The date line (see).

In·ter·na·tio·nale (ĭn′tər-năsh′ən-əl; French ăN-tĕr-nȧ-syô-nàl′) n. A revolutionary song adopted at different times by various syndicalist and communist movements as the hymn of the world proletariat. [French, "the International."]

in·ter·na·tion·al·ism (ĭn′tər-năsh′ən-ə-lĭz′əm) n. **1.** The state or quality of being international in character, principles, concern, or attitude. **2.** A theory that promotes cooperation among nations, especially in politics and economy. —**in′ter·na′tion·al·ist** n. —**in′ter·na′tion·al′i·ty** n.

in·ter·na·tion·al·ize (ĭn′tər-năsh′ən-ə-līz′) tr.v. **-ized, -izing, -izes.** To make international; put under international control. —**in′ter·na′tion·al·i·za′tion** n.

International Labor Organization. Abbr. **ILO** A specialized agency of the United Nations originally established in 1919 to standardize and improve international labor conditions.

international law. A set of rules generally regarded and accepted as binding in relations between states and nations. Also called "law of nations."

international Morse code. The **continental code** (see).

International Phonetic Alphabet. Abbr. **IPA, I.P.A.** A phonetic alphabet sponsored by the International Phonetic Association to provide a uniform, universally comprehensible system of letters and symbols for writing the speech sounds of all languages.

international pitch. A standard of tuning of 440 vibrations per second for A above middle C.

International System. Abbr. **SI** A complete, coherent system of units used for scientific work, based on the metric system with the addition of units of time, electric current, temperature, and luminous intensity. See **measurement.**

in·terne. Variant of **intern.**

in·ter·ne·cine (ĭn′tər-nĕs′ēn′, -ən, -nē′sīn′) adj. **1.** Mutually destructive; ruinous or fatal to both sides. **2.** Characterized by bloodshed or carnage. **3.** Relating to struggle within a nation or organization. See Usage note. [Latin internecīnus, from internecio, massacre, from internecāre, to slaughter, massacre : inter (intensive) + necāre, to kill (see **nek-¹** in Appendix*).]

Usage: The newer sense of internecine that relates to internal struggle does not necessarily imply fatal or mutually destructive conflict. Examples of internecine in this newer sense, dealing with struggles within a political party and a labor union, are acceptable to 91 per cent of the Usage Panel.

in·tern·ee (ĭn′tûr-nē′) n. One who is interned, especially during a war.

in·ter·nist (ĭn-tûr′nĭst) n. A physician who specializes in internal medicine. [INTERN(AL MEDICINE) + -IST.]

in·tern·ment (ĭn-tûrn′mənt) n. The act of interning or the state of being interned.

internment camp. A camp for confining prisoners of war or enemy aliens during a war.

in·ter·node (ĭn′tər-nōd′) n. A section or part between two nodes, as of a nerve or stem. —**in′ter·no′dal** (-nōd′l) adj.

in·ter nos (ĭn′tər nōs′). Latin. Between ourselves.

in·ter·nun·ci·o (ĭn′tər-nŭn′shē-ō′, -sē-ō′) n., pl. **-os. 1.** A Vatican diplomatic envoy or representative ranking just beneath a nuncio. **2.** A messenger or agent; a go-between. [Italian internunzio, from Latin internuntius, go-between : inter-, between + nūntius, messenger, NUNCIO.]

in·ter·o·cep·tor (ĭn′tə-rō-sĕp′tər) n. A specialized sensory nerve receptor responding to stimuli originating in internal organs. [From INTER(IOR) + (RE)CEPTOR.] —**in′ter·o·cep′tive** adj.

interp. interpreter.

in·ter·pel·late (ĭn′tər pĕl′āt′, ĭn-tûr′pə-lāt′) tr.v. **-lated, -lating, -lates.** To question formally about government policy or ac-

tion. [Latin interpellāre, to interrupt by speaking. See **pel-⁶** in Appendix.*] —**in′ter·pel·la′tion** n. —**in′ter·pel′la·tor** (-lā′tər) n.

in·ter·pen·e·trate (ĭn′tər-pĕn′ə-trāt′) v. **-trated, -trating, -trates.** —tr. To penetrate between. —intr. To penetrate mutually. —**in′ter·pen′e·tra′tion** n. —**in′ter·pen′e·tra′tive** adj.

in·ter·phase (ĭn′tər-fāz′) n. A period or stage between two successive mitotic divisions of a cell nucleus.

in·ter·phone (ĭn′tər-fōn′) n. A telephone system connecting the different parts of a unit, such as a home, ship, or aircraft.

in·ter·plan·e·tar·y (ĭn′tər-plăn′ə-tĕr′ē) adj. Between planets.

in·ter·play (ĭn′tər-plā′) n. Reciprocal action and reaction; interaction. —intr.v. **interplayed, -playing, -plays.** To act or react on each other; interact.

in·ter·plead (ĭn′tər-plēd′) intr.v. **-pleaded, -pleading, -pleads.** Law. To go to court together to establish a dispute involving a third party. [Norman French entrepleder : INTER- + pleder, to plead, from Old French plaidier, pleidier, PLEAD.]

in·ter·plead·er (ĭn′tər-plē′dər) n. Law. **1.** A legal procedure to determine which of two persons bringing the same suit against a third person is the rightful claimant. **2.** One who interpleads.

in·ter·po·late (ĭn-tûr′pə-lāt′) v. **-lated, -lating, -lates.** —tr. **1.** To insert or introduce between other things or parts; intercalate. **2.** To insert (additional or false material) in a text. **3.** To change or falsify (a text) by introducing new or false material. **4.** Mathematics. To determine a value of (a function) between known values by a procedure or algorithm different from that specified by the function itself. —intr. To make insertions or additions. [Latin interpolāre : inter-, between + polīre, to adorn, furbish, POLISH.] —**in·ter′po·la′tion** n. —**in·ter′po·la′tive** adj. —**in·ter′po·lat′or** (-lā′tər) n.

in·ter·pose (ĭn′tər-pōz′) v. **-posed, -posing, -poses.** —tr. **1.** To insert or introduce between parts. **2.** To introduce or interject (a remark, question, or digression) during a conversation or speech. **3.** To exert (influence or authority) in order to interfere or intervene. —intr. **1.** To come between; intervene. **2.** To introduce a remark, question, or argument. [Old French interposer, from Latin interpōnere (past participle interpositus), to place between : inter-, between + pōnere, to put, place (see apo- in Appendix*).] —**in′ter·po′sal** n. —**in′ter·pos′er** n. —**in′ter·po·si′tion** (-pə-zĭsh′ən) n.

in·ter·pret (ĭn-tûr′prĭt) v. **-preted, -preting, -prets.** —tr. **1.** To clarify the meaning of; elucidate. **2.** To expound the significance of. **3.** To represent the meaning of through art. **4.** To translate. —intr. **1.** To offer an explanation. **2.** To translate orally. —See Synonyms at **explain.** [Middle English interpreten, from Old French interpreter, from Latin interpretārī, from interpres, interpreter, negotiator. See **per-⁷** in Appendix.*] —**in·ter′pret·a·ble** adj. —**in·ter′pret·a·bil′i·ty, in·ter′pret·a·ble·ness** n.

in·ter·pre·ta·tion (ĭn-tûr′prə-tā′shən) n. **1.** The act or process of interpreting; an explanation. **2.** The result of interpretation; an explanation. **3.** A concept of a work of art as expressed by the character and style of its representation or performance. —**in·ter′pre·ta′tion·al** adj.

in·ter·pre·ta·tive (ĭn-tûr′prə-tā′tĭv) adj. Also **in·ter·pre·tive** (-prə-tĭv). Expository; explanatory. —**in·ter′pre·ta′tive·ly** adv.

    Usage: Interpretative and interpretive are both used. Although interpretative was usually preferred in earlier usage, interpretive is acceptable to 78 per cent of the Usage Panel, and is considered to be no less appropriate to a formal level than the longer form by 70 per cent of the Panel.

in·ter·pret·er (ĭn-tûr′prə-tər) n. Abbr. **interp. 1.** One who translates orally from one language into another. **2.** One who makes and expounds an interpretation: medieval interpreters of Aristotle.

in·ter·reg·num (ĭn′tər-rĕg′nəm) n., pl. **-nums** or **-na** (-nə). **1.** The interval of time between the end of a sovereign's reign and the accession of a successor. **2.** Temporary suspension of the usual functions of government or control. **3.** A gap in continuity. [Latin interregnum : inter-, between + regnum, REIGN.] —**in′ter·reg′nal** adj.

in·ter·re·late (ĭn′tər-rĭ-lāt′) v. **-lated, -lating, -lates.** —tr. To place in mutual relationship. —intr. To come into mutual relationship. —**in′ter·re·la′tion** n. —**in′ter·re·la′tion·ship′** n.

in·ter·rex (ĭn′tər-rĕks′) n., pl. **interreges** (ĭn′tər-rē′jēz′). One who holds supreme state power during an interregnum. [Latin interrex : inter-, between + rēx, king (see **reg-¹** in Appendix*).]

interrog. interrogative.

in·ter·ro·gate (ĭn-tĕr′ə-gāt′) tr.v. **-gated, -gating, -gates.** To examine by formal questioning. See Synonyms at **ask.** [Latin interrogāre, to consult, question : inter-, between + rogāre, to ask (see **reg-¹** in Appendix*).] —**in·ter′ro·ga′tion** n. —**in·ter′ro·ga′tion·al** adj.

interrogation point. A **question mark** (see).

in·ter·rog·a·tive (ĭn′tə-rŏg′ə-tĭv) adj. Abbr. **interrog. 1.** Of the nature of a question; asking a question. **2.** Designating a word or form used in asking a question: an interrogative pronoun. —n. **1.** A word or form used in asking a question. **2.** An interrogative sentence or expression. —**in′ter·rog′a·tive·ly** adv.

in·ter·ro·ga·tor (ĭn′tər′ə-gā′tər) n. One that interrogates.

in·ter·rog·a·to·ry (ĭn′tə-rŏg′ə-tôr′ē, -tōr′ē) adj. Interrogative. —n., pl. **interrogatories.** Law. A formal question, as to an accused person. —**in·ter·rog′a·tor′i·ly** adv.

in·ter·rupt (ĭn′tə-rŭpt′) v. **-rupted, -rupting, -rupts.** —tr. **1.** To break the continuity or uniformity of. **2.** To hinder or stop the action or discourse of (someone) by breaking in upon. —intr. To break in upon an action or discourse. [Middle English interrupten, from Latin interrumpere (past participle interruptus), to break in : inter, between + rumpere, to break (see **reup-**

in Appendix*).] —**in′ter·rup′tion** *n.* —**in′ter·rup′tive** *adj.*

in·ter·rupt·ed (ĭn′tə-rŭp′tĭd) *adj.* **1.** Broken in continuity; discontinuous. **2.** *Botany.* Having an uneven arrangement, as of leaflets along a stem. —**in′ter·rup′ted·ly** *adv.*

in·ter·rupt·er (ĭn′tə-rŭp′tər) *n.* Also **in·ter·rup·tor.** **1.** One that interrupts. **2.** *Electricity.* A device for periodically and automatically opening or closing an electric circuit.

in·ter·scho·las·tic (ĭn′tər-skə-lăs′tĭk) *adj.* Existing or conducted between or among schools.

in·ter se (ĭn′tər sē′, sā′). *Latin.* Between or among themselves.

in·ter·sect (ĭn′tər-sĕkt′) *v.* **-sected, -secting, -sects.** —*tr.* **1.** To cut across or through. **2.** To form an intersection with. —*intr.* **1.** To cut across or overlap each other. **2.** To form an intersection. [Latin *intersecāre* (past participle *intersectus*) : *inter-*, mutually + *secāre*, to cut (see **sek-** in Appendix*).]

in·ter·sec·tion (ĭn′tər-sĕk′shən) *n.* **1.** *Mathematics.* **a.** The point or locus of points common to two or more geometric figures. **b.** A set, every member of which is an element of each of two or more given sets. Compare **union.** **2. a.** The act or process of intersecting. **b.** A place where things intersect.

in·ter·ses·sion (ĭn′tər-sĕsh′ən) *n.* The time between two academic sessions or semesters. —**in′ter·ses′sion·al** *adj.*

in·ter·sex (ĭn′tər-sĕks′) *n.* An intersexual individual.

in·ter·sex·u·al (ĭn′tər-sĕk′sho͞o-əl) *adj.* **1.** Existing or occurring between the sexes. **2.** Having sexual characteristics intermediate between those of a typical male and a typical female. —**in′ter·sex′u·al′i·ty** *n.* —**in′ter·sex′u·al·ly** *adv.*

in·ter·space (ĭn′tər-spās′) *tr.v.* **-spaced, -spacing, -spaces.** To make or occupy a space between. —*n.* (ĭn′tər-spās′). A space between two things; an interval. —**in′ter·spa′tial** (-spā′shəl) *adj.* —**in′ter·spa′tial·ly** *adv.*

in·ter·sperse (ĭn′tər-spûrs′) *tr.v.* **-spersed, -spersing, -sperses.** **1.** To scatter or distribute among other things at irregular intervals. **2.** To supply or diversify with things distributed at irregular intervals. [Latin *interspergere* (past participle *interspersus*), to scatter among : *inter-*, among + *spargere*, to scatter (see **sphereg-** in Appendix*).] —**in′ter·spers′ed·ly** (-spûr′sĭd-lē) *adv.* —**in′ter·sper′sion** (-spûr′zhən, -shən) *n.*

in·ter·state (ĭn′tər-stāt′) *adj.* Pertaining to, existing between, or connecting two or more states.

Interstate Commerce Commission. *Abbr.* **ICC** An agency of the U.S. government for the regulation and supervision of interstate commerce.

in·ter·stel·lar (ĭn′tər-stĕl′ər) *adj.* Between the stars.

in·ter·stice (ĭn-tûr′stĭs) *n., pl.* **-stices** (-stĭ-sēz′, -sĭz). A narrow or small space between things or parts; crevice. [French, from Late Latin *interstitium*, from Latin *intersistere* (past participle *interstitus*), to stand in the middle of : *inter-*, in the middle of, between + *sistere*, to stand (see **stā-** in Appendix*).]

in·ter·sti·tial (ĭn′tər-stĭsh′əl) *adj.* **1.** Of or occurring in interstices. **2.** Affecting or based on interstices. —**in′ter·sti′tial·ly** *adv.*

in·ter·strat·i·fy (ĭn′tər-străt′ə-fī′) *v.* **-fied, -fying, -fies.** —*tr.* To alternate or vary with other strata. Used in the passive. —*intr.* To lie or be formed as strata between other strata. —**in′ter·strat′i·fi·ca′tion** *n.*

in·ter·tex·ture (ĭn′tər-tĕks′chər) *n.* **1.** The act of interweaving or the state of being interwoven. **2.** Something interwoven.

in·ter·tid·al (ĭn′tər-tīd′l) *adj.* Of, pertaining to, or being the region between the extremes of high and low tide.

in·ter·tri·bal (ĭn′tər-trī′bəl) *adj.* Existing between tribes.

in·ter·trop·i·cal (ĭn′tər-trŏp′ĭ-kəl) *adj. Geography.* **1.** Between or within the tropics. **2.** Of or pertaining to the tropics.

in·ter·twine (ĭn′tər-twīn′) *v.* **-twined, -twining, -twines.** —*tr.* To twist or braid together. —*intr.* To interweave with one another. Also "intertwist." —**in′ter·twine′ment** *n.*

in·ter·ur·ban (ĭn′tər-ûr′bən) *adj.* Pertaining to or connecting urban areas: *an interurban railroad.*

in·ter·val (ĭn′tər-vəl) *n. Abbr.* **int.** **1.** A space between two objects, points, or units. **2.** The temporal duration between two specified instants, events, or states. **3.** *Mathematics.* **a.** A set consisting of all the numbers between a pair of given numbers. **b.** Such a set including the endpoints. Also called "closed interval." **c.** Such a set not including the endpoints. Also called "open interval." **d.** A line segment representing such a set. **e.** A set of numbers greater than or less than a given number and including or excluding the given number. **4.** *British.* An intermission. **5.** The difference in pitch between two tones on a given scale. [Middle English *intervalle*, from Latin *intervallum*, space between ramparts : *inter-*, between + *vallum*, rampart (see **walso-** in Appendix*).]

in·ter·vale (ĭn′tər-vāl′) *n. Regional.* A tract of low-lying land, especially along a river. [Middle English *intervalle* (influenced in meaning by VALE), INTERVAL.]

in·ter·vene (ĭn′tər-vēn′) *intr.v.* **-vened, -vening, -venes.** **1.** To enter or occur extraneously. **2.** To come, appear, or lie between two things. **3.** To occur or come between two periods or points of time. **4.** To come in or between so as to hinder or modify. **5.** To interfere, usually through force or threat of force, in the affairs of another nation. **6.** *Law.* To enter into a suit as a third party for the protection of an alleged interest. [Latin *intervenīre*, to come between : *inter-*, between + *venīre*, to come (see **gwā-** in Appendix*).] —**in′ter·ven′er** *n.* —**in′ter·ven′tion** (-vĕn′shən) *n.*

in·ter·ven·tion·ism (ĭn′tər-vĕn′shə-nĭz′əm) *n.* The policy of intervening in the affairs of another sovereign state. —**in′ter·ven′tion·ist** *adj.* & *n.*

in·ter·view (ĭn′tər-vyo͞o′) *n.* **1. a.** A face-to-face meeting. **b.** Such a meeting arranged for the formal discussion of some matter. **2. a.** A conversation between a reporter and a person from whom he seeks facts or statements. **b.** An account or reproduction of such a conversation. —*tr.v.* **interviewed, -viewing, -views.** To obtain an interview from. [Earlier *entervewe*, from Old French *entrevue*, from *entrevu*, past participle of *(s′)entrevoir*, to see each other : *entre-*, mutually, each other + *voir*, to see, from Latin *vidēre* (see **weid-** in Appendix*).]

in·ter·vo·cal·ic (ĭn′tər-vō-kăl′ĭk) *adj. Phonetics.* Immediately followed and immediately preceded by a vowel.

in·ter·volve (ĭn′tər-vŏlv′) *v.* **-volved, -volving, -volves.** —*tr.* To wind or coil together. —*intr.* To intertwine mutually.

in·ter·weave (ĭn′tər-wēv′) *v.* **-wove** (-wōv′) or *rare* **-weaved, -woven** (-wō′vən) or *rare* **-wove, -weaving, -weaves.** —*tr.* **1.** To weave together. **2.** To intermix. —*intr.* To intertwine.

in·tes·tate (ĭn-tĕs′tāt′, -tĭt) *adj.* **1.** Having made no legal will. **2.** Not disposed of by a legal will. —*n.* One who dies without a legal will. [Middle English, from Latin *intestātus* : *in-*, not + *testātus*, TESTATE.] —**in·tes′ta·cy** (-tə-sē) *n.*

in·tes·tine (ĭn-tĕs′tən) *n.* The portion of the **alimentary canal** *(see)* extending from the stomach to the anus. See **small intestine, large intestine.** [Latin *intestīnum*, from *intestīnus*, internal, from *intus*, within. See **en** in Appendix.*] —**in·tes′ti·nal** *adj.* —**in·tes′ti·nal·ly** *adv.*

intestinal fortitude. Courage; endurance.

in·thrall. Variant of **enthrall.**

in·throne. Variant of **enthrone.**

in·ti·ma (ĭn′tə-mə) *n., pl.* **-mae** (-mē′) or **-mas.** *Anatomy.* The innermost layer of an organ or part, especially the wall of a lymphatic vessel, artery, or vein. [New Latin, from Latin, feminine of *intimus*, innermost. See **intimate** (hint).]

in·ti·ma·cy (ĭn′tə-mə-sē) *n., pl.* **-cies.** **1.** The condition of being intimate. **2.** An instance of being intimate. **3.** *Often plural.* Illicit sexual intercourse. [From INTIMATE.]

in·ti·mate¹ (ĭn′tə-mĭt) *adj.* **1.** Marked by close acquaintance, association, or familiarity. **2.** Pertaining to or indicative of one's deepest nature. **3.** Essential; innermost. **4.** Characterized by informality and privacy: *an intimate nightclub.* **5.** Very personal; private; secret. —See Synonyms at **familiar.** —*n.* A close friend or confidant. [Late Latin *intimātus*, past participle of *intimāre*, to put in, announce, INTIMATE (to hint).] —**in′ti·mate·ly** *adv.* —**in′ti·mate·ness** *n.*

in·ti·mate² (ĭn′tə-māt′) *tr.v.* **-mated, -mating, -mates.** **1.** To communicate with a hint or other indirect sign; imply subtly. **2.** *Rare.* To announce; proclaim. —See Synonyms at **suggest.** [Late Latin *intimāre*, to put or bring in, publish, announce, from Latin *intimus*, inmost, deepest. See **en** in Appendix.*] —**in′ti·mat′er** *n.* —**in′ti·ma′tion** *n.*

in·tim·i·date (ĭn-tĭm′ə-dāt′) *tr.v.* **-dated, -dating, -dates.** **1.** To make timid; frighten. **2.** To discourage or inhibit by or as if by threats. —See Synonyms at **dismay, threaten.** [Medieval Latin *intimidāre* : Latin *in-* (causative) + *timidus*, TIMID.] —**in·tim′i·da′tion** *n.* —**in·tim′i·da′tor** (-dā′tər) *n.*

in·tinc·tion (ĭn-tĭngk′shən) *n. Ecclesiastical.* The administration of the Eucharist by dipping the host into the consecrated wine and offering both simultaneously to the communicant. [Late Latin *intinctiō*, from Latin *intingere* (past participle *intinctus*), to dip in : *in-*, in + *tingere*, to wet, moisten, dip, dye (see **teng-** in Appendix*).]

in·tit·ule (ĭn-tĭt′yo͞ol) *tr.v.* **-uled, -uling, -ules.** *British.* To entitle. [Old French *intituler*, from Late Latin *intitulāre* : Latin *in-*, in + *titulus*, TITLE.]

intl. international.

in·to (ĭn′to͞o) *prep.* **1.** To the inside of. **2.** To the action or occupation of: *go into banking.* **3.** To the condition or form of: *break into pieces.* **4.** So as to be in or within: *enter into an agreement.* **5.** To a time or place in the course of: *well into the week.* **6.** Against: *ram into a tree.* **7.** Toward; in the direction of: *look into the distance.* —See Usage note at **in.** [Middle English *into*, Old English *intō* : IN + TO.]

in·tol·er·a·ble (ĭn-tŏl′ər-ə-bəl) *adj.* **1.** Insupportable; unbearable. **2.** Inordinate; extravagant. —**in·tol′er·a·bil′i·ty, in·tol′er·a·ble·ness** *n.* —**in·tol′er·a·bly** *adv.*

in·tol·er·ance (ĭn-tŏl′ər-əns) *n.* Also **in·tol·er·an·cy** (-ən-sē). **1.** The quality or condition of being intolerant. **2.** Inability to withstand or consume.

in·tol·er·ant (ĭn-tŏl′ər-ənt) *adj.* Not tolerant, especially: **a.** Bigoted. **b.** Irritable. **c.** Unable to endure. —**in·tol′er·ant·ly** *adv.*

in·to·nate (ĭn′tō-nāt′) *tr.v.* **-nated, -nating, -nates.** **1.** To intone. **2.** To utter with a particular tone of voice.

in·to·na·tion (ĭn′tō-nā′shən) *n.* **1. a.** The act of intoning or chanting. **b.** An intoned utterance. **2.** A manner of producing or uttering tones, especially with regard to accuracy of pitch. **3. a.** The use of pitch as an element of meaning in language. **b.** A use of pitch characteristic of a speaker or dialect: *"He could hear authority, the old parish intonation coming back into his voice"* (Graham Greene).

in·tone (ĭn-tōn′) *v.* **-toned, -toning, -tones.** —*tr.* **1.** To recite in a singing voice. **2.** To utter in a monotone. —*intr.* To speak with a given intonation. [Middle English *entonen*, from Old French *entoner*, from Medieval Latin *intonāre*, to utter in a musical tone : Latin *in-*, in + *tonus*, TONE.] —**in·ton′er** *n.*

in to·to (ĭn tō′tō). *Latin.* Totally; altogether.

in·tox·i·cant (ĭn-tŏk′sĭ-kənt) *n.* An agent that intoxicates; especially, an alcoholic beverage. —*adj.* Intoxicating.

in·tox·i·cate (ĭn-tŏk′sĭ-kāt′) *tr.v.* **-cated, -cating, -cates.** **1.** To induce, especially by the effect of ingested alcohol, any of a series of progressively deteriorating states ranging from exhilaration to stupefaction. **2.** To stimulate or excite: *"a man whom life intoxicates, who has no need of wine"* (Anaïs Nin). **3.** To

ă pat/ā pay/âr care/ä father/b bib/ch church/d deed/ĕ pet/ē be/f fife/g gag/h hat/hw which/ĭ pit/ī pie/îr pier/j judge/k kick/l lid, needle/m mum/n no, sudden/ng thing/ŏ pot/ō toe/ô paw, for/oi noise/ou out/o͝o took/o͞o boot/p pop/r roar/s sauce/sh ship, dish/

poison. [Medieval Latin *intoxicare*, to put poison in, poison : Latin *in-*, in + *toxicum*, poison (see **toxic**).] —**in·tox′i·ca′tion** *n.* —**in·tox′i·ca′tive** *adj.* —**in·tox′i·ca′tor** (-kā′tər) *n.*

intr. intransitive.

intra–. Indicates in, within, or inside of; for example, **intracostal, intramuscular.** ***Note:*** Many compounds other than those entered here may be formed with *intra-*. In forming compounds, *intra-* is normally joined with the following element without space or hyphen: *intraorbital.* However, if the second element begins with a capital letter or with the letter *a*, it is separated with a hyphen: *intra-European, intra-atomic.* [Late Latin, from Latin *intrā*, on the inside, within. See **en** in Appendix.*]

in·tra·a·tom·ic (ĭn′trə-ə-tŏm′ĭk) *adj.* Within an atom.

in·tra·car·di·ac (ĭn′trə-kär′dē-ăk′) *adj.* Within a chamber of the heart.

in·tra·car·ti·lag·i·nous (ĭn′trə-kär′tə-lăj′ə-nəs) *adj.* Within cartilage.

in·tra·cel·lu·lar (ĭn′trə-sĕl′yə-lər) *adj.* Within a cell or cells.

in·tra·cos·tal (ĭn′trə-kŏs′təl) *adj.* On the inner surface of a rib or ribs. [From INTRA- + COSTA.]

in·tra·cra·ni·al (ĭn′trə-krā′nē-əl) *adj.* Within the skull.

in·trac·ta·ble (ĭn-trăk′tə-bəl) *adj.* **1.** Difficult to manage or govern; stubborn. **2.** Difficult to mold or manipulate. **3.** Difficult to alleviate, remedy, or cure. —See Synonyms at **unruly.** —**in·trac′ta·bil′i·ty, in·trac′ta·ble·ness** *n.* —**in·trac′ta·bly** *adv.*

in·tra·cu·ta·ne·ous (ĭn′trə-kyo͞o-tā′nē-əs) *adj.* Within the skin.

in·tra·dos (ĭn-trā′dŏs′, -dōs′) *n., pl.* **intrados** (-dōz′, -dōz′) or **-doses.** *Architecture.* The inner curve of an arch. [French, "inside back" : INTRA- + *dos*, back, from Old French, from Latin *dorsum* (see **dorsum** in Appendix*).]

in·tra·mo·lec·u·lar (ĭn′trə-mə-lĕk′yə-lər) *adj.* Within a molecule.

in·tra·mu·ral (ĭn′trə-myo͝or′əl) *adj.* **1.** Existing within bounds of an institution, especially a school. **2.** *Anatomy.* Within the wall of a cavity or organ. —**in′tra·mu′ral·ly** *adv.*

in·tra·mus·cu·lar (ĭn′trə-mŭs′kyə-lər) *adj.* Within a muscle.

in·tran·si·gent (ĭn-trăn′sə-jənt) *adj.* Also **in·tran·si·geant.** Refusing to moderate an extreme position; uncompromising. [French *intransigeant*, from Spanish *los intransigentes*, "the uncompromising" (name of a party of extreme republicans) : *in-*, not, from Latin + *transigente*, present participle of *transigir*, to compromise, from Latin *trānsigere*, to drive through, come to an understanding : *trāns-*, through + *agere*, to drive (see **ag-** in Appendix*).] —**in·tran′si·gence, in·tran′si·gen·cy** *n.* —**in·tran′si·gent** *n.* —**in·tran′si·gent·ly** *adv.*

in·tran·si·tive (ĭn-trăn′sə-tĭv) *adj. Abbr.* **intr., i.** Designating a verb or verb construction that does not require a direct object to complete its meaning. —*n.* An intransitive verb. [Late Latin *intransitīvus* : *in-*, not + *transitīvus*, TRANSITIVE.] —**in·tran′si·tive·ly** *adv.* —**in·tran′si·tive·ness** *n.*

in·tra·nu·cle·ar (ĭn′trə-no͞o′klē-ər, -nyo͞o′klē-ər) *adj.* Within a nucleus.

in·tra·state (ĭn′trə-stāt′) *adj.* Within the boundaries of a state.

in·tra·u·ter·ine (ĭn′trə-yo͞o′tər-ĭn, -tə-rīn′) *adj.* Within the uterus.

intrauterine device. *Abbr* **IUD** A stainless steel or plastic loop, ring, or spiral inserted into the uterus as a contraceptive.

in·tra·va·sa·tion (ĭn-trăv′ə-sā′shən) *n.* The entry of foreign matter into a blood vessel. [INTRA- + VAS + -ATION.]

in·tra·vas·cu·lar (ĭn′trə-văs′kyə-lər) *adj.* Within the blood vessels or lymphatics.

in·tra·ve·na·tion (ĭn′trə-vē-nā′shən) *n.* The entry of foreign matter into a vein.

in·tra·ve·nous (ĭn′trə-vē′nəs) *adj. Abbr.* **IV** Within a vein or veins. —**in′tra·ve′nous·ly** *adv.*

in·treat. Variant of **entreat.**

in·trench. Variant of **entrench.**

in·trench·ment. Variant of **entrenchment.**

in·trep·id (ĭn-trĕp′ĭd) *adj.* Resolutely courageous; fearless; bold: *"thinking is but the intrepid effort of the soul to keep the open independence of her sea"* (Melville). See Synonyms at **brave.** [French, *intrépide*, from Latin *intrepidus* : *in-*, not + *trepidus*, agitated, alarmed (see **trep-**[1] in Appendix*).] —**in′tre·pid′i·ty** (-trə-pĭd′ə-tē), **in·trep′id·ness** *n.* —**in·trep′id·ly** *adv.*

in·tri·ca·cy (ĭn′trĭ-kə-sē) *n., pl.* **-cies. 1.** The condition or quality of being intricate. **2.** Something intricate.

in·tri·cate (ĭn′trĭ-kĭt) *adj.* **1.** Having many complexly arranged elements. **2.** Soluble or comprehensible only with painstaking effort. —See Synonyms at **complex, hard.** [Middle English *interkat*, from Latin *intricātus*, past participle of *intricāre*, to entangle : *in-*, in + *tricae*, trifles, troubles, perplexities (see **extricate**).] —**in′tri·cate·ly** *adv.* —**in′tri·cate·ness** *n.*

in·tri·gant (ĭn′trə-gənt) *n.* Also **in·tri·guant.** *Feminine* **in·tri·gante** (ĭn′trə-gănt′, -gänt′). An intriguer. [French, "intriguing," from Italian *intrigante*, present participle of *intrigare*, to INTRIGUE.]

in·trigue (ĭn′trēg′, ĭn-trēg′) *n.* **1.** A covert maneuver to achieve an unavowed purpose; a secret or underhand scheme. **2.** The use of or involvement in such schemes. **3.** A clandestine love affair. **4.** Mystery; suspense. —See Synonyms at **conspiracy.** —*v.* (ĭn-trēg′) **intrigued, -triguing, -trigues.** —*intr.* To engage in covert schemes; to plot. —*tr.* **1.** To insinuate (one's way, for example) by scheming. **2.** To arouse the interest or curiosity of. See Usage note. [French, from Italian *intrigo*, from *intrigare*, to perplex, from Latin *intricāre*, to entangle. See **intricate.**] —**in·tri′guer** *n.*

Usage: *Intrigue*, as a transitive verb in the sense of arousing interest or curiosity, has been established on a popular level since the 1920's. It has been resisted by writers on usage, however, usually on the ground that it tends to displace words that would convey the desired sense more sharply. The following example is acceptable to 52 per cent of the Usage Panel: *The announcement of a special press conference intrigued the correspondents in the manner of a good suspense novel.*

in·trin·sic (ĭn-trĭn′sĭk) *adj.* Also *archaic* **in·trin·si·cal** (-sĭ-kəl). **1.** Pertaining to the essential nature of a thing; inherent: *"the exploitive and oppressive relationships intrinsic to capitalism."* (E.P. Thompson). **2.** *Anatomy.* Situated within or belonging solely to a body part, as certain nerves and muscles. [Old French *intrinseque*, inner, from Late Latin *intrinsecus*, inward, from Latin, inwardly, on the inside : *intrim* (unattested), inward, from *intrā*, within (see **en** in Appendix*) + *secus*, alongside (see **sekw-**[1] in Appendix*).] —**in·trin′si·cal·ly** *adv.*

intro–. Indicates: **1.** In or into; for example, **introjection. 2.** Inward; for example, **introvert.** [Latin, from *intrō*, to the inside, inwardly. See **en** in Appendix.*]

intro. introduction; introductory.

in·tro·duce (ĭn′trə-do͞os′, -dyo͞os′) *tr.v.* **-duced, -ducing, -duces. 1.** To identify and present; especially, to make (a stranger or strangers) acquainted. **2.** To present and recommend (a plan, for example) for consideration. **3.** To bring into currency, use, or practice; originate. **4.** To bring in and establish: *introduce exotic birds.* **5.** To insert or inject. **6.** To inform of something for the first time. **7.** To preface; to open. [Latin *intrōdūcere*, to lead in : *intrō-*, in + *dūcere*, to lead (see **deuk-** in Appendix*).] —**in′tro·duc′er** *n.* —**in′tro·duc′i·ble** *adj.*

in·tro·duc·tion (ĭn′trə-dŭk′shən) *n. Abbr.* **intro. 1.** The act of introducing. **2.** The fact of being introduced. **3.** A means of presenting one person to another, as a personal presentation or formal letter. **4.** Something recently introduced: *"He loathed a fork; it is a modern introduction which has still scarcely reached common people."* (D.H. Lawrence). **5.** Anything spoken, written, or otherwise presented in introducing, especially: **a.** A preface, as in a book. **b.** A short preliminary movement in a musical work. **6.** A basic instructive text or course of study. [Middle English *introduccion*, from Old French *introduction*, from Latin *intrōductiō*, from *intrōdūcere*, INTRODUCE.]

in·tro·duc·to·ry (ĭn′trə-dŭk′tə-rē) *adj.* Also **in·tro·duc·tive** (-tĭv). *Abbr.* **intro** Serving to introduce. —**in′tro·duc′to·ri·ly** *adv.*

in·tro·it (ĭn-trō′ĭt) *n.* Also **Introit.** *Ecclesiastical.* **1.** A hymn or psalm sung at the opening of a service, especially in the Anglican Church. **2.** The beginning of the proper of the Mass in the Roman Catholic Church, usually consisting of a psalm verse, antiphon, and the Gloria Patri. [Middle English, "entrance," beginning, from Old French *introït*, from Latin *introitus*, from the past participle of *introīre*, to go in, enter : *intrō-*, into + *īre*, to go (see **ei-**[1] in Appendix*).]

in·tro·jec·tion (ĭn′trə-jĕk′shən) *n.* **1.** The ascribing of living characteristics to inanimate objects. **2.** The unconscious incorporation into one's personality of the characteristics of another person or of an inanimate object. [INTRO- + (PRO)JECTION.]

in·tro·mis·sion (ĭn′trə-mĭsh′ən) *n.* Introduction; admission. [Medieval Latin *intrōmissiō*, from Latin *intrōmittere*, INTROMIT.] —**in·tro·mis′sive** *adj.*

in·tro·mit (ĭn′trə-mĭt′) *tr.v.* **-mitted, -mitting, -mits.** To cause or permit to enter; introduce or admit. [Middle English *intromitten*, from Latin *intrōmittere*, to send or put in, introduce : *intrō-*, in + *mittere*, to send (see **smeit-** in Appendix*).] —**in′tro·mit′tent** *adj.* —**in′tro·mit′ter** *n.*

in·trorse (ĭn-trôrs′) *adj. Botany.* Facing inward; turned toward the axis. Said especially of anthers. [Latin *introrsus*, contracted from *intrōversus*, turned inward : *intrō-*, inward + *versus*, past participle of *vertere*, to turn (see **wer-**[3] in Appendix*).]

in·tro·spect (ĭn′trə-spĕkt′) *intr.v.* **-spected, -specting, -spects.** To turn one's thoughts inward; examine one's own feelings. [Latin *intrōspicere* (past participle *intrōspectus*), to look into : *intrō-*, into + *specere*, to look (see **spek-** in Appendix*).]

in·tro·spec·tion (ĭn′trə-spĕk′shən) *n.* Contemplation of one's own thoughts and sensations; self-examination.

in·tro·spec·tive (ĭn′trə-spĕk′tĭv) *adj.* **1.** Of or pertaining to introspection. **2.** Given to private thought; contemplative. —**in′tro·spec′tive·ly** *adv.* —**in′tro·spec′tive·ness** *n.*

in·tro·ver·sion (ĭn′trə-vûr′zhən, -shən) *n.* **1.** The act of introverting or the condition of being introverted. **2.** The directing of one's thoughts and interests inward. Compare **extroversion. 3.** *Medicine.* The turning of one part within another. —**in′tro·ver′sive** *adj.*

in·tro·vert (ĭn′trə-vûrt′) *v.* **-verted, -verting, -verts.** —*tr.* **1.** To turn or direct inward. **2.** To concentrate (one's interests) upon oneself. **3.** To turn (a tubular organ or part) inward upon itself. —*intr.* To exhibit introversion. —*n.* (ĭn′trə-vûrt′). **1.** A person whose thoughts and interests are directed inward. Compare **extrovert. 2.** An anatomic structure, such as the intestine, that is turned inward upon itself. [New Latin *introvertere* : INTRO- + Latin *vertere*, to turn (see **wer-**[3] in Appendix*).]

in·trude (ĭn-tro͞od′) *v.* **-truded, -truding, -trudes.** —*tr.* **1.** To interpose (oneself or something) without invitation, fitness, or leave. **2.** *Geology.* To thrust (molten rock) into a stratum. —*intr.* To come in rudely or inappropriately; enter as an improper or unwanted element: *"The flute would be intruding here like a delicate lady at a club smoker."* (Leonard Bernstein). [Latin *intrūdere*, to thrust in : *in-*, in + *trūdere*, to thrust (see **treud-** in Appendix*).] —**in·trud′er** *n.*

Synonyms: *intrude, obtrude, interlope.* These verbs mean to force oneself or something upon other persons without their consent or approval. *Intrude* is more often found in the sense of violating another's privacy, and *obtrude* in the transitive sense of forcing opinions, ideas, or the like on another's attention. *Interlope* implies intermeddling in another's affairs; sometimes it also implies depriving another of what is his by right.

in·tru·sion (ĭn-tro͞o′zhən) *n.* **1.** The act of intruding, or the fact of being intruded upon; imposition. **2.** An inappropriate or unwelcome addition: *"The fields were a timid intrusion on a landscape hardly marked by man"* (Doris Lessing). **3.** *Law.* Illegal entry upon or appropriation of the property of another. **4.** *Geology.* **a.** The forcing of molten rock into an earlier formation. **b.** The intrusive mass so produced.

in·tru·sive (ĭn-tro͞o′sĭv) *adj.* **1.** Intruding or tending to intrude. **2.** *Geology.* Designating igneous rock forced into another stratum while in molten state; irruptive. **3.** *Linguistics.* Constituting an **epenthesis** *(see).* —See Synonyms at **curious.** —**in·tru′sive·ly** *adv.* —**in·tru′sive·ness** *n.*

in·trust. Variant of **entrust.**

in·tu·bate (ĭn′to͞o-bāt′, -tyo͞o-bāt′) *tr.v.* **-bated, -bating, -bates** To insert a tube into (an organ or passage). —**in′tu·ba′tion** *n*

in·tu·it (ĭn-to͞o′ĭt, -tyo͞o′ĭt) *v.* **-ited, -iting, -its.** —*tr.* To know or sense by intuition. —*intr.* To acquire knowledge by intuition. [Back-formation from INTUITION.]

in·tu·i·tion (ĭn′to͞o-ĭsh′ən, ĭn′tyo͞o-) *n.* **1. a.** The act or faculty of knowing without the use of rational processes; immediate cognition. **b.** Knowledge so gained; a sense of something not evident or deducible. **2.** A capacity for guessing accurately; sharp insight. —See Synonyms at **reason.** [Middle English *intuycion,* contemplation, from Old French *intuition,* from Late Latin, view, contemplation, from Latin *intuērī,* to look at or toward, contemplate : *in-,* on, toward + *tuērī,* to look at, watch (see **teu-** in Appendix*).]

in·tu·i·tion·al (ĭn′to͞o-ĭsh′ən-əl, ĭn′tyo͞o-) *adj.* Of, pertaining to, or based on intuition. —**in′tu·i′tion·al·ly** *adv.*

in·tu·i·tion·al·ism (ĭn′to͞o-ĭsh′ən-ə-lĭz′əm, ĭn′tyo͞o-) *n.* Intuitionism. —**in′tu·i′tion·al·ist** *n.*

in·tu·i·tion·ism (ĭn′to͞o-ĭsh′ən-ĭz′əm, ĭn′tyo͞o-) *n.* **1.** The theory that basic truths are known by intuition rather than reason. **2.** The theory that objects of perception are known to be real by intuition. **3.** The theory that ethical principles are known to be valid and universal through intuition. —**in′tu·i′tion·ist** *n.*

in·tu·i·tive (ĭn-to͞o′ə-tĭv, ĭn-tyo͞o′-) *adj.* **1.** Of or pertaining to intuition; intuitional. **2.** Known or arising from intuition. **3.** Possessing or demonstrating intuition. —**in·tu′i·tive·ly** *adv.* —**in·tu′i·tive·ness** *n.*

in·tu·i·tiv·ism (ĭn-to͞o′ə-tĭ-vĭz′əm, ĭn-tyo͞o′-) *n.* The theory of intuitionism in ethics. —**in·tu′i·tiv·ist** *n.*

in·tu·mesce (ĭn′to͞o-mĕs′, ĭn′tyo͞o-) *intr.v.* **-mesced, -mescing, -mesces.** To swell or expand; enlarge. [Latin *intumēscere,* to swell up : *in-* (intensive) + *tumēscere,* to begin to swell, from *tumēre,* to swell (see **teue-** in Appendix*).]

in·tu·mes·cence (ĭn′to͞o-mĕs′əns, ĭn′tyo͞o-) *n.* Also **in·tu·mes·cen·cy** (-ən-sē) *pl.* **-cies. 1.** The process or condition of swelling. **2.** A swollen organ or part. —**in′tu·mes′cent** *adj.*

in·turn (ĭn′tûrn′) *n.* A curving inward. —**in′turned′** *adj.*

in·tus·sus·cept (ĭn′təs-sə-sĕpt′) *tr.v.* **-cepted, -cepting, -cepts.** To fold or turn inward; invaginate. [Probably back-formation from INTUSSUSCEPTION.] —**in′tus·sus·cep′tive** *adj.*

in·tus·sus·cep·tion (ĭn′təs-sə-sĕp′shən) *n.* Invagination; especially, an infolding of one part of the intestine into another. [New Latin *intussusceptio* : Latin *intus,* within (see **en** in Appendix*) + *susceptiō,* taking up, from *suscipere,* to take up : *sub-,* up from under + *capere,* to take, seize (see **kap-** in Appendix*).]

in·twine. Variant of **entwine.**

in·twist. Variant of **entwist.**

in·u·lin (ĭn′yə-lĭn) *n.* A carbohydrate, $(C_6H_{10}O_5)_3$ or $(C_6H_{10}O_5)_4$, found in the roots of many plants and used to manufacture fructose. [Probably from German *Inulin,* from New Latin *Inula,* genus of plants from which it is derived, from Latin *inula,* elecampane, from Greek *helenion,* perhaps from *helenē,* wicker basket. See **wel-³** in Appendix.*]

in·unc·tion (ĭn-ŭngk′shən) *n.* **1.** *Medicine.* The process of applying and rubbing in an ointment. **2.** A liniment, lubricant, ointment, or the like. **3.** The act of anointing, as in religious ceremony. [Middle English, from Latin *inunctiō,* from *inunguere,* to smear oil on, anoint : *in-,* on + *unguere,* to smear, anoint (see **ongw-** in Appendix*).]

in·un·date (ĭn′ŭn-dāt′) *tr.v.* **-dated, -dating, -dates. 1.** To cover with water, especially flood water; overflow. **2.** To overwhelm as if with a flood; to swamp: *inundated with requests.* [Latin *inundāre,* "to flow in" : *in-,* in + *undāre,* to flow, from *unda,* wave (see **wed-¹** in Appendix*).] —**in′un·da′tor** (-dā′tər) *n.* —**in·un′da·to′ry** (-də-tôr′ē, -tōr′ē) *adj.*

in·un·da·tion (ĭn′ŭn-dā′shən) *n.* The act of inundating or the condition of being inundated; a flooding.

in·ur·bane (ĭn′ûr-bān′) *adj.* Uncouth; rude. [Latin *inurbānus* : *in-,* not + *urbānus,* URBANE.] —**in′ur·ban′i·ty** (-băn′ə-tē) *n.*

in·ure (ĭn-yo͝or′) *tr.v.* **-ured, -uring, -ures.** Also **en·ure.** To make used to something undesirable by prolonged subjection: *"though the food became no more palatable, he soon became sufficiently inured to it"* (John Barth). [Middle English *enewren* : *en-* (causative) + *ure,* use, custom, from Old French *uevre, euvre,* custom, work, from Latin *opera,* work (see **op-¹** in Appendix*).] —**in·ure′ment** *n.*

in·urn (ĭn-ûrn′) *tr.v.* **-urned, -urning, -urns. 1.** To put or seal in an urn, as the ashes of the dead. **2.** To bury or entomb; inter.

in·u·tile (ĭn-yo͞ot′l, -tīl) *adj.* Useless. [Middle English, from Old French, from Latin *inūtilis* : *in-,* not + *ūtilis,* useful, from *ūtī,* use (see **use**).] —**in·u′tile·ly** *adv.* —**in′u·til′i·ty** (-tĭl′ə-tē) *n.*

inv. 1. invented; invention; inventor. **2.** invoice.

in·vade (ĭn-vād′) *v.* **-vaded, -vading, -vades.** —*tr.* **1.** To enter by force in order to conquer or overrun. **2.** To encroach or intrude upon; violate: *"a security . . . nothing but the beasts of the forest could invade"* (James Fenimore Cooper). **3.** To overrun or infest: *"About 1917 the shipworm invaded the harbor of San Francisco"* (Rachel Carson). **4.** To enter and spread harm through. —*intr.* To make an invasion. [Middle English *invaden,* from Latin *invādere,* "to go in" : *in-,* in + *vādere,* to go (see **wādh-** in Appendix*).] —**in·vad′er** *n.*

in·vag·i·nate (ĭn-văj′ə-nāt′) *v.* **-nated, -nating, -nates.** —*tr.* **1.** To enclose in or as in a sheath. **2.** To turn within; introvert. —*intr.* To become enclosed or turned within. [Medieval Latin *invāgināre* : Latin *in-,* in + *vāgina,* sheath (see **wag-** in Appendix*).] —**in·vag′i·na·ble** (-nə-bəl) *adj.*

in·vag·i·na·tion (ĭn-văj′ə-nā′shən) *n.* **1.** The act or process of invaginating or the condition of being invaginated. **2.** Something invaginated, as an organ or part. **3.** *Embryology.* The infolding of the blastula to form the gastrula.

in·va·lid¹ (ĭn′və-lĭd) *n.* A chronically ill or disabled person. —*adj.* **1.** Disabled by illness or injury; sickly or infirm. **2.** Of, pertaining to, or for invalids. —*v.* **invalided, -liding, -lids.** —*tr.* **1.** To make an invalid of; disable physically. **2.** *Chiefly British.* To release or exempt from duty because of ill health. —*intr.* *Rare.* To become invalided. [Latin *invalidus,* not strong, ineffective : *in-,* not + *validus,* strong, VALID.]

in·val·id² (ĭn-văl′ĭd) *adj.* **1.** Null; legally ineffective. **2.** Falsely based or reasoned; unjustified: *an invalid conclusion.* [Latin *invalidus,* ineffective, INVALID (infirm).] —**in·val′id·ly** *adv.*

in·val·i·date (ĭn-văl′ə-dāt′) *tr.v.* **-dated, -dating, -dates.** To make void; render invalid. See Synonyms at **nullify.** —**in·val′i·da′tion** *n.* —**in·val′i·da′tor** (-dā′tər) *n.*

in·va·lid·ism (ĭn′və-lĭd-ĭz′əm) *n.* The condition of being chronically ill or disabled.

in·va·li·di·ty (ĭn′və-lĭd′ə-tē) *n.* The condition or quality of being void or unjustifiable; lack of validity.

in·val·u·a·ble (ĭn-văl′yo͞o-ə-bəl) *adj.* **1.** Having great value; priceless: *invaluable paintings.* **2.** Of inestimable use or help; indispensable; much appreciated: *an invaluable service.* —See Synonyms at **costly.** —**in·val′u·a·bly** *adv.*

In·var (ĭn-vär′) *n.* A trademark for an iron alloy containing 36 per cent nickel with an extremely low coefficient of expansion, and used chiefly in measuring rods and tapes, pendulums, balance wheels, tuning forks, and in temperature-regulating devices. [From INVARIABLE.]

in·var·i·a·ble (ĭn-vâr′ē-ə-bəl) *adj.* Not changing or subject to change; constant. —**in·var′i·a·bil′i·ty, in·var′i·a·ble·ness** *n.* —**in·var′i·a·bly** *adv.*

in·var·i·ant (ĭn-vâr′ē-ənt) *adj.* **1.** Not varying; constant. **2.** Unaffected by a designated mathematical operation, such as a transformation of coordinates. —*n.* An invariant quantity, function, configuration, or system. —**in·var′i·ance** *n.*

in·va·sion (ĭn-vā′zhən) *n.* **1.** The act of invading; especially, entrance by force. **2.** The onset of something injurious or harmful, as of a disease. **3.** Any intrusion or encroachment; infringement. [Middle English *invasioune,* from Old French *invasion,* from Late Latin *invāsiō,* from Latin *invādere,* INVADE.]

in·va·sive (ĭn-vā′sĭv) *adj.* **1.** Tending to spread; especially, tending to invade healthy tissue. **2.** *Archaic.* Of, relating to, or given to armed aggression.

in·vec·tive (ĭn-vĕk′tĭv) *n.* **1.** A denunciatory or abusive expression. **2.** Vehement denunciation; vituperation. —*adj.* Characterized by abuse and insult. [Middle English *invectiff,* abusive, vituperative, from Old French *invectif,* from Late Latin *invectīvus (ōrātiō),* "abusive (speech)," from Latin *invehere,* to attack, INVEIGH.] —**in·vec′tive·ly** *adv.* —**in·vec′tive·ness** *n.*

in·veigh (ĭn-vā′) *intr.v.* **-veighed, -veighing, -veighs.** To give vent to angry censure; protest vehemently; to rail: *"It is a layman's guide to health, and was inveighed against by doctors"* (Tucker Brooke). [Latin *invehī,* passive infinitive of *invehere,* to carry in, sail into, assail, attack : *in-,* in + *vehere,* to carry (see **wegh-** in Appendix*).] —**in·veigh′er** *n.*

in·vei·gle (ĭn-vē′gəl, ĭn-vā′-) *tr.v.* **-gled, -gling, -gles. 1.** To lead astray or win over by deceitful flattery or persuasion. **2.** To obtain by cajolery. —See Synonyms at **lure.** [Earlier *invegle,* from Norman French *envegler,* alteration of Old French *aveugler,* to blind, from *aveugle,* blind, from Medieval Latin *ab oculis,* without eyes : Latin *ab,* out of + *oculus,* eye (see **okw-** in Appendix*).] —**in·vei′gle·ment** *n.* —**in·vei′gler** *n.*

in·vent (ĭn-vĕnt′) *tr.v.* **-vented, -venting, -vents. 1.** To conceive of or devise first; originate. **2.** To fabricate; to make up. [Middle English *inventen,* to come upon, find, from Latin *invenīre* (past participle *inventus*) : *in-,* on + *venīre,* to come (see **gwā-** in Appendix*).] —**in·vent′i·ble** *adj.*

in·ven·tion (ĭn-vĕn′shən) *n. Abbr.* **inv. 1.** The act or process of inventing. **2.** A new device or process developed from study and experimentation. **3.** A mental fabrication; falsehood. **4.** Skill in inventing; inventiveness: *"very unlearned, neither savouring of poetry, wit, nor invention"* (Shakespeare). **5.** A short musical piece developing a single theme contrapuntally. **6.** *Archaic.* A discovery; a finding. —**in·ven′tion·al** *adj.*

in·ven·tive (ĭn-vĕn′tĭv) *adj.* **1.** Of or characterized by invention. **2.** Adept or skillful at inventing; creative; ingenious. **3.** Of an invention: *the basic inventive concept.* —**in·ven′tive·ly** *adv.* —**in·ven′tive·ness** *n.*

in·ven·tor (ĭn-vĕn′tər) *n.* Also **in·ven·ter.** *Abbr.* **inv.** One who contrives a previously unknown device, method, or process.

in·ven·to·ry (ĭn′vən-tôr′ē, -tōr′ē) *n., pl.* **-ries. 1.** A detailed list of things in one's view or possession; especially, a periodic survey of all goods and materials in stock. **2.** The process of making such a survey. **3.** The items so listed. **4.** The quantity of goods and materials so determined. **5.** Broadly, an evaluation or survey. —*tr.v.* **inventoried, -rying, -ries. 1.** To make an inventory of. **2.** To include in an inventory. [Medieval Latin *inventōrium,* list, altered from Late Latin *inventārium,* "a finding out," "enumeration," from Latin *invenīre,* to come upon, find, INVENT.] —**in'ven·to'ri·al** *adj.* —**in'ven·to'ri·al·ly** *adv.*

in·ve·rac·i·ty (ĭn'və-răs'ə-tē) *n., pl.* **-ties. 1.** Lack of veracity; untruthfulness. **2.** An untruth; falsehood.

In·ver·car·gill (ĭn'vər-kär'gĭl). A city and port of extreme southern South Island, New Zealand. Population, 44,000.

in·ver·ness (ĭn'vər-nĕs') *n.* Also **In·ver·ness. 1.** A loose overcoat with a detachable cape. **2.** The cape of such a coat. Also called "Inverness cape." [First popularized in INVERNESS.]

In·ver·ness (ĭn'vər-nĕs'). **1.** Also **In·ver·ness·shire** (-shĭr, -shər). The largest county of Scotland, 4,211 square miles in area, located in the northwest. Population, 81,000. **2.** The county seat of this county, a port in the north on the Caledonian Canal. Population, 30,000. [Scottish Gaelic *Ionarnis, Inbhirnis,* "mouth of the river Ness" : *inbhir,* mouth of a river, from Old Irish *in(d)ber,* "a carrying in," estuary (see **bher-¹** in Appendix*) + *Nis,* the river Ness.]

in·verse (ĭn-vûrs', ĭn'vûrs') *adj.* **1.** Reversed in order, nature, or effect. **2.** Turned upside down; inverted. —*n.* **1.** That which is opposite, as in sequence or character; the reverse. **2.** *Mathematics.* An element x^* in a set S related to a designated element x in S such that $x^* \cdot x = x \cdot x^* = I$, where $\cdot$ is a binary operation defined in S and I is the identity element; especially: **a.** The reciprocal of a designated quantity. Also called "multiplicative inverse." **b.** The negative of a designated quantity. Also called "additive inverse." [Latin *inversus,* past participle of *invertere,* INVERT.] —**in·verse'ly** *adv.*

in·ver·sion (ĭn-vûr'zhən, -shən) *n.* **1.** The act of inverting or the state of being inverted. **2.** An interchange of position, especially of adjacent objects in a sequence. **3.** A change in normal word order, as the placing of a verb before its subject. **4.** *Music.* **a.** A rearrangement of tones in which upper and lower voices are transposed, as in counterpoint, or in which each interval in a single melody is applied in the opposite direction. **b.** An interval, chord, or melody resulting from such rearrangement. **5.** Homosexuality. **6.** *Chemistry.* Conversion from the dextrorotatory to the levorotatory or from the levorotatory to the dextrorotatory form. **7.** *Meteorology.* A state in which the air temperature increases with increasing altitude, holding surface air down along with its pollutants. [Latin *inversiō,* from *invertere,* INVERT.]

in·vert (ĭn-vûrt') *v.* **-verted, -verting, -verts.** —*tr.* **1.** To turn inside out or upside down. **2.** To reverse the position, order, or condition of. **3.** To subject to or produce inversion. —*intr.* To be subjected to inversion. —See Synonyms at **reverse.** —*n.* (ĭn'vûrt'). **1.** Something inverted. **2.** A homosexual. [Latin *invertere,* to turn inside out or upside down : *in-,* in, inward + *vertere,* to turn (see **wer-³** in Appendix*).] —**in·vert'i·ble** *adj.*

in·ver·tase (ĭn-vûr'tās') *n.* A plant and animal enzyme that catalyzes the conversion of sucrose to glucose and fructose. Also called "sucrase," "saccharase." [INVERT + -ASE.]

in·ver·te·brate (ĭn-vûr'tə-brĭt, -brāt') *adj.* Having no backbone or spinal column; not vertebrate. —*n.* An invertebrate animal. [New Latin *Invertebrata,* neuter plural of *invertebratus,* having no backbone : IN- (no) + VERTEBRATE.]

inverted commas. *Chiefly British.* Quotation marks.

inverted mordent. *Music.* A **pralltriller** (*see*).

in·vert·er (ĭn-vûr'tər) *n.* **1.** One that inverts. **2.** A device used to convert direct current into alternating current.

invert sugar. A hygroscopic mixture of equal parts of glucose and fructose resulting from the hydrolysis of sucrose and used chiefly in brewing and in medicine. [Commercially produced by inversion of sucrose.]

in·vest (ĭn-vĕst') *v.* **-vested, -vesting, -vests.** —*tr.* **1.** To commit (money or capital) in order to gain profit or interest, as by purchasing property, securities, or bonds. **2.** To spend or utilize (time, money, or effort) for future advantage or benefit. Often used with *in.* **3.** To endow with rank, authority, or power. **4.** To inaugurate with ceremony; install in office. **5.** To provide with some enveloping or pervasive quality: *"A charm invests a face/Imperfectly beheld"* (Emily Dickinson). **6.** *Rare.* To clothe; adorn. **7.** To cover completely; envelop; shroud. **8.** *Military.* To surround with hostile troops or ships; besiege. —*intr.* To invest money; make an investment. [Old French *investir,* from Medieval Latin *investīre,* from Latin, to clothe in, surround : *in-,* in + *vestīre,* to clothe, from *vestis,* clothes (see **wes-⁴** in Appendix*).] —**in·ves'tor** (-vĕs'tər) *n.*

in·ves·ti·gate (ĭn-vĕs'tĭ-gāt') *v.* **-gated, -gating, -gates.** —*tr.* To observe or inquire into in detail; examine systematically. —*intr.* To make an investigation. [Latin *investigāre,* to trace out, search into : *in-,* in + *vestigāre,* to trace, track, from *vestīgium,* trace, footprint, VESTIGE.] —**in·ves'ti·ga·ble** (-gə-bəl), **in·ves'ti·ga'tive, in·ves'ti·ga·to'ry** (-gə-tôr'ē, -tōr'ē) *adj.*

in·ves·ti·ga·tion (ĭn-vĕs'tĭ-gā'shən) *n.* The act, process or an instance of investigating; inquiry.

in·ves·ti·ga·tor (ĭn-vĕs'tĭ-gā'tər) *n.* **1.** One who investigates. **2.** A detective. —**in·ves'ti·ga·to'ri·al** (-tôr'ē-əl, -tōr'ē-əl) *adj.*

in·ves·ti·tive (ĭn-vĕs'tə-tĭv) *adj.* Of or pertaining to investiture.

in·ves·ti·ture (ĭn-vĕs'tə-cho͝or') *n.* **1.** The act or formal ceremony of conferring upon one the authority and symbols of a high office. **2.** A thing that covers or adorns, as a garment. [Middle English, from Medieval Latin *investītūra,* from *investīre,* INVEST.]

in·vest·ment (ĭn-vĕst'mənt) *n.* **1.** The act of investing or the state of being invested. **2.** An amount invested. **3.** Property or another possession acquired for future income or benefit. **4.** Investiture. **5.** *Archaic.* A garment; vestment. **6.** An outer covering or layer. **7.** *Military.* A siege.

in·vet·er·ate (ĭn-vĕt'ər-ĭt) *adj.* **1.** Firmly established by long standing; deep-rooted. **2.** Persisting in an ingrained habit; habitual: *an inveterate liar.* [Latin *inveterātus,* past participle of *inveterāre,* to render old : *in-* (causative) + *vetus* (stem *veter-*), old (see **wet-** in Appendix*).] —**in·vet'er·a·cy** (-ər-ə-sē), **in·vet'er·ate·ness** *n.* —**in·vet'er·ate·ly** *adv.*

in·vid·i·ous (ĭn-vĭd'ē-əs) *adj.* **1.** Tending to rouse ill will or animosity; offensive. **2.** Containing or implying a slight; discriminatory: *"he had the privilege of going to see them . . . through some invidious distinction, which was denied to us"* (Lamb). **3.** *Obsolete.* Envious. [Latin *invidiōsus,* envious, hostile, from *invidia,* ENVY.] —**in·vid'i·ous·ly** *adv.* —**in·vid'i·ous·ness** *n.*

in·vig·or·ate (ĭn-vĭg'ə-rāt') *tr.v.* **-ated, -ating, -ates.** To impart vigor, strength, or vitality to: *"A few whiffs of the raw, strong scent of phlox invigorated her."* (D.H. Lawrence). [IN- (causative) + VIGOR + -ATE.] —**in·vig'or·at'ing·ly, in·vig'or·a'tive·ly** *adv.* —**in·vig'or·a'tion** *n.* —**in·vig'or·a'tive** *adj.* —**in·vig'or·a'tor** (-ə-rā'tər) *n.*

in·vin·ci·ble (ĭn-vĭn'sə-bəl) *adj.* Unconquerable. [Middle English, from Latin *invincibilis* : *in-,* not + *vincibilis,* VINCIBLE.] —**in·vin'ci·bil'i·ty, in·vin'ci·ble·ness** *n.* —**in·vin'ci·bly** *adv.*

in·vi·o·la·ble (ĭn-vī'ə-lə-bəl) *adj.* **1.** Safe from or secured against violation or profanation; kept sacred. **2.** Impregnable to assault or trespass. —**in·vi'o·la·bil'i·ty, in·vi'o·la·ble·ness** *n.* —**in·vi'o·la·bly** *adv.*

in·vi·o·late (ĭn-vī'ə-lĭt) *adj.* Not violated; intact: *"The great inviolate place had an ancient permanence which the sea cannot claim."* (Hardy). [Middle English *invyolat,* from Latin *inviolātus* : *in-,* not + *violātus,* past participle of *violāre,* VIOLATE.] —**in·vi'o·la·cy** (-lə-sē), **in·vi'o·late·ness** *n.* —**in·vi'o·late·ly** *adv.*

in·vis·i·ble (ĭn-vĭz'ə-bəl) *adj.* **1.** Incapable of being seen; not visible. **2.** Not accessible to view; hidden. **3.** Not easily noticed or detected; inconspicuous: *"the poor are politically invisible"* (Michael Harrington). **4.** Not published in financial statements: *an invisible asset.* —*n.* One that is invisible. —**in·vis'i·bil'i·ty, in·vis'i·ble·ness** *n.* —**in·vis'i·bly** *adv.*

invisible ink. Ink that is colorless and invisible until treated by a chemical, heat, or special light. Also called "sympathetic ink."

in·vi·ta·tion (ĭn'və-tā'shən) *n.* **1.** The act of inviting. **2.** A spoken or written request for one's presence or participation. **3.** An allurement, enticement, or attraction.

in·vi·ta·tion·al (ĭn'və-tā'shən-əl) *adj.* Restricted to invited participants: *an invitational golf tournament.*

in·vi·ta·to·ry (ĭn-vī'tə-tôr'ē, -tōr'ē) *n., pl.* **-ries.** A psalm or other piece sung as an invitation to prayer in church services. [Middle English *invytatory,* from Medieval Latin *invītātōrium,* from the neuter of Late Latin *invītātōrius,* inviting, antiphonal, from Latin *invītāre,* INVITE.]

in·vite (ĭn-vīt') *v.* **-vited, -viting, -vites.** —*tr.* **1.** To request the presence or participation of. **2.** To request formally. **3.** To welcome. **4.** To tend to bring on; provoke: *"divisions at home would invite dangers from abroad"* (John Jay). **5.** To lure; entice; tempt. —*intr.* To give an invitation. —*n. Informal.* An invitation. [Old French *inviter,* from Latin *invītāre*†.]

in·vit·ing (ĭn-vī'tĭng) *adj.* Attractive; tempting: *an inviting dessert.* —**in·vit'ing·ly** *adv.* —**in·vit'ing·ness** *n.*

in vi·tro (ĭn vē'trō). In an artificial environment outside the living organism. [New Latin, "in glass."]

in vi·vo (ĭn vē'vō). Within the living organism. [New Latin, "in a living body."]

in·vo·cate (ĭn'və-kāt') *tr.v.* **-cated, -cating, -cates.** *Archaic.* To invoke. [Latin *invocāre,* INVOKE.] —**in·voc'a·tive** (ĭn-vŏk'ə-tĭv) *adj.* —**in'vo·ca'tor** (-kā'tər) *n.*

in·vo·ca·tion (ĭn'və-kā'shən) *n.* **1.** The act of invoking; especially, an appeal to a higher power for assistance. **2.** A prayer or other formula used in invoking, as at the opening of a religious service. **3. a.** A conjuring or calling up of a spirit by incantation. **b.** The incantation used in conjuring. [Middle English, from Old French, from Latin *invocātiō,* from *invocāre,* INVOKE.]

in·voc·a·to·ry (ĭn-vŏk'ə-tôr'ē, -tōr'ē) *adj.* Of, pertaining to, or having the nature of an invocation.

in·voice (ĭn'vois') *n. Abbr.* **inv. 1.** A detailed list of goods shipped or services rendered, with an account of all costs; a bill. **2.** The goods or services so itemized. —*tr.v.* **invoiced, -voicing, -voices.** To make an invoice of; to bill. [Originally *invoyes,* plural of *invoy,* invoice, from Old French *envoy,* a sending, shipment of goods. See **envoi.**]

in·voke (ĭn-vōk') *tr.v.* **-voked, -voking, -vokes. 1.** To call upon (a higher power) for assistance: *"Stretching out her hands she had the air of a Greek woman who invoked a deity"* (Ford Madox Ford). **2.** To appeal to; to petition. **3.** To call for earnestly; solicit. **4.** To summon with incantations; conjure. **5.** To cite in support or justification of one's cause. [Old French *invoquer,* from Latin *invocāre,* "to call upon" : *in-,* in, on + *vocāre,* to call (see **wekw-** in Appendix*).] —**in·vok'er** *n.*

in·vol·u·cel (ĭn-vŏl'yo͞o-sĕl') *n. Botany.* A secondary involucre, as at the base of an umbellule in a compound umbel. [New Latin *involucellum,* diminutive of *involucrum,* INVOLUCRE.]

in·vo·lu·crate (ĭn'və-lo͞o'krĭt, -krāt') *adj. Botany.* Having an involucre.

in·vo·lu·cre (ĭn'və-lo͞o'kər) *n.* A whorl or series of leaflike scales or bracts beneath or around a flower or flower cluster. [New Latin *involucrum,* from Latin, wrapper, case, envelope, from *involvere,* to enwrap, INVOLVE.] —**in'vo·lu'cral** *adj.*

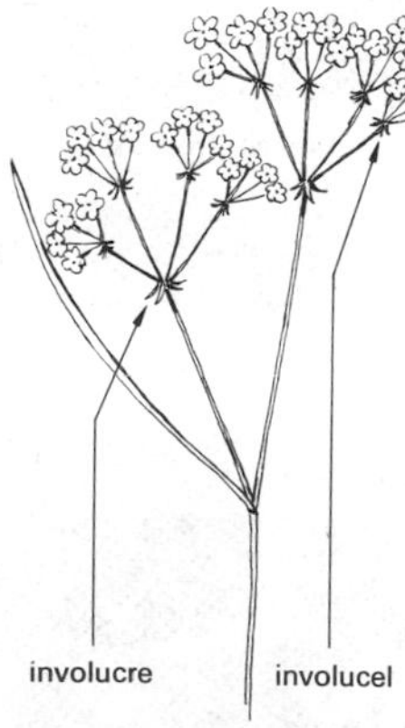

involucel
Compound umbel

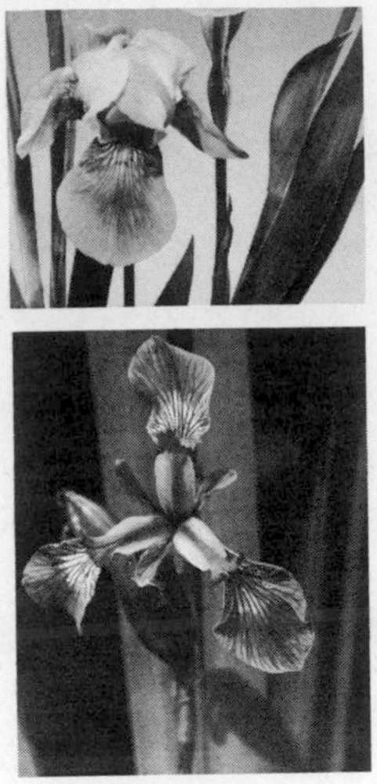

iris
Above: Cultivated bearded iris
Below: Wild iris

in·vo·lu·crum (ĭn′və-lo͞o′krəm) *n., pl.* **-cra** (-krə). An enveloping sheath or envelope. [New Latin, INVOLUCRE.]

in·vol·un·tar·y (ĭn-vŏl′ən-tĕr′ē) *adj.* **1.** Not performed willingly. **2.** Not subject to control. —See Synonyms at **spontaneous.** —**in·vol′un·tar′i·ly** *adv.* —**in·vol′un·tar′i·ness** *n.*

in·vo·lute (ĭn′və-lo͞ot′) *adj.* Also **in·vo·lut·ed** (-lo͞o′tĭd). **1.** Intricate; complex. **2.** *Botany.* Having the margins rolled inward. **3.** Having whorls that obscure the axis or other volutions, as the shell of a cowry. —*n. Mathematics.* **1.** The locus of a fixed point on a taut, inextensible string as it unwinds from a fixed plane curve. **2.** The locus of any point on a tangent line as it rolls but does not slide around a fixed curve. [Latin *involutus*, past participle of *involvere*, to enwrap, INVOLVE.]

in·vo·lu·tion (ĭn′və-lo͞o′shən) *n.* **1.** The act of involving or the state of being involved. **2.** Anything that is internally complex or involved. **3.** A complicated grammatical construction. **4.** *Mathematics.* The multiplying of a quantity by itself a specified number of times; raising to a power. In this sense, compare **evolution.** [Latin *involūtiō*, from *involvere*, INVOLVE.]

in·volve (ĭn-vŏlv′) *tr.v.* **-volved, -volving, -volves. 1.** To contain or include as a part. **2.** To have as a necessary feature or consequence. **3.** To draw in as an associate or participant; embroil. **4.** To occupy or engross completely; absorb. **5.** To make complex or intricate; complicate. **6.** To wrap; envelop: *a castle involved in mist.* **7.** *Archaic.* To wind or coil about. **8.** *Mathematics.* To raise (a number) to a specified degree. —See Synonyms at **include.** [Middle English *involven*, from Latin *involvere*, to enwrap, "roll in" : *in-*, in + *volvere*, to roll, turn (see **wel-**[3] in Appendix*).] —**in·volve′ment** *n.* —**in·volv′er** *n.*

in·volved (ĭn-vŏlvd′) *adj.* **1.** Complicated; intricate. **2.** Involute; twisted. **3.** Confused; tangled. —See Synonyms at **complex.**

in·vul·ner·a·ble (ĭn-vŭl′nər-ə-bəl) *adj.* **1.** Immune to attack; impregnable: *an invulnerable position.* **2.** Incapable of being damaged, injured, or wounded. [Latin *invulnerābilis* : *in-*, not + *vulnerāre*, to wound (see **vulnerable**).] —**in·vul′ner·a·bil′i·ty, in·vul′ner·a·ble·ness** *n.* —**in·vul′ner·a·bly** *adv.*

in·ward (ĭn′wərd) *adj.* **1.** Located inside; inner. **2.** Directed or moving toward the interior. **3.** Existing in thought or mind. **4.** Intimate; familiar. —*adv.* Also **in·wards** (-wərdz). **1.** Toward the inside or center. **2.** Toward the mind or the self: *thoughts turned inward.* —*n.* **1.** An inner or central part. **2.** An inner essence or spirit. **3.** *Plural.* Entrails; innards. [Middle English *inward*, Old English *inweard.* See **wer-**[3] in Appendix.*]

in·ward·ly (ĭn′wərd-lē) *adv.* **1.** On or in the inside; within. **2.** Privately; to oneself: *"kept his lips closed with the expression of a man inwardly laughing"* (T.S. Stribling).

in·ward·ness (ĭn′wərd-nĭs) *n.* **1.** Intimacy; familiarity. **2.** Self-preoccupation; introspection. **3.** Essential or fundamental nature. **4.** Internal quality or essence.

in·weave (ĭn-wēv′) *tr.v.* **-wove** (-wōv′) or **-weaved, -woven** (-wō′vən) or *rare* **-wove, -weaving, -weaves.** To weave into a fabric or design.

in·wind. Variant of **enwind.**

in·wrap. Variant of **enwrap.**

in·wreathe. Variant of **enwreathe.**

in·wrought (ĭn-rôt′) *adj.* **1.** Worked or woven in. **2.** Having a decorative pattern worked or woven in.

I·o (ī′ō). *Greek Mythology.* A maiden who was loved by Zeus and transformed by Hera into a heifer.

i·o·date (ī′ə-dāt′) *tr.v.* **-dated, -dating, -dates.** To iodize. —*n.* A salt of iodic acid. [IOD(O)- + -ATE.]

i·od·ic acid (ī-ŏd′ĭk). A colorless or white crystalline powder, HIO_3, used as an antiseptic and deodorant. [French *iodique*, from *iode*, IODINE.]

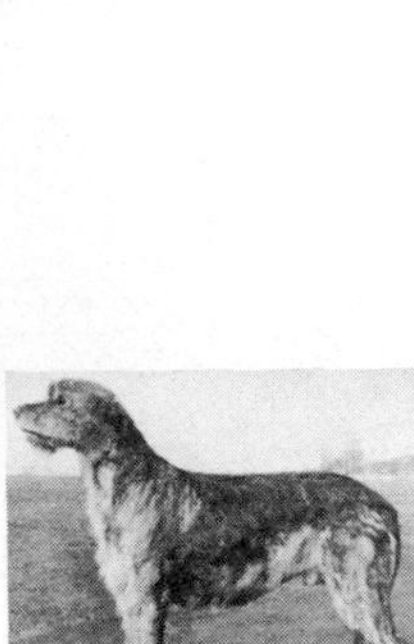

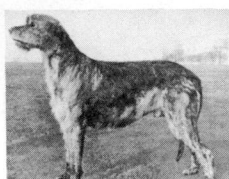

Irish wolfhound

i·o·dide (ī′ə-dīd′) *n.* A binary compound of iodine with a more electropositive atom or group. [IOD(O)- + -IDE.]

i·o·dine (ī′ə-dīn′, -dĭn, -dēn′) *n. Symbol* **I 1.** A lustrous, grayish-black, corrosive, poisonous halogen element having radioactive isotopes, especially I 131, used as tracers and in thyroid disease diagnosis and therapy, and compounds used as germicides, antiseptics, and dyes. Atomic number 53, atomic weight 126.9044, melting point 113.5°C, boiling point 184.35°C, specific gravity (solid, 20°C) 4.93, valences 1, 3, 5, 7. See **element. 2.** A **tincture** *(see)* of iodine and sodium iodide, NaI, or potassium iodide, KI, used as an antiseptic for wounds. [French *iode*, from Greek *iōdēs, ioeidēs*, violet-colored : *ion*, violet, of Mediterranean origin + -OID + -INE.]

i·o·dism (ī′ə-dĭz′əm) *n.* Poisoning by iodine or iodine compounds. [IOD(O)- + -ISM.]

i·o·dize (ī′ə-dīz′) *tr.v.* **-dized, -dizing, -dizes.** To treat or combine with iodine or an iodide. [IOD(O)- + -IZE.]

iodo–, iod–. Indicates iodine; for example, **iodoform, iodide.** [From French *iode*, IODINE.]

i·o·do·form (ī-ō′də-fôrm′, ī-ŏd′ə-) *n.* A yellowish iodine compound, CHI_3, used as an antiseptic. [IODO- + FORM(YL).]

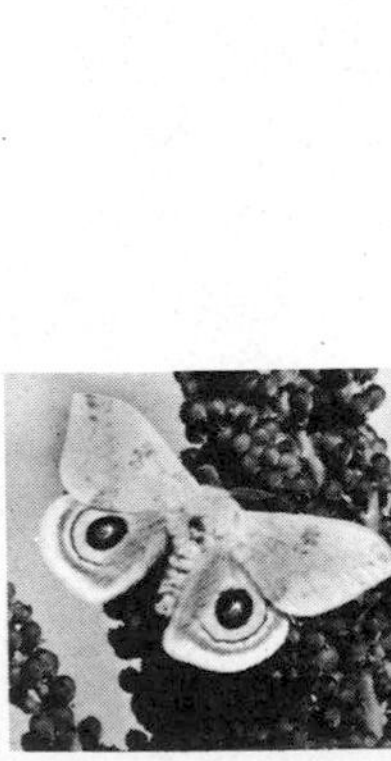

io moth

i·o moth (ī′ō). A large yellowish moth, *Automeris io*, of North America, having prominent eyelike spots on the hind wings. [After Io, alluding to the gadfly sent by Hera to torment her (the moth's larva stings).]

i·on (ī′ən, ī′ŏn′) *n.* An atom, group of atoms, or molecule that has acquired or is regarded as having acquired a net electric charge by gaining electrons in or losing electrons from an initially electrically neutral configuration. [From Greek *ion*, "going particle" (referring to the passage of ions to either of the electrodes in electrolysis), neuter present participle of *ienai*, to go. See **ei-**[1] in Appendix.*]

–ion. Indicates: **1.** An act or process or the outcome of an act or process; for example, **indention. 2.** A state of being; for example, **cohesion.** [Middle English *-io(u)n*, from Old French *-ion*, from Latin *-iō* (stem *-iōn-*).]

Ion. Ionic.

I·o·na (ī-ō′nə). An island, six square miles in area, of the southern Inner Hebrides, Scotland; site of St. Columba's abbey (founded A.D. 563).

ion engine. A rocket engine that develops thrust by expelling ions rather than gaseous combustion products. Also called "ion rocket." See **ionic propulsion.**

Io·nes·co (yə-nĕs′kō, ē′ə-), **Eugene.** Born 1912. Rumanian-born French dramatist.

ion exchange. A reversible chemical reaction between a solid and a fluid mixture by means of which ions may be interchanged, used in water softening and separation of radioactive isotopes.

I·o·ni·a (ī-ō′nē-ə). The Aegean coast of western Asia Minor, settled by the Ionians.

I·o·ni·an (ī-ō′nē-ən) *adj.* Of or pertaining to Ionia or the Ionians. —*n.* One of a Hellenic people who settled in Attica and on the northern coast of the Peloponnesus about 1100 B.C. and founded colonies on the western coast of Asia Minor and adjacent islands.

Ionian Islands. A group of seven Greek islands, 853 square miles in area, in the Ionian Sea.

Ionian Sea. A section of the Mediterranean between southern Italy and western Greece.

i·on·ic (ī-ŏn′ĭk) *adj.* Of, containing, or involving ions.

I·on·ic (ī-ŏn′ĭk) *adj.* **1.** Ionian. **2.** *Architecture.* Pertaining to or designating the Ionic order. **3.** *Greek Metrics.* **a.** Designating a metrical foot consisting of two long syllables followed by two short ones, or two short syllables followed by two long ones. **b.** Designating a verse or meter having such feet. —*n. Abbr.* **Ion. 1.** The ancient Greek dialect of Ionia, belonging to Attic-Ionic, early developed as a medium for scientific and historical prose. **2.** *Greek Metrics.* An Ionic foot, verse, or meter. **3.** *Printing.* A style of heavy-faced type.

ionic bond. A chemical bond characteristic of salts and formed by the complete transfer of one or more electrons from one kind of atom to another. Also called "electrovalent bond."

Ionic order. An order of classical Greek architecture characterized by two opposed volutes in the capital. Compare **Corinthian order, Doric order.**

ionic propulsion. Propulsion by the reactive thrust of a high-speed beam of similarly charged ions ejected by an ion engine. Also called "ion propulsion."

i·on·i·za·tion (ī′ə-nə-zā′shən) *n.* **1.** The formation of one or more ions by the addition of electrons to or the removal of electrons from an electrically neutral atomic or molecular configuration by heat, electrical discharge, radiation, or chemical reaction. **2.** The state or condition of being ionized.

ionization chamber. A gas-filled enclosure fitted with electrodes between which electric current flows upon ionization of the gas by incident radiation, the electrodes being maintained at a potential difference just sufficient to collect ions thus produced without causing further ionization.

ionization potential. The energy required to remove completely the weakest bound electron from its ground state in an atom or molecule so that the resulting ion is also in its ground state.

i·on·ize (ī′ə-nīz′) *v.* **-ized, -izing, -izes.** —*tr.* To convert totally or partially into ions. —*intr.* To become converted totally or partially into ions.

ionizing radiation. Radiation capable of producing ionization, including energetic charged particles such as alpha and beta rays, nonparticulate radiation such as x rays, and neutrons.

i·o·none (ī′ə-nōn′) *n.* Either of two yellowish to colorless liquid isomers, $C_{13}H_{20}O$, having a strong odor of violets and used in perfumes. [Greek *ion*, violet (see **iodine**) + -ONE.]

i·on·o·sphere (ī-ŏn′ə-sfîr′) *n.* An electrically conducting set of layers of the earth's atmosphere, extending from altitudes of approximately 30 miles to more than 250 miles, caused by ionization of rarefied atmospheric gases by incident solar radiation. [ION + -SPHERE.]

ion rocket. 1. A rocket using ionic propulsion. **2.** An **ion engine** *(see).*

I.O.O.F. Independent Order of Odd Fellows.

i·o·ta (ī-ō′tə) *n.* **1.** The ninth letter in the Greek alphabet, written *I, ι.* Transliterated in English as *I, i.* See **alphabet. 2.** A very small amount. Often used in the phrase *not one iota.* [Greek *iōta*, of Semitic origin, akin to Hebrew *yōdh*, YOD.]

i·o·ta·cism (ī-ō′tə-sĭz′əm) *n.* The conversion of other vowel sounds in Greek to the sound of iota. [Late Latin *iotacismus*, from Greek *iotakismos*, from *iōta*, IOTA.]

IOU (ī′ō-yo͞o′) *n., pl.* **IOU's, IOUs.** A promise to pay a debt. [Short for *I owe you.*]

–ious. Indicates characterized by or full of; for example, **sagacious, edacious.** [Middle English, partly from Latin *-ius*, and partly from Old French *-ieus, -ieux*, from Latin *-iōsus* : *-i-*, stem + *-ōsus*, -OUS.]

I·o·wa[1] (ī′ə-wə). **1.** A Midwestern state of the United States, 56,290 square miles in area; admitted to the Union in 1846. Population, 2,760,000. Capital, Des Moines. See map at **United States of America. 2.** A river rising in the north-central part of this state and flowing 329 miles generally southeast to the Mississippi. [Dakota *Ayuhwa*, "sleepy ones."]

I·o·wa[2] (ī′ə-wə) *n., pl.* **Iowa** or **-was. 1.** A tribe of Siouan-speaking North American Indians formerly inhabiting the region of Minnesota, Iowa, and Missouri. **2.** A member of this tribe. **3.** The Siouan language of this tribe. —**I′o·wa** *adj.*

IPA 1. International Phonetic Alphabet. 2. International Phonetic Association. 3. isopropyl alcohol.
I.P.A. 1. International Phonetic Alphabet. 2. International Phonetic Association.
I·pa·tieff (ĭ-pä′tyĕf, -tē-ĕf′), **Vladimir Nikolaevich.** 1867–1952. Russian-born American chemist; improved gasoline.
ip·e·cac (ĭp′ə-kăk′) *n.* Also **ip·e·cac·u·an·ha** (ĭp′ə-kăk′yo͞o-ăn′ə). 1. A low-growing South American shrub, *Cephaelis ipecacuanha,* having roots used medicinally. 2. The dried roots of this shrub. [Shortened from Portuguese *ipecacuanha,* from Tupi *ipekaaguéne.*]
Iph·i·ge·ni·a (ĭf′ə-jə-nī′ə, -nē′ə). *Greek Mythology.* The daughter of Clytemnestra and Agamemnon, offered as a sacrifice to Artemis to enable the Greek fleet to sail for Troy.
I·pin (ē′pĭn′). A city of southeast-central Szechwan, China. Population, 190,000.
I·poh (ē′pō). A city of Perak State, Malaysia, on the western coast of the Malay Peninsula. Population, 126,000.
ip·se dix·it (ĭp′sē dĭk′sĭt). 1. An unsupported assertion, usually by a person of standing. 2. An arbitrary statement; dictum. [Latin, he himself said (it), translation of Doric Greek *autos epha,* expression used by the Pythagoreans of dogmatic assertions of Pythagoras.]
ip·sis·si·ma ver·ba (ĭp-sĭs′ə-mə vûr′bə). *Latin.* The very words.
ip·so fac·to (ĭp′sō făk′tō). *Latin.* By the fact itself; by that very fact: *An alien, ipso facto, has no right to a U.S. passport.*
ip·so ju·re (ĭp′sō jo͝or′ē). *Latin.* By the law itself.
Ips·wich (ĭps′wĭch). The county seat of East Suffolk, England. Population, 120,000.
IQ, I.Q. intelligence quotient.
I·qui·que (ē-kē′kā). A city and port of northwestern Chile. Population, 51,000.
I·qui·tos (ē-kē′tōs). A city of Peru, in the northeast on the Amazon. Population, 58,000.
Ir The symbol for the element iridium.
Ir. Irish.
I.R.A. Irish Republican Army.
I·ran (ĭ-răn′, ē-rän′). Formerly **Per·sia** (pûr′zhə, -shə). A kingdom, 628,000 square miles in area, of southwestern Asia. Population, 22,860,000. Capital, Teheran. [Persian *Īrān,* from Old Persian *āriya,* noble. See **aryo-** in Appendix.*]
I·ra·ni·an (ĭ-rā′nē-ən) *adj.* Of or pertaining to Iran, its inhabitants, or their language. —*n.* 1. A native or inhabitant of Iran. 2. A group of languages including Persian, Kurdish, and Pashto, spoken principally in Iran, Afghanistan, and westernmost West Pakistan, and forming a subbranch of the Indo-Iranian branch of the Indo-European language family.
I·raq (ĭ-răk′, ē-räk′). Also **I·rak.** A republic, 116,000 square miles in area, of southwestern Asia. Population, 8,262,000. Capital, Baghdad.
I·ra·qi (ē-rä′kē) *adj.* Of or pertaining to Iraq, its inhabitants, or their language. —*n., pl.* **Iraqi** or **-qis.** 1. A native or inhabitant of Iraq. 2. The Arabic dialect spoken in Iraq.
i·ras·ci·ble (ĭ-răs′ə-bəl, ī-răs′-) *adj.* 1. Prone to outbursts of temper; easily angered. 2. Characterized by or resulting from anger. [Old French, from Late Latin *īrāscibilis,* from Latin *īrāscī,* to get angry, from *īra,* anger, IRE.] —**i·ras′ci·bil′i·ty, i·ras′ci·ble·ness** *n.* —**i·ras′ci·bly** *adv.*
i·rate (ī′rāt, ī-rāt′) *adj.* 1. Angry; enraged. 2. Characterized or occasioned by anger: *an irate phone call.* [Latin *īrātus,* from *īra,* anger, IRE.] —**i′rate·ly** *adv.*
I·ra·zú (ē-rä-so͞o′). A volcano rising to 11,260 feet in central Costa Rica.
IRBM Intermediate Range Ballistic Missile.
ire (īr) *n.* Wrath; anger. See Synonyms at **anger.** [Middle English, from Old French, from Latin *īra,* anger. See **eis-**[1] in Appendix.*]
Ire. Ireland.
ire·ful (īr′fəl) *adj.* Full of ire; angry; wrathful. —**ire′ful·ly** *adv.* —**ire′ful·ness** *n.*
Ire·land (īr′lənd). *Abbr.* **Ire.** 1. One of the British Isles, 31,839 square miles in area, in the Atlantic west of Britain, divided into the Republic of Ireland and **Northern Ireland** *(see).* 2. *Gaelic* **Eir·e** (âr′ə). Formerly **Irish Free State.** Officially, Republic of Ireland. A republic, 26,601 square miles in area, occupying most of Ireland. Population, 2,849,000. Capital, Dublin. [Middle English *Ireland,* Old English *Īr(a)land* : *Īras,* the Irish (see **Iveriū** in Appendix*) + LAND.]
I·rene (ī-rēn′). A feminine given name. [French *Irène,* from Latin *Irene,* from Greek *Eirēnē,* from *eirēnē,* peace. See **irenic.**]
i·ren·ic (ī-rĕn′ĭk, ī-rē′nĭk) *adj.* Also **i·ren·i·cal** (ī-rĕn′ĭk-əl, ī-rē′-). Promoting peace; conciliatory; pacific. [Greek *eirēnikos,* from *eirēnē*†, peace.] —**i·ren′i·cal·ly** *adv.*
i·ren·ics (ī-rĕn′ĭks, ī-rē′nĭks) *n.* Plural in form, used with a singular verb. Theology dealing with the promotion of peace and unity among Christian churches.
ir·i·dec·to·my (ĭr′ə-dĕk′tə-mē, ī′rə-) *n., pl.* **-mies.** The surgical removal of part of the iris of the eye. [Latin *īris* (stem *īrido-*), IRIS + -ECTOMY.]
ir·i·des·cence (ĭr′ə-dĕs′əns) *n.* The state or quality of being iridescent; a display of rainbowlike colors.
ir·i·des·cent (ĭr′ə-dĕs′ənt) *adj.* Producing a display of lustrous, rainbowlike colors: *"The prelude was as iridescent as a prism in a morning room."* (Carson McCullers). [Latin *īris* (stem *īrid-*), rainbow, IRIS + -ESCENT.]
i·rid·ic (ĭ-rĭd′ĭk, ī-rĭd′-) *adj.* Pertaining to the iris of the eye.
i·rid·i·um (ĭ-rĭd′ē-əm, ī rĭd′-) *n.* *Symbol* **Ir** A very hard and brittle, exceptionally corrosion-resistant, whitish-yellow metallic element occurring in platinum ores and used principally to harden platinum and in high-temperature materials, electrical contacts, and wear-resistant bearings. Atomic number 77, atomic weight 192.2, melting point 2,410°C, boiling point 4,527°C, specific gravity 22.42 (17°C), valences 3, 4. See **element.** [New Latin, from Latin *īris* (stem *īrid-*), rainbow, IRIS (from the variety of colors it gives in solutions).]
ir·i·dos·mine (ĭr′ə-dŏz′mĭn, -dŏs′mĭn, ī′rə-) *n.* An alloy, **osmiridium** *(see).* [German *Iridosmin* : IRID(IUM) + OSM(IUM) + -INE.]
i·ris (ī′rĭs) *n., pl.* **irises** or **irides** (ĭr′ə-dēz′, ĭr′ə-). 1. The pigmented, round, contractile membrane of the eye, situated between the cornea and lens, and perforated by the pupil. 2. Any of numerous plants of the genus *Iris,* having narrow sword-shaped leaves and showy, variously colored flowers. 3. A rainbow or rainbowlike display of colors. [Middle English *iris, yris,* rainbow, kind of prismatic crystal, from Latin *īris,* from Greek *iris,* rainbow, iris of the eye. See **wei-**[1] in Appendix.*]
I·ris (ī′rĭs). *Greek Mythology.* The goddess of the rainbow and messenger of the gods.
iris diaphragm. A metallic diaphragm adjustable to vary the diameter of a central aperture, commonly used on cameras to regulate the amount of light admitted to a lens.
I·rish (ī′rĭsh) *adj. Abbr.* **Ir.** Of or relating to Ireland, its people, or their language. —*n. Abbr.* **Ir.** 1. a. The inhabitants of Ireland. b. People of immediate Irish descent. 2. The Celtic language spoken in Ireland, **Irish Gaelic** *(see).* 3. The English spoken in Ireland; Irish English. 4. *Informal.* Fieriness of temper or passion; high spirit. —**get one's Irish up.** *Informal.* To become angry. [Middle English *Irisc(h),* from Old English *Īras,* the Irish. See **Iveriū** in Appendix.*]
Irish coffee. A beverage of sweetened hot coffee and Irish whiskey, topped with whipped cream.
Irish elk. A large extinct European deer of the genus *Megaceros,* of the Pliocene and Pleistocene epochs, having very large palmate antlers.
Irish English. The English spoken in Ireland.
Irish Free State. A former name (1921–37) for the Republic of **Ireland.**
Irish Gaelic. The Goidelic language of Ireland. Also called "Erse," "Irish."
I·rish·ism (ī′rĭsh-ĭz′əm) *n.* An Irish idiom or custom.
I·rish·man (ī′rĭsh-mən) *n., pl.* **-men** (-mĭn). A man of Irish birth or descent.
Irish moss. An edible North Atlantic seaweed, *Chondrus crispus,* that yields a mucilaginous substance used medicinally and in preparing jellies. Also called "carrageen."
Irish Republican Army. *Abbr.* **I.R.A.** A secret Irish nationalist organization formed to oppose the partition of Ireland, active in anti-British terrorist acts chiefly in the 1920's and 1930's.
Irish Sea. The sea between Britain and Ireland.
Irish setter. A setter having a silky reddish-brown coat.
Irish stew. A stew of meat and vegetables.
Irish terrier. A terrier having a wiry brown coat.
Irish whiskey. Whiskey made by the distillation of barley.
Irish wolfhound. A large dog of an ancient breed, having a rough, shaggy coat.
I·rish·wom·an (ī′rĭsh-wo͝om′ən) *n., pl.* **-women** (-wĭm′ĭn). A woman of Irish birth or descent.
i·ri·tis (ī-rī′tĭs) *n.* Inflammation of the iris of the eye. [New Latin : IR(IS) + -ITIS.]
irk (ûrk) *tr.v.* **irked, irking, irks.** To vex; to weary; irritate. See Synonyms at **annoy.** [Middle English *irken, yrken,* possibly from Old Norse *yrkja,* to work. See **werg-**[1] in Appendix.*]
irk·some (ûrk′səm) *adj.* Causing annoyance or bother; wearisome; tedious: *irksome restrictions.* See Synonyms at **boring.** —**irk′some·ly** *adv.* —**irk′some·ness** *n.*
Ir·kutsk (ĭr-ko͞otsk′). A city of the southern Russian S.F.S.R., on the Angara near Lake Baikal. Population, 390,000.
IRO International Refugee Organization.
i·ron (ī′ərn) *n.* 1. *Symbol* **Fe** A silvery-white, lustrous, malleable, ductile, magnetic or magnetizable, metallic element occurring abundantly in combined forms, notably in hematite, limonite, magnetite, and taconite, and used alloyed in a wide range of important structural materials. Atomic number 26, atomic weight 55.847, melting point 1,535°C, boiling point 3,000°C, specific gravity 7.874 (20°C), valences 2, 3, 4, 6. See **element.** 2. Great hardness or strength; firmness: *a will of iron.* 3. An implement made of iron alloy or similar metal; especially, a bar heated for use in branding, curling hair, or cauterizing. 4. A golf club with a metal head, numbered from one to nine according to the degree of slant of the face of the club. 5. A metal appliance with a handle and a weighted flat bottom, used when heated to press wrinkles from fabric. 6. A harpoon. 7. *Plural.* Fetters; shackles. 8. A tonic, pill, or other medication containing iron as a dietary supplement. —**have an iron in the fire.** To be engaged in an undertaking. —**in irons.** 1. Fettered. 2. *Nautical.* Lying head to the wind and unable to turn either way. —**strike while the iron is hot.** To seize an opportunity to act. —*adj.* 1. Made of or containing iron. 2. Extremely hard and strong: *an iron fist.* 3. Hardy; robust: *an iron constitution.* 4. Inflexible; unyielding: *an iron will.* 5. Base; degraded: *an iron age of incessant wars.* —*v.* **ironed, ironing, irons.** —*tr.* 1. a. To press and smooth with a heated iron. b. To remove (creases) by pressing. 2. To put in irons; to fetter. 3. To fit or clad with iron. —*intr.* To iron clothes. —**iron out.** To settle through discussion or compromise; work out: *iron out our problems.* [Middle English *yren, yron, iren,* Old English *īren,* earlier *īsern, īsen.* See **eis-**[1] in Appendix.*]
Iron Age. The generally prehistoric period succeeding the

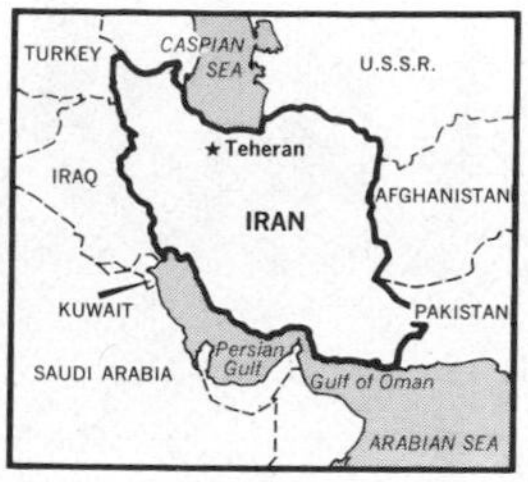

Iran

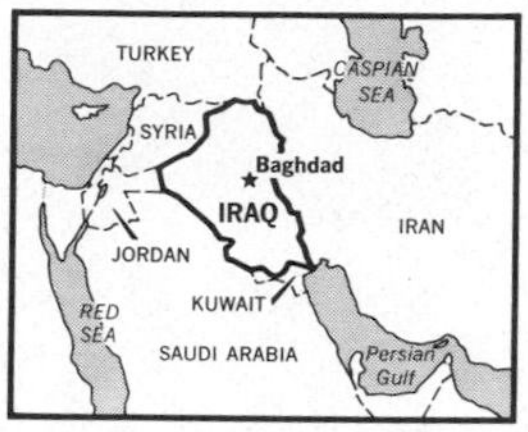

Iraq

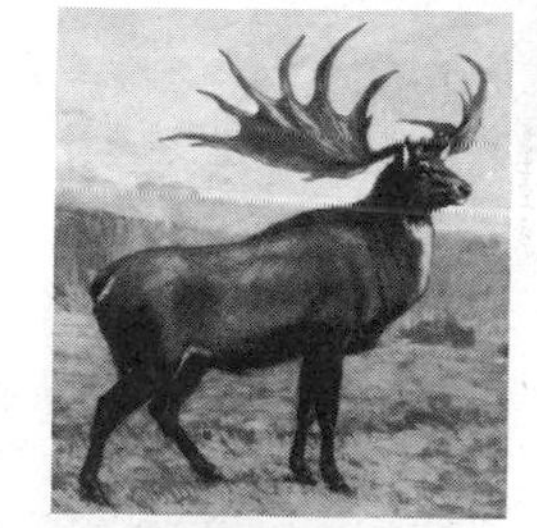
Irish elk

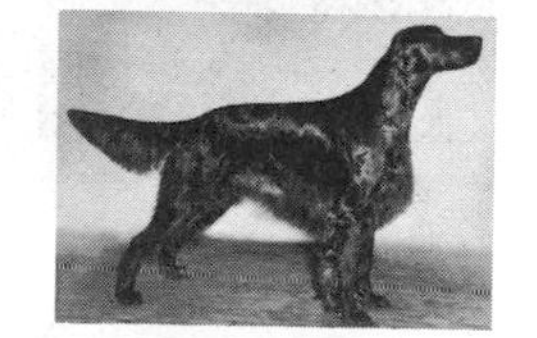
Irish setter

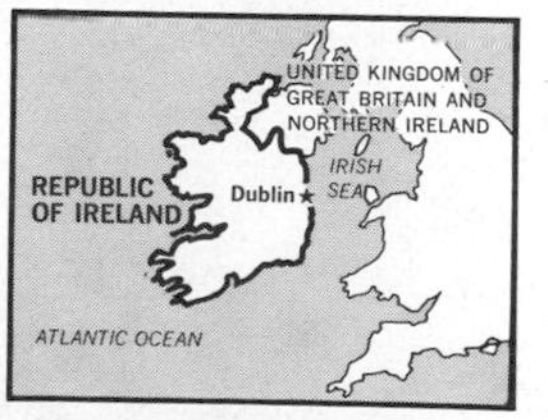

Republic of Ireland

Bronze Age, characterized by the introduction of iron metallurgy, in Europe beginning around the eighth century B.C.

i·ron·bark (ī′ərn-bärk′) *n.* Any of several Australian trees of the genus *Eucalyptus,* often having hard, rough bark.

iron blue. Any of various light- and heat-resistant, semitransparent blue pigments of powerful tinctorial strength, used chiefly in permanent industrial finishes, printing inks, and artists' colors. Also called "Prussian blue."

i·ron·bound (ī′ərn-bound′) *adj.* **1.** Bound with iron. **2.** Rigid and unyielding. **3.** Bound with rocks and cliffs, as a coast.

i·ron·clad (ī′ərn-klăd′) *adj.* **1.** Sheathed with iron plates for protection. **2.** Rigid: *an ironclad rule.* —*n.* A 19th-century warship having sides armored with metal plates.

Iron Curtain. A barrier that prevents free exchange or communication; specifically, the political and ideological barrier between the Soviet bloc and western Europe after World War II. [Popularized (1946) by Winston Churchill.]

iron hand. Rigorous or despotic control: *ruling with an iron hand.* —**i′ron-hand′ed** (ī′ərn-hăn′dĭd) *adj.*

iron horse. *Informal.* A railroad locomotive.

i·ron·ic (ī-rŏn′ĭk) *adj.* Also **i·ron·i·cal** (ī-rŏn′ĭ-kəl). **1.** Characterized by or constituting irony. **2.** Given to the use of irony. —See Synonyms at **sarcastic.** —**i·ron′i·cal·ly** *adv.* —**i·ron′i·cal·ness** *n.*

i·ron·ing (ī′ər-nĭng) *n.* **1.** The pressing of clothes with a heated iron. **2.** The clothing to be pressed.

ironing board. A long narrow padded board on a collapsible support, used as a working surface for ironing.

i·ron·ist (ī′rə-nĭst) *n.* A notable user of irony.

iron lung. A tank in which the entire body except the head is enclosed and by means of which pressure is regularly increased and decreased to provide artificial respiration.

i·ron·mas·ter (ī′ərn-măs′tər, -mäs′tər) *n. British.* A manufacturer of iron.

i·ron·mon·ger (ī′ərn-mŭng′gər, -mŏng′gər) *n. British.* A hardware merchant.

i·ron·mon·ger·y (ī′ərn-mŭng′gə-rē, -mŏng′gə-rē) *n., pl.* **-ies.** *British.* **1.** Ironware. **2.** The shop or business of an ironmonger.

iron pyrites. *Chemistry.* **Pyrite** *(see).*

i·ron·smith (ī′ərn-smĭth′) *n.* One who works in iron; blacksmith.

i·ron·stone (ī′ərn-stōn′) *n.* **1.** One of several kinds of iron ore with admixtures of silica and clay. **2.** A hard white pottery.

i·ron·ware (ī′ərn-wâr′) *n.* Iron utensils and other products made of iron; hardware.

i·ron·weed (ī′ərn-wēd′) *n.* Any plant of the genus *Vernonia,* having clusters of purplish flowers. [From its hard stem.]

i·ron·wood (ī′ərn-wo͝od′) *n.* **1.** Any of various trees having very hard wood, such as the **hornbeam** and the **hop hornbeam** *(both of which see).* **2.** The wood of such a tree.

i·ron·work (ī′ərn-wûrk′) *n.* Work in iron, as gratings and rails.

i·ron·works (ī′ərn-wûrks′) *n.* Plural in form, usually used with a singular verb. A building or establishment where iron is smelted or where heavy iron products are made.

i·ro·ny[1] (ī′rə-nē) *n., pl.* **-nies.** **1.** The use of words to convey the opposite of their literal meaning. **2.** An expression or utterance marked by such a deliberate contrast between apparent and intended meaning. **3.** A literary style employing such contrasts for humorous or rhetorical effect. **4.** Incongruity between what might be expected and what actually occurs: *"Hyde noted the irony of Ireland's copying the nation she most hated."* (Richard Kain). **5.** An occurrence, result, or circumstance notable for such incongruity. **6.** The dramatic effect achieved by leading an audience to understand an incongruity between a situation and the accompanying speeches, while the characters in the play remain unaware of the incongruity. **7.** Feigned ignorance, as in the Socratic method of instruction. —See Synonyms at **wit.** [Latin *īrōnia,* from Greek *eirōneia,* dissembling, feigned ignorance, from *eirōn,* dissembler, "one who says less than he thinks," from *eirein,* to say. See **wer-**[6] in Appendix.*]

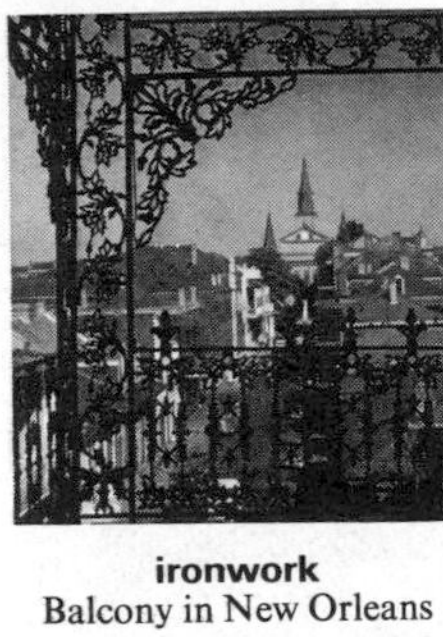

ironwork
Balcony in New Orleans

i·ron·y[2] (ī′ər-nē) *adj.* Of, like, or containing iron.

Ir·o·quoi·an (ĭr′ə-kwoi′ən) *n.* **1.** A family of North American Indian languages spoken in Canada and eastern United States by such tribes as the Iroquois, Cherokee, Conestoga, Erie, and Wyandot. **2.** A member of a tribe using a language of this family. —*adj.* Of or constituting this language family.

Ir·o·quois (ĭr′ə-kwoi′, -kwoiz′) *n., pl.* **Iroquois.** **1.** Any of several Iroquoian-speaking North American Indian tribes formerly inhabiting New York State, and forming the confederacy known as the **Five Nations,** including the Cayuga, Mohawk, Oneida, Onondaga, and Seneca peoples. After 1722 the confederacy was joined by the Tuscaroras to form the **Six Nations.** **2.** A member of any of these tribes. **3.** Any of the languages spoken among these tribes. [French, from Algonquin *Irinakhoiw,* "real adder."] —**Ir′o·quois** *adj.*

ir·ra·di·ant (ĭ-rā′dē-ənt) *adj.* Sending forth radiant light. [Latin *irradiāns,* present participle of *irradiāre,* IRRADIATE.] —**ir·ra′di·ance, ir·ra′di·an·cy** *n.*

ir·ra·di·ate (ĭ-rā′dē-āt′) *v.* **-ated, -ating, -ates.** —*tr.* **1. a.** To expose to radiation. **b.** To treat with radiation. **2.** To emit in a manner analogous to the emission of light. —*intr. Archaic.* **1.** To send forth rays; radiate. **2.** To become radiant. [Latin *irradiāre,* to shine forth : *in-,* toward + *radiāre,* to shine, RADIATE.] —**ir·ra′di·a′tive** *adj.* —**ir·ra′di·a′tor** (-ā′tər) *n.*

ir·ra·di·a·tion (ĭ-rā′dē-ā′shən) *n.* **1.** The act of irradiating or the condition of being irradiated. **2.** Therapy or treatment by exposure to radiation.

ir·ra·tion·al (ĭ-răsh′ən-əl) *adj.* **1. a.** Not endowed with reason. **b.** Affected by loss of usual or normal mental clarity; incoherent, as from shock. **c.** Contrary to reason; illogical: *an irrational dislike.* **2. a.** Designating a syllable in Greek and Latin prosody whose length does not fit the metrical pattern. **b.** Designating a metrical foot containing such a syllable. **3.** *Mathematics.* Incapable of being expressed as an integer or a quotient of integers. —**ir·ra′tion·al·ly** *adv.* —**ir·ra′tion·al·ness** *n.*

ir·ra·tion·al·ism (ĭ-răsh′ən-ə-lĭz′əm) *n.* Irrational thought, expression, or behavior.

ir·ra·tion·al·i·ty (ĭ-răsh′ə-năl′ə-tē) *n., pl.* **-ties.** **1.** The state or quality of being irrational. **2.** An irrational idea or action.

irrational number. A member of the set of real numbers which is not a member of the set of rational numbers. See **number.**

Ir·ra·wad·dy (ĭr′ə-wä′dē). A river rising in northern Burma and flowing 1,350 miles generally south to its vast delta on the Andaman Sea.

ir·re·claim·a·ble (ĭr′ĭ-klā′mə-bəl) *adj.* Incapable of being reclaimed: *irreclaimable wasteland.* —**ir′re·claim′a·bil′i·ty, ir′re·claim′a·ble·ness** *n.* —**ir′re·claim′a·bly** *adv.*

ir·rec·on·cil·a·ble (ĭ-rĕk′ən-sī′lə-bəl, ĭ-rĕk′ən-sī′-) *adj.* **1.** Not capable of being reconciled; implacably hostile. **2.** Incompatible; incongruous. —*n.* **1.** A person who will not compromise, adjust, or submit. **2.** *Plural.* Conflicting ideas or beliefs that cannot be brought into harmony.

ir·re·cov·er·a·ble (ĭr′ĭ-kŭv′ər-ə-bəl) *adj.* Incapable of being recovered; irreparable: *irrecoverable losses.* —**ir′re·cov′er·a·ble·ness** *n.* —**ir′re·cov′er·a·bly** *adv.*

ir·re·cu·sa·ble (ĭr′ĭ-kyo͞o′zə-bəl) *adj.* Not subject to challenge or objection; unexceptionable; undeniable. [French *irrécusable,* from Late Latin *irrecūsābilis* : *in-,* not + *recūsābilis,* that should be rejected, from Latin *recūsāre,* to reject (see **recusant**).] —**ir′re·cu′sa·bly** *adv.*

ir·re·deem·a·ble (ĭr′ĭ-dē′mə-bəl) *adj.* **1.** Incapable of being bought back or paid off: *irredeemable annuity.* **2.** Not convertible into coin. **3.** Incapable of being remedied. **4.** Incapable of being saved or reformed. —**ir′re·deem′a·bly** *adv.*

ir·re·den·tist (ĭr′ĭ-dĕn′tĭst) *n.* One who advocates the recovery of lands of which his nation has been deprived, or of territory culturally or historically related to his nation but now subject to a foreign government. [Italian *irredentista,* from *(Italia) irredenta,* "unredeemed (Italy)" (Italian-speaking areas subject to other countries), from *irredento,* not redeemed : *in-,* not, from Latin + *redento,* redeemed, from Latin *redemptus,* past participle of *redimere,* REDEEM.] —**ir′re·den′tist** *adj.* —**ir′re·den′tism′** *n.*

ir·re·duc·i·ble (ĭr′ĭ-do͞o′sə-bəl, -dyo͞o′sə-bəl) *adj.* Incapable of being reduced to a desired, simpler, or smaller form or amount. —**ir′re·duc′i·bil′i·ty, ir′re·duc′i·ble·ness** *n.* —**ir′re·duc′i·bly** *adv.*

ir·ref·ra·ga·ble (ĭ-rĕf′rə-gə-bəl) *adj.* Incapable of being refuted or controverted; indisputable. [Late Latin *irrefrāgābilis* : Latin *in-,* not + *refrāgārī,* to oppose, akin to *frangere,* to break (see **bhreg-** in Appendix*).] —**ir·ref′ra·ga·bil′i·ty** *n.* —**ir·ref′ra·ga·bly** *adv.*

ir·re·fran·gi·ble (ĭr′ĭ-frăn′jə-bəl) *adj.* **1.** Incapable of being broken; indestructible. **2.** *Optics.* Incapable of being refracted. —**ir′re·fran′gi·bly** *adv.*

ir·ref·u·ta·ble (ĭ-rĕf′yə-tə-bəl, ĭr′ĭ-fyo͞o′tə-bəl) *adj.* Incapable of being refuted or disproved; incontrovertible: *irrefutable arguments.* —**ir·ref′u·ta·bil′i·ty** *n.* —**ir·ref′u·ta·bly** *adv.*

irreg. irregular; irregularly.

ir·re·gard·less (ĭr′ĭ-gärd′lĭs) *adv. Nonstandard.* Regardless.
Usage: *Irregardless,* a double negative, is never acceptable except when the intent is clearly humorous.

ir·reg·u·lar (ĭ-rĕg′yə-lər) *adj. Abbr.* **irreg.** **1.** Not according to rule, accepted order, or general practice: *a bit irregular to promote a man so soon.* **2.** Not conforming to legality, moral law, or social convention: *an irregular marriage.* **3.** Not straight, uniform, or symmetrical: *a path of irregular width; irregular facial features.* **4.** Of uneven rate, occurrence, or duration: *an irregular heartbeat.* **5.** Deviating from type; asymmetrically arranged or atypical. **6.** *Botany.* Having differing floral parts, especially petals. **7.** Falling below the manufacturer's standard or usual specifications; flawed; imperfect. **8.** *Grammar.* Departing from the usual set of inflectional forms. An example of an irregular verb is *be.* **9.** Not belonging to a permanent, organized military force: *irregular troops.* —*n.* **1.** A person or thing that is irregular. **2.** A soldier, such as a guerrilla, who is not a member of a regular military force. —**ir·reg′u·lar·ly** *adv.*

ir·reg·u·lar·i·ty (ĭ-rĕg′yə-lăr′ə-tē) *n., pl.* **-ties.** **1.** The quality or state of being irregular. **2.** That which is irregular.

ir·rel·a·tive (ĭ-rĕl′ə-tĭv) *adj.* **1.** Having no correlative relationship; unconnected. **2.** Irrelevant. —**ir·rel′a·tive·ly** *adv.*

ir·rel·e·vance (ĭ-rĕl′ə-vəns) *n.* Also **ir·rel·e·van·cy** (-vən-sē) *pl.* **-cies.** **1.** The quality or state of being irrelevant. **2.** That which is irrelevant.

ir·rel·e·vant (ĭ-rĕl′ə-vənt) *adj.* Having no applications or effects in a specified circumstance. —**ir·rel′e·vant·ly** *adv.*

ir·re·lig·ion (ĭr′ĭ-lĭj′ən) *n.* Hostility or indifference to religion.

ir·re·lig·ious (ĭr′ĭ-lĭj′əs) *adj.* Indifferent or hostile to religion; ungodly. —**ir′re·lig′ious·ly** *adv.* —**ir′re·lig′ious·ness** *n.*

ir·rem·e·a·ble (ĭ-rĕm′ē-ə-bəl, ĭ-rē′mē-) *adj. Archaic.* Affording no possibility of return. [Latin *irremeābilis* : *in-,* not + *remeāre,* to return : *re-,* back + *meāre,* to go (see **mei-**[1] in Appendix*).]

ir·re·me·di·a·ble (ĭr′ĭ-mē′dē-ə-bəl) *adj.* Impossible to remedy, correct, or repair; incurable. —**ir′re·me′di·a·bly** *adv.*

ir·re·mis·si·ble (ĭr′ĭ-mĭs′ə-bəl) *adj.* Not remissible; unpardonable. —**ir′re·mis′si·bil′i·ty** *n.* —**ir′re·mis′si·bly** *adv.*

ir·re·mov·a·ble (ĭr′ĭ-mo͞o′və-bəl) *adj.* Not removable. —**ir′re·mov′a·bil′i·ty** *n.* —**ir′re·mov′a·bly** *adv.*
ir·rep·a·ra·ble (ĭ-rĕp′ər-ə-bəl) *adj.* Incapable of being repaired, rectified, or amended; beyond repair: *irreparable harm.* —**ir·rep′a·ra·bil′i·ty, ir·rep′a·ra·ble·ness** *n.* —**ir·rep′a·ra·bly** *adv.*
ir·re·peal·a·ble (ĭr′ĭ-pē′lə-bəl) *adj.* Not repealable.
ir·re·place·a·ble (ĭr′ĭ-plā′sə-bəl) *adj.* Incapable of being replaced.
ir·re·pres·si·ble (ĭr′ĭ-prĕs′ə-bəl) *adj.* Not repressible; impossible to control or restrain. —**ir′re·pres′si·bil′i·ty, ir′re·pres′si·ble·ness** *n.* —**ir′re·pres′si·bly** *adv.*
ir·re·proach·a·ble (ĭr′ĭ-prō′chə-bəl) *adj.* Beyond reproach. —**ir′re·proach′a·ble·ness** *n.* —**ir′re·proach′a·bly** *adv.*
ir·re·sis·ti·ble (ĭr′ĭ-zĭs′tə-bəl) *adj.* **1.** Impossible to resist. **2.** Having an overpowering appeal: *"an irresistible urge to hand banknotes to everyone in sight"* (Carter Dickson). —**ir′re·sis′ti·bil′i·ty, ir′re·sis′ti·ble·ness** *n.* —**ir′re·sis′ti·bly** *adv.*
ir·res·o·lu·ble (ĭ-rĕz′əl-yə-bəl, ĭr′ĭ-zŏl′-) *adj.* Not capable of being solved.
ir·res·o·lute (ĭ-rĕz′ə-lo͞ot′) *adj.* **1.** Unresolved as to action or procedure: *"greatly oppressed in my mind, irresolute, and not knowing what to do"* (Defoe). **2.** Lacking in resolution; vacillating; wavering; indecisive. —**ir·res′o·lute′ly** *adv.* —**ir·res′o·lute′ness, ir·res′o·lu′tion** *n.*
ir·re·solv·a·ble (ĭr′ĭ-zŏl′və-bəl) *adj.* **1.** Incapable of being resolved. **2.** Not capable of being separated into component parts; irreducible.
ir·re·spec·tive (ĭr′ĭ-spĕk′tĭv) *adj. Archaic.* Characterized by disregard; heedless. —**irrespective of.** Regardless of; without consideration of. —**ir′re·spec′tive·ly** *adv.*
ir·re·spir·a·ble (ĭr′ĭ-spīr′ə-bəl, ĭ-rĕs′pər-) *adj.* Not fit for breathing; not respirable.
ir·re·spon·si·ble (ĭr′ĭ-spŏn′sə-bəl) *adj.* **1.** Not liable to be called to account by a higher authority. **2.** Not mentally or financially fit to assume responsibility. **3.** Showing no sense of responsibility; undependable; unreliable; untrustworthy. —*n.* An irresponsible person. —**ir′re·spon′si·bil′i·ty, ir′re·spon′si·ble·ness** *n.* —**ir′re·spon′si·bly** *adv.*
ir·re·spon·sive (ĭr′ĭ-spŏn′sĭv) *adj.* **1.** Not responsive, as to treatment or stimuli. **2.** Not responding or answering readily. —**ir′re·spon′sive·ly** *adv.* —**ir′re·spon′sive·ness** *n.*
ir·re·triev·a·ble (ĭr′ĭ-trē′və-bəl) *adj.* Not capable of being retrieved or recovered. —**ir′re·triev′a·ble·ness, ir′re·triev′a·bil′i·ty** *n.* —**ir′re·triev′a·bly** *adv.*
ir·rev·er·ence (ĭ-rĕv′ər-əns) *n.* **1.** Want of reverence or due respect. **2.** A disrespectful act or remark.
ir·rev·er·ent (ĭ-rĕv′ər-ənt) *adj.* **1.** Lacking in reverence; disrespectful: *an irreverent person.* **2.** Proceeding from irreverence: *an irreverent act.* —**ir·rev′er·ent·ly** *adv.*
ir·re·vers·i·ble (ĭr′ĭ-vûr′sə-bəl) *adj.* Incapable of being reversed. —**ir′re·vers′i·bil′i·ty, ir′re·vers′i·ble·ness** *n.* —**ir′re·vers′i·bly** *adv.*
ir·rev·o·ca·ble (ĭ-rĕv′ə-kə-bəl) *adj.* Incapable of being retracted or revoked; irreversible. —**ir·rev′o·ca·bil′i·ty, ir·rev′o·ca·ble·ness** *n.* —**ir·rev′o·ca·bly** *adv.*
ir·ri·ga·ble (ĭr′ĭ-gə-bəl) *adj.* Admitting of irrigation.
ir·ri·gate (ĭr′ĭ-gāt′) *tr.v.* **-gated, -gating, -gates. 1.** To supply (dry land) with water by means of ditches, pipes, or streams. **2.** To wash out (a canal or wound) with water or a medicated fluid. **3.** To vitalize or make fertile. [Latin *irrigāre,* to lead water to : *in-,* in + *rigāre,* to wet, water (see **reg-[2]** in Appendix*).] —**ir′ri·ga′tion** *n.* —**ir′ri·ga′tion·al** *adj.* —**ir′ri·ga′tor** (-gā′tər) *n.*
ir·ri·ta·bil·i·ty (ĭr′ə-tə-bĭl′ə-tē) *n.* **1.** The quality or state of being irritable; testiness; petulance. **2.** *Pathology.* Excessive sensitivity. **3.** *Biology.* The capacity to respond to stimuli.
ir·ri·ta·ble (ĭr′ə-tə-bəl) *adj.* **1.** Easily annoyed; ill-tempered. **2.** *Pathology.* Abnormally sensitive. **3.** *Biology.* Responsive to stimuli. [Latin *irrītābilis,* from *irrītāre,* IRRITATE.] —**ir′ri·ta·ble·ness** *n.* —**ir′ri·ta·bly** *adv.*
ir·ri·tant (ĭr′ə-tənt) *adj.* Causing irritation; irritating, physically or mentally. —*n.* Something that causes irritation. [Latin *irrītāns,* present participle of *irrītāre,* IRRITATE.]
ir·ri·tate (ĭr′ə-tāt′) *tr.v.* **-tated, -tating, -tates. 1. a.** To exasperate; vex. **b.** To provoke. **2.** To chafe or inflame. —See Synonyms at **annoy.** [Latin *irrītāre*†.] —**ir′ri·tat′ing·ly** *adv.* —**ir′ri·ta′tor** (-tā′tər) *n.*
ir·ri·ta·tion (ĭr′ə-tā′shən) *n.* **1.** The act of irritating. **2.** A source of annoyance. **3.** The condition of being irritated; vexation. **4.** *Pathology.* Incipient inflammation, soreness, roughness, or irritability of a bodily part.
ir·ri·ta·tive (ĭr′ə-tā′tĭv) *adj.* Involving irritation.
ir·ro·ta·tion·al (ĭr′ō-tā′shən-əl) *adj.* Not involving rotation.
ir·rupt (ĭ-rŭpt′) *intr.v.* **-rupted, -rupting, -rupts. 1.** To break or burst in; make an incursion or invasion. **2.** *Ecology.* To irregularly increase in number. Said of a population. [Latin *irrumpere* (past participle *irruptus*) : *in-,* in + *rumpere,* to break, burst (see **reup-** in Appendix*).] —**ir·rup′tion** *n.*
ir·rup·tive (ĭ-rŭp′tĭv) *adj.* **1.** Irrupting or tending to irrupt. **2.** *Geology.* Intrusive. **3.** Characterized by irruption.
IRS Internal Revenue Service.
Ir·tish (ĭr′tĭsh). Also **Ir·tysh.** A river rising in the northern Sinkiang-Uigur Autonomous Region of China and flowing 1,844 miles west and northwest through the Kazakh S.S.R. to the Ob in the west-central Russian S.F.S.R.
Ir·ving (ûr′vĭng), **Washington.** 1783–1859. American author.
Ir·ving·ton (ûr′vĭng-tən). A city and manufacturing center of northeastern New Jersey. Population, 60,000.
is (ĭz). The third person singular present indicative of the verb **be.** —**as is.** In its present state; as it stands.

is. island.
Is. 1. Isaiah (Old Testament). **2.** island.
Isa. Isaiah (Old Testament).
I·saac (ī′zək). A Hebrew patriarch, the son of Abraham and Sarah and the father of Jacob. Genesis 21:1–4. [Late Latin *Isaacus,* from Greek *Isaak,* from Hebrew *Yiṣḥāq,* "he laughs."]
Is·a·bel (ĭz′ə-bĕl′). A feminine given name. [Spanish, probably altered from Late Latin *Elizabeth,* ELIZABETH.]

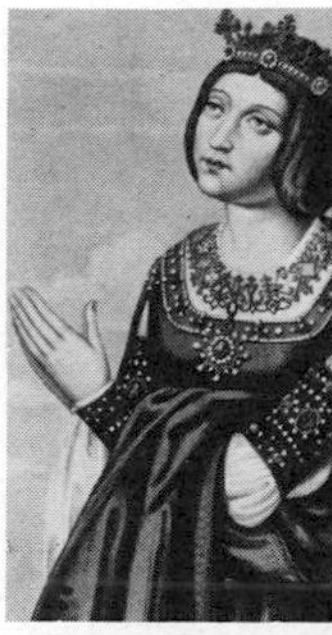
Isabella I

I·sa·be·la (ĭz′ə-bĕl′ə). The largest (1,650 square miles) of the Galápagos Islands of Ecuador.
Is·a·bel·la I (ĭz′ə-bĕl′ə). Called "the Catholic." 1451–1501. Queen of Castile and Aragon as wife of Ferdinand V.
I·sa·iah[1] (ī-zā′ə, ī-zī′ə). Also in Douay Bible **I·sa·ias** (ī-zā′yəs, ī-zī′əs). A Hebrew prophet of the eighth century B.C. in Judah. [Hebrew *Yəsha'yāh(u),* "salvation of the Lord" : *yēsha',* *yəshū'āh,* salvation + *yāh(u),* the Lord.]
I·sa·iah[2] (ī-zā′ə, ī-zī′ə) *n. Abbr.* **Is., Isa.** A book in the Old Testament attributed to Isaiah.
i·sal·lo·bar (ī-săl′ə-bär′) *n.* A line on a weather map connecting places exhibiting equal changes in barometric pressure within a given period of time. [IS(O)- + ALLO- + Greek *baros,* weight (see **gwer-[2]** in Appendix*).]
I·sar (ē′zär). A river rising near Innsbruck, Austria, flowing 163 miles generally northeast through Bavaria, West Germany, to the Danube, bisecting Munich on its course.
I·sau·ri·a (ī-sôr′ē-ə). An ancient district of south-central Asia Minor between the Taurus Mountains and the Mediterranean.
Is·car·i·ot. See **Judas Iscariot.**
is·che·mi·a (ĭ-skē′mē-ə) *n.* A local anemia caused by mechanical obstruction of the blood supply. [New Latin *ischaemia,* from Greek *iskhaimos,* stanching, stopping blood : *iskhein,* to keep back, hold, restrain (see **segh-** in Appendix*) + *haima,* blood (see **hemo-**).]
Is·chia (ēs′kyä). An island of Italy, 18 square miles in area, at the entrance to the Bay of Naples.
is·chi·um (ĭs′kē-əm) *n., pl.* **-chia** (-kē-ə). The lowest of three major bones comprising each half of the pelvis. [Latin, hip joint, from Greek *iskhion*†.]
-ise. Variant of **-ize.**
I·se Bay (ē′sĕ). An inlet of the Philippine Sea, extending 15 miles into the south-central coast of Honshu, Japan.
is·en·trop·ic (ī′sĕn-trŏp′ĭk, -trō′pĭk) *adj.* Without change in entropy; at constant entropy. [IS(O)- + ENTROP(Y) + -IC.]
I·sère (ē-zâr′). A river rising in the Graian Alps of southeast-central France and flowing 180 miles generally west to the Rhône.
I·seult (ĭ-so͞olt′). Also **I·solde** (ĭ-sōld′). *Arthurian Legend.* An Irish princess who married the king of Cornwall and had a hopeless love affair with his knight Tristan.
Is·fa·han (ĭs′fə-hän′, -hăn′). Also **Es·fa·han** (ĕs′-), **Is·pa·han** (ĭs′pə-). A city of west-central Iran. Population, 340,000.
-ish. Indicates: **1. a.** Of the nationality of; for example, **Swedish, Finnish. b.** Having the qualities or character of; for example, **childish, sheepish, womanish. c.** Tending to or preoccupied with; for example, **bookish, selfish. d.** Somewhere near or approximately. Used informally in naming hours or years: *She's fortyish.* **2.** Somewhat or rather; for example, **greenish.** [Middle English *-is(c)h,* Old English *-isc,* from Common Germanic *-iskaz* (unattested), corresponding to Greek *-iskos,* diminutive noun suffix.]
I·shim (ĭ-shĭm′). A river rising in the north-central Kazakh S.S.R. and flowing 1,123 miles west, then north, to the Irtish in the southwest-central Russian S.F.S.R.
Ish·i·kar·i Bay (ē′shē-kä′rē). An inlet of the Sea of Japan extending about 50 miles into western Hokkaido, Japan.
Ish·ma·el[1] (ĭsh′mē-əl). The son of Abraham by Sarah's handmaid, Hagar. Genesis 16:1–16. [Late Latin *Ismaēl,* from Hebrew *Yishmā'ēl,* "God hears" : *yishmā,* he hears, from *shāma',* he heard + *'Ēl,* God.]
Ish·ma·el[2] (ĭsh′mē-əl) *n.* An outcast. [From ISHMAEL.]
Ish·ma·el·ite (ĭsh′mē-ə-līt′) *n.* **1.** One of a group of desert-dwelling people believed by the ancient Hebrews to be descended from Ishmael. **2.** One at odds with society. —**Ish′ma·el·it′ism′** *n.*
Ish·tar (ĭsh′tär′). *Assyrian & Babylonian Mythology.* The goddess of love and fertility, and also of war; identified with the Phoenician Astarte. [Akkadian *Ishtar,* akin to Hebrew *'Ashtōreth,* ASHTORETH.]

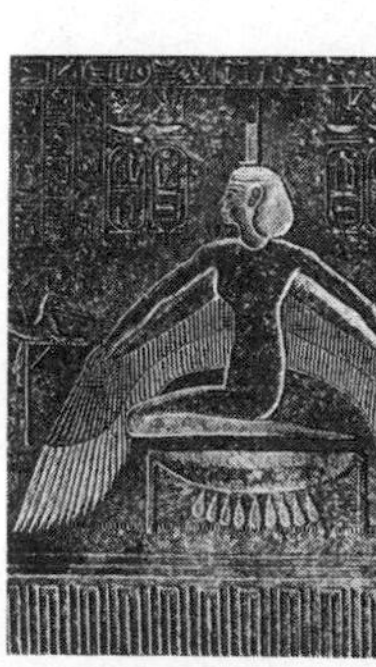
Isis[1]
Detail from relief on sarcophagus of Rameses III

i·sin·glass (ī′zĭng-glăs′, -gläs′, ī′zən-) *n.* **1.** A transparent, almost pure gelatin prepared from the air bladder of certain fishes, as the sturgeon. **2. Muscovite** *(see).* [Alteration (influenced by GLASS) of obsolete Dutch *huizenblas,* from Middle Dutch *huusblase* : *huus,* sturgeon, from Germanic *hūsōn-* (unattested) + *blase,* bladder (see **bhle-[2]** in Appendix*).]
I·sis[1] (ī′sĭs). An ancient Egyptian goddess of fertility and sister and wife of Osiris.
I·sis[2]. See **Oxford.**
Is·kar (ĭs′kär′). Also **Is·ker** (ĭs′kər). A river rising in northwest-central Bulgaria and flowing 249 miles north, through Sofia, then northeast to the Danube.
Is·ken·de·run (ĭs-kĕn′də-ro͞on′). Formerly **Al·ex·an·dret·ta** (ăl′ĭg-zăn-drĕt′ə). A port of southern Turkey, on the northeastern corner of the Mediterranean. Population, 62,000.
isl. island.
Is·la de Pas·cu·a. The Spanish name for **Easter Island.**
Is·la de Pi·nos. The Spanish name for the Isle of **Pines.**
Is·lam (ĭs′ləm, ĭz′-, ĭs-läm′) *n.* **1.** A religion based upon the teachings of the prophet Mohammed, believing in one God (Allah) and in Paradise and Hell, and having a body of law put

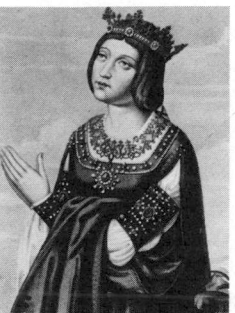

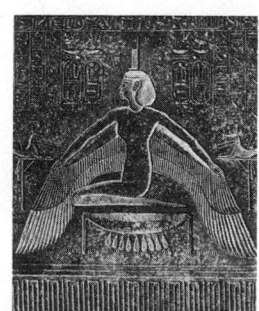

forth in the Koran and the Sunna; the Moslem religion.
2. a. All those nations of the world, specifically in Asia and Africa, whose populations are Moslem. **b.** Islamic civilization. **3.** Moslems collectively. [Arabic *islām*, "submission (to God)," from *aslama*, he surrendered, he resigned himself, from *salama*, he was safe. See **slm** in Appendix.*] **—Is·lam·ic** *adj.*

Is·lam·a·bad (ĭs-lä′mə-bäd′, ĭz-). The capital of Pakistan, located in northern West Pakistan near Rawalpindi. Population, 50,000.

Is·lam·ize (ĭs′lə-mīz′) *tr.v.* **-ized, -izing, -izes.** To convert to Islam.

is·land (ī′lənd) *n.* **1.** *Abbr.* **i., I., is., Is., isl.** A land mass, especially one smaller than a continent, entirely surrounded by water. **2.** Anything completely isolated or regarded as resembling such an isolated land mass. **3.** *Anatomy.* A tissue or cluster of cells separated from surrounding tissue by a groove or differing from surrounding tissue in structure. **—tr.v. islanded, -landing, -lands.** To make into or as into an island; insulate. [Middle English *eland, ilond, ylond* (influenced by ISLE), Old English *ī(e)gland, īland.* See **akwā-** in Appendix.*]

Ís·land. The Icelandic name for **Iceland.**

is·land·er (ī′lən-dər) *n.* An inhabitant of an island.

islands of Lang·er·hans (läng′ər-häns′). Also **islets of Lang·er·hans.** Irregular masses of small cells that lie in the interstitial tissue of the pancreas and secrete insulin. [After Paul *Langerhans* (1847–1888), German physician.]

Is·las Ba·le·ar·es. The Spanish name for the **Balearic Islands.**

Is·las Ca·nar·i·as. The Spanish name for the **Canary Islands.**

Is·las Mal·vi·nas. The Spanish name for the **Falkland Islands.**

Is·lay (ī′lā). An island, 234 square miles in area, at the southern extremity of the Inner Hebrides, Scotland.

isle (īl) *n. Abbr.* **i., I.** An island, especially a small one. Used poetically, and in place names. [Middle English *i(s)le,* from Old French, from Latin *īnsula†.*]

Isle of E·ly. See **Ely, Isle of.**

Isle of Man. See **Man, Isle of.**

Isle of Pines. See **Pines, Isle of.**

Isle of Wight. See **Wight, Isle of.**

Isle Roy·ale (roi′əl). An island of Michigan occupying 209 square miles in northwestern Lake Superior.

Isles of the Blest. The Hesperides.

is·let (ī′lĭt) *n.* A little island.

Is·ling·ton (ĭz′lĭng-tən). A borough of London, England, comprising the former administrative divisions of Islington and Finsbury. Population, 262,000.

ism (ĭz′əm) *n. Informal.* A distinctive doctrine, system, or theory. Generally used disparagingly. [From -ISM.]

–ism. Indicates: **1.** An action, practice, or process; for example, **terrorism, favoritism. 2.** A state or condition of being; for example, **pauperism, parallelism. 3.** A characteristic behavior or quality; for example, **heroism, individualism. 4.** A distinctive usage or feature, especially of language; for example, **malapropism, Latinism. 5.** A doctrine, theory, system, or principle; for example, **Platonism, expressionism, capitalism, Platonism.** [Middle English *-isme,* from Old French, from Latin *-ismus,* from Greek *-ismos,* suffix used to form nouns of action from verbs in *-izein,* -IZE.]

Is·ma·il·i, Is·ma·i·li (ĭs-mā-ĭl′ē) *n.* Also **Is·ma·i·li·an** (ĭs′mä-ĭl′ē-ən). A Moslem of a Shiah sect. [Arabic *Ismaʿīliy,* after *Ismaʿil* (died A.D. 760), son of the sixth Imam Jafar.]

Is·ma·i·li·a (ĭs′mä-ē′lē-ä). Also **Is·ma·i·li·ya** (-yä). A city of northeastern Egypt, on the Suez Canal. Population, 285,000.

isn't (ĭz′ənt). Contraction of *is not.*

iso-, is-. Indicates: **1.** Equal, identical, or similar; for example, **isallobar, isogon. 2.** *Chemistry.* Isomeric; for example, **isopropyl alcohol.** [Greek, from *isos†,* equal.]

i·so·ag·glu·ti·na·tion (ī′sō-ə-glōōt′n-ā′shən) *n.* The agglutination of an agglutinogen by the serum of another individual of the same species.

i·so·ag·glu·tin·in (ī′sō-ə-glōōt′n-ĭn) *n.* An isoantibody that causes agglutination of cells. [ISO- + AGGLUTININ.]

i·so·ag·glu·tin·o·gen (ī′sō-ăg′lōō-tĭn′ə-jən) *n.* An isoantigen that on exposure to its isoantibody induces agglutination of cells to which it is attached. [ISOAGGLUTIN(IN) + -GEN.]

i·so·an·ti·bod·y (ī′sō-ăn′tē-bŏd′ē) *n., pl.* **-ies.** An antibody that occurs in only some individuals of a species and reacts specifically with the corresponding isoantigen.

i·so·an·ti·gen (ī′sō-ăn′tĭ-jən, -jĕn′) *n.* An antigen that occurs in only some individuals of a species and never in those having cells that contain the corresponding isoantibody.

i·so·bar (ī′sə-bär′) *n.* **1.** A line on a map connecting points of equal pressure. **2.** Any of two or more nuclides having the same mass number but different atomic numbers. [ISO- + Greek *baros,* weight (see **gwer-²** in Appendix*).] **—i′so·bar′ic** *adj.*

i·so·chro·mat·ic (ī′sə-krō-măt′ĭk) *adj.* **1. a.** Having the same color. **b.** Of uniform color. **2.** *Photography.* Orthochromatic.

i·soch·ro·nal (ī-sŏk′rə-nəl) *adj.* Also **i·soch·ro·nous** (-nəs), **i·so·chron·ic** (ī′sō-krŏn′ĭk). **1.** Equal in duration. **2.** Characterized by or occurring at equal intervals of time. [From Greek *isokhronos,* ISOCHRONOUS.] **—i·soch′ro·nal·ly** *adv.* **—i·soch′ro·nism′** *n.*

i·soch·ro·nize (ī-sŏk′rə-nīz′) *tr.v.* **-nized, -nizing, -nizes.** To make isochronal.

i·soch·ro·ous (ī-sŏk′rō-əs) *adj.* Having the same color throughout. [ISO- + -CHROUS.]

i·so·cli·nal (ī′sə-klī′nəl) *adj.* Also **i·so·clin·ic** (ī′sə-klĭn′ĭk). Having the same inclination or dip. *—n.* Also **i·so·clin·ic.** An isoclinic line.

i·so·cline (ī′sə-klīn′) *n.* An anticline or syncline with strata so

tightly folded as to have the same dip. [ISO- + -CLINE.]

isoclinic line. A line on a map connecting points of equal magnetic dip.

i·so·di·a·met·ric (ī′sō-dī′ə-mĕt′rĭk) *adj.* Having equal diameters.

i·so·di·mor·phism (ī′sō-dī-môr′fīz′əm) *n.* Isomorphism between crystalline forms of two dimorphic substances.

i·so·dy·nam·ic (ī′sō-dī-năm′ĭk) *adj.* Having equal force or strength.

i·so·e·lec·tric (ī′sō-ĭ-lĕk′trĭk) *adj.* Having equal electric potential.

i·so·e·lec·tron·ic (ī′sō-ĭ-lĕk′trŏn′ĭk) *adj.* Having equal numbers of electrons or the same electronic configuration.

i·so·gam·ete (ī′sō-găm′ēt′, -gə-mēt′) *n.* A gamete that is morphologically indistinguishable from one with which it unites.

i·sog·a·my (ī-sŏg′ə-mē) *n.* Conjugation of isogametes or of identical cells. [ISO- + -GAMY.] **—i·sog′a·mous** *adj.*

i·so·gloss (ī′sə-glôs′, -glŏs′) *n.* A geographical boundary line delimiting the area in which a given linguistic feature occurs. [ISO- + Greek *glōssa,* language, tongue (see **glōgh-** in Appendix*).] **—i′so·gloss′al** *adj.*

i·so·gon (ī′sə-gŏn′) *n.* An equiangular polygon. [ISO- + -GON.]

i·so·gon·ic (ī′sə-gŏn′ĭk) *adj.* Also **i·sog·o·nal** (ī-sŏg′ə-nəl). Having equal angles. *—n.* Also **i·sog·o·nal.** An isogonic line.

isogonic line. A line on a map connecting points of equal magnetic declination.

i·so·gram (ī′sə-grăm′) *n.* A line on a map, chart, or graph connecting points of equal value. [ISO- + -GRAM.]

i·so·hel (ī′sə-hĕl′) *n.* A line drawn on a map connecting points receiving equal sunlight. [ISO- + Greek *hēlios,* sun (see **sāwel-** in Appendix*).]

i·so·hy·et (ī′sə-hī′ət) *n.* A line drawn on a map connecting points receiving equal rainfall. [ISO- + Greek *huetos,* rain (see **seu-⁴** in Appendix*).]

i·so·la·ble (ī′sə-lə-bəl, ĭs′ə-) *adj.* Capable of being isolated.

i·so·late (ī′sə-lāt′, ĭs′ə-) *tr.v.* **-lated, -lating, -lates. 1.** To separate from a group or whole and set apart. **2.** To place in quarantine. **3.** *Chemistry.* To obtain (a substance) in an uncombined form. **4.** To render free of external influence; insulate. [Back-formation from *isolated,* from French *isolé,* from Italian *isolato,* from Late Latin *īnsulātus,* converted into an island, from Latin *insula,* island. See **isle.**] **—i′so·la′tor** (-lā′tər) *n.*

i·so·la·tion (ī′sə-lā′shən, ĭs′ə-) *n.* **1.** The act of isolating. **2.** The condition of being isolated. **—See Synonyms at solitude.**

i·so·la·tion·ism (ī′sə-lā′shə-nĭz′əm, ĭs′ə-) *n.* A national policy of remaining aloof from political or economic entanglements with other countries. **—i′so·la′tion·ist** *n. & adj.*

I·solde. Variant of **Iseult.**

I·so·le E·ga·di. The Italian name for the **Egadi Islands.**

i·so·leu·cine (ī′sō-lōō′sēn′) *n.* An essential amino acid, C_6H_{13}-NO_2, isomeric with leucine.

i·so·mag·net·ic (ī′sō-măg-nĕt′ĭk) *adj.* Designating or pertaining to points of equal magnetic induction.

i·so·mer (ī′sə-mər) *n.* **1.** *Chemistry.* **a.** A compound having the same percentage composition and molecular weight as another compound but differing in chemical or physical properties. **b.** Such a compound so differing because of the manner of linkage of its constituent atoms. Also called "structural isomer." **c.** Such a compound so differing because of the manner of arrangement of its constituent atoms in space. Also called "stereoisomer." **d.** A stereoisomer manifesting one of two structures that rotate the plane of polarization of polarized light either to the left or to the right. Also called "optical isomer." **e.** A stereoisomer having no effect on polarized light but exhibiting isomerism because of a structural asymmetry about a double bond in the molecule. Also called "geometric isomer." **2.** *Physics.* An atom the nucleus of which can exist in any of several bound excited states for a measurable period of time. In this sense, also called "nuclear isomer." [Greek *isomerēs,* equally divided, equal : ISO- + *meros,* part (see **smer-²** in Appendix*).] **—i′so·mer′ic** *adj.*

i·som·er·ism (ī-sŏm′ə-rĭz′əm) *n.* **1.** The phenomenon of the existence of isomers. **2.** The complex of chemical and physical phenomena characteristic of or attributable to isomers. **3.** The state or condition of being an isomer.

i·som·er·ous (ī-sŏm′ər-əs) *adj.* **1.** Having an equal number of parts, as organs or markings. **2.** Having or designating floral whorls with equal numbers of parts. [ISO- + -MEROUS.]

i·so·met·ric (ī′sə-mĕt′rĭk) *adj.* Also **i·so·met·ri·cal** (-rĭ-kəl). **1.** Of or exhibiting equality in dimensions or measurements. **2.** *Crystallography.* Of or being a crystal system of three equal and mutually orthogonal axes. **3.** *Physiology.* Of or involving muscular contraction occurring when the ends of the muscle are fixed in place so that significant increases in tension occur without appreciable increases in length. *—n.* **1.** A line connecting isometric points. **2.** *Plural.* Isometric exercise. Used with a singular verb. [From Greek *isometros,* of equal measure : ISO- + *metron,* measure (see **mē-²** in Appendix*).]

isometric exercise. Exercise involving isometric contraction; isometrics.

i·so·me·tro·pi·a (ī′sō-mə-trō′pē-ə) *n.* Equality of refraction in both eyes. [New Latin : Greek *isometros,* of equal measure, ISOMETRIC + -OPIA.]

i·som·e·try (ī-sŏm′ə-trē) *n.* **1.** Equality of measure. **2.** *Geography.* Equality of elevation above sea level. [ISO- + -METRY.]

i·so·morph (ī′sə-môrf′) *n.* An object, organism, or group exhibiting isomorphism. [ISO- + -MORPH.]

i·so·mor·phism (ī′sə-môr′fĭz′əm) *n.* **1.** *Biology.* Similarity in form, as in different kinds of organisms. **2.** *Mathematics.* **a.** A one-to-one correspondence between the elements of two sets such that the result of an operation on elements of one set corresponds to the result of the analogous operation on their images in the other set. **b.** A mapping * of a group G onto another group H such that $(ab)^* = (a^*)(b^*)$ for all a, b in G. **3.** *Crystallography.* The existence or an instance of the existence of two or more different substances having closely similar crystalline structure, crystalline dimensions, and chemical composition. —**i'so·mor'phic, i'so·mor'phous** *adj.*

i·so·oc·tane (ī'sō-ŏk'tān') *n.* A highly flammable liquid, C_8H_{18}, used to determine the octane numbers of fuels.

i·so·pi·es·tic (ī'sō-pī-ĕs'tĭk) *adj.* Marked by or indicating equal pressure; isobaric. —*n.* An isobar. [ISO- + Greek *piestos,* capable of being compressed, from *piezein,* to press tight, compress (see **sed-**[1] in Appendix*).]

i·so·pod (ī'sə-pŏd') *n.* Any of numerous crustaceans of the order Isopoda, which includes the sow bugs and gribbles. —*adj.* Of or belonging to the Isopoda. [New Latin *Isopoda,* "those having pairs of legs" : ISO- + *-poda,* plural of -POD.]

i·so·prene (ī'sə-prēn') *n.* A colorless volatile liquid, C_5H_8, used chiefly to make synthetic rubber. [ISO- + PR(OPYL) + -ENE.]

i·so·pro·pyl alcohol (ī'sə-prō'pəl). *Abbr.* **IPA** A clear, colorless, mobile flammable liquid, C_3H_8O, used in antifreeze compounds, lotions and cosmetics, and as a solvent for gums, shellac, and essential oils. [ISO- + PROPYL.]

i·sos·ce·les (ī-sŏs'ə-lēz') *adj.* *Geometry.* Having two equal sides: *isosceles triangle; isosceles trapezoid.* [Late Latin *isoscelēs,* from Greek *isoskelēs,* "having equal legs" : ISO- + *skelos,* leg (see **skel-**[3] in Appendix*).]

i·so·seis·mic (ī'sō-sīz'mĭk) *adj.* Also **i·so·seis·mal** (-məl). Of, pertaining to, or exhibiting equal seismic intensities.

i·sos·mot·ic (ī'sŏz-mŏt'ĭk, ī'sŏs-) *adj.* Of or exhibiting equal osmotic pressure. Also "isotonic." [IS(O)- + OSMOTIC.]

i·so·spin (ī'sə-spĭn') *n.* *Symbol* **I** A quantum number related to the number of charge states of a subatomic particle by the equation $2I + 1 = M$, where M is the number of such states. Also called "isotopic spin." [Short for *isotopic spin.*]

i·sos·ta·sy (ī-sŏs'tə-sē) *n.* Any equilibrium condition resulting from isotropic equalization of pressure. [ISO- + Greek *stasis,* a standing, standstill (see **stā-** in Appendix*).]

i·so·therm (ī'sə-thûrm') *n.* A line drawn on a weather map or chart linking all points having identical mean temperature for a given period or identical temperature at a given time. [French *isotherme,* having the same temperature : ISO- + -THERM.]

i·so·ther·mal (ī'sə-thûr'məl) *adj.* **1.** Of, pertaining to, or indicating equal temperatures. **2.** Of or designating changes of pressure and volume at constant temperature. **3.** Of or pertaining to an isotherm. —*n.* An isotherm.

i·so·ton·ic (ī'sə-tŏn'ĭk) *adj.* **1.** Of equal tension. **2.** **Isosmotic** *(see).* [ISO- + Greek *tonos,* tension, stretching, TONE.]

i·so·tone (ī'sə-tōn') *n.* One of two or more atoms, the nuclei of which have the same number of neutrons but different numbers of protons. [ISO- + Greek *tonos,* stretching, TONE.]

i·so·tope (ī'sə-tōp') *n.* One of two or more atoms, the nuclei of which have the same number of protons but different numbers of neutrons. Compare **nuclide.** [ISO- + Greek *topos,* place, "position in the periodic table" (see **topic**).] —**i'so·top'ic** (-tŏp'ĭk) *adj.* —**i'so·top'ic·al·ly** *adv.*

i·so·trop·ic (ī'sə-trŏp'ĭk) *adj.* Identical in all directions; invariant with respect to direction. [ISO- + -TROPIC.] —**i·sot'ro·py** (ī-sŏt'rə-pē), **i·sot'ro·pism'** (-pĭz'əm) *n.*

Is·pa·han. See **Isfahan.**

Is·ra·el[1] (ĭz'rē-əl). **1.** *Abbr.* **Isr.** A republic, founded in 1948, occupying 7,993 square miles in Palestine on the eastern seaboard of the Mediterranean. Population, 2,565,000. Capital, Jerusalem. **2.** The northern kingdom of ten tribes founded by Jeroboam in 933 B.C. and destroyed by the Assyrians in 721 B.C. —**Is'ra·el** *adj.*

Usage: English-speaking Israelis often prefer the adjective *Israel* to denote "pertaining to the state of Israel." *Israeli,* however, is perhaps better established in the English-speaking world at large in this sense, and more especially so in cultural rather than political contexts; it is the only noun denoting "a native or inhabitant of the state of Israel."

Is·ra·el[2] (ĭz'rē-əl) *n.* **1.** The descendants of Jacob. **2.** The whole Hebrew people, past, present, and future, regarded as the chosen people of Jehovah by virtue of the covenant of Jacob. **3.** The Christian church, regarded as the heir to the ancient covenant. [Latin *Israēl,* from Greek, from Hebrew *Yisrā'ēl,* the name given to Jacob by the angel with whom he wrestled (Genesis 32:28), perhaps literally "God struggles" : *sārāh,* he fought or contended + *Ēl,* God.]

Is·ra·el[3]. A name of the patriarch **Jacob** *(see).*

Is·rae·li (ĭz-rā'lē) *adj.* Of or relating to the state of Israel or its people. See Usage note at **Israel.** —*n., pl.* **Israeli** or **-lis.** A native or inhabitant of the state of Israel.

Is·ra·el·ite (ĭz'rē-ə-līt') *n.* **1.** A Hebrew. **2.** A member of any of various Christian groups regarded as heirs of the covenant of Jacob. —*adj.* Also **Is·ra·el·it·ic** (ĭz'rē-əl-ĭt'ĭk). Of or relating to Israel or the Israelites.

Is·sa·char[1] (ĭs'ə-kär'). One of the patriarchs of Israel, son of Jacob and Leah. Genesis 30:18.

Is·sa·char[2] (ĭs'ə-kär') *n.* The tribe descended from Issachar.

Is·sei (ēs'sā') *n., pl.* **Issei** or **-seis.** A Japanese immigrant to the United States or Canada. Compare **Nisei, Kibei.** [Japanese, "first generation," from Chinese (Mandarin) *i*[1]*shih*[4] : *i*[1], one, first + *shih*[4], lifetime, generation.]

is·su·a·ble (ĭsh'ōō-ə-bəl) *adj.* **1.** Capable of issuing or being issued. **2.** Capable of being established as an issue; open to debate or litigation. **3.** Authorized for issue.

is·su·ance (ĭsh'ōō-əns) *n.* An act of issuing; issue.

is·su·ant (ĭsh'ōō-ənt) *adj.* **1.** Emerging. **2.** *Heraldry.* Designating an animal with only the upper part depicted.

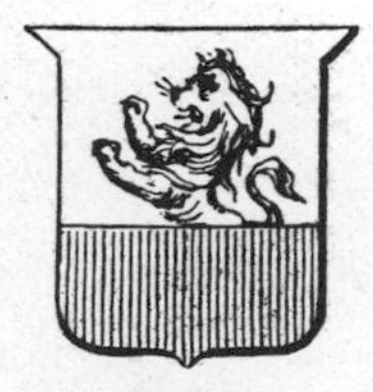

issuant
A lion issuant

is·sue (ĭsh'ōō) *n.* **1. a.** An act or instance of flowing, passing, or giving out. **b.** An act of circulating, distributing, or publishing by an office or official group: *government issue of new bonds.* **2.** Something produced, published, or offered, as: **a.** An item or set of items, as stamps or coins, made available at one time by an office or bureau. **b.** A single copy of a periodical. **c.** A distinct set of copies of an edition of a book distinguished from others of that edition by variations in the printed matter. **d.** The result of an action. **e.** Proceeds from estates or fines. **f.** Something proceeding from a specified source: *suspicions that were the issue of a deranged mind.* **3.** Offspring; progeny. **4. a.** A point of discussion, debate, or dispute. **b.** A matter of wide public concern. **c.** The essential point; crux: *the real issue.* **d.** A culminating point leading to a decision: *bring a case to an issue.* **5.** A place of egress; an outlet: *a lake with no issue to the sea.* **6.** *Pathology.* **a.** A discharge, as of blood. **b.** A suppurating sore. **7.** *Archaic.* Termination; close. —**at issue. 1.** In question; in dispute. **2.** At variance; in disagreement. —**join issue. 1.** To enter into controversy. **2.** *Law.* To submit an issue jointly for decision. —**take issue.** To take an opposing point of view; disagree. —*v.* **issued, -suing, -sues.** —*intr.* **1.** To go or come out. **2.** To accrue as proceeds or profit: *Little money issued from the stocks.* **3.** To be born or be descended. **4.** To be circulated or published. **5.** To spring or result from. **6.** To terminate or result in. —*tr.* **1.** To cause to flow out; emit. **2.** To circulate or distribute in an official capacity: *The school issued uniforms to the players.* **3.** To publish. [Middle English, from Old French *(e)issue,* from Vulgar Latin *exūta* (unattested), "exit," altered from Latin *exita,* feminine of *exitus,* past participle of *exire,* to go out : *ex-,* out + *ire,* to go (see **ei-**[1] in Appendix*).] —**is'su·er** *n.*

Is·sus (ĭs'əs). The site, near Iskenderun, Turkey, of a battle in which Alexander the Great defeated the Persians in 333 B.C.

Is·syk-Kul (ē'sĭk-kōōl'). A lake occupying 2,395 square miles in the Tien Shan Mountains of the northeastern Kirghiz S.S.R.

–ist. Indicates: **1.** A person who does, makes, produces, operates, plays, or sells a specified thing; for example, **dramatist, lobbyist, motorist, organist, tobacconist. 2.** A person who is skilled, trained, or employed in a specified field; for example, **machinist, radiologist, industrialist. 3.** An adherent or proponent of a doctrine, system, or school of thought; for example, **anarchist, federalist, Platonist. 4.** A person characterized by a certain trait or predilection; for example, **romanticist, sadist.** [Middle English *-iste,* from Old French, from Latin *-ista, -istēs,* from Greek *-istēs,* agential suffix for verbs in *-izein,* -IZE.]

IST Airport code for Istanbul, Turkey.

Is·tan·bul (ĭs'tăn-bōōl', ĭs'tän-). Also **Stam·bul** (stäm-bōōl'), **Stam·boul.** Formerly **Con·stan·ti·no·ple** (kŏn'stăn-tə-nō'pəl). Originally **By·zan·ti·um** (bĭ-zăn'shē-əm, -tē-əm). The largest city of Turkey, located on the European side of the Bosporus and the Sea of Marmara. Population, 1,467,000.

isth·mi·an (ĭs'mē-ən) *adj.* **1.** Of, pertaining to, or forming an isthmus. **2.** *Capital* **I.** Of or pertaining to the Isthmus of Corinth, especially with regard to the biennial pan-Hellenic games held there in antiquity. **3.** *Capital* **I.** Of or pertaining to the Isthmus of Panama.

isth·mus (ĭs'məs) *n., pl.* **-muses** or **-mi** (-mī'). **1.** A narrow strip of land connecting two larger masses of land. **2.** *Anatomy.* **a.** A narrow strip of tissue joining two larger organs or parts of an organ. **b.** A narrow passage connecting two larger cavities. [Latin, from Greek *isthmos*†.]

is·tle (ĭs'lē, ĭst'-) *n.* Also **ix·tle.** A plant, **pita** *(see),* or its fiber. [Mexican Spanish *ixtle,* from Nahuatl *ichtli.*]

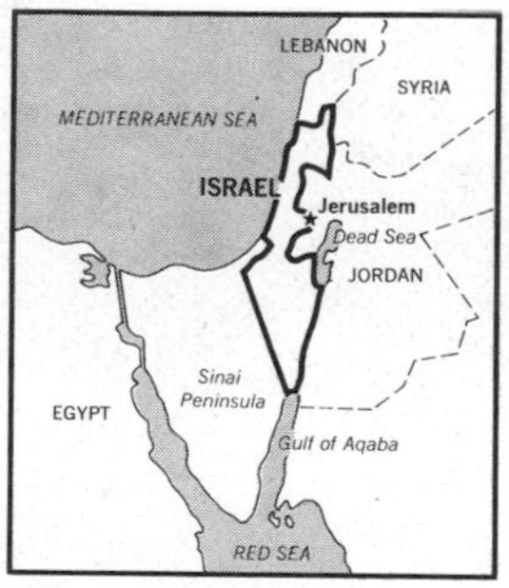

Israel[1]

Is·tri·a (ĭs'trē-ə). Also **Is·tri·an Peninsula** (-ən). A peninsula, 1,908 square miles in area, in Italy and Yugoslavia, extending 60 miles south from Trieste into the Adriatic.

it (ĭt) *pron.* The third person singular pronoun, neuter gender. **1.** Used to represent the thing or nonhuman being last mentioned or implied. **2.** Used without antecedent as an expletive: *It is raining. Live it up.* **3.** Used to represent a word, phrase, or clause that follows: *It is he. It's certain that he'll win.* **4.** Used to represent a situation, topic for consideration, or any other item of discourse that the speaker assumes the hearer will comprehend without antecedent: *Always try to do it right the first time.* **5.** Used to represent all the experience that can be endured or desired. *He'd had it; he quit.* **6.** Used to represent the crucial moment upon which an outcome depends: *This is it! he thought as the plane's engine sputtered.* **7.** Used to represent a human life: *The old man's eyes closed; it was all over.* **8. a.** Used to represent desirable qualities: *They had it all over the other team.* **b.** *Informal.* Used to represent the best or ultimate: *That steak was really it!* [Middle English *(h)it, (h)yt,* Old English *hit, hyt.* See **ko-** in Appendix.*]

It. Italian; Italy.

it·a·col·u·mite (ĭt'ə-kŏl'yə-mīt') *n.* A variety of sandstone that is flexible when cut into thin slabs. [Found in *Itacolumi,* a mountain in Brazil.]

ital. italic.

Ital. Italian; Italy.

I·ta·li·a. The Italian name for **Italy.**

I·tal·ian (ĭ-tăl'yən) *adj. Abbr.* **It., Ital.** Pertaining to Italy, its people, or their language. —*n. Abbr.* **It., Ital. 1.** A native or citizen of Italy, or a person of Italian descent. **2.** The Romance language of Italy and one of the three official languages of

Switzerland. [Middle English, from Italian *Italiano*, from *Italia*, ITALY.]

I·tal·ian·ate (ĭ-tăl′yə-nāt′, -nĭt) *adj.* Italian in character. [Italian *Italianato*, from *Italiano*, ITALIAN.]

Italian hand. A forward-slanting script employed by 15th-century Italian calligraphers and used as a model for modern English penmanship. —**fine Italian hand.** Subtlety; cunning; craftiness.

I·tal·ian·ism (ĭ-tăl′yə-nĭz′əm) *n.* **1.** An Italian custom, trait, or expression. **2.** A quality characteristic of Italy or its people.

I·tal·ian·ize (ĭ-tăl′yə-nīz′) *v.* **-ized, -izing, -izes.** —*tr.* To give an Italian aspect to. —*intr.* To become Italian; adopt Italian speech, manners, or customs. —**I·tal′ian·i·za′tion** *n.*

Italian So·ma·li·land (sō-mä′lē-lănd′). *Italian* **So·ma·li·a I·ta·li·a·na** (sō-mä′lyä ē-tä-lyä′nä). A former Italian colony, occupying 194,000 square miles in eastern Africa; united with former British Somaliland in 1960 to form the independent Republic of Somalia.

Italian sonnet. A Petrarchan sonnet.

i·tal·ic (ĭ-tăl′ĭk, ī-tăl′-) *adj. Abbr.* **ital.** Being a style of printing type patterned upon a Renaissance script with the letters slanting to the right, now chiefly used to set off a word or passage within a text printed in roman type, indicating that the word or passage is emphatic, or in a foreign language, or has a structurally independent function within the main text: *This sentence is printed in italic type.* Compare **roman.** —*n.* Italic print or typeface. Usually used in the plural, sometimes with a singular verb. [Introduced in the Aldine Virgil printed in Venice in 1501, which was dedicated to Italy.]

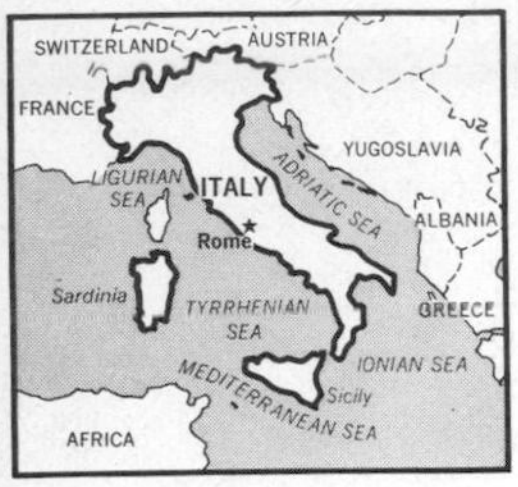

Italy

I·tal·ic (ĭ-tăl′ĭk) *adj.* **1.** Of or pertaining to ancient Italy or its peoples. **2.** Of or pertaining to a branch of Indo-European languages that includes the Latino-Faliscan and Osco-Umbrian groups. —*n.* The Italic branch of the Indo-European family of languages. [Latin *Italicus*, from Greek *Italikos*, from *Italia*, Italy, from Latin. See **Italy.**]

I·tal·i·cism (ĭ-tăl′ĭ-sĭz′əm) *n.* Italianism; especially, a word or idiom borrowed from or suggestive of the Italian language.

i·tal·i·cize (ĭ-tăl′ĭ-sīz′) *v.* **-cized, -cizing, -cizes.** —*tr.* **1.** To print in italic type. **2.** To underscore (written matter) with a single line to indicate italics. —*intr.* To print or put words in italics; use italics. —**i·tal′i·ci·za′tion** *n.*

It·a·ly (ĭt′ə-lē). *Italian* **I·ta·li·a** (ē-tä′lyä). *Abbr.* **It., Ital.** A republic, 116,224 square miles in area, of southern Europe, projecting into the Mediterranean Sea. Population, 50,849,000. Capital, Rome. [Latin *Italia*, from Oscan *Viteliu!.*]

I·tas·ca (ī-tăs′kə). A lake occupying two square miles in northwest-central Minnesota; the source of the Mississippi.

itch (ĭch) *n.* **1.** A skin sensation causing a desire to scratch. **2.** Any of various contagious skin diseases marked by intense irritation, eruptions, and itching. **3.** A restless desire or craving for something: *"I am tormented with an everlasting itch for things remote."* (Melville). —*v.* **itched, itching, itches.** —*intr.* **1.** To feel, have, or produce an itch; have a desire to scratch. **2.** To have a persistent restless craving. —*tr.* To cause to itch. [Middle English *(y)icchen*, Old English *giccan*, from Germanic *juk-* (unattested).]

itch mite. A parasitic mite, *Sarcoptes scabiei*, that causes scabies.

itch·y (ĭch′ē) *adj.* **-ier, -iest.** Having or causing an itching sensation: *"that itchy particular red velvet that one associates with hot days on a train"* (Truman Capote). —**itch′i·ness** *n.*

-ite[1]. Indicates: **1.** A person who is a native or resident of a specified place; for example, **New Jerseyite. 2.** An adherent of someone specified; for example, **Luddite. 3.** *Biology.* A part of an organ or body; for example, **somite. 4.** A mineral or rock; for example, **graphite. 5.** A commercial product; for example, **Lucite.** [Middle English, from Old French, from Latin *-ita*, *-itēs*, from Greek *-itēs.*]

-ite[2]. Indicates a salt or ester of an acid whose adjectival denomination ends in *-ous;* for example, **sulfite.** [French, arbitrarily altered from -ATE.]

i·tem (ī′təm) *n.* **1.** A single article or unit included in a collection, enumeration, or series and specified separately. **2.** A clause of a bill, charter, or other document. **3.** An entry in an account. **4. a.** A bit of information; a detail. **b.** A short piece in a newspaper or magazine. **5.** A member of a set of minimal units: *a lexical item.* —*tr.v.* **itemed, iteming, items.** *Archaic.* To compute. —*adv.* Also; likewise. Used to introduce each article in an enumeration or list. [Middle English, also, likewise, from Latin, from *ita*, so. See **i-** in Appendix.*]

i·tem·ize (ī′tə-mīz′) *tr.v.* **-ized, -izing, -izes.** To set down item by item; to list. —**i′tem·i·za′tion** *n.* —**i′tem·iz′er** *n.*

I·té·nez. See **Guaporé.**

it·er·ance (ĭt′ər-əns) *n.* Iteration.

it·er·ant (ĭt′ər-ənt) *adj.* Iterating; repeating.

it·er·ate (ĭt′ə-rāt′) *tr.v.* **-ated, -ating, -ates.** To say or perform again; repeat. [Latin *iterāre*, from *iterum*, again. See **i-** in Appendix.*] —**it′er·a′tion** *n.*

it·er·a·tive (ĭt′ə-rā′tĭv, -ər-ə-tĭv) *adj.* **1.** Repetitious. **2.** *Grammar.* Frequentative.

Ith·a·ca (ĭth′ə-kə). **1.** *Greek* **I·thá·kē** (ē-thä′kyē). An island of Greece, 36 square miles in area, in the Ionian Sea. **2.** A city and manufacturing center of south-central New York State. Population, 29,000.

I·thunn, I·thun (ē′thōōn′). Also **I·dun** (ē′thōōn′). *Norse Mythology.* The wife of Bragi, goddess of youth and spring. [Old Norse *Idhunn*, probably from *idh*, again, anew. See **i-** in Appendix.*]

ith·y·phal·lic (ĭth′ə-făl′ĭk) *adj.* **1.** Of or pertaining to the phallus carried in the ancient festival of Bacchus. **2.** Relating to or composed in the trochaic meter of the hymns to Bacchus. **3.** Having the penis erect. Said of graphic and sculptural representations. **4.** Lascivious; salacious; obscene. —*n.* **1.** A poem in ithyphallic meter. **2.** An indecent or obscene verse. [Late Latin *īthyphallicus*, from Greek *ithuphallikos*, from *ithuphallos*, erect phallus : *ithus*†, straight + *phallos*, phallus (see **bhel-**[2] in Appendix*).]

I·tim·bi·ri (ē′tĭm-bîr′ē). A river rising in the northeast-central Democratic Republic of the Congo (Kinshasa) and flowing 350 miles west, then southwest, to the Congo River.

i·tin·er·an·cy (ī-tĭn′ər-ən-sē, ĭ-tĭn′-) *n.* Also **i·tin·er·a·cy** (-ər-ə-sē). A state or system of itinerating, especially in the role or office of public speaker, minister, or judge.

i·tin·er·ant (ī-tĭn′ər-ənt, ĭ-tĭn′-) *adj.* Traveling from place to place, especially to perform some duty or work: *an itinerant judge; itinerant labor.* —*n.* One who so travels. [Late Latin *itinerāns*, present participle of *itinerārī*, ITINERATE.]

i·tin·er·ar·y (ī-tĭn′ə-rĕr′ē, ĭ-tĭn′-) *n.* **1.** A route or proposed route of a journey. **2.** An account or record of a journey. **3.** A travelers' guidebook. —*adj.* **1.** Of or pertaining to a journey or to a route. **2.** Traveling from place to place; itinerant. [Middle English *itinerarie*, from Late Latin *itinerārium*, course of travel, from *itinerārius*, of traveling, from Latin *iter* (stem *itiner-*), journey. See **ei-**[1] in Appendix.*]

i·tin·er·ate (ī-tĭn′ə-rāt′, ĭ-tĭn′-) *intr.v.* **-ated, -ating, -ates.** *Rare.* To travel from place to place. [Late Latin *itinerārī*, from Latin *iter* (stem *itiner-*), journey. See **itinerary.**] —**i·tin′er·a′tion** *n.*

-itis. Indicates inflammation of or inflammatory disease; for example, **laryngitis, bronchitis.** [New Latin, from Greek *-itis*, feminine of *-itēs*, -ITE (pertaining to, native).]

it'll (ĭt′l). **1.** Contraction of *it will.* **2.** Contraction of *it shall.*

ITO International Trade Organization.

-itol. *Chemistry.* Indicates alcohols containing more than one hydroxyl group; for example, **mannitol.** [-ITE + -OL.]

its (ĭts) *adj.* The possessive form of the pronoun *it.* Used to indicate possession, agency, or reception of an action by the thing or nonhuman being spoken of: **1.** Used attributively: *its forepaw.* **2.** Used absolutely: *The appeal of the plain girl in the fancy bonnet was more its than hers.* [Originally *it's* : IT + *-'s*, possessive ending.]

Usage: Its, the pronominal, or possessive, adjective, is now never written with an apostrophe. The contraction *it's* (*it is* or *it has*) always has an apostrophe: *It's almost five o'clock. It's been raining all day.*

it's (ĭts). **1.** Contraction of *it is.* **2.** Contraction of *it has.*

it·self (ĭt-sĕlf′) *pron.* A specialized form of the third person singular neuter pronoun. It is used: **1.** As a reflexive pronoun, forming the direct or indirect object of a verb or the object of a preposition: *This record player turns itself off.* **2.** For emphasis, after a noun or *it: The trouble is in the machine itself.* **3.** As an emphasizing substitute for *it: It works well within the system but itself was not made to do the job.* **4.** In an absolute construction: *Itself no great painting, it still reveals talent.* **5.** As an indication of its real identity or normal, healthy condition: *The computer is acting itself again since the program was corrected.* [Middle English *itself*, Old English *hit self* : IT + SELF.]

ITU **1.** International Telecommunication Union. **2.** International Typographical Union.

I·tu·ri (ĭ-tōōr′ē). The name of the Aruwimi River in its upper course.

I·tu·rup (ē′tər-əp). An island of the Soviet Union, the largest (2,657 square miles) of the Kurile group, in the southern part of the archipelago.

-ity. Indicates a state or quality; for example, **authenticity, jollity.** [Middle English *-it(i)e*, from Old French *-ite*, from Latin *-itās* : thematic vowel *-i-* + *-tās*, -TY.]

IUD intrauterine device.

-ium. *Chemistry & Physics.* Indicates the name of an element or chemical group; for example, **barium, ammonium.** [New Latin, from Latin, from Greek *-ion*, diminutive suffix.]

IV intravenous; intravenously.

I·van (ī′vən; *Russian* ĭ-văn′). A masculine given name. [Russian, from Old Russian *Ioannŭ*, from Greek *Iōannēs*, JOHN.]

I·van III Va·sil·ie·vich (ī′vən; *Russian* ĭ-vän′; vä-sēl′yə-vĭch). Called "the Great." 1440–1505. Grand Duke of Muscovy (1462–1505); expanded territory and centralized government; grandfather of Ivan IV.

I·van IV Va·sil·ie·vich (ī′vən; *Russian* ĭ-vän′; vä-sēl′yə-vĭch). Called "the Terrible." 1530–1584. Grand Duke of Muscovy (1533–84); first czar (1547–84).

I·va·no·vo (ĭ-vä′nô-vô). Formerly **I·va·no·vo Voz·ne·sensk** (vôz′nə-sĕnsk′). A city and industrial center of the west-central Russian S.F.S.R. Population, 368,000.

I've (īv). Contraction of *I have.*

-ive. Indicates having a tendency toward or inclination to perform some action; for example, **degenerative, disruptive.** [Middle English *-if*, *-ive*, from Old French *-if* (feminine *-ive*), from Latin *-ivus* (feminine *-iva*, neuter *-ivum*).]

Ives (īvz), **Charles Edward.** 1874–1954. American composer.

Ives (īvz), **Frederick Eugene.** 1856–1937. American inventor of halftone photography.

i·vied (ī′vēd) *adj.* Overgrown or cloaked with ivy.

I·vi·za. See **Ibiza.**

i·vo·ry (ī′və-rē, īv′rē) *n., pl.* **-ries. 1. a.** The hard, smooth, yellowish-white dentine forming the main part of the tusks of the elephant, and used as an ornamental material. **b.** A similar substance forming the tusks or teeth of certain other animals,

such as the walrus. **2.** A tusk, especially an elephant's tusk. **3.** A substance resembling ivory. **4.** Pale or grayish yellow to yellowish white. See **color. 5.** An article made of ivory. **6.** *Usually plural. Slang.* **a.** Piano keys. **b.** Dice. **c.** The teeth. —*adj.* **1.** Made of or resembling ivory. **2.** Of the color ivory. [Middle English *ivor(ie), yvory*, from Old French *ivurie, ivoire*, from Vulgar Latin *eboreus* (unattested), from neuter of Latin *eboreus*, of ivory, from *ebur* (stem *ebor-*), ivory, probably of Egyptian origin, akin to Egyptian *abu*, Coptic *ebu*. See also **elephant, eburnation.**]

i·vo·ry-billed woodpecker (ī′və-rē-bĭld′, ĭv′rē-). A large, probably extinct North American woodpecker, *Campephilus principalis*, having a white bill. Also called "ivorybill."

ivory black. A black pigment prepared from charred ivory.

Ivory Coast, Republic of the. A republic of western Africa, occupying 124,471 square miles on the Gulf of Guinea between Ghana and Liberia; a former French colony, independent since 1960. Population, 3,750,000. Capital, Abidjan.

ivory nut. The hard seed of an American palm *Phytelephas macrocarpa*, yielding an ivorylike substance.

ivory tower. A place or attitude of retreat, especially, preoccupation with lofty, remote, or intellectual considerations rather than with practical everyday life. [Translation of French *tour d'ivoire*, first used by C.A. Sainte-Beuve with reference to Alfred de Vigny, who was anxious to preserve the purity of his inspiration unmixed with practical matters.]

i·vy (ī′vē) *n., pl.* **ivies. 1.** Any of several woody, climbing or trailing plants of the genus *Hedera*, native to the Old World, especially *H. helix*, having lobed, evergreen leaves and berrylike black fruit. **2.** Any of various other climbing or creeping plants, such as Boston ivy or poison ivy. [Middle English *ivi, ivye*, Old English *ifig*, from Germanic *ibahs* (unattested), obscurely related to Latin *ibex*, "climber," IBEX.]

Ivy League. An association of eight colleges in the northeastern United States, comprising Brown, Columbia, Cornell, Dartmouth, Harvard, Princeton, the University of Pennsylvania, and Yale. —*adj.* Of or resembling the traditions of the Ivy League. [Coined by New York sports editor Stanley Woodward, probably with reference to the old, ivy-covered school buildings.]

i·wis (ĭ-wĭs′) *adv.* Also **y·wis.** *Archaic.* Certainly; assuredly. [Middle English *iwis(se), gewis*, Old English *gewis*, certain. See **weid-** in Appendix.*]

I·wo (ē′wō). A city of southwestern Nigeria, near Ibadan. Population, 159,000.

I·wo Ji·ma (ē′wō jē′mə). The largest (eight square miles) of the Volcano Islands in the western Pacific; captured by the U.S. in World War II; returned to Japan in 1968.

IWW, I.W.W. Industrial Workers of the World.

Ix·elles (ēk-sĕl′). A southeastern suburb of Brussels, Belgium. Population, 94,000.

Ix·i·on (ĭk-sī′ən). *Greek Mythology.* A Thessalian king whom Zeus punished for his temerity in seeking Hera's love by having him bound to a perpetually revolving wheel in Hades.

Ix·ta·ci·hua·tl (ēs′tä-sē′wät′l). Also **Iz·tac·ci·hua·tl** (ēs′täk-sē′-). A dormant volcano rising to 17,342 feet in central Mexico.

ix·tle. Variant of **istle.**

I·yar (ē-yär′, ē′yär) *n.* Also **Iy·yar.** The eighth month of the year on the Hebrew calendar. See **calendar.** [Hebrew *iyyār.*]

iz·ar (ĭ-zär′) *n.* A long cotton outer garment, usually white, worn by women in many Moslem countries. [Arabic '*izār*, '*izr*, veil, covering.]

–ize. Also **–ise.** Indicates: **1. a.** To cause to be or to become; make into; for example, **dramatize. b.** To make conform with; for example, **Hellenize, Anglicize. c.** To treat or regard as; for example, **idolize. 2.** To cause to acquire a specified quality; for example, **legalize, modernize, sterilize. 3.** To become or become similar to; for example, **crystallize, oxidize, materialize. 4. a.** To subject to; for example, **jeopardize, anesthetize. b.** To affect with; for example, **magnetize, galvanize. 5.** To do or follow some practice; for example, **pasteurize, bowdlerize.** *Note:* For most words, the American spelling of this suffix is *-ize* and the British spelling is *-ise*. The British variant is not entered as such in this Dictionary. Note, however, that for certain words the spelling *-ise* is preferred in America; for example, *advertise*, which also has the acceptable American variant *advertize*; in certain cases, as in *baptize*, there is no variant spelling. [Middle English *-isen*, from Old French *-iser*, from Late Latin *-izāre*, from Greek *-izein*.]

I·zhevsk (ē′zhĭfsk). The capital of the Udmurt A.S.S.R., an industrial center located in the southeast. Population, 330,000.

Iz·mir (ĭz-mîr′). Formerly **Smyr·na** (smûr′nə). A port city of Turkey, on the Gulf of Izmir, an inlet of the Aegean extending 40 miles into western Turkey. Population, 297,000.

Iz·mit (ĭz-mĭt′). Also **Iz·mid.** A city and port of northwestern Turkey, on the Sea of Marmara. Population, 73,000.

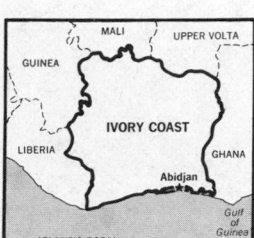

Ivory Coast

---

t tight/th thin, path/*th* this, bathe/ŭ cut/ûr **urge**/v valve/w with/y yes/z zebra, size/zh vision/ə about, item, edible, gallop, circus/ à *Fr.* ami/œ *Fr.* feu, *Ger.* schön/ü *Fr.* tu, *Ger.* über/ᴋʜ *Ger.* ich, *Scot.* loch/ɴ *Fr.* bon. ***Follows main vocabulary. †Of obscure origin.**

Ivan the Terrible

Jj

1 2 Phoenician 3 4 5 6 Greek 7 8 Roman 9 10 11 Medieval 12 13 14 15 Modern

Around 1000 B.C. the Phoenicians and other Semites of Syria and Palestine began to use a graphic sign in the forms (1,2). They gave it the name yōdh, meaning "hand," and used it for a semiconsonant y, as in English boy, boys. *After 900 B.C. the Greeks borrowed the sign from the Phoenicians, using at first various angular versions (3,4,5), and then a simplified form (6). They also changed its name to* iōta *and made it stand for their vowel* i. *The Greek form (6) passed unchanged via Etruscan to the Roman alphabet (7,8). The Romans used the sign both for the vowel* i *and for the semiconsonant* y, *as in* IECIT. *When subsequently the need arose to differentiate the two sounds, an unsystematic habit grew up of adding a tail to the* i *for the semiconsonant, as in the late Roman and medieval Uncial (9,10) and Cursive (11). The distinction was not fully established until the 17th century, when the capital (12,13) and small letter (14,15) took their modern forms. The dot on the small letter was carried over from the letter* i.

j, J (jā) *n., pl.* **j's** *or rare* **js, J's** *or* **Js. 1.** The tenth letter of the modern English alphabet. See **alphabet. 2.** Any of the speech sounds represented by this letter. **3.** Anything shaped like the letter J.

j, J, j., J. *Note:* As an abbreviation or symbol, *j* may be a small or capital letter, with or without a period. Established forms or those generally preferred precede the definition. When no form is given, all four forms are in general use in that sense. **1.** J current density. **2.** J joule. **3.** J. journal. **4.** J. judge; justice. **5.** The tenth in a series.

J.A. 1. joint account. **2.** judge advocate.

jab (jăb) *v.* **jabbed, jabbing, jabs.** —*tr.* **1.** To poke abruptly, especially with something sharp. **2.** To stab or pierce. **3.** To thrust into or against something with a rough, abrupt movement: *"He laughed and jabbed his spectacles back on his nose."* (John Barth). **4.** To punch with short blows. —*intr.* **1.** To make an abrupt jabbing motion. **2.** To deliver a quick punch. —*n.* A quick stab or blow. [Variant of JOB.]

Ja·bal·pur. See Jubbulpore.

jab·ber (jăb'ər) *v.* **-bered, -bering, -bers.** —*intr.* To talk rapidly, unintelligibly, or idly. —*tr.* To utter rapidly or unintelligibly. —*n.* Rapid or babbling talk. [Middle English *jaberen* (imitative).] —**jab'ber·er** *n.*

jab·i·ru (jăb'ə-rōō') *n.* A large tropical American wading bird, *Jabiru mycteria,* having white plumage and a naked neck. [Portuguese *jabirú,* from Tupi-Guarani.]

jab·o·ran·di (jăb'ə-răn'dē) *n., pl.* **-dis. 1.** Either of two tropical American shrubs, *Pilocarpus jaborandi* or *P. microphyllus,* the dried leaves of which yield **pilocarpine** (*see*). **2.** The dried leaves of these shrubs. [Portuguese, from Tupi *yaborandí.*]

jab·ot (zhă-bō', jă-) *n.* A cascade of frills down the front of a shirt. [French, from Auvergne or Limousin dialect, akin to Old French dialectal *gave,* throat, gullet, from a Romance root *gab-* (unattested), crop, gullet, perhaps from Gaulish.]

jac·al (hä-käl') *n., pl.* **-als** *or* **jacales** (hä-kä'lās). A thatch-roofed hut made of wattle and daub in Mexico and the southwestern United States. [Mexican Spanish, from Nahuatl *xacalli : xamitl,* adobe + *calli,* house.]

jac·a·mar (jăk'ə-mär') *n.* Any of various tropical American birds of the family Galbulidae, having iridescent plumage and a long bill. [French, from Tupi-Guarani *jacamaciri.*]

ja·ca·na (zhä'sə-nä') *n.* Any of several tropical marsh birds of the family Jacanidae, having long toes adapted for walking on floating vegetation. Also called "lily-trotter." [From Portuguese *jaçaná,* from Tupi-Guarani *jasaná.*]

jac·a·ran·da (jăk'ə-răn'də) *n.* **1.** Any of several trees of the genus *Jacaranda,* native to tropical America, having compound leaves and clusters of pale-purple flowers. **2.** The wood of such a tree. **3.** A similar wood. [Portuguese *jacarandá,* from Tupi *yacarandá.*]

ja·cinth (jā'sĭnth, jăs'ĭnth) *n.* **1.** A reddish-orange variety of zircon, **hyacinth** (*see*). **2.** *Obsolete.* A hyacinth. [Middle English *iacynth, iacin(c)t,* from Old French *iacinte,* from Medieval Latin *jacintus,* from Latin *hyacinthus,* HYACINTH.]

jack (jăk) *n.* **1.** *Usually capital* J. A man; fellow; chap. Often used in direct address. **2.** One who does odd or heavy jobs; a laborer. Usually used in combination: *lumberjack.* **3.** A sailor; tar. **4.** A playing card showing the figure of a knave and ranking below a queen. **5. a.** Any of several devices or contrivances replacing human labor. Often used in combination: *bootjack.* **b.** A usually portable device for raising heavy objects by means of force applied with a lever, screw, or hydraulic press. **c.** A wooden wedge for cleaving rock. **d.** A support or brace, especially the iron crosstree on a topgallant masthead. **6.** The male of certain animals, especially the ass. **7.** Any of several food and game fishes chiefly of the genus *Caranx,* of Atlantic and Pacific waters. **8.** A piece of wood holding the leather or quill pluck in a harpsichord or the hammer in other keyboard instruments, such as the piano. **9.** A pin in some bowling games. **10. a.** *Plural.* A game played with a set of small six-pointed metal pieces and a small ball, the object being to pick up the pieces in various combinations. Used with a singular verb. Also called "jackstones." **b.** One of the metal pieces used. Also called "jackstone." **11.** A socket that accepts a plug at one end and attaches to electric circuitry at the other. **12.** A jacklight. **13.** A small flag flown at the bow of a ship, usually to indicate nationality. **14.** *Slang.* Money. **15.** Applejack. —**every man jack.** Every single person of a group. —*v.* **jacked, jacking, jacks.** —*tr.* To hunt or fish for with a jacklight. —*intr.* To jacklight. —**jack up. 1.** To hoist with or as if with a jack. **2.** To raise: *jack prices up.* **3.** To bolster confidence in; support. [Transferred use of the name JACK.]

Jack (jăk). A masculine given name. [Middle English *Jacke, Iakke,* from *Jankin,* diminutive of *Jan, John,* JOHN.]

jack·al (jăk'əl, -ôl') *n.* **1.** Any of several doglike carnivorous mammals of the genus *Canis,* of Africa and Asia. **2.** An accomplice or lackey characterized by the voracity and baseness attributed to the jackal. [Turkish *chakāl,* from Persian *shagāl, shaghāl†.*]

jack·a·napes (jăk'ə-nāps') *n.* **1.** A cheeky fellow; bounder; coxcomb. **2.** A mischievous child. **3.** *Archaic.* A monkey or ape: *"Dressing him out like a jackanapes, and giving him money to play the fool with"* (Lord Chesterfield). [Earlier, "an ape," originally (about 1450) *Jack Napes,* nickname of William de la Pole, first Duke of Suffolk, whose badge was a figure of an ape's ball and chain.]

jack·ass (jăk'ăs') *n.* **1.** A male ass or donkey. **2.** A foolish or stupid person; blockhead. [JACK ("male") + ASS.]

jackass rig. *Nautical.* Any nonstandard combination of square rig and fore-and-aft rig on a sailing ship having two or more masts. Also called "hermaphrodite rig."

jack bean. A tropical American plant, *Canavalia ensiformis,* having clusters of purple flowers and long pods.

jack·boot (jăk'bōōt') *n.* Also **jack boot.** A stout boot extending above the knee.

jack·daw (jăk'dô') *n.* A Eurasian bird, *Corvus monedula,* related to and resembling the crow. Also called "daw."

jack·et (jăk'ĭt) *n.* **1.** A short coat, usually hip-length, worn by men or women. **2.** An outer covering or casing, especially:

jacana
Jacana spinosa

ă pat/ā pay/âr care/ä father/b bib/ch church/d deed/ĕ pet/ē be/f fife/g gag/h hat/hw which/ĭ pit/ī pie/îr pier/j judge/k kick/l lid/ needle/m mum/n no, sudden/ng thing/ŏ pot/ō toe/ô paw, for/oi noise/ou out/ŏŏ took/ōō boot/p pop/r roar/s sauce/sh ship, dish/

a. The skin of a potato. **b.** The dust jacket of a book. **c.** Insulation covering a steam pipe, wire, boiler, or the like. **d.** A paper or thin cardboard envelope for a phonograph record. **e.** An open envelope or folder for filing papers. **f.** The outer metal shell or case of a bullet. —*tr.v.* **jacketed, -eting, -ets.** To supply or cover with a jacket. [Middle English *jaket*, from Old French *jacquet, jaquet*, diminutive of *jaque*, short jacket, perhaps from the given name *Jacques*.]

Jack Frost. Frost or cold weather personified.

jack·fruit (jăk′fro͞ot′) *n.* **1.** A tree, *Artocarpus heterophyllus*, of tropical Asia, bearing large, edible fruit. **2.** The fruit of this tree. [Portuguese *jaca*, from Malayalam *chakka* + FRUIT.]

jack·ham·mer (jăk′hăm′ər) *n.* A hand-held pneumatic machine for drilling rock.

jack-in-the-box (jăk′ĭn-*th*ə-bŏks′) *n., pl.* **jack-in-the-boxes** or **jacks-in-the-box.** A toy consisting of a grotesque puppet that springs up out of a box when the lid is opened.

jack-in-the-pul·pit (jăk′ĭn-*th*ə-po͝ol′pĭt, -pŭl′pĭt) *n.* A plant, *Arisaema triphyllum*, of eastern North America, having a leaflike spathe enclosing a clublike spadix. Also called "Indian turnip."

jack·knife (jăk′nīf′) *n., pl.* **-knives** (-nīvz′). **1.** A large clasp pocketknife. **2.** A dive executed by jumping headfirst and then bending the body at the waist to form a 90-degree angle and, with the legs straight, touching the feet with the hands before straightening out to enter the water, hands first. —*v.* **jackknifed, -knifing, -knifes.** —*tr.* To fold or double like a jackknife. —*intr.* **1.** To bend or fold up like a jackknife. **2.** To form a 90-degree angle. [Probably JACK + KNIFE.]

jack·light (jăk′līt′) *n.* A light used as a lure in night hunting or fishing. —*intr.v.* **jacklighted, -lighting, -lights.** To hunt or fish with a jacklight.

jack mackerel. A food and game fish, *Trachurus symmetricus*, of Pacific coastal waters. Also called "saurel."

jack-of-all-trades (jăk′əv-ôl′trādz′) *n., pl.* **jacks-of-all-trades.** A person who can do many different kinds of work.

jack-o′-lan·tern (jăk′ə-lăn′tərn) *n.* **1. a.** A lantern made from a hollowed pumpkin with a carved face. **b.** A commercial imitation of this. **2.** An ignis fatuus or similar phenomenon.

jack pine. An evergreen tree, *Pinus banksiana*, of northern North America, having short, twisted needles and soft wood.

jack·plane (jăk′plān′) *n.* A bench plane for rough surfacing. [JACK (given name) + PLANE.]

jack·pot (jăk′pŏt′) *n.* **1. a.** The accumulated stakes in a kind of poker that requires one to hold a pair of jacks or better in order to open the betting. **b.** Any cumulative pool or kitty in various games and competitions. **2.** A top prize or reward. —**hit the jackpot.** *Informal.* To experience great success or sudden good fortune. [JACK (playing card) + POT.]

jack rabbit. Any of several large long-eared, long-legged hares of the genus *Lepus*, of western North America. [JACK(ASS) (from its long ears) + RABBIT.]

jack·screw (jăk′skro͞o′) *n.* A jack for lifting, operated by a screw.

jack·shaft (jăk′shăft′, -shäft′) *n.* A short shaft that transmits motion from a motor to a machine, especially in an automobile.

jack·snipe (jăk′snīp′) *n., pl.* **jacksnipe** or **-snipes.** **1.** An Old World wading bird, *Limnocryptes minima*, having brownish plumage and a long bill. **2.** Any of several similar birds. [JACK + SNIPE.]

Jack·son (jăk′sən). **1.** The capital of Mississippi, on the Pearl River. Population, 144,000. **2.** A city of Michigan on the Grand River. Population, 51,000.

Jack·son (jăk′sən), **Andrew.** 1767–1845. Seventh President of the United States (1829–37).

Jack·son (jăk′sən), **Thomas Jonathan.** Called "Stonewall." 1824–1863. American military leader; commanded Confederate troops at Bull Run and Shenandoah Valley.

Jack·so·ni·an (jăk-sō′nē-ən) *adj.* Of or pertaining to Andrew Jackson's concepts of popular government or his Presidency. —*n.* A supporter of Andrew Jackson.

Jack·son·ville (jăk′sən-vĭl). A city of northern Florida, near the mouth of the St. Johns River. Population, 201,000.

jack·stay (jăk′stā′) *n.* **1.** A stay for racing or cruising vessels used to steady the mast against the strain of the gaff. **2.** A rope, rod, or batten along the upper side of a yard, gaff, or boom to which a sail is fastened. **3.** A rope or rod running vertically on the forward side of the mast on which the yard moves.

jack·stone (jăk′stōn′) *n.* **1.** *Plural.* The game of **jacks** *(see)*. Used with a singular verb. **2.** A **jack** *(see)*. [Alteration of earlier *chackstone*, from *checkstone*, plural *checkstones*, a similar game, perhaps from *check*, short for CHECKER.]

jack·straw (jăk′strô′) *n.* **1.** *Plural.* A game played with a pile of straws or thin sticks, with the players attempting in turn to remove a single stick without disturbing the others. Used with a singular verb. Also called "spilikins." **2.** One of the straws or sticks used in this game. Also called "spilikin." [JACK + STRAW.]

jack-tar (jăk′tär′) *n.* Also **Jack-tar.** A sailor. [JACK (given name) + TAR.]

Ja·cob[1] (jā′kəb). A masculine given name. [Late Latin *Jacōbus*, from Greek *Iakōbos*, from Hebrew *Ya'aqōbh*, "he who takes by the heel or overreaches," from *'aqēbh*, heel.]

Ja·cob[2] (jā′kəb). Hebrew patriarch; son of Isaac and grandson of Abraham; father of 12 sons, ancestors of the 12 tribes of Israel. See **Israel.**

Jac·o·be·an (jăk′ə-bē′ən) *adj.* **1.** Of or pertaining to the reign of James I of England or his times. **2.** *Architecture.* Designating a style of the 17th century in England blending late Gothic and Palladian elements. —*n.* A prominent figure of this period. [From New Latin *Jacobaeus*, from *Jacobus*, JAMES.]

Jac·o·bin (jăk′ə-bĭn) *n.* **1.** A radical republican during the French Revolution. **2.** A leftist. Sometimes used as an abusive epithet. **3.** A Dominican friar. [French, from Late Latin *Jacōbus*, after the church of *Saint-Jacques*, near which the Jacobin friars built their first convent. The French political group was founded (1789) in this convent.] —**Jac′o·bin′ic, Jac′o·bin′i·cal** *adj.* —**Jac′o·bin·ism′** *n.*

Jac·o·bin·ize (jăk′ə-bĭ-nīz′) *tr.v.* **-ized, -izing, -izes.** To imbue with or convert to the revolutionary ideas of the Jacobins.

Jac·o·bite (jăk′ə-bīt′) *n.* A supporter of James II of England or of the Stuart pretenders following 1688. [From New Latin *Jacobus*, JAMES.] —**Jac′o·bit′i·cal** (-bĭt′ĭ-kəl) *adj.* —**Jac′o·bit·ism′** (-bī-tĭz′əm) *n.*

Jacob's ladder. **1.** *Nautical.* A rope or chain ladder with rigid rungs. **2.** A plant of the genus *Polemonium*, having blue flowers and numerous paired leaflets. [From the ladder seen by the patriarch JACOB in a dream. Genesis 28:12.]

ja·co·bus (jə-kō′bəs) *n.* A gold coin issued during the reign of James I. [From New Latin *Jacobus*, JAMES.]

jac·o·net (jăk′ə-nĕt′) *n.* **1.** A cotton cloth with a hard finish similar to lawn. **2.** A cloth with a soft finish resembling nainsook. [Urdu *jagannāthī*, first made in *Jagannath*, India.]

jac·quard (jăk′ärd′, jə-kärd′) *adj.* Also **Jac·quard.** Designating a special loom or other apparatus or the method employed in the weaving of a figured fabric. —*n.* Also **Jac·quard.** A fabric with an intricately woven pattern made on a jacquard loom. [After Joseph JACQUARD.]

Jac·quard (zhȧ-kȧr′), **Joseph Marie.** 1752–1834. French inventor of mechanical loom.

Jac·que·line (jăk′wə-lĭn′, -lēn′, jăk′ə-). A feminine given name. [French, diminutive of *Jacques*, James, from Late Latin *Jacōbus*, JACOB.]

Jac·que·rie (zhä-krē′) *n.* **1.** The uprising of the French peasants against the nobility in 1358. **2.** *Often small* **j.** A peasant revolt, especially a very bloody one. [French, from Old French, from *jacques*, "peasant," from *Jacques*, James. See **Jacqueline.**]

jac·ta·tion (jăk-tā′shən) *n.* Bragging; boasting. [Latin *jactātiō*, from *jactāre*, "to toss about," discuss, boast, frequentative of *jacere* (past participle *jactus*), to throw. See **yē-** in Appendix.*]

jac·ti·ta·tion (jăk′tə-tā′shən) *n.* **1.** A boasting; fanfaronade. **2.** *Law.* A false boast or claim, as of marriage, detrimental to the interests of another. **3.** *Pathology.* Extreme restlessness or tossing in bed. [Medieval Latin *jactitātiō*, a false assertion made to the injury of another, from *jactitāre*, frequentative of Latin *jactāre*, to boast, declare publicly. See **jactation.**]

jade[1] (jād) *n.* Either of two distinct minerals, **nephrite** and **jadeite** *(both of which see)*, that are generally pale green or white and are used mainly as gemstones or in carving. [French *jade*, *ejade*, from Spanish *ijada*, shortened from *(piedra de) ijada*, "(stone of the) flank" (from the belief that it was a cure for renal colic), from Vulgar Latin *iliata* (unattested), flanks, from Latin *īlia*, plural of *īlium*, flank, ILEUM.]

jade[2] (jād) *n.* **1.** A broken-down or useless horse; a nag. **2. a.** A worthless woman. **b.** A willful girl. —*v.* **jaded, jading, jades.** —*tr.* To exhaust or wear out. —*intr.* To become weary or spiritless. [Middle English *jade*†, a broken-down horse.]

jad·ed (jā′dĭd) *adj.* **1.** Wearied; spiritless with fatigue: *"My father's words had left me jaded and depressed."* (William Styron). **2.** Dulled as by surfeit; sated: *"the sickeningly sweet life of the amoral, jaded, bored upper classes."* (John Simon). —See Synonyms at **tired.** [From JADE (verb).] —**jad′ed·ly** *adv.* —**jad′ed·ness** *n.*

jade·ite (jā′dīt′) *n.* A rare, emerald to light-green, white, red-brown, yellow-brown, or violet jade, $NaAlSi_2O_6$, used as a gem and for ornamental carvings. [French : JADE + -ITE.]

Ja·dot·ville (zhȧ′dō′vēl′). A city of the Democratic Republic of the Congo (Kinshasa) in the southeast. Population, 80,000.

jae·ger (yā′gər; *also* jā′gər *for sense 1*) *n.* **1.** Any of several sea birds of the genus *Stercorarius*, that snatch food from other birds. See **skua.** **2.** A huntsman or hunting attendant. [German *Jäger*, "hunter," from Old High German *jagāri*, from *jagōn*, to hunt, from Germanic *jagōjan* (unattested).]

Ja·én (hä-ān′). A city of Spain, situated in the southeast. Population, 75,000.

Jaf·fa (jăf′ə, yä′fə). Ancient name **Jop·pa** (jŏp′ə). A seaport of west-central Israel, constituting with Tel Aviv one municipality. Combined population, 394,000.

Jaff·na (jăf′nə). A seaport of north Ceylon. Population, 94,000.

jag[1] (jăg) *n.* Also **jagg.** **1.** A sharp projection; barb. **2. a.** A hanging flap along the edge of a garment. **b.** A slash or slit in a garment exposing material of a different color. —*tr.v.* **jagged, jagging, jags.** Also **jagg.** **1.** To cut jags in; notch. **2.** To cut unevenly; make (an edge) ragged. **3.** *Scottish.* To prick; jab sharply. [Middle English *jagge*†.]

jag[2] (jăg) *n.* **1.** *Slang.* A bout or spree: *a shopping jag; a crying jag.* **2.** *Regional.* A small load or portion. —**have a jag on.** Be high, as on alcohol or drugs. [Origin unknown.]

J.A.G. Judge Advocate General.

Jag·a·tai. Variant of **Chagatai.**

jag·ged (jăg′ĭd) *adj.* Toothed or serrated; having jags. See Synonyms at **rough.** —**jag′ged·ly** *adv.* —**jag′ged·ness** *n.*

jag·ger·y (jăg′ə-rē) *n.* Unrefined sugar made from palm sap. [From Indo-Portuguese *jagara*, from Kanarese *sharkare*, from Sanskrit *śarkarā*†, "gravel," sugar. See **sugar.**]

jag·gy (jăg′ē) *adj.* **-gier, -giest.** Having jags; jagged.

jag·uar (jăg′wär′, -yo͞o-är′) *n.* A large feline mammal, *Panthera onca*, of tropical America, having a tawny coat spotted with

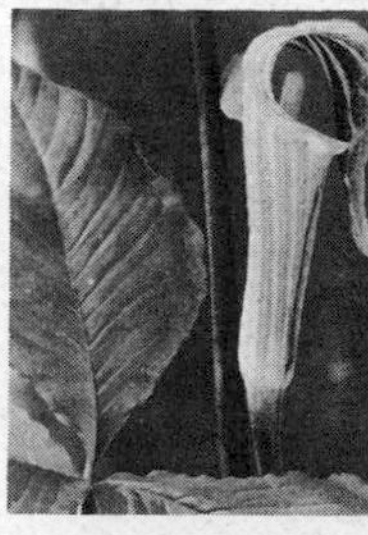

jack-in-the-pulpit

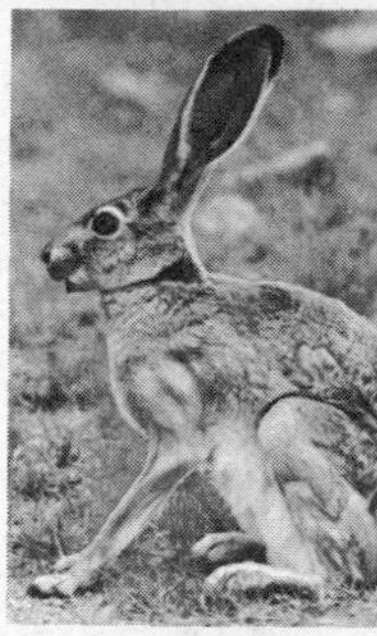

jack rabbit
Lepus californicus

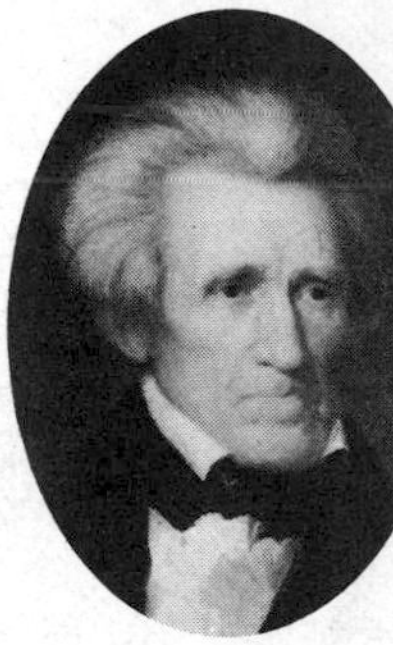

Andrew Jackson
Portrait by
Asher B. Durand

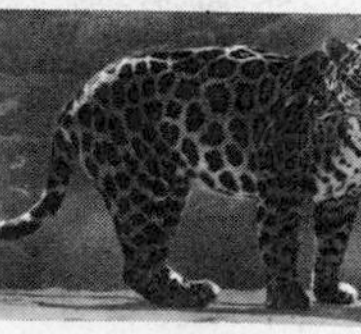

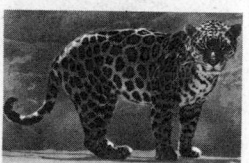

jaguar

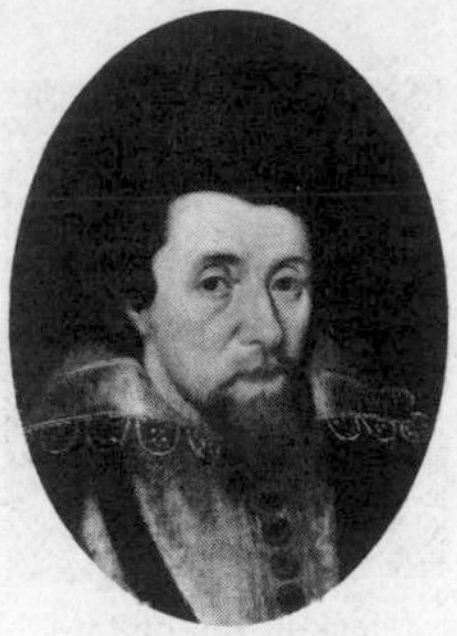

James I

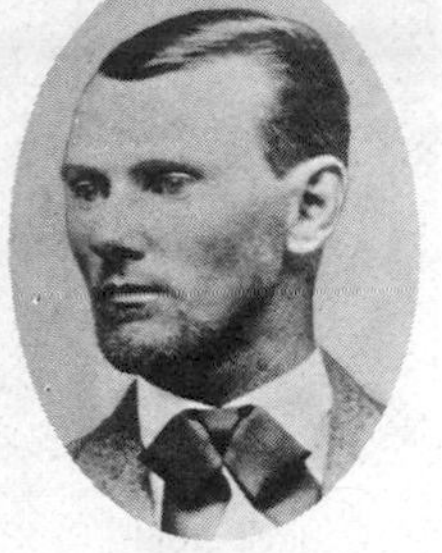

Jesse James

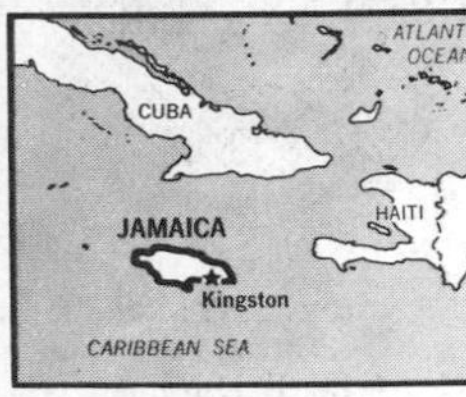

Jamaica

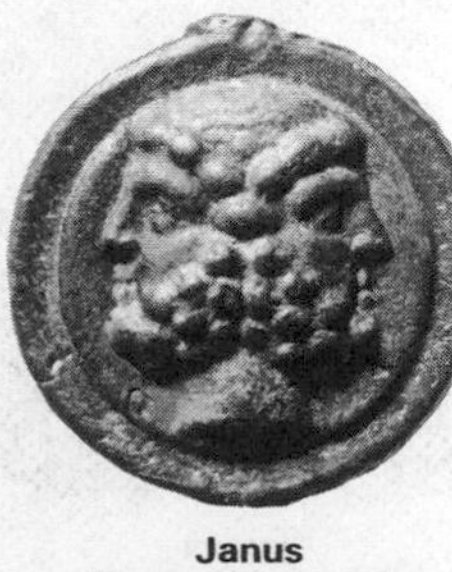

Janus
Bronze Roman coin from about 350 B.C.

black rosettelike markings. [Spanish *jaguar, yaguar* and Portuguese *jaguar*, from Tupi-Guarani *jaguara, yaguara.*]
ja·gua·ron·di (jăg′wə-rŭn′dē, jä′gwə-) *n., pl.* **-dis.** Also **ja·gua·run·di.** A long-tailed grayish-brown wild cat, *Felis yagouaroundi*, of tropical America. [American Spanish and Portuguese, from Tupi-Guarani *jaguarundi, yaguarundi.*]
Jah·veh, Jah·weh. Variants of **Yahweh.**
Jah·vist, Jah·wist. Variants of **Yahwist.**
jai a·lai (hī′ lī′, hī′ ə-lī′, hī′ ə-lī′). An extremely fast court game popular in Spain, Latin America, and the Philippines, in which players use a long hand-shaped basket strapped to the wrist to propel the ball against a wall. Also called "pelota." [Spanish, from Basque : *jai*, festival + *alai*, joyous.]
jail (jāl) *n.* Also *chiefly British* **gaol.** A place for the confinement of persons in lawful detention; prison. —*tr.v.* **jailed, jailing, jails.** Also *chiefly British* **gaol.** To detain in custody; imprison. [*Jail* and *gaol*, respectively from Middle English *jaiole* and *gayole*, from Old French *jaiole* and Norman French *gaiole*, both from Vulgar Latin *gaviola* (unattested), variant of *caveola* (unattested), diminutive of Latin *cavea*, a hollow, den, coop. See **keu-**[3] in Appendix.*]
jail·bait (jāl′bāt′) *n. Slang.* A girl below the age of consent with whom fornication can constitute statutory rape.
jail·bird (jāl′bûrd′) *n. Informal.* A prisoner or ex-convict.
jail delivery. 1. *British Law.* The clearing of a jail by bringing all the prisoners to trial. **2.** A mass escape or forcible freeing of prisoners from a jail.
jail·er (jā′lər) *n.* Also **jail·or.** The keeper of a jail.
Jain (jīn) *n.* Also **Jai·na** (jī′nə). A believer or follower of Jainism. —*adj.* Also **Jai·na.** Of or pertaining to Jainism or the Jains. [Hindi *jaina*, from Sanskrit *jainas*, saintly, from *jinas*, saint, "overcomer," from *jayati*, to conquer. See **gweyə-** in Appendix.*]
Jain·ism (jī′nĭz′əm) *n.* An ascetic religion of India, founded in the sixth century B.C., that teaches the immortality and transmigration of the soul and denies the existence of a perfect or supreme being.
Jai·pur (jī′po͝or′). The capital of Rajasthan, Republic of India, a commercial center in the eastern part of the state. Population, 403,000.
Ja·kar·ta. See **Djakarta.**
jake (jāk) *adj. Slang.* Fine; suitable; all right. [Origin unknown.]
jakes (jāks) *n.* Plural in form, used with a singular verb. *Regional.* A privy. [Perhaps from the French given name *Jacques.*]
jal·ap (jăl′əp) *n.* **1.** A Mexican plant, *Exogonium purga*, having a tuberous rootstock that is dried, powdered, and used medicinally as a cathartic. **2.** Any of several similar or related plants. **3.** The dried rootstock of such a plant. [French *jalap*, from Mexican Spanish *jalapa*, short for *(purga de) Jalapa*, "(purgative of) JALAPA."]
Ja·la·pa (hä-lä′pä). Also **Ja·la·pa En·rí·quez** (ān-rē′kās). The capital of Veracruz, Mexico, a city in the center of the state. Population, 67,000.
Ja·lis·co (hä-lēs′kō). A state occupying 31,152 square miles in west-central Mexico. Population, 2,707,000. Capital, Guadalajara.
ja·lop·y (jə-lŏp′ē) *n., pl.* **-ies.** Also **ja·lop·py.** *Informal.* An old, dilapidated automobile or airplane. [Origin unknown.]
ja·lou·sie (jăl′o͞o-sē; *chiefly British* zhăl′o͞o-zē′) *n.* A blind or shutter having adjustable horizontal slats for regulating the passage of air and light. [French, "jealousy" (probably because one sees through it without being seen), from Old French *jelousie*, from *jelous*, JEALOUS.]
Ja·lu·it (jăl′o͞o-ĭt). The largest atoll (30 miles long and about 20 miles wide) of the Marshall Islands.
jam[1] (jăm) *v.* **jammed, jamming, jams.** —*tr.* **1.** To drive or wedge forcibly; squeeze into a tight position. **2.** To activate or apply suddenly: *jam the brakes on.* **3.** To cause to lock in an unworkable position: *jam the typewriter keys.* **4.** To fill or pack to excess; cram: *He jammed the drawer with old socks.* **5.** To block, congest, or clog: *The drain was jammed by debris.* **6.** To crush; smash; bruise. **7.** *Electronics.* To interfere with or prevent the clear reception of (broadcast signals) by electronic means. —*intr.* **1.** To become wedged; stick. **2.** To become inoperable because of jammed parts. **3.** To force into or through a limited space. **4.** To play jazz improvisations. —*n.* **1.** The act of jamming or the condition of being jammed. **2.** A crush or congestion of people or things in a limited space: *a traffic jam.* **3.** *Informal.* A predicament: *in a jam with the police.* [Expressive formation.]
jam[2] (jăm) *n.* A preserve made from whole fruit boiled to a pulp with sugar. [Probably from JAM (act of jamming).]
Ja·mai·ca (jə-mā′kə). *Abbr.* **Jam. 1.** An island, 4,411 square miles in area, in the Caribbean, south of Cuba; a former British possession independent since 1962. Population, 1,613,000. Capital, Kingston. **2.** A section of the borough of Queens, New York City. —**Ja·mai′can** *n.* & *adj.*
jamb (jăm) *n.* **1.** The vertical posts or pieces of a door or window frame. **2.** A jambeau. [Middle English *jambe*, from Old French, "leg," jamb, from Late Latin *gamba*, hoof, from Greek *kampē*, joint. See **kamp-** in Appendix.*]
jam·beau (jăm′bō) *n., pl.* **-beaux** (-bōz). A piece of armor for the leg below the knee. Also called "jambe." [Middle English, from Norman French *jambeau* (unattested), from Old French *jambe*, leg. See **jamb.**]
jam·bo·ree (jăm′bə-rē′) *n.* **1.** A noisy celebration. **2.** A large assembly, often international, as of Boy Scouts. Compare **camporee. 3.** A mass gathering or assembly, as of a political party or association. [Origin unknown.]
James[1] (jāmz). *Abbr.* **Jas.** A masculine given name. [Middle English *James, Jame*, from Old French *James*, from Late Latin *Jacomus*, variant of *Jacōbus*, JACOB.]
James[2] (jāmz) *n. Abbr.* **Jas.** The 20th book of the New Testament, attributed to Saint James the Lesser.
James I (jāmz). 1566–1625. First Stuart king of England (1603–25); as James VI, king of Scotland (1567–1625); son of Mary, Queen of Scots; patron of the King James Bible.
James II (jāmz). 1633–1701. King of England, Scotland, and Ireland (1685–88); second son of Charles I; exiled in France (from 1688).
James (jāmz), **Henry.** 1843–1916. American novelist and critic; resident in England; brother of William James.
James (jāmz), **Jesse Woodson.** 1847–1882. American outlaw.
James (jāmz), **Saint**[1]. Called "the Less." Traditionally regarded as the brother of Jesus, author of the Epistle of James, and first bishop of Jerusalem.
James (jāmz), **Saint**[2]. Called "the Greater." One of the Twelve Apostles; son of Zebedee and brother of John; traditionally supposed to have been martyred by Herod Agrippa (A.D. 44?).
James (jāmz), **Saint**[3]. One of the Twelve Apostles; often identified with Saint James the Less.
James (jāmz), **William.** 1842–1910. American philosopher and psychologist; brother of Henry James.
James Bay (jāmz). An arm of Hudson Bay extending southward 275 miles between Ontario and Quebec, Canada.
James River (jāmz). **1.** Also **Da·ko·ta River** (də-kō′tə). A river rising in central North Dakota and flowing 750 miles generally southeast to the Mississippi in southeastern South Dakota. **2.** A river rising in western Virginia and flowing 340 miles generally east to Hampton Roads in the southeast.
James·town (jāmz′toun). **1.** The first permanent English settlement in the New World, founded in 1607 and now a restored village on the James River in Virginia. **2.** The capital of St. Helena. Population, 2,000.
Jam·mu (jŭm′o͞o). The winter capital of the northern Indian state Jammu and Kashmir, a city in the southwest near the West Pakistan border. Population, 108,000.
Jam·mu and Kash·mir (jŭm′o͞o; kăsh-mîr′, kăsh′mîr′). A territory occupying 86,024 square miles north of the Republic of India and between West Pakistan and China; claimed as a state by India and partially occupied by Pakistan in a dispute dating from 1947. Population, 3,560,000. Capitals, Srinagar (summer) and Jammu (winter).
Jam·na·gar (jäm-nŭg′ər). A city of the Republic of India, in west-central Gujarat. Population, 152,000.
jam-pack (jăm′păk′) *tr.v.* **-packed, -packing, -packs.** *Informal.* To crowd to capacity: *a road jam-packed with cars.*
jam session. 1. An impromptu gathering of jazz musicians to play improvisations together. **2.** Any jazz concert.
Jam·shed·pur (jäm′shĕd-po͝or′). A city in southeastern Bihar State, Republic of India. Population, 292,000.
jam-up (jăm′ŭp′) *n. Informal.* **1.** A situation in which a flow or action is blocked as by congestion. **2.** Any hindrance, malfunction, or obstruction.
JAN Airport code for Jackson, Mississippi.
Jan. January.
Jane (jān). A feminine given name. [Middle English, from Old French *Jehane*, JOAN.]
Jan·et (jăn′ĭt). A feminine given name. [Middle English *Janeta*, diminutive of JANE.]
jan·gle (jăng′gəl) *v.* **-gled, -gling, -gles.** —*intr.* To make a harsh, metallic sound. —*tr.* **1.** To cause (something metallic) to sound with audible, often discordant, effect: *"Like sweet bells jangled, out of tune and harsh."* (Shakespeare). **2.** To grate on or jar (the nerves). —*n.* A harsh, metallic sound. [Middle English *janglen*, from Old French *jangler*, probably from Germanic, akin to Middle Dutch *jangelen*†.] —**jan′gler** *n.*
jan·is·sar·y (jăn′ĭ-sĕr′ē) *n., pl.* **-ies.** Also **jan·i·zar·y** (-zĕr′ē). A soldier in an elite guard of Turkish troops organized in the 14th century and abolished in 1826. [French *janissaire*, from Turkish *yeniçeri* : *yeni*, new + *çeri*, militia.]
jan·i·tor (jăn′ə-tər) *n.* **1.** One who attends to the maintenance or cleaning of a building. **2.** *Rare.* A doorman. [Latin *jānitor*, from *jānua*, door, from *jānus*, arched passage. See **Janus.**] —**jan′i·to′ri·al** (-tôr′ē-əl, -tōr′ē-əl) *adj.*
Jan May·en (yän′ mī′ən). An island of Norway, 144 square miles in area, in the Greenland Sea midway between northern Norway and Greenland.
Jan·sen (jăn′sən; *Dutch* yän′sən), **Cornelis.** *Latin* Cornelius Jansenius. 1585–1638. Dutch Roman Catholic theologian.
Jan·sen·ism (jăn′sə-nĭz′əm) *n.* The theological principles of Cornelis Jansen, condemned as heretical by the Roman Catholic Church, which emphasize predestination, deny free will, and maintain that human nature is incapable of good. —**Jan′sen·ist** *n.* & *adj.* —**Jan′sen·is′tic** *adj.*
Jan·u·ar·y (jăn′yo͞o-ĕr′ē) *n., pl.* **-ies.** *Abbr.* **Jan.** The first month of the year in the Gregorian calendar. January has 31 days. See **calendar.** [Middle English *Januarie*, from Latin *Jānuārius (mensis)*, "(month of) Janus," from *Jānus*, JANUS.]
Ja·nus (jā′nəs). *Mythology.* An ancient Roman god of gates and doorways, depicted with two faces looking in opposite directions, whose festival month was January. [Latin *Jānus*. See **ei-**[1] in Appendix.*]
Ja·nus-faced (jā′nəs-fāst′) *adj.* Hypocritical.
Jap (jăp) *n. Slang.* Japanese. Usually used disparagingly.
Jap. Japan; Japanese.

ă pat/ā pay/âr care/ä father/b bib/ch church/d deed/ĕ pet/ē be/f fife/g gag/h hat/hw which/ĭ pit/ī pie/îr pier/j judge/k kick/l lid, needle/m mum/n no, sudden/ng thing/ŏ pot/ō toe/ô paw, for/oi noise/ou out/o͝o took/o͞o boot/p pop/r roar/s sauce/sh ship, dish/

ja·pan (jə-păn′) *n.* **1.** A black enamel or lacquer of a type originating in the Orient, used to produce a durable glossy finish. **2.** Any object decorated and varnished in the Japanese manner. —*adj.* Relating to or varnished with japan. —*tr.v.* **japanned, -panning, -pans. 1.** To enamel with japan. **2.** To coat with a glossy finish. [From JAPAN.]

Ja·pan (jə-păn′). *Japanese* **Ni·hon** (nē-hôn′), **Nip·pon** (nĭ-pŏn′). *Abbr.* **Jap.** A country of Asia occupying an archipelago of 142,706 square miles off the northeastern coast of the continent, and comprising the main islands of Hokkaido, Honshu, Shikoku, and Kyushu, with numerous smaller islands. Population, 93,419,000. Capital, Tokyo, on Honshu. [Probably from Malay *Japang,* from Chinese *Jih*[4]*-pen*[3], "(Land of the) Rising Sun." See **Nihon, Nippon.**]

Ja·pan, Sea of (jə-păn′). That part of the Pacific Ocean lying between Japan and the Asian mainland.

Japan clover. A leguminous plant, *Lespedeza striata,* native to Asia, cultivated as a forage plant and for soil improvement.

Ja·pan Current (jə-păn′). *Japanese* **Ku·ro·shi·o** (ko͞o′rō-shē′ō). A warm ocean current flowing northeast from the Philippine Sea past southeastern Japan to the North Pacific.

Jap·a·nese (jăp′ə-nēz′, -nēs′) *adj. Abbr.* **Jap.** Of or pertaining to Japan, or to the people, language, or culture of Japan. —*n., pl.* **Japanese. 1.** A native or inhabitant of Japan. **2.** *Abbr.* **Jap.** The language of Japan, having no proved affinities to any other language.

Japanese andromeda. A shrub, *Pieris japonica,* native to Japan, having small, early-blooming white flowers.

Japanese beetle. A metallic-green and brownish beetle, *Popillia japonica,* native to eastern Asia, the larvae and adults of which are serious plant pests in North America.

Japanese cedar. A tree, the **cryptomeria** *(see),* or its wood.

Japanese iris. A plant, *Iris kaempferi,* native to Asia, and cultivated in many horticultural varieties for its large, flat, showy flowers.

Japanese ivy. Boston ivy *(see).*

Japanese leaf. A plant, the **Chinese evergreen** *(see).*

Japanese maple. A shrub or small tree, *Acer palmatum,* native to eastern Asia and widely cultivated for its decorative, deeply lobed, often reddish foliage.

Japanese river fever. *Pathology.* **Scrub typhus** *(see).*

Japanese spurge. A plant, **pachysandra** *(see).*

Japan paper. A strong fibrous paper made in Japan, and often used for printing etchings.

Japan Trench. A depression in the floor of the North Pacific off northeastern Japan, extending from the Bonin to the Kurile islands and reaching depths of over 30,000 feet.

Japan wax. A pale-yellow solid wax obtained from the berries of certain plants of the genus *Rhus* and used in wax matches, soaps, food packaging, and as a substitute for beeswax.

jape (jāp) *v.* **japed, japing, japes.** *Archaic.* —*intr.* To joke or quip. —*tr.* To joke about; make sport of. —*n.* A joke or quip. [Middle English *japen,* to trick, joke, from Old French *japper,* to yap (imitative).] —**jap′er** *n.* —**jap′er·y** *n.*

Ja·pheth (jā′fĭth). Also **Ja·phet** (-fĭt). The third son of Noah, in some traditions considered the ancestor of the Indo-European race. Genesis 5:32.

Ja·phet·ic (jə-fĕt′ĭk) *adj.* **1.** Of or pertaining to Japheth or his descendants. **2.** Designating a discredited linguistic grouping that attempted to associate Basque, Etruscan, and sometimes Sumerian and Elamite with the Caucasian languages.

ja·pon·i·ca (jə-pŏn′ĭ-kə) *n.* **1.** A shrub, the **camellia** *(see).* **2.** A shrub, *Chaenomeles japonica,* native to Japan, cultivated for its red flowers. In this sense, also called "Japanese quince." [New Latin, "Japanese," from *Japonia,* JAPAN.]

Jap·o·nism (jăp′ə-nĭz′əm) *n.* Something characteristically Japanese. [French *Japonisme,* from *Japon,* JAPAN.]

Ja·pu·rá (zhä′po͞o-rä′). A river of South America, rising in southwestern Colombia and flowing 1,500 miles generally southeast to the Amazon in northwestern Brazil.

jar[1] (jär) *n.* **1.** A cylindrical glass or earthenware vessel with a wide mouth and usually without handles. **2.** The contents of such a vessel; a jarful. [French *jarre,* from Provençal *jarra,* from Arabic *jarrah,* large earthen vase.]

jar[2] (jär) *v.* **jarred, jarring, jars.** —*intr.* **1.** To make or utter a harsh sound. **2.** To disturb or irritate; grate: *His voice jarred on her nerves.* **3.** To shake or shiver from impact. **4.** To clash or conflict: *"We ourselves . . . often jar with the landscape."* (Isak Dinesen). —*tr.* **1.** To bump or cause to move or shake from impact. **2.** To startle or unsettle; to shock. —*n.* **1.** A jolt; shock. **2.** A harsh or grating sound; discord. [Probably imitative.]

jar·di·nière (järd′n-îr′; *French* zhȧr-dē-nyâr′) *n.* **1.** A large, decorative stand or pot for plants. **2.** Diced, cooked vegetables served as a garnish with meat. [French, feminine of *jardinier,* gardener, from *jardin,* garden, from Old French, from Vulgar Latin *gardīnus* (unattested), GARDEN.]

Jar·ed·ite (jâr′ə-dīt′) *n.* A member of the ancient people believed by the Mormons to have migrated to America under God's protection after the dispersal from Babel. [After their eponymous ancestor *Jared.*] —**Jar′ed·ite′** *adj.*

jar·ful (jär′fo͝ol′) *n., pl.* **-fuls. 1.** The amount a specified jar will hold. **2.** The contents of a jar.

jar·gon[1] (jär′gən) *n.* **1.** Nonsensical, incoherent, or meaningless utterance; gibberish: *"Wholly a blessed time: when jargon might abate, and . . . genuine speech begin"* (Carlyle). **2.** A hybrid language or dialect; pidgin. **3.** The specialized or technical language of a trade, profession, class, or fellowship; cant: *"She could not follow the ugly academic jargon"* (Virginia Woolf). Compare **argot, slang.** —See Synonyms at **dialect.** —*intr.v.* **jargoned, -goning, -gons.** To speak in or use jargon. [Middle English *iargoun, gargoun,* meaningless chatter, from Old French *jargoun, gargon,* "twittering" (probably imitative).]

jar·gon[2] (jär-gŏn′) *n.* Also **jar·goon** (jär-go͞on′). A smoky, yellow, or colorless variety of zircon. [French, ZIRCON.]

jar·gon·ize (jär′gə-nīz′) *v.* **-ized, -izing, -izes.** —*tr.* To debase or translate into jargon. —*intr.* To talk in jargon.

jarl (yärl) *n.* A great chieftain or nobleman of the medieval Scandinavians. [Old Norse, from Common Germanic *erilaz* (unattested), EARL.]

Jas. 1. James. **2.** James (New Testament).

jas·mine (jăz′mən) *n.* Also **jes·sa·mine** (jĕs′ə-mĭn) (especially for sense 2). **1.** Any of several vines or shrubs of the genus *Jasminum;* especially, *J. officinalis,* native to Asia, having fragrant white flowers used in making perfume. **2.** Any of several woody vines of the genus *Gelsemium;* especially, *G. sempervirens,* of the southeastern United States, having fragrant yellow flowers. **3.** Any of several other plants or shrubs having fragrant flowers. **4.** Light to brilliant yellow. See **color.** [French *jasmin,* from Arabic *yās(a)mīn,* from Persian *yasmīn, yāsman*†.]

Ja·son (jā′sən). *Greek Mythology.* The leader of the Argonauts in quest of the Golden Fleece; husband of Medea.

jas·per (jăs′pər) *n.* **1.** An opaque variety of quartz, reddish, brown, or yellow in color. **2.** Chalcedony, especially green chalcedony. [Middle English *jaspre,* from Old French *jasp(r)e,* from Latin *jaspis,* from Greek *iaspis,* from Semitic, akin to Assyrian *ashpū,* Aramaic *yashb,* and Hebrew *yashpāh.*]

Jas·pers (yäs′pərs), **Karl.** 1883–1969. German philosopher.

jasper ware. A fine white porcelain or stoneware invented by Josiah Wedgwood, often colored by metallic oxides with raised designs remaining white.

Jas·sy. See **Iaşi.**

Jat (jät, jôt) *n.* A member of an Indo-Aryan people of the Punjab and Uttar Pradesh. [Hindi *jāṭ*†.]

ja·to (jā′tō) *n.* **1.** A takeoff aided by an auxiliary jet or rocket. **2.** An auxiliary unit providing thrust for such a takeoff. [From JATO.]

JATO jet assisted takeoff.

jaun·dice (jôn′dĭs, jän′-) *n.* Yellowish discoloration of tissues and bodily fluids with bile pigment caused by any of several pathological conditions in which normal processing of bile is interrupted. Also called "icterus." [Middle English *jaun(d)is,* from Old French *jaunice,* from *jaune,* yellow, from Latin *galbinus,* greenish yellow, pale green, from *galbus*†.]

jaun·diced (jôn′dĭst, jän′-) *adj.* **1.** Affected with jaundice. **2.** Yellow or yellowish. **3.** Affected by envy, jealousy, prejudice, or hostility; embittered.

jaunt (jônt, jänt) *n.* A short trip or excursion, usually pleasurable; an outing: *"He set off for a three-day bachelor jaunt to Capri"* (Morris L. West). —*intr.v.* **jaunted, jaunting, jaunts.** To make a short journey, especially for pleasure. [Origin unknown.]

jaunting car. A light, open cart with seats hung back to back over its two wheels, used in Ireland. Also called "jaunty car."

jaun·ty (jôn′tē, jän′-) *adj.* **-tier, -tiest. 1.** Crisp and dapper in appearance; natty. **2.** Having a buoyant or self-confident air; brisk; carefree. **3.** *Obsolete.* Well-bred. [Earlier *jentee, jantee,* elegant, "genteel," from French *gentil.* See **gentle.**] —**jaun′ti·ly** *adv.* —**jaun′ti·ness** *n.*

Jav. Javanese.

ja·va (jăv′ə, jä′və) *n. Informal.* Brewed coffee. [From JAVA.]

Ja·va (jä′və, jăv′ə). An island of Indonesia, 48,842 square miles in area, lying between the Indian Ocean and the Java Sea; site of Djakarta, the country's capital. Population, 63,000,000.

Java man. Pithecanthropus *(see).*

Jav·a·nese (jăv′ə-nēz′, -nēs′) *adj. Abbr.* **Jav.** Of or pertaining to Java, or to the people, language, or culture of Java. —*n., pl.* **Javanese.** *Abbr.* **Jav. 1.** A native or inhabitant of Java. **2.** The Indonesian language spoken in Java.

Ja·va·rí (zhä′və-rē′). *Spanish* **Ya·va·rí** (yä′vä-rē′). A river rising in eastern Peru and flowing about 650 miles northeast along the border between Peru and Brazil to the Amazon.

Ja·va Sea (jä′və, jăv′ə). The part of the Pacific Ocean lying between the islands of Java and Borneo.

Java sparrow. A small grayish bird, *Padda oryzivora,* native to tropical Asia and often kept as a cage bird.

jave·lin (jăv′lən, jăv′ə-) *n.* **1.** A light spear thrown with the hand and used as a weapon. **2.** A metal or metal-tipped spear, generally not less than 8½ feet in length for men, used in contests of distance throwing. **3.** The athletic field event in which such a spear is thrown. In this sense, also called "javelin throw." [French *javeline,* from Old French, variant of *javelot,* from Celtic. See **ghabholo-** in Appendix.*]

Ja·velle water (zhə-vĕl′). Also **Ja·vel water.** An aqueous solution of potassium or sodium hypochlorite, used as a disinfectant and bleaching agent. [From *Javel,* former town, now part of Paris, France.]

jaw (jô) *n.* **1.** Either of two bony or cartilaginous structures in most vertebrates forming the framework of the mouth and holding the teeth. **2.** The anatomical parts forming the wall of the mouth and serving to open and close it. **3.** Either of two opposed hinged parts in a mechanical device. **4.** *Plural.* The walls of a pass, canyon, or cavern. **5.** *Plural.* A dangerous situation or confrontation: *the jaws of death.* **6.** *Slang.* **a.** Impudent argument or expression of opposition; back talk: *Don't give me any jaw.* **b.** Chatter. —*intr.v.* **jawed, jawing, jaws.** *Slang.* To talk vociferously; jabber. [Middle English *iawe, iowe*†.]

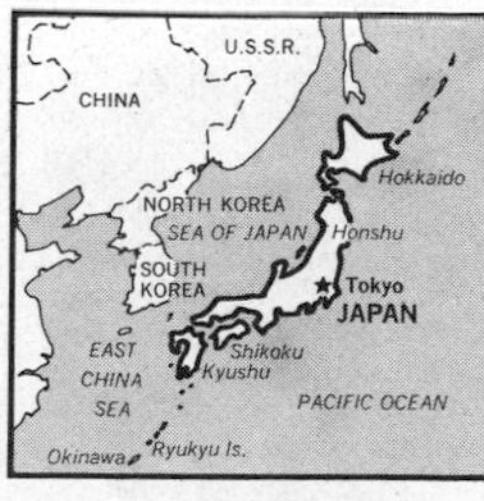

Japan

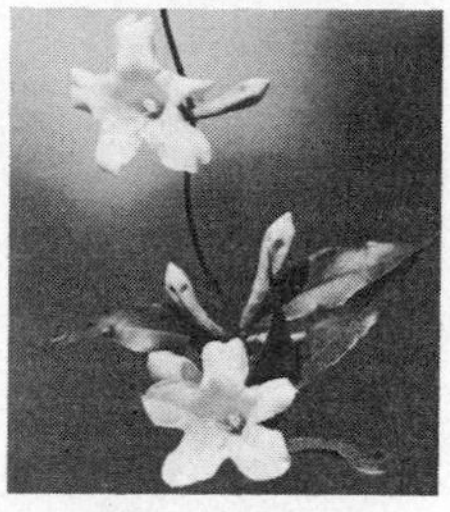
jasmine
Gelsemium sempervirens

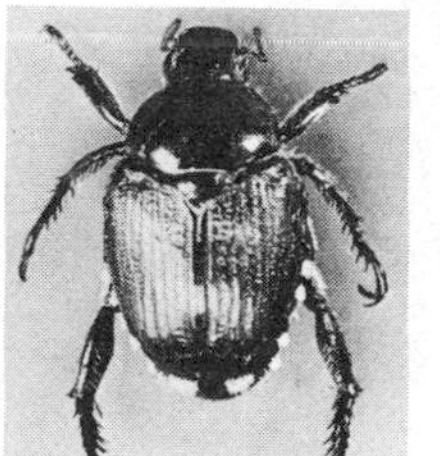
Japanese beetle

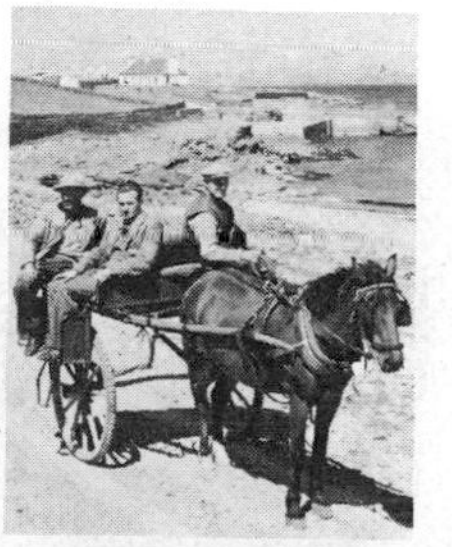
jaunting car

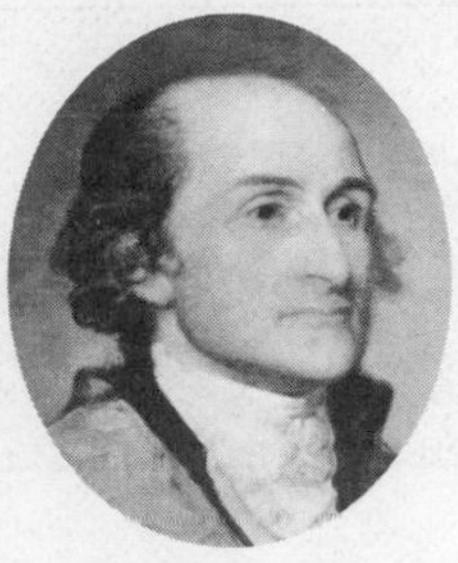
John Jay
Portrait by Gilbert Stuart

jaw·bone (jô′bōn′) *n.* **1.** Any bone of the jaw; especially, the bone of the lower jaw. **2.** *Slang.* Credit.
jaw·break·er (jô′brā′kər) *n.* **1.** A kind of very hard candy. **2.** *Slang.* A word which is difficult to pronounce. **3.** A machine that crushes rock or ore. Also called "jawcrusher."
jay[1] (jā) *n.* The letter *j.*
jay[2] (jā) *n.* **1.** Any of various often crested birds of the genera *Garrulus, Cyanocitta, Aphelocoma,* and related genera within the family Corvidae, often having a loud, harsh call. **2.** A noisy or talkative person; chatterbox. **3.** *Slang.* A newcomer or inexperienced person. [Middle English, from Old French, from Late Latin *gāius* and *gāia*†.]
Jay (jā), **John.** 1745–1829. American statesman, diplomat, and first Chief Justice of the United States.
jay·hawk·er (jā′hô′kər) *n.* **1.** One of the free-soil guerrilla raiders in Kansas or Missouri during the border disputes of 1857–59. **2.** Any Unionist guerrilla soldier. **3.** *Usually capital* **J.** *Informal.* A Kansan. [From the imaginary bird the *jayhawk.*]
jay·vee (jā′vē′) *n. Informal.* **1.** A junior varsity. **2.** A member of a junior varsity. [*Jay,* the letter *J* + *vee,* the letter *V.*]
jay·walk (jā′wôk′) *intr.v.* **-walked, -walking, -walks.** To cross a street illegally or recklessly. [From JAY (newcomer).] **—jay′walk′er** *n.*
jazz (jăz) *n.* **1.** A kind of native American music first played extemporaneously by Negro bands in Southern towns at the turn of the century and in most styles having a strong but flexible rhythmic understructure with solo and ensemble improvisations on basic tunes and chord patterns, and, in more recent styles, a highly sophisticated harmonic idiom. **2.** Big-band dance music, popular especially in the 1920's and 1930's. **3.** *Slang.* Animation; enthusiasm. **4.** *Slang.* **a.** Extreme exaggeration: *all that jazz about his big deals.* **b.** Nonsense. *—v.* **jazzed, jazzing, jazzes.** *—tr.* **1.** To play in a jazz style. **2.** *Slang.* To lie or exaggerate to. *—intr. Slang.* To lie or exaggerate. **—jazz up.** *Informal.* **1.** To play in a more lively or improvisational way, as by a jazz arrangement. **2.** To make more interesting; enliven. [Origin uncertain.] **—jazz′er** *n.*
jazz·y (jăz′ē) *adj.* **-ier, -iest.** **1.** Resembling jazz; rhythmical. **2.** *Slang.* Showy; flashy: *a jazzy red car.* **—jazz′i·ly** *adv.* **—jazz′i·ness** *n.*
J-bar (jā′bär′) *n.* A device by which a skier is towed uphill leaning on a J-shaped bar suspended from an overhead cable.
J.C.B. Bachelor of Canon Law (Latin *Juris Canonici Baccalaureus*).
J.C.D. Doctor of Canon Law (Latin *Juris Canonici Doctor*).
J.C.S. Joint Chiefs of Staff.
jct. junction.
J.D. **1.** Doctor of Laws (Latin *Jurum Doctor*). **2.** juvenile delinquent.
jeal·ous (jĕl′əs) *adj.* **1.** Fearful or wary of being supplanted; apprehensive of loss of position or affection. **2.** Resentful or bitter in rivalry; envious. Often used with *of.* **3.** Possessively watchful; vigilant: *He kept a jealous guard on what he had hoarded.* **4.** Protective; solicitous. Used with *of* or *for: jealous for his daughter's welfare.* **5.** Concerning or arising from feelings of envy, apprehension, or bitterness: *jealous thoughts.* **6.** Intolerant of disloyalty or infidelity; autocratic: *a jealous God.* [Middle English *gelus, ielus,* jealous, zealous for, from Old French *gelos, jelos,* from Medieval Latin *zēlōsus,* from Late Latin *zēlus,* from Greek *zēlos,* zeal. See **yā-** in Appendix.*] **—jeal′ous·ly** *adv.* **—jeal′ous·ness** *n.*
jeal·ous·y (jĕl′ə-sē) *n., pl.* **-ies.** **1.** A jealous attitude, especially toward a rival. **2.** Close watchfulness.
jean (jēn) *n.* **1.** A heavy, strong, twilled cotton, used in making uniforms and work clothes. **2.** *Plural.* Clothes, especially pants, made of such fabric. In this sense, also called "blue jeans." [Earlier *iene fustian, geane fustian,* from Middle English *Jene, Gene,* Genoa, where it was first made.]
Jean[1] (jēn). A feminine given name. [Scottish, from Old French *Jehane,* JOAN.]
Jean[2] (jēn). A masculine given name. [French, JOHN.]
Jeanne d'Arc. See **Joan of Arc.**
Jeans (jēnz), Sir **James Hopwood.** 1877–1946. British astronomer and mathematician.
Je·bel esh Shar·qi. The Arabic name for **Anti-Lebanon.**
Je·bel Ha·run. The Arabic name for Mount **Hor.**
Je·bel Ka·ther·i·na (jĕb′əl kăth′ə-rē′nə). *English* **Mount Cath·e·rine** (kăth′rĭn, -ər-ĭn). The highest point (8,651 feet) on the Sinai Peninsula, near its southern end.
Je·bel Mu·sa (jĕb′əl mōō′sə). *Ancient name* **Ab·il·a** (ăb′ə-lə). A mountain 2,790 feet high in northern Morocco on the Strait of Gibraltar; one of the Pillars of Hercules.
Jed·da. See **Jidda.**
jee. Variant of **gee** (mild expletive).
jeep (jēp) *n.* A small, durable motor vehicle with four-wheel drive and quarter-ton capacity, used as an all-purpose vehicle by the armed forces. [Originally *G.P.,* "general purpose."]
jeer (jîr) *v.* **jeered, jeering, jeers.** *—intr.* To speak or shout derisively; mock. *—tr.* To abuse openly; to taunt. *—n.* A scoffing or taunting remark or shout. Usually used in the plural. [Origin unknown.] **—jeer′er** *n.* **—jeer′ing·ly** *adv.*
Jefferson, Mount (jĕf′ər-sən). **1.** A mountain rising to 10,495 feet in the Cascade Range in northwest-central Oregon. **2.** A mountain rising to 5,725 feet in the White Mountains of north-central New Hampshire.
Jef·fer·son (jĕf′ər-sən), **Thomas.** 1743–1826. Third President of the United States (1801–09).
Jef·fer·son City (jĕf′ər-sən). The capital of Missouri, in the center of the state on the Missouri River. Population, 28,000.
Jef·fer·so·ni·an (jĕf′ər-sō′nē-ən) *adj.* Pertaining to or typical of Thomas Jefferson or his political attitudes and theories. *—n.* A follower of Jefferson or a proponent of his politics. **—Jef′fer·so′ni·an·ism′** *n.*
Jef·frey (jĕf′rē). Also **Geof·frey.** A masculine given name. [Middle English *Ge(o)ffrey,* from Old French *Geoffroi,* from Medieval Latin *Galfridus,* from Germanic. See **pri-** in Appendix.*]
je·had. Variant of **jihad.**
Je·han. See **Shah Jahan.**
Jeh·lam. See **Jhelum.**
Je·hol. The former name for **Chengteh.**
Je·ho·vah (jĭ-hō′və). God, especially in Christian translations of the Old Testament. See **Tetragrammaton.** [From the Hebrew Tetragrammaton YHWH with the addition of the vowel points of ADONAI.]
Jehovah's Witnesses. A religious sect founded in the United States during the late 19th century, the followers of which practice active evangelism, preach the imminent approach of the millennium, and are strongly opposed to war and to the authority of organized government in matters of conscience.
Je·ho·vist (jĭ-hō′vĭst) *n.* The author of portions of the Hexateuch, **Yahwist** *(see).*
je·june (jə-jōōn′) *adj.* **1.** Not nourishing; insubstantial. **2.** Not interesting; insipid or weak; dull: *"and there pour forth jejune words and useless empty phrases"* (Trollope). **3.** Childish; immature; unsophisticated. [From Latin *jējūnus,* hungry, fasting. See **dine.**] **—je·june′ly** *adv.* **—je·june′ness** *n.*
je·ju·num (jə-jōō′nəm) *n., pl.* **-na** (-nə). The section of the small intestine between the duodenum and the ileum. [Medieval Latin *jējūnum (intestīnum),* "the fasting (intestine)," from *jējūnus,* fasting, JEJUNE; a translation of Greek *nēstis,* the jejunum, from *nēstis,* fasting, so named because it was always found (in dissection) empty.]
Je·kyll and Hyde (jē′kəl, jĕk′əl; hīd). *Informal.* One who has quasi-schizophrenic alternating phases of pleasantness and unpleasantness. [After *The Strange Case of Dr. Jekyll and Mr. Hyde* (1886), story by R.L. Stevenson.]
jell (jĕl) *v.* **jelled, jelling, jells.** *—intr.* **1.** To become firm or gelatinous; congeal. **2.** *Informal.* To take shape or fall into place; become clear and definite; crystallize: *My ideas on the subject haven't jelled yet.* *—tr.* **1.** To cause to become firm or gelatinous; jelly. **2.** *Informal.* To give shape to; make clear and definite. *—n.* Jelly. [Back-formation from JELLY.]
jel·lied (jĕl′ēd) *adj.* **1.** Chilled or otherwise congealed into jelly. **2.** Coated with jelly. **3.** Made or served within jelly.
jel·li·fy (jĕl′ə-fī′) *v.* **-fied, -fying, -fies.** *—intr.* To become jelly. *—tr.* To make into jelly. **—jel′li·fi·ca′tion** *n.*
Jell-O (jĕl′ō) *n.* A trademark for a gelatin dessert.
jel·ly (jĕl′ē) *n., pl.* **-lies.** **1.** A soft, semisolid food substance with a resilient consistency, made by the setting of a liquid containing pectin or gelatin, or by the addition of gelatin to a liquid; specifically, such a substance made of fruit juice containing pectin boiled with sugar. **2.** Any substance with the consistency of jelly, such as a petroleum ointment. **3.** Anything similar or likened to jelly. *—v.* **jellied, -lying, -lies.** *—tr.* **1.** To make or cause to become jelly. **2.** To spread or prepare with jelly. *—intr.* To become jelly; to set. [Middle English *geli, gely,* from Old French *gelee,* frost, jelly, from Vulgar Latin *gelāta* (unattested), from Latin, feminine past participle of *gelāre,* to freeze. See **gel-**[3] in Appendix.*]
jel·ly·bean (jĕl′ē-bēn′) *n.* A small ovoid candy with a hardened sugar coating over a chewy center.
jelly doughnut. A rounded cake of deep-fried dough with a jelly center.
jel·ly·fish (jĕl′ē-fĭsh′) *n., pl.* **jellyfish** or **-fishes.** **1.** Any of numerous usually free-swimming marine coelenterates of the class Scyphozoa, characteristically having a gelatinous, tentacled, often bell-shaped medusoid stage as the dominant or only phase of its life cycle. **2.** Any of various similar or related coelenterates or other organisms. **3.** *Informal.* A person who lacks force of character, resiliency, or self-control; a weakling.
jem·a·dar (jĕm′ə-där′) *n.* **1.** An officer of the army of India with a rank corresponding to lieutenant. **2.** Any of several officials of the Indian government. [Urdu *jamaʻdār* : Persian *jamaʻat,* body of men, from Arabic *jamʻ,* collection + *dār,* holder, from Old Persian (see **dher-**[2] in Appendix*).]
jem·my. *Chiefly British.* Variant of **jimmy.**
Je·na (yā′nä). A city of southern East Germany near the site of a Napoleonic victory over Prussia (1806). Population, 83,000.
Jen·ghis, Jen·ghiz. See **Genghis Khan.**
Jen·ner (jĕn′ər), **Edward.** 1749–1823. British physician; discovered vaccination.
jen·net (jĕn′ĭt) *n.* Also **gen·et.** A small Spanish saddle horse. [Middle English *jennett, genett,* from Old French *genet,* from Spanish *jinete,* light horseman, from Arabic *Zenetī,* Berber tribe famed for horsemanship.]
jen·ny (jĕn′ē) *n., pl.* **-nies.** **1.** A female donkey. **2.** A female wren. **3.** A spinning jenny. [From *Jenny,* pet form of JANE.]
Jen·sen (yĕn′zən, jĕn′sən), **J. Hans Daniel.** Born 1907. German nuclear physicist.
jeop·ard·ize (jĕp′ər-dīz′) *tr.v.* **-dized, -dizing, -dizes.** To invite loss of or injury to; make vulnerable or precarious; imperil.
jeop·ard·y (jĕp′ər-dē) *n., pl.* **-ies.** **1.** Danger or risk of loss or injury; peril; vulnerability. **2.** *Law.* The defendant's risk or danger of conviction when put on trial. [Middle English *jeopartie,* even chance, from Old French *jeu parti,* "divided play, even chance" : *jeu,* game, from Latin *jocus,* jest, game (see

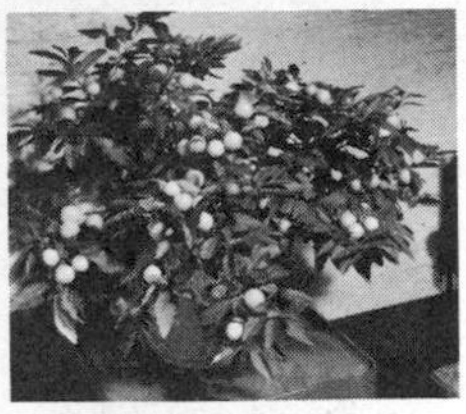
Jerusalem cherry

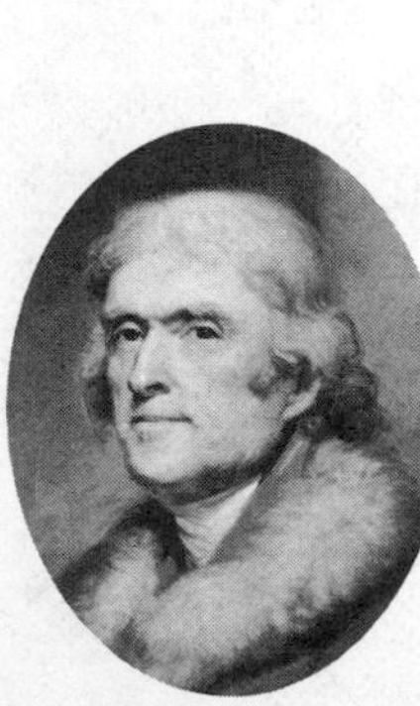
Thomas Jefferson
Portrait by
Rembrandt Peale

yek- in Appendix*) + *parti,* past participle of *partir,* to divide, from Latin *partīre,* from *pars* (stem *part-*), PART.]

Jeph·thah (jĕf′thə, jĕp′-). A judge of Israel who sacrificed his daughter to fulfill a rash vow. Judges 11-12.

je·quir·i·ty bean (jĭ-kwîr′ə-tē). The **rosary pea** *(see),* or one of its seed. [From Tupi-Guarani *jekirití.*]

Je·qui·tin·hon·ha (zhĕ-kĕ′tē-nyō′nyä). A river of Brazil, rising in central Minas Gerais and flowing 500 miles generally northeast through southern Bahia to the Atlantic.

Jer. Jeremiah (Old Testament).

jer·bo·a (jər-bō′ə) *n.* Any of various small, leaping rodents of the family Dipodidae, of Asia and northern Africa, having long hind legs and a long, tufted tail. [New Latin, from Medieval Latin *jerbōa,* from Arabic *yerbō′, yarbu′,* flesh of the loins (from the animal's highly developed thighs).]

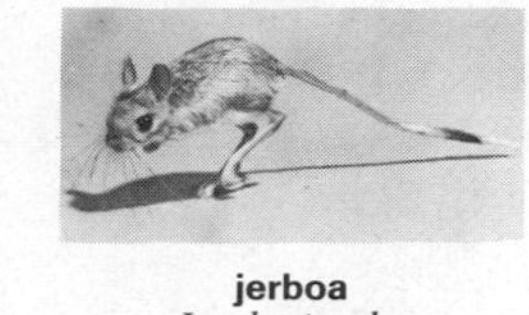

jerboa
Jaculus jaculus

jer·e·mi·ad (jĕr′ə-mī′əd) *n.* An elaborate and prolonged lamentation or a tale of woe. [French *jérémiade,* after *Jérémie,* JEREMIAH (who lamented the decline of morals).]

Jer·e·mi·ah[1] (jĕr′ə-mī′ə). Also in Douay Bible **Jer·e·mi·as** (-mī′əs). A Major Prophet of the seventh and sixth centuries B.C. [Late Latin *Jeremias,* from Hebrew *Yirmayāh(ū),* "the Lord is exalted."]

Jer·e·mi·ah[2] (jĕr′ə-mī′ə) *n.* Also in Douay Bible **Jer·e·mi·as** (-mī′əs). *Abbr.* **Jer.** A book in the Old Testament containing the prophecies of Jeremiah.

Je·rez (hĕ-rāth′). In full **Jerez de la Fron·te·ra** (*thĕ* lä frōn-tär′ä). Formerly **Xe·res** (hā′rās). A city of Spain, in the southwest, 14 miles northeast of Cádiz. Population, 140,000.

Jer·i·cho (jĕr′ĭ-kō′). **1.** An ancient city of Jordan, situated at 800 feet below sea level near the northern end of the Dead Sea; captured by the Israelites in the 13th century B.C. Joshua 2:6. **2.** A modern village on the site of ancient Jericho.

jerk[1] (jûrk) *v.* **jerked, jerking, jerks.** —*tr.* **1.** To move (something) by a sharp, suddenly abrupt motion; give an abrupt thrust, push, pull, or twist to: *He jerked his head as a signal.* **2.** To throw or toss with a quick abrupt motion. **3.** To utter abruptly or sharply. Used with *out.* —*intr.* **1.** To move in sudden abrupt motions; jolt: *The train jerked ahead.* **2.** To make spasmodic motions: *His legs jerked from fatigue.* —**jerk off.** *Vulgar Slang.* To masturbate. —*n.* **1.** A sudden, abrupt motion, such as a yank, tug, or twist. **2.** A jolting or lurching motion. **3.** *Physiology.* A sudden spasmodic, muscular movement. **4.** *Plural.* Violent convulsive twitching and shaking often resulting from excitement. **5.** *Plural. Slang.* Chorea. **6.** *Slang.* A dull, stupid, or fatuous person; numbskull. [Origin obscure.] —**jerk′er** *n.*

jerk[2] (jûrk) *tr.v.* **jerked, jerking, jerks.** To cut (meat) into long strips and dry in the sun or cure by exposing to smoke. [Back-formation from JERKY (cured meat).]

jer·kin (jûr′kən) *n.* **1.** A sleeveless waistcoat; vest. **2.** A short, close-fitting coat or jacket, usually of leather. [Origin unknown.]

jerk·wa·ter (jûrk′wô′tər, -wŏt′ər) *adj.* **1.** *Informal.* Remote, small, and insignificant: *a jerkwater town.* **2.** Contemptibly trivial. [An early railroad term for a remote place where water had to be "jerked" or drawn and carried to trains.]

jerk·y[1] (jûr′kē) *adj.* **-ier, -iest. 1.** Characterized by jerks or jerking. **2.** *Slang.* Foolish; silly. —**jerk′i·ly** *adv.* —**jerk′i·ness** *n.*

jerk·y[2] (jûr′kē) *n.* Meat, especially beef, cured by jerking. Also called "charqui." [Earlier *jerkin beef,* from CHARQUI.]

jer·o·bo·am (jĕr′ə-bō′əm) *n.* A wine bottle holding about 4/5 of a gallon. [Humorously after *Jeroboam I,* king of northern Israel, who was a "mighty man of valor" (I Kings 11:28), and who "made Israel to sin" (I Kings 14:16).]

Je·rome (jə-rōm′). A masculine given name. [French *Jérôme,* from Greek *Hierōnumos,* "holy name" : Greek *hieros,* sacred (see **eis-[1]** in Appendix*) + *-ōnumos,* -ONYM.]

Jerome (jə-rōm′), **Saint.** A.D. 340?–420. Latin scholar and Doctor of the Church; prepared the Vulgate.

Jer·ry (jĕr′ē) *n., pl.* **-ries.** *Chiefly British Slang.* A German; especially, a German soldier. [Alteration of GERMAN.]

jer·ry-build (jĕr′ē-bĭld′) *tr.v.* **-built** (-bĭlt′), **-building, -builds.** To build shoddily, flimsily, and cheaply. [Origin obscure.] —**jer′ry-build′er** *n.*

jer·sey (jûr′zē) *n., pl.* **-seys. 1.** A soft, plain-knitted fabric used for clothing. **2.** Any garment made of this fabric. **3.** A knitted pullover shirt worn for certain sports. **4.** A close-fitting knitted jacket or sweater. [Originally a woolen sweater peculiar to the fishermen of JERSEY.]

Jer·sey[1] (jûr′zē). The largest (45 square miles) of the Channel Islands. Capital, St. Helier.

Jer·sey[2] (jûr′zē) *n.* Any of a breed of fawn-colored dairy cattle developed on the island of Jersey.

Jer·sey City (jûr′zē). A city of New Jersey, a river port on the Hudson in the northeast. Population, 276,000.

Je·ru·sa·lem (jə-rōō′sə-ləm, -zə-ləm). Ancient names **Sa·lem** (sā′ləm), **Hi·er·o·sol·y·ma** (hī′ə-rō-sŏl′ə-mə). The capital of ancient and modern Israel, regarded as holy by Jews, Christians, and Moslems. Population, 248,000.

Jerusalem artichoke. 1. A North American sunflower, *Helianthus tuberosus,* having yellow, rayed flowers and edible tuberous roots. **2.** The tuber of this plant, eaten as a vegetable. [By folk etymology from Italian *girasole,* sunflower, GIRASOL.]

Jerusalem cherry. A small shrub, *Solanum pseudo-capsicum,* native to the Old World, bearing inedible reddish fruit and used as a house plant.

Jerusalem cross. A cross with four arms, each terminating in a crossbar.

Jerusalem oak. A weedy North American plant, *Chenopodium botrys,* having lobed leaves and a characteristic odor suggestive of turpentine.

Jerusalem thorn. A spiny tropical American tree, *Parkinsonia aculeata,* having clusters of yellow flowers. [After Christ's crown of thorns.]

Jer·vis Bay (jär′vĭs, jûr′-). An inlet of the Pacific in eastern New South Wales, Australia, constituting part of the Australian Capital Territory.

jess (jĕs) *n.* A short strap fastened around the leg of a hawk or other bird used in falconry, and to which a leash may be fastened. —*tr.v.* **jessed, jessing, jesses.** To put jesses on (a hawk). [Middle English *ges(se),* from Old French *ges,* "a throwing," "something thrown around," from Vulgar Latin *jectus* (unattested), variant of Latin *jactus,* from *jacere,* to throw. See **yē-** in Appendix.*]

jes·sa·mine. Variant of **jasmine.**

Jes·se[1] (jĕs′ē). A masculine given name. [Latin, from Greek *Iessai,* from Hebrew *Yishay.*]

Jes·se[2] (jĕs′ē). Father of King David.

Jes·sel·ton. The former name for **Kota Kinabalu.**

Jes·si·ca (jĕs′ĭ-kə). A feminine given name. [Probably from Late Latin *Jesca,* from Greek (Septuagint) *Ieskha,* from Hebrew *Yiskāh,* Biblical name rendered as *Iscah* in the Authorized Version (Genesis 11:29), probably "shut up," "confined."]

jest (jĕst) *n.* **1.** Something said or done to provoke amusement and laughter. **2.** A frolicsome attitude; a frivolous mood: *spoken in jest.* **3.** A jeering remark; a taunt. **4.** An object of ridicule; laughingstock. **5.** *Obsolete.* **a.** An exploit. **b.** A tale of exploits. —See Synonyms at **joke.** —*v.* **jested, jesting, jests.** —*intr.* **1.** To act or speak playfully; make sport; to joke. **2.** To make witty or amusing remarks. **3.** To utter scoffs or jeers; to gibe. —*tr.* To make fun of; ridicule. [Middle English *geste,* deed, tale, from Old French *geste, jeste,* from Latin *gesta,* exploits, from *gerere,* to do. See **gerere** in Appendix.*]

jest·er (jĕs′tər) *n.* One given to jesting; especially, a fool or buffoon at medieval courts.

jest·ing (jĕs′tĭng) *n.* The action of one who jests. —*adj.* **1.** Given to making jests. **2.** Occasioning jests; trivial; unimportant. —**jest′ing·ly** *adv.*

Je·su (jē′zōō; *Latin* yā′sōō). Liturgical vocative of **Jesus.** [Late Latin *Jēsū,* vocative of *Jēsūs,* JESUS.]

Jes·u·it (jĕzh′ōō-ĭt, jĕz′yōō-) *n.* **1.** A member of the Society of Jesus, a Roman Catholic order founded by Saint Ignatius Loyola in 1534. **2.** *Often small* **j.** One given to subtle casuistry. [French *Jésuite,* from New Latin *Jesuita,* from JESUS.] —**Jes′u·it′i·cal** (-ĭ-kəl) *adj.* —**Jes′u·it′i·cal·ly** *adv.*

Je·sus (jē′zəs) 4?B.C.–A.D.29? **1.** Son of Mary; founder of Christianity; regarded by Christians as the son of God and the Messiah. Also, in various contexts, "Jesus Christ," "Christ," "Christ Jesus," or "Jesus of Nazareth." **2.** *Christian Science.* "The highest human corporeal concept of the divine idea" (Mary Baker Eddy). [Late Latin *Jēsūs,* from Greek *Iēsous,* from Hebrew *yēshūa′,* from *Yəhōshūa′,* JOSHUA.]

jet[1] (jĕt) *n.* **1.** A dense black coal that takes a high polish and is used for jewelry. **2.** A deep black. —*adj.* **1.** Made of or resembling jet. **2.** Black as jet. [Middle English *ge(e)t, jeet,* from Old French *jayet* and Norman French *geet,* from Latin *gagātēs,* from Greek *gagatēs,* "stone of *Gagai*" (town in Lycia).]

jet[2] (jĕt) *n.* **1.** A high-velocity fluid stream forced under pressure out of a small-diameter opening or nozzle. **2.** Something emitted in or as if in such a stream: *"such myriad and such vivid jets of images"* (Henry Roth). **3.** An outlet, such as a spout or nozzle, for emitting such a stream. **4. a.** A jet-propelled vehicle; especially, a jet-propelled aircraft. **b.** A jet engine. —*v.* **jetted, jetting, jets.** —*intr.* **1.** To move quickly; to dart. **2.** To travel by jet plane. —*tr.* To propel outward or squirt, as under pressure: *"Any man might . . . hang around outside of it, jetting tobacco juice."* (Ross Lockridge, Jr.). [Old French, from *jeter,* to spout forth, "to throw," from Vulgar Latin *jectāre* (unattested), from Latin *jactāre,* frequentative of Latin *jacere* (past participle *jactus*), to throw. See **yē-** in Appendix.*]

jet engine. 1. Any engine that develops thrust by ejecting a jet, especially by ejecting a jet of gaseous combustion products. **2.** Such an engine equipped to consume atmospheric oxygen, used especially in aircraft, and distinguished from rocket engines with self-contained fuel-oxidizer systems.

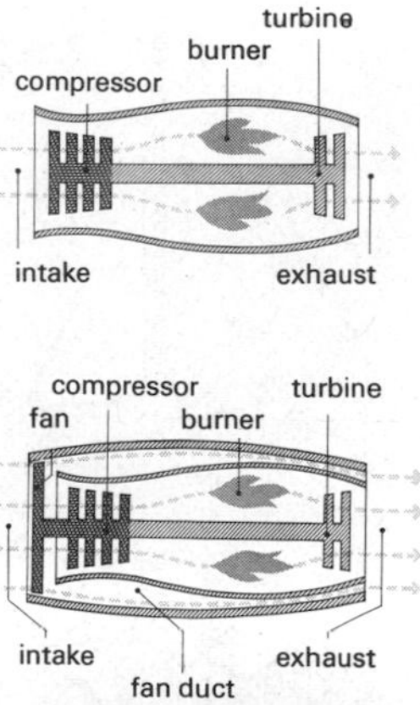

jet engine
Schematic of turbojet *(above)* and turbofan *(below)* jet engines

jet·lin·er (jĕt′lī′nər) *n.* A large passenger-carrying jet airplane.

jet·port (jĕt′pôrt′, -pōrt′) *n.* An airport equipped for jet aircraft.

jet propulsion. Propulsion derived from the expulsion of matter in a jet stream; especially, propulsion by jet engines.

jet·sam (jĕt′səm) *n.* **1.** Cargo or equipment thrown overboard to lighten a ship in distress. **2.** Discarded cargo or equipment found washed ashore. Used in the phrase *flotsam and jetsam.* **3.** Discarded odds and ends. [Earlier *jetson,* from JETTISON.]

jet set. A social set made up of people who spend much of their time aboard jetliners, traveling from one fashionable place to another. —**jet setter.**

jet stream. 1. A high-speed wind near the troposphere, generally moving from a westerly direction at speeds often exceeding 250 miles an hour. **2.** A high-speed stream; a jet.

jet·ti·son (jĕt′ĭ-sən, -zən) *tr.v.* **-soned, -soning, -sons. 1.** To cast off or overboard. **2.** To discard (unwanted or burdensome articles). —*n.* **1.** The act of jettisoning. **2.** Jetsam. [From Middle English *jetteson,* a throwing overboard, from Norman French *getteson,* from Latin *jactātiō,* from *jactāre,* to throw. See **jet** (to dart).]

jet·ty[1] (jĕt′ē) *n., pl.* **-ties. 1.** A pier or other structure projecting into a body of water to influence the current or tide or protect a harbor or shoreline. **2.** A wharf. [Middle English *jette,* from

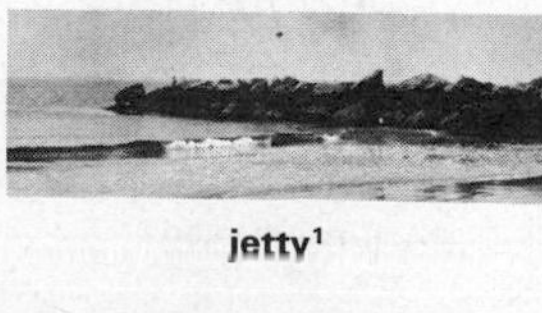

jetty[1]

t tight/th thin, path/*th* this, bathe/ŭ cut/ûr urge/v valve/w with/y yes/z zebra, size/zh vision/ə about, item, edible, gallop, circus/ à *Fr.* ami/œ *Fr.* feu, *Ger.* schön/ü *Fr.* tu, *Ger.* über/KH *Ger.* ich, *Scot.* loch/N *Fr.* bon. ***Follows main vocabulary. †Of obscure origin.**

Old French *jetee*, a jutting, projection, from the feminine past participle of *jeter*, to throw, project. See **jet** (to dart).]

jet·ty^{2} (jĕt′ē) *adj.* **1.** Resembling jet. **2.** Having the color of jet. **—jet′ti·ness** *n.*

jeu d'es·prit (zhœ dĕs-prē′) *pl.* **jeux d'esprit** (zhœ dĕs-prē′). *French.* A display or stroke of wit.

Jew (jo͞o) *n.* **1.** An adherent of Judaism. **2.** A descendant of the Hebrew people. *—adj.* Jewish. Considered offensive. **—jew down.** To best in bargaining by haggling or shrewd practices. An offensive expression, used derogatorily. [Middle English *Giw, Ju,* from Old French *giu, juiu,* from Latin *Jūdaeus,* from Greek *Ioudaios,* from Aramaic *Yəhūdāy* and Hebrew *Yəhūdī,* after the tribe of *Yəhūdāh,* JUDAH.]

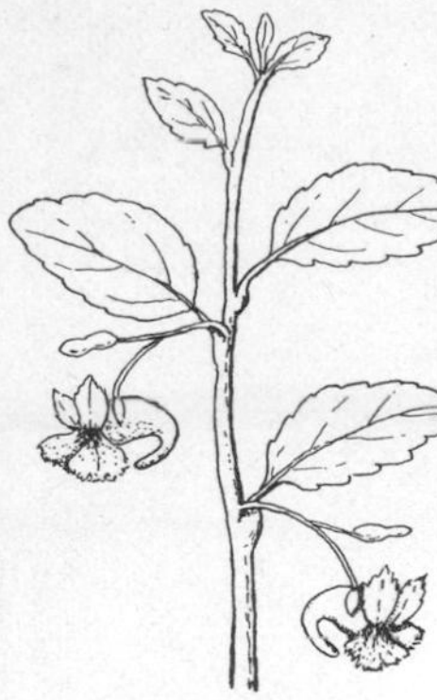

jewelweed
Impatiens biflora

Jew-bait·ing (jo͞o′bā′tĭng) *n.* Systematic persecution of Jews. **—Jew′-bait′ing** *adj.* **—Jew′-bait′er** *n.*

jew·el (jo͞o′əl) *n.* **1.** A costly ornament of precious metal or gems used as adornment. **2.** A precious stone; a gem. **3.** A small gem or gem substitute used as a bearing in a watch. **4.** A person or thing that is treasured or esteemed. *—tr.v.* **jeweled, -eling, -els.** Also *chiefly British* **-elled, -elling. 1.** To adorn with jewels. **2.** To fit with jewels, as a watch. [Middle English *iuel, gewel,* from Norman French *juel,* perhaps from *jeu,* game, jest, from Latin *jocus.* See **yek-** in Appendix.*]

jew·el·er (jo͞o′ə-lər) *n.* Also *chiefly British* **jew·el·ler.** *Abbr.* **jwlr.** A person who makes, repairs, or deals in jewelry.

jew·el·fish (jo͞o′əl-fĭsh′) *n., pl.* **jewelfish** or **-fishes.** A small, brilliantly colored freshwater fish, *Hemichromis bimaculatus,* of tropical Africa, popular in home aquariums.

jew·el·ry (jo͞o′əl-rē) *n.* Jewels collectively.

jew·el·weed (jo͞o′əl-wēd′) *n.* Any of several plants of the genus *Impatiens,* having yellowish, spurred flowers and seed pods that burst open at a touch when ripe. Also called "touch-me-not."

Jew·ess (jo͞o′ĭs) *n.* A Jewish woman or girl. Considered offensive.

jew·fish (jo͞o′fĭsh′) *n. pl.* **jewfish** or **-fishes.** Any of several large marine fishes of the family Serranidae; especially, *Epinephelus itajara,* of tropical Atlantic waters.

Jew·ish (jo͞o′ĭsh) *adj.* **1.** Of, concerning, or characteristic of the Jews, their customs, or their religion. **2.** Yiddish. *—n.* Yiddish. **—Jew′ish·ly** *adv.* **—Jew′ish·ness** *n.*

Jewish Autonomous Oblast. See **Birobidzhan.**

Jewish calendar. See **calendar.**

Jew·ry (jo͞o′rē) *n.* **1.** Jews collectively; the Jewish community. **2.** A section of a medieval city inhabited by Jews; ghetto.

jew's-harp (jo͞oz′härp′) *n.* Also **jews'-harp.** A small musical instrument with a lyre-shaped metal frame and a projecting steel tongue that is held between the teeth when played.

jez·e·bel (jĕz′ə-bĕl′, -bəl) *n.* Also **Jez·e·bel.** A scheming, wicked woman. [After JEZEBEL, who was known for her wickedness.]

Jez·e·bel (jĕz′ə-bĕl′, -bəl). Also in Douay Bible **Jez·a·bel.** Phoenician princess of the ninth century B.C.; queen of Israel as wife of Ahab. I Kings 16:29–31.

Jez·re·el, Plain of (jĕz′rē-əl, jĕz-rēl′). Also **Es·dra·e·lon** (ĕz′drə-ē′lŏn, ĕs′drā-). A fertile plain in northern Israel.

JFK 1. John Fitzgerald Kennedy. **2.** Airport code for John F. Kennedy International Airport, New York, New York.

jg junior grade.

Jhe·lum (jā′ləm). Also **Jeh·lam.** A river rising in the Himalayas of Jammu and Kashmir and flowing 480 miles first northwest and then southwest to the Chenab in West Pakistan.

JHVH, JHWH. Variants of **YHWH.**

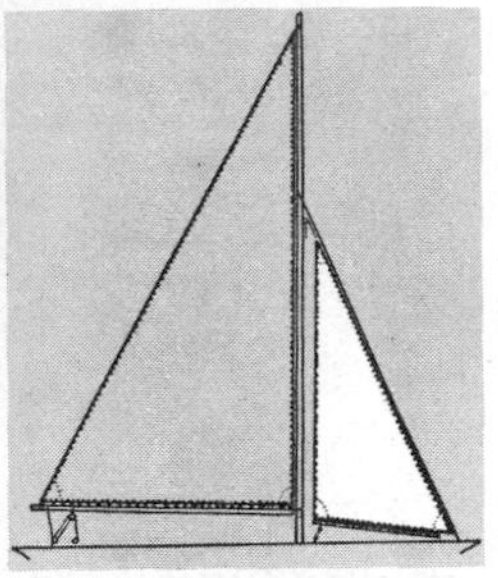

jib^{1}

jib^{1} (jĭb) *n.* **1.** A triangular sail stretching from the foretopmast head to the jib boom and in small craft to the bowsprit or the bow. **2. a.** The arm of a mechanical crane. **b.** The boom of a derrick. **—the cut of one's jib.** *Informal.* One's appearance, style, or manner. *—v.* **jibbed, jibbing, jibs.** *—intr.* To jibe. *—tr.* To cause to jibe. [Origin unknown.]

jib^{2} (jĭb) *intr.v.* **jibbed, jibbing, jibs. 1.** To stop short and turn restively from side to side; balk. Used of an animal. **2.** To draw back, balk, or shy. *—n.* Also **jib·ber** (jĭb′ər). An animal that jibs. [Origin unknown.]

jib^{3}. Variant of **jibe** (to shift).

jib boom. A spar forming a continuation of the bowsprit.

jibe^{1} (jīb) *v.* **jibed, jibing, jibes.** Also **gybe.** *—intr.* To shift a fore-and-aft sail from one side of a vessel to the other while sailing before the wind; to jib. *—tr.* To cause to jibe. *—n.* The act of jibing. [From obsolete Dutch *gijben*†.]

jibe^{2} (jīb) *intr.v.* **jibed, jibing, jibes.** *Informal.* To be in accord; harmonize; agree. [Origin unknown.]

jibe^{3}. Variant of **gibe** (taunt).

Ji·bu·ti. See **Djibouti.**

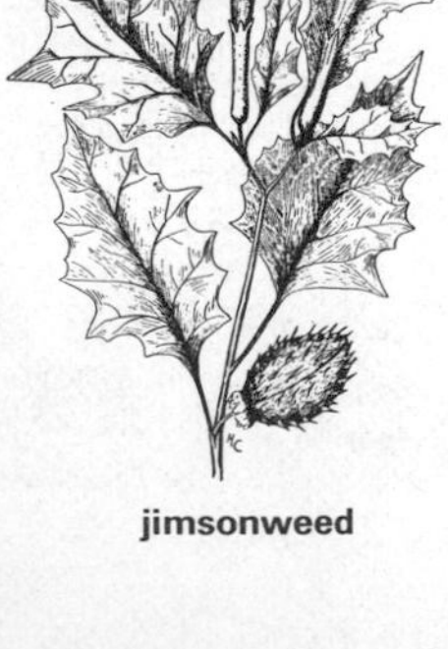

jimsonweed

Jid·da (jĭd′ə). Also **Jid·dah, Jed·da** (jĕd′ə). A city of west-central Saudi Arabia, a port on the Red Sea. Population, 148,000.

jif·fy (jĭf′ē) *n., pl.* **-fies.** Also **jiff** (jĭf). *Informal.* A moment; no time at all. See Synonyms at **moment.** [Origin unknown.]

jig (jĭg) *n.* **1. a.** Any of various lively dances in triple time. Also called "gigue." **b.** The music for such a dance. **2.** A joke or trick. **3.** A typically metal fishing lure with one or more hooks, usually fished on or near the bottom with a jiggling retrieve. **4.** An apparatus for cleaning or separating ore by agitation in water. **5.** A device for guiding a tool or for holding machine work in place. **—the jig is up.** *Slang.* The game is up; all hope is gone. *—v.* **jigged, jigging, jigs.** *—intr.* **1.** To dance or play a jig. **2.** To move or bob up and down jerkily and rapidly. **3.** To operate a jig, as in fishing, machine work, or refining ore. *—tr.* **1.** To bob or jerk up and down or to and fro. **2.** To machine with the aid of a jig. **3.** To separate or clean (ore) by shaking a jig. [Origin unknown.]

jig·a·boo (jĭg′ə-bo͞o′) *n., pl.* **-boos.** *Slang.* A Negro. An offensive term used derogatorily. Often shortened to "jig." [Origin unknown.]

jig·ger^{1} (jĭg′ər) *n.* **1.** A person who jigs or operates a jig. **2. a.** A small measure for liquor, usually holding 1½ ounces. **b.** This amount of liquor. **3.** *Golf.* A short club with an iron head. **4.** In fishing, mining, or mechanics, a jig. **5.** Any device that operates with a jerking or jolting motion, as a drill. **6.** *Nautical.* **a.** A light tackle. **b.** A small sail set in the stern of a yawl, for example. **c.** A boat having such a sail. **d.** A **jigger mast** *(see).* **7.** Some trivial article or device whose name eludes one.

jig·ger^{2} (jĭg′ər) *n.* **1.** A mite, the **chigger** *(see).* **2.** A flea, the **chigoe** *(see).* [Variant of CHIGOE.]

jigger mast. *Nautical.* **1.** The short after mast from which the jigger sail is set on a ketch or yawl. Also called "mizzenmast." **2.** The fourth mast aft on a four-masted ship. Also called "jigger."

jig·gle (jĭg′əl) *v.* **-gled, -gling, -gles.** *—intr.* To move or rock lightly up and down or to and fro in an unsteady, jerky manner. *—tr.* To cause to move in this manner. *—n.* A jiggling motion. [Frequentative of JIG (verb).]

jig·saw (jĭg′sô′) *n.* A saw, often power-driven with a narrow vertical reciprocating blade, used to cut sharp curves.

jigsaw puzzle. A game consisting of the reassembly of a picture on cardboard or wood that has been cut into numerous interlocking pieces.

ji·had (jĭ-häd′) *n.* Also **je·had. 1.** A Moslem holy war against infidels. **2.** A crusade. [Arabic *jihād.*]

jill. Variant of **gill** (sweetheart).

jilt (jĭlt) *tr.v.* **jilted, jilting, jilts.** To deceive or cast aside (a lover). *—n.* A woman who discards a lover. [Probably from earlier *jillet,* from JILL (girl).]

jim-crow (jĭm′krō′) *adj. Slang.* Also **Jim-Crow. 1.** Favoring or promoting the segregation of Negroes: *jim-crow policies.* **2.** For Negroes only: *a jim-crow waiting room.* [From JIM CROW.]

Jim Crow. *Slang.* The systematic practice of segregating and suppressing Negro people. [After *Jim Crow,* a character in an act by Thomas D. Rice (died 1860), American entertainer who based it on an anonymous 19th-century song called *Jim Crow.*] **—Jim′-Crow′ism′** *n.*

jim-jams (jĭm′jămz′) *pl.n. Slang.* **1.** A state of extreme nervousness; the jitters. **2.** Delirium tremens. [Expressive formation.]

jim·my (jĭm′ē) *n., pl.* **-mies.** Also *chiefly British* **jem·my** (jĕm′ē). A short crowbar with curved ends, often regarded as a burglar's tool. *—tr.v.* **jimmied, -mying, -mies.** Also *chiefly British* **jemmy.** To pry open with or as if with a jimmy. [*Jimmy,* pet form of JAMES.]

jim·son·weed (jĭm′sən-wēd′) *n.* A coarse, poisonous plant, *Datura stramonium,* having large, trumpet-shaped white or purplish flowers and prickly fruit. Also called "stramonium," "thorn apple." [From archaic *Jamestown weed,* named for JAMESTOWN, Virginia.]

Jin·ghiz. See **Ghengis Khan.**

jin·gle (jĭng′gəl) *v.* **-gled, -gling, -gles.** *—intr.* **1.** To make a tinkling or ringing metallic sound. **2.** To have the sound of a poetic jingle. *—tr.* To cause to jingle. *—n.* **1. a.** The sound produced by bits of metal striking together: *the jingle of sleigh bells.* **b.** Something resembling or suggesting this. **2.** A simple, repetitious, catchy rhyme or doggerel. [Middle English *ginglen* (probably imitative).]

jingle shell. The thin, translucent, rounded, yellowish or grayish shell of any of several marine bivalve mollusks of the genus *Anomia.* [From the jingling sound made when the shells are shaken together.]

jin·go (jĭng′gō) *n., pl.* **-goes.** One who vociferously supports his country, especially one who supports a belligerent foreign policy; a blatant patriot; chauvinist. *—adj.* **1.** Of or pertaining to a jingo. **2.** Characterized by jingoism. **—by jingo.** Used to express surprise or for emphasis. [From the refrain of a music-hall song sung by those in England ready to fight Russia in 1878: *"We don't want to fight, yet by Jingo! if we do,/we've got the ships, we've got the men, and got the money too."* Origin unknown.] **—jin′go·ish, jin′go·is′tic** *adj.* **—jin′go·ism′** *n.* **—jin′go·ist** *n.* & *adj.*

jink (jĭngk) *intr.v.* **jinked, jinking, jinks.** To make a quick, evasive turn. *—n.* **1.** A sudden evasive turn. **2.** *Plural.* Rambunctious play; frolic: *high jinks.* [Origin unknown.]

Jin·nah (jĭn′ə), **Mohammed Ali.** 1876–1948. Moslem leader; first governor general of Pakistan (1947–48).

jin·ni (jĭn′ē, jĭ-nē′) *n., pl.* **jinn** (jĭn). Also **jin·nee, djin·ni** *pl.* **djinn, djin·ny, ge·nie** (jē′nē). In Moslem legend, a spirit capable of assuming human or animal form and exercising supernatural influence over men. [Arabic *jinnīy.*]

jin·rik·sha, jin·rick·sha (jĭn-rĭk′shô) *n.* Also **jin·rik·i·sha** (-rĭk′shô). A small, two-wheeled, oriental carriage drawn by one or two men. Also called "rickshaw." [Japanese *jinrikisha* : *jin,* man, from Ancient Chinese *ńźiĕn* (Mandarin *jên^{2}*) + *riki,* strength, from Ancient Chinese *liək* (Mandarin *li^{4}*) + *sha,* vehicle, from Ancient Chinese *tś'ia* (Mandarin *ch'ê^{1}*).]

jinx (jĭngks) *n. Informal.* Something or someone believed to bring bad luck. *—tr.v.* **jinxed, jinxing, jinxes.** *Informal.* To bring bad luck or misfortune to. [Possibly from *Jynx,* genus name of the wryneck, from Greek *iunx,* wryneck (a bird used in magic), from *iuzein,* to call, cry. See **yu-^{2}** in Appendix.*]

ji·pi·ja·pa (hē′pē-hä′pä) *n.* A palmlike plant, *Carludovica palmata,* of Central and South America, having long-stalked, fanlike leaves used to make Panama hats. [Spanish, after *Jipijapa,* Ecuador.]

jit·ney (jĭt′nē) *n. Informal.* **1.** A small bus or automobile that

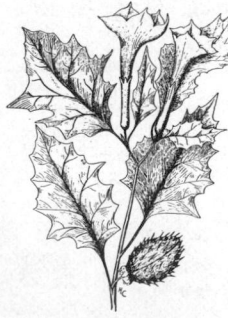

transports passengers on a route for a small fare. **2.** *Archaic.* A nickel. [Origin unknown.]

jit·ter (jĭt′ər) *intr.v.* **-tered, -tering, -ters.** *Informal.* To be nervous or uneasy; to fidget. [Origin unknown.]

jit·ter·bug (jĭt′ər-bŭg′) *n. Slang.* **1.** A strenuous dance performed to quick-tempo jazz or swing music and consisting of various two-step patterns embellished with twirls and sometimes acrobatic maneuvers, especially popular in the 1940's. **2.** A person who does such a dance. —*intr.v.* **jitterbugged, -bugging, -bugs.** To dance the jitterbug. [JITTER + BUG.]

jit·ters (jĭt′ərz) *pl.n. Informal.* A fit of nervousness.

jiu·jit·su, jiu·jut·su. Variants of **jujitsu.**

jive (jīv) *n. Slang.* **1.** Jazz or swing music. **2.** The jargon of jazz musicians and enthusiasts. **3.** Deceptive, nonsensical, or glib talk. [Origin unknown.]

JKT Airport code for Djakarta, Indonesia.

JNB Airport code for Johannesburg, South Africa.

jnt. joint.

JNU Airport code for Juneau, Alaska.

Joan (jōn). A feminine given name. [Middle English *Johne, Johan,* from Old French *Jehane,* from Medieval Latin *Jō(h)anna,* feminine of *Jō(h)annēs,* JOHN.]

Joan of Arc (jōn′; ärk′), **Saint.** French name **Jeanne d'Arc** (zhän därk′). Called "the Maid of Orléans," "La Pucelle." 1412–1431. French heroine and military leader; condemned for witchcraft and heresy and burned at the stake; canonized 1920.

João Pes·so·a (ZHWOUN′ pĕ-sō′ä). The capital of Paraíba, a state of northeastern Brazil, in the eastern part of the state. Population, 136,000.

job[1] (jŏb) *n.* **1.** An action requiring some exertion; a task; an undertaking. **2.** An activity performed in exchange for payment; especially, one performed regularly as one's trade, occupation, or profession. **3. a.** A specific piece of work to be done for a set fee. **b.** The object to be worked on. **c.** Anything resulting from or produced by work. **4.** A position in which one is employed. **5.** An assigned or assumed duty or responsibility: *It was her job to get her younger brother ready for school.* **6.** *Informal.* A difficult or strenuous task. **7.** *Informal.* A damaging piece of work. **8.** *Informal.* A state of affairs: *Their marriage turned out to be a bad job.* **9.** *Informal.* A criminal act, especially a robbery: *pull a bank job.* **10.** Something done ostensibly for the public welfare, but actually for improper private gain. —See Synonyms at **task.** —**lie down on the job.** *Informal.* To neglect the responsibilities of one's job. —**on the job.** *Informal.* **1.** Working at one's occupation or task; at work. **2.** Paying close attention to one's work or responsibilities. —*v.* **jobbed, jobbing, jobs.** —*intr.* **1.** To work at odd jobs. **2.** To work by the piece. **3.** To act as a middleman or jobber. **4.** To exploit one's position for private profits. —*tr.* **1.** To purchase (merchandise) from manufacturers and sell it to retailers. **2.** To arrange for (contracted work) to be done in portions by others; to subcontract. **3.** To transact (official business) dishonestly for private profit. [Originally a piece of work, perhaps from obsolete *job*†, "piece."] —**job′less** *adj.* —**job′less·ness** *n.*

job[2] (jŏb) *v.* **jobbed, jobbing, jobs.** *Archaic.* —*tr.* To jab. —*intr.* To make a jab. —*n. Archaic.* A jab. [Middle English *jobben*†.]

Job[1] (jōb). In the Old Testament, an upright man whose faith in God survived the test of repeated calamities. [Hebrew *Iyyōbh,* "hated, persecuted," from *ayabh,* be hostile.]

Job[2] (jōb) *n.* A book of the Old Testament, recounting the story of Job.

job·ber (jŏb′ər) *n.* **1.** One who buys merchandise from manufacturers and sells it to retailers. **2.** A person who works by the piece or at odd jobs. **3.** A public official who exploits his position for personal gain. **4.** *Chiefly British.* A middleman in the exchange of stocks and securities among brokers.

job·ber·y (jŏb′ə-rē) *n.* Corruption among public officials. [From JOB (seek graft).]

job·hold·er (jŏb′hōl′dər) *n.* One who has a regular job.

job lot. **1.** Miscellaneous merchandise sold in one lot. **2.** Any collection of cheap items.

job printer. A printer who does miscellaneous work, as circulars and cards.

Job's comforter. One who discourages or saddens while seemingly offering sympathy or comfort. [From *Job,* who was treated in such a way by his friends.]

Job's-tears (jōbz′tîrz′) *n.* Plural in form, used with a singular or plural verb. **1.** A grass, *Coix lacryma-jobi,* of tropical Asia, having white, beadlike seeds. **2.** The edible seeds of this plant.

job stick. A **composing stick** *(see).*

Jo·cas·ta (jō-kăs′tə). *Greek Mythology.* A Theban queen who unknowingly married her own son, Oedipus.

jock·ey (jŏk′ē) *n., pl.* **-eys.** A person who rides horses in races, especially as a profession. —*v.* **jockeyed, -eying, -eys.** —*tr.* **1.** To ride (a horse) as jockey. **2.** To direct or maneuver by cleverness or skill. **3.** To trick; to cheat. —*intr.* **1.** To ride a horse in a race. **2.** To maneuver for a certain position or advantage. **3.** To employ trickery; to cheat; swindle. [Originally "lad," diminutive of Scottish *Jock,* pet form of JACK.] —**jock′ey·ism′** *n.*

jock·strap (jŏk′străp′) *n.* Also **jock strap.** An **athletic supporter** *(see).* [Slang *jock,* "penis," earlier *jockum*† + STRAP.]

jo·cose (jō-kōs′) *adj.* **1.** Given to good-humored joking; merry. **2.** Characterized by joking; humorous. [Latin *jocōsus,* from *jocus,* jest, joke. See **yek-** in Appendix.*] —**jo·cose′ly** *adv.*

jo·cos·i·ty (jō-kŏs′ə-tē) *n., pl.* **-ties.** **1.** The state or quality of being jocose. **2.** A jocose remark or act; a jest.

joc·u·lar (jŏk′yə-lər) *adj.* **1.** Given to or characterized by joking. **2.** Meant in jest; facetious. —See Synonyms at **jolly.** [Latin *joculāris,* from *joculus,* diminutive of *jocus,* jest, joke. See **yek-** in Appendix.*] —**joc′u·lar·ly** *adv.*

joc·u·lar·i·ty (jŏk′yə-lăr′ə-tē) *n., pl.* **-ties.** **1.** The state or quality of being jocular. **2.** Playful humor. **3.** A jocular remark or act.

joc·und (jŏk′ənd, jō′kənd) *adj.* Having a cheerful disposition or quality; merry; gay. [Middle English, from Old French, from Late Latin *jōcundus,* from Latin *jūcundus,* agreeable, pleasant, from *juvāre,* to entertain, delight, AID.] —**joc′und·ly** *adv.*

jo·cun·di·ty (jō-kŭn′də-tē) *n., pl.* **-ties.** **1.** The state or quality of being jocund. **2.** A jocund remark or act.

Jodh·pur (jŏd′po͝or′). **1.** A former princely state of India. Also called "Marwar." **2.** A city in central Rajasthan, Republic of India. Population, 225,000.

jodh·pur boots (jŏd′pər). Short ankle-height leather boots worn with jodhpurs for riding.

jodh·purs (jŏd′pərz) *pl.n.* Wide-hipped riding breeches of heavy cloth, fitting tightly at the knees and ankles. Also called "jodhpur breeches." [From JODHPUR.]

Jo·el[1] (jō′əl). A masculine given name. [Hebrew *Yō'ēl,* "the Lord is God."]

Jo·el[2] (jō′əl). A Hebrew Minor Prophet.

Jo·el[3] (jō′əl) *n.* A book of the Old Testament containing Joel's prophecies of the judgment of Judah.

joe-pye weed (jō′pī′). Any of several tall North American plants of the genus *Eupatorium,* having whorled leaves and terminal clusters of small pinkish or purplish flowers. [Origin uncertain.]

jo·ey (jō′ē) *n., pl.* **-eys.** *Australian.* A young kangaroo or other animal. [Native Australian name.]

Jof·fre (zhôf′r′), **Joseph Jacques Césaire.** 1852–1931. French marshal; World War I commander of Allied armies in France.

jog[1] (jŏg) *v.* **jogged, jogging, jogs.** —*tr.* **1.** To jar or move by shoving, bumping, or jerking. **2.** To give a slight push or shake to; to nudge. **3.** To stimulate; stir (one's memory, for example). —*intr.* **1.** To run or ride at a steady slow trot. **2.** To proceed leisurely with or as if with occasional bumps: *"While his life was thus jogging easily along"* (Duff Cooper). —*n.* **1.** A slight jolt or shake. **2.** A nudge. **3.** A slow steady pace; a trot. [Origin obscure.] —**jog′ger** *n.*

jog[2] (jŏg) *n.* **1.** A protruding or receding part in a surface or line. **2.** An abrupt change in direction. —*intr.v.* **jogged, jogging, jogs.** To turn sharply; veer. [Perhaps variant of JAG.]

jog·gle[1] (jŏg′əl) *v.* **-gled, -gling, -gles.** —*tr.* To shake or jar slightly. —*intr.* To move with a shaking or jolting motion. —*n.* A shaking or jolting motion. [Frequentative of JOG.]

jog·gle[2] (jŏg′əl) *n.* **1.** A joint between two pieces of building material formed by a notch and a fitted projection. **2.** The notch or the projecting piece used in such a joint. —*tr.v.* **joggled, -gling, -gles.** To join or attach by means of a joggle. [From JOG (protruding part).]

jog trot. **1.** A slow, steady, jolting pace; a jog. **2.** A regular, humdrum way of living or of doing something.

Jo·han·nes·burg (jō-hăn′ĭs-bûrg′, yō-hä′nĭs-). The largest city of the Republic of South Africa, in southern Transvaal. Population, 1,153,000 (metropolitan area).

john (jŏn) *n. Slang.* A toilet. [From JOHN (given name).]

John[1] (jŏn). A masculine given name. [Middle English *John, Iohn,* earlier *Iohan, Ion,* from Medieval Latin *Jōhannēs* and Late Latin *Jōannēs,* from Greek *Iōannēs,* from Hebrew *Yōḥānān,* "the Lord is gracious."]

John[2] (jŏn). Known as John Lackland. 1167?–1216. King of England (1199–1216); son of Henry II and brother of Richard I; signed the Magna Carta.

John[3] (jŏn) *n.* A book of the New Testament, the fourth Gospel, attributed to Saint John.

John XXIII (jŏn). Original name, Angelo Giuseppe Roncalli. 1881–1963. Pope (1958–63).

John (jŏn), **Saint.** Called "the Evangelist," "the Divine." One of the Twelve Apostles; reputed author of the fourth Gospel, three epistles, and Book of Revelation.

John Bar·ley·corn (jŏn′ bär′lē-kôrn′). A personification of malt liquor or of alcoholic beverages in general.

John Birch Society (jŏn′ bûrch′). An ultraconservative anticommunist organization established by Robert Welch in 1958.

John Bull (jŏn′ bo͝ol′). **1.** A personification of England or the English. **2.** A typical Englishman. [From a character in *Law is a Bottomless Pit* (1712), a satire by John Arbuthnot (1667–1735), Scottish writer.]

John Day (jŏn′ dā′). A river rising in east-central Oregon and flowing about 280 miles generally northwest to the Columbia on the Washington border.

John Doe (jŏn′ dō′). **1.** A name used in legal proceedings to designate a fictitious or unidentified person. **2.** Any average, undistinguished man. Also called "Richard Roe."

John Do·ry (jŏn′ dôr′ē, dōr′ē). Either of two fishes, *Zenopsis ocellata,* of the western Atlantic, or *Zeus faber,* of the eastern Atlantic, having spiny fins and a laterally compressed body.

John Han·cock (jŏn′ hăn′kŏk′). *Informal.* A person's signature. [After John HANCOCK, whose signature appears prominently on the Declaration of Independence.]

John·ny Ap·ple·seed. See John **Chapman.**

john·ny·cake (jŏn′ē-kāk′) *n.* **Corncake** *(see).*

John·ny-come-late·ly (jŏn′ē-kŭm′lāt′lē) *n., pl.* **-lies.** *Informal.* A newcomer or latecomer; especially, a tardy adherent to a cause or fashion.

John·ny-jump-up (jŏn′ē-jŭmp′ŭp′) *n.* A plant, the **heartsease** *(see).* [From its quick growth.]

John·ny-on-the-spot (jŏn′ē-ŏn′*th*ə-spŏt′, jŏn′ē-ôn′-) *n. Infor-*

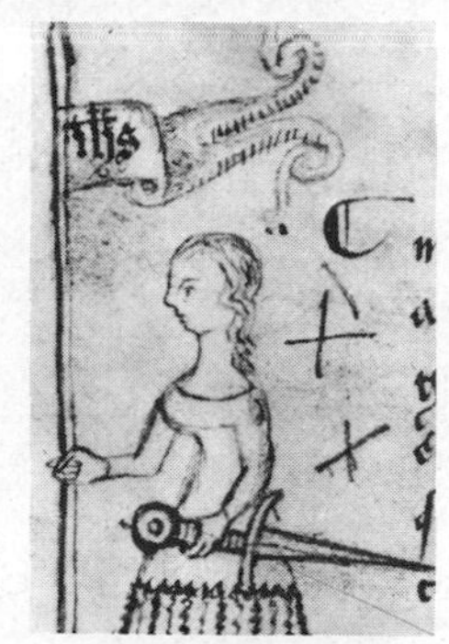

Joan of Arc
The only known contemporary portrait

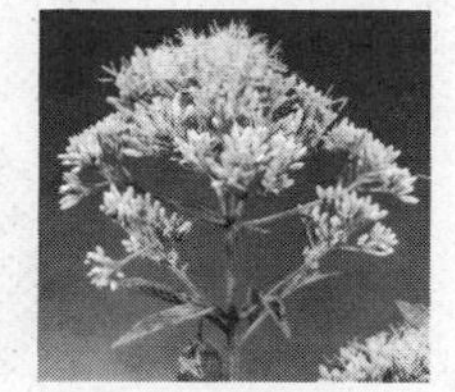

joe-pye weed
Eupatorium maculatum

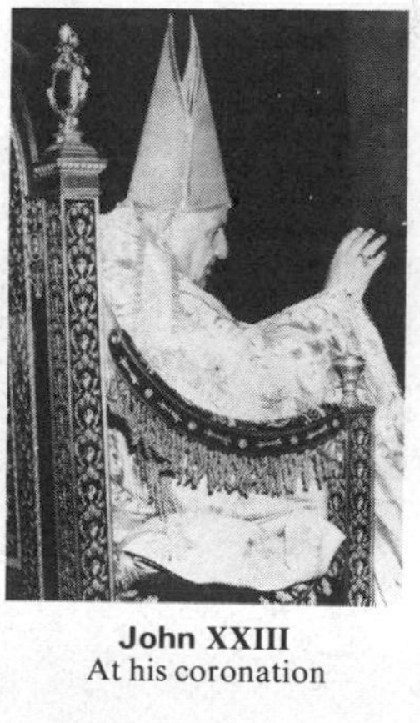

John XXIII
At his coronation

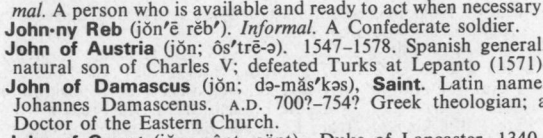

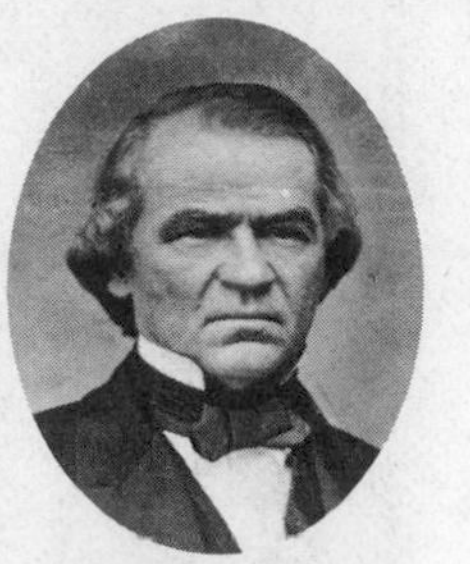
Andrew Johnson

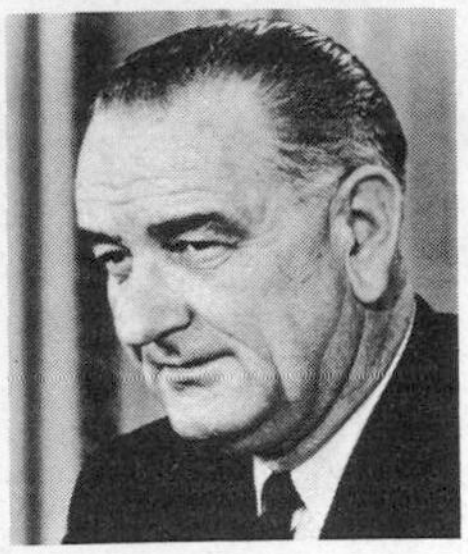
Lyndon Baines Johnson

mal. A person who is available and ready to act when necessary.

John·ny Reb (jŏn′ē rĕb′). *Informal.* A Confederate soldier.

John of Austria (jŏn; ôs′trē-ə). 1547–1578. Spanish general; natural son of Charles V; defeated Turks at Lepanto (1571).

John of Damascus (jŏn; də-măs′kəs), **Saint.** Latin name, Johannes Damascenus. A.D. 700?–754? Greek theologian; a Doctor of the Eastern Church.

John of Gaunt (jŏn; gônt, gänt). Duke of Lancaster. 1340–1399. Son of Edward III and brother of the Black Prince.

John of the Cross (jŏn), **Saint.** 1542–1591. Spanish mystic and founder of discalced Carmelites with Saint Theresa.

John o' Groat's (jŏn′ ə grōts′). A point on the northern coast of Caithness, Scotland; traditionally regarded as the northern limit of Great Britain.

John·son (jŏn′sən), **Andrew.** 1808–1875. Seventeenth President of the United States (1865–69); impeached and acquitted by a margin of one vote (1868).

John·son (jŏn′sən), **James Weldon.** 1871–1938. American author and educator; secretary of the NAACP (1916–30).

John·son (jŏn′sən), **Lyndon Baines.** Born 1908. Thirty-sixth President of the United States (1963–69).

John·son (jŏn′sən), **Philip Cortelyou.** Born 1906. American architect.

John·son (jŏn′sən), **Richard Mentor.** 1780–1850. Vice President of the United States under Martin Van Buren (1837–41).

John·son (jŏn′sən), **Samuel.** Known as Dr. Johnson. 1709–1784. English lexicographer, critic, author, and conversationalist.

John·son grass (jŏn′sən). A coarse grass, *Sorghum halepense,* native to the Mediterranean area, cultivated for forage but often a troublesome weed. [Developed by William *Johnson,* 19th-century American agriculturalist.]

John·so·ni·an (jŏn-sō′nē-ən) *adj.* Of, resembling, or relating to Samuel Johnson or his writings. —*n.* An admirer or student of Samuel Johnson or his work.

John·ston (jŏn′stən), **Albert Sidney.** 1803–1862. American army officer; commanded Confederate troops in Civil War.

John·ston (jŏn′stən), **Joseph Eggleston.** 1807–1891. American army officer; commanded Confederate troops in Civil War.

Johns·town (jŏnz′toun). A city of Pennsylvania, in the southwest-central part of the state. Population, 54,000.

John the Baptist (jŏn), **Saint.** Son of Elizabeth and Zacharias; cousin of Jesus, whom he baptized; executed by Herod Antipas.

Jo·hore (jō-hôr′, -hōr′). A state of Malaysia, occupying 7,321 square miles at the southern end of the Malay Peninsula. Population, 1,179,000. Capital, Johore Bahru.

Jo·hore Bah·ru (jō-hôr′ bə-ro͞o′, -hōr′). The capital of Johore State, Malaysia, at the southern end of the Malay Peninsula opposite Singapore Island. Population, 75,000.

joie de vi·vre (zhwȧ də vē′vr′) *French.* Hearty or carefree enjoyment of life.

join (join) *v.* **joined, joining, joins.** —*tr.* **1.** To put or bring together; unite or make continuous: *The children joined hands in a circle.* **2.** To put or bring into close association or relationship: *joined in marriage.* **3.** *Geometry.* To connect (points), as with a straight line. **4.** To form a junction with; combine with. **5.** To become a part or member of. **6.** To take a place among, in, or with; enter into the company of: *I shall join you later.* **7.** *Informal.* To adjoin. —*intr.* **1.** To come or act together; form a connection, junction, or alliance. **2.** To become a member of a group. **3.** To take part; participate: *He joined in the singing.* —**join battle.** To enter into a conflict or battle. —**join up.** To enlist, especially in the armed forces. —*n.* A joint; junction. [Middle English *joinen,* from Old French *joindre* (stem *joign-*), from Latin *jungere.* See **yeug-** in Appendix.*]

Synonyms: *join, combine, unite, consolidate, link, connect, relate, associate.* These verbs refer to the bringing or coming together of persons or things. *Join* is applied to the physical attachment of things and to the coming together of persons, usually in a close relationship. *Combine* suggests mixing or merging of related components to effect a specific purpose. *Unite* stresses the coherence or oneness of persons or things joined. *Consolidate* implies a particular compactness or closeness of merged components. *Link* and especially *connect* imply a looser relationship in which individual units retain their identities while coming together at some point, either through physical contact or mental association. *Relate* refers to attachment of persons through kinship or to connection of things through logical association. *Associate* implies a relationship of persons having common aims, interests, or the like, or a relationship of things that are similar, complementary, or have connection in one's thoughts.

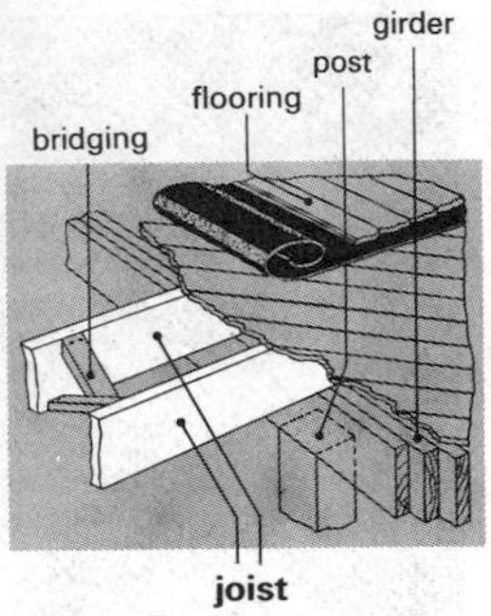

join·der (join′dər) *n.* **1.** The act of joining. **2.** *Law.* **a.** A joining of causes of action or defense in a suit. **b.** A joining of parties in a suit. **c.** The formal acceptance of an issue offered. [From French *joindre* (mistaken as a substantive), to JOIN.]

join·er (joi′nər) *n.* **1.** One that joins. **2.** *Chiefly British.* A carpenter; especially, a cabinetmaker. **3.** *Informal.* A person given to joining groups, organizations, or causes.

joint (joint) *n. Abbr.* **jnt. 1. a.** A point or position at which two or more things are joined. **b.** A configuration in or by which two or more things are joined. **2.** The manner of joining. **3.** *Anatomy.* A point of connection or articulation between more or less movable parts, as between bones or between segments in the leg of an arthropod. **4.** *Botany.* A point on a stem from which a leaf or branch may grow; a node. **5.** *Geology.* A fracture or crack in a rock mass along which no appreciable movement has occurred. **6.** A large cut of meat, such as the shoulder or leg, used for roasting. **7.** *Slang.* A cheap or disreputable gathering place, such as a restaurant or bar. **8.** *Slang.* Any public establishment or dwelling. **9.** *Slang.* A marijuana cigarette. —**out of joint. 1.** Dislocated, as a bone. **2.** Not harmonious; inconsistent. **3.** Out of order; unsatisfactory. **4.** In bad spirits or humor; out of sorts. —*adj.* **1.** Shared by or common to two or more: *a joint income-tax return.* **2.** Sharing with another or others. **3.** Formed or characterized by cooperation or united action. **4.** Involving both houses of a legislature: *a joint session.* **5.** *Law.* Regarded as one legal body; united in identity of interest or liability. —See Usage note at **mutual.** —*tr.v.* **jointed, jointing, joints. 1.** To combine or attach at a joint or joints. **2.** To provide or construct with joints. **3.** To cut (meat) into joints. [Middle English, from Old French, from the past participle of *joindre,* to JOIN.] —**joint′ly** *adv.*

Joint Chiefs of Staff. *Abbr.* **J.C.S.** The principal military advisory group to the President of the United States, composed of the chiefs of the Army, Navy, and Air Force.

joint·ed (join′tĭd) *adj.* **1.** Having a joint or joints. **2.** Having a specified type of joint. Often used in compounds: *double-jointed.*

joint·er (join′tər) *n.* **1.** One that joints; especially, a machine or tool used in making joints. **2.** A sharp triangular device connected to the beam of a plow to bury trash.

joint resolution. A resolution passed by both houses of a bicameral legislature and eligible to become a law if signed by the chief executive or passed over his veto. Compare **concurrent resolution.**

joint stock. Stock or capital funds of a company held jointly or in common by its owners.

joint-stock company (joint′stŏk′). A business whose capital is held in transferable shares of stock by its joint owners.

join·ture (join′chər) *n.* **1.** *Law.* **a.** An arrangement by which a man may set aside property to be used for the support of his wife after his death. **b.** The property so designated. **2.** *Obsolete.* The act of joining, or the state of being joined. —*tr.v.* **jointured, -turing, -tures.** *Law.* To arrange a jointure for. [Middle English, from Old French, from Latin *junctūra,* JUNCTURE.]

joint·worm (joint′wûrm′) *n.* The larva of certain wasps of the family Eurytomidae, and especially of *Harmolita tritici,* infesting wheat and causing hard swellings in the stems.

joist (joist) *n.* Any of the parallel horizontal beams set from wall to wall to support the boards of a floor or ceiling. —*tr.v.* **joisted, joisting, joists.** To construct with joists. [Middle English *gyste, giste,* from Old French *giste,* beam supporting a bridge, from Latin *jacitum,* from the past participle of *jacēre,* to lie down. See **yē-** in Appendix.*]

joke (jōk) *n.* **1.** An amusing story, especially one with a punch line. **2.** An amusing or jesting remark; a witticism, quip, or pun. **3.** A mischievous trick; prank. **4.** An amusing or ludicrous incident or situation. **5.** Something not to be taken seriously; a triviality: *His accident was no joke.* **6.** An object of amusement or laughter; a laughingstock. —*v.* **joked, joking, jokes.** —*intr.* **1.** To tell or play jokes; to jest. **2.** To speak in fun; be facetious. —*tr.* To make fun of; to tease. [Latin *jocus,* jest, joke. See **yek-** in Appendix.*] —**jok′ing·ly** *adv.*

Synonyms: *joke, jest, witticism, quip, sally, crack, wisecrack, gag.* These nouns refer to forms of humorous sayings or actions. *Joke* and *jest,* which can denote something said or done, are approximately interchangeable, though *jest* now occurs infrequently in this sense. *Witticism* refers to verbal humor, usually with an intellectual flavor and neatly phrased. *Quip* suggests a light, pointed, bantering remark, and *sally* a sudden, clever, or witty statement. *Crack* and *wisecrack* refer less formally to flippant or mocking retorts or to impromptu remarks in response to a specific situation. *Gag* is principally applicable to a broadly comic remark, or, less often, to comic by-play in a theatrical routine.

jok·er (jō′kər) *n.* **1. a.** A person who tells or plays jokes; a clown; a prankster. **b.** An insolent person who seeks to make a show of cleverness. **2.** A playing card, usually printed with a picture of a jester, used in certain games as the highest ranking card or as a wild card. **3.** A minor clause in a document such as a legislative bill that voids or changes its original or intended purpose. **4.** An unseen or unpredicted difficulty. **5.** A deceptive means of getting the better of someone.

Jok·ja·kar·ta. See **Djokjakarta.**

jole. Variant of **jowl** (jaw).

Jo·li·et (jō′lē-ĕt′, jō′lē-ĕt′). A city of northeastern Illinois, 30 miles southwest of Chicago. Population, 66,000.

Jo·li·et (jō′lē-ĕt′; *French* zhô-lyĕ′), **Louis.** Also **Jol·li·et.** 1645–1700. French-Canadian explorer of Mississippi River and Canada.

Jo·liot-Cu·rie (zhô-lyō′kü-rē′), **Frédéric.** Original surname, Joliot. 1900–1958. French physicist; discovered artificial radioactivity with his wife Irène Joliot-Curie.

Jo·liot-Cu·rie (zhô-lyō′kü-rē′), **Irène.** 1897–1956. French physicist; daughter of Pierre and Marie Curie.

jol·li·fi·ca·tion (jŏl′ə-fĭ-kā′shən) *n.* Festivity; revelry; merrymaking. [From JOLLY.]

jol·li·fy (jŏl′ə-fī′) *v.* **-fied, -fying, -fies.** —*tr.* To cause to become jolly; cheer up. —*intr.* To make merry; celebrate.

jol·li·ty (jŏl′ə-tē) *n.* Gaiety; merriment: *"the jollity of aged men has much in common with the mirth of children"* (Hawthorne).

jol·ly (jŏl′ē) *adj.* **-lier, -liest. 1.** Full of merriment and good spirits; fun-loving; gay. **2.** Exhibiting or occasioning happiness or mirth; cheerful; festive. **3.** Greatly pleasing; enjoyable. —*adv. British Informal.* Very; extremely: *a jolly good cook.* —*v.*

ă pat/ā pay/âr care/ä father/b bib/ch church/d deed/ĕ pet/ē be/f fife/g gag/h hat/hw which/ĭ pit/ī pie/îr pier/j judge/k kick/l lid, needle/m mum/n no, sudden/ng thing/ŏ pot/ō toe/ô paw, for/oi noise/ou out/o͝o took/o͞o boot/p pop/r roar/s sauce/sh ship, dish/

jollied, -lying, -lies. —*tr.* 1. To keep amused or diverted for one's own purposes; to humor. 2. To poke fun at good-naturedly; to tease. —*intr.* To amuse oneself with humorous or teasing banter. —*n., pl.* jollies. *Slang.* Amusement; fun. Used in the plural. [Middle English *jolif, joli,* from Old French, gay, pleasant, probably from Old Norse *jōl,* name of the midwinter festival, yule, from Common Germanic *jegol* (unattested), YULE.] —jol′li·ly *adv.* —jol′li·ness *n.*

Synonyms: *jolly, jovial, merry, blithe, jocular, convivial.* These adjectives describe persons who show good humor or high spirits or who are companionable in general. *Jolly* and *jovial* are especially associated with outward display of good cheer that invites friendship and promotes camaraderie. *Merry* suggests love of fun and laughter, and *blithe* implies buoyancy and freedom from care. *Jocular* refers to one who is sportive or given to joking, and *convivial* to one who derives great pleasure from the cheerful companionship of others.

jol·ly·boat (jŏl′ē-bōt′) *n.* A small boat kept by the stern of a larger ship. [Probably an alteration of earlier *jolywat*†.]

Jolly Rog·er (rŏj′ər). A black flag bearing the emblematic white skull and crossbones of a pirate ship.

Jo·lo (hō′lō, hō-lō′). 1. The chief island (345 square miles) of the Sulu Archipelago, Republic of the Philippines. 2. The capital of Sulu Province, on the northwestern coast of Jolo.

jolt (jōlt) *v.* jolted, jolting, jolts. —*tr.* 1. To bump into; to jostle. 2. To shake or knock about; to jiggle. 3. To jar with or as if with a sudden, sharp blow. 4. To put into a specified condition by or as if by a blow: *"now and then he jolted a nodding reader awake by inserting a witty paragraph"* (Walter Blair). —*intr.* To proceed in an irregular, bumpy, or jerky fashion. —*n.* 1. A sudden jarring or jerking, as from a blow. 2. An abrupt or unexpected shock or reversal: *"For jolts to preconceptions let us be grateful."* (Stanley Kauffman). [Origin uncertain.] —jolt′er *n.* —jolt′i·ly *adv.* —jolt′i·ness *n.* —jolt′y *adj.*

Jo·ma·da. Variant of Jumada.

Jo·nah[1] (jō′nə). An Old Testament prophet who was thrown overboard during a storm at sea caused by his disobedience to God. He was swallowed by a great fish and disgorged unharmed three days later. [Hebrew *Yōnāh,* "the moaning one," dove, pigeon, akin to *ānāh,* "moan."]

Jo·nah[2] (jō′nə) *n.* A book of the Old Testament containing the story of Jonah.

Jo·nah[3] (jō′nə) *n.* One thought to bring bad luck. [After JONAH.]

Jon·a·than[1] (jŏn′ə-thən). A masculine given name. [Hebrew *Yōnāthān, Yəhōnāthān,* "the Lord has given."]

Jon·a·than[2] (jŏn′ə-thən). Eldest son of King Saul of Israel and friend of David. I Samuel 20.

Jon·a·than[3] (jŏn′ə-thən) *n.* A variety of red, late-ripening apple. [After *Jonathan* Hasbrouck (died 1846), American jurist.]

Jon·a·than[4] (jŏn′ə-thən) *n.* Brother Jonathan *(see).*

Jones (jōnz), **Anson.** 1789–1858. American lawyer; president of Republic of Texas (1844–46).

Jones (jōnz), **Inigo.** 1573–1652. English architect and designer.

Jones (jōnz), **James.** Born 1921. American novelist.

Jones (jōnz), **John Paul.** Original name, John Paul. 1747–1792. Scottish-born American naval officer in Revolutionary War.

Jones Sound (jōnz). An arm of Baffin Bay lying between Ellesmere and Devon islands, Northwest Territories, Canada.

jon·gleur (jŏng′glər; *French* zhôN-glœr′) *n.* A wandering minstrel and storyteller in Medieval England and France. [French, from Old French, variant of *joglere,* JUGGLER.]

jon·quil (jŏng′kwĭl, jŏn′-) *n.* A widely cultivated plant, *Narcissus jonquilla,* having long, narrow leaves and short-tubed, fragrant yellow flowers. [New Latin *jonquilla,* from Spanish *junquillo,* diminutive of *junco,* rush, reed, from Latin *juncus*†.]

Jon·son (jŏn′sən), **Ben(jamin).** 1573–1637. English poet and dramatist.

Jop·pa. The ancient name for Jaffa.

Jor·dan (jôrd′n). The principal river of Israel and Jordan, flowing 200 miles south from extreme northern Israel through the Sea of Galilee to the Dead Sea.

Jor·dan, Hash·e·mite Kingdom of (hăsh′ə-mīt′; jôrd′n). Also Jor·dan. Formerly Trans-Jor·dan (trăns′-, trănz′-), Trans·jor·da·nia (-jôr-dā′nē-ə). A kingdom occupying 36,700 square miles in northwestern Arabia. Population, 1,935,000. Capital, Amman. —Jor·da′ni·an (jôr-dā′nē-ən) *adj.* & *n.*

Jordan almond. 1. A large variety of almond from Málaga, Spain, used widely in confections. 2. An almond covered with a hard, colored and flavored sugar coating. [By folk etymology from Middle English *jardin,* probably from Old French *jardin,* from Vulgar Latin *gardīnus* (unattested), GARDEN + ALMOND.]

jo·rum (jôr′əm) *n.* 1. A large drinking bowl. 2. The amount such a bowl contains. [Perhaps after *Joram* (II Samuel 8:10), who brought vessels of silver, gold, and brass to King David.]

jo·seph (jō′zəf) *n.* A long riding coat with a small cape, worn by women in the 18th century. [Probably after Joseph's (son of Jacob) "coat of many colors" (Genesis 37:3).]

Jo·seph[1] (jō′zəf). A masculine given name. [Hebrew *Yōsēph,* he adds, increases, from *yāsaph,* add.]

Jo·seph[2] (jō′zəf). Son of Jacob and Rachel, sold into slavery in Egypt. Genesis 3; 37; 41; 45.

Jo·seph[3] (jō′zəf). Husband of Mary the mother of Jesus. Matthew 1:16.

Jo·sé·phine de Beau·har·nais (zhō-zā-fēn′ də bō-är-nĕ′). Original name Marie Joséphine Tascher de la Pagerie. 1763–1814. Empress of the French as wife of Napoleon I (1804–09).

Jo·seph of Ar·i·ma·the·a (jō′zəf; âr′ə-mə-thē′ə, ăr′-). Israelite who provided tomb for Jesus; subject of many legends.

Joseph's coat. A tropical plant, *Amaranthus tricolor,* cultivated for variously colored foliage. [From JOSEPH. See joseph.]

Jo·se·phus (jō-sē′fəs), **Flavius.** Original name, Joseph ben Matthias. A.D. 37–100? Jewish historian and general.

josh (jŏsh) *v.* joshed, joshing, joshes. —*tr.* To tease (someone) good-humoredly. —*intr.* To banter; to joke. —*n.* A teasing or joking remark. [Origin unknown.]

Josh. Joshua (Old Testament).

Josh·u·a[1] (jŏsh′o͞o-ə). A masculine given name. [Hebrew *Yəhōshūa′,* "the Lord is salvation."]

Josh·u·a[2] (jŏsh′o͞o-ə). Also in Douay Bible Jos·u·e (-yo͞o-ē). Successor of Moses in the Exodus.

Josh·u·a[3] (jŏsh′o͞o-ə) *n.* Also in Douay Bible Jos·u·e (-yo͞o-ē). *Abbr.* Josh. An Old Testament book with the narrative of Joshua.

Joshua tree. A treelike plant, *Yucca brevifolia,* of the southwestern United States, having sword-shaped leaves and greenish-white flowers. [From the greatly extended branches, recalling the outstretched arm of the prophet Joshua as he pointed with his spear to the city of Ai. Joshua 8:18.]

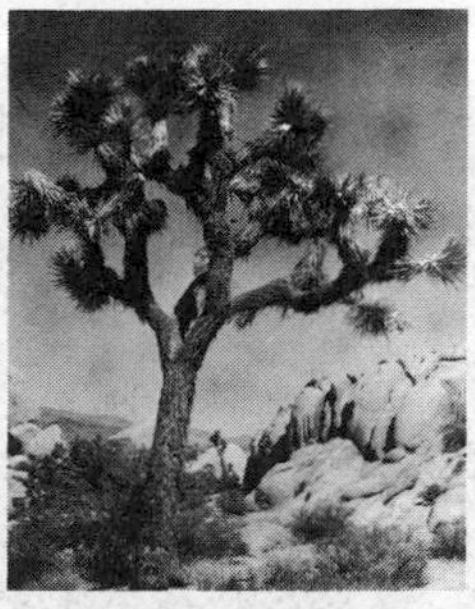

Joshua tree

Jo·si·ah (jō-sī′ə). Also in Douay Bible Jo·si·as (jō-sī′əs). King of Judah (638?–608? B.C.).

joss (jŏs) *n.* A Chinese idol. [Pidgin English, from Portuguese *deos,* god, from Latin *deus.* See deiw- in Appendix.*]

joss house. A Chinese temple or shrine containing idols.

joss stick. A stick of incense burned before a joss.

jos·tle (jŏs′əl) *v.* -tled, -tling, -tles. Also jus·tle (jŭs′-). —*intr.* 1. To come in contact or collide; knock or push together. 2. To make one's way by pushing or elbowing. 3. To vie for an advantage or favorable position. 4. To be in close proximity. —*tr.* 1. To force by pushing, shoving, and elbowing. 2. To come into close contact or collision with. 3. To vie with for an advantage or favorable position. 4. To be in close proximity with: *"books written in all languages by men and women of all tempers, races, and ages jostle each other on the shelf"* (Virginia Woolf). —*n.* Also jus·tle. A rough shove or push. [Earlier *justle,* from Middle English *justlen,* to come against in combat, frequentative of *justen,* from Old French *juster,* to JOUST.]

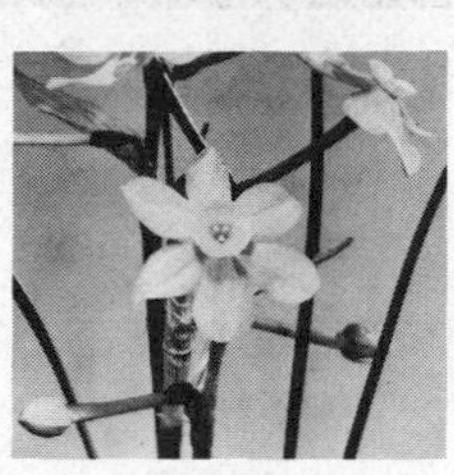

jonquil

jot (jŏt) *n.* The smallest bit or particle; iota. —*tr.v.* jotted, jotting, jots. To write down briefly and hastily: *jot down an address.* [Earlier *iote,* from Latin *iōta,* from Greek, IOTA.]

jot·ting (jŏt′ĭng) *n.* A brief note or memorandum.

Jo·tun·heim (yô′to͝on-hām′). Also Jö·tunn·heim (yœ′-), Jo·tunn·heim, Jo·tunn·heim·r (-hā′mər). *Norse Mythology.* Utgard *(see).*

joule (joul, jo͞ol) *n. Abbr.* J 1. The International System unit of energy, equal to the work done when a current of 1 ampere is passed through a resistance of 1 ohm for 1 second. 2. A unit of energy, equal to the work done when the point of application of a force of 1 newton is displaced 1 meter in the direction of the force. See measurement. [After James P. JOULE.]

Joule (joul, jo͞ol), **James Prescott.** 1818–1889. British physicist.

jounce (jouns) *v.* jounced, jouncing, jounces. —*intr.* To move with bumps and jolts. —*tr.* To cause to jounce. —*n.* A rough, jolting bounce. [Middle English *jouncen*†.]

jour. 1. journal; journalist. 2. journeyman.

jour·nal (jûr′nəl) *n. Abbr.* J., jour. 1. A daily record of occurrences or transactions, especially: a. A personal record of experiences and reflections; a diary. b. An official record of daily proceedings, as of a legislative body. c. A ship's log. 2. *Bookkeeping.* a. A daybook. b. A book of original entry in a double-entry system, listing all transactions and indicating the accounts to which they belong. 3. A newspaper. 4. A periodical presenting news in a particular area: *a medical journal.* 5. *Machinery.* The part of a shaft or axle supported by a bearing. [Middle English, from Old French *jurnal, jornal,* from *journal, jornel,* "daily," from Late Latin *diurnālis,* diurnal, from *diurnus,* daily, from *diēs,* day. See deiw- in Appendix.*]

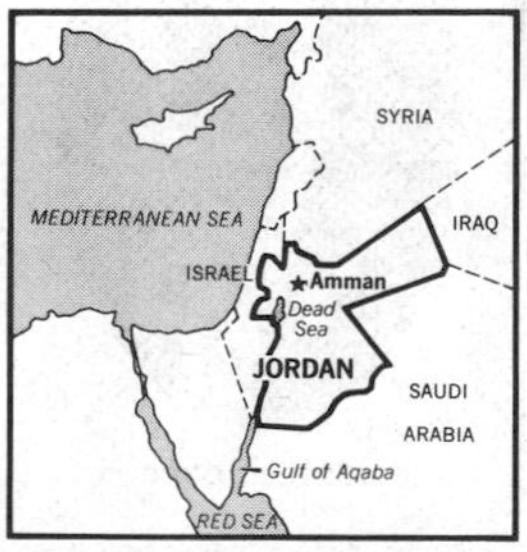

Hashemite Kingdom of Jordan

journal box. A housing enclosing a journal and its bearings.

jour·nal·ese (jûr′nə-lēz′, -lēs′) *n.* The slick, superficial style of writing often held to be characteristic of newspapers and magazines. [JOURNAL + -ESE.]

jour·nal·ism (jûr′nə-lĭz′əm) *n.* 1. The collecting, writing, editing, and publishing of news or news articles through newspapers or magazines. 2. Material written for publication in a newspaper or magazine. 3. The style of writing characteristic of material in newspapers and magazines, consisting of the direct presentation of facts or occurrences with little attempt at analysis or interpretation. 4. Newspapers and magazines collectively. 5. An academic course training one in journalism. 6. Written material of current interest or wide popular appeal.

jour·nal·ist (jûr′nə-lĭst) *n.* 1. *Abbr.* jour. A person whose occupation is journalism. 2. A person who keeps a journal.

jour·nal·is·tic (jûr′nə-lĭs′tĭk) *adj.* Pertaining to or characteristic of journalism or journalists. —jour′nal·is′ti·cal·ly *adv.*

jour·nal·ize (jûr′nə-līz′) *v.* -ized, -izing, -izes. —*tr.* To record in a journal. —*intr.* To keep a journal. —jour′nal·iz′er *n.*

jour·ney (jûr′nē) *n., pl.* -neys. 1. a. Travel from one place to another; a trip. b. A long overland trip as distinguished from a voyage or a flight. 2. a. The distance to be traveled on a journey. b. The time required for such a trip. —*v.* journeyed, -neying, -neys. —*intr.* To travel; make a trip. —*tr.* To travel over or through. [Middle English *journey, jorne,* period of travel, a day's traveling, from Old French *jornee,* from Vulgar Latin *diurnāta* (unattested), from Latin *diurnum,* daily portion,

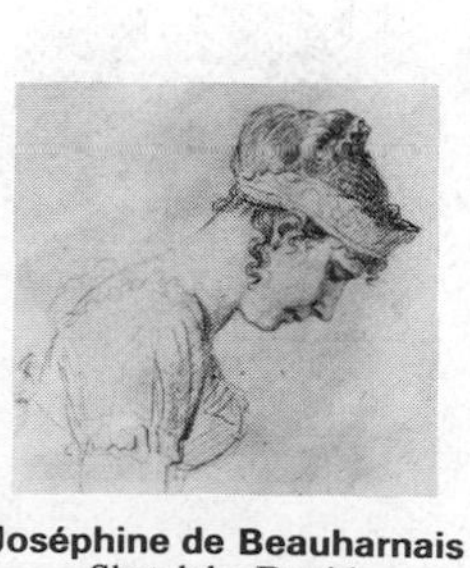

Joséphine de Beauharnais
Sketch by David

neuter of *diurnus,* daily, from *diēs,* day. See **deiw-** in Appendix.*] —**jour′ney·er** *n.*

jour·ney·man (jûr′nē-mən) *n., pl.* **-men** (-mĭn). **1.** *Abbr.* **jour.** One who has fully served his apprenticeship in a trade or craft and is a qualified worker in another's employ. **2.** Any competent workman. [Middle English : JOURNEY (in the dialectal sense of "a day's work") + MAN.]

jour·ney·work (jûr′nē-wûrk′) *n.* The work of a journeyman.

joust (jŭst, joust, jo͞ost) *n.* Also **just** (jŭst). **1.** A combat with lances between two mounted knights or men-at-arms; a tilting match. **2.** *Plural.* A series of these matches; a tournament. **3.** Any combat suggestive of a joust. —*intr.v.* **jousted, jousting, jousts.** Also **just.** To engage in such combat; tilt. [Middle English, from Old French *juste, jouste,* from *juster,* to join battle, joust, from Vulgar Latin *juxtāre* (unattested), to come together, from Latin *juxtā,* close together. See **yeug-** in Appendix.*]

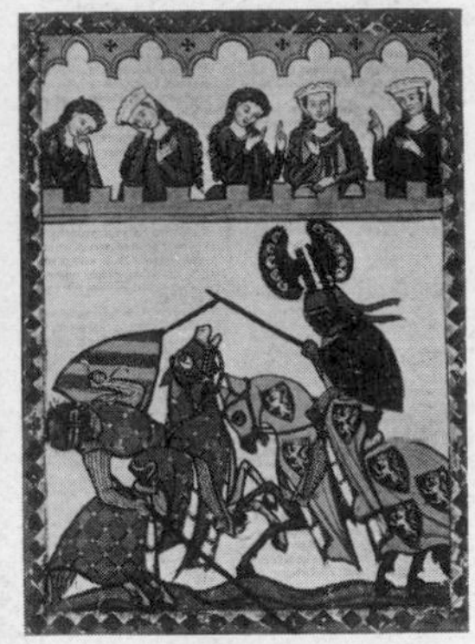

joust
Illustration from a 12th-century German manuscript

Jove (jōv) *n.* **1.** The god **Jupiter** *(see).* **2.** *Poetic.* The planet Jupiter. —**by Jove.** A mild oath used to express surprise or emphasis. [Middle English, from Latin *Jov-,* stem of the oblique cases of Old Latin *Jovis.* See **deiw-** in Appendix.*]

jo·vi·al (jō′vē-əl) *adj.* Marked by hearty conviviality. See Synonyms at **jolly.** [Originally "born under the influence of Jupiter" (the planet, regarded as the source of happiness), from French *jovial,* from Italian *gioviale,* from *Giove,* Jove, from Latin *Jov-.* See **Jove.**] —**jo′vi·al′i·ty** *n.* —**jo′vi·al·ly** *adv.*

Jo·vi·an (jō′vē-ən) *adj.* Of, pertaining to, or resembling Jove.

jowl[1] (joul) *n.* Also **jole** (jōl). **1.** The jaw, especially the lower jaw. **2.** The cheek. [Middle English *chawle, chauel,* Old English *ceafl.* See **geph-** in Appendix.*]

jowl[2] (joul) *n.* **1.** The flesh under the lower jaw, especially when plump or flaccid. **2.** A similar fleshy part, as a dewlap or a wattle. [Middle English *cholle,* probably Old English *ceole, ceolu,* throat. See **gwel-**[5] in Appendix.*]

joy (joi) *n.* **1.** A condition or feeling of high pleasure or delight; happiness; gladness. **2.** The expression or manifestation of such feeling. **3.** A source or object of pleasure or satisfaction. —See Synonyms at **pleasure.** —*v.* **joyed, joying, joys.** —*intr.* To take pleasure; rejoice: *"Joying frankly in excess, the fiery noontide hour had a special charm for him."* (Ronald Firbank). —*tr. Archaic.* **1.** To fill with joy. **2.** To enjoy. [Middle English *joy(e),* from Old French *joie, joye,* from Vulgar Latin *gaudia* (unattested), from Latin, plural of *gaudium,* gladness, delight, from *gaudēre,* to rejoice. See **gāu-** in Appendix.*]

joy·ance (joi′əns) *n.* **1.** Enjoyment; delight. **2.** Merrymaking; festivity. [JOY + -ANCE.]

Joyce (jois), **James.** 1882–1941. Irish novelist.

joy·ful (joi′fəl) *adj.* Feeling, causing, or indicating joy. See Synonyms at **glad.** —**joy′ful·ly** *adv.* —**joy′ful·ness** *n.*

joy·less (joi′lĭs) *adj.* Destitute of joy; cheerless; dismal. —**joy′less·ly** *adv.* —**joy′less·ness** *n.*

joy·ous (joi′əs) *adj.* Feeling or causing joy; joyful. See Synonyms at **glad.** —**joy′ous·ly** *adv.* —**joy′ous·ness** *n.*

joy ride. 1. An automobile ride taken simply for fun and often for the thrills provided by reckless driving. **2.** A hazardous, reckless, and often costly venture.

joy-ride (joi′rīd′) *intr.v.* **-rode** (-rōd′), **-ridden** (-rĭd′n), **-riding, -rides.** To take a joy ride.

joy stick. *Slang.* The control stick of an airplane.

J.P. justice of the peace.

jr., Jr. junior.

J.R.C. Junior Red Cross.

JRS Airport code for Jerusalem.

J.S.D. Doctor of Juristic Science.

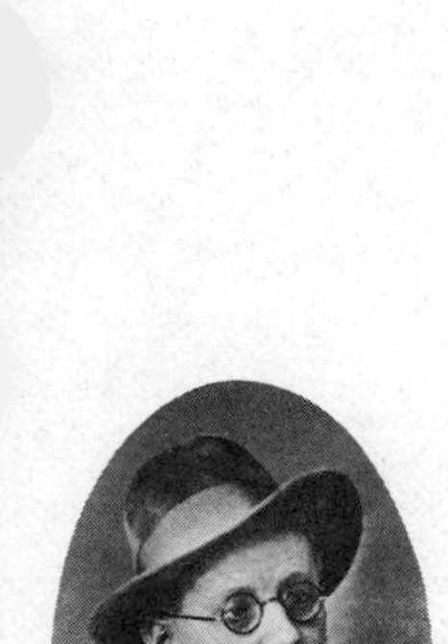

James Joyce

Juan de Fu·ca Strait (hwän′ də fo͞o′kə). An inlet of the Pacific extending for 100 miles between northwestern Washington and Vancouver Island, British Columbia, Canada.

Juan Fer·nán·dez Islands (jo͞o′ən fər-năn′dēz; *Spanish* hwän′ fĕr-nän′dās). A group of three volcanic islands of Chile, in the Pacific, 400 miles west of Valparaiso.

Juá·rez. See **Ciudad Juárez.**

Juá·rez (hwä′rās), **Benito Pablo.** 1806–1872. Mexican revolutionary statesman; president (1861–65 and 1867–72).

ju·ba (jo͞o′bə) *n.* A group dance of probable West African origin characterized by complex rhythmic clapping and body movements and practiced on plantations in the South during the 18th and 19th centuries. [Origin obscure.]

Ju·ba (jo͞o′bä). A river of Africa, rising in south-central Ethiopia and flowing 545 miles generally south through Somalia to the Indian Ocean.

Ju·bal (jo͞o′bəl). A descendant of Cain and inventor of musical instruments. Genesis 4:21.

Jub·bul·pore (jŭb′əl-pōr′, -pôr′, -po͝or′). Also **Ja·bal·pur.** A city of the Republic of India, near the Narmada River in central Madhya Pradesh. Population, 326,000.

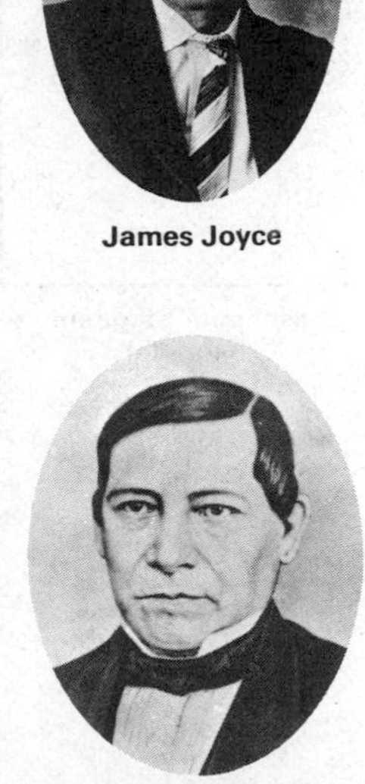

Benito Pablo Juárez

ju·bi·lant (jo͞o′bə-lənt) *adj.* **1.** Exultingly joyful. **2.** Expressing joy. [Latin *jūbilāns,* present participle of *jūbilāre,* to JUBILATE.] —**ju′bi·lance, ju′bi·lan·cy** *n.* —**ju′bi·lant·ly** *adv.*

ju·bi·late (jo͞o′bə-lāt′) *intr.v.* **-lated, -lating, -lates.** To rejoice; exult. [Latin *jūbilāre,* to raise a shout of joy. See **yu-**[2] in Appendix.*]

Ju·bi·la·te (jo͞o′bə-lä′tē, -lä′tē) *n.* **1.** The 100th Psalm in the King James Bible, or the 99th in the Vulgate and the Douay Bible. **2.** A musical setting of the Jubilate. **3.** The third Sunday after Easter. **4.** A song or outburst of joy and triumph. [Latin *jūbilāte!,* rejoice! (the first word in the Jubilate), imperative of *jūbilāre,* to JUBILATE.]

ju·bi·la·tion (jo͞o′bə-lā′shən) *n.* **1.** The state of being jubilant; exultation. **2.** A celebration or other expression of joy.

ju·bi·lee (jo͞o′bə-lē′) *n.* **1. a.** A special anniversary; especially, a 25th, 50th, 60th, or 75th anniversary. **b.** The celebration of such an anniversary. **2.** A season or occasion of joyful celebration. **3.** Jubilation; rejoicing. **4.** In the Old Testament, a year of rest to be observed by the Israelites every 50th year, during which slaves were to be set free, alienated property restored to the former owners, and the lands left untilled. Leviticus 25:8–17. **5.** *Roman Catholic Church.* A year during which plenary indulgence may be obtained by the performance of certain pious acts. [Middle English, from Old French *jubilé,* from Late Latin *jūbilaeus (annus),* "(year) of jubilee," alteration (influenced by Latin *jūbilāre,* to JUBILATE) of Late Greek *iōbēlaios,* from *iōbēlos,* jubilee, from Hebrew *yōbhēl,* "ram's horn" (used to proclaim the jubilee), originally, "leading animal," akin to *hōbhīl,* lead, conduct.]

Jú·car (ho͞o′kär). A river rising in east-central Spain and flowing about 300 miles south and east to the Mediterranean.

Ju·dah[1] (jo͞o′də). Son of Jacob and Leah; ancestor of one of the twelve tribes of Israel. [Hebrew *Yəhūdāh,* "praised."]

Ju·dah[2] (jo͞o′də) *n.* The tribe of Israel descended from Judah.

Ju·dah[3] (jo͞o′də). An ancient kingdom in southern Palestine, occupied by the tribes of Judah and Benjamin and governed by the descendants of Solomon. I Kings 11:31, 12:17–21.

Ju·da·ic (jo͞o-dā′ĭk) *adj.* Also **Ju·da·i·cal** (-ĭ-kəl). Of or pertaining to Jews or Judaism. [Latin *Jūdaicus,* from Greek *Ioudaikos,* from *Ioudaios,* JEW.] —**Ju·da′i·cal·ly** *adv.*

Ju·da·ism (jo͞o′dē-ĭz′əm) *n.* **1.** The monotheistic religion of the Jewish people, tracing its origins to Abraham, having its spiritual and ethical principles embodied chiefly in the Bible and the Talmud. **2.** Conformity to the traditional ceremonies and rites of the Jewish religion. **3.** The cultural, spiritual, and social way of life of the Jewish people. [Late Latin *Jūdaismus,* from Greek *Ioudaismos,* from *Ioudaios,* JEW.]

Ju·da·ize (jo͞o′dē-īz′) *v.* **-ized, -izing, -izes.** —*tr.* To bring into conformity with Judaism. —*intr.* To adopt Jewish customs and beliefs. —**Ju′da·i·za′tion** *n.* —**Ju′da·iz′er** *n.*

Ju·das[1] (jo͞o′dəs). Called "Judas Iscariot." One of the Twelve Apostles; betrayer of Jesus. [Late Latin *Jūdas,* from Greek *Ioudas,* from Hebrew *Yəhūdāh,* JUDAH.]

Ju·das[2] (jo͞o′dəs). Known as Saint Jude to distinguish him from Judas Iscariot. One of the Twelve Apostles.

Ju·das[3] (jo͞o′dəs) *n.* **1.** One who betrays under the appearance of friendship. **2.** *Usually small* **j.** A one-way peephole in a door. [From JUDAS (Iscariot).]

Ju·das Mac·ca·bae·us. See **Maccabaeus.**

Judas tree. The **redbud** *(see).* [From a belief that Judas Iscariot hanged himself on such a tree.]

Jude (jo͞od) *n.* The Epistle of Jude, a book of the New Testament often attributed to Saint Jude.

Ju·de·a (jo͞o-dē′ə). Also **Ju·dae·a.** The southern section of ancient Palestine, now comprising southern Israel and southwestern Jordan. —**Ju·de′an** *n.* & *adj.*

Ju·de·o-Span·ish (jo͞o-dā′ō-spăn′ĭsh) *n.* **Ladino** *(see).*

Judg. Judges (Old Testament).

judge (jŭj) *v.* **judged, judging, judges.** —*tr.* **1. a.** To pass judgment upon in a court of law. **b.** To sit in judgment upon; to try; hear. **c.** *Obsolete.* To pass sentence upon; condemn. **2.** To determine authoritatively after deliberation, especially: **a.** To decide or settle (a controversy, for example). **b.** To appraise discriminatingly as an expert: *"You can always judge the quality of a cook or a restaurant by roast chicken."* (Julia Child). **c.** To declare after determination: *They judged her a witch.* **3.** To form an opinion about: *judge character; judge distances.* **4.** To criticize; to censure. **5.** *Informal.* To think; consider; suppose. **6.** *Obsolete.* To govern; to rule. —*intr.* **1.** To act or decide as a judge; pass judgment. **2.** To form an opinion or estimation; make a critical determination or appraisal. —*n.* **1.** *Abbr.* **J.** A public official who hears and decides cases brought before a court of law for the purpose of administering justice; a justice; magistrate. **2.** An appointed arbiter in a contest or competition. **3.** One whose critical judgment or opinion is sought; a connoisseur. **4.** A leader of the Israelites during a period of about 400 years between the death of Joshua and the accession of Saul. [Middle English *jugen,* from Old French *jugier,* from Latin *jūdicāre,* from *jūdex* (stem *jūdic-*), judge. See **yewo-**[1] in Appendix.*]

Synonyms: *judge, arbitrator, arbiter, referee, umpire.* These nouns denote persons empowered to make decisions that determine points at issue. A *judge* is either the presiding officer in a court of justice or, in a nonlegal sense, anyone in a position to make such decisions because he has authority or knowledge recognized as authoritative. An *arbitrator* usually works, singly or with associates, to settle disputes, especially in labor-management relations, and derives his authority by advance consent of the disputants, who choose him or approve his selection for the job. An *arbiter* is usually one who has no official status but is recognized as pre-eminent in a given nonlegal area, such as fashion or literature. Less often *arbiter* is used interchangeably with *arbitrator.* In legal terminology, a *referee* is an attorney appointed by a court to make a determination of a case or to investigate and report on it, and an *umpire* is a person called upon to settle an issue that arbitrators are unable to resolve. In sports, *referee* and *umpire* refer to officials who enforce the rules and settle points at issue.

judge advocate *pl.* **judge advocates.** *Abbr.* **J.A. 1.** A commissioned officer in the U.S. Army assigned to the Judge Advocate General's Corps. **2.** A staff officer serving as legal adviser to a commander. **3.** An officer acting as prosecutor at a court-martial.

ă pat/ā pay/âr care/ä father/b bib/ch church/d deed/ĕ pet/ē be/f fife/g gag/h hat/hw which/ĭ pit/ī pie/îr pier/j judge/k kick/l lid, needle/m mum/n no, sudden/ng thing/ŏ pot/ō toe/ô paw, for/oi noise/ou out/o͝o took/o͞o boot/p pop/r roar/s sauce/sh ship, dish/

Judge Advocate General *pl.* **Judge Advocates General** or **Judge Advocate Generals.** *Abbr.* **J.A.G.** A major general in the U.S. Army or Air Force who serves as senior legal officer.

Judg·es (jŭj′ĭz) *n.* Plural in form, used with a singular verb. *Abbr.* **Judg.** A book of the Old Testament containing the history of the Israelites during the rule of the judges.

judge·ship (jŭj′shĭp′) *n.* The office or jurisdiction of a judge.

judg·mat·ic (jŭj-măt′ĭk) *adj.* Also **judg·mat·i·cal** (-ĭ-kəl). *Informal.* Judicious. [From JUDGMENT.] —**judg·mat′i·cal·ly** *adv.*

judg·ment (jŭj′mənt) *n.* Also **judge·ment.** **1. a.** The mental ability to perceive and distinguish relationships or alternatives; the critical faculty; discernment. **b.** The capacity to make reasonable decisions, especially in regard to the practical affairs of life; good sense; wisdom. **c.** The exercise of this capacity. **2.** A formal decision, as of an arbiter in a contest. **3.** A discriminating appraisal; authoritative opinion. **4.** Estimation: *make a judgment of the distance.* **5.** An assertion of something believed; idea; opinion; thought: *It's my judgment that we ought to leave soon.* **6.** Criticism; censure. **7.** *Law.* **a.** A determination of a court of law; a judicial decision. **b.** A court act creating or affirming an obligation, such as a debt. **c.** A writ in witness of such an act. —See Synonyms at **opinion, reason.** [Middle English *jugement,* from Old French, from *jugier,* to JUDGE.]

Judgment Day. **1.** In the teleology of Judaism, Christianity, and Islam, the day of God's final judgment. **2.** Any day of reckoning or final judgment. Also called "Day of Judgment."

ju·di·ca·ble (jo͞o′dĭ-kə-bəl) *adj.* **1.** Capable of being judged. **2.** Liable to be judged. [Late Latin *jūdicābilis,* from Latin *jūdicāre,* to JUDGE.]

ju·di·ca·tive (jo͞o′dĭ-kā′tĭv, -kə-tĭv) *adj.* Having the capacity to judge; judicial. [Medieval Latin *jūdicātivus,* from Latin *jūdicāre,* to JUDGE.]

ju·di·ca·tor (jo͞o′dĭ-kā′tər) *n.* One who acts as judge. [Late Latin *jūdicātor,* from Latin *jūdicāre,* to JUDGE.]

ju·di·ca·to·ry (jo͞o′dĭ-kə-tôr′ē, -tōr′ē) *n., pl.* **-ries.** **1.** A court of justice; a tribunal. **2.** A system of courts of law for the administration of justice; a judiciary. —*adj.* Of or pertaining to the administration of justice. [Medieval Latin *jūdicātōrium,* from Latin *jūdicāre,* to JUDGE.]

ju·di·ca·ture (jo͞o′dĭ-kə-cho͝or′) *n.* **1.** The administering of justice. **2.** The position, function, or authority of a judge. **3.** The jurisdiction of a law court or a judge. **4.** A court of law. **5.** A system of law courts and their judges. [Old French, from Medieval Latin *jūdicātūra,* from Latin *jūdicāre,* to JUDGE.]

ju·di·cial (jo͞o-dĭsh′əl) *adj.* **1.** Of, pertaining to, or proper to courts of law or to the administration of justice: *the judicial branch of the government.* Compare **executive, legislative.** **2.** Decreed by or proceeding from a court of justice. **3.** Pertaining or appropriate to the office of a judge. **4.** Relative to, characterized by, or expressing judgment. **5.** *Theology.* Proceeding from a divine judgment. [Middle English, from Old French, from Latin *jūdiciālis,* from *jūdicium,* judgment, from *jūdex* (stem *jūdic-*), JUDGE.] —**ju·di′cial·ly** *adv.*

judicial separation. A court order recognizing that husband and wife are living apart and regulating their mutual rights and liabilities. Also called "legal separation."

ju·di·ci·ar·y (jo͞o-dĭsh′ē-ĕr′ē) *adj.* Of or pertaining to courts, judges, or judicial decisions. —*n., pl.* **judiciaries.** **1.** The judicial branch of government. **2.** A system of courts of justice. **3.** Judges collectively. [Latin *jūdiciārius,* from *jūdicium,* judgment. See **judicial.**]

ju·di·cious (jo͞o-dĭsh′əs) *adj.* Having or exhibiting sound judgment. [Old French *judicieux,* from Latin *jūdicium.* See **judicial.**] —**ju·di′cious·ly** *adv.* —**ju·di′cious·ness** *n.*

Ju·dith¹ (jo͞o′dĭth) A feminine given name. [Latin, from Greek *Ioudith,* from Hebrew *Yəhūdīth,* probably feminine of *Yəhūdī,* JEW.]

Ju·dith² (jo͞o′dĭth). In the Apocrypha, a Jewish woman who rescued her people by slaying the Assyrian general Holofernes.

Ju·dith³ (jo͞o′dĭth) *n.* A book of the Apocrypha and the Douay Bible relating the story of Judith.

ju·do (jo͞o′dō) *n.* A modern form of jujitsu applying principles of balance and leverage, often used as a method of physical training. [Japanese *jūdō* : *jū,* soft (see **jujitsu**) + *dō,* way.]

Jud·son (jŭd′sən), **Edward Zane Carroll.** Pen name, Ned Buntline. 1823–1886. American author of adventure stories.

Ju·dy¹ (jo͞o′dē). A feminine given name. [Pet form of JUDITH.]

Ju·dy² (jo͞o′dē). A character in a puppet show. See **Punch.**

jug (jŭg) *n.* **1.** A small pitcher. **2. a.** A tall, often rounded vessel of earthenware, glass, or metal with a small mouth, a handle, and usually a stopper or cap, made for holding liquids. **b.** The contents of a jug. **c.** The amount of liquid a jug will hold. **3.** *Slang.* A jail. —*tr.v.* **jugged, jugging, jugs.** **1.** To stew (a hare, for example) in an earthenware jug or jar. **2.** *Slang.* To put in jail. [From *Jug,* pet form of JOAN or JUDITH.]

ju·gate (jo͞o′gĭt, -gāt′) *adj.* Joined in or forming a pair or pairs. [From New Latin *jugum,* yoke, from Latin. See **yeug-** in Appendix.*]

jug·ger·naut (jŭg′ər-nôt′) *n.* Anything that draws blind and destructive devotion, or to which people are ruthlessly sacrificed, such as a belief or institution. [From JUGGERNAUT.]

Jug·ger·naut (jŭg′ər-nôt′). A title of the Hindu deity Krishna, whose idol is drawn in an annual procession on a huge car or wagon under the wheels of which worshipers are said to have thrown themselves to be crushed. [Hindi *Jagannath,* from Sanskrit *Jagaṇātha,* "Lord of the world" : *jagat,* "the moving," world, from *jigāti,* goes (see **gwā-** in Appendix*) + *nātha-*†, "protector," lord.]

jug·gle (jŭg′əl) *v.* **-gled, -gling, -gles.** —*tr.* **1.** To keep (two or more balls, plates, or other objects) in the air at one time by alternately tossing and catching them. **2.** To keep (more than one activity) in motion or progress at one time. **3.** To attempt to balance or otherwise cope with: *juggle a handbag and glass at a cocktail party.* **4.** To manipulate in order to deceive: *juggle figures in a ledger.* —*intr.* **1.** To perform tricks with sleight of hand. **2.** To make juggling motions. **3.** To use trickery to deceive. —*n.* **1.** An act of juggling. **2.** A piece of trickery for some dishonest purpose. [Middle English *jogelen,* from Old French *jogler,* from Latin *joculārī,* to jest. See **juggler.**]

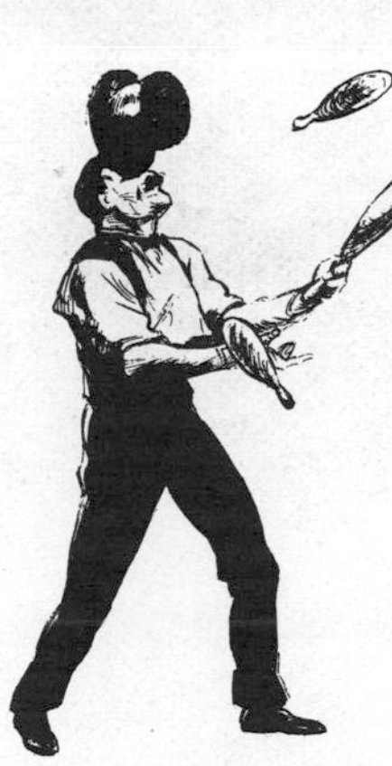

juggler

jug·gler (jŭg′lər) *n.* **1.** An entertainer who performs tricks of dexterity; especially, one who juggles balls or other objects. **2.** One who uses tricks, deception, or fraud. [Middle English *iugelere, iugelour,* jester, magician, from Old French *joglere, juglere,* from Latin *joculātor,* from *joculārī,* to jest, from *joculus,* diminutive of *jocus,* jest, joke. See **yek-** in Appendix.*]

jug·gler·y (jŭg′lə-rē) *n., pl.* **-ies.** **1.** The art or performance of a juggler. **2.** Trickery; deception.

jug·head (jŭg′hĕd′) *n. Slang.* **1.** A horse that is stupid and hard to train. **2.** A dull, slow-witted person.

Ju·go·sla·vi·a. See **Yugoslavia.**

Ju·go·sla·vi·ja. The Serbo-Croatian name for **Yugoslavia.**

jug·u·lar (jŭg′yə-lər) *adj.* Of, pertaining to, or located in the region of the neck or throat. —*n.* A jugular vein. [Late Latin *jugulāris,* from Latin *jugulum,* collarbone, diminutive of *jugum,* yoke. See **yeug-** in Appendix.*]

jugular vein. Any of various large veins of the neck.

ju·gum (jo͞o′gəm) *n., pl.* **-ga** (-gə) or **-gums.** A paired or yokelike structure, such as a pair of opposite leaflets or a lobe joining the bases of the forewings and hind wings of certain insects. [New Latin, from Latin *jugum,* yoke. See **yeug-** in Appendix.*]

juice (jo͞os) *n.* **1. a.** Any fluid naturally contained in plant or animal tissue. **b.** Any bodily secretion. **2.** *Slang.* Vigorous life and vitality. **3.** *Slang.* **a.** Electric current. **b.** Fuel for an engine. —*tr.v.* **juiced, juicing, juices.** To extract the juice from. [Middle English *iuys, jus,* from Old French *jus,* from Latin *jūs,* broth, sauce, juice. See **yeu-¹** in Appendix.*]

juic·er (jo͞o′sər) *n.* A kitchen appliance for extracting juice from fruits and vegetables.

juic·y (jo͞o′sē) *adj.* **-ier, -iest.** **1.** Full of juice; succulent. **2.** Richly interesting; lively; racy: *a juicy bit of gossip.* **3.** Yielding wealth; lucrative. —**juic′i·ly** *adv.* —**juic′i·ness** *n.*

Juiz de Fo·ra (zhwēzh′ də fôr′ə, fōr′ə). A city of Brazil, in southeastern Minas Gerais. Population, 125,000.

ju·jit·su (jo͞o-jĭt′so͞o) *n.* Also **ju·jut·su, jiu·jit·su, jiu·jut·su.** A Japanese art of self-defense or hand-to-hand combat based on set maneuvers that force an opponent to use his weight and strength against himself. [Japanese *jūjitsu* : *jū,* soft, yielding, from Ancient Chinese *ńźiəu* (Mandarin *jou²*) + *jitsu,* art, from Ancient Chinese *dź'iuət* (Mandarin *shu⁴*).]

ju·ju (jo͞o′jo͞o) *n.* **1.** An object used as a fetish, charm, or amulet in West Africa. **2.** Supernatural power ascribed to such an object. [Probably of West African origin.] —**ju′ju·ism′** *n.*

ju·jube (jo͞o′jo͞ob′) *n.* **1. a.** Any of several spiny trees of the genus *Ziziphus;* especially, *Z. jujuba,* native to the Old World, having small yellowish flowers and dark-red fruit. **b.** The fleshy, edible fruit of this tree. Also called "Chinese date." **2.** A fruit-flavored, usually chewy candy or lozenge. [Middle English *iuiube,* from Old French *jujube* or Medieval Latin *jujuba,* both from Latin *zizyphum,* from Greek *zizuphon*†.]

juke box (jo͞ok). A coin-operated phonograph, typically encased in a gaudy cabinet and equipped with push buttons for the selection of records. [From earlier *juke-house,* a brothel, from Gullah, disorderly.]

Jukes (jo͞oks) *n.* Used with a singular or plural verb. A family, group, or rarely, a person regarded as inferior to the surrounding society. Often used in the phrase *the Jukes and the Kallikaks.* [From *The Jukes,* a fictitious name given to a 19th-century New York State family whose history revealed a high incidence of crime and disease.]

ju·lep (jo͞o′lĭp) *n.* **1.** A **mint julep** *(see).* **2.** A sweet syrupy drink, especially one to which medicine may be added. [Middle English *iulep,* from Old French *julep,* from Arabic *julāb,* from Persian *gulāb,* "rose water" : *gul,* rose (see **wrod-** in Appendix*) + *āb,* water (see **ap-²** in Appendix*).]

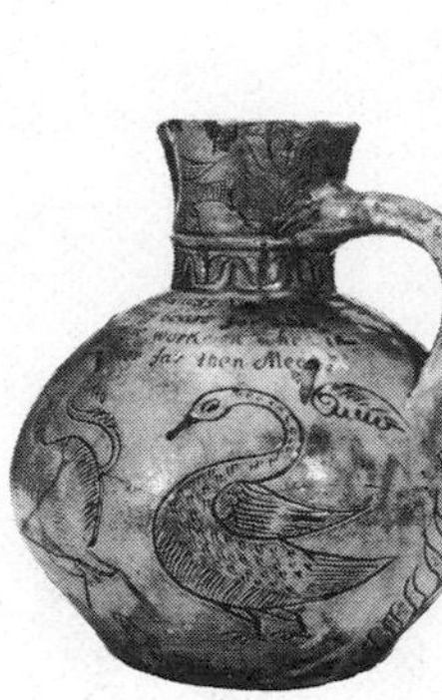

jug
Late 17th-century
English

Jul·ia (jo͞ol′yə). A feminine given name. [Feminine of JULIUS.]

Jul·ian (jo͞ol′yən). Latin name, Flavius Claudius Julianus. A.D. 331–363. Roman emperor (361–363); opponent of Christianity. [Middle English, from Latin *Jūliānus,* from JULIUS.]

Ju·li·an·a (jo͞o′lē-ăn′ə). Born 1909. Queen of the Netherlands (since 1948).

Jul·ian Alps (jo͞ol′yən). A section of the Alps in northeastern Italy and northwestern Yugoslavia. Highest elevation, Triglav (9,395 feet).

Jul·ian calendar (jo͞ol′yən). The calendar introduced by Julius Caesar in Rome in 46 B.C., eventually replaced by the Gregorian calendar. See **calendar.**

ju·li·enne (jo͞o′lē-ĕn′; *French* zhü-lyĕn′) *adj.* Cut into long thin strips: *julienne potatoes.* —*n.* Consommé or broth garnished with strips of julienne vegetables. [From French *à la julienne,* probably from the given name *Julien* or *Jules.*]

Jul·ius (jo͞ol′yəs). A masculine given name. [Latin *Jūlius,* name of a Roman gens. See **deiw-** in Appendix.*]

Jul·ius II (jo͞ol′yəs). 1443–1513. Pope (1503–13); patron of Raphael, Michelangelo, and Bramante.

Jul·ius Cae·sar. See **Caesar.**

Jul·lun·dur (jŭl′ən-dər). A city in northwestern Punjab, Republic of India. Population, 223,000.

Ju·ly (jo͞o-lī′, jo͞o-) *n., pl.* **-lys.** The seventh month of the year

according to the Gregorian calendar. July has 31 days. See **calendar.** [Middle English *Julie,* from Norman French, from Latin *Jūlius (mēnsis),* (month of) Julius Caesar.]

Ju·ma (jo͞o′mä) *n.* The Islamic Sabbath, falling on Friday.

Ju·ma·da (jo͞o-mä′dä) *n.* Also **Jo·ma·da.** **1.** The fifth month of the year in the Moslem calendar, having 30 days. See **calendar.** **2.** The sixth month of the year in the Moslem calendar, having 29 days. See **calendar.** [Arabic *Jumādā.*]

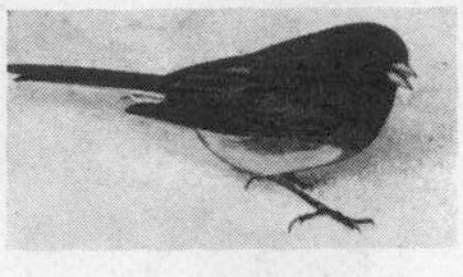

junco
Junco hyemalis

jum·ble (jŭm′bəl) *v.* **-bled, -bling, -bles.** —*intr.* To move, mix, or mingle in a confused, disordered manner. —*tr.* **1.** To stir or mix in a disordered mass. **2.** To muddle; confuse: *The rapid-fire questioning jumbled his thoughts.* —*n.* **1.** A confused or disordered mass: *a jumble of sales goods.* **2.** A disordered state; a muddle. [Origin obscure.]

jum·bo (jŭm′bō) *n., pl.* **-bos.** An unusually large person, animal, or thing. —*adj.* Larger than average: *jumbo shrimp.* [After *Jumbo,* a large elephant exhibited by P.T. Barnum.]

jum·buck (jŭm′bŭk) *n. Australian.* A sheep. [From a native Australian name.]

Jum·na (jŭm′nə). A river rising in the Himalayas of north-central India and flowing 860 miles southeast to the Ganges.

jump (jŭmp) *v.* **jumped, jumping, jumps.** —*intr.* **1. a.** To spring off the ground or other base by a muscular effort of the legs and feet: *jumped three feet into the air.* **b.** To perform this movement repeatedly or rhythmically, as for exercise. **2.** To throw oneself down, off, out, or into something: *He jumped into the political fray.* **3.** To spring at with the intent to assail or censure: *He jumped at me for saying such a thing.* **4.** To arrive at hastily or haphazardly. Used with *to: jump to conclusions.* **5.** To grab at eagerly; respond with alacrity. Used with *at: jump at a bargain.* **6.** To start involuntarily: *jump at a loud noise.* **7.** To rise suddenly and pronouncedly: *Prices jumped.* **8. a.** To skip over space or material, leaving a break in continuity. **b.** To be displaced vertically or laterally because of improper alignment: *The film jumped during projection.* **9.** *Checkers.* To move over an opponent's playing piece. **10.** *Bridge.* To make a jump bid. **11.** *Informal.* To show enterprise and quickness. **12.** *Slang.* To have a lively, pulsating quality: *a nightclub that jumps.* —*tr.* **1.** To leap over or across: *jump the rope.* **2.** To leap aboard; jump on; to catch: *jump a bus.* **3.** To spring upon in sudden attack: *The muggers jumped him.* **4.** To cause to leap: *jump a horse over a hurdle.* **5.** To cause to increase suddenly and markedly. **6.** To skip: *The typewriter jumped a space.* **7.** To promote, especially by more than one level: *He was jumped to head foreman.* **8.** *Bridge.* To raise (a partner's bid) by more than is necessary. **9.** *Checkers.* To take (an opponent's piece) by moving over it with one's own checker. **10.** To leave (a course or track) through mishap: *The train jumped the rail.* —**jump a claim.** To take land or rights from another by violence or fraud. —**jump bail.** To forfeit one's bail by absconding. —**jump down one's throat.** To answer sharply or angrily. —**jump ship.** To desert. —**jump the gun.** To start something too soon. —*n.* **1.** The act of jumping; a leap. **2.** The space or distance covered by a leap: *a jump of seven feet.* **3.** A hurdle, barrier, or span to be jumped. **4.** A track sport featuring skill in jumping: *the high jump.* **5. a.** A sudden, pronounced rise, as in price or salary. **b.** An impressive promotion. **6.** A step or level: *a jump ahead of the others.* **7.** A major transition, as from one career to another. **8. a.** A short trip: *just a hop, skip, and a jump to the shore.* **b.** One in a series of moves and stopovers, as with a circus or road show. **9.** *Checkers.* A move made by jumping. **10. a.** An involuntary nervous movement, as when startled. **b.** *Informal. Plural.* The fidgets. —**get** (or **have**) **a jump on one.** *Informal.* To have a head start over another. —**on the jump.** *Informal.* **1.** Energetically busy. **2.** On the go; constantly dashing about. [Probably imitative.]

jump bid. *Bridge.* A bid at a higher level than that required to exceed the preceding bid.

jump·er¹ (jŭm′pər) *n.* **1.** One that jumps. **2.** A type of coasting sled. **3.** *Electricity.* A short length of wire used temporarily to complete or by-pass a circuit.

jum·per² (jŭm′pər) *n.* **1.** A sleeveless dress worn over a blouse or sweater. **2.** A loose, protective garment worn over other clothes. **3.** A child's garment consisting of straight-legged pants attached to a biblike bodice. [Probably from British dialectal *jump, jup,* man's loose jacket, woman's underbodice, from French *juppe,* variant of *jupe,* skirt, from Arabic *jubbah.*]

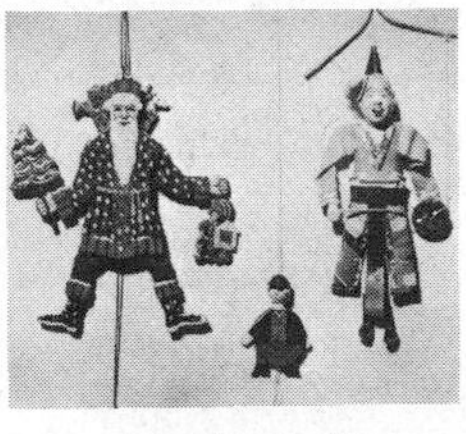

jumping jack
Left: French
Center: Swiss
Right: Chinese

jumper cable. A **booster cable** *(see).* Also called "jump cable."

jumping bean. A seed, as of certain Mexican shrubs or plants of the genera *Sebastiana* and *Sapium,* containing the larva of a moth, *Laspeyresia saltitans,* the movements of which cause the seed to jerk or roll.

jumping jack. A toy figure with jointed limbs that can be made to dance by pulling an attached string.

jumping mouse. Any of various small rodents of the family Zapodidae, having a long tail and long hind legs.

jump·ing-off place (jŭm′pĭng-ôf′, -ŏf′). **1.** A very remote spot; an isolated outpost. **2.** A beginning point for an enterprise.

jump-off (jŭmp′ôf′, -ŏf′) *n.* The commencement of a race or of a planned military attack.

jump seat. **1.** A portable or collapsible seat in the entrance or flight deck of an airplane or in an automobile between the front and rear seats. **2.** A small rear seat in a sports car.

jump-start (jŭmp′stärt′) *tr.v.* **-started, -starting, -starts.** **1.** To start (an automobile engine) by pushing or rolling and suddenly releasing the clutch. **2.** To start (an automobile engine) using a booster cable connected to the battery of another automobile. —*n.* The process of jump-starting.

jump·y (jŭm′pē) *adj.* **-ier, -iest.** **1.** Characterized by fitful, jerky movements. **2.** Easily unsettled or alarmed; nervous or on edge, as with apprehension. —**jump′i·ness** *n.*

jun (jo͝on) *n., pl.* **jun.** A coin equal to 1/100 of the won of North Korea. See table of exchange rates at **currency.** [Korean.]

jun., Jun. junior.

junc. junction.

jun·co (jŭng′kō) *n., pl.* **-cos.** Any of various North American birds of the genus *Junco,* having predominantly gray plumage. [Spanish, "rush," junco. See **jonquil.**]

junc·tion (jŭngk′shən) *n.* **1.** The act or process of joining or the condition of being joined. **2.** *Abbr.* **jct., junc.** The place where two things join or meet; specifically, the place where two roads or railway routes join or cross paths. **3.** A transition layer or boundary between two different materials or between physically different regions in a single material, especially: **a.** A connection between conductors or sections of a transmission line. **b.** The interface between a region of predominantly positive charge carriers and another of predominantly negative charge carriers in a semiconductor. **c.** A mechanical or alloyed contact between different metals or other materials, as in a thermocouple. [Latin *junctiō,* from *junctus,* past participle of *jungere,* to join. See **yeug-** in Appendix.*] —**junc′tion·al** *adj.*

junction box. An enclosed panel used to connect or branch electric circuits without making permanent splices.

junc·ture (jŭngk′chər) *n.* **1.** The act of joining, or the condition of being joined. **2.** The line or point where two things are joined; junction; joint; hinge. **3.** A point or interval in time; especially, a crisis or similar turning point. **4.** The transition or mode of transition from one sound to another in speech. [Middle English, from Latin *junctūra,* from *junctus,* past participle of *jungere,* to join. See **yeug-** in Appendix.*]

June (jo͞on) *n.* The sixth month of the year according to the Gregorian calendar. June has 30 days. See **calendar.** [Middle English, from Old French *juin,* from Latin *Jūnius (mēnsis),* (month consecrated to) the goddess JUNO.]

Ju·neau (jo͞o′nō). The capital of Alaska, in the southeast near the border of British Columbia, Canada. Population, 7,000.

June beetle. Any of various North American beetles of the subfamily Melolonthinae, having larvae that are often destructive to crops. Also called "June bug," "May beetle."

June·ber·ry (jo͞on′bĕr′ē) *n., pl.* **-ries.** The **shadbush** *(see),* or its fruit.

Jung (yo͝ong), **Carl Gustav.** 1875–1961. Swiss psychologist.

Jung·frau (yo͝ong′frou′). A mountain rising to 13,653 feet in the Bernese Alps, in south-central Switzerland.

Jung·i·an (yo͝ong′ē-ən) *adj.* **1.** Of or pertaining to Carl G. Jung or his theories. **2.** Maintaining Jung's psychological theories; specifically, stressing the contributions of racial and cultural inheritance to the psychology of an individual. —**Jung′i·an** *n.*

jun·gle (jŭng′gəl) *n.* **1.** Land densely overgrown with tropical vegetation and trees. **2.** Any dense thicket or growth. **3.** *Slang.* A place of rendezvous for hoboes, often a clearing near a railroad. **4.** A milieu characterized by intense, often ruthless competition. **5.** Any maze, entanglement, or confusion, especially one that is fruitless or leads nowhere. [Originally, "wasteland," from Hindi and Marathi *jangal,* from Sanskrit *jāṅgala*†, "dry," desert.]

jungle fever. A pernicious malaria occurring in the East Indies.

jungle fowl. Any of several birds of the genus *Gallus,* of southeastern Asia; especially, *G. gallus,* considered to be the ancestor of the common domestic fowl.

Jungle gym. A trademark for a structure of poles and bars on which children can play.

jun·gly (jŭng′glē) *adj.* **-glier, -gliest.** Resembling or suggestive of a jungle.

Ju·nín (ho͞o-nēn′). A town in west-central Peru; the site of a decisive defeat of the Spaniards by Bolívar and Sucre (1824).

jun·ior (jo͞on′yər) *adj.* **1.** *Abbr.* **Jr., Jun.** Younger. Used to distinguish the son from the father of the same name, and written after the full name: *William Jones, Jr.* **2.** Designed for or including youthful persons: *a junior tennis match; junior dress sizes.* **3.** Lower in rank or shorter in length of tenure: *the junior senator.* **4.** Designating the third or penultimate year of a U.S. high school or college. **5.** Lesser in scale than the usual. —*n. Abbr.* **Jr., jr., Jun., jun.** **1.** A younger person or individual. **2.** A person lesser in rank or time of participation or service; subordinate. **3.** An undergraduate in his third or penultimate year of a U.S. high school or college. [Latin *jūnior,* from pre-classical *juvenior* (unattested), comparative of *juvenis,* young. See **yeu-²** in Appendix.*]

junior college. An educational institution offering a two-year course that is generally the equivalent of the first two years of a four-year undergraduate course.

junior high school. A school in the U.S. system intermediate between grammar school and high school, and generally including the seventh, eighth, and sometimes ninth grades. Also called "junior high."

jun·ior·i·ty (jo͞on-yôr′ə-tē, jo͞on-yŏr′-) *n.* The rank or condition of being a junior.

junior varsity. *Abbr.* **J.V.** A high-school or college team that competes in interschool sports on the level below varsity.

ju·ni·per (jo͞o′nə-pər) *n.* Any of various evergreen trees or shrubs of the genus *Juniperus,* having scalelike, often prickly foliage and aromatic, bluish-gray, berrylike fruit. [Middle English *junipere,* from Latin *jūniperus*†.]

junk¹ (jŭngk) *n.* **1.** Scrapped materials such as glass, rags, paper, or metals that can be converted into usable stock. **2.** *Informal.* **a.** Anything worn-out or fit to be discarded. **b.** Anything of inferior quality; something cheap or shoddy. **c.** Anything

ă pat/ā pay/âr care/ä father/b bib/ch church/d deed/ĕ pet/ē be/f fife/g gag/h hat/hw which/ĭ pit/ī pie/îr pier/j judge/k kick/l lid, needle/m mum/n no, sudden/ng thing/ŏ pot/ō toe/ô paw, for/oi noise/ou out/o͝o took/o͞o boot/p pop/r roar/s sauce/sh ship, dish/

meaningless, fatuous, or unbelievable; nonsense. **3.** *Slang.* Heroin. **4.** *Nautical.* **a.** Hard salt beef. **b.** Old cordage, reused for gaskets, oakum, and mats. —*tr.v.* **junked, junking, junks.** To throw away or desert as useless; to scrap. [Originally (until the 20th century) a nautical term meaning old, worn-out pieces of rope or cable, from Middle English *jonke*†.]

junk² (jŭngk) *n.* A Chinese flat-bottomed ship with a high poop and battened sails. [Chiefly from Portuguese *junco* and Dutch *jonk,* from Malay *jong,* sea-going ship.]

Jun·ker (yŏŏng′kər) *n.* A member of the Prussian landed aristocracy, especially of its ultrareactionary section. [German, from Old High German *junchērro* : *jung,* young (see **yeu-²** in Appendix*) + *hērro,* comparative of *hēr,* worthy, exalted (see **kei-²** in Appendix*).] —**Jun′ker·dom** *n.*

Jun·kers (yŏŏng′kərs), **Hugo.** 1859–1935. German pioneer aircraft designer and transportation executive.

jun·ket (jŭng′kĭt) *n.* **1.** A sweet food made from flavored milk and rennet. **2.** A party, banquet, or outing. **3.** A trip taken by an official and underwritten with public funds. **4.** An excursion or tour; especially, a trip covering some professional circuit. —*v.* **junketed, -keting, -kets.** —*intr.* **1.** To hold a party or banquet. **2.** To make an excursion using public funds. —*tr.* To fete at a party or banquet. [Middle English *jonket,* a kind of egg custard served on rushes or made in a rush mat, from *junket,* rush basket, from Old North French *jonquette,* from *jonc,* rush, from Latin *juncus.* See **jonquil.**] —**jun′ket·er** *n.*

junk·ie (jŭng′kē) *n.* Also **junk·y** *pl.* **-ies.** *Slang.* A narcotics addict, especially one using heroin.

junk·man (jŭngk′măn′) *n., pl.* **-men** (-mĕn′). A man who makes an occupation of buying and selling junk.

Ju·no (jōō′nō). *Roman Mythology.* The principal goddess of the Pantheon, wife and sister of Jupiter, patroness primarily of marriage and the well-being of women, identified with the Greek goddess Hera. [Latin *Jūno*†.]

Ju·no·esque (jōō′nō-ĕsk′) *adj.* Having the stately bearing and imposing beauty of the goddess Juno.

jun·ta (hŏŏn′tə, hōōn′-, jŭn′-) *n.* **1.** A group of military officers holding state power in a country after a coup d'état. **2.** A council or small legislative body in a government, especially in Central and South American countries. **3.** Variant of **junto.** [Spanish and Portuguese, from Vulgar Latin *juncta* (unattested), "joined," from Latin, feminine past participle of *jungere,* to join. See **yeug-** in Appendix.*]

jun·to (jŭn′tō) *n., pl.* **-tos.** Also **jun·ta.** A small, usually secret group or committee that gathers for some common interest or aim; cabal; clique; faction. [Variant of JUNTA.]

Ju·pi·ter¹ (jōō′pə-tər). *Roman Mythology.* The supreme god, patron of the Roman state, brother and husband of Juno, identified with the Greek god Zeus. Also called "Jove." [Middle English, from Latin *Jūpiter, Jūppiter.* See **deiw-** in Appendix.*]

Ju·pi·ter² (jōō′pə-tər) *n. Astronomy.* The fifth planet from the sun, the largest and most massive in the solar system, having a diameter of approximately 86,000 miles, a mass approximately 318 times that of Earth, and a sidereal period of revolution about the sun of 11.86 years at a mean distance of 483 million miles. See **solar system.** [After JUPITER.]

ju·ra. Plural of **jus.**

Ju·ra (jŏŏr′ə; *French* zhü-rȧ′). Also **Ju·ra Mountains.** A range extending for about 200 miles along the French-Swiss border. Highest elevation, Crêt de la Neige (5,652 feet).

ju·ral (jŏŏr′əl) *adj.* **1.** Of or pertaining to law. **2.** Of, pertaining to, or arising from rights and obligations. [From Latin *jūs* (stem *jūr-*), right, law. See **yewo-¹** in Appendix.*] —**ju′ral·ly** *adv.*

ju·rant (jŏŏr′ənt) *adj.* Taking oath. —*n.* A person who takes an oath. [Latin *jūrāns,* from *jūrāre,* to swear. See **jury.**]

Ju·ras·sic (jōō-răs′ĭk) *adj. Geology.* Of, belonging to, or designating the time and deposits of the second period of the Mesozoic era, characterized by the existence of dinosaurs and the appearance of primitive mammals and birds. See **geology.** —*n. Geology.* The Jurassic period. Preceded by *the.* [French *jurassique,* after the JURA Mountains.]

ju·rat (jŏŏr′ăt′) *n.* A certification on an affidavit declaring when, where, and before whom it was sworn. [Latin *jūrātum (est),* "(it has been) sworn," from *jūrāre,* to swear. See **jury.**]

ju·ra·to·ry (jŏŏr′ə-tôr′ē, -tōr′ē) *adj. Law.* Of or pertaining to an oath. [Latin *jūrātōrius,* from *jūrāre,* to swear. See **jury.**]

ju·rid·i·cal (jōō-rĭd′ĭ-kəl) *adj.* Also **ju·rid·ic** (-ĭk). Of or pertaining to the law and its administration. [From Latin *jūridicus* : *jūs* (stem *jūr-*), law (see **yewo-¹** in Appendix*) + *dīcere,* to say (see **deik-** in Appendix*).] —**ju·rid′i·cal·ly** *adv.*

juridical days. The days on which court is in session.

ju·ris·con·sult (jŏŏr′əs-kŏn′sŭlt′) *n.* A person learned in law; jurist. [Latin *jūrisconsultus* : *jūris,* genitive of *jūs,* law (see **yewo-¹** in Appendix*) + *consultus,* past participle of *consulere,* to CONSULT.]

ju·ris·dic·tion (jŏŏr-əs-dĭk′shən) *n.* **1.** The right and power to interpret and apply the law. **2.** Authority or control. **3.** The extent of authority or control. **4.** The territorial range of authority or control. [Middle English *jurisdiccioun,* from Old French *juridiction,* from Latin *jūrisdictiō* : *jūris,* genitive of *jūs,* law (see **yewo-¹** in Appendix*) + *dictiō,* declaration (see **dic-tion**).] —**ju′ris·dic′tion·al** *adj.* —**ju′ris·dic′tion·al·ly** *adv.*

ju·ris·pru·dence (jŏŏr′əs-prōōd′əns) *n.* **1.** The philosophy of law or the formal science of law. **2.** A division or department of law. [Originally "skill in law," from Late Latin *jūrisprūdentia* : *jūris,* genitive of *jūs,* law (see **yewo-¹** in Appendix*) + *prūdentia,* foresight, knowledge, from *prūdēns,* knowing, PRUDENT.] —**ju′ris·pru·den′tial** (-dĕn′shəl) *adj.* —**ju′ris·pru·den′tial·ly** *adv.*

ju·ris·pru·dent (jŏŏr′əs-prōōd′ənt) *adj.* Versed in jurisprudence. —*n.* A jurist.

ju·rist (jŏŏr′əst) *n.* A person who is skilled in the law, especially an eminent judge, lawyer, or legal scholar. [Old French, from Medieval Latin *jūrista,* from Latin *jūs* (stem *jūr-*), law. See **yewo-¹** in Appendix.*]

ju·ris·tic (jōō-rĭs′tĭk) *adj.* Also **ju·ris·ti·cal** (-tĭ-kəl). **1.** Of or pertaining to a jurist or to jurisprudence. **2.** Of or pertaining to law or legality. —**ju·ris′ti·cal·ly** *adv.*

ju·ror (jŏŏr′ər, -ôr′) *n.* **1. a.** A person serving as a member of a body sworn to hear and hand down a verdict on a case. **b.** A person called or designated for jury duty. **2.** A person who serves on any body acting in a capacity analogous to that of a jury, as when judging the entries in a competition. [Middle English *juroure,* from Norman French *jurour,* from Latin *jūrātor,* "swearer," from *jūrātus,* past participle of *jūrāre,* to swear. See **jury.**]

Ju·ruá (zhōō-rwä′). A river of South America, rising in the Peruvian Andes and flowing 1,200 miles northeast to the Amazon in northwestern Brazil.

Ju·rue·na (zhōō-rwā′nä). A river rising in southwestern Mato Grosso, Brazil, and flowing 500 miles north to the Tapajós.

ju·ry¹ (jŏŏr′ē) *n., pl.* **-ries.** **1.** A group of persons forming a body sworn to judge and give a verdict on some matter; specifically, a body of persons summoned by law and sworn to hear and hand down a verdict upon a case presented in court. See **grand jury, petit jury.** **2.** A group of persons forming a committee to judge, for example, a competition and award prizes. [Middle English *jurie,* from Norman French *juree,* from Old French *juree,* oath, inquest, from Latin *jūrāta,* "thing sworn," from the feminine past participle of *jūrāre,* to swear, from *jūs* (stem *jūr-*), law. See **yewo-¹** in Appendix.*]

ju·ry² (jŏŏr′ē) *adj. Nautical.* Intended or designed for emergency or temporary use; makeshift: *a jury rig.* [Origin obscure.]

ju·ry·man (jŏŏr′ē-mən) *n., pl.* **-men** (-mĭn). A person serving on a jury; juror.

ju·ry-rigged (jŏŏr′ē-rĭgd′) *adj. Nautical.* Rigged for emergency or temporary use.

jus (yōōs) *n., pl.* **jura** (yōō′rə). *Latin.* **1.** Right; justice; law. **2.** A given right; legal power.

jus gen·ti·um (yōōs gĕn′tē-əm). *Latin.* The law of nations; international law.

jus·sive (jŭs′ĭv) *adj. Grammar.* Expressing or used to express a command. —*n.* A word, mood, or construction used to express command. [From Latin *jussus,* past participle of *jubēre,* to command. See **yeudh-** in Appendix.*]

just¹ (jŭst) *adj.* **1.** Honorable and fair in one's dealings and actions. **2.** Consistent with moral right; fair; equitable. **3.** Properly due or merited: *just deserts.* **4.** Valid within the law; legitimate. **5.** Suitable; fitting. **6.** Sound; well-founded: *a just appraisal.* **7.** Exact; accurate: *a just measure.* **8.** Upright before God; righteous. —See Synonyms at **fair.** —*adv.* (jŭst; *unstressed* jəst, jĭst). **1.** Precisely; exactly: *That's just what I was going to say.* **2.** At the exact moment of: *It's just six.* **3.** Only a moment ago: *He just came.* **4.** By a narrow margin; barely: *You just missed Tom.* **5.** But a little distance: *You'll find it just down the road.* **6.** Merely; only: *I just meant that I agree.* **7.** Simply; certainly. Used as an intensive: *It's just beautiful!* —**just about.** **1.** On the point of: *I was just about to go.* **2.** Almost; very nearly: *I've just about had enough.* —**just now.** **1.** At this very moment. **2.** Only a moment ago. [Middle English *just(e),* from Old French *juste,* from Latin *jūstus.* See **yewo-¹** in Appendix.*] —**just′ly** *adv.* —**just′ness** *n.*

just². Variant of **joust.**

jus·tice (jŭs′tĭs) *n.* **1.** Moral rightness; equity. **2.** Honor; fairness. **3.** Good reason: *He's very angry, and with justice.* **4.** Fair handling; due reward or treatment. **5.** The administration and procedure of law. **6.** *Abbr.* **J.** A judge. **7.** A justice of the peace. —**bring to justice.** To effect the apprehension and trial of (a lawbreaker). —**do justice to.** **1.** To approach with proper appreciation; enjoy fully. **2.** To show to full advantage: *The picture doesn't do justice to her eyes.* [Middle English, from Old French, from Latin *jūstitia,* from *jūstus,* JUST.]

Justice, Department of. The legal department of the executive branch of the U.S. government, headed by the Attorney General and having as its jurisdiction the legal representation of the government, the enforcement of antitrust and civil-rights laws, and the supervision of immigration and naturalization.

justice of the peace. *Abbr.* **J.P.** A magistrate of the lowest level of the state court system, having authority chiefly to act upon minor offenses, commit cases to a higher court for trial, perform marriages, and administer oaths.

jus·tice·ship (jŭs′tĭs-shĭp′) *n.* The office of a justice.

jus·ti·ci·a·ble (jŭ-stĭsh′ə-bəl) *adj.* Appropriate for or subject to court trial; liable for court decision. [French, from Old French, from *justicier,* to try, from *justice,* JUSTICE.]

jus·ti·ci·ar·y (jŭ-stĭsh′ē-ĕr′ē) *adj.* Pertaining to the administration of the law. —*n., pl.* **justiciaries.** Also **jus·ti·ci·ar** (jŭ-stĭsh′ē-ər). A high judicial officer in medieval England. [Medieval Latin *jūstitiārius,* from Latin *jūstitia,* JUSTICE.]

jus·ti·fi·a·ble (jŭs′tə-fī′ə-bəl, jŭs′tə-fī′-) *adj.* Capable of being justified. —**jus′ti·fi′a·bil′i·ty, jus′ti·fi′a·ble·ness** *n.* —**jus′ti·fi′a·bly** *adv.*

jus·ti·fi·ca·tion (jŭs′tə-fĭ-kā′shən) *n.* **1.** The act of justifying. **2.** The condition or fact of being justified. **3.** The fact, circumstance, or evidence that justifies; ground of defense: *"There are few justifications for a revolution"* (Burke).

jus·ti·fi·ca·tive (jŭ-stĭf′ĭ-kə-tĭv) *adj.* Also **jus·ti·fi·ca·to·ry** (-tôr′ē, -tōr′ē). Serving as justification.

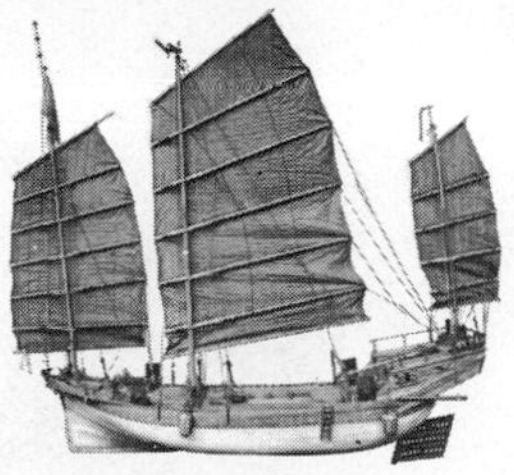

junk²
Model of a South China trading junk

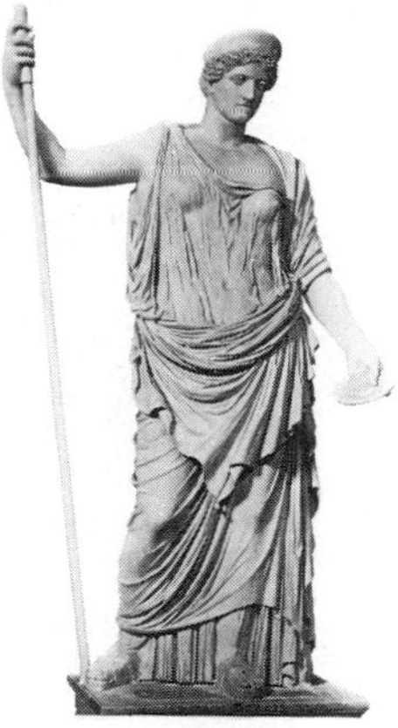

Juno
Roman statue in the Vatican Museum

jus·ti·fi·er (jŭs'tə-fī'ər) *n.* **1.** One that justifies. **2.** In phototypesetting, a space that varies as necessary to justify a line.
jus·ti·fy (jŭs'tə-fī') *v.* **-fied, -fying, -fies.** —*tr.* **1.** To demonstrate or prove to be just, right, or valid. **2.** To show to be well-founded; to warrant. **3.** To declare free of blame; absolve. **4.** *Theology.* To free (man) of the guilt and penalty attached to grievous sin. Said only of God. **5.** *Law.* **a.** To demonstrate good reason for (an action taken). **b.** To prove to be qualified as a bondsman. **6.** *Printing.* To adjust or space (lines) to the proper length. —*intr. Printing.* To be or become properly spaced and of the correct length. Said óf a line of type. [Middle English *justifien*, originally, to judge, punish, from Old French *justifier*, from Late Latin *jūstificāre*, to do justice toward, to forgive, pardon : *jūstus*, JUST + *facere*, to do (see dhē-¹ in Appendix*).]
Jus·tin·i·an I (jŭ-stĭn'ē-ən). Called "the Great." A.D. 483–565. Roman emperor of the East (527–565).
Justinian's Code. The codification of Roman law, legislative records, and legal opinions made by order of Justinian I and published in 529 A.D.
jus·tle. Variant of **jostle.**
jut (jŭt) *intr.v.* **jutted, jutting, juts.** To project, usually sharply, beyond the limits of the main body; protrude. Often used with *out:* "*He had a sharp crooked nose jutting out of a lean dancer's face*" (Graham Greene). —*n.* Something that protrudes; a projection. [Variant of JET (to project).]
jute (jōōt) *n.* **1.** Either of two Asian plants, *Corchorus capsularis* or *C. olitorius,* yielding a fiber used for sacking and cordage. **2.** The fiber obtained from such a plant. [Bengali *jhōṭo, jhuṭo,* from Sanskrit *jūṭa*†.]
Jute (jōōt) *n.* A member of any of several Germanic tribes, some of whom invaded Britain and settled in Kent in the fifth century A.D. [Middle English *Iutes* (plural), Old English *Eotas, Iotas,* akin to Old Norse *Iōtar*†, people of Jutland.]
Jut·land (jŭt'lənd). *Danish* **Jyl·land** (yül'län). A peninsula of northern Europe, comprising mainland Denmark in the north and Schleswig-Holstein, West Germany, in the south.
Jut·land, Battle of (jŭt'lənd). The only major naval engagement between the British and German fleets in World War I (1916), fought about 70 miles west of Jutland.
juv. juvenile.

ju·ve·nal (jōō'və-nəl) *adj.* Of or pertaining to a young bird having its first plumage of true feathers though often lacking the adult characteristics of its species: *juvenal plumage.* [Latin *juvenālis,* juvenile, young, from *juvenis,* young. See yeu-² in Appendix.*]
Ju·ve·nal (jōō'və-nəl). Latin name, Decimus Junius Juvenalis. A.D. 60?–140? Roman satirist.
ju·ve·nes·cent (jōō'və-nĕs'ənt) *adj.* Becoming young or youthful. [JUVEN(AL) + -ESCENT.] —**ju've·nes'cence** *n.*
ju·ve·nile (jōō'və-nəl, -nīl') *adj. Abbr.* **juv. 1.** Young; youthful. **2. a.** Not fully developed; not yet adult. Said of animals. **b.** Juvenal. **3.** Characteristic of youth or children; immature: *juvenile behavior.* **4.** Intended for or appropriate to children or young persons: *juvenile fashions.* —*n. Abbr.* **juv. 1. a.** A young person; child. **b.** A young animal that has not reached sexual maturity. **2.** An actor who plays children or young persons. **3.** A children's book. —See Synonyms at **young.** [Latin *juvenīlis,* from *juvenis,* young, a youth. See yeu-² in Appendix.*] —**ju've·nile·ly** *adv.* —**ju've·nile·ness** *n.*
juvenile delinquency. Antisocial or criminal behavior by children or adolescents.
juvenile delinquent. *Abbr.* **J.D.** A child or adolescent who exhibits antisocial or criminal behavior.
ju·ve·nil·i·a (jōō'və-nīl'ē-ə) *pl.n.* Works, particularly written or artistic works, produced in childhood or youth. [Latin *juvenīlia,* neuter plural of *juvenīlis,* JUVENILE.]
ju·ve·nil·i·ty (jōō'və-nīl'ə-tē) *n., pl.* **-ties. 1.** The quality or condition of being foolishly juvenile; immaturity. **2.** The quality or condition of being young or youthful. **3.** *Plural.* A manifestation of youth; juvenile or immature acts or characteristics. **4.** Young persons collectively.
jux·ta·pose (jŭk'stə-pōz') *tr.v.* **-posed, -posing, -poses.** To situate side by side; place together. [French *juxtaposer,* probably from JUXTAPOSITION.]
jux·ta·po·si·tion (jŭk'stə-pə-zĭsh'ən) *n.* The act of juxtaposing or the state of being juxtaposed. [French : Latin *juxtā,* close together (see yeug- in Appendix*) + POSITION.] —**jux'ta·po·si'tion·al** *adj.*
J.V. junior varsity.
jwlr. jeweler.
Jyl·land. The Danish name for **Jutland.**

ă pat/ā pay/âr care/ä father/b bib/ch church/d deed/ĕ pet/ē be/f fife/g gag/h hat/hw which/ĭ pit/ī pie/îr pier/j judge/k kick/l lid/ needle/m mum/n no, sudden/ng thing/ŏ pot/ō toe/ô paw, for/oi noise/ou out/ŏŏ took/ōō boot/p pop/r roar/s sauce/sh ship, dish/

Justinian I
Detail from a mosaic
in San Vitale, Ravenna

K k

∀ ∀ Ꮶ 𝖐 𝖐 k k K k k K K k k

1	2	3	4	5	6	7	8	9	10	11	12	13	14

Phoenician　　　　Greek　　　　Roman　　　Medieval　　　Modern

Around 1000 B.C. the Phoenicians and other Semites of Syria and Palestine began to use a graphic sign in the forms (1,2), later in the form (3). They gave it the name kaph, *meaning "(hollow of the) hand," and used it for the consonant k. After 900 B.C. the Greeks borrowed the sign from the Phoenicians (4), later reversing its orientation and giving it a symmetrical form (5,6). They also changed its name to* kappa. *The Greek form passed unchanged via the Etruscans to the Roman alphabet (7), in which it was rarely used. The Roman Monumental Capital (8) is the prototype of our modern capital, printed (11) and written (12). The written Roman form (7) developed into the late Roman and medieval Uncial (9) and Cursive (10), which are the bases of our modern small letter, printed (13) and written (14).*

k, K (kā) *n., pl.* **k's** or *rare* **ks, K's** or **Ks. 1.** The 11th letter of the modern English alphabet. See **alphabet. 2.** Any of the speech sounds represented by this letter.

k, K, k., K. *Note:* As an abbreviation or symbol, *k* may be a small or a capital letter, with or without a period. Established forms or those generally preferred precede the definition. When no form is given, all four forms are in general use in that sense. **1. K** kaon. **2. k** karat. **3. K a.** kelvin (temperature unit). **b.** Kelvin (temperature scale). **4. k** kilo-. **5. k., K.** king. **6. K** *Chess.* king. **7.** *Card Games.* **K.** king. **8. k., K.** knight. **9. k., K** kopeck. **10. k., K.** koruna. **11. k., K.** krona. **12. k., K.** krone. **13. K** The symbol for the element potassium. **14.** The 11th in a series; 10th when *J* is omitted.

K2. See **Godwin Austen.**

Ka·a·ba (kä'ə-bə, kä'bə) *n.* Also **Ca·a·ba.** A Moslem shrine in Mecca which houses a sacred black stone said to have been given to Abraham by the archangel Gabriel, and toward which followers of Mohammed face when praying. [Arabic *ka'bah,* "square building," from *ka'b, Ka'ba,* cube.]

Kaap·land. The Afrikaans name for **Cape of Good Hope Province.**

kab. Variant of **cab** (measure).

kab·a·la. Variant of **cabala.**

Kab·ar·din-Bal·kar Autonomous Soviet Socialist Republic (käb'ər-dēn'bôl'kär', -bäl'kär'). Also **Kab·ar·di·no-Bal·kar A.S.S.R.** (käb'ər-dē'nō-). An administrative division, 4,825 square miles in area, of the southwestern Russian S.F.S.R. Population, 507,000. Capital, Nalchik.

kab·ba·la. Variant of **cabala.**

ka·bob (kə-bŏb') *n.* **Shish kebab** (*see*).

ka·bu·ki (kä-bōō'kē, kə-) *n.* A type of popular Japanese drama, evolved from the older No theater, in which elaborately costumed performers, usually male, enact both tragedies and comedies using stylized movements, dances, and songs. [Japanese, "art of singing and dancing" : *kabu,* singing and dancing, from Ancient Chinese *kâ miu* (Mandarin *kê¹ wu³*) + *ki,* art, artist, from Ancient Chinese *g'jie* (Mandarin *chi⁴*).]

Ka·bul (kä'bool). **1.** The capital of Afghanistan, on the Kabul River in the east-central part of the country. Population, 450,000. **2.** A river rising west of Kabul, Afghanistan, and flowing about 300 miles generally east to the Indus River in West Pakistan.

Ka·byle (kə-bīl') *n., pl.* **Kabyle** or **-byles. 1.** A member of one of the Berber tribes inhabiting Tunisia or Algeria. **2.** The Hamitic Berber dialect spoken by these people. [French, from Arabic *qabā'il,* plural of *qabīlah,* tribe.]

Ká·dár (kä'där), **János.** Born 1912. Premier of Hungary (1956–58 and since 1961).

Kad·dish (kä'dĭsh) *n. Judaism.* A prayer in praise of God, recited in the daily synagogue services and by mourners after the death of a close relative. [Aramaic *qaddish.*]

Ka·di·koy (kä-dĭ-koi'). A city of Turkey, at the southern end of the Bosporus opposite Istanbul. Population, 129,000.

Ka·du·na (kə-dōō'nə). The capital of the Northern Region of Nigeria, on the Kaduna River. Population, 150,000.

Kae·song (kā'sŏng'). A city of North Korea, in the southwest just across the border from South Korea. Population, 140,000.

kaf·fee klatsch. Variant of **coffee klatch.**

kaf·fir (käf'ər) *n.* Also **kaf·ir.** A variety of sorghum, *Sorghum vulgare caffrorum,* of Africa, cultivated in dry regions for its grain and as fodder. Also called "kaffir corn." [From KAF-FIR.]

Kaf·fir (käf'ər) *n., pl.* **Kaffir** or **-firs. 1.** A member of one of the Bantu-speaking tribes inhabiting South Africa. **2.** The language spoken by these people. **3.** A non-Moslem. Used disparagingly by Arabic Moslems. **4.** Variant of **Kafir.** [Arabic *kāfir,* "infidel," present participle of *kafara,* to deny, be skeptical.]

Ka·fir (kä'fər, käf'ər) *n., pl.* **Kafir** or **-firs. 1.** A people of ancient Iranian stock living in Nuristan in northeastern Afghanistan. **2.** A member of the Kafir people. **3.** Variant of **Kaffir.** [Arabic *kāfir,* infidel, KAFFIR.]

Ka·fi·ri (kä-fîr'ē) *n.* The Indic language of the Iranian Kafirs.

Kaf·ka (käf'kä), **Franz.** 1883–1924. Austrian novelist.

kaf·tan. Variant of **caftan.**

Ka·fu·e (kä-fōō'ā). A river of Zambia, rising in the northwest and flowing about 600 miles first south and then east to the Zambezi on the Rhodesian border.

Ka·ge·ra (kä-gā'rä). A river of Africa, the chief head stream of the Nile, flowing 250 miles first north along the Rwanda-Tanzania border and then east to Lake Victoria from which it emerges as the Victoria Nile. See **Nile.**

Ka·go·shi·ma (kä'gō-shē'mä). A city of Japan, a seaport in southern Kyushu. Population, 328,000.

Ka·ho·o·la·we (kä-hō'ō-lä'vē, -wē). An island of Hawaii, 45 square miles in area, lying southwest of Maui.

kai·ak. Variant of **kayak.**

Kai·e·teur Falls (kī'ə-tōor'). A waterfall, 750 feet high, in Guyana.

Kai·feng (kī'fŭng'). The capital of Honan, China, in the northeastern part of the province. Population, 318,000.

Kai Islands. The former name for the **Ewab Islands.**

kail. Variant of **kale.**

kain (kān) *n.* Also **cain, kane.** Tax or rent payments made in kind. [Middle English *cain,* from Scottish Gaelic *cāin,* rent, fine, probably from Late Latin *canōn,* tribute, decree, from Latin, rule, law, CANON.]

kai·nite (kī'nīt', kā'ə-nīt') *n.* A mineral, essentially $KCl \cdot MgSO_4 \cdot 3H_2O$, used mainly as fertilizer and as a source of potassium compounds. [German *Kainit* : Greek *kainos,* new, recently formed (see ken-³ in Appendix*) + -ITE.]

Kair·ouan (kīr'wän'; *French* kĕr-wän'). *Arabic* **Qair·wan** (kīr'wän). A city of northeastern Tunisia, a pilgrimage center and holy city of the Moslems. Population, 35,000.

Kai·ser (kī'zər) *n.* A title designating the emperors of the Holy Roman Empire (A.D. 962–1806), Austria (1804–1918), and Germany (1871–1918). [German *Kaiser,* from Old High German *Keisar,* from Latin *Caesar,* CAESAR.]

Kai·ser (kī'zər), **Henry J(ohn).** 1882–1967. American industrialist.

Kai-shek, Chiang. See **Chiang Kai-shek.**

Kai·shu. The Japanese name for **Haeju.**

kabuki
Woodblock print of
kabuki actor

---

t tight/th thin, path/*th* this, bāthe/u cut/ür urge/v valve/w with/y yes/z zebra, size/zh vision/ə about, item, edible, gallop, circus/ à *Fr.* ami/œ *Fr.* feu, *Ger.* schön/ü *Fr.* tu, *Ger.* über/KH *Ger.* ich, *Scot.* loch/N *Fr.* bon. *Follows main vocabulary. †Of obscure origin.

ka·ka (kä′kə) *n.* A brownish or greenish parrot, *Nestor meridionalis,* of New Zealand. [Maori, imitative of its cry.]
ka·ka·po (kä′kə-pō′) *n., pl.* **-pos.** A ground-dwelling nocturnal parrot, *Strigops habroptilus,* of New Zealand, having greenish plumage. [Maori KAKA (parrot) + *po,* night.]
ka·ke·mo·no (kä′kə-mō′nō) *n., pl.* **-nos.** A Japanese scroll painting on silk or paper. [Japanese, "hanging thing," scroll : *kake,* hanging + *mono,* thing.]
ka·la-a·zar (kä′lä-ä-zär′) *n.* A chronic, usually fatal disease occurring in Asia, especially in India, caused by a protozoan parasite, *Leishmania donovani,* and characterized by irregular fever, enlargement of the spleen, hemorrhages, dropsy, and extreme emaciation. [Hindi *kālā-āzār,* "black disease" : *kālā,* black, from Sanskrit *kālaḥ,* blue-black, black, from Dravidian + *āzār,* disease, from Persian *āzār*†.]
Ka·la·ha·ri Desert (kä′lə-här′ē). An arid plateau in southern Africa extending over western Botswana and eastern South-West Africa.
Ka·lakh (kä′läKH′). Biblical name **Ca·lah** (kā′lə). The ancient capital of Assyria, antedating Nineveh.
Kal·a·ma·zoo (kăl′ə-mə-zo͞o′). A city of Michigan, a manufacturing center in the southwest. Population, 82,000.
Ka·lat (kə-lät′). Also **Khe·lat.** A former princely state of Baluchistan, in West Pakistan since 1948.
kale (kāl) *n.* Also **kail. 1.** A variety of cabbage, *Brassica oleracea acephala,* having ruffled or crinkled leaves that do not form a tight head. Also called "borecole." **2.** *Slang.* Money. [Middle English (northern dialect) *cal(e),* variant of *col,* COLE.]
ka·lei·do·scope (kə-lī′də-skōp′) *n.* **1.** A small tube in which patterns of colors are optically produced and viewed for amusement, especially one in which mirrors reflect light transmitted through bits of loose colored glass contained at one end, causing them to appear as symmetrical designs when viewed at the other. **2.** A constantly changing set of colors. **3.** A series of changing phases or events. [Greek *kalos,* beautiful (see **kal-**^{2} in Appendix*) + *eidos,* form (see **weid-** in Appendix*) + -SCOPE.] —**ka·lei′do·scop′ic** (-skŏp′ĭk), **ka·lei′do·scop′i·cal** *adj.* —**ka·lei′do·scop′i·cal·ly** *adv.*

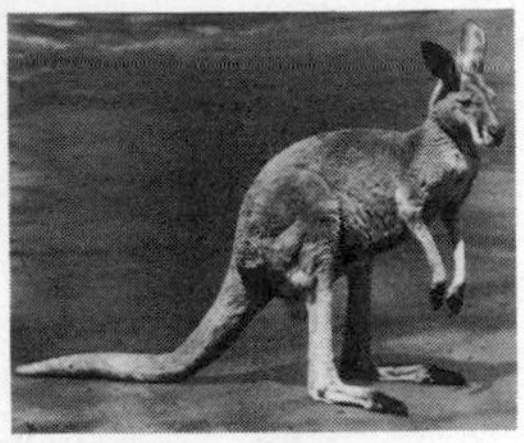

kangaroo
Macropus rufus

kal·ends. Variant of **calends.**
Kal·gan (käl′gän′). A city of China in northwestern Hopei Province, 95 miles northwest of Peking. Population, 480,000.
Kal·goor·lie (kăl-go͝or′lē). A city in southern Western Australia, in the gold-mining region. Population, 10,000.
Ka·li·man·tan (kä′lē-män′tän′). Formerly **Dutch Bor·ne·o** (bôr′nē-ō′, bōr′-) The Indonesian sector of Borneo.
Ka·li·nin (kə-lē′nĭn). Formerly **Tver** (tə-vĕr′). A city of the Soviet Union, northwest of Moscow. Population, 306,000.
Ka·li·nin·grad (kə-lē′nĭn-grăd). Formerly **Kö·nigs·berg** (kā′-nĭgz-bûrg′; *German* kœ′nĭks-bĕrk′). A city of the Soviet Union, a seaport in the extreme west on the Baltic Sea; formerly the capital of East Prussia. Population, 253,000.
Kal·li·kaks (kăl′ĭ-kăks′) *n.* Used with a singular or plural verb. A family, group, or rarely, a person regarded as inferior to the surrounding society. Often used in the phrase: *the Jukes and the Kallikaks.* [From *Kallikak,* a fictitious name given to a New Jersey family whose sociological history revealed two lines of descendants, one of respectable citizens, the other of mental deficients and social misfits.]
Kal·mar (kăl′mär). A city of Sweden, a port on Kalmar Sound, an arm of the Baltic Sea between the mainland and Öland. Population, 32,000.
Kal·muck (kăl′mŭk′, kăl-mŭk′) *n., pl.* **Kalmuck** or **-mucks.** Also **Kal·muk, Kal·myk** (-mĭk, -mĭk′). **1.** A member of one of the Buddhist Mongol peoples originally inhabiting northwestern China, and later migrating westward to the lower Volga. **2.** The Mongolian language spoken by the Kalmucks. [Turkish *kalmuk,* probably "that part (of the tribe) remaining (at home)," from the past participle of *kalmak,* to remain.]

kangaroo rat
Dipodomys deserti

Kal·muck Autonomous Soviet Socialist Republic (kăl′mŭk′, kăl-mŭk′). Also **Kal·muk A.S.S.R., Kal·myk A.S.S.R.** (-mĭk, -mĭk′). An administrative division, 29,300 square miles in area, of the southwestern Russian S.F.S.R.; partitioned among adjacent divisions in 1943, it was reconstituted in 1958. Population, 239,000. Capital, Elista.
kal·pak. Variant of **calpac.**
kal·so·mine. Variant of **calcimine.**
Ka·ma (kä′mə). A river of the Soviet Union, rising in the northern Udmurt A.S.S.R. and flowing 1,262 miles in a winding course to the Volga below Kazan.
Ka·ma·ku·ra (kä′mə-ko͝or′ə). A city and religious center of southeastern Honshu, Japan. Population, 110,000.
ka·ma·la (kăm′ə-lə, kə-mä′lə) *n.* **1.** An Asian tree, *Mallotus philippinensis,* having hairy, capsular fruit. **2.** A purgative powder obtained from the capsules of this tree. [Sanskrit *kamala,* probably from Dravidian, akin to Kanarese *kōmaḷe.*]
Ka·ma·su·tra (kä′mə-so͞o′trə). A treatise written in Sanskrit (4th–7th centuries A.D.), setting forth rules for love and marriage in accordance with Hindu law. [Sanskrit, "book on love" : *kāma,* love, desire (see **kā-** in Appendix*) + *sūtra,* warp, "warp of life" (see **syū-** in Appendix*).]

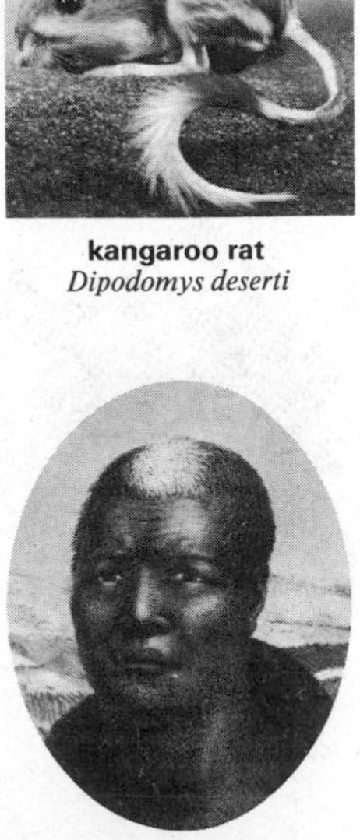

Kamehameha I

Kam·chat·ka Peninsula (kăm-chăt′kə; *Russian* kəm-chät′kə). A peninsula of northeastern Siberia, 104,200 square miles in area, between the Sea of Okhotsk and the Bering Sea.
kame (kām) *n.* A small conical hill or short ridge of sand and gravel deposited during the melting of glacial ice. [Scottish, from Middle English *camb,* northern variant of *comb,* COMB.]
Ka·me·ha·me·ha I (kä-mā′hä-mā′hä). 1737?–1819. King of Sandwich Islands (1795–1819).
Ka·met (kŭm′āt′). A mountain 25,447 feet high, in northern Uttar Pradesh, Republic of India, near the Tibetan border.
ka·mi·ka·ze (kä′mĭ-kä′zē) *n.* **1.** During World War II, a Japanese pilot trained to make a suicidal crash attack. **2.** An airplane loaded with explosives to be piloted in such an attack. [Japanese, "divine wind" : *kami,* God + *kaze,* wind.]
Kam·pa·la (käm-pä′lə). The capital of Uganda, in the east on Lake Victoria. Population, 45,000.
kam·seen, kam·sin. Variants of **khamsin.**
Kan (kän). A river of China, flowing 540 miles northward through Kiangsi to the Yangtze.
ka·na (kä′nə) *n.* Either of two Japanese syllabaries, **hiragana** or **katakana** *(both of which see).* Compare **kanji.** [Japanese, "pseudocharacters" (as distinguished from *kanji,* which are regarded as being composed of real characters) : *ka,* false, from Chinese (Mandarin) *chia*^{3} + *na,* name, character.]
Ka·nak·a (kə-năk′ə, -nä′kə, kăn′ə-kə) *n.* A native of the South Sea Islands. [Hawaiian, "person."]
Ka·na·ra (kä′nər-ə). A region of the Republic of India, occupying 60,000 square miles in the southern Deccan Plateau.
Ka·na·rese (kăn′ə-rēz′, -rēs′) *adj.* Of or relating to Kanara, its people, or its language. —*n., pl.* **Kanarese. 1.** One of the Dravidian peoples of Kanara. **2.** The Dravidian language of the Kanarese.
Ka·na·za·wa (kä′nə-zä′wə, kə-nä′zə-wə). A port city of west-central Honshu, Japan. Population, 386,000.
Kan·chen·jun·ga (kŭn′chən-jŭng′gə). The third-highest mountain in the world (28,146 feet), in the Himalayas of Nepal, near the Sikkim border.
Kan·da·har (kän′də-här′). Also **Qan·da·har.** A city of Afghanistan, in the southeast near the border of West Pakistan. Population, 115,000.
Kan·din·ski (kăn-dĭn′skē), **Vasili.** 1866–1944. Russian painter.
Kan·dy (kăn′dē). A city of Ceylon, formerly the capital, situated in the center of the country. Population, 68,000.
kane. Variant of **kain.**
kan·ga·roo (kăng′gə-ro͞o′) *n., pl.* **-roos.** Any of various herbivorous marsupials of the family Macropodidae, of Australia and adjacent areas, characteristically having short forelimbs, large hind limbs adapted for leaping, and a long, tapered tail. [Probably from a native name in Queensland, Australia.]
kangaroo court. 1. A mock court set up in violation of established legal procedure. **2.** A court characterized by dishonesty or incompetence. [By allusion to its irregular procedures suggesting the leaps of a kangaroo.]
Kangaroo Island. An island, 1,680 square miles in area, of South Australia, in the Indian Ocean south of Adelaide.
kangaroo rat. Any of various long-tailed rodents of the genera *Dipodomys* and *Microdipodops,* of arid areas of western North America, having long hind legs adapted for jumping.
kangaroo vine. A climbing or trailing vine, *Cissus antarctica,* native to Australia, and often grown as a house plant for its glossy green foliage.
kan·ji (kän′jē) *n., pl.* **kanji** or **-jis. 1.** A Japanese system of writing based upon borrowed or modified Chinese characters. **2.** A character used in the kanji system of writing. Compare **kana.** [Japanese, from Chinese (Mandarin) *han*^{4}*tzû*^{4} : *han*^{4}, Chinese (originally a dynastic name) + *tzû*^{4}, word.]
Kan·ka·kee (kăng′kə-kē′). A river rising in northwestern Indiana and flowing 225 miles generally southwest through Illinois to the Des Plaines with which it forms the Illinois River.
Kan-ko. The Japanese name for the **Han.**
Kan·na·da (kä′nə-də) *n.* A Dravidian language spoken in the state of Mysore, Republic of India. —**Kan′na·da** *adj.*
Ka·no (kä′nō). A city of Nigeria, the leading commercial center of the Northern Region. Population, 295,000.
Kan·pur (kän′po͝or). Formerly **Cawn·pore** (kôn′pōr). A city of the Republic of India, on the Ganges in south-central Uttar Pradesh. Population, 895,000.
Kan·sas (kăn′zəs). **1.** *Abbr.* **Kans.** A Central state of the United States, 82,276 square miles in area, bounded on the northeast by the Missouri River; admitted to the Union in 1861. Population, 2,179,000. Capital, Topeka. See map at **United States of America. 2.** A river of northeastern Kansas, flowing 169 miles from Junction City eastward to the Missouri.
Kan·sas City (kăn′zəs). **1.** A city of Kansas, in the northeast on the Missouri River. Population, 122,000. **2.** A city of Missouri, in the northwest across the Missouri River from Kansas City, Kansas. Population, 476,000.
Kan·su (kăn′so͞o′; *Chinese* gän′so͞o′). A province, 150,000 square miles in area, of north-central China. Population, 12,800,000. Capital, Lanchow.
Kant (kănt, känt), **Immanuel.** 1724–1804. German philosopher.
kan·tar (kän-tär′) *n.* Any of various units of weight in some Mediterranean countries, corresponding approximately to the hundredweight. [Arabic *qinṭār,* from Aramaic *qinṭ(īn)ārā,* from Late Greek *kentēnarion,* from Late Latin *centēnārium (pondus),* "hundredweight," hundred pounds, from Latin *centēnārius,* of a hundred, from *centēnī,* a hundred each, from *centum,* hundred. See **dekm̥** in Appendix.*]
Kant·i·an (kăn′tē-ən, kän′-) *adj.* Of or characteristic of Kant's philosophy. —**Kant′i·an·ism′** *n.*
Kao·hsiung (gou′shyo͞ong′). A city of Taiwan, a seaport on the southwestern coast. Population, 371,000.
Kao·lan. The former name for **Lanchow.**
ka·o·lin (kā′ə-lĭn) *n.* Also **ka·o·line.** A fine white to yellowish or grayish clay, mostly kaolinite, used in ceramics and refractories, and as a filler or coating for paper and textiles. Also called "terra alba." [French, from Mandarin Chinese *kao*^{1} *ling*^{3},

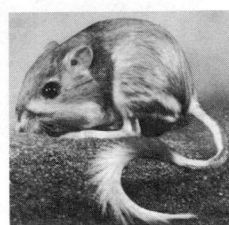

name of a hill in Kiangsi Province where it was first obtained, "high mountain" : *kao[1]*, high + *ling[3]*, mountain, peak.]

ka·o·lin·ite (kā′ə-lĭ-nīt′) *n.* A mineral, essentially $Al_2O_3 \cdot 2SiO_2 \cdot 2H_2O$, the principal constituent of kaolin.

ka·on (kā′ŏn′) *n. Symbol* **K** *Physics.* Either of two mesons. See **particle.** [*ka,* the letter *k* + (MES)ON.]

Ka·pell·meis·ter (kä-pĕl′mīs′tər) *n., pl.* **Kapellmeister.** The leader of a choir or orchestra. [German, "choir master."]

kaph (käf) *n.* Also **caph.** The 11th letter in the Hebrew alphabet. Transliterated in English as *K, k.* See **alphabet.** [Hebrew *kāph,* "palm of the hand" (from the ancient form of this letter).]

Ka·pi·tza (kə-pyĭt′sə), **Peter Leonidovich.** Born 1894. Soviet physicist.

ka·pok (kā′pŏk′) *n.* A silky fiber obtained from the fruit of the silk-cotton tree, and used for insulation and as padding in pillows, mattresses, and life preservers. [Malay.]

kap·pa (kăp′ə) *n.* The tenth letter in the Greek alphabet, written Κ, κ. Transliterated in English as *K, k.* See **alphabet.** [Greek, from Semitic, akin to Hebrew *kāph,* KAPH.]

Kap·teyn (käp-tīn′), **Jacobus Cornelis.** 1851–1922. Dutch astronomer.

Ka·pu·as (kä′po͞o-äs′). A river of Borneo, rising in north-central Kalimantan and flowing 710 miles generally west to the South China Sea.

ka·put (kä-po͝ot′) *adj.* Also **ka·putt.** *Informal.* **1.** Destroyed; wrecked. **2.** Incapacitated. [German *kaputt,* from French *capot,* as in the expression *être capot,* to have lost all tricks at cards, "be hoodwinked," from *capot,* cloak with hood, from *cape,* CAPE (garment).]

kar·a·bi·ner (kăr′ə-bē′nər) *n.* An oblong steel ring that is snapped to the eye of a piton and through which a rope is run, used in mountaineering. [German *Karabiner(haken),* "carbine hook" (originally used to fasten carbines to belt) : *Karabiner,* carbine, from French *carabine,* CARBINE + *Haken,* hook.]

Ka·ra·chay-Cher·kess Autonomous Region (kăr′ə-chī′chĕr-kĕsh′). Also **Ka·ra·cha·ev-Cher·kess Autonomous Region** (kăr′-ə-chī′əf-). An administrative division, 5,442 square miles in area, of the southwestern Russian S.F.S.R. Population, 320,000. Capital, Cherkessk.

Ka·ra·chi (kə-rä′chē). A city of southern West Pakistan, a sea-port on the Arabian Sea and formerly the capital of Pakistan (1948–59). Population, 1,913,000.

Ka·ra·de·niz Bo·ğa·zı. The Turkish name for the **Bosporus.**

Kar·a·fu·to. See **Sakhalin.**

Ka·ra·gan·da (kăr′ə-gən-dä′). A city of the Soviet Union, an industrial center in the coal-mining area of the central Kazakh S.S.R. Population, 482,000.

Ka·ra·kal·pak (kăr′ə-kăl-păk′) *n., pl.* **Karakalpak** or **-paks. 1.** A member of a Turkic people inhabiting the Kara-Kalpak region of the Uzbek S.S.R. **2.** The Turkic language spoken by the Karakalpaks.

Ka·ra-Kal·pak Autonomous Soviet Socialist Republic (kăr′-ə-kăl-păk′). An administrative division, 63,920 square miles in area, of the northwestern Uzbek S.S.R. Population, 606,000. Capital, Nukus.

Kar·a·kor·am (kăr′ə-kōr′əm). A mountain range of northern Jammu and Kashmir, along the border with China. Highest elevation, Godwin Austen (28,250 feet).

kar·a·kul (kăr′ə-kəl) *n.* Also **car·a·cul. 1.** One of a breed of sheep of central Asia, having wool that is curled and glossy in the young and wiry and coarse in the adult. Also called "broad-tail." **2.** Fur made from the pelt of a karakul lamb. Compare **broadtail, Persian lamb.** [Originally bred near *Kara Kul,* "black lake," lake in Tadzhik S.S.R.]

Ka·ra Kum (kăr′ə ko͞om′). A desert of the southwestern Soviet Union, in the Turkmen S.S.R. between the Caspian Sea and the Amu Darya River.

Ka·ra Sea (kăr′ə). An arm of the Arctic Ocean off the north-western coast of the Soviet Union, between the Barents and Laptev seas.

kar·at (kăr′ət) *n.* Also **car·at.** *Abbr.* **k, kt.** A measure comprising 24 units used to specify the proportion of pure gold in an alloy; for example, 12 karat gold is 50 per cent pure gold. [Old French *carat,* unit of weight for precious stone, CARAT.]

ka·ra·te (kə-rä′tē, kä-rä′tā) *n.* A Japanese system of unarmed self-defense that stresses efficiently struck blows. [Japanese, "empty-handed" : *kara,* empty + *te,* hand.]

Ka·re·li·an Autonomous Soviet Socialist Republic (kə-rē′lē-ən, -rēl′yən). An administrative division, 66,560 square miles in area, of the northwestern Russian S.F.S.R. Population, 697,000. Capital, Petrozavodsk. Also called "Karelia."

Ka·re·li·an Isthmus (kə-rē′lē-ən, -rēl′yən). A land bridge in the northwestern Soviet Union, between Lake Ladoga and the Gulf of Finland.

Ka·re·lo-Fin·nish Soviet Socialist Republic (kə-rē′lō-fĭn′ĭsh). A former constituent republic of the Soviet Union, demoted in 1956 to the status of autonomous republic. See **Karelian A.S.S.R.**

Karl (kärl). A masculine given name. [German form for CHARLES.]

Karl-Marx-Stadt (kärl-märk′shtät′). Formerly **Chem·nitz** (kĕm′nĭts). A city of East Germany, an industrial center in the southeast. Population, 286,000.

Kar·lo·vy Va·ry (kär′lō-vē vä′rē). *German* **Carls·bad** (kärls′bät′), **Karls·bad.** A city and health resort of Czechoslovakia, in Bohemia in the northwest. Population, 43,000.

Karls·ru·he (kärls′ro͞o′ə). Also **Carls·ru·he.** A city of West Germany, a port on the Rhine in west-central Baden-Württemburg. Population, 252,000.

kar·ma (kär′mə, kûr′mə) *n.* **1.** *Hinduism & Buddhism.* The sum and the consequences of a person's actions during the successive phases of his existence, regarded as determining his destiny. **2.** Fate; destiny. [Sanskrit *karman* (nominative *karma*), act, deed, work, from *karoti,* he makes, he does. See **kwer-[1]** in Appendix.*] —**kar′mic** (-mĭk) *adj.*

Kár·mán (kär′män), **Theodor von.** 1881–1963. Hungarian-born American physicist and aeronautical engineer.

karn. Variant of **cairn.**

Kar·nak (kär′năk). A village on the Nile in east-central Egypt, on part of the site once occupied by Thebes.

Kar·na·phu·li (kär′nə-po͞o′lē). A river rising in Assam, Republic of India, and flowing 146 miles south and southwest through East Pakistan to the Bay of Bengal.

Kar·ni·sche Al·pen. The German name for the **Carnic Alps.**

Kärn·ten. The German name for **Carinthia.**

Kar·rer (kär′ər), **Paul.** Born 1889. Swiss chemist.

kar·roo (kə-ro͞o′, kă-) *n., pl.* **-roos.** Also **ka·roo.** An arid plateau of southern Africa. [Afrikaans *karo,* perhaps from Hottentot *garo,* desert.]

Kar·roo (kə-ro͞o′, kă-). A vast (100,000 square miles) tableland of South Africa, in Cape of Good Hope Province, divided into the Great or Central Karroo, the Upper or Northern Karroo along the Orange River, and the Southern Karroo along the coast.

Ka·run (kə-ro͞on′). A river rising in southwestern Iran and flowing about 500 miles southwest to the Shatt-al-Arab.

karyo–, caryo–. Indicates the nucleus of a living cell; for example, **karyogamy, caryopsis.** [New Latin, from Greek *karuon,* kernel, nut. See **kar-[1]** in Appendix.*]

kar·y·og·a·my (kăr′ē-ŏg′ə-mē) *n.* The coming together and fusing of gamete nuclei. [KARYO- + -GAMY.]

kar·y·o·lymph (kăr′ē-ə-lĭmf′) *n.* The clear homogeneous liquid portion of nuclear protoplasm. [KARYO- + LYMPH.]

kar·y·o·plasm (kăr′ē-ə-plăz′əm) *n.* Nuclear protoplasm, **nucleoplasm** *(see).* [KARYO- + -PLASM.] —**kar′y·o·plas′mic** *adj.*

kar·y·o·some (kăr′ē-ə-sōm′) *n.* A spherical aggregation of chromatin in a resting nucleus during mitosis. Also called "net knot." [KARYO- + -SOME (body).]

kar·y·o·type (kăr′ē-ə-tīp′) *n.* **1.** The chromosomal complement of an individual or of a species. **2.** A photomicrograph of metaphase chromosomes in a standard array. [KARYO- + TYPE.] —**kar′y·o·typ′ic** (-tĭp′ĭk), **kar′y·o·typ′ic·al** *adj.*

Ka·sai (kä-sī′). A river of Africa, rising in central Angola and flowing 1,200 miles east, north, and finally northwest to the Congo River in the Democratic Republic of the Congo.

Kas·bah. See **Casbah.**

ka·sha (kä′shə) *n.* Buckwheat groats. [Russian *kasha,* from Slavic *kasyā* (unattested).]

ka·sher. Variant of **kosher.**

kash·mir. Variant of **cashmere** (wool).

Kash·mir. Also **Cash·mere.** See **Jammu and Kashmir.**

Kashmir goat. Variant of **Cashmere goat.**

Kash·mi·ri (kăsh-mîr′ē) *n.* An Indic language spoken in Jammu and Kashmir.

Kas·kas·ki·a River (kăs-kăs′kē-ə). A river rising in east-central Illinois and flowing 520 miles southwest to the Mississippi.

Kas·sel (kä′sĕl). Also **Cas·sel.** An industrial center of West Germany, in northern Hesse. Population, 231,000.

Kast·ler (kăst′lər), **Alfred.** Born 1902. French physicist.

ka·ta·ka·na (kä′tä-kä′nä) *n.* A phonetic Japanese syllabary used for writing foreign words or documents, such as telegrams. Also called "kana." See **hiragana.** [Japanese : *kata,* one, one-sided + KANA.]

Ka·tan·ga (kə-tăng′gə). A former province of the Democratic Republic of the Congo, with its capital at Elisabethville (now Lubumbashi), divided in 1963 into the three provinces of North Katanga, Lualaba, and East Katanga. —**Kat′an·gese′** (kăt′-ăng-gēs′, -gēz′) *adj. & n.*

Ka·tha·re·vu·sa (kä′thə-rĕv′ə-sä′). Also **Ka·tha·re·vou·sa.** The official form of Modern Greek, exhibiting many morphological and lexical characteristics restored from Classical Greek. [Modern Greek *kathareuousa,* from Greek, feminine present participle of *kathareuein,* to be pure, from *katharos,* pure. See **catharsis.**]

Kath·e·rine. Variant of **Catherine.**

Ka·thi·a·war (kä′tē-ä-wär′). A peninsula of northwestern India, part of Gujarat State projecting into the Arabian Sea.

Kath·leen. Variant of **Cathleen.**

Kat·mai National Monument (kăt′mī). An area of 4,214 square miles on the northern end of the Alaska Peninsula, containing the Valley of Ten Thousand Smokes and the active Katmai Volcano (7,000 feet).

Kat·man·du (kät′män-do͞o′). The capital of Nepal, in a valley of the Himalayas about 100 miles southwest of Mount Everest. Population, 123,000.

Ka·to·wi·ce (kä′tō-vēt′sĕ). A city of southern Poland, 40 miles northwest of Kraków. Population, 285,000.

Kat·te·gat (kăt′ə-găt′). Also **Cat·te·gat.** A strait of the North Sea extending for 137 miles between eastern Jutland, Denmark, and southwestern Sweden.

Ka·tun (kə-to͞on′). A river rising in the Altai Mountains of the south-central Soviet Union, and flowing 386 miles generally northwest to the Ob.

ka·ty·did (kā′tē-dĭd′) *n.* Any of various green insects of the genus *Microcentrum* and related genera, related to the grass-hoppers and the crickets, and having specialized organs in the wings of the male that when rubbed together produce a distinctive sound. [Imitative.]

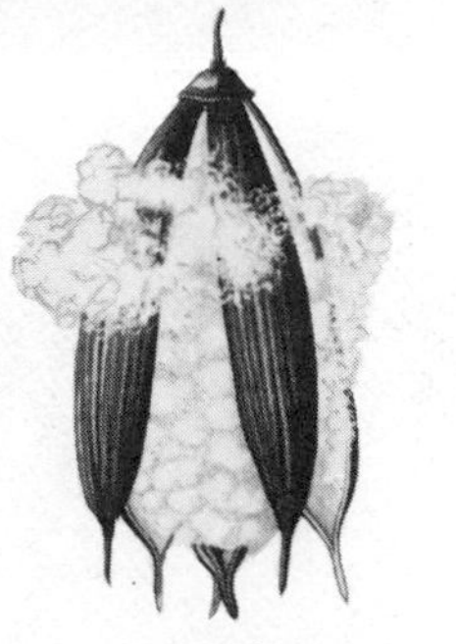

kapok
Open seed pod of silk-cotton tree, showing kapok

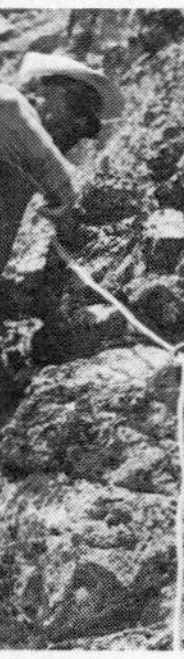

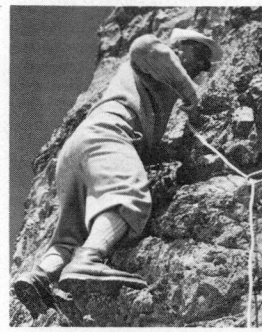

karabiner
Climber using karabiner, piton, and rope

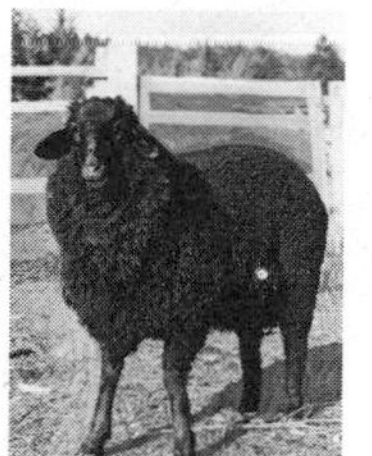

karakul

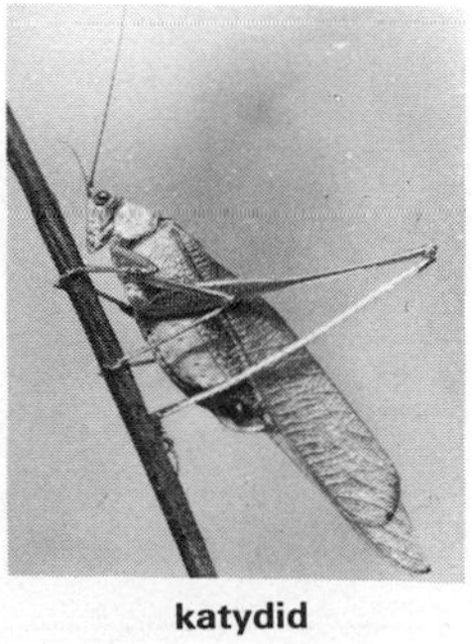

katydid

t tight/th thin, path/*th* this, bathe/ŭ cut/ûr urge/v valve/w with/y yes/z zebra, size/zh vision/ə about, item, edible, gallop, circus/ à *Fr.* ami/œ *Fr.* feu, *Ger.* schön/ü *Fr.* tu, *Ger.* über/KH *Ger.* ich, *Scot.* loch/N *Fr.* bon. ***Follows main vocabulary. †Of obscure origin.**

katz·en·jam·mer (kăt′sən-jăm′ər; *German* kät′sĕn-yäm′ĕr) *n.* **1.** A loud discordant noise. **2.** A hangover. **3.** A state of depression or bewilderment. [German *Katzenjammer* : *Katzen*, plural of *Katze*, cat, from Old High German *kazza*, from Common Germanic *kattuz* (unattested), CAT + *Jammer*, lamentation, misery, from Old High German *jāmar*, from *jāmar*, sad, akin to Old English *geōmor* (probably imitative).]

Kau·ai (kou′ī). The fourth largest (551 square miles) of the islands of Hawaii, northwest of Oahu.

Kau·nas (kou′näs). A city of Lithuania, on the Neman in the south-central part of the republic. Population, 269,000.

kau·ri (kou′rē) *n.* **1.** Any of several coniferous trees of the genus *Agathis;* especially, *A. australis*, of New Zealand, having close-grained, durable wood. **2.** The wood of such a tree. **3.** A resin obtained from the kauri or from deposits of fossilized exudations of such trees, used in varnishes and enamels. In this sense, also called "kauri gum." [Maori *kawri.*]

ka·va (kä′və) *n.* **1.** A shrub, *Piper methysticum*, of tropical Pacific islands, the dried roots of which are used to make an intoxicating beverage. **2.** The beverage made from this plant. Also called "kava-kava." [Tongan *kava*, "bitter."]

Ka·ve·ri. See **Cauvery.**

Ka·vir Desert. See **Dasht-i-Kavir.**

Ka·wa·sa·ki (kä′wə-sä′kē). A city of Japan, on the west shore of Tokyo Bay in central Honshu. Population, 768,000.

kay (kā) *n.* The letter *k.*

Kay (kā), **Sir.** *Arthurian Legend.* The foster brother and steward of King Arthur.

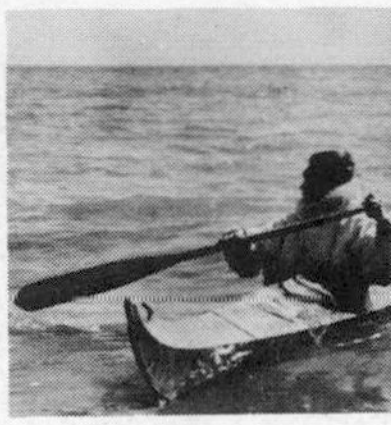

kayak
Eskimo kayak

kay·ak (kī′ăk′) *n.* Also **kai·ak. 1.** A watertight Eskimo canoe made of skins stretched over a light wooden frame and having a deck covering that closes around the waist of the paddler. Compare **umiak. 2.** A lightweight and highly maneuverable, usually canvas-covered canoe popular for sports. [Eskimo *qajaq.*]

kay·o (kā′ō, kā′ō′) *n., pl.* **-os.** Also **KO** *pl.* **KO's; K.O., k.o.** *Slang.* In boxing, a **knockout** *(see). —tr. v.* **kayoed, -oing, -os.** *Slang.* To knock out; put out of commission. [Pronunciation of the initial letters in *knock out.*]

Kay·se·ri (kī′sə-rē′). Ancient name **Cae·sa·rea Maz·a·ca** (sē′zə-rē′ə măz′ə-kə). An ancient city of central Turkey in Asia.

Ka·zakh (kə-zäk′) *n., pl.* **Kazakh** or **-zakhs.** A member of a Kirghiz people dwelling chiefly in Kazakh S.S.R. [Turki, "free person, adventurer."]

Ka·zakh Soviet Socialist Republic (kə-zäk′). Also **Ka·zakh·stan** (kə-zäk′stän′). The second largest (1,064,000 square miles) of the constituent republics of the Soviet Union, northeast of the Caspian Sea. Population, 10,934,000. Capital, Alma Ata.

Ka·zan (kə-zän′). The capital of the Tatar A.S.S.R., on the Volga 450 miles east of Moscow. Population, 762,000.

Kaz·bek, Mount (kəz-bĕk′). A volcanic mountain, 16,541 feet high, in the Georgian S.S.R., in the western Soviet Union.

Kaz·da·gi. The Turkish name for the **Ida Mountains.**

ka·zoo (kə-zōō′) *n., pl.* **-zoos.** A toy musical instrument in which a paper membrane is vibrated by the performer's voice. [Probably imitative of its sound.]

KB *Chess.* king's bishop.

KBL Airport code for Kabul, Afghanistan.

KBP *Chess.* king's bishop's pawn.

kc kilocycle.

K.C. 1. King's Counsel. **2.** Knights of Columbus.

kcal kilocalorie.

K.D. *Commerce.* knocked down.

ke·a (kē′ə, kā′ə) *n.* A brownish-green parrot, *Nestor notabilis*, of mountainous areas of New Zealand, reputed to kill sheep by pecking at their fat and flesh. [Maori, imitative of its cry.]

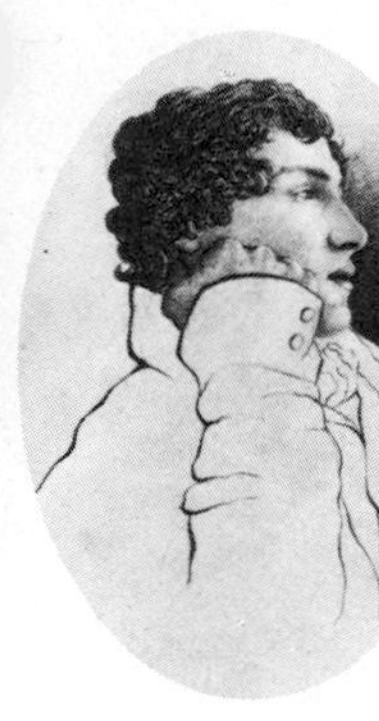

John Keats

Keats (kēts), **John.** 1795–1821. English poet.

ke·bab (kə-bŏb′) *n.* Also **ke·bob. Shish kebab** *(see).*

Kech·ua. Variant of **Quechua.**

keck (kĕk) *intr.v.* **kecked, kecking, kecks.** To retch. **—keck at.** To refuse or shrink from with an expression of disgust: *"If they can sit with us at table, why do they keck at our cookery?"* (Lamb). [Imitative.]

keck·le (kĕk′əl) *tr.v.* **-led, -ling, -les.** *Nautical.* To wrap (a cable) with rope against chafing. [Origin unknown.]

Ke·dah (kā′dä). A state of Malaysia, occupying 3,660 square miles on the west-central coast of the Malay Peninsula. Population, 850,000. Capital, Alor Star.

kedge (kĕj) *n.* A light anchor used for warping a vessel. *—v.* **kedged, kedging, kedges.** *—tr.* To warp (a vessel) by means of a kedge. *—intr.* To move by means of a kedge. Used of a ship. [From *kedge*, earlier *cadge*, to warp a ship, perhaps from Middle English *caggen*†, to tie, bind.]

ked·ger·ee (kĕj′ə-rē′) *n.* **1.** An Indian dish of rice, lentils, onions, eggs, and condiments. **2.** An English dish of leftover flaked fish, boiled rice, and eggs, served hot. [Hindi *khichṛī*, from Sanskrit *khiccā*†.]

ke·ef. Variant of **kif.**

keel[1]

keel[1] (kēl) *n.* **1.** The principal structural member of a ship, running fore and aft on the center line, extending from bow to stern, and forming the backbone of the vessel to which the frames are attached. **2.** *Poetic.* A ship. **3.** A structure that resembles a ship's keel in function or shape, such as the fin extending lengthwise at the bottom of an airship. **4.** *Biology.* A structure having a longitudinal ridge suggestive of a ship's keel, as: **a.** The anterior part of the breastbone of a flying bird. **b.** A pair of united petals in certain flowers, as those of the pea. **—on an even keel.** Balanced; steady. *—v.* **keeled, keeling, keels.** *—tr.* To capsize (a vessel). *—intr.* To roll on her keel. Used of a ship. **—keel over. 1.** To capsize. **2.** To drop as in a faint from fatigue or shock. [Middle English *ke(o)le*, from Old Norse *kjölr.* See **ku-** in Appendix.*]

keel[2] (kēl) *n.* **1. a.** A freight barge; especially, one for carrying coal on the Tyne in England. **b.** The load capacity of this barge. **2.** A British unit of weight formerly used for coal, equal to 21.2 long tons. [Middle English *kele*, from Middle Dutch *kiel*, ship. See **ku-** in Appendix.*]

keel[3] (kēl) *v.* **keeled, keeling, keels.** *—tr. Archaic & Regional.* To cool (a hot liquid), as by stirring in order to prevent boiling over. Used chiefly in the phrase *keel the pot. —intr. Obsolete.* To become cool. [Middle English *kelen*, Old English *cēlan.* See **gel-**[3] in Appendix.*]

keel·boat (kēl′bōt′) *n.* A large covered flat-bottomed boat with a keel but without sails, used for river freight.

keel·haul (kēl′hôl′) *tr.v.* **-hauled, -hauling, -hauls. 1.** To punish by dragging under the keel of a ship from one side to the other or from stem to stern. **2.** To castigate. [Dutch *kielhalen* : Middle Dutch *kiel*, keel of a ship (see **ku-** in Appendix*) + *halen*, to pull, haul (see **kel-**[3] in Appendix*).]

Kee·ling Islands. See **Cocos Islands.**

keel·son (kēl′sən, kĕl′-) *n.* Also **kel·son** (kĕl′-). *Nautical.* A timber or girder placed parallel with and bolted to the keel for additional strength. [Probably from Low German *kielswīn* : Middle Low German *kiel*, keel of a ship (see **ku-** in Appendix*) + *swīn*, swine, "timber" (see **su-**[1] in Appendix*).]

Kee·lung (kē′lōōng′). Also **Chi·lung** (jē′-). A city of Taiwan, a seaport in the extreme north. Population, 197,000.

keen[1] (kēn) *adj.* **keener, keenest. 1.** Having a fine, sharp cutting edge or point. **2.** Intellectually acute; penetrating; trenchant. **3.** Acutely sensitive. Said of the senses. **4.** Sharp; vivid; strong: *"His entire body hungered for keen sensation, something exciting"* (Richard Wright). **5.** Intense; piercing: *a keen wind.* **6.** Pungent; acrid. **7. a.** Ardent; enthusiastic. **b.** Eagerly desirous of: *keen on going.* **8.** *Slang.* Great; splendid; fine. —See Synonyms at **eager, sharp.** [Middle English *kene*, Old English *cēne*, wise, bold, powerful, from Common Germanic *kōnjaz* (unattested).] **—keen′ly** *adv.* **—keen′ness** *n.*

keen[2] (kēn) *n.* A loud wailing lamentation for the dead. *—intr.v.* **keened, keening, keens.** To wail over the dead. See Synonyms at **cry.** [Irish Gaelic *caoine*, lamentation, from *caoinim*, I wail, I lament, from Old Irish *coīnim*, from Common Celtic *koinyo-* (unattested), to wail.] **—keen′er** *n.*

keep (kēp) *v.* **kept** (kĕpt), **keeping, keeps.** *—tr.* **1.** To retain possession of. **2.** To store; put customarily: *Where do you keep your saw?* **3.** To take in one's charge temporarily: *Keep this for me until I return.* **4.** To provide with the necessities of life; support: *"There's little to earn and many to keep."* (Charles Kingsley). **5. a.** To supply with room and board for a charge: *keep boarders.* **b.** To raise and feed: *keep chickens.* **6.** To have the resources to retain for pleasure or use: *"It is not too much for me now, in degree or cost, to keep a coach."* (Pepys). **7.** To have in ready supply. **8.** To manage; tend: *keep shop.* **9.** To maintain by making current entries in: *keep records.* **10.** To cause to continue in some condition or position: *keep a man in office.* **11.** To preserve and protect; save. **12.** To detain. **13.** To confine: *keep in quarantine.* **14.** To prevent or deter. Used with *from: keep ice from melting.* **15.** To maintain: *keep late hours.* **16.** To adhere to; fulfill: *keep a schedule; keep one's word.* **17.** To refrain from divulging: *keep a secret; keep counsel.* **18.** To celebrate; observe: *—intr.* **1.** To remain in a given position, place, or condition; stay: *keep in line; keep quiet.* **2.** To persevere in some action; continue: *keep guessing.* **3.** To remain fresh or unspoiled: *The dessert won't keep.* —See Synonyms at **observe. —keep at it.** To persevere in an action or work. **—keep back. 1.** To refuse to tell or give; withhold. **2.** To hold back; restrain. **—keep from.** To desist from or prevent. Used with the present participle: *I can't keep from worrying.* **—keep in. 1.** To detain, especially after school. **2.** To cause to stay indoors. **—keep off.** To refrain from approaching, discussing, or the like. **—keep on. 1.** To continue in an action. Used with the present participle: *keep on smiling.* **2.** To continue to employ: *keep on five men.* **—keep out.** To prevent from entering and taking control or possession: *keep out the unions.* **—keep to.** To adhere to: *keep to the original purpose.* **—keep to oneself. 1.** To shun company. **2.** To refrain from sharing or divulging: *He's keeping the news to himself.* **—keep up. 1.** To maintain in good condition. **2.** To persevere in; carry on. **3.** To maintain at the same level or pace. **4.** To cause to stay up late at night. **—keep up with. 1.** To stay in touch with. **2.** To maintain the same pace or status as. **—keep up with the Joneses.** To strive competitively with one's neighbors or associates. **—keep with.** To persevere in: *Keep with your studies. —n.* **1.** Care; charge: *The child is in my keep for the day.* **2. a.** A living; subsistence: *earn one's keep.* **b.** The means by which one is supported. **3. a.** The main tower or donjon of a castle; a stronghold. **b.** A jail. —See Synonyms at **livelihood. —for keeps. 1.** To keep forever: *He gave it to me for keeps.* **2.** Seriously and permanently: *We're separating for keeps.* [Middle English *kepen*, Old English *cēpan*†, to seize, hold, guard.]

Synonyms: *keep, retain, withhold, reserve, grasp, clutch.* These verbs mean to have something in one's possession or control. *Keep* is the most general and imprecise. *Retain* sometimes indicates mere possession but often in the face of loss: *what the mind retains; seeking to retain control. Withhold* implies a deliberate holding back of something in one's possession. *Reserve* refers to a holding back for the future or for a special purpose. In a related sense *reserve* refers to keeping for oneself the right to act in a certain way. *Grasp* and *clutch* apply to securing firm physical possession.

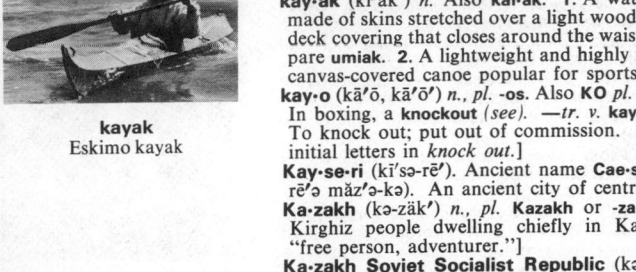

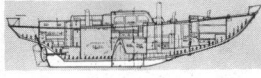

keep·er (kē′pər) *n.* **1.** One who keeps, especially: **a.** An attendant, guard, or warden. **b.** One who has the charge or care of something. **2.** A device for keeping something in place.

keep·ing (kē′pĭng) *n.* **1.** The action of holding, guarding, supporting, or the like. **2.** Custody; care; guardianship. **3.** Harmony; conformity.

keep·sake (kēp′sāk′) *n.* Something given or kept as a reminder of the giver; a memento. [KEEP + SAKE.]

kees·hond (kās′hŏnd′) *n., pl.* **-honden** (-hŏn′dən) or **-honds.** A dog of a breed originating in the Netherlands, having a thick grayish-black coat. [Dutch : probably *Kees,* pet form of name *Cornelis,* from Latin *Cornēlius*†, name of a Roman gens + *hond,* dog, from Middle Dutch (see **kwon-** in Appendix*).]

Kee·wa·tin (kē-wāt′n). A district of 228,160 square miles in the eastern Northwest Territories, Canada. Population, 2,500.

kef. Variant of **kif.**

keg (kĕg) *n.* A small cask or barrel, usually with a capacity of five to ten gallons. [Earlier *cag,* Middle English *kag,* from Old Norse *kaggi*†.]

keg·ler (kĕg′lər) *n. Informal.* A bowler. [German *Kegler,* from *kegeln,* to bowl, from *Kegel,* bowling pin, from Old High German *kegil*†, stick, peg.]

Kei·jo. The Japanese name for **Seoul.**

keir. Variant of **kier.**

keist·er (kē′stər) *n. Slang.* The buttocks or anus. [Perhaps from Yiddish, from German *Kiste,* box, chest, from Old High German *kista,* from Germanic *kistā* (unattested), from Latin *cista,* from Greek *kistē.* See **kista** in Appendix.*]

Ke·ku·lé von Stra·do·nitz (kā′ko͞o-lā′ fən shträ′dō-nĭts′), **Friedrich August.** 1829–1896. German chemist.

Ke·lan·tan (kə-lăn′tăn). A state of Malaysia, occupying 5,746 square miles in east-central Malay Peninsula. Population, 619,000. Capital, Kota Bharu.

Kel·ler (kĕl′ər), **Helen Adams.** 1880–1968. American author and lecturer, deaf and blind from infancy.

Kel·ler·wand (kĕl′ər-vänt). *Italian* **Mon·te Co·glians** (mōn′tā kō-lyäns′). The highest elevation (9,220 feet) of the Carnic Alps, on the border between Italy and Austria.

ke·loid (kē′loid′) *n.* Also **che·loid.** A mass of hyperplastic, fibrous, connective tissue, usually at the site of a scar. [French *kéloïde* : Greek *khēlē,* claw, CHELA + -OID.]

kelp (kĕlp) *n.* **1.** Any of various brown, often very large seaweeds of the order Laminariales. **2.** The ash of such seaweeds, used as a source of potash and iodine. [Middle English *cülpe*†.]

kel·pie (kĕl′pē) *n.* Also **kelp·y** *pl.* **-ies.** A water spirit in Scottish legend, usually having the shape of a horse and causing or rejoicing in drownings. [Probably of Celtic origin, akin to Scottish Gaelic *cailpeach, colpach*†, bullock, heifer.]

kel·son. Variant of **keelson.**

Kelt. Variant of **Celt.**

Kelt·ic. Variant of **Celtic.**

kel·vin (kĕl′vĭn) *n. Symbol* **K** The unit of thermodynamic temperature, equal to $1/_{273.16}$ of the thermodynamic temperature of the triple point of water. [After Lord KELVIN.]

Kel·vin (kĕl′vĭn) *adj. Abbr.* **K** Of or pertaining to an **absolute scale** *(see)* of temperature, the zero point of which is approximately −273.16°C.

Kel·vin (kĕl′vĭn), **First Baron.** Title of William Thomson. 1824–1907. British physicist, mathematician, and inventor.

Ke·mal A·ta·türk (kĕ-mäl′ ä-tä-türk′, kə-mäl′ ăt′ə-tûrk′). Original name, Mustafa Kemal. 1881–1938. Founder of Turkish Republic; president (1923–38).

Ke·me·ro·vo (kĕm′ər-ə-və, -ə-rō′vō). A city of the south-central Soviet Union, north of Novosibirsk. Population, 351,000.

Kem·pis (kĕm′pĭs), **Thomas à.** 1380–1471. German ecclesiastic and writer.

ken (kĕn) *v.* **kenned** or **kent** (kĕnt), **kenning, kens.** —*tr.* **1.** *Chiefly Scottish.* To know (a person or thing). **2.** *Chiefly Scottish.* To recognize. **3.** *Archaic.* To descry. —*intr. Chiefly Scottish.* To have an understanding of something. —*n.* **1.** Perception; understanding. **2. a.** Range of vision. **b.** View; sight: *"he was on the point of letting go the ladder to swim away beyond my ken"* (Conrad). [Middle English *kennen,* Old English *cennan,* to make known (probably influenced in sense by Old Norse cognate *kenna,* to know). See **gnō-** in Appendix.*]

Ken. Kentucky (unofficial).

Ke·nai Peninsula (kē′nī). A peninsula approximately 160 miles long and 130 miles wide in south-central Alaska.

Ken·dal green (kĕnd′l). **1.** A coarse green woolen fabric originally manufactured in Kendal, England. Also called "Kendal." **2.** The color of this fabric. [Originally manufactured at *Kendal,* borough of Westmorland, England.]

Ken·il·worth (kĕn′əl-wûrth). A town in central Warwickshire, England; site of Kenilworth Castle ruins. Population, 14,000.

Kenilworth ivy. A trailing or climbing vine, *Cymbalaria muralis,* having lobed leaves and pale-purple flowers.

Ken·ne·bec (kĕn′ə-bĕk). A river of Maine, flowing 150 miles generally south from Moosehead Lake to the Atlantic Ocean.

Ken·ne·dy, Cape (kĕn′ə-dē). Formerly **Cape Ca·nav·er·al** (kə-năv′ər-əl). A cape on the east-central coast of Florida, the site of the U.S. Air Force Missile Test Center.

Ken·ne·dy (kĕn′ə-dē), **John Fitzgerald.** 1917–1963. Thirty-fifth President of the United States (1961–63); assassinated.

Ken·ne·dy (kĕn′ə-dē), **Robert Francis.** 1925–1968. U.S. Attorney General (1961-64) and senator from New York (1965–68); assassinated; brother of John Fitzgerald Kennedy.

ken·nel[1] (kĕn′əl) *n.* **1.** A shelter for a dog or dogs. **2.** A pack of dogs, especially hounds. **3.** An establishment where dogs are bred, trained, or boarded. **4.** The lair of a fox or other wild animal. —See Synonyms at **flock.** —*v.* **kenneled** or **-nelled, -neling** or **-nelling, -nels.** —*tr.* To keep or place in or as in a kennel. —*intr.* To take cover or lie in or as in a kennel. [Middle English *kenel,* from Old North French *kenil* (unattested), variant of Old French *chenil,* from Vulgar Latin *canile* (unattested), from Latin *canis,* dog. See **kwon-** in Appendix.*]

ken·nel[2] (kĕn′əl) *n.* A gutter along a street. [Variant of *cannel,* Middle English *canel, canal,* CANAL.]

Ken·nel·ly-Heav·i·side layer (kĕn′ə-lē-hĕv′ē-sīd′). The **E layer** *(see)* of the ionosphere. [Discovered by Arthur Edwin *Kennelly* (1861–1939), American electrical engineer, and Oliver *Heaviside* (1850–1925), English physicist.]

Ken·ne·saw Mountain (kĕn′ə-sô). A lone peak, 1,809 feet high, in northwestern Georgia; the site of a Civil War battle during Sherman's drive on Atlanta (1864).

Ken·neth (kĕn′ĭth). A masculine given name. [Scottish Gaelic *Coinneach*†, "handsome."]

ken·ning (kĕn′ĭng) *n.* A metaphorical, usually compound expression substituted for the name of something, especially in Old English and Old Norse poetry. [Old Norse *kenning,* "naming," symbol, from *kenna,* to know, name (with a kenning). See **gnō-** in Appendix.*]

Ken·ny (kĕn′ē), **Elizabeth.** 1886–1952. Called "Sister Kenny." Australian nurse; developed treatment of paralysis resulting from poliomyelitis.

ke·no (kē′nō) *n.* A game of chance similar to lotto, but using balls rather than counters. [Probably from French *quine,* set of five (winning numbers), back-formation from Old French *quines,* five each, from Latin *quīnī* (accusative *quīnas*). See **penkwe** in Appendix.*]

Ke·no·sha (kĭ-nō′shə). A city of southeastern Wisconsin, a port and industrial center on Lake Michigan. Population, 68,000.

ke·no·sis (kĭ-nō′sĭs) *n. Theology.* The relinquishment of the form of God by Christ in becoming man and suffering death. Philippians 2:5–8. [Late Greek *kenōsis,* from Greek, an emptying, from *kenoun,* to empty, from *kenos,* empty. See **ken-**[4] in Appendix.*] —**ke·not′ic** (-nŏt′ĭk) *adj.* & *n.*

Ken·sing·ton (kĕn′zĭng-tən). A former administrative division of London, England, now part of Kensington and Chelsea.

Ken·sing·ton and Chel·sea (kĕn′zĭng-tən; chĕl′sē). A borough of London, England, comprising the two former administrative divisions of Kensington and Chelsea. Population, 218,000.

kent. Alternate past tense and past participle of **ken.**

Kent (kĕnt). A county of England, occupying 1,525 square miles in the southeast. Population, 1,702,000. County seat, Maidstone. [Middle English *Kent,* Old English *Cent,* from Latin *Cantium,* probably from Celtic *cantos* (attested by Welsh *cant*), border, borderland, coast. See **kantho-** in Appendix.*]

Kent (kĕnt), **Rockwell.** Born 1882. American artist.

Kent·ish (kĕn′tĭsh) *adj.* Of or relating to the county of Kent. —*n.* The dialect of Kent.

kent·ledge (kĕnt′lĭj) *n.* Pig iron used as permanent ballast. [Old French *quintelage,* ballast, from *quintal,* hundredweight, from Medieval Latin *quintale,* from Arabic *qinṭār,* KANTAR.]

Ken·tuck·y (kən-tŭk′ē). *Abbr.* **Ky.** A state of the United States, occupying 40,395 square miles in the east-central part of the country; admitted to the Union in 1792. Population, 3,038,000. Capital, Frankfort. See map at **United States of America.**

Kentucky bluegrass. See **bluegrass.**

Kentucky coffee tree. A deciduous North American tree, *Gymnocladus dioica,* having flat, pulpy pods containing seeds formerly used as a coffee substitute.

Kentucky Derby. An annual horse race for three-year-olds run since 1875 at Churchill Downs in Louisville, Kentucky.

Ken·tuck·y River (kən-tŭk′ē). A navigable river of Kentucky, flowing 250 miles northwest across the state to the Ohio.

Ken·ya (kĕn′yə, kĕn′-). A republic occupying 224,960 square miles in east-central Africa; a former British colony independent since 1963. Population, 9,365,000. Capital, Nairobi.

Ken·ya, Mount (kĕn′yə, kĕn′-). The second-highest mountain (17,040 feet) of Africa, an extinct volcano in central Kenya.

Ken·yat·ta (kĕn-yä′tə), **Jomo.** Original name, Kamau Johnstone. Born 1893? Kenya nationalist leader and anthropologist; president of Kenya (since 1963).

Ke·os (kē′ŏs). Ancient name **Ce·os** (sē′ŏs). An island of Greece, 60 square miles in area; one of the Cyclades.

keph·a·lin. Variant of **cephalin.**

Ke·phal·li·ni·a. The Greek name for **Cephalonia.**

kep·i (kā′pē, kĕp′ē) *n., pl.* **-is.** A French military cap with a flat, circular top and a visor. [French *képi,* from Swiss German *käppi,* diminutive of German *Kappe,* cap, from Old High German *kappa,* cloak, from Late Latin *cappa,* hood, cloak, probably from Latin *caput,* head. See **kaput** in Appendix.*]

Kep·ler (kĕp′lər), **Johannes.** 1571–1630. German astronomer, physicist, and mathematician.

kept. Past tense and past participle of **keep.**

Ke·ra·la (kā′rə-lə). A state of the Republic of India, occupying 15,002 square miles in the extreme southwest. Population, 16,904,000. Capital, Trivandrum.

ker·a·tin (kĕr′ə-tən) *n.* A tough, fibrous protein containing sulfur and forming the outer layer of epidermal structures such as hair, nails, horns, and hoofs. [Greek *keras* (stem *kerat-*), horn (see **ker-**[1] in Appendix*) + -IN.] —**ke·rat′i·nous** (kə-răt′n-əs) *adj.*

ker·a·tin·ize (kĕr′ə-tə-nīz′) *v.* **-ized, -izing, -izes.** —*tr.* To form keratin in or on. —*intr.* To form a keratinous layer. —**ker′a·tin·i·za′tion** *n.*

kerb. *British.* Variant of **curb.**

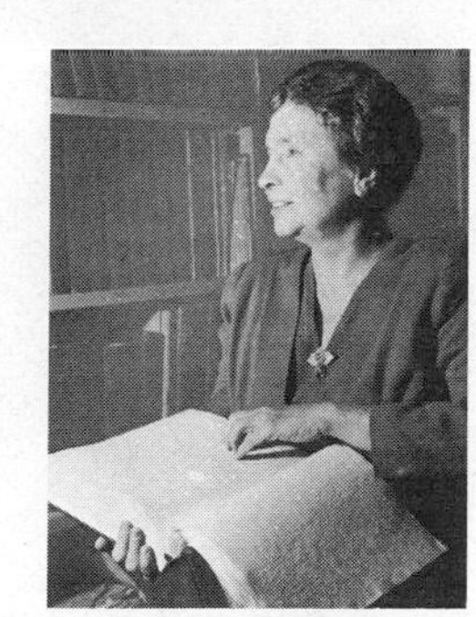

Helen Keller

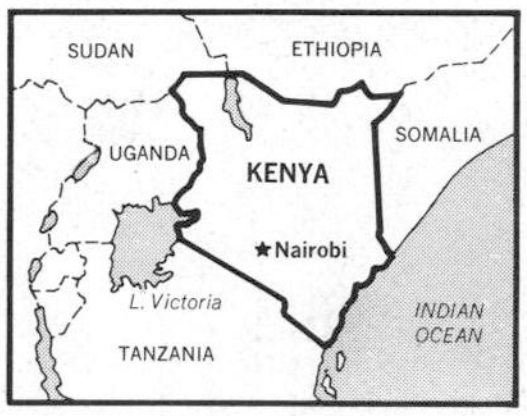

Kenya

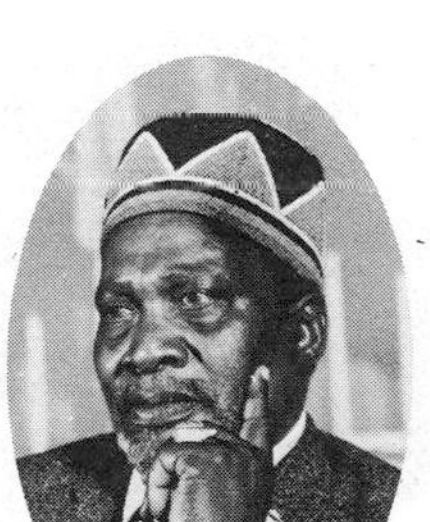

Jomo Kenyatta

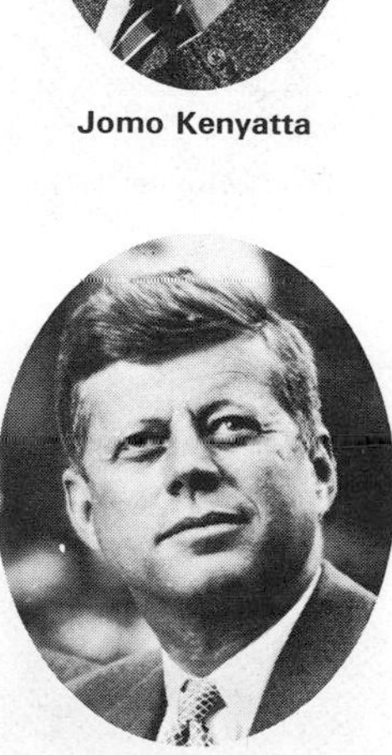

John F. Kennedy

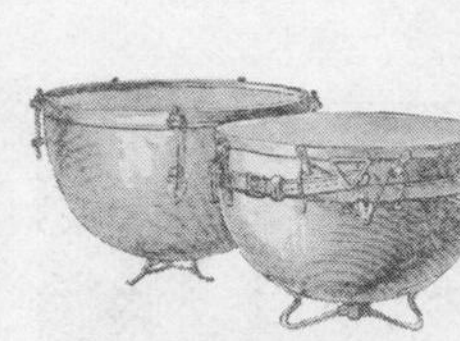

kettledrum
A pair of kettledrums

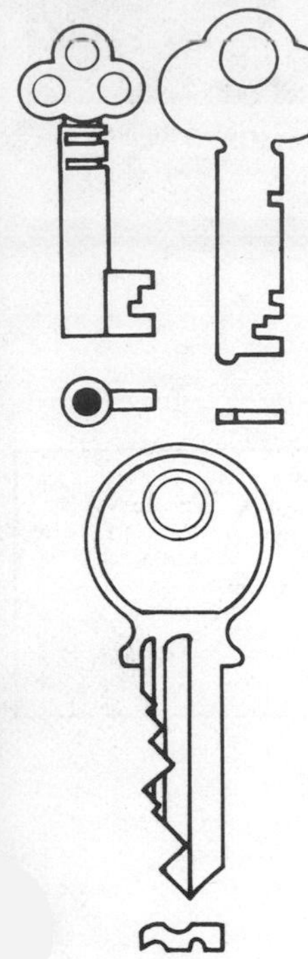

key¹
A variety of keys and keyholes

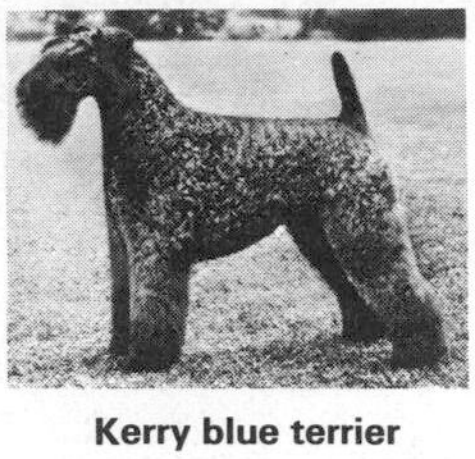

Kerry blue terrier

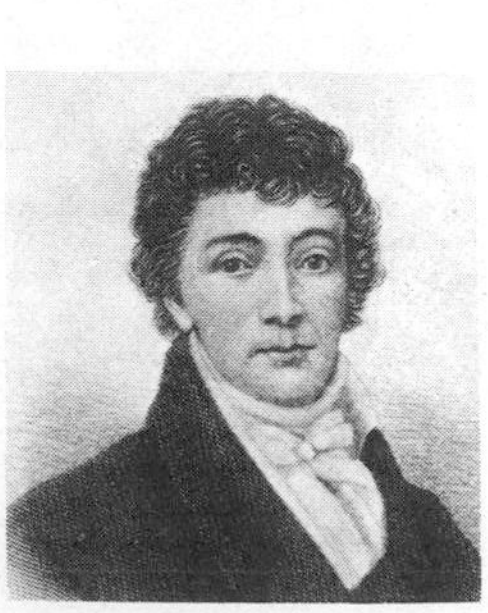

Francis Scott Key

Kerch (kĕrch). A city of the Soviet Union in the southwest at the eastern end of the Crimea. Population, 107,000.

ker·chief (kûr′chĭf) *n.* **1.** A woman's square scarf, often worn as a head covering. **2.** A handkerchief. [Middle English *c(o)urchef, kercheffe,* from Old French *couvrechef, cuerchief,* "head covering" : *co(u)vrir,* to COVER + *ch(i)ef,* head, from Latin *caput* (see **kaput** in Appendix*).]

Ke·ren·sky (kə-rĕn′skē), **Alexander Feodorovich.** Born 1881. Russian revolutionary leader; premier (July to November 1917); resident in America (since 1946).

kerf (kûrf) *n.* **1.** A groove or notch made by a saw, ax, or the like. **2.** The width of such a cut. [Middle English *kyrf, kerf,* Old English *cyrf,* act of cutting. See **gerebh-** in Appendix.*]

Ker·gue·len Islands (kûr′gə-lən). An island group in the southern Indian Ocean, 2,700 square miles in area, administered as part of the French Southern and Antarctic lands.

Ke·rin·chi, Mount (kə-rĭn′chē). The highest mountain (12,467 feet) of Indonesia, in southwest-central Sumatra.

Ker·ky·ra. The Greek name for **Corfu.**

Ker·man. Variant of **Kirman.**

Ker·man·shah (kĕr-män′shä′). A city in west-central Iran on an ancient caravan route. Population, 167,000.

ker·mes (kûr′mēz) *n.* The dried bodies of the females of various scale insects of the genus *Kermes,* used as a red dyestuff. [French *kermès,* short form for *alkermès,* from Spanish *alkermez,* from Arabic *al-qirmiz,* "the kermes," from Sanskrit *krmija-,* (red dye) produced by a worm : *kṛmi-,* worm (see **kwrmi-** in Appendix*) + *ja-,* born, produced (see **gene-** in Appendix*).]

ker·mis (kûr′məs) *n.* Also **ker·mess, kir·mess. 1.** An annual outdoor fair in the Low Countries. **2.** A fund-raising fair or carnival. [Dutch *kermis(se),* from Middle Dutch *kercmisse* : *kerke, kerc,* church, from West Germanic *kirika* (unattested), from Late Greek *kurikon,* CHURCH + *misse,* Mass, church festival, from Late Latin *missa* (see **Mass**).]

kern¹ (kûrn) *n.* Also **kerne. 1.** A medieval Scottish or Irish foot soldier. **2.** A loutish person. [Middle English *kerne,* from Middle Irish *ceithern,* from Old Irish, band of foot soldiers, possibly from *cath,* battle, troop. See **kat-²** in Appendix.*]

kern² (kûrn) *n. Printing.* The portion of a typeface that projects beyond the body or shank of a character. —*tr.v.* **kerned, kerning, kerns.** *Printing.* To provide (a type) with a kern. [French *carne,* corner, salient angle, from Latin *cardō* (stem *cardin-*), hinge. See **cardinal.**]

Kern (kûrn), **Jerome David.** 1885–1945. American composer of scores for musical comedies and films.

ker·nel (kûr′nəl) *n.* **1.** A grain or seed, as of a cereal grass, enclosed in a hard husk. **2.** The inner, usually edible part of a nut or fruit stone. **3.** A nucleus; essence; core: *"that hard kernel of gaiety that never breaks"* (Evelyn Waugh). [Middle English *kirnel, kernell,* Old English *cyrnel,* seed, kernel, diminutive of *corn,* corn, berry, seed. See **grə-no-** in Appendix.*]

kern·ite (kûr′nīt′) *n.* A colorless to white crystalline compound, $Na_2B_4O_7 \cdot 4H_2O$, that is a major source of borax and boron compounds. [Found in Kern County, California.]

ker·o·sene (kĕr′ə-sēn′, kĕr′ə-sēn′) *n.* Also **ker·o·sine.** A thin oil distilled from petroleum or shale oil, used as a fuel and alcohol denaturant. Also called "coal oil" and in British usage "paraffin." [Greek *kēros,* wax (see **ceruse**) + -ENE (from the use of paraffin in its distillation).]

Ker·ou·ac (kĕr′o͞o-ăk′), **Jack.** Original name, Jean-Louis Lefris de Kérouac. Born 1922. Canadian-born American novelist.

Ker·ry¹ (kĕr′ē). A county of the Republic of Ireland, occupying 1,815 square miles in the southwest. Population, 116,000. County seat, Tralee.

Ker·ry² (kĕr′ē) *n., pl.* **-ries.** One of a breed of small, black dairy cattle originally raised in the county of Kerry, Ireland.

Kerry blue terrier. One of a breed of terriers of Irish origin, having a dense, wavy bluish-gray coat.

ker·sey (kûr′zē) *n., pl.* **-seys. 1.** A woolen fabric, often ribbed, formerly used for hose and trousers. **2.** A twilled woolen fabric, sometimes with a cotton warp, used for coats. **3.** *Often plural.* A garment made of one of these fabrics. [Middle English, probably after *Kersey,* village in Suffolk, England.]

ker·sey·mere (kûr′zē-mîr′) *n.* A type of fine woolen cloth with a fancy weave. Also called "cassimere." [Altered from CASSIMERE (by association with KERSEY).]

Ker·u·len (kĕr′o͞o-lĕn). A river of Mongolia, rising 120 miles northeast of Ulan Bator and flowing 785 miles south and then northeast to Lake Hulun Nor in China's Inner Mongolian Autonomous Region.

kes·trel (kĕs′trəl) *n.* **1.** A small Old World falcon, *Falco tinnunculus,* having brown and gray plumage. **2.** Any of several similar birds. [Middle English *castrell,* alteration of Old French *cresserelle, crecelle,* "rattle," kestrel (from its cry), from Vulgar Latin *crepicella* (unattested), diminutive formation from Latin *crepitāre,* to rattle, creak, crackle, frequentative of *crepāre,* to crack. See **ker-²** in Appendix.*]

ketch (kĕch) *n.* A two-masted fore-and-aft-rigged sailing vessel with a mizzen or jigger mast stepped aft of a taller mainmast but forward of the rudder. [Earlier *catch,* Middle English *cache,* probably from *cachen, cacchen,* to hunt, CATCH.]

ketch·up (kĕch′əp, kăch′-) *n.* Also **catch·up** (kăch′əp, kĕch′-), **cat·sup** (kăt′səp, kăch′əp, kĕch′-). A condiment consisting of a thick, smooth-textured, spicy sauce usually made with tomatoes. [Malay *kechap,* from Chinese (Amoy) *kōetsiap, kētsiap,* brine of fish : *kōe,* minced seafood + *tsiap,* brine, sauce, juice, corresponding to Mandarin Chinese *chih³.*]

ke·tene (kē′tēn′) *n.* A pungent, toxic, colorless gas, H_2C_2O, used chiefly as an acetylation agent. [KET(O)- + -ENE.]

keto–, ket–. *Chemistry.* Indicates a ketone or ketonic properties; for example, **ketosis.** [From KETONE.]

ke·tone (kē′tōn′) *n.* Any of a class of organic compounds having a carbonyl group linked to a carbon atom in each of two hydrocarbon radicals and having the general formula $R_1(CO)R_2$, where R_1 may be the same as R_2. [German *Keton,* from *Aketon, Azeton,* ACETONE.] —**ke·ton′ic** (kē-tŏn′ĭk) *adj.*

ketone body. Any of several substances, such as acetoacetic acid, increasing in the blood in certain diabetic and other pathological conditions. Also called "acetone body."

ke·tose (kē′tōs′) *n.* Any of various carbohydrates containing a ketone group in each molecule. [KET(O)- + -OSE.]

ke·to·sis (kē-tō′sĭs) *n.* A pathological accumulation of ketone bodies in the body. [New Latin : KET(O)- + -OSIS.]

Ket·ter·ing (kĕt′ər-ĭng), **Charles Franklin.** 1876–1958. American engineer, inventor, and automotive manufacturer.

ket·tle (kĕt′l) *n.* **1.** A metal pot, usually with a lid, for boiling or stewing; especially, a teakettle. **2.** A pothole. **3.** A kettledrum. [Middle English *ketel,* from Old Norse *ketill,* from Common Germanic *katilaz* (unattested), from Latin *catillus,* small bowl or dish, from *catinus*†, bowl, dish, pot.]

ket·tle·drum (kĕt′l-drŭm′) *n.* A large copper or brass hemispherical drum with a parchment head that may be tuned by adjusting the tension.

Keu·ka, Lake (kyo͞o′kə, kā-o͞o′kə). One of the Finger Lakes, about 18 miles long, in west-central New York State.

keV kiloelectron volt.

ke·va·zin·go (kĕv′ə-zĭng′gō, kā′və-) *n., pl.* **-gos. 1.** A tree, *Didelotia africana,* of western Africa, having hard reddish or purplish wood. **2.** The wood of this tree, used for veneer and in cabinetwork. Also called "bubinga." [A native West African word.]

kev·el (kĕv′əl) *n.* A sturdy belaying cleat or pin for the heavier cables of a ship. [Middle English *kevile,* peg, from Old North French *keville,* from Late Latin *clāvicula,* bolt, bar, from Latin, small key, from *clāvis,* key. See **klēu-** in Appendix.*]

Kew (kyo͞o). A suburb of western London, England, the site of the Royal Botanic Gardens. Population, 6,000.

Ke·wee·naw Peninsula (kē′wē-nô′). A peninsula of northwestern Michigan, extending 60 miles northeast into Lake Superior.

Kew·pie (kyo͞o′pē) *n.* A trademark for a small fat-cheeked wide-eyed doll with a curl of hair on top. Also called "Kewpie doll." [Probably from CUPID.]

key¹ (kē) *n., pl.* **keys. 1.** An implement designed to open a lock; especially, a mounted, metallic, notched and grooved piece inserted into and turned to open or close a lock. **2.** Any means of control, especially of entry or possession. **3. a.** A small instrument for winding a spring. **b.** A slotted metal strip used to open cans. **4. a.** New or vital information or a crucial fact. **b.** A set of answers to a test. **c.** A table, gloss, or cipher for decoding or interpreting. **5.** A pin inserted to lock together mechanical or structural parts. **6.** The keystone in the crown of an arch. **7. a.** A control button or lever on a machine that is operated with the fingers. **b.** A button or lever on a musical instrument, such as a clarinet or piano, that is pressed with the fingers to produce or modulate a sound. **8.** *Music.* **a.** A tonal system consisting of seven tones in fixed relationship to a tonic, having a characteristic key signature, and being since the Renaissance the structural foundation of the bulk of Western music; tonality. **b.** The principal tonality of a musical work: *an etude in the key of E.* **9.** The pitch of a voice or other sound: *She spoke in a high key.* **10.** A general tone, or level of intensity, as of a speech, theatrical performance, or sales campaign. **11.** *Botany.* A key fruit; a samara. —**in** (or **out of**) **key.** In (or out of) tune with other factors: *"The one exception is an episode that is both out of key and intrinsically false"* (Stanley Kauffman). —*tr.v.* **keyed, keying, keys. 1.** To lock together with pins, bolts, wedges, or the like. **2.** To furnish (an arch) with a keystone. **3.** To supply with a key or keys. **4.** To bring into harmony; coordinate. **5.** To coordinate or identify by means of a key. —**key up.** To raise to a high pitch; make intense. —*adj.* Of crucial importance: *"The Channel was a key factor in English history as a center of communications."* (Christopher Brooke). [Middle English *key(e), kay,* Old English *cǣg(e)*†.]

key² (kē) *n., pl.* **keys.** A low offshore island or reef, often of coral or sand; a cay. [Spanish *cayo,* CAY.]

Key (kē), **Francis Scott.** 1779–1843. American lawyer; author of "The Star-Spangled Banner."

key·board (kē′bôrd′, -bōrd′) *n.* A set of keys, as on a piano, an organ, or a typewriter. —*tr.v.* **keyboarded, -boarding, -boards.** To set (copy) by means of a keyed typesetting machine.

keyed (kēd) *adj.* **1.** Equipped with keys. **2.** Strengthened or secured with a key. **3.** Built with or reinforced by a keystone: *a keyed arch.*

key fruit. A **samara** *(see).* [The fruit resembles a key.]

key·hole (kē′hōl′) *n.* The hole in a lock into which a key fits.

key money. 1. Money paid as a bribe to a landlord or superintendent by someone seeking an apartment. **2.** Advance rent or security requested of a new tenant in exchange for his key.

Keynes (kānz), **John Maynard.** First Baron Keynes. 1883–1946. British economist.

Keynes·i·an (kān′zē-ən) *adj.* Of or pertaining to the economic theories or policies of John M. Keynes or his supporters. —*n.* A supporter of Keynes's economic views.

key·note (kē′nōt′) *n.* **1.** The tonic of a musical key. **2.** A prime or crucial element: *"the keynote of the revolution settlement was personal freedom under the law"* (G.M. Trevelyan). **3.** An underlying or general tone, spirit, or idea: *"Liveliness is the keynote of all Dunbar's work."* (Tucker Brooke). —*tr.v.* **key-noted, -noting, -notes.** To give or set the keynote of.

keynote address. An opening address, as at a political convention, that outlines the issues to be considered. Also called "keynote speech."

key·not·er (kē′nō′tər) *n.* One who gives a keynote address.

key punch. A keyboard machine that is used to punch holes in cards or tapes for data-processing systems.

key signature. The group of sharps or flats placed to the right of the clef on a musical staff to identify the key.

key·stone (kē′stōn′) *n. Architecture.* The central wedge-shaped stone of an arch that locks the others together.

Keystone State. The nickname for Pennsylvania.

key·way (kē′wā′) *n., pl.* **-ways. 1.** A slot in a wheel hub or shaft for a key. **2.** The keyhole of a cylinder lock.

Key West. The southernmost city of the continental United States, a seaport of Florida on Key West Island, the westernmost of the Florida Keys. Population, 34,000.

kg kilogram.

K.G. Knight of the Garter.

KGB, K.G.B. The Commission of State Security (Russian *Komitět Gosudarstvĕnnoi Bezopasnost'i*), an intelligence agency of the Soviet Union analogous to the Central Intelligence Agency of the United States. See **Cheka.**

Kha·ba·rovsk (kə-bär′əfsk). A city of the Soviet Union, on the Amur in southeastern Siberia. Population, 349,000.

Kha·kass Autonomous Region (kə-käs′). An administrative division, 23,855 square miles in area, of the south-central Russian S.F.S.R. Population, 458,000. Capital, Abakan.

khak·i (kăk′ē, kä′kē) *n., pl.* **khakis. 1.** A color ranging from light olive brown to a moderate or light yellowish brown. **2.** A sturdy wool or cotton cloth of this color. **3.** *Plural.* A uniform of this cloth. —*adj.* Of the color khaki. [Urdu *khākī,* dusty, dust-colored, from *khāk,* dust, from Persian *khāk†.*]

kha·lif. Variant of **caliph.**

Kha·li·fa (khă-lē′fä), **The.** 1846?–1899. Sudanese Arab leader; defeated at Omdurman (1898) by Kitchener.

Khal·ki·di·kí (käl′kĭ-thĭ-kē′). **1.** The capital of Euboea, Greece. **2.** The Greek name for **Chalcidice.**

Khal·kis. The Modern Greek name for **Chalcis.**

kham·sin (kăm-sēn′) *n.* Also **kham·seen, kam·seen, kam·sin.** A generally southerly hot wind from the Sahara that blows across Egypt from late March to early May. [Arabic *(rīḥ al-)khamsīn,* (wind of the) 50 (days), from *khamsūn,* 50.]

khan¹ (kän, kăn) *n.* **1.** A title of respect for rulers, officials, or important persons in India and some central Asian countries. **2.** Formerly, a title given to the rulers of Mongol, Tartar, or Turkish tribes who succeeded Genghis Khan, as well as to emperors of China. [Middle English *caan, c(h)an,* from Old French, from Medieval Latin *caanus,* from Turkish *khān,* contraction of *khāqān,* sovereign, ruler.]

khan² (kän, kăn) *n.* A caravansary in the East. [Middle English, from Arabic and Persian *khān,* inn.]

khan·ate (kä′nāt, kăn′āt′) *n.* **1.** The realm of a khan. **2.** The position of a khan.

Khan·ba·lik (kän′bä-lēk′). The capital of Kublai Khan's China, on the site now occupied by Peking. Called "Cambaluc" by Marco Polo.

Kha·ni·a. The Greek name for **Canea.**

Khan·ka, Lake (kăng′kə). Also **Han·ka** (häng′-). A lake occupying 1,700 square miles on the Sino-Soviet eastern border, 100 miles north of Vladivostok.

Khar·kov (kär′kôf, -kôv). A city of the Soviet Union in the eastern Ukrainian S.S.R., of which it was once the capital (1920–34). Population, 1,702,000.

Khar·toum (kär-tōōm′). Also **Khar·tum.** The capital of Sudan, in the east-central part of the country at the confluence of the Blue Nile and the White Nile. Population, 584,000.

Khay·yám, Omar. See **Omar Khayyám.**

khe·dive (kə-dēv′) *n.* The title of the Turkish viceroys of Egypt from 1867 to 1914.

Khe·lat. See **Kalat.**

Kher·son (kĕr-sôn′). A city of the Soviet Union, near the mouth of the Dnieper in the southern Ukrainian S.S.R. Population, 210,000.

KHI Airport code for Karachi, Pakistan.

Khing·an Mountains (shĭng′än′). A mountain range extending for 700 miles in western Manchuria. Highest elevation, 5,670 feet. Also called "Great Khingan Mountains."

Khir·bet Qum·ran (kir-bĕt′ kōōm-rän′). The site in Jordan, at the northwestern end of the Dead Sea, of the caves in which the Dead Sea Scrolls were found.

Khi·va (kē′və). An oasis of the Soviet Union, along the Amu Darya in southern Uzbekistan.

Khmer (kmĕr) *n., pl.* **Khmer** or **Khmers. 1. a.** A people of Cambodia whose culture flourished during the Middle Ages. **b.** A member of this people. **2.** The Mon-Khmer language of this people. —**Khmer′i·an** *adj.*

Khoi·san (koi′sän) *n.* A family of languages of southwestern Africa including those of the Bushmen and Hottentots.

Khond (kŏnd) *n., pl.* **Khond** or **Khonds. 1.** One of a hill people of Dravidian stock of east-central India. **2.** The Dravidian language of this people.

Kho·tan (kō′tän′). A river of China, rising in the Kunlun Mountains and flowing 400 miles north through Sinkiang-Uigur Autonomous Region to the Yarkand to form the Tarim.

Khru·shchev (krōōsh-chôf′, -chôv′, krōōsch′chôf′, -chôv′, -chĕf′), **Nikita Sergeyevich.** Born 1894. First secretary of the Russian Communist Party (1953–64); premier of the Soviet Union (1958–64).

Khub·su·gul (khœb′sœ-gœl′). A lake of the Mongolian People's Republic, occupying 1,010 square miles in the north-central part of the republic.

Khu·fu. See **Cheops.**

Khur·ram·shahr (khōōr′räm-shär′). The capital of Khuzistan, Iran, in the southwestern part of the province. Population, 43,000.

Khu·zi·stan (khōō′zĭ-stän′). A province of Iran, occupying 34,027 square miles in the southwest. Population, 1,855,000. Capital, Khurramshahr.

Khwa·riz·mi, al-. See **al-Khwarizmi.**

Khy·ber Pass (kī′bər). A pass extending for about 30 miles through the mountains between Afghanistan and West Pakistan.

Kia·ling Kiang (jyä′lĭng′ jyäng′). A river of China, rising in southern Kansu and flowing about 500 miles generally south through Szechwan to the Yangtze.

Kia·mu·sze (jyä′mōō′sœ′). *Japanese* **Chia·mus·su** (chyä-mōōs′sōō). A city of China in eastern Manchuria. Population, 232,000.

ki·ang (kē-äng′) *n.* A wild ass, *Equus hemionus kiang,* of the mountains of eastern Asia. [Tibetan *rkyaṅ.*]

Kiang·si (jyäng′sē′). A province of China, occupying 65,000 square miles in the southeastern part of the country. Population, 18,610,000. Capital, Nanchang.

Kiang·su (jyäng′sōō′). A province occupying 35,000 square miles in east-central China. Population, 45,250,000. Capital, Nanking.

Kiao·chow (jyou′jō′). A territory of some 400 square miles in southeastern Shantung, China, formerly leased to Germany (1898–1914).

kiaugh (kyäкн) *n. Scottish.* Trouble; anxiety. [Probably from Scottish Gaelic *cabhag†,* hurry.]

kib·butz (kĭ-bōōts′) *n., pl.* **-butzim** (-bōōt′sēm′). A collective farm or settlement in modern Israel. [Hebrew *qibbūtz,* "gathering," from *qibbētz,* he gathered.]

kibe (kīb) *n.* An ulcerated chilblain, especially one on the heel. [Middle English *kybe,* possibly from Welsh *cibi, cibwst†.*]

Ki·bei (kē-bā′) *n., pl.* **Kibei** or **-beis.** A native American citizen of Japanese immigrant parents, educated largely in Japan. Compare **Issei, Nisei.** [Japanese, "(one who) returns to America" : *ki,* to return, from Ancient Chinese *kjwei* (Mandarin *kwei¹*) + *bei,* America (a character meaning "rice," but used to transliterate the stressed syllable in the word *America*), from Ancient Chinese *miei* (Mandarin *mi³*).]

kib·itz (kĭb′ĭts) *intr.v.* **-itzed, -itzing, -itzes.** *Informal.* To act as a kibitzer. [Yiddish *kibitsen,* from German *kiebitzen,* to look on, from *Kiebitz,* lapwing, plover, hence a meddlesome person, looker on (at a card game), from Middle High German *gībiz,* plover (imitative of its cry).]

kib·itz·er (kĭb′ĭt-sər) *n. Informal.* **1.** An onlooker at a card game who gives unwanted advice to the players. **2.** Any meddler who offers gratuitous advice. [Yiddish *kibitser,* from German *Kiebitzer,* from *kiebitzen,* KIBITZ.]

kib·lah (kĭb′lä) *n.* **1.** The direction toward which Moslems face when they pray. **2.** A niche in the wall of a mosque indicating this direction. [Arabic *qiblah,* from *qābilah,* he lay opposite.]

ki·bosh (kī′bŏsh, kĭ-bŏsh′) *n. Informal.* A restraint; a check. Used chiefly in the phrase *put the kibosh on.* [Origin unknown.]

kick (kĭk) *v.* **kicked, kicking, kicks.** —*intr.* **1.** To strike out with the foot or feet. **2.** *Football.* **a.** To score or gain ground by kicking the ball. **b.** To punt. **3.** To recoil, as a gun when fired. **4.** *Informal.* To object vigorously; complain; protest. —*tr.* **1.** To strike with the foot. **2.** To drive or move by striking with the foot. **3.** To spring back against suddenly, as a gun when fired. **4.** *Football.* To score (a goal or point) by kicking the ball. —See Synonyms at **object.** —**kick around.** *Informal.* **1.** To treat roughly; neglect. **2.** To move from place to place. **3.** To give consideration or thought to (an idea). —**kick in.** *Slang.* **1.** To contribute (one's share). **2.** To die. —**kick out.** *Slang.* To eject; dismiss. —**kick the bucket.** *Slang.* To die. —**kick the habit.** *Slang.* To free oneself of narcotic addiction. —**kick up.** *Informal.* To raise trouble: *The motor began to kick up a storm. Slang.* To stir up trouble; make a fuss. —**kick up one's heels.** *Slang.* To cast off one's inhibitions; enjoy oneself. —*n.* **1. a.** A vigorous thrust or blow with the foot. **b.** The motion of the legs used in swimming. **2.** The jolting recoil of a gun. **3.** *Slang.* A complaint or protest. **4.** *Slang.* Power; force: *still a lot of kick in that engine.* **5.** *Slang.* Stimulating or intoxicating impact: *quite a kick in that martini.* **6.** *Slang.* **a.** A feeling of excitement or pleasure. **b.** *Plural.* Fun; thrills: *just for kicks.* **7.** *Slang.* A temporary concentration of interest: *He's on a science-fiction kick.* **8.** *Slang.* A sudden or revealing surprise. **9.** *Football.* **a.** A kicking of a football. **b.** The kicked ball. **c.** The distance spanned by a kicked ball: *a 47-yard kick.* [Middle English *kiken, kyken†.*]

Kick·a·poo (kĭk′ə-pōō′) *n., pl.* **Kickapoo** or **-poos. 1.** A member of a tribe of Algonquian-speaking Indians formerly of northern Illinois and southern Wisconsin. **2.** The language of the Kickapoos. [Kickapoo *kiwĕgapawa,* "he stands about."]

kick back. 1. To recoil unexpectedly and violently. **2.** *Slang.* To return (stolen items). **3.** *Slang.* To pay a kickback.

kick·back (kĭk′băk′) *n.* **1.** A sharp response or reaction; repercussion. **2.** *Slang.* **a.** A percentage payment to a person able to influence or control a source of income, as by confidential arrangement or coercion. **b.** The money paid.

keystone

Nikita Khrushchev
Addressing the United Nations General Assembly in 1960

kick off. 1. *Football.* To put the ball in play by place kicking it toward the opposing team. 2. *Slang.* To die.

kick·off (kĭk′ôf′, -ŏf′) *n.* 1. A place kick in football or soccer with which play is begun. 2. A beginning.

kick plate. A protective sheet of metal attached to the bottom of a door.

kick·shaw (kĭk′shô′) *n.* Also **kick·shaws** (-shôz′). 1. A fancy food; a delicacy. 2. A trinket or trifle; a gewgaw. [Earlier *kickshose, quelkchose,* from French *quelque chose,* something.]

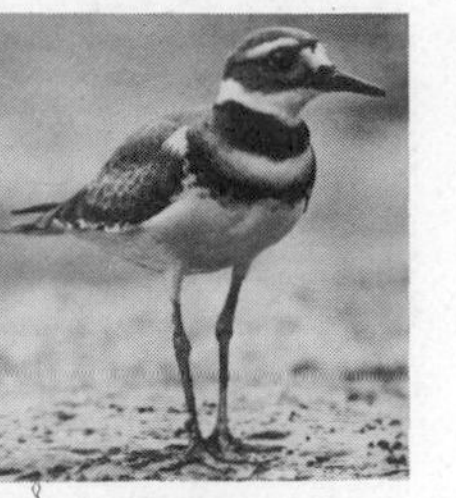

killdeer

kid[1] (kĭd) *n.* 1. a. A young goat. b. The young of a similar animal, such as an antelope. 2. The flesh of a young goat. 3. Leather made from the skin of a young goat. 4. An article made from this leather. 5. *Slang.* a. A child. b. A young person. —*adj.* 1. Made of kid. 2. *Informal.* Younger: *my kid brother.* —*v.* **kidded, kidding, kids.** —*tr. Informal.* 1. To mock playfully; to tease. 2. To deceive in fun; to fool. —*intr.* 1. *Informal.* To engage in teasing or good-humored fooling. 2. To bear young. Used of a goat or an antelope. [Middle English *kide, kyde,* from Old Norse *kidh,* young goat, from Germanic *kidhja-* (unattested).] —**kid′der** *n.*

kid[2] (kĭd) *n.* A small wooden tub; especially, a tub used as a sailor's mess container. [Probably variant of KIT (tub).]

Kidd (kĭd), **William.** Known as Captain Kidd. 1645?–1701. Scottish-born pirate; hanged.

Kid·der·min·ster (kĭd′ər-mĭn′stər) *n.* An ingrain carpet. [Originally manufactured at *Kidderminster,* borough in Worcestershire, England.]

Kid·dush (kĭd′əsh, kĭ-do͞osh′) *n. Judaism.* The traditional blessing and prayer recited over a cup of wine or bread on the eve of the Sabbath or a festival. [Hebrew *qiddūsh,* sanctification, from *qiddesh,* he sanctified.]

kid·dy (kĭd′ē) *n., pl.* **-dies.** Also **kid·die.** *Slang.* A small child.

kid glove. A glove made of fine, soft leather, especially kidskin. —**handle with kid gloves.** To treat tactfully and cautiously.

kid·nap (kĭd′năp′) *tr.v.* **-naped** or **-napped, -naping** or **-napping, -naps.** To abduct and detain (a person or animal), often for ransom. [Back-formation from *kidnaper* : KID (child) + *napper,* (slang) thief, from *nap,* to seize, probably from Scandinavian, akin to Swedish *nappa*†, to snatch.] —**kid′nap′er, kid′nap′per** *n.*

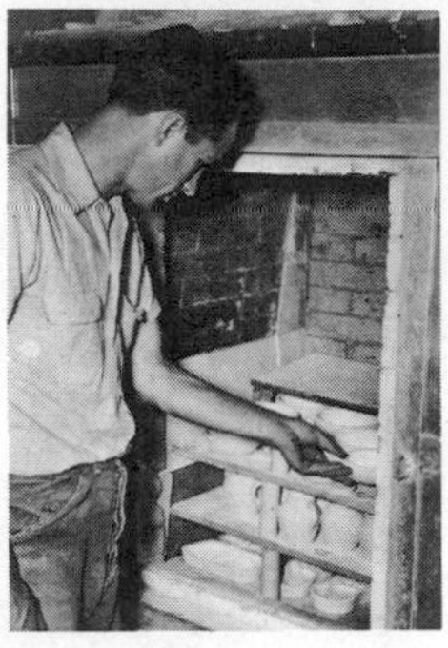

kiln

kid·ney (kĭd′nē) *n., pl.* **-neys.** 1. *Anatomy.* Either of a pair of structures in the dorsal region of the vertebrate abdominal cavity, functioning to maintain proper water balance, regulate acid-base concentration, and excrete metabolic wastes as urine. 2. The kidney of certain animals, eaten as food. 3. An excretory organ of certain invertebrates. 4. Disposition; temperament. [Middle English *kidenei, kydney* : possibly *kiden-* (an obscure element) + *ei,* egg, Old English *ǣg* (see **awi-** in Appendix*).]

kidney bean. 1. A bean, *Phaseolus vulgaris,* cultivated in many forms for its edible seeds. 2. The reddish seed of this bean.

kidney stone. *Pathology.* A renal **calculus** *(see).*

kidney vetch. A plant, *Anthyllis vulneraria,* native to Europe, having grayish-green leaves and small yellow flowers. [Formerly used to treat kidney disorders.]

kid·skin (kĭd′skĭn′) *n.* Soft leather made from the skin of a young goat.

Kiel (kēl). The capital of Schleswig-Holstein, West Germany, a seaport in the east on the Baltic. Population, 271,000.

Kiel Canal (kēl). A canal extending some 60 miles across central Schleswig-Holstein, West Germany, connecting the North Sea with the Baltic.

Kiel·ce (kyĕlt′sĕ). A city of Poland, a railroad junction in the southeast. Population, 98,000.

kier (kîr) *n.* Also **keir.** A vat for boiling, dyeing, or bleaching fabric, yarn, or fiber. [Earlier *keare,* from Old Norse *ker,* tub, akin to Old High German *char,* Gothic *kas*†, vessel.]

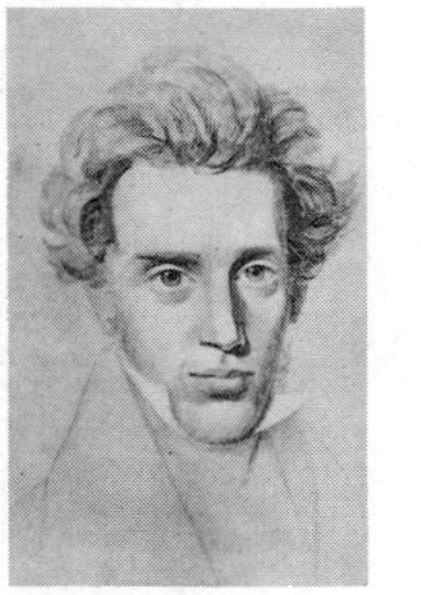

Sören Kierkegaard
At the age of 27

Kier·ke·gaard (kîr′kə-gärd′; *Danish* kîr′kə-gôr′), **Sören Aabye.** 1813–1855. Danish philosopher and theologian.

kie·sel·guhr (kē′zəl-go͝or′) *n. Mineralogy.* **Diatomite** *(see).*

kie·ser·ite (kē′zə-rīt′) *n.* A whitish to yellowish hydrous magnesium sulfate mineral. [German *Kieserit,* after Dietrich G. *Kieser* (died 1862), German physicist.]

Kies·ing·er (kē′sĭng-ər; *German* kē′zĭng-ər), **Kurt Georg.** Born 1904. Chancellor of West Germany (since 1966).

Ki·ev (kē-ĕv′, kē′ĕf′). The capital of the Ukrainian S.S.R., an industrial city on the Dnieper in the north-central part of the republic. Population, 1,348,000.

kif (kēf) *n.* Also **keef, kef** (kāf). 1. Indian hemp or other related material prepared for smoking, especially in the Maghreb. 2. The odd euphoria often associated with its use. [Arabic *kef,* informal form of *kayf,* pleasure, well-being.]

Ki·ga·li (kĭ-gä′lē). The capital of Rwanda. Population, 4,000.

kike (kīk) *n. Slang.* A Jew. An offensive term used derogatorily. [Perhaps from *kiki,* reduplication of *-(s)ki, -(s)ky,* ending in names common among Jews from Slavic countries.]

Ki·kla·dhes. A Greek name for the **Cyclades.**

Ki·ku·yu (kĭ-ko͞o′yo͞o) *n., pl.* **Kikuyu** or **-yus.** 1. A member of a Bantu people of Kenya. 2. The Bantu language of this people.

Ki·lau·e·a (kē′lou-ā′ə). A large, active volcanic crater on Mauna Loa, Hawaii.

Kil·dare (kĭl-dâr′). A county of the Republic of Ireland, occupying 654 square miles in the east. Population, 64,000. County seat, Naas.

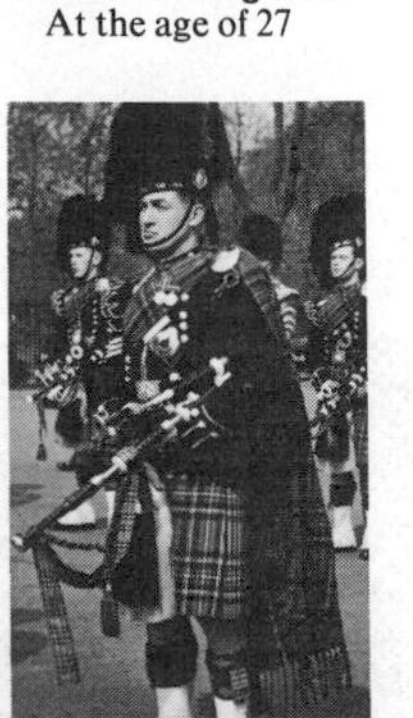

kilt
Worn by a member of the Scots Guards

kil·der·kin (kĭl′dər-kən) *n.* 1. A cask. 2. An obsolete English measure of capacity equal to 18 gallons. [Middle English *kilderkyn,* earlier *kyn(d)erkyn,* from Middle Dutch *kinderkin, kinnekijn,* diminutive of *kintal,* hundredweight, from Medieval Latin *quintāle.* from Arabic *qinṭār,* KANTAR.]

ki·lim (kē-lēm′) *n.* An oriental tapestry-woven rug or other textile piece. [Turkish, from Persian *kilīm*†.]

Kil·i·man·ja·ro (kĭl′ə-mən-jär′ō). The highest mountain (19,565 feet) in Africa, in northeastern Tanzania near the border with Kenya.

Kil·ken·ny (kĭl-kĕn′ē). 1. A county of the Republic of Ireland, occupying 796 square miles in the southeast. Population, 62,000. 2. The county seat of this county. Population, 10,000.

kill[1] (kĭl) *v.* **killed, killing, kills.** —*tr.* 1. a. To put to death; slay. b. To deprive of life: *Famine killed thousands.* 2. To put an end to; extinguish. 3. To harm greatly; to ruin: *killed the taste.* 4. To pass (time) idly or unproductively. 5. To consume entirely; finish off: *kill a bottle of whiskey.* 6. To cause extreme pain or discomfort to: *My shoes are killing me.* 7. To mark for deletion; rule out. 8. To thwart; veto: *kill a congressional bill.* 9. To cause to stop; turn off. 10. *Tennis.* To hit (a ball) with such force as to make a return impossible. —*intr.* 1. To be fatal; cause death or extinction: *"the letter killeth, but the spirit giveth life"* (II Corinthians 3:6). 2. To commit murder. —*n.* 1. The act of killing. 2. The animal or animals killed, especially in hunting. —**in at the kill.** Present at the moment of triumph. [Middle English *kullen, killen, kellen,* Old English *cyllan* (unattested). See **gwel-**[2] in Appendix.*]

kill[2] (kĭl) *n.* A creek, stream, or channel. Used in place names; for example, *Wallkill, Bushkill.* [Dutch *kil,* from Middle Dutch *kille.* See **gei-**[1] in Appendix.*]

Kil·lar·ney (kĭ-lär′nē). A town in central County Kerry, Republic of Ireland. Population, 7,000.

kill·deer (kĭl′dîr′) *n., pl.* **-deers** or **killdeer.** A New World bird, *Charadrius vociferus,* of inland ponds, streams, and fields, having a distinctive cry. [Imitative of its cry.]

kill·er (kĭl′ər) *n.* 1. One that kills. 2. The killer whale.

killer whale. A black and white predatory whale, *Orcinus orca,* of cold seas. Sometimes called "grampus," "orc."

kil·lick (kĭl′ĭk) *n.* Also **kil·lock** (-ək). A small anchor, especially one made of a stone in a wooden frame. [Origin unknown.]

kil·li·fish (kĭl′ĭ-fĭsh′) *n., pl.* **killifish** or **-fishes.** Any of numerous small fishes of the family Cyprinodontidae, chiefly of fresh and brackish waters of warm regions. [KILL (creek) + FISH.]

kil·li·ki·nick. Variant of **kinnikinnick.**

kill·ing (kĭl′ĭng) *n.* 1. A murder; homicide. 2. Quarry; kill. 3. A sudden large profit. —*adj.* 1. Designed or apt to kill; fatal. 2. Exhausting: *a killing ordeal.* 3. *Informal.* Hilarious.

kill·joy (kĭl′joi′) *n.* A person who spoils the enthusiasm or fun of others.

Kil·mer (kĭl′mər), **Alfred Joyce.** 1886–1918. American poet.

kiln (kĭl, kĭln) *n.* Any of various ovens for hardening, burning, or drying substances, such as grain, meal, or clay; especially, a brick-lined oven used to bake or fire ceramics. —*tr.v.* **kilned, kilning, kilns.** To process in a kiln. [Middle English *kylne,* Old English *cyline, cylen,* from Latin *culīna,* kitchen, deformed variant of *coquīna,* cookery, from *coquīnus,* of cooking, from *coquere,* to cook. See **pekw-** in Appendix.*]

ki·lo (kē′lō, kĭl′ō) *n., pl.* **-los.** 1. A kilogram. 2. A kilometer.

kilo-. *Symbol* **k** Indicates 1,000 (10^3); for example, **kilowatt, kilocalorie.** [French, arbitrarily from Greek *khilioi,* thousand. See **gheslo-** in Appendix.*]

kil·o·cal·o·rie (kĭl′ə-kăl′ə-rē) *n. Abbr.* **kcal** A kilogram calorie.

kil·o·cy·cle (kĭl′ə-sī′kəl) *n. Abbr.* **kc** 1. A unit equal to 1,000 cycles. 2. Loosely, 1,000 cycles per second.

kil·o·gram (kĭl′ə-grăm′) *n. Abbr.* **kg** 1. The fundamental unit of mass in the International System, about 2.2046 pounds. See **measurement.** 2. A force equal to a kilogram weight, that is, the product of a kilogram mass with the acceleration of gravity.

kilogram calorie. A **calorie** *(see).*

kil·o·gram-me·ter (kĭl′ə-grăm′mē′tər) *n.* A meter-kilogram-second unit of work, equal to the work performed by a one-kilogram force acting through a distance of one meter.

kil·o·me·ter (kĭl′ə-mē′tər, kĭ-lŏm′ə-tər) *n. Abbr.* **km** One thousand meters, approximately 0.62137 mile. —**kil′o·met′ric** (-mĕt′rĭk) *adj.*

kil·o·ton (kĭl′ə-tŭn′) *n.* 1. One thousand tons. 2. An explosive force equivalent to that of 1,000 tons of TNT.

kil·o·watt (kĭl′ə-wŏt′) *n. Abbr.* **kW** One thousand watts.

kil·o·watt-hour (kĭl′ə-wŏt′our′) *n. Abbr.* **kWh** The total energy developed by a power of one kilowatt acting for one hour, a common unit of electric power consumption.

kilt (kĭlt) *n.* A knee-length skirt with deep pleats, usually of a tartan wool, worn especially as part of the dress for men in the Scottish Highlands. —*tr.v.* **kilted, kilting, kilts.** To tuck up around the body. [From dialectal verb *kilt,* to fasten up, tuck up, Middle English (northern dialect) *kilten,* from Scandinavian, akin to Danish *kilte,* to tuck up, Old Norse *kjalta*†, shirt.]

Usage: *Kilts* as a singular form is sometimes used in designating a woman's skirt designed in imitation of a Scotsman's kilt.

kil·ter (kĭl′tər) *n.* Good condition; proper form. Used chiefly in the phrase *out of kilter.* [Origin unknown.]

Kim·ber·ley (kĭm′bər-lē). 1. A city of South Africa, a diamond-mining center in northern Cape of Good Hope Province. Population, 79,000. 2. A gold field in northeastern Western Australia.

Kim·bun·du (kĭm-bo͞on′do͞o) *n.* A language of the Bantu family, spoken in Angola.

ki·mo·no (kə-mō′nə, -nō) *n., pl.* **-nos.** 1. A long, loose, wide-sleeved Japanese robe, worn with a broad sash. 2. A bathrobe or dressing gown modeled after this. [Japanese, "thing for wearing" : *ki,* to wear + *mono,* person, thing.]

ă pat/ā pay/âr care/ä father/b bib/ch church/d deed/ĕ pet/ē be/f fife/g gag/h hat/hw which/ĭ pit/ī pie/îr pier/j judge/k kick/l lid, needle/m mum/n no, sudden/ng thing/ŏ pot/ō toe/ô paw, for/oi noise/ou out/o͝o took/o͞o boot/p pop/r roar/s sauce/sh ship, dish/

kin (kĭn) *n.* One's relatives collectively; family; kindred; kinsfolk. —**next of kin.** The person or persons closest in blood relationship. —*adj.* Related; akin. [Middle English *kin(n), kyn,* Old English *cyn(n).* See **gene-** in Appendix.*]

-kin. Indicates small or diminutive; for example, **bodkin, lambkin.** [Middle English, from Middle Dutch *-kin, -kijn,* from West Germanic *-kin* (unattested).]

KIN Airport code for Kingston, Jamaica.

Kin·a·ba·lu (kĭn'ə-bə-lo͞o'). The highest mountain (13,455 feet) on the island of Borneo, situated in Sabah, Malaysia.

kin·aes·the·sia, kin·aes·the·sis. Variants of **kinesthesia.**

kin·ase (kĭn'ās', kī'nās') *n.* An enzyme that catalyzes the activation of an enzyme. [KIN(ETIC) + -ASE.]

Kin·car·din·shire (kĭn-kärd'n-shĭr, -shər). Also **Kin·car·dine** (kĭn-kärd'n). Formerly **The Mearns** (mûrnz). A county in east-central Scotland. Population, 25,000. County seat, Stonehaven.

kind¹ (kīnd) *adj.* **kinder, kindest.** **1.** Of a friendly nature; generous or hospitable; warmhearted; good. **2.** Charitable; helpful; showing sympathy or understanding: *a kind word.* **3.** Humane; considerate: *kind to animals.* **4.** Forbearing; tolerant; charitable: *very kind about the broken window.* **5.** Courteous; thoughtful: *Thank you for your kind reply.* **6.** Generous; liberal: *his kind words of praise.* **7.** *Informal.* Agreeable; beneficial: *a soap kind to the skin.* [Middle English *kynde, kind,* Old English *gecynde,* natural, innate. See **gene-** in Appendix.*]

Synonyms: *kind, kindly, kindhearted, benign, benevolent, gracious, compassionate.* These adjectives apply to persons and their actions when they show evidence of concern or sympathy for others. *Kind* and *kindly* are approximately interchangeable in describing persons and their natures; with reference to acts that reflect consideration or sympathy, *kindly* is more common. *Kindhearted* especially suggests an innate tendency to behave in such manner. *Benign* implies gentleness by nature; *benevolent,* charitableness and desire to promote others' welfare; *gracious,* courtesy and warmth, especially to those at a disadvantage; and *compassionate,* a tendency to be moved to pity easily.

kind² (kīnd) *n.* **1.** Variety; sort; type: *the kind of people who are cheerful in the morning.* **2.** A class or category of similar or related individuals: *What kind of dog is that?* **3.** *Rare.* Mode of action; manner; way: *He was successful in his kind.* **4.** *Archaic.* Nature within an order. —See Synonyms at **type.** —**a kind of.** A rough approximation of the category expressed: *a kind of shelter.* —**differ in kind.** To differ in nature, not simply in degree. —**in kind. 1.** With produce or commodities rather than with money: *pay in kind.* **2.** In the same manner or with something equivalent; accordingly: *returned the slight in kind.* —**kind of.** *Informal.* Somewhat: *I'm kind of hungry.* [Middle English *kynd(e), kind(e),* Old English *cynd, gecynd(e),* birth, nature, race. See **gene-** in Appendix.*]

Usage: *Kind,* as a singular classifying noun, is preferably preceded by a singular demonstrative adjective and followed by a singular noun and verb in examples such as *This kind of book has little value.* Informally, and especially in speech, plural elements often occur with *kind: These kind of books have little value.* Although the plural construction has a long history in written usage as well, it is avoided by many writers and editors. A similar sentence, considered as an example in writing on a formal level, is termed unacceptable by 90 per cent of the Usage Panel: *Those kind of buildings seem old-fashioned* (preferably *Buildings of that kind seem old-fashioned*). The alternative phrasing *that kind of buildings seem* is unacceptable on a formal level to 75 per cent of the Panel. A more acceptable use of *kind,* with an accompanying plural noun and verb, occurs in interrogative constructions introduced by *what* or *which: What kind of books are these?* (accepted by 76 per cent of the Panel). The plural *kinds* is sometimes resorted to by writers in an effort to justify accompanying plural elements, but *kinds* is possible only when the desired sense involves more than one class or variety. *Kinds* is always used, with plural verbs, in the following typical sentences: *All kinds of plants were displayed. All kinds of difficulty were involved.*

kin·der·gar·ten (kĭn'dər-gärt'n) *n.* A program or class for four- to six-year-old children that serves as an orientation for school by accustoming them to a new social environment through varied experiences planned to develop manipulative skill, motor coordination, and social awareness. [German *Kindergarten,* "children's garden" : *Kinder,* plural of *Kind,* child, from Old High German *kind* (see **gene-** in Appendix*) + *Garten,* garden, from Middle High German *garte,* from Old High German *garto* (see **gher-²** in Appendix*).]

kin·der·gart·ner (kĭn'dər-gärt'nər) *n.* Also **kin·der·gar·ten·er** (-gärt'n-ər). **1.** A child who attends kindergarten. **2.** A teacher in a kindergarten.

kind·heart·ed (kīnd'här'tĭd) *adj.* Having or proceeding from a kind heart; sympathetic; generous; helpful. See Synonyms at **kind.** —**kind'heart'ed·ly** *adv.* —**kind'heart'ed·ness** *n.*

kin·dle¹ (kĭnd'l) *v.* **-dled, -dling, -dles.** —*tr.* **1. a.** To build or fuel (a fire); to start; tend. **b.** To set fire to; ignite. **2.** To cause to glow; light up: *The sunset kindled the skies.* **3. a.** To inflame; make ardent. **b.** To arouse; inspire: *"no spark had yet kindled in him an intellectual passion"* (George Eliot). —*intr.* **1.** To catch fire; burst into flame. **2.** To become bright; to glow. **3. a.** To become inflamed. **b.** To be stirred up; rise. [Middle English *kind(e)len,* from Old Norse *kynda,* to kindle, catch fire (but influenced in form by Old Norse *kyndill,* torch), akin to Middle High German *künden*†, to set on fire.] —**kin'dler** *n.*

kin·dle² (kĭnd'l) *n.* A brood or litter, especially of kittens. See Synonyms at **flock.** [Middle English *kindle,* perhaps from *kinde,* a KIND.]

kind·less (kīnd'lĭs) *adj.* **1.** Heartless. **2.** *Obsolete.* Inhuman.

kind·li·ness (kīnd'lē-nĭs) *n.* **1.** The quality of being kindly. **2.** A kindly deed; a good turn; kindness.

kin·dling (kĭnd'lĭng) *n.* Easily ignited material, such as dry sticks of wood, used to start a fire.

kindling point. **Ignition point** *(see).*

kind·ly (kīnd'lē) *adj.* **-lier, -liest. 1.** Expressive of a sympathetic, helpful, or benevolent nature or impulse: *a kindly interest.* **2.** Characterizing a person who customarily shows kindness: *a gentle, kindly soul.* **3.** Agreeable; pleasant. **4.** *Archaic.* Natural to its kind. —See Synonyms at **kind.** —*adv.* **1.** Out of kindness: *He kindly overlooked their mistake.* **2.** In a kind manner; graciously; cordially: *She spoke kindly to him.* **3.** Pleasantly; agreeably: *The sun shone kindly.* **4.** Please; accommodatingly. Often used to imply formality, tolerance, or impatience: *Would you kindly refrain from doing that?* **5.** *Obsolete.* In a way or course that is natural; fittingly. —**take kindly (of).** To accept pleasantly or as well-intentioned: *I take it kindly of you.* —**take kindly to. 1.** To be receptive to: *take kindly to new methods.* **2.** To be naturally attracted or fitted to; thrive on.

kind·ness (kīnd'nĭs) *n.* **1.** The quality or state of being kind: *We relied upon their kindness.* **2.** An instance of kind behavior.

kin·dred (kĭn'drĭd) *n.* **1.** A group of related persons; a family, clan, tribe, or the like. **2.** A person's relatives; kinsfolk; family. —*adj.* **1.** Of the same ancestry or family: *kindred clans.* **2.** Having a similar or related origin, nature, character, or the like: *"The youth studied the faces of his companions, ever on the watch to detect kindred emotions"* (Stephen Crane). [Middle English *kin(d)red(e), kinraden* : KIN + *-rede,* from Old English *rǣden,* condition, rule, from *rǣdan,* to advise, rule, read (see **ar-** in Appendix*).] —**kin'dred·ness** *n.*

kine. *Archaic.* Plural of **cow.**

kin·e·mat·ics (kĭn'ə-măt'ĭks) *n.* Plural in form, used with a singular verb. *Physics.* The study of motion exclusive of the influences of mass and force. [From Greek *kinēma* (stem *kinēmat-*), motion, from *kinein,* to move. See **kei-³** in Appendix.*]

kin·e·scope (kĭn'ə-skōp') *n.* **1.** A cathode-ray tube in a television receiver that translates received electrical signals into a visible picture on a luminescent screen. **2.** A film of a transmitted television program. [KINE(TIC) + -SCOPE.]

-kinesis. Indicates: **1.** Division; for example, **cytokinesis. 2.** Movement or motion; for example, **photokinesis.** [New Latin, from Greek *kinēsis,* movement, from *kinein,* to move. See **kinetic.**]

kin·es·the·sia (kĭn'əs-thē'zhə) *n.* Also **kin·aes·the·sia, kin·aes·the·sis** (-sĭs). The sensation of bodily position, presence, or movement resulting chiefly from stimulation of sensory nerve endings in muscles, tendons, and joints. [Greek *kinēma,* motion (see **kinematics**) + ESTHESIA.]

ki·net·ic (kĭ-nĕt'ĭk) *adj.* Of, relating to, or produced by motion. [Greek *kinētikos,* from *kinētos,* moving, from *kinein,* to move. See **kei-³** in Appendix.*]

kinetic energy. Energy associated with motion, equal for a body in pure translational motion at nonrelativistic speeds to one-half the product of its mass and the square of its speed. Compare **potential energy.**

ki·net·ics (kĭ-nĕt'ĭks) *n.* Plural in form, used with a singular verb. *Physics.* **1.** The study of all aspects of motion, comprising both kinematics and dynamics. **2.** The study of the relationship between motion and the forces affecting motion.

kinetic theory. A theory of the thermodynamic behavior of matter, especially of pressure-volume-temperature relationships in gases, based in its simplest form on the identification of heat with the kinetic energy of a substance's rapid, randomly moving molecules and on a classical dynamic analysis of molecular motion under simplifying assumptions including the conservation of energy and momentum in all collisions and the applicability of statistical analysis for large numbers of molecules.

kin·folk, kin·folks. Variants of **kinsfolk.**

king (kĭng) *n.* **1.** *Abbr.* **k, K.** A male monarch. **2.** One that is the most powerful or eminent of a particular group, category, or place. **3.** *Capital* **K.** God or Christ. **4.** *Abbr.* **K.** A playing card bearing a picture of a king. **5.** *Chess. Abbr.* **K** The principal piece, capable of being moved one square in any direction. **6.** *Checkers.* A piece that has reached the opponent's side of the board and been crowned. [Middle English *king,* Old English *cyning.* See **gene-** in Appendix.*]

King (kĭng), **Martin Luther, Jr.** 1929–1968. American Baptist minister and civil-rights leader; awarded Nobel Peace Prize (1964); assassinated.

King (kĭng), **William Lyon Mackenzie.** 1874–1950. Prime minister of Canada (1921–26, 1926–30, and 1935–48).

King (kĭng), **William Rufus DeVane.** 1786–1853. Vice President of the United States under Franklin Pierce (1853).

king·bird (kĭng'bûrd') *n.* Any of various chiefly gray New World birds of the genus *Tyrannus,* especially *T. tyrannus.*

king·bolt (kĭng'bōlt') *n.* A vertical bolt used for such purposes as joining the body of a wagon to the front axle, and usually serving as a pivot. Also called "kingpin."

King Charles spaniel. A variety of toy spaniel having a curly black and tan coat and long ears. [After King CHARLES II of England.]

king cobra. A large venomous snake, *Ophiophagus hannah,* of tropical Asia. Also called "hamadryad."

king crab. 1. A large crab, *Paralithodes camtschatica,* of coastal waters of Alaska, Japan, and Siberia, valued commercially for its edible flesh. **2.** A marine arthropod, the **horseshoe crab** *(see).*

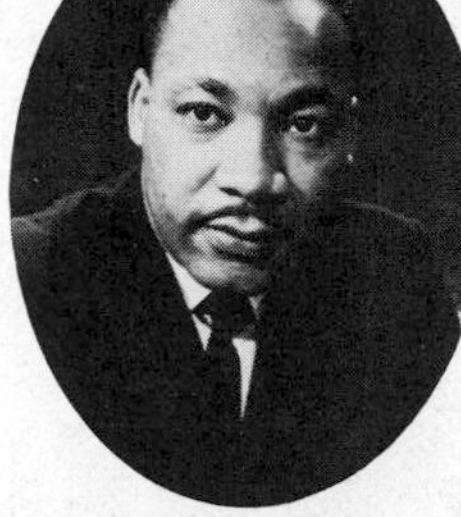

Martin Luther King, Jr.

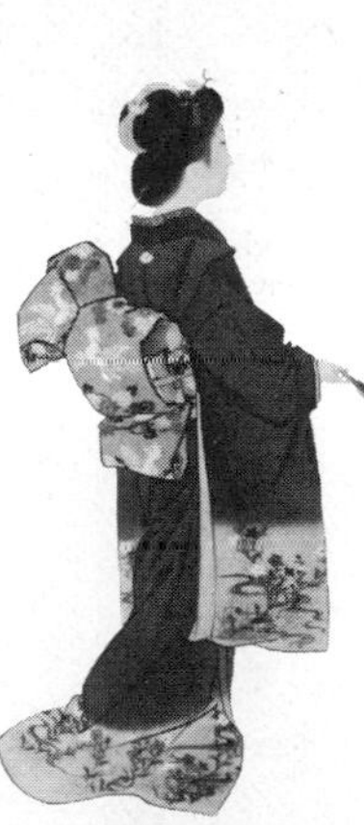

kimono

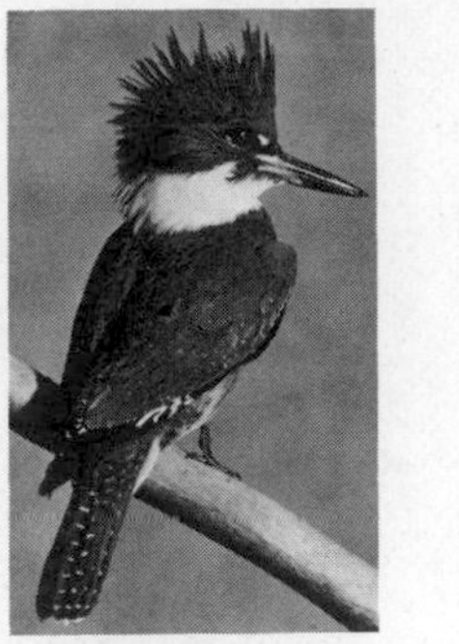

kingfisher
Megaceryle alcyon

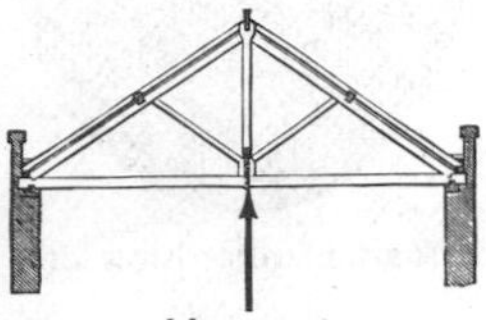

king post

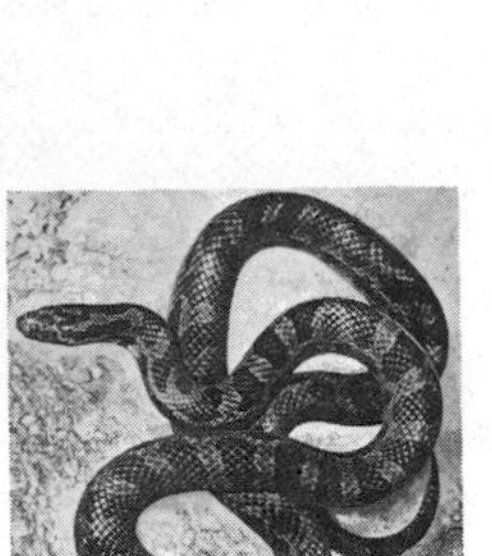

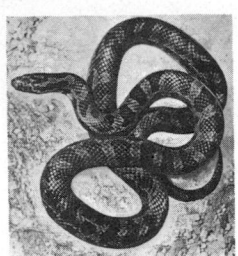

king snake
Lampropeltis calligaster

king·craft (kĭng′krăft′, -kräft′) *n.* The art, style, or method used by a king to rule.
king·cup (kĭng′kŭp′) *n. Chiefly British.* Any of several plants having yellow flowers; especially, the **marsh marigold** *(see).*
king·dom (kĭng′dəm) *n.* **1.** A government, country, state, or population that is nominally or actually ruled by a king or queen. **2. a.** The eternal spiritual sovereignty of God. **b.** The realm over which this sovereignty extends. **3.** An area, province, or realm in which one thing is dominant: *the kingdom of the imagination.* **4. a.** The broadest, most inclusive taxonomic category of organisms having certain basic characteristics: *the animal kingdom; the plant kingdom.* **b.** Any such large general category of natural forms: *the mineral kingdom.* [Middle English *kingdom,* Old English *cyningdōm* : KING + -DOM.]
king·fish (kĭng′fĭsh′) *n., pl.* **kingfish** or **-fishes.** **1.** Any of several food and game fishes of the genus *Menticirrhus,* of warm Atlantic waters. **2.** Any of several similar or related fishes. **3.** *Informal.* Any pre-eminent or powerful person; especially, a prominent political leader.
king·fish·er (kĭng′fĭsh′ər) *n.* Any of various birds of the family Alcedinidae, characteristically having a crested head. [Originally *king's fisher,* Middle English *kyngys fischare.*]
King George's Falls. The former name for **Aughrabies Falls.**
King James Bible. An Anglican translation of the Bible from Hebrew and Greek into English published in 1611 under the auspices of James I. Also called "Authorized Version," "King James Version."
King Lear. See **Lear.**
king·let (kĭng′lĭt) *n.* Either of two small, grayish North American birds, ***Regulus satrapa*** or *R. calendula,* having a yellowish or reddish patch on the crown of the head. [Diminutive of KING (from the patch on its crown).]
king·ly (kĭng′lē) *adj.* **-lier, -liest.** **1.** Having the status or rank of king. **2.** Relating to or suitable for a king; majestic; regal. *—adv.* As a king; regally; royally. **—king′li·ness** *n.*
king mackerel. A food and game fish, *Scomberomorus cavalla,* of warm Atlantic waters. Also called "cavalla," "cero."
king-of-arms (kĭng′əv-ärmz′) *n., pl.* **kings-of-arms.** The title of a high-ranking heraldic officer in England.
king·pin (kĭng′pĭn′) *n.* **1.** *Bowling.* The foremost or central pin of the arrangement of pins to be knocked down. Also called "head pin." **2.** The most important or essential person or thing. **3.** A **kingbolt** *(see).*
king post. Also **king·post** (kĭng′pōst′). A supporting post extending vertically from a crossbeam to the apex of a triangular truss. Compare **queen post.**
Kings (kĭngz) *n.* **1.** Either of the two Old Testament books, I Kings or II Kings, which tell the history of the kings of Israel and Judah. **2.** A group of four books, I, II, III, and IV Kings, in the Douay version of the Old Testament corresponding to I Samuel, II Samuel, I Kings, and II Kings in the King James Bible.
King salmon. The **Chinook salmon** *(see).*
King's Counsel. *Abbr.* **K.C.** **1.** A group of pre-eminent barristers appointed to serve as counsel to the British crown. Also called "Queen's Counsel" during the reign of a queen. **2.** A member of this group of barristers.
King's English. A style of speaking or writing English that is held up as a standard when another style or usage is being disapproved. Usually used facetiously.
king's evidence. Evidence given for the crown by an accused person against an accomplice in a British legal proceeding. Also called "queen's evidence" during the reign of a queen.
king·ship (kĭng′shĭp′) *n.* **1.** The position, power, province, or prerogative of a king. **2.** The domain ruled by a king; a kingdom. **3.** The period or tenure of a king; reign. **4.** A monarchy.
Kings·ley (kĭngz′lē), **Charles.** 1819–1875. English author.
king snake. Any of various nonvenomous New World snakes of the genus *Lampropeltis,* having yellow or reddish markings.
Kings Peak. The highest (13,498 feet) of the Uinta Mountains and the highest point in the state of Utah.
Kings·ton (kĭngz′tən). **1.** A former administrative division of London, England, now part of **Kingston-on-Thames** *(see).* **2.** The capital of Jamaica, a seaport on the southeastern coast. Population, 123,000. **3.** A city of Ontario, Canada, at the northeastern end of Lake Ontario. Population, 53,000.
Kings·ton-on-Thames (kĭngz′tən-ŏn-tĕmz′). A borough of London, England, comprising the former administrative divisions of Kingston, of Maldens and Coombe, and of Surbiton. Population, 166,000.
Kings·ton-up·on-Hull. See **Hull.**
Kings·town (kĭngz′toun). The capital of St. Vincent, West Indies, a seaport on the southwestern coast of the island. Population, 4,000.
King Wil·liam Island (wĭl′yəm). An island, 6,200 miles in area, of the Northwest Territories, Canada, lying southwest of the Boothia Peninsula.
king·wood (kĭng′wo͝od′) *n.* **1.** A South American tree, *Dalbergia cearensis,* having hard, fine-textured, purplish-brown wood used in cabinetmaking. **2.** The wood of this tree.
kink (kĭngk) *n.* **1.** A tight curl, as in a hair, or a sharp twist in a line or wire, typically caused by the tensing of a looped section. **2.** A painful muscle spasm, as in the neck or back; a crick. **3.** A slight difficulty or flaw, as in a plan or system. **4.** A quirk of personality. **5.** A clever idea for doing something. *—v.* **kinked, kinking, kinks.** *—tr.* To cause to have a kink or kinks. *—intr.* To form kinks. [Low German *kinke,* a twist in a rope, from Middle Low German *kinke*†.] **—kink′y** *adj.*
kink·a·jou (kĭng′kə-jo͞o′) *n.* An arboreal mammal, *Potos flavus,* of tropical America, having brownish fur and a long, prehensile tail. Also called "honey bear." [French *quincajou,* from Algonquian, akin to Ojibwa *quingwâage,* wolverine.]
Kin·men. The Chinese name for **Quemoy.**
Kin·ne·ret (kĭn-ĕ′rĕt). The Sea of Galilee. Also called "Yam Kinneret."
kin·ni·kin·nick (kĭn′ĭ-kĭ-nĭk′) *n.* Also **kin·ni·kin·nic, kil·li·ki·nick** (kĭl′-). **1.** A tobaccolike preparation made from the dried leaves or bark of various plants and used for smoking, especially by American Indians. **2.** A plant having leaves or bark used in such a preparation, such as the **bearberry** *(see).* [From Algonquian, akin to Natick *kinukkinuk,* mixture.]
ki·no (kē′nō) *n., pl.* **-nos.** A reddish resin obtained from several Old World tropical trees of the genera *Pterocarpus* and *Butea.* [A West African word, akin to Mandingo *keno.*]
Ki·no (kē′nō), **Eusebio Francisco.** 1645?–1711. Italian Jesuit missionary and explorer in the American Southwest.
Kin·ross (kĭn-rôs′). Also **Kin·ross·shire** (-rôs′shîr, -shər). A county, 82 square miles in area, in east-central Scotland. Population, 7,000.
Kin·sey (kĭn′zē), **Alfred Charles.** 1894–1956. American sociologist and biologist; studied human sexual behavior.
kins·folk (kĭnz′fōk′) *pl.n.* Also *informal* **kin·folk** (kĭn′-), **kin·folks** (kĭn′fōks). Members of a family; kindred.
Kin·sha·sa (kĭn-shä′sä). Formerly **Lé·o·pold·ville** (lē′ə-pōld-vĭl, lā′ō-pôld-vēl′). The capital of the Democratic Republic of the Congo, situated in the west on the Congo River opposite Brazzaville. Population, 1,000,000.
kin·ship (kĭn′shĭp′) *n.* **1.** The state of being kin or related by blood. **2.** An analogous relationship, as of cognate words.
kins·man (kĭnz′mən) *n., pl.* **-men** (-mĭn). **1.** A male blood relation or, loosely, a relation by marriage. **2.** Someone of the same racial, cultural, or national background. [Middle English *kynnes-man,* Old English *cynnes mannum* (dative) : *cynnes,* genitive of *cynn,* KIN + *mannum,* dative of *mann,* MAN.] **—kins′wo′man** *n.*
Ki·o·ga (kē-ō′gə). Also **Ky·o·ga.** A lake of eastern Africa, occupying about 1,000 square miles in south-central Uganda.
ki·osk (kē-ŏsk′, kē′ŏsk′) *n.* **1.** An open gazebo or pavilion. **2.** A small, sometimes ornamental, structure used as a newsstand, refreshment booth, or the like. **3.** A cylindrical structure, common on European sidewalks, on which advertisements are posted. [French *kiosque,* from Turkish *kōshk,* pavilion, from Persian *kūshk*†, palace.]
Kio·to. See **Kyoto.**
Ki·o·wa (kī′ō-wā′, -ə-wə) *n., pl.* **Kiowa** or **-was.** Also **Ki·o·way** (-ō-wā′). **1.** A member of a tribe of Plains Indians originally inhabiting parts of Colorado, Oklahoma, Kansas, New Mexico, and Texas. **2.** The Uto-Aztecan language of this tribe. [Kiowa *Gâ-i-gwŭ, Kâ-i-gwŭ,* "chief people."]
kip¹ (kĭp) *n., pl.* **kip.** The basic monetary unit of Laos, equal to 100 at. See table of exchange rates at **currency.** [Thai.]
kip² (kĭp) *n.* The untanned hide of a small or young animal, such as a calf. [Obsolete Dutch *kip,* bundle (of hides), from Middle Dutch, akin to Old Norse *kippi*†, bundle.]
kip³ (kĭp) *n. British Slang.* **1.** A rooming house. **2.** A room or bed in a rooming house. **3.** A bed. **4.** Sleep. *—intr.v.* **kipped, kipping, kips.** *British Slang.* To sleep. [Danish *kippe*†, cheap inn.]
kip⁴ (kĭp) *n.* A 1,000-pound unit of weight. [KI(LO)- + P(OUND).]
Kip·ling (kĭp′lĭng), **Rudyard.** 1865-1936. English author.
kip·per (kĭp′ər) *n.* **1.** A male salmon or sea trout in the spawning season. **2.** A herring that has been split, salted, and smoked. *—tr.v.* **kippered, -pering, -pers.** To cure (fish) in this manner. [Middle English *kypre,* Old English *cypera,* perhaps from *coper,* COPPER (from the color of the salmon).]
Kir·by-Smith (kûr′bē-smĭth′), **Edmund.** 1824–1893. American army officer; commanded Confederate troops in Civil War.
Kirch·hoff (kĭr′KHôf′), **Gustav Robert.** 1824–1887. German physicist; worked in spectrum analysis, optics, and electricity.
Kir·ghiz (kĭr-gēz′) *n., pl.* **Kirghiz** or **-ghizes** (-gē′zĭz). Also **Kir·giz.** **1.** One of a nomadic Mongolian people inhabiting the western part of Central Asia between the Volga and Irtish rivers. **2.** The Western Turkic language of these people.
Kir·ghiz Soviet Socialist Republic (kĭr-gēz′). Also **Kir·giz S.S.R.** A constituent republic of the Soviet Union, occupying 76,640 square miles in the south on the Chinese border.
Kir·ghiz Steppe (kĭr-gēz′). A large steppe area of the Soviet Union, in the central Kazakh S.S.R. Also called "The Steppes." Population, 2,318,000. Capital, Frunze.
ki·ri·ga·mi (kĭ′rĭ-gä′mē) *n.* The Japanese art of making ornamental designs by cutting and folding paper. Compare **origami.** [Japanese : *kiri,* to cut + *-gami,* from *kami,* paper.]
Ki·rin (kē′rĭn′). **1.** A province of China, occupying 72,000 square miles in the northeast. Population, 12,550,000. Capital, Ch'angchun. **2.** A city in this province, in the east-central part on the Sungari River. Population, 568,000.
kirk (kûrk) *n.* **1.** *Chiefly Scottish.* A church. **2.** *Capital* **K.** The Presbyterian Church of Scotland. So called in England. [Middle English *kirk(e),* from Old Norse *kirkja,* from Old English *cir(i)ce,* CHURCH.]
Kirk·cud·bright (kûr′kə-brē′). Also **Kirk·cud·bright·shire** (-brē′shîr, -shər). A county of Scotland, occupying 899 square miles in the southwest and forming part of Galloway district. Population, 28,000.
Kir·kuk (kĭr-ko͞ok′). A city of northeastern Iraq, in an oil-bearing region. Population, 177,000.

Kirk·wall (kûrk′wôl). The county seat of Orkney, Scotland, and chief town of the Orkney Islands. Population, 4,000.

Kir·man (kər-män′) *n.* Also **Ker·man.** A Persian rug with an elaborate border pattern and muted colors. [After *Kirman,* province of Iran, where such rugs were originally made.]

kir·mess. Variant of **kermis.**

Ki·rov (kē′rəf). A city of the Soviet Union, an industrial center 265 miles northeast of Gorkiy. Population, 284,000.

Ki·ro·va·bad (kĭ-rō′və-băd). Formerly **Gan·dzha** (gän′jä). A city of the Soviet Union, in northwestern Azerbaijan S.S.R. Population, 166,000.

kirsch (kîrsh) *n.* A colorless brandy made from the fermented juice of cherries. Also called "kirschwasser." [German *Kirsch(wasser),* "cherry (water)," from Old High German *kirsa,* cherry, from Vulgar Latin *cerasia* (unattested). See **cherry.**]

kir·tle (kûrt′l) *n. Archaic.* **1.** A knee-length tunic or coat for a man. **2.** A woman's long dress or skirt. [Middle English *ki(e)rtel, curtle,* Old English *cyrtel,* from Germanic *kurtilaz* (unattested), "short coat," diminutive of *kurt-* (unattested), short, from Latin *curtus,* cut short. See **sker-¹** in Appendix.*]

Ki·san·ga·ni (kē′säng-gä′nē). Formerly **Stan·ley·ville** (stăn′lē-vĭl). A city of the Democratic Republic of the Congo, in the northeast on the Congo River. Population, 127,000.

Ki·shi·nev (kĭsh′ĭ-nĕf, kĭ-shĭ-nyôf′). *Rumanian* **Chi·şi·nău** (kē′shē-nou′). The capital of the Moldavian S.S.R., a city in the center of the republic; formerly in Rumania (1918–40). Population, 282,000.

kish·ke (kĭsh′kə) *n.* A food, **derma** *(see).* [Yiddish, probably from Russian *kishka,* gut. See **skeu-** in Appendix.*]

Kis·ka (kĭs′kə). An island of Alaska, about 20 miles long, near the western end of the Aleutian chain; occupied by the Japanese in World War II (1942–43).

Kis·lev (kĭs-lĕf′, kĭs′lĕf) *n.* Also **Kis·lew.** The third month of the Hebrew year. See **calendar.** [Hebrew *kislēw,* from Akkadian *kislīmu, kislīwu.*]

kis·met (kĭz′mĭt, kĭs′-) *n.* Fate; fortune. [Turkish *kısmet,* from Arabic *qismah,* lot, from *qasama,* he divided, he allotted.]

kiss (kĭs) *v.* **kissed, kissing, kisses.** —*tr.* **1.** To touch or caress with the lips as a sign of sexual passion, affection, greeting, or respect. **2.** To touch lightly; brush against. —*intr.* To touch or caress someone or something with the lips. —*n.* **1.** A caress or touching with the lips. **2.** A slight or gentle touching. **3.** A small piece of candy, especially of chocolate. **4.** A baked confection made of meringue. [Middle English *kissen, cussen,* Old English *cyssan.* See **kus-** in Appendix.*]

kiss·er (kĭs′ər) *n.* **1.** A person who kisses. **2.** *Slang.* The mouth. **3.** *Slang.* The face.

kissing bug. An assassin bug, *Melanolestes picipes,* that inflicts a painful bite, often on the lips of a sleeping person.

kiss of death. That which is ruinous while superficially harmless. [From Judas' kiss that betrayed Jesus.]

kiss off. To dismiss; get rid of.

kiss-off (kĭs′ôf′, -ŏf′) *n.* A dismissal.

kist. Variant of **cist** (coffin).

Kist·na (kĭst′nə). Also **Krish·na** (krĭsh′-). A river of the Republic of India, rising in the Western Ghats and flowing 800 miles generally east to the Bay of Bengal.

kit¹ (kĭt) *n.* **1. a.** A set of instruments or equipment used for a specific purpose: *a survival kit.* **b.** A container for such a set. **2.** A set of parts or materials to be assembled: *a model airplane kit.* **3.** A collection of personal effects, especially for travel; an outfit. **4.** A container such as a box, bag, valise, or knapsack. —**the whole kit and caboodle.** *Informal.* The entire collection or lot. [Middle English *kytt, kitt,* wooden tub, from Middle Dutch *kitte*†, jug, tankard.]

kit² (kĭt) *n.* A kitten or other young fur-bearing animal. [Short for KITTEN.]

kit³ (kĭt) *n.* A small three-stringed violin. [Perhaps shortened from Latin *cithara,* CITHER.]

Ki·ta Ky·u·shu (kē′tä kyōō′shōō). A city of northern Kyushu, Japan, formed in 1963 by the merger of Kokura, Moji, Wakamatsu, Tobata, and Yahata. Population, 1,700,000.

kitch·en (kĭch′ən) *n.* **1.** A room or area in which food is cooked or prepared. **2.** The facilities and equipment used in the preparation and serving of food. **3.** A department that prepares, cooks, and serves food. [Middle English *kichene, kuchene,* Old English *cycene,* from West Germanic *kocina* (unattested), from Late Latin *coquina,* from Latin, feminine of *coquīnus,* of cooking, from *coquere,* to cook. See **pekw-** in Appendix.*]

kitch·en·er (kĭch′ə-nər) *n.* **1.** A kitchen manager, especially in a monastery. **2.** *British.* A large cooking stove.

Kitch·e·ner (kĭch′ə-nər). A city of Canada, in Ontario, about 55 miles west of Toronto. Population, 60,000.

Kitch·e·ner (kĭch′ə-nər), **Horatio Herbert.** First Earl Kitchener of Khartoum. 1850–1916. British military leader and colonial official in Africa and India.

kitch·en·ette (kĭch′ə-nĕt′) *n.* A small kitchen.

kitchen garden. A garden in which vegetables and fruits are grown for household consumption.

kitchen midden. A refuse heap or mound of the Mesolithic or later periods, containing numerous artifacts, shells, and often animal bones. [Translation of Danish *køkkenmødding.*]

kitchen police. *Abbr.* **KP, K.P.** *Military.* **1.** Enlisted men assigned to work in the kitchen. **2.** The work of this assignment.

kitch·en·ware (kĭch′ən-wâr′) *n.* Utensils for use in the kitchen, such as pots and pans.

kite (kīt) *n.* **1.** A flying toy made up of one or more cloth or paper surfaces stretched over a flexible framework, designed to climb and hover in a steady breeze at the end of a long string. **2.** Any of the light sails of a ship, used in a light wind. **3.** Any of various predatory birds of the subfamilies Milvinae and Elaninae, having a long, often forked tail. **4.** In business, any negotiable paper representing a fictitious transaction, as a bad check, used temporarily to sustain credit or raise money. —*v.* **kited, kiting, kites.** —*intr.* **1.** To fly like a kite; soar or glide. **2.** In business, to get money or credit through kites. —*tr.* In business, to issue as a kite. [Middle English *kyte, kete,* kite (bird), Old English *cȳta,* from Common German *kūtja-* (unattested), probably imitative of its cry.]

kith (kĭth) *n.* Friends and neighbors. Now used only in the phrase *kith and kin.* [Middle English *kith, kyth,* Old English *cȳth(the), cȳththu,* "knowledge," "acquaintance," friend. See **gnō-** in Appendix.*]

Ki·thi·ra. The modern Greek name for **Cythera.**

Kitt·a·tin·ny Mountain (kĭt′ə-tĭn′ē). A mountain ridge of the Appalachians, extending from southeastern New York State into northwestern New Jersey along the Delaware River and into Pennsylvania. Highest elevation, about 1,800 feet.

kit·ten (kĭt′n) *n.* A young cat. —*intr.v.* **kittened, -tening, -tens.** To bear kittens. [Middle English *kitoun,* from Old North French *caton* (unattested), diminutive of *cat,* cat, from Late Latin *cattus,* CAT.]

kit·ten·ish (kĭt′n-ĭsh) *adj.* Playful; flirtatious; coy. —**kit′ten·ish·ly** *adv.* —**kit′ten·ish·ness** *n.*

kit·ti·wake (kĭt′ē-wāk′) *n.* Either of two gulls, *Rissa tridactyla* or *R. brevirostris,* of northern regions. [Imitative of its cry.]

kit·tle (kĭt′l) *adj. Scottish.* Unpredictable; capricious; touchy. [From Scottish *kittle,* to tickle, Middle English (Scottish) *kytyllen,* probably from Old Norse *kitla.* See **tit-** in Appendix.*]

kit·ty¹ (kĭt′ē) *n., pl.* **-ties. 1.** An extra hand or part of a hand in some card games to be used by the highest bidder. **2.** A fund made up of a portion of each player's winnings in a card game, used to pay the game expenses. **3.** Any pool of money or things. [Originally "small bowl," diminutive of KIT (tub).]

kit·ty² (kĭt′ē) *n., pl.* **-ties.** *Informal.* A kitten or cat. [From *kit,* short for KITTEN.]

kit·ty-cor·nered (kĭt′ē-kôr′nərd) *adj.* Cater-cornered.

Kitty Hawk. A village in northeastern North Carolina; the site of the first successful flight of a power-driven airplane, made by Orville and Wilbur Wright (1903).

Kiu·shu. See **Kyushu.**

ki·va (kē′və) *n.* An underground or partly underground room in a Pueblo Indian village, used by the men especially for ceremonies or councils. [Hopi.]

Ki·vu, Lake (kē′vōō). A lake occupying 1,100 square miles in east-central Africa, just north of Lake Tanganyika.

Ki·wa·ni·an (kĭ-wä′nē-ən, kĭ-wô′-) *n.* A member of Kiwanis. —*adj.* Of or pertaining to Kiwanis.

Ki·wa·nis (kĭ-wä′nĭs, kĭ-wô′-) *n.* An organization of men's clubs throughout North America founded in Detroit in 1915 to promote community service and higher standards of business and professional ethics. Also called "Kiwanis Clubs."

ki·wi (kē′wē) *n.* **1.** Any of several flightless birds of the genus *Apteryx,* of New Zealand, having vestigial wings and a long, slender bill. **2.** A vine, *Actinidia chinensis,* native to Asia, bearing fuzzy, edible fruit. In this sense, also called "Chinese gooseberry." [Maori, imitative of its cry.]

Kiz·il·Ir·mak (kĭ-zĭl′ĭr-mäk′). Ancient name **Ha·lys** (hā′lĭs). A river rising in the mountains of central Turkey and flowing 715 miles first southwest and then northeast to the Black Sea.

Kjö·len (chœ′lən). A mountain range along the northern border between Sweden and Norway. Highest elevation, 6,963 feet.

K.K.K. Ku Klux Klan.

Klai·pe·da (klī′pə-də). *German* **Mem·el** (mā′məl). A city and seaport on the Baltic in the western Lithuanian S.S.R. Population, 89,000.

Klam·ath Mountains (klăm′əth). A mountain range of northwestern California and southwestern Oregon. Highest elevation, 8,038 feet, in California.

Klam·ath River (klăm′əth). A river rising in southern Oregon and flowing 263 miles generally southwest through northern California to the Pacific.

Klan (klăn) *n.* The **Ku Klux Klan** *(see).*

Klans·man (klănz′mən) *n., pl.* **-men** (-mĭn). A member of the Ku Klux Klan.

Klap·roth (kläp′rōt′), **Martin Heinrich.** 1743–1817. German analytical chemist.

Klau·sen·burg. The German name for **Cluj.**

klav·ern (klăv′ərn) *n.* A local organizational unit of the Ku Klux Klan. [KL(AN) + (C)AVERN.]

Klax·on (klăk′sən) *n.* A trademark for a loud horn formerly used on automobiles. [From Greek *klazein,* to roar. See **klēg-** in Appendix.*]

Klee (klā, klē), **Paul.** 1879–1940. Swiss painter.

Kleen·ex (klē′nĕks′) *n.* A trademark for a soft cleansing tissue.

Klein bottle (klīn). A one-sided topological surface having no inside or outside, formed by inserting the small open end of a tapered tube through the side of the tube and making it contiguous with the larger open end. [After Felix *Klein* (1849–1925), German mathematician.]

klep·to·ma·ni·a (klĕp′tə-mā′nē-ə) *n.* Also **clep·to·ma·ni·a.** An obsessive impulse to steal, especially in the absence of economic necessity or personal desire. [New Latin : Greek *kleptein,* to steal (see **klep-** in Appendix*) + -MANIA.] —**klep′to·ma′ni·ac′** *n.*

klieg light (klēg). A powerful carbon-arc lamp producing an intense light, used especially in making movies. [Invented by the brothers John H. Kliegl (1869–1959) and Anton T. *Kliegl* (1872–1927), American lighting experts.]

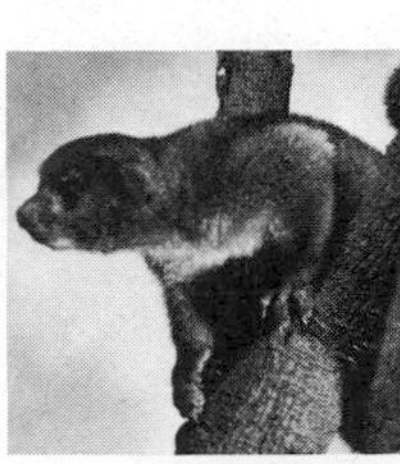

kinkajou

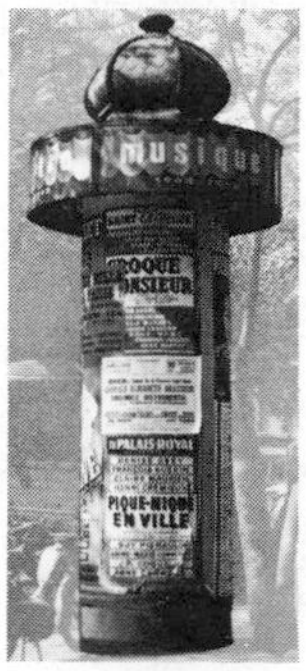

kiosk
Paris, France

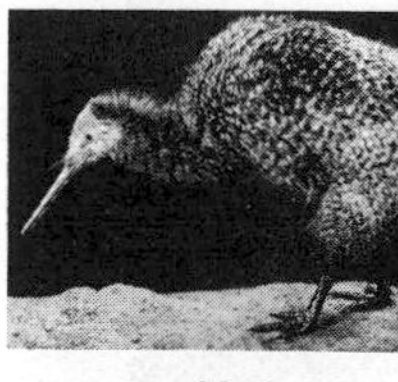

kiwi
Apteryx australis

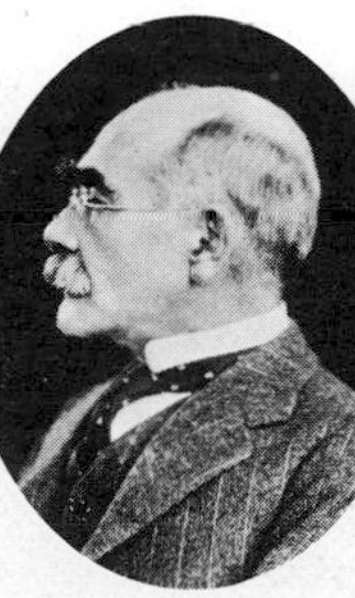

Rudyard Kipling

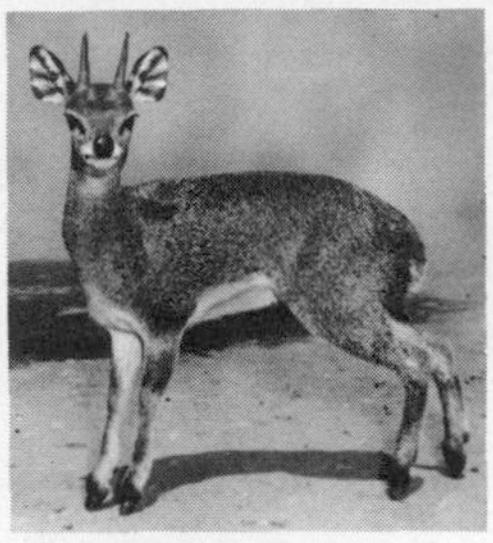
klipspringer

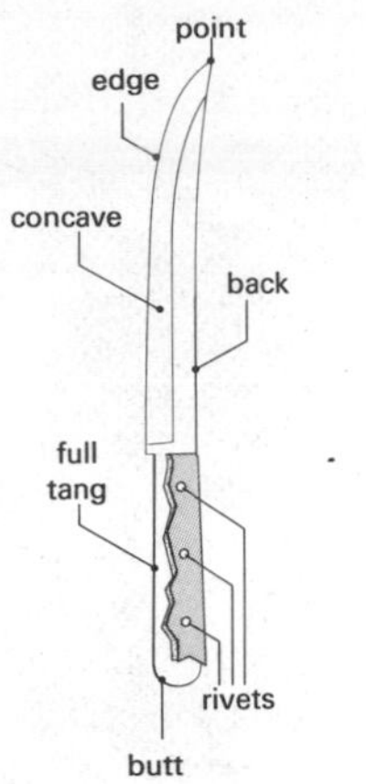
point
edge
concave
back
full
tang
rivets
butt
knife

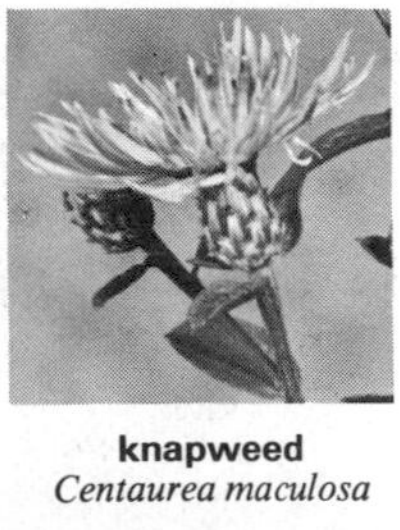
knapweed
Centaurea maculosa

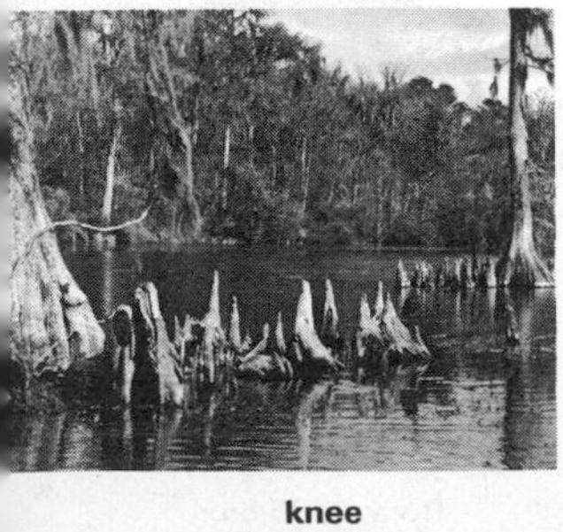
knee
Cypress knees

klip·spring·er (klĭp′sprĭng′ər) *n.* A small, hoofed African mammal, *Oreotragus oreotragus,* having large ears. [Afrikaans, "cliff springer" : Dutch *klip,* cliff, from Middle Dutch *klippe,* from Germanic *klibam* (unattested), CLIFF + *springer,* from *springen,* to leap, from Middle Dutch (see **spergh-** in Appendix*).]

Klon·dike (klŏn′dīk′). A region in the Yukon Territory, northwestern Canada; the site of abundant gold deposits on both sides of the Klondike River, a tributary of the Yukon.

kloof (kloof) *n.* In South Africa, a deep ravine. [Afrikaans, from Dutch, from Middle Dutch *clove,* cleft. See **gleubh-** in Appendix*.]

klutz (klŭts) *n. Slang.* A clumsy or dull-witted person. [German *Klotz,* clod, "block," from Middle High German *kloz,* block, lump. See **gel-**[1] in Appendix.*]

klys·tron (klĭs′trŏn′, -trən, klī′strŏn′, -strən) *n.* An electron tube used to amplify or generate radio waves of microwave range frequencies by means of velocity modulation. [Greek *klustēr,* syringe, clyster pipe, from *kluzein,* to wash out (see **kleu-**[2] in Appendix*) + (ELECTR)ON.]

km kilometer.

kn. **1.** knot. **2.** krona. **3.** krone.

knack (năk) *n.* **1.** A clever, expedient way of doing something. **2.** A specific talent for something, especially one difficult to explain or teach. **3.** *Rare.* A trinket; knickknack. **—get the knack of.** To learn how to do skillfully and quickly. [Middle English *knak(ke),* probably identified with *knak,* sharp blow, from Dutch and Low German *knak.* See **gen-** in Appendix.*]

knack·er (năk′ər) *n. British.* **1.** A person who buys useless or worn-out livestock and sells the meat or hides. **2.** A person who buys up discarded structures and dismantles them to sell the materials. [Originally "harness maker," saddler, probably from Scandinavian, akin to Old Norse *hnakkur,* saddle. See **ken-**[5] in Appendix.*] **—knack′er·y** *n.*

knack·wurst (nŏk′wûrst′, -wŏŏrst′) *n.* Also **knock·wurst.** A short, thick sausage resembling a frankfurter. [German *Knackwurst,* "sausage whose skin cracks open when bitten" : *knacken,* to crack, from Middle High German (see **gen-** in Appendix*) + *Wurst,* sausage, WURST.]

knap[1] (năp) *v.* **knapped, knapping, knaps.** *British Regional.* **—tr.** **1.** To strike sharply; to rap. **2.** To break or chip with a sharp blow, as flints. **3.** To snap at or bite. **—intr.** **1.** To strike sharply. **2.** To break stones by striking sharply. **3.** To snap or bite; to nibble. [Middle English *knappen,* probably from Low German, akin to Middle Dutch *cnappen,* Low German *knappen.* See **gen-** in Appendix.*]

knap[2] (năp) *n. Regional.* The crest of a hill; summit. [Middle English *knap,* Old English *cnæpp.* See **gen-** in Appendix.*]

knap·sack (năp′săk′) *n.* A case or bag, usually of canvas or leather, worn on the back to carry supplies and equipment, especially on a hike or march. [Low German *knappsack* : probably *knappen,* to snap, bite, eat (see **gen-** in Appendix*) + *sack,* bag, from Middle Low German, from Germanic, from Latin *saccus,* SACK (bag).]

knap·weed (năp′wēd′) *n.* Any of various plants of the genus *Centaurea,* having purplish, thistlelike flowers. [Middle English *knopwed* : KNOP (from the knobby head of its flower) + WEED.]

knar (när) *n.* A knot or burl on a tree or in wood. [Middle English *knarre,* probably from Scandinavian, akin to Norwegian *knart.* See **gen-** in Appendix.*]

knave (nāv) *n.* **1.** An unprincipled, crafty man: *knaves and fools.* **2.** *Archaic.* A male servant. **3.** *Card Games.* The jack. [Middle English *knave,* Old English *cnafa,* boy, lad, from Common Germanic *knabōn-* (unattested).]

knav·er·y (nā′və-rē) *n., pl.* **-ies.** **1.** Dishonest or crafty dealing. **2.** A piece of mischief or trickery.

knav·ish (nā′vĭsh) *adj.* Like or characteristic of a knave; roguish; unprincipled. **—knav′ish·ly** *adv.* **—knav′ish·ness** *n.*

knawel (nôl) *n.* A low-growing, weedy plant, *Scleranthus annuus,* native to Eurasia, having narrow leaves and inconspicuous green flowers. [German *Knäuel,* knot, knob, ball of yarn, from Middle High German *kniuwel, kliuwel(in),* from Old High German *kliuwilin,* from *kliuwa,* ball. See **gel-**[1] in Appendix.*]

knead (nēd) *tr.v.* **kneaded, kneading, kneads.** **1.** To mix and work (a substance) into a uniform mass, especially to fold, press, and stretch dough with the hands. **2.** To make (bread) by kneading. **3.** To squeeze, press, or roll with the hands, as in massaging. [Middle English *kneden,* Old English *cnedan.* See **gen-** in Appendix.*] **—knead′er** *n.*

knee (nē) *n.* **1.** *Anatomy.* The joint or region of the human leg that is the articulation for the tibia, fibula, and patella. **2.** A corresponding joint of a leg of other animals, as in the forelimb of a hoofed animal. **3.** One of the woody projections arising from the roots of the bald cypress and emerging above the surface of the water of a swamp or pond. [Middle English *kne(e), kn(e)ow,* Old English *cnēo.* See **genu-**[1] in Appendix.*]

knee action. An automotive front-wheel suspension that permits independent vertical motion of each wheel.

knee breeches. Breeches extending to just below the knee.

knee·cap (nē′kăp′) *n.* **1.** A bone, the **patella** *(see).* Also called "kneepan." **2.** A kneepad.

knee-deep (nē′dēp′) *adj.* **1.** As high as the knees; reaching to the knees; knee-high. **2.** Submerged to the knees. **3.** Deeply occupied or engaged.

knee-high (nē′hī′) *adj.* As tall or high as the knee.

knee·hole (nē′hōl′) *n.* A space or opening for the knees, as under a desk or counter.

knee jerk. A sudden, involuntary kick forward produced by a smart tap to the tendon below the patella as the leg hangs relaxed forming a right angle with the thigh.

kneel (nēl) *intr.v.* **knelt** (nĕlt) or **kneeled, kneeling, kneels.** To fall or rest on bent knees. [Middle English *kne(w)len,* Old English *cnēowlian.* See **genu-**[1] in Appendix.* Knelt (past tense and past participle) is an analogous formation after FEEL, FELT.]

kneel·er (nē′lər) *n.* **1.** One who kneels. **2.** Something to kneel on, such as a stool, cushion, or board.

knee·pad (nē′păd′) *n.* A protective covering for the knee.

knell (nĕl) *v.* **knelled, knelling, knells.** **—intr.** **1.** To ring or sound a bell, especially for a funeral; to toll. **2.** To sound mournfully or ominously. **—tr.** To signal, summon, or proclaim by tolling. **—n.** **1.** The slow, solemn sounding of a bell; passing bell; a toll. **2.** An omen or signal of sorrow or death. **3.** Any deep, mournful sound. [Middle English *knillen, knellen,* Old English *cnyllan.* See **gen-** in Appendix.*]

Knes·set (knĕs′ĕt′) *n.* The Israeli parliament. [Hebrew (Mishnaic) *Kəneseth,* "assembly," from *kānas,* he gathered.]

knew. Past tense of **know.**

Knick·er·bock·er (nĭk′ər-bŏk′ər) *n.* **1.** A descendant of the Dutch settlers of New York. **2.** A New Yorker. [From Diedrich *Knickerbocker,* fictitious Dutch settler and pretended author of Washington Irving's *History of New York* (1809).]

knick·er·bock·ers (nĭk′ər-bŏk′ərz) *pl.n.* Full breeches gathered and banded just below the knee. Also called "knickers." [Supposed to have been worn by Dutch settlers.]

knick·ers (nĭk′ərz) *pl.n.* **1.** Long bloomers formerly worn as underwear by women and girls. **2.** **Knickerbockers** *(see).*

knick·knack (nĭk′năk′) *n.* Also **nick·nack.** A small, ornamental article; trinket. [Reduplication of KNACK (device).]

knife (nīf) *n., pl.* **knives** (nīvz). **1.** A cutting instrument consisting of a sharp blade with a handle. **2.** Any cutting edge or blade. **—v.** **knifed, knifing, knifes.** **—tr.** **1.** To use a knife on, especially to cut, stab, or wound. **2.** *Informal.* To hurt, defeat, or betray by underhand means. **—intr.** To cut or slash a way through, with, or as with a knife. [Middle English *knyf, knif,* Old English *cnīf.* See **gen-** in Appendix.*]

knife-edge (nīf′ĕj′) *n.* **1.** The cutting edge of a blade. **2.** Any sharp, knifelike edge. **3.** A wedge of metal used as a low-friction fulcrum for a balancing beam or lever.

knight (nīt) *n. Abbr.* **k., K., Knt, Kt** **1.** A medieval tenant giving military service as a mounted man-at-arms to a feudal landholder. **2.** A medieval gentleman-soldier, usually of high birth, raised by a sovereign to privileged military status after training as a page and squire. **3.** The holder of a nonhereditary dignity conferred by a sovereign in recognition of personal merit or services rendered to the country. **4.** A member of any of several orders or brotherhoods that call their members *knights.* **5. a.** A defender, champion, or zealous upholder of a cause or principle. **b.** The devoted champion of a lady. **6.** *Abbr.* **N** A chess piece usually representing a horse's head and able to be moved two squares horizontally and one vertically, or two vertically and one horizontally. **—tr.v.** **knighted, knighting, knights.** To raise (a person) to knighthood; make a knight. [Middle English *cniht, knyght,* Old English *cniht,* originally "boy," "lad," "servant," from West Germanic *knihtas* (unattested).]

knight banneret. See **banneret.**

knight errant *pl.* **knights errant.** **1.** A knight of medieval romance who wandered in search of adventure. **2.** One given to adventurous or quixotic conduct. **—knight′-er′rant·ry** *n.*

knight·head (nīt′hĕd′) *n.* Either of two timbers rising from the keel of a sailing ship to support the inner end of the bowsprit. [They were sometimes adorned with a carved knight's head.]

knight·hood (nīt′hŏŏd′) *n.* **1.** The rank, profession, or dignity of a knight. **2.** The behavior of or qualities befitting a knight; chivalry. **3.** Knights as a body or class.

knight·ly (nīt′lē) *adj.* Of, pertaining to, or befitting a knight. **—knight′li·ness** *n.*

Knights of Columbus. *Abbr.* **K.C.** A benevolent society of Roman Catholic men, founded in the United States in 1882.

Knights of Malta. The religious and military order of Hospitalers.

Knights of Pythias. *Abbr.* **K.P.** A secret fraternal order founded in Washington, D.C., in 1864 for philanthropic purposes.

Knights of the Round Table. The knights of the court of King Arthur.

Knight Templar *pl.* **Knights Templars** (for sense 1) or **Knights Templar** (for sense 2). **1.** A member of an order of knights founded in 1119 to protect pilgrims in the Holy Land during the second Crusade and suppressed in 1312. Also called "Templar." **2.** A member of an order of Freemasons claiming descent from these medieval knights.

knish (knĭsh) *n.* A piece of dough stuffed with potato or other filling and baked or fried. [Yiddish, from Russian, akin to Ukrainian *knyš,* Polish *knysz*†.]

knit (nĭt) *v.* **knit** or **knitted, knitting, knits.** **—tr.** **1.** To make (a fabric or garment) by intertwining yarn or thread in a series of connected loops either on a machine or by hand with knitting needles. **2.** To make (yarn or thread) into a fabric or garment in this manner. **3.** To join closely; unite securely. **4.** To draw (the brows) together in wrinkles; to furrow. **—intr.** **1.** To make a fabric or garment by intertwining yarn or thread in connected loops. **2.** To come or grow together securely. **3.** To come together in wrinkles or furrows. **—n.** A fabric or garment made by knitting. [Middle English *knitten,* Old English *cnyttan,* to tie in a knot. See **gen-** in Appendix.*] **—knit′ter** *n.*

knit·ting (nĭt′ĭng) *n.* **1.** The process of producing something knitted. **2.** Knitted work.

ă pat/ā pay/âr care/ä father/b bib/ch church/d deed/ĕ pet/ē be/f fife/g gag/h hat/hw which/ĭ pit/ī pie/îr pier/j judge/k kick/l lid, needle/m mum/n no, sudden/ng thing/ŏ pot/ō toe/ô paw, for/oi noise/ou out/ŏŏ took/oo boot/p pop/r roar/s sauce/sh ship, dish/

knitting needle. A long, thin, pointed rod used in knitting.
knives. Plural of **knife.**
knob (nŏb) *n.* **1. a.** A rounded protuberance on a surface or extremity. **b.** A rounded handle or dial. **2.** A prominent rounded hill or mountain. [Middle English *knobbe,* from Middle Low German, tree knot, knob. See **gen-** in Appendix.*] **—knobbed** *adj.* **—knob'by** *adj.*
knob·ker·rie (nŏb'kĕr'ē) *n.* A short club with one knobbed end, used as a weapon by South African tribesmen. [Afrikaans *knopkierie* : *knop,* knob, from Middle Dutch *cnoppe* (see **gen-** in Appendix*) + *kieri,* club, from Hottentot *kĭrri.*]
knock (nŏk) *v.* **knocked, knocking, knocks.** *—tr.* **1.** To strike with a hard blow; hit. **2.** To put into a specified place or condition with a blow: *knocked senseless.* **3.** To send into collision; cause to collide. **4.** To produce by hitting or striking: *She knocked a hole in the wall.* **5.** To instill with or as if with blows: *Try to knock some sense into his head.* **6.** *Slang.* To criticize adversely; disparage. *—intr.* **1.** To strike a blow or series of blows; to rap; to pound. **2.** To collide; to bump. **3.** To make the pounding or clanking noise of a laboring or defective engine. **—knock about** (or **around**). *Informal.* **1.** To be rough or brutal with; maltreat. **2.** To wander aimlessly from place to place. **3.** To discuss or consider. **—knock for a loop.** *Slang.* To surprise tremendously; astonish. **—knock off. 1.** *Informal.* **a.** To take a break or rest from; to stop. **b.** To cease work. **2.** *Informal.* To make, accomplish, or consume hastily or easily. **3.** *Informal.* To eliminate; deduct: *The grocer knocked off a little from the bill.* **4.** *Slang.* To kill. **5.** *Slang.* To hold up or burglarize. **—knock out of the box.** *Baseball.* To force the removal of (an opposing pitcher) by heavy hitting. **—knock together.** To make or assemble quickly or carelessly. **—knock up. 1.** *British Informal.* To gain the attention of or wake up by knocking at the door. **2.** *British Informal.* To exhaust; wear out. **3.** *Vulgar Slang.* To make pregnant. *—n.* **1.** An instance of knocking; a blow. **2.** The sound of a sharp tap on a hard surface; a rap. **3.** A pounding, clanking noise made by an engine, especially one in poor operating condition. **4.** *Slang.* A criticism or insult; a cutting remark. [Middle English *knokken,* Old English *cnocian.* See **gen-** in Appendix.*]
knock·a·bout (nŏk'ə-bout') *n. Nautical.* A small sloop with a mainsail, a jib, and a keel, but no bowsprit. *—adj.* **1.** Rough; boisterous; rowdy. **2.** Appropriate for rough wear or use.
knock down. 1. To disassemble into parts, as for storage or shipping. **2.** To declare as sold at an auction, as by striking a blow with a gavel. **3.** *Informal.* To reduce (a purchase price). **4.** *Slang.* To receive as wages; earn.
knock·down (nŏk'doun') *adj.* **1.** Strong enough to knock down or overwhelm; powerful. **2.** Designed to be assembled or disassembled quickly and easily: *knockdown furniture.* *—n.* **1.** The act of knocking down; a toppling or overwhelming. **2.** An overwhelming blow or shock. **3.** An apparatus designed to be easily and quickly assembled and disassembled.
knock·er (nŏk'ər) *n.* **1.** One that knocks; especially, a fixture used for knocking on a door. **2.** *Vulgar Slang.* A female breast.
knock-knee (nŏk'nē') *n.* An abnormal condition in which one knee is turned toward the other, or in which each is turned toward the other. **—knock'-kneed'** *adj.*
knock out. 1. To render unconscious. **2.** *Boxing.* To defeat (an opponent) by knocking him to the canvas for a count of ten. **3.** *Informal.* To defeat or overcome. **4.** *Informal.* To exert or exhaust (oneself or another) to the utmost.
knock·out (nŏk'out') *n.* **1.** A blow that induces unconsciousness. Also called "kayo." **2.** *Boxing.* The knocking out of an opponent. Also called "kayo." **3.** *Slang.* Something very impressive or attractive. *—adj.* Effecting a knockout.
knockout drops. *Slang.* A solution, as of chloral hydrate, put into a drink to render the drinker unconscious.
knock·wurst. Variant of **knackwurst.**
knoll[1] (nōl) *n.* A small rounded hill or mound; a hillock. [Middle English *knol(le),* Old English *cnoll.* See **gen-** in Appendix.*]
knoll[2] (nōl) *v.* **knolled, knolling, knolls.** *Archaic.* *—tr.* To knell. *—intr.* To toll. *—n. Archaic.* A knell. [Middle English *knollen,* probably variant of *knellen,* KNELL.]
knop (nŏp) *n. Archaic.* A decorative knob; a boss. [Middle English *knoppe,* probably from Middle Low German or Middle Dutch. See **gen-** in Appendix.*]
Knos·sos (nŏs'əs). Also **Cnos·sos.** A city of ancient Crete, metropolis of the Minoan civilization.
knot[1] (nŏt) *n.* **1.** A more or less complex, compact intersection of interlaced cord, ribbon, rope, or the like. **2.** A fastening made by tying together lengths, as of rope, in a prescribed way. **3.** A decorative bow of ribbon, fabric, or braid. **4.** Any tie or bond, especially a marriage bond. **5.** A tight cluster of persons or things. **6.** A difficulty; problem. **7. a.** A hard place or node, especially of a tree, at a point from which a stem or branch grows. **b.** The circular contrastingly dark-colored cross section of such a node as it appears cross-grained on a piece of cut lumber. **8.** A growth on or enlargement of a gland, muscle, or the like. **9.** *Nautical.* **a.** A division on a log line used to measure the speed of a ship. **b.** *Abbr.* **kn.** A unit of speed, one nautical mile per hour, about 1.15 statute miles per hour. **c.** A distance of one nautical mile. See Usage note below. **—tie the knot.** *Slang.* To get married. *—v.* **knotted, knotting, knots.** *—tr.* **1.** To tie in or fasten with a knot or knots. **2.** To entangle. **3.** To cause to form knots. *—intr.* **1.** To become snarled or entangled. **2.** To form a knot or knots. [Middle English *knot(te),* Old English *cnotta.* See **gen-** in Appendix.*]
Usage: In strict nautical usage, *knot* is a unit of speed, not of distance, and has a built-in sense of "per hour." Therefore a ship may be said to travel at ten knots (not knots per hour) and to cover ten nautical miles in an hour.
knot[2] (nŏt) *n.* Either of two shore birds, *Calidris canutus* or *C. tenuirostris,* related to the sandpipers. [Origin unknown.]
knot garden. A formal garden having the flower beds arranged in an intricate, usually geometrical pattern.
knot·grass (nŏt'grăs', -gräs') *n.* **1.** A low-growing, weedy plant *Polygonum aviculare,* having very small greenish flowers. Also called "allseed." **2.** Any of several similar plants.
knot·hole (nŏt'hōl') *n.* A hole in a piece of lumber where a knot has dropped out or been removed.
knot·ted (nŏt'ĭd) *adj.* **1.** Tied or fastened in or with a knot or knots. **2.** Intricate; knotty. **3.** Characterized by knots and knobs; gnarled: *a knotted branch.* **4. a.** Decorated with bosses. **b.** Laid out in the form of a knot garden.
knot·ty (nŏt'ē) *adj.* **-tier, -tiest. 1.** Tied or snarled in knots: *a knotty cord.* **2.** Covered with knots or knobs; gnarled: *a knotty board.* **3.** Difficult to understand or solve; intricate; puzzling. —See Synonyms at **complex.** **—knot'ti·ness** *n.*
knot·weed (nŏt'wēd') *n.* Any of several plants of the genus *Polygonum,* having jointed stems and inconspicuous flowers.
knout (nout) *n.* A leather scourge formerly used for flogging criminals in Russia. *—tr.v.* **knouted, knouting, knouts.** To flog with a knout. [French, from Russian *knut,* from Old Norse *knūtr,* knot. See **gen-** in Appendix.*]
know (nō) *v.* **knew** (nōō, nyōō), **known, knowing, knows.** *—tr.* **1.** To perceive directly with the senses or mind; apprehend with clarity or certainty: *"Wise Nicodemus saw such light/As made him know his God by night."* (Henry Vaughan). **2.** To be certain of; regard or accept as true beyond doubt. **3.** To be capable of; have the skill to. Used with *how: know how to swim.* **4.** To have a practical understanding of or thorough experience with. **5.** To be subjected to; to experience: *"a black stubble that had known no razor"* (Faulkner). **6.** To have firmly secured in the mind or memory. **7.** To be able to distinguish; recognize: *Do you know him from his twin brother?* **8.** To be acquainted or familiar with. **9.** *Archaic.* To have sexual intercourse with: *"And Adam knew Eve his wife; and she conceived"* (Genesis 4:1). *—intr.* **1.** To possess knowledge. **2.** To be cognizant or aware. **—in the know.** Possessing correct or secret information. [Know, knew, known; Middle English *knowen, knew, knowe(n),* Old English *(ge)cnāwan, (ge)cnēow, (ge)cnāwen.* See **gnō-** in Appendix.*] **—know'a·ble** *adj.* **—know'er** *n.*
Usage: *Know,* especially in negative constructions, is often followed by clauses introduced by *that, whether,* or *if,* but not by *as: I don't know that* (not *as*) *I can.*
know-how (nō'hou') *n. Informal.* Skill or ingenuity.
know·ing (nō'ĭng) *adj.* **1.** Possessing knowledge or understanding. **2.** Suggestive of secret or private information: *a knowing glance.* **3.** Clever; shrewd. **4.** Planned; deliberate. —See Synonyms at **intelligent.** **—know'ing·ly** *adv.* **—know'ing·ness** *n.*
know-it-all (nō'ĭt-ôl') *n. Informal.* A person who arrogantly claims to know everything.
knowl·edge (nŏl'ĭj) *n.* **1.** The state or fact of knowing. **2.** Familiarity, awareness, or understanding gained through experience or study. **3.** That which is known; the sum or range of what has been perceived, discovered, or inferred. **4.** Learning; erudition: *men of knowledge.* **5.** Specific information about something. **6.** *Obsolete.* Sexual intercourse; copulation. Now used only in the phrase *carnal knowledge.* [Middle English *knowlege, know(e)lech,* from *cnawlechen, know(e)lechen,* to confess, recognize, Old English *cnāwlǣcan* (unattested), from *cnāwan,* to KNOW.]
Synonyms: *knowledge, information, learning, erudition, lore, scholarship, wisdom, enlightenment.* These nouns refer to cognitive or intellective mental components acquired and retained through study and experience. *Knowledge* includes both empirical material and that derived by inference or interpretation. *Information* is usually construed as narrower in scope and implies a random collection of material rather than orderly synthesis. *Learning* usually refers to what is gained by schooling and study, and *erudition* adds to this the idea of profound knowledge often in a specialized area. *Lore* is knowledge gained by tradition or intuition rather than formally. The remaining terms refer to qualities possessed by persons rather than directly to what is stored in their minds. *Scholarship* is the distinctive mark of one who has mastered some area of learning, as reflected in the quality of his work, especially with respect to scope, thoroughness, and care. *Wisdom* involves sound judgment and the ability to apply what has been acquired mentally to the conduct of one's affairs. *Enlightenment* is the state of possessing knowledge and truth.
knowl·edge·a·ble (nŏl'ĭ-jə-bəl) *adj.* Well-informed.
known (nōn). Past participle of **know.** *—adj.* Proved, satisfactorily specified, or completely understood. *—n.* Something that is known, such as the presence of a certain substance or the occurrence of a certain event, especially in relation to one or more unknown factors.
know-noth·ing (nō'nŭth'ĭng) *n.* **1.** An ignoramus. **2.** An agnostic. **3.** An anti-intellectual.
Know-Noth·ing (nō'nŭth'ĭng) *n.* A member of an American political movement active in the 1850's that was antagonistic toward immigrants and Roman Catholics. *—adj.* Of or relating to this party or its policies. **—Know'-Noth'ing·ism'** *n.*
Knox (nŏks), **John.** 1505–1572. Scottish Protestant reformer, author, and political leader.
Knox·ville (nŏks'vĭl). A city of Tennessee, in the east on the Tennessee River. Population, 172,000.
Knt knight.

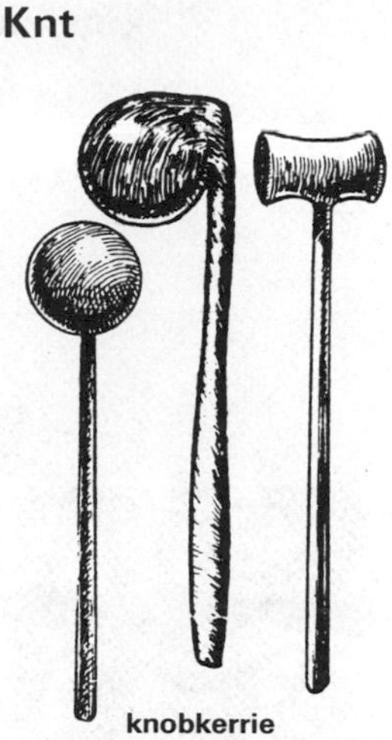
knobkerrie
Three types of knobkerrie

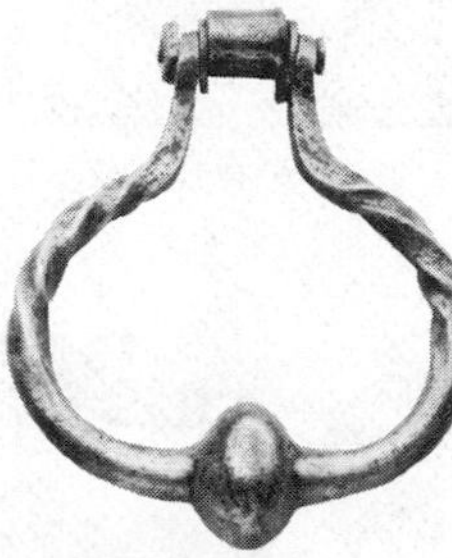
knocker
Mid-18th-century American

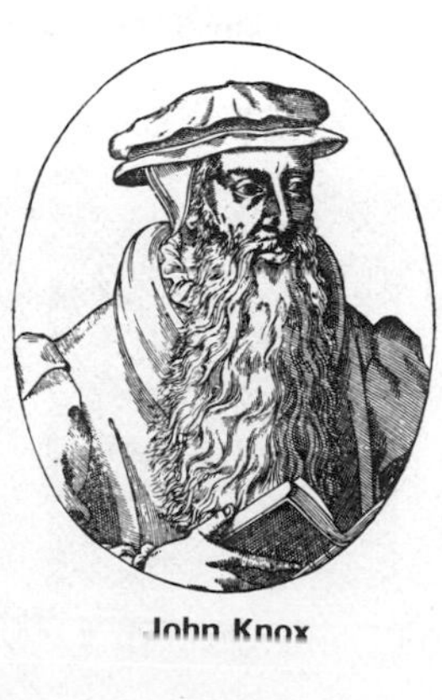
John Knox

knuck·le (nŭk′əl) n. **1.** Anatomy. **a.** Any joint or region around a joint of a finger, especially one of the joints connecting the fingers to the hand. **b.** Any of the rounded protuberances formed by the bones in such a joint. **2.** A cut of meat centering on the carpal joint, as of a pig. **3.** The part of a hinge through which the pin passes. **4.** Plural. **Brass knuckles** (see). —tr.v. **knuckled, -ling, -les. 1.** To press, rub, or hit with the knuckles of the fist: "They stared gaping, and knuckling their brows" (Mary Renault). **2.** To shoot (a marble) with the thumb over the bent forefinger. —**knuckle down.** To apply oneself earnestly to a task. —**knuckle under.** To yield to pressure; give in. [Middle English knokel, from Middle. Low German knökel. See gen- in Appendix.*]

knuckle ball. A typically slow, fluttering baseball pitch thrown by gripping the ball with the knuckles of two or three fingers. Also called "knuckler."

knuck·le·bone (nŭk′əl-bōn′) n. **1.** A knobbed bone, as of a knuckle or joint. **2.** Plural. A game formerly played by tossing such bones.

knuck·le·dust·ers (nŭk′əl-dŭs′tərz) pl.n. Slang. Brass knuckles.

knuckle joint. A hinged, flexible joint formed by the juncture of two rods or projections, one fitted within the other and the two locked by a pin that functions like an axle.

knur (nûr) n. A bump or knot, as on a tree trunk. [Middle English knorre, swelling, from Germanic, akin to Middle Low German and Middle High German knorre, knot, knob. See gen- in Appendix.*]

knurl (nûrl) n. **1.** A knob, knot, or similar protuberance. **2.** One of a series of small ridges or beads placed along the edge of a metal object such as a thumbscrew as an aid in gripping. —tr.v. **knurled, knurling, knurls.** To provide with knurls; to mill. [Probably from KNUR (influenced by GNARL).] —**knurl′y** adj.

Knut. See **Canute.**

KO (kā′ō′) tr.v. **KO′d, KO′ing, KO′s.** Also **K.O., k.o.** Slang. To knock out. —n. Slang. Variant of **kayo.**

ko·a·la (kō-ä′lə) n. An arboreal marsupial, Phascolarctos cinereus, of Australia, having dense grayish fur and feeding chiefly on the leaves and bark of eucalyptus trees. [Earlier koola, from native Australian name kūlla.]

Ko·bar·id (kō′bä-rēd′). A town in northwestern Yugoslavia, formerly in Italy; the site of a decisive Austro-German victory over the Italians in World War I (1917).

Ko·be (kō′bē, -bā′). A city of Japan, a seaport on Osaka Bay in southern Honshu. Population, 1,181,000.

Kø·ben·havn. The Danish name for **Copenhagen.**

Ko·blenz. See **Coblenz.**

ko·bold (kō′bōld′) n. German Folklore. **1.** A mischievous household elf. **2.** A gnome that haunts underground places such as mines and caves. [German Kobold, from Middle High German kobolt. See ku- in Appendix.*]

Koch (kōKH), **Robert.** 1843–1910. German pioneer bacteriologist.

Ko·chi (kō′chē). A city of Japan, a seaport on south-central Shikoku. Population, 217,000.

Ko·dak (kō′dăk′) n. A trademark for a hand camera.

Ko·di·ak (kō′dē-ăk′). An island of Alaska, 3,465 square miles in area, lying in the Gulf of Alaska, southeast of the Alaska Peninsula.

Kodiak bear. A form of the brown bear, Ursus arctos, of islands and coastal areas of Alaska, sometimes considered a separate species, U. middendorffi.

Ko·fu (kō′fōō). A city of Japan, in central Honshu, 70 miles west of Tokyo. Population, 172,000.

Ko·hi·ma (kō′hē-mä). The capital of Nagaland, in northeastern Republic of India, in the south-central part of the state. Population, 7,000.

Koh·i·noor (kō′ĭ-noor′) n. Also **Koh·i·nor, Koh·i·nur.** A 109-carat diamond discovered in India and added to the British crown jewels in 1849. [Persian Kōh-i-nūr, "mountain of light" : kōh, mountain, from Old Persian kaufa-† + Arabic nūr, light.]

kohl (kōl) n. A preparation used in Moslem and Asian countries as a cosmetic around the eyes. [Arabic kuḥl, kohl, powder of antimony. See also **alcohol.**]

kohl·ra·bi (kōl-rä′bē, kōl′rä′-) n., pl. **-bies.** A plant, Brassica caulorapa, with a thickened basal part that is eaten as a vegetable. Also called "turnip cabbage." [German Kohlrabi (influenced by Kohl, cabbage), from Italian cavoli rape, plural of cavolo rapa : cavolo, cole, cabbage, from Latin caulis (see kaul- in Appendix*) + rapa, turnip, from Latin rāpa, rāpum (see rāp- in Appendix*).]

koi·ne (koi-nā′) n. A lingua franca that develops out of a mixture of several languages. [From KOINE.]

Koi·ne (koi-nā′) n. A dialect of Ancient Greek during the Hellenistic age, developed primarily from Attic and eventually replacing the local dialects, forming a common language used throughout the Hellenistic world from which the later stages of Greek are descended. [Greek koinē (dialektos), "common (language)," from koinos, common. See kom in Appendix.*]

Ko·ko Nor (kō′kō′ nôr′). Also **Ku·ku Nor** (kōō′kōō′). A salt lake occupying 2,300 square miles in northeastern Tsinghai Province, central China.

kok·sa·ghyz (kŏk′sə-gēz′) n. A dandelion, Taraxacum koksaghyz, of central Asia, having fleshy roots that yield a form of rubber. [Russian kok-saghyz, from Turkish kok-sagiz : kok, root + sagiz, rubber.]

Ko·ku·ra (kō-kōōr′ə, kō′kōō-rä′). A former city of Japan on northern Kyushu; part of Kita Kyushu since 1963.

ko·la (kō′lə) n. Also **co·la.** Either of two African trees, Cola nitida or C. acuminata, bearing nuts used in the manufacture of

koala

Komodo dragon

kohlrabi

beverages and medicinally. [A native West African name, akin to Mandingo kolo, nut.]

ko·lac·ky (kə-lä′kē, -chē) n., pl. **kolacky.** A pastry of eastern European origin consisting of a rich, sweet bun with a fruit or poppyseed filling. [Czech koláč, "wheel-shaped cake," from Old Church Slavonic kolo, wheel. See kwel-¹ in Appendix.*]

kola nut. Also **cola nut.** The nut of a kola tree, containing caffeine and theobromine, and yielding an extract used in carbonated beverages and in pharmaceutical products.

Ko·la Peninsula (kō′lə). A peninsula of the Soviet Union, occupying 50,000 square miles in the northwest between the White and Barents seas.

Ko·lar Gold Fields (kō-lär′). A city of the Republic of India, a gold-mining center in southeastern Mysore. Population, 147,000.

Kol·ha·pur (kō′lə-pŏŏr′). A city of the Republic of India, in southern Maharashtra. Population, 204,000.

ko·lin·sky (kə-lĭn′skē) n., pl. **-skies. 1.** Any of several minks of northern Eurasia, especially Mustela siberica. **2.** The fur of such an animal. [Russian kolinskiĭ, "(mink) of Kola," from Kola, district in northwestern U.S.S.R.]

Kol·khi·da. The Russian name for **Colchis.**

kol·khoz (kŏl-KHôz′) n. Also **kol·koz.** A Soviet collective farm. [Russian, contraction of kollektivnoe khozyaĭstvo : kollektivnoe, neuter of kollektivnyĭ, collective + khozyaĭstvo, household, farm.]

Kol·mar. The German name for **Colmar.**

Köln. The German name for **Cologne.**

Kol Ni·dre (kōl′ nĭd′rä, -rē, -rə). Judaism. The opening prayer recited on the eve of Yom Kippur, containing a declaration of the annulment of all personal vows of the preceding year. [Aramaic kol nidhrē, "all vows," from the opening words of the prayer.]

Ko·lom·na (kə-lôm′nä). A city of the Soviet Union, an industrial center 65 miles southeast of Moscow. Population, 125,000.

Ko·ly·ma (kə-lē′mə). A river of the Soviet Union, rising in the Kolyma Range of northeastern Siberia, and flowing 1,335 miles generally north to the East Siberian Sea.

Ko·ly·ma Range (kə-lē′mə). A range extending about 700 miles through northeastern Siberia. Highest elevation, about 6,000 feet.

Ko·man·dor·skie Islands (kŏm′ən-dôr′skē). Also **Ko·man·dor·skye.** English **Com·mand·er Islands** (kə-măn′dər). An island group of the Soviet Union, 850 square miles in area, lying in the Bering Sea east of the Kamchatka Peninsula.

Ko·ma·ti (kō-mä′tē). A river rising in southeastern Transvaal, South Africa, and flowing about 500 miles generally east through Swaziland and Mozambique to the Indian Ocean.

Ko·men·ský, Jan. See John **Comenius.**

Ko·mi Autonomous Soviet Socialist Republic (kō′mē). An administrative division, 160,540 square miles in area, of the northwestern Russian S.F.S.R. Population, 953,000. Capital, Syktyvkar.

Ko·mo·do dragon (kə-mō′dō). A large monitor lizard, Varanus komodoensis, of the Indonesian islands of Komodo and Flores.

Kom·so·molsk (kŏm′sə-môlsk′). A city and industrial center of the Soviet Union, on the Amur in the southeastern Russian S.F.S.R. Population, 192,000.

Ko·nan. The Japanese name for **Hungnam.**

Kon·go (kŏng′gō) n. A Bantu language spoken in the region of the lower Congo River.

Kö·nigs·berg. The former name for **Kaliningrad.**

ko·ni·ol·o·gy (kō′nē-ŏl′ə-jē) n. Also **co·ni·ol·o·gy.** The scientific study of atmospheric dust and its effects. [Greek konia, dust (see keni- in Appendix*) + -LOGY.]

Kon·stanz. The German name for **Constance.**

Kon·ya (kôn-yä′). Also **Kon·ia.** A city of Turkey, in the southwest-central part of the country. Population, 120,000.

koo·doo. Variant of **kudu.**

kook (kōōk) n. Slang. An amusingly eccentric or zany person. [Perhaps from CUCKOO.] —**kook′y** adj. —**kook′i·ness** n.

kook·a·bur·ra (kōōk′ə-bûr′ə) n. A large kingfisher, Dacelo novaeguineae (or D. gigas), of Australia and adjacent areas, having a call resembling raucous laughter. Also called "laughing jackass." [Native Australian name.]

Koo·te·nay (kōōt′n-ā′). Also **Koo·te·nai.** A river rising in southeastern British Columbia, Canada, and flowing about 450 miles first south into Montana and then north through Idaho and back into British Columbia, passing through Lake Kootenay (221 square miles) to the Columbia River.

ko·peck (kō′pĕk′) n. Also **co·peck.** Abbr. **k., K., kop.** A coin equal to 1/100 of the rouble of the Union of Soviet Socialist Republics. See table of exchange rates at **currency.** [Russian kopeĭka, from kop′e, lance (from the figure of the czar with a lance in his hand originally stamped on the coin), from kopat′, to hack. See skep- in Appendix.*]

kop·pa (kŏp′ə) n. A letter occurring in certain early forms of the Greek alphabet, later mostly replaced by kappa (see). Transliterated in English as q. [Greek, from Semitic, akin to Hebrew qôph, ΚΟΡΗ.]

kor (kôr, kōr) n. A homer (see). [Hebrew kōr, "a measure."]

Ko·ran (kō-răn′, -rän′, kō-) n. The sacred text of Islam, believed to contain the revelations made by Allah to Mohammed. Also called "Alcoran." [Arabic qur'ān, reading, recitation, from qara'a, to read, recite.] —**Ko·ran′ic** adj.

Kor·do·fan (kôr′dō-făn′). A province occupying 146,930 square miles in central Sudan. Population, 2,952,000. Capital, El Obeid.

Ko·re·a (kô-rē′ə, kō-). Formerly **Cho·sen** (chō′sĕn′). A former country occupying a peninsula of east-central Asia, opposite Japan, divided since 1948 into two political entities, the People's Democratic Republic of Korea (unofficially, North Korea), 46,768 square miles in area with a population of 10,930,000 and its capital at Pyongyang; and the Republic of Korea (unofficially, South Korea), 30,031 square miles in area, with a population of 28,155,000 and its capital at Seoul. [From *Koryo,* name of an ancient state in Korea.]

Ko·re·a Bay (kô-rē′ə, kō-). An inlet of the Yellow Sea lying between mainland China and northwestern North Korea.

Ko·re·an (kô-rē′ən, kō-) *adj.* Of or relating to Korea, its inhabitants, or their language. —*n.* **1.** A native or inhabitant of Korea. **2.** The language of Korea, unclassified linguistically but containing many words of Chinese origin.

Korean War. A military action between North Korea and United Nations forces (1950–53).

Ko·re·a Strait (kô-rē′ə, kō-). A channel about 110 miles wide between South Korea and Japan, and connecting the Sea of Japan with the East China Sea.

Ko·rin·thos. The Greek name for **Corinth.**

Korn·berg (kôrn′bûrg′), **Arthur.** Born 1918. American biochemist.

ko·ru·na (kôr′ŏŏ-nä′) *n., pl.* **-ny** (-nē) or **-nas.** *Abbr.* **k., K. 1.** The basic monetary unit of Czechoslovakia, equal to 100 halers. See table of exchange rates at **currency. 2.** A coin worth one koruna. [Czech, "crown," from Latin *corōna,* CROWN.]

Kos (kŏs, kôs). *Latin* **Cos** (kŏs). The second-largest of the Greek Dodecanese Islands (111 square miles), at the entrance to the Gulf of Kos, an inlet of the Aegean on the coast of southwestern Turkey.

Kos·ci·us·ko, Mount (kŏs′ē-ŭs′kō). The highest mountain (7,316 feet) of Australia, in southeastern New South Wales.

Kos·ci·us·ko (kŏs′ē-ŭs′kō), **Thaddeus.** 1746–1817. Polish patriot and commander of American troops in Revolutionary War.

ko·sher (kō′shər) *adj.* Also **ka·sher** (kä′shər). **1.** Conforming to or prepared in accordance with Jewish dietary laws, as: **a.** Slaughtered or prepared for eating according to rabbinic law; ritually pure: *kosher meat.* **b.** Specializing in the preparation or sale of such food: *a kosher delicatessen.* Compare **tref. 2.** *Slang.* **a.** Proper; correct; permissible. **b.** Genuine; legitimate. —**keep kosher.** To obey the Jewish dietary laws. —*n.* Food prepared and served according to the Jewish dietary laws. —*tr.v.* **koshered, -shering, -shers.** To make kosher. [Yiddish, from Hebrew *kāshēr,* proper.]

Ko·ši·ce (kô′shĭ-tsĕ). A city of northeastern Czechoslovakia. Population, 88,000.

Kos·sel (kô′səl), **Albrecht.** 1853–1927. German biochemist; worked on nucleic acids and proteins.

Kos·tro·ma (kə-strə-mä′, kôs′trə-). A city of the Soviet Union, on the Volga in the west-central Russian S.F.S.R. Population, 202,000.

Ko·sy·gin (kə-sē′gĭn), **Aleksei Nikolayevich.** Born 1904. Premier of the Soviet Union (since 1964).

Ko·ta Bha·ru (kō′tə bär′ŏŏ). The capital of Kelantan, Malaysia, a city in the northern part of the state. Population, 38,000.

Ko·ta Kin·a·ba·lu (kō′tə kĭn′ə-bə-lŏŏ′). Formerly **Jes·sel·ton** (jĕs′əl-tən). The capital of Sabah, Malaysia, a seaport on the northwestern coast of Borneo. Population, 21,000.

ko·to (kō′tō) *n.* A Japanese musical instrument that has 13 strings stretched over an oblong box. [Japanese.]

kou·mis, kou·miss. Variants of **kumiss.**

Kow·loon (kou′lŏŏn′). A city of Hong Kong, on Kowloon Peninsula opposite Hong Kong Island. Population, 729,000.

kow·tow (kou′tou′, kō′-) *n.* Also **ko·tow** (kō′-). **1.** A Chinese salutation in which one touches the forehead to the ground as an expression of respect or submission. **2.** An obsequious act. —*intr.v.* **kowtowed, -towing, -tows. 1.** To perform a kowtow. **2.** To show servile deference; to fawn. [Mandarin Chinese *k'o¹ t'ou² : k'o¹,* to knock, bump + *t'ou²,* head.]

Ko·zhi·kode (kō′zhĭ-kōd′). Formerly **Cal·i·cut** (kăl′ĭ-kŭt′, -kət). A city of the Republic of India, a seaport in west-central Kerala. Population, 204,000.

KP 1. *Chess.* king's pawn. **2.** kitchen police.

K.P. 1. kitchen police. **2.** Knights of Pythias.

Kr The symbol for the element krypton.

KR *Chess.* king's rook.

kr. 1. krona. **2.** krone.

Kra, Isthmus of (krä). The narrow strip of land (about 40 miles wide) linking the Malay Peninsula and the mainland in southern Thailand.

kraal (kräl) *n.* Also **craal. 1.** A village of southern African natives, typically consisting of huts surrounded by a stockade. **2.** An enclosure for livestock in southern Africa. —*tr.v.* **kraaled, kraaling, kraals.** To put or keep livestock in a kraal. [Afrikaans, "enclosure for cattle," from Portuguese *curral,* perhaps of Hottentot origin. See **corral.**]

Krafft-E·bing (kräft′ĕb′ĭng, kräft′-; *German* kräft′ä′bĭng), Baron **Richard von.** 1840–1902. German neurologist and psychiatrist; author of *Psychopathia Sexualis* (1886).

kraft (kräft, kräft) *n.* A tough wrapping paper made from sulfate wood pulp. [German *Kraft,* force, strength, from Old High German, from Germanic *kraftaz* (unattested). See **craft.**]

Krain. The German name for **Carniola.**

krait (krīt) *n.* Any of several venomous snakes of the genus *Bungarus,* of southeastern Asia. [Hindi *karait*†.]

Kra·ka·to·a (krăk′ə-tō′ə). Also **Kra·ka·tau** (-tou′). A small volcanic island of Indonesia between Java and Sumatra, virtually obliterated in 1883 by explosive eruptions.

kra·ken (krä′kən) *n.* A legendary sea monster said to dwell in Norwegian waters. [Dialectal Norwegian : *krake*†, kraken + -*n,* suffix used as the definite article.]

Kra·ków (krä′kou′, krăk′ou′, krä′kō; *Polish* krä′kŏŏf). *English* **Crac·ow** (krä′kō). A city in southern Poland. Population, 509,000.

Kranj. The Slovene name for **Carniola.**

Kras·no·dar (krăs′nə-där′). Formerly **E·ka·te·ri·no·dar** (ĭ-kăt′ə-rē′nə-där′). A city of the Soviet Union in the southwestern Russian S.F.S.R. Population, 385,000.

Kras·no·yarsk (kräs′nə-yärsk′). A city of the Soviet Union in the south-central Russian S.F.S.R. Population, 501,000.

K ration. A U.S. Army emergency field ration used in World War II, consisting of a single tightly packaged meal.

kraut (krout) *n.* **1.** Sauerkraut. **2.** *Slang.* A German. Used disparagingly.

Krebs (krĕbz), Sir **Hans Adolf.** Born 1900. German-born British biochemist.

Krebs cycle (krĕbz). A series of enzymatic reactions occurring in most aerobic organisms, involving oxidative metabolism of acetyl units, especially during respiration, to provide the main source of cellular energy in the form of phosphate-rich ATP. [After Hans KREBS.]

Kre·feld (krā′fĕlt). A city of West Germany, in east-central North Rhine-Westphalia. Population, 219,000.

Krem·lin (krĕm′lĭn) *n.* **1.** The citadel of Moscow, housing the offices of the Soviet government. **2.** The Soviet government. [French, from Russian *kreml',* citadel, of Tatar origin.]

Kre·te. The Greek name for **Crete.**

kreu·zer (kroit′sər) *n.* Also **kreut·zer.** Any of several small coins of low value formerly in currency in Austria and Germany. [German *Kreuzer,* from Middle High German *kriuzer,* from *kriuze,* a cross (originally stamped with a cross), from Old High German *krūzi,* from Latin *crux,* CROSS.]

krieg·spiel (krēg′spēl′, -shpēl′) *n.* A war game played with miniature figures or markers on a large map or terrain model. [German *Kriegspiel,* "war game" : *Krieg,* war (see **blitzkrieg**) + *Spiel,* game (see **spiel**).]

Kriem·hild (krēm′hĭld′; *German* krēm′hĭlt′). Also **Kriem·hil·de** (krēm-hĭl′də). In the Nibelungenlied, the wife of Siegfried and avenger of his murder.

krill (krĭl) *pl.n.* Small marine crustaceans of the order Euphausiacea, constituting the principal food of whalebone whales. [Norwegian *kril*†, young of fish.]

Krim. The Russian name for **Crimea.**

krim·mer (krĭm′ər) *n.* Gray, curly fur made from the pelts of lambs of the Crimean region. [German *Krimmer,* from *Krim,* the Crimean peninsula.]

kris (krēs) *n.* Also **creese, cris.** A sword of Malayan origin having a wavy double-edged blade. [Malay *kĕris.*]

Krish·na¹ (krĭsh′nə). *Hinduism.* The eighth and principal avatar of Vishnu, often depicted as a handsome young man playing a flute. [Hindi, "the black one," from Sanskrit *kṛṣṇáh,* black. See **kers-¹** in Appendix.*] —**Krish′na·ism** *n.*

Krish·na². See **Kistna.**

Kriss Krin·gle (krĭs′ krĭng′gəl). Santa Claus. [German *Christkindl,* Christ child : *Christ,* Christ + *Kindl,* diminutive of *Kind,* child, from Old High German *kind* (see **geno-** in Appendix*).]

Kri·voi Rog (krĭv′oi rōg′, rôk′). A city of the Soviet Union, in the southeastern Ukrainian S.S.R. Population, 488,000.

kro·na¹ (krō′nə) *n., pl.* **-nur** (-nər). *Abbr.* **k., K., kn., kr. 1.** The basic monetary unit of Iceland, equal to 100 aurar. See table of exchange rates at **currency. 2.** A coin worth one krona. [Icelandic *króna,* from Old Norse *krūna,* crown, from Middle Low German, from Latin *corōna,* CROWN.]

kro·na² (krō′nə) *n., pl.* **-nor** (-nôr′). *Abbr.* **k., K., kn., kr. 1.** The basic monetary unit of Sweden, equal to 100 öre. See table of exchange rates at **currency. 2.** A coin worth one krona. [Swedish, "crown," from Old Swedish *krūna, krōna,* from Latin *corōna,* wreath, CROWN.]

kro·ne (krō′nə) *n., pl.* **-ner** (-nər). *Abbr.* **k., K., kn., kr. 1.** The basic monetary unit of Denmark and Norway, equal to 100 öre. See table of exchange rates at **currency. 2.** A coin worth one krone. [Danish *krone* and Norwegian *krune,* "crown," from Old Norse *krūna,* crown, from Latin *corōna,* CROWN.]

Kro·nos. Variant of **Cronus.**

Kron·stadt. The German name for **Brașov.**

kroon (krŏŏn) *n., pl.* **kroons** or **krooni** (krŏŏ′nē). **1.** A former monetary unit of Estonia, equivalent to the Swedish krona. **2.** A coin or note worth one kroon. [Estonian *kron,* from German *Krone,* crown, from Old High German *corōna,* from Latin, CROWN.]

KRP *Chess.* king's rook's pawn.

KRT Airport code for Khartoum, Sudan.

Kru·ger National Park (krŏŏ′gər). An 8,000 square mile wildlife preserve in northeastern South Africa.

krul·ler. Variant of **cruller.**

Krung Thep. The Thai name for **Bangkok.**

Krupp (krŭp; *German* krŏŏp). A German family of steel and ordnance manufacturers, including **Friedrich** (1787–1826); his grandson, **Friedrich Alfred** (1854–1902); and the latter's son-in-law, **Gustav Krupp von Bohlen und Halbach** (1870–1950).

Krup·ska·ya (krŏŏp′skə-yə, krŏŏp′-), **Nadezhda Konstantinovna.** 1869–1939. Russian revolutionary; wife of Lenin; author of *Memories of Lenin* (1930).

Krůs·né Ho·ry. The Czech name for **Erzgebirge.**

kryp·ton (krĭp′tŏn′) *n. Symbol* **Kr** A whitish, inert, gaseous element used chiefly in gas-discharge lamps, fluorescent lamps, and electronic flash tubes. Atomic number 36, atomic weight

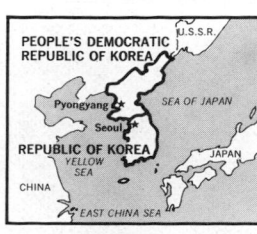

Korea

Krishna¹
Twelfth-century Indian statuette of Krishna dancing

koto
Late 18th-century Japanese woodcut

83.80, melting point −156.6°C, boiling point −152.30°C, density 3.73 grams per liter (0°C). See **element**. [New Latin, "hidden (element)," from Greek *krupton*, neuter of *kruptos*, hidden, from *kruptein*, to hide. See **krāu-** in Appendix.*]

KS Kansas (with Zip Code).

Ksha·tri·ya (kshăt′rē-ə, shăt′-) *n.* **1.** A major Hindu caste, including the professional, governing, and military occupations. **2.** A member of this caste. See also **caste**. [Sanskrit *kṣatriya*, "ruling, ruler," from *kṣatra*, rule, dominion, from *kṣayati*, he possesses, he rules. See **ksei-²** in Appendix.*]

Kt knight.

kt. karat.

Kua·la Li·pis (kwä′lə lē′pĭs). The capital of Pahang, Malaysia, in the central part of the state. Population, 9,000.

Kua·la Lum·pur (kwä′lə lŏŏm′pŏŏr). The capital of Malaysia, in southeastern Selangor State, of which it is also the capital. Population, 316,000.

Kua·la Treng·ga·nu (kwä′lə trĕng-gä′nŏŏ). The capital of Trengganu, Malaysia, a seaport in the east-central part of the state. Population, 29,000.

Kuang·chow. The Chinese name for **Canton**.

Ku·ban (kŏŏ-băn′). A river of the Soviet Union, rising in the Georgian S.S.R. and flowing 584 miles north and northwest through the Russian S.F.S.R. to the Sea of Azov.

Ku·blai Khan (kŏŏ′blī kän′). Also **Ku·bla Khan** (kŏŏ′blə). 1216–1294. Mongol khan; founder of the Mongol dynasty and conqueror of China; grandson of Genghis Khan.

ku·chen (kŏŏ′KHən) *n.* A German yeast-raised coffee cake containing fruits and nuts and usually crusted with sugar and spices. [German *Kuchen*, from Middle High German *kuoche*, cake, from Old High German *kuocho*. See **kak-²** in Appendix.*]

Ku·ching (kŏŏ′chĭng). The capital of Sarawak, Malaysia, in the southwest on the South China Sea. Population, 51,000.

ku·dos (kyŏŏ′dŏs′, -dōs′) *n.* Acclaim or prestige as a result of achievement or position: *"all the kudos of the Presidency of the United States"* (Eric F. Goldman). [Originally British university slang, from Greek *kudos*, glory, fame. See **keu-¹** in Appendix.*]

Usage: Kudos is construed as singular in the choice of a verb: *Kudos is due him.* The singular term *kudo*, which is not acceptable in standard usage, is the invention of those who misconstrue *kudos* as exclusively plural.

Kud·run. Variant of **Gudrun**.

ku·du (kŏŏ′dŏŏ). Also **koo·doo**. Either of two African hoofed mammals, *Tragelaphus strepsiceros* or *T. imberbis*, having a brownish coat with narrow white vertical stripes and long, spirally curved horns in the male. [Afrikaans *koedoe*, from Bantu (Xhosa) *iqudu*.]

kud·zu (kŏŏd′zŏŏ) *n.* A vine, *Pueraria lobata*, native to Japan, having compound leaves and clusters of reddish-purple flowers and grown for fodder and forage. [Japanese *kuzu*, from Ancient Chinese *kât* (Mandarin *ko²*).]

kue (kyŏŏ) *n.* The letter *q*.

Ku·fic (kŏŏ′fĭk, kyŏŏ′-) *adj.* Also **Cu·fic**. Designating or pertaining to an early form of the Arabic alphabet used for making fine copies of the Koran. [From Arabic *Al Kufah*, town in south-central Iraq, where such copies of the Koran were made.]

Kui·by·shev (kwē′bə-shĕf′, -shĕv′). Formerly **Sa·ma·ra** (sə-mär′ə). A city of the Soviet Union, a river port on the Volga 530 miles southeast of Moscow. Population, 948,000.

Ku Klux Klan (kŏŏ′ klŭks′ klăn′, kyŏŏ′). *Abbr.* **K.K.K. 1.** A secret society organized in the South after the Civil War to reassert white supremacy with terroristic methods. **2.** Full name, Knights of the Ku Klux Klan. A secret organization founded in Georgia in 1915 and modeled upon the earlier society. [Said to be Greek *kuklos*, circle, CYCLE + *klan*, from CLAN. (The word "circle" appears in names of many secret societies supporting the Confederacy, such as the Knights of the Golden Circle.)] —**Ku Kluxer, Ku Klux Klanner.** —**Ku Kluxism.**

Ku·ku Nor. See **Koko Nor**.

KUL Airport code for Kuala Lumpur, Malaysia.

ku·lak (kŏŏ-läk′, -lăk′) *n.* **1.** In Czarist Russia and during the October Revolution, a rich peasant or village usurer notorious as an exploiter. **2.** One of a class of Russian peasants disenfranchised by the revolution. [Russian, "fist," "tight-fisted person," from Turkic, akin to Turkish *kol*, arm.]

Kul·tur (kŏŏl-tŏŏr′) *n.* Culture; especially, German culture and civilization as idealized by the exponents of German imperialism during the period 1900–45: *"Kultur, in fact, has become the exact opposite of 'culture.'"* (London Times). [German, from Latin *cultūra*, CULTURE.]

Kul·tur·kampf (kŏŏl-tŏŏr′kämpf′) *n.* **1.** The struggle (1872–87) between the Roman Catholic Church and the German government for control over civil marriage and school and church appointments. **2.** Any conflict between secular and religious authorities: *"The 1920's proved to be the focal decade in the Kulturkampf of American Protestantism."* (Richard Hofstadter). [German, "culture struggle" : KULTUR + *Kampf*, fight, struggle, from Old High German *kamph*, from Germanic, from Latin *campus*, field, battlefield (see **camp**).]

Ku·ma·mo·to (kŏŏ′mə-mō′tō). A city of Japan, a seaport in west-central Kyushu. Population, 403,000.

Ku·ma·si (kŏŏ-mä′sē). Formerly **Coo·mas·sie** (-măs′ĭ). A city of Ghana, the historic capital of the Ashanti kingdom, situated 125 miles northwest of Accra. Population, 190,000.

ku·miss (kŏŏ′mĭs) *n.* Also **kou·mis, kou·miss**. The fermented milk of a mare or camel, drunk by people of western and central Asia. [Russian *kumys*, from Kazan Tatar *kumyz*.]

küm·mel (kĭm′əl; *German* kü′məl) *n.* A colorless liqueur flavored with caraway, anise, or cumin. [German *Kümmel*, "cumin seed," from Old High German *kumil, kumin*, from Latin *cumīnum*, CUMIN.]

kum·mer·bund. Variant of **cummerbund**.

kum·quat (kŭm′kwŏt′) *n.* Also **cum·quat. 1.** Any of several trees of the genus *Fortunella*, native to China, having small, edible, orangelike fruit. **2.** The fruit of such a tree, having acid pulp and a thin, edible rind. [Cantonese *kam kwat, kam kat*, corresponding to Mandarin Chinese *chin¹ chü²*, "golden orange" : *chin¹*, gold, golden + *chü²*, orange.]

Ku·na·shir (kŏŏ′nə-shĭr′). The southernmost and largest (1,548 square miles) of the Kurile Islands.

Ku·ne·ne. See **Cunene**.

Kung (kŏŏng), **H.H.** Original name, K'ung Hsiang-hsi. 1881–1967. Nationalist Chinese statesman and financier.

Kung Fu-tse. See **Confucius**.

Kun·gur, Mount (kŏŏn′gŏŏr). The highest elevation (25,325 feet) of the Pamirs, a peak in western China.

Kun·lun (kŏŏn′lŏŏn′). A mountain system of western China, between Tibet and the Sinkiang-Uigur Autonomous Region. Highest elevation, Ulugh Muztagh (25,340 feet).

Kun·ming (kŏŏn′mĭng′). The capital of Yunnan, China, in the central part of the province. Population, 900,000.

kunz·ite (kŏŏnts′īt′) *n.* A transparent lilac-colored spodumene, used as a gemstone. [After George F. *Kunz* (1856–1932), American gem expert.]

Kuo·min·tang (kwō′mĭn′tăng′) *n.* The official ruling party of the Republic of China (Taiwan), originally founded as an anti-imperialist program by Sun Yat-sen (1911) and subsequently developed under his leadership as an instrument of the democratic revolution in China. [Mandarin Chinese *kuo² min² tang³*, "Nationalist Party" : *kuo²*, nation + *min²*, people + *tang³*, party.]

Kuo·yu (gwō′ü′) *n.* **Mandarin Chinese** (*see*). [Mandarin Chinese *kuo² yü³* : *kuo²*, nation, national + *yü*, language.]

Ku·ra (kŏŏ-rä′). Ancient name **Cy·rus** (sī′rəs). A river rising in northeastern Turkey and flowing 940 miles first northeast and then southeast through the Soviet republics of Georgia and Azerbaijan to the Caspian Sea.

Kur·cha·tov (kŏŏr-chä′tôf′, -tôv′), **Igor Vasilevich.** 1903–1960. Soviet physicist; head of Soviet atomic and hydrogen bomb programs.

Kurd (kûrd, kŏŏrd) *n.* One of a nomadic Moslem people living chiefly in Kurdistan.

Kurd·ish (kûr′dĭsh, kŏŏr′-) *adj.* Of or pertaining to the Kurds, their culture, or their language. —*n.* The northwestern Iranian language of the Kurds.

Kurd·i·stan (kûr′dĭ-stăn′, kŏŏr′dĭ-stän′). A plateau and mountain region of southwestern Asia, comprising southeastern Turkey and adjoining parts of Iraq and Iran.

Ku·re (kŏŏ′rĕ). A city of Japan, a shipbuilding center in southern Honshu on the Inland Sea. Population, 210,000.

Ku·rile Islands (kŏŏr′ĭl, kŏŏ-rēl′, -rĭl′). Also **Ku·ril Islands**. *Japanese* Chi·shi·ma Ret·to (chē-shē′mä rĕt′tō); *Russian* Ku·ril·ski·ye Os·tro·va (kŏŏ-rēl′skē-ə ŏ-strŏ-vä′). A chain of islands of the Soviet Union, extending about 700 miles between the Kamchatka Peninsula and northern Hokkaido, Japan. Also called "Kuriles." —**Ku·ril′i·an** *adj. & n.*

Ku·ro·sa·wa (kŏŏr′ə-sä′wə), **Akira.** Born 1910. Japanese film director.

Ku·ro·shi·o. The Japanese name for the **Japan Current**.

kur·ra·jong (kûr′ə-jŏng′) *n.* An Australian tree, *Brachychiton populneum*, having evergreen leaves and yellowish or reddish flowers. [Native Australian name.]

Kursk (kŏŏrsk). A city of the Soviet Union, in the western Russian S.F.S.R. just north of the Ukrainian border. Population, 245,000.

kur·to·sis (kər-tō′sĭs) *n.* The general form or a quantity indicative of the general form of a statistical frequency curve near the distribution's mean. [Greek *kurtōsis*, convexity, curvature, from *kurtos*, convex. See **sker-³** in Appendix.*]

Kush. See **Cush**.

Kush·it·ic. Variant of **Cushitic**.

Kus·ko·kwim (kŭs′kə-kwĭm′). A river of Alaska, rising in the Alaska Range and flowing about 600 miles generally southwest to the Bering Sea.

Kutch. 1. See **Cutch. 2.** See **Rann of Cutch**.

Ku·wait (kŏŏ-wät′, -wĭt′). **1.** A republic occupying 5,800 square miles on the Arabian Peninsula at the head of the Persian Gulf; a former British protectorate independent since 1961. Population, 468,000. **2.** Also **Al Ku·wait** (ăl). The capital of the republic, a seaport on the Persian Gulf. Population, 100,000.

Kuz·netsk Basin (kŏŏz-nĕtsk′). A coal-producing region of the south-central Russian S.F.S.R.

kvass (kväs) *n.* Also **kvas**. A fermented Russian beverage similiar to beer, made from rye or barley. [Russian *kvas*. See **kwath-** in Appendix.*]

kvetch (kvĕch) *intr.v.* **kvetched, kvetching, kvetches.** *Slang.* To complain or find fault in a persistent, querulous manner. —*n. Slang.* A chronic and annoying complainer. [Yiddish, from German *quetschen*, to crush, squeeze, from Middle High German *quetzen*. See **gwedh-** in Appendix.*]

kW kilowatt.

Kwa (kwä) *n.* A branch of the Niger-Congo language family, including Ibo, Yoruba, and other languages spoken in West Africa. —**Kwa** *adj.*

kwa·cha (kwä′chä′) *n.* The basic monetary unit of Zambia, equal to 100 ngwee. See table of exchange rates at **currency**. [Native word in Zambia.]

kumquat

kudu
Tragelaphus imberbis

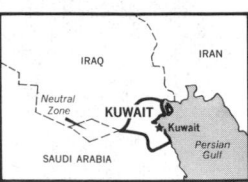

Kuwait

Kwa·ja·lein (kwŏj'ə-lən, -lān'). A small atoll in the Marshall Islands; site of an American naval base since 1945.

Kwa·ki·utl (kwä'kē-ōōt'l) *n., pl.* **Kwakiutl** or **-utls. 1.** A Wakashan-speaking North American people of northern Vancouver Island and the adjacent British Columbia coast. **2.** A member of this people. **3.** The language of this people.

Kwan·do (kwän'dō). A river of Africa, rising in central Angola and flowing 600 miles generally southeast to the Zambezi.

Kwang·chow. The Chinese name for **Canton.**

Kwang·cho·wan (gwäng'jō'wän'). A coastal region of Kwantung Province, China, occupied by France in 1898 and returned in 1943.

Kwang·ju (gwäng'jōō'). A city of South Korea, a textile center in the southwest. Population, 313,000.

Kwang·si-Chuang Autonomous Region (gwäng'sē'chwäng'). An administrative division of China, occupying 85,000 square miles in the southeast. Population, 19,390,000. Capital, Nanning.

Kwang·tung (gwäng'dŏŏng'). A province of China, occupying 85,000 square miles in the southeast. Population, 37,960,000. Capital, Canton.

Kwan·tung Leased Territory (gwän'dŏŏng'). The territory constituted by Port Arthur (now Lüshun) and its suburbs in Liaotung Peninsula, China, under Japanese administration (1905–45).

kwash·i·or·kor (kwäsh'ē-ôr'kôr, kwä'shē-) *n.* Severe malnutrition, occurring especially in African children, characterized by anemia, edema, potbelly, depigmentation of the skin, and loss of hair or change in hair color. [Native word in Ghana.]

Kwei·chow (gwä'jō'). A province occupying 65,000 square miles in south-central China. Population, 16,890,000. Capital, Kweiyang.

Kwei·sui. See **Huhehot.**

Kwei·yang (gwä'yäng'). The capital of Kweichow, China, situated in the center of the province. Population, 530,000.

kWh kilowatt-hour.

KWI Airport code for Kuwait, Kuwait.

Ky (kē), **Nguyen Kao.** Born 1930. Premier of South Vietnam (1965–67); vice president (since 1967).

KY Kentucky (with Zip Code).

Ky. Kentucky.

ky·ack (kī'ăk') *n.* A packsack that hangs on either side of a packsaddle. [Origin unknown.]

ky·a·nite (kī'ə-nīt') *n.* Also **cy·a·nite** (sī'-). A bluish, greenish, or colorless mineral, essentially Al_2SiO_5, used as a refractory. [German *Zyanit* : *zyan(o)-*, CYANO- + -ITE.]

kyat (kyät, kē-ät') *n.* **1.** The basic monetary unit of Burma, equal to 100 pyas. See table of exchange rates at **currency. 2.** A coin worth one kyat. [Burmese.]

Kyd (kĭd), **Thomas.** 1557?–1595. English playwright.

Ky·kla·des. A Greek name for the **Cyclades.**

ky·lix (kī'lĭks, kĭl'ĭks) *n., pl.* **kylikes** (kī'lĭ-kēz', kĭl'ĭ-). Also **cy·lix** (sī'lĭks, sĭl'ĭks). A shallow, typically tall-stemmed drinking cup used in ancient Greece. [Greek *kulix,* cup. See **kal-¹** in Appendix.*]

ky·mo·graph (kī'mə-grăf', -gräf') *n.* Also **cy·mo·graph** (sī'-). An instrument for recording pressure variations, especially in blood pressure. [*Kymo-,* variant of *cymo-,* from CYME + -GRAPH.]

Kym·ric. Variant of **Cymric.**

Kym·ry. Variant of **Cymry.**

Kyn·e·wulf. See **Cynewulf.**

Ky·o·ga. See **Kioga.**

Kyong·song. See **Seoul.**

Kyo·to (kyō'tō, kē-ō'-). Also **Kio·to.** A city and industrial center of Japan, in southern Honshu; the capital of Japan until 1868. Population, 1,376,000. [Japanese *kyōtō,* "capital city," from Ancient Chinese *kiang tuo* (Mandarin *ching¹tu¹*) : *kiang,* the capital + *tuo,* metropolis, capital, city.]

ky·pho·sis (kī-fō'sĭs) *n.* Abnormal curvature of the spine with rearward convexity. Also called "humpback," "hunchback." [Greek *kuphōsis,* from *kuphos,* bent, hunchbacked. See **keu-²** in Appendix.*] **—ky·phot·ic** (-fŏt'ĭk) *adj.*

Kyr·i·e e·le·i·son (kĭr'ē-ā' ĭ-lā'ə-sən). **1.** A liturgical prayer in the liturgical Christian churches beginning with or composed of the words "Lord, have mercy." **2.** A musical setting for such a prayer, as in a choral mass. Also called "Kyrie." [Late Latin, from Greek *Kurie eleēson,* "Lord, have mercy" : *Kurie,* vocative of *kurios,* lord, master, "powerful (one)," from *kuros,* power, supreme authority (see **keu-³** in Appendix*) + *eleēson,* aorist imperative of *elein,* to show mercy, from *eleos,* pity, mercy (see **alms**).]

Kyu·shu (kyōō'shōō). Also **Kiu·shu.** The southernmost and third-largest (13,770 square miles) of the four main islands of Japan.

Ky·zyl (kĭ-zĭl'). The capital of the Tuva A.S.S.R., in the south-central Russian S.F.S.R. Population, 34,000.

---

t tight/th thin, path/*th* this, bathe/ŭ cut/ûr urge/v valve/w with/y yes/z zebra, size/zh vision/ə about, item, edible, gallop, circus/ à *Fr.* ami/œ *Fr.* feu, *Ger.* schön/ü *Fr.* tu, *Ger.* über/KH *Ger.* ich, *Scot.* loch/N *Fr.* bon. *Follows main vocabulary. †Of obscure origin.

Kublai Khan
Portrait from a
Chinese manuscript

L1

CL CL LLNT LL L LL L Ll
1 2   3 4 5 6 7   8 9 10   11 12   13 14 15 16
Phoenician   Greek   Roman   Medieval   Modern

Around 1000 B.C. *the Phoenicians and other Semites of Syria and Palestine began to use a graphic sign in the forms (1,2). They gave the sign the name* lāmedh *and used it for their consonant* l. *After 900* B.C. *the Greeks borrowed the sign from the Phoenicians, writing it in several different forms (3,4,5,6) before developing their standard symmetrical form (7). They also changed its name to* lambda. *The Greek form (3) passed via Etruscan to the Roman alphabet (8), later developing the form (9) peculiar to the Latin writing. The Roman Monumental Capital (10) is the prototype of our modern capital; printed (13) and written (14). The written Roman form (8) developed into the late Roman and medieval Uncial (11) and Cursive (12), which are the bases of our modern small letter, printed (15) and written (16).*

l, L (ĕl) *n., pl.* **l's** *or rare* **ls, L's** *or* **Ls. 1.** The 12th letter of the modern English alphabet. See **alphabet. 2.** Any of the speech sounds represented by this letter. **3.** Anything shaped like the letter **L.**

l, L, l., L. *Note:* As an abbreviation or symbol, *l* may be a small or a capital letter, with or without a period. Established forms or those generally preferred precede the definition. When no form is given, all four forms are in general use in that sense. **1.** l., L. lake. **2.** L lambert. **3.** L large. **4.** L. Latin. **5.** l. left. **6.** l. length. **7.** L. licentiate (in titles). **8.** l. line. **9.** L. Linnaean. **10.** l. lira. **11.** l liter. **12.** L. lodge (society). **13.** L The Roman numeral for 50. **14.** The 12th in a series; 11th when *J* is omitted.

la¹ (lä) *n. Music.* **1.** The syllable used to represent the sixth tone of the diatonic scale. **2.** The tone A. [Short for Latin *labii*, word sung in hymn to Saint John the Baptist. See **gamut.** Latin *labii*, genitive of singular *labium*, lip. See **labial.**]

la² (lä) *interj. Obsolete.* Used to express emphasis or to indicate surprise. [Perhaps variant of LO.]

La The symbol for the element lanthanum.

LA Louisiana (with Zip Code).

La. Louisiana.

L.A. 1. Legislative Assembly. **2.** local agent. **3.** Los Angeles.

laa·ger (lä′gər) *n.* Also **la·ger.** A defensive encampment encircled by wagons or armored vehicles. —*v.* **laagered, -gering, -gers.** Also **la·ger.** —*tr.* To form into a laager. —*intr.* To camp in a laager. [Obsolete Afrikaans *lager*, from German *Lager*, lair, from Old High German *legar*, bed, lair. See **legh-** in Appendix.*]

Laa·land (lô′län′). Also **Lol·land.** An island of Denmark, 479 square miles in area, in the Baltic Sea between Sjaelland and northern West Germany.

lab (lăb) *n. Informal.* A **laboratory** *(see).*

lab. laboratory.

Lab. Labrador.

La·ban (lā′bən). The father of Leah and Rachel. Genesis 29:16.

lab·a·rum (lăb′ər-əm) *n., pl.* **-ara** (-ər-ə). **1.** An ecclesiastical banner. **2.** The banner adopted by Constantine the Great after his conversion to Christianity. [Late Latin *labarum*.]

lab·da·num (lăb′də-nəm) *n.* Also **lad·a·num** (lăd′n-əm). A resinous exudation of certain Old World plants of the genus *Cistus*, yielding a fragrant essential oil used in flavorings and perfumes. [Medieval Latin, from Latin *lādanum*, from Greek *ladanon, lēdanon*, from *lēdon*, shrub from which labdanum exudes, from Semitic, akin to or possibly ultimately from Akkadian *ladunu*.]

La·be. The Czech name for the **Elbe.**

la·bel (lā′bəl) *n.* **1.** Anything functioning as a means of identification; especially, a small piece of paper or cloth attached to an article to designate its origin, owner, contents, use, or destination. **2.** A descriptive term; an epithet. **3.** A molding over a door or window; a dripstone. —*tr.v.* **labeled** or **-belled, -beling** or **-belling, -bels. 1.** To attach a label to. **2.** To describe, classify, or designate. [Middle English, label, narrow strip, from Old French, ribbon, strip, from Germanic. See **leb-¹** in Appendix.*] —**la′bel·er, la′bel·ler** *n.*

la·bel·lum (lə-bĕl′əm) *n., pl.* **-bella** (-bĕl′ə). The often enlarged lip of an orchid. [New Latin, from Latin, "small lip," diminutive of *labrum*, lip. See **leb-²** in Appendix.*]

la·bi·al (lā′bē-əl) *adj.* **1.** Of or pertaining to the lips or labia. **2.** Resembling or serving as a lip. **3.** *Music.* Producing tones by the impact of a stream of air upon the edge of a lip, as in a flute or the flue pipes of an organ. **4.** *Phonetics.* Formed mainly by closing or partly closing the lips, as *b, m, v, w,* or a rounded vowel. —*n.* **1.** A flue pipe. **2.** A labial sound. [Medieval Latin *labiālis*, from Latin *labium*, lip. See **leb-²** in Appendix.*] —**la′bi·al·ly** *adv.*

la·bi·al·ize (lā′bē-ə-līz′) *tr.v.* **-ized, -izing, -izes.** *Phonetics.* To round (a vowel). —**la′bi·al·ism′, la′bi·al·i·za′tion** *n.*

labia ma·jo·ra (mə-jôr′ə, -jōr′ə). Two rounded folds of tissue that form the external lateral boundaries of the vulva. [New Latin, "greater lips."]

labia mi·no·ra (mə-nôr′ə, -nōr′ə). Two narrow folds of tissue enclosed within the cleft of the labia majora. Also called "nympha." [New Latin, "lesser lips."]

la·bi·ate (lā′bē-ĭt, -āt′) *adj.* **1.** Having lips or liplike parts. **2.** *Botany.* **a.** Having or characterizing flowers with the corolla divided into two liplike parts. **b.** Of or belonging to the family Labiatae, which includes the mints. —*n.* A labiate plant. [New Latin *labiatus*, from Latin *labium*, lip. See **labial.**]

labio-. Indicates formed with the lips and (another organ); for example, **labiodental.** [From Latin *labium*, lip. See **labial.**]

la·bi·o·den·tal (lā′bē-ō-dĕnt′l) *adj. Phonetics.* Articulated with the lip or lips and teeth. —*n. Phonetics.* A labiodental sound.

la·bi·o·na·sal (lā′bē-ō-nā′zəl) *adj. Phonetics.* Simultaneously labial and nasal. —*n. Phonetics.* A labionasal sound.

la·bi·o·ve·lar (lā′bē-ō-vē′lər) *adj. Phonetics.* Simultaneously labial and velar. —*n. Phonetics.* A labiovelar sound.

la·bi·um (lā′bē-əm) *n., pl.* **-bia** (-bē-ə). **1.** *Anatomy.* Any of four folds of tissue of the female external genitalia. **2.** *Zoology.* A liplike structure, such as that forming the floor of the mouth in insects. **3.** *Botany.* One of the liplike divisions of a labiate corolla. [New Latin, from Latin, lip. See **leb-²** in Appendix.*]

la·bor (lā′bər) *n.* Also *chiefly British* **la·bour. 1.** Physical or mental exertion of a practical nature, as distinguished from exertion for the sake of amusement; work. **2.** A specific task. **3.** Work for wages, as distinguished from work for profits. **4.** Workers collectively; the laboring class. **5.** *Capital* L. A political party claiming to represent the interest of workers especially. **6.** Something produced by labor. **7.** The physical efforts of childbirth; parturition. —See Synonyms at **work.** —*v.* **labored, -boring, -bors.** Also *chiefly British* **la·bour.** —*intr.* **1.** To work; toil. **2.** To strive painstakingly. **3. a.** To proceed slowly; plod. **b.** To pitch and roll. **4.** To be hampered. Used with *under: labor under a misconception.* **5.** To undergo the pangs of childbirth. —*tr.* **1.** To deal with in exhaustive detail; treat laboriously: *labor a point.* **2.** To burden. **3.** *Archaic.* To cultivate; till. —*adj.* Also *chiefly British* **la·bour. 1.** Of or pertaining to labor. **2.** *Capital* L. Of or pertaining to a political party claiming to represent the interests of the working class. [Middle English *labour, labor*, from Old French, from Latin *labor*, labor, exertion. See **leb-¹** in Appendix.*] —**la′bor·er** *n.*

lab·o·ra·to·ry (lăb′rə-tôr′ē, -tōr′ē; *British* lə-bŏr′ə-tə-rē) *n.*, *pl.* **-ries.** *Abbr.* **lab.** **1.** A room or building equipped for scientific experimentation, research, or testing. **2.** A place where drugs and chemicals are manufactured. **3.** Any observation point or testing ground. **4.** A period devoted to work or study in a laboratory. Also informally called "lab." [Medieval Latin *labōrātōrium*, workshop, from Latin *labōrātus*, past participle of *labōrāre*, to labor, from *labor*, LABOR.]

Labor Day. Also *Canadian* **Labour Day.** The first Monday in September, a legal holiday observed in the United States and Canada in honor of the workingman.

la·bored (lā′bərd) *adj.* **1.** Done or produced with labor. **2.** Showing labor; lacking natural ease; overworked.

la·bo·ri·ous (lə-bôr′ē-əs, lə-bōr′-) *adj.* **1.** Requiring long, hard work. **2.** Hard-working; industrious. [Middle English, from Old French *laborieux*, from Latin *labōriōsus*, from *labor*, LABOR.] —**la·bo′ri·ous·ly** *adv.* —**la·bo′ri·ous·ness** *n.*

la·bor·ite (lā′bə-rīt′) *n.* Also *chiefly British* **la·bour·ite.** **1.** A member or supporter of a labor movement or union. **2.** *Capital* **L.** A member of a political party representing labor.

la·bor·sav·ing (lā′bər-sā′vĭng) *adj.* Conserving labor.

labor union. An organization of wage earners formed for the purpose of serving their class interests with respect to wages and working conditions; a trade union.

Lab·ra·dor (lăb′rə-dôr). *Abbr.* **Lab.** **1.** A peninsula of northeastern Canada, over 500,000 square miles in area, divided between Newfoundland and Quebec, where the northern section is known as Ungava Peninsula. **2.** The mainland territory of Newfoundland, Canada, occupying 112,926 square miles.

Lab·ra·dor Current (lăb′rə-dôr). A cold ocean current flowing southward from Baffin Bay along the coast of Labrador and turning east after intersecting with the Gulf Stream.

lab·ra·dor·ite (lăb′rə-dôr′īt, -dô-rīt′) *n.* A plagioclase feldspar, found in igneous rocks, and characterized by brilliant colors in some specimens. [It is found in LABRADOR.]

Labrador retriever. A dog of a breed originating in Newfoundland, having a short, dense coat and a tapering tail.

Lab·ra·dor Sea (lăb′rə-dôr). A section of the North Atlantic between Labrador and southwestern Greenland.

la·bret (lā′brĕt) *n.* An ornament inserted in a perforation in the lip. [Latin *labrum*, lip (see **leb-²** in Appendix*) + -ET.]

la·brum (lā′brəm) *n.*, *pl.* **-bra** (-brə). A lip or liplike structure, such as that forming the roof of the mouth in insects. [New Latin, from Latin, lip. See **leb-²** in Appendix.*]

La Bru·yère (lȧ brü-yâr′), **Jean de.** 1645–1696. French moralist; author of *Caractères* (1688).

La·bu·an (lä′bo͞o-än′, lə-bo͞o′ən). An island of Malaysia, 35 square miles in area, off the western coast of Sabah.

la·bur·num (lə-bûr′nəm) *n.* Any of several trees or shrubs of the genus *Laburnum;* especially, *L. anagyroides*, cultivated for its drooping clusters of yellow flowers. Also called "golden chain." [Latin *laburnum*, perhaps from Etruscan.]

lab·y·rinth (lăb′ə-rĭnth′) *n.* **1. a.** An intricate structure of interconnecting passages. **b.** *Capital* **L.** *Greek Mythology.* The maze in which the Minotaur was confined. **2.** Something highly intricate in composition or construction. **3.** *Anatomy.* **a.** A group of communicating anatomical cavities. **b.** The internal ear, comprising the semicircular canals, vestibule, and cochlea. [Learned respelling of Middle English *laborintus*, from Latin *labyrinthus*, from Greek *laburinthos*, probably akin to Greek *labrus*, double ax, perhaps a word borrowed from Caria.]

lab·y·rin·thi·an (lăb′ə-rĭn′thē-ən) *adj.* Labyrinthine.

lab·y·rin·thine (lăb′ə-rĭn′thĭn′, -thēn′) *adj.* **1.** Of, pertaining to, or constituting a labyrinth. **2.** Intricate; complicated.

lac¹ (lăk) *n.* A resinous secretion of the **lac insect** *(see)*, used in making shellac. [Dutch *lak* or French *laque*, from Hindi *lākh*, from Prakrit *lakkha*, from Sanskrit *lākshā*. See **reg-³** in Appendix.*]

lac² (lăk) *n.* Also **lakh.** In India: **1.** The sum of 100,000: *12 lacs of rupees.* **2.** A very large number. [Hindi *lākh*, from Sanskrit *lākshā*, "mark," "sign." See **reg-³** in Appendix.*]

Lac·ca·dive, Mi·ni·coy, and A·min·di·vi Islands (lăk′ə-dīv′; mĭn′ĭ-koi′; ŭm′ən-dē′vē). A group of small islands in the Arabian Sea off the southwestern coast of the Republic of India; a union territory of India since 1956.

lace (lās) *n.* **1.** A cord or ribbon threaded through eyelets or around hooks on two opposite edges for drawing and tying them together. **2.** A delicate fabric woven of silk, cotton, nylon, or other thread in an open weblike pattern. **3.** Gold or silver braid ornamenting an officer's uniform. —*v.* **laced, lacing, laces.** —*tr.* **1.** To thread a cord through the eyelets or around the hooks of: *lace shoes.* **2. a.** To draw together and tie the laces of. **b.** To cinch in the waist of by tightening corset laces. **3.** To intertwine: *lace garlands through a trellis.* **4.** To apply lace to. **5.** To add liquor to (a beverage). **6.** To streak with color. **7.** To give a beating to; thrash. —*intr.* To be fastened with lace. —**lace into.** To attack; assail. [Middle English *lace, laas, las*, ornamental braid, cord, from Old French *laz, las*, from Vulgar Latin *lacium* (unattested), from Latin *laqueus*, noose, trap, probably related to *lacere*, to allure. See **delight.**] —**lac′er** *n.*

Lac·e·dae·mon. See **Sparta.**

lac·er·ate (lăs′ə-rāt′) *tr.v.* **-ated, -ating, -ates.** **1.** To tear. **2.** To distress deeply. —*adj.* Also **lac·er·at·ed** (-rā′tĭd). **1.** Torn; mangled. **2.** Wounded. **3.** Having jagged, deeply cut edges: *lacerate leaves.* [Latin *lacerāre*, from *lacer*, torn, rent, mangled. See **lēk-** in Appendix.*] —**lac′er·a′tion** *n.* —**lac′er·a′tive** *adj.*

La·cer·ta (lə-sûr′tə) *n.* A constellation in the Northern Hemisphere near Cygnus and Andromeda. [New Latin, from Latin, LIZARD.]

la·cer·til·i·an (lăs′ər-tĭl′ē-ən) *adj.* *Rare.* Of, pertaining to, or characteristic of lizards and closely related reptiles. [From New Latin *Lacertilia*, a former suborder of lizardlike reptiles, from Latin *lacerta*, LIZARD.]

lace·wing (lās′wĭng′) *n.* Any of various greenish or brownish insects of the families Chrysopidae and Hemerobiidae, having four gauzy wings, threadlike antennae, and larvae that feed on insect pests such as aphids and scale insects.

lach·es (lăch′ĭz, lā′chĭz) *n.*, *pl.* **laches.** *Law.* Culpable negligence; especially, delay in asserting a right or a claim. [Middle English *lachesse*, from Old French, from *lasche*, lax, from Vulgar Latin *lascus* (unattested), from Latin *laxus*, LAX.]

Lach·e·sis (lăk′ə-sĭs). *Greek Mythology.* One of the three Fates. [Greek *Lakhesis*, "disposer of lots," from *lakhein*, aoristic infinitive of *lankhanain*†, to obtain by lot.]

Lach·lan (läk′lən). A river of Australia, rising in the Eastern Highlands and flowing 922 miles northwest and then southwest to the Murrumbidgee in southwestern New South Wales.

lach·ry·mal (lăk′rə-məl) *adj.* Also **lac·ri·mal.** **1.** Of or pertaining to tears. **2.** Of or pertaining to the glands that produce tears. —*n.* Also **lac·ri·mal.** **1.** A lachrymatory. **2.** *Plural.* The lachrymal glands. [Medieval Latin *lachrymālis, lacrimālis*, from Latin *lacrima, lacruma*, tear. See **dakru-** in Appendix.*]

lach·ry·ma·tor (lăk′rə-mā′tər) *n.* **Tear gas** *(see).* [From Latin *lacrimatiō*, weeping, from *lacrimāre*, to cry. See **lachrymatory.**]

lach·ry·ma·to·ry (lăk′rə-mə-tôr′ē, -tōr′ē) *n.*, *pl.* **-ries.** A vase or phial for holding the tears of mourners. —*adj.* Of, pertaining to, or causing tears. [Medieval Latin *lachrymatōrium*, from Late Latin *lacrimatōrius*, of tears, from Latin *lacrimāre*, to cry, from *lacrima*, tear. See **lachrymal.**]

lach·ry·mose (lăk′rə-mōs′) *adj.* **1.** Weeping or inclined to weep; tearful. **2.** Causing tears; sorrowful. [Latin *lacrimōsus*, from *lacrima*, tear. See **lachrymal.**] —**lach′ry·mose′ly** *adv.*

la·cin·i·ate (lə-sĭn′ē-āt′) *adj.* Also **la·cin·i·a·ted** (-ā′tĭd). **1.** Fringed. **2.** Having edges cut into narrow, fringelike segments or lobes: *laciniate petals.* [From Latin *lacīnia*, fringe, tuft. See **lēk-** in Appendix.*] —**la·cin′i·a′tion** *n.*

lac insect. Any of various insects of the subfamily Lacciferinae; especially, *Laccifer lacca*, of southern Asia, the female of which secretes the resinous substance lac.

lack (lăk) *n.* **1.** A deficiency or absence; want: *a lack of money.* **2.** A need. —*v.* **lacked, lacking, lacks.** —*tr.* **1.** To be entirely without or have very little of. **2.** To need. —*intr.* **1.** To be wanting or deficient. **2.** To be missing; be unobtainable. —See Usage note below. [Middle English *lac, lacke*, perhaps from Middle Dutch, deficiency, fault. See **leg-²** in Appendix.*]

Synonyms: *lack, want, need.* These verbs mean to be without, or deficient in, something, usually what is necessary or highly desirable. *Lack* emphasizes the void or deficiency that results from the absence of the thing in question or from the inadequacy of its supply. *Want* and *need* put the stress on the urgent necessity for filling the void or remedying the inadequacy.

Usage: *Lack* is used as a transitive verb in *You will not lack support from me.* Intransitively, *lack* is often followed by *in: what you lack in ready cash; you will not be lacking in support from me.* The variant construction *lack for* is less well established in such examples. The following is acceptable to only 42 per cent of the Usage Panel: *You will not lack for support from me.*

lack·a·dai·si·cal (lăk′ə-dā′zĭ-kəl) *adj.* Lacking spirit or interest; languid. [From earlier *lackadaisy*, extended form of LACKADAY.] —**lack′a·dai′si·cal·ly** *adv.* —**lack′a·dai′si·cal·ness** *n.*

lack·a·day (lăk′ə-dā′) *interj.* *Archaic.* Used to express regret or disapproval. [From the phrase *alack the day.*]

lack·ey (lăk′ē) *n.*, *pl.* **-eys.** Also **lac·quey.** **1.** A liveried male servant; footman. **2.** A servile follower; toady. —*v.* **lackeyed, -eying, -eys.** Also **lac·quey.** —*tr.* To attend as a lackey. —*intr.* To act in a servile manner; fawn. [French *laquais*, from Old French, from Catalan *alacay*, perhaps akin to Spanish *alcalde*, ALCALDE.]

lack·lus·ter (lăk′lŭs′tər) *adj.* Also *chiefly British* **lack·lus·tre.** Lacking luster, brightness, or vitality; dull.

La Col·um·na. See **Pico Bolívar.**

La·co·ni·a (lə-kō′nē-ə). The ancient region of the Peloponnesus of which Sparta was the metropolis.

la·con·ic (lə-kŏn′ĭk) *adj.* Terse; concise; succinct. See Synonyms at **concise.** [Latin *laconicus*, from Greek *Lakōnikos*, of or resembling the Spartans (known for their brevity of speech), from *Lakōn*†, native of Laconia, Spartan.] —**la·con′i·cal·ly** *adv.*

lac·o·nism (lăk′ə-nĭz′əm) *n.* Also **la·con·i·cism** (lə-kŏn′ĭ-sĭz′əm). **1.** Succinctness of expression. **2.** A laconic expression.

La Co·ru·ña (lä kō-ro͞o′nyä). A city of Spain, a seaport in the northwest on the Atlantic. Population, 161,000.

lac·quer (lăk′ər) *n.* **1.** Any of various clear or colored synthetic coatings, made by dissolving nitrocellulose or other cellulose derivatives together with plasticizers and pigments in a mixture of volatile solvents, and used to give wood and metal surfaces a high gloss. **2.** Any glossy, often resinous material used as a surface coating, such as the exudation of the lacquer tree. **3.** A baked-on finish on the inside of food and beverage cans. —*tr.v.* **lacquered, -quering, -quers.** **1.** To coat with lacquer. **2.** To give a sleek, glossy finish to. [Earlier *lacker*, from obsolete French *lacre*, sealing wax, from Spanish *laca*, resin, from Hindi *lākh*, LAC (resin).] —**lac′quer·er** *n.*

lacquer tree. A tree, *Rhus verniciflua*, of eastern Asia, having a toxic exudation from which a black lacquer is obtained.

lac·ri·mal. Variant of **lachrymal.**

lac·ri·ma·tion (lăk′rə-mā′shən) *n.* The secretion of tears, especially in excess.

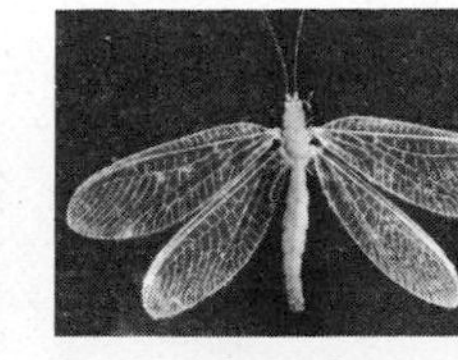
lacewing
Genus *Chrysopa*

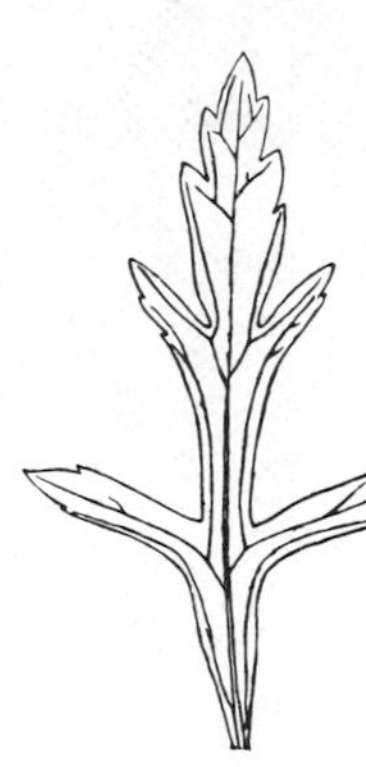
laciniate
Laciniate leaf

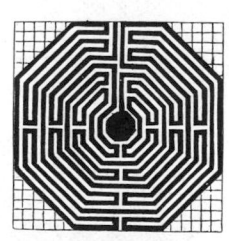

labyrinth

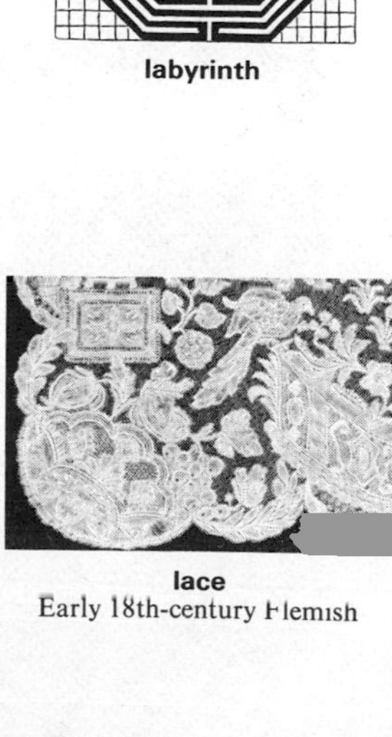
lace
Early 18th-century Flemish

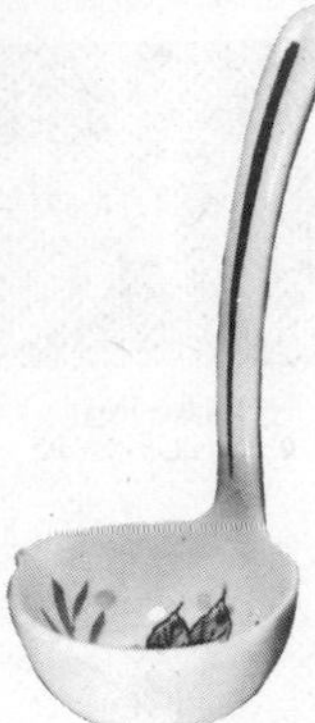

ladle

la·crosse (lə-krôs′, -krŏs′) *n.* A game of American Indian origin resembling field hockey, played with a lacrosse stick, a long-handled racquet, and requiring ten players on each team. [Canadian French, from French *(le jeu de) la crosse,* (the game of) the hooked stick, from Old French *crosse, croce,* staff, crosier, from Germanic. See **ger-**[3] in Appendix.*]
Lac Saint-Jean. The French name for Lake **Saint John.**
lac·tal·bu·min (lăk′tăl-byōō′mən) *n.* The albumin contained in milk. [LACT(O)- + ALBUMIN.]
lac·ta·ry (lăk′tə-rē) *adj.* Of or pertaining to milk. [Latin *lactārius,* from *lac* (stem *lact-*), milk. See **melg-** in Appendix.*]
lac·tase (lăk′tās′) *n.* An enzyme occurring in certain yeasts and in the intestinal juices of mammals that catalyzes the conversion of lactose into glucose and galactose. [LACT(O)- + -ASE.]
lac·tate (lăk′tāt′) *intr.v.* **-tated, -tating, -tates.** To secrete or produce milk. —*n.* A salt or ester of lactic acid. [Latin *lactāre,* to suckle, from *lac* (stem *lact-*), milk. See **melg-** in Appendix.*] —**lac·ta′tion** *n.*
Lac Tchad. The French name for Lake **Chad.**
lac·te·al (lăk′tē-əl) *adj.* **1.** Of, pertaining to, or like milk; milky. **2.** *Anatomy.* Of or pertaining to the lacteals. —*n. Anatomy.* Any of numerous minute lymph-carrying vessels that convey chyle from the intestine to the thoracic duct. [From Latin *lacteus,* of milk, from *lac* (stem *lact-*), milk. See **melg-** in Appendix.*] —**lac′te·al·ly** *adv.*
lac·tes·cent (lăk-tĕs′ənt) *adj.* **1.** Becoming milky. **2.** Milky. **3.** *Biology.* Secreting or yielding a milky juice, as certain plants and insects. [Latin *lactescēns,* present participle of *lactescere,* to become milky, from *lactēre,* to be milky, from *lac* (stem *lact-*), milk. See **melg-** in Appendix.*] —**lac·tes′cence** *n.*
lac·tic (lăk′tĭk) *adj.* Pertaining to or derived from milk. [French *lactique,* from Latin *lac* (stem *lact-*), milk. See **lacteal.**]
lactic acid. A hygroscopic syrupy liquid, $C_3H_6O_3$, present in sour milk, molasses, various fruits, and wines, and used in foods and beverages as an acidulant, flavoring, and preservative, and in adhesives, plasticizers, and pharmaceuticals.
lac·tif·er·ous (lăk-tĭf′ər-əs) *adj.* **1.** Producing, secreting, or conveying milk. **2.** *Botany.* Yielding latex or a similar milky juice. [Late Latin *lactifer* : LACT(O)- + *-fer,* -FEROUS.]
lacto-, lact-. Indicates milk; for example, **lactoprotein, lactone.** [French, from Late Latin, from Latin *lac* (stem *lact-*), milk. See **melg-** in Appendix.*]
lac·to·ba·cil·lus (lăk′tō-bə-sĭl′əs) *n., pl.* **-cilli** (-sĭl′ī′). Any of various bacilli of the genus *Lactobacillus,* that ferment lactic acid from carbohydrates. [New Latin : LACTO- + BACILLUS.]
lac·to·fla·vin (lăk′tə-flā′vĭn, lăk′tə-flā′-) *n. Chemistry.* **Riboflavin** *(see).* [LACTO- + FLAVIN.]
lac·to·gen·ic (lăk′tə-jĕn′ĭk) *adj.* Inducing lactation. [LACTO- + -GENIC.]
lac·tone (lăk′tōn′) *n.* A cyclic ester of a hydroxyl acid, formed by removing the constituents of water from a molecule of the acid. [LACT(O)- + -ONE.] —**lac·ton′ic** (-tŏn′ĭk) *adj.*
lac·to·pro·te·in (lăk′tō-prō′tē-ən, -prō′tēn′) *n.* Any protein normally present in milk.
lac·tose (lăk′tōs′) *n.* A white crystalline disaccharide, $C_{12}H_{22}O_{11}$, made from whey, and used in pharmaceuticals, infant foods, bakery products, and confections. Also called "milk sugar," "sugar of milk." [French : LACT(O)- + -OSE.]
la·cu·na (lə-kyōō′nə) *n., pl.* **-nae** (-nē) or **-nas.** **1.** An empty space or missing part; a gap: *"self-centered in opinion, with curious lacunae of astounding ignorance"* (Frank Norris). **2.** *Anatomy.* A cavity or depression. [Latin *lacūna,* pool. See **lagoon.**] —**la·cu′nal, la·cu′nar, la·cu′nar·y** *adj.*
la·cu·nar (lə-kyōō′nər) *n., pl.* **-nars** or **lacunaria** (lăk′yōō-nâr′ē-ə). *Architecture.* **1.** A ceiling or soffit decorated with a pattern of recessed panels. **2.** A panel in such a pattern. [Latin *lacūnar,* from *lacūna,* cavity, cleft, pool. See **lagoon.**]
la·cus·trine (lə-kŭs′trən) *adj.* **1.** Of or pertaining to a lake. **2.** Living or growing in or along the edges of lakes. [From French *lacustre,* of a lake, from Latin *lacus,* LAKE (influenced in form by Latin *palūster,* marshy, from *palus,* swamp).]
lac·y (lā′sē) *adj.* **-ier, -iest.** Of, pertaining to, or resembling lace. —**lac′i·ness** *n.*
lad (lăd) *n.* **1.** A young man. **2.** *Informal.* A man of any age. Used familiarly. [Middle English *ladde*†.]
lad·a·num. Variant of **labdanum.**
lad·der (lăd′ər) *n.* **1.** A device consisting of two long structural members crossed by parallel, equally spaced rungs, used to climb or descend vertically. **2.** Something resembling a ladder, as a run in a stocking. **3. a.** A means of ascent and descent: *ascending the social ladder.* **b.** A series of ranked stages or levels: *high on the executive ladder.* [Middle English *ladder,* Old English *hlǣd(d)er.* See **klei-** in Appendix.*]
lad·der-back (lăd′ər-băk′) *n.* **1.** A chair back consisting of two upright posts connected by horizontal slats. **2.** A chair with this type of back. —**lad′der-back′** *adj.*
lad·die (lăd′ē) *n.* A young lad. [From LAD.]
lade (lād) *v.* **laded, laden** (lād′n) or **laded, lading, lades.** —*tr.* **1. a.** To load with or as if with cargo. **b.** To place as a load for or as if for shipment. **2.** To weigh down; to burden; oppress. **3.** To take up or remove water with a ladle or the like; to bale. —*intr.* **1.** To take on cargo. **2.** To ladle a liquid. [Lade (infinitive), laden (past participle); Middle English *laden, laden,* Old English *hladan, gehladen.* See **klā-** in Appendix.*]
lad·en (lād′n) *adj.* **1.** Weighed down with a load; heavy: *"the warmish air, laden with the rains of those thousands of miles of western sea"* (Hilaire Belloc). **2.** Oppressed; burdened: *laden with grief.*
la-di-da (lä′dē-dä′) *adj.* Also **la-de-da.** *Informal.* Affectedly genteel; pretentious. —*n. Informal.* Also **la-de-da.** A person showing such affectation. [Perhaps imitative of affected speech.]

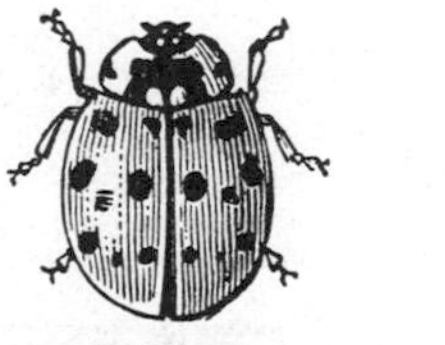

ladybug
Anatis quindecimpunctatum

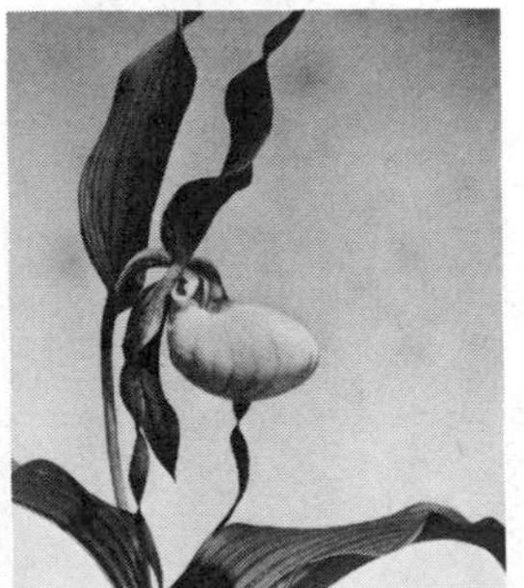

lady's-slipper
Cypripedium pubescens

la·dies′ man. Variant of **lady's man.**
la·dies′-tress·es (lā′dēz-trĕs′ĭz) *n.* Also **la·dy's-tress·es.** Plural in form, used with a singular or plural verb. Any of various orchids of the genus *Spiranthes,* having a spike of small white flowers usually in a twisted or spiral arrangement.
La·din (lə-dēn′) *n.* **1.** The Rhaeto-Romanic dialect spoken in southeastern Switzerland, contiguous parts of northern Italy, and the Tyrol, forming a distinct Romance language. **2.** An inhabitant of this region who speaks Ladin. [Italian *Ladino,* from Latin *Latinus,* LATIN.]
lad·ing (lā′dĭng) *n.* **1.** An act of lading. **2.** Cargo; freight: *a bill of lading.*
La·di·no (lə-dē′nō) *n.* A Romance language, derived from Spanish with Hebrew elements and modifications, spoken by Sephardic Jews, especially in the Balkans. Also called "Judeo-Spanish." [Spanish, "Latin," from Latin *Latinus,* LATIN.]
la·dle (lād′l) *n.* A long-handled spoon with a deep bowl for serving liquids. —*tr.v.* **ladled, -dling, -dles.** To lift out or convey with a ladle. [Middle English *ladel,* Old English *hlædel,* from *hladan,* to draw out, LADE.]
La·do·ga (lăd′ə-gə, lä′də-). The largest lake in Europe (7,100 square miles), in the northwestern Russian S.F.S.R. about 30 miles south of the Finnish border.
La·drone Islands, La·drones. Former names for the **Mariana Islands.**
la·dy (lā′dē) *n., pl.* **-dies.** **1.** A woman having the refined habits, gentle manners, and sense of responsibility often associated with breeding, culture, and high station; the feminine equivalent of a gentleman. **2.** The female head of a household. Now chiefly used in the phrase *the lady of the house.* **3. a.** A polite term for any adult member of the feminine sex; woman. **b.** *Informal.* Madam. Used in direct address: *Carry your bags, lady?* **4. a.** A woman to whom a man is romantically attached; ladylove. **b.** *Informal.* A wife. **5.** *Capital* **L.** *British.* The general feminine title of nobility and of other rank, used in the following specific ways: **a.** For the wife of a knight or baronet: *Lady Smith* (wife of Sir Harry Smith); **b.** Semiformally for a marchioness, countess, or viscountess: *Lady Salisbury* (the Marchioness of Salisbury); **c.** As the usual style for the wife of a baron: *Lady Snow* (wife of Lord Snow); **d.** Semiformally for a baroness in her own right: *Lady Ruthven* (daughter of a baron deceased without male issue, holding a rare barony that can descend in the female line); **e.** As a courtesy title for the daughter of a duke, marquis, or earl: *Lady Hester Stanhope* (daughter of Earl Stanhope); **f.** As a courtesy title for the wife of a younger son of a duke or marquis: *Lady John Russell* (wife of Lord John Russell, third son of the Duke of Bedford). ***Note:*** In direct address, *my lady* or *your ladyship* are deferential substitutes for any of the above. In direct address and in informal reference, **e** and **f** above may be shortened to *Lady Hester* and *Lady John* respectively; but these may never be given as *Lady Stanhope* and *Lady Russell,* while **a, b, c,** and **d** may never be used with baptismal names. With all except **a,** the more formal usage (as in addressing a letter), is *The Lady Snow, The Lady Ruthven,* and the like. [Middle English *la(ve)di, lafdi,* Old English *hlǣfdige,* "kneader of bread," lady. See **dheigh-** in Appendix.*]
la·dy·bug (lā′dē-bŭg′) *n.* Any of numerous small beetles of the family Coccinellidae, often reddish with black spots, and feeding on insect pests such as aphids and scale insects. Also called "ladybird," "lady beetle." [After OUR LADY.]
Lady Chapel. Also **lady chapel.** A chapel in a cathedral, usually located behind the sanctuary, dedicated to the Virgin Mary.
la·dy·fin·ger (lā′dē-fĭng′gər) *n.* Also **la·dys·fin·ger** (lā′dēz-). A small, oval sponge cake, suggestive of a finger.
lady in waiting *pl.* **ladies in waiting.** A lady of a court appointed to serve or attend a queen or princess.
la·dy-kill·er (lā′dē-kĭl′ər) *n. Slang.* A man reputed to be exceptionally successful and often ruthless with women.
la·dy·like (lā′dē-līk′) *adj.* **1.** Characteristic of a lady; delicate; refined; well-bred. **2.** Appropriate for or becoming a lady. **3.** Unduly sensitive to matters of propriety or decorum. **4.** Lacking virility or strength. —See Synonyms at **feminine.**
la·dy·love (lā′dē-lŭv′) *n.* A beloved woman; sweetheart.
la·dy·ship (lā′dē-shĭp′) *n.* **1.** A form of address employed in speaking or referring to a woman holding the rank of lady. Used with *Your* or *Her.* See Note at **lady.** **2.** The condition of being a lady.
lady's man. Also **ladies' man.** A man who enjoys and attracts the company of ladies.
La·dy·smith (lā′dē-smĭth). A city of South Africa, in west-central Natal; the subject of a prolonged siege against the British by the Boers (1899–1900). Population, 23,000.
la·dy's-slip·per (lā′dēz-slĭp′ər) *n.* Any of various orchids of the genus *Cypripedium,* having variously colored flowers with an inflated, pouchlike lip. See **moccasin flower.**
la·dy's-smock (lā′dēz-smŏk′) *n.* A plant, the **cuckooflower** *(see).*
la·dy's-thumb (lā′dēz-thŭm′) *n.* A plant, *Polygonum persicaria,* native to Europe, having clusters of very small pinkish flowers.
la·dy's-tress·es. Variant of **ladies'-tresses.**
La·er·tes (lā-ûr′tēz). *Greek Mythology.* The father of Odysseus.
La·fay·ette (lä′fē-ĕt′, lăf′ē-). A city of Louisiana, in the south-central part of the state. Population, 50,000.
La Fa·yette (là fâ-yĕt′), **Comtesse de.** Called "Madame de La Fayette." 1634–1693. French novelist.
La·fay·ette (lä′fē-ĕt′, lăf′ē-; *French* là-fâ-yĕt′), **Marquis de.** Title of Marie Joseph Paul Yves Roch Gilbert du Motier.

1757–1834. French military and political leader; commanded American troops in the Revolutionary War.

Laf·fitte (là-fēt′), **Jean.** Also **La·fitte.** 1780?–1826. French pirate in America.

La Fol·lette (lə fŏl′ĭt), **Robert Marion.** 1855–1925. American political leader; U.S. senator (1906–25) and Progressive Party candidate for President (1924).

La Fon·taine (là fôn-tĕn′), **Jean de.** 1621–1695. French poet and fabulist.

lag[1] (lăg) v. **lagged, lagging, lags.** —*intr.* **1.** To fail to keep up a pace; fall behind; straggle; loiter. **2.** To proceed or develop slowly or abnormally slowly. **3.** To fail, weaken, or slacken gradually; to flag. **4.** *Billiards.* To determine the order of play by successively hitting the cue ball against the end rail, the ball rebounding closest to the head rail indicating the player to shoot first. —*tr.* **1.** To fall or lag behind. **2.** To shoot, throw, or pitch (a marble or coin, for example) at a mark. —*n.* **1.** One that lags. **2.** The act, process, or condition of lagging. **3.** A condition of slowness or retardation. **4.** An extent or duration of lagging: *"he wondered darkly at how great a lag there was between his thinking and his actions"* (Thomas Wolfe). **5.** Any interval between events or phenomena. [Origin obscure.]

lag[2] (lăg) n. **1.** A barrel stave. **2.** Any covering for a cylindrical object. —*tr.v.* **lagged, lagging, lags.** To furnish or cover with lags. [Perhaps from Scandinavian, akin to Swedish *lagg*, barrel stave. See **leu-**[1] in Appendix.*]

lag[3] (lăg) *tr.v.* **lagged, lagging, lags.** *Slang.* **1.** To arrest. **2.** To send to prison. —*n. Slang.* **1.** A convict. **2.** A term of imprisonment. [Origin unknown.]

lag·an (lăg′ən) n. Also **li·gan** (lī′gən), **lag·end** (lăg′ənd). *Maritime Law.* Cargo or equipment thrown into the sea from a ship in distress, but attached to a float or buoy to enable its recovery. [Old French, perhaps from Old Norse *lögn* (stem *lagn-*), dragnet. See **legh-** in Appendix.*]

Lag b'O·mer (läg′ bō′mər). A Jewish holiday, originating as an agricultural festival, celebrated on the 33rd day after the 2nd day of Passover, on the 18th day of Iyar. [Hebrew, "thirty-third (day) of the Omer."]

la·ger[1] (lä′gər) n. A type of beer, originally brewed in Germany, that contains a relatively small amount of hops and is aged from six weeks to six months to allow sedimentation. Also called "lager beer." [Short for German *Lager(bier)*, (beer) for storing, from *lager*, store, lair, from Old High German *legar*, lair. See **legh-** in Appendix.*]

la·ger[2]. Variant of **laager.**

lag·gard (lăg′ərd) n. A person who lags behind; a straggler. —*adj.* Falling or lingering behind; retarded; backward. See Synonyms at **slow.** [LAG (fall behind) + -ARD.] —**lag′gard·ly** *adv.* —**lag′gard·ness** *n.*

lag·ger (lăg′ər) n. One that lags.

lag·ging (lăg′ĭng) n. **1.** Insulation used to prevent heat diffusion from steam pipes, boilers, and the like. **2.** A wooden frame built to support the sides of an arch until the keystone is positioned. **3.** The act or process of covering or supporting with lagging. [From LAG (barrel stave).]

la·gniappe (lăn-yăp′, lăn′yăp′) n. **1.** A small gift presented to a customer with his purchase by a store owner. **2.** *Informal.* An extra or unexpected gift; a gratuity. [Louisiana French, from American Spanish *la ñapa* : *la*, the + *ñapa*, lagniappe, from Quechua *yápa*, addition.]

La·go·a dos Pa·tos (lä-gō′ä dōōsh pä′tōōs). A tidal lagoon, extending for about 150 miles in southeastern Brazil.

La·go di Gar·da. The Italian name for **Lake Garda.**

lag·o·morph (lăg′ə-môrf′) n. Any of various gnawing mammals of the order Lagomorpha, which includes the rabbits, hares, and pikas. [New Latin *Lagomorpha* : Greek *lagōs*, hare (see **slēg-** in Appendix*) + -MORPH.] —**lag′o·mor′phic** *adj.*

la·goon (lə-gōōn′) n. Also **la·gune, la·gu·na** (-gōō′nə). A body of brackish water, especially one separated from the sea by sandbars or coral reefs. [French *lagune* and Italian or Spanish *laguna*, from Latin *lacūna*, pool, cavity, from *lacus*, LAKE.]

La·goon Islands. The former name for the **Ellice Islands.**

La·gos (lā′gŏs, -gəs). The capital of Nigeria, a seaport in the southwest on the Gulf of Guinea. Population, 450,000.

La·grange (lə-grănj′; *French* là-gränzh′), **Comte Joseph Louis.** 1736–1813. French astronomer, mathematician, and educator.

lag screw. A heavy wood screw having a square bolt head. [Originally used in securing barrel staves.]

Lag·ting, Lag·thing (läg′tĭng) n. The upper house in the Storthing, or parliament, of Norway. [Norwegian : *lag*, society, from Old Norse, due place (influenced in meaning by plural *lög*, law) (see **legh-** in Appendix*) + *ting*, parliament, from Old Norse *thing*, parliament, assembly (see **tenk-**[1] in Appendix*).]

La Guar·di·a (lə gwär′dē-ə), **Fiorello H(enry).** 1882–1947. American political leader; mayor of New York City (1934–45).

La Ha·ba·na. The Spanish name for **Havana.**

La Hague, Cape (lə häg′). A promontory of France, in the northwest on the English Channel.

La·hore (lə-hôr′, -hōr′). The capital of West Pakistan in the northeast of the province. Population, 1,296,000.

la·ic (lā′ĭk) adj. Also **la·i·cal** (-ĭ-kəl). Of or relating to the laity; secular. —*n.* A layman. [Late Latin *lāicus*, LAY (nonclergy).] —**la′i·cal·ly** *adv.*

la·i·cize (lā′ĭ-sīz′) *tr.v.* **-cized, -cizing, -cizes. 1.** To free from ecclesiastical control; give over to laymen. **2.** To render lay; secularize. —**la′i·ci·za′tion** *n.*

laid. Past tense and past participle of **lay** (verb).

laid lines. The close thin lines detectable in laid paper, produced by the parallel wires of the mold.

laid paper. 1. A paper made on wire molds that give it a characteristic watermark of laid lines. Compare **wove paper. 2.** A machine-made paper imitating this.

lain. Past participle of **lie** (to rest).

lair (lâr) n. **1.** The den or dwelling of a wild animal. **2.** *Obsolete.* A resting place; a couch. **3.** *Scottish.* A tomb or grave. —*v.* **laired, lairing, lairs.** —*tr.* **1.** To put in a lair. **2.** To be a lair for. —*intr.* To retreat to or lie in a lair. [Middle English *lair, leir*, Old English *leger*. See **legh-** in Appendix.*]

laird (lârd) n. *Scottish.* The owner of a landed estate. [Scottish, variant of LORD.]

lais·sez faire (lĕs′ā fâr′). Also **lais·ser faire. 1.** The doctrine that government should not interfere with commerce. **2.** *Informal.* Noninterference in the affairs of others. [French, "allow (them) to do."] —**lais′sez-faire′** *adj.* —**lais′sez-faire′ism** *n.*

lais·sez-pas·ser (lĕs′ā-pä-sā′) n. A pass; especially, one used in lieu of a passport. [French, "allow (them) to pass."]

la·i·ty (lā′ə-tē) n., pl. **-ties. 1.** Laymen collectively, as distinguished from the clergy. **2.** All those persons outside a given profession, art, or other specialization; nonprofessionals. [From LAY (nonclergy).]

La·ius (lā′əs). *Greek Mythology.* The king of Thebes who was mistakenly killed by his own son, Oedipus.

lake[1] (lāk) n. *Abbr.* **L., l. 1.** A large inland body of fresh or salt water. **2.** A scenic pond as in a park. **3.** A large pool of any liquid. [Middle English *lac*, from Old French *lac*, from Latin *lacus*, basin for water. See **laku-** in Appendix.*]

lake[2] (lāk) n. A pigment consisting of organic coloring matter with an inorganic base or carrier. [Variant of LAC (resin).]

lake[3] (lāk) *tr.v.* **laked, laking, lakes.** To cause (blood plasma) to become red by releasing hemoglobin from erythrocytes, as by suspending the erythrocytes in water. [From LAKE (pigment).]

Lake, Lake of. For names of lakes, see the specific element of the name; for example, **Victoria, Lake; Constance, Lake of.** Other names beginning with Lake are entered under **Lake.**

Lake Aral. See **Aral Sea.**

Lake Charles (chärlz). A city of Louisiana, a commercial center in the southwest. Population, 63,000.

Lake District. An area in northwestern England, noted for its scenery and many lakes.

lake dwelling. A dwelling built on piles in a shallow lake.

lake herring. A food fish, *Coregonus artedii* (or *Leucichthys artedi*), of the Great Lakes region, related to the whitefishes.

Lake Poets. Coleridge, Wordsworth, and Southey, grouped as a school because they lived for a time in the Lake District.

lak·er (lā′kər) n. **1.** A lake fish, such as the lake trout. **2.** A ship used on lakes.

Lake Success. A village of New York State, in the southeast on Long Island; the early headquarters of the United Nations Security Council (1946–51). Population, 3,000.

lake trout. A freshwater food fish, *Salvelinus namaycush*, of the Great Lakes. Also called "Mackinaw trout," "togue."

Lake·wood (lāk′wŏŏd′). A city of southwestern California, southeast of Los Angeles. Population, 67,000.

lakh. Variant of **lac** (sum of money).

lak·y (lā′kē) adj. **-ier, -iest.** Of the color of lake or of blood.

la·la·pa·loo·za, la·la·pa·loo·za. Variants of **lollapalooza.**

Lal·lan (lăl′ən) n. Also **Lal·lans** (lăl′ənz). *Scottish.* **1.** The Lowlands of Scotland. **2.** The dialect of Scottish English spoken in the Lowlands. [Scottish, variant of LOWLANDS.] —**Lal′lan** *adj.*

lal·la·tion (lă-lā′shən) n. The substitution of the phoneme (l) for (r). [From Latin *lallāre*, to make lulling sounds. See **lā-** in Appendix.*]

Lal·ly (lăl′ē) n. A trademark for a concrete-filled steel cylinder used as a supporting member in a building.

lam[1] (lăm) v. **lammed, lamming, lams.** *Slang.* —*tr.* To thrash; wallop. —*intr.* To strike. Used with *out.* —**lam into.** To thrash. [Of Scandinavian origin, akin to Old Norse *lemja*, to flog, to cripple by beating. See **lem-**[1] in Appendix.*]

lam[2] (lăm) *intr.v.* **lammed, lamming, lams.** *Slang.* To depart swiftly or escape, as from prison. —**on the lam.** In flight, especially from the law. [Origin obscure.]

Lam. Lamentations (Old Testament).

la·ma (lä′mə) n. A Buddhist monk of Tibet or Mongolia. [Tibetan *blama*.]

La·ma·ism (lä′mə-ĭz′əm) n. The religion of Tibet and Mongolia and neighboring areas, a form of Mahayana Buddhism with an admixture of indigenous animism, having elaborate rituals and stressing celibacy. [From LAMA (priest).] —**La′ma·ist** *n.* & *adj.* —**La′ma·is′tic** *adj.*

La Man·cha (lə män′chə; *Spanish* lä män′chä). A historic region of south-central Spain; the scene of Cervantes' *Don Quixote de La Mancha.*

La Manche. The French name for the **English Channel.**

La·mar (lə-mär′), **Mirabeau Buonaparte.** 1825–1893. President of the Republic of Texas (1838–41).

La·marck (lə-märk′; *French* là-màrk′), **Chevalier de.** Title of Jean Baptiste Pierre Antoine de Monet. 1744–1829. French naturalist.

La·marck·i·an (lə-mär′kē-ən) adj. Of or relating to Lamarck or Lamarckism. —*n.* A supporter of Lamarckism.

La·marck·ism (lə-mär′kĭz′əm) n. The theory that adaptive responses to environment cause structural changes capable of being inherited. [Developed by Chevalier de LAMARCK.]

La·mar·tine (lä-mär-tēn′), **Alphonse Marie Louis de Prat de.** 1790–1869. French poet.

la·ma·ser·y (lä′mə-ser′ē) n., pl. **-ies.** A Lamaist monastery.

lake trout

Marquis de Lafayette

Fiorello H. La Guardia

ă pat/ā pay/âr care/ä father/b bib/ch church/d deed/ĕ pet/ē be/f fife/g gag/h hat/hw which/ĭ pit/ī pie/îr pier/j judge/k kick/l lid, needle/m mum/n no, sudden/ng thing/ŏ pot/ō toe/ô paw, for/oi noise/ou out/ōō took/ōō boot/p pop/r roar/s sauce/sh ship, dish/t tight/th thin, path/th this, bathe/ŭ cut/ûr urge/v valve/w with/y yes/z zebra, size/zh vision/ə about, item, edible, gallop, circus/ à *Fr.* ami/œ *Fr.* feu, *Ger.* schön/ü *Fr.* tu, *Ger.* über/кн *Ger.* ich, *Scot.* loch/N *Fr.* bon. *Follows main vocabulary. †Of obscure origin.

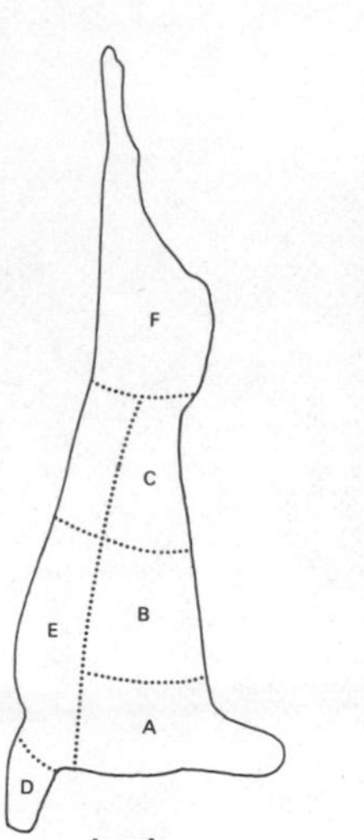

lamb
A. Shoulder
B. Ribs
C. Loin
D. Shank
E. Breast
F. Leg

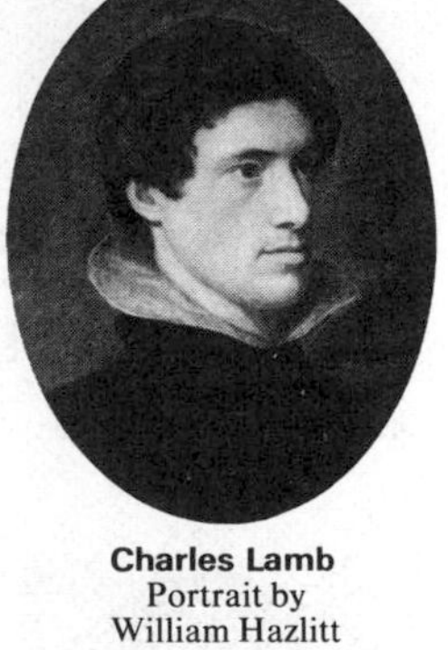

Charles Lamb
Portrait by
William Hazlitt

lamb (lăm) *n.* **1.** A young sheep, especially one not yet weaned. **2.** The flesh of a young sheep used as meat. **3.** Lambskin. **4.** A sweet, mild-mannered person; a dear. **5.** One who can be fleeced, especially in financial matters; a dupe. **6.** A member of a Christian flock. **7.** *Capital* **L.** Christ. Used with *the.* In this sense, also called "Lamb of God." —*intr.v.* **lambed, lambing, lambs.** To give birth to a lamb. [Middle English *lamb,* Old English *lamb,* from Germanic *lambiz-* (unattested).]
Lamb (lăm), **Charles.** Pen name **E·li·a** (ē′lē-ə). 1775–1834. English essayist.
Lamb (lăm), **Willis Eugene.** Born 1913. American physicist.
lam·baste (lăm-bāst′) *tr.v.* **-basted, -basting, -bastes.** *Slang.* **1.** To give a thrashing to; whip; beat. **2.** To scold sharply; berate. [Perhaps LAM (beat) + BASTE (beat).]
lamb·da[1] (lăm′də) *n.* The 11th letter in the Greek alphabet, written Λ, λ. Transliterated in English as *L, l.* See **alphabet.** [Greek *lambda,* of Semitic origin, akin to Hebrew *lāmedh,* LAMED.]
lamb·da[2] (lăm′də) *n. Symbol* Λ *Physics.* An electrically neutral subatomic particle in the baryon family, having a mass 2,183 times that of the electron and a mean lifetime of approximately 2.5×10^{-10} second. See **particle.** [From LAMBDA.]
lambda point. 1. The temperature at which the transition from helium I to superfluid helium II occurs, approximately 2.19°K. **2.** The temperature of any phase transition in which the specific heat regarded as a function of temperature has a logarithmic singularity.
lamb·doid (lăm′doid′) *adj.* Also **lamb·doi·dal** (lăm-doid′l) (for sense 2). **1.** Having the shape of the Greek letter lambda. **2.** Designating the deeply serrated suture in the skull between the two parietal bones and the occipital bone. [French *lambdoïde,* from Greek *lambdoeidēs,* "lambda-shaped" : LAMBDA + -OID.]
lam·bent (lăm′bənt) *adj.* **1.** Flickering lightly and gently over a surface: *"a sheet of lambent fire"* (Ruskin). **2.** Flitting over subjects with effortless brilliance: *a lambent wit.* **3.** Having a gentle glow; luminous: *"his eyes soft and lambent but wild, like a stag's."* (Katherine Anne Porter). —See Synonyms at **bright.** [Latin *lambens,* present of *lambere,* to lick, tap. See **lab-** in Appendix.*] —**lam′ben·cy** *n.* —**lam′bent·ly** *adv.*
Lam·bert (lăm′bərt; *German* läm′bĕrt′), **Johann Heinrich.** 1728–1777. German physicist, mathematician, and astronomer.
lam·bert (lăm′bərt) *n. Symbol* **L** A unit of brightness equal to $1/\pi$ candle per square centimeter. [After Johann LAMBERT.]
Lam·beth (lăm′bəth). A borough of London, England, comprising the former administrative division of Lambeth and part of the former administrative division of Wandsworth. Population, 341,000.
lamb·kill (lăm′kĭl′) *n.* A shrub, **sheep laurel** *(see).* [From its poisonous effect on sheep.]
lamb·kin (lăm′kĭn) *n.* **1.** A small lamb. **2.** A small endearing child. Used as a term of affection.
lam·bre·quin (lăm′bər-kĭn, -brə-kĭn) *n.* **1.** A short piece of drapery ornamenting the top of a window or door or the edge of a shelf. **2.** A heavy, protective cloth or other material worn over a helmet in medieval times. **3.** A scalloped band of color ornamenting the top of a piece of porcelain. [French, from Dutch *lamperkin* (unattested), diminutive of *lamper,* veil, from Middle Dutch *lamper*†.]
lamb·skin (lăm′skĭn′) *n.* **1.** The skin of a lamb, especially when dressed without removing the fleece, as for a garment. **2.** Leather made from the dressed hide of a lamb.
lamb's-let·tuce (lămz′lĕt′əs) *n.* A plant, **corn salad** *(see).*
lamb's-quar·ters (lămz′kwôr′tərz) *n.* Also **lamb's quarters.** Plural in form, used with a singular or plural verb. A species of **pigweed** *(see).*
lamb's wool. 1. Wool shorn from a lamb. **2.** A fabric or yarn made from this wool.
lame[1] (lām) *adj.* **lamer, lamest. 1. a.** Disabled or crippled in one or more limbs, especially in a leg or foot so that ability to walk is impaired. **b.** Limping because of such impairment. **2.** Weak and ineffectual; unsatisfactory: *a lame attempt to apologize.* —*tr.v.* **lamed, laming, lames. 1.** To cause to become lame. **2.** To cripple. [Middle English *lame,* Old English *lama.* See **lem-[1]** in Appendix.*] —**lame′ly** *adv.* —**lame′ness** *n.*
lame[2] (lām) *n.* A thin metal plate; especially, one of the overlapping steel plates in medieval armor. [Old French, from Latin *lāmina,* thin plate. See **stel-[2]** in Appendix.*]
la·mé (lă-mā′) *n.* A fabric having metallic threads in the warp or in the filling. [French, from adjective, "worked with silver and gold thread," from Old French *lame,* thin metal plate, LAME.]
la·med (lä′mĕd′, -mĭd) *n.* Also **la·medh.** The 12th letter in the Hebrew alphabet. See **alphabet.** [Hebrew *lāmedh,* "ox goad" (from the shape of the letter).]
lame duck. 1. An elected officeholder or an assembly continuing in office during the period between the election and the inauguration of a successor. **2.** An ineffective or helpless person; a weakling. **3.** A speculator who has overbought.
la·mel·la (lə-mĕl′ə) *n., pl.* **-mellae** (-mĕl′ē′) or **-las.** A thin scale, plate, or layer, as in the gills of a bivalve mollusk or forming one of the gills of a mushroom. [New Latin, from Latin *lāmella,* diminutive of *lāmina,* thin plate. See **stel-[2]** in Appendix.*] —**la·mel′lar** *adj.* —**la·mel′lar·ly** *adv.*
la·mel·late (lăm′ə-lāt′, lə-mĕl′āt′) *adj.* **1.** Having, composed of, or arranged in thin layers or lamellae. **2.** Resembling a lamella. —**lam′el·la′ted** *adj.* —**lam′el·la′tion** *n.*
lamelli-. Indicates a lamella or lamellae; for example, **lamellibranch.** [From LAMELLA.]
la·mel·li·branch (lə-mĕl′ə-brănk′) *n.* Any of the mollusks of the class Pelecypoda (or Lamellibranchia), having a hinged bivalve shell, and including the clams, mussels, and oysters. —*adj.* Of or pertaining to lamellibranchs. [New Latin *Lamellibranchia,* "plate gilled" : LAMELLI- + BRANCHIA.]
la·mel·li·corn (lə-mĕl′ĭ-kôrn′) *adj.* Of or belonging to the superfamily Lamellicornia (or Scarabaeoidea), which includes the scarabs and other beetles having antennae tipped with movable leaflike plates. —*n.* A lamellicorn beetle. [New Latin *Lamellicornia,* "plate horned" : LAMELLI- + Latin *cornū,* horn (see **ker-[1]** in Appendix*).]
la·mel·li·form (lə-mĕl′ə-fôrm′) *adj.* Having the form of a thin plate or lamella. [LAMELLI- + -FORM.]
la·ment (lə-mĕnt′) *v.* **-mented, -menting, -ments.** —*tr.* **1.** To express grief for or about; mourn over: *lament a death.* **2.** To regret deeply; deplore. —*intr.* **1.** To grieve: *"And add this to them —that all Asia laments to see the folly of their king."* (Marlowe). **2.** To wail; complain: *" 'Doesn't she know,' she lamented, 'that black's bad luck for weddings?' "* (Mary McCarthy). —*n.* **1.** A feeling or expression of sorrow or grief; a lamentation. **2.** A song or poem expressing grief; an elegy; a dirge. [French *lamenter,* from Old French, from Latin *lāmentārī,* from *lāmentum,* expression of sorrow. See **lā-** in Appendix.*] —**la·ment′er** *n.*
lam·en·ta·ble (lăm′ən-tə-bəl, lə-mĕn′-) *adj.* **1.** To be lamented; deplorable. **2.** *Archaic.* Exhibiting sorrow or grief; mournful. —See Synonyms at **pathetic.** —**lam′en·ta·bly** *adv.*
lam·en·ta·tion (lăm′ən-tā′shən) *n.* **1.** The act of lamenting. **2.** An instance of such expression of grief; a lament.
Lam·en·ta·tions (lăm′ən-tā′shənz) *n.* Plural in form, used with a singular verb. *Abbr.* **Lam.** A book of the Old Testament, attributed to Jeremiah.
la·ment·ed (lə-mĕn′tĭd) *adj.* Mourned for. —**la·ment′ed·ly** *adv.*
la·mi·a (lā′mē-ə) *n., pl.* **-as** or **-ae** (-ē′). **1.** *Greek Mythology.* A monster, represented as a serpent with the head and breasts of a woman, reputed to prey upon humans and suck the blood of children. **2.** A sorceress; vampire. [Middle English, from Latin, from Greek. See **lem-[2]** in Appendix.*]
lam·i·na (lăm′ə-nə) *n., pl.* **-nae** (-nē′) or **-nas. 1.** A thin plate, sheet, or layer. **2.** *Botany.* The expanded area, or blade, of a leaf. **3.** *Zoology.* A scalelike or platelike structure, as one of the thin layers of sensitive tissue in the hoof of a horse. [New Latin, from Latin *lāmina,* thin plate. See **stel-[2]** in Appendix.*] —**lam′i·nar, lam′i·nal** *adj.*
laminar flow. Nonturbulent flow of a viscous fluid in layers near a boundary, as of lubricating oil in bearings.
lam·i·nate (lăm′ə-nāt′) *v.* **-nated, -nating, -nates.** —*tr.* **1.** To beat or compress into a thin plate or sheet. **2.** To divide into thin layers. **3.** To make by uniting several layers. **4.** To cover with thin sheets. —*intr.* To split into thin layers or sheets. —*adj.* (lăm′ə-nĭt, -nāt′). Also **lam·i·nose** (-nōs′), **lam·i·nous** (-nəs). Consisting of, arranged in, or covered with a lamina or laminae. —*n.* A laminated product, as plywood. [LAMIN(A) + -ATE.] —**lam′i·na′tor** (-nā′tər) *n.*
lam·i·nat·ed (lăm′ə-nā′tĭd) *adj. Abbr.* **lam. 1.** Composed of layers bonded together. **2.** Arranged in laminae; laminate.
lam·i·na·tion (lăm′ə-nā′shən) *n.* **1.** The process or state of being laminated. **2.** Something laminated. **3.** A lamina.
lam·i·ni·tis (lăm′ə-nī′tĭs) *n.* Inflammation of the sensitive laminae in the hoof of a horse. Also called "founder." [New Latin : LAMIN(A) + -ITIS.]
Lam·mas (lăm′əs) *n.* **1.** *Roman Catholic Church.* A festival on August 1 commemorating Saint Peter's deliverance from prison. **2.** A harvest festival formerly held in England on August 1 when bread baked from the season's first ripe grain was consecrated. In this sense, also called "Lammas Day." [Middle English *Lammasse,* Old English *hlāfmæsse* : *hlāf,* LOAF + *mæsse,* MASS.]
Lam·mas·tide (lăm′əs-tīd′) *n.* The season of Lammas.
lam·mer·gei·er (lăm′ər-gī′ər) *n.* Also **lam·mer·geir** (-gīr′), **lam·mer·gey·er** (-gī′ər). A large predatory bird, *Gypaetus barbatus,* of mountainous regions of the Old World. Also called "bearded vulture" and sometimes "ossifrage." [German *Lämmergeier* : *Lämmer,* genitive plural of *Lamm,* lamb, from Old High German *lamb,* from Germanic *lambiz-* (unattested), LAMB + *Geier,* vulture, from Old High German *gīr* (see **ghei-** in Appendix*).]
lamp (lămp) *n.* **1. a.** Any device that generates light, heat, or therapeutic radiation. **b.** A vessel containing oil or alcohol burned through a wick for illumination. **2.** *Poetic.* A star, planet, meteor, or other celestial body regarded as lighting the heavens. **3.** That which illumines the mind or the soul. [Middle English *lampe,* from Old French, from Latin *lampas,* from Greek, torch, from *lampein,* to shine. See **lap-** in Appendix.*]
lamp·black (lămp′blăk′) *n.* A gray or black pigment made from the soot collected from incompletely burned carbonaceous materials, used as a pigment, and in matches, explosives, lubricants, and fertilizers.
lam·pi·on (lăm′pē-ən) *n.* An oil-burning lamp, often of colored glass, for outdoor use. [French, from Italian *lampione,* augmentative of *lampa,* lamp, from Old French *lampe,* LAMP.]
lamp·light (lămp′līt′) *n.* The light shed by a lamp.
lamp·light·er (lămp′lī′tər) *n.* **1.** A person employed to light street lamps. **2.** Something, as a torch, used to light lamps.
lam·poon (lăm-po͞on′) *n.* **1.** A broad satirical piece that is strongly personal in its flavor and ridicule. **2.** A light, good-humored satire. —See Synonyms at **caricature.** —*tr.v.* **lampooned, -pooning, -poons.** To assail in a satiric composition; write a lampoon concerning. [French, perhaps from *lampons,*

let us drink (used as a refrain in 17th-century poetry), first person plural imperative of *lamper*, to gulp down, guzzle, from Germanic. See **lab-** in Appendix.*] **—lam·poon′er, lam·poon′ist** *n.* **—lam·poon′er·y** *n.*

lamp·post (lămp′pōst′) *n.* A post supporting a street lamp.

lam·prey (lăm′prē) *n., pl.* **-preys.** Any of various primitive elongated freshwater or anadromous fishes of the family Petromyzontidae, characteristically having a jawless sucking mouth with a rasping tongue. Also called "lamper eel." [Middle English *lamprei*, from Old French *lampreie*, from Medieval Latin *lamprēda*†. See also **limpet.**]

lamp shell. A marine invertebrate, a **brachiopod** *(see).* [From the shape of one of the valves in certain species.]

la·na·i (lə-nī′; *Hawaiian* lä-nä′ē) *n., pl.* **-is.** A verandah. [Hawaiian.]

La·na·i (lä-nä′ē). An island of Hawaii, 141 square miles in area, lying about seven miles west of Maui.

Lan·ark (lăn′ərk). **1.** Also **Lan·ark·shire** (-shîr, -shər). A county occupying 879 square miles in south-central Scotland. Population, 1,595,000. **2.** Its county seat. Population, 8,000.

la·nate (lā′nāt′) *adj.* Having or consisting of woolly hairs. [Latin *lānātus*, from *lāna*, wool. See **wel-**[5] in Appendix.*]

Lan·ca·shire (lăng′kə-shîr, -shər). *Abbr.* **Lancs.** A county occupying 1,818 square miles in northwestern England. Population, 5,129,000. County seat, Lancaster.

Lan·cas·ter[1] (lăng′kə-stər). Family name of rulers of England (1399–1461).

Lan·cas·ter[2] (lăng′kə-stər; *also* lăng′kăs′tər *for sense 2*). **1.** The county seat of Lancashire, England. Population, 48,000. **2.** A city in southeastern Pennsylvania. Population, 61,000.

Lan·cas·ter Sound (lăng′kə-stər). A channel about 50 miles wide between northern Baffin Island and southern Devon Island, Northwest Territories, Canada.

Lan·cas·tri·an (lăng-kăs′trē-ən) *adj.* **1.** Of or pertaining to the English royal house of Lancaster. **2.** Of or pertaining to Lancashire or its inhabitants. *—n.* **1.** A member of the Lancastrian faction, the Red Rose party, in the Wars of the Roses (1455–85). **2.** An inhabitant of Lancashire.

lance (lăns, läns) *n.* **1.** A thrusting weapon with a long wooden shaft and a sharp metal head. **2.** A similar implement for spearing fish. **3.** A lancer. **4.** A lancet. *—tr.v.* **lanced, lancing, lances. 1.** To pierce with a lance. **2.** *Surgery.* To make an incision in with a lancet; cut into: *lance a boil.* [Middle English *la(u)nce*, from Old French *lance*, from Latin *lancea*†.]

lance corporal. 1. In the U.S. Marine Corps, an enlisted man ranking above a private first class and below a corporal. **2.** In the British Army, a private acting as a corporal. [From obsolete *lancepesade*, from Old French *lancepessade*, from Old Italian *lancia spezzata*, old soldier, "broken lance" : *lancia*, lance, from Latin *lancea*, LANCE + *spezzata*, feminine past participle of *spezzare*, to break in pieces : *s-*, from Latin *dis-* + *pezza*, piece, from Medieval Latin *petia*, PIECE.]

lance·let (lăns′lĭt, läns′-) *n.* Any of various small, flattened marine organisms of the subphylum Cephalochordata, allied to the vertebrates but having a notochord rather than a true vertebral column. Also called "amphioxus." [LANCE + -LET.]

Lan·ce·lot (lăn′sə-lət, -lŏt′, län′-). Also **Laun·ce·lot.** *Arthurian Legend.* A knight of the Round Table whose love affair with Queen Guinevere resulted in a war with King Arthur.

lan·ce·o·late (lăn′sē-ə-lāt′) *adj.* Narrow and tapering at each end: *lanceolate leaves.* [Late Latin *lanceolātus*, from Latin *lanceola*, diminutive of *lancea*, LANCE.]

lanc·er (lăn′sər, län′-) *n.* A cavalryman armed with a lance. [French *lancier*, from Old French, from *lance*, LANCE.]

lanc·ers (lăn′sərz, län′-) *n.* Also **lan·ciers** (lăn-sîrz′, län-). Plural in form, used with a singular verb. **1.** A form of quadrille. **2.** The music for this dance.

lan·cet (lăn′sĭt, län′-) *n.* **1.** A surgical knife with a short, wide, pointed, double-edged blade. **2.** *Architecture.* **a.** A **lancet arch** *(see).* **b.** A **lancet window** *(see).* [Middle English *lancette*, from Old French, diminutive of *lance*, LANCE.]

lancet arch. *Architecture.* An arch that is narrow and pointed like the head of a spear. Also called "lancet."

lancet fish. Either of two large marine fishes, *Alepisaurus ferox*, of the Atlantic, or *A. richardsoni*, of the Pacific, having long, sharp teeth and a large dorsal fin.

lancet window. *Architecture.* A tall narrow window set in a lancet arch. Also called "lancet."

lance·wood (lăns′wo͝od′, läns′-) *n.* **1.** Any of several tropical American trees, such as one of the genera *Calycophyllum* or *Mimusops*, having hard, durable, uniformly grained wood. **2.** The wood of such a tree.

Lan·chow (län′jō′). Formerly **Kao-lan** (gou′län′). The capital of Kansu, China, a city in the south-central part of the province. Population, 732,000.

Lancs. Lancashire.

land (lănd) *n.* **1.** The solid ground of the earth, especially as distinguished from the sea. **2. a.** The soil; the earth: *till the land.* **b.** A topographically or functionally distinguished tract: *desert land.* **3. a.** A nation. **b.** A district or region inhabited by a particular people. **c.** *Plural.* Territorial possessions. **4.** Public or private landed property; real estate. **5.** *Law.* **a.** Any tract of land that may be owned, together with everything growing or constructed upon it. **b.** A landed estate. **6.** The raised portion of a grooved surface. —See Synonyms at **nation.** *—v.* **landed, landing, lands.** *—tr.* **1. a.** To bring to and unload on land: *land cargo.* **b.** To set down on land or other surface: *land an airplane.* **2.** To cause to arrive; set down; place: *"Having one's own way landed one completely at sea."* (D.H. Lawrence). **3. a.** To catch and pull in (a fish). **b.** To win; to secure: *land a big contract.* **4.** To deliver: *land a blow on the head.* *—intr.* **1. a.** To come to shore. **b.** To disembark. **2.** To descend toward and settle on the ground or other surface. **3.** To arrive at a destination: *They landed at the theater too late.* **4.** To come to rest in a certain way or place: *land on one's feet.* [Middle English *land*, Old English *land.* See **lendh-**[2] in Appendix.*]

-land. Indicates: **1.** A region of a particular quality or kind; for example, **grassland. 2.** A realm of a specified nature; for example, **dreamland.**

Land (lănd), **Edwin Herbert.** Born 1909. American inventor of Polaroid products.

lan·dau (lăn′dô, -dou′) *n.* **1.** A four-wheeled closed carriage with facing front and back passenger seats and a roof made in two sections for lowering or detachment. **2.** A former style of automobile with a roof similar to this. [First manufactured in *Landau*, Bavaria, Germany.]

Lan·dau (län-dou′), **Lev Davidovich.** 1908–1968. Soviet physicist.

lan·dau·let, lan·dau·lette (lăn′dô-lĕt′) *n.* **1.** A small landau. **2.** An automobile having a collapsible roof over the back seat and an open driver's seat. [LANDAU + -LET.]

land bank. A bank that issues long-term loans on real estate in return for mortgages.

land·ed (lăn′dĭd) *adj.* **1.** Owning land: *landed gentry.* **2.** Consisting of land or real estate: *a landed estate.*

land·fall (lănd′fôl′) *n.* **1.** The sighting or reaching of land on a voyage or flight. **2.** The land sighted or reached.

land grant. A government grant of public land for a railroad, highway, or state college.

land-grant (lănd′grănt′, -gränt′) *adj.* Being a state educational institution given land by the Federal government under provision of the Morrill Act of 1862 on the condition that it offer courses in agriculture and the mechanical arts.

land·grave (lănd′grāv′) *n.* **1.** In medieval Germany, a count having jurisdiction over a particular territory. **2.** The title of certain German princes. [German *Landgraf*, from Middle High German *lantgrāve* : *lant*, land, from Old High German (see **lendh-**[2] in Appendix*) + *grāve*, count, from Old High German *grāvo* (see **gravo-** in Appendix*).]

land·gra·vi·ate (lănd-grā′vē-ĭt, -āt′) *n.* The office, jurisdiction, or territory of a landgrave.

land·gra·vine (lănd′grə-vēn′) *n.* **1.** The wife of a landgrave. **2.** The female ruler of a landgraviate. [German *Landgräfin*, from Middle High German *lantgrævinne*, from *lantgrāve*, LANDGRAVE.]

land·hold·er (lănd′hōl′dər) *n.* A person who owns or holds land. **—land′hold′ing** *n.*

land·ing (lăn′dĭng) *n. Abbr.* **ldg. 1. a.** The act or process of coming to land or rest, especially after a voyage or flight. **b.** A termination, especially of a voyage or flight. **2.** A site for landing. **3. a.** An intermediate platform on a flight of stairs. **b.** The area at the top or bottom of a staircase.

landing craft. *Abbr.* **LC.** A flat-bottomed naval craft specifically designed to convey troops and equipment from ship to shore.

landing field. A tract of land providing a runway for aircraft.

landing gear. The undercarriage of an aircraft, designed to support the weight of the craft and its load on the ground.

landing strip. An aircraft runway without airport facilities.

land·la·dy (lănd′lā′dē) *n., pl.* **-dies. 1.** A woman who owns and rents real estate, especially dwelling units. **2.** A woman who runs a rooming house or inn. **3.** The wife of a landlord.

länd·ler (lĕnt′lər) *n.* **1.** An Austrian country dance for couples in triple time. **2.** The music for this dance. [German, from (dialectal) *Landl*, Upper Austria, where the dance originated.]

land·less (lănd′lĭs) *adj.* Owning or having no land.

land·locked (lănd′lŏkt′) *adj.* **1.** Surrounded or nearly surrounded by land. **2.** Confined to inland waters, as certain salmon.

land·lord (lănd′lôrd′) *n.* **1.** A person from whom a tenant leases land, buildings, or dwelling units. **2.** A man who runs a rooming house or inn; innkeeper.

land·lord·ism (lănd′lôr-dĭz′əm) *n.* **1.** Land management in which ownership of land is vested in a private individual or group that leases it to tenants. **2.** The principles and practices of landlords collectively.

land·lub·ber (lănd′lŭb′ər) *n.* A person unfamiliar with the sea or seamanship. [LAND + LUBBER.]

land·mark (lănd′märk′) *n.* **1.** A fixed marker, as a concrete block, indicating a boundary line. **2.** A prominent and identifying feature of a landscape. **3.** An event marking an important stage of development or a turning point in history. **4.** A building or site having historical significance and marked for preservation by a municipal or national government.

land mine. An explosive mine laid usually just below the surface of the ground.

land office. A government office that handles and keeps records of any sale or transfer of public land.

land-of·fice business (lănd′ô′fĭs, -ŏf′ĭs). A thriving, extensive, or rapidly moving business.

Land of Nod (nŏd). **1.** The land east of Eden where Cain lived after killing Abel. Genesis 4:16. **2.** *Informal.* Sleep.

Land of the Midnight Sun. 1. Land lying north of the Arctic circle and having continuous daylight throughout the short summer. **2.** Norway.

Land of the Rising Sun. Japan.

land·own·er (lănd′ō′nər) *n.* One who owns land. **—land′own′er·ship′** *n.* **—land′own′ing** *n. & adj.*

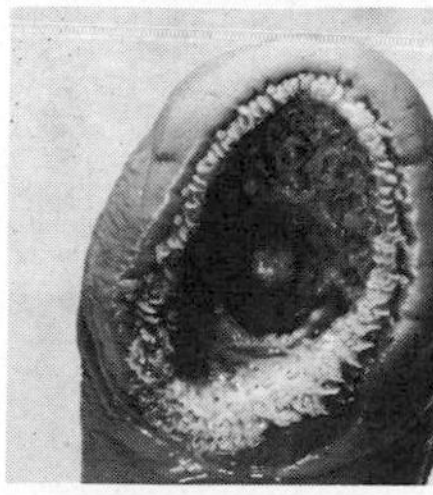

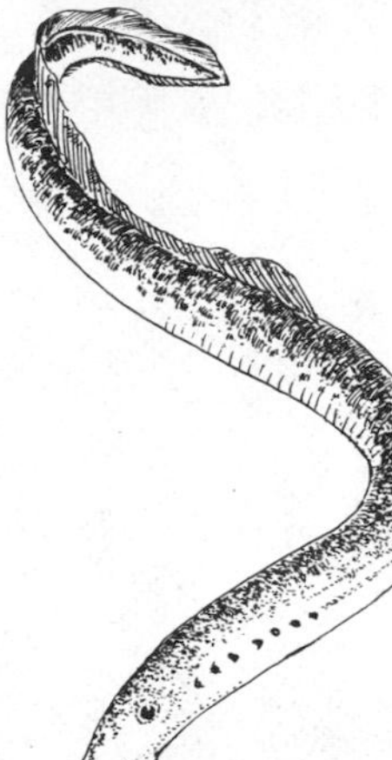

lamprey
Petromyzon marinus
Above: Detail of mouth

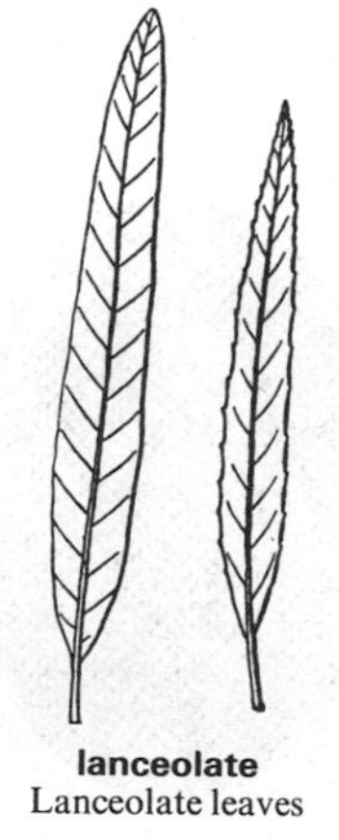

lanceolate
Lanceolate leaves

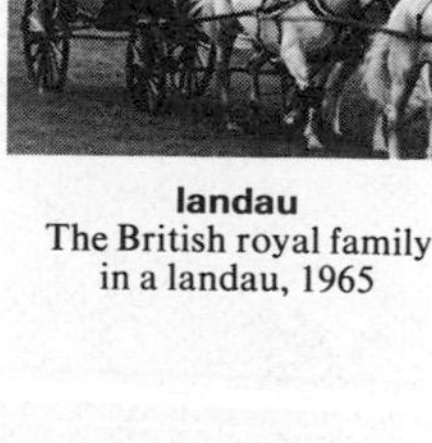

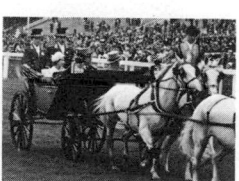

landau
The British royal family in a landau, 1965

land-poor (lănd′po͝or′) *adj.* Owning much unprofitable land but lacking the capital to improve or maintain it.

land·scape (lănd′skāp′) *n.* **1.** A view or vista of scenery on land: *a desert landscape.* **2.** A painting, photograph, or the like depicting such a scene. **3.** The branch of art dealing with the representation of natural scenery. **4.** The aspect of the land characteristic of a particular region: *a New England landscape.* **5.** An extensive mental view; prospect; vista: *"They occupy the whole landscape of my thought"* (James Thurber). *—v.* **land-scaped, -scaping, -scapes.** *—tr.* To adorn or improve (a section of ground) by contouring the land and planting flowers, shrubs, or trees. *—intr.* To arrange grounds artistically as a profession. [Dutch *landschap,* from Middle Dutch *landschap, lantscap,* landscape, region : *land,* land (see **lendh-²** in Appendix*) + *-schap, -scap,* suffix indicating condition (see **skop** in Appendix*).]

landscape architect. One whose professional skill is the decorative and functional alteration and planting of grounds, especially at or around a building site. **—landscape architecture.**

land·scap·ist (lănd′skā′pĭst) *n.* A painter of landscapes.

Land·seer (lănd′sîr′, -syər), Sir **Edwin Henry.** 1802–1873. British painter of animals and portraits.

Land's End. The southwestern tip of England, a promontory in western Cornwall.

land·side (lănd′sīd′) *n.* The flat side of a plow opposite the furrow.

land·slide (lănd′slīd′) *n.* Also *chiefly British* **land·slip** (-slĭp′) (for sense 1). **1. a.** The dislodging and fall of a mass of earth and rock. **b.** The dislodged mass. **2. a.** An overwhelming majority of votes for a political party or candidate. **b.** An election that sweeps a party or person into office. **c.** Any great victory.

Lands·mål (länts′môl′) *n.* One of two officially recognized forms of Norwegian incorporating various dialects. Compare **Riksmål.** [Norwegian *Landsmål,* "country speech."]

lands·man¹ (lăndz′mən) *n., pl.* **-men** (-mĭn). One who lives and works on land as distinguished from a seaman.

lands·man² (länts′mən) *n., pl.* **landsleit** (länts′līt′). A fellow Jew coming from one's own district or town in Eastern Europe. [Yiddish, compatriot, from Middle High German *lantsman* : Old High German *lant,* land (see **lendh-²** in Appendix*) + *man,* man (see **man-¹** in Appendix*).]

Land·stei·ner (lănd′stī′nər; *German* länt′shtī′nər), **Karl.** 1868–1943. Austrian-born American pathologist.

Land·tag (länt′täk′) *n.* Formerly, the legislative assembly of Prussia and other German states. [German, "land-day."]

land·ward (lănd′wərd) *adv.* Also **land·wards** (-wərdz). Toward the land or the interior. *—adj.* Being toward the land.

Land·wehr (länt′vâr′) *n.* In Germany and some other European countries, a trained military reserve. [German, "land defense."]

lane (lān) *n.* **1. a.** A narrow way or passage between walls, hedges, or fences. **b.** A narrow country road. **2.** Any narrow passage, course, or track, as: **a.** A prescribed course for ships or aircraft. **b.** A strip delineated on a street or highway to accommodate a single line of automobiles. **c.** One of a set of parallel courses marking the bounds for contestants in a race. **d.** A bowling alley. [Middle English *lane,* Old English *lane,* akin to Old Frisian *lana,* Middle Dutch *lāne*†.]

Lan·franc (lăn′frăngk′). 1005?–1089. Italian-born Archbishop of Canterbury (1070–89) and counselor of William I.

lang (lăng) *adj. Scottish.* Long.

lang. language.

Lang·er·hans, islands of. See **islands of Langerhans.**

Lang·land (lăng′lənd), **William.** Also **Lang·ley** (-lē). 1332?–1400? English poet, probable author of *Piers Plowman.*

lang·lauf (läng′louf′) *n.* A cross-country ski run. [German *Langlauf,* "long race" : *lang,* long, from Old High German (see **del-¹** in Appendix*) + *Lauf,* a running, from Old High German *hlouf,* a leap, from *hlouffan,* to leap (see **klou-** in Appendix*).] **—lang′lauf′er** *n.*

lang·ley (lăng′lē) *n.* A unit of illumination used to measure temperature, as of a star, equal to one gram calorie per square centimeter of irradiated surface. [After Samuel LANGLEY.]

Lang·ley (lăng′lē), **Samuel Pierpont.** 1834–1906. American astronomer, inventor, and aeronautical pioneer.

Lang·muir (lăng′myo͝or′), **Irving.** 1881–1957. American physical chemist and inventor.

Lan·go·bard (lăng′gō-bärd′) *n., pl.* **-bardi** (-bär′dē). A **Lombard** *(see).* **—Lan′go·bar′dic** *adj.*

lan·gouste (län-go͞ost′) *n.* The **spiny lobster** *(see).* [French, from Old French, from Old Provençal *langosta,* from Vulgar Latin *lacusta* (unattested), perhaps variant of Latin *lōcusta,* lobster, LOCUST.]

lan·grage (lăng′grĭj) *n.* Also **lan·grel** (-grəl), **lan·gridge** (-grĭj). A type of case shot loaded with iron scrap, formerly used in naval warfare to damage sails and rigging. [Origin unknown.]

lang·syne (lăng-sīn′, -zīn′) *adv.* Also **lang syne.** *Scottish.* Long ago; long since. *—n. Scottish.* Time long past; times past. [Middle English *lang sine* : *lang,* LONG + *sine,* contraction of *sithen,* SINCE.]

lan·guage (lăng′gwĭj) *n. Abbr.* **lang. 1.** The aspect of human behavior that involves the use of vocal sounds in meaningful patterns and, when they exist, corresponding written symbols to form, express, and communicate thoughts and feelings. **2.** A historically established pattern of such behavior that offers substantial communication only within the culture it defines: *the English language.* **3.** Any method of communicating ideas, as by a system of signs, symbols, gestures, or the like: *the language of algebra.* **4.** The transmission of meaning, feeling, or intent by significance of act or manner: *"There's language in her eye"* (Shakespeare). **5.** The special vocabulary and usages of a scientific, professional, or other group. **6.** A characteristic style of speech or writing: *Miltonic language.* **7. a.** Abusive, violent, or profane utterance; bad language: *"language that would make your hair curl"* (W.S. Gilbert). **b.** Any particular manner of utterance: *gentle language.* **8.** The manner or means of communication between living creatures other than man: *the language of dolphins.* **9. a.** Language as a subject of study. **b.** Linguistics. **10.** *Law.* The wording of a document or statute as distinct from the spirit. **—speak the same language.** To have the same background, experience, or understanding as another person. [Middle English *language, langage,* from Old French *langage,* from Gallo-Roman *linguāticum* (unattested), from Latin *lingua,* tongue, language. See **dn̥ghū** in Appendix.*]

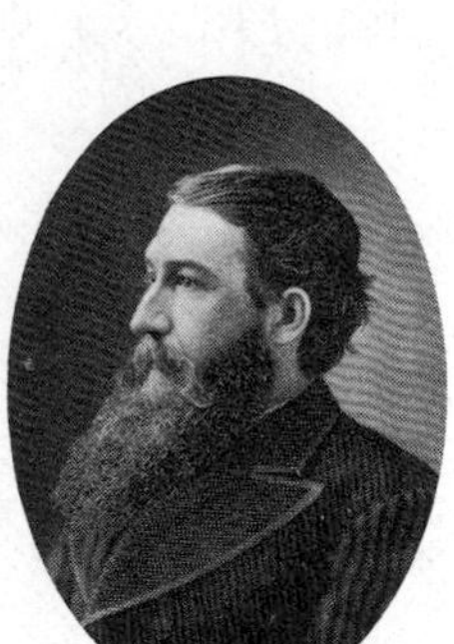

Sidney Lanier

langue d'oc (läNg dôk′). The form of Old French surviving in Provençal. [French, from Old French, "language of *oc.*" *Oc* is the word for "yes" in Provençal.]

Langue·doc (läng-dôk′). A former province of southern France, now a leading wine-producing region.

langue d'o·ïl (läNg dô-ēl′). The Romance language of Gaul north of the Loire that formed the base of modern French. [French, "language of *oïl.*" *Oïl* is the word used for "yes" in northern France.]

lan·guet (lăng′gwĭt, lăng-gwĕt′) *n.* A tonguelike thing or part. [Middle English, from Old French *languette,* diminutive of *langue,* tongue, language, from Latin *lingua.* See **dn̥ghū** in Appendix.*]

lan·guid (lăng′gwĭd) *adj.* **1.** Lacking energy or vitality; faint; weak. **2.** Unwilling to stir or exert oneself: *"From O'Connell to Parnell, . . . the Irish had been languid in their demands for autonomy."* (Sean O'Faolain). **3.** Showing little or no spirit or animation; listless. **4.** Slow of movement; sluggish. [Old French *languide,* from Latin *languidus,* from *languēre,* to LANGUISH.] **—lan′guid·ly** *adv.* **—lan′guid·ness** *n.*

lan·guish (lăng′gwĭsh) *intr.v.* **-guished, -guishing, -guishes. 1. a.** To become weak or feeble; sag with loss of strength or vigor; to flag: *All life languished under the tropic sun.* **b.** To continue in a state of apathy, debility, or suffering; exist under miserable or disheartening conditions. **2.** To fall off; fade. **3.** To become listless as with longing; to pine. Often used with *for.* **4.** To affect a mawkish air of nostalgia, tenderness, or wistfulness. [Middle English *languishen,* from Old French *languir* (stem *languiss-*), from Vulgar Latin *languīre* (unattested), from Latin *languēre,* to be faint or weak. See **slēg-** in Appendix.*] **—lan′guish·er** *n.* **—lan′guish·ment** *n.*

lan·guish·ing (lăng′gwĭ-shĭng) *adj.* **1.** Becoming weak; fading. **2.** Slow; lingering. **3.** Expressing languor; full of sentimentality: *"truly, she has got a languishing eye, and reads romances"* (Smollett). **—lan′guish·ing·ly** *adv.*

lan·guor (lăng′gər) *n.* **1.** Languidness; lassitude; sluggishness: *"The train slowed up with midsummer languor"* (F. Scott Fitzgerald). **2.** Oppressive quiet or stillness. **3.** An air of soft or wistful tenderness: *"It was hot, yet with a sweet languor about it all."* (Dreiser). **4.** *Archaic.* Debility; sickness. —See Synonyms at **lethargy.** [Middle English, from Old French, from Latin, from *languēre,* to LANGUISH.] **—lan′guor·ous** *adj.* **—lan′guor·ous·ly** *adv.* **—lan′gour·ous·ness** *n.*

lan·gur (lŭng-go͝or′) *n.* Any of various slender, long-tailed Asian monkeys of the genus *Presbytis* and related genera. [Hindi *langūr,* perhaps from Sanskrit *lāṅgūla*†, "tailed."]

lan·iard. Variant of **lanyard.**

La·nier (lə-nîr′), **Sidney.** 1842–1881. American poet.

la·nif·er·ous (lə-nĭf′ər-əs) *adj.* Also **la·nig·er·ous** (lə-nĭj′-). Having wool or woollike hair. [From Latin *lānifer,* "wool-bearing" : *lāna,* wool (see **wel-⁵** in Appendix*) + -FEROUS.]

lank (lăngk) *adj.* **1.** Long and lean; gaunt. **2.** Long, straight, and limp: *lank hair.* —See Synonyms at **lean.** [Ultimately from Old English *hlanc,* loose, hollow. See **kleng-** in Appendix.*] **—lank′ly** *adv.* **—lank′ness** *n.*

lank·y (lăng′kē) *adj.* **-ier, -iest.** Tall, thin, and ungainly. See Synonyms at **lean.** **—lank′i·ly** *adv.* **—lank′i·ness** *n.*

lan·ner (lăn′ər) *n.* **1.** A falcon, *Falco biarmicus,* of Africa and the Mediterranean region. **2.** *Archaic.* The female of this species, used in falconry. [Middle English *laner,* from Old French *lanier (faucon),* cowardly (falcon), scornful application of *lanier,* weaver, from Latin *lānārius,* wool worker, from *lāna,* wool. See **wel-⁵** in Appendix.*]

lan·ner·et (lăn′ə-rĕt′) *n. Archaic.* A male lanner, smaller than the female, used in falconry. [Middle English *lanerette,* from Old French *laneret,* diminutive of *lanier,* LANNER.]

lan·o·lin (lăn′ə-lən) *n.* A yellowish-white fatty substance obtained from wool and used in soaps, cosmetics, and ointments. Also called "wool fat." [German *Lanolin* : Latin *lāna,* wool (see **wel-⁵** in Appendix*) + -OL (hydrocarbon) + -IN.]

la·nose (lā′nōs′) *adj.* Woolly. [Latin *lānōsus,* from *lāna,* wool. See **wel-⁵** in Appendix.*] **—la·nos′i·ty** (-nŏs′ə-tē) *n.*

Lan·sing (lăn′sĭng). The capital of Michigan, in the south-central part of the state. Population, 113,000.

lan·ta·na (lăn-tā′nə) *n.* Any of various aromatic, chiefly tropical shrubs of the genus *Lantana,* having dense clusters of small, variously colored flowers. [New Latin *Lantana*†.]

lan·tern (lăn′tərn) *n.* Also *obsolete* **lant·horn** (lănt′hôrn′, lăn′tərn). **1.** A case that has transparent or translucent sides for holding and protecting a light, and is either fixed or portable. **2. a.** A lighthouse. **b.** The room at the top of a lighthouse where the light is located. **3.** *Architecture.* A structure built on top of a roof with open or windowed walls to let in light and air. **4.** A slide projector. [Middle English *lanterne,* from Old

French, from Latin *lanterna,* from Greek *lamptēr,* lantern, torch, from *lampein,* to shine. See **lāp-** in Appendix.*]

lantern fish. Any of numerous small deep-sea fishes of the family Myctophidae, having phosphorescent light organs.

lantern fly. Any of various chiefly tropical insects of the subfamily Fulgorinae, having an enlarged, elongated head. [They were once erroneously thought to be luminous.]

lantern jaw. A jaw that is undershot. **—lan'tern-jawed'** *adj.*

lantern wheel. A small pinion consisting of circular disks connected by cylindrical bars that serve as teeth, used now chiefly in inexpensive clocks. Also called "lantern pinion."

lan·tha·nide (lăn'thə-nīd') *n.* A **rare-earth element** *(see).* [LANTHAN(UM) + -IDE.]

lanthanide series. The set of chemically related elements with atomic numbers from 57 to 71; the rare-earth elements.

lan·tha·num (lăn'thə-nəm) *n. Symbol* **La** A soft, silvery-white, malleable, ductile, metallic, rare-earth element, obtained chiefly from monazite and bastnaesite, used in glass manufacture and with other rare earths in carbon lights for motion-picture and television studio lighting. Atomic number 57, atomic weight 138.91, melting point 920°C, boiling point 3,469°C, specific gravity 5.98 to 6.186, valence 3. See **element.** [New Latin, from Greek *lanthanein,* to hide (from the finding of lanthanum concealed in cerium oxide). See **lādh-** in Appendix.*]

Lan·tsang. The Chinese name for the **Mekong.**

la·nu·gi·nous (lə-no͞o'jə-nəs, lə-nyo͞o'-) *adj.* Also **la·nu·gi·nose** (-nōs'). Covered with soft, short hair; downy. [Latin *lānūginōsus,* from *lānūgō,* down, LANUGO.] **—la·nu'gi·nous·ness** *n.*

la·nu·go (lə-no͞o'gō, lə-nyo͞o'-) *n., pl.* **-gos.** Fine, soft hair. [Latin *lānūgō,* down, from *lāna,* wool. See **wel-**[5] in Appendix.*]

La·nús (lä-no͞os'). A city of eastern Argentina, just south of Buenos Aires. Population, 382,000.

lan·yard (lăn'yərd) *n.* Also **lan·iard. 1.** *Nautical.* A short rope or gasket for seizing a ladder or the like or to secure rigging. **2.** A cord worn around the neck for carrying a knife, keys, or a whistle. **3.** A cord with a hook at one end used to fire a cannon. [Middle English *lanyer,* from Old French *laniere, lasniere,* from *lasne,* thong, strap : perhaps *laz,* LACE + *nasle,* string, from Germanic (see **ned-** in Appendix*).]

Lao (lou) *n., pl.* **Lao** or **Laos.** Also **La·o·tian** (lā-ō'shən, lou'shən). **1. a.** One of a Buddhist people of Thai stock living in the area of the Mekong River in Laos and Thailand. **b.** The Lao people. **2.** The Thai language of these people, the official language of Laos. *—adj.* Of the Lao or their language.

La·oc·o·on (lā-ŏk'ō-ŏn'). *Greek Mythology.* A Trojan priest of Apollo who was killed with his two sons by two serpents for having warned his people against the Trojan horse.

La·od·i·ce·an (lā-ŏd'ə-sē'ən) *adj.* Indifferent or lukewarm. [After *Laodicea,* ancient city in Asia Minor whose early church is reproved in Revelation 3:14–16 as being "lukewarm, and neither hot nor cold."] **—La·od'i·ce'an** *n.*

Laoigh·is (lā'ĭsh). Also **Leix** (lāks). Formerly **Queen's** (kwēnz). A county of the Republic of Ireland, occupying 664 square miles in western Leinster. Population, 45,000. County seat, Maryborough.

La·om·e·don (lā-ŏm'ə-dŏn'). *Greek Mythology.* The founder and king of Troy and father of Priam.

La·os (lä'ōs, lous, lā'ŏs'). A landlocked kingdom of southeastern Asia, occupying 91,400 square miles west of North Vietnam. Population, 3,000,000. Capitals, Luang Prabang (royal) and Vientiane (administrative).

Lao-tse (lou'dzŭ'). Also **Lao-tsze, Lao-tsu.** 604?–531 B.C. Chinese philosopher; regarded as founder of Taoism. [Mandarin Chinese *Lao*[3] *tze*[3], "the old Master."]

lap[1] (lăp) *n.* **1.** The front region or area of a seated person extending from the lower trunk to the knees. **2. a.** The portion of a garment that covers this area: *"Mrs. Dai Bread Two is looking into a crystal ball which she holds in the lap of her dirty yellow petticoat"* (Dylan Thomas). **b.** *Obsolete.* A hanging or flapping part of a garment. **3.** A hollow in the land. **4. a.** A secure place or environment: *a lap of luxury.* **b.** Control; custody: *the lap of the gods.* [Middle English *lappe,* Old English *læppa,* flap of a garment. See **leb-**[1] in Appendix.*]

lap[2] (lăp) *v.* **lapped, lapping, laps.** *—tr.* **1.** To fold, wrap, or wind over or around something: *lap pie crust over a filling.* **2.** To envelop in something; enwrap; swathe: *lapped in sables.* **3. a.** To place (a thing) so as to overlap another. **b.** To lie partly over (something underneath); project onto or over the edge of. **4.** In cabinetwork, to join as by scarfing. **5.** To get ahead of (an opponent) in a race by one or more complete circuits of the course. **6.** To polish until smooth. **7.** To convert (cotton or other fibers) into a sheet or layer. *—intr.* **1.** To fold or wind around something. **2.** To extend beyond an edge; overlap. *—n.* **1.** A part that overlaps. **2. a.** One complete turn or circuit, especially of a racetrack. **b.** A segment or stage of a race, trip, or comparable undertaking. **3.** A length as of rope required to encircle a drum, wheel, or the like to make one complete turn. **4.** A continuous band, layer, or sheet of cotton, flax, or other fibers ready for further processing. **5.** A wheel, disk, or slab of leather or metal, either stationary or rotating, for polishing stone, glass, or the like. [Middle English *lappen,* probably from *lappe,* LAP.]

lap[3] (lăp) *v.* **lapped, lapping, laps.** *—tr.* **1.** To take in (a liquid or food) with the tongue. **2.** To wash against with a gentle intermittent slapping sound. Used of waves or a body of water. *—intr.* **1.** To drink by lifting a liquid with the tongue. **2.** To dash or slap softly against a shore or other surface. **—lap up. 1.** To drink or eat by lapping. **2.** *Informal.* To receive eagerly: *lap up praise.* *—n.* **1.** The act or process of lapping. **2.** A watery food for animals. **3.** An amount ingested by a lap. **4.** The sound of lapping water. [Middle English *lappen,* Old English *lapian.* See **lab-** in Appendix.*] **—lap'per** *n.*

La Pal·ma (lä päl'mä). An island of Spain, 280 square miles in area, in the northwestern Canary Islands.

lap·a·rot·o·my (lăp'ə-rŏt'ə-mē) *n., pl.* **-mies.** Surgical incision into any part of the abdominal wall. [Greek *lapara,* flank, from *laparos,* soft (see **lep-**[1] in Appendix*) + -TOMY.]

La Paz (lə păz', päz'; *Spanish* lä päs'). **1.** The administrative capital of Bolivia, 30 miles east of Lake Titicaca. Population, 361,000. **2.** The capital of Baja California Sur Territory, Mexico, on the Gulf of California. Population, 24,000.

lap·board (lăp'bôrd', -bōrd') *n.* A flat board to hold on the lap as a substitute for a table or desk.

lap dissolve. A cinematic technique of overlapping a fade-out and a fade-in so that one scene dissolves into the next.

lap dog. A small, easily held dog kept as a pet.

la·pel (lə-pĕl') *n.* Either of two parts of a garment that are an extension of the collar and fold back against the breast. [From LAP (flap of a garment).]

La Pé·rouse (lȧ pā-ro͞oz'), **Comte de.** Title of Jean François de Galaup. 1741–1788. French explorer of western Pacific Ocean.

La Pé·rouse Strait (lȧ pā-ro͞oz'). A strait between Sakhalin Island, U.S.S.R., and northern Hokkaido, Japan, joining the Sea of Okhotsk and the Sea of Japan.

lap·ful (lăp'fo͝ol') *n.* As much as the lap can support or hold.

lap·i·dar·i·an (lăp'ə-dâr'ē-ən) *adj.* Cut in or inscribed on stone. [Latin *lapidārius,* of stone, from *lapis* (stem *lapid-*), stone, perhaps akin to Greek *lepas,* of Mediterranean origin.]

lap·i·dar·y (lăp'ə-dĕr'ē) *n., pl.* **-ies. 1.** A person who works at cutting, polishing, or engraving gems. **2.** A dealer in precious or semiprecious stones. *—adj.* **1.** Of or relating to precious stones or the art of working with them. **2.** Engraved in stone. **3.** Of an elegance suitable for inscription in stone: *lapidary prose.* [Latin *lapidārius,* stoneworker, from *lapis* (stem *lapid-*), stone. See **lapidarian.**]

la·pil·lus (lə-pĭl'əs) *n., pl.* **-pilli** (-pĭl'ī'). A small solidified fragment of lava. Usually used in the plural. [Latin *lapillus,* small stone, diminutive of *lapis,* stone. See **lapidarian.**]

lap·in (lăp'ən; *French* lȧ-păN') *n.* **1.** A rabbit. **2.** Rabbit fur, especially when sheared. [French, perhaps of Iberian origin.]

lap·is laz·u·li (lăp'ĭs lăz'yo͞o-lē). **1.** An opaque, azure-blue to deep-blue gemstone of lazurite. **2.** A mineral, **lazurite** *(see).* [Middle English, from Medieval Latin : Latin *lapis,* stone (see **lapidarian**) + Medieval Latin *lazuli,* genitive of *lazulum,* lapis lazuli, from Arabic *lāzaward,* from Persian *lāzhuward*†.]

Lap·ith (lăp'ĭth) *n., pl.* **-ithae** (-ə-thē') or **-iths.** *Greek Mythology.* One of a Thessalonian tribe who, at the disastrous wedding of their king, defeated the drunken centaurs.

lap joint. A joint in which the ends or edges are overlapped and fastened together. **—lap'-joint'ed** *adj.*

La·place (lȧ-plȧs'), **Marquis de.** Title of Pierre Simon. 1749–1827. French mathematician and astronomer.

Lap·land (lăp'lănd). A region of some 150,000 square miles comprising the areas of northern Scandinavia and Finland, and the northwestern Soviet Union lying above the Arctic Circle.

La Pla·ta (lä plä'tä). **1.** A city of Argentina southeast of Buenos Aires. Population, 330,000. **2.** See **Río de la Plata.**

Lapp (lăp) *n.* Also **Lap·land·er** (lăp'lăn'dər) (for sense 1) or **Lap·pish** (lăp'ĭsh) (for sense 2). **1.** One of a people of nomadic tradition who inhabit Lapland. **2.** The Finno-Ugric language of this people. [Swedish *Lapp*†.]

lap·pet (lăp'ĭt) *n.* **1.** A decorative flap or loose fold on a garment or headdress. **2.** A flaplike structure, such as the wattle of a bird. [From LAP (fold or flap).]

lapse (lăps) *v.* **lapsed, lapsing, lapses.** *—intr.* **1. a.** To fall away by degrees; decline; vanish: *My enthusiasm soon lapsed.* **b.** To subside gradually; drift: *lapse into dreaminess.* **c.** *Obsolete.* To fall into ruin. **d.** *Obsolete.* To fall from grace. **2.** To elapse: *Years had lapsed since we last met.* **3. a.** *Law.* To pass to another through neglect or omission. Said of a right or privilege, a benefice, or an estate. **b.** To become void or ineffective: *The guarantee lapsed.* *—tr. Obsolete.* To allow to lapse. *—n.* **1.** The act of lapsing; a gradual or imperceptible falling or sliding away. **2. a.** A minor slip or failure: *"his errors of aesthetic judgment are merely lapses of taste"* (Lionel Trilling). **b.** A fall from rectitude; moral error. **3.** A slipping into a lower state or degree; a decline: *lapse into premature senility.* **4. a.** The passage of time. **b.** An interval. **5.** *Law.* The termination of a right or privilege through disuse, a death, or other failure. [Latin *lapsus,* error, a sliding, from *lābī* (past participle *lapsus*), to slide. See **leb-**[1] in Appendix.*] **—laps'er** *n.*

lap·strake (lăp'strāk') *adj.* Also **lap·streak** (-strēk'). *Nautical.* Built with each strake overlapping the one below; clinker-built. *—n.* Also **lap·streak.** A clinker-built boat. [LAP (to overlap) + STRAKE.]

lap·sus (lăp'səs) *n. Latin.* A lapse; a slip.

Lap·tev Sea (lăp'tĕf). Formerly **Nor·don·skjöld Sea** (no͞or'dən-shœld'). A section of the Arctic Ocean lying north of the central Russian S.F.S.R.

La·pu·ta (lə-pyo͞o'tə). In Swift's *Gulliver's Travels,* a flying island inhabited by philosophers engaged in absurdly impractical enterprises. **—La·pu'tan** (-pyo͞ot'n) *n. & adj.*

lap·wing (lăp'wĭng') *n.* Any of several Old World birds of the genus *Vanellus,* related to the plovers; especially, *V. vanellus,* having a narrow crest. Also called "pewit," "green plover." [Middle English *lapwinge,* variant (influenced by *winge,* wing, and *lappen,* to overlap) of *lappewinke,* Old English *hlēapewince.* See **klou-** in Appendix.*]

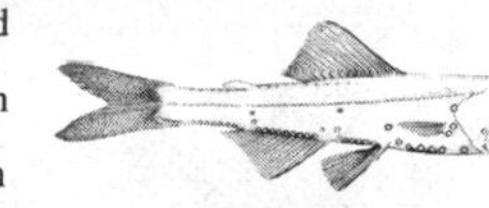

lantern fish
Lampanyctus nicholsi

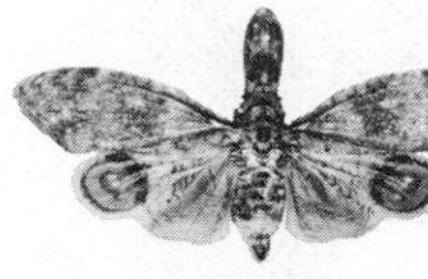

lantern fly
Fulgora lanternaria

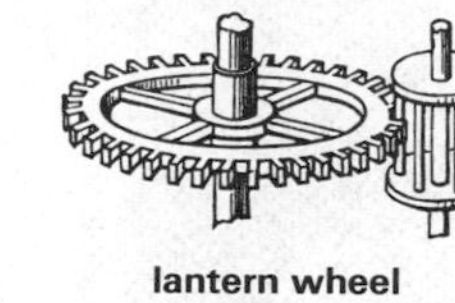

lantern wheel

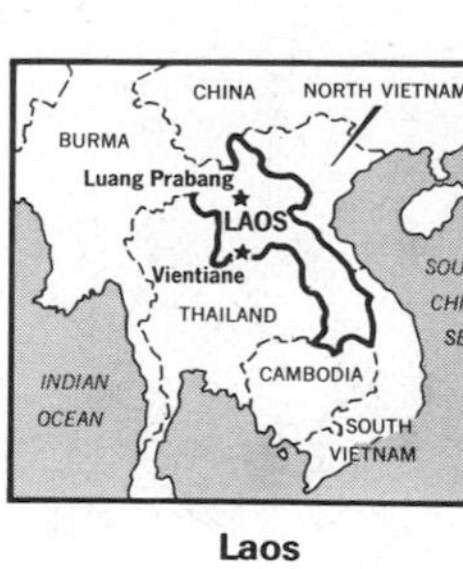

Laos

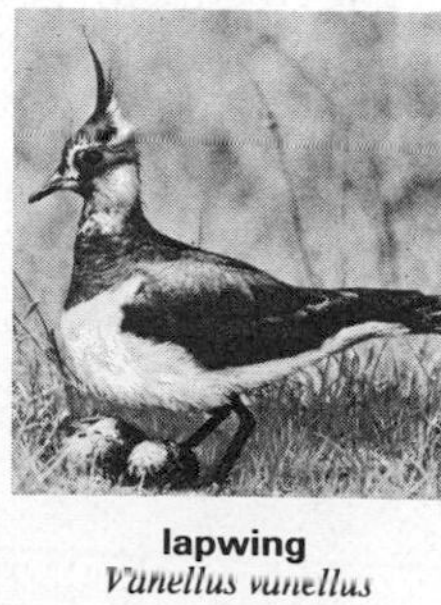

lapwing
Vanellus vanellus

larch
Above: Needles and cones
of *Larix laricina*
Below: Larix siberica

lar (lär) *n., pl.* **lares** (lâr′ēz) or **lars.** Also **Lar.** A tutelary deity or spirit of an ancient Roman household. [Latin *Lār*† (plural *Larēs*), household gods.]

Lar·a·mie (lăr′ə-mē). A city of Wyoming, a livestock-raising center in the southeast. Population, 18,000.

lar·board (lär′bərd) *n. Nautical.* The port side. —*adj. Nautical.* On the port side. [Middle English *lathebord, lad(d)borde,* probably "the loading side" (but influenced by STARBOARD) : *laden,* to load, LADE + *bord,* ship's side, BOARD.]

lar·ce·nist (lär′sə-nĭst) *n.* Also **lar·ce·ner** (-nər). One who commits larceny.

lar·ce·ny (lär′sə-nē) *n., pl.* **-nies.** The felonious taking and removing of another's personal property with the intent of permanently depriving the owner. See **grand larceny, petit larceny.** [Middle English, from Old French *larcin,* from Latin *latrōcinium,* military service for pay, freebooting, from *latrō,* mercenary soldier, from Greek *latron,* pay. See **lēi-**¹ in Appendix.*] —**lar′ce·nous** *adj.*

larch (lärch) *n.* **1.** Any of several coniferous trees of the genus *Larix,* having deciduous needles and heavy, durable wood. See **tamarack. 2.** The wood of a larch. [German *Lärche,* from Middle High German *larche, lerche,* from Old High German *larihha* (unattested), from Latin *larix*† (stem *laric-*).]

lard (lärd) *n.* The white solid or semisolid rendered fat of a hog. —*tr.v.* **larded, larding, lards. 1.** To cover or coat with fat. **2.** To insert strips of bacon or the like in (lean meat or poultry) before cooking. **3. a.** To make richer with or as if with fat. **b.** To enrich (speech or writing) with salient additions. [Middle English, from Old French, from Latin *lārdum, lāridum*†.] —**lard′y** *adj.*

lard·er (lär′dər) *n.* A room, cupboard, or the like where meat and other foods are kept. [Middle English, from Old French *lardier,* from *lard,* LARD.]

lar·don (lärd′n) *n.* Also **lar·doon** (lär-dōōn′). A strip of fat for larding meat. [French, from Old French, from *lard,* LARD.]

La·re·do (lə-rā′dō). A city of Texas, in the southwest on the Rio Grande. Population, 60,000.

lares and penates. Esteemed household possessions. [From two kinds of Roman household gods. See **lar, penates.**]

large (lärj) *adj.* **larger, largest.** *Abbr.* **L, lg., lge. 1.** Of considerable size, extent, quantity, capacity, or amount; big; not small: *a large house.* **2.** Important; major: *a large role.* **3. a.** Of wide scope or capacity: *a large mind.* **b.** Having breadth or sweep; comprehensive. **4. a.** Liberal; generous: *a large heart.* **b.** Prodigal. **5. a.** Pretentious; big. Said of speech or manners. **b.** *Rare.* Unrestrained; loose; gross. Said of speech or language. **6.** *Nautical.* Designating a favorable wind. —**at large. 1.** At liberty; free. **2.** At length; copiously; comprehensively: *He spoke at large on the housing problem.* **3.** As an entity or whole; in general. **4.** Representing a nation, state, or district as a whole. **5.** Not assigned to any particular country: *ambassador at large.* —**in the large.** On a broad scale; in entirety. [Middle English, from Old French, from Latin *largus*†, generous, bountiful.] —**large′ness** *n.*

Synonyms: *large, big, great.* These adjectives are applied to what is notably above the average of its kind in size, degree, or the like. *Large* and *big* are interchangeable in many contexts. However, *large* is more often found in references to physical dimensions, quantity, and capacity: *a large building; a large estate; a large sum; a large glass. Big* is especially applicable to physical bulk or mass, volume of sound, and figurative magnitude: *big ears; a big noise; a big heart; big problems. Great* implies impressiveness or distinctiveness in references involving physical size: *a great ocean liner.* Often the term is used figuratively to express degree: *great sorrow.*

large calorie. A calorie (*see*).

large-heart·ed (lärj′här′tĭd) *adj.* Having a generous disposition; sympathetic. —**large′-heart′ed·ness** *n.*

large intestine. The portion of the intestine that extends from the ileum to the anus, forming an arch around the convolutions of the small intestine, and including the cecum, colon, rectum, and anal canal.

large·ly (lärj′lē) *adv.* **1.** In a large manner; on a large scale. **2.** To a large extent; mainly.

large-mind·ed (lärj′mīn′dĭd) *adj.* Having a breadth of ideas; of liberal view; open-minded. —**large′-mind′ed·ness** *n.*

large-mouth bass (lärj′mouth′). A North American freshwater food and game fish, *Micropterus salmoides.*

large-scale (lärj′skāl′) *adj.* **1.** Of large scope; extensive. **2.** Drawn or made large to show detail. Said of maps and models.

lar·gess (lär-jĕs′, lär′jĭs, -jĕs′) *n.* Also **lar·gesse. 1. a.** Liberality in giving. **b.** The money or gifts bestowed. **2.** A bounty, dole, or tip. **3.** Generosity of attitude. **4.** *Archaic.* Generosity; munificence. [Middle English *largesse,* from Old French, from *large,* generous, LARGE.]

lar·ghet·to (lär-gĕt′ō) *adv. Music.* Moderately slow in tempo. Used as a direction. —*n., pl.* **larghettos.** *Music.* A movement or passage played larghetto. —*adj. Music.* Moderately slow. [Italian, diminutive of *largo,* LARGO.]

larg·ish (lär′jĭsh) *adj.* Fairly large.

lar·go (lär′gō) *adv. Music.* In a slow, solemn manner. Used as a direction to a performer. —*adj. Music.* Slow and solemn. —*n., pl.* **largos.** *Music.* A largo movement or passage. [Italian, slow, "broad," from Latin *largus,* LARGE.]

lar·i·at (lăr′ē-ət) *n.* **1.** A long rope with a running noose for catching wild livestock; a lasso. **2.** A rope for picketing grazing horses or mules. [Spanish *la reata,* lasso, rope used for tying mules : *la,* the + *reatar,* to tie again : *re-,* again, from Latin +

atar, to tie, from Latin *aptāre,* to fit, from *aptus,* APT.]

La·ri·sa (lä′rē-sä′). Also **La·ris·sa** (lə-rĭs′ə). A city of Greece, in eastern Thessaly. Population, 55,000.

lark¹ (lärk) *n.* **1.** Any of various chiefly Old World birds of the family Alaudidae, having a sustained, melodious song. **2.** Any of several similar birds, such as the meadowlark. [Middle English *larke,* Old English *lāwerce, lǣwerce,* from West Germanic *larw(a)rikōn* (unattested).]

lark² (lärk) *n.* **1.** A carefree adventure. **2.** A harmless prank. —*intr.v.* **larked, larking, larks.** To go on a merry spree. [Probably variant of dialectal *lake,* to play, from Middle English *leiken,* from Old Norse *leika.* See **leig-**³ in Appendix.*]

lark·spur (lärk′spûr′) *n.* Any of various plants of the genus *Delphinium,* having spurred, variously colored flowers.

La Roche·fou·cauld (là rôsh-fōō-kō′), **Duc François de.** 1613–1680. French author of maxims and memoirs.

La Ro·chelle (là rô-shĕl′). A fishing and tourist center of France, in the west on the Bay of Biscay; a former Huguenot center, captured by Cardinal Richelieu after a 15-month siege (1627–28). Population, 66,000.

La·rousse (là-rōōs′), **Pierre Athanase.** 1817–1875. French lexicographer, encyclopedist, and educator.

lar·ri·gan (lăr′ĭ-gən) *n.* Also **Lar·ri·gan.** A moccasin with knee-high leggings made of oiled leather. [Origin unknown.]

lar·rup (lăr′əp) *tr.v.* **-ruped, -ruping, -rups.** *Regional.* To beat; flog; thrash. —*n. Regional.* A blow. [Origin uncertain.]

lar·um (lăr′əm) *n. Archaic.* An alarm. [Short for ALARUM.]

lar·va (lär′və) *n., pl.* **-vae** (-vē). **1.** The wingless, often wormlike form of a newly hatched insect before undergoing metamorphosis. **2.** The newly hatched, earliest stage of any of various animals that undergo metamorphosis, differing markedly in form and appearance from the adult. [Latin *lārva*†, disembodied spirit, mask.] —**lar′val** *adj.*

lar·vi·cide (lär′vĭ-sīd′) *n.* An insecticide designed to kill larval pests. [LARV(A) + -CIDE.] —**lar′vi·ci′dal** (-sīd′l) *adj.*

la·ryn·ge·al (lə-rĭn′jē-əl, -jəl, lăr′ən-jē′əl) *adj.* Also **la·ryn·gal** (lə-rĭng′gəl). **1.** Of, pertaining to, affecting, or near the larynx. **2.** *Phonetics.* Produced in or with the larynx; glottal. —*n.* **1.** A part of the larynx. **2.** *Phonetics.* A laryngeal sound. **3.** Any of a set of sounds reconstructed for Proto-Indo-European, of uncertain character (but originally thought to be laryngeal in nature), manifested in various environments, typically involving loss of the original sound in most languages of the family. [From New Latin *laryngeus,* from *larynx* (stem *laryng-*), LARYNX.]

lar·yn·gi·tis (lăr′ən-jī′tĭs) *n.* Inflammation of the larynx, causing hoarseness and sometimes temporary loss of speech. [New Latin : LARYNG(O)- + -ITIS.] —**lar′yn·git′ic** (-jĭt′ĭk) *adj.*

laryngo-, laryng-. Indicates the larynx or pertaining to the larynx; for example, **laryngoscope, laryngitis.** [New Latin, from Greek *larungo-,* from *larunx* (stem *larung-*), LARYNX.]

lar·yn·gol·o·gy (lăr′ĭng-gŏl′ə-jē) *n.* The medical study, treatment, or speciality of the larynx and its diseases. [LARYNGO- + -LOGY.] —**lar·yn′go·log′i·cal** (lə-rĭng′gə-lŏj′ĭ-kəl) *adj.*

la·ryn·go·scope (lə-rĭng′gə-skōp′) *n.* A tubular instrument or apparatus used to observe the interior of the larynx. [LARYNGO- + -SCOPE.] —**la·ryn′go·scop′ic** (-skŏp′ĭk), **la·ryn′go·scop′i·cal** *adj.* —**la·ryn′go·scop′i·cal·ly** *adv.* —**lar′yn·gos′co·py** (lăr′ĭng-gŏs′kə-pē) *n.*

lar·ynx (lăr′ĭngks) *n., pl.* **larynges** (lə-rĭn′jēz) or **-ynxes.** The upper part of the respiratory tract between the pharynx and the trachea, having cartilaginous walls and containing the vocal cords enveloped in folds of mucous membrane attached to the sides. [New Latin, from Greek *larunx*†.]

La·sa. See Lhasa.

la·sa·gna (lə-zän′yə) *pl.n.* Also **la·sa·gne. 1.** Flat wide noodles. **2.** A dish made by baking such noodles with layers of ground meat, tomato sauce, and cheese. [Italian, from Latin *lasanum,* cooking pot, originally "chamber pot," from Greek *lasanon*†.]

La Salle (lə săl′; *French* là sàl′), **Sieur de.** Title of Robert Cavalier. 1643–1687. French explorer of North America.

las·car (lăs′kər) *n.* An East Indian sailor. [Hindi *lashkarī,* soldier, from *lashkar,* army, from Persian, from Arabic *al-'askar,* the army.]

Las Ca·sas (läs kä′säs), **Bartolomé de.** 1474–1566. Spanish Dominican missionary, historian, and supporter of the Indians of Latin America.

las·civ·i·ous (lə-sĭv′ē-əs) *adj.* **1.** Of or characterized by lust; lewd; lecherous: *"the chief reading of the population consisted of lascivious novels"* (C.L.R. James). **2.** Exciting sexual desires. [Late Latin *lascīvīōsus,* from Latin *lascivia,* licentiousness, wantonness, from *lascīvus,* wanton, lustful. See **las-** in Appendix.*] —**las·civ′i·ous·ly** *adv.* —**las·civ′i·ous·ness** *n.*

lase (lāz) *intr.v.* **lased, lasing, lases.** To function as a laser; emit coherent radiation by the action of a laser. [Back-formation from LASER.]

la·ser (lā′zər) *n.* **1.** Any of several devices that convert incident electromagnetic radiation of mixed frequencies to one or more discrete frequencies of highly amplified and coherent visible radiation. Also called "optical maser." **2.** Any such device, including the **maser** (*see*), the output of which is in an invisible region of the electromagnetic spectrum. [L(IGHT) A(MPLIFICATION BY) S(TIMULATED) E(MISSION OF) R(ADIATION).]

lash¹ (lăsh) *n.* **1.** A stroke or blow with or as if with a whip. **2.** A whip or its thong. **3.** A remark that insults, reprimands, or ridicules. **4.** A powerful impact: *The lash of rain on the windows.* **5.** An eyelash. —*v.* **lashed, lashing, lashes.** —*tr.* **1.** To strike with or as if with a whip. **2.** To strike against with force or violence: *"Rainstorm Lashes a Forest on Coast"* (New York

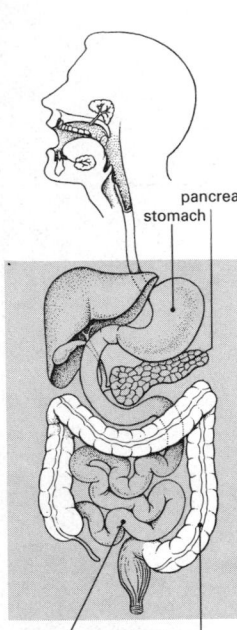

pancreas
stomach

small intestine   large intestine

large intestine

ă pat/ā pay/âr care/ä father/b **bib**/ch **church**/d **deed**/ĕ pet/ē be/f **fife**/g **gag**/h **hat**/hw **which**/ĭ pit/ī **pie**/îr **pier**/j **judge**/k **kick**/l **lid,** needle/m **mum**/n **no,** sudden/ng **thing**/ŏ pot/ō **toe**/ô paw, for/oi **noise**/ou **out**/ŏŏ **took**/ōō **boot**/p **pop**/r **roar**/s **sauce**/sh **ship,** dish/

Times). **3.** To move or wave rapidly to and fro: *like an angry lion lashing his tail.* **4.** To make a violent verbal or written attack against. **5.** To incite or goad. —*intr.* **1.** To move rapidly or violently; to dash. **2.** To make a verbal or written attack. **—lash out.** To attack with sudden violence. [Middle English *lashe*†.] **—lash′er** *n.*

lash[2] (lăsh) *tr.v.* **lashed, lashing, lashes.** To secure or bind, as with a rope, cord, or chain. [Middle English *lasshen*, from Old French *lac(h)ier*, from Latin *laqueāre*, to ensnare, from *laqueus*, snare. See **lace.**] **—lash′er** *n.*

lash·ing (lăsh′ĭng) *n.* Something used for securing or binding, as a rope or cord.

lash·ings (lăsh′ĭngz) *pl.n. Chiefly British.* Lavish quantities. [From LASH (whip) in an obsolete sense "lavish."]

La·shio (lə-shō′). A town in northern Shan State, Burma; the southern terminus of the Burma Road. Population, 5,000.

La Sou·fri·ère. See **Grande Soufrière.**

Las Pal·mas (läs päl′mäs). The largest city of Spain's Canary Islands, situated on the northeastern coast of Grand Canary Island. Population, 166,000.

La Spe·zia (lä spā′tsyä). A city of Italy, a major port and naval base in the northwest on the Ligurian Sea. Population, 128,000.

lass (lăs) *n.* **1.** A girl or young woman. **2.** A sweetheart. [Middle English *lasce, lasse*†.]

Las·sen Peak (lăs′ən). The only active volcano in the continental United States, rising to 10,453 feet at the southern end of the Cascade Range of northern California.

las·sie (lăs′ē) *n.* A lass. [Diminutive of LASS.]

las·si·tude (lăs′ə-to͞od′, -tyo͞od′) *n.* A state of exhaustion or torpor. See Synonyms at **lethargy.** [Latin *lassitūdō*, from *lassus*, tired, weary. See **lēi-[2]** in Appendix.*]

las·so (lăs′ō) *n., pl.* **-sos** or **-soes.** A long rope or leather thong with a running noose at one end used especially to catch horses and cattle; lariat. —*tr.v.* **lassoed, -soing, -sos** or **-soes.** To catch with or as if with a lasso; to rope. [Spanish *lazo*, from Latin *laqueus*, snare. See **lace.**]

Las·so (läs′sō), **Orlando di.** Also **Orlandus Las·sus** (läs′əs). 1532?–1594. Belgian composer.

last[1] (lăst, läst). Alternate superlative of **late.** —*adj.* **1.** Being or coming after all others. **2.** Being the only remaining part of a collection or sequence. **3.** Most recent; latest: *last year.* **4.** Newest; most fashionable: *the last thing in evening clothes.* **5.** Highest; greatest; utmost: *the last degree.* **6.** Most valid, authoritative, or conclusive. **7.** Least appropriate; most unexpected: *He was the last man we would have suspected.* **8.** The lowest in rank, size, or importance: *the last prize.* **9.** *Ecclesiastical.* Administered just before death: *the last sacraments.* —See Usage note at **first.** —*adv.* **1.** After all others in chronology or sequence. **2.** At a time just previous to the present. **3.** In conclusion; finally; lastly. —*n.* **1.** One that is last: *The last of the Plantagenets.* **2.** The end: *He held out until the last.* **3.** The final mention or appearance of something: *I fear we haven't seen the last of her.* **—at (long) last.** After a considerable length of time; finally. **—breathe one's last.** To die. [Middle English *last*, Old English *latost.* See **lēi-[2]** in Appendix.*]

Synonyms: *last, final, terminal, eventual, ultimate.* These adjectives refer to that which marks an end or conclusion. *Last* applies to that which brings a series, sequence, or any collection of like things to an end: *the last day of the month; the last piece of candy. Final* refers to the end of a progression or process, and stresses the definiteness of the conclusion: *his final remark; our final offer. Terminal* is applied to that which marks a limit or boundary in space, time, development, or operativeness: *the terminal point of enemy penetration; the terminal stage of tuberculosis. Eventual* refers to an outcome or issue: *eventual date of publication;* sometimes it implies a foreseeable or inevitable result: *the eventual downfall of a corrupt government. Ultimate* is applied to that which marks the termination of a lengthy progression and beyond which there exists no other: *our ultimate fate; an ultimate goal; the ultimate authority.*

last[2] (lăst, läst) *intr.v.* **lasted, lasting, lasts. 1.** To continue in existence; endure; go on: *The war lasted four years.* **2.** To remain in good condition; endure: *Clay lasts longer than paper.* **3.** To remain in adequate supply: *Will our water last?* [Middle English *lasten*, Old English *lǣstan.* See **leis-** in Appendix.*] **—last′er** *n.*

last[3] (lăst, läst) *n.* A block or form shaped like a human foot, used by shoemakers in making or repairing shoes. —*tr.v.* **lasted, lasting, lasts.** To mold or shape on a last. **—stick to one's last.** To do one's own work. [Middle English *laste*, Old English *lǣste*, from *lāst*, sole, footprint. See **leis-** in Appendix.*]

last[4] (lăst, läst) *n. Chiefly British.* A unit of weight or volume varying for different commodities and in different districts, and approximating 80 bushels, 640 gallons, or 2 tons. See **measurement.** [Middle English *last*, "load," "burden," Old English *hlæst.* See **klā-** in Appendix.*]

Las·tex (lăs′tĕks) *n.* A trademark for a yarn having a core of elastic rubber wound with rayon, nylon, silk, or cotton threads. [(E)LAS(TIC) + TEX(TILE).]

last·ing[1] (lăs′tĭng, läs′-) *adj.* Continuing for a long time; durable. **—last′ing·ly** *adv.* **—last′ing·ness** *n.*

last·ing[2] (lăs′tĭng, läs′-) *n.* A durable twilled fabric.

Last Judgment. The final judgment by God of all mankind.

last·ly (lăst′lē) *adv.* In the end; in conclusion; finally.

Last Supper. Christ's supper with his disciples on the night before his Crucifixion. Also called "Lord's Supper."

last word. 1. The final statement in a verbal argument. **2. a.** A conclusive or authoritative statement or treatment: *the last word in automobile safety.* **b.** The power or authority of ultimate decision. **3.** *Informal.* The newest in fashion; the latest thing.

Las Ve·gas (läs vā′gəs). A city of Nevada, a resort in the southeastern part of the state. Population, 64,000.

lat. latitude.

Lat. Latin.

lat·a·ki·a (lăt′ə-kē′ə) *n.* A grade of Turkish tobacco.

La·ta·ki·a (lăt′ə-kē′ə). A city of Syria, a Mediterranean seaport opposite Cyprus. Population, 72,000.

latch (lăch) *n.* A fastening or lock, usually consisting of a bar that enters a notch or cavity. —*v.* **latched, latching, latches.** —*tr.* To close or lock with a latch. —*intr.* To have a latch for closing or locking. **—latch on to.** *Informal.* **1.** To attach oneself to; cling to. **2.** To get possession of; obtain. **3.** To understand; perceive. [Middle English *lache*, from *lachen*, to latch, seize, Old English *læccan*, to grasp. See **slagw-** in Appendix.*]

latch·et (lăch′ĭt) *n.* A thong used to fasten a shoe or sandal: "*Milton wore latchets in his shoes instead of buckles.*" (Boswell). [Middle English, from Old French *lachet, lacet*, shoestring, from *las*, noose, snare. See **lace.**]

latch·key (lăch′kē′) *n.* A key for opening a latch, especially one on an outside door or gate. Also called "passkey."

latch·string (lăch′strĭng′) *n.* A cord attached to a latch and often passed through a hole in the door to allow lifting of the latch from the outside.

late (lāt) *adj.* **later** or **latter** (lăt′ər), **latest** or **last** (lăst, läst). **1.** Coming, occurring, or remaining after the correct, usual, or expected time; delayed. **2. a.** Beginning at or lasting until an advanced hour: *a late supper.* **b.** Occurring, being, or continuing toward the end: *the late 19th century.* **3.** Having recently begun or occurred; just previous to the present: *the latest developments.* **4.** Having recently occupied a position or place: *the company's late president.* **5.** Dead, especially if only recently deceased: *the late Mr. Foster.* —See Synonyms at **tardy.** —*adv.* **later, latest. 1.** After the correct, usual, or expected time; tardily. **2.** At or far into an advanced period of time: *undertaken late in his life.* **3.** In the recent past: *As late as last week, he was still alive.* **—of late.** In the near past; lately. [Middle English *late*, Old English *læt.* See **lēi-[2]** in Appendix.*] **—late′ness** *n.*

lat·ed (lā′tĭd) *adj. Poetic.* Belated. [From LATE.]

la·teen (lă-tēn′) *adj. Nautical.* **1.** Being a triangular sail hung on a long yard attached at an angle to a short mast. **2.** Rigged with such a sail. —*n.* A lateen-rigged boat. [French *(voile) Latine*, "Latin (sail)" (from its use in the Mediterranean), from Old French, feminine of *Latin*, LATIN.]

Late Greek. Greek during the early Byzantine Empire, from the fourth to the ninth century A.D.

Late Latin. Latin from the third to the seventh century A.D.

late·ly (lāt′lē) *adv.* Not long ago; recently.

la·ten·cy (lāt′n-sē) *n.* The state or quality of being latent.

la·tent (lā′tənt) *adj.* Present or potential, but not manifest: *latent talent.* [Latin *latēns*, present participle of *latēre*, to lie hidden, be concealed. See **lādh-** in Appendix.*] **—la′tent·ly** *adv.*

Synonyms: *latent, dormant, quiescent.* These adjectives describe what is existent or capable of existence but is not manifesting itself. What is *latent* is not clearly visible: *latent energy.* What is *dormant* is inactive, as if sleeping or in suspended animation: *a dormant volcano; dormant legislative proposals.* Persons or things are *quiescent* when they cease to be active or marked by activity; sometimes the term suggests temporary inactivity: *a quiescent interlude between school terms.*

latent heat. The quantity of heat absorbed or released by a substance undergoing a change of state, as by ice changing to water or water to steam.

latent period. 1. The incubation period of an infectious disease. **2.** The interval between stimulus and response.

lat·er (lā′tər). Comparative of **late.** **—later on.** Subsequently.

lat·er·al (lăt′ər-əl) *adj.* **1.** Of, relating to, or situated at or on the side or sides. **2.** Designating a sound produced by breath passing along one or both sides of the tongue. —*n.* **1.** A lateral part, projection, passage, or appendage. **2.** *Football.* A lateral pass. **3.** A lateral sound, such as (l). [Latin *laterālis*, from *latus*† (stem *later-*), side.] **—lat′er·al·ly** *adv.*

lateral line. A linear series of sensory pores and tubes extending along the side of a fish or certain other aquatic animals.

lateral pass. *Football.* A pass thrown sideways, parallel to the line of scrimmage.

Lat·er·an (lăt′ər-ən) *n.* **1.** The church of Saint John Lateran, the cathedral church of the pope as bishop of Rome. **2.** The palace, now a museum, adjoining this church.

lat·er·ite (lăt′ə-rīt′) *n.* A red residual soil in humid tropical and subtropical regions, containing concentrations of iron and aluminum hydroxides, and sometimes used as an ore of iron, aluminum, manganese, or nickel. [Latin *later*†, brick, tile + -ITE.]

la·tex (lā′tĕks′) *n., pl.* **latices** (lăt′ə-sēz′) or **-texes. 1.** The usually milky, viscous sap of certain trees and plants, such as the rubber tree, that coagulates on exposure to air. **2.** An emulsion of rubber or plastic globules in water, used in paints, adhesives, and various synthetic rubber products. [New Latin, from Latin *latex*, fluid. See **lat-** in Appendix.*] **—la′tex′** *adj.*

latex paint. A paint having a binder that is a latex. Also called "rubber-base paint."

lath (lăth, läth) *n., pl.* **laths** (lăthz, läthz, lăths, läths). **1.** A narrow, thin strip of wood or metal, used especially in making a supporting structure for plaster, shingles, slates, or tiles. **2.** Any other building material, such as a sheet of metal mesh, used for similar purposes. **3.** Lathing. **4.** Work made with or from laths. —*tr.v.* **lathed, lathing, laths.** To build, cover, or line with laths. [Middle English *lat, lathe*, Old English *lætt.* See **legwh-** in Appendix.*]

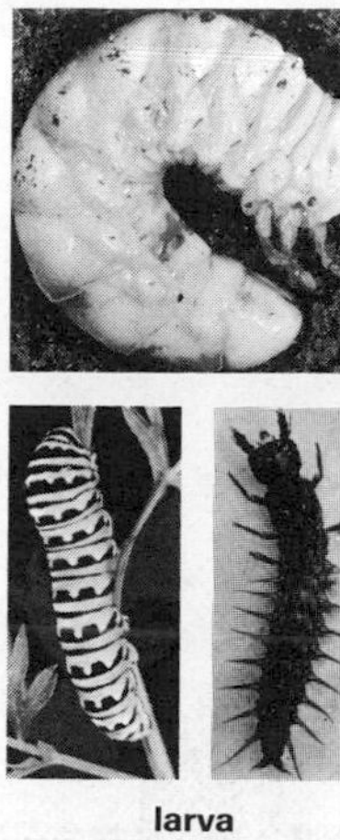

larva
Insect larvae
Above: Cockchafer
Below: Left, black swallowtail; right, dobson fly

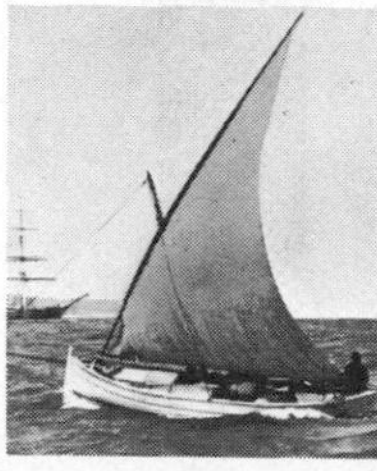

lateen

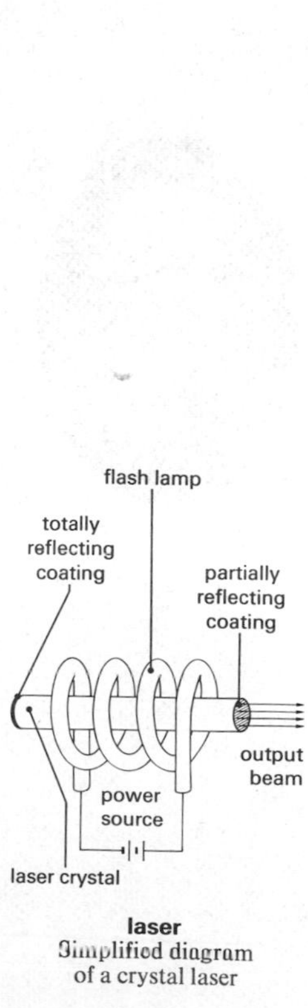
flash lamp
totally reflecting coating
partially reflecting coating
output beam
power source
laser crystal

laser
Simplified diagram of a crystal laser

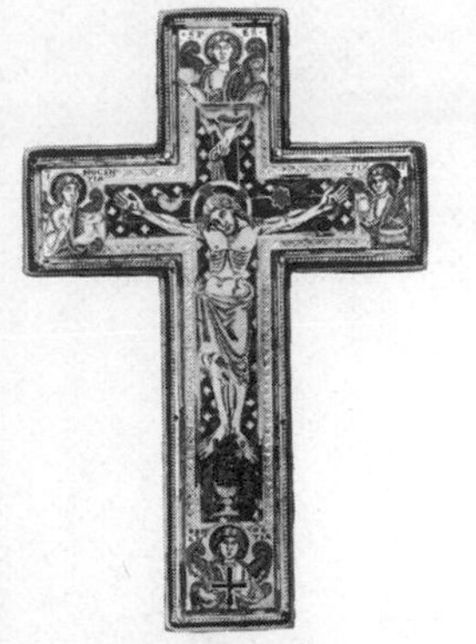

Latin cross
Twelfth-century German

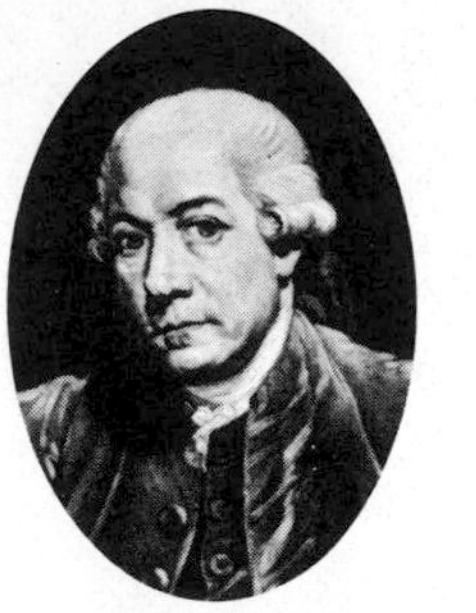

Henry Laurens
Engraving from a portrait by John Singleton Copley

lathe (lāth) *n.* **1.** A machine on which a piece is spun on a horizontal axis and shaped by a fixed cutting or abrading tool. **2.** A potter's wheel. —*tr.v.* **lathed, lathing, lathes.** To cut or shape on a lathe. [Perhaps Middle English *lath,* perhaps from Old Danish *lad,* supporting stand, perhaps a special use of *lad,* pile, from Old Norse *hladh.* See **klā-** in Appendix.*]

lath·er (lăth'ər) *n.* **1.** A light foam formed by soap or detergent agitated in water. **2.** Froth formed by profuse sweating, as on a horse. —**in a lather.** *Slang.* Highly excited or upset; agitated. —*v.* **lathered, -ering, -ers.** —*tr.* **1.** To put lather on; coat with lather. **2.** *Informal.* To give a beating to; to whip. —*intr.* **1.** To produce lather; to foam. **2.** To become coated with lather, as a horse. [Revival of Old English *lēathor,* washing soda. See **lou-** in Appendix.*] —**lath'er·er** *n.* —**lath'er·y** *adj.*

lath·ing (lăth'ĭng, läth'-) *n.* **1.** The act or process of building with laths. **2.** Work made of or using laths.

lat·i·cif·er·ous (lăt'ə-sĭf'ər-əs) *adj.* Secreting or exuding latex. [New Latin *latex* (stem *latic-*), LATEX + -FEROUS.]

lat·i·fun·di·um (lăt'ə-fŭn'dē-əm) *n., pl.* **-dia** (-dē-ə). A great landed estate, especially of the ancient Romans. [Latin *lātifundium* : *lātus,* broad (see **latitude**) + *fundus,* estate, piece of land, bottom (see **bhudh-** in Appendix*).]

Lat·i·mer (lăt'ə-mər), **Hugh.** 1485?–1555. English Protestant martyr; executed for heresy.

Lat·in (lăt'n) *adj.* **1.** *Abbr.* **L., Lat.** Of or relating to Latium, its people, or its culture. **2.** Of or relating to ancient Rome, its people, or its culture. **3.** Of, relating to, or composed in the language of ancient Rome and Latium. **4.** Of or relating to those countries or peoples using Romance languages, especially the countries of Latin America. **5.** Of or relating to the Roman Catholic Church, as distinguished from the Eastern Orthodox Church. —*n. Abbr.* **L., Lat. 1.** The ancient Italic dialect of Latium, which through the political and cultural expansion of Rome became dominant in western Europe, remaining until early modern times the official language of church and state. **2.** A native or resident of ancient Latium. **3.** A member of a Latin people, especially of Latin America. **4.** A Roman Catholic. [Middle English, from Old French or Old English, both from Latin *Latīnus,* from *Latium,* LATIUM.]

La·ti·na (lə-tē'nə; *Italian* lä-tē'nä). A city of west-central Italy, south of Rome. Population, 149,000.

Latin alphabet. The Roman alphabet adopted from the Greek by way of the Etruscan alphabet, consisting of 23 letters upon which are founded the modern western European alphabets. Also called "Roman alphabet."

Latin America. The countries of the Western Hemisphere south of the United States, having Spanish or Portuguese as their official languages.

Lat·in·ate (lăt'n-āt') *adj.* Freighted with Latinisms: *Latinate English prose.*

Latin Church. The Roman Catholic Church.

Latin cross. A cross with the lower limb longest.

Lat·in·ism (lăt'n-ĭz'əm) *n.* An idiom, structure, or word derived from or in imitation of Latin.

Lat·in·ist (lăt'n-ĭst) *n.* A Latin scholar.

La·tin·i·ty (lə-tĭn'ə-tē) *n.* **1.** The use of Latin. **2.** The manner in which Latin is used in speaking or writing; Latin style.

Lat·in·ize (lăt'n-īz') *v.* **-ized, -izing, -izes.** —*tr.* **1.** To translate into Latin. **2.** To transliterate into the characters of the Latin alphabet; Romanize. **3.** To cause to adopt or acquire Latin characteristics or customs. **4.** To cause to follow or resemble the Roman Catholic Church in dogma or practices. —*intr.* To use Latinisms. —**Lat'in·i·za'tion** *n.* —**Lat'in·iz'er** *n.*

La·ti·no-Fa·lis·can (lə-tē'nō-fə-lĭs'kən) *n.* A subdivision of the Italic languages, including Latin and Faliscan. —**La·ti'no-Fa·lis'can** *adj.*

Latin Quarter. A section of Paris on the south bank of the Seine, a student center for many centuries.

lat·ish (lā'tĭsh) *adj. Informal.* Fairly late. —**lat'ish** *adv.*

lat·i·tude (lăt'ə-to͞od', -tyo͞od') *n. Abbr.* **lat. 1.** Extent; breadth; range. **2.** Freedom from normal restraints, limitations, or regulations. **3.** *Geography.* The angular distance north or south of the equator, measured in degrees along a meridian, as on a map or globe. **4.** A region of the earth considered in relation to its distance from the equator: *temperate latitudes.* **5.** *Astronomy.* The angular distance of a celestial body north or south of the ecliptic. [Middle English, from Latin *lātitūdō,* from *lātus,* wide, broad. See **stel-²** in Appendix.*] —**lat'i·tu'din·al** *adj.*

lat·i·tu·di·nar·i·an (lăt'ə-to͞od'n-âr'ē-ən, -tyo͞od'n-âr'ē-ən) *adj.* Favoring freedom of thought and behavior, especially in religion. —*n.* A latitudinarian person. [Latin *lātitūdō* (stem *lātitūdin-*), LATITUDE + -ARIAN.] —**lat'i·tu'di·nar'i·an·ism'** *n.*

La·ti·um (lā'shē-əm). **1.** An ancient country in west-central Italy. **2.** A region of modern Italy, occupying 6,480 square miles in the west along the Tyrrhenian Sea. Population, 3,923,000. Capital, Rome. [Latin *Latium*†.]

La Tor·tue. The French name for **Tortuga.**

la·trine (lə-trēn') *n.* A communal toilet in use by a barracks, camp, or the like. [French, from Latin *latrīna,* contraction of *lavātrīna,* bath. See **lou-** in Appendix.*]

La·trobe (lə-trōb'), **Benjamin Henry.** 1764–1820. British-born American engineer and architect.

-latry. Indicates the worship of; for example, **bibliolatry.** [From Greek *latreia,* service, worship. See **lēi-¹** in Appendix.*]

lat·ten (lăt'n) *n.* **1.** An alloy formerly made of or made to resemble brass, hammered thin, and used in the manufacture of church vessels. **2.** Any thin sheet of metal, especially of tin. [Middle English *laton,* from Old French *leiton, laton,* from Arabic *lāṭūn,* copper, from Turkish dialectal *altan,* gold.]

lat·ter (lăt'ər). Alternate comparative of **late.** —*adj.* **1.** Designating the second of two persons or things mentioned. See Usage note below. **2.** Further advanced in time or sequence; later. **3.** Closer to the end: *the latter part of the book.* [Middle English *latter,* Old English *lætra.* See **lēi-²** in Appendix.*] —**lat'ter·ly** *adv.*

Usage: Latter, in the sense in which it contrasts with *former,* is appropriate only in referring to the second of two previously mentioned: *Jones and Smith have been nominated, but the latter may decline the post. Latter* sometimes appears when reference is made to the last of three or more, but not acceptably so, according to 69 per cent of the Usage Panel. In such examples, *last-named* is often an acceptable substitute. Neither *latter* nor *last-named* is ever appropriate where there is doubt as to the referent. Repetition of the name avoids ambiguity.

lat·ter-day (lăt'ər-dā') *adj.* Belonging to present or recent time; modern.

Latter-day Saint. A **Mormon** *(see).*

lat·ter·most (lăt'ər-mōst') *adj.* Last.

lat·tice (lăt'ĭs) *n.* **1.** An open framework made of strips of metal, wood, or the like interwoven to form regular, patterned spaces. **2.** A screen, window, gate, or the like made of such a framework. **3.** Something, such as a decorative motif or heraldic bearing, that resembles such a framework. **4.** *Physics.* A regular, periodic configuration of points, particles, or objects throughout an area or space; especially, the arrangement of ions or molecules in a crystalline solid. —*tr.v.* **latticed, -ticing, -tices.** To construct or furnish with a lattice or latticework. [Middle English *latis,* from Old French *lattis,* from *latte,* lath, from Germanic, akin to Old English *lætt,* LATH.] —**lat'ticed** *adj.*

lat·tice·work (lăt'ĭs-wûrk') *n.* **1.** A lattice or something resembling a lattice; trelliswork. **2.** A structure made of lattices.

Lat·vi·a (lăt'vē-ə). Officially, Latvian Soviet Socialist Republic. A constituent republic of the Soviet Union, occupying 24,095 square miles in Europe on the Baltic Sea. Population, 2,241,000. Capital, Riga. [Latvian *Latvija*†.]

Lat·vi·an (lăt'vē-ən) *adj.* Of or relating to Latvia, its people, or its language. —*n.* **1.** A native or resident of Latvia. **2.** The Baltic language of these people. Also called "Lettish."

laud (lôd) *tr.v.* **lauded, lauding, lauds.** To give praise or express devotion to; glorify. See Synonyms at **praise.** —*n.* **1.** Praise; glorification. **2.** A hymn or song of praise. **3.** *Plural. Usually capital* **L.** *Ecclesiastical.* **a.** An early-morning church service at which psalms of praise are sung. **b.** The service of prayers following the matins and constituting with them the first of the seven canonical hours. [Latin *laudāre,* to praise, from *laus* (stem *laud-*), praise. See **lēu-²** in Appendix.*] —**laud'er** *n.*

Laud (lôd), **William.** 1573–1645. English prelate; archbishop of Canterbury. Executed for treason.

laud·a·ble (lô'də-bəl) *adj.* Deserving approbation; commendable; praiseworthy. —**laud'a·bil'i·ty, laud'a·ble·ness** *n.* —**laud'a·bly** *adv.*

lau·da·num (lôd'n-əm) *n.* A tincture of opium. [New Latin *laudanum* (coined by Paracelsus), possibly from Latin *lādanum, labdanum,* resin, LABDANUM.]

laud·a·tion (lô-dā'shən) *n.* The act of lauding; praise.

laud·a·tive (lô'də-tĭv) *adj.* Laudatory.

laud·a·to·ry (lô'də-tôr'ē, -tōr'ē) *adj.* Including, expressing, or bestowing praise; eulogistic. [Late Latin *laudātōrius,* from Latin *laudāre* (past participle *laudātus*), to praise, LAUD.]

Lau·e (lou'ə), **Max Theodor Felix von.** 1879–1960. German physicist; worked on x rays and relativity.

laugh (lăf, läf) *v.* **laughed, laughing, laughs.** —*intr.* **1.** To express emotion, typically mirth, by a series of inarticulate sounds, characteristically with the mouth open in a wide smile. **2.** To produce sounds or cries resembling laughter. **3.** To manifest or resemble the manifestation of joy in any way. —*tr.* To drive, induce, or effect with or by laughter: *They laughed him from the stage.* —**laugh at. 1.** To exhibit amusement at. **2.** To poke fun at; ridicule; deride. **3.** To refuse to consider seriously. —**laugh away** (or **off**). To dismiss with laughter. —**laugh down.** To silence with laughter. —**laugh up** (or **in**) **one's sleeve.** To be secretly amused, especially over the discomfiture of another. —*n.* **1.** A burst or sound of laughter. **2.** *Informal.* Something amusing, improbable, or ridiculous; a joke or absurdity: *That's a laugh.* —**have the last laugh.** To enjoy vindication. [Middle English *laughen,* Old English *hliehhan, hlæhhan.* See **klēg-** in Appendix.*] —**laugh'er** *n.* —**laugh'ing·ly** *adv.*

laugh·a·ble (lăf'ə-bəl, läf'-) *adj.* Causing or deserving of laughter or derision. —**laugh'a·ble·ness** *n.* —**laugh'a·bly** *adv.*

laughing gas. An anesthetic, **nitrous oxide** *(see).*

laughing jackass. A bird, the **kookaburra** *(see).*

laugh·ing·stock (lăf'ĭng-stŏk', läf'-) *n.* An object of jokes, laughter, or ridicule; a butt; a fool.

laugh·ter (lăf'tər, läf'-) *n.* **1.** The act of laughing. **2.** The sound produced by laughing. **3.** The experience or appearance of joy, merriment, amusement, or the like. **4.** *Archaic.* A cause or subject for laughter. [Middle English *laughter,* Old English *hleahtor.* See **klēg-** in Appendix.*]

launce (lăns, läns, lôns) *n.* A fish, the **sand lance** *(see).* [Perhaps variant of LANCE.]

Laun·ce·lot. Variant of **Lancelot.**

launch¹ (lônch, länch) *v.* **launched, launching, launches.** —*tr.* **1.** To move or set in motion with force; propel: *launch a missile; launched a volley of snowballs.* **2.** To slide or lower (a boat) into the water, especially for the first time. **3.** To put into action; inaugurate; initiate. **4.** To set or start (someone) on a particular course of action. —*intr.* **1.** To begin a new project or venture; start out on a new course of action. Usually used with *forth,*

ă pat/ā pay/âr care/ä father/b bib/ch church/d deed/ĕ pet/ē be/f fife/g gag/h hat/hw which/ĭ pit/ī pie/îr pier/j judge/k kick/l lid, needle/m mum/n no, sudden/ng thing/ŏ pot/ō toe/ô paw, for/oi noise/ou out/o͝o took/o͞o boot/p pop/r roar/s sauce/sh ship, dish/

into, on or out. **2.** To make a beginning. Used with *into: "The loud soldier launched then into the subject of the anticipated fight"* (Stephen Crane). **3.** To move out to sea. Used with *forth, into, on,* or *out.* —*n.* **1.** An act of launching. **2.** A dock or slip from which a ship is launched. [Middle English *launchen,* to hurl, pierce, from Old North French *lancher,* variant of Old French *lancier,* from *lance,* LANCE.]

launch² (lônch, länch) *n.* **1.** A large ship's boat formerly sloop-rigged but now powered. **2.** Any large, open motorboat. [Portuguese *lancha,* from Malay, akin to Malay *lancharan,* boat.]

launch·er (lôn′chər, län′-) *n.* One that launches, as: **a.** A device for firing grenades. **b.** A device for firing rockets.

launch pad. Also **launching pad.** The base or platform from which a rocket or space vehicle is launched.

launch vehicle. *Aerospace.* A **booster** *(see).*

laun·der (lôn′dər, län′-) *v.* **-dered, -dering, -ders.** —*tr.* **1.** To wash (clothes or linens). **2.** To wash and iron (clothes or linens). —*intr.* **1.** To withstand or emerge from washing in a specified way: *It laundered well.* **2.** To wash, or wash and iron, clothes or linens. —*n. Mining.* A wooden trough for water, used for washing ore. [From obsolete *launder,* launderer, from Middle English *launder,* variant of *lavender,* from Old French *lavandier,* launderer, from Vulgar Latin *lavandārius* (unattested), from Latin *lavanda,* things that need washing, from the gerundive of *lavāre,* to wash, LAVE.] —**laun′der·er** *n.*

laun·dress (lôn′drĭs, län′-) *n.* A woman employed to wash and iron clothes or linens.

Laun·dro·mat (lôn′drə-măt′, län′-) *n.* A trademark for a commercial establishment equipped with washing machines and dryers, usually coin-operated and self-service. [LAUNDR(Y) + -OMAT.]

laun·dry (lôn′drē, län′-) *n., pl.* **-dries. 1.** Soiled or laundered clothes and linens; wash. **2.** A place where laundering is done. [From obsolete *launder,* launderer. See **launder.**]

Laur·a·sia (lô-rā′zhə, -shə). A hypothetical continent of the Mesozoic era thought by geologists to have linked land masses that later separated to form North America, Greenland, and northern Eurasia. [LAUR(ENTIAN) + (EUR)ASIA.]

lau·re·ate (lôr′ē-ĭt) *adj.* **1.** Worthy of laurels for one's achievements; pre-eminent. **2.** Crowned or decked with laurel as a mark of honor. **3.** *Archaic.* Made of laurel sprigs, as a wreath or crown. —*n.* **1.** A poet laureate. **2.** One honored with a crown of laurel. [Latin *laureātus,* crowned with laurel, from *laurea,* laurel tree or crown, from *laureus,* of laurel, from *laurus,* LAUREL.] —**lau′re·ate·ship′** *n.*

lau·rel (lôr′əl, lŏr′-) *n.* **1.** A shrub or tree, *Laurus nobilis,* native to the Mediterranean region, having aromatic evergreen leaves and small blackish berries. Also called "bay." **2.** Any of several similar or related shrubs or trees, such as the **mountain laurel** *(see).* **3.** *Often plural.* Leaves or twigs of a laurel, especially *L. nobilis,* formed into a wreath and conferred as a mark of honor in ancient times upon poets, heroes, and victors in athletic contests. **4.** *Usually plural.* Honor and glory won for achievement. —**look to one's laurels.** To protect one's position of eminence against rivals. —**reap** (or **win**) **laurels.** To receive honors and acquire glory. —**rest on one's laurels.** To be content with past achievements and cease effort. —*tr.v.* **laureled** or **-relled, -reling** or **-relling, -rels.** To crown with laurel. [Middle English *lorel, laurer,* laurel tree, from Old French *lorier,* from *lor,* laurel, from Latin *laurus,* perhaps of Mediterranean origin.]

Lau·rence, Law·rence (lôr′əns, lŏr′-). A masculine given name. [Middle English, from Latin *Laurentius,* of Laurentium, name of a city, perhaps from *laurus,* LAUREL.]

Lau·ren·cin (lô-räɴ-săɴ′), **Marie.** 1885–1956. French painter.

Lau·rens (lôr′əns, lŏr′-), **Henry.** 1724–1792. American Revolutionary statesman and diplomat.

Lau·rent (lô-räɴ′), **Auguste.** 1807–1853. French chemist; advanced nucleus theory of organic radicals.

Lau·ren·tian (lô-rĕn′shən) *adj.* **1.** Of, pertaining to, or in the vicinity of the St. Lawrence River. **2.** *Geology.* Of or relating to the gneissic granite of the early Precambrian (Archeozoic).

Laurentian Mountains. *French* **Lau·ren·tides** (lô-räɴ-tēd′). A low-lying range in Quebec, Canada, extending from the St. Lawrence River to Hudson Bay. Highest elevation, 3,905 feet.

Laurentian Plateau. Also **Laurentian Shield.** A Precambrian plateau extending over half of Canada from Labrador southwest around Hudson Bay and northwest to the Arctic Ocean. Also called "Canadian Shield."

lau·ric acid (lôr′ĭk, lŏr′-). A fatty acid, $C_{12}H_{24}O_2$, obtained chiefly from coconut oil, and used in making soaps, cosmetics, insecticides, and alkyd resins. [From Latin *laurus,* LAUREL (from its occurrence in some laurel).]

Lau·rier (lô-ryā′), Sir **Wilfred.** 1841–1919. Prime minister of Canada (1896–1911).

Lau·sanne (lō-zăn′, -zän′). A city of Switzerland, in the west on the northern shore of Lake Geneva. Population, 132,000.

lav. lavatory.

la·va (lä′və, lăv′ə) *n.* **1.** Molten rock that issues from a volcano or a fissure in the earth's surface. **2.** The rock formed by the cooling and solidifying of this substance. [Italian, lava stream from Vesuvius, stream caused by rain, from *lavare,* to wash, from Latin *lavāre,* to LAVE.]

la·va·bo (lə-vā′bō, -vä′bō) *n., pl.* **-boes. 1.** *Often capital* **L.** In the Roman Catholic and Anglican churches, the ceremonial washing of the hands and recitation from the Psalms by the celebrant before the Eucharist. **2.** The passage recited, Psalm 26: 6–12 (in the Douay and Vulgate versions, Psalm 25: 6–12). **3.** The basin or small towel used in this ritual. **4.** A washbowl and water tank with a spout used for ablutions in monasteries. [Latin *lavābo,* "I will wash" (first word in Psalm 26:6), from *lavāre,* to wash, LAVE.]

lav·age (lăv′ĭj; *French* là-vàzh′) *n.* A washing, especially of a hollow organ, such as the stomach or lower bowel, with repeated injections of water. [French, a washing, from Old French, from *laver,* to wash, from Latin *lavāre,* to wash, LAVE.]

la·va-la·va (lä′və-lä′və) *n.* A draped, kiltlike garment of cotton print worn by Polynesians, especially Samoans. [Samoan *lava-lava.*]

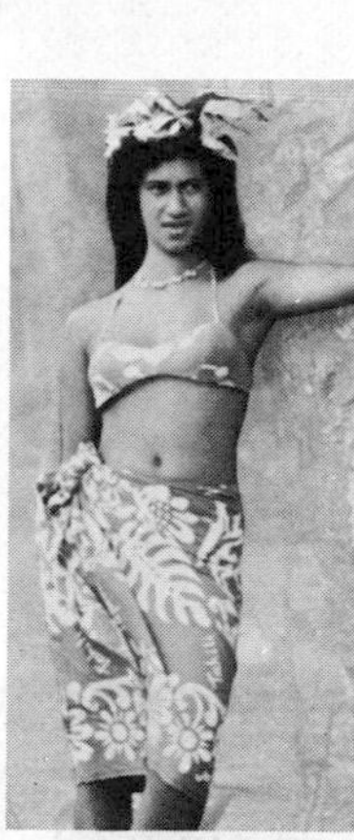

lava-lava

lav·a·liere (lăv′ə-lîr′) *n.* Also *French* **la·val·lière** (là-và-lyâr′). A pendant worn on a chain around the neck. [French *lavallière,* after Louise de *La Vallière,* a mistress of Louis XIV.]

la·va·tion (lă-vā′shən, lā-) *n.* The process of washing; a cleansing. [Latin *lavātiō,* from *lavātus,* LAVE.]

lav·a·to·ry (lăv′ə-tôr′ē) *n., pl.* **-ries.** *Abbr.* **lav. 1.** A room equipped with washing and, usually, toilet facilities. **2.** A basin or bowl, usually one permanently installed with running water, for washing the face and hands. **3.** A bathroom. **4.** *Ecclesiastical.* The ritual washing of the celebrant's hands; lavabo. [Middle English *lavatorie,* from Late Latin *lavātorium,* washing place, washing vessel, from Latin *lavāre,* LAVE.]

lave (lāv) *v.* **laved, laving, laves.** —*tr.* **1.** To wash; bathe. **2.** To lap or wash against: *The stream laved the rocks.* —*intr.* To bathe oneself: *"In her chaste current oft the Goddess laves"* (Pope). [Middle English *laven,* from Old French *laver,* from Latin *lavāre.* See **lou-** in Appendix.*]

lav·en·der (lăv′ən-dər) *n.* **1.** Any of various aromatic Old World plants of the genus *Lavandula;* especially, *L. officinalis* (or *L. spica* or *L. vera*), having clusters of small purplish flowers and yielding an oil used in perfumery. **2.** The fragrant dried leaves, stems, and flowers of such a plant. **3.** Pale to light or moderate purple, to very light or very pale violet. See **color.** [Middle English *lavendre,* from Norman French, from Medieval Latin *lavendula, livendula*†.] —**lav′en·der** *adj.*

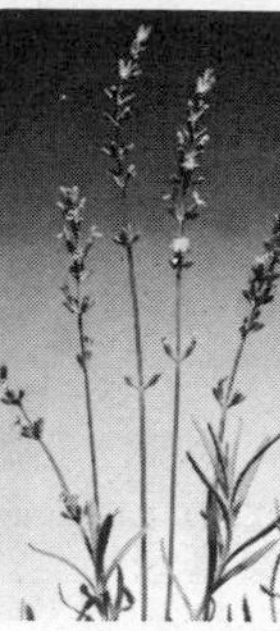

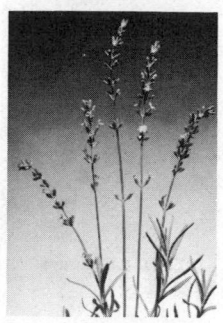

lavender
Lavandula officinalis

la·ver¹ (lā′vər) *n.* **1.** A large basin used in ancient Judaism by the priest for ablutions before making a sacrificial offering. **2.** *Archaic.* A vessel, stone basin, or trough used for washing. [Middle English *laver, lavor,* from Old French *laveoir,* perhaps from Late Latin *lavātorium,* LAVATORY.]

la·ver² (lā′vər) *n.* Any of several edible seaweeds of the genus *Porphyra.* [New Latin, from Latin *laver*†.]

La Vé·ren·drye (là vā-räɴ-drē′), **Sieur de.** Title of Pierre Gaultier de Varennes. 1685–1749. Canadian explorer of New France and the Northwest.

lav·er·ock (lăv′ər-ək) *n. Scottish & Archaic.* A skylark. [Middle English *laverok,* Old English *lǣwerce,* LARK.]

lav·ish (lăv′ĭsh) *adj.* **1.** Extravagant; prodigal: *"a lavish expenditure on looking glass and marble"* (Evelyn Waugh). **2.** Characterized by or produced with extravagance and profusion: *a lavish buffet.* —See Synonyms at **ornate.** —*tr.v.* **lavished, -ishing, -ishes.** To give or pour forth unstintingly: *"the . . . loving care they lavished on their bodies"* (Pauline Kael). [Middle English *lavas,* from noun, "an outpouring," profusion, from Old French *lavasse,* torrent of rain, from *laver,* to wash, LAVE.] —**lav′ish·er** *n.* —**lav′ish·ly** *adv.* —**lav′ish·ness** *n.*

La·voi·sier (là-vwà-zyā′), **Antoine Laurent.** 1743–1794. French chemist, regarded as founder of modern chemistry.

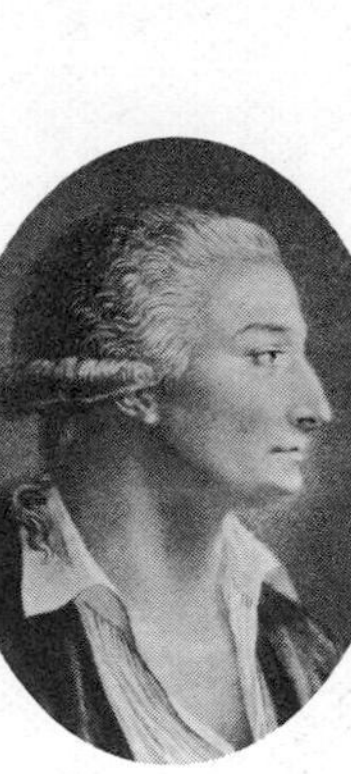

Antoine Lavoisier

law (lô) *n.* **1.** A rule established by authority, society, or custom. **2. a.** The body of rules governing the affairs of man within a community or among states; social order: *the common law; the law of nations.* **b.** A declaration or position which is not to be questioned or disputed: *His word is law.* **3.** A set of rules or customs governing a discrete field or activity: *the law of contracts; criminal law.* **4.** The body of rules originally enforced by the common law courts, in distinction to the rules and decisions given by the chancellor in England and the courts of equity. **5. a.** The system of courts, judicial processes, and legal officers giving effect to the laws of a society: *resort to the law in defense of one's interests.* **b.** An impromptu organization substituted for established juridical procedure: *lynch law.* **6.** The science and study of law; jurisprudence. **7.** Knowledge of law: *His law is good.* **8.** The profession of a lawyer. **9.** *Capital* **L.** *Often plural.* A code of behavior of divine origin: *Mosaic Law.* **10. a.** *Often plural.* Principles of conduct conceived to be of natural origin: *the laws of decency.* **b.** A way of life: *"who knew no law but the law of club and fang"* (Jack London). **11.** A code of principles and regulations observed by a profession or association or by sportsmen: *the law of the turf.* **12. a.** *Often plural.* A formulation of the observed recurrence, order, relationship, or interaction of natural phenomena: *laws of motion.* **b.** A generalization based on the observation of repeated events: *Parkinson's law.* **13.** *Mathematics.* A general principle or rule that is obeyed in all cases to which it is applicable. **14.** *Often plural.* The rules of art; principles or elements: *the laws of harmony; the laws of grammar.* **15.** The police or a policeman. Preceded by *the.* —**go to law.** To take a complaint to court for settlement. —**lay down the law.** To stipulate firmly. —**read law.** *Chiefly British.* To study law. —*intr.v.* **lawed, lawing, laws.** To go to law. [Middle English *law(e),* binding custom or practice, Old English *lagu,* code of rules. See **legh-** in Appendix.*]

law·a·bid·ing (lô′ə-bī′dĭng) *adj.* Abiding by the law.

law·break·er (lô′brā′kər) *n.* A person who breaks the law. —**law′break′ing** *n.* & *adj.*

law·ful (lô′fəl) *adj.* **1.** Within the law; allowed by law: *lawful methods.* **2.** Established or recognized by the law; legally acknowledged: *the lawful heir.* **3.** Legally sanctioned; legitimate: *a lawful marriage.* —**law′ful·ly** *adv.* —**law′ful·ness** *n.*

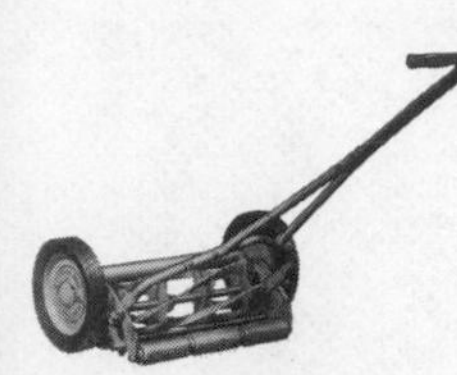
lawn mower

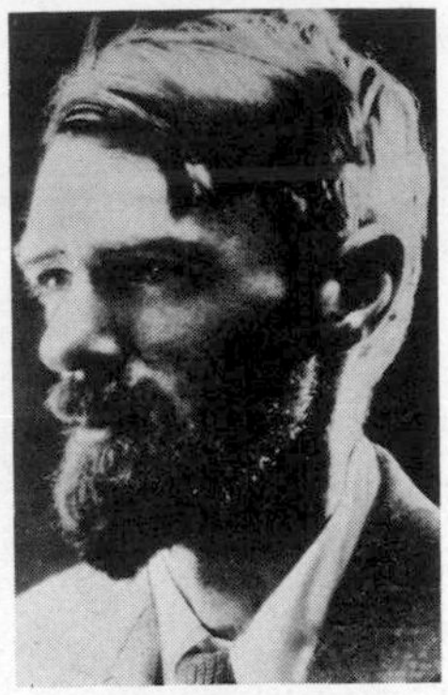
D. H. Lawrence

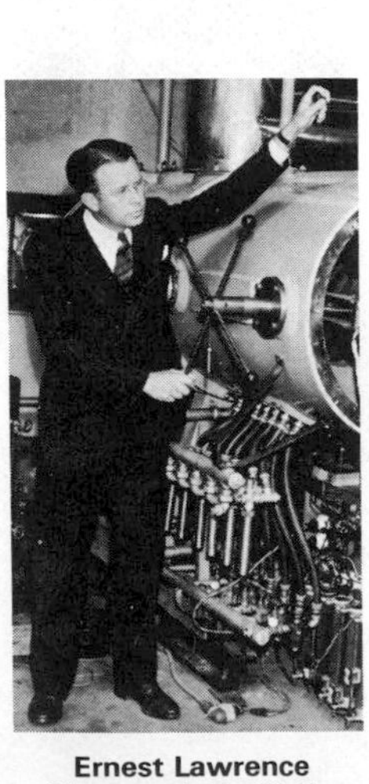
Ernest Lawrence
Photographed with the cyclotron at the University of California

law·giv·er (lô′gĭv′ər) *n.* **1.** One who gives a code of laws to a people. **2.** A lawmaker; legislator. —**law′giv′ing** *n.* & *adj.*
law·less (lô′lĭs) *adj.* **1. a.** Unrestrained by law; disobedient: *a lawless person.* **b.** Unbridled: *lawless passion.* **2.** Heedless of or contrary to the law: *a lawless act.* **3.** Not governed by law: *the lawless frontier.* —**law′less·ly** *adv.* —**law′less·ness** *n.*
law·mak·er (lô′mā′kər) *n.* One who drafts or helps enact laws; a legislator. —**law′mak′ing** *n.* & *adj.*
law merchant. The rules and regulations applied to trade and commerce, drawn from the customs of merchants in the past.
lawn[1] (lôn) *n.* A usually closely mown plot or area planted with grass or similar plants. [Variant of obsolete *laund,* from Middle English *launde, lawnde,* from Old French *launde,* heath, from Germanic. See **lendh-**[2] in Appendix.*] —**lawn′y** *adj.*
lawn[2] (lôn) *n.* A very fine, thin fabric of cotton or linen. [Middle English, probably from *Laon,* France, linen-manufacturing town.] —**lawn′y** *adj.*
lawn mower. A rotary-blade machine for cutting grass.
lawn tennis. Tennis played on a grass court.
law of large numbers. Bernoulli's law *(see).*
Law of Moses. Mosaic Law *(see).*
law of nations. International law *(see).*
Law·rence[1] (lôr′əns, lŏr′-). A city of Massachusetts, in the northeast on the Merrimack River. Population, 71,000.
Law·rence[2]. Variant of **Laurence.**
Law·rence (lôr′əns, lŏr′-), **D(avid) H(erbert).** 1885–1930. English author.
Law·rence (lôr′əns, lŏr′-), **Ernest Orlando.** 1901–1958. American physicist; inventor of the cyclotron.
Law·rence (lôr′əns, lŏr′-), **James.** 1781–1813. American naval officer in the War of 1812.
Law·rence (lôr′əns, lŏr′-), Sir **Thomas.** 1769–1830. British portraitist.
Law·rence (lôr′əns, lŏr′-), **T(homas) E(dward).** Known as Lawrence of Arabia. Later assumed the name T.E. Shaw. 1888–1935. British soldier and writer.
law·ren·ci·um (lô-rĕn′sē-əm, lō-) *n. Symbol* **Lw** A synthetic transuranic element having a single isotope with mass number 257 and a half-life of 8 seconds. Atomic number 103. See **element.** [After Ernest O. LAWRENCE.]
law·suit (lô′so͞ot′) *n.* A case brought before court.
Law·ton (lôt′n). A city of Oklahoma. Population, 62,000.
law·yer (lô′yər) *n.* **1.** One whose profession is to give legal advice and assistance to clients and represent them in court. **2.** *Regional.* A burbot. [Middle English *lawyere,* from *lawe,* LAW.]
Synonyms: *lawyer, attorney, counselor, counsel, barrister, solicitor, advocate.* These nouns denote persons who practice law. *Lawyer* is the general and most comprehensive term for one authorized to manage the legal affairs of a client, give legal advice, and plead cases in court. *Attorney* is often used interchangeably with *lawyer* but in a narrower sense refers to a legal agent for a client in the transaction of business. In a still narrower sense, *attorney* denotes anyone legally appointed to transact another's business. *Counselor* and *counsel* are terms for persons who give legal advice and serve as trial lawyers; *counsel* is also applied to a team of lawyers employed in conducting a case. *Barrister* refers principally to an English trial lawyer, and *solicitor* to an English lawyer whose practice is devoted largely to serving as a legal agent, representing clients in minor courts, and preparing cases for trial in superior courts. *Advocate* is largely restricted to military usage; in Scotland and France, it has the approximate sense of trial lawyer.
lax (lăks) *adj.* **1. a.** Showing little concern; remiss; negligent: *lax about paying bills.* **b.** Not strict; unenforced. **2.** Not taut, firm, or compact; slack. **3.** Loose and not easily retained or controlled. Said of bowel movements. **4.** *Phonetics.* Pronounced with the muscles of the tongue and jaw partially relaxed; wide. Said of certain vowel sounds, such as *e* in *let* or *i* in *hide.* Compare **tense.** [Middle English, from Latin *laxus,* slack, loose. See **slēg-** in Appendix.*] —**lax′ly** *adv.* —**lax′ness** *n.*
LAX Airport code for Los Angeles, California.
lax·a·tive (lăk′sə-tĭv) *n.* **1.** *Medicine.* A drug that stimulates evacuation of the bowels. **2.** Something that induces catharsis. —*adj.* **1.** Stimulating evacuation of the bowels. **2.** Unrestrained. [Middle English *laxatif,* from adjective, "producing looseness," from Old French, from Latin *laxātīvus,* from *laxāre,* to relax, from *laxus,* loose, LAX.]
lax·i·ty (lăk′sə-tē) *n.* The state or quality of being lax.
lay[1] (lā) *v.* **laid** (lād), **laying, lays.** —*tr.* **1.** To cause to lie; put in a recumbent position: *lay a child in its crib.* **2.** To place or rest in a particular state or position. **3.** To put or set down; deposit. **4.** To produce and deposit: *lay eggs.* **5.** To cause to settle or subside. **6.** To put or apply: *lay an ear to the door.* **7.** To assign or attribute: *laid the blame on him.* **8.** To put in a setting; locate: *The story was laid in northern Italy.* **9.** To bury; sink in the ground: *lay a cable.* **10.** To place in the proper position or spot: *lay a carpet.* **11.** To arrange in a required order for use; put in readiness: *lay a trap.* **12.** To devise; make: *lay plans.* **13.** To apply in a thick layer or coat: *lay paint on a canvas.* **14.** To place or give (importance): *lay stress on clarity of expression.* **15.** To impose as a burden or punishment. Usually used with *upon: lay a penalty upon him.* **16.** To put forth for examination; present; submit: *lay a case before a committee.* **17.** To place (a bet); to stake; wager: *lay ten dollars on a horse.* **18.** To bring down forcefully: *laid a blow on his jaw.* **19.** *Vulgar Slang.* To have sexual intercourse with. **20.** *Military.* To aim (a gun or cannon). **21. a.** To place together (strands) to be twisted into rope. **b.** To make in this manner. Used with *up: lay up cable.* **22.** To inlay: *The floor was laid in semiprecious stones.* **23.** To bring (a ship) to a specified position: *lay the vessel alongside the wharf.* —*intr.* **1.** To produce and deposit eggs. **2.** To bet; wager. **3. a.** *Nonstandard.* To lie; recline. **b.** *Nautical.* To lie in a specified position: *The ship laid aft.* —**lay about (one). 1.** To hit out in all directions; fight vigorously. **2.** To rouse oneself into activity; bestir oneself. —**lay a course. 1.** *Nautical.* To go in a certain course or direction without tacking. **2.** To plan some action. —**lay aloft.** *Nautical.* To go up into the rigging of a ship. —**lay aside. 1.** To put off to one side; abandon: *lay aside hope of rescue.* **2.** To put aside for the future; save. —**lay away. 1.** To reserve for the future; save. **2.** In merchandising, to hold for future delivery. **3.** *Informal.* To bury; inter. —**lay bare.** To expose to view; reveal. —**lay before.** To put forth for consideration; bring to the attention of. —**lay by. 1.** To keep on hand for future needs; save. **2.** *Nautical.* To lay to. —**lay claim to.** To insist upon as a right; assert a claim. —**lay down. 1.** To store, as provisions in a cellar. **2.** To place (a bet); to wager. —**lay down one's arms.** To surrender. —**lay down one's life.** To sacrifice one's life. —**lay down the law. 1.** To assert authoritatively what is to be done or observed. **2.** To scold vehemently. —**lay (fast) by the heels.** To seize and prevent from escaping. —**lay for.** *Informal.* To wait for an opportune time to attack (another), as in revenge. —**lay heads together.** To confer. —**lay hold of.** To seize; grasp. —**lay in.** To obtain and stock (provisions or other supplies); to store. —**lay into. 1.** To thrash. **2.** To scold sharply. —**lay it on.** *Informal.* To be effusive with praise, flattery, excuses, or the like; cajole with exaggeration. —**lay low. 1.** To prostrate. **2.** *Slang.* To stay out of sight; to hide. —**lay oneself open.** To make oneself vulnerable; expose oneself to criticism, blame, or the like. —**lay open. 1.** To cut open. **2.** To expose; reveal. —**lay the land.** *Nautical.* To sail away from the land so that it appears to sink below the horizon. —**lay to. 1.** To apply oneself vigorously. **2.** To attribute to; attach (responsibility, blame, or credit) to. **3. a.** *Nautical.* To bring (a sailing ship) to a stop in open water, steadying her with a jib or other small sail. **b.** To remain stationary, facing into the wind. —**lay to rest.** To bury (a person). —**lay waste.** To ravage. —*n.* **1.** A share of the profits of a whaling or fishing expedition allotted in place of wages. **2. a.** The direction the strands of a rope or cable are twisted in: *a left lay.* **b.** The amount of such twist. **3.** *Vulgar Slang.* **a.** A partner in sexual intercourse. **b.** An act of sexual intercourse. **4.** *Chiefly British Slang.* A line of activity, especially one of a questionable nature. —**in lay.** In a period of ovulation. Said of laying hens. —**lay of the land. 1.** The nature, surface, or form of an area of land. **2.** *Informal.* An arrangement. [Lay, laid, laid; Middle English *leggen, leide, leid,* Old English *lecgan, lēde, gelēd.* See **legh-** in Appendix.*]
Usage: *Lay* (to put, place or prepare) and *lie* (to recline or be situated) are often confused in their application. In the senses noted, *lay* always takes a direct object; *lie* never does. The following are representative examples where errors are likely to occur: *He laid* (not *lay*) *the newspaper on the cabinet an hour ago. The table was laid for four. The hen lays* (or *laid* or *has laid*) *an egg. Mother often lies* (not *lays*) *down after lunch. When I lay* (not *laid*) *down last night, I fell asleep immediately. The rubbish had lain* (not *laid*) *there nearly a week. I was lying* (not *laying*) *in bed when he called. The site lies between Seattle and Everett. He was accused of lying* (not *laying*) *down on the job. They decided to lie low* (not *lay low*), *but lying low was not possible.*
lay[2] (lā) *adj.* **1.** Pertaining to, coming from, or serving the laity; secular: *a lay preacher.* **2.** Practicing psychoanalysis but not having a medical degree: *a lay analyst.* **3.** Of or typical of the average or common man: *lay opinion.* [Middle English *laie,* from Old French *lai,* from Late Latin *lāicus,* from Greek *laikos,* from *laos*†, the people.]
lay[3] (lā) *n.* A ballad. [Middle English, from Old French *lai,* akin to Provençal *lais*†.]
lay[4]. Past tense of **lie** (recline).
lay day. *Commerce.* One of a certain number of days in port allowed the lessee of a ship without charge; a free day. [Perhaps from LAY (verb).]
lay·er (lā′ər) *n.* **1.** A single thickness, coating, or stratum spread out or covering a surface. **2.** One that lays, especially a hen. **3.** *Horticulture.* A stem that is covered with soil for rooting while still part of a living plant. —*v.* **layered, -ering, -ers.** —*tr.* *Horticulture.* To propagate (a plant) by layering. —*intr.* **1.** To separate or split into layers. **2.** *Horticulture.* To take root as a result of layering. [Middle English *leyer,* from *leyen, leggen,* to LAY.]
layer cake. A usually frosted cake of two or more layers separated by a filling, as of jelly or cream.
lay·er·ing (lā′ər-ĭng) *n.* Also **lay·er·age** (-ĭj). The process of rooting branches, twigs, or stems that are still attached to a parent plant, as by placing a specially treated part in moist soil.
lay·ette (lā-ĕt′) *n.* Clothing and other equipment for a newborn child. [French, from Old French, diminutive of *laie,* box, from Middle Dutch *laege*†.]
lay figure. 1. A jointed model of the human body used by artists, especially to demonstrate the arrangement of drapery. Also called "mannequin." **2.** A subservient person.
lay·man (lā′mən) *n., pl.* **-men** (-mĭn). **1.** A member of a congregation as distinguished from the clergy. **2.** One who does not have special or advanced training or skill.
lay off. 1. To suspend from employment, as during a slack period. **2.** To mark off; to chart: *lay off sales jurisdictions.* **3.** *Slang.* **a.** To give up or quit (something one has customarily done or consumed). **b.** To desist.

ă pat/ā pay/âr care/ä father/b bib/ch church/d deed/ĕ pet/ē be/f fife/g gag/h hat/hw which/ĭ pit/ī pie/îr pier/j judge/k kick/l lid, needle/m mum/n no, sudden/ng thing/ŏ pot/ō toe/ô paw, for/oi noise/ou out/o͝o took/o͞o boot/p pop/r roar/s sauce/sh ship, dish/

lay·off (lā′ôf′, -ŏf′) *n.* **1.** The suspension or dismissal of employees. **2.** The interval for which employment has been suspended. **3.** Any period of temporary inactivity or rest.
lay out. **1.** To put or spread out in readiness, as for wear, packing, or inspection. **2.** To arrange according to plan: *He laid out the day's work for his employees.* **3.** *Informal.* To spend; supply (money). **4.** To clothe and prepare (a corpse) for burial. **5.** *Informal.* To knock down; to prostrate.
lay·out (lā′out′) *n.* **1.** The laying out of something. **2.** The arrangement, plan, or structuring of something laid out; overall picture or form: *the layout of a factory.* **3. a.** The spread and juxtaposition of printed matter, as of a newspaper or magazine page. **b.** A dummy, sketch, or paste-up for matter to be printed. **4.** *Informal.* Establishment or quarters: *The company has quite a layout in London.* **5.** A set of tools or implements.
lay over. **1.** To stop at some place in the course of a journey because of scheduling requirements. **2.** To overlay.
lay·o·ver (lā′ō′vər) *n.* A stop, usually of short duration, imposed by the scheduling of a carrier or carriers.
lay reader. A layman in the Anglican and Episcopal churches authorized by a bishop to read some parts of the service.
lay up. **1.** To stock (supplies) for future needs. **2.** *Informal.* To confine as an invalid. **3.** To put (a ship) in dock, as for repairs.
lay-up (lā′ŭp′) *n. Basketball.* A usually one-handed, banked shot made close to the basket after driving in.
la·zar (lā′zər, lăz′ər) *n. Archaic.* A beggar afflicted with some loathsome disease, especially leprosy; a leper. [Middle English, from Medieval Latin *Lazarus,* LAZARUS.]
laz·a·ret·to (lăz′ə-rĕt′ō) *n., pl.* **-tos.** Also **laz·a·ret, laz·a·rette** (lăz′ə-rĕt′). **1.** A hospital treating contagious diseases. **2.** A building or ship used as a quarantine station. **3.** A storage space between the decks of a ship. [Italian *lazaretto,* from *lazzaro,* leper, beggar, from Medieval Latin *Lazarus,* LAZARUS.]
Laz·a·rus (lăz′ər-əs). **1.** The brother of Mary and Martha whom Jesus raised from the dead. John 11:1–44. **2.** The diseased beggar in the parable of the rich man and the beggar. Luke 16:19–31.
Laz·a·rus (lăz′ər-əs), **Emma.** 1849-1887. American poet and philanthropist.
laze (lāz) *v.* **lazed, lazing, lazes.** *—intr.* To be lazy; to loaf. *—tr.* To spend (time) in loafing. [Back-formation from LAZY.]
laz·u·li (lăz′yŏŏ-lē) *n.* **Lapis lazuli** *(see).*
laz·u·lite (lăz′yŏŏ-līt′) *n.* A relatively rare, light- to deep-blue mineral, essentially $(Mg, Fe)Al_2(PO_4)_2(OH)_2$. [From Medieval Latin *lazulum,* LAPIS LAZULI + -ITE.]
laz·u·rite (lăz′yŏŏ-rīt′) *n.* A relatively rare, blue, violet-blue, or greenish-blue mineral, essentially $Na_{4-5}Al_3Si_3O_{12}S$. Also called "lapis lazuli." [German *Lasurit,* from Medieval Latin *lazur,* from Arabic *lāzaward,* LAPIS LAZULI.]
la·zy (lā′zē) *adj.* **-zier, -ziest.** **1.** Resistant to work or exertion; disposed to idleness; slothful. **2.** Slow-moving; sluggish: *a lazy river.* **3.** Conducive to languor or indolence: *a lazy summer day.* **4.** Depicted as reclining or lying on its side. Said of a livestock brand. [Origin obscure.] **—la′zi·ly** *adv.* **—la′zi·ness** *n.*
la·zy·bones (lā′zē-bōnz′) *n., pl.* **lazybones.** *Slang.* A lazy person.
lazy Susan. A revolving tray for condiments or food.
lazy tongs. Tongs having a jointed extensible framework operated by scissorslike handles for grasping an object at a distance.
lb pound (Latin *libra*).
LBJ Lyndon Baines Johnson.
l.c. *Printing.* lower-case.
L.C. **1.** landing craft. **2.** Library of Congress.
L/C letter of credit.
L.C.D. lowest common denominator.
l.c.m. least common multiple.
LCT local civil time.
ld. **1.** *Printing.* lead. **2.** load.
Ld. **1.** limited. **2.** Lord (English title).
lea (lē, lā) *n.* Also **ley** (lā, lē). *Poetic.* Grassland; meadow. [Middle English *ley(e),* Old English *lēah, lēa.* See **leuk-** in Appendix.*]
lea. **1.** league (unit of distance). **2.** leather.
leach (lēch) *v.* **leached, leaching, leaches.** *—tr.* **1.** To remove soluble constituents from (a substance) by the action of a percolating liquid. **2.** To remove (soluble constituents) from a substance by the action of a percolating liquid. *—intr.* **1.** To be dissolved and washed out by a percolating liquid. **2.** To lose or yield soluble matter to a percolating liquid. *—n.* **1.** The process of leaching. **2.** A porous, perforated, or sievelike vessel that holds material to be leached. **3.** The substance through which a liquid is leached. **4.** The solution thus leached. [Variant of obsolete *letch,* to wet, probably ultimately from Old English *leccan,* to moisten. See **leg-**[2] in Appendix.*] **—leach′er** *n.*
lead[1] (lēd) *v.* **led** (lĕd), **leading, leads.** *—tr.* **1.** To show the way to by going in advance; conduct, escort, or direct. **2.** To guide by taking by the hand or by a rope: *lead a horse.* **3.** To serve as a route for; conduct on a particular course: *The path led him to a cemetery.* **4.** To cause to follow some course of action or line of thought; induce: *led him to believe otherwise.* **5.** To direct the performance or activities of: *lead an orchestra; lead a battalion.* **6.** To assume leadership in; to steer; to guide: *lead a discussion.* **7.** To be at the head of: *His name led the list.* **8.** To be ahead of: *led the runner-up by three strides.* **9.** To pursue; to live: *leading a hectic life.* **10.** *Card Games.* To begin a round of play by putting down (a card): *led an ace.* **11.** To aim in front of (a moving target). *—intr.* **1.** To be first; be ahead. **2.** To go first as a guide. **3.** To act as commander, director, or conductor. **4.** To maneuver a partner in dance steps. **5.** To be guided: *The horse leads easily.* **6.** To afford a passage, course, or route. **7.** To tend toward a certain goal or result. Used with *to: led to complications.* **8.** To make the initial play, as in a card game. **—lead astray.** To lead into error or wrongdoing. **—lead on.** To draw along; lure; entice. **—lead the way.** To show or point the way by going first or by setting an example. **—lead up to.** **1.** To result in by a series of steps. **2.** To proceed toward (one's true purpose or subject) with lengthy or evasive preliminary remarks. *—n.* **1.** The first place; foremost position. **2.** The margin by which one is ahead. **3. a.** A piece of information of possible use in a search: *several good leads for a job.* **b.** A clue; a hint. **4. a.** Command; leadership: *take the lead.* **b.** Ability to guide or steer. **5.** An example; precedent. **6. a.** The principal role in a dramatic production. **b.** The person playing such a part. **7.** *Journalism.* **a.** The opening line or paragraph of a news story. **b.** A prominently displayed news story. **8.** *Card Games.* **a.** The first play. **b.** The prerogative or turn to make the first play. **c.** The card played. **9.** *Baseball.* A position taken by a base runner away from his base toward the next. **10.** A leash, rope, or strap for leading an animal. **11.** *Nautical.* The direction in which a rope runs. **12.** *Mining.* **a.** A deposit of gold ore in an old riverbed. **b.** A lode. **13.** *Electricity.* A conductor by which one circuit element is electrically connected to another or to the circuit. [Middle English *leden,* Old English *lǣdan, lǣdde, lǣded.* See **leith-** in Appendix.*]
lead[2] (lĕd) *n.* **1.** *Symbol* **Pb** A soft, malleable, ductile, bluish-white, dense metallic element, extracted chiefly from galena and used in containers and pipes for corrosives, in solder and type metal, bullets, radiation shielding, paints, and antiknock compounds. Atomic number 82, atomic weight 207.19, melting point 327.5°C, boiling point 1,744°C, specific gravity 11.35, valences 2, 4. **2.** A plumb bob suspended by a line, used to make soundings. **3.** *Plural. British.* **a.** A flat or slightly pitched roof covered with sheets of lead. **b.** The sheets of lead used for such a roof. **4.** Bullets from or for firearms; shot. **5.** *Plural.* Strips of lead used in fitting windows with small panes or stained glass pieces. **6.** *Printing. Abbr.* **ld.** A thin strip of type metal used to separate lines of type. **7. a.** Any of various, often graphitic, compositions used as the writing substance in pencils. **b.** A thin stick of such material. *—adj.* Containing or made of lead. *—v.* **leaded, leading, leads.** *—tr.* **1.** To cover, line, weight, fill, or treat with lead. **2.** *Printing.* To provide space between (lines of type) with leads. **3.** To secure (window glass) with leads. *—intr.* To become filled, covered, or clogged with lead. [Middle English *lead, lęd,* Old English *lēad,* from West Germanic *lauda* (unattested), akin to Gaelic *luaidh*†.]

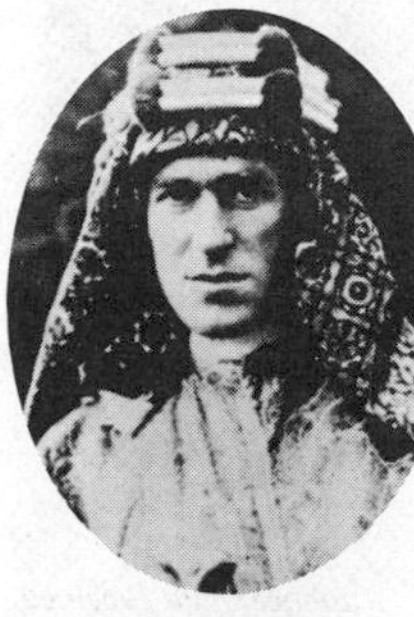

T. E. Lawrence
Photographed in 1919

lead acetate (lĕd). A poisonous white crystalline compound, $Pb(C_2H_3O_2)_2 \cdot 3H_2O$, used in dyes, waterproofing compounds, and varnishes. Also called "sugar of lead."
lead arsenate (lĕd). A poisonous white crystalline compound, $Pb_3(AsO_4)_2$, used in insecticides and herbicides.
lead carbonate (lĕd). A poisonous white amorphous powder, $PbCO_3$, used as a paint pigment.
lead chromate (lĕd). A poisonous yellow crystalline compound, $PbCrO_4$, used as a paint pigment.
lead colic (lĕd). *Pathology.* **Painter's colic** *(see).*
lead·en (lĕd′n) *adj.* **1.** Made of or containing lead. **2.** Heavy and inert like lead. **3.** Dull and listless; sluggish. **4.** Burdened; weighted down; depressed: *a leaden heart.* **5.** Dull, dark gray: *a leaden sky.* **—lead′en·ly** *adv.* **—lead′en·ness** *n.*
lead·er (lē′dər) *n.* **1.** A person who leads others along a way; a guide. **2.** One in charge or in command of others. **3. a.** The head of a political party or organization. **b.** One who has an influential voice in politics. **4. a.** The conductor of an orchestra, band, or choral group. **b.** The principal performer of an orchestral section, as the first violinist. **5.** The foremost horse or other draft animal in a harnessed team. **6.** A **loss leader** *(see).* **7.** *Chiefly British.* The main newspaper editorial. **8.** *Plural. Printing.* Dots or dashes in a row leading the eye across a page, as in an index entry. **9.** A pipe for conveying rainwater from the roof to the ground. **10.** A short length of gut, wire, or the like by which the hook is attached to a fishing line. **11.** *Botany.* The growing apex or main shoot of a shrub or tree.

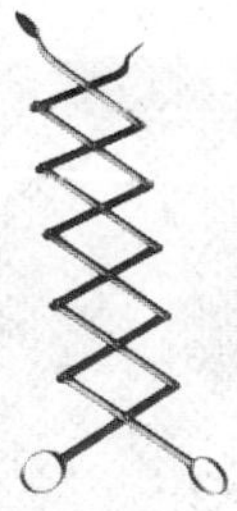

lazy tongs

lead·er·ship (lē′dər-shĭp′) *n.* **1.** The position, office, or term of a leader. **2.** A group of leaders. **3.** The capacity to be a leader; ability to lead.
lead glass. **Flint glass** *(see).*
lead·ing[1] (lē′dĭng) *adj.* **1.** Major; principal: *a leading factor.* **2.** At the head; in the lead; foremost: *the leading candidate.* **3.** Playing one of the leads in a theatrical production: *a leading lady.* **4.** Phrased to elicit a desired response: *a leading question.* —See Synonyms at **chief.** **—lead′ing·ly** *adv.*
lead·ing[2] (lĕd′ĭng) *n.* **1.** A border or rim of lead, as around a windowpane. **2.** *Printing.* The spacing between lines.
lead·ing edge (lē′dĭng). **1.** The edge of a sail that faces the wind. **2.** The front edge of an airplane propeller blade or wing.
lead·ing strings (lē′dĭng). **1.** Strings or straps used to support and guide a child learning to walk. **2.** Close control or guidance.
lead·ing tone (lē′dĭng). *Music.* The seventh tone, or degree, of a scale, a half tone below the tonic; a subtonic.
lead line (lĕd). *Nautical.* A sounding line.
lead monoxide (lĕd). *Chemistry.* **Litharge** *(see).*
lead off (lēd). **1.** To make the initial play or move; to start. **2.** *Baseball.* To be the first batter in an inning or a line-up.
lead·off (lēd′ôf′, -ŏf′) *adj.* Opening; beginning: *leadoff pitch.* *—n.* **1.** An opening play or move; start; beginning. **2.** A player who starts the action of a game; especially, the first batter in a baseball line-up or in an inning.

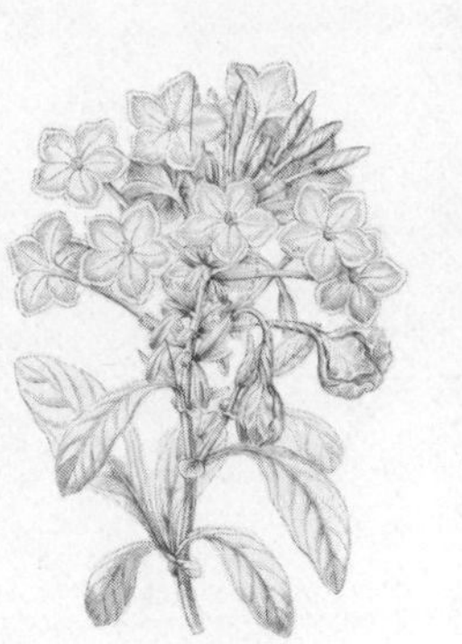

leadwort
Plumbago capensis

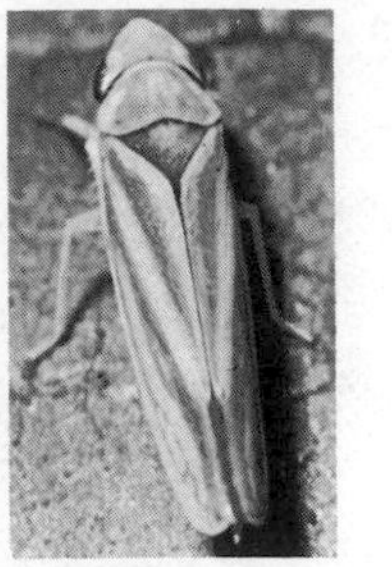

leafhopper
Graphocephala coccinea

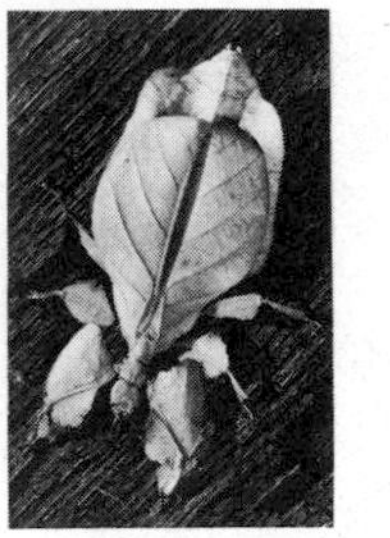

leaf insect
Genus *Phyllium*

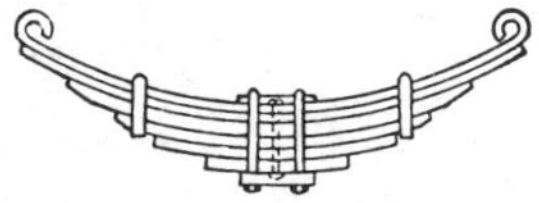

leaf spring

lead pencil (lĕd). A pencil that contains a thin stick of graphite as its marking substance.

lead·plant (lĕd′plănt′, -plänt′) *n.* A shrub, *Amorpha canescens,* of central North America, having leaves covered with whitish hairs. [Once thought to indicate the presence of lead.]

lead poisoning (lĕd). Acute or chronic poisoning by lead or any of its salts, the acute form causing severe gastroenteritis, and the chronic form anemia, abdominal pain, constipation, partial paralysis, and convulsions. Also called "saturnism."

leads·man (lĕdz′mən) *n., pl.* **-men** (-mĭn). *Nautical.* The man who uses the lead line in taking soundings.

lead tetraethyl (lĕd). **Tetraethyl lead** *(see).*

lead·wort (lĕd′wûrt′, -wôrt′) *n.* **1.** Any of various chiefly tropical plants of the genus *Plumbago,* having clusters of variously colored flowers. **2.** Any of several similar plants. [Some species were thought to cure lead poisoning.]

leaf (lēf) *n., pl.* **leaves** (lēvz). **1.** A usually green, flattened structure of vascular plants, characteristically consisting of a bladelike expansion attached to a stem, and functioning as a principal organ of photosynthesis and transpiration. **2.** A leaflike organ or structure. **3.** Leaves collectively; foliage. **4.** The leaves of a plant used or processed for a specific purpose: *tobacco leaf.* **5.** One of the sheets of paper bound in a volume, each side of which constitutes a page. **6.** A very thin sheet of metal: *gold leaf.* **7.** A hinged or removable section for a table top. **8.** A hinged or otherwise movable section of a folding door, shutter, or gate. **9.** One of several metal strips forming a leaf spring. **—in leaf.** Having sprouted or produced leaves; green with foliage. **—turn over a new leaf.** To start a new chapter in one's life by mending one's ways. **—***v.* **leafed, leafing, leafs.** **—***intr.* **1.** To produce leaves; put forth foliage. **2.** To turn pages rapidly; glance: *leafed through the catalogue.* **—***tr.* To turn over one by one. [Middle English *le(e)f,* Old English *lēaf.* See **leup-** in Appendix.*]

leaf·age (lē′fĭj) *n.* Leaves; foliage.

leaf beet. A vegetable, **chard** *(see).*

leaf beetle. Any of numerous beetles of the family Chrysomelidae, many of which feed on plant leaves.

leaf fat. A layer of fat sheathing the kidneys, especially of a hog.

leaf·hop·per (lēf′hŏp′ər) *n.* Any of numerous insects of the family Cicadellidae, that suck juices from plants.

leaf insect. Any of various chiefly Asiatic insects of the genus *Phyllium* and related genera, that resemble leaves.

leaf lard. High-grade lard made from the leaf fat of a hog.

leaf·less (lēf′lĭs) *adj.* Having or putting forth no leaves.

leaf·let (lēf′lĭt) *n.* **1.** One of the segments of a compound leaf. **2.** A small leaf or leaflike part. **3.** A printed, usually folded handbill or flier, such as an advertising circular.

leaf miner. Any of numerous small flies and moths that in the larval state dig into and feed on leaf tissue.

leaf mold. Humus or compost consisting of decomposed leaves and other organic material.

leaf spot. Any of various plant diseases resulting in well-defined necrotic areas on the leaves.

leaf spring. A composite spring, used especially in automotive suspensions, consisting of several layers of flexible metallic strips joined to act as a single unit.

leaf·stalk (lēf′stôk′) *n.* The stalk by which a leaf is attached to a stem; a petiole.

leaf·worm (lēf′wûrm′) *n.* See **cotton leafworm.**

leaf·y (lē′fē) *adj.* **-ier, -iest.** **1.** Having or covered with leaves. **2.** Consisting of leaves. **3.** Leaflike. **—leaf′i·ness** *n.*

league[1] (lēg) *n.* **1.** An association of states, organizations or individuals for common action; alliance. **2.** An association of sports teams or clubs that compete chiefly among themselves. **3.** *Informal.* A class of competition: *out of his league.* **—in league.** Allied; in close cooperation. **—***v.* **leagued, leaguing, leagues.** **—***intr.* To come together for a common purpose; unite. **—***tr.* To bring together under a common agreement; join. [Middle English *ligg,* from Old French *ligue,* from Italian *liga, lega,* from *legare,* to bind, from Latin *ligāre.* See **leig-**[1] in Appendix.*]

league[2] (lēg) *n. Abbr.* **lea. 1. a.** A unit of distance equal to three statute miles. **b.** Any of various other units of about the same length. **2.** A square league. [Middle English *leg(h)e,* from Late Latin *leuca, leuga,* perhaps from Gaulish.]

League of Nations. A world organization of nations established in 1920 and dissolved in 1946.

lea·guer[1] (lē′gər) *n. Archaic.* **1.** A siege; beleaguerment. **2.** A besieging army or its camp. **—***tr.v.* **leaguered, -guering, -guers.** To besiege; beleaguer. [Dutch *leger,* camp, siege, from Middle Dutch, camp, lair. See **legh-** in Appendix.*]

lea·guer[2] (lē′gər) *n.* A person who belongs to a league.

Le·ah (lē′ə). The elder daughter of Laban and first wife of Jacob. Genesis 29:16–23. [Hebrew, "wild cow."]

Lea·hy (lā′hē), **William Daniel.** 1875–1959. American Admiral of the Fleet and diplomat.

leak (lēk) *n.* **1.** An escape from normal or proper confinement; especially, an accidental escape from a container or conduit. **2.** Something escaping normal or proper confines, as: **a.** A liquid or gas abnormally flowing out of a pipe or reservoir. **b.** An electric current diverted through faulty insulation. **c.** Visible light or other radiation passing through an accidental opening. **3.** A flaw, crack, hole, or passage through which an escape occurs. **4.** The path followed by the escaping material. **5. a.** A disclosure of confidential information, either unauthorized or deliberate. **b.** The information disclosed. **c.** The source of such information. **—spring a leak.** To contract or develop an opening or other flaw that allows the escape or entrance of a substance. **—***v.* **leaked, leaking, leaks.** **—***intr.* **1.** To permit the escape or passage of something through a breach or flaw. **2.** To escape or pass through a breach or flaw. **3.** To become publicly known through a breach of secrecy. Often used with *out: The news leaked out.* **—***tr.* **1.** To permit (a substance) to escape or pass through a breach or flaw. **2.** To disclose (information) without authorization or official sanction. [Middle English *leke,* perhaps from Old Norse *leki.* See **leg-**[2] in Appendix.*]

leak·age (lē′kĭj) *n.* **1.** The process of leaking. **2.** That which escapes by leaking. **3.** An allowance made for loss by leaking.

leak·y (lē′kē) *adj.* **-ier, -iest.** Having leaks or tending to leak.

lean[1] (lēn) *v.* **leaned** or **leant** (lĕnt), **leaning, leans.** **—***intr.* **1.** To bend or slant away from the vertical; to incline. **2.** To incline the weight of the body so as to be supported: *leaning against the railing.* **3.** To rely for assistance or support: *He leans on his wife for encouragement.* **4.** To have a tendency or preference. Used with *to* or *toward: She leans more to the group approach.* **—***tr.* **1.** To set or place so as to be resting or supported. **2.** To cause to incline; to bend: *Lean your head back.* **—***n.* A tilt or inclination away from the vertical; a list. [Middle English *lenen,* Old English *hleonian, hlinian.* See **klei-** in Appendix.*]

lean[2] (lēn) *adj.* **leaner, leanest.** **1.** Not fleshy or fat; thin. **2.** Containing little or no fat. Said of meat. **3.** Not productive or abundant: *lean years.* **4. a.** Lacking mineral value: *lean ore.* **b.** Lacking a high proportion of combustible material; containing much air: *lean fuel.* **—***n.* Meat with little or no fat. [Middle English *lene,* Old English *hlæne,* from Germanic *hlainjaz* (unattested).] **—lean′ly** *adv.* **—lean′ness** *n.*

Synonyms: *lean, spare, skinny, scrawny, lank, lanky, rawboned, gaunt.* These adjectives describe persons who are thin of body. *Lean* and *spare* often suggest desirable absence of flesh in one who is athletic and vigorous; sometimes, however, they have no particular connotation. *Skinny* and *scrawny* imply unattractive thinness associated with underdevelopment or undernourishment. *Lank* describes one who is thin in proportion to height, and *lanky* one who is thin, tall, and loose-jointed. *Rawboned* suggests the lankiness or spareness of an outdoorsman. *Gaunt* implies thinness that gives undue prominence to the bones and may suggest illness or hardship.

Le·an·der (lē-ăn′dər). *Greek Mythology.* A youth who loved Hero and swam the Hellespont each night to be with her.

lean·ing (lē′nĭng) *n.* A tendency; proclivity; inclination.

lean-to (lēn′to͞o′) *n., pl.* **-tos.** **1.** A shed with a single-pitch roof attached to the side of a building. **2.** A shelter made from planks or branches raised in the front on poles.

leap (lēp) *v.* **leaped** or **leapt** (lĕpt, lēpt), **leaping, leaps.** **—***intr.* **1.** To jump off the ground with a spring of the legs. **2.** To jump forward; to vault; bound. **3.** To move quickly, abruptly, or impulsively: *He leaps from loyalty to loyalty with each new election.* **—***tr.* **1.** To jump over; to hurdle: *I can't leap the brook.* **2.** To cause to vault or jump: *leap a horse.* **—***n.* **1.** The act of springing up or forward; vault; bound: *"methinks it were an easy leap/To pluck bright honor from the pale-fac'd moon"* (Shakespeare). **2.** The distance cleared in a forward spring. **3.** An abrupt or precipitous passage, shift or transition. **—by leaps and bounds.** Very quickly and by large degrees. [Middle English *le(a)pen,* Old English *hlēapan.* See **klou-** in Appendix.*] **—leap′er** *n.*

leap·frog (lēp′frôg′, -frŏg′) *n.* A game in which one player kneels or bends over while the next in line jumps over him straddle-legged. **—***v.* **leapfrogged, -frogging, -frogs.** **—***tr.* **1.** To jump over in or as if in leapfrog. **2.** *Military.* To advance (two military units) by engaging one with the enemy while moving the other to a forward position. **—***intr.* To move forward or progress by or as if by alternating leaps.

leap year. **1.** A year in the Gregorian calendar having 366 days, with the extra day, February 29, intercalated to compensate for the quarter-day difference between an ordinary year and the astronomical year. Every year whose number is divisible by 4 is a leap year, with the exception of centennial numbers, which are leap years only when divisible by 400. See **calendar.** **2.** An intercalary year in any calendar.

Lear (lîr). The protagonist in Shakespeare's tragedy *King Lear.*

Lear (lîr), **Edward.** 1812–1888. English author of nonsense verse.

learn (lûrn) *v.* **learned** or **learnt** (lûrnt), **learning, learns.** **—***tr.* **1.** To gain knowledge, comprehension, or mastery of through experience or study. **2.** To fix in the mind or memory; memorize: *learned the poem by heart.* **3.** To acquire through experience: *learned humility in the hands of his captors.* **4.** To become informed of; find out. **5.** *Obsolete.* To give information of. **—***intr.* **1.** To gain knowledge, comprehension or skill. **2.** To become informed. Used with *of* or *about.* [Middle English *lernen,* Old English *leornian.* See **leis-** in Appendix.*] **—learn′er** *n.*

Usage: *Learn* in modern usage is never acceptable in the sense of *teach* (to instruct or to impart knowledge) except in contexts clearly representing uneducated speech.

learn·ed (lûr′nĭd) *adj.* **1.** Having or demonstrating profound knowledge or scholarship; erudite; scholarly. **2.** Directed toward scholars: *a learned journal.*

learn·ing (lûr′nĭng) *n.* **1.** Instruction; education. **2.** Acquired wisdom, knowledge, or skill. —See Synonyms at **knowledge.**

lear·y. Variant of **leery.**

lease (lēs) *n.* **1.** A contract granting use or occupation of land or holdings during a specified period in exchange for rent. **2.** The term or duration of use or occupation granted by such a contract. **3.** Property used or occupied by contract in exchange for rent. **4.** An extension under improved circumstances: *a new lease on life.* —*tr.v.* **leased, leasing, leases. 1.** To grant use or occupation of under contract in exchange for rent. **2.** To use or occupy by contract in exchange for rent. [Middle English *les,* from Norman French, from *lesser,* to lease, from Old French *laissier,* to let go, leave, from Latin *laxāre,* to let go, loosen, from *laxus,* LAX.] —**leas'a·ble** *adj.*

lease·hold (lēs'hōld') *n.* **1.** Possession by lease. **2.** Property held by lease. —*adj.* Held by lease. —**lease'hold'er** *n.*

leash (lēsh) *n.* **1.** A chain, rope, or strap attached to the collar or harness of an animal and used to hold it in check. **2.** Control; check: *kept in leash.* **3.** A set of three hounds or other animals. —*tr.v.* **leashed, leashing, leashes.** To restrain with or as if with a leash. [Middle English *lees, leshe,* from Old French *laisse,* from *laissier,* to loosen, let (a dog run slack). See **lease.**]

leas·ing (lē'sĭng) *n. Archaic.* A lie, or the act of lying; falsehood. [Middle English *le(e)sing,* Old English *lēasung,* from *lēasian,* to lie, from *lēas,* untrue, false. See **leu-¹** in Appendix.*]

least (lēst). Alternate superlative of **little.** —*adj.* **1.** Lowest in importance or rank. **2.** Smallest in magnitude or degree. —*adv.* To or in the smallest degree. —**at least. 1.** According to the lowest possible assessment; no less than. **2.** In any event; anyway: *You might at least answer.* —*n.* The smallest; slightest. —**in the least.** At all: *I don't mind in the least.* [Middle English *leest, least,* Old English *lǣst,* from Germanic *loisiz* (unattested), little. See **less.**]

least common denominator. *Mathematics.* **Lowest common denominator** *(see).*

least common multiple. *Abbr.* **l.c.m.** The least quantity that is exactly divisible by each of two or more designated quantities; for example, 12 is the least common multiple of 2, 3, 4, and 6. Also called "lowest common multiple."

least flycatcher. A small grayish North American bird, *Empidonax minimus.* Also called "chebec."

least squares. A method of determining the line or curve that best fits a relation between two experimental sets of data, using the criterion that the sums of the squares of deviations of experimental points from curve ordinates be a minimum.

least·wise (lēst'wīz') *adv.* Also *regional* **least·ways** (-wāz'). *Informal.* Anyway; at least. [LEAST + -WISE.]

leath·er (lĕth'ər) *n. Abbr.* **lea. 1.** The dressed or tanned hide of an animal, usually with the hair removed. **2.** Any of various articles or parts made of leather, as a strap or boot. **3.** The flap of a dog's ear. —*adj.* Of or made of leather. —*tr.v.* **leathered, -ering, -ers. 1. a.** To cover wholly or in part with leather. **b.** To add leather parts to. **2.** *Informal.* To beat with a leather strap. [Middle English *lether, leder,* Old English *lether-.* See **letro-** in Appendix.*]

leath·er·back (lĕth'ər-băk') *n.* A large, chiefly tropical marine turtle, *Dermochelys coriacea,* having a leathery, longitudinally ridged carapace.

Leath·er·ette (lĕth'ər-rĕt') *n.* A trademark for a paper or cloth imitation leather.

leath·er·head (lĕth'ər-hĕd') *n.* The **friarbird** *(see).*

leath·er·jack·et (lĕth'ər-jăk'ĭt) *n.* A fish, *Oligoplites saurus,* of Atlantic and Pacific waters, having tough, leathery skin and venomous spines on the anal fin.

leath·ern (lĕth'ərn) *adj. Archaic.* **1.** Made of or covered with leather. **2.** Resembling leather.

leath·er·neck (lĕth'ər-nĕk') *n. Slang.* A marine. [The marine uniform used to have a leather neckband.]

leath·er·wood (lĕth'ər-wŏŏd') *n.* **1.** A shrub, *Dirca palustris,* of eastern North America, having tough, pliable bark and small yellow flowers. Also called "wicopy." **2.** A shrub, the **titi** *(see).*

leath·er·y (lĕth'ə-rē) *adj.* Having the texture or appearance of leather; tough or weathered: *"the leathery fissures of* [*Lincoln's*] *face"* (Carl Sandburg).

leave¹ (lēv) *v.* **left** (lĕft), **leaving, leaves.** —*tr.* **1.** To go out of or away from. **2.** To go without taking or removing: *left his book on the subway.* **3.** To have as a result, consequence, or remainder: *left a trail of smoke.* **4.** To forgo moving, changing, or interfering with; let remain: *Leave the dishes in the sink.* See Usage note below. **5.** To have remaining after death: *He leaves a son.* **6.** To bequeath. **7.** To submit to another to be done, acted upon, or accomplished: *Leave the hard work for Jones to do.* **8.** To abandon; forsake: *She's leaving home.* **9.** To submit as identification in one's absence: *I left my number with the operator.* —*intr.* To depart; set out; go. —**leave off. 1.** To stop; cease. **2.** To stop doing or using: *leave off alcohol.* —**leave out.** To omit. [Leave, left, left; Middle English *leven, left, lefte,* Old English *lǣfan, lǣfde, lǣfed.* See **leip-** in Appendix.*]

Usage: *Leave* and *let* are interchangeable only when they are followed by a noun or pronoun and *alone: Leave* (or *let*) *John alone.* The intended sense here is "refrain from disturbing or interfering," and both *leave alone* and *let alone* are capable of expressing it acceptably. Some writers and speakers use only *let alone* in such examples and restrict *leave alone* to the sense of "depart and leave one in solitude." However, in the following sentences, considered as examples in writing, *leave alone* is accepted by majorities of the Usage Panel in the sense of "refrain from disturbing": *Leave him alone and he will produce. Left alone, he was quite productive.* The first is acceptable to 63 per cent; the second, employing *left,* to 81 per cent. *Leave* is not interchangeable with *let* in other senses of "allow" or "permit," as illustrated in the following examples. In all of them, only *let* is acceptable: *Let me be. Let him go. Let us not quarrel. Let it lie.*

leave² (lēv) *n. Abbr.* **lv. 1.** Permission. **2.** Official permission to be absent from work or duty for a considerable length of time; especially, such permission granted to military personnel. **3.** The duration of absence granted by such permission. **4.** Formal or verbal farewell: *took leave of her with a heavy heart.* —**on leave.** Absent with official permission. [Middle English *leve,* Old English *lēaf.* See **leubh-** in Appendix.*]

leave³ (lēv) *intr.v.* **leaved, leaving, leaves.** To put forth foliage; leaf. [Middle English *leven,* from *le(e)f,* LEAF.]

leaved (lēvd) *adj.* **1.** Having or bearing a leaf or leaves. **2.** Having a specified number or kind of leaves. Usually used in combination: *three-leaved; wide-leaved.*

leav·en (lĕv'ən) *n.* **1. a.** A substance, such as yeast or cream of tartar, used as an ingredient in batters and doughs to produce fermentation. **b.** A portion of fermented dough used to produce fermentation in a new batch of dough. **2.** Any element or influence which works subtly to lighten or enliven the whole. —*tr.v.* **leavened, -ening, -ens. 1.** To add yeast or other fermenting agent to. **2.** To produce fermentation in. **3.** To pervade with a lightening or enlivening influence: *"the mild ethics of Buddhism and Jainism had gradually leavened Indian society"* (A.L. Basham). [Middle English *levain,* from Old French *levain,* probably from Latin *levāmen,* alleviation, hence (in Vulgar Latin) "that which raises," from *levāre,* to raise. See **legwh-** in Appendix.*]

leaves. Plural of **leaf.**

leave-tak·ing (lēv'tā'kĭng) *n.* A departure or farewell.

leav·ings (lē'vĭngz) *pl.n.* Scraps or remains; leftovers; residue. See Synonyms at **remainder.**

Leb·a·nese (lĕb'ə-nēz', -nēs') *adj.* Of or pertaining to Lebanon, its people, or their culture. —*n., pl.* **Lebanese.** A native or inhabitant of Lebanon.

Leb·a·non (lĕb'ə-nən). A republic occupying 4,000 square miles between Syria and Israel on the eastern shore of the Mediterranean. Population, 2,152,000. Capital, Beirut.

Leb·a·non Mountains (lĕb'ə-nən). A range extending for 100 miles along the length of Lebanon. Highest elevation, Qurnet es Sauda (10,131 feet).

Le·bens·raum (lā'bəns-roum') *n.* Additional territory deemed necessary to a nation for its economic well-being. [German, "living space."]

Le·brun (lə-brœɴ'), **Charles.** Also **Le Brun.** 1619–1690. French painter.

Lech (lĕk). A river rising in extreme western Austria and flowing about 175 miles north through Bavaria, West Germany, to the Danube.

Le Cha·te·lier (lə shä-tə-lyā'), **Henri Louis.** 1850–1936. French chemist.

lech·er (lĕch'ər) *n.* A man given to excessive or promiscuous sexual indulgence. [Middle English *lech(o)ur,* from Old French *lecheor, lecheur,* from *lechier,* to live in debauchery, to lick, from Frankish *likkōn* (unattested). See **leigh-** in Appendix.*]

lech·er·ous (lĕch'ər-əs) *adj.* Given to, characterized by, or inciting lechery. —**lech'er·ous·ly** *adv.* —**lech'er·ous·ness** *n.*

lech·er·y (lĕch'ə-rē) *n., pl.* **-ies. 1.** Excessive indulgence in sexual activity. **2.** Prurience; lasciviousness.

lec·i·thin (lĕs'ə-thən) *n.* Any of a group of phosphatides found in all plant and animal tissues, produced commercially from egg yolks, soybeans, and corn, and used in the processing of foods, pharmaceuticals, cosmetics, paints and inks, and rubber and plastics. [Greek *lekithos*†, egg yolk + -IN.]

Le·conte de Lisle (lə-kôɴt' də lēl'), **Charles Marie.** Original surname, Leconte. 1818–1894. French poet.

Le Cor·bu·sier (lə kôr-bü-zyā'). Pseudonym of Charles Edouard Jenneret. 1887–1965. Swiss-born architect.

lec·tern (lĕk'tərn) *n.* **1.** A reading desk with a slanted top holding the books from which Scriptural passages are read during a church service. **2.** Any stand that serves as a support for the notes or books of a speaker. [Middle English *lectorn, lettron,* from Old French *lettrun,* from Medieval Latin *lectrinum,* from *lectrum,* from Latin *lectus,* past participle of *legere,* to read. See **leg-** in Appendix.*]

lec·tion (lĕk'shən) *n.* **1.** A variant reading or transcription of a text as given in a particular edition or copy. **2.** A reading from Scripture that forms a part of a church service. [Latin *lectiō,* "a reading," from *legere,* to read. See **lectern.**]

lec·tion·ar·y (lĕk'shə-nĕr'ē) *n., pl.* **-ies.** A book containing lessons or a list of lessons from Scripture to be read at services. [Late Latin *lectiōnārium,* from Latin *lectiō,* LECTION.]

lec·tor (lĕk'tər) *n.* **1.** A cleric of the second lowest of the four minor orders in the early Christian church and titularly in the Roman Catholic Church, having the office of reading the sacred books in church. **2.** A person who reads aloud certain of the Scriptural passages used in a church service; a reader. **3.** A public lecturer or reader in certain universities. [Late Latin, from Latin, "reader," from *legere,* to read. See **lecture.**]

lec·ture (lĕk'chər) *n.* **1.** An exposition of a given subject delivered before an audience or class for the purpose of instruction; discourse. **2.** A method of teaching by discourse, especially as opposed to teaching by conversation or seminar. **3.** A sober admonition or correction; solemn scolding; sermon. —*v.* **lectured, -turing, -tures.** —*intr.* To deliver a lecture. —*tr.* **1.** To give a lecture to (a class or audience). **2.** To scold soberly and at length. [Middle English, "a reading," from Old French, from Medieval Latin *lectūra,* from *lectus,* past participle of *legere,* to read. See **leg-** in Appendix.*]

lec·tur·er (lĕk'chər-ər) *n.* **1.** A person who gives a lecture. **2. a.** A member of the faculty of a college or university usually

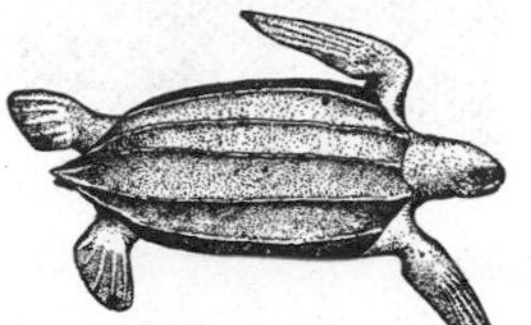

leatherback

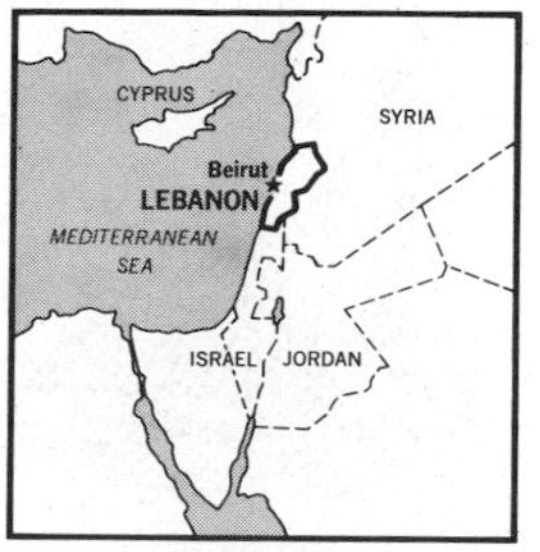

Lebanon

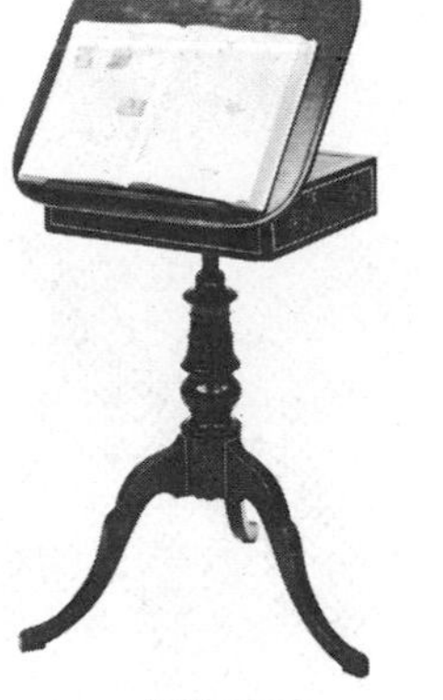

lectern
Late 18th-century American

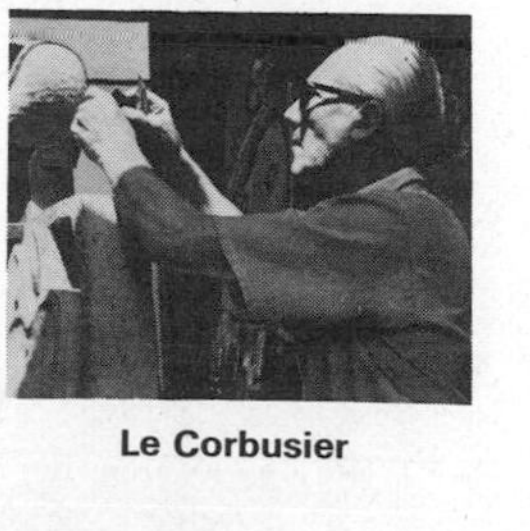

Le Corbusier

having qualified status without rank or tenure. **b.** The rank or position of such a faculty member.

lec·ture·ship (lĕk′chər-shĭp′) *n.* **1.** The status or position of a lecturer. **2.** An endowment or foundation supporting a series or course of lectures.

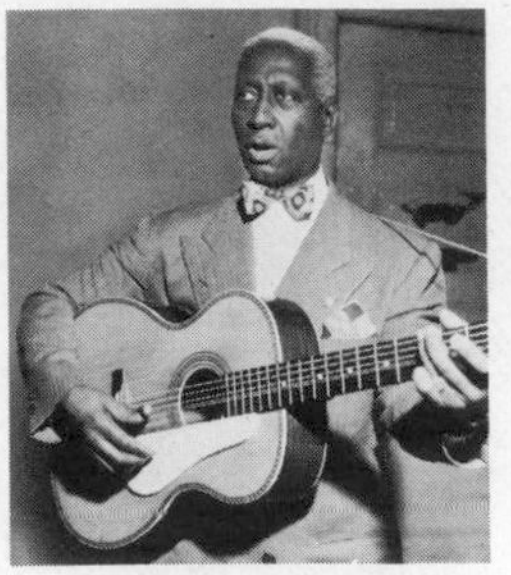
Huddie Ledbetter

led. Past tense and past participle of **lead.**

Le·da (lē′də). *Greek Mythology.* A queen of Sparta and the mother, by Zeus in the form of a swan, of Helen and Pollux and by her husband of Castor and Clytemnestra.

Led·bet·ter (lĕd′bĕt′ər), **Huddie.** Known as Leadbelly. 1888?–1949. American folk singer and guitarist.

ledge (lĕj) *n.* **1.** A horizontal projection forming a narrow shelf on a wall. **2.** A cut or projection forming a shelf on a cliff or rock wall. **3.** A ridge or rock shelf under water. **4.** A level of rock bearing ore; vein. [Middle English *legge,* a raised strip or bar, perhaps from *leggen,* to lay, Old English *lecgan.* See **legh-** in Appendix.*]

ledg·er (lĕj′ər) *n.* Also **leg·er** (for sense 4). **1. a.** A book in which the monetary transactions of a business are posted in the form of debits and credits. **b.** A book to which the record of accounts is transferred as final entry from original postings. **c.** Any list or record in which the transactional elements of a business are posted. **2.** A slab of stone laid flat over a grave. **3.** A horizontal timber in a scaffold, attached to the uprights and supporting the putlogs. **4.** Ledger bait, line, or tackle. [Middle English *legger,* book remaining in one place, probably from Middle Dutch *legger, ligger,* respectively from *leggen,* to lay and *liggen,* to lie. See **legh-** in Appendix.*]

ledger bait. Fishing bait that rests on the bottom.

ledger board. The top railing of a fence or balustrade.

ledger line. Also **leger line. 1.** *Music.* A short line placed above or below a staff to accommodate notes higher or lower than the staff's range. **2.** A fishing line used with ledger bait.

ledger tackle. Fishing tackle used with ledger bait.

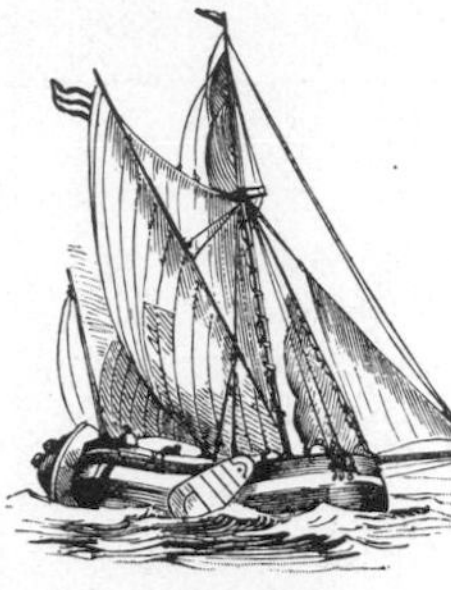
leeboard
Sailing vessel
with leeboard

lee (lē) *n.* **1.** The side or quarter away from the direction from which the wind blows; the side sheltered from the wind. **2.** Any place sheltered from the wind. **3.** Cover; shelter. —*adj.* Located on or moving toward the side toward which the wind blows. Compare **weather.** [Middle English *le(e),* from Old English *hlēo,* covering, shelter. See **kel-**[1] in Appendix.*]

Lee (lē). A river of the Republic of Ireland flowing about 50 miles eastward through central County Cork to the Atlantic.

Lee (lē), **Ann.** 1736–1784. British religious leader; founded first Shaker colony in America (1776).

Lee (lē), **Charles.** 1731–1782. British-born American general in the Revolutionary War; relieved of command (1778).

Lee (lē), **Henry.** Known as Light-Horse Harry. 1756–1818. American statesman and Revolutionary War commander; father of Robert E. Lee.

Lee (lē), **Richard Henry.** 1732–1794. American Revolutionary statesman; U.S. senator from Virginia (1789–92).

Lee (lē), **Robert E(dward).** 1807–1870. Commander in chief of Confederate armies in the Civil War; son of Henry Lee.

Lee (lē), **T(sung) D(ao).** Born 1926. Chinese-born American physicist; proposed with C.N. Yang the violation of conservation of parity in weak interactions.

lee·board (lē′bôrd′, -bōrd′) *n.* One of a pair of movable boards or plates attached to the sides of certain kinds of flat-bottomed sailing vessels, the leeward of which is lowered into the water when the vessel is sailing to windward to prevent slippage down wind.

leech[1] (lēch) *n.* **1.** Any of various chiefly aquatic bloodsucking or carnivorous annelid worms of the class Hirudinea, of which one species, *Hirudo medicinalis,* was formerly used by physicians to bleed their patients. **2.** One who preys on or clings to another; a parasite. **3.** *Archaic.* A physician. —*tr.v.* **leeched, leeching, leeches.** *Medicine.* **1.** To bleed (someone) with leeches. **2.** *Archaic.* To heal. [Middle English *leche,* from Old English *lǣce,* leech, akin to Middle Dutch *leke*† and *lǣce,* physician (see **leg-** in Appendix*).]

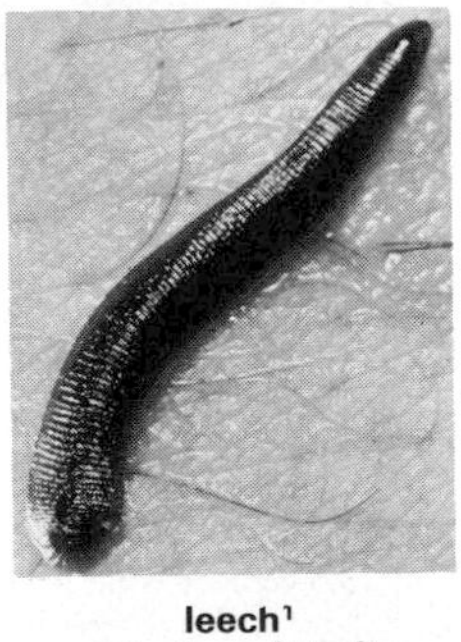
leech[1]
Hirudo medicinalis

leech[2] (lēch) *n. Nautical.* **1.** Either vertical edge of a square sail. **2.** The after edge of a fore-and-aft sail. [Middle English *leche,* earlier *liche,* probably from Middle Low German *līk,* leech line. See **leig-**[1] in Appendix.*]

Leeds (lēdz). A city of England, a textile-manufacturing center in the West Riding, Yorkshire. Population, 509,000.

leek (lēk) *n.* A plant, *Allium porrum,* related to the onion and having a white, slender bulb and dark-green leaves. [Middle English *le(e)k,* Old English *lēac.* See **leug-**[1] in Appendix.*]

leer (lîr) *intr.v.* **leered, leering, leers.** To look obliquely or roll the eyes suggestively, as with prurient interest, malicious intent, or insidious triumph: *"The men said it blissfully, leering at each other with dirty smiles."* (Stephen Crane). —*n.* A suggestive or cunning look. [Probably from obsolete *leer,* cheek, Middle English *ler(e),* Old English *hlēor.* See **kleu-**[1] in Appendix.*]

leer·y (lîr′ē) *adj.* **-ier, -iest.** Also **lear·y.** *Informal.* Suspicious or distrustful; wary. [From LEER, sly look.]

lees (lēz) *pl.n.* Sediment settling during fermentation, especially in wine dregs. [Plural of obsolete *lee,* sediment, from Middle English *lie,* from Old French, from Medieval Latin *lia,* from Celtic. See **legh-** in Appendix.*]

lee shore. A shore toward which the wind is blowing and toward which a ship is likely to be driven.

leet (lēt) *n.* A former manorial court in England. Also called "court-leet." [Middle English *lete,* from Norman French *lete* and Medieval Latin *leta*†.]

Leeu·war·den (lā′wär′dn). The capital of Friesland, the Netherlands, in the northern part of the province. Population, 86,000.

Leeu·wen·hoek (lā′wən-ho͝ok′), **Anton van.** 1632–1723. Dutch naturalist; pioneer in microscopy.

lee·ward (lē′wərd, lo͞o′ərd) *adj.* Located on or moving toward the side toward which the wind is blowing. —*n.* The lee side or quarter. —*adv.* Toward the lee side. Compare **windward.**

Lee·ward Islands (lē′wərd). **1.** A former British colony in the Caribbean, comprising the islands of Anguilla, Antigua, St. Kitts, Nevis, Montserrat, and the British Virgin Islands. **2.** An island group of the northern Lesser Antilles, including Guadeloupe, Saba, the Virgin Islands of the United States, and the former British Leeward Islands colony.

lee·way (lē′wā′) *n.* **1.** The drift of a ship or plane to leeward of true course. **2.** A margin of freedom or variation, as of activity, time, or expenditure; play; latitude.

left[1] (lĕft) *adj.* **1.** *Abbr.* **l.** Designating, belonging to, or located on the side of the body to the north when the subject is facing east. **2.** *Abbr.* **l. a.** Designating or located on the corresponding side of anything that can be said to have a front. **b.** Designating or located on the side nearest to the left hand of the subject or agent. **3.** *Sometimes capital* **L.** Of or belonging to the political or intellectual Left. —*n.* **1.** The direction or position on the left side of the person or thing in question. **2.** The left side or hand. **3.** A turn in the direction of the left hand or side. **4.** *Often capital* **L. a.** The individuals and groups pursuing generally egalitarian political goals by reformist or revolutionary means, in opposition to broadly conservative, established, or reactionary interests. **b.** The relative degree of commitment to such goals, considered as part of a measurable political continuum: *moving further to the left.* **5.** *Boxing.* The left hand or a blow struck by the left hand. —*adv.* Toward or on the left. [Middle English *luft, lift, left,* Old English *left, lyft* (attested only in *lyftādl,* paralysis, "left-disease"), akin to Middle Dutch *luft, lucht*†, weak, useless.]

left[2]. Past tense and past participle of **leave.**

left-hand (lĕft′hănd′) *adj.* **1.** Of, pertaining to, or located on the left. **2.** Moving, swinging, or turning to the left. **3.** Intended for the left hand or for use by a left-handed person.

left-hand·ed (lĕft′hăn′dĭd) *adj.* **1.** Having more dexterity in the left hand, or using the left hand more easily than the right. **2.** Executed with the left hand. **3.** Designed for wear on or use by the left hand. **4.** Awkward; maladroit. **5.** Obliquely derisive; dubious; insincere: *left-handed flattery.* **6.** Of, pertaining to, or born of a morganatic marriage. **7.** Turning or spiraling from right to left; counterclockwise. —*adv.* With the left hand. —**left′-hand′ed·ly** *adv.* —**left′-hand′ed·ness** *n.*

left-hand·er (lĕft′hăn′dər) *n.* **1.** One who is left-handed or uses the left hand. **2.** A blow with the left hand.

left·ism (lĕf′tĭz′əm) *n.* Also **Left·ism.** The ideology of the Left. —**left′ist** *n.* & *adj.*

left·o·ver (lĕft′ō′vər) *adj.* Being an unused remnant.

left·o·vers (lĕft′ō′vərz) *n.* **1.** An unused portion or remnant of something, especially of food. **2.** A dish made out of leftovers. —*adj.* Of or pertaining to something left over.

left wing. Also **Left Wing.** The leftist faction of a group. —**left′-wing′** *adj.* —**left′-wing′er** *n.*

left·y (lĕf′tē) *n., pl.* **-ies.** *Slang.* A left-handed person.

leg (lĕg) *n.* **1.** A limb or appendage of an animal, used for locomotion or support. **2. a.** The lower or hind limb in man and primates. **b.** The part of the limb between the knee and foot in vertebrates. **3.** The back part of the hindquarter of a food animal. **4.** Any supporting part resembling a leg in shape or function. **5.** One of the branches of a forked or jointed object. **6.** Any part of a garment, especially of a pair of trousers, that covers all or part of the leg. **7.** *Geometry.* Either side of a right triangle that is not the hypotenuse. **8.** A stage of a journey or course. **9.** *Nautical.* The distance traveled by a sailing vessel on a single tack. **10.** *Aviation.* That part of an air route or flight pattern that is between two successive stops, positions, or changes in direction. **11.** *Bridge.* The first game of a rubber. **12.** *Cricket.* The right side of the field when the batsman is right-handed, or vice versa. —**give a leg up.** To assist or aid by boosting or providing support. —**not have a leg to stand on.** To have no justifiable or logical basis for a defense or proposition. —**on one's last legs.** On the verge of failure, collapse, or death. —**pull one's leg.** *Informal.* To tease, make fun of, or fool someone. —**shake a leg.** *Slang.* **1.** To hasten; hurry. **2.** To dance. —**stretch one's legs.** To stand or walk, especially after sitting for a long time. —*intr.v.* **legged, legging, legs.** *Informal.* To walk or run. Usually used with *it.* [Middle English *leg, legge,* from Old Norse *leggr*†.]

leg. **1.** legal. **2.** legate. **3.** *Music.* legato. **4.** legislation; legislative; legislature.

leg·a·cy (lĕg′ə-sē) *n., pl.* **-cies. 1.** Money or property bequeathed to someone by will. **2.** Something handed down from an ancestor or predecessor, or from the past. [Middle English *legacie,* from Old French, from Medieval Latin *lēgantia,* from Latin *lēgāre,* to depute, commission, bequeath. See **leg-** in Appendix.*]

le·gal (lē′gəl) *adj. Abbr.* **leg. 1.** Of, relating to, or concerned with law: *legal papers.* **2. a.** Authorized by or based on law: *a legal act.* **b.** Established by law; statutory. **3.** In conformity with or permitted by law. **4.** Recognized or enforced by law rather than by equity. **5.** In terms of or created by the law: *a legal offense.* **6.** Applicable to or characteristic of lawyers or their profession. —*n.* Securities in which investors such as trustees or savings banks may invest. Usually used in the plural. [Old French, from Latin *lēgālis,* from *lēx* (stem *lēg-*), law. See **leg-** in Appendix.*] —**le′gal·ly** *adv.*

legal age. The age of legal responsibility. See **age.**

legal cap. A white, often ruled writing paper measuring 8½ by 13 to 16 inches, generally used by lawyers.
legal holiday. Any holiday authorized by law and characterized by a limit or ban on work or official business.
le·gal·ism (lē′gə-lĭz′əm) *n.* Strict, literal adherence to law. —**le′gal·ist** *n.* —**le′gal·is′tic** *adj.* —**le′gal·is′ti·cal·ly** *adv.*
le·gal·i·ty (lē-găl′ə-tē) *n., pl.* **-ties. 1.** The state or quality of being legal; lawfulness. **2.** Adherence to or observance of the law. **3.** A requirement of law: *legalities prevented the merger.*
le·gal·ize (lē′gə-līz′) *tr.v.* **-ized, -izing, -izes.** To make legal or lawful. —**le′gal·i·za′tion** *n.*
legal memory. *Law.* A period of time, **memory** *(see).*
legal reserve. The sum of money that a bank or insurance company is required by law to set aside as security.
legal separation. Judicial separation *(see).*
legal tender. Currency in certain denominations or amounts that may legally be offered in payment of a debt and that a creditor must accept.
leg·ate (lĕg′ĭt) *n. Abbr.* **leg.** An official emissary, especially an official representative of the pope. [Middle English, from Old French, from Latin *lēgātus,* from the past participle of *lēgāre,* to depute, commission, send on an embassy. See **leg-** in Appendix.*] —**leg′ate·ship′** *n.* —**leg′a·tine′** (-tēn′, -tīn′, -tĭn) *adj.*
leg·a·tee (lĕg′ə-tē′) *n.* The inheritor of a legacy.
le·ga·tion (lə-gā′shən) *n.* **1.** The sending of a legate. **2.** The mission on which a legate is sent. **3.** A diplomatic mission in a foreign country, ranking below an embassy. **4.** The legate and staff of such a mission. **5.** The premises occupied by a legation. [Middle English *legacioun,* from Old French *legation,* from Latin *lēgātiō,* from *lēgātus,* LEGATE.]
le·ga·to (lə-gä′tō) *adv. Abbr.* **leg.** *Music.* In an even, smooth style. Used as a direction. —*n., pl.* **legatos.** A smooth, even style, performance, or passage. [Italian, "connected, continuous, bound," from *legare,* to bind, from Latin *ligāre.* See **leig-**[1] in Appendix.*] —**le·ga′to** *adj.*
le·ga·tor (lə-gā′tər, lĕg′ə-tôr′) *n.* A person who makes a will; a testator. [Latin *lēgātor,* from *lēgāre,* to bequeath. See **legacy.**]
leg·end (lĕj′ənd) *n.* **1.** An unverified popular story handed down from earlier times. **2.** A body or collection of such stories. **3.** A romanticized or popularized myth of modern times. **4.** A person who achieves legendary fame. **5.** An inscription or title on an object, such as a coat of arms or coin. **6.** An explanatory caption accompanying a map, chart, or illustration. [Middle English *legende,* originally, story of a saint's life, from Old French, from Medieval Latin *legenda,* "things for reading," from Latin *legendus,* gerundive of *legere,* to collect, gather, read. See **leg-** in Appendix.*]
leg·en·dar·y (lĕj′ən-dĕr′ē) *adj.* **1.** Of, constituting, based on, or of the nature of a legend. **2.** Famous or described in legend.
leg·er. Variant of **ledger.**
Lé·ger (lā-zhā′), **Fernand.** 1881–1955. French painter.
leg·er·de·main (lĕj′ər-də-mān′) *n.* **1.** Sleight of hand. **2.** Any deception or trickery; hocus-pocus. [Middle English *legerdemayn,* from Old French *leger de main,* "light of hand" : *leger,* light, from Vulgar Latin *leviārius* (unattested), from Latin *levis* (see **legwh-** in Appendix*) + *main,* hand, from Latin *manus* (see **man-**[2] in Appendix*).]
le·ges. Plural of **lex.**
leg·ged (lĕg′ĭd, lĕgd) *adj.* Having a specified number or kind of legs. Used in combination: *bowlegged; six-legged.*
leg·ging (lĕg′ĭng) *n.* A leg covering of material such as canvas or leather, usually extending from the knee to the foot. Usually used in the plural.
leg·gy (lĕg′ē) *adj.* **-gier, -giest. 1.** Having disproportionately long legs: *a leggy colt.* **2.** *Informal.* Having attractively long and slender legs. **3.** Having long, spindly, often leafless stems.
leg·horn (lĕg′hôrn′, -ərn) *n.* **1.** The dried and bleached straw of an Italian variety of wheat. **2.** A plaited fabric made from this straw. **3.** A hat made from this fabric. **4.** *Often capital* **L.** One of a breed of domestic fowl of Mediterranean origin, noted for prolific production of eggs. [After LEGHORN.]
Leg·horn (lĕg′hôrn). *Italian* **Li·vor·no** (lē-vôr′nō). A city of northwestern Italy, on the Ligurian Sea. Population, 168,000.
leg·i·ble (lĕj′ə-bəl) *adj.* Capable of being read or deciphered. [Middle English *legibille,* from Late Latin *legibilis,* from Latin *legere,* to read. See **leg-** in Appendix.*] —**leg′i·bil′i·ty, leg′i·ble·ness** *n.* —**leg′i·bly** *adv.*
le·gion (lē′jən) *n.* **1.** The major unit of the Roman army consisting of 3,000 to 6,000 infantry troops and 100 to 200 cavalrymen. **2.** Any large number; a multitude: *Their numbers are legion.* **3.** *Usually capital* **L.** Any of several honorary or military awards or organizations. —See Synonyms at **multitude.** [Middle English *legioun,* from Old French *legion,* from Latin *legiō,* from *legere,* "to gather," levy troops. See **leg-** in Appendix.*]
le·gion·ar·y (lē′jə-nĕr′ē) *adj.* Of, relating to, or constituting a legion. —*n., pl.* **legionaries.** A soldier of a legion.
legionary ant. An army ant *(see).*
le·gion·naire (lē′jə-nâr′) *n.* A member of a legion. [French *légionnaire,* from Old French *legion,* LEGION.]
Legion of Honor. A high French civilian and military decoration, instituted in 1802.
Legion of Merit. A U.S. military decoration awarded for exceptionally meritorious conduct in the performance of outstanding services.
legis. legislation; legislative; legislature.
leg·is·late (lĕj′ĭs-lāt′) *v.* **-lated, -lating, -lates.** —*intr.* To pass a law or laws. —*tr.* To create or bring about by legislation; enact into law. [Back-formation from LEGISLATOR.]
leg·is·la·tion (lĕj′ĭs-lā′shən) *n. Abbr.* **leg., legis. 1.** The act or procedure of legislating; lawmaking. **2.** A law or laws made by such a procedure.
leg·is·la·tive (lĕj′ĭs-lā′tĭv) *adj. Abbr.* **leg., legis. 1.** Of or relating to legislation. **2.** Resulting from or decided by legislation. **3.** Having the power to create laws; designed to legislate. **4.** Of or relating to a legislature. Compare **executive, judicial.** —*n.* The legislative body of a government. —**leg′is·la′tive·ly** *adv.*
leg·is·la·tor (lĕj′ĭs-lā′tər) *n.* **1.** A person who creates or enacts laws. **2.** A member of a legislative body. [Latin *lēgis lātor,* "proposer of law" : *lēgis,* genitive of *lēx,* law (see **leg-** in Appendix*) + *lātor,* bearer, proposer, from *lātus,* "carried" (see **tel-**[1] in Appendix*).]
leg·is·la·ture (lĕj′ĭs-lā′chər) *n. Abbr.* **leg., legis.** An officially selected body of persons vested with the responsibility and the power to legislate for a political unit, such as a nation or state.
le·gist (lē′jĭst) *n.* A specialist in law. [Medieval Latin *lēgista,* from Latin *lēx,* law. See **leg-** in Appendix.*]
le·git (lə-jĭt′) *n. Slang.* Legitimate drama; theatrical production as opposed to motion pictures. —*adj. Slang.* Legitimate.
le·git·i·mate (lə-jĭt′ə-mĭt) *adj.* **1.** In compliance with the law; lawful. **2.** In accordance with traditional or established patterns and standards. **3.** Based on logical reasoning; reasonable: *a legitimate solution.* **4.** Authentic; genuine. **5.** Born in wedlock. **6.** Of, relating to, or ruling by hereditary right. **7.** *Theater.* **a.** Of or pertaining to drama performed on a stage as opposed to other media, such as motion pictures or television. **b.** Of or pertaining to drama of high professional quality, as opposed to burlesque, vaudeville, and the like. —*tr.v.* (lə-jĭt′ə-māt′) **legitimated, -mating, -mates. 1.** To justify as legitimate; authorize. **2.** To make, establish, or declare legitimate. [Middle English, born in wedlock, from Medieval Latin *lēgitimātus,* past participle of *lēgitimāre,* to make lawful, from Latin *lēgitimus,* lawful, legal, from *lēx* (stem *lēg-*), law. See **leg-** in Appendix.*] —**le·git′i·ma·cy** (-mə-sē) *n.* —**le·git′i·mate·ly** *adv.*
le·git·i·mist (lə-jĭt′ə-mĭst) *n.* A person who believes in or supports rule by hereditary right. —**le·git′i·mism′** *n.*
leg-of-mut·ton (lĕg′ə-mŭt′n, lĕg′əv-) *adj.* Resembling a leg of mutton in shape; tapering sharply from one large end to a point or smaller end, as a sleeve or sail.
Le·gree, Simon. See **Simon Legree.**
leg·ume (lĕg′yo͞om′, lə-gyo͞om′) *n.* **1.** A pod, such as that of a pea or bean, that splits into two valves with the seeds attached to the lower edge of one of the valves. **2.** Such a pod or seed, used as food. **3.** Any plant of the family Leguminosae, characteristically bearing such pods. [French *légume,* from Latin *legūmen*†, pulse, bean.]
le·gu·mi·nous (lə-gyo͞o′mə-nəs) *adj.* **1.** Of, belonging to, or characteristic of the family Leguminosae, which includes peas, beans, clover, alfalfa, and other plants. **2.** Resembling or of the nature of a legume. [New Latin *leguminosus,* from Latin *lugūmen,* bean, LEGUME.]
Le·hár (lā′här′), **Franz.** 1870–1948. Hungarian composer of operettas.
Le Ha·vre (lə hä′vrə; *French* lə â′vr′). A city and port of northern France on the English Channel. Population, 183,000.
Le·high River (lē′hī). A river rising in the Pocono Mountains of eastern Pennsylvania and flowing 100 miles southwest, southeast, and east to the Delaware.
Lehm·bruck (lām′bro͝ok′), **Wilhelm.** 1881–1919. German sculptor and graphic artist.
le·hu·a (lā-ho͞o′ə) *n.* A tree, *Metrosideros collina,* of Hawaii and other Pacific islands, having showy red flowers. [Hawaiian.]
lei[1] (lā, lā′ē) *n., pl.* **leis.** A garland of flowers. [Hawaiian.]
lei[2]**.** Plural of **leu.**
Leib·nitz (līb′nĭts′; *German* lĭp′nĭts′), Baron **Gottfried Wilhelm von.** Also **Leib·niz.** 1646–1716. German philosopher and mathematician.
Leices·ter[1] (lĕs′tər) *n.* A sheep of a breed developed in Leicestershire, England, having long, fine wool.
Leices·ter[2] (lĕs′tər). **1.** Also **Leices·ter·shire** (-shîr, -shər). A county occupying 832 square miles in central England. Population, 683,000. **2.** The county seat of this county. Population, 267,000.
Leices·ter (lĕs′tər), **First Earl of.** Title of Robert Dudley. 1532?–1588. English courtier and general.
Lei·den (līd′n). Also **Ley·den.** A city of the southwestern Netherlands, northeast of The Hague. Population, 99,000.
Lein·ster (lĕn′stər). A province of the Republic of Ireland, occupying 7,580 square miles in the southeast.
Leip·zig (līp′sĭg, -sĭk; *German* līp′tsĭk). A city of East Germany 90 miles southwest of Berlin. Population, 595,000.
leish·man·i·a·sis (lēsh′mə-nī′ə-sĭs) *n.* **1.** Infection with flagellate protozoans of the genus *Leishmania.* **2.** A disease, such as kala-azar or either of two clinically distinct, ulcerative skin diseases, caused by such infection. [New Latin, from *Leishmania,* genus of protozoans, identified by Sir William B. *Leishman* (died 1926), British medical officer.]
leis·ter (lēs′tər) *n.* A three-pronged spear used for fishing. —*tr.v.* **leistered, -tering, -ters.** To spear (a fish) with a leister. [Old Norse *ljōstr*†.]
lei·sure (lē′zhər, lĕzh′ər) *n.* Freedom from time-consuming duties, responsibilities, or activities. See Synonyms at **rest.** —**at leisure. 1.** Having free time. **2.** Not employed, occupied, or engaged. **3.** Unhurried. —**at one's leisure.** When one has free time; at one's convenience. —*adj.* **1.** Not spent in work or compulsory activity; free. **2.** Having much leisure: *the leisure class.* [Middle English *leisour, leiser,* freedom, opportunity, from Norman French *leisour,* variant of Old French *leisir,* to be

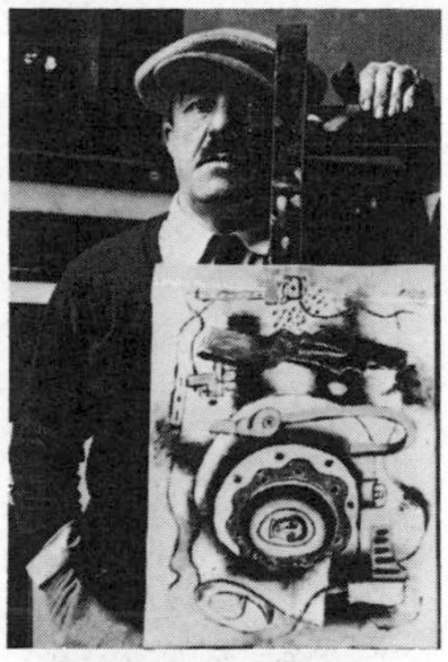
Fernand Léger

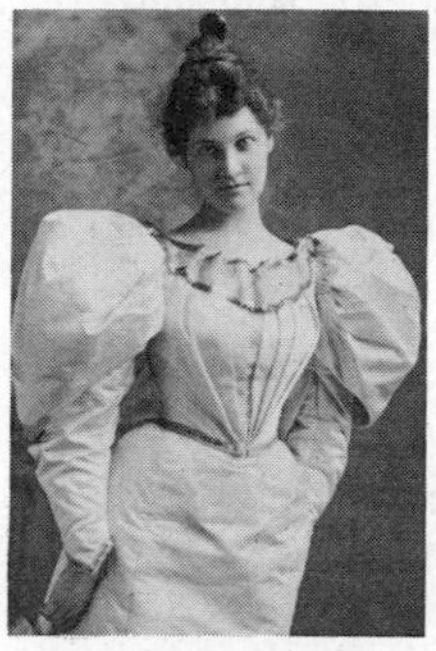
leg-of-mutton
Late 19th-century dress with leg-of-mutton sleeves

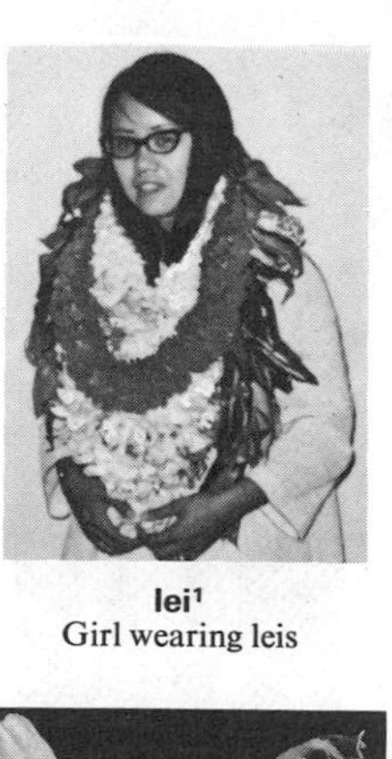
lei[1]
Girl wearing leis

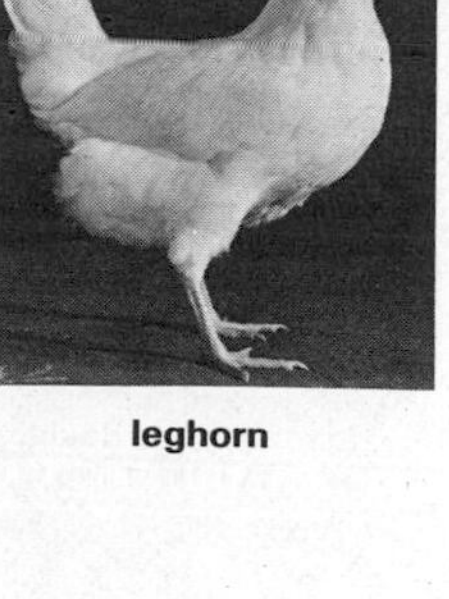
leghorn

permitted, from Latin *licēre*†, to be lawful, be permitted.]

lei·sured (lē′zhərd, lĕzh′ərd) *adj.* Characterized by or having leisure.

lei·sure·ly (lē′zhər-lē, lĕzh′ər-) *adj.* Without haste; unhurried: *a leisurely meal.* See Synonyms at **slow.** —*adv.* In an unhurried, relaxed manner; slowly. —**lei′sure·li·ness** *n.*

leit·mo·tif (līt′mō-tēf′) *n.* Also **leit·mo·tiv. 1.** A thematic passage in Wagnerian opera associated with a specific character, thing, or element. **2.** A dominant theme, as in a novel. [German *Leitmotiv,* "leading motif" : *leiten,* to lead, from Old High German (see **leith-** in Appendix*) + *motiv,* from French *motif,* MOTIF.]

Lei·trim (lē′trĭm). A county of the Republic of Ireland, occupying 589 square miles in the northwest. Population, 33,000. County seat, Carrick-on-Shannon.

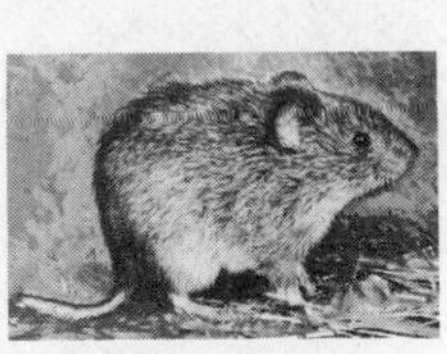

lemming
Synaptomys cooperi

Leix. See **Laoighis.**

lek (lĕk) *n.* **1.** The basic monetary unit of Albania, equal to 100 quintars. See table of exchange rates at **currency. 2.** A coin worth one lek. [Albanian *lek.*]

Lek (lĕk). A northern tributary of the Rhine, flowing for 40 miles through the central Netherlands.

Le·maî·tre (lə-mĕ′tr′), **Abbé Georges Édouard.** Born 1894. Belgian astrophysicist.

lem·an (lĕm′ən, lē′mən) *n. Archaic.* **1.** A lover. **2.** A mistress. [Middle English *leofman, lemman* : *lef, leof,* dear, from Old English *lēof* (see **leubh-** in Appendix*) + MAN.]

Lé·man, Lake. See Lake of **Geneva.**

Le Mans (lə mäN′). A city of west-central France; the site of an annual 24-hour automobile race. Population, 129,000.

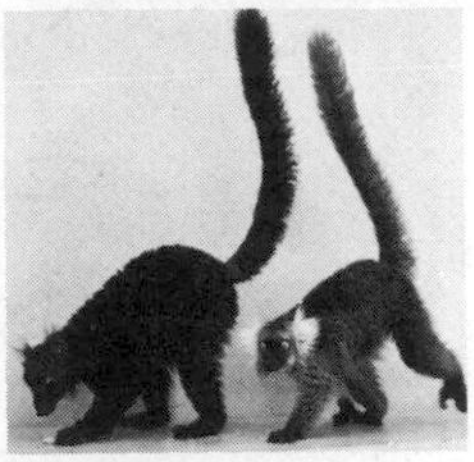

lemur
Lemur macaco
Male *(left)* and female

lem·ma[1] (lĕm′ə) *n., pl.* **-mas** or **lemmata** (lĕm′ə-tə). **1.** *Logic.* A subsidiary proposition assumed to be valid and used to demonstrate a principal proposition. **2. a.** A theme, argument, or subject indicated in a title. **b.** A glossed word in a glossary or other listing, as in the Appendix of this Dictionary. [Latin, from Greek *lēmma,* anything received, argument, proof, from *lambanein* (past perfect *eilēmmai*), to grasp, take. See **slagw-** in Appendix.*]

lem·ma[2] (lĕm′ə) *n. Botany.* The outer, lower bract enclosing the flower in a grass spikelet. [Greek *lemma,* rind, husk, from *lepein,* to peel. See **lep-**[1] in Appendix.*]

lem·ming (lĕm′ĭng) *n.* Any of various rodents of the genus *Lemmus* and related genera, of northern regions, such as the European species *L. lemmus,* noted for its mass migrations as a result of periodic population increases. [Norwegian *lemming, lemende,* akin to Swedish *lemmel*†.]

lem·nis·cus (lĕm-nĭs′kəs) *n., pl.* **-nisci** (-nĭs′ī′, -nĭs′kē). A bundle of nerve fibers located in the brain. [New Latin, from Latin *lēmniscus,* ribbon, from Greek *lēmniskos*†.]

Lem·nos (lĕm′nŏs). Also **Lim·nos** (lēm′nôs). An island of Greece, 186 square miles in area, lying in the Aegean northwest of Lesbos.

lem·on (lĕm′ən) *n.* **1.** A spiny evergreen tree, *Citrus limonia,* native to Asia, widely cultivated for its yellow, egg-shaped fruit. **2.** The fruit of this tree, having an aromatic rind and acid, juicy pulp. **3. Lemon yellow** *(see).* **4.** *Informal.* Something or someone that is or proves to be defective or unsuitable. [Middle English *lymon,* from Old French *limon,* from Arabic *laymūn,* variant of *līmūn,* from Persian *līmūn*†.] —**lem′on** *adj.*

lem·on·ade (lĕm′ə-nād′) *n.* A drink made of lemon juice, water, and sugar. [French *limonade* : obsolete *limon,* LEMON + -ADE.]

lemon balm. A plant, **balm** *(see).*

lem·on·grass (lĕm′ən-grăs′, -gräs′) *n.* Any of several tropical grasses of the genus *Cymbopogon;* especially, *C. citratus,* yielding an aromatic oil used in perfumery and as flavoring.

lemon verbena. An aromatic plant, *Lippia citriodora,* native to South America, cultivated for its fragrant foliage and flowers.

lem·on·wood (lĕm′ən-wo͝od′) *n.* A tree, the **degame** *(see),* or its wood.

lem·on·y (lĕm′ə-nē) *adj.* Having the characteristic odor or flavor of lemons.

lemon yellow. Brilliant, vivid yellow to greenish yellow. See **color.** —**lem′on-yel′low** *adj.*

lem·pi·ra (lĕm-pîr′ə) *n.* **1.** The basic monetary unit of Honduras, equal to 100 centavos. See table of exchange rates at **currency. 2.** A coin or note worth one lempira. [After *Lempira,* Indian leader who resisted the Spanish.]

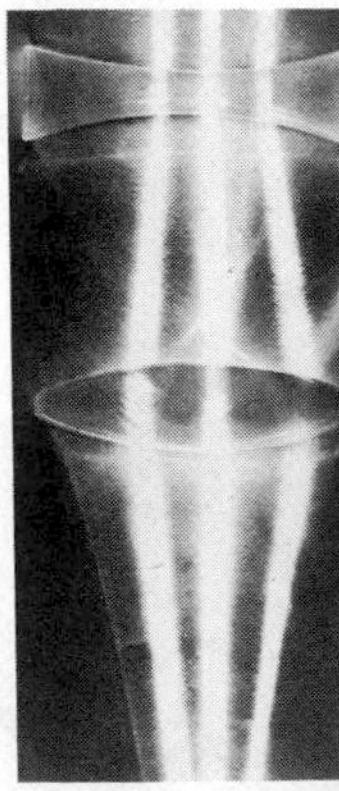

lens
Rays diverge after traversing concave lens *(above)* and converge after traversing double convex lens *(below)*

le·mur (lē′mər) *n.* Any of several arboreal primates chiefly of the family Lemuridae, of Madagascar and adjacent islands, having large eyes, soft fur, and a long tail. [New Latin, coined by Linnaeus after Latin *lemurēs,* LEMURES, from the ghostly appearance of its face and its nocturnal habits.]

lem·u·res (lĕm′yo͞o-rēz′) *pl.n.* In ancient Rome, the spirits of the dead considered as frightening specters. Compare **manes.** [Latin *lemurēs.* See **lem-**[2] in Appendix.*]

Le·na (lē′nə, lā′-). A river of the Soviet Union, rising in Lake Baikal in southern Siberia, and flowing 2,648 miles generally north to the Laptev Sea.

Len·a·pe (lĕn′ə-pē) *n.* Also **Len·i-Len·a·pe** (lĕn′ē-), **Len·ni-Len·a·pe.** A tribe, the **Delaware** *(see).* —**Len′a·pe** *adj.*

Le·nard (lā′närt′), **Philipp Eduard Anton.** 1862–1947. German physicist.

lend (lĕnd) *v.* **lent** (lĕnt), **lending, lends.** —*tr.* **1.** To give out or allow the use of (something) temporarily on the condition that it or its equivalent in kind will be returned. **2.** To provide (money) temporarily on the condition that the amount borrowed will be returned, often with an interest fee. **3.** To contribute or impart, especially a desirable attribute or quality; add; grace with. **4.** To put at another's service or needs; give: *lend a helping hand.* **5.** To accommodate or offer (itself) to something; be suitable for. Used reflexively: *This medium lends itself to many styles.* —*intr.* To make one or more loans. —See Usage note at **loan.** [Middle English *len(d)en,* Old English *lǣnan,* to lend, give. See **leikw-** in Appendix.*] —**lend′er** *n.*

lending library. A library from which books may be borrowed or rented for a minimal fee. Also called "circulating library."

lend-lease (lĕnd′lēs′) *n.* The aid program during World War II through which the United States provided food, munitions, and other goods to countries whose defense against Germany and Italy was considered necessary to the United States according to the Lend-Lease Act passed on March 11, 1941. —*tr.v.* **lend-leased, -leasing, -leases.** To provide (aid) to a country according to the provisions of the Lend-Lease Act.

L'En·fant (läN-fäN′), **Pierre Charles.** 1754–1825. French-born engineer in America; made original plan for Washington, D.C.

length (lĕngkth, lĕngth) *n. Abbr.* **l. 1.** The state, quality, or fact of being long. **2. a.** The measurement of the extent of something along its greatest dimension. **b.** The measurement of the extent of something from back to front as distinguished from its width or height. **3.** A piece of something, often of a standard size, normally measured along the greatest dimension: *a length of cloth.* **4.** A unit of measurement based on the approximate extent from front to back of an animal or vehicle in a race. **5.** The extent of a thing from start to finish as measured by space or words: *the length of a story.* **6.** The amount of time between specified moments; duration; period. **7.** The distance between specified locations: *the length of their journey.* **8.** The state or quality of extending greatly in time or space. **9.** *Phonetics.* **a.** The quantity of a vowel. **b.** Loosely, the quality of a vowel. **10.** *Prosody.* The quantity of a syllable. —**at length. 1.** After some time; eventually. **2.** For a considerable time; fully. —**go to any (great) length (or lengths).** To take great trouble. —**keep at arm's length.** To refuse to become close with. [Middle English *lengthe,* Old English *lengthu.* See **del-**[1] in Appendix.*]

length·en (lĕngk′thən, lĕng′-) *v.* **-ened, -ening, -ens.** —*tr.* To make longer. —*intr.* To become longer.

length·wise (lĕngkth′wīz′, lĕngth′-) *adv.* Also **length·ways** (-wāz′). Of, along, or referred to the direction of length; longitudinally. —**length′wise′** *adj.*

length·y (lĕngk′thē, lĕng′-) *adj.* **-ier, -iest.** Of considerable length, especially in time; drawn-out.

le·ni·en·cy (lē′nē-ən-sē, lēn′yən-) *n., pl.* **-cies.** Also **le·ni·ence** (lē′nē-əns, lēn′yəns). **1.** The condition or quality of being lenient. **2.** A lenient action. —See Synonyms at **mercy.**

le·ni·ent (lē′nē-ənt, lēn′yənt) *adj.* **1.** Merciful, restrained, or forgiving; gentle or understanding in dispensation. **2.** Not austere or strict; liberal; generous: *lenient rules.* [Latin *lēniens,* present participle of *lēnire,* to soothe, make soft, from *lēnis,* soft. See **lēi-**[2] in Appendix.*] —**le′ni·ent·ly** *adv.*

Len·i-Len·a·pe, Len·ni-Len·a·pe. Variants of **Lenape.**

Le·nin (lĕn′ĭn, -ēn′), **Nikolai.** Original name, Vladimir Ilich Ulyanov. 1870–1924. Russian revolutionary statesman; first premier of U.S.S.R. (1918–24).

Len·in·grad (lĕn′ĭn-grăd′). Formerly **St. Pe·ters·burg** (sānt′ pē′tərz-bûrg′) (1703–1914), **Pet·ro·grad** (pĕt′rō-grăd′) (1914–1924). A city of the Soviet Union, a seaport in the west-central Russian S.F.S.R. on the Gulf of Finland. Population, 3,641,000.

Len·in·ism (lĕn′ə-nĭz′əm) *n.* The theory and practice of proletarian revolution as developed by Lenin. See **Marxism-Leninism.**

Len·in·ist (lĕn′ə-nĭst) *n.* A follower of Lenin or Leninism. —*adj.* Of or relating to Lenin or Leninism.

Le·nin Peak (lĕn′ĭn, -ēn′). The highest mountain (23,382 feet) of the Trans Alai Range of the Soviet Union, on the border between the Kirghiz and Tadzhik republics.

le·nis (lē′nĭs, lā′-) *adj. Phonetics.* Articulated with little or no aspiration; weak; soft. The consonants *b* and *d* are lenis compared with *p* and *t.* Compare **fortis.** —*n., pl.* **lenes** (lē′nēz, lā′-). *Phonetics.* A speech sound pronounced with little or no aspiration; a lenis consonant. [Latin *lēnis,* soft, mild, smooth. See **lēi-**[2] in Appendix.*]

len·i·tive (lĕn′ə-tĭv) *adj.* Capable of easing pain or discomfort. —*n.* A lenitive medicine. [Old French *lenitif,* from Medieval Latin *lēnītīvus,* from Latin *lēnīre,* to soothe, soften, from *lēnis,* soft. See **lēi-**[2] in Appendix.*]

len·i·ty (lĕn′ə-tē) *n., pl.* **-ties. 1.** The state, condition, or quality of being lenient; leniency. **2.** A lenient action. [Latin *lēnitas,* gentleness, mildness, from *lēnis,* soft, mild. See **lēi-**[2] in Appendix.*]

le·no (lē′nō) *n., pl.* **-nos. 1.** A type of weaving in which the warp yarns are paired and twisted. **2.** A fabric having this type of weave. [Probably from French *linon,* fine linen, from *lin,* flax, linen, from Latin *līnum.* See **lino-** in Appendix.*]

Le·noir (lə-nwär′), **(Jean Joseph) Étienne.** 1822–1900. Belgian-born French inventor of an internal-combustion engine.

lens (lĕnz) *n.* **1.** A carefully ground or molded piece of glass, plastic, or other transparent material, having opposite surfaces either or both of which are curved, by means of which light rays are refracted so that they converge or diverge to form an image. **2.** A combination of two or more such lenses, sometimes with other optical devices such as prisms, used to form an image for viewing or photographing. Also called "compound lens." **3.** Any device that causes radiation other than light to converge or diverge by an action analogous to that of an optical lens. **4.** A transparent, biconvex body of the eye between the iris and the vitreous humor, that focuses light rays entering through the pupil to form an image on the retina. In this sense, also called "crystalline lens." [New Latin, from Latin *lēns,* LENTIL (from the resemblance of an optical lens to a lentil seed).]

lent. Past tense and past participle of **lend.**

Lent (lĕnt) *n.* The 40 weekdays before Easter (beginning on Ash Wednesday), observed as a season of penitence. [Middle English *lente, lenten,* originally "spring," Old English *lengten.* See **del-**[1] in Appendix.*]

Lent·en (lĕn′tən) *adj.* **1.** Of or pertaining to Lent. **2.** Characteristic of or appropriate to Lent; meager; somber.

len·ti·cel (lĕn′tə-sĕl′) *n. Botany.* One of the small pores on the surface of the stems of woody plants, allowing the passage of gases to and from the interior tissue. [New Latin *lenticella,* diminutive of Latin *lēns* (genitive *lentis*), LENTIL.] **—len′ti·cel′·late** (-sĕl′ĭt) *adj.*

len·tic·u·lar (lĕn-tĭk′yə-lər) *adj.* **1.** Shaped like a biconvex lens. **2.** Of or pertaining to a lens. [Latin *lenticulāris,* like a lentil, from *lenticula,* LENTIL (compare **lens**).]

len·ti·go (lĕn-tī′gō) *n., pl.* **-tigines** (-tĭj′ə-nēz′). **1.** A freckle. **2.** A nevus. [Latin *lentīgo,* freckles, from *lēns,* LENTIL.] **—len·tig′i·nous** (-tĭj′ə-nəs), **len·tig′i·nose′** (-nōs′) *adj.*

len·til (lĕn′təl) *n.* **1.** A leguminous plant, *Lens esculenta* (or *L. culinaris*), native to the Old World, having pods containing edible seeds. **2.** The round, flattened seed of this plant. [Middle English, from Old French *lentille,* from Vulgar Latin *lenticula* (unattested), variant of Latin *lenticula,* diminutive of *lēns*†, lentil.]

len·tisk (lĕn′tĭsk′) *n.* The **mastic tree** *(see).* [Middle English, from Latin *lentiscus*†.]

len·to (lĕn′tō) *adv. Music.* Slowly. Used as a direction. *—adj. Music.* Slow. [Italian, from Latin *lentus,* pliant, sticky, tenacious, slow. See **lento-** in Appendix.*]

Le·o (lē′ō) *n.* **1.** A constellation in the Northern Hemisphere near Cancer and Virgo, containing the bright stars Regulus and Denebola. **2.** The fifth sign of the **zodiac** *(see).* Also called the "Lion." [New Latin, from Latin *leō,* LION.]

Le·o I (lē′ō), **Saint.** Called "the Great." A.D. 390?–461. Pope (A.D. 440–461).

Le·o III (lē′ō), **Saint.** A.D. 750?–816. Pope (A.D. 795–816); crowned Charlemagne as emperor of the West (A.D. 800).

Le·o X (lē′ō). Original name, Giovanni de' Medici. 1475–1521. Pope (1513–21); son of Lorenzo de' Medici.

Le·o XIII (lē′ō). 1810–1903. Pope (1878–1903).

Leo Minor. A constellation in the Northern Hemisphere near Leo and Ursa Major.

Le·ón (lā-ôn′). **1.** A region and ancient kingdom of northwestern Spain. **2.** A city of Spain, situated in the northwest; the capital of the ancient kingdom. Population, 56,000. **3.** A city of central Mexico, in west-central Guanajuato. Population, 275,000. **4.** A city of Nicaragua, northwest of Lake Managua; the former capital of Nicaragua (1570–1855). Population, 55,000.

Leon·ard (lĕn′ərd). A masculine given name. [Middle English, from Old French, from Old High German *Lewenhart* (unattested), "bold as a lion" : *lewo,* lion, from Latin *leō,* LION + *hart,* hardy, bold (see **kar-**[1] in Appendix*).]

Le·o·nar·do da Vin·ci (lē′ə-när′dō də vĭn′chē; *Italian* lā′ō-när′dō dä vēn′chē). 1452–1519. Florentine artist and engineer.

le·one (le-ōn′) *n.* **1.** The basic monetary unit of Sierra Leone, equal to 100 cents. See table of exchange rates at **currency. 2.** A note worth one leone. [From SIERRA LEONE.]

Le·o·ne, Mount (lā-ō′nā). The highest (11,683 feet) of the Lepontine Alps, on the Swiss-Italian border.

Le·on·i·das I (lē-ŏn′ə-dəs). King of Sparta (490?–480 B.C.); killed at Thermopylae.

le·o·nine (lē′ə-nīn′) *adj.* Of, pertaining to, or characteristic of a lion: *"The old man emitted a huge leonine sigh"* (Trollope). [Middle English, from Old French *leonin(e),* from Latin *leōninus,* from *leō* (stem *leōn-*), LION.]

leop·ard (lĕp′ərd) *n.* **1.** A large feline mammal, *Panthera pardus,* of Africa and Asia, having a tawny coat with dark rosettelike markings, and also a black color phase. See **panther. 2.** Any of several similar felines, such as the cheetah or the snow leopard. **3.** The pelt or fur of a leopard. **4.** *Heraldry.* A lion in side view, having one forepaw raised and the head facing the observer. [Middle English *leopard, leupard,* from Old French, from Late Latin *leopardus,* from Late Greek *leopardos, leontopardos,* "lion pard" (it was thought to be a hybrid) : *leōn* (genitive *leontos*), LION + *pardos,* PARD.]

leop·ard·ess (lĕp′ər-dĭs) *n.* A female leopard.

leopard lily. A tall plant, *Lilium pardalinum,* of the western United States, having orange-red, dark-spotted flowers.

leopard moth. A moth, *Zeuzera pyrina,* having spotted wings and larvae that damage trees by boring into the wood.

leop·ard's-bane (lĕp′ərdz-bān′) *n.* **1.** Any of several widely cultivated plants of the genus *Doronicum,* having rayed yellow flowers. **2.** Any of several similar or related plants.

Le·o·pold (lē′ə-pōld′). A masculine given name. [French *Léopold* and German *Leopold,* from Old High German *Leutpald, Liutbald* : *liut,* people (see **leudh-**[2] in Appendix*) + *bald,* bold (see **bhel-**[2] in Appendix*).]

Le·o·pold II, Lake (lē′ə-pōld′). A lake occupying about 900 square miles in the west-central Democratic Republic of the Congo (Kinshasa).

Lé·o·pold·ville. The former name for **Kinshasa.**

le·o·tard (lē′ə-tärd′) *n.* **1.** *Often plural.* A snugly fitting elastic garment originally worn by dancers or acrobats. **2.** *Plural.* Tights. [Popularized by Jules *Léotard,* 19th-century French aerialist.]

Le·pan·to, Battle of (lĭ păn′tō; *Italian* lĕ-pän′tō). A naval battle, fought in 1571 in a strait between the Gulf of Corinth and the Ionian Sea, in which Ottoman sea power was temporarily destroyed by a Christian armada.

Le·pan·to, Gulf of. See Gulf of **Corinth.**

Lep·cha (lĕp′chə) *n., pl.* **Lepcha** or **-chas. 1.** Any of a Mongoloid people living in Sikkim, India. **2.** The Tibeto-Burman language of this people.

lep·er (lĕp′ər) *n.* A person afflicted with leprosy. [Middle English, from *leper,* leprosy, from Old French *lepre,* from Late Latin *lepra,* from Greek *lepra,* from *lepros,* scaly, from *lepos, lepis,* a scale. See **lep-**[1] in Appendix.*]

lepido-. Indicates scale or flake; for example, **lepidopteran.** [From Greek *lepis* (stem *lepid-*), scale. See **lep-**[1] in Appendix.*]

le·pid·o·lite (lĭ-pĭd′l-īt′) *n.* A lilac or pink to gray mica, $K_2Li_3Al_4Si_7O_2(OH, F)_3$, used as lithium ore and in glass and ceramic production. [German *Lepidolith* : LEPIDO- + -LITH.]

lep·i·dop·ter·an (lĕp′ə-dŏp′tər-ən) *n.* Also **lep·i·dop·ter·on** (-tə-rŏn′, -tər-ən) *pl.* **-tera** (-tə-rə). A lepidopterous insect. [From New Latin *Lepidoptera,* "scale-winged ones" : LEPIDO- + -PTER.]

lep·i·dop·ter·ist (lĕp′ə-dŏp′tər-ĭst) *n.* An entomologist specializing in the study of butterflies and moths.

lep·i·dop·ter·ous (lĕp′ĭ-dŏp′tər-əs) *adj.* Of or belonging to the order Lepidoptera, which includes insects such as the butterflies and moths, having four wings covered with small scales.

lep·i·dote (lĕp′ə-dōt′) *adj.* Covered with small, scurfy scales. [Greek *lepidōtos,* from *lepis,* scale. See **lep-**[1] in Appendix.*]

Lep·i·dus (lĕp′ə-dəs), **Marcus Aemilius.** Died 13 B.C. Roman triumvir from 43 to 36 B.C.

Le·pon·tine Alps (lə-pŏn′tən). The section of the Alps in southern Switzerland and along the Swiss-Italian border.

lep·o·rine (lĕp′ə-rīn′, -ər-ən) *adj.* Of or characteristic of rabbits or hares. [Latin *leporinus,* from *lepus* (stem *lepor-*), hare, probably from a Mediterranean language.]

lep·re·chaun (lĕp′rə-kôn′, -kŏn′) *n. Irish Folklore.* One of a race of elves who are cobblers and have hidden treasure. [Earlier *lubrican,* from Irish *lupracán, leipracán,* from Middle Irish *luchrupán,* from Old Irish *luchorpán* : *lū,* small (see **legwh-** in Appendix*) + *corp,* body, from Latin *corpus* (see **krep-** in Appendix*).]

lep·ro·sar·i·um (lĕp′rə-sâr′ē-əm) *n., pl.* **-ums** or **-ia** (-ē-ə). A hospital for the treatment of lepers. [Medieval Latin, from Late Latin *leprōsus,* LEPROUS.]

lep·rose (lĕp′rōs′) *adj.* Scurfy or scaly; leprous. [Late Latin *leprōsus,* LEPROUS.]

lep·ro·sy (lĕp′rə-sē) *n.* A chronic, infectious, granulomatous disease occurring almost exclusively in tropical and subtropical regions, caused by a bacillus, *Mycobacterium leprae,* and ranging in severity from noncontagious and spontaneously remitting forms to contagious, malignant forms with progressive anesthesia, paralysis, ulceration, nutritive disturbances, gangrene, and mutilation. Also called "Hansen's disease." [From LEPROUS.] **—lep·rot′ic** (lĕ-prŏt′ĭk) *adj.*

lep·rous (lĕp′rəs) *adj.* **1.** Having leprosy. **2.** Of, relating to, or resembling leprosy: *"the marks the bullets made, white leprous scars in the flesh-pink wall of a near-by house"* (Gore Vidal). **3.** *Biology.* Having or consisting of loose, scurfy scales. [Middle English *lepro(u)s,* from Late Latin *leprōsus,* from *lepra,* leprosy. See **leper.**] **—lep′rous·ly** *adv.*

-lepsy. Indicates a fit or seizure; for example, **narcolepsy.** [Greek *-lēpsia,* from *lēpsis,* taking, seizure, from *lambanein* (future stem *leps-*), to take, seize. See **slagw-** in Appendix.*]

lepto-, lept-. Indicates slender, thin, fine; for example, **leptocephalus, lepton.** [From Greek *leptos,* peeled, fine, small, thin, from *lepein,* to peel. See **lep-**[1] in Appendix.*]

lep·to·ceph·a·lus (lĕp′tə-sĕf′ə-ləs) *n., pl.* **-li** (-lī′). One of the slender, transparent larvae of eels and certain other fishes. [New Latin, "slender-headed" : LEPTO- + -CEPHALOUS.]

lep·ton[1] (lĕp′tŏn′) *n., pl.* **-ta** (-tə). A monetary unit equal to $^1/_{100}$ of the drachma of Greece. See table of exchange rates at **currency.** [Modern Greek, from Greek, small coin, from *leptos,* fine, small, from *lepein,* to peel. See **lep-**[1] in Appendix.*]

lep·ton[2] (lĕp′tŏn′) *n., pl.* **-tons.** Any of a family of subatomic particles including the electron, the muon, and their associated neutrinos, all having spin equal to $^1/_2$ and masses less than those of the mesons. See **particle.** [LEPT(O)- + -ON.]

lep·to·some (lĕp′tə-sōm′) *n. Physiology.* A person with a slender, thin, or frail body. [German *Leptosom* : LEPTO- + -SOME (body).] **—lep′to·so·mat′ic** *adj.*

Le·pus (lē′pəs) *n.* A constellation in the Southern Hemisphere near Orion and Columba. [New Latin, from Latin, hare. See **leporine.**]

Le·ri·da (lā′rē-*thä*). A city of northeastern Spain, the site of Caesar's victory over Pompey (49 B.C.). Population, 72,000.

Ler·wick (lûr′wĭk, lĕr′ĭk). The capital of the Shetland Islands, a seaport on Mainland Island. Population, 6,000.

Le·sage (lə-sȧzh′), **Alain René.** 1668–1747. French novelist; author of *Gil Blas.*

Les·bi·an (lĕz′bē-ən) *n.* **1.** A native or resident of Lesbos. **2.** The Ancient Greek dialect of Lesbos, belonging to Aeolic, used in the lyric poetry of Sappho and Alcaeus. **3.** *Usually small* **l.** A female homosexual. *—adj.* **1.** Of or relating to Lesbos or its people. **2.** Of or relating to the Ancient Greek dialect of Lesbos. **3.** Of, relating to, or characteristic of Sappho, or her poetry. **4.** *Usually small* **l.** Relating to, or characteristic of female homosexuals.

les·bi·an·ism (lĕz′bē-ə-nĭz′əm) *n.* Also **Les·bi·an·ism.** Female homosexuality.

Les·bos (lĕz′bəs, -bŏs). Also **Les·vos** (lĕz′vôs). An island of

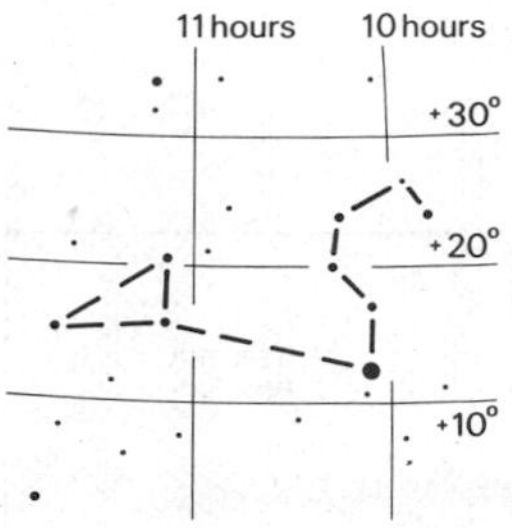

11 hours
10 hours
+30°
+20°
+10°

Leo

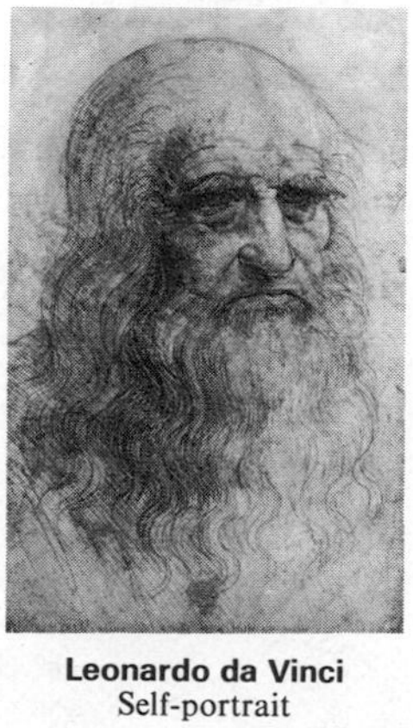
Leonardo da Vinci
Self-portrait

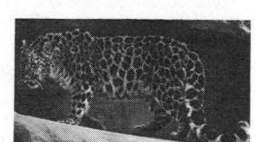

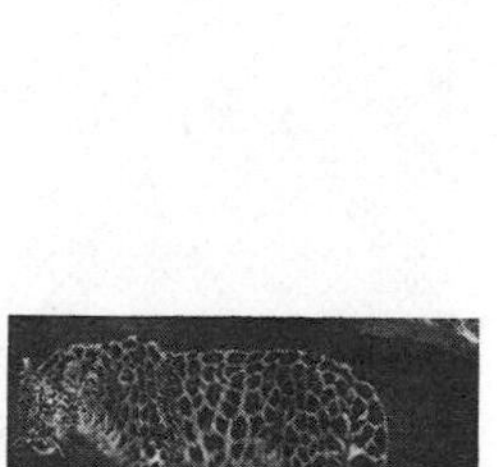
leopard
Panthera pardus

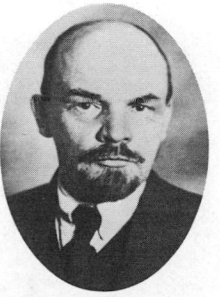

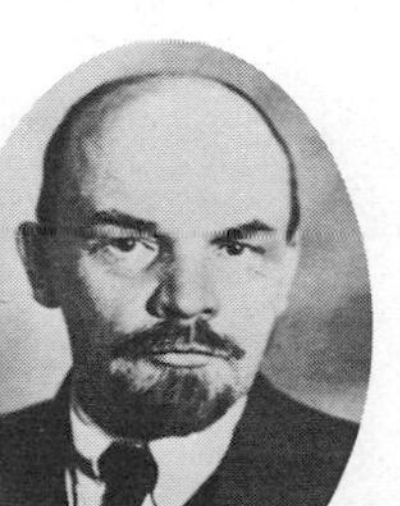
Lenin

Greece, 632 square miles in area, in the Aegean off the western coast of Turkey. Also called "Mytilene."

Les Cayes (lā kā′). A city of Haiti, a seaport on the southwestern coast. Population, 14,000.

lese majesty (lēz′) *pl.* **lese majesties.** Also *French* **lèse ma·jes·té** (lĕz mà-zhĕs-tā′). **1.** An offense or crime committed against the ruler or supreme power of a state; treason. **2.** Any affront to another's dignity or an overstepping of authority. [From Old French *lese-majeste,* from Latin *laesa mājestās,* "violated majesty" : *laesa,* past participle of *laedere,* to injure, damage, offend (see **lesion**) + MAJESTY.]

le·sion (lē′zhən) *n.* **1.** A wound or injury. **2.** A circumscribed pathological alteration of tissue. **3.** A point or patch of a skin disease. [Middle English *lesioun,* from Old French *lesion,* from Latin *laesiō,* from *laedere*†, to injure, damage.]

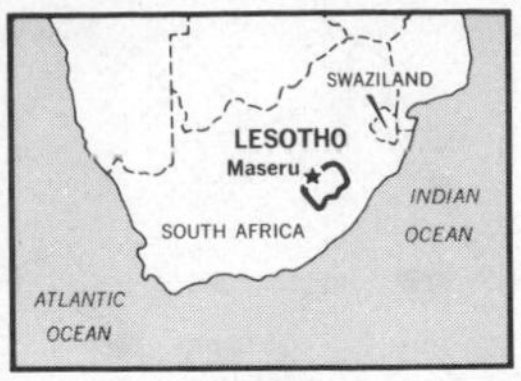

Lesotho

Le·so·tho (lə-sō′tō). Formerly **Ba·su·to·land** (bə-sōō′tō-lănd′). A kingdom of southern Africa, occupying 11,700 square miles within the Republic of South Africa; formerly a British protectorate. Population, 745,000. Capital, Maseru.

les·pe·de·za (lĕs′pə-dē′zə) *n.* Any plant of the genus *Lespedeza,* which includes the bush clovers. [New Latin; named after Vicente Manuel de *Céspedes,* misspelled *Léspedes* (died 1785), Spanish governor of East Florida.]

less (lĕs). Alternate comparative of **little.** —*adj.* **1.** Not as great in magnitude or degree. **2.** Lower in importance, esteem, or rank. —*adv.* To a smaller extent, degree, or frequency. —*n.* A smaller amount. —*prep.* Minus; subtracting: *five dollars less two.* See Usage note at **fewer.** [Middle English *less(e),* Old English *lǣssa* (adjective) and *lǣs* (adverb and noun), from Germanic *loisiz* (unattested), little.]

-less. Indicates lack of, free of, or not having; without; for example, **toothless, sleepless, blameless.** [Middle English *-les(se),* Old English *-lēas,* from *lēas,* lacking, free from. See **leu-**[1] in Appendix.*]

les·see (lĕ-sē′) *n.* A tenant holding a lease. [Middle English, from Norman French *lessee,* variant of Old French *lesse,* past participle of *lesser,* to LEASE.]

less·en (lĕs′ən) *v.* **-ened, -ening, -ens.** —*tr.* **1.** To cause to decrease; make less. **2.** To make little of; minimize; belittle. —*intr.* To become less; to decrease. —See Synonyms at **decrease.** [Middle English *lessenen,* from *lesse,* LESS.]

Les·seps (lĕs′əps; *French* lĕ-sĕps′), Vicomte **Ferdinand Marie de.** 1805–1894. French diplomat; promoted Suez Canal.

less·er (lĕs′ər) *adj.* Smaller or less in size, amount, value, or importance, especially in a comparison between two things. [Middle English double comparative, from LESS.]

Lesser An·til·les (ăn-tĭl′ēz). An island group in the West Indies extending in an arc from Curaçao to the Virgin Islands.

lesser celandine. A plant, *Ranunculus ficaria,* having heart-shaped leaves and yellow flowers. Also called "pilewort."

lesser doxology. The **Gloria Patri** *(see).*

lesser panda. See **panda.**

Lesser Slave Lake. A lake occupying 461 square miles in central Alberta, Canada.

Lesser Sun·da Islands. The former name for **Nusa Tenggara.**

Les·sing (lĕs′ĭng), **Gotthold Ephraim.** 1729–1781. German dramatist and critic.

les·son (lĕs′ən) *n.* **1.** Something to be learned. **2. a.** A period of instruction; a class. **b.** The material taught in one such period. **3. a.** An experience or observation that imparts beneficial new knowledge or wisdom. **b.** The knowledge or wisdom learned in such a manner. **4.** A reprimand or punishment. **5.** A reading from the Bible or other sacred writing as part of a religious service. —*tr.v.* **lessoned, -soning, -sons.** *Rare.* **1.** To teach a lesson or lessons to; instruct. **2.** To reprimand or punish. [Middle English *lesso(u)n,* a reading, lesson, from Old French *lecon,* from Latin *lectiō,* LECTION.]

les·sor (lĕs′ôr′, lĕ-sôr′) *n.* One who lets property under a lease; a landlord. [Middle English *lessour,* from Norman French, from *lesser,* to LEASE.]

lest (lĕst) *conj.* **1.** So as to prevent the possibility that; for fear that: *Tiptoe lest the guard should hear you.* **2.** That. Used after phrases denoting fear, worry, or the like: *anxious lest he should become ill.* [Middle English *leste,* short for *les the,* whereby less, Old English *thȳ lǣs the,* from *lǣs,* LESS.]

Les·vos. See **Lesbos.**

let[1] (lĕt) *v.* **let, letting, lets.** —*tr.* **1.** Used as an auxiliary verb followed by an infinitive omitting *to:* **a.** To grant permission to; allow: *She let him continue.* **b.** To cause to. Used with *know* or *hear: He let me know the results.* **2.** Used as an auxiliary verb in the imperative: **a.** In order to convey a command, request, or proposal: *Let's finish the job!* **b.** In order to convey a warning or threat: *Just let her try!* **c.** In order to convey an assumption or hypothesis: *Let x equal y.* **d.** In order to convey acceptance of or resignation to the inevitable: *Let the future come!* **3.** To permit to move or change in a specified manner: *let the dog in.* **4.** To free from confinement; permit to escape: *let the air out of the balloon.* **5.** To rent or lease: *let a room to a bachelor.* **6.** To assign, especially after bids have been submitted: *let the construction job to a new firm.* —*intr.* **1.** To become rented or leased. **2.** To be or become assigned, as to a contractor. —See Synonyms at **allow.** —**let alone.** Not to speak of; much less: *Don't whisper, let alone speak.* —**let in on. 1.** To take into confidence; inform: *Were they let in on the secret?* **2.** To allow to participate: *Let him in on the robbery.* —**let loose. 1.** To release from confinement; free. **2.** To release a grip. —**let off. 1.** To emit or release: *let off steam.* **2.** To excuse or dismiss: *let the workmen off early.* **3.** To give little or no punishment for an offense: *He was let off with a year on probation.* —**let on. 1.** To allow it to be known: *Don't let on that you know me.* **2.** To pretend. —**let out. 1.** To release from confinement. **2.** To give forth; emit: *The dog let out a yelp.* **3.** To make known, as a secret; reveal: *Who let that story out?* **4.** To increase the size of (a garment, for example). —**let up on.** *Informal.* To reduce the pressure on; be more lenient to. [Middle English *leten,* Old English *lǣtan,* to leave behind, leave undone. See **lēi-**[2] in Appendix.*]

Usage: *Let* (verb) is followed by objective pronouns in constructions such as: *Let Pamela and me* (not *I*) *decide. Let you and her* (not *she*) *do it.* See also Usage note at **leave.**

let[2] (lĕt) *n.* **1.** Obstacle. Used in the phrase *without let or hindrance.* **2.** *Sports.* A stroke in tennis, volleyball, or a similar net game that is invalid and must be repeated. —*tr.v.* **letted** or **let, letting, lets.** *Archaic.* To obstruct or hinder. [Middle English *let(te),* a hindrance, from *letten,* to hinder, prevent, Old English *lettan.* See **lēi-**[2] in Appendix.*]

-let. Indicates: **1.** Diminutive size or minor status; for example, **brooklet, starlet. 2.** An article worn on some part of the body; for example, **bracelet, anklet.** [Middle English *-lette,* from Old French *-elet* : noun ending *-el* + *-et(te),* -ETTE.]

letch (lĕch) *n.* Also **lech.** A strong desire or craving, especially of a sexual nature. [Perhaps back-formation from earlier *letcher,* variant of LECHER.]

let down. 1. To take down; lower: *let down the sails.* **2.** To fail to satisfy; disappoint: *The mayor let down the electorate.*

let·down (lĕt′doun′) *n.* **1.** A slowing down, relaxing, or decrease, as of effort or energy. **2.** A disappointment. **3.** The descent made by an airplane in order to land.

le·thal (lē′thəl) *adj.* **1.** Sufficient to cause or capable of causing death. **2.** Of, pertaining to, or causing death. —See Synonyms at **fatal.** [Latin *lethālis,* from *lēthum,* death, variant of *lētum.* See **ol-** in Appendix.*] —**le·thal′i·ty** (lē-thăl′ə-tē) *n.*

le·thar·gic (lə-thär′jĭk) *adj.* Of, causing, or characterized by lethargy. —**le·thar′gi·cal·ly** *adv.*

lethargic encephalitis. *Pathology.* **Encephalitis lethargica** *(see).*

leth·ar·gy (lĕth′ər-jē) *n., pl.* **-gies. 1.** Sluggish indifference. **2.** A state of unconsciousness resembling deep sleep, from which an individual can be roused but into which he at once relapses. [Middle English *litargie, letargie,* from Old French *litargie,* from Latin *lēthargia,* drowsiness, from Greek, from *lēthargos,* forgetful, from *lēthē,* forgetfulness. See **lādh-** in Appendix.*]

Synonyms: *lethargy, lassitude, sluggishness, torpor, stupor, languor.* These nouns refer to conditions in which a person is unable or disinclined to be active, physically or mentally. *Lethargy* often implies the operation of physically disabling factors, such as illness or overwork, or it can reflect apathy or indifference. *Lassitude* implies inactivity or loss of vigor resulting from physical or mental strain. *Sluggishness* is slowness of body or mind, produced by ailments or indolence. *Torpor* suggests the suspension of physical and mental activity characteristic of an animal in hibernation. *Stupor* is marked by cessation or great decrease of mental activity or feeling, often produced by sleepiness, illness, or the effect of alcohol or narcotics. *Languor* is lack of vigor or spirit characteristic of one who is indolent or satiated by overindulgence in luxury or pleasure.

Le·the (lē′thē) *n.* **1.** The river of forgetfulness in Hades. **2.** Oblivion; loss of memory. [Greek *lēthē,* forgetfulness (later personified). See **lādh-** in Appendix.*] —**Le′the·an** (lē′thē-ən) *adj.*

Le·to (lē′tō′). *Greek Mythology.* A consort of Zeus and the mother of Apollo and Artemis.

let's (lĕts). Contraction of *let us.*

Lett (lĕt) *n.* A Latvian.

let·ter (lĕt′ər) *n.* **1.** A written symbol or character representing a speech sound; a component of an alphabet. **2.** A written or printed communication directed to an individual or organization. **3.** *Often plural.* A certified document granting rights to its bearer. **4.** The literal meaning of something: *the letter of the law.* **5.** *Plural.* Literary culture or learning; literature as a discipline or profession. Used with a singular verb. **6.** *Printing.* **a.** A piece of type that prints a single character. **b.** A specific style of type. **c.** The characters in one style of type. **7.** An emblem in the shape of the initial of a school awarded to athletes. —*v.* **lettered, -tering, -ters.** —*tr.* **1.** To write letters on. **2.** To write in letters. —*intr.* To write or form letters. [Middle English *letter, lettre,* from Old French *lettre,* from Latin *littera,* letter (of the alphabet), letter, document (in plural only). See **deph-** in Appendix.*] —**let′ter·er** *n.*

let·ter·box (lĕt′ər-bŏks′) *n. Chiefly British.* A **mailbox** *(see).*

letter carrier. A mailman.

let·tered (lĕt′ərd) *adj.* **1. a.** Educated to read and write; literate. **b.** Erudite; learned. **2.** Of or relating to literacy or learning. **3.** Inscribed or marked with letters.

let·ter·head (lĕt′ər-hĕd′) *n.* **1.** The heading atop a sheet of letter paper, usually consisting of a name and address. **2.** Stationery with such a heading.

let·ter-high (lĕt′ər-hī′) *adj.* **Type-high** *(see).*

let·ter·ing (lĕt′ər-ĭng) *n.* **1.** The act, process, or art of forming letters. **2.** Letters collectively.

letter of advice. A letter containing specific information about a commercial transaction, as from a consignor to a consignee.

letter of credit. *Abbr.* **L/C** A letter issued by a bank authorizing the bearer to draw a stated amount of money from the issuing bank, its branches, or other associated banks or agencies.

let·ter-per·fect (lĕt′ər-pûr′fĭkt) *adj.* Correct to the last detail.

let·ter·press (lĕt′ər-prĕs′) *n.* **1. a.** The process of printing from a raised inked surface. **b.** Anything printed in this fashion. **2.** The text distinct from illustrations or other ornamentation.

letters of administration. A legal document entrusting an individual with the administration of the estate of a decedent.
letters of credence. Also **letter of credence.** An official document conveying the credentials of a diplomatic envoy to a foreign government.
letters of marque. Also **letter of marque.** **1.** A document issued by a nation allowing a private citizen to seize citizens or goods of another nation. **2.** A document issued by a nation allowing a private citizen to equip a ship with arms in order to attack enemy ships. Also called "letter of marque and reprisal," "letters of marque and reprisal." [Middle English, from Old French *marque,* reprisal, from Old Provençal *marca,* from *marcar,* to seize as a pledge, from Germanic. See **merg-** in Appendix.*]
letters patent. *Law.* A document issued by a government granting a patent to an inventor.
letters testamentary. *Law.* A document issued by a probate court or officer informing an executor of a will of his appointment and authority.
Let·tish (lĕt′ĭsh) *adj.* Of or relating to the Latvians or their language. *—n.* **Latvian** *(see).*
let·tuce (lĕt′əs) *n.* **1.** Any of various plants of the genus *Lactuca;* especially, *L. sativa,* cultivated for its edible leaves. **2.** The leaves of *L. sativa,* eaten as salad. **3.** *Slang.* Paper money. [Middle English *letus(e),* from Old French *laitues,* plural of *laitue,* from Latin *lactūca,* from *lac* (stem *lact-*), milk (from its milky juice). See **melg-** in Appendix.*]
let up. **1.** To diminish; slacken; lessen. **2.** To stop.
let·up (lĕt′ŭp′) *n.* **1.** A slackening of pace, force, intensity, or the like; a slowdown. **2.** A temporary stop; a pause.
le·u (lĕ′o͞o) *n., pl.* **lei** (lĕ′ī). **1.** The basic monetary unit of Rumania, equal to 100 bani. See table of exchange rates at **currency.** **2.** A coin worth one leu. [Rumanian, "lion," from Latin *leō* (stem *leōn-*), LION.]
leu·cine (lo͞o′sēn′) *n.* An essential amino acid, $C_6H_{13}NO_2$, derived from the hydrolysis of protein by pancreatic enzymes and used as a nutrient. [LEUC(O)- + -INE.]
leu·cite (lo͞o′sīt′) *n.* A white or gray mineral, essentially KAl$(SiO_3)_2$. [German *Leucit* : LEUC(O)- + -ITE.]
leu·co-. Variant of **leuko-.**
leu·co·plast (lo͞o′kə-plăst′) *n.* Also **leu·co·plas·tid** (lo͞o′kə-plăs′tĭd). A colorless plastid in the cytoplasm of plant cells, around which starch collects. [LEUCO- + PLAST(ID).]
Leu·kas. See **Levkas.**
leu·ke·mi·a (lo͞o-kē′mē-ə) *n.* Any of a group of usually fatal diseases of the reticuloendothelial system, involving uncontrolled proliferation of leukocytes. [New Latin : LEUK(O)- + -EMIA.]
leuko-, leuk-, leuco-. Indicates: **1.** White or colorless; for example, **leukoderma, leucoplast.** **2.** Leukocyte; for example, **leukemia, leukopenia.** [New Latin, from Greek *leukos,* clear, white. See **leuk-** in Appendix.*]
leu·ko·cyte (lo͞o′kə-sīt′) *n.* Also **leu·co·cyte.** Any of the white or colorless nucleated cells occurring in blood. Also called "white blood cell," "white corpuscle." [LEUKO- + -CYTE.] *—***leu′ko·cyt′ic** (-sĭt′ĭk) *adj.*
leu·ko·cy·to·sis (lo͞o′kō-sī-tō′sĭs) *n., pl.* **-ses** (-sēz′). Also **leu·co·cy·to·sis.** A large increase in the number of leukocytes in the blood. [New Latin : LEUKOCYT(E) + -OSIS.] *—***leu′ko·cy·tot′ic** (-tŏt′ĭk) *adj.*
leu·ko·der·ma (lo͞o′kō-dûr′mə) *n.* Also **leu·co·der·ma.** Partial or total lack of skin pigmentation. [New Latin : LEUKO- + -DERMA.] *—***leu′ko·der′mal, leu′ko·der′mic** *adj.*
leu·ko·ma (lo͞o-kō′mə) *n.* Also **leu·co·ma.** A dense, white opacity of the cornea of the eye. [New Latin *leucoma,* from Greek *leukōma* : LEUK(O)- + -OMA.]
leu·ko·pe·ni·a (lo͞o′kə-pē′nē-ə) *n.* Also **leu·co·pe·ni·a.** An abnormally low number of leukocytes in the circulating blood. [New Latin : LEUKO- + -PENIA.]
leu·ko·poi·e·sis (lo͞o′kō-poi-ē′sĭs) *n.* Also **leu·co·poi·e·sis.** The formation and development of leukocytes. [New Latin : LEUKO- + -POIESIS.] *—***leu′ko·poi·et′ic** (-ĕt′ĭk) *adj.*
leu·kor·rhe·a (lo͞o′kə-rē′ə) *n.* Also **leu·cor·rhe·a.** A vaginal discharge containing mucus and pus cells. [New Latin : LEUKO- + -RRHEA.]
lev (lĕf) *n., pl.* **leva** (lĕv′ə). The basic monetary unit of Bulgaria, equal to 100 stotinki. See table of exchange rates at **currency.** [Bulgarian, "lion," from Old Bulgarian *livu,* probably from Old High German *lewo,* from Latin *leō,* LION.]
Lev. Leviticus (Old Testament).
Lev·al·loi·si·an (lĕv′ə-loi′zē-ən) *adj.* Of or related to a western European stage in lower Paleolithic culture, known from the method of striking off flake tools from pieces of flint. [After *Levallois*-Perret, district near Paris.]
le·vant (lə-vănt′) *n.* A type of heavy, coarse-grained morocco leather often used in bookbinding. Also called "Levant morocco." [Originally imported from the LEVANT.]
Le·vant (lə-vănt′). The countries bordering on the eastern Mediterranean. [Middle English *levaunt,* "the Orient," from Old French *levant,* "rising" (said of the sun), present participle of *lever,* to rise, raise. See **lever.**]
le·vant·er (lə-văn′tər) *n.* **1.** A strong easterly wind of the Mediterranean area. **2.** *Capital* **L.** A Levantine.
le·van·tine (lə-văn′tĭn, lĕv′ən-tēn′, -tīn′) *n.* A sturdy, closely woven silk fabric. [Originally made in the LEVANT.]
Le·van·tine (lə-văn′tĭn, lĕv′ən-tēn′, -tīn′) *adj.* Of or relating to the Levant. *—n.* **1.** A native or resident of the Levant. **2.** A ship from the Levant.
le·va·tor (lə-vā′tər) *n., pl.* **levatores** (lĕv′ə-tôr′ēz, -tōr′ēz). **1.** *Anatomy.* A muscle that raises a part. **2.** *Surgery.* An instrument for lifting the depressed part of a fractured skull. [New Latin, from Latin *levāre,* to raise. See **lever.**]
lev·ee[1] (lĕv′ē) *n.* **1.** An embankment raised to prevent a river from overflowing. **2.** A small ridge or raised area bordering an irrigated field. **3.** A landing place on a river; pier. [French *levée,* from Old French *levee,* "raising," from the past participle of *lever,* to raise. See **lever.**]
lev·ee[2] (lĕv′ē, lə-vē′) *n.* **1.** A reception held by a monarch or other high-ranking person upon his arising from bed. **2.** A formal reception, as at a court. [French *levé,* variant of *lever,* rising, from *lever,* to rise. See **lever.**]
lev·el (lĕv′əl) *n.* **1.** Relative position or rank on a scale: *a high level of achievement.* **2.** A natural or proper position, place, or stage: *finally found his own level.* **3.** Position along a vertical axis; elevation; height: *the level of the windows.* **4. a.** A horizontal line or plane at right angles to the plumb. **b.** The position or height of such a line or plane: *eye level.* **5.** A flat, horizontal surface. **6.** A tract of land of uniform elevation. **7. a.** An instrument for ascertaining whether a surface is horizontal consisting essentially of an encased, liquid-filled tube containing an air bubble that moves to a center window when the instrument is set on a horizontal plane. Also called "spirit level." **b.** Such a device combined with a telescope, used in surveying. **c.** A computation of the difference in elevation between two points, using such a device. *—***on the level.** *Informal.* Without deception. *—adj.* **1.** Having a flat, smooth surface. **2.** On a horizontal plane. **3.** Being at the same height as another; even. **4.** Poured or measured into a container so as to be even with its rim: *a level teaspoon.* **5.** Being of the same degree or rank as another; equal. **6.** Without abrupt variations; uniform; consistent. *—***level best.** Conscientious best. *—v.* **leveled** or **-elled, -eling** or **-elling, -els.** *—tr.* **1.** To make horizontal, flat, or even. Often used with *off.* **2.** To tear down; raze. **3.** To knock down with or as if with a blow. **4.** To put (two persons or things) in the same rank, degree, or plane. **5.** To aim along a horizontal plane: *level a gun at her head.* **6.** To direct emphatically or forcefully toward someone. **7.** To measure the different elevations of (a tract of land) with a level. *—intr.* **1.** To render persons or things equal, as in rank, importance, or size. **2.** To achieve or come to a level. **3.** To aim a weapon horizontally. **4.** *Informal.* To be frank. Used with *with: Level with me on what happened last night.* *—***level off.** **1.** To move toward stability or consistency. **2.** To maneuver an aircraft into flight that is parallel to the surface of the earth after gaining or losing altitude. *—adv.* Along a flat or even line or plane. [Middle English *level, livel,* from Old French *livel,* from Vulgar Latin *libellum* (unattested), variant of Latin *lībella,* level, water level, plummet line, diminutive of *lībra,* "a pound," balance, level. See **līthrā** in Appendix.*] *—***lev′el·ly** *adv.* *—***lev′el·ness** *n.*
Synonyms: *level, flat, plane, even, smooth, flush.* These adjectives are applicable to surfaces in which there are no variations, or no significant variations, in the form of elevations or depressions. *Level* implies being horizontal, or parallel with the line of the horizon. *Flat* often refers to such a horizontal surface, but can also be applied to one that is oblique or even vertical. *Plane* and *even* refer to flat surfaces that are wholly without elevations or depressions and demonstrably so either by the application of scientific principles, in the case of *plane,* or by observation, in the case of *even. Smooth* describes a surface in which the absence of even slight irregularities can be established by sight or touch. *Flush* is applied to a surface that is on an exact level with an adjoining one, forming a continuous surface.
level crossing. *British.* A **grade crossing** *(see).*
lev·el·er (lĕv′ə-lər) *n.* Also **lev·el·ler.** **1.** One that levels. **2.** One who advocates the abolition of social inequities.
lev·el·head·ed (lĕv′əl-hĕd′ĭd) *adj.* Characteristically self-composed and sensible. *—***lev′el·head′ed·ness** *n.*
leveling rod. A graduated pole or stick with a movable marker, used with a surveyor's level to measure differences in elevation. Also called "leveling staff," "leveling pole."
Lev·el·ler (lĕv′ə-lər) *n.* A member of an English radical political movement active in the 1640's that advocated universal male suffrage, parliamentary democracy, and religious tolerance.
Le·ven, Loch (lē′vən). A lake occupying eight square miles in east-central Scotland.
le·ver (lĕv′ər, lē′vər) *n.* **1.** A simple **machine** *(see)* consisting of a rigid body, typically a metal bar, pivoted on a fixed fulcrum. **2.** A projecting handle used to adjust or operate a mechanism. **3.** A means of accomplishment. *—tr.v.* **levered, -vering, -vers.** To move or lift with a lever. [Middle English *lever, levour,* from Old French *levier, leveor,* from *lever,* to raise, from Latin *levāre,* from *levis,* light. See **legwh-** in Appendix.*]
le·ver·age (lĕv′ər-ĭj, lē′vər-) *n.* **1.** The action of a lever. **2.** The mechanical advantage of a lever. **3.** Positional advantage; power to act effectively.
lev·er·et (lĕv′ər-ĭt) *n.* A young hare, especially one less than a year old. [Middle English, from Norman French *leveret,* diminutive of *levre,* variant of Old French *lievre,* hare, from Latin *lepus* (stem *lepor-*). See **leporine.**]
Le·ver·ku·sen (lā′vər-ko͞o′zən). A city of West Germany, in southwestern North Rhine-Westphalia. Population, 103,000.
Le·ver·rier (lə-vĕ-ryā′), **Urbain Jean Joseph.** 1811–1877. French astronomer.
Le·vi[1] (lē′vī′). A son of Jacob and Leah. Genesis 29:34. [Hebrew, "joining."]
Le·vi[2] (lē′vī′) *n.* A tribe of Israel descended from Levi.
lev·i·a·ble (lĕv′ē-ə-bəl) *adj.* Liable to be levied or levied on.

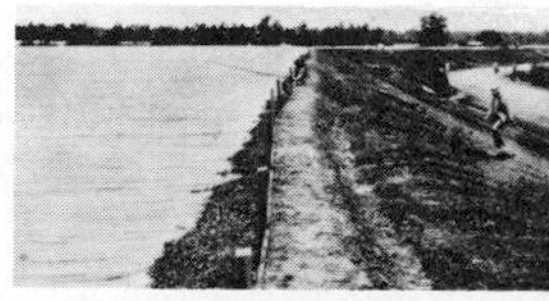
levee[1]
Mississippi River, Louisiana

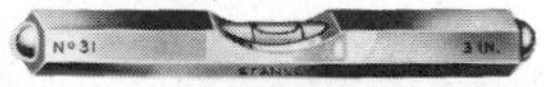
level
Level for gauging horizontal surfaces

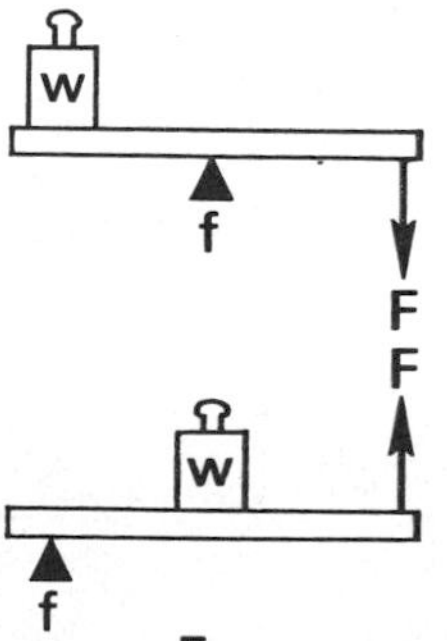

lever
Three basic types of lever; f is the fulcrum and F is the force needed to raise a weight W

le·vi·a·than (lə-vī′ə-thən) n. 1. A monstrous sea creature mentioned in the Old Testament. Job 41:1. 2. Any very large animal. 3. Anything unusually large for its kind. [Middle English, from Late Latin, from Hebrew libhyāthān.]

lev·i·gate (lĕv′ĭ-gāt′) tr.v. -gated, -gating, -gates. 1. To make into a smooth, fine powder, as by grinding when moist. 2. To suspend in a liquid. 3. To make smooth; to polish. —adj. (lĕv′ĭ-gāt′, -gĭt). Smooth. [Latin lēvigāre : lēvis, smooth (see legwh- in Appendix*) + agere, to do, make (see ag- in Appendix*).] —lev′i·ga′tion n.

lev·in (lĕv′ən) n. Archaic. Lightning. [Middle English leven(e), levin, probably from Scandinavian, akin to Old Swedish liughn(elder), lightning (flash). See leuk- in Appendix*.]

lev·i·rate (lĕv′ə-rāt′, -ər-ĭt) n. The practice of marrying the widow of one's brother, as required by ancient Hebrew law. Compare sororate. [From Latin lēvir, husband's brother. See daiwer in Appendix*.] —lev′i·rat′ic (-răt′ĭk), lev′i·rat′i·cal adj.

Le·vis (lē′vīz′) pl.n. A trademark for snugly fitting trousers of heavy denim with rivets reinforcing points of strain.

lev·i·tate (lĕv′ə-tāt′) v. -tated, -tating, -tates. —intr. To rise into the air and float, in apparent defiance of gravity. —tr. To cause to rise into the air and float. [From LEVITY.] —lev′i·ta′tion n. —lev′i·ta′tor (-tā′tər) n.

Le·vite (lē′vīt′) n. One of the tribe of Levi, assistants to the Temple priests. [Middle English, from Late Latin Levītēs, from Greek Leuitēs, from Leui, Levi, from Hebrew Lēwī.]

Le·vit·i·cal (lə-vĭt′ĭ-kəl) adj. Also **Le·vit·ic** (-vĭt′ĭk). 1. Of or relating to the Levites. 2. Of or relating to Leviticus.

Le·vit·i·cus (lə-vĭt′ĭ-kəs) n. Abbr. **Lev.** The third book of the Old Testament, containing the Hebrew ceremonial laws.

Lev·it·town (lĕv′ĭt-toun′). An urban area constructed on southeastern Long Island, New York State. Population, 65,000.

lev·i·ty (lĕv′ə-tē) n., pl. **-ties.** 1. Lack of weight; lightness; buoyancy. 2. Lightness of speech or manner, especially when inappropriate; frivolity. 3. Changeableness; inconstancy. [Latin levitās, from levis, light. See legwh- in Appendix*.]

Lev·kas (lĕf-käs′). Also **Leu·kas** (loo′kəs). An Ionian Island of Greece, 114 square miles in area, off the western mainland.

le·vo (lē′vō) adj. Levorotatory.

le·vo·ro·ta·tion (lē′vō-rō-tā′shən) n. A counterclockwise rotation, especially of the plane of polarized light. [Latin laevus, left (see laiwo- in Appendix*) + ROTATION.]

le·vo·ro·ta·to·ry (lē′vō-rō′tə-tôr′ē, -tōr′ē) adj. Also **le·vo·ro·ta·ry** (-rō′tə-rē). 1. Optics. Turning or rotating the plane of polarization of light to the left or counterclockwise. 2. Chemistry. Of or pertaining to a solution that so rotates the plane of polarized light. Compare **dextrorotatory.** [Latin laevus, left (see laiwo- in Appendix*) + ROTATORY.]

lev·u·lose (lĕv′yə-lōs′) n. A sugar, fructose (see). [LEV(OROTATORY) + -UL(E) + -OSE.]

lev·y (lĕv′ē) v. **-ied, -ying, -ies.** —tr. 1. To impose or collect (a tax, for example). 2. To draft into military service. 3. To declare, begin, or wage (a war). —intr. To confiscate property, especially in accordance with a legal judgment. —n. 1. The act or process of levying. 2. The money, property, or troops levied. [Middle English leve(e), levie, from Old French levee, a raising, from lever, to raise. See lever.] —lev′i·er n.

Sinclair Lewis

lewd (lood) adj. **lewder, lewdest.** 1. Licentious; lustful. 2. Obscene. 3. Obsolete. Wicked. [Middle English lewd(e)d, originally, ignorant, vulgar, Old English lǣwede†, lay (nonclergy).] —lewd′ly adv. —lewd′ness n.

Lew·es River (loo′ĭs). A river of Canada, rising in the southern Yukon Territory and flowing 338 miles northwest to the Pelly with which it forms the Yukon River.

lew·is (loo′ĭs) n. A dovetailed iron tenon made of several parts and designed to fit into a dovetail mortise in a large stone so that it can be lifted by a hoisting apparatus. Also called "lewisson." [Origin uncertain.]

lewis

Lew·is (loo′ĭs) n. A masculine given name. [Middle English Lewis, from Old French Louis, from Medieval Latin Ludovicus, from Old High German Hluodowig. See weik-5 in Appendix*.]

Lew·is (loo′ĭs), **C(live) S(taples).** 1898-1963. English novelist.

Lew·is (loo′ĭs), **(Harry) Sinclair.** 1885-1951. American novelist.

Lew·is (loo′ĭs), **John L(lewellyn).** 1880-1969. American labor leader; organizer and president (1935-40) of the CIO.

Lew·is (loo′ĭs), **Meriwether.** 1774-1809. American explorer; led overland expedition to the Pacific Ocean (1804-06) with William Clark (see).

Lew·i·sham (loo′ə-shəm, -səm). A borough of London, England, comprising the former administrative divisions of Lewisham and Deptford. Population, 290,000.

lew·is·ite (loo′ĭ-sīt′) n. An oily, colorless to violet or brown liquid, $C_2H_2AsCl_3$, used to make a highly toxic military gas. [After Winford Lee Lewis (died 1943), American chemist.]

Lew·is Range (loo′ĭs). A range of the Rocky Mountains, extending about 160 miles through northwestern Montana. Highest elevation, Mount Cleveland (10,448 feet).

Lew·is·ton (loo′ĭ-stən). The second-largest city of Maine, on the Androscoggin River in the southwest. Population, 40,000.

Lew·is with Har·ris (loo′ĭs; hăr′ĭs). The largest (825 square miles) and northernmost island of the Outer Hebrides, Scotland.

lex (lĕks) n., pl. **leges** (lē′jēz). Law. [Latin lēx. See leg- in Appendix*.]

lex. lexicon.

lex·i·cal (lĕk′sĭ-kəl) adj. 1. Of or relating to the vocabulary, words, or morphemes of a language. 2. Of, relating to, or appropriate to lexicography or a lexicon. [From LEXICON.]

lex·i·cog·ra·pher (lĕk′sĭ-kŏg′rə-fər) n. One who writes or compiles a dictionary.

lex·i·cog·ra·phy (lĕk′sĭ-kŏg′rə-fē) n. The writing or compilation of a dictionary or dictionaries. [LEXICO(N) + -GRAPHY.] —lex′i·co·graph′ic (-kō-grăf′ĭk), lex′i·co·graph′i·cal adj. —lex′i·co·graph′i·cal·ly adv.

lex·i·col·o·gy (lĕk′sĭ-kŏl′ə-jē) n. The study of the lexical component of language. —lex′i·co·log′i·cal adj. —lex′i·co·log′i·cal·ly adv. —lex′i·col′o·gist n.

lex·i·con (lĕk′sĭ-kŏn′) n. Abbr. **lex.** 1. A dictionary. 2. A stock of terms used in or of a particular profession, subject, or style; vocabulary: the lexicon of the sports page. 3. Linguistics. The morphemes of a language. [New Latin, from Greek lexikon (biblion), (book) pertaining to words, from lexis, speech, word, phrase, from legein, to speak. See leg- in Appendix*.]

Lex·ing·ton (lĕk′sĭng-tən). 1. A city of Kentucky, in the Bluegrass Country. Population, 63,000. 2. A town and suburb of Boston, Massachusetts; the site of an armed encounter of Minutemen and British soldiers that started the American Revolution (April 19, 1775). Population, 28,000.

ley. Variant of **lea.**

Ley·den. See **Leiden.**

Ley·den jar (līd′n). An early form of capacitor consisting of a glass jar lined inside and out with tinfoil and having a conducting rod connected to the inner foil lining and passing out of the jar through an insulated stopper. [Invented in LEYDEN.]

Ley·te (lā′tē, -tā). An island of the Republic of the Philippines, 2,785 square miles in area, in the Visayan group north of Mindanao. Population, 1,973,000.

Ley·te Gulf (lā′tē, -tā). An inlet of the Pacific between the islands of Leyte and Samar, Republic of the Philippines; the site of a naval battle in World War II in which the Americans defeated the Japanese (1944).

Ley·ton (lāt′n). A former administrative division of London, England, now part of **Waltham Forest** (see).

lf 1. Printing. lightface. 2. low frequency.

LG, L.G. Low German.

lg., lge. large.

LGA Airport code for La Guardia Airport, New York.

Lha·sa (lä′sə, läs′ə). Also **La·sa.** The capital of Tibet, in the southeast at an altitude of 12,050 feet. Population, 80,000.

Lhasa ap·so (äp′sō). A small dog of a Tibetan breed, having a long, straight coat. [LHASA + Tibetan apso, Lhasa apso.]

li (lē) n., pl. **li.** A Chinese measure of distance measuring about one-third of a mile. [Chinese li³.]

Li The symbol for the element lithium.

L.I. Long Island.

li·a·bil·i·ty (lī′ə-bĭl′ə-tē) n., pl. **-ties.** 1. Something for which one is liable; an obligation or debt. 2. Plural. The financial obligations entered in the balance sheet of a business enterprise. Compare **assets.** 3. A hindrance; handicap. 4. Likelihood.

li·a·ble (lī′ə-bəl) adj. 1. Legally obligated; responsible: liable for military service. 2. Susceptible; subject: "How liable she would become not only to their contempt, but to their outrage" (John Jay). 3. Likely; apt: "The more simple anything is, the less liable it is to be disordered" (Thomas Paine). —See Synonyms at **responsible.** —See Usage note at **apt.** [Perhaps from Norman French liable (unattested), from Old French lier, to bind, from Latin ligāre. See leig-1 in Appendix*.]

li·ai·son (lē′ā-zŏn′, lē-ā′zŏn′, lē′ə-; French lyĕ-zôn′) n., pl. **-sons** (-zŏnz′, -zŏnz′; French -zôn′). 1. An instance or means of communication between bodies, groups, or units. 2. a. A close relationship: "the blissful liaison,/Between himself and his environment" (Wallace Stevens). b. An adulterous relationship. 3. The pronunciation of the usually silent final consonant of a word when followed by a word beginning with a vowel. [French liaison, "binding," from Old French, from lier, to bind. See **liable.**]

Liá·kou·ra. The modern name for Mount **Parnassus.**

li·an·a (lē-ăn′ə, -ä′nə) n. Also **li·ane** (-än′). Any of various high-climbing, usually woody vines common in the tropics. [French liane, perhaps from lier, to bind. See **liable.**]

liang (lyăng) n., pl. **liang** or **liangs.** A former Chinese unit of weight, equivalent to 1/16 of the catty, approximately 1⅓ ounces. Compare **tael.** [Mandarin Chinese liang³.]

Liao (lyou). A river of northeastern China, rising on the southern Inner Mongolian plateau and flowing 900 miles first northeast and then southwest to the Gulf of Liaotung.

Liao·ning (lyou′nĭng′). Formerly **Sheng·king** (shŭn′jĭng′). A province of China, occupying 58,301 square miles in the northeast. Population, 24,050,000. Capital, Shenyang.

Liao·tung, Gulf of (lyou′dŏong′). An arm of the Gulf of Po Hai in northeastern China.

Liao·tung Peninsula (lyou′dŏong′). A peninsula in northeastern China projecting into the Yellow Sea.

li·ar (lī′ər) n. One who tells lies.

Li·ard (lē′ärd). A river of Canada, rising in the southeastern Yukon Territory and flowing 570 miles southeast and then northeast to the Mackenzie River in the Northwest Territories.

lib. 1. liberal. 2. librarian; library.

Lib. Liberal.

li·ba·tion (lī-bā′shən) n. 1. a. The pouring of a liquid offering as a religious ritual. b. The liquid poured. 2. Informal. An intoxicating beverage. [Middle English libacioun, from Latin lībātiō, from lībāre, to taste, pour out as an offering. See lei-³ in Appendix*.]

Lib·by (lĭb′ē), **Willard Frank.** Born 1908. American chemist; devised carbon-14 dating technique.

li·bec·cio (lī-bĕch′ē-ō′; Italian lē-bĕt′chō) n. A southwest wind in Italy. [Italian, from Latin *Libs*, the southwest wind, from Greek *Lips* (stem *lib-*).]

li·bel (lī′bəl) *n.* **1.** *Law.* **a.** Any written, printed, or pictorial statement that damages a person by defaming his character or exposing him to ridicule. **b.** The act of presenting such a statement to the public. Compare **slander.** **2.** Any slighting statement. **3.** The written claims presented by a plaintiff in an action at admiralty law or to an ecclesiastical court. —*tr.v.* **libeled** or **-belled, -beling** or **-belling, -bels. 1.** To make or publish a defamatory statement about. **2.** To speak slightingly of. —See Synonyms at **malign.** [Middle English, formal written claim of a plaintiff, from Old French *libel*, from Latin *libellus*, a little book, diminutive of *liber*, book. See **library.**] —**li′bel·er, li′bel·ist** *n.*

li·bel·ant (lī′bə-lənt) *n.* Also **li·bel·lant.** The plaintiff in a case of ecclesiastical or admiralty libel.

li·bel·ee (lī′bə-lē′) *n.* Also **li·bel·lee.** The defendant in a case of ecclesiastical or admiralty libel.

li·bel·ous (lī′bə-ləs) *adj.* Also **li·bel·lous.** Containing or constituting a libel; defamatory. —**li′bel·ous·ly** *adv.*

lib·er·al (lĭb′ər-əl, lĭb′rəl) *adj. Abbr.* **lib. 1.** Having, expressing, or following social or political views or policies that favor nonrevolutionary progress and reform. **2.** Having, expressing, or following views or policies that favor the freedom of individuals to act or express themselves in a manner of their own choosing. **3.** *Capital* **L.** *Abbr.* **Lib.** Of, designating, or belonging to a Liberal political party. **4.** Of, relating to, or characteristic of representational forms of government. **5.** Tolerant of the ideas or behavior of others. **6. a.** Tending to give freely; generous: *a liberal benefactor.* **b.** Generously given; bountiful: *a liberal serving.* **7.** Not literal: *a liberal translation.* **8.** *Obsolete.* **a.** Permissible or appropriate for a free man. **b.** Unrestrained. **9.** Relating to or based on a liberal arts education. —*n.* **1.** A person with liberal ideas or opinions. **2.** *Capital* **L.** *Abbr.* **Lib.** A member of a Liberal political party. [Middle English, from Old French, from Latin *līberālis*, of freedom, from *līber*, free. See **leudh-²** in Appendix.*] —**lib′er·al·ly** *adv.* —**lib′er·al·ness** *n.*

liberal arts. Academic disciplines, such as languages, history, philosophy, and abstract science, that are presumed to develop general intellectual ability and judgment and provide information of general cultural concern, as distinguished from more narrowly practical training, as for a profession.

lib·er·al·ism (lĭb′ər-ə-lĭz′əm, lĭb′rə-) *n.* **1.** Liberal views and policies, especially in regard to social or political questions. **2.** A liberalizing movement within Protestantism.

lib·er·al·i·ty (lĭb′ə-răl′ə-tē) *n., pl.* **-ties. 1.** The quality or state of being liberal. **2.** A generous gift.

lib·er·al·ize (lĭb′ər-ə-līz′, lĭb′rə-) *v.* **-ized, -izing, -izes.** —*tr.* To make liberal. —*intr.* To become liberal.

Liberal Party. A political party advocating liberalism; especially, a party formed in Great Britain in about 1830.

lib·er·ate (lĭb′ə-rāt′) *tr.v.* **-ated, -ating, -ates. 1.** To give liberty to; set free, especially to free (a country) from foreign control. **2.** *Chemistry.* To release from combination, as a gas. **3.** *Military Slang.* To obtain by looting. [Latin *līberāre*, from *līber*, free. See **leudh-²** in Appendix.*] —**lib′er·a′tor** (-ā′tər) *n.*

Li·be·ri·a (lī-bîr′ē-ə). A republic of Africa, occupying 43,000 square miles on the Gulf of Guinea; founded by freed U.S. slaves in 1847. Population, 1,066,000. Capital, Monrovia.

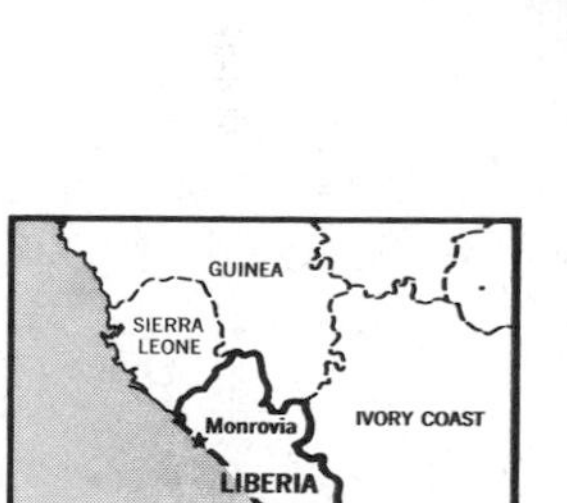

Liberia

lib·er·tar·i·an (lĭb′ər-târ′ē-ən) *n.* **1.** One who believes in freedom of action and thought. **2.** One who believes in free will. [From LIBERTY.] —**lib′er·tar′i·an·ism′** *n.*

lib·er·tine (lĭb′ər-tēn′) *n.* **1.** One who acts without moral restraint; a dissolute person. **2.** One standing in defiance of established religious or moral precepts, as during the Enlightenment or the ensuing revolutionary period in Europe. —*adj.* Morally unrestrained. [Middle English *libertyn* (only in the sense "freed slave"), from Latin *lībertīnus*, from *lībertus*, set free, from *līber*, free. See **leudh-²** in Appendix.*]

lib·er·tin·ism (lĭb′ər-tē-nĭz′əm) *n.* Also **lib·er·tin·age** (-tē′nĭj). **1.** Promiscuity. **2.** *Rare.* Freedom of thought.

lib·er·ty (lĭb′ər-tē) *n., pl.* **-ties. 1. a.** The condition of being not subject to restriction or control. **b.** The right to act in a manner of one's own choosing. **2.** The state of not being in confinement or servitude. **3.** Permission to do a specific thing; privilege. **4.** *Often plural.* **a.** A social action regarded as more familiar than polite convention permits: *Is it a liberty to use your first name?* **b.** A statement, attitude, or action not warranted by conditions or actualities: *a historical novel that takes liberties with chronology.* **5.** Authorized leave from naval duty. —See Synonyms at **freedom.** —**at liberty. 1.** Not in confinement or under constraint; free. **2.** Not occupied or in use. [Middle English *liberte*, from Old French, from Latin *lībertās*, from *līber*, free. See **leudh-²** in Appendix.*]

liberty cap. A brimless cap that fits snugly around the head and has a soft conical crown. Compare **Phrygian cap.**

Liberty Island. Formerly **Bed·loe's Island** (bĕd′lōz), **Bed·loe Island** (bĕd′lō). An island occupying about ten acres in New York Bay; the site of the Statue of Liberty.

Liberty Ship. A type of large American cargo ship produced in large numbers during World War II.

li·bid·i·nous (lĭ-bĭd′n-əs) *adj.* Characterized by or having lustful desires; licentious; lascivious. [Middle English *lybydynous*, from Latin *libīdinōsus*, from *libīdō*, desire, LIBIDO.]

li·bi·do (lĭ-bē′dō, -bī′dō) *n., pl.* **-dos. 1.** The psychic and emotional energy associated with instinctual biological drives. **2. a.** Sexual desire. **b.** Manifestation of the sexual drive. [Latin *libīdō*, desire, lust. See **leubh-** in Appendix.*] —**li·bid′i·nal** (lĭ bĭd′n əl) *adj.*

li·bra (lī′brə *for sense 1;* lē′brä *for sense 2*) *n., pl.* **-brae** (-brē′) (for sense 1) or **-bras** (-bräs) (for sense 2). **1.** A unit of weight in ancient Rome corresponding to a pound and equivalent to approximately 12 ounces. **2.** A former gold coin of Peru. [Latin *lībra*, "pound," balance. See **līthrā** in Appendix.*]

Li·bra (lī′brə, lē′-) *n.* **1.** A constellation in the Southern Hemisphere near Scorpius and Virgo. **2.** The seventh sign of the zodiac *(see).* Also called the "Scales," the "Balance." [New Latin, from Latin *lībra*, balance. See **libra.**]

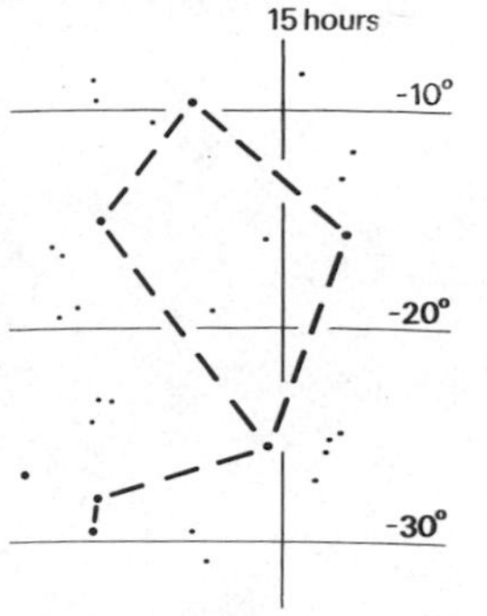

Libra

li·brar·i·an (lī-brâr′ē-ən) *n. Abbr.* **lib. 1.** A custodian of a library. **2.** One trained in library science. —**li·brar′i·an·ship′** *n.*

li·brar·y (lī′brĕr′ē) *n., pl.* **-ies.** *Abbr.* **lib. 1.** A repository for literary and artistic materials, such as books, periodicals, newspapers, pamphlets, and prints, kept for reading or reference. **2.** A collection of such material, especially when systematically arranged for reference. **3.** An institution or foundation maintaining such a collection. **4.** A commercial establishment that lends books for a fee. **5.** A series or set of books issued by a publisher. [Middle English *librarie*, from Old French *librairie*, from Vulgar Latin *librāriā* (unattested), alteration of Latin *librāria (taberna)*, book (shop), from *liber*†, book.]

Library of Congress. *Abbr.* **L.C.** The national library of the United States in Washington, D.C., founded in 1800.

library service. The principles or practice of library administration; the care, storage, and retrieval of printed and other library matter. Also called "library science."

li·bra·tion (lī-brā′shən) *n.* A real or apparent very slow oscillation of a satellite as viewed from the larger celestial body around which it revolves. —**li′bra·to′ry** (-brə-tôr′ē, -tōr′ē) *adj.*

li·bret·tist (lĭ-brĕt′ĭst) *n.* The author of a libretto.

li·bret·to (lĭ-brĕt′ō) *n., pl.* **-tos** or **-bretti** (-brĕt′ē). **1.** The text of an opera or other dramatic musical work. **2.** A book containing such a text. Also called "book." [Italian, diminutive of *libro*, book, from Latin *liber*. See **library.**]

Li·bre·ville (lē′brə-vēl′). The capital of Gabon, a seaport in the northwest on the Gulf of Guinea. Population, 46,000.

Lib·y·a (lĭb′ē-ə). A kingdom occupying 680,000 square miles in northern Africa. Population, 1,617,000. Capitals, Tripoli and Bengasi.

Lib·y·an (lĭb′ē-ən) *adj.* Of or relating to Libya, its people, or its language. —*n.* **1.** A native or resident of Libya. **2.** The extinct Hamitic language used in ancient Libya.

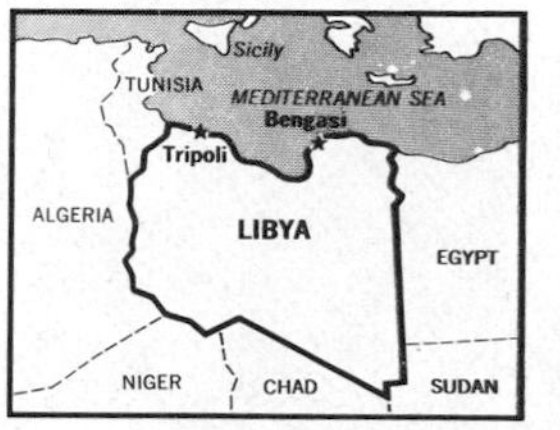

Libya

Libyan Desert. The northeastern part of the Sahara, about 750,000 square miles in area.

lice. Plural of **louse.**

li·cense (lī′səns) *n.* Also *chiefly British* **li·cence. 1.** Official or legal permission to do or own a specified thing. **2.** Proof of permission granted, usually in the form of a document, card, plate, or tag: *a driver's license.* Compare **certificate. 3.** Deviation from normal rules, practices, or methods in order to achieve a certain end or effect. **4.** An instance of such deviation. **5.** Freedom from strict rules, especially concerning behavior or speech. **6.** Excessive or undisciplined freedom constituting an abuse of a privilege. **7.** Lust; licentiousness. —See Synonyms at **freedom.** —*tr.v.* **licensed, -censing, -censes.** Also *chiefly British* **li·cence. 1.** To give or yield permission to or for. **2.** To grant a license to or for; authorize. [Middle English *licence*, from Old French *licence*, from Latin *licentia*, freedom, from *licēre*, to be lawful, be permitted. See **leisure.**] —**li′cens·a·ble** *adj.* —**li′cen·ser, li′cen·sor′** (lī′sən-sər, lī′sən-sôr′) *n.*

li·cen·see (lī′sən-sē′) *n.* One to whom a license is granted.

li·cen·ti·ate (lī-sĕn′shē-ĭt, -āt′) *n.* **1.** A person who is granted a license by an authorized body to practice a specified profession. **2.** *Abbr.* **L.** A degree from certain European universities ranking just below that of a doctor. **3.** One holding such a degree. [Medieval Latin *licentiātus*, from *licentiāre*, to allow, from Latin *licentia*, freedom, LICENSE.]

li·cen·tious (lī-sĕn′shəs) *adj.* **1.** Lacking moral discipline or sexual restraint. **2.** Having no regard for accepted rules or standards. [Latin *licentiōsus*, from *licentia*, freedom, dissoluteness, LICENSE.] —**li·cen′tious·ly** *adv.* —**li·cen′tious·ness** *n.*

li·chee. Variant of **litchi.**

li·chen (lī′kən) *n.* **1.** Any of numerous plants consisting of a fungus, usually of the class Ascomycetes, in close combination with certain of the green or blue-green algae, characteristically forming a crustlike, scaly, or branching growth on rocks or tree trunks. **2.** *Pathology.* Any of various skin eruptions occurring primarily in lichenlike patches. —*tr.v.* **lichened, -chening, -chens.** To cover with lichens. [Latin *līchēn*, from Greek *leikhēn*, "licker," from *leikhein*, to lick. See **leigh-** in Appendix.*] —**li′chen·ous, li′chen·ose′** *adj.*

li·chen·in (lī′kə-nĭn) *n.* A white, starchlike, gelatinous compound, $C_6H_{10}O_5$, obtained from a lichen, Iceland moss. [LICHEN + -IN.]

li·chen·ol·o·gy (lī′kə-nŏl′ə-jē) *n.* The botanical study of lichens. [LICHEN + -LOGY.] —**li′chen·ol′o·gist** *n.*

lich gate (lĭch). Also **lych gate.** A roofed gateway to a churchyard used originally as a resting place for the bier before burial. [Middle English *lycheyate* : *lich*, body, corpse, Old English *līc* (see **līk-** in Appendix*) + *gate, yate*, GATE.]

lic·it (lĭs′ĭt) *adj.* Within the law; legal. [Middle English, from Latin *licitus*, from the past participle of *licēre*, to be permitted. See **leisure.**] —**lic′it·ly** *adv.* —**lic′it·ness** *n.*

lick (lĭk) *v.* **licked, licking, licks.** —*tr.* **1.** To pass the tongue over or along. **2.** To lap up. **3.** To move or flicker like a tongue: *The waves licked the rocks lining the shore.* **4.** To thrash. **5.** To get the better of; to defeat. —*intr.* To pass or move quickly and rapidly: *The flames licked at our feet.* —**lick into shape.** To bring into satisfactory condition or appearance. —**lick one's**

chops. To anticipate delightedly. **—lick one's wounds.** To recuperate after a defeat. *—n.* **1.** The act or process of licking. **2.** A small quantity; a bit. **3.** A place frequented by animals that lick the exposed natural salt deposits. **4.** A blow. **—last licks.** A last chance or turn. [Middle English *licken,* Old English *liccian.* See **leigh-** in Appendix.*] **—lick'er** *n.*

lick·er·ish (lĭk'ər-ĭsh) *adj.* Also **li·quor·ish.** *Archaic.* **1.** Lascivious; lecherous. **2.** Relishing pleasurable sensations. **3.** Greedy. **4.** Arousing hunger; appetizing. [Alteration of Middle English *lickerous,* from Norman French *likerous* (unattested), variant of Old French *lechereus,* from *lecheor,* LECHER.] **—lick'er·ish·ly** *adv.*

lick·e·ty-split (lĭk'ə-tē-splĭt') *adv.* With great speed. [Formed from LICK and SPLIT.]

lick·ing (lĭk'ĭng) *n.* **1.** An act of one that licks. **2.** A beating.

Licking River. A river of Kentucky, rising in the east-central part of the state and flowing 320 miles generally northwest to the Ohio opposite Cincinnati.

lick·spit·tle (lĭk'spĭt'l) *n.* A fawning underling; toady.

lic·o·rice (lĭk'ər-ĭs, -ĭsh) *n.* Also *chiefly British* **li·quo·rice.** **1.** A plant, *Glycyrrhiza glabra,* of the Mediterranean region, having blue flowers and a sweet, distinctively flavored root. **2.** The root of this plant, used as a flavoring in candy, liquors, tobacco, and medicines. **3.** A confection made from or flavored with this root. **4.** Any of various plants resembling licorice. [Middle English *licoris, licorice,* from Norman French *lycorys* and Old French *licoresse, licorece,* from Late Latin *liquiritia,* alteration (influenced by Latin *liquor,* LIQUOR) of Greek *glukurrhiza,* "sweetroot" : *glukus,* sweet (see **dl̥ku-** in Appendix*) + *rhiza,* root (see **werād-** in Appendix*).]

lic·tor (lĭk'tər) *n.* A Roman functionary who carried fasces in attendance on a magistrate. [Middle English *littour,* from Latin *lictor.* See **leig-**[1] in Appendix.*]

lid (lĭd) *n.* **1.** A removable or hinged cover for any hollow receptacle. **2.** An eyelid. **3.** *Biology.* A flaplike covering, such as an operculum. **4.** A curb or restraint: *put the lid on crime.* **5.** *Slang.* A hat. **—flip one's lid.** *Slang.* To lose one's composure. [Middle English *lid,* Old English *hlid,* covering, gate, opening. See **klei-** in Appendix.*] **—lid'ded** *adj.*

Li·di·ce (lĭd'ə-sē', -ət-sē'). A village of Czechoslovakia, in west-central Bohemia; entirely destroyed by the Nazis (1942) and since rebuilt as a national memorial.

lid·less (lĭd'lĭs) *adj.* **1.** Having no lid. **2.** Sleepless; watchful.

Li·do (lē'dō). An island off Venice.

lie[1] (lī) *intr.v.* **lay** (lā), **lain** (lān), **lying, lies. 1.** To be in or place oneself in a prostrate or recumbent position; rest; recline. **2.** To be placed on or supported by a surface that is usually horizontal. **3.** To be or remain in a specific condition: *The conflict lies dormant.* **4.** To exist; be inherent: *His good nature lies within him.* **5.** To occupy a place: *The spring lies several miles beyond this mesa.* **6.** To be buried or entombed. **7.** To extend: *Our land lies between these trees and the river.* **8.** *Archaic.* To stay for a night or short while: *The regiment is lying not far from here.* **9.** *Law.* To be admissible or maintainable. —See Usage note at **lay.** **—lie down on the job.** To do less than one is capable of. **—lie in.** To be in confinement for childbirth. **—lie in wait.** To lie in ambush. **—lie low.** To keep oneself or one's plans hidden. **—lie over.** To remain and wait until a future time. **—lie to.** *Nautical.* To remain stationary while facing the wind. **—lie with. 1.** To be decided by, dependent upon, or up to: *The choice lies with you.* **2.** *Archaic.* To have sexual intercourse with. *—n.* **1.** The manner or position in which something is situated. **2.** A haunt or hiding place of an animal. **3.** *Golf.* The position of a ball that has come to a stop. [Lie, lay, lain; Middle English *lien* (or *lig(g)en*), *lay, ley(e)n,* Old English *licgan, læg, legen.* See **legh-** in Appendix.*]

lie[2] (lī) *n.* **1.** A false statement or piece of information deliberately presented as being true; a falsehood. **2.** Anything meant to deceive or give a wrong impression. **—give the lie to. 1.** To accuse of lying; contradict. **2.** To prove to be untrue; belie. *—v.* **lied, lying, lies.** *—intr.* **1.** To present false information with the intention of deceiving. **2.** To convey a false image or impression: *Appearances often lie.* *—tr.* To put in a specific condition through deceit: *lied himself into trouble.* [Middle English *ligen, lien,* Old English *lēogan.* See **leugh-** in Appendix.*]

Lie·big (lē'bĭk), Baron **Justus von.** 1803–1873. German organic chemist and educator.

Liech·ten·stein (lĭKH'tən-shtīn). A principality occupying 62 square miles in central Europe between Austria and Switzerland. Population, 19,000. Capital, Vaduz.

lied (lēd; *German* lēt) *n., pl.* **lieder** (lē'dər). A German art song. [German *Lied,* song, from Old High German *liod.* See **leu-**[2] in Appendix.*]

Lie·der·kranz (lē'dər-kränts', -krănts') *n.* A trademark for a soft cheese resembling a mild Limburger. [German, "song collection."]

lie detector. A **polygraph** *(see)* used to detect lying.

lief (lēf) *adv.* Readily; willingly: *I would as lief go now as later.* *—adj. Archaic.* **1.** Beloved; dear. **2.** Ready or willing. [Middle English *le(e)f, lif,* from *le(e)f,* "beloved," Old English *lēof.* See **leubh-** in Appendix.*]

liege (lēj) *n.* **1.** A lord or sovereign in feudal law. **2.** A vassal or subject owing allegiance and services to a lord or sovereign under feudal law. *—adj.* **1.** Of, relating to, or characteristic of the relationship between a vassal or subject and his lord. **2.** Entitled to the loyalty and services of his vassals or subjects. Said of a feudal lord. **3.** Bound to give such allegiance and services to a lord or monarch. Said of a feudal vassal or subject. **4.** Loyal. [Middle English *li(e)ge, lege,* from Old French *li(e)ge,* from Medieval Latin *lēticus, laeticus,* from *lētus, lītus,* serf, from Germanic. See **lēi-**[2] in Appendix.*]

lifeboat

Li·ège (lē-ĕzh', -āzh'). *Flemish* **Luik** (loik). **1.** A province occupying 1,526 square miles in eastern Belgium. Population, 1,004,000. **2.** The capital of this province, a river port on the Meuse. Population, 153,000.

liege·man (lēj'mən) *n., pl.* **-men** (-mĭn). **1.** A feudal vassal or subject. **2.** A loyal supporter or follower.

lien (lēn, lē'ən) *n. Law.* The right to take and hold or sell the property of a debtor as security or payment for a debt. [Old French *l(o)ien,* bond, tie, from Latin *ligāmen,* from *ligāre,* to bind. See **leig-**[1] in Appendix.*]

li·e·nal (lī-ē'nəl) *adj.* Of or relating to the spleen. [From Latin *liēn,* spleen. See **spelgh-** in Appendix.*]

li·erne (lē-ûrn') *n.* A reinforcing secondary rib used in Gothic vaulting to connect the intersections and bosses of the primary ribs. [French, from Old French, from *lier,* to bind, from Latin *ligāre.* See **lien.**]

lieu (lo͞o) *n.* Place; stead. **—in lieu of.** In place of; instead of. [Middle English *liue,* from Old French *lieu,* from Latin *locus,* place, LOCUS.]

lieu·ten·ant (lo͞o-tĕn'ənt; *British* lĕf-tĕn'ənt) *n.* **1.** *Abbr.* **Lt.** *Military.* One of two ranks held by commissioned officers: **a.** A *second lieutenant,* the lowest-ranking commissioned officer; **b.** A *first lieutenant,* an officer ranking above a second lieutenant and below a captain. **2.** *Abbr.* **Lt.** *U.S. Navy.* One of two ranks held by commissioned officers: **a.** A *lieutenant junior grade,* an officer ranking just above an ensign; **b.** A *lieutenant senior grade,* an officer ranking above a lieutenant junior grade and below a lieutenant commander. **3.** *British & Canadian Navy.* A commissioned officer ranking just below a lieutenant-commander. **4.** One who acts in place of his superior; a deputy. [Originally, "officer who acts for a superior," from Middle English *lieutenaunt,* vice regent, from Old French *lieutenant* : *lieu,* LIEU + *tenant,* present participle of *tenir,* to hold, from Vulgar Latin *tenīre* (unattested), from Latin *tenēre* (see **ten-** in Appendix*).] **—lieu·ten'an·cy** *n.*

lieutenant colonel. *Abbr.* **Lt. Col.** *Military.* A commissioned officer ranking above a major and below a colonel.

lieutenant commander. Also *British & Canadian* **lieu·ten·ant-com·man·der.** *Abbr.* **Lt. Comdr.** A commissioned naval officer ranking above a lieutenant and below a commander.

lieutenant general. Also *British & Canadian* **lieu·ten·ant-gen·er·al.** *Abbr.* **Lt. Gen.** A commissioned army officer ranking above a major general and below a general.

lieutenant governor. *Abbr.* **Lt. Gov. 1.** An elected state official ranking just below the governor. **2.** The nonelective chief of government of a Canadian province.

life (līf) *n., pl.* **lives** (līvz). **1.** The property or quality manifested in functions such as metabolism, growth, response to stimulation, and reproduction, by which living organisms are distinguished from dead organisms or from inanimate matter. **2.** The characteristic state or condition of a living organism. **3.** Living organisms collectively: *plant life.* **4.** A living being, especially a person, contrasted with one no longer alive: *lives lost in battle.* **5.** The interval between the birth or inception of an organism and its death. **6.** The interval or amount of time during which anything exists or functions: *the operating life of a machine.* **7.** A spiritual state regarded as a transcending of death. **8.** An account of a person's life; a biography. **9.** Human activities, relationships, and interests collectively: *everyday life.* **10.** A manner of activity or a characteristic of existence: *country life.* **11.** A pleasant, easy, or luxurious manner of existence: *That's the life.* **12.** An animating force; a source of vitality. **13.** Animation, spirit, or liveliness: *full of life.* **14.** Strength or freshness of flavor. **15.** *Fine Arts.* **a.** A living person or model regarded as an artistic subject: *painted from life.* **b.** Actual environment or reality; nature. **16.** *Capital* **L.** *Christian Science.* God. **—as big (or large) as life.** Life-size. **—bring to life. 1.** To cause to regain consciousness. **2.** To put spirit into; to animate. **3.** To make lifelike. **—come to life. 1.** To regain consciousness. **2.** To become animated; grow lively. **—for dear life.** Desperately or urgently. **—for life. 1.** Until the end of one's life. **2.** So as to save one's life. **—for the life of me** (or **him** or **her**). *Informal.* Though trying hard. Used with negative expressions: *For the life of me I couldn't remember his name.* **—not on your life.** *Informal.* Not for any reason; definitely not. **—take a life.** To kill. **—the life of Riley.** *Informal.* An easy or good life. **—the life of the party.** An animated or amusing person who enlivens a social gathering. **—to the life.** Exactly or closely resembling a model or original. **—true to life.** Not deviating from reality; faithfully representing real life. [Middle English *lif(e),* Old English *līf.* See **leip-** in Appendix.*]

life belt. A life preserver worn like a belt.

life·blood (līf'blŭd') *n.* **1.** Blood regarded as essential for life. **2.** The indispensable vital part of a thing.

life·boat (līf'bōt') *n.* **1.** A boat carried on a ship to sustain persons abandoning the ship. **2.** A boat used for rescue service.

life buoy. A **buoy** *(see).*

life cycle. 1. The course of developmental changes through which an organism passes from its inception as a fertilized zygote to the mature state in which another zygote may be produced. **2.** A progression through a series of differing stages of development, as in insect metamorphosis.

life expectancy. The statistically determined number of years that an individual is expected to live.

life·guard (līf'gärd') *n.* An expert swimmer trained and employed to safeguard swimmers or bathers.

life history. 1. The history of changes undergone by an organ-

ă pat/ā pay/âr care/ä father/b bib/ch church/d deed/ĕ pet/ē be/f fife/g gag/h hat/hw which/ĭ pit/ī pie/îr pier/j judge/k kick/l lid, needle/m mum/n no, sudden/ng thing/ŏ pot/ō toe/ô paw, for/oi noise/ou out/o͝o took/o͞o boot/p pop/r roar/s sauce/sh ship, dish/

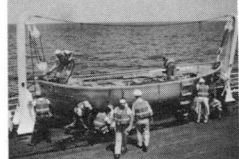

ism from inception or conception to death. **2.** The developmental history of an individual or group in its social environment.

life insurance. Insurance that guarantees a specific sum of money to a designated beneficiary upon the death of the insured or to the insured should he live beyond a certain age.

life jacket. A life preserver in the form of a jacket or vest.

life·less (līf′lĭs) *adj.* **1.** Having no life; inanimate. **2.** Incapable of sustaining life; not inhabited by living beings. **3.** Having lost life; dead. **4.** Lacking vitality or animation; dull; listless. —See Synonyms at **dead.** —**life′less·ly** *adv.* —**life′less·ness** *n.*

life·like (līf′līk′) *adj.* **1.** Resembling a living thing. **2.** Accurately representing real life. —**life′like′ness** *n.*

life line. **1.** An anchored line thrown as a support to someone falling or drowning. **2.** A line shot to a ship in distress either to connect it with the shore or for hauling aboard other lifesaving devices such as heavier lines or breeches buoys. **3.** A line used to raise and lower deep-sea divers. **4.** Any means or route by which necessary supplies are transported. **5.** A diagonal line crossing the palm of the hand and alleged to indicate the length and major events of one's life.

life·long (līf′lông′, -lŏng′) *adj.* Continuing for a lifetime.

life preserver. **1.** A buoyant device, usually in the shape of a ring, belt, or jacket, designed to keep a person afloat in the water. **2.** *British.* A weapon such as a blackjack or bludgeon.

lif·er (lī′fər) *n. Slang.* A prisoner serving a life sentence.

life raft. A raft usually made of wood or inflatable material and used as a lifeboat.

life·sav·er (līf′sā′vər) *n.* **1.** One that saves a life. **2.** A lifeguard. **3.** One that provides help in a minor crisis or emergency. **4.** A life preserver shaped like a ring. —**life′sav′ing** *n.* & *adj.*

Life Saver. A trademark for a candy shaped like a life preserver.

life-size (līf′sīz′) *adj.* Also **life-sized** (-sīzd′). Being of the same size as the person, animal, or thing represented.

life span. The period of time during which an organism remains alive under normal or optimum conditions.

life-sup·port system (līf′sə-pôrt′, -pōrt′). The equipment that provides a viable environment in a spacecraft.

life·time (līf′tīm′) *n.* **1.** The period of time during which an individual is alive. **2.** The interval or amount of time during which an object, property, process, or phenomenon exists or functions. —*adj.* Continuing or lasting for such a period of time: *a lifetime guarantee.*

life·work (līf′wûrk′) *n.* The chief work of one's lifetime.

Lif·fey (lĭf′ē). A river of the Republic of Ireland, rising in County Wicklow and flowing 50 miles to Dublin Bay.

lift (lĭft) *v.* **lifted, lifting, lifts.** —*tr.* **1.** To direct or carry from a lower to a higher position; raise; elevate: *lift one's eyes; lift the shades.* **2.** To pick up for the purpose of moving or removing: *lift the child from the sandbox.* **3. a.** To take back or remove; revoke; rescind: *lift a ban.* **b.** To bring an end to (a blockade or siege) by removing forces. **c.** To cease (artillery fire) on an area. **4.** To raise in condition, rank, esteem, or value; exalt: *His courage lifted him in their eyes.* **5.** To remove (plants) from the ground for transplanting. **6.** To project or sound in loud, clear tones: *They lifted their voices in song.* **7.** *Informal.* To steal; pilfer. **8.** *Informal.* To plagiarize. **9.** To pay off or clear (a debt or mortgage, for example). **10.** To perform cosmetic surgery on (the face), especially to remove wrinkles. **11.** *Golf.* **a.** To hit (the ball) very high into the air. **b.** To pick up (the ball) in the hand to put in a better position. —*intr.* **1.** To rise; ascend: *"the moon lifted with slow majesty"* (Kenneth Grahame). **2.** To disappear or disperse by or as if by rising: *By afternoon, the clouds had lifted.* **3.** To use force or energy in or as if in lifting something. **4.** To yield to upward force: *The window doesn't lift.* **5.** To stop temporarily. —*n.* **1.** The act or process of raising or rising to a higher position. **2.** Power or force available for raising: *the lift of a pump.* **3.** An amount or weight raised or capable of being raised at one time; a load. **4.** The extent or height something is raised; the amount of elevation. **5.** The distance or space through which something is raised. **6.** A rising of the level of the ground. **7.** A rising of spirits; mood of exhilaration or happiness. **8.** A raised, high, or erect position: *the lift of his chin.* **9.** A machine or device designed to pick up, raise, or carry something. **10.** One of the layers of leather, rubber, or other material making up the heel of a shoe. **11.** *Chiefly British.* An **elevator** *(see).* **12.** A ride given to help someone reach a destination. **13.** Any kind of assistance or help. **14.** *Mining.* A set of pumps used in a mine. **15.** *Aviation.* The component of the total aerodynamic force acting on an airfoil, or on an entire aircraft or winged missile, perpendicular to the relative wind and normally exerted in an upward direction, opposing the pull of gravity. [Middle English *liften,* from Old Norse *lypta.* See **leup-** in Appendix.*] —**lift′er** *n.*

Synonyms: *lift, raise, rear, elevate, hoist, heave, boost.* These verbs mean to move or bring something from a lower level to a higher one. *Lift* stresses the expenditure of effort thus involved. *Raise* often implies movement to a position that is approximately vertical, or figurative movement to a higher plane or level. *Rear* is interchangeable with *raise* in the sense of bringing to an upright position, though it is now infrequently so used. *Elevate* refers to movement to a markedly higher level; figuratively it often suggests exalting, ennobling, or increasing in rank. *Hoist* is applied principally to the lifting of heavy objects by mechanical means, and *heave* to lifting or raising that requires great exertion. *Boost* refers informally to upward movement effected by pushing from below; figuratively it is applied to increase or advance in amount, degree, status, or favor.

lift·off (lĭft′ôf′, -ŏf′) *n.* The initial movement by which or instant in which a rocket or other craft commences flight.

lig·a·ment (lĭg′ə-mənt) *n.* **1.** *Anatomy.* A sheet or band of tough, fibrous tissue connecting two or more bones or cartilages, or supporting an organ, fascia, or muscle. **2.** Any unifying or connecting tie or bond. [Middle English, from Latin *ligāmentum,* bond, bandage, from *ligāre,* to bind, LIGATE.] —**lig′a·men′tal, lig′a·men′ta·ry, lig′a·men′tous** *adj.*

li·gan. Variant of **lagan.**

li·gate (lī′gāt′) *tr.v.* **-gated, -gating, -gates.** To tie up, bind, or constrict with a ligature. [Latin *ligāre.* See **leig-**[1] in Appendix.*]

li·ga·tion (lī-gā′shən) *n.* **1.** The act of binding. **2.** The state of being bound. **3.** Something that binds; a ligature.

lig·a·ture (lĭg′ə-cho͝or′) *n.* **1.** The act of tying together, binding, or constricting. **2.** A cord, wire, or bandage used for tying, binding, or constricting. **3.** Something that unites; a bond. **4.** *Surgery.* A thread, wire, cord, or the like, applied in a tight loop, as to close vessels or tie off ducts. **5.** A character or type combining two or more letters, such as *fi.* **6.** *Music.* **a.** A group of notes intended to be played or sung as one phrase. **b.** A curved line indicating such a phrase; a slur. —*tr.v.* **ligatured, -turing, -tures.** To ligate. [Middle English, from Latin *ligātūra,* from *ligāre,* to bind, LIGATE.]

light[1] (līt) *n.* **1.** *Physics.* **a.** Electromagnetic radiation that has a wavelength in the range from about 3,900 to about 7,700 angstroms and that may be perceived by the unaided, normal human eye. **b.** Any electromagnetic radiation. **2.** The sensation of the perception of such radiation; brightness. **3.** A source of illumination, such as the sun or an electric lamp. **4.** The illumination derived from such a source. **5.** Daylight. **6.** Dawn; daybreak. **7.** The period of duration of daylight. **8.** A specific amount, supply, or emission of illumination. **9.** Something that admits light, as a window. **10.** A means or agent, as a match or cigarette lighter, for igniting a fire. **11.** Spiritual or intellectual comprehension or awareness; enlightenment. **12.** Public attention; general knowledge. **13.** A way of regarding something; angle; aspect: *She saw the situation in a different light.* **14.** *Archaic & Poetic.* Eyesight. **15.** *Plural.* One's individual opinions, choices, or life philosophy: *They acted according to their own lights.* **16.** A person who inspires or is adored by another: *His granddaughter is the light of his life.* **17.** A prominent or distinguished person, especially one serving as an example for others; a notable or luminary: *one of the brighter lights of Irish literature.* **18.** An expression of the eyes, usually indicative of animation or liveliness. **19.** *Capital* **L.** In Quaker doctrine, the guiding spirit or divine presence in each man. **20. a.** The representation of light in art. **b.** An area of pronounced illumination as rendered in a painting or photograph. —**in (the) light of.** In consideration of; in relationship to. —**see the light (of day).** **1.** To be born; come into existence. **2.** To become known to the public. **3.** To comprehend or perceive the meaning of something. —**shed** (or **throw**) **light on.** To provide information about; make more comprehensible. —*v.* **lighted** or **lit** (lĭt), **lighting, lights.** —*tr.* **1.** To set on fire; ignite; kindle. **2.** To cause to give out light; make luminous. **3.** To provide, cover, or fill with light; illuminate. **4.** To signal, direct, or indicate with or as if with lights. **5.** To enliven or animate: *A smile lights his face.* —*intr.* To start to burn; be ignited or kindled: *Green wood will not light easily.* —**light up.** **1.** To become or cause to become light, radiant, or bright. **2.** To become or cause to become animated or cheerful. **3.** *Informal.* To start smoking a cigarette, cigar, or pipe. —*adj.* **lighter, lightest.** *Abbr.* **lt.** **1.** Having a greater rather than lesser degree of **lightness** *(see).* Said of a color. See **color.** **2.** Characterized by or filled with light; radiant; bright. **3.** Being mixed with white; pale; fair: *light colors.* [Middle English *liht, light,* Old English *lēoht, līht.* See **leuk-** in Appendix.*]

light[2] (līt) *adj.* **lighter, lightest.** **1.** Of relatively low weight; not heavy. **2.** Of relatively low density. **3.** Of less than the correct, standard, or lawful weight; underweight: *a light pound.* **4.** Exerting little pressure; having less force or impact than normal: *a light kick.* **5. a.** Having less quantity, intensity, length, or volume than normal: *a light snow; a light murmur; a light turnout.* **b.** Moderate; abstemious: *a light eater; a light smoker.* **6.** Having little importance or value; insignificant: *light chatter.* **7.** Intended as entertainment; not serious or profound: *a light comedy.* **8.** Free from worries or troubles; blithe. **9.** Characterized by frivolity; silly; trivial. **10.** Quick to change or be swayed or diverted; fickle. **11.** Having little moral discipline; wanton. **12.** Suffering from mild delirium or faintness; dizzy. **13.** Moving quickly and easily; graceful; buoyant. **14.** Designed for ease and quickness of movement with a slim structure and little weight. **15.** Carrying little weight; unencumbered. **16.** *Military.* Carrying little equipment or arms: *a light brigade.* **17.** Without a weighty or massive appearance; airy; delicate. **18.** Easily digested. **19.** Having a spongy or flaky texture; well-leavened: *light pastries.* **20.** Having a loose, porous consistency; not packed together or solid: *light earth.* **21.** Containing a relatively small amount of alcohol: *a light wine.* **22.** *Phonetics & Prosody.* Designating a vowel or syllable pronounced with little or no stress. —See Synonyms at **easy.** —**make light of.** To regard or treat as insignificant or petty. —*adv.* **1.** Lightly. **2.** Without additional weight or burdens; in an unencumbered manner: *traveling light.* —*intr.v.* **lighted** or **lit** (lĭt), **lighting, lights.** **1.** To get down, as from a mount or vehicle; dismount; alight. **2.** To descend to the ground after flight; perch; land. **3.** To come upon one unexpectedly; strike suddenly, as a blow or stroke of luck. Often used with *on* or *upon:*

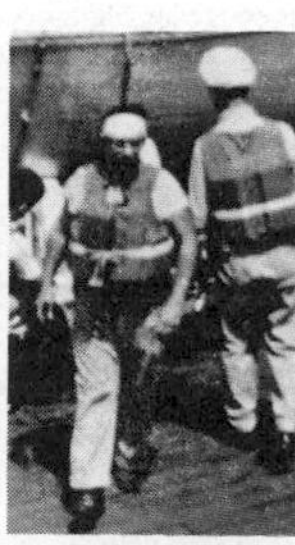

life jacket

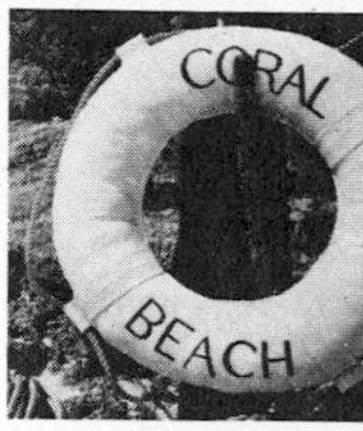

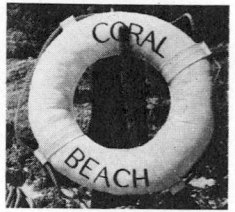

life preserver

lighthouse
Portland, Maine

Misfortune lighted upon him. **4.** To come upon by chance or accident. Often used with *on* or *upon.* —**light into.** To attack verbally or physically; assail. —**light out.** *Informal.* To leave hastily; run off. [Middle English *liht, light,* Old English *lēoht, liht.* See **legwh-** in Appendix.*]

light·en¹ (līt'n) *v.* **-ened, -ening, -ens.** —*tr.* **1. a.** To make light or lighter; illuminate; brighten. **b.** To make lighter (a color). **2.** *Archaic.* To enlighten mentally or spiritually, as by imparting knowledge or wisdom. —*intr.* **1.** To become light or lighter; brighten. **2.** To be luminous; glow; shine. **3.** To produce or give off flashes of lightning.

light·en² (līt'n) *v.* **-ened, -ening, -ens.** —*tr.* **1.** To make less heavy, as by a reduction in weight or load. **2.** To lessen the oppressiveness, trouble, or severity of. **3.** To relieve of cares or worries; gladden. —*intr.* **1.** To become lighter. **2.** To become less oppressive, severe, or troublesome. **3.** To become cheerful. —See Synonyms at **relieve.**

light·er¹ (līt'ər) *n.* **1.** One that ignites something. **2.** A mechanical device for lighting a cigarette, cigar, or pipe.

light·er² (līt'ər) *n.* *Nautical.* A large barge used to transport goods over short distances or to deliver to or unload from a larger cargo ship unable to navigate in shallow water. —*v.* **lightered, -ering, -ers.** —*tr.* To convey (cargo) in a lighter. —*intr.* To use a lighter for the transportation of cargo. [Middle English, from Middle Dutch *lichter* (unattested), from *lichten,* to lighten, unload. See **legwh-** in Appendix.*]

light·er³. **1.** Comparative of **light** (not dark). **2.** Comparative of **light** (not heavy).

light·er·age (līt'ər-ĭj) *n.* **1.** The transportation of goods on a lighter. **2.** The fee charged for such service.

light·er-than-air (līt'ər-thən-âr') *adj.* Having a weight less than that of the air displaced. Said of certain aircraft.

light·face (līt'fās') *n.* *Printing.* *Abbr.* **lf** A typeface or font of characters having relatively thin, light lines. —**light'faced'** *adj.*

light-fin·gered (līt'fĭng'gərd) *adj.* **1.** Having quick and nimble fingers. **2.** Skilled at petty thievery. —**light'-fin'gered·ness** *n.*

light-foot·ed (līt'fŏŏt'ĭd) *adj.* Also *Poetic* **light-foot** (-fŏŏt'). Treading with light and nimble ease. —**light'-foot'ed·ly** *adv.* —**light'-foot'ed·ness** *n.*

light-head·ed (līt'hĕd'ĭd) *adj.* **1.** Delirious, giddy, or faint: *lightheaded with wine.* **2.** Given to frivolity; fanciful; silly. —**light'head'ed·ly** *adv.* —**light'head'ed·ness** *n.*

light-heart·ed (līt'här'tĭd) *adj.* Blithe; carefree; gay. See Synonyms at **glad.** —**light'heart'ed·ly** *adv.* —**light'heart'ed·ness** *n.*

light heavyweight. *Boxing & Wrestling.* A fighter weighing between 161 and 175 pounds.

light·house (līt'hous') *n.* A tall structure topped by a powerful light used as a beacon or signal to aid marine navigation.

light·ing (līt'tĭng) *n.* **1.** The state of being lighted; illumination. **2. a.** The method or equipment used to provide artificial illumination. **b.** The illumination so provided. **3.** The act or process of igniting.

light·ly (līt'lē) *adv.* **1.** With little weight or force; gently. **2.** To a slight extent or amount; sparingly; little: *use lightly.* **3.** With buoyancy or ease; quickly and gracefully. **4.** In a carefree manner; cheerfully; blithely: *take the news lightly.* **5.** Without enough care or serious consideration; thoughtlessly; indifferently. **6.** Depreciatingly; slightingly.

light meter. *Photography.* An **exposure meter** *(see).*

light-mind·ed (līt'mīn'dĭd) *adj.* Frivolous, silly, or inanely giddy. —**light'-mind'ed·ly** *adv.* —**light'-mind'ed·ness** *n.*

light·ness¹ (līt'nĭs) *n.* **1.** The state or quality of having little weight or force. **2.** Ease or quickness of movement; agility; nimbleness; buoyancy. **3.** Freedom from worry or trouble; blitheness; gaiety. **4.** Lack of appropriate seriousness; levity.

light·ness² (līt'nĭs) *n.* The dimension of the color of an object by which the object appears to reflect or transmit more or less of the incident light, varying from black to white for surface colors, and from black to colorless for transparent volume colors. See **color.**

light·ning (līt'nĭng) *n.* **1.** A large-scale high-tension natural electric discharge in the atmosphere. **2.** The visible flash of light accompanying such a discharge. —*intr.v.* **lightninged** (-nĭngd), **-ning, -nings.** To discharge a flash or flashes of lightning. —*adj.* Moving with extreme alacrity; very fast or sudden, like a flash of lightning. [Middle English *light(e)ning,* from *light-enen,* to illuminate, from **LIGHT** (illumination).]

lightning arrester. A protective device for electrical equipment that reduces excessive voltage resulting from lightning to a safe level by grounding the discharge.

lightning bug. A firefly.

lightning rod. A grounded metal rod placed high on a structure to prevent damage by conducting lightning to ground.

light opera. An **operetta** *(see).* See Synonyms at **musical comedy.**

light ratio. The ratio of the brightness of a star to that of any other star one magnitude fainter, equal to approximately 2.512.

lights (līts) *pl.n.* The lungs, especially of an animal used for food. [Middle English *lihte,* from *liht,* **LIGHT** (not heavy).]

light·ship (līt'shĭp') *n.* A ship with a powerful light or warning signals anchored in dangerous waters to alert other vessels.

light·some¹ (līt'səm) *adj.* **1.** Providing light; illuminating; luminous. **2.** Covered with or full of light; bright. —**light'some·ly** *adv.* —**light'some·ness** *n.*

light·some² (līt'səm) *adj.* **1.** Light, nimble, or graceful in movement; buoyant. **2.** Carefree; blithe; cheerful. **3.** Frivolous; silly. —**light'some·ly** *adv.* —**light'some·ness** *n.*

light-struck (līt'strŭk') *adj.* Fogged by accidental exposure. Said of photosensitive materials.

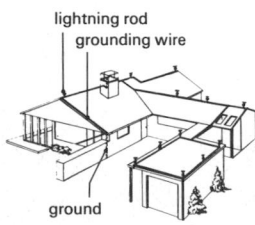

lightning rod
grounding wire

ground

lightning rod

light·weight (līt'wāt') *n.* **1.** A person, animal, or thing that weighs relatively little. **2.** *Boxing & Wrestling.* A fighter weighing between 127 and 135 pounds. **3.** A person of little ability, intelligence, influence, or importance. —*adj.* Weighing relatively little; not heavy: *lightweight wool.*

light·wood (līt'wŏŏd') *n.* Dry, easily ignited, often resinous wood, as of a pine, used for kindling or fuel.

light-year (līt'yîr') *n.* Also **light year.** The distance that light covers traveling in a vacuum for a period of one year, approximately 5.878 trillion (5.878 × 10¹²) miles.

lign aloes (līn). Also **lign-al·oes** (lī-năl'ōz, lĭg-). *Archaic.* The wood of a tree, *Aquilaria agallocha,* mentioned in the Old Testament. Numbers 24:6. [Middle English *ligne aloes,* from Late Latin *lignum aloēs,* "wood of the aloe" : Latin *lignum,* wood (see **ligneous**) + *aloēs,* genitive of *aloē,* **ALOE.**]

lig·ne·ous (lĭg'nē-əs) *adj.* Consisting of or having the texture or appearance of wood; woody. [Latin *ligneus,* from *lignum,* wood. See **leg-** in Appendix.*]

ligni-, ligno-, lign-. Indicates wood; for example, **lignocellulose, lignin.** [From Latin *lignum,* wood. See **leg-** in Appendix.*]

lig·ni·fy (lĭg'nə-fī') *v.* **-fied, -fying, -fies.** —*intr.* To form or turn into wood through the formation and deposit of lignin in cell walls. —*tr.* To make woody or woodlike by the deposit of lignin. [French *lignifier* : **LIGNI-** + **-FY.**] —**lig'ni·fi·ca'tion** *n.*

lig·nin (lĭg'nĭn) *n.* The chief noncarbohydrate constituent of wood, a polymer that functions as a natural binder and support for the cellulose fibers of woody plants. [**LIGN**(I)- + **-IN.**]

lig·nite (lĭg'nīt') *n.* A low-grade, brownish-black coal. Also called "brown coal." [French : **LIGN**(I)- + **-ITE.**] —**lig·nit'ic** (-nĭt'ĭk) *adj.*

lig·no·cel·lu·lose (lĭg'nō-sĕl'yə-lōs') *n.* Any combination of lignin and cellulose that strengthens woody cells. [*Ligno-,* variant of **LIGNI-** + **CELLULOSE.**]

lig·num vi·tae (lĭg'nəm vī'tē) *pl.* **lignum vitaes.** Also **lig·num-vi·tae, lig·num·vi·tae.** **1.** Either of two tropical American trees, *Guaiacum officinale* or *G. sanctum,* having evergreen leaves and heavy, durable, resinous wood. **2.** The wood of either of these trees, used for bearing surfaces. **3.** Any of several similar or related trees. [New Latin, from Late Latin, "tree or wood of life" : *lignum,* wood (see **ligni-**) + *vītae,* genitive of *vīta,* life (see **gwei-** in Appendix*).]

lig·ro·in (lĭg'rō-ĭn) *n.* A volatile, flammable fraction of petroleum, obtained by distillation, and used as a solvent. Also called "benzine." [Origin unknown.]

lig·u·la (lĭg'yə-lə) *n., pl.* **-lae** (-lē') or **-las.** A strap-shaped structure, especially a mouth part in certain insects. [New Latin, **LIGULE.**]

lig·u·late (lĭg'yə-lĭt, -lāt') *adj.* **1.** Strap-shaped. **2.** Having a ligule. [New Latin *ligula,* **LIGULE** + **-ATE.**]

lig·ule (lĭg'yŏōl) *n.* A straplike structure, such as a ray flower of a daisy, or a sheathlike organ at the base of a grass leaf. [New Latin *ligula,* from Latin, tongue of a shoe, shoe-strap, variant of *lingula,* from *lingua,* tongue. See **dnghū** in Appendix.*]

lig·ure (lĭg'yŏŏr') *n.* A precious stone of ancient Israel. Exodus 28:19. [Middle English *lugre, ligurie,* from Late Latin *ligūrius,* from Greek *ligurion†,* a precious stone.]

Li·gu·ri·a (lĭ-gyŏŏr'ē-ə). A region of Italy, occupying 2,090 square miles along the northwestern coast. Population, 1,708,000. Capital, Genoa.

Li·gu·ri·an (lĭ-gyŏŏr'ē-ən) *adj.* Of or relating to Liguria, its people, or its language. —*n.* **1.** A native of Liguria. **2.** The Italian dialect spoken by these people.

Ligurian Sea. The Mediterranean between Liguria and Corsica.

lik·a·ble (lī'kə-bəl) *adj.* Also **like·a·ble.** Pleasing; attractive. —**lik'a·ble·ness, like'a·ble·ness** *n.*

like¹ (līk) *v.* **liked, liking, likes.** —*tr.* **1.** To find pleasant; enjoy. **2.** To want, wish, or prefer. **3.** To feel toward or respond to; to view; to regard: *How do you like that!* **4.** To feel an attraction, tenderness, or affection for; be fond of. —*intr.* **1.** To have an inclination or preference; to desire; choose; to wish: *If you like, we can meet you there.* **2.** *Obsolete.* To agree with; suit or please. Used with the dative: *This likes me not.* —See Usage note below. —*n. Plural.* Preferences or predilections. Used in the phrase *likes and dislikes.* [Middle English *lik(i)en,* Old English *līcian,* to please, be sufficient. See **līk-** in Appendix.*] —**lik'er** *n.*

Synonyms: like, love, enjoy, relish, fancy, dote. These verbs mean to be attracted to or to take pleasure in. *Like,* the least forceful, usually suggests only mild interest or regard. *Love,* in careful use, implies much stronger attachment or affection and deeper involvement on an emotional or, less often, intellectual level. *Enjoy* is applied to what gives personal satisfaction or fulfillment; *relish,* to what moves one to keen or zestful appreciation and thus brings great personal gratification; and *fancy,* to what appeals to one's taste, inclination, caprice, or notion of what a person or thing should be. *Dote* implies infatuation, or foolish and extravagant attachment.

Usage: Like (verb) is frequently followed by an infinitive preceded by a noun or pronoun: *He would like you to run an errand* (not *like for you to run*). In conditional sentences, *would have liked* and *should have liked* are usually followed by the present infinitive, not by the perfect infinitive: *They would have liked to come* (not *to have come*).

like² (līk) *prep.* **1.** Possessing the characteristics of; resembling closely; similar to. **2.** In the typical manner of: *It's not like you to take offense.* **3.** Desirous of; disposed to: *He felt like running away.* **4.** As if the probability exists for; indicative of: *It looks like a bad season for the Yankees.* —*adj.* **1.** Possessing the same

ă pat/ā pay/âr care/ä father/b bib/ch church/d deed/ĕ pet/ē be/f fife/g gag/h hat/hw which/ĭ pit/ī pie/îr pier/j judge/k kick/l lid/needle/m mum/n no, sudden/ng thing/ŏ pot/ō toe/ô paw, for/oi noise/ou out/ŏŏ took/ōō boot/p pop/r roar/s sauce/sh ship, dish/

or almost the same characteristics; similar: *on this and like occasions.* **2.** Equivalent; equal. **3.** *Rare.* Alike: *They are as like as two brothers.* **—like** (one), **like** (another). The characteristics of (one) are also those of (the other): *Like mother, like daughter.* —*adv.* **1.** *Informal.* In the manner of being; as if: *He ran like crazy.* **2.** *Informal.* Probably; likely: *Like as not she'll change her mind.* **3.** *Nonstandard.* Used as an expletive to provide an emphasis or pause: *He was like over the hill before he saw the other car. The accident was like horrible.* —*n.* **1.** Similar or related persons or things. Used with *the: He was subject to fevers, coughs, asthma, and the like.* **2.** *Often plural. Informal.* An equivalent or similar person or thing; an equal or match: *I've never seen the likes of this before.* —*conj. Nonstandard.* **1.** In the same way that; as: *Tell it like it is.* **2.** As if: *It rained like the skies were falling.* —See Usage note below. [Middle English *lic, lik,* Old English *līc* (unattested), short for *gelīc.* See **līk-** in Appendix.*]

Usage: *Like,* as a conjunction, is not appropriate to formal usage, especially written usage, except in certain constructions noted below. On other levels it occurs frequently, especially in casual speech and in writing representing speech. In formal usage the conjunctive *like* is most acceptable when it introduces an elliptical clause in which a verb is not expressed: *He took to politics like a fish to water. The dress looked like new.* Both examples, which are acceptable on a formal level to 76 per cent of the Usage Panel, employ such elliptical, or shortened, expressions following *like.* If they were recast to include full clauses containing verbs, *like* would preferably be replaced, in formal usage, by *as, as if,* or *as though: took to politics as a fish takes to water; dress looked as if it were new.* The examples that follow illustrate the difference. All employ *like* to introduce full clauses containing verbs; all are termed unacceptable by more than 75 per cent of the Usage Panel, and in every case a more desirable construction is indicated: *He manipulates an audience like* (preferably *as*) *a virtuoso commands a musical instrument. The engine responds now like* (preferably *as*) *good machinery should. It looks like* (preferably *as if*) *they will be finished earlier than usual. He had no authority, but he always acted like* (preferably *as if*) *he did.* The restriction on *like* as a conjunction does not affect its other uses. Fear of misusing *like* often causes writers to use *as* in its place in constructions where *like* is not only acceptable but clearly called for. It is always used acceptably when it functions prepositionally, followed by a noun or pronoun as object: *works like a charm; sings like an angel; looking for a girl like me* (not *I*); *spoke like one who had authority* (but not *like he had authority*). Used prepositionally, *like* indicates comparison; in modern usage *as,* in place of *like,* would imply the assumption of another role: *He behaved like* (not *as*) *a child. She treated him like* (not *as*) *a fool. John, like* (not *as*) *his grandfather earlier, chose to ignore politics.*

like³ (līk) *v.* Also **liked** (līkt). *Nonstandard.* Used as a verbal auxiliary with a perfect infinitive to indicate doing or undergoing something: *I like* (or *liked* or *had liked*) *to have killed him when he said that.* [From LIKE (adjective).]

Usage: Use of *like* as a verbal auxiliary disappeared from standard English during the late 18th century, but is still widely heard in some dialects. It is now considered nonstandard in formal usage.

-like. Indicates: **1.** A resemblance or similarity to something specified; for example, **lifelike. 2.** A characteristic of or appropriateness to something specified; for example, **childlike, ladylike.** [From LIKE (preposition).]

like·li·hood (līk′lē-ho͝od′) *n.* **1.** The state of being likely or probable; probability. **2.** Something that is probable.

like·ly (līk′lē) *adj.* **-lier, -liest. 1.** Having, expressing, or exhibiting an inclination or probability; apt. Used with an infinitive: *They are likely to become angry with him.* **2.** Logically or expectedly about to occur; imminent. **3.** Within the realm of credibility; seeming to be true; plausible: *a likely excuse.* **4.** Apparently appropriate; suitable: *a likely place.* **5.** Apparently capable of doing well or becoming successful; promising: *a likely lad.* See Usage note at **apt. 6.** Attractive; pleasant; enjoyable. —*adv.* Probably. [Middle English *likely,* from Old Norse *līkligr,* from *līkr,* like. See **līk-** in Appendix.*]

Usage: *Likely,* as an adverb, is preferably preceded by a qualifying word such as *quite, very,* or *most: He will very likely arrive on Friday. The new government quite likely will be more receptive to change.* Without qualifiers, the preceding examples are both unacceptable to more than 70 per cent of the Usage Panel. No qualifier is needed when *likely* is used as an adjective: *She called it a likely story.*

like-mind·ed (līk′mīn′dĭd) *adj.* Of the same turn of mind.

lik·en (lī′kən) *tr.v.* **-ened, -ening, -ens.** To see, mention, or show as like or similar; compare. [Middle English *lik(n)en,* from *lik,* LIKE (adjective).]

like·ness (līk′nĭs) *n.* **1.** The state or quality of resembling or being like something. **2.** An imitative appearance; a semblance or guise. **3.** A pictorial, graphic, or sculptured representation of something; an image.

Synonyms: *likeness, similarity, similitude, resemblance, analogy, affinity.* These nouns are applied to the relationship between persons or things that are in agreement or conformity in some respect. *Likeness* can refer to any degree of correspondence, but in the absence of a qualifying term usually implies close agreement. *Similarity* and *similitude* suggest agreement in certain details, but not close overall correspondence. *Resemblance* refers to correspondence in appearance or in some other external, or surface, detail. *Analogy* is correspondence between unlike things that are otherwise not comparable. The correspondence consists not in the fundamental nature or appearance of the things involved but in the similarity of certain of their properties or functions: *the analogy between the working of the human heart and the distribution of goods and services under an economic system. Affinity* is correspondence based on kinship or on the possession of properties, characteristics, or sympathies that cause persons or things to be compatible or to have attraction for one another.

like·wise (līk′wīz′) *adv.* **1.** In the same way; similarly: *"Some have little power to do good, and have likewise little strength to resist evil."* (Samuel Johnson). **2.** As well; also; too. —See Synonyms at **also.**

Usage: *Likewise,* not being a conjunction, cannot take the place of connectives such as *and* and *together with: The applicant's poor record and his evasiveness led to his rejection* (but not *poor record, likewise his evasiveness, led to his rejection*).

lik·ing (lī′kĭng) *n.* **1.** The state or act of someone who likes. **2.** A feeling of attraction, tenderness, or love; fondness; affection. **3.** Preference; inclination; taste.

li·ku·ta (lē-ko͞o′tä) *n., pl.* **makuta** (mä-ko͞o′tä). A coin equal to 1/100 of the zaire of the Democratic Republic of the Congo (Kinshasa). See table of exchange rates at **currency.** [Native word in the Congo.]

li·lac (lī′lək, -lŏk′) *n.* **1.** Any of various shrubs of the genus *Syringa;* especially, *S. vulgaris,* widely cultivated for its clusters of fragrant purplish or white flowers. **2.** Pale to light or moderate purple. See **color.** [Obsolete French, from Spanish, from Arabic *līlak,* from Persian, variant of *nīlak,* from *nīl,* indigo, blue. See **nei-¹** in Appendix.*] —**li′lac** *adj.*

Li·li·en·thal (lē′lē-ən-täl′), **Otto.** 1848–1896. German inventor and pilot of gliders.

Lil·ith (lĭl′ĭth). **1.** In ancient Semitic legend, an evil female spirit or demon alleged to haunt lonely, deserted places and attack children. **2.** In Hebrew folklore, the first wife of Adam, believed to have been in existence before the creation of Eve. [Hebrew *līlīth.*]

Li·li·u·o·ka·la·ni (lē-lē′o͞o-ō-kä-lä′nē), **Lydia Kamekeha.** 1838–1917. Queen of Hawaiian Islands (1891–93); deposed.

Lille (lēl). A city of France, a major textile-producing center in the north near the Belgian border. Population, 196,000.

Lil·li·an (lĭl′ē-ən). A feminine given name. [Perhaps a pet form of ELIZABETH.]

Lil·li·pu·tian (lĭl′ə-pyo͞o′shən) *n.* **1.** One of the tiny inhabitants of an island in Jonathan Swift's *Gulliver's Travels.* **2.** *Often small* **l.** A very small person or being. **3.** *Often small* **l.** A person of little intelligence, worth, or significance. —*adj. Often small* **l. 1.** Very small; diminutive. **2.** Trivial; petty.

Li·long·we (lē-lông′wā′). The designated capital of Malawi, to replace Zomba.

lilt (lĭlt) *n.* **1.** A light, happy tune or song. **2.** A cheerful or lively manner of speaking, in which the pitch of the voice varies pleasantly. **3.** A light or resilient manner of moving or walking. —*v.* **lilted, lilting, lilts.** —*tr.* To say, sing, or play in a cheerful, rhythmic manner. —*intr.* **1.** To speak, sing, or play with liveliness or rhythm. **2.** To move with lightness and buoyancy. [Middle English *lulten†,* to sound, sing.]

lil·y (lĭl′ē) *n., pl.* **-ies. 1.** Any of various plants of the genus *Lilium,* having showy, variously colored, often trumpet-shaped flowers. **2.** Any of various similar or related plants, such as the day lily or the water lily. **3.** The flower of such a plant. —*adj.* Like a lily in beauty, purity, or whiteness. [Middle English *lilie,* Old English *lilie,* from Latin *līlium,* akin to Greek *leirion,* probably of Mediterranean origin.]

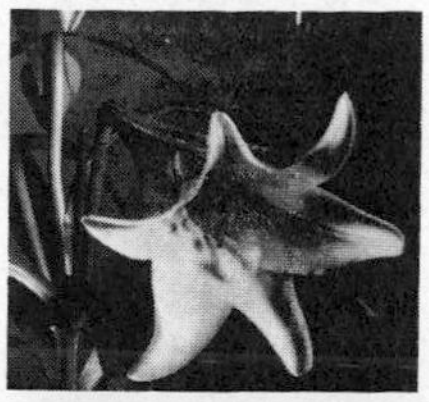

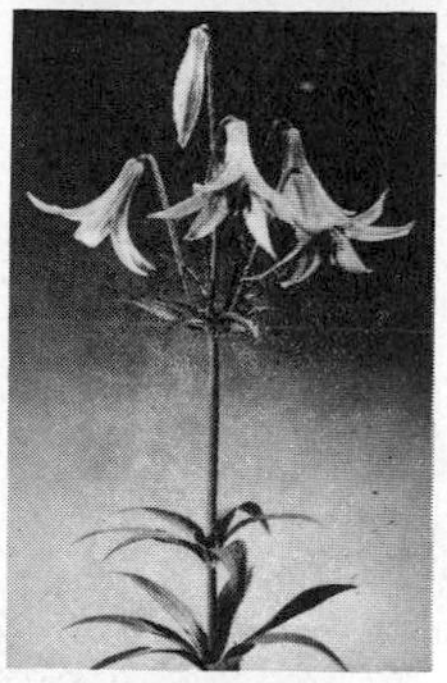

lily
Above: Lilium candidum
Madonna lily
Below: Lilium canadense
Meadow lily

lily iron. A harpoon with a barbed head that may be detached. [From its shape.]

lily leek. A plant, *Allium moly,* of southern Europe, having a cluster of yellow flowers. Sometimes called "moly."

lil·y-liv·ered (lĭl′ē-lĭv′ərd) *adj.* Cowardly; timid.

lily of the valley *pl.* **lilies of the valley.** A widely cultivated plant, *Convallaria majalis,* having a cluster of fragrant, bell-shaped white flowers.

lily pad. One of the broad, floating leaves of a water lily.

lil·y-trot·ter (lĭl′ē-trŏt′ər) *n.* A bird, the **jacana** *(see).*

lil·y-white (lĭl′ē-hwīt′) *adj.* **1.** White as a lily. **2.** Beyond reproach; blameless; pure. **3.** *Informal.* **a.** Designating or describing political groups or social organizations that discriminate against Negroes. **b.** Racially segregated.

LIM Airport code for Lima, Peru.

lim. limit.

Li·ma (lē′mə). **1.** The capital and largest city of Peru, in the west-central part of the country, eight miles inland from the Pacific. Population, 1,716,000. **2.** A city of Ohio, an industrial center in the northwest. Population, 51,000.

li·ma bean (lī′mə). **1.** Any of several varieties of a tropical American plant, *Phaseolus limensis,* having flat pods containing large, light-green, edible seeds. **2.** The seed of such a plant. Sometimes called "butter bean." [From LIMA, Peru.]

lim·a·cine (lĭm′ə-sēn′, lī′mə-) *adj.* Of, pertaining to, or resembling a slug. [New Latin *limacinus* : Latin *līmax* (stem *līmac-*), slug, snail, from *līmus,* slime (see **lei-** in Appendix*) + -INE.]

Li·mas·sol (lĭm′ə-sôl′). A city of Cyprus, a seaport on the southern coast. Population, 47,000.

Li·may (lī-mī′). A river of Argentina, rising in Lake Nahuel Huapí near the Chilean border and flowing 250 miles northeast to the Neuquén with which it forms the Río Negro.

limb¹ (lĭm) *n.* **1.** One of the larger branches of a tree. **2.** One of the jointed appendages of an animal, used for locomotion or grasping, as an arm, leg, wing, or flipper. **3.** Any extension or projecting part. **4.** One that is considered to be an extension,

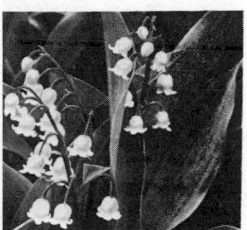

lily of the valley

member, or representative of a larger body, group, or the like. **5.** *Informal.* An impish or naughty child. **—out on a limb.** *Informal.* In a difficult, awkward, or vulnerable position. *—tr.v.* **limbed, limbing, limbs.** To dismember. [Middle English *lim, lymm,* Old English *lim,* akin to Old Norse *limr*†.]

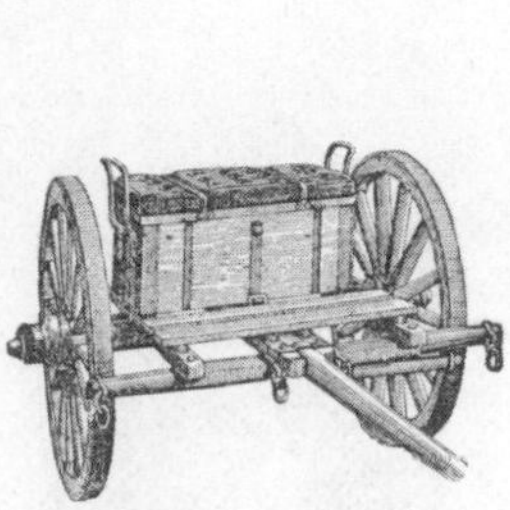
limber[2]

limb² (lĭm) *n.* **1.** *Astronomy.* The circumferential edge of the apparent disk of a celestial body. **2.** The edge of a graduated arc or circle used in an instrument to measure angles. **3.** *Botany.* The expanded tip of a petal or the expanded upper part of a united corolla. [French *limbe,* from Latin *limbus,* border, hem, seam. See **limbus.**]

lim·bate (lĭm′bāt′) *adj. Botany.* Having an edge or margin of a different color. [Late Latin *limbātus,* bordered, from *limbus,* border. See **limbus.**]

lim·ber¹ (lĭm′bər) *adj.* **1.** Bending or flexing readily; pliable. **2.** Capable of moving, bending, or contorting easily; agile; supple. *—v.* **limbered, -bering, -bers.** *—tr.* To make limber. Often used with *up.* *—intr.* To make oneself limber. Used with *up: The football players limbered up before the game.* [Origin uncertain.] **—lim′ber·ly** *adv.* **—lim′ber·ness** *n.*

lim·ber² (lĭm′bər) *n.* A two-wheeled horse-drawn vehicle that carries ammunition and behind which a field gun may be towed. *—v.* **limbered, -bering, -bers.** *—tr.* To fasten a limber to (a gun). Often used with *up.* *—intr.* To fasten a limber and a gun together. Often used with *up.* [Middle English *lymo(u)r,* shaft of a carriage, possibly from Medieval Latin *limōnārius,* of a shaft, from *limō,* shaft, perhaps from Celtic.]

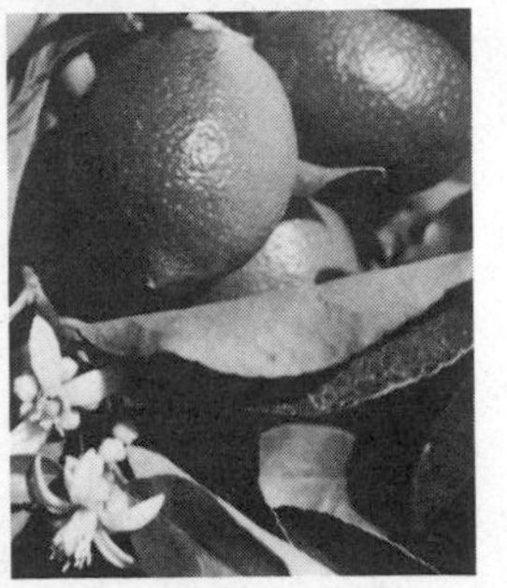
lime[1]

lim·bo (lĭm′bō) *n., pl.* **-bos.** **1.** *Often capital* **L.** *Theology.* The abode of souls kept from Heaven through circumstance, such as lack of baptism. **2.** A region or condition of oblivion or neglect. **3.** A state or place of confinement. **4.** An intermediate place or state. [Middle English, from Medieval Latin *in limbō,* "(region) on the border (of hell)," : *in,* on + *limbus,* border (see **limbus**).]

Lim·burg (lĭm′bûrg′). **1.** Also **Lim·bourg** (-bo͝org′). A province occupying 930 square miles in eastern Belgium. Population, 615,000. Capital, Hasselt. **2.** A province of the Netherlands, occupying 840 square miles in the southeast. Population, 954,000.

Lim·burg·er cheese (lĭm′bûr′gər). A soft white cheese with a very strong odor and flavor, originally produced in Limburg, Belgium. Also called "Limburger."

lim·bus (lĭm′bəs) *n., pl.* **-bi** (-bī′). *Biology.* A distinctive border or edge. [Latin *limbus*†, border, hem, seam.]

lime¹ (līm) *n.* **1.** A spiny tree, *Citrus aurantifolia,* native to Asia, having evergreen leaves, fragrant white flowers, and edible, egg-shaped fruit with a green rind and acid juice used as flavoring. **2.** The fruit of this tree. [French *lime,* from Provençal *limo,* from Arabic *līmah.*]

lime² (līm) *n.* Any of several Old World linden trees. [Variant of *line,* dialectal variant of obsolete *lind,* LINDEN.]

lime³ (līm) *n.* **1. a.** *Chemistry.* **Calcium oxide** *(see).* **b.** Any of various mineral and industrial forms of calcium oxide differing chiefly in water content and percentage of such constituents as silica, alumina, and iron. **2.** A sticky substance smeared on twigs and used to catch small birds; birdlime. *—tr.v.* **limed, liming, limes.** **1.** To treat with lime. **2.** To smear with birdlime. **3.** To catch or snare with or as with birdlime. [Middle English *lim,* Old English *līm.* See **lei-** in Appendix.*]

lime·ade (līm′ād′) *n.* A sweetened beverage of lime juice and plain or carbonated water.

lime·kiln (līm′kĭl′, -kĭln′) *n.* A furnace used to reduce naturally occurring forms of calcium carbonate to lime.

lime·light (līm′līt′) *n.* **1.** A stage light in which lime is heated to incandescence producing brilliant illumination. **2.** The brilliant light so produced. Also called "calcium light." **3.** A focus of public attention or notoriety. Preceded by *the.*

li·men (lī′mən) *n., pl.* **-mens** or **limina** (lĭm′ə-nə). The threshold of a physiological or psychological response. [From Latin *līmen,* threshold, akin to *līmes,* boundary, LIMIT.] **—lim′i·nal** (lĭm′ə-nəl) *adj.*

lim·er·ick (lĭm′ər-ĭk) *n.* A light humorous or nonsensical verse of five anapestic lines usually with the rhyme scheme *aabba.* [From the line "Will you come up to Limerick?" (the refrain of a convivial verse in a similar form).]

Lim·er·ick (lĭm′ər-ĭk). A county of the Republic of Ireland, occupying 1,037 square miles in the southwest. Population, 133,000.

li·mes (lī′mēz′) *n., pl.* **limites** (lĭm′ə-tēz′). A fortified boundary, as of the Roman Empire. [Latin *līmes,* boundary, LIMIT.]

lime·stone (līm′stōn′) *n.* A shaly or sandy sedimentary rock, chiefly $CaCO_3$, containing variable quantities of magnesium carbonate and quartz, used as a building stone, and in the manufacture of lime, carbon dioxide, and cement.

lime-twig (līm′twĭg′) *n.* **1.** A twig covered with birdlime to catch birds. **2.** A snare.

lime·wa·ter (līm′wô′tər, -wŏt′ər) *n.* A clear colorless alkaline aqueous solution of calcium hydroxide, used in calamine lotion and other skin preparations and sometimes as an antacid.

lim·ey (lī′mē) *n., pl.* **-eys.** *Slang.* **1.** A British seaman. **2.** An Englishman.

li·mic·o·line (lī-mĭk′ə-līn′, -lĭn) *adj.* Of or pertaining to shore birds, such as sandpipers, of the suborder Charadrii. [From New Latin *Limicolae* (former order name), "mud dwellers" : Latin *līmus,* slime, mud (see **lei-** in Appendix*) + *-colae,* from *-colus,* -COLOUS.]

lim·it (lĭm′ĭt) *n. Abbr.* **lim.** **1.** The point, edge, or line beyond which something cannot or may not proceed; the final or furthest confines, bounds, or restriction of something. **2.** *Usually plural.* The boundary surrounding a specific area; bounds: *within the city limits.* **3.** The greatest amount or number allowed. **4.** In games of chance, the largest amount which may be bet at one time. **5.** *Obsolete.* A region or section enclosed within or as if within boundaries. **6.** *Mathematics.* A number k that is approached by a function $f(x)$ as x approaches a if, for every positive number ϵ, there exists a number δ such that $|f(x)-k|<\epsilon$ if $0<|x-a|<\delta$. —See Synonyms at **boundary.** **—off limits.** Prohibited, especially to military personnel not on official business. **—the limit.** *Informal.* One that approaches or exceeds certain limits, as of credibility, forbearance, or acceptability. *—tr.v.* **limited, -iting, -its.** To confine or restrict within a limit or limits. [Middle English *limite,* from Latin *līmes*† (stem *līmit-*), borderline between fields, boundary.] **—lim′it·a·ble** *adj.* **—lim′i·ta′tive** *adj.* **—lim′it·er** *n.*

Synonyms: *limit, restrict, confine, circumscribe, bound.* These verbs mean to keep or contain within a specified area. *Limit* refers principally to establishing a maximum, as in quantity, degree, space, or time, beyond which a person or thing cannot or may not go. It is sometimes interchangeable with *restrict* and *confine,* but *restrict* and *confine* more often refer to keeping persons, things, or activities within a prescribed area: *messages limited to 50 words; a sale limited* (or *confined*) *to two days; a soldier restricted* (or *confined*) *to his quarters; wiretapping restricted* (or *confined*) *to cases involving national security. Circumscribe* is applied to encircling in a literal sense or, more often, to keeping something intangible, such as power, law, or influence, within specified and often narrow limits. *Bound* refers largely to setting geographical limits.

lim·i·tar·y (lĭm′ə-tĕr′ē) *adj. Archaic.* **1. a.** Of or relating to a limit or boundary. **b.** Limiting; restrictive. **2.** Limited.

lim·i·ta·tion (lĭm′ə-tā′shən) *n.* **1.** The act of limiting or the state of being limited. **2.** A restriction. **3.** *Law.* A limited period during which, by statute, an action may be brought.

lim·it·ed (lĭm′ə-tĭd) *adj. Abbr.* **Ld., Ltd., ltd.** **1. a.** Having a limit or limits. **b.** Confined or restricted. **2.** Not attaining the highest goals or achievement: *a limited success.* **3.** Having governmental or ruling powers restricted by enforceable limitations, as a constitution or legislative body. **4.** *Chiefly British.* Limiting the liability of each stockholder or partner in a business to his actual investment: *a limited company.* **5.** Designating transportation facilities, such as trains or buses that make few stops and carry relatively few passengers. *—n. Abbr.* **Ltd., ltd., Ld.** A limited train or bus. **—lim′i·ted·ly** *adv.* **—lim′i·ted·ness** *n.*

limited edition. An edition, as of a book or set of books, limited to a specified number of copies.

limited monarchy. A **constitutional monarchy** *(see).*

li·mites. Plural of **limes.**

lim·it·less (lĭm′ĭt-lĭs) *adj.* **1.** Having no limit or limits. **2.** Unconfined or unrestricted. —See Synonyms at **infinite.**

limn (lĭm) *tr.v.* **limned, limning, limns.** **1.** *Archaic.* To describe. **2.** *Archaic.* To depict by painting or drawing. **3.** *Obsolete.* To illuminate with paintings or drawing. [Middle English *limnen,* to illuminate (manuscript), shortened from *luminen,* from Old French *luminer,* from Latin *lūmināre,* from *lūmen,* light. See **leuk-** in Appendix.*] **—lim′ner** (lĭm′nər) *n.*

lim·net·ic (lĭm-nĕt′ĭk) *adj.* Of or occurring in the deeper, open waters of lakes or ponds. [From Greek *limnē*†, pool, lake.]

lim·nol·o·gy (lĭm-nŏl′ə-jē) *n.* The scientific study of the life and phenomena of lakes, ponds, and streams. [Greek *limnē,* pool, lake (see **limnetic**) + -LOGY.] **—lim′no·log′i·cal** (-nə-lŏj′ĭ-kəl) *adj.* **—lim′no·log′i·cal·ly** *adv.* **—lim·nol′o·gist** *n.*

Lim·nos. See **Lemnos.**

Li·moges¹ (lĭ-mōzh′; *French* lē-môzh′) *n.* A variety of fine porcelain made at Limoges. Also called "Limoges ware."

Li·moges² (lĭ-mōzh′; *French* lē-môzh′). An industrial city of west-central France. Population, 118,000.

lim·o·nene (lĭm′ə-nēn′) *n.* A liquid, $C_{10}H_{16}$, with a characteristic lemonlike fragrance, used as a solvent, wetting agent, and dispersing agent, and in the manufacture of resins. [French *limon,* lime, from Old French, LEMON + -ENE.]

li·mo·nite (lī′mə-nīt′) *n.* A widely occurring yellowish-brown to black natural iron oxide, essentially $FeO(OH)\cdot nH_2O$, used as an ore of iron. [German *Limonit,* "meadow ore," bog iron ore : Greek *leimōn*†, meadow + -ITE.] **—li′mo·nit′ic** (-nĭt′ĭk) *adj.*

Li·mou·sin (lē-mo͞o-zăN′). A region and former province of west-central France.

lim·ou·sine (lĭm′ə-zēn′, lĭm′ə-zēn′) *n.* Any of various large passenger vehicles; especially, an automobile with an enclosed passenger compartment and an open but roofed driver's seat. [Originally a kind of flowing mantle or coat, popularized in LIMOUSIN.]

limp (lĭmp) *intr.v.* **limped, limping, limps.** **1.** To walk lamely, especially with irregularity, as if favoring one leg. **2.** To move or proceed haltingly or unsteadily. *—n.* An irregular, jerky, or awkward gait. *—adj.* **limper, limpest.** **1.** Lacking or having lost rigidity; flaccid; flabby. **2.** Lacking strength or firmness of character; weak. **—limp′ly** *adv.* **—limp′ness** *n.* [Probably shortened from obsolete *limphalt,* lame, ultimately from Old English *lemphealt,* *læmpihalt.* See **leb-¹** in Appendix.*]

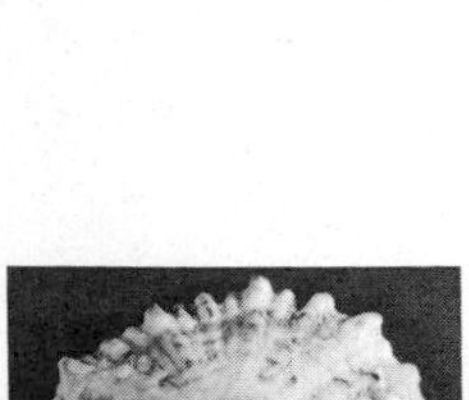

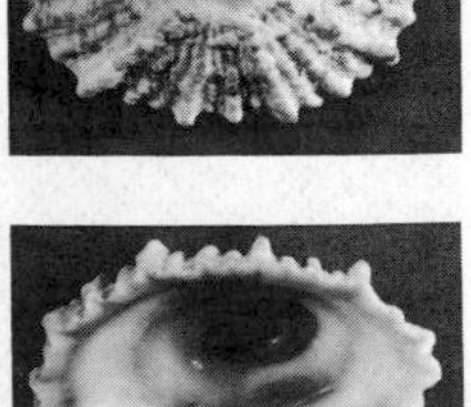
limpet
Fissurella barbadoensis

lim·pet (lĭm′pĭt) *n.* **1.** Any of numerous marine gastropod mollusks, as of the families Acmaeidae and Patellidae, characteristically having a tent-shaped shell and adhering to rocks of tidal areas. **2.** One who clings persistently. **3.** A type of explosive designed to cling to the hull of a ship and detonate on contact or signal. [Middle English *lempet,* Old English *lempedu,* from Medieval Latin *lamprēda,* LAMPREY.]

lim·pid (lĭm′pĭd) *adj.* **1.** Characterized by transparent clearness; pellucid. **2.** Easily intelligible; clear. **3.** Calm and untroubled;

ă pat/ā pay/âr care/ä father/b bib/ch church/d deed/ĕ pet/ē be/f fife/g gag/h hat/hw which/ĭ pit/ī pie/îr pier/j judge/k kick/l lid, needle/m mum/n no, sudden/ng thing/ŏ pot/ō toe/ô paw, for/oi noise/ou out/o͝o took/o͞o boot/p pop/r roar/s sauce/sh ship, dish/

serene: *"the early mornings and evenings were limpid and restful"* (Isak Dinesen). [French *limpide,* from Latin *limpidus*†.] —**lim·pid′i·ty, lim′pid·ness** *n.* —**lim′pid·ly** *adv.*

limp·kin (lĭmp′kĭn) *n.* A brownish wading bird, *Aramus guarauna,* of warm, swampy regions of the New World, having a distinctive, wailing call. Also called "courlan."

Lim·po·po (lĭm-pō′pō). A river of southeastern Africa, rising near Johannesburg, South Africa, and flowing about 1,000 miles in a wide northeast-southeast arc to the Indian Ocean. Also called "Crocodile."

lim·y (lī′mē) *adj.* **-ier, -iest.** Of, resembling, or containing lime.

lin. 1. lineal. 2. linear.

lin·age (lī′nĭj) *n.* Also **line·age.** 1. The number of lines of printed or written material. 2. Payment for written work according to the number of such lines.

lin·al·o·ol (lĭ-năl′ō-ôl′, -ōl′) *n.* Also **lin·al·ol** (lĭn′ə-lôl′, -lōl′). A colorless, fragrant liquid, $C_{10}H_{18}O$, distilled from the oils of rosewood, bergamot, and other plants and trees, and used in perfume manufacture. [Earlier *linaloe,* the fragrant wood of a Mexican tree, from Mexican Spanish *lináloe,* from Spanish, from Late Latin *lignum aloēs,* "wood of the aloe" : Latin *lignum,* wood (see **ligni-**) + *aloē,* ALOE.]

linch·pin (lĭnch′pĭn′) *n.* 1. A locking pin inserted in the end of a shaft, as in an axle to prevent a wheel from slipping off. 2. A central or cohesive element: *" 'The Dead' is a linchpin in Joyce's work."* (Richard Ellmann). [Middle English *lynspin* : *lins,* linchpin, Old English *lynis,* akin to Old Saxon *lunisa*† + PIN.]

Lin·coln (lĭng′kən). 1. Also **Lin·coln·shire** (-shîr, -shər). *Abbr.* **Lincs.** A county occupying 2,663 square miles in east-central England. Population, 744,000. 2. The county seat of this county. Population, 77,000. 3. The capital of Nebraska, in the southeastern part of the state. Population, 129,000.

Lin·coln (lĭng′kən), **Abraham.** 1809–1865. Sixteenth President of the United States (1861–65); assassinated.

Lin·coln, Mount (lĭng′kən). The highest elevation (14,284 feet) of the Park Range in central Colorado.

Lin·coln·esque (lĭng′kə-nĕsk′) *adj.* Suggestive of Abraham Lincoln, his life, or his character.

Lincoln's Inn. One of the four **Inns of Court** *(see).*

Lind (lĭnd), **Jenny.** In full, Johanna Maria Lind-Goldschmidt. 1820–1887. Swedish-born British coloratura soprano.

Lind·bergh (lĭnd′bûrg′, lĭn′-), **Charles Augustus.** Born 1902. American aviator; first to make solo nonstop transatlantic flight (1927).

lin·den (lĭn′dən) *n.* Any of various trees of the genus *Tilia,* having heart-shaped leaves and yellowish, often fragrant flowers, and often planted for shade. See **basswood.** [Perhaps from Middle English *linden,* made of linden wood, Old English *linden,* from *linde,* the linden. See **lento-** in Appendix.*]

Lind·say (lĭnd′zē, lĭn′-), **John V(liet).** Born 1921. American political leader; mayor of New York City (from 1966).

Lind·say (lĭn′zē), **(Nicholas) Vachel.** 1879–1931. American poet.

line[1] (līn) *n. Abbr.* **l.** 1. *Geometry.* a. The locus of a point having one degree of freedom; a curve. b. A set of points (x, y) that satisfy the linear equation $ax + by + c = 0$, where a and b are not both zero. 2. A thin, continuous mark, as that made by a pen, pencil, or brush applied to a surface. 3. A similar mark cut or scratched into a surface. 4. An indentation or crease in the skin, especially on the face or palm; a wrinkle. 5. *Sports.* a. A mark on a playing court or field indicating a boundary of play. b. A mark or imaginary point at which a race starts or ends. 6. A border or limit: *the county line.* 7. Any demarcation. 8. A contour or outline. 9. *Art.* a. A mark used to define a shape or represent a contour. b. Any of the marks that make up the formal design of a picture. 10. A cable, rope, string, cord, or wire, as one used aboard a ship or for catching fish. 11. A pipe or system of pipes for distribution or drainage, as of water. 12. An electric-power transmission cable. 13. An open or functioning telephone connection. 14. a. A passenger or cargo system of transportation, usually over a definite route. b. A company owning or managing such a system. 15. A railway track or system of tracks. 16. A course of progress or movement: *the line of flight.* 17. A general method, manner, or course of procedure: *different lines of thought.* 18. An official or prescribed policy: *the party line.* 19. Alignment; agreement: *brought the front wheels into line.* 20. a. One's trade or occupation. b. The range of one's competence or preferred activity: *out of my line.* 21. Merchandise of a similar or related nature: *This store carries a line of small tools.* 22. A group of persons or things arranged in a row or series, especially abreast. 23. A series of persons who succeed each other chronologically: *a line of rulers.* 24. a. A row of words printed or written across a page or a column. b. A unit of verse made up of such a row, or formed of a certain number of metrical feet characteristic of the verse. 25. A brief letter; a note. 26. *Often plural.* The dialogue of a play or other theatrical presentation: *learning his lines.* 27. A calculated or glib way of speaking, usually to obtain some undeclared end. 28. *Plural. British Informal.* A marriage certificate. 29. *Advertising.* An **agate line** *(see).* 30. *Bridge.* A horizontal demarcation dividing categories of points scored. 31. *Music.* One of the five parallel marks composing a staff. 32. *Military.* a. A formation in which elements, such as troops, tanks, or ships, are arranged abreast of each other. b. The battle area closest to the enemy. c. The troops in this area. d. Combatant troops. e. The officers in direct command of warships. f. A bulwark or trench. g. An extended system of such fortifications or defenses. 33. *Football.* a. A line of scrimmage. b. The linemen. —**all along the line.** 1. In every place. 2. At every moment. —**get a line on.** *Informal.* To acquire information about. —**hard lines.** *British Slang.* An unhappy fate or lot. —**hold the line.** 1. *Football.* To prevent the opposing team from carrying the ball forward. 2. To maintain a firm position. —**in line.** 1. In a series or row. 2. In conjunction, harmony, or agreement. 3. In restraint against waywardness; in conformity. —**in line for.** Next in order for: *in line for the presidency.* —**on a line.** In conjunction or alignment; even. —**on line.** In a series or row. Usually said of persons waiting: *We stood on line for an hour.* —**on the line.** *Informal.* 1. Ready or available for immediate payment. 2. In jeopardy; so as to be risked: *put his reputation on the line.* —**out of line.** 1. Not in place. 2. Not in agreement or conformity. 3. Unruly. —*v.* **lined, lining, lines.** —*tr.* 1. To mark or incise with a line or lines. 2. To represent or depict with a line or lines. 3. To place in a series or row. 4. To form a bordering line along; to edge: *Small stalls lined the alleys.* 5. *Baseball.* To hit (a ball) sharply so that its path is roughly a straight line. —*intr.* 1. To form a line. Usually used with *up.* 2. *Baseball.* To hit a line drive: *lined out to shortstop.* [Middle English *ligne, line,* cord, stroke, mark, line, partly from Old French *ligne,* from Vulgar Latin *linja* (unattested), from Latin *līnea,* thread, line, from *līnum,* flax (see **lino-** in Appendix*), and partly from Old English *līne,* cord, rope, series, representing a Common Germanic borrowing of Latin *līnea.*]

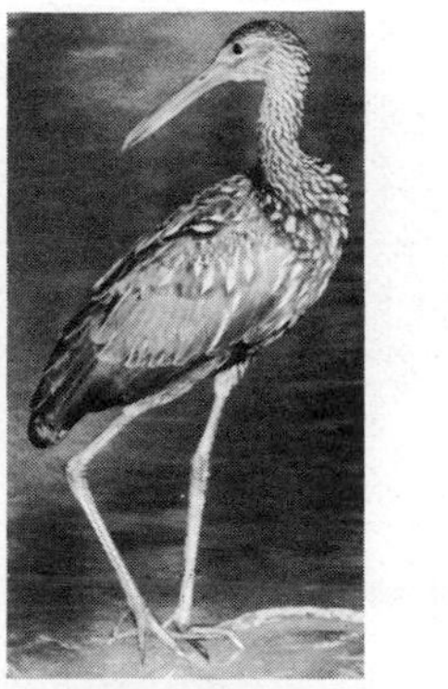

limpkin

line[2] (līn) *tr.v.* **lined, lining, lines.** 1. To sew or fit a covering to the inside surface of: *a coat lined with fur.* 2. To cover the inner surface of: *Moisture lined the cave's walls.* 3. To fill plentifully, as with money or food. [Middle English *linen,* from *line,* flax, Old English *līn,* from Germanic *līnam* (unattested), from Latin *līnum,* flax. See **lino-** in Appendix.*]

lin·e·age[1] (lĭn′ē-ĭj) *n.* 1. Direct descent from a particular ancestor; ancestry. 2. Derivation. 3. The descendants of a certain ancestor considered as the founder of the line. [Middle English *linage,* from Old French *li(g)nage,* from *ligne,* LINE.]

line·age[2]. Variant of **linage.**

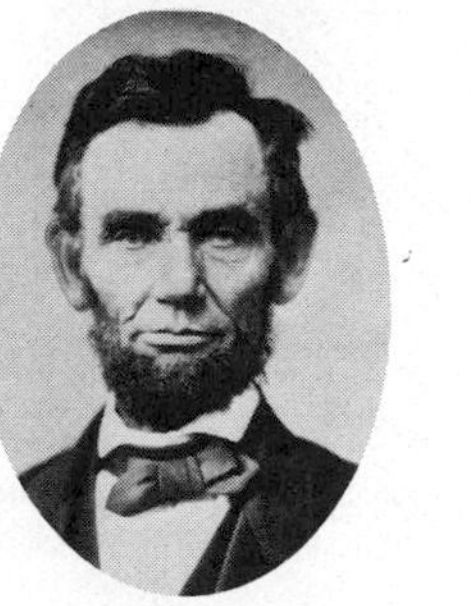

Abraham Lincoln

lin·e·al (lĭn′ē-əl) *adj. Abbr.* **lin.** 1. Belonging to or being in the direct line of descent from an ancestor. 2. Derived from or relating to a particular line of descent: *the lineal rights of royalty.* 3. Linear. [Middle English, from Old French, from Late Latin *lineālis,* from Latin *līnea,* LINE.] —**lin′e·al·ly** *adv.*

lin·e·a·ment (lĭn′ē-ə-mənt) *n.* 1. A distinctive shape, contour, or line, especially of the face. 2. A definitive or characteristic mark or feature. [Middle English *liniament,* from Latin *līneāmentum,* from *līneāre,* to make straight, from *līnea,* LINE.]

lin·e·ar (lĭn′ē-ər) *adj. Abbr.* **lin.** 1. Of, relating to, or resembling a line or lines; straight. 2. *Geometry.* a. In, of, describing, described by, or related to a straight line. b. Having only one dimension. 3. *Art.* Characterized chiefly by forms and shapes that are precisely defined by line. Compare **painterly.** 4. Narrow and elongated: *a linear leaf.* [Latin *līneāris,* from *līnea,* LINE.] —**lin′e·ar·ly** *adv.*

linear accelerator. An electron, proton, or heavy-ion **accelerator** *(see)* in which the paths of the particles accelerated are essentially straight lines rather than circles or spirals.

Linear B. A syllabic script used in Mycenaean Greek documents of Crete and Pylos from the 14th to the 12th century B.C.

linear equation. An algebraic equation, such as $x + y + 5 = 0$, in which the highest degree term in the variable or variables is of the first degree.

linear measure. 1. Measurement of length. 2. A unit or system of units for measuring length. Also called "long measure."

linear momentum. *Physics.* **Momentum** *(see).*

linear perspective. A form of **perspective** *(see).*

lin·e·ate (lĭn′ē-ĭt, -āt′) *adj.* Also **lin·e·at·ed** (-ā′tĭd). Marked with lines or stripes; striated. [Medieval Latin *līneātus,* past participle of *līneāre,* from Latin, to make straight, from *līnea,* LINE.]

lin·e·a·tion (lĭn′ē-ā′shən) *n.* 1. A marking or outlining with lines. 2. An outline. 3. An arrangement of lines.

line·back·er (līn′băk′ər) *n. Football.* Any of three defensive players forming a second line of defense usually just behind the ends and tackles. —**line′back′ing** *n.*

line breeding. Selective breeding to perpetuate certain qualities or characteristics in a strain of stock.

line cut. A letterpress printing plate made from a line drawing by a photoengraving process. Also called "line engraving."

line drawing. A drawing made with lines only, especially one used as copy for a line cut.

line drive. *Baseball.* A batted ball hit sharply so that its path roughly describes a straight line. Also called "liner."

line engraving. *Printing.* 1. A metal plate, used in intaglio printing, on the surface of which design lines have been hand engraved. 2. The process of making such an engraving. 3. A print made from such an engraving. 4. A **line cut** *(see).*

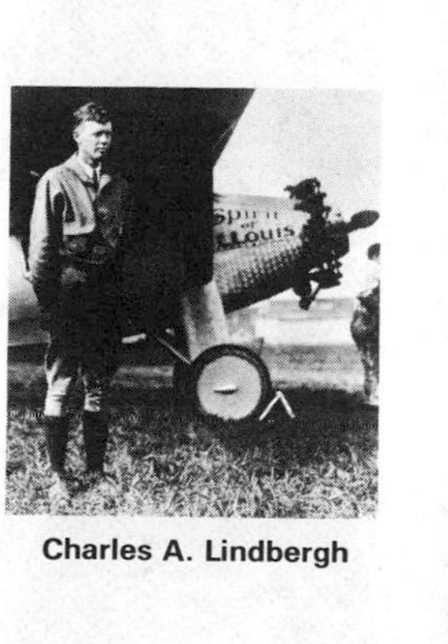

Charles A. Lindbergh

Line Islands. A group of islands in the Pacific Ocean, south of Hawaii on the equator; under British and U.S. administration. Also called "Equatorial Islands."

line·man (līn′mən) *n., pl.* **-men** (-mĭn). 1. One employed to install or repair telephone, telegraph, or other electric power lines. Also called "linesman." 2. *Surveying.* A chainman. 3. One employed to inspect and repair railroad tracks. 4. *Football.* A player positioned on the forward line.

lin·en (lĭn′ən) *n.* 1. Thread made from fibers of the flax plant. 2. Cloth woven from this thread. 3. Garments or articles made from this cloth, or from similar material. 4. Paper made from flax fibers, or given a linenlike luster. —*adj.* 1. Made of flax or linen. 2. Resembling linen. [Middle English *linen,* Old English *līnen, linnen,* "made of flax" (not used of linen cloth), from

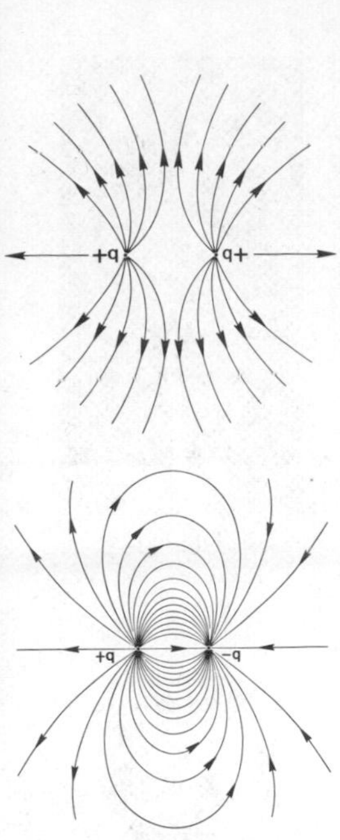

line of force
Electric lines of force
Above: Equal and similar charges (+*q*, +*q*)
Below: Equal but opposite charges (+*q*, −*q*)

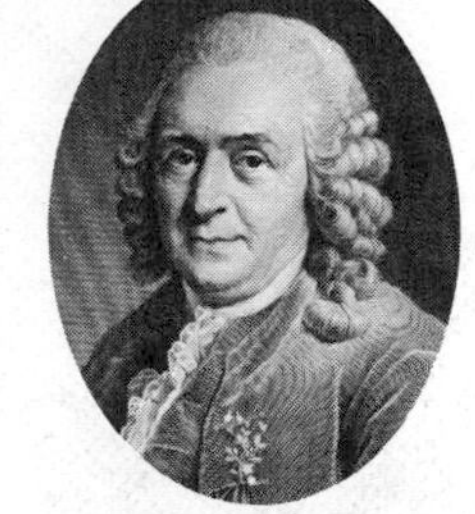

Carolus Linnaeus

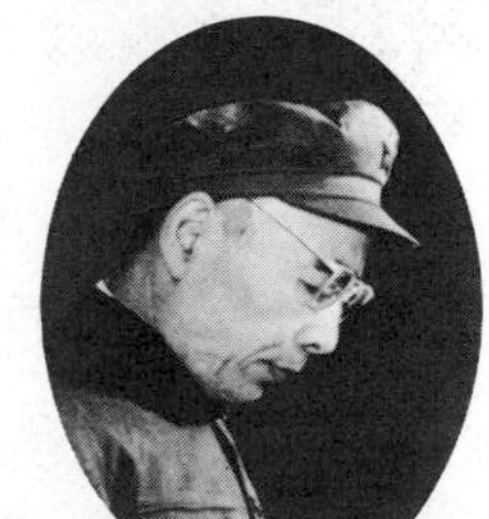

Lin Piao

Germanic *līnin* (unattested), from *līnam* (unattested), flax, from Latin *līnum*. See **lino-** in Appendix.*]

line of credit. A **credit line** *(see).*

line of force. A theoretical line in a field of force, any tangent to which gives the direction of the field at the point of tangency.

line of scrimmage. *Football.* See **scrimmage.**

line of sight. **1.** An imaginary line from the eye to the object being looked at. **2.** *Electronics.* An unobstructed path between sending and receiving antennas.

lin·e·o·late (lĭn′ē-ə-lāt′) *adj.* Marked with fine lines. [New Latin *lineolatus*, from Latin *līneola*, diminutive of *līnea*, LINE.]

lin·er¹ (lī′nər) *n.* **1.** One that draws or makes a line or lines. **2.** A commercial ship or airplane, especially one carrying passengers on a regular route. **3.** *Baseball.* A **line drive** *(see).*

lin·er² (lī′nər) *n.* **1.** One who makes or puts in linings. **2.** Something used as a lining.

lines·man (līnz′mən) *n., pl.* **-men** (-mĭn). **1.** *Sports.* **a.** A football official who marks the downs and the position of the ball and watches for certain violations from the sidelines. **b.** An official in various court games whose chief duty is to call shots that fall out of bounds. **2.** A **lineman** *(see).*

line spectrum. A spectrum consisting of a set of discrete, fairly narrow lines.

line squall. A squall or squalls occurring along a narrow band of thunderstorms. Now usually limited to nautical use.

line storm. A violent storm or series of storms of rain and wind popularly supposed to take place during the equinoxes.

line up. **1.** To form or take a place in a line. **2.** To put into a line or into alignment. **3.** To assemble, organize, or prepare: *lined up a lot of evidence against him.* **4.** To take sides.

line-up (līn′ŭp′) *n.* Also **line·up.** **1.** A line of persons formed for inspection or identification. **2. a.** The members of a team chosen to start a game: *a football line-up.* **b.** A list of such players. **3.** A group of persons, organizations, or things enlisted or arrayed for a specific purpose.

lin·ey. Variant of **liny.**

ling¹ (lĭng) *n., pl.* **ling** or **lings.** Any of various marine food fishes related to or resembling the cod, such as *Molva molva*, of northern European Atlantic waters, or a burbot or hake. [Middle English *leng(e)*, probably of Low German origin, akin to Dutch *lenghe, linghe.* See **del-¹** in Appendix.*]

ling² (lĭng). A plant, **heather** *(see).* [Middle English *lyng*, from Old Norse *lyng.* See **lenk-** in Appendix.*]

-ling¹. Indicates: **1.** One who belongs to or is connected with; for example, **worldling, hireling.** Often used disparagingly. **2.** One who has a specified quality; for example, **underling. 3.** A diminutive; for example, **duckling, nursling, princeling.** Often used contemptuously. [Middle English *-ling*, Old English *-ling*, from Common Germanic *-linga-* (unattested) : noun ending *-ilaz* (unattested) + patronymic ending *-inga-*.]

-ling². Indicates: **1.** Direction or position; for example, **sideling, flatling. 2.** Condition; for example, **firstling, darkling.** [Middle English *-ling*, from Old English *-ling*, from West Germanic *-ling-, -lang-* (unattested).]

ling. linguistics.

lin·gam (lĭng′gəm) *n.* Also **lin·ga** (-gə). A stylized phallus worshiped as a symbol of the Hindu god Shiva. [Sanskrit *liṅgaṁ*, "distinctive mark," penis.]

Lin·ga·yen Gulf (lĭng′gä-yĕn′). An inlet of the South China Sea in west-central Luzon, Republic of the Philippines; the site of Japanese and U.S. landing operations (1941 and 1945).

ling·cod (lĭng′kŏd′) *n., pl.* **lingcod** or **-cods.** A food fish, *Ophiodon elongatus*, of northern Pacific waters.

lin·ger (lĭng′gər) *v.* **-gered, -gering, -gers.** —*intr.* **1.** To delay departure; be slow and reluctant to leave; tarry. **2.** To hover between life and death for some time before dying. **3.** To persist: *The memory still lingers.* **4.** To proceed slowly; saunter. **5.** To be tardy in acting; procrastinate. —*tr.* To pass (a period of time) in a leisurely or aimless manner. —See Synonyms at **stay.** [Middle English (northern dialect) *lengeren*, frequentative of *lengen*, to tarry, from Old Norse *lengja.* See **del-¹** in Appendix.*] —**lin′ger·er** *n.* —**lin′ger·ing·ly** *adv.*

lin·ge·rie (län′zhə-rā′, län′zhə-rē; *French* lăNzh-rē′) *n.* **1.** Women's underwear. **2.** *Archaic.* Linen articles, especially garments. [French, "linen garments," from *linge*, linen, from Latin *lineus*, made of linen, from *līnum*, flax. See **lino-** in Appendix.*]

Ling·ga (lĭng′gə). An archipelago of Indonesia, about 840 square miles in area, lying off the east-central coast of Sumatra.

lin·go (lĭng′gō) *n., pl.* **-goes.** Language that is unintelligible or unfamiliar through being foreign or a special jargon. See Synonyms at **dialect.** [Portuguese *lingoa*, "tongue," language, from Latin *lingua*, LINGUA.]

lin·gon·ber·ry (lĭng′gən-bĕr′ē) *n., pl.* **-ries.** The **cowberry** *(see).*

lin·gua (lĭng′gwə) *n., pl.* **-guae** (-gwē′). A tongue or tonguelike organ. [Latin. See **dṇghū** in Appendix.*]

lingua fran·ca (frăng′kə). **1.** *Capital* **L.** A mixture of Italian with French, Spanish, Arabic, Greek, and Turkish, spoken in the Mediterranean area, especially in the Levant. **2.** Any hybrid language used as a medium of communication between peoples of different languages. [Italian, "the Frankish tongue."]

lin·gual (lĭng′gwəl) *adj.* **1.** Of, pertaining to, or resembling the tongue or a tonguelike organ. **2.** *Phonetics.* With the tongue in conjunction with other organs of speech. **3.** Linguistic. —*n.* *Phonetics.* A sound that is pronounced with the tongue in conjunction with other organs of speech, as the sounds (t), (l), (n). —**lin′gual·ly** *adv.*

lin·gui·form (lĭng′gwə-fôrm′) *adj.* Having the form of a tongue.

lin·gui·ni (lĭng-gwē′nē) *n.* Plural in form, usually treated as a collective. Pasta in the form of long, flat, thin strands. [Italian, plural of *linguino*, "small tongue," from *lingua*, tongue, from Latin. See **lingua.**]

lin·guist (lĭng′gwĭst) *n.* **1.** A person who speaks several languages fluently. **2.** A specialist in linguistics. [From Latin *lingua*, tongue, language, LINGUA.]

lin·guis·tic (lĭng-gwĭs′tĭk) *adj.* Of or relating to language or linguistics. —**lin·guis′ti·cal·ly** *adv.*

linguistic form. Any meaningful unit of speech, such as an affix, word, phrase, or sentence.

lin·guis·tics (lĭng-gwĭs′tĭks) *n.* Plural in form, used with a singular verb. *Abbr.* **ling.** The science of language; the study of the nature and structure of human speech.

linguistic stock. A family of languages including a parent language and all offshoots.

lin·gu·late (lĭng′gyə-lāt′) *adj.* Tongue-shaped. [Latin *lingulātus*, from *lingula*, diminutive of *lingua*, tongue, LINGUA.]

lin·i·ment (lĭn′ə-mənt) *n.* A medicinal fluid applied to the skin by rubbing as an anodyne or counterirritant. [Middle English *lynyment*, from Late Latin *linīmentum*, from Latin *linere*, to anoint. See **lei-** in Appendix.*]

li·nin (lī′nən) *n.* The filamentous, achromatic material in the nucleus of a cell that interconnects the chromatin granules. [Latin *līnum*, flax (see **lino-** in Appendix*) + -IN.]

lin·ing (lī′nĭng) *n.* **1. a.** An interior covering or coating. **b.** Material that may be used for such covering or coating. **2.** The act or process of applying a lining to something.

link¹ (lĭngk) *n.* **1.** One of the rings or loops forming a chain. **2.** Anything resembling a chain link in its physical arrangement or its connecting function, as: **a.** One of several sausages strung together. **b.** A bridge or other unit in a transportation or communications system. **c.** A single connecting element in a narrative. **3.** A cuff link. **4.** *Surveying.* A unit of length used in surveying, equal to 0.01 chain or 7.92 inches. **5.** A rod or lever transmitting motion in a machine. —*v.* **linked, linking, links.** —*tr.* To connect or couple with or as if with links. —*intr.* To become connected with or as with links. —See Synonyms at **join.** [Middle English *link*, from Old Norse *hlenkr* (unattested), variant of *hlekkr*, link, ring. See **kleng-** in Appendix.*]

link² (lĭngk) *n.* A torch formerly used for lighting one's way in the streets. [Possibly from Medieval Latin *linchinus*, variant of *lichinus*, from Latin *lychnus*, from Greek *lukhnos*, lamp. See **leuk-** in Appendix.*]

link·age (lĭng′kĭj) *n.* **1.** The act or process of linking. **2.** The state or condition of being linked. **3.** *Machinery.* A system of interconnected machine elements, such as rods, springs, and pivots, used to transmit power or motion. **4.** *Electricity.* A measure of the induced voltage in a circuit caused by a magnetic flux, and equal to the flux times the number of turns in the coil that surrounds it. **5.** *Genetics.* A relationship between two or more nonallelic genes occupying the same chromosome that causes them to have closely associated inherited effects.

link·boy (lĭngk′boi′) *n.* A boy hired to carry a torch to light persons along dark streets.

linked (lĭngkt) *adj.* **1.** Connected, especially by or as if by links. **2.** *Genetics.* Exhibiting linkage.

linking verb. A verb, such as *appear, be, feel, grow,* or *seem*, that connects a subject and a predicate adjective or predicate nominative; a copulative verb.

links (lĭngks) *pl.n.* **1.** *Chiefly Scottish.* Relatively flat or undulating sandy turf-covered ground usually along a seashore. **2.** A golf course. [Middle English *links*, from Old English *hlincas*, plural of *hlinc*, ridge. See **kleng-** in Appendix.*]

link·work (lĭngk′wûrk′) *n.* **1.** Mesh, chain, or the like consisting of joined links. **2.** A mechanical device or system operated by or consisting of a series of links.

linn (lĭn) *n. Chiefly Scottish.* **1.** A waterfall. **2.** A steep ravine. [Scottish Gaelic *linne.* See **pleu-** in Appendix.*]

Lin·nae·an (lĭ-nē′ən) *adj.* Also **Lin·ne·an.** *Abbr.* **L.** Of or pertaining to Linnaeus or to the system of taxonomic classification and nomenclature originated by him.

Lin·nae·us (lĭ-nē′əs), **Carolus.** Original name, Carl von Linné. 1707–1778. Swedish botanist and originator of system of taxonomic classification.

lin·net (lĭn′ĭt) *n.* **1.** A small Old World songbird, *Acanthis cannabina*, having brownish plumage. **2.** A similar bird, *Carpodacus mexicanus*, of western North America. [Old French dialectal *linette*, from *lin*, flax (so called because the bird feeds on linseeds), from Latin *līnum.* See **lino-** in Appendix.*]

lin·o·le·ic acid (lĭn′ə-lē′ĭk). A colorless to straw-colored liquid, $C_{18}H_{32}O_2$, an important component of drying oils and an essential fatty acid in the human diet. [Greek *linon*, flax (see **lino-** in Appendix*) + OLEIC ACID (so called because found in linseed oil).]

lin·o·len·ic acid (lĭn′ə-lĕn′ĭk). A colorless liquid, $C_{18}H_{30}O_2$, an important component of natural drying oils and an essential fatty acid in the human diet. [Arbitrarily from LINOLEIC ACID.]

li·no·le·um (lĭ-nō′lē-əm) *n.* A durable, washable material made in sheets by pressing a mixture of heated linseed oil, rosin, powdered cork, and pigments onto a burlap or canvas backing, used as a floor and counter-top covering. [Latin *līnum*, flax (see **lino-** in Appendix*) + *oleum*, OIL.]

linoleum block print. A relief print taken from a block of linoleum on which a design has been carved.

Li·no·type (lī′nə-tīp′) *n.* A trademark for a machine that can set an entire line of type on a single metal slug and is operated by a keyboard similar to that of a typewriter. —*v.* **Linotyped, -typing, -types.** —*tr.* To typeset on such a machine. —*intr.* To use a Linotype. [LINE + TYPE.] —**Li′no·typ′er, Li′no·typ′ist** *n.*

Lin Pi·ao (lĭn′ byou′). Born 1908. Vice-chairman of Chinese

ă pat/ā pay/âr care/ä father/b bib/ch church/d deed/ĕ pet/ē be/f fife/g gag/h hat/hw which/ĭ pit/ī pie/îr pier/j judge/k kick/l lid, needle/m mum/n no, sudden/ng thing/ŏ pot/ō toe/ô paw, for/oi noise/ou out/ŏŏ took/ōō boot/p pop/r roar/s sauce/sh ship, dish/

Communist Party; designated as successor to Mao Tse-tung (1969).

lin·sang (lĭn′săng′) *n.* Any of several Asian or African carnivorous mammals of the genera *Poiana* and *Prionodon,* having a spotted coat and a long banded tail. [Malay.]

lin·seed (lĭn′sēd′) *n.* The seed of flax, especially when used as the source of linseed oil; flaxseed. [Middle English *linseed,* Old English *līnǣd* : Old English *līn,* flax, from Latin *līnum* (see **lino-** in Appendix*) + SEED.]

linseed oil. A golden-yellow, amber, or brown oil that thickens and hardens on exposure to air, extracted from the seeds of flax, and used as a drying oil in paints and varnishes, and in linoleum, printing inks, and synthetic resins.

lin·sey-wool·sey (lĭn′zē-wo͝ol′zē) *n., pl.* **-seys.** A coarse fabric of cotton or linen woven with wool. [Middle English *lynsy-wolsye* : probably *Lindsey,* village in Suffolk, England (where it was originally manufactured) + WOOL.]

lin·stock (lĭn′stŏk′) *n.* A long forked stick for holding a match, formerly used to fire cannon. [Dutch *lontstok* : *lont,* match, wick, akin to Middle Low German *lunte*† + *stok,* stick.]

lint (lĭnt) *n.* **1.** Clinging bits of fiber and fluff; fuzz. **2.** Downy material obtained by scraping linen cloth and used for dressing wounds. **3.** The mass of soft fibers surrounding the seeds of unginned cotton. [Middle English *lynet,* from Latin *linteum,* linen cloth, from *linteus,* made of linen, from *līnum,* flax. See **lino-** in Appendix.*]

lin·tel (lĭnt′l) *n.* The horizontal beam that forms the upper member of a window or door frame and supports part of the structure above it. [Middle English, from Old French *lintel, lintier,* from Vulgar Latin *līmitāris* (unattested), alteration (influenced by Latin *līmes,* stem *līmit-,* boundary, LIMIT) of Latin *līmināris,* of a threshold, from *līmen,* threshold, LIMEN.]

lint·er (lĭn′tər) *n.* **1.** A machine that removes linters from the seeds of cotton. **2.** *Plural.* The short fibers that cling to cotton seeds after the first ginning.

lint·white (lĭnt′hwīt′) *n. Poetic.* A linnet. [Middle English *lynkwhyte,* Old English *līnetwige,* "linseed eater" : *līn,* flax (see **linseed**) + *-twige,* "plucker," "eater," from West Germanic *twig-* (unattested), to pluck.]

lin·y (lī′nē) *adj.* Also **lin·ey.** **1.** Resembling a line; thin or narrow. **2.** Marked with or full of lines.

Linz (lĭnts). The capital of Upper Austria, an industrial center and river port on the Danube. Population, 196,000.

li·on (lī′ən) *n.* **1.** A large, carnivorous feline mammal, *Panthera leo,* of Africa and India, having a short tawny coat and a long, heavy mane around the neck and shoulders in the male. **2.** Any of several related animals or animals considered to resemble a lion in some way. **3.** A person resembling a lion, as in bravery or ferocity. **4.** One whose eminence, as in arts and letters, has given him social prestige. **5.** The national emblem of Great Britain. **—beard the lion in his den.** To face or defy the opposition in its territory or home. **—the lion's share.** The greatest or best part of the whole. **—twist the lion's tail.** To irritate or insult the people or government of Great Britain. [Middle English *li(o)un, leoun,* from Norman French *liun* and Old French *lion,* both from Latin *leō* (stem *leōn-*), from Greek *leōn,* perhaps from Semitic, akin to Hebrew *lābhī′,* lion, and *lāyish,* lion (whence probably Homeric form *lis*).]

Li·on (lī′ən) *n. Astronomy.* The constellation and sign of the zodiac, **Leo** *(see).* Preceded by *the.*

li·on·ess (lī′ə-nĭs) *n.* A female lion. [Middle English *leonesse,* from Old French *lionnesse,* from *lion,* LION.]

li·on·heart·ed (lī′ən-här′tĭd) *adj.* Extraordinarily courageous.

li·on·ize (lī′ə-nīz′) *tr.v.* **-ized, -izing, -izes.** To look upon or treat (a person) as a celebrity. **—li′on·i·za′tion** *n.* **—li′on·iz′er** *n.*

Li·ons, Gulf of (lī′ənz). A wide inlet of the Mediterranean on the southern coast of France.

lip (lĭp) *n.* **1.** *Anatomy.* Either of two fleshy, muscular folds that together surround the opening of the mouth. **2.** Any structure or part that similarly encircles or bounds an orifice, as: **a.** *Anatomy.* A labium. **b.** The margin of flesh around a wound. **c.** Either of the margins of the aperture of a gastropod shell. **d.** The rim of a vessel, bell, crater, or the like. **3.** *Botany.* One of the protruding divisions of an irregular corolla or calyx, either paired, as in the snapdragon, or single, as in an orchid. **4.** The tip of a pouring spout. **5.** *Slang.* Insolent talk. **—bite one's lip.** **1.** To hold back one's anger or other feeling. **2.** To show vexation. **—button one's lip.** *Slang.* To stop talking. **—smack one's lips.** To relish or gloat over something anticipated or remembered. **—*tr.v.*** **lipped, lipping, lips.** **1. a.** To touch the lips to. **b.** *Poetic.* To kiss. **2.** To utter; especially, to whisper or murmur. **3.** To lap. Used of water. **4.** To serve as a lip or rim to. **5.** *Golf.* To hit the ball so that it stops just at the edge of the hole. **—*adj.*** **1.** *Phonetics.* Formed or uttered with the help of the lips; labial. **2.** Uttered insincerely: *lip admiration.* [Middle English *lip(pe),* Old English *lippa.* See **leb-²** in Appendix.*]

Lip·a·ri Islands (lĭp′ə-rē). A group of islands of Italy, in the Tyrrhenian Sea off the northeastern coast of Sicily. Also called "Aeolian Islands."

lip·ase (lĭp′ās′, lī′pās′) *n.* An enzyme that hydrolyzes fats to form glycerol and fatty acids. [LIP(O)- + -ASE.]

Li·petsk (lē′pĕtsk). A city of the Soviet Union, in the southwestern Russian S.F.S.R. Population, 226,000.

lip·id (lĭp′ĭd, lī′pĭd) *n.* Also **lip·ide** (lĭp′īd′, lī′pīd′). Any of numerous fats and fatlike materials that are generally insoluble in water but soluble in common organic solvents, that are related to the fatty acid esters, and that together with carbohydrates and proteins constitute the principal structural material of living cells. [French *lipide* : LIP(O)- + -ID.]

Lip·mann (lĭp′mən), **Fritz Albert.** Born 1899. German-born American biochemist; worked on enzymes.

Li Po (lē′ bô′). Chinese poet of the eighth century A.D.

lipo-, lip-. Indicates fat or fatty; for example, **lipolysis, lipoma.** [New Latin, from Greek *lipos,* fat. See **leip-** in Appendix.*]

lip·oid (lĭp′oid′) *adj.* Also **lip·oi·dal** (lĭ-poid′l). Resembling fat; fatty. [LIP(O)- + -OID.] **—lip′oid′** *n.*

li·pol·y·sis (lĭ-pŏl′ə-sĭs) *n.* Hydrolysis of fat. [LIPO- + -LYSIS.]

li·po·ma (lĭ-pō′mə) *n., pl.* **-mata** (-mə-tə) or **-mas.** A benign tumor of chiefly fatty cells. [LIP(O)- + -OMA.] **—li·pom′a·tous** (-pŏm′ə-təs) *adj.*

lip·o·pro·tein (lĭp′ō-prō′tēn′, -tē-ĭn) *n.* A conjugated protein consisting of a simple protein combined with a lipid group.

lip·o·trop·ic (lĭp′ō-trŏp′ĭk) *adj.* Preventing abnormal or excessive accumulation of fat in the liver. [LIPO- + -TROPIC.] **—li·pot′ro·py** (lĭ-pŏt′rə-pē), **li·pot′ro·pism′** *n.*

Lip·pe (lĭp′ə). A former state of Germany, included in North Rhine-Westphalia, West Germany, since 1945.

Lip·pi (lĭp′ē; *Italian* lēp′pē), Fra **Filippo** or **Lippo.** 1406?–1469. With his son, **Filippino** (1457?–1504), Florentine painter.

Lipp·mann (lĭp′mən), **Walter.** Born 1889. American journalist.

lip-read (lĭp′rēd′) *v.* **-read** (-rĕd′), **-reading, -reads.** —*tr.* To interpret (another's utterance) by lip reading. —*intr.* To use lip reading.

lip reading. A technique used, especially by the deaf, to understand inaudible speech by interpreting lip and facial movements. **—lip reader.**

lip service. Insincere agreement or payment of respect.

lip·stick (lĭp′stĭk′) *n.* A stick of waxy or pastelike lip coloring enclosed in a small cylindrical case.

liq. **1.** liquid. **2.** liquor.

li·quate (lī′kwāt′) *tr.v.* **-quated, -quating, -quates.** To separate (the metals in an alloy) by melting some constituents while leaving others solid. [Latin *liquāre,* to melt, dissolve. See **leikw-** in Appendix.*] **—li·qua′tion** *n.*

liq·ue·fac·tion (lĭk′wə-făk′shən) *n.* **1.** The process of liquefying. **2.** The state of being liquefied.

liq·ue·fi·er (lĭk′wə-fī′ər) *n.* One that liquefies.

liq·ue·fy (lĭk′wə-fī′) *v.* **-fied, -fying, -fies.** Also **liq·ui·fy.** —*tr.* To cause to become liquid, especially: **a.** To melt (a solid) by heating. **b.** To condense (a gas) by cooling. —*intr.* To become liquid. —See Synonyms at **melt.** [Old French *liquefier,* from Latin *liquefacere* : *liquēre,* to be liquid (see **leikw-** in Appendix*) + *facere,* to make (see **dhē-¹** in Appendix*).]

li·ques·cent (lĭ-kwĕs′ənt) *adj.* Becoming or tending to become liquid; melting. [Latin *liquescēns,* present participle of *liquescere,* to become liquid, from *liquēre,* to be liquid. See **leikw-** in Appendix.*] **—li·ques′cence, li·ques′cen·cy** *n.*

li·queur (lĭ-kûr′, -kyo͝or′) *n.* A sweet syrupy alcoholic beverage often with a brandy base. Also called "cordial." [French, from Old French *licour,* liquid, LIQUOR.]

liq·uid (lĭk′wĭd) *n. Abbr.* **liq.** **1.** The state of matter in which a substance exhibits a characteristic readiness to flow, little or no tendency to disperse, and relatively high incompressibility. **2.** Matter or a specific body of matter in this state. **3.** *Phonetics.* The sounds of *l* and *r,* which are nonfrictional and vowellike. —*adj.* **1.** Of or being a liquid. **2.** Liquefied, especially: **a.** Melted by heating: *liquid wax.* **b.** Condensed by cooling: *liquid oxygen.* **3.** Transparent; shining: *"the beauty of the hawk's eye . . . full, liquid, and piercing."* (Richard Jefferies). **4. a.** Flowing and clear; musical; limpid: *liquid prose.* **b.** Not guttural and harsh; smooth; fluent. Said of a speech sound. **5.** Flowing gracefully in motion. **6.** Readily converted into cash: *liquid assets.* [From Middle English *liquide* (adjective), from Old French, from Latin *liquidus,* from *liquēre,* to be liquid. See **leikw-** in Appendix.*]

liquid air. Air in the liquid state, condensed from the gas by cooling and sometimes pressure.

liq·uid·am·bar (lĭk′wĭd-ăm′bər) *n.* A tree of the genus *Liquidambar,* such as the sweet gum. [New Latin *Liquidambar,* "liquid amber" (from its aromatic resin) : LIQUID + Medieval Latin *ambar,* ambergris, AMBER.]

liq·ui·date (lĭk′wə-dāt′) *v.* **-dated, -dating, -dates.** —*tr.* **1.** To pay off or settle (a debt, claim, or obligation). **2.** To wind up the affairs of (a business firm, a bankrupt estate, or the like) by determining the liabilities and applying the assets to their discharge. **3.** To convert (assets) into cash. **4.** To abolish. **5.** To kill. —*intr.* To go into liquidation. [Late Latin *liquidāre,* to make clear, melt, from Latin *liquidus,* LIQUID.]

liq·ui·da·tion (lĭk′wə-dā′shən) *n.* **1.** The action or process of liquidating. **2.** The state of being liquidated.

liquid crystal. Any of various liquids in which the atoms or molecules are regularly arrayed in either one dimension or two dimensions, the order giving rise to optical properties, such as anisotropic scattering, associated with the crystals.

liquid measure. **1.** A unit or system of units of liquid capacity. **2.** A measure for liquids. See **measurement.**

liq·uor (lĭk′ər) *n. Abbr.* **liq.** **1.** An alcoholic beverage made by distillation rather than by fermentation. **2.** A liquid substance, such as broth or juice, produced in cooking. **3.** *Pharmacy.* An aqueous solution of a nonvolatile substance. **4.** A solution, emulsion, or suspension for industrial use. —*tr.v.* **liquored, -uoring, -uors.** *Slang.* **1.** To cause to become drunk with alcoholic liquor. Used with *up.* **2. a.** To treat (leather) with grease. **b.** To steep (malt or the like). [Middle English *lic(o)ur,* liquid, beverage, from Old French, from Latin *liquor,* from *liquēre,* to be liquid. See **leikw-** in Appendix.*]

li·quo·rice. *Chiefly British.* Variant of **licorice.**

li·quor·ish. Variant of **lickerish.**

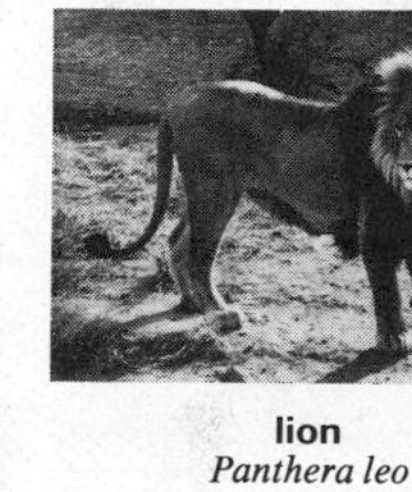

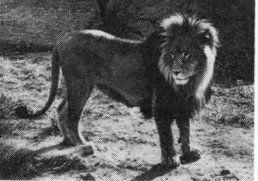

lion
Panthera leo

li·ra (lîr′ə; *Italian* lē′rä) *n., pl.* **lire** (lîr′ā; *Italian* lē′rā) or **-ras.** *Abbr.* **l.** **1.** The basic monetary unit of Italy, equal to 100 centesimi. See table of exchange rates at **currency.** **2.** A coin or note worth one lira. [Italian, from Latin *lībra,* balance, measure. See **līthrā** in Appendix.*]

lir·i·pipe (lîr′ə-pīp′) *n.* A long scarf or cord attached to and hanging from a hood. [Medieval Latin *liripipium*†.]

LIS Airport code for Lisbon, Portugal.

Li·sa (lē′sə, -zə). A feminine given name. [Diminutive of Elizabeth.]

Lis·bon (lĭz′bən). *Portuguese* **Lis·bo·a** (lēzh-vō′ə). The capital of Portugal, a port on the Tagus River estuary, eight miles inland from the Atlantic. Population, 802,000.

lisle (līl) *n.* **1.** A fine, smooth, tightly twisted thread spun from long-stapled cotton and used especially for hosiery and underwear. Also called "lisle thread." **2.** Fabric knitted of lisle. [From *Lisle,* earlier form of Lille, where it was originally made.]

lisp (lĭsp) *n.* **1.** A speech defect or mannerism characterized by the failure to produce normal sibilants, especially by the substitution of the sounds (th) and (*th*) for the sibilants (s) and (z). **2.** The act or habit of lisping. **3.** The sound of a lisp. *—v.* **lisped, lisping, lisps.** *—intr.* **1.** To speak with a lisp. **2.** To speak imperfectly, as a child does. *—tr.* To pronounce with a lisp. [Middle English *(w)lispen,* Old English *wlispian* (attested only in compound *awlispian*), from *wlisp,* a lisping, akin to Old High German *lisp* (imitative).] **—lisp′er** *n.*

lis pen·dens (lĭs′ pĕn′dĕnz′). *Law.* A pending suit. [Latin, "pending lawsuit."]

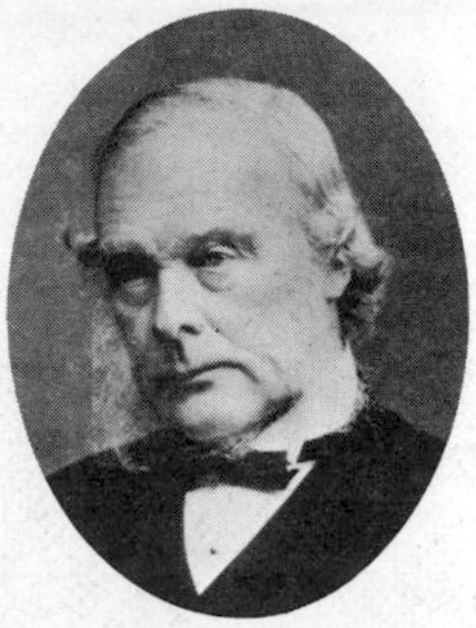

Joseph Lister

lis·some (lĭs′əm) *adj.* Also **lis·som.** **1.** Lithe; supple. **2.** Capable of moving with ease; limber; nimble. [Variant of lithesome.] **—lis′some·ly** *adv.* **—lis′some·ness** *n.*

list[1] (lĭst) *n.* An item-by-item printed or written entry of persons or things, often arranged in a particular order, and usually of a specified nature or category: *a shopping list; a guest list.* *—v.* **listed, listing, lists.** *—tr.* **1.** To make a list of; itemize. **2.** To enter in a list; register or catalogue. **3.** *Archaic.* To enlist. *—intr. Archaic.* To enlist in the armed forces. [Old French *liste,* band, border, strip of paper, list, from Old Italian *lista,* from Germanic. See **leizd-** in Appendix.*]

list[2] (lĭst) *n.* **1. a.** A narrow strip, especially of wood. **b.** A listel. **c.** A border or selvage of cloth. **2.** A stripe or band of color. **3.** *Obsolete.* A boundary; border. **4.** *Plural.* **a.** An arena for tournaments or other contests. **b.** A place of combat. **5.** A ridge thrown up between two furrows by a lister in plowing. *—tr.v.* **listed, listing, lists.** **1.** To cover, line, or edge with list. **2.** To cut a thin strip from the edge of. **3.** To furrow or plant (land) with a lister. [Middle English *liste,* border, edge, strip, Old English *līste.* See **leizd-** in Appendix.*]

list[3] (lĭst) *n.* An inclination to one side, as of a ship; a tilt. *—v.* **listed, listing, lists.** *Nautical.* *—intr.* To lean or tilt to the side; careen. *—tr.* To heel (a ship) over. [Origin unknown.]

list[4] (lĭst) *v.* **listed, listing, lists.** *Poetic.* *—tr.* To listen to. *—intr.* To listen. [Middle English *listen, lusten,* Old English *hlystan.* See **kleu-**[1] in Appendix.*]

list[5] (lĭst) *v.* **listed, listing, lists.** *—tr.* To be pleasing to; satisfy; please. *—intr.* To be disposed; choose. *—n.* A desire or inclination. [Middle English *listen,* Old English *lystan.* See **las-** in Appendix.*]

lis·tel (lĭs′təl) *n. Architecture.* A narrow border, molding, or fillet. [Old French, from Old Italian *listello,* diminutive of *lista,* band, border, list.]

lis·ten (lĭs′ən) *intr.v.* **-tened, -tening, -tens.** **1.** To apply oneself to hearing something. **2.** To pay attention; give heed. **—listen in.** **1.** To tune in and listen to a broadcast. **2.** To listen to a conversation, sometimes surreptitiously. [Middle English *listnen,* Old English *hlysnan.* See **kleu-**[1] in Appendix.*] **—lis′ten·er** *n.*

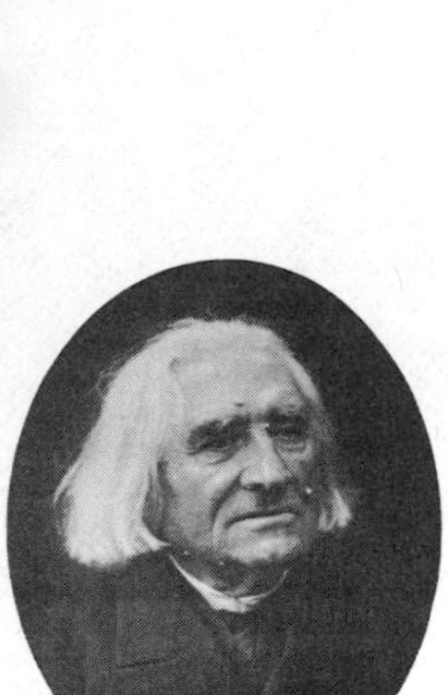

Franz Liszt

listening post. A strategic spot for gathering information.

list·er (lĭs′tər) *n.* A plow equipped with a double moldboard that turns up the soil on each side of the furrow, often having an attached drill for seed planting. [From list (border).]

Lis·ter (lĭs′tər), **Joseph.** First Baron Lister. 1827–1912. British surgeon; founder of antiseptic surgery.

list·ing (lĭs′tĭng) *n.* **1.** An act or instance of making a list or entering in a list. **2.** An entry in a list. **3.** A list.

list·less (lĭst′lĭs) *adj.* Marked by a lack of energy or enthusiasm; disinclined toward any effort; indifferent; languid. [Middle English *listles* : *list,* desire, from *listen,* to be pleasing, to list + -less.] **—list′less·ly** *adv.* **—list′less·ness** *n.*

list price. A basic published or advertised price, often subject to discount.

Liszt (lĭst), **Franz.** 1811–1886. Hungarian composer and pianist.

lit. **1.** Alternate past tense and past participle of **light** (to illuminate). **2.** Alternate past tense and past participle of **light** (to descend).

LIT Airport code for Little Rock, Arkansas.

lit. **1.** literal; literally. **2.** literary; literature.

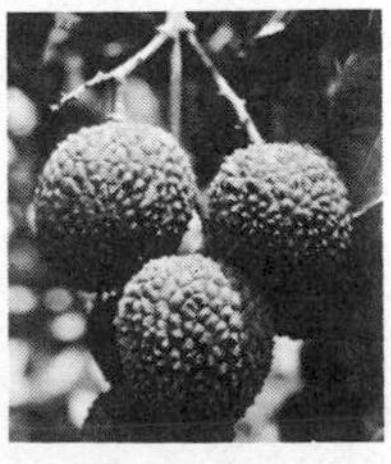

litchi

lit·a·ny (lĭt′n-ē) *n., pl.* **-nies.** **1.** A liturgical prayer consisting of phrases recited by a leader alternating with responses by the congregation. **2.** *Capital* **L.** The set of prayers in this form in the Book of Common Prayer. **3.** Any repetitive or incantatory recital. [Middle English *letanie,* from Old French, from Late Latin *litania,* from Greek *litaneia,* entreaty, from *litanuein,* to entreat, from *litanos,* entreating, from *litē*†, supplication.]

li·tchi (lē′chē) *n.* Also **li·chee, ly·chee.** **1.** A Chinese tree, *Litchi chinensis,* bearing edible fruit. **2.** The fruit of this tree. In this sense, also called "litchi nut." [Cantonese *lai chi,* corresponding to Mandarin Chinese *li⁴chih¹*.]

-lite. Indicates stone. Used in names of minerals; for example, **cryolite, actinolite.** [French *-lite* and German *-lit,* variants of *-lithe* and *-lith,* from Greek *lithos,* stone. See **litho-.**]

li·ter (lē′tər) *n.* Also *chiefly British* **li·tre.** *Abbr* **l** A metric unit of volume equal to a cubic decimeter, approximately 1.056 liquid quart or 0.908 dry quart. See **measurement.** [French *litre,* from obsolete *litron,* old measure of capacity, from Medieval Latin *lītra,* from Greek *litra,* a unit of weight, a pound, a silver coin of Sicily. See **līthrā** in Appendix.*]

lit·er·a·cy (lĭt′ər-ə-sē) *n.* The condition or quality of being literate, especially the ability to read and write.

lit·er·al (lĭt′ər-əl) *adj. Abbr.* **lit.** **1.** In accordance with, conforming to, or upholding the explicit or primary meaning of a word or the words of a text. **2.** Word for word; verbatim: *a literal translation.* **3.** Concerned chiefly with facts; prosaic: *a literal mind.* **4.** Avoiding exaggeration, metaphor, or embellishment; plain: *a literal statement.* **5.** Consisting of, using, or expressed by letters: *literal notation.* [Middle English *lit(t)eral,* of letters, written, from Old French *literal,* from Late Latin *litterālis,* from Latin *littera,* letter. See **deph-** in Appendix.*] **—lit′er·al·ness** *n.*

lit·er·al·ism (lĭt′ər-ə-lĭz′əm) *n.* **1.** Adherence to the explicit sense of a given text or doctrine. **2.** Literal portrayal; realism. **—lit′er·al·ist** *n.* **—lit′er·al·is′tic** *adj.*

lit·er·al·ize (lĭt′ər-ə-līz′) *tr.v.* **-ized, -izing, -izes.** To make literal.

lit·er·al·ly (lĭt′ər-ə-lē) *adv. Abbr.* **lit.** **1.** In a literal or strict sense. **2.** Really; actually: *"There are people in the world who literally do not know how to boil water."* (Craig Claiborne).

lit·er·ar·y (lĭt′ə-rĕr′ē) *adj. Abbr.* **lit.** **1.** Of, relating to, or dealing with literature. **2. a.** Found in or appropriate to literature: *a literary style.* **b.** Employed chiefly in writing rather than speaking: *a literary language.* **3.** Versed in or fond of literature or learning: *a literary man.* **4.** Of or relating to writers or the profession of literature: *literary circles.* **5.** Bookish; pedantic. [French *littéraire,* from Latin *litterārius,* of writing, from *litterae,* epistle, writing, plural of *littera,* letter. See **literate.**]

literary epic. An **epic** *(see).*

lit·er·ate (lĭt′ər-ĭt) *adj.* **1.** Able to read and write. **2.** Knowledgeable; educated. **3.** Familiar with literature; literary. *—n.* **1.** Someone who can read and write. **2.** A well-informed, educated person. [Middle English *litterate,* from Latin *lit(t)erātus,* acquainted with writings, learned, from *litterae,* epistle, writing, plural of *littera,* letter. See **deph-** in Appendix.*]

lit·e·ra·ti (lĭt′ə-rä′tē, -rā′tī′) *pl.n.* The literary intelligentsia. [Italian, from Latin *litterātī,* plural of *litterātus,* literate.]

lit·e·ra·tim (lĭt′ə-rā′tĭm, -rä′tĭm) *adv.* Literally; letter for letter. [Medieval Latin, from *lit(t)era,* letter. See **literate.**]

lit·er·a·ture (lĭt′ər-ə-cho͝or′) *n. Abbr.* **lit.** **1.** A body of writings in prose or verse. **2.** Imaginative or creative writing; belles-lettres. **3.** The art or occupation of a literary writer. **4.** The body of written work produced by scholars or researchers in a given field: *medical literature.* **5.** Printed material of any kind, as for a political or advertising campaign. **6.** *Music.* The aggregate of compositions, especially for a specific instrument or ensemble. [Middle English *litterature,* from Old French, from Latin *litterātūra,* writing, learning, from *litterātus,* learned, literate.]

-lith. Indicates stone or rock; for example, **paleolith.** [Greek *lithos,* stone. See **litho-.**]

lith. lithograph; lithographic; lithography.

lith·arge (lĭth′ärj′, lĭ-thärj′) *n.* A yellow lead oxide, PbO, used in storage batteries, glass, and as a pigment. Also called "lead monoxide." Compare **massicot.** [Middle English *lit(h)arge,* from Old French, from Latin *lithargyrus,* from Greek *litharguros,* "silver stone" : lith(o)- + *arguros,* silver (see **arg-** in Appendix*).]

lithe (līth) *adj.* **1.** Readily bent; supple; limber. **2.** Marked by effortless grace. [Middle English *lith(e), lythe,* meek, mild, flexible, Old English *līthe.* See **lento-** in Appendix.*] **—lithe′ly** *adv.* **—lithe′ness** *n.*

lithe·some (līth′səm) *adj.* Lithe; lissome.

lith·i·a (lĭth′ē-ə) *n. Chemistry.* **Lithium oxide** *(see).*

li·thi·a·sis (lĭ-thī′ə-sĭs) *n.* The pathological formation of calculi in the body. [New Latin, from Greek : lith(o)- + -iasis.]

lithia water. Mineral water containing some lithium salts.

lith·ic (lĭth′ĭk) *adj.* **1.** Pertaining to stone. **2.** Pertaining to lithium. [Greek *lithikos,* from *lithos,* stone. See **litho-.**]

-lithic. Indicates the use of stone; for example, **Neolithic.**

lith·i·um (lĭth′ē-əm) *n. Symbol* **Li** A soft, silvery, highly reactive metallic element that is used as a heat transfer medium, in thermonuclear weapons, and in various alloys, ceramics, and optical forms of glass. Atomic number 3, atomic weight 6.939, melting point 179°C, boiling point 1,317°C, specific gravity 0.534, valence 1. See **element.** [New Latin : lith(o)- (from its mineral origin) + -ium.]

lithium oxide. A strongly alkaline white powder, Li_2O, used in ceramics and glass. Also called "lithia."

litho-, lith-. Indicates stone; for example, **lithosphere, lithia.** [Latin, from Greek, from *lithos*†, stone.]

litho., lithog. lithograph; lithographic; lithography.

lith·o·graph (lĭth′ə-grăf′, -gräf′) *n. Abbr.* **lith., litho., lithog.** A print produced by lithography. *—tr.v.* **lithographed, -graphing, -graphs.** To produce by lithography. [Back-formation from lithography.] **—li·thog′raph·er** (lĭ-thŏg′rə-fər) *n.* **—lith′o·graph′ic, lith′o·graph′i·cal** *adj.* **—lith′o·graph′i·cal·ly** *adv.*

li·thog·ra·phy (lĭ-thŏg′rə-fē) *n. Abbr.* **lith., litho., lithog.** A printing process in which the image configuration to be printed is rendered on a flat surface, as on stone or now chiefly on sheet zinc or aluminum, and treated so that it will retain ink while the nonimage areas are treated to repel ink. [German *Lithographie* : litho- + -graphy.]

li·thol·o·gy (lĭ-thŏl′ə-jē) *n.* **1.** The gross physical character of a rock. **2.** The microscopic study, description, and classification of rock. [New Latin *lithologia* : LITHO- + -LOGY.] —**lith′o·log′ic, lith′o·log′i·cal** *adj.* —**lith′o·log′i·cal·ly** *adv.* —**li·thol′o·gist** *n.*

lith·o·phyte (lĭth′ə-fīt′) *n.* **1.** *Botany.* A plant that grows on a rocky surface. **2.** An organism, such as coral, having a stony structure. [French : LITHO- + -PHYTE.] —**lith′o·phyt′ic** (-fĭt′ĭk) *adj.*

lith·o·pone (lĭth′ə-pōn′) *n.* A white pigment consisting of a mixture of zinc sulfide, zinc oxide, and barium sulfate. [LITHO- + Greek *ponos,* work, product. See **spen-** in Appendix.*]

lith·o·sphere (lĭth′ə-sfîr′) *n.* **1.** The solid part of the earth, as distinguished from the hydrosphere and atmosphere. **2.** The rocky crust of the earth.

lith·o·stra·tig·ra·phy (lĭth′ō-strə-tĭg′rə-fē) *n.* **1.** Stratigraphy based on the physical and petrographic properties of rocks. **2.** The interpretation of the physical characters of sedimentary rocks. —**lith′o·strat′i·graph′ic** (-străt′ĭ-grăf′ĭk) *adj.*

li·thot·o·my (lĭ-thŏt′ə-mē) *n., pl.* **-mies.** Surgery to remove calculi. [Late Latin *lithotomia,* from Greek : LITHO- + -TOMY.]

li·thot·ri·ty (lĭ-thŏt′rə-tē) *n., pl.* **-ties.** The surgical operation of pulverizing calculi in the bladder or urethra. [Irregularly from Greek *lithōn thrutika,* "stone-crushing (drug)" : *lithōn,* genitive plural of *lithos,* stone (see **litho-**) + *thrutikos,* crushing, from *thruptein,* to crush (see **dhreu-** in Appendix*).]

Lith·u·a·ni·a (lĭth′o͞o-ā′nē-ə). Officially, Lithuanian Soviet Socialist Republic. A constituent republic of the Soviet Union, formerly independent (1918–40), occupying 26,173 square miles in the northwest on the Baltic Sea. Population, 2,949,000. Capital, Vilnius. [Latinized form of Lithuanian *Lietuva.*]

Lith·u·a·ni·an (lĭth′o͞o-ā′nē-ən) *adj.* Of or pertaining to Lithuania, its people, or their language. —*n.* **1.** An inhabitant or native of Lithuania. **2.** The Baltic language of the Lithuanians.

lit·i·ga·ble (lĭt′ĭ-gə-bəl) *adj.* Capable of being litigated.

lit·i·gant (lĭt′ĭ-gənt) *n.* One who is engaged in a lawsuit. —*adj.* Engaged in a lawsuit. [Latin *lītigāns,* present participle of *lītigāre,* LITIGATE.]

lit·i·gate (lĭt′ĭ-gāt′) *v.* **-gated, -gating, -gates.** —*tr.* To subject (something) to legal proceedings. —*intr.* To engage in legal proceedings. [Latin *lītigāre,* to dispute, quarrel, sue : *līs*† (stem *līt-*), lawsuit + *agere,* to drive, lead, act (see **ag-** in Appendix*).] —**lit′i·ga′tor** (-gā′tər) *n.*

lit·i·ga·tion (lĭt′ĭ-gā′shən) *n.* Legal action or process.

li·ti·gious (lĭ-tĭj′əs) *adj.* Given to or characterized by litigation. —**li·ti′gious·ly** *adv.* —**li·ti′gious·ness** *n.*

lit·mus (lĭt′məs) *n.* A blue, amorphous powder derived from certain lichens, that changes to red with increasing acidity and to blue with increasing alkalinity. [Perhaps from Old Norse *litmosi,* "dye moss" : *litr,* a dye, color (see **wel-¹** in Appendix*) + *mosi,* moss (see **meu-** in Appendix*).]

litmus paper. An unsized white paper impregnated with litmus and used as an acid-base indicator.

li·to·tes (lī′tə-tēz′, lĭt′ə-) *n.* A figure of speech in which an affirmative is expressed by the negation of its opposite: *This is no small problem.* [Greek *litotēs,* from *litos,* simple, plain, unadorned. See **lei-** in Appendix.*]

li·tre. *Chiefly British.* Variant of **liter.**

lit·ter (lĭt′ər) *n.* **1.** A conveyance carried by men or animals, typically consisting of an enclosed couch mounted on shafts. **2.** A stretcher for the sick or wounded. **3.** Straw or other material used as bedding for animals. **4.** The young produced at one birth by a multiparous mammal. **5.** A disorderly accumulation of objects, especially carelessly discarded waste materials or scraps. **6.** The uppermost layer of the forest floor consisting chiefly of decaying organic matter. —See Synonyms at **flock.** —*v.* **littered, -tering, -ters.** —*tr.* **1.** To give birth to (young). **2.** To make untidy by discarding rubbish carelessly. **3.** To scatter about. **4.** To supply (animals) with litter for bedding. —*intr.* **1.** To give birth to a litter. **2.** To scatter litter. [Middle English *litere,* bed, offspring at birth, from Norman French, variant of Old French *litiere,* from Medieval Latin *lectāria,* from Latin *lectus,* bed. See **legh-** in Appendix.*]

lit·té·ra·teur (lĭt′ər-ə-tûr′; *French* lē-tā-rà-tœr′) *n.* Also **lit·ter·a·teur.** A man of letters. [French, from Latin *litterātor,* elementary teacher, grammarian, from *littera,* LETTER.]

lit·ter·bug (lĭt′ər-bŭg′) *n. Slang.* One who litters public areas with discarded materials.

lit·tle (lĭt′l) *adj.* **littler** or **less** (lĕs) (especially for senses 2, 3, 4), **littlest** or **least** (lēst) (especially for senses 2, 3, 4). **1.** Small, or smaller in comparison. **2.** Short in extent or duration; brief: *little time.* **3.** Small in quantity or degree: *little money.* **4.** Unimportant; trivial; insignificant: *little trouble.* **5.** Without much force; weak. **6.** Narrow; petty. **7.** Without much power or influence; of minor status. **8.** Being at an early stage of growth. Said of children and animals. **9.** Appealing; affectionate; endearing: *the little rascal.* —See Synonyms at **small.** —*adv.* **less, least. 1.** Not much; scarcely: *He sleeps little.* **2.** Not at all; not in the least. Used before a verb: *They little expected such trouble.* —*n.* **1.** A small quantity: *Give me a little.* **2.** An insignificant amount. **3.** A short distance or time: *a little down the road; a little past four o'clock.* —**in little.** On a small scale. —**little by little.** By small degrees or increments; gradually. —**make little of.** To regard or treat as not very important; dismiss. —**think little of. 1.** To have no hesitancy about. **2.** To think of as relatively unimportant or valueless. [Middle English *litel, lutel,* Old English *lȳtel.* See **leud-** in Appendix.*] —**lit′tle·ness** *n.*

Little A·mer·i·ca (ə-mĕr′ĭ-kə). Any of five American bases for polar exploration on the Ross Shelf Ice in Antarctica, the first of which was established by Richard Byrd (1929).

little auk. A bird, the **dovekie** *(see).*

Little Bear. A constellation, **Ursa Minor** *(see).*

Little Big·horn (bĭg′hôrn′). A river rising in northern Wyoming and flowing northward about 90 miles to join the Bighorn in southern Montana; on its shores Custer and his men were defeated by Indians (1876).

Little Col·o·ra·do (kŏl′ə-rä′dō, -răd′ō). A river rising in east-central Arizona and flowing 325 miles to the Colorado.

Little Dipper. A constellation, **Ursa Minor** *(see).*

Little Mis·sou·ri (mĭ-zo͝or′ē). A river rising in northeastern Wyoming and flowing 560 miles generally northeast to the Missouri in North Dakota.

lit·tle·neck (lĭt′l-nĕk′) *n.* A clam, the quahog, when small and suitable for eating raw. [From *Littleneck* Bay, Long Island.]

little owl. A small Old World owl, *Athene noctua,* having streaked brownish plumage.

Little Rhod·y (rō′dē). The nickname for Rhode Island.

Little Rock. The capital of Arkansas, on the Arkansas River in the center of the state. Population, 129,000.

Little Russian. Ukrainian *(see).*

little slam. See **slam.**

Little St. Ber·nard Pass. See **St. Bernard Pass.**

little theater. A small theater usually for a community, collegiate, or experimental drama group.

lit·to·ral (lĭt′ər-əl) *adj.* Of or existing on a shore. —*n.* A shore or coastal region. [Latin *littorālis, lītorālis,* from *lītus* (stem *lītor-*), shore. See **lēi-³** in Appendix.*]

li·tur·gi·cal (lĭ-tûr′jĭ-kəl) *adj.* Also **li·tur·gic** (-tûr′jĭk). Of, relating to, or characteristic of liturgy. —**li·tur′gi·cal·ly** *adv.*

li·tur·gics (lĭ-tûr′jĭks) *n.* Plural in form, used with a singular verb. The study of liturgies.

li·tur·gi·ol·o·gy (lĭ-tûr′jē-ŏl′ə-jē) *n.* Liturgics.

lit·ur·gist (lĭt′ər-jĭst) *n.* **1.** One who uses or advocates the use of liturgical forms. **2.** A scholar in liturgics.

lit·ur·gy (lĭt′ər-jē) *n., pl.* **-gies. 1.** The rite of the Eucharist. **2. a.** The system of public worship in the Christian church. **b.** The Book of Common Prayer. [Late Latin *litūrgia,* from Greek *leitourgia,* public service, service of a priest, from *leitourgos,* public servant, minister, priest : *leōs* (stem *leit-*), variant of *laos,* people, multitude (see **lay**) + *ergon,* work (see **werg-¹** in Appendix*).]

Liu Shao-ch'i (lyo͞o′ shou′chē′). Born 1898. Chinese Communist political leader; chief of state (1959–68).

liv·a·ble (lĭv′ə-bəl) *adj.* Also **live·a·ble. 1.** Fit to live in; habitable. Said of a living space. **2.** Worth living.

live¹ (lĭv) *v.* **lived, living, lives.** —*intr.* **1.** To exhibit the characteristic signs of life. **2.** To continue to remain alive. **3.** To be maintained; subsist: *living on rice and fish; lived on inherited income.* **4.** To reside. **5.** To conduct one's existence in a particular manner: *lived by the old code of personal honor.* **6.** To pursue a positive, satisfying existence: *He really lived.* **7.** To remain in human memory, usage, or general acceptance: *He lives in the minds of us all.* —*tr.* **1.** To go through (existence or experience in various forms): *lived a nightmare.* **2.** To embody in one's manner of existence: *He lived his beliefs.* —**live and let live.** To be tolerant. —**live down.** To overcome (an adversity) by acceptance over a period of time. —**live it up.** *Informal.* To have ebullient fun. —**live together.** To reside together, especially in sexual intimacy. —**live up to. 1.** To guide one's life by: *live up to Christian ideals.* **2.** To show oneself as good as: *live up to a great reputation.* —**live with. 1.** To reside with, especially in sexual intimacy. **2.** To put up with (a continuing adverse factor). [Middle English *liven,* Old English *libban, lifian.* See **leip-** in Appendix.*]

live² (līv) *adj.* **1.** Having life. **2.** Characteristic of life. **3.** Of current interest: *a live topic.* **4.** Glowing; burning: *a live coal.* **5.** Ignitable or explosible: *live ammunition.* **6.** *Electricity.* Carrying current. **7.** Brilliant; vivid. **8.** Native; not mined or quarried. Said of rocks and ores. **9.** *Radio & Television.* Carried on or present at a broadcast made at the time of occurrence. **10.** *Printing.* Not yet set into type: *live copy.* **11.** *Sports.* Being or capable of being in play: *a live ball.* [Short for ALIVE.]

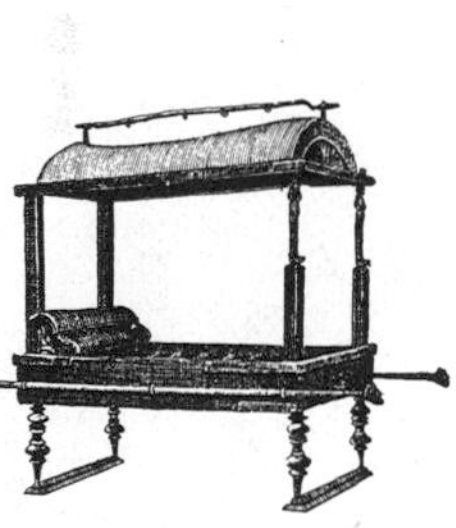

litter
Ancient Roman

live-bear·er (līv′bâr′ər) *n.* An ovoviviparous fish, such as a guppy. —**live′-bear′ing** *adj.*

live-for·ev·er (lĭv′fər-ĕv′ər) *n.* A plant, the **orpine** *(see).*

live·li·hood (līv′lē-ho͝od′) *n.* Means of support; subsistence. [Variant (influenced by LIVELY and -HOOD) of Middle English *liv(e)lode,* course of life, sustenance, Old English *līflād* : *līf,* LIFE + *lād,* course (see **leith-** in Appendix*).]

Synonyms: *livelihood, living, subsistence, sustenance, maintenance, support, keep.* These nouns refer to that which provides the necessities of life. *Livelihood* and *living* usually specify the occupation, work, or other means by which one earns his income. *Subsistence* refers to that which barely supports life, and *sustenance* to the means by which one exists on any economic level. *Maintenance, support,* and *keep* are usually reckoned as the equivalent in money of what is needed to provide necessities such as food, lodging, and clothing. *Support* is also applied to one who, or that which, provides the means for obtaining the necessities of life.

live load (līv). A moving, variable weight added to the dead load or intrinsic weight of a structure or vehicle. Compare **dead load.**

live·long (lĭv′lông′, -lŏng′) *adj.* **1.** Long or seemingly long in passing. **2.** Complete; whole. [Middle English *lefe longe,* "dear long" : *lef,* "dear" (here used only as an intensive), Old English *lēof* (see **leubh-** in Appendix*) + LONG.]

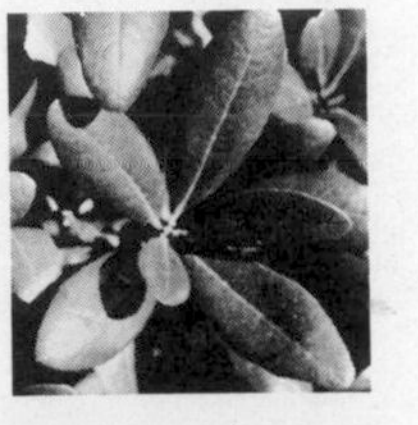

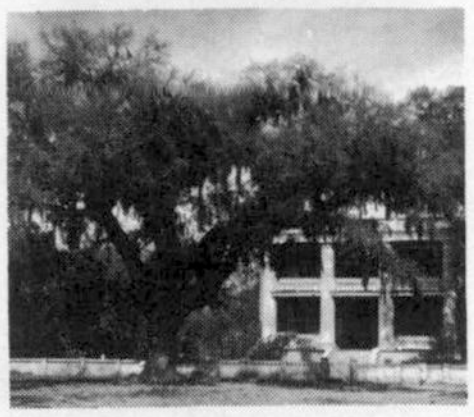

live oak
Quercus virginiana
Above: Foliage

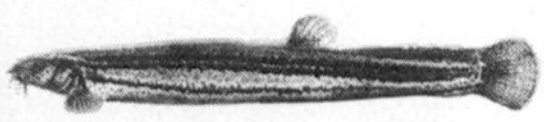

loach
Misgurnus fossilis

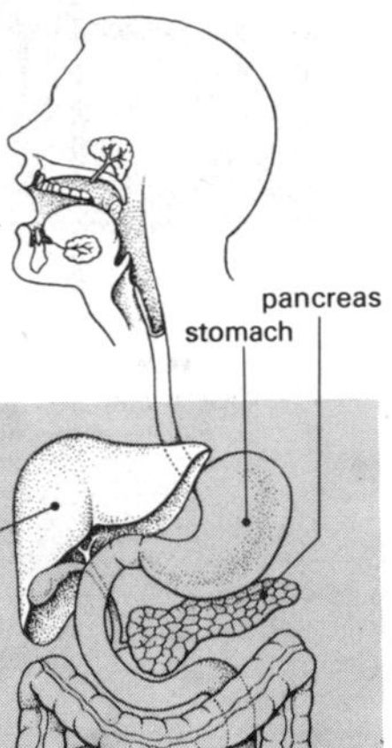

live·ly (līv′lē) *adj.* **-lier, -liest. 1.** Full of life; vigorous; energetic. **2.** Full of activity, spirit, or excitement. **3.** Exhibiting or characterized by intellectual or emotional activity; intense; keen. **4.** Exhibiting or inspiring liveliness; gay; cheerful. **5.** Effervescent; sparkling. **6.** Invigorating; brisk. **7.** Bouncing readily upon impact; resilient, as a ball. **8.** *Rare.* Lifelike. —See Synonyms at **active.** —*adv.* In a vigorous, energetic, or spirited manner. —**step lively.** To move quickly or briskly. [Middle English *lifliche,* Old English *līflic,* living, vital, from *līf,* life. See **leip-** in Appendix.*] —**live′li·ly** *adv.* —**live′li·ness** *n.*

li·ven (lī′vən) *v.* **-vened, -vening, -vens.** —*tr.* To cause to become lively. —*intr.* To become lively.

live oak (līv). Any of several evergreen American oaks, such as *Quercus virginiana,* of the southeastern United States, or *Q. agrifolia,* of southwestern North America.

liv·er[1] (lĭv′ər) *n.* **1.** *Anatomy.* A large compound, tubular, vertebrate gland that secretes bile and that acts in the formation of blood and in the metabolism of carbohydrates, fats, proteins, minerals, and vitamins. **2.** A similar invertebrate organ. **3.** The liver of an animal, used as food. [Middle English *liver,* Old English *lifer.* See **leip-** in Appendix.*]

liv·er[2] (lĭv′ər) *n.* One who lives in a specified manner.

liver extract. A dry, brownish powder containing the soluble thermolabile fraction of mammalian livers that is capable of increasing the number of red blood corpuscles in persons afflicted with pernicious anemia.

liver fluke. 1. Any of several parasitic trematode worms, such as *Fasciola hepatica* or *Opisthorchis sinensis* (or *Clonorchis sinensis*), that infest the liver of various animals, including man. **2.** Infestation with such parasites. Also called "liver rot," "rot."

liv·er·ied (lĭv′ə-rēd) *adj.* Wearing livery, especially as a servant.

liv·er·ish (lĭv′ər-ĭsh) *adj.* **1.** Resembling liver, particularly in color. **2.** Having a liver disorder; bilious. **3.** Having a disagreeable disposition; irritable.

liv·er·leaf (lĭv′ər-lēf′) *n.* A plant, the **hepatica** *(see).*

Liv·er·pool (lĭv′ər-po͞ol). A city of England, a port on the Mersey estuary in southwestern Lancashire. Population, 722,000. —**Liv′er·pud′li·an** (-pŭd′lē-ən) *adj.* & *n.*

liver starch. A carbohydrate, **glycogen** *(see).*

liv·er·wort (lĭv′ər-wûrt′, -wôrt′) *n.* **1.** Any of numerous green nonflowering plants of the class Hepaticae within the division Bryophyta. Also called "hepatic." **2.** The **hepatica** *(see).*

liv·er·wurst (lĭv′ər-wûrst′) *n.* A type of sausage made with or containing chopped liver.

liv·er·y (lĭv′ə-rē) *n., pl.* **-ies. 1.** The costume or insignia worn by the retainers of a feudal lord. **2.** The costume or uniform worn by male servants. **3.** The distinctive dress or garb worn by the members of a particular organization or group. **4.** Persons wearing such costumes or uniforms. **5.** The boarding and care of horses for a fee. **6.** The hiring out of horses and carriages. **7.** A livery stable. **8.** *Law.* The official delivery of property, especially land, to a new owner. [Middle English *livere, liverye,* from Norman French *livere,* variant of Old French *livree,* "something delivered or given," allowance (later clothes) granted to servants, from the feminine past participle of *livrer,* to deliver, relieve, from Latin *līberāre,* to set free, from *līber,* free. See **leudh-**[2] in Appendix.*]

liv·er·y·man (lĭv′ə-rē-mən) *n., pl.* **-men** (-mĭn). **1.** A keeper or employee of a livery stable. **2.** A member of one of the livery companies of the City of London.

livery stable. A stable that boards horses and keeps horses and carriages for hire.

lives. Plural of **life.**

live steam (līv). Steam coming from a boiler at full pressure.

live·stock (līv′stŏk′) *n.* Domestic animals, such as cattle, horses, sheep, hogs, or goats, raised for home use or for profit.

live wire (līv). **1.** A wire carrying electric current. **2.** *Slang.* A vivacious, alert, or energetic person.

liv·id (lĭv′ĭd) *adj.* **1.** Having discoloration of the skin, as from a bruise. **2.** Ashen or pallid, as with anger, rage, or illness. **3.** Extremely angry; furious. [French *livide,* from Latin *līvidus,* from *līvēre,* to be bluish. See **slī-** in Appendix.*] —**li·vid′i·ty, liv′id·ness** *n.* —**liv′id·ly** *adv.*

liv·ing (lĭv′ĭng) *adj.* **1.** Possessing life; alive. **2.** In active function or use. **3.** Of or relating to persons who are alive. **4.** Of, relating to, or characteristic of daily life: *living standards.* **5.** Of or relating to the maintenance of existence. **6.** *Informal.* True to life; real: *the living image of her mother.* **7.** In contemporary use or operation; currently active or valid. —*n.* **1.** The act, state, or condition of being alive. **2.** A manner or means of maintaining life; livelihood. **3.** A manner or style of life: *plain living.* **4.** Those who are alive. Preceded by *the: the living and the dead.* **5.** *British.* A church benefice, including the revenue attached to it. —See Synonyms at **livelihood.**

Synonyms: *living, alive, extant.* These adjectives are applied to what has continuing existence. *Living* and *alive* refer principally to organisms that have life. *Extant* describes something in existence, often a single or limited surviving example of its kind.

living room. A room in a private residence intended for the general use of the members of the household and for the reception and entertainment of guests.

Liv·ing·ston (lĭv′ĭng-stən), **Robert.** 1654–1728. Scottish colonist (from 1673) and legislator in New York.

Liv·ing·ston (lĭv′ĭng-stən), **Robert R.** 1746–1813. American statesman; an author of the Declaration of Independence.

Liv·ing·stone (lĭv′ĭng-stən), **David.** 1813–1873. Scottish medical missionary and explorer in Central Africa.

living wage. A wage sufficient to provide minimally satisfactory living conditions. Also called "minimum wage."

Li·vo·ni·a (lĭ-vō′nē-ə). **1.** A region of the Soviet Union comprising southern Latvia and northern Estonia. **2.** A city of Michigan, in the southeast near Detroit. Population, 67,000.

Li·vor·no. The Italian name for **Leghorn.**

li·vre (lē′vər; *French* lē′vr′) *n. Abbr.* **lv.** A former French money of account originally worth a pound of silver. [French, from Latin *lībra,* a pound. See **līthrā** in Appendix.*]

Liv·y (lĭv′ē). Latin name, Titus Livius. 59 B.C.–A.D. 17. Roman historian.

lix·iv·i·ate (lĭk-sĭv′ē-āt′) *tr.v.* **-ated, -ating, -ates.** To wash or percolate the soluble matter from. [From Late Latin *lixīvium,* lye, from the neuter of Latin *lixīvius,* of lye, from *lixa,* lye. See **leikw-** in Appendix.*] —**lix·iv′i·al** *adj.* —**lix·iv′i·a′tion** *n.*

liz·ard (lĭz′ərd) *n.* **1.** Any of numerous reptiles of the suborder Sauria (or Lacertilia), characteristically having an elongated, scaly body, four legs, and a tapering tail. **2.** Broadly, any reptile or amphibian resembling a lizard. **3.** Leather made from the skin of a lizard. [Middle English *liserd, lesard(e),* from Old French *lesard, laisarde,* from Latin *lacertus, lacerta*†.]

lizard fish. Any of various bottom-dwelling fishes of the family Synodontidae, of warm seas, having a lizardlike head.

Lju·blja·na (lyo͞o′blyə-nä). The capital of Slovenia, Yugoslavia, on the Sava. Population, 157,000.

ll. lines.

lla·ma (lä′mə) *n.* A South American ruminant mammal, *Lama peruana,* domesticated as a beast of burden and for its soft, fleecy wool. [Spanish, from Quechua.]

lla·no (lăn′ō, lä′nō) *n., pl.* **-nos.** A large, grassy, almost treeless plain, as one of those of Latin America and the southwestern United States. [Spanish, from Latin *plānum,* a plain, from the neuter of *plānus,* level. See **pelə-**[1] in Appendix.*]

Lla·no Es·ta·ca·do (lăn′ō ĕs′tə-kä′dō, lä′nō). A southern section of the Great Plains, extending over southeastern New Mexico and northwestern Texas. Also called "Staked Plain."

LL.B. Bachelor of Laws (Latin *Legum Baccalaureus*).

LL.D. Doctor of Laws (Latin *Legum Doctor*).

LL.M. Master of Laws (Latin *Legum Magister*).

Lloyd (loid). A masculine given name. [Welsh *llwyd,* "gray." See **pel-**[2] in Appendix.*]

Lloyd George (loid′ jôrj′), **David.** First Earl of Dwyfor. 1863–1945. Prime minister of Great Britain (1916–22).

Lloyd's (loidz) *n.* An association of underwriters founded in London in 1688, originally specializing in marine insurance and shipping data and now noted for the variety of insurance written. [After *Lloyd's* Coffee House in London, a gathering place of marine underwriters.]

Lloyd's Register. A compilation of data about oceangoing vessels of all nations, published annually by Lloyd's.

Llu·llai·lla·co (yo͞o′yī-yä′kō). A volcanic peak, 22,057 feet high, in the Andes of northern Chile.

lm lumen.

LM lunar module.

LMT local mean time.

ln Napierian logarithm.

lo (lō) *interj.* Used to attract attention or to show surprise: *lo and behold.* [Middle English *lo, la,* Old English *lā.*]

loach (lōch) *n.* Any of various Old World freshwater fishes of the family Cobitidae, having barbels around the mouth. [Middle English *loch(e),* from Old French *loche*†.]

load (lōd) *n. Abbr.* **ld. 1. a.** A supported weight or mass. **b.** The overall force to which a structure is subjected in supporting a weight or mass, or in resisting externally applied forces. **2. a.** Material transported by an automotive vehicle, ship, or aircraft, or carried by a man or pack animal. **b.** The quantity of such material. **3. a.** The share of work allocated to or required of an individual, machine, group, or organization. **b.** The demand for services or performance made on a machine or system. **4.** The amount that can be loaded into a machine or device at one time. **5.** A single charge of ammunition for a firearm. **6. a.** Mental or emotional stress regarded as a depressing weight. **b.** A responsibility regarded as an oppressive weight. **7.** The external mechanical resistance against which a machine acts. **8. a.** The power output of a generator or power plant. **b.** A device, or the resistance of a device, to which power is delivered. **9.** The sales charge added to the price of a share in a mutual fund. **10.** *Usually plural. Informal.* Any large amount or quantity. —**get a load of.** *Slang.* **1.** To look at or take notice of. **2.** To listen to or overhear: *Get a load of what she is saying.* —*v.* **loaded, loading, loads.** —*tr.* **1.** To put or place (a load) in or on a structure, device, or conveyance. **2.** To put or place in or on (a structure, device, or conveyance). **3.** To provide with plenty; give a lot of a thing to. **4.** To weigh down with; burden; oppress. **5.** To charge (a firearm) with ammunition. **6. a.** To insert (film, tape, or the like) into a holder or magazine. **b.** To insert film, tape, or the like into (a holder or magazine). **7.** To tamper with; especially, to make (dice) heavier on one side by adding weight. **8. a.** To twist or bias (evidence). **b.** To distort (a question or questions) so as to elicit a desired response. **9.** To dilute, adulterate, or doctor. **10.** *Electricity.* To raise the power demand in (a circuit), as by adding resistance. **11.** To increase (an insurance premium or a mutual-fund share price) by adding expenses or sale costs. —*intr.* **1.** To receive a load; put on cargo. **2.** To be charged with ammunition. **3.** To insert ammunition, film, tape, or the like. —**load the dice. 1.** To tamper with dice. **2.** To arrange beforehand for an outcome. [Middle English *lode* (influenced in sense by Middle English *laden,* to load, LADE), Old English *lād,* way, course, conveyance. See **leith-** in Appendix.*] —**load′er** *n.*

load displacement. The displacement of a fully loaded ship.

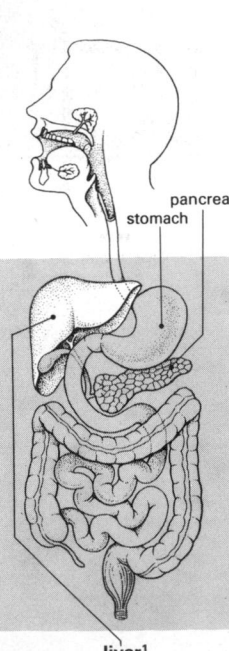

load·ed (lō′dĭd) *adj.* **1.** Having a load. **2.** Filled with ammunition, film, tape, or the like. **3.** Weighted or tampered with, as fraudulent dice. **4.** Meant to trick or trap: *a loaded question.* **5.** *Slang.* Intoxicated. **6.** *Slang.* Having much money.

load·ing (lō′dĭng) *n. Abbr.* **ldg. 1.** A weight, stress, or burden. **2.** The act of supplying a load. **3.** A substance added to something; filler. **4.** An addition to an insurance premium to cover extra costs. **5.** *Electricity.* The addition of inductance to a transmission line to improve its transmission characteristics.

load line. *Nautical.* Plimsoll mark (*see*).

load·star. Variant of **lodestar.**

load·stone. Variant of **lodestone.**

loaf¹ (lōf) *n., pl.* **loaves** (lōvz). **1.** A shaped mass of bread baked in one piece. **2.** Any shaped mass of food: *veal loaf.* [Middle English *lo(o)f, laf,* Old English *hlāf,* loaf, bread, from Germanic *hlaibaz* (unattested). See also **lord, lady.**]

loaf² (lōf) *v.* **loafed, loafing, loafs.** *—intr.* **1.** To spend time lazily or aimlessly. **2.** To waste time on a job; dawdle. *—tr.* To spend (time) lazily or idly. Usually used with *away.* [Probably back-formation from LOAFER.]

loaf·er (lō′fər) *n.* **1.** One who loafs. **2.** A casual or informal moccasinlike shoe.

loam (lōm) *n.* **1.** Soil consisting mainly of sand, clay, silt, and organic matter. **2.** A mixture of moist clay and sand, together with straw, used principally in making bricks and foundry molds. *—tr.v.* **loamed, loaming, loams.** To fill, cover, or coat with loam. [Middle English *lome, lame,* Old English *lām.* See **lei-** in Appendix.*] **—loam′y** *adj.*

loan (lōn) *n.* **1.** A sum of money lent at interest. **2.** Anything lent for temporary use. **3.** The action of lending. **—on loan. 1.** Borrowed: *He has my coat on loan.* **2.** Transferred temporarily to some duty or place away from a regular position or location. *—tr.v.* **loaned, loaning, loans.** To lend. [Middle English *lone, lane,* from Old Norse *lān.* See **leikw-** in Appendix.*]
Usage: Loan has long been established as a verb, especially in business usage. *Lend* is considered by many to be preferable to *loan* in general usage, however, and particularly in formal writing. More than 70 per cent of the Usage Panel express such a preference for *lend* in each of these examples: *If you loan money to a friend, he may cease to be your friend. When I refused to loan him my pen, he became very angry.*

Lo·an·da. See **Luanda.**

loan shark. *Slang.* A usurer, especially one who is financed and supported by gangsters.

loan translation. A form of borrowing from one language to another, whereby the semantic components of a given term are literally translated into their equivalents in the borrowing language; for example, **superman** is a loan translation of German *Übermensch* (*über,* over = *super-; Mensch,* man = *man*). Also called "calque."

loan·word (lōn′wûrd′) *n.* Also **loan word, loan·word.** A word adopted from another language that has become at least partly naturalized; for example, *encore, kindergarten, hors d'oeuvre.*

loath (lōth, lō*th*) *adj.* Also **loth.** Unwilling; reluctant; disinclined. Usually used with an infinitive: *loath to go.* [Middle English *loth(e), lath,* Old English *lāth,* hateful, loathsome. See **leit-** in Appendix.*]

loathe (lō*th*) *tr.v.* **loathed, loathing, loathes.** To detest greatly; abhor. [Middle English *lothen,* Old English *lāthian.* See **leit-** in Appendix.*] **—loath′er** *n.*

loath·ing (lō′*th*ĭng) *n.* Abhorrence. **—loath′ing·ly** *adv.*

loath·ly (lōth′lē, lō*th*′-) *adv.* Loathsome. [Middle English *lothly,* Old English *lāthlic : lāth,* loathsome (see **loath**) + -LY.]

loath·some (lōth′səm, lō*th*′-) *adj.* Abhorrent; repulsive; disgusting. [Middle English *lothsum : loth,* hatred, Old English *lāth,* from adjective (see **loath**) + -SOME.] **—loath′some·ly** *adv.*

lob¹ (lŏb) *v.* **lobbed, lobbing, lobs.** *—tr.* To hit, toss, or propel (something) slowly in or as if in a high arc. *—intr.* To hit a ball in a high arc. *—n.* **1.** A ball hit or thrown in a high arc. **2.** A cricket ball thrown underhand in a slow arc. **3.** A tennis ball hit in a slow high arc. [Of Low German origin, akin to Low German *lubbe,* awkward person, Flemish *lobbe,* fool, Middle Low German *lobbe†,* hanging lip.]

lob² (lŏb) *intr.v.* **lobbed, lobbing, lobs.** To move heavily or clumsily. *—n.* A clumsy, dull person; a lout. [Probably from LOB (to toss heavily).]

Lo·ba·chev·ski (lō′bə-chĕf′skē, -chĕv′skē, lŏb′ə-), **Nikolai Ivanovich.** 1793–1856. Russian mathematician.

lo·bar (lō′bər, -bär′) *adj.* Of or relating to a lobe, such as one of those in the lungs: *lobar pneumonia.*

lo·bate (lō′bāt′) *adj.* Also **lo·bat·ed** (-bā′tĭd). **1.** Having lobes. **2.** Resembling a lobe.

lo·ba·tion (lō-bā′shən) *n.* **1.** The state of being lobed. **2.** A lobe or part resembling a lobe.

lob·by (lŏb′ē) *n., pl.* **-bies. 1.** A hall, foyer, or waiting room at or near the entrance to buildings, such as hotels, apartment houses, or theaters. **2.** A public room next to the assembly chamber of a legislative body. **3.** A group of private persons engaged in influencing legislation. *—v.* **lobbied, -bying, -bies.** *—intr.* To seek to influence legislators in favor of some special interest. *—tr.* To seek to influence legislators to pass (legislation). [Medieval Latin *lobium, lobia, laubia,* a monastic cloister, from Germanic. See **leup-** in Appendix.*] **—lob′by·er** *n.*

lob·by·ist (lŏb′ē-ĭst) *n.* One employed to influence legislators to introduce or vote for measures favorable to the interest he represents. **—lob′by·ism′** *n.*

lobe (lōb) *n.* **1.** A rounded projection; especially, a rounded, projecting anatomical part such as the fatty lobule of the auricle

of the human ear. **2.** A subdivision of an organ or part bounded by fissures, connective tissue, or other structural boundaries. [Old French, from Late Latin *lobus,* from Greek *lobos,* lobe (of the ear or liver). See **leb-¹** in Appendix.*]

lo·bec·to·my (lō-bĕk′tə-mē) *n., pl.* **-mies.** Surgical excision of a lobe. [LOB(E) + -ECTOMY.]

lobed (lōbd) *adj.* Having lobes: *lobed leaves.*

lobe·fin (lōb′fĭn′) *n.* Any of various mostly extinct bony fishes of the subclass Sarcopterygii, of which the coelacanth is a living representative.

lo·be·li·a (lō-bē′lē-ə, -bēl′yə) *n.* Any of numerous plants of the genus *Lobelia,* having terminal clusters of variously colored flowers. [New Latin, after Matthias de *Lobel* (1538–1616), Flemish botanist.]

lob·lol·ly (lŏb′lŏl′ē) *n., pl.* **-lies.** *Regional.* **1.** A mudhole; a mire. **2.** A lout. [Originally "a thick gruel" : perhaps dialectal *lob†,* to bubble, boil + *lolly†,* broth.]

loblolly pine. A pine, *Pinus taeda,* of the southeastern United States, having strong wood used as lumber and for paper pulp.

Lob Nor Basin. See **Lop Nor Basin.**

lo·bo (lō′bō) *n., pl.* **-bos.** *Western U.S.* The gray or timber wolf, *Canis lupus.* [Spanish, from Latin *lupus,* wolf. See **wļkwo-** in Appendix.*]

lo·bot·o·my (lō-bŏt′ə-mē, lə-) *n., pl.* **-mies. 1.** Surgical division of one or more cerebral nerve tracts. **2.** Surgical incision into a lobe. [LOB(E) + -TOMY.]

lob·scouse (lŏb′skous′) *n.* A seaman's stew made of meat, vegetables, and hardtack. [Perhaps dialectal *lob,* to bubble, boil (see **loblolly**) + *scouse†,* broth.]

lob·ster (lŏb′stər) *n.* **1.** Any of several relatively large marine crustaceans of the genus *Homarus,* having five pairs of legs, the first pair modified into large claws. **2.** Any of several related crustaceans, such as the **spiny lobster** (*see*). **3.** The flesh of any of these crustaceans, used as food. [Middle English *lobster, lopster,* Old English *loppestre, lopystre,* from Latin *locusta,* locust, lobster (influenced by Old English *loppe,* spider). See **lek-** in Appendix.*]

lobster New·burg, lobster New·burgh (nōō′bûrg′, nyōō′-). A dish consisting of pieces of cooked lobster in a rich cream sauce containing sherry.

lobster pot. A slatted cage with an opening covered by a funnel-shaped net, used for trapping lobsters.

lobster ther·mi·dor (thûr′mə-dôr′). A dish consisting of cooked lobster meat mixed with a cream sauce and then returned to its shell, sprinkled with cheese, and browned.

lob·u·late (lŏb′yə-lĭt, -lāt′) *adj.* Also **lob·u·lat·ed** (-lā′tĭd). Having or consisting of lobules. **—lob′u·la′tion** *n.*

lob·ule (lŏb′yōōl) *n.* **1.** A small lobe. **2.** A section or subdivision of a lobe. [French, from New Latin *lobulus,* diminutive of Late Latin *lobus,* LOBE.] **—lob′u·lar** (-yə-lər), **lob′u·lose′** *adj.* **—lob′u·lar·ly** *adv.*

lob·worm (lŏb′wûrm′) *n.* A lugworm (*see*). [LOB (obsolete sense "lump") + WORM.]

lo·cal (lō′kəl) *adj.* **1.** Of or relating to a place. **2.** Pertaining to, existing in, of interest to, peculiar to, or serving a locality: *local government.* **3.** Not broad or general; confined. **4.** *Medicine.* Of or affecting a limited part of the body; not systemic: *a local disease.* **5.** Making many stops; not express: *a local train. —n.* **1.** A public conveyance that makes all possible or scheduled stops. **2.** A local or regional chapter or branch of an organization, especially of a labor union. **3.** A local person. [Middle English, from Old French, from Late Latin *locālis,* from Latin *locus,* place, LOCUS.]

local anesthetic. An injected or topically applied drug that induces local anesthesia. Compare **general anesthetic.**

local color. The interest or flavor of a locality imparted by the customs and sights peculiar to it.

lo·cale (lō-kăl′, -käl′) *n.* **1.** A locality, with reference to some event. **2.** The scene or setting, as of a novel. [French *local,* locality, from Old French, LOCAL.]

lo·cal·ism (lō′kə-lĭz′əm) *n.* **1.** An idiom, mannerism, custom, or the like peculiar to a locality. **2.** Provincialism.

lo·cal·i·ty (lō-kăl′ə-tē) *n., pl.* **-ties. 1.** A neighborhood, place, or district. **2.** A site, as of an event. **3.** The fact or quality of having position in space. See Synonyms at **area.** [French *localité,* from Late Latin *locālitās,* from Latin *locālis,* LOCAL.]

lo·cal·ize (lō′kə-līz′) *v.* **-ized, -izing, -izes.** *—tr.* **1.** To make local. **2.** To confine or restrain to a particular area or part. **3.** To attribute to a locality or determine the origin or source of: *localize a dialect. —intr.* To become local; especially, to become fixed in one area or part.

local option. Option granted usually by a state government to a community or a local government in such issues as whether to keep stores open on Sundays or to sell liquor.

lo·cate (lō′kāt′, lō-kāt′) *v.* **-cated, -cating, -cates.** *—tr.* **1.** To determine or specify the position and boundaries of: *locate Albany on the map.* **2.** To find by searching, examining, or experimenting: *locate the source of error.* **3.** To station, situate, or place: *locate an agent in Rochester. —intr.* To become established in some spot; settle. [Latin *locāre,* to place, from *locus,* place, LOCUS.]

lo·ca·tion (lō-kā′shən) *n.* **1.** The act or process of locating. **2.** The fact of being located or settled. **3.** A place where something is or might be located. **4. a.** A site or situation. **b.** Position in a series. **5.** *Motion Pictures.* A site away from the studio grounds, where a scene is shot: *make a movie on location.* **6.** A tract of land that has been surveyed and marked off. [Latin *locātio,* a placing, from *locāre,* to place, LOCATE.]

loc·a·tive (lŏk′ə-tĭv) *adj. Grammar.* Being a noun case in certain

lizard
Sceloporus magister
Spiny lizard

llama

lobster
Homarus americanus

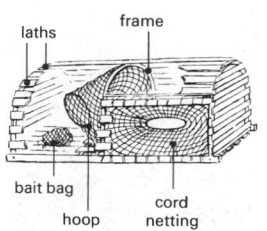

lobster pot
Diagram showing trap interior

ă pat/ā pay/â care/ä father/b bib/ch church/d deed/ĕ pet/ē be/f fife/g gag/h hat/hw which/ĭ pit/ī pie/î pier/j judge/k kick/l lid, needle/m mum/n no, sudden/ng thing/ŏ pot/ō toe/ô paw, for/oi noise/ou out/ōō took/ōō boot/p pop/r roar/s sauce/sh ship, dish/t tight/th thin, path/*th* this, bathe/ŭ cut/ûr urge/v valve/w with/y yes/z zebra, size/zh vision/ə about, item, edible, gallop, circus/ à Fr. ami/œ Fr. feu, Ger. schön/ü Fr. tu, Ger. über/KH Ger. ich, Scot. loch/N Fr. bon. *Follows main vocabulary. †Of obscure origin.

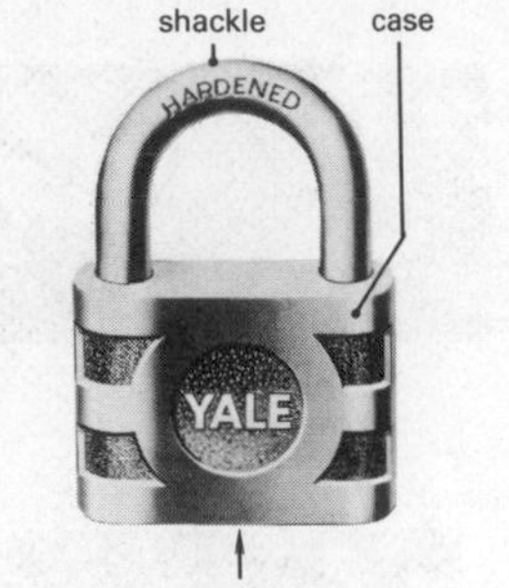

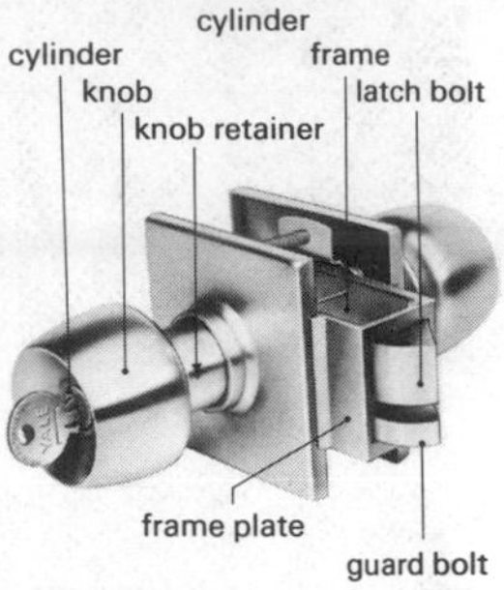

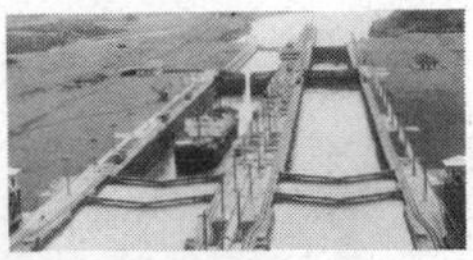

lock[1]
Above: Padlock
Center: Doorlock
Below: The Miraflores locks of the Panama Canal

Indo-European languages such as Sanskrit, that denotes place or the place where. —*n. Grammar.* **1.** The locative case. **2.** A word in this case. [French *locatif,* from Old French, from Latin *locāre,* LOCATE.]

lo·ca·tor (lō′kā′tər) *n.* One that locates, as a person who fixes the boundaries of a mining claim or other land.

loc. cit. In the place cited (Latin *locō citātō*).

loch (lŏKH, lŏk) *n. Scottish.* **1.** A lake. **2.** An arm of the sea similar to a fjord. [Middle English (Scottish) *louch,* from Scottish Gaelic *loch,* probably from Old Irish. See **laku-** in Appendix.*]

lo·chi·a (lō′kē-ə, lŏk′ē-ə) *pl.n.* The normal discharge of blood, tissue, and mucus from the vagina after childbirth. [New Latin, from Greek *lokhia,* from neuter plural of *lokhios,* of childbirth, from *lokhos,* childbirth, "ambush," "place for lying in wait." See **legh-** in Appendix.*] —**lo′chi·al** *adj.*

lo·ci. Plural of **locus.**

lock[1] (lŏk) *n.* **1.** A device used to provide restraint; especially, a key- or combination-operated mechanism used to fasten shut a door, lid, or the like. **2.** Such a device used to prevent unauthorized operation of a machine. **3.** A section of a canal closed off with gates and in which a vessel may be raised or lowered by the raising or lowering of the section's water level. **4.** A mechanism in a firearm for exploding its charge of ammunition. Usually used in combination: *a flintlock.* **5.** A jamming or locking together of elements or parts. **6.** Any of several holds in wrestling. —**under lock and key.** Safely locked up. —*v.* **locked, locking, locks.** —*tr.* **1. a.** To fasten with a lock to secure against passage or entry: *lock a door.* **b.** To shut by fastening all locks: *lock up a house.* **2. a.** To confine or safeguard by putting behind a lock. Used with *in* or *up: lock the dog in for the night.* **b.** To put in jail. Used with *up.* **3.** To engage and fix together securely; intertwine. **4.** To clasp or embrace tightly. **5.** To entangle in struggle or battle. **6.** To jam or force together so as to make unmovable. **7.** To equip (a canal or other waterway) with locks. **8. a.** To pass (a vessel) through a lock. **b.** To furnish or section off (a waterway) with locks. **9.** *Printing.* **a.** To secure (letterpress type) in a chase or press bed by tightening the quoins. **b.** To fasten (a curved plate) to the cylinder of a rotary press. Usually used with *up.* **10.** To invest (funds) in such a way that they cannot be easily converted into cash. Used with *up.* —*intr.* **1.** To become fastened by or as if by a lock. **2.** To become entangled; interlock. **3.** To become rigid or unmovable. **4.** To pass or flow through a lock. —**lock horns.** To become embroiled. —**lock on.** To find, fasten onto, and automatically follow a target, especially with radar. [Middle English *lo(c)k,* Old English *loc.* See **leug-[1]** in Appendix.*]

lock[2] (lŏk) *n.* **1.** A strand or curl of hair; tress; ringlet. **2.** *Plural.* The hair of the head. **3.** A small wisp or tuft, as of wool or cotton. [Middle English *lock, lok(k),* Old English *locc.* See **leug-[1]** in Appendix.*]

lock·age (lŏk′ĭj) *n. Nautical.* **1.** The passage of a vessel through a lock by operation of the lock. **2.** The toll for the use of a lock. **3. a.** A system of locks. **b.** The works of a lock. **4.** The amount of the rise and fall undertaken by a lock or a system of locks.

Locke (lŏk), **David Ross.** Pen name, Petroleum V. Nasby. 1833–1888. American journalist and humorist.

Locke (lŏk), **John.** 1632–1704. English philosopher.

lock·er (lŏk′ər) *n.* **1.** One that locks. **2.** An enclosure that may be locked, especially one used by a person at a gymnasium or public place, for the safekeeping of clothing and valuables. **3.** A flat trunk for storing things. **4.** A heavily insulated refrigerated cabinet, compartment, or room for storing frozen foods for extended periods.

locker room. 1. A room in a gymnasium, school, clubhouse, or the like, walled with metal lockers. **2.** A room for changing one's clothes, as at a public swimming place.

lock·et (lŏk′ĭt) *n.* A small ornamental case for a picture or keepsake usually worn as a pendant. [Old French *locquet,* latch, small lock, diminutive of Norman French *loc,* lock, probably from Old English *loc,* lock. See **leug-[1]** in Appendix.*]

lock·jaw (lŏk′jô′) *n. Pathology.* **1. Tetanus** *(see).* **2.** A symptom of tetanus, in which the jaw is locked closed because of a tonic spasm of the muscles of mastication. Also called "trismus."

lock·nut (lŏk′nŭt′) *n.* Also **lock nut. 1.** A usually thin nut screwed down on a primary nut to keep the latter from loosening. **2.** A self-locking nut.

lock out. 1. To bar or shut out by locking a door. **2.** To refuse work to (employees) during a dispute.

lock·out (lŏk′out′) *n.* The closing down of a plant by an employer to coerce the workers into meeting his terms or modifying theirs. Also called "shutout."

lock·smith (lŏk′smĭth′) *n.* One who makes or repairs locks.

lock step. A marching technique in which the marchers follow each other as closely as possible.

lock stitch. A stitch made on a sewing machine by the interlocking of the upper thread and the bobbin thread.

lock, stock, and barrel. Completely; the whole lot.

lock·up (lŏk′ŭp′) *n.* **1.** *Informal.* A jail, especially a local one in which offenders are held while awaiting a court hearing. **2.** An act of locking up or the state of being locked up.

Lock·yer (lŏk′yər), Sir **Joseph Norman.** 1836–1920. British astronomer; studied spectra.

lo·co (lō′kō) *n., pl.* **-cos. 1.** Locoweed. **2.** Loco disease. —*tr.v.* **locoed, -coing, -cos. 1.** To poison with locoweed. **2.** *Slang.* To craze. —*adj. Slang.* Mad; insane. [Mexican Spanish *loco,* locoweed, from Spanish *loco*†, crazy, insane.]

loco disease. A disease of livestock caused by locoweed poisoning, and characterized by dullness, lack of coordination, and partial paralysis. Also called "locoweed disease," "locoism."

Lo·co·fo·co (lō′kə-fō′kō) *n., pl.* **-cos.** A member of a radical faction of the New York Democratic Party organized in 1835. [From *Locofoco,* trade name of a match (because in 1835 members of this group carried matches to a meeting to foil a plot to put out the lights) : probably LOCO(MOTIVE), "self-propelled" + Italian *f(u)oco,* fire, from Latin *focus,* fireplace, hearth (see **fuel**).]

lo·co·ism (lō′kō-ĭz′əm) *n.* **Loco disease** *(see).*

lo·co·mo·tion (lō′kə-mō′shən) *n.* **1.** The act of moving or ability to move from place to place. **2.** Locomotive power. [Latin *locō,* ablative of *locus,* place, LOCUS + MOTION.]

lo·co·mo·tive (lō′kə-mō′tĭv) *n.* A self-propelled engine, now usually electric or diesel-powered, that pulls or pushes freight or passenger cars on railroad tracks. —*adj.* **1.** Of or involved in locomotion. **2.** Able to move independently from place to place. **3.** Of or relating to travel. [Old French, capable of moving from place to place : Latin *locō* (see **locomotion**) + MOTIVE.]

lo·co·mo·tor (lō′kə-mō′tər) *adj.* Locomotive. [Latin *locō* (see **locomotion**) + *mōtor,* mover, MOTOR.]

locomotor ataxia. *Pathology.* **Tabes dorsalis** *(see).*

lo·co·weed (lō′kō-wēd′) *n.* Any of several plants of the genera *Oxytropis* and *Astragalus,* of the western and central United States, causing severe poisoning when eaten by livestock. Also called "crazyweed."

loc·u·lar (lŏk′yə-lər) *adj.* Also **loc·u·late** (-lāt′, -lĭt), **loc·u·lat·ed** (-lā′tĭd). Having, formed of, or divided into small cells or cavities. —**loc′u·la′tion** *n.*

loc·ule (lŏk′yo͞ol) *n.* Also **loc·u·lus** (-yə-ləs) *pl.* **-li** (-lī′). A small cavity or compartment within an organ or part, such as a plant ovary. [Latin, diminutive of *locus,* place, LOCUS.]

lo·cum te·nens (lō′kəm tē′nĕnz′, tĕn′ĭnz). *Chiefly British.* A substitute physician or clergyman. [Medieval Latin *locum tenēns,* "(one) holding the place."]

lo·cus (lō′kəs) *n., pl.* **-ci** (-sī′). **1.** A place. **2.** *Geometry.* The set or configuration of all points satisfying specified geometric conditions. **3.** *Genetics.* The position that a gene occupies on a chromosome. [Latin *locus*†, place.]

locus clas·si·cus (klăs′ĭ-kəs) *pl.* **loci classici** (klăs′ĭ-sī′). A passage from a classic or standard work that is cited as an illustration or instance. [Latin, "classical place."]

lo·cust[1] (lō′kəst) *n.* **1.** Any of numerous grasshoppers of the family Locustidae, often traveling in swarms and causing damage to vegetation. **2.** A cicada such as the **seventeen-year locust** *(see).* [Middle English, from Old French *locuste,* from Latin *lōcusta,* locust, lobster. See **lek-** in Appendix.*]

lo·cust[2] (lō′kəst) *n.* **1.** A North American tree, *Robinia pseudoacacia,* having compound leaves, drooping clusters of fragrant white flowers, and hard, durable wood. **2.** Any of several similar or related trees, such as the honey locust or the carob. **3.** The wood of such a tree. [From the locust-shaped pods of some species.]

lo·cu·tion (lō-kyo͞o′shən) *n.* **1.** A particular word, phrase, or expression considered from the point of view of style. **2.** Style of speaking; phraseology. [Middle English *locucion,* from Latin *locūtiō,* speech, utterance, from *loquī* (past participle *locūtus*), to speak. See **tolkw-** in Appendix.*]

lode (lōd) *n.* **1.** *Mining.* **a.** A fissure in a rock formation that is filled with a metalliferous ore. **b.** A vein of mineral ore deposited between clearly demarcated, nonmetallic layers of rock. **2.** A rich source or supply. [Middle English *lode, lade,* course, way, Old English *lād.* See **leith-** in Appendix.*]

lode·star (lōd′stär′) *n.* Also **load·star. 1.** A star that is used as a point of reference; especially, the North Star. **2.** A guiding principle, interest, or ambition: *"his devotion to poetry was his one constant lodestar"* (Philip Horton). [Middle English *lo(o)de sterre,* "guiding star" : *lode, lade,* course, guidance (see **lode**) + STAR.]

lode·stone (lōd′stōn′) *n.* Also **load·stone. 1.** A magnetized piece of magnetite. **2.** One that attracts or magnetizes. [From its use by sailors to guide their course.]

lodge (lŏj) *n.* **1.** A cottage or cabin, often rustic and usually located in deep country or the mountains, used as a temporary abode or shelter: *a skiing lodge.* **2.** A small house on the grounds of an estate or park for a caretaker, gatekeeper, or the like. **3.** An inn. **4. a.** A North American Indian living unit such as a hogan, wigwam, or long house. **b.** The group living in such a unit. **5. a.** *Abbr.* **L.** A local chapter of certain fraternal organizations. **b.** The meeting hall of such a society. **c.** A meeting of a society. **6.** The den of certain animals, as the dome-shaped structure built by beavers. —*v.* **lodged, lodging, lodges.** —*tr.* **1.** To provide with quarters temporarily, especially for sleeping. **2.** To rent a room or rooms to; take in as a paying guest. **3.** To place or establish in quarters: *lodge children with relatives.* **4.** To serve as a depository for; to harbor. **5.** To place, leave, or deposit for safety. **6.** To fix, force, or implant. **7.** To register (a charge) in court or with an appropriate party: *lodge a complaint.* **8.** To vest (authority or power, for example). Used with *in* or *with.* **9.** *Archaic.* To beat down (crops). Used of wind or rain: *"If rye or wheat be lodged, cut it though it be not ripe."* (Robert Browning). —*intr.* **1.** To reside temporarily: *"Coleridge, Southey, and Burnett lodged together at 48 College Street."* (J.D. Campbell). **2.** To rent accommodations, especially for sleeping. **3.** To take shelter. **4.** To be or become embedded. [Middle English *log(g)e,* from Old French *loge,* shed, small house, from Frankish *laubja* (unattested). See **leup-** in Appendix.*]

lodge·pole pine (lŏj′pōl′). A pine, *Pinus contorta,* of western North America, having light wood used in construction.

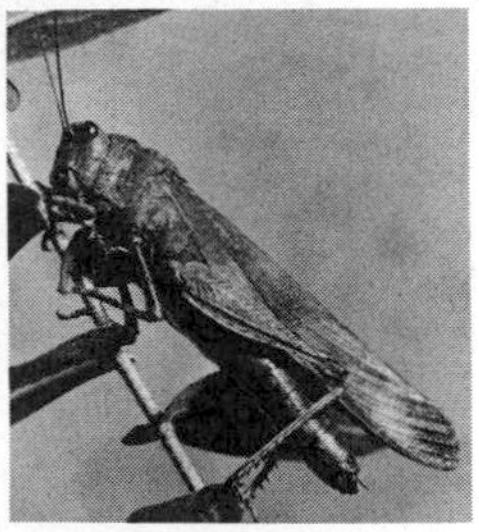

locust[1]
Dissosteira carolina

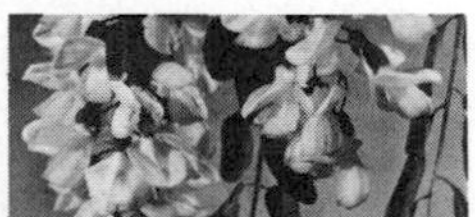

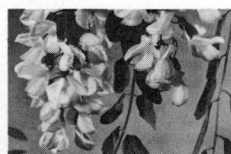

locust[2]
Flowers and foliage of
Robinia pseudo-acacia

ă pat/ā pay/âr care/ä father/b bib/ch church/d deed/ĕ pet/ē be/f fife/g gag/h hat/hw which/ĭ pit/ī pie/îr pier/j judge/k kick/l lid, needle/m mum/n no, sudden/ng thing/ŏ pot/ō toe/ô paw, for/oi noise/ou out/o͝o took/o͞o boot/p pop/r roar/s sauce/sh ship, dish/

lodg·er (lŏj′ər) *n.* A person who rents and lives in a furnished room or rooms; roomer.

lodg·ing (lŏj′ĭng) *n.* **1.** *Often plural.* Sleeping accommodations. **2.** *Plural.* Rented rooms.

lodg·ment (lŏj′mənt) *n.* Also **lodge·ment. 1. a.** The act of lodging. **b.** The state of being lodged. **2.** A place for lodging. **3.** An accumulation or deposit. **4.** *Military.* A foothold, beachhead, or salient gained in enemy or neutral territory.

lod·i·cule (lŏd′ĭ-kyo͞ol′) *n. Botany.* One of the small scales at the base of each flower in grasses. [Late Latin *lōdīcula,* diminutive of *lōdix* (stem *lōdic-*), covering, perhaps from Celtic.]

Łódź (lo͞oj). A city of central Poland about 75 miles southwest of Warsaw. Population, 700,000.

lo·ess (lō′ĕs, lĕs, lŭs) *n.* A buff to gray, fine-grained, calcareous silt or clay, thought to be a deposit of wind-blown dust. [German *Löss,* from Swiss German *Lösch,* from *lösch,* loose. See **leu-**[1] in Appendix.*]

Loe·wi (lō′ē), **Otto.** 1873–1961. German-born American physiologist; worked on chemical transmission of nerve impulses.

Loe·wy (lō′ē), **Raymond Fernand.** Born 1893. French-born American industrial designer.

Lo·fo·ten Islands (lō′fōt′n). An island group of Norway, 550 square miles in area, lying off the northwestern coast.

loft (lôft, lŏft) *n.* **1.** A large, usually unpartitioned floor over a commercial or industrial space. **2.** An open space under a roof; attic. **3.** A gallery or balcony, as in a church: *a choir loft.* **4.** A **hayloft** *(see).* **5. a.** A coop in which pigeons are kept. **b.** A flock of pigeons kept in such a coop. **6.** *Nautical.* A large room where full-scale plans of a vessel are laid out or where rigging is assembled. **7.** *Golf.* **a.** The backward slant of the face of a club head, designed to drive the ball in a high arc. **b.** A golf stroke that lofts the ball. **c.** The upward course of a lofted ball. —*v.* **lofted, lofting, lofts.** —*tr.* **1.** To put, store, or keep in a loft. **2.** To send (a ball) in a high arc. **3.** To lay out a drawing of (the parts of a ship's engine, for example). —*intr.* To loft a golf ball. [Middle English *lofte,* upper room, sky, Old English *loft,* sky, air, from Old Norse *lopt,* air, attic. See **leup-** in Appendix.*]

loft·er (lôf′tər, lŏf′-) *n.* A golf club designed to loft the ball. Also called "lofting iron."

loft·y (lôf′tē, lŏf′-) *adj.* **-ier, -iest. 1.** Of imposing height; towering. **2.** Elevated in character; exalted; noble. **3.** High-flown; affecting grandness; pompous. **4.** Arrogant; haughty. —See Synonyms at **high.** [Middle English, from *lofte,* raised, elevated, from *lofte,* sky, LOFT.] —**loft′i·ly** *adv.* —**loft′i·ness** *n.*

log (lôg, lŏg) *n.* **1. a.** A usually large trunk of a fallen or felled tree. **b.** A long, thick section of trimmed but unhewn timber. **2.** *Nautical.* A device trailed from a ship to determine its speed through the water. **3. a.** A record of a ship's speed, progress, and shipboard events of navigational importance. **b.** The book in which this record is kept. Also called "logbook." **c.** Any record of performance such as the flight record of an aircraft. —**sleep like a log.** To sleep soundly without much turning or twisting. —*v.* **logged, logging, logs.** —*tr.* **1. a.** To cut down the timber of (a section of land). **b.** To cut (trees) into logs. **2.** *Nautical & Aviation.* **a.** To enter (something) in a ship's or aircraft's log. **b.** To travel (a specified distance, time, or speed). **3.** To chalk up creditably: *He's logged 25 years with his company.* —*intr.* To cut down, trim, and haul timber. [Middle English *logge*†.]

log logarithm.

Lo·gan, Mount (lō′gən). The highest (19,850 feet) of the St. Elias Mountains in the southwestern Yukon Territory, Canada.

lo·gan·ber·ry (lō′gən-bĕr′ē) *n., pl.* **-ries. 1.** A trailing, prickly plant, *Rubus loganobaccus,* cultivated for its acid, edible fruit. **2.** The red fruit of this plant. [First grown by James H. *Logan* (1841–1928), American judge and horticulturist.]

log·a·rithm (lô′gə-rĭth′əm, lŏg′ə-) *n. Abbr.* **log** The exponent indicating the power to which a fixed number, the base, must be raised to produce a given number. For example, if $n^x = a$, the logarithm of *a,* with *n* as the base, is *x;* symbolically, $\log_n a = x$. See **common logarithm, Napierian logarithm.** [New Latin *logarithmus* : Greek *logos,* reckoning, reason, ratio (see **leg-** in Appendix*) + *arithmos,* number (see **ar-** in Appendix*).] —**log′a·rith′mic** (-rĭth′mĭk), **log′a·rith′mi·cal** *adj.* —**log′a·rith′mi·cal·ly** *adv.*

log·book (lôg′bo͝ok′, lŏg′-) *n.* Also **log book.** The official record book of a ship or aircraft.

loge (lōzh) *n.* **1.** A small compartment; especially, a box in a theater. **2.** The front rows of a theater's mezzanine. [French, from Old French, shed, small house. See **lodge.**]

log·ger (lô′gər, lŏg′ər) *n.* **1.** A lumberjack. **2.** A tractor, crane, or other machine used for hauling or loading logs.

log·ger·head (lô′gər-hĕd′, lŏg′ər-) *n.* **1.** A marine turtle, *Caretta caretta,* having a large, beaked head. **2.** An iron tool consisting of a long handle with a bulbous end, used when heated to melt tar or to warm liquids. **3.** *Nautical.* A post on a whaleboat used to help secure a rope holding a harpooned whale. **4. a.** *Informal.* A blockhead; dolt. **b.** A disproportionately large head. **5.** The loggerhead shrike. —**at loggerheads.** In a head-on dispute. [Dialectal *logger,* wooden block, from LOG + HEAD.]

loggerhead shrike. A North American bird, *Lanius ludovicianus,* having gray and white plumage and a hooked beak.

log·gi·a (lô′jē-ə, lŏj′ē-ə; *Italian* lôd′jä) *n.* **1.** A roofed but open gallery or arcade along the front or side of a building, often at an upper level. **2.** An open balcony in a theater. [Italian, from French *loge,* LOGE.]

log·ging (lô′gĭng, lŏg′ĭng) *n.* The work or business of felling and trimming trees and transporting the logs to a mill.

log·ic (lŏj′ĭk) *n.* **1.** The study of the principles of reasoning, especially of the structure of propositions as distinguished from their content and of method and validity in deductive reasoning. **2. a.** A system of reasoning. **b.** A mode of reasoning. **c.** The formal, guiding principles of a discipline, school, or science. **3.** Valid reasoning, especially as distinguished from invalid or irrational argumentation. **4.** The relationship of element to element to whole in a set of objects, individuals, principles, or events. [Middle English *logik,* from Old French *logique,* from Late Latin *logica,* from Greek *logikē (tekhnē),* "(art) of reasoning," from the feminine of *logikos,* of speech, of reasoning, from *logos,* speech, reason. See **leg-** in Appendix.*]

log·i·cal (lŏj′ĭ-kəl) *adj.* **1.** Pertaining to, in accordance with, or of the nature of logic. **2.** Showing consistency of reasoning. **3.** Reasonable on the basis of earlier statements or events: *"He did something so logical that it is impossible that no one else should have thought of it"* (Randall Jarrell). **4.** Able to reason clearly: *a logical thinker.* —**log′i·cal′i·ty, log′i·cal·ness** *n.* —**log′i·cal·ly** *adv.*

logical positivism. A philosophy asserting the primacy of observation in assessing the truth of statements of fact and holding that metaphysical and subjective arguments not based on observable data are meaningless, meaningful statements being either a priori and analytic or a posteriori and synthetic.

lo·gi·cian (lō-jĭsh′ən) *n.* A practitioner of a system of logic.

lo·gi·on (lō′gē-ŏn′) *n., pl.* **-gia** (-gē-ä′). One of the sayings of Jesus not recorded in the Gospels but supposed to have belonged to the source material from which they were compiled. [Greek, "saying."]

lo·gis·tic[1] (lō-jĭs′tĭk) *adj. Rare.* Of or skilled in arithmetic calculation. —*n. Rare.* Calculation by arithmetic. Used in the plural. [French *logistique,* from Late Latin *logisticus,* of reason, from Greek *logistikos,* skilled in calculation, from *logistēs,* calculator, from *logizein,* to calculate, from *logos,* reckoning. See **leg-** in Appendix.*] —**lo·gis′ti′cian** (-jĭ′stĭsh′ən) *n.*

lo·gis·tic[2] (lō-jĭs′tĭk) *adj.* Also **lo·gis·ti·cal** (-tĭ-kəl). Of or pertaining to logistics.

lo·gis·tics (lō-jĭs′tĭks) *n.* Plural in form, used with a singular verb. The procurement, distribution, maintenance, and replacement of materiel and personnel.

log·jam (lôg′jăm′, lŏg′-) *n.* Also **log-jam, log jam. 1.** A mass of floating logs crowded immovably together. **2.** A deadlock in the progress of negotiations, debates, or the like.

logo-. Indicates word or speech; for example, **logogram.** [Greek, from *logos,* speech, word, reason, account. See **leg-** in Appendix.*]

log·o·gram (lô′gə-grăm′, lŏg′ə-) *n.* A symbol or letter representing an entire word, such as ¢ for cents or *e* for energy (in physics). [LOGO- + -GRAM.] —**log′o·gram·mat′ic** (-grə-măt′ĭk) *adj.* —**log′o·gram·mat′i·cal·ly** *adv.*

log·o·graph (lô′gə-grăf′, -gräf′) *n.* A logogram. [LOGO- + -GRAPH.] —**log′o·graph′ic** *adj.* —**log′o·graph′i·cal·ly** *adv.*

lo·gog·ra·pher (lō-gŏg′rə-fər) *n.* Any of the Greek historians before Herodotus. [Late Latin *logographus,* from Greek *logographos* : *logos,* word (see **leg-** in Appendix*) + *-graphos,* writer, -GRAPH.]

lo·gog·ra·phy (lō-gŏg′rə fē) *n.* The use of logotypes in design and printing. Also called "logotypy." [LOGO- + -GRAPHY.]

log·o·griph (lô′gə-grĭf′, lŏg′ə-) *n.* A word puzzle, as an anagram or one in which clues are given in a set of verses. [French *logogriphe* : LOGO- + Greek *griphos*†, fishing basket.]

lo·gom·a·chy (lō-gŏm′ə-kē) *n., pl.* **-chies.** Argument about words. [Greek *logomakhia* : LOGO- + -MACHY.]

Log·os (lŏg′ŏs′, lō′gŏs′) *n.* **1.** *Often small* **l. a.** Cosmic reason, affirmed in ancient Greek philosophy as the source of world order and intelligibility. **b.** Reason or an expression of reason in words or things. **2.** The self-revealing thought and will of God, as set forth in the Gospel of John, often associated with the second person of the Trinity. [Greek *logos,* speech, word, reason. See **leg-** in Appendix.*]

log·o·type (lô′gə-tīp′, lŏg′ə-) *n.* A piece of type having two or more usually separate elements cast in one piece. [LOGO- + TYPE.]

log·roll (lôg′rōl′, lŏg′-) *v.* **-rolled, -rolling, -rolls.** —*tr.* To work toward the passage of (legislation) by logrolling. —*intr.* To engage in political logrolling.

log·roll·ing (lôg′rō′lĭng, lŏg′-) *n.* Also **log-roll·ing. 1. Birling** *(see).* **2.** The exchanging of political favors; especially, the trading of influence or votes among legislators to achieve passage of projects of interest to one another. —**log′roll′er** *n.*

-logue, -log. Indicates speech, discourse, or recitation; for example, **travelogue, travelog.** [Greek *-logos,* from *legein,* to speak. See **legend.**]

log·wood (lôg′wo͝od′, lŏg′-) *n.* **1.** A tropical American tree, *Haematoxylon campechianum,* having dark heartwood from which a dyestuff is obtained. **2.** The wood of this tree. **3.** The blackish or brownish dye obtained from this wood.

lo·gy (lō′gē) *adj.* **-gier, -giest.** Sluggish; lethargic. [Perhaps from Dutch *log,* heavy, sluggish. See **sleu-** in Appendix.*]

-logy. Indicates: **1.** Discourse or expression; for example, **phraseology. 2.** The science, theory, or study of; for example, **paleontology.** [Middle English *-logie,* from Old French, from Latin *-logia,* from Greek, from *logos,* word, speech. See **leg-** in Appendix.*]

loin (loin) *n.* **1.** *Usually plural. Anatomy.* The part of the side and back between the ribs and the pelvis. **2.** A cut of meat taken from this part of an animal. **3.** *Plural.* **a.** The region of the thighs and groin. **b.** The reproductive organs. —**gird up**

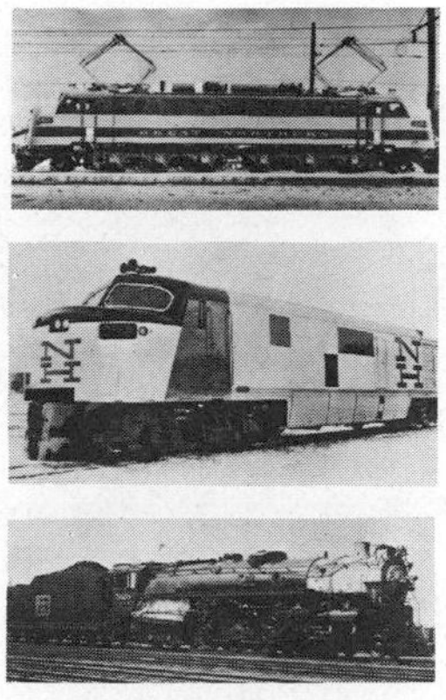

locomotive
Above: Electric locomotive
Center: Diesel locomotive
Below: Steam locomotive

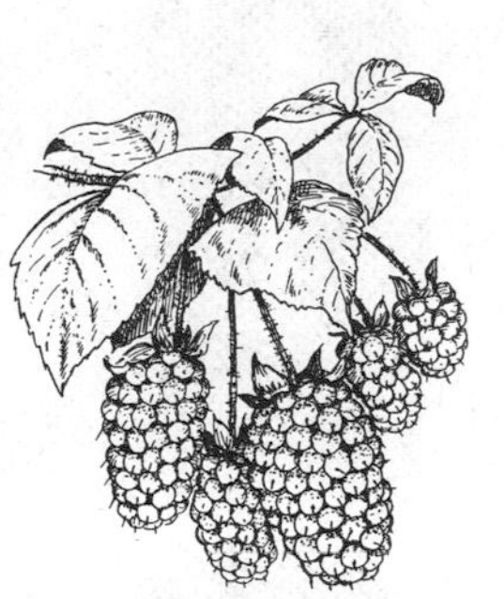

loganberry

one's loins. To prepare oneself for strenuous effort. [Middle English *loyne*, from Old French *loigne*, dialectal form for *longe*, from Vulgar Latin *lumbia* (unattested), from feminine of *lumbeus* (unattested), of the loin, from Latin *lumbus*, loin. See **lendh-**[1] in Appendix.*]

loin·cloth (loin′klôth′, -klŏth′) *n., pl.* **-cloths** (-klôths′, -klô*th*z′, -klŏths′, -klŏ*th*z′). A strip of cloth worn around the loins.

Loire (lwär). The longest river of France, rising in the southeast and flowing 625 miles northwest to the Bay of Biscay.

loi·ter (loi′tər) *intr. v.* **-tered, -tering, -ters. 1.** To stand idly about; linger aimlessly; loaf. **2.** To proceed slowly or with many stops. **3.** To dawdle: *loiter over a job.* [Middle English *loyteren*, perhaps from Middle Dutch *loteren*, to shake, totter. See **leud-** in Appendix.*] —**loi′ter·er** *n.*

Lo·ki (lō′kē). *Norse Mythology.* A god who created discord, especially among his fellow gods. [Old Norse, probably related to *logi*, flame, fire. See **leuk-** in Appendix.*]

loll (lŏl) *v.* **lolled, lolling, lolls.** —*intr.* **1.** To move, stand, or recline in an indolent or relaxed manner. **2.** To hang or droop laxly. —*tr.* To permit to hang or droop laxly. —*n. Archaic.* An act or attitude of lolling. [Middle English *lollen*, probably of Low German origin, akin to Middle Dutch *lollen*, to lull to sleep. See **lā-** in Appendix.*] —**loll′er** *n.* —**loll′ing·ly** *adv.*

Lol·land. See **Laaland.**

lol·la·pa·loo·za (lŏl′ə-pə-lo͞o′zə) *n.* Also **lol·la·pa·loo·sa, lal·la·pa·loo·za, la·la·pa·loo·za.** *Slang.* Something outstanding of its kind. [Origin unknown.]

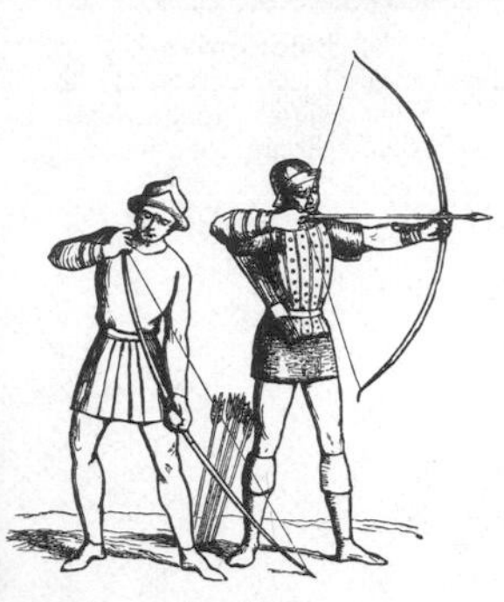
longbow

Lol·lard (lŏl′ərd) *n.* One of a sect of reformers who were followers of John Wycliffe in the 14th and 15th centuries. [Middle English, from Middle Dutch *lollaerd*, "mumbler (of prayers)," from *lollen*, to mutter. See **lā-** in Appendix.*]

lol·li·pop (lŏl′ē-pŏp′) *n.* Also **lol·ly·pop.** A piece of hard candy on the end of a stick. [Perhaps northern English dialect *lolly*, the tongue, from LOLL, to hang out (the tongue) + POP.]

Lo·lo (lō′lō) *n.* A group of Tibeto-Burman dialects spoken in southwestern China. —**Lo′lo** *adj.*

Lo·ma·mi (lō-mä′mē). A river of the Democratic Republic of the Congo, rising in the southeast and flowing 900 miles north to the Congo River.

Lo·mas de Za·mo·ra (lō′mäs *th*ā sä-mō′rä). A city of eastern Argentina, south of Buenos Aires, of which it is a suburb. Population, 275,000.

Lo·max (lō′măks′), **John Avery.** 1867–1948. With his son, **Alan** (born 1915), American folklorists and musicologists.

Lom·bard (lŏm′bərd, -bärd′, lŭm′-) *n.* **1.** One of a Germanic people that invaded northern Italy in A.D. 568 and established a kingdom in the Po Valley. **2.** A native of Lombardy. **3.** *Archaic.* A banker or pawnbroker. Also called "Langobard," "Longobard." —*adj.* Also **Lom·bar·dic** (lŏm-bär′dĭk, lŭm-). Of or relating to the Lombards or to Lombardy. [Middle English *Lumbarde*, from Old French *lombard*, from Italian *lombardo*, from Medieval Latin *lombardus*, from Late Latin *langobardus, longobardus*. See **del-**[1] in Appendix.*]

Lombard Street. The British banking and financial world. [After the moneychangers and bankers from LOMBARDY who once occupied one London street.]

Lom·bar·dy (lŏm′bər-dē, lŭm′-). A region occupying 9,188 square miles in northern Italy. Population, 7,339,000. Capital, Milan.

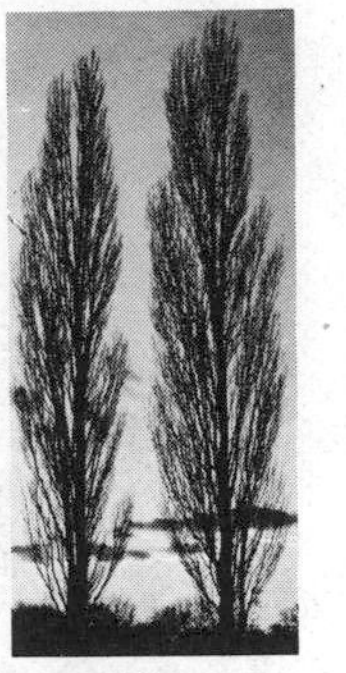
Lombardy poplar

Lombardy poplar. A tree, *Populus nigra italica*, having upward-pointing branches that form a slender, columnar outline.

Lom·bok (lŏm-bŏk′). An island of Indonesia, 1,825 square miles in area, lying east of Bali.

Lom·bro·so (lôm-brō′sō), **Cesare.** 1836–1909. Italian physician; founder of the science of criminology.

Lo·mé (lô′mā′). The capital of Togo, a seaport in the south on the Gulf of Guinea. Population, 80,000.

lo·ment (lō′mĕnt′) *n.* A pod, as of the tick trefoil or similar leguminous plants, having a series of constrictions separating the individual seeds. [New Latin *lomentum*, from Latin *lōmentum, lōvimentum*, a bean meal used by Roman women as a wash or cosmetic, from *lavāre*, to wash. See **lou-** in Appendix.*]

Lo·mond, Loch (lō′mənd). The largest lake (about 20 miles long and 5 miles wide) in Scotland, in the east-central part between Dunbarton and Stirling counties.

LON Airport code for London, England.

Lon·don (lŭn′dən). **1.** The capital of England and of the United Kingdom, on the Thames in southeastern England. Population, 7,990,000. **2.** A city in southern Ontario, Canada. Population, 170,000. [Middle English *Lundin, London*, Old English *Lundenne, Lundres*, from Latin *Londinium*, from Celtic *londos* (unattested), "wild," akin to Old Irish *lond*, wild.]

Lon·don, City of (lŭn′dən). The financial center of London, occupying about one square mile north and west of the Tower of London. Also called "the City."

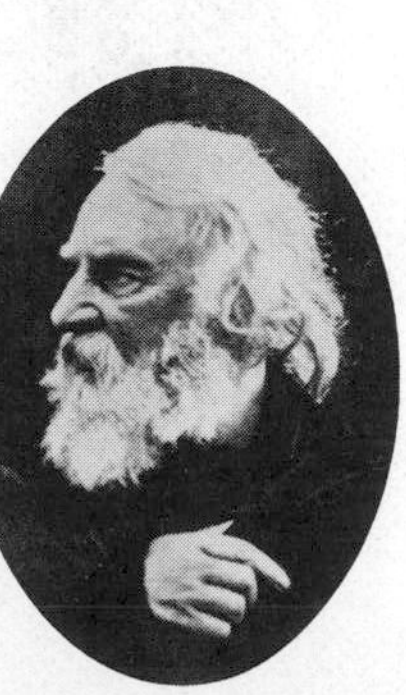
Henry Wadsworth Longfellow

Lon·don (lŭn′dən), **Jack.** 1876–1916. American author and adventurer.

London broil. Broiled flank steak, cut into thin slices.

Lon·don·der·ry (lŭn′dən-dĕr′ē). **1.** A county of Northern Ireland, occupying 804 square miles in the northwest. Population, 116,000. **2.** The county seat of this county. Population, 56,000. Also called "Derry."

lone (lōn) *adj.* **1.** Companionless; solitary: *a lone tree.* **2.** Isolated; unfrequented; sequestered; lonely. **3.** Unmarried or widowed. [Shortened from ALONE (*a-* is taken for the indefinite article).]

lone hand. 1. In some card games, a hand played without help from a partner's hand. **2.** A cardplayer without a partner. **3.** One who operates alone.

lone·ly (lōn′lē) *adj.* **-lier, -liest. 1. a.** Without companions; lone. **b.** Characterized by aloneness; solitary: *a lonely existence.* **2.** Unfrequented; empty of people; desolate: *a lonely crossroads.* **3. a.** Dejected by the awareness of being alone. **b.** Producing such dejection: *the loneliest night of the week.* —See Synonyms at **alone.** [From LONE.] —**lone′li·ly** *adv.* —**lone′li·ness** *n.*

lon·er (lō′nər) *n. Informal.* One who avoids other people.

lone·some (lōn′səm) *adj.* **1.** Dejected by being lonely. **2.** Inducing the sense of loneliness: *a lonesome trip.* **3.** Offering solitude; secluded. **4.** Deserted; unfrequented: *a lonesome valley.* **5.** Lone: *a lonesome pine.* —See Synonyms at **alone.** —*n. Informal.* Self: *He ate all by his lonesome.*

Lone Star State. The nickname for Texas.

long[1] (lông, lŏng) *adj.* **longer, longest. 1. a.** Having great length. **b.** *Rare.* Tall. **2.** Of relatively great duration: *a long time.* **3.** Of a specified linear extent or duration: *a mile long; an hour long.* **4.** Extending beyond an average or a standard: *a long game.* **5.** Tediously protracted; lengthy: *a long speech.* **6.** Concerned with distant issues; far-reaching: *a long view.* **7.** Risky; chancy: *long odds.* **8.** Having an abundance or an excess of. Used with *on: long on hope.* **9.** *Finance.* Having a large holding of a security or commodity in expectation of a rise in price: *long on steel.* **10.** *Phonetics.* Having a comparatively protracted sound: *a long vowel.* **11. a.** *Prosody.* Being of relatively great duration, as *feed* compared with *feet.* **b.** Stressed: *a long syllable.* —**in the long run.** Ultimately; eventually. —*adv.* **1.** During or for an extended period of time: *The promotion was long due.* **2.** Far: *He read long into the night.* **3.** For or throughout a specified period: *They talked all night long.* **4.** At a point of time distant from that referred to: *long before we were born.* —**as** (or **so**) **long as. 1.** Since; inasmuch as. **2.** During the time that. —**no longer.** Not now as formerly; no more: *He no longer smokes.* —*n.* **1.** A long time. **2.** A long syllable, vowel, or consonant. **3.** *Finance.* One who acquires large holdings of a security expecting a rise in price. **4. a.** A garment size for a tall person. **b.** *Plural.* Full-length trousers. —**before long.** Soon. —**the long and the short of.** The substance; gist: *The long and short of it is they won.* [Middle English *long, lang*, Old English *long, lang*. See **del-**[1] in Appendix.*]

long[2] (lông, lŏng) *intr.v.* **longed, longing, longs.** To yearn; wish earnestly; desire greatly: *He longed to go home.* See Synonyms at **yearn.** [Middle English *longen*, Old English *langian*, "to seem long (to some)," to yearn for. See **del-**[1] in Appendix.*]

long. longitude.

Long (lông, lŏng), **Huey Pierce.** 1893–1935. American political leader; governor of (1928–31) and U.S. senator from (1931–35) Louisiana; assassinated.

Long (lông, lŏng), **Stephen Harriman.** 1784–1864. American engineer and explorer of the West.

lon·ga·nim·i·ty (lŏng′gə-nĭm′ə-tē) *n.* Equanimity in the face of suffering and adversity; forbearance. [Middle English *longanimyte*, from Late Latin *longanimitās*, from *longanimis*, "long-souled," patient : Latin *longus*, long (see **del-**[1] in Appendix*) + *animus*, soul, mind (see **ane-** in Appendix*).]

Long Beach. A city of southwestern California, on San Pedro Bay 20 miles south of Los Angeles. Population, 344,000.

long·boat (lông′bōt′, lŏng′-) *n.* The longest boat carried by a sailing ship, especially by a merchantman.

long·bow (lông′bō′, lŏng′-) *n.* **1.** A wooden bow roughly five to six feet long. **2.** A powerful hand-drawn bow, sometimes exceeding six feet in length, much used in medieval England.

Long·den (lông′dən, lŏng′-), **John Eric ("Johnny").** Born 1910. British-born American jockey.

long distance. 1. An operator or system that places long-distance telephone calls. **2.** A long-distance telephone call.

long-dis·tance (lông′dĭs′təns, lŏng′-) *adj.* **1.** Located or from far away. **2.** Covering a long distance. **3.** Of or involving telephone communications to a distant station. —*adv.* By long-distance telephone.

long division. A process of division in arithmetic, usually used when the divisor has more than one digit, in which the remainders leading to succeeding steps of the procedure are recorded in a determinate pattern.

long dozen. Thirteen; a baker's dozen.

long-drawn (lông′drôn′, lŏng′-) *adj.* Prolonged. Also "long-drawn-out."

lon·ge·ron (lŏn′jər-ən) *n.* A structural member that runs from front to rear of an aircraft's fuselage. [French, from *longer*, to pass along, extend along, from Late Latin *longāre*, to lengthen, from Latin *longus*, long. See **del-**[1] in Appendix.*]

lon·gev·i·ty (lŏn-jĕv′ə-tē) *n.* **1.** A long duration of life. **2.** Long duration, as in an occupation or political office. [Late Latin *longevitās*, from Latin *longaevus*, living to a great age : *longus*, long (see **del-**[1] in Appendix*) + *aevum*, age (see **aiw-** in Appendix*).] —**lon·ge′vous** (-jē′vəs) *adj.*

long face. A discontented or sullen facial expression.

Long·fel·low (lông′fĕl′ō, lŏng′-), **Henry Wadsworth.** 1807–1882. American poet.

Long·ford (lông′fərd, lŏng′-). **1.** A county of north-central Republic of Ireland, 403 square miles in area. Population, 31,000. **2.** The county seat of this county. Population, 4,000.

long green. *Slang.* Paper money.

long·hair (lông′hâr′, lŏng′-) *n.* **1.** One dedicated to the arts and especially to classical music. **2.** One whose taste in the arts is held to be overrefined. —**long′hair′, long′haired′** *adj.*

long·hand (lông′hănd′, lŏng′-) *n.* Cursive writing.

long·head (lông′hĕd′, lŏng′-) *n.* **1.** A head having a cephalic index of less than 75.9. **2.** A person having such a head.

long·head·ed (lông′hĕd′ĭd, lŏng′-) *adj.* Also **long·head·ed.**

1. Dolichocephalic. **2.** Foresighted; shrewd; astute; cunning.

long·horn (lông'hôrn', lŏng'-) *n.* One of a breed of long-horned cattle formerly bred in the southwestern United States.

long-horned beetle (lông'hôrnd', lŏng'-). Any of numerous beetles of the family Cerambycidae, having long legs and long antennae. Also called "longicorn."

long house. A long wooden dwelling of the Iroquois.

longi–. Indicates long; for example, **longicorn**. [Latin, from *longus*, long. See **del-**[1] in Appendix.*]

lon·gi·corn (lŏn'jĭ-kôrn') *n.* A long-horned beetle *(see).* —*adj.* **1.** Having long antennae. **2.** Of or belonging to the family Cerambycidae, which includes the long-horned beetles. [New Latin *Longicornia* (former classification) : LONGI- + Latin *cornū*, horn (see **ker-**[1] in Appendix*).]

long·ing (lông'ing, lŏng'-) *n.* A persistent yearning or desire that cannot be fulfilled. —*adj.* Affected by such a yearning: *look with longing eyes.* —**long'ing·ly** *adv.*

long·ish (lông'ish, lŏng'-) *adj.* Fairly long.

Long Island. *Abbr.* **L.I.** An island, 1,401 square miles in area, of southeastern New York State, adjacent to and including sections of New York City.

Long Island Sound. An arm of the Atlantic Ocean extending for 90 miles between Long Island and Connecticut.

lon·gi·tude (lŏn'jə-tōōd', -tyōōd') *n. Abbr.* **long. 1.** *Geography.* The angular distance on the earth or on a globe or map, east or west of the prime meridian at Greenwich, England, to the point on the earth's surface for which the longitude is being ascertained, expressed either in degrees or in hours, minutes, and seconds. **2.** *Astronomy.* The angular distance, measured in degrees eastward along the ecliptic from the vernal equinox to the great circle passing through the pole of the ecliptic and the celestial point being measured. [Middle English, from Latin *longitūdō*, from *longus*, LONG.]

lon·gi·tu·di·nal (lŏn'jə-tōōd'n-əl, -tyōōd'n-əl) *adj.* **1.** Of or pertaining to length. **2.** Placed or running lengthwise. **3.** Pertaining to longitude. —**lon'gi·tu'di·nal·ly** *adv.*

long johns. *Informal.* Long, warm underwear.

long jump. The broad jump.

long-leaf pine (lông'lēf', lŏng'-). An evergreen tree, *Pinus australis* (or *P. palustris*), of the southeastern United States, having long needles and heavy, tough, resinous wood valued as timber and as a source of turpentine.

long-lived (lông'līvd', -livd', lŏng'-) *adj.* **1.** Having a long life. **2.** Persistent: *a long-lived rumor.* —**long'-lived'ness** *n.*

long measure. Linear measure *(see).*

Lon·go·bard (lŏng'gō-bärd') *n., pl.* **-bards** or **-bardi** (-bär'dē). A Lombard *(see).* [Latin *Longobardī, Langobardī*, the Lombards. See Lombard.] —**Lon'go·bar'di·an, Lon'go·bar'dic** *adj.*

Long Parliament. The English Parliament that was convened in 1640, dismissed by Cromwell in 1653, and reconvened in 1659–1660. See **Rump Parliament.**

long pig. A human being used for meat by cannibals.

long-play·ing (lông'plā'ing, lŏng'-) *adj. Abbr.* **LP** Relating to or being a microgroove phonograph record; especially, one turning at 33⅓ revolutions per minute.

long purples. A plant, purple loosestrife *(see).*

long-range (lông'rānj', lŏng'-) *adj.* **1.** Requiring or involving a span of years; not immediate: *long-range planning.* **2.** Of, suitable for, or covering long distances.

long·shore (lông'shôr', -shōr', lŏng'-) *adj.* Occurring, living, or working along a seacoast. [Short for ALONGSHORE.]

long·shore·man (lông'shôr'mən, -shōr'mən, lŏng'-) *n., pl.* **-men** (-min). A dock worker who loads and unloads ships.

long shot. 1. An entry, as in a horse race, with only a slight chance of winning. **2. a.** A bet made at and against great odds. **b.** A risky venture that will pay off handsomely if successful. **3.** A motion-picture sequence taken at some distance from the subject. —**by a long shot.** By a great extent or amount.

long-sight·ed (lông'sī'tid, lŏng'-) *adj.* **1.** Afflicted with **hyperopia** *(see)*; hyperopic. **2.** Farsighted. —**long'-sight'ed·ness** *n.*

long·some (lông'səm, lŏng'-) *adj.* Tiresomely long.

Longs Peak (lôngz, lŏngz). A mountain rising to 14,255 feet in the Rocky Mountains of north-central Colorado.

long·spur (lông'spûr', lŏng'-) *n.* Any of several birds of the genera *Calcarius* and *Rhynchophanes*, of northern regions, having brownish plumage and long-clawed hind toes.

long-stand·ing (lông'stăn'dĭng, lŏng'-) *adj.* Of long duration.

Long·street (lông'strēt', lŏng'-), **James.** 1821–1904. American army officer; commanded Confederate troops in the Civil War.

long-suf·fer·ing (lông'sŭf'ər-ĭng, lŏng'-) *adj.* Patiently enduring wrongs or difficulties. —*n.* Also **long-suf·fer·ance** (-əns). Patient endurance. —**long'-suf'fer·ing·ly** *adv.*

long suit. 1. *Card Games.* A suit containing more cards than any of the other suits in a hand. **2.** The personal quality or talent that is one's strongest asset; a selling point.

long-term (lông'tûrm', lŏng'-) *adj.* In effect, involving, or maturing after a number of years: *a long-term investment.*

long-time (lông'tīm', lŏng'-) *adj.* Having existed or persisted for a long time: *a long-time acquaintance.*

long ton. A ton *(see).*

long-wind·ed (lông'wĭn'dĭd, lŏng'-) *adj.* **1.** Wearisomely verbose: *a long-winded bore.* **2.** Not subject to quick loss of breath. —**long'wind'ed·ly** *adv.* —**long'wind'ed·ness** *n.*

long·wise (lông'wīz', lŏng'-) *adv.* Lengthwise.

loo (lōō) *n., pl.* **loos.** A card game in which each player contributes stakes to a pool. [Shortened from *lanterloo*, from French *lanturlu*, originally the refrain of a popular song.]

loo·by (lōō'bē) *n., pl.* **-bies.** A big, gangling, clumsy fellow; lubber. [Middle English *loby*, probably of Low German origin, akin to Middle Low German *lobbe*, loose-hanging lip, bumpkin. See **lob**.]

loo·fa, loo·fah (lōō'fə) *n.* Also **luf·fa** (lŭf'ə). **1. a.** Any of several Old World tropical vines of the genus *Luffa.* **b.** The fruit of such a vine, having a fibrous, spongelike interior. Also called "dishcloth gourd." **2.** The dried, fibrous part of this fruit, used as a washing sponge or as a filter. Also called "vegetable sponge." [New Latin *Luffa*, from Arabic *lūf, lūfah.*]

look (lōōk) *v.* **looked, looking, looks.** —*intr.* **1.** To employ one's eyes in seeing. **2. a.** To turn one's glance. **b.** To turn one's attention. **3.** To seem or appear to be: *look morose.* See Usage note at **bad.** **4.** To face in a specified direction: *The cottage looks on the river.* **5.** *Informal.* To hope or expect. Used with an infinitive: *He looked to hear from her.* —*tr.* **1.** To turn one's eyes on. **2.** To express by one's appearance: *She looked her joy.* **3.** To have an appearance in conformity with: *look one's age.* —**look after.** To take care of. —**look alive.** To act or respond quickly. —**look down on** (or **upon**). To regard with contempt or condescension. —**look for. 1.** To search for. **2.** To expect. —**look forward to.** To anticipate eagerly. —**look into.** To investigate. —**look on. 1.** To be a spectator. **2.** To consider; regard. —**look oneself.** To exhibit one's normal or usual appearance. —**look over.** To inspect; especially, to inspect casually. —**look to. 1.** To expect. **2.** To attend to. **3.** To rely upon. —**look up. 1.** To search for and find, as in a reference book. **2.** To locate and call upon; to visit. **3.** *Informal.* To improve. —**look up and down. 1.** To inspect critically, coldly, or disdainfully. **2.** To search everywhere. —**look up to.** To admire. —*n.* **1.** The action of looking; a gaze or glance. **2.** Appearance or aspect. **3.** *Plural.* Physical appearance, especially when pleasing. [Middle English *loken*, to look, have the appearance, Old English *lōcian*, to look, from West Germanic *lōkōjan* (unattested).]

longhorn

look·down (lōōk'doun') *n.* A marine fish, *Selene vomer*, of Atlantic waters, having a steep frontal profile.

look·er (lōōk'ər) *n.* **1.** One who looks. **2.** *Slang.* A very pretty woman or a very handsome man.

look·er-on (lōōk'ər-ŏn', -ôn') *n., pl.* **lookers-on.** A spectator.

look in. To drop in; make a brief visit.

look-in (lōōk'ĭn') *n.* **1.** A short visit. **2.** A quick glance.

looking glass. A mirror.

look out. 1. To be careful or protective: *looking out for one's interests.* **2.** To be on the watch: *Look out for the slippery floor.*

look·out (lōōk'out') *n.* **1.** The act of observing or keeping watch. **2.** A high place or structure commanding a wide view for observation. **3.** One who keeps watch. **4.** Outlook. **5.** Something worthy of concern or worry; a problem.

Lookout Mountain. A ridge in southeastern Tennessee, the site of a Union victory in the Civil War (1863).

look-see (lōōk'sē') *n. Slang.* A quick survey or glance.

loom[1] (lōōm) *intr.v.* **loomed, looming, looms. 1.** To come into view as a massive, distorted, or indistinct image. **2.** To appear to the mind in a magnified and threatening form. **3.** To seem imminent; to impend. —*n.* A distorted, threatening appearance of something, as through fog or darkness. [Probably of Low German origin, akin to East Frisian *lōmen*, to move slowly, *lōm*, lame, crippled. See **lem-**[1] in Appendix.*]

loom[2] (lōōm) *n.* **1.** A machine or device from which cloth is produced by interweaving thread or yarn at right angles. **2.** *Nautical.* The shaft of an oar. [Middle English *lome*, Old English *gelōma*, utensil, tool : *ge-* (collective prefix) + *-lōma*, akin to Middle Dutch *allame*†, tool.]

L.O.O.M. Loyal Order of Moose.

loon[1] (lōōn) *n.* Any of several diving birds of the genus *Gavia*, of northern regions, having a laughlike cry. Also called "diver." [Probably from Old Norse *lomr.* See **lā-** in Appendix.*]

loon[2] (lōōn) *n.* **1.** A simple-minded or mad person. **2.** An idler. [Middle English *loun, lownt*†.]

loon·y (lōō'nē) *adj.* **-ier, -iest.** Also **lun·y.** *Informal.* So odd as to appear demented. —*n., pl.* **loonies.** Also **lun·y.** *Informal.* A loony person.

loop[1] (lōōp) *n.* **1.** A length of line, as of wire, thread, rope, or ribbon, that is folded over and joined at the ends. **2.** The opening formed by such a doubled line. **3.** Any roughly oval, closed, or nearly closed turn or figure. **4.** Something having such a turn or figure. **5.** *Electricity.* A closed circuit. **6.** A flight maneuver in which an aircraft flies a circular path in a vertical plane with the lateral axis of the aircraft remaining horizontal. —*v.* **looped, looping, loops.** —*tr.* **1.** To form (thread, for example) into a loop or loops. **2.** To fasten, join, or encircle with a loop or loops. **3.** To fly (an aircraft) in a loop. **4.** *Electricity.* To join (conductors) so as to complete a circuit. —*intr.* **1.** To form a loop or loops. **2.** *Aviation.* To make a loop or loops. —**loop the loop.** To make a vertical loop or loops in the air. Used of an aircraft. [Middle English *loupe*†.]

loop[2] (lōōp) *n. Archaic.* A small opening in a wall; loophole. [Middle English *loupe*†.]

Loop, the. The central business district of Chicago.

loop·er (lōō'pər) *n.* **1.** One that makes loops. **2.** A **measuring worm** *(see).*

loop·hole (lōōp'hōl') *n.* **1.** A small hole or slit in a wall, especially one through which small arms may be fired. **2.** A way of escaping a difficulty; especially, an omission or an ambiguity, as in the wording of a contract or law, that provides a means of evasion. [LOOP (opening) + HOLE.]

loose (lōōs) *adj.* **looser, loosest. 1.** Not fastened or restrained; unbound. **2.** Not taut or drawn up tightly; slack. **3.** Free from confinement or imprisonment; unfettered. **4.** Not tight-fitting or tightly fitted. **5.** Calm; unruffled. **6.** Not bound, bundled,

lookdown

loon[1]
Gavia immer

ă pat/ā pay/âr care/ä father/b bib/ch church/d deed/ĕ pet/ē be/f fife/g gag/h hat/hw which/ĭ pit/ī pie/îr pier/j judge/k kick/l lid, needle/m mum/n no, sudden/ng thing/ŏ pot/ō toe/ô paw, for/oi noise/ou out/ōō took/

t tight/th thin, path/th this, bathe/ŭ cut/ûr urge/v valve/w with/y yes/z zebra, size/zh vision/ə about, item, edible, gallop, circus/
à *Fr.* ami/œ *Fr.* feu, *Ger.* schön/ü *Fr.* tu, *Ger.* über/KH *Ger.* ich, *Scot.* loch/N *Fr.* bon. *Follows main vocabulary. †Of obscure origin.

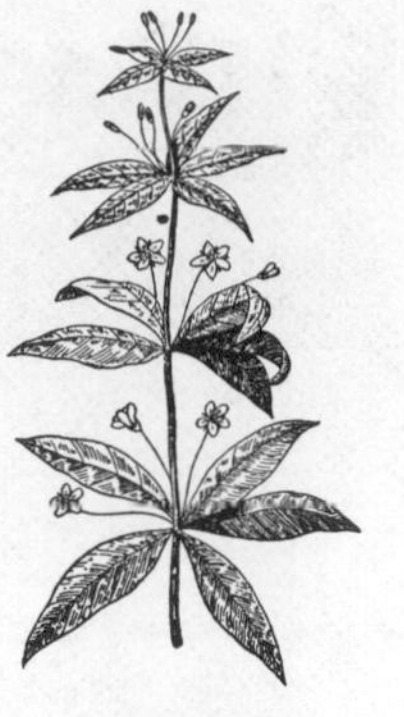

loosestrife
Lysimachia quadrifolia
Whorled loosestrife

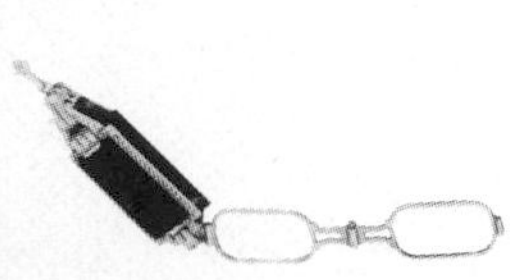

lorgnette

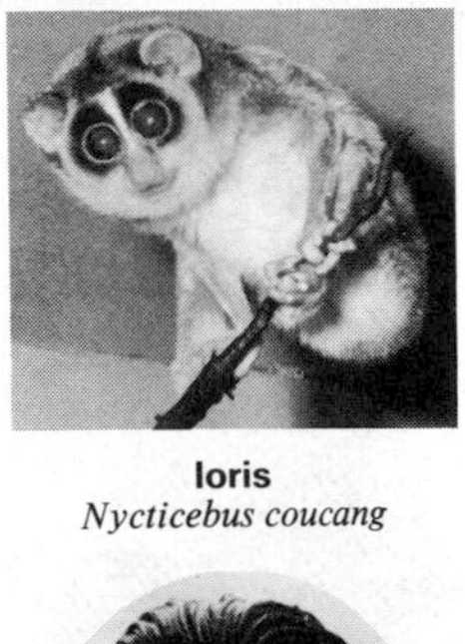

loris
Nycticebus coucang

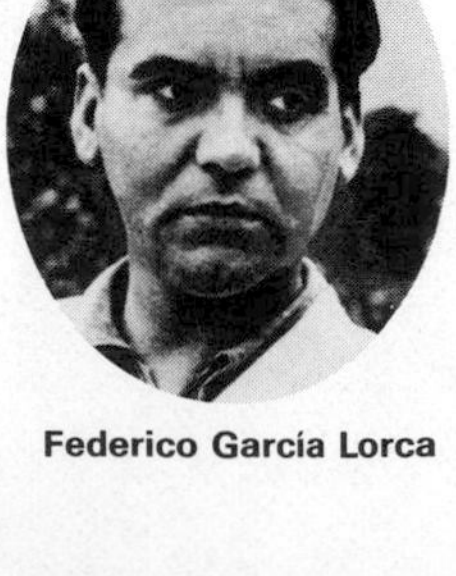

Federico García Lorca

stapled, or gathered together. **7.** Not compact or dense. **8.** Not fast: *a loose dye.* **9.** Lacking a sense of restraint or responsibility; idle: *loose talk.* **10.** Licentious; unchaste; immoral. **11.** Not literal or exact: *a loose translation.* **12.** Not completed; unfinished. **—at loose ends.** Without plans or direction. **—on the loose.** *Informal.* **1.** At large; free. **2.** Acting in an uninhibited or licentious fashion. *—adv.* In a loose manner. **—cut loose.** **1.** To untie; release. **2.** To behave in an uninhibited or licentious manner. *—v.* **loosed, loosing, looses.** *—tr.* **1.** To let loose; set free; release. **2.** To undo, untie, or unwrap. **3.** To release pressure on; make less tight, firm, or compact. **4.** To relax (rules or regulations); make less strict. **5.** To let fly (a missile). *—intr.* **1.** To become loose. **2.** To discharge a missile; to fire. [Middle English *lous(e), lo(o)s,* from Old Norse *lauss, louss.* See **leu-**[1] in Appendix.*] **—loose′ly** *adv.* **—loose′ness** *n.*

loose-joint·ed (lo͞os′join′tĭd) *adj.* **1.** Having freely articulated joints. **2.** Limber in movement. **—loose′-joint′ed·ness** *n.*

loos·en (lo͞o′sən) *v.* **-ened, -ening, -ens.** *—tr.* **1.** To untie or make looser. **2.** To free from restraint, pressure, or strictness. **3.** To free (the bowels) from constipation. *—intr.* To become loose or looser. [Middle English *lo(o)snen,* from *lo(o)s,* LOOSE.]

loose·strife (lo͞os′strīf′) *n.* **1.** Any of various plants of the genus *Lysimachia,* having usually yellow flowers. **2.** Any of various plants of the genus *Lythrum.* See **purple loosestrife.** [LOOSE + STRIFE (literal translation of Latin *lysimachia,* from Greek *lusimakheion,* said to be named after its discoverer, *Lusimakhos,* a doctor).]

loot (lo͞ot) *n.* **1.** Valuables pillaged in time of war; spoils. **2.** Stolen goods. **3.** *Informal.* Goods illicitly obtained, as by bribery. **4.** *Slang.* Money. *—v.* **looted, looting, loots.** *—tr.* **1.** To pillage. **2.** To take as spoils. *—intr.* To engage in pillage. —See Synonyms at **rob.** [Hindi *lūṭ,* from Sanskrit *lō(p)tra,* booty. See **leup-** in Appendix.*]

lop[1] (lŏp) *tr.v.* **lopped, lopping, lops.** **1.** To cut off branches or twigs from; to trim. **2.** To cut off from a tree or shrub: *"superfluous branches / We lop away that bearing boughs may live"* (Shakespeare). **3.** To cut off (a part), especially with a single swift blow. **4.** To eliminate or excise as superfluous. [Origin obscure.] **—lop′per** *n.*

lop[2] (lŏp) *v.* **lopped, lopping, lops.** *—intr.* To hang loosely; to droop. *—tr.* To let hang loosely. [Obscurely related to LOB.]

lope (lōp) *intr.v.* **loped, loping, lopes.** To run or ride with a steady, easy gait. *—n.* A steady, easy gait. [Middle English *lo(u)pen,* from Old Norse *hlaupa,* to leap. See **klou-** in Appendix.*] **—lop′er** *n.*

lop-eared (lŏp′îrd′) *adj.* Having bent or drooping ears.

Lop Nor Basin (lôp′ nôr′). Also **Lob Nor Basin.** A shallow, saline marshy depression, in east-central Sinkiang-Uigur Autonomous Region, China.

lop·py (lŏp′ē) *adj.* **-pier, -piest.** Hanging limp; pendulous.

lop·sid·ed (lŏp′sī′dĭd) *adj.* **1.** Heavier, larger, or higher on one side than on the other; not symmetrical. **2.** Sagging or leaning to one side. **—lop′sid′ed·ly** *adv.* **—lop′sid′ed·ness** *n.*

loq. loquitur.

lo·qua·cious (lō-kwā′shəs) *adj.* Very talkative. See Synonyms at **talkative.** [From Latin *loquāx* (stem *loquāc-*), from *loquī,* to speak. See **tolkw-** in Appendix.*] **—lo·qua′cious·ly** *adv.* **—lo·qua′cious·ness, lo·quac′i·ty** (lō-kwăs′ə-tē) *n.*

lo·quat (lō′kwŏt′, -kwăt′) *n.* **1.** A small tree, *Eriobotrya japonica,* native to eastern Asia, having fragrant white flowers and yellow, pear-shaped fruit. **2.** The edible fruit of this tree. [Cantonese *lō kwat, lō kat,* corresponding to Mandarin Chinese *lu*[2]*chü*[2], "rush orange" : *lu*[2], rush + *chü*[2], orange.]

lo·qui·tur (lō′kwə-to͝or′, lŏk′wə-tər). *Abbr.* **loq.** Begins to speak. Used as a stage direction. [Latin.]

Lo·rain (lô-rān′, lō-). A city of Ohio, a port in the north on Lake Erie. Population, 69,000.

lo·ran (lôr′ăn′, lōr′-) *n.* A long-range navigational system based on pulsed radio signals from two or more pairs of ground stations of known position, with which a navigator can establish his own position by an analysis involving the time intervals between pulses. [LO(NG-)RA(NGE) N(AVIGATION).]

Lor·ca (lôr′kä), **Federico García.** 1899–1936. Spanish poet and dramatist.

lord (lôrd) *n.* **1.** A man of high rank in a feudal society or in one that retains feudal forms and institutions, as: **a.** A king. **b.** A territorial magnate. **c.** The proprietor of a manor. **2.** *Capital* **L.** *British. Abbr.* **Ld.** The general masculine title of nobility and other rank, used in the following specific ways: **a.** Semiformally for any peer other than a duke: *Lord Cardigan* (the Earl of Cardigan). **b.** As the usual style for a baron: *Lord Morrison* (titularly, Baron Morrison of Lambeth). **c.** As a courtesy title for a younger son of a duke or marquis: *Lord Randolph Churchill* (third son of the Duke of Marlborough). **d.** As part of the titles of certain high officials and dignitaries, as *the Lord Mayor of London, the Lord Chancellor, the Lords of the Admiralty.* **e.** As a nominal title for a bishop. ***Note:*** In direct address, *my lord* and *your lordship* are deferential appellations for any of the above. *My lord,* usually pronounced (mə-lŭd′), is also used in addressing a British judge in court. In direct address and in informal reference, **c** may be shortened to *Lord Randolph,* but it may never be given as *Lord Churchill,* while **a** and **b** may never be used with baptismal names. With **b** and **c,** the formal usage (as in addressing a letter) is *The Lord Morrison.* **3. a.** *Capital* **L.** God. Also used in exclamations, as *Lord!, Good Lord!, My Lord!* **b.** *Archaic.* The head of a household. **c.** A husband. **d.** A man of renowned power. **e.** A man who has mastery in some field or activity. **4.** *Capital* **L.** *Plural.* The House of Lords. *—intr.v.* **lorded, lording, lords.** To play the lord; domineer. Used with *over* and often with *it: lording it over the newcomers.* [Middle English *lord, loverd,* Old English *hlāford, hlāfweard,* "keeper of the bread" (in the symbolic formal role of supplier of food to his retainers and companions) : *hlāf,* LOAF + *weard,* keeper, WARD.]

Lord Chancellor *pl.* **Lords Chancellor.** The presiding officer of the House of Lords. Also called "Lord High Chancellor."

lord·ing (lôr′dĭng) *n.* **1.** *Archaic & Poetic.* Lord; sir. Used chiefly as a form of address. **2.** *Obsolete.* A lordling.

lord·ling (lôrd′lĭng) *n.* An immature or insignificant lord.

lord·ly (lôrd′lē) *adj.* **-lier, -liest.** **1.** Of or pertaining to a lord. **2.** Dignified; noble. **3.** Arrogant; overbearing; haughty. *—adv.* In a lordly fashion. **—lord′li·ness** *n.*

Lord of Hosts. Jehovah; God.

Lord of Misrule. Master of traditional Christmas revelry in England during the 15th and 16th centuries.

lor·do·sis (lôr-dō′sĭs) *n.* An abnormal forward curvature of the spine in the lumbar region. Also called "lordoma." [New Latin, from Greek *lordōsis* : *lordos,* bent backward (see **lerd-** in Appendix*) + -OSIS.] **—lor·dot′ic** (-dŏt′ĭk) *adj.*

lords-and-la·dies (lôrdz′ən-lā′dēz) *n.* A plant, the **cuckoopint** *(see).* [From its dark (for lords) and light (for ladies) spadices.]

Lord's Day, Lord's day. The Sabbath; Sunday.

lord·ship (lôrd′shĭp′) *n.* **1.** *Usually capital* **L.** A form of address or a title for a British nobleman, judge, or bishop. Used with *your* or *his.* See Note at **lord.** **2.** The position or authority of a lord. **3.** The territorial fief of a feudal lord.

Lord's Prayer. The prayer taught by Jesus to his disciples. Matthew 6:9–13. Also called "paternoster."

Lord's Supper. **1.** The **Last Supper** *(see).* **2.** The Eucharist.

Lord's Table. The Communion table.

lore[1] (lôr, lōr) *n.* **1.** Accumulated fact, tradition, or belief about a particular subject: *"We were wiser in the lore of survival"* (John Hersey). **2.** Knowledge acquired through education or experience. **3.** *Archaic.* Anything taught or learned. —See Synonyms at **knowledge.** [Middle English *lore,* Old English *lār.* See **leis-** in Appendix.*]

lore[2] (lôr, lōr) *n.* The area between a bird's eye and the base of the bill. [New Latin *lorum,* from Latin *lōrum*†, thong.]

Lo·re·lei (lôr′ə-lī′; *German* lō′rə-lī′). *Germanic Mythology.* A siren of the Rhine whose singing lures sailors to shipwreck.

Lo·rentz (lō′rĕnts′), **Hendrik Antoon.** 1853–1928. Dutch physicist.

Lorentz contraction. The contraction in length of a moving body, as measured by an observer at rest with respect to the body, by the factor $(1 - v^2/c^2)^{1/2}$, where *v* is the relative speed of the moving body and *c* the speed of light. Also called "Lorentz-Fitzgerald contraction." [After Hendrik LORENTZ.]

Lo·renz (lō′rĕnts′), **Konrad Zacharias.** Born 1903. Austrian psychologist.

lor·gnette (lôrn-yĕt′) *n.* Eyeglasses or opera glasses with a short handle. Also called "lorgnon." [French, from *lorgner,* to leer at, from Old French, from *lorgne*†, squinting.]

lo·ri·ca (lô-rī′kə, lō-) *n., pl.* **-cae** (-sē′). *Zoology.* A protective external shell or case, as of a rotifer, diatom, or certain protozoans. [Latin *lōrica,* leather cuirass, from *lōrum,* thong. See **lore.**] **—lor′i·cate′** (lôr′ĭ-kāt′, lŏr′-), **lor′i·ca′ted** (-kā′tĭd) *adj.*

lor·i·keet (lôr′ĭ-kēt′, lŏr′-) *n.* Any of several small Australasian parrots of the subfamily Loriinae. [LOR(Y) + (PARA)KEET.]

lo·ris (lôr′ĭs, lōr′-) *n.* Any of several small, nocturnal, arboreal primates of the genera *Loris* and *Nycticebus,* of tropical Asia, having dense, woolly fur, large eyes, and a vestigial tail. [French, probably from obsolete Dutch *loeris*†, simpleton, clown.]

lorn (lôrn) *adj. Poetic.* Bereft of; forlorn. [Middle English *lorn, loren,* lost, Old English *-loren,* past participle of *-lēosan,* to lose. See **leu-**[1] in Appendix.*]

Lor·rain (lô-răN′), **Claude.** Also **Lor·raine** (-rĕn′). Pseudonym of Claude Gelée. 1600–1682. French landscape artist and engraver.

Lor·raine (lô-rān′, lō-; *French* lô-rĕn′). *German* **Loth·ring·en** (lō′trĭng-ən). A region and former province of eastern France, ceded to Germany in 1871 and returned to France in 1919. See **Alsace-Lorraine.**

lor·ry (lôr′ē, lŏr′ē) *n., pl.* **-ries.** **1.** A low, horse-drawn, four-wheeled wagon. **2.** *Chiefly British.* A motor truck. **3.** A flatbed freight car that runs on rails. [Origin obscure.]

lo·ry (lôr′ē, lōr′ē) *n., pl.* **-ries.** Any of various brightly colored Australasian parrots of the subfamily Loriinae, having a tongue with a brushlike tip. [Malay *luri, nuri.*]

LOS Airport code for Lagos, Nigeria.

Los A·la·mos (lôs ăl′ə-mōs′, lŏs). A town in northern New Mexico, the site of a research center where the first atomic bomb was developed. Population, 13,000.

Los An·ge·les (lôs ăn′jə-ləs, -lēz′, lŏs). *Abbr.* **L.A.** A city of southwestern California, the largest city in the state and the third largest in the United States. Population, 2,479,000.

lose (lo͞oz) *v.* **lost** (lôst, lŏst), **losing, loses.** *—tr.* **1.** To be unable to find; mislay. **2.** To be unable to maintain, sustain, or keep: *lose one's balance.* **3. a.** To be deprived of: *lose a friend.* **b.** To be deprived of through death. **4.** To fail to win: *lose the game.* **5.** To fail to use or take advantage of: *lose a chance.* **6.** To fail to hear, see, or understand. **7.** To remove (oneself), as from everyday reality into a fantasy world. **8.** To rid oneself of: *lose ten pounds.* **9.** To stray or wander from: *lose one's way.* **10.** To make (oneself) disappear or fade from view: *He lost himself in the crowd.* **11.** To elude or outdistance: *lose one's pursuers.*

12. To cause or result in the loss of: *Failure to reply lost her a job.* 13. To cause to die or be destroyed. Used passively: *Both planes were lost in the crash.* —*intr.* 1. To suffer loss. 2. To be defeated. 3. To run slow. Used of a timepiece. —**lose out.** To be defeated. —**lose out on.** To miss. [*Lose, lost, lost;* Middle English *losen, lost, loste,* Old English *lōsian, lōsode, gelōsod,* from *los,* loss, perdition, destruction. See **leu-¹** in Appendix.*]

lo·sel (lō′zəl, lo͞o′-, lŏz′əl) *n.* One that is worthless. [Middle English, profligate, "lost one," from *losen,* alternate past participle of *losen,* to lose, Old English *-lēosan.* See **leu-¹** in Appendix.*]

loss (lôs, lŏs) *n.* 1. The act or an instance of losing. 2. Something or someone that is lost. 3. The harm or suffering caused by losing or by being lost. 4. *Plural.* Casualties. 5. *Electricity.* The power decrease in a circuit, circuit element, or device caused by resistance. 6. The amount of a claim on an insurer by an insured. —**at a loss.** Perplexed; puzzled. [Middle English *los,* probably back-formation from *loste,* past participle of *losen,* to lose, Old English *lōsian,* to perish, be destroyed or ruined, from *los,* destruction, loss. See **leu-¹** in Appendix.*]

loss leader. A commodity offered by a retail store at cost or less to attract customers. Also called "leader."

loss ratio. The ratio between the premiums paid to an insurance company and the claims settled by the company.

loss·y (lô′sē, lŏs′ē) *adj.* Tending to damp undesirable oscillations while having no effect on desirable oscillations. Said of a material or medium. [From LOSS.]

lost (lôst, lŏst) *adj.* 1. Strayed or misplaced; missing. 2. Gone in time; passed away: *lost youth.* 3. Gone morally astray; fallen: *a lost woman.* 4. Bewildered or bemused. 5. Unable to function, act, or make progress; helpless. 6. No longer possessed or practiced: *a lost art.* [From the past participle of LOSE.]

lot (lŏt) *n.* 1. An object used in making a determination or choice by chance. 2. The use of lots for selection. 3. The selections made. 4. That which befalls an individual as a result of such a selection. 5. One's fortune in life; fate. 6. A number of people or things. 7. Kind, type, or sort. 8. A **job lot** *(see).* 9. A large amount or number. 10. a. A piece of land. b. A piece of land having fixed boundaries. c. A motion-picture studio. —**cast** (or **draw**) **lots.** To arrive at a decision or selection by means of lots. —**the lot.** All of a specific collection, quantity, or group. —**throw** (or **cast**) **in one's lot with.** To join with voluntarily. —*adv.* Very much. —*v.* **lotted, lotting, lots.** —*tr.* 1. To apportion by lots; allot. 2. To draw lots for. 3. To divide (land) into lots. —*intr.* To cast lots. [Middle English *lot(te),* Old English *hlot.* See **klēu-** in Appendix.*]

Lot¹ (lŏt). Abraham's nephew, whose wife was turned into a pillar of salt when she looked back as they fled from Sodom. Genesis 29:1–26. [Hebrew *lōṭ,* "covering."]

Lot² (lôt). A river of France, rising in the southeast and flowing 300 miles west to the Garonne.

lo·tah (lō′tə) *n.* Also **lo·ta.** A rounded copper or brass container used in India to carry water or store food. [Hindi *loṭā*†.]

loth. Variant of **loath.**

Lo·thar·i·o (lō-thâr′ē-ō) *n., pl.* **-os.** A seducer. [Name of a seducer in *The Fair Penitent,* by Nicholas ROWE.]

Lo·thi·ans, The (lō′*th*ē-ənz, lō′thē-). A region of Scotland divided into West Lothian, Midlothian, and East Lothian.

Loth·ring·en. The German name for **Lorraine.**

lo·tion (lō′shən) *n.* 1. A medicated liquid for external application, especially one containing a substance in suspension. 2. Any of various externally applied cosmetic liquids. [Middle English *loscion,* from Old French *lotion,* from Latin *lōtiō,* washing, from *lavere* (past participle *lautus, lōtus*), to wash. See **lou-** in Appendix.*]

lot·ter·y (lŏt′ə-rē) *n., pl.* **-ies.** 1. A contest in which tokens are distributed or sold, the winning token or tokens being secretly predetermined or ultimately selected in a chance drawing. 2. An activity or event regarded as having an outcome depending on fate. [Old French *loterie,* from Middle Dutch *loterije,* from *lot,* lot. See **klēu-** in Appendix.*]

lot·to (lŏt′ō) *n.* A game of chance played with numbered counters selected by lot to be placed upon the corresponding numbers on the players' boards. Compare **bingo.** [French *loto,* from Italian *lotto,* from Old French *lot,* lot, from Frankish *lot* (unattested). See **klēu-** in Appendix.*]

lo·tus (lō′təs) *n.* Also **lo·tos.** 1. a. An aquatic plant, *Nelumbo nucifera,* native to southern Asia, having large leaves, fragrant, pinkish flowers, and a broad, rounded, perforated seed pod. b. Any of several similar or related plants, such as certain water lilies. 2. A representation of such a plant in classical, usually Egyptian, sculpture, architecture, and art. 3. Any of several leguminous plants of the genus *Lotus.* 4. a. A small tree or shrub, *Zizyphus lotus,* of the Mediterranean region, the fruit of which is said to be that eaten by the lotus-eaters. b. The fruit of this tree. [Latin *lōtus,* from Greek *lōtos,* fruit eaten by the lotus-eaters, of Semitic origin, akin to Hebrew *lōṭ,* myrrh.]

lo·tus-eat·er (lō′təs-ē′tər) *n.* 1. One of a North African people described in the *Odyssey* who lived on the lotus, in a drugged, indolent state. 2. An indolent sybarite.

loud (loud) *adj.* **louder, loudest.** 1. Characterized by high volume and intensity of sound: *a loud crash.* 2. Producing or capable of producing a sound of high volume and intensity. 3. Clamorous and insistent: *loud denials.* 4. a. Having offensively bright colors: *a loud necktie.* b. Having an offensively strong odor. c. Offensive in manner. —*adv.* **louder, loudest.** In a loud manner. See Usage note below. [Middle English *l(o)ud, lowde,* Old English *hlūd.* See **kleu-¹** in Appendix.*] —**loud′ly** *adv.* See Usage note. —**loud′ness** *n.*

Usage: Loud (adverb) and *loudly* are often used interchangeably after certain common verbs, such as *laugh, play, roar, say, scream, shout, sing,* and *talk. Loudly* occurs more frequently in formal usage, especially in writing. *Loudly* is the idiomatic form after verbs such as *boast, brag, insist,* and *proclaim.*

loud·en (loud′n) *v.* **-ened, -ening, -ens.** —*tr.* To make louder. —*intr.* To become louder.

loud·mouth (loud′mouth′) *n.* One whose speech is loud and irritating or indiscreet. —**loud′mouthed′** (-mou*th*d′, -moutht′) *adj.*

loud-speak·er (loud′spē′kər) *n.* Also **loud·speak·er.** A device that converts electric signals to audible sound. Also called "speaker."

lough (lŏKH, lŏk) *n. Irish.* 1. A lake. 2. A bay or inlet of the sea. [Middle English *lough, lowe,* perhaps from Old English *luh,* from Old Irish *loch.* See **laku-** in Appendix.*]

lou·is (lo͞o′ē) *n.* A **louis d'or** *(see).*

Lou·is (lo͞o′ĭs, lo͞o′ē). A masculine given name. [French, from Old French *Louis,* LEWIS.]

Lou·is IX (lo͞o′ē; *French* lwē). Known as Saint Louis. 1214–1270. King of France (1226–70).

Lou·is XI (lo͞o′ē; *French* lwē). 1423–1483. King of France (1461–83).

Lou·is XIII (lo͞o′ē; *French* lwē). 1601–1643. King of France (1610–43).

Lou·is XIV (lo͞o′ē; *French* lwē). Called "the Sun King." 1638–1715. King of France (1643–1715).

Lou·is XV (lo͞o′ē; *French* lwē). 1710–1774. King of France (1715–74).

Lou·is XVI (lo͞o′ē; *French* lwē). 1754–1793. King of France (1774–92).

Lou·is XVIII (lo͞o′ē; *French* lwē). 1755–1824. King of France (1814–15 and 1815–24); brother of Louis XVI.

Lou·is (lo͞o′ĭs), **Joe.** Original name, Joseph Louis Barrow. Born 1914. World heavyweight boxing champion (1937–49).

Lou·is·burg (lo͞o′ĭs-bûrg). Also **Lou·is·bourg.** A town on Cape Breton Island, Nova Scotia, Canada, the site of a former French fortress captured by New England volunteers (1745) and by the British (1758).

lou·is d'or (lo͞o′ē dôr′; *French* lwē dôr′). 1. A gold coin of France from 1640 until the Revolution. 2. A 20-franc gold coin of post-Revolutionary France. Also called "louis." [French, "gold Louis," first minted in the reign of Louis XIII.]

Lou·ise (lo͞o-ēz′). Also **Lou·is·a** (-ē′zə). A feminine given name. [French, feminine of *Louis,* LEWIS.]

Lou·ise, Lake (lo͞o-ēz′). A scenic lake in a recreation area in the Rocky Mountains, southwestern Alberta, Canada.

Lou·i·si·an·a (lo͞o-ē′zē-ăn′ə). *Abbr.* **La.** A Southern state of the United States, 48,523 square miles in area, with a long (397 miles) coastline on the Gulf of Mexico; admitted to the Union in 1812. Population, 3,534,000. Capital, Baton Rouge. See map at **United States of America.**

Louisiana French. French as spoken by descendants of the original French settlers of Louisiana.

Louisiana Purchase. The territory extending west from the Mississippi to the Rocky Mountains between the Mexican and Canadian borders, purchased by the United States from France in 1803 for $15,000,000.

Lou·is Na·po·le·on. See **Napoleon III.**

Lou·is Phi·lippe (lo͞o′ē fĭ-lēp′; *French* lwē fē-lēp′). 1773–1850. Called "the Citizen King." King of France (1830–48).

Lou·is Qua·torze (lo͞o′ē kă-tôrz′). Pertaining to the baroque style of architecture, furniture, and decoration of the reign of Louis XIV. [French, "Louis XIV."]

Lou·is Quinze (lo͞o′ē kăNz′). Pertaining to the rococo style in architecture, furniture, and decoration of the reign of Louis XV. [French, "Louis XV."]

Lou·is Seize (lo͞o′ē sĕz′). Pertaining to the neoclassic style in architecture, furniture, and decoration of the reign of Louis XVI. [French, "Louis XVI."]

Lou·is Treize (lo͞o′ē trĕz′). Pertaining to the heavy late-Renaissance style in architecture, furniture, and decoration of the reign of Louis XIII. [French, "Louis XIII."]

Lou·is·ville (lo͞o′ē-vĭl). A city of Kentucky, on the Ohio River in the northern part of the state. Population, 389,000.

lounge (lounj) *v.* **lounged, lounging, lounges.** —*intr.* 1. To stand, lean, sit, or lie in a lazy, relaxed way; loll. 2. To walk in a leisurely way; saunter: *"I lounged about the streets insufficiently and unsatisfactorily fed."* (Dickens). 3. To pass time idly. —*tr.* To pass (time) in lounging. —*n.* 1. The act of lounging. 2. A period of lounging. 3. A lounging walk or gait. 4. A public waiting room, as in a hotel, theater, or air terminal, often having smoking or lavatory facilities. 5. a. A living room. b. A lobby. 6. A long couch, especially one having no back and a headrest at one end. [Origin obscure.] —**loung′er** *n.*

loupe (lo͞op) *n.* A small magnifying glass usually set in an eyepiece and used chiefly by watchmakers and jewelers. [French, from Old French *loupe*†, imperfect gem.]

loup-ga·rou (lo͞o′gə-ro͞o′; *French* lo͞o-gȧ-ro͞o′) *n., pl.* **loups-ga·rous** (lo͞o′gə-ro͞oz′; *French* lo͞o-gȧ-ro͞o′). A werewolf. [French, from Old French *leu garoul* : *leu,* wolf, from Latin *lupus* (see **wlkwo-** in Appendix*) + *garoul, garulf,* werewolf, from Frankish *werwulf* (unattested), "man wolf" (see **wiros** in Appendix*).]

loup·ing ill (lou′pĭng, lō′-). A disease of sheep. See **tremble.** [From earlier *loup,* to leap, Middle English *loupen,* to LOPE.]

lour. Variant of **lower** (scowl).

Lourdes (lo͝ord; *French* lo͞ord). A town at the foot of the Pyrenees in southwestern France; site of a shrine and grotto of the Virgin (Our Lady of Lourdes). Population, 16,000.

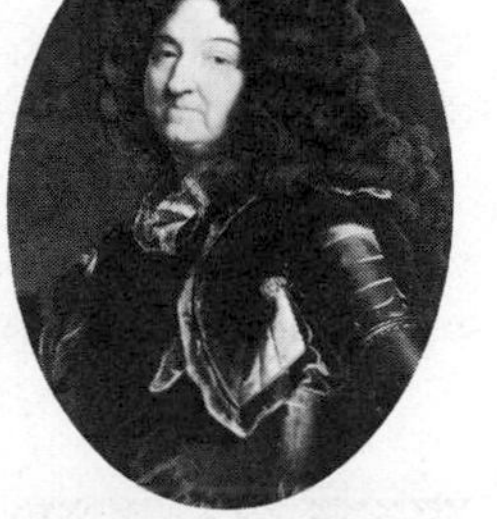
Louis XIV

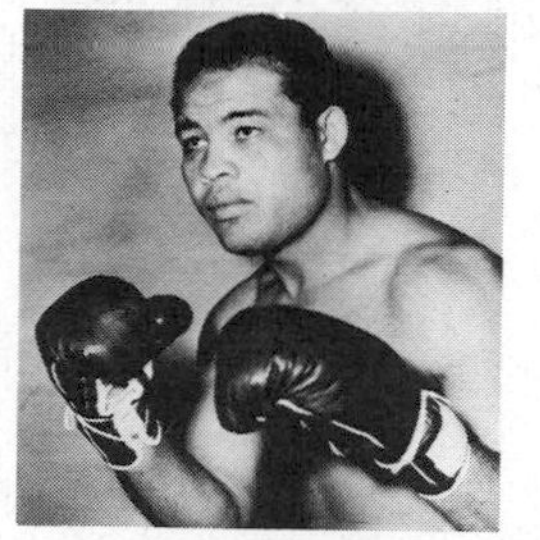
Joe Louis

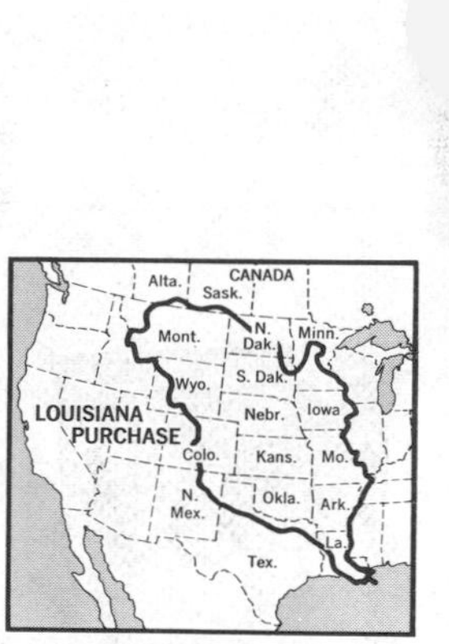

Louisiana Purchase
The approximate original claim of 1803, before modifications and later treaties

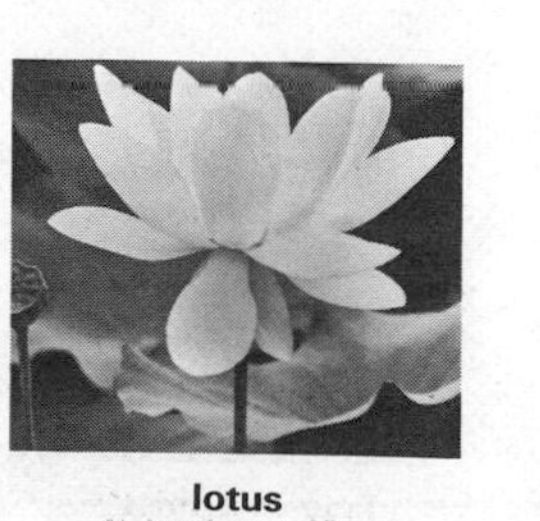
lotus
Nelumbo nucifera

t tight/th thin, path/*th* this, bathe/ŭ cut/ûr urge/v valve/w with/y yes/z zebra, size/zh vision/ə about, item, edible, gallop, circus/ à *Fr.* ami/œ *Fr.* feu, *Ger.* schön/ü *Fr.* tu, *Ger.* über/KH *Ger.* ich, *Scot.* loch/N *Fr.* bon. ***Follows main vocabulary. †Of obscure origin.**

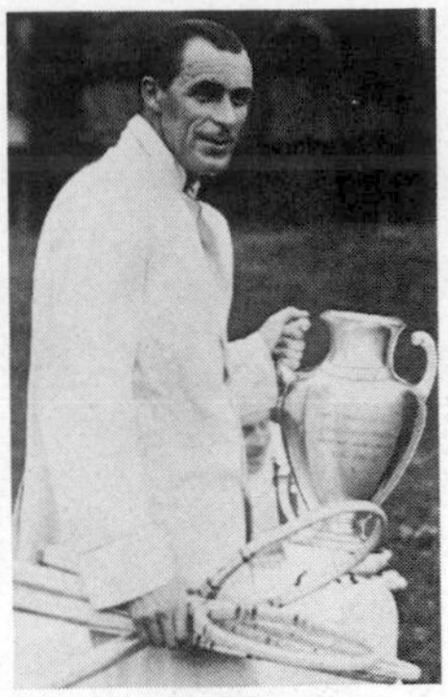

loving cup
Tennis champion
William Tilden with trophy

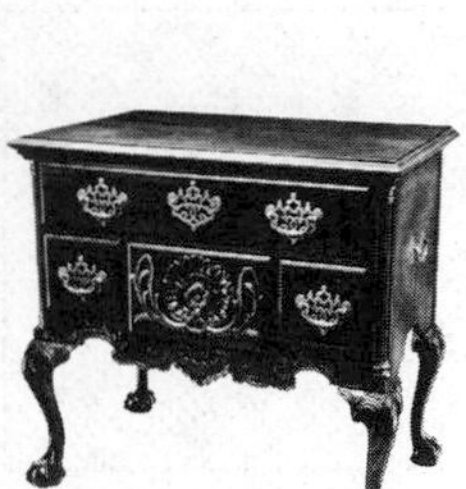

lowboy

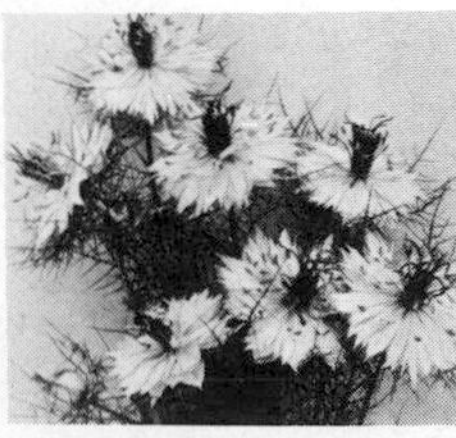

love-in-a-mist

Lou·ren·ço Mar·ques (lō-rāɴ′so͞o mər-kāsh′). The capital of Mozambique, a seaport in the extreme south on an inlet of the Mozambique Channel. Population, 79,000.

louse (lous) *n., pl.* **lice** (līs) or **louses** (for sense 2). **1.** Any of numerous small, flat-bodied, wingless, biting or sucking insects of the order Anoplura, many of which are external parasites on various animals, including man. **2.** *Slang.* A mean or despicable person. —*tr.v.* **loused, lousing, louses.** *Slang.* To bungle. Often used with *up: louse up a deal.* [Louse, lice; Middle English *lous, lys,* Old English *lūs, lȳs.* See **lus** in Appendix.*]

louse·wort (lous′wûrt′, -wôrt′) *n.* Any of numerous plants of the genus *Pedicularis,* having clusters of irregular, variously colored flowers. Also called "betony," "wood betony." [Sheep feeding on it were believed to be subject to vermin.]

lous·y (lou′zē) *adj.* **-ier, -iest. 1.** Infested with lice: *"By this time we were as lousy as rooks."* (Frank Richards). **2.** *Slang.* Mean; nasty; contemptible: *a lousy trick.* **3.** *Slang.* Painful; unpleasant: *a lousy headache.* **4.** *Slang.* Inferior; worthless. **5.** *Slang.* Abundantly supplied; having a surfeit of. Used with *with: lousy with money.* —**lous′i·ly** *adv.* —**lous′i·ness** *n.*

lout¹ (lout) *n.* An awkward, stupid fellow; boor; oaf. [Perhaps ultimately from Old Norse *lūtr,* bent low, from *lūta,* to bend down, bow. See **leud-** in Appendix.*]

lout² (lout) *intr.v.* **louted, louting, louts.** *Archaic.* **1.** To bow or curtsy. **2.** To bend or stoop. [Middle English *l(o)uten,* Old English *lūtan,* to bend down, bow. See **leud-** in Appendix.*]

Louth (louth). A county of the Republic of Ireland, occupying 307 square miles in the northeast. Population, 67,000. County seat, Dundalk.

lout·ish (lou′tĭsh) *adj.* Having the characteristics of a lout; stupid; clumsy; boorish. —**lout′ish·ly** *adv.* —**lout′ish·ness** *n.*

lou·ver (lo͞o′vər) *n.* Also **lou·vre. 1.** A framed opening in a wall, fitted with fixed or movable slanted slats. **2.** One of the slats used in a louver. **3.** *Architecture.* A lantern-shaped cupola on the roof of many medieval buildings to admit air and provide for the escape of smoke. **4.** Any slatted ventilating opening, as on an automobile hood. [Middle English *luver, lover,* from Old French *lov(i)er*†.] —**lou′vered** *adj.*

L'Ou·ver·ture, Toussaint. See **Toussaint L'Ouverture.**

lov·a·ble (lŭv′ə-bəl) *adj.* Also **love·a·ble.** Having characteristics that attract love or affection; adorable; endearing. —**lov′a·bil′i·ty, lov′a·ble·ness** *n.* —**lov′a·bly** *adv.*

lov·age (lŭv′ĭj) *n.* A plant, *Levisticum officinale,* having small, aromatic seeds used as seasoning. [Middle English *lov(e)ache,* from Old French *luvesche, levesche,* from Late Latin *levisticum (apium),* "Ligurian (parsley)," variant of *ligusticum,* neuter of *ligusticus,* of LIGURIA.]

love (lŭv) *n.* **1.** An intense affectionate concern for another person. **2.** An intense sexual desire for another person. **3.** A beloved person. Often used as a term of endearment. **4.** A strong fondness or enthusiasm for something: *a love of the woods.* **5.** *Capital* **L.** Eros or Cupid, the god of love in classical mythology. **6.** *Theology.* **a.** God's benevolence and mercy toward man. **b.** Man's devotion to or adoration of God. **c.** The benevolence, kindness, or brotherhood that man should rightfully feel toward others. **7.** *Capital* **L.** *Christian Science.* God. **8.** A zero score in tennis. —**fall in love.** To become enamored of or sexually attracted to someone. —**for love.** As a favor; out of fondness; without payment. —**for love or money.** Under any circumstances. Usually used in the negative: *He would not do that for love or money.* —**for the love of.** With loving regard for; for the sake of. —**in love.** Feeling love for someone or something; enamored. —**make love. 1.** To copulate. **2.** To embrace and caress. —*v.* **loved, loving, loves.** —*tr.* **1.** To feel love for. **2.** To desire (another person) sexually. **3.** To embrace or caress. **4.** To like or desire enthusiastically; delight in. **5.** To thrive on; need: *The cactus loves hot, dry air.* —*intr.* To experience loving tenderness or sexual desire for another; be in love. —See Synonyms at **like.** [Middle English *love,* Old English *lufu.* See **leubh-** in Appendix.*]

Synonyms: *love, affection, devotion, fondness, infatuation.* These nouns refer to feelings of attraction and attachment experienced by persons. *Love* suggests a feeling more intense and less susceptible to control than that associated with the other words of this group. *Affection* is a more unvarying feeling of warm regard for another person. *Devotion* is dedication and attachment to a person or thing; contrasted with *love,* it implies a more selfless and often a more settled feeling. *Fondness,* in its most common modern sense, is rather strong liking for a person or thing. *Infatuation* is extravagant attraction or attachment to a person or thing, usually short in duration and indicative of folly or faulty judgment.

love affair. 1. An intimate sexual relationship or episode between lovers. **2.** An enthusiastic liking or desire.

love apple. *Archaic.* A tomato.

love·bird (lŭv′bûrd′) *n.* Any of various small Old World parrots, chiefly of the genus *Agapornis,* often kept as a cage bird.

love feast. 1. Among early Christians, a meal eaten with others as a symbol of love. **2.** A similar symbolic meal among certain modern Christian sects. **3.** A gathering intended to promote good will among the participants.

love game. A tennis game in which the winner loses no points.

love-in-a-mist (lŭv′ĭn-ə-mĭst′) *n.* A plant, *Nigella damascena,* native to Europe, having blue or whitish flowers surrounded by numerous threadlike bracts.

love-in-i·dle·ness (lŭv′ĭn-īd′l-nĭs) *n.* *Archaic.* A plant, heartsease.

love knot. A stylized knot regarded as a symbol of the constancy of two lovers.

Love·lace (lŭv′lās′), **Richard.** 1618–1658. English Cavalier poet.

love·less (lŭv′lĭs) *adj.* **1.** Characterized by an absence of love. **2.** Feeling no love; unloving. **3.** Receiving no love; unloved.

love-lies-bleed·ing (lŭv′līz′blē′dĭng) *n.* A tropical plant, *Amaranthus caudatus,* having clusters of small red flowers.

love·lock (lŭv′lŏk′) *n.* **1.** A lock of hair, often curled separately and tied with ribbon, worn by courtiers and men of fashion during the 17th and 18th centuries. **2.** Any similar lock of hair.

love·lorn (lŭv′lôrn′) *adj.* Bereft of love or one's lover.

love·ly (lŭv′lē) *adj.* **-lier, -liest. 1.** Full of love; loving: *"completed after the first lovely gush of his inspiration"* (D.B. Wyndham Lewis). **2.** Inspiring love or affection. **3.** Having pleasing or attractive qualities; beautiful; graceful: *a lovely girl.* **4.** Enjoyable; delightful: *a lovely party.* —See Synonyms at **beautiful.** —*n., pl.* **lovelies.** *Informal.* **1.** A beautiful woman, especially an entertainer or model. **2.** A lovely object: *all the lovelies in the boutique.* —**love′li·ness** *n.* —**love′ly** *adv.*

love·mak·ing (lŭv′mā′kĭng) *n.* **1.** Sexual activity between lovers; especially, sexual intercourse. **2.** Courtship.

lov·er (lŭv′ər) *n.* **1.** Someone who loves another; especially, a man in love with a woman. **2.** *Plural.* A couple in love with each other. **3. a.** A paramour. **b.** A sexual partner. **4.** One who is fond of or devoted to something. —**lov′er·ly** *adj.* & *adv.*

lovers' knot. A **true lovers' knot** *(see).*

love seat. A small sofa or double chair that seats two people.

love set. *Tennis.* A set in which the winner loses no games.

love·sick (lŭv′sĭk′) *adj.* **1.** Stricken, as if with illness, by love. **2.** Exhibiting a yearning with love. —**love′sick′ness** *n.*

lov·ing (lŭv′ĭng) *adj.* **1.** Feeling love; affectionate; devoted. **2.** Indicative of or exhibiting love.

loving cup. 1. A large, ornamental wine vessel, usually made of silver and having two or more handles, formerly used at ceremonial banquets. **2.** A similar cup given as an award in modern sporting events and similar affairs.

lov·ing-kind·ness (lŭv′ĭng-kīnd′nĭs) *n.* Affection or tenderness stemming from sincere love for someone.

low¹ (lō) *adj.* **lower, lowest. 1. a.** Having little relative height; not tall. **b.** Rising only slightly above surrounding surfaces: *low relief.* **c.** Situated or placed below normal height: *a low lighting fixture.* **d.** Situated below the surrounding surfaces: *water standing in low spots.* **e.** *Archaic.* Dead and buried: *"And wilt thou weep when I am low?"* (Byron). **f.** Cut to show the wearer's chest, back, and neck; décolleté. **2.** Near or at the horizon: *The sun is low in the sky.* **3.** *Phonetics.* Sounded with all or part of the tongue depressed. Said of a vowel. The vowel (ä) in *large* is low. **4.** Of less than usual or average depth; shallow: *The river is low.* **5. a.** Of inferior quality or character: *low intelligence.* **b.** Of relatively simple structure in the scale of living organisms. **6. a.** Morally base. **b.** Having inferior social, moral, or cultural status. **7. a.** Wanting vigor; weak. **b.** Emotionally or mentally depressed. **c.** Giving little nourishment. **8. a.** Below average in degree or intensity: *a low temperature.* **b.** Below an average or standard figure: *low wages.* See Usage note at **nominal. c.** Pertaining to or designating latitudes nearest to the equator. **d.** Of relatively small price: *The cost is low.* See Usage note at **nominal. e.** Not flourishing or advancing. **9. a.** *Music.* Being a sound produced by a relatively small frequency of vibrations: *a low tone.* **b.** Hushed; not loud: *a low voice.* **10.** Being almost without money: *low in funds.* **11.** Not adequately provided with or equipped for. **12.** Of small value or quality; depreciatory; disparaging: *a low opinion of his qualities.* **13.** Brought down or reduced in health or wealth. **14.** Overthrown; defeated. **15.** Staying in hiding; biding one's time. —See Synonyms at **mean** (ignoble). —*adv.* **1. a.** In a low position, level, or space. **b.** In a low condition or rank; humbly: *You value yourself too low.* **2.** In or to a reduced, humbled, or degraded condition: *"A woman too brought Parnell low."* (Joyce). **3.** Softly; quietly: *speak low.* **4.** With a deep pitch. **5.** At a small price: *bought low, sold high.* —*n.* **1.** A low level, position, or degree: *The stock market fell to a new low.* **2.** *Meteorology.* A region of depressed barometric pressure. **3.** The gear configuration or setting that produces the lowest range of output speeds, as in an automotive transmission. **4.** In some card games, the lowest trump. **5.** In some other games, the lowest score. [Middle English *low(e), lah,* from Old Norse *lāgr.* See **legh-** in Appendix.*] —**low′ness** *n.*

low² (lō) *n.* The characteristic sound uttered by cattle; a moo. —*v.* **lowed, lowing, lows.** —*intr.* To utter a low; to moo. —*tr.* To indicate or utter by lowing. [Middle English *loowen,* Old English *hlōwan.* See **kel-³** in Appendix.*]

Low (lō), Sir **David.** 1891–1963. British political cartoonist.

Low Archipelago. See **Tuamotu Archipelago.**

low area. *Meteorology.* A **low** *(see).*

low·born (lō′bôrn′) *adj.* Of humble birth.

low·boy (lō′boi′) *n.* A low, tablelike chest of drawers.

low·bred (lō′brĕd′) *adj.* **1.** Lowborn. **2.** Coarse; vulgar.

low·brow (lō′brou′) *n.* *Informal.* One having uncultivated tastes. Compare **highbrow, middlebrow.** —*adj.* Also **low·browed** (lō′broud′). Uncultivated; vulgar. —**low′brow′ism′** *n.*

Low-Church (lō′chûrch′) *adj.* Of or relating to a faction in the Anglican Church that is opposed to excessive ritualism and favors a more evangelical doctrine. Compare **Broad-Church, High-Church.** —**Low′-Church′man** *n.*

low comedy. Comedy characterized by slapstick, burlesque, and horseplay.

Low Countries. The region of western Europe occupied by Belgium, the Netherlands, and Luxembourg.

low-down (lō′doun′) *adj.* Mean; unfair; despicable.

ă pat/ā pay/âr care/ä father/b bib/ch church/d deed/ĕ pet/ē be/f fife/g gag/h hat/hw which/ĭ pit/ī pie/îr pier/j judge/k kick/l lid, needle/m mum/n no, sudden/ng thing/ŏ pot/ō toe/ô paw, for/oi noise/ou out/o͝o took/o͞o boot/p pop/r roar/s sauce/sh ship, dish/

low·down (lō'doun') *n. Slang.* All the facts; the whole truth.

Low Dutch. The language of the Netherlands, **Dutch** (*see*).

Low·ell (lō'əl). A city of northeastern Massachusetts, a textile center on the Merrimack. Population, 92,000.

Low·ell (lō'əl), **Amy.** 1874–1925. American poet.

Low·ell (lō'əl), **James Russell.** 1819–1891. American poet, essayist, and diplomat.

low·er[1] (lou'ər) *intr.v.* **-ered, -ering, -ers.** Also **lour, loured, louring, lours.** **1.** To look angry, sullen, or threatening; to scowl. **2.** To appear dark or threatening, as the sky or weather. —*n.* Also **lour.** **1.** A threatening, sullen, or angry look. **2.** A dark and ominous look, as of thunderheads. [Middle English *l(o)uren.*] —**low'er·ing·ly** *adv.*

low·er[2] (lō'ər). Comparative of **low.** —*adj.* **1.** Below someone or something in rank, position, or authority. **2.** Below a similar or comparable thing: *a lower shelf.* **3.** *Capital* L. *Geology & Archaeology.* Being an earlier division of the period named. **4.** Denoting the larger and usually more representative house of a bicameral legislature. —*n.* One that is beneath another; especially, a lower berth. —*v.* **lowered, -ering, -ers.** —*tr.* **1.** To let, bring, or move something down to a lower level. **2.** To reduce in value, degree, or quality. **3.** To weaken; undermine: *lower one's energy.* **4.** To reduce in standing or respect. —*intr.* To diminish; become less.

Lower Aus·tri·a (ôs'trē-ə). A province of Austria, occupying 7,299 square miles in the northeast. Population, 1,374,000. Capital, Vienna.

lower bound. *Mathematics.* A number that is not greater than any number in a set.

Lower Bur·ma (bûr'mə). The districts of Burma, particularly those of the Irrawaddy River delta, incorporated with Upper Burma in 1886 to form the Burma province of India.

Lower Cal·i·for·nia (kăl'ə-fôrn'yə, -fôr'nē-ə). A peninsula of northwestern Mexico, extending 760 miles southward from the U.S. border and divided into Baja California State and Baja California Sur Territory.

Lower Can·a·da (kăn'ə-də). A former administrative division of Canada, now the province of Quebec.

Lower Carboniferous. *Geology.* **Mississippian** (*see*).

low·er·case (lō'ər-kās') *adj. Abbr.* **l.c.** *Printing.* Of or pertaining to small letters as distinguished from capitals: *a, b,* and *c* are *lower-case letters.* —*tr.v.* **lower-cased, -casing, -cases.** To set (type) in lower case. —**lower case.**

lower class. The class or classes of lower than middle rank in a society. Often used in the plural. —**low'er-class'** *adj.*

low·er·class·man (lō'ər-klăs'mən, -kläs'mən) *n., pl.* **-men** (-mĭn). An underclassman.

Lower Cretaceous. Comanchean (*see*).

lower criticism. Textual criticism and verbal examination of a written work, especially of the Bible. Compare **higher criticism.**

Lower E·gypt (ē'jĭpt). The section of northern Egypt comprising the Nile Delta.

low·er·most (lō'ər-mōst') *adj.* Lowest.

Lower Peninsula. The section of the state of Michigan lying south of the Straits of Mackinac and between Lakes Michigan and Huron.

Lower Sax·o·ny (săk'sə-nē). A state of West Germany, occupying 18,293 square miles in the north. Population, 6,855,000. Capital, Hanover.

Lower Si·le·sia (sī-lē'zhə, -shə, sĭ-). A former province of Germany, part of Poland since 1945.

lower world. 1. The abode of the dead, considered in ancient times to be beneath the surface of the earth. **2.** The earth.

low·er·y (lou'ə-rē) *adj.* Overcast; threatening: *a lowery sky.*

lowest common denominator. *Abbr.* **L.C.D.** The least common multiple of the denominators of a set of fractions. Also called "least common denominator."

lowest common multiple. Least common multiple (*see*).

low frequency. *Abbr.* **lf** A radio frequency (*see*) in the range from 30 to 300 kilocycles per second.

Low German. *Abbr.* **LG, L.G. 1.** Any of several German dialects spoken in northern Germany. **2.** All of the West Germanic languages except High German. See **High German.**

low-key (lō'kē') *adj.* **1.** Having low intensity; low-keyed. **2.** *Photography.* Having or producing uniformly dark tones with little contrast.

low-keyed (lō'kēd') *adj.* Restrained, as in style or quality.

low·land (lō'lənd) *n.* An area of land that is low in relation to the surrounding country. —*adj.* Pertaining to or characteristic of low, usually level, land.

Low·land (lō'lənd) *n.* The English dialect of the Scottish Lowlands; Lallan. —*adj.* Of or from the Scottish Lowlands.

low·land·er (lō'lən-dər) *n.* **1.** A native or inhabitant of a lowland. **2.** *Capital* L. An inhabitant of the Scottish Lowlands.

Low·lands, The (lō'ləndz). The lowlands of eastern and southern Scotland.

low·ly (lō'lē) *adj.* **-lier, -liest. 1.** Having or suited for a low rank or position. **2.** Humble; meek. **3.** Plain; simple; undistinguished. —See Synonyms at **humble.** —*adv.* **1.** In a low manner, condition, or position. **2.** Humbly; meekly. —**low'li·ness** *n.*

Low Mass. A Mass of nonelaborate ceremonial form that is recited rather than sung by the priest.

low-mind·ed (lō'mīn'dĭd) *adj.* Exhibiting a coarse, vulgar character. —**low'-mind'ed·ly** *adv.* —**low'-mind'ed·ness** *n.*

low-necked (lō'někt') *adj.* Also **low-neck** (-něk'). Having a low-cut neckline; décolleté.

low-pitched (lō'pĭcht') *adj.* **1.** Low in tone or tonal range. **2.** Having a moderate slope: *a low-pitched roof.*

low-pres·sure (lō'prěsh'ər) *adj.* **1.** Having, working under, or exerting little pressure. **2.** Relaxed; calm; easygoing.

low relief. Sculptural relief that projects very little from the background. Also called "bas-relief," "basso-relievo." [Translation of French *bas-relief.*]

low-spir·it·ed (lō'spĭr'ə-tĭd) *adj.* In low spirits; depressed.

Low Sunday. The Sunday following Easter.

low-ten·sion (lō'těn'shən) *adj. Electricity.* **1.** Of or at low potential or voltage. **2.** Operating at low voltage.

low-test (lō'těst') *adj.* Having low volatility and a high boiling point. Said of gasoline.

low tide. 1. The tide at its lowest ebb. **2.** The time of this ebb.

low water. *Abbr.* **L.W. 1.** The lowest level of water in a body of water, such as rivers, lakes, or reservoirs. **2.** Low tide.

lox[1] (lŏks) *n.* Smoked salmon, often eaten on a bagel. [Yiddish *laks,* from Middle High German *lahs,* salmon, from Old High German. See **laks-** in Appendix.*]

lox[2] (lŏks) *n.* Liquid oxygen, especially as a rocket fuel oxidizer. [L(IQUID) OX(YGEN).]

lox·o·drom·ic (lŏk'sə-drŏm'ĭk) *adj.* Also **lox·o·drom·i·cal** (-ĭ-kəl). *Nautical.* Pertaining to sailing on a rhumb line. [From Greek *loxos†,* slanting + *dromos,* a running, course (see **der-**[1] in Appendix*).] —**lox'o·drom'i·cal·ly** *adv.*

loxodromic curve. A rhumb line (*see*).

loy·al (loi'əl) *adj.* **1.** Steadfast in allegiance to one's homeland, government, or sovereign. **2.** Faithful to a person, ideal, or custom. **3.** Of or professing loyalty. —See Synonyms at **faithful.** [Old French *loyal, loial, leial,* faithful to obligations, legal, from Latin *lēgālis,* legal, from *lēx* (stem *lēg-*), law. See **leg-** in Appendix.*] —**loy'al·ism'** *n.* —**loy'al·ly** *adv.*

loy·al·ist (loi'ə-lĭst) *n.* **1.** One who maintains loyalty to a lawful government, political party, or sovereign, especially during war or revolutionary change. **2.** *Capital* L. A Tory. **3.** *Capital* L. One who supported the lawful government of Spain during the Spanish Civil War.

loy·al·ty (loi'əl-tē) *n., pl.* **-ties. 1.** The state or quality of being loyal. **2.** *Plural.* Feelings of devoted attachment and affection: *"Loyalties flow deep between girl friends until they want the same man."* (J.P. Donleavy). —See Synonyms at **fidelity.**

Loyalty Islands. A chain of coral islands in the southwestern Pacific, administered as part of New Caledonia.

Lo·yang (lō'yäng'). Formerly **Ho·nan·fu** (hō'nän'fōō'). A city of eastern China in northern Honan. Population, 500,000.

Loy·o·la, Saint Ignatius. See **Saint Ignatius Loyola.**

loz·enge (lŏz'ĭnj) *n.* **1.** A four-sided planar figure with a diamondlike shape; a rhombus that is not a square. **2.** A lozenge-shaped, medicated drop for local medication of the mouth or throat. [Middle English *losenge,* from Old French, originally a diamond-shaped figure in heraldic design, from Gaulish *lausa* (unattested), flat stone. See **leu-**[1] in Appendix.*]

LP (ĕl'pē') *adj.* Long-playing. —*n., pl.* **LP's** or **LPs.** A trademark for a long-playing record.

LPB Airport code for La Paz, Bolivia.

LPG liquefied petroleum gas.

l.s. letter signed.

L.S. the place of the seal (Latin *locus sigilli*).

LSD Lysergic acid diethylamide (*see*); specifically, this chemical taken as a hallucinogen. Also called "acid."

LSS lifesaving service.

l.s.t. local standard time.

lt. light.

Lt. lieutenant.

l.t. local time.

Lt. Col. lieutenant colonel.

Lt. Comdr. lieutenant commander.

ltd., Ltd. limited.

Lt. Gen. lieutenant general.

Lt. Gov. lieutenant governor.

Lu The symbol for the element lutetium.

Lu·a·la·ba (lōō'ä-lä'bä). A river of Africa, rising near the Congo-Zambia border and flowing about 400 miles north to form, with other tributaries, the Congo River near Kisangani.

Lu·an·da (lōō-än'də). Also **Lo·an·da** (lō-än'də; *Portuguese* lwänn'də). Formerly **São Pau·lo de Lo·an·da** (souɴ pou'lōō də). The capital of Angola, a seaport in the west on the Atlantic. Population, 245,000.

Luang Pra·bang (lwäng' prä-bäng'). The royal capital of Laos, a city on the Mekong in the northwest. Population, 8,000.

Lu·ang·wa (lōō-äng'wä). A river rising in northeastern Zambia and flowing 500 miles southwest to the Zambezi.

lu·au (lōō-ou') *n.* An elaborate Hawaiian feast. [Hawaiian *lu'au.*]

lub. lubricant; lubrication.

Lu·ba (lōō'bə) *n., pl.* **Luba. 1.** A member of a Negroid people of the southeastern Congo (Kinshasa). **2.** The language of this people. —**Lu'ba** *adj.*

lub·ber (lŭb'ər) *n.* **1.** A clumsy fellow. **2.** An inexperienced sailor; a landlubber. [Middle English *lobur, lobre†.*]

lubber line. Also **lubber's line.** A line or mark on a compass or cathode-ray indicator that represents the heading of a ship or aircraft.

lubber's hole. A hole through the platform surrounding the upper part of a ship's mast, through which one may climb to go aloft.

Lub·bock (lŭb'ək). A city of Texas, in the northwest in the center of a rich oil-producing region. Population, 129,000.

Lü·beck (lōō'běk; *German* lü'běk). A city of northern West Germany, in eastern Schleswig-Holstein. Population, 239,000.

Lu·bi·lash (lōō-bē'läsh). The upper course of the Sankuru

Amy Lowell

James Russell Lowell

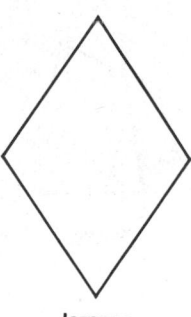

lozenge

River, flowing 285 miles north and northwest through southeastern Democratic Republic of the Congo.

Lu·blin (lo͞o′blĭn, -blĕn′). *Russian* **Lyu·blin** (lyo͞o′blĭn). A city in southeast Poland. Population, 199,000.

lu·bri·cant (lo͞o′brĭ-kənt) *n. Abbr.* **lub.** **1.** Any of various usually oily liquids or solids, such as grease, machine oil, or graphite, that reduce friction, heat, and wear when applied as a surface coating to moving parts. **2.** Something or someone that helps reduce difficulty or conflict. [Latin *lūbricāns,* present participle of *lūbricāre,* LUBRICATE.] **—lu′bri·cant** *adj.*

lu·bri·cate (lo͞o′brĭ-kāt′) *v.* **-cated, -cating, -cates.** *—tr.* **1.** To apply a lubricant to. **2.** To make slippery. *—intr.* To act as a lubricant. [Latin *lūbricāre,* from *lūbricus,* slippery. See **sleubh-** in Appendix.*] **—lu′bri·ca′tion** *n.* **—lu′bri·ca′tive** *adj.*

lu·bri·ca·tor (lo͞o′brĭ-kā′tər) *n.* **1.** One who lubricates. **2.** A lubricant. **3.** A device for applying a lubricant.

lu·bric·i·ty (lo͞o-brĭs′ə-tē) *n.* **1.** Lewdness; salaciousness. **2.** Shiftiness; trickiness. **3.** Slipperiness. [Late Latin *lūbricitās,* slipperiness, from Latin *lūbricus,* slippery. See **sleubh-** in Appendix.*]

lu·bri·cous (lo͞o′brĭ-kəs) *adj.* Also **lu·bri·cious** (lo͞o-brĭsh′əs). **1.** Characterized by lewdness. **2.** Elusive. **3.** Slippery. [From Latin *lūbricus,* slippery. See **sleubh-** in Appendix.*]

Lu·bum·ba·shi (lo͞o′bo͝om-bä′shē). Formerly **E·lis·a·beth·ville** (ĭ-lĭz′ə-bəth-vĭl). A city of the Democratic Republic of the Congo, in the southeast near Zambia. Population, 184,000.

Lu·can (lo͞o′kən). Latin name, Marcus Annaeus Lucanus. A.D. 39–65. Roman poet.

Lu·ca·nia. The ancient name for **Basilicata.**

lu·carne (lo͞o-kärn′) *n.* A dormer window. [Variant (influenced by French *lucarne*) of earlier *lucane,* Old French *lucanne,* from Frankish *lukinna* (unattested), from *lūk* (unattested), something that closes. See **leug-[1]** in Appendix.*]

lu·cent (lo͞o′sənt) *adj.* **1.** Giving off light; luminous. **2.** Translucent. [Latin *lūcēns,* present participle of *lūcēre,* to shine. See **leuk-** in Appendix.*] **—lu′cen·cy** *n.* **—lu′cent·ly** *adv.*

lu·cerne (lo͞o-sûrn′) *n. Chiefly British.* A plant, **alfalfa** *(see).* [French *luzerne,* from Provençal *luzerno,* special use of *luzerno,* glowworm (from its shiny seeds), perhaps from Latin *lucerna,* lamp. See **leuk-** in Appendix.*]

Lu·cerne (lo͞o-sûrn′; *French* lü-sĕrn′). *German* **Lu·zern** (lo͞o-tsĕrn′). A city of Switzerland, on the northwestern shore of the Lake of Lucerne. Population, 73,000.

Lucerne, Lake of (lo͞o-sûrn′; *French* lü-sĕrn′). A lake occupying 44 square miles in central Switzerland.

lu·ces. Alternate plural of **lux.**

Lu·chow. The former name for **Hofei.**

Lu·cian (lo͞o′shən). Greek satirist of the second century A.D.

lu·cid (lo͞o′sĭd) *adj.* **1.** Easily understood; clear: *a lucid speech.* **2.** Sane; rational: *a lucid speaker.* [French *lucide* and Italian *lucido,* from Latin *lūcidus,* from *lūcēre,* to shine. See **leuk-** in Appendix.*] **—lu·cid′i·ty, lu′cid·ness** *n.* **—lu′cid·ly** *adv.*

lu·ci·fer (lo͞o′sə-fər) *n.* A friction match. [After LUCIFER.]

Lu·ci·fer[1] (lo͞o′sə-fər). The archangel cast from Heaven for leading a revolt of the angels; Satan. [Middle English *Lucifer,* Old English *Lucifer,* from Latin *Lūcifer,* "light-bearer" : *lūx* (stem *lūc-*), light (see **leuk-** in Appendix*) + -FER.]

Lu·ci·fer[2] (lo͞o′sə-fər) *n.* The planet Venus in its appearance as the morning star.

lu·cif·er·ase (lo͞o-sĭf′ə-rās′) *n.* An enzyme that catalyzes the oxidation of luciferin. [LUCIFER(IN) + -ASE.]

lu·cif·er·in (lo͞o-sĭf′ər-ən) *n.* A pigment in bioluminescent animals, such as fireflies or certain marine crustaceans, that produces an almost heatless, bluish-green light when oxidized. [From Latin *lūcifer,* "light-bearer." See **Lucifer.**]

Lu·ci·na (lo͞o-sī′nə) *n. Archaic.* A midwife. [Latin *Lūcīna,* goddess of childbirth, from *lūcīnus,* "bringing to light," from *lūx* (stem *lūc-*), light. See **leuk-** in Appendix.*]

Lu·cite (lo͞o′sīt′) *n.* A trademark for a transparent, thermoplastic, acrylic resin.

lugsail

luck (lŭk) *n.* **1.** The fortuitous happening of fortunate or adverse events; fortune; lot. **2.** Good fortune; prosperity; success: *I wish you luck.* **—down on one's luck.** To undergo misfortune. **—try one's luck.** To attempt something with no assurance of success. [Middle English *lucke,* perhaps from Low German *luk* or Middle Dutch *luc,* akin to Middle High German *gelücke*†.]

luck·i·ly (lŭk′ə-lē) *adv.* With or by favorable chance.

luck·less (lŭk′lĭs) *adj.* Unlucky; having poor luck.

Luck·now (lŭk′nou). The capital of Uttar Pradesh, Republic of India, situated in the center of the state. Population, 595,000.

luck·y (lŭk′ē) *adj.* **-ier, -iest.** **1.** Having or resulting in good luck. **2.** Occurring by chance. **3.** Believed to bring good luck: *a lucky number.* —See Usage note at **fortuitous.** **—luck′i·ness** *n.*

lu·cra·tive (lo͞o′krə-tĭv) *adj.* Producing wealth; profitable. [Middle English *lucratif,* from Old French, from Latin *lucrātīvus,* from *lucrārī,* to profit, from *lucrum,* gain, LUCRE.]

lu·cre (lo͞o′kər) *n.* Money; profits. [Middle English, from Latin *lucrum,* gain, profit. See **lāu-** in Appendix.*]

Lu·cre·tius (lo͞o-krē′shəs). Full name, Titus Lucretius Carus. 96?–55 B.C. Roman poet and philosopher.

lu·cu·brate (lo͞o′kyo͞o-brāt′) *intr.v.* **-brated, -brating, -brates.** To write in a scholarly fashion. [Latin *lūcubrāre,* to work at night by lamplight. See **leuk-** in Appendix.*]

lu·cu·bra·tion (lo͞o′kyo͞o-brā′shən) *n.* **1.** Laborious study or writing. **2.** Pedantry in speech or writing.

lu·cu·lent (lo͞o′kyo͞o-lənt) *adj.* Easily understood; clear; lucid. [Middle English, full of light, clear, from Latin *lūculentus,* from *lūx* (stem *lūc-*), light. See **leuk-** in Appendix.*]

Lu·cul·lan (lo͞o-kŭl′ən) *adj.* **1.** Of or pertaining to Lucullus or his luxurious banquets. **2.** Lavish; luxurious.

Lu·cul·lus (lo͞o-kŭl′əs), **Lucius Licinius.** 110?–57? B.C. Roman general, consul, and patron of art and literature.

Lu·cy (lo͞o′sē). A feminine given name. [Middle English, from Latin *Lūcia,* feminine of *Lūcius,* probably from *lūx* (stem *lūc-*), light. See **leuk-** in Appendix.*]

Lud·dite (lŭd′īt′) *n.* Any of a group of British workmen who, between 1811 and 1816, rioted and destroyed textile machinery in the belief that it would diminish employment. [Probably after Ned *Lud(d),* a late 18th-century worker who destroyed stocking frames in England.]

Lud·hi·a·na (lo͝od′hē-ä′nə). A city of the Republic of India, in east-central Punjab. Population, 244,000.

lu·di·crous (lo͞o′dĭ-krəs) *adj.* Laughable or hilarious through obvious absurdity or incongruity. See Synonyms at **foolish.** [Latin *lūdicrus,* done playfully, from *lūdus,* game. See **leid-** in Appendix.*] **—lu′di·crous·ly** *adv.* **—lu′di·crous·ness** *n.*

Lud·wigs·ha·fen (lo͞ot′vĭkhs-hä′fən). A city of West Germany, in southeastern Rhineland Palatinate. Population, 175,000.

lu·es (lo͞o′ēz) *n., pl.* **lues.** *Pathology.* **1.** Syphilis. **2.** A plague; pestilence. [New Latin, from Latin *luēs,* plague. See **leu-[1]** in Appendix.*] **—lu·et′ic** (-ĕt′ĭk) *adj.* **—lu·et′i·cal·ly** *adv.*

luff (lŭf) *n.* **1.** The act of sailing closer into the wind. **2.** The forward side of a fore-and-aft sail. **3.** The fullest part of the bow of a ship. *—intr.v.* **luffed, luffing, luffs.** **1.** To steer a sailing vessel nearer into the wind, especially with the sails flapping. **2.** To flap while losing wind. Used of a sail. [Earlier *loufe,* Middle English *luff, lof,* from Old French *lof,* perhaps from Middle Dutch *loef* (unattested). See **lep-[2]** in Appendix.*]

luf·fa. Variant of **loofa.**

Luft·waf·fe (lo͝oft′väf′ə) *n.* The German air force before and during World War II. [German, "air weapon."]

lug[1] (lŭg) *n.* **1.** An earlike handle or projection on a vessel or machine, used as a hold or support. **2.** *Machinery.* A nut, especially one that is closed at one end to serve as a cap. **3.** A loop, usually of leather, at the side of the saddle of a harness rig through which one of the shafts of a cart or other conveyance passes. **4.** A copper or brass fitting to which electrical wires can be soldered or otherwise connected. **5.** *Slang.* A clumsy fool; blockhead. [Middle English (Scottish) *lugge,* flap, ear, perhaps from *luggen,* to LUG (to pull as the ear).]

lug[2] (lŭg) *v.* **lugged, lugging, lugs.** *—tr.* **1.** To drag or haul (something) laboriously. **2.** To pull or drag with short jerks. *—intr.* **1.** To pull with difficulty; tug. **2.** To move by jerks or as if under a heavy burden. *—n.* **1.** The act or task of lugging. **2.** Something that is lugged. **3.** A **lugsail** *(see).* **4.** *Slang.* An extortion of money. Used chiefly in the phrase *put the lug on.* [Middle English *luggen,* to pull, perhaps from Scandinavian, akin to Swedish *lugga*†, to pull one's hair.]

Lu·gan·da (lo͞o-găn′də) *n.* The Bantu language of the Ganda, a people of Uganda. **—Lu·gan′da** *adj.*

Lu·ga·no, Lake of (lo͞o-gä′nō). A lake occupying about 19 square miles in southern Switzerland and northern Italy.

Lu·gansk (lo͞o-gänsk′). Formerly **Vo·ro·shi·lov·grad** (vôr′ə-shē′ləf-grăd′). A city of the Soviet Union, a manufacturing center in the eastern Ukrainian S.S.R. Population, 330,000.

Lu·ger (lo͞o′gər) *n.* A trademark for a German automatic pistol.

lug·gage (lŭg′ĭj) *n.* **1.** Something that one lugs. **2.** Baggage. [Probably LUG (to drag) + (BAG)GAGE.]

lug·ger (lŭg′ər) *n.* A small boat used for fishing, sailing, or coasting and having two or three masts, each with a lugsail, and two or three jibs set on the bowsprit. [From LUG(SAIL).]

lug·sail (lŭg′səl) *n.* A quadrilateral sail lacking a boom and having the foot larger than the head, bent to a yard hanging obliquely on the mast. Also called "lug." [Perhaps from LUG (obsolete sense "flap," "ear").]

lu·gu·bri·ous (lo͞o-go͞o′brē-əs, lo͞o-gyo͞o′-) *adj.* Mournful or doleful, especially to a ludicrous degree. [Latin *lūgubris,* mournful, from *lūgēre,* to mourn. See **leug-[2]** in Appendix.*] **—lu·gu′bri·ous·ly** *adv.* **—lu·gu′bri·ous·ness** *n.*

lug·worm (lŭg′wûrm′) *n.* Any of various segmented, burrowing marine worms of the genus *Arenicola;* especially, *A. marina,* often used as fishing bait. Also called "lobworm." [Origin uncertain.]

Lui·chow Peninsula (lā′jō′). A projection of southern Kwangtung Province, China, extending southward north of Hainan between the Gulf of Tonkin and the South China Sea.

Luik. The Flemish name for **Liège.**

Luke[1] (lo͝ok). A masculine given name. [Middle English *Luke, Luck,* from Latin *Lucas,* from Greek *Loukas,* "of Lucania."]

Luke[2] (lo͝ok) *n.* A book of the New Testament, the first Gospel, attributed to Saint Luke.

Luke (lo͝ok), **Saint.** A companion of the Apostle Paul, traditionally regarded as author of the third Gospel and The Acts of the Apostles.

luke·warm (lo͞ok′wôrm′) *adj.* **1.** Mildly warm; tepid. **2.** Lacking in enthusiasm; indifferent. [Middle English : *luke,* perhaps from *lew,* tepid, Old English *hlēow,* warm (see **kel-[1]** in Appendix*) + WARM.] **—luke′warm′ly** *adv.* **—luke′warm′ness** *n.*

lull (lŭl) *v.* **lulled, lulling, lulls.** *—tr.* **1.** To cause to sleep or rest; soothe. **2.** To deceive into trustfulness: *"that honeyed charm that he used so effectively to lull his victims"* (S.J. Perelman). *—intr.* To become calm. *—n.* **1.** A relatively calm interval in a storm or other turbulence. **2.** An interval of lessened activity: *a lull in sales.* [Middle English *lullen,* perhaps of German origin, akin to Middle Low German *lollen.* See **lā-** in Appendix.*]

lull·a·by (lŭl′ə-bī′) *n., pl.* **-bies.** A soothing song with which to lull a child to sleep. *—tr.v.* **lullabied, -bying, -bies.** To quiet

with or as if with a lullaby. [Perhaps LULL + (GOOD-)BY.]
Lul·ly (lü-lē′), **Jean Baptiste.** Also **Lul·li.** 1632–1687. Italian-born French composer of operas.
lu·lu[1] (lo͞o′lo͞o) *n. Slang.* An object, action, or idea that is remarkable. [Perhaps from *Lulu,* pet form of LOUISE.]
lu·lu[2] (lo͞o′lo͞o) *n. Slang.* A flat payment to members of a legislature in lieu of itemized payments. [Reduplication of LIEU.]
lum·ba·go (lŭm-bā′gō) *n.* A painful, inflammatory rheumatism of the tendons and muscles of the lumbar region. [Latin *lumbāgo,* from *lumbus,* loin. See **lendh-**[1] in Appendix.*]
lum·bar (lŭm′bər, -bär′) *adj.* Of or situated in the part of the back and sides between the lowest ribs and the pelvis. —*n.* A lumbar artery, nerve, vertebra, or part. [New Latin *lumbaris,* from *lumbus,* loin. See **lendh-**[1] in Appendix.*]
lum·ber[1] (lŭm′bər) *n.* **1.** Timber sawed into boards, planks, or structural members of standard or specified length. **2.** *Chiefly British.* Miscellaneous stored articles. **3.** Anything useless or cumbersome. —*v.* **lumbered, -bering, -bers.** —*tr.* **1. a.** To cut down (trees) and prepare as marketable timber. **b.** To cut down the timber of. **2.** *Chiefly British.* To clutter with or as if with unused articles. —*intr.* To cut and prepare timber for the market. [Possibly a blend of LUMBER (to move clumsily, hence something clumsy) and LOMBARD (in the sense of a storehouse or pawnshop, from the moneychangers of Lombardy).] —**lum′ber** *adj.* —**lum′ber·er, lum′ber·man** (-mən) *n.*
lum·ber[2] (lŭm′bər) *intr.v.* **-bered, -bering, -bers. 1.** To walk or move with heavy clumsiness: *"Lennie lumbered to his feet and disappeared in the bush"* (Steinbeck). **2.** To move with a rumbling noise: *The trucks lumbered up from the excavation.* [Middle English *lomeren,* perhaps from Scandinavian, akin to Swedish dialectal *loma,* to move heavily. See **lem-**[1] in Appendix.*]
lum·ber·jack (lŭm′bər-jăk′) *n.* **1.** One who fells trees and transports the timber to a mill; a logger. **2.** A short, warm outer jacket resembling that worn by a lumberjack. [LUMBER (wood) + JACK (man).]
lum·ber·yard (lŭm′bər-yärd′) *n.* An establishment that sells lumber and other building materials from a yard.
lum·bri·coid (lŭm′brĭ-koid′) *adj.* Resembling an earthworm. —*n.* A parasitic roundworm, *Ascaris lumbricoides,* that infests the human intestine. [New Latin *lumbricoides* : Latin *lumbricus,* earthworm (see **sleidh-** in Appendix*) + -OID.]
lu·men (lo͞o′mən) *n., pl.* **-mens** or **-mina** (-mə-nə). **1.** *Anatomy.* The inner open space of a tubular organ, as of a blood vessel or an intestine. **2.** *Abbr.* **lm** *Physics.* The unit of luminous flux in the International System, equal to the luminous flux emitted in a solid angle of one steradian by a uniform point source having an intensity of one candela. See **measurement.** [New Latin, from Latin *lūmen,* light, eye, opening. See **leuk-** in Appendix.*] —**lu′men·al, lu′min·al** *adj.*
Lu·mière (lü-myâr′), **Auguste Marie Louis Nicolas.** 1862–1954. With his brother, **Louis Jean** (1864–1948), French chemist, inventor, and pioneer in cinematography.
lu·mi·nance (lo͞o′mə-nəns) *n.* **1.** The condition or quality of being luminous. **2.** *Physics.* The luminous intensity per unit projected area of a given surface viewed from a given direction. [Latin *lūmen* (stem *lūmin-*), light (see **luminary**) + -ANCE.]
lu·mi·nar·y (lo͞o′mə-nĕr′ē) *n., pl.* **-ies. 1.** An object, as a celestial body, that gives light. **2.** A source of intellectual or spiritual light. **3.** A notable person in a specific field. [Middle English *luminarye,* from Old French *luminarie,* from Late Latin *lūminăre,* lamp, heavenly body, from Latin *lūmen* (stem *lūmin-*), light. See **leuk-** in Appendix.*] —**lu′mi·nar′y** *adj.*
lu·mi·nesce (lo͞o′mə-nĕs′) *intr.v.* **-nesced, -nescing, -nesces.** To be or become luminescent. [Back-formation from LUMINESCENT.]
lu·mi·nes·cence (lo͞o′mə-nĕs′əns) *n.* **1.** The emission of light, as in phosphorescence, fluorescence, and bioluminescence, by processes that derive energy from essentially nonthermal sources such as chemical, biochemical, or crystallographic changes, the motion of subatomic particles, or the excitation of an atomic system by radiation; especially, such emission distinguished from incandescence. **2.** The light so emitted.
lu·mi·nes·cent (lo͞o′mə-nĕs′ənt) *adj.* Capable of, exhibiting, or suitable for the emission of luminescence. [Latin *lūmen* (stem *lūmin-*), light (see **luminous**) + -ESCENT.]
lu·mi·nif·er·ous (lo͞o′mə-nĭf′ər-əs) *adj.* Generating, yielding, or transmitting light. [Latin *lūmen* (stem *lūmin-*), light (see **luminous**) + -FEROUS.]
lu·mi·nos·i·ty (lo͞o′mə-nŏs′ə-tē) *n.* **1.** The condition or quality of being luminous. **2.** Something luminous. **3.** The ratio of luminous flux at a specific wavelength to the radiant flux at the same wavelength. In this sense, also called "luminosity factor."
lu·mi·nous (lo͞o′mə-nəs) *adj.* **1.** Emitting light; especially, emitting self-generated light. **2.** Full of light; illuminated. **3.** Intelligible; clear. —See Synonyms at **bright.** [Middle English, from Old French *lumineux,* from Latin *lūminōsus,* full of light, from *lūmen* (stem *lūmin-*), light. See **leuk-** in Appendix.*] —**lu′min·ous·ly** *adv.* —**lu′min·ous·ness** *n.*
luminous efficiency. The ratio of the total luminous flux to the total radiant flux of an emitting source.
luminous energy. The radiant energy of electromagnetic waves in the visible portion of the electromagnetic spectrum.
luminous flux. The rate of flow of light per unit time; especially, the flux of visible light expressed in lumens.
luminous intensity. The luminous flux density per solid angle as measured in a given direction relative to the emitting source.
luminous paint. A paint containing a phosphorescent or fluorescent substance that makes it glow in the dark.
lum·mox (lŭm′əks) *n.* An oaf; lout. [Origin unknown.]
lump[1] (lŭmp) *n.* **1.** An irregularly shaped mass or piece. **2.** A small cube of sugar. **3.** *Pathology.* A swelling or small, palpable mass. **4.** An aggregate; collection; totality. **5.** An ungainly or dull-witted person. **6.** A piece of coal or coke suitable for use in a stove or fireplace. **7.** *Plural.* **a.** Punishment in the form of beatings: *take one's lumps.* **b.** One's just deserts. —**a lump in the throat.** A feeling of constriction in the throat caused by emotion. —*adj.* Formed into lumps: *lump sugar.* —*v.* **lumped, lumping, lumps.** —*tr.* **1.** To put together or amass in a single group or pile. **2.** To move with heavy clumsiness. **3.** To make lumpy. —*intr.* **1.** To become lumpy. **2.** To move heavily. [Middle English, perhaps of Low German origin, akin to Dutch *lomp,* rag, Low German *lump,* coarse. See **leb-**[1] in Appendix.*]
lump[2] (lŭmp) *tr.v.* **lumped, lumping, lumps.** *Informal.* To tolerate (what must be endured): *like it or lump it.* [Origin unknown.]
lump·er (lŭm′pər) *n.* A laborer employed to load and unload ships; a stevedore. [From LUMP ("to put together," "load").]
lump·fish (lŭmp′fĭsh′) *n., pl.* **lumpfish** or **-fishes.** A fish, *Cyclopterus lumpus,* of Atlantic waters, having a body covered with tuberous excrescences. [Obsolete *lump,* lumpfish, from Middle Dutch *lumpe* (see **leb-**[1] in Appendix*) + FISH.]

lumpfish

lump·ish (lŭm′pĭsh) *adj.* **1.** Stupid; dull. **2.** Clumsy; heavy; cumbersome. —**lump′ish·ly** *adv.* —**lump′ish·ness** *n.*
lump sum. A sum of money as complete payment.
lump·y (lŭm′pē) *adj.* **-ier, -iest. 1.** Covered with lumps. **2.** Full of lumps. **3.** Thickset or cumbersome in appearance. **4.** Characterized by short, jumbled waves, as a tidal rip.
lumpy jaw. *Pathology.* **Actinomycosis** *(see).*
Lu·mum·ba (lo͞o-mo͝om′bə), **Patrice Emergy.** 1925–1961. Premier of the Republic of Congo (1960–61).
lu·na (lo͞o′nə) *n.* An alchemical designation for silver. [Middle English, from Medieval Latin *lūna,* from Latin, moon (from its color). See **leuk-** in Appendix.*]
Lu·na (lo͞o′nə). The Roman goddess of the moon. [Latin *Lūna,* personification of *lūna,* moon. See **leuk-** in Appendix.*]
lu·na·cy (lo͞o′nə-sē) *n., pl.* **-cies. 1.** *Archaic.* Mental derangement associated with certain phases of the moon. **2.** Insanity. **3.** Foolish and irresponsible conduct. —See Synonyms at **insanity.** [From LUNATIC.]

luna moth

luna moth. A large, pale-green North American moth, *Actias luna,* having a long projection on each hind wing. [From Latin *lūna,* moon (from the yellow rings on its wings). See **lunar.**]
lu·nar (lo͞o′nər) *adj.* **1.** Of, involving, caused by, or affecting the moon. **2.** Measured by the revolution of the moon: *a lunar month; a lunar year.* **3.** Of or relating to silver. [Latin *lūnāris,* from *lūna,* moon. See **leuk-** in Appendix.*]
lunar caustic. Silver nitrate used in cauterization.
lunar month. A **month** *(see).*
lunar year. An interval of 12 lunar months. See **month.**
lu·nate (lo͞o′nāt′) *adj.* Also **lu·nat·ed** (-nā′tĭd). Crescent-shaped. [Latin *lūnātus,* from *lūnāre,* to form into a crescent, from *lūna,* moon. See **leuk-** in Appendix.*]
lunate bone. The second of three bones forming the upper row of bones in the wrist. Also called "semilunar bone."
lu·na·tic (lo͞o′nə-tĭk) *adj.* **1.** Suffering from lunacy; insane. **2.** Of or for the insane: *a lunatic asylum.* **3.** Wildly or giddily foolish: *a lunatic decision.* [Middle English *lunatik,* from Old French *lunatique,* from Latin *lūnāticus,* "moonstruck," crazy, from *lūna,* moon. See **leuk-** in Appendix.*] —**lu′na·tic** *n.*
lunatic fringe. The fanatic or irrational members of a society or group.
lu·na·tion (lo͞o-nā′shən) *n.* The time elapsing between two successive new moons, averaging 29 days, 12 hours, 44 minutes, 28 seconds. [Middle English *lunacioun,* from Medieval Latin *lūnātiō,* from Latin *lūna,* moon. See **lunar.**]
lunch (lŭnch) *n.* **1.** A meal eaten at midday. **2.** The food provided for this meal. —*intr.v.* **lunched, lunching, lunches.** To have one's lunch. [Originally "chunk, thick piece of food," perhaps from Spanish *lonja*†, slice.] —**lunch′er** *n.*
lunch·eon (lŭn′chən) *n.* **1.** A noonday meal; a lunch. **2.** An early afternoon party at which a light meal is served. [Probably an extension of LUNCH.]
lunch·eon·ette (lŭn′chə-nĕt′) *n.* A small restaurant that serves simple, easily prepared meals. Also called "lunchroom."
Lund (lŭnd). A city of Sweden, in the southeast about ten miles northeast of Malmö; the capital of the kings of Denmark in the early Middle Ages. Population, 50,000.
lune (lo͞on) *n.* A portion of a sphere enclosed between two semicircles having their common end points at opposite poles. [From Latin *lūna,* moon. See **leuk-** in Appendix.*]
lunes (lo͞onz) *pl.n. Archaic.* Fits of lunacy. [French, from Old French *lune,* "moon," whim, from Latin *lūna,* moon. See **lunar.**]
lu·nette (lo͞o-nĕt′) *n.* Also **lu·net** (lo͞o′nĭt). **1.** *Architecture.* **a.** A small, circular or crescent-shaped opening in a vaulted roof. **b.** A crescent-shaped or semicircular space, usually over a door or window, that may contain another window, a sculpture, or a mural. **2.** *Military.* A type of fieldwork that has two projecting faces and two parallel flanks. [Old French *lunette,* crescent, from Latin *lūna,* moon. See **lunar.**]
lung (lŭng) *n.* **1.** Either of two spongy, saclike respiratory organs in most vertebrates, occupying the chest cavity together with the heart, and functioning to remove carbon dioxide from the blood and provide it with oxygen. **2.** A comparable invertebrate structure, as in terrestrial snails. [Middle English *lunge,* from Old English *lungen.* See **legwh-** in Appendix.*]
lunge[1] (lŭnj) *n.* **1.** A sudden thrust or pass, as with a sword or rapier. **2.** Any sudden forward movement or plunge. —*v.* **lunged, lunging, lunges.** —*intr.* **1.** To make a thrust or pass. **2.** To move with a lunge. —*tr.* To cause (someone) to lunge,

[Earlier *allonge, elonge,* from French *allonger, alongier,* to lengthen, extend, from Vulgar Latin *allongāre* (unattested) : Latin *ad-* (toward) + *longus,* long (see **del-**[1] in Appendix*).]

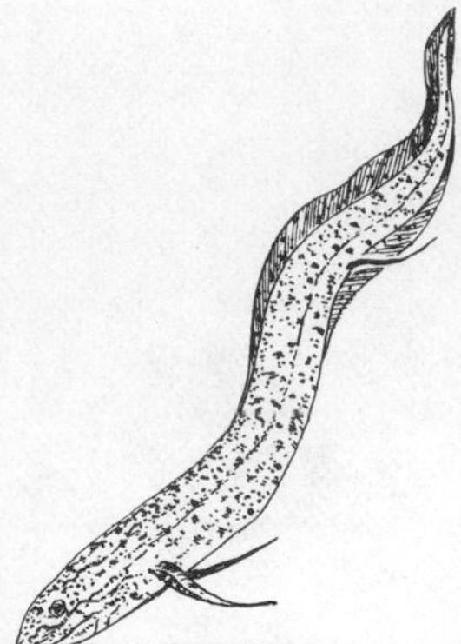

lungfish
Protopterus annectens

lunge[2] (lŭnj) *n.* A long rope or leather rein used for schooling or exercising a horse by someone on foot. Also called "lunging rein." —*tr.v.* **lunged, lunging, lunges.** To school or exercise (a horse) by means of a lunge. [French *longe,* "long (rein)," from Latin *longus,* long. See **del-**[1] in Appendix.*]

lung·er[1] (lŭn′jər) *n.* One that lunges.

lung·er[2] (lŭng′ər) *n. Informal.* One who has tuberculosis of the lungs.

lung·fish (lŭng′fĭsh′) *n., pl.* **lungfish** or **-fishes.** Any of several elongated tropical freshwater fishes of the order Dipnoi (or Dipneusti), having lungs as well as gills, and in certain species constructing a mucus-lined mud covering in which to withstand an extended drought.

lun·gi (lo͝ong′gē) *n.* Also **lun·gee. 1.** A loincloth in India. **2.** The long piece of fabric used to form a loincloth, turban, or scarf. [Hindi, from Persian *lungi*†.]

Lung·shi (lo͝ong′shē′). Formerly **Chang·chow** (chäng′jō′). A city of China, in southern Fukien Province. Population, 81,000.

lung·wort (lŭng′wûrt′, -wôrt′) *n.* **1.** Any of various plants of the genus *Mertensia,* having drooping clusters of tubular, usually blue flowers. **2.** Any of several plants of the genus *Pulmonaria,* native to Europe, with long-stalked leaves and coiled clusters of blue or purple flowers. [Formerly used to treat lung diseases.]

lu·ni·so·lar (lo͞o′nĭ-sō′lər) *adj.* Of or caused by both the sun and the moon. [Latin *lūna,* moon (see **lunar**) + SOLAR.]

lu·ni·ti·dal (lo͞o′nĭ-tīd′l) *adj.* Of or pertaining to tidal phenomena caused by the moon. [Latin *lūna,* moon (see **lunar**) + TIDAL.]

lunitidal interval. The time elapsing between the moon's transit of a particular meridian and the next high tide at that meridian.

lunk·er (lŭng′kər) *n. Informal.* Something unusually large of its kind, especially a large game fish. [Origin unknown.]

lunk·head (lŭngk′hĕd′) *n. Slang.* A stupid person. [Probably formed from LUMP and HEAD.] —**lunk′head′ed** *adj.*

lu·nu·la (lo͞on′yə-lə) *n., pl.* **-lae** (-lē′). Also **lu·nule** (-yo͞ol). A small crescent-shaped structure or marking. [Latin *lūnula,* crescent-shaped ornament, "little moon," from *lūna,* moon. See **leuk-** in Appendix.*]

lu·nu·lar (lo͞on′yə-lər) *adj.* Crescent-shaped.

lu·nu·late (lo͞on′yə-lāt′, -lĭt) *adj.* Also **lu·nu·lat·ed** (-lā′tĭd). **1.** Small and lunular. **2.** Having crescent-shaped markings.

lu·ny. Variant of **loony.**

Lu·per·ca·li·a (lo͞o′pər-kā′lē-ə) *n.* A fertility festival in ancient Rome, celebrated on February 15 in honor of the pastoral god Lupercus. —**Lu′per·ca′li·an** *adj.*

lupine[1]
Lupinus perennis

lu·pine[1] (lo͞o′pən) *n.* Also **lu·pin.** Any of various plants of the genus *Lupinus,* having clusters of variously colored flowers. [Middle English, from Latin *lupīnum,* from *lupīnus,* LUPINE (wolflike), from the ancient belief that it destroyed the soil.]

lu·pine[2] (lo͞o′pīn′) *adj.* **1.** Wolflike. **2.** Rapacious; ravenous. [Latin *lupīnus,* from *lupus,* wolf. See **wlkwo-** in Appendix.*]

lu·pu·lin (lo͞op′yə-lən) *n.* Minute yellowish-brown hairs from the strobiles of the hop plant, formerly used as a sedative. [New Latin *lupulus,* hop plant, diminutive of Latin *lupus,* wolf, hop plant (see **lupine**) + -IN.]

lu·pus (lo͞o′pəs) *n.* Any of several diseases of the skin and mucous membranes, many causing disfiguring lesions, especially: **a.** *Lupus vulgaris,* characterized by ulcerating, nodular facial lesions, especially around the nose and ears. **b.** *Lupus erythematosus,* characterized by eruption of atrophic scarred lesions with chronically inflamed margins. Also called "noli-me-tangere." [New Latin, from Latin, wolf. See **lupine.**]

Lu·pus (lo͞o′pəs) *n.* A constellation in the Southern Hemisphere near Centaurus and Scorpius. [Latin *lupus,* wolf. See **lupine.**]

Lu·qui·llo Mountains (lo͞o-kē′yō). A mountain range in eastern Puerto Rico. Highest elevation, El Yunque (3,496 feet).

lurch[1] (lûrch) *intr.v.* **lurched, lurching, lurches. 1.** To stagger. **2.** To roll or pitch suddenly or erratically, as a ship during a storm. —*n.* **1.** A staggering or tottering movement or gait. **2.** An abrupt rolling or pitching. [Origin obscure.]

lurch[2] (lûrch) *n.* **1.** A position of difficulty or discomfort. Now used only in the phrase *to leave (someone) in the lurch.* **2.** In the game of cribbage, the losing position of a player who scores 30 points or less to the winner's 61. [From French *lourche,* a game resembling backgammon, "defeat," probably from Middle High German *lurz,* left, wrong, "defeat." See **lerd-** in Appendix.*]

lurch·er (lûr′chər) *n.* **1.** *Archaic.* A lurker; sneak thief. **2.** *Chiefly British.* A crossbred dog used by poachers. [From obsolete *lurch,* to lurk, Middle English *lorchen,* variant of *lurken,* LURK.]

lure
Fishing lures

lure (lo͝or) *n.* **1. a.** Anything that entices, tempts, or attracts with the promise of gaining a pleasure or reward. **b.** An attraction or appeal. **2.** Any decoy used in catching animals; especially, an artificial bait used in catching fish. **3.** A bunch of feathers attached to a long cord, used in falconry to recall the hawk. —*tr.v.* **lured, luring, lures. 1.** To attract by wiles or temptation; entice. **2.** To recall (a falcon) with a lure. [Middle English, from Old French *loirre,* bait, from Germanic *lōthr* (unattested).]

Synonyms: *lure, entice, inveigle, decoy, tempt, seduce, beguile.* These verbs refer to leading or attempting to lead a person from his course, usually into harm or wrong, by exerting a strong attraction. *Lure* strongly implies capture by calculated and deliberate means. *Entice* involves drawing one on skillfully by making attractive promises; *inveigle,* winning over by coaxing, flattery, or specious talk; and *decoy,* trapping or ensnaring by false appearances or deception. *Tempt* and *seduce* both imply an effort to overcome moral resistance by means that are otherwise not explicit. Unlike *tempt, seduce* clearly connotes success in leading astray, and in one sense means causing another to surrender chastity. *Beguile* implies deluding or victimizing by craft, charm, or any device that diverts attention.

lu·rid (lo͝or′ĭd) *adj.* **1.** Causing shock or horror. **2.** Glowing or glaring through a haze. **3.** Sallow in color; pallid. —See Synonyms at **ghastly.** [Latin *lūridus,* pallid, ghastly, from *lūror*†, pale yellow, ghastliness.] —**lu′rid·ly** *adv.*

lurk (lûrk) *intr.v.* **lurked, lurking, lurks. 1.** To lie in wait, as in ambush. **2.** To move furtively; to sneak; slink. **3.** To exist unobserved or unsuspected; be concealed. [Middle English *lurken,* probably frequentative of *luren,* LOWER (to frown).]

Lu·sa·ka (lo͞o-sä′kə). The capital of Zambia, in the southeast-central part of the country. Population, 122,000.

Lu·sa·tia (lo͞o-sā′shə). A region of Europe, extending over southeastern East Germany and southwestern Poland.

Lu·sa·tian (lo͞o-sā′shən) *n.* A language, **Wendish** *(see).*

lus·cious (lŭsh′əs) *adj.* **1.** Sweet and pleasant to taste or smell; delicious: *a luscious melon.* **2.** Having strong sensory appeal. **3.** *Archaic.* Excessively sweet; cloying. [Perhaps from Middle English *lucius, licius,* possibly shortened from DELICIOUS.]

lush[1] (lŭsh) *adj.* **lusher, lushest. 1.** Having or characterized by luxuriant growth or vegetation. **2.** Luxurious; opulent: *lush carpets.* **3.** Delicious. **4.** Overelaborate or extravagant: *lush rhetoric.* [Middle English *lusch,* lax, soft, perhaps variant of *lasche,* soft, watery, from Old French, lax, slack, from Latin *laxus,* spacious, loose. See **slēg-** in Appendix.*]

lush[2] (lŭsh) *n. Slang.* **1.** A drunkard. **2.** Intoxicating liquor. —*intr.v.* **lushed, lushing, lushes.** *Slang.* To drink liquor to excess. [Origin unknown.]

Lü·shun (lü′sho͞on′). Formerly **Port Ar·thur** (är′thər). A city of China, now part of the municipal district of Lüta.

Lu·si·ta·ni·a. The ancient name for **Portugal.**

lust (lŭst) *n.* **1.** Sexual craving, especially excessive or unrestrained. **2.** Any overwhelming desire or craving: *a lust for power.* **3.** *Obsolete.* Pleasure; delight; relish. —*intr.v.* **lusted, lusting, lusts.** To have an inordinate or obsessive desire, especially sexual desire. Usually used with *after* or *for.* [Middle English *lust,* Old English *lust.* See **las-** in Appendix.*]

lus·ter (lŭs′tər) *n.* Also *chiefly British* **lus·tre. 1.** Soft reflected light; sheen; gloss. **2.** Brilliance or radiance of light; brightness. **3.** Glorious or radiant quality; splendor. **4.** A glass pendant, especially on a chandelier. **5.** A decorative object, as a chandelier having glass pendants. **6.** Any of various substances, as wax, used to give an object a gloss or polish. **7.** A fabric, as alpaca, having a glossy surface. **8.** *Mineralogy.* The appearance of a mineral surface judged by its brilliance and ability to reflect light in comparison with metals, glasses, diamonds, and other materials regarded as standards. —*v.* **lustered, -tering, -ters.** Also *chiefly British* **lus·tre, -tred, -tring, -tres.** —*tr.* To give a gloss or sheen to. —*intr.* To become or be lustrous. [French *lustre,* from Italian *lustro,* from *lustrare,* to brighten, from Latin *lūstrāre,* to purify, make bright, from *lūstrum,* purification. See **leuk-** in Appendix.*]

lus·ter·ware (lŭs′tər-wâr′) *n.* Pottery having a metallic sheen.

lust·ful (lŭst′fəl) *adj.* **1.** Excited by lust. **2.** *Archaic.* Vigorous.

lus·tral (lŭs′trəl) *adj.* **1.** Of, pertaining to, or used in a rite of purification. **2.** Pertaining to a lustrum. [Latin *lustrālis,* from *lustrum,* LUSTRUM.]

lus·trate (lŭs′trāt′) *tr.v.* **-trated, -trating, -trates.** To purify by means of ceremony. [Latin *lustrāre,* to purify, from *lustrum,* LUSTRUM.] —**lus·tra′tion** *n.* —**lus′tra·tive** (-trə-tĭv) *adj.*

lus·trous (lŭs′trəs) *adj.* **1.** Having a sheen. **2.** Radiant. —See Synonyms at **bright.** —**lus′trous·ly** *adv.* —**lus′trous·ness** *n.*

lus·trum (lŭs′trəm) *n.* **1.** A ceremonial purification of the entire ancient Roman population after the census every five years. **2.** A period of five years. [Latin *lustrum.* See **leuk-** in Appendix.*]

lust·y (lŭs′tē) *adj.* **-ier, -iest. 1.** Full of vigor; robust. **2.** Powerful: *a lusty drink.* **3.** Lustful. **4.** *Archaic.* Merry; joyous.

lu·sus na·tu·rae (lo͞o′səs nə-to͝or′ē, -tyo͝or′ē). A freak of nature. [Latin *lūsus nātūrae,* "a joke of nature."]

Lü·ta (lo͞o′dä′). A municipal district of northeastern China, on the tip of the Liaotung Peninsula, and including the port cities of Talien and Lüshun. Population, 1,590,000.

lu·ta·nist (lo͞ot′n-ĭst) *n.* A lute player. [From Medieval Latin *lūtānista,* from *lūtāna,* from Old French *lut,* LUTE.]

Lut Desert. See **Dasht-i-Lut.**

lute[1] (lo͞ot) *n.* A musical stringed instrument having a body shaped like half a pear and usually a bent neck with a fretted fingerboard with pegs for tuning. [Middle English, from Old French *lut,* earlier *leut,* from Arabic *al-'ud,* "the wood."]

lute[2] (lo͞ot) *n.* A substance, such as dried clay or cement, used to pack and seal joints and other connections or coat a porous surface to make it tight. [Middle English, from Old French *lut,* from Latin *lutum,* mud, clay. See **leu-**[2] in Appendix.*]

lu·te·al (lo͞o′tē-əl) *adj.* Of or relating to the **corpus luteum** *(see).*

lu·te·in (lo͞o′tē-ən) *n.* A yellow pigment isolated from the corpus luteum and found in body fats and egg yolk. [Latin *lūteum,* egg yolk, from *lūteus,* yellow, from *lūtum,* yellowweed (see **luteous**) + -IN.]

lu·te·ous (lo͞o′tē-əs) *adj.* Of a light or moderate greenish yellow. [From Latin *lūteus,* yellow, from *lūtum*†, yellowweed.]

lu·te·ti·um (lo͞o-tē′shē-əm) *n.* Also **lu·te·ci·um.** *Symbol* **Lu** A silvery-white rare-earth element that is exceptionally difficult to separate from the other rare-earth elements, used in nuclear technology. Atomic number 71, atomic weight 174.97, melting point 1,652°C, boiling point 3,327°C, specific gravity 9.872, valence 3. See **element.** [New Latin, from *Lūtētia,* Latin name for Paris, native city of its discoverer, Georges Urbains (1872–1938), French chemist.]

Lu·ther (loo'thər), **Martin.** 1483–1546. German monk; a founder of Protestantism.

Lu·ther·an (loo'thər-ən) *adj.* **1.** Of or relating to Martin Luther or his religious teachings and especially to the doctrine of justification by faith alone. **2.** Of or relating to the branch of the Protestant Church adhering to the views of Martin Luther. —*n.* A member of the Lutheran Church. —**Lu'ther·an·ism'** *n.*

Lutheran Church. The Protestant denomination founded in Germany in the 16th century by Martin Luther.

Lu·thu·li (loo-too'lē), **Albert John.** 1898?–1967. South African Negro leader; Zulu chieftain (1936–53).

lu·tist (loo'tist) *n.* **1.** A maker of lutes. **2.** A lute player.

Lu·ton (loot'n). An industrial city in southeastern Bedford, England. Population, 151,000.

lux (lŭks) *n., pl.* **luxes** or **luces** (loo'sēz). *Abbr.* **lx** The International System unit of illumination, equal to one lumen per square meter. See **measurement.** [Latin *lūx,* light. See **leuk-** in Appendix.*]

lux·ate (lŭk'sāt') *tr.v.* **-ated, -ating, -ates.** To put out of joint; dislocate. [Latin *luxāre,* from *luxus,* dislocated. See **leug-¹** in Appendix.*] —**lux·a'tion** *n.*

luxe (looks, lŭks; *French* lüks) *n.* The condition of being elegantly sumptuous. Usually used in the phrase *de luxe.* [From French *luxe,* from Latin *luxus,* luxury.]

Lux·em·bourg (lŭk'səm-bûrg; *French* lük'sän-boor'). Also **Lux·em·burg** (lŭk'səm-bûrg; *German* look'səm-boork). **1.** A constitutional monarchy and grand duchy occupying 999 square miles in western Europe, and bordered by France, Belgium, and West Germany. Population, 331,000. **2.** Also **Luxembourg City.** The capital of this grand duchy. Population, 77,000. **3.** A province occupying 1,706 square miles in southeastern Belgium. Population, 219,000. Capital, Arlon.

Lux·or (lŭk'sôr', look'-). A city of Egypt, on the east bank of the Nile 415 miles south of Cairo. Population, 35,000.

lux·u·ri·ant (lŭg-zhoor'ē-ənt, lŭk-shoor'-) *adj.* **1.** Growing abundantly, vigorously, or lushly. **2.** Exuberantly elaborate; ornate; florid. **3.** Abundantly fertile or productive. [Latin *luxuriāns,* present participle of *luxuriāre,* to grow profusely, LUXURIATE.] —**lux·u'ri·ance** *n.* —**lux·u'ri·ant·ly** *adv.*

lux·u·ri·ate (lŭg-zhoor'ē-āt', lŭk-shoor'-) *intr.v.* **-ated, -ating, -ates.** **1.** To take luxurious pleasure; indulge oneself. Used with *in.* **2.** To proliferate. **3.** To grow profusely. [Latin *luxuriāre,* to grow profusely, from *luxuria,* excess, LUXURY.]

lux·u·ri·ous (lŭg-zhoor'ē-əs, lŭk-shoor'-) *adj.* **1.** Fond of or given to luxury. **2.** Characterized by or contributing to luxury. —See Synonyms at **sensuous.**

lux·u·ry (lŭg'zhə-rē, lŭk'shə-) *n., pl.* **-ries. 1.** Anything conducive to physical comfort. **2.** The enjoyment of sumptuous living. [Middle English *luxurie,* from Old French, from Latin *luxuria,* excess, rankness, from *luxus,* excess, extravagance. See **leug-¹** in Appendix.*]

Lu·zern. The German name for **Lucerne.**

Lu·zon (loo-zŏn'; *Spanish* loo-sôn'). The largest island (40,420 square miles) of the Republic of the Philippines, lying at the northern end of the archipelago.

lv. 1. leave. **2.** livre.

Lvov (lə-vôf', -vôv'). Also **L'vov.** A city of the Soviet Union, in the west-central Ukrainian S.S.R. Population, 496,000.

Lw The symbol for the element lawrencium.

L.W. low water.

lx lux.

LXX Septuagint.

–ly¹. Indicates: **1.** A characteristic or resemblance; for example, **sisterly. 2.** Appearance or occurrence at specified intervals; for example, **weekly, monthly.** [Middle English *-li, -lich,* Old English *-lic,* "having the form of." See **lîk-** in Appendix.*]

–ly². Indicates: **1.** In a specified manner; for example, **gradually, partly. 2.** At every specified interval; for example, **hourly, daily.** [Middle English *-li, -liche,* Old English *-lice,* from *-lic,* -LY (adjectival suffix).]

Ly·all·pur (lī'əl-poor). A city of northeastern West Pakistan, 75 miles west of Lahore. Population, 425,000.

ly·can·thrope (lī'kən-thrōp', lī-kăn'-) *n.* A werewolf. [New Latin *lycanthropus,* from Greek *lukanthrōpos,* werewolf : *lukos,* wolf (see **wl̥kwo-** in Appendix*) + *anthrōpos,* man (see **ner-²** in Appendix*).]

ly·can·thro·py (lī-kăn'thrə-pē) *n.* The magical ability to assume the form and characteristics of a wolf.

Ly·ca·o·ni·a (lī'kā-ō'nē-ə, lĭk'ā-). An ancient territory in south-central Asia Minor around modern Konya, Turkey.

ly·ce·um (lī-sē'əm) *n.* **1.** A hall in which lectures, concerts, and the like are presented. **2.** An organization sponsoring such presentations. [Greek *Lukeion,* the school outside Athens where Aristotle taught from 335 to 323 B.C., named after the nearby temple of *Apollō Lukeios; Lukeios,* a title of uncertain origin.]

ly·chee. Variant of **litchi.**

lych gate. Variant of **lich gate.**

lych·nis (lĭk'nĭs) *n.* Any of various plants of the genus *Lychnis,* which includes the campions. [New Latin *Lychnis,* from Latin, a kind of rose of fiery color, from Greek *lukhnis,* from *lukhnos,* lamp. See **leuk-** in Appendix.*]

Lyc·i·a (lĭsh'ē-ə, lĭsh'ə). An ancient country and later a Roman province on the southwestern coast of Asia Minor.

Lyc·i·an (lĭsh'ē-ən, lĭsh'ən) *n.* **1.** An inhabitant of ancient Lycia.

2. The Anatolian language of the Lycians. —*adj.* Of or pertaining to the Lycians or their language.

ly·co·po·di·um (lī'kə-pō'dē-əm) *n.* **1.** Any plant of the genus *Lycopodium,* which includes the club mosses. **2.** The yellowish powdery spores of certain club mosses, especially *Lycopodium clavatum,* used in fireworks and explosives, and as a covering for pills. [New Latin *Lycopodium,* "wolf foot" (from its claw-shaped roots) : Greek *lukos,* wolf (see **wl̥kwo-** in Appendix*) + *pous* (stem *pod-*), foot (see **ped-¹** in Appendix*).]

lyd·dite (lĭd'īt') *n.* An explosive consisting chiefly of picric acid. [From *Lydd,* town in England where it was first tested.]

Lyd·gate (lĭd'gāt', -gĭt), **John.** 1370?–1451? English court poet.

Lyd·i·a¹ (lĭd'ē-ə). A feminine given name. [From Greek *Ludia,* "a Lydian woman."]

Lyd·i·a² (lĭd'ē-ə). An ancient Aegean country of Asia Minor.

Lyd·i·an (lĭd'ē-ən) *n.* **1.** One of a people of ancient Lydia. **2.** The Anatolian language of these people. —*adj.* Of or pertaining to the Lydians, their language, or their music.

lye (lī) *n.* **1.** The liquid obtained by leaching wood ashes. **2.** Potassium hydroxide *(see).* **3.** Sodium hydroxide *(see).* [Middle English *lye, ley(e),* Old English *lēag.* See **lou-** in Appendix.*]

Ly·ell (lī'əl), **Sir Charles.** 1797–1875. British geologist.

ly·ing (lī'ĭng) *adj.* Untruthful. See Synonyms at **dishonest.**

ly·ing-in (lī'ĭng-ĭn') *n.* The confinement of a woman in childbirth.

Lyl·y (lĭl'ē), **John.** 1554?–1606. English novelist and dramatist.

lymph (lĭmf) *n.* **1.** *Physiology.* A clear, transparent, watery, sometimes faintly yellowish liquid that contains white blood cells and some red blood cells, travels through the lymphatic system to return to the venous blood stream through the thoracic duct, and acts to remove bacteria and certain proteins from the tissues, to transport fat from the intestines, and to supply lymphocytes to the blood. **2.** *Archaic.* A spring or stream of pure, clear water. [Latin *lympha,* earlier *lumpa, limpa,* water, possibly from earlier *dumpa* (unattested), akin to Oscan *Diumpais,* "for the Nymphs."]

lym·phad·e·ni·tis (lĭm-făd'n-ī'tĭs, lĭm'fə-də-nī'-) *n.* Inflammation of the lymph nodes. [New Latin : *lympha,* LYMPH + Greek *adēn,* gland (see **engw-** in Appendix*) + -ITIS.]

lym·phat·ic (lĭm-făt'ĭk) *adj.* **1.** Of or relating to lymph, a lymph vessel, or a lymph node. **2.** Sluggish; indifferent; phlegmatic. —*n.* A vessel that conveys lymph. [New Latin *lymphaticus,* from *lympha,* LYMPH.]

lymphatic system. The interconnected system of spaces and vessels between tissues and organs by which lymph is circulated throughout the body.

lym·pha·tism (lĭm'fə-tĭz'əm) *n.* A pathological condition of infancy and childhood characterized by hyperplasia of the lymphatic structures, spleen, and bone marrow.

lym·pha·ti·tis (lĭm'fə-tī'tĭs) *n.* Inflammation of lymph nodes or vessels. [LYMPHAT(IC) + -ITIS.]

lymph follicle. Any of the round masses of lymphocytes in the cortex of a lymph node. Also called "lymph nodule."

lymph node. Any of numerous oval or round bodies, located along the lymphatic vessels, that supply lymphocytes to the circulatory system and remove bacteria and foreign particles from the lymph. Also called "lymph gland."

lympho–, lymph–. Indicates lymph or lymphatic system; for example, **lymphocyte, lymphoma.** [From LYMPH.]

lym·pho·blast (lĭm'fə-blăst') *n.* An immature lymphocyte. [LYMPHO- + -BLAST.]

lym·pho·cyte (lĭm'fə-sīt') *n.* A white blood cell formed in lymphoid tissue, as in the lymph nodes, spleen, thymus, and tonsils, and constituting between 22 to 28 per cent of all leukocytes in the normal adult human's blood. Also called "lymph cell." [LYMPHO- + -CYTE.]

lym·pho·cy·to·sis (lĭm'fō-sī'tō'sĭs) *n. Pathology.* A form of leukocytosis in which lymphocytes are greatly increased in number. —**lym'pho·cy·tot'ic** (-tŏt'ĭk) *adj.*

lym·phoid (lĭm'foid') *adj.* Of or pertaining to lymph, lymphatic tissue, or the lymphatic system. [LYMPH(O)- + -OID.]

lym·pho·ma (lĭm-fō'mə) *n., pl.* **-mata** (-mə-tə) or **-mas.** Any of various abnormally proliferative diseases of lymphoid tissue. —**lym·pho'ma·toid', lym·phom'a·tous** (-fŏm'ə-təs) *adj.*

lym·pho·poi·e·sis (lĭm'fō-poi·ē'sĭs) *n., pl.* **-ses** (-sēz'). The formation of lymphocytes. [New Latin : LYMPHO- + -POIESIS.] —**lym'pho·poi·et'ic** *adj.*

lyn·ce·an (lĭn-sē'ən) *adj.* Sharp-sighted. [From Latin *lyncēus,* from Greek *Lunkeios,* pertaining to Lynceus (an Argonaut noted for his keenness of sight), from *Lunkeos,* Lynceus.]

lynch (lĭnch) *tr.v.* **lynched, lynching, lynches.** To execute without due process of law; especially, to hang. [After Charles *Lynch* (1736–1796), Virginia planter and justice of the peace.]

Lynch·burg (lĭnch'bûrg). A city of Virginia, on the James River in the south-central part of the state. Population, 55,000.

lynch law. The punishment of persons suspected of crime without due process of law. Also called "swamp law."

Ly·nen (lē'nən), **Feodor.** Born 1911. German biochemist.

Lynn (lĭn). A city of Massachusetts. Population, 94,000.

lynx (lĭngks) *n.* Any of several wild cats of the genus *Lynx;* especially, *L. canadensis,* of northern North America, or *L. lynx,* of Eurasia, having thick, soft fur, a short tail and tufted ears. [Latin, from Greek *lunx.* See **leuk-** in Appendix.*]

Lynx (lĭngks) *n.* A constellation in the Northern Hemisphere near Ursa Major and Auriga.

lynx-eyed (lĭngks'īd') *adj.* Keen of vision.

lyo–. Indicates dispersion or dissolution; for example, **lyophilic.** [From Greek *luein,* to loosen, to dissolve. See **leu-¹** in Appendix.*]

Martin Luther
Portrait by Lucas Cranach

Luxembourg

lynx
Lynx canadensis

ă pat/ā pay/âr care/ä father/b bib/ch church/d deed/ĕ pet/ē be/f fife/g gag/h hat/hw which/ĭ pit/ī pie/îr pier/j judge/k kick/l lid, needle/m mum/n no, sudden/ng thing/ŏ pot/ō toe/ô paw, for/oi noise/ou out/oo took/oo boot/p pop/r roar/s sauce/sh ship, dish/t tight/th thin, path/th this, bathe/ŭ cut/ûr urge/v valve/w with/y yes/z zebra, size/zh vision/ə about, item, edible, gallop, circus/ à *Fr.* ami/œ *Fr.* feu, *Ger.* schön/ü *Fr.* tu, *Ger.* über/KH *Ger.* ich, *Scot.* loch/N *Fr.* bon. *Follows main vocabulary. †Of obscure origin.

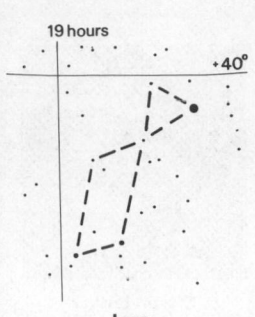

19 hours

+40°

Lyra

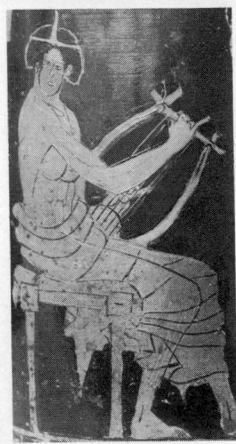

lyre
Detail from ancient
Greek vase painting

Ly·on (lē′ôN′; *French* lyôN). A city and industrial center of east-central France, at the confluence of the Saône and Rhône rivers. Population, 529,000.

Ly·on·nais (lē-ô-nā′; *French* lyô′ně′). A region and former province of France.

ly·on·naise (lī′ə-nāz′; *French* lyô′něz′) *adj.* Cooked with onions: *lyonnaise potatoes.* [From French *à la Lyonnaise,* in the manner of LYON.]

ly·o·phil·ic (lī′ə-fĭl′ĭk) *adj. Chemistry.* Of, relating to, or exhibiting a strong affinity between the dispersed phase and the dispersing medium of a colloid. [LYO- + -PHILIC.]

ly·o·pho·bic (lī′ə-fō′bĭk) *adj. Chemistry.* Of, relating to, or exhibiting a lack of strong affinity between the dispersed phase and the dispersing medium of a colloid. [LYO- + PHOBIC.]

lyr. lyric.

Ly·ra (lī′rə) *n.* A constellation in the Northern Hemisphere near Cygnus and Hercules, and containing the star Vega. [Latin *lyra,* LYRE.]

ly·rate (lī′rāt′, -rĭt) *adj.* Having a form or curvature suggestive of a lyre. [New Latin *lyratus,* from Latin *lyra,* LYRE.]

lyre (līr) *n.* A stringed instrument of the harp family used to accompany a singer or reader of poetry, especially in ancient Greece. [Middle English *lire,* Old French, from Latin *lyra,* from Greek *lura†.*]

lyre·bird (līr′bûrd′) *n.* Either of two Australian birds, *Menura superba* (or *M. novaehollandae*) or *M. alberti,* of which the male has a long tail spread during courtship in a lyre-shaped display.

lyr·ic (lĭr′ĭk) *adj. Abbr.* **lyr.** **1. a.** Of or relating to a category of poetic literature that is distinguished from the narrative and dramatic, is most representational of music in its sound patterns, and is generally characterized by subjectivity and sensuality of expression. **b.** Relating to or constituting a poem in this category, as a sonnet, ode, hymn, or elegy. **c.** Being a poet of lyric verse. **2.** Highly enthusiastic or emotional; exuberant. **3. a.** Of or pertaining to the lyre or harp. **b.** Appropriate for accompaniment by the lyre. **4.** Having a singing voice of light volume and modest range. —*n.* **1.** A lyric poem or poet. **2.** *Plural.* The words of a song. [Old French *lyrique,* of a lyre, from Latin *lyricus,* from Greek *lurikos,* from *lura,* LYRE.]

lyr·i·cism (lĭr′ə-sĭz′əm) *n.* **1.** The character or quality of subjectivism and sensuality of expression, especially in the arts. **2.** An intense outpouring of exuberant emotion.

lyr·i·cist (lĭr′ə-sĭst) *n.* A writer of lyrics for a musical.

lyr·ism (lĭr′ĭz′əm) *n.* Lyricism. [French *lyrisme,* from Greek *lurismos,* played on the lyre, from *lura,* LYRE.]

lyr·ist (lĭr′ĭst *for sense 1;* lī′rĭst *for sense 2*) *n.* **1.** A lyricist. **2.** One who plays a lyre. [Latin *lyristēs,* one who plays a lyre, from Greek *luristēs,* from *lura,* LYRE.]

lyse (līs) *v.* **lysed, lysing, lyses.** —*tr.* To cause (something) to undergo lysis. —*intr.* To undergo lysis. [From LYSIS.]

Ly·sen·ko (lĭ-sěng′kō), **Trofim Denisovich.** Born 1898. Soviet biologist.

Ly·sen·ko·ism (lĭ-sěng′kō-ĭz′əm) *n.* The biological doctrine of Trofim Lysenko that maintains the possibility of inheriting environmentally acquired characteristics.

ly·ser·gic acid (lĭ-sûr′jĭk, lī-). A crystalline alkaloid, $C_{16}H_{16}N_2O_2$, derived from ergot and used in medical research. [From LYS(O)- + ERG(OT) + -IC.]

lysergic acid di·eth·yl·am·ide (dī′ěth-əl-ăm′īd′). A hallucinogenic drug, $C_{20}H_{25}N_3O$, derived from lysergic acid. Also called "LSD."

ly·sin (lī′sĭn) *n.* A specific antibody that acts to destroy blood cells, tissues, or microorganisms. [LYS(O)- + -IN.]

ly·sine (lī′sēn′, -sĭn) *n.* An essential, crystalline amino acid, $C_6H_{14}N_2O_2$, used in nutrition studies, in culture media, and to fortify foods and feeds. [LYS(O)- + -INE.]

ly·sis (lī′sĭs) *n.* **1.** *Biochemistry.* The dissolution or destruction of red blood cells, bacteria, or other antigens by a specific lysin. **2.** *Medicine.* The gradual subsiding of the symptoms of an acute disease. [New Latin, from Greek *lusis,* a loosing, deliverance, from *luein,* to loosen, unbind. See **leu-¹** in Appendix.*]

–lysis. Indicates dissolving or decomposition; for example, **hydrolysis.** [New Latin, from Greek *lusis.* See **lysis.**]

lyso–, lys–. Indicates an instance or act of loosening, dissolving, or freeing; for example, **lysin, lysogenesis.** [From Greek *lusis,* a loosening. See **lysis.**]

ly·so·gen·e·sis (lī′sō-jěn′ə-sĭs) *n.* The production of lysins. [New Latin : LYSO- + -GENESIS.]

Ly·sol (lī′sôl′, -sōl′, -sŏl′) *n.* A trademark for a liquid antiseptic and disinfectant. [LYS(O)- + -OL (phenol).]

ly·so·zyme (lī′sə-zīm′) *n.* An enzyme occurring naturally in tears, capable of destroying the cell walls of certain bacteria, thereby acting as a mild antiseptic. [LYSO- + -ZYME.]

–lyte. Indicates a substance that can be decomposed by a specific process; for example, **electrolyte.** [From Greek *lutos,* soluble, from *luein,* to loosen. See **leu-¹** in Appendix.*]

lyt·ic (lĭt′ĭk) *adj.* **1.** Of, pertaining to, or causing lysis. **2.** Of or relating to a lysin. [Greek *lutikos,* able to loose, laxative, from *lutos,* capable of being untied, from *luein,* to untie, loosen. See **lysis.**]

–lytic. Indicates a loosening or dissolving; for example, **hydrolytic.** [From Greek *lutikos,* able to loose. See **lytic.**]

lyt·ta (lĭt′ə) *n., pl.* **lyttae** (lĭt′ē′). A thin cartilaginous strip on the underside of the tongue of certain carnivorous mammals, such as dogs. [Latin, "worm under a dog's tongue" (believed to cause madness), from Greek *lutta, lussa,* madness, frenzy. See **leuk-** in Appendix.*]

Lyu·blin. The Russian name for **Lublin.**

–lyze. Indicates the causing of chemical decomposition; for example, **pyrolyze.** [From -LYSIS.]

ă pat/ā pay/âr care/ä father/b bib/ch church/d deed/ě pet/ē be/f fife/g gag/h hat/hw which/ĭ pit/ī pie/îr pier/j judge/k kick/l lid, needle/m mum/n no, sudden/ng thing/ŏ pot/ō toe/ô paw, for/oi noise/ou out/oŏ took/ōō boot/p pop/r roar/s sauce/sh ship, dish/

lyrebird
Menura superba

Mm

Around 1000 B.C. the Phoenicians and other Semites of Syria and Palestine began to use a graphic sign representing the consonant m, first in form (1), later in form (2). They named the sign mēm, meaning "water." After 900 B.C. the Greeks borrowed the sign from the Phoenicians in the modified form (3), altering its name to mu. They later reversed its orientation (4), and gradually eliminated its "tail," giving it a symmetrical form (5). The Greek forms passed unchanged via Etruscan to the Romans (6,7); they developed the Monumental Capital (8) that is the basis of our modern capital, printed (11) and written (12). The written Roman forms (6,7) developed into the late Roman and medieval Uncial (9) and Cursive (10), which are the bases of our modern small letter, printed (13) and written (14).

m, M (ĕm) *n., pl.* **m's** or *rare* **ms, M's** or **Ms. 1.** The 13th letter of the modern English alphabet. See **alphabet. 2.** Any of the speech sounds represented by the letter **M**.

m, M, m., M. *Note:* As an abbreviation or symbol, *m* may be a small or a capital letter, with or without a period. Established forms or those generally preferred precede the definition. When no form is given, all four forms are in general use in that sense. **1. m, M** *Printing.* **a.** em. **b.** pica em. **2. M** *Physics.* Mach number. **3. M.** majesty (in titles). **4.** male. **5. M.** mark (currency). **6. m, M** *Physics.* mass. **7. M.** master (in titles). **8. M.** medieval. **9.** medium. **10. M** mega-. **11. M.** member (in titles). **12. m., M.** meridian. **13. M** *Chemistry.* metal. **14. m** meter (measure). **15. M** *Logic.* middle term of a syllogism. **16. m.** mile. **17. M** mill (currency). **18. m** milli-. **19. M.** minim (liquid measure). **20. m, M** *Physics.* modulus. **21. M** *Chemistry.* molar. **22. M** *Physics.* moment. **23. M.** Monday. **24. M.** *French.* Monsieur. **25.** month. **26. M** *Physics.* mutual inductance. **27. m., M.** noon (Latin *meridies*). **28. M** Roman numeral for 1,000 (Latin *mille*). **29.** The 13th in a series; 12th when *J* is omitted.

ma (mä, mô) *n. Informal.* Mother. [Shortened form of MAMA.]

mA milliampere.

MA 1. Maritime Administration. **2.** Massachusetts (with Zip Code). **3.** mental age.

M.A. 1. Master of Arts (Latin *Magister Artium*). **2.** mental age.

MAA Airport code for Madras, India.

Ma'am (măm). A contraction of **Madam** (*see*).

maar (mär) *n* A flat-bottomed, roughly circular volcanic crater of explosive origin, often filled with water. [Dialectal North German *maar*, from Middle Low German *mare*, lake. See **mori-** in Appendix.*]

Maas. The Dutch name for the **Meuse** River.

Maas·tricht (màs-trĭкнт'). Also **Maes·tricht**. A city of the Netherlands between the Meuse River and the Belgian border. Population, 94,000.

Ma·bel (mā'bəl). A feminine given name. [Middle English, shortened from *Amabel*, from Latin *amābilis*, lovely, amiable, from *amāre*, to love. See **amma** in Appendix.*]

Mab·i·no·gi·on (măb'ĭ-nō'gē-ən) *n.* A collection of medieval Welsh folk tales translated by Lady Charlotte Guest in 1838–49. [Welsh, plural of *mabinogi*, bardic instruction, "tales of youth," from *mab*, youth, son, from Old Welsh *map*, from Common Celtic *makkwos* (unattested). Compare **Mac-**.]

mac (măk) *n. Chiefly British Informal.* A mackintosh.

Mac-, M'-, Mc-. Indicates son of. Used in surnames. [Irish and Gaelic *Mac-*, from Common Celtic *makkos* (unattested), son. Compare **Mabinogion**.]

Mac. Maccabees (books of the Apocrypha).

ma·ca·bre (mə-kä'brə, -bər) *adj.* **1.** Suggesting the horror of death and decay; gruesome; ghastly. **2.** Associated with or sug-

gestive of the danse macabre, in which an allegorical figure of death summons those about him to dance with him to their deaths. —See Synonyms at **ghastly.** [French, ghastly, from Old French *Danse Macabre*, the Dance of Death, probably originally *Danse Macabé*, "the Maccabean Dance," translation of Medieval Latin *Chorea Maccabaeorum*, dance of the Maccabees; a traditional feature of morality plays, probably representing the slaughter of the Maccabees.] —**ma·ca'bre·ly** *adv.*

mac·ad·am (mə-kăd'əm) *n.* A pavement of layers of compacted small stones, now usually bound with tar or asphalt. [Developed by John L. *McAdam* (1756–1836), Scottish engineer.]

mac·a·da·mi·a (măk'ə-dā'mē-ə) *n.* Any tree of the genus *Macadamia*, native to Australia; especially, *M. ternifolia*, having clusters of small white flowers and edible, nutlike seeds called *macadamia nuts*. [After John *Macadam* (died 1865), Australian chemist.]

mac·ad·am·ize (mə-kăd'ə-mīz') *tr.v.* **-ized, -izing, -izes.** To construct or pave (a road) with **macadam** (*see*). —**mac·ad'am·i·za'tion** *n.* —**mac·ad'am·iz'er** *n.*

Ma·cao (mə-kou'). Portuguese **Ma·cau** (mä-kou'). **1.** *Chinese* **Ao·men** (ou'mən). An island of the South China Sea near the mouth of the Chu Kiang, and 40 miles west of Hong Kong. **2.** A Portuguese colony consisting of this island and two small offshore islands. Population, 188,000. **3.** The principal town of this colony.

Ma·ca·pá (mä-kä-pä'). The capital of Amapá, Brazil, in the southeastern part of the territory. Population, 20,000.

ma·caque (mə-kăk', -käk') *n.* Any of several short-tailed monkeys of the genus *Macacu*, of southeastern Asia, Japan, Gibraltar, and northern Africa. See **Barbary ape, rhesus monkey.** [French, from Portuguese *macaco*, a Congolese monkey, possibly from Fiot *makaku*, "some monkeys" : *ma*, numerical sign + *kaku*, monkey.]

mac·a·ro·ni (măk'ə-rō'nē) *n., pl.* **macaroni** (for sense 1), **-nis** or **-nies** (for sense 2). Also **mac·ca·ro·ni. 1.** A paste of wheat flour pressed into hollow tubes or other shapes, dried, and prepared for eating by boiling. **2.** *Obsolete.* A fashionable fop. [Obsolete Italian *maccaroni*, plural of *maccarone†*, macaroni, macaroon.]

mac·a·ron·ic (măk'ə-rŏn'ĭk) *adj.* Also **mac·a·ron·i·cal** (-ĭ-kəl). **1.** Of or pertaining to a literary composition containing a mixture of vernacular words with Latin words or with non-Latin words that are humorously given Latin terminations: *macaronic verse.* **2.** Of or involving a mixture of two or more languages. **3.** *Archaic.* Having the qualities or characteristics of a medley; mixed; jumbled. —*n. Usually plural.* A macaronic composition. [New Latin *macaronicus*, "like macaroni" (i.e., a crude rustic mixture), from Italian *maccaroni*, MACARONI.]

mac·a·roon (măk'ə-rōōn', măk'ə-rōōn') *n.* A chewy cooky made with sugar, egg whites, and almond paste or coconut. [French *macaron*, from Italian *maccarone*, MACARONI.]

Mac·Ar·thur (mək-är'thər), **Douglas.** 1880–1964. American General of the Army; supreme commander Allied forces in Southwest Pacific (World War II), occupational forces in Japan (1945–51), and United Nations forces in Korea (1950–51).

Ma·cas·sar. See **Makassar.**

Macassar oil. Hair pomade, first made of oils from Makassar.

Ma·cau. The Portuguese name for **Macao.**

Ma·cau·lay (mə-kô'lē), **Thomas Babington.** First Baron Macaulay. 1800–1859. English historian and statesman.

ma·caw (mə-kô') *n.* Any of various tropical American parrots of the genera *Ara* and *Anodorhynchus*, including the largest parrots, characterized by long saber-shaped tails, curved powerful

macaw
Anodorhynchus hyacinthinus

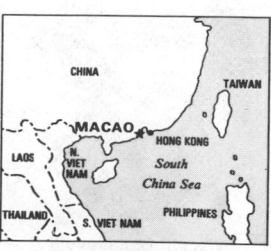

Macao

bills, and usually brilliant plumage. [Portuguese *macaú*, perhaps from *macaúba*, a kind of palm (on whose fruit the parrot feeds), from Tupi *macahuba, macahiba* : probably *maca-*, thorn (of African origin) + *-yba*, tree.]

Macc. Maccabees (books of the Apocrypha).

Mac·ca·be·an (măk'ə-bē'ən) *adj.* Of or pertaining to Judas Maccabeus or to the Maccabees.

Mac·ca·bees (măk'ə-bēz'). **1.** Original name, Hasmoneans. A Jewish dynasty of patriots, high priests, and kings of the second and first centuries B.C. See Judas **Maccabeus**. **2.** *Abbr.* **Mac., Macc.** Four books in the Old Testament Apocrypha, the first two of which tell about the feats of this family. In the Protestant churches, all four books are apocryphal; in the Roman Catholic and Eastern Orthodox churches, the first two are canonical. Also called in the Douay Bible "Machabees."

Mac·ca·be·us (măk'ə-bē'əs), **Judas.** Died 160 B.C. Jewish patriot, most famous of the **Maccabees** *(see)*; his rededication of the Temple at Jerusalem (164 B.C.) is commemorated by the Feast of Chanukah.

mac·ca·boy (măk'ə-boi') *n.* Also **mac·ca·baw** (măk'ə-bô'). A perfumed snuff made in Martinique. [From French *macouba;* made at *Macouba*, district of Martinique.]

mac·ca·ro·ni. Variant of **macaroni.**

Mac·cles·field (măk'əlz-fēld') *n.* A type of silk having a variety of small, allover patterns, used for men's neckties. [Originally produced in *Macclesfield*, England.]

Mac·don·ald (mək-dŏn'əld), **Dwight.** Born 1906. American author and editor.

Mac·Don·ald (mək-dŏn'əld), **Flora.** 1722–1790. Scottish Jacobite heroine; rescuer of Prince Charles Edward.

Mac·Don·ald (mək-dŏn'əld), **(James) Ramsay.** 1866–1937. Prime minister of Great Britain (1924; 1929–35).

Mac·don·ald (mək-dŏn'əld), Sir **John Alexander.** 1815–1891. First prime minister of Canada (1867–73); again prime minister (1878–91).

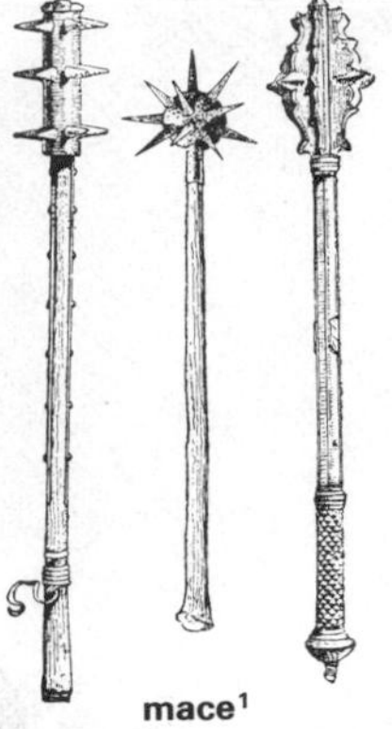

mace[1]

mace[1] (mās) *n.* **1.** A heavy medieval war club with a spiked or flanged metal head, used to crush armor. **2.** A ceremonial staff borne or displayed as the symbol of authority of a legislative body. **3.** A **macebearer** *(see)*. [Middle English, from Old French *mace, masse*, from Vulgar Latin *mattea* (unattested), club, from Latin *mateola*, rod, club. See **mat-** in Appendix.*]

mace[2] (mās) *n.* An aromatic spice made from the dried, waxy, scarlet or yellowish covering that partly encloses the kernel of the nutmeg. [Middle English, formed as singular of *macis*, mace (wrongly taken to be plural), from Medieval Latin *macis*, misreading of *macir*, from Greek *makir*, an Indian spice (of oriental origin).]

Mace (mās) *n.* **Chemical Mace** *(see)*.

mace·bear·er (mās'bâr'ər) *n.* An official who carries a mace of office. Also called "mace," "macer."

Maced. Macedonia; Macedonian.

mac·é·doine (măs'ə-dwän', măs'ə-dwän') *n.* **1.** A mixture of finely cut vegetables or fruits, sometimes jellied, served as a salad, dessert, or appetizer. **2.** Any mixture; a medley; hodgepodge. [French *macédoine*, "Macedonian" (the population of Macedonia is a mixture of various peoples).]

Mac·e·do·ni·a (măs'ə-dō'nē-ə). *Abbr.* **Maced. 1.** Also **Mac·e·don** (măs'ə-dŏn'). An ancient kingdom, north of Greece, that reached the height of its power under the rule of Alexander the Great (336–323 B.C.). **2.** A Balkan region consisting of parts of Greece, Bulgaria, and Yugoslavia. **3.** A constituent People's Republic of Yugoslavia, occupying 10,229 square miles in the southern part of the country. Population, 1,406,000. Capital, Skoplje. **4.** A geographic region comprising most of northern Greece. [Greek *Makedonia*, from *Makedōn*, a Macedonian, "highlander." See **māk-** in Appendix.*]

Mac·e·do·ni·an (măs'ə-dō'nē-ən) *adj. Abbr.* **Maced.** Of or pertaining to ancient or modern Macedonia, or the people or languages of these regions. —*n. Abbr.* **Maced. 1.** A native or inhabitant of ancient or modern Macedonia. **2.** The language of ancient Macedonia, having characteristics regarded as Indo-European. **3.** The Slavic language of modern Macedonia.

Ma·cei·ó (mà'sā-ô'). The capital city of Alagoas State in eastern Brazil. Population, 154,000.

mac·er (mā'sər) *n.* A **macebearer** *(see)*.

mac·er·ate (măs'ə-rāt') *v.* **-ated, -ating, -ates.** —*tr.* **1.** To soften (a solid substance) by soaking or steeping in a liquid, often with heat. **2.** To separate (a solid substance) into constituents by soaking. **3.** To cause to become lean; emaciate, usually by starvation. —*intr.* To become macerated; undergo macerating. —*n.* (măs'ər-ĭt). A substance prepared or produced by macerating. [Latin *mācerāre*, to soften. See **mag-** in Appendix.*] —**mac'er·a'tion** *n.* —**mac'er·a·tor, mac'er·a·ter** *n.*

Mach (mäKH), **Ernst.** 1836–1916. Austrian physicist and philosopher.

Mach (mäk) *n.* Also **mach.** Short for **Mach number** *(see)*.

mach. machine; machinery; machinist.

Mach·a·bees. In the Douay Bible, **Maccabees** *(see)*.

ma·chet·e (mə-shĕt'ē, -chĕt'ē) *n.* A large, heavy knife with a broad blade, used for cutting vegetation and as a weapon. [American Spanish, from Spanish, diminutive of *macho*, ax, club, probably from a Mozarabic variant of *maza*, mace, from Vulgar Latin *mattea* (unattested), club, from Latin *mateola*, rod, club. See **mat-** in Appendix.*]

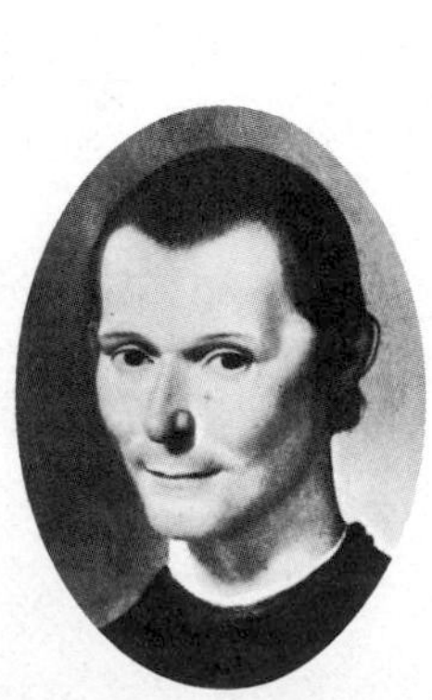

Niccolò Machiavelli
Detail of a portrait
by Santi di Tito

Mach·i·a·vel·li (măk'ē-ə-vĕl'ē; *Italian* mä'kyä-vĕl'lē), **Niccolò.** 1469–1527. Italian statesman and political theorist; author of *The Prince* (1513).

Mach·i·a·vel·li·an (măk'ē-ə-vĕl'ē-ən) *adj.* **1.** Of or pertaining to Niccolò Machiavelli. **2.** Of or pertaining to Machiavellianism. **3.** Suggestive of or characterized by the principles of expediency attributed to Machiavelli; wily; deceitful; unscrupulous. —*n.* Also **Mach·i·a·vel·list** (-ĭst). One who believes in Machiavellianism.

Mach·i·a·vel·li·an·ism (măk'ē-ə-vĕl'ē-ən-ĭz'əm) *n.* Also **Mach·i·a·vel·lism** (-ĭz'əm). The political doctrine of Machiavelli, which denies the relevance of morality in political affairs and holds that craft and deceit are justified in pursuing and maintaining political power; political opportunism.

ma·chic·o·la·tion (mə-chĭk'ə-lā'shən) *n.* **1. a.** A projecting gallery at the top of a castle wall, supported by a row of corbeled arches, having openings in the floor through which stones and boiling liquids could be dropped on attackers. **b.** One of these openings. **c.** One of these corbeled arches. **2.** *Usually plural.* A row of small corbeled arches used as an ornamental architectural feature. [Medieval Latin *machicolātiō*, from Old French *machicoulis*, machicolation, "crushing flow" : *macher*, to crush, from Latin *masticāre*, to chew, from Greek *mastikhan*, to grind the teeth, from *mastax*, mouth (see **menth-** in Appendix*) + *coulis*, flow, from *couler*, to flow, from Latin *cōlāre*, to filter (see **kagh-** in Appendix*).]

mach·i·nate (măk'ĭ-nāt', măsh'ĭ-) *v.* **-nated, -nating, -nates.** —*tr.* To devise (a plot). —*intr.* To plot. [Latin *māchinārī*, from *māchina*, contrivance, MACHINE.] —**mach'i·na'tor** *n.*

mach·i·na·tion (măk'ĭ-nā'shən, măsh'ĭ-) *n.* **1.** The act of plotting. **2.** A plot; a hostile intrigue: *"Be frustrate all ye stratagems of hell,/And devilish machinations come to nought."* (Milton). —See Synonyms at **conspiracy.**

ma·chine (mə-shēn') *n. Abbr.* **mach. 1. a.** Any system, usually of rigid bodies, formed and connected to alter, transmit, and direct applied forces in a predetermined manner to accomplish a specific objective, such as the performance of useful work. **b.** A simple device, such as a lever, pulley, or inclined plane, that alters the magnitude or direction or both, of an applied force. In this sense, also called "simple machine." **2.** Any such system or device together with its power source and auxiliary equipment, for example, an automobile, aircraft, or jackhammer. **3.** Any system or device, such as an electronic computer, that performs or assists in the performance of a human task. **4. a.** An intricate natural system or organism, such as the human body. **b.** A functional unit of such a system, for example, an organ, such as the heart or kidney. **5.** A person who acts in a rigid, mechanical, or unconscious manner. **6.** An organized group of persons whose members appear to be under the control of one or more leaders. Applied disparagingly to political organizations in U.S. cities and states. **7. Deus ex machina** *(see)*. —*v.* **machined, -chining, -chines.** —*tr.* To cut, shape, or finish by machine. —*intr.* To be cut, shaped, or finished by machine: *This metal machines easily.* [French, from Old French, from Latin *māchina*, engine, contrivance, from Doric Greek *mākhanā*, from *mākhos*, contrivance, means. See **magh-[1]** in Appendix.*] —**ma·chin'a·ble** *adj.*

machine finish. A finish on metal surfaces, **mill finish** *(see)*.

machine gun. A gun, usually mounted, that fires rapidly and repeatedly when the trigger is pressed. Compare **submachine gun.** —**machine gunner.**

ma·chine-gun (mə-shēn'gŭn') *tr.v.* **-gunned, -gunning, -guns.** To fire at or kill with a machine gun. —*adj.* Fast and staccato.

machine language. Any of various systems of symbols used to code input information so that a computer can perform the desired operations with it.

ma·chin·er·y (mə-shē'nər-ē, -shēn'rē) *n., pl.* **-ies.** *Abbr.* **mach. 1.** Collectively, machines or machine parts. **2.** The working parts of a particular machine. **3.** Any system of related elements that operates in a definable manner: *"Many languages are burdened with unnecessary machinery, such as grammatical gender."* (E.H. Sturtevant). **4.** A generally unsubtle device in literature for bringing about a calculated effect such as a happy ending. See **deus ex machina.**

machine shop. A workshop where power-driven tools are used for making, finishing, or repairing machines or machine parts.

machine tool. A power-driven tool for machining.

ma·chin·ist (mə-shē'nĭst) *n. Abbr.* **mach. 1.** One skilled in operating machine tools. **2.** One who makes, operates, or repairs machines. **3.** *U.S. Navy & Coast Guard.* **a.** A warrant officer who assists the engineer officer in the engine room. **b.** A machinist's mate, a petty officer in this specialty. **4.** *Archaic.* A person in charge of stage machinery.

Mach·me·ter (mäk'mē'tər) *n.* Also **mach·me·ter.** An aircraft instrument that indicates speed in Mach numbers.

Mach number. Also **mach number.** *Abbr.* **M** The ratio of the speed of an object to the speed of sound in the surrounding medium. For example, an aircraft moving twice as fast as sound is said to be traveling at Mach 2. [After Ernst MACH.]

ma·chree (mə-krē') *n. Anglo-Irish.* My dear. A term of endearment. [Irish *mo chroidhe*, "my heart" : *mo*, my, from Old Irish (see **me-[1]** in Appendix*) + *chroidhe*, heart, from Old Irish *cride* (see **kerd-[1]** in Appendix*).]

Ma·chu Pic·chu (mä'cho͞o pēk'cho͞o). An ancient fortress city in the Peruvian Andes, about 50 miles northwest of Cuzco.

mac·in·tosh. Variant of **mackintosh.**

Mack (măk), **Connie.** Original name, Cornelius McGillicuddy. 1862–1956. American baseball player, manager, and executive.

Mac·ken·zie (mə-kĕn'zē). **1.** A district of the Northwest Territories, Canada. **2.** A Canadian mountain range of the northern Rocky Mountains, extending some 500 miles along the border of the Yukon Territory and the Northwest Territories. **3.** The second-longest river in North America, rising in the Northwest Territories, and flowing more than 2,500 miles to the

ă pat/ā pay/âr care/ä father/b bib/ch church/d deed/ĕ pet/ē be/f fife/g gag/h hat/hw which/ĭ pit/ī pie/îr pier/j judge/k kick/l lid, needle/m mum/n no, sudden/ng thing/ŏ pot/ō toe/ô paw, for/oi noise/ou out/o͝o took/o͞o boot/p pop/r roar/s sauce/sh ship, dish/

Mackenzie Bay on the Beaufort Sea, a part of the Arctic Ocean.
Mac·ken·zie (mə-kĕn′zē), Sir **Alexander.** 1764–1820. Scottish explorer of the Canadian northwest.
mack·er·el (măk′ər-əl, măk′rəl) *n., pl.* **mackerel** or **-els. 1.** Any of several marine fishes of the family Scombridae, found worldwide. Some species are important food fishes, especially the Atlantic mackerel, *Scomber scombrus,* which has dark, wavy bars on the back and a silvery belly. **2.** Any of the smaller fishes of the suborder Scombroidea, such as the **Spanish mackerel** *(see).* **3.** Any of various fishes resembling mackerel. [Middle English *makerel,* from Old French *maquerel*†.]
mackerel gull. A sea bird, the **tern** *(see).*
mackerel sky. A formation of cirrocumulus or altocumulus clouds suggesting the bars on a mackerel's back.
Mack·i·nac (măk′ĭ-nô′). An island in Michigan on the Lake Huron side of the Straits of Mackinac. Population, 11,000. [Canadian French, short for *Michilimackinac,* from early Ojibwa *Mĭšĭlimaahkinaank,* "at the territory of the Mishinimaki" (an extinct division of the Ojibwa formerly living there).]
Mack·i·nac, Straits of (măk′ĭ-nô′). A channel between Michigan's Upper and Lower peninsulas.
mack·i·naw (măk′ə-nô′) *n.* **1.** A short, double-breasted coat of heavy woolen material, usually plaid. **2.** The cloth from which such a coat is made, usually of wool, often with a heavy nap. [From MACKINAC (the cloth and the coat were trading items through the entrepôt on the island in the 19th century).]
Mackinaw blanket. A thick blanket formerly used in northern and western North America by Indians, traders, and trappers.
Mackinaw boat. A flat-bottomed boat formerly common in the upper Great Lakes area.
Mack·i·naw City (măk′ə-nô′). A resort city of Michigan, on the Straits of Mackinac, opposite St. Ignace. Population, 900.
Mackinaw trout. The **lake trout** *(see).*
mack·in·tosh (măk′ĭn-tŏsh′) *n.* Also **mac·in·tosh.** *Chiefly British.* **1.** *Obsolete.* **a.** A raincoat of patented rubberized cloth. **b.** This cloth. **2.** Any raincoat. Also informally called "mac." [Invented by Charles *Macintosh* (1766–1843), Scottish chemist.]
mack·le (măk′əl) *n.* Also **mac·ule** (măk′yōōl). *Printing.* A spot, especially a blurred or double impression caused by a slipping of the type or wrinkle in the paper. *—v.* **mackled, -ling, -les.** Also **mac·ule, -uled, -uling, -ules.** *—tr.* To blur or double (a printed impression). *—intr.* To become blurred. [French *macule,* from Latin *macula,* spot. See **macula** in Appendix.*]
mac·le (măk′əl) *n.* **1.** A mineral, **chiastolite** *(see).* **2.** A crystalline form, **twin** *(see).* **3.** A spot or discoloration in a mineral. [French, double crystal, from Old French *macle,* heraldic term for a "voided lozenge" (one diamond shape within another), originally a stylized mesh of a net, from Latin *macula,* mesh, hole in a net, spot. See **macula** in Appendix.*]
Mac·Leish (mək-lēsh′), **Archibald.** Born 1892. American poet, dramatist, and Librarian of Congress.
Mac·leod (mə-kloud′), **John James Rickard.** 1876–1935. Scottish physiologist; participated in development of insulin.
Mac·Mil·lan (mək-mĭl′ən), **Donald Baxter.** Born 1874. American Arctic explorer; first to use aircraft in exploration.
Mac·mil·lan (mək-mĭl′ən), **(Maurice) Harold.** Born 1894. Prime minister of the United Kingdom (1957–63).
Ma·con (mā′kən). A city and industrial center of Georgia, 78 miles southeast of Atlanta. Population, 69,000.
Mâ·con (mä-kôN′) *n.* A red or white Burgundy wine made in France. [Produced near *Mâcon,* city in east-central France.]
Mac·pher·son (mək-fûr′sən), **James.** 1736–1796. Scottish poet and historian; self-proclaimed translator of **Ossian** *(see).*
Mac·quar·ie (mə-kwŏr′ē). **1.** A river in New South Wales, Australia, flowing 590 miles from the Blue Mountains to the Darling River. **2.** A group of small islands in the South Pacific, some 800 miles southeast of Tasmania, Australia.
mac·ra·mé (măk′rə-mā′) *n.* Coarse lacework made by weaving and knotting cords into a pattern, used as a fringe or trimming for furniture. [French, from Italian *macramè,* from Turkish *makrama,* napkin, towel, from Arabic *miqramah,* striped cloth.]
mac·ren·ceph·a·ly (măk′rĕn-sĕf′ə-lē) *n.* Also **mac·ren·ce·pha·li·a** (-sə-fā′lē-ə). *Pathology.* Abnormal enlargement of the brain. [MACR(O)- + ENCEPHAL(O) + -Y.] —**mac′ren·ce·phal′ic** (măk′rĕn-sĭ-făl′ĭk), **mac′ren·ceph′a·lous** *adj.*
macro–, macr–. Indicates: **1.** Largeness or longness in extent, duration, or size; for example, **macronucleus. 2.** Abnormal largeness or overdevelopment, especially in some part; for example, **macrencephaly.** Compare **micro-.** [From Greek *makros,* large, long. See **māk-** in Appendix.*]
mac·ro·bi·o·sis (măk′rō-bī-ō′sĭs) *n.* Longevity. [Late Greek *makrobiōsis* : MACRO- + -BIOSIS.]
mac·ro·ceph·a·ly (măk′rō-sĕf′ə-lē) *n.* Also **mac·ro·ce·pha·li·a** (-sĭ-fā′lē-ə). *Pathology.* Abnormally large cranial capacity, often observed in the mentally retarded. Also called "megacephaly," "megalocephaly." [French *macrocéphalie,* from *macrocéphale,* having a long head, from Greek *makrokephalos* : MACRO- + -CEPHALOUS.] —**mac′ro·ce·phal′ic** (-sĭ-făl′ĭk), **mac′ro·ceph′a·lous** *adj.*
mac·ro·chem·is·try (măk′rō-kĕm′ĭs-trē) *n.* Chemistry requiring neither microscopy nor microanalysis. Compare **microchemistry.** —**mac′ro·chem′i·cal** *adj.*
mac·ro·cli·mate (măk′rō-klī′mĭt) *n. Meteorology.* The climate of a large geographical area. Compare **microclimate.** —**mac′ro·cli·mat′ic** (-klī-măt′ĭk) *adj.*
mac·ro·cosm (măk′rō-kŏz′əm) *n.* **1.** The universe itself, or the concept of universe. **2.** A system regarded as an entity containing subsystems. Compare **microcosm.** [French *macrocosme,* from Medieval Latin *macrocosmus,* from Late Greek *makros* *kosmos,* the great world : MACRO- + *kosmos,* world (see **kosmos** in Appendix*).] —**mac′ro·cos′mic** *adj.*
mac·ro·cyte (măk′rō-sīt′) *n. Pathology.* An abnormally large red blood cell associated with some forms of anemia. [MACRO- + (ERYTHRO)CYTE.] —**mac′ro·cyt′ic** (-sĭt′ĭk) *adj.*
mac·ro·cy·to·sis (măk′rō-sī-tō′sĭs) *n. Pathology.* A condition in which the blood contains macrocytes. —**mac′ro·cy·tot′ic** (-tŏt′ĭk) *adj.*
mac·ro·ev·o·lu·tion (măk′rō-ĕv′ə-lōō′shən) *n.* Evolution involving whole species, or larger groups, of organisms. —**mac′ro·ev′o·lu′tion·ar·y** *adj.*
mac·ro·ga·mete (măk′rō-gə-mēt′, -găm′ēt′) *n. Biology.* The larger of two conjugating cells, usually female, in protozoans. Compare **microgamete.**
mac·ro·graph (măk′rō-grăf′, -gräf′) *n.* A representation of an object at least as large as the object. [MACRO- + -GRAPH.]
ma·crog·ra·phy (mə-krŏg′rə-fē) *n.* **1.** Examination of objects with the unaided eye. Compare **micrography. 2.** Abnormally large handwriting, sometimes indicating a nervous disorder. [MACRO- + -GRAPHY.]
mac·ro·mol·e·cule (măk′rō-mŏl′ə-kyōōl) *n.* **1.** A polymer, especially one composed of more than 100 repeated monomers. **2.** Any crystal, such as diamond or common salt, in which individual atoms or molecules cannot be distinguished.
ma·cron (mā′krŏn′, -krən) *n.* **1.** A diacritical mark placed above a vowel to indicate a long sound or phonetic value in pronunciation, such as (ā) in the word *make.* Compare **breve. 2.** The horizontal mark (—) used to indicate a stressed or long syllable in a foot of verse. [Greek *makron,* neuter of *makros,* long. See **māk-** in Appendix.*]
mac·ro·nu·cle·us (măk′rō-nōō′klē-əs) *n., pl.* **-clei** (-klē-ī). A large, trophic, nonreproductive nucleus in the cells of ciliated protozoans. Compare **micronucleus.**
mac·ro·nu·tri·ent (măk′rō-nōō′trē-ənt) *n. Botany.* An element, such as carbon, hydrogen, oxygen, or nitrogen, required in large proportion for the growth and development of plants.
mac·ro·phys·ics (măk′rō-fĭz′ĭks) *n.* Plural in form, used with a singular verb. The physics of macroscopic phenomena.
ma·crop·ter·ous (mə-krŏp′tər-əs) *adj. Zoology.* Having unusually large fins or wings. [Greek *makropteros* : MACRO- + -PTEROUS.]
mac·ro·scop·ic (măk′rə-skŏp′ĭk) *adj.* Also **mac·ro·scop·i·cal** (-ĭ-kəl). **1.** Large enough to be perceived or examined without instrumentation, especially as by the unaided eye. **2.** Pertaining to observations made without magnifying instruments, especially as by the unaided eye. Also "megascopic." [MACRO- + -SCOP(Y) + -IC.] —**mac′ro·scop′i·cal·ly** *adv.*
mac·ro·spo·ran·gi·um (măk′rō-spə-răn′jē-əm) *n., pl.* **-gia** (-jē-ə). *Botany.* A **megasporangium** *(see).*
mac·ro·spore (măk′rə-spôr, -spōr′) *n. Botany.* A **megaspore** *(see).*
mac·u·la (măk′yōōl-ə) *n., pl.* **-lae** (-lē). **1.** A spot, stain, blemish, or pit; especially, a discoloration of the skin caused by excess or lack of pigment. **2.** A sunspot. [Latin *macula,* spot, blemish. See **macula** in Appendix.*] —**mac′u·lar** (-lər) *adj.*
macula lu·te·a (lōō′tē-ə) *pl.* **maculae luteae** (lōō′tē-ē). *Anatomy.* An area in the eye near the center of the retina at which visual perception is most acute. [New Latin, "yellow spot."]
mac·u·late (măk′yōō-lāt′) *tr.v.* **-lated, -lating, -lates.** To spot, blemish, or pollute. *—adj.* (măk′yə-lĭt). **1.** Spotted or blotched. **2.** Stained; impure. Compare **immaculate.** [Middle English *maculaten,* to stain, from Latin *maculāre,* from *macula,* spot, blemish. See **macula** in Appendix.*]
mac·u·la·tion (măk′yōō-lā′shən) *n.* **1.** The act of spotting or staining. **2.** A spotted or stained condition. **3.** The spotted markings of a plant or animal, such as the spots of the leopard.
mac·ule (măk′yōōl) *v.* **-uled, -uling, -ules.** *—tr.* To blur; mackle. *—intr.* To become blurred or mackled. *—n. Printing.* Variant of **mackle.** [Middle English, from Old French, from Latin *macula,* spot, blemish. See **macula** in Appendix.*]
mad (măd) *adj.* **madder, maddest. 1.** Suffering from a disorder of the mind; insane: *"Honora was eccentric, but Maggie told everyone in the village that she was mad."* (John Cheever). **2.** As if insane; temporarily or apparently deranged by violent sensations, emotions, or ideas: *"I tell thee I am mad / In Cressid's love."* (Shakespeare). **3.** *Informal.* Feeling or showing strong liking or enthusiasm. Used with *about, for,* or *over: "You probably know how mad he is about sports."* (Peter Taylor). **4.** *Informal.* Angry; resentful: *"He'd be so mad he missed it he wouldn't speak to me for days."* (Harper Lee). **5.** Lacking restraint or reason; wildly foolish; senseless: *"Ah, will you stop telling me your mad dreams."* (Eugene O'Neill). **6.** Marked by extreme excitement, confusion, or agitation; frantic: *a mad scramble for the bus.* **7.** Boisterously gay; hilarious: *have a mad time.* **8.** *Slang.* Delightfully unusual; humorously pointless: *mad conversation in double talk.* **9.** Affected by rabies; rabid. —**have a mad on.** *Slang.* To sulk; be angry. —**like mad.** *Slang.* Wildly; impetuously: *He drove like mad.* *—v.* **madded, madding, mads.** *—tr. Rare.* To madden or make mad. *—intr. Rare.* To act, be, or become mad. [Middle English *madd,* Old English *gemǣdd,* past participle of *gemǣdan,* to madden, from *gemād,* mad. See **mei-**[1] in Appendix.*]
MAD Airport code for Madrid, Spain.
Mad·a·gas·car (măd′ə-găs′kər). The fourth-largest island (227,602 square miles) in the world. Lying in the Indian Ocean, about 250 miles off the southeastern coast of Africa, it is coextensive with the Malagasy Republic.
Madagascar periwinkle. A plant, *Vinca rosea,* native to Madagascar, having pink or white flowers.

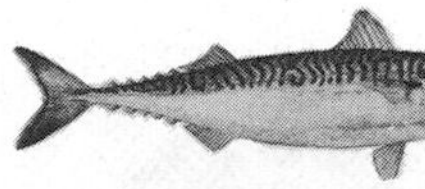
mackerel
Scomber scombrus
Atlantic mackerel

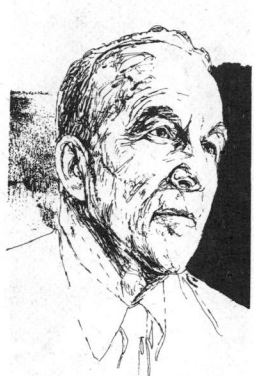

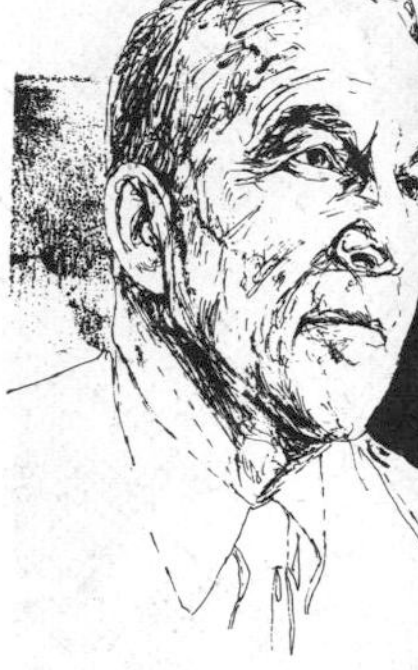
Archibald MacLeish

t tight/th thin, path/*th* this, bathe/ŭ cut/ûr urge/v valve/w with/y yes/z zebra, size/zh vision/ə about, item, edible, gallop, circus/ à *Fr.* ami/œ *Fr.* feu, *Ger.* schön/ü *Fr.* tu, *Ger.* über/KH *Ger.* ich, *Scot.* loch/N *Fr.* bon. ***Follows main vocabulary.** †**Of obscure origin.**

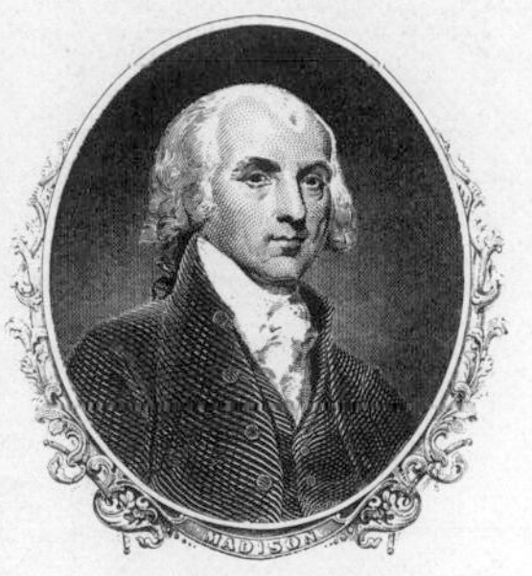

James Madison
Nineteenth-century engraving used on $5,000 bills

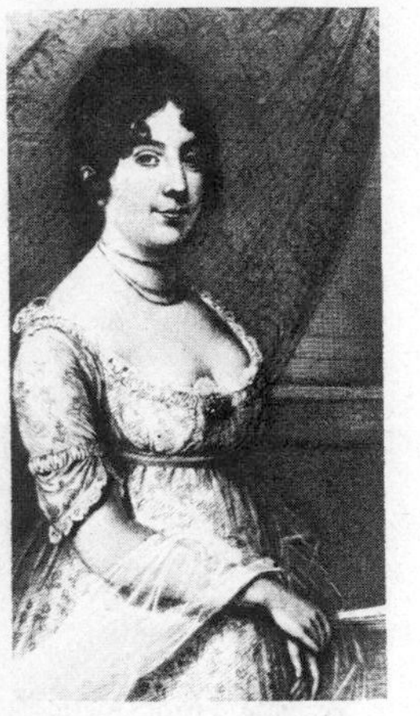

Dolley Madison
Engraving after a portrait by Gilbert Stuart

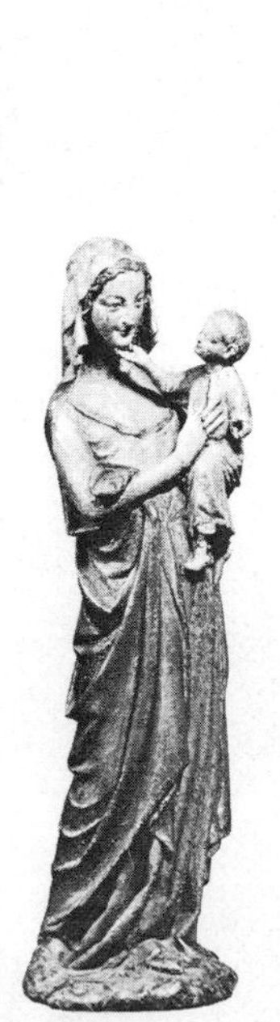

Madonna
Thirteenth-century French polychrome woodcarving

Mad·am (măd′əm) *n., pl.* **Mesdames** (mā-däm′) (for senses 1 and 2) or **madams** (for senses 3 and 4). **1.** A title of courtesy used alone as a form of address to a woman, originally to a woman of rank or position, now to any woman. Used both in speech and in writing. **2.** A title of courtesy formerly prefixed to a given name but now only prefixed to a surname or to a title indicating rank or office: *Madam Ambassador.* **3.** *Small* **m.** *Informal.* The mistress of a household. Often preceded by *the.* **4.** *Small* **m.** A woman who manages a brothel. [Middle English, from MADAME.]

Mad·ame (măd′əm, mə-dăm′; *French* må-dåm′) *n., pl.* **Mesdames** (mā-däm′; *French* mā-dåm′). *Abbr.* **Mme., Mme** **1. a.** The French title of courtesy for a married woman. **b.** A title of courtesy prefixed to the surname of a foreign married woman. Roughly equivalent to, but more formal than the English **Mrs. 2.** A title of courtesy or distinction prefixed to the full name or surname of a woman or to a title indicating rank or office: *Madame Tebaldi.* [Middle English, from Old French *ma dame,* my lady : *ma,* my, from Latin *mea,* feminine of *meus,* my (see **me-**[1] in Appendix*) + *dame,* lady, from Latin *domina,* feminine of *dominus,* lord (see **demə-**[1] in Appendix*).]

mad·cap (măd′kăp′) *n.* A rash or impulsive person, especially a girl. —*adj.* Rash; impulsive; wild. [MAD + CAP (head).]

mad·den (măd′n) *v.* **-dened, -dening, -dens.** —*tr.* **1.** To make mad; drive insane. **2.** *Informal.* To make angry; excite or irritate. —*intr.* To become infuriated. —**mad′den·ing·ly** *adv.*

mad·der[1] (măd′ər) *n.* **1.** Any of various plants of the genus *Rubia;* especially, a Eurasian species, *R. tinctoria,* having small, yellow flowers and a red, fleshy root. **2.** The root of this plant, formerly an important source of dye. **3.** A red dye obtained from the madder root. **4.** Medium to strong red or reddish orange. See **color.** [Middle English *mader,* Old English *mædere.* See **modhro-** in Appendix.*]

mad·der[2]. Comparative of **mad.**

madder lake. A bluish-red pigment used in stains, inks, and artists' oil paints.

mad·ding (măd′ĭng) *adj. Obsolete.* Acting as if mad; frenzied: *"She, mixing with the throng / Of madding matrons, bears the bride along."* (Dryden).

mad·dish (măd′ĭsh) *adj.* Somewhat mad.

mad-dog skullcap (măd′dôg′, -dŏg′). A North American plant, *Scutellaria lateriflora,* having one-sided clusters of two-lipped, blue or white flowers. [Formerly used as an antispasmodic.]

made (mād). The past tense and past participle of **make.** —*adj.* **1.** Produced or manufactured by constructing, shaping, forming, etc. Used in combination: *handmade.* **2.** Produced or created artificially; not found naturally. **3.** Invented; designed; contrived. **4.** Assured of success or fortune: *a made man.* —**made for.** Perfectly suited for: *made for each other.*

Ma·dei·ra[1] (mə-dîr′ə; *Portuguese* mä-dā′rä). **1.** An archipelago in the Atlantic Ocean about 400 miles west of Morocco, constituting the Funchal District of Portugal. Population, 596,000. Capital, Funchal. **2.** The main island of this archipelago. **3.** A river of northwestern Brazil, rising at the Bolivian border, and flowing about 2,000 miles northeast to the Amazon. [Portuguese, from Latin *māteria,* timber (the island was thickly wooded). See **māter-** in Appendix.*] —**Ma·dei′ran** *adj.* & *n.*

Ma·dei·ra[2] (mə-dîr′ə) *n.* A fortified white dessert wine from the island of Madeira.

Madeira vine. A tropical American vine, *Boussingaultia baselloides,* having small, white, fragrant flowers.

mad·e·leine (măd′ə-lĕn′) *n.* A small, rich cake, baked in a shell-shaped mold. [Invented by *Madeleine* Paulmier, 19th-century French pastry cook.]

Mad·e·line (măd′l-ĭn). A feminine given name. [French *Madeleine,* after MARY MAGDALENE.]

mad·e·moi·selle (măd′ə-mə-zĕl′) *n., pl.* **mademoiselle** or **-selles.** Any of several marine fishes of the genus *Bairdiella,* especially *B. chrysura,* of the U.S. Atlantic and Gulf coasts. Also called "silver perch," "yellowtail." [Fanciful use of MADEMOISELLE.]

Mad·e·moi·selle (măd′ə-mə-zĕl′; *French* måd-mwå-zĕl′) *n., pl.* **Mesdemoiselles** (mād-mwå-zĕl′). *Abbr.* **Mlle., Mlle** **1.** The French title of courtesy for a young girl or unmarried woman, equivalent to the English *Miss.* It may be used separately or prefixed to either a first or last name. **2.** *Usually small* **m.** A French governess. [French, from Old French *ma demoiselle* : *ma,* my, from Latin *mea,* feminine of *meus,* my (see **me-**[1] in Appendix*) + *demoiselle,* young lady, from Gallo-Roman *dom(i)nicella* (unattested), diminutive of Latin *domina,* lady, feminine of *dominus,* lord (see **demə-**[1] in Appendix*).]

Ma·de·ro (mä-thā′rō), **Francisco Indalecio.** 1873–1913. Mexican statesman and revolutionary martyr; president (1911–13).

made-to-or·der (măd′tōō-ôr′dər) *adj.* **1.** Made in accordance with particular instructions to fill the requirements of a customer; custom-made. Compare **ready-made. 2.** Very suitable.

made-up (mād′ŭp′) *adj.* **1.** Fabricated; fictitious; imaginary; invented: *a made-up story.* **2.** Changed or adorned by the application of cosmetics or make-up: *a made-up actress.* **3. a.** Complete; finished: *a made-up package.* **b.** Put together; assembled; arranged: *a made-up page of type.*

mad·house (măd′hous′) *n.* **1.** An asylum for the mentally ill. Not in technical use. **2.** *Informal.* A place of great disorder.

Ma·dhya Pra·desh (mŭ′dyə prə-dāsh′). Formerly **Central Provinces and Be·rar** (bā-rär′). A state of the Republic of India, occupying 171,201 square miles in the central part of the country. Population, 32,372,000. Capital, Bhopal.

Mad·i·son (măd′ĭ-sən). The capital of Wisconsin, located in the southern part of the state. Population, 127,000.

Mad·i·son (măd′ĭ-sən), **Dolley.** Often wrongly **Dolly.** 1768–1849. Wife of James Madison; celebrated hostess.

Mad·i·son (măd′ĭ-sən), **James.** 1751–1836. Fourth President of the United States (1809–17).

Mad·i·son Avenue (măd′ĭ-sən). **1.** A street in New York City known as a center of the American advertising business. **2.** The principles, attitudes, ideas, and methods of advertising and mass communications. Often used disparagingly.

mad·ly (măd′lē) *adv.* **1.** Insanely. **2.** Wildly; furiously; frantically. **3.** Foolishly; rashly.

mad·man (măd′măn′, -mən) *n., pl.* **-men** (-mĕn′). **1.** A man who is mentally ill; a maniac. Not in technical use. **2.** A frantic man.

mad money. *Slang.* **1.** Carfare carried by a girl on a date to pay her way home in the event of a quarrel with her escort. **2.** A small sum of money kept by a female for unlikely contingencies.

mad·ness (măd′nĭs) *n.* **1.** Insanity. **2.** Great folly: *"O madness, to think use of strongest wines / And strongest drinks our chief support of health."* (Milton). **3.** Fury; rage: *"But the hunger madness made them terrifying, irresistible."* (Jack London). **4.** Enthusiasm; excitement. —See Synonyms at **insanity.**

Ma·doer·a. The Dutch name for **Madura.**

ma·don·na (mə-dŏn′ə; *Italian* mä-dôn′nä) *n.* Formerly, an Italian title for a married woman, equivalent to **Madam.** It has been replaced in current usage by **signora.** [Italian : *ma,* my, from Latin *mea,* feminine of *meus,* my (see **me-**[1] in Appendix*) + *donna,* lady, from Latin *domina,* feminine of *dominus,* lord (see **demə-**[1] in Appendix*).]

Ma·don·na (mə-dŏn′ə) *n.* **1.** The Virgin Mary. Usually preceded by *the.* **2.** An artistic representation of the Virgin Mary.

Madonna lily. A plant, *Lilium candidum,* native to Eurasia, having white, trumpet-shaped flowers. Also called "Annunciation lily."

Ma·dras (mə-drăs′, -dräs′). **1.** A state of the Republic of India, occupying over 50,000 square miles in the southeast. Population, 33,687,000. **2.** The capital city and principal seaport of this state, on the Bay of Bengal. Population, 1,729,000.

ma·dras (măd′rəs, mə-drăs′, -dräs′) *n.* **1.** A cotton cloth of fine texture, usually with a plaid, striped, or checked pattern. **2.** A silk cloth, generally striped. **3. a.** A light cotton cloth used for drapery. **b.** A similar cloth of rayon. **4.** A large handkerchief of brightly colored silk or cotton, often worn as a turban. [Originally produced in MADRAS, India.]

Madras hemp. A plant, **sunn** *(see),* or its fiber.

Ma·dre de Dios (mä′thrā thā thyōs′). A river rising in southern Peru, and flowing 700 miles to the Beni River in Bolivia.

mad·re·pore (măd′rə-pôr′, -pōr′) *n.* Any of various corals of the genus *Madrepora,* including the reef builders of tropical seas. [French, from Italian *madrepora,* "mother-stone," referring to the manner in which polyps produce coral : *madre,* mother, from Latin *māter* (see **māter-** in Appendix*) + Latin *pōrus,* tufa, from Greek *pōros*†.] —**mad′re·por′ic** *adj.*

Ma·drid (mə-drĭd′; *Spanish* mä-thrēth′). **1.** A province of Spain, occupying about 3,000 square miles in the central plateau. **2.** The capital city of Spain and of this province. Population, 2,559,000.

mad·ri·gal (măd′rĭ-gəl) *n.* **1.** An unaccompanied vocal composition for two or three voices in simple harmony, following a strict poetic form, developed in Italy in the late 13th and early 14th centuries. **2.** A polyphonic part song, usually unaccompanied and with parts for four to six voices, using a secular text and sometimes an accompaniment by strings that either doubles or replaces one or more of the vocal parts. This form was developed in Italy in the 16th century, and became very popular in England in the 16th and early 17th centuries. **3.** A lyric poem with a pastoral, idyllic, or amatory subject, developed from the lyrics of the 13th-century Italian madrigal. **4.** Any part song. [Italian *madrigale,* earlier *madriale,* "(piece) without accompaniment," probably from Latin *mātrīcālis,* "of the womb," newly sprung from the womb, simple, from *mātrix,* womb, from *māter,* mother. See **māter-** in Appendix.*] —**mad′ri·gal·ist** *n.*

ma·dri·lène (măd′rĭ-lĕn′) *n.* Also **ma·dri·lene.** A consommé flavored with tomato, generally chilled. [Abbreviation of French *consommé madrilène,* from Spanish *madrileño,* of or pertaining to Madrid.]

ma·dro·ña (mə-drō′nyə) *n.* Also **ma·dro·ño** (mə-drō′nyō), **ma·dro·ne** (mə-drō′nə). A tree, *Arbutus Menziesi,* of western North America, having glossy, evergreen leaves, white flowers, and red-orange fruit. [Spanish *madroño*†.]

mad tom. Any of several small freshwater North American catfishes of the genus *Noturus,* common in the east-central United States, having poisonous spines. [MAD + TOM (cat).]

Ma·dur·a[1] (mə-dōōr′ä). *Dutch* **Ma·doer·a. 1.** An Indonesian island in the Java Sea, near the northeast coast of Java. **2.** A strait between Java and the island of Madura.

Ma·dur·a[2]. The former name for **Madurai.**

Ma·du·rai (mŭ′dōō-rī′). Also **Mat·hu·rai** (mŭt′hōō-rī′). Formerly **Ma·du·ra** (mə-dōōr′ə). A city of the state of Madras, Republic of India. Population, 425,000.

Mad·u·rese (măd′yōō-rēz′, -rēs′) *n., pl.* **Madurese. 1.** The Malayan people inhabiting the Indonesian island of Madura. **2.** The Austronesian language of the Malayans of Madura and eastern Java. —**Mad′u·rese′** *adj.*

ma·du·ro (mə-dōōr′ō) *n., pl.* **-ros.** A strong-flavored cigar with a dark wrapper. [Spanish *maduro,* "ripe," "mellow," from Latin *mātūrus,* ripe. See **mā-**[1] in Appendix.*] —**ma·du′ro** *adj.*

mad·wo·man (măd′wōōm′ən) *n., pl.* **-women** (-wĭm′ĭn). **1.** An insane woman. Not in technical use. **2.** A frantic woman.

mad·wort (măd′wûrt′) *n.* **1.** A low-growing plant, *Asperugo procumbens,* native to Eurasia, having rough stems and small

ă pat/ā pay/âr care/ä father/b bib/ch church/d deed/ĕ pet/ē be/f fife/g gag/h hat/hw which/ĭ pit/ī pie/îr pier/j judge/k kick/l lid, needle/m mum/n no, sudden/ng thing/ŏ pot/ō toe/ô paw, for/oi noise/ou out/ōō took/ōō boot/p pop/r roar/s sauce/sh ship, dish/

blue flowers. **2.** Any of several plants of the genus *Alyssum.* [Formerly believed to cure madness.]
mad·zoon. Variant of **matzoon.**
Mae (mā). A feminine given name. [Variant of MAY (name).]
Mae·an·der. The ancient name for the **Menderes** River.
Mae·ce·nas (mī-sē′nəs, mī-) *n.* A patron, especially one generous to artists. [From Gaius *Maecenas,* Roman statesman of the first century B.C., patron of Horace and Virgil.]
Mael·strom, the (māl′strəm). A notoriously dangerous whirlpool, off the northwest coast of Norway.
mael·strom (māl′strəm) *n.* **1.** A whirlpool of extraordinary size or violence. **2.** A situation that resembles such a whirlpool in violence, turbulence, or power to engulf: *caught in the maelstrom of war.* [Early Modern Dutch *maelstrom,* "whirlstream" : *malen,* to whirl, grind, from Middle Dutch (see **melə-** in Appendix*) + *stroom,* stream (see **sreu-** in Appendix*).]
mae·nad (mē′năd′) *n., pl.* **-nads** or **maenades** (mĕn′ə-dēz′). Also **me·nad. 1.** *Greek Mythology.* A woman member of the orgiastic cult of Dionysus. **2.** A frenzied woman. [Latin *maenas* (stem *maenad-*), from Greek *mainas,* "she who is mad," from *mainesthai,* to be mad. See **men-**[1] in Appendix.*] **—mae·nad′ic** (mē-năd′ĭk) *adj.*
Mae Nam (mä′ näm′). Also **Me·nam.** See the **Chao Phraya** River.
ma·es·to·so (mä′ĕs-tō′sō, -zō) *adv. Music.* In a majestic and stately manner. Used as a direction. *—adj. Music.* Majestic; stately: *a maestoso march. —n., pl.* **maestosos.** *Music.* A maestoso passage or movement. [Italian, majestic, from *maestà,* majesty, from Latin *mājestās.* See **meg-** in Appendix.*]
Maes·tricht. See **Maastricht.**
maes·tro (mīs′trō; *Italian* mä-ĕs′trō) *n., pl.* **-tros** or **-tri** (-trē). A master in any art, especially a composer, a leader of a group of musical performers, or a music teacher. [Italian, from Latin *magister,* master. See **meg-** in Appendix.*]
Mae·ter·linck (mā′tər-lĭngk′), Count **Maurice.** 1862–1949. Belgian poet, naturalist, and author of symbolist drama.
Mae West (mā′ wĕst′). An inflatable, vestlike life preserver. [After *Mae West,* born 1892, U.S. actress.]
Maf·e·king (măf′ə-kĭng′). The former administrative capital of Bechuanaland (now Botswana), in Cape of Good Hope Province, Republic of South Africa. Population, about 8,000.
maf·fick (măf′ĭk) *intr.v.* **-ficked, -ficking, -ficks.** *British.* To rejoice or celebrate with boisterous public demonstrations. [Back-formation from MAFEKING, referring to the wild celebration of the raising of the siege of Mafeking (1900).]
Ma·fi·a (mä′fē-ə) *n.* Also **Maf·fi·a. 1.** A secret terrorist organization in Sicily, operating since the early 19th century in opposition to legal authority. **2.** An alleged international criminal organization believed active, especially in Italy and the United States, since the late 19th century. Compare **Black Hand, Camorra, Cosa Nostra. 3.** Any organization using terrorist methods to control an activity. [Italian (Sicilian dialect) *mafia,* lawlessness, "boldness," from Arabic *mahyah,* boasting.]
mag. 1. magazine. **2.** magnetism. **3.** magnitude.
Ma·ga·dha (mŭ′gə-də). An ancient kingdom and center of Buddhism in northeastern India.
Ma·ga·lla·nes (mä′gä-yä′näs). Formerly **Pun·ta A·re·nas** (po͞on′tä ä-rā′näs). A port city of extreme southern Chile on the Strait of Magellan, called the southernmost city in the world.
mag·a·zine (măg′ə-zēn′, măg′ə-zēn′) *n. Abbr.* **mag. 1. a.** A place where goods are stored; especially, a building (as in a fort) or storeroom (as on a warship) where ammunition is stored. **b.** The contents of a storehouse; a stock of ammunition. **2.** A periodical containing a collection of articles, stories, pictures, or other features. **3. a.** A compartment in some types of firearms, often a small, detachable box, in which cartridges are held to be fed into the firing chamber. **b.** A compartment in a camera in which rolls or cartridges of film are held for feeding through the exposure mechanism. **c.** Any of various other compartments attached to machines, for storing or supplying necessary material. [Old French *magazin,* storehouse, from Italian *magazzino,* from Arabic *makhāzin,* plural of *makhzan,* storehouse, from *khazana,* to store up.]
mag·da·len (măg′də-lən) *n.* Also **mag·da·lene** (măg′də-lēn′). *Rare.* **1.** A reformed prostitute. **2.** A reformatory for prostitutes. [From MARY MAGDALENE.]
Mag·da·len[1] (môd′lən). A college of Oxford University.
Mag·da·len[2] (măg′də-lən). **Mary Magdalene** *(see).*
Mag·da·le·na (mäg′*thä*-lā′nä). A river rising in the Andes in southwestern Colombia, and flowing north to the Caribbean.
mag·da·lene. Variant of **magdalen.**
Mag·da·lene[1] (môd′lən). A college of Cambridge University.
Mag·da·lene[2] (măg′də-lēn′). **Mary Magdalene** *(see).*
Mag·da·le·ni·an (măg′də-lē′nē-ən) *adj. Archaeology.* Of or pertaining to the last upper Paleolithic culture of Europe, succeeding the Aurignacian. [French *magdalénien.* The artifacts from which the culture was classified were found near the village of *La Madeleine,* France, named after MARY MAGDALENE.]
Mag·de·burg (măg′də-bûrg′; *German* mäg′də-bo͝orkh′). A city in East Germany, 80 miles southwest of Berlin. Population, 265,000.
mage (māj) *n. Archaic.* **1.** A magician. **2.** One of the Magi. [Middle English, from Latin *magus,* sorcerer. See **Magi.**]
Ma·gel·lan (mə-jĕl′ən), **Ferdinand.** *Portuguese* Fernão de Magalhães. 1480?–1521. Portuguese navigator; commander of the Spanish expedition that was first to circumnavigate the world.
Ma·gel·lan, Strait of (mə-jĕl′ən). *Spanish* **Es·tre·cho de Ma·ga·lla·nes** (ās-trā′chō *thä* mä′gä-yä′näs). A navigable channel, about 350 miles long, between the southern tip of mainland South America and Tierra del Fuego and other islands.
Mag·el·lan·ic cloud (măj′ə-lăn′ĭk). Either of two small galaxies, the closest to the Milky Way, faintly visible near the south celestial pole. [After Ferdinand MAGELLAN.]
Ma·gen Da·vid (mä′gən dä′vĭd, mŭ′gən dŭ′vĭd). Also **Mo·gen Da·vid** (mō′gən dä′vĭd, mŭ′gən dŭ′vĭd). A six-pointed star, or hexagram, formed by placing two triangles together, one upon the other or interlaced. It is a symbol of Judaism, and appears on the Israeli flag. Also known as "Shield of David," "Star of David." [Hebrew *māgen Dāwīd,* shield of (King) David.]

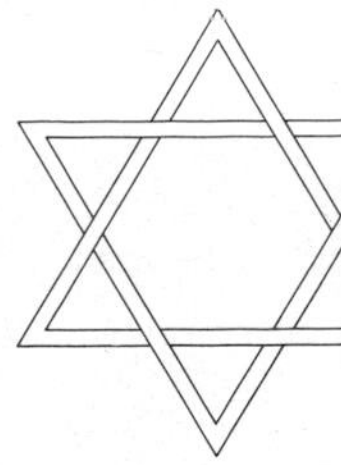
Magen David

Ma·gen·die (ma-zhäɴ-dē′), **François.** 1783–1855. French physician; pioneer in experimental physiology and nutrition.
ma·gen·ta (mə-jĕn′tə) *n.* **1.** A coal-tar dye, **fuchsin** *(see).* **2.** Moderate to vivid purplish red, or dark to strong reddish purple. See **color.** [The dye was discovered in the year of the battle of *Magenta* (1859), and named for its bloodiness.]
Mag·gio·re, La·go (lä′gō mäd-jō′rā). A lake, 40 miles long and 82 square miles in area, in Italy and southern Switzerland.
mag·got (măg′ət) *n.* **1.** The legless, soft-bodied larva of any of various insects of the order Diptera, especially of the housefly and the bluebottle fly, usually found in decaying matter or as a parasite. **2.** *Rare.* An extravagant notion; a whim. [Middle English *magot, maked,* earlier *maddock, madhek.* See **math-** in Appendix.*]
mag·got·y (măg′ət-ē) *adj.* **1.** Infested with maggots. **2.** *Rare.* Full of strange whims.
Ma·ghreb (mŭ′grĭb). The region of Africa north of the Sahara between Egypt and the Atlantic, including the northern areas of Libya, Tunisia, Algeria, and Morocco. [Arabic, "West."]
Ma·gi (mā′jī′) *pl.n.* The singular **Magus** is rare. **1.** *Sometimes small* **m.** The Zoroastrian priestly caste of the Medes and Persians. **2.** The "wise men from the East" who traveled to Bethlehem to pay homage to the infant Jesus. Matthew 2:1–12. [Middle English, from Latin, plural of *magus,* sorcerer, from Greek *magos,* from Persian *maguš.* See **magh-**[1] in Appendix.*] **—Ma′gi·an** (mā′jē-ən) *adj. & n.*
mag·ic (măj′ĭk) *n.* **1.** The art that purports to control or forecast natural events, effects, or forces by invoking the supernatural. **2.** The practice of using charms, spells, or rituals to attempt to produce supernatural effects or to control events in nature. **3.** The exercise of sleight of hand or conjuring for entertainment; the use of premeditated deception or concealed equipment to produce baffling effects. **4.** Any mysterious and overpowering quality that lends singular distinction and enchantment: *"For me the names of those men breathed the magic of the past, just as it was breathed for me by Swinburne's presence."* (Max Beerbohm). *—adj.* **1.** Pertaining to the supernatural; having to do with magic and its practice: *"stubborn unlaid ghost, / That breaks his magic chains at curfew time"* (Milton). **2.** Possessing distinctive qualities that produce unaccountable or baffling effects: *a magic wand.* [Middle English, from Old French *magique,* from Late Latin *magicē,* from Greek *magikē (tekhnē),* the sorcerer's art, from *magikos,* pertaining to sorcery, from *magos,* sorcerer, from Old Persian *maguš.* See **magh-**[1] in Appendix.*]
Synonyms: *magic, black magic, sorcery, voodoo, witchcraft, necromancy, alchemy. Magic* is the most inclusive of these related nouns; it pertains to all supposedly supernatural powers that affect natural events, but is often used broadly in the sense of that which seems to transcend rational explanation. *Black magic,* which is practiced with intent to do harm, is the approximate equivalent of *sorcery;* these specifically involve the use of charms and spells. *Voodoo* is a form of primitive sorcery that originated in Africa, and is generally associated with fetishes. *Witchcraft* is associated with evil intent and with power derived from evil spirits; it is generally practiced by women, and suggests a broader set of techniques than that used in *sorcery. Necromancy* signifies forecasting of the future through supposed communication with the dead. *Alchemy* is now applied figuratively to any seemingly miraculous change for the better an extension of the original sense of transmutation.
mag·i·cal (măj′ĭ-kəl) *adj.* Pertaining to or produced by magic. **—mag′i·cal·ly** *adv.*
ma·gi·cian (mə-jĭsh′ən) *n.* **1.** A sorcerer; wizard. **2.** A person who performs magic for entertainment or diversion. **3.** One whose skill or art seems to be magical: *a magician with words.*
magic lantern. An optical device formerly used to project the enlarged image of a picture.
magic number. *Physics.* Any of the numbers 2, 6, 8, 14, 20, 28, 50, 82, 126, that represent the number of neutrons or protons in strongly bound, exceptionally stable, and abundant atomic nuclei.
Ma·gi·not Line (măzh′ĭ-nō′). A line of fortifications built by France along its eastern border before World War II. [After André *Maginot* (1877–1932), French minister of war.]
mag·is·te·ri·al (măj′ĭs-tîr′ē-əl) *adj.* **1.** Pertaining to a master, teacher, or person in a similar position of authority. **2. a.** Characteristic of a master; authoritative; commanding: *"She would appear on the porch and reign over the street in magisterial beauty."* (Harper Lee). **b.** Dictatorial; dogmatic; overbearing: *offended by his magisterial manner of giving advice.* **3.** Of or pertaining to a magistrate or his official functions: *"my magisterial duties, which you, as a brother magistrate, can imagine are frequently very distasteful"* (Rudyard Kipling). Also "magistral." [Latin *magisterius,* from *magister,* master. See **meg-** in Appendix.*] **—mag′is·te′ri·al·ly** *adv.*
mag·is·ter·y (măj′ĭs-tĕr′ē) *n., pl.* **-ies.** Also **ma·gis·ter** (mə-jĭs′tər). *Alchemy.* A power in nature associated with transmuta-

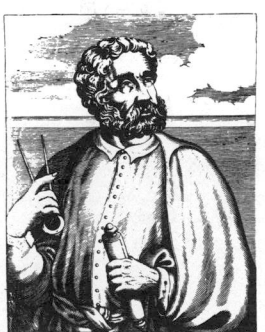

Ferdinand Magellan
Woodcut by
Nicholas De L'Armessin

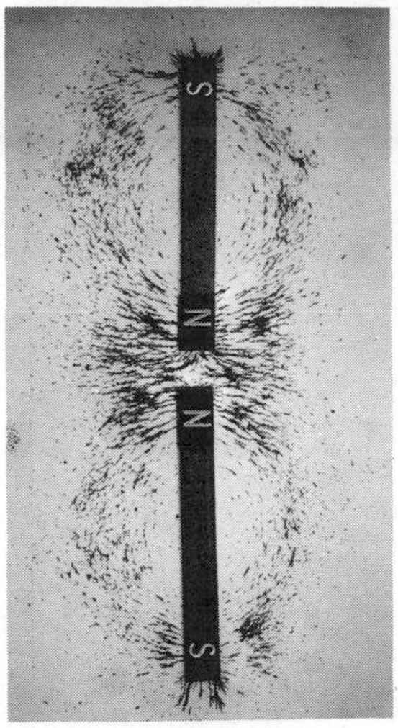

magnetic field
Iron filings aligned by magnetic fields of bar magnets

tion; the philosopher's stone. [Medieval Latin *magisterium*, from Latin, position of a master, from *magister*, master. See **meg-** in Appendix.*]

mag·is·tra·cy (măj′ĭs-trə-sē) *n., pl.* **-cies.** Also **mag·is·tra·ture** (măj′ĭs-trə-cho͝or′). **1.** The position, function, or term of office of a magistrate. **2.** A body of magistrates. **3.** The district under jurisdiction of a magistrate.

mag·is·tral (măj′ĭs-trəl) *adj.* **1. Magisterial** *(see).* **2.** *Pharmacology.* **a.** Formulated by a physician. **b.** Prepared as specified by a physician's prescription. Compare **officinal. 3.** Principal; main: *the magistral line of fortifications.* [Latin *magistrālis*, masterful, from *magister*, master. See **meg-** in Appendix.*]

mag·is·trate (măj′ĭs-trāt′, -trĭt) *n.* **1.** A civil officer with power to administer and enforce law. **2.** A minor official with limited judicial authority, such as a justice of the peace or the judge of a police court. [Latin *magistrātus*, magistracy, magistrate, from *magister*, master. See **meg-** in Appendix.*]

Ma·gle·mo·si·an (mä′glə-mō′zē-ən) *adj. Archaeology.* Of or pertaining to a Mesolithic forest culture of northern Europe. [The archaeological evidence from which the culture was classified was found at *Maglemose*, Denmark.]

mag·ma (măg′mə, mäg′-) *n., pl.* **magmata** (măg′mä′tə, mäg′-) or **-mas. 1.** A mixture of finely divided solids with enough liquid to produce a pasty mass. **2.** *Geology.* The molten matter under the earth's crust, from which igneous rock is formed by cooling. **3.** *Pharmacology.* A suspension of particles in a liquid, such as milk of magnesia. **4.** The residue of fruits after expressing the juice; pomace. [Middle English, dregs of a liquid, from Latin, sediment, from Greek *magma*, unguent. See **mag-** in Appendix.*] **—mag·mat′ic** *adj.*

Mag·na Char·ta, Mag·na Car·ta (măg′nə kär′tə). **1.** The great charter of English political and civil liberties granted by King John at Runnymede on June 15, 1215. **2.** Any document or piece of legislation that serves as a guarantee of basic rights. [Medieval Latin, "Great Charter."]

mag·na cum lau·de (măg′nä ko͝om lou′dā, măg′nə ko͝om lôd′). *Latin.* With great praise. Used to designate a college or university degree, awarded with high honors, or the recipient of such a degree. Compare **cum laude, summa cum laude.**

Mag·na Grae·ci·a (măg′nä grī′kē-ä, măg′nə grē′shə). The colonies of ancient Greece in southern Italy and Sicily. [Latin, "Great Greece."]

mag·na·nim·i·ty (măg′nə-nĭm′ĭ-tē) *n.* The quality of being magnanimous: *"Magnanimity in politics is not seldom the truest wisdom."* (Burke).

mag·nan·i·mous (măg-năn′ə-məs) *adj.* Noble of mind and heart; generous in forgiving; above revenge or resentment; unselfish; gracious: *"Daring and magnificent in war, Israel now has an unprecedented opportunity to be magnanimous in peace."* (New York Times). [Latin *magnanimus*, "great-souled" : *magnus*, great (see **meg-** in Appendix*) + *animus*, soul (see **ane-** in Appendix*).] **—mag·nan′i·mous·ly** *adv.* **—mag·nan′i·mous·ness** *n.*

mag·nate (măg′nāt′) *n.* A powerful or influential man, especially in business or industry: *a railroad magnate.* [Middle English *magnates* (plural only), from Late Latin *magnātēs*, plural of *magnās*, "great man," from Latin *magnus*, great. See **meg-** in Appendix.*]

mag·ne·sia (măg-nē′zhə, -shə) *n.* **Magnesium oxide** *(see)*, especially when processed for purity. [Middle English, from Medieval Latin, from Late Greek *magnēsia*, name of various minerals, from *Magnēsia*, name of a metalliferous region of Thessaly.] **—mag·ne′sian** *adj.*

mag·ne·site (măg′nə-sīt′) *n.* **1.** A white, yellowish, or brown, usually crystalline mineral of magnesium carbonate, $MgCO_3$, used in the manufacture of magnesium oxide and carbon dioxide. **2.** Any of several grades of magnesium oxide obtained from this material. [MAGNES(IUM) + -ITE.]

mag·ne·si·um (măg-nē′zē-əm, -shəm) *n. Symbol* **Mg** A light, silvery, moderately hard, metallic element which in ribbon or powder form burns with a brilliant white flame. It is used in structural alloys, pyrotechnics, flash photography, and incendiary bombs. Atomic number 12, atomic weight 24.312, melting point 651°C, boiling point 1,107°C, specific gravity 1.74, valence 2. See **element.** [New Latin, from MAGNESIA.]

magnesium carbonate. A very light, odorless, white powdery compound, $MgCO_3$, used in a wide variety of manufactured products including inks, glass, dentifrices, and cosmetics.

magnesium oxide. A white, powdery compound, MgO, having a high melting point (2,800°C), and used in high-temperature refractories, electric insulation, food packaging, and semiconductor devices. Also called "magnesia."

magnesium sulfate. A colorless, crystalline compound, $MgSO_4$, used in fireproofing, ceramics, matches, explosives, and fertilizers. The hydrate, $MgSO_4 \cdot 7H_2O$, is **Epsom salt** *(see).*

mag·net (măg′nĭt) *n.* **1.** A body that attracts iron and certain other materials by virtue of a surrounding field of force produced by the motion of its atomic electrons and the alignment of its atoms. **2.** An **electromagnet** *(see).* **3.** A person, place, object, or situation that exerts attraction: *"Morse was the magnet that attracted to Japan not only Fenollosa but Percival Lowell."* (Van Wyck Brooks). [Middle English *magnete*, from Old French, from Latin *magnēs* (stem *magnēt-*), from Greek *magnēs*, short for *Magnēs lithos*, "the Magnesian stone," from *Magnēs*, pertaining to *Magnēsia*. See **magnesia.**]

mag·net·ic (măg-nĕt′ĭk) *adj.* Also *rare* **mag·net·i·cal** (-ĭ-kəl). **1.** Of or relating to magnetism or magnets. **2.** Having the properties of a magnet; exhibiting magnetism. **3.** Relating to the magnetic poles of the earth: *a magnetic compass bearing.* **4.** Capable of being magnetized or of being attracted by a magnet. **5.** Operating by means of magnetism: *a magnetic recorder.* **6.** Exerting powers of attraction upon persons: *a magnetic personality.* **—mag·net′i·cal·ly** *adv.*

magnetic compass. An instrument using a **magnetic needle** *(see)* to show direction relative to the earth's magnetic field.

magnetic declination. The angle between the geographic meridian and the local magnetic meridian, in navigation indicated as degrees plus (+) to the east, or degrees minus (−) to the west, of the geographic meridian. Also called "declination," "magnetic variation."

magnetic dip. The angle that the earth's magnetic field makes with the horizontal plane at any specific location. Also called "magnetic inclination."

magnetic equator. A line connecting all points on the earth's surface where there is no magnetic dip. Also called "aclinic line." Compare **geomagnetic equator.**

magnetic field. A condition in a region of space, established by the presence of a magnet, or of an electric current, and characterized by the existence of a detectable magnetic force at every point in the region.

magnetic field strength. 1. Magnetic intensity *(see).* **2. Magnetic induction** *(see).*

magnetic flux. The total number of magnetic lines°of force passing through a bounded area in a magnetic field. Also loosely called "magnetism."

magnetic flux density. Magnetic induction *(see).*

magnetic force. 1. The force on a **magnetic pole** *(see)* in a magnetic field. **2.** The force on an electrically charged particle, or on an electric current, in a magnetic field.

magnetic head. A device, as in a tape recorder, that converts electric impulses into variations in the magnetism of a surface for storage and subsequent retrieval. See **magnetic recording.**

magnetic hysteresis. The failure of the **magnetization** *(see)* in a body to return to its original value when the external field is reduced.

magnetic inclination. Magnetic dip *(see).*

magnetic induction. 1. A vector quantity that specifies the direction and magnitude of magnetic force at every point in a magnetic field. Also called "magnetic field strength," "magnetic flux density." **2.** The temporary conversion of a piece of iron or of certain other materials into a magnet by a magnetic field.

magnetic intensity. That part of a magnetic field related solely to external currents as a cause, without reference to the presence of matter. Also called "magnetic field strength."

magnetic line of force. A curve whose tangent at any point is along the direction of magnetic force at that point. The number of lines of force per unit area in the neighborhood of a point is proportional to the **magnetic induction** *(see)* at that point.

magnetic meridian. A meridian passing through the earth's magnetic poles.

magnetic mine. A marine mine detonated by a mechanism that responds to a mass of magnetic material, such as the steel hull of a ship.

magnetic moment. The ratio of the maximum torque exerted on a magnet, or on an electric current loop, in a magnetic field to the magnetic induction of the field.

magnetic needle. A needle-shaped bar magnet usually suspended on a low-friction mounting and used in various instruments, especially in the magnetic compass, to indicate the alignment of a local magnetic field.

magnetic north. The direction of the earth's magnetic pole, to which the north-seeking pole of a magnetic needle points when free from local magnetic influence.

magnetic permeability. A measure of the ability of a medium to modify a magnetic field, equal to the ratio of magnetic induction to magnetic intensity.

magnetic pickup. A type of phonograph pickup that utilizes a coil in a magnetic field to receive vibrations from the stylus and convert them into electric impulses. Compare **crystal pickup.**

magnetic pole. 1. Either of two limited regions in a magnet at which the magnet's field is most intense, each of which is designated by the approximate geographic direction to which it is attracted: *a north, or north-seeking pole; a south, or south-seeking pole.* **2.** Either of two variable points on the earth, close to but not coinciding with the geographic poles, where the earth's magnetic field is most intense.

magnetic pole strength. A measure of the effectiveness of a magnet, equal to the quotient of the magnetic moment by the length of the magnet.

magnetic pyrites. A mineral, **pyrrhotite** *(see).*

magnetic recording. 1. The recording of a signal, such as sound or computer instructions, in the form of a magnetic pattern on a magnetizable surface for storage and subsequent retrieval. **2.** A surface containing such a magnetic pattern.

magnetic storm. A severe but transitory fluctuation in the earth's magnetic field believed to be produced by currents of charged particles and gamma rays, resulting from abnormal solar activity.

magnetic susceptibility. The ratio of the magnetic permeability of a medium to that of a vacuum, minus one. It is positive for a paramagnetic or ferromagnetic medium, negative for a diamagnetic medium.

magnetic tape. A plastic tape coated with iron oxide for use in **magnetic recording** *(see).*

magnetic variation. Magnetic declination *(see).*

mag·net·ism (măg′nə-tĭz′əm) *n. Abbr.* **mag. 1.** The class of phenomena exhibited by the field of force produced by a magnet or by an electric current. **2.** The study of magnets and

ă pat/ā pay/âr care/ä father/b bib/ch church/d deed/ĕ pet/ē be/f fife/g gag/h hat/hw which/ĭ pit/ī pie/îr pier/j judge/k kick/l lid, needle/m mum/n no, sudden/ng thing/ŏ pot/ō toe/ô paw, for/oi noise/ou out/o͝o took/o͞o boot/p pop/r roar/s sauce/sh ship, dish/

their effects. **3.** The force exerted by a magnetic field. **4.** Loosely, **magnetic flux** *(see).* **5.** Unusual power to attract, fascinate, or influence: *the magnetism of money.* **6. Animal magnetism** *(see).*

mag·net·ite (măg′nə-tīt′) *n.* The mineral form of black iron oxide, Fe_3O_4, often occurring with titanium or magnesium, and an important ore of iron. A magnetically polarized piece of this mineral is called a **lodestone** *(see).* [German *Magnetit* : MAGNET + -ITE.]

mag·net·i·za·tion (măg′nə-tĭ-zā′shən) *n.* **1.** The process of making a substance temporarily or permanently magnetic, as by insertion in a magnetic field. **2.** The magnetic moment per unit volume induced in a body by an external field. **3.** The property of being magnetic. **4.** Suddenly heightened attentiveness, especially of an audience.

mag·net·ize (măg′nə-tīz′) *tr.v.* **-ized, -izing, -izes.** **1.** To make magnetic. **2.** To exert strong influence upon (a person). —**mag′net·iz′a·ble** *adj.* —**mag′net·iz′er** *n.*

magnetizing force. The magnetic intensity at any point in a substance capable of being magnetized.

mag·ne·to (măg-nē′tō) *n., pl.* **-tos.** A small generator of alternating current using permanent magnets, used in the ignition systems of some internal-combustion engines. [Short for *magnetoelectric machine.*]

magneto–. Indicates magnetic properties; for example, **magnetometer, magnetohydrodynamics.**

mag·ne·to·chem·is·try (măg-nē′tō-kĕm′ĭs-trē) *n.* The study of the interrelation of magnetic and chemical phenomena.

mag·ne·to·graph (măg-nē′tō-grăf′) *n.* A magnetometer equipped for recording, as by photography. [MAGNETO- + -GRAPH.]

mag·ne·to·hy·dro·dy·nam·ics (măg-nē′tō-hī′drō-dī-năm′ĭks) *n.* The study of electrically conducting fluids, such as molten metal or plasma, in electric and magnetic fields.

mag·ne·tom·e·ter (măg′nə-tŏm′ə-tər) *n.* An instrument for comparing the intensity and direction of magnetic fields. [MAGNETO- + -METER.]

mag·ne·to·mo·tive force (măg-nē′tō-mō′tĭv). *Abbr.* **mmf, m.m.f.** **1.** The agency that produces **magnetic flux** *(see)* in a magnetic circuit. **2.** The strength of such an agency, equal to the work required to carry a hypothetical isolated magnetic pole of unit strength completely around the circuit.

mag·ne·ton (măg′nə-tŏn′) *n.* A unit of the magnetic moment of a subatomic particle, equal to $eh/4\pi mc$, where *e* is the particle's electric charge, *m* its mass, *h* Planck's constant, and *c* the speed of light; especially: **a.** The *Bohr magneton,* calculated using the mass and charge of the electron. **b.** The *nuclear magneton,* calculated using the mass of the nucleon. [French *magnéton* : MAGNET + (ELECTR)ON.]

mag·ne·to·sphere (măg-nē′tō-sfîr) *n.* An asymmetric region surrounding the earth, extending from about four hundred to several thousand miles above the surface, in which charged particles are trapped and their behavior dominated by the earth's magnetic field. [MAGNETO- + -SPHERE.]

mag·ne·to·stric·tion (măg-nē′tō-strĭk′shən) *n.* The deformation of a ferromagnetic material subjected to a magnetic field.

mag·ne·tron (măg′nə-trŏn′) *n.* A thermionic tube in which the electron beam is controlled by electromagnetic fields and generates high-power microwaves. [MAGNE(T) + (ELEC)TRON.]

mag·nif·ic (măg-nĭf′ĭk) *adj. Obsolete.* Magnificent. [Middle English *magnifyque,* from Old French *magnifique,* from Latin *magnificus,* "great in deeds" : *magnus,* great (see **meg-** in Appendix*) + -FIC.] —**mag·nif′i·cal·ly** *adv.*

Mag·nif·i·cat (măg-nĭf′ĭ-kăt′, -kät′) *n.* **1.** The canticle beginning *Magnificat anima mea Dominum* ("My soul doth magnify the Lord"). The text is Luke 1:46-55. **2.** A musical setting of this text. **3.** *Small* **m.** Any hymn or song of praise.

mag·ni·fi·ca·tion (măg′nĭ-fĭ-kā′shən) *n.* **1. a.** The act of magnifying or the state of being magnified. **b.** The process of enlarging the size of something, as an optical image. **c.** Something that has been magnified; an enlarged representation, image, or model. **2.** *Optics.* The ratio of image size to object size.

mag·nif·i·cence (măg-nĭf′ĭ-səns) *n.* **1.** Greatness or lavishness of surroundings or dress; splendor; sumptuousness. **2.** Grand or imposing beauty: *the magnificence of the scenery.*

mag·nif·i·cent (măg-nĭf′ĭ-sənt) *adj.* **1.** Great in splendor; lavish: *"My lord could not take the trouble to be magnificent."* (Boswell). **2.** Grand or imposing to the mind; marked by nobility of thought or deed; exalted. **3.** Outstanding of its kind; superlative: *" 'It's a magnificent place for sailing,' said Davies."* (Erskine Childers). See Synonyms at **grand.** [Latin *magnificent-,* variant stem of *magnificus,* MAGNIFIC.] —**mag·nif′i·cent·ly** *adv.*

mag·nif·i·co (măg-nĭf′ĭ-kō′) *n., pl.* **-coes.** **1.** A nobleman of the Venetian Republic. **2.** A person of distinguished rank, importance, or appearance: *"He is both an old-world and a new-world figure, a feudal magnifico and a modern technocrat."* (Observer, London). [Italian, from *magnifico,* magnificent, from Latin *magnificus,* MAGNIFIC.]

mag·ni·fi·er (măg′nĭ-fī′ər) *n.* **1. a.** A **magnifying glass** *(see).* **b.** Broadly, any system of optical components that magnifies. **2.** A person who magnifies.

mag·ni·fy (măg′nĭ-fī′) *v.* **-fied, -fying, -fies.** —*tr.* **1.** To make greater in size; enlarge; amplify; intensify; heighten: *"Plato's error was magnified by the Christian transvaluation of Plato."* (Walter Kaufmann). **2.** To cause to appear greater or seem more important; exaggerate: *"My wife . . . used every art to magnify the merit of her daughter."* (Goldsmith). **3.** To increase the apparent size of, especially by means of a lens. **4.** To glorify: *"What is man, that thou shouldest magnify him?"* (Job 7:17). —*intr.* To increase or have the power to increase the size or volume of an image or sound. —See Synonyms at **increase.** [Middle English *magnifien,* from Old French *magnifier,* from Latin *magnificāre,* to make great, from *magnificus,* MAGNIFIC.]

magnifying glass. A converging lens that enlarges the image of an object. Also called "magnifier."

mag·nil·o·quent (măg-nĭl′ə-kwənt) *adj.* Lofty and extravagant in speech; grandiloquent. [Latin *magniloquus* : *magnus,* great (see **meg-** in Appendix*) + *loqui,* to speak (see **tolkw-** in Appendix*).] —**mag·nil′o·quence** *n.* —**mag·nil′o·quent·ly** *adv.*

Mag·ni·to·gorsk (măg-nē′tə-gôrsk′). A city on the Ural River in the Soviet Union, in Asia. Population, 348,000.

mag·ni·tude (măg′nĭ-to͞od′, -tyo͞od′) *n. Abbr.* **mag. 1. a.** Greatness of rank or position: *"such duties as were expected of a landowner of his magnitude"* (Anthony Powell). **b.** Greatness in size or extent. **c.** Greatness in significance or influence: *"One could see the magnitude of the achievement."* (Thomas Wolfe). **2.** *Astronomy.* The relative brightness of a celestial body designated on a numerical scale, originally integers from 1 (brightest) through 6 (faintest visible), now extended to include negative integers, integers above 6, and decimals, with the scale rule that a decrease of 1 unit represents an increase in apparent brightness by a factor of 2.512. Also called "apparent magnitude." **3.** *Mathematics.* **a.** A number assigned to a member of a set to form the basis of comparison with other members of the same set. **b.** A property that can be quantitatively described, such as the volume of a sphere, or the length of a vector. [Middle English, from Latin *magnitūdō,* greatness, from *magnus,* great. See **meg-** in Appendix.*]

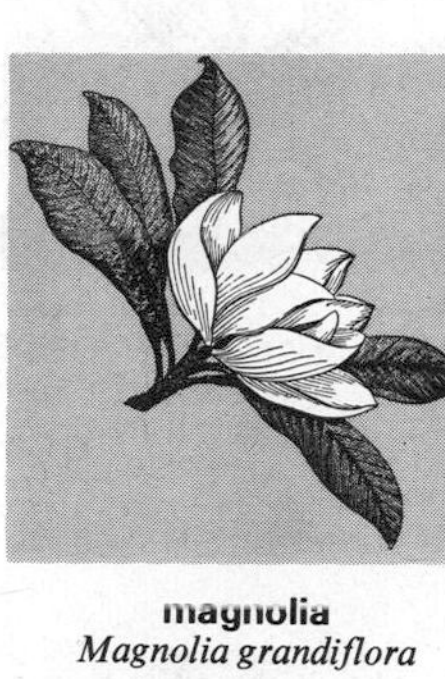

magnolia
Magnolia grandiflora

mag·no·lia (măg-nōl′yə) *n.* **1.** Any of various evergreen or deciduous trees and shrubs of the genus *Magnolia,* of the Western Hemisphere and Asia, many of which are cultivated for their showy white, pink, purple, or yellow flowers. **2.** The flower of any of these trees or shrubs. [New Latin, after Pierre *Magnol* (1638–1715), French botanist.]

magnolia warbler. A black-and-yellow, ground-nesting songbird, *Dendroica magnolia,* of North America.

mag·num (măg′nəm) *n.* **1.** A bottle, holding about two-fifths of a gallon, for wine or liquor. **2.** The amount of liquid contained in such a bottle. [Latin, "a big one," neuter of *magnus,* great. See **meg-** in Appendix.*]

mag·num o·pus (măg′nəm ō′pəs). **1.** A great work, especially a literary or artistic masterpiece. **2.** The greatest single work of an artist, writer, or composer. [Latin, "great work."]

mag·nus hitch (măg′nəs). A clove hitch with one extra turn. See **knot.** [Apparently from Latin *magnus,* "large."]

Ma·gog. See **Gog and Magog.**

ma·got (mä-gō′, măg′ət) *n.* **1.** The **Barbary ape** *(see).* **2.** A Chinese or Japanese figurine, usually grotesque and rendered in a crouching position. [French *magot, magog,* a monstrous or grotesque figure, from the Biblical giant Magog.]

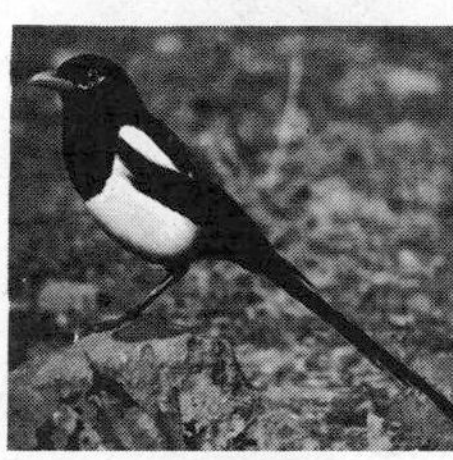

magpie
Pica pica

mag·pie (măg′pī) *n.* **1.** Any of various birds of the family Corvidae, found worldwide, having a long, graduated tail, and black, blue, or green coloring with white markings, noted for their chattering call. The species *Pica pica,* the black-billed magpie, is widespread in the Northern Hemisphere. **2.** Any of various birds resembling the magpie. **3.** Any of several piping crows and bell magpies of the family Cracticidae, of Australia. **4.** A person who chatters. [*Mag,* a dialectal name for a chatterbox in proverbs (probably from *Mag,* pet form of MARGARET) + PIE (magpie).]

M. Agr. Master of Agriculture.

Mag·say·say (mäg-sī′sī′), **Ramon.** 1907–1957. President of the Republic of the Philippines (1953–57).

ma·guey (mə-gā′, măg′wā) *n.* **1.** Any of various plants of the genus *Agave,* native to tropical America; especially, any yielding a fiber or beverage. Also called "mescal." **2.** Any plant of the related genus *Furcraea.* **3.** The fiber obtained from any of these plants. [Spanish, from Taino.]

Ma·gus (mā′gəs) *n., pl.* **-gi** (-jī). *Rare.* One of the **Magi** *(see).*

Mag·yar (măg′yär′, mäg′-; *Hungarian* mŭd′yär′) *n.* **1.** A member of the principal ethnic group of Hungary. **2.** The Finno-Ugric language of the Magyars, the official language of Hungary; Hungarian. [Hungarian *Magyar*†.] —**Mag′yar** *adj.*

Mag·yar·or·szág. The Hungarian name for **Hungary.**

Ma·ha·bha·ra·ta (mə-hä′bä′rə-tə). Also **Ma·ha·bha·ra·tam** (-təm). One of the two great epics of ancient India. Compare **Ramayana.** [Sanskrit *Mahābhārata,* "the great story" : *mahā,* great (see **meg-** in Appendix*) + *bhārata,* story (see **bher-**[1] in Appendix*).]

Ma·hal·la el Ku·bra (mə-hăl′ə ĕl ko͞o′brə). A leading textile-producing city of Egypt, on the Nile delta, 65 miles north of Cairo. Population, 178,000.

Ma·han (mə-hăn′), **Alfred Thayer.** 1840–1914. American naval officer; author of influential works on naval operations.

Ma·ha·na·di (mə-hä′nə-dē). A river of the Republic of India, flowing 560 miles from the Eastern Ghats to the Bay of Bengal.

ma·ha·ra·jah, ma·ha·ra·ja (mä′hə-rä′jä, -zhä) *n.* A king or prince in India, especially the sovereign of one of the former native states. [Hindi *mahārājā,* from Sanskrit : *mahā,* great (see **meg-** in Appendix*) + *rājā,* king (see **reg-**[1] in Appendix*).]

ma·ha·ra·ni, ma·ha·ra·nee (mä′hə-rä′nē) *n.* **1.** The wife of a maharajah. **2.** A queen or princess in India, especially the sovereign ruler of one of the former native states. [Hindi *mahārānī,* from Sanskrit *mahārājñī* : *mahā,* great (see **meg-** in Appendix*) + *rājñī,* queen (see **reg-**[1] in Appendix*).]

Ma·ha·rash·tra (mä-hä′răsh′trä). A state of the Republic of India, occupying 119,000 square miles in the west, bordering on the Arabian Sea. Population, 39,554,000. Capital, Bombay.

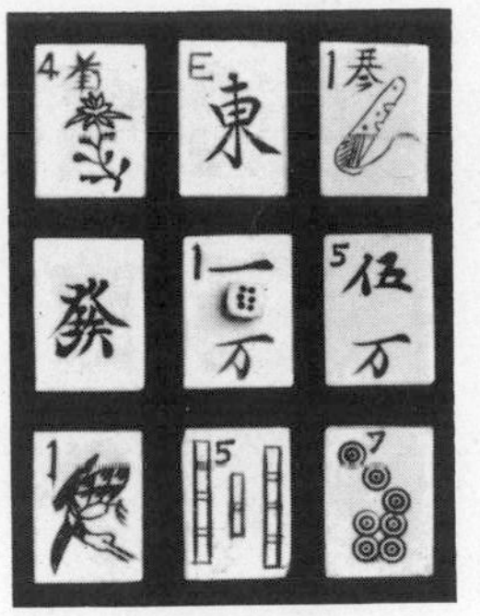

mahjong
Tiles, with "house sparrow" at lower left

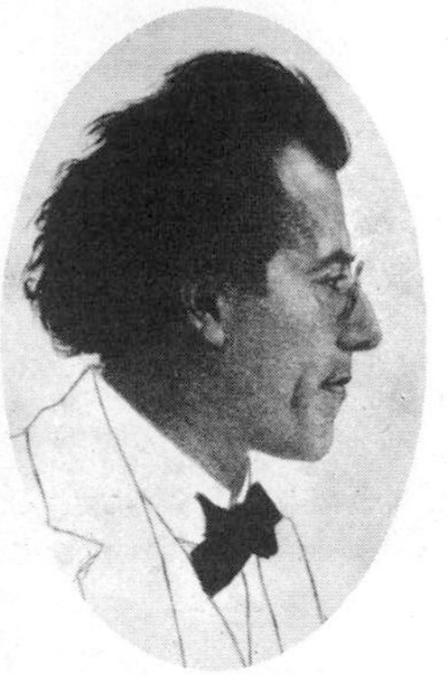

Gustav Mahler
Contemporary mezzotint

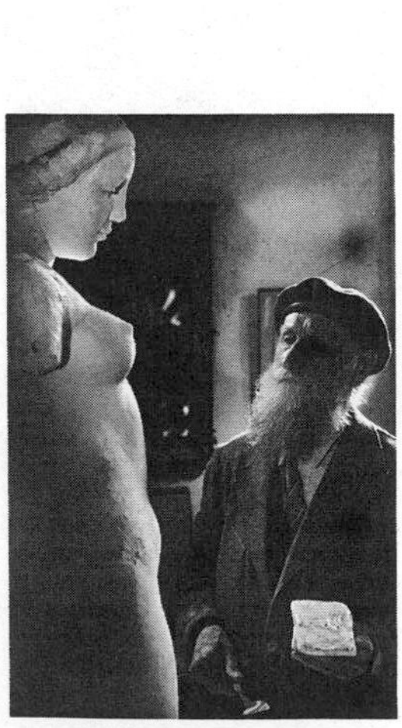

Aristide Maillol
At work on his last statue, "Harmonie"

ma·hat·ma (mä-hät′mä, mə-hăt′mə) *n.* **1.** *Theosophy.* In India and Tibet, one of a class of persons venerated for great knowledge and love of humanity. **2.** *Capital* **M.** A Hindu title of respect for a man renowned for spirituality and high-mindedness, such as Mohandas K. Gandhi, often called "Mahatma Gandhi." [Sanskrit *mahātman* : *mahā,* great (see **meg-** in Appendix*) + *ātman,* soul (see **ētmen-** in Appendix*).]

Ma·ha·ya·na (mä′hə-yä′nə). One of the major schools of Buddhism, active in Japan, Korea, Nepal, Tibet, Mongolia, and China. Compare **Hinayana.** [Sanskrit *mahāyāna,* "the great vehicle" : *mahā,* great (see **meg-** in Appendix*) + *yāna,* vehicle (see **ei-**[1] in Appendix*).]

Mah·di (mä′dē). **1.** The Islamic messiah who, it is believed, will appear at the world's end and establish a reign of peace and righteousness. **2.** A title assumed by various Islamic religious leaders; especially, Mohammed Ahmed (1843?–1885), Sudanese leader of a religious war against the British and Egyptians. [Arabic *mahdīy,* "rightly guided (one)," past participle of *madā,* to lead rightly.] —**Mah′dism** *n.* —**Mah′dist** *adj.* & *n.*

Ma·hé (mä-hā′). An island of the Seychelles in the Indian Ocean, northeast of Madagascar. Population, 33,478.

Ma·hi·can (mə-hē′kən) *n., pl.* **Mahican** or **-cans.** Also **Mo·hi·can** (mō-hē′kən, mə-). **1.** A tribe or confederacy of Algonquian-speaking Indians that formerly lived between the upper Hudson River Valley and Lake Champlain. **2.** A member of this tribe or confederacy.

mah·jong (mä′zhŏng′, -zhông′). Also **mah·jongg** *n.* A game of Chinese origin usually played by four persons. Tiles, resembling dominoes and bearing various designs, are drawn and discarded until one player wins with a hand of four combinations of three tiles each and a pair of matching tiles. [Cantonese *ma chiung,* from Chinese (Mandarin) *ma*[2] *chiang*[4], *ma*[2] *ch'iao*[4], "house sparrow" (from the figure of a house sparrow on the leading piece of one of the suits) : *ma*[2], spotted + *ch'iao*[4], bird, sparrow.]

Mah·ler (mä′lĕr), **Gustav.** 1860–1911. Bohemian-born Austrian composer and conductor.

mahl·stick. Variant of **maulstick.**

ma·hog·a·ny (mə-hŏg′ə-nē) *n., pl.* **-nies. 1. a.** Any of various tropical American trees of the genus *Swietenia,* valued for their hard, reddish-brown wood. **b.** The wood of any of these trees; especially, that of *S. mahogani,* much used for making furniture. **2. a.** Any of several trees having wood resembling true mahogany. **b.** The wood of any of these trees. See **African mahogany, Philippine mahogany. 3.** Moderate reddish brown. See **color.** [Probably from an indigenous language of Honduras.]

Ma·hom·et. Variant of **Mohammed.**

Ma·hom·et·an. Variant of **Mohammedan.**

Ma·hom·et·an·ism. Variant of **Mohammedanism.**

Ma·hound (mə-hound′, -ho͝ond′). *Archaic.* Mohammed.

ma·hout (mə-hout′) *n.* The keeper and driver of an elephant. [Hindi *mahāut, mahāwat,* from Sanskrit *mahāmātra,* "of great measure," originally an honorific title : *mahā,* great (see **meg-** in Appendix*) + *mātra,* measure (see **med-** in Appendix*).]

Mah·rat·i. Variant of **Marathi.**

Mah·rat·ta. Variant of **Maratha.**

Mah·rat·ti. Variant of **Marathi.**

ma·huang (mä′hwăng′) *n.* Any of various Asiatic plants or shrubs of the genus *Ephedra;* especially, *E. sinica,* from which ephedrine is obtained. [Chinese *ma*[2] *huang*[2], "yellow hemp" : *ma*[2], hemp + *huang*[2], yellow.]

mah·zor (mäкн′zôr) *n., pl.* **mahzorim** (mäкн-zôr′ĭm) or **-zors.** The Hebrew prayer book containing rituals prescribed for holidays. Compare **siddur.** [Hebrew *maḥzor,* cycle.]

Mai·a[1] (mā′ə, mī′ə). *Greek Mythology.* A goddess, the eldest of the **Pleiades** *(see).* [Greek, from *maia,* mother, nurse. See **mā-**[2] in Appendix.*]

Mai·a[2] (mā′ə, mī′ə) *n.* The brightest star in the **Pleiades** *(see).*

Mai·a[3] (mā′ə, mī′ə). *Roman Mythology.* A goddess of spring, daughter of Faunus and wife of Vulcan. [Latin *Maia,* "the great one." See **meg-** in Appendix.*]

maid (mād) *n.* **1. a.** A girl or an unmarried woman. **b.** A virgin: " *'Well,' said Mercy, 'if nobody will have me I will die a maid.'* " (Bunyan). **2.** A female servant. [Middle English *maide,* shortening of MAIDEN.]

maid·en (mād′n) *n.* **1. a.** An unmarried girl or woman. **b.** A virgin. **2.** A machine resembling the guillotine, used to behead criminals in the 16th and 17th centuries in Scotland. **3.** A racehorse that has never won a race. **4.** *Cricket.* A **maiden over** *(see).* **5.** A one-year-old woody plant. —*adj.* **1.** Of, pertaining to, or befitting a maiden: *a maiden blush.* **2.** Unmarried. Said only of women: *a maiden aunt.* **3.** Inexperienced; untried. **4.** Designating a racehorse that has never won a race. **5.** First or earliest: *a maiden voyage.* [Middle English *maiden,* Old English *mægden.* See **maghu-** in Appendix.*]

maid·en·hair (mād′n-hâr′) *n.* Any of various ferns of the genus *Adiantum,* having dark stems and light-green, feathery fronds with fan-shaped leaflets. Also called "maidenhair fern." [From the fineness of the stems.]

maidenhair tree. The **ginkgo** *(see).*

maid·en·head (mād′n-hĕd′) *n.* **1.** The hymen. **2.** *Rare.* Maidenhood; virginity. [Middle English *maidenhed* : MAIDEN + *-hed,* variant of -HOOD.]

maid·en·hood (mād′n-ho͝od′) *n.* The condition or time of being a maiden.

maid·en·ly (mād′n-lē) *adj.* Pertaining to or suitable for a maiden. —**maid′en·li·ness** *n.*

maiden name. A woman's family name before marriage.

maiden over. *Cricket.* An over during which no runs are scored. Also called "maiden."

maid in waiting *pl.* **maids in waiting.** An unmarried woman attending a queen or princess.

Maid Mar·i·an (mâr′ē-ən). **1.** The Queen of the May in morris dances and May Day games. **2.** Robin Hood's sweetheart.

maid of honor *pl.* **maids of honor. 1.** An unmarried noblewoman attendant upon a queen or princess. **2.** The chief unmarried female attendant of a bride. Compare **bridesmaid, matron of honor.**

maid·ser·vant (mād′sûr′vənt) *n.* A female servant.

Maid·stone (mād′stən, -stōn′). The county seat of Kent, in southeastern England. Population, 54,000.

Mai·du (mī′do͞o) *n., pl.* **Maidu** or **-dus. 1.** A Penutian-speaking Indian tribe, formerly living in the Sacramento Valley area of California. **2.** A member of this tribe. **3.** The Penutian language of this tribe. [Maidu, "man."] —**Mai′du** *adj.*

ma·ieu·tic (mā-yo͞o′tĭk, mī-) *adj.* Also **ma·ieu·ti·cal** (-tĭk-əl, mī-). Pertaining to that aspect of the Socratic method that induces a pupil or respondent to formulate latent concepts and show their connections with reality through a dialectic or logical sequence of questions. [Greek *maieutikos,* obstetric, "bringing ideas to birth," from *maieuesthai,* to act as midwife, from *maia,* midwife, nurse. See **mā-**[2] in Appendix.*]

mai·gre (mā′gər) *adj.* **1.** Not containing flesh or its juices: *a maigre diet.* **2.** *Roman Catholic Church.* Formerly, of or designating a day of abstinence on which only maigre food was permitted. [French, thin, from Old French, from Latin *macer,* thin. See **māk-** in Appendix.*]

mai·hem. Variant of **mayhem.**

Mai·kop (mī′kôp). Also **May·kop.** An industrial city of the Soviet Union, the capital of the Adygey Autonomous Region. Population, 82,000.

mail[1] (māl) *n.* **1. a.** The bulk of letters, packages, and other material handled in a postal system. **b.** Postal material for a specific person or organization: *I received my mail today.* **c.** Material processed for distribution from a post office at a specified time: *the morning mail.* **2.** A system by which letters, packages, and other postal materials are transported. Sometimes plural and preceded by *the: He was appointed to take charge of the mails.* **3.** A vehicle by which mail is transported: *The ship is a fast mail.* —*adj.* Of, pertaining to, carrying, or used in the handling of mail: *mail delivery.* —*v.* **mailed, mailing, mails.** —*tr.* To send by mail. —*intr.* To send letters and other postal material by mail. [Middle English *male,* mailbag, from Old French *male,* pouch, bag, from Old High German *malha.* See **molko-** in Appendix.*] —**mail′a·ble** *adj.*

mail[2] (māl) *n.* **1.** Flexible armor composed of small overlapping metal rings, loops of chain, or scales. See **chain mail, coat of mail. 2.** The protective shell or covering of certain animals, such as the turtle. **3.** The full-grown breast feathers of a hawk. —*tr.v.* **mailed, mailing, mails.** To cover or armor with mail. [Middle English *maille,* from Old French, from Latin *macula,* spot, mesh. See **macula** in Appendix.*]

mail·bag (māl′băg′) *n.* **1.** A large canvas sack used for transporting mail. **2.** A leather or canvas bag suspended from the shoulder, used by mailmen for carrying mail.

mail·box (māl′bŏks′) *n.* **1.** A public box for deposit of outgoing mail. **2.** A private box for incoming mail. Also *chiefly British* "letterbox."

mail call. Distribution of mail to members of a military unit.

mail car. A railroad car designed to carry mail, and usually having facilities for sorting and processing mail.

mail carrier. 1. Any vehicle or other device used for transporting mail. **2.** A **mailman** *(see).*

mail catcher. A device used for catching bags of mail suspended from a **mail crane** *(see).*

mail clerk. A worker in a business office responsible for mail.

mail crane. A hooklike device on a pole alongside a railroad track, used to transfer mailbags to and from a moving train.

mail drop. 1. Any receptacle for holding mail at the address of delivery. **2.** A slot for the insertion of mail. **3.** An address at which a person receives mail but does not reside.

mailed (māld) *adj.* **1.** Covered with or made of plates of mail. **2.** Having a hard covering of scales, spines, or horny plate, as an armadillo or lobster.

mailed fist. The threat of the use of force, as between nations.

mail·er (mā′lər) *n.* **1.** One who uses the mails. **2. a.** A person who addresses, stamps, or otherwise prepares mail. **b.** A **mailing machine** *(see).* **3.** *Rare.* A ship that carries mail. **4.** A container, especially a cardboard tube, to hold material to be mailed. **5.** An advertising leaflet included with a letter.

Mail·er (mā′lər), **Norman.** Born 1923. American writer.

mailing machine. Any of various machines that stamp, address, or seal material for mailing. Also called "mailer."

Mail·lol (mä-yôl′), **Aristide.** 1861–1944. French sculptor of heroic female nudes.

mail·lot (mī-yō′) *n.* **1.** A coarsely knitted, stretchable, jersey fabric. **2. a.** A gymnastic suit, pair of tights, or similar article of clothing made of this material. **b.** A bathing suit of this material, usually of one piece. [French *maillot,* tight garment, originally a child's swaddling bands, from Old French, from *maille,* band of cloth, mail, from Latin *macula,* spot, mesh. See **macula** in Appendix.*]

mail·man (māl′măn′, -mən) *n., pl.* **-men** (-mĕn, -mən). One who carries and delivers mail. Also called "postman."

mail order. *Abbr.* **m. o., M. O.** A request for goods or services that is received, and often filled, through the mail.

mail-or·der house (māl′ôr′dər). A business establishment that is primarily organized to promote, receive, and fill requests for merchandise or services through the mail.

ă pat/ā pay/âr care/ä father/b bib/ch church/d deed/ĕ pet/ē be/f fife/g gag/h hat/hw which/ĭ pit/ī pie/îr pier/j judge/k kick/l lid, needle/m mum/n no, sudden/ng thing/ŏ pot/ō toe/ô paw, for/oi noise/ou out/o͝o took/o͞o boot/p pop/r roar/s sauce/sh ship, dish/

maim (mām) *tr.v.* **maimed, maiming, maims. 1.** To deprive (a person) of, or of the use of, a limb or bodily member; mutilate; disable; cripple. **2.** To make imperfect or defective; impair: *The bill was maimed by extensive amendments.* [Middle English *maymen, mayhaymen,* to wound, from Old French *mahaignier,* from Common Romance *mahagnāre* (unattested), probably from Germanic. See **mai-**[1] in Appendix.*]

Mai·mon·i·des (mī-mŏn′ə-dēz′), **Moses.** Also called Moses ben Maimon. 1135–1204. Spanish-born Jewish philosopher and physician; codifier of the Talmud; rabbi of Cairo.

main[1] (mān) *adj.* **1.** Most important; principal; major: *the main building on the campus.* **2.** Exerted to the utmost; sheer; utter: *"They took her off the sled by main strength."* (Jack London). **3.** Of or relating to a continuous area or stretch, as of land or water: *the main ocean.* **4.** *Obsolete.* Very great or considerable of its kind; remarkable: *"I am a main bungler at a long story."* (Sheridan). **5.** *Obsolete.* Highly important; momentous: *"by this main accident of time"* (Bacon). **6.** *Obsolete.* Showing or having great strength; mighty: *"soaring on main wing"* (Milton). **7.** *Grammar.* Denoting the principal clause, verb, or phrase referring to the subject in a complex sentence. **8.** *Nautical.* Connected to or located near the mainmast: *a main skysail.* —*n.* **1.** The principal or most important part or point: *"The main of life is composed of small incidents."* (Samuel Johnson). **2.** The principal pipe or conduit in a system for conveying water, gas, oil, or other utility. **3.** Physical strength. Used chiefly in the phrase *might and main.* **4.** *Rare.* The mainland, as distinguished from islands. This historical use survives chiefly in the phrase **Spanish Main** *(see).* **5.** *Poetic.* The open ocean: *on the high main.* **6.** *Nautical.* **a.** The **mainsail** *(see).* **b.** The **mainmast** *(see).* —**in the main.** Mostly; on the whole; chiefly: *"Wyatt's sonnets are in the main hard reading."* (Tucker Brooke). —See Synonyms at **chief.** [Middle English, from Old English *mægen,* strength, and *mægn-* (used in compounds), "strong," "great." See **magh-**[1] in Appendix.*]

main[2] (mān) *n.* **1.** In dice playing, a throw of the dice. **2.** A series of cockfights consisting of an odd number of matches. [Origin uncertain.]

Main (mān; *German* mīn). A river of West Germany rising in northern Bavaria, and flowing 305 miles westward to the Rhine.

main chance. One's most advantageous opportunity.

main clause. *Grammar.* The clause in a complex sentence that can stand syntactically by itself; an independent clause.

main deck. The principal deck of a ship or other large vessel.

main drag. *Slang.* The principal street of a city or town.

Maine[1] (mān). The northeasternmost state of the United States, 33,215 square miles in area, bordered on the east by the Atlantic Ocean. It joined the Union in 1820. Population, 914,000. Capital, Augusta. See map at **United States of America.** [After *Maine,* former province of France.]

Maine[2] (mān). A U.S. battleship blown up in the harbor of Havana, Cuba, on February 15, 1898, with the loss of 260 lives. The explosion was a cause of the Spanish-American War.

main·land (mān′lănd′, -lənd) *n.* The principal land mass of a country, territory, or continent, as distinguished from an island or peninsula.

Main·land (mān′lənd). **1.** Pomona, the largest of the Orkney Islands. **2.** The largest of the Shetland Islands. **3.** Honshu, Japan.

main line. 1. A principal section of a railroad line. **2.** *Slang.* A principal and easily accessible vein, usually in the arm or leg, into which narcotics can be injected.

main·line (mān′līn′) *intr.v.* **-lined, -lining, -lines.** *Slang.* To inject narcotics directly into a major vein.

Main Line. The fashionable suburbs west of Philadelphia, Pennsylvania, along the railroad line to Paoli.

main·ly (mān′lē) *adv.* Most importantly; for the most part.

main·mast (mān′məst) *n.* **1.** The principal mast of a vessel. **2.** The taller mast, whether forward or aft, of any two-masted sailing vessel. **3.** The second mast aft of any sailing ship with three or more masts.

main roy·al·mast (roi′əl-məst). The section of the mainmast of a square-rigged vessel above the main topgallantmast.

main·sail (mān′səl) *n.* **1.** The principal sail of a vessel. **2.** A quadrilateral or triangular sail set from the after part of the mainmast on a fore-and-aft rigged vessel. **3.** A square sail set from the main yard on a square-rigged vessel.

main sequence. A major grouping of stars, containing the sun and 90 per cent of the known stars in the vicinity of the sun, characterized by an approximately uniform average increase of luminosity with surface temperature as represented by a single band on the **Hertzsprung-Russell diagram** *(see).*

main·sheet (mān′shēt′) *n.* The rope that controls the angle at which the mainsail is trimmed and set.

main·spring (mān′spring′) *n.* **1.** The principal spring in a mechanical device, especially in a watch or clock, that drives the mechanism by uncoiling. **2.** A motivating force; an impelling cause: *He was the mainspring of the reform movement.*

main·stay (mān′stā′) *n.* **1.** A strong rope that serves to steady and support the mainmast of a sailing vessel. **2.** A principal support: *Agriculture is a mainstay of the economy.*

main stem. *Slang.* The principal street in a town or city.

main·stream (mān′strēm′) *n.* The prevailing current or direction of a movement or influence: *writers in the mainstream of 18th-century thought.*

main street. 1. The principal street of an American town or city. **2.** *Capital* **M,** *capital* **S.** The culture of smug, materialistic, and provincial small towns. [Sense 2, chiefly from *Main Street* (1920), novel by Sinclair LEWIS.]

main·tain (mān-tān′) *tr.v.* **-tained, -taining, -tains. 1.** To continue; carry on; keep up: *maintain good relations; maintain a custom.* **2.** To preserve or retain: *"the presence of mind to maintain a composed exterior"* (Saki). **3.** To keep in a condition of good repair or efficiency: *maintain public roads.* **4. a.** To provide for; bear the expenses of: *maintain a family.* **b.** To keep in existence; sustain: *food to maintain life.* **5.** To defend or sustain; hold against attack: *"Perhaps the Germans could not maintain the corridor."* (Winston Churchill). **6.** To declare to be true; defend against dispute: *The defendant maintains his innocence.* **7.** To assert in or as if in an argument; state; declare: *"Descartes maintained that thought was the essence of the mind."* (David Hume). —See Synonyms at **support.** [Middle English *mainteine,* from Old French *maintenir,* from Medieval Latin *manūtenēre,* from Latin *manū tenēre,* "to hold in the hand," support, know : *manū,* ablative of *manus,* hand (see **man-**[2] in Appendix*) + *tenēre,* to hold (see **ten-** in Appendix*).] —**main·tain′a·ble** *adj.* —**main·tain′er** *n.*

main·te·nance (mān′tə-nəns) *n.* **1. a.** The action of continuing, carrying on, preserving, or retaining something: *maintenance of the peace.* **b.** The state of being continued, carried on, preserved, or retained: *the maintenance of tribal custom.* **2.** The support or defense of an opinion, action, or cause: *an appeal to law in the maintenance of his opinions.* **3.** The work of keeping something in proper condition: *the maintenance of roads.* **4. a.** The provision of support or livelihood: *maintenance of serfs by a feudal lord.* **b.** Means of support or livelihood: *His income barely provided maintenance.* —See Synonyms at **livelihood.** [Middle English *maintenaunce,* from Old French *maintenance,* from *maintenir,* to MAINTAIN.]

Main·te·non (măɴt-nôɴ′), **Marquise de.** Title of Françoise d'Aubigné. 1635–1719. Mistress of Louis XIV and (from 1685) his second wife.

main·top (mān′tŏp′) *n.* A platform at the head of the mainmast on a square-rigged vessel.

main top·gal·lant (tə-găl′ənt). A sail or yard set from the topgallant section of a mainmast.

main top·gal·lant·mast (tə-găl′ən-məst). The section of the mainmast next above the main topmast on a square-rigged vessel.

main top·mast (tŏp′məst). The section of the mainmast on a square-rigged sailing vessel between the lower mast and the main topgallantmast.

main top·sail (tŏp′səl). The sail that is set above the mainsail.

main yard. The lower yard on a mainmast.

Mainz (mīnts). Also *French* **Ma·yence** (mȧ-yäɴs′). A city and port of West Germany, at the confluence of the Main and Rhine rivers, 20 miles southwest of Frankfurt. Population, 141,000.

maî·tre d'hô·tel (mĕ′tr′ dō-tĕl′) *pl.* **maîtres d'hôtel** (mĕ′tr′ dō-tĕl′). **1.** A head steward or butler, **major-domo** *(see).* **2.** A **headwaiter** *(see).* Also informally called "maître d'." **3.** A sauce of melted butter, chopped parsley, lemon juice, salt, and pepper. [French, "master of hotel."]

maize (māz) *n.* **1.** A grain native to the New World, **corn** *(see).* **2.** Light yellow to moderate orange yellow. See **color.** [Spanish *maíz,* from Taino *mahiz.*] —**maize** *adj.*

Maj. major.

ma·jes·tic (mə-jĕs′tĭk) *adj.* Also **ma·jes·ti·cal** (-tĭ-kəl). Having or exhibiting stateliness or great dignity; royal; dignified: *"Mrs. Crupp . . . thanked me with a majestic curtsey."* (Dickens). See Synonyms at **grand.** —**ma·jes′ti·cal·ly** *adv.*

maj·es·ty (măj′ĭs-tē) *n., pl.* **-ties. 1. a.** The greatness and dignity of a sovereign. **b.** The sovereignty and power of God. **2.** The supreme authority or power: *the majesty of the law.* **3. a.** A royal personage. **b.** *Capital* **M.** *Abbr.* **M.** A title used in speaking of or to a sovereign monarch: *His Majesty's wish; Your Majesty.* **4. a.** Royal dignity of bearing or aspect; grandeur: *"Edith was there in all her majesty of brow and figure."* (Dickens). **b.** Stateliness, splendor, or magnificence, as of appearance, style, or character; imposing quality: *the Greek statue in all the majesty of its classical beauty.* [Middle English *maieste, mageste,* from Old French *majeste,* from Latin *mājestās,* authority, grandeur. See **meg-** in Appendix.*]

Maj. Gen. major general.

ma·jol·i·ca (mə-jŏl′ĭ-kə, -yŏl′-) *n.* **1.** A type of richly colored and decorated Italian Renaissance pottery that is enameled and glazed. **2.** A modern pottery made in imitation of this. [Italian *maiolica,* from *Majolica,* medieval form of MAJORCA, where the ceramic style originated.]

ma·jor (mā′jər) *adj.* **1.** Greater in importance, rank, or stature: *a major writer; a major scientific discovery.* **2.** Serious or dangerous; requiring great attention or concern: *major difficulties; a major illness.* **3.** *Law.* Having attained full legal age. **4.** Designating the senior or older of two pupils with the same surname. Used especially in English public schools. **5.** Designating or relating to the principal field of academic specialization chosen by students in a college or university. **6.** *Logic.* More inclusive in scope, broader, as the **major premise** and **major term** *(both of which see).* **7.** *Music.* **a.** Designating a scale or mode having half steps between the third and fourth and the seventh and eighth degrees. **b.** Equivalent to the distance between the tonic note and the second or third or sixth or seventh degrees of a major scale or mode: *a major interval.* **c.** Based on a major scale: *major key.* Compare **minor.** —*n.* **1.** *Abbr.* **Maj. a.** An officer in the U.S. Army, Air Force, or Marine Corps ranking next above a captain and next below a lieutenant colonel. **b.** An officer of similar rank in other military or paramilitary organizations. **2.** *Law.* One who has reached full legal age (21 years

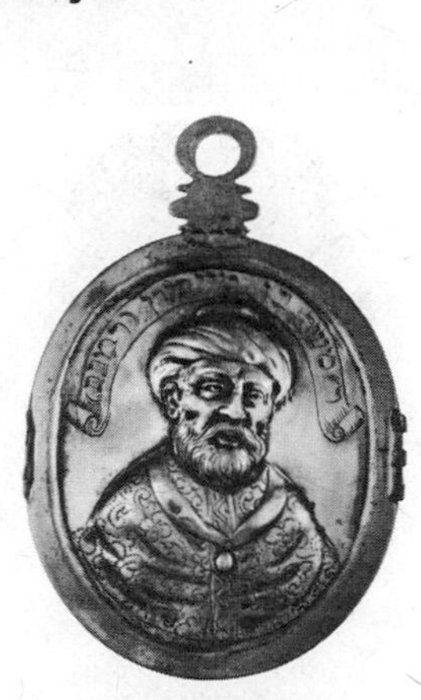

Moses Maimonides
Eighteenth-century
Italian medallion

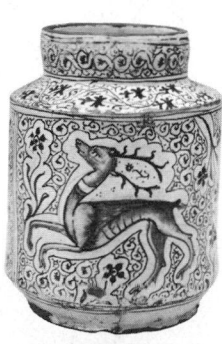

majolica
Made in 15th-century
Florence, Italy

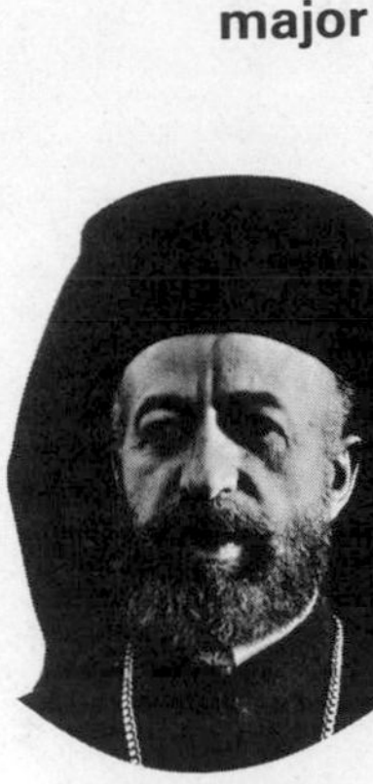

Makarios III
In Nicosia, Cyprus,
March 1964

in most of the United States). **3. a.** The principal field of academic specialization of a candidate for a degree in a college or university: *His major is chemistry.* **b.** A student specializing in such a field: *a history major.* **4.** A **major premise** or **major term** *(both of which see).* **5.** *Music.* A major scale, key, interval, or mode. **6.** *Plural. Sports.* The major leagues. —*intr.v.* **ma·jored, -joring, -jors.** To pursue academic studies in a major field. Used with *in.* [As adjective, Middle English, from Latin *mājor,* greater. See **meg-** in Appendix.* As noun (in military sense), from French, shortened from SERGEANT MAJOR.]

major axis. *Geometry.* **1.** The line intersecting an ellipse and passing through both of its focuses. **2.** The longest axis of an ellipsoid.

Ma·jor·ca (mə-yôr′kə, mə-jôr′kə). *Spanish* **Ma·llor·ca** (mä-yôr′-kä). The largest (1,405 square miles) of Spain's Balearic Islands, lying in the Mediterranean Sea, about 120 miles southeast of Barcelona. Population, 363,000. Capital, Palma. [Italian, from Latin *mājor,* larger. See **meg-** in Appendix.*] —**Ma·jor′can** *adj. & n.*

ma·jor-do·mo (mā′jər-dō′mō) *n., pl.* **-mos. 1.** The head steward or butler in the household of a sovereign or great nobleman. **2.** Any steward or butler. [Italian *maggiordomo* and Spanish *mayordomo,* from Medieval Latin *mājor domūs,* "head of the house," "mayor of the palace" : *mājor,* substantive use of Latin *mājor,* greater (see **meg-** in Appendix*) + *domūs,* genitive of Latin *domus,* house (see **demə-¹** in Appendix*).]

ma·jor·ette (mā′jər-ĕt′) *n.* A **drum majorette** *(see).*

major gene. A gene, **oligogene** *(see).*

major general. *Abbr.* **Maj. Gen.** An officer in the U.S. Army, Air Force, or Marine Corps, who ranks next above a brigadier general and next below a lieutenant general. [French *major-général* : MAJOR (officer) + *général* (adjective), "of general rank," from Old French *general,* GENERAL.]

major generalcy. The commission or rank of a major general. Also called "major generalship."

ma·jor·i·ty (mə-jôr′ĭ-tē, mə-jŏr′-) *n., pl.* **-ties. 1.** The greater number or part of something: *the majority of the consumers.* See Usage note below. **2. a.** A number more than half of the total number of a given group. Compare **minority. b.** The number of votes cast in any election above the total number of all other votes cast. Compare **plurality. 3.** The status of legal age (21 years in most states of the United States) when full civil and personal rights may be exercised legally. **4.** The political party, group, or faction having the most power by virtue of its larger representation or electoral strength. **5.** The military rank, commission, or office of a major. **6.** *Obsolete.* The fact or state of being greater; superiority. [Old French *majorite,* from Medieval Latin *mājōritās,* the state of being greater, greater number, from Latin *mājor,* greater. See **meg-** in Appendix.*]

Usage: *Majority* is often preceded by *great* (but not by *greater*) in expressing, emphatically, the sense of *most of: The great majority approved.* The construction *greater majority* is used only with reference to a comparison of two specific numbers (two majorities). When *majority* signifies a specific numerical figure, it takes a singular verb: *His majority was five votes.* When it signifies the larger of two groups, it is either singular or plural, depending on the sense involved. When the sense is that of oneness or unity, the verb is singular: *The majority is determined;* when the sense stresses the individuality of members, the verb is plural: *The majority are of different minds on this issue.* When *majority* signifies most of a given group, it takes a plural verb: *The majority of the employees oppose the rule.*

majority leader. The leader of the majority party in a legislature, as in the U.S. Senate and House of Representatives. Compare **minority leader.**

majority rule. A political doctrine by which a numerical majority of the voters holds the power to make decisions binding on all the voters.

major league. 1. Either of the two principal groups of professional baseball teams in the United States: the **American League** or the **National League** *(both of which see).* **2.** Any league of principal importance in other professional sports, such as basketball, football, or ice hockey.

ma·jor-league (mā′jər-lēg′) *adj.* In a leading position; holding high rank: *Car rental is now a major-league business.* Also "big-league."

major orders. See **holy orders.**

major party. A political party able to gain control of a government with comparative regularity. Compare **third party.**

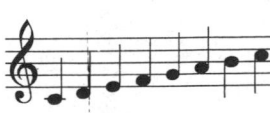

major scale
Key of C

major premise. *Logic.* In a syllogism, the premise containing the **major term** *(see).*

Major Prophets. 1. The Hebrew prophets Isaiah, Jeremiah, and Ezekiel. **2.** In the Old Testament, the books of these prophets.

major scale. *Music.* A diatonic scale having half steps between the third and fourth and the seventh and eighth tones. Compare **minor scale.**

major suit. In the game of bridge, a suit of superior scoring value, either spades or hearts.

major term. *Logic.* A term of a syllogism that forms the predicate of the conclusion and the subject or predicate of the major premise.

ma·jus·cule (mə-jŭs′kyōōl) *n.* **1.** A large letter, either capital or uncial, used in writing or printing. **2.** Writing that uses such letters. Compare **minuscule.** [French *majuscule,* from Medieval Latin *(littera) mājuscula,* largish (script), from *mājusculus,* somewhat larger, diminutive of *mājor,* larger. See **meg-** in Appendix.*] —**ma·jus′cule, ma·jus′cu·lar** (-kyə-lər) *adj.*

Ma·ka·lu (mŭk′ə-lōō′). A mountain rising to over 27,700 feet in the Himalayas, in northeastern Nepal on the border with Tibet near Mount Everest.

Ma·kar·i·os III (mä-kä′rē-ōs). Original name, Michael Christedoulos Mouskos. Born 1913. Cypriot statesman and Greek Orthodox prelate; president of Cyprus (since 1960).

Ma·kas·sar (mə-kăs′ər). Also **Ma·cas·sar. 1.** The largest city on the island of Sulawesi, Indonesia. Population, 360,000. **2.** A strait extending 600 miles between Borneo and Sulawesi.

make (māk) *v.* **made** (mād), **making, makes.** —*tr.* **1.** To create; construct; form; shape: *make a ladder from scrap lumber.* **2.** To give a new form or use to: *make a stone into a weapon.* **3.** To cause to become: *The club made him president.* **4.** To cause to acquire a stated characteristic or property: *make a stone sharp.* **5. a.** To cause to behave in a particular manner: *Heat makes a gas expand.* **b.** To compel: *make him obey.* **6.** To use or adopt for a specified purpose: *make Chicago one's home.* **7.** To bring about; cause: *make trouble.* **8.** To engage in: *make war.* **9.** To perform: *make a phone call.* **10.** To arrive at; come around to: *make a decision.* **11.** To form as one's own; acquire: *make a friend.* **12. a.** To score; achieve: *make a run in baseball; make two tricks in bridge.* **b.** To earn: *make money.* **c.** To manage to come within reach of; attain: *make a train.* **13.** *Informal.* To achieve the rank of: *make lieutenant.* **14.** To set into proper condition; prepare: *make the bed for a guest.* **15.** To prepare and start: *make a fire.* **16.** To regard as the nature or meaning. Used with *of: We don't know what to make of his behavior.* **17.** To allow provision for; provide: *make room.* **18.** To admit to transformation into: *Oak makes good building material.* **19.** To constitute: *Twenty members make a quorum.* **20.** To be the completion or satisfaction of: *That makes my day.* **21.** To succeed in becoming a member of: *make the basketball team.* **22.** To calculate as being; estimate: *We make the distance 20 miles.* **23. a.** To proceed over; traverse: *They expect to make 200 miles before sunset.* **b.** To travel at the rate of: *His car was making 80 miles an hour.* **24.** To develop into: *He will make a fine doctor.* **25.** To cause to be or seem: *The beard makes him quite distinguished.* **26.** *Slang.* To persuade to have sexual intercourse. —*intr.* **1. a.** To give an appearance: *She made as if to shake my hand.* **b.** To behave or act in a specified manner: *make merry.* **2.** To head in the direction; set out: *a ship making for shore.* —**make a face.** To distort the features of the face; grimace. —**make away with.** To carry off; especially, to steal. —**make bold.** To venture straightforwardly: *May I make bold to offer an opinion.* —**make book.** To accept bets on a contest or race. —**make do.** To manage or get along with something, although it may be no longer satisfactory: *She made do with her old hat until she could afford a new one.* —**make eyes.** To give amorous glances; ogle. —**make good. 1.** To carry out successfully; achieve: *He made good his plan.* **2.** To pay back: *make good one's debts.* **3.** To succeed: *make good in the big city.* —**make hay.** To take advantage of every opportunity. —**make like.** *Slang.* To imitate: *make like a bird.* —**make love. 1.** To pay court to; woo. **2.** To caress; pet. **3.** To engage in sexual intercourse. —**make out. 1. a.** To discern or see, especially with difficulty: *He could barely make out the lighthouse through the fog.* **b.** To decipher: *I can't make out his handwriting.* **2.** To understand or comprehend: *I can't make out what he is saying.* **3. a.** To write out or draw up: *He made out the invoices.* **b.** To fill in by writing: *make out an application.* **4.** To attempt to prove or imply: *He makes me out a liar.* **5.** *Slang.* To get along well; succeed: *He has made out in business.* **6.** *Slang.* To neck; pet. —**make over. 1.** To change or redo; renovate: *We made over the cellar into a playroom.* **2.** To change or transfer the ownership of, usually by means of a legal document: *He made over the property to his son.* —**make public.** To disclose to public knowledge: *He made public his attitudes.* —**make sail. 1.** To begin a voyage. **2.** To set the sails of a ship. —**make time. 1.** To travel at a specified rate of speed: *We didn't make very good time on the highway.* **2.** To move fast: *We'll have to make time, if we're going to keep the appointment.* **3.** *Slang.* To engage in flirtation: *make time with the stewardess.* —**make tracks.** *Slang.* To move with haste. —**make way.** To give room for passage. —**make whoopee.** *Slang.* To have a riotously good time. —**make with.** *Slang.* To perform; produce. Usually followed by *the: a flirt making with the eyes; start making with the hard work.* —*n.* **1.** The act or process of making. **2.** The style or manner in which a thing is made: *I dislike the make of this coat.* **3. a.** A manufacturing style. **b.** A specific line of manufactured goods, identified by the maker's name or the registered trademark: *a famous make of shirt.* **4.** The physical or moral nature of a person: *Let's see what make of man you are.* **5.** The amount produced; the yield or output, especially of a factory. —**on the make. 1.** Applying oneself brashly to social or financial self-improvement. **2.** *Slang.* Sexually active and aggressive. [Make (infinitive), made (past tense), made (past participle); Middle English *maken, mad, mad,* Old English *macian, macode, macod.* See **mag-** in Appendix.*]

make believe. To feign; pretend.

make-be·lieve (māk′bĭ-lēv′) *n.* **1. a.** Playful pretense or fanciful belief, as in the conscious suspension of reality in a child's game. **b.** One who makes believe or feigns. **2.** *Psychology.* A tendency to live in a world of fantasy. —**make′-be·lieve′** *adj.*

make fast. *Nautical.* To tie up to (a buoy, post, pile, or the like).

make·fast (māk′făst′, -făst′) *n. Nautical.* An object, such as a buoy, post, or pile, to which a boat is tied.

make-peace (māk′pēs′) *n. Rare.* A peacemaker.

mak·er (mā′kər) *n.* **1.** One that makes. **2.** *Law.* An individual who signs a promissory note. **3.** *Capital* **M.** God. Usually used with a possessive pronoun: *our Maker.* **4.** *Archaic.* A poet.

make ready. *Printing.* To prepare and adjust a printing form and press.

make-read·y (māk′rĕd′ē) *n. Printing.* The operation of preparing a form for printing by adjusting and leveling the plates to insure a clear impression.

make·shift (māk′shĭft′) *n.* Something used or assembled as a temporary or expedient substitute. —**make′shift′** *adj.*

make up. **1.** To construct something by fitting materials together or from prefabricated parts: *make up a model from a kit.* **2.** To organize something for use by adjustments: *make up the beds.* **3.** To apply cosmetics to the face. **4.** To construct fictionally or falsely: *make up an excuse.* **5.** To compose one's thoughts; come to a decision: *make up one's mind to do something.* **6.** To form a number or quantity: **a.** To collect or combine units: *make up a consignment of 50 parcels.* **b.** To comprise the units and come together: *make up a table at bridge.* **c.** To amount to: *Guerrillas make up a formidable striking force.* **7.** To make a number or quantity higher, as by adding or joining: *One vote would make up a majority.* **8. a.** To fill up a remaining deficit: *make up the difference.* **b.** To resolve a personal difference: *They made up after their quarrel.* **c.** To make ingratiating overtures to someone, especially with amorous intent. Used with *to.* **d.** To satisfy a grievance or debt: *I'll make it up to him.* **e.** To compensate generally for a mistake, offense, or omission: *make up for lost time.* **f.** To repeat (an examination or course one has failed). **g.** To take (an examination one has missed) at a later time.

make-up (māk′ŭp′) *n.* Also **make·up.** **1.** The way in which something is composed or arranged; construction: *the complex make-up of a large corporation.* **2.** *Printing.* The arrangement or composition, as of type or illustrations, on a page or in a book. **3.** The qualities or temperament that constitute a personality; disposition: *He has an easygoing make-up.* **4.** Cosmetics applied especially to the face. **5.** The cosmetics, costumes, wigs, and the like, that an actor uses in portraying a role. **6.** A special examination prepared for a student who has been absent from or has failed a previous examination.

make·weight (māk′wāt′) *n.* **1.** Something added on a scale in order to meet a required weight. **2.** A counterweight; counterbalance.

make-work (māk′wûrk′) *n.* Work of little or no value done only to keep someone busy; busy-work.

Ma·ke·yev·ka (mə-kā′yəf-kə). A city of the Soviet Union, in southeastern Ukraine. Population, 358,000.

Ma·khach·ka·la (mä′kăch-kə-lä′). Formerly **Pe·trovsk** (pə-trôfsk′). The capital of the Dagestan A.S.S.R, a port on the Caspian Sea. Population, 140,000.

mak·ing (mā′kĭng) *n.* **1.** The act of one that makes or the process of being made. **2.** A means of gaining success: *The job will be the making of him.* **3. a.** Something made. **b.** The amount or quantity of something made at one time: *the baker's largest making of pastry for the week.* **4.** *Often plural.* The materials or substances necessary for making or doing something: *We have the makings of a fine organization.* **5.** *Plural. Slang.* The paper and tobacco for rolling a cigarette.

ma·ku·ta. Plural of **likuta.**

mal–. Indicates: bad, badly, or wrongly; for example, **maladminister, malodorous.** [Middle English *mal-*, from Old French *mal-* (prefix) and *mal* (adverb and adjective), from Latin *mal-, male-* (prefix), *male* (adverb), ill, and *malus* (adjective), bad. See **mel-**[5] in Appendix.*]

Mal. **1.** Malachi (Old Testament). **2.** Malay; Malayan.

Mal·a·bar (măl′ə-bär′). A coastal region of India, extending 450 miles along the Arabian Sea northwestward from Cape Comorin, and between 30 and 70 miles inland to the Western Ghats. Also called "Malabar Coast."

Ma·lac·ca[1] (mə-lăk′ə). **1.** A state of Malaysia, 633 square miles in area, on the west coast of the Malay Peninsula. Population, 372,000. **2.** The capital and a port city of this state. Population, 70,000. **3.** A strait 500 miles long between Sumatra and the Malay Peninsula, joining the Andaman and South China seas.

Ma·lac·ca[2] (mə-lăk′ə) *n.* The stem of the rattan palm of Asia, used for walking sticks. [From MALACCA.]

Mal·a·chi[1] (măl′ə-kī′). A Hebrew prophet of the fifth century B.C., the last of the **Minor Prophets** *(see).*

Mal·a·chi[2] (măl′ə-kī′) *n. Abbr.* **Mal.** A prophetic book of the Old Testament attributed to Malachi.

mal·a·chite (măl′ə-kīt′) *n.* A green to nearly black mineral carbonate of copper, $CuCO_3 \cdot Cu(OH)_2$, used as a source of copper and for ornamental stoneware. [French *malachite*, from Old French *melochite*, from Latin *molochītēs*, from Greek *molokhitis*, malachite, "the mallow-green stone," from *molokhē*, variant of *malakhē*, mallow. See **malakhē** in Appendix.*]

mal·a·col·o·gy (măl′ə-kŏl′ə-jē) *n.* The scientific study of mollusks. [French *malacologie*, abbreviation of *malacozoologie;* New Latin *Malacozoa*, mollusks : Greek *malakos*, soft (see **mel-**[1] in Appendix*) + -ZOA + -LOGY.]

mal·ad·just·ment (măl′ə-jŭst′mənt) *n.* **1.** Faulty adjustment, as in a machine. **2.** *Psychology.* Inability to adjust personality needs to the demands of the environment. **3.** Imbalance in social and economic relations, as between city and country or supply and demand. —**mal′ad·just′ed** *adj.*

mal·ad·min·is·ter (măl′əd-mĭn′ĭs-tər) *tr.v.* **-tered, -tering, -ters.** To administer or manage inefficiently or dishonestly. —**mal′ad·min′is·tra′tion** (măl′əd-mĭn′ĭs-trā′shən) *n.*

mal·a·droit (măl′ə-droit′) *adj.* **1.** Characterized by a lack of dexterity; clumsy. **2.** Characterized by a lack of perception or judgment; tactless. —See Synonyms at **awkward.** [French, from Old French : MAL- + ADROIT.] —**mal′a·droit′ly** *adv.*

mal·a·dy (măl′ə-dē) *n., pl.* **-dies.** **1.** A disease, disorder, or ailment: *"There were many sick of a malady that would not be healed."* (J.R.R. Tolkien). **2.** Any unwholesome condition. [Middle English *maladie*, from Old French, from *malade*, sick, from Latin *male habitus*, "ill-kept," "in poor condition" : *male*, ill, from *malus*, bad (see **mel-**[5] in Appendix*) + *habitus*, past participle of *habēre*, to have, keep (see **ghabh-** in Appendix*).]

ma·la fi·de (mā′lə fī′dē). *Latin.* In bad faith. Compare **bona fide.**

Mál·a·ga (măl′ə-gə; *Spanish* mä′lä-gä). A city of Spain on the Mediterranean Sea, about 60 miles northeast of Gibraltar. Population, 325,000.

Mal·a·ga (măl′ə-gə) *n.* A sweet wine originally from Málaga.

Mal·a·gas·y (măl′ə-găs′ē) *n.* **1.** A native of the Malagasy Republic. **2.** The Austronesian language spoken in the Malagasy Republic. —**Mal′a·gas′y** *adj.*

Mal·a·gas·y Republic (măl′ə-găs′ē). A country occupying the island of Madagascar, independent since 1960; a former French colony. Population, 5,862,000. Capital, Tananarive.

ma·la·gue·ña (mä′lä-gā′nyä) *n.* **1.** A dance native to Málaga. It is a variety of fandango. **2.** The music for such a dance. [Spanish, feminine of *malagueño*, of MÁLAGA.]

mal·aise (măl-āz′; *French* mà-lĕz′) *n.* A feeling of illness or depression. [French, from Old French : MAL- + *aise*, EASE.]

ma·la·mute, ma·le·mute (mä′lə-myōōt′, măl′ə-) *n.* Also **ma·le·miut.** A powerful dog of a breed developed in Alaska as a sled dog, having a thick gray, black, or white coat. Also called "Alaskan malamute." [Innuit Eskimo *Mahlemut*, name of the Alaskan tribe that bred the dog.]

Ma·lan (mə-lăn′, -län′), **Daniel François.** 1874–1959. South African journalist and statesman; prime minister (1948–54).

Ma·lang (mä-läng′). A city in east-central Java, Indonesia. Population, 342,000.

mal·a·pert (măl′ə-pûrt′) *adj. Rare.* Saucy in speech or manner; impudent; bold. —*n. Rare.* An impudent, saucy person. [Middle English, from Old French : MAL- + *apert*, clever, from Latin *apertus*, open, from past participle of *aperīre*, to open (see **wer-**[5] in Appendix*).] —**mal′a·pert′ly** *adv.* —**mal′a·pert′ness** *n.*

mal·a·prop·ism (măl′ə-prŏp-ĭz′əm) *n.* A humorous misuse of a word; for example, "a shrewd awakening." [From Mrs. Malaprop in Sheridan's play *The Rivals;* from MALAPROPOS.] —**mal′a·prop′i·an** (măl′ə-prŏp′ē-ən) *adj.*

mal·a·pro·pos (măl′ăp-rə-pō′) *adj.* Inappropriate; out of place. —*adv.* In an inappropriate or inopportune manner. [French *mal à propos*, "not to the purpose."]

ma·lar (mā′lər) *adj. Anatomy.* Of or pertaining to the cheekbone or the cheek. —*n. Anatomy.* The zygomatic bone in the cheek. [Latin *mālāris*, from *māla*†, cheekbone, upper jaw. See also **maxilla.**]

Mä·lar, Lake (mā′lär′). *Swedish* **Mä·lar·en** (mĕ′lär′ən). A lake of Sweden, extending 70 miles westward from Stockholm.

ma·lar·i·a (mə-lâr′ē-ə) *n.* **1.** An infectious disease characterized by cycles of chills, fever, and sweating, transmitted by the bite of the infected female anopheles mosquito. Also called "paludism," "swamp fever." **2.** *Obsolete.* Bad or foul air. [Italian *mal'aria*, foul air (hence, also the fever once erroneously associated with it) : *mal(a)*, feminine of *malo*, bad, from Latin *malus* (see **mel-**[5] in Appendix*) + *aria*, air, from Latin *āēr*, from Greek *aēr* (see **wē-** in Appendix*).] —**ma·lar′i·al, ma·lar′i·an, ma·lar′i·ous** *adj.*

ma·lar·key (mə-lär′kē) *n.* Also **ma·lar·ky.** *Slang.* Exaggerated or meaningless talk; nonsense. [Origin unknown.]

Mal·a·spi·na (măl′ə-spē′nə). A glacier covering 1,500 square miles on the slopes of St. Elias Range, in southeastern Alaska.

mal·as·sim·i·la·tion (măl′ə-sĭm′ə-lā′shən) *n. Pathology.* Incomplete assimilation of food.

mal·ate (măl′āt′, mā′lāt′) *n.* A salt or an ester of malic acid. [MAL(IC ACID) + -ATE.]

Mal·a·thi·on (măl′ə-thī′ŏn′) *n.* A trademark for an organic compound, $C_{10}H_{19}O_6PS_2$, used as an insecticide.

Ma·la·wi, Republic of (mä-lä′wē). A country of southeastern Africa, independent since 1964. Formerly, the British protectorate of Nyasaland. Population, 3,900,000. Capital, Zomba.

Ma·lay (mā′lā′, mə-lā′) *n. Abbr.* **Mal.** **1.** One of a people inhabiting the Malay Peninsula, other parts of Malaysia, Indonesia, and some adjacent areas. **2.** The Austronesian language of the Malays. **3.** One of a breed of fowl with red and black plumage, domesticated in Asia. —*adj.* **1.** Of, pertaining to, or characteristic of the Malays or their language. **2.** Of or pertaining to Malaya or Malaysia. [Obsolete Dutch *Malayo*, from Malay *Mĕlayu*, ethnic name.] —**Ma·lay′an** *adj.* & *n.*

Ma·lay·a (mə-lā′ə). **1.** The **Malay Peninsula** *(see).* **2.** Officially, Federation of Malaya. Formerly, Malay States, Malayan Union. A former independent federation of 11 Malay states (1957–63); a British protectorate (1948–57). Compare **Malaysia.**

Mal·a·ya·lam (măl′ə-yä′ləm) *n.* A Dravidian language spoken on the Malabar coast in southwestern India.

Ma·lay Archipelago (mā′lā′, mə-lā′). A group of islands in the Indian and Pacific oceans, including Sumatra, Java, Borneo, Sulawesi (formerly Celebes), Timor, Nusa Tenggara, the Moluccas, the Philippines, and sometimes New Guinea.

Ma·lay·o-Pol·y·ne·sian (mə-lā′ō-pŏl′ə-nē′zhən, -shən) *n.* **Austronesian** *(see).* —**Ma·lay′o-Pol′y·ne′sian** *adj.*

Ma·lay Peninsula (mā′lā′, mə-lā′). A narrow southward extension of Asia, composed of the Malayan states of Malaysia and segments of Thailand and Burma. Also called "Malaya."

Ma·lay·sia (mə-lā′zhə, -shə). A country of southeast Asia independent since 1963. It is composed of the states of the

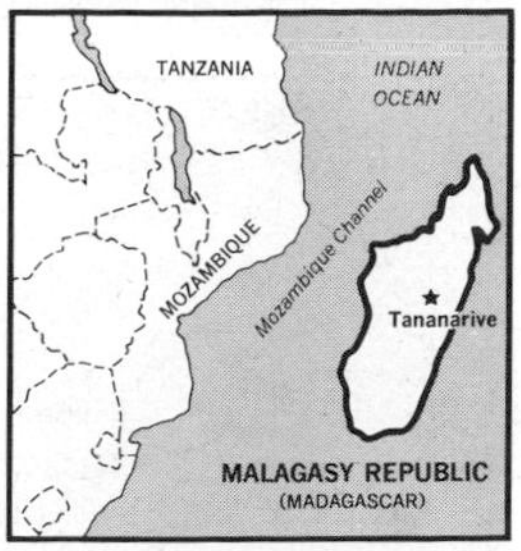

Malagasy Republic

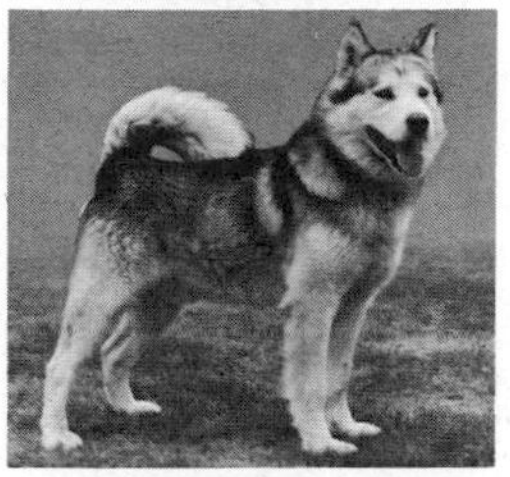

malamute

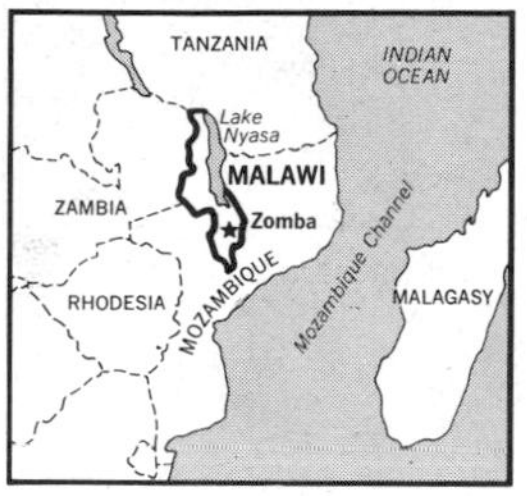

Malawi

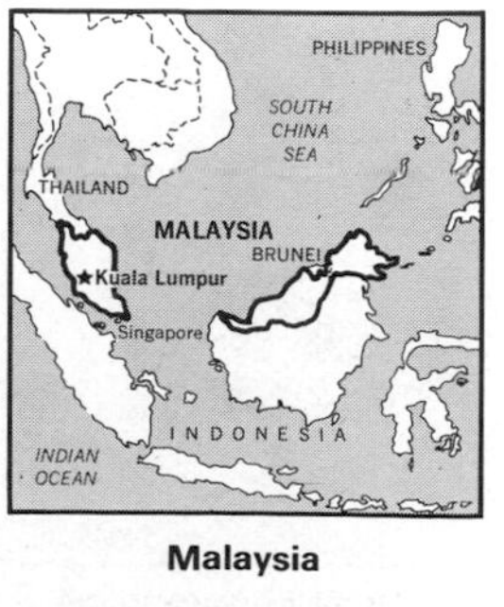

Malaysia

t tight/th thin, path/*th* this, bathe/ŭ cut/ûr urge/v valve/w with/y yes/z zebra, size/zh vision/ə about, item, edible, gallop, circus/ à *Fr.* ami/œ *Fr.* feu, *Ger.* schön/ü *Fr.* tu, *Ger.* über/KH *Ger.* ich, *Scot.* loch/N *Fr.* bon. ***Follows main vocabulary.** **†Of obscure origin.**

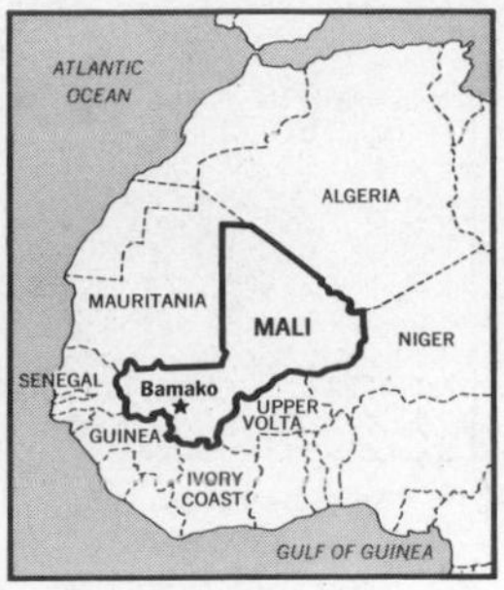

Mali

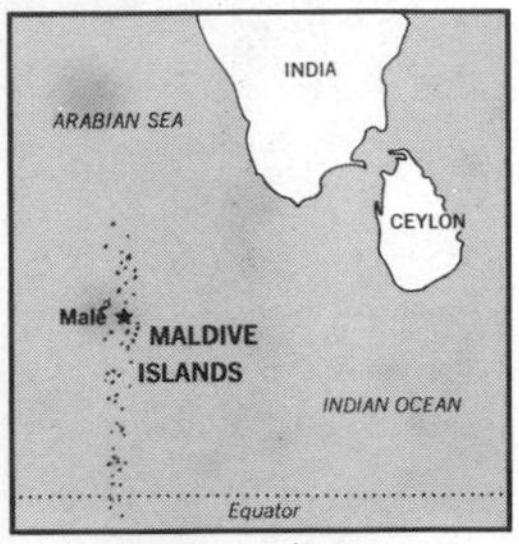

Maldive Islands

former Federation of Malaya and the former British colonies of Sarawak and British North Borneo (now Sabah). Population, 9,137,000. Capital, Kuala Lumpur. —**Ma·lay′sian** *adj.* & *n.*

Mal·colm (măl′kəm). A masculine given name. [Gaelic *Maelcolm*, from Old Gaelic *máel Coluim*, "servant of (Saint) Columba" : *máel*, bald, hence (because Celtic servants had shaved heads), servant (see **mai-¹** in Appendix*) + *Coluim*, of (Saint) COLUMBA.]

Mal·colm X (măl′kəm ĕks). Original name, Malcolm Little. Also called Al Hajj Malik Shabazz. 1925–1965. A leader of the **Nation of Islam** *(see)* until he founded his own movement (1964); assassinated.

mal·con·tent (măl′kən-tĕnt′) *adj.* Discontented with or in rebellion against established conditions. —*n.* A discontented person. [French : MAL- + CONTENT.]

Mal·den (môl′dən). A city in Massachusetts, five miles north of Boston. Population, 58,000.

Mal·dive Islands (măl′dīv′). An island group in the Indian Ocean, southwest of India, constituting a self-governing sultanate since 1965. Formerly a British protectorate. Population, 96,000. Principal island and capital, Malé. —**Mal·div′i·an** (măl-dĭv′ē-ən), **Mal·di′van** (-dī′vən) *adj.* & *n.*

male (māl) *adj. Abbr.* **m, M, m., M.** **1.** Of, pertaining to, or designating the sex that has organs to produce spermatozoa for fertilizing ova. **2.** Of or characteristic of the male sex; masculine: *"It was the immemorial male reply to the restless woman."* (Sinclair Lewis). **3.** Virile; manly. **4.** Composed of men or boys, or both: *a male choir.* **5.** *Botany.* **a.** Pertaining to or designating organs, such as stamens or anthers, that are capable of fertilizing female organs. **b.** Bearing stamens but not pistils; staminate: *male flowers.* **6.** Designating an object, such as an electric plug, designed for insertion into a fitted bore or socket. —*n. Abbr.* **m, M, m., M.** **1.** An individual of the sex that begets young by fertilizing ova. **2.** A plant having only staminate flowers. [Middle English, from Old French *male, masle*, from Latin *masculus*, diminutive of *mas*, male. See **mas** in Appendix.*] —**male′ness** *n.*

Synonyms: *male, masculine, manlike, manly, manful, virile, mannish.* The adjective *male* is confined to categorizing by sex, and applies to more than human beings. *Masculine*, when limited to human beings, pertains to qualities characteristic of males: *masculine charm. Manlike*, when applied to human beings, pertains to men as opposed to women and children; said of other animals, it indicates resemblance to a human being. *Manly* pertains broadly to admirable qualities of men. *Manful* suggests braveness, resoluteness, or forcefulness. *Virile* stresses physical prowess or sexual potency. *Mannish* usually indicates affectation of masculine traits or style by women.

Ma·lé (mä′lā). **1.** The principal island of the Maldive Islands. **2.** The capital of the Maldive Islands. Population, 11,000.

Male·branche (mál-bräNsh′), **Nicolas de.** 1638–1715. French metaphysical philosopher.

Mal·e·cite (măl′ə-sīt′) *n., pl.* **Malecite** or **-cites.** Also **Mal·i·seet** (măl′ə-sēt′). **1.** A tribe of Algonquian-speaking Indians formerly inhabiting what is now New Brunswick, Canada, and northeastern Maine. **2.** A member of this tribe. **3.** The Algonquian language of this tribe. [Probably from Micmac *Maliisit*, "he talks lazily."] —**Mal′e·cite′** *adj.*

mal·e·dict (măl′ə-dĭkt′) *adj. Rare.* Accursed. —*tr.v.* **maledicted, -dicting, -dicts.** *Rare.* To pronounce a curse against. [Middle English, from Latin *maledictus*, past participle of *maledīcere*, to speak ill of, curse : *male*, ill, from *malus*, bad (see **mel-⁵** in Appendix*) + *dīcere*, to say (see **deik-** in Appendix*).]

mal·e·dic·tion (măl′ə-dĭk′shən) *n.* **1.** A curse. **2.** Slander; calumny. —**mal′e·dic′to·ry** *adj.*

mal·e·fac·tor (măl′ə-făk′tər) *n.* **1.** One who has committed a crime; a criminal. **2.** An evildoer. [Middle English, from Latin *malefactor*, from *malefacere*, to do wrong : *male*, ill, from *malus*, bad (see **mel-⁵** in Appendix*) + *facere*, to do (see **dhē-¹** in Appendix*).] —**mal′e·fac′tion** (măl′ə-făk′shən) *n.*

mal·e·fac·tress (măl′ə-făk′trĭs) *n.* A woman who is an evildoer.

male fern. A fern, *Dryopteris filix-mas*, that yields the drug used to treat tapeworm infestation.

ma·lef·ic (mə-lĕf′ĭk) *adj.* Producing or causing evil; causing disaster. [Latin *maleficus*, wrongdoing (adjective) : *male*, ill, from *malus*, bad (see **mel-⁵** in Appendix*) + -FIC.]

ma·lef·i·cence (mə-lĕf′ə-səns) *n.* **1.** Evil or harm; mischief; evildoing. **2.** Harmful or evil nature or quality. [Latin *maleficentia*, from *maleficus*, MALEFIC.] —**ma·lef′i·cent** *adj.*

ma·le·mute, ma·le·miut. Variants of **malamute.**

Ma·len·kov (mä′lĕn-kôf′), **Georgi Maximilianovich.** Born 1902. Premier of U.S.S.R. (1953–55).

ma·lev·o·lence (mə-lĕv′ə-ləns) *n.* **1.** Ill will toward others; rancor; malice: *"that malevolence of disposition, of which at our birth we partake in common with the savage creation"* (Fielding). **2.** Evil influence, especially supernatural: *"the old belief in the malevolence of the dead body"* (Ambrose Bierce).

ma·lev·o·lent (mə-lĕv′ə-lənt) *adj.* **1.** Having or exhibiting ill will; wishing harm to others; malicious: *"the lynx, which looked like a huge and exceedingly malevolent pussy-cat"* (Theodore Roosevelt). **2.** Having an evil influence: *"Our malevolent stars have struggled hard, / And held us long asunder."* (Dryden). [Latin *malevolēns* : *male*, ill, from *malus*, bad (see **mel-⁵** in Appendix*) + *volēns*, present participle of *velle*, to will; wish (see **wel-²** in Appendix*).] —**ma·lev′o·lent·ly** *adv.*

mal·fea·sance (măl-fē′zəns) *n. Law.* Misconduct or wrongdoing; especially, wrongdoing that is illegal or contrary to official obligations. Compare **misfeasance, nonfeasance.** [MAL- + Old French *faisance*, doing, from Medieval Latin *faciēntia*, from Latin *facere*, to do (see **dhē-¹** in Appendix*).] —**mal·fea′sant** *adj.* & *n.*

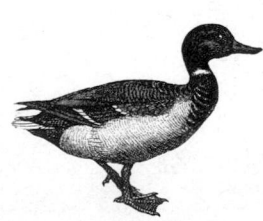

mallard
A male of the species

mal·for·ma·tion (măl′fôr-mā′shən) *n.* **1.** The condition of being malformed. **2.** An abnormal structure or form.

mal·formed (măl-fôrmd′) *adj.* Abnormally or faultily formed.

mal·func·tion (măl-fŭngk′shən) *intr.v.* **-tioned, -tioning, -tions.** **1.** To fail to function. **2.** To function abnormally; perform imperfectly. —*n.* The act or an instance of malfunctioning.

Mal·herbe (mál-ĕrb′), **François de.** 1555–1628. French court poet; founder of French classical poetics.

Ma·li (mä′lē). A republic of Africa, 464,873 square miles in area; independent since 1960; formerly part of French West Africa. Population, 4,485,000. Capital, Bamako. —**Ma′li** *adj.*

mal·ic acid (măl′ĭk, mā′lĭk). A colorless, crystalline compound, $COOHCH_2CH(OH)COOH$, that occurs naturally in a wide variety of unripe fruit, including apples, cherries, and tomatoes, and is used as a flavoring and to aid in aging wine. [French *acide malique; malique* from Latin *mālum*, apple, from Doric Greek *malon*, variant of Attic *mēlon*. See **mēlon** in Appendix.*]

mal·ice (măl′ĭs) *n.* **1.** The desire to harm others, or to see others suffer; ill will; spite: *"A well-meaning man is one who often does a great deal of mischief without any kind of malice."* (William Hazlitt). **2.** *Law.* The intent, without just cause or reason, to commit an unlawful act that will result in injury to another or others. Often used in the phrases *malice aforethought* and *malice prepense.* [Middle English, from Old French, from Latin *malitia*, from *malus*, bad. See **mel-⁵** in Appendix.*]

ma·li·cious (mə-lĭsh′əs) *adj.* **1.** Resulting from or having the nature of malice: *"Malicious whispers began to circulate the neighborhood at our expense."* (Goldsmith). **2.** Motivated by or experiencing malice: *"You might, if you felt malicious, call me a cold fish."* (Morris West). —**ma·li′cious·ly** *adv.* —**ma·li′cious·ness** *n.*

ma·lign (mə-līn′) *tr.v.* **-ligned, -ligning, -ligns.** To speak evil of; slander; defame. See Synonyms below. —*adj.* **1.** Evil in nature or intent. **2.** Evil in influence; injurious; baleful. —See Synonyms at **sinister.** [Middle English *maligne*, evil, baleful, from Old French, from Latin *malignus*, from *malus*, bad. See **mel-⁵** in Appendix.*] —**ma·lign′er** *n.* —**ma·lign′ly** *adv.*

Synonyms: *malign, defame, traduce, vilify, revile, vituperate, asperse, slander, calumniate, libel.* The verb *malign* applies in general to the expression of evil with malicious intent, and connotes falsehood or misrepresentation. *Defame* and *traduce* imply more open circulation of evil, maliciously motivated, and definite injury to character or reputation. *Vilify* pertains to open, deliberate, and forceful defaming or degrading. *Revile* and *vituperate* stress gross verbal abuse, which may be more spontaneous than calculated and may not involve falsehood. *Asperse* involves falsehood and calculated, malicious intent, usually expressed orally but obliquely, as by innuendo. *Slander* and *calumniate* apply to malicious oral expression which is false and defamatory. *Libel* generally involves written or pictorial expression injurious to character or reputation.

ma·lig·nan·cy (mə-lĭg′nən-sē) *n., pl.* **-cies.** Also **ma·lig·nance** (-nəns). **1.** The state or quality of being malignant. **2.** A malignant tumor.

ma·lig·nant (mə-lĭg′nənt) *adj.* **1.** Showing great malevolence; actively evil in nature. **2.** Highly injurious; pernicious. **3.** *Pathology.* **a.** Designating an abnormal growth that tends to metastasize. Compare **benign. b.** Threatening to life or health; virulent: *a malignant disease.* —**ma·lig′nant·ly** *adv.*

ma·lig·ni·ty (mə-lĭg′nə-tē) *n., pl.* **-ties.** **1. a.** Intense ill will or hatred; great malice. **b.** An act or feeling of great malice. **2.** The condition or quality of being highly evil or injurious; deadliness.

ma·li·hi·ni (mä′lĭ-hē′nē) *n.* A newcomer, foreigner, or stranger among the natives of Hawaii. [Hawaiian.]

ma·lines (mə-lēn′) *n.* **1.** A thin, stiff veiling woven in a hexagonal pattern. **2.** Also **ma·line.** A fine lace, **Mechlin** *(see).* [French, from MALINES, where the lace was originally woven.]

Ma·lines. The French name for **Mechlin.**

ma·lin·ger (mə-lĭng′gər) *intr.v.* **-gered, -gering, -gers.** To pretend to be ill or injured in order to avoid duty or work. [From French *malingre*, sickly, from Old French *malingre*†] —**ma·lin′ger·er** *n.*

Ma·lin·ke (mə-lĭng′kē) *n., pl.* **Malinke** or **-kes.** **1.** A people of western Africa related to the Mandingoes. **2.** A member of this people. **3.** The language of the Malinke.

Ma·li·now·ski (mä′lĭ-nôf′skē), **Bronislaw Kasper.** 1884–1942. Polish-born English anthropologist.

Mal·i·seet. Variant of **Malecite.**

mal·i·son (măl′ə-sən, -zən) *n. Archaic.* A curse. [Middle English *malisoun*, from Old French *maleison*, from Latin *maledictiō*, from *maledīcere*, MALEDICT.]

mall¹ (môl, măl) *n.* **1.** A shady public walk or promenade. **2.** A street lined with shops and closed to vehicles. **3.** A median strip dividing a road or highway. [From The *Mall*, a tree-lined street in London that was originally a *mall* (obsolete term for a pall-mall lane), shortened from PALL-MALL.]

mall². Variant of **maul.**

mal·lard (măl′ərd) *n., pl.* **-lards** or **mallard.** A wild duck, *Anas platyrhynchos*, of which the male has a green head and neck. It is the ancestor of most domestic ducks. [Middle English, from Old French *mallart*†.]

Mal·lar·mé (má-lár-mā′), **Stéphane.** 1842–1898. French lyric poet; leader of the symbolist school.

mal·le·a·ble (măl′ē-ə-bəl) *adj.* **1.** Capable of being shaped or formed, as by hammering or pressure: *a malleable metal.* **2.** Capable of being altered or influenced; tractable; pliable: *the*

malleable mind of the pragmatist. —See Synonyms at **flexible.** [Middle English *malliable,* from Old French *malleable,* from Medieval Latin *malleābilis,* from *malleāre,* to hammer, from *malleus,* a hammer. See **melə-** in Appendix.*] —**mal'le·a·bil'i·ty, mal'le·a·ble·ness** *n.* —**mal'le·a·bly** *adv.*

mal·lee (măl'ē) *n.* **1.** Any of several low, scrubby, evergreen trees of the genus *Eucalyptus,* of western Australia. **2.** A thicket or growth of these trees. [Native Australian name.]

mal·le·muck (măl'ə-mŭk') *n.* Any of several sea birds, such as the fulmar, the albatross, or the shearwater. [Dutch *mallemok,* fulmar : Middle Dutch *mal,* silly (see **mel-⁷** in Appendix*) + *mocke,* thing (see **muk-** in Appendix*).]

mal·let (măl'ĭt) *n.* **1. a.** A short-handled hammer, usually with a cylindrical head of wood, used chiefly to drive a chisel or wedge. **b.** Any of various specialized forms of the tool. **2.** *Sports.* A longer handled, similar implement used to strike the ball, as in croquet and polo. [Middle English *maillet,* from Old French, from *mailler,* to hammer, from *mail,* a hammer, from Latin *malleus,* hammer. See **melə-** in Appendix.*]

mal·le·us (măl'ē-əs) *n., pl.* **mallei** (măl'ē-ī', -ē-ē'). The largest of three small bones in the middle ear. Also called "hammer." See **ear.** [Latin, "hammer." See **melə-** in Appendix.*]

Ma·llor·ca. The Spanish name for **Majorca.**

mal·low (măl'ō) *n.* **1.** Any plant of the widely distributed genus *Malva,* characteristically having pink or white flowers. **2.** Any of various related plants, such as the **rose mallow** *(see).* [Middle English *malwe,* Old English *mealuwe, mealwe,* from Latin *malva,* mallow. See **malakhē** in Appendix.*]

malm (mäm) *n.* **1. a.** A soft, easily crumbled limestone. **b.** Loam formed by the disintegration of such limestone. **2.** A mixture of clay and chalk used in making bricks. [Middle English *malme,* Old English *mealm-* (only in compounds). See **melə-** in Appendix.*]

Malmes·bur·y (mämz'bər-ē), **William of.** English historian of the early 12th century.

Mal·mö (măl'mō). A seaport and the third-largest city of Sweden, on the Öresund. Population, 233,000.

malm·sey (mäm'zē) *n., pl.* **-seys.** A sweet fortified white wine originally made in Greece, but now also produced in Madeira, the Canary Islands, the Azores, and Spain. [Middle English, from Medieval Latin *Malmasia,* alteration of Greek *Monembasia,* Greek seaport from which it was shipped.]

mal·nour·ished (măl-nûr'ĭsht) *adj.* Suffering from improper nutrition or insufficient food.

mal·nu·tri·tion (măl'nōō-trĭsh'ən, măl'nyōō-) *n.* Poor nutrition because of insufficient or poorly balanced diet or because of defective digestion or defective utilization of foods.

mal·oc·clu·sion (măl'ə-klōō'zhən) *n.* Faulty closure of teeth.

mal·o·dor·ous (măl-ō'dər-əs) *adj.* Having a bad odor; ill-smelling: *"As we were opening the door a faint, malodorous air seemed to exhale through the gaps."* (Bram Stoker). —**mal·o'dor·ous·ly** *adv.* —**mal·o'dor·ous·ness** *n.*

Ma·lone (mə-lōn'), **Edmond** or **Edmund.** 1741–1812. Irish scholar, critic, and editor of Shakespeare.

Mal·o·ry (măl'ə-rē), Sir **Thomas.** English author of the 15th century; compiler of *Le Morte d'Arthur.*

Mal·pi·ghi (mäl-pē'gē), **Marcello.** 1628–1694. Italian anatomist; discoverer of the capillary system.

Mal·pigh·i·an corpuscle (măl-pĭg'ē-ən). *Anatomy.* **1.** A mass of arterial capillaries enveloped in a capsule and attached to a tubule in the kidney. Also called "Malpighian body." **2.** A lymph nodule surrounding the smaller arteries in the spleen. [Discovered by Marcello MALPIGHI.]

Malpighian layer. *Anatomy.* The deepest layer of the epidermis, from which the outer layers develop.

Malpighian tube. *Entomology.* One of the excretory tubes leading from the digestive tract in insects.

mal·po·si·tion (măl'pə-zĭsh'ən) *n.* An abnormal position, especially of a fetus.

mal·prac·tice (măl-prăk'tĭs) *n.* Also **mal·prax·is** (măl-prăk'sĭs). **1.** Improper or negligent treatment of a patient by a physician, resulting in damage or injury. **2.** Improper or unethical conduct by the holder of an official or professional position. **3.** An improper practice. —**mal'prac·ti'tion·er** *n.*

Mal·raux (măl-rō'), **André.** Born 1901. French statesman and adventurer; author of novels and works on aesthetics.

malt (môlt) *n.* **1.** Grain, usually barley, that has been allowed to sprout, used chiefly in brewing and distilling. **2.** Any alcoholic beverage brewed from malt. **3.** *Informal.* A drink made with **malted milk** *(see).* —*v.* **malted, malting, malts.** —*tr.* **1.** To process (grain) into malt. **2.** To treat or to mix with malt or a malt extract. —*intr.* To become malt. [Middle English *malt,* Old English *mealt.* See **mel-¹** in Appendix.*]

Mal·ta (môl'tə). **1.** Ancient name **Mel·i·ta** (mĕl'ĭ-tə). The chief island of a group of three in the Mediterranean Sea, just south of Sicily. **2.** A country composed of these islands, 122 square miles in area, formerly a British colony, and independent since 1964. Population, 324,000. Capital, Valletta.

Malta fever. **Undulant fever** *(see).*

mal·tase (môl'tās', -tāz') *n.* An enzyme that hydrolyzes maltose to glucose.

mal·ted milk (môl'tĭd). **1.** A soluble powder made of dried milk, malted barley, and wheat flour. **2.** A beverage made by mixing milk with this powder and adding ice cream and flavoring. In this sense, also called "malt," "malted."

Mal·tese (môl-tēz', -tēs') *adj.* **1.** Of or pertaining to Malta, its inhabitants, or the language spoken in Malta. **2.** Of or pertaining to the **Knights of Malta** *(see).* —*n., pl.* **Maltese. 1.** A native or inhabitant of Malta. **2.** The language spoken in Malta, a dialect of North Arabic with elements of Italian. **3.** A Maltese cat or dog.

Maltese cat. A domestic cat with short, silky, bluish-gray hair.

Maltese cross. A cross having the form of four arrowheads placed with their points toward the center of a circle.

Maltese dog. A small spaniel with long, white hair.

mal·tha (măl'thə) *n.* A black, viscous natural bitumen. [Latin, from Greek *maltha,* a mixture of wax and pitch. See **mel-¹** in Appendix.*]

Mal·thus (măl'thəs), **Thomas Robert.** 1766–1834. English economist.

Mal·thu·sian (măl-thōō'zhən, môl-) *adj.* Of or pertaining to the theory of Thomas Malthus that population tends to increase faster than food supply, with inevitably disastrous results unless the increase in population can be checked. —*n.* A believer in the theory of Thomas Malthus. —**Mal·thu'sian·ism** *n.*

malt liquor. Beer, ale, or other alcoholic liquor made by fermentation of malt.

mal·tose (môl'tōs', -tōz') *n.* A sugar, $C_{12}H_{22}O_{11} \cdot H_2O$. Also called "malt sugar." [French : English MALT + -OSE.]

mal·treat (măl-trēt') *tr.v.* **-treated, -treating, -treats.** To treat cruelly; handle roughly. See Synonyms at **abuse.** [French *maltraiter* : MAL- + *traiter,* to TREAT.] —**mal·treat'ment** *n.*

mal·va·si·a (măl'və-sē'ə) *n.* **1.** A grape from which malmsey wine is made. **2.** Malmsey wine. [Italian, from Medieval Greek *Monemvasia, Monembasia,* MALMSEY.]

mal·ver·sa·tion (măl'vər-sā'shən) *n.* Misconduct in public office. [Old French, from *malverser,* to misbehave, from Latin *male versārī* : *male,* ill, from *malus,* bad (see **mel-⁵** in Appendix*) + *versārī,* to behave (see **wer-³** in Appendix*).]

mal·voi·sie (măl'vwə-zē) *n.* Malmsey wine, or a grape from which it is made. [Middle English *malvesie,* from Old French, from Medieval Greek *Monemvasia,* MALVASIA.]

ma·ma (mä'mə, mə-mä' *for sense 1;* mä'mə *for sense 2*) *n.* Also **mam·ma. 1.** Mother. Used familiarly, chiefly by children. Also shortened to **ma. 2.** *Slang.* A voluptuous woman: *the last of the red-hot mamas.* [Baby talk. See **mā-²** in Appendix.*]

mam·ba (mäm'bə) *n.* Any of several venomous snakes of the genus *Dendraspis,* found in tropical Africa; especially, *D. angusticeps,* a green or black tree snake. [Zulu *im-amba.*]

mam·bo (mäm'bō) *n., pl.* **-bos. 1.** A dance of Latin-American origin, resembling the rumba. **2.** The syncopated music for this dance, in 4/4 time. —*intr.v.* **mamboed, -boing, -boes.** To dance the mambo. [American Spanish, from Haitian Creole *mambo,* a voodoo priestess.]

Mam·e·luke (măm'ə-lōōk') *n.* A member of a former military caste, originally composed of slaves from Turkey, that held the Egyptian throne from about 1250 until 1517 and remained powerful until 1811.

mam·ma (măm'ə) *n., pl.* **mammae** (măm'ē', măm'ī'). An organ of female mammals that contains milk-producing glands; a breast or udder. [Latin. See **mā-²** in Appendix.*]

mam·mal (măm'əl) *n.* A member of the class **Mammalia** *(see).* —**mam·mal'i·an** (mă-mā'lē-ən) *adj.* & *n.*

Mam·ma·li·a (mă-mā'lē-ə, -māl'yə) *pl.n.* A class of vertebrate animals of more than 15,000 species, including man, distinguished by self-regulating body temperature, hair, and, in the females, milk-producing mammae. [New Latin, from Latin *mammalis,* of the breast, from *mamma,* breast. See **mā-²** in Appendix.*]

mam·mal·o·gy (mă-măl'ə-jē) *n.* The branch of zoology dealing with the study of Mammalia. [Irregular compound of MAMMA(L) + -LOGY.] —**mam'ma·log'i·cal** (măm'ə-lŏj'ĭ-kəl) *adj.* —**mam·mal'o·gist** (mă-măl'ə-jĭst) *n.*

mam·ma·ry (măm'ər-ē) *adj.* Of or pertaining to a breast or **mamma** *(see).*

mammary gland. A milk-producing organ in female mammals, consisting of clusters of alveoli or small cavities with ducts terminating in a nipple or teat.

mam·mee apple (mă-mē'). **1.** A tree, *Mammea americana,* of the American tropics, cultivated for its large, edible fruit. **2.** The fruit of this tree, having a reddish rind and yellow pulp. Also called "mamey." [Spanish *mamey,* from Taino.]

mam·mif·er·ous (mă-mĭf'ər-əs) *adj.* Having mammary glands. [French *mammifère* : Latin *mamma,* breast (see **mā-²** in Appendix*) + -FEROUS.]

mam·mil·la (mă-mĭl'ə) *n., pl.* **-millae** (-mĭl'ē). **1.** A nipple or teat. **2.** Any nipple-shaped protuberance. [Latin, diminutive of *mamma,* breast. See **mā-²** in Appendix.*] —**mam'mil·lar'y** (măm'ə-lĕr'ē) *adj.*

mam·mil·late (măm'ĭ-lāt') *adj.* Also **mam·mil·lat·ed** (măm'ə-lāt'ĭd). **1.** Having nipples or mammillae. **2.** Shaped like a nipple or mammilla. —**mam'mil·la'tion** *n.*

Mam·mon (măm'ən) *n.* **1.** In the New Testament, riches, avarice, and worldly gain personified as a false god. Matthew 6:24; Luke 16:9,11,13. **2.** *Often small* **m.** Riches regarded as an object of worship or an evil influence. [Middle English *Mammona,* from Medieval Latin *mammōna,* from Greek *mamōnas,* from Aramaic *māmōnā,* riches.]

mam·moth (măm'əth) *n.* **1.** An extinct elephant of the genus *Mammuthus,* once found throughout the Northern Hemisphere. The best-known species is the woolly mammoth, *M. primigenius,* of northern Eurasia and North America. **2.** Something of great size. —*adj.* Of enormous size; huge; gigantic. See Synonyms at **enormous.** [Obsolete Russian *mammot',* from Tartar *mamont,* "earth" (probably because mammoths were believed to have burrowed).]

Mammoth Cave National Park. A national park of 79 square miles in central Kentucky, noted for limestone caverns.

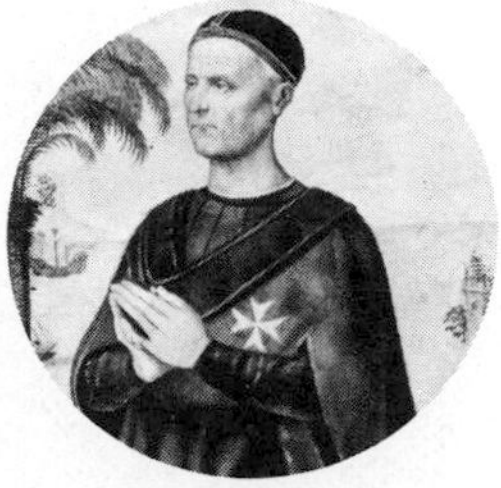

Maltese cross
Worn as a badge by a Hospitaler in a painting by Pinturicchio

mallet

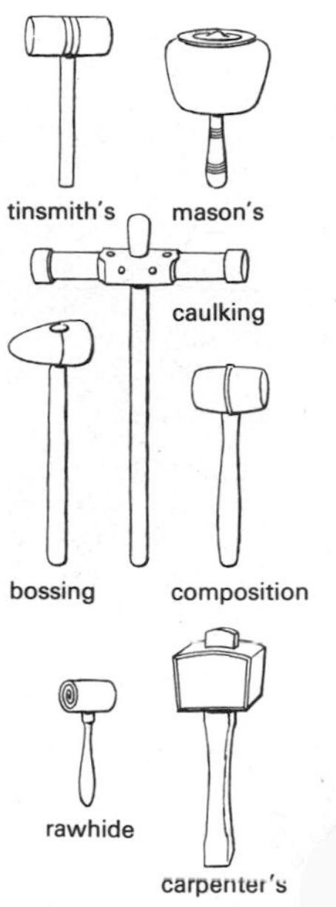
tinsmith's
mason's
caulking
bossing
composition
rawhide
carpenter's

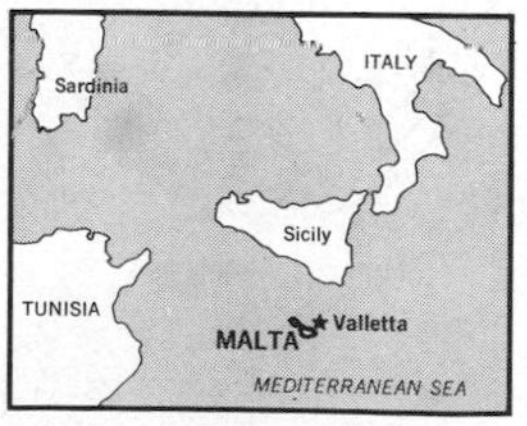
Sardinia
ITALY
Sicily
TUNISIA
MALTA
Valletta
MEDITERRANEAN SEA

Malta

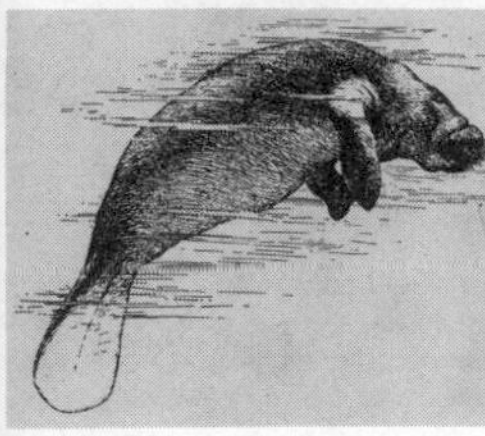

manatee
Trichechus manatus

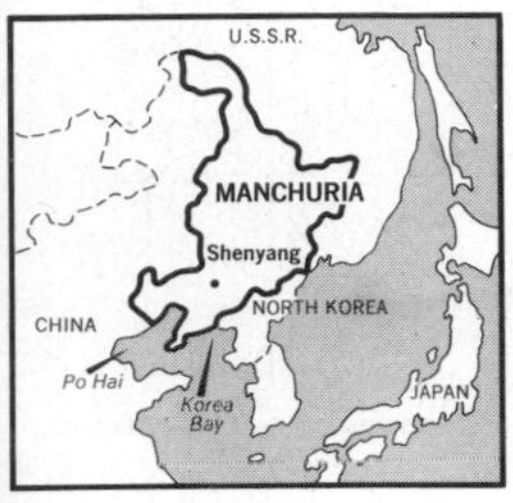

Manchuria

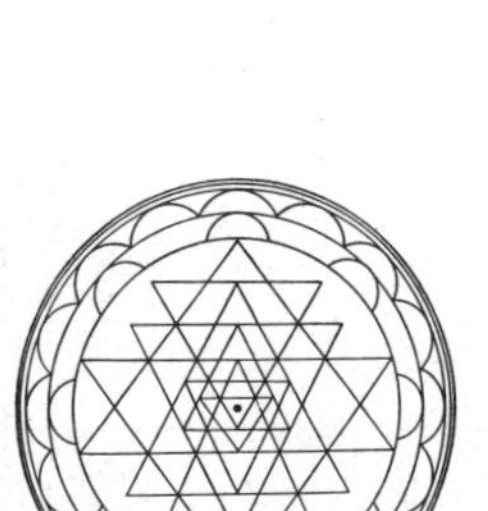

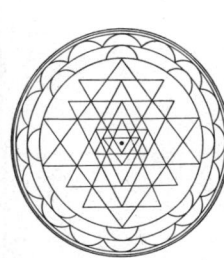

mandala

mam·my (măm′ē) *n., pl.* **-mies.** Also **mam·mie. 1.** Mother. Used familiarly, especially by children. **2.** *Chiefly Southern U.S.* A Negro nurse for white children. Often used disparagingly. [Baby talk, variant of MAMA.]

Ma·mo·ré (mä′mō-rā′). A river rising in north-central Bolivia, and flowing 700 miles to and along the Brazilian border until, with the Beni, it forms the Madeira.

man (măn) *n., pl.* **men** (mĕn). **1.** An adult male human being, as distinguished from a female. **2.** Any human being, regardless of sex or age; a member of the human race; a person. **3.** The human race; mankind. Used without an article: *the accomplishments of man.* **4.** *Zoology.* A member of the genus *Homo,* family Hominidae, order Primates, class Mammalia, characterized by erect posture and an opposable thumb; especially, a member of the only extant species, *Homo sapiens,* distinguished by the ability to communicate by means of organized speech and to record information in a variety of symbolic systems. **5.** A male human being endowed with such qualities as courage, strength, and fortitude, considered characteristic of manhood. **6.** *Theology.* In Christianity and Judaism, a being composed of a body and a soul or spirit. **7.** A husband, lover, or sweetheart. Now used chiefly informally, except in the phrase *man and wife.* **8.** An enlisted serviceman of the armed forces. Used chiefly in the plural: *officers and men.* **9.** Any workman, servant, or subordinate, as opposed to an employer or master. **10.** *Informal.* Fellow. Used as a term of address. **11.** One who swore allegiance to a lord in the Middle Ages; a liegeman; vassal. **12.** Any of the pieces used in chess, checkers, backgammon, and other board games. **13.** *Nautical.* A ship. Used in combination: *merchantman; man-of-war.* **—as one man.** Unanimously: *They answered him as one man.* **—be one's own man.** To be independent in judgment and action. **—man and boy.** From childhood on: *Man and boy, I've lived here 40 years.* **—The Man.** *Negro Slang.* A white man. Used disparagingly. **—to a man.** Including everyone; without exceptions. *—tr.v.* **manned, manning, mans. 1.** To supply or furnish with men for defense, support, or service: *manning a ship.* **2.** To be stationed at in order to defend, care for, or operate: *man the guns.* *—adj.* Male. *—interj.* Used as an expletive to indicate excitement or to draw attention: *Man! it's hot in here.* [Middle English *man* (plural *men*), Old English *mann* (plural *menn*). See **man-**[1] in Appendix.*]

Man, Isle of (măn). A British island, 220 square miles in area, in the Irish Sea. Population, 48,000. Capital, Douglas. **—Manx** *adj. & n.*

Man. Manitoba.

ma·na (mä′nə) *n.* An impersonal supernatural force inherent in gods and sacred objects, in the native religions of Oceania. [Polynesian, akin to Hawaiian *mana,* divine power.]

man about town *pl.* **men about town.** A worldly and socially knowledgeable man who frequents fashionable places.

man·a·cle (măn′ə-kəl) *n.* Usually plural. **1.** A device for confining the hands, usually consisting of two metal rings that are fastened about the wrists and joined by a metal chain; a handcuff. **2.** Anything that confines or restrains. *—tr.v.* **manacled, -cling, -cles. 1.** To restrain with manacles. **2.** To confine or restrain as if with manacles; shackle; fetter. [Middle English *manicle,* from Old French, from Latin *manicula,* little hand, handle, diminutive of *manus,* hand. See **man-**[2] in Appendix.*]

man·age (măn′ĭj) *v.* **-aged, -aging, -ages.** *—tr.* **1.** To direct or control the use of; handle, wield, or use (a tool, machine, or weapon). **2.** To exert control over; make submissive to one's authority, discipline, or persuasion. **3.** To direct or administer (the affairs of an organization, estate, household, or business). **4.** To contrive or arrange; succeed in doing or accomplishing, especially with difficulty: *I'll manage to come on Friday.* *—intr.* **1.** To direct, supervise, or carry on business affairs; perform the duties of a manager. **2.** To carry on; get along: *I don't know how they manage without him.* —See Synonyms at **conduct.** [Italian *maneggiare,* to handle (a horse), probably from Vulgar Latin *manidiāre* (unattested), to handle, from Latin *manus,* hand. See **man-**[2] in Appendix.*] **—man′age·a·ble** *adj.* **—man′age·a·bil′i·ty, man′age·a·ble·ness** *n.* **—man′age·a·bly** *adv.*

managed currency. A monetary system in which the money supply and its buying power are regulated by a governmental agency or central bank, rather than automatically regulated by the gold standard.

man·age·ment (măn′ĭj-mənt) *n.* **1.** The act, manner, or practice of managing, handling, or controlling something. **2.** The person or persons who manage a business establishment, organization, or institution. **3.** Skill in managing; executive ability.

man·ag·er (măn′ĭj-ər) *n. Abbr.* **mgr., Mgr. 1.** A person who manages a business or other enterprise. **2.** A person who is in charge of the business affairs of an entertainer or group of entertainers. **3.** *Sports.* **a.** A person in charge of the training and performance of an athlete or team. **b.** A student in charge of the equipment and records of a school or college team. **—man′ag·er·ship** *n.*

man·a·ger·i·al (măn′ə-jîr′ē-əl) *adj.* Of, pertaining to, or characteristic of a manager or management. **—man′a·ge′ri·al·ly** *adv.*

managing editor. An executive who supervises editorial work.

Ma·na·gua (mä-nä′gwä). **1.** A lake, 390 square miles in area, in western Nicaragua. **2.** The capital of Nicaragua, on the southern shore of this lake. Population, 275,000.

man·a·kin (măn′ə-kĭn) *n.* **1.** Any of various small, colorful birds of the family Pipridae, found in forests of Central and South America. **2.** Variant of **manikin.**

Ma·na·ma (mă-nă′mə). The capital and chief port of Bahrein. Population, 79,000.

ma·ña·na (mä-nyä′nä) *adv.* **1.** Tomorrow. **2.** At some unspecified future time. *—n.* Some indefinite time in the future. [Spanish, tomorrow, from Vulgar Latin *(cras) māneāna* (unattested), "early tomorrow" : *crās,* tomorrow (see **procrastinate**) + *māneāna,* early, from Latin *māne,* in the morning (see **mā-**[1] in Appendix*).]

Ma·nas·sas (mə-năs′əs). A town of Virginia near the site of the Civil War battles of Bull Run (1861 and 1862), which the Confederates called the battles of Manassas. Population, 3,600.

Ma·nas·seh[1] (mə-năs′ə). The elder son of Joseph. Genesis 41:51.

Ma·nas·seh[2] (mə-năs′ə) *n.* A tribe of Israel descended from Manasseh, son of Joseph.

Ma·nas·seh[3] (mə-năs′ə). A king of Judah in the seventh century B.C. II Kings 21:1–18.

man-at-arms (măn′ət-ärmz′) *n., pl.* **men-at-arms.** A soldier, especially a medieval cavalryman supplied with heavy arms.

man·a·tee (măn′ə-tē′) *n.* Any aquatic mammal of the genus *Trichechus,* found in Atlantic coastal waters of the tropical Americas and Africa. [Spanish *manati,* of South American origin, perhaps akin to Cariban *manati,* breast.]

Ma·naus (mä-nous′). Formerly **Ma·náos.** A city of northwestern Brazil and capital of Amazonas, on the Rio Negro. Population, 154,000.

Man·ches·ter (măn′chĕs′tər, -chĭs-tər). **1.** A city in England, 30 miles northeast of Liverpool. Population, 638,000. **2.** A city of southeastern New Hampshire. Population, 88,000. **—Man·cu′ni·an** *n. & adj.*

Manchester terrier. A short-haired, black-and-tan dog of a breed that originated in Manchester, England. Formerly called "black-and-tan terrier."

man·chi·neel (măn′chĭ-nēl′) *n.* A tropical American tree, *Hippomane Mancinella,* having poisonous milky sap that causes skin blisters on contact, and poisonous fruit. [French *mancenille,* from Spanish *manzanilla,* "small apple," MANZANILLA.]

Man·chu (măn′cho͞o, măn-cho͞o′) *n., pl.* **Manchu** or **-chus. 1.** One of a nomadic Mongoloid people, native to Manchuria, who conquered China in 1644 and established a dynasty that was overthrown by revolution in 1911. Also called "Ch'ing." **2.** The Tungusic language of the Manchu. *—adj.* **1.** Of or pertaining to the Manchus, their dynasty, language, or culture. **2.** Of or pertaining to Manchuria. [Manchu.]

Man·chu·kuo (măn′cho͞o′kwō′). Also **Man·chou·kuo.** A former state of eastern Asia (1932–45), established by the Japanese and dissolved after World War II.

Man·chu·ri·a (măn-cho͝or′ē-ə). The northernmost region and an administrative division of China, composed of three provinces and covering 585,000 square miles. Population, 51,500,000. Principal city, Shenyang. **—Man·chu′ri·an** *adj. & n.*

Man·cu·ni·an (măn-kyo͞o′nē-ən) *n.* A native or inhabitant of Manchester, England. [From *Mancunium,* Medieval Latin name for MANCHESTER.] **—Man·cu′ni·an** *adj.*

-mancy. Indicates divination by a specific means or in a particular manner; for example, **chiromancy, necromancy.** [Middle English, from Old French *-mancie,* from Late Latin *-mantia,* from Greek *manteia,* divination, from *manteuesthai,* to prophesy, from *mantis,* a prophet. See **men-**[1] in Appendix.*]

Man·dae·an. Variant of **Mandean.**

man·da·la (mŭn′də-lə) *n.* In Oriental art and religion, any of various designs symbolic of the universe. [Sanskrit *maṇḍala,* circle, probably from Tamil *muṭalai.*]

Man·da·lay (măn′də-lā′). The second-largest city of Burma, in Upper Burma on the Irrawaddy River. Population, 322,000.

man·da·mus (măn-dā′məs) *n. Law.* A writ issued by a superior court ordering a public official or body or a lower court to perform a specified duty. *—tr.v.* **mandamused, -musing, -muses.** To serve with a mandamus. [Latin *mandāmus,* "we order," from *mandāre,* to order. See **man-**[2] in Appendix.*]

Man·dan (măn′dăn) *n., pl.* **Mandan** or **-dans. 1.** A tribe of Siouan-speaking Indians that inhabited the Missouri River Valley in North Dakota. **2.** A member of this tribe. **3.** The Siouan language of this tribe.

man·da·rin (măn′də-rĭn) *n.* **1.** In imperial China, a member of any of the nine ranks of high public officials. **2.** A high civil servant thought to exercise large undefined powers without publicity or political control. **3.** *Capital* **M. Mandarin Chinese** *(see).* **4.** *Capital* **M.** In imperial China, the dialect used by mandarins and other officials of the empire. *—adj.* **1.** Of or like a mandarin. **2.** Marked by elaborate and intricate language or literary style. [Portuguese *mandarin,* from Malay *mĕntĕri,* from Hindi *mantrī,* from Sanskrit *mantrin,* counselor, from *mantra,* counsel. See **men-**[1] in Appendix.*]

Mandarin Chinese. *Chinese* **kuo-yü** (gwô′ü′). The national language of China, based on the principal dialect spoken in the area around Peking.

mandarin duck. A waterfowl, *Aix galericulata,* of Asia, having brightly colored plumage and a crested head.

mandarin orange. The **tangerine** *(see).* [French *mandarine,* from Spanish *naranja mandarina,* from *mandarin,* a mandarin (so named because the tangerine was imported from China), from Portuguese *mandarin,* MANDARIN.]

man·da·tar·y (măn′də-târ′ē) *n., pl.* **-ies.** One that receives a mandate.

man·date (măn′dāt′) *n.* **1.** An authoritative command or instruction. **2.** The wishes of a political electorate, expressed by election results to its representatives in government. **3. a.** A commission from the League of Nations authorizing a nation to administer a territory. **b.** Any region under such administration. Compare **trusteeship, trust territory. 4.** *Law.* **a.** An order issued by a superior court of law to a lower court. **b.** A contract by which an individual agrees to perform services for another without payment. —*tr.v.* **mandated, -dating, -dates.** To assign (a colony or territory) to a specified nation under a mandate. [Latin *mandātum,* a command, from *mandāre,* to command. See **man-²** in Appendix.*]

man·da·tor (măn′dā′tər) *n.* One who gives a mandate.

man·da·to·ry (măn′də-tôr′ē, -tōr′ē) *adj.* **1.** Of, pertaining to, having the nature of, or containing a mandate. **2.** Required as if by mandate; obligatory. **3.** Holding a mandate over some region.

man-day (măn′dā′) *n., pl.* **man-days.** The work performed by one man during one day.

Man·de (män′dā) *n., pl.* **Mande** or **-des. 1.** A people of West Africa in the upper Niger valley. **2.** A branch of the Niger-Congo language family. [Mandingo : *ma-,* "mother" + *-nde,* diminutive suffix. See also **Mandingo.**]

Man·de·an (măn-dē′ən) *n.* Also **Man·dae·an. 1.** A member of an ancient Gnostic sect of Mesopotamia. **2.** An ancient form of Aramaic used by the Mandeans. —*adj.* Also **Man·dae·an.** Of or pertaining to the Mandeans. [From Mandean *mandaya,* "having knowledge," from *mandā,* knowledge.]

Man·de·ville (măn′də-vĭl′), Sir **John.** Pen name of the unknown compiler of a book describing fantastic travels in the East (India and Palestine), published 1357–71.

man·di·ble (măn′də-bəl) *n.* A jaw, especially: **a.** The lower jaw in vertebrates. **b.** Either the upper or lower part of the beak in birds. **c.** Any of various mouth parts in insects. [Old French, from Latin *mandibula,* from *mandere,* to chew. See **menth-** in Appendix.*] —**man·dib′u·lar** (măn-dĭb′yə-lər) *adj.*

man·dib·u·late (măn-dĭb′yə-lĭt, -lāt′) *n.* An animal having mandibles. —**man·dib′u·late′** (-lāt) *adj.*

Man·din·go (măn-dĭng′gō) *n., pl.* **-gos** or **-goes. 1.** A member of any of various Negroid peoples inhabiting the region of the upper Niger River valley of western Africa. **2.** Any language or dialect of the Mandingos. [Mandingo : *ma-,* "mother" + *-ndi, -nde,* diminutive suffix + *-ngo,* variant of *-ko,* suffix of nationality or tribe.]

man·do·lin (măn′də-lĭn′, măn′də-lĭn′) *n.* A musical instrument with a usually pear-shaped wooden body and a fretted neck over which several pairs of metal strings are stretched. [French *mandoline,* from Italian *mandolino,* diminutive of *mandola, mandora,* lute, from Greek *pandoura.* See **pandoura** in Appendix.*] —**man′do·lin′ist** *n.*

man·drag·o·ra (măn-drăg′ə-rə) *n. Chiefly Poetic.* The mandrake, or a narcotic prepared from it: *"not poppy, nor mandragora, nor all the drowsy syrups of the world"* (Shakespeare).

man·drake (măn′drāk′) *n.* **1.** A Eurasian plant, *Mandragora officinarum,* having purplish flowers and a branched root thought to resemble the human body, from which a narcotic was formerly prepared. This plant was once widely believed to have magical powers. **2.** A North American plant, the **May apple** *(see).* [Middle English *mandragge, mandrake* (probably influenced by DRAKE, dragon), from Middle Dutch *mandragre* and Old English *mandragora,* both from Latin *mandragoras,* from Greek *mandragoras*†.]

man·drel, man·dril (măn′drəl) *n.* **1.** A spindle or axle used to secure or support material being machined or milled. **2.** A metal core around which wood and other materials may be cast and shaped. **3.** A shaft on which a working tool is mounted, as in dental drills. [Probably alteration of French *mandrin,* a lathe, from Provençal *mandre,* axle, crank, from Old Provençal, beam of a balance, from Latin *mamphur,* bow-drill, probably from Oscan.]

man·drill (măn′drĭl) *n.* A large, fierce baboon, *Mandrillus sphinx,* of western Africa, having a beard, a crest, and a mane, tawny-greenish body hair with yellowish hair on underparts, and brilliant blue, purple, and scarlet facial markings in the adult male. [MAN + DRILL (baboon).]

mane (mān) *n.* **1. a.** The long hair along the top and sides of the neck of such mammals as the horse and the male lion. **b.** The feathers on the back of the neck and head of some pigeons. **2.** A long, thick growth of human hair. [Middle English *mane,* Old English *manu.* See **mon-** in Appendix.*]

man-eat·er (măn′ē′tər) *n.* **1.** An animal that eats human flesh. **2.** *Informal.* A woman who habitually dominates and discards lovers. —**man′-eat′ing** *adj.*

ma·nège (mă-nĕzh′) *n.* Also **ma·nege. 1.** The art and practice of training a horse in the more difficult exercises of the **haute école** *(see).* **2.** A riding academy. [French *manège,* from Italian *maneggio,* from *maneggiare,* to MANAGE.]

ma·nes, Ma·nes (mā′nēz, mä′nās) *pl.n.* In ancient Rome: **1.** The spirits of the dead, especially ancestors, deified as minor gods. **2.** Any revered spirit of one who has died. Used with a singular verb. Compare **lemures.** [Latin *mānēs,* probably "the good ones," from *mānis,* good. See **mā-¹** in Appendix.*]

Ma·net (mă-nā′), **Edouard.** 1832–1883. French painter; forerunner of impressionism.

ma·neu·ver (mə-no͞o′vər, -nyo͞o′-) *n.* Also *chiefly British* **ma·noeu·vre. 1. a.** A strategic or tactical military movement. **b.** *Often plural.* A large-scale military training exercise simulating combat. **2. a.** A movement or way of doing something generally requiring skill and dexterity. **b.** A controlled change in flight path of an aircraft, rocket, or space vehicle. **3.** A calculated and skillful movement, act, or stratagem: *devious political maneuvers.* See Synonyms at **artifice.** —*v.* **maneuvered, -vering, -vers.** Also *chiefly British* **ma·noeu·vre, -vred, -vring, -vres.** —*intr.* **1.** To perform or carry out a military maneuver. **2.** To make a change, or a series of changes, in position for some desired end. **3.** To shift ground or location; change tactics: *His opposition had no room in which to maneuver.* **4.** To attempt to bring about something by planning or scheming. —*tr.* **1.** To alter the tactical placement of (troops or warships). **2.** To manipulate into a desired position or toward a predetermined goal. [French *manoeuvre,* from Old French *maneuvre,* from Medieval Latin *man(u)opera,* manual work, from Latin *manū operārī,* to work by hand : *manū,* ablative of *manus,* hand (see **man-²** in Appendix*) + *operārī,* to work, from *opus,* work (see **op-¹** in Appendix*).] —**ma·neu′ver·a·bil′i·ty** *n.* —**ma·neu′ver·a·ble** *adj.*

man Friday. Any devoted male servant, aide, or employee, especially one having a high degree of responsibility. [After *Man Friday,* the devoted native servant in Daniel Defoe's novel *Robinson Crusoe.*]

man·ful (măn′fəl) *adj.* Having or displaying qualities befitting a man; brave and resolute; manly. See Synonyms at **male.** —**man′ful·ly** *adv.* —**man′ful·ness** *n.*

man·ga·bey (măng′gə-bā′, -bē′) *n.* Any monkey of the genus *Cercocebus,* of equatorial Africa, having a long tail and a relatively long muzzle. [After *Mangaby,* a region of Madagascar.]

Man·ga·lore (măng′gə-lôr′). A seaport of India, on the Malabar Coast. Population, 143,000.

man·ga·nate (măng′gə-nāt′) *n.* Any salt containing manganese in its anion, especially a salt containing the MnO_4 radical. [MANGAN(ESE) + -ATE (salt).]

man·ga·nese (măng′gə-nēz′, -nēs′) *n. Symbol* **Mn** A gray-white or silvery, brittle metallic element, occurring in several allotropic forms, found worldwide, especially in the ore pyrolusite. Manganese is alloyed with steel to increase strength, hardness, wear resistance, and other properties, and with other metals to form highly ferromagnetic materials. Atomic number 25, atomic weight 54.9380, melting point 1,244°C, boiling point 2,097°C, specific gravity 7.21 to 7.44, valences 1,2,3,4,6,7. See **element.** [French *manganèse,* from Italian *manganese,* probably alteration of Medieval Latin *magnēsia,* manganese, magnesia, from Late Greek *magnēsia.* See **magnesia.**]

manganese spar. 1. A mineral, **rhodonite** *(see).* **2.** A mineral, **rhodochrosite** *(see).*

man·gan·ic (măn-găn′ĭk) *adj.* Pertaining to trivalent manganese or any compound containing it.

man·ga·nite (măng′gə-nīt′) *n.* A steel-gray to black mineral form of manganese oxide, $Mn_2O_3 \cdot H_2O$, found in North America and Europe. It is an important ore of manganese. [MANGAN(ESE) + -ITE.]

man·ga·nous (măng′gə-nəs) *adj.* Pertaining to bivalent manganese or to any compound containing it.

mange (mānj) *n.* A contagious skin disease of many mammals, occasionally including man. It is caused by parasitic mites and characterized by itching and loss of hair. [Middle English *maniewe,* from Old French *manjue,* "eating," itch, from *mangier,* to eat, from Latin *mandūcāre,* to eat, chew, from *mandūcō,* glutton, from *mandere,* to chew. See **menth-** in Appendix.*]

man·gel-wur·zel (măng′gəl-wûr′zəl) *n.* A variety of the common beet having a large yellowish root, used chiefly as cattle feed. Also called "mangel," "mangold." [German, (properly) *Mangold-wurzel,* "beet-root" : *Mangold,* beet, from Old High German *mānegolt*† + *Wurzel,* root, from Old High German *wurzala* (see **werad-** in Appendix*).]

man·ger (mān′jər) *n.* A trough or open box in which feed for horses or cattle is placed. [Middle English *maniure, ma(w)nger,* from Old French *mangeoire, manjeure,* from Vulgar Latin *mandūcātōria* (unattested), feeding place, from *mandūcāre,* to chew. See **mange.**]

man·gle¹ (măng′gəl) *tr.v.* **-gled, -gling, -gles. 1.** To mutilate or disfigure by battering, hacking, cutting, or tearing. **2.** To ruin or spoil through ineptitude or ignorance: *mangle a speech.* [Middle English *manglen,* from Norman French *mangler, mahangler,* probably frequentative of Old French *mahaignier,* to wound, from Common Romance *mahagnāre* (unattested). See **mai-¹** in Appendix.*] —**man′gler** *n.*

man·gle² (măng′gəl) *n.* **1.** A laundry machine for pressing fabrics. **2.** *Chiefly British.* A clothes wringer. —*tr.v.* **mangled, -gling, -gles.** To smooth or press with a mangle. [Dutch *mangel,* from German, diminutive of Middle High German *mange,* mangle, from Late Latin *manganum,* MANGONEL.]

man·go (măng′gō) *n., pl.* **-goes** or **-gos. 1.** A tropical evergreen tree, *Mangifera indica,* native to Asia, cultivated for its edible fruit. **2.** The ovoid fruit of this tree, having a smooth rind and sweet, juicy, yellow-orange flesh. **3.** Any of various types of pickle; especially, a pickled, stuffed sweet pepper. [Portuguese *manga,* from Malay *mangā,* from Tamil *mānkāy* : *mān,* mango tree + *kāy,* fruit.]

man·go·nel (măng′gə-nĕl′) *n.* A military machine used during the Middle Ages for hurling stones and other missiles. [Middle English, from Old French, from Medieval Latin *mangonellus, manganellus,* diminutive of Late Latin *manganum,* mangonel, from Greek *manganon,* enchantment, contrivance, war machine. See **meng-** in Appendix.*]

man·go·steen (măng′gə-stēn′) *n.* **1.** A tropical tree, *Garcinia Mangostana,* having thick, leathery leaves and edible fruit. **2.** The fruit of this tree, having a hard rind and segmented, sweet, juicy pulp. [Malay *manggustan.*]

man·grove (măn′grōv′, măng′grōv′) *n.* **1.** Any of various tropical evergreen trees or shrubs of the genus *Rhizophora,* having stiltlike roots and stems, and forming dense thickets along tidal shores. **2.** Any of various similar shrubs or trees, especially one of the genus *Avicennia.* [From Portuguese *mangue* (influenced by GROVE), from Taino *mangle.*]

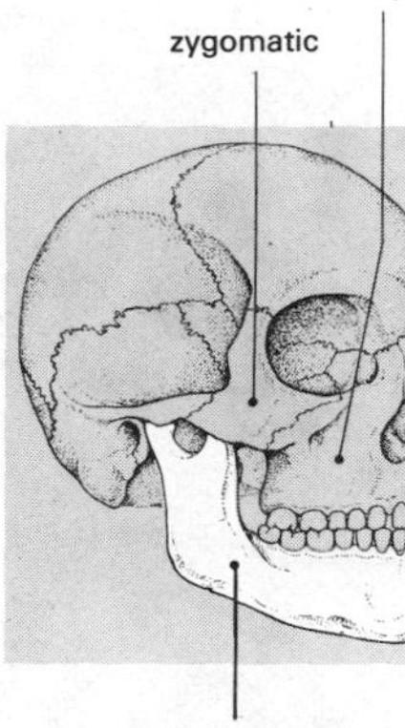
maxilla
zygomatic
mandible

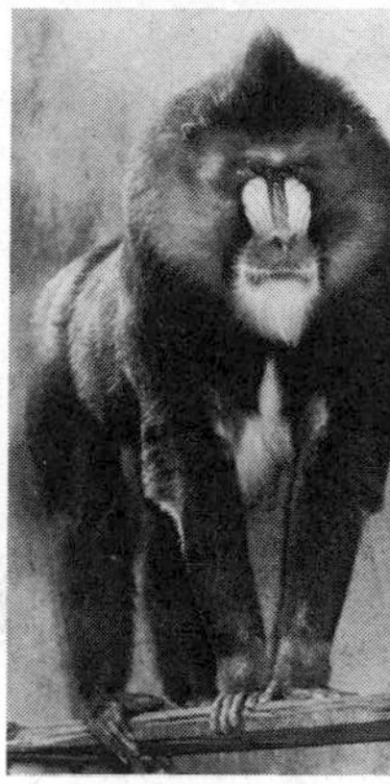
mandrill

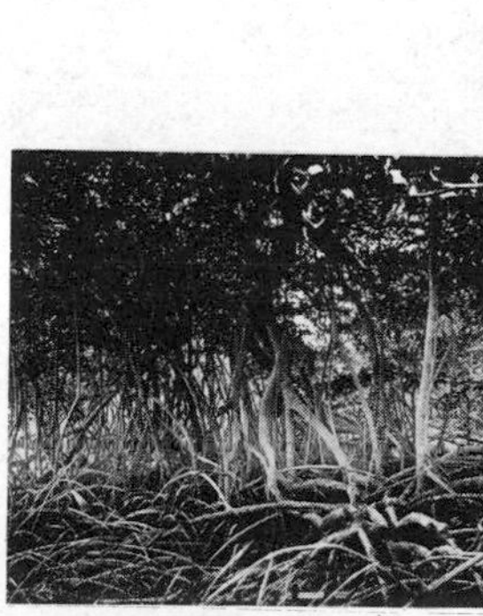
mangrove
Thicket of mangroves

man·gy (măn′jē) *adj.* **-gier, -giest. 1.** Having, resembling, or caused by mange. **2.** Having many bare spots; shabby: *a mangy old mink coat.* **3.** Having a squalid appearance; wretched: *mangy tenements.* —**man′gi·ly** *adv.* —**man′gi·ness** *n.*

man·han·dle (măn′hăn′dəl) *tr.v.* **-dled, -dling, -dles. 1.** To handle roughly. **2.** To move by manpower, without machinery.

Man·hat·tan[1] (măn-hăt′n, mən-) *n., pl.* **Manhattan** or **-tans. 1.** A tribe of Algonquian-speaking Indians, formerly inhabiting the area that is now roughly New York City. **2.** A member of this tribe. [From Proto-Algonquian *menahanwi* (unattested), "isolated thing in the water," island.]

Man·hat·tan[2] (măn-hăt′n, mən-). **1.** An island in New York City, 22 square miles in area, bounded by the Hudson, Harlem, and East rivers, and upper New York Bay. **2.** A borough of New York City, contained mainly on this island and coextensive with New York County. Population, 1,698,000.

Man·hat·tan[3] (măn-hăt′n, mən-) *n.* A cocktail made from vermouth and whiskey. [After MANHATTAN, New York.]

Manhattan clam chowder. See **clam chowder.**

Manhattan District. In World War II, the name given to a unit of the U.S. Army Corps of Engineers established in 1942 to administer the nuclear energy project that produced the atomic bomb. Also unofficially called "Manhattan Project."

man·hole (măn′hōl′) *n.* A hole through which a man may enter a sewer, boiler, pipe, conduit, or drain.

man·hood (măn′hŏŏd) *n.* **1.** The state or condition of being an adult male as distinguished from being a child or a woman: *Boys grow to manhood.* **2.** The composite of qualities, such as courage, determination, and vigor, ordinarily attributed to an adult male. **3.** Men collectively. **4.** The state or condition of being part of or endowed with humanity.

man·hour (măn′our′) *n., pl.* **man-hours.** An industrial unit of production equal to the work a man can produce in one hour.

man·hunt (măn′hŭnt′) *n., pl.* **manhunts.** An organized and extensive search for a man, usually a fugitive criminal.

ma·ni·a (mā′nē-ə, măn′yə) *n.* **1.** An inordinately intense desire or enthusiasm for something; craze. **2.** A manifestation of manic-depressive psychosis, characterized by profuse and rapidly changing ideas, exaggerated gaiety, and physical overactivity. **3.** Any violent abnormal behavior. [Middle English, madness, from Late Latin, from Greek *mania.* See **men-**[1] in Appendix.*] —**man′ic** (măn′ĭk) *adj.*

-mania. Indicates an exaggerated desire for or pleasure in, or a pathological excitement induced by (something); for example, **monomania.**

In the following list, the English meaning is indicated for the form with which -mania is combined:

acromania (heights)	necromania (death)
ailuromania (cats)	noctimania (night)
automania (solitude)	ochlomania (crowds)
cynomania (dogs)	ophidiomania (reptiles)
gymnomania (nudity)	ornithomania (birds)
hedonomania (pleasure)	pharmacomania (medicines)
heliomania (sunbathing)	sitomania (food)
hippomania (horses)	xenomania (foreigners)
hypnomania (sleep)	zoomania (animals)

ma·ni·ac (mā′nē-ăk′) *n.* **1.** An insane person; a lunatic. **2.** A person who has excessive enthusiasm or desire for something: *a bridge maniac.* —*adj.* Maniacal. [Greek *maniakos,* from *mania,* madness. See **men-**[1] in Appendix.*]

ma·ni·a·cal (mə-nī′ə-kəl) *adj.* **1.** Insane: *a maniacal killer.* **2.** *Informal.* Characterized by excessive enthusiasm: *a maniacal fondness for gambling.* Also "maniac." —**ma·ni′a·cal·ly** *adv.*

man·ic-de·pres·sive (măn′ĭk-dĭ-prĕs′ĭv) *adj. Psychiatry.* Designating or afflicted with a psychosis in which periods of manic excitation alternate with melancholic depression. —*n. Psychiatry.* A person so afflicted.

Man·i·chae·an, Man·i·che·an (măn′ĭ-kē′ən) *n.* Also **Manichee** (măn′ĭ-kē′). A believer in Manichaeism. —*adj.* Of or pertaining to Manichaeism. [Middle English, from Medieval Latin *Manichaeus,* from Late Greek *Manikhaios,* a follower of *Manikhaios,* or *Manes,* the prophet of the philosophy.]

Man·i·chae·ism, Man·i·che·ism (măn′ĭ-kē-ĭz′əm) *n.* Also **Man·i·chae·an·ism, Man·i·che·an·ism** (măn′ĭ-kē′ən-ĭz′əm). **1.** A syncretic religious philosophy of Zoroastrian, classical, pagan, Christian, and Gnostic thought, taught by the Persian prophet Manes about the third century A.D. **2.** Any similar dualistic philosophy, especially one considered a heresy by the Roman Catholic Church.

man·i·cot·ti (măn′ĭ-kŏt′ē) *n.* An Italian dish consisting of pasta with a filling of chopped ham and ricotta cheese, usually served hot with a tomato sauce. [Italian, "sleeves," plural of *manicotto,* augmentative of *mánica,* sleeve, from Latin *manica,* sleeve, from *manus,* hand. See **man-**[2] in Appendix.*]

man·i·cure (măn′ĭ-kyŏŏr′) *n.* Treatment of the hands and fingernails, including shaping, cleaning, and polishing of the nails. —*tr.v.* **manicured, -curing, -cures. 1.** To care for (the fingernails) by shaping, cleaning, and polishing. **2.** To clip or trim evenly and closely: *He manicured the hedge.* [French *manicure,* "hand-care" : Latin *manus,* hand (see **man-**[2] in Appendix.*) + *cūra,* care (see *cūra* in Appendix.*).] —**man′i·cur′ist** *n.*

man·i·fest (măn′ə-fĕst′) *adj.* Clearly apparent to the sight or understanding; obvious: *"It became manifest that the invaders had come not only to ravage but to settle."* (Winston Churchill). See Synonyms at **evident.** —*v.* **manifested, -festing, -fests.** —*tr.* **1.** To show or demonstrate plainly; reveal: *"Mercedes . . . manifested the chaotic abandonment of hysteria."* (Jack London). **2.** To be evidence of; prove. **3. a.** To record or list in a ship's manifest. **b.** To display or present a manifest of (cargo). —*intr.*

Spiritualism. Of a spirit, to appear: *"seances . . . at which good and holy spirits manifested."* (Hawthorne). —*n.* **1. a.** A list of cargo or passengers. **2.** A list of railroad cars, according to owner and location. **2.** A fast freight train, usually one that carries perishable goods. [Middle English, from Latin *manifestus, manufestus,* palpable, "grasped by hand" : *manus,* hand (see **man-**[2] in Appendix*) + *-festus,* "gripped" (see **dhers-** in Appendix*).] —**man′i·fest′a·ble** *adj.* —**man′i·fest·ly** *adv.*

man·i·fes·tant (măn′ə-fĕs′tənt) *n.* A participant in a manifestation or a public demonstration.

man·i·fes·ta·tion (măn′ə-fĕs-tā′shən) *n.* **1. a.** The act of manifesting or the state of being manifested. **b.** The demonstration of the existence, reality, or presence of a person, object, or quality: *a manifestation of ill will.* **c.** One of the forms in which someone or something, such as an individual, a divine being, or an idea, is revealed. **2.** A public demonstration, usually of a political nature.

Manifest Destiny. *U.S. History.* The 19th-century doctrine that the United States had the right and duty to expand throughout the North American continent.

man·i·fes·to (măn′ə-fĕs′tō) *n., pl.* **-toes** or **-tos.** A public declaration of principles or intentions, especially of a political nature. —*intr.v.* **manifestoed, -toing, -toes.** To issue a manifesto. [Italian, "manifestation," from adjective, manifest, from Latin *manifestus,* MANIFEST.]

man·i·fold (măn′ə-fōld) *adj.* **1.** Of many kinds; varied; multiple: *"under the manifold exasperations of life"* (Thomas Mann). **2.** Having many features or forms: *manifold intelligence.* **3.** Consisting of or operating several of one kind. —*n.* **1.** A whole composed of diverse elements. **2.** Any one of many copies; a copy made by manifolding. **3.** *Mechanics.* A pipe so fitted that it has several apertures for making multiple connections. **4.** *Mathematics.* A set of elements sharing a number of properties, usually of a topologic nature, such as orientability, differentiability, and dimensionality. A circle is a one-dimensional manifold. —*tr.v.* **manifolded, -folding, -folds. 1.** To make several copies of. **2.** To make manifold; multiply. [Middle English *manifold,* Old English *manig-feald* : MANY + -FOLD.] —**man′i·fold·ly** *adv.* —**man′i·fold·ness** *n.*

man·i·fold·er (măn′ə-fōl′dər) *n.* A machine for making manifold copies of documents or other writings.

man·i·kin, man·ni·kin (măn′ĭ-kĭn) *n.* **1.** Also **man·a·kin.** A dwarf *(see).* **2.** An anatomical model of the human body, used primarily for study in medical and art schools. **3.** Variant of **mannequin.** [Middle Dutch *mannekin,* diminutive of *man,* man. See **man-**[1] in Appendix.*]

Ma·nil·a (mə-nĭl′ə). The largest city and former capital of the Philippines, on Luzon Island. Population, 1,139,000. [Tagalog *Ma(y)nila,* from *doon sa may nila,* there where the nila (flowers) are.]

ma·nil·a, ma·nil·la (mə-nĭl′ə) *n. Often capital* **M. 1.** A cheroot made in Manila. **2.** A fiber, **Manila hemp** *(see).* **3.** Manila paper. **4.** Light yellow brown. See **color.**

Manila hemp. The fiber of a tropical plant, the **abaca** *(see),* used for making rope, cordage, and paper.

Manila paper. Strong paper or thin cardboard with a smooth finish, usually buff in color, made from Manila hemp or wood fibers similar to it.

man in the moon. The face or shape of a man in the light and dark areas of the moon's surface as viewed from the earth.

man in the street. The ordinary citizen; the common man.

man·i·oc (măn′ē-ŏk′) *n.* Also **man·i·o·ca** (măn′ē-ō′kə). A tropical plant, the **cassava** *(see).* [French, of Tupian origin, akin to Tupi *manioca.*]

man·i·ple (măn′ə-pəl) *n.* **1.** An ornamental silk band hung as an ecclesiastical vestment on the left arm near the wrist. **2.** A subdivision of an ancient Roman legion, containing 60 or 120 men. [Sense 1, Middle English, from Old French handkerchief, from Latin *manipulus,* handful. Sense 2, direct from Latin *manipulus,* handful, hence, a bundle of hay on a pole used as a standard, hence a detachment of troops : *manus,* hand (see **man-**[2] in Appendix*) + an obscure second element.]

ma·nip·u·lar (mə-nĭp′yə-lər) *adj.* **1.** Of or pertaining to an ancient Roman maniple. **2.** Of or relating to manipulation. —*n.* A Roman soldier in a maniple.

ma·nip·u·late (mə-nĭp′yə-lāt′) *tr.v.* **-lated, -lating, -lates. 1.** To operate or control by skilled use of the hands; handle. **2.** To influence or manage shrewdly or deviously: *He manipulated public opinion in his favor.* **3.** To tamper with or falsify (financial records) for personal gain. —See Synonyms at **handle.** [Back-formation, from MANIPULATION.] —**ma·nip′u·la·bil′i·ty** *n.* —**ma·nip′u·la·ble, ma·nip′u·lat′ive, ma·nip′u·la·to′ry** (-lə-tôr′ē, -tōr′ē) *adj.* —**ma·nip′u·la′tor** (-lā′tər) *n.*

ma·nip·u·la·tion (mə-nĭp′yə-lā′shən) *n.* **1.** The act of manipulating. **2.** Shrewd or devious management, especially for one's own advantage. **3.** The state of being manipulated. [From Latin *manipulus,* handful. See **maniple.**]

Ma·ni·pur (mŭn′ĭ-pŏŏr′). A northeastern territory of India, 8,620 square miles in area. Population, 780,000. Capital, Imphal.

Man·i·to·ba (măn′ĭ-tō′bə). *Abbr.* **Man. 1.** A south-central province of Canada, 246,512 square miles in area. Population, 958,000. Capital, Winnipeg. See map at **Canada. 2.** A lake, 1,817 square miles in area, in the southern part of this province. [Perhaps from Cree *manitoopeek,* "divine water."] —**Man′i·to′ban** *adj. & n.*

man·i·tou, man·i·tu (măn′ĭ-tōō′) *n.* Also **man·i·to** (măn′ə-tō′). **1.** A spirit or force of nature, either good or bad, deified in the religion of the Algonquian Indians. **2.** A representation or image of such a spirit. [French, from Ojibwa *manitoo,* from Proto-Algonquian *manetoowa* (unattested).]

Man·i·tou·lin Island (măn′ĭ-to͞o′lĭn). An island of Ontario, Canada, in Lake Huron. It is the world's largest lake island (1,600 square miles).

Ma·ni·za·les (mä′nē-sä′lās). A city of Colombia, at an altitude of over 7,000 feet in the Cordillera Central, about 125 miles northeast of Buenaventura. Population, 222,000.

man·kind (măn′kīnd′, -kīnd′ *for sense 1;* măn′kīnd′ *for sense 2*) *n.* **1.** The human race. **2.** Men as distinguished from women.

man·like (măn′līk′) *adj.* **1.** Resembling a man. **2.** Belonging to or befitting a man. —See Synonyms at **male.**

man·ly (măn′lē) *adj.* **-lier, -liest. 1.** Having qualities generally attributed to a man: *manly courage.* **2.** Belonging to or befitting a man; masculine: *manly clothes.* —See Synonyms at **male.** —*adv. Rare.* In a manly manner. —**man′li·ness** *n.*

Mann (măn), **Horace.** 1796–1859. American educator and political leader; reformer and advocate of public schools.

Mann (män), **Thomas.** 1875–1955. German author of novels, plays, and essays; awarded the Nobel Prize in literature (1929); naturalized American citizen (1940).

man·na (măn′ə) *n.* **1.** The food miraculously provided for the Israelites in the wilderness during their flight from Egypt. Exodus 16:14–36. **2.** Any spiritual nourishment of divine origin. **3.** Something of value that a person receives unexpectedly. **4.** The dried exudate of certain plants; especially, that of a Eurasian ash tree, *Fraxinus ornus,* formerly used as a laxative. [Aramaic *mannā,* from Hebrew *mān.*]

Mann Act. A U.S. law (1910) prohibiting transportation of women across state lines for immoral purposes. [After James Robert *Mann* (1856–1922), U.S. Congressman.]

Man·nar, Gulf of (mə-när′). An inlet, about 100 miles long and 80 to 170 miles wide, of the Indian Ocean between Ceylon and the southeastern tip of the Republic of India.

man·ne·quin (măn′ĭ-kĭn) *n.* Also **man·i·kin. 1.** A life-size, full or partial representation of the human body, used for the fitting or displaying of clothes; dummy. **2.** A **lay figure** *(see).* **3.** A woman who models clothes; a model. [French, from Middle Dutch *mannekīn,* MANIKIN.]

man·ner (măn′ər) *n.* **1.** A way of doing something, or the way in which a thing is done or happens: *"The Spaniards according to their usual manner, fill the world with their vain-glorious vaunts."* (Sir Walter Raleigh). **2.** A way of acting; a person's bearing or behavior: *"She adopted towards Erridge a decidedly flirtatious manner."* (Anthony Powell). **3.** *Plural.* **a.** The socially correct way of acting; polite bearing or behavior; etiquette: *"Captain Harville, though not equalling Captain Wentworth in manners, was a perfect gentleman."* (Jane Austen). **b.** The prevailing systems or modes of social conduct of a specific society, period, or group, especially as the subject of a literary work: *"Removed from the polite, they still retained a primeval simplicity of manners."* (Goldsmith). **4.** Practice, style, execution, or method in the arts: *This fresco is typical of the painter's early manner.* **5.** Kind or sort: *"I thought also of the manner of the death with which this place destroyeth men."* (Bunyan). —See Synonyms at **bearing, method.** —**by all manner of means.** Of course; surely. —**by no manner of means.** In no way whatever. —**in a manner of speaking.** In a way; so to speak. —**to the manner born. 1.** Born to follow or obey usual practices or customs. **2. a.** Fitted by birth, education, or experience to occupy a specific position, usually one of leadership. **b.** Accustomed by family background to a preferred mode of behavior. [Middle English *manere,* from Norman French, from Old French *maniere,* from Vulgar Latin *manuāria* (unattested), "way of handling," manner, from Latin *manuārius,* of the hand, from *manus,* hand. See **man-²** in Appendix.*]

man·nered (măn′ərd) *adj.* **1.** Having a manner or manners of a specific kind. Often used in combination: *ill-mannered.* **2.** Artificial or affected: *His mannered speech made everyone uncomfortable.* **3.** Of, pertaining to, or exhibiting mannerisms. Said of art or literature.

man·ner·ism (măn′ər-ĭz′əm) *n.* **1.** A distinctive behavioral trait; idiosyncrasy: *"a mannerism of scratching his chin that suggested our own more nervous era"* (Louis Auchincloss). **2.** Exaggerated or affected style or habit, as in dress, speech, or art: *"The analyst . . . had adopted a number of speech mannerisms from Middle European big-wheel psychoanalysts"* (Lillian Ross). **3.** *Capital* **M.** An artistic style of the late 16th century characterized by distortion of such elements as scale and perspective. —See Synonyms at **affectation.** —**man′ner·ist** *n.* —**man′ner·is′tic** *adj.*

man·ner·less (măn′ər-lĭs) *adj.* Having bad manners.

man·ner·ly (măn′ər-lē) *adj.* Having good manners; well-behaved; polite: *"very handsome and goodly people, and in their behaviour as mannerly and civil as any in Europe"* (Arthur Barlowe). —*adv.* With good manners; politely.

Mann·heim (măn′hīm′; *German* män′hīm′). A river port and city in West Germany, at the junction of the Rhine and Neckar rivers. Population, 323,000.

man·ni·kin. Variant of **manikin.**

man·nish (măn′ĭsh) *adj.* **1.** Of or befitting a man. **2.** Resembling a man: *"A woman impudent and mannish grown / Is not more loathed than an effeminate man."* (Shakespeare). —See Synonyms at **male.** —**man′nish·ly** *adv.* —**man′nish·ness** *n.*

man·ni·tol (măn′ĭ-tôl′, -tōl′) *n.* An alcohol, $C_6H_8(OH)_6$, used as a nutrient, a dietary supplement, and as the basis of dietetic sweets. [MANN(A) + -IT(E) + -OL.]

ma·noeu·vre. *Chiefly British.* Variant of **maneuver.**

man of the world. A sophisticated, worldly man.

man-of-war (măn′ə-wôr′) *n., pl.* **men-of-war. 1.** A warship. **2.** A jellyfish, the **Portuguese man-of-war** *(see).*

Man·o·let·e (män′ō-lā′tā). Original name, Manuel Laureano Rodríguez y Sánchez. 1917–1947. Spanish bullfighter.

ma·nom·e·ter (mă-nŏm′ə-tər) *n.* **1.** An instrument for measuring the pressure of liquids and gases. **2.** An instrument for measuring blood pressure, a **sphygmomanometer** *(see).* [French *manomètre* : Greek *manos,* sparse (here used of gaseous conditions) (see **men-⁴** in Appendix*) + -METER.] —**man′o·met′ric** (măn′ə-mĕt′rĭk), **man′o·met′ri·cal** *adj.* —**man′o·met′ri·cal·ly** *adv.* —**ma·nom′e·try** *n.*

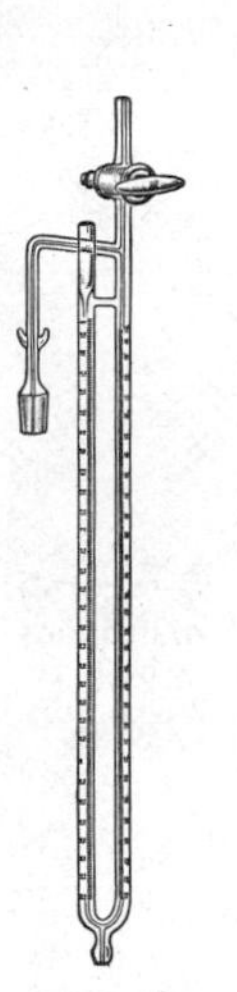

manometer

man·or (măn′ər) *n.* **1. a.** The district over which a lord had domain in medieval western Europe. **b.** The lord's residence in such a district. **2.** Any landed estate. **3.** The main house on any estate; mansion. **4.** In certain North American colonies, a tract of land with hereditary rights granted by royal charter. [Middle English *maner,* from Norman French *manere,* from Old French *maneir,* "dwelling place," from *maneir,* to dwell, from Latin *manēre,* to dwell, remain. See **men-³** in Appendix.*] —**ma·no′ri·al** (mă-nôr′ē-əl, mă-nōr′-) *adj.*

man-o'-war bird. The **frigate bird** *(see).*

man·pow·er (măn′pou′ər) *n.* **1.** The power of human physical strength. **2.** Power in terms of the men available to a particular group, or required for a particular task.

man·qué (mäɴ-kā′) *adj.* Unfulfilled; frustrated; unsuccessful. Placed after the noun it modifies: *an artist manqué.* [French, from *manquer,* to fail, lack, from Italian *mancare,* from *manco,* lacking, defective, from Latin *mancus,* maimed. See **man-²** in Appendix.*]

man·rope (măn′rōp′) *n. Nautical.* A rope rigged as a handrail on a gangplank or ladder.

man·sard (măn′särd) *n.* **1.** A roof having two slopes on all four sides, with the lower slope almost vertical, and the upper almost horizontal. Also called "mansard roof." **2.** The upper story formed by the lower slope of a mansard roof. [French *(toit en) mansarde,* "mansard (roof)"; originally designed by François *Mansart* (1598–1666), French architect.]

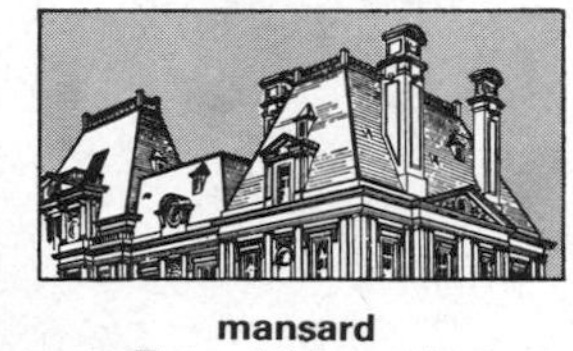

mansard
Francois Mansart's
Château de Maisons-Laffitte

manse (măns) *n.* **1.** *Chiefly Scottish.* A clergyman's house and land. **2.** *Rare.* A mansion. [Medieval Latin *mansa, mansus, mansum,* dwelling place, from Latin *manēre,* to dwell, remain. See **men-³** in Appendix.*]

man·ser·vant (măn′sûr′vənt) *n., pl.* **menservants** (mĕn′sûr′vəntz). A male servant, especially a valet.

Mans·field, Mount (mănz′fēld′). The highest peak (4,393 feet) of the Green Mountains in north-central Vermont.

man·sion (măn′shən) *n.* **1.** A large, stately house. **2.** A manor house. **3.** *Archaic.* A dwelling; abode. **4.** *Astrology.* **a.** A **house** *(see).* **b.** Any one of the 28 divisions of the moon's monthly path. [Middle English, house, from Old French, from Latin *mānsiō,* dwelling, from *manēre,* to dwell, remain. See **men-³** in Appendix.*]

man-sized (măn′sīzd′) *adj. Informal.* Large enough for a man; hefty: *a man-sized piece of pie.*

man·slaugh·ter (măn′slô′tər) *n.* **1.** The taking of human life without premeditation. **2.** *Law.* The unlawful killing of one human being by another without express or implied intent to do injury. Compare **murder.**

man·slay·er (măn′slā′ər) *n.* A person or animal who kills a human being. —**man′slay′ing** *n.* & *adj.*

man·sue·tude (măn′swĭ-to͞od′, -tyo͞od′) *n.* Gentleness of manner; mildness: *"Our Lord Himself, made all of mansuetude."* (Robert Browning). [Middle English, from Latin *mānsuētūdō,* from *mānsuēscere,* to tame, "to accustom to the hand" : *manus,* hand (see **man-²** in Appendix*) + *suēscere,* to accustom (see **seu-²** in Appendix*).]

man·ta (măn′tə) *n.* **1.** A rough-textured cotton fabric or blanket made and used in Spanish America and the southwestern U.S. **2.** Any of several fishes of the family Mobulidae, having large, extremely flattened bodies with winglike pectoral fins. Also called "devilfish," "manta ray." [Spanish *manta,* cape, blanket, (hence, in American Spanish) fish trap shaped like a blanket, manta ray (caught with such a fish trap), from Vulgar Latin *manta* (unattested), cloak, variant of Latin *mantus,* shortened from *mantellum*†, MANTLE.]

man·teau (măn-tō′) *n., pl.* **-teaus** (-tōz′) or **-teaux** (-tō′). A loose cloak or mantle. [French, from Old French *mantel,* from Latin *mantellum*†, MANTLE.]

Man·te·gna (män-tā′nyä), **Andrea.** 1431–1506. Italian painter, muralist, and engraver; leader of the Paduan school.

man·tel (măn′təl) *n.* Also **man·tle. 1.** An ornamental facing around a fireplace. **2.** The protruding shelf over a fireplace. Also called "mantelpiece." [Middle English *mantel,* cloak, covering, from Old French, from Latin *mantellum*†, MANTLE.]

man·tel·et (măn′təl-ĕt′, mănt′lĭt) *n.* **1.** A short cape. **2.** Also **mant·let** (mănt′lĭt). A mobile screen or shield formerly used to protect soldiers. [Middle English, from Old French, diminutive of *mantel,* mantle, from Latin *mantellum*†, MANTLE.]

man·tel·let·ta (măn′tə-lĕt′ə) *n.* A knee-length, sleeveless vestment worn by Roman Catholic prelates. [Italian, from Old French *mantelet,* MANTELET.]

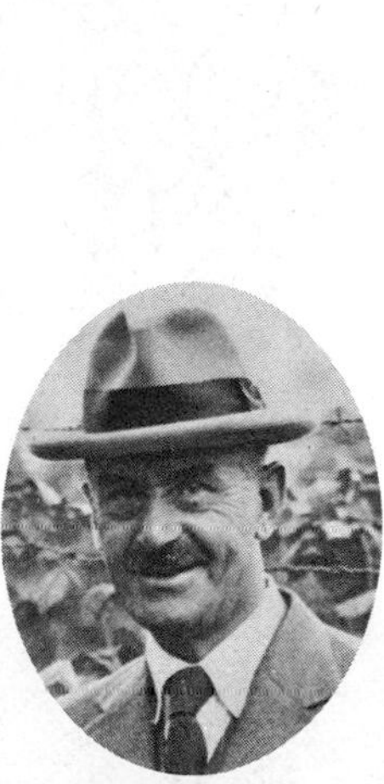

Thomas Mann
In Munich, Germany,
before World War II

man·tel·piece (măn′təl-pēs′) *n.* Also **man·tle·piece.** The shelf over a fireplace, a **mantel** *(see).*

man·tel·tree (măn′təl-trē′) *n.* A beam, stone, or arch that functions as a lintel on a fireplace, supporting the masonry above. [Middle English : MANTEL + TREE (beam).]

man·tic (măn′tĭk) *adj.* Of, pertaining to, or having the power of divination; prophetic: *"Nor is the discussion closed on the subject of mantic or prophetic dreams."* (Nathan Rapport). [Greek *mantikos,* from *mantis,* prophet. See **men-¹** in Appendix.*]

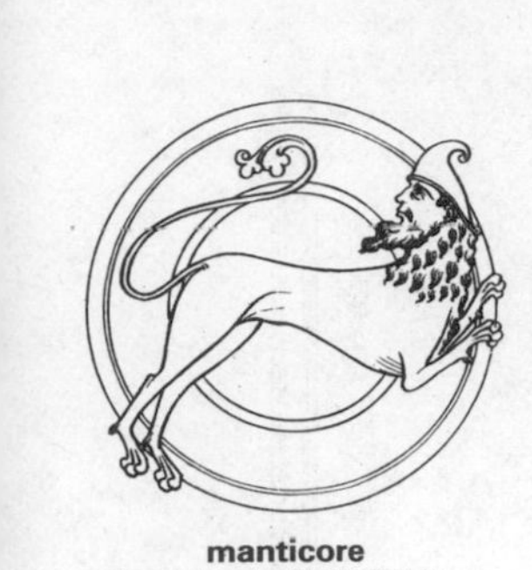
manticore
Drawing by T. H. White
from a 12th-century bestiary

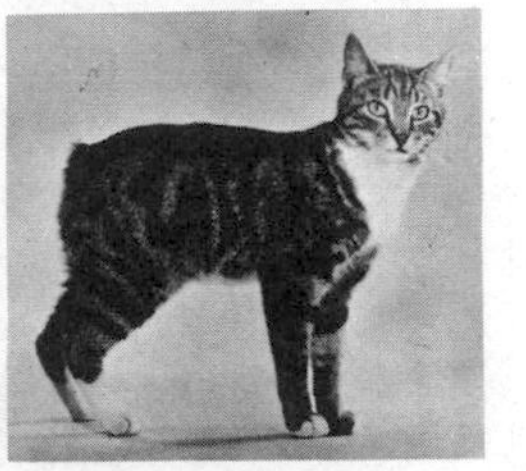
Manx cat

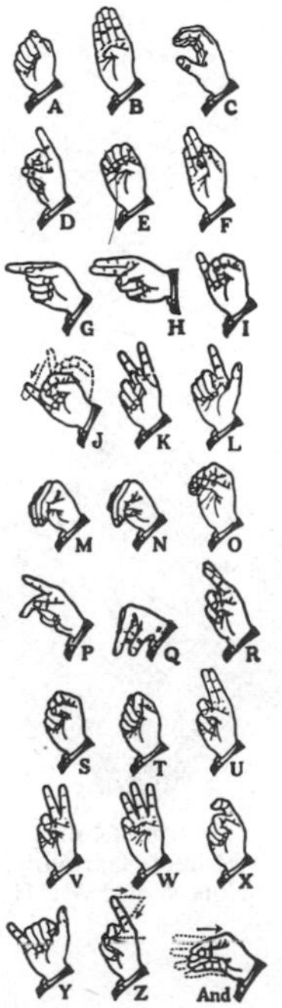

manual alphabet

man·ti·core (măn′tĭ-kôr′, -kōr′) *n.* A fabulous monster having the head of a man, body of a lion, and the tail of a dragon or scorpion. [Middle English, from Latin *mantichōra*, from Greek *mantikhōras*, a misreading for *martikhoras*, a fabulous Oriental beast, from an unattested Old Iranian word meaning "man-eater" : represented by Old Persian *martīya-*, man (see **mer-**[2] in Appendix*) + Avestan **khvar-**, to eat (see **swel-**[1] in Appendix*).]

man·til·la (măn-tē′yə, -tĭl′ə) *n.* **1.** A scarf, usually of lace, worn over the head and shoulders, often over a high comb, by women in Spain and Latin America. **2.** A short cloak or cape. [Spanish, diminutive of *manta*, cape, MANTA.]

man·tis (măn′tĭs) *n., pl.* **-tises** or **-tes** (-tēz). Any of various insects of several genera, primarily tropical but including a few Temperate Zone species. They are usually pale-green and have two pairs of walking legs and shorter forelimbs that are often folded in a praying position. See **praying mantis.** [New Latin, from Greek *mantis*, prophet, diviner, hence (from its prayerful appearance) mantis. See **men-**[1] in Appendix.*]

mantis crab. A burrowing crustacean, the **squilla** *(see).*

man·tis·sa (măn-tĭs′ə) *n. Mathematics.* The decimal part of a common logarithm when the logarithm is written as the sum of an integer and a decimal. [Latin *mantissa*, makeweight, probably from Etruscan.]

mantis shrimp. A burrowing crustacean, the **squilla** *(see).*

man·tle (măn′təl) *n.* **1.** A loose, sleeveless coat worn over outer garments. **2.** Anything that covers, envelops, or conceals: *"On a summer night . . . a mantle of dust hangs over the gravel roads."* (John Dollard). **3.** Variant of **mantel. 4.** The outer covering of a wall. **5.** A zone of hot gases around a flame. **6.** A device in gas lamps consisting of a sheath of threads that gives off brilliant illumination when heated by the flame. **7.** *Anatomy.* The covering of the brain, **cerebral cortex** *(see).* **8.** *Geology.* The layer of the earth between the crust and the core. See **Mohorovičić discontinuity. 9.** *Ornithology.* The wings, shoulder feathers, and back of a bird, when differently colored from the rest of the body. **10.** *Zoology.* In mollusks and brachiopods, a membrane between the body and the shell. —*v.* **mantled, -tling, -tles.** —*tr.* To cover with or as if with a mantle; to cloak; conceal: *"all the high points about the valley were mantled in fresh snow"* (John Muir). —*intr.* **1.** To spread or become extended over a surface. **2.** To become covered with a coating, such as scum or froth on the surface of a liquid. **3.** To be or become covered or overspread by blushes or colors: *Her face mantled in joy.* [Middle English, from Old English *mentel*, cloak, and Old French *mantel*, cloak, both from Latin *mantellum*†, cloak.]

man·tle·piece. Variant of **mantelpiece.**

mantle rock. Loose rock material, **regolith** *(see).*

mant·let. Variant of **mantelet.**

man·tra (mŭn′trə) *n. Hinduism.* A sacred formula believed to embody the divinity invoked and to possess magical power. It is used in prayer and incantation. [Sanskrit *mantra*, "prayer," "hymn." See **men-**[1] in Appendix.*]

man·tu·a (măn′tōō-ə, -tyōō-ə) *n.* A loose gown, open in front to reveal an underskirt, worn in the 17th and 18th centuries. [From French *manteau*, mantle (influenced by MANTUA, Italy, formerly famous for silks), from Old French *mantel*, from Latin *mantellum*, MANTLE.]

Man·tu·a (măn′tōō-ə, -tyōō-ə). A city of northern Italy; the birthplace of Virgil. Population, 43,000. —**Man′tu·an** *adj.* & *n.*

man·u·al (măn′yōō-əl) *adj.* **1. a.** Of, pertaining to, or done by the hands. **b.** Used by or operated with the hands, as a weapon, tool, or simple machine: *manual controls.* **c.** Employing human rather than mechanical energy: *manual labor.* **2.** Of, pertaining to, or resembling a manual or guidebook. —*n.* **1.** Any small reference book, especially one giving instructions; guidebook; handbook. **2.** A keyboard of an organ played with the hands. **3.** *Military.* Prescribed movements in the handling of a weapon, especially a rifle. [Middle English *manuel*, from Old French, from Latin *manuālis*, of the hand, from *manus*, hand. See **man-**[2] in Appendix.*] —**man′u·al·ly** *adv.*

manual alphabet. An alphabet of hand signals used for communication by deaf-mutes.

ma·nu·bri·um (mə-nōō′brē-əm) *n., pl.* **-bria** (-brē-ə). *Anatomy.* **1.** The upper part of the breastbone or sternum. **2.** The handle-shaped projection of the malleus in the ear. [New Latin, from Latin *manubrium*, handle : *manus*, hand (see **man-**[2] in Appendix*) + an obscure second element.]

man·u·fac·to·ry (măn′yə-făk′tər-ē) *n., pl.* **-ries.** A factory. [MANUFACT(URE) + (FACT)ORY.]

man·u·fac·ture (măn′yə-făk′chər) *v.* **-tured, -turing, -tures.** —*tr.* **1. a.** To make or process (a raw material) into a finished product, especially by means of a large-scale industrial operation. **b.** To make or process (a product), especially with the use of industrial machines. **2.** To create, produce, or turn out in a mechanical manner: *"His books seem to have been manufactured rather than composed."* (Dwight Macdonald). **3.** To concoct or invent; fabricate. —*intr.* To make or process goods, especially in large quantities and by means of industrial machines. —*n. Abbr.* **manuf., manufac., mfg., mfr. 1.** The act, craft, or process of manufacturing. **2.** A product that is manufactured. [Old French *manufacture*, a making by hand, handiwork, from Late Latin *manūfactus*, handmade : Latin *manū*, by hand, from *manus*, hand (see **man-**[2] in Appendix*) + *factus*, made, from *facere*, to make (see **dhē-**[1] in Appendix*).] —**man′u·fac′tur·a·ble** *adj.*

manufactured gas. A gaseous fuel made from various petroleum products or from soft coal.

man·u·fac·tur·er (măn′yə-făk′chər-ər) *n. Abbr.* **mfr.** A person or enterprise that manufactures; especially, the owner or operator of a factory.

man·u·mit (măn′yōō-mĭt′) *tr.v.* **-mitted, -mitting, -mits.** To free from slavery or bondage; emancipate. [Middle English *manumitten*, from Old French *manumitter*, from Latin *manumittere*, from *manū ēmittere*, to liberate, release from one's hand : *manū*, ablative of *manus*, hand (see **man-**[2] in Appendix*) + *ēmittere*, to EMIT.] —**man′u·mit′ter** *n.* —**man′u·mis′sion** (-mĭsh′ən) *n.*

ma·nure (mə-nŏŏr′, -nyŏŏr′) *n.* Animal dung, compost, or other material used to fertilize soil. —*tr.v.* **manured, -nuring, -nures.** To apply manure to. [Middle English *manour*, cultivation of soil, from *manouren*, to till, from Norman French *mainoverer*, from Old French *manoeuvrer*, to till, "work by hand," from Medieval Latin *manuoperārī* : *manū*, by hand, from Latin *manus*, hand (see **man-**[2] in Appendix*) + *operārī*, to work (see **op-**[1] in Appendix*).] —**ma·nur′er** *n.*

ma·nus (mā′nəs, mä′-) *n., pl.* **manus.** *Zoology.* The end of the forelimb in vertebrates, such as the hand, claw, or hoof. [Latin *manus*, hand. See **man-**[2] in Appendix.*]

Ma·nus (mä′nōōs). The largest (633 square miles) of the Admiralty Islands, in the Southwest Pacific.

man·u·script (măn′yə-skrĭpt′) *n. Abbr.* **ms, MS, ms., MS. 1.** A book, document, or other composition written by hand. **2.** A typewritten or handwritten version of a book, article, document, or other work, especially the author's own copy, prepared and submitted for publication in print. **3.** Handwriting, as opposed to printing. —*adj.* Handwritten or typewritten. [Medieval Latin *manūscrīptus*, handwritten : Latin *manū*, by hand, from *manus*, hand (see **man-**[2] in Appendix*) + *scrīptus*, written, from *scrībere*, to write (see **skeri-** in Appendix*).]

Ma·nu·ti·us (mə-nōō′shē-əs, mə-nyōō′-, -shəs), **Aldus.** Original name, Aldo Manucci. 1450–1515. Italian scholar, printer, and publisher; founder of the Aldine press.

man·ward (măn′wərd) *adv.* Also **man·wards** (măn′wərdz). *Rare.* Toward man. —*adj.* Pertaining to or directed toward man.

man·wise (măn′wīz′) *adv.* In a manner characteristic of man.

Manx (măngks) *adj.* Of or pertaining to the Isle of Man or the Manx language. —*n., pl.* **Manx. 1.** A native or resident of the Isle of Man. **2.** The nearly extinct Goidelic Celtic language spoken on the Isle of Man. **3.** A Manx cat.

Manx cat, manx cat. A breed of domestic cat, having short hair, usually solid color, and an internal vestigial tail. Also shortened to "Manx." [Originally bred on the Isle of Man.]

man·y (mĕn′ē) *adj.* **more, most. 1.** Being one of a large, indefinite number; numerous. Sometimes used before *a, an,* or *another: many a man; many another day.* **2.** Amounting to or consisting of a large, indefinite number: *many friends.* —*n.* Singular in form, used with a plural verb. **1.** A large, indefinite number of persons or things. Followed by *of: Many of the children were ill.* **2.** The great body of the people; the masses. Usually preceded by *the: "The many fail; the one succeeds."* (Tennyson). —*pron.* Used with a plural verb. A large number of persons or things: *"Many are called, but few are chosen."* (Matthew 22:14). [Middle English *many*, Old English *manig*, *mænig*. See **menegh-** in Appendix.*]

man·y·plies (mĕn′ĭ-plīz′) *n.* The third stomach of a cud-chewing mammal, the **omasum** *(see).*

man·za·ni·lla (măn′zə-nĭl′ə; *Spanish* män′thä-nē′lyä, -nē′yä) *n.* A pale dry sherry from Spain. [Spanish *manzanilla*, small apple, hence (from its aromatic bouquet) manzanilla sherry, diminutive of *manzana*, apple, from Old Spanish, from Latin *(māla) Matiāna*, "(apples) of *Matius*," a particular kind of apple, probably named after Caius *Matius* Calvena, Roman author of a cookbook (first century B.C.).]

man·za·ni·ta (măn′zə-nē′tə) *n.* Any of several evergreen shrubs of the genus *Arctostaphylos*, of the Pacific coast of North America; especially, *A. Manzanita*, bearing white or pink flowers in clusters. [American Spanish, diminutive of Spanish *manzana*, apple. See **manzanilla.**]

Man·zo·ni (män-dzō′nē), **Alessandro.** 1785–1873. Italian novelist; author of *I Promessi Sposi* (1825–26).

Mao·ism (mou′ĭzm) *n.* The Communist political philosophy and practice developed in China chiefly by Mao Tse-tung.

Ma·o·ri (mou′rē) *n., pl.* **Maori** or **-ris. 1.** A member of the aboriginal people of New Zealand, of Polynesian-Melanesian descent. **2.** The Austronesian language of the Maori. [Maori *Maori*, "native to New Zealand."] —**Ma′o·ri** *adj.*

Mao Tse-tung (mou′tsĭ-tŏŏng′, mou′dzŭ′dŏŏng′). Born 1893. Chinese Communist leader and chief theorist of the Chinese Revolution; head of state (1949–59); party chairman.

map (măp) *n.* **1.** A representation, usually on a plane surface, of a region of the earth or heavens. **2.** Something that suggests a map in clarity of representation. **3.** *Slang.* The face. —**put on the map.** To make famous or known. —**wipe off the map.** To destroy completely; annihilate. —*tr.v.* **mapped, mapping, maps. 1.** To make a map of. **2.** To explore or make a survey of (a region) for the purpose of making a map. **3.** To plan or delineate, especially in detail; arrange. Often followed by *out: families mapping out their vacation plans.* **4.** *Mathematics.* To establish a mapping of (a set or aggregate). [Medieval Latin *mappa (mundī)*, map (of the world), from *mappa*, napkin, sheet, cloth. See **mappa** in Appendix.*] —**map′per** *n.*

ma·ple (mā′pəl) *n.* **1.** Any tree or shrub of the genus *Acer*, found in the North Temperate Zone. Most are tall, deciduous trees, having lobed leaves and winged seeds borne in pairs. **2.** The wood of a maple, especially the hard, close-grained wood of the **sugar maple** *(see)*, much used for furniture and flooring. **3.** The flavor of the concentrated sap of the sugar maple. [Middle English *maple,* Old English *mapel(treow),* maple (tree). See **smē-** in Appendix.*]

maple sugar. A sugar made by boiling down maple syrup.

maple syrup. 1. A sweet syrup made from the sap of the sugar maple *(see).* **2.** Syrup made from other sugars and flavored with maple syrup or artificial maple flavoring.

map·ping (măp'ĭng) *n. Mathematics.* A rule of correspondence established between two sets that associates each member of the first set with a single member of the second.

ma·qui (mä'kē) *n.* **1.** An evergreen shrub, *Aristotelia Macqui,* of Chile, bearing purple berries. **2.** A Chilean wine made from these berries. [Spanish, from Chilean Araucan (Mapuche).]

ma·quis (mà-kē') *n., pl.* **maquis.** In the Mediterranean area, a dense growth of small trees and shrubs. [French (via Corsica), from Italian *macchia,* "spot," (hence) scrub bushes dotting a hillside, from Latin *macula,* spot. See **macula** in Appendix.*]

Ma·quis (mà-kē') *n., pl.* **Maquis. 1.** The French underground organization that fought against German occupation forces during World War II; the resistance. **2.** A member of this organization. [French, from *maquis,* MAQUIS, "bush" (referring to undergrowth as a hiding place).]

mar (mär) *tr.v.* **marred, marring, mars. 1.** To damage or deface. **2.** To spoil the quality of: *"Mend your speech lest it mar your fortunes."* (Shakespeare). —See Synonyms at **injure.** —*n.* A mark that disfigures; blemish. [Middle English *marren, merran,* Old English *merran, mierran.* See **mer-⁴** in Appendix.*]

mar. 1. maritime. **2.** married.

Mar. March.

mar·a·bou (măr'ə-boo) *n.* Also **mar·a·bout. 1.** Any of several large, Old World birds of the genus *Leptoptilus,* having a soft down used to trim women's garments. Also called "adjutant," "adjutant stork." **2.** A neckpiece, hat, dress, or coat trimmed with the down of the marabou. **3. a.** A raw silk that can be dyed without being separated from the gum. **b.** A fabric or an article of apparel made from such silk. [French *marabout,* from Portuguese *marabuto,* from Arabic *murābit,* stork, "holy man," "hermit" (the stork is a sacred bird in Islam). See **marabout.**]

mar·a·bout¹ (măr'ə-boo', -boot') *n.* **1.** A Moslem hermit or saint. Used especially in northern Africa. **2.** The tomb of a marabout or a shrine to his memory. [French, from Portuguese *marabuto,* from Arabic *murābit,* hermit, holy man, "(one) stationed (at a frontier post)," from *rabata,* to make fast, fix.]

mar·a·bout². Variant of **marabou.**

ma·ra·ca (mə-rä'kə) *n.* A percussion instrument consisting of a hollow-gourd rattle containing pebbles or beans. Maracas are often played in pairs. [Brazilian Portuguese, from Tupi.]

Ma·ra·cai·bo (mä'rä-kī'bō). **1.** A seaport of Venezuela, between Lake Maracaibo and the Gulf of Venezuela. Population, 421,000. **2.** The largest lake (about 5,000 square miles) in South America, in Venezuela, south of the Gulf of Venezuela.

Ma·ra·cay (mär'ə-kī'). A city of northern Venezuela, 50 miles southwest of Caracas. Population, 135,000.

Mar·a·jó (mä-rä-jō'). An island occupying 18,500 square miles in the Amazon delta in Brazil. Population, 125,000.

Ma·ra·nhão (mä'räN-youN'). A state of Brazil, occupying 129,252 square miles in the northeast. Population, 3,097,000. Capital, São Luis.

Ma·ra·ñón (mä'rä-nyōn'). A river rising in the Peruvian Andes and flowing about 1,000 miles to join the Ucayali, with which it forms the Amazon.

ma·ran·ta (mə-răn'tə) *n.* **1.** Any plant of the tropical American genus *Maranta,* one species of which yields arrowroot. Several species are cultivated for their ornamental appearance. **2.** A starch made from arrowroot. [New Latin, after Bartolommeo *Maranta* (died 1571), Italian herbalist.]

ma·ras·ca (mə-răs'kə) *n.* A European cherry tree, *Prunus Cerasus Marasca,* bearing bitter red fruit from which maraschino is made. [Italian, shortened from *amarasca (ciliegio),* bitter (cherry), from *amaro,* bitter, from Latin *amārus,* bitter. See **om-** in Appendix.*]

mar·a·schi·no (măr'ə-skē'nō, -shē'nō) *n.* A cordial made from the fermented juice and crushed pits of the marasca cherry. [Italian, from *marasca,* MARASCA.]

maraschino cherry. A maraschino-flavored preserved cherry.

ma·ras·mus (mə-răz'məs) *n. Pathology.* A wasting away of the body, associated with inadequate or inadequately assimilated food. [Late Latin, from Greek *marasmos,* from *marainein,* to waste away. See **mer-²** in Appendix.*] —**ma·ras'mic** *adj.*

Ma·rat (mà-rà'), **Jean Paul.** 1743–1793. Swiss-born French revolutionary leader and journalist; assassinated.

Ma·ra·tha (mə-rä'tə) *n., pl.* **Maratha** or **-thas.** Also **Mah·rat·ta** (mə-răt'ə). **1.** A Scytho-Dravidian people of southwestern India. **2.** A member of the Maratha people. [Native name.]

Ma·ra·thi (mə-rä'tē) *n.* Also **Mah·rat·i, Mah·rat·ti** (mə-rä'tē, mə-răt'ē). The major Indic language in the state of Maharashtra, India. [Marathi, from MARATHA.]

Mar·a·thon (măr'ə-thŏn'). A plain in eastern Attica, Greece, where the Persians were defeated by the Athenians and Plataeans in 490 B.C.

mar·a·thon (măr'ə-thŏn') *n.* **1.** A cross-country footrace of 26 miles, 385 yards. It is an event in the Olympic games. **2.** Any long-distance race: *a swimming marathon.* **3.** A contest of endurance: *a dance marathon.* **4.** A task or action that requires endurance: *a marathon of greetings.* [Named in commemoration of the messenger who ran to Athens, bringing the news of the Greek victory at MARATHON.] —**mar'a·thon'** *adj.*

ma·raud (mə-rôd') *v.* **-rauded, -rauding, -rauds.** —*intr.* To rove in search of booty; raid for plunder. —*tr.* To invade for loot; raid or pillage. —*n. Archaic.* A raid. [French *marauder,* from *maraud,* vagabond, rogue, perhaps from dialectal *maraud,* tomcat (imitative of purring).] —**ma·raud'er** *n.*

mar·ble (mär'bəl) *n.* **1.** A metamorphic rock, chiefly calcium carbonate, $CaCO_3$, often irregularly colored by impurities. It is used for architectural and ornamental purposes. **2.** A piece of marble. **3.** A sculpture of marble: *the Elgin marbles.* **4.** A hard ball used in children's games. **5.** *Plural.* A game played with marbles. Used with a singular verb. —**lose one's marbles.** *Slang.* To take leave of one's senses. —*tr.v.* **marbled, -bling, -bles.** To mottle and streak with colors and veins in imitation of marble. —*adj.* **1.** Consisting of marble. **2.** Resembling marble in consistency, texture, venation, color, or coldness: *a marble heart.* [Middle English *marbel,* from Old French *marbre,* from Latin *marmor,* from Greek *marmaros†,* marble, originally any hard stone.] —**mar'bly** *adj.*

Mar·ble·head (mär'bəl-hĕd', -hĕd'). A resort town in Massachusetts, about 15 miles northeast of Boston, on Massachusetts Bay. Population, 19,000.

mar·ble·ize (mär'bəl-īz') *tr.v.* **-ized, -izing, -izes.** To give a veined or mottled appearance to: *"An aged yellow eye . . . encrusted within a sphere of marbleized pink skin."* (Octavia Waldo).

mar·ble·wood (mär'bəl-wood') *n.* An Asian tree, *Diospyros Kurzii,* having mottled gray wood used in cabinetwork.

mar·bling (mär'blĭng) *n.* **1.** A mottling or streaking that resembles marble. **2.** The process or operation of giving something the surface appearance of marble. **3.** *Bookbinding.* The decorative imitation of marble patterns printed on page edges and endpapers.

Mar·burg (mär'bûrg'; *German* mär'boŏrk'). A city in West Germany; site of Germany's oldest Protestant university (established in 1527). Population, 48,000.

marc (märk) *n.* **1.** The pulpy residue left after the juice has been pressed from grapes, apples, or other fruits. **2.** Brandy distilled from grape or apple residue. [French *marc,* from Old French *marcher,* to trample (grapes), to MARCH.]

mar·ca·site (mär'kə-sīt', -zīt') *n.* **1.** A mineral of iron disulfide, FeS_2, having the same composition as pyrite but differing in crystalline structure. Also called "white iron pyrites." **2.** An ornament of pyrite, polished steel, or white metal. **3.** Any of several minerals resembling iron disulfide. [Middle English *marchasite,* from Medieval Latin *marcasīta,* from Arabic *marqashīṭā,* probably from Persian.]

mar·cel (mär-sĕl') *n.* A former hair style characterized by regular waves. —*tr.v.* **marcelled, -celling, -cels.** To style (the hair) in a marcel. [Originated by *Marcel* Grateau (died 1936), French hairdresser.]

mar·ces·cent (mär-sĕs'ənt) *adj. Botany.* Withering but not falling off, as a blossom that persists on a twig after flowering. [Latin *marcēscēns,* present participle of *marcēscere,* inceptive of *marcēre,* to wither. See **merk-** in Appendix.*]

march¹ (märch) *v.* **marched, marching, marches.** —*intr.* **1. a.** To walk in a formal military manner with measured steps at a steady rate. **b.** To begin to move in such a manner: *The troops will march at dawn.* **2.** To advance or proceed with steady movement. —*tr.* **1.** To cause to march: *soldiers being marched into battle.* **2.** To traverse by marching: *They marched the route in a day.* —*n.* **1.** The act of marching: *The steady forward movement of a body of troops.* **b.** A long tiring journey on foot. **2.** Forward movement; advancement; progression: *the march of time.* **3.** A regulated pace: *quick march.* **4.** The distance covered by marching: *a week's march away.* **5.** *Music.* A musical composition in regularly accented, usually duple, meter, to accompany marching. —**on the march.** Advancing; progressing: *Science is on the march.* —**steal a march on.** To get ahead of, especially by quiet enterprise. [Old French *marcher, marchier,* to walk, tramp, trample, from Frankish *markôn* (unattested), to mark out with footprints. See **merg-** in Appendix.*]

march² (märch) *n.* **1.** The border or boundary of a country or area of land. **2.** A tract of land bordering on two countries and claimed by both: *"The whole valley of the Thames was a devastated march."* (Alfred Duggan). —*intr.v.* **marched, marching, marches.** To border upon or have a common boundary (with): *England marches with Scotland.* [Middle English *marche,* from Old French *marche, marc,* borderland, from Germanic. See **merg-** in Appendix.*]

March¹ (märch) *n. Abbr.* **Mar.** The third month of the Gregorian calendar. March has 31 days. See **calendar.** [Middle English, from Old French *Marche, Marz,* from Latin *Mārtius (mēnsis),* (month) of Mars, from *Mārs* (stem *Mārt-*), Mars. See **Māwort-** in Appendix.*]

March². The German name for the **Morava** River.

March. marchioness.

Mär·chen (mĕr'KHən) *n., pl.* **Märchen.** *German.* A folk tale or fairy story.

Marches, The (mär'chĭz). **1.** A region of central Italy on the Adriatic Sea, 3,744 square miles in area. **2.** *Small* t. Border districts between England and Wales or between England and Scotland.

mar·che·sa (mär-kā'zä) *n., pl.* **-se** (-zä). A wife or widow of a marchese. [Italian, feminine of *marchese,* MARCHESE.]

mar·che·se (mär-kā'zä) *n., pl.* **-si** (-zē). An Italian nobleman ranking above a count and below a prince. [Italian, from Late Latin *marcēnsis,* "ruler of a march," from *marca,* boundary, march. See **merg-** in Appendix.*]

Mar·chesh·van, Mar·ches·van. Heshvan *(see).*

marabou
Leptoptilus crumeniferus

maple
Acer rubrum
Above: Red maple in winter
Below: Detail showing leaves, flowers, and fruit

ă pat/ā pay/âr care/ä father/b bib/ch church/d deed/ĕ pet/ē be/f fife/g gag/h hat/hw which/ĭ pit/ī pie/îr pier/j judge/k kick/l lid, needle/m mum/n no, sudden/ng thing/ŏ pot/ō toe/ô paw, for/oi noise/ou out/oŏ took/ōō boot/p pop/r roar/s sauce/sh ship, dish/
t tight/th thin, path/*th* this, bathe/ŭ cut/ûr urge/v valve/w with/y yes/z zebra, size/zh vision/ə about, item, edible, gallop, circus/
à *Fr.* ami/œ *Fr.* feu, *Ger.* schön/ü *Fr.* tu, *Ger.* über/KH *Ger.* ich, *Scot.* loch/N *Fr.* bon. *Follows main vocabulary. †Of obscure origin.

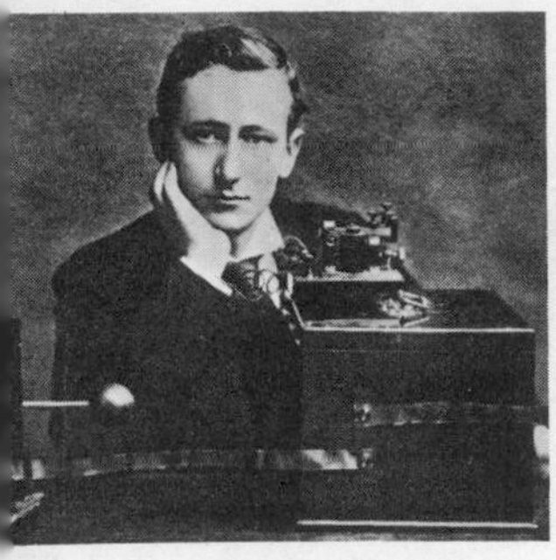

Guglielmo Marconi
In 1896 with his first wireless receiver

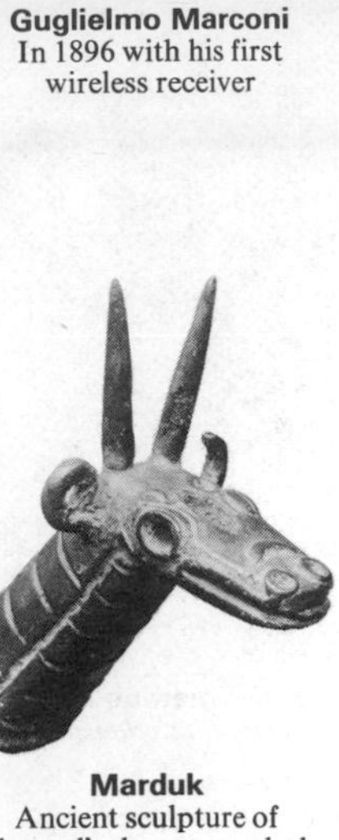

Marduk
Ancient sculpture of the god's dragon symbol

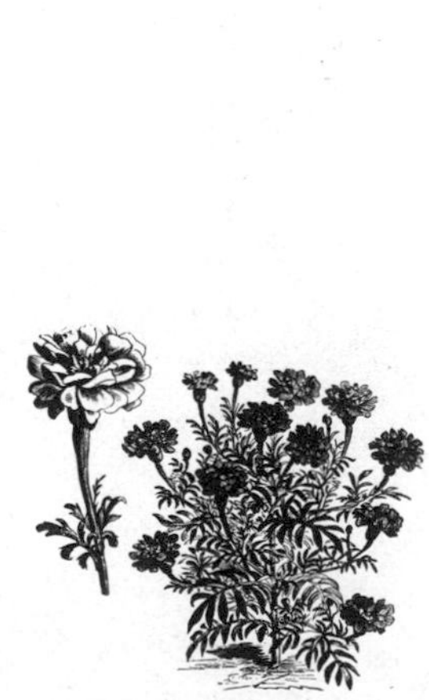

marigold
Tagetes patula

marching orders. Orders to move on or depart.

mar·chion·ess (mär′shən-ĭs, mär′shə-nĕs′) *n., pl.* **-esses.** *Abbr.* **March. 1.** The wife or widow of a marquis. **2.** A peeress of the rank of marquis in her own right. Also called "marquise." [Medieval Latin *marchionissa,* feminine of *marchiō,* marquis, "ruler of the march," from *marca,* borderland, march. See **merg-** in Appendix.*]

march·land (märch′lănd′) *n.* A borderland; a march.

march·pane (märch′pān′) *n.* A confection, **marzipan** *(see).*

Mar·cia (mär′shə). A feminine given name. [Latin, feminine of *Mārcius,* name of a Roman gens. See **Māwort-** in Appendix.*]

Mar·cio·nism (mär′shə-nĭzm) *n.* A Gnostic movement of the second and third centuries A.D. that rejected the Old Testament. [Founded by *Marcion* of Sinope.]

Mar·co·ni (mär-kō′nē), Marchese **Guglielmo.** 1874–1937. Italian electrical engineer; developer of wireless telegraphy.

Marconi rig. A **Bermuda rig** *(see).* [From MARCONI, since the rig resembles an early radio transmitting aerial.]

Mar·co Po·lo. See **Polo, Marco.**

Mar·cos (mär′kōs), **Ferdinand Edralin.** Born 1917. President of the Philippine Republic (since 1965).

Mar·cus (mär′kəs). A masculine given name. [Latin. See **Māwort-** in Appendix.*]

Mar·cus Au·re·li·us An·to·ni·nus (mär′kəs ô-rē′lē-əs ăn′tə-nī′nəs). Original name, Marcus Annius Verus. 121–180 A.D. Roman emperor and Stoic philosopher.

Mar·cy, Mount (mär′sē). The highest mountain (5,344 feet) in New York State, in the Adirondacks.

Mar del Pla·ta (mär dĕl plä′tə). A city, resort, and naval base on the Atlantic coast of Argentina. Population, 114,000.

Mar·di gras (mär′dē grä′). Shrove Tuesday, the last day before Lent. It is celebrated by carnivals, masquerade balls, and parades of costumed merrymakers. [French, "fat Tuesday."]

Mar·duk (mär′dŏŏk) *n.* The chief god of ancient Babylon.

mare¹ (mâr) *n.* A female horse or the female of other equine species. [Middle English *mare, mere,* Old English *mere, miere.* See **marko-** in Appendix.*]

ma·re² (mä′rā) *n., pl.* **-ria** (-rē-ə). *Astronomy.* Any of the large dark areas on the moon or Mars. [New Latin, from Latin *mare,* sea. See **mori-** in Appendix.*]

ma·re clau·sum (mâr′ē klô′səm; *Latin* mä′rā klou′sŏŏm). A sea that is under the jurisdiction of one nation and closed to all others. [Latin, "closed sea."]

ma·re li·be·rum (mâr′ē lĭb′ər-əm; *Latin* mä′rā lē-bä′rŏŏm). A sea open to navigation by all nations. [Latin, "free sea."]

Ma·ren·go (mə-rĕng′gō) *adj.* Browned in oil and sautéed in a sauce of tomatoes, mushrooms, garlic or onion, and white wine: *chicken Marengo; veal Marengo.* [Said to be from the chicken dish served to Napoleon after the battle of Marengo (1800).]

mare's nest. 1. A hoax or fraud. **2.** An extraordinarily complicated situation. [From the proverbial expression "to find a mare's nest" (*i.e.,* an impossible fantasy).]

mare's-tail (mârz′tāl′) *n.* An aquatic plant, *Hippuris vulgaris,* of the North Temperate Zone, having minute flowers and whorls of tapering leaves.

Mar·gar·et (mär′gə-rət, mär′grət). A feminine given name. [Middle English, from Old French *Margarete,* from Latin *Margarīta* (after St. *Margaret* of Antioch, third-century martyr), from Greek *margaritēs,* pearl. See **margaritēs** in Appendix.*]

Mar·gar·et of An·jou (mär′gə-rət; äɴ-zhōō′). 1430–1482. Queen of Henry VI of England; a leader of the Lancastrians during the Wars of the Roses.

Mar·gar·et of Na·varre (mär′gə-rət; nȧ-vär′). Also known as Margaret of Angoulême. 1492–1549. Queen of Navarre; writer.

Mar·gar·et of Val·ois (mär′gə-rət; vȧl-wä′). Also known as Queen Margot. 1553–1615. Queen of Henry IV of France, whom she divorced (1599); author of *Mémoires* (1628).

mar·gar·ic (mär-găr′ĭk). Also **mar·ga·rit·ic** (mär′gə-rĭt′ĭk) *adj.* Resembling pearl; pearly. [French *margarique,* from Greek *margaron,* pearl. See **margaritēs** in Appendix.*]

mar·ga·rine (mär′jə-rĭn). Also **mar·ga·rin** *n.* A fatty solid consisting of a blend of hydrogenated vegetable oils mixed with emulsifiers, vitamins, coloring matter, and other ingredients. It is used as a butter substitute. Also called "oleomargarine." [French, from *margarique,* MARGARIC (from the color of an acid from which margarine is obtained).]

mar·ga·ri·ta (mär′gə-rē′tə) *n.* A cocktail made of tequila, lemon or lime juice, and Triple Sec, usually served with salt encrusted on the rim of the glass. [Mexican Spanish, probably from *Margarita,* Margaret, from Latin *Margarīta,* MARGARET.]

Mar·ga·ri·ta (mär′gä-rē′tä). An island of Venezuela, 444 square miles in area, in the Caribbean Sea.

mar·ga·rite (mär′gə-rīt′) *n.* **1.** A mineral, $CaAl_2(Si_2Al_2)O_{10}(OH)_2$, related to mica, with a pearly, translucent luster, formed in sheets of monoclinic crystals. **2.** *Archaic.* A pearl. **3.** A rock formation that resembles beads. [In sense 1, from German *Margarit,* from Greek *margaritēs,* pearl. In sense 2, Middle English, from Old French, from Latin *margarīta,* from Greek *margaritēs,* pearl. See **margaritēs** in Appendix.*]

Mar·gate (mär′gĭt, -gāt′). A seaport and summer resort in Kent, England. Population, 46,000.

mar·gay (mär′gā′, mär-gā′) *n.* A spotted wildcat, *Felis weidii,* resembling a small, long-tailed ocelot, found from Texas to Brazil. [French or Spanish, from Tupi *marakaya.*]

Mar·ger·y (mär′jər-ē). Also **Mar·jor·ie, Mar·jo·ry.** A feminine given name. [Middle English, from Old French, variant of *Marguerite,* MARGUERITE.]

mar·gin (mär′jən) *n.* **1.** An edge and the area immediately adjacent to it; border; rim; verge. **2.** The blank space bordering the written or printed area on a page. **3.** A limit of a state or process: *the margin of reality.* **4.** An amount allowed beyond what is needed; a surplus measure or amount: *a margin of safety.* **5.** A measure, quantity, or degree of difference: *a margin of 500 votes.* **6.** *Economics.* **a.** The minimum return that an enterprise may earn and still pay for itself. **b.** The difference between the cost and the selling price of securities or commodities. **7.** *Finance.* An amount in money, or represented by securities, deposited by a customer with his broker as a provision against loss on transactions made on account. **8.** *Botany.* The border of a leaf. **9.** *Entomology.* The boundary area of an insect's wing. —See Synonyms at **border.** —*tr.v.* **margined, -gining, -gins. 1.** To provide with a margin. **2.** *Finance.* To deposit a margin upon. [Middle English, from Latin *margō* (stem *margin-*). See **merg-** in Appendix.*]

mar·gin·al (mär′jə-nəl) *adj.* **1.** Of, pertaining to, or constituting a margin: *the marginal strip of beach.* **2.** Geographically adjacent: *states marginal to Canada.* **3.** Written or printed in the margin of a book: *marginal notes.* **4.** Barely within a lower standard or limit of quality: *marginal writing ability.* **5.** *Economics.* **a.** Designating enterprises that produce goods or are capable of producing goods at a rate that barely covers production costs. **b.** Pertaining to commodities thus manufactured and sold. **6.** *Psychology.* Pertaining to the **fringe of consciousness** *(see).* [Medieval Latin *margināl̄is,* from Latin *margō* (stem *margin-*), margin. See **merg-** in Appendix.*] —**mar′gin·al′i·ty** (mär′jə-năl′ə-tē) *n.* —**mar′gin·al·ly** *adv.*

mar·gi·na·li·a (mär′jə-nā′lē-ə) *pl.n.* Notes in a book margin. [New Latin, neuter plural of Medieval Latin *marginālis,* MARGINAL.]

mar·gin·ate (mär′jə-nāt′) *tr.v.* **-ated, -ating, -ates.** To provide with margins or a margin. —*adj.* (mär′jə-nāt′). Also **mar·gin·at·ed** (-nā′tĭd). *Biology.* Having a border or edge of distinctive color or pattern. —**mar′gin·a′tion** *n.*

mar·grave (mär′grāv′) *n.* **1.** The lord or military governor of a medieval German border province. **2.** A hereditary title of certain princes in the Holy Roman Empire. [Middle Dutch *markgrave,* "count of the march" : *mark,* march, border (see **merg-** in Appendix*) + *grave,* count (see **gravo-** in Appendix*).]

mar·gra·vi·ate (mär-grā′vē-ĭt, -āt′) *n.* Also **mar·gra·vate** (mär′grə-vāt′). The territory governed by a margrave.

mar·gra·vine (mär′grə-vēn′) *n.* The wife or widow of a margrave. [Middle Dutch *markgravin,* feminine of *markgrave,* MARGRAVE.]

Mar·gue·rite (mär′gə-rēt′, mär′gyə-). A feminine given name. [French, from Old French, from Latin *Margarīta,* from Greek *margaritēs,* pearl. See **margaritēs** in Appendix.*]

mar·gue·rite (mär′gə-rēt′, mär′gyə-) *n.* **1.** A plant, *Chrysanthemum frutescens,* native to the Canary Islands, having white or pale-yellow flowers that resemble those of the common American daisy. Also called "Paris daisy." **2.** Any of several similar or related plants having daisylike flowers. [French, from Old French *margarite,* daisy, from Latin *margarīta,* pearl, from Greek *margaritēs,* pearl. See **margaritēs** in Appendix.*]

ma·ri·a. *Astronomy.* Plural of **mare.**

Ma·ri·a (mə-rē′ə, mə-rī′ə). A feminine given name. [Late Latin *Maria,* MARY.]

Mar·i·an¹ (mâr′ē-ən, măr′-). A feminine given name. [Variant of MARION.]

Mar·i·an² (mâr′ē-ən, măr′-) *n.* **1.** A devotee of the Virgin Mary. **2. a.** A supporter of Queen Mary I of England. **b.** An adherent of Mary, Queen of Scots. —*adj.* Of or pertaining to the Virgin Mary, Queen Mary I of England, or Mary, Queen of Scots.

Mar·i·an·a Islands (mâr′ē-ăn′ə, -ä′nə). Formerly **La·drone Islands** (lä-drōn′) or **La·drones** (lä-drōnz′). A western Pacific island chain, 370 square miles in area, lying 1,500 miles east of the Republic of the Philippines and constituting part of the Trust Territory of the Pacific under U.S. administration. Also called "Marianas."

Ma·ria·na·o (mä′ryä-nä′ō). A manufacturing and resort city of northwestern Cuba. Population, 230,000.

Mar·i·an·as Trench (mâr′ē-ăn′əs, -än′əs). A depression in the floor of the Pacific Ocean southeast of the Marianas, where the greatest depths have been recorded (37,800 feet in 1960).

Ma·ri·as (mə-rī′əs). **1.** A river rising in northwestern Montana and flowing 210 miles southeast to the Missouri. **2.** A pass over 5,000 feet high, in the Lewis Range of the Rocky Mountains.

Ma·ri·a The·re·sa (mə-rē′ə tə-rā′zə, tə-rā′sə). 1717–1780. Queen of Hungary and Bohemia and Archduchess of Austria; wife of Emperor Francis I and mother of Marie Antoinette.

Ma·ri Autonomous Soviet Socialist Republic (mä′rē). An administrative division, 8,900 square miles in area, of west-central Russian S.F.S.R. Population, 662,000. Capital, Ioshkar Ola.

Ma·rie (mə-rē′). A feminine given name. [French *Marie,* MARY.]

Ma·rie An·toi·nette (mə-rē′ ăn′twə-nĕt′). 1755–1793. Queen of France; daughter of Maria Theresa and Francis I; wife (1770) of Louis XVI; executed by the Revolutionary Tribunal.

Ma·ri·e·hamn (mä-rē′ə-hä′mən). The capital of the Åland Islands, a seaport on the southwestern coast of Åland island. Population, 7,000.

Ma·rie-Lou·ise (mə-rē′lōō-ēz′). 1791–1847. Second wife of Napoleon I; mother of Napoleon II.

mar·i·gold (măr′ə-gōld′, mâr′-) *n.* **1.** Any plant of the genus *Tagetes,* native to tropical America. Several species are widely cultivated for their showy yellow or orange flowers. **2.** Any of several plants having similar flowers, such as the **corn marigold** and the **marsh marigold** *(both of which see).* [Middle English *marygould* : MARY (with some reference to the Virgin Mary) + *gold,* a marigold, Old English *gold,* probably from *gold,* GOLD.]

mar·i·jua·na, mar·i·hua·na (măr′ə-wä′nə) *n.* **1.** A plant, **hemp** *(see).* **2.** The dried flower clusters and leaves of the hemp plant, especially when taken to induce euphoria. Slang equivalents include "weed," "pot," "Mary Jane," "tea," "gage," "grass," and as a cigarette, "reefer," "joint." See **hashish, bhang.** [Mexican Spanish *mariguana, marihuana*†.]

Mar·i·lyn (măr′ə-lĭn, mâr′-). A feminine given name. [Probably a diminutive of MARY.]

ma·rim·ba (mə-rĭm′bə) *n.* A large xylophone with resonators. [Kimbundu.]

Mar·in (măr′ĭn), **John.** 1872–1953. American painter of landscapes, seascapes, and city scenes, primarily in water color.

ma·ri·na (mə-rē′nə) *n.* A boat basin that has docks, moorings, supplies, and other facilities for small boats. [Italian, feminine of *marino,* marine, from Latin *marīnus,* MARINE.]

mar·i·nade (măr′ə-nād′) *n.* A pickling liquid of vinegar or wine and oil, with various spices and herbs, in which meat and fish are soaked before cooking. —*tr.v.* **marinaded, -nading, -nades.** To marinate. [French, from Spanish *marinada,* from *marinar,* to marinate, from *marino,* "briny," marine, from Latin *marīnus,* MARINE.]

mar·i·nate (măr′ə-nāt′) *tr.v.* **-nated, -nating, -nates.** To soak (meat or fish) in a marinade. [Alteration of MARINADE.]

Ma·rin·du·que (mä′rĭn-do͞o′kä). An island of the Republic of the Philippines, 346 square miles in area, between southern Luzon and eastern Mindoro. Population, 112,000.

ma·rine (mə-rēn′) *adj.* **1. a.** Of or pertaining to the sea: *marine exploration.* **b.** Native to or formed by the sea: *marine life.* **2.** Of or pertaining to shipping or maritime affairs: *marine bureau.* **3.** Of or pertaining to sea navigation; nautical: *marine chart.* **4.** Designating or pertaining to troops that serve at sea as well as on land, specifically the U.S. Marine Corps. —*n.* **1.** Shipping in general; maritime interests as represented by ships: *"In our marine the case is entirely the reverse."* (Henry Fielding). Rare except in the phrase *merchant marine.* **2. a.** A soldier serving on a ship or at a naval installation. **b.** *Capital* **M.** A member of the U.S. Marine Corps. **3.** In some nations, the governmental department in charge of naval affairs. **4.** A painting or photograph of the sea. [Middle English, from Old French *marin,* from Latin *marīnus,* from *mare,* sea. See **mori-** in Appendix.*]

Marine Corps. *Abbr.* **MC, USMC, U.S.M.C.** Officially, United States Marine Corps. A branch of the U.S. Armed Forces composed chiefly of amphibious troops under the authority of the Secretary of the Navy.

mar·i·ner (măr′ə-nər) *n.* **1.** One who navigates a ship; a sailor or seaman: *"I grew familiarly acquainted with . . . the best mariners of our nation."* (Richard Hakluyt). **2.** A senior Girl Scout specializing in seamanship and water skills. [Middle English, from Old French *marinier,* from *marin,* MARINE.]

Mar·i·ol·o·gy (mâr′ē-ŏl′ə-jē) *n.* Also **Mar·y·ol·o·gy.** The body of belief relating to the Virgin Mary. [MARY + -LOGY.]

Mar·i·on (măr′ē-ən, mâr′-). A masculine or feminine given name. [Middle English, from Old French, diminutive of *Marie,* MARY.]

Mar·i·on (măr′ē-ən, mâr′-), **Francis.** Called "the Swamp Fox." 1732?–1795. American general; guerrilla leader in the Revolutionary War.

mar·i·o·nette (măr′ē-ə-nĕt′) *n.* A jointed puppet manipulated by strings or wires attached to its limbs. [French, diminutive of *Marion,* MARION.]

mar·i·po·sa lily (mâr′ĭ-pō′zə). Any of several bulbous plants of the genus *Calochortus,* of the southwestern United States and Mexico, having variously colored, tuliplike flowers. Sometimes called "mariposa tulip." See **sego lily.** [From Spanish *mariposa,* butterfly : probably *María,* MARIA + *posar,* to perch, alight, from Late Latin *pausāre,* to stop, pause, from Latin *pausa,* pause. See **pauein** in Appendix.*]

Mar·ist (mâr′ĭst, măr′-) *n.* **1.** A member of the Society of Mary, a congregation of Roman Catholic missionary priests founded in 1824. **2.** A member of the Little Brothers of Mary, a Roman Catholic teaching order founded in 1817. —**Mar′ist** *adj.*

Ma·ri·tain (mà-rē-tăN′), **Jacques.** Born 1882. French Thomist philosopher and critic; taught in America.

mar·i·tal (măr′ə-təl) *adj.* **1.** Of or pertaining to marriage. **2.** *Rare.* Of or pertaining to a husband. [Latin *marītālis,* from *marītus,* married, husband. See **mari-** in Appendix.*] —**mar′i·tal·ly** *adv.*

mar·i·time (măr′ə-tīm′) *adj. Abbr.* **mar. 1.** Located on or near the sea. **2.** Of or concerned with shipping or navigation. [French, from Latin *maritimus,* from *mare,* sea. See **mori-** in Appendix.*]

Maritime Alps. A part of the western Alps extending 120 miles between France and Italy.

Maritime Provinces. Nova Scotia, New Brunswick, and Prince Edward Island. Also called "the Maritimes." See map at **Canada.**

Ma·ri·tsa (mä-rē′tsä). Also **Ma·ri·tza.** A river rising in central Bulgaria and flowing 300 miles to the Aegean Sea. It forms the Greco-Turkish border for 115 miles of its course.

Ma·riu·pol. Former name for **Zhdanov.**

Mar·i·us (mâr′ē-əs), **Gaius.** 155?–86 B.C. Roman general; seven times consul.

mar·jo·ram (mär′jər-əm) *n.* **1.** An aromatic plant, *Majorana hortensis,* having small purplish-white flowers and leaves used as seasoning. Also called "sweet marjoram." **2.** A similar plant, *Origanum vulgare,* having spikes of pinkish flowers, and leaves used in cooking. Also called "pot marjoram," "wild marjoram." [Middle English *majorane,* from Old French, from Medieval Latin *majorāna*†.]

Mar·jo·rie, Mar·jo·ry. Variants of **Margery.**

mark[1] (märk) *n. Abbr.* **mk. I.** A sign, symbol, or visible impression. **1.** A visible trace or impression on something, as a spot, dent, or line. **2.** A cross or other sign made in lieu of a signature: *"Dost thou sign thy name or make thy mark?"* (Herman Melville). **3.** A written or printed symbol used for punctuation; punctuation mark. **4.** A number, letter, or symbol used to indicate various grades of scholastic achievement: *A mark of 95 is excellent.* **5. a.** An inscription, name, stamp, label, or seal placed on an article to signify ownership, quality, manufacture, or origin. Compare **trademark, hallmark. b.** A notch in an animal's ear or hide indicating ownership. **6.** *Nautical.* **a.** A knot or piece of material placed at various measured lengths on a lead line to indicate the depth of the water. **b. Plimsoll mark** *(see).* **II.** A quality; an impression or type of quality. **1. a.** A visible indication of some quality, property, or feature: *"The old Fort Prince George now bears no marks of a fortress, but is used as a trading house."* (William Bartram). **b.** A visible sign or symbol, as a badge or brand adopted by or imposed on a person: *"He was indeed a man whom trouble had set its mark on."* (Mary Renault). **c.** *Capital* **M.** A particular mode, brand, size, or quality of a product. Usually followed by a designation such as a numeral and used attributively: *This automobile is the Mark X model.* **2.** A recognized standard or criterion of quality: *schoolwork that is not up to the mark.* **3.** Quality; note; importance. Usually preceded by *of: "A fellow of no mark nor likelihood."* (Shakespeare). **4.** Notice; attention; heed. Usually preceded by *of: "Little matter worthy of mark occurred."* (Scott). **III.** Something aimed at or desired. **1.** A target: *"A mounted officer would be a conspicuous mark."* (Ambrose Bierce). **2.** That which one wishes to achieve; a goal. **3.** An object or point that serves as a guide. **4.** *Slang.* A person who is an easy target for a swindler; dupe. **5.** The place from which racers begin and sometimes end their contest. **6.** A stationary ball in bowls; the jack. **IV.** A boundary, or an area enclosed by a boundary. **1.** A boundary between countries. **2.** In medieval England and Germany, a tract of land held in common by a community. **3.** *Statistics.* The numerical value given for computational convenience to a statistical observation falling within one of a number of intervals. —See Synonyms at **sign.** —**beside the mark.** Beside the point; irrelevant. —**God** (or **Heaven**) **save** (or **bless**) **the mark!** Used to express ironic deprecation: *"The crisis of apathetic melancholy from which . . . he emerged by the reading of Marmontel's Memoirs (Heaven save the mark!) and Wordsworth's poetry."* (William James). —*v.* **marked, marking, marks.** —*tr.* **1.** To make a visible impression on, as with a spot, line, or dent. **2.** To form, make, or depict by making a visible impression on, as with a spot, line, or dent: *He marked a square on the board.* **3. a.** To distinguish or indicate by making a visible impression: *He marked the spot where the treasure is buried.* **b.** To distinguish, indicate, or characterize: *This year marks the tenth anniversary.* **4.** To set off by or separate as if by a mark. **5.** To attach price tags, maker's labels, or other identification to articles for sale. **6.** To grade and correct (scholastic work) by evaluating it according to an established scale of letters and numbers. **7. a.** To give attention to; notice: *"Mark what radiant state she spreads."* (Milton). **b.** To take note of in writing; write down. **8.** To consider; study; observe: *Mark my word.* **9.** To keep (score) in various games. —*intr.* **1.** To make a visible impression: *This pen will mark under water.* **2.** To receive a visible impression: *The floor marks easily.* **3.** *Poetic.* To notice; pay attention: *"Pray you, mark."* (Shakespeare). **4.** To keep score. Used of various games. **5.** To determine scholastic grades: *His teacher marks strictly.* [Middle English *mark,* Old English *mearc,* boundary, hence landmark, sign, trace. See **merg-** in Appendix.*]

mark[2] (märk) *n. Abbr.* **M. 1.** A former English and Scottish monetary unit equal to 13 shillings and 4 pence. **2.** A monetary unit, the **Deutsche mark, ostmark,** or **reichsmark** *(all of which see).* **3.** Any of several former European units of weight equal to about eight ounces, used especially for weighing gold and silver. **4.** A Finnish monetary unit, a **markka** *(see).* [Sense 1, Middle English *mark,* Old English *marc.* Sense 2, German *Mark,* from Middle High German *marke.* (The word exists in all Germanic and Romance languages; the source is probably identical with that of MARK (sign), in a sense such as "a mark on a bar of metal.") See **merg-** in Appendix.*]

Mark[1] (märk). A masculine given name. [Middle English, from Old French *Marc,* from Latin *Mārcus.* See **Māwort-** in Appendix.*]

Mark[2] (märk). *Arthurian Legend.* The king of Cornwall who was the husband of Iseult and the uncle of Tristan.

Mark[3] (märk) *n.* A book of the New Testament, the second Gospel, attributed to Saint Mark.

Mark[4] (märk), **Saint.** The author of the second Gospel of the New Testament.

Mark An·to·ny. See Marcus Antonius.

marked (märkt) *adj.* **1.** Having a mark or marks. **2.** Having a noticeable character or trait; distinctive; clearly defined: *"certain strongly marked variations, which no one would rank as mere individual differences"* (Charles Darwin). **3.** Singled out, especially for a dire fate: *a marked man.* —**mark′ed·ly** (mär′kĭd-lē) *adv.* —**mark′ed·ness** (mär′kĭd-nĭs) *n.*

mark·er (mär′kər) *n.* **1.** Something that marks or distinguishes,

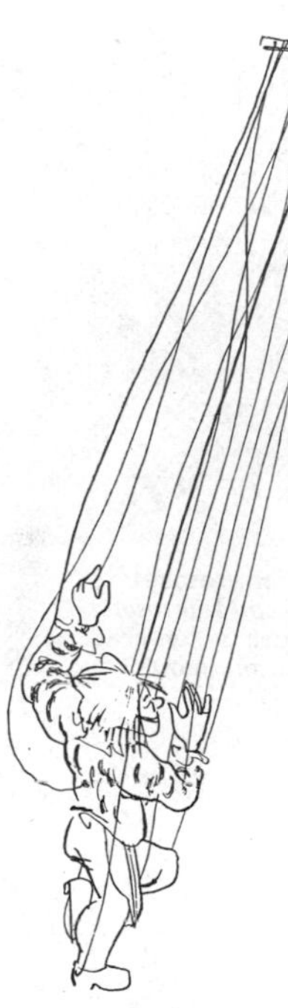

marionette

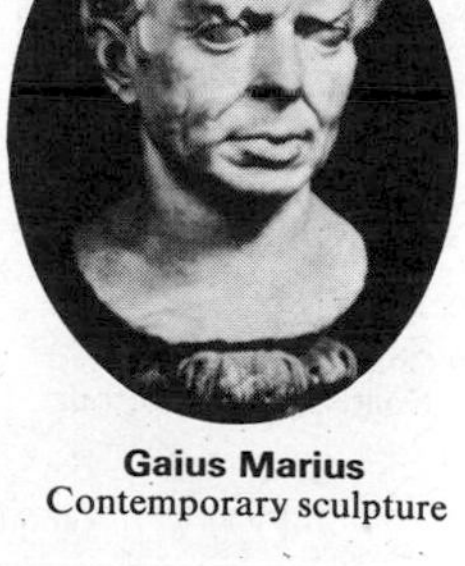

Gaius Marius
Contemporary sculpture

as a bookmark, tombstone, or milestone. **2.** A person who marks objects, especially for industrial purposes. **3.** A person who grades scholastic papers. **4.** *Sports.* A line, stake, flag, or other device on a playing field that shows playing or scoring position. **5. a.** A person or device that keeps score in various games. **b.** A score in a game. **6.** *Slang.* A written, signed promissory note; an IOU.

mar·ket (mär′kĭt) *n. Abbr.* **mkt. 1.** A public gathering held at regular intervals for buying and selling merchandise. **2.** An open place or building where goods are offered for sale. Also called "marketplace." **3.** A store or shop that sells a particular type of merchandise: *a meat market.* **4. a.** The business of buying and selling a specified commodity. **b. Market price** *(see).* **c.** The buying or selling of a particular type of product, as a business carried on by a specific group of persons or persons living in a particular area or involved with a specific institution: *the college market.* **5.** The opportunity to buy or sell; demand for availability of merchandise. **6. a.** An exchange for buying and selling stocks or commodities: *securities sold on the New York market.* **b.** The entire enterprise of buying and selling commodities and securities. Usually preceded by *the.* **—at the market.** At the price prevailing when a customer's order to buy or sell is placed. **—be in the market for.** To desire to acquire or buy. **—play the market.** To speculate on the stock exchange. **—put on the market.** To put up for sale. **—***v.* **marketed, -keting, -kets.** **—***tr.* **1.** To offer for sale. **2.** To sell. **—***intr.* **1.** To deal in a market. **2.** To buy household supplies: *She marketed for Sunday dinner.* [Middle English *market,* Old English *market,* from Vulgar Latin *marcātus* (unattested), variant of Latin *mercātus,* from the past participle of *mercārī,* to trade, from *merx,* merchandise. See **merc-** in Appendix.*] **—mar′ket·er** *n.*

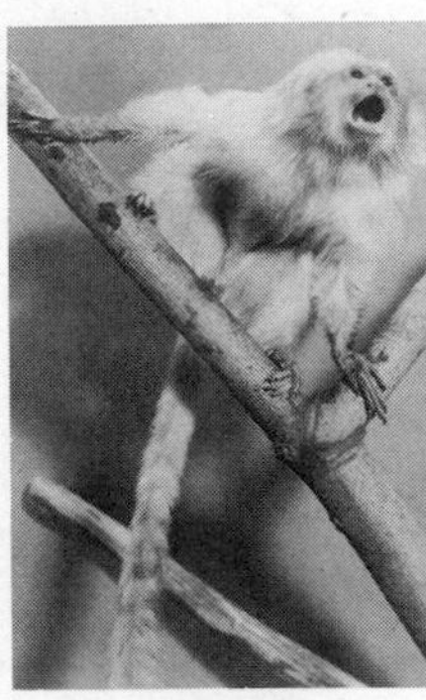

marmoset
Leontideus rosalia
Golden or lion-headed marmoset

mar·ket·a·ble (mär′kĭt-ə-bəl) *adj.* **1.** Fit to be offered for sale. **2.** Salable: *"Naturally he asked if he had any marketable manuscript, and Goldsmith dug out* The Vicar of Wakefield." (J.H. Plumb). **3.** Relating to selling or buying. **—mar′ket·a·bil′i·ty** *n.*

market order. An order to buy or sell stocks or commodities at the prevailing market price.

mar·ket·place (mär′kĭt-plās′) *n.* Also **market place. 1.** A public square or other place in which a market is set up. **2.** The figurative place of assembly where works, opinions, and ideas are debated and exchanged. Usually used with *the: the marketplace of ideas.* Also called "market."

market price. The prevailing price at which merchandise, securities, or commodities are sold. Also called "market."

mar·ket-ripe (mär′kĭt-rīp′) *adj.* Not quite ripe. Said of produce picked so that it will be ripe and fit to eat when sold.

market value. The amount that a seller may expect to obtain for merchandise, services, or securities in the open market.

Mark·ham (mär′kəm), **(Charles) Edwin.** 1852–1940. American poet.

Mark·ham, Mount (mär′kəm). A mountain, with peaks up to 15,100 feet, in Victoria Land, Antarctica.

mark·ing (mär′kĭng) *n.* **1.** The act of making a mark or marks. **2.** A mark or marks. **3.** The arrangement or pattern of characteristic coloration of a plant or animal.

mark·ka (mär′kä′) *n., pl.* **-kaa** (-kä′). *Abbr.* **mk.** The basic monetary unit of Finland equal to 100 pennis. Also called "mark." See table of exchange rates at **currency.** [Finnish, from Swedish *mark.* See **mark** (money).]

marks·man (märks′mən) *n., pl.* **-men** (-mən). **1.** A person skilled at shooting a gun or other weapon. **2.** A classification in the U.S. Army and Marine Corps for the lowest of three ratings of rifle proficiency. **3.** A soldier in the U.S. Army who rates as a marksman. Compare **sharpshooter, expert.** [*Mark's man;* from MARK (target).] **—marks′man·ship′** *n*

Mark Twain. Pen name of Samuel Langhorne **Clemens** *(see).*

mark·up (märk′ŭp′) *n.* **1.** A raise in price. **2.** The amount added to the cost of an item when figuring the selling price.

marl (märl) *n.* A mixture of clays, carbonates of calcium and magnesium, and remnants of shells, forming a loam used as fertilizer. **—***tr.v.* **marling, marled, marls.** To fertilize with marl. [Middle English *marl,* Old English *marle,* from Late Latin *margila,* diminutive of *marga*†, marl.]

Marl·bor·ough (märl′bər-ə, môl′-, -brə), **First Duke of.** Title of John Churchill. 1650–1722. English general and statesman during the War of the Spanish Succession.

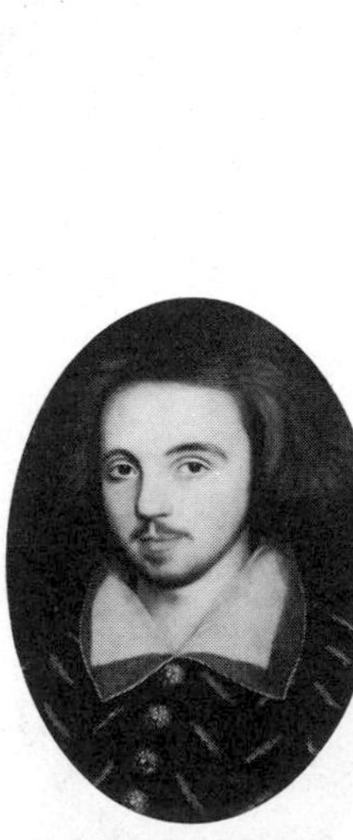

Christopher Marlowe
Contemporary portrait

Mar·lene (mär-lēn′; *German* mär-lā′nə). A feminine given name. [German, probably ultimately from Latin *Magdalēna,* MARY MAGDALENE.]

mar·lin (mär′lən) *n.* Any of several large game fish of the genus *Makaira,* of the Atlantic and Pacific oceans. [Short for MARLINESPIKE (from the pointed shape of the snout).]

mar·line (mär′lən) *n.* Also **mar·lin, mar·ling** (-lĭng). *Nautical.* A light rope made of two loosely twisted strands. [*Marline,* Middle English *marline,* from Middle Dutch *marlijn,* "tie-line" : *marren,* to tie (see **mer-³** in Appendix*) + *lijn,* line, from Latin *līnea,* LINE.]

mar·line·spike (mär′lən-spīk′) *n.* Also **mar·lin·spike, mar·ling·spike** (-lĭng-spīk′). *Nautical.* A pointed metal spike, used to separate strands of rope in splicing.

mar·lite (mär′līt′) *n.* A marl containing 25 to 75 per cent clay, the remainder being calcium carbonate, that is resistant to decomposition in air. Also called "marlstone." [MARL (loam) + -ITE.] **—mar·lit′ic** (mär-lĭt′ĭk) *adj.*

Mar·lowe (mär′lō), **Christopher.** 1564–1593. English dramatist and poet.

marl·stone (märl′stōn′) *n.* **Marlite** *(see).*

mar·ma·lade (mär′mə-lād′) *n.* A preserve made from the pulp and rind of fruits, especially citrus fruits. [French *marmelade,* from Portuguese *marmelada,* "quince jam," from *marmelo,* quince, from Latin *melimēlum,* from Greek *melimēlon,* "honey-apple," the fruit of an apple tree grafted on a quince : *meli,* honey (see **melit-** in Appendix*) + *mēlon,* apple, fruit (see **mēlon** in Appendix*).]

marmalade box. A tree, the **genipap** *(see).*

marmalade plum. A tree, *Calocarpum zapota,* of the American tropics, having edible fruit.

Mar·ma·ra, Sea of (mär′mə-rə). Also **Mar·mo·ra.** Ancient name **Pro·pon·tis** (prō-pŏn′tĭs). A sea, about 4,300 square miles in area, between European and Asiatic Turkey.

mar·mite (mär-mēt′, -mīt) *n.* **1. a.** A large covered kettle, usually made of earthenware or metal. **b.** A small, covered earthenware casserole designed to hold an individual serving. **2.** The broth made in such a kettle or served in such a casserole. In this sense, also called "petite marmite." [Old French, kettle, pot, from *marmite,* hypocritical (because the cover keeps children from seeing inside) : *marmouser,* to murmur (see **mormor-** in Appendix*) + *mite,* term of endearment for cats (imitative).]

Mar·mo·la·da (mär′mō-lä′dä). The highest mountain in the Dolomites, rising to 10,964 feet in northeastern Italy.

mar·mo·re·al (mär-môr′ē-əl, -mōr′ē-əl) *adj.* Also **mar·mo·re·an** (mär-môr′ē-ən, -mōr′ē-ən). Cold, smooth, white, and hard, as a marble statue: *a complexion of marmoreal lustre.* [Latin *marmoreus,* from *marmor,* MARBLE.]

mar·mo·set (mär′mə-sĕt′, -zĕt′) *n.* Any of various small monkeys of the genera *Callithrix, Cebuella, Saguinus,* and *Leontideus,* found in tropical forests of the Americas. They have soft, dense fur, tufted ears, and long tails. [Middle English, from Old French *marmoset*†, grotesque figure.]

mar·mot (mär′mət) *n.* Any of various stocky, coarse-furred rodents of the genus *Marmota,* having short legs and ears, and bushy tails, found throughout the Northern Hemisphere. See **woodchuck, whistler.** [French *marmotte,* from earlier *marmottaine,* from Medieval Latin *mormotāna,* representing Latin *mūs* (stem *mūr-*), mouse (see **mū-¹** in Appendix*) + *montānus,* mountain (adjective), from *mons,* mountain (noun) (see **men-²** in Appendix*).]

Marne (märn). A river in northeastern France; scene of battles in World War I (1914, 1918) and in World War II (1944).

Ma·roc. The French name for **Morocco.**

Ma·ro·ni (mə-rō′nē). A river of northern South America, flowing 450 miles north to the Atlantic Ocean along the border between Surinam and French Guiana.

ma·roon¹ (mə-ro͞on′) *tr.v.* **-rooned, -rooning, -roons. 1.** To put (a person) ashore on a deserted island or coast. **2.** To abandon or isolate (a person) with little hope of rescue or escape. **—***n.* **1. a.** A fugitive Negro slave in the West Indies in the 17th and 18th centuries. **b.** A descendant of such a slave. **2.** A person who is marooned. [French *marron,* alteration of American Spanish *cimarrón,* fugitive slave, originally, "living on the mountain tops," possibly from *cima,* summit, from Latin *cȳma,* sprout, from Greek *kuma.* See **keu-³** in Appendix.*]

ma·roon² (mə-ro͞on′) *n.* Dark reddish brown to dark purplish red. See **color.** [Originally, "chestnut," from French *marron*†.] **—ma·roon′** *adj.*

Ma·ros. The Hungarian name for **Mureş.**

mar·plot (mär′plŏt′) *n.* A stupid and officious meddler whose interference compromises the success of any undertaking. [After *Marplot,* character in *The Busy Body* (1709), a comedy by Susanna Centlivre (1667?–1723), English author.]

marque, letters of. See **letters of marque.**

mar·quee (mär-kē′) *n.* **1.** A large tent with open sides, used chiefly for outdoor entertainment. **2.** A rooflike structure, often bearing a signboard, projecting over an entrance to a building. Also called "marquise." [French *marquise,* a linen tent pitched atop an officer's tent to distinguish it from others, from *marquis,* MARQUIS (disparagingly).]

Mar·que·san (mär-kā′zən, -sən) *n.* **1.** An inhabitant of the Marquesas Islands. **2.** The Austronesian language of the Marquesans. **—***adj.* Of or pertaining to the Marquesas Islands, their inhabitants, or their language.

Mar·que·sas Islands (mär-kā′zəs, -səs). An archipelago of 11 volcanic islands of French Polynesia, 492 square miles in area, in the South Pacific. Population, 85,000. Capital, Atuona.

mar·que·try (mär′kə-trē) *n., pl.* **-tries.** Also **mar·que·terie.** An inlay of wood, ivory, or the like, used chiefly for decorating furniture. [French *marqueterie,* from *marqueter,* to checker, from *marqué,* "a mark," pattern, variant of Old French *merc, merche,* from Old Norse *merki.* See **merg-** in Appendix.*]

Mar·quette (mär-kĕt′), **Jacques.** Known as Père Marquette. 1637–1675. French Jesuit missionary and explorer of New France and the Mississippi River.

mar·quis (mär′kwĭs; *French* mȧr-kē′) *n., pl.* **marquis** or **-quises.** Also *chiefly British* **mar·quess** (mär′kwĭs). The title of a nobleman ranking below a duke and above an earl or count. [Middle English *marchis, markis,* from Old French *marquis, marchis,* "count of the march (frontier)," from *marche,* frontier country. See **merg-** in Appendix.*]

Mar·quis (mär′kwĭs), **Don(ald Robert Perry).** 1878–1937. American journalist; author of *archy and mehitabel* (1927).

mar·quis·ate (mär′kwĭ-zĭt, -sĭt) *n.* The rank or territory of a marquis.

mar·quise (mär-kēz′) *n.* **1.** A **marchioness** *(see).* **2.** A **marquee** *(see).* **3. a.** A finger ring set with a pointed oval stone or cluster of pointed oval stones. **b.** A pointed oval shape of diamonds or other gems. [French, feminine of *marquis,* MARQUIS.]

ă pat/ā pay/âr care/ä father/b bib/ch church/d deed/ĕ pet/ē be/f fife/g gag/h hat/hw which/ĭ pit/ī pie/îr pier/j judge/k kick/l lid, needle/m mum/n no, sudden/ng thing/ŏ pot/ō toe/ô paw, for/oi noise/ou out/o͝o took/o͞o boot/p pop/r roar/s sauce/sh ship, dish/

mar·qui·sette (mär'kĭ-zĕt', mär'kwĭ-) *n.* A sheer fabric of cotton, rayon, silk, or nylon, used for clothing, curtains, and mosquito nets. [From MARQUISE (in the sense "marquee").]
Marquis of Queensberry Rules. A boxing code of fair play developed in 1869 by the eighth Marquis of Queensberry.
Mar·ra·kesh, Mar·ra·kech (mə-rä'kĕsh, măr'ə-kĕsh', mär'ə-kĕsh'). A city and former capital of Morocco. Population, 255,000.
mar·ram (măr'əm) *n.* A beach grass, *Ammophila arenaria,* much planted to stabilize shifting dunes. [East Anglian dialect, from Old Norse *maralmr* : *marr,* sea (see **mori-** in Appendix*) + *halmr,* grass (see **koləm-** in Appendix*).]
mar·riage (măr'ĭj) *n.* **1. a.** The state of being husband and wife; wedlock. **b.** The legal union of a man and woman as husband and wife. **2.** The act of marrying or the ceremony of being married; a wedding. **3.** Any close union: *a true marriage of minds.* **4.** The combination of the king and queen of the same suit, as in pinochle. [Middle English *mariage,* from Old French, from *marier,* to MARRY.]
Synonyms: marriage, matrimony, wedlock, wedding, nuptials. Marriage is applied broadly to the state or process of being married, to the ceremony thus entailed, and to a union of inanimate objects (as music and drama in opera). *Matrimony* applies to the state of being married, with emphasis on its religious nature. *Wedlock* applies to the state, primarily from a legal standpoint. *Wedding* pertains to the ceremony, with connotations of social festivity. *Nuptials,* also applied to the act of being married, may emphasize the religious aspects.
mar·riage·a·ble (măr'ĭj-ə-bəl) *adj.* Suitable for marriage: *of marriageable age.* —**mar'riage·a·bil'i·ty, mar'riage·a·ble·ness** *n.*
mar·ried (măr'ēd) *adj. Abbr.* **mar. 1. a.** Having a spouse: *"No married woman ever trusts her husband absolutely."* (H.L. Mencken). **b.** United in matrimony: *a married couple.* **2.** Of or pertaining to the state of marriage.
mar·ron (măr'ən; *French* mà-rôN') *n.* A tree, the **Spanish chestnut** *(see),* or its fruit. [French. See **maroon** (color).]
mar·row (măr'ō) *n.* **1.** The soft material that fills bone cavities, consisting, in varying proportions, of fat cells and maturing blood cells, together with supporting connective tissue and numerous blood vessels. **2.** Spinal marrow; the spinal cord. **3. a.** The inmost, choicest, or essential part; pith: *"I wanted to live deep and suck out all the marrow of life."* (Thoreau). **b.** Strength or vigor; vitality. **4.** *British.* A squash, the **vegetable marrow** *(see).* [Middle English *marowe, margh,* Old English *mærg, mærh.* See **mozgo-** in Appendix.*]
mar·row·bone (măr'ō-bōn') *n.* A bone for flavoring soup.
mar·row·fat (măr'ō-făt') *n.* One of several varieties of pea that produces large seeds. Also called "marrow pea."
marrow squash. The **vegetable marrow** *(see).*
Mar·ru·e·cos. The Spanish name for **Morocco.**
mar·ry[1] (măr'ē) *v.* **-ried, -rying, -ries.** —*tr.* **1. a.** To become united with in matrimony: *They married each other in June.* **b.** To take as a husband or wife: *He married his sweetheart.* **c.** To give in marriage. **2.** To perform the marriage ceremony for. **3.** To obtain by marriage: *marry wealth.* **4.** *Nautical.* To join (two ropes) end to end by interweaving their strands. —*intr.* **1.** To take a husband or wife; wed: *They married in their twenties.* **2.** To enter into a close relationship; unite. [Middle English *marien,* from Old French *marier,* from Latin *maritare,* from *maritus,* husband. See **mari-** in Appendix.*]
mar·ry[2] (măr'ē) *interj. Obsolete.* An exclamation of surprise or emphasis. [Middle English *Marie,* "Mary!" (the Virgin).]
Mar·ry·at (măr'ē-ĭt), **Frederick.** 1792–1848. English naval officer and author of novels about the sea.
Mars[1] (märz). *Roman Mythology.* The god of war, identified with the Greek god Ares. [Middle English, from Latin *Mārs.* See **Māwort-** in Appendix.*]
Mars[2] (märz) *n.* The fourth planet from the sun, having a sidereal period of revolution about the sun of 687 days at a mean distance of 141.6 million miles, a mean radius of approximately 2,090 miles, and a mass approximately 0.15 that of Earth. See **solar system.**
Mar·sa·la (mär-sä'lə) *n.* A pale-brown sweet dessert wine, originally exported from Marsala, Sicily.
Mar·seil·laise (mär'sā-yĕz', -sə-lĕz') *n.* The French national anthem, written in 1792 by Claude Joseph Rouget de Lisle. [French *(chanson) Marseillaise,* (song) of Marseilles.]
mar·seille (mär-săl') *n.* Also **mar·seilles** (mär-sălz'). A heavy cotton fabric with a raised pattern of stripes or figures. [Short for *Marseille quilting,* originally made in MARSEILLE.]
Mar·seille (mär-sā'). Also **Mar·seilles** (mär-sā'). The oldest and second-largest city of France and its principal seaport, situated in the southeast on the Mediterranean coast. Population, 778,000. —**Mar'seil·lais'** (mär'sā-yĕ', -sə-lĕz') *adj.*
marsh (märsh) *n.* An area of low-lying, wet land; a fen, swamp, or bog. [Middle English *mersh,* Old English *mersc, merisc.* See **mori-** in Appendix.*]
Marsh (märsh), **Reginald.** 1898–1954. American painter, illustrator, and muralist.
mar·shal (mär'shəl) *n.* **1.** In some countries, a military officer of the highest rank. See **field marshal. 2.** In the United States: **a.** A Federal officer who carries out court orders. **b.** A city officer who carries out court orders. **c.** The head of a police or fire department. **3.** A person in charge of a ceremony. **4.** A high official in a royal court, especially one aiding the sovereign in military affairs. —*v.* **marshaled, -shaling, -shals.** Also *chiefly British* **-shalled, -shalling.** —*tr.* **1.** To arrange or place (soldiers) in line for a parade, maneuver, or review. **2.** To arrange, place, or set in methodical order: *"Marshalled facts and reasoned analyses tend to cover up human nature."* (Edith Hamilton). **3.** To enlist and organize: *"our interests in marshalling the French colonies against Germany"* (Winston Churchill). **4.** To guide (a person) ceremoniously; conduct or usher. —*intr.* To take form or order; especially, take up positions in or as if in a military formation. —See Synonyms at **gather.** [Middle English *mareschal,* marshal, farrier, from Old French *mareschal,* from Old High German *marahscalc,* "keeper of the horses," marshal. See **marko-** in Appendix.*] —**mar'shal·cy, mar'shal·ship'** *n.*
Mar·shall (mär'shəl), **George Catlett.** 1880–1959. American General of the Army, statesman, and diplomat.
Mar·shall (mär'shəl), **John.** 1755–1835. American statesman and jurist; Chief Justice of the United States for 35 years.
Mar·shall (mär'shəl), **Thomas Riley.** 1854–1925. Vice President of the United States under Woodrow Wilson (1913–21).
Mar·shall (mär'shəl), **Thurgood.** Born 1908. American jurist; first Negro appointed to the U.S. Supreme Court (1967).
Mar·shall Islands (mär'shəl). An archipelago consisting of two island chains with a total land area of 70 square miles, about 2,500 miles north of New Zealand. They are part of the United Nations Trust Territory of the Pacific Islands, administered by the United States. Population, 18,000.
Marshall Plan. See **European Recovery Program.**
marsh elder. Any of several shrubs of the genus *Iva,* of eastern and central North America, often growing in salt marshes.
marsh gas. Methane *(see).*
marsh hawk. A hawk, *Circus cyaneus,* found in marshy areas of North America and Eurasia. Also called "hen harrier."
marsh hen. Any of various marsh birds of the family Rallidae, which includes the gallinules, coots, and rails.
marsh mallow. A plant, *Althaea officinalis,* native to Europe and naturalized in marshes of eastern North America. It has showy pink flowers and a mucilaginous root used as a demulcent and in confectionery. [Middle English *mershmalwe,* Old English *merscmealwe* : MARSH + MALLOW.]
marsh·mal·low (märsh'mĕl'ō, -măl'ō) *n.* **1.** A confection of sweetened paste, formerly made from the root of the marsh mallow. **2.** A confection made of corn syrup, gelatin, sugar, and starch, and dusted with powdered sugar.
marsh marigold. Any plant of the genus *Caltha;* especially, *C. palustris,* growing in swampy places and having bright yellow flowers. Also called "cowslip," "king-cup."
Mar·ston Moor (mär'stən). The site in Yorkshire, England, of the first decisive battle of the English Civil War (July 2, 1644), won by the Parliamentarians.
mar·su·pi·al (mär-sōō'pē-əl) *n.* Any mammal of the order Marsupialia, including kangaroos, opossums, bandicoots, and wombats, found principally in the Australian region and South and Central America. The female of most species lacks a placenta and possesses a **marsupium** *(see).* [New Latin *marsupialis,* from *marsupium,* MARSUPIUM.] —**mar·su'pi·al** *adj.*
mar·su·pi·um (mär-sōō'pē-əm) *n., pl.* **-pia** (-pē-ə). **1.** An external abdominal pouch in female marsupials that contains mammary glands and that shelters the young until fully developed. **2.** A temporary egg pouch in various animals. [From Latin *marsupium,* pouch, from Greek *marsupion, marsipion,* diminutive of *marsipos,* purse, probably from Avestan *maršu*†, belly.]
mart (märt) *n.* **1.** A market; trading center: *"London was the true mart where abilities of every kind were sure of meeting distinction and reward."* (Goldsmith). **2.** *Archaic.* A fair. [Middle English, shortened from Old English *market,* MARKET.]
Mar·ta·ban, Gulf of (mär'tä-băn'). A part of the Andaman Sea, extending northward into Lower Burma.
mar·ta·gon (mär'tə-gən) *n.* A lily, *Lilium martagon,* having pinkish-purple, spotted flowers. Also called "martagon lily," "Turk's-cap lily." [Middle English, from Old French, from Spanish *martagón,* from Turkish *martagān,* a kind of turban.]
Mar·tel, Charles. See **Charles Martel.**
Mar·tel·lo tower (mär-tĕl'ō). A small circular fort, formerly used in Europe for coastal defense. Also called "martello." [Alteration of *Mortella Tower,* a fort on Corsica.]
mar·ten (märt'n) *n., pl.* **marten** or **-tens. 1.** Any carnivore of the genus *Martes,* found in northern wooded areas. **2.** The fur of the marten. See **sable.** [Middle English *martren,* marten, marten's fur, from Old French *martrine,* marten's fur, from *martre,* marten, from (unattested) Common Germanic *marthuz.*]
mar·ten·site (mär'tən-zīt') *n.* A solid solution of iron and up to one per cent of carbon, the chief constituent of hardened carbon tool steels. [After Adolf *Marten* (born 1914), German metallurgist.] —**mar'ten·sit'ic** (mär'tən-zĭt'ĭk) *adj.*
Mar·tha[1] (mär'thə). A feminine given name. [Latin and Greek, from Aramaic *Mārthā,* lady, feminine of *mare,* lord.]
Mar·tha[2] (mär'thə). A sister of Lazarus and Mary, and friend of Jesus. Luke 10:38–41.
Mar·tha's Vineyard (mär'thəz). An island of Massachusetts, about 100 square miles in area, 15 miles off the coast.
Mar·tí (mär-tē'), **José Julián.** 1853–1895. Cuban hero; revolutionary leader and writer; killed in war for independence.
mar·tial (mär'shəl) *adj.* **1.** Of, pertaining to, or suggesting war. **2.** Pertaining to or connected with the armed forces or the military profession: *court martial.* **3.** Characteristic of or befitting a warrior: *"a bull-necked, martial-looking man"* (Dickens). **4.** *Capital* **M.** *Astrology.* Under the evil influence of the planet Mars. [Middle English, from Latin *mārtiālis,* from *Mārs* (stem *Mārt-*), Mars. See **Māwort-** in Appendix.*] —**mar'tial·ism'** *n.* —**mar'tial·ist** *n.* —**mar'tial·ly** *adv.*
Mar·tial (mär'shəl). Full name, Marcus Valerius Martialis. Roman poet and epigrammatist of the first century A.D.

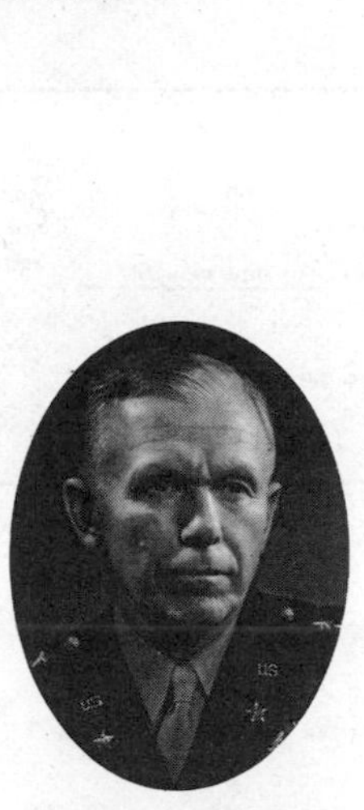
George C. Marshall
Portrait by Yousuf Karsh

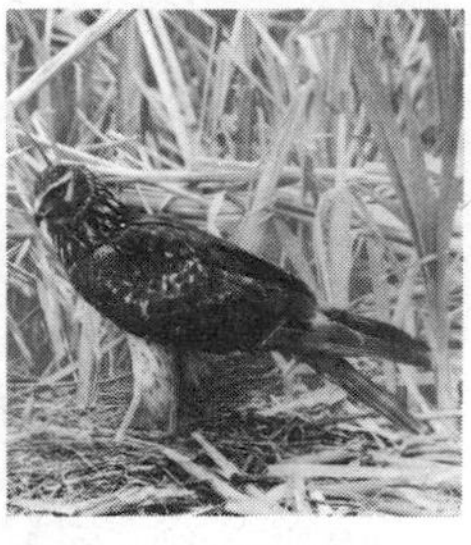
marsh hawk

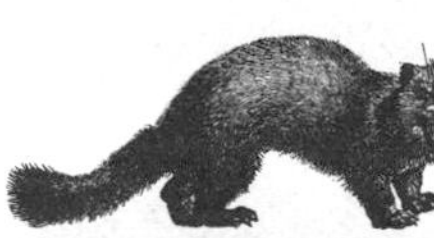
marten
Martes americana

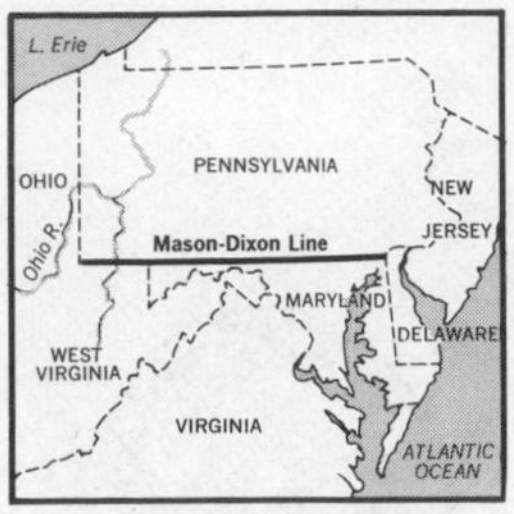

Mason-Dixon line

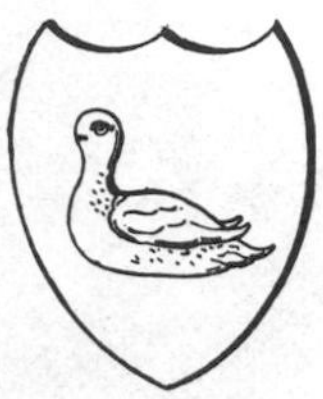

martlet

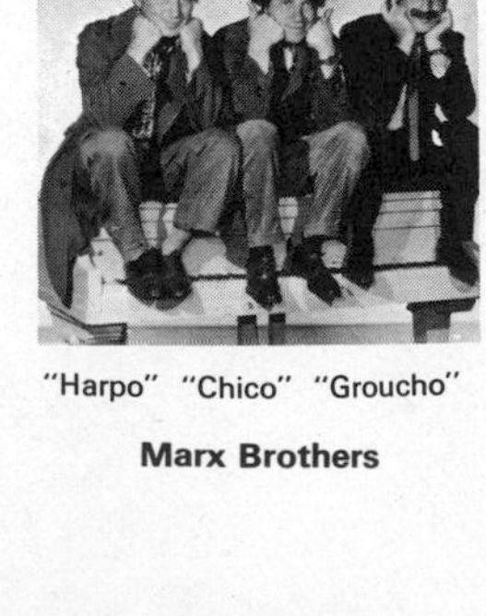

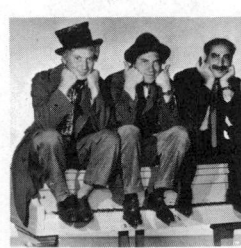

"Harpo" "Chico" "Groucho"

Marx Brothers

martial law. Temporary rule by military authorities imposed upon a civilian population in time of war or when civil authority has ceased to function. Compare **military law.**

Mar·tian (mär′shən) *adj.* Of or pertaining to the planet Mars. —*n.* An inhabitant of the planet Mars, especially as a stock fictional character. [Middle English, from Latin *mārtius,* from *Mārs* (stem *Mārt-*), MARS.]

mar·tin (märt′n) *n.* Any of several birds resembling and closely related to the swallows, such as the **house martin** and the **purple martin** *(both of which see).* [Middle English, after Saint MARTIN (the birds migrate from England near the time of Martinmas).]

Mar·tin (märt′n). A masculine given name. [Middle English, from Medieval Latin *Mārtinus,* (Saint) Martin, probably from Latin *mārtius,* warlike, from *Mārs* (stem *Mārt-*), Mars. See **māwort-** in Appendix.*]

Mar·tin (märt′n, *French* mår-tăɴ′), **Saint.** Also called "Saint Martin of Tours." A.D. 315?–399? Patron saint of France.

mar·ti·net (mär′tə-nĕt′) *n.* **1.** A rigid military disciplinarian. **2.** A person who demands absolute adherence to rules: *"James O'Neill . . . was a martinet about his children's schooling."* (B. and A. Gelb). [After Jean *Martinet,* 17th-century French general.]

mar·tin·gale (mär′tən-gāl′) *n.* Also **mar·tin·gal** (-găl′). **1.** A part of a harness designed to prevent a horse from throwing back its head. **2.** *Nautical.* Any of several parts of standing rigging strengthening bowsprit and jib boom against the force of the head stays. **3.** A method of gambling in which one doubles the stakes after each loss. **4.** A loose half belt or strap placed on the back of a garment, such as a coat or jacket. [French, from *(chausses à la) martingale,* (trousers in the manner of a) native of *Martigue,* a small village in Provençe (whose natives fasten their trousers at the back), from Provençal *martegalo,* feminine of *martegal,* native of Martigue. Sense 3 derives from *à la martingale,* "in a ridiculous manner" (since the customs of Martigue differ from those of other Provençals, and are often held up to ridicule by their neighbors).]

mar·ti·ni (mär-tē′nē) *n., pl.* **-nis.** A cocktail usually made of three or more parts of gin to one part of dry vermouth. [Origin uncertain.]

Mar·ti·nique (mär′tĭ-nēk′). An island and overseas department of France, 427 square miles, in the West Indies. Population, 292,000. Capital, Fort-de-France. —**Mar′ti·ni′can** *n.*

Mar·tin·mas (mär′tən-məs) *n.* A Christian festival celebrated annually on Saint Martin's Day, November 11.

mart·let (märt′lĭt) *n.* **1.** A bird, the **martin** *(see).* **2.** *Heraldry.* A representation of a bird without feet, used as a crest or bearing to indicate a fourth son. [French *martelet,* probably an alteration of *martinet,* diminutive of *martin,* MARTIN.]

mar·tyr (mär′tər) *n.* **1.** One who chooses to suffer death rather than renounce religious principles. **2.** One who sacrifices something very important to him in order to further a belief, cause, or principle. **3.** A person who endures great suffering. **4.** A person who makes a great show of suffering in order to arouse sympathy: *"For to feel oneself a martyr, as everybody knows, is a pleasurable thing."* (Erskine Childers). —*tr.v.* **martyred, -tyring, -tyrs. 1.** To make a martyr of (a person). **2.** To inflict great pain upon; torment: *"martyr'd by the gout"* (Pope). [Middle English *martir,* Old English *martyr,* from Late Latin *martyr,* from Greek *martus*† (stem *martur-*), witness, witness (of Christ).]

mar·tyr·dom (mär′tər-dəm) *n.* **1.** The state of being a martyr; the suffering of death by a martyr. **2.** Extreme suffering.

mar·tyr·ize (mär′tə-rīz′) *tr.v.* **-ized, -izing, -izes.** To martyr.

mar·vel (mär′vəl) *n.* **1.** Something that evokes surprise, admiration, or wonder. **2.** A sense of profound wonder or astonishment. —*v.* **marveled, -veling, -vels.** Also *chiefly British* **-velled, -velling.** —*intr.* To become filled with wonder or astonishment. —*tr.* To wonder at or about: *I marvel the fact that he came through safely.* [Middle English *marveile,* from Old French *merveille,* from Vulgar Latin *mīrābilia* (unattested), marvel, originally "wonderful things," Latin neuter plural of *mīrābilis,* wonderful, from *mīrārī,* to wonder, from *mīrus,* wonderful. See **smei-** in Appendix.*]

Mar·vell (mär′vəl), **Andrew.** 1621–1678. English poet, satirist, and political writer.

mar·vel-of-Pe·ru (mär′vəl-əv-pə-ro͞o′) *n.* A plant, the **four-o'clock** *(see).* [Originally found in Peru.]

mar·vel·ous (mär′vəl-əs) *adj.* Also **mar·vel·lous. 1.** Causing wonder or astonishment: *a marvelous cure.* **2.** Miraculous; supernatural: *"the Lord's doing; it is marvellous in our eyes"* (Psalm 118:23). **3.** Of the highest or best kind or quality: *a marvelous recipe.* —**mar′vel·ous·ly** *adv.* —**mar′vel·ous·ness** *n.*

Mar·war. See **Jodhpur.**

Marx (märks), **Karl.** 1818–1883. German philosopher and political economist; founder of world Communism.

Marx Brothers (märks). American family of comedians; principal members **Julius ("Groucho") Marx** (born 1895), **Adolph Arthur ("Harpo") Marx** (1893–1964), and **Leonard ("Chico") Marx** (1891–1961).

Marx·i·an (märk′sē-ən) *n.* One who studies or makes use of Karl Marx's philosophical or other concepts as a method of analysis and interpretation, as in political economy, or historical or literary criticism. —**Marx′i·an** *adj.* —**Marx′i·an·ism′** *n.*

Marx·ism (märk′sĭz′əm) *n.* The political and economic ideas of Karl Marx and Friedrich Engels as developed into a system of thought that gives class struggle a primary role in leading society from bourgeois democracy under capitalism to a socialist society and thence to communism.

Marx·ism-Len·in·ism (märk′sĭz′əm-lĕn′ĭ-nĭz′əm) *n.* The expansion of Marxism to include Lenin's concept of imperialism as the final form of capitalism, and a shift in the focus of struggle from the developed to the underdeveloped countries.

Marx·ist (märk′sĭst) *n.* One who believes in or follows the ideas of Marx and Engels; especially, a militant Communist. —*adj.* Of or pertaining to Marxism.

Mar·y[1] (mâr′ē). A feminine given name. [Middle English *Mary,* from Old English *Maria, Marie* and Old French *Marie,* both from Latin *Maria,* from Greek *Mariám,* from Hebrew *Miryām,* "rebellion." See **Miryām** in Appendix.*]

Mar·y[2] (mâr′ē). The mother of Jesus. Matthew 1:18–25. Also called "the Virgin Mary," "Saint Mary."

Mar·y I (mâr′ē). Title of Mary Tudor. Called "Bloody Mary." 1516–1558. Queen of England and Ireland (1553–58).

Mar·y II (mâr′ē). 1662–1694. Queen of England, Scotland, and Ireland (1689–94); ruled jointly with her husband, **William III** *(see).*

Mar·y·land (mâr′ə-lənd). *Abbr.* **Md.** Officially, the Commonwealth of Maryland. A state of the United States, 10,577 square miles in area; admitted to the Union in 1788 as one of the original 13 states. Population, 2,343,000. Capital, Annapolis. See map at **United States of America.** [After Queen Henrietta *Maria* of England (1609–1669).]

Marylebone. See **Saint Marylebone.**

Mar·y Mag·da·lene (mâr′ē măg′də-lēn′, -lən, măg′də-lē′nē). Also **Mar·y Mag·da·len** (măg′də-lən). A woman in the New Testament (Luke 8:2) whom Jesus cured of evil spirits. She is usually considered identical with the repentant prostitute in Luke 7:36–50. Also called "the Magdalene."

Mar·y·ol·o·gy. Variant of **Mariology.**

Mar·y Queen of Scots (mâr′ē). Title of Mary Stuart. 1542–1587. Queen of Scotland; abdicated (1567); beheaded on charges of sedition against her cousin Elizabeth I.

mar·zi·pan (mär′zə-păn′, märt′sə-pän′) *n.* A confection including ground almonds, molded into decorative forms. Also called "marchpane." [German *Marzipan,* from Italian *marzapane,* fine box for confections, originally a box containing a tenth of a load, from Venetian *matapan,* coin bearing a seated Christ figure, originally, a ten per cent tax, from Arabic *mawthabān,* "seated king," name given to similar coins in circulation since the Crusades.]

-mas. Indicates a Christian festival; for example, **Christmas.** [Middle English *-masse,* Old English *mæsse,* festival mass, MASS.]

Ma·sac·cio (mä-zät′chō). Original name, Tommaso Guidi. 1401–1428. Italian painter of the Florentine school.

Ma·sai (mä-sī′) *n., pl.* **Masai** or **-sais. 1.** A member of a people of Kenya and parts of Tanzania. **2.** The language of these people. —**Ma·sai′** *adj.*

Ma·san (mä′sän′). A port city of southeastern South Korea on an inlet of Korea Strait. Population, 157,000.

Ma·sa·ryk (măs′ə-rĭk), **Jan Garrigue.** 1886–1948. Czech statesman and diplomat; son of Tomáš Garrigue Masaryk.

Ma·sa·ryk (măs′ə-rĭk), **Tomáš Garrigue.** 1850–1937. Czech statesman; first president of Czechoslovakia (1918–35).

Mas·ba·te (mäs-bä′tā). One of the Visayan Islands, 1,262 square miles in area, of the Republic of the Philippines.

masc. masculine.

Mas·ca·gni (mäs-kä′nyē), **Pietro.** 1863–1945. Italian composer of operas.

mas·ca·longe. Variant of **muskellunge.**

mas·car·a (măs-kăr′ə) *n.* A cosmetic applied to darken the eyelashes. [Spanish *máscara,* "mask," from Italian *maschera,* possibly from Arabic *maskharah,* "buffoon." See also **mask.**]

mas·cot (măs′kŏt, -kət) *n.* A person, animal, or object believed to bring good luck; especially, one kept as the symbol of an athletic team or other organization. [French *mascotte,* from Provençal *mascoto,* sorcery, talisman, from *masco, masca,* sorcerer, from Late Latin *masca,* witch, from Langobard *masca.* See **mezg-**[2] in Appendix.*]

mas·cu·line (măs′kyə-lĭn) *adj. Abbr.* **masc. 1.** Of or pertaining to men or boys; male. **2.** Mannish; unwomanly: *a masculine hairdo.* **3.** Of, designating, or constituting the gender of words or grammatical forms denoting or referring normally to males: *a masculine suffix.* —See Synonyms at **male.** —*n. Abbr.* **masc. 1.** The masculine gender. **2.** A word or word form of the masculine gender. [Middle English *masculin,* from Old French, from Latin *masculīnus,* from *masculus,* male, diminutive of *mas,* male. See **mas** in Appendix.*] —**mas′cu·line·ly** *adv.* —**mas′cu·lin′i·ty** (măs′kyə-lĭn′ə-tē), **mas′cu·line·ness** *n.*

masculine ending. The ending of a line of verse with a stressed syllable. Compare **feminine ending.**

masculine rhyme. A rhyme of only a single terminal syllable always stressed, as in *cat, hat* and *annoy, enjoy.* Compare **feminine rhyme.**

Mase·field (mās′fēld′), **John.** 1878–1967. English author of poems, novels, and short stories; poet laureate (1930–67).

ma·ser (mā′zər) *n. Physics.* Any of several devices that convert incident electromagnetic radiation from a wide range of frequencies to one or more discrete frequencies of highly amplified and coherent microwave radiation. Compare **laser.** [M(ICROWAVE) A(MPLIFICATION BY) S(TIMULATED) E(MISSION OF) R(ADIATION).]

Mas·er·u (măz′ə-ro͞o′). The capital of Lesotho, in the west near the border of South Africa. Population, 9,000.

mash (măsh) *n.* **1.** Any fermentable starchy mixture from which alcohol or spirits can be distilled. **2.** A mixture of ground grain and nutrients fed to livestock and fowl. **3.** Any soft, pulpy mixture or mass. *—tr.v.* **mashed, mashing, mashes. 1.** To convert (malt or grain) into mash. **2.** To convert (something) into a soft, pulpy mixture resembling mash: *mash potatoes.* **3.** To crush or grind. **4.** *Slang.* To flirt with. [Middle English *mash,* Old English *māsc.* See **meik-** in Appendix.*]

Mash·ar·brum (mŭsh'ər-brŏŏm'). Also **Mash·er·brum.** A mountain peak, 25,660 feet high, in the Karakoram Mountains in Kashmir.

mash·er (măsh'ər) *n.* **1.** A kitchen utensil for mashing vegetables or fruit. **2.** *Slang.* A man who attempts to force his amorous attentions upon a woman: *"It was Soapy's design to assume the role of the despicable and execrated 'masher.'"* (O. Henry). [Sense 2 originally "a flirt," from *mash* (verb), to flirt, make advances, from *mash* (noun), a "crush."]

Mash·had. The Iranian name for **Meshed.**

mash·ie (măsh'ē) *n., pl.* **-ies.** Also **mash·y.** A golf club of medium loft. Also called "five iron." [Origin unknown.]

mas·jid (mŭs'jĭd) *n.* A **mosque** *(see).*

mask (măsk, mäsk) *n.* **1.** A covering worn on the face to conceal one's identity; as: **a.** A cloth covering that has openings for the eyes, entirely or partly conceals the face, and is worn especially at a masquerade ball. **b.** A representation of a grotesque face. **c.** A facial covering worn for ritual. **d.** A figure of a head worn by actors in Greek and Roman drama to identify a trait. **2.** A protective covering for the face or head. **3.** A **gas mask** *(see).* **4.** A representation of a face or head: **a.** A mold of a person's face, usually made after death. See **death mask. b.** An often grotesque representation of a head and face, used for ornamentation. **5.** The face or facial markings of certain animals, such as a fox or dog. **6.** A face having a blank, fixed, or enigmatic expression. **7.** Something, often a trait, that disguises or conceals: *"If ever I saw misery under a mask, it was on her face."* (Erskine Childers). **8.** A natural or artificial feature of terrain that conceals and protects military forces or installations. **9. a.** An opaque border or pattern placed between a source of light and a photosensitive surface to prevent exposure of specified portions of the surface. **b.** The translucent border framing a television picture tube and screen. **10.** A cosmetic preparation applied as a covering and removed. **11.** A **masque** *(see).* **12.** A person wearing a mask. *—v.* **masked, masking, masks.** *—tr.* **1.** To cover with a decorative or protective mask. **2.** To disguise; especially, to make indistinct or blurred to the senses: *The spice masks the meat's strong flavor.* **3.** To cover up for concealment or protection: *"their rifles protruding from the green boughs with which they had masked their small defenses"* (Ambrose Bierce). **4.** To block the view of: *Undergrowth masked the entrance.* **5.** To cover (a part of a photographic film) by the application of an opaque border. **6.** *Chemistry.* To inhibit (a compound or radical) with a reagent more active in a specific reaction. *—intr.* **1.** To put on a mask, especially at a masquerade ball; disguise oneself. **2.** To conceal one's real personality, character, or intentions. [French *masque,* from Italian *maschera,* perhaps from Arabic *maskharah,* "buffoon." See also **mascara.**]

mas·ka·longe. Variant of **muskellunge.**

masked (măskt, mäskt) *adj.* **1.** Wearing a mask. **2.** Disguised; concealed. **3.** Latent or hidden, as a symptom or disease. **4.** *Botany.* Resembling a mask, **personate** *(see).* **5.** *Zoology.* Having masklike markings on the head or face.

mas·keg. Variant of **muskeg.**

mask·er (măs'kər, mäs'-) *n.* Also **mas·quer.** A participant in a masquerade or masque.

mask·ing (măs'kĭng, mäs'-) *n.* **1.** The act of concealing the face with a mask. **2.** *Psychology.* The concealment or screening of one sensory process by another. **3.** *Theater.* A piece of scenery used to conceal a part of the stage from the audience.

mas·ki·nonge. Variant of **muskellunge.**

mas·o·chism (măs'ə-kĭz'əm) *n.* **1.** *Psychiatry.* An abnormal condition in which sexual excitement and satisfaction depend largely on being subjected to abuse or physical pain, whether by oneself or by another. **2. a.** The deriving of pleasure from being offended, dominated, or mistreated in some way. **b.** The tendency to seek such mistreatment. **3.** The turning of any sort of destructive tendencies inward or upon oneself. Compare **sadism.** [After Leopold von Sacher-*Masoch* (1836–1895), Austrian novelist, who described it.] **—mas'o·chist** *n.* **—mas'o·chis'tic** (măs'ə-kĭs'tĭk) *adj.* **—mas'o·chis'ti·cal·ly** *adv.*

ma·son (mā'sən) *n.* **1.** A person who builds or works with stone or brick. **2.** A **stonecutter** *(see).* **3.** *Capital* **M.** A **Freemason** *(see).* *—tr.v.* **masoned, -soning, -sons.** To build of or strengthen with masonry. [Middle English *masoun, machoun,* from Norman French *machun,* from Old French *masson,* from Frankish *makjo* (unattested), from *makōn,* to make (unattested). See **mag-** in Appendix.*]

mason bee. Any of various solitary bees of the genus *Anthidium,* found worldwide, that build clay nests.

Ma·son-Dix·on line (mā'sən-dĭk'sən). The boundary between Pennsylvania and Maryland, as surveyed by Charles Mason and Jeremiah Dixon (1763–67). It was regarded as the division between the free and the slave states before the Civil War. Also called "Mason and Dixon's line."

Ma·son·ic (mə-sŏn'ĭk) *adj.* Of or pertaining to Freemasons or Freemasonry.

Mason jar. A wide-mouthed glass jar with a screw top, used widely for home canning and preserving. [Patented by John L. *Mason* (1832–1902), American inventor.]

ma·son·ry (mā'sən-rē) *n., pl.* **-ries. 1.** The trade of a mason. **2.** Stonework or brickwork. **3.** *Capital* **M. Freemasonry** *(see).*

Ma·so·ra (mə-sôr'ə, -sōr'ə) *n.* Also **Ma·so·rah. 1.** The body of tradition relating to correct textual reading of the Old Testament. **2.** The critical notes in which this tradition is embodied, made by Jewish scholars before the tenth century A.D. [Middle Hebrew *māsōrāh,* "tradition," from Hebrew *māsar,* to hand over, transmit.] **—Mas'o·ret'ic** (măs'ə-rĕt'ĭk) *adj.*

Mas·qat. The Arabic name for **Muscat.**

masque (măsk, mäsk) *n.* Also **mask. 1.** A dramatic entertainment, usually based on a mythological or allegorical theme, popular in England in the 16th and early 17th centuries. **2.** A dramatic verse composition written for a masque production. **3.** A **masquerade** *(see).* [Variant of MASK.]

mas·quer. Variant of **masker.**

mas·quer·ade (măs'kə-rād') *n.* **1.** A costume ball or party at which masks are worn; masked ball. Also called "masque." **2.** The costume for such a party or ball. **3.** Any disguise or false outward show; pretense: *a masquerade of humility.* *—intr.v.* **masqueraded, -ading, -ades. 1.** To wear a mask or disguise, as at a masquerade: *She masqueraded as a shepherdess.* **2.** To go about as if in disguise; have or put on a deceptive appearance: *He masqueraded as the ship's surgeon.* [French *mascarade,* from Italian *mascherata* or Spanish *mascarada,* from Italian *maschera,* MASK.] **—mas'quer·ad'er** *n.*

Masr-el-Ge·di·da. The Arabic name for **Heliopolis.**

mass (măs) *n.* **1.** A unified body of matter with no specific shape: *"It was not a bird; it was a flattened mass of dusty feathers."* (Nadine Gordimer). **2.** A grouping of individual parts or elements that compose a unified body of unspecified size or quantity: *"the heterogeneous, indistinguishable mass of college boys"* (F. Scott Fitzgerald). **3.** Any large but nonspecific amount or number: *a mass of bruises.* **4.** The major part of something; majority. **5.** The physical volume or bulk of a solid body. **6.** *Physics. Abbr.* **m, M** The measure of a body's resistance to acceleration. The mass of a body is different from but proportional to its **weight** *(see),* is independent of the body's position but dependent on its motion with respect to other bodies, and may be expressed in mass units, such as kilograms or slugs, or corresponding energy units, by means of the mass-energy relationship of the special theory of relativity. **7.** *Painting.* An area of unified light, shade, or color. **8.** *Pharmacology.* A thick, pasty mixture of drugs used to form pills. **9.** *Mining.* A mineral deposit with no specific shape. Compare **bed, vein. —the masses.** The body of common people; the many. *—v.* **massed, massing, masses.** *—tr.* To gather or form into a mass. *—intr.* To assemble in a mass. *—adj.* **1.** Of, pertaining to, characteristic of, or attended by a large number of people: *mass education.* **2.** Done on a large scale; involving great numbers or large amounts: *mass production.* **3.** Total; complete: *The mass result is impressive.* [Middle English, from Old French *masse,* from Latin *massa,* from Greek *maza,* barley cake, lump, mass. See **mag-** in Appendix.*]

Mass (măs) *n.* Also **mass. 1.** In Roman Catholic and some Protestant churches, the celebration of the Eucharist. See **High Mass, Low Mass. 2.** A musical setting of certain parts of the Mass, especially the Kyrie, Gloria, Credo, Sanctus, Benedictus, and Agnus Dei. [Middle English *masse,* Old English *mæsse, messe,* from Late Latin *missa,* eucharist, possibly deriving from phrases such as *Ite, missa est,* "Go, it is the dismissal," from *mittere* (past participial stem *miss-*), to send away. See **smeit-** in Appendix.*]

Mass. Massachusetts.

Mas·sa·chu·set (măs'ə-chōō'sĭt, -zĭt) *n.* Also **Mas·sa·chu·sett. 1.** A large tribe of Algonquian-speaking Indians who lived on or near Massachusetts Bay. **2.** A member of this tribe. **3.** The Algonquian language of these Indians. [Native name, "at the big hill," from (unattested) Proto-Algonquian *me'th-,* big + *-aĉiiw-,* hill + *-ehs-,* a diminutive + *-enki,* locative ending.]

Mas·sa·chu·setts (măs'ə-chōō'sĭts, -zĭts). *Abbr.* **Mass.** Officially, the Commonwealth of Massachusetts. A New England state of the United States, 8,257 square miles in area, with an Atlantic coastline of about 190 miles. It was admitted to the Union in 1788 as one of the original 13 states. Population, 4,691,000. Capital, Boston. See map at **United States of America.** [After the MASSACHUSET Indians.]

Mas·sa·chu·setts Bay (măs'ə-chōō'sĭts, -zĭts). An inlet of the Atlantic Ocean on the Massachusetts coast, extending about 65 miles from Cape Ann to Cape Cod.

Massachusetts Bay Company. A company originally organized in 1628 as the New England Company and confirmed by royal charter in 1629 for the purpose of establishing a colony on Massachusetts Bay.

mas·sa·cre (măs'ə-kər) *n.* **1.** Savage and indiscriminate killing. **2.** *Informal.* A severe defeat, as in sports. *—tr.v.* **massacred** (-kərd), **-cring** (-krĭng, -kər-ĭng), **-cres. 1.** To kill indiscriminately and wantonly; to slaughter. **2.** *Informal.* To defeat decisively, as in sports. [French, from Old French *maçacre, macecle,* from *massacrer, macelcler* (verb), probably from Vulgar Latin *matteucculāre* (unattested), from *matteūca* (unattested), club, from *mattea* (unattested), club, from Latin *mateola,* a kind of mallet. See **mat-** in Appendix.*] **—mas'sa·crer** (-kər-ər, -krər) *n.*

mas·sage (mə-säzh') *n.* The rubbing or kneading of parts of the body to aid circulation or to relax the muscles. *—tr.v.* **massaged, -saging, -sages. 1.** To give a massage to. **2.** To treat by means of a massage. [French, from *masser,* to massage, probably from Arabic *mass,* to touch, handle.]

mas·sa·sau·ga (măs'ə-sô'gə) *n.* A brown and white venomous rattlesnake, *Sistrurus catenatus,* of North America. [After the *Missisauga* River, Ontario, Canada, where it was first discovered.]

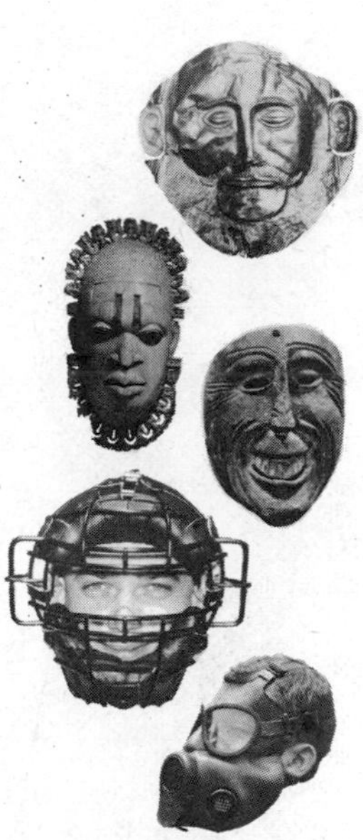

mask
From top:
Mycenaean death mask,
Nigerian ivory mask,
Mexican carnival mask,
baseball catcher's mask,
U.S. Army gas mask

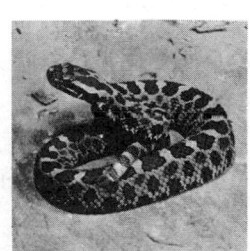

massasauga

Mas·sa·soit (măs′ə-soit′, măs′ə-soit′). 1580?–1661. Wampanoag Indian chief; aided and signed a peace treaty with the Pilgrims.

mass communication. Communication directed at or reaching many people.

Mass·cult (măs′kŭlt′) *n.* Culture at the level of the masses: *American films, in the main, are Masscult.* Compare **Midcult.** [*Mass* + *cult*(ure). Coined by Dwight Macdonald in 1965.]

mass defect. The amount by which the mass of an atomic nucleus is less than the sum of the masses of its constituent particles. It is equivalent to the **binding energy** *(see)* of the nucleus. Also called "mass deficiency."

mas·sé (mă-sā′) *n. Billiards.* A stroke made by hitting the cue ball on its side with the cue held nearly perpendicular, so the cue ball will curve around one of the object balls. [French, from *masser,* to cue, from *masse,* cue, club, MACE.]

mass-energy equivalence. The physical principle that a measured quantity of energy is equivalent to a measured quantity of mass. The equivalence is expressed by Einstein's equation, $E = mc^2$, where E represents energy, m the equivalent mass, and c the speed of light.

Mas·se·net (măs′ə-nā′; *French* mȧs-nĕ′), **Jules Émile Frédéric.** 1842–1912. French composer.

mas·seur (mă-sûr′) *n. Feminine* **mas·seuse** (-sœz′). A man who gives massages professionally. [French, from *masser,* to MASSAGE.]

mas·si·cot (măs′ə-kŏt′, -kō′) *n.* The yellow crystalline mineral form of lead monoxide, PbO. Compare **litharge.** [Middle English *masticot,* from Old French, akin to Italian *marzacotto,* ointment, cosmetic, from Spanish *mazacote,* from Arabic *šabb qubṭi,* "Egyptian alum."]

mas·sif (mă-sēf′) *n.* A large mountain mass or compact group of connected mountains forming an independent portion of a range. [French, from *massif,* MASSIVE.]

Mas·sif Cen·tral (mă-sēf′ sĕn-träl′). A plateau region in southeastern and southern France, covering about 33,000 square miles, with an average elevation of 2,500 feet.

Mas·sin·ger (măs′ən-jər), **Philip.** 1583–1640. English dramatist; author or co-author of comedies and romantic dramas.

mas·sive (măs′ĭv) *adj.* **1.** Consisting of or making up a large mass; bulky; heavy; solid: *a massive piece of furniture.* **2.** Unusually large or impressive: *a massive head.* **3.** Large or imposing in quantity, scope, degree, intensity, or scale: *"a massive book, characteristic of American scholarship at its most serious"* (Times Literary Supplement). **4.** *Medicine.* Large in comparison with the usual amount. Said of dosage. **5.** *Pathology.* Affecting a large area of bodily tissue; widespread and severe: *massive gangrene.* **6.** Pertaining to rock lacking obvious layering, banding, or foliation, or to rocks with very thick layers. **7.** Lacking crystalline structure; amorphous. —See Synonyms at **heavy.** [Middle English, from Old French *massif,* alteration of earlier *massiz,* from Vulgar Latin *massīceus* (unattested), from Latin *massa,* MASS (amount).] —**mas′sive·ly** *adv.* —**mas′sive·ness** *n.*

Mas·sive, Mount (măs′ĭv). A mountain rising to 14,418 feet in the Sawatch Mountains of central Colorado.

mass medium *pl.* **mass media.** Any means of public communication reaching a large audience.

mass number. The total number of neutrons and protons in an atomic nucleus. Also called "nucleon number." See **atomic number, atomic mass.**

mass production. The manufacture of goods in large quantities, using standardized designs and often assembly-line techniques. —**mass′-pro·duced′** *adj.*

mass spectrograph. *Physics.* An instrument used to separate charged particles from a prepared beam by means of an electromagnetic field and to photograph the resulting distribution or spectrum of masses.

mass·y (măs′ē) *adj.* **-ier, -iest.** *Archaic.* Massive; solid; having great mass or bulk: *"his massy and elaborate dictionary"* (Macaulay).

mast¹ (măst, mäst) *n.* **1.** A tall vertical spar, sometimes sectioned, that rises from the keel of a sailing vessel to support the sails and running rigging. **2.** Any vertical pole. —**before the mast.** Serving as an unlicensed seaman or common sailor (seamen's quarters were forward of the foremast). [Middle English *maste,* Old English *mæst.* See **mazdo-** in Appendix.*]

mast² (măst, mäst) *n.* The nuts of forest trees accumulated on the ground, used especially as food for swine. [Middle English *maste,* Old English *mæst.* See **mad-** in Appendix.*]

mas·ta·ba (măs′tə-bə) *n.* Also **mas·ta·bah.** An ancient Egyptian tomb with a rectangular base and sloping sides. [Arabic *maṣṭabah,* stone bench.]

mas·tec·to·my (măs-tĕk′tə-mē) *n., pl.* **-mies.** *Surgery.* Removal of a breast. [MAST(O)- + -ECTOMY.]

mas·ter (măs′tər, mäs′-) *n.* **1.** A man having control over the action of another or others. **2.** The captain of a merchant ship. Also called "master mariner." **3.** *Often capital* **M.** A person who employs another in his service: *"and that he shall be well instructed in the art or profession of his Master"* (Benjamin Franklin). **4.** The owner of a slave or an animal: *"As I would not be a slave, so I would not be a master."* (Abraham Lincoln). **5.** The man who serves as the head of a household. **6.** One who has control over something; owner; possessor: *"I was now master of near a thousand pounds."* (Hume). **7.** One who defeats another; a victor. **8.** A teacher, schoolmaster, or tutor. **9. a.** A person whose teachings or doctrines are accepted by followers. **b.** *Capital* **M.** Preceded by *our* or *the.* Christ. **10.** A man of great learning; scholar. **11.** *Abbr.* **M.** A person holding a master's degree. **12.** A workman qualified to teach apprentices and to carry on his craft independently. **13.** An **old master** *(see).* **14.** A former title for a man holding a naval office ranking next below a lieutenant on a warship. **15.** The title of the head or presiding officer of certain societies, clubs, orders, or institutions. **16.** *Chiefly British.* The title of any of various law court officers. **17.** *Capital* **M.** The title of any of various officers having specified duties concerning the management of the British royal household: *Master of the Horse.* **18.** *Capital* **M.** A man who owns a pack of hounds or is a chief officer of a hunt. **19.** *Archaic.* A form of address for any man, **mister** *(see).* **20.** *Capital* **M.** A prefix to the name of a boy or youth not considered old enough to be addressed as Mister. **21.** An original from which copies can be made. —*adj.* **1.** Of, pertaining to, or characteristic of a master. **2.** Being the principal or leading force: *a master plot.* **3.** Being something specified in a superlative degree: *a master thief.* **4.** Being a part of a mechanism that controls all other parts: *a master control switch.* **5.** Being an original from which copies are made. —*tr.v.* **mastered, -tering, -ters.** **1.** To act as or be the master of. **2.** To make oneself a master of (an art, craft, or science). **3.** To overcome or defeat: *"I had mastered the tyranny of opium."* (De Quincey). **4.** To reduce to subjugation; break or tame (a person or animal). **5.** To season or age (dyed goods). [Middle English, from Old English *mægister, magister* and Old French *maistre,* both from Latin *magister.* See **meg-** in Appendix.*] —**mas′ter·dom** *n.* —**mas′ter·hood′** *n.*

mas·ter-at-arms (măs′tər-ət-ärmz′, mäs′-) *n., pl.* **masters-at-arms.** A naval petty officer assigned to maintain order.

mas·ter·ful (măs′tər-fəl, mäs′-) *adj.* **1.** Given to playing the master; imperious; domineering. **2.** Fit to command; vigorous; powerful. **3.** Revealing mastery: *"His technique is genuinely masterful."* (Henry R. Winkler). **4.** Expert; skillful: *masterful moviemaking.* —**mas′ter·ful·ly** *adv.* —**mas′ter·ful·ness** *n.*

master key. A key that opens several different locks whose keys are not the same. Also called "passkey."

mas·ter·ly (măs′tər-lē, mäs′-) *adj.* Like a master; especially, indicating the knowledge or skill of a master. —*adv.* With the skill of a master. —**mas′ter·li·ness** *n.*

master mason. **1.** An expert mason. **2.** *Capital* **M,** *capital* **M.** The third degree of Freemasonry.

mas·ter·mind (măs′tər-mīnd′, mäs′-) *n.* A highly intelligent person; especially, one who plans and directs a project. —*tr.v.* **masterminded, -minding, -minds.** To direct, plan, or supervise (a project or activity).

Master of Arts. *Abbr.* **A.M., M.A.** **1.** A degree granted by a U.S. college or university to a person who has completed at least one year of prescribed study beyond the bachelor's degree, especially in the liberal arts. **2.** A person holding such a degree. Compare **Bachelor of Arts, Doctor of Philosophy.**

master of ceremonies. *Abbr.* **m.c., M.C.** **1.** A person who acts as host at a formal event, making the welcoming speech and introducing other speakers. **2.** A performer who conducts a program of varied entertainment by introducing other performers to the audience. Also called informally "emcee."

Master of Science. *Abbr.* **M.S.** **1.** A degree granted by a U.S. college or university to a person who has completed at least one year of prescribed study in the sciences beyond the bachelor's degree. **2.** A person holding such a degree. Compare **Bachelor of Science, Doctor of Philosophy.**

mas·ter·piece (măs′tər-pēs′, mäs′-) *n.* **1.** An outstanding work of art or craft. **2.** Anything superlative: *a masterpiece of hypocrisy.* [Probably translation of Dutch *meesterstuk* or German *Meisterstück,* the piece of work presented to a guild by a craftsman for admission to the rank of master.]

Mas·ters (măs′tərz, mäs′-), **Edgar Lee.** 1869–1950. American poet; author of *Spoon River Anthology.*

master sergeant. *Abbr.* **MSgt, M. Sgt.** A noncommissioned officer of the next to highest rating in the U.S. Army, Air Force, and Marine Corps.

mas·ter·ship (măs′tər-shĭp′, mäs′-) *n.* **1.** The office, function, or authority of a master. **2.** The skill or dexterity of a master.

mas·ter·sing·er (măs′tər-sĭng′ər, mäs′-) *n.* A **Meistersinger** *(see).*

Mas·ter·son (măs′tər-sən, mäs′-), **William Barclay ("Bat").** 1853–1921. American frontier figure; gambler and marshal.

mas·ter·stroke (măs′tər-strōk′, mäs′-) *n.* A masterly achievement or action: *a masterstroke of statesmanship.*

mas·ter·work (măs′tər-wûrk′, mäs′-) *n.* A masterpiece.

master workman. **1.** An expert workman. **2.** An overseer.

mas·ter·wort (măs′tər-wûrt′, mäs′-) *n.* **1.** A plant, *Astrantia major,* of Europe, having compound leaves and clusters of pink or white flowers. **2.** A plant, the **cow parsnip** *(see).* [Translation of German *Meisterwurz;* reason for naming unknown.]

mas·ter·y (măs′tər-ē, mäs′-) *n., pl.* **-ies.** **1.** Possession of consummate skill. **2.** The status of master or ruler; dominion; control: *mastery of the seas.* **3.** Full command of some subject of study: *a poet's mastery of the language.*

mast·head (măst′hĕd′, mäst′-) *n.* **1.** The top of a ship's mast. **2.** The listing in a newspaper, magazine, or other publication of information about its staff and operation.

mas·tic (măs′tĭk) *n.* **1.** The **mastic tree** *(see).* **2.** The aromatic resin of the mastic tree, used in varnishes and lacquers and as an astringent. **3.** A Near Eastern liquor, flavored with mastic resin and aniseed. **4.** A pastelike cement, especially one made with powdered lime or brick and tar. [Middle English *mastyk,* from Old French *mastic,* from Late Latin *mastichum,* variant of *mastichē,* from Greek *mastikhē,* mastic, "chewing gum," from *mastikhān,* to grind the teeth. See **menth-** in Appendix.*]

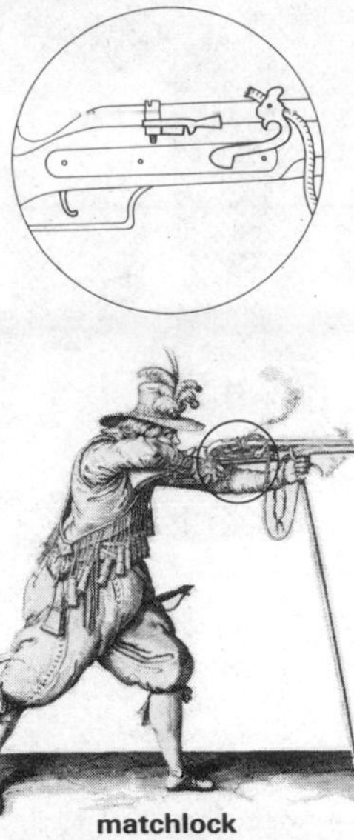

matchlock
Above: Detail of mechanism
Below: Man firing a gun equipped with a matchlock

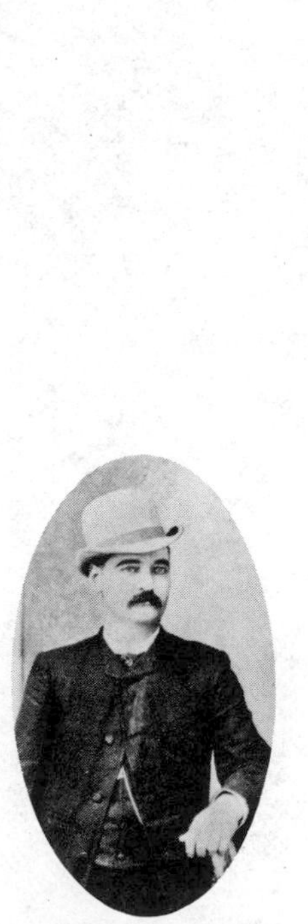

"Bat" Masterson
In 1886, as deputy marshal of Dodge City, Kansas

ă pat/ā pay/âr care/ä father/b bib/ch church/d deed/ĕ pet/ē be/f fife/g gag/h hat/hw which/ĭ pit/ī pie/îr pier/j judge/k kick/l lid, needle/m mum/n no, sudden/ng thing/ŏ pot/ō toe/ô paw, for/oi noise/ou out/ŏŏ took/ōō boot/p pop/r roar/s sauce/sh ship, dish/

mas·ti·cate (măs′tə-kāt′) *tr.v.* **-cated, -cating, -cates. 1.** To chew. **2.** To grind and knead. [Late Latin *masticāre,* from Greek *mastikhān,* to grind the teeth. See **menth-** in Appendix.*] **—mas′ti·ca′tion** *n.* **—mas′ti·ca′tor** (-kā′tər) *n.*

mas·ti·ca·to·ry (măs′tĭ-kə-tôr′ē, -tōr′ē) *adj.* **1.** Of, pertaining to, or used in mastication. **2.** Being adapted for chewing. *—n., pl.* **masticatories.** A substance chewed to increase salivation.

mastic tree. 1. A small evergreen tree, *Pistacia lentiscus,* of the Mediterranean region. It yields a resin, **mastic** *(see).* Also called "lentisk." **2.** See **pepper tree.**

mas·tiff (măs′tĭf) *n.* A large dog of an ancient breed, probably originating in Asia, having a short fawn-colored coat. [Middle English *mastif,* from Old French *mastin,* from Vulgar Latin *mānsuētīnus* (unattested), "tame," from Latin *mānsuētus,* tamed, "accustomed to the hand" : *manus,* hand (see **man-**[2] in Appendix*) + *suēscere,* to accustom (see **seu-**[2] in Appendix*).]

mastiff bat. Any of various bats of the family Molossidae, found in the tropics, having narrow wings and brown, gray, or black fur. [From the superficially doglike ears.]

mas·ti·goph·o·ran (măs′tĭ-gŏf′ə-rən) *n.* Also **mas·tig·o·phore** (măs-tĭg′ə-fôr′, -fōr′). Any member of the class Mastigophora, which includes protozoans with one or more flagella. [From New Latin *Mastigophora,* "whip bearers" : Greek *mastix*† (stem *mastig-*), whip, lash + *-phora* (neuter plural), -PHORE.] **—mas′ti·goph′o·ran** *adj.*

mas·ti·tis (măs-tī′tĭs) *n.* Inflammation of the breast or udder. [MAST(O)- + -ITIS.]

masto-, mast-. Indicates the breast or protuberances resembling a breast or nipple; for example, **mastitis.** [New Latin, from Greek *mastos*†, breast.]

mas·to·don (măs′tə-dŏn′) *n.* Any of several extinct mammals of the genus *Mammut* (sometimes called *Mastodon*), resembling the elephant. [New Latin, "breast-tooth" : MAST(O)- + -ODON; from the nipple-shaped protuberances on the teeth.]

mas·to·dont (măs′tə-dŏnt′) *adj.* **1.** Having teeth like those of a mastodon. **2.** Of, pertaining to, or characteristic of mastodons.

mas·toid (măs′toid′) *n.* **1.** The **mastoid process** *(see).* **2. Mastoiditis** *(see).* Not used technically. *—adj.* **1.** Pertaining to the mastoid process. **2.** Shaped like a breast or nipple. [New Latin *mastoides,* "breast-shaped" : MAST(O)- + -OID.]

mas·toid·ec·to·my (măs′toid-ĕk′tə-mē) *n., pl.* **-mies.** *Surgery.* Removal of part or all of the mastoid process.

mas·toid·i·tis (măs′toid-ī′tĭs) *n. Pathology.* Inflammation of part or all of the mastoid process.

mastoid process. *Anatomy.* The rear portion of the temporal bone on each side of the head behind the ear in man and many other vertebrates. Also called "mastoid," "mastoid bone."

mas·tur·bate (măs′tər-bāt′) *v.* **-bated, -bating, -bates.** *—intr.* To perform an act of masturbation. *—tr.* To perform an act of masturbation on. [Latin *masturbārī*†.]

mas·tur·ba·tion (măs′tər-bā′shən) *n.* Excitation of the genital organs, usually to orgasm, by means other than sexual intercourse. **—mas′tur·ba′tion·al, mas′tur·ba·to′ry** (măs′tər-bə-tôr′ē, -tōr′ē) *adj.* **—mas′tur·ba′tor** (-bā′tər) *n.*

Ma·su·ri·a (mə-zŏŏr′ē-ə, -sŏŏr′ē-ə). *German* **Ma·su·ren** (mä-zōō′rən). *Polish* **Ma·zu·ry** (mä-zōō′rē). A region in northeastern Poland, dotted with numerous lakes. **—Ma·su′ri·an** *adj.*

mat[1] (măt) *n.* **1.** A flat piece of fabric or other material used for wiping one's shoes or feet, or in various other forms as a floor covering. **2.** A small, flat piece of decorated material placed under a lamp, dish of food, or other object. **3.** A floor pad to protect athletes, as in wrestling or gymnastics. **4.** Any densely woven or thickly tangled mass: *a mat of hair.* **5.** The solid part of a lace design. **6.** A heavy, woven net of rope or wire cable placed over a blasting site to keep debris from scattering. *—v.* **matted, matting, mats.** *—tr.* **1.** To cover, protect, or decorate with a mat or mats. **2.** To interweave into or cover with a thick mass: *A heavy growth of vines matted the tree.* *—intr.* To be interwoven into a thick mass; become entangled. [Middle English *mat,* Old English *matt-(e),* from Late Latin *matta,* mat, possibly from Phoenician (Punic) *matta.*]

mat[2] (măt) *n.* **1.** A decorative border of cardboard or similar material placed around a picture to serve as a frame or act as a contrast between the picture and the frame. **2.** Also **matte. a.** A dull, often rough, finish, as on glass, metal, or paper. **b.** A special tool for producing such a surface or finish. **3.** *Printing.* A type mold or an impression of type, **matrix** *(see).* *—tr.v.* **matted, matting, mats. 1.** To put a mat around (a picture). **2.** To produce a dull finish on. *—adj.* Also **matte.** Having a dull finish. [French *mat,* dull, from Old French, from Latin *mattus,* dull, vague, originally, drunk, probably variant of *maditus,* drunk, from *madēre,* to be sodden, to be drunk. See **mad-** in Appendix.*]

mat. matinee.

M.A.T. Master of Arts in Teaching.

Mat·a·be·le (măt′ə-bē′lē) *n., pl.* **Matabele** or **-les. 1.** A Zulu tribe driven out of the Transvaal by the Boers in 1837. **2.** A member of this tribe. **3.** The Bantu language of the Matabele.

Mat·a·be·le·land (măt′ə-bē′lē-lănd′). A region of Rhodesia inhabited by the Matabele people since 1837.

Ma·ta·di (mə-tä′dē). The most important port of the Congo (Kinshasa), 100 miles from the mouth of the Congo River and 230 miles southwest of Kinshasa. Population, 48,000.

mat·a·dor (măt′ə-dôr′) *n.* **1.** A bullfighter who performs the **faena** *(see)* and kills the bull. **2.** One of the highest trumps in certain card games. [Spanish, "killer," from *matar,* to kill, from Old Spanish, from Latin *mactāre,* to sacrifice, from *mactus,* sacred. See **meg-** in Appendix.*]

Ma·ta Ha·ri (mä′tə hä′rē). Original name, Gertrud Margarete Zelle. 1876–1917. German spy in France during World War I.

Ma·ta·mo·ros (măt′ə-môr′əs, -mōr′əs; *Spanish* mä′tä-mō′rōs). A seaport of northeastern Mexico, near the mouth of the Rio Grande, opposite Brownsville, Texas. Population, 132,000.

Ma·tan·zas (mə-tăn′zəs; *Spanish* mä-tän′säs). **1.** A province of northern Cuba. Population, 361,000. **2.** The capital of this province, on Matanzas Bay. Population, 83,000.

Mat·a·pan, Cape (măt′ə-păn′). *Greek* **Taí·na·ron** (tā′nə-rŏn′). The southern tip of mainland Greece.

match[1] (măch) *n.* **1. a.** A person or thing that is exactly like another; counterpart. **b.** A person or thing that is like another in one or more specified qualities: *He is John's match for bravery.* **2. a.** A person or thing that closely resembles or harmonizes with another: *The napkins were a nice match for the tablecloth.* **b.** A pair made up of two things or persons that resemble or harmonize with each other: *The colors were a close match.* **3.** A person or thing equal in qualities or able to compete with another of the same class or type: *The boxer had met his match.* **4.** *Sports.* **a.** An athletic contest or game in which two or more persons, animals, or teams oppose and compete with each other: *a boxing match.* **b.** A race between horses belonging to two different owners who have set the terms and conditions of the race. **c.** A tennis contest decided on the basis of victory in a specified number of sets, usually two out of three or three out of five. **5.** A marriage or an arrangement of marriage: *"She had rejected several matches that had been made her."* (Goldsmith). **6.** A person viewed as a prospective marriage partner. *—v.* **matched, matching, matches.** *—tr.* **1. a.** To be exactly like; correspond exactly; equal. **b.** To be like with respect to specified qualities: *The markings on the stamps matched each other.* **2.** To resemble or harmonize with: *The coat matches the dress.* **3.** To adapt or suit so that a balanced or harmonious result is achieved; cause to correspond: *"Let poets match their subject to their strength."* (Earl Roscommon). **4.** To fit together or cause to fit together; especially, to cut (boards) with a tongue and groove. **5.** To join or give in marriage. **6.** To place in opposition or competition with; to pit: *"The only way that power can be overcome is to match organization with organization."* (Ann D. Gordon). **7.** To provide with an adversary or competitor. **8.** To set in comparison; measure; compare: *beauty that could never be matched.* **9.** To flip or toss (coins) and compare the sides that land face up. **10.** To couple (electric circuits) by means of a transformer. *—intr.* To be a close counterpart; correspond. —See Synonyms at **rival.** [Middle English *macche,* match, mate, Old English *gemæcca,* mate. See **mag-** in Appendix.*] **—match′a·ble** *adj.* **—match′er** *n.*

match[2] (măch) *n.* **1.** A narrow strip of wood, cardboard, or wax coated on one end with a compound that ignites easily by friction. **2.** An easily ignited cord or wick, formerly used for detonating powder charges or firing cannons and muzzle-loading firearms. [Middle English *macche, mecche,* lamp wick, candle, from Old French *meiche,* from Medieval Latin *myxa,* lamp wick, from Latin, nozzle of a lamp, from Greek *muxa,* lamp wick, originally, mucus. See **meug-**[2] in Appendix.*]

match·board (măch′bôrd′, -bōrd′) *n.* Also **matched board.** A board cut with a tongue on one side and a matching groove on the other to fit with other boards of identical cut.

match·book (măch′bŏŏk′) *n.* A small cardboard folder containing safety matches.

match·box (măch′bŏks′) *n.* A box for keeping matches.

match·less (măch′lĭs) *adj.* Having no match or equal; peerless; unsurpassed: *"that small, matchless quarter of London where peace and dignity do still reign"* (Max Beerbohm). **—match′less·ly** *adv.* **—match′less·ness** *n.*

match·lock (măch′lŏk′) *n.* **1.** A gunlock in which powder is ignited by a match. **2.** A musket having such a gunlock.

match·mak·er (măch′mā′kər) *n.* **1.** One who habitually tries to arrange marriages. **2.** One who arranges athletic competitions. **—match′mak′ing** *n.* & *adj.*

match play. *Golf.* A method of scoring the game by counting only the number of holes won by each side rather than the number of strokes taken. Compare **medal play.**

match point. The final point needed to win a sports match.

match·wood (măch′wŏŏd′) *n.* **1.** Wood in small pieces or splinters suitable especially for making matches. **2.** Splinters: *The vessel was beaten to matchwood when it came ashore.*

mate[1] (māt) *n.* **1.** One of a matched pair: *the mate to this glove.* **2.** A spouse. **3. a.** One of a conjugal pair of animals or birds. **b.** One of a pair of animals brought together for breeding. **4.** A person with whom one is in close association. **5.** A deck officer on a merchant ship ranking below the master. **6.** *U.S. Navy.* A petty officer who is an assistant to the warrant officer. *—v.* **mated, mating, mates.** *—tr.* **1.** To join closely; pair; couple. **2.** To unite in marriage. **3.** To pair (animals) for breeding. *—intr.* **1.** To become joined in marriage. **2.** To become mated; breed. [Middle English, from Middle Low German *mate, gemate,* companion. See **mad-** in Appendix.*]

mate[2] (māt) *n. Chess.* A checkmate. *—v.* **mated, mating, mates.** *Chess.* *—tr.* To checkmate. *—intr.* To achieve a checkmate: *White mated in 20 moves.* [Middle English *mat,* from Old French, short for *eschec mat,* CHECKMATE.]

ma·té (mä′tā′) *n.* **1.** An evergreen tree, *Ilex paraguayensis,* of South America, where it is widely cultivated. **2.** A mildly stimulant beverage, popular in South America, made from the dried leaves of this tree. Also called "Paraguay tea," "yerba maté." [American Spanish *maté,* alteration (influenced by *té,* tea) of *mate* (with initial stress), from Quechua.]

mat·e·lote (măt′ə-lōt′) *n.* Also **mat·e·lotte** (măt′ə-lŏt′). **1.** A wine sauce for fish. **2.** Fish stewed in such a sauce. [French

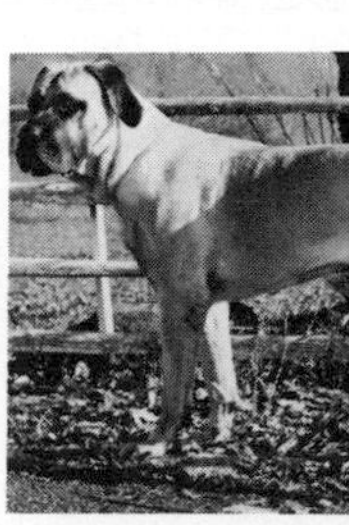

mastiff

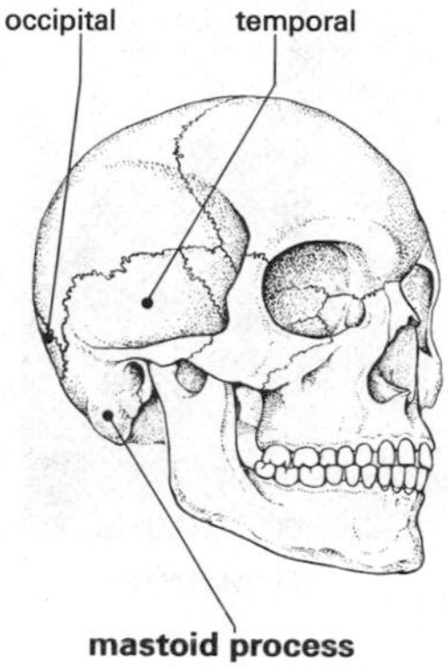

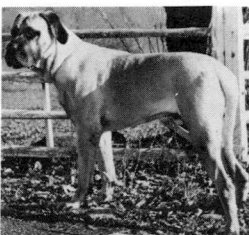

(sauce) matelote, "sailor (sauce)," from *matelot,* sailor, from Old French *matenot, mathenot,* probably from Middle Dutch *mattenoot,* earlier *mātghenōt,* messmate : *māt,* meat (see **mad-** in Appendix*) + *ghenōt,* fellow (see **neud-** in Appendix*).]

ma·ter (mā'tər) *n. Chiefly British Obsolete.* Mother. [Latin *māter.* See **māter-** in Appendix.*]

ma·ter·fa·mil·i·as (mā'tər-fə-mĭl'ē-əs) *n.* The mother of a family. [Latin : *māter,* mother (see **māter-** in Appendix*) + *familias,* archaic genitive of *familia,* FAMILY.]

ma·te·ri·al (mə-tîr'ē-əl) *n.* **1.** The substance or substances out of which a thing is or may be constructed: *"Simple ideas, the materials of all our knowledge, are suggested to the mind only by sensation and reflection."* (Locke). **2.** A precursory element, such as an idea or sketch, to be refined and made or incorporated into a finished effort: *material for a comedy.* **3.** *Plural.* Tools or apparatus for the performance of a given task: *writing materials.* **4.** Yard goods or cloth. —*adj.* **1.** Composed of or pertaining to physical substances; relating to matter; corporeal. **2.** Of, pertaining to, or affecting the enjoyment of physical well-being: *material comfort.* **3.** Of or concerned with the physical as distinct from the intellectual or spiritual. **4.** Substantial; noticeable; especially, of importance to an argument: *"I shall therefore endeavor . . . to lay before you some of the most material circumstances"* (Burke). **5.** *Law.* Relevant to the case: *material testimony.* **6.** *Philosophy.* Of or pertaining to the matter of reasoning, rather than the form. —See Synonyms at **relevant.** [Middle English, from Old French *materiel,* from Late Latin *māteriālis,* from *māteria,* matter. See **māter-** in Appendix.*] —**ma·te'ri·al·ness** *n.*

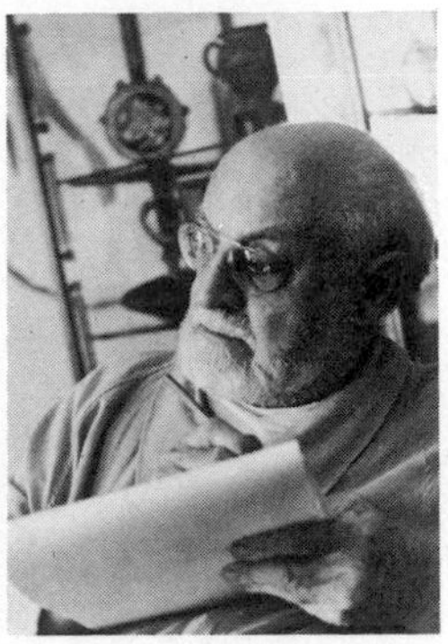

Henri Matisse

ma·te·ri·al·ism (mə-tîr'ē-əl-ĭz'əm) *n.* **1.** The philosophical opinion that physical matter in its movements and modifications is the only reality and that everything in the universe, including thought, feeling, mind, and will, can be explained in terms of physical laws. Compare **idealism.** **2.** The theory or doctrine that physical well-being and worldly possessions constitute the greatest good and highest value in life. **3.** Undue regard for worldly concerns: *"His thinking was distorted by the materialism of the time."* (George F. Kennan). —**ma·te'ri·al·ist** *adj.* & *n.* —**ma·te'ri·al·is'tic** *adj.* —**ma·te'ri·al·is'ti·cal·ly** *adv.*

ma·te·ri·al·i·ty (mə-tîr'ē-ăl'ə-tē) *n., pl.* **-ties. 1.** The state or quality of being material. **2.** Matter; physical substance.

ma·te·ri·al·ize (mə-tîr'ē-əl-īz') *v.* **-ized, -izing, -izes.** —*tr.* To invest with material or physical characteristics; cause to become real or actual: *By building the house, he materialized his dream.* —*intr.* **1.** To assume material or effective form: *"French support on the eastern flank did not materialise."* (Winston Churchill). **2.** To take form or shape. —**ma·te'ri·al·i·za'tion** *n.* —**ma·te'ri·al·iz'er** *n.*

Usage: *Materialize* (intransitive) is not a proper substitute for the more general *happen* or *occur,* as in *Nothing new materialized during the hearing.* The preceding example is approved by only 33 per cent of the Usage Panel, but 69 per cent accept the more specific sense of *The plans materialized.*

ma·te·ri·al·ly (mə-tîr'ē-əl-ē) *adv.* **1.** With regard to matter as distinguished from form. **2.** To a significant extent or degree; importantly. **3.** With regard to the physical world.

ma·te·ri·a med·i·ca (mə-tîr'ē-ə mĕd'ĭ-kə). *Medicine.* **1.** The study of remedies and their sources, preparation, and use. **2.** A substance used in preparing remedies or as a medicine. [Latin, "medical material."]

ma·te·ri·el, ma·té·ri·el (mə-tîr'ē-ĕl') *n.* **1.** The equipment, apparatus, and supplies, such as guns and ammunition, of a military force. **2.** The equipment, apparatus, and supplies of any organization. [French, from *matériel,* MATERIAL (adjective).]

ma·ter·nal (mə-tûr'nəl) *adj.* **1.** Relating to or characteristic of a mother or motherhood; motherly: *maternal instinct.* **2.** Inherited from one's mother: *a maternal trait.* **3.** Related to through one's mother: *my maternal uncle.* **4.** Of one's mother: *the maternal bosom.* [Middle English, from Old French *maternel,* from Latin *māternus,* from *māter,* mother. See **māter-** in Appendix.*] —**ma·ter'nal·ly** *adv.*

ma·ter·ni·ty (mə-tûr'nə-tē) *n.* **1.** The state of being a mother; motherhood. **2.** The feelings or characteristics associated with being a mother; motherliness. —*adj.* Associated with pregnancy and childbirth: *a maternity dress; a maternity ward.* [French *maternité,* from Medieval Latin *māternitās,* from *māternus,* MATERNAL.]

ma·tey (mā'tē) *adj.* Sociable; friendly.

math (măth) *n.* Mathematics.

math. mathematical; mathematician; mathematics.

math·e·mat·i·cal (măth'ə-măt'ĭ-kəl) *adj.* Also **math·e·mat·ic.** *Abbr.* **math. 1.** Of or pertaining to mathematics. **2.** Precise; rigorous; exact. [Old French *mathematique,* from Latin *mathēmaticus,* from Greek *mathēmatikos,* from *mathēma,* science, from *manthanein* (stem *math-*), to learn. See **mendh-** in Appendix.*] —**math'e·mat'i·cal·ly** *adv.*

mathematical induction. A principle and method of proof in mathematics. See **induction.**

mathematical logic. Symbolic logic *(see).*

math·e·ma·ti·cian (măth'ə-mə-tĭsh'ən) *n. Abbr.* **math.** A person skilled or learned in mathematics.

math·e·mat·ics (măth'ə-măt'ĭks) *n. Abbr.* **math.** Plural in form, used with a singular verb. The study of number, form, arrangement, and associated relationships, using rigorously defined literal, numerical, and operational symbols. [Probably from French *(les) mathématiques,* from Latin *mathēmatica* (neuter plural), from Greek *(ta) mathēmatika.* See **mathematical.**]

Math·er (măth'ər, măth'ər), **Cotton.** 1663–1728. American Congregational clergyman and author; son of Increase Mather.

Math·er (măth'ər, măth'ər), **Increase.** 1639–1723. American Congregational clergyman; father of Cotton Mather.

Math·ew·son (măth'yōō-sən), **Christopher ("Christy").** 1880–1925. American baseball pitcher and manager.

Ma·thu·ra (mŭt'ə-rə). Formerly **Mut·tra** (mŭt'rə). A city of the Republic of India, in Uttar Pradesh State, sacred to the Hindus as the birthplace of Krishna. Population, 106,000.

Ma·thu·rai. See **Madurai.**

Ma·til·da (mə-tĭl'də). A feminine given name. [Middle English, from Medieval Latin, from Common Germanic *Mahthildis,* "mighty in battle." See **magh-¹** in Appendix.*]

mat·il·i·ja poppy (mə-tĭl'ē-hä'). A shrubby plant, *Romneya Coulteri,* of California and Mexico, having very large, solitary white flowers. [From *Matilija* Canyon, California.]

mat·in (măt'ĭn) *adj.* Also **mat·in·al** (-əl). Of or pertaining to matins or to the early part of the day: *"Fear thou no more the matin frost."* (Coleridge). [From MATINS.]

mat·i·nee, mat·i·née (măt'n-ā') *n. Abbr.* **mat.** A dramatic or musical performance given in the daytime, usually in the afternoon. [French *matinée,* "morning," early performance, from Old French *matinee,* from *matin,* morning, from Latin *(tempus) mātūtīnum,* morning (time), from *mātūtīnus,* of the morning, from *Mātūta,* goddess of dawn. See **mā-¹** in Appendix.*]

mat·ins (măt'ĭnz) *n.* Plural in form, used with a singular or plural verb. Also *chiefly British* **mat·tins. 1.** *Roman Catholic Church.* The office that, together with lauds, constitutes the first of the seven **canonical hours** *(see).* **2.** *Sometimes capital* **M. Morning Prayer** *(see).* [Middle English *matines,* from Old French, from Medieval Latin *(vigiliae) mātūtīnae,* morning (watches, vigils), from Latin *mātūtīnus,* of the morning, from *Mātūta,* goddess of dawn. See **mā-¹** in Appendix.*]

Ma·tisse (mà-tēs'), **Henri.** 1869–1954. French postimpressionist painter and sculptor; a leader of Les Fauves.

Ma·to Gros·so (măt'ə grō'sō; *Portuguese* mä'tōō grō'sōō). Also **Mat·to Gros·so.** The second-largest state of Brazil, 487,451 square miles in area, in the central and western part of the country. Population, 910,000. Capital, Cuiabá.

matri-. Indicates motherhood; for example, **matriclinous.** [From Latin *māter,* mother. See **māter-** in Appendix.*]

ma·tri·arch (mā'trē-ärk') *n.* **1.** A woman who rules a family, clan, or tribe. **2.** A woman who dominates any group or activity. [MATRI- + -ARCH.] —**ma'tri·ar'chal** (mā'trē-är'kəl), **ma'tri·ar'chic** (-är'kĭk) *adj.* —**ma'tri·ar'chal·ism'** *n.*

ma·tri·ar·chate (mā'trē-är'kĭt, -kāt') *n.* **1.** A society, tribe, or state in which the dominant authority is held by women. **2.** The authority held by matriarchs in such a society. **3.** A hypothetical stage in the evolution of primitive society in which authority is held by matriarchs.

ma·tri·ar·chy (mā'trē-är'kē) *n., pl.* **-chies. 1.** A social system in which descent is traced through the mother's side of the family. **2.** A **matriarchate** *(see).*

mat·ri·cide (măt'rə-sīd') *n.* **1.** The act of killing one's mother. **2.** One who kills his mother. [Latin *mātricīda* (person), and *mātricīdium* (act) : MATRI- + -CIDE.] —**mat'ri·ci'dal** (-sīd'l) *adj.*

mat·ri·cli·nous (măt'rə-klī'nəs) *adj.* Also **mat·ro·cli·nous.** Having predominantly maternal hereditary traits. [MATRI- + *-clinous,* from Greek *-klinēs,* "leaning," from *klinein,* to lean (see **klei-** in Appendix*).]

ma·tric·u·lant (mə-trĭk'yə-lənt) *n.* A person who matriculates or is a candidate for matriculation.

ma·tric·u·late (mə-trĭk'yə-lāt') *v.* **-lated, -lating, -lates.** —*tr.* To enroll (a person) in a group, especially a college or university. —*intr.* To become so enrolled. —*n.* A matriculant. [Medieval Latin *mātriculāre,* to enroll, from *mātricula,* list, roll, from *mātrīx,* list, originally, womb, source. See **matrix.**] —**ma·tric'u·la'tion** *n.*

mat·ri·lin·e·al (măt'rə-lĭn'ē-əl) *adj.* Relating to, based upon, or tracing ancestral descent through the maternal line rather than through the paternal.

mat·ri·lo·cal (măt'rə-lō'kəl) *adj. Anthropology.* Pertaining to the home territory of a wife's kin group or clan in primitive societies. —**mat'ri·lo'cal·ly** *adv.*

mat·ri·mo·ny (măt'rə-mō'nē) *n., pl.* **-nies. 1.** The act or state of being married; the sacrament or rite of marriage: *"I would approach matrimony as cheerfully as I would the tomb."* (Dodie Smith). **2. a.** A card game. **b.** The combination of a king and queen in this card game. —See Synonyms at **marriage.** [Middle English, from Norman French *matrimonie,* from Latin *mātrimōnium,* marriage, "motherhood" : *māter,* mother (see **māter-** in Appendix*) + *-mōnium,* abstract noun suffix.] —**mat'ri·mo'ni·al** *adj.* —**mat'ri·mo'ni·al·ly** *adv.*

matrimony vine. Any of various often thorny shrubs of the genus *Lycium,* some species of which are cultivated for their purplish flowers and brightly colored berries. Sometimes called "boxthorn." [The reason for naming is unknown.]

ma·trix (mā'trĭks) *n., pl.* **matrices** (mā'trə-sēz', măt'rə-) or **-trixes. 1.** A situation or surrounding substance within which something originates, develops, or is contained: *"Folklore must be maintained in the matrix of the culture for some time before it can be accepted as genuine."* (Horace Beck). **2.** The womb. **3.** *Anatomy.* The formative cells of a fingernail or tooth. **4.** *Geology.* **a.** The solid matter in which a fossil or crystal is embedded. **b.** The impression left in a rock when an object, such as a gemstone, has been removed. **5.** A mold or die. **6.** The principal metal in an alloy, for example, the iron in steel. **7.** A binding substance, such as cement in concrete. **8.** *Mathematics.* A rectangular array of numerical or algebraic quantities treated as an algebraic entity. **9.** The network of intersections between input and output leads in a computer, func-

tioning as an encoder or decoder. **10.** *Printing.* **a.** A metal plate used for casting type faces. **b.** A mold used in stereotyping and designed to receive positive impressions of type or illustrations from which metal plates can be cast. In this sense, also called "mat." [Latin *mātrix*, womb, originally, pregnant animal, from *māter*, mother. See **māter-** in Appendix.*]

mat·ro·cli·nous. Variant of **matriclinous.**

ma·tron (mā′trən) *n.* **1.** A married woman; especially, a mother of mature age with established dignity and social position. **2.** A woman who supervises a public institution, such as a school, hospital, or prison. [Middle English, from Old French *matrone*, from Latin *mātrōna*, matron, wife, from *māter*, mother. See **māter-** in Appendix.*] —**ma′tron·ly** *adj. & adv.* —**ma′tron·li·ness** *n.* —**ma′tron·al** *adj.*

matron of honor *pl.* **matrons of honor.** A married woman serving as chief attendant of the bride at a wedding. Compare **bridesmaid, maid of honor.**

mat·ro·nym·ic. Variant of **metronymic.**

Ma·tsu (mä′tsōō′). An island group of the Republic of China, about six square miles in land area, situated in Formosa Strait, 12 miles east of the southeastern Chinese mainland.

Ma·tsu·mo·to (mä′tsōō-mō′tō). An industrial city of central Honshu, Japan. Population, 145,000.

Ma·tsu·ya·ma (mä′tsōō-yä′mä). A city near the northwestern coast of Shikoku, Japan. Population, 281,000.

Matt. Matthew (New Testament).

matte[1]. Variant of **mat** (finish).

matte[2] (măt) *n. Metallurgy.* A mixture of a metal with its oxides and sulfides, produced by smelting certain sulfide ores. Also called "regulus." [French, from dialectal French *mate*, a lump, probably deriving from Late Latin *matta*, mat of rushes, MAT (floor covering).]

mat·ted (măt′ĭd) *adj.* **1.** Covered with or made from mats. **2.** Tangled in a dense mass: *"through weeds and thorns, and matted underwood"* (Coleridge). —**mat′ted·ly** *adv.*

mat·ter (măt′ər) *n.* **1. a.** That which occupies space, can be perceived by one or more senses, and constitutes any physical body or the universe as a whole. **b.** *Physics.* Any entity displaying gravitation and inertia when at rest as well as when in motion. **2.** A specific type of substance: *inorganic matter.* **3.** Discharge or waste from a living organism, as pus or feces. **4.** The actual substance of thought or expression; the thesis or theme of what is expressed as distinguished from the manner in which it is stated or conveyed. **5.** *Philosophy.* In Aristotelian and scholastic use, that which is in itself undifferentiated and formless and which, as the subject of change and development, receives form and becomes substance and experience. **6.** *Christian Science.* That which is postulated by the mortal mind, regarded as illusion and as the opposite of substance or God. **7.** Something that is the subject of concern, feeling, or action: *"For leaving of all is a hard matter, yea, a harder matter than many are aware of."* (Bunyan). **8.** Business, affair, or thing. **9.** An unpleasant or disagreeable situation or circumstance; trouble; difficulty. Used with *the: What's the matter with you?* **10.** An indefinite but approximated quantity, amount, or extent: *a matter of a few cents.* **11.** Something that is printed or otherwise set down in writing: *reading matter.* **12.** Something that is sent by mail. **13.** *Printing.* **a.** Composed, or set, type. **b.** Material to be set in type. —See Synonyms at **subject.** —*intr.v.* **mattered, -tering, -ters.** To be of importance: *It matters very much.* [Middle English *matere*, from Norman French, from Latin *māteria*, matter. See **māter-** in Appendix.*]

Mat·ter·horn (măt′ər-hôrn′). A mountain peak, 14,701 feet high, on the Italian-Swiss frontier.

matter of course. A natural or logical outcome. —**mat′ter-of-course′** (măt′ər-əv-kôrs′, -kōrs′) *adj.*

mat·ter-of-fact (măt′ər-əv-făkt′) *adj.* Pertaining to or adhering to facts; prosaic; literal: *a matter-of-fact description of a fanciful affair.* —**mat′ter-of-fact′ly** *adv.* —**mat′ter-of-fact′ness** *n.*

Mat·thew[1] (măth′yōō). A masculine given name. [Middle English *Mathew*, from Norman French *Mathiu*, from Old French *Matheu*, from Latin *Matthaeus*, from Greek *Matthaios*, from Hebrew *Mattathyāh*, "gift of Jehovah" : *mattat*, gift, from a root *ntn*, to give + *yāh*, Yah (Jehovah).]

Mat·thew[2] (măth′yōō) *n. Abbr.* **Matt.** A book of the New Testament, the first Gospel, attributed to Saint Matthew.

Mat·thew (măth′yōō), **Saint.** One of the Apostles of Christ and author of the first Gospel.

Mat·thi·as (mə-thī′əs), **Saint.** One of the Apostles of Christ, chosen by lot to take the place of Judas Iscariot. Acts 1:23–26.

mat·ting[1] (măt′ĭng) *n.* **1.** A coarsely woven fabric used for covering floors and similar purposes. **2.** Mat-making.

mat·ting[2] (măt′ĭng) *n.* **1.** A dull surface or finish. **2.** The process of dulling a surface, as of metal. **3.** A border or mat used for framing a picture.

mat·tins. *Chiefly British.* Variant of **matins.**

mat·tock (măt′ək) *n.* A digging tool with a blade set at right angles to the handle and used with a downward motion. [Middle English *mattok*, Old English *mattuc*. See **mat-** in Appendix.*]

Mat·to Gros·so. See **Mato Grosso.**

mat·tress (măt′rĭs) *n.* **1.** A rectangular pad of heavy cloth filled with soft material, used as or on a bed. **2.** A closely woven mat of brush and poles used to protect an embankment, dike, or dam from erosion. [Middle English *materas*, from Old French, from Old Italian *materasso*, from Arabic *maṭraḥ*, place where something is thrown, from *taraha*, to throw, fling.]

mat·u·rate (măch′ōō-rāt′) *v.* **-rated, -rating, -rates.** —*intr.* **1.** To mature or ripen. **2.** To suppurate. —*tr.* **1.** To cause to mature or ripen. **2.** To cause to suppurate. [Latin *mātūrāre*, to mature, from *mātūrus*, MATURE.] —**mat′u·ra′tive** *adj.*

mat·u·ra·tion (măch′ōō-rā′shən) *n.* **1.** The process of becoming mature; a ripening: *"Maturation plays a large role in emotional development."* (Norman L. Munn). **2.** Discharge of pus, **suppuration** *(see).* **3.** *Biology.* **a.** Formation of a sex cell, **gametogenesis** *(see).* **b.** The final differentiation processes in biological systems, such as the final ripening of a seed.

maturation division. **Meiosis** *(see).*

ma·ture (mə-tyŏŏr′, -tŏŏr′, -chŏŏr′) *adj.* **-turer, -turest.** **1. a.** Complete and finished in natural growth or development: *a mature cell.* **b.** Fully developed; ripe: *a mature cheese.* **2.** Of, pertaining to, or characteristic of full development, either mental or physical: *"She had magnificent shoulders and arms, rare in a young girl. She was probably mature for her age."* (Joyce Cary). **3.** Worked out fully by the mind; completed; perfected: *a mature plan of action.* **4.** *Commerce.* Having reached the limit of its time; payable; due: *a mature bond.* **5.** *Geology.* Being a landscape in which hills and valleys predominate over flat areas as a result of erosion. —*v.* **matured, -turing, -tures.** —*tr.* **1.** To bring to full development; ripen. **2.** To work out fully in the mind: *"to be able to digest and mature my thoughts for my own mind only"* (J.S. Mill). —*intr.* **1.** To evolve toward full development: *The child's judgment matures as he grows older.* **2.** *Commerce.* To become due. Used only of notes and bonds. [Middle English, from Latin *mātūrus*. See **mā-**[1] in Appendix.*] —**ma·ture′ly** *adv.* —**ma·ture′ness** *n.*

ma·tur·i·ty (mə-tyŏŏr′ə-tē, -tŏŏr′ə-tē, -chŏŏr′ə-tē) *n., pl.* **-ties.** **1. a.** The state or quality of being mature; ripeness. **b.** The state or quality of being fully grown. **2. a.** The time at which a note, bill, or bond is due. **b.** The state of a note, bill, or bond being due. **3.** *Geology.* The state of being mature. Used of eroded landscape. [Middle English *maturite*, from Latin *mātūritās*, from *mātūrus*, MATURE.]

ma·tu·ti·nal (mə-tōō′tə-nəl, -tyōō′tə-nəl, măch′ōō-tī′nəl) *adj.* Of, pertaining to, or occurring in the morning; early: *"At such a matutinal hour only trashy errand-boys . . . might be expected to call."* (Ronald Firbank). [Late Latin *mātūtīnālis*, from Latin *mātūtīnus*, from *Mātūta*, goddess of dawn. See **mā-**[1] in Appendix.*] —**ma·tu′ti·nal·ly** *adv.*

mat·zo (mät′sə) *n., pl.* **-zoth** (-sōth′, -sōt′, -sōs′) or **-zos** (-səz, -səs, -sōz′) or **-zot** (-sōt′). A brittle, flat piece of unleavened bread, eaten especially during the Passover. [Yiddish *matse*, from Hebrew *maṣṣah*, probably from the same root as Arabic *massa*, to touch, handle. See also **massage.**]

mat·zoon (mät-sōōn′) *n.* Also **mad·zoon** (mäd-zōōn′). A fermented milk product similar to yogurt. [Armenian *madzun*, from Old Armenian *matsun*. See **mag-** in Appendix.*]

Maud, Maude (môd). A feminine given name. [Middle English, from Old French *Maud, Mahault, Mahhild*, from Common Germanic *Mahthildis*, MATILDA.]

maud·lin (môd′lĭn) *adj.* Effusively sentimental: *"Goering and Hitler displayed an almost maudlin concern for the welfare of animals."* (Aldous Huxley). [From *Maudlin*, Mary Magdalene (typifying tearful repentance), from Old French *Madelaine*, from Late Latin *Magdalēna*, from Greek *Magdalēnē*, (MARY) MAGDALENE.] —**maud′lin·ly** *adv.* —**maud′lin·ness** *n.*

Maugham (môm), **W(illiam) Somerset.** 1874–1965. English author of novels, short stories, and plays.

Mau·i (mou′ē). The second-largest island and one of the five counties of Hawaii, 728 square miles in area, lying between Hawaii and Molokai. Population, 36,000.

maul (môl) *n.* Also **mall** (môl). A heavy, long-handled hammer used to drive stakes, piles, or wedges. —*tr.v.* **mauled, mauling, mauls.** Also **mall.** **1.** To split (wood) with a maul and wedge. **2.** To handle roughly; bruise or tear: *a hunter mauled by a bear.* **3.** To injure by or as if by beating. [Middle English *meall, mal*, from Old French *mail*, from Latin *malleus*, hammer. See **melə-** in Appendix.*] —**maul′er** *n.*

Maul·din (môl′dĭn), **William Henry ("Bill").** Born 1921. American editorial cartoonist.

Maul·main. Variant of **Moulmein.**

maul·stick (môl′stĭk′) *n.* Also **mahl·stick** (môl′stĭk′). A long wooden stick used by painters to support the hand that holds the brush. [After Dutch *maalstok* : *maalen*, to paint, from Middle Dutch *malen* (see **melə-** in Appendix*) + STICK, translation of Dutch *stok.*]

Mau Mau (mou′ mou′) *n., pl.* **Mau Mau** or **Mau Maus.** **1.** A secret organization of Kikuyu tribesmen in Kenya that used revolutionary terrorism during the 1950's in a rebellion against British colonial rule. **2.** A member of this organization.

Mau·na Ke·a (mou′nä kā′ä). An inactive volcano, rising to 13,825 feet, on the island of Hawaii. It is the world's highest island mountain.

Mau·na Lo·a (mou′nä lō′ä). A volcanic mountain, rising to 13,675 feet, in the south-central area of the island of Hawaii. Several of its craters are still active.

maund (mônd) *n.* A unit of weight varying in different countries of Asia from 24.7 to 82.286 pounds avoirdupois, the latter being the official maund in India. [Hindi *mān*, from Persian, from Akkadian *manū*, designating a unit of weight. See **mina.**]

maun·der (môn′dər, män′-) *intr.v.* **-dered, -dering, -ders.** **1.** To talk incoherently or aimlessly. **2.** To move or act aimlessly or vaguely; wander. [Originally, "to grumble"†.]

Maundy Thursday. The Thursday before Easter, commemorating Jesus' Last Supper. In the Roman Catholic Church, also called "Holy Thursday."

Mau·pas·sant (mō-pä-säN′), **(Henri René Albert) Guy de.** 1850–1893. French author of short stories and novels.

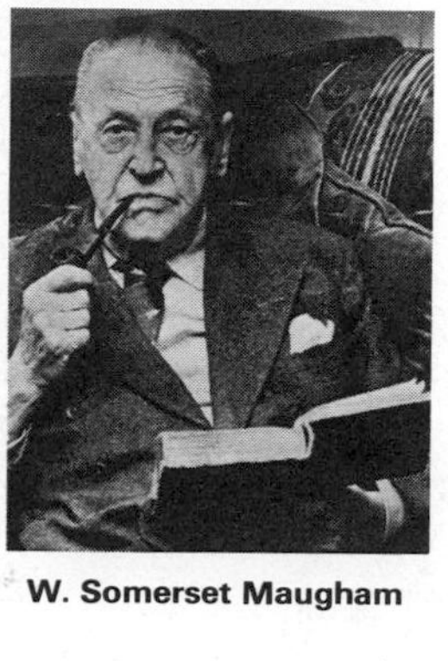

W. Somerset Maugham

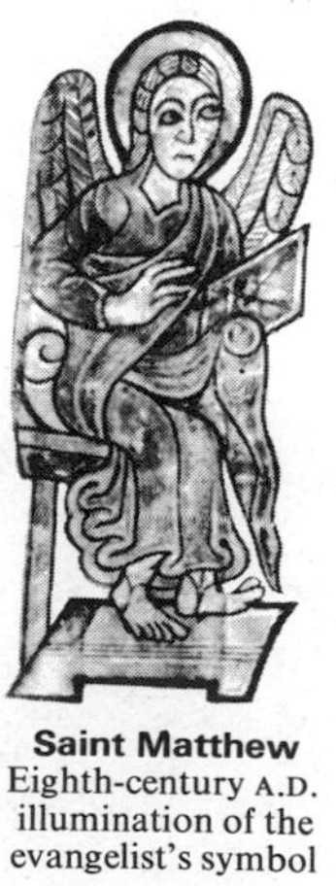

Saint Matthew
Eighth-century A.D. illumination of the evangelist's symbol

t tight/th thin, path/*th* this, bathe/ŭ cut/ûr urge/v valve/w with/y yes/z zebra, size/zh vision/ə about, item, edible, gallop, circus/ à *Fr.* ami/œ *Fr.* feu, *Ger.* schön/ü *Fr.* tu, *Ger.* über/KH *Ger.* ich, *Scot.* loch/N *Fr.* bon. ***Follows main vocabulary. †Of obscure origin.**

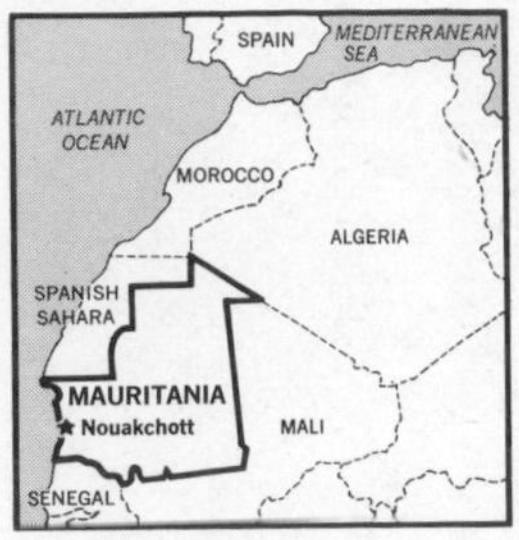

Mauritania

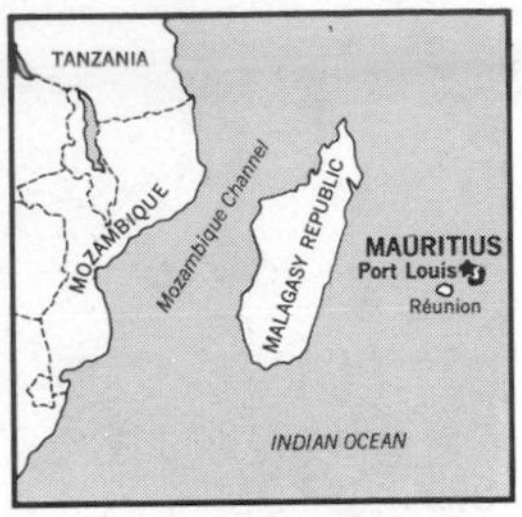

Mauritius

May apple

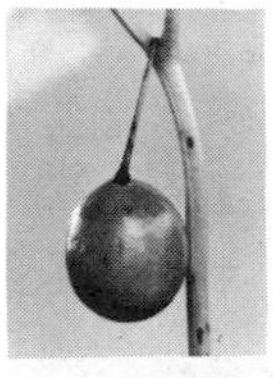
fruit

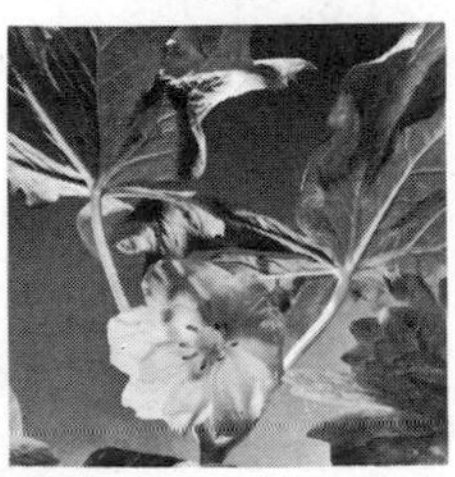
flower

Mau·per·tuis (mō-pĕr-twē′), **Pierre Louis Moreau de.** 1698–1759. French scientist; known for theory of least action.

Mau·reen (mô-rēn′). A feminine given name. [Irish *Mairin,* diminutive of *Maire,* from Old Irish, from Latin *Maria,* MARY.]

Mau·re·ta·ni·a (môr′ə-tā′nē-ə). An ancient country of northern Africa including parts of modern Morocco and Algeria.

Mau·riac (mô-ryàk′), **François.** Born 1885. French novelist.

Mau·rice (mô-rēs′, môr′ĭs, mŏr′ĭs). A masculine given name. [French, from Old French, from Latin *Mauritius,* "Moorish," name of a third-century martyr, from *Maurus,* Moor, from Greek *Mauros,* MOOR.]

Mau·ri·ta·ni·a (môr′ə-tā′nē-ə). Officially, Islamic Republic of Mauritania. A republic of northwestern Africa with an area of 419,299 square miles. Independent since 1960. Population, 900,000. Capital, Nouakchott. —**Mau′ri·ta′ni·an** *adj. & n.*

Mau·ri·ti·us (mô-rĭsh′ē-əs, -rĭsh′əs). Formerly **Île de France** (ēl də fräns′). **1.** An island nation occupying 804 square miles in the Indian Ocean, formerly a British crown colony, and since 1968 an independent member of the Commonwealth. Population, 734,000. Capital, Port Louis. **2.** The principal island of this colony, 720 square miles in area. —**Mau·ri′ti·an** (mô-rĭsh′ən) *adj. & n.*

Mau·rois (mô-rwà′), **André.** Pen name of Émile Herzog. 1885–1967. French biographer, novelist, and historian.

Mau·ry (môr′ē), **Matthew Fontaine.** 1806–1873. American naval officer, meteorologist, and pioneer oceanographer.

Mau·ser (mou′zər) *n.* A trademark for a repeating rifle or pistol. [Invented by Peter Paul *Mauser* (1838–1914), German arms manufacturer.]

mau·so·le·um (mô′sə-lē′əm, mô′zə-) *n., pl.* **-leums** or **-lea** (-lē′ə). A large and stately tomb, or a building housing such a tomb or tombs. [Latin *mausōlēum,* from Greek *mausōleion,* originally, the tomb of *Mausōlos,* satrap of Caria (died 353 B.C.), at Halicarnassus.] —**mau′so·le′an** *adj.*

mauve (mōv) *n.* Brilliant violet to strong or brilliant purple to moderate reddish purple. See **color.** [French *mauve,* "mallow(-colored)," from Latin *malva,* mallow. See **malakhē** in Appendix.*] —**mauve** *adj.*

mav·er·ick (măv′ər-ĭk, măv′rĭk) *n.* **1.** An unbranded or orphaned range calf or colt, traditionally considered the property of the first person who brands it. **2.** A horse or steer that has escaped from a herd. **3. a.** One who refuses to abide by the dictates of his group; a dissenter: *"Pitt was a maverick among Whig politicians in that he adhered to Tory diplomacy and strategy."* (W.L. Morton). **b.** One who resists adherence to or affiliation with any single organized group or faction; an independent. Often used attributively: *maverick politicians.* [After Samuel A. *Maverick* (1803–1870), Texas cattleman who did not brand his calves.]

mav·er·ick·er (măv′ər-ĭk-ər, măv′rĭk-ər) *n.* **1.** One who claimed any unbranded calf. **2.** A cattle thief.

ma·vis (mā′vĭs) *n.* Also **ma·vie** (mā′vē). A bird, the **song thrush** *(see).* [Middle English *mavys,* from Old French *mauvis,* akin to Middle Breton *milhuyt*†, thrush.]

Ma·vis (mā′vĭs). A feminine given name. [After the bird MAVIS.]

ma·vour·neen (mə-vo͝or′nēn′) *n.* Also **ma·vour·nin** (mə-vo͝or′nēn′). *Irish.* My darling. [Irish *mo mhuirnín : mo,* my (see **me-¹** in Appendix*) + *muirnín,* darling, diminutive of *muirn,* delight, from Old Irish, revels, banquet, tumult (see **mormor-** in Appendix.]

maw (mô) *n.* **1.** The stomach, mouth, or gullet of a voracious animal. **2.** An opening that gapes as if with voracious appetite: *"Rome and Greece swept Art into their maw and destroyed it."* (Blake). [Middle English *mawe,* Old English *maga.* See **mak-²** in Appendix.*]

mawk·ish (mô′kĭsh) *adj.* Excessively and objectionably sentimental. [Earlier senses "nauseating," "nauseated," from Northern dialectal *mawk,* maggot, whim, fastidious person, from Middle English *mathek,* variant of *magot,* MAGGOT.] —**mawk′ish·ly** *adv.* —**mawk′ish·ness** *n.*

Max (măks). A masculine given name. [Shortened from *Maximilian.*]

max. maximum.

max·il·la (măk-sĭl′ə) *n., pl.* **-lae** (-sĭl′ē) or **-las.** **1.** *Anatomy.* One of a pair of bones forming the upper jaw of mammals. See **skull.** **2.** *Zoology.* Either of two laterally moving appendages behind the mandibles in insects and most other arthropods. [Latin, "lower jaw," akin to *māla*†, upper jaw. See also **malar.**] —**max′il·lar** (măk′sə-lər, măk-sĭl′ər) *adj.*

max·il·lar·y (măk′sə-lĕr′ē) *n., pl.* **-ies.** A jaw or jawbone. —**max′il·lar′y** *adj.*

max·im (măk′sĭm) *n.* A succinct formulation of some fundamental principle or rule of conduct: *"Their respective maxims of conduct were the dictates of nature."* (J.S. Mill). —See Synonyms at **saying.** [Middle English, from Old French *maxime,* from Medieval Latin *(prōpositiō) maxima,* "greatest proposition," philosophical term for a fundamental axiom, from *maximus,* greatest. See **meg-** in Appendix.*]

max·i·mal (măk′sə-məl) *adj.* **1.** Of, pertaining to, or consisting of a maximum. **2.** The greatest or highest possible. **3.** *Mathematics.* Designating the maximal of an ordered set. —*n. Mathematics.* An element, in an ordered set, that is followed by no other. —**max′i·mal·ly** *adv.*

max·i·mal·ist (măk′sə-məl-ĭst) *n.* One who advocates direct, immediate revolutionary action to secure social and political gains. [French *maximaliste* (probably from English MAXIMAL).]

Max·im gun (măk′sĭm). The first automatic repeating gun. [Invented by Sir Hiram *Maxim* (1840–1916), British engineer.]

Max·i·mil·ian (măk′sə-mĭl′yən). Full name, Ferdinand Maximilian Joseph. 1832–1867. Austrian archduke; named emperor of Mexico (1864); executed by forces of Benito Juárez.

Max·i·mil·ian I (măk′sə-mĭl′yən). 1459–1519. Holy Roman Emperor (1493–1519).

max·i·mize (măk′sə-mīz′) *tr.v.* **-mized, -mizing, -mizes.** **1.** To make as great as possible; increase to a maximum: *"the ideal of maximizing opportunity through the equalizing of educational opportunity"* (Robert J. Havighurst). **2.** *Mathematics.* To find a maximum value of (a function). —**max′i·mi·za′tion** *n.* —**max′i·miz′er** *n.*

max·i·mum (măk′sə-məm) *n., pl.* **-mums** or **-ma** (-mə). *Abbr.* **max.** **1. a.** The greatest possible quantity, degree, or number. **b.** The time or period during which the highest point or degree is attained. **2.** An upper limit stipulated by law or other authority. **3.** *Astronomy.* **a.** The moment when a variable star is most brilliant. **b.** The magnitude of the star at such a moment. **4.** *Mathematics.* **a.** The value of a function that is not exceeded by neighboring values. **b.** The greatest value assumed by a function within some subset of its domain of definition. **c.** The largest number in a set. —*adj. Abbr.* **max.** **1.** Having or being the greatest quantity or the highest degree that has been or can be attained: *maximum temperature.* **2.** Of, pertaining to, or making up a maximum or maximums: *a maximum number in a series.* [Latin *maximum,* "greatest (quantity)," neuter of *maximus,* greatest. See **meg-** in Appendix.*]

Max·ine (măk-sēn′). A feminine given name. [French, feminine diminutive of *Max,* MAX.]

ma·xi·xe (mə-shēsh′, măk′sĕks, mə-shē′shā) *n.* A Brazilian dance similar to the two-step. [Brazilian Portuguese *maxixe*†.]

max·well (măks′wĕl′, -wəl) *n. Abbr.* **Mx** A unit of magnetic flux in the centimeter-gram-second electromagnetic system, equal to the flux perpendicularly intersecting an area of one square centimeter in a region where the magnetic induction is one gauss. See **measurement.** [After James MAXWELL.]

Max·well (măks′wĕl′, -wəl), **James Clerk.** 1831–1879. Scottish physicist; propounded the electromagnetic theory.

may¹ (mā) *v.* Past **might** (mīt) (see Usage note below), present **may** *archaic* **mayest** (mā′ĭst) or **mayst** (māst) for second person singular. Used as an auxiliary followed by an infinitive without *to,* or, in reply to a question or suggestion, with the infinitive understood. It can indicate: **1.** A requesting or granting of permission: *May I take a swim? You may.* See Usage note at **can.** **2.** Possibility: *It may rain this afternoon.* **3.** Ability or capacity, with the force of *can: If I may be of service.* See Usage note at **can.** **4.** Obligation or function, with the force of *must* or *shall,* in statutes, deeds, and other legal documents: *"Congress may determine the time of choosing the electors."* (Constitution). **5.** Desire or fervent wish. Used chiefly in exclamatory phrases: *Long may he live!* **6.** Contingency, purpose, or result, in clauses introduced by *that* or *so that: expressing ideas so that the average man may understand.* **7.** Less abrupt or pointed questioning: *How old may this little boy be?* [Middle English *may,* past *mighte, moghte,* Old English *maeg* (first and third person singular), past *mighte, moghte,* infinitive *magan,* to be strong, be able, have permission. See **magh-¹** in Appendix.*]

Usage: *May* and *might* are basically alike in meaning, in the senses of possibility and permission; they differ principally in intensity, not in time. (This is because, in modern usage, these words are treated as subjunctive verbs, each capable of expressing present and future time, although *might* is, grammatically, the past tense of *may.*) *May* is stronger than *might* in both senses: *He may leave* suggests greater likelihood than *He might leave;* and *May I go?* is more forceful than the less importunate *Might I go? Might* is also used to signify obligation, in statements containing a mild reproof: *You might show some gratitude.* In the past perfect, *might* sometimes signifies a condition opposed to fact: *He might have succeeded, if he had tried harder.*

may² (mā) *n. British.* The blossoms of the hawthorn: *Here we go gathering nuts and may.* [From MAY (month).]

May¹ (mā) *n.* **1.** The fifth month of the year according to the Gregorian calendar. May has 31 days. See **calendar.** **2.** The springtime of life; youth. **3.** The celebration of May Day. [Middle English *May,* from Old French *Mai,* from Latin *Maius (mēnsis),* (the month) of *Maia,* Italic goddess. See **meg-** in Appendix.*]

May² (mā). A feminine given name. [Short for MARGARET, MARY, or MABEL. Sometimes also from MAY (month).]

May, Cape (mā). A peninsula in southernmost New Jersey, between Delaware Bay and the Atlantic Ocean.

ma·ya (mä′yə) *n. Hinduism.* **1.** The origin of the world. **2.** The illusory appearance of the world. [Sanskrit *māyā*†.]

Ma·ya (mä′yə) *n., pl.* **Mayas** or **Maya.** **1.** A member of a race of Indians in southern Mexico and Central America whose civilization reached its height around A.D. 1000. **2.** The language spoken by these Indians; Mayan. [Mayan place name for Northern Yucatán.] —**Ma′ya** *adj.*

Ma·yan (mä′yən) *adj.* Of or pertaining to the Mayas, their culture, their language or the language group to which it belongs. —*n.* **1.** A Maya. **2.** A family of Central American languages, including the language of the Mayas.

Ma·ya·pán (mä′yä-pän′). A village in Yucatán, Mexico, on the site of the capital of the Mayan empire.

May apple. **1.** A plant, *Podophyllum peltatum,* of eastern North America, having a single, nodding white flower and oval yellow fruit. Although the pulp of the ripe fruit is edible, the roots, leaves, and seeds of this plant are poisonous. Also called "mandrake." **2.** The fruit of this plant.

ă pat/ā pay/âr care/ä father/b bib/ch church/d deed/ĕ pet/ē be/f fife/g gag/h hat/hw which/ĭ pit/ī pie/îr pier/j judge/k kick/l lid, needle/m mum/n no, sudden/ng thing/ŏ pot/ō toe/ô paw, for/oi noise/ou out/o͝o took/o͞o boot/p pop/r roar/s sauce/sh ship, dish/

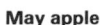

may·be (mā'bē) *adv.* Perhaps; possibly.
May beetle. The June beetle *(see)*.
May Day. 1. The first day of May, marked by the celebration of spring. **2.** May 1, regarded in a number of places as an international holiday to celebrate labor organizations.
may·day (mā'dā') *n.* An international radio-telephone signal word used by aircraft and ships in distress. [Phonetic rendering of French *m'aider*, help me.]
Ma·yence. The French name for **Mainz**.
May·er (mī'ər), **Julius Robert von.** 1814–1878. German physicist and physician; experimented with thermodynamics.
May·er (mā'ər), **Louis B(urt).** 1885–1957. Russian-born American motion-picture executive.
may·flow·er (mā'flou'ər) *n.* **1.** Broadly, any of a wide variety of plants that bloom in May. **2.** The **trailing arbutus** *(see)*.
May·flow·er (mā'flou'ər). The ship on which the Pilgrims sailed to America in 1620.
Mayflower Compact. An agreement signed by the male passengers aboard the *Mayflower* on November 11, 1620, constituting the signers and their families as a body politic and providing for the establishment of a local government.
may·fly (mā'flī') *n., pl.* **-flies.** Any of various fragile, winged insects of the order Ephemeroptera that develop from aquatic nymphs and live in the adult stage for only a few hours. Also called "dayfly," "shadfly." [Because it swarms in May.]
may·hap (mā'hăp', mā-hăp') *adv.* Archaic. Perhaps; perchance. [From the phrase *it may hap*.]
may·hem (mā'hĕm', mā'əm) *n.* Also **mai·hem. 1.** *Law.* The offense of willfully maiming or crippling a person. **2.** The infliction of violent injury upon a person or thing; wanton destruction: *children committing mayhem in the flower beds.* **3.** A state of violent disorder or riotous confusion; havoc. [Middle English, from Norman French *maihem, mahaym*, injury, from Old French *mahaignier*, MAIM.]
may·ing (mā'ĭng) *n.* Poetic. The gathering of spring flowers, especially during a May festival. [From MAY (month).]
May·kop. See **Maikop**.
may·n't (mā'ənt, mānt). Contraction of *may not.*
May·o (mā'ō). A county of the Republic of Ireland, in the northwest, 2,084 square miles in area. Population, 123,000.
May·o (mā'ō), **Charles Horace.** 1865–1939. American surgeon; with his brother, **William James** (1861–1939), established the Mayo Clinic at Rochester, Minnesota (1889).
Ma·yon, Mount (mä-yōn'). An active volcano (erupted in 1968) rising to 7,926 feet in Luzon, the Philippines.
may·on·naise (mā'ə-nāz') *n.* A dressing made of beaten raw egg yolk, butter or olive oil, lemon juice or vinegar, and seasonings. [French, possibly named in commemoration of the capture in 1756 of the city of *Mahon*, capital of Minorca, by the Duke of Richelieu.]
may·or (mā'ər, mâr) *n.* The chief magistrate of a city, town, borough, or municipal corporation. [Middle English *mair*, from Old French *maire*, from Medieval Latin *mājor*, title of various officials, from Latin *mājor*, "greater." See **meg-** in Appendix.*] —**may'or·al** *adj.* —**may'or·ship'** *n.*
may·or·al·ty (mā'ər-əl-tē, mâr'əl-) *n., pl.* **-ties. 1.** The office of a mayor. **2.** The term of office of a mayor. [Middle English, from Old French *mairalté*, from *maire*, MAYOR.]
may·or·ess (mā'ər-ĭs, mâr'ĭs) *n.* **1.** A woman holding the office of mayor. **2.** *Rare.* The wife of a mayor.
Mayor of the Palace. One of the hereditary chief administrators under the Merovingian monarchy who during the seventh and eighth centuries usurped both the royal power in the three Frankish kingdoms and at last the title (751) with the founding of the Carolingian dynasty. Also called "palatine."
Ma·yotte (mə-yôt'). The easternmost of the Comoro Islands, 140 square miles in area, in the Indian Ocean at the northern entrance to the Mozambique Channel.
May·pole (mā'pōl'). Also **may·pole.** A pole decorated with streamers that May Day celebrants hold while dancing.
may·pop (mā'pŏp') *n.* **1.** A vine, *Passiflora incarnata*, of the southeastern United States, having purple and white flowers and edible yellow fruit. **2.** The fruit of this plant. [Originally *maycock*, from Powhatan *mahcawq*.]
may tree. *British.* The hawthorn.
may·weed (mā'wēd') *n.* A widespread weed, *Anthemis cotula*, having rank-smelling leaves and white flowers. Also called "dog fennel," "stinking chamomile."
May wine. 1. A still white wine with woodruff flavoring, often containing orange or pineapple slices. **2.** A punch of champagne, claret, and Moselle or Rhine wine, flavored with woodruff. [Translation of German *Maiwein*, after the month of May, when the woodruff blooms.]
Maz·a·rin (măz'ə-rĭn; *French* mà-zà-răn'), **Jules.** Original name, Giulio Mazarini. 1602–1661. Italian-born French cardinal; tutor and first chief minister to Louis XIV.
Ma·za·tlán (mä'sä-tlän'). A resort city and seaport of western Mexico. Population, 76,000.
Maz·da·ism (măz'də-ĭz'əm) *n.* Also **Maz·de·ism.** A religion, Zoroastrianism *(see)*. [From Avestan *Mazdah-*, Zoroastrian deity. See **mendh-** in Appendix.*]
maze (māz) *n.* **1. a.** An intricate, usually confusing, network of walled or hedged pathways; labyrinth. **b.** Any physical situation resembling such a network, in which it is easy to get lost: *"The traffic was a gadfly maze in which he wandered stricken."* (Dolores Hitchens). **2.** Any of various similar networks of pathways, some blind and some leading to a goal, used experimentally to investigate learning in animals. **3.** A graphic puzzle, the solution of which is an uninterrupted path through

an intricate pattern of line segments from a starting point to a goal. **4.** Anything made up of many confused or conflicting elements; a tangle. **5.** A mental state of confusion or perplexity: *"We've trod the maze of error round."* (George Crabbe). —**mazed, mazing, mazes.** *Archaic & Regional.* To stupefy; daze; bewilder. [Middle English *maze*, a maze, earlier, "delusion," from *mazen*, to bewilder, amaze, from Old English *ā-masian†*. See also **amaze**.] —**ma'zy** *adj.*
ma·zel tov (mä'zəl tôf') *interj.* Also **ma·zal tov.** *Hebrew.* Congratulations. [Late Hebrew *mazáltob* : *mazál*, luck + *tob*, good.]
ma·zer (mā'zər) *n.* A large drinking bowl or goblet made of hard wood or metal. [Middle English *mazer*, originally, "an outgrowth of maple wood from which a mazer was made," from Old English *maser*, "knot in wood, outgrowth." See **smē-** in Appendix.*]
ma·zu·ma (mə-zōō'mə) *n.* *Slang.* Money; cash. [Yiddish *mezumen*, "ready" (*i.e.*, "ready cash"), from Hebrew *məzumān*, from Chaldean, "the ready necessary."]
ma·zur·ka (mə-zûr'kə, -zōōr'kə) *n.* Also **ma·zour·ka. 1.** A lively Polish dance resembling the polka, frequently adopted as a ballet form. **2.** A piece of music for such a dance, written in $\frac{3}{4}$ or $\frac{3}{8}$ time with the second beat heavily accented. [French, from Polish *Mazurka*, oblique form of *mazurek*, diminutive of *mazur*, one from Mazovia province.]
Ma·zu·ry. The Polish name for **Masuria**.
maz·zard (măz'ərd) *n.* A wild sweet cherry, *Prunus avium*, often used as grafting stock. [Perhaps akin to MAZER.]
Maz·zi·ni (mät-tsē'nē), **Giuseppe.** 1805–1872. Italian patriot and republican revolutionary.
M.B.A. Master of Business Administration.
Mba·bane (əm-bä-bän'). The capital of Swaziland, near the western border of the country, and 200 miles east of Johannesburg, South Africa. Population, 8,400.
Mbo·mu. See **Bomu River**.
Mc-. Variant of **Mac-**.
Mc megacycle.
MC 1. Marine Corps. **2.** Medical Corps. **3.** Member of Congress.
m.c. master of ceremonies.
M.C. 1. Master of Ceremonies. **2.** Member of Congress.
Mc·Car·thy (mə-kär'thē), **Eugene Joseph.** Born 1916. U.S. senator from Minnesota (since 1958).
Mc·Car·thy (mə-kär'thē), **Mary Therese.** Born 1912. American critic and novelist.
Mc·Car·thy·ism (mə-kär'thē-ĭz'əm) *n.* **1.** The political practice of publicizing accusations of disloyalty or subversion with insufficient regard to evidence. **2.** The use of methods of investigation and accusation regarded as unfair, in order to suppress opposition. [Coined and used by opponents of Joseph R. *McCarthy* (1909–1957), U.S. Senator from Wisconsin (1946–57).] —**Mc·Car'thy·ist** *n. & adj.*
Mc·Clel·lan (mə-klĕl'ən), **George Brinton.** 1826–1885. U.S. general in the Civil War; Presidential candidate (1864).
Mc·Cor·mick (mə-kôr'mĭk), **Cyrus Hall.** 1809–1884. American manufacturer and inventor of a reaping machine (1834).
Mc·Coy, the (real) (mə-koi'). *Slang.* The authentic thing or quality; something that is not an imitation or substitute. [After Kid *McCoy*, professional name of Norman Selby (1873–1940), American boxer.]
Mc·Cul·lers (mə-kŭl'ərz), **Carson (Smith).** 1917–1967. American author of novels, short stories, and plays.
Mc·Graw (mə-grô'), **John J(oseph).** 1873–1934. American baseball manager and third baseman.
Mc·Guf·fey (mə-gŭf'ē), **William Holmes.** 1800–1873. American educator; editor of *McGuffey's Eclectic Readers*.
Mc·In·tosh (măk'ĭn-tŏsh') *n.* A variety of red eating apple, grown commercially in the northern United States. [First cultivated, in 1796, by John *McIntosh*, of Ontario, Canada.]
Mc·Kim (mə-kĭm'), **Charles Follen.** 1847–1909. American architect; member of the firm of McKim, Mead, and White.
Mc·Kin·ley, Mount (mə-kĭn'lē). The highest mountain in North America (20,320 feet), in Alaska.
Mc·Kin·ley (mə-kĭn'lē), **William.** 1843–1901. Twenty-fifth President of the United States (1897–1901); assassinated.
MCM Airport code for Monte Carlo, Monaco.
Mc·Mil·lan (mək-mĭl'ən), **Edwin Mattison.** Born 1907. American physicist; studied transuranium elements.
Mc·Na·ma·ra (măk'nə-măr'ə), **Robert Strange.** Born 1916. American business executive; Secretary of Defense (1961–68).
Md The symbol for the element mendelevium.
MD Maryland (with Zip Code).
Md. Maryland.
M.D. Doctor of Medicine (Latin *Medicinae Doctor*).
M-day (ĕm'dā') *n. Military.* Mobilization day; the day on which national mobilization for war is ordered.
M.D.S. Master of Dental Surgery.
mdse. merchandise.
MDW Airport code for Midway Airport, Chicago, Illinois.
me (mē) *pron.* The objective case of the first person pronoun *I*. It is used: **1.** As the direct object of a verb: *He assisted me.* **2.** As the indirect object of a verb: *They offered me a ride.* **3.** As the object of a preposition: *This letter is addressed to me.* **4.** After *than* or *as* in comparisons in which the first term is in the objective case: *The judges praised you more than me.* **5.** *Informal.* In place of the reflexive pronoun *myself*, as the indirect object of a verb: *I'm going to buy me a car.* **6.** In various elliptical, absolute, or interjectional phrases in which it is neither subject nor object: *Goodness me! Unlucky me. Who,*

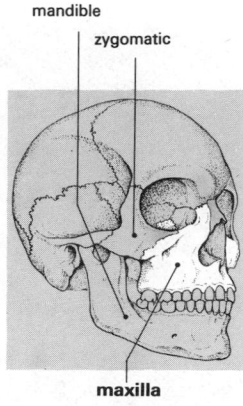

mandible
zygomatic
maxilla

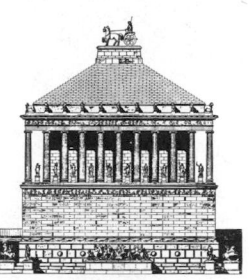

mausoleum
Built about 350 B.C.
for King Mausolos of Caria

maze

me? [Middle English *me*, Old English *mē*, *mĕ*. See **me-**[1] in Appendix.*]

Usage: *I*, rather than *me*, is the grammatically prescribed first person pronoun for use after the verb *be*: *It is I*. In formal writing, *it is I* is the construction specified by 78 per cent of the Usage Panel. The variant *it is me* (or *it's me*) is felt by many persons to be much more natural in speech, and this form is termed acceptable in speech on all levels by 60 per cent of the Panel. See Usage note at **but**.

ME **1.** Maine (with Zip Code). **2.** Middle English.

Me. Maine (unofficial).

ME. Middle English.

M.E. **1.** mechanical engineer; mechanical engineering. **2.** Middle English. **3.** military engineer. **4.** mining engineer.

me·a cul·pa (mā′ə kŭl′pə, mē′ə). *Latin.* My fault; I am at fault.

mead[1] (mēd) *n.* An alcoholic beverage made from fermented honey and water. [Middle English *mede*, Old English *medu*, *meodu*. See **medhu-** in Appendix.*]

mead[2] (mēd) *n. Archaic.* A meadow. [Middle English *mede*, Old English *mǣd*. See **mē-**[4] in Appendix.*]

meadowlark
Sturnella neglecta

Mead, Lake (mēd). An artificial lake, 247 square miles in area, formed in the Colorado River by Hoover Dam.

Mead (mēd), **Margaret.** Born 1901. American anthropologist.

Meade (mēd), **George Gordon.** 1815–1872. General of the U.S. Army of the Potomac in the Civil War.

mead·ow (mĕd′ō) *n.* A tract of grassland, either natural or used as pasture or for growing hay. [Middle English *medwe*, Old English *mǣdwe*, oblique case of *mǣd*, MEAD.] —**mead′ow·y** *adj.*

meadow beauty. Any plant of the genus *Rhexia*, of eastern North America, growing in wet ground and having showy purple flowers. Also called "deer grass."

meadow fescue. A grass, *Festuca eliator*, used for hay.

meadow hen. Any of various birds of the family Rallidae, especially a rail or coot.

mead·ow·lark (mĕd′ō-lärk′) *n.* Any bird of the genus *Sturnella*, with two species, *S. magna*, the eastern meadowlark, and *S. neglecta*, the western meadowlark, found in North America. Both are noted for their song.

meadow mouse. The **field mouse** *(see)*.

meadow rue. Any of various plants of the genus *Thalictrum*, having clusters of small white, yellowish, or purplish flowers.

meadow saffron. A plant, the **autumn crocus** *(see)*.

mead·ow·sweet (mĕd′ō-swēt′) *n.* Any of several plants of the genus *Spiraea*; especially, *S. alba* or *S. latifolia*, of eastern North America, having pyramidal clusters of flowers.

mea·ger (mē′gər) *adj.* Also **mea·gre.** **1.** Having little flesh; thin; lean. **2.** Conspicuously deficient in quantity, fullness, or extent; scanty. **3.** Conspicuously deficient in richness, fertility, or vigor; barren; feeble: *the meager soil of an eroded plain.* [Middle English *megre*, from Norman French *megre* and Old French *maigre*, from Latin *macer* (stem *macr-*), thin. See **māk-** in Appendix.*] —**mea′ger·ly** *adv.* —**mea′ger·ness** *n.*

Synonyms: *meager, spare, sparse, skimpy, scanty, scant. Meager* indicates deficient supply, often of general or intangible requisites: *meager resources; meager education. Spare* implies bare sufficiency, free of all excess. It is often applied to physical characteristics of persons *(spare of build)* and to manner of speech or writing: *spare style. Sparse* indicates lack of density and a spatial separation of units: *sparse vegetation; sparse hair. Skimpy* emphasizes conspicuous smallness or brevity: *skimpy dress; skimpy allowance. Scanty* conveys the same sense, most often of physical extent: *scanty living quarters. Scant* applies to what is barely enough or just short of a minimal amount: *a scant hour; scant measure.*

meal[1] (mēl) *n.* **1.** The edible seed or other edible part of any grain, coarsely ground. **2.** Any granular substance produced by grinding. [Middle English *mele*, Old English *melu*, flour. See **melə-** in Appendix.*]

meal[2] (mēl) *n.* **1.** The food served and eaten in one sitting. **2.** A customary time or occasion of eating food. [Middle English *meel*, Old English *mǣl*, "mark," "measure," fixed time, mealtime. See **mē-**[2] in Appendix.*]

meal·ie (mē′lē) *n. South African.* **1.** An ear of corn. **2.** *Plural.* Corn; maize. [Afrikaans *milie*, from Portuguese *milho*, millet, from Latin *milium*. See **melə-** in Appendix.*]

meal ticket. **1.** A card or ticket entitling the holder to a meal or meals. **2.** *Slang.* A person or thing depended on as a source of financial support.

meal·time (mēl′tīm′) *n.* The usual time for eating a meal.

meanders

meal·worm (mēl′wûrm′) *n.* The larva of any of several beetles of the genus *Tenebrio* that infest flour and other grain products and are raised for bird feed.

meal·y (mē′lē) *adj.* **-ier, -iest.** **1.** Resembling meal in texture or consistency; granular: *mealy potatoes.* **2. a.** Made of or containing meal. **b.** Sprinkled or covered with meal or a similar granular substance. **3.** Flecked with spots; mottled. **4.** Lacking healthy coloring; pale. **5.** Mealy-mouthed. —**meal′i·ness** *n.*

meal·y·bug (mē′lē-bŭg′) *n.* Any insect of the genus *Pseudococcus*. Some species are destructive to plants, especially citrus trees. [So named because they are covered with a white powdery substance.]

meal·y-mouthed (mē′lē-mouthd′, -moutht′) *adj.* Unwilling to state facts or opinions simply and directly.

mean[1] (mēn) *v.* **meant** (mĕnt), **meaning, means.** —*tr.* **1. a.** To be defined or described as; denote: *The word "dog" means a certain species of mammal.* **b.** To convey the same sense as; refer to the same thing as: *The French word "chien" means "dog."* **c.** To act as a symbol of; signify; represent: *In this poem, the budding flower means youth.* **2.** To intend to convey or indicate: *What do you mean by that look?* **3.** To have as a purpose or intention; intend; want: *"Most of the girls who were not betrothed meant to be teachers."* (Sinclair Lewis). **4.** To design or intend for a certain purpose or end: *a building meant for storage.* **5.** To have as a consequence; bring about: *Friction means heat.* **6.** To be attended by; be associated with; imply: *Red sky at night means fair weather.* —*intr.* **1.** To be of a specified importance or significance; to matter: *The opinions of critics meant little to him.* **2.** To have intentions of a specified kind; be disposed. Followed by *well* or *ill*: *She means well, despite her blunders.* [Middle English *menen*, Old English *mǣnan*, to intend, tell, signify. See **mei-no-** in Appendix.*]

Synonyms: *mean, signify, import, denote, represent, purport. Mean* is the least specific of the verbs considered here; it is used in the sense of conveying something meaningful. *Signify* is properly used after terms that are themselves objectively representative or symbolic of the ideas conveyed: *The Statue of Liberty signifies a haven for the oppressed. Import* makes this implication more strongly; it is often employed when what is conveyed is not merely an idea but associated ideas or implications. *Denote* is used when the idea transmitted is capable of precise statement, as a definition apart from connotations; it is also used after terms that are themselves clear indications (but not objective symbols) of the ideas conveyed: *Serenity denotes a clear conscience,* but *His crown signifies royal power. Represent* is employed when symbols convey the idea: *The shaded part of the map represents free soil,* or when a specific case serves as an example of the idea: *Crossing our borders represents aggression. Purport* may imply doubtful authenticity or pretense.

Usage: The construction *mean for* is nonstandard in conveying purpose, as in *I did not mean for you to go.* A clause introduced by *that* should be used instead: *I did not mean that you should go.*

mean[2] (mēn) *adj.* **meaner, meanest.** **1.** Low in quality or grade; inferior. **2.** Low in social status; of humble origin or rank. **3.** Characteristic of humble folk; common or poor in appearance; shabby: *"The boy was in very mean clothes, but of a very fresh and well-favoured countenance."* (Bunyan). **4.** Ignoble; base; petty: *a mean motive.* **5.** Low in value or amount; paltry. **6.** Miserly; stingy. **7.** Lacking elevating human qualities, as kindness and good will: **a.** Reluctant to oblige or accommodate. **b.** Cruel; malicious; spiteful. **8.** *Informal.* Ill-tempered. Said often of animals. **9.** *Informal.* In poor health; out of sorts; sick: *I always feel mean in wet weather.* **10.** *Slang.* **a.** Hard to cope with; difficult; troublesome: *a mean street to cross.* **b.** Hard to defeat: *He plays a mean game of bridge.* [Middle English *mene, imene*, Old English *gemǣne*, "common." See **mei-**[1] in Appendix.*]

Synonyms: *mean, low, base, abject, infamous, ignoble. Mean,* originally applied to persons of lowly birth, now emphasizes lack of those qualities that make man a superior form of life; it specifically pertains to pettiness, spite, and niggardliness. *Low* may indicate lack of refinement or apply to that which is deliberately pitched beneath a decent level, with evil intent: *a low trick. Base* emphasizes lack of honor or moral fiber. *Abject* stresses low condition without emotional connotation; it often indicates starkness or hopelessness: *abject squalor. Infamous* emphasizes bad reputation and its causes. *Ignoble* pertains to lack of qualities that give man distinction of mind and soul.

mean[3] (mēn) *n.* **1.** The middle point, quantity, state, or person regarded as between two extremes. **2.** The avoidance of extremes of behavior; moderation: *"Every virtue, as we were taught in youth, is a mean between two extremes."* (Max Beerbohm). **3.** *Mathematics.* **a.** A number that represents a set of numbers in any of several ways determined by a rule involving all members of the set; average. **b.** The **arithmetic mean** *(see)*. Compare **geometric mean.** **4.** *Logic.* The middle term in a syllogism. **5.** *Plural.* A method, course of action, or instrument by which some act can be accomplished or some end achieved: *"Means are always in our power; ends are very seldom so."* (Fielding). **6.** *Plural.* Money, property, or other wealth. —**by all means.** Without fail; certainly. —**by any means.** In any way possible; in any case: *not by any means an easy opponent.* —**by means of.** With the use of; owing to: *They succeeded by means of patience and sacrifice.* —**by no means.** In no sense; certainly not. —*adj.* **1.** Occupying a middle or intermediate position between two extremes. **2.** Intermediate in size, extent, quality, time, or degree; medium. [Middle English *mene*, from Norman French *meen* and Old French *meien*, from Latin *mediānus*, median, from *medius*, middle. See **medhyo-** in Appendix.*]

Usage: *Means*, signifying resources (money, property), takes a plural verb. *Means*, signifying a way to an end, is used in the plural, but may be either singular or plural in construction and sense. The choice of a modifying word generally determines the number of a verb following *means*. For example, *the means* can be followed by either a singular or plural verb. *A means, one means, any means, every means,* and the like are followed by singular verbs. *All means, several means, such means* (but not *such a means*) are followed by plural verbs.

me·an·der (mē-ăn′dər) *intr.v.* **-dered, -dering, -ders.** **1.** To follow a winding and turning course: *Streams tend to meander through level land.* **2.** To wander aimlessly and idly without fixed direction: *vagabonds meandering through life.* —See Synonyms at **wander.** —*n.* **1.** *Plural.* Circuitous windings or sinuosities (of a stream or path). **2.** *Usually plural.* A circuitous journey or excursion; a ramble. **3.** The Greek fret or key pattern, used in art and architecture. [Originally as a noun, from Latin *maeander*, from Greek *maiandros*, from *Maiandros*, a

ă pat/ā pay/âr care/ä father/b bib/ch church/d deed/ĕ pet/ē be/f fife/g gag/h hat/hw which/ĭ pit/ī pie/îr pier/j judge/k kick/l lid, needle/m mum/n no, sudden/ng thing/ŏ pot/ō toe/ô paw, for/oi noise/ou out/o͝o took/o͞o boot/p pop/r roar/s sauce/sh ship, dish/

river in Phrygia noted for its windings.] —**me·an′der·er** *n.* —**me·an′der·ing·ly** *adv.* —**me·an′drous** (-drəs) *adj.*

mean deviation. *Statistics.* The arithmetic mean of the absolute values of deviations from the arithmetic mean, or from the median, in a statistical distribution.

mean·ing (mē′nǐng) *n.* **1.** That which is signified by something; what something represents; sense; import; semantic content: *"Pending a satisfactory explanation of the notion of meaning, linguists in the semantic field are in the situation of not knowing what they are talking about."* (Willard V. Quine). **2.** That which one wishes to convey: *I listened carefully to grasp his meaning.* **3.** That which is interpreted to be the goal; intent, or end. **4.** That which is felt to be the inner significance of something: *"But who can comprehend the meaning of the voice of the city?"* (O. Henry). **5.** Functional value; efficacy; significance: *customs now empty of all meaning.* —*adj.* **1.** Full of meaning; expressive. **2.** Intentioned or disposed in a specified manner. Used in combination with *well* or *ill: a well-meaning fellow.*
   Synonyms: *meaning, sense, significance, signification, acceptation, import, purport.* Meaning, being nonspecific, overlaps each of the following. *Sense,* in this context, may be used generally, as the equivalent of meaning (comprehensibility), or specifically, to denote a particular meaning (one of a group of meanings conveyed by a single word, symbol, or idea): *"Vision" has the distinct senses of sight and foresight. Significance* stresses meaning beyond immediate comprehension (underlying or long-range meaning); besides perception, it implies evaluation. In contrast, *signification* and *acceptation* apply to accepted or established meaning, directly conveyed. *Import* also pertains to ostensible meaning. *Purport* applies to broad understanding, often of an extensive subject.

mean·ing·ful (mē′nǐng-fəl) *adj.* Having meaning, function, or purpose; significant. —**mean′ing·ful·ly** *adv.*

mean·ing·less (mē′nǐng-lǐs) *adj.* Having no meaning or significance; senseless. —**mean′ing·less·ly** *adv.*

mean·ly (mēn′lē) *adv.* In a poor, mean, or base manner: *"Still we live meanly, like ants."* (Thoreau).

mean·ness (mēn′nǐs) *n.* **1.** The state of being inferior in quality, character, or value; poorness; commonness. **2.** Selfishness; stinginess; malice. **3.** A spiteful or malicious act.

mean solar day. The period of time between two successive transits of the **mean sun** *(see);* the standard for the 24-hour day, measured from midnight to midnight. Also called "civil day."

mean square. *Mathematics.* The arithmetic mean of the squares of a set of numbers.

mean sun. A hypothetical sun defined as moving at a uniform rate along the celestial equator so that it completes its orbit in the same period as the apparent sun. It is used in computing the mean solar day.

meant. Past tense and past participle of **mean.**

mean time. Time measured with reference to the **mean sun** *(see),* giving equal 24-hour days throughout the year. Also called "civil time," "mean solar time."

mean·time (mēn′tīm′) *n.* The time between one occurrence and another; interval. —*adv.* During a period of intervening time; meanwhile: *"Meantime, let wonder seem familiar."* (Shakespeare).
   Usage: *Meantime* serves principally as a noun: *In the meantime, we waited.* In expressing the same sense by a single adverb, *meanwhile* is more common than *meantime: Meanwhile, we waited.* In the sense of intervening time, *meantime* is now always written as one word.

mean·tone system (mēn′tōn′). *Music.* A former system for tuning keyboard instruments. It has now been replaced by **equal temperament** *(see).*

mean·while (mēn′hwīl′) *n.* The intervening time. —*adv.* **1.** During or in the intervening time: *Meanwhile, life goes on.* **2.** At the same time: *The court is deliberating; meanwhile, we must be patient.* See Usage note at **meantime.**

Mean·y (mē′nē), **George.** Born 1894. American labor leader.

Mearns, The. The former name for **Kincardineshire.**

meas. measurable; measure.

mea·sles (mē′zəlz) *n.* Plural in form, used with a singular verb. **1.** An acute, contagious virus disease, usually occurring in childhood. Its symptoms include the eruption of red spots. It is usually self-immunizing. Also called "rubeola." **2.** Any of certain other diseases displaying similar but milder symptoms, especially **German measles** *(see).* **3.** A disease of cattle and swine, caused by tapeworm larvae. **4.** A plant disease, usually caused by fungi, and producing minute spots on leaves and stems. [Middle English *maseles,* plural of *masel,* from Middle Dutch *māsel,* blemish. See *smē-* in Appendix.*]

mea·sly (mēz′lē) *adj.* -slier, -sliest. **1.** Infected or spotted with measles; measled. **2.** Infected with larval tapeworms. Said of meat. **3.** *Slang.* Contemptibly small; meager: *a measly tip.*

meas·ur·a·ble (mĕzh′ər-ə-bəl) *adj. Abbr.* **meas.** **1.** Capable of being measured. **2.** Of distinguished importance; significant: *a measurable figure in literature.* **3.** Not so great as to escape all measure or comparison; moderate: *"The fire of Insurrection gets damped . . . into measurable, manageable heat."* (Carlyle).

meas·ure (mĕzh′ər) *n. Abbr.* **meas.** See also the tables and explanations at **measurement.** **1.** The dimensions, quantity, or capacity of anything as ascertained by measuring: *Length, area, volume, and mass are basic measures of material properties.* **2.** A reference standard or sample used for the quantitative comparison of properties: *The standard kilogram is maintained as a measure of mass.* **3.** A unit specified by a scale, as an inch, or by variable conditions, as a day's march. **4.** A system of measurement, such as the metric system. **5.** A device, such as a marked

tape or a graduated container, used for measuring. **6.** An act of measurement. **7.** An evaluation or basis of comparison: *"Long survival is no more self-evidently the final measure of the worth of a society than it is of an individual."* (Joseph Wood Krutch). **8.** The extent or degree of something: *"For never was from Heaven granted / Measure of strength so great to mortal seed."* (Milton). **9.** A fitting amount: *a measure of recognition.* **10.** A limited amount or degree: *"a measure of serenity"* (John Updike). **11.** Limit; bounds: *a generosity knowing no measure.* **12.** Appropriate restraint; moderation: *criticism in measure.* **13.** An action taken as a means to an end; expedient: *a desperate measure.* **14.** A legislative bill or enactment: *"I have opposed measures, not men."* (Lord Chesterfield). **15.** Poetic meter. **16.** *Often plural.* Discourse having poetic rhythm or cadence: *"And so I mocked her in magnificent measure."* (Wallace Stevens). **17.** *Music.* The metrical unit between two bars on the staff; a bar. —**beyond measure. 1.** In excess. **2.** Without limit. —**for good measure.** In addition to the required amount. —**in (a) great (or large) measure.** To a great extent: *"also here he in great measure lost his senses"* (Bunyan). —**in a (or some) measure.** To a degree: *The new law was in some measure harmful.* —*v.* **measured, -uring, -ures.** —*tr.* **1.** To ascertain the dimensions, quantity, or capacity of. **2.** To mark, lay out, or establish dimensions for by measuring. Often followed by *off: measure off an area.* **3.** To estimate by evaluation or comparison: *"I gave them an account . . . of the situation as far as I could measure it."* (Winston Churchill). **4.** To bring into opposition: *She measured her power with that of a dangerous adversary.* **5.** To mark off, usually with reference to some unit of measurement; dole out. Often followed by *out: measure out a pint of milk.* **6.** To serve as a measure of: *The inch measures length.* **7.** To allot or distribute as if by measuring; mete. Often followed by *out: The revolutionary tribunal measured out harsh justice.* **8.** To consider or choose with care; weigh: *He measures his words with pedantic caution.* **9.** *Archaic.* To travel over or through: *"We must measure much ground today."* (Shakespeare). —*intr.* **1.** To have a measurement of: *The room measures 10 by 12 feet.* **2.** To allow of measurement: *White sugar measures more easily than brown.* —**measure one's length.** To fall flat: *He measured his length on the wet pavement.* [Middle English *mesure,* from Old French *mesure,* from Latin *mēnsūra,* a measure, from *mētīrī* (past participial stem *mēns-*), to measure. See *mē-²* in Appendix.*] —**meas′ur·er** *n.*

meas·ured (mĕzh′ərd) *adj.* **1.** Determined by measurement: *The measured distance was less than a mile.* **2.** Regular in rhythm and number: *"a clock struck slowly in the house with a measured, solemn chime"* (Thomas Wolfe). **3.** Careful; moderate; restrained: *measured words.* **4.** Calculated; deliberate: *with measured irony.* **5.** Slow and stately. **6.** Written in meter. **7.** *Music.* Mensural. **8.** Limited: *a measured capacity for action.* —**meas′ured·ly** *adv.* —**meas′ured·ness** *n.*

meas·ure·less (mĕzh′ər-lǐs) *adj.* Limitless; immeasurable; infinite: *"Through caverns measureless to man"* (Coleridge). See Synonyms at **infinite.** —**meas′ure·less·ly** *adv.*

meas·ure·ment (mĕzh′ər-mənt) *n.* **1.** The act of measuring or the process of being measured. **2.** A system of measuring: *measurement in miles.* **3.** The dimension, quantity, or capacity determined by measuring: *room measurements.* See the tables and their explanation.

measure
First measure of
"Frère Jacques"

MEASUREMENT

There are three major systems of measurement units in wide use: the U.S. Customary System, the British Imperial System, and the International (Metric) System.

The fundamental quantities of each system, together with their relationships to derived units within the same system and conversion to similar quantities in other systems, are shown in Table I. This table is confined to units of "weights and measures," that is, measurements of length, mass (or weight), and capacity. Table II is a separate tabulation of some of the most common units of scientific measurement and other miscellaneous units.

Measurement of a quantity implies that a number is assigned to represent its magnitude. Usually the assignment can be made by a simple comparison. The magnitude of the quantity is compared to a "standard" quantity, the magnitude of which is arbitrarily chosen to have the measure 1.

Quantities having a scale of measurement chosen in this way, arbitrarily and independently of the scales of other quantities, are called "fundamental." All other quantities are measured in units defined in relation to, or "derived" from, fundamental quantities. The foot, defined as ⅓ of a yard, is an example of a derived unit. Another example is provided by the relationship between the weight and mass of a body. In the equation $W = mg$, W is the weight, m the mass, and g the acceleration of gravity at the place where the body is located. The units for g are derived units, given in terms of the fundamental quantities length and time. Thus, if mass is chosen as a fundamental quantity, the units for weight follow naturally from the above equation and are derived units. (It is, of course, possible to choose weight rather than mass as the fundamental quantity. This is in fact done when the resulting units are convenient for calculation.)

There is an important distinction between a "unit of measurement" and a "standard of measurement."

Measurement (continued)

A *unit of measurement* is a precisely defined quantity in terms of which the magnitudes of all other quantities of the same kind can be stated.

A *standard of measurement* is an *object* which, under specified conditions, serves to define, represent, or record the magnitude of a unit.

In the U.S. Customary System, the fundamental units are the *yard* and the (avoirdupois) *pound*. There are no primary standards as such in the U.S. System. The fundamental units are defined in terms of standards used in the Metric System. The U.S. System has its origins in the British System, but they are not identical.

The fundamental units in the British Imperial System also are the yard and the pound. Until 1959, these were defined not by reference to a Metric standard, as in the United States, but by reference to primary standards created specifically for that purpose. In that year, by agreement between the United States and the British Commonwealth, the International Yard and the International Pound were defined in terms of the Metric standards (as given in Table I) in the U.S. Customary System.

There are, however, significant differences between the U.S. and British systems. In the British System the units of dry measure (capacity) are the same as those of liquid measure. In the U.S. System they are not. In 1824 the British Imperial gallon was defined as the volume of 10 pounds of water at a temperature of 62°F (= 277.42 cubic inches, by calculation). The bushel was defined as 8 gallons. In 1879 the troy pound was abolished in England, only the troy ounce being retained. The troy pound, however, is still a legal, although infrequently used, unit.

The Metric System is the system used in most of the civilized world, and the one used almost exclusively for scientific work. With the addition of units of time (the second), electric current (the ampere), temperature (kelvin, or alternatively degree Kelvin), and luminous intensity (candela), the Metric System provides a complete coherent system of units used for all physical measurements. It is called the International System of Units and its units are called SI units. The International System was adopted for scientific use by the U.S. National Bureau of Standards in February 1964.

The Metric System was first proposed in France by Gabriel Mouton, Vicar of Lyons, in 1670. However, it was not possible to introduce this entirely new system of weights and measures until the French Revolution provided the opportunity. The new system was presented to the National Assembly in 1790, and it was adopted in France by legislative action in April 1795.

In the United States the Metric System is the only system that has ever received specific legislative sanction by Congress (in 1866). Acceptance and use of the Metric System in the United States have steadily grown until at present it is of nearly equal importance with the Customary System.

The fundamental units of the Metric System are the meter and the kilogram. The meter was defined in 1960 by the Eleventh General Conference on Weights and Measures to be equal to 1,650,763.73 wavelengths of the orange-red radiation in vacuum of krypton 86. The kilogram is defined as the mass of a platinum-iridium standard, the International Prototype Kilogram, kept at the International Bureau of Weights and Measures in Sèvres, France.

The International Kilogram is a standard of *mass*. Consequently, units such as the pound and gram derived from it should be regarded as units of mass. In common practice, however, the terms kilogram, pound, gram, etc., are used to designate the *weights* of these masses. This is permissible because equal masses have equal weights under identical conditions. Standards of mass (or "weights") are ordinarily calibrated (or "weighed") on an equal-arm analytical balance. On this instrument two identical masses balance each other independently of the local value of the acceleration of gravity (which determines weight). Thus standards of mass can also be used as standards of weight.

The Metric System is a decimal system, that is, one in which all derived units are multiples of ten. The prefixes at the top of the next column, in combination with the basic unit names, provide the multiples and submultiples in the International System. For example the unit *meter* with the prefix *kilo-* produces *kilometer*, meaning "1,000 meters."

Prefix	Symbol	Multiple*			
deka-	da	10	deci-	d	10^{-1}
hecto-	h	10^2	centi-	c	10^{-2}
kilo-	k	10^3	milli-	m	10^{-3}
mega-	M	10^6	micro-	μ	10^{-6}
giga-	G	10^9	nano-	n	10^{-9}
tera-	T	10^{12}	pico-	p	10^{-12}
			femto-	f	10^{-15}
			atto-	a	10^{-18}

* 10^{-1} means 0.1. Similarly, 10^{-6} = 0.000001, etc.; 10^3 = 1,000. 10^6 = 1,000,000, etc.

Table I. Measurement Units

Length

U.S. Customary Unit	U.S. Equivalents	Metric Equivalents
inch	0.083 foot	2.54 centimeters
foot	⅓ yard, 12 inches	0.3048 meter
yard	3 feet, 36 inches	0.9144 meter
rod	5½ yards, 16½ feet	5.0292 meters
mile (statute, land)	1,760 yards, 5,280 feet	1.609 kilometers
mile (nautical, international)	1.151 statute miles	1.852 kilometers

Area

U.S. Customary Unit	U.S. Equivalents	Metric Equivalents
square inch	0.007 square foot	6.4516 square centimeters
square foot	144 square inches	929.030 square centimeters
square yard	1,296 square inches, 9 square feet	0.836 square meter
acre	43,560 square feet, 4,840 square yards	4.047 square meters
square mile	640 acres	2.590 square kilometers

Volume or Capacity

U.S. Customary Unit	U.S. Equivalents	Metric Equivalents
cubic inch	0.00058 cubic foot	16.387 cubic centimeters
cubic foot	1,728 cubic inches	0.028 cubic meter
cubic yard	27 cubic feet	0.765 cubic meter

U.S. Customary Liquid Measure	U.S. Equivalents	Metric Equivalents
fluid ounce	8 fluid drams, 1.804 cubic inches	29.573 milliliters
pint	16 fluid ounces, 28.875 cubic inches	0.473 liter
quart	2 pints, 57.75 cubic inches	0.946 liter
gallon	4 quarts, 231 cubic inches	3.785 liters
barrel	varies from 31 to 42 gallons, established by law or usage	

measuring worm. A caterpillar that moves in alternate contractions and expansions suggestive of measuring. Also called "inchworm," "looper," "spanworm."

meat (mēt) *n.* **1.** The edible flesh of mammals, as distinguished from that of fish or poultry. **2.** Any edible flesh: *crab meat.* **3.** Edible flesh cooked and prepared to be eaten. **4.** The edible portions of eggs, fruits, or nuts. **5.** The essence or principal part of something: *the meat of the editorial.* **6.** *Slang.* Something one enjoys or excels in; forte: *Tennis is his meat.* **7.** Anything eaten for nourishment; food. Now chiefly used in the phrase *meat and drink.* [Middle English *mete,* "food," meat, Old English *mete,* food. See **mad-** in Appendix.*]

meat-ball (mēt'bôl') *n.* **1.** A small ball of ground meat variously combined and cooked. **2.** *Slang.* A stupid fellow.

Meath (mēth, mĕth). A county in eastern Republic of Ireland, 903 square miles in area. Population, 65,000. Capital, Trim.

meat-less (mēt'lĭs) *adj.* **1.** Lacking meat or food. **2.** When meat is not to be eaten: *meatless days.*

meat loaf. A mounded or molded dish, usually baked, of ground beef or a combination of meats and other ingredients.

me·a·tus (mē-ā'təs) *n., pl.* **meatuses** or **meatus.** A body canal or passage, such as the opening of the ear or the urethral canal. [Latin *meātus,* passage, from *meāre* (past participial stem *meāt-*), to pass. See **mei-¹** in Appendix.*]

meat·y (mē'tē) *adj.* **-ier, -iest. 1.** Of or pertaining to meat; having the flavor or smell of meat. **2.** Full of or containing meat. **3.** Heavily fleshed. **4.** Supplying ample food for thought; pithy; substantial: *a meaty theme for study and debate.* **—meat'i·ness** *n.*

MEB Airport code for Melbourne, Australia.

Mec·ca (mĕk'ə). The birthplace of Mohammed and the most holy city of Islam. It is a capital of Saudi Arabia. Population,

ă pat/ā pay/âr care/ä father/b bib/ch church/d deed/ĕ pet/ē be/f fife/g gag/h hat/hw which/ĭ pit/ī pie/îr pier/j judge/k kick/l lid/needle/m mum/n no, sudden/ng thing/ŏ pot/ō toe/ô paw, for/oi noise/ou out/ŏŏ took/ōō boot/p pop/r roar/s sauce/sh ship, dish/

Table I. (continued)

U.S. Customary Dry Measure	U.S. Equivalents	Metric Equivalents
pint	½ quart, 33.6 cubic inches	0.551 liter
quart	2 pints, 67.2 cubic inches	1.101 liters
peck	8 quarts, 537.605 cubic inches	8.810 liters
bushel	4 pecks, 2,150.42 cubic inches	35.238 liters

British Imperial Liquid and Dry Measure	U.S. Customary Equivalents	Metric Equivalents
fluid ounce	0.961 U.S. fluid ounce, 1.734 cubic inches	28.412 milliliters
pint	1.032 U.S. dry pints, 1.201 U.S. liquid pints, 34.678 cubic inches	568.26 milliliters
quart	1.032 U.S. dry quarts, 1.201 U.S. liquid quarts, 69.354 cubic inches	1.136 liters
gallon	1.201 U.S. gallons, 277.420 cubic inches	4.546 liters
peck	554.84 cubic inches	0.009 cubic meter
bushel	1.032 U.S. bushels, 2,219.36 cubic inches	0.036 cubic meter

Weight

U.S. Customary Unit (Avoirdupois)	U.S. Equivalents	Metric Equivalents
grain	0.036 dram, 0.002285 ounce	64.79891 milligrams
dram	27.344 grains, 0.0625 ounce	1.772 grams
ounce	16 drams, 437.5 grains	28.350 grams
pound	16 ounces, 7,000 grains	453.59237 grams
ton (short)	2,000 pounds	0.907 metric ton (1,000 kilograms)
ton (long)	1.12 short tons, 2,240 pounds	1.016 metric tons

Apothecary Weight Unit	U.S. Customary Equivalents	Metric Equivalents
scruple	20 grains	1.296 grams
dram	60 grains	3.888 grams
ounce	480 grains, 1.097 avoirdupois ounces	31.103 grams
pound	5,760 grains, 0.823 avoirdupois pound	373.242 grams

Scientific Measurement

The units tabulated in Table II are commonly used in science and engineering. They are primarily chosen from the fields of mechanics and electricity and magnetism and are a representative, not an exhaustive, selection.

SI units are given for all physical quantities listed. For those units having a special name in the International System, the name appears, along with the derivation of the unit from the fundamental SI quantities, which are defined as: meter (m), kilogram (kg), second (s), ampere (A), kelvin (K) or alternatively degree Kelvin (°K), and candela (cd). Two supplementary units, the radian (rad), for measuring plane angles, and the steradian (sr), for measuring solid angles, are used. These are "geometrical" rather than "physical" units, in the sense that their definitions are based on abstract geometrical concepts rather than on physical standards.

In some instances, it is customary practice to measure a quantity in units other than SI units; in such cases the appropriate unit is given in the right-hand column, along with a conversion to SI units.

Additional information on individual units, including those not tabulated, should be sought at the unit names in text.

Table II. Scientific Units

Quantity	SI Unit	Symbol	Derivation	Other Units
acceleration	meter per second squared	m/s²		
angular acceleration	radian per second squared	rad/s²		
angular velocity	radian per second	rad/s		
density	kilogram per cubic meter	kg/m³		
electric capacitance	farad	F	(A·s/V)	
electric charge	coulomb	C	(A·s)	electrostatic unit (esu) = ⅓ × 10⁻⁹ C
electric current	ampere	A		
electric field strength	volt per meter	V/m		
electric resistance	ohm	Ω	(V/A)	
energy, work, quantity of heat	joule	J	(N·m)	electronvolt (eV) = 1.60207×10^{-19} J calorie (cal) = 4.186 J British thermal unit (Btu) = 1,054.8 J erg = 10^{-7} J foot-pound (ft-lb) = 1.3558 J
flux of light	lumen	lm	(cd·sr)	
force	newton	N	(kg·m/s²)	dyne (dyn) = 10^{-5} N
frequency	hertz	Hz	(s⁻¹)	formerly cycle per second (cps, c/sec)
illumination	lux	lx	(lm/m²)	
inductance	henry	H	(V·s/A)	
length	meter	m		angstrom (Å) = 10^{-10} m
luminance	candela per square meter	cd/m²		
magnetic field strength	ampere per meter	A/m		oersted (Oe) = $(1/4\pi) \times 10^3$ A/m
magnetic flux	weber	Wb	(V·s)	maxwell (Mx) = 10^{-8} Wb
magnetic flux density	tesla	T	(Wb/m²)	gauss (G) = 10^{-4} T
magnetomotive force	ampere	A		
mass	kilogram	kg		
power	watt	W	(J/s)	horsepower (hp) = 745.7 W
pressure	newton per square meter	N/m²		atmosphere (atm) = 1.01325×10^5 N/m² bar = 10^5 N/m²
velocity	meter per second	m/s		
voltage, potential difference, electromotive force	volt	V	(W/A)	

200,000. —**Mec'can** adj. & n.

mec·ca (mĕk'ə) n. Sometimes capital **M.** **1.** A place regarded as the center of an activity or interest; a goal to which adherents of a faith or practice fervently aspire. **2.** Any place visited by many people. [From MECCA as a goal of pilgrims.]

mech. **1.** mechanical; mechanics. **2.** mechanism.

me·chan·ic (mǐ-kăn'ǐk) n. A worker skilled in making, using, or repairing machines and tools. [From mechanic, earlier form of MECHANICAL.] —**me·chan'ic** adj.

me·chan·i·cal (mǐ-kăn'ǐ-kəl) adj. Abbr. **mech.** **1.** Of or pertaining to machines or tools. **2.** Operated or produced by a machine. **3.** Of, pertaining to, or governed by mechanics. **4.** Acting or performing like a machine; automatic: The speaker's delivery was mechanical. **5.** Pertaining to, produced by, or dominated by physical forces. **6.** Interpreting and explaining the phenomena of the universe by referring to causally deter-

mined material forces; mechanistic. **7.** Rare. Of or pertaining to manual labor, its tools, and its skills. —n. Printing. A layout consisting of type proofs, artwork, or both, exactly positioned and prepared for making an offset or other printing plate. Also called "paste-up." [Middle English, pertaining to manual labor, earlier mechanic, from Latin mēchanicus, from Greek mēkhanikos, from mēkhunē, contrivance, machine, from mēkhos, means, expedient. See magh-¹ in Appendix.*] —**me·chan'i·cal·ly** adv. —**me·chan'i·cal·ness** n.

mechanical advantage. The ratio of the output force of a machine to the input force.

mechanical drawing. **1. Drafting** (see). **2.** Any drawing that enables measurements to be interpreted, for example, an architect's plans.

mechanical engineering. Abbr. **M.E.** The branch of engineering that encompasses the generation and application of heat

---

† tight/th thin, path/th this, bathe/ŭ cut/ûr urge/v valve/w with/y yes/z zebra, size/zh vision/ə about, item, edible, gallop, circus/ à Fr. ami/œ Fr. feu, Ger. schön/ü Fr. tu, Ger. über/KH Ger. ich, Scot. loch/N Fr. bon. *Follows main vocabulary. †Of obscure origin.

and mechanical power and the design, production, and use of machines and tools. —**mechanical engineer.**

mech·a·ni·cian (mĕk'ə-nĭsh'ən) *n.* A person who makes, uses, or repairs machines and tools.

me·chan·ics (mĭ-kăn'ĭks) *n.* Plural in form, used with a singular verb. *Abbr.* **mech. 1.** The analysis of the action of forces on matter or material systems. **2.** The design, construction, operation, and application of machinery or mechanical structures.

Me·chan·ics·ville (mĭ-kăn'ĭks-vĭl'). A village in north-central Virginia, near the site of the Battle of Mechanicsville (June 26, 1862) in the Civil War.

mech·a·nism (mĕk'ə-nĭz'əm) *n.* **1.** *Abbr.* **mech. a.** A machine or mechanical appliance. **b.** The arrangement of connected parts in a machine. **2.** Any system of parts that operate or interact like those of a machine: *the mechanism of the solar system.* **3.** An instrument or process, physical or mental, by which something is done or comes into being: *"The mechanism of oral learning is largely that of continuous repetition."* (T.G.E. Powell). **4.** *Psychology.* **a.** The automatic and consistent response of an organism to various stimuli. **b.** Any habitual manner of acting to achieve some end. **5.** *Psychoanalysis.* A usually unconscious mental and emotional pattern that dominates behavior: *defense mechanism.* **6.** *Abbr.* **mech.** *Chemistry.* The sequence of steps in a chemical reaction. **7.** *Philosophy.* The doctrine that all natural phenomena are explicable by material causes and mechanical principles. [Late Latin *mēchanisma,* from Greek *mēkhanē,* machine. See **mechanical.**]

mech·a·nist (mĕk'ə-nĭst) *n.* **1.** A person who believes in or employs in his work or thinking the philosophical doctrine of mechanism. **2.** A mechanician.

mech·a·nis·tic (mĕk'ə-nĭs'tĭk) *adj.* **1.** Of or pertaining to mechanics as a branch of physics. **2.** Of or pertaining to the philosophy of mechanism; specifically, tending to explain phenomena only by reference to physical or biological causes: *"Advertising, not culture, is the most characterisitic product of the study of the mind on mechanistic principles."* (Joseph Wood Krutch). —**mech'a·nis'ti·cal·ly** *adv.*

mech·a·nize (mĕk'ə-nīz') *tr.v.* **-nized, -nizing, -nizes. 1.** To equip with machinery: *mechanize a factory.* **2.** To equip (a military unit) with motor vehicles, such as tanks and trucks. **3.** To make automatic or unspontaneous; render mechanical, routine, or monotonous. **4.** To produce by machines or as if by machines. [From MECHAN(ICAL).] —**mech'a·ni·za'tion** *n.*

mech·a·no·chem·i·cal coupling (mĕk'ə-nō-kĕm'ĭ-kəl). *Biophysics.* The reversible conversion of chemical energy into mechanical work: *The control of muscle contraction and relaxation by ATP is an example of mechanochemical coupling.*

mech·a·no·ther·a·py (mĕk'ə-nō-thĕr'ə-pē) *n.* Medical treatment by mechanical methods, such as massage.

Mech·lin¹ (mĕk'lĭn). *French* **Ma·lines** (mà-lēn'). *Flemish* **Me·che·len** (mĕkH'ə-lən). A city in north-central Belgium, formerly noted for its lace. Population, 65,000.

Mech·lin² (mĕk'lĭn) *n.* A delicate lace in which the pattern details are defined by a flat thread. Also called "malines." [From MECHLIN.]

Meck·len·burg (mĕk'lən-bûrg'; *German* mĕk'lən-bŏork'). **1.** A former state in northern Germany. **2.** A state of East Germany from 1945 to 1952, formed by the union of the foregoing territory with western Pomerania.

me·co·ni·um (mĭ-kō'nē-əm) *n.* Excrement in the fetal intestinal tract that is discharged at birth. [Latin *mecōnium,* from Greek *mēkōneion,* "poppy juice," the greenish excrement of a newborn child, from *mēkōn,* poppy. See **mak-¹** in Appendix.*]

med. 1. medical; medicine. **2.** medieval. **3.** medium.

M. Ed. Master of Education.

me·da·ka (mĭ-dä'kə) *n.* **1.** The Japanese rice fish, *Oryzias latipes,* much used in biological research. **2.** Any fish of the Asiatic and Indo-Malayan genus *Oryzias.* [Japanese, killifish.]

med·al (mĕd'l) *n.* **1.** A piece of metal, stamped with a design or inscription commemorating an event or person, often given as an award. **2.** A piece of metal stamped with a religious device, used as an object of veneration or commemoration. —*tr.v.* **medaled, -aling, -als.** Also *chiefly British* **-alled, -alling.** To honor or decorate with a medal. [French *médaille,* from Italian *medaglia,* from Common Romance *medallia* (unattested), from Vulgar Latin *metallea* (unattested), from Latin *metallum,* METAL.]

Medal for Merit. A decoration awarded by the United States to civilians for outstanding services in peace or war.

med·al·ist (mĕd'l-ĭst) *n.* Also *chiefly British* **med·al·list. 1.** One who designs, makes, or collects medals. **2.** One who has received a medal. **3.** *Golf.* The winner at **medal play** *(see)* in a tournament.

me·dal·lion (mə-dăl'yən) *n.* **1.** A large medal. **2.** Any of various large ancient Greek coins. **3.** Something resembling a large medal, such as an oval or circular design used as decoration. [French *médaillon,* from Italian *medaglione,* augmentative of *medaglia,* MEDAL.]

Medal of Honor. *Abbr.* **MH** The highest U.S. military decoration, awarded in the name of Congress to members of the armed forces for gallantry and bravery beyond the call of duty in action against the enemy. Also called "Congressional Medal of Honor."

medal play. *Golf.* Competition in which the total number of strokes taken is the basis of the score. Compare **match play.**

Me·dan (mā-dän'). A city and trade center of northeastern Sumatra, Indonesia. Population, 310,000.

med·dle (mĕd'l) *intr.v.* **-dled, -dling, -dles. 1.** To intrude in other people's affairs or business; interfere. Used with *in* or *with:* "*But

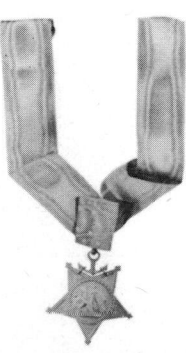

Medal of Honor

I will meddle no more with that." (Izaak Walton). **2.** To handle something idly or ignorantly; tamper. Followed by *with.* —See Synonyms at **interfere.** [Middle English *medlen,* "to mix," meddle, from Old French *medler, mesdler,* to mix in, variants of *mesler,* from Vulgar Latin *misculāre* (unattested), frequentative of Latin *miscēre,* to mix. See **meik-** in Appendix.*] —**med'dler** (mĕd'lər, mĕd'l-ər) *n.*

med·dle·some (mĕd'l-səm) *adj.* Inclined to meddle or interfere. —**med'dle·some·ly** *adv.* —**med'dle·some·ness** *n.*

Mede (mēd) *n.* A native or inhabitant of ancient Media. [Middle English, from Latin *Mēdus,* from Greek *Mēdos,* from Old Persian *mada†.*]

Me·de·a (mĭ-dē'ə). *Greek Mythology.* A princess and sorceress of Colchis who helped Jason obtain the Golden Fleece.

Me·de·llín (mĕd'l-ēn'; *Spanish* mā'thā-yēn'). A city of central Colombia, the country's second-largest city and foremost manufacturing and commercial center. Population, 773,000.

Med·ford (mĕd'fərd; mĕd'fərd *for sense 2*). **1.** A city in northeastern Massachusetts, northwest of Boston. Population, 65,000. **2.** A city in southwestern Oregon. Population, 24,000.

Med. Gr. Medieval Greek.

me·di·a. Alternate plural of **medium.**

Me·di·a (mē'dē-ə). An ancient country of southwestern Asia, now the northwestern region of Iran. —**Me'di·an** *adj. & n.*

me·di·a·cy (mē'dē-ə-sē) *n.* **1.** The state or quality of being mediate. **2.** Mediation.

me·di·ae·val. Variant of **medieval.**

me·di·ae·val·ism. Variant of **medievalism.**

me·di·al (mē'dē-əl) *adj.* **1.** Pertaining to, situated in, or extending toward the middle; median. **2.** *Phonetics.* Being a sound, syllable, or letter occurring between the initial and final positions in a word or morpheme. **3.** Being or pertaining to a mathematical average or mean. **4.** Average; ordinary. —*n. Phonetics.* **1.** A voiced stop, as *b, d,* or *g.* Also called "media." **2.** An element used in the middle of a word, such as a sound, letter, or form of a letter. [From Late Latin *mediālis,* from Latin *medius,* middle. See **medhyo-** in Appendix.*] —**me'di·al·ly** *adv.*

me·di·an (mē'dē-ən) *adj.* **1.** Pertaining to, located in, or directed toward the middle; medial. **2.** *Anatomy & Zoology.* Of, pertaining to, or lying in the plane that divides a bilaterally symmetrical animal into right and left halves; mesial. **3.** *Statistics.* Relating to or constituting the middle value in a distribution. —*n.* **1.** A median point, plane, line, or part. **2.** *Statistics.* The middle value in a distribution, above and below which lie an equal number of values. **3.** *Geometry.* **a.** A line that joins a vertex of a triangle to the midpoint of the opposite side. **b.** The line that joins the midpoints of the nonparallel sides of a trapezoid. [Latin *mediānus,* from *medius,* middle. See **medhyo-** in Appendix.*] —**me'di·an·ly** *adv.*

median plane. A plane dividing a bilaterally symmetrical animal into right and left halves.

median point. The intersection of the medians of a triangle.

median strip. The dividing area, often paved or landscaped, between opposing traffic on some highways.

me·di·ant (mē'dē-ənt) *n.* The third tone in a diatonic musical scale between the tonic and the dominant and traditionally related harmonically to them.

me·di·as·ti·num (mē'dē-ăs-tī'nəm) *n., pl.* **-na** (-nə). The septum that divides the pleural sacs in mammals, containing all the thoracic viscera except the lungs. [New Latin, from neuter of Latin *mediastīnus,* median, from *medius,* middle. See **medhyo-** in Appendix.*] —**me'di·as·ti'nal** *adj.*

me·di·ate (mē'dē-āt') *v.* **-ated, -ating, -ates.** —*tr.* **1.** To resolve or settle (differences) by acting as an intermediary agent between two or more conflicting parties. **2.** To bring about (a settlement, agreement, or the like) by action as an intermediary. **3.** To serve as a vehicle for bringing about (a result) or for conveying (information) to others. —*intr.* **1.** To occupy an intermediate or middle position. **2.** To intervene between two or more disputing parties in order to effect an agreement, settlement, or compromise. —*adj.* (mē'dē-ĭt). **1.** Acting through an intervening agency. **2.** Involving or dependent upon some intervening agency. [Latin *mediāre,* to be in the middle, from *medius,* middle. See **medhyo-** in Appendix.*] —**me'di·ate·ly** *adv.* —**me'di·a'tor** (-ā'tər) *n.*

me·di·a·tion (mē'dē-ā'shən) *n.* **1.** The act of mediating; intervention. **2.** The state of being mediated. **3.** *International Law.* The attempt to bring about a peaceful settlement or compromise between disputing nations through the benevolent intervention of a neutral power.

Synonyms: mediation, conciliation, arbitration. *Mediation* denotes only intervention in a dispute with intent to settle it equitably, but generally implies a favorable result. *Conciliation* stresses the settlement of difference and the assuaging of ill feeling. *Arbitration,* often the last resort among these processes, emphasizes finality and decision, usually achieved through legal apparatus and procedure agreed upon in advance.

me·di·a·tive (mē'dē-ā'tĭv) *adj.* Mediating; mediatory.

me·di·a·tize (mē'dē-ə-tīz') *tr.v.* **-tized, -tizing, -tizes. 1.** To annex (a small or weak state or ruler) to a large or powerful one as a means of permitting the ruler of the smaller or weaker power to retain his title and part of his former authority: "*'the Kaisers and Krupps, Hindenburgs and mediatized princes'*" (Anthony Powell). **2.** To place in a middle or intermediate position. [From German *mediatisieren,* from *mediat,* mediate, from Latin *mediāre,* to be in the middle, MEDIATE.] —**me'di·a·ti·za'tion** *n.*

me·di·a·tor (mē'dē-ā'tər) *n.* One that mediates; especially, a

---

ă pat/ā pay/âr care/ä father/b bib/ch church/d deed/ĕ pet/ē be/f fife/g gag/h hat/hw which/ĭ pit/ī pie/îr pier/j judge/k kick/l lid, needle/m mum/n no, sudden/ng thing/ŏ pot/ō toe/ô paw, for/oi noise/ou out/ŏŏ took/ōō boot/p pop/r roar/s sauce/sh ship, dish/

person who serves as an intermediary to reconcile differences.
me·di·a·tor·y (mē′dē-ə-tôr′ē, -tōr′ē) *adj.* Also **me·di·a·to·ri·al.** **1.** Of or pertaining to mediation. **2.** Tending or serving to mediate. **—me′di·a·to′ri·al·ly** *adv.*
med·ic¹, med·ick (mĕd′ĭk) *n.* Any of several plants of the genus *Medicago,* native to the Old World and having clusters of small, usually yellow flowers and compound leaves with three leaflets. [Middle English *medike,* from Latin *Mēdica,* from Greek *Mēdikē (poa),* Median (grass), from *Mēdikos,* Median, from *Mēdos,* a MEDE.]
med·ic² (mĕd′ĭk) *n. Informal.* **1.** A physician or surgeon. **2.** A medical student or intern. **3.** A military medical corpsman. [Latin *medicus,* doctor. See **medical.**]
med·i·ca·ble (mĕd′ĭ-kə-bəl) *adj.* Potentially responsive to treatment with medicine; curable.
med·i·cal (mĕd′ĭ-kəl) *adj. Abbr.* **med. 1.** Of or pertaining to the study or practice of medicine. **2.** Requiring medical as distinct from surgical treatment. **3.** *Archaic.* Medicinal; curative. *—n. Informal.* A thorough physical examination. [French *médical,* from Medieval Latin *medicālis,* from Latin *medicus,* doctor, from *medērī,* to heal. See **med-** in Appendix.*]
medical examiner. 1. A public official whose function is to ascertain the causes and circumstances of the deaths of those who die violently or by crime. Compare **coroner. 2.** A physician who examines applicants for life insurance.
me·dic·a·ment (mĭ-dĭk′ə-mənt, mĕd′ĭ-kə-mənt) *n.* An agent that promotes recovery from injury or ailment; medicine. [Latin *medicāmentum,* from *medicārī,* to MEDICATE.]
Med·i·care (mĕd′ə-kâr′) *n.* Also **med·i·care.** A program under the Social Security Administration that provides medical care for the aged. [MEDI(CAL) + CARE.]
med·i·cate (mĕd′ə-kāt′) *tr.v.* **-cated, -cating, -cates. 1.** To treat medicinally. **2.** To tincture or permeate with a medicinal substance. [Latin *medicārī,* from *medicus,* a doctor, from *medērī,* to heal. See **med-** in Appendix.*] **—med′i·ca′tive** *adj.*
med·i·ca·tion (mĕd′ə-kā′shən) *n.* **1.** A medicine; medicament. **2.** The act or process of being medicated. **3.** The administration of medicine.
Med·i·ci (mĕ′dē-chē′). An Italian family that dominated Florence and Tuscany during the Renaissance. **—Med′i·ce′an** (mĕd′ə-chē′ən) *adj.*
Med·i·ci, Caterina de′. See **Catherine de Médicis.**
Med·i·ci (mĕ′dē-chē′), **Cosimo de′.** Called "Cosimo the Elder." 1389–1464. Florentine banker, art patron, and ruler of Tuscany; grandfather of Lorenzo de' Medici.
Med·i·ci, Giovanni de′. See Pope **Leo X.**
Med·i·ci, Giulio de′. See Pope **Clement VII.**
Med·i·ci (mĕ′dē-chē′), **Lorenzo de′.** Called "Lorenzo the Magnificent." 1449–1492. Florentine art patron and author; ruler of Tuscany; grandson of Cosimo the Elder.
me·dic·i·nal (mə-dĭs′ə-nəl) *adj.* Pertaining to or having the properties of medicine; healing; curative. **—me·dic′i·nal·ly** *adv.*
med·i·cine (mĕd′ə-sən) *n.* **1.** *Abbr.* **med.** The science of diagnosing, treating, or preventing disease and other damage to the body or mind. **2.** The branch of this science encompassing treatment by drugs, diet, exercise, and other nonsurgical means. **3.** The practice of medicine. **4.** Any drug or other agent used to treat disease or injury. **5.** Among North American Indians, something believed to control natural or supernatural powers and to serve as a preventive or remedy. **—take one's medicine.** To endure deserved punishment. [Middle English, from Old French, from Latin *medicīna,* the art of a physician, from *medicus,* doctor, from *medērī,* to heal. See **med-** in Appendix.*]
medicine ball. A large, heavy ball used for exercise.
Medicine Bow. A river rising in south-central Wyoming and flowing about 120 miles to join the North Platte.
Medicine Bow Mountains. A range in south-central Wyoming and north-central Colorado. Highest elevation, Medicine Bow Peak (12,005 feet).
medicine dance. A ritual dance performed by some Plains Indians of North America to obtain supernatural assistance.
medicine lodge. A large wooden structure used by some North American Indian tribes for various ritualistic ceremonies.
medicine man. 1. A person believed among preliterate peoples to possess supernatural powers for healing, invoking spirits, and other purposes; sorcerer; shaman. **2.** A hawker of brews and potions among the audience in a medicine show.
medicine show. A traveling show, popular especially in 19th-century America, that offered varied entertainment, between the acts of which medicines were peddled.
med·ick. Variant of **medic** (the plant).
med·i·co (mĕd′ĭ-kō′) *n., pl.* **-cos.** *Informal.* A doctor or medical student. [Italian and Spanish, from Latin *medicus,* doctor, from *medērī,* to heal. See **med-** in Appendix.*]
me·di·e·val (mē′dē-ē′vəl, mĕd′ē′vəl) *adj.* Also **me·di·ae·val.** *Abbr.* **M., med.** Pertaining or belonging to the Middle Ages. [From New Latin *Medium Aevum,* the Middle Age : Latin *medium,* neuter of *medius,* middle (see **medhyo-** in Appendix*) + *aevum,* age (see **aiw-** in Appendix*).] **—me′di·e′val·ly** *adv.*
Medieval Greek. *Abbr.* **Med. Gr.** Greek from about A.D. 700 to 1500. Also called "Middle Greek."
me·di·e·val·ism (mē′dē-ē′vəl-ĭz′əm, mĕd′ē-) *n.* Also **me·di·ae·val·ism. 1.** The spirit, or the body of beliefs, customs, or practices, of the Middle Ages. **2.** Devotion to or acceptance of the ideas of the Middle Ages. **3.** Scholarly study of the Middle Ages. **—me′di·e′val·ist** *n.*
Medieval Latin. *Abbr.* **ML, M.L.** Latin as used throughout Europe in the Middle Ages, from about A.D. 700 to 1500.
Me·di·na (mə-dē′nə). *Arabic* **Al-Ma·di·na** (ăl′mă-dē′nə). A city of northwestern Saudi Arabia, in Hejaz about 250 miles north of Mecca. It is the site of Mohammed's tomb and a sacred center of Islam. Population, 30,000.
me·di·o·cre (mē′dē-ō′kər) *adj.* Neither good nor bad; average; ordinary; commonplace. Usually used disparagingly. See Synonyms at **average.** [From Latin *mediocris,* "halfway up the mountain," in a middle state : *medius,* middle (see **medhyo-** in Appendix*) + *ocris,* mountain, peak (see **ak-** in Appendix*).]
me·di·oc·ri·ty (mē′dē-ŏk′rə-tē) *n., pl.* **-ties. 1.** The state or quality of being mediocre: *"the almost general mediocrity of fortune that prevails in America"* (Benjamin Franklin). **2.** Mediocre ability, achievement, or performance: *"He had little patience with collective mediocrity."* (Charles Wharton Stork). **3.** A person who displays mediocre qualities: *"These mediocrities, as they often were, had been great successes."* (Van Wyck Brooks).
Medit. Mediterranean Sea.
med·i·tate (mĕd′ə-tāt′) *v.* **-tated, -tating, -tates.** *—tr.* **1.** To reflect upon; ponder; contemplate: *He meditated the sorry state of his affairs.* **2.** To plan or intend in the mind: *He meditated a just revenge.* *—intr.* To engage in contemplation. [Latin *meditārī.* See **med-** in Appendix.*] **—med′i·ta′tor** (-tā′tər) *n.*
med·i·ta·tion (mĕd′ə-tā′shən) *n.* **1. a.** The act of meditating. **b.** A devotional exercise of contemplation. **2.** A contemplative discourse, usually on a religious or philosophical subject.
med·i·ta·tive (mĕd′ə-tā′tĭv) *adj.* Devoted to, characterized by, or expressing meditation. See Synonyms at **pensive. —med′i·ta′tive·ly** *adv.* **—med′i·ta′tive·ness** *n.*
med·i·ter·ra·ne·an (mĕd′ə-tə-rā′nē-ən, -rān′yən) *adj.* **1.** Surrounded nearly or completely by dry land. Said of large bodies of water, as lakes or seas. **2.** *Capital* **M.** Of, pertaining to, or characteristic of the Mediterranean Sea, or the countries and their people that border the Mediterranean Sea. **3.** *Capital* **M.** Designating languages spoken in the Mediterranean region before the coming of the Indo-Europeans, items of which may be seen in borrowings into attested languages such as Greek and Latin. *—n. Capital* **M. 1.** A collective designation for the Mediterranean languages. **2.** The Mediterranean Sea. [From Latin *mediterrāneus* : *medius,* middle (see **medhyo-** in Appendix*) + *terra,* land (see **ters-** in Appendix*).]
Mediterranean fever. A disease, **undulant fever** *(see).*
Mediterranean flour moth. A small, pale-gray moth, *Ephestia kuehniella,* now found worldwide, the larvae of which destroy flour, whole grains, and beehive pollen.
Mediterranean fruit fly. A black and white, two-winged fly, *Ceratitis capitata,* found in most subtropical countries except North America. It attacks citrus and other fruits.
Med·i·ter·ra·ne·an Sea (mĕd′ə-tə-rā′nē-ən, -rān′yən). *Abbr.* **Medit.** The world's largest inland sea (965,000 square miles), bounded by Africa in the south, Asia in the east, and Europe in the north and west. It has access to the Atlantic Ocean through the Strait of Gibraltar, to the Black Sea through the Dardanelles and the Bosporus, and to the Red Sea and the Indian Ocean through the Suez Canal.
me·di·um (mē′dē-əm) *n., pl.* **-dia** (-dē-ə) or **-ums** (only form for sense 5). *Abbr.* **m, M, m., M., med. 1.** Something occupying a position or having a condition midway between extremes, such as an intermediate course of action; a compromise: *"The common situation of society is a medium amidst all these extremes."* (Hume). **2.** An intervening substance through which something is transmitted or carried on, such as an agency for transmitting energy. **3.** An agency, such as a person, object, or quality, by means of which something is accomplished, conveyed, or transferred: *"The principal use of money is as a medium of exchange."* (Melville Ullmer). **4.** A means of mass communication, such as newpapers, magazines, or television. See Usage note below. **5.** A person thought to have powers of communicating with the spirits of the dead. **6.** A surrounding environment in which something functions and thrives: **a.** The substance in which a specific organism lives and thrives. **b.** A substance in which bacteria are cultivated for scientific purposes. Also called "culture." **7. a.** A specific type of artistic technique or means of expression as determined by the materials used or the creative methods involved: *the medium of lithography.* **b.** The materials used. **8.** Any solvent with which paint is thinned to the proper consistency. **9.** *Chemistry.* A filtering substance, such as filter paper. **10.** A size of paper, usually 18 × 23 inches or 17½ × 22 inches. —See Synonyms at **average.** *—adj. Abbr.* **m, M, m., M., med. 1.** Occurring or being between two degrees, amounts, or quantities; intermediate: *a medium steak.* **2.** Average; mean: *a medium-grade ore.* [Latin *medium,* the middle, from *medius,* middle. See **medhyo-** in Appendix.*]
Usage: *Media* (means of mass communication) is often used as a singular noun: *Television is an unpredictable media.* This is unacceptable in writing to 90 per cent of the Usage Panel, and in speech to 88 per cent. The use of *medias* as a plural form is condemned even more severely.
medium of exchange. Anything that is commonly used in a specific area or among a certain group of people as money. See **circulating medium, money.**
med·lar (mĕd′lər) *n.* **1.** A tree, *Mespilus germanica,* cultivated for its fruit. **2.** The fruit of this tree. [Middle English *medler,* from Old French *medler,* a medlar tree, from *medle* (unattested), variant of *mesle,* a medlar fruit, from Latin *mespila,* from Greek *mespilē*†, medlar. See **naseberry.**]
med·ley (mĕd′lē) *n., pl.* **-leys. 1.** A jumbled assortment; mixture: *"Pigeons and rabbits and a parrot made a medley of insolent noises at her."* (F. Scott Fitzgerald). **2.** A musical arrangement

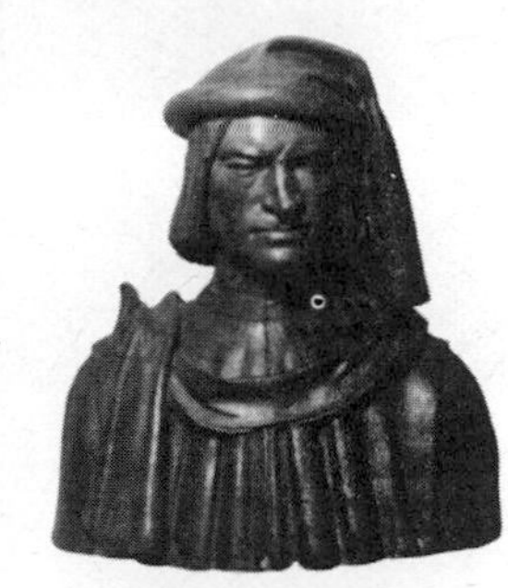

Lorenzo de' Medici
Contemporary
terra-cotta bust
by Andrea del Verrocchio

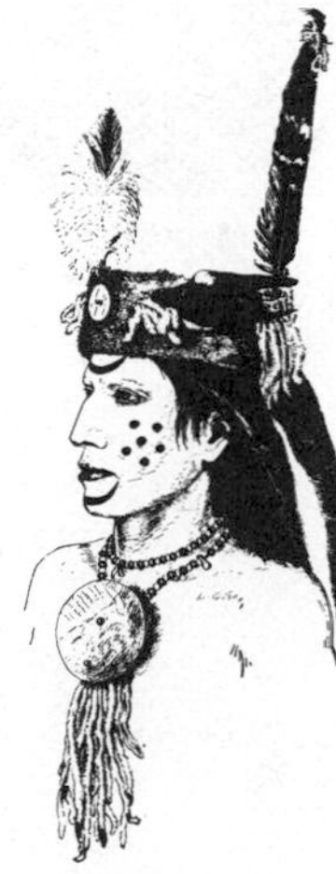

medicine man
American Blackfoot Indian

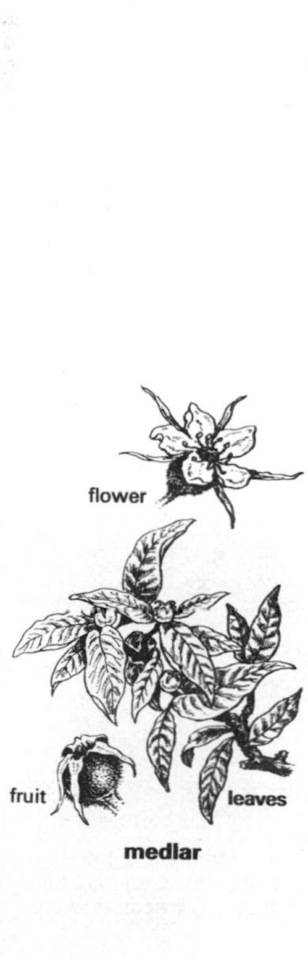

medlar

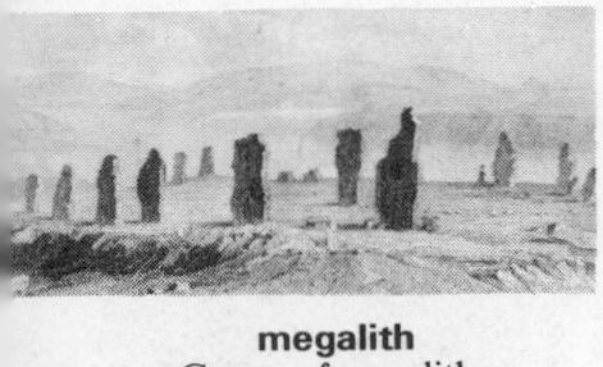
megalith
Group of megaliths in Carnac, Brittany

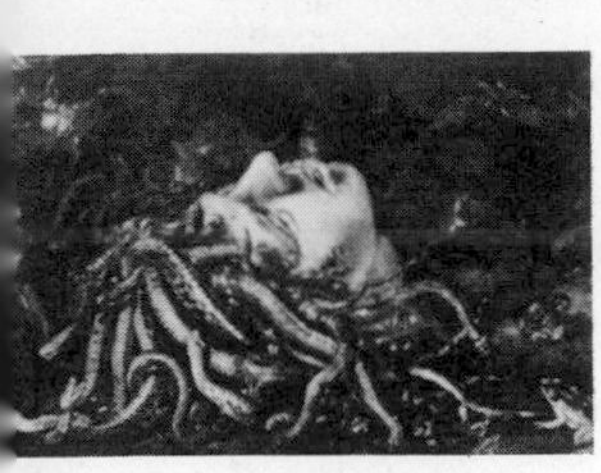
Medusa
Sixteenth-century Flemish painting

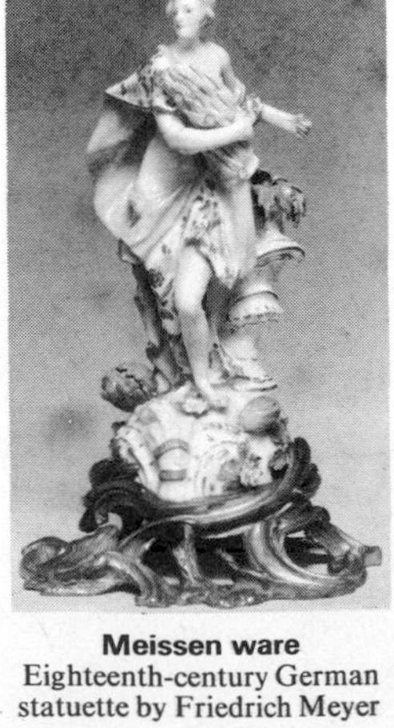
Meissen ware
Eighteenth-century German statuette by Friedrich Meyer

made from a series of melodies from various sources. —*adj.* Of, pertaining to, or made up of a jumbled mixture of elements. [Middle English *medlee,* from Old French *medlee,* variant of *meslee,* from Vulgar Latin *misculāta* (unattested), from Late Latin *misculāre,* to mix up, frequentative of *miscēre,* to mix. See **meik-** in Appendix.*]

Mé·doc (mā-dôk′, -dŏk′) *n.* A red Bordeaux wine made in Médoc, a region of southwestern France.

me·dul·la (mə-dŭl′ə) *n., pl.* **-las** or **-lae** (-ē). **1.** *Anatomy.* The inner core of certain vertebrate body structures, such as the marrow of bone. **2.** The **medulla oblongata** *(see).* **3.** *Botany.* The pith or central tissue in stems of certain plants. [Latin *medulla,* marrow. See **smer-**[3] in Appendix.*] —**me·dul′lar** (mə-dŭl′ər), **med′ul·lar′y** (mĕd′ə-lĕr′ē, mə-dŭl′ə-rē) *adj.*

medulla ob·lon·ga·ta (ŏb′lông-gä′tə) *pl.* **medulla oblongatas** or **medullae oblongatae** (-gä′tē). The nervous tissue at the bottom of the brain that controls respiration, circulation, and certain other bodily functions. [New Latin, "elongated marrow."]

medullary sheath. 1. *Anatomy.* **Myelin** *(see).* **2.** *Botany.* A layer of thick-walled cells surrounding the pith in the stems of various plants.

med·ul·lat·ed (mĕd′ə-lā′tĭd) *adj.* **Myelinated** *(see).* [From Late Latin *medullātus,* having a marrow, from Latin *medulla,* MEDULLA.] —**med′ul·la′tion** (mĕd′ə-lā′shən, mĕj′o͞o-) *n.*

med·ul·li·za·tion (mĕd′ə-lə-zā′shən, mĕj′o͞o-) *n.* Replacement of bone tissue by marrow, as in inflammatory bone disease.

me·du·sa (mə-do͞o′sə, mə-dyo͞o′sə, -zə) *n., pl.* **-sas** or **-sae** (-sē, -zē). A jellyfish. [New Latin.] —**me·du′san** *adj.*

Me·du·sa (mə-do͞o′sə, mə-dyo͞o′sə, -zə). *Greek Mythology.* One of the three Gorgons.

me·du·soid (mə-do͞o′soid′, mə-dyo͞o′-, -zoid′) *n.* **1.** A shape resembling a jellyfish. **2.** Any jellyfish. —**me·du′soid′** *adj.*

meed (mēd) *n. Archaic.* A merited gift or reward. [Middle English *mede,* Old English *mēd.* See **mizdho-** in Appendix.*]

meek (mēk) *adj.* **meeker, meekest. 1.** Showing patience and humility; long-suffering. **2.** Easily imposed upon; submissive; spineless: *"He was the meekest of his sex, the mildest of little men."* (Dickens). **3.** *Archaic.* Kind; gentle: *"I am meek and gentle with these butchers."* (Shakespeare). —See Synonyms at **humble.** [Middle English *mēk, mēoc,* from Old Norse *mjūkr,* soft. See **meug-**[2] in Appendix.*] —**meek′ly** *adv.*

meer·schaum (mîr′shəm, -shôm) *n.* **1.** A tough, compact, usually white mineral of hydrous magnesium silicate, $H_4Mg_2Si_3O_{10}$, found in the Mediterranean area and used in fashioning tobacco pipes and as a building stone. Also called "sepiolite." **2.** A tobacco pipe with a bowl of meerschaum. [German *Meerschaum,* sepiolite, originally the name of a kind of coral (Alcyonium digitatum), literally "sea-foam," translation of Latin *spūma maris* and Greek *halos hakhnē,* "foam of the sea" (the coral was thought to be formed from congealed foam) : *Meer,* sea, from Old High German *meri, mari* (see **mori-** in Appendix*) + *Schaum,* foam, from Old High German *scūm* (see **skeu-** in Appendix*).]

Mee·rut (mā′rət, mîr′ət). A city in Uttar Pradesh State in the Republic of India. Population, 200,000.

meet[1] (mēt) *v.* **met** (mĕt), **meeting, meets.** —*tr.* **1.** To come upon; encounter by chance or arrangement. **2.** To be present at the arrival of: *I will try my best to meet the train.* **3.** To be introduced to; make the acquaintance of: *We'd like to meet your sister.* **4.** To come into association or conjunction with; join: *where the sea meets the sky.* **5.** To come into the company or presence of, as for a conference. **6.** To come to the notice of (the senses): *more than meets the eye.* **7.** To experience; undergo: *"He resolved that he would meet his fate more manly."* (Ambrose Bierce). **8.** To deal with; oppose; fight: *"We have met the enemy and they are ours."* (Oliver Hazard Perry). **9.** To cope or contend effectively with. **10.** To come into conformity with the views, wishes, or opinions of: *The firm has done its best to meet us on that point.* **11.** To satisfy (a demand, need, obligation); fulfill: *meet a need.* **12.** To pay; settle: *enough money to meet the expenses.* —*intr.* **1.** To come together: *"now that we are so happily met"* (Bunyan). *Let's meet tonight.* **2.** To come into conjunction; be joined: *"East is East, and West is West, and never the twain shall meet"* (Kipling). **3.** To come together as opponents; contend. **4.** To become introduced. **5.** To assemble. **6.** To experience or undergo. Often used with *with: The housing bill met with approval.* **7.** To occur together, especially in one person or entity: *"The hopes and fears of all the years / Are met in thee tonight."* (Phillips Brooks). —*n.* A meeting or contest, especially an athletic competition. [Middle English *meten,* Old English *mētan.* See **mōd-** in Appendix.*]

meet[2] (mēt) *adj. Archaic.* Fitting; proper: *"It is not meet, nor wholesome to my place."* (Shakespeare). See Synonyms at **fit.** [Middle English *mete, y-mete,* Old English *gemǣte.* See **med-** in Appendix.*] —**meet′ly** *adv.*

meet·ing (mēt′ĭng) *n. Abbr.* **mtg. 1. a.** A coming together; an assembly. **b.** The persons so assembled. **2.** A joining or conjunction. **3.** A hostile encounter, such as a duel.

mega–. Indicates: **1.** *Abbr.* **M** One million (10^6); for example, **megacycle. 2.** Large; for example, **megalith.** [Greek, from *megas,* great. See **meg-** in Appendix.*]

meg·a·buck (mĕg′ə-bŭk) *n. Slang.* One million dollars.

meg·a·ceph·a·ly (mĕg′ə-sĕf′ə-lē) *n.* Enlargement of the head, **macrocephaly** *(see).* [MEGA- + -CEPHALY.] —**meg′a·ce·phal′ic** (-sə-făl′ĭk), **meg′a·ceph′a·lous** (-sĕf′ə-lĕs) *adj.*

meg·a·cy·cle (mĕg′ə-sī′kəl) *n. Physics.* **1.** *Abbr.* **Mc** One million cycles. **2. Megahertz** *(see).*

meg·a·death (mĕg′ə-dĕth) *n.* One million human deaths regarded as a measure of the effectiveness of nuclear warfare.

Me·gae·ra (mə-jîr′ə). *Greek Mythology.* One of the Furies.

meg·a·hertz (mĕg′ə-hûrtz) *n. Abbr.* **MHz** *Physics.* One million cycles per second, used especially as a radio-frequency unit.

meg·a·lith (mĕg′ə-lĭth′) *n.* A very large stone used in various prehistoric architectures or monumental styles, notably in western Europe during the second millennium B.C. See **dolmen, menhir.** [MEGA- + -LITH.] —**meg′a·lith′ic** *adj.*

megalo–. Indicates largeness, greatness, or exaggerated size; for example, **megalocephaly, megalomania.** [Greek, from *megas* (extended stem *megal-*), great. See **meg-** in Appendix.*]

meg·a·lo·car·di·a (mĕg′ə-lō-kär′dē-ə) *n. Pathology.* Enlargement of the heart. Also called "cardiomegaly." [MEGALO- + Greek *kardia,* heart (see **kerd-**[1] in Appendix*).]

meg·a·lo·ceph·a·ly (mĕg′ə-lō-sĕf′ə-lē) *n.* Enlargement of the head, **macrocephaly** *(see).* [MEGALO- + -CEPHALY.] —**meg′a·lo·ce·phal′ic** (-sə-făl′ĭk), **meg′a·lo·ceph′a·lous** (-sĕf′ə-ləs) *adj.*

meg·a·lo·ma·ni·a (mĕg′ə-lō-mā′nē-ə, -mān′yə) *n. Psychiatry.* A psychopathological condition in which fantasies of wealth, power, or omnipotence predominate. —**meg′a·lo·ma′ni·ac′** *adj.* & *n.* —**meg′a·lo·ma·ni′a·cal** (-mə-nī′ə-kəl) *adj.*

meg·a·lop·o·lis (mĕg′ə-lŏp′ə-lĭs) *n.* A region made up of several large cities and their surrounding areas in sufficiently close proximity to be considered a single urban complex. [MEGALO- + Greek *polis,* city (see **pele**[2] in Appendix*).] —**meg′a·lo·pol′i·tan** (-lō-pŏl′ə-tən) *adj.*

meg·a·lo·saur (mĕg′ə-lə-sôr′) *n.* An extinct gigantic carnivorous dinosaur, genus *Megalosaurus,* of the Jurassic period. [New Latin *Megalosaurus* : MEGALO- + -SAURUS.] —**meg′a·lo·saur′i·an** *n.* & *adj.*

Me·gan·thro·pus (mĭ-găn′thrə-pəs) *n.* An extinct manlike primate, genus *Meganthropus,* known only from jawbone fragments found in Pleistocene deposits of Java. [New Latin : MEG(A)- + -ANTHROPUS.]

meg·a·phone (mĕg′ə-fōn′) *n.* A funnel-shaped device used to direct and amplify the voice. Compare **bullhorn.** —**meg′a·phon′ic** (mĕg′ə-fŏn′ĭk) *adj.* —**meg′a·phon′i·cal·ly** *adv.*

meg·a·pode (mĕg′ə-pōd′) *n.* Any bird of the family Megapodiidae, found in Australia and many South Pacific islands. [New Latin *Megapodius* : MEGA- + -PODE.]

Meg·a·ra (mĕg′ə-rə). An ancient Greek city on the isthmus of Corinth. —**Me·gar′i·an** (mĭ-gâr′ē-ən) *adj.* & *n.*

meg·a·scop·ic (mĕg′ə-skŏp′ĭk) *adj.* Visible to the naked eye, **macroscopic** *(see).* —**meg′a·scop′i·cal·ly** *adv.*

meg·a·spo·ran·gi·um (mĕg′ə-spə-răn′jē-əm) *n., pl.* **-gia** (-jē-ə). *Botany.* A structure that encloses a megaspore. Sometimes called "macrosporangium."

meg·a·spore (mĕg′ə-spôr′, -spōr′) *n. Botany.* **1.** The larger of two types of spores formed by heterosporous plants, such as ferns, giving rise to the female gametophyte. Compare **microspore. 2.** A spore that forms the embryo sac in seed plants. Sometimes called "macrospore." —**meg′a·spor′ic** *adj.*

meg·a·spo·ro·phyll (mĕg′ə-spôr′ə-fĭl′, -spōr′ə-fĭl′) *n. Botany.* A leaflike structure that produces megasporangia. [MEGA- + SPOROPHYLL.]

meg·a·there (mĕg′ə-thîr′) *n.* A member of the extinct family Megatheriidae, composed of large ground sloths of the Miocene and Pleistocene epochs. [New Latin *Megatherium* : MEGA- + -THERE.] —**meg′a·ther′i·an** (mĕg′ə-thîr′ē-ən) *adj.*

meg·a·ton (mĕg′ə-tŭn′) *n.* A unit of explosive force equal to one million tons of TNT. —**meg′a·ton′ic** (-tŏn′ĭk) *adj.*

Me·gid·do (mĭ-gĭd′ō). An ancient city of northwestern Palestine that flourished from about 2500 to 300 B.C., and may have been the Armageddon mentioned in Revelation 16:16.

Me·gil·lah (mə-gĭl′ə) *n.* **1.** The Judaic scroll containing the Biblical narrative of the Book of Esther, traditionally read in synagogues to celebrate the festival of Purim. **2.** *Small* **m.** *Slang.* A prolix, tediously detailed or embroidered account. [Hebrew *məgillāh,* "scroll," from *gālal,* to roll.]

Me·grez (mē′grĕz′) *n.* A star in the Big Dipper.

me·grim (mē′grĭm) *n.* **1.** A severe headache, **migraine** *(see).* **2.** *Often plural.* A caprice or fancy: *"Can't one work for sober truth as well as for megrims?"* (George Eliot). **3.** *Plural.* Depression or unhappiness: *"If these megrims are the effect of Love, thank Heaven, I never knew what it was."* (Samuel Richardson). **4.** *Plural.* A disease of cattle and horses. In this sense, also called "blind staggers." [Middle English *mygreyme, mygreyn,* from Old French *migraine,* MIGRAINE.]

Me·hem·et A·li. See **Mohammed Ali.**

Mei·ji (mā′jē) *n.* The reign of Emperor Mutsuhito of Japan, lasting from 1867 to 1912 and held to represent an era in modern Japanese history. [Japanese, "enlightened government" : Ancient Chinese *ming* (Mandarin *ming*[2]), enlightened + *dji* (Mandarin *chih*[4]), government.]

Mein Kampf (mīn′ kämpf′). A book (1924–26) by Adolf Hitler, setting forth the doctrines and program of National Socialism. [German, "my battle."]

mei·o·sis (mī-ō′sĭs) *n., pl.* **-ses** (-sēz′). **1.** *Biology.* The cell division in sexually reproducing organisms that reduces the number of chromosomes in reproductive cells, leading to the production of gametes in animals and spores in plants. Also called "reduction division," "maturation division." Compare **mitosis. 2.** Rhetorical understatement; litotes. [New Latin, from Greek *meiōsis,* diminution, from *meioun,* to diminish, from *meiōn,* less. See **mei-**[2] in Appendix.*] —**mei·ot′ic** (mī-ŏt′ĭk) *adj.* —**mei·ot′i·cal·ly** *adv.*

Meis·sen (mīs′ən). A city of East Germany, on the Elbe northwest of Dresden. Population, 48,000.

Meissen ware. A delicate porcelain ware made in Meissen, Germany. Also called "Dresden china."

Meis·ter·sing·er (mīs′tər-sĭng′ər) *n., pl.* **Meistersinger** or **-ers.** *German.* A member of one of the guilds organized in the principal cities of Germany in the 14th, 15th, and 16th centuries for the purpose of establishing competitive standards for the composition and performance of music and poetry. Also in English "mastersinger." [German, from Middle High German : *meister,* master, from Old High German *meistar,* from Latin *magister,* MASTER + *singer,* singer, from *singen,* to sing, from Old High German *singan,* to sing (see **sengwh-** in Appendix*).]

Meit·ner (mīt′nər), **Lise.** 1878–1968. Austrian-born Swedish physicist; pioneer in the study of nuclear fission.

Mé·ji·co. The Spanish name for **Mexico.**

Mek·nès (mĕk-nĕs′). One of the traditional capital cities of Morocco, 33 miles southwest of Fez. Population, 185,000.

Me·kong (mā′kŏng′). *Chinese* **Lan·tsang** (län′tsäng′). A river of southeastern Asia, rising in the Tibetan Highlands and flowing 2,600 miles southeast, forming the borders between Laos and Burma and between Laos and Thailand, and continuing through Cambodia and South Vietnam to the South China Sea.

mel·a·mine resin (mĕl′ə-mēn′). A thermosetting resin used for molded products, adhesives, and surface coatings.

mel·an·cho·li·a (mĕl′ən-kō′lē-ə) *n.* A mental disorder characterized by feelings of dejection and usually by withdrawal. It is often a phase of manic-depressive psychosis. [New Latin, from Late Latin *melancholia,* MELANCHOLY.] **—mel′an·cho′li·ac** *adj. & n.*

mel·an·chol·ic (mĕl′ən-kŏl′ĭk) *adj.* **1.** Afflicted with or subject to melancholy; gloomy; depressed. **2.** Of, pertaining to, subject to, or afflicted with melancholia. **—mel′an·chol′ic** *n.* **—mel′an·chol′i·cal·ly** *adv.*

mel·an·chol·y (mĕl′ən-kŏl′ē) *n.* **1.** Sadness or depression of the spirits; gloom: *"A melancholy numbs my limbs."* (Keats). **2.** Pensive reflection or contemplation. **3.** *Archaic.* **a.** Black bile, one of the four humors of ancient or medieval physiology. **b.** An emotional state characterized by sullenness and outbreaks of violent anger, believed to arise from the bile. *—adj.* **1.** Sad; depressed; gloomy: *"He passed the evening, in much melancholy contemplation."* (Fielding). **2.** Tending to promote sadness or gloom. **3.** Pensive; thoughtful: *"He had a pleasing face and a melancholy air."* (Jane Austen). —See Synonyms at **sad.** [Middle English *malencolie, melancholye,* from Old French *melancolie,* from Late Latin *melancholia,* from Greek *melankholia,* sadness, "(an excess of) black bile" : *melas* (stem *melan-*), black (see **mel-**[2] in Appendix*) + *kholē,* bile (see **ghel-**[2] in Appendix*).] **—mel′an·chol′i·ly** *adv.* **—mel′an·chol′i·ness** *n.*

Me·lanch·thon (mə-lăngk′thən), **Philipp.** Original name, Philipp Schwarzerd. 1497–1560. German theologian and humanist; associate of Martin Luther and a leader in the Lutheran Reformation.

Mel·a·ne·sia (mĕl′ə-nē′zhə, -shə). An island group in the southwestern Pacific Ocean, extending southeastward from the Admiralty Islands to the Fiji Islands. [New Latin : MELA(NO)- + Greek *nēsos,* island (see **snā-** in Appendix*).]

Mel·a·ne·sian (mĕl′ə-nē′zhən, -shən) *adj.* Of or pertaining to Melanesia, its people, or their languages. *—n.* **1.** An indigenous inhabitant of Melanesia. **2.** A subfamily of Austronesian languages spoken in Melanesia.

mé·lange (mā-läNzh′) *n.* Also **me·lange.** A mixture. [French, from Old French, from *mesler,* to mix, from Vulgar Latin *misculāre* (unattested), from Latin *miscēre,* to mix. See **meik-** in Appendix.*]

me·la·ni·an (mə-lā′nē-ən) *adj.* Pertaining to dark or black pigmentation. [French *mélanien* : MELAN(O)- + -IAN.]

me·lan·ic (mə-lăn′ĭk) *adj.* **1.** Of, pertaining to, or exhibiting melanism. **2.** Afflicted with melanosis.

mel·a·nin (mĕl′ə-nĭn) *n.* A dark pigment found in the skin, retina, and hair. [MELAN(O)- + -IN.]

mel·a·nism (mĕl′ə-nĭz′əm) *n.* **1.** *Pathology.* **Melanosis** *(see).* **2.** Any darkness of the skin, hair, or eyes resulting from high pigmentation. [MELAN(O)- + -ISM.] **—mel′a·nist** *n.* **—mel′a·nis′tic** (mĕl′ə-nĭs′tĭk) *adj.*

mel·a·nite (mĕl′ə-nīt′) *n.* A black variety of garnet. [German *Melanit* : MELAN(O)- + -ITE.] **—mel′a·nit′ic** (mĕl′ə-nĭt′ĭk) *adj.*

melano–, melan–. Indicates blackness or darkness; for example, **melanocyte, melanoma.** [New Latin, from Greek, from *melas* (stem *melan-*), black. See **mel-**[2] in Appendix.*]

Mel·a·noch·ro·i (mĕl′ə-nŏk′rō-ī′, -nŏk′roi′) *pl.n.* Caucasians with dark hair and light skin. [New Latin, "the dark-pale (people)" : MELAN(O)- + Greek *ōkhroi,* plural of *ōkhros,* pale (see **ocher**).] **—Mel′a·noch′roid′** (-nŏk′roid′) *adj.*

mel·a·no·cyte (mĕl′ə-nō-sīt′) *n. Zoology.* An epidermal cell capable of synthesizing the black pigment melanin, and responsible for color variations in the skin of many animals including man. [MELANO- + -CYTE.]

mel·a·noid (mĕl′ə-noid′) *adj.* **1.** Black-pigmented. **2.** Afflicted with melanosis. [Greek *melanoeidēs,* black-looking : MELAN(O)- + -OID.] **—mel′a·noid′** *n.*

mel·a·no·ma (mĕl′ə-nō′mə) *n., pl.* **-mas** or **-mata** (-mə-tə). A dark-pigmented malignant tumor. [New Latin : MELAN(O)- + -OMA.]

mel·a·no·sis (mĕl′ə-nō′sĭs) *n. Pathology.* Abnormally dark pigmentation of the skin or other tissues, resulting from sunburn and various dermatoses. Also called "melanism." [New Latin : MELAN(O)- + -OSIS.] **—mel′a·not′ic** (-nŏt′ĭk) *adj.*

mel·a·nous (mĕl′ə-nəs) *adj.* Having a swarthy or black complexion and black hair. Compare **xanthous.** [MELAN(O)- + -OUS.] **—mel′a·nos′i·ty** (mĕl′ə-nŏs′ə-tē) *n.*

mel·a·phyre (mĕl′ə-fīr′) *n.* A dark, igneous porphyry embedded with feldspar crystals. [French *mélaphyre* : MELA(NO)- + *(por)phyre,* porphyry, from Medieval Latin *porphyrium,* PORPHYRY.]

Mel·ba toast (mĕl′bə). Very thinly sliced crisp toast. [After Dame Nellie *Melba* (1861–1931), Australian soprano.]

Mel·bourne (mĕl′bərn). A seaport and industrial center, capital city of the state of Victoria, Australia. Population, 2,122,000. [After Viscount MELBOURNE.]

Mel·bourne (mĕl′bərn), **Second Viscount.** Title of William Lamb. 1779–1848. Prime Minister of Britain (1834; 1835–41).

Mel·chi·or (mĕl′kē-ôr′). One of the three Magi, the other two being Caspar and Balthasar, who came to the infant Jesus.

Mel·chiz·e·dek[1] (mĕl-kĭz′ə-dĕk′). Also **Mel·chis·e·dec.** The king of Salem and high priest who blessed Abraham. Genesis 14:18.

Mel·chiz·e·dek[2] (mĕl-kĭz′ə-dĕk′) *n.* The higher order of priesthood of the Mormon Church.

meld[1] (mĕld) *v.* **melded, melding, melds.** *—tr.* To declare or display (a card or combination of cards in a hand) for inclusion in one's score in a game such as pinochle. *—intr.* To present a meld. *—n.* A combination of cards to be declared for a score. [German *melden,* to declare, from Old High German *meldōn.* See **meldh-**[1] in Appendix.*]

meld[2] (mĕld) *v.* **melded, melding, melds.** *—tr.* To cause to unite, blend, or combine. *—intr.* To become blended or combined: *"The hard water of the melting snows . . . fans out to meld with the teeming salt depths of the Bay of Bengal."* (Wheeler Hall). [Blend of *melt* + *weld.*]

Mel·e·a·ger (mĕl′ē-ā′jər). Greek author of the first century B.C.; epigrammatist and anthologist.

me·lee (mā′lā′, mā-lā′) *n.* Also **mê·lée** (mĕ-lā′). **1. a.** The confused, hand-to-hand fighting in a pitched battle. **b.** A violent free-for-all: *"He . . . struck his aunt and wife, and during the melee the baby also suffered scratches."* (Atlanta Constitution). **2.** Any confused and tumultuous mingling, as of a crowd: *the rush-hour melee.* —See Synonyms at **conflict.** [French *mêlée,* a mixture, from Old French *meslee,* MEDLEY.]

mel·i·lot (mĕl′ə-lŏt′) *n.* Any of several plants of the genus *Melilotus,* native to the Old World, having compound leaves and narrow clusters of small, fragrant, white or yellow flowers. Also called "sweet clover." [Middle English *mellilot,* from French *melilot,* from Latin *melilōtus,* from Greek *melilōtos,* sweet clover, "honey-lotus" : *meli,* honey (see **melit-** in Appendix*) + *lōtos,* LOTUS.]

mel·i·nite (mĕl′ə-nīt′) *n.* A high explosive made with picric acid. [French *mélinite,* from Greek *mēlinos,* quince-yellow, pertaining to quinces or apples, from *mēlon,* fruit, apple. See **mēlon** in Appendix.*]

mel·io·rate (mēl′yə-rāt′, mē′lē-ə-) *v.* **-rated, -rating, -rates.** *—tr.* To make better; improve. *—intr.* To grow better; evolve toward higher forms: *"The races meliorate, and man is born."* (Emerson). [Latin *meliōrāre,* from *melior,* better. See **mel-**[4] in Appendix.*] **—mel′io·ra·ble** (-rə-bəl) *adj.* **—mel′io·ra′tive** *adj. & n.* **—mel′io·ra′tor** (-rā′tər) *n.*

mel·io·ra·tion (mēl′yə-rā′shən, mē′lē-ə-) *n.* **1. a.** The act or process of improving something or the state of being improved: *"I could not . . . effect any melioration of the noxious quality of this kind of air."* (Joseph Priestley). **b.** A specific instance of this; an improvement: *"I should like to think that this melioration came through our sense of justice."* (Max Beerbohm). **2.** The linguistic process by which a word grows more elevated in meaning, or more positive in connotation, over a period of time. *Pretty,* meaning "sly" in Old English and coming to mean "beautiful" in Modern English, is an example of melioration. In this sense, compare **pejoration.**

mel·io·rism (mēl′yə-rĭz′əm, mē′lē-ə-) *n.* The belief that society has an innate tendency toward improvement and that this tendency may be furthered through conscious human effort. [From Latin *melior,* better. See **mel-**[4] in Appendix.*] **—mel′io·rist** *adj. & n.* **—mel′io·ris′tic** (mēl′yə-rĭs′tĭk, mē′lē-ə-) *adj.*

me·lis·ma (mə-lĭz′mə, -lĭs′mə) *n., pl.* **-mata** (-mə-tə) or **-mas.** *Music.* A passage sung to one syllable of text, as in Gregorian chant. [Greek, from *melizein,* to sing, from *melos,* song. See **mel-**[3] in Appendix.*] **—mel′is·mat′ic** (mĕl′ĭz-măt′ĭk) *adj.*

Me·lis·sa (mə-lĭs′ə). A feminine given name. [New Latin, from Greek, bee, from *meli,* honey. See **melit-** in Appendix.*]

mel·lif·er·ous (mə-lĭf′ər-əs) *adj.* Also **mel·lif·ic** (mə-lĭf′ĭk). Forming or bearing honey. [From Latin *mellifer* : *mel,* honey (see **melit-** in Appendix*) + -FER.]

mel·lif·lu·ous (mə-lĭf′lo͞o-əs) *adj.* **1.** Flowing with honey or sweetness. **2.** Smooth and sweet; honeyed. Used especially of sounds and utterances. [From Latin *mellifluus* : *mel,* honey (see **melit-** in Appendix*) + *-fluus,* flowing (see **bhleu-** in Appendix*).] **—mel·lif′lu·ous·ly** *adv.* **—mel·lif′lu·ous·ness** *n.*

Mel·lon (mĕl′ən), **Andrew William.** 1855–1937. American industrialist and financier; Secretary of the Treasury (1921–32).

mel·lo·phone (mĕl′ō-fōn′) *n.* A brass musical wind instrument, sometimes used as a substitute for the French horn, which it resembles in tone. [MELLO(W) + -PHONE.]

mel·low (mĕl′ō) *adj.* **-lower, -lowest. 1. a.** Soft, sweet, juicy, and full-flavored because of ripeness. Said of fruit. **b.** Suggesting any of these qualities: *"The mellow air brought in the feel of imminent autumn."* (Thomas Hardy). **2.** Rich and soft in quality; not harsh: *a mellow sound; a mellow wine.* **3.** Having the gentleness, wisdom, or dignity often characteristic of maturity: *"A mellow and aristocratic flavour clung to these pink dwellings."* (Norman Douglas). **4.** Relaxed and at ease; genial. **5.** Slightly and pleasantly intoxicated. **6.** Moist, rich, soft, and loamy. Said of soil. *—v.* **mellowed, -lowing, -lows.** *—tr.* To bring to maturity; ripen. *—intr.* **1. a.** To become ripe; mature.

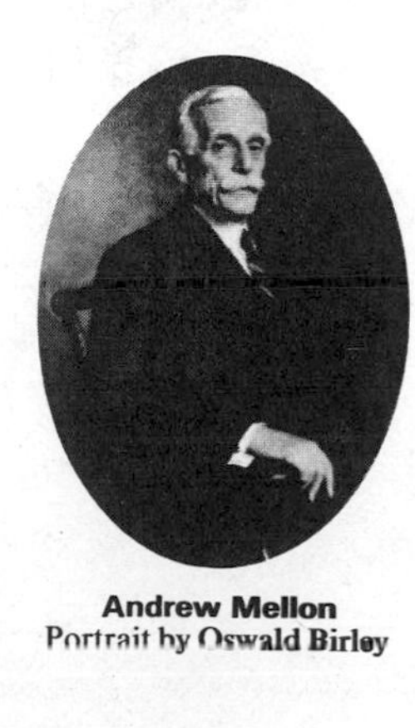

Andrew Mellon
Portrait by Oswald Birley

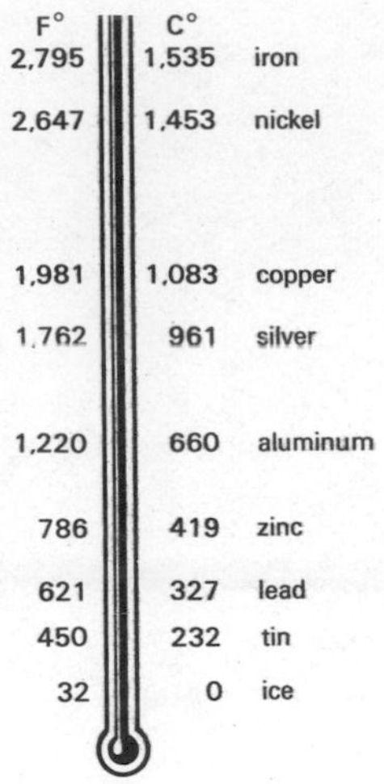

melting point

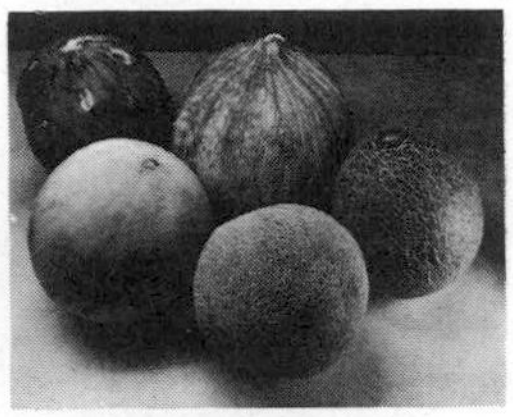

melon
Top row, left to right:
Cranshaw, casaba, Persian
Bottom row, left to right:
Honeydew, cantaloupe

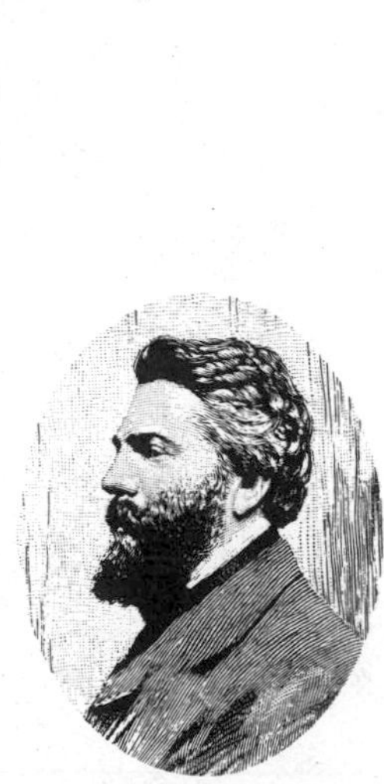

Herman Melville

b. To become overripe; rot: *"Prosperity begins to mellow and drop into the rotten mouth of death."* (Shakespeare). 2. To become gentle and sympathetic: *His outlook mellowed with advancing age.* [Middle English *mel(o)we,* probably from an attributive use of Old English *melu,* meal, "soft and rich, like meal." See **mela-** in Appendix.*] —**mel'low·ly** *adv.* —**mel'low·ness** *n.*

me·lo·de·on (mə-lō'dē-ən) *n.* A small reed organ. [Alteration of earlier *melodium,* from MELODY (by analogy with HARMONIUM).]

me·lod·ic (mə-lŏd'ĭk) *adj.* Pertaining to or containing melody. —**me·lod'i·cal·ly** *adv.*

me·lo·di·ous (mə-lō'dē-əs) *adj.* 1. Containing or pertaining to a pleasing succession of sounds; tuneful. 2. Agreeable to hear. —**me·lo'di·ous·ly** *adv.* —**me·lo'di·ous·ness** *n.*

mel·o·dize (mĕl'ə-dīz') *v.* **-dized, -dizing, -dizes.** —*tr.* 1. To write a melody for (a song lyric). 2. To make melodious: *"The words and thought lead, and the lyre . . . melodizes them."* (Ruskin). —*intr.* 1. To make melody; play on a musical instrument. Often used humorously. 2. *Poetic.* To mingle or blend melodiously. Followed by *with:* *"To murmur through the . . . groves, and melodize with man's blest nature there."* (Shelley). —**mel'o·diz'er, mel'o·dist** *n.*

mel·o·dra·ma (mĕl'ə-drä'mə, -drăm'ə) *n.* 1. A dramatic presentation characterized by heavy use of suspense, sensational episodes, romantic sentiment, and a conventionally happy ending. 2. The dramatic genre characterized by this treatment: *"Noble or hideous visitations . . . took tawdry refuge among the gaslights of melodrama."* (George Steiner). 3. Behavior or occurrences, in fiction or real life, having melodramatic characteristics: *"My idea of heaven is that there is no melodrama in it at all."* (Emerson). [French *mélodrame,* originally "musical drama" : Greek *melos,* song (see **mel-**³ in Appendix*) + French *drame,* drama, from Late Latin *drāma,* DRAMA.]

mel·o·dra·mat·ic (mĕl'ə-drə-măt'ĭk) *adj.* 1. Having the excitement and emotional appeal of melodrama: *"a melodramatic account of two perilous days spent among the planters"* (Frank O. Gatell). 2. Exaggeratedly emotional or sentimental; histrionic: *"Accuse me, if you will, of melodramatic embroidery."* (Erskine Childers). 3. Characterized by false pathos and sentiment. —**mel'o·dra·mat'i·cal·ly** *adv.*

mel·o·dra·mat·ics (mĕl'ə-drə-măt'ĭks) *pl.n.* 1. Melodramatic theatrical performance. 2. Melodramatic actions.

mel·o·dy (mĕl'ə-dē) *n., pl.* **-dies.** 1. A pleasing succession or arrangement of sounds. 2. Musical quality: *the melody of verse.* 3. *Music.* a. A rhythmically organized sequence of single tones so related to one another as to make up a particular musical phrase or idea. b. The structure of music with respect to the arrangement of single notes in succession. Together with harmony and rhythm, melody is one of the three basic elements of traditional Western music. c. The leading part or the air in a harmonic composition. 4. A poem suitable for setting to music or singing. [Middle English *melodie,* from Old French, from Late Latin *melōdia,* from Greek *melōidia,* choral song : *melos,* tune (see **mel-**³ in Appendix*) + *-ōidia,* "singing," from *aoidein,* to sing (see **wed-**² in Appendix*).]

mel·oid (mĕl'oid', mĕl'ō-ĭd) *n.* A blister beetle. —*adj.* Of or pertaining to blister beetles. [New Latin *meloidae* (family), from *Meloe*† (genus name).]

mel·on (mĕl'ən) *n.* 1. Any of several varieties of two related vines, *Cucumis melo* or *Citrullus vulgaris,* widely cultivated for their edible fruit. 2. The fruit of any of these vines, characteristically having a hard rind and juicy flesh. See **cantaloupe, honeydew melon, watermelon.** —**cut a melon.** *Slang.* To distribute profits, winnings, or dividends. [Middle English, from Old French, from Late Latin *mēlo* (stem *mēlōn-*), shortening of *mēlo(pepōn),* from Greek *mēlo(pepōn),* melon, "apple(-gourd)," from *mēlon,* apple. See **mēlon** in Appendix.*]

Me·los (mē'lŏs'). A Greek island of the Cyclades group in the Aegean Sea.

Mel·pom·e·ne (mĕl-pŏm'ə-nē'). *Greek Mythology.* The Muse of tragedy. [Latin *Melpomenē,* from Greek, "the singing one," from the feminine present participle of *melpesthai,* to sing, to sing of, from *melpein*†, to sing.]

melt (mĕlt) *v.* **melted, melted** or *archaic* **molten** (mōl'tən), **melting, melts.** —*intr.* 1. To be changed from a solid to a liquid state by the application of heat, pressure, or both. 2. To dissolve: *Sugar melts in water.* 3. To disappear or vanish gradually as if by dissolving. Often used with *away:* *"Like snow in sunshine his capital had melted."* (Ian Fleming). 4. To pass or merge imperceptibly into something else; blend gradually. Used with *into:* *"Objects at a little distance grew indistinct and melted bafflingly into each other."* (R.L. Stevenson). 5. To become softened in feeling by compassion or the like; be made gentle: *Her heart melted at the child's tears.* 6. *Archaic.* To be absorbed into something: *"Like fiery dews that melt into the bosom of a frozen bud."* (Shelley). 7. *Obsolete.* To be overcome, prostrated, or crushed by grief, dismay, fear, or the like. 8. To be extremely hot; perspire from heat: *He stood by the fire, melting in his ski outfit.* —*tr.* 1. a. To reduce from a solid to a liquid state by the application of heat, pressure, or both. b. To reduce (manufactured metal articles) to the state of raw material, usually for making other metal articles. Used with *down:* *They melted down everything from statues to pots and pans for shell casings.* 2. To dissolve: *melting honey in hot milk.* 3. To cause to disappear gradually; disperse: *The sun melted the fog.* 4. To cause (units) to blend: *"Here individuals of all races are melted into a new race of men"* (H.J.S. Crevecoeur). 5. To cause to pass or merge imperceptibly; blend (colors, sounds, or outlines): *"This effect is produced by melting . . . the shadows in a ground still darker."* (Sir Joshua Reynolds). 6. To soften (someone's feelings); make gentle or tender: *"O ye critics! will nothing melt you?"* (Sterne). —*n.* 1. A melted solid; fused mass. 2. The state of being melted. 3. a. The act or operation of melting. b. The quantity melted at a single operation or in one period. [Melt (infinitive), molten (past participle); Middle English *melten, molten,* Old English *meltan, gemolten.* See **mel-**¹ in Appendix.*] —**melt'a·bil'i·ty** *n.* —**melt'a·ble** *adj.* —**melt'er** *n.*

Synonyms: *melt, fuse, liquefy, thaw, dissolve, deliquesce. Melt* is applied to physical liquefaction (caused usually by heat) and, figuratively, to gradual disappearance or transformation. *Fuse* is largely restricted to the process whereby metals are joined by melting, and to figurative unions produced under stress: *courage and resolve fused by threat of conquest. Liquefy* is restricted to physical processes, but is said of both gases and solids, whereas the other terms apply only to solids. *Thaw* is applicable to that which is frozen and subjected to heat, but does not necessarily indicate complete liquefaction; figuratively it may refer to the softening of a harsh emotion or attitude. *Dissolve* specifies liquefaction by means of a solvent (a liquid that mingles its components with those of the original solid in a resultant liquid); figuratively it applies to melting, as by emotion. In both senses the term stresses complete transformation. *Deliquesce* refers to physical melting, usually gradual, through absorption of moisture from the air.

melt·age (mĕl'tĭj) *n.* 1. The quantity or substance produced by a melting process. 2. The process or act of melting.

melting point. *Abbr.* **m.p., mp** 1. The temperature at which a solid becomes a liquid at standard atmospheric pressure. 2. The temperature at which a solid and its liquid are in equilibrium, at any fixed pressure.

melting pot. 1. A container in which a substance is melted or fused. 2. A place where immigrants of different cultures or races form an integrated society.

mel·ton (mĕl'tən) *n.* A heavy, woolen cloth used chiefly for making overcoats and hunting jackets. [From *Melton* Mowbray, Leicestershire, England.]

Me·lun·geon (mə-lŭn'jən) *n.* One of a small group of dark-skinned people of uncertain origin living in the mountains of eastern Tennessee. [Origin uncertain.]

Mel·ville (mĕl'vĭl), **Herman.** 1819–1891. American novelist; author of *Moby Dick.*

Mel·ville, Lake (mĕl'vĭl). A lake about 25 miles wide and 120 miles long, in southeastern Labrador, Canada.

Mel·ville Island (mĕl'vĭl). 1. An Australian island, 2,400 square miles in area, off the northwest coast. 2. An island of the Canadian Northwest Territories, 16,503 square miles.

Mel·ville Peninsula (mĕl'vĭl). A peninsula, 24,156 square miles in area, projecting northward 250 miles from the eastern Northwest Territories, Canada.

Mel·vin, Mel·vyn (mĕl'vĭn). A masculine given name. [Adopted from Old English *Mǣlwine,* "friend of the council" : *mǣl,* council (see **mōd-** in Appendix*) + *wine,* friend, protector (see **wen-** in Appendix*).]

mem (mĕm) *n.* The thirteenth letter of the Hebrew alphabet. See **alphabet.** [Hebrew, perhaps from *mavim,* water.]

MEM Airport code for Memphis, Tennessee.

mem. 1. member. 2. memoir. 3. memorandum. 4. memorial.

mem·ber (mĕm'bər) *n.* 1. A distinct part of a whole, such as a clause in a sentence, a proposition of a syllogism, or one of the expressions in a mathematical equation. 2. A part or organ of a human or animal body: a. A limb, such as an arm or leg. b. The penis. 3. A part of a plant. 4. *Abbr.* **mem., M.** A person who belongs to a group or organization. 5. *Abbr.* **mem., M.** One who serves on or is elected to a political body such as Congress. 6. *Mathematics.* a. The expression on either side of an equality sign. b. An element of a set. [Middle English, from Old French *membre,* from Latin *membrum.* See **mēms-** in Appendix.*]

mem·ber·ship (mĕm'bər-shĭp') *n.* 1. The state of being a member. 2. The total number of members in a group.

mem·brane (mĕm'brān') *n.* 1. *Biology.* A thin, pliable layer of tissue covering surfaces or separating or connecting regions, structures, or organs of an animal or plant. 2. A piece of parchment. 3. *Chemistry.* A thin sheet of natural or synthetic material that is permeable to substances in solution. [Latin *membrāna,* membrane, "skin covering an organ or member of the body," from *membrum,* member. See **mēms-** in Appendix.*]

membrane bone. A bone formed directly in the connective tissue, as some cranial bones. Compare **cartilage bone.**

mem·bra·nous (mĕm'brə-nəs) *adj.* Also **mem·bra·na·ce·ous** (mĕm'brə-nā'shəs). 1. Made of or similar to a membrane. 2. *Pathology.* Characterized by membrane formation.

Mem·el. 1. The German name for **Klaipeda.** 2. The German name for the **Neman River.**

me·men·to (mə-mĕn'tō) *n., pl.* **-tos** or **-toes.** 1. Any reminder of the past; a keepsake, souvenir, or relic. 2. *Capital* **M.** *Roman Catholic Church.* Either of the two prayers in the canon of the Mass starting with the word "Memento." [Middle English, from Latin *mementō,* "remember," imperative of *meminisse,* to remember. See **men-**¹ in Appendix.*]

me·men·to mo·ri (mə-mĕn'tō môr'ē, mōr'ī'). Any reminder of death or mortality, such as a death's-head or an ornament bearing symbols of death. [Latin, "remember that you must die."]

Mem·ling (mĕm'lĭng), **Hans.** Also **Mem·linc** (mĕm'lĭngk). 1430?–1495. Flemish painter of religious subjects and portraits.

Mem·non¹ (mĕm'nŏn'). *Greek Mythology.* An Ethiopian king

ă pat/ā pay/âr care/ä father/b bib/ch church/d deed/ĕ pet/ē be/f fife/g gag/h hat/hw which/ĭ pit/ī pie/îr pier/j judge/k kick/l lid, needle/m mum/n no, sudden/ng thing/ŏ pot/ō toe/ô paw, for/oi noise/ou out/ŏŏ took/ōō boot/p pop/r roar/s sauce/sh ship, dish/

killed by Achilles and made immortal by Zeus.
Mem·non[2] (mĕm′nŏn′) *n.* A huge statue of the Egyptian Pharaoh Amenhotep III at Thebes.
mem·o (mĕm′ō) *n., pl.* **-os.** A memorandum.
mem·oir (mĕm′wär′, -wôr′) *n. Abbr.* **mem. 1. a.** A narrative of experiences that the writer has lived through. **b.** *Usually plural.* An autobiography. **c.** A biography or biographical sketch. **2.** A written reminder; memorandum. **3.** A monograph: *"a remarkable memoir . . . on the oaks of the whole world"* (Charles Darwin). **4.** *Plural.* The report of the proceedings of a learned society. [French *mémoire,* from Old French *memoire,* memory, from Latin *memoria,* MEMORY.]
mem·o·ra·bil·i·a (mĕm′ər-ə-bĭl′ē-ə, -bĭl′yə) *pl.n.* Things worthy of remembrance. [Latin *memorābilia,* from *memorābilis,* MEMORABLE.]
mem·o·ra·ble (mĕm′ər-ə-bəl) *adj.* Worth being remembered or noted; remarkable: *"We may now review up to this point the course of this memorable battle."* (Winston Churchill). [Middle English, from Latin *memorābilis,* from *memorāre,* to remember, from *memor,* mindful. See **smer-**[1] in Appendix.*] **—mem′o·ra·bil′i·ty, mem′o·ra·ble·ness** *n.* **—mem′o·ra·bly** *adv.*
mem·o·ran·dum (mĕm′ə-răn′dəm) *n., pl.* **-dums** or **-da** (-də). *Abbr.* **mem. 1.** A short note written as a reminder. **2.** A written record or communication, as in a business office. **3.** *Law.* A short, written statement outlining the terms of an agreement, transaction, or contract. **4.** A business statement made by a consignor about a shipment of goods that may be returned. **5.** A brief, unsigned diplomatic communication. [Middle English, "let it be remembered," from Latin, from *memorāre,* to remember, from *memor,* mindful. See **smer-**[1] in Appendix.*]
me·mo·ri·al (mə-môr′ē-əl, mə-mōr′-) *n. Abbr.* **mem. 1.** Something, such as a monument or a holiday, designed or established to serve as a remembrance of a person or an event. **2.** A written statement of facts or a petition presented to a legislative body or an executive. *—adj.* **1.** Serving as a remembrance of a person or event; commemorative. **2.** Of, pertaining to, or in memory. [Middle English, from Latin *memoriālis,* belonging to memory, from *memoria,* MEMORY.] **—me·mo′ri·al·ly** *adv.*
Memorial Day. A day designated in the United States for honoring dead servicemen, May 30 in most states. Also called "Decoration Day."
me·mo·ri·al·ist (mə-môr′ē-əl-ĭst, mə-mōr′-) *n.* **1.** A person who writes memoirs. **2.** A person who writes or signs a memorial.
me·mo·ri·al·ize (mə-môr′ē-əl-īz′, mə-mōr′-) *tr.v.* **-ized, -izing, -izes. 1.** To commemorate. **2.** To present a memorial to; petition. **—me·mo′ri·al·i·za′tion** *n.* **—me·mo′ri·al·iz′er** *n.*
mem·o·rize (mĕm′ə-rīz′) *tr.v.* **-rized, -rizing, -rizes.** To commit to memory; learn by heart. **—mem′o·riz′a·ble** *adj.* **—mem′o·ri·za′tion** *n.* **—mem′o·riz′er** *n.*
mem·o·ry (mĕm′ər-ē) *n., pl.* **-ries. 1.** The mental faculty of retaining and recalling past experience; the ability to remember. **2.** An act or instance of remembrance; a recollection: *"He fell into pleasant memories of his childhood."* (Ambrose Bierce). **3.** All that a person can remember. **4.** Something remembered of a person, thing, or event: *"The memory of the just is blessed."* (Proverbs 10:7). **5.** The fact of being remembered; remembrance; recollection. **6.** The period of time covered by the remembrance or recollection of a person or group of persons: *within the memory of man.* **7.** *Law.* The period of time required for certain customs to attain legal significance. In British common law and in most states of the United States, about 20 years. Also called "legal memory." **8.** *Biology.* Persistent modification of behavior resulting from the organism's experience. See **instinct. 9.** A unit of a computer that preserves data for retrieval. **10.** *Statistics.* The set of past events affecting a given event in a stochastic process. [Middle English *memorie,* from Old French, from Latin *memoria,* from *memor,* mindful. See **smer-**[1] in Appendix.*]
Synonyms: *memory, remembrance, recollection, reminiscence, retrospect. Memory* overlaps each of these terms without having all of their specific senses; the plural *memories* sometimes implies a personal, cherished quality. *Remembrance* generally applies to a specific act of recall; in all senses (including the physical one of memento or keepsake) it usually connotes intimate associations. *Recollection* also is limited to a specific instance, which is deliberate and practical (rather than sentimental). *Reminiscence* stresses pleasurable, casual recall of intimate matters; generally it involves the sharing of what is recalled. *Retrospect (retrospection)* emphasizes purposeful recall, often accompanied by evaluation.
Mem·phis (mĕm′fĭs). **1.** The ruined capital of ancient Egypt, on the Nile about 12 miles south of Cairo. **2.** A city on the Mississippi River in southwestern Tennessee. Population, 498,000. **—Mem′phi·an** (mĕm′fē-ən) *adj. & n.*
mem·sa·hib (mĕm′sä′ĭb) *n.* A title of respect applied to a white European woman in colonial India. [From MA'AM + SAHIB.]
men. Plural of **man.**
men·ace (mĕn′ĭs) *n.* **1. a.** A threat: *"the prophecy and menace of the bullet"* (Ambrose Bierce). **b.** The act of threatening: *"A large alligator floated close by the ship, its jaws open in menace."* (H.M. Tomlinson). **2.** A troublesome or annoying person: *She has become a menace by her gossip. —v.* **menaced, -acing, -aces.** *—tr.* To threaten: *The storm menaced the countryside. —intr.* To make threats; indicate danger or coming harm. —See Synonyms at **threaten.** [Middle English *manace,* from Old French, from Latin *minācia,* menace, originally "threatening things," neuter plural of *minax* (stem *minac-*), threatening, from *minārī,* to threaten, from *minae,* threats. See **men-**[2] in Appendix.*] **—men′ac·er** *n.* **—men′ac·ing·ly** *adv.*
men·a·di·one (mĕn′ə-dī′ōn′) *n.* A yellow crystalline powder, $C_{10}H_5CH_3O_2$, having physiological effects similar to vitamin K. It is used as a medicine and as a fungicide. [ME(THYL) + NA(PHTHA) + DI- + -ONE.]
mé·nage (mā-näzh′) *n.* Also **me·nage. 1.** Persons living together as a unit; a household. **2.** The management of a household. [French, from Old French *menage,* from Vulgar Latin *mansiōnāticum* (unattested), household, from *mansiō,* house, dwelling, from *manēre,* to dwell. See **men-**[3] in Appendix.*]
me·nag·er·ie (mə-năj′ə-rē, mə-näzh′-) *n.* **1.** A collection of live wild animals on exhibition. **2.** The enclosure in which such animals are kept. [French *ménagerie,* originally "the management of domestic animals," from *ménage,* MÉNAGE.]
Me·nam. See **Chao Phraya** River.
Me·nan·der (mə-năn′dər). Athenian author of comedies of contemporary manners in the fourth century B.C.

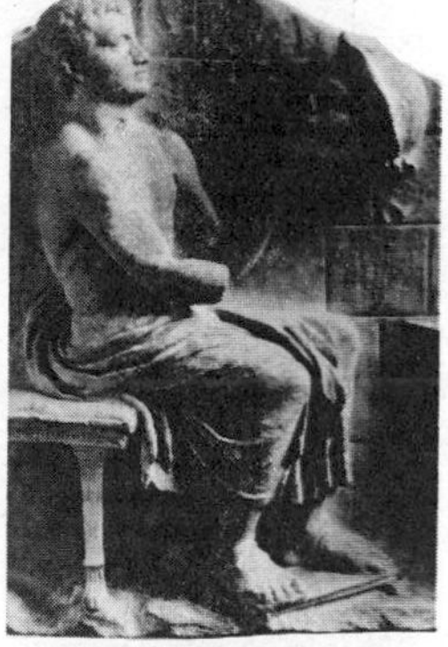

Menander
Marble relief of Menander holding a theatrical mask

me·nar·che (mə-när′kē) *n.* The first occurrence of menstruation. [New Latin : Greek *mēn,* moon (see **mē-**[2] in Appendix*) + *arkhē,* beginning (see **arkhein** in Appendix*).] **—me·nar′che·al** (mə-när′kē-əl) *adj.*
Men·ci·us (mĕn′shē-əs, -shəs). Original name, Meng Ko. Long known in China as Meng-tse. Chinese philosopher of the fourth century B.C.
Menck·en (mĕng′kən), **H(enry) L(ouis).** 1880–1956. American editor, critic, and author of works on the American language.
mend (mĕnd) *v.* **mended, mending, mends.** *—tr.* **1.** To make right or correct; repair. **2.** To reform or improve. Used chiefly in the phrase *mend one's ways. —intr.* **1.** To undergo a moral improvement; reform. **2. a.** To improve in health: *He is mending well.* **b.** To heal: *The bone mended in a month.* **3.** To correct errors; set right: *Least said, soonest mended.* **—mend one's fences.** To strengthen one's reputation by personal negotiation or maneuvering. *—n.* **1.** The act of mending. **2.** A mended place. **—on the mend.** Improving, especially in health; recuperating. [Middle English *menden,* shortening of *amenden,* to AMEND.] **—mend′a·ble** *adj.* **—mend′er** *n.*
men·da·cious (mĕn-dā′shəs) *adj.* **1.** Lying; untruthful: *a mendacious child.* **2.** False; untrue: *a mendacious statement.* —See Synonyms at **dishonest.** [From Latin *mendāx* (stem *mendāc-*). See **mend-** in Appendix.*] **—men·da′cious·ly** *adv.* **—men·dac′i·ty** (mĕn-dăs′ə-tē) *n.*
Men·del (mĕn′dəl), **Gregor Johann.** 1822–1884. Austrian monk; founder of the science of genetics.
Men·de·le·ev (mĕn′də-lā′əf), **Dmitri Ivanovich.** 1834–1907. Russian chemist; first devised and published the periodic table of the elements (1869).
men·de·le·vi·um (mĕn′də-lē′vē-əm) *n. Symbol* **Md** A radioactive transuranium element of the actinide series. Atomic number 101, mass numbers 255 and 256, half-lives approximately 30 minutes (Md^{255}) and 1.5 hours (Md^{256}). [New Latin, after Dmitri MENDELEEV.]
Men·de·li·an (mĕn-dē′lē-ən, -dēl′yən) *adj.* Of or pertaining to Gregor Mendel or his theories of genetics.
Men·del·ism (mĕn′dəl-ĭz′əm) *n.* Also **Men·de·li·an·ism** (mĕn-dē′lē-ən-ĭz′əm). The theoretical principles of heredity formulated by Gregor Mendel. See **Mendel's laws.**
Mendel's laws. The principles of heredity of sexually reproducing organisms formulated by Gregor Mendel, now usually summarized in three laws: **a.** *Law of Segregation:* Certain paired characteristics, one from each parent, do not blend with or alter each other in the offspring, thus accounting for contrasting traits in successive generations. **b.** *Law of Independent Combination:* The genes determining such pairs of traits combine in the offspring according to the statistics of chance. **c.** *Law of Dominance:* If one of a pair of genes is dominant and the other recessive, the recessive trait may appear in an offspring only if both genes of its pair are recessive.
Men·dels·sohn (mĕn′dəl-sən), **Felix.** Full name, Jakob Ludwig Felix Mendelssohn-Bartholdy. 1809–1847. German composer, pianist, and conductor; grandson of Moses Mendelssohn.
Men·dels·sohn (mĕn′dəl-sən), **Moses.** 1729–1786. German-Jewish philosopher and translator.
Men·de·res (mĕn′də-rĕs′). **1.** Ancient name **Mae·an·der** (mē-ăn′dər). A river of western Turkey, flowing 250 miles from Dinar to the Aegean Sea. **2.** Ancient name **Sca·man·der** (skə-măn′dər). A river of northwestern Turkey, flowing about 60 miles to the Dardanelles.
Men·dès-France (mäN-dĕs-fräNs′), **Pierre.** Born 1907. French socialist leader; premier and foreign minister (1954–55).
men·di·cant (mĕn′dĭ-kənt) *adj.* Depending upon alms for a living; practicing begging: *"The popular preaching of the mendicant friars encouraged emotional religion."* (George L. Mosse). *—n.* **1.** A beggar. **2.** A member of a mendicant order of friars. [Latin *mendīcāns* (stem *mendīcant-*), present participle of *mendīcāre,* to beg, from *mendīcus,* beggar, poor man, originally "injured," from *mendum,* physical defect. See **mend-** in Appendix.*] **—men′di·can·cy, men·dic′i·ty** (mĕn-dĭs′ə-tē) *n.*
mend·ing (mĕn′dĭng) *n.* Articles to be mended.
Men·do·za (mĕn-dō′sä). A city and wine-making and oil-refining center of west-central Argentina. Population, 109,000.
Men·e·la·us (mĕn′ə-lā′əs). *Greek Mythology.* The king of Sparta, husband of Helen and brother of Agamemnon.
me·ne, me·ne, tek·el, u·phar·sin (mē′nē mē′nē tĕk′əl yōō-fär′sĭn). Aramaic words meaning, literally, "numbered, numbered, weighed, divided," which appeared on the wall at Belshazzar's feast. Daniel 5:25–28. The phrase was interpreted by Daniel to mean that God had doomed Belshazzar's kingdom.
Me·nén·dez de A·vi·lés (mə-nĕn′dās dā ä′vē-lās′), **Pedro.**

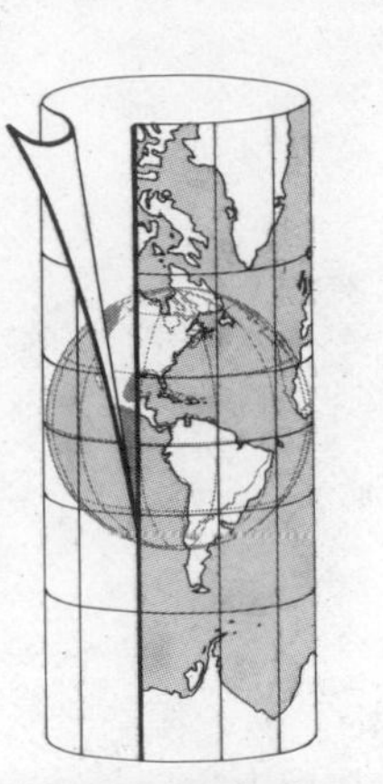

Mercator projection
Cylindrical projection showing meridians and North and South American continents

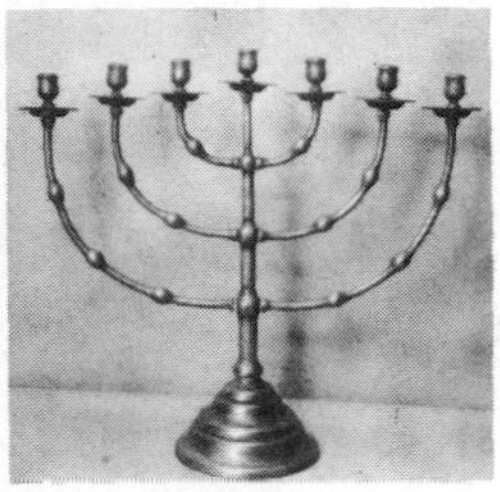

Menorah

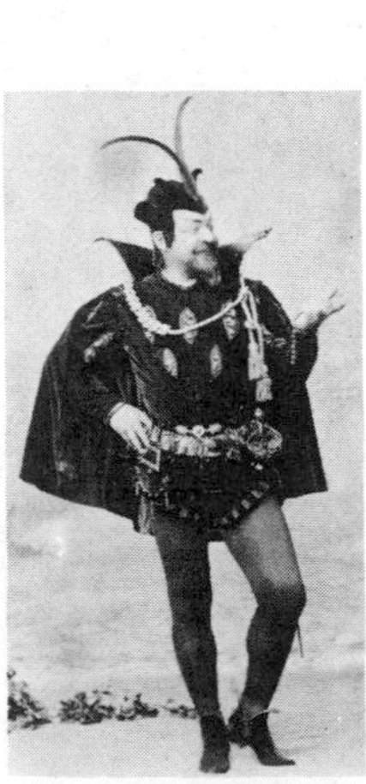

Mephistopheles
Édouard de Reszke as Mephistopheles in the opera *Faust*

1519–1574. Spanish founder of St. Augustine, Florida.
Me·nes (mē′nēz). Egyptian king; founder (about 3000 B.C.) of the first dynasty, uniting Upper and Lower Egypt.
Meng-tse. See **Mencius.**
men·ha·den (mĕn-hăd′n) *n., pl.* **menhaden** or **-dens.** An abundant inedible fish, *Brevoortia tyrannus,* of American Atlantic and Gulf waters, used as a source of fish oil, fish meal, fertilizer, and bait. Also called "mossbunker," "oldwife," "pogy." [Narraganset *munnawhatteaug,* menhaden, perhaps akin to Natick *munnohquohteau,* "he fertilizes" (menhaden were used by the Algonquins as fertilizer for corn).]
men·hir (mĕn′hîr′) *n.* A prehistoric monument of a class found chiefly in the British Isles and northern France, consisting of a single tall, upright megalith. Compare **dolmen.** [French, from Breton *men hir,* "long stone" : *men,* stone, from Middle Breton, from (unattested) Celtic *magino-,* stone (compare **dolmen**) + *hir,* long, from Middle Breton (see **sē-²** in Appendix*).]
me·ni·al (mē′nē-əl, mēn′yəl) *adj.* **1.** Of, pertaining to, or appropriate for a servant. **2.** Of or pertaining to work or a job regarded as servile. —*n.* **1.** A servant, especially a domestic servant. **2.** A person who has a servile or low nature. [Middle English *meynial,* from Norman French *menial,* from Old French *meinie, mesne,* servant, from Vulgar Latin *mānsiōnatā* (unattested), household, from *mānsiō,* house dwelling. See **mansion.**] —**me′ni·al·ly** *adv.*
me·nin·ge·al (mə-nĭn′jē-əl) *adj.* Of, relating to, or concerned with a meninx or meninges.
men·in·gi·tis (mĕn′ĭn-jī′tĭs) *n. Pathology.* Inflammation of any or all of the meninges of the brain and the spinal cord, usually caused by a bacterial infection. [New Latin : MENING(ES) + -ITIS.] —**men′in·git′ic** (-jĭt′ĭk) *adj.*
me·ninx (mē′nĭngks) *n., pl.* **meninges** (mə-nĭn′jēz). Any of the membranes enclosing the brain and spinal cord in vertebrates. [New Latin (plural *meninges*), from Greek *mēninx* (stem *mēning-*), membrane. See **mēms-** in Appendix.*]
me·nis·cus (mə-nĭs′kəs) *n., pl.* **menisci** (-nĭs′ī′) or **-cuses. 1.** A crescent-shaped body. **2.** A concavo-convex lens. **3.** The curved upper surface of a nonturbulent liquid in a container. It is concave if the liquid wets the container walls and convex if it does not. **4.** *Anatomy.* A cartilage disk that acts as a cushion between the ends of bones that meet in a joint. [New Latin, from Greek *mēniskos,* crescent, diminutive of *mēnē,* moon. See **mē-²** in Appendix.*] —**me·nis′cal** (-kəl), **me·nis′cate′** (-kāt′), **me·nis′coid′** (-koid′), **men′is·coi′dal** (mĕn′ĭs-koid′l) *adj.*
Men·ning·er (mĕn′ĭng-ər), **Charles F.** 1862–1953. American psychiatrist; with his sons, **Karl Augustus,** born 1893, and **William Claire,** 1899–1966, he established the Menninger psychiatric clinic in Topeka, Kansas.
Men·non·ite (mĕn′ə-nīt′) *n.* A member of an Evangelical Protestant Christian sect opposed to taking oaths, holding public office, or performing military service. [German *Mennonit,* after *Menno* Simons (1492–1559), religious reformer.]
me·nol·o·gy (mə-nŏl′ə-jē) *n., pl.* **-gies. 1.** An ecclesiastical calendar of the months with important religious events recorded. **2.** A collection of short biographies of the lives of the saints arranged in the form of a calendar. [Medieval Greek *mēnologion,* "list of months" : Greek *mēn,* month (see **mē-²** in Appendix*) + -LOGY.]
men·o·pause (mĕn′ə-pôz′) *n.* The period of cessation of menstruation, occurring usually between the ages of 45 and 50. Also called "change of life," "climacteric." [French : Greek *mēn,* moon (from the monthly cycle of the menses) (see **mē-²** in Appendix*) + PAUSE.] —**men′o·paus′al** *adj.*
Me·no·rah (mə-nôr′ə, -nōr′ə) *n.* **1.** A ceremonial seven-branched candelabrum of the Jewish Temple symbolizing the seven days of the Creation. Exodus 37:17–24. **2.** A nine-branched candelabrum used in the celebration of Chanukah. [Hebrew *mənōrāh,* candlestick.]
Me·nor·ca. The Spanish name for **Minorca.**
men·or·rha·gi·a (mĕn′ə-rā′jē-ə) *n. Pathology.* Abnormally heavy menstrual flow. [New Latin : Greek *mēn,* moon (see **mē-²** in Appendix*) + -RRHAGIA.]
Me·not·ti (mə-nŏt′ē), **Gian Carlo.** Born 1911. Italian-born American composer and librettist of operas and ballets.
Men·sa (mĕn′sə) *n.* A southern constellation between Hydrus and Volans. [Latin *mēnsa*†, table.]
men·sal¹ (mĕn′səl) *adj.* Belonging to or used at the table. [Late Latin *mēnsālis,* from *mēnsa,* table. See **Mensa.**]
men·sal² (mĕn′səl) *adj.* Monthly. [From Latin *mēnsis,* month. See **mē-²** in Appendix.*]
mensch (mĕnsh) *n. Informal.* A person having admirable characteristics, such as fortitude and firmness of purpose. [Yiddish *mens(c)h,* from Middle High German *mensch,* man, from Old High German *mennisco.* See **man-¹** in Appendix.*]
men·ses (mĕn′sēz) *pl.n. Physiology.* Blood and dead cell debris that is discharged from the uterus through the vagina by adult women at approximately monthly intervals between puberty and menopause. [Latin *mēnsēs,* months, hence also "monthly periods," plural of *mēnsis,* month. See **mē-²** in Appendix.*]
Men·she·vik (mĕn′shə-vĭk) *n., pl.* **-viks** or **-viki** (-vē′kē). **1. a.** A member of the liberal minority faction of the Russian Social Democratic Party which struggled against the more radical majority element, the Bolsheviks, from 1903 until the Russian Revolution in 1917. **b.** A member of a liberal socialist group established after the Russian Revolution to oppose the activities of the Bolshevik Party. **2.** A person having views in accord with the Menshevik faction. Compare **Bolshevik.** [Russian *men′shevik,* a member of the smaller (faction), from *men′she,* less, from Old Church Slavonic *mĭnĭshĭ,* less. See **mei-²** in Appendix.*] —**Men′she·vism** *n.* —**Men′she·vist** *adj.* & *n.*
Men·shi·kov (mĕn′shĭ-kôf′), Prince **Aleksandr Danilovich.** 1672–1729. Russian soldier and statesman; exiled to Siberia.
men·stru·al (mĕn′strōō-əl) *adj.* Also **men·stru·ous** (mĕn′strōō-əs). **1.** *Physiology.* Relating to menstruation. **2.** Taking place monthly; having a monthly duration. [Middle English *menstruall,* from Latin *mēnstruālis,* from *mēnstruus,* menstrual, monthly, from *mēnsis,* month. See **mē-²** in Appendix.*]
men·stru·ate (mĕn′strōō-āt′) *intr.v.* **-ated, -ating, -ates.** *Physiology.* To undergo menstruation. [Latin *mēnstruāre,* from *mēnstruus,* MENSTRUAL.]
men·stru·a·tion (mĕn′strōō-ā′shən) *n.* The process or an instance of discharging the menses.
men·stru·um (mĕn′strōō-əm) *n., pl.* **-ums** or **-strua** (-strōō-ə). A solvent, especially one used in extracting and preparing drugs. [Middle English, from Medieval Latin *mēnstruum,* solvent, originally "menstrual blood" (alchemists regarded the gold-transmuting solvent as similar to menstrual blood, which they believed transformed sperm in the womb into an embryo), from Latin *mēnstruus,* MENSTRUAL.]
men·su·ra·ble (mĕn′sər-ə-bəl, mĕn′shər-ə-) *adj.* **1.** Capable of being measured. **2.** Having fixed rhythm and measure, as in music; mensural. —**men′su·ra·bil′i·ty** *n.*
men·su·ral (mĕn′sər-əl, mĕn′shər-) *adj.* **1.** Of or pertaining to measure. **2.** *Music.* Having notes of fixed rhythmic value. [Latin *mēnsurālis,* from *mēnsūra,* MEASURE.]
men·su·ra·tion (mĕn′sə-rā′shən, mĕn′shə-) *n.* **1.** The process, act, or art of measuring. **2.** The measurement of geometric quantities. —**men′su·ra′tive** *adj.*
-ment. Indicates product, means, action, or state; for example, **casement, appeasement, measurement, environment.** [Middle English, from Old French, from Latin *-mentum,* abstract noun suffix originally added only to verbs.]
men·tal (mĕn′təl) *adj.* **1.** Of or pertaining to the mind; intellectual. **2.** Done or performed by the mind; existing in the mind. **3.** Relating to the mind. [Middle English, from Old French, from Latin *mentālis,* from *mēns* (stem *ment-*), mind. See **men-¹** in Appendix.*] —**men′tal·ly** *adv.*
mental age. *Abbr.* **MA, M.A.** A measure of mental development, as determined by intelligence tests, generally restricted to children and expressed as the age at which that level is average.
mental deficiency. Subnormal intellectual development, either congenital or induced by brain injury or disease, characterized broadly by deficiencies ranging in severity from impaired learning ability through social and vocational inadequacy to inability to learn connected speech or guard against common dangers.
men·tal·i·ty (mĕn-tăl′ə-tē) *n., pl.* **-ties. 1.** The sum of a person's intellectual capabilities or endowment; mental capacity; intelligence. **2.** Cast or turn of mind; mental status or inclination: *"his was a Tory mentality and he supported harsh measures"* (Samuel Chew). —See Synonyms at **mind.**
mental retardation. Mental deficiency *(see).*
mental telepathy. Telepathy *(see).*
men·thol (mĕn′thôl′) *n.* A white, crystalline, organic compound, $CH_3C_6H_9(C_3H_7)OH$, obtained from peppermint oil or synthesized. It is used in perfumes, as a mild anesthetic, and as a flavoring. Also called "peppermint camphor." [German *Menthol* : Latin *mentha,* MINT + -OL.] —**men′tho·lat′ed** *adj.*
men·tion (mĕn′shən) *tr.v.* **-tioned, -tioning, -tions.** To cite or refer to incidentally. —**Don't mention it.** A formula of courtesy used to deprecate proffered thanks or apology. —*n.* **1. a.** The act of briefly or casually referring to something. **b.** An incidental reference or allusion. **2. Honorable mention** *(see).* [Middle English *mencioun,* from Old French *mention,* from Latin *mentiō,* remembrance, mention. See **men-¹** in Appendix.*] —**men′tion·a·ble** *adj.* —**men′tion·er** *n.*
Men·tor (mĕn′tôr′, -tər). *Greek Mythology.* Odysseus' trusted counselor, under whose disguise Athena became the guardian and teacher of Telemachus. [Latin *Mentōr,* from Greek *Mentōr,* name probably meaning "adviser," "wise man." See **men-¹** in Appendix.*]
men·tor (mĕn′tôr′, -tər) *n.* A wise and trusted counselor or teacher: *"Moore and Kierkegaard have become mentors of two different philosophic movements."* (Walter Kaufmann). [French, from *Mentor,* a character in Fénelon's *Télémaque* (1699), modeled after MENTOR.]
men·u (mĕn′yōō, mān′yōō) *n.* **1.** A list of the dishes to be served or available for a meal; bill of fare. **2.** The dishes served or available. [French, menu, list, from *menu,* detailed, small, from Latin *minūtus,* minute, diminished, past participle of *minuere,* to diminish. See **mei-²** in Appendix.*]
me·ow (mē-ou′) *n.* Also **mi·aow, mi·aou.** The cry of a cat. —*intr.v.* **meowed, -owing, -ows.** Also **mi·aow, mi·aou.** To make the crying sound of a cat. [Imitative.]
mep, m.e.p. mean effective pressure.
me·per·i·dine hydrochloride (mə-pĕr′ə-dēn′). An organic compound, $C_{15}H_{21}NO_2 \cdot HCl$, used as an analgesic and sedative. [From ME(THYL) + (PI)PERIDINE.]
Meph·i·stoph·e·les (mĕf′ə-stŏf′ə-lēz′). The devil in the Faust legend to whom Faust sold his soul. —**Me·phis′to·phe′le·an, Me·phis′to·phe′li·an** (mə-fĭs′tō-fē′lē-ən, -fēl′yən, mĕf′ə-stə-) *adj.*
me·phi·tis (mə-fī′tĭs) *n.* **1.** An offensive smell; stench. **2.** A poisonous or foul-smelling gas emitted from the earth. [Latin *mefitis*†, stench.] —**me·phit′ic** (mə-fĭt′ĭk), **me·phit′i·cal** *adj.* —**me·phit′i·cal·ly** *adv.*
me·pro·ba·mate (mĕp′rō-băm′āt, mĕ-prō′bə-māt′) *n.* A white, bitter powder, $CH_3(C_3H_7)C(CH_2OOCNH_2)_2$, used as a tranquilizer. [ME(THYL) + PRO(PYL) + (DICAR)BAMATE.]
meq. milliequivalent.

ă pat/ā pay/âr care/ä father/b bib/ch church/d deed/ĕ pet/ē be/f fife/g gag/h hat/hw which/ĭ pit/ī pie/îr pier/j judge/k kick/l lid, needle/m mum/n no, sudden/ng thing/ŏ pot/ō toe/ô paw, for/oi noise/ou out/ŏŏ took/ōō boot/p pop/r roar/s sauce/sh ship, dish/

mer. meridian.
mer·bro·min (mər-brō′mĭn) *n.* A green, crystalline, organic compound, $C_{20}H_8Br_2HgNa_2O_6$, that forms a red aqueous solution used as a germicide and antiseptic under the trademark Mercurochrome. [MER(CURIC + DI)BROM(OFLORESCE)IN.]
mer·can·tile (mûr′kən-tēl′, -tīl′, -tĭl) *adj.* **1.** Of or pertaining to merchants or trade. **2.** Of or pertaining to mercantilism. [French, from Italian, from *mercante, mercatante,* merchant, from Vulgar Latin *mercātāns* (unattested), MERCHANT.]
mer·can·til·ism (mûr′kən-tēl′ĭz′əm, -tĭl′ĭz′əm, -tĭl-ĭz′əm) *n.* The theory and system of political economy prevailing in Europe after the decline of feudalism, based on national policies of accumulating bullion, establishing colonies and a merchant marine, and developing industry and mining to attain a favorable balance of trade. [French *mercantilisme,* from *mercantile,* MERCANTILE.] —**mer′can·til′ist** *n.*
mer·cap·tan (mər-kăp′tăn′) *n.* Any sulfur-containing organic compound with the general formula RSH, R being any radical, for example, ethyl mercaptan, C_2H_5SH. Also called "thiol." [German *Mercaptan,* from Danish, from Medieval Latin *(corpus) mercurium captans,* "(substance) seizing mercury" : *mercurium,* from *mercurius,* MERCURY + *captāns,* present participle of *captāre,* frequentative of *capere,* to take (see **kap-** in Appendix*).]
Mer·ca·tor projection (mər-kā′tər). Also **Mer·ca·tor's projection.** A map projection in which the meridians and parallels of latitude appear as lines crossing at right angles and in which areas appear greater farther from the equator. [Invented by Gerhardus *Mercator* (1512–1594), Flemish cartographer.]
Mer·ce·da·rio (mĕr′sā-*thä′*ryō). A mountain in the Andes of Argentina rising to 22,210 feet, near the Chilean border.
Mer·ce·des (mər-sā′dēz). A feminine given name. [Spanish, shortened from *(Maria de) Mercedes,* "Mary of mercies," plural of *merced,* mercy, from Late Latin *mercēs,* reward. See **merc-** in Appendix.*]
mer·ce·nar·y (mûr′sə-nĕr′ē) *adj.* **1.** Motivated solely by a desire for monetary or material gain; greedy; venal. **2.** Hired for service in a foreign army. —*n., pl.* **mercenaries. 1.** A person who serves or works merely for monetary gain; hireling. **2.** A professional soldier who is hired by a foreign country. [Middle English *mercenarie,* from Latin *mercēnārius,* from *mercēs,* pay. See **merc-** in Appendix.*] —**mer′ce·nar′i·ly** *adv.* —**mer′ce·nar′i·ness** *n.*
mer·cer (mûr′sər) *n. British.* A dealer in textiles, especially silks. [Middle English, from Old French *mercier,* trader, from Vulgar Latin *merciārius* (unattested), from *merx* (stem *merc-*), merchandise. See **merc-** in Appendix.*]
mer·cer·ize (mûr′sə-rīz′) *tr.v.* **-ized, -izing, -izes.** To treat (cotton thread) with sodium hydroxide, so as to shrink the fiber and increase its color absorption and luster. [Process invented by John *Mercer* (1791–1866), English textile maker.]
mer·chan·dise (mûr′chən-dīz′, -dīs′) *n.* Also **mer·chan·dize.** *Abbr.* **mdse.** The bulk of commodities of commerce; goods that may be bought or sold. —*v.* (mûr′chən-dīz′) **merchandised, -dising, -dises.** Also **mer·chan·dize.** —*tr.* **1.** To buy and sell (commodities). **2.** To promote the sale of, as by advertising or display. —*intr.* To trade commercially: *"Merchandizing was at a full stop, for very few ships ventured to come up the river, and none at all went out."* (Defoe). [Middle English *mercheaundise,* from Old French *marcheandise,* from *marcheant,* MERCHANT.] —**mer′chan·dis′er** *n.*
mer·chant (mûr′chənt) *n.* **1.** A person whose occupation is the wholesale purchase and retail sale of goods for profit. **2.** A person who runs a retail business; shopkeeper. —*adj.* **1.** Of or pertaining to a merchant, merchandise, or commercial trade; dealing in commerce: *a merchant guild.* **2.** Of or pertaining to the **merchant marine** *(see).* [Middle English *marchaund,* from Old French *marcheant,* trader, from Vulgar Latin *mercātāns* (unattested), present participle of *mercātāre* (unattested), to trade, from Latin *mercārī,* to trade, from *merx* (stem *merc-*), merchandize. See **merc-** in Appendix.*]
mer·chant·a·ble (mûr′chənt-ə-bəl) *adj.* Suitable for buying and selling; marketable.
mer·chant·man (mûr′chənt-mən) *n., pl.* **-men** (-mən). **1.** A ship used in commerce. **2.** *Archaic.* A merchant.
merchant marine. 1. A nation's ships that are engaged in commerce. **2.** The personnel of such ships.
Mer·ci·a (mûr′shē-ə, -shə). An Anglo-Saxon kingdom extending over most of central England from the middle of the seventh to the late eighth century. [Medieval Latin, from Old English *Mierce,* the Mercians, "men of the border" (i.e., the Anglo-Saxon border with Wales). See **merg-** in Appendix.*]
Mer·ci·an (mûr′shē-ən, -shən) *n.* **1.** A native or inhabitant of Mercia. **2.** The dialect of Old English used in Mercia. —**Mer′ci·an** *adj.*
mer·ci·ful (mûr′sĭ-fəl) *adj.* Full of mercy; compassionate; lenient: *"for I am merciful, saith the Lord"* (Jeremiah 3:12). —**mer′ci·ful·ly** *adv.* —**mer′ci·ful·ness** *n.*
mer·ci·less (mûr′sĭ-lĭs) *adj.* Having no mercy; pitiless; cruel: *"the most merciless of all the wars"* (Winston Churchill). —**mer′ci·less·ly** *adv.* —**mer′ci·less·ness** *n.*
mer·cu·ri·al (mər-kyŏŏr′ē-əl) *n.* A medical or chemical preparation containing mercury. —*adj.* **1.** *Usually capital* **M.** Of or pertaining to the Roman god Mercury or the planet Mercury. **2.** Having the characteristics of eloquence, shrewdness, swiftness, and thievishness attributed to the god Mercury in Roman mythology. **3.** Containing or caused by the action of the element mercury. **4.** Being quick and changeable in character: *a mercurial temperament.* [Latin *mercuriālis,* from *Mercurius,* the god MERCURY.] —**mer·cu′ri·al·ly** *adv.*
mer·cu·ri·al·ism (mər-kyŏŏr′ē-əl-ĭz′əm) *n.* Poisoning caused by mercury or its compounds. Also called "hydrargyrism."
mer·cu·ric (mər-kyŏŏr′ĭk) *adj. Chemistry.* Pertaining to or containing bivalent mercury.
mercuric chloride. A poisonous white crystalline compound, $HgCl_2$, used as an antiseptic and disinfectant and in insecticides, preservatives, and batteries, and in metallurgy and photography. Also called "corrosive sublimate."
mercuric sulfide. A poisonous compound, HgS, having two forms: **a.** *Black mercuric sulfide,* a black powder obtained from mercury salts or by the reaction of mercury with sulfur, used as a pigment. **b.** *Red mercuric sulfide,* a bright scarlet powder derived from heating mercury with sulfur, used as a pigment. In this form, also called "artificial cinnabar," "vermilion."
Mer·cu·ro·chrome (mər-kyŏŏr′ə-krōm′) *n.* A trademark for a solution of **merbromin** *(see),* used as an antiseptic.
mer·cu·rous (mər-kyŏŏr′əs, mûr′kyə-rəs) *adj. Chemistry.* Pertaining to or containing monovalent mercury.
Mer·cu·ry (mûr′kyə-rē). *Roman Mythology.* A god, often identified with the Greek god **Hermes** *(see),* serving as messenger to the other gods and being the god of commerce, travel, and thievery. [Middle English *Mercurie,* from Middle Latin *Mercurius,* the god, the planet, from Latin. See **merc-** in Appendix.*]

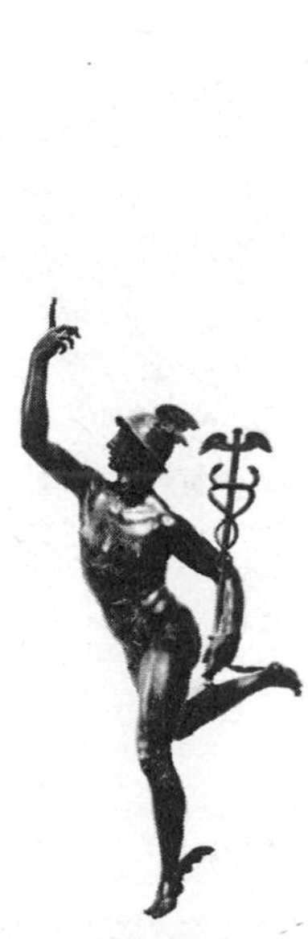

Mercury
Sixteenth-century statue by Giovanni Bologna

mer·cu·ry (mûr′kyə-rē) *n., pl.* **-ries. 1.** Symbol **Hg** A silvery-white poisonous metallic element, liquid at room temperature. It is used in thermometers, barometers, vapor lamps, and batteries, and in the preparation of chemical pesticides. Atomic number 80, atomic weight 200.59, melting point −38.87°C, boiling point 356.58°C, specific gravity 13.546, valences 1, 2. Also called "quicksilver." See **element. 2.** Temperature. A figurative use from the mercury in some thermometers. **3.** Any of several weedy plants of the genera *Mercurialis* or *Acalypha.* See **dog's mercury. 4.** The smallest of the planets and the one nearest the Sun, having a sidereal period of revolution about the Sun of 88.0 days at a mean distance of 36.2 million miles, a mean radius of approximately 1,500 miles, and a mass approximately 0.05 that of Earth. See **solar system.** [Middle English *Mercurie,* god, planet, metal, and plant (after Greek *Hermou poa,* "herb of Hermes"), from Medieval Latin *Mercurius,* MERCURY.]
mer·cu·ry-va·por lamp (mûr′kyə-rē-vā′pər). A lamp in which ultraviolet and yellowish-green to blue visible light is produced by an electric discharge through mercury vapor. It is used as a source of ultraviolet light and for outdoor lighting.
mer·cy (mûr′sē) *n., pl.* **-cies. 1.** Kind and compassionate treatment of an offender, enemy, prisoner, or other person under one's power; clemency. **2.** A disposition to be kind and forgiving: *I threw myself on his mercy.* **3.** Something for which to be thankful; a fortunate occurrence: *It's a mercy he survived.* **4.** Alleviation of distress; relief: *Her death was a mercy.* [Middle English *merci,* from Old French *merci,* compassion, forbearance (to someone in one's power), from Late Latin *merces,* reward, God's gratuitous compassion, from Latin *mercēs,* pay, reward. See **merc-** in Appendix.*]
Synonyms: *mercy, leniency, clemency, forbearance, charity. Mercy* emphasizes compassion in a general way; it suggests reprieve from a fate of considerable severity, without further implication. *Leniency* applies to a specific act of indulgence. *Clemency* is usually applied to a specific act of a person or agency charged with administering justice; the recipient therefore is considered an offender. *Forbearance,* especially in its legal sense, is allied to *clemency* in denoting the act of foregoing the execution of a right. *Charity,* in this context, is a nonspecific term denoting benevolence.
mercy killing. Euthanasia.
mercy seat. 1. The golden covering of the ark of the covenant regarded as the resting place of God. Exodus 25:12–22. Also called "propitiatory." **2.** The throne of God.
mere[1] (mîr) *adj.* Superlative **merest. 1.** Being nothing more than what is specified: *"His fee was a mere twenty guineas."* (Peter Quennell). **2.** *Archaic.* Pure; unadulterated. [Latin *merus,* clear, pure, unmixed. See **mer-**[1] in Appendix.*]
mere[2] (mîr) *n.* A small lake, pond, or marsh. [Middle English *mere,* Old English *mere,* sea, lake. See **mori-** in Appendix.*]
mere[3] (mîr) *n. Archaic.* A boundary. [Middle English *mere,* Old English *mǣre, gemǣre,* boundary. See **mei-**[3] in Appendix.*]
-mere, -mer. *Zoology.* Indicates a part or segment; for example, **blastomere, elastomer.** [French *-mere,* from Greek *meros,* a part. See **smer-**[2] in Appendix.*]
Mer·e·dith (mĕr′ə-dĭth), **George.** 1828–1909. English writer.
mere·ly (mîr′lē) *adv.* **1.** Nothing more than what is specified; only: *"Although he seems so firm to us / He is merely flesh and blood."* (T.S. Eliot). **2.** *Obsolete.* Absolutely; completely.
mer·e·tri·cious (mĕr′ə-trĭsh′əs) *adj.* **1.** Pertaining to or resembling a prostitute. **2. a.** Attracting attention in a vulgar manner: *meretricious ornamentation.* **b.** Lacking sincerity: *a meretricious argument.* [Latin *meritricius,* from *meretrix,* a prostitute, from *merere,* to earn pay. See **smer-**[2] in Appendix.*] —**mer′e·tri′cious·ly** *adv.* —**mer′e·tri′cious·ness** *n.*
mer·gan·ser (mər-găn′sər) *n.* Any fish-eating duck of the genus *Mergus,* having a slim, hooked bill. Also called "sheldrake." See **hooded merganser.** [New Latin *merganser,* "diver-goose" : Latin *mergus,* diver (bird) (see **mezg-**[1] in Appendix*) + *anser,* goose (see **ghans-** in Appendix*).]

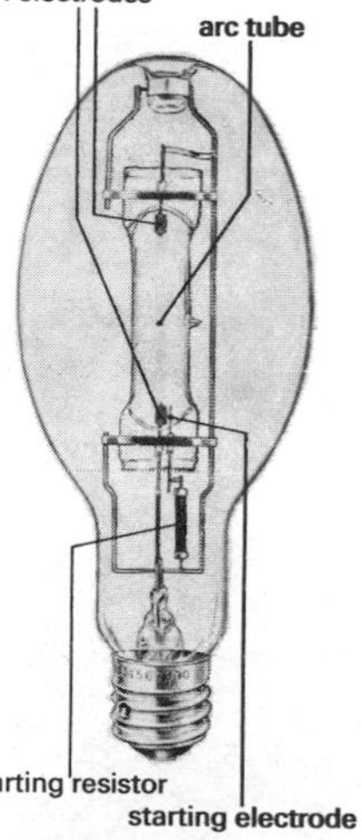
main electrodes
arc tube
starting resistor
starting electrode

mercury-vapor lamp

merge (mûrj) *v.* **merged, merging, merges.** —*tr.* To cause to be absorbed so as to lose identity. —*intr.* To blend together so as to lose identity: *"By slow degrees our sickness and dizziness and*

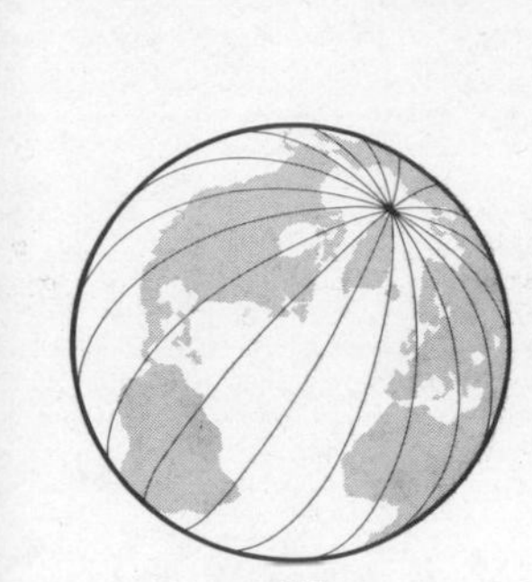

meridian
Earth encircled by meridians

horror become merged in a cloud of unnamable feeling." (Poe). —See Synonyms at **mix.** [From Latin *mergere,* to dive, plunge. See **mezg-**[1] in Appendix.*] —**mer'gence** *n.*

merg·er (mûr'jər) *n.* **1.** The union of two or more commercial interests or corporations. **2.** *Law.* The absorption of a lesser estate, liability, right, action, or offense into a greater one.

Mer·gui Archipelago (mər-gwē'). An island group in the Andaman Sea off the west coast of Burma.

Mé·ri·da (mā'rē-*th*ä). The capital of Yucatán, Mexico. Population, 187,000.

me·rid·i·an (mə-rĭd'ē-ən) *n. Abbr.* **M., m., mer. 1.** *Geography.* **a.** A great circle on the earth's surface passing through both geophysical poles. **b.** Either half of such a great circle lying between the poles. **2.** *Astronomy.* A great circle passing through the two poles of the celestial sphere and the observer's zenith; the celestial meridian. **3.** *Mathematics.* **a.** A curve on a surface of revolution, formed by the intersection of a plane containing the axis of revolution with the surface. **b.** A plane section of a surface of revolution containing the axis of revolution. **4.** The highest point or stage of development of anything; zenith: *"Men come to their meridian at various periods of their lives."* (J.H. Newman). **5.** *Obsolete.* Noon. —**me·rid'i·an** *adj.* [Middle English *meridien,* noon, meridian circle, from Old French, from Latin *merīdiānus,* from *merīdiēs,* midday, dissimulated variant of *medidiēs* : *medius,* middle (see **medhyo-** in Appendix*) + *diēs,* day (see **deiw-** in Appendix*).]

me·rid·i·o·nal (mə-rĭd'ē-ə-nəl) *adj.* **1.** Of or pertaining to a meridian. **2.** Characteristic of southern areas or people. **3.** Located in the south; southerly. —*n.* An inhabitant of a southern region, especially of France. [Middle English, from Old French *meridionel,* from Late Latin *merīdiōnālis,* variant extension of Latin *merīdiānus,* MERIDIAN.]

Mé·ri·mée (mā'rē-mā'), **Prosper.** 1803–1870. French novelist.

me·ringue (mə-răng') *n.* **1.** A topping for pastry or pies made of beaten and baked egg whites. **2.** A small pastry shell or cake made of meringue, often containing fruit or nutmeats. [French *méringue*†.]

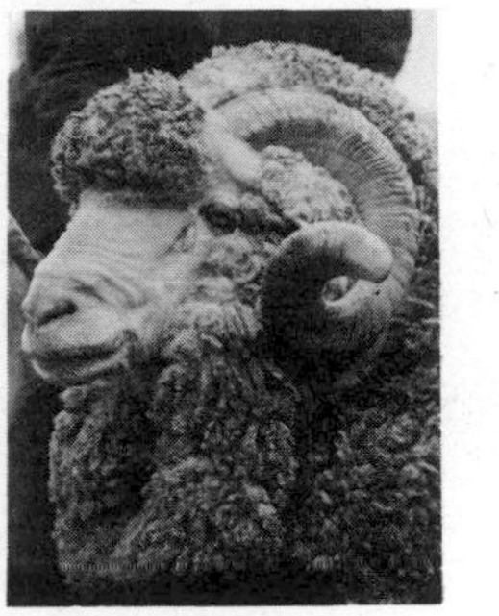

merino

me·ri·no (mə-rē'nō) *n., pl.* **-nos. 1. a.** A sheep of a breed originally from Spain. **b.** The fine wool of this sheep. **2.** A soft, lightweight fabric made originally of merino wool but now of any fine wool. **3. a.** A type of fine wool and cotton yarn used for knitting underwear, hosiery, and other articles of apparel. **b.** A knitted fabric made from merino yarn. —*adj.* Made of merino yarn, wool, or cloth. [Spanish, from Berber *Benī Merīn,* name of the tribe that developed the breed.]

Mer·i·on·eth·shire (mĕr'ē-ŏn'ĭth-shîr). Also **Mer·i·on·eth.** A county of Wales occupying 600 square miles in the northwest. Population, 39,000. County seat, Dolgellau.

mer·i·stem (mĕr'ə-stĕm') *n. Botany.* The growing point or area of rapidly dividing cells at the tip of a stem, root, or branch. [From Greek *meristos,* divided, divisible, from *merizein,* to divide, from *meris,* a division, part. See **smer-**[2] in Appendix.*]

me·ris·tic (mə-rĭs'tĭk) *adj. Biology.* **1.** Made up of segments, as some worms. **2.** Modified by changes in the number or placement of entire body parts, as contrasted with modification by gradual change of the entire organism. [From Greek *meristos,* divided, divisible. See **meristem.**]

mer·it (mĕr'ĭt) *n.* **1.** Value, excellence, or superior quality: *a play of merit.* **2.** An aspect of a person's character or behavior deserving approval or disapproval: *to each according to his merits.* **3.** *Theology.* Spiritual credit granted for good works. **4.** *Plural. Law.* **a.** A party's strict legal rights, excluding jurisdictional or technical aspects. **b.** The factual substance of a case as distinguished from its form and procedural aspects. **5.** The intrinsic right or wrong of any matter; the actual facts of a matter. —*v.* **merited, -iting, -its.** —*tr.* **1.** To earn; deserve; warrant: *"How can the unknown merit reverence?"* (Harold Pinter). **2.** *Theology.* To have the right to claim (a divine reward). —*intr. Theology.* To gain merit. [Middle English, from Old French *merite,* that which is deserved, from Latin *meritum,* recompense, desert, from *merēre* (past participle *meritus*), to earn, deserve. See **smer-**[2] in Appendix.*] —**mer'it·ed·ly** *adv.*

mer·i·to·ri·ous (mĕr'ə-tôr'ē-əs, -tōr'ē-əs) *adj.* Deserving reward or praise; having merit. [Latin *meritōrius,* earning money, from *merēre* (past participle *meritus*), to earn, MERIT.] —**mer'i·to'ri·ous·ly** *adv.*

merit system. In the U.S. Civil Service, a system of appointing and promoting personnel on the basis of merit, determined by competitive examinations. Compare **spoils system.**

merle (mûrl) *n.* Also **merl.** The European blackbird, *Turdus merula.* See **blackbird.** [Middle English, from Old French *merle,* from Latin *merulus, merula,* blackbird. See **ames-** in Appendix.*]

Merle (mûrl). A masculine or feminine given name. [French, probably from *merle,* blackbird, from Old French, MERLE.]

mer·lin (mûr'lĭn) *n. Falconry.* The **pigeon hawk** *(see).* [Middle English *meriloun,* from Norman French *merilun,* from Old French *esmerillon, esmeril,* merlin, from Old High German *smiril*†.]

Mer·lin (mûr'lən). In Arthurian legend, a magician and prophet serving as counselor to King Arthur.

mer·lon (mûr'lən) *n.* The solid portion of a crenelated wall between two open spaces. [French, from Italian *merlone,* from *merlo,* blackbird, battlement (probably from ranks of blackbirds perched on castle walls), from Latin *merulus, merula,* blackbird. See **ames-** in Appendix.*]

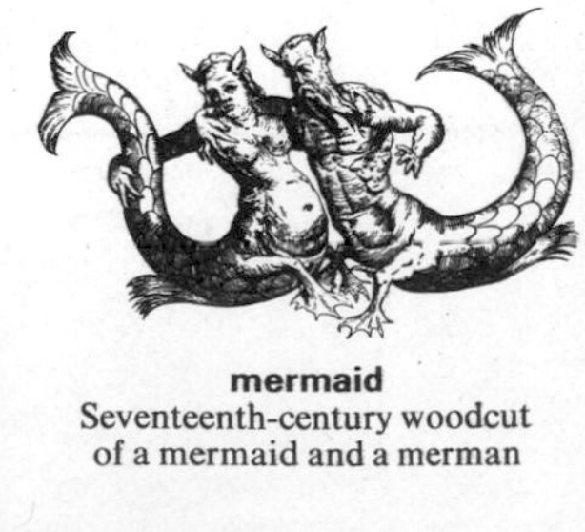

mermaid
Seventeenth-century woodcut of a mermaid and a merman

mer·maid (mûr'mād') *n.* A fabled creature of the sea with the head and upper body of a woman and the tail of a fish. [Middle English *meremaide* : MERE (sea) + MAID.]

mer·man (mûr'măn', -mən) *n., pl.* **-men** (-mĕn', -mĭn). A fabled creature of the sea with the head and upper body of a man and the tail of a fish. [After MERMAID.]

mero-. Indicates parts or segments; for example, **meroblastic, merocrine.** [New Latin, from Greek *meros,* part, division. See **smer-**[2] in Appendix.*]

mer·o·blas·tic (mĕr'ə-blăs'tĭk) *adj. Biology.* Undergoing partial cleavage. Said of an egg with a large yolk. Compare **holoblastic.** [MERO- + -BLASTIC.] —**mer'o·blas'ti·cal·ly** *adv.*

mer·o·crine (mĕr'ə-krĭn, -krīn', -krēn') *adj.* Of or pertaining to a gland the cells of which remain intact during secretion. Compare **holocrine.** [Literally, "partly separating" (referring to the cells) : MERO- + Greek *krinein,* to separate (see **skeri-** in Appendix*).]

Mer·o·ë (mĕr'ō-ē'). The ruined capital of Cush (ancient Ethiopia) on the Nile about 50 miles east of Khartoum, Sudan.

Me·rom, Waters of. See **Hula, Lake.**

Mer·o·pe[1] (mĕr'ə-pē'). *Greek Mythology.* One of the **Pleiades** *(see),* who, after marrying a mortal, hid her face in shame.

Mer·o·pe[2] (mĕr'ə-pē') *n.* The seventh star in the Pleiades cluster and the only one not visible to the naked eye.

me·ro·pi·a (mə-rō'pē-ə) *n.* Partial blindness. [New Latin : MER(O)- + -OPIA.] —**me·ro'pic** (mə-rō'pĭk, -rŏp'ĭk) *adj.*

-merous. *Biology.* Having (a specified number or kind of) parts; for example, **pentamerous.** [New Latin *-merus,* from Greek *-meres,* from *meros,* a part. See **smer-**[2] in Appendix.*]

Mer·o·vin·gi·an (mĕr'ə-vĭn'jē-ən, -jən) *adj.* Of or pertaining to the first dynasty of Frankish kings that ruled over Gaul from about A.D. 500 until A.D. 751. —*n.* A member of the first dynasty of Frankish kings. [French *mérovingien,* from Medieval Latin *Merovingī,* "the descendants of Merovaeus," from Frankish *Merowig,* the eponymous ancestor.]

mer·o·zo·ite (mĕr'ə-zō'īt') *n.* A cell produced by fission of a sporozoan. [MERO- + ZO- + -ITE.]

Mer·ri·mack[1] (mĕr'ə-măk') *n.* A frigate captured from Union forces by the Confederacy during the Civil War, fitted with iron plating, and used under the name *Virginia* against the Union's **Monitor** *(see)* at Hampton Roads on March 9, 1862.

Mer·ri·mack[2] (mĕr'ə-măk'). Also **Mer·ri·mac.** A river rising in central New Hampshire and flowing about 110 miles through northeastern Massachusetts to the Atlantic Ocean.

mer·ri·ment (mĕr'ĭ-mənt) *n.* Gay conviviality; hilarity. See Synonyms at **mirth.**

mer·ry (mĕr'ē) *adj.* **-rier, -riest. 1.** Full of high-spirited gaiety; jolly: *"the merry Greek, tart Aristophanes"* (Ben Jonson). **2.** Marked by or offering fun and gaiety; festive. **3.** Pleasurable; delightful; entertaining. —See Synonyms at **jolly.** [Middle English *merie,* Old English *mirige,* pleasant. See **mreghu-** in Appendix.*] —**mer'ri·ly** *adv.* —**mer'ri·ness** *n.*

mer·ry-an·drew (mĕr'ē-ăn'drōō) *n.* A prankster, jester, or clown. [Original reference unknown.]

mer·ry-bells (mĕr'ē-bĕlz') *n.* Plural in form, sometimes used as the singular. A plant, the **bellwort** *(see).*

mer·ry-go-round (mĕr'ē-gō-round') *n.* **1.** A circular platform fitted with seats, often in the form of wooden animals, revolved mechanically, usually to music, and ridden for amusement. **2.** A piece of playground equipment consisting of a small circular platform that revolves when pushed or pedaled. **3.** Any whirl or swift round: *a merry-go-round of parties.*

mer·ry·mak·ing (mĕr'ē-mā'kĭng) *n.* **1.** Participation in a revel. **2.** A festivity; revelry. —**mer'ry·mak'er** *n.*

mer·ry·thought (mĕr'ē-thôt') *n. Archaic.* A wishbone.

Mer·sey (mûr'zē). A river rising in northwestern England and flowing 70 miles northwest to Liverpool. [Middle English *Merse,* Old English *Mǣresēa,* "boundary-river" (i.e., between Mercia and Northumbria) : *mǣre,* boundary (see **mei-**[3] in Appendix*) + *ēa,* river (see **akwa-** in Appendix*).]

Mer·thi·o·late (mər-thī'ə-lāt') *n. Pharmacology.* A trademark for **thimerosal** *(see).*

Mer·thyr Tyd·fil (mûr'thər tĭd'vĭl'). A borough of southern Wales, about 20 miles northwest of Cardiff. Population, 58,000.

Mer·ton (mûrt'n). A borough of London, England, comprising the former administrative divisions of Merton and Morden, Mitcham, and Wimbledon. Population, 189,000.

me·sa (mā'sə) *n.* A flat-topped elevation with one or more clifflike sides, common in the southwestern United States. [Spanish, from Old Spanish, from Latin *mēnsa*†, table.]

Me·sa·bi Range (mə-sä'bē). A narrow range of low hills in Minnesota, noted for vast deposits of iron ore and taconite.

mé·sal·li·ance (mā-zăl'ē-əns; *French* mā-zà-lyäNs') *n.* A marriage with a person of inferior social position. [French : *més-,* MIS- + *alliance,* ALLIANCE.]

Me·sa Ver·de National Park (mā'sə vûrd', vĕr'dē). An area of about 80 square miles in southwestern Colorado, noted for its ruins of prehistoric cliff dwellings.

mes·cal (mĕs-kăl') *n.* **1.** A spineless, globe-shaped cactus, *Lophophora williamsii,* of Mexico and the southwestern United States, having buttonlike tubercles that are dried and chewed as a drug by certain Indian tribes. Also called "peyote." See **mescaline. 2.** A Mexican liquor distilled from the fermented juice of certain species of **agave** *(see).* **3.** A plant, **maguey** *(see).* [Spanish *mescal, mezcal, mexcal,* from Nahuatl *mexcalli.*]

mes·ca·line (mĕs'kə-lēn') *n.* An alkaloid drug, $(CH_3O)_3C_6H_2(CH_2CH_2NH_2)$, that produces hallucinations and other psychedelic effects. [MESCAL + -INE.]

Mes·dames. *Abbr.* **Mmes.** Plural of **Madame** or **Madam.**

Mes·de·moi·selles. *Abbr.* **Mlles.** Plural of **Mademoiselle.**

ă pat/ā pay/âr care/ä father/b bib/ch church/d deed/ĕ pet/ē be/f fife/g gag/h hat/hw which/ĭ pit/ī pie/îr pier/j judge/k kick/l lid, needle/m mum/n no, sudden/ng thing/ŏ pot/ō toe/ô paw, for/oi noise/ou out/ōō took/ōō boot/p pop/r roar/s sauce/sh ship, dish/

mes·en·ceph·a·lon (mĕs′ĕn-sĕf′ə-lŏn′) *n.* Also **mes·o·ceph·a·lon** (mĕs′ō-). The middle section of the embryonic brain. Also called "midbrain." See **brain.** [New Latin : MES(O)- + ENCEPHALON.] —**mes′en·ce·phal′ic** (-sə-făl′ĭk) *adj.*

mes·en·chyme (mĕs′ən-kīm′) *n.* Also **mes·en·chy·ma** (mĕs-ĕng′kĭ-mə). The part of the embryonic mesoderm from which develop connective tissue, skeletal tissue, and the circulatory and lymphatic systems. [German *Mesenchym* : MESO- + ENCHYMA.] —**mes·en′chy·mal** (mĕs-ĕng′kĭ-məl, mĕz-), **mes′en·chym′a·tous** (mĕs′ən-kĭm′ə-təs, mĕz′-) *adj.*

mes·en·ter·i·tis (mĕs-ĕn′tə-rī′tĭs) *n.* Inflammation of the mesentery. [New Latin : *mesenterium,* MESENTERY + -ITIS.]

mes·en·ter·on (mĕs-ĕn′tə-rŏn′) *n. Biology.* **1.** The embryonic intestinal cavity, the **midgut** *(see).* **2.** The middle section of the gastrovascular cavity in anthozoans. [New Latin : MES(O)- + ENTERON.] —**mes·en′ter·on′ic** *adj.*

mes·en·ter·y (mĕs′ən-tĕr′ē) *n., pl.* **-ies.** Also **mes·en·ter·i·um** (mĕs′ən-tîr′ē-əm) *pl.* **-ia** (-ē-ə). Any of several peritoneal folds that connect the intestines to the dorsal abdominal wall. [New Latin *mesenterium,* from Greek *mesenterion, mesenteron* : *mes(o)-,* middle + *enteron,* ENTERON.]

mesh (mĕsh) *n.* **1.** Any of the open spaces in a cord, thread, or wire network. **2.** *Usually plural.* The cords, threads, or wires surrounding these spaces. **3.** A net or network. **4.** Something that snares or entraps: *"Arabia had become entangled in the meshes of . . . politics."* (W. Montgomery Watt). **5.** *Machinery.* The engagement of gear teeth. —**in mesh.** In gear. —*v.* **meshed, meshing, meshes.** —*tr.* **1.** To entangle or ensnare. **2.** To cause (gear teeth) to become engaged. **3.** To cause to work closely together. —*intr.* **1.** To be or become entangled. **2.** To be or become engaged or interlocked, as gear teeth. **3. a.** To coordinate or fit harmoniously and effectively: *" 'I just couldn't seem to mesh with the job,' he says."* (New York Times). **b.** To accord with another; harmonize. [Earlier *meash, mash,* from Middle Dutch *masche, maesche.* See **mezg-²** in Appendix.*] —**mesh′y** *adj.*

Me·shach (mē′shăk′). A Hebrew captive who, with Shadrach and Abednego, miraculously escaped death in Nebuchadnezzar's fiery furnace. Daniel 3.

Me·shed (mə-shĕd′). Also **Mesh·hed.** Iranian **Mash·had** (mä-shäd′). A city of Iran, a trade center in the extreme northeast. Population, 312,000.

mesh·work (mĕsh′wûrk′) *n.* Meshes; network.

me·si·al (mē′zē-əl, mĕz′ē-, mē′zhəl, mĕs′ē-əl) *adj.* Of, in, near, or toward the middle. [MES(O)- + -IAL.] —**me′si·al·ly** *adv.*

me·sit·y·lene (mə-sĭt′ə-lēn′) *n.* A hydrocarbon, $(CH_3)_3C_6H_3$, occurring in petroleum and coal tar and synthesized from acetone. [MESITYL(OXIDE) + -ENE.]

mes·i·tyl oxide (mĕs′ə-tĭl). An oily liquid, $(CH_3)_2C{:}CHCOCH_3$, obtained from acetones and used as a solvent and insect repellent. [From Greek *mesitēs,* mediator, from *mesos,* middle (see **medhyo-** in Appendix*) + -YL.]

mes·mer·ism (mĕz′mə-rĭz′əm) *n.* Hypnotism as practiced by F.A. Mesmer. See **animal magnetism.** [After Franz Anton *Mesmer* (1734–1815), Austrian physician.] —**mes·mer′ic** (mĕz-mĕr′ĭk) *adj.*

mes·mer·ize (mĕz′mə-rīz′, mĕs′-) *tr.v.* **-ized, -izing, -izes. 1.** To hypnotize. **2.** To enthrall: *"He could mesmerize an audience by the sheer force of his presence."* (Justin Kaplan). —**mes′mer·iz′er** *n.*

mesne (mēn) *adj. Law.* Intermediate; intervening. [Middle English, from Norman French *mesne, meen,* from Old French *meien,* from Latin *mediānus,* median, from *medius,* middle. See **medhyo-** in Appendix.*]

mesne lord. A feudal lord intermediate between a superior lord and his own vassals or tenants.

meso–, mes–. Indicates middle, center, or intermediate; for example, **mesoblast, mesoderm.** [Greek, from *mesos,* middle. See **medhyo-** in Appendix.*]

mes·o·blast (mĕz′ə-blăst′, mĕs′-) *n.* The middle germinal layer of the embryo; the mesoderm in its early stage of development. [MESO- + -BLAST.] —**mes′o·blas′tic** *adj.*

mes·o·carp (mĕz′ə-kärp′, mĕs′-) *n. Botany.* The middle, usually fleshy layer of a **pericarp** *(see).* [MESO- + -CARP.]

mes·o·ceph·a·lon. Variant of **mesencephalon.**

mes·o·derm (mĕz′ə-dûrm′, mĕs′-) *n.* The embryonic germ layer, lying between the ectoderm and the endoderm, from which develop connective tissue, muscles, and the urogenital and vascular systems. [MESO- + -DERM.] —**mes′o·der′mal, mes′o·der′mic** *adj.*

Mes·o·lith·ic (mĕz′ə-lĭth′ĭk, mĕs′-) *adj. Archaeology.* Designating the cultural period between the Paleolithic and Neolithic Ages, marked by the appearance of the bow and of cutting tools. Also "Miolithic." —*n. Archaeology.* The Mesolithic Age. Preceded by *the.* [MESO- + -LITHIC.]

mes·o·morph (mĕz′ə-môrf′, mĕs′-) *n.* A human body characterized by powerful musculature and a predominantly bony framework. Compare **ectomorph, endomorph.** [MESO- + -MORPH.]

mes·o·mor·phic (mĕz′ə-môr′fĭk, mĕs′-) *adj.* **1.** Also **mes·o·mor·phous** (-fəs). Of, pertaining to, or existing in a state of matter intermediate between liquid and crystal. **2.** Of or pertaining to a mesomorph. —**mes′o·mor′phy** *n.*

mes·on (mĕz′ŏn′, mē′zŏn′, mĕs′ŏn′, mē′sŏn′) *n. Physics.* Any of several subatomic particles, having integral spins and masses generally intermediate between leptons and baryons. See **particle.** Formerly called "mesotron." [MES(O)- + -ON.] —**me·son′ic** (mĕ-zŏn′ĭk, mē-, -sŏn′ĭk) *adj.*

mes·o·neph·ros (mĕz′ə-nĕf′rŏs, -rŏs′, mĕs′-) *n.* The midpart of the embryonic excretory system in vertebrates that becomes the functioning kidney in fish and amphibians. Also called "Wolffian body." Compare **metanephros, pronephros.** [New Latin : MESO- + Greek *nephros,* kidney (see **negwhro-** in Appendix*).] —**mes′o·neph′ric** *adj.*

mes·o·pause (mĕz′ə-pôz′, mĕs′-) *n.* The atmospheric zone, about 50 miles above the earth, forming the upper limit of the mesosphere. [MESO- + PAUSE.]

mes·o·phyll (mĕz′ə-fĭl′, mĕs′-) *n.* The soft tissue of a leaf, between the top and bottom epidermis. [New Latin *mesophyllum* : MESO- + -PHYLL.] —**mes′o·phyl′lic, mes′o·phyl′lous** *adj.*

mes·o·phyte (mĕz′ə-fīt′, mĕs′-) *n.* A land plant that grows in an environment having a moderate amount of moisture. Compare **xerophyte, hydrophyte.** [MESO- + -PHYTE.] —**mes′o·phyt′ic** (-fĭt′ĭk) *adj.*

Mes·o·po·ta·mi·a (mĕs′ə-pə-tā′mē-ə). The ancient country between the Tigris and Euphrates rivers. [Latin, from Greek *Mesopotamia (khōra),* "(the land) between (two) rivers" : *mesos,* middle (see **medhyo-** in Appendix*) + *potamos,* river (see **pet-¹** in Appendix*).] —**Mes′o·po·ta′mi·an** *adj.* & *n.*

mes·o·sphere (mĕz′ə-sfîr′, mĕs′-) *n.* The portion of the atmosphere from about 20 to 50 miles above the earth, characterized by a temperature range that decreases from 50°F to −130°F with increasing altitude. See **atmosphere.** [MESO- + -SPHERE.] —**mes′o·spher′ic** (-sfîr′ĭk, -sfĕr′ĭk) *adj.*

mes·o·the·li·um (mĕz′ə-thē′lē-əm, mĕs′-) *n., pl.* **-lia** (-lē-ə). **1.** The layer of flat cells lining the embryonic body cavity. **2.** A layer of squamous cells of the epithelium lining the peritoneum, pericardium, and pleura. [New Latin : MESO- + (EPI)THELIUM.] —**mes′o·the′li·al** *adj.*

mes·o·tho·rax (mĕz′ə-thôr′ăks, -thōr′ăks, mĕs′-) *n., pl.* **-raxes** or **-thoraces** (-thôr′ə-sēz′, -thōr′ə-sēz′). The midsection of an insect's thoracic region, bearing the middle legs and the rear wings. [New Latin : MESO- + THORAX.]

mes·o·tho·ri·um (mĕz′ə-thôr′ē-əm, -thōr′ē-əm, mĕs′-) *n.* Either of two decay products of thorium: **a.** mesothorium I, an isotope of radium. **b.** mesothorium II, an isotope of actinium. [New Latin : MESO- + THORIUM.]

mes·o·tron (mĕz′ə-trŏn′, mĕs′-) *n. Physics.* An obsolete term for **meson** *(see).* [MESO- + (ELEC)TRON.]

Mes·o·zo·ic (mĕz′ə-zō′ĭk, mĕs′-) *adj.* Of, belonging to, or designating the third era of geologic time, which includes the Cretaceous, Jurassic, and Triassic periods, and is characterized by the predominance of reptilian life forms. See **geology.** —*n.* Preceded by *the.* The Mesozoic era. [MESO- + -ZOIC.]

mes·quite (mĕs-kēt′, mə-skēt′) *n.* Also **mes·quit.** Any of several shrubs or small trees of the genus *Prosopis;* especially, *P. juliflora,* of the southwestern United States and Mexico. Its pods are used as forage. Also called "algarroba," "honey locust." See **screw bean.** [Spanish *mezquite,* from Nahuatl *mizquitl.*]

mess (mĕs) *n.* **1.** A disorderly accumulation of items. **2.** A cluttered, untidy, usually dirty state or condition. **3. a.** A disturbing, confusing, and troublesome state of affairs; muddle. **b.** Senseless confusion and discontinuity; chaos. **4.** An amount of food for a meal, course, or dish: *"at their savory dinner set / Of herbs, and other country messes"* (Milton). **5.** A serving of soft, semiliquid food. **6.** A distasteful and unappetizing concoction. **7.** An amount or number acquired, usually of something edible: *a mess of fish.* **8. a.** A group of persons, usually in the military, who regularly eat meals together. **b.** The place where such meals are served. **c.** A meal eaten there. —*v.* **messed, messing, messes.** —*tr.* **1.** To make disorderly and soiled; clutter. Often used with *up: messed up the kitchen with pots and pans.* **2.** To bungle, mismanage, or botch. Usually used with *up: He messed up the test.* **3.** *Slang.* To be rough with; manhandle. Usually used with *up: a mugger messing up his victim.* —*intr.* **1.** To cause or make a mess. **2.** To interfere; meddle. **3.** To take a meal in a military mess. —**mess around (or about).** *Informal.* To occupy time by puttering or tinkering; work aimlessly: *"there is nothing . . . half so much worth doing as simply messing about in boats"* (Kenneth Grahame). [Middle English *mes,* course of a meal, dish of food, group of messmates, from Old French, from Latin *missus,* "placement," course of a meal, from *mittere* (past participle *missus*), to send, place, put. See **smeit-** in Appendix.*]

mes·sage (mĕs′ĭj) *n. Abbr.* **msg. 1.** A communication transmitted by spoken or written words, by signals, or by other means from one person or group to another. **2.** A statement made or read before a gathering: *a farewell message.* **3.** The basic theme or significance of something: *"the life of Britain, her message, and her glory"* (Winston Churchill). [Middle English, from Old French, from Vulgar Latin *missāticum* (unattested), "something sent," "a communication," from Latin *mittere* (past participle *missus*), to send. See **smeit-** in Appendix.*]

mes·sa·line (mĕs′ə-lēn′) *n.* A lightweight, soft, shiny silk cloth with a twilled or satin weave. [French *messaline*†.]

Mes·sei·gneurs. Plural of **Monseigneur.**

mes·sen·ger (mĕs′ən-jər) *n.* **1.** One who is charged with transmitting messages or performing errands: **a.** A person employed to carry telegrams, letters, or parcels. **b.** A military or other official dispatch bearer; courier. **c.** An angel: *Gabriel, messenger of the Annunciation.* **d.** An envoy; especially, a chosen prophet: *a messenger of Allah.* **2.** A bearer of news: *"Strange faces come through the streets to me/like messengers"* (Archibald MacLeish). **3.** *Archaic.* A forerunner; harbinger. **4.** *Nautical.* A chain or rope used for hauling in a cable. [Middle English *messager, messanger,* from Old French *messagier,* from *message,* MESSAGE.]

messenger RNA. A **ribonucleic acid** *(see)* that carries the

mesquite
Prosopis juliflora

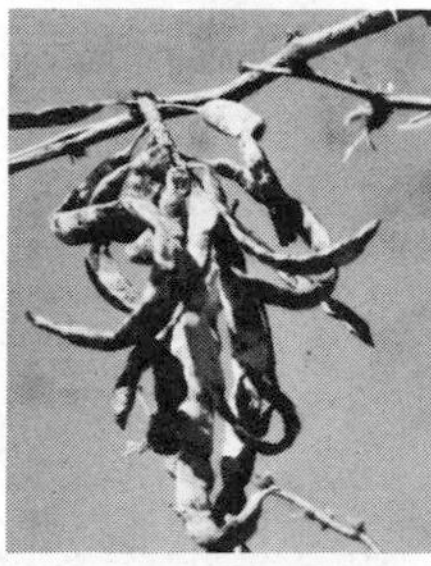

branch with pods

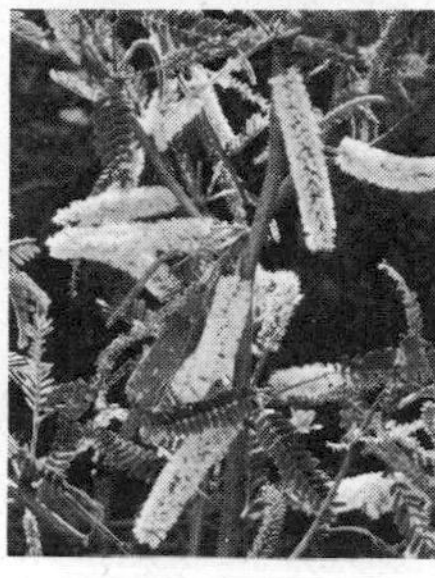

flowers and foliage

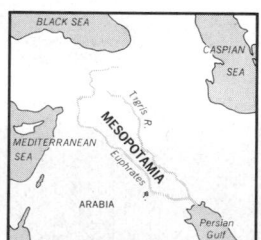

Mesopotamia

genetic information required for protein synthesis in cells. Also called "messenger ribonucleic acid," "mRNA."

Mes·si·ah (mə-sī′ə) n. Also **Mes·si·as** (mə-sī′əs). **1.** Judaism. The anticipated deliverer and king of the Jews. **2.** Jesus Christ. **3.** Small **m.** Any expected deliverer or liberator. [Aramaic məshīḥa or Hebrew māshiaḥ, "the anointed," the Messiah.]

mes·si·an·ic (mĕs′ē-ăn′ĭk) adj. Also **Mes·si·an·ic. 1.** Of or pertaining to a messiah. **2.** Invoking the aura of a messiah.

Mes·sieurs. Abbr. **Messrs., M.M.** Plural of **Monsieur.**

Mes·si·na (mə-sē′nə). A seaport on the extreme northeastern tip of Sicily. Population, 262,000.

Mes·si·na, Strait of (mə-sē′nə). The strait between Sicily and Italy.

mess jacket. A man's fitted, waist-length jacket, worn chiefly on semiformal occasions. Also called "monkey jacket."

mess·mate (mĕs′māt′) n. A person with whom one eats regularly, as in a military or naval mess.

Messrs. 1. Messieurs. **2.** Plural of **Mr.**

mes·suage (mĕs′wĭj) n. Law. A dwelling house with its outbuildings and adjoining lands. [Middle English, from Norman French, household, probably based on a misreading of Old French me(s)nage, MÉNAGE.]

mess·y (mĕs′ē) adj. **-i·er, -i·est.** Like, being in, or causing a mess; untidy; dirty; disordered. —**mess′i·ly** adv. —**mess′i·ness** n.

mes·ti·zo (mĕs-tē′zō) n., pl. **-zos** or **-zoes.** Feminine **mes·ti·za** (-zə). American Spanish & Portuguese. A person of mixed European and Indian ancestry. [Spanish, from mestizo, mixed, from Old Spanish, from Vulgar Latin mixtīcius (unattested), of mixed race, from Latin mixtus, from the past participle of miscēre, to mix. See meik- in Appendix.*]

met. Past tense and past participle of **meet.**

met. 1. metaphor. **2.** metaphysics. **3.** meteorological; meteorology. **4.** metropolitan.

me·ta (mā′tə) adj. Chemistry. **1.** Of, pertaining to, or designating positions in a benzene ring separated by one carbon atom. **2.** Designating closely related, especially isomeric, compounds.

Me·ta (mā′tə; Spanish mā′tä). A river rising in west-central Colombia, flowing 685 miles generally northeast. It forms part of the Colombia-Venezuela border before joining the Orinoco.

meta-, met-. Indicates: **1.** Anatomy. Situated behind; for example, **metacarpus. 2.** Occurring later; for example, **metazoan. 3.** Beyond; transcending; for example, **metalinguistics. 4.** Changed or involving change; for example, **metachromatism. 5.** Alternating; for example, **metagenesis. 6.** Geology. Having undergone metamorphic change. [In borrowed Greek compounds, meta- indicates: **1.** Between, as in **metope; 2.** After, following, as in **method; 3.** Behind, backward, hence reversed, changed, as in **metathesis, metamorphosis; 4.** Intensified action, as in **meteor.** Meta- is the preverbal form of the preposition meta, between, with, beside, after. See me-² in Appendix.*]

met·a·bol·ic (mĕt′ə-bŏl′ĭk) adj. **1.** Biology. Of, pertaining to, or exhibiting metabolism. **2.** Zoology. Of, pertaining to, or undergoing metamorphosis. [Greek metabolikos, changeable, from metabolē, change. See **metabolism.**] —**met′a·bol′i·cal·ly** adv.

me·tab·o·lism (mə-tăb′ə-lĭz′əm) n. Biology. **1.** The complex of physical and chemical processes involved in the maintenance of life. See **anabolism, catabolism. 2.** The functioning of any specific substance within the living body: water metabolism; iodine metabolism. [From Greek metabolē, change, from metaballein, to change : meta (denoting change) + ballein, to throw (see gwel-¹ in Appendix*).]

me·tab·o·lite (mə-tăb′ə-līt′) n. Any of various organic compounds produced by metabolism. [METABOL(ISM) + -ITE.]

me·tab·o·lize (mə-tăb′ə-līz′) v. **-lized, -lizing, -lizes.** —tr. To subject (a substance) to metabolism. —intr. To undergo change by metabolism.

met·a·car·pal (mĕt′ə-kär′pəl) adj. Anatomy. Pertaining to the metacarpus. —n. Anatomy. Any of the bones of the metacarpus.

met·a·car·pus (mĕt′ə-kär′pəs) n. Anatomy. The part of the hand or forefoot that includes the five bones between the phalanges and the carpus. [New Latin : META- (behind) + CARPUS.]

met·a·cen·ter (mĕt′ə-sĕn′tər) n. Also chiefly British **met·a·cen·tre.** The intersection of the verticals through the center of buoyancy of a floating body when in equilibrium and when tilted. This point must be above the center of gravity for stability. —**met′a·cen′tric** (mĕt′ə-sĕn′trĭk) adj.

met·a·chro·ma·tism (mĕt′ə-krō′mə-tĭz′əm) n. A change in color caused by variation of the physical conditions to which a body is subjected, as in heating. [META- (denoting change) + CHROMAT(O)- + -ISM.] —**met′a·chro·mat′ic** (-krō-măt′ĭk) adj.

Met·a·com·et. See King Philip.

met·a·gal·ax·y (mĕt′ə-găl′ək-sē) n., pl. **-ies.** The total physical universe including all galaxies.

met·age (mē′tĭj) n. **1.** The official measurement of weight or contents, as of trucks using state roads. **2.** The fee charged for metage. [From METE (to measure).]

met·a·gen·e·sis (mĕt′ə-jĕn′ə-sĭs) n. Biology. The occurrence in certain organisms of alternating sexual (gametophyte) and asexual (sporophyte) reproductive cycles. Also called "alternation of generations," "digenesis," "heterogenesis." [New Latin : META- + GENESIS.] —**met′a·ge·net′ic** (-jə-nĕt′ĭk) adj.

me·tag·na·thous (mə-tăg′nə-thəs) adj. Ornithology. Having a beak in which the tips of the mandibles cross, as the crossbill. [META- + -GNATHOUS.] —**me·tag′na·thism** n.

met·al (mĕt′l) n. **1.** Symbol **M** Any of a category of electropositive elements that are usually whitish, lustrous, and, in the transition metals, typically ductile and malleable with high tensile strength. Typical metals form salts with nonmetals, basic oxides with oxygen, and alloys with one another. **2.** An alloy of two or more metallic elements. **3.** An object made of metal. **4.** Basic character; mettle. **5.** British. Broken stones used for road surfaces or railroad beds. **6.** Molten glass, especially when used in glassmaking. **7.** Molten cast iron. **8.** Printing. Type made of metal. **9.** Heraldry. Either of the tinctures or (gold) and argent (silver), as distinguished from the colors and the furs. —tr.v. **metaled, -aling, -als.** Also chiefly British **-alled, -alling.** To make (a road) with metals. [Middle English, from Old French, from Latin metallum, from Greek metallon†, a mine, mineral, metal.]

metal. metallurgical; metallurgy.

met·a·lin·guis·tics (mĕt′l-lĭng-gwĭs′tĭks) n. Plural in form, used with a singular verb. The study of the interrelationship between language and other cultural behavioral phenomena.

met·al·ist (mĕt′l-ĭst) n. Also **met·al·list. 1.** A worker in metals. **2.** One who advocates metal money instead of paper currency.

met·al·ize (mĕt′l-īz′) tr.v. **-ized, -izing, -izes.** Also **met·al·lize.** To make metallic; coat with metal. —**met′al·i·za′tion** n.

metall. metallurgical; metallurgy.

me·tal·lic (mə-tăl′ĭk) adj. **1.** Of, pertaining to, or having the characteristics of a metal. **2.** Containing a metal: a metallic compound. **3.** Having a quality characteristic of metal: "the strange metallic note of the meadow lark, suggesting the clash of vibrant blades" (Ambrose Bierce). —**me·tal′li·cal·ly** adv.

metallic bond. The chemical bond characteristic of metals, produced by the sharing of valence electrons between atoms in a usually stable crystalline structure.

metallic soap. A soft, waxlike organic compound composed of a metal oxide and a fatty acid, used as a drier or lubricant.

met·al·lif·er·ous (mĕt′l-ĭf′ər-əs) adj. Containing metal. [From Latin metallifer : metallum, METAL + -FEROUS.]

met·al·line (mĕt′l-ĭn, -īn′) adj. **1.** Of, resembling, or having the properties of a metal. **2.** Containing metal ions.

met·al·log·ra·phy (mĕt′l-ŏg′rə-fē) n. The study of the structure of metals and their compounds, especially with a microscope. —**met′al·log′ra·pher** n. —**me·tal′lo·graph′ic** (mə-tăl′ə-grăf′ĭk) adj. —**me·tal′lo·graph′i·cal·ly** adv.

met·al·loid (mĕt′l-oid′) n. A nonmetallic element, such as arsenic, that has some of the chemical properties of a metal, or one, such as carbon, that can form an alloy with metals. —adj. Also **met·al·loi·dal** (mĕt′l-oid′l). **1.** Relating to or having the properties of a metalloid. **2.** Having the appearance of a metal.

me·tal·lo·ther·a·py (mə-tăl′ō-thĕr′ə-pē) n. Medicine. The use of metals or metal compounds in the treatment of disease.

met·al·lur·gy (mĕt′l-ûr′jē) n. Abbr. **metal., metall. 1.** The science or procedures of extracting metals from their ores, of purifying metals, and of creating useful objects from metals. **2.** The knowledge and study of metals and their properties in bulk and at the atomic level. [New Latin metallurgia, from Greek metallourgos, a miner : metallon†, a mine + -ourgos, agent suffix of ergon, work (see werg-¹ in Appendix*).] —**met′al·lur′gic, met′al·lur′gi·cal** adj. —**met′al·lur′gi·cal·ly** adv. —**met′al·lur′gist** (mĕt′l-ûr′jĭst) n.

met·al·work (mĕt′l-wûrk) n. Artistic work done in metal.

met·al·work·ing (mĕt′l-wûr′kĭng) n. The art of shaping things out of metal. —**met′al·work′er** n.

met·a·math·e·mat·ics (mĕt′ə-măth′ə-măt′ĭks) n. The study of the principles, conceptual elements, consistency, and other aspects of logical systems, especially of mathematical systems. —**met′a·math′e·mat′i·cal** adj. —**met′a·math′e·ma·ti′cian** (mĕt′-ə-măth′ə-mə-tĭsh′ən) n.

met·a·mere (mĕt′ə-mîr′) n. One of a series of homologous body segments, as in worms and lobsters. Also called "somite." [META- + -MERE.] —**met′a·mer′ic** (mĕt′ə-mĕr′ĭk, -mîr′ĭk) adj. —**met′a·mer′i·cal·ly** adv.

met·a·mor·phic (mĕt′ə-môr′fĭk) adj. Also **met·a·mor·phous** (mĕt′ə-môr′fəs). **1.** Of or relating to metamorphosis. **2.** Geology. Characteristic of, pertaining to, or changed by metamorphism. [From METAMORPHOSIS.]

met·a·mor·phism (mĕt′ə-môr′fĭz′əm) n. **1.** Geology. Any alteration in composition, texture, or structure of rock masses, caused by great heat or pressure. **2.** Metamorphosis (of an insect). [METAMORPH(OSIS) + -ISM.]

met·a·mor·phose (mĕt′ə-môr′fōz′, -fōs′) v. **-phosed, -phosing, -phoses.** —tr. **1.** To transform, as by sorcery: "His eyes turned bloodshot, and he was metamorphosed into a raging fiend." (Jack London). **2.** To cause to change in form, structure, or character; subject to metamorphosis or metamorphism. —intr. To be changed or transformed by or as if by metamorphosis or metamorphism. [Old French metamorphoser, from metamorphose, transformation, from Latin metamorphōsis, METAMORPHOSIS.]

met·a·mor·pho·sis (mĕt′ə-môr′fə-sĭs) n., pl. **-ses** (-sēz′). **1.** A transformation, as by magic or sorcery. **2.** A marked change in appearance, character, condition, or function. **3.** Biology. Change in the structure and habits of an animal during normal growth, usually in the postembryonic stage. Metamorphosis includes, in insects, the emerging of an adult fly from a maggot or of a butterfly from a caterpillar, and, in amphibians, the changing of a tadpole into a frog: "the metamorphoses of many organs show what wonderful changes in function are at least possible" (Darwin). Compare **epimorphosis. 4.** Pathology. Transformation of one kind of tissue into another; especially, degeneration. [Latin metamorphōsis, from Greek : meta- (involving change) + morphōsis, MORPHOSIS.]

met·a·neph·ros (mĕt′ə-nĕf′rŏs′) n. The embryonic vertebrate kidney, in its third stage, which becomes the adult kidney.

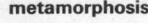
metamorphosis

eggs

larva and egg

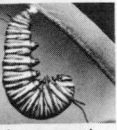
larva on twig

pupa

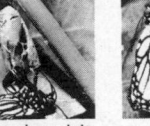
emerging adult

adult

Metamorphosis of the monarch butterfly from egg to adult

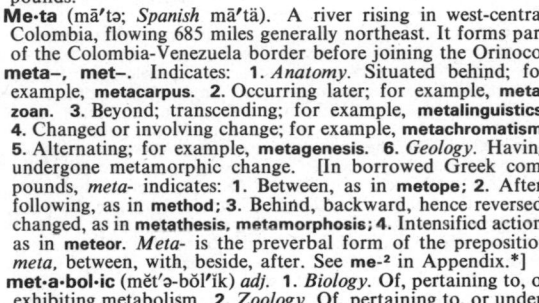

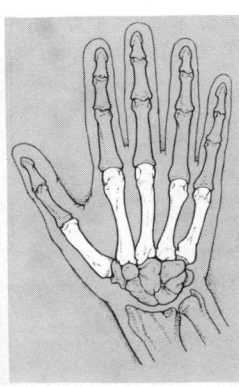
metacarpus

Compare **mesonephros, pronephros.** [New Latin : META- + Greek *nephros,* kidney (see **negwhro-** in Appendix*).]

metaph. **1.** metaphor; metaphorical. **2.** metaphysics.

met·a·phase (mĕt′ə-fāz′) *n. Biology.* The stage of mitosis during which the chromosomes are aligned along the equator of the mitotic spindle. [META- + PHASE.]

met·a·phor (mĕt′ə-fôr′, -fər) *n.* **1.** *Abbr.* **met., metaph.** A figure of speech in which a term is transferred from the object it ordinarily designates to an object it may designate only by implicit comparison or analogy, as in the phrase *evening of life.* **2.** Figurative language; allegory; parable: *"The prophets used much by metaphors to set forth truth"* (Bunyan). Compare **simile.** [Old French *metaphore,* from Latin *metaphora,* from Greek, transference, from *metapherein,* to transfer : *meta-* (involving change) + *pherein,* to bear (see **bher-**[1] in Appendix*).] —**met′a·phor′ic** (mĕt′ə-fôr′ĭk, -fŏr′ĭk), **met′a·phor′i·cal** *adj.* —**met′a·phor′i·cal·ly** *adv.*

met·a·phos·phate (mĕt′ə-fŏs′fāt′) *n.* The inorganic anion PO_3^-, or a compound containing it.

met·a·phos·phor·ic acid (mĕt′ə-fŏs-fôr′ĭk, -fŏr′ĭk). An inorganic compound, HPO_3, used as a dehydrating agent and in dental cements.

met·a·phrase (mĕt′ə-frāz′) *n.* A word-for-word translation. Compare **paraphrase.** —*tr.v.* **metaphrased, -phrasing, -phrases.** To manipulate the wording of (a text), especially as a means of subtly altering the sense: *Reformists were accused of metaphrasing certain Marxian texts in order to justify their views.* [New Latin *metaphrasis,* from Greek, from *metaphrazein,* to translate : *meta-* (involving change) + *phrazein,* to relate, tell (see **phrazein** in Appendix*).] —**met′a·phras′tic** (-frăs′tĭk) *adj.*

met·a·phrast (mĕt′ə-frăst′) *n.* One who renders a text into a different form, as by recasting prose in verse. [Middle Greek *metaphrastēs,* from Greek *metaphrazein,* to METAPHRASE.]

met·a·phys·i·cal (mĕt′ə-fĭz′ĭ-kəl) *adj.* Also *rare* **met·a·phys·ic** (mĕt′ə-fĭz′ĭk). **1.** Of or pertaining to metaphysics. **2.** Based on speculative or abstract reasoning. **3.** Too abstract; excessively subtle: *"like most metaphysical speculations [it] has very little reference at all to the abstract facts of life, as we know them"* (Oscar Wilde). **4. a.** Immaterial; incorporeal. **b.** Supernatural. **5.** *Usually capital* **M.** Of or designating 17th-century poets of the school of Donne whose verse is characterized by complex imagery and an abundance of conceits. —*n. Usually capital* **M.** One of the Metaphysical poets or their imitators: *"corn-belt metaphysicals, present blight of poetic professors"* (Kenneth Rexroth). [Middle English, from Medieval Latin *metaphysicālis,* from *metaphysica,* METAPHYSICS.] —**met′a·phys′i·cal·ly** *adv.*

met·a·phy·si·cian (mĕt′ə-fə-zĭsh′ən) *n.* One who is specialized or skilled in metaphysics: *"Samuel Taylor Coleridge—Logician, Metaphysician, Bard!"* (Charles Lamb).

met·a·phys·ics (mĕt′ə-fĭz′ĭks) *n.* Plural in form, used with a singular verb. Also *rare* **met·a·phys·ic** (-ĭk). **1.** *Abbr.* **met., metaph.** The branch of philosophy that systematically investigates the nature of first principles and problems of ultimate reality. Metaphysics includes the study of being (ontology) and, often, the study of the structure of the universe (cosmology). See **epistemology.** **2.** Speculative or critical philosophy in general. [Medieval Latin *metaphysica,* metaphysics, from Greek *Ta meta ta phusika,* "the things after the physics," Aristotle's treatise on transcendental philosophy, so called because it followed his work on physics : *meta-,* after + *phusika,* physics, from *phusikos,* natural (see **physic**).]

met·a·pla·sia (mĕt′ə-plā′zhə, -zhē-ə) *n.* **1.** The metamorphosis of tissue from one type to another, as in ossification. **2.** The change of cells from a normal to an abnormal state. [New Latin : META- + -PLASIA.]

met·a·plasm (mĕt′ə-plăz′əm) *n.* **1.** *Biology.* Inert material in the protoplasm of a cell, such as the yolk of an egg. **2.** *Grammar.* The changing of a word by adding, subtracting, or transposing letters or syllables. [Sense 1, META- + PLASM; sense 2, Latin *metaplasmus,* transformation, from Greek *metaplasmos,* from *metaplassein,* to remold : *meta-* (involving change) + *plassein,* to mold (see **pele-**[1] in Appendix*).] —**met′a·plas′mic** (mĕt′ə-plăz′mĭk) *adj.*

met·a·pro·tein (mĕt′ə-prō′tēn′, -prō′tē-ĭn) *n.* Any of various organic compounds resulting from a reaction between an acid or alkali and a protein. Metaproteins are soluble in weak acids or alkalis, and insoluble in neutral solutions.

met·a·psy·chol·o·gy (mĕt′ə-sī-kŏl′ə-jē) *n.* Philosophical speculation on the origin, structure, and function of the mind, and on the relationship between the mind and objective reality.

met·a·so·ma·tism (mĕt′ə-sō′mə-tĭz′əm) *n.* Also **met·a·so·ma·to·sis** (mĕt′ə-sō′mə-tō′sĭs). *Geology.* Metamorphism in which chemical as well as physical changes occur as a result of reaction with external material. [META- + SOMAT(O)- + -ISM.]

met·a·sta·ble (mĕt′ə-stā′bəl) *adj.* Designating a relatively unstable, transient, but significant state or condition of a chemical or physical system, as of a supersaturated solution or an energetically excited atom. —**met′a·sta·bil′i·ty** (-stə-bĭl′ə-tē) *n.*

me·tas·ta·sis (mə-tăs′tə-sĭs) *n., pl.* **-ses** (-sēz′). **1.** *Pathology.* Transmission of disease from an original site to one or more sites elsewhere in the body, as in tuberculosis or cancer. **2.** *Rhetoric.* A sudden transition from one point to another. **3.** A geological process, **paramorphism** *(see).* [New Latin, from Late Latin, transition, from Greek, from *methistanai,* to change : *meta-* (involving change) + *histanai,* cause to stand (see **stā-** in Appendix*).] —**met′a·stat′ic** (mĕt′ə-stăt′ĭk) *adj.*

me·tas·ta·size (mə-tăs′tə-sīz′) *intr.v.* **-sized, -sizing, -sizes.** To be transmitted, transferred, or transformed by metastasis.

met·a·tar·sal (mĕt′ə-tär′səl) *adj.* Of or pertaining to the metatarsus. —*n.* Any of the bones of the metatarsus.

met·a·tar·sus (mĕt′ə-tär′səs) *n., pl.* **-si** (-sī′). **1.** The middle part of the foot in man, composed of the five bones between the toes and the tarsus, that forms the instep. **2.** A corresponding part of the hind foot in four-legged animals, or of the foot in birds. [New Latin : META- + TARSUS.]

me·tath·e·sis (mə-tăth′ə-sĭs) *n., pl.* **-ses** (-sēz′). **1.** Transposition within a word of letters, sounds, or syllables, as in the change from Old English *brid* to modern English *bird,* or in the confusion of *revelant* for *relevant.* **2.** *Chemistry.* **Double decomposition** *(see).* [Late Latin, from Greek, from *metatithenai,* to transpose : *meta-* (involving change) + *tithenai,* to place (see **dhē-**[1] in Appendix*).] —**met′a·thet′ic** (mĕt′ə-thĕt′ĭk), **met′a·thet′i·cal** *adj.*

me·tath·e·size (mə-tăth′ə-sīz′) *v.* **-sized, -sizing, -sizes.** —*tr.* To subject to metathesis. —*intr.* To undergo metathesis.

met·a·tho·rax (mĕt′ə-thôr′ăks, -thōr′ăks) *n., pl.* **-raxes** or **-thoraces** (-thôr′ə-sēz′, -thōr′ə-sēz′). The hindmost of the three thoracic segments of an insect. [New Latin : META- + THORAX.]

met·a·zo·an (mĕt′ə-zō′ən) *n.* A member of one of two divisions of the animal kingdom, the Metazoa, which includes all animals more complex than the one-celled protozoan. [From New Latin *Metazoa* : META- + -ZOA.] —**met′a·zo′an, met′a·zo′ic** *adj.*

Metch·ni·koff (mĕch′nĭ-kôf′), **Élie.** Also known as Ilya Mechnikov. 1845–1916. Russian-born French bacteriologist.

mete[1] (mēt) *tr.v.* **meted, meting, metes.** **1.** To distribute by or as if by measure; deal out; allot: *"I mete and dole / Unequal laws unto a savage race."* (Tennyson). **2.** *Archaic.* To measure. —*n. Archaic.* A measure. [Middle English *meten,* Old English *metan.* See **med-** in Appendix.*]

mete[2] (mēt) *n.* A boundary line or limit. Used chiefly in the phrase *metes and bounds.* [Norman French, from Latin *mēta.* See **mei-**[3] in Appendix.*]

me·tem·psy·cho·sis (mə-tĕm′sĭ-kō′sĭs, mĕt′əm-sī-kō′sĭs) *n., pl.* **-ses** (-sēz′). The transmigration of souls. [Greek *metempsukhōsis,* from *metempsukhousthai,* (of the soul) to transmigrate : *meta-* (involving transfer) + *empsukhos,* animate : *en-,* in + *psukhē,* soul (see **bhes-**[2] in Appendix*).]

met·en·ceph·a·lon (mĕt′ĕn-sĕf′ə-lŏn′, -lən) *n., pl.* **-la** (-lə). The part of the embryonic hindbrain from which the cerebellum and the pons develop. [New Latin : MET(A)- + ENCEPHALON.] —**met′en·ce·phal′ic** (-sə-făl′ĭk) *adj.*

me·te·or (mē′tē-ər, -ôr′) *n.* **1.** The luminous trail or streak that appears in the sky when a meteoroid is made incandescent by friction with the earth's atmosphere. Also called "shooting star." **2.** A meteoroid. **3.** *Obsolete.* Any atmospheric phenomenon, such as a rainbow, lightning, or snow. [Middle English, from Old French *meteore,* from Medieval Latin *meteōrum,* from Greek *meteōron,* astronomical phenomenon, from *meteōros,* high in the air : *meta-* (intensifier) + *aeirein,* to raise (see **wer-**[2] in Appendix*).]

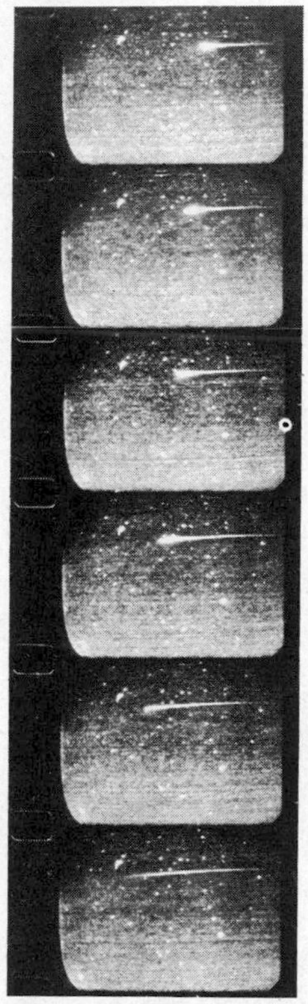

meteor
Photographed at 24 frames per second from a television monitor in 1963

meteor. meteorological; meteorology.

me·te·or·ic (mē′tē-ôr′ĭk, -ŏr′ĭk) *adj.* **1.** Of, pertaining to, or formed by a meteor or meteors. **2.** Resembling a meteor in speed and brilliance: *a meteoric rise to fame.* **3.** Of or pertaining to the earth's atmosphere. —**me′te·or′i·cal·ly** *adv.*

me·te·or·ite (mē′tē-ə-rīt′) *n.* The stony or metallic material of a meteoroid that survives passage through the atmosphere and reaches the earth's surface. [METEOR + -ITE.] —**me′te·or·it′ic** (mē′tē-ə-rĭt′ĭk) *adj.*

me·te·or·o·graph (mē′tē-ôr′ə-grăf′, -ŏr′ə-grăf′, -gräf′) *n.* An instrument that records simultaneously several meteorological conditions, such as temperature, barometric pressure, and moisture. [French *météorographe* : METEOR + -GRAPH.]

me·te·or·oid (mē′tē-ə-roid′) *n.* Any of numerous celestial bodies, ranging in size from specks of dust to asteroids weighing thousands of tons, which appear as meteors when entering the earth's atmosphere.

me·te·or·ol·o·gy (mē′tē-ə-rŏl′ə-jē) *n. Abbr.* **meteorol., meteor., met.** The science dealing with the phenomena of the atmosphere, especially weather and weather conditions. [Greek *meteōrologia,* discussion of astronomical phenomena : *meteōron,* METEOR + -LOGY.] —**me′te·or′o·log′i·cal** (mē′tē-ôr′ə-lŏj′ĭ-kəl, -ŏr′ə-lŏj′ĭ-kəl), **me′te·or′o·log′ic** *adj.* —**me′te·or′o·log′i·cal·ly** *adv.* —**me′te·or·ol′o·gist** *n.*

meteor shower. Any group of meteors that appear together and have an apparent common origin.

me·ter[1] (mē′tər) *n.* Also *chiefly British* **me·tre.** **1. a.** The measured rhythm characteristic of verse. **b.** A specified rhythmic pattern of verse, usually determined by the number and kinds of metric units in a typical line. See **foot** (prosody). **2. a.** The division of music into measures or bars. **b.** A specific musical rhythm determined by the number of beats and the time value assigned to each note in a measure. —See Synonyms at **rhythm.** [Middle English *meter, metre,* from Old English *mēter* and Old French *metre,* both from Latin *metrum,* measure, from Greek *metron.* See **mē-**[2] in Appendix.*]

me·ter[2] (mē′tər) *n.* Also *chiefly British* **me·tre.** *Abbr.* **m** The fundamental unit of length (equivalent to 39.37 inches) in the metric system. It was defined in 1790 as one ten-millionth (10^{-7}) of the earth's quadrant passing through Paris, but was redefined in 1960 as the length equal to 1,650,763.73 wavelengths in a vacuum of the orange-red radiation of krypton 86. See **measurement.** [French *mètre,* from Greek *metron,* meter, measure. See **mē-**[2] in Appendix.*]

me·ter[3] (mē′tər) *n.* Any of various devices designed to measure time, distance, speed, or intensity, or to indicate and record or

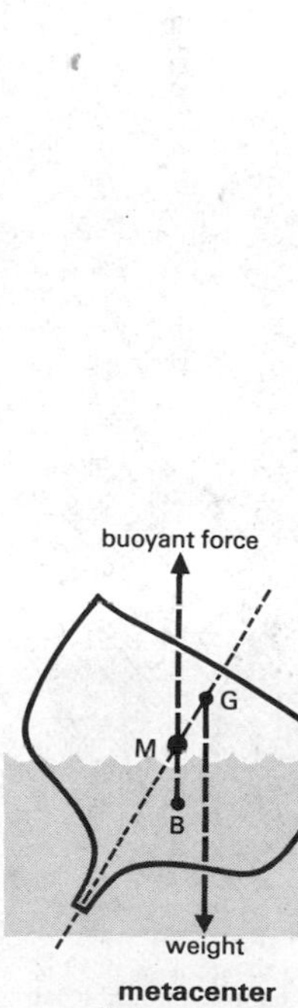

metacenter
B. Center of buoyancy
G. Center of gravity
M. Metacenter

t tight/th thin, path/*th* this, bathe/ŭ cut/ûr urge/v valve/w with/y yes/z zebra, size/zh vision/ə about, item, edible, gallop, circus/ à *Fr.* ami/œ *Fr.* feu, *Ger.* schön/ü *Fr.* tu, *Ger.* über/KH *Ger.* ich, *Scot.* loch/N *Fr.* bon. ***Follows main vocabulary. †Of obscure origin.**

regulate the amount or volume of something, such as a flow of gas or an electric current. —*tr.v.* **metered, -tering, -ters.** **1.** To measure or regulate with a metering device. **2.** To imprint with postage or other revenue stamps by means of a postage meter or similar device. [From -METER.]

-meter. Indicates a measuring device; for example, **barometer, speedometer.** [New Latin *-metrum*, or French *-mètre*, both from Greek *metron*, meter, measure. See mē-² in Appendix.*]

meter-kilogram-second-ampere system. *Abbr.* **mksA** A coherent system of units for mechanics, electricity, and magnetism, using the meter, the kilogram, the second, and the ampere as basic units for length, mass, time, and current intensity.

meter-kilogram-second system. *Abbr.* **mks** A coherent system of units for mechanics, using the meter, the kilogram, and the second as basic units of length, mass, and time. See **centimeter-gram-second system.**

met·es·trus (mĕt-ĕs′trəs) *n.* The period of sexual inactivity that follows estrus in the mammalian female. [New Latin : MET(A)- + ESTRUS.] —**met·es′trous** (-trəs) *adj.*

meth-. Indicates chemical compounds containing methyl; for example, **methacrylate.** [From METHYL.]

Meth. Methodist.

meth·ac·ry·late (mĕth-ăk′rə-lāt′) *n.* **1.** An ester of methacrylic acid, CH₂:C(CH₃)COOR, R being an organic radical. It is used in the manufacture of plastics. **2.** A resin derived from methacrylic acid. [METH- + ACRYL(IC) + -ATE.]

meth·a·cryl·ic acid (mĕth′ə-krĭl′ĭk). A colorless liquid, CH₂:C(CH₃)COOH, used in the manufacture of resins and plastics. [From METH- + ACRYLIC.]

meth·a·done hydrochloride (mĕth′ə-dōn′). An organic compound, $C_{21}H_{27}NO \cdot HCL$, used as an analgesic and in treating heroin addiction. [From (DI)METH(YL) + A(MINO)- + D(IPHENYL) + (heptan)one, from HEPTANE + -ONE.]

meth·ane (mĕth′ān′) *n.* An odorless, colorless, flammable gas, CH₄, that is the major constituent of natural gas. It is used as a fuel and is an important source of hydrogen and a wide variety of organic compounds. [METH- + -ANE.]

methane series. A group of hydrocarbons of similar structure, the **paraffin series** *(see).*

meth·a·nol (mĕth′ə-nôl′, -nōl′) *n.* Methyl alcohol *(see).* [METHAN(E) + -OL.]

me·theg·lin (mə-thĕg′lĭn) *n.* A kind of spiced mead. [Welsh *meddyglyn : meddyg*, medicinal, from Latin *medicus*, MEDICAL + *llyn*, liquor, from Old Irish *linn* (see **pleu-** in Appendix).]

met·he·mo·glo·bin (mĕt-hē′mə-glō′bĭn, -hĕm′ə-glō′bĭn) *n.* A brownish-red, crystalline, organic compound formed by oxidation of hemoglobin and found in the blood after poisoning by chlorates, nitrates, ferricyanides, or various other substances. [MET(A)- + HEMOGLOBIN.]

me·the·na·mine (mə-thē′nə-mēn′, -mĭn) *n.* An organic compound, (CH₂)₆N₄, used as a urinary tract antiseptic and in rubber vulcanizing. Also called "hexamethylenetetramine." [METH- + -EN(E) + AMINE.]

me·thinks (mĭ-thĭngks′) *v.* Past tense **me·thought** (mĭ-thôt′). *Archaic.* It seems to me. [Middle English *me thinketh*, Old English *mē thyncth : mē*, ME + *thyncth*, third person singular present of *thyncan*, to seem (see **tong-** in Appendix*).]

me·thi·o·nine (mə-thī′ə-nēn′) *n.* An organic compound, C₅H₁₁NO₂S, derived from protein and used as a dietary supplement and in pharmaceuticals. [ME(TH)- + THION- + -INE.]

meth·od (mĕth′əd) *n.* **1.** A means or manner of procedure; especially, a regular and systematic way of accomplishing anything. **2.** Orderly and systematic arrangement; orderliness; regularity: *"While Lady Elliott lived, there had been method, moderation, and economy"* (Jane Austen). **3.** The procedures and techniques characteristic of a particular discipline or field of knowledge. —**the Method.** A system of acting in which the actor recalls emotion and reactions from his past experience and utilizes them in the role he is playing. [French *méthode*, from Latin *methodus*, from Greek *methodos*, "a going after," pursuit (as of knowledge) : *met(a)-*, after + *hodos*, journey (see sed-² in Appendix*).]

Synonyms: method, system, routine, manner, mode, fashion, way. Method emphasizes procedures according to a detailed, logically ordered plan. *System*, broader in scope, stresses order and regularity affecting all parts of a relatively complex procedure. *Routine* stresses procedure from the standpoint of detail and rather rigid sequence; it involves only the mechanical skills necessary for unvarying practice. *Manner* emphasizes personal behavior and distinctive procedure more strongly than it does logic and order. *Mode* often applies to distinctive procedure characteristic of a group and influenced by local tradition and customs. *Fashion* usually applies to individual, highly personal behavior; *after a fashion* and *in one's fashion* suggest (unfavorably) idiosyncrasies or mannerisms. *Way* is most often an inclusive synonym for these terms, but it can indicate highly individual procedure, as in *It's just his way.*

me·thod·i·cal (mə-thŏd′ĭ-kəl) *adj.* Also **me·thod·ic.** **1.** Arranged or proceeding in regular, systematic order. **2.** Characterized by ordered and systematic habits or behavior. —See Synonyms at **orderly.** —**me·thod′i·cal·ly** *adv.* —**me·thod′i·cal·ness** *n.*

Meth·od·ism (mĕth′ə-dĭz′əm) *n.* **1.** The beliefs, worship, and system of organization of the Methodists. **2.** *Small* m. Emphasis on systematic procedure.

Meth·od·ist (mĕth′ə-dĭst) *n.* **1.** *Abbr.* **Meth.** A member of a Protestant Christian denomination (in the United States, the United Methodist Church) with a theology developed from the teachings of John and Charles Wesley and others in England in

the early 18th century, and characterized by an emphasis on the doctrines of free grace and individual responsibility. **2.** *Small* m. *Rare.* One who emphasizes or insists on systematic methods. [From METHOD.] —**Meth′od·ist, Meth′od·is′tic** *adj.*

meth·od·ize (mĕth′ə-dīz′) *tr.v.* **-ized, -izing, -izes.** To reduce to or organize according to a method; systematize. —**meth′od·i·za′tion** *n.* —**meth′od·iz′er** *n.*

meth·od·ol·o·gy (mĕth′ə-dŏl′ə-jē) *n., pl.* **-gies. 1.** The system of principles, practices, and procedures applied to any specific branch of knowledge. **2.** The branch of logic dealing with the general principles of the formation of knowledge. —**meth′od·o·log′i·cal** (mĕth′ə-də-lŏj′ĭ-kəl) *adj.* —**meth′od·o·log′i·cal·ly** *adv.*

me·thought. Past tense of **methinks.**

Me·thu·se·lah (mə-thōō′zə-lə). A Biblical patriarch said to have lived 969 years. Genesis 5:27.

me·thu·se·lah (mĕ·thōō′zə-lə) *n.* An extremely old man. [After METHUSELAH.]

meth·yl (mĕth′əl) *n.* The univalent organic radical CH₃, derived from methane, and occurring in many important organic compounds. [French *méthyle*, back-formation from *méthylène*, METHYLENE.] —**me·thyl′ic** (mə-thĭl′ĭk) *adj.*

methyl acetate. An organic compound, C₃H₆O₂, used as a paint remover, general solvent, and in the manufacture of perfumes.

meth·yl·al (mĕth′ə-lăl′) *n.* A colorless flammable liquid, CH₂(OCH₃)₂, used in the manufacture of perfumes, adhesives, and protective coatings. [METHYL + -AL.]

methyl alcohol. A colorless flammable liquid, CH₃OH, used as an antifreeze, general solvent, fuel, and denaturant for ethyl alcohol. Also called "methanol," "wood alcohol," "wood spirits."

meth·yl·a·mine (mĕth′əl-ə-mēn′, -ăm′ēn′, mə-thĭl′ə-mēn′) *n.* A flammable gas, CH₃NH₂, produced by the decomposition of organic matter, and synthesized for use as a solvent and in the manufacture of many products, such as dyes and insecticides.

meth·yl·ate (mĕth′ə-lāt′) *n.* An organic compound in which the hydrogen of the hydroxyl group (OH) of methyl alcohol is replaced by a metal. —*tr.v.* **methylated, -lating, -lates. 1.** To mix or combine with methyl alcohol. **2.** To combine with the methyl radical. —**meth′yl·a′tion** (mĕth′ə-lā′shən) *n.*

methylated spirit. *Often plural.* A denatured alcohol consisting of a mixture of ethyl alcohol and methyl alcohol.

methyl chloride. An explosive gas, CH₃Cl, used in organic synthesis and polymerization, as a refrigerant, and as an anesthetic.

meth·yl·ene (mĕth′ə-lēn′) *n.* A bivalent organic radical, CH₂, a component of unsaturated hydrocarbons. [French *méthylène* : Greek *methu*, wine, mead (see **medhu-** in Appendix*) + *hulē*, wood (see **hulē** in Appendix*) + -ENE.]

methylene blue. An organic compound, C₁₆H₁₈N₃SCl·3H₂O, the dark-green crystals or powder of which forms a deep-blue solution when dissolved in water. It is used as an antidote for cyanide poisoning and as a bacteriological stain.

methyl ethyl ketone. *Chemistry.* Butanone *(see).*

methyl methacrylate. A colorless liquid, CH₂:C(CH₃)-COOCH₃, that is used as a monomer in plastics.

meth·yl·naph·tha·lene (mĕth′əl-năf′thə-lēn′, -năp′thə-lēn′) *n.* An organic compound, C₁₀H₇CH₃, obtained from coal tar in two isomeric forms, one a liquid, the other a solid. The liquid is used to standardize diesel fuels, the solid for insecticides, and both are used in organic synthesis.

me·tic·u·lous (mə-tĭk′yə-ləs) *adj.* **1.** Extremely careful and precise. **2.** Excessively concerned with details; overscrupulous. [Latin *meticulōsus*, overly concerned, fearful : *metus†*, fear + (*per*)*īculus*, perilous, from *perīculum*, PERIL.] —**me·tic′u·los′i·ty** (mə-tĭk′yə-lŏs′ə-tē), **me·tic′u·lous·ness** *n.*

Synonyms: meticulous, conscientious, scrupulous, fastidious, punctilious. Meticulous stresses extreme care, and sometimes exaggerated care for small details. *Conscientious* combines diligence with the dictates of conscience, thus involving duty and a sense of right and wrong. *Scrupulous* likewise implies strong concern for moral rectitude. *Fastidious*, said of personal tastes and appearance, stresses concern, often excessive, for niceties. *Punctilious* specifically applies to care in matters of etiquette.

mé·tier (mā-tyā′) *n.* **1.** An occupation, trade, or profession; especially, the work for which one is especially suited. **2.** One's specialty: *"His 'métier' was the American tropics, and he had lived all over Latin America"* (Van Wyck Brooks). [French, from Old French *mestier*, from Vulgar Latin *misterium* (unattested), from Latin *ministerium*, MYSTERY (trade).]

mé·tis (mā-tēs′) *n., pl.* **métis.** *Feminine* **mé·tisse** (mā-tēs′). A man of mixed Indian and French-Canadian ancestry. [Canadian French, from Old French *metis*, mongrel, from Vulgar Latin *mixtīcius* (unattested). See **mestizo.**]

Me·ton·ic cycle (mə-tŏn′ĭk). A period of 235 lunar months or about 19 Julian years, at the end of which the phases of the moon recur in the same order and on the same days as in the preceding cycle. [Discovered by *Meton*, Athenian astronomer of the fifth century B.C.]

met·o·nym (mĕt′ə-nĭm′) *n.* A word used in metonymy.

me·ton·y·my (mə-tŏn′ə-mē) *n., pl.* **-mies.** A figure of speech in which an idea is evoked or named by means of a term designating some associated notion. The words *sword* and *sex* are metonymical designations for *military career* and *womankind* in the example *"He abandoned the sword and the sex together"* (Sterne). [Late Latin *metōnymia*, from Greek *metōnumia*, "substitute naming" : *meta-* (involving transfer) + *onoma*, name (see **nomen-** in Appendix*).] —**met′o·nym′i·cal** (mĕt′ə-nĭm′ĭ-kəl) *adj.*

me-too (mē′tōō′) *adj. Informal.* Advocating principles or prac-

Prince Metternich
Portrait engraved in 1852
by Johann Leonhard Raab

tices closely similar to those of a rival: *a me-too political campaign.* —**me′-too′er** *n.* —**me′-too′ism′** *n.*

met·o·pe (mĕt′ə-pē, mĕt′ōp′) *n.* One of the spaces between triglyphs on a Doric frieze. [Latin *metopa,* from Greek *metopē,* area between two beam-ends : *meta,* between + *opē,* opening (see **okw-** in Appendix*).]

me·top·ic (mə-tŏp′ĭk) *adj. Anatomy.* Of or pertaining to the forehead. [Greek *metōpikos,* from *metōpon,* forehead : *meta,* between + *ōps,* eye (see **okw-** in Appendix*).]

Met·ra·zol (mĕt′rə-zôl′, -zōl′) *n.* A trademark for **pentylenetetrazol** *(see).*

me·tre. *Chiefly British.* Variant of **meter.**

met·ric¹ (mĕt′rĭk) *adj.* Designating, pertaining to, or using the **metric system** *(see).* [French *métrique,* from *mètre,* METER (unit of length).]

met·ric² (mĕt′rĭk) *n.* **1.** A standard of measurement. **2.** *Geometry.* A function defined for a coordinate system such that the distance between any two points in that system may be determined from their coordinates.

met·ric³ (mĕt′rĭk) *n. Rare.* A branch of prosody, **metrics** *(see).* [Greek *metrikē,* from *metrikos,* METRICAL.]

met·ri·cal (mĕt′rĭ-kəl) *adj.* **1.** Pertaining to or characterized by versification or measure in music or poetry. **2.** Composed in or making up a unit of poetic meter: *Chaucer, Scott, and Byron are masters of the metrical romance.* **3.** Pertaining to measurement. [From Latin *metricus,* from Greek *metrikos,* from *metron,* measure, meter. See **mē-²** in Appendix.*] —**met′ri·cal·ly** *adv.*

metric centner. A unit of mass equal to 100 kilograms.

metric hundredweight. A unit of mass equal to 50 kilograms.

me·tri·cian (mə-trĭsh′ən) *n.* A student or composer of poetic meters. [French *métricien,* from *mètre,* METER.]

met·rics (mĕt′rĭks) *n.* Plural in form, used with a singular verb. Also *rare* **metric.** The branch of prosody dealing with measure and metrical structures: *Greek metrics.*

metric system. A decimal system of weights and measures based on the meter as a unit length and the kilogram as a unit mass. Derived units include the liter for liquid volume, the stere for solid volume, and the are for area. See **measurement.**

metric ton. *Abbr.* **m.t., M.T.** A unit of mass equal to 1,000 kilograms. See **measurement.**

me·tri·tis (mə-trī′tĭs) *n.* Inflammation of the uterus. [New Latin : METR(O)- + -ITIS.]

met·ro, Mét·ro (mĕt′rō; *French* mā-trō′) *n.* The subway system of Paris. [French, short for *(chemin de fer) métropolitain,* "metropolitan (railway)."]

metro–, metr–. Indicates the uterus or things pertaining to the uterus; for example, **metritis, metrorrhagia.** [New Latin, from Greek *mētro-, mētr-,* from *mētra,* womb, uterus, from *mētēr,* mother. See **māter-** in Appendix.*]

me·trol·o·gy (mĕ-trŏl′ə-jē) *n., pl.* **-gies. 1.** The science that deals with systems of measurement. **2.** A system of measurement. [French *métrologie,* from Greek *metrologia,* theory of measurements : *metron,* measure (see **mē-²** in Appendix*) + -LOGY.] —**met′ro·log′i·cal** (mĕt′rə-lŏj′ĭ-kəl) *adj.* —**me·trol′o·gist** *n.*

met·ro·nome (mĕt′rə-nōm′) *n.* A device to mark time at a steady beat in adjustable intervals. [Greek *metron,* measure (see **mē-²** in Appendix*) + *nomos,* rule, law (see **nem-²** in Appendix*).] —**met′ro·nom′ic** (mĕt′rə-nŏm′ĭk) *adj.*

me·tro·nym·ic (mē′trə-nĭm′ĭk, mĕt′rə-) *adj.* Also **mat·ro·nym·ic** (măt′-). Of, pertaining to, or derived from the name of one's mother or female ancestor. —*n.* A metronymic name. [Medieval Greek *mētronumikos* : Greek *mētēr,* mother (see **māter-** in Appendix*) + *onoma,* name (see **nomen-** in Appendix*).]

me·trop·o·lis (mə-trŏp′ə-lĭs) *n., pl.* **-lises. 1.** A major city; especially, the capital, largest, or most important city of a particular country, state, or region. **2.** A large urban center of culture, trade, or other activity. **3.** The chief see of a metropolitan bishop; especially, the main diocese of a specific ecclesiastical province. **4.** The mother city of a state or colony in ancient Greece. **5.** *Zoology.* A region or area where a particular kind of organism lives and thrives. [Late Latin *mētropolis,* from Greek : *mētēr,* mother (see **māter-** in Appendix*) + *polis,* city (see **pelə-²** in Appendix*).]

met·ro·pol·i·tan (mĕt′rə-pŏl′ə-tən) *adj. Abbr.* **met. 1. a.** Of, pertaining to, or characteristic of a metropolis. **b.** Making up a metropolis. **2.** Pertaining to or comprising the home territory of a sovereign state, as distinguished from its dependencies, protectorates, or overseas territories and provinces. **3.** Of or pertaining to a metropolitan. —*n.* **1.** In the Roman Catholic and other episcopal churches, an archbishop who has authority over bishops. **2.** In the Eastern Orthodox Church, a bishop ranking next below the patriarch who serves as the head of an ecclesiastical province. [Middle English, from Late Latin *mētropolītānus,* from Greek *mētropolitēs,* a citizen of a metropolis, from *mētropolis,* METROPOLIS.]

me·tror·rha·gi·a (mē′trə-rā′jē-ə, mĕt′rə-) *n.* An abnormal hemorrhage of the uterus, especially between menstrual flows. [New Latin : METRO- + -RRHAGIA.]

–metry. Indicates the science or process of measuring; for example, **calorimetry, photometry.** [Middle English *-metrie,* from Old French, from Latin *-metria,* from Greek, from *metron,* meter, measure. See **mē-²** in Appendix.*]

Met·ter·nich (mĕt′ər-nĭKH), Prince **Klemens Wenzel Nepomuk Lothar von.** 1773–1859. Austrian statesman.

met·tle (mĕt′l) *n.* **1.** Inherent quality of character and temperament. **2.** Courage and fortitude; spirit: *show one's mettle in combat.* —See Synonyms at **courage.** —**on one's mettle.** Putting one's spirit, courage, or energy to the test. [Middle English *metel,* fortitude, metal, variant of *metal,* METAL.]

met·tle·some (mĕt′l-səm) *adj.* Full of mettle; high-spirited; plucky. See Synonyms at **brave.**

Metz (mĕts; *French* mĕs). A city on the Moselle River in northeastern France. Population, 103,000.

Meuse (myōōz; *French* mœz). *Dutch* **Maas** (mäs). A river rising in eastern France and flowing 560 miles in a northerly direction through Belgium and the Netherlands to the North Sea.

mew¹ (myōō) *n.* **1.** A cage for hawks, especially when molting. **2.** A secret place; hideaway. —*v.* **mewed, mewing, mews.** —*tr.* To confine in a cage or as if in a cage. Often followed by *up.* —*intr.* To molt. Used of a hawk. [Middle English *mewe,* cage for molting hawks, from Old French *mue,* a molting, from *muer,* to molt, from Latin *mūtāre,* to change. See **mei-¹** in Appendix.*]

mew² (myōō) *intr.v.* **mewed, mewing, mews.** To make the high-pitched, crying sound of a cat; to meow. —*n.* The crying sound of a cat; a meow. [Middle English *mewen* (imitative).]

mew³ (myōō) *n.* A sea bird, *Larus canus,* one of the gulls. It is found in northern Eurasia and western North America. [Middle English *mew,* Old English *mǣw,* from Germanic *maiwa-* (unattested), possibly a pre-Indo-European Atlantic borrowing.]

mewl (myōōl) *n.* A whimper or weak cry. —*intr.v.* **mewled, mewling, mewls.** To cry weakly: *"The infant, mewling and puking in his nurse's arms"* (Shakespeare). [Imitative.]

mews (myōōz) *n.* Plural in form, used with a singular verb. A small street behind a residential street, containing private stables for town houses; now mostly converted into small apartments. [After the *Mews* at Charing Cross, London, medieval royal stables built on a site previously used for the royal hawk cages, plural of MEW (cage).]

Mex. Mexican; Mexico.

Mex·i·cal·i (mĕk′sĭ-kăl′ē; *Spanish* mĕ′hē-kä′lē). The capital of Baja California, Mexico, in the north near the U.S.-Mexican border. Population, 289,000.

Mex·i·can (mĕk′sĭ-kən) *n.* A native or inhabitant of Mexico. —*adj. Abbr.* **Mex.** Of or pertaining to Mexico or to its inhabitants, their language, or their culture.

Mexican bean beetle. A spotted beetle, *Epilachna varivestis,* found in the southern United States and Mexico. It causes serious damage to bean crops.

Mexican hairless. A small dog of a breed of unknown origin, found in Mexico, having a smooth hairless body except for tufts on the head and tail.

Mexican Spanish. The form of Spanish spoken in Mexico.

Mexican War. A war between the United States and Mexico (1846–48) settled by the Treaty of Guadalupe Hidalgo.

Mex·i·co (mĕk′sĭ-kō′). *Mexican Spanish* **Mé·xi·co** (mĕ′hē-kō); *Spanish* **Mé·ji·co** (mĕ′hē-kō). *Abbr.* **Mex. 1.** Officially, Estados Unidos Mexicanos. A republic of southwestern North America, occupying 760,373 square miles between the United States and Central America. Population, 39,643,000. Capital, Mexico City. **2.** A state of south-central Mexico, 8,268 square miles in area. Population, 1,898,000. Capital, Toluca. [Spanish *Méjico,* from Nahuatl *mexihco, meshi'ko,* "at Mexico City" : *meshi'-,* place name + *-ko,* a locative.]

Mex·i·co, Gulf of (mĕk′sĭ-kō′). An extensive inlet of the Atlantic Ocean south of North America and surrounded by the United States, Mexico, and Cuba.

Mex·i·co City (mĕk′sĭ-kō′). Officially, México, D.F. The capital of Mexico and of the Distrito Federal (Federal District), at the southern end of the central plateau at an altitude of 7,800 feet. Population, 3,193,000.

Mey·er·beer (mī′ər-bîr′, -bâr′), **Giacomo.** Real name, Jakob Liebmann Beer. 1791–1864. German composer of operas.

Mey·er·hof (mī′ər-hŏf′), **Otto.** 1884–1951. German physiologist; worked on energy conversion.

me·ze·re·on (mə-zîr′ē-ən) *n.* **1.** A shrub, *Daphne mezereum,* native to Eurasia, having fragrant lilac-purple flowers and small scarlet fruit. **2.** A bark, mezereum. [Middle English *mizerion,* from Medieval Latin *mezereon,* from Arabic *māzaryūn.*]

me·ze·re·um (mə-zîr′ē-əm) *n.* **1.** A shrub, the mezereon. **2.** The dried bark of certain shrubs of the genus *Daphne,* once used externally as a vesicant and internally for arthritis. [New Latin, variant of Medieval Latin *mezereon,* MEZEREON.]

me·zu·zah (mə-zōōz′ə, -zōōz′ə) *n., pl.* **mezuzoth** (mə-zōōz′ōth) or **-zahs.** Also **me·zu·za.** *Judaism.* A small piece of parchment inscribed with the Biblical passages Deuteronomy 6:4–9 and 11:13–21 and marked with the word "Shaddai," a name of the Almighty. The parchment is rolled up in a container and affixed to a door frame as a sign that a Jewish family lives within. It may also be carried as an amulet. [Hebrew *məzūzāh,* "a doorpost."]

mez·za·nine (mĕz′ə-nēn′, mĕz′ə-nēn′) *n.* **1.** A partial story occurring between two main stories of a building. **2.** The lowest balcony in a theater or its first few rows. [French, from Italian *mezzanino,* from *mezzano,* middle, from Latin *mediānus,* in the middle, from *medius,* middle. See **medhyo-** in Appendix.*]

mez·zo (mĕt′sō, mĕd′zō, mĕz′ō) *n., pl.* **-zos.** A **mezzo-soprano** *(see).* [By shortening.]

mez·zo-re·lie·vo (mĕt′sō-rĭ-lē′vō, mĕz′ō-) *n., pl.* **-vos.** Also *Italian* **mez·zo-ri·lie·vo** (mĕt′sō-rē-lyā′vō) *pl.* **-vi** (-vē). *Sculpture.* **Half relief** *(see).* [Italian *mezzorilievo* : *mezzo,* half, from Latin *medius* (see **medhyo-** in Appendix*) + *rilievo,* relief, from *rilevare,* to raise, from Latin *relevāre* : *re-,* again + *levāre,* to raise (see **legwh-** in Appendix*).]

mez·zo-so·pran·o (mĕt′sō-sə-prăn′ō, -prä′nō, mĕd′zō-, mĕz′ō-) *n., pl.* **-os, -prani** (-prä′nē). **1.** A voice or voice part having a range between soprano and contralto. **2.** A woman having such a voice. [Italian : *mezzo,* half (see **mezzo-relievo**) + SOPRANO.]

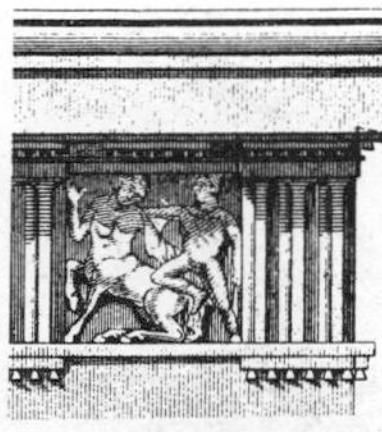

metope

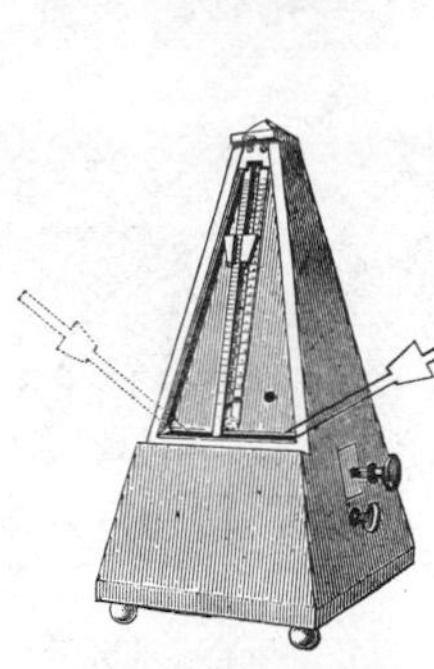

metronome
Example of the device manufactured after 1816 by Johann Mälzel

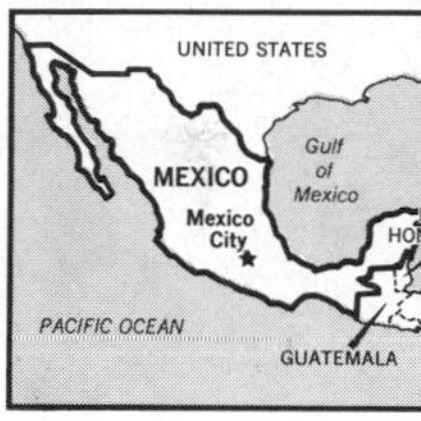

Mexico

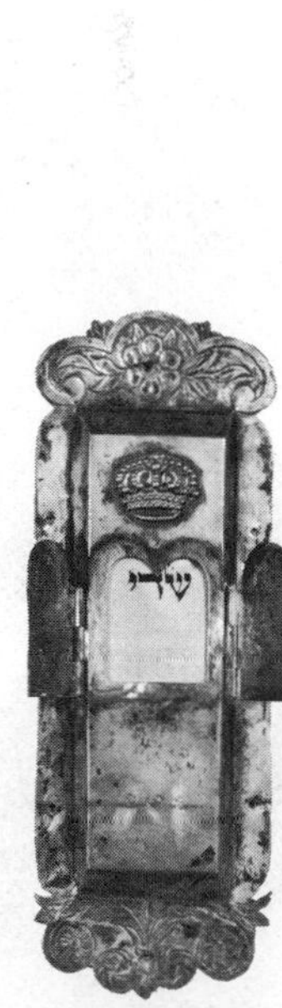

mezuzah
In 19th-century German silver case

mez·zo·tint (mĕt′sō-tĭnt′, mĕd′zō-, mĕz′ō-) *n.* **1.** A method of engraving a copper or steel plate by scraping and burnishing areas to produce effects of light and shadow. **2.** A print made from a plate so treated. [Italian *mezzotinto* : *mezzo,* half (see **mezzo-relievo**) + *tinto,* tint, from Latin *tingere* (past participle stem *tinctus*), to TINT.]

mF millifarad.

m.f. *Music.* mezzo-forte.

M.F. medium frequency.

M.F.A. Master of Fine Arts.

mfg. manufacture; manufactured; manufacturing.

mfr. manufacture; manufacturer.

mg milligram.

Mg The symbol for the element magnesium.

M.G. Major General.

MGM Airport code for Montgomery, Alabama.

mgr. manager.

Mgr. **1.** manager. **2.** Monseigneur; Monsignor.

mH millihenry.

MH Medal of Honor.

mho (mō) *n., pl.* **mhos.** *Electricity.* A unit of conductance, reciprocal to the ohm. [Backward spelling of OHM.]

MHT Airport code for Manchester, New Hampshire.

MHz megahertz.

mi (mē) *n. Music.* The third tone of the diatonic scale in solfeggio. [Medieval Latin, from Latin *mīra,* "wonders," a word sung to this note in a hymn to Saint John the Baptist (see **gamut**), from Latin *mīrārī,* to be amazed at, from *mīrus,* wonderful. See **smei-** in Appendix.*]

MI Michigan (with Zip Code).

mi. **1.** mile. **2.** mill (monetary unit).

Mi·am·i[1] (mī-ăm′ē, -ăm′ə) *n., pl.* **Miami** or **-is.** One of an Algonquian tribe of Indians who lived in what is now Ohio, Indiana, Illinois, and Wisconsin.

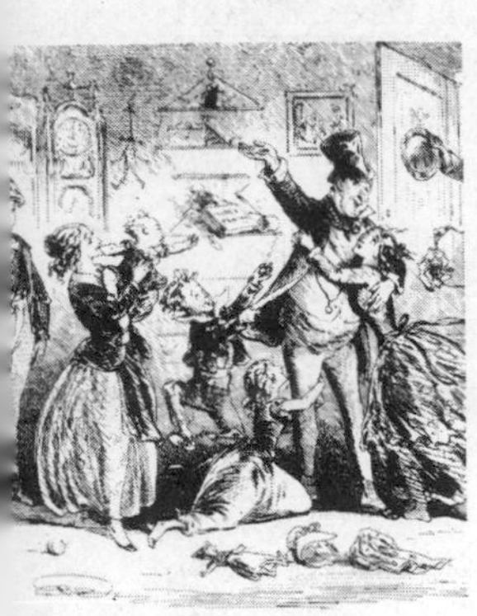

micawber
Nineteenth-century etching by "Phiz" of Wilkins Micawber *(center)* and family

Mi·am·i[2] (mī-ăm′ē, -ăm′ə). **1.** A resort city on the southeastern coast of Florida, on Biscayne Bay. Population, 292,000. **2.** A river rising in west-central Ohio and flowing 160 miles southward to the Ohio River.

Mi·am·i Beach (mī-ăm′ē, -ăm′ə). A resort city on the southeastern coast of Florida. Population, 63,000.

mi·aou, mi·aow. Variants of **meow.**

mi·as·ma (mī-ăz′mə, mē-) *n., pl.* **-mas** or **-mata** (-mə-tə). **1. a.** A poisonous atmosphere formerly thought to rise from swamps and putrid matter and cause disease: *"they have their ghastly origin in the rank miasma of the tarn"* (Poe). **b.** A thick, vaporous atmosphere: *"a perpetually burning city dump, contributing its miasmas and choking vapors to the murky sky"* (Loren Eiseley). **2.** Any noxious atmosphere or influence: *"A miasma of evil suddenly enveloped Profane from behind"* (Thomas Pynchon). [New Latin, from Greek, from *miainein,* to pollute. See **mai-**[2] in Appendix.*] —**mi·as′mal** (-məl), **mi′as·mat′ic** (mī′əz-măt′ĭk), **mi·as′mic** *adj.*

Mic. Micah (Old Testament).

mi·ca (mī′kə) *n.* Any of a group of chemically and physically related mineral silicates, common in igneous and metamorphic rocks, each containing hydroxyl, alkali, and aluminum silicate groups, characteristically splitting into flexible sheets used in insulation. [New Latin (meaning influenced by Latin *micāre,* to shine), from Latin *mīca,* grain. See **smē-** in Appendix.*] —**mi·ca′ceous** (-kā′shəs) *adj.*

Mi·cah[1] (mī′kə). Also **Mi·che·as** (mī-kē′əs). A Hebrew prophet of the eighth century B.C.

Mi·cah[2] (mī′kə) *n.* Also **Mi·che·as** (mī-kē′əs). *Abbr.* **Mic.** The sixth of the Old Testament books of the Minor Prophets.

mi·caw·ber (mə-kô′bər) *n.* An improvident person who, despite constant adversity, remains doggedly optimistic about a change in his luck. [From Wilkins *Micawber,* a character in Charles Dickens' novel *David Copperfield* (1849–50).]

mice. Plural of **mouse.**

mi·celle (mĭ-sĕl′) *n., pl.* **-celles.** Also **mi·cel·la** (mĭ-sĕl′ə) *pl.* **-cellae** (-sĕl′ē), **mi·cell** *pl.* **-cells.** **1.** A submicroscopic aggregation of molecules such as a droplet in a colloidal system. **2.** An organic particle of colloidal size found in coal. **3.** A coherent strand or structure in natural or synthetic fibers. **4.** A submicroscopic structural unit of protoplasm. [New Latin *micella,* from Latin *mīca,* grain, MICA.] —**mi·cel′lar** (mĭ-sĕl′ər) *adj.*

Mich. Michigan.

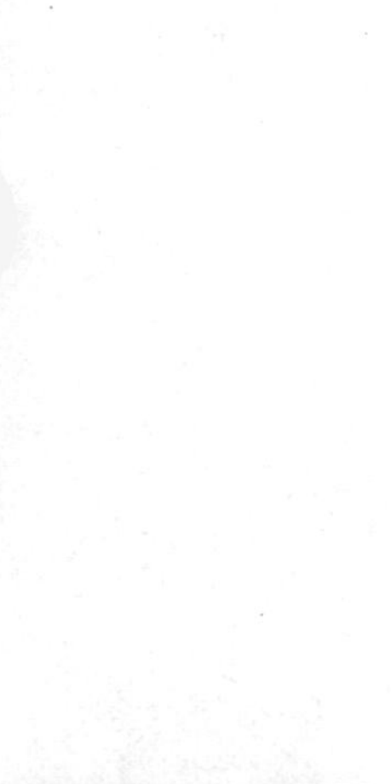

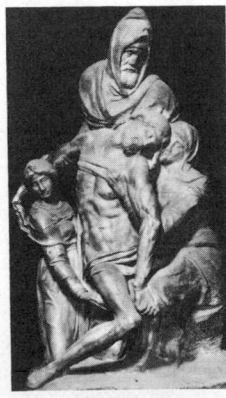

Michelangelo
Unfinished Pietà by Michelangelo (figure at rear is considered a self-portrait)

Mi·chael[1] (mī′kəl). A masculine given name. [Middle English *Michael,* Old English *Michael,* the archangel Michael, from Late Latin *Michaēl,* from Greek *Mikhaēl,* from Hebrew *Mīkāēl,* "who is like God" : *mī,* who + *ka,* like + *ēl,* god.]

Mi·chael[2] (mī′kəl). The guardian archangel of the Jews in the Old Testament. Daniel 10:13; Revelation 12:7–9.

Mich·ael·mas (mĭk′əl-məs) *n.* A church festival celebrated on September 29 in honor of the archangel Michael. [Middle English *mychelmesse,* Old English *Michaeles mæsse* : *Michaeles,* genitive of *Michael,* MICHAEL + *mæsse,* MASS.]

Michaelmas daisy. Any of several hybrid asters derived primarily from North American species such as the **New England aster** and the **New York aster** *(both of which see).*

Mi·chel·an·ge·lo (mī′kəl-ăn′jə-lō′, mĭk′əl-; *Italian* mē′kāl-än′jā-lō). Full name, Michelangelo Buonarroti. 1475–1564. Italian sculptor, painter, architect, and poet of the High Renaissance.

Mi·chel·son (mī′kəl-sən), **Albert Abraham.** 1852–1931. German-born American physicist.

Mi·chel·son-Mor·ley experiment (mī′kəl-sən-môr′lē). An experiment performed (1887) in an attempt to detect the motion of the earth through the ether by measuring the difference in velocity of two perpendicular beams of light. [After Albert Abraham MICHELSON and Edward Williams MORLEY.]

Mich·i·gan (mĭsh′ĭ-gən). *Abbr.* **Mich.** A Midwestern state of the United States, about 58,000 square miles in area, admitted to the Union in 1837. It is the center of automotive industries. Population, 6,372,000. Capital, Lansing. See map at **United States of America.** [After Lake MICHIGAN.] —**Mich′i·gan′der** (mĭsh′ĭ-găn′dər) *n.*

Mich·i·gan, Lake (mĭsh′ĭ-gən). The third largest (22,400 square miles) of the Great Lakes, lying between the states of Michigan and Wisconsin. [Ojibwa *mišsikamaa,* "it is a big lake" : Proto-Algonquian *me′th-* (unattested), big + *-kam-* (unattested), body of water + *-yaa* (unattested), inanimate intransitive suffix.]

Mi·cho·a·cán (mē′chō-ä-kän′). A state, 23,202 square miles in area, of central Mexico on the Pacific coast. Population, 2,009,000. Capital, Morelia.

mick (mĭk) *n.* Also **Mick.** An Irishman. Used disparagingly. [Probably from *Mick,* nickname for MICHAEL.]

Mick·ey Finn (mĭk′ē fĭn′). *Slang.* An alcoholic beverage that is surreptitiously drugged to induce diarrhea or to stupefy, render unconscious, or otherwise incapacitate its imbiber. Also called "Mickey." [Origin unknown.]

mick·le (mĭk′əl) *adj.* Also **muck·le** (mŭk′-). *Scottish.* Great. —*adv.* Also **muck·le.** *Scottish.* Greatly. [Middle English *mikell,* from Old Norse *mikill.* See **meg-** in Appendix.*]

Mic·mac (mĭk′măk′) *n., pl.* **Micmac** or **-macs.** **1.** An Algonquian tribe of North American Indians formerly inhabiting the areas that are now Nova Scotia and New Brunswick. **2.** A member of this tribe. **3.** The Algonquian language of the Micmac. [Micmac *miigemuag,* tribal name.]

mi·cra. Alternate plural of **micron.**

micro–. Indicates: **1.** The smaller, inner, or more detailed of two contrasting things; for example, **microcosm.** Compare **macro-.** **2.** An instrument or technique for working with small quantities; for example, **microchemistry.** **3.** Use of a microscope and related tools; for example, **microscopy.** **4.** Abnormally small size; for example, **microcephaly.** **5.** Amplification or enlargement; for example, **microphone.** **6.** *Symbol* μ One-millionth (10^{-6}) part of a unit in the metric or related measurement systems. ***Note:*** Many compounds other than those entered here may be formed with *micro-.* In forming compounds, *micro-* is normally joined to the following word or element without space or hyphen: *micrometer.* However, if the second element begins with a capital letter, it is separated with a hyphen: *micro-America.* If the second element begins with *o,* a hyphen is normally used, but as the compound grows widely familiar, the hyphen may be dropped. An example is the word *microorganism,* which the usage of scientists has established in that form. [Middle English, from Latin *micro-,* from Greek *mikro-, mikr-,* from *mikros,* small. See **smē-** in Appendix.*]

mi·cro·a·nal·y·sis (mī′krō-ə-năl′ə-sĭs) *n. Chemistry.* The analysis of quantities weighing one milligram or less. —**mi′cro·an′a·lyst** (-ăn′ə-lĭst) *n.* —**mi′cro·an′a·lyt′ic** (-ăn′ə-lĭt′ĭk), **mi′cro·an′a·lyt′i·cal** *adj.*

mi·crobe (mī′krōb′) *n.* A minute life form; a microorganism, especially one that causes disease. Not in technical use. See Synonyms at **germ.** [MICRO- + Greek *bios,* life (see **gwei-** in Appendix*).] —**mi·cro′bi·al** (mī-krō′bē-əl), **mi·cro′bic** *adj.*

mi·cro·bi·ol·o·gy (mī′krō-bī-ŏl′ə-jē) *n.* The science that deals with microorganisms, and especially their effects on other forms of life. [MICRO- + BIOLOGY.] —**mi′cro·bi′o·log′i·cal** (-bī′ə-lŏj′ĭ-kəl) *adj.* —**mi′cro·bi′o·log′i·cal·ly** *adv.* —**mi′cro·bi·ol′o·gist** *n.*

mi·cro·ceph·a·ly (mī′krō-sĕf′ə-lē) *n.* Abnormal smallness of the head, often associated with pathological mental conditions. [From Greek *mikrokephalos,* small-headed : MICRO- + -CEPHALOUS.] —**mi′cro·ce·phal′ic** (-sə-făl′ĭk) *n.* & *adj.* —**mi′cro·ceph′a·lous** (-sĕf′ə-ləs) *adj.*

mi·cro·chem·is·try (mī′krō-kĕm′ĭs-trē) *n.* Chemistry that deals with minute quantities of materials, weighing one milligram or less. Compare **macrochemistry.** —**mi′cro·chem′i·cal** *adj.*

mi·cro·cir·cuit (mī′krō-sûr′kĭt) *n.* An electric circuit consisting of miniaturized components. —**mi′cro·cir′cuit·ry** (-rē) *n.*

mi·cro·cli·mate (mī′krō-klī′mĭt) *n.* The climate of a specific place within an area, contrasted with the climate of the area as a whole. Compare **macroclimate.** —**mi′cro·cli·mat′ic** (-măt′ĭk) *adj.* —**mi′cro·cli′ma·to·log′ic** (-mə-tə-lŏj′ĭk), **mi′cro·cli′ma·to·log′i·cal** *adj.* —**mi′cro·cli′ma·tol′o·gy** (-mə-tŏl′ə-jē) *n.*

mi·cro·cline (mī′krō-klīn′) *n.* A mineral of the feldspar group, chiefly $KAlSi_3O_8$, used in making pottery. [German *Mikroklin* : MICRO- + CLINE.]

mi·cro·coc·cus (mī′krō-kŏk′əs) *n., pl.* **-cocci** (-kŏk′sī′, -kŏk′ī′). A spherical bacterium of several species of the genus *Micrococcus,* found in irregular clusters. [New Latin : MICRO- + COCCUS.]

mi·cro·cop·y (mī′krō-kŏp′ē) *n., pl.* **-ies.** A greatly reduced photographic copy, usually reproduced by projection.

mi·cro·cosm (mī′krə-kŏz′əm) *n.* A diminutive, representative world; a system more or less analogous to a much larger system in constitution, configuration, or development: *The town meeting is a microcosm of American democracy.* Compare **macrocosm.** [Middle English *microcosme,* from Medieval Latin *mīcro(s)cosmus,* from Greek *mikros kosmos,* small world : MICRO- + COSMOS.] —**mi′cro·cos′mic, mi′cro·cos′mi·cal** *adj.*

mi·cro·cyte (mī′krə-sīt′) *n.* An abnormally small red blood cell, less than five microns in diameter. [MICRO- + (ERYTHRO)CYTE.]

mi·cro·e·lec·tron·ics (mī′krō-ĭ-lĕk-trŏn′ĭks) *n.* Plural in form, used with a singular verb. The branch of electronics that deals with components of miniature size. —**mi′cro·e·lec·tron′ic** *adj.*

ă pat/ā pay/âr care/ä father/b bib/ch church/d deed/ĕ pet/ē be/f fife/g gag/h hat/hw which/ĭ pit/ī pie/îr pier/j judge/k kick/l lid, needle/m mum/n no, sudden/ng thing/ŏ pot/ō toe/ô paw, for/oi noise/ou out/o͝o took/o͞o boot/p pop/r roar/s sauce/sh ship, dish/

mi·cro·fiche (mī′krō-fēsh′) *n. Library Service.* A sheet of microfilm, usually of the same dimensions as a filing card, used in the preservation of records. [French : MICRO- + *fiche,* index card, slip of paper, peg, from Old French, point, from *fichier,* to fasten to, pin to, from Vulgar Latin *figicāre* (unattested), from Latin *fīgere,* to fasten. See **dhigw-** in Appendix.*]

mi·cro·film (mī′krə-fĭlm′) *n.* **1.** A film upon which documents are photographed greatly reduced in size. **2.** A reproduction on microfilm. —*tr.v.* **microfilmed, -filming, -films.** To reproduce (documents or other materials) on microfilm.

mi·cro·form (mī′krə-fôrm′) *n. Library Service.* Any arrangement of images reduced in size, as on microfilm.

mi·cro·ga·mete (mī′krō-gə-mēt′, -găm′ēt′) *n. Biology.* The smaller of a pair of conjugating gametes, the male gamete. Compare **macrogamete.** [MICRO- + GAMETE.]

mi·crog·ra·phy (mī-krŏg′rə-fē) *n.* The representation, study, or description of microscopic objects. Compare **macrography.** [MICRO- + -GRAPHY.] —**mi′cro·graph′ic** (mī′krə-grăf′ĭk) *adj.*

Mi·cro·groove (mī′krō-gro͞ov′) *n.* A trademark for a long-playing phonograph record.

mi·cro·hab·i·tat (mī′krō-hăb′ə-tăt′) *n.* The smallest unit of a habitat, as in a clump of grass or a space between rocks.

mi·cro·me·te·or·ite (mī′krō-mē′tē-ə-rīt′) *n.* A micrometeoroid, especially one found on the earth or the moon.

mi·cro·me·te·or·oid (mī′krō-mē′tē-ə-roid′) *n.* Any of numerous relatively small meteoroids distinguished by increasing occurrence as meteors with decreasing meteoric mass.

mi·cro·me·te·or·ol·o·gy (mī′krō-mē′tē-ə-rŏl′ə-jē) *n.* The study of meteorologic conditions in a small region, usually a shallow layer up to a few hundred feet above ground in which temperature and humidity extremes are found.

mi·crom·e·ter (mī-krŏm′ə-tər) *n.* Any device for measuring minute distances, especially one based on the rotation of a finely threaded screw, as in relation to a microscope. [French *micromètre* : MICRO- + -METER.]

mi·crom·e·try (mī-krŏm′ə-trē) *n.* Measurement with a micrometer. —**mi′cro·met′ric** (mī′krō-mĕt′rĭk), **mi′cro·met′ri·cal** *adj.* —**mi′cro·met′ri·cal·ly** *adv.*

mi·cron (mī′krŏn′) *n., pl.* **-crons** or **-cra** (-krə). Also **mi·kron.** *Symbol* μ A unit of length equal to one-millionth (10^{-6}) of a meter. [New Latin, from Greek, from *mikros,* small. See **smē-** in Appendix.*]

Mi·cro·ne·sia (mī′krō-nē′zhə, -shə). The island groups in the Pacific Ocean east of the Philippines and north of the equator. They include the Mariana, Marshall, Caroline, and Gilbert islands and have a land area of about 1,335 square miles. [New Latin : MICRO- + Greek *nēsos,* island (see **snā-** in Appendix*).]

Mi·cro·ne·sian (mī′krō-nē′zhən, -shən) *adj.* Of or pertaining to Micronesia, its inhabitants, their languages, or their culture. —*n.* **1.** A native or inhabitant of Micronesia. **2.** A subfamily of Austronesian languages spoken in Micronesia.

mi·cro·nu·cle·us (mī′krō-no͞o′klē-əs, -nyo͞o′klē-əs) *n., pl.* **-clei** (-klē-ī′) or **-uses.** The smaller nuclear mass in ciliated and suctorial protozoans, distinguished from the macronucleus in such animals. [New Latin : MICRO- + NUCLEUS.]

mi·cro·nu·tri·ent (mī′krō-no͞o′trē-ənt, -nyo͞o′trē-ənt) *n.* A substance that in minute amounts is essential to life.

mi·cro·or·gan·ism (mī′krō-ôr′gən-ĭz′əm) *n.* Also **mi·cro-or·gan·ism.** An animal or plant of microscopic size, especially a bacterium or a protozoan.

mi·cro·pa·le·on·tol·o·gy (mī′krō-pā′lē-ŏn-tŏl′ə-jē, -ən-tŏl′ə-jē) *n.* The scientific study of microscopic fossils. —**mi′cro·pa′le·on·to·log′ic** (-tə-lŏj′ĭk), **mi′cro·pa′le·on·to·log′i·cal** *adj.*

mi·cro·phone (mī′krə-fōn′) *n.* An instrument that converts acoustical waves into an electric current, usually fed into an amplifier, recorder, or broadcast transmitter. [MICRO- + -PHONE.] —**mi′cro·phon′ic** (mī′krə-fŏn′ĭk) *adj.*

mi·cro·pho·to·graph (mī′krō-fō′tə-grăf′, -gräf′) *n.* **1.** A photograph requiring magnification for viewing. **2.** A photograph on microfilm. **3.** A photomicrograph. —**mi′cro·pho′to·graph′ic** *adj.* —**mi′cro·pho·tog′ra·phy** (-fə-tŏg′rə-fē) *n.*

mi·cro·phys·ics (mī′krō-fĭz′ĭks) *n.* Plural in form, used with a singular verb. The physics of molecular, atomic, nuclear, and subnuclear systems. —**mi′cro·phys′i·cal** *adj.*

mi·cro·phyte (mī′krə-fīt′) *n.* Any plant of microscopic size. [MICRO- + -PHYTE.] —**mi′cro·phyt′ic** (-fĭt′ĭk) *adj.*

mi·cro·print (mī′krə-prĭnt′) *n.* The printed or positive reproduction of a microphotograph.

mi·cro·pyle (mī′krə-pīl′) *n.* **1.** *Botany.* A minute opening in the ovule of a plant, through which the pollen tube usually enters. **2.** *Zoology.* A pore in the membrane of the ova of some animals, through which the spermatozoon enters. [MICRO- + Greek *pulē,* gate (see **pulē** in Appendix*).] —**mi′cro·py′lar** (-pī′lər) *adj.*

mi·cro·scope (mī′krə-skōp′) *n.* An optical instrument that uses a combination of lenses to produce magnified images of small objects, especially of objects too small to be seen by the unaided eye. See **simple microscope, compound microscope, electron microscope, x-ray microscope.** [New Latin *microscopium* : MICRO- + -SCOPE.]

mi·cro·scop·ic (mī′krə-skŏp′ĭk) *adj.* Also **mi·cro·scop·i·cal** (-ĭ-kəl). **1.** Too small to be seen by the unaided eye but large enough to be studied under a microscope. **2.** Exceedingly small; minute: *"The activities of men . . . were reduced to a microscopic scale."* (John Hersey). **3.** Characterized by or done with extreme attention to detail: *a microscopic investigation.* **4.** Of, pertaining to, or concerned with a microscope. **5.** Like or resembling a microscope; having the ability to observe very small objects. —**mi′cro·scop′i·cal·ly** *adv.*

Mi·cro·sco·pi·um (mī′krə-skō′pē-əm) *n.* A constellation in the Southern Hemisphere. [New Latin, MICROSCOPE.]

mi·cros·co·py (mī-krŏs′kə-pē) *n.* **1. a.** The study of microscopes. **b.** The use of microscopes. **2.** Investigation employing a microscope. —**mi·cros′co·pist** *n.*

mi·cro·seism (mī′krə-sī′zəm) *n.* A faint, recurrent tremor of the earth's crust. [MICRO- + SEISM.] —**mi′cro·seis′mic** (mī′krə-sīz′mĭk, -sīs′mĭk), **mi′cro·seis′mi·cal** *adj.*

mi·cro·some (mī′krə-sōm′) *n.* A cell particle, a **ribosome** *(see).* [German *Mikrosom* : MICRO- + -SOME.] —**mi′cro·so′mi·al** (-sō′mē-əl), **mi′cro·so′mic** *adj.*

mi·cro·spo·ran·gi·um (mī′krō-spə-răn′jē-əm) *n., pl.* **-gia** (-jē-ə). A structure or receptacle in which microspores are formed. [New Latin : MICRO- + SPORANGIUM.]

mi·cro·spore (mī′krə-spôr′, -spōr′) *n.* **1.** *Botany.* The smaller of two types of spores produced by heterosporous plants, such as ferns, giving rise to the male gametophyte. Compare **megaspore. 2.** The smaller of two spores formed by Radiolaria and certain other protozoans. —**mi′cro·spor′ic, mi′cro·spo′rous** (mī-krŏs′pə-rəs) *adj.*

mi·cro·spo·ro·phyll (mī′krə-spôr′ə-fĭl′, -spōr′ə-fĭl′) *n.* A structure that produces microsporangia. [MICRO- + SPOROPHYLL.]

mi·cro·tome (mī′krə-tōm′) *n.* An instrument used to cut tissue into thin sections for microscopic examination. [MICRO- + -TOME.]

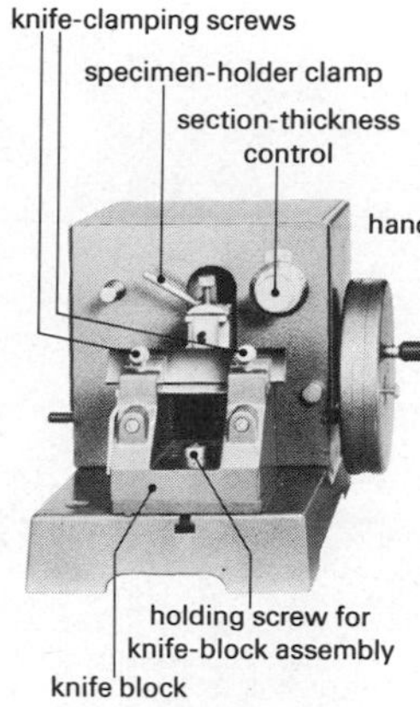
knife-clamping screws
specimen-holder clamp
section-thickness control
handle
holding screw for knife-block assembly
knife block
microtome

mi·crot·o·my (mī-krŏt′ə-mē) *n.* The preparation of specimens with a microtome. —**mi′cro·tom′ic** (mī′krə-tŏm′ĭk) *adj.*

mi·cro·tone (mī′krə-tōn′) *n. Music.* An interval smaller than a half tone.

mi·cro·wave (mī′krə-wāv′) *n.* Any electromagnetic radiation having a wavelength in the approximate range from one millimeter to one meter, the region between infrared and short-wave radio wavelengths.

mic·tu·rate (mĭk′chə-rāt′, mĭk′tə-) *intr.v.* **-rated, -rating, -rates.** To urinate. [Latin *micturīre,* to want to urinate, from *meiere* (past participle stem *mictus*), to urinate. See **meigh-** in Appendix.*]

mic·tu·ri·tion (mĭk′chə-rĭsh′ən, mĭk′tə-) *n.* The act of urinating. [From Latin *micturītiō,* from *micturīre,* to MICTURATE.]

mid[1] (mĭd) *adj.* **1.** Middle; central. **2.** Being the part in the middle or center: *in the mid Pacific.* **3.** *Phonetics.* Pronounced with the tongue approximately intermediate between high and low, as in the *u* in *cut* or the *e* in *pet.* Said of vowel sounds. —*n. Archaic.* The middle. [Middle English *mid, midde,* Old English *midd.* See **medhyo-** in Appendix.*]

mid[2] (mĭd) *prep. Chiefly Poetic.* Amid: *mid smoke and flame.*

mid–. Indicates a middle part, time, or location; for example, **midship, midway.** ***Note:*** Many compounds other than those entered here may be formed with *mid-.* In forming compounds, *mid-* is normally joined to the following word or element without space or hyphen: *midday.* However, if the second element begins with a capital letter, it is always separated with a hyphen: *mid-May.* It is always acceptable to separate the elements with a hyphen to avoid possible confusion with another form; for example, *mid-den* (the middle of a den) as distinct from the word *midden.* Note that the adjective *mid*[1] above is a separate word, though, as with any adjective, it may be joined to another word with a hyphen when used as a unit modifier: *in the mid Pacific,* but *a mid-Pacific island.* [From MID (middle).]

mid. middle.

mid·air (mĭd′âr′) *n.* A point or region in the middle of the air; space: *floating in midair.*

Mi·das (mī′dəs). The fabled king of Phrygia to whom Dionysus gave the power of turning to gold all that he touched.

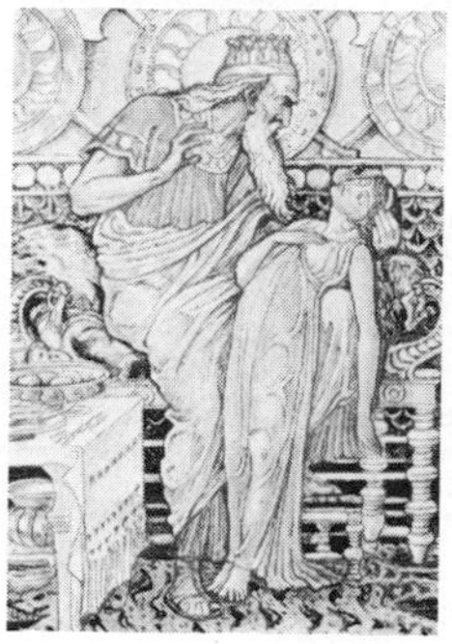
Midas
The king with his daughter as she turns into gold

mid·brain (mĭd′brān′) *n.* **1.** The middle region of the embryonic vertebrate brain, the **mesencephalon** *(see).* **2.** The parts that develop from this region.

mid·course (mĭd′kôrs′, -kōrs′) *n. Aerospace.* The part of a missile's flight between burnout and re-entry, during which corrective maneuvers are made.

Mid·cult (mĭd′kŭlt′) *n.* An intermediate form of culture with qualities of high culture and mass culture. [MID(DLEBROW) + CULT(URE). Coined by Dwight Macdonald.]

mid·day (mĭd′dā′) *n.* The middle of the day; noon. —*adj.* Of, pertaining to, or occurring in the middle of the day or at noon: *a midday snack.* [Middle English *midday,* Old English *middæg* : *midd,* MID (middle) + *dæg,* DAY.]

mid·den (mĭd′n) *n.* **1.** A dunghill or refuse heap, especially of a primitive habitation. **2.** A **kitchen midden** *(see).* [Middle English *myddung,* from Old Norse *myki-dyngja* (unattested) : *myki-,* muck (see **meug-**[2] in Appendix*) + *dyngja,* heap (see **dung**).]

mid·dle (mĭd′l) *adj. Abbr.* **mid. 1.** Equally distant from extremes or limits; central; mean: *the middle point on a line.* **2.** Intermediate; in-between: *the middle piece of cake.* **3.** Medium; moderate: *"He was about the middle height."* (Dickens). **4.** Intervening between an earlier and later period of time; part of a sequence or series: *the middle years.* **5.** *Capital* **M.** Designating a stage in the development of a language or literature between earlier and later stages: *Middle English.* **6.** *Logic.* Designating a term that appears in both premises of a syllogism but not in the conclusion. **7.** *Grammar.* Intermediate between active and passive voice. Said of verb forms in Sanskrit and Greek in which the subject is represented as acting on, for, or with reference to itself. —*n.* **1.** An area or point equidistant between extremes; the center: *the middle of a circle.* **2.** Something intermediate between extremes; a mean. **3.** The interior portion: *the middle of the chain.* **4.** The middle part of the human body; waist. **5.** *Logic.* The **middle term** *(see).* **6.** *Grammar.* The middle voice. —*tr.v.* **middled, -dling, -dles. 1.** To place in the middle. **2.** *Nau-*

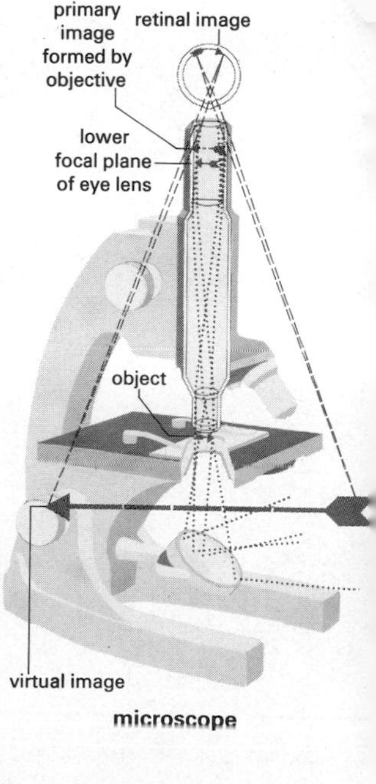
primary image formed by objective
retinal image
lower focal plane of eye lens
object
virtual image
microscope

tical. To fold in the middle: *middle the sail.* [Middle English *middel,* Old English *middel.* See medhyo- in Appendix.*]

middle age. The time of human life between youth and old age, usually reckoned as the years between 40 and 60.

Middle Ages. The period in European history between Antiquity and the Renaissance, often dated from A.D. 476, when Romulus Augustulus, the last emperor of the Western Roman Empire, was deposed, to A.D. 1453, when Constantinople was conquered by the Turks. Compare **Dark Ages.**

Middle America. Mexico and Central America. Sometimes the designation includes the West Indies.

Middle Atlantic States. Those states of the United States having Atlantic Ocean ports and lying between New England and Virginia. They are New York, Pennsylvania, New Jersey, Delaware, and Maryland. Also called "Middle States."

Middle Breton. Breton from the 5th century to the 16th.

mid·dle·brow (mĭd′l-brou′) *n. Informal.* A person of mediocre culture. Compare **highbrow, lowbrow.** —**mid′dle·brow′** *adj.*

middle C. *Music.* The musical tone represented by the first ledger line below the treble (G) clef or the first ledger line above the bass (F) clef.

middle class. The members of society occupying an intermediate social and economic position between the laboring classes and those who are wealthy in land or money.

mid·dle-class (mĭd′l-klăs′, -kläs′) *adj.* Of, pertaining to, or characteristic of the middle class.

Middle Congo. Formerly, a French colony and later an overseas territory in French Equatorial Africa. See **Congo, Republic of (Brazzaville).**

Middle Danish. Danish in the 16th and 17th centuries.

middle distance. **1.** The area between the foreground and background in a painting, drawing, or photograph. **2.** *Track & Field.* A division of competition in racing with events usually ranging from 440 yards to 1 mile.

Middle Dutch. Dutch from the middle of the 12th century through the 15th.

middle ear. The space between the tympanic membrane and the inner ear. It contains the auditory ossicles that convey vibrations to the auditory tube. Also called "tympanum." See **ear.**

Middle East. **1.** The area in Asia and Africa between and including Libya in the west, Pakistan in the east, Turkey in the north, and the Arabian Peninsula in the south. **2.** *British.* This same region, excluding Turkey and including Ethiopia, Sudan, and Somaliland in Africa, and sometimes India, Burma, and Tibet in Asia. Also called "Mideast."

Middle Empire. The **Middle Kingdom** *(see)* of Egypt.

Middle English. *Abbr.* **M.E., ME., ME** English from the 12th century through the 15th. It is distinguished from Old English by a tendency to weaken unaccented syllables, which resulted in the gradual attrition of inflectional endings, greater reliance on word order, the reduction of Old English prefixes, and an increase of French and Scandinavian loan words. The five main dialects of Middle English were: Kentish (southeastern), Southern (southwestern), East Midland, West Midland, and Northern. Late in the 14th century, the southern branch of East Midland, spoken in London, emerged as the national written language that became Modern English.

Middle French. A former classification of French in use from the 14th century to the middle of the 16th; now regarded as the final period of Old French.

Middle Greek. **Medieval Greek** *(see).*

Middle High German. High German from the 11th century through the 15th.

Middle Irish. Irish from the 10th century through the 13th.

Middle Kingdom. **1.** A kingdom of ancient Egypt lasting from about 2100 to about 1600 B.C. Capitals, Heracleopolis, later Thebes. Also called "Middle Empire." **2. a.** The former Chinese empire, considered by its inhabitants to be the center of the world. **b.** The original 18 provinces of China. Often called "China Proper." [In sense 2, an improper translation of Chinese (Mandarin) *chung¹ kuo²,* "middle nation," Chinese name for China : *chung¹,* middle + *kuo²,* nation.]

Middle Low German. Low German from the middle of the 13th century through the 15th.

mid·dle·man (mĭd′l-măn′) *n., pl.* **-men** (-mĕn′). **1.** A trader who buys from producers and sells to retailers or consumers. **2.** An intermediary or go-between.

mid·dle·most (mĭd′l-mōst′) *adj.* Midmost. [Middle English *middelmast : middel,* MIDDLE + *-mast,* -MOST.]

Middle Norwegian. Norwegian from the late 14th century to the early 16th.

middle passage. A former slave-trade route from West Africa to the West Indies or the Americas.

Middle Persian. The language of the Sassanians, from the third century A.D. to the seventh.

Mid·dles·brough (mĭd′əlz-brə). A borough in the North Riding of Yorkshire, England. Population, 157,000.

Mid·dle·sex (mĭd′l-sĕks′). **1.** *Abbr.* **Middlx., Midx., Mx.** A county of southeastern England, containing part of London's metropolitan area. Population, 2,235,000. **2.** A county of eastern Massachusetts, where the first engagement of the Revolutionary War (April 19, 1775) was fought. [Middle English *Midelsexe,* Old English *Middelseaxan,* "the Middle Saxons" : *middel,* MIDDLE + *Seaxan,* SAXON(S).]

Middle Swedish. Swedish from the late 14th century to the early 16th.

Middle Temple. **1.** A society of lawyers in London, England. **2.** The buildings of this society; one of the Inns of Court.

middle term *Logic. Abbr.* **M** The term in a syllogism presented in both premises but not appearing in the conclusion.

Mid·dle·town (mĭd′l-toun′) *n.* A hypothetical community regarded as representative of American middle-class culture: *The candidates heeded Middletown.*

mid·dle·weight (mĭd′l-wāt′) *n.* A boxer or wrestler weighing between 147 and 160 pounds.

Middle Welsh. Welsh from the 12th century through the 15th.

Middle West. A cultural and historical region of the United States extending roughly from Ohio westward through Iowa, and from the Ohio and Missouri rivers northward through the Great Lakes. Also called "Midwest." —**Middle Western.** —**Middle Westerner.**

mid·dling (mĭd′lĭng, -lĭn) *adj.* Of medium size, quality, or state; mediocre; ordinary. See Synonyms at **average.** —*n.* **1.** *Often plural. Chiefly Southeastern U.S.* Pork or bacon cut from between the ham and shoulder of a pig. **2.** *Plural.* Products that are intermediate in quality, size, price, or grade. **3.** *Plural.* Coarsely ground wheat mixed with bran. —*adv. Informal.* Fairly; moderately. [Middle English (Scottish) *mydlyn : midde,* MID (middle) + -LING (small).] —**mid′dling·ly** *adv.*

mid·dy (mĭd′ē) *n., pl.* **-dies. 1.** *Informal.* A midshipman: "*And the seasick little middy strikes the bell.*" (Masefield). **2.** A middy blouse.

middy blouse. A woman's or child's loose blouse with a sailor collar.

Mid·east (mĭd′ēst′) *n.* **Middle East** *(see).*

Mid·gard (mĭd′gärd). Also **Mid·garth** (mĭd′gärth′), **Mith·gar·thr** (mĭth′gär′thər). *Norse Mythology.* The part of the world inhabited by men, imagined as a fortress encircled by a huge serpent, built by the gods around the middle region of the universe. [From Old Norse *Midhgardhr.* See medhyo- in Appendix.*]

midge (mĭj) *n.* **1.** Any of various gnatlike flies of the family Chironomidae, found worldwide. **2.** Any small person. [Middle English *migge,* Old English *mycg.* See mū-² in Appendix.*]

midg·et (mĭj′ĭt) *n.* **1.** An extremely small person who is otherwise normally proportioned. **2.** A small or miniature version of something. **3.** A class of small objects, such as a class of very small sailboats or racing automobiles. —*adj.* **1.** Miniature; diminutive; dwarfed. **2.** Belonging to a type or class much smaller than what is considered standard: *a midget automobile.* [Diminutive of MIDGE.]

mid·gut (mĭd′gŭt′) *n.* The middle section of the digestive tract in the vertebrate embryo, from which the ileum and the jejunum develop. Also called "mesenteron."

Mi·di (mē-dē′) *n. French.* The south of France.

Mid·i·an (mĭd′ē-ən). An ancient region in the northwest of the Arabian Peninsula, east of the Gulf of Aqaba.

Mid·i·an·ite (mĭd′ē-ən-ĭt′) *n.* One of the ancient Arabian tribe of Midian. Exodus 2:15–22; Judges 6–8. —**Mid′i·an·ite′** *adj.*

mid·i·ron (mĭd′ī′ərn) *n.* An iron golf club that has more loft than a driver and less than a mashie, used for medium fairway shots and long approach shots. Now called "two iron."

mid·land (mĭd′lənd) *n.* The middle or interior part of a specific country or region. —*adj.* Of or in a midland.

Mid·land¹ (mĭd′lənd) *n.* The dialect of Middle English spoken in the Midlands, which formed the basis of Modern English.

Mid·land² (mĭd′lənd). A city of west-central Texas. Population, 62,000.

Mid·lands (mĭd′ləndz). The middle counties of England.

Mid·lo·thi·an (mĭd-lō′thē-ən). A county of Scotland, 366 square miles in area, in the southeast on the Firth of Forth. Population, 566,000. County seat, Edinburgh.

mid·most (mĭd′mōst′) *adj.* **1.** Situated in the exact middle; middlemost. **2.** Situated nearest the middle. —*adv.* In the middle. [Middle English *midmest,* Old English *midmest : midd,* MID + -*mest,* -MOST.]

mid·night (mĭd′nīt′) *n.* **1.** The middle of the night; specifically, twelve o'clock at night. **2. a.** Intense darkness or gloom. **b.** A period of darkness and gloom. —*adj.* **1.** Of or pertaining to the middle of the night. **2.** Resembling the middle of the night; dark; gloomy; dreary. —**burn the midnight oil.** To work or study very late at night. [Middle English *midnight,* Old English *midniht : midd,* MID + *niht,* NIGHT.]

midnight sun. The sun as seen at midnight during the summer within the Arctic or Antarctic Circle.

mid·point (mĭd′point′) *n.* **1.** The point of a line segment or curvilinear arc that divides it into two parts of the same length. **2.** A position midway between two extremes.

Mid·rash (mĭd′räsh′) *n., pl.* **Midrashim** (mĭd-räsh′ĭm), **Midrashoth** (mĭd-räsh′ōth). Any of a group of Jewish commentaries on the Hebrew Scriptures, written between A.D. 400 and 1200. [Late Hebrew *midhrāsh,* commentary, from *dārash,* to investigate, seek.] —**Mid·rash′ic** (mĭd-räsh′ĭk) *adj.*

mid·rib (mĭd′rĭb′) *n.* The central or principal vein of a leaf.

mid·riff (mĭd′rĭf′) *n.* **1.** A part of the body, the **diaphragm** *(see).* **2.** The middle, outer portion of the front of the human body, extending roughly from just below the breast to the waistline. [Middle English *midrif,* Old English *midhrif : midd,* MID + *hrif,* belly (see **krep-** in Appendix*).] —**mid′riff** *adj.*

mid·ship (mĭd′shĭp′) *adj.* Pertaining to the middle of a ship.

mid·ship·man (mĭd′shĭp′mən, mĭd-shĭp′mən) *n., pl.* **-men** (-mĭn). **1.** Formerly a naval cadet on British ships of war whose battle station was amidships or abreast of the mainmast. **2.** A student training to be commissioned as an officer in the U.S. Navy or Coast Guard. **3.** A noncommissioned officer ranking below sublieutenant in the Royal and British Commonwealth navies. **4.** Any of various fishes of the genus *Porichthys,* having several rows of light-producing organs along their bodies.

ă pat/ā pay/âr care/ä father/b bib/ch church/d deed/ĕ pet/ē be/f fife/g gag/h hat/hw which/ĭ pit/ī pie/îr pier/j judge/k kick/l lid, needle/m mum/n no, sudden/ng thing/ŏ pot/ō toe/ô paw, for/oi noise/ou out/ŏŏ took/ōō boot/p pop/r roar/s sauce/sh ship, dish/

[From earlier *midshipsman* : MIDSHIPS + MAN.]
mid·ships (mĭd′shĭps′) *adv.* **1.** Amidships. **2.** In the center position. Said of the helm. —*n.* The middle part of a ship. [Short for AMIDSHIPS.]
midst (mĭdst, mĭtst) *n.* **1.** The middle position or part; center. **2.** The condition of being in the interior of, surrounded by, or enveloped in something. Used chiefly in the phrases *in the midst of* and *in our (their, your) midst: "There can be no very black melancholy to him who lives in the midst of nature"* (Thoreau). —*prep.* Among. [Middle English *middest,* variant of *middes,* from phrases such as *in middes,* variant of *in middan,* dative of *midde,* MID.]
mid·sum·mer (mĭd′sŭm′ər) *n.* **1.** The middle of the summer. **2.** The summer solstice, about June 21. —**mid′sum′mer** *adj.*
mid·term (mĭd′tûrm′) *n.* **1.** The middle of an academic term or a political term of office. **2. a.** An examination given at the middle of a school term. **b.** *Plural.* A series of such examinations. —**mid′term′** *adj.*
mid-Vic·to·ri·an (mĭd′vĭk-tôr′ē-ən, -tōr′ē-ən) *adj.* Pertaining to, occurring in, or characteristic of the middle period of the reign of Queen Victoria in Great Britain (1837–1901), a period known for rigid social standards. —*n.* **1.** A person living in the mid-Victorian period. **2.** A person having mid-Victorian ideas.
mid·way (mĭd′wā′) *n.* **1.** The area of any fair, carnival, circus, or exposition where side shows and other amusements are located. **2.** *Obsolete.* **a.** The middle of a way or distance. **b.** A middle way or course of action or thought. —*adv.* In the middle of a way or distance; halfway. —**mid′way′** *adj.*
Midway Islands. A coral atoll consisting of two islets, two square miles in area, in the Pacific Ocean 1,200 miles northwest of Hawaii, near which U.S. naval forces won a decisive battle of the Pacific war against the Japanese (June, 1942).
mid·week (mĭd′wēk′) *n.* The middle of the week. —*adj.* Happening in the middle of the week. —**mid′week′ly** *adj.* & *adv.*
Mid·west (mĭd′wĕst′) *n.* The **Middle West** *(see).* —**Mid′west′, Mid′west′ern** *adj.* —**Mid′west′ern·er** *n.*
mid·wife (mĭd′wīf′) *n., pl.* **-wives** (-wīvz′). A woman who assists women in childbirth. [Middle English *midwif* : *mid,* with, Old English *mid* (see **me-**[2] in Appendix*) + *wif,* WIFE.]
mid·wife·ry (mĭd′wīf′rē, -wĭ′fər-ē) *n.* The practice of a midwife.
mid·win·ter (mĭd′wĭn′tər) *n.* **1.** The middle of the winter. **2.** The period of the winter solstice, about December 22.
Midx. Middlesex.
mid·year (mĭd′yîr′) *n.* **1.** The middle of the calendar or academic year. **2. a.** A scholastic examination given in the middle of the school year. **b.** *Plural.* A series of such examinations.
mien (mēn) *n.* **1.** One's bearing or manner; expression: *a person of noble mien.* **2.** An appearance or aspect: *"Vice is a monster of so frightful mien,/As, to be hated, needs but to be seen"* (Pope). See Synonyms at **bearing.** [From earlier *meane, mine* (influenced by French *mine,* appearance), short for DEMEAN.]
Mies van der Ro·he (mēs′ vän dər rō′ə), **Ludwig.** Born 1886. German-born American architect.
miff (mĭf) *n.* **1.** A petulant, bad-tempered mood; huff. **2.** A petty quarrel or argument; tiff. —*tr.v.* **miffed, miffing, miffs.** To cause (a person) to become offended or annoyed. [Perhaps imitative of an expression of disgust.]
mif·fy (mĭf′ē) *adj.* **-fier, -fiest. 1.** *Informal.* Easily offended; overly sensitive. **2.** *Botany.* Difficult to raise except under perfect conditions. Said of certain plants. —**mif′fi·ness** *n.*
might[1] (mīt) *n.* **1. a.** Tremendous power held by an individual or group: *"with twenty-five squadrons of fighters he could defend the island against the whole might of the German Air Force"* (Winston Churchill). **b.** Supreme power attributed to a divine being: *the might of God.* **2.** Physical or bodily strength. —See Synonyms at **strength.** —**with might and main.** With all one's strength; with the utmost effort. [Middle English *might,* Old English *miht.* See **magh-**[1] in Appendix.*]
might[2]. Past tense of **may.**
might·i·ly (mī′tə-lē) *adv.* **1.** In a mighty manner; forcefully; powerfully. **2.** To a great degree; greatly.
might·y (mī′tē) *adj.* **-ier, -iest. 1. a.** Having might; powerful; strong: *"The smith, a mighty man is he."* (Longfellow). **b.** Having great intellectual or artistic ability: *"the mighty sage"* (Boswell). **2.** Exerting great force; violent: *a mighty blow of his ax.* **3.** Awesomely huge: *"the city stood on a mighty hill"* (Bunyan). —*adv. Informal.* In a great degree; very; extremely. See Usage note below. —**might′i·ness** *n.*
Usage: The use of *mighty* for *very* in writing is condemned by 89 per cent of the Usage Panel; however, 56 per cent accept this usage in speech on all levels.
mi·gnon·ette (mĭn′yən-ĕt′) *n.* A plant, *Reseda odorata,* native to the Mediterranean region but widely cultivated for its clusters of fragrant but inconspicuous greenish flowers. [French, feminine of obsolete *mignonnet,* diminutive of *mignon,* dainty, small, MINION.]
mi·graine (mī′grān′) *n.* Severe, recurrent headache, usually affecting only one side of the head, characterized by sharp pain and often accompanied by nausea. Also called "megrim." [French, from Old French, from Late Latin *hēmicrānia,* pain in half of the head, from Greek *hēmikrania* : HEMI- + *kranion,* CRANIUM.] —**mi′grain′oid′** (-noid′), **mi′grain′ous** (-nəs) *adj.*
mi·grant (mī′grənt) *n.* **1.** A person, animal, bird, or fish that moves from one region to another by chance, instinct, or plan. **2.** An itinerant worker who travels from one area to another in search of work. —*adj.* Migratory: *"The migrant people looked humbly for pleasure on the roads."* (Steinbeck). [Latin *migrāns,* present participle of *migrāre,* to MIGRATE.]
mi·grate (mī′grāt′) *intr.v.* **-grated, -grating, -grates. 1.** To move from one country or region and settle in another. **2.** To change location periodically; move seasonally from one region to another: *"The birds that fish the cold sea for a living must either migrate or starve."* (Rachel Carson). [Latin *migrāre.* See **mei-**[1] in Appendix.*]
Usage: *Migrate* is used with reference both to the place of departure and the destination, and can be followed by *from* or *to.* It is said of persons, animals, and birds, and sometimes implies lack of permanent settlement (notably seasonal movement). *Emigrate* pertains to a single move by persons, and implies permanence. It has specific reference to the place of departure, emphasizes movement from that place, and is usually followed by *from. Immigrate* specifies a single move by persons, and implies permanence. But it refers to the destination, emphasizes movement there, and is followed by *to.*
mi·gra·tion (mī-grā′shən) *n.* **1.** The action or an act of migrating. **2.** A group migrating together. **3.** *Chemistry.* **a.** The movement of one or more atoms from one position in a molecule to another. **b.** The movement of ions toward one electrode or the other during electrolysis. —**mi·gra′tion·al** *adj.*
mi·gra·to·ry (mī′grə-tôr′ē, -tōr′ē) *adj.* **1.** Characterized by migration; migrating periodically: *migratory birds.* **2.** Of or relating to a migration. **3.** Roving; nomadic.
mijn·heer. *Dutch* for **Mynheer.**
mi·ka·do (mĭ-kä′dō) *n., pl.* **-dos.** *Often capital* **M.** The emperor of Japan. The title is not used by Japanese people, who use "Tenno." [Japanese, "exalted gate" : *mi* (honorific prefix) + *kado,* gate. Probably originally said of the imperial court.]
mike (mīk) *n. Informal.* A microphone.
Mi·ko·yan (mĭk′ə-yän′), **Anastas Ivanovich.** Born 1895. Soviet political leader.
mi·kron. Variant of **micron.**
mil[1] (mĭl) *n.* **1.** A unit of length equal to one-thousandth (10^{-3}) of an inch. Used chiefly to specify the diameter of wire. **2.** A milliliter, or one cubic centimeter. **3.** A unit of angular measurement used in artillery and equal to $^1/_{6400}$ of a complete revolution. [Short for Latin *millēsimus,* thousandth, from *mīlle,* thousand. See **gheslo-** in Appendix.*]
mil[2] (mĭl) *n.* A coin equal to $^1/_{1000}$ of the pound of Cyprus. See table of exchange rates at **currency.** [Latin *mīlle,* a thousand. See **gheslo-** in Appendix.*]
mil. military; militia.
mi·la·dy (mĭ-lā′dē) *n., pl.* **-dies.** Also **mi·la·di** *pl.* **-dis. 1.** My lady. A title of respect formerly used in Europe when speaking of or addressing an English noblewoman or gentlewoman. **2.** A chic or fashionable woman. [French, from English *my lady.*]
mil·age. Variant of **mileage.**
Mi·lan (mĭ-lăn′, -län′). *Italian* **Mi·la·no** (mē-lä′nō). The second-largest city of Italy, in Lombardy. Population, 1,666,000.
Mil·an·ese (mĭl′ə-nēz′, -nēs′) *n., pl.* **Milanese.** A native or inhabitant of Milan. —*adj.* **1.** Of or pertaining to Milan or its people, culture, or products. **2.** *Cookery.* Coated with bread crumbs or flour and fried in oil or butter.
milch (mĭlch) *adj.* Giving milk: *a milch cow.* [Middle English *milche,* Old English *-milce.* See **melg-** in Appendix.*]
mild (mīld) *adj.* **milder, mildest. 1.** Gentle or kind in disposition, manners, or behavior: *a strong but mild man.* **2.** Moderate in type, degree, effect, or force: *a mild punishment.* **3.** Not very harmful; light: *a mild fever.* **4.** Having no extremes in temperature; temperate: *"In regions mild of calm and serene air"* (Milton). **5.** Not sharp, bitter, or strong in taste or odor: *a mild cheese; mild tobacco.* [Middle English *mild,* Old English *milde.* See **mel-**[1] in Appendix.*] —**mild′ly** *adv.* —**mild′ness** *n.*
mil·dew (mĭl′do͞o′, -dyo͞o′) *n.* **1.** A plant disease in which a fungus forms a superficial growth on the plant. See **downy mildew, powdery mildew. 2.** A superficial coating or discoloring of organic materials, such as paint, paper, cloth, leather, and the like, caused by fungi, especially under damp conditions. Compare **mold.** —*v.* **mildewed, -dewing, -dews.** —*tr.* To affect with mildew. —*intr.* To become affected with mildew. [Middle English *mildew,* Old English *mildēaw.* See **melit-** in Appendix.*] —**mil′dew·y** *adj.*
Mil·dred (mĭl′drĭd). A feminine given name. [Middle English *Mildred,* Old English *Mildthryth,* "mild strength" : *milde,* MILD + *thryth,* strength. (See **treu-** in Appendix.*)]
mile (mīl) *n. Abbr.* **m., mi. 1.** A unit of length, equal to 5,280 feet, 1,760 yards, or 1,609.34 meters, used in the United States and other English-speaking countries. Also called "statute mile." See **measurement. 2.** A **nautical mile** *(see).* **3.** An **air mile** *(see).* **4.** A race of a mile. **5.** Any relatively great distance. [Middle English *mile,* Old English *mīl,* from West Germanic *mīlja* (unattested), from Latin *mīlia, mīllia,* plural of *mīle, mīlle,* thousand. See **gheslo-** in Appendix.*]
mile·age (mī′lĭj) *n.* Also **mil·age. 1.** Total length, extent, or distance measured or expressed in miles. **2.** Total miles covered or traveled in a given time. **3.** The amount of service, use, or wear estimated by miles used or traveled: *This tire will give very good mileage.* **4.** The number of miles traveled by a motor vehicle on a certain quantity of fuel. **5.** *Informal.* The amount of service something has yielded or may yield in the future; usefulness; benefit; advantage: *get full mileage out of a typewriter.* **6.** An allowance for travel expenses established at a specified rate per mile. **7.** Expense per mile, as for the use of a car.
mile·post (mīl′pōst′) *n.* A post set up to indicate distance in miles, as along a highway.
mil·er (mī′lər) *n.* One trained to race a mile.
Miles (mīlz). A masculine given name. [Middle English *Mile* (genitive *Miles*), Old English *Milo.* See **mei-** in Appendix.*]
Miles (mīlz), **Nelson Appleton.** 1839–1925. American general.

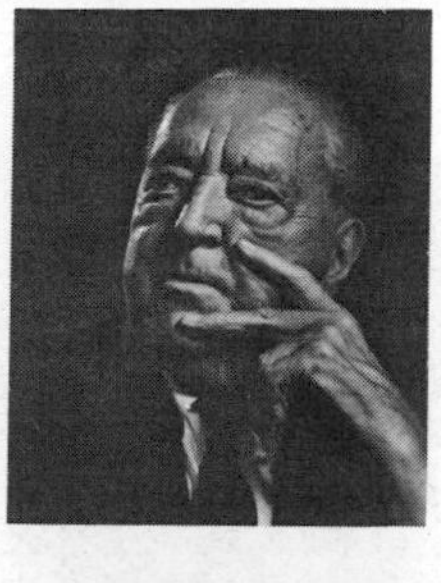

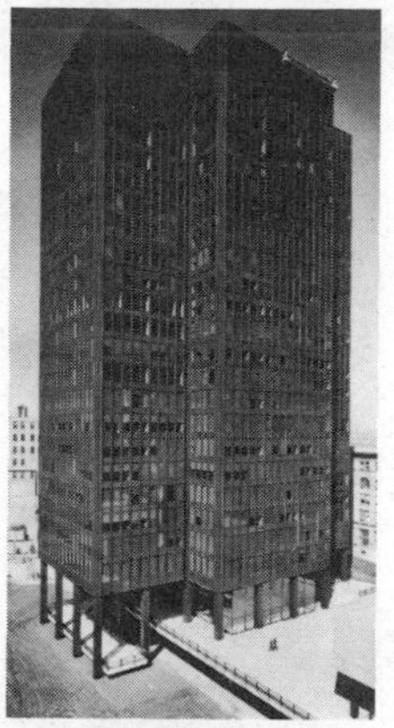

Ludwig Mies van der Rohe
Above: Portrait by Yousuf Karsh
Below: His building at 1 Charles Center, Baltimore, Maryland

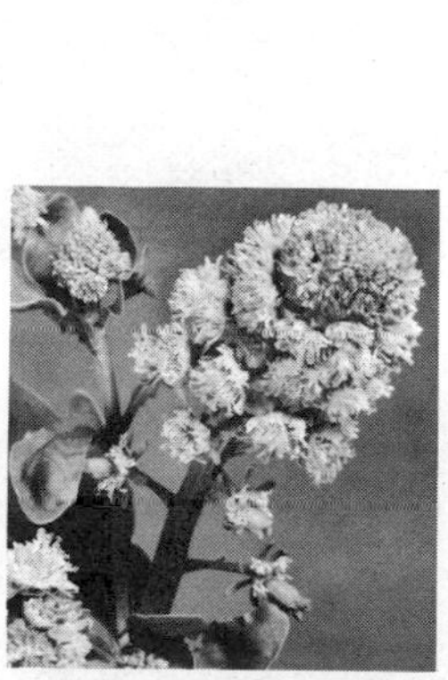

mignonette

milkweed
Asclepias syriaca

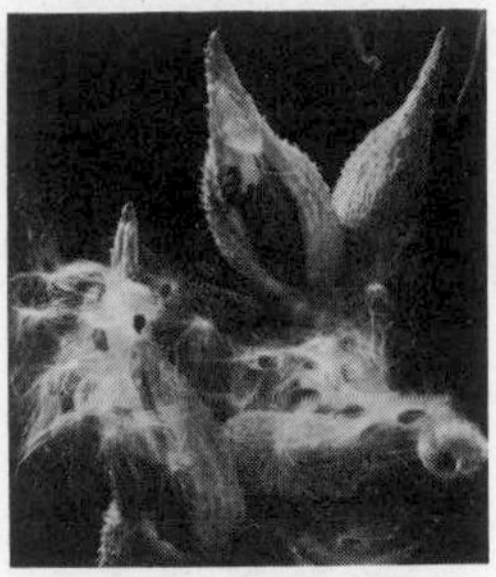

seed pods

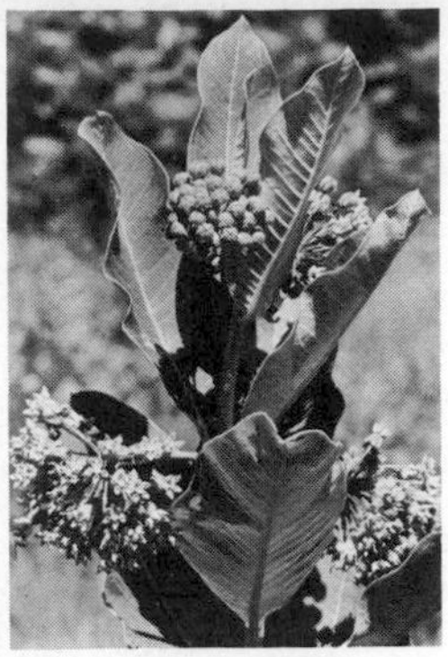

leaves and flowers

mi·les glo·ri·o·sus (mē′lās′ glôr′ē-ō′səs, glō′rē-) *pl.* **milites gloriosi** (mē′lə-tās′ glôr′ē-ō′sē, glō′rē-). *Latin.* A bragging, swaggering soldier, especially as a stock character in comedy. [After *Miles Gloriosus,* a comedy (circa 206 B.C.) by Plautus.]
Mi·le·sian[1] (mī-lē′zhən, -shən) *adj.* Of or pertaining to Miletus or its inhabitants. —*n.* A native or inhabitant of Miletus.
Mi·le·sian[2] (mī-lē′zhən, -shən) *n.* A native of Ireland; an Irishman. —*adj.* Of or pertaining to Ireland or its people; Irish. [After *Milesius (Miledh),* legendary Spanish king who was supposedly an ancestor of the Irish people.]
mile·stone (mīl′stōn′) *n.* **1.** A stone marker set up on a roadside to indicate the distance in miles from a given point. **2.** An important event or turning point in one's history or career.
Mi·le·tus (mī-lē′təs). An ancient Ionian city on the west coast of Asia Minor, near the mouth of the Menderes.
mil·foil (mĭl′foil′) *n.* **1.** A plant, the **yarrow** *(see).* **2.** See **water milfoil.** [Middle English, from Old French, from Latin *millefolium,* "thousand-leafed" (from the fine divisions of the leaves) : *mille,* thousand (see **gheslo-** in Appendix*) + *folium,* leaf (see **bhel-**[3] in Appendix*).]
Mil·haud (mē-yō′), **Darius.** Born 1892. French composer.
mil·i·ar·i·a (mĭl′ē-âr′ē-ə) *n. Pathology.* A skin disease caused by an inflammation of the sweat glands and characterized by blebs, redness, and a prickling or burning sensation. Also called "prickly heat," "heat rash." [New Latin *(fēbris) miliaria,* "miliary (fever)," from Latin *mīliārius,* MILIARY.]
mil·i·ar·y (mĭl′ē-ĕr′ē) *adj.* **1.** Designating a lesion or growth about one-eighth inch in diameter. **2.** Designating a disease marked by small skin lesions that look like millet seeds. [Latin *mīliārius,* of millet, having the appearance of millet seeds (as lesions), from *milium,* MILLET.]
miliary tuberculosis. An acute form of tuberculosis characterized by very small tubercles in various body organs, caused by the spread of tubercle bacilli through the blood stream.
mi·lieu (mē-lyœ′) *n.* Environment or surroundings. [French, environment, midst, from Old French, midst, center : *mi,* middle, from Latin *medius* (see **medhyo-** in Appendix*) + *lieu,* place, from Latin *locus,* place, LOCUS.]
mil·i·tant (mĭl′ə-tənt) *adj.* **1.** Fighting or warring. **2.** Having a combative character; aggressive, especially in the service of some cause: *the church militant.* —*n.* A militant person; especially, a political activist. [Middle English, from Old French, from Latin *mīlitāns,* present participle of *mīlitāre,* to MILITATE.] —**mil′i·tan·cy** (mĭl′ə-tən-sē) *n.* —**mil′i·tant·ly** *adv.*
mil·i·ta·rism (mĭl′ə-tə-rĭz′əm) *n.* **1.** The glorification of the ideals of a professional military class. **2.** Predominance of the military in the administration or policy of the state.
mil·i·ta·rist (mĭl′ə-tə-rĭst) *n.* **1.** One who supports or advocates militarism or warlike policies. **2.** *Obsolete.* One devoted to the study of or skilled in military science. —**mil′i·ta·ris′tic** *adj.* —**mil′i·ta·ris′ti·cal·ly** *adv.*
mil·i·ta·rize (mĭl′ə-tə-rīz′) *tr.v.* **-rized, -rizing, -rizes.** **1.** To make military; equip or train for war. **2.** To imbue with militarism.
mil·i·tar·y (mĭl′ə-tĕr′ē) *adj. Abbr.* **mil.** **1.** Of, pertaining to, characteristic of, or performed by a soldier or soldiers; soldierly: *"his hat, which was cocked with much military fierceness on his head"* (Fielding). **2.** Characteristic of or befitting the armed forces. **3.** Of or pertaining to war. —*n., pl.* **military** or **-ies.** *Abbr.* **mil.** Soldiers generally; armed forces. Used with *the: ruled by the military.* [French *militaire,* from Latin *mīlitāris,* from *mīles*† (stem *mīlit-*), soldier.] —**mil′i·tar′i·ly** *adv.*
military attaché. An army officer on the official staff of an ambassador, consul general, or minister to a foreign country.
military intelligence. **1.** Any information important for its military value. **2.** The branch of the army that procures, analyzes, and uses information of military value.
military law. Regulations and rules pertaining to the discipline and administration of the armed forces. Compare **martial law.**
military police. *Abbr.* **MP, M.P.** Members of the armed forces assigned to perform police duties. —**military policeman.**
mil·i·tate (mĭl′ə-tāt′) *intr.v.* **-tated, -tating, -tates.** To have force as evidence. Used with *against* or, rarely, *for: The facts available to us militate against this interpretation.* [Latin *mīlitāre,* to serve as a soldier, from *mīles*†, soldier.]
mi·li·tia (mə-lĭsh′ə) *n. Abbr.* **mil.** **1. a.** A citizen army, as distinct from a body of professional soldiers. **b.** The armed citizenry, as distinct from the regular army. **2.** The able-bodied male citizens in a state who are not members of regular armed forces, but who are called to military service in cases of emergency. **3.** The whole body of physically fit male civilians eligible by law for military service. [Original sense, "military organization," from Latin *mīlitia,* warfare, from *mīles*†, soldier.] —**mi·li′tia·man** *n.*
mil·i·um (mĭl′ē-əm) *n., pl.* **-ia** (-ē-ə). *Pathology.* A small, hard, white or yellowish mass just below the surface of the skin, caused by retention of the secretion of a sebaceous gland. [Middle English, from Latin, millet (from the resemblance of the lesions to millet seeds). See **melo-** in Appendix.*]
milk (mĭlk) *n.* **1. a.** A whitish liquid that is produced by the mammary glands of all mature female mammals after they have given birth and is used for feeding their young until weaned. **b.** The milk of cows, goats, or other animals, used as food by man. **2.** Any liquid similar to milk in appearance, such as coconut milk, milkweed sap, or plant latex. **3.** Any of various medicinal emulsions. —*v.* **milked, milking, milks.** —*tr.* **1.** To draw milk from the teat or udder of (a female mammal). **2.** To press out, drain off, or remove by or as if by milking: *He milked the snake of its venom.* **3.** To draw out or extract something from as if by milking: *milk information from a person.* **4.** To use for one's own benefit; exploit: *corrupt officials milking the company's treasury.* —*intr.* **1.** To yield or supply milk. **2.** To draw milk from a female mammal. [Middle English *milk,* Old English *milc, meolc.* See **melg-** in Appendix.*] —**milk′er** *n.*

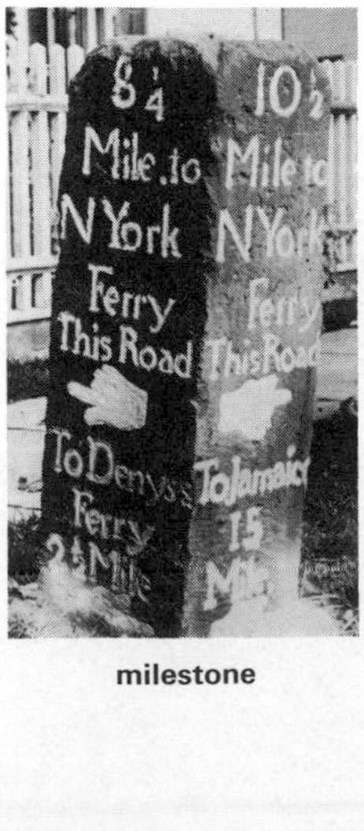

milestone

milk adder. The **milk snake** *(see).*
milk-and-wa·ter (mĭlk′ən-wô′tər, -wŏt′ər) *adj.* Lacking forcefulness; insipid; feeble.
milk chocolate. Sweetened chocolate made with milk and other ingredients to give it a milky taste or appearance.
milk fever. **1.** A mild fever, usually occurring at the beginning of lactation, associated with infection following childbirth. **2.** A disease affecting dairy cows and occasionally sheep or goats, especially soon after giving birth.
milk·fish (mĭlk′fĭsh′) *n., pl.* **-fish** or **-fishes.** A large fish, *Chanos chanos,* of the South Pacific and Indian oceans, widely used for food. [From its milky color.]
milk glass. An opaque or translucent whitish glass.
milking machine. An apparatus fitted with suction devices, used for milking cows mechanically.
milk leg. *Pathology.* A painful swelling of the leg, occurring in women after childbirth as a result of clotting and inflammation of the femoral veins.
milk-liv·ered (mĭlk′lĭv′ərd) *adj.* Lacking courage.
milk·maid (mĭlk′mād′) *n.* A girl or woman who milks cows.
milk·man (mĭlk′măn′) *n., pl.* **-men** (-mĕn′). A man who sells or delivers milk to customers.
milk of magnesia. A liquid suspension of magnesium hydroxide, $Mg(OH)_2$, used as an antacid and laxative.
milk run. *Slang.* A military aerial mission that is either of short duration or lacking in danger. [From the suggestion that it is as monotonous as the daily delivery of milk.]
milk shake. A beverage made of milk, flavoring, and usually ice cream, shaken or whipped until foamy.
milk sickness. **1.** An acute disease characterized by trembling, vomiting, and severe intestinal pain. It is caused by eating the dairy products or flesh of cattle poisoned by eating white snakeroot. **2.** A disease of cattle, the **trembles** *(see).*
milk snake. A nonvenomous grayish or tan snake, *Lampropeltis doliata,* also *L. triangulum,* of the northeastern United States. It grows to 30 inches in length, has black-rimmed brown splotches, and feeds on frogs and mice, not on milk as once commonly believed. Also called "milk adder," "house snake."
milk·sop (mĭlk′sŏp′) *n.* A boy or man lacking in courage and manliness; weakling. —**milk′sop′py, milk′sop′ping** *adj.*
milk sugar. A constituent of milk, **lactose** *(see).*
milk tooth. Any of the temporary first teeth of a young mammal. Also called "baby tooth."
milk vetch. Any of various plants of the genus *Astragalus,* having compound leaves and clusters of purple, white, or yellowish flowers. [From its supposed ability to increase a goat's yield of milk.]
milk·weed (mĭlk′wēd′) *n.* **1.** Any plant of the genus *Asclepias,* most of which have milky juice. *A. syriaca,* the common milkweed of eastern North America, has clusters of fragrant, dull-purple flowers, and pointed pods that split open to release seeds with downy tufts. This species is also called "silkweed." **2.** Broadly, any of various other plants having milklike juice.
milkweed butterfly. A butterfly, the **monarch** *(see).*
milk white. The white or somewhat blue-white color of milk.
milk·wort (mĭlk′wûrt′) *n.* Any plant of the genus *Polygala,* having variously colored, usually small flowers. See **fringed polygala, Seneca snakeroot.** [From its supposed ability to increase human lactation.]
milk·y (mĭl′kē) *adj.* **-ier, -iest.** **1.** Like milk in color or consistency; opaque-white: *milky glass.* **2.** Filled with, consisting of, or yielding milk or a fluid resembling milk: *a milky kernel of corn.* **3.** Subdued; insipid: *a milky character.* —**milk′i·ly** *adv.*
Milky Way. The galaxy in which the solar system is located, visible as a luminous band in the night sky. [Middle English (translation of Latin *via lactea*).]
mill[1] (mĭl) *n.* **1.** A building or establishment equipped with machinery for grinding grain into flour or meal. **2.** A device or mechanism, such as rotating millstones, that grinds grain. **3.** A mechanical appliance or machine that reduces a solid or coarse substance into a pulp or minute grains by crushing, grinding, or pressing: *a pepper mill.* **4.** A machine that releases the juice of fruits and vegetables by pressing or grinding: *a cider mill.* **5. a.** Any machine that produces something by the repetition of a simple process, such as a machine for stamping coins. **b.** Any of various machines for shaping, cutting, polishing, or dressing metal surfaces. **6. a.** A building or group of buildings equipped with machinery for processing materials such as wood, hay, textile fibers, and iron ore into paper, fodder, cloth, and steel: *a textile mill.* **b.** Any building or collection of buildings that has machinery for manufacture; factory. **7.** An agency, institution, process, or the like, that operates in a routine way or turns out products in the manner of a factory: *The college was only a diploma mill.* **8.** A slow or laborious process: *It took three years for the bill to get through the legislative mill.* **9.** A steel roller bearing a raised design, used for making a die, a banknote printing plate, or the like, by pressure. **10.** *Slang.* A fist fight. —**run of the mill.** Ordinary; commonplace. —**through the mill.** Through a difficult experience, usually having a definite effect on personality or character. —*v.* **milled, milling, mills.** —*tr.* **1.** To grind, pulverize, or break down into smaller particles in a mill. **2.** To transform or process mechanically in a mill. **3.** To shape, polish, dress, or finish in a mill or with a milling tool. **4. a.** To produce a ridge around the edge of (a coin). **b.** To groove or flute the rim of (a coin). **5.** To agitate or stir until

foamy. —*intr.* **1.** To move around in churning confusion: *"There was a long line outside, milling and pushing and squirming to get at the ticket window"* (Henry Miller). **2.** *Slang.* To fight with the fists; box. **3.** To undergo milling. [Middle English *mille*, Old English *mylen*, from West Germanic *mulīna* (unattested), from Late Latin *molīna*, from *molīnus*, of a mill, from Latin *mola*, millstone. See **melə-** in Appendix.*]
mill[2] (mĭl) *n. Abbr.* **M., mi.** A monetary unit equal to $\frac{1}{1000}$ of the dollar of the United States. [Short for Latin *millēsimus*, thousandth. See **mil.**]
Mill (mĭl), **John Stuart.** 1806–1873. English economist, philosopher, and political theorist.
Mil·lay (mĭ-lā′), **Edna St. Vincent.** 1892–1950. American poet and playwright.
mill·board (mĭl′bôrd′, -bōrd′) *n.* A stiff, heavy paperboard used primarily for book covers. [Alteration of *milled board.*]
mill·dam (mĭl′dăm′) *n.* **1.** A dam constructed across a stream to raise the water level so the overflow will have sufficient power to turn a mill wheel. **2.** A millpond.
milled (mĭld) *adj.* **1.** Processed or manufactured in a mill. **2.** Fluted or grooved around the edge, as certain coins.
mil·le·nar·i·an (mĭl′ə-nâr′ē-ən) *adj.* **1.** Of or pertaining to a thousand, especially to a thousand years. **2.** Of, pertaining to, or believing in the doctrine of the millennium. —*n.* One who believes the millennium will occur. [Late Latin *millēnārius*, MILLENARY.] —**mil′le·nar′i·an·ism′** *n.*
mil·le·nar·y (mĭl′ə-nĕr′ē, mə-lĕn′ə-rē) *adj.* **1.** Of or pertaining to a thousand; millenarian. **2.** Of or relating to the doctrine of the millennium or the millenarians. —*n., pl.* **millenaries. 1.** A sum or total of one thousand, especially a thousand years. **2.** A **millenarian** *(see).* [Late Latin *millēnārius*, of a thousand, from Latin *millēnī*, a thousand each, from *mīlle*, thousand. See **gheslo-** in Appendix.*]
mil·len·ni·um (mə-lĕn′ē-əm) *n., pl.* **-ums** or **-lennia** (-lĕn′ē-ə). **1.** A span of one thousand years; a millenary. **2.** A thousand-year period of holiness during which Christ is to rule on earth. Revelation 20:1–5. **3.** A hoped-for period of joy, serenity, prosperity, and justice. [New Latin (influenced by BIENNIUM) : Latin *mīlle*, thousand (see **gheslo-** in Appendix*) + *annus*, year (see **at-** in Appendix*).] —**mil·len′ni·al** (mə-lĕn′ē-əl) *adj.* —**mil·len′ni·al·ist** *n.* —**mil·len′ni·al·ly** *adv.*
mil·le·ped, mil·le·pede. Variants of **millipede.**
mil·le·pore (mĭl′ə-pôr′, -pōr′) *n.* Any of various reef-building hydrocorals of the genus *Millepora*, of tropical marine waters, forming white or yellowish calcareous formations, and resembling the true corals of the class Anthozoa. [New Latin *Millepora* (genus), "thousand-pored" : Latin *mīlle*, thousand (see **gheslo-** in Appendix*) + *porus*, PORE.]
mill·er (mĭl′ər) *n.* **1.** One who works in, operates, or owns a mill for grinding grain. **2.** A milling machine. **3.** Any of various moths having wings and bodies covered with a powdery substance.
Mil·ler (mĭl′ər), **Arthur.** Born 1915. American playwright, novelist, and short-story writer.
Mil·ler (mĭl′ər), **Henry.** Born 1891. American novelist, essayist, and critic.
Mil·ler (mĭl′ər), **Joaquin.** Pen name of Cincinnatus Hiner Miller. 1839–1913. American poet and eccentric.
mil·ler·ite (mĭl′ə-rīt′) *n.* A mineral of nickel sulfide, NiS, usually occurring in long slender crystals, and used as a nickel ore. [German *Millerit*, after William Hallowes *Miller* (1801–1880), English mineralogist.]
Mil·ler·ite (mĭl′ə-rīt′) *n.* A member of the Adventist Church led by William Miller (1782–1849), who predicted in 1831 the end of the world and Christ's second coming in 1843.
miller's thumb *pl.* **miller's thumbs.** Any of several freshwater fishes of the genus *Cottus*, found in Europe and North America. They have spiny heads and fins, and are mainly bottom dwellers. Also called "bullhead." [Middle English *millarys thowmbe* (because of its stocky, thumblike shape). The phrase "miller's thumb" was originally a proverbial expression about the dishonesty of millers, who gave short weight by tipping the scales with their thumbs.]
Mil·les (mĭl′əs), **Carl.** Original name, Vilhelm Carl Emil Anderson. 1875–1955. Swedish sculptor.
mil·les·i·mal (mə-lĕs′ə-məl) *adj.* **1.** Thousandth. **2.** Consisting of a thousandth, or pertaining to thousandths. —*n.* A thousandth. [From Latin *millēsimus*, from *mīlle*, thousand. See **gheslo-** in Appendix.*]
mil·let (mĭl′ĭt) *n.* **1.** A grass, *Panicum miliaceum*, cultivated in Eurasia for its seed and in North America for hay. **2.** The white seeds of this plant, widely used as a food grain in the Old World. **3.** Any of several milletlike grasses, or their seeds. [Middle English *milet*, from Old French, from *mil*, millet, from Latin *milium*. See **melə-** in Appendix.*]
Mil·let (mĭ-lā′; *French* mē-lĕ′), **Jean François.** 1814–1875. French painter of the Barbizon school.
mill finish. A smooth surface on various papers, made by machine. Also called "machine finish."
milli–. *Abbr.* **m** Indicates one-thousandth (10^{-3}) of a unit in the International (Metric) System of measurement. For example, a *millimeter* is one-thousandth (0.001) of a meter. See **measurement.** [French, from Latin *milli-*, from *mīlle*, thousand. See **gheslo-** in Appendix.*]
mil·liard (mĭl′yərd, -yärd′, mĭl′ē-ärd′) *n. British.* **Billion** *(see).* [French, from Old French *miliart*, from *milion*, MILLION.]
mil·li·ar·y (mĭl′ē-ĕr′ē) *adj.* Pertaining to or marking the distance of an ancient Roman mile, which equaled 1,000 paces. [Latin *milliārius*, consisting of a thousand, one mile long, from *mīlle*, thousand. See **gheslo-** in Appendix.*]
Mil·li·cent (mĭl′ə-sənt). A feminine given name. [Middle English *Melisent*, from Old French, from Old High German *Amalaswintha*, "strong work" : *amal*, work (see **omə-** in Appendix*) + *swintha*, strong (see **swento-** in Appendix*).]
mil·lieme (mēl-yĕm′, mē-yĕm′) *n.* A coin equal to $\frac{1}{1000}$ of the dinar of Tunisia. See table of exchange rates at **currency.** [Perhaps from French *millième*, a thousandth, from *mille*, a thousand, from Old French *milie*, from Latin *milia*, plural of *mīlle*. See **gheslo-** in Appendix.*]
Mil·li·kan (mĭl′ĭ-kən), **Robert Andrews.** 1868–1953. American nuclear physicist.
mil·line (mĭl′līn′, mĭl′līn′) *n.* **1.** A unit of advertising copy equal to one agate line, one column wide, printed in one million copies of a publication. **2.** The cost of such a unit.
mil·li·ner (mĭl′ə-nər) *n.* **1.** A person who makes, trims, designs, or sells women's hats. **2.** *Obsolete.* A seller of ribbons, laces, and notions. [Alteration of obsolete *Milaner*, native of Milan, importer of goods, such as women's finery, from MILAN.]
mil·li·ner·y (mĭl′ə-nĕr′ē) *n.* **1.** Articles, especially women's hats, sold by a milliner. **2.** The profession or business of a milliner.
mill·ing (mĭl′ĭng) *n.* **1.** The act or process of grinding, especially grain into flour or meal. **2.** The operation of cutting, shaping, finishing, or working metal, cloth, or any other product manufactured in a mill. **3.** The ridges cut on the edges of coins. **4.** *Western U.S.* The process of halting a cattle stampede by turning the lead animals in a wide arc, so they form the center of a gradually tightening spiral.
mil·lion (mĭl′yən) *n., pl.* **-lion** or **-lions.** The plural **millions** is rarely used with a specific number. **1.** The cardinal number written 1,000,000 or 10^6. See **number. 2.** A million monetary units, as of dollars: *He made a million in the stock market.* **3.** *Often plural.* An indefinitely large number: *"There are millions of truths that a man is not concerned to know."* (Locke). —**the million** or **the millions.** The masses; the common people. [Middle English *milioun*, from Old French *milion*, from Old Italian *milione*, augmentative of *mille*, thousand, from Latin *mīlle*. See **gheslo-** in Appendix.*] —**mil′lion** *adj.*
mil·lion·aire (mĭl′yə-nâr′) *n.* Also **mil·lion·naire. 1.** A person whose wealth amounts to a million or more dollars, or the equivalent in some other currency. **2.** A very wealthy person. [French *millionnaire*, from *million*, million, from Old French *milion*, MILLION.]
mil·lionth (mĭl′yənth) *n.* **1.** The ordinal number one million in a series. **2.** One of a million equal parts. See **number.** —**mil′lionth** *adj.*
mil·li·pede, mil·le·pede (mĭl′ə-pēd′) *n.* Also **mil·li·ped, mil·le·ped** (mĭl′ə-pĕd′). Any crawling, herbivorous arthropod of the class Diplopoda, found worldwide. They have wormlike bodies with legs attached in double pairs to most body segments. Compare **centipede.** [Latin *millepeda*, woodlouse, "thousand-feet" : *mīlle*, thousand (see **gheslo-** in Appendix*) + *pēs* (stem *ped-*), foot (see **ped-**[1] in Appendix*).]
mill·pond (mĭl′pŏnd′) *n.* A pond formed by a milldam to supply power for operating a mill.
mill·race (mĭl′rās′) *n.* The fast-moving stream of water that drives a mill wheel. Also called "millrun."
mill-run (mĭl′rŭn′) *adj.* Being in the state in which a product leaves a mill; unsorted; uninspected: *mill-run fabric.*
mill·run (mĭl′rŭn′) *n.* **1.** A **millrace** *(see).* **2.** The output of a sawmill. **3. a.** A test of the mineral quality or content of a rock or ore by the process of milling. **b.** The mineral yielded by this test.
mill·stone (mĭl′stōn′) *n.* **1.** One of a pair of cylindrical stones used in a mill for grinding grain. **2.** A heavy weight; burden.
mill·stream (mĭl′strēm′) *n.* **1.** The water flowing in a millrace. **2.** A stream whose flow is used to run a mill.
mill wheel. A wheel, generally a water wheel, that drives a mill.
mill·wright (mĭl′rīt′) *n.* A person who designs, builds, or repairs mills or mill machinery.
Milne (mĭln), **A(lan) A(lexander).** 1882–1956. English author of children's books, novels, plays, and poems.
Milne (mĭln), **John.** 1850–1913. British mining engineer and geologist; inventor of the seismograph.
mi·lo (mī′lō) *n., pl.* **-los.** An early-growing grain sorghum, resembling millet. Some varieties are drought-resistant. Compare **durra, feterita, kaffir.** [Sotho *maili.*]
mi·lord (mĭ-lôrd′) *n.* My lord. A title of respect formerly used in Europe when speaking of or addressing an English nobleman or gentleman. [French, from English *my lord.*]
milque·toast (mĭlk′tōst′) *n.* Any person with a meek, timid, and retiring nature. [After Caspar *Milquetoast*, a character in the newspaper cartoon *The Timid Soul*, by H(arold) T(ucker) Webster (1885–1952), from *milk toast*, a bland dish of hot buttered toast in warm milk, often associated with frail persons.]
mil·reis (mĭl′rās′) *n., pl.* **milreis. 1.** A former coin and monetary unit of Brazil, worth 1,000 reis. **2.** A former Portuguese coin and monetary unit. [Portuguese *milréis* : *mil*, thousand, from Latin *mīlle* (see **gheslo-** in Appendix*) + *réis*, plural of *real*, royal, from Latin *rēgālis*, REGAL.]
milt (mĭlt) *n.* **1.** Fish sperm, including the seminal fluid. **2.** The reproductive glands of male fishes when filled with this fluid. **3.** *Zoology.* The **spleen** *(see).* —*tr.v.* **milted, milting, milts.** To fertilize (fish roe) with milt. [As fish sperm, probably from Middle Dutch *milte*, milt, spleen; as the spleen, Middle English *milte*, Old English *milte*. See **mel-**[1] in Appendix.*]
milt·er (mĭl′tər) *n.* A male fish that is ready to breed.
Mil·ti·a·des (mĭl-tī′ə-dēz′). 540?–489 B.C. Athenian general; defeated the Persians at the Battle of Marathon (490 B.C.).

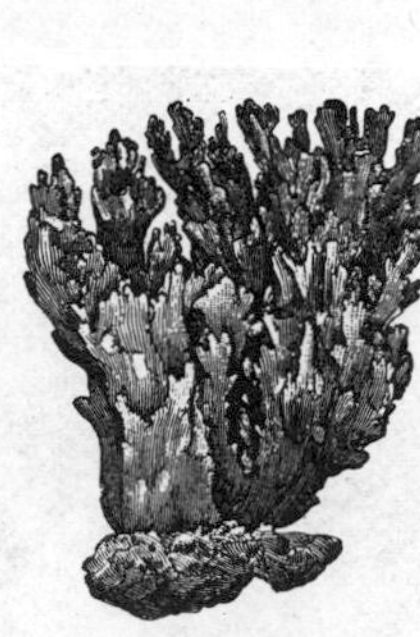
millepore
Millepora alcicornis

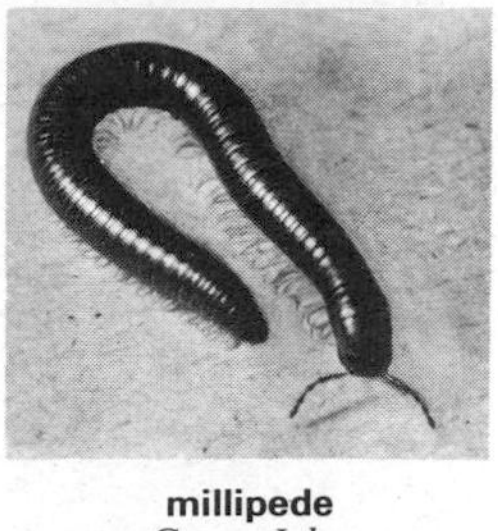
millipede
Genus *Julus*

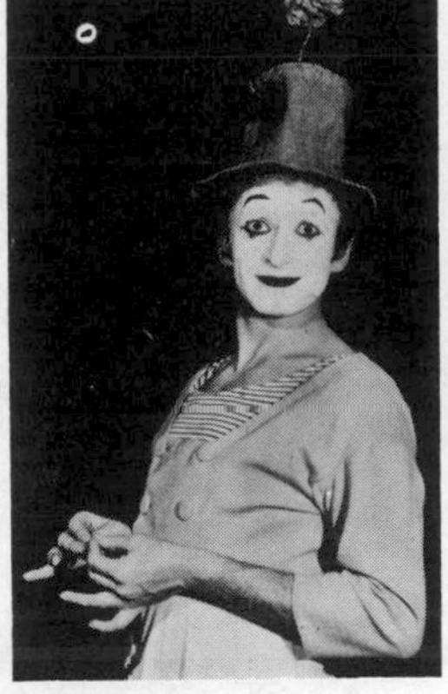

mime
Marcel Marceau as his character Bip

minaret
Mosque in Ankara, Turkey

Mil·ton (mĭl′tən), **John.** 1608–1674. English poet.

Mil·ton·ic (mĭl-tŏn′ĭk) *adj.* Also **Mil·to·ni·an** (mĭl-tō′nē-ən). Characteristic of the poet John Milton, his works, or his literary style; especially, majestic or exalted.

Mil·wau·kee (mĭl-wô′kē). The largest city of Wisconsin, situated on Lake Michigan. Population, 741,000. [Perhaps from Proto-Algonquian *melw-* (unattested), good + *-axky-* (unattested), land.]

mime (mīm) *n.* **1. a.** A form of ancient Greek and Roman drama in which realistic characters and situations were farcically portrayed and actual persons mimicked on the stage. **b.** A performance of, or dialogue for, such a comic drama. **c.** An actor in such a drama. **2.** A modern actor or comedian who specializes in comic mimicry; buffoon; clown. **3. a.** The art of **pantomime** *(see).* **b.** A performance of pantomime. **c.** An actor skilled in pantomime. —*v.* **mimed, miming, mimes.** —*tr.* **1.** To ridicule by imitation; mimic; ape. **2.** To portray in pantomime; act out with gestures and body movements. —*intr.* **1.** To act as a mimic. **2.** To portray characters and situations by wordless gesture and body movement. [Latin *mīmus,* from Greek *mimos,* imitator. See **mimos** in Appendix.*] —**mim′er** *n.*

mim·e·o·graph (mĭm′ē-ə-grăf′, -gräf′) *n.* **1.** A duplicator that makes copies of written, drawn, or typed material from a stencil that is fitted around an inked drum. **2.** A copy made by such a duplicator. —*v.* **mimeographed, -graphing, -graphs.** —*tr.* To make (copies) on a mimeograph. —*intr.* To use a mimeograph. [Originally a trademark : from Greek *mimeomai,* first person singular of *mimeisthai,* to imitate, from *mimos,* imitator (see **mimos** in Appendix*) + -GRAPH.]

mi·me·sis (mĭ-mē′sĭs, mī-) *n.* **1.** The imitation or representation of nature, especially in art and literature: *"The earliest theory of art . . . proposed that art was mimesis, imitation of reality."* (Susan Sontag). **2.** *Biology.* **Mimicry** *(see).* **3.** *Medicine.* The appearance, often due to hysteria, of symptoms of a disease not actually present. [Greek *mimēsis,* from *mimeisthai,* to imitate, from *mimos,* imitator. See **mimos** in Appendix.*]

mi·met·ic (mĭ-mĕt′ĭk, mī-) *adj.* **1.** Pertaining to, characteristic of, or showing mimicry. **2. a.** Of or pertaining to an imitation; imitative. **b.** Using imitative means of representation: *a mimetic dance.* [Greek *mimētikos,* from *mimeisthai,* to imitate. See **mimesis.**] —**mi·met′i·cal·ly** *adv.*

mim·ic (mĭm′ĭk) *tr.v.* **-icked, -icking, -ics. 1.** To copy or imitate closely, especially in external characteristics, as speech, expression, and gesture; to ape. **2.** To copy or imitate so as to ridicule; mock. **3.** To resemble closely; simulate: *an insect mimicking a twig.* —See Synonyms at **imitate.** —*n.* **1.** One who imitates: **a.** A performer skilled in mimicking. **b.** A person who copies or mimics others, as for amusement. **2.** A copy or imitation of some person or object. —*adj.* **1.** Pertaining to, acting as, resembling, or characteristic of a mimic or mimicry; imitative. **2.** Imitating a person or object, often for amusement: *"to devise mimic and fabulous worlds of their own"* (Bacon). [Latin *mīmicus,* imitative, from Greek *mimikos,* from *mimos,* imitator. See **mimos** in Appendix.*] —**mim′ick·er** *n.*

mim·ic·ry (mĭm′ĭk-rē) *n., pl.* **-ries. 1. a.** The act, practice, or art of mimicking. **b.** An instance of mimicking. **2.** *Biology.* The resemblance, through natural selection, of one organism to another or to a natural object, as a natural aid in concealment. Also called "mimesis."

Mi·mir (mē′mîr′). *Norse Mythology.* A giant who dwelt by the roots of Yggdrasil, where he guarded the well of wisdom. [Old Norse. See **smer-**[1] in Appendix.*]

mi·mo·sa (mĭ-mō′sə, -zə) *n.* **1.** Any of various mostly tropical plants, shrubs, and trees of the genus *Mimosa,* having ball-like clusters of small flowers, and compound leaves that are often sensitive to touch or light. See **sensitive plant. 2.** Loosely, any of several similar or related plants or trees, such as the **silk tree** *(see).* [New Latin, from Latin *mīmus,* MIME, from its imitation of animal sensitivity.]

min minute (unit of time).

min. 1. mineralogical; mineralogy. **2.** minimum. **3.** mining.

mi·na[1] (mī′nə) *n., pl.* **-nas** or **-nae** (-nē). A varying unit of weight or money, used in ancient Greece and Asia. [Latin, from Greek *mna,* from Akkadian *manū,* designating a unit of weight, from Sumerian *mana.*]

mi·na[2]. Variant of **myna.**

mi·na·cious (mĭ-nā′shəs) *adj.* Of a menacing or threatening nature. [From Latin *mināx* (stem *mināc-*), from *minārī,* to menace, from *minae,* threats, projecting points. See **men-**[2] in Appendix.*] —**mi·na′cious·ness, mi·nac′i·ty** (mĭ-năs′ə-tē) *n.*

min·a·ret (mĭn′ə-rĕt′) *n.* A tall, slender tower on a mosque with one or more projecting balconies from which a muezzin summons the people to prayer. [French, from Spanish *minarete,* from Turkish *minārat,* from Arabic *manārat,* lamp.]

Mi·nas Basin (mī′nəs). A 25-mile-long southeastern extension of the Bay of Fundy in Nova Scotia.

Mi·nas Ge·rais (mē′nəzh zhə-rīs′). Formerly spelled **Mi·nas Ge·raes.** A landlocked state of eastern Brazil, 224,701 square miles in area. Population, 9,799,000. Capital, Belo Horizonte.

min·a·to·ry (mĭn′ə-tôr′ē, -tōr′ē) *adj.* Also **min·a·to·ri·al** (mĭn′ə-tôr′ē-əl, -tōr′ē-əl). Menacing; threatening. [French *minatoire,* from Late Latin *minātōrius,* from Latin *minārī,* to menace. See **minacious.**] —**min′a·to′ri·ly** *adv.*

mince (mĭns) *v.* **minced, mincing, minces.** —*tr.* **1.** To cut or chop into very small pieces. **2.** To pronounce in an affected way, as with forced elegance and refinement: *He minced his phrases in the presence of the rich.* **3.** To moderate or restrain for the sake of politeness and decorum; euphemize: *"I know no ways to mince it in love, but directly to say 'I love you.'"* (Shakespeare). —*intr.* **1.** To walk with very short steps or with excessive primness. **2.** To speak in an affected way, as with forced elegance and refinement. —*n.* Food that is finely chopped; mincemeat. [Middle English *mincen,* from Old French *mincier,* to diminish, from Vulgar Latin *minūtiāre* (unattested), from Late Latin *minūtia,* minutia, from Latin *minuere,* to diminish. See **mei-**[2] in Appendix.*] —**minc′er** *n.*

mince·meat (mĭns′mēt′) *n.* **1.** *Obsolete.* Finely chopped meat. **2.** A mixture of finely chopped apples, spices, suet, and sometimes meat, used especially as a pie filling. Also called "mince." —**make mincemeat of.** *Slang.* To destroy utterly, as if by cutting into little pieces.

mince pie. A pie filled with mincemeat.

minc·ing (mĭn′sĭng) *adj.* Affectedly refined or dainty. Also "mincy." —**minc′ing·ly** *adv.*

mind (mīnd) *n.* **1.** The human consciousness that originates in the brain and is manifested especially in thought, perception, feeling, will, memory, or imagination. **2.** The totality of conscious and unconscious processes of the brain and central nervous system that directs the mental and physical behavior of a sentient organism. **3.** The principle of intelligence; the spirit of consciousness regarded as an aspect of reality: *mind over matter.* **4.** The faculty of the intellect as distinguished from emotion or will: *Follow your mind, not your heart.* **5.** A person considered with reference to his intellect: *the greatest mind of the century.* **6. a.** Individual consciousness, memory, or recollection: *I'll bear the problem in mind.* **b.** Collective memory; the entire span of time covered by remembrance: *time out of mind.* **7.** A character or inclination of intellect: *"an elegance of mind and sweetness of character"* (Jane Austen). **8.** Opinion or sentiment: *I may change my mind when I hear the facts.* **9.** A desire or purpose: *I have a mind to spend my vacation in the mountains.* **10.** Focus of thought; attention. **11.** A healthy mental state; sanity: *losing one's mind.* **12.** *Capital* **M.** *Christian Science.* The Deity, regarded as the perfect intelligence ruling over all of divine creation. **13.** A Roman Catholic Mass said in remembrance of a deceased person, often held one month or one year after his death. —**make up one's mind.** To decide between alternatives; come to a definite decision or opinion. —**piece of one's mind.** *Informal.* One's bluntly expressed opinion; especially, a strongly worded rebuke or condemnation. —**put one in mind.** *Informal.* To fill one with memories; remind one: *The novel put her in mind of her youth.* —*v.* **minded, minding, minds.** —*tr.* **1.** *Rare.* **a.** To put (a person) in mind of something; remind. **b.** To bring (an object or idea) to mind; remember. **2.** To become aware of; perceive; notice. **3.** To obey: *The children minded their mother.* **4.** To make sure: *"And before you let the sun in, mind it wipes its shoes."* (Dylan Thomas). **5.** To attend to; heed to: *Mind closely what I tell you.* **6.** To be careful about; take heed of or watch out for. **7.** To object to; dislike. **8.** To take care or take charge of; look after. **9.** To care about; be concerned about. —*intr.* **1.** To take notice; give heed. **2.** To behave obediently. **3.** To be concerned or troubled; care: *"Not minding about bad food has become a national obsession"* (Times Literary Supplement). **4.** To be cautious or careful. —**never mind.** *Informal.* Disregard it; it doesn't matter. [Middle English *minde,* Old English *gemynd,* memory, mind. See **men-**[1] in Appendix.*]

Synonyms: *mind, intellect, intelligence, mentality, brains, wits, sense, reason. Mind,* which overlaps all of these terms, pertains broadly to capacities not distinctly physical and not associated with the heart, soul, or spirit. *Intellect* denotes capacity for knowing and thinking, as contrasted with feeling and willing, and emotion generally; it is closely allied to judgment and reason. *Intelligence* applies to adaptive behavior, as in solving problems, learning from experience, and reasoning abstractly. *Mentality* is now used most often in the sense of *intellect* (and *mental* and *cerebral* in the sense of *intellectual*). *Brains* is said of intellect, often with intent of emphasis. *Wits* pertains to intelligence, and stresses quickness or facility of comprehension. *Sense* involves natural power of understanding, reasonableness, and capacity for sound perception and judgment. *Reason,* the capacity for logical and analytic thought, embraces comprehending, evaluating, and drawing conclusions.

Min·da·na·o (mĭn′də-nä′ō). The second largest island (36,537 square miles) of the Republic of the Philippines, at the southeastern extremity of the archipelago. Population, 1,997,000. Principal cities, Davao and Zamboanga.

Min·da·na·o Deep (mĭn′də-nä′ō). A Pacific Ocean depth of 35,400 feet, off Mindanao, Republic of the Philippines.

Min·da·na·o Sea (mĭn′də-nä′ō). The expanse of water between Mindanao and the Visayan Islands.

mind·ed (mīn′dĭd) *adj.* **1.** Having an intention; disposed; inclined: *I am not minded to answer any of your questions.* **2.** Having a specified kind of mind. Used in combination: *evil-minded.*

mind·ful (mīnd′fəl) *adj.* Attentive; heedful. Used with *of: "The mother, always mindful of small responsibilities"* (Nadine Gordimer). —**mind′ful·ly** *adv.* —**mind′ful·ness** *n.*

mind·less (mīnd′lĭs) *adj.* **1. a.** Lacking intelligence or good sense; foolish. **b.** Without intelligent purpose, meaning, or direction: *mindless violence.* **2.** Giving or showing little attention or care; heedless. Usually used with *of: They proceeded, mindless of the dangers.* —**mind′less·ly** *adv.* —**mind′less·ness** *n.*

Min·do·ro (mĭn-dôr′ō, -dōr′ō). An island, 3,759 square miles in area, of the Republic of the Philippines, separated from Luzon in the northeast by Verde Island Passage. Population, 132,000.

Min·do·ro Strait (mĭn-dôr′ō, -dōr′ō). The strait between Mindoro and the Calamian Islands.

mind reading. 1. The guessing of what someone is thinking by

ă pat/ā pay/âr care/ä father/b bib/ch church/d deed/ĕ pet/ē be/f fife/g gag/h hat/hw which/ĭ pit/ī pie/îr pier/j judge/k kick/l lid, needle/m mum/n no, sudden/ng thing/ŏ pot/ō toe/ô paw, for/oi noise/ou out/o͝o took/o͞o boot/p pop/r roar/s sauce/sh ship, dish/

observing facial expressions and other signs. Also called "thought reading." **2.** The supposed faculty of discerning another's thoughts through extrasensory means of communication; telepathy. —**mind reader.**

mine[1] (mīn) *n.* **1. a.** An excavation in the earth for the purpose of extracting free metals, coal, salt, or other minerals. **b.** The site of such an excavation, with its surface buildings, elevator shafts, and equipment. **2.** Any deposit of ore or minerals in the earth or on its surface. **3.** An abundant supply or source of something valuable: *Her guidebook is a mine of information.* **4.** *Military.* **a.** A tunnel dug under an enemy emplacement to gain an avenue of attack or to lay explosives. **b.** An explosive device used to destroy enemy personnel, fortifications, or equipment, usually placed in a concealed position and designed to be detonated by contact or by a time fuse. **5.** A burrow, tunnel, or gallery made by an insect. —*v.* **mined, mining, mines.** —*tr.* **1. a.** To extract (ores or minerals) from the earth. **b.** To dig a mine or mines in (the earth) to obtain ores or minerals. **2. a.** To dig under (the earth, or a surface feature); tunnel under. **b.** To make (a tunnel) by digging. **3.** *Military.* To lay explosive mines in or under. **4.** To attack, damage, or destroy by underhanded means; undermine; subvert. **5.** To delve into and make use of; exploit: *Mine the archives for detailed information.* —*intr.* **1.** To excavate the earth for the purpose of extracting minerals or ores; work in a mine. **2.** To dig a tunnel or tunnels under the earth; especially, to dig under an enemy emplacement or fortification. **3.** *Military.* To lay explosive mines. [Middle English, from Old French, from Vulgar Latin *mina* (unattested), from Common Celtic *meini-*† (unattested), ore.] —**min'a·ble, mine'a·ble** *adj.*

mine[2] (mīn). Possessive pronoun, absolute form of *my.* **1.** Belonging to me; my own. Used predicatively: *The green boots are mine.* **2.** The one or ones that belong to me. Used substantively: *If you can't find your hat, take mine.* **3.** *Archaic.* Used to modify: **a.** A following noun beginning with a vowel or *h: mine honor.* **b.** A preceding noun: *Mother mine.* —**of mine.** Belonging or pertaining to me: *a friend of mine.* [Middle English *min,* Old English *mīn.* See **me-**[1] in Appendix.*]

mine detector. Any of various electromagnetic devices used to locate explosive mines. —**mine detection.**

mine·field (mīn'fēld') *n.* An area in which explosive mines have been anchored or sunk in water or buried on land.

mine·lay·er (mīn'lā'ər) *n.* A ship equipped for laying explosive underwater mines.

min·er (mī'nər) *n.* **1.** One whose trade or business it is to extract minerals from the earth. **2.** A machine for the automatic extraction of minerals, especially of coal. **3.** A member of a military unit engaged in laying explosive mines. **4.** Any of various insects that burrow in leaves; **leaf miner** *(see).*

min·er·al (mĭn'ər-əl) *n.* **1.** Any naturally occurring, homogeneous inorganic substance having a definite chemical composition and characteristic crystalline structure, color, and hardness. **2.** Any of various natural substances: **a.** An element, such as gold or silver. **b.** A mixture of inorganic compounds, such as hornblende or granite. **c.** An organic derivative, such as coal or petroleum. **3.** Any substance that is neither animal nor vegetable; inorganic matter. **4.** An ore. **5.** *Plural. British.* Carbonated beverages. —*adj.* **1.** Of or pertaining to minerals: *a mineral deposit.* **2.** Impregnated with minerals: *mineral water.* [Middle English, from Medieval Latin *minerāle* (noun), from *minerālis* (adjective), from Old French *miniere,* from *mine,* MINE.]

min·er·al·ize (mĭn'ər-əl-īz') *v.* **-ized, -izing, -izes.** —*tr.* **1.** To convert to a mineral substance; petrify. **2.** To transform a metal into a mineral by oxidation. **3.** To impregnate with minerals. —*intr.* To develop or hasten mineral formation. —**min'er·al·i·za'tion** *n.* —**min'er·al·iz'er** *n.*

mineral kingdom. The group of objects and substances that are composed only of inorganic matter. Compare **animal kingdom, vegetable kingdom.**

min·er·al·o·gist (mĭn'ə-rŏl'ə-jĭst, -răl'ə-jĭst) *n.* An expert or specialist in the study of minerals.

min·er·al·o·gy (mĭn'ə-rŏl'ə-jē, -răl'ə-jē) *n. Abbr.* **min.** The study of minerals, including their distribution, identification, and properties. [MINERA(L) + -LOGY.] —**min'er·a·log'i·cal** (mĭn'ər-ə-lŏj'ĭ-kəl) *adj.* —**min'er·a·log'i·cal·ly** *adv.*

mineral oil. 1. Any of various light hydrocarbon oils, especially a distillate of petroleum. **2.** A refined distillate of petroleum, used medicinally as a laxative.

mineral pitch. A bituminous material, **asphalt** *(see).*

mineral tar. A petroleum product, **maltha** *(see).*

mineral water. Naturally occurring or prepared water that contains dissolved minerals or gases, often used therapeutically.

mineral wax. A mixture of hydrocarbons, **ozocerite** *(see).*

mineral wool. Any inorganic fibrous material produced by steam blasting and cooling molten silicate or a similar substance. It is used as an insulator and filtering medium.

miner's lettuce. A plant, **winter purslane** *(see).*

Mi·ner·va (mĭ-nûr'və). *Roman Mythology.* The goddess of wisdom, invention, the arts, and martial prowess, identified with the Greek Athena. [Latin. See **men-**[1] in Appendix.*]

min·e·stro·ne (mĭn'ə-strō'nē) *n.* A soup of Italian origin containing assorted vegetables, vermicelli, and herbs in a meat or vegetable broth. [Italian, augmentative of *minestra,* from *minestrare,* to serve, dish out, from Latin *ministrāre,* to serve, from *minister,* servant, minister. See **mei-**[2] in Appendix.*]

mine sweeper. A ship equipped for destroying, removing, or neutralizing explosive marine mines.

Ming (mĭng). A Chinese dynasty that ruled from 1368 to 1644, noted for its achievements in scholarship and the arts. [Mandarin Chinese *ming*[2], "luminous," "enlightened."]

min·gle (mĭng'gəl) *v.* **-gled, -gling, -gles.** —*tr.* **1.** To mix or bring together in close association; combine. **2.** To mix (things) so that the components become united; merge: *"I desired my dust to be mingled with yours"* (Ezra Pound). —*intr.* **1.** To be or become mixed or united. **2.** To become closely associated; join or take part with others: *Servants mingled freely with guests.* —See Synonyms at **mix.** [Middle English *menglen,* frequentative of *mengen,* to mix, Old English *mengan.* See **mag-** in Appendix.*] —**min'gler** *n.*

Ming T'ai Tsu (mĭng' tī' dzōō'). Title of Chu Yüan-chang. 1328–1398. Chinese emperor (1368–98); founder of the Ming dynasty.

Mi·nho (mē'nyōō). Spanish **Mi·ño** (mē'nyō). A river rising in northwest Spain, flowing 171 miles southwestward to the Atlantic, and forming part of the Portuguese-Spanish frontier.

min·i (mĭn'ē) *n.* Something distinctively smaller or shorter than other members of its class. Used especially as a shortening of compounds such as **minicar, miniskirt.** —**min'i** *adj.*

mini-. Indicates something distinctively smaller or shorter than other members of its class; for example, **minicar, miniskirt.** [Probably from both MINIATURE and MINIMUM.]

min·i·a·ture (mĭn'ē-ə-chŏŏr', mĭn'ə-chŏŏr', -chər) *n.* **1.** A copy or model that represents or reproduces something in a greatly reduced size. **2. a.** A small painting executed with great detail, often on a surface such as ivory or vellum. **b.** A small portrait, picture, or decorative letter on an illuminated manuscript. **c.** The art of making such paintings, portraits, or letters. —*adj.* On a small or greatly reduced scale from the usual: *miniature furniture.* See Synonyms at **small.** [Italian *miniatura,* painting (especially the miniature illuminations in Medieval manuscripts), from *miniare,* to illuminate, from Latin *miniāre,* to color with red lead, from *minium,* MINIUM.]

min·i·a·tur·ize (mĭn'ē-ə-chə-rīz', mĭn'ə-chə-rīz') *tr.v.* **-ized, -izing, -izes.** To plan or make on a greatly reduced scale. —**min'i·a·tur'i·za'tion** *n.*

min·i·cab (mĭn'ē-kăb') *n.* A minicar used as a taxicab, especially in England. [MINI- + CAB.]

min·i·car (mĭn'ē-kär') *n.* A diminutive automobile, especially one made in England. [MINI- + CAR.]

min·ié ball (mĭn'ē, mĭn'ē-ā'; *French* mē-nyā'). *Often capital* **M.** A conical rifle bullet manufactured in the 19th century and designed with a hollow base that expands when fired to fit the spiral grooves of the bore. [After its inventor, Captain Claude Étienne *Minié* (1814–1879), French Army officer.]

min·i·fy (mĭn'ə-fī') *tr.v.* **-fied, -fying, -fies.** To make smaller or less significant; reduce. [From MINIMUM, after MAGNIFY.]

min·i·kin (mĭn'ĭ-kən) *n. Rare.* A very small or delicate creature. —*adj.* **1.** *Obsolete.* Diminutive. **2.** Affectedly dainty; mincing. [Middle Dutch *minneken,* darling, diminutive of *minne,* love. See **men-**[1] in Appendix.*]

min·im (mĭn'əm) *n.* **1.** *Abbr.* **M.** A unit of fluid measure: **a.** In the United States, $\frac{1}{60}$ of a fluid dram or 0.00376 cubic inches. **b.** In Great Britain, $\frac{1}{20}$ of a scruple or 0.00361 cubic inches. **2.** *Music.* A half note. **3.** An insignificantly small portion or thing; a jot. **4.** A downward vertical stroke in handwriting. [In music, Middle English *mynym,* from Medieval Latin *minimus,* from Latin, least; other senses, from Medieval Latin *minimus,* least, from Latin. See **minimum.**]

min·i·mal (mĭn'ə-məl) *adj.* Smallest in amount or degree; least possible. —*n. Mathematics.* In an ordered set, a member that precedes all others. —**min'i·mal·ly** *adv.*

min·i·max (mĭn'ə-măks') *adj. Mathematics.* Of or pertaining to the strategic principle in game theory by which a player selects the strategy to minimize an opponent's greatest possible gain and maximize his own. [MINI(MUM) + MAX(IMUM).]

min·i·mize (mĭn'ə-mīz') *tr.v.* **-mized, -mizing, -mizes. 1.** To reduce to the smallest possible amount, extent, size, or degree. **2.** To represent as having the least degree of importance, value, or size; depreciate. [From MINIMUM.] —**min'i·mi·za'tion** *n.* —**min'i·miz'er** *n.*

Usage: *Minimize* is an absolute term; as such it cannot properly be qualified by adverbs such as *greatly* and *somewhat,* which are appropriate to the verb *reduce.*

min·i·mum (mĭn'ə-məm) *n., pl.* **-mums** or **-ma** (-mə). *Abbr.* **min. 1.** The least possible quantity or degree. **2.** The lowest quantity, degree, or number reached or recorded; the lower limit of variation. **3.** *Mathematics.* **a.** A number not greater than any other in a finite set of numbers. **b.** A value of a function that is exceeded for any sufficiently small increase or decrease in the function's variables. —*adj. Abbr.* **min.** Of, consisting of, or representing the lowest possible amount or degree permissible or attainable. [Latin, from *minimus,* least, superlative of *minor,* minor. See **mei-**[2] in Appendix.*]

minimum wage. 1. The lowest wage, determined by law or contract, that an employer may pay an employee for a specified job. **2.** A **living wage** *(see).*

min·ing (mī'nĭng) *n. Abbr.* **min. 1.** The process or business of extracting coal, minerals, or ore from a mine. **2.** The process of laying explosive mines.

min·ion (mĭn'yən) *n.* **1.** One who is esteemed; a favorite. **2. a.** An obsequious follower or dependent; sycophant. **b.** A subordinate of an individual or organization: *Internal Revenue Service minions.* **3.** *Printing.* A size of type, 7-point. —*adj. Rare.* Endearingly dainty; delicate. [French *mignon,* darling, from Old High German *minna,* love. See **men-**[1] in Appendix.*]

min·i·skirt (mĭn'ē-skûrt') *n.* A short skirt hemmed several inches above the knees. [MINI- + SKIRT.] —**min'i·skirt·ed** *adj.*

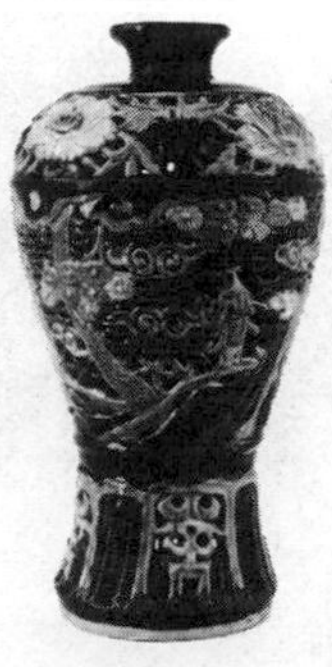

Ming
Fifteenth-century vase

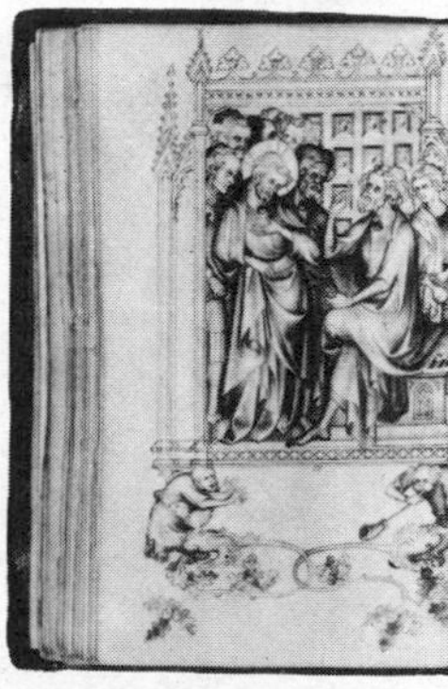

miniature
Page in Jeanne d'Evreux's book of hours, illuminated by Jean Pucelle. Actual size $3\frac{1}{2}$ by $2\frac{7}{10}$ inches

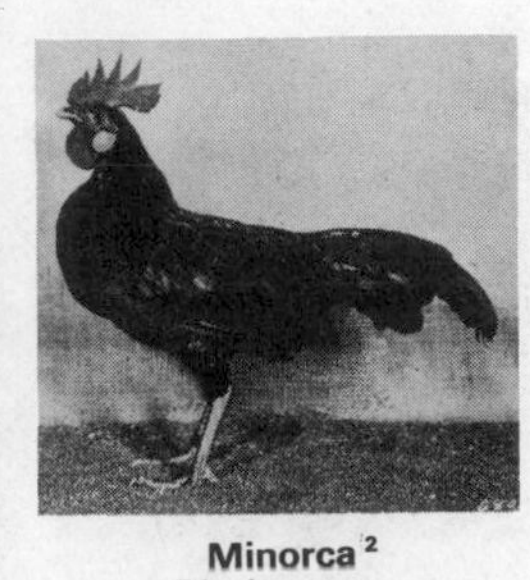

Minorca[2]
Black rooster

min·is·ter (mĭn′ĭ-stər) *n.* **1.** A person serving as an agent for another by carrying out specified orders or functions. **2.** A person authorized to perform religious functions in a church; clergyman; pastor. **3.** A high officer of state appointed to head an executive or administrative department of government. **4.** A person authorized to represent his government in diplomatic dealings with other governments, usually ranking next below an ambassador. *—v.* **ministered, -tering, -ters.** *—intr.* To attend to the wants and needs of others. Usually followed by *to: Volunteers ministered to the homeless after the flood.* *—tr.* **1.** To administer or dispense: *The Cardinal himself ministered the Sacrament.* **2.** *Archaic.* To furnish or provide. [Middle English *ministre,* from Old French, from Latin *minister,* attendant, servant. See **mei-[2]** in Appendix.*]

min·is·te·ri·al (mĭn′ĭ-stîr′ē-əl) *adj.* **1.** Of, pertaining to, or characteristic of a minister of religion or of the ministry. **2.** Of or pertaining to administrative and executive duties and functions of government. **3.** *Law.* Of or designating a mandatory act or duty admitting of no personal discretion or judgment in its performance. Compare **judicial. 4.** Acting or serving as an agent; instrumental. *—***min′is·te′ri·al·ly** *adv.*

minister plenipotentiary. A diplomatic representative with full authority to speak and act for his government; plenipotentiary.

minister resident. A diplomatic agent ranking below a minister plenipotentiary.

min·is·trant (mĭn′ĭ-strənt) *adj.* Serving as a minister. *—n.* One who ministers. [Latin *ministrāns,* present participle of *ministrāre,* to serve, from *minister,* MINISTER.]

min·is·tra·tion (mĭn′ĭ-strā′shən) *n.* **1.** The act or process of serving or aiding. **2.** The act of performing the duties of a minister of religion. [Latin *ministrātiō,* from *ministrāre,* to serve, from *minister,* MINISTER.] *—***min′is·tra′tive** *adj.*

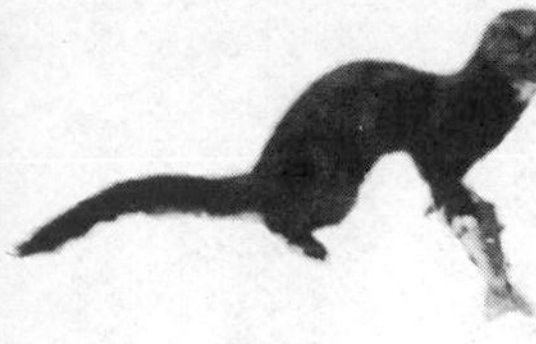

mink
Mustela vison

min·is·try (mĭn′ĭ-strē) *n., pl.* **-tries. 1.** The act of serving; ministration. **2. a.** The profession, duties, and services of a minister of religion. **b.** Ministers of religion as a group; the clergy. **c.** The period of service of a minister of religion. **3. a.** A governmental department presided over by a minister. **b.** The building in which such a department is housed. **c.** The duties, functions, or term of a governmental minister and his staff. **d.** *Often capital* **M.** Governmental ministers as a group. [Middle English *ministerie,* from Latin *ministerium,* functions of a minister, from *minister,* minister. See **mei-[2]** in Appendix.*]

min·i·track (mĭn′ē-trăk′) *n.* A trademark for an electronic measuring system designed to follow the course of satellites and rockets and to correlate radio signals received by a network of ground stations. [MINI- + TRACK.]

min·i·um (mĭn′ē-əm) *n. Chemistry.* **Red lead** *(see).* [Latin *minium,* cinnabar, red lead, probably of Iberian origin, akin to Basque *arminea,* cinnabar. See also **miniature.**]

min·i·ver (mĭn′ə-vər) *n.* **1.** A white or light-gray fur of uncertain origin, used as a rich trim on medieval robes. **2.** The ermine used in the ceremonial robes of peers. [Middle English *meniver,* from Old French *menu vair,* small vair : *menu,* small, from Latin *minūtus,* small, MINUTE + *vair,* variegated fur, from Latin *varius,* varied (see **various**).]

mink (mĭngk) *n., pl.* **mink** or **minks. 1.** Any semiaquatic carnivore of the genus *Mustela,* especially *M. vison* of North America, resembling the weasel and having short ears, a pointed snout, short legs, and partly webbed toes. **2.** The soft, thick, lustrous fur of this animal. **3.** A coat or stole made of this fur. [Middle English *mynk,* from Scandinavian, akin to Danish *mink*†.]

Minn. Minnesota.

Min·ne·ap·o·lis (mĭn′ē-ăp′ə-lĭs). The largest city of Minnesota, in the southeast on the Mississippi River. Population, 483,000.

min·ne·sing·er (mĭn′ĭ-sĭng′ər, mĭn′ə-zĭng′ər) *n. German.* One of the German lyric poets and singers in the troubadour tradition who flourished from the 12th to the 14th centuries. [German, "love singer," from Middle High German : *minne,* love, from Old High German *minna* (see **men-[1]** in Appendix*) + *singer,* singer, from *singen,* to sing, from Old High German *singan* (see **sengwh-** in Appendix*).]

Min·ne·so·ta (mĭn′ə-sō′tə). **1.** *Abbr.* **Minn.** A state in the north-central United States, with a land area of 80,009 square miles, a 166-mile coastline on Lake Superior, and with Canada as its northern border. It joined the Union in 1858. Population, 2,982,000. Capital, St. Paul. See map at **United States of America. 2.** A river rising near the Minnesota-South Dakota border and flowing generally eastward 332 miles to join the Mississippi River near St. Paul. [From Dakota *minisota,* "clear water."] *—***Min′ne·so′tan** (mĭn′ə-sō′tən) *n.* & *adj.*

Min·new·it, Peter. See **Minuit.**

min·now (mĭn′ō) *n., pl.* **minnow** or **-nows. 1.** Any of a large number of small, freshwater fishes of the family Cyprinidae, widely used as live bait. **2.** Any small, silver-colored fish. [Middle English *menawe,* Old English *mynwe.* See **men-[4]** in Appendix.*]

Mi·ño. The Spanish name for the **Minho** River.

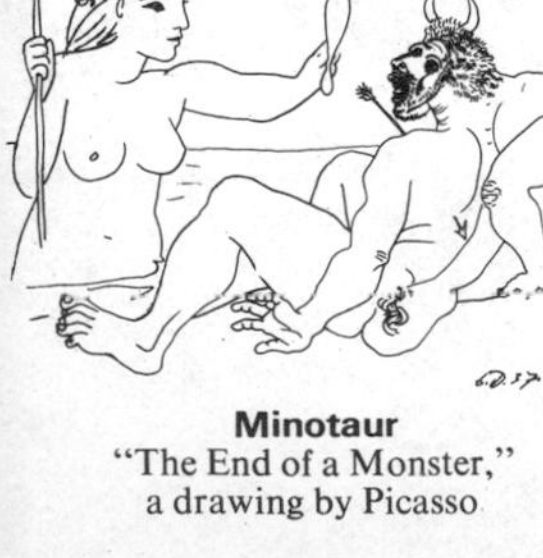

Minotaur
"The End of a Monster,"
a drawing by Picasso

Mi·no·an (mĭ-nō′ən) *adj.* Of or pertaining to the advanced Bronze Age culture that flourished in Crete from about 3000 to 1100 B.C. [From Latin *Mīnōus,* of Minos, from Greek *Minōios,* from *Minōs,* MINOS.]

mi·nor (mī′nər) *adj.* **1.** Lesser or smaller in amount, extent, quantity, or size. **2.** Lesser in importance, rank, or stature: *a minor essayist.* **3.** Lesser in seriousness or danger; requiring comparatively little attention or concern: *minor difficulties; a minor injury.* **4.** *Law.* Under legal age; not yet a legal adult. **5.** Designating the junior or younger of two pupils with the same surname. Used especially in English public schools. **6.** Designating or relating to a field of academic specialization requiring fewer class hours or credits than a major field. **7.** *Logic.* Dealing with a more restricted category; narrower. **8.** *Music.* **a.** Designating a **minor scale** *(see).* **b.** Less in distance by a half step than the corresponding major interval. **c.** Based on a minor scale: *minor key.* *—n.* **1.** A person or thing that is lesser in comparison to others of the same class. **2.** *Law.* One who has not reached full legal age (twenty-one years in most U.S. states). **3. a.** An area of specialized study of a degree candidate in a college or university that requires fewer class hours or credits than his major. **b.** One studying a minor: *a chemistry minor.* **4.** A **minor premise** or **minor term** *(both of which see).* **5.** *Music.* A minor key, scale, or interval. **6.** *Sports.* **a.** A **minor league** *(see).* **b.** *Plural.* The minor leagues of a sport, as a group. *—intr.v.* **minored, -noring, -nors.** To pursue academic studies in a minor field. Used with *in.* [Middle English, from Latin *minor,* less. See **mei-[2]** in Appendix.*]

Mi·nor·ca[1] (mĭ-nôr′kə). *Spanish* **Me·nor·ca** (mā-nôr′kä). The second largest (271 square miles) of the Balearic islands, 23 miles northeast of Majorca. *—***Mi·nor′can** *n.* & *adj.*

Mi·nor·ca[2] (mĭ-nôr′kə) *n.* A domestic fowl of a breed originating in the Mediterranean region, having white or black plumage.

Mi·nor·ite (mī′nə-rīt′) *n.* Also **Mi·nor·ist** (mī′nər-ĭst). A Franciscan friar. [From *Friars Minor* (Medieval Latin *Frātrēs Minōrēs*), name given to the Franciscan order by its founder, Saint Francis of Assisi, as a title of humility.]

mi·nor·i·ty (mə-nôr′ə-tē, -nŏr′ə-tē, mī-) *n., pl.* **-ties. 1.** The smaller in number of two groups forming a whole; a group of persons or things numbering less than half of a total. Compare **majority. 2.** A racial, religious, political, national, or other group regarded as different from the larger group of which it is part. **3.** The state or period of being under legal age: *an heir still in his minority.* [French *minorité,* from Medieval Latin *minōritās,* from Latin *minor,* MINOR.]

minority leader. The head of the minority party in a legislative body. Compare **majority leader.**

minor league. Any league of professional sports clubs, especially baseball, not belonging to the major leagues.

minor-league (mī′nər-lēg′) *adj.* **1.** Pertaining or belonging to a minor sports league. **2.** Being of subordinate position or importance: *a minor-league politician.* *—***mi′nor-lea′guer** *n.*

minor orders. *Roman Catholic Church.* The orders of acolyte, exorcist, reader or lector, and doorkeeper. See **holy orders.**

minor premise. The premise in a syllogism containing the minor term, which will form the subject of the conclusion.

Minor Prophets. 1. The Hebrew prophets Hosea, Joel, Amos, Obadiah, Jonah, Micah, Nahum, Habakkuk, Zephaniah, Haggai, Zechariah, and Malachi. **2.** In the Old Testament, the group of books containing their prophecies.

minor scale. *Music.* A diatonic scale having a minor third between the first and third tones. It has several forms with different intervals above the fifth. Compare **major scale.**

minor suit. In bridge, the suit of clubs or of diamonds, so called because of their lower scoring value.

minor term. The term in a syllogism that is stated in the minor premise and forms the subject of the conclusion.

Mi·nos (mī′nəs, -nŏs′). *Greek Mythology.* A king of Crete, the son of Zeus and Europa.

Mi·not (mī′nŏt′). A city of northern North Dakota, 100 miles north of Bismarck. Population, 31,000.

Mi·not (mī′nət), **George Richards.** 1885–1950. American physician; worked on anemia.

Min·o·taur (mĭn′ə-tôr′, mīn′ə-tôr′). *Greek Mythology.* The son of Pasiphaë by a sacred bull, in body half man, half bull, slain by Theseus.

Minsk (mĭnsk; *Russian* myĕnsk). Capital of the Byelorussian S.S.R., 400 miles southwest of Moscow. Population, 717,000.

min·ster (mĭn′stər) *n. British.* **1.** A monastery church. **2.** The title of certain cathedrals, as that of York. [Middle English *minster,* Old English *mynster,* from Vulgar Latin *monisterium* (unattested), variant of Late Latin *monastērium,* MONASTERY.]

min·strel (mĭn′strəl) *n.* **1.** A medieval musician who traveled from place to place singing and reciting poetry. **2.** Any lyric poet or musician. **3.** A performer in a minstrel show. [Middle English *ministral,* from Old French *menestral,* entertainer, servant, from Late Latin *ministeriālis,* household officer, from Latin *ministerium,* MINISTRY.]

minstrel show. A variety show, formerly popular in the United States, in which performers, some in blackface, sing, dance, and tell jokes, often reflecting a travesty of Negro life.

min·strel·sy (mĭn′strəl-sē) *n., pl.* **-sies. 1.** The art or profession of a minstrel. **2.** A troupe of minstrels. **3.** A group of ballads and lyrics sung by minstrels.

mint[1] (mĭnt) *n.* **1.** A place where the coins of a country are manufactured by authority of the government. **2.** An abundant amount or repository, especially of money: *He is worth a mint.* **3.** Anything that may be exploited as a source of money or ideas: *a mint of useful ideas.* *—tr.v.* **minted, minting, mints. 1.** To produce (money) by stamping metal; to coin. **2.** To invent or fabricate: *a phrase minted for one occasion and audience.* *—adj.* In original condition; freshly minted; unused: *a mint stamp.* [Middle English *mynt,* Old English *mynet,* money, from West Germanic *munita* (unattested), from Latin *monēta,* money, mint, from *Monēta,* epithet of Juno, whose palace housed the mint in Ancient Rome. See **monēta** in Appendix.*]

mint[2] (mĭnt) *n.* **1.** Any of various plants of the genus *Mentha,* characteristically having aromatic foliage and two-lipped flowers. Many species are cultivated for their aromatic oil, used for

ă pat/ā pay/âr care/ä father/b bib/ch church/d deed/ĕ pet/ē be/f fife/g gag/h hat/hw which/ĭ pit/ī pie/îr pier/j judge/k kick/l lid, needle/m mum/n no, sudden/ng thing/ŏ pot/ō toe/ô paw, for/oi noise/ou out/ŏŏ took/ōō boot/p pop/r roar/s sauce/sh ship, dish/

flavoring. See **peppermint, spearmint. 2.** Any of various similar or related plants, such as **mountain mint** and **stone mint** *(both of which see).* **3.** A candy flavored with mint. [Middle English *minte,* Old English *minte,* from West Germanic *minta* (unattested), from Latin *menta, mentha,* from Greek *minthē,* from Mediterranean.] **—mint'y** *adj.*

mint·age (mĭn'tĭj) *n.* **1.** The act or process of minting coins. **2.** Money manufactured in a mint. **3.** The fee paid to a mint by the government. **4.** The impression stamped on a coin.

mint jelly. A clear green jelly, usually made with apples or crab apples, chopped mint, and green vegetable coloring.

mint julep. A tall, frosted drink made of bourbon whiskey, sugar, crushed mint leaves, and shaved ice.

mint sauce. A sauce, traditionally served with roast lamb, made of chopped mint leaves combined with vinegar and water.

min·u·end (mĭn'yo͞o-ĕnd') *n.* The quantity from which another quantity, the subtrahend, is to be subtracted. [Latin *minuendum,* something to be diminished, from *minuendus,* to be diminished, from *minuere,* to lessen. See **mei-**[2] in Appendix.*]

min·u·et (mĭn'yo͞o-ĕt') *n.* **1.** A slow, stately, pattern dance for groups of couples, originated in 17th-century France. **2.** The music for or in the rhythm of this dance, in ¾ time. [French, from obsolete *menuet,* dainty, small, from Old French *menu,* small, from Latin *minūtus,* small, MINUTE.]

Min·u·it (mĭn'yo͞o-ĭt), **Peter.** Also **Min·ne·wit** (mĭn'ə-wĭt). 1580–1638. Dutch colonial official; established New Netherland and New Sweden; served as governor of both.

mi·nus (mī'nəs) *prep.* **1.** *Mathematics.* Reduced by the subtraction of; less: *Seven minus four equals three.* **2.** *Informal.* Lacking; deprived of; without. *—adj.* **1.** *Mathematics.* Negative or on the negative part of a scale: *a minus value; minus five degrees.* **2.** Designating one subdivision of a grade less than; slightly less than: *a grade of B minus.* *—n.* **1.** The minus sign (−). **2.** A negative quantity. **3.** A loss, deficiency, or disadvantage. [Middle English *mynus,* from Latin *minus,* less, from *minor,* less, minor. See **mei-**[2] in Appendix.*]

min·us·cule (mĭn'ə-skyo͞ol', mĭ-nŭs'kyo͞ol) *n.* **1.** A small, cursive script developed from uncial between the seventh and ninth centuries A.D. and used in medieval manuscripts. **2.** A letter written in this script. **3.** A lower-case letter. Compare **majuscule.** *—adj.* **1.** Of, pertaining to, or written in minuscule. **2.** Very small; tiny; minute. —See Synonyms at **small.** [French, from Latin *minuscula (littera),* minuscule (letter), from *minusculus,* less, from *minor* (stem *minus-*), less, minor. See **mei-**[2] in Appendix.*] **—mi·nus'cu·lar** (-kyə-lər) *adj.*

minus sign. *Mathematics.* The symbol (−) as in $4-2=2$. It is used to indicate subtraction or a negative quantity. Compare **plus sign.**

min·ute[1] (mĭn'ĭt) *n.* **1.** *Abbr.* **min** *Symbol* **′** **a.** A unit of time equal to one-sixtieth of an hour, or to 60 **seconds** *(see).* **b.** A unit of angular measurement equal to one-sixtieth of a degree, or to 60 seconds. Also called "minute of arc." **2.** Any short interval of time; a moment. **3.** A specific point in time. **4.** A note or summary covering points to be remembered; memorandum. **5.** *Plural.* An official record of proceedings at the meeting of an organization. —See Synonyms at **moment.** **—up to the minute.** Having the most recent information, style, or standard: *a fashion up to the minute; up-to-the-minute news.* *—tr.v.* **minuted, -uting, -utes. 1.** To record exactly, as speed or time elapsed. **2.** To record in a memorandum or other notation. **3.** To record in the minutes of a meeting. [Middle English, from Old French, from Medieval Latin *minūta,* minute, small note, from Late Latin, from *minūtus,* small, MINUTE.]

mi·nute[2] (mī-no͞ot', -nyo͞ot', mĭ-) *adj.* **1.** Exceptionally small; tiny: *minute spores carried by the wind.* **2.** Beneath notice; insignificant; trifling. **3.** Characterized by careful scrutiny and close examination: *"we are in a great measure indebted to his minute and accurate researches"* (Macaulay). —See Synonyms at **small.** [Latin *minūtus,* small, from the past participle of *minuere,* to lessen. See **mei-**[2] in Appendix.*]

min·ute hand (mĭn'ĭt). The long hand on a clock or watch that indicates the minutes.

min·ute·ly[1] (mĭn'ĭt-lē) *adj.* At intervals of one minute.

mi·nute·ly[2] (mī-no͞ot'lē, -nyo͞ot'lē, mĭ-) *adv.* **1.** With attention to minutiae. **2.** On a very small scale.

min·ute·man (mĭn'ĭt-măn') *n., pl.* **-men** (-mĕn'). *Sometimes Capital* **M.** A Revolutionary War militiaman or any armed civilian pledged to be ready to fight on a minute's notice.

mi·nute·ness (mī-no͞ot'nĭs, -nyo͞ot'nĭs, mĭ-) *n.* **1.** The state or quality of being extremely small. **2.** Precise attention to small details; rigorous exactness.

minute of arc. A unit of angular measurement, a **minute** *(see).*

minute steak. A small, thin steak, often scored or cubed, that can be cooked quickly.

mi·nu·ti·a (mĭ-no͞o'shē-ə, -nyo͞o'shē-ə, -shə) *n., pl.* **-tiae** (-shē-ē'). A small or trivial detail: *"all the particulars of past sad scenes, all the minutiae of distress upon distress"* (Jane Austen). Usually used in the plural. [Latin *minūtia,* smallness, from *minūtus,* small, MINUTE.]

minx (mĭngks) *n., pl.* **minxes. 1.** A pert, impudent, or flirtatious young girl. **2.** *Archaic.* A prostitute or promiscuous woman. [Low German *minsk,* hussy. See **man-**[1] in Appendix.*]

Mi·o·cene (mī'ə-sēn') *adj. Geology.* Of, belonging to, or characteristic of the geologic time, rock series, and sedimentary deposits of the fourth epoch of the Tertiary period, characterized by the appearance of primitive apes, whales, and grazing animals. See **geology.** *—n. Geology.* **1.** The Miocene epoch. Preceded by *the.* **2.** The deposits of this epoch. [Greek *meiōn,* less (see **mei-**[2] in Appendix*) + -CENE.]

Mi·o·lith·ic (mī'ə-lĭth'ĭk) *adj.* See **Mesolithic.** [Greek *meiōn,* less (see **mei-**[2] in Appendix*) + -LITHIC.]

mi·o·sis (mī-ō'sĭs) *n., pl.* **-ses** (-sēz'). Also **my·o·sis.** *Pathology.* Excessive contraction of the pupil of the eye. [New Latin : Greek *muein,* to close the eyes (see **mu-** in Appendix*) + -OSIS.]

mi·ot·ic (mī-ŏt'ĭk) *n.* An agent that causes contraction of the pupil of the eye. *—adj.* Pertaining to or causing miosis. [From MIOSIS.]

Mi·que·lon. See **St. Pierre and Miquelon.**

mir (mîr) *n.* A prerevolutionary Russian peasant commune. [Russian, commune, peace, world, from Old Church Slavonic *mirŭ,* joy, peace. See **mei-** in Appendix.*]

Mi·ra·beau (mîr'ə-bō'; *French* mē'rà-bō'), **Comte de.** Title of Honoré G.V. Riqueti. 1749–1791. French revolutionist.

mi·ra·bi·le dic·tu (mĭ-rä'bĭ-lā' dĭk'to͞o). *Latin.* Wonderful to relate.

mir·a·cle (mĭr'ə-kəl) *n.* **1.** An event that appears unexplainable by the laws of nature and so is held to be supernatural in origin or an act of God. **2.** A person, thing, or event that excites admiring awe. **3.** A **miracle play** *(see).* [Middle English, from Old French, from Latin *mīrāculum,* from *mīrārī,* to wonder at, from *mīrus,* wonderful. See **smei-** in Appendix.*]

miracle play. A form of religious drama of the Middle Ages in which scenes and events in the lives of miracle-working saints and martyrs were represented. Compare **mystery play.**

mi·rac·u·lous (mĭ-răk'yə-ləs) *adj.* **1.** Of the nature of a miracle. **2.** Caused by or as if by a miracle: *a miraculous cure.* **3.** Having the power to work miracles. [Old French *miraculeux,* from Medieval Latin *mīrāculōsus,* from Latin *mīrāculum,* MIRACLE.] **—mi·rac'u·lous·ly** *adv.* **—mi·rac'u·lous·ness** *n.*

mir·a·dor (mĭr'ə-dôr', -dōr') *n.* In Spanish architecture, a window or balcony that commands a view. [Spanish, from Catalan, "watchtower," from *mirar,* to look at, from Latin *mīrārī,* to wonder at. See **miracle.**]

Mir·a·flo·res Lake (mîr'ə-flôr'əs; *Spanish* mē'rä-flō'räs). An artificial lake that forms part of the Panama Canal system.

mi·rage (mĭ-räzh') *n.* **1.** An optical phenomenon that creates the illusion of water, often with inverted reflections of distant objects. It results from distortion of light by alternate layers of hot and cool air. Also called "fata morgana." **2.** Something that is illusory or insubstantial like a mirage. [French, from *mirer,* to look at, from Latin *mīrārī,* to wonder at, from *mīrus,* wonder. See **smei-** in Appendix.*]

mire (mīr) *n.* **1.** An area of wet, soggy, and muddy ground; a bog. **2.** Deep, slimy soil or mud. *—v.* **mired, miring, mires.** *—tr.* **1.** To cause to sink or become stuck in mire. **2.** To soil with mud. **3.** To trap or entangle as if in mire. *—intr.* To sink or become stuck in mire. [Middle English, from Old Norse *mȳrr,* a bog. See **meu-** in Appendix.*]

Mir·i·am[1] (mĭr'ē-əm). A feminine given name. [Hebrew *Miryām,* "rebellion." See **Miryām** in Appendix.*]

Mir·i·am[2] (mĭr'ē-əm). The sister of Moses. Exodus 15:20.

mirk. Variant of **murk.**

mirk·y. Variant of **murky.**

Mi·ró (mē-rō'), **Joan.** Born 1893. Spanish artist.

mir·ror (mĭr'ər) *n.* **1.** Any surface capable of reflecting sufficient undiffused light to form a virtual image of an object placed in front of it. **2.** Anything that faithfully reflects or gives a true picture of something else: *"the mind of man . . . (is) . . . the mirror of the fairest and most interesting qualities of nature"* (Wordsworth). **3.** Something worthy of imitation; a model. *—tr.v.* **mirrored, -roring, -rors.** To reflect in or as if in a mirror: *"Under the October twilight the water/Mirrors a still sky"* (Yeats). [Middle English *mirour,* from Old French *miroir, mirour,* from *mirer,* to look at, from Latin *mīrārī,* to wonder at, from *mīrus,* wonderful. See **smei-** in Appendix.*]

mirth (mûrth) *n.* **1.** Rejoicing or enjoyment, especially when expressed in merrymaking: *"which time was taken up in innocent mirth between my wife and daughters"* (Goldsmith). **2.** Gladness and gaiety, especially when expressed by laughter: *"She cackled with mirth, showing the stumps of betel-stained teeth."* (C.T. Sommers). [Middle English *mirthe,* Old English *myrgth.* See **mreghu-** in Appendix.*]

Synonyms: *mirth, merriment, hilarity, glee. Mirth* stresses lightheartedness and suggests easy laughter. *Merriment* strongly implies sociability and conviviality. *Hilarity* suggests also group activity; in modern usage it implies lack of restraint in expression of gaiety. *Glee* applies especially to reaction to particular circumstances, such as a sudden victory or an adversary's bad fortune; it emphasizes intensity of spirits, sometimes unworthily motivated, as by spite.

mirth·ful (mûrth'fəl) *adj.* **1.** Full of mirth. **2.** Characterized by or expressing mirth. **—mirth'ful·ly** *adv.* **—mirth'ful·ness** *n.*

mirth·less (mûrth'lĭs) *adj.* Without mirth; humorless; melancholy. **—mirth'less·ly** *adv.* **—mirth'less·ness** *n.*

mir·y (mīr'ē) **-ier, -iest** *adj.* **1.** Full of or resembling mire; swampy. **2.** Smeared with mire; muddy. **—mir'i·ness** *n.*

mir·za (mîr'zä) *n.* A Persian title of honor used after the name of a prince and before the name of a hero, scholar, or high official. [Persian *mīrzā,* short for *mīrzād,* "son of a lord" : *mīr,* prince, from Arabic, *amīr,* prince, EMIR + *zād,* born, from *zādan,* to be born (see **genə-** in Appendix*).]

mis–. Indicates: **1.** Error or wrongness; for example, **misspell. 2.** Badness or impropriety; for example, **misbehave, misdeed. 3.** Unsuitableness; for example, **misalliance. 4.** Opposite or lack of; for example, **mistrust. 5.** Failure; for example, **misfire.** ***Note:*** Many compounds other than those entered here may be formed with *mis-.* In compounds *mis-* is normally joined to the following word or element without space or hyphen: *miscast.*

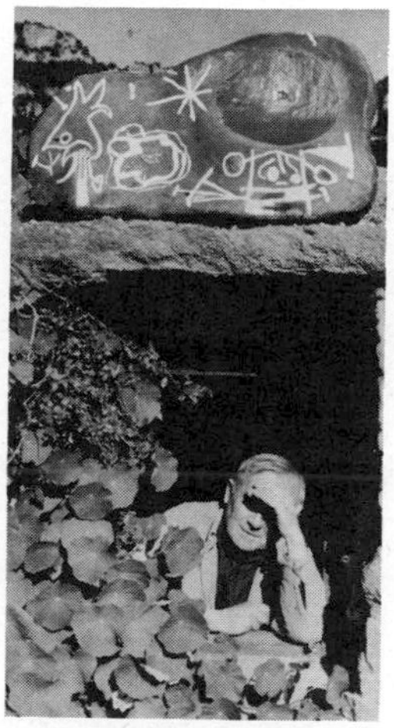

Joan Miró
At window below one of his ceramic sculptures

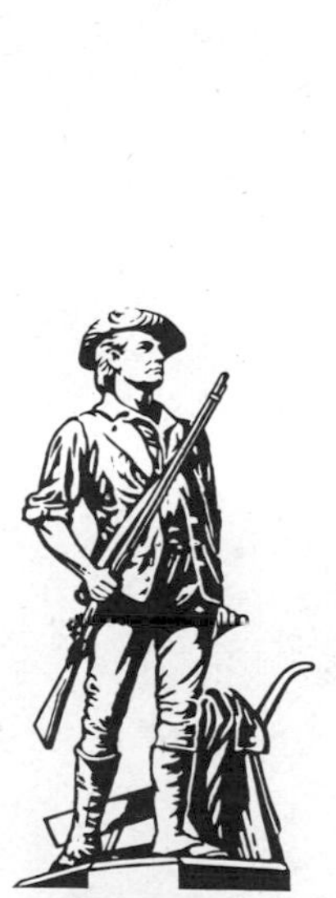

minuteman
Drawing of the minuteman statue in Concord, Massachusetts

However, in forming an unusual compound, it may be desirable to separate the elements with a hyphen to avoid misreading, especially if the second element begins with *h: mis-hit.* [There are two separate developments of *mis-* that became confused in Modern English: 1. Middle English *mis-*, wrong, Old English *mis-*. See **mei-**[1] in Appendix.* 2. Middle English *mes-*, bad, wrong, from Old French, from Vulgar Latin *minus-* (unattested), from Latin *minus*, MINUS.]

mis·ad·ven·ture (mĭs′əd-vĕn′chər) *n.* Also **mis·ven·ture** (mĭs-vĕn′chər). An instance of great misfortune; disaster. See Synonyms at **misfortune.** [Middle English *misaventure*, from Old French *mesaventure*, from *mesavenir*, to result in misfortune : *mes-*, badly, mis- + *avenir*, to turn out, from Latin *advenīre*, to come to : *ad*, to + *venīre*, to come (see **gwā-** in Appendix*).]

mis·ad·vise (mĭs′əd-vīz′) *tr.v.* **-vised, -vising, -vises.** To advise wrongly.

mis·al·li·ance (mĭs′ə-lī′əns) *n.* An unsuitable alliance, especially in marriage. [French *mésalliance* : *més-*, improper, mis- + *alliance*, alliance, from Old French *aliance*, ALLIANCE.]

mis·al·ly (mĭs′ə-lī′) *tr.v.* **-lied, -lying, -lies.** To ally badly.

mis·an·thrope (mĭs′ən-thrōp′, mĭz′-) *n.* Also **mis·an·thro·pist** (mĭs-ăn′thrə-pĭst, mĭz-). A person who hates or distrusts mankind. [Greek *misanthrōpos*, hating mankind : MISO- + *anthrōpos*, man (see **ner-**[2] in Appendix*).]

mis·an·throp·ic (mĭs′ən-thrŏp′ĭk, mĭz′-) *adj.* Also **mis·an·throp·i·cal** (-ĭ-kəl). Of or characteristic of a misanthrope: *"Such ruminations naturally produced a streak of misanthropic bitterness."* (George Eliot). —**mis′an·throp′i·cal·ly** *adv.*

mis·an·thro·py (mĭs-ăn′thrə-pē, mĭz-) *n.* Hatred of mankind.

mis·ap·ply (mĭs′ə-plī′) *tr.v.* **-plied, -plying, -plies. 1.** To apply wrongly. **2.** To make wrong use of; especially, to misappropriate (funds). —**mis′ap·pli·ca′tion** (mĭs′ăp-lĭ-kā′shən) *n.*

mis·ap·pre·hend (mĭs′ăp-rĭ-hĕnd′) *tr.v.* **-hended, -hending, -hends.** To fail to interpret correctly; misunderstand.

mis·ap·pre·hen·sion (mĭs′ăp-rĭ-hĕn′shən) *n.* A failure to interpret correctly; misunderstanding.

mis·ap·pro·pri·ate (mĭs′ə-prō′prē-āt′) *tr.v.* **-ated, -ating, -ates. 1. a.** To appropriate wrongly. **b.** To appropriate dishonestly for one's own use; embezzle. **2.** To use for illegal purposes.

mis·be·come (mĭs′bĭ-kŭm′) *tr.v.* **-came** (-kām′), **-coming, -comes.** To be unsuitable or inappropriate for: *"what I have done that misbecame my place"* (Shakespeare).

mis·be·got·ten (mĭs′bĭ-gŏt′n) *adj.* Also **mis·be·got** (-bĭ-gŏt′). Illegally or abnormally begotten; especially, illegitimate.

mis·be·have (mĭs′bĭ-hāv′) *v.* **-haved, -having, -haves.** —*intr.* To behave badly. —*tr.* To conduct oneself badly.

mis·be·hav·ior (mĭs′bĭ-hāv′yər) *n.* Also *chiefly British* **mis·be·hav·iour.** Improper, rude behavior.

mis·be·lief (mĭs′bĭ-lēf′) *n.* **1.** A wrong or faulty belief; erroneous opinion. **2.** A heretical or unorthodox religious belief.

mis·be·lieve (mĭs′bĭ-lēv′) *intr.v.* **-lieved, -lieving, -lieves.** *Obsolete.* To believe wrongly; hold a false or erroneous opinion.

misc. miscellaneous.

mis·cal·cu·late (mĭs-kăl′kyə-lāt′) *v.* **-lated, -lating, -lates.** —*tr.* To calculate wrongly; make a wrong estimate of. —*intr.* To commit an error in calculation. —**mis′cal·cu·la′tion** *n.*

mis·call (mĭs-kôl′) *tr.v.* **-called, -calling, -calls. 1.** To call by a wrong name. **2.** *Regional.* To call by a bad name; revile.

mis·car·riage (mĭs-kăr′ĭj) *n.* **1. a.** Mismanagement; bad administration: *a miscarriage of justice.* **b.** Failure to attain the right or desired end: *the miscarriage of a cherished plan.* **2.** Premature expulsion of a nonviable fetus from the uterus. In this sense, also called "spontaneous abortion."

mis·car·ry (mĭs-kăr′ē) *intr.v.* **-ried, -rying, -ries. 1.** To go astray; be lost in transit. **2.** To go wrong; fail to reach the proper conclusion: *"very artful men sometimes miscarry by fancying others wiser"* (Fielding). **3.** To bring forth a fetus prematurely; abort.

mis·cast (mĭs-kăst′, -käst′) *tr.v.* **-cast, -casting, -casts. 1.** To cast in an unsuitable role. **2.** To cast (a role or a theatrical production) inappropriately.

mis·ce·ge·na·tion (mĭs′ĭ-jə-nā′shən, mĭ-sĕj′ə-nā′shən) *n.* The interbreeding of what are presumed to be distinct human races, especially marriage between white and nonwhite persons. [From Latin *miscēre*, to mix (see **meik-** in Appendix*) + *genus*, race (see **genə-** in Appendix*).] —**mis′ce·ge·net′ic** (mĭs′ĭ-jə-nĕt′ĭk, mĭ-sĕj′ə-) *adj.*

mis·cel·la·ne·a (mĭs′ə-lā′nē-ə) *pl.n.* A conglomeration of items, especially a collection of written works. [Latin *miscellānea*, from the neuter plural of *miscellāneus*, MISCELLANEOUS.]

mis·cel·la·ne·ous (mĭs′ə-lā′nē-əs) *adj. Abbr.* **misc. 1.** Made up of a variety of parts or ingredients. **2.** Having a variety of characteristics, abilities, or appearances: *miscellaneous opinions.* **3.** Concerned with diverse subjects or aspects: *"various miscellaneous objections . . . against my views"* (Darwin). [Latin *miscellāneus*, from *miscellus*, mixed, from *miscēre*, to mix. See **meik-** in Appendix.*] —**mis′cel·la′ne·ous·ly** *adv.*

Synonyms: *miscellaneous, heterogeneous, motley, mixed, varied, assorted. Miscellaneous* things are similar in kind but sufficiently unlike on secondary levels to defy orderly classification. *Heterogeneous* applies to large collections of persons or things that differ in basic kind. *Motley*, said of persons or things, emphasizes differences to the point of contradiction and discordance; it often expresses contempt. *Mixed* may indicate differences between persons or things in a general way, or specify the presence of both sexes, two or more races, or the like: *mixed doubles. Varied* emphasizes differences between things, emphatically but not specifically. *Assorted* is used when the differences are calculated and purposeful: *assorted nails for the job.*

mis·cel·la·nist (mĭs′ə-lā′nĭst; *British* mĭ-sĕl′ə-nĭst) *n.* One who compiles or edits a miscellany; a writer of miscellanies.

mis·cel·la·ny (mĭs′ə-lā′nē; *British* mĭ-sĕl′ə-nē) *n., pl.* **-nies. 1.** A collection of various items, parts, or ingredients, especially one composed of diverse literary works. **2.** *Plural.* A book or other publication containing a variety of literary works. [Latin *miscellānea*, MISCELLANEA.]

mis·chance (mĭs-chăns′, -chäns′) *n.* **1.** An unfortunate occurrence; unlucky incident. **2.** Bad luck. —See Synonyms at **misfortune.** [Middle English *mischaunce*, from Old French *mescheance* : *mes-*, ill, mis- + *cheaunce*, CHANCE.]

mis·chief (mĭs′chĭf) *n.* **1.** An act or behavior that causes discomfiture or annoyance in another: *"We were often in mischief simply because we were a crowd of children in our own world"* (Joyce Cary). **2.** An inclination or tendency to play pranks or cause embarrassment: *full of mischief.* **3.** One that causes minor trouble or a disturbance: *The child was a mischief in school.* **4.** Damage, destruction, or injury caused by a specific person or thing: *"the evil of his attentions last night, the irremediable mischief he might have done"* (Jane Austen). [Middle English *meschief*, from Old French *meschief, meschef*, from *meschever*, to meet with misfortune : *mes-*, amiss, ill, mis- + *chever*, "to come to a head," happen, from Common Romance *capāre* (unattested), from Latin *caput*, head. See **kaput** in Appendix.*]

mis·chie·vous (mĭs′chə-vəs) *adj.* **1.** Causing mischief. **2.** Playful; teasing. **3.** Troublesome; irritating: *a mischievous prank.* **4.** Causing harm, injury, or damage: *"one of the most evil and mischievous falsehoods existent in society"* (Dickens). —See Synonyms at **playful.** [Middle English *mischevous*, unfortunate, harmful, from Norman French *meschevous*, from Old French *meschever*, to meet with misfortune. See **mischief.**] —**mis′chie·vous·ly** *adv.* —**mis′chie·vous·ness** *n.*

mis·ci·ble (mĭs′ə-bəl) *adj. Chemistry.* Capable of being mixed in all proportions. [Medieval Latin *miscibilis*, from Latin *miscēre*, to mix. See **meik-** in Appendix.*] —**mis′ci·bil′i·ty** *n.*

mis·con·ceive (mĭs′kən-sēv′) *tr.v.* **-ceived, -ceiving, -ceives.** To interpret incorrectly; misunderstand. —**mis′con·ceiv′er** *n.*

mis·con·cep·tion (mĭs′kən-sĕp′shən) *n.* An incorrect interpretation or understanding; a delusion.

mis·con·duct (mĭs-kŏn′dŭkt) *n.* **1.** Behavior not conforming to prevailing standards or laws; impropriety; immorality. **2.** Dishonest or bad management, especially by persons entrusted or engaged to act on another's behalf. **3.** Malfeasance, especially by public officials. —*tr.v.* (mĭs′kən-dŭkt′) **misconducted, -ducting, -ducts. 1.** To behave (oneself) improperly. **2.** To administer or manage poorly or dishonestly.

mis·con·struc·tion (mĭs′kən-strŭk′shən) *n.* **1.** An inaccurate explanation, interpretation, or report; a misunderstanding. **2.** A faulty construction, especially of a sentence or clause.

mis·con·strue (mĭs′kən-strōō′) *tr.v.* **-strued, -struing, -strues.** To mistake the meaning of; misinterpret; misunderstand.

mis·count (mĭs-kount′) *v.* **-counted, -counting, -counts.** —*tr.* To count or figure up incorrectly; miscalculate. —*intr.* To err in counting. —*n.* (mĭs′kount′). An inaccurate count.

mis·cre·ant (mĭs′krē-ənt) *n.* **1.** An evildoer or villain. **2.** An infidel or heretic. [Middle English *miscreaunt*, heretical, unbelieving, from Old French *mescreant*, present participle of *mescroire*, to disbelieve : *mes-*, MIS- + *croire*, to believe, from Latin *crēdere* (see **kerd-**[1] in Appendix*).] —**mis′cre·ant** *adj.*

mis·cre·ate (mĭs′krē-āt′) *tr.v.* **-ated, -ating, -ates.** To make or shape badly. —*adj.* (mĭs′krē-ĭt, -āt′). *Rare.* Formed unnaturally; deformed. —**mis′cre·a′tion** *n.*

mis·cue (mĭs-kyōō′) *n.* **1.** In billiards, a stroke that misses or just brushes the ball due to a slip of the cue. **2.** A blunder or mistake. —*intr.v.* **miscued, -cuing, -cues. 1.** To make a miscue. **2.** *Theater.* To miss one's own cue or mistake someone else's cue for one's own.

mis·deal (mĭs-dēl′) *v.* **-dealt** (-dĕlt′), **-dealing, -deals.** —*tr.* To deal (playing cards) in the wrong order or improperly. —*intr.* To deal cards improperly. —**mis′deal′** *n.* —**mis·deal′er** *n.*

mis·deed (mĭs-dēd′) *n.* A wicked, immoral, or illegal deed.

mis·de·mean·ant (mĭs′dĭ-mē′nənt) *n.* One who is guilty of, or has been convicted and sentenced for, a misdemeanor.

mis·de·mean·or (mĭs′dĭ-mē′nər) *n.* Also *chiefly British* **mis·de·mean·our. 1.** *Archaic.* Misbehavior. **2.** *Law.* An offense of lesser gravity than a felony, for which punishment may be a fine or imprisonment in a local rather than a state institution. Compare **crime, felony.**

mis·di·rect (mĭs′dĭ-rĕkt′, -dī-rĕkt′) *tr.v.* **-rected, -recting, -rects. 1.** To instruct incorrectly. **2.** To put a wrong address on.

mis·di·rec·tion (mĭs′dĭ-rĕk′shən, -dī-rĕk′shən) *n.* **1.** Inaccurate or wrong instructions or guidance. **2.** *Law.* An error made by a judge in charging a jury.

mis·do (mĭs-dōō′) *v.* **-did** (-dĭd′), **-done** (-dŭn′), **-doing, -does** (-dŭz′). —*tr.* To do wrongly or awkwardly; botch. —*intr. Obsolete.* To do wrong or harm. —**mis·do′er** *n.*

mis·doubt (mĭs-dout′) *v.* **-doubted, -doubting, -doubts.** —*tr.* To suspect; fear; feel wary of. —*intr.* To have doubts or be fearful.

mise en scène (mēz äN sĕn′). *French.* **1. a.** The properties used to stage a play or a scene in a play or motion picture. **b.** The arrangement of the performers and of such properties. **2.** Any physical environment. [French, "placing on stage."]

mis·em·ploy (mĭs′ĕm-ploi′) *tr.v.* **-ployed, -ploying, -ploys.** To put to a wrong use; abuse. —**mis′em·ploy′ment** *n.*

mi·ser (mī′zər) *n.* **1.** One who deprives himself of all but the barest essentials in order to hoard money. **2.** A greedy or avaricious person. [Originally, "wretch," from Latin *miser*, wretched, unfortunate. See **miser** in Appendix.*]

mis·er·a·ble (mĭz′ər-ə-bəl, mĭz′rə-bəl) *adj.* **1.** Very uncomfortable or unhappy; wretched. **2.** Causing or accompanied by wretchedness or other discomfort: *a miserable climate.* **3.** *Informal.* Suffering from an ailment. **4.** Skimpy or inadequate. **5.** Lacking quality; of little value; inferior. —See Synonyms at **sad.** [Middle English, from Old French *miserable,* from Latin *miserābilis,* pitiable, from *miserārī,* to have pity, from *miser,* wretched, unfortunate. See **miser** in Appendix.*] **—mis′er·a·ble·ness** *n.* **—mis′er·a·bly** *adv.*

mis·e·re·re (mĭz′ə-râr′ē, -rîr′ē) *n.* **1.** Part of a church seat, a **misericord** *(see).* **2.** A prayer for mercy. [From MISERERE.]

Mis·e·re·re (mĭz′ə-râr′ē, -rîr′ē) *n.* **1.** The 51st Psalm, which opens with *"Miserere mei Deus"* (Have mercy upon me, O God). **2.** A musical setting of this Psalm.

mis·er·i·cord, mis·er·i·corde (mĭz′ər-ĭ-kôrd′, mĭ-zĕr′ĭ-kôrd′) *n.* **1.** In a monastery, the relaxation of a rule, such as a dispensation from fasting. **2.** The room in a monastery used by monks granted such a dispensation. **3.** A bracket attached to the underside of a hinged seat in a church stall, against which a standing person may lean. Also called "miserere." **4.** A narrow dagger used in medieval times to deliver the death stroke to a seriously wounded knight. [Middle English, pity, mercy, dagger, from Old French, from Latin *misericordia,* from *misericors,* pitiful : *miserērī,* to have pity (see **Miserere**) + *cors* (stem *cord-*), heart (see **kerd-**[1] in Appendix*).]

mi·ser·ly (mī′zər-lē) *adj.* Characteristic of a miser; tending to hoard money or possessions: *too miserly to leave a tip.* See Synonyms at **stingy.** **—mi′ser·li·ness** *n.*

mis·er·y (mĭz′ər-ē) *n., pl.* **-ies.** **1.** Prolonged or extreme suffering; a state of great mental, emotional, or physical pain; wretchedness. **2.** A cause or source of suffering or pain, such as an affliction or deprivation. **3.** *Informal.* A physical ache or ailment. [Middle English *miserie,* from Norman French, from Latin *miseria,* from *miser,* wretched. See **miser** in Appendix.*]

mis·es·teem (mĭs′ĕ-stēm′, -ə-stēm′) *tr.v.* **-teemed, -teeming, -teems.** To fail to regard with deserved esteem; disrespect.

mis·es·ti·mate (mĭs-ĕs′tə-māt′) *tr.v.* **-mated, -mating, -mates.** To estimate or appraise inaccurately or wrongly. —*n.* (mĭs-ĕs′tə-mĭt). An inaccurate estimate or appraisal.

mis·fea·sance (mĭs-fē′zəns) *n. Law.* The improper and unlawful execution of some act that in itself is lawful and proper. Compare **malfeasance, nonfeasance.** [Old French *mesfaisance,* from *mesfaire,* to misdo : *mes-,* wrongly, mis- + *faire,* to do, from Latin *facere* (see **dhē-**[1] in Appendix*).]

mis·fea·sor (mĭs-fē′zər) *n. Law.* One guilty of misfeasance.

mis·fire (mĭs-fīr′) *intr.v.* **-fired, -firing, -fires.** **1.** To fail to explode or ignite when expected, as a gun or internal-combustion engine. **2.** To fail to achieve the anticipated result: *a scheme that misfired.* **—mis′fire** *n.*

mis·fit (mĭs′fĭt′, mĭs-fĭt′) *n.* **1.** Something of the wrong size or shape for its purpose. **2.** A person who is maladjusted or disturbingly different from those with whom he wishes to associate. —*v.* (mĭs-fĭt′) **misfitted, -fitting, -fits.** *Rare.* —*tr.* To fit poorly. —*intr.* To be of the wrong size or shape.

mis·for·tune (mĭs-fôr′chən) *n.* **1.** Bad fortune or ill luck. **2.** An instance of this; a distressing occurrence.

Synonyms: *misfortune, adversity, mishap, mischance, misadventure. Misfortune* applies broadly to bad fortune, usually over a long period and involving circumstances beyond the victim's control. *Adversity* differs principally in being more intense. (The related *calamity, catastrophe, cataclysm, debacle,* and *disaster* are much stronger still.) *Mishap* and *mischance* denote single instances of bad fortune having light consequences; *mischance* especially suggests that the victim was not at fault. *Misadventure* applies to a single instance; it is nonspecific as to severity, but implies some measure of fault or responsibility.

mis·give (mĭs-gĭv′) *v.* **-gave** (-gāv′), **-given** (-gĭv′ən), **-giving, -gives.** —*tr.* To arouse suspicion or apprehension in. —*intr.* To be suspicious, apprehensive, or doubtful. [Originally, to suggest doubt (used of the mind) : MIS- (wrongly) + GIVE (in the Middle English sense of "to suggest").]

mis·giv·ing (mĭs-gĭv′ĭng) *n. Often plural.* A feeling of uncertainty or apprehension: *"Modern historians of science usually approach Kepler with some misgiving"* (M.H. Nicholson). See Synonyms at **apprehension, qualm.**

mis·gov·ern (mĭs-gŭv′ərn) *tr.v.* **-erned, -erning, -erns.** To govern or administrate inefficiently or badly. **—mis·gov′ern·ment** *n.* **—mis·gov′er·nor** *n.*

mis·guide (mĭs-gīd′) *tr.v.* **-guided, -guiding, -guides.** To give wrong or misleading direction to; lead astray. **—mis·guid′ance** *n.* **—mis·guid′ed·ly** *adv.* **—mis·guid′er** *n.*

mis·han·dle (mĭs-hăn′dəl) *tr.v.* **-dled, -dling, -dles.** To treat or deal with clumsily or inefficiently.

mis·hap (mĭs′hăp′, mĭs-hăp′) *n.* **1.** Bad luck or misfortune. **2.** An unfortunate accident. —See Synonyms at **misfortune.**

mis·hear (mĭs-hîr′) *tr.v.* **-heard** (-hûrd′), **-hearing, -hears.** To hear wrongly or badly.

mish·mash (mĭsh′măsh′, -mŏsh′) *n.* A collection or mixture of unrelated things; hodgepodge. [Reduplication of MASH.]

Mish·nah (mĭsh′nə, -nä) *n., pl.* **Mish·na·yoth** (mĭsh′nə-yōth′). Also **Mish·na.** **1.** The first section of the Talmud, comprising a collection of early oral interpretations of the scriptures as compiled about A.D. 200. **2.** A paragraph from this collection. **3.** The teaching of a rabbi or other noted authority on Jewish laws. [Rabbinical Hebrew *mishnāh,* repetition, instruction, from *shānāh,* to repeat.] **—Mish·na′ic** (mĭsh-nā′ĭk) *adj.* **—Mish′nic** (mĭsh′nĭk), **Mish′ni·cal** *adj.*

mis·in·form (mĭs′ĭn-fôrm′) *tr.v.* **-formed, -forming, -forms.** To give wrong or inaccurate information to. **—mis′in·form′ant** (-fôr′mənt), **mis′in·form′er** *n.* **—mis′in·for·ma′tion** *n.*

mis·in·ter·pret (mĭs′ĭn tûr′prĭt) *tr.v.* **-preted, -preting, -prets.** **1.** To explain inaccurately. **2.** To err in understanding. **—mis′in·ter′pre·ta′tion** *n.* **—mis′in·ter′pret·er** *n.*

mis·join·der (mĭs-join′dər) *n.* Improper joining of different causes of action or different parties to a lawsuit.

mis·judge (mĭs-jŭj′) *v.* **-judged, -judging, -judges.** —*tr.* To make a mistake in the judgment of. —*intr.* To be wrong in judging. **—mis·judg′ment** *n.*

mis·lay (mĭs-lā′) *tr.v.* **-laid** (-lād′), **-laying, -lays.** **1.** To place or put down incorrectly: *mislay linoleum.* **2.** To put in a place that is afterward forgotten: *She mislaid her hat.* **—mis·lay′er** *n.*

mis·lead (mĭs-lēd′) *tr.v.* **-led** (-lĕd′), **-leading, -leads.** **1.** To lead or guide in the wrong direction. **2.** To lead into error or wrongdoing in action or thought. —See Synonyms at **deceive.**

mis·lead·ing (mĭs-lē′dĭng) *adj.* Tending to mislead; deceptive. **—mis·lead′ing·ly** *adv.*

Synonyms: *misleading, deceptive, delusive. Misleading* is the most nonspecific of these terms; it makes no clear implication regarding intent. *Deceptive* applies almost exclusively to surface appearance, and may imply deliberate misrepresentation. *Delusive* stresses calculated misrepresentation or sham.

mis·like (mĭs-līk′) *tr.v.* **-liked, -liking, -likes.** **1.** *Archaic.* To be displeasing to. **2.** To disapprove of; dislike. —*n.* Dislike; disapproval. [Middle English *misliken,* Old English *mislīcian* : *mis-,* ill + *līcian,* to LIKE.]

mis·man·age (mĭs-măn′ĭj) *tr.v.* **-aged, -aging, -ages.** To manage badly or carelessly. **—mis·man′age·ment** *n.*

mis·match (mĭs-măch′) *tr.v.* **-matched, -matching, -matches.** To match unsuitably or inaccurately, especially in marriage. **—mis′match** *n.*

mis·mate (mĭs-māt′) *tr.v.* **-mated, -mating, -mates.** To mate or match unsuitably: *Fate mismated them.*

mis·name (mĭs-nām′) *tr.v.* **-named, -naming, -names.** To call by a wrong name.

mis·no·mer (mĭs-nō′mər) *n.* **1.** An error in naming a person or place. **2.** A name wrongly or unsuitably applied to a person or object. [Middle English, from Norman French, from Old French *mesnommer,* to misname : *mes-,* wrongly, mis- + *nommer,* to name, from Latin *nōmināre,* from *nōmen,* name (see **nomen** in Appendix*).]

miso–. Indicates hating or hatred; for example, **misogamy.** [Greek, from *misein,* to hate, and *misos*†, hatred.]

mi·sog·a·my (mĭ-sŏg′ə-mē) *n.* Hatred of marriage. [MISO- + -GAMY.] **—mi·sog′a·mist** *n.*

mi·sog·y·ny (mĭ-sŏj′ə-nē) *n.* Hatred of women. [Greek *misogunia* : MISO- + -GYNY.] **—mi·sog′y·nist** *n.* **—mi·sog′y·nis′tic, mi·sog′y·nous** *adj.*

mi·sol·o·gy (mĭ-sŏl′ə-jē) *n.* Hatred of reason, argument, or enlightenment. [Greek *misologia* : MISO- + -LOGY.]

mis·o·ne·ism (mĭs′ə-nē′ĭz′əm) *n.* Hatred of change or innovation. [Italian *misoneismo* : MISO- + Greek *neos,* new (see **newo-** in Appendix*).] **—mis′o·ne′ist** *n.*

mis·pick·el (mĭs′pĭk′əl) *n.* The mineral **arsenopyrite** *(see).* [German, variant of earlier *Mispūtl, Mispilt*†.]

mis·place (mĭs-plās′) *tr.v.* **-placed, -placing, -places.** **1. a.** To put in a wrong place. **b.** To lose; mislay. **2.** To bestow (faith, affection, or confidence, for example) on an improper, unsuitable, or unworthy person or idea. **—mis·place′ment** *n.*

mis·play (mĭs′plā) *n.* A mistaken action in a game. —*tr.v.* (mĭs-plā′) **misplayed, -playing, -plays.** To make a misplay of.

mis·plead·ing (mĭs-plē′dĭng) *n. Law.* An error in pleading.

mis·print (mĭs-prĭnt′) *tr.v.* **-printed, -printing, -prints.** To print incorrectly. —*n.* (mĭs′prĭnt′, mĭs-prĭnt′). An error in printing.

mis·pri·sion (mĭs-prĭzh′ən) *n. Law.* **1.** Maladministration of public office. **2.** Neglect in preventing or reporting a crime. [Middle English, from Norman French *mesprisioun,* from *mesprendre* : *mes-,* wrongly, mis- + *prendre,* to take, from Latin *praehendere,* to grasp, seize (see **ghend-** in Appendix*).]

mis·prize (mĭs-prīz′) *tr.v.* **-prized, -prizing, -prizes.** To undervalue; disparage.

mis·pro·nounce (mĭs′prə-nouns′) *v.* **-nounced, -nouncing, -nounces.** —*tr.* To pronounce badly or incorrectly. —*intr.* To make a poor pronunciation. **—mis′pro·nun′ci·a′tion** (mĭs′prə-nŭn′sē-ā′shən) *n.*

mis·quote (mĭs-kwōt′) *tr.v.* **-quoted, -quoting, -quotes.** To quote incorrectly. **—mis′quo·ta′tion** (mĭs′kwō-tā′shən) *n.*

Misr. The Arabic name for **Egypt.**

mis·read (mĭs-rēd′) *tr.v.* **-read** (-rĕd′), **-reading, -reads.** **1.** To read inaccurately. **2.** To misinterpret.

mis·reck·on (mĭs-rĕk′ən) *v.* **-oned, -oning, -ons.** —*tr.* To miscalculate. —*intr.* To make an erroneous reckoning.

mis·re·mem·ber (mĭs′rĭ-mĕm′bər) *v.* **-bered, -bering, -bers.** —*tr.* **1.** To recollect incorrectly. **2.** *Regional.* To forget.

mis·re·port (mĭs′rĭ-pôrt′) *tr.v.* **-ported, -porting, -ports.** To report mistakenly or falsely. —*n.* An inaccurate or wrong report. **—mis′re·port′er** *n.*

mis·rep·re·sent (mĭs′rĕp-rĭ-zĕnt′) *tr.v.* **-sented, -senting, -sents.** **1.** To give an incorrect or misleading representation of. **2.** To serve incorrectly or dishonestly as an official representative of. **—mis′rep·re·sen·ta′tion** *n.* **—mis′rep·re·sen′ta·tive** *adj.* **—mis′rep·re·sent′er** *n.*

mis·rule (mĭs-ro͞ol′) *tr.v.* **-ruled, -ruling, -rules.** To rule wrongly, unjustly, or unwisely; misgovern. —*n.* **1.** Misgovernment. **2.** Disorder or lawless confusion.

miss[1] (mĭs) *v.* **missed, missing, misses.** —*tr.* **1.** To fail to hit, reach, attain, catch, meet, or otherwise make contact with (a specific object): *miss the target.* **2.** To fail to perceive, understand, or otherwise experience: *One misses the subtle shading in the painting.* **3.** To fail to accomplish, achieve, or attain one's goal: *He missed winning the race.* **4.** To fail to attend or per-

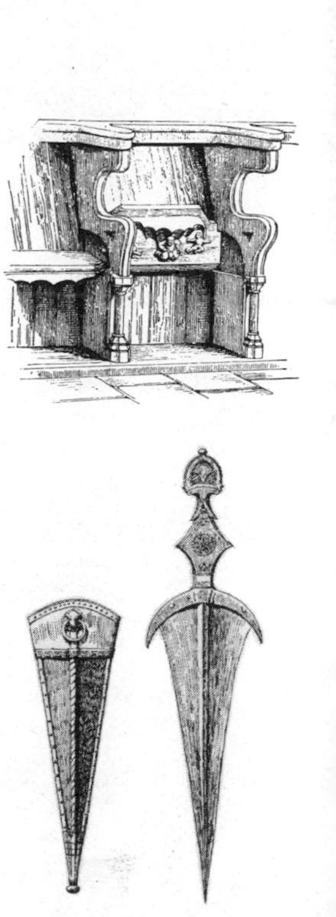

misericord
Above: Raised seat at right shows carving underneath
Below: Fifteenth-century scabbard and dagger

form: *We don't want to miss a day of work.* **5. a.** To leave out or omit: *He missed a name in typing the list.* **b.** To overlook or let go by; let slip: *miss a chance.* **6.** To escape or avoid. **7.** To discover the absence or loss of. **8.** To feel the lack or loss of: *He missed his wife.* —*intr.* **1.** To fail to hit or otherwise make contact with something: *He fired his final shot and missed again.* **2.** *Archaic.* To fail to get, secure, or achieve a specified goal. Usually used with *of: "a project which had very narrowly missed of success"* (Macaulay). **3.** To be unsuccessful; fail. Often used with *out* or *out on: He missed making the dean's list. She missed out on getting a promotion.* —*n.* **1.** A failure to hit, succeed, or find. **2.** *Obsolete.* A loss or lack. [Middle English *missen,* Old English *missan.* See **mei-**[1] in Appendix.*]

miss[2] (mĭs) *n., pl.* **misses. 1.** *Capital* **M.** A title of address when speaking to or of an unmarried woman or girl, used before her name. **2.** A title used in speaking to or of an unmarried woman or girl, used without her name. **3.** An unmarried woman or girl. **4.** *Plural.* A range in size of garments for girls and women. [Short for MISTRESS.]

Miss. Mississippi.

mis·sal (mĭs′əl) *n.* **1.** A book containing all the prayers and responses necessary for celebrating the Roman Catholic Mass throughout the year. **2.** Any prayer book. [Middle English *messel,* from Medieval Latin *missāle,* from *missālis,* pertaining to the mass, from Late Latin *missa,* MASS.]

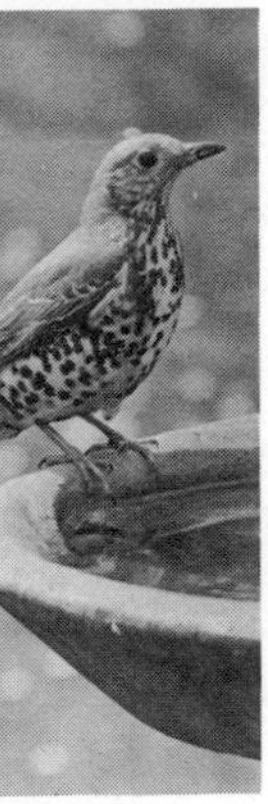

missel thrush

mis·sel thrush (mĭs′əl). Also **mis·tle thrush.** A European thrush, *Turdus viscivorus,* that eats berries, mainly of the mistletoe. [Earlier *missel-bird,* from *missel,* mistletoe, from Middle English *mistel,* MISTLETOE.]

mis·shape (mĭs-shāp′) *tr.v.* **-shaped** or **-shapen** (-shā′pən), **-shaping, -shapes.** To shape badly; deform. —**mis·shap′en** *adj.*

mis·sile (mĭs′əl; *British* mĭs′īl′) *n.* **1.** Any object or weapon that is fired, thrown, dropped, or otherwise projected at a target; projectile. **2.** A **guided missile** *(see).* **3.** A **ballistic missile** *(see).* [From Latin *missilis,* from *mittere* (past participle *missus*), to let go, send. See **smeit-** in Appendix.*]

mis·sile·man (mĭs′əl-mən) *n., pl.* **-men** (-mĭn). A person skilled in the design, building, or launching of guided missiles.

mis·sile·ry (mĭs′əl-rē) *n.* Also **mis·sil·ry.** The art and science of making and using guided or ballistic missiles.

miss·ing (mĭs′ĭng) *adj.* Not present; absent; lost; lacking.

missing link. 1. A theoretical primate postulated to bridge the evolutionary gap between the anthropoid apes and man. **2.** Something lacking but needed to complete a series.

mis·sion (mĭsh′ən) *n.* **1. a.** A body of persons sent to conduct negotiations or establish relations with a foreign country. **b.** The business with which such a body of persons is charged. **2. a.** A body of persons sent to do religious work in a foreign land. **b.** An establishment of missionaries abroad. **c.** The district assigned to a missionary. **d.** Missionary duty or work. **e.** A missionary building or compound. **f.** An organization for carrying on missionary work in any territory. **3.** A permanent diplomatic office in a foreign country. **4.** *Military.* A combat operation assigned to an individual or unit; especially, an air operation against the enemy: *"'The colonel wants forty missions,' he repeated."* (Joseph Heller). **5.** A welfare or educational organization set up for the poor, usually in a large city. **6.** A church or congregation with no priest of its own. **7.** A series of special religious services for purposes of proselytizing. **8.** A self-imposed duty. —*adj.* **1.** Of or pertaining to a mission. **2.** In the style of early Spanish missions of the southwestern United States: *mission furniture.* —*tr.v.* **missioned, -sioning, -sions. 1.** To send on a mission. **2.** To organize or establish a mission among (a people) or in (a territory). [French, from Latin *missiō,* from *mittere* (past participle *missus*), to let go, send. See **smeit-** in Appendix.*] —**mis′sion·er** *n.*

mis·sion·ar·y (mĭsh′ə-nĕr′ē) *n., pl.* **-ies. 1.** One who is sent on a mission; especially, a person sent to do religious or charitable work in some territory or foreign country. **2.** A propagandist. —*adj.* **1.** Of or pertaining to missions or missionaries. **2.** Engaged in the activities of a mission or missionary. **3.** Tending to propagandize or use insistent persuasion: *missionary fervor.*

Missionary Ridge. A ridge in Georgia and Tennessee where Union forces defeated the Confederates in 1863.

mis·sis, mis·sus (mĭs′ĭz, mĭs′ĭs) *n. Informal.* **1.** The mistress of a household. Usually used with *the.* **2.** One's wife. Used with *the, my,* or *his.* [Slurring of MISTRESS.]

Mis·sis·sip·pi (mĭs′ə-sĭp′ē). *Abbr.* **Miss.** A Southern state of the United States, 47,420 square miles in area, on the Gulf of Mexico and the Mississippi River. It entered the Union in 1817. Population, 2,179,000. Capital, Jackson. See map at **United States of America.** [After the MISSISSIPPI RIVER.]

Mis·sis·sip·pi·an (mĭs′ə-sĭp′ē-ən) *adj.* **1.** *Geology.* Of, belonging to, or designating the geologic time, system of rocks, and sedimentary deposits of the fifth period of the Paleozoic era characterized by the submergence of extensive land areas under shallow seas. In Europe, called "Lower Carboniferous." See **geology. 2.** Of or concerned with the state of Mississippi. —*n.* **1.** *Geology.* The Mississippian period. Preceded by *the.* **2.** A native or inhabitant of Mississippi.

Mis·sis·sip·pi River (mĭs′ə-sĭp′ē). A river of the central United States, rising in Lake Itasca in northwestern Minnesota and flowing 2,350 miles southeastward to the Gulf of Mexico. [Ojibwa *missi-,* "big" + *-siippii,* "river" : from Proto-Algonquian *me'si-siipiiwi* (unattested).]

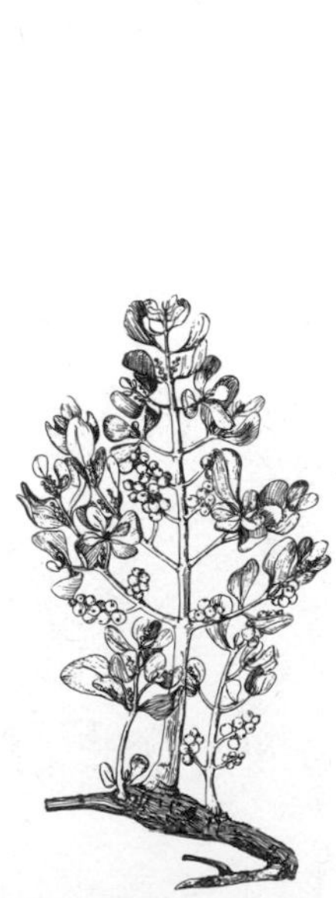

mistletoe
Phoradendron flavescens
American mistletoe

mis·sive (mĭs′ĭv) *n.* A letter or message. —*adj.* Sent or dispatched; intended for sending. [Noun, Middle English phrase *letter missive,* letter sent by superior authority, from Medieval Latin *litterae missīvae* (plural); adjective, Medieval Latin *missīvus,* from Latin *mittere* (past participle *missus*), to let go, send. See **smeit-** in Appendix.*]

Mis·sou·ri[1] (mĭ-zo͝or′ē, -zo͝or′ə) *n., pl.* **Missouri** or **-ris. 1.** A tribe of North American Indians of the Siouan language family, formerly inhabiting what is now northern Missouri. **2.** A member of this tribe. **3.** The language of this tribe. [Tribal name, from American Colonial French *ouémissourites,* "those who have canoes," based on Illinois *missouri,* canoe.]

Mis·sou·ri[2] (mĭ-zo͝or′ē, -zo͝or′ə). *Abbr.* **Mo.** A Midwestern state of the United States, 69,270 square miles in area; most of its eastern border is formed by the Mississippi River. It joined the Union in 1821. Population, 3,955,000. Capital, Jefferson City. See map at **United States of America.** —**from Missouri.** *Informal.* Doubting until given proof; skeptical: *I'm from Missouri: show me.* [After the MISSOURI RIVER.] —**Mis·sou′ri·an** (mĭ-zo͝or′ē-ən) *adj.* & *n.*

Missouri Compromise. A set of U.S. laws adopted in 1820 to maintain the balance between slave and nonslave states.

Mis·sou·ri River (mĭ-zo͝or′ē, -zo͝or′ə). The longest river of the United States, rising in the Rocky Mountains in western Montana and flowing 2,714 miles to join the Mississippi River north of St. Louis. [After the MISSOURI Indians.]

mis·spell (mĭs-spĕl′) *tr.v.* **-spelled** or **-spelt** (-spĕlt′), **-spelling, -spells.** To spell incorrectly. —**mis·spell′ing** *n.*

mis·spend (mĭs-spĕnd′) *tr.v.* **-spent** (-spĕnt′), **-spending, -spends.** To spend improperly or extravagantly; squander.

mis·state (mĭs-stāt′) *tr.v.* **-stating, -stated, -states.** To state wrongly or falsely. —**mis·state′ment** *n.*

mis·step (mĭs-stĕp′) *n.* **1.** A misplaced or awkward step. **2.** An instance of wrong or improper conduct.

mis·sus. Variant of **missis.**

miss·y (mĭs′ē) *n., pl.* **-ies.** *Often capital* **M.** *Informal.* A familiar and diminutive form of **miss** *(see).*

mist (mĭst) *n.* **1.** A mass of fine droplets of water in the atmosphere, near or in contact with the earth. **2.** Water vapor condensed on and clouding the appearance of a surface. **3.** Fine drops of any liquid, such as perfume, sprayed into the air. **4.** A colloidal suspension of a liquid in a gas. **5.** Something that dims or conceals sight or judgment, such as a haze from tears in the eyes. **6.** Something that produces or gives the impression of dimness or obscurity. —*v.* **misted, misting, mists.** —*intr.* **1.** To be or become obscured or misty; be blurred or concealed by or as if by a mist. **2.** To rain in a fine shower. —*tr.* To conceal or veil as if with a mist. [Middle English *mist,* Old English *mist.* See **meigh-** in Appendix.*]

mis·tak·a·ble (mĭ-stā′kə-bəl) *adj.* Capable of being mistaken or misunderstood. —**mis·tak′a·bly** *adv.*

mis·take (mĭ-stāk′) *n.* **1.** An error or fault. **2.** A misconception or misunderstanding. —See Synonyms at **error.** —*v.* **mistook,** (-to͝ok′), **-taken** (-tā′kən), **-taking, -takes.** —*tr.* **1.** To understand wrongly; misinterpret: *"Aziz overrated hospitality, mistaking it for intimacy"* (E.M. Forster). **2.** To recognize or identify incorrectly: *He mistook her for her sister.* —*intr.* To make a mistake. [Middle English *mistaken,* from Old Norse *mistaka,* to take in error : *miss-,* wrongly + *taka,* to TAKE.]

mis·tak·en (mĭ-stā′kən) *adj.* **1.** Wrong or incorrect in opinion, understanding, or perception. **2.** Based on error; wrong: *a mistaken view of the situation.* —**mis·tak′en·ly** *adv.*

Mis·tas·si·ni Lake (mĭs′tə-sē′nē). A lake, 840 square miles in area, in central Quebec, Canada.

Mis·ter (mĭs′tər) *n.* **1.** *Abbr.* **Mr.** A title of respect used when speaking to or of a man. It is usually written in its abbreviated form and placed before a man's surname or title of office: *Mr. Jones; Mr. Secretary.* **2.** *Abbr.* **Mr.** The official term of address for certain U.S. military and naval personnel: **a.** A warrant officer. **b.** A flight officer. **c.** A cadet at one of the service academies. **d.** Any naval officer below the rank of commander. **3.** *Small* **m.** *Informal.* A form of address used without a name. [Weakened form of MASTER.]

mist·flow·er (mĭst′flou′ər) *n.* A plant, *Eupatorium coelestinum,* of southeastern North America, having clusters of small, blue flowers.

Mis·ti, El. See **El Misti.**

mistle thrush. Variant of **missel thrush.**

mis·tle·toe (mĭs′əl-tō′) *n.* **1.** A Eurasian parasitic shrub, *Viscum album,* having leathery evergreen leaves and waxy white berries. **2.** Any of several related American parasitic shrubs, such as *Phoradendron flavescens,* of eastern North America. **3.** A mistletoe sprig, often used as a Christmas decoration. Traditionally, a man is privileged to kiss a woman standing under such a sprig. [Middle English *mistilto,* Old English *misteltān* : *mistel,* mistletoe (see **meigh-** in Appendix*) + *tān,* twig, from Germanic *tainaz* (unattested).]

mistletoe cactus. A leafless, epiphytic, tropical American cactus, *Rhipsalis cassytha.*

mis·took. Past tense of **mistake.**

mis·tral (mĭs′trəl, mĭ-sträl′; *French* mē-strȧl′) *n.* A dry, cold northerly wind that blows in squalls through the Rhône Valley and nearby areas toward the Mediterranean coast of southern France. [French, from Provençal, from Latin *magistrālis (ventus),* "master (wind)"; *magistrālis,* MAGISTRAL.]

mis·treat (mĭs-trēt′) *tr.v.* **-treated, -treating, -treats.** To handle or treat roughly or wrongly; abuse. See Synonyms at **abuse.** —**mis·treat′ment** *n.*

mis·tress (mĭs′trĭs) *n.* **1.** A woman in a position of authority, such as the head of a household or estate: *"Thirteen years had seen her mistress of Kellynch Hall"* (Jane Austen). **2.** A woman owning an animal or, formerly, a slave. **3.** A woman who has ultimate control over something: *the mistress of his heart.*

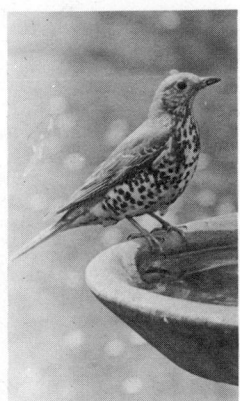

4. *Often capital* **M.** Any idea or object personified as a woman having control or authority over something: *"The independence of America is as fixed as fate; she is mistress of her own fortune"* (Thomas Pownall). 5. A woman who has mastered a skill: *a mistress of cooking.* 6. A woman who has a continuing sexual relationship with a man to whom she is not married, especially one who receives financial support from the man. 7. *Capital* **M.** Formerly, a title of courtesy when speaking to or of a woman. 8. *British.* A female schoolteacher. [Middle English *maistresse,* from Old French *maistresse,* from *maistre,* MASTER.]

mis·tri·al (mĭs-trī′əl, -trīl′) *n. Law.* 1. A trial that becomes invalid because of basic error in procedure. 2. An inconclusive trial, such as one in which the jurors fail to agree on a verdict.

mis·trust (mĭs-trŭst′) *n.* Lack of trust; suspicion; doubt. —*v.* **mistrusted, -trusting, -trusts.** —*tr.* To regard without confidence. —*intr.* To be wary or doubtful. —See Synonyms at **uncertainty.** —**mis·trust′ful** *adj.* —**mis·trust′ing·ly** *adv.*

mist·y (mĭs′tē) *adj.* **-ier, -iest.** 1. Consisting of or resembling mist: *a misty rain.* 2. Obscured or clouded by or as if by mist. 3. Lacking in clarity; vague. —**mist′i·ly** *adv.* —**mist′i·ness** *n.*

mis·un·der·stand (mĭs′ŭn-dər-stănd′) *tr.v.* **-stood** (-stŏŏd′), **-standing, -stands.** To understand incorrectly; misinterpret.

mis·un·der·stand·ing (mĭs′ŭn-dər-stăn′dĭng) *n.* 1. A failure to understand correctly. 2. A disagreement or quarrel.

mis·un·der·stood (mĭs′ŭn-dər-stŏŏd′) *adj.* 1. Understood wrongly or incorrectly. 2. Not appreciated or given sympathetic understanding: *a misunderstood child.*

mis·use (mĭs-yōōs′) *n.* 1. Improper use; misapplication. 2. *Obsolete.* Abuse. —*tr.v.* (mĭs-yōōz′) **-used, -using, -uses.** 1. To use wrongly or incorrectly. 2. To mistreat or abuse. —See Synonyms at **abuse.**

mis·val·ue (mĭs-văl′yōō) *tr.v.* **-ued, -uing, -ues.** To value or estimate incorrectly.

mis·ven·ture. Variant of **misadventure.**

mis·word (mĭs-wûrd′) *tr.v.* **-worded, -wording, -words.** To express incorrectly; word improperly.

Mitch·am (mĭch′əm). A former administrative division of London, England, now part of the borough of Merton.

Mitch·ell (mĭch′əl), **John.** 1870–1919. American labor leader.

Mitch·ell (mĭch′əl), **Margaret.** 1900–1949. American author of the popular novel *Gone with the Wind.*

Mitch·ell (mĭch′əl), **Mount.** The highest elevation (6,684 feet) of the Appalachian Mountain system. It is in North Carolina.

Mitch·ell (mĭch′əl), **William ("Billy").** 1879–1936. American military leader; early commander and advocate of the air forces.

mite[1] (mīt) *n.* Any of various small arachnids that are often parasitic. They may infest foods and carry disease. [Middle English *mite,* Old English *mīte.* See **mai-**[1] in Appendix.*]

mite[2] (mīt) *n.* 1. a. A very small amount of money or contribution. b. A **widow's mite** *(see).* 2. A coin of very small value, especially an obsolete British coin worth half a farthing. 3. Any very small object, creature, or particle: *"little Sulie, a bedraggled mite somewhere out in this wide bush"* (Conrad Richter). [Middle English (originally in the phrase "not worth a mite"), from Middle Dutch *mīte.* See **mai-**[1] in Appendix.*]

mi·ter (mī′tər) *n.* Also *chiefly British* **mi·tre.** 1. A tall, pointed hat with peaks in front and back, worn by bishops and some other ecclesiastics. 2. a. A thong for binding the hair, worn by women in ancient Greece. b. The ceremonial headdress worn by ancient Jewish high priests. 3. A covering or top of a chimney that permits the release of smoke while keeping out rain and debris. 4. a. A **miter joint** *(see).* b. The edge of a piece of material that has been beveled preparatory to making a miter joint. c. A **miter square** *(see).* —*v.* **mitered, -tering, -ters.** Also *chiefly British* **mi·tre, -tred, -tring, -tres.** —*tr.* 1. To bestow a miter upon; raise to a rank entitled to wear a miter. 2. To make join with a miter joint. —*intr.* To meet in a miter joint. [Middle English *mitre,* from Old French, from Latin *mitra,* from Greek *mitra,* headband, kind of oriental turban, hence, headdress of the Jewish high priest (in the Septuagint). See **mei-**[4] in Appendix.*]

miter box. 1. A box open at the ends, with sides slotted to guide a saw in cutting miter joints. 2. A device for handsaws that may be set to guide cuts in lumber at various degrees.

miter joint. A joint made by beveling each of two surfaces to be joined, usually at a 45° angle, to form a 90° corner.

miter square. A carpenter's square with a blade set at a 45-degree angle or adjustable.

mi·ter·wort (mī′tər-wûrt′) *n.* Any of several North American plants of the genus *Mitella* having heart-shaped leaves and clusters of small white flowers. Also called "bishop's-cap." [Because its capsule resembles a bishop's miter.]

mith·er (mĭ*th*′ər) *n. Scottish.* Mother.

Mith·gar·thr. *Norse Mythology.* Variant of **Midgard.**

Mith·ra·ism (mĭth′rə-ĭz′əm, mĭth′rā-) *n.* A Persian religious cult that flourished in the late Roman Empire, rivaling Christianity. See **Mithras.** —**Mith·ra′ic** (mĭth-rā′ĭk) *adj.* —**Mith′ra·ist** (mĭth′rə-ĭst, mĭth′rā-, mĭth-rā′ĭst) *n. & adj.*

Mith·ras (mĭth′rəs). Also **Mith·ra** (mĭth′rə). *Persian Mythology.* The god of light and guardian against evil, often identified with the sun. [Latin, from Greek, from Old Persian *mithra-.* See **mei-**[4] in Appendix.*]

Mith·ri·da·tes VI (mĭth′rə-dā′tēz). Called "Eupator" or "The Great." 132?–63 B.C. King of Pontus; fought Mithridatic Wars against Rome; defeated by Pompey (67 B.C.).

mith·ri·da·tism (mĭth′rə-dā′tĭz′əm) *n.* Tolerance of a poison, acquired by taking gradually larger doses of it. [After MITHRIDATES VI, said to have thus immunized himself.] —**mith′ri·dat′ic** (-dăt′ĭk) *adj.*

mit·i·gate (mĭt′ə-gāt′) *v.* **-gated, -gating, -gates.** —*tr.* To moderate (a quality or condition) in force or intensity; alleviate: *"do what he could to mitigate the Emperor's displeasure"* (Robert Graves). —*intr.* To become milder. —See Synonyms at **relieve.** [Middle English *mitigaten,* from Latin *mītigāre,* from *mītis,* gentle, mild. See **mēi-** in Appendix.*] —**mit′i·ga·ble** (mĭt′ĭ-gə-bəl) *adj.* —**mit′i·ga′tion** *n.* —**mit′i·ga′tive, mit·i·ga·to·ry** (mĭt′ĭ-gə-tôr′ē, -tōr′ē) *adj.* —**mit′i·ga′tor** *n.*

mi·to·chon·dri·on (mī′tə-kŏn′drē-ən) *n., pl.* **-dria** (-drē-ə). *Biology.* A microscopic body found in the cells of almost all living organisms. It contains enzymes responsible for the conversion of food to usable energy. See **adenosine triphosphate, oxidative phosphorylation.** Also called "chondriosome." [New Latin : Greek *mitos,* thread (see **mei-**[4] in Appendix*) + *khondrion,* small grain, diminutive of *khondros* (see **ghren-** in Appendix*).] —**mi′to·chon′dri·al** (-kŏn′drē-əl) *adj.*

mi·to·sis (mī-tō′sĭs) *n. Biology.* 1. The sequential differentiation and segregation of replicated chromosomes in a cell nucleus that precedes complete cell division. 2. The entire sequence of processes in cell division in which the diploid number of chromosomes is retained in both daughter cells. See **prophase, metaphase, anaphase, telophase.** Compare **meiosis.** [New Latin : Greek *mitos,* a thread (see **mei-**[4] in Appendix*) + -OSIS.] —**mi·tot′ic** (mī-tŏt′ĭk) *adj.* —**mi·tot′i·cal·ly** *adv.*

mi·tral (mī′trəl) *adj.* 1. Pertaining to or resembling a miter. 2. Pertaining to a mitral valve. [New Latin *mitrālis,* from Latin *mitra,* MITER.]

mitral valve. The heart valve between the left auricle and the left ventricle that regulates blood flow from the auricle to the ventricle.

mi·tre. *Chiefly British.* Variant of **miter.**

mitt (mĭt) *n.* 1. A woman's glove that extends over the hand but only partially covers the fingers. 2. A **mitten** *(see).* 3. A large leather padded mitten worn by baseball catchers and first basemen. 4. Any of various hand coverings, as for protection from heat. 5. *Usually plural. Slang.* A hand or fist. —**tip one's mitt.** *Slang.* To betray oneself. [Short for MITTEN.]

mit·ten (mĭt′n) *n.* A covering for the hand that encases the thumb separately and the four fingers together. Also called "mitt." [Middle English *mytayne,* from Old French *mitaine,* from Common Romance *medietāna* (unattested), "skin-lined glove cut off at the middle," from Latin *medietās,* half, from *medius,* middle. See **medhyo-** in Appendix.*]

mit·ti·mus (mĭt′ə-məs) *n., pl.* **-muses.** 1. *Law.* A writ instructing a jailer to hold a prisoner. 2. *British.* A dismissal, especially from a job or office. [Latin, "we send," the first word of such a writ, from *mittere,* to send. See **smeit-** in Appendix.*]

mitz·vah (mĭts′və, -vä) *n., pl.* **mitzvoth** (mĭts′vōth′) or **-vahs.** Also **mits·vah.** *Judaism.* 1. A command of the Law. 2. The fulfillment of such a command. 3. Any worthy deed. [Hebrew *miṣwāh,* "(divine) commandment," from *ṣiwwāh,* to command.]

mix (mĭks) *v.* **mixed** or *Archaic* **mixt** (mĭkst), **mixing, mixes.** —*tr.* 1. a. To combine or blend (ingredients or elements) into one mass or mixture so that the constituent parts are indistinguishable: *mix sugar and egg yolks.* b. To create or form by adding ingredients together: *mix a cake.* c. To add (an ingredient or element) to another: *mix flour in water.* 2. To combine or join: *mix joy with sorrow.* 3. To bring into social contact: *mix boys and girls in a coeducational school.* 4. To crossbreed. —*intr.* 1. a. To become mixed or blended together. b. To be capable of being blended together: *Oil does not mix with water.* 2. To associate socially or get along with others: *He does not mix well at parties.* 3. To be crossbred. —**get (or become) mixed up in (or with).** To participate in, often unwillingly or improperly. —**mix it up.** *Slang.* To fight. —*n.* 1. An act of mixing. 2. A mixture, especially of ingredients packaged and sold commercially: *a cake mix.* [Back-formation from *mixed, mixt,* from Middle English, from Norman French *mixte,* from Latin *miscēre* (past participle *mixtus*), to mix. See **meik-** in Appendix.*] —**mix′a·ble, mix′i·ble** *adj.*

Synonyms: *mix, blend, mingle, coalesce, merge, amalgamate, combine, compound, fuse.* The verb *mix* is nonspecific, implying only components capable of existing together. *Blend* (transitive) denotes purposeful mixing; intransitively, it suggests that the components shade into each other. In either case the result is harmonious, and the components lose some or all of their original definition. *Mingle* implies no such loss of individual characteristics. *Coalesce* involves a union slowly achieved, with a distinct new identity. *Merge* also stresses new identity. *Amalgamate* implies a looser union, akin to a federation. *Combine* is usually applied to the union of a small number of elements, and implies resultant homogeneity. *Compound* stresses studious care in mixing distinct elements, which when united assume a new and independent character. *Fuse* emphasizes enduring union, as of molten metals, achieved under stress and strongly marked by loss of identity of parts.

mixed (mĭkst) *adj.* 1. Blended together into one unit or mass; intermingled. 2. Composed of a variety of differing, sometimes conflicting, entities: *mixed emotions.* 3. Made up of people of different sex, race, or social class. 4. *Informal.* Being in a state of confusion; muddled. Usually followed by *up.* —See Synonyms at **miscellaneous.**

mixed grill. A dish consisting of a variety of broiled meats and vegetables, typically including a lamb chop.

mixed marriage. Marriage between persons of different races or religions.

mixed metaphor. A succession of metaphors that produce an incongruous and ludicrous effect, for example: *His mounting ambition was soon bridled by a wave of opposition.*

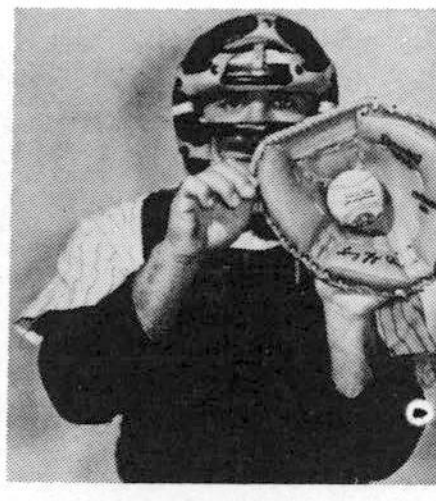

mitt
Baseball catcher's mitt

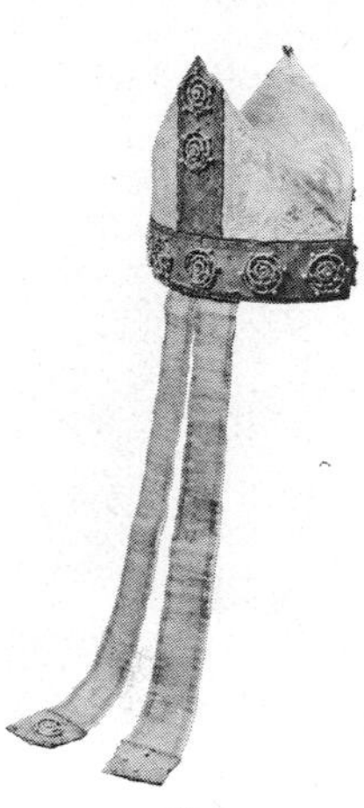

miter
Made in 13th-century Austria

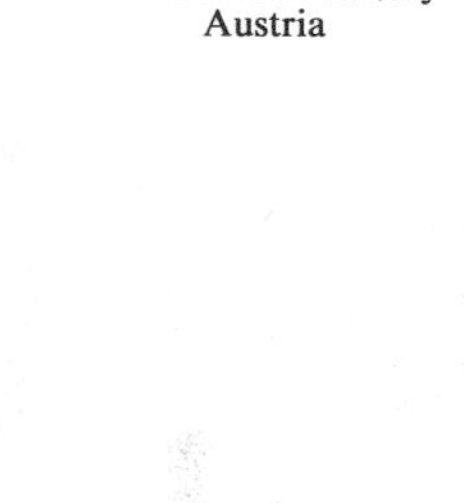

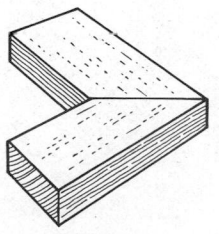

miter joint

mixed number. A number, such as 7¼, equal to the sum of an integer and a fraction.

mix·er (mĭk′sər) n. **1.** One that mixes. **2.** A sociable person: *"He was a good mixer, and in three days knew everyone on board."* (Maugham). **3.** An informal dance or party arranged for the purpose of giving members of a group an opportunity to get acquainted in an atmosphere of ease and conviviality. **4.** Any device that blends or mixes substances or ingredients, especially by mechanical agitation. **5.** A beverage, such as soda water or ginger ale, used in diluting alcoholic drinks.

mixt. Archaic alternate past tense and past participle of mix.

mix·ture (mĭks′chər) n. **1.** Something produced by mixing. **2.** Anything consisting of diverse elements: *"There was among the pilgrims a mixture of joy and trembling"* (Bunyan). **3.** A fabric made of different kinds of thread or yarn. **4.** The act or process of mixing or of being mixed. **5.** *Chemistry.* Any composition of two or more substances that are not chemically bound to each other. [French, from Latin *mixtūra*, from *miscēre* (past participle *mixtus*), to mix. See **meik-** in Appendix.*]

Synonyms: mixture, blend, admixture, combination, compound, composite, amalgam. *Mixture,* being nonspecific, overlaps, in nontechnical use, all of these terms. *Blend* denotes a harmonious mixture in which the original components are modified substantially. *Admixture* applies when one ingredient is not in harmony with the fundamental quality of the new union. *Combination* applies broadly to any union of rather few components. *Compound* stresses careful, purposeful mixing; the new product has an independent identity not necessarily deducible from its components. *Composite* implies more components and less deliberation in mixing; the new product lacks the unity of a compound, since the components do not wholly lose their identities. *Amalgam* implies a union more homogeneous than a composite but less sharply defined than a compound.

mix up. To confuse; confound.

mix-up (mĭks′ŭp′) n. **1.** A state of confusion; muddle. **2.** *Informal.* A fight or melee.

Mi·zar (mī′zär′) n. The star at the crook of the handle of the Big Dipper. [Arabic *mi′zar*, veil, cloak.]

miz·zen, miz·en (mĭz′ən) n. **1.** A fore-and-aft sail set on the mizzenmast. **2.** A mizzenmast. [Middle English *mesan, meseyn,* from Old French *misaine,* later variant (influenced by Italian *mezzana*) of *migenne,* from Old Catalan *mitjana,* "middle (sail)," feminine of *mitjan,* from Common Romance *medietāna* (unattested), from Latin *medietās,* half, from *medius,* middle. See **medhyo-** in Appendix.*]

miz·zen·mast, miz·en·mast (mĭz′ən-məst, -măst′, -mäst′) n. **1.** The third mast aft on sailing ships carrying three or more masts. **2.** A jigger mast *(see).*

miz·zle (mĭz′əl) intr.v. **-zled, -zling, -zles.** *Regional.* To rain in fine, mistlike droplets. —n. *Regional.* A mistlike rain. [Late Middle English *misellen,* from Middle Dutch *mieselen.* See **meigh-** in Appendix.*]

mk. 1. mark. **2.** markka.

MKC Airport code for Kansas City, Missouri.

MKE Airport code for Milwaukee, Wisconsin.

mks meter-kilogram-second (system of units).

mksA meter-kilogram-second-ampere (system of units).

mkt. market.

ml milliliter.

ML, M.L. Medieval Latin.

MLA Airport code for Malta.

M.L.A. Modern Language Association.

MLD minimum lethal dose.

Mlle. Mademoiselle.

Mlles. Mesdemoiselles.

M.L.S. Master of Library Science.

mm millimeter.

MM. Messieurs.

m.m. with the necessary changes having been made (Latin *mutatis mutandis*).

Mme. Madame.

Mmes. Mesdames.

mmf, m.m.f. magnetomotive force.

Mn The symbol for the element manganese.

MN Minnesota (with Zip Code).

mne·mon·ic (nĭ-mŏn′ĭk) adj. Relating to, assisting, or designed to assist the memory. —n. A device, such as a formula or rhyme, used as an aid in remembering. [Medieval Latin *mnēmonicus,* from Greek *mnēmonikos,* from *mnēmōn,* mindful. See **men-¹** in Appendix.*] —**mne·mon′i·cal·ly** adv.

mne·mon·ics (nĭ-mŏn′ĭks) n. Plural in form, used with a singular verb. A system to improve or develop the memory.

Mne·mos·y·ne (nĭ-mŏs′ə-nē, nĭ-mŏz′-). *Greek Mythology.* The goddess of memory, mother of the Muses. [Latin, from Greek *mnēmosunē,* memory, from *mnasthai,* to remember. See **men-¹** in Appendix.*]

Mngr. Monseigneur; Monsignor.

MNL Airport code for Manila, Philippines.

-mo. *Bookbinding.* Indicates leaves formed by folding a larger sheet of paper, and used after numerals or the names of numerals; for example, **duodecimo,** which is generally written "12 mo" and called by printers "twelvemo." [Latin ablative ending of ordinals, after the preposition *in,* in, as in *duodecimo,* from *duodecimus,* twelfth.]

Mo The symbol for the element molybdenum.

MO Missouri (with Zip Code).

mo. month.

Mo. Missouri.

m.o., M.O. 1. mail order. **2.** medical officer. **3.** money order.

mo·a (mō′ə) n. Any of various large, long-necked, flightless birds of the order Dinorthiformes, native to New Zealand and extinct for over a century. [Maori.]

Mo·ab (mō′ăb′). An ancient kingdom east of the Dead Sea, in an area that is now part of Jordan.

Mo·ab·ite (mō′ə-bīt′) n. **1.** A descendant of Moab, the son of Lot. Genesis 19:37. **2.** An inhabitant or native of Moab. **3.** The Semitic language of Moab. —adj. Of or pertaining to Moab, its people, or their language.

moan (mōn) n. **1.** A low, sustained, mournful sound, usually indicative of sorrow or pain. **2.** Any similar sound: *the moan of the wind.* **3.** *Rare.* Lamentation. —v. **moaned, moaning, moans.** —intr. **1.** To utter a moan or moans. **2.** To make a sound resembling a moan: *The wind moaned through the trees.* **3.** To complain, lament, or grieve. —tr. **1.** To bewail: *He moaned his misfortunes to anyone who would listen.* **2.** To utter with a moan or moans. —See Synonyms at **cry.** [Middle English *mone,* complaint, from Old English *mān* (unattested), complaint. See **mei-no-** in Appendix.*]

moat (mōt) n. A wide, deep ditch, usually filled with water, surrounding a medieval town, fortress, or castle as a protection against assault. —tr.v. **moated, moating, moats.** To surround with or as if with a moat. [Middle English *mote,* originally, "mound," "embankment," from Old French *mote, motte,* clod, hill, mound, probably from (unattested) Gaulish *mutt(a)†.*]

mob (mŏb) n. **1.** A large, disorderly crowd or throng: *"A mob is a society of bodies voluntarily bereaving themselves of reason"* (Emerson). **2.** The mass of common people, regarded as ignorant or otherwise deficient. **3.** *Informal.* An organized gang of hoodlums; a crime syndicate. —tr.v. **mobbed, mobbing, mobs. 1.** To crowd around and jostle or annoy, especially in anger or excessive enthusiasm: *The audience mobbed the singer as he came through the stage door.* **2.** To crowd into (a place): *Crowds mobbed the fairgrounds.* **3.** To attack violently, usually in a crowd or mob. [Shortening of earlier *mobile,* from Latin *mōbile (vulgus),* "the fickle (crowd)," neuter of *mōbilis,* MOBILE.]

mob·cap (mŏb′kăp′) n. A large, high cap trimmed with frills and ribbons, worn by women in the 18th and early 19th centuries. [From earlier *mob,* "negligee," "informal attire," earlier, "slattern," "loose woman," variant of *mab,* short for MABEL.]

mo·bile¹ (mō′bəl, -bēl′, -bīl′) adj. **1.** Capable of moving or of being moved from place to place. See usage note at **movable. 2.** Moving quickly from one state to another: *"His mouth was wide and mobile, the mouth of an actor or preacher."* (Joyce Cary). **3.** Marked by the easy intermixing of different social groups: *a mobile society.* **4.** Flowing freely: *a mobile liquid.* [Old French *mobile,* from Latin *mōbilis,* from the root of *movēre,* to move. See **mew-** in Appendix.*] —**mo·bil′i·ty** n.

mo·bile² (mō′bēl′) n. A type of sculpture consisting of parts that move, especially in response to air currents.

Mo·bile (mō′bēl′). A port city and manufacturing center in southwestern Alabama on Mobile Bay. Population, 203,000.

-mobile. Indicates a specialized kind of vehicle; for example **bloodmobile, bookmobile.** [From AUTOMOBILE.]

Mobile Bay (mō′bēl′). An inlet of the Gulf of Mexico in southwestern Alabama; site of a Civil War Union naval victory (1864).

mo·bi·lize (mō′bə-līz′) v. **-lized, -lizing, -lizes.** —tr. **1.** To make mobile or capable of movement. **2.** To assemble, prepare, or put into operation for war or a similar emergency: *mobilize troops.* —intr. To become prepared for war or similar emergency. [French *mobiliser.*] —**mo·bi·li·za′tion** n.

Mö·bi·us strip (mœ′bē-əs). *Topology.* A one-sided surface that can be formed from a rectangular strip by rotating one end 180° and attaching it to the other end. Also called "Möbius band." [After its inventor August *Möbius* (1790–1868), German mathematician.]

mob·oc·ra·cy (mŏb-ŏk′rə-sē) n., pl. **-cies.** Political control by a mob. —**mob′o·crat** (mŏb′ə-krăt) n. —**mob′o·crat′ic** (mŏb′ə-krăt′ĭk), **mob′o·crat′i·cal** adj.

mob·ster (mŏb′stər) n. *Slang.* A member of a criminal gang.

Mo·bu·tu (mō-bōō′tōō), **Joseph Désiré.** Born 1930. Congolese general and president of the Congo (Kinshasa) (since 1965).

Mo·çam·bi·que. The Portuguese name for **Mozambique.**

moc·ca·sin (mŏk′ə-sĭn) n. **1.** A soft leather slipper worn by American Indians. **2.** A shoe or slipper resembling an Indian moccasin. **3.** A snake, the **water moccasin** *(see).* [Natick *mohkussin,* from Proto-Algonquian *maxkeseni* (unattested).]

moccasin flower. Any of several North American orchids of the genus *Cypripedium;* especially, *C. acaule,* of eastern North America, having a solitary flower with a pouchlike pink lip. Also called "lady's-slipper."

mo·cha (mō′kə) n. **1.** A rich, pungent Arabian coffee. **2.** Coffee of high quality. **3.** A flavoring made of coffee often mixed with chocolate. **4.** A soft, thin glove leather usually made from goatskin. **5.** Dark olive brown. See **color.** [Originally exported from *Mocha,* a port of Yemen.] —**mo′cha** adj.

mo·chi·la (mō-chē′lə) n. A leather saddle covering with cutouts allowing the horn and cantle to protrude. [Spanish, saddlebag, probably from *mochil,* errand boy, from Basque *mutil,* servant boy, from Latin *mutilus,* maimed. See **mut-** in Appendix.*]

mock (mŏk) v. **mocked, mocking, mocks.** —tr. **1.** To treat with scorn or contempt; deride; ridicule. **2. a.** To mimic, as in sport or derision. **b.** To imitate; counterfeit. **3.** To frustrate the hopes of; disappoint. —intr. To express scorn or ridicule. Often used with *at: They mocked at the idea.* —See Synonyms

moccasin
Blackfoot Indian styles

moccasins with
quills and beads

beaded legging
moccasins

moccasin flower
Cypripedium acaule

at **ridicule.** —*n.* **1. a.** An act of mocking: *"Fools make a mock at sin."* (Proverbs 14:9). **b.** Mockery; derision. **2.** Something deserving of derision. **3.** Something simulated; an imitation or counterfeit. —*adj.* Simulated; false; sham: *a mock battle.* [Middle English *mokken, mocquen,* from Old French *mocquer,* to deride, from Common Romance *moccāre* (unattested), probably from a root *mok-,* imitative of laughter.] —**mock'er** *n.* —**mock'ing·ly** *adv.*

mock·er·y (mŏk'ər-ē) *n., pl.* **-ies. 1.** Scornful contempt; ridicule; derision. **2.** A specific action of ridicule or derision. **3.** An object of scorn or ridicule. **4.** A false, derisive, or impudent imitation; travesty: *The trial was a mockery of justice.* **5.** Something that is ludicrously futile or unsuitable: *"I leave/no pallid ghost or mockery of a man"* (Yeats).

mock-he·ro·ic (mŏk'hĭ-rō'ĭk) *n., pl.* **mock-heroics.** A satirical imitation or burlesque of the heroic manner or style. Usually in the plural. —**mock'-he·ro'ic** *adj.* —**mock'-he·ro'i·cal·ly** *adv.*

mock·ing·bird (mŏk'ĭng-bûrd') *n.* Any of several species of New World birds of the family Mimidae, especially *Mimus polyglottos,* a gray and white bird of the southern United States. They are noted for their ability to mimic other birds.

mock moon. A **paraselene** *(see).*

mock orange. 1. Any of several deciduous shrubs of the genus *Philadelphus,* having white, usually fragrant flowers. Also called "syringa." **2.** Any of various other shrubs or trees having flowers or fruit resembling those of the orange.

mock pennyroyal. A species of **pennyroyal** *(see).*

mock sun. A **parhelion** *(see).*

mock turtle soup. Soup made from calf's head or veal and spiced to taste like green turtle soup.

mock up. To make a mockup of.

mock·up (mŏk'ŭp') *n.* Also **mock-up. 1.** A scale model, usually full-sized, of a building, machine, or structure, used for demonstration, study, or testing. **2.** A layout of printed matter.

Moc·te·zu·ma. See **Montezuma II.**

mod[1] (mŏd) *n.* A fashionable style of dress that originated in England in the 1960's. —*adj.* **1.** In or characteristic of this style. **2.** Stylishly up-to-date, especially in dress. [Probably after *the Mods,* name of a gang of English youths, shortening of MODERN (noun).]

mod[2] *Mathematics.* modulus.

mod. 1. moderate. **2.** *Music.* moderato. **3.** modern.

mo·dal (mōd'l) *adj.* **1.** Of, pertaining to, or characteristic of a mode. **2.** *Grammar.* Of, pertaining to, or expressing the mood of a verb. **3.** *Music.* Of, pertaining to, characteristic of, or composed in any of the modes typical of medieval church music. **4.** *Philosophy.* Of or pertaining to mode or form as opposed to substance. **5.** *Logic.* Expressing or characterized by modality. **6.** *Statistics.* Of or pertaining to a statistical mode; most frequent, common, or typical. [Medieval Latin *modālis,* from Latin *modus;* measure, mode. See **med-** in Appendix.*] —**mo'dal·ly** *adv.*

modal auxiliary. One of a set of English verbs, including *can, may, must, ought, shall, should, will,* and *would,* that are characteristically used with other verbs to express mood or tense.

mo·dal·i·ty (mō-dăl'ə-tē) *n., pl.* **-ties. 1.** The fact, state, or quality of being modal. **2.** The persistence of a general pattern among individuals. **3.** *Logic.* The classification of propositions on the basis of whether they assert or deny the possibility, impossibility, contingency, or necessity of their content. **4.** *Medicine.* **a.** A method of therapy, usually physical, such as massage. **b.** An apparatus for such a therapy.

mode (mōd) *n.* **1. a.** Manner, way, or method of doing or acting: *"The modern mode of travelling cannot compare with the old mail-coach system in grandeur and power."* (De Quincey). **b.** A particular form, variety, or manner: *"He had his mode of religion for every fresh occasion"* (Bunyan). **2.** The current or customary fashion or style. **3.** *Music.* **a.** Any of certain arrangements of the diatonic tones of an octave. The two chief modes in Western music have been the **major** and **minor** *(both of which see).* **b.** One of several patterned arrangements characteristic of classical Greek and medieval church music. **4.** *Philosophy.* The particular form or manner in which an underlying substance, or some permanent aspect or attribute of it, is manifested. **5.** *Logic.* **a.** The arrangement or order of the propositions in a syllogism according to both quality and quantity. **b.** The **modality** *(see)* of a proposition. **6.** *Statistics.* The value or item occurring most frequently in a series of observations or statistical data. **7.** *Geology.* The mineral composition of a specific sample of igneous rock expressed in percentages of weight. **8.** *Physics.* Any of numerous patterns of wave motion, as of acoustic or electromagnetic waves. —See Synonyms at **fashion, method.** [Middle English *moede* (and French *mode,* fashion), from Latin *modus,* measure, manner, size, harmony, melody. See **med-** in Appendix.*]

mod·el (mŏd'l) *n.* **1.** A small object, usually built to scale, that represents some existing object. **2.** A preliminary pattern representing an item not yet constructed, and serving as the plan from which the finished work, usually larger, will be produced. **3.** A tentative ideational structure used as a testing device: *"two conflicting models of generative grammar"* (Noam Chomsky). **4.** A style or design of an item: *His car is last year's model.* **5.** A person or object serving as an example to be imitated or compared: *"in her temper, manners, mind, a model of female excellence"* (Jane Austen). **6.** A person or object serving as the subject for an artist or photographer. **7.** A person employed to display clothing by wearing it. —See Synonyms at **ideal.** —*v.* **modeled, -eling, -els.** Also *chiefly British* **-elled, -elling.** —*tr.* **1.** To make or construct a model of. **2.** To plan or fashion according to a model. **3.** To make by shaping a plastic substance. **4.** To make conform to a chosen standard: *He modeled his manners on his father's.* **5.** To display by wearing or posing. **6.** In painting and drawing, to give a three-dimensional appearance to, as by shading. —*intr.* **1.** To make a model. **2.** To serve as a model: *She models for a living.* —*adj.* **1.** Serving as or used as a model. **2.** Serving as a standard of excellence; worthy of imitation: *a model child.* [Obsolete French *modelle,* from Italian *modello,* from Vulgar Latin *modellus*° (unattested), from Latin *modulus,* little measure, diminutive of *modus,* measure, rhythm, harmony. See **med-** in Appendix.*] —**mod'el·er** *n.*

mod·el·ing (mŏd'l-ĭng) *n.* Also *chiefly British* **mod·el·ling. 1.** The act, art, or condition of producing or being a model. **2. a.** Representation of depth and solidity in painting or drawing. **b.** Visual shape and texture of something regarded aesthetically, especially the human form or face.

Model T. A trademark for Ford automobiles of 1908–28. Referred to formerly as a symbol of simplicity, economy, and dependability and later as a symbol of the old-fashioned. Also *slang* "tin lizzie."

Mo·de·na (mô'dā-nä). A city of northern Italy, in central Emilia-Romagna. Population, 153,000.

mod·er·ate (mŏd'ər-ĭt) *adj. Abbr.* **mod. 1.** Within reasonable limits; not excessive or extreme: *a moderate price.* **2.** Not violent; mild; calm: *a moderate climate.* **3.** Of medium or average quantity, quality, or extent; mediocre. **4.** Opposed to radical or extreme views or measures, especially in politics and religion. —*n.* One who holds moderate views or opinions, especially in politics or religion. —*v.* (mŏd'ə-rāt') **moderated, -ating, -ates.** —*tr.* **1.** To make less violent, severe, or extreme. **2.** To preside over: *He was chosen to moderate the convention.* —*intr.* **1.** To become less violent, severe, or extreme; abate. **2.** To act as a moderator. [Latin *moderātus,* from the past participle of *moderārī, moderāre,* to reduce, regulate, control. See **med-** in Appendix.*] —**mod'er·ate·ly** *adv.* —**mod'er·a'tion** *n.*

***Synonyms:** moderate, temperate. Moderate* indicates absence of extremes over a wide range of application. *Temperate* is said principally of climate and personal conduct; in the latter use it indicates conscious self-control.

mod·e·ra·to (mŏd'ə-rä'tō) *adv. Abbr.* **mod.** *Music.* In moderate tempo; slower than allegretto but faster than andante. Used as a direction to the performer. —**mod·e·ra'to** *adj.* & *n.* [Italian, from Latin *moderātus,* MODERATE.]

mod·er·a·tor (mŏd'ə-rā'tər) *n.* **1.** One that moderates. **2.** The officer who presides over a synod or general assembly of the Presbyterian Church. **3.** A substance, such as water or graphite, that is used in a nuclear reactor to decrease the speed of fast neutrons and increase the likelihood of fission.

mod·ern (mŏd'ərn) *adj. Abbr.* **mod. 1.** Of or pertaining to recent times or the present; not ancient: *modern history.* **2.** Characteristic of recent times or the present; modish; contemporary: *"The apartment into which we were shown was perfectly elegant and modern"* (Goldsmith). —*n.* **1.** One who lives in modern times. **2.** One who has modern ideas, standards, or beliefs. **3.** *Printing.* Any of a variety of type faces characterized by strongly contrasted heavy and thin parts. [Old French *moderne,* from Late Latin *modernus,* from *modō,* "just now," originally "exactly," "to the measure," from *modus,* measure. See **med-** in Appendix.*] —**mod'ern·ly** *adv.* —**mod·ern'i·ty** *n.*

Modern English. English since the early 16th century.

Modern Greek. Greek since the early 16th century, divided into **Dhimotiki** and **Katharevusa** *(both of which see).*

mod·ern·ism (mŏd'ər-nĭz'əm) *n.* **1.** Modern thought, character, or practice; sympathy with modern ideas, practices, or standards. **2.** Something, as a peculiarity of usage or style, that is characteristic of modern times. **3.** *Often capital* **M.** In Christian Churches, the name given to movements that attempt to define church teachings in the light of modern revolutions in science and philosophy. **4.** The theory and practice of modern art. —**mod'ern·ist** *n.* —**mod'ern·ist'ic** *adj.*

mod·ern·ize (mŏd'ər-nīz') *v.* **-ized, -izing, -izes.** —*tr.* To make modern in appearance, style, or character. —*intr.* To accept or adopt modern ways, ideas, or style. —**mod'ern·i·za'tion** *n.*

modern pentathlon. A **pentathlon** *(see).*

mod·est (mŏd'ĭst) *adj.* **1.** Having or showing a moderate estimation of one's own talents, abilities, and value. **2.** Having a shy and retiring nature; reserved. **3.** Having a regard for decencies of behavior or dress. **4.** Quiet and humble in appearance; unpretentious: *a modest house.* **5.** Moderate; not extreme: *a modest charge.* —See Synonyms at **humble, shy.** [Old French *modeste,* from Latin *modestus,* "keeping due measure." See **med-** in Appendix.*] —**mod'est·ly** *adv.*

mod·es·ty (mŏd'ĭs-tē) *n., pl.* **-ties. 1.** The state or quality of being modest. **2.** Reserve or propriety in speech, dress, or behavior. **3.** Lack of pretentiousness.

mod·i·cum (mŏd'ĭ-kəm) *n., pl.* **-cums** or **-ca** (-kə). A small or moderate amount or quantity. [Latin, short way, short time, from *modicus,* moderate, from *modus,* (due) measure. See **med-** in Appendix.*]

mod·i·fi·ca·tion (mŏd'ə-fĭ-kā'shən) *n.* **1.** The act of modifying or the condition of being modified. **2.** The result of modifying. **3.** A small alteration, adjustment, or limitation. **4.** *Biology.* A physical change in an organism due to environment or activity, but not transmitted to the organism's descendants. **5.** *Linguistics.* **a.** A change undergone by a word as it passes from language to language. **b.** The linguistic change of a morpheme from one construction to another. **c.** The raising of a vowel sound produced by the existence of a high vowel in the following syllable; umlaut. —**mod'i·fi·ca'to·ry** (mŏd'ə-fĭ-kā'tər-ē),

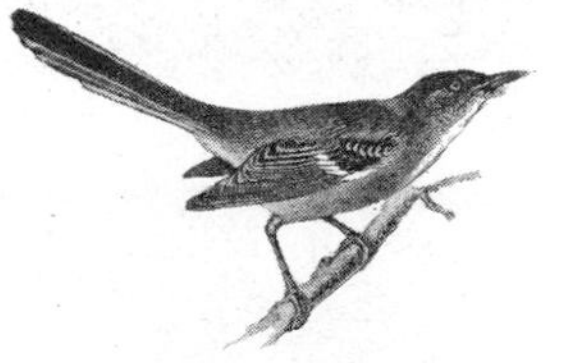

mockingbird
Mimus polyglottos

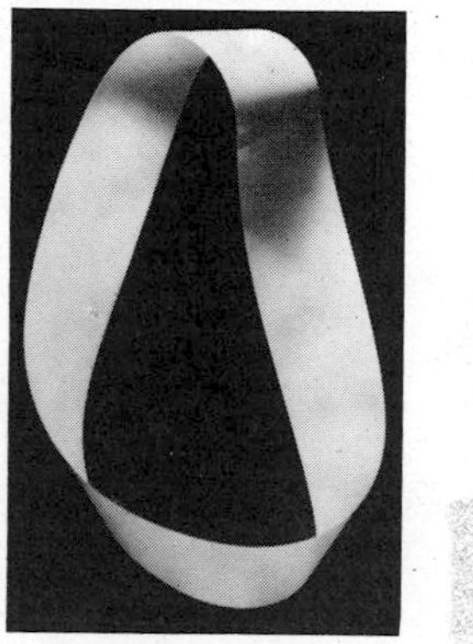

Möbius strip

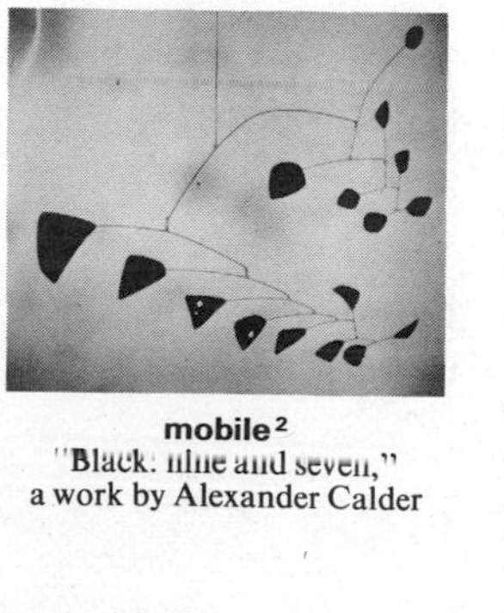

mobile[2]
"Black: nine and seven,"
a work by Alexander Calder

moiré effect

mod'i·fi·ca'tive (-kā'tĭv) adj. —mod'i·fi·ca'tor (-tər) n.
mod·i·fi·er (mŏd'ə-fī'ər) n. 1. One that modifies. 2. *Grammar.* A word, phrase, or clause that limits or qualifies the sense of another word or word group.
mod·i·fy (mŏd'ə-fī') v. -fied, -fying, -fies. —tr. 1. To change in form or character; alter: *"the first tools must have been natural objects only slightly modified"* (V. Gordon Childe). 2. To make less extreme, severe, or strong: *"taking the barest suggestion of whiskey and modifying it with seltzer"* (Dreiser). 3. *Grammar.* To qualify or limit the meaning of. For example, *"wet"* modifies *"day"* in the phrase *a wet day.* 4. *Linguistics.* To change (a vowel) by umlaut. —intr. To be or become modified. —See Synonyms at **change.** [Middle English *modifien,* to limit, moderate, from Old French *modifier,* from Latin *modificāre : modus,* a measure (see **med-** in Appendix*) + *facere,* to do, make (see **dhē-¹** in Appendix*).] —mod'i·fi'a·ble adj.
Mo·di·glia·ni (mō'dē-lyä'nē), Amedeo. 1884–1920. Italian painter and sculptor.
mo·dil·lion (mō-dĭl'yən) n. *Architecture.* An ornamental bracket used in series under the cornice of the Corinthian, Composite, or Roman Ionic orders. [French *modillon,* earlier *modiglion,* from Italian *modiglione,* from Vulgar Latin *mutellione* (unattested), from *mutellus* (unattested), alteration of Latin *mutulus,* from Etruscan *mut-* (unattested root), to stand out.]
mo·di·o·lus (mō-dī'ə-ləs) n., pl. -li (-lī') *Anatomy.* The central, conical, bony shaft of the cochlea. See **ear.** [New Latin, from Latin, hub of a wheel, bucket of a water wheel, diminutive of *modius,* a measure for grain. See **med-** in Appendix.*]
mod·ish (mō'dĭsh) adj. Being in or conforming to the prevailing or current fashion; stylish. [From MODE (fashion).] —mod'ish·ly adv. —mod'ish·ness n.
mo·diste (mō-dēst') n. One who produces, designs, or deals in ladies' fashions. [French, from *mode,* MODE (fashion).]
Mo·dred (mō'drĭd). Also Mor·dred (môr'drĭd). King Arthur's wicked nephew.
mod·u·late (mŏj'oō-lāt', mŏd'yə-) v. -lated, -lating, -lates. —tr. 1. To adjust or adapt to a certain proportion; regulate; temper. 2. To change or vary the pitch, intensity, or tone of: *"and modulated his voice to such a degree that what he said seemed wholly confidential"* (Dreiser). 3. To sing or intone, as a chant or prayer. 4. *Electronics.* To vary the frequency, amplitude, phase, or other characteristic of (any carrier wave). —intr. 1. *Music.* To pass from one key or tonality to another by means of a regular melodic chord or progression. 2. *Electronics.* To vary the frequency, amplitude, phase, or other characteristic of any carrier wave. In this sense, see **modulation.** [Latin *modulārī,* to measure off, set to a measure, play music, from *modulus,* diminutive of *modus,* measure, rhythm. See **med-** in Appendix.*] —mod'u·la·tive, mod'u·la·to'ry adj.
mod·u·la·tion (mŏj'oō-lā'shən, mŏd'yə-) n. 1. The act or process of modulating. 2. The state of being modulated. 3. *Music.* A passing from one tonality to another by means of a regular melodic or chord progression. 4. a. A change in pitch or loudness of the voice; an inflection of the voice. b. The use of a particular intonation or inflection of the voice to convey meaning. 5. The harmonious use of language, as in poetry or prose. 6. *Architecture.* Proportion determined by a module. 7. *Electronics.* The variation of a property of an electromagnetic wave or signal, such as its amplitude, frequency, or phase, in a manner determined by another wave or signal, especially for the purpose of transferring information from an audible signal, such as the human voice, to a carrier wave suitable for radio or telephonic transmission.
mod·u·la·tor (mŏj'oō-lā'tər, mŏd'yə-) n. 1. One that modulates. 2. *Electronics.* A device or electric circuit used to modulate a carrier wave. See **modulation.** 3. *Anatomy.* A nerve fiber in the retina of the eye, related to color discrimination.
mod·ule (mŏj'oōl, mŏd'yoōl) n. 1. A standard or unit of measurement. 2. *Architecture.* a. The part of a construction used as a standard to which the rest is proportioned. b. A uniform structural component used repeatedly in a building. 3. *Electronics.* A self-contained assembly of electronic components and circuitry, such as a stage in a computer. 4. *Aerospace.* A self-contained unit of a spacecraft that performs a specific task or class of tasks in support of the major function of the craft. [Latin *modulus,* MODULUS.] —mod'u·lar adj.
mod·u·lus (mŏj'oō-ləs, mŏd'yə-) n., pl. -li (-lī'). *Abbr.* m, M 1. *Physics.* A constant or coefficient that expresses the degree to which a substance possesses some property. 2. *Mathematics.* a. The absolute value (*see*) of a complex number. b. *Abbr.* mod A number or quantity that produces the same remainder when divided into each of two quantities. c. The number by which a logarithm in one system must be multiplied to obtain the corresponding logarithm in another system. 3. A standard; norm. [New Latin, from Latin, small measure, a measure, diminutive of *modus,* measure. See **med-** in Appendix.*] —mod'u·lar adj.
mo·dus op·er·an·di (mō'dəs ŏp'ə-răn'dē). *Latin.* 1. The manner in which something operates. 2. A person's manner of working.
mo·dus vi·ven·di (mō'dəs vĭ-věn'dē, -věn'dī'). *Latin.* 1. A way of living. 2. A temporary agreement between contending parties pending a final settlement; a practical compromise.
Moe·so·goth (mē'sō-gŏth') n. Also Moe·so·Goth. A Goth of Moesia, an ancient region in Bulgaria.
Moe·so·goth·ic (mē'sō-gŏth'ĭk) n. Also Moe·so·Goth·ic. The language of the Moesogoths, the only documented form of Gothic (*see*). —Moe'so·goth'ic adj.
mo·fette (mō-fět') n. Also mof·fette. 1. An opening in the earth from which carbon dioxide and other gases escape, usually marking the last stage of volcanic activity. 2. The gases escaping from such a fissure. [French, "fetid exhalation," from Italian *moffetta,* from *muffa,* mustiness, from (unattested) Lombardic *muff* (probably imitative).]
Mog·a·dish·u (mŏg'ə-dĭsh'ōō). The capital of Somalia, a port on the Indian Ocean. Population, 100,000.
Mog·a·dor. The former name for **Essaouira.**
Mo·gen Da·vid. Variant of **Magen David.**
Mo·gi·lev (mō'gĭ-lĕf', mŏg'ĭ-; *Russian* mŏ-gĭ-lyôf'). A city in eastern Byelorussia, U.S.S.R. Population, 121,000.
mo·gul¹ (mō'gəl) n. A small mound on a ski slope. [Possibly of Scandinavian origin, akin to Old Norse *mūgi,* heap. See **muk-** in Appendix.*]
mo·gul² (mō'gəl) n. 1. A very rich or powerful person: *a movie mogul.* 2. A kind of heavy steam locomotive.
Mo·gul (mō'gəl, mō-gŭl') n. 1. Also Mo·ghul, Mu·ghal (moō-gŭl'), Mu·ghul. a. One of the followers of Baber who conquered India in 1526 and founded a Moslem empire that formally lasted until 1857. See **Great Mogul.** b. A descendant of a follower of Baber. 2. A Mongol or Mongolian. [Probably from German dialectal (Austro-Bavarian) *Mugl, Mugel.* See **muk-** in Appendix.*] —Mo'gul adj.
Mo·hács (mō'häch'). A city in southern Hungary, on the Danube; site of an Ottoman victory (1526) over the Hungarians that marked the beginning of 150 years of Turkish rule. Population, 16,000.
mo·hair (mō'hâr') n. 1. The hair of the Angora goat. 2. A shiny, heavy, woolly fabric made of this hair, often with a mixture of cotton. 3. An upholstery fabric with mohair pile. [Variant (influenced by HAIR) of earlier *moochary, mocayare,* from Italian *moccaiaro,* from Arabic *mukhayyar,* "select," "choice," cloth of goat's hair, from *khayyara,* to choose.]
Mo·ham·med (mō-hăm'ĭd, -hä'mĭd). Also Mo·ham·mad (mō-hăm'ĭd, -hä'mĭd), Ma·hom·et (mə-hŏm'ĭt). A.D. 570?–632. Prophet and founder of Islam. [Arabic *Muḥammad,* "praiseworthy," from *hamida,* to praise.]
Mo·ham·med II (mō-hăm'ĭd, -hä'mĭd). Called "the Conqueror," "the Great." 1429?–1481. Sultan of Turkey (1451–81); captured Constantinople in 1453, ending the Byzantine Empire.
Mo·ham·med A·li (mō-hăm'ĭd ä-lē', -hä'mĭd). Also Me·he·met A·li (mĕ-mĕt' ä-lē'). 1769–1849. Viceroy of Egypt (1805–48).
Mo·ham·med·an (mō-hăm'ə-dən) adj. Also Mu·ham·mad·an (moō-hăm'ə-dən), Mu·ham·med·an, Ma·hom·et·an (mə-hŏm'ə-tən). Of or pertaining to Mohammed or Islam; Moslem. —n. A follower of Mohammed; one who believes in Islam; a Moslem.
Mo·ham·med·an·ism (mō-hăm'ə-də-nĭz'əm) n. Also Mu·ham·mad·an·ism (moō-), Ma·hom·et·an·ism (mə-hŏm'ə-tən-). The Mohammedan religion, **Islam** (*see*).
Mo·ham·med Ri·za Pah·la·vi. See **Pahlavi.**
Mo·har·ram. Variant of **Muharram.**
Mo·ha·ve (mō-hä'vē) n., pl. Mohave or -ves. Also Mo·ja·ve (mō-hä'vē). 1. A tribe of Yuman-speaking Indians, formerly living along the Gila and Colorado rivers. 2. A member of this tribe. [Mohave *hamokhava,* "three mountains," i.e., three peaks near Needles, California.] —Mo·ha've adj.
Mo·ha·ve Desert. See **Mojave Desert.**
Mo·hawk (mō'hôk') n., pl. Mohawk or -hawks. 1. The most easterly tribe of the Iroquian-speaking Five Nations. They occupied the territory from the Mohawk River to the St. Lawrence. 2. A member of this tribe. 3. The language of this tribe. [Narraganset *mohowaugsuck,* from earlier *mohowaug* (unattested), "man-eaters" : Proto-Eastern-Algonquian *məhw-* (unattested), eat + *-awee-* unattested), animate object + *-w-,* nominal ending + *-aki,* animate plural.] —Mo'hawk' adj.
Mo·hawk River (mō'hôk'). A river of New York State, rising near Utica and flowing 148 miles to join the Hudson at Troy.
Mo·he·gan (mō-hē'gən) n., pl. Mohegan or -gans. 1. A tribe of Algonquian-speaking Indians, formerly living in the area around the Thames River, Connecticut. 2. A member of this tribe. [Tribal name possibly meaning "seaside people."] —Mo·he'gan adj.
Mo·hen·jo-Da·ro (mō-hĕn'jō-dä'rō). A ruined ancient city on the Indus River in West Pakistan.
Mo·hi·can. Variant of **Mahican.**
Mo·ho (mō'hō') n. The **Mohorovičić discontinuity** (*see*).
Mo·hock (mō'hŏk') n. One of a band of young aristocrats who vandalized London in the early 18th century. [Variant of MOHAWK.]
Mo·holy-Nagy (mō'hoi-nŏd'y'), Laszlo or Ladislaus. 1895–1946. Hungarian-born American artist and educator.
Mo·ho·ro·vi·čić discontinuity (mō'hə-rō'və-chĭch'). The boundary between the earth's crust and the subjacent mantle rock, ranging in depth from 6 to 8 miles under ocean basins to 20 to 25 miles under continents. Also called "Moho." [After Andrija *Mohorovičić* (1857–1936), Yugoslav geologist.]
Mohs scale (mōz). A scale for determining the relative hardness of a mineral according to its resistance to scratching by one of the following minerals, arranged in order of increasing hardness: 1. talc; 2. gypsum; 3. calcite; 4. fluorite; 5. apatite; 6. feldspar; 7. vitreous silica; 8. quartz; 9. topaz; 10. garnet; 11. fused zirconia; 12. fused alumina; 13. silicon carbide; 14. boron carbide; 15. diamond. [Devised by Friedrich *Mohs* (1773–1839), German mineralogist.]
mo·hur (mō'ər, mō'hoor') n. A gold coin, formerly used in India, equal to 15 rupees. [Hindi *muhur, muhr,* gold coin, seal, from Persian *muhr,* a seal, from Middle Persian, from Old Iranian *mudrā* (unattested), probably from *muzrā* (unattested), from Akkadian *musarûm,* document, from Sumerian *mu-sar-.*]

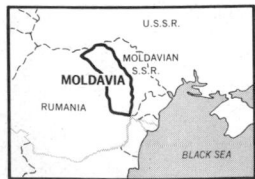

Moldavia

moi·dore (moi′dôr′, -dōr′, moi-dôr′, -dōr′) *n.* A former Portuguese or Brazilian gold coin. [Earlier *moyodore,* from Portuguese *moeda d'ouro,* "coin of gold" : *moeda,* money, from Latin *monēta,* mint, MONEY + *d'ouro,* "of gold" : *de,* of + *ouro,* gold, from Latin *aurum,* AURUM.]
moi·e·ty (moi′ə-tē) *n., pl.* **-ties.** **1.** A half. **2.** A part, portion, or share of indefinite size. **3.** Either of two basic units that make up a tribe on the basis of unilateral descent. [Middle English *moite, moitie,* from Old French *moite,* from Latin *medietās,* half, from *medius,* middle. See **medhyo-** in Appendix.*]
moil (moil) *intr.v.* **moiled, moiling, moils.** **1.** To toil or slave. **2.** To churn about. —*n.* **1.** Toil; drudgery. **2.** Confusion; turmoil. [Middle English *moillen,* to moisten, smear, from Old French *moillier,* to moisten, paddle in mud, from Vulgar Latin *molliāre* (unattested), from Latin *mollis,* soft. See **mel-**[1] in Appendix.*]
moire (mwär) *n.* Cloth, especially silk, that has a watered or wavy pattern. [French, earlier *mouaire,* from English MOHAIR.]
moi·ré (mwä-rā′) *n.* A watered pattern produced on cloth by engraved rollers. [French, from *moiré,* MOIRE.] —**moi·ré** *adj.*
moiré effect. The effect of superimposing a repetitive design, such as a grid, on the same or a different design to produce a pattern distinct from its components.
Mois·san (mwä-säN′), **(Ferdinand Frédéric) Henri.** 1852–1907. French chemist; isolated fluorine.
moist (moist) *adj.* **moister, moistest.** **1.** Slightly wet or damp; humid. **2.** Filled with moisture. **3.** Tearful. —See Synonyms at **wet.** [Middle English *moiste,* fresh, moist, from Old French, from Vulgar Latin *muscidus* (unattested), moldy, wet, alteration of Latin *mūcidus,* from *mūcus,* mucus. See **meug-**[2] in Appendix.*] —**moist′ly** *adv.* —**moist′ness** *n.*
mois·ten (mois′ən) *v.* **-tened, -tening, -tens.** —*tr.* To make moist. —*intr.* To become moist. —**mois′ten·er** *n.*
mois·ture (mois′chər) *n.* Diffuse wetness that can be felt as vapor in the atmosphere or as condensed liquid on the surfaces of objects; dampness. [Middle English, from Old French *moistour,* from *moiste,* MOIST.]
mo·jar·ra (mō-här′ə) *n., pl.* **mojarra** or **-ras.** **1.** Any of several species of small American marine fishes of the family Gerridae, having extremely protrusile mouths. **2.** Any of several tropical American freshwater fishes of the family Cichlidae. [American Spanish, from Spanish, "lance head" (a fish), from Arabic *muḥarrab,* pointed, from *ḥarrab,* to sharpen, fight.]
Mo·ja·ve. Variant of **Mohave.**
Mo·ja·ve Desert (mō-hä′vē). Also **Mo·ha·ve Desert.** A desert region of southern California, about 15,000 square miles.
Mo·ji (mō′jē). One of five cities in northern Kyushu, Japan, combined in 1963 to form the city of **Kita Kyushu** *(see).*
moke (mōk) *n. Slang.* **1.** A Negro. Used disparagingly. **2.** *British.* A donkey. **3.** A dull or boring person. **4.** *Australian.* An old, broken-down horse. [Origin obscure.]
Mo·ki (mō′kē) *n.* Also **Mo·qui.** An Indian, a **Hopi** *(see).* [Spanish *moqui,* from Hopi *môokwi,* a tribal name.]
MOL Manned Orbital Laboratory.
mol. *Chemistry.* Variant of **mole.**
mol. molecular; molecule.
mo·lal (mō′ləl) *adj. Chemistry.* Of or designating a solution containing one mole of solute in 1,000 grams of solvent, usually water. Compare **molar.** [From MOLE (chemistry).]
mo·lal·i·ty (mō-lăl′ə-tē) *n., pl.* **-ties.** *Chemistry.* The molal concentration of a solute, usually expressed as the number of moles of solute per 1,000 grams of solvent. See **molal.**
mo·lar[1] (mō′lər) *adj.* **1.** *Physics.* Of or pertaining to a body of matter as a whole, perceived apart from molecular or atomic properties. **2.** *Abbr.* **M** *Chemistry.* **a.** Containing one mole of a substance. **b.** Pertaining to or designating a solution that contains one mole of solute per liter of solution. In this sense, compare **molal.** [From MOLE (quantity).]
mo·lar[2] (mō′lər) *n.* A tooth with a broad crown for grinding food, located behind the bicuspids. Man has twelve molars, three in each jaw quadrant. —*adj.* **1.** Of or pertaining to the molar teeth. **2.** Capable of grinding. [Latin *molāris,* millstone, molar tooth, from *mola,* millstone. See **mele-** in Appendix.*]
mo·lar·i·ty (mō-lăr′ə-tē) *n., pl.* **-ties.** *Chemistry.* The molar concentration of a solute, usually expressed as the number of moles of solute per liter of solution. See **molar.**
mo·las·ses (mə-lăs′ĭz) *n., pl.* **molasses.** Any of various thick syrups produced in refining sugar. [Earlier *melasus, malassos,* from Portuguese *melaço,* from Late Latin *mellāceum,* must, from Latin *mel,* honey. See **melit-** in Appendix.*]
mold[1] (mōld) *n.* Also *chiefly British* **mould.** **1.** A form or matrix for shaping a fluid or plastic substance. **2.** A frame or model around or on which something is formed or shaped. **3.** Something that is made in or shaped on a mold. **4.** The pattern of a mold. **5.** General shape or form: *the oval mold of her face.* **6.** Distinctive shape, character, or type: *in the mold of his ancestors.* **7.** *Architecture.* **Molding** *(see).* —*tr.v.* **molded, molding, molds.** Also *chiefly British* **mould.** **1.** To shape in or on a mold. **2. a.** To form into a desired shape. **b.** To guide or determine the growth or development of; influence. **3.** To make a mold of or from, prior to casting. [Middle English *molde,* alteration of Old French *modle,* from Latin *modulus,* a small measure, diminutive of *modus,* measure. See **med-** in Appendix.*] —**mold′a·ble** *adj.*
mold[2] (mōld) *n.* Also *chiefly British* **mould.** **1.** Any of various fungous growths often causing disintegration of organic matter. **2.** A fungus that causes mold. Compare **mildew.** —*intr.v.* **molded, molding, molds.** Also *chiefly British* **mould.** To become moldy; grow musty. [From Northern English dialectal *mouled,* moldy, from the past participle of *moul,* to become moldy, probably from Old Danish *mul,* mold, from Old Norse *mugla, mygla,* mold. See **meug-**[2] in Appendix.*]
mold[3] (mōld) *n.* Also *chiefly British* **mould.** **1.** Loose, friable soil, rich in humus, and fit for planting. **2.** *Poetic.* **a.** The earth; the ground. **b.** The earth of the grave. **3.** *Obsolete.* Earth as the substance of the human body: *"Be merciful great Duke to men of mould."* (Shakespeare). [Middle English *molde,* Old English *molde.* See **mela-** in Appendix.*]
Mol·da·vi·a (mŏl-dā′vē-ə, -vyə). **1.** A historic region of eastern Rumania, 14,690 square miles in area. **2.** The Moldavian Soviet Socialist Republic.
Mol·da·vi·an (mŏl-dā′vē-ən, -vyən) *n.* **1.** A native or inhabitant of Moldavia. **2.** The language of Moldavia, a form of Rumanian. —**Mol·da′vi·an** *adj.*
Moldavian Soviet Socialist Republic. The second smallest republic of the Soviet Union, 13,000 square miles in area, in the southwest between Rumania and the Ukrainian S.S.R. Population, 3,300,000. Capital, Kishinev. Also called "Moldavia."
mold·board (mōld′bôrd′, -bōrd′) *n.* The curved plate of a plow that turns over the furrow slice. [MOLD (earth) + BOARD.]
mold·er (mōl′dər) *v.* **-ered, -ering, -ers.** Also *chiefly British* **mould·er.** —*intr.* To become dust gradually, by natural decay; crumble. —*tr.* To cause to decay or crumble. —See Synonyms at **decay.** [Probably from Scandinavian, akin to dialectal Norwegian *muldra,* from Old Norse *muldhra* (unattested). See **mela-** in Appendix.*]
mold·ing (mōl′dĭng) *n.* Also *chiefly British* **mould·ing.** **1.** Anything that is molded. **2.** *Architecture.* An embellishment in strip form used to decorate a surface.
mold·y (mōl′dē) *adj.* **-ier, -iest.** Also *chiefly British* **mould·y.** **1.** Covered with or containing mold: *moldy bread.* **2.** Musty or stale, as from age or decay. —**mold′i·ness** *n.*
mole[1] (mōl) *n.* A small congenital growth on the human skin, usually slightly raised and dark, and sometimes hairy; especially, a pigmented **nevus** *(see).* [Middle English *mool, mole,* Old English *māl.* See **mai-**[2] in Appendix.*]
mole[2] (mōl) *n.* **1.** Any of various small, insectivorous, burrowing mammals having thickset bodies with silky light-brown to dark-gray fur, rudimentary eyes, tough muzzles, and strong forefeet for digging. Most live underground. See **desman, shrew mole, star-nosed mole.** **2.** The pelt of the mole, **moleskin** *(see).* **3.** Dark gray. See **color.** [Middle English *molle, mulle, mole,* from Middle Dutch *mol* and Medieval Latin *mulus,* both from an unknown Germanic source.]
mole[3] (mōl) *n.* **1.** A massive stone wall used as a breakwater or jetty, or to enclose an anchorage or harbor. **2.** The anchorage or harbor enclosed by such a barrier. [French *môle,* from Medieval Greek *mōlos,* from Latin *mōlēs,* pier, dam, massive structure, heavy bulk. See **mō-** in Appendix.*]
mole[4] (mōl) *n.* A mass or tumor in the uterus, caused by the degeneration or abortive development of an ovum. [French *môle,* from Latin *mola,* "millstone" (since it is a hardened mass), mole. See **mela-** in Appendix.*]
mole[5] (mōl) *n.* Also **mol** (mōl). *Chemistry.* The amount of a substance that has a weight in grams numerically equal to the molecular weight of the substance. Also called "gram-molecular weight," "gram molecule." [German *Mol,* short for *Molekulargewicht,* molecular weight.]
mo·le[6] (mō′lē) *n.* A Mexican hot sauce of chili, other spices, and sometimes chocolate. It is served with various meats. [Mexican Spanish, from Nahuatl *molli,* sauce.]
Mo·lech. Variant of **Moloch.**
mole cricket. Any of various burrowing crickets, with short wings and front legs well adapted for digging and shearing.
mo·lec·u·lar (mə-lĕk′yə-lər) *adj. Abbr.* **mol.** Pertaining to, consisting of, caused by, or existing between molecules.
molecular beam. *Physics.* A highly collimated, internally collisionless stream of molecules that is used to study electromagnetic phenomena as the stream traverses an evacuated chamber.
molecular biology. The field of biology in which the structure and development of biological systems are analyzed in terms of the physics and chemistry of their molecular constituents.
molecular film. A surface film of thickness comparable to that of a single molecule.
molecular weight. *Abbr.* **mol. wt.** *Chemistry.* The sum of the atomic weights of a molecule's constituent atoms.
mol·e·cule (mŏl′ə-kyōōl′) *n. Abbr.* **mol.** **1.** A stable configuration of atomic nuclei and electrons bound together by electrostatic and electromagnetic forces. It is the simplest structural unit that displays the characteristic physical and chemical properties of a compound. **2.** A small particle; tiny bit. [French *molécule,* from New Latin *molecula,* diminutive of Latin *mōlēs,* mass, bulk, burden. See **mō-** in Appendix.*]
mole·hill (mōl′hĭl′) *n.* A small mound of loose earth thrown up by a burrowing mole. —**make a mountain out of a molehill.** To exaggerate a minor problem.
mole-rat (mōl′răt′) *n.* A rodent, the **bandicoot** *(see).*
mole·skin (mōl′skĭn′) *n.* **1.** The short, soft, silky fur of the mole. Also called "mole." **2. a.** A heavy-napped cotton twill fabric. **b.** *Plural.* Clothing, especially trousers, of this fabric.
mo·lest (mə-lĕst′) *tr.v.* **-lested, -lesting, -lests.** **1.** To disturb, interfere with, or annoy; inconvenience: *"to go on dreaming and not to be molested by the world"* (James Baldwin). **2.** To accost and harass sexually. [Middle English *molesten,* to vex, molest, from Old French *molester,* from Latin *molestāre,* to annoy, from *molestus,* troublesome. See **mō-** in Appendix.*] —**mo′les·ta′tion** *n.* —**mo·lest′er** *n.*
Mo·lière (mōl-yâr′; *French* mô-lyâr′). Pen name of Jean Bap-

mold[1]

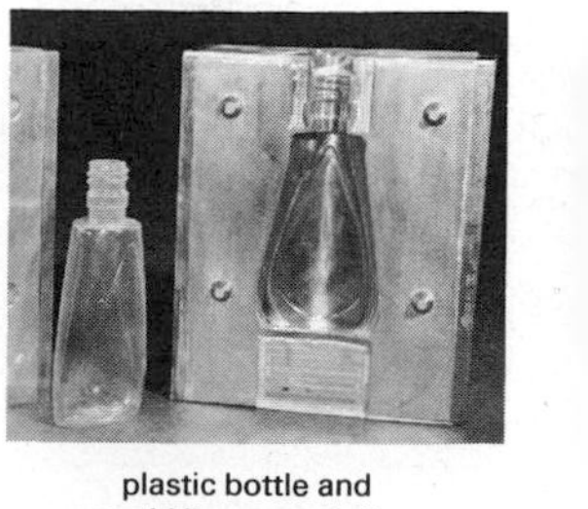

plastic bottle and mold it was made in

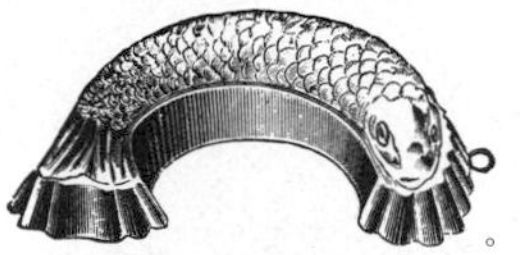

cooking mold for making a fish mousse

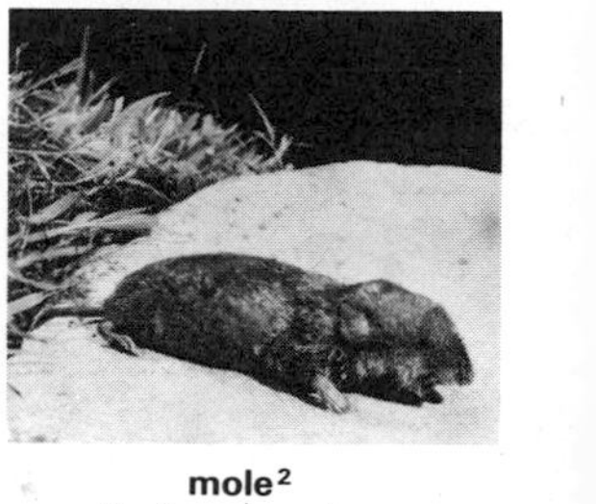

mole[2]
Scalopus aquaticus
Eastern American mole

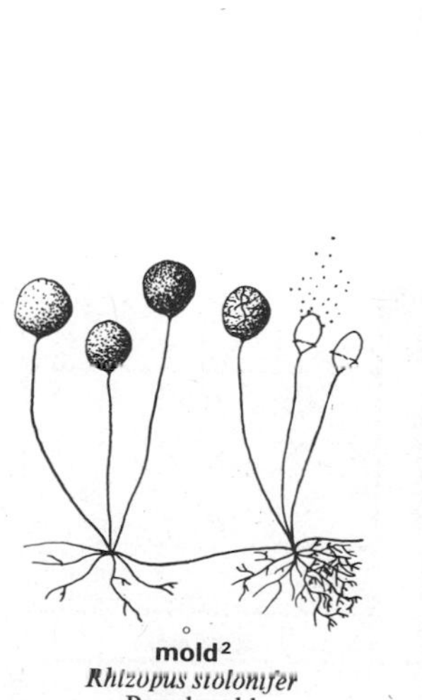

mold[2]
Rhizopus stolonifer
Bread mold

tiste Poquelin. 1622–1673. French playwright, actor, and theatrical manager; author of farces and comedies of manners.

moll (mŏl) *n. Slang.* **1.** A female companion of a thief or gangster. **2.** A prostitute. [From MOLL, pet form for MARY.]

mol·lah. Variant of **mullah.**

mol·li·fy (mŏl′ə-fī′) *tr.v.* **-fied, -fying, -fies. 1.** To allay (the anger of); placate; calm: *"This confession . . . did not mollify Mrs. Deborah, who now pronounced a second judgment."* (Fielding). **2.** To make gentler; soften or ease: *"with a countenance greatly mollified by the softening influence of tobacco"* (Dickens). —See Synonyms at **pacify.** [Middle English *mollifien,* from Old French *mollifier,* from Latin *mollificāre,* to make soft : *mollis,* soft (see **mel-**[1] in Appendix*) + *facere,* to make, to do (see **dhē-**[1] in Appendix*).] —**mol′li·fi′a·ble** *adj.* —**mol′li·fi·ca′tion** (mŏl′ə-fĭ-kā′shən) *n.* —**mol′li·fi′er** *n.* —**mol′li·fy′ing·ly** *adv.*

mol·lus·can (mə-lŭs′kən) *adj.* Also **mol·lus·kan.** Of or relating to the mollusks. —*n.* Also **mol·lus·kan.** A mollusk.

mol·lusk (mŏl′əsk) *n.* Also **mol·lusc.** Any member of the phylum Mollusca, of largely marine invertebrates, including the edible shellfish and some 100,000 other species. [French *mollusque,* from New Latin *Mollusca,* "the soft ones," from Latin *molluscus,* extension of *mollis,* soft. See **mel-**[1] in Appendix.*] —**mol·lus′cous** (mə-lŭs′kəs) *adj.*

mol·ly (mŏl′ē) *n., pl.* **-lies.** Also **mol·lie.** Any of several tropical and subtropical fishes of the genus *Mollienesia.* The males of some species have saillike dorsal fins and are raised in aquaria. [From New Latin *Mollienesia* (genus), after Comte François N. *Mollien* (1758–1850), French statesman.]

Mol·ly (mŏl′ē). Also **Mol·lie.** A feminine given name. [Pet form of MARY.]

mol·ly·cod·dle (mŏl′ē-kŏd′l) *n.* A person of weak character who seeks to be pampered and protected: *"I was resolved . . . not to be a mollycoddle waiting for life but to seize life by the throat."* (Virgilia Peterson). —*tr.v.* **mollycoddled, -dling, -dles.** To be overprotective and indulgent toward; spoil by pampering and coddling. [Obsolete British slang *molly,* "milksop," from MOLLY + CODDLE.] —**mol′ly·cod′dler** *n.*

mol·ly·grubs. Variant of **mulligrubs.**

Molly Ma·guire (mə-gwīr′). **1.** A member of a secret society in Ireland that terrorized law officers attempting to evict tenants in the 1840's. **2.** A member of a secret society of Pennsylvania miners who terrorized mine owners from about 1865 to 1877 in order to secure better working conditions and better pay.

Mol·nár (mōl′när′), **Ferenc.** 1878–1952. Hungarian playwright, novelist, short-story writer, and journalist.

Mo·loch[1] (mō′lŏk′, mŏl′ək). Also **Mo·lech** (mō′lĕk′, mŏl′ək). In the Old Testament, a god of the Ammonites and Phoenicians to whom children were sacrificed by burning. [Late Latin *Moloch,* from Greek *Molokh,* from Hebrew *Molekh.*]

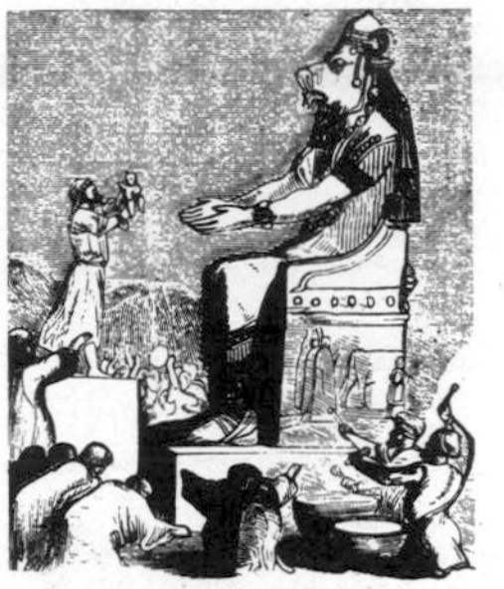

Moloch[1]
Sacrifice of a child to the idol

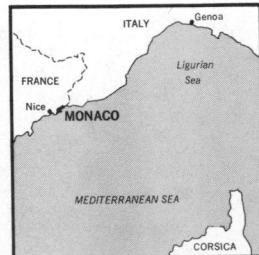

Mo·loch[2] (mō′lŏk′, mŏl′ək) *n.* Also **Mo·lech** (mō′lĕk′, mŏl′ək). Anything regarded as demanding a terrible sacrifice.

Mo·lo·kai (mō′lō-kī′, mō′lō-kī′). One of the islands of Hawaii, 259 square miles in area. Population, 5,000.

Mo·lo·po (mə-lō′pō). A South African river rising near Mafeking and flowing westward about 600 miles to the Orange River.

Mo·lo·tov. The former name for **Perm.**

Mo·lo·tov (mŏl′ə-tôf′, mō′lə-), **Vyacheslav Mikhailovich.** Original surname, Skriabin. Born 1890. Foreign minister of U.S.S.R. (1939–49, 1953–56); purged from governmental service (1961).

Molotov cocktail. A makeshift incendiary bomb made of a breakable container filled with flammable liquid and provided with a rag wick. [After V.M. MOLOTOV.]

molt (mōlt) *v.* **molted, molting, molts.** Also *chiefly British* **moult.** —*intr.* To shed part or all of a coat or outer covering, such as feathers, cuticle, or skin, which is replaced periodically by a new growth. —*tr.* To shed or cast off by the process of molting. —*n.* Also *chiefly British* **moult. 1.** The process of molting, most common among arthropods, birds, and reptiles. Compare **ecdysis, exuviae. 2.** The material cast off during molting. [Middle English *mouten,* Old English *mūtian* (unattested), from Latin *mūtāre,* to change. See **mei-**[1] in Appendix.*]

mol·ten (mōlt′n). Archaic past participle of **melt.** —*adj.* **1.** Made liquid by heat; melted. **2.** Made by melting and casting: *a molten image.* **3.** Brilliantly glowing: *"A huge red bed of coals blazed and quivered with molten fury."* (Richard Wright).

mol·to (mōl′tō) *adv. Music.* Very; much. Used with directions to the performer. [Italian, from Latin *multum,* much (adverb), from *multus,* much (adjective). See **mel-**[4] in Appendix.*]

Mo·luc·ca Islands (mə-lŭk′ə). Formerly **Spice Islands** (spīs). An island group of Indonesia, 33,315 square miles in area, lying between Sulawesi and New Guinea. Population, 600,000. Capital, Amboina. Also called "Moluccas."

mol. wt. molecular weight.

mo·ly (mō′lē) *n., pl.* **-lies. 1.** In the *Odyssey,* a magic herb with black roots and white flowers, given to Odysseus by Hermes to nullify the spells of Circe. **2.** A plant, the **lily leek** *(see).* [Latin *mōly,* from Greek *mōlu.* See **mōulo-** in Appendix.*]

Monaco

mo·lyb·de·nite (mə-lĭb′də-nīt′) *n.* A mineral form of molybdenum sulfide, MoS_2, that is the principal ore of molybdenum. [MOLYBDEN(UM) + -ITE.]

mo·lyb·de·num (mə-lĭb′də-nəm) *n. Symbol* **Mo** A hard, gray, metallic element used to toughen alloy steels and soften tungsten alloy. It is also used in fertilizers, dyes, enamels, and reagents. Atomic number 42, atomic weight 95.94, melting point 2,620°C, boiling point 4,800°C, specific gravity 10.2, valences 2, 3, 4, 5. See **element.** [New Latin, from obsolete *molybdena,* from Latin *molybdaena,* galena, from Greek *molubdaina,* a lead (of a plumb line), from *molubdos,* lead. See **plumbum** in Appendix.*]

mo·lyb·dic (mə-lĭb′dĭk) *adj.* Designating molybdenum or a compound containing molybdenum in its higher valences.

mo·lyb·dous (mə-lĭb′dəs) *adj.* Designating molybdenum or a compound containing molybdenum in its lower valences.

mom (mŏm) *n. Informal.* Mother. [Short for *momma,* from baby talk. See **mā-**[2] in Appendix.*]

Mom·ba·sa (mŏm-bä′sə). The leading seaport of Kenya, in the southeastern part of the country. Population, 178,000.

mo·ment (mō′mənt) *n.* **1.** A brief, indefinite interval of time: *He'll join you in a moment.* **2.** A specific point in time, especially the present time: *He is reading at the moment.* **3.** The appropriate or right point in time: *This is the moment to reappraise the situation.* **4.** A particular period of importance, significance, excellence, enjoyment, or the like: *"Swinburne's entry was for me a great moment."* (Max Beerbohm). **5.** Outstanding significance or value; importance: *"Thus was a voyage of great moment and adventure settled for me."* (H.M. Tomlinson). **6.** *Philosophy.* **a.** An essential or constituent element; an important factor. **b.** A phase or aspect of a thing. **7.** *Physics. Abbr.* **M a.** The product of a quantity and its perpendicular distance from a reference point. **b.** The rotation produced in a body when a force is applied; torque. **8.** *Statistics.* The expected value of a positive integral power of a random variable. The first moment is the mean of the density function. —See Synonyms at **importance.** [Middle English, from Old French, from Latin *mōmentum,* movement, MOMENTUM.]

Synonyms: *moment, minute, instant, second, trice, jiffy, flash. Moment* pertains to an indefinitely short but usually not insignificant period; the sense of importance is strengthened when the term specifies a point in time: *great moment in history. Minute,* used strictly, is specific; informally it is interchangeable with *moment.. Instant* denotes a period shorter than the foregoing; although imprecise, it implies haste and usually urgency, especially as a specific point in time: *Come this instant! Second* may be used specifically or loosely as the equivalent of *instant. Trice,* a literary term, and *jiffy* and *flash,* used informally, appear in combinations preceded by *in a* (as *in a trice*); they are imprecise but approximately equal in duration to *instant,* and imply haste but not necessarily urgency.

mo·men·tar·i·ly (mō′mən-tĕr′ə-lē) *adv.* **1.** For only an instant or moment. **2.** Very soon. **3.** *Rare.* From moment to moment.

mo·men·tar·y (mō′mən-tĕr′ē) *adj.* **1.** Lasting only a brief time. **2.** Occurring or present at every moment: *in momentary fear of being exposed.* **3.** Short-lived; ephemeral. Said of a living creature. —See Synonyms at **transient.** [Latin *mōmentārius,* from *mōmentum,* MOMENT.] —**mo′men·tar′i·ness** *n.*

mo·ment·ly (mō′mənt-lē) *adv.* **1.** Every moment; from moment to moment: *"The throng momently increased."* (Poe). **2.** At any moment. **3.** For a moment.

moment of inertia. *Physics.* **1.** A measure of a body's resistance to angular acceleration, equal to: **a.** The product of the mass of a particle and the square of its distance from a reference. **b.** The sum of the products of each mass element of a body multiplied by the square of its distance from an axis. **2.** The sum of the products of each element of an area multiplied by the square of its distance from a coplanar axis.

moment of momentum. Angular momentum *(see).*

mo·men·tous (mō-mĕn′təs) *adj.* Of utmost importance or outstanding significance; having grave implications or consequences: *"the decision to initiate thermonuclear war is . . . a momentous one"* (Herman Kahn). —**mo·men′tous·ly** *adv.* —**mo·men′tous·ness** *n.*

mo·men·tum (mō-mĕn′təm) *n., pl.* **-ta** (-tə) or **-tums. 1.** *Symbol* **p** *Physics.* The product of a body's mass and linear velocity. Also called "linear momentum." See **angular momentum. 2. a.** The force of motion, **impetus** *(see).* **b.** Impetus in human affairs: *"Even as the voyage was about to end, I sensed that its momentum might endure."* (Sterling Hayden). **3.** *Philosophy.* A constituent or essential element; moment. [Latin *mōmentum,* motion, movement, from *movimentum* (unattested), from *movēre,* to move. See **mew-** in Appendix.*]

mo·mus (mō′məs) *n., pl.* **-muses** or **-mi** (-mī′). One who finds fault; a critic of petty details. [From MOMUS.]

Mo·mus (mō′məs). *Greek Mythology.* The god of blame and ridicule.

mon (mŏn) *n. Scottish.* Man.

Mon (mōn) *n.* **1. a.** The principal native people of the Pegu region in Burma. **b.** A member of this people. **2.** The Mon-Khmer language of this people.

mon. 1. monastery. **2.** monetary.

Mon. Monday.

Mo·na (mō′nə). A feminine given name. [Irish *Muadhnait,* diminutive of *muadh,* noble, from Middle Irish *muad.* See **meu-** in Appendix.*]

mon·a·chism (mŏn′ə-kĭz′əm) *n.* Monasticism. [Middle English, from Medieval Latin *monachismus,* from Late Greek *monakhismos,* from *monakhos,* MONK.]

mon·ac·id, mon·a·cid·ic. Variants of **monoacid.**

Mon·a·co (mŏn′ə-kō′, mə-nä′kō; *French* mô-nȧ-kō′). An independent principality occupying 370 acres on the Mediterranean coast in the south of France. Population, 22,000. Largest town, Monte Carlo. Capital, Monaco-Ville. —**Mon′a·can** *adj.* & *n.*

mo·nad (mō′năd′, mŏn′ăd′) *n.* **1.** In the philosophy of Leibnitz, an indivisible and impenetrable unit of substance viewed as the basic constituent element of physical reality. **2.** *Biology.* Any single-celled microscopic organism, especially a flagellate protozoan. Also called "monas." **3.** *Chemistry.* An atom or radical with a valence of 1. [Late Latin *monas* (stem *monad-*), unit, from Greek *monas*, from *monos*, single. See **men-⁴** in Appendix.*] —**mo·nad'ic, mo·nad'i·cal** *adj.* —**mo·nad'i·cal·ly** *adv.*

mon·a·del·phous (mŏn'ə-dĕl'fəs, mō'nə-) *adj. Botany.* **a.** United by the filaments into a single tubelike group. Said of stamens. **b.** Having stamens thus united. Compare **diadelphous**. [MON(O)- + -ADELPHOUS.]

mo·nad·nock (mə-năd'nŏk') *n.* A mountain or rocky mass that has resisted erosion and stands isolated in a plain or peneplain. [After Mt. *Monadnock* in New Hampshire.]

Mon·a·ghan (mŏn'ə-gən, -ə-hăn'). **1.** A county, 498 square miles in area, in northeastern Ireland. Population, 47,000. **2.** Its county seat.

mo·nan·drous (mə-năn'drəs) *adj. Botany.* **1.** Having a single stamen. **2.** Having flowers bearing a single stamen. [MON(O)- + -ANDROUS.]

mo·nan·dry (mə-năn'drē) *n.* **1.** The custom of having one husband at a time. Compare **polyandry**. **2.** *Botany.* The condition of being monandrous. [MON(O)- + -ANDRY.]

mo·nan·thous (mə-năn'thəs) *adj. Botany.* Bearing a single flower. [MON(O)- + Greek *anthos*, flower (see **andh-** in Appendix*).]

Mo·na Passage (mō'nə). A strait about 75 miles wide joining the Atlantic Ocean and the Caribbean Sea between Puerto Rico and the Dominican Republic.

mon·arch (mŏn'ərk) *n.* **1.** A sole and absolute ruler of a state. **2.** A sovereign, such as a king or emperor. **3.** One that presides over or rules: *"Monarch is night/Of all eldest things"* (William Rose Benét). **4.** One that surpasses others in power or preeminence: *"Mont Blanc is the monarch of the mountains."* (Byron). **5.** A large orange and black butterfly, *Danaus plexippus*, having a wingspread of up to four inches. Also called "milkweed butterfly." [Late Latin *monarcha*, from Greek *monarkhēs* : *mono-*, sole + *-arkhes*, -ARCH.] —**mo·nar'chal, mon·ar'chic, mo·nar'chi·al, mon·ar'chi·cal** *adj.* —**mo·nar'chal·ly, mon·ar'chi·cal·ly** *adv.*

mo·nar·chi·an·ism (mə-när'kē-ə-nĭz'əm) *n.* A Christian heresy of the second and third centuries that denied the doctrine of the Trinity. [From Late Latin *monarchiāni*, "the monarchians," from *monarchia*, MONARCHY.] —**mo·nar'chi·an** (mə-när'kē-ən) *n. & adj.*

mon·ar·chism (mŏn'ər-kĭz'əm) *n.* **1.** The principles of monarchy. **2.** Belief in or advocacy of monarchy. —**mon'ar·chist** (-kĭst) *n. & adj.* —**mon'ar·chis'tic** *adj.*

mon·ar·chy (mŏn'ər-kē) *n., pl.* **-chies.** **1.** Government by a monarch. **2.** A state ruled by a monarch. [Middle English *monarchie*, from Old French, from Late Latin *monarchia*, from Greek *monarkhia*, from *monarkhēs*, MONARCH.]

mo·nar·da (mə-när'də) *n.* Any aromatic plant of the genus *Monarda*, such as the Oswego tea. [New Latin, after N. *Monardes*, 16th-century Spanish botanist and physician.]

mo·nas (mō'năs, mŏn'ăs) *n., pl.* **monades** (mŏn'ə-dēz'). Any single-celled organism, a **monad** *(see).* [Late Latin *monas* (stem *monad-*), MONAD.]

mon·as·ter·y (mŏn'ə-stĕr'ē) *n., pl.* **-ies.** *Abbr.* **mon. 1.** The dwelling place of a community of persons under religious vows, especially monks. **2.** The community of monks living in such a place. [Middle English *monasterie*, from Late Latin *monasterium*, from Late Greek *monastērion*, from Greek *monazein*, to live alone, from *monos*, alone. See **men-⁴** in Appendix.*] —**mon·as·te'ri·al** (-stîr'ē-əl, -stĕr'ē-əl) *adj.*

mo·nas·tic (mə-năs'tĭk) *adj.* Also **mo·nas·ti·cal** (mə-năs'tĭ-kəl). Pertaining to or characteristic of monasteries or persons living in religious or contemplative seclusion. —*n.* A monk. [Late Latin *monasticus*, from Late Greek *monastikos*, from Greek *monazein*, to live alone. See **monastery**.] —**mo·nas'ti·cal·ly** *adv.*

mo·nas·ti·cism (mə-năs'tə-sĭz'əm) *n.* The monastic life or system, especially as practiced in a monastery.

mon·a·tom·ic (mŏn'ə-tŏm'ĭk) *adj.* **1.** Occurring as single atoms, as, for example, helium. **2.** Having one replaceable atom or radical. **3.** Univalent. [MON(O)- + ATOMIC.]

mon·au·ral (mŏn-ôr'əl, mō-nôr'əl) *adj.* **1.** Designating sound reception by one ear. **2.** Relating to a system of transmitting, recording, or reproducing sound whereby one or more sources are channeled into a single carrier. [MON(O)- + AURAL.]

mon·ax·i·al (mŏn-ăk'sē-əl, mō-năk'-) *adj.* **Uniaxial** *(see).*

mon·a·zite (mŏn'ə-zīt') *n.* A reddish-brown mineral phosphate of rare-earth metals, chiefly cerium and lanthanum, usually together with thorium. [German *Monazit*, from Greek *monazein*, to live alone (because it is rare). See **monastery**.]

Mön·chen Glad·bach (mœn'кнən glät'bäкн'). A city and textile center of West Germany, about 20 miles east of the southern border of the Netherlands. Population, 154,000.

Monck, George. See **Monk.**

Mon·day (mŭn'dē, -dā') *n. Abbr.* **Mon., M.** The second day of the week, occurring after Sunday and before Tuesday. [Middle English *monday*, Old English *mōnan dæg*, moon's day (translation of Late Latin *lūnae diēs*) : *mona*, MOON + *dæg*, DAY.]

Mon·di·no de'Luz·zi (mōn-dē'nō dā lōot'tsē). 1275?–1326. Italian anatomist; wrote the first textbook on anatomy.

Mon·dri·an (môn'drē-än'), **Piet.** 1872–1944. Dutch painter.

mo·ne·cious. Variant of **monoecious.**

Mo·né·gasque (mô-nā-gàsk') *n.* A citizen of Monaco; Monacan. [French, from Provençal *Mounegasc*, from *Mounegue*, MONACO.] —**Mo·né·gasque'** *adj.*

mo·nel metal (mō-nĕl') *n.* A corrosion-resistant alloy of nickel, copper, iron, and manganese. [After Ambrose *Monel*, president of International Nickel Co. (1873–1921).]

Mo·net (mō nā'), **Claude.** 1840–1926. French painter; a founder of and one of the great masters of impressionism.

mon·e·tar·y (mŏn'ə-tĕr'ē, mŭn'-) *adj. Abbr.* **mon. 1.** Of or pertaining to money. **2.** Of or pertaining to a nation's currency or coinage. —See Synonyms at **financial.** [Late Latin *monētārius*, from Latin *monēta*, MONEY.] —**mon'e·tar'i·ly** *adv.*

mon·e·tize (mŏn'ə-tīz', mŭn'-) *tr.v.* **-tized, -tizing, -tizes. 1.** To establish as legal tender. **2.** To make into money; to coin. [From Latin *monēta*, MONEY.] —**mon'e·ti·za'tion** *n.*

mon·ey (mŭn'ē) *n., pl.* **-eys** or **-ies. 1.** A commodity such as gold or silver that is legally established as an exchangeable equivalent of all other commodities and is used as a measure of their comparative values on the market. **2.** The official currency, coins and negotiable paper notes, issued by a government. **3.** Assets and property that may be converted into actual currency. **4.** Pecuniary profit or loss: *He made money on the sale.* **5.** Any unspecified amount of currency: *money for groceries.* —**in the money.** *Slang.* Having plenty of money. —**put money on.** To place a bet on. [Middle English *moneye*, from Old French *moneie*, from Latin *monēta*, money, mint, from *Monēta*, epithet of Juno, whose temple in Rome housed the mint. See **monēta** in Appendix.*]

Usage: Moneys (rather than *monies*) is the preferred plural form. It is used in referring to the mediums of exchange of two or more countries or, within one country, in designating particular forms of money or specific sums.

mon·ey·bag (mŭn'ē-băg') *n.* **1.** A bag for holding money. **2.** *Plural.* Wealth. Used with a singular or plural verb. **3.** *Plural.* A rich and greedy person. Used with a singular verb.

mon·ey·chang·er (mŭn'ē-chān'jər) *n.* **1.** A person who exchanges money, as from one currency to another. **2.** A machine that holds and dispenses coins.

money cowry, money cowrie. A small shell used as money by certain primitive people. See **cowry.**

mon·ey·ed (mŭn'ēd) *adj.* Also **mon·ied. 1.** Having a great deal of money: *"Christian symbols, having been taken over by the moneyed classes, are now agents of corruption."* (Carolyn See). **2.** Representing or arising from the possession of money: *the triumph of moneyed interests over landed interests.*

mon·ey·er (mŭn'ē-ər) *n.* **1.** A person authorized to coin or mint money. **2.** *Obsolete.* A banker or broker. [Middle English *monyer*, from Old French *monier*, from Late Latin *monētārius*, minter, from *monēta*, MONEY.]

mon·ey·lend·er (mŭn'ē-lĕn'dər) *n.* One whose business is lending money at an interest rate.

mon·ey·mak·ing (mŭn'ē-mā'kĭng) *n.* The acquisition of money or other wealth. —*adj.* **1.** Engaged in acquiring wealth. **2.** Actually or potentially profitable. —**mon'ey·mak'er** *n.*

money of account. Any of the various monetary units in which accounts are kept, which may or may not correspond to actual current denominations.

money order. *Abbr.* **m.o., M.O.** An order for the payment of a specified amount of money, usually issued and payable at a bank or post office.

mon·ey·wort (mŭn'ē-wûrt', -wôrt) *n.* A creeping plant, *Lysimachia nummularia*, of Europe and eastern North America, having rounded, opposite leaves and yellow flowers. Also called "creeping Charlie," "creeping Jennie." [So named from its round, coinlike leaves.]

mon·ger (mŭng'gər, mŏng'-) *n.* **1.** A dealer in a specific commodity. Usually used in combination: *ironmonger.* **2.** A person promoting something undesirable. Usually used in combination: *scandalmonger, warmonger.* —*tr.v.* **mongered, -gering, -gers.** To peddle. [Middle English *mongere*, Old English *mangere*, from *mangian*, to traffic, from Common Germanic *mangojan* (unattested), from Latin *mangō*, (fraudulent) dealer. See **meng-** in Appendix.*]

Mon·gol (mŏng'gəl, -gōl') *n.* **1.** A member of one of the nomadic tribes of Mongolia. **2.** A native of Mongolia. **3.** Any of the languages of Mongolia. **4.** A member of the Mongoloid ethnic group. [Mongol *Mongol*.] —**Mon'gol** *adj.*

Mon·go·li·a (mŏng-gō'lē-ə, -gōl'yə, mŏn-). A region of east-central Asia, some 1,000,000 square miles in area, now consisting of the Mongolian People's Republic (Outer Mongolia), the Inner Mongolian Autonomous Region of China (Inner Mongolia), and the Buryat A.S.S.R.

mon·go·li·an (mŏng-gō'lē-ən, -gōl'yən, mŏn-) *adj.* Of, pertaining to, or exhibiting mongolism.

Mon·go·li·an (mŏng-gō'lē-ən, -gōl'yən, mŏn-) *n.* **1.** A native or inhabitant of Mongolia. **2.** A member of the Mongoloid race. **3. a.** The Mongolic subfamily of the Altaic languages. **b.** Any of the Mongolic languages of Mongolia. —**Mon·go'li·an** *adj.*

Mongolian People's Republic. A nation of 600,000 square miles, between the Soviet Union and China. Population, 1,050,000. Capital, Ulan Bator. Also called "Outer Mongolia."

Mon·go·lic (mŏng-gŏl'ĭk, mŏn-) *n.* The Altaic subfamily that includes the various languages of Mongolia. —*adj.* Of or pertaining to the Mongoloid ethnic division or to the subfamily of Altaic languages spoken in Mongolia.

mon·gol·ism (mŏng'gə-lĭz'əm, mŏn'-) *n.* Also **Mon·gol·ism.** A congenital idiocy in which a child is born with a skull, flattened skull, slanting eyes, and other anomalies. [From a supposed resemblance to the features of ethnic Mongoloids.]

mon·gol·oid (mŏng'gə-loid', mŏn'-) *adj.* Characterized by or relating to mongolism.

Mon·gol·oid (mŏng'gə-loid', mŏn'-) *adj. Anthropology.* **1.** Of, pertaining to, or designating a major ethnic division of the human species whose members are characterized by yellowish-brown to white pigmentation, coarse straight black hair, dark eyes with pronounced epicanthic folds, and prominent cheek-

monarch
Butterflies on milkweed pods

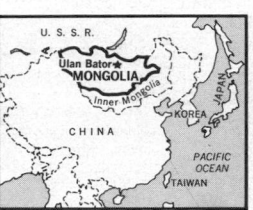

Mongolian People's Republic

Mondrian
The artist in 1944, seated before his painting "Trafalgar Square"

ă pat/ā pay/â care/ä father/b bib/ch church/d deed/ĕ pet/ē be/f fife/g gag/h hat/hw which/ĭ pit/ī pie/î pier/j judge/k kick/l lid/m mum/n no, sudden/ng thing/ŏ pot/ō toe/ô paw, for/oi noise/ou out/oo took/oo boot/p pop/r roar/s sauce/sh ship, dish/

t tight/th thin, path/*th* this, bathe/ŭ cut/û urge/v valve/w with/y yes/z zebra, size/zh vision/ə about, item, edible, gallop, circus/
à *Fr.* ami/œ *Fr.* feu, *Ger.* schön/ü *Fr.* tu, *Ger.* über/кн *Ger.* ich, *Scot.* loch/N *Fr.* bon. *Follows main vocabulary. †Of obscure origin.

mongoose
Dologale dybowskii

monkey puzzle

tree

tip of a branch

monkey wrench

bones. This division is considered to include the Chinese, Japanese, Malayans, Mongolians, Siberians, Eskimos, and American Indians. **2.** Characteristic of or like a Mongol. —*n.* A member of the Mongoloid ethnic division of the human species.

mon·goose (mŏng′gōōs′, mŏn′-) *n., pl.* **-gooses.** Any of various ferretlike, carnivorous Old World mammals having slender bodies, long tails, and brown or black coats. Mongooses are noted for their ability to kill venomous snakes. See **ichneumon.** [Marathi *mangūs,* from Dravidian, akin to Telugu *mangisu.*]

mon·grel (mŭng′grəl, mŏng′-) *n.* **1.** An animal or plant, especially a dog, resulting from various interbreedings. **2.** A person of mixed racial stock. Usually used disparagingly or facetiously: *"Europe is a continent of energetic mongrels."* (H.A.L. Fisher). **3.** A cross between one thing and another: *"Some cart, or dilapidated mongrel between cart and basket"* (Carlyle). —*adj.* Of mixed origin or character. Chiefly used disparagingly. [Probably diminutive of Middle English *mong,* Old English *gemang,* mixture. See **mag-** in Appendix.*]

mon·grel·ize (mŭng′grə-līz′, mŏng′-) *tr.v.* **-ized, -izing, -izes.** To make mongrel in race, nature, or character. Usually disparaging when applied to human beings.

Mon·i·ca (mŏn′ĭ-kə). A feminine given name. [Late Latin, possibly of African origin.]

mon·ied. Variant of **moneyed.**

mon·i·ker, mon·ick·er (mŏn′ĭ-kər) *n. Slang.* A personal name or nickname: *"No one but Pinky and Sister Heavenly knew his straight monicker."* (Chester Himes). See Synonyms at **name.** [Origin unknown.]

mo·nil·i·form (mō-nĭl′ə-fôrm′) *adj. Biology.* Resembling a string of beads, as various plant roots, the antennae of certain insects, and the nuclei of some members of the Ciliata. [Latin *monīle,* necklace (see **mon-** in Appendix*) + -FORM.]

mon·ish (mŏn′ĭsh) *tr.v.* **-ished, -ishing, -ishes.** *Archaic.* To admonish. [Middle English *monisshen,* variant of *monesten,* from Old French *monester,* from Vulgar Latin *monestāre* (unattested), extension of Latin *monēre,* to warn. See **men-**[1] in Appendix.*]

mo·nism (mō′nĭz′əm, mŏn′ĭz′əm) *n. Philosophy.* A metaphysical system in which reality is conceived as a unified whole. Compare **dualism, pluralism.** [German *Monismus* : MON(O)- + -ISM.] —**mo′nist** *n.* & *adj.* —**mo·nis′tic** (mō-nĭs′tĭk, mŏ-) *adj.* —**mo·nis′ti·cal·ly** *adv.*

mo·ni·tion (mō-nĭsh′ən, mə-) *n.* **1.** A warning or intimation of some impending danger. **2. a.** An admonition. **b.** A piece of advice; an admonitory counsel: *"I should feel that this was rather a tantalizing monition"* (Henry James). **3.** A formal order from a bishop or ecclesiastical court to refrain from some specified offense. **4.** *Law.* A summons directing the recipient to appear and answer. [Middle English *monicioun,* from Old French *monition,* from Latin *monitiō,* from *monēre,* to warn. See **men-**[1] in Appendix.*]

mon·i·tor (mŏn′ə-tər) *n.* **1.** One that admonishes, cautions, or reminds. **2.** A pupil who assists a teacher in routine duties. **3.** Any device used to record or control a process. **4.** An articulated device holding a rotating nozzle, used in mining and fire-fighting. **5.** A heavily ironclad warship of the 19th century with a low, flat deck and one or more gun turrets; specifically, the first such ship, the Union vessel *Monitor,* which fought the Confederate ironclad *Merrimack* on March 9, 1862. **6.** Any tropical carnivorous lizard of the genus *Varanus,* ranging in length from several inches to ten feet. See **Komodo dragon.** —*v.* **monitored, -toring, -tors.** —*tr.* **1.** To check (the transmission quality of a signal) by means of a receiver. **2.** To test (a surface) for radiation intensity. **3.** To keep track of by means of an electronic device. **4.** To check by means of a receiver for significant content: *"In modern war, message-sending must be monitored."* (Dan McLachlan, Jr.). **5.** To scrutinize or check systematically with a view to collecting certain specified categories of data. **6.** To keep watch over; supervise: *monitor an examination.* **7.** To direct as a monitor: *"white Chastity shall . . . monitor me nightly to lone slumber"* (Keats). —*intr.* To act as a monitor. [Latin, one who warns, from *monēre,* to warn. See **men-**[1] in Appendix.*]

mon·i·to·ri·al (mŏn′ə-tôr′ē-əl, -tōr′ē-əl) *adj.* Of, pertaining to, or performed by monitors. —**mon′i·to′ri·al·ly** *adv.*

mon·i·to·ry (mŏn′ə-tôr′ē, -tōr′ē) *adj.* Conveying an admonition or warning: *a monitory glance.* —*n., pl.* **monitories.** A letter of admonition. [Latin *monitōrius,* from *monitor,* MONITOR.]

Mo·niz (mōō-nēsh′), **Antonio Caetano de Abreu Freire Egas.** 1874–1955. Portuguese neurologist; worked on the development of prefrontal lobotomy.

monk (mŭngk) *n.* A member of a religious brotherhood living in a monastery and devoted to a discipline prescribed by his order. [Middle English *munk,* Old English *munuc,* from Late Latin *monachus,* from Late Greek *monakhos,* solitary, monk, from Greek *monos,* alone. See **men-**[4] in Appendix.*]

Monk (mŭngk), **George.** Also **Monck.** First Duke of Albemarle. 1608–1670. English general; instrumental in restoration of Charles II; supervised London during the Plague (1665).

Monk (mŭngk), **Thelonius (Sphere).** Born 1918? American jazz pianist and composer.

monk·er·y (mŭng′kər-ē) *n., pl.* **-ies. 1.** Monastic life or practices. **2.** Monks collectively. **3.** A monastery.

mon·key (mŭng′kē) *n., pl.* **-keys. 1.** Any member of the order Primates except man; specifically, most long-tailed primates, including the Old and New World monkeys and the marmosets, and usually excluding the anthropoid apes and the lemurs, lorises, tree shrews, and tarsiers. **2.** A mischievous, playful child or young person. Used familiarly. **3.** The iron block of a pile driver. **4.** A narrow passageway or opening in a coal mine. **5.** *Slang.* A person who is mocked, duped, or made to appear a fool. **6.** *Slang.* Drug addiction, regarded as a burdensome affliction: *have a monkey on one's back.* —*v.* **monkeyed, -keying, -keys.** —*intr. Informal.* To play or fiddle with something idly. Usually used with *around* or *with* or *around with.* —*tr.* To imitate or mimic; ape. [Possibly from Middle Low German *Moneke,* the name of the ape's son in *Reynard the Fox.*]

monkey bread. The fruit of the **baobab** *(see).*

monkey business. *Slang.* Silly, mischievous, or deceitful acts.

mon·key-flow·er (mŭng′kē-flou′ər) *n.* Any of various plants of the genus *Mimulus,* having variously colored, two-lipped flowers. [From the resemblance of the flower to a simian face.]

monkey jacket. 1. A short, tight-fitting jacket, formerly worn by sailors. **2.** A **mess jacket** *(see).* [From its similarity to the jackets worn by performing monkeys.]

monkey pot. 1. The large, urn-shaped lidded pod of tropical trees of the genus *Lecythis.* **2.** Any tree bearing this type of pod. **3.** A cylindrical or barrel-shaped melting pot used in making flint glass. [Reason for the name uncertain.]

monkey puzzle. An evergreen tree, *Araucaria araucana,* native to Chile, having intricately ramifying branches covered with stiff, prickle-tipped leaves. [Because its branches make it difficult for a monkey to climb.]

mon·key·shine (mŭng′kē-shīn′) *n. Usually plural. Slang.* A playful, mischievous trick. [MONKEY + SHINE (prank).]

monkey suit. *Slang.* **1.** A man's suit for formal wear; dress suit. **2.** A full-dress military uniform. **3.** Any uniform. [Probably extended from **monkey jacket.**]

monkey wrench. 1. A hand tool with adjustable jaws for turning nuts of varying sizes. **2.** *Informal.* Something that disrupts: *He threw a monkey wrench into the plans.* [Origin obscure.]

monk·fish (mŭngk′fĭsh′) *n., pl.* **-fish** or **-fishes.** The **goosefish** *(see).* [From the cowled appearance of the head.]

Mon-Khmer (mōn′kmĕr′) *n.* A subfamily of the Austro-Asiatic languages, spoken primarily in Indochina.

monk·hood (mŭngk′hŏŏd′) *n.* **1.** The state or profession of a monk; monasticism. **2.** Monks collectively.

monk·ish (mŭng′kĭsh) *adj.* Of, relating to, or characteristic of monks or monasticism.

monk's cloth. A heavy cotton cloth in a coarse basket weave. [Originally used for the habits of monks.]

monk seal. A seal of the nearly extinct genus *Monachus,* formerly much hunted in Mediterranean and Caribbean waters for its fur, which may be gray or yellow with black spots or uniformly brown. [From the cowled appearance of its head.]

monks·hood (mŭngks′hŏŏd′) *n.* Any of various plants of the genus *Aconitum,* having hooded flowers of various colors. Most species are poisonous. Also called "aconite," "wolfsbane."

Mon·mouth (mŏn′məth; *also* mŭn′məth *for sense 2*). **1.** A county in New Jersey, scene of the Battle of Monmouth Court House (June 28, 1778). **2. Monmouthshire** *(see).*

Mon·mouth (mŏn′məth, mŭn′-), **Duke of.** Title of James Scott. 1649–1685. English pretender to the throne; reputed illegitimate son of Charles II; beheaded by James II.

Mon·mouth·shire (mŏn′məth-shîr′, -shər, mŭn′-). Also **Monmouth.** A county in southeastern Wales, 546 square miles in area. Population, 445,000. County seat, Newport.

Mon·net (mō-nā′; *French* mô-nĕ′), **Jean.** Born 1888. French economist and political figure; principal founder of the European Common Market.

mono–, mon–. Indicates: **1.** One; single; alone; for example, **monophonic. 2.** The presence of a single atom, radical, or group in a compound; for example, **monohydric.** [Middle English, from Old French, from Latin, from Greek, from *monos,* single, sole, alone. See **men-**[4] in Appendix.*]

mon·o·ac·id (mŏn′ō-ăs′ĭd) *adj.* Also **mon·o·a·cid·ic** (mŏn′ō-ə-sĭd′ĭk), **mon·ac·id** (mŏn-ăs′ĭd), **mon·a·cid·ic** (mŏn′ə-sĭd′ĭk). *Chemistry.* Having only one hydroxyl group to react with acids.

mon·o·ba·sic (mŏn′ə-bā′sĭk) *adj. Chemistry.* **1. Monoprotic** *(see).* **2.** Having only one metal ion or positive radical.

mon·o·carp (mŏn′ə-kärp′) *n. Botany.* A monocarpic plant. [MONO- + -CARP.]

mon·o·car·pel·lar·y (mŏn′ə-kär′pə-lĕr′ē) *adj. Botany.* Consisting of only one carpel.

mon·o·car·pic (mŏn′ə-kär′pĭk) *adj.* Also **mon·o·car·pous** (mŏn′ə-kär′pəs). *Botany.* Flowering and bearing fruit only once. Annuals and biennials are monocarpic. [MONO- + -CARPIC.]

Mo·noc·er·os (mə-nŏs′ər-əs) *n.* **1.** A constellation near Canis Major and Canis Minor. Also called "Unicorn." **2.** *Small* **m.** *Obsolete.* **a.** A one-horned fish, such as the swordfish. **b.** A unicorn. [Middle English, from Old French, from Latin, from Greek *monokeros,* "one-horned" : MONO- + *keras,* horn (see **ker-**[1] in Appendix*).]

mon·o·cha·si·um (mŏn′ə-kā′zē-əm, -zhē-əm) *n., pl.* **-sia** (-zē-ə, -zhē-ə). *Botany.* A **cyme** *(see)* having a single main stem. —**mon′o·cha′si·al** *adj.* [MONO- + (DI)CHASIUM.]

mon·o·chord (mŏn′ə-kôrd′) *n. Music.* An acoustical instrument consisting of a sounding box with one string and a movable bridge, used to study musical tones. [Middle English *monocorde,* from Old French, from Medieval Latin *monochordum,* from Greek *monokhordon* : MONO- + *khordē,* CHORD.]

mon·o·chro·mat·ic (mŏn′ə-krō-măt′ĭk) *adj.* Also **mon·o·chro·ic** (-krō′ĭk). **1.** Having only one color. **2.** Having or producing light of only one wavelength. [From Greek *monokhrōmatos* : MONO- + *khrōma,* -CHROME.] —**mon′o·chro·mat′i·cal·ly** *adv.*

mon·o·chrome (mŏn′ə-krōm′) *n.* **1.** A painting done in different shades of one color. **2.** The technique of executing such paintings. [Medieval Latin *monochrōma,* from Greek *monokhrōmos,* of one color : MONO- + *khrōma,* -CHROME.] —**mon′o·chro′mic** (-krō′mĭk) *adj.*

mon·o·cle (mŏn′ə-kəl) *n.* An eyeglass for one eye. [French, from Late Latin *monoculus,* one-eyed : MONO- + *oculus,* eye (see **okw-** in Appendix*).] —**mon′o·cled** (-kəld) *adj.*

mon·o·cline (mŏn′ə-klīn′) *n.* A geologic formation in which all strata are inclined in the same direction. Compare **isocline.** [MONO- + CLINE.] —**mon′o·cli′nal** *adj.*

mon·o·clin·ic (mŏn′ə-klĭn′ĭk) *adj. Crystallography.* Of or pertaining to three unequal crystal axes, two of which intersect obliquely and are perpendicular to the third. [MONO- + Greek *-klinēs,* leaning, from *klinein,* to lean (see **klei-** in Appendix*).]

mon·o·cli·nous (mŏn′ə-klī′nəs) *adj. Botany.* Having pistils and stamens in the same flower. [New Latin *monoclinus,* monoclinous, "hermaphroditic" : MONO- + Greek *klinē,* couch (see **klei-** in Appendix*).]

mon·o·coque (mŏn′ə-kōk′, -kŏk′) *n.* A metal structure, as of an aircraft or automobile, in which the covering absorbs a large part of the stresses to which the body is subjected. [French : MONO- + *coque,* shell, from Latin *coccum,* berry, from Greek *kokkos* (see **kokkos** in Appendix*).]

mon·o·cot·y·le·don (mŏn′ə-kŏt′l-ēd′n) *n.* Also **mon·o·cot** (mŏn′ə-kŏt′). *Botany.* Any plant of the Monocotyledonae, one of the two major divisions of angiosperms, characterized by a single embryonic seed leaf that appears at germination. Included among the monocotyledons are such plants as grasses, orchids, and lilies. Compare **dicotyledon.** [New Latin : MONO- + COTYLEDON.] —**mon′o·cot′y·le′don·ous** *adj.*

mo·noc·ra·cy (mō-nŏk′rə-sē, mō-, mə-) *n.* Government or rule by a single person; autocracy. [MONO- + -CRACY.]

mon·o·crat (mŏn′ə-krăt′) *n.* One who favors autocracy: *"The war between France and England has brought forward the Republicans and Monocrats in every State."* (Jefferson). —**mon′o·crat′ic** *adj.*

mo·noc·u·lar (mŏ-nŏk′yə-lər, mə-) *adj.* **1.** Having or pertaining to one eye. **2.** Adapted for the use of only one eye. [From Late Latin *monoculus,* one-eyed. See **monocle.**]

mon·o·cy·cle (mŏn′ə-sī′kəl) *n.* A vehicle having a single wheel, a **unicycle** *(see).*

mon·o·cyte (mŏn′ə-sīt′) *n.* A large white blood corpuscle, having a pale, oval nucleus and more protoplasm than a lymphocyte. [MONO- + -CYTE.] —**mon′o·cyt′ic** (mŏn′ə-sĭt′ĭk), **mon′o·cy′toid′** (mŏn′ə-sī′toid′) *adj.*

mon·o·dac·tyl (mŏn′ə-dăkt′l) *n.* An animal having only one claw on each extremity. [French *mondactyle,* from Greek *monodaktulos,* one-toed, one-fingered : MONO- + *daktulos,* DACTYL.] —**mon′o·dac′ty·lous** *adj.*

mon·o·dra·ma (mŏn′ə-drä′mə, -drăm′ə) *n.* A dramatic composition written for one performer. —**mon′o·dra·mat′ic** (-drə-măt′ĭk) *adj.*

mon·o·dy (mŏn′ə-dē) *n., pl.* **-dies. 1.** *Greek prosody.* An ode for one voice or actor. **2.** An elegiac verse expressing personal lament. **3.** *Music.* **a.** A style of composition in which one vocal part or melodic line predominates. **b.** A composition in this style. [Late Latin *monōdia,* from Greek *monōidia* : MONO- + *ōidē,* song (see **wed-²** in Appendix*).] —**mo·nod′ic** (mə-nŏd′ĭk), **mo·nod′i·cal** *adj.* —**mo·nod′i·cal·ly** *adv.* —**mon′o·dist** (mŏn′ə-dĭst) *n.*

mo·noe·cious (mə-nē′shəs) *adj.* Also **mo·ne·cious. 1.** *Botany.* Having male and female reproductive organs in separate flowers on a single plant. Compare **dioecious. 2.** *Zoology.* Hermaphroditic. [From New Latin *Monoecia* : MON(O) + Greek *oikia,* dwelling, from *oikos,* house (see **weik-¹** in Appendix*).] —**mo·noe′cious·ly** *adv.*

mon·o·fu·el (mŏn′ō-fyōō′əl) *n.* A **monopropellant** *(see).*

mo·nog·a·my (mə-nŏg′ə-mē) *n.* **1.** The custom or condition of being married to only one person at a time. **2.** The state of having one mate for life. [French *monogamie,* from Late Latin *monogamia,* from Greek : MONO- + -GAMY.] —**mo·nog′a·mous** *adj.* —**mo·nog′a·mous·ly** *adv.* —**mo·nog′a·mist** *n.*

mon·o·gen·e·sis (mŏn′ə-jĕn′ə-sĭs) *n.* **1.** The theory that all living organisms are descended from a single cell. Compare **polygenesis. 2.** Asexual reproduction, as by sporulation. **3.** The development of an ovum into an organism resembling the parent, without metamorphosis. [New Latin : MONO- + -GENESIS.] —**mo·nog′e·nous** (mə-nŏj′ə-nəs) *adj.*

mon·o·ge·net·ic (mŏn′ō-jə-nĕt′ĭk) *adj.* **1.** Pertaining to or showing monogenesis. **2.** Asexual. **3.** Arising from a single formation process, as a mountain range.

mon·o·gen·ic (mŏn′ə-jĕn′ĭk) *adj.* **1.** Having a common or single origin, as igneous rocks composed of a single mineral. **2. a.** Of or pertaining to monogenesis; monogenetic. **b.** Relating to monogenism. **3.** Of or regulated by one gene or one of a pair of allelic genes. **4.** Producing offspring mostly of one sex. [MONO- + -GENIC.] —**mon′o·gen′i·cal·ly** *adv.*

mo·nog·e·nism (mə-nŏj′ə-nĭz′əm) *n.* The theory that mankind has descended from a single pair of ancestors. Compare **polygenism.** [MONO- + -GEN + -ISM.] —**mo·nog′e·nist** *n.* —**mo·nog′e·nis′tic** *adj.*

mon·o·gram (mŏn′ə-grăm′) *n.* A design composed of one or more letters, usually the initials of a name. —*tr.v.* **monogrammed** or **-gramed, -gramming** or **-graming, -grams.** To mark with a monogram. [Late Latin *monogramma* : MONO- + -GRAM.] —**mon′o·gram·mat′ic** (mŏn′ə-grə-măt′ĭk) *adj.*

mon·o·graph (mŏn′ə-grăf′, -gräf′) *n.* A scholarly book, article, or pamphlet on a specific and usually limited subject. [MONO- + -GRAPH.] —**mo·nog′ra·pher** (mə-nŏg′rə-fər) *n.* —**mon′o·graph′ic** *adj.* —**mon′o·graph′i·cal·ly** *adv.*

mo·nog·y·ny (mə-nŏj′ə-nē) *n.* The practice or condition of having only one wife at a time. [MONO- + -GYNY.] —**mo·nog′y·nist** *n.* —**mo·nog′y·nous** *adj.*

mon·o·hy·brid (mŏn′ə-hī′brĭd) *n.* Hybrid offspring of parents differing in a single characteristic or genetic factor.

mon·o·hy·drate (mŏn′ə-hī′drāt′) *n. Chemistry.* A compound of singly hydrated molecules. —**mon′o·hy′drat′ed** *adj.*

mon·o·hy·dric (mŏn′ə-hī′drĭk) *adj. Chemistry.* Containing one replaceable hydroxyl radical.

mo·noi·cous (mə-noi′kəs) *adj. Botany.* Having archegonia and antheridia on the same plant; bisexual. [Variant of MONOECIOUS.]

mo·nol·a·try (mə-nô′lə-trē) *n.* The worship of one god without denying the existence of others. Compare **henotheism.**

mon·o·lay·er (mŏn′ə-lā′ər) *n.* **1.** A film or stratum of a compound one molecule thick; monomolecular layer. **2.** A layer one atom thick; monatomic layer.

mon·o·lith (mŏn′ə-lĭth′) *n.* A large block of stone used in architecture or sculpture. [French *monolithe,* from Greek *monolithos,* "consisting of a single stone" : MONO- + -LITH.]

mon·o·lith·ic (mŏn′ə-lĭth′ĭk) *adj.* **1.** Consisting of a monolith. **2.** Like a monolith; massive, solid, and uniform: *"Pétain's prestige grew to monolithic proportions"* (New York Times).

mon·o·logue (mŏn′ə-lôg′, -lŏg′) *n.* Also **mon·o·log. 1.** A long speech or talk made by one person, often monopolizing conversation. **2. a.** A soliloquy or any literary composition in the form of a soliloquy. **b.** A continuous series of jokes or comic stories delivered by a single comedian. [French : MONO- + (DIA)LOGUE.] —**mon′o·log′ic** (mŏn′ə-lŏj′ĭk), **mon′o·log′i·cal** *adj.* —**mo·nol′o·gist** (mə-nŏl′ə-jĭst, mŏn′ə-lôg′ĭst, -lŏg′ĭst) *n.*

mon·o·ma·ni·a (mŏn′ō-mā′nē-ə, -mān′yə) *n.* **1.** Pathological obsession with one idea. Not in technical use. See **paranoia. 2.** Intent concentration on, or exaggerated enthusiasm for, a subject or an idea. [New Latin : MONO- + -MANIA.] —**mon′o·ma′ni·ac′** (-ăk′) *n.* —**mon′o·ma·ni′a·cal** (-mə-nī′ə-kəl) *adj.*

mon·o·mer (mŏn′ə-mər) *n.* Any molecule that can be chemically bound as a unit of a **polymer** *(see): Ethylene is a monomer of polyethylene.* [MONO- + Greek *meros,* part (see **smer-²** in Appendix*).] —**mon′o·mer′ic** (mŏn′ə-mĕr′ĭk) *adj.*

mon·o·me·tal·lic (mŏn′ō-mə-tăl′ĭk) *adj.* **1.** Consisting of or containing one metal. **2.** Pertaining to monometallism.

mon·o·met·al·lism (mŏn′ō-mĕt′l-ĭz′əm) *n.* Also **mon·o·met·al·ism. 1.** The use of only one metal, usually gold or silver, as a standard of money. **2.** The economic theory supporting the use of one metallic monetary standard. —**mon′o·met′al·list** *n.*

mo·no·mi·al (mō-nō′mē-əl, mō-, mə-) *n.* **1.** *Algebra.* An expression consisting of only one term. **2.** *Biology.* A taxonomic name consisting of a single word. [MON(O)- + (BIN)OMIAL.] —**mo·no′mi·al** *adj.*

mon·o·mo·lec·u·lar (mŏn′ō-mə-lĕk′yə-lər) *adj.* **1.** Of or pertaining to a single molecule. **2.** Of or consisting of a layer one molecule thick.

mon·o·mor·phic (mŏn′ə-môr′fĭk) *adj.* Also **mon·o·mor·phous** (-fəs). **1.** *Chemistry.* Having but one form, as one crystal form. **2.** *Zoology.* Having a basic structure remaining unchanged through a series of developmental changes. [MONO- + -MORPHIC.] —**mon′o·mor′phism** *n.*

Mo·non·ga·he·la (mə-nŏng′gə-hē′lə). A river rising in West Virginia and flowing 128 miles northward to Pittsburgh, Pennsylvania, where it joins the Allegheny to form the Ohio.

mon·o·nu·cle·o·sis (mŏn′ō-nōō′klē-ō′sĭs, -nyōō′klē-ō′sĭs) *n.* **1.** The presence of an abnormally large number of leucocytes with single nuclei in the bloodstream. **2.** A disease producing this condition. In this sense, also called "infectious mononucleosis." [New Latin : MONO- + NUCLE(US) + -OSIS.]

mon·o·pet·al·ous (mŏn′ə-pĕt′l-əs) *adj.* Having petals united to form one corolla; gamopetalous. [MONO- + PETALOUS.]

mo·noph·a·gous (mə-nŏf′ə-gəs) *adj.* Eating only one kind of food. Said especially of insects. [MONO- + -PHAGOUS.]

mon·o·pho·bi·a (mŏn′ō-fō′bē-ə) *n.* Excessive fear of solitude. [New Latin : MONO- + -PHOBIA.] —**mon′o·pho′bic** (-fō′bĭk) *adj.*

mon·o·phon·ic (mŏn′ə-fŏn′ĭk) *adj.* **1.** *Music.* Of the nature of monophony; having a single melodic line; monodic. **2.** *Electronics.* Using one channel to carry or reproduce sounds through audio devices; monaural. [MONO- + PHONIC.]

mo·noph·o·ny (mə-nŏf′ə-nē) *n.* Music consisting of a single melodic line. Compare **polyphony, homophony.**

mon·oph·thong (mŏn′əf-thông′, -thŏng′) *n.* **1.** A single vowel sound made while the supraglottal speech organs are in a fixed position. **2.** Two written vowels representing a single sound; for example, *oa* in *boat* is a monophthong. [Late Greek *monophthongos* : MONO- + *phthongos*†, vowel. See **diphthong.**] —**mon′oph·thon′gal** (-thông′gəl, -thŏng′gəl) *adj.*

mon·o·phy·let·ic (mŏn′ō-fī-lĕt′ĭk) *adj.* **1.** Of or concerning a single phylum of plants or animals. **2.** Descended or derived from one stock or source. [MONO- + PHYLETIC.]

Mo·noph·y·site (mə-nŏf′ə-sīt′) *n. Theology.* An adherent of the doctrine that in the person of Christ there was but a single, divine nature. Coptic and Syrian Christians profess this doctrine. [Medieval Latin *monophysīta,* from Medieval Greek *monophusitēs* : MONO- + *phusis,* nature (see **bheu-** in Appendix*).] —**Mo·noph′y·sit′ic** (mə-nŏf′ə-sĭt′ĭk) *adj.* —**Mo·noph′y·sit·ism′** *n.*

mon·o·plane (mŏn′ə-plān′) *n.* An airplane with only one pair of wings. Compare **biplane.**

mon·o·ple·gi·a (mŏn′ə-plē′jē-ə, -plē′jə) *n.* Paralysis of a single limb or part of the body, such as one side of the face. [MONO- + -PLEGIA.] —**mon′o·ple′gic** (-plē′jĭk, -plĕj′ĭk) *adj.*

mon·o·pode (mŏn′ə-pōd′) *n.* **1.** A creature having only one

monogram

Queen Anne of Great Britain and Ireland

Albrecht Dürer

James Monroe
Posthumous painting
by Thomas Sully

monster
Sixteenth-century
encyclopedia illustration

monstrance

foot; specifically, a member of a fabled people in Africa. **2.** *Botany.* Variant of **monopodium.** [Late Latin *monopodius,* one-footed. See **monopodium.**]

mon·o·po·di·um (mŏn′ə-pō′dē-əm) *n., pl.* **-dia** (-dē-ə). Also **mon·o·pode** (mŏn′ə-pōd′). *Botany.* A main axis of a plant, such as the trunk of certain conifers, that maintains a single line of growth, giving off lateral branches. [New Latin, from Late Latin *monopodius,* one-footed, from Greek *monopous* (stem *monopod-*) : MONO- + *pous,* foot (see **ped-**[1] in Appendix*).] —**mon′o·po′di·al** (-dē-əl) *adj.*

mo·nop·o·lize (mə-nŏp′ə-līz′) *tr.v.* **-lized, -lizing, -lizes. 1.** To acquire or maintain a monopoly of. **2.** To dominate by excluding others. —**mo·nop′o·li·za′tion** *n.* —**mo·nop′o·liz′er** *n.*

mo·nop·o·ly (mə-nŏp′ə-lē) *n., pl.* **-lies. 1.** *Economics.* Exclusive control by one group of the means of producing or selling a commodity or service. Compare **oligopoly. 2.** *Law.* A right granted by a government, giving exclusive control over a specified commercial activity to a single party. **3. a.** A company or group having exclusive control over a commercial activity. **b.** A commodity or service controlled exclusively by one company or group. **4.** Exclusive possession of or control over anything: *"the lexicographer had no monopoly of the problem of meaning"* (William V. Quine). [From Latin *monopōlium,* from Greek *monopōlion,* sole selling rights : MONO- + *pōlein,* to sell (see **pel-**[6] in Appendix*).] —**mo·nop′o·lism′** *n.* —**mo·nop′o·list** *n.* & *adj.* —**mo·nop′o·lis′tic** *adj.*

Synonyms: *monopoly, corner, pool, trust, cartel, syndicate, combination, combine. Monopoly* is a general term applicable to a condition or organization and the service or commodity involved; in none of these senses is illegality necessarily implied. *Corner* denotes only a condition. It is a short-term speculative monopoly created by individuals (not necessarily illegally) to control a market. *Pool* and *trust* denote intercorporate organizations (now illegal) designed to restrict competition within specific areas and industries over a long period. *Cartel* usually denotes an international pool or trust; in Europe the term often also applies to a pool or trust operating within a single country. *Syndicate* pertains to any group engaged in a short-term commercial venture involving large capital; monopoly is no longer usually implied. *Combination* denotes any sizable, relatively permanent intercorporate association; the term no longer indicates monopoly unless so qualified, as in *combination in restraint of trade. Combine* is used informally for a combination, and generally implies monopolistic practice for private gain.

mon·o·pro·pel·lant (mŏn′ō-prə-pĕl′ənt) *n.* A rocket propellant in which fuel and oxidizer are combined, such as a mixture of hydrogen peroxide and alcohol. Also called "monofuel."

mon·o·pro·tic (mŏn′ō-prŏt′ĭk) *adj. Chemistry.* Having only one hydrogen ion to donate to a base in an acid-base reaction. Also "monobasic." [MONO- + PROT(ON) + -IC.]

mo·nop·so·ny (mə-nŏp′sə-nē) *n., pl.* **-nies.** A market situation in which the product or service of several sellers is sought by only one buyer. Compare **oligopsony.** [MON(O)- + Greek *opsōnia,* a buying, from *opsōnein,* to buy food (see **opsonin**).]

mon·o·rail (mŏn′ə-rāl′) *n.* **1.** A single rail on which a vehicle or train of cars travels. **2.** A railway system with such a track.

mon·o·sac·cha·ride (mŏn′ə-săk′ə-rīd′, -rĭd) *n.* A simple sugar that cannot be decomposed by hydrolysis, especially one of the hexoses, having the general formula $C_6H_{12}O_6$.

mon·o·sep·al·ous (mŏn′ə-sĕp′ə-ləs) *adj. Botany.* Having sepals united to form a single calyx; gamosepalous. [MONO- + -SEPALOUS.]

mon·o·so·di·um glu·ta·mate (mŏn′ə-sō′dē-əm glo͞o′tə-māt′). A chemical, **sodium glutamate** *(see).*

mon·o·some (mŏn′ə-sōm′) *n.* **1.** A cell lacking one or more chromosomes. **2.** An unpaired X chromosome. See **sex chromosome.** [MONO- + -SOME (body).] —**mon′o·so′mic** (mŏn′ə-sŏm′ĭk) *adj.*

mon·o·sper·mous (mŏn′ə-spûr′məs) *adj.* Also **mon·o·sper·mal** (-məl). Having a single seed. [MONO- + -SPERMOUS.]

mon·o·stome (mŏn′ə-stōm′) *adj.* Also **mo·nos·to·mous** (mə-nŏs′tə-məs). Having one oral sucker only, as certain flatworms. —*n.* A trematode worm. [From Greek *monostomos,* having one mouth : MONO- + *stoma,* mouth, -STOME.]

mon·o·sty·lous (mŏn′ə-stī′ləs) *adj. Botany.* Having one style.

mon·o·syl·lab·ic (mŏn′ə-sĭ-lăb′ĭk) *adj.* **1.** Having only one syllable. **2.** Characterized by or consisting of monosyllables.

mon·o·syl·la·ble (mŏn′ə-sĭl′ə-bəl) *n.* A word or utterance of one syllable. [Late Latin *monosyllabum,* from Greek *monosullabon* : MONO- + *sullabē,* SYLLABLE.]

mon·o·the·ism (mŏn′ə-thē-ĭz′əm) *n.* The doctrine or belief that there is only one God. [MONO- + THEISM.] —**mon′o·the′ist** *n.* & *adj.* —**mon′o·the·is′tic** *adj.* —**mon′o·the·is′ti·cal·ly** *adv.*

mon·o·the·mat·ic (mŏn′ō-thē-măt′ĭk) *adj. Music.* Having but one theme.

mon·o·tint (mŏn′ə-tĭnt′) *n.* A picture, a **monochrome** *(see).*

mon·o·tone (mŏn′ə-tōn′) *n.* **1.** A succession of sounds or words uttered in a single tone of voice. **2.** *Music.* **a.** A single tone repeated with different words or time values, as in plainsong. **b.** A chant in a single tone. **3.** Sameness, dull repetition, or lack of variety in sound, style, manner, or color. —*adj.* **1.** Of, pertaining to, or characteristic of sounds emitted at a single pitch. **2.** Monotonous. **3.** Also **mon·o·ton·ic** (mŏn′ə-tŏn′ĭk). *Mathematics.* Designating sequences the successive members of which either consistently increase or decrease but do not oscillate in relative value. Each member of a *monotone increasing* sequence is greater than or equal to the preceding member; each member of a *monotone decreasing* sequence is less than or equal to the preceding member. See **sequence.** [From Greek *monotonos,* having one tone : MONO-, single + *tonos,* TONE.]

mo·not·o·nous (mə-nŏt′n-əs) *adj.* **1.** Unvarying in vocal inflection or pitch; sounded in one persistent tone: *"The monotonous beat from the jukebox invades the room persistently."* (John Rechy). **2.** Without variation or variety; repetitiously dull: *"It was a monotonous life, operating with machinelike regularity."* (Jack London). —See Synonyms at **boring.** [From Greek *monotonos,* having one tone : MONO-, single + *tonos,* TONE.] —**mo·not′o·nous·ly** *adv.*

mo·not·o·ny (mə-nŏt′n-ē) *n.* **1.** Uniformity or lack of variation in pitch, intonation, or inflection. **2.** Wearisome sameness. [Greek *monotonia,* from *monotonos,* MONOTONOUS.]

mon·o·treme (mŏn′ə-trēm′) *n.* A member of the Monotremata, an order of egg-laying mammals restricted to Australia and New Guinea, and including the platypus and the echidna. [From New Latin *Monotremata* (order) : MONO- + Greek *trēma* (stem *trēmat-*), hole (see **ter-**[2] in Appendix*).]

mo·not·ri·chous (mə-nŏt′rĭ-kəs) *adj.* Also **mon·o·trich·ic** (mŏn′ə-trĭk′ĭk). Having one flagellum at only one pole or end, as certain bacteria. [MONO- + TRICH(O)- + -OUS.]

mon·o·troph·ic (mŏn′ə-trŏf′ĭk, -trō′fĭk) *adj.* Requiring only one kind of food; monophagous. [MONO- + TROPHIC.]

mon·o·type (mŏn′ə-tīp′) *n. Biology.* The sole member of its group, such as a species that also constitutes a genus. —**mon′o·typ′ic** *adj.*

Mon·o·type (mŏn′ə-tīp′) *n.* A trademark for a typesetting machine operated from a keyboard which activates a unit that casts individual letters from matrices and assembles them.

mon·o·va·lent (mŏn′ə-vā′lənt) *adj.* **1.** *Chemistry.* Possessing a valence of 1; univalent. **2.** *Pathology.* Able to resist a specific pathogen because the proper antibodies or antigens are present. —**mon′o·va′lence, mon′o·va′len·cy** *n.*

mon·ox·ide (mŏ-nŏk′sīd′, mə-) *n.* An oxide with each molecule containing one oxygen atom. [MON(O)- + OXIDE.]

Mon·roe (mən-rō′), **James.** 1758–1831. Fifth President of the United States (1817–25).

Monroe Doctrine. The U.S. policy of opposition to outside interference in the Americas. [After a foreign policy statement (1823) by President MONROE.]

Mon·ro·vi·a (mən-rō′vē-ə). The capital and principal seaport of Liberia. Population, 80,000.

mons (mŏnz) *n., pl.* **montes** (mŏn′tēz). A protuberance of the human body; especially, that formed by the pubic bones, called "mons pubis" in the male and "mons veneris" in the female. [New Latin, from Latin *mōns,* mountain. See **men-**[2] in Appendix.*]

Mon·sei·gneur (môN-sĕ-nyœr′) *n., pl.* **Messeigneurs** (mā-sĕ-nyœr′). *Abbr.* **Mgr., Mngr., Msgr.** *French.* A title of princes and prelates. [French, "my lord."]

Mon·sieur (mə-syœ′) *n., pl.* **Messieurs** (mĕs′ərz; *French* mā-syœ′). *Abbr.* **M.** *French.* **1.** A title of courtesy prefixed to the name or nobiliary or professional title of a Frenchman, equivalent to the English "Mister," "Sir," or "my Lord," according to the rank of the person. **2.** Since the 16th century, the oldest brother of a king of France. [French, "my lord."]

Mon·si·gnor (mŏn-sēn′yər) *n., pl.* **-gnors.** *Italian* **Mon·si·gno·re** (môn′sē-nyô′rā) *pl.* **-ri** (-rē). Also **mon·si·gnor.** *Abbr.* **Mgr., Mngr., Monsig., Msgr. 1.** A title of certain officials of the Roman Catholic Church. **2.** A person holding this title. [Italian, from French *monseigneur,* MONSEIGNEUR.]

mon·soon (mŏn-so͞on′) *n.* A wind system that influences large climatic regions and reverses direction seasonally; specifically, the Asiatic monsoon that produces dry and wet seasons in India and southern Asia. [Obsolete Dutch *monssoen,* from Portuguese *monção,* from Arabic *mausim,* season, monsoon season.]

mons pu·bis (pyo͞o′bĭs). The male **mons** *(see).*

mon·ster (mŏn′stər) *n.* **1.** A fabulous being compounded of elements from various human or animal forms. **2.** An animal or plant having structural defects or deformities. **3.** *Pathology.* A fetus or infant that is grotesquely abnormal. **4.** Any very large animal, plant, or object. **5.** One who inspires horror or disgust. Often used in rhetorical overstatement: *a monster of selfishness.* —*adj.* Gigantic; huge; enormous. [Middle English *monstre,* from Old French, from Latin *mōnstrum,* prodigy, portent, from *monēre,* to warn. See **men-**[1] in Appendix.*]

mon·strance (mŏn′strəns) *n. Roman Catholic Church.* A receptacle in which the Host is held. [Middle English, from Old French, from Medieval Latin *mōnstrantia,* from Latin *mōnstrāre,* to show, from *mōnstrum,* portent, MONSTER.]

mon·stros·i·ty (mŏn-strŏs′ə-tē) *n., pl.* **-ties. 1.** One that is monstrous. **2.** The quality or character of being monstrous.

mon·strous (mŏn′strəs) *adj.* **1.** Deviating from the norm in appearance or structure; grotesquely unnatural. **2.** Exceptionally large; enormous: *"Just then flew down a monstrous crow"* (Lewis Carroll). **3.** Hideous; frightful; shocking: *"a monstrous tyranny, never surpassed in the dark, lamentable catalogue of human crime"* (Winston Churchill). **4.** Of, pertaining to, or like a fabulous monster: *"Harpies and Hydras, or all the monstrous forms / 'Twixt Africa and Ind"* (Milton). —See Synonyms at **outrageous.** [Middle English *monstrows,* from Old French *monstruex,* from Latin *mōnstruōsus,* from *mōnstrum,* MONSTER.] —**mon′strous·ly** *adv.* —**mon′strous·ness** *n.*

mons ve·ne·ris (vĕn′ə-rĭs). The female **mons** *(see).*

Mont. Montana.

mon·tage (mŏn-täzh′; *French* môN-tȧzh′) *n.* **1. a.** The art, style, or process of making one pictorial composition from many pictures or designs, closely arranged or superimposed upon each other. **b.** A picture so made. **2.** *Motion Pictures & Television.* **a.** A rapid sequence of thematically related short scenes or

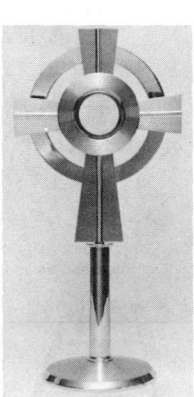

images that exhibits different aspects of the same idea or situation. **b.** A portion of a motion picture or television program employing such a special effect. **3.** In various other art forms, a sequence using different sensuous elements presented at short intervals. [French, "mounting," from *monter*, to mount, from Old French, to MOUNT.]

Mon·ta·gu (mŏn'tə-gyōō'), Lady **Mary Wortley**. 1689-1762. English poet and writer of letters.

Mon·taigne (mŏn-tān'; *French* môN-tĕn'y'), **Michel Eyquem de**. 1533-1592. French author of three books of essays.

Mon·tan·a (mŏn-tăn'ə). *Abbr.* **Mont.** A Western state of the United States, 147,138 square miles in area, bordered in the north by Canada. The state joined the Union in 1889. Population, 591,000. Capital, Helena. See map at **United States of America.** —**Mon·tan'an** *adj. & n.*

mon·tane (mŏn'tān') *adj.* Of, growing in, or inhabiting mountain areas. [Latin *montānus*, from *mōns* (stem *mont-*), mountain. See men-² in Appendix.*]

mon·tan wax (mŏn'tən, -tăn'). A hard, white wax obtained from lignite and used in the manufacture of polishes, candles, and insulators. [From Latin *montānus*, MONTANE.]

Mon·tauk Point (mŏn'tôk'). The easternmost point of New York State, at the eastern tip of Long Island.

Mont Blanc (môN bläN'). The highest mountain in the Alps (15,781 feet) near the French-Italian border.

Mont·calm (mŏnt-käm'; *French* môN-kȧlm'), **Marquis de**. In full, Louis Joseph, Marquis de Montcalm de Saint-Véran. 1712-1759. French commander in chief in New France; defeated by General Wolfe (1759).

mon·te (mŏn'tē) *n.* A game of Spanish origin in which each player bets that one of two cards will be matched by the dealer before the other one. Also called "monte bank." See **three-card monte.** [Spanish, "mountain," referring to the pile of unplayed cards, from Latin *mōns* (stem *mont-*), mountain. See men-² in Appendix.*]

Mon·te Al·ban (môn'tä äl-bän'). A ruined Zapotec city.

Mon·te Car·lo (mŏn'tē kär'lō; *Italian* môn'tä kär'lō). A resort town and site of the casino in Monaco.

Mon·te·go Bay (mŏn-tē'gō). A seaport and resort town on the northwestern coast of Jamaica, in the West Indies. Population, 24,000.

Mon·te·ne·gro (mŏn'tə-nē'grō). A constituent republic of Yugoslavia, 5,343 square miles, on the Adriatic. Population, 472,000. Capital, Titograd. —**Mon'te·ne'grin** *adj. & n.*

Mon·te·rey (mŏn'tə-rā'). A city on the coast of California about 100 miles south of San Francisco. Population, 23,000.

mon·te·ro (mŏn-târ'ō) *n., pl.* -**ros.** A huntsman's cap with side flaps. [Spanish, "hunter," from *monte*, forest region, mountain. See **monte.**]

Mon·ter·rey (mŏn'tə-rā'; *Spanish* môn'tĕr-rā'). The capital of Nuevo León State, Mexico. Population, 774,000.

mon·tes. Plural of **mons.**

Mon·tes·quieu (mŏn'təs-kyōō', mŏn-tĕs'kyōō; *French* môN-tĕs-kyœ'), **Baron de la Brède et de**. Title of Charles de Secondat. 1689-1755. French political philosopher, writer, and jurist.

Mon·tes·so·ri (mŏn'tə-sôr'ē, -sōr'ē; *Italian* môn'tĕs-sô'rē), **Maria**. 1870-1952. Italian physician and educator.

Montessori method. A method of instructing young children that stresses development of a child's own initiative. Also called "Montessori system." [After Maria MONTESSORI.]

Mon·te·ver·di (mŏn'tə-vâr'dē; *Italian* môn'tä-vĕr'dē), **Claudio**. 1567-1643. Italian composer of operas and madrigals.

Mon·te·vi·de·o (mŏn'tə-vĭ-dā'ō; *Spanish* môn'tä-vē-thä'ō). The capital of Uruguay, a seaport at the mouth of the Río de la Plata. Population, 1,204,000.

Mon·te·zu·ma II (mŏn'tə-zōō'mə). Also **Moc·te·zu·ma** (*Spanish* môk'tä-sōō'mä). 1480?-1520. Last Aztec emperor in Mexico; overthrown by Hernando Cortés.

Montezuma cypress. A tree, the **ahuehuete** (*see*).

Mont·fort (mŏnt'fərt; *French* môN-fôr'), **Simon de**[1]. 1160?-1218. French crusader; father of S. de Montfort.

Mont·fort (mŏnt'fərt; *French* môN-fôr'), **Simon de**[2]. 1208?-1265. English statesman and soldier; son of S. de Montfort.

Mont·gol·fi·er (mŏnt-gŏl'fē-ər, -fē-ā'; *French* môN-gôl-fyā'), **Joseph Michel**. 1740-1810. French inventor; with his brother, **Jacques Étienne** (1745-1799), built and ascended (1783) in first practical balloon.

Mont·gom·er·y[1] (mŏnt-gŭm'ər-ē, -gŭm'rē, mənt-). The capital of Alabama, in the central part of the state on the Alabama River. Population, 134,000.

Mont·gom·er·y[2]. Variant of **Montgomeryshire.**

Mont·gom·er·y (mənt-gŭm'rē), **Sir Bernard Law**. First Viscount Montgomery of Alamein. Born 1887. British army officer; World War II commander in North Africa.

Mont·gom·er·y·shire (mənt-gŭm'rē-shĭr). Also **Mont·gom·er·y** (-ər-ē). A county in Wales, 797 square miles in area. Population, 44,000. County seat, Welshpool.

month (mŭnth) *n. Abbr.* **mo., m, M, M., m.** **1.** One of the 12 divisions of a year as determined by the Gregorian calendar. Also called "calendar month." **2.** Any period extending from a date in one calendar month to the corresponding date in the following month. **3. a.** A period of four weeks. **b.** A period of 30 days. **4.** The average period of revolution of the moon around the earth determined by using a fixed star as a reference point and equal to 27 days 7 hours 43 minutes. Also called "sidereal month." **5.** The average time between successive new, or full, moons; equal to 29 days 12 hours 44 minutes. Also called "synodic month," "lunar month." **6.** One twelfth of a tropical year, totaling 30 days 10 hours 29 minutes 3.8 seconds.

Also called "solar month." See **calendar.** —**month of Sundays.** *Informal.* An indefinitely long period of time. [Middle English *moneth*, Old English *mōnath*. See me-² in Appendix.*]
Usage: The singular *month*, preceded by a numeral (or number) and a hyphen, is used as a compound attributive: *a three-month vacation.* The plural possessive form without a hyphen is also possible: *a three months' vacation.*

month·ly (mŭnth'lē) *adj.* **1.** Occurring, appearing, or coming due every month. **2.** Continuing or lasting for a month. **3.** *Informal.* Of or pertaining to the menses; menstrual. —*adv.* Once a month; by the month; every month. —*n., pl.* **monthlies.** **1.** A periodical publication appearing once each month. **2.** *Plural. Informal.* The menses.

Mon·ti·cel·lo (mŏn'tə-chĕl'ō, -sĕl'ō). Thomas Jefferson's estate, near Charlottesville, Virginia.

mon·ti·cule (mŏn'tĭ-kyōōl') *n.* A secondary volcanic cone of a volcano. [French, from Late Latin *monticulus*, diminutive of Latin *mōns* (stem *mont-*), mountain. See men-² in Appendix.*]

Mont·mar·tre (môN-mȧr'tr'). A district in northern Paris noted for its cafés and nightclubs.

Mont·par·nasse (môN-pȧr-nȧs'). A district of southern Paris, on the left bank of the Seine, noted as a gathering place for intellectuals and artists.

Mont·pe·lier (mŏnt-pēl'yər). The capital of Vermont, situated in the center of the state. Population, 9,000.

Mont·pel·lier (môN-pĕ-lyā'). A city in southern France, about 80 miles northwest of Marseille. Population, 119,000.

Mon·tre·al (mŏn'trē-ôl', môn'-). *French* **Mont·ré·al** (môN-rā-äl'). Canada's largest city, located at the head of the St. Lawrence Seaway in Quebec. Population, 1,191,000.

Mon·treux (môN-trœ'). A resort area comprising a group of villages at the eastern end of Lake Geneva, Switzerland.

Mont-Saint-Mi·chel (môN-săN-mē-shĕl'). A small island off the coast of Brittany, celebrated for its Benedictine abbey.

Mont·ser·rat (mŏnt'sə-răt'). One of the Leeward Islands, a British colony in the West Indies. Population, 14,000.

mon·u·ment (mŏn'yə-mənt) *n.* **1.** A structure, such as a building, tower, or sculpture, erected as a memorial. **2.** An inscribed stone or other marker placed at a grave or tomb; tombstone. **3.** Any structure venerated for its enduring significance. **4.** Any place or region officially designated as having special interest or significance, and maintained and preserved by a government. **5. a.** An outstanding and enduring achievement viewed as a model for later generations. **b.** Something that commemorates by association: *"Although Henry Hudson himself was gone, his bay, his strait and his river remained as monuments to his life."* (Virginia S. Eifert). **c.** An exceptional example of something: *"Thousands of them wrote texts, some of them monuments of dullness."* (Robert L. Heilbroner). [Middle English, from Latin *monumentum*, from *monēre*, to remind, warn. See men-¹ in Appendix.*]

mon·u·men·tal (mŏn'yə-mĕn'təl) *adj.* **1.** Of, resembling, or serving as a monument. **2.** Impressively large, sturdy, and enduring. **3.** Of outstanding significance: *"Thorndike's contributions to the science of education have been monumental."* (V.T. Thayer). **4.** Enormous and astounding: *"the monumental unimaginativeness of German scholarship"* (Herbert J. Muller). **5.** *Fine Arts.* Larger than life-size. —**mon'u·men'tal·ly** *adv.*

mon·zo·nite (mŏn-zō'nīt', mŏn'zə-nīt') *n.* An igneous rock composed chiefly of plagioclase and orthoclase, with small amounts of other minerals. [French, from Mount *Monzoni* in northeast Italy, where it was discovered.]

moo (mōō) *intr.v.* **mooed, mooing, moos.** To emit the deep, bellowing sound made by a cow; to low. —*n., pl.* **moos.** The lowing of a cow, or a similar sound. [Imitative.]

mooch (mōōch) *v.* **mooched, mooching, mooches.** Also *chiefly British* **mouch** (mōōch). *Slang.* —*tr.* **1.** To obtain free of charge by cajolery or begging. **2.** To steal or filch. —*intr.* **1.** To dawdle or wander around aimlessly. **2.** To lurk or skulk about. [Middle English *mowche*, from Old French *muchier.* See meug-¹ in Appendix.*] —**mooch'er** *n.*

mood¹ (mōōd) *n.* **1.** A temporary state of mind or feeling, as evidenced by the tendency of one's thoughts: *a gloomy mood.* **2.** A pervading impression on the feelings of an observer: *the somber mood of the painting.* **3.** *Plural.* Spells of sulking or morose behavior. —**in the mood.** Inclined; disposed. [Middle English *mod*, Old English *mōd.* See me-¹ in Appendix.*]
Synonyms: mood, humor, temper. *Mood* suggests greater duration than the other terms here. It pertains to persons and nonliving things (such as art and the times), and can indicate any segment of the emotional range, although when applied without qualification to a person, it generally implies antisocial behavior. *Humor,* said only of persons, emphasizes transitoriness; it sometimes implies variability of emotion. *Temper,* restricted to persons, stresses brief intensity of anger.

mood² (mōōd) *n.* **1.** *Grammar.* A set of verb forms used to indicate the speaker's attitude toward the factuality or likelihood of the action or condition expressed. In English, the indicative mood is used for factual statements, the subjunctive mood to indicate doubt or unlikelihood, and the imperative mood to express a command. Compare **aspect.** **2.** *Logic.* The arrangement or form of a proposition. [Alteration (influenced by MOOD¹) of MODE.]

mood·y (mōō'dē) *adj.* -**ier,** -**iest.** **1.** Given to changeable emotional states, especially of gloom. **2.** Gloomy; uneasy; glum: *a moody silence.* —**mood'i·ly** *adv.* —**mood'i·ness** *n.*

Moo·dy (mōō'dē), **Dwight Lyman**. 1837-1899. American evangelist.

moo goo gai pan (mōō' gōō' gī' păn'). A Cantonese dish of

Montezuma II
From 16th-century genealogical codex of the Montezuma clan

chicken, mushrooms, vegetables, and spices, steamed together. [Cantonese, for Mandarin *mo^{2}ku^{1}chi^{1}p'ien^4* : *mo^{2}ku^1*, mushroom (from Mongolian *mugu*) + *chi^1*, chicken + *p'ien^4*, a slice.]

moo·la, moo·lah (mo͞o′lə) *n. Slang.* Money. [Origin unknown.]

Mool·tan. See **Multan.**

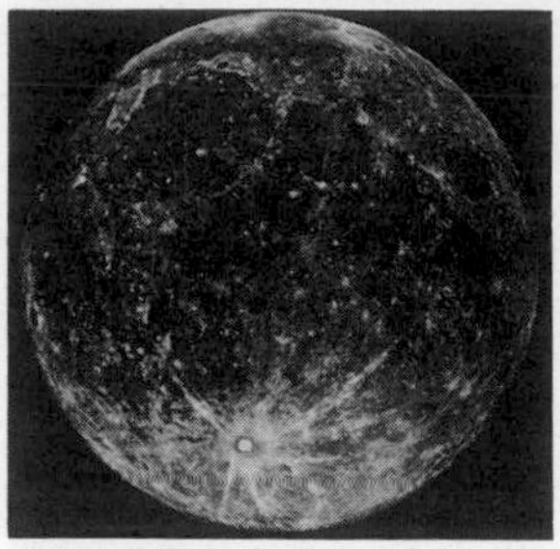

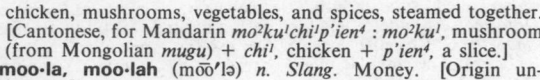

moon
Showing crater Tycho and its ray system

moon (mo͞on) *n.* **1.** The natural satellite of the earth, visible by reflection of sunlight, having a slightly elliptical orbit, approximately 221,600 miles distant at perigee and 252,950 miles at apogee. Its mean diameter is 2,160 miles, its mass approximately one-eightieth that of the earth, and its average period of revolution around the earth 29 days 12 hours 44 minutes calculated with respect to the sun. **2.** Any natural satellite revolving around a planet. **3.** The moon as it appears at a particular time in its cycle of phases: *the full moon; a half moon.* **4.** A month, especially a lunar month. **5.** Any disk, globe, or crescent resembling the moon. **6.** Moonlight. *—intr.v.* **mooned, mooning, moons. 1.** To wander about or pass time languidly and aimlessly. **2.** To exhibit infatuation. [Middle English *moone, mon,* Old English *mōna.* See **mē-^{2}** in Appendix.*]

moon·beam (mo͞on′bēm′) *n.* A ray of moonlight.

moon·blind (mo͞on′blīnd′) *adj.* Suffering from moon blindness.

moon blindness. 1. Recurrent inflammation of horses' eyes, often resulting in eventual blindness. Also called "mooneye." **2.** A defect of human vision, **nyctalopia** *(see).*

moon·calf (mo͞on′kăf′, -käf′) *n.* **1.** A fool from birth; stupid creature. **2.** A freak. [From the supposed maleficent influence of the moon on the unborn.]

moon dog. A bright spot on a lunar halo, a **paraselene** *(see).*

moon·eye (mo͞on′ī′) *n.* **1.** A silvery freshwater fish, *Hiodon tergisus,* of northern North America. **2.** An eye inflammation, **moon blindness** *(see).*

moon-faced (mo͞on′fāst′) *adj.* Having a round face.

moon·fish (mo͞on′fĭsh′) *n., pl.* **moonfish** or **-fishes. 1.** Either of two marine fishes of the family Carangidae, found in the warm coastal waters of the Americas. They have short, compressed bodies, and are silver to yellowish in color. Also called "dollarfish." **2.** A large marine fish, the **opah** *(see).*

moon·flow·er (mo͞on′flou′ər) *n.* Any of several night-blooming vines related to the morning-glories.

moon·light (mo͞on′līt′) *n.* The light reflected from the surface of the moon, principally that originating at the sun. *—adj.* **1.** Of moonlight. **2.** Under moonlight. *—intr.v.* **moonlighted, -lighting, -lights.** *Informal.* To work at a spare-time job, often at night, in addition to one's full-time job. **—moon′light′er** *n.*

moon·lit (mo͞on′lĭt′) *adj.* Lighted by the moon.

Moon, Mountains of the. See **Ruwenzori.**

moon·seed (mo͞on′sēd′) *n.* Any of several climbing vines of the genus *Menispermum* or related genera, having clusters of small, greenish or whitish flowers and red or blackish fruit with crescent-shaped or ring-shaped seeds.

moon·shine (mo͞on′shīn′) *n.* **1.** Moonlight. **2.** *Informal.* Foolish or nonsensical talk, thought, or action. **3.** *Slang.* Illegally distilled whiskey. *—v.* **moonshined, -shining, -shines.** *—tr.* To distill (liquor) illegally. *—intr.* To operate an illegal still. **—moon′shine′** *adj.* **—moon′shin′er** *n.*

moon·stone (mo͞on′stōn′) *n.* A mineral valued as a gem for its pearly translucence. It is a **feldspar,** commonly **albite, labradorite,** or **orthoclase** *(all of which see),* and is found worldwide.

moon·struck (mo͞on′strŭk′) *adj.* Also **moon·strick·en** (mo͞on′-strĭk′ən). **1.** Afflicted with insanity; crazed; deranged. **2.** Dazed or distracted with romantic sentiment; lovelorn. [From the belief that moonlight causes insanity.]

Moon type. A system of printing for the blind that uses embossed letters instead of the raised dots of Braille, and that requires less sensitivity of the fingers. [Devised by William *Moon* (1819–1894), British inventor.]

moon·wort (moon′wûrt′, -wôrt) *n.* A **grape fern** *(see).* [From the moonlike parts.]

moon·y (mo͞o′nē) *adj.* **-ier, -iest. 1.** Resembling the moon. **2.** Moonlit. **3.** Resembling moonlight; giving soft light. **4.** Dreamy in mood or nature; absent-minded; distracted: *"a graceless gawk with a moony face"* (Frank O'Connor).

moor^1 (mo͝or) *v.* **moored, mooring, moors.** *—tr.* **1.** To secure or make fast (a vessel or aircraft) by means of cables, anchors, or other contrivances. **2.** To fix in place; secure. *—intr.* **1.** To secure a vessel or aircraft. **2.** To be secured, as a vessel or aircraft. [Middle English *moren,* from Middle Low German *mōren.* See **mer-^{3}** in Appendix.*]

moor^2 (mo͝or) *n.* A broad tract of open land, often high but poorly drained, with patches of heath and peat bogs. [Middle English *mor,* Old English *mōr.* See **mā-^{3}** in Appendix.*]

Moor (mo͝or) *n.* **1.** One of a Moslem people of mixed Berber and Arab descent, now living chiefly in northern Africa. **2.** One of the Saracens who invaded Spain in the eighth century A.D. [Middle English *More,* from Old French, from Latin *Maurus,* from Greek *Mauros,* probably of North African origin.]

moor·age (mo͝or′ĭj) *n.* **1.** A place where a ship may be moored. **2.** The act of mooring or state of being moored. **3.** A charge for the use of mooring facilities.

Moore (mo͝or), **Clement Clarke.** 1779–1863. American scholar; author of the ballad *A Visit from Saint Nicholas.*

Moore (mo͝or), **George.** 1852–1933. Irish author and art critic.

Moore (mo͝or), **Henry.** Born 1898. English sculptor and artist.

Moore (mo͝or), **Marianne Craig.** Born 1887. American poet.

Moore (mo͝or), **Thomas.** 1779–1852. Irish poet and satirist.

moor·hen (mo͝or′hĕn′) *n. British.* A common, widely distributed gallinule, *Gallinula chloropus.*

moor·ing (mo͝or′ĭng) *n.* **1.** Equipment, such as anchors, chains, or lines, for holding fast a vessel or aircraft. **2.** The act of securing a vessel or aircraft. **3.** A place at which a vessel or aircraft can be moored. **4.** *Usually plural.* Elements providing stability or security: *lost his emotional moorings at the trial.*

Moor·ish (mo͝or′ĭsh) *adj.* Of or characteristic of the Moors or their culture: *Moorish architecture.*

moor·land (mo͝or′lănd′) *n. British.* A tract of moors.

moor·wort (mo͝or′wûrt′) *n.* A plant, the **bog rosemary** *(see).*

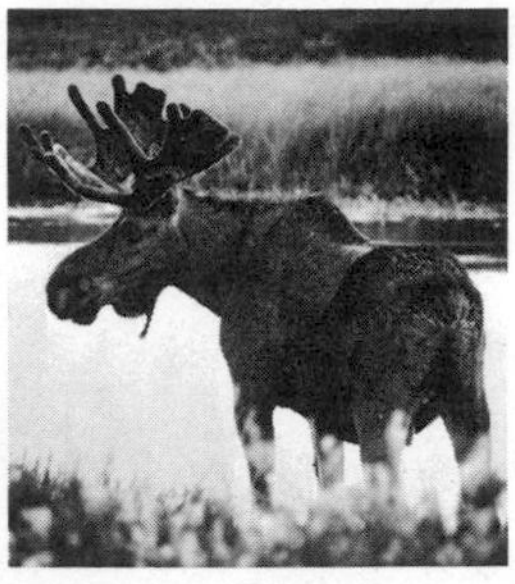

moose
A bull moose

moose (mo͞os) *n., pl.* **moose.** A hoofed mammal, *Alces alces* (also known as *A. americana*), of the deer family, found in forests of northern North America, and also in Eurasia, where it is usually called "elk." It has a broad, pendulous muzzle, and the male has large, flat antlers. [Natick *moos,* from Proto-Algonquian *mooswa* (unattested).]

moose·bird (mo͞os′bûrd′) *n.* A bird, the **Canada jay** *(see).*

Moose·head (mo͞os′hĕd′). A lake occupying about 120 square miles in west-central Maine.

moose·wood (mo͞os′wo͝od′) *n.* A slender maple, *Acer pennsylvanicum,* of eastern North America, having smooth bark with vertical whitish or greenish stripes. Also called "striped maple."

moot (mo͞ot) *n.* **1.** An ancient English meeting, especially a representative meeting of the freemen of a shire. **2.** An imaginary case argued by law students as an exercise. *—tr.v.* **mooted, mooting, moots. 1. a.** To offer as a subject for debate; bring up for discussion. **b.** To discuss or debate. **2.** To plead or argue (a case) in a moot court. *—adj.* **1.** Subject to debate; arguable; unresolved: *a moot question.* **2.** *Law.* Without legal significance, through having been previously decided or settled; of only academic importance. [Middle English *mot, moot,* Old English *mōt,* moot, assembly. See **mōd-** in Appendix.*]

moot court. A mock court where hypothetical cases are tried for the training of law students.

mop (mŏp) *n.* **1.** A household implement made of absorbent material attached to a handle and used for dusting, washing, and drying floors. **2.** Any loosely tangled bunch or mass: *a mop of hair.* *—tr.v.* **mopped, mopping, mops.** To wash, scrub, or wipe with, or as if with, a mop. **—mop up. 1.** *Military.* To destroy remaining enemy resistance after an initial victory. **2.** *Informal.* To complete a task. [Middle English *mappe,* perhaps from *mappel,* from Medieval Latin *mappula,* towel, cloth, diminutive of Latin *mappa,* cloth. See **mappa** in Appendix.*]

mop·board (mŏp′bôrd′, -bōrd′) *n.* The baseboard around a room next to the floor.

mope (mōp) *intr.v.* **moped, moping, mopes. 1.** To be gloomy or dejected. **2.** To give oneself up to brooding or sulking. **3.** To move in a leisurely or aimless manner; dawdle. *—n.* **1.** A person given to gloomy or dejected moods. **2.** *Plural.* Low spirits; the blues. [Originally, to move as in a daze, perhaps from Middle Dutch *mopen.* See **mu-** in Appendix.*] **—mop′er** *n.* **—mop′ing·ly** *adv.* **—mop′ish** *adj.* **—mop′ish·ly** *adv.*

mop·pet (mŏp′ĭt) *n.* A young child; especially, a little girl. [Diminutive of *mop,* child, fool, Middle English *mop,* probably of Low German origin, akin to Low German *mops,* fool. See **mu-** in Appendix.*]

mo·quette (mō-kĕt′) *n.* **1.** A heavy fabric with a thick nap, used for upholstery. **2.** A type of carpet with a deep, tufted pile. [French, variant of obsolete *moucade*†.]

Mo·qui. Variant of **Moki.**

mor. morocco (leather)

Mor. Morocco.

mo·ra (môr′ə, mōr′ə) *n., pl.* **morae** (môr′ē, mōr′ē) or **-ras.** *Prosody.* In quantitative verse, the unit of metrical time equal to the short syllable. [Latin, "pause." See **(s)mer-** in Appendix.*]

Mo·rad·a·bad (mə-räd′ə-bäd′, mə-răd′ə-băd′). A city of India, in northern Uttar Pradesh. Population, 180,000.

mo·raine (mə-rān′) *n.* An accumulation of boulders, stones, or other debris carried and deposited by a glacier. [French, from Savoyard *morena*†.] **—mo·rain′al. mo·rain′ic** *adj.*

mor·al (môr′əl, mŏr′-) *adj.* **1.** Of or concerned with the judgment of the goodness or badness of human action and character; pertaining to the discernment of good and evil: *moral philosophy.* **2.** Designed to teach goodness or correctness of character and behavior; instructive of what is good and bad: *"the highest precepts and the strongest examples of moral and religious endurances"* (Jane Austen). **3.** Being or acting in accordance with standards and precepts of goodness or with established codes of behavior, especially with regard to sexual conduct. **4.** Arising from conscience or the sense of right and wrong: *a moral obligation.* **5.** Having psychological rather than physical or tangible effects: *"The aggressiveness of our pilots soon established a complete moral ascendancy."* (Winston Churchill). **6.** Based upon strong likelihood or firm conviction, rather than upon the actual evidence or demonstration: *a moral certainty.* *—n.* **1.** The lesson or principle contained in or taught by a fable, story, or event. **2.** A concisely expressed precept or general truth; maxim. **3.** *Plural.* Rules or habits of conduct, especially sexual conduct, with reference to standards of right and wrong: *a woman of loose morals.* [Middle English, from Old French, from Latin *mōrālis,* from *mōs* (stem *mōr-*), custom. See **mē-^{1}** in Appendix.*]

Synonyms: *moral, ethical, virtuous, righteous. Moral* pertains to personal behavior (especially sexual) measured by prevailing standards of rectitude. *Ethical* approaches behavior from a philosophical standpoint; it stresses more objectively defined, but essentially idealistic, standards of right and wrong, such as those applicable to the practices of lawyers, doctors, and businessmen. *Virtuous* pertains to sexual continence, especially of women, or to loftiness of character in general. *Righteous* emphasizes one's credentials for salvation, especially the absence

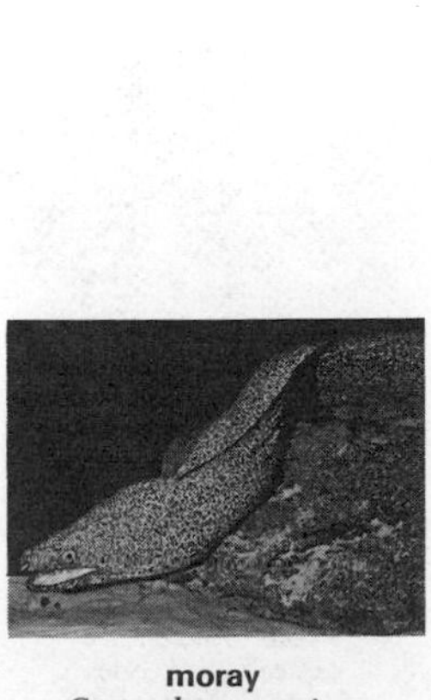

moray
Gymnothorax moringa
Spotted moray

of guilt or sin, and implies zealousness and uprightness.

mo·rale (mə-răl′) *n.* The state of the spirits of an individual or group, as shown in willingness to perform assigned tasks, confidence, cheerfulness, and discipline. [French, feminine of *moral,* moral, from Old French, MORAL.]

moral hazard. *Insurance.* A risk resulting from uncertainty about the insured's honesty.

mor·al·ism (môr′ə-lĭz′əm, mŏr′-) *n.* **1.** A conventional moral maxim or attitude. **2.** The act or practice of moralizing. **3.** The practice of or belief in a system of principles governing conduct, as distinguished from a religion.

mor·al·ist (môr′ə-lĭst, mŏr′-) *n.* **1.** A teacher or student of ethics. **2.** A person who follows a system of moral principles as distinguished from an established religion.

mor·al·is·tic (môr′ə-lĭs′tĭk, mŏr′-) *adj.* Characterized by or given to moralizing. —**mor′al·is′ti·cal·ly** *adv.*

mo·ral·i·ty (mə-răl′ə-tē, mô-) *n., pl.* **-ties. 1.** The quality of being moral. **2.** The evaluation of or means of evaluating human conduct, as: **a.** A set of ideas of right and wrong: *Christian morality.* **b.** A set of customs of a given society, class, or social group which regulate relationships and prescribe modes of behavior to enhance the group's survival: *middle-class morality.* **3.** Virtuous conduct, especially in compliance with approved codes for sexual behavior. **4.** A rule or lesson in moral conduct; a moral. **5.** A morality play.

morality play. A dramatic genre of the 15th and 16th centuries that essayed moral instruction through allegorically personifying virtues and vices in stories drawn from popular legend.

mor·al·ize (môr′ə-līz′, mŏr′-) *v.* **-ized, -izing, -izes.** —*tr.* **1.** To derive a moral lesson from; explain in moral terms: *"I was going to moralize this fable"* (Goldsmith). **2.** To improve the morals of; reform. —*intr.* To think about or discuss moral or ethical issues. —**mor′al·i·za′tion** *n.* —**mor′al·iz′er** *n.*

mor·al·ly (môr′ə-lē, mŏr′-) *adv.* **1.** In accordance with accepted rules of conduct; virtuously. **2.** With reference to moral law; ethically. **3.** In all probability; virtually: *morally certain.*

moral philosophy. The science of morality, **ethics** *(see).*

mo·rass (mə-răs′, mô-) *n.* **1.** An area of low-lying, soggy ground; a bog or marsh. **2.** Any difficult or perplexing situation. [Dutch *moeras,* variant (influenced by *moer,* moorland) of Middle Dutch *marasch,* from Old French *marasc,* from Germanic. See **mori-** in Appendix.*]

mor·a·to·ri·um (môr′ə-tôr′ē-əm, -tōr′ē-əm, mŏr′-) *n., pl.* **-ums** or **-toria** (-tôr′ē-ə, -tōr′ē-ə). **1.** *Law.* An authorization to a debtor, such as a bank or nation, permitting temporary suspension of payments. **2.** A deferment or delay of any action. [New Latin, from Late Latin *morātōrius,* MORATORY.]

mor·a·to·ry (môr′ə-tôr′ē, -tōr′ē, mŏr′-) *adj.* Authorizing delay in payment; postponing: *a moratory contract.* [French *moratoire,* from Late Latin *morātōrius,* from Latin *morārī,* to delay, from *mora,* delay. See **merə-** in Appendix.*]

Mo·ra·va (môr′ä-vä). **1.** *German* **March** (märkh). A river rising on the Polish-Czech border and flowing southward about 225 miles to join the Danube near Bratislava. **2.** A major river of Yugoslavia, flowing from central Serbia about 130 miles north to the Danube. **3.** The Czech name for **Moravia.**

Mo·ra·vi·a (mə-rā′vē-ə). *German* **Mäh·ren** (mâr′ən); *Czech* **Mo·ra·va** (mô′rä vä). A historic region and former province of central Czechoslovakia.

Mo·ra·vi·an (mə-rā′vē-ən) *n.* **1.** A native or inhabitant of Moravia. **2.** The Czech dialect spoken in Moravia. **3.** A member of the Moravian Church, a Protestant denomination founded in Saxony in 1722 by Hussite emigrants from Moravia. —*adj.* Of, pertaining to, or characteristic of Moravia, the Moravians, or the Moravian Church.

Moravian Gate. A gap between the Sudetes and Carpathian mountains.

Mo·rav·ska O·stra·va. The former name for **Ostrava.**

mo·ray (môr′ā, mōr′ā, mə-rā′) *n.* Any of various often voracious marine eels of tropical and temperate coastlines. [Portuguese *moreia,* from Latin *mūrēna,* from Greek *murainat*†.]

Mor·ay (mûr′ē). Formerly **El·gin** (ĕl′gĭn), **El·gin·shire** (ĕl′gĭn-shîr, -shər). A county of Scotland, 476 square miles, on the northeastern coast. Population, 51,000. County seat, Elgin.

Moray Firth. An inlet of the North Sea extending 39 miles into northeastern Scotland.

mor·bid (môr′bĭd) *adj.* **1. a.** Of, relating to, or caused by disease. **b.** Psychologically unhealthy: *"She had a morbid fear of dance floors"* (Eric Berne). **2.** Susceptible to or characterized by preoccupation with unwholesome matters: *"he suffered much from a morbid acuteness of the senses"* (Poe). **3.** Gruesome; grisly. [Latin *morbidus,* diseased, from *morbus,* disease. See **mer-²** in Appendix.*] —**mor′bid·ly** *adv.* —**mor′bid·ness** *n.*

mor·bid·i·ty (môr-bĭd′ə-tē) *n., pl.* **-ties. 1.** The state or quality of being morbid. **2.** Morbidity rate.

mor·bif·ic (môr-bĭf′ĭk) *adj.* Causing or producing disease; pathogenic. [New Latin *morbificus* : Latin *morbus,* disease (see **mer-²** in Appendix*) + *-ficus,* -FIC.]

mor·ceau (môr-sō′) *n., pl.* **-ceaux** (-sō′). *French.* A short literary or musical composition. [French, "morsel."]

mor·da·cious (môr-dā′shəs) *adj.* **1.** Given to biting; biting. **2.** Caustic; sarcastic. [From Latin *mordāx* (stem *mordāc-*), caustic, biting, from *mordēre,* to bite. See **mer-²** in Appendix.*] —**mor·da′cious·ly** *adv.* —**mor·dac′i·ty** (môr-dăs′ə-tē) *n.*

mor·dant (môr′dənt) *adj.* **1. a.** Bitingly sarcastic. **b.** Incisive and trenchant. **2.** Bitingly painful. **3.** Serving to fix colors in dyeing. —*n.* **1.** A reagent, such as tannic acid, used to fix coloring matter in textiles, leather, or other materials. **2.** A corrosive substance, such as an acid, used to etch treated areas on a metal or other surface. —*tr.v.* **mordanted, -danting, -dants.** To treat with a mordant. [French, from Old French, from the present participle of *mordre,* to bite, from Latin *mordēre.* See **mer-²** in Appendix.*] —**mor′dan·cy** *n.* —**mor′dant·ly** *adv.*

Mor·den (môr′dən). A former administrative division of London, England, now included in Merton *(see).*

mor·dent (môr′dənt, môr-dĕnt′) *n. Music.* A melodic ornament in which a principal note is rapidly alternated with a note a half or full step below. [German, from Italian *mordente,* a musical grace, from *mordere,* to bite (in allusion to the sharpness of attack with which it is executed), from Latin *mordēre.* See **mer-²** in Appendix.*]

Mor·dred. Variant of **Modred.**

Mord·vin·i·an Autonomous Socialist Soviet Republic (môrd-vĭn′ē-ən). An autonomous administrative division, 10,010 square miles in area, of west-central Russian S.F.S.R. Population, 1,003,000. Capital, Saransk.

more (môr, mōr) *adj. Superlative* **most. 1. a.** Greater in number. Comparative of **many. b.** Greater in size, amount, extent, or degree. Comparative of **much. 2.** Additional; extra: *They need more food.* —*n.* **1.** A greater or additional quantity, number, degree, or amount. Used with *of* and a plural verb: *More of them are coming.* **2.** Something that exceeds or surpasses expectation: *more than necessary.* —*adv.* **1.** To or in a greater extent or degree. Used to form the comparative of many adjectives and adverbs: *more difficult; more intelligently.* **2.** In addition; besides; further; again; longer. —**more or less. 1.** About; approximately. **2.** To an undetermined degree. [Middle English *more,* Old English *māra* (adjective), *māre* (adverb and noun). See **mē-³** in Appendix.*]

More (môr, mōr), **Hannah.** 1745–1833. English religious writer and social reformer.

More (môr, mōr), **Saint** (Sir) **Thomas.** 1478–1535. English statesman and author; upheld the Roman Catholic Church in defiance of Henry VIII and was beheaded; canonized 1935.

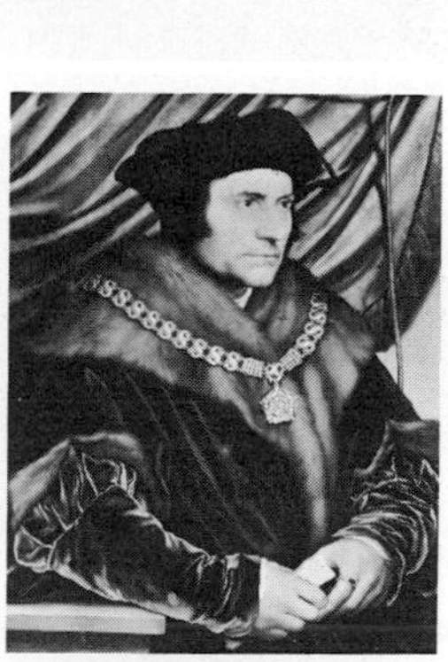

Saint Thomas More
Contemporary portrait by Hans Holbein the Younger

Mo·re·a. The medieval name for the **Peloponnesus.**

mo·reen (mə-rēn′, mô-) *n.* A sturdy ribbed fabric of wool or cotton, often with an embossed finish, used for clothing and upholstery. [Perhaps blend of MOIRE and VELVETEEN or SATEEN.]

mo·rel (mə-rĕl′, mô-) *n.* Any of various edible mushrooms of the genus *Morchella* and related genera, characterized by a brownish, spongelike cap. Also called "sponge mushroom." [French *morille,* from Old French, from Vulgar Latin *mauricula* (unattested), dark brown, from Latin *Maurus,* Moor, from Greek, *Mauros*†, MOOR.]

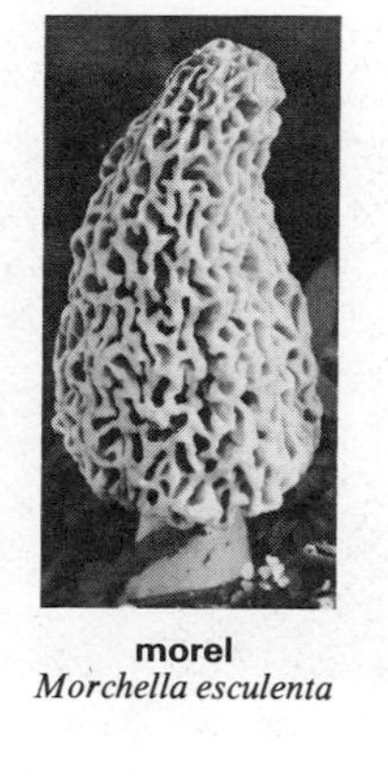

morel
Morchella esculenta

Mo·re·lia (mō-rā′lyä). Formerly **Va·lla·do·lid** (vä′yä-dō-lēd′). The capital of Michoacán, Mexico. Population, 128,000.

mo·rel·lo (mə-rĕl′ō) *n., pl.* **-los.** A variety of the sour cherry, *Prunus cerasus austera,* having fruit with dark-red skin. [Probably from Italian *amarello,* from Medieval Latin *amārellum,* diminutive of Latin *amārus,* bitter. See **om-** in Appendix.*]

Mo·re·los (mō-rā′lōs). A state of Mexico, 1,917 square miles in area, centrally located just south of the Federal District. Population, 430,000. Capital, Cuernavaca.

more·o·ver (môr-ō′vər, mōr-, môr′ō′vər, mōr′-) *adv.* Beyond what has been stated; further; besides. See Synonyms at **also.**

mo·res (môr′āz, mōr′-, -ēz) *pl.n.* **1.** The accepted traditional customs and usages of a particular social group that come to be regarded as essential to its survival and welfare, thence often becoming, through general observance, part of a formalized legal code. **2.** Moral attitudes. **3.** Manners; ways. [Latin *mōrēs,* plural of *mōs,* custom. See **mē-¹** in Appendix.*]

Mo·resque (mô-rĕsk′, mə-) *adj.* Moorish. Said of decoration and architecture. —*n.* An ornament or decoration in Moorish style. [French, from Spanish *Morisco,* MORISCO.]

Mor·gan (môr′gən) *n.* One of a breed of American saddle and trotting horses. [After Justin *Morgan* (1747–1798), owner of the stallion from which the breed is descended.]

Mor·gan (môr′gən), Sir **Henry.** 1635?–1688. Welsh buccaneer in the Caribbean; acting governor of Jamaica (1680–82).

Mor·gan (môr′gən), **John Hunt.** 1825–1864. American commander of Confederate raiders in the Civil War.

Mor·gan (môr′gən), **J(ohn) P(ierpont).** 1837–1913. American financier, steel and railroad magnate, and philanthropist.

Mor·gan (môr′gən), **Lewis Henry.** 1818–1881. American anthropologist and ethnologist; authority on American Indians.

Mor·gan (môr′gən), **Thomas Hunt.** 1866–1945. American biologist; studied heredity.

mor·ga·nat·ic (môr′gə-năt′ĭk) *adj.* Of or pertaining to a type of legal marriage between a man or woman of royal or noble birth and a partner of lower rank, in which agreement is made that any titles or estates of the royal or noble partner will not be shared by the commoner or by any of their offspring. [New Latin *morganaticus,* from Medieval Latin *matrimonium ad morganaticam,* "marriage for (no dowry but) the morning-gift" (i.e., the husband's token gift to the wife on the morning after the wedding night), from Old High German *morgan,* morning. See **mer-¹** in Appendix.*] —**mor′ga·nat′i·cal·ly** *adv.*

mor·gan·ite (môr′gə-nīt′) *n.* A rosy-pink silicate of beryllium and aluminum valued as a semiprecious gem. [After J.P. MORGAN.]

Mor·gan le Fay (môr′gən lə fā′). Also **Mor·gain le Fay** (môr′gān, -gən). The sorceress sister and enemy of King Arthur.

mor·gen (môr′gən) *n., pl.* **morgen** or **-gens.** A Dutch unit of land area equal to 2.116 acres, still in use in South Africa. [Dutch, from Middle Dutch *morghen,* morning, i.e., "a morning's plowing." See **mer-¹** in Appendix.*]

morgue (môrg) *n.* **1.** A place in which the bodies of persons

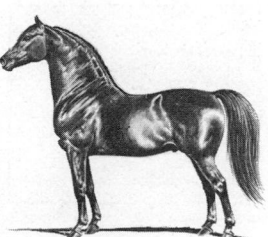

Morgan
Stallion

t tight/th thin, path/*th* this, bathe/ŭ cut/ûr urge/v valve/w with/y yes/z zebra, size/zh vision/ə about, item, edible, gallop, circus/ à *Fr.* ami/œ *Fr.* feu, *Ger.* schön/ü *Fr.* tu, *Ger.* über/KH *Ger.* ich, *Scot.* loch/N *Fr.* bon. ***Follows main vocabulary. †Of obscure origin.**

found dead are kept for identification and arrangement of burial. **2.** A reference file in a newspaper or magazine office. [French, from *le Morgue,* the mortuary building in Paris.]

mor·i·bund (môr′ə-bŭnd′, mŏr′-) *adj.* **1.** At the point of death; about to die. **2.** Approaching an end; obsolescent: *"a commendable instinct for hastening the demise of moribund words"* (New Yorker). [Latin *moribundus,* from *morī,* to die. See **mer-**[2] in Appendix.*] —**mor′i·bun′di·ty** *n.* —**mor′i·bund′ly** *adv.*

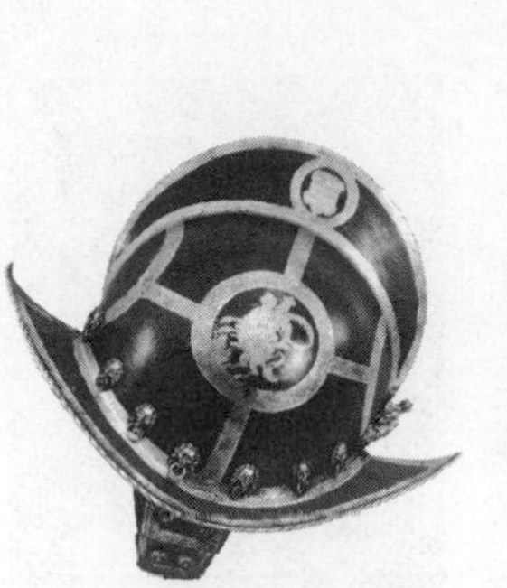

morion[1]
Made in early
17th-century Germany

mo·ri·on[1] (môr′ē-ŏn′, mōr′-) *n.* A crested metal helmet with a curved peak in front and back, worn by soldiers in the 16th and 17th centuries. [French, from Spanish *morrion,* from *morro,* crown of the head, from Vulgar Latin *murrum*† (unattested), round thing.]

mo·ri·on[2] (môr′ē-ŏn′, mōr′-) *n.* A variety of smoky quartz, often nearly black. [Manuscript error for Latin *mormorion*†.]

Mo·ris·co (mə-rĭs′kō) *n., pl.* **-cos** or **-coes.** A Spanish Moor. —*adj.* Moorish. Said of a style of architecture. [Spanish, from *Moro,* Moor, from Latin *Maurus,* MOOR.]

mo·ri·tu·ri te sa·lu·ta·mus (mō′rĭ-tōō′rē tä sä′lōō-tä′mōōs; môr′ĭ-tyŏŏr′ī tē săl′yōō-tā′məs). *Latin.* We who are about to die salute you. The gladiators' salutation to the Roman emperor.

Mor·ley (môr′lē), **Edward Williams.** 1838–1923. American chemist; collaborated in the **Michelson-Morley experiment** *(see).*

Mor·mon[1] (môr′mən). *Mormon Church.* An American prophet, warrior, and historian of the fourth century A.D., who was revealed to Joseph Smith as the author of a sacred history of the Americas, engraved on golden tablets, which Smith translated as the Book of Mormon.

Mor·mon[2] (môr′mən) *n.* **1.** A member of the Church of Jesus Christ of Latter-day Saints, founded by Joseph Smith in 1830 at Fayette, New York. **2.** A member of one of numerous sects deriving from Smith's original church that accept the Book of Mormon as the word of God. —*adj.* Of or pertaining to the Mormons, their religion, or their church. —**Mor′mon·ism′** *n.*

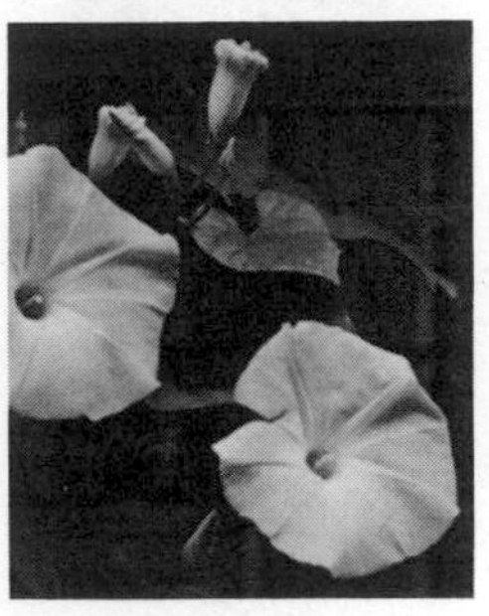

morning-glory
Ipomoea tricolor

morn (môrn) *n. Poetic.* The morning. [Middle English *morwen, morn,* Old English *morgen.* See **mer-**[1] in Appendix.*]

Mor·nay (môr-nā′) *n.* A white sauce flavored with grated Swiss or Parmesan cheese. [Probably after Philippe de *Mornay* (1549–1623), French Huguenot leader.]

morn·ing (môr′nĭng) *n.* **1.** The first or early part of the day, lasting from midnight to noon or from sunrise to noon. **2.** The hour from daybreak to sunrise; dawn. **3.** The first or early part of anything. [Middle English *morwening,* from *morwen,* MORN (by analogy with EVENING).] —**morn′ing** *adj.*

morn·ing-glo·ry (môr′nĭng-glôr′ē, -glōr′ē) *n., pl.* **-ries.** Any of various, usually twining vines of the genus *Ipomoea,* having funnel-shaped, variously colored flowers that close late in the day.

Morning Prayer. *Anglican Church.* The service of morning worship in the Book of Common Prayer. Also called "matins."

morning sickness. Nausea and vomiting upon rising in the morning, often one of the earlier symptoms of pregnancy.

morning star. A planet visible in the east just before sunrise, especially Venus.

Mo·ro (môr′ō, mōr′ō) *n., pl.* **-ros.** A member of any of the Moslem Malay tribes of the southern Philippines. [Spanish, from Latin *Maurus,* MOOR.] —**Mo′ro** *adj.*

mo·roc·co (mə-rŏk′ō) *n., pl.* **-cos.** *Abbr.* **mor. 1.** A soft, fine leather of goatskin tanned with sumac, made originally in Morocco. It is used chiefly for bookbindings and shoes. **2.** Any imitation of this. Also called "morocco leather."

Mo·roc·co (mə-rŏk′ō). *French* **Ma·roc** (mȧ-rôk′); *Spanish* **Mar·rue·cos** (mär-rwā′kōs). *Abbr.* **Mor.** A kingdom of northwestern Africa, independent since 1956. It has an area of about 172,000 square miles. Population, 11,598,000. Capital, Rabat. [Italian *Marocco,* from Arabic *Magrib-al-aqṣa,* "the extreme west" : *magrib,* west + *al,* the + *aqṣa,* extreme.] —**Mo·roc′can** (mə-rŏk′ən) *adj. & n.*

Mo·ro Gulf (môr′ō, mōr′ō). A wide inlet of the Celebes Sea in southwestern Mindanao, Republic of the Philippines.

mo·ron (môr′ŏn′, mōr′-) *n.* **1.** A mentally retarded person, specifically one having a mental age between 7 and 12 years or an intelligence quotient between 50 and 75. See **mental deficiency. 2.** A remarkably stupid or oafish person. [Greek *mōron,* neuter of *mōros,* foolish. See **mōuro-** in Appendix.*] **mo·ron′ic** (mə-rŏn′ĭk, mô-) *adj.* —**mo·ron′i·cal·ly** *adv.* —**mo′ron′·ism, mo·ron′i·ty** (mə-rŏn′ə-tē, mô-) *n.*

mo·rose (mə-rōs′, mô-) *adj.* Sullenly melancholy; gloomy; ill-humored. See Synonyms at **glum.** [Latin *mōrōsus,* captious, fretful, from *mōs* (stem *mōr-*), custom, manner, humor, caprice. See **mē-**[1] in Appendix.*] —**mo·rose′ly** *adv.* —**mo·rose′ness** *n.*

-morph. Indicates: **1.** A specified form, shape, or structure; for example, **endomorph. 2.** A morpheme; for example, **allomorph.** [Greek *-morphos,* from *morphē,* shape, form. See **mer-bh-** in Appendix.*]

morph. morphological; morphology.

mor·phal·lax·is (môr′fə-lăk′sĭs) *n. Biology.* The regeneration of a part, or the transformation of one part into another, by means of structural reorganization with only limited production of new cells, a process observed primarily in invertebrate organisms, such as certain lobsters. [New Latin, "structure exchange" : MORPH(O)- + Greek *allaxis,* exchange, from *allassein,* to exchange, from *allos,* other (see **al-**[1] in Appendix*).]

Morocco

mor·pheme (môr′fēm′) *n.* A linguistic unit of relatively stable meaning that cannot be divided into smaller meaningful parts, as words such as *man* or *most,* or word elements such as *-ly* or *al-* as found in *manly* and *almost.* [French *morphème,* from Greek *morphē,* form (by analogy with PHONEME). See **mer-bh-** in Appendix.*]

Mor·phe·us (môr′fē-əs, -fyōōs′). In Ovid's *Metamorphoses,* the god of dreams and of the forms dreaming sleepers see, now existing in popular literary allusion as the god of sleep, or sleep itself. —**Mor′phe·an** (-fē-ən) *adj.*

mor·phi·a (môr′fē-ə) *n. Obsolete.* Morphine. [New Latin : obsolete *morphium,* from *Morpheus* (see **morphine**) + -IA.]

mor·phic (môr′fĭk) *adj.* Pertaining to form; morphological. [MORPH(O)- + -IC.] —**mor′phi·cal·ly** *adv.*

-morphic, -morphous. Indicates possession of (some specified) shape or form; for example, **polymorphic, amorphous.** [From -MORPH.]

mor·phine (môr′fēn′) *n.* An organic compound, $C_{17}H_{19}NO_3$, extracted from opium, the soluble salts of which are used in human and veterinary medicine as a light anesthetic or as a sedative. Repeated dosage causes addiction. [French, from MORPHEUS.]

mor·phin·ism (môr′fē-nĭz′əm, môr′fə-) *n.* **1.** Morphine addiction. **2.** Poisoning caused by sustained or immoderate dosage of morphine, a chronic condition.

morpho-, morph-. Indicates: **1.** Shape, form, or structure; for example, **morphogenesis, morphology. 2.** Morpheme; for example, **morphophonemics.** [German, from Greek, from *morphē,* shape. See **mer-bh-** in Appendix.*]

mor·pho·gen·e·sis (môr′fō-jĕn′ə-sĭs) *n.* **1.** Evolutionary development of the structure of an organism or part. **2.** Embryological development of the structure of an organism or part. [New Latin : MORPHO- + GENESIS.] —**mor′pho·ge·net′ic** (-jə-nĕt′ĭk), —**mor′pho·gen′ic** *adj.*

morphol. morphological; morphology.

mor·phol·o·gy (môr-fŏl′ə-jē) *n. Abbr.* **morph., morphol. 1.** The biological study of the form and structure of living organisms. **2.** The structure and form of an organism, excluding its functions. **3.** *Geology.* The study of the structure of earth features, **geomorphology** *(see).* **4.** *Linguistics.* The study of word formation, including the origin and function of inflections and derivations. [German *Morphologie* : MORPHO- + -LOGY.] —**mor′pho·log′i·cal** (môr′fə-lŏj′ĭ-kəl), **mor′pho·log′ic** *adj.* —**mor′pho·log′i·cal·ly** *adv.* —**mor·phol′o·gist** *n.*

mor·pho·phone (môr′fə-fōn′) *n. Linguistics.* A family of different phonemes that are non-contrasting in the same words. [MORPHO- + PHONE.] —**mor′pho·phon′ics** (-fŏn′ĭks) *n.*

mor·pho·pho·ne·mics (môr′fō-fə-nē′mĭks) *n.* Plural in form, used with a singular verb. **1.** Linguistic structure in terms of the phonological patterning of morphemes, as through variations, such as the addition, loss, or substitution of phonemes, including stress shifts, which determine the different articulated shapes of morphemically related words. **2.** The study of relationships constituting this structure. [MORPHO- + PHONEMICS.] —**mor′pho·pho·ne′mic** *adj.*

mor·pho·sis (môr-fō′sĭs) *n., pl.* **-ses** (-sēz). The manner in which an organism or one of its parts changes form or the manner or order of its development. [New Latin, from Greek *morphōsis,* formation, from *morphoun,* to form, from *morphē,* form. See **mer-bh-** in Appendix.*]

-morphous. Variant of **-morphic.**

mor·ris (môr′ĭs, mŏr′-) *n.* An English folk dance in which a story is acted by costumed dancers. Also called "morris dance." [Middle English *Moreys,* Moorish, from *More,* MOOR.]

Mor·ris (môr′ĭs, mŏr′-), **Gouverneur.** 1752–1816. American diplomat and political leader.

Mor·ris (môr′ĭs, mŏr′-), **Robert.** 1734–1806. American Revolutionary War financier and political leader.

Mor·ris (môr′ĭs, mŏr′-), **William.** 1834–1896. English poet, artist, craftsman, and utopian socialist.

Morris chair. A large easy chair with arms, an adjustable back, and removable cushions. [Designed by William MORRIS.]

Mor·ris Jes·up, Cape (môr′ĭs jĕs′əp, mŏr′ĭs). The world's northernmost point of land, in northern Greenland on the Arctic Ocean, 440 miles from the North Pole. [After *Morris Ketchum Jesup* (1830–1908), American banker and philanthropist, sponsor of Perry's Arctic expeditions.]

Mor·ri·son, Mount. (môr′ə-sən, mŏr′-). *Chinese* **Sin·kao Shan** (shĭn′kou′shän′). The highest peak (over 13,000 feet) on Taiwan.

mor·row (môr′ō, mŏr′ō) *n.* **1.** The day following some specified day. **2.** The time immediately subsequent to some particular event. **3.** *Archaic.* The morning. [Middle English *morwe,* Old English *morgen.* See **mer-**[1] in Appendix.*]

Morse (môrs), **Samuel F(inley) B(reese).** 1791–1872. American artist; promoter of the telegraph (patented 1840).

Morse code. A system of communication in which letters of the alphabet and numbers are represented by short and long patterns, which may be conveyed as sounds, flashes of light, written dots and dashes, or wigwags of a flag. Also called "Morse," "Morse alphabet." [Invented by Samuel MORSE.]

mor·sel (môr′səl) *n.* **1.** A small piece or bite of food. **2.** A light meal; snack. **3.** A small piece or amount of anything. **4.** A tasty tidbit. [Middle English, from Old French *mors,* a bite, from Latin *morsum, mordēre,* to bite. See **mer-**[2] in Appendix.*]

mort[1] (môrt) *n. Hunting.* The note sounded on a horn to announce the death of the deer. [Middle English, death, from Old French, from Latin *mortem,* from *mors,* death. See **mer-**[2] in Appendix.*]

mort[2] (môrt) *n. British Regional.* A great number or quantity: *a mort of money.* [Possibly from MORTAL (extremely).]

mor·tal (môrt′l) *adj.* **1.** Liable or subject to death. **2.** Of or pertaining to man as a being who must die. **3.** Of, pertaining to, or accompanying death: *mortal throes.* **4.** Causing death; fatal; deadly: *"This wound is mortal and is mine."* (Aldous Hux-

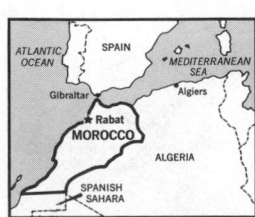

ley). **5.** Fought to the death: *"with victorious Germany and Italy engaged in mortal attack upon us"* (Winston Churchill). **6.** Unrelenting; implacable: *"Skyris Bolgolam . . . hath been your mortal enemy almost ever since your arrival."* (Swift). **7.** Of or like the fear of death; dire; grievous: *in mortal terror.* **8.** *Roman Catholic Church.* Entailing or causing spiritual death. Said of sins, crimes, or transgressions: *Suicide is a mortal sin.* Compare **venial.** **9.** Explicable in terms of this world; earthly; conceivable: *There is no mortal reason for us to go.* **10.** Very great; extreme: *"I go there a mortal sight of times"* (Dickens). **11.** Very long and tedious: *"Six mortal hours did I endure her loquacity."* (Scott). *—n.* A human being. *—adv. Regional.* Extremely; very: *"Never had she seen her sister look so mortal pretty."* (Conrad Richter). [Middle English, from Old French *mortal, mortel,* from Latin *mortālis,* from *mors* (stem *mort-*), death. See **mer-²** in Appendix.*] **—mor'tal·ly** *adv.*

mor·tal·i·ty (môr-tăl'ə-tē) *n., pl.* **-ties. 1.** The condition of being subject to death. **2.** Frequency of number of deaths in proportion to a population; death rate. **3.** Deadliness. **4.** The quality of being mortal. Said of a sin.

mor·tar (môr'tər) *n.* **1.** A receptacle made of a hard material in which substances are crushed or ground with a pestle. **2.** Any machine in which materials are ground and blended or crushed. **3.** *Military.* A muzzle-loading cannon used to fire shells at low velocities, short ranges, and great angular elevation. Also called "trench mortar." **4.** Any of several similar devices used for various purposes, such as shooting life lines across a stretch of water. **5.** A mixture of cement or lime with sand and water that is used in building. *—v.* **mortared, -taring, -tars.** *—tr.* **1.** To plaster or join with mortar. **2.** To bombard with a mortar; hit with mortar shells. *—intr.* To fire mortars. [Middle English *morter,* partly from Old English *mortere* and partly from Old French *mortier,* both from Latin *mortārium,* a mortar and the substance made in it. See **mer-²** in Appendix.*]

mor·tar·board (môr'tər-bôrd', -bōrd') *n.* **1.** A square board with a handle, for holding and carrying mortar. **2.** An academic cap topped by a flat square covered with cloth.

Morte d'Ar·thur, Le (lə môrt' där'thər). A collection of Arthurian stories compiled and translated from Old French by Sir Thomas Malory, and printed by William Caxton in 1485.

mort·gage (môr'gĭj) *n. Abbr.* **mtg., mtge.** *Law.* **1.** A temporary and conditional pledge of property to a creditor as security against a debt. **2.** A contract or deed specifying the terms of such a pledge. **3.** The claim that the mortgagee or creditor has upon property pledged in this manner. *—tr.v.* **mortgaged, -gaging, -gages. 1.** To pledge (property) by mortgage. **2.** To pledge or stake against future success or failure; place an advance liability upon. [Middle English *morgage,* from Old French *mortgage,* "dead pledge" : *mort,* dead, from Latin *mortuus,* from *mors* (stem *mort-*), death (see **mer-²** in Appendix*) + *gage,* GAGE (pledge).]

mort·ga·gee (môr'gĭ-jē') *n.* The holder of a mortgage.

mort·ga·gor (môr'gĭ-jôr', môr'gĭ-jər) *n.* Also **mort·gag·er** (môr'gĭ-jər). A person who mortgages his property.

mor·ti·cian (môr-tĭsh'ən) *n.* A funeral director; undertaker. [MORT(UARY) + -ICIAN.]

mor·ti·fi·ca·tion (môr'tə-fĭ-kā'shən) *n.* **1.** A feeling of shame, humiliation, or wounded pride. **2.** Mortifying of the body and appetites. **3.** The death or decay of one part of a living body; gangrene.

mor·ti·fy (môr'tə-fī') *v.* **-fied, -fying, -fies.** *—tr.* **1.** To cause to experience shame, humiliation, or wounded pride; humiliate. **2.** To discipline (one's body and appetites) by self-denial and austerity: *"to subdue and mortify all lusts and affections"* (George Herbert). **3.** To cause (a bodily part) to die, as by gangrene. *—intr.* **1.** To practice ascetic discipline or punishment of the body. **2.** To become gangrenous or necrosed, as a part of the body. —See Synonyms at **degrade.** [Middle English *mortifien,* from Old French *mortifier,* from Late Latin *mortificāre,* to cause to die : *mors* (stem *mort-*), death (see **mer-²** in Appendix*) + *-ficāre,* -FY.] **—mor'ti·fy'ing** *adj.*

mor·tise (môr'tĭs) *n.* Also **mor·tice. 1.** A cavity, usually rectangular, in a piece of wood, stone, or other material, prepared to receive a similarly shaped projection or **tenon** *(see)* of another piece, to hold the two together. **2.** *Printing.* A hole cut in a plate for the insertion of type. *—tr.v.* **mortised, -tising, -tises.** Also **mor·tice. 1.** To join or fasten securely, as with a mortise and tenon. **2.** To cut or make a mortise in. **3.** *Printing.* **a.** To cut a hole in (a plate) for the insertion of type. **b.** To cut such a hole and insert (type). [Middle English *mortays,* from Old French *mortoise*†.]

mort·main (môrt'mān') *n. Law.* Perpetual ownership of real estate by institutions such as churches that cannot transfer or sell them. Also called "dead hand." [Middle English *mortemayne,* from Old French *mortemain,* "dead hand" (i.e., institutional possession) : *morte,* feminine of *mort,* dead, from Latin *mortuus,* from *mors* (stem *mort-*), death (see **mer-²** in Appendix*) + *main,* hand, from Latin *manus* (see **man-²** in Appendix*).]

Mor·ton (môrt'n), **Ferdinand Joseph La Menthe ("Jelly Roll").** 1885–1941. American jazz pianist and composer.

Mor·ton (môrt'n), **Levi Parsons.** 1824–1920. Vice President of the United States under Benjamin Harrison (1889–93).

Mor·ton (môrt'n), **Thomas.** 1622?–1647? American colonial leader; established anti-Puritan community.

Mor·ton (môrt'n), **William Thomas Green.** 1819–1868. American dentist; first to use ether as an anesthetic (1846).

mor·tu·ar·y (môr'chōō-ĕr'ē) *n., pl.* **-ies.** A place where dead bodies are prepared or kept prior to burial or cremation. *—adj.* Of or pertaining to death or to the burial of the dead. [Middle English *mortuarie,* from Norman French, from Late Latin *mortuārium,* from *mortuārius,* of burial, from Latin *mortuus,* dead, from *mors* (stem *mort-*), death. See **mer-²** in Appendix.*]

mor·u·la (môr'ə-lə) *n., pl.* **-lae** (-lē'). **1.** The spherical embryonic mass of blastomeres formed before complete blastulation. Compare **gastrula. 2.** A spherical mass of developing male gametes occurring especially in certain annelid worms. [New Latin, from Latin *mōrum,* mulberry tree, from Greek *moron.* See **moro-** in Appendix.*] **—mor'u·lar** (-lər) *adj.*

mos. months.

mo·sa·ic (mō-zā'ĭk) *n.* **1.** A picture or decorative design made by setting small colored pieces, such as tile, in mortar. **2.** Anything that resembles a piece of mosaic work: *"I have tried to arrange these chunks and splinters so that they form a sort of personal mosaic."* (Kenneth Tynan). **3.** A virus disease of plants, resulting in light and dark areas in the leaves, which often become shriveled and dwarfed. **4.** Overlapping photographs, usually aerial, assembled into a composite picture. **5.** A photosensitive surface in the iconoscope of a television camera. *—tr.v.* **mosaicked, -icking, -ics. 1.** To make by mosaic or as if by mosaic. **2.** To adorn with mosaic or as if with mosaic. [Middle English *musycke,* from Old French *mosaique,* from Old Italian *mosaico,* from Medieval Latin *mosaicus, musaicus,* irregularly from Late Greek *mouseion,* a mosaic, from *mouseios,* belonging to the Muses, from *Mousa,* Muse. See **Mousa** in Appendix.*] **—mo·sa'ic** *adj.* **—mo·sa'i·cist** (mō-zā'ə-sĭst) *n.*

Mo·sa·ic (mō-zā'ĭk) *adj.* Also **Mo·sa·i·cal.** Of or pertaining to Moses or the laws and writings attributed to him. [New Latin *Mosaicus,* from MOSES.]

mosaic gold. An alloy resembling gold, **ormolu** *(see).*

Mosaic Law. The ancient law of the Hebrews, traditionally attributed to Moses and contained mainly in the Pentateuch. Also called "Law of Moses."

Mos·by (môz'bē), **John Singleton.** 1833–1916. American commander of Confederate raiders in the Civil War.

mos·cha·tel (mŏs'kə-tĕl', mŏs'kə-tĕl') *n.* A plant, *Adoxa moschatellina,* of northern regions, having greenish-white, musk-scented flowers. [French *moscatelle,* from Italian *moscatella,* from *moscato,* musk, from Late Latin *muscus,* MUSK.]

Mos·cow (mŏs'kou', -kō). *Russian* **Mos·kva** (mŏs-kvä'). The capital and largest city of the Soviet Union, in the western Russian S.F.S.R., of which it is also the capital. Population, 6,433,000.

Mos·cow River (mŏs'kou', -kō). A river rising in the eastern Smolensk-Moscow Upland, and flowing generally east 315 miles to join the Oka River near Kolomna.

Mose·ley (mōz'lē), **Henry Gwyn-Jeffreys.** 1887–1915. British physicist; developed modern form of the periodic table.

Mo·selle¹ (mō-zĕl'). *German* **Mo·sel** (mō'zəl). A river rising in northeastern France and flowing 320 miles to join the Rhine.

Mo·selle² (mō-zĕl') *n.* A light, dry white wine produced in the valley of the Moselle River.

Mo·ses¹ (mō'zĭz, -zĭs). A masculine given name. [Middle English *Moyse,* after MOSES.]

Mo·ses² (mō'zĭz, -zĭs). The lawgiver who led the Israelites out of Egypt. [Latin and Greek *Mōses,* from Hebrew *Mosheh,* possibly from Egyptian *mes,* child.]

mo·sey (mō'zē) *intr.v.* **-seyed, -seying, -seys.** *Informal.* **1.** To jog along. **2.** To get going; move along. [Origin obscure.]

Mos·lem (mŏz'ləm, mŏs'-) *n.* Also **Mus·lim, Mus·lem** (mŭz'ləm, mōōz'-, mŭs'-, mōōs'-), *archaic* **Mus·sul·man** (mŭs'əl-mən, mōōs'-). A believer in or adherent of Islam. [Arabic *muslim,* MUSLIM.] **—Mos'lem** *adj.*

Usage: *Moslem* is the form predominantly preferred in journalism and popular usage. *Muslim* is preferred by scholars and by English-speaking adherents of Islam; it is considered the only correct form by members of the **Nation of Islam** *(see).*

Moslem calendar. The lunar calendar used in Moslem countries. See **calendar.**

mosque (mŏsk) *n.* A Moslem house of worship. Also called "masjid," "musjid." [French *mosquée,* from Italian *moschea,* from Arabic *masjid,* a place of worship, from *sajada,* to worship.]

mos·qui·to (mə-skē'tō) *n., pl.* **-toes** or **-tos.** Any of various winged insects of the family Culicidae, in which the female of most species is distinguished by a long proboscis for sucking blood. Some species are vectors of diseases such as malaria and yellow fever. [Spanish, from *mosca,* fly, from Latin *musca.* See **mū-²** in Appendix.*]

Mos·qui·to (mŏ-skē'tō) *n., pl.* **Mosquito** or **-tos. 1.** A South American Indian people living on the Atlantic coast of Nicaragua and Honduras. **2.** The languages of this people.

mosquito boat. *Chiefly British.* A **PT boat** *(see).*

mosquito hawk. 1. A bird, the **nighthawk** *(see).* **2.** An insect, the **dragonfly** *(see).*

mosquito net. A fine net used to cover windows and beds to keep out mosquitoes.

moss (môs, mŏs) *n.* **1.** Any of various green, usually small plants of the class Musci within the division Bryophyta. **2.** A patch or covering of such plants. **3.** Any of various other plants that are similar in appearance or manner of growth, such as **club moss, Irish moss,** and **Spanish moss** *(all of which see).* **4.** *Chiefly Scottish.* A peat bog or moor. [Middle English *moss, mos,* Old English *mos.* See **meu-** in Appendix.*]

moss·back (môs'băk', mŏs'-) *n.* **1.** An old shellfish or turtle with a growth of algae on its back. **2.** *Slang.* An extremely conservative or old-fashioned person. **—moss'backed'** *adj.*

Möss·bau·er (mœs'bou'ər, mŏs'-), **Rudolf Ludwig.** Born

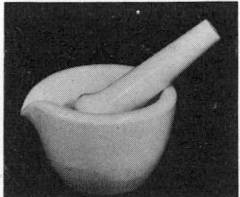

mortar
Porcelain mortar and pestle

A	·–	V	···–
B	–···	W	·––
C	–·–·	X	–··–
D	–··	Y	–·––
E	·	Z	––··
F	··–·	Á	·––·–
G	––·	Ä	·–·–
H	····	É	··–··
I	··	Ñ	––·––
J	·–––	Ö	–––·
K	–·–	Ü	··––
L	·–··	1	·––––
M	––	2	··–––
N	–·	3	···––
O	–––	4	····–
P	·––·	5	·····
Q	––·–	6	–····
R	·–·	7	––···
S	···	8	–––··
T	–	9	––––·
U	··–	0	–––––
, (comma)	––··––		
. (period)	·–·–·–		
?	··––··		
;	–·–·–·		
:	–––···		
/	–··–·		
- (hyphen)	–····–		
apostrophe	·––––·		
parenthesis	–·––·–		
underline	··––·–		

Morse code

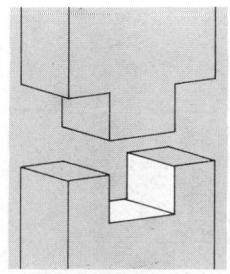

mortise

motion picture
Section of film showing
a football being kicked
toward the camera

mountain laurel

1929. German physicist; made experiments with gamma rays.
Mössbauer effect. *Physics.* The recoilless fluorescence of gamma rays having an extremely narrow frequency range from atomic nuclei bound in solids. [After Rudolf MÖSSBAUER.]
moss·bunk·er (môs'bŭng'kər, mŏs'-) *n.* Also **moss·bank·er** (môs'băng'kər, mŏs'-). A fish, the **menhaden** *(see).* [Dutch *marsbanker†.*]
moss campion. A low-growing plant, *Silene acaulis,* of cool regions, having purplish-red flowers and forming dense, cushionlike mats. Also called "cushion pink."
moss green. Moderate yellow green to grayish or moderate olive or dark yellowish green. See color. —**moss'-green'** *adj.*
moss-grown (môs'grōn', mŏs'-) *adj.* 1. Overgrown with moss. 2. Old-fashioned; antiquated.
mos·so (môs'sō) *adv. Music.* With motion or animation. Used as a direction. [Italian, from the past participle of *muovere,* to move, from Latin *movēre.* See mew- in Appendix.*]
moss pink. A low-growing plant, *Phlox subulata,* forming dense, mosslike mats. It is widely cultivated for its profuse pink or white flowers. Also called "ground pink."
moss rose. A variety of rose, *Rosa centifolia muscosa,* having fragrant pink flowers with a mossy flower stalk and calyx.
moss-troop·er (môs'trōō'pər, mŏs'-) *n.* 1. One of a band of raiders operating in the bogs on the borders of England and Scotland during the 17th century. 2. A raider or marauder.
moss·y (môs'ē, mŏs'ē) *adj.* **-ier, -iest.** 1. Covered with moss or something like moss. 2. Resembling moss. —**moss'i·ness** *n.*
most (mōst) *adj.* 1. a. Superlative of **many.** Greatest in number or quantity. b. Superlative of **much.** Largest or greatest in amount, size, or degree. 2. In the greatest number of instances: *Most fish have fins.* —*n.* 1. The greatest amount, quantity, or degree; the largest part: *Most of his land was fertile.* 2. The greatest number (of a group or classification); the majority. Used with a plural verb: *Most of her novels have been well received.* —**at (the) most.** Not over; at the absolute limit: *I walked four miles at the most.* —**make the most of.** 1. To use as advantageously as possible. 2. To attach undue importance to. —**the most.** *Slang.* A person or thing that produces great excitement or satisfaction. —*adv.* 1. In the highest degree, quantity, or extent. Used with many adjectives and adverbs to form the superlative degree: *most honest; most impatiently.* 2. Very: *a most impressive piece of writing.* 3. *Informal.* Almost: *Most everyone agrees.* See Usage note. [Middle English *most, mest, mast,* Old English *mǣst.* See mē-³ in Appendix.*]
Usage: The adverb *most,* in the sense of *almost,* is properly so written, not *'most.* However, 92 per cent of the Usage Panel term this usage unacceptable in writing, and 53 per cent condemn it in speech. In the sense of *very,* as an intensive where no explicit comparison is involved, 86 per cent accept *most* in written usage, and 96 per cent approve it in speech. "This has value as emphasis," Paul Horgan noted. "Adds emphasis to speech, weakness to writing," Virgil Thomson declared. See also Usage note at **mostly.**
-most. Forms the superlative degree of adverbs and adjectives; for example, **foremost, innermost.** [Middle English **-most,** **-mast,** Old English **-mǣst, -mest,** originally an independent superlative suffix, later erroneously regarded as being from the adverb **mǣst,** most.]
most·ly (mōst'lē) *adv.* For the most part; almost entirely.
Usage: Mostly cannot replace *most* when the desired sense is *to the greatest degree, very,* or *extremely: Those most* (not *mostly) affected are farmers.*
Mo·sul (mō-sōōl') *n.* A city in northern Iraq, on the Tigris opposite Nineveh. Population, 954,000.
mot (mō) *n.* A witticism or short, clever saying. [French, from Old French, from Vulgar Latin *mottum* (unattested), from Latin *muttum,* grunt, from *muttīre,* to mutter. See mu- in Appendix.*]
mote¹ (mōt) *n.* A speck, especially of dust. [Middle English *mot, moot,* Old English *mot.* See meu- in Appendix.*]
mote² (mōt) *intr.v. Archaic.* May; might. [Middle English *moten,* Old English *mōtan,* to be allowed. See med- in Appendix.*]
mo·tel (mō-tĕl') *n.* A hotel for motorists, usually with blocks of rooms opening directly on a parking area. Also called "motor court." [Blend of MOTOR and HOTEL.]
mo·tet (mō-tĕt') *n.* A polyphonic musical composition based on a text of a sacred nature and usually sung without accompaniment. [Middle English, from Old French, from *mot,* phrase, word, MOT.]
moth (môth, mŏth) *n., pl.* **moths** (môthz, mŏthz, môths, mŏths). 1. Any of numerous insects of the order Lepidoptera, generally distinguished from butterflies by their nocturnal activity, hairlike or feathery antennae, and stout bodies. 2. The clothes moth *(see).* [Middle English *motthe,* Old English *moththe.* See math- in Appendix.*]
moth ball. 1. A marble-sized ball, originally of camphor but now of naphthalene, stored with clothes to repel moths. 2. *Plural.* A condition of long storage: *warships put into moth balls.*
moth-ball (môth'bôl', mŏth'-) *tr.v.* **-balled, -balling, -balls.** To preserve with moth balls or some other method of storage.
moth-eat·en (môth'ēt'ən, mŏth'-) *adj.* 1. Eaten away by moths. 2. Old and timeworn: *a moth-eaten phrase.*
moth·er¹ (mŭth'ər) *n.* 1. A female that has borne an offspring. 2. A female who has adopted a child or otherwise established a maternal relationship with another person. 3. A creative or environmental source: *"Religion is the mother of the sciences."* (Tobias Dantzig). 4. A woman having some of the responsibilities of a mother: *a house mother.* 5. Qualities attributed to a mother, such as capacity to love: *a baby that appealed to the*

mother in her. 6. An affectionate, familiar term for addressing an elderly woman. —*adj.* 1. Being or resembling a mother: *a mother hen.* 2. Characteristic of a mother: *mother love.* 3. Having a maternal relationship: *the mother church.* 4. Derived from or as if from one's mother; native: *one's mother tongue.* —*tr.v.* **mothered, -ering, -ers.** 1. To give birth to; be the mother of. 2. To create and care for; instigate and carry through. 3. To watch over, nourish, and protect. [Middle English *moder,* Old English *mōdor.* See māter- in Appendix.*] —**moth'er·less** *adj.*
moth·er² (mŭth'ər) *n.* A stringy slime composed of yeast cells and bacteria that forms on the surface of fermenting liquids. It is added to wine or cider to start production of vinegar. Also called "mother of vinegar." [Probably from MOTHER, partly by association with afterbirth.]
Mother Car·ey's chicken (kâr'ēz). Any of various petrels, especially the **storm petrel** *(see).* [Possibly from Latin *Mater Cara,* "Dear Mother," title of the Virgin Mary as patroness of seamen.]
Mother Goose. The eponym of *"Mother Goose's Tales,"* title of the traditional collection of the main bulk of English nursery rhymes, first collected in the 18th century.
moth·er·hood (mŭth'ər-hŏŏd') *n.* 1. The state or condition of being a mother. 2. The feelings or qualities characteristic of a mother. 3. Mothers collectively.
Mother Hub·bard (hŭb'ərd). 1. The title of a well-known nursery rhyme. 2. A woman's long, loose, unbelted dress.
moth·er-in-law (mŭth'ər-ĭn-lô') *n., pl.* **mothers-in-law.** The mother of one's wife or husband.
moth·er·land (mŭth'ər-lănd') *n.* 1. The land or country of one's birth. 2. The native land of one's ancestors.
moth·er·ly (mŭth'ər-lē) *adj.* Of, befitting, resembling, or characteristic of a mother; maternal. —*adv.* In the manner of a mother. —**moth'er·li·ness** *n.*
moth·er-of-pearl (mŭth'ər-əv-pûrl') *n.* The pearly internal layer of certain mollusk shells, used to make decorative objects. Also called "nacre." —**moth'er-of-pearl'** *adj.*
Mother's Day. An annual day of commemoration of mothers and motherhood observed the second Sunday in May.
mother superior. A woman in charge of a female religious community.
mother tongue. 1. One's native language. 2. The language from which another is derived.
mother wit. Innate intelligence; common sense.
moth·er·wort (mŭth'ər-wûrt', -wôrt) *n.* Any of several plants of the genus *Leonurus;* especially, *L. cardiaca,* a weed having clusters of small purple or pink flowers. [Middle English *moderwort : moder,* MOTHER (from its once reputed power to cure diseases of the uterus) + WORT.]
moth mullein. A plant, *Verbascum blattaria,* native to Eurasia, having spikelike clusters of yellow or white flowers.
moth-proof (môth'prōōf', mŏth'-) *adj.* Resistant to damage by moths. —*tr.v.* **mothproofed, -proofing, -proofs.** To make resistant to damage by moths.
moth·y (mô'thē, mŏth'ē) *adj.* **-ier, -iest.** Infested by moths.
mo·tif (mō-tēf') *n.* Also **mo·tive** (mō'tĭv, mō-tēv'). 1. A recurrent thematic element used in the development of an artistic or literary work. 2. A short significant phrase in a musical composition. 3. A repeated figure or design in architecture or decoration. [French, from Old French, MOTIVE.]
mo·tile (mōt'l, mō'tĭl') *adj.* Moving or having the power to move spontaneously, as certain spores and microorganisms. —*n. Psychology.* A person whose mental imagery chiefly consists of his own bodily motion. [From MOTION.] —**mo·til'i·ty** (mō-tĭl'ə-tē) *n.*
mo·tion (mō'shən) *n.* 1. The action or process of change of position. 2. A meaningful or expressive change in the position of the body or a part of the body; a gesture or movement. 3. The way in which a body moves; gait. 4. The ability or power to move. 5. A prompting from within; an impulse or inclination. 6. *Music.* Melodic ascent and descent of pitch. 7. *Law.* An application to a court for a ruling. 8. A formal proposal put to the vote under parliamentary procedures. —*v.* **motioned, -tioning, -tions.** —*tr.* To signal to or direct by making a gesture. —*intr.* To make a gesture signifying something, such as agreement. [Middle English *mocioun,* from Old French *motion,* from Latin *mōtiō,* from *movēre* (past participle *mōtus),* to move. See mew- in Appendix.*]
mo·tion·less (mō'shən-lĭs) *adj.* Not moving. —**mo'tion·less·ly** *adv.* —**mo'tion·less·ness** *n.*
motion picture. 1. A series of filmed images viewed in sufficiently rapid succession to create the illusion of motion and continuity. 2. The thematically connected content of images so filmed and viewed. Also called "moving picture," "cinema," and informally "movie."
motion sickness. A malady induced by motion, as in travel by airplane, car, ship, or other vehicle, and characterized by nausea, vomiting, and often dizziness.
motion study. **Time and motion study** *(see).*
mo·ti·vate (mō'tə-vāt') *tr.v.* **-vated, -vating, -vates.** To stimulate to action; provide with an incentive or motive; impel; incite. [From MOTIVE.]
mo·ti·va·tion (mō'tə-vā'shən) *n.* 1. The act or process of motivating. 2. An incentive, inducement, or motive, especially for an act. —**mo'ti·va'tion·al** *adj.*
motivational research. The use of certain techniques borrowed from psychology and sociology, especially by advertisers and marketers, to assess consumer attitudes toward products and services. Also "motivation research."
mo·tive (mō'tĭv; *also* mō-tēv' *for sense 2) n.* 1. An emotion,

desire, physiological need, or similar impulse acting as an incitement to action. **2.** A **motif** *(see)*. *—adj.* **1.** Causing or able to cause motion: *motive pleas.* **2.** Of, pertaining to, or constituting a motive. *—tr.v.* **motived, -tiving, -tives.** To provide with an incentive; motivate. [Middle English, from Old French *motif,* from adjective, "causing to move," from Late Latin *mōtīvus,* from Latin *movēre* (past participle *mōtus*), to move. See **mew-** in Appendix.*] **—mo·tiv′i·ty** *n.*

mot juste (mō zhüst′) *pl.* **mots justes** (mō zhüst′). *French.* The most suitable word or expression.

mot·ley (mŏt′lē) *adj.* **1.** Having components of great variety; heterogeneous: *"I did not realize how motley are the qualities that go to make up a human being."* (Maugham). **2.** Exhibiting or having many colors; multicolored. —See Synonyms at **miscellaneous.** *—n.* **1.** The professional attire of a court jester. **2.** A heterogeneous mixture or assemblage. [Middle English *motteley*†.]

Mot·ley (mŏt′lē), **John Lothrop.** 1814–1877. American historian and diplomat; specialized in history of the Netherlands.

mot·mot (mŏt′mŏt′) *n.* Any of several tropical American birds of the family Momotidae, usually having green and blue plumage. [American Spanish *mot-mot* (imitative).]

mo·to·neu·ron (mō′tə-no͝or′ŏn′, -nyo͝or′ŏn′) *n. Anatomy.* A neuron that stimulates motion; motor nerve cell. [MOTO(R) + NEURON.]

mo·tor (mō′tər) *n.* **1.** Something that imparts or produces motion, such as a machine or engine. **2.** A device that converts any form of energy into mechanical energy, especially an **internal-combustion engine** *(see)*, or an arrangement of coils and magnets that converts electric current into mechanical power. **3.** A motorized conveyance, especially an automobile. *—adj.* **1.** Causing or producing motion: *motor power.* **2.** Driven by or having a motor: *a motor scooter.* **3.** Of, pertaining to, or for motor vehicles: *motor oil.* **4.** Of, pertaining to, or designating nerves carrying impulses from the nerve centers to the muscles. **5.** Of or relating to movements of the muscles: *motor coordination.* *—v.* **motored, -toring, -tors.** *—intr.* To drive or travel in a motor vehicle. *—tr.* To carry by motor vehicle. [Latin *mōtor,* agential noun of *movēre* (past participle *mōtus*), to move. See **mew-** in Appendix.*]

mo·tor·bike (mō′tər-bīk′) *n.* **1.** A lightweight motorcycle. **2.** A pedal bicycle that has an attached motor.

mo·tor·boat (mō′tər-bōt′) *n.* A boat propelled by an internal-combustion engine. Also called "powerboat."

mo·tor·bus (mō′tər-bŭs′) *n., pl.* **-buses** or **-busses.** A bus that is powered by an internal-combustion engine or other type of motor. Also called "motor coach."

mo·tor·cade (mō′tər-kād′) *n.* A procession of automobiles or other motor vehicles. [MOTOR + (CAVAL)CADE.]

mo·tor·car (mō′tər-kär′) *n.* An automobile.

motor court. A type of hotel, a **motel** *(see)*.

mo·tor·cy·cle (mō′tər-sī′kəl) *n.* A vehicle with two wheels in tandem, propelled by an internal-combustion engine, and sometimes having a side car with a third wheel. *—intr.v.* **motorcycled, -cycling, -cycles.** To ride on or drive a motorcycle. **—mo′tor·cy′clist** (-sī′klĭst) *n.*

motor drive. A system consisting of an electric motor and accessory parts, used to power machinery.

mo·tor·ist (mō′tər-ĭst) *n.* One who travels in an automobile.

mo·tor·ize (mō′tə-rīz′) *tr.v.* **-ized, -izing, -izes. 1.** To equip with a motor or motors. **2.** To supply with motor-driven vehicles in substitution for ones drawn by horses or other animals. **3.** To provide motor vehicle transportation for. **—mo′tor·i·za′tion** *n.*

mo·tor·man (mō′tər-mən) *n., pl.* **-men** (-mĭn). One who drives an electrically powered streetcar, locomotive, or subway train.

motor scooter. A two-wheeled vehicle with small wheels and a low-powered gasoline engine geared to the rear wheel.

mo·tor·ship (mō′tər-shĭp′) *n.* A ship powered by an internal-combustion engine.

motor vehicle. Any self-propelled, wheeled conveyance that does not run on rails.

Mott (mŏt), **Lucretia Coffin.** 1793–1880. American Quaker advocate of abolitionism, women's rights, and temperance.

motte (mŏt) *n.* Also **mott.** *Western U.S.* A copse or small stand of trees on a prairie. [Mexican Spanish *mata,* from Spanish, shrub, probably from Late Latin *matta,* MAT.]

mot·tle (mŏt′l) *tr.v.* **-tled, -tling, -tles.** To cover (a surface) with spots or streaks of different shades or colors. *—n.* **1.** A spot of color or shading contrasting with the rest of the surface on which it is found. **2.** A variegated pattern, as on marble. [Probably back-formation from MOTLEY.]

mot·to (mŏt′ō) *n., pl.* **-toes** or **-tos. 1.** A brief sentence, phrase, or single word used to express a principle, goal, or ideal; maxim. **2.** A briefly stated sentiment of appropriate character inscribed on or attached to an object. —See Synonyms at **saying.** [Italian, "a word," from Gallo-Roman *mottum* (unattested), a sound uttered, from Latin *muttum,* a mutter, grunt, from *muttīre,* to mutter. See **mu-** in Appendix.*]

mouch. *Chiefly British.* Variant of **mooch.**

moue (mo͞o) *n.* A grimace; a pout. [French, from Old French, from (unattested) Frankish *mauwa* (probably imitative).]

mou·flon (mo͞of′lŏn′) *n., pl.* **mouflon** or **-flons.** Also **mouf·flon.** A wild sheep, *Ovis musimon,* of Sardinia and Corsica. [French, from Italian *muflone,* from Sardinian *muvrone,* from Late Latin *mufrō*†, sheep.]

mouil·lé (mo͞o-yā′) *adj. Phonetics.* Pronounced palatally; palatalized, for example, the *ll* in the word *mouillé.* [French, past participle of *mouiller,* to moisten, palatalize, from Old French *moullier,* to soften by soaking, from Vulgar Latin *molliāre* (unattested), from Latin *mollis,* soft. See **mel-¹** in Appendix.*]

mou·jik. Variant of **muzhik.**

mou·lage (mo͞o-läzh′) *n.* **1.** The making of a mold of a mark, such as a footprint, especially for identification. **2.** A mold of this kind. [French, from Old French, from *mouler,* to mold, from *moule, modle,* a mold, from Latin *modulus,* diminutive of *modus,* a measure, manner. See **med-** in Appendix.*]

mould. *Chiefly British.* Variant of **mold.**

mou·lin (mo͞o-lăN′) *n.* A vertical shaft in a glacier, kept open by falling water and rock debris. [French, "mill," from Old French, from Late Latin *molīnum,* from Latin *molīnus,* of a mill, from *mola,* mill, millstone. See **melə-** in Appendix.*]

Moul·mein (mo͞ol-mān′, mōl-). Also **Maul·main** (mōl-mān′, môl-). The capital of Tenasserim, Burma; a seaport in the south on the Gulf of Martaban. Population, 190,000.

moult. *Chiefly British.* Variant of **molt.**

mound (mound) *n.* **1.** A pile of earth, gravel, sand, rocks, or debris heaped for protection or concealment. **2.** A natural elevation, such as a small hill. **3.** Any raised mass, as of hay. **4.** *Baseball.* The slightly elevated pitcher's area in the center of the diamond. *—tr.v.* **mounded, mounding, mounds. 1.** To fortify or conceal with a mound. **2.** To heap in a mound. [Originally "an enclosing hedge or fence," perhaps from Dutch *mond,* protection, or from Old Norse *mund.* See **man-²** in Appendix.*]

Mound Builder. A member of one of the prehistoric North American Indian tribes who built burial and effigy mounds, mainly in the Mississippi valley.

mount¹ (mount) *v.* **mounted, mounting, mounts.** *—tr.* **1.** To climb or ascend. **2.** To get up on; place oneself upon: *mount a horse.* **3.** To get up on in order to copulate. Used of male animals. **4.** To provide with a riding horse or horses: *The stable mounted all the riders.* **5.** To prepare, place, or fix on or in an appropriate or convenient setting, as for display, study, or use: *mount pictures on cardboard.* **6.** To provide with scenery, costumes, and other accessories: *mount a theatrical performance.* **7.** *Military.* **a.** To set (guns) in position. **b.** To put in readiness and start to carry out: *mount an attack.* **c.** To be furnished with or carry: *The warship mounted ten guns.* **d.** To post (a guard): *mount sentries.* *—intr.v.* **1.** To go or move upward. **2.** To get or climb up on a horse or vehicle. **3.** To increase, as in amount, degree, extent, intensity, or number. —See Synonyms at **rise.** *—n.* **1. a.** A horse, other animal, or vehicle on which to ride. **b.** The opportunity to ride a horse, especially in a race. **2.** An object to which another is affixed or on which another is placed for accessibility, display, or use. [Middle English *mounten,* from Old French *monter,* from Vulgar Latin *montāre* (unattested), "to climb a mountain," from Latin *mōns* (stem *mont-*), mountain. See **men-²** in Appendix.*] **—mount′a·ble** *adj.*

mount² (mount) *n.* **1.** *Abbr.* **Mt., mt.** A mountain or hill. Used chiefly as part of a proper name or in poetry. **2.** In palmistry, any of the seven fleshy cushions around the edges of the palm of the hand. [Middle English *mont, munt,* from Old French *mont* and Old English *munt,* both from Latin *mōns* (stem *mont-*), mountain. See **men-²** in Appendix.*]

Mount, Mount of. For names of actual mountains, see the specific element of the name; for example, **McKinley, Mount; Olives, Mount of.** Names of places other than mountains beginning with *Mount* are entered under **Mount**; for example, **Mount Vernon.**

moun·tain (moun′tən) *n. Abbr.* **Mt., mt., mtn. 1.** A natural elevation of the earth's surface having considerable mass, generally steep sides, and a height greater than that of a hill. **2. a.** A large heap: *a mountain of ironing.* **b.** A huge quantity: *a mountain of trouble.* **3.** *Capital* **M.** The extreme revolutionary party of the French Revolution, so called because its members occupied the uppermost seats in the National Convention Hall in 1793. Used with *the.* [Middle English *mountaine,* from Old French *montaigne,* from Vulgar Latin *montānea* (unattested), from Latin *montānus,* mountainous, from *mōns* (stem *mont-*), mountain. See **men-²** in Appendix.*] **—moun′tain** *adj.*

mountain ash. 1. Any of various deciduous trees of the genus *Sorbus,* such as the **rowan** *(see)*, or *S. americana,* of eastern North America, having clusters of small white flowers and bright orange-red berries. **2.** An ash tree, *Fraxinus texensis,* of Texas. **3.** Any of several Australian eucalyptus trees.

mountain cranberry. A plant, the **cowberry** *(see)*.

mountain dew. *Slang.* Illegally distilled corn liquor.

moun·tain·eer (moun′tən-îr′) *n.* **1.** An inhabitant of a mountainous area. **2.** One who climbs mountains for sport. *—intr.v.* **mountaineered, -eering, -eers.** To climb mountains for sport.

mountain goat. A hoofed mammal, *Oreamnos americanus,* of the northwestern North American mountains, having short, curved black horns and yellowish-white hair and beard. Also called "Rocky Mountain goat."

mountain laurel. An evergreen shrub, *Kalmia latifolia,* of eastern North America, having leathery, poisonous leaves and clusters of pink or white flowers. Also called "calico bush."

mountain lion. A large, powerful, wild cat, *Felis concolor,* of mountainous regions of the Western Hemisphere, having an unmarked tawny body. Also called "catamount," "cougar," "mountain cat," "panther," "puma."

mountain mint. Any of various aromatic North American plants of the genus *Pycnanthemum,* having clusters of small white or purplish flowers.

moun·tain·ous (moun′tən-əs) *adj.* **1.** Of or pertaining to a region having many mountains. **2.** Of impressive size or height.

mountain sheep. 1. The **bighorn** *(see)*. **2.** Any wild sheep native to a mountainous area.

mountain ash
Sorbus americana
Foliage and berries

motorcycle

mountain goat

mountain sickness. Shortness of breath, nausea, headache, nosebleed, and other symptoms caused by insufficient oxygen at high altitudes.
Mountains of the Moon. See **Ruwenzori.**
Mountain Standard Time. *Abbr.* **MST, M.S.T.** Time at the 105th meridian west of Greenwich, England, and in the seventh time zone based on it in North America. It is seven hours earlier than Greenwich time. See **standard time.**
Mount Ath·os (ăth′əs, ā′thŏs). An autonomous monastic republic located on a peninsula in northeastern Greece.
Mount·bat·ten (mount-băt′n), **Louis.** First Earl Mountbatten of Burma. Born 1900. British naval officer; supreme Allied commander in Southeast Asia (1943–46); last viceroy and first governor general of India (1947).
Mount Des·ert (dĕz′ərt, dĭ-zûrt′). An island summer resort, about 100 square miles in area, off the southern coast of Maine.
moun·te·bank (moun′tə-băngk′) *n.* **1.** A hawker of quack medicines and nostrums who attracts customers with stories, jokes, or tricks. **2.** Any charlatan or trickster. —See Synonyms at **impostor.** [Italian *montambanco, montimbanco,* "one who climbs on a bench" : *montare,* to mount, from Vulgar Latin *montāre* (unattested), from Latin *mōns,* mountain (see **men-**[2] in Appendix*) + *in,* in, on, from Latin (see **en** in Appendix*) + *banco, banca,* bench (see **bheg-** in Appendix*).]
mount·ed (moun′tĭd) *adj.* **1.** Seated upon or riding on a horse, bicycle, or other means of conveyance. **2.** Serving on horseback, or equipped with a horse or horses: *a mounted policeman.* **3.** Fitted into or set in a backing or support.
mount·ing (moun′tĭng) *n.* **1.** The act of rising or getting up on something. **2.** That which provides a backing or appropriate setting for something else: *a mounting for a gem.*
Mount Mc·Kin·ley National Park (mə-kĭn′lē). A national park, 3,030 square miles in area, in the Alaska Range in south-central Alaska.
Mount Rai·nier National Park (rə-nîr′, rā-). A national park, 378 square miles in area, in the Cascade Range of west-central Washington.
Mount Rush·more National Memorial (rŭsh′môr′, -mōr′). Portraits 60 feet high of George Washington, Thomas Jefferson, Abraham Lincoln, and Theodore Roosevelt, sculptured in the side of Mount Rushmore in South Dakota's Black Hills.
Mount Ver·non (vûr′nən). **1.** The estate of George and Martha Washington, situated on the banks of the Potomac River near Washington, D.C. **2.** A city of New York, located just north of the Bronx, New York City. Population, 76,000.
Mount·y (moun′tē) *n., pl.* **-ies.** Also **Mount·ie.** *Informal.* A Royal Canadian Mounted Policeman.
mourn (môrn, mōrn) *v.* **mourned, mourning, mourns.** —*intr.* **1.** To express or feel grief or sorrow, especially for someone who has died. **2.** To express public grief for a death by conventional signs; be in mourning. —*tr.* To feel or express sorrow for; bewail; deplore. [Middle English *mournen,* Old English *murnan.* See **smer-**[1] in Appendix.*] —**mourn′er** *n.*
mourn·ful (môrn′fəl, mōrn′-) *adj.* **1.** Feeling or expressing grief: *"Sweet I hear the mournful song"* (Blake). **2.** Arousing or suggesting grief: *"the mournful notes of a whippoorwill"* (James Fenimore Cooper). —**mourn′ful·ly** *adv.* —**mourn′ful·ness** *n.*
mourn·ing (môr′nĭng, mōr′-) *n.* **1.** The actions or expressions of one who has suffered a bereavement. **2.** The symbols or conventional outward signs of grief for the dead. **3.** The period during which a death is mourned. —**in mourning. 1.** Wearing clothes conventionally expressive of mourning, as a black tie or armband, or entirely black clothes. **2.** Abiding by appropriate conduct during a period of mourning. —**mourn′ing·ly** *adv.*
mourning cloak. A butterfly, *Nymphalis antiopa,* of Europe and North America, having purplish-brown wings with a broad yellow border. Also called "Camberwell beauty."
mourning dove. A wild dove, *Zenaidura macroura,* of North America, noted for its plaintive call. Also called "turtledove."
mourning warbler. A warbler, *Oporornis philadelphia,* of eastern North America, noted for its plaintive song.
mouse (mous) *n., pl.* **mice** (mīs). **1. a.** Any of numerous small rodents of the families Muridae and Cricetidae, such as the common house mouse, *Mus musculus,* or the harvest mouse, *Reithrodontomys humilis* and related species, characteristically having a long, naked or almost hairless tail. **b.** Any of various similar or related animals, such as the **jumping mouse** or the **pocket mouse** *(both of which see).* **2.** *Informal.* **a.** An affectionate term for a little girl or young woman. **b.** A cowardly or timid person. **3.** *Slang.* A black eye. **4.** A mousing on a hook. —*intr.v.* (mouz) **moused, mousing, mouses. 1.** To hunt, stalk, or catch mice. **2.** To search furtively for something; prowl. [Mouse, mice; Middle English *mous, mys,* Old English *mūs, mȳs.* See **mū-**[1] in Appendix.*]
Mouse. *Regional.* The **Souris** River *(see).*
mouse deer. A **chevrotain** *(see).*
mous·er (mou′zər) *n.* An animal that catches mice
mouse·tail (mous′tāl′) *n.* Any plant of the genus *Myosurus,* especially *M. minimus,* having a taillike flower spike.
mouse·trap (mous′trăp′) *n.* A trap for catching mice.
mous·ing (mou′zĭng) *n. Nautical.* **1.** A binding around the point and shank of a hook to prevent it from slipping from an eye. **2.** A metal shackle used for the same purpose.
mousse (mo͞os) *n.* **1.** Any of various chilled desserts made with whipped cream, gelatin, and flavoring. **2.** A molded dish made from a purée of meat, fish, or shellfish with whipped cream. [French *mousse*†, "froth."]
mousse·line (mo͞os-lēn′) *n.* A fine cotton fabric originally made in Mosul, Iraq. [French, MUSLIN.]

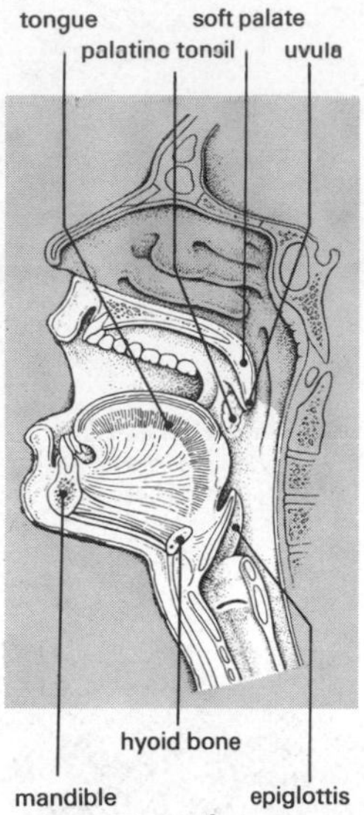

mouth

mourning dove

Mous·sorg·sky (mə-zôrg′skē), **Modest Petrovich.** Also **Mussorg·sky.** 1835–1881. Russian composer of operas, songs, and piano and orchestral works.
mous·tache. *Chiefly British.* Variant of **mustache.**
Mous·te·ri·an, Mous·tie·ri·an (mo͞o-stîr′ē-ən) *adj. Archaeology.* Designating or belonging to a Middle Paleolithic culture following the Acheulian. [French *moustérien, moustiérien,* from *Le Moustier,* village in southwestern France near which archaeological specimens were found.]
mous·y (mou′sē, -zē) *adj.* **-ier, -iest.** Also **mous·ey.** Mouselike in color, features, or shyness: *mousy hair; a mousy person.*
mouth (mouth) *n., pl.* **mouths** (mouthz). **1.** *Anatomy.* **a.** The body opening through which an animal takes in food; the oral cavity. **b.** The system of related organs including the lips, teeth, tongue, and associated parts, with which food is chewed and swallowed and sounds and speech are articulated. **2.** The part of the lips visible on the human face. **3.** A person viewed as a consumer of food: *"Mouths without hands, maintained at vast expense."* (Dryden). **4.** A pout, grimace, or similar expression. **5. a.** Capacity of speech; propensity for speaking: *"A fool's mouth is his destruction."* (Proverbs 18:7). **b.** A manner of speech. Used disparagingly: *a foul mouth; a big mouth.* **6.** A natural opening, such as the part of a stream or river that empties into a larger body of water, or the entrance to a harbor, canyon, valley, or cave. **7.** The opening through which any container is filled or emptied. **8.** An opening in tools and devices whose function is to hold or grip. **9. a.** An opening in the pipe of an organ. **b.** The opening in the mouthpiece of a flute across which the player blows. —**down in** (or **at**) **the mouth.** *Informal.* Crestfallen; unhappy. —**shut** (or **stop**) **one's mouth.** To desist from speaking. —*v.* (mouth). **mouthed, mouthing, mouths.** —*tr.* **1.** To utter in a meaninglessly declamatory manner: *"the mouthing of a man whose praise would be as insolent as his slander is impotent"* (Oscar Wilde). **2.** To put, take, or move around in the mouth. —*intr.* **1.** To orate affectedly; declaim; rant. **2.** To grimace. [Middle English *mouth,* Old English *mūth.* See **menth-** in Appendix.*]
mouth·breed·er (mouth′brē′dər) *n.* Any of various unrelated fishes that carry their eggs and young in the mouth.
mouth·ful (mouth′fo͝ol′) *n., pl.* **mouthfuls. 1.** The amount of food or other material that can be placed or held in the mouth at one time. **2.** A small amount to be tasted or eaten. **3.** *Informal.* An utterance that is complicated or difficult to pronounce. —**say a mouthful.** *Slang.* To utter an important or especially perceptive remark or observation.
mouth organ. Either of two musical instruments, a **harmonica** or a **panpipe** *(both of which see).*
mouth·piece (mouth′pēs′) *n.* **1.** A part, as of a musical instrument or a telephone, that functions in or near the mouth. **2.** A protective rubber device worn over the teeth by boxers. **3.** *Informal.* A spokesman. **4.** *Slang.* A defense lawyer.
mouth·y (mou′thē, -thē) *adj.* **-ier, -iest.** Given to ranting; grandiloquent; bombastic. —**mouth′i·ly** *adv.* —**mouth′i·ness** *n.*
mou·ton (mo͞o′tŏn′) *n.* Sheepskin sheared and processed to resemble beaver or seal, and used for garments. [French, "sheep," from Old French *mo(u)ton,* MUTTON.]
mou·ton·née (mo͞o′tə-nā′) *adj.* Also **mou·ton·néed** (-nād′). *Geology.* Rounded by glacial action to a shape likened to a sheep's back, as a rock formation. See **roche moutonnée.**
mov·a·ble (mo͞o′və-bəl) *adj.* Also **move·a·ble. 1.** Capable of being moved. **2.** Varying in date from year to year: *a movable feast.* **3.** *Law.* Of or pertaining to personal property that can be moved, as opposed to real property such as land. —*n. Usually plural.* **1.** Something that can be moved, especially furniture, as opposed to permanent fixtures. **2.** *Law.* Personal property, as distinguished from real property such as land. —**mov′a·bil′i·ty, mov′a·ble·ness** *n.* —**mov′a·bly** *adv.*
Usage: *Movable* denotes capacity for being moved, without implying great facility for movement. *Mobile* stresses such facility. Thus, *mobile equipment* is designed expressly for ready movement.
move (mo͞ov) *v.* **moved, moving, moves.** —*intr.* **1.** To change in position from one point to another. **2.** To march, as an army or procession. **3.** To progress in sequence, as in the development of a literary or musical composition. **4.** To follow some specified course: *The earth moves in orbit around the sun.* **5. a.** To be transferred from one position to another in a board game. **b.** To transfer a piece in a board game. **6.** To settle in a new place of residence or business; relocate. **7.** To change hands commercially: *Furs move slowly in summer.* **8.** To change posture or position; stir: *"On his bench in Madison Square Soapy moved uneasily."* (O. Henry). **9.** To be stirred: *The foliage moved in the breeze.* **10.** To stir the emotions: *High art must teach, delight, and move.* **11.** To be put into motion or to turn according to a prescribed motion. Used of machinery. **12.** To hum with activity; be busy. **13.** To initiate some action: *We will wait for the election returns before we move.* **14.** To behave or proceed in a certain manner. **15.** To live or be active in a particular environment: *move in diplomatic circles.* **16.** To make a formal motion in parliamentary procedure: *move for an adjournment.* **17.** To evacuate; void. Used of the bowels. —*tr.* **1. a.** To change the place of; shift; remove; displace: *move one's household.* **b.** To change the position of: *move one's fingers.* **2.** To dislodge from a fixed point of view, especially by persuasion. **3.** To prompt (someone) to some action; actuate: *"I am not moved by the power of ambition or avarice."* (William Penn). **4.** To set or maintain in motion. **5.** To set astir; agitate; shake: *The wind moved the blossoms.* **6.** To arouse or upset (a person): *"We have been moved already beyond endurance, and need rest."*

(John Maynard Keynes). **7.** To excite or provoke to the expression of some feeling: *"far too freely moved to tears"* (Hilaire Belloc). **8.** To affect deeply. **9.** *Archaic.* To arouse (someone's feelings): *"But Jack so moved their patience, they shot him."* (Captain John Smith). **10.** To propose or request in formal parliamentary procedure: *move adjournment.* **11.** To cause (the bowels) to evacuate. —See Synonyms at **affect.** —**move heaven and earth.** To make a tremendous effort. —*n.* **1.** An act of moving: *Nobody dared make a move.* **2.** A change of residence or place of business. **3.** In board games: **a.** An act of transferring a piece from one position to another. **b.** The prescribed manner in which a piece may be maneuvered. **c.** A player's turn to maneuver one of his pieces. **4.** One of a series of calculated actions undertaken to achieve some end. —**get a move on.** *Informal.* To get started; get going. —**on the move. 1.** In the process of moving about; traveling. **2.** Making progress; advancing. [Middle English *moven,* from Norman French *mover,* variant of Old French *moveir,* from Latin *movēre,* to move. See **mew-** in Appendix.*]

move·a·ble. Variant of **movable.**

move·ment (mōōv'mənt) *n.* **1. a.** An act of moving; a change in position. **b.** *Military.* A change in the location of troops, ships, or aircraft for tactical or strategic purposes; a maneuver. **2. a.** The activities of a group of people to achieve a specific goal: *the labor movement.* **b.** A tendency or trend. **3.** Activity, especially in business or commerce. **4. a.** An evacuation of the bowels. **b.** The matter so evacuated. **5.** *Fine Arts.* The effect or illusion of motion. **6.** *Literature.* The progression of events in the development of the plot. **7.** *Prosody.* The rhythmical or metrical structure of a poetic composition. **8.** *Music.* A self-contained component section of a composition. **9.** A mechanism that produces or transmits motion, as the works of a watch. [Middle English, from Old French, from Medieval Latin *movimentum,* from Latin *movēre,* to move. See **mew-** in Appendix.*]

mov·er (mōō'vər) *n.* **1.** One that moves. **2.** One whose occupation is transporting furnishings.

mov·ie (mōō'vē) *n. Informal.* **1.** A motion picture *(see).* **2.** A theater that shows motion pictures. **3.** *Plural.* **a.** A showing of a motion picture. Used with *the.* **b.** The motion picture industry. [Shortened from MOVING PICTURE.]

mov·ing (mōō'vĭng) *adj.* **1.** Changing or capable of changing position. **2.** Causing or producing motion. **3.** Affecting the emotions: *a moving tale.* —**mov'ing·ly** *adv.* —**mov'ing·ness** *n.*
  Synonyms: moving, stirring, poignant, touching, pathetic, affecting. These words all refer to emotional reaction. *Moving* applies to that which calls forth any deeply felt emotion. *Stirring* stresses strong emotion, and is related to stimulation and inspiration. *Poignant* describes that which pierces or penetrates; it has wide-ranging application, from grief to sarcasm and (less often) to delight. *Touching* emphasizes sympathy and compassion. *Pathetic* stresses pity, and sometimes mild scorn (for that which is hopelessly inept or inadequate). *Affecting* applies to anything capable of moving the feelings, but usually pertains to that which inspires pity and tenderness.

moving picture. A motion picture *(see).*

moving staircase. An escalator *(see).*

mow¹ (mō) *v.* **mowed, mowed** or **mown** (mōn), **mowing, mows.** —*tr.* **1.** To cut down (grain, grass, or similar growth) with a scythe or a mechanical device such as a lawn mower or mowing machine. **2.** To cut (such growth) from: *mow the lawn.* —**mow down.** To fell in great numbers, as in battle: *"our brave fellows . . . were mown down with volleys of grape and musquetry"* (Edward Brenton). [Mow, mown; Middle English *mowen, mowen,* Old English *māwan, māwen.* See **mē-⁴** in Appendix.*] —**mow'er** (mō'ər) *n.*

mow² (mou) *n.* **1.** A place for storing hay or grain. **2.** Feed so stored. [Middle English *mough, mow,* stack of hay, Old English *mūga, mūha, mūwa.* See **muk-** in Appendix.*]

MOW Airport code for Moscow, U.S.S.R.

mowing machine. A machine for cutting hay, grass, or grain.

Mox·ie (mŏk'sē) *n.* **1.** A trademark for a soft drink. **2.** *Small m. Slang.* The ability to face difficulty with spirit; pluck. [Origin uncertain.]

Mo·zam·bique (mō'zăm-bēk'). *Portuguese* **Mo·çam·bi·que** (mōō'səm-bē'kə). Formerly **Portuguese East Africa.** An overseas province of Portugal, 302,328 square miles in area, situated on the southeastern coast of Africa. Population, 6,872,000. Capital, Lourenço Marques.

Mo·zam·bique Channel (mō'zăm-bēk'). The strait lying between Mozambique and the Malagasy Republic.

Moz·ar·ab (mō-zăr'əb) *n.* One of a group of Spanish Christians who practiced a modified form of their religion under the Moslems. [Spanish *Mozárabe,* from Arabic *Musta'rib,* "a would-be Arab," from *'arab,* ARAB.] —**Moz·ar'a·bic** *adj.*

Mo·zart (mōt'särt'), **Wolfgang Amadeus.** 1756–1791. Austrian composer of more than 600 works.

mo·zet·ta (mō-zĕt'ə, mōt-sĕt'ə) *n.* Also **moz·zet·ta.** *Roman Catholic Church.* A short, hooded cape worn by bishops. [Italian, short for *almozzetta,* irregular diminutive formed from Medieval Latin *almūtia,* ALMUCE.]

mo·zo (mō'zō) *n., pl.* **-zos.** *Western U.S.* A man who helps with a pack train or acts as a porter. [Spanish, "a boy," from Old Spanish *moço* (origin unknown).]

moz·za·rel·la (mōt'sə-rĕl'ə, mŏt'-) *n.* A soft, white Italian curd cheese, often melted in cookery. [Italian, diminutive of *mozza,* "slice," (sliced) cheese, from *mozzare,* to cut off, perhaps from Vulgar Latin *mutiāre* (unattested), from Latin *mutilāre,* to mutilate, cut up, from *mutilus,* cut short. See **mut-** in Appendix.*]

MP military police; military policeman; mounted police.

mp, m.p. 1. melting point. **2.** *Music.* mezzo-piano.

M.P. 1. Member of Parliament. **2.** military police; military policeman.

M.P.A. 1. Master of Public Administration. **2.** Master of Public Accounting.

M. Pd. Master of Pedagogy.

M.P.E. Master of Physical Education.

mpg, m.p.g. miles per gallon.

mph, m.p.h. miles per hour.

M.P.H. Master of Public Health.

MPV Airport code for Montpelier, Vermont.

Mr. (mĭs'tər) *n., pl.* **Messrs.** The abbreviated form of the title **Mister** when used with a name.

Mrs. (mĭs'ĭz) *n., pl.* **Mmes.** A title of courtesy used in speaking to or of a married woman, preceding the woman's surname. [Abbreviation of **mistress.**]

ms 1. manuscript. **2.** millisecond.

MS 1. manuscript. **2.** Mississippi (with Zip Code). **3.** multiple sclerosis.

ms., MS. manuscript.

M.S. Master of Science (Latin *Magister Scientiae*).

msec millisecond.

msg. message.

Msgr. Monseigneur; Monsignor.

MSgt, M. Sgt. master sergeant.

M.S. in L.S. Master of Science in Library Science.

m.s.l., M.S.L. mean sea level.

MSN Airport code for Madison, Wisconsin.

MSP Airport code for Minneapolis and St. Paul, Minnesota.

mss, MSS, mss., MSS. manuscripts.

MST, M.S.T. Mountain Standard Time.

M.S.W. Master of Social Work.

MSY Airport code for New Orleans, Louisiana.

MT Montana (with Zip Code).

mt., Mt. mount; mountain.

m.t., M.T. 1. metric ton. **2.** Mountain Time.

mtg. 1. meeting. **2.** mortgage.

mtge. mortgage.

mtn. mountain.

MTO Mediterranean Theater of Operations.

mu (myōō, mōō) *n.* The 12th letter in the Greek alphabet, written M, μ. It has been transliterated in English as *M, m.* See **alphabet.**

much (mŭch) *adj.* **more, most.** Great in quantity, degree, or extent: *much rain.* —*n.* **1.** A large quantity or amount. **2.** Anything remarkable or important: *As a leader, he is not much.* —**make much of.** To pay great attention to. —**think much of.** To esteem highly. —*adv.* **more, most. 1.** To a great degree; to a large extent: *much impressed.* **2.** Just about; almost: *much the same.* [Middle English *muche, miche,* shortened from *muchel, michel,* Old English *mycel, micel,* great, large, greatly, much. See **meg-** in Appendix.*]

mu·cic acid (myōō'sĭk). An organic acid, HOOC(CHOH)₄-COOH, often derived from milk sugar. [From MUCUS.]

mu·ci·lage (myōō'sə-lĭj) *n.* **1.** A sticky substance used as an adhesive. **2.** A gummy substance obtained from certain plants. [Middle English *muscilage,* from Old French *mucilage,* from Late Latin *mūcilāgō,* musty juice, from Latin *mūcus,* MUCUS.] —**mu'ci·lag'i·nous** (-lăj'ə-nəs) *adj.*

mu·cin (myōō'sən) *n.* Any of a group of organic compounds produced by mucous membranes. [MUC(O)- + -IN.] —**mu'cin·oid'** (-sə-noid'), **mu'cin·ous** (-sə-nəs) *adj.*

muck (mŭk) *n.* **1.** A moist, sticky mixture, especially of mud and filth. **2.** Moist animal dung mixed with decayed vegetable matter and used as a fertilizer; manure. **3.** Dark, fertile soil containing putrid vegetable matter. **4.** Anything regarded as filthy or disgusting. **5.** Earth, rocks, or clay excavated in mining. —**make a muck of.** *Informal.* To botch or mismanage. —*tr.v.* **mucked, mucking, mucks. 1.** To fertilize with manure or compost. **2.** *Informal.* To soil or make dirty with or as if with muck. **3.** To remove muck or dirt from (a mine or site). —**muck about.** *Chiefly British Informal.* To spend time idly; putter. —**muck up.** *Informal.* **1.** To make dirty or untidy. **2.** To mismanage or interfere with (a plan or project). [Middle English *muk,* from Old Norse *mykr.* See **meug-²** in Appendix.*] —**muck'y** *adj.* —**muck'i·ly** *adv.*

muck·a·muck (mŭk'ə-mŭk') *n.* Also **muck·et·y·muck** (mŭk'ə-tē-mŭk'). *Slang.* A person of importance. Usually used scornfully, often in the phrase *high muckamuck.* [Shortened from HIGH MUCKAMUCK.]

muck·le. Variant of **mickle.**

muck·rake (mŭk'rāk') *intr.v.* **-raked, -raking, -rakes.** To search for and expose political or commercial corruption. —*n.* A rake used for gathering and spreading muck. [Back-formation from *muckraker,* used in 1906 by Theodore Roosevelt in allusion to the "man with a Muck-rake" in Bunyan's *Pilgrim's Progress.*] —**muck'rak'er** *n.*

muck·worm (mŭk'wûrm') *n.* Any worm or larva found in mud and animal droppings.

muco–, muc–. Indicates mucus or something pertaining to the mucous membrane; for example, **mucoprotein, mucin.** [From Latin *mūcus,* MUCUS.]

mu·coid (myōō'koid') *n.* Any of a group of organic compounds similar to the mucins and found in connective tissue. [MUC(O)- + -OID.] —**mu'coid, mu·coi'dal** (myōō-koid'l) *adj.*

mu·co·pol·y·sac·cha·ride (myōō'kō-pŏl'ē-săk'ə-rīd') *n.* Any of the polysaccharides that form chemical bonds with water to produce mucilaginous and lubricating fluids

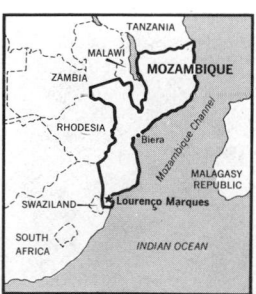

Mozambique

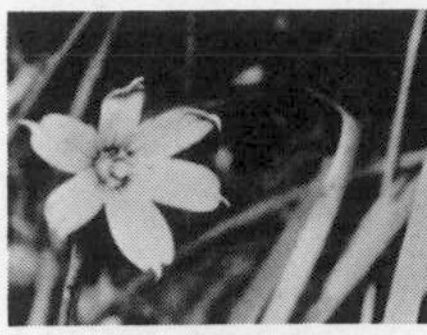
mucronate
Mucronate petals of blue-eyed grass

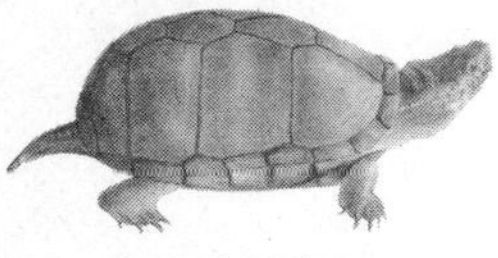
mud turtle
Kinosternon subrubrum

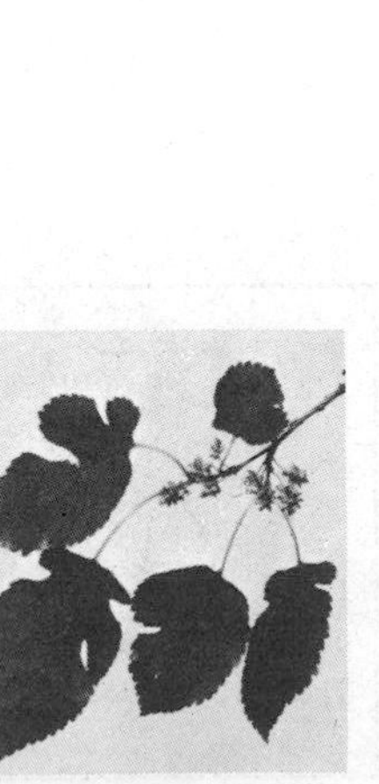
mulberry
Morus rubra
Red mulberry

mu·co·pro·tein (myōō'kō-prō'tēn', -prō'tē-ĭn) *n.* Any of a group of organic compounds, such as the mucins, that contain proteins and mucopolysaccharides.

mu·co·sa (myōō-kō'sə) *n., pl.* **-sae** (-sē) or **-sas.** A mucous membrane. [New Latin *mūcōsa (membrana),* from *mūcōsus,* MUCOUS.] —**mu·co'sal** *adj.*

mu·cous (myōō'kəs) *adj.* Also **mu·cose** (-kōs'). **1.** Producing or secreting mucus. **2.** Pertaining to, consisting of, or resembling mucus. [Latin *mūcōsus,* from *mūcus,* MUCUS.]

mucous membrane. The membrane lining all bodily channels that communicate with the air, such as the respiratory and alimentary tracts, the glands of which secrete mucus.

mu·cro (myōō'krō) *n., pl.* **mucrones** (myōō-krō'nēz). *Biology.* A sharp tip of some plant and animal organs. [New Latin, from Latin *mucrō*†, a sharp point, sword's point.]

mu·cro·nate (myōō'krə-nāt') *adj. Biology.* Having a **mucro** *(see).* [Latin *mucronātus,* from *mucrō,* a point, MUCRO.]

mu·cus (myōō'kəs) *n.* The viscous suspension of mucin, water, cells, and inorganic salts secreted as a protective, lubricant coating by glands in the mucous membrane. [Latin *mūcus, muccus.* See **meug-²** in Appendix.*]

mud (mŭd) *n.* **1.** Wet, sticky, soft earth. **2.** Slanderous or defamatory charges. **3.** That which is degrading: *His name was dragged in the mud.* —**Here's mud in your eye.** A humorous drinking toast. —**one's name is mud.** One is in bad favor. —*tr.v.* **mudded, mudding, muds.** To soil or bury with or as if with mud. [Middle English *mudde, mode*†.]

mud cat. Any of several large American catfish of the Mississippi valley and southeastern U.S. streams.

mud dauber. Any of several wasps having long hind legs and a slender abdomen terminating in a bulb. The female lays eggs in paralyzed insect larvae, which are placed in a nest of mud.

mud·der (mŭd'ər) *n. Racing.* A horse that runs well on a wet or muddy track.

mud·dle (mŭd'l) *v.* **-dled, -dling, -dles.** —*tr.* **1.** To make turbid; muddy. **2.** To mix confusedly; jumble. **3.** To mix up (the mind), as with alcohol; confuse or befuddle. **4.** To mismanage or bungle. **5.** To stir or mix (a beverage) gently. —*intr.* To act or think in a confused manner. —**muddle through.** *Chiefly British.* To push on to a successful conclusion in a disorganized way. —*n.* A confusion, jumble, or mess. [Perhaps from Middle Dutch *moddelen,* to make muddy, from *modde,* mud. See **meu-** in Appendix.*] —**mud'dler** *n.*

mud·dle-head·ed (mŭd'l-hĕd'ĭd) *adj.* Mentally confused; stupid; dull. —**mud'dle-head'ed·ness** *n.*

mud·dy (mŭd'ē) *adj.* **-dier, -diest.** **1.** Covered, full of, or spattered with mud. **2.** Not clear or pure, as a color or liquid. **3.** Dull: *a muddy complexion.* **4.** Confused, vague, or obscure, as in expression or meaning: *a muddy style of writing.* —*tr.v.* **muddied, -dying, -dies.** **1.** To make muddy or dirty. **2.** To make dull or cloudy. **3.** To make obscure or confused. —**mud'di·ly** *adv.* —**mud'di·ness** *n.*

mud eel. An amphibian, *Siren lacertina,* found in swamps of the southeastern United States. It is eellike in appearance, having only front legs, which are inconspicuous.

mud·fish (mŭd'fĭsh') *n., pl.* **mudfish** or **-fishes.** Any of various fishes found in mud or muddy water, such as the **bowfin** and the **mud minnow** *(both of which see).*

mud flat. Land covered at high tide and exposed at low tide.

mud·guard (mŭd'gärd') *n.* A shield over a vehicle's wheel.

mud hen. Any of various birds inhabiting marshy or coastal regions, such as a coot, gallinule, or rail.

mud·lark (mŭd'lärk') *n. British Slang.* A street urchin.

mud minnow. Any fish of the genus *Umbra,* brown in color and found in the muddy areas of North American and European lakes and ponds.

mud puppy. Any of various aquatic salamanders of the genus *Necturus,* especially *N. maculosus,* of North America, having conspicuous clusters of external gills. Also called "water dog."

mu·dra (mə-drä') *n.* In East Indian classical dancing, a code of body postures and hand movements with which a dancer enacts a narrative.

mud·sill (mŭd'sĭl') *n.* The lowest sill, block, or timber supporting a building, located at or below ground level.

mud·skip·per (mŭd'skĭp'ər) *n.* Any of several species of fishes of the family Gobiidae that are found along the western coast of tropical Africa and in the Indo-Pacific region and are noted for their ability to maneuver on land.

mud·sling·er (mŭd'slĭng'ər) *n.* One who makes malicious charges against an opponent. —**mud'sling'ing** *n.*

mud snake. A burrowing snake, *Farancia abacura,* of the southeastern United States, having black scales with reddish markings. Sometimes called "hoop snake."

mud·stone (mŭd'stōn') *n.* A dark-gray, fine-grained shale that decomposes into mud when exposed to the atmosphere.

mud turtle. Any turtle of the genus *Kinosternon,* found in sluggish fresh waters throughout the Western Hemisphere. Also called "mud terrapin," "mud tortoise."

mud wasp. The **potter wasp** *(see).*

Muen·ster, Mun·ster (mŏŏn'stər, mŭn'-, mĭn'-) *n.* A semisoft, creamy, yellow fermented Alsatian cheese of mild flavor. [Originally made at *Munster,* city in northeastern France.]

mu·ez·zin (myōō-ĕz'ĭn, mōō-) *n. Islam.* The crier who calls the faithful to prayer five times a day, usually from a minaret. [Arabic *mu'adhdhin,* active participle of *adhana,* to cause to listen, from *adhina,* to listen.]

muff¹ (mŭf) *v.* **muffed, muffing, muffs.** —*tr.* **1.** To perform (an act) clumsily; bungle: *He muffed his chance for the job.* **2.** *Sports.* To fail to catch (the ball). —*intr.* **1.** To perform some act clumsily; bungle. **2.** *Sports.* To fail to catch a ball. —*n.* A clumsy or bungled act. [Origin uncertain.]

muff² (mŭf) *n.* A small cylindrical fur or cloth cover, open at both ends, in which the hands are placed to keep them warm. [Dutch *mof,* from Middle Dutch *moffel,* from Old French *moufle,* glove, MUFFLE (wrap).]

muf·fin (mŭf'ĭn) *n.* A small, cup-shaped bread, often sweetened and usually served hot. [Probably from Low German *muffen,* plural of *muffe*†, cake.]

muf·fle¹ (mŭf'əl) *tr.v.* **-fled, -fling, -fles.** **1.** To wrap up in a blanket, shawl, or scarf for warmth, protection, or secrecy: *"passers-by were muffled to their puckered eyes"* (Kipling). **2.** To wrap or pad in order to deaden a sound: *"we heard . . . fifes and a muffled drum—a dirge"* (Ambrose Bierce). **3.** To deaden (a sound): *"the soft, muffled fall of a horse's hoof in the thick dust of the highway"* (Bret Harte). **4.** To make vague or obscure: *"his message was so muffled by learning and 'artiness' "* (Walter Blair). —*n.* **1.** Anything that muffles. **2.** A kiln or part of a kiln in which pottery can be fired without being exposed to direct flame. [Middle English *muflen,* from Old French *enmoufler,* "to put on a muff or mittens," from *moufle,* mitten, from Medieval Latin *muffula*†.]

muf·fle² (mŭf'əl) *n.* The hairless snout of certain mammals. [French *mufle*†.]

muf·fler (mŭf'lər) *n.* **1.** A heavy scarf worn around the neck for warmth. **2.** Any device that absorbs noise, especially that of an internal-combustion engine.

muf·ti¹ (mŭf'tē, mōōf'-) *n., pl.* **-tis.** A judge who interprets Moslem religious law. [Arabic *muftī,* "one who decides," from *aftā,* to decide (by legal opinion).]

muf·ti² (mŭf'tē) *n.* Civilian dress; especially, such clothing when worn by one whose regular garb is a military or other uniform. [Probably an obscure slang use of MUFTI (judge).]

mug¹ (mŭg) *n.* **1.** A cylindrical drinking vessel often with a handle. **2.** The liquid contained in such a vessel. [Origin obscure.]

mug² (mŭg) *n. Slang.* **1.** The face of a person. **2.** The area of the mouth, chin, and jaw. **3.** A photograph of the face, especially one used by police for identification. Also called "mug shot." **4.** A grimace. **5.** A rough or ugly man; hoodlum. **6.** *British.* A victim or dupe. —*v.* **mugged, mugging, mugs.** *Slang.* —*tr.* **1.** To photograph (a person's face) for police files. **2.** To waylay and beat severely, usually with intent to rob. —*intr.* To grimace; especially, to overact as a performer by means of exaggerated facial expressions. [Probably from MUG (vessel); some old tankards were shaped like grotesque human faces.] —**mug'ger** *n.*

mug·ger (mŭg'ər) *n.* Also **mug·gar, mug·gur.** A large crocodile, *Crocodilus palustris,* of southwestern Asia, having an exceptionally broad, wrinkled snout. [Hindi *magar,* from Sanskrit *makara,* a crocodile, from Dravidian.]

mug·ging (mŭg'ĭng) *n. Informal.* An aggravated assault usually by surprise and with intent to rob.

mug·gy (mŭg'ē) *adj.* **-gier, -giest.** Warm and extremely humid. [From English dialectal *mug,* fine rain, from Middle English *muggen,* to drizzle, from Old Norse *mugga.* See **meug-²** in Appendix.*] —**mug'gi·ness** *n.*

Mu·ghal, Mu·ghul. Variants of **Mogul.**

mug·wort (mŭg'wûrt', -wôrt) *n.* Any of several plants of the genus *Artemisia;* especially, *A. vulgaris,* native to Eurasia, having clusters of small greenish-yellow flowers. [Middle English *mugwort,* Old English *mucgwyrt* : *mucg-,* a midge, fly (see **mū-²** in Appendix*) + *wyrt,* WORT.]

mug·wump (mŭg'wŭmp') *n.* **1.** *Often capital* **M.** A Republican who bolted his party in 1884, refusing to support James G. Blaine as candidate for the U.S. presidency. **2.** Any person who acts independently, especially in politics. [Natick *mugquomp, mugwomp,* "captain."] —**mug'wump'er·y** *n.*

Mu·ham·mad. See **Mohammed.**

Mu·ham·mad A·li. See Cassius Marcellus **Clay.**

Mu·ham·ma·dan, Mu·ham·me·dan. Variants of **Mohammedan.**

Mu·ham·ma·dan·ism. Variant of **Mohammedanism.**

Mu·har·ram (mōō-hăr'əm) *n.* Also **Mo·har·ram** (mō-hăr'əm), **Mu·har·rum** (mōō-hăr'əm). **1.** The first month of the Moslem calendar. See **calendar. 2.** A festival held during the first ten days of this month.

Müh·len·berg (myōō'lən-bûrg'), **Henry Melchior.** 1711–1787. German-born American clergyman; established the first synod of the Lutheran Church in America.

Muir (myŏŏr), **John.** 1838–1914. Scottish-born American naturalist, explorer, conservationist, and writer.

Muir Glacier (myŏŏr). A glacier covering an area of about 350 square miles in the St. Elias Mountains of southeastern Alaska.

Muir Woods (myŏŏr). A national monument occupying 424 acres of redwood forest in California, north of San Francisco.

mu·jik. Variant of **muzhik.**

Muk·den. Former name for **Shenyang.**

muk·luk (mŭk'lŭk') *n.* **1.** A soft Eskimo boot made of reindeer skin or sealskin. **2.** A slipper like this boot. [Eskimo *muklok,* "large seal."]

mu·lat·to (mōō-lăt'ō, -lä'tō, myōō-) *n., pl.* **-tos** or **-toes. 1.** A person having one white and one Negro parent. **2.** Any person of mixed Caucasian and Negro ancestry. —*adj.* Pertaining to or characteristic of a mulatto. [Spanish *mulato,* young mule, mulatto, from *mulo,* mule, from Latin *mūlus,* MULE.]

mul·ber·ry (mŭl'bĕr'ē, -bə-rē) *n., pl.* **-ries. 1.** Any of several trees of the genus *Morus,* having edible fruit. See **red mulberry, white mulberry. 2.** The sweet, berry-like fruit of any of these

ă pat/ā pay/âr care/ä father/b bib/ch church/d deed/ĕ pet/ē be/f fife/g gag/h hat/hw which/ĭ pit/ī pie/îr pier/j judge/k kick/l lid, needle/m mum/n no, sudden/ng thing/ŏ pot/ō toe/ô paw, for/oi noise/ou out/ŏŏ took/ōō boot/p pop/r roar/s sauce/sh ship, dish/

trees. **3.** Any of several related or similar trees, such as the **paper mulberry** *(see).* **4.** Grayish to dark purple. Also "murrey." See **color.** [Middle English *mulberrie, murberie,* Old English *mōrberie* : *mōr-*, a Germanic borrowing, from Latin *mōrum,* mulberry (see **moro-** in Appendix*) + Old English *berie,* BERRY.] **—mul′ber·ry** *adj.*

mulch (mŭlch) *n.* A protective covering of various substances, especially organic, placed around plants to prevent evaporation of moisture and freezing of roots and to control weeds. *—tr.v.* **mulched, mulching, mulches.** To cover with a mulch. [Originally "rotten hay," probably extended use of Middle English *mulsh,* soft, yielding, variant of *melsh,* Old English *mel(i)sc, mylsc,* mild, mellow. See **mel-**[1] in Appendix.*]

mulct (mŭlkt) *n.* A fine or similar penalty. *—tr.v.* **mulcted, mulcting, mulcts. 1.** To penalize by fining or demanding forfeiture. **2.** To acquire or take away from by trickery or deception. [Latin *mulcta, multa,* a fine, of Italic origin.]

mule[1] (myo͞ol) *n.* **1.** A sterile hybrid of a male ass and a female horse. Compare **hinny. 2.** Any sterile hybrid, as between a canary and other birds, or between certain plants. **3.** *Informal.* A stubborn person. **4.** A type of spinning machine that makes thread or yarn from fibers. Also called "mulejenny." **5.** A small, usually electric, tractor or locomotive for hauling short distances. [Middle English *mul,* from Old English *mūl* and Old French *mul,* both from Latin *mūlus,* mule, probably from Mediterranean, akin to Albanian *mušk,* mule.]

mule[2] (myo͞ol) *n.* A slipper that has no counter or strap to fit around the heel of the foot. [Old French, slipper, from Latin *mulleus (calceus),* "red (shoe)." See **mel-**[2] in Appendix.*]

mule deer. A hoofed mammal, *Odocoileus hemionus,* of western North America. It has long ears and two-pronged antlers, and is brownish gray. Also called "black-tailed deer."

mule·skin·ner (myo͞ol′skĭn′ər) *n. Informal.* A driver of mules.

mu·le·ta (mo͞o-lā′tə, -lĕt′ə) *n.* A short red cape, suspended from a hollow staff, that is used by the matador to maneuver the bull during the **faena** *(see).* [Spanish, crutch, support, "small mule," from *mula,* "she-mule," from Latin *mūla,* feminine of *mūlus,* MULE.]

mu·le·teer (myo͞o′lə-tîr′) *n.* A mule driver. [Old French *muletier,* from *mulet,* diminutive of *mul,* MULE.]

mule train. 1. A train of wagons pulled by mules. **2.** A line of mules carrying packs.

mu·ley (myo͞o′lē, mo͞ol′ē, mo͞o′lē) *adj.* Hornless. Said of cattle. *—n., pl.* **muleys.** A hornless animal. [Variant of dialectal *moiley,* from *moil,* hornless, a hornless cow, from Irish *maol,* from Old Irish *máel,* bald, hornless. See **mai-**[1] in Appendix.*]

Mul·ha·cén (mo͞o′lä-thān′). The highest mountain peak in Spain (11,411 feet), in the Sierra Nevada.

Mül·heim (mül′hīm′). An industrial city of West Germany, on the Ruhr southwest of Essen. Population, 192,000.

Mul·house (mü-lo͞oz′). A city and textile center of northeastern France, on the Rhône-Rhine Canal. Population, 109,000

mu·li·eb·ri·ty (myo͞o′lē-ĕb′rə-tē) *n.* **1.** The state or condition of being a woman. **2.** The qualities characteristic of women. [Late Latin *muliebritās,* from Latin *muliebris,* womanly, from *mulier*†, a woman.]

mul·ish (myo͞o′lĭsh) *adj.* Characteristic of a mule; stubborn. See Synonyms at **obstinate. —mul′ish·ly** *adv.* **—mul′ish·ness** *n.*

mull[1] (mŭl) *tr.v.* **mulled, mulling, mulls.** To heat and spice (a beverage, such as wine or ale). [Perhaps from Middle English *mul,* dust, meal, powdered spice, from Middle Dutch *mol, mul.* See **melə-** in Appendix.*]

mull[2] (mŭl) *v.* **mulled, mulling, mulls.** *—tr.* To consider or go over mentally: *mulling each of the proposed courses. —intr.* To ponder or ruminate on. Followed by *over.* [Originally "to grind," Middle English *mullen,* to pulverize, from *mul,* dust, from Middle Dutch *mol, mul.* See **melə-** in Appendix.*]

mull[3] (mŭl) *n.* A soft, thin kind of muslin used in dresses and for trimmings. [Short for *mulmull,* from Hindi *malmal,* from Persian *malmal*†.]

Mull (mŭl). An island, about 350 square miles in area, of the Inner Hebrides.

mul·lah (mŭl′ə, mo͞ol′ə) *n.* Also **mul·la, mol·lah** (mô′lə). A Moslem religious teacher or leader. Used as a title. [Turkish *mulla* and Persian *mullā,* from Arabic *mawlā,* "master."]

mul·lein (mŭl′ən) *n.* **1.** Any plant of the genus *Verbascum;* especially, *V. thapsus,* native to Eurasia, a tall plant having leaves covered with dense, woolly down, and closely clustered yellow flowers. This species is also called "flannel-leaf," "velvet plant." **2.** The **Cretan mullein** *(see).* [Middle English *moleyne,* from Old French *moleine,* probably from *mol,* soft, from Latin *mollis.* See **mel-**[1] in Appendix.*]

mullein pink. A plant, the **rose campion** *(see).*

Mul·lens (mŭl′ənz), **Priscilla.** Also **Mul·lins.** American Puritan colonist; married John Alden (1623?).

mul·ler (mŭl′ər) *n.* **1.** Any of several manual or mechanical devices used for grinding. **2.** A device with a stone or other hard base, used manually or mechanically to grind paints or drugs. [Middle English *molour,* probably from *mullen,* to grind, pulverize. See **mull** (to consider).]

Mul·ler (mŭl′ər), **Hermann Joseph.** 1890–1967. American geneticist; worked on x rays and mutation rates.

Mül·ler, Johann. See **Regiomontanus.**

Mül·ler (myo͞o′lər, mŭl′ər; *German* mül′ər), **Johannes Peter.** 1801–1858. German physiologist; studied the nervous system.

Mül·ler (myo͞o′lər, mŭl′ər; *German* mül′ər), **Paul Herman.** 1899–1965. Swiss chemist; developed DDT.

Mül·ler-Ly·er illusion (mül′ər-lē′ər, mŭl′ər-lī′ər). An optical illusion in which two lines of the same length are made to appear unequal. [After Franz *Müller-Lyer* (1857–1916), German philosopher.]

mul·let (mŭl′ĭt) *n., pl.* **mullet** or **-lets.** Any of various edible fishes of the family Mugilidae found worldwide in tropical and temperate coastal waters and some freshwater streams. Also called "gray mullet" in Europe. See **red mullet.** [Middle English *molet,* from Old French *mulet,* from Latin *mullus,* red mullet, from Greek *mullos.* See **mel-**[2] in Appendix.*]

mul·li·gan (mŭl′ĭ-gən) *n.* A stew of various meats and vegetables. Also called "mulligan stew." [Probably from the Irish surname *Mulligan.*]

mul·li·ga·taw·ny (mŭl′ĭ-gə-tô′nē) *n.* An East Indian meat soup strongly flavored with curry. [Tamil *milagutanni(r),* "pepper-water."]

mul·li·grubs, mul·ly·grubs (mŭl′ĭ-grŭbz′) *pl.n.* Also **mol·ly·grubs** (mŏl′ĭ-grŭbz′). **1.** A stomach ache; griping of the intestines; colic. **2.** Ill temper. [Alteration of earlier *mulligrums,* perhaps alteration of MEGRIM.]

Mul·li·kan (mŭl′ĭ-kən), **Robert Sanderson.** Born 1896. American nuclear physicist.

mul·lion (mŭl′yən) *n.* A vertical strip dividing the panes of a window. [Variant of obsolete *monial,* a mullion, Middle English *moniel,* from Old French *moynel,* from *moyen,* middle, from Latin *mediānus,* median, from *medius,* middle. See **medhyo-** in Appendix.*] **—mul′lioned** *adj.*

Mul·tan (mo͞ol-tän′). Also **Mool·tan.** A city of West Pakistan, about 200 miles southwest of Lahore. Population, 190,000.

multi–. Indicates: **1.** Many or much; for example, **multicolored. 2.** More than one; for example, **multiparous.** ***Note:*** Many compounds other than those entered here may be formed with *multi-.* In forming compounds, *multi-* is normally joined to the following word or element without space or hyphen: *multiangular.* However, if the second element begins with *i,* it is separated with a hyphen: *multi-infection.* [Middle English, from Latin, from *multus,* much. See **mel-**[4] in Appendix.*]

mul·ti·ad·dress (mŭl′tē-ăd′rĕs, mŭl′tī-) *adj.* Designating a storage system of data-processing computers in which it is possible to store instructions or quantities in more than one position.

mul·ti·col·ored (mŭl′tĭ-kŭl′ərd) *adj.* Having many colors.

mul·ti·far·i·ous (mŭl′tə-fâr′ē-əs) *adj.* Having great variety; made up of many parts or kinds: *"multifarious produce, supply for human want in every kind"* (Carlyle). [Latin *multifārius* : MULTI- + *-fārius,* doing (see **dhē-**[1] in Appendix*).] **—mul′ti·far′i·ous·ly** *adv.* **—mul′ti·far′i·ous·ness** *n.*

mul·ti·fid (mŭl′tə-fĭd′) *adj. Biology.* Having many clefts forming lobes or segments: *multifid leaves.* [Latin *multifidus* : MULTI- + -FID.] **—mul′ti·fid′ly** *adv.*

mul·ti·flo·ra rose (mŭl′tə-flôr′ə, -flōr′ə). A climbing or sprawling shrub, *Rosa multiflora,* native to Asia, having clusters of small, fragrant flowers. It is the origin of many horticultural varieties. [New Latin *Rosa multiflōra,* "multiflorous rose."]

mul·ti·flo·rous (mŭl′tə-flôr′əs, -flōr′əs) *adj. Botany.* Bearing many flowers. [Latin *multiflōrus* : MULTI- + -FLOROUS.]

mul·ti·foil (mŭl′tə-foil′) *n.* Any flat object or opening with scalloped edges or ornaments. See **scallop.**

mul·ti·fold (mŭl′tə-fōld′) *adj.* Many times doubled; manifold. [MULTI- + -FOLD.]

mul·ti·form (mŭl′tə-fôrm′) *adj.* Occurring in or having many forms, shapes, or appearances. [Latin *multiformis* : MULTI- + -FORM.] **—mul′ti·for′mi·ty** *n.*

Mul·ti·graph (mŭl′tə-grăf′, -gräf′) *n.* A trademark for an office machine for typesetting and rotary printing. *—tr.v.* **Multigraphed, -graphing, -graphs.** To reproduce by Multigraph. [MULTI- + -GRAPH.]

mul·ti·grav·i·da (mŭl′tĭ-grăv′ə-də) *n.* A pregnant woman who has had at least two previous pregnancies. Compare **multipara.** [New Latin : MULTI- + Latin *gravida,* pregnant woman, feminine of *gravidus,* pregnant, GRAVID.]

mul·ti·lat·er·al (mŭl′tə-lăt′ər-əl) *adj.* **1.** Having many sides. **2.** *Government.* Involving more than two nations; multipartite. **—mul′ti·lat′er·al·ly** *adv.*

Mul·ti·lith (mŭl′tə-lĭth′) *n.* A trademark for a small rotary offset press. *—tr.v.* **Multilithed, -lithing, -liths.** To reproduce by Multilith. [MULTI- + LITH(OGRAPH).]

mul·ti·mil·lion·aire (mŭl′tə-mĭl′yə-nâr′) *n.* A person whose financial assets equal many millions of dollars.

mul·ti·no·mi·al (mŭl′tə-nō′mē-əl) *n.* A **polynomial** *(see).* [MULTI- + (BI)NOMIAL.] **—mul′ti·no′mi·al** *adj.*

multinomial theorem. *Mathematics.* The theorem that establishes the rule for forming the terms of a polynomial expansion. See **binomial theorem, expansion, polynomial.**

mul·tip·a·ra (mŭl-tĭp′ər-ə) *n., pl.* **-rae** (-rē′). A pregnant woman who has borne at least one child. Compare **multigravida.** [New Latin, feminine of *multiparus,* MULTIPAROUS.]

mul·tip·a·rous (mŭl-tĭp′ər-əs) *adj.* **1.** Having borne more than one child. **2.** Giving birth to more than one offspring at one time. [New Latin *multiparus* : MULTI- + -PAROUS.] **—mul′ti·par′i·ty** *n.*

mul·ti·par·tite (mŭl′tə-pär′tīt′) *adj.* **1.** Having many parts. **2.** Multilateral. [Latin *multipartitus* : MULTI- + PARTITE.]

mul·ti·ped (mŭl′tə-pĕd′) *adj.* Also **mul·ti·pede** (-pēd′). Having many feet. [Late Latin *multipedes* : MULTI- + -PED.]

mul·ti·ple (mŭl′tə-pəl) *adj.* Having, pertaining to, or consisting of more than one individual, element, part, or other component; manifold. Also "multiplicate." *—n. Mathematics.* A quantity into which another quantity may be divided with zero remainder: *4, 6, and 12 are multiples of 2.* A *common multiple* is a quantity into which each of two or more other quantities may be divided with zero remainder: *6, 12, and 24 are common mul-*

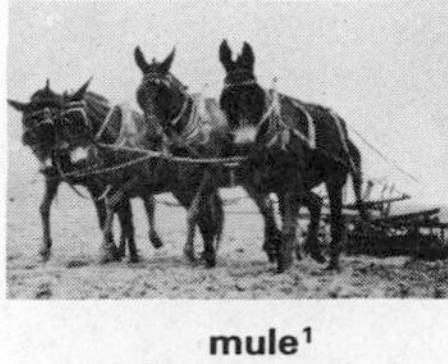

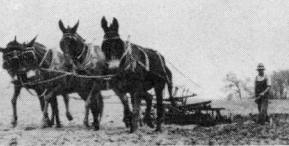

mule[1]
Team of mules pulling a disk harrow

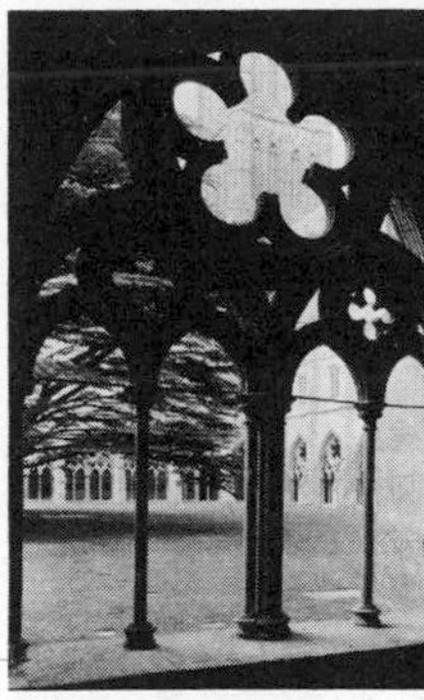

multifoil

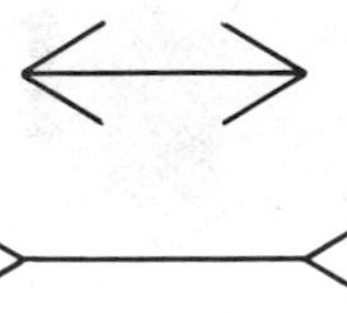

Müller-Lyer illusion

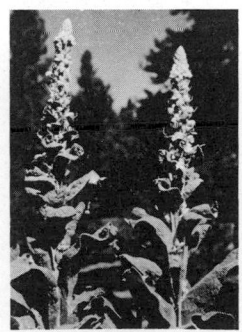

mullein
Verbascum thapsus

tiples of 2 and 3. A *least common multiple* is the least quantity into which two or more other quantities may be divided with zero remainder: *6 is the least common multiple of all common multiples of 2 and 3.* [Old French, from Late Latin *multiplus* : MULTI- + *-plus,* "-fold" (see **pel-**[3] in Appendix*).]
multiple allele. *Genetics.* A set of three or more alleles, or alternative states of a gene, only two of which can be present in a **somatic cell** *(see)* at the same time. Also called "multiple allelomorph."
mul·ti·ple-choice (mŭl′tə-pəl-chois′) *adj.* Offering a number of solutions from which one correct one is to be chosen.
multiple factor. *Genetics.* A combination of two or more genes acting as a unit to produce a quantitative inheritance trait, such as leaf shape or eye color.
multiple fruit. A fruit, such as a pineapple or mulberry, in which the fruits of several flowers are combined into a single structure. Also called "collective fruit." Compare **aggregate fruit.**
multiple neuritis. Inflammation of more than one nerve at a time. See **neuritis.**
multiple root. *Mathematics.* A **root** *(see).*
multiple sclerosis. *Abbr.* **MS** A degenerative disease of the central nervous system, in which hardening of tissue occurs throughout the brain or spinal cord or both. Also called "Charcot's disease," "insular sclerosis."
multiple star. Three or more stars, usually with a common gravitational center, that appear as one to the naked eye.
mul·ti·plet (mŭl′tə-plĕt′, -plĭt) *n. Physics.* **1.** A spectral line having more than one component representing slight variations in energy states characteristic of an atom. **2.** Any of several classes or groupings of subatomic particles, such as the nucleon, each member of which has the same set of **quantum numbers** *(see)* except for electric charge. [From MULTIPLE.]
mul·ti·plex (mŭl′tə-plĕks′) *adj.* **1.** Multiple; manifold: *"The whole complex and multiplex detail of the noble science of dinner."* (Peacock). **2.** Designating or being a simultaneous communication of two or more messages on the same wire or radio channel. **3.** Designating a method of making topographic maps with three cameras arranged to employ stereoscopic principles. —*v.* **multiplexed, -plexing, -plexes.** —*intr.* To send messages or signals in a multiplex system. —*tr.* To send simultaneously (more than one signal) using one radio frequency. [Latin : MULTI- + *-plex,* "-fold" (see **plek-** in Appendix*).]
mul·ti·pli·a·ble (mŭl′tə-plī′ə-bəl) *adj.* Also **mul·ti·plic·a·ble** (mŭl′tə-plĭk′ə-bəl). Capable of being multiplied.
mul·ti·pli·cand (mŭl′tə-plĭ-kănd′) *n.* The number that is or is to be multiplied by another. [Latin *multiplicandum,* neuter of *multiplicandus,* gerundive of *multiplicāre,* to MULTIPLY.]
mul·tip·li·cate (mŭl-tĭp′lĭ-kĭt) *adj.* **1.** Having more than one layer or fold, as some shells or leaves. **2.** Multiple. [Middle English, from Latin *multiplicātus,* past participle of *multiplicāre,* to MULTIPLY.]
mul·ti·pli·ca·tion (mŭl′tə-plĭ-kā′shən) *n.* **1.** The act of multiplying or the process of being multiplied. **2.** The propagation of plants and animals. **3.** *Mathematics.* **a.** The conjunction of two real numbers in which the number of times either is taken in summation is determined by the value of the other. **b.** Any of certain analogous operations conjoining expressions other than real numbers. Compare **division.** **4.** An increase or buildup achieved by adding. —**mul′ti·pli·ca′tion·al** *adj.*
multiplication sign. *Mathematics.* The sign ×, placed between multiplicand and multiplier, or operand and operator, as $a \times b$.
multiplication table. A table listing the products of certain numbers multiplied together, usually the numbers 1 to 12.
mul·ti·pli·ca·tive (mŭl′tə-plĭ-kā′tĭv, mŭl′tə-plĭk′ə-tĭv) *adj.* **1.** Tending to multiply or capable of multiplying or increasing. **2.** Having to do with multiplication. —**mul′ti·pli·ca′tive·ly** *adv.*
mul·ti·plic·i·ty (mŭl′tə-plĭs′ə-tē) *n., pl.* **-ties.** **1.** The state of being various or manifold. **2.** A large number: *a multiplicity of ideas.* **3.** *Physics.* The number of subatomic particles in a **multiplet** *(see).* [French *multiplicité,* from Latin *multiplicitās,* from *multiplex* (stem *multiplic-*), having folds, MULTIPLEX.]
mul·ti·pli·er (mŭl′tə-plī′ər) *n.* **1.** One that multiplies. **2.** *Mathematics.* The number by which the multiplicand is multiplied. If 3 is multiplied by 2, 3 is the multiplicand, 2 is the multiplier, and 6 is the product. **3.** *Physics.* Any device, such as a phototube, used to enhance or increase an effect.
mul·ti·ply (mŭl′tə-plī′) *v.* **-plied, -plying, -plies.** —*tr.* **1.** To increase the amount, number, or degree of; make more numerous. **2.** *Mathematics.* To perform multiplication on. —*intr.v.* **1.** To become more in number, amount, or degree. **2.** To breed; propagate. **3.** *Mathematics.* To perform multiplication. [Middle English *multiplien,* from Old French *multiplier,* from Latin *multiplicāre,* from *multiplex* (stem *multiplic-*), having many folds, MULTIPLEX.]
mul·ti·stage (mŭl′tə-stāj′) *adj.* Functioning by stages.
multistage rocket. A rocket composed of two or more stages, each stage firing in succession. Also called "step rocket."
mul·ti·tude (mŭl′tə-to͞od′, -tyo͞od′) *n.* **1.** The condition or quality of being numerous. **2.** A great, indefinite number: *"there certainly were a dreadful multitude of ugly women in Bath"* (Jane Austen). **3.** The masses; the populace. Preceded by *the.* [Middle English, from Old French, from Latin *multitūdō,* a great number, from *multus,* many. See **mel-**[4] in Appendix.*]
Synonyms: *multitude, host, legion, army, array. Multitude* denotes only great numbers; it applies to persons and things, but *in the multitude* indicates the people. The remaining terms suggest, besides numbers, some measure of orderliness and purposeful association. *Host,* applied to persons and things, and *legion,* largely confined to persons, stress impressiveness. *Army,* said chiefly of persons, emphasizes order and common purpose. *Array* primarily denotes imposing arrangement, but also applies to the persons and things thus arranged, with lesser emphasis on sheer numbers.

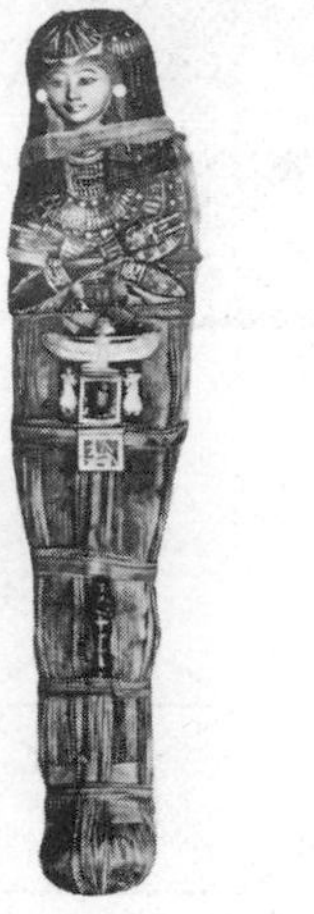
mummy case
Theban, about 1300 B.C.

mul·ti·tu·di·nous (mŭl′tə-to͞od′n-əs, -tyo͞od′n-əs) *adj.* **1.** Very numerous; existing in great numbers. **2.** Consisting of many parts. **3.** Crowded. —**mul′ti·tu′di·nous·ly** *adv.*
mul·ti·va·lent (mŭl′tə-vā′lənt, mŭl-tĭv′ə-lənt) *adj.* **1.** *Chemistry.* **Polyvalent** *(see).* **2.** *Biology.* Of or pertaining to homologous chromosomes in synapsis. **3.** Having various meanings or values. —**mul′ti·va′lence** *n.*
mul·ti·ver·si·ty (mŭl′tə-vûr′-sĭ-tē) *n., pl.* **-ties.** A university that has numerous constituent and affiliated institutions such as separate colleges and campuses and research centers. [MULTI- + (UNI)VERSITY.]
mum[1] (mŭm) *adj.* Not talking. [Middle English *mum, mom,* probably from Low German, akin to Middle Low German *mummen,* to be silent. See **mu-** in Appendix.*]
mum[2] (mŭm) *intr.v.* **mummed, mumming, mums.** To act or play in a mask; especially, to act as a mummer. [Middle English *mummen, mommen,* from Old French *momer.* See **mu-** in Appendix.*]
mum[3] (mŭm) *n. Informal.* **1.** **Ma'am** *(see).* **2.** *Chiefly British.* Mama.
mum[4] (mŭm) *n. Informal.* A chrysanthemum.
mum·ble (mŭm′bəl) *v.* **-bled, -bling, -bles.** —*tr.* **1.** To utter indistinctly by lowering the voice or partially closing the mouth. **2.** *Rare.* To chew slowly or painfully without or as if without teeth. —*intr.* **1.** To speak indistinctly, as by lowering the voice or partially closing the mouth. **2.** *Rare.* To chew food slowly or painfully, as if without teeth. —See Synonyms at **mutter.** —*n.* A low, indistinct sound or speech. [Middle English *momelen,* frequentative of *mom,* inarticulate sound, MUM.] —**mum′bler** *n.*
mum·ble·ty-peg (mŭm′bəl-tē-pĕg′, mŭm′blē-pĕg′) *n.* Also **mum·ble-the-peg** (mŭm′bəl-*thə*-pĕg′). A children's game in which the players throw a knife from various positions with the object of having the blade stick firmly in the ground. [Traditionally, the loser's penalty was to pull up with his teeth a peg driven into the ground : *"mumble the peg."*]
mum·bo jum·bo (mŭm′bō jŭm′bō). **1.** *Capital* **M** and **J.** In some Mandingo peoples of the western Sudan, a priest believed to have power to protect his village from evil. **2.** An object believed to have supernatural powers; a fetish. **3.** Confusing or meaningless activity; unintelligible incantation; obscure ritual. **4.** Gibberish. [Mandingo *mā-mā-gyo-mbō,* "magician who makes the troubled spirits of ancestors go away" : *mā-mā,* grandmother + *gyo,* trouble + *mbō,* to leave.]
mu meson. *Physics. Obsolete.* A particle, the **muon** *(see).*
mum·mer (mŭm′ər) *n.* **1.** One who acts or plays in a mask or costume. **2.** Any actor. [Middle English *mummar,* from Middle Dutch *mommer,* from Old French *mommeur,* from *momer,* to MUM.]
mum·mer·y (mŭm′ə-rē) *n., pl.* **-ies.** **1.** A performance by mummers. **2.** A pretentious or hypocritical show or ceremony.
mum·mi·fy (mŭm′ə-fī′) *v.* **-fied, -fying, -fies.** —*tr.* To make into a mummy by embalming and drying. —*intr.* To shrivel or dry up like a mummy. —**mum′mi·fi·ca′tion** *n.*
mum·my[1] (mŭm′ē) *n., pl.* **-ies.** **1.** The body of a human being or animal embalmed after death, as practiced by the ancient Egyptians. **2.** Any withered or shrunken body, living or dead, that resembles a preserved mummy. [Middle English *mummie,* from Old French *momie,* embalming ointment, mummy, from Medieval Latin *mumia,* from Arabic *mūmiyā,* mummy, bitumen, from *mūm,* wax.]
mum·my[2] (mŭm′ē) *n., pl.* **-ies.** *Informal.* Mother. [Alteration of MAMMY.]
mummy case. A container for a mummy, often decorated with a likeness of the dead and with other ornamentation.
mumps (mŭmps) *n.* Plural in form, used with a singular verb. An acute, inflammatory, contagious disease of the salivary glands, especially the parotids, and, sometimes, of the pancreas, ovaries, or testes. It is caused by a virus, *Rubula inflans.* [Plural of dialectal *mump,* grimace, from verb *mump,* to mumble, grimace, probably from Scandinavian, akin to Icelandic *mumpa,* to eat greedily. See **mu-** in Appendix.*]
mun. municipal; municipality.
Mu·na (mo͞o′nə). An island, 659 square miles in area, of the Republic of Indonesia, lying just south of southeastern Sulawesi in the Flores Sea.
munch (mŭnch) *tr.v.* **munched, munching, munches.** To chew steadily with a crunching sound. [Middle English *monchen* (imitative).] —**munch′er** *n.*
Mun·chau·sen (mŭn′chou′zən, mo͞on′-), **Baron.** Original name, Karl Friedrich Hieronymus von Münchhausen. 1720–1797. German soldier; subject of exaggerated tales.
Mun·cie (mŭn′sē). A city of eastern Indiana, 50 miles northeast of Indianapolis. Population, 69,000.
mun·dane (mŭn′dān′, mŭn′dān′) *adj.* **1.** Bound to earth; worldly: *"mundane pleasures dominated those of the spirit"* (George L. Mosse). **2.** Typical of or concerned with the ordinary: *"the sublime style . . . was to be found in classical poets, even the most mundane like Horace"* (Josephine Miles). —See Synonyms at **earthly.** [Middle English *mondeyne,* from Old French *mondain,* from Late Latin *mundānus,* from Latin *mundus,* the world. See **mundus** in Appendix.*] —**mun·dane′ly** *adv.*
mung bean (mŭng). A bean, *Phaseolus aureus,* of eastern Asia. It is the source of bean sprouts used in Oriental cookery.
mun·go (mŭng′gō) *n.* Reclaimed wool used for cheap cloth. See

shoddy. [Possibly from Yorkshire dialect *mungo*†.]
Mu·nich (myo͞o′nĭk). *German* **Mün·chen** (mün′KHən). The capital of Bavaria, West Germany. Population, 1,193,000.
mu·nic·i·pal (myo͞o-nĭs′ə-pəl) *adj.* *Abbr.* **mun. 1. a.** Of or pertaining to a city or its government. **b.** Having local self-government: *a municipal borough.* **2.** Of or pertaining to the internal affairs of a nation, as distinguished from its international affairs. [Latin *mūnicipālis*, from *mūnicipium*, a franchized city, from *mūniceps*, citizen of a *mūnicipium* (who could perform public offices but not hold magistracies) : *mūnus*, public office (see **mei-**[1] in Appendix*) + *-ceps*, "-taker," from *capere*, to take (see **kap-** in Appendix*).] —**mu·nic′i·pal·ly** *adv.*
mu·nic·i·pal·i·ty (myo͞o-nĭs′ə-păl′ə-tē) *n., pl.* **-ties.** *Abbr.* **mun. 1.** A city, town, village, borough, or other district incorporated for local self-government. **2.** A body of officials appointed to manage the affairs of such a community.
mu·nic·i·pal·ize (myo͞o-nĭs′ə-pə-līz′) *tr.v.* **-ized, -izing, -izes. 1.** To place under municipal ownership. **2.** To make a municipality of. —**mu·nic′i·pal·i·za′tion** *n.*
mu·nif·i·cence (myo͞o-nĭf′ə-səns) *n.* **1.** A disposition to bestow lavish benefits; a generous nature. **2.** The lavish bestowal of gifts, entertainment, hospitality, or other benefits.
mu·nif·i·cent (myo͞o-nĭf′ə-sənt) *adj.* **1.** Extremely liberal in giving; very generous. **2.** Showing great generosity: *a munificent gift.* [Latin *mūnificens*, from *mūnificus*, "present-making," generous, bountiful : *mūnus*, office, duty, gift (see **mei-**[1] in Appendix*) + *-ficus*, -FIC.] —**mu·nif′i·cent·ly** *adv.*
mu·ni·ment (myo͞o′nə-mənt) *n.* **1.** *Plural. Law.* Documentary evidence of ownership; written proof by which a person defends his ownership of property or maintains rights. **2.** *Rare.* A means of defense or protection. [Middle English, from Old French, from Medieval Latin *mūnīmentum*, from Latin, defense, from *mūnīre*, to defend, fortify. See **mei-**[3] in Appendix.*]
mu·ni·tion (myo͞o-nĭsh′ən) *n.* *Usually plural.* War materiel, especially weapons and ammunition. —*tr.v.* **munitioned, -tioning, -tions.** To supply with munitions. [Originally, "fortification," from Old French, from Latin *mūnītiō*, from *mūnīre*, to defend, fortify. See **mei-**[3] in Appendix.*]
Mu·ñoz Ma·rín (mo͞o-nyōs′ mä-rēn′), **Luis.** Born 1898. Puerto Rican political leader and journalist; governor (1948–64).
Mun·ro (mən-rō′), **H(ector) H(ugh).** Pen name **Saki** (sä′kē). 1870–1916. English author of short stories.
Mun·ster[1] (mŭn′stər). A province of the Republic of Ireland, occupying 9,317 square miles in the southern part of the country. Population, 917,000.
Mun·ster[2]. Variant of **Muenster.**
Mün·ster (mo͝on′stər, mŭn′-, mĭn′-; *German* mün′stər). A city and port on the Dortmund-Ems Canal in North Rhine-Westphalia, West Germany. Population, 194,000.
Mün·ster·berg (mo͝on′stər-bûrg′, mŭn′-), **Hugo.** 1863–1916. German-born American psychologist and author.
munt·jac (mŭnt′jăk′) *n.* Also **munt·jak.** Any of several small deer of the genus *Muntiacus*, of southeastern Asia and the East Indies. Also called "barking deer." [Malay *menjangan*, deer.]
mu·on (myo͞o′ŏn′) *n.* *Symbol* μ *Physics.* A subatomic particle in the lepton family, having a mass 207 times that of the electron, a negative electric charge, and a mean lifetime of 2.2×10^{-6} second. Formerly called "mu meson." See **particle.**
Mur (mo͝or). *Hungarian & Serbo-Croatian* **Mu·ra** (mo͞o′rä). A river rising in southern Austria and forming part of the Yugoslav border in its 300-mile course to the Drava.
mu·ral (myo͝or′əl) *n.* A picture or decoration, usually a very large one, applied directly to a wall or ceiling. —*adj.* **1.** Of, pertaining to, or like a wall. **2.** Painted on or affixed to a wall. [Old French, from Latin *mūrālis*, from *mūrus*, a wall. See **mei-**[3] in Appendix.*] —**mu′ral·ist** *n.*
Mu·ra·sa·ki (mo͞o′rä-sä′kē), **Baroness.** In full, Murasaki Shikibu. Japanese novelist of the 11th century; author of *Genji Monogatari*, or *The Tale of Genji*.
Mu·rat (mo͞o-rät′). Also **Mu·rad** (mo͞o-rät′). A river rising in east-central Turkey and flowing 380 miles generally westward to join the Euphrates.
Mu·rat (myo͞o-rä′; *French* mü-rȧ′), **Joachim.** 1767?–1815. French marshal; king of Naples (1808–15); brother-in-law of Napoleon Bonaparte.
Mur·chi·son Falls (mûr′chĭ-sən). A series of cascades in north-western Uganda, formed as the Victoria Nile drops 400 feet through a narrow cleft to Lake Albert.
Mur·chi·son River (mûr′chĭ-sən). An intermittent river rising in Western Australia and flowing 400 miles southwest to the Indian Ocean.
Mur·cia (mûr′shə, -shē-ə; *Spanish* mo͞or′thyä). **1.** A region of southeastern Spain, 10,100 square miles in area, on the Mediterranean Sea. **2.** A city in this region. Population, 256,000.
mur·der (mûr′dər) *n.* Also *obsolete* **mur·ther** (mûr′*th*ər). **1.** The unlawful killing of one human being by another, especially with malice aforethought. Compare **homicide, manslaughter. 2.** *Slang.* Something that is very difficult or hazardous or that causes extreme discomfort: *This heat is murder.* —**get away with murder.** *Informal.* To escape punishment for or detection of a blameworthy act. —*v.* **murdered, -dering, -ders.** Also *obsolete* **mur·ther.** —*tr.* **1.** To kill (a human being) unlawfully. **2.** To kill (one or more human beings) brutally or inhumanly. **3.** To destroy or put an end to. **4.** To mar or spoil by ineptness: *"Four little Japanese waitresses were murdering the English language at the counter."* (Alan R. Bosworth). **5.** *Slang.* To defeat decisively; trounce: *The new show was murdering the competition.* —*intr.* To commit murder. [Middle English *murther*, *mordre*, Old English *morthor*. See **mer-**[2] in Appendix.*] —**mur′der·er** (mûr′dər-ər), **mur′der·ess** (mûr′də-rəs) *n.*
mur·der·ous (mûr′dər-əs) *adj.* **1.** Capable of, guilty of, or intending murder: *"but nothing is known . . . that could have caused such a murderous rage"* (Edward D. Radin). **2.** Characteristic of murder; involving bloodshed; deadly; brutal: *a murderous ambush.* **3.** *Informal.* Very difficult or dangerous: *a murderous exam.* —**mur′der·ous·ly** *adv.* —**mur′der·ous·ness** *n.*
Mur·dock (mûr′dŏk′), **William.** 1754–1839. British engineer and inventor; first to use coal gas for illumination.
mure (myo͝or) *tr.v.* **mured, muring, mures.** *Rare.* To immure; confine; wall in. [Middle English *muren*, from Old French *murer*, from Late Latin *mūrāre*, to wall in, from Latin *mūrus*, a wall. See **mei-**[3] in Appendix.*]
Mu·res (mo͞o′rĕsh′). *Hungarian* **Ma·ros** (mô′rōsh′). A river rising in central Rumania and flowing first northward and then westward 550 miles to join the Tisza at Szeged, in southern Hungary.
mu·rex (myo͝or′ĕks′) *n., pl.* **murices** (myo͝or′ə-sēz′) or **-rexes.** Any of various marine gastropods of the genus *Murex*, with rough, spiny shells, common in warm seas. One species, *M. trunculus*, was the source of royal purple dye. [New Latin, from Latin *mūrex*, the purple-fish, of Mediterranean origin.]
Mur·frees·bor·o (mûr′frēz-bûr′ō). A city of central Tennessee near the site of a Civil War battle (December 31, 1862 to January 2, 1863). Population, 19,000.
mu·ri·cate (myo͝or′ə-kāt′) *adj.* Also **mu·ri·cat·ed** (-kā′-tĭd). Having a roughened surface because of many short spines. [Latin *mūricātus*, murex-shaped, pointed, from *mūrex*, MUREX.]
Mu·ri·el (myo͝or′ē-əl). A feminine given name. [Probably from a Celtic cognate of Irish *Muirgheal* : Old Irish *muir*, sea (see **mori-** in Appendix*) + *geal*, bright, from Old Irish *gel* (see **gel-**[2] in Appendix*).]
Mu·ri·llo (mo͞o-rē′lyō), **Bartolomé Esteban.** 1617–1682. Spanish painter, chiefly of religious subjects.
mu·rine (myo͝or′īn′) *adj.* **1.** Of or pertaining to a member of the rodent family Muridae, including rats and mice. **2.** Caused, transmitted, or affected by rodents of the family Muridae: *a murine plague.* —*n.* A murine rodent. [Latin *mūrinus*, from *mūs* (stem *mūr-*), mouse. See **mū-**[1] in Appendix.*]
murk (mûrk) *n.* Also **mirk.** Darkness; gloom. —*adj.* Also **mirk.** *Archaic.* Dark; gloomy. [Middle English *mirke*, from an oblique case of Old English *mirce*, darkness. See **mer-**[1] in Appendix.*]
murk·y (mûr′kē) *adj.* **-ier, -iest.** Also **mirk·y. 1.** Dark or gloomy: *"Haste to Pluto's murky abode."* (Cowper). **2. a.** Heavy and thick with smoke, mist, or the like; foggy; hazy. **b.** Turbid with sediment: *murky waters.* **3. a.** Cloudy in color; having no brightness: *"His colors are dark and murky"* (Time Magazine). **b.** Cloudy in mind; confused; muddled: *"and transcending her murky self she felt at last the passion of a great moral decision"* (Bessie Brever). **4.** Hard to understand; obscure. —See Synonyms at **dark.** —**murk′i·ly** *adv.* —**murk′i·ness** *n.*
Mur·mansk (mo͝or-mänsk′). A city and ice-free seaport of the Soviet Union, on the northern shore of the Kola Peninsula. Population, 272,000.
mur·mur (mûr′mər) *n.* **1.** A low, indistinct, and continuous sound or succession of sounds: *the murmur of the waves.* **2.** An indistinct complaint; mutter. **3.** A whispered utterance: *a murmur of approval.* **4.** *Medicine.* An abnormal sound, usually in the thoracic cavity, derived from the heart or lungs and detected by the ear or a device such as a stethoscope. —*v.* **murmured, -muring, -murs.** —*intr.* **1.** To make a low, continuous, and indistinct sound or succession of sounds. **2.** To complain in low mumbling tones; grumble. —*tr.* To say in a low indistinct voice; utter indistinctly. —See Synonyms at **mutter.** [Middle English *murmure*, from Old French, from Latin *murmur*, rumble, murmur. See **mormor-** in Appendix.*] —**mur′mur·er** *n.* —**mur′mur·ing·ly** *adv.* —**mur′mur·ous** *adj.* —**mur′mur·ous·ly** *adv.*
Mu·ro·ran (mo͞o′rō-rän′). An industrial seaport in southwestern Hokkaido, Japan. Population, 124,000.
mur·phy (mûr′fē) *n., pl.* **-phies.** *Slang.* A potato. [From the Irish surname *Murphy* (the potato was a staple Irish food).]
Mur·phy (mûr′fē), **William Parry.** Born 1892. American physician; worked on pernicious anemia.
Murphy bed. A bed that folds or swings into a closet for concealment. [Designed by William Lawrence *Murphy* (1876–1959), U.S. inventor.]
Murphy's Law. An axiom of engineers and scientists: "If anything can go wrong, it will." [Origin obscure.]
mur·ra (mûr′ə) *n.* Also **mur·rha.** A precious substance, variously conjectured to have been jade, fluorite, or porcelain, obtained by the Romans from Parthia to make cups and bowls. [Latin *murr(h)a*, probably from Parthian.] —**mur′rine, mur′rhine** (mûr′ĭn, -īn′) *adj.*
mur·rain (mûr′ĭn) *n.* **1.** Any highly infectious and malignant disease of domestic plants or animals, such as potato blight or anthrax. **2.** *Archaic.* Any pestilence or dire disease: *"a murrain to her"* (Steele). [Middle English *moreyne*, from Old French *morine*, from *morir*, to die, from Vulgar Latin *morīre* (unattested), variant of Latin *morī*, to die. See **mer-**[2] in Appendix.*]
Mur·ray (mûr′ē), **(George) Gilbert (Aimé).** 1866–1957. British classical scholar, educator, and translator of Greek drama.
Mur·ray (mûr′ē), Sir **James Augustus Henry.** 1837–1915. British philologist; original editor of the Oxford English Dictionary.
Mur·ray River (mûr′ē). A river of Australia, rising in the Australian Alps and flowing westward 1,600 miles to the Indian Ocean, about 100 miles south of Adelaide, South Australia.

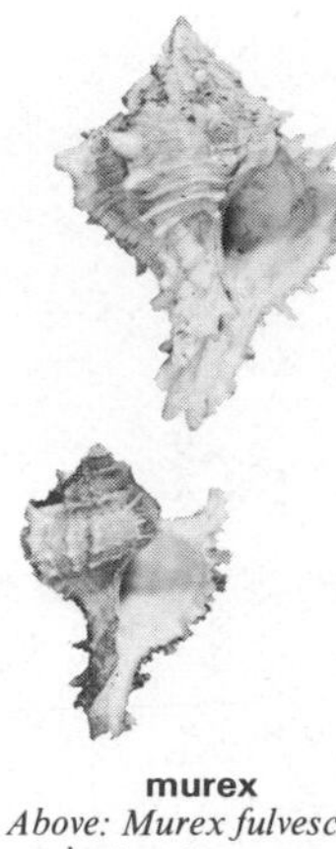

murex
Above: Murex fulvescens, giant eastern murex
Below: Murex brevifrons, West Indian murex

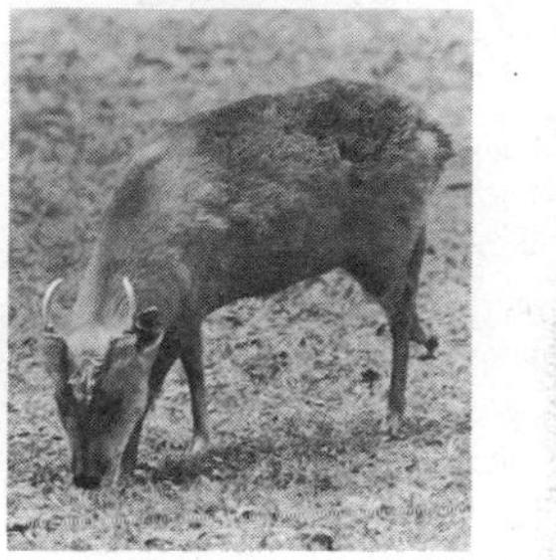

muntjac
Muntiacus muntjak

murre (mûr) *n., pl.* **murre** or **murres.** Any of various sea birds of the genus *Uria,* found in north temperate and arctic regions. [Origin unknown.]

mur·rey (mûr′ē) *n.* A color, **mulberry** (*see*). [Middle English *morreye,* from Old French *more,* from Medieval Latin *morātum,* from *morātus,* mulberry-colored, from Latin *morum,* mulberry, from Greek *moron.* See **moro-** in Appendix.*] —**mur′rey** *adj.*

murrhine glass. Also **murrine glass. 1.** Glassware believed to resemble ancient Roman vessels of murra. **2.** Glassware embedded with precious stones, or with colored metals and glass. [Latin *murr(h)inus,* from *murr(h)a,* MURRA.]

Mur·row (mûr′ō), **Edward R(oscoe).** 1908–1965. American radio-television journalist, producer, and correspondent.

Mur·rum·bidg·ee (mûr′əm-bĭj′ē). A river of New South Wales, Australia, rising in the Eastern Highlands just south of the Australian Capital Territory and flowing generally westward 1,050 miles to join the Murray River on the Victoria border.

mur·ther. *Obsolete.* Variant of **murder.**

Mur·vie·dro. The former name for **Sagunto.**

mus. 1. museum. **2.** music; musical; musician.

Mus. B. Bachelor of Music (Latin *Musicae Baccalaureus*).

Mus·ca (mŭs′kə) *n.* A constellation in the polar region of the Southern Hemisphere near Apus and Carina. [Latin, "the fly." See **mū-²** in Appendix.*]

mus·ca·dine (mŭs′kə-dĭn′, -dĭn) *n.* **1.** A woody vine, *Vitis rotundifolia,* of the southeastern United States. **2.** The fruit of this vine, a purple grape used to make wine. Also called "bullace grape," "scuppernong." [Variant of MUSCATEL.]

mus·cae vo·li·tan·tes (mŭs′ē vŏl′ĭ-tăn′tēz). Small motes and threads that seem to move about the field of vision, due to the presence of cell fragments or other defects in the vitreous humor and the lens of the eye. [Latin, "fluttering flies."]

mus·ca·rine (mŭs′kə-rēn′, -rĭn) *n.* A highly toxic organic compound, $C_9H_{21}O_3N$, related to the cholines, derived from the red form of the mushroom *Amanita muscaria* and occurring in dead animal tissue. [From New Latin (*Amanita*) *muscaria,* from Latin *muscārius,* of a fly, from *musca,* a fly. See **mū-²** in Appendix.*]

mus·cat (mŭs′kăt, -kət) *n.* **1.** Any of various sweet white grapes used for making wine or raisins. **2.** A wine, **muscatel** (*see*). [Old French, from Old Provençal *muscat,* "musky" (flavor), from *musc,* musk, from Late Latin *muscus,* MUSK.]

Mus·cat (mŭs′kăt). *Arabic* **Mas·qat** (mŏs′kŏt). The capital of the sultanate of Muscat and Oman on the Gulf of Oman. Population, 6,000.

Mus·cat and O·man. See **Oman.**

mus·ca·tel (mŭs′kə-tĕl′) *n.* Also **mus·ca·del** (mŭs′kə-dĕl′). **1.** A rich, sweet wine made from muscat grapes. **2.** A muscat grape or raisin. [Middle English *muscadelle,* from Old French *muscadel,* from Old Provençal *muscadel,* diminutive of *muscat,* musky, MUSCAT.]

mus·cle (mŭs′əl) *n.* **1.** A tissue composed of fibers capable of contracting and relaxing to effect bodily movement. The principal types are **striated muscle** and **smooth muscle,** with **cardiac muscle** (*all of which see*) intermediate between them. **2.** A contractile organ consisting of muscle tissue. **3.** Muscular strength: *enough muscle to be a high jumper.* **4.** Power or authority: *put some muscle into law enforcement.* —*intr.v.* **mus·cled, -cling, -cles.** To force one's way into a place or situation where one is not wanted. Usually used with *in.* [Old French, from Latin *mūsculus,* "little mouse," muscle (from the shape of certain muscles), from *mūs,* mouse. See **mū-¹** in Appendix.*]

mus·cle-bound (mŭs′əl-bound′) *adj.* **1.** Having stiff, overdeveloped muscles, usually as the result of excessive exercise. **2.** Unable to act flexibly; rigid: *"the greatest military establishment . . . might easily have been muscle-bound during the 15 fateful minutes of warning time"* (William Manchester).

muscle fiber. An elongated, contractile cell having highly striated cytoplasm.

muscle sense. A sense through which muscular movement is perceived. It arises from nerve ends in the skin, tendons, muscles, and joints.

muscle sugar. A natural sugar, **inositol** (*see*).

mus·co·va·do (mŭs′kə-vä′dō) *n.* Also **mus·ca·va·do.** Unrefined sugar obtained from the juice of sugar cane by evaporation and extraction of the molasses. [Portuguese (*açúcar*) *mascavado,* unrefined (sugar), from *mascavar,* to adulterate, depreciate, from Vulgar Latin *minuscapāre* (unattested) : *minus,* less, from *minor,* smaller (see **mei-²** in Appendix*) + *capāre* (unattested), "to bring to a head," cause, from Latin *caput,* head (see **kaput** in Appendix*).]

mus·co·vite (mŭs′kə-vīt′) *n.* A mineral, the most common form of mica, consisting essentially of hydrous potassium aluminum silicate, $KAl_2(AlSi_3O_{10})(OH)_2$. It ranges from colorless or pale yellow to gray and brown, has a pearly luster, and is used as an insulator. Also called "isinglass," "white mica." [Formerly called *Muscovy* glass.]

Mus·co·vite (mŭs′kə-vīt′) *n.* A native or resident of Moscow or of Muscovy. —**Mus′co·vite′** *adj.*

Mus·co·vy¹ (mŭs′kə-vē). **1.** The principality of Moscow (12th–16th century). **2.** *Poetic.* Russia.

Mus·co·vy² (mŭs′kə-vē, -kō-vē) *n.* A waterfowl, *Cairina moschata,* found wild from Mexico to Brazil, but domesticated around the world for its succulent flesh. It is greenish-black with heavy red wattles. Also called "Muscovy duck," "musk duck." [Folk etymology from *musk duck* (by mistaken association with MUSCOVY).]

mus·cu·lar (mŭs′kyə-lər) *adj.* **1.** Pertaining to or consisting of muscle or muscles. **2.** Accomplished with the use of muscle or

muscles. **3.** Having strong muscles. [From Latin *mūsculus,* MUSCLE.] —**mus′cu·lar′i·ty** (-lăr′ə-tē) *n.* —**mus′cu·lar·ly** *adv.*

muscular dystrophy. A chronic, noncontagious disease of unknown cause, in which complete incapacitation follows gradual but irreversible muscular deterioration.

mus·cu·la·ture (mŭs′kyə-lə-chŏŏr′) *n.* The system of muscles of an animal or a body part. [French, from Latin *mūsculus,* MUSCLE.]

Mus. D., Mus. Dr. Doctor of Music.

muse (myōōz) *v.* **mused, musing, muses.** —*intr.* To ponder or meditate; consider or deliberate at length. Often followed by *over, on,* or *upon:* "*Beneath the waning moon I walk at night/And muse on human life"* (Bryant). —*tr.* **1.** To meditate on; consider reflectively: *muse the problem.* **2.** To wonder: *"The maiden paused, musing what this might mean."* (Coleridge). —*n.* A state of musing or deep meditation. [Middle English *musen,* from Old French *muser,* to muse, "to sniff around," "cast about for a scent," from *mus,* snout, from Medieval Latin *mūsum.* See **mūsum** in Appendix.*] —**muse′ful** *adj.* —**muse′ful·ly** *adv.*

Muse (myōōz) *n.* **1.** *Greek Mythology.* Any of the nine daughters of Mnemosyne and Zeus, each of whom presided over a different art or science. The Muses are Calliope, Clio, Erato, Euterpe, Melpomene, Polyhymnia, Terpsichore, Thalia, and Urania. **2.** *Small* **m.** The spirit or power regarded as inspiring and watching over poets, musicians, and artists; a source of inspiration. [Middle English, from Old French, from Latin *Mūsa,* from Greek *Mousa.* See **Mousa** in Appendix.*]

mu·sette (myōō-zĕt′) *n.* **1.** A small French bagpipe with a soft sound. **2.** A soft, pastoral air that imitates the sound of a bagpipe. **3.** A kind of dance performed to such an air. **4.** A small canvas or leather bag with a shoulder strap, used especially by soldiers. Also called "musette bag." [Middle English, from Old French, from *muser,* to MUSE, dawdle, play the musette.]

mu·se·um (myōō-zē′əm) *n. Abbr.* **mus.** A place or building in which works of artistic, historical, and scientific value are cared for and exhibited. [Latin *mūsēum,* library, study, museum, from Greek *mouseion,* "place of the Muses," from *mouseios,* of the Muses, from *Mousa,* a Muse. See **Mousa** in Appendix.*]

mush¹ (mŭsh) *n.* **1.** Boiled cornmeal. **2.** Anything thick, soft, and pulpy in texture. **3.** *Informal.* Maudlin sentimentality or amorousness. [Probably alteration of MASH.]

mush² (mŭsh) *interj.* A command to a team of sled dogs to start or go faster. —*intr.v.* **mushed, mushing, mushes.** To travel with a dog sled. —*n.* A journey by dog sled. [Canadian French *mouche!* "run!" from *moucher,* to fly, hasten, from French *mouche,* a fly, from Latin *musca.* See **mū-²** in Appendix.*] —**mush′er** *n.*

mush·room (mŭsh′rōōm′, -rŏŏm′) *n.* **1.** Any of various fleshy fungi of the class Basidiomycetes, characteristically having an umbrella-shaped cap borne on a stalk; especially, any of the edible varieties. Compare **toadstool. 2.** Something resembling a mushroom in shape. —*intr.v.* **mushroomed, -rooming, -rooms. 1.** To multiply, grow, or expand rapidly: *The demonstration mushroomed into a riot.* **2.** To spread out, flatten, or swell into a mushroomlike shape. [Middle English *musseroun, muscheron,* from Old French *mousseron, moisseron,* from Gallo-Roman *mussiro†* (unattested), agaric.]

mush·y (mŭsh′ē) *adj.* **-ier, -iest. 1.** Like mush; soft and pulpy. **2.** *Informal.* Excessively sentimental. —**mush′i·ly** *adv.* —**mush′i·ness** *n.*

mu·sic (myōō′zĭk) *n. Abbr.* **mus. 1.** The art of organizing tones to produce a coherent sequence of sounds intended to elicit an aesthetic response in a listener. **2.** Vocal or instrumental sounds having some degree of rhythm, melody, and harmony. **3. a.** A musical composition. **b.** A body of such compositions: *the music of Béla Bartók; French music.* **c.** The written or printed score for a musical composition. **d.** Such scores collectively. **4.** A musical accompaniment. **5.** The study of musicology. **6.** Any aesthetically pleasing or harmonious sound or combination of sounds: *the music of her voice.* **7.** A group of musicians. Now used chiefly of a military band. —**face the music.** *Slang.* To accept the consequences, especially of one's own actions. [Middle English *musik,* from Old French *musique,* from Latin *mūsica,* from Greek *mousikē (tekhnē),* (art) of the Muses, i.e., poetry, literature, music, etc., from *mousikos,* of the Muses, from *Mousa,* a Muse. See **Mousa** in Appendix.*]

mu·si·cal (myōō′zĭ-kəl) *adj. Abbr.* **mus. 1.** Of, pertaining to, or capable of producing music: *a musical instrument.* **2.** Characteristic of or resembling music; melodious: *a musical speaking voice.* **3.** Set to or accompanied by music: *a musical revue.* **4.** Devoted to or skilled in music. —*n.* **1.** A **musical comedy** (*see*). **2.** *Rare.* A musicale. —**mu′si·cal·ly** *adv.*

musical chairs. A game in which the players walk to music around a row of chairs containing one chair fewer than the number of players. When the music stops, the players rush to sit down, and the one left without a chair is eliminated.

musical comedy. A play in which dialogue is interspersed with songs and dances, usually based upon a rather sketchy plot.

Synonyms: musical comedy, revue, operetta, light opera, vaudeville. A *musical comedy* differs from a *revue* principally in having a plot. A *revue* is a plotless series of comic sketches and songs, often topical and satiric. *Operetta,* used interchangeably with *light opera,* is a form having a plot with spoken dialogue; the libretto and the music are generally more serious and substantial than those of *musical comedy.* In modern usage, *vaudeville* denotes a plotless program of unrelated specialty acts; the approximate British equivalents are *music hall* and *variety.*

mu·si·cale (myōō′zĭ-kăl′) *n.* A program of music performed at

Muse
Sculpture
of the Muse Calliope

a party or social gathering. [French *(soirée) musicale,* "musical (evening)," from *musical,* musical, from Old French, from *musique,* MUSIC.]
musical glasses. An instrument, the **glass harmonica** *(see).*
mu·si·cal·i·ty (myo͞o′zĭ-kăl′ə-tē) *n.* **1.** Musical quality: *"the musicality, accuracy, and infectious charm of these performances"* (New York Times). **2.** Skill in the performance of, ability to respond to, or talent for music.
music box. A box containing a device, activated by clockwork, which produces musical sounds.
music drama. An opera in which the musical and dramatic continuity is not interrupted by arias, recitatives, or ensembles, while its text is set to continuously expressive music often based extensively on leitmotifs. See **opera.**
music hall. 1. An auditorium for musical performances. **2.** *Chiefly British.* **a.** A vaudeville theater. **b.** Vaudeville.
mu·si·cian (myo͞o-zĭsh′ən) *n. Abbr.* **mus.** A person skilled in composing or performing music, especially a professional. [Middle English *musicien,* from Old French, from Latin *mūsica,* MUSIC.] —**mu·si′cian·ly** *adj.*
mu·si·cian·ship (myo͞o-zĭsh′ən-shĭp′) *n.* Skill, taste, and artistry in performing or composing music.
music of the spheres. An inaudible harmony thought by Pythagoras to be produced by the movements of celestial bodies.
mu·si·col·o·gy (myo͞o′zĭ-kŏl′ə-jē) *n.* The historical and scientific study of music. —**mu′si·col′o·gist** *n.*
mus·ing (myo͞o′zĭng) *adj.* Absorbed in thought; contemplative. —*n.* Contemplation; meditation: *"cold midnight musings on the Breton shore"* (Jack Kerouac). —**mus′ing·ly** *adv.*
mus·jid (mŭs′jĭd) *n.* A **mosque** *(see).*
musk (mŭsk) *n.* **1.** A greasy secretion with a powerful odor, produced in a glandular sac beneath the skin of the abdomen of the male musk deer and used in perfumery. **2.** Any similar secretion of certain other vertebrates, such as the otter or civet. **3.** Any synthetic chemical resembling natural musk in odor or use. **4.** The odor of musk or an odor resembling it. **5.** The **musk deer** *(see).* [Middle English *muske,* from Old French *musc,* from Late Latin *muscus,* from Greek *moskhos,* from Persian *mushk,* probably from Sanskrit *muṣka,* testicle, scrotum (from the scrotum-shaped musk bag of a musk deer), "little mouse," from *mūṣ,* mouse. See **mū-¹** in Appendix.*] —**musk′y** *adj.* —**musk′i·ness** *n.*
musk beaver. The **muskrat** *(see).*
musk deer. A small, hornless deer, *Moschus moschiferus,* of central and northeastern Asia. The male secretes musk.
musk duck. 1. A waterfowl, the **Muscovy** *(see).* **2.** A waterfowl, *Biziura lobata,* of Australia. The male has a leathery chin lobe, and emits a musky odor during the breeding season.
mus·keg (mŭs′kĕg′) *n.* Also **mas·keg** (măs′kĕg′). A swamp or bog formed by an accumulation of sphagnum moss, leaves, and decayed matter resembling peat. [Cree *maskeek,* from Proto-Algonquian *maškyeekwi* (unattested), swamp.]
mus·kel·lunge (mŭs′kə-lŭnj′) *n., pl.* **muskellunge** or **-lunges.** Also **mus·kal·lunge, mas·ka·longe** (măs′kə-lŏnj′), **mas·ca·longe, mas·ki·nonge** (măs′kə-nŏnj′). A large game fish, *Esox masquinongy,* similar to the pike, found in the cooler fresh waters of North America. Also called "muskie." [Of Algonquian origin, akin to Algonquian *maskinonge,* "big pike."]
mus·ket (mŭs′kĭt) *n.* A smoothbore shoulder gun used from the late 16th through the 18th centuries. [French *mousquet,* from Italian *moschetto,* crossbolt, later musket, diminutive of *mosca,* a fly, from Latin *musca.* See **mū-²** in Appendix.*]
mus·ket·eer (mŭs′kĭ-tîr′) *n.* **1.** A soldier armed with a musket. **2.** A member of the French royal household bodyguard in the 17th and 18th centuries. [French *mousquetaire,* from *mousquet,* MUSKET.]
mus·ket·ry (mŭs′kĭ-trē) *n.* **1.** Muskets collectively. **2.** The fire of muskets. **3.** The technique of using small arms.
Mus·kho·ge·an (mŭs-kō′gē-ən) *n.* Also **Mus·ko·ge·an.** A North American Indian language family, including Chickasaw, Choctaw, Creek, and Seminole.
musk mallow. 1. A plant, *Malva moschata,* native to Europe, having finely divided leaves and pink or white flowers with a faint scent of musk. **2.** A plant, the **abelmosk** *(see).*
musk·mel·on (mŭsk′mĕl′ən) *n.* **1.** Any of several varieties of the melon *Cucumis melo,* such as the cantaloupe, having fruit characterized by a netted rind and flesh with a musky aroma. **2.** The fruit of any of these plants.
musk ox. A large, hoofed mammal, *Ovibos moschatus,* of northern Canada and Greenland, that emits a musky odor. It has a long, shaggy, brown-to-black coat and horns. Also called "ovibos."
musk·rat (mŭsk′krăt′) *n., pl.* **muskrat** or **-rats. 1.** An aquatic rodent, *Ondatra zibethica,* of North America, having a brown coat that is widely used as a fur. It has partly webbed hind feet, and musk glands under a broad, flat tail. Also called "musk beaver," "musquash." See **water rat. 2.** The fur of this rodent. [MUSK + RAT (possibly influenced by Algonquian (Natick) *musquash,* MUSQUASH).]
musk rose. A prickly shrub, *Rosa moschata,* native to the Mediterranean region, cultivated for its clustered, musk-scented white flowers.
musk turtle. Any small freshwater turtle of the genus *Sternotherus,* of the eastern United States and Canada, having a musky odor.
Mus·lim (mŭz′ləm, mo͝os′-, mo͞oz′-) *n.* Also **Mus·lem** (mŭz′ləm, mo͝os′-, mo͞oz′-). **1.** See **Moslem. 2.** A member of the **Nation of Islam** *(see).* —See Usage note at **Moslem.** —*adj.* **1.** Moslem. **2.** Pertaining or belonging to the Nation of Islam. [Arabic *muslim,* "one who surrenders (to God)," active participle of *salama,* to surrender. See **slm** in Appendix.*]
mus·lin (mŭz′lĭn) *n.* **1.** Any of various sturdy, plain-weave cotton fabrics, used especially for sheets. **2.** A prototype of a garment or other cloth article to be fitted and used as a pattern. [French *mousseline,* from Italian *mussolina,* "cloth of Mosul," from Arabic *mūṣlin,* originally made in *Al-Mawṣil,* MOSUL.]
Mus. M. Master of Music (Latin *Magister Musicae*).
mus·quash. The **muskrat** *(see).* [Algonquian (Natick).]
muss (mŭs) *tr.v.* **mussed, mussing, musses.** To make messy or untidy; rumple. Often followed by *up.* —*n.* **1.** A state of disorder; a mess. **2.** *Archaic.* A squabble; disturbance; row. [Perhaps alteration of MESS.] —**muss′y** *adj.* —**muss′i·ly** *adv.*
mus·sel (mŭs′əl) *n.* **1.** Any of several marine bivalve mollusks, especially the edible *Mytilus edulis,* having a blue-black shell. **2.** Any of several freshwater bivalve mollusks of the genera *Anodonta* and *Unio,* found in central United States, whose shells provide mother-of-pearl. [Middle English *muscle,* Old English *mus(c)le,* from West Germanic *muskul* (unattested), from Latin *mūsculus,* "little mouse," muscle, mussel (from its mouselike shape), from *mūs,* mouse. See **mū-¹** in Appendix.*]
Mus·sel·shell (mŭs′əl-shĕl′). A river rising in central Montana and flowing 300 miles first east and then north to the Missouri.
Mus·set (mü-sĕ′), **Alfred de.** 1810–1857. French Romantic poet and dramatist.
Mus·so·li·ni (mo͞os′sō-lē′nē), **Benito.** 1883–1945. Fascist dictator of Italy (1922–43); executed by partisans.
Mus·sorg·sky, Modest Petrovich. See **Moussorgsky.**
Mus·sul·man (mŭs′əl-mən) *n., pl.* **-men** (-mĭn) or **-mans.** *Archaic.* A Moslem. [Turkish *musulmān,* probably from Arabic *mushmūn,* plural of *muslim,* MUSLIM.]
must¹ (mŭst) *v.* Used as an auxiliary followed by an infinitive without *to,* or, in reply to a question or suggestion, with the infinitive understood. Indicates: **1.** Compulsion or obligation: *When duty calls, you must answer.* **2.** Requirement or prerequisite: *You must register in order to vote.* **3.** Probability, expectation, or supposition: *It must be nearly midnight.* **4.** Inevitability or certainty: *To each of us, death must come.* **5. a.** In the first person, insistence or fixed resolve: *I must finish this tonight.* **b.** In the second and third persons, insistence imputed by the speaker to others: *Have another drink, if you must.* **6.** Unpleasant inevitability. Used as a past or historical present: *The rain was bad enough, now it must snow.* —*n.* **1.** An absolute requirement; unavoidable responsibility: *Promptness on the job is a must.* **2.** Something that should without fail be done, seen, or otherwise acted upon: *If you visit Yugoslavia, the Dalmatian Coast is a must.* —*adj. Informal.* Of cardinal importance; absolutely necessary: *Let the other work go; this is a must job.* [Middle English *moste* (past tense), Old English *mōste,* past tense of *mōtan,* to be allowed. See **med-** in Appendix.*]
must² (mŭst) *n.* Staleness; mustiness. [Back-formation from MUSTY.]
must³ (mŭst) *n.* The unfermented or fermenting juice being processed for wine; new wine. [Middle English *must,* Old English *must, moste,* from Latin *mustum,* "new wine," from neuter of *mustus,* new, newborn. See **meu-** in Appendix.*]
mus·tache (mŭs′tăsh′, mə-stăsh′). Also *chiefly British* **mous·tache** *n.* **1.** *Sometimes plural.* The hair growing on the upper lip, especially when it is cultivated and groomed. **2.** Something similar to a mustache in appearance and position, especially: **a.** A group of bristles or hair about the mouth of an animal. **b.** Distinctive coloring or feathers near the beak of a bird. [Old French *mo(u)stache,* from Italian *mustaccio,* from Medieval Greek *moustaki,* from Greek (Doric) *mustax,* the upper lip, mustache. See **menth-** in Appendix.*]
mus·ta·chio (mə-stăsh′ō, -stăsh′ē-ō′, -stä′shō, -shē-ō′) *n., pl.* **-chios.** *Often plural.* A mustache, especially a luxuriant one. Usually used jocosely. [Spanish *mostaccho* and Italian *mustaccio,* MUSTACHE.]
Mus·ta·fa Ke·mal. See **Kemal Atatürk.**
mus·tang (mŭs′tăng′) *n.* A wild horse of the North American plains, descended from Spanish stock. [Mexican Spanish *mesten(g)o,* from Spanish, stray (animal), from *mesta,* meeting of owners of stray animals, from Medieval Latin *(animalia) mixta,* wild or stray animals that mixed with and became attached to a grazier's herd, "mixed animals," from Latin *mixtus,* past participle of *miscēre,* to mix. See **meik-** in Appendix.*]
mus·tard (mŭs′tərd) *n.* **1.** Any of various plants of the genus *Brassica,* native to Eurasia, having four-petaled yellow flowers and slender pods. Some species, especially *B. nigra* and *B. alba,* are cultivated for their pungent seeds. **2. a.** Powdered mustard seeds used medicinally. See **mustard plaster. b.** A condiment consisting of a paste made from powdered mustard seeds mixed with wine, vinegar, or water, and various spices, such as turmeric. **3.** Dark yellow to light olive brown. See **color.** [Middle English *mustarde,* condiment, later also plant, from Old French *mo(u)starde,* from Common Romance *mosto* (unattested), from Latin *mustum,* MUST, "new wine" (because mustard paste was originally made by mixing grape juice with mustard powder).]
mustard gas. An oily, volatile liquid, $(ClCH_2CH_2)_2S$, used in warfare as a gaseous blistering agent. [From its mustardlike odor.]
mustard oil. Any oil obtained from mustard seeds.
mustard plaster. A pastelike mixture of powdered mustard, flour, and water, spread on cloth or paper, and applied as a poultice.
mus·te·line (mŭs′tə-līn′, -lĭn) *adj.* Of or pertaining to fur-bearing mammals of the family Mustelidae, which includes

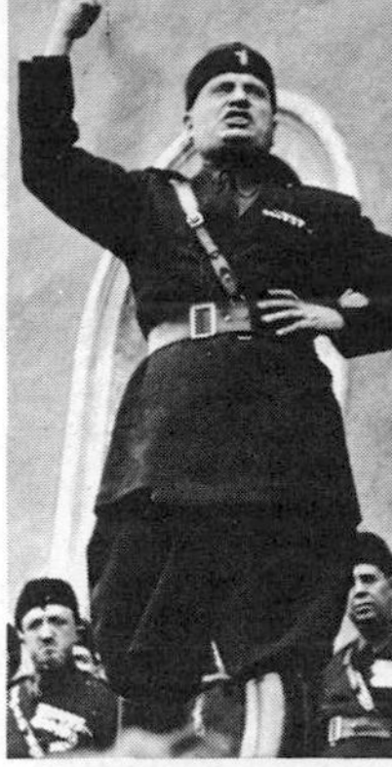
Benito Mussolini

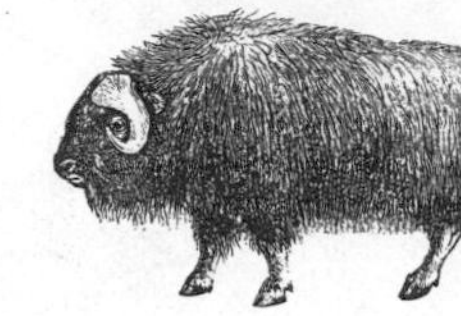
musk ox

pod

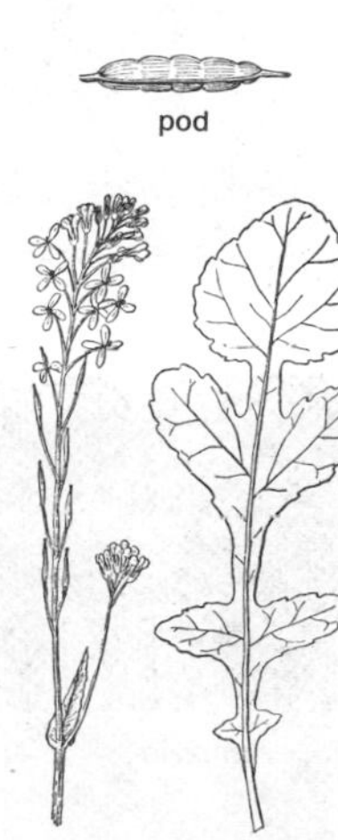
flowers leaf
mustard
Brassica nigra

badger, mink, otter, and weasel. [Latin *mustēlīnus,* of a weasel, from *mustēla,* weasel, probably from *mūs,* mouse. See **mū-**[1] in Appendix.*]

mus·ter (mŭs′tər) *v.* **-tered, -tering, -ters.** —*tr.* **1.** To summon or assemble (troops): *The men were mustered for roll call.* **2.** To collect or gather. Often used with *up: Muster up your courage.* —*intr.* To assemble or gather: *mustering for inspection.* —**muster in** or **out.** To enlist (someone) in, or discharge (someone) from, military service: *He was mustered in at the age of eighteen.* —*n.* **1. a.** A gathering, especially of troops, for service, inspection, review, or roll call. **b.** The persons assembled for such a gathering. **2.** The official roll of men in a military or naval unit. Also called "muster roll." **3.** Any gathering or collection: *a muster of business leaders at a luncheon.* **4.** A flock of peacocks. —See Synonyms at **flock.** —**pass muster.** To be acceptable. [Middle English *mostren, mustren,* from Old French *mo(u)strer,* from Latin *monstrāre,* to show, indicate (originally by an omen), from *mōnstrum,* an omen, prodigy, probably from *monēre,* to warn. See **men-**[1] in Appendix.*]

must·y (mŭs′tē) *adj.* **-ier, -iest.** **1.** Having a stale or moldy odor or taste. **2.** Hackneyed; dull; antiquated; stale. [Variant (influenced by MUST, juice) of obsolete *moisty,* from MOIST.] —**must′i·ly** *adv.* —**must′i·ness** *n.*

mut. Variant of **mutt.**

mu·ta·ble (myōō′tə-bəl) *adj.* **1.** Subject to change or alteration. **2.** Prone to frequent change; inconstant; fickle. [Latin *mūtābilis,* from *mūtāre,* to change, MUTATE.] —**mu′ta·bil′i·ty, mu′ta·ble·ness** *n.* —**mu′ta·bly** *adv.*

mu·ta·gen (myōō′tə-jən, -jĕn′) *n.* Any agent, including radioactive elements, ultraviolet light, and certain chemicals, that causes biological mutation. [MUTA(TION) + -GEN.] —**mu′ta·gen′ic** *adj.* —**mu′ta·gen′i·cal·ly** *adv.*

mu·tant (myōō′tənt) *n. Biology.* An individual or organism differing from the parental strain or strains as a result of mutation. [Latin *mūtans,* changing, present participle of *mūtāre,* to change, MUTATE.] —**mu′tant** *adj.*

mu·tate (myōō′tāt′, myōō-tāt′) *v.* **-tated, -tating, -tates.** —*tr.* To cause to undergo alteration, especially by mutation. —*intr.* To undergo change by mutation. [Latin *mūtāre.* See **mei-**[1] in Appendix.*] —**mu′ta·tive** (myōō′tā′tĭv, myōō′tə-) *adj.*

mu·ta·tion (myōō-tā′shən) *n.* **1.** The act or process of being altered or changed. **2.** An alteration or change, as in nature, form, or quality. **3.** *Biology.* **a.** Any heritable alteration of the genes or chromosomes of an organism. **b.** A mutant. **4.** *Linguistics.* The change that is caused in the sound of one vowel by its assimilation to another vowel; especially, **umlaut** *(see).* [Middle English *mutacioun,* from Old French *mutation,* from Latin *mūtātiō,* from *mūtāre,* to change, MUTATE.] —**mu·ta′tion·al** *adj.* —**mu·ta′tion·al·ly** *adv.*

mu·ta·tis mu·tan·dis (mōō-tä′tēs mōō-tän′dēs; myōō-tā′tĭs myōō-tăn′dĭs). *Abbr.* **m.m.** *Latin.* The necessary changes having been made; substituting new terms.

mutch·kin (mŭch′kĭn) *n. Scottish.* A unit of liquid measure equal to 0.9 U.S. pint. [Middle English (Scottish) *muchekyn,* from obsolete Dutch *mudseken,* diminutive of *mudde,* bushel, from Latin *modius.* See **med-** in Appendix.*]

mute (myōōt) *adj.* **muter, mutest.** **1.** Refraining from producing speech or vocal sound. **2. a.** Unable to speak. **b.** Unable to vocalize, as certain animals. **3.** *Law.* Refusing, as a defendant, to plead either guilty or not guilty when under arraignment. Used chiefly in the phrase *stand mute.* **4.** *Phonetics.* **a.** Not pronounced; silent, as the *e* in *house.* **b.** Pronounced with a temporary stoppage of breath, as the sounds of *p* and *b;* plosive; stopped. —See Synonyms at **dumb.** —*n.* **1.** A person incapable of speech; especially, one both deaf and mute. **2.** *Law.* A defendant who refuses to plead either guilty or not guilty when under arraignment. **3.** *Music.* Any of various devices used to muffle or soften the tone of a musical instrument. **4.** *Phonetics.* **a.** A silent or unpronounced letter. **b.** A plosive; a stop. —*tr.v.* **muted, muting, mutes.** **1.** To muffle or soften the sound of. **2.** To soften the tone, color, shade, or hue of. [Middle English *muet,* from Old French, diminutive of *mu,* mute, from Latin *mūtus,* silent, dumb. See **mu-** in Appendix.*] —**mute′ly** *adv.* —**mute′ness** *n.*

mu·ti·late (myōōt′l-āt′) *tr.v.* **-lated, -lating, -lates.** **1.** To deprive (a person or animal) of a limb or other essential part. **2.** To render imperfect by damaging or excising a part. [Latin *mutilāre,* cut off, from *mutilus,* maimed. See **mut-** in Appendix.*] —**mu′ti·la′tion** *n.* —**mu′ti·la′tor** *n.* —**mu′ti·la′tive** *adj.*

mu·ti·neer (myōōt′n-îr′) *n.* A person, especially a soldier or sailor, who takes part in a mutiny. [Obsolete French *mutinier,* from Old French *mutin,* MUTINY.]

mu·ti·nous (myōōt′n-əs) *adj.* **1.** Pertaining to, engaged in, or disposed toward mutiny: *a mutinous crew.* **2.** Rebellious; disaffected: *a mutinous child.* **3.** Turbulent and uncontrollable: *"Mutinous passions, and conflicting fears."* (Shelley). —See Synonyms at **insubordinate.** [From obsolete *mutine,* MUTINY.] —**mu′ti·nous·ly** *adv.* —**mu′ti·nous·ness** *n.*

mu·ti·ny (myōōt′n-ē) *n., pl.* **-nies.** Open rebellion against constituted authority; especially, rebellion of sailors or soldiers against superior officers. See Synonyms at **rebellion.** —*intr.v.* **mutinied, -nying, -nies.** To rebel thus. [From obsolete *mutine,* mutiny, from Old French *mutin,* rebellious, rebellion, from *meute,* revolt, "movement," from Vulgar Latin *movita* (unattested), from Latin *movēre,* to move. See **mew-** in Appendix.*]

mut·ism (myōō′tĭz′əm) *n.* The condition of being mute.

Mu·tsu·hi·to (mōō′tsōō-hē′tō). Reign name, Meiji. 1852–1912. Emperor of Japan (1867–1912); abolished feudalism and launched westernizing reforms.

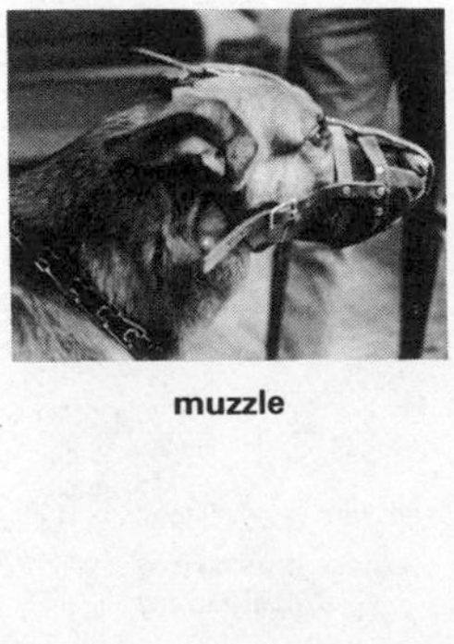

muzzle

mutt (mŭt) *n.* Also **mut.** *Slang.* **1.** A mongrel dog. **2.** A fool. [Shortened from MUTTONHEAD.]

mut·ter (mŭt′ər) *v.* **-tered, -tering, -ters.** —*intr.* **1.** To speak indistinctly in low tones. **2.** To complain or grumble morosely: *"He muttered against the men who wear helmets and carry clubs."* (O. Henry). —*tr.* To utter or say in low, indistinct tones. —*n.* A low, indistinct uttering or utterance, often of discontent. [Middle English *muteren,* akin to Old Norse *mudhla.* See **mu-** in Appendix.*] —**mut′ter·er** *n.*

Synonyms: *mutter, mumble, murmur. Mutter* pertains to human speech uttered through compressed lips, and generally suggests muted resentment or dissatisfaction. *Mumble,* applicable to speech, stresses indistinctness resulting from nearly closed lips, which may merely indicate carelessness. *Murmur,* applied to speech, wind, or water, stresses continuous, low-pitched sound, which may be pleasant. It may suggest a mingled drone.

mut·ton (mŭt′n) *n.* The flesh of fully grown sheep. [Middle English *moto(u)n,* from Old French *moton,* sheep, from Medieval Latin *multō* (stem *multōn-*). See **mel-**[1] in Appendix.*]

mutton chop. **1.** A thick chop cut from the loin section of mutton. **2.** *Plural.* Side whiskers shaped like chops of meat.

mut·ton·fish (mŭt′n-fĭsh′) *n., pl.* **muttonfish** or **-fishes.** A species of **eelpout** *(see).*

mut·ton·head (mŭt′n-hĕd′) *n. Slang.* A stupid person. [From the stupidity of sheep.] —**mut′ton·head′ed** *adj.*

Mut·tra. The former name for **Mathura.**

mu·tu·al (myōō′chōō-əl) *adj.* **1.** Having the same relationship each to the other: *mutual friends.* **2.** Directed and received in equal amount: *"The best league between princes, is a mutual fear of each other."* (Donne). See Usage note below. **3.** Possessed in common: *mutual interests.* See Usage note below. [Middle English *mutuall,* from Old French *mutuel,* from Latin *mūtuus,* exchanged, reciprocal, mutual. See **mei-**[1] in Appendix.*] —**mu′tu·al′i·ty** (-ăl′ə-tē) *n.* —**mu′tu·al·ly** *adv.*

Usage: *Mutual,* in strict usage, is properly applied to what two persons do, feel, or represent to each other. Major exceptions to this rule are the expressions *mutual friend,* which is often used instead of "common friend" to denote a third party, and *mutual aid,* which usually suggests the participation of many persons. The first is accepted by 86 per cent of the Usage Panel, and the second by 83 per cent. *Mutual* often pertains to intangibles of a personal nature, such as fear, respect, and obligation. *Reciprocal* also indicates two parties, in strict usage, and often modifies nouns with impersonal, tangible senses, such as trade or tariff. But it stresses a balanced relationship in which one action is taken in return for another. Thus it is applicable to a single action of one partner, whereas *mutual* always pertains to both partners. *Common,* as in *common interest,* is applied to what is shared by each of two or more persons or things, without implying any further relationship. *Joint,* as in *joint control,* suggests a venture of two or more persons or groups acting in concert, and usually stresses an active, equal relationship.

mutual fund. A company without fixed capitalization, freely buying and selling its own shares and using its capital to invest in other companies. Also called "open-end investment company." Compare **closed-end investment company.**

mutual inductance. *Abbr.* **M** *Physics.* **1.** The ratio expressed by the flux linking one circuit with a neighboring circuit divided by the current in the neighboring circuit. **2.** The ratio expressed by the electromagnetic force induced in a circuit by a neighboring circuit divided by the corresponding change of current in the neighboring circuit. See **inductance.**

mutual insurance. An insurance system in which the insured persons become company members, each paying specified amounts into a common fund from which members are entitled to indemnification in case of loss.

mu·tu·al·ism (myōō′chōō-ə-lĭz′əm) *n. Biology.* Any association between two organisms, such as **parasitism** or **symbiosis** *(both of which see).*

mu·tu·al·ize (myōō′chōō-ə-līz′) *tr.v.* **-ized, -izing, -izes.** **1.** To make mutual. **2.** To set up or reorganize (a corporation) so that the majority of common stock is owned by customers or employees. —**mu′tu·al·i·za′tion** *n.*

muu·muu (mōō′mōō′) *n.* A long, loose dress that hangs free from the shoulders. [Hawaiian *mu'u mu'u.*]

mu·zhik (mōō-zhēk′, -zhĭk′) *n.* Also **mou·jik, mu·jik, mu·zjik.** A peasant in czarist Russia. [Russian *muzhik,* a peasant, diminutive of *muzh,* man, from Old Church Slavonic *mǫzhi.* See **man-**[1] in Appendix.*]

Muz·tagh (mōōs-tä′). A mountain rising to 23,890 feet in southwestern Sinkiang-Uigur Autonomous Region, China.

Muz·tagh-Kar·a·ko·ram Range. See **Karakoram.**

muz·zle (mŭz′əl) *n.* **1.** The forward, projecting part of the head, including the jaws and nose, of certain animals. **2.** A leather or wire device that, when fitted over an animal's snout, prevents biting and eating. **3.** The forward, discharging end of the barrel of a firearm. —*tr.v.* **muzzled, -zling, -zles.** **1.** To put a muzzle on (an animal). **2. a.** To restrain (someone) from expressing opinions. **b.** To restrain (something) from being expressed. [Middle English *mosel, musell,* from Old French *musel,* from Gallo-Roman *mūsellum* (unattested), diminutive of Late Latin *mūsum,* snout. See **mūsum** in Appendix.*] —**muz′zler** *n.*

muz·zle·load·er (mŭz′əl-lō′dər) *n.* A firearm loaded through the muzzle. —**muz′zle·load′ing** *adj.*

muz·zy (mŭz′ē) *adj.* **-zier, -ziest.** *Informal.* **1.** Muddled; confused. **2.** Blurred; indistinct. [Origin obscure.] —**muz′zi·ly** *adv.* —**muz′zi·ness** *n.*

mV millivolt.

MV 1. megavolt. **2.** motor vessel.
M.V. motor vessel.
MVA Missouri Valley Authority.
MVD, M.V.D. Ministry of Internal Affairs (Russian *Minis-teyrstvo Vnutreynnikh Deyl*), a former administrative branch of the Soviet government functioning as a successor to the **Cheka** and corresponding to the later **KGB** (*both of which see*).
mW milliwatt.
MW megawatt.
Mwe·ru (mwā′rōō). A lake, about 173 square miles in area, on the border between Zambia and the Democratic Republic of the Congo (Kinshasa).
Mx *Physics.* maxwell.
Mx. Middlesex.
my (mī) *adj.* The possessive form of the pronoun *I.* **1.** Used attributively to indicate possession, agency, or reception of an action by the speaker: *my wallet; pursuing my tasks; suffered my first rebuff.* **2.** Used preceding various forms of polite, affectionate, or familiar address: *my lord; my dear Dr. Dressner; my good man.* **3.** Used in various interjectional phrases: *My word! My goodness!* —*interj.* Used as an exclamation of surprise, pleasure, or dismay: *Oh, my!* [Middle English *my, mi, min,* Old English *mīn.* See **me-¹** in Appendix.*]
my·al·gi·a (mī-ăl′jē-ə, -jə) *n. Pathology.* **1.** Muscular rheumatism. **2.** Muscular pain. [New Latin : MY(O)- + -ALGIA.]
my·a·sis. Variant of **myiasis.**
my·as·the·ni·a (mī′əs-thē′nē-ə) *n.* Abnormal muscular weakness or fatigue. [New Latin : MY(O)- + ASTHENIA.] —**my′as·then′ic** (-thĕn′ĭk) *adi.*
myc. mycological; mycology.
my·ce·li·um (mī-sē′lē-əm) *n., pl.* -**lia** (-lē-ə). The vegetative part of a fungus, consisting of a mass of branching, threadlike filaments called hyphae. [New Latin, "nail of fungus" : MYC(O)- + Greek *hēlos,* nail, wart (see **wel-³** in Appendix*).] —**my·ce′li·al** *adj.*
My·ce·nae (mī-sē′nē). An ancient city of Greece, located in the northeastern Peloponnesus.
My·ce·nae·an (mī′sə-nē′ən) *adj.* Of, pertaining to, or designating the Aegean civilization that spread its influence from Mycenae to many parts of the Mediterranean region from about 1400 B.C. to 1150 B.C. —**My′ce·nae′an** *n.*
Mycenaean Greek. The early East Greek dialect of the Mycenaeans, attested in documents in Linear B script.
-**mycete.** Indicates a member of a specified class of fungi; for example, **basidiomycete.** [From New Latin -*mycetes* (class), from Greek *mukētes,* plural of *mukēs,* fungus. See **meug-²** in Appendix.*]
my·ce·to·ma (mī′sə-tō′mə) *n., pl.* -**mas** or -**mata** (-mə-tə). **1.** A chronic fungous infection usually affecting the foot, characterized by nodules that discharge oily pus. **2.** A mycetoma nodule. [New Latin : Greek *mukētes,* fungi (see -**mycete**) + -OMA.] —**my′ce·tom′a·tous** (-tŏm′ə-təs, -tō′mə-təs) *adj.*
my·ce·to·zo·an (mī-sē′tə-zō′ən) *n.* A slime mold (*see*). —*adj.* Of or relating to slime molds. [From New Latin *Mycetozoa* "fungus-animals" (formerly classed in the animal kingdom) : Greek *mukētes,* fungi (see -**mycete**) + -ZOA.]
-**mycin.** Indicates derivation of a specified substance from bacteria or fungi; for example, **streptomycin.** [MYC(O)- + -IN.]
myco-, myc-. Indicates fungus; for example, **mycelium, mycology.** [New Latin, from Greek *mukēs,* fungus. See **meug-²** in Appendix.*]
my·co·bac·te·ri·um (mī′kō-băk-tîr′ē-əm) *n., pl.* -**teria** (-tîr′ē-ə). Any slender, rod-shaped bacterium of the genus *Mycobacterium,* which includes the bacterium that causes tuberculosis.
mycol. mycological; mycology.
my·col·o·gy (mī-kŏl′ə-jē) *n. Abbr.* **myc., mycol. 1.** The branch of botany that deals with fungi. **2.** The fungi native to a region. [New Latin *mycologia* : MYCO- + -LOGY.] —**my′co·log′i·cal** (mī′kə-lŏj′ĭ-kəl), **my′co·log′ic** *adj.* —**my·col′o·gist** *n.*
my·cor·rhi·za, my·co·rhi·za (mī′kə-rī′zə) *n., pl.* -**zae** (-zē) or -**zas.** *Botany.* The symbiotic association of the mycelium of a fungus with the roots of certain plants, such as conifers, beeches, or orchids. [New Latin : MYCO- + Greek *rhiza,* a root (see **werād-** in Appendix*).] —**my·cor·rhi′zal** *adj.*
my·co·sis (mī-kō′sĭs) *n., pl.* -**ses** (-sēz′). **1.** A fungous growth in the body. **2.** A disease caused by a fungous growth. [New Latin : MYC(O)- + -OSIS.]
my·dri·a·sis (mĭ-drī′ə-sĭs, mī-) *n.* Prolonged and abnormal dilatation of the pupil of the eye as a result of disease or a drug. [Latin, from Greek *mudriasis*†.]
myd·ri·at·ic (mĭd′rē-ăt′ĭk) *n.* A drug that produces dilatation of the pupils. [From MYDRIASIS.] —**myd′ri·at′ic** *adj.*
myel-. Indicates the spinal cord or bone marrow; for example, **myelencephalon, myelitis.** [New Latin, from Greek *muelos,* marrow, from *mus,* muscle. See **mū-¹** in Appendix.*]
my·el·en·ceph·a·lon (mī′ə-lĕn-sĕf′ə-lŏn′) *n.* The rear part of the embryonic hindbrain from which the medulla oblongata develops. [New Latin : MYEL- + ENCEPHALON.] —**my′el·en·ce·phal′ic** (-sə-făl′ĭk) *adj.*
my·e·lin (mī′ə-lĭn) *n.* Also **my·e·line** (mī′ə-lĭn, -lēn′). **1.** A white, fatty material encasing some nerve fibers. Also called "medullary sheath." **2.** One of several fatlike substances found in body tissues. [MYEL- + -IN.] —**my′e·lin′ic** *adj.*
my·e·li·nat·ed (mī′ə-lĭ-nā′tĭd) *adj.* Having a myelin sheath. Said of nerves. Also "medullated."
my·e·li·ni·za·tion (mī′ə-lĭ-nə-zā′shən) *n.* Also **my·e·li·na·tion** (mī′ə-lĭ-nā′shən). **1.** The process of growing a myelin sheath; becoming myelinated. **2.** The condition of having a myelin sheath.

my·e·li·tis (mī′ə-lī′tĭs) *n.* Inflammation of the spinal column or bone marrow. [New Latin : MYEL- + -ITIS.]
my·e·loid (mī′ə-loid′) *adj.* **1.** Of, related to, or derived from bone marrow. **2.** Of or pertaining to the spinal cord. [MYEL- + -OID.]
my·e·lo·ma (mī′ə-lō′mə) *n., pl.* -**mas** or -**mata** (-mə-tə). A malignant tumor of the bone marrow. [New Latin : MYEL- + -OMA.] —**my′e·lo′ma·toid** *adj.*
my·i·a·sis (mī′ə-sĭs, mī-ī′ə-sĭs) *n.* Also **my·a·sis** (mī′ə-sĭs). *Pathology.* Infestation of human tissue by fly maggots or flies, or a disease resulting from it. [New Latin : Greek *muia, mua,* fly (see **mū-²** in Appendix*) + -IASIS.]
my·lo·nite (mī′lə-nīt′) *n.* A fine-grained laminated rock formed by the shifting of rock layers. [Greek *mulōn,* mill, from *mulē, mulos,* mill, millstone (see **melə-** in Appendix*) + -ITE.]
my·na (mī′nə) *n.* Also **my·nah, mi·na.** Any of various birds of the family Sturnidae, of southeastern Asia. They are related to the starlings, and are blue-black to dark-brown with yellow bills. Certain species are known for mimicry of human speech. [Hindi *mainā,* from Sanskrit *madana.* See **mad-** in Appendix.*]
myn·heer (mĭn-hâr′, -hîr′) *n.* **1.** Also *Dutch* **mijn·heer** (mə-nîr′). *Often capital* **M.** The Dutch title of courtesy and respect equivalent to the English *sir* or *Mr.* **2.** *Informal.* A Dutchman. [Dutch *mynheer,* obsolete variant of *mijnheer,* "my lord" : *mijn,* my, from Middle Dutch *mijn* (see **me-¹** in Appendix*) + *heer,* lord, sir, master, from Middle Dutch (see **kei-²** in Appendix*).]
myo-, my-. Indicates muscle; for example, **myograph, myasthenia.** [New Latin, from Greek *mus,* muscle. See **mū-¹** in Appendix.*]
my·o·car·di·o·graph (mī′ō-kär′dē-ə-grăf′, -gräf′) *n.* An instrument for graphing the action of the heart muscle.
my·o·car·di·tis (mī′ō-kär-dī′tĭs) *n.* Inflammation of the myocardium. [MYOCARD(IUM) + -ITIS.]
my·o·car·di·um (mī′ō-kär′dē-əm) *n.* The muscle tissue of the heart. [New Latin : MYO- + Greek *kardia,* the heart (see **kerd-¹** in Appendix*).] —**my′o·car′di·al** *adj.*
my·o·gen·ic (mī′ō-jĕn′ĭk) *adj.* Also **my·o·ge·net·ic** (mī′ō-jə-nĕt′-ĭk). **1.** Giving rise to or forming muscle tissue. **2.** Of muscular origin. [MYO- + -GENIC.]
my·o·glo·bin (mī′ō-glō′bĭn) *n.* The form of hemoglobin found in muscle fibers.
my·o·graph (mī′ə-grăf′, -gräf′) *n.* An instrument for graphing muscular contractions. [MYO- + -GRAPH.]
my·ol·o·gy (mī-ŏl′ə-jē) *n.* The scientific study of muscles. [MYO- + -LOGY.] —**my′o·log′ic** *adj.* —**my·ol′o·gist** *n.*
my·o·ma (mī-ō′mə) *n., pl.* -**mas** or -**mata** (-mə-tə). A tumor composed of muscle tissue. [MY(O)- + -OMA.] —**my·om′a·tous** (mī-ŏm′ə-təs, -ō′mə-təs) *adj.*
my·ope (mī′ōp′) *n.* One who has myopia. [French, from Late Latin *myops,* myopic, from Greek *muōps.* See **myopia.**]
my·o·pi·a (mī-ō′pē-ə) *n.* **1.** *Pathology.* A visual defect in which distant objects appear blurred because their images are focused in front of the retina rather than on it; nearsightedness. **2.** Shortsightedness or lack of discernment in thinking or planning: *"For Lorca, New York is a symbol of spiritual myopia, where man . . . has lost sight of those elemental natural forces"* (Edwin Honig). [New Latin, from Greek *muōpia,* from *muōps,* myopic, "closing or contracting the eyes" : *muein,* to close (see **mu-** in Appendix*) + *ōps,* eye (see **okw-** in Appendix*).] —**my·op′ic** (mī-ŏp′ĭk, -ō′pĭk) *adj.* —**my·op′i·cal·ly** *adv.*
my·o·sin (mī′ə-sĭn) *n.* The commonest protein in muscle; with actin it forms **actomyosin** (*both of which see*). [Greek *muos,* genitive of *mus,* muscle (see **mū-¹** in Appendix*) + -IN.]
my·o·sis. *Pathology.* Variant of **miosis.**
my·o·so·tis (mī′ə-sō′tĭs) *n.* Any plant of the genus *Myosotis,* such as the forget-me-not. [New Latin, from Latin *myosotis,* from Greek *muosōtis,* "mouse-ear" (from its furry leaves) : *muos,* genitive of *mus,* mouse (see **mū-¹** in Appendix*) + *ous* (stem *ōt-*), ear (see **ous-** in Appendix*).]
my·o·to·ni·a (mī′ə-tō′nē-ə) *n. Pathology.* Tonic spasm or temporary muscular rigidity. [MYO- + -TONIA.] —**my′o·ton′ic** (-tŏn′ĭk) *adj.*
myria-. Indicates: **1.** A very large or countless number; for example, **myriapod. 2.** Ten thousand, as combined with names of metric units; for example, *myriameter* equals 10,000 meters. [From Greek *murios,* countless, and its plural *murioi,* ten thousand. See **meu-** in Appendix.*]
myr·i·ad (mĭr′ē-əd) *adj.* Amounting to a very large, indefinite number: *"The forests, with their myriad tongues, / Shouted of liberty"* (Longfellow). —*n.* **1.** *Archaic.* Ten thousand. **2.** A vast number; a great multitude. [Late Latin *myrias* (stem *myriad-*), from Greek *murias,* from *murios,* countless, and its plural *murioi,* ten thousand. See **meu-** in Appendix.*]
myr·i·a·pod (mĭr′ē-ə-pŏd′) *n.* Any of several arthropods, such as the centipede, having segmented bodies and many legs. [New Latin *myriapoda* : MYRIA- + -POD.] —**myr′i·ap′o·dan** (mĭr′ē-ăp′ə-dən) *adj.* & *n.* —**myr′i·ap′o·dous** (-ăp′ə-dəs) *adj.*
my·ris·tic acid (mə-rĭs′tĭk, mī-). An organic compound, $CH_3(CH_2)_{12}COOH$, occurring in animal and vegetable fats. It is used in cosmetics and flavors. [Greek *muristikos,* fragrant, from *muron,* perfume. See **Myron.**]
myrmeco-. Indicates ant; for example, **myrmecophile.** [Greek, from *murmēx,* ant. See **morwi-** in Appendix.*]
myr·me·col·o·gy (mûr′mə-kŏl′ə-jē) *n.* The study of ants. [MYRMECO- + -LOGY.] —**myr′me·co·log′i·cal** (mûr′mə-kə-lŏj′ĭ-kəl) *adj.* —**myr′me·col′o·gist** *n.*
myr·me·coph·a·gous (mûr′mə-kŏf′ə-gəs) *adj.* Feeding on ants. [MYRMECO- + -PHAGOUS.]
myr·me·co·phile (mûr′mə-kə-fīl′) *n.* Any organism that habitu-

ally shares the nest of an ant colony. [MYRMECO- + -PHILE.] —myr'me·coph'i·lous (mûr'mə-kŏf'ə-ləs) *adj.* —myr'me·coph'i·ly (-kŏf'ə-lē) *n.*

Myr·mi·don (mûr'mə-dŏn', -dən) *n.* One of a legendary Greek warrior people of ancient Thessaly who followed their king Achilles on the expedition against Troy.

myr·mi·don (mûr'mə-dŏn', -dən) *n.* A faithful follower who carries out orders without question. [After MYRMIDON.]

Myr·na (mûr'nə). A feminine given name. [Origin uncertain.]

my·rob·a·lan (mī-rŏb'ə-lən, mə-) *n.* **1.** A tree, *Prunus cerasifera,* native to Asia, bearing edible red or yellow fruit. Also called "cherry plum." **2.** A tree, the **Indian almond** *(see).* **3.** The fruit of either of these trees. [Old French *mirobolan,* from Latin *myrobalanus,* from Greek *murobalanos* : *muron,* perfume, unguent (see **Myron**) + *balanos,* acorn, date (see **gwel-**[3] in Appendix*).]

My·ron[1] (mī'rən). A masculine given name. [Greek, from *muron*†, sweet oil, perfume, "something delightful."]

My·ron[2] (mī'rən). Greek sculptor of the fifth century B.C.; most celebrated work the *Discobolus.*

myrrh (mûr) *n.* **1.** An aromatic gum resin obtained from several trees and shrubs of the genus *Commiphora,* of India, Arabia, and eastern Africa. It is used in perfume and incense, and was one of the gifts of the Magi to the infant Jesus. **2.** Any shrub or tree that exudes such a gum resin. **3.** A plant, **sweet cicely** *(see).* [Middle English *myrre,* Old English *myrrha,* from Common Germanic *murra* (unattested), from Latin *myrrha,* from Greek *murrha,* perhaps from Semitic, akin to Arabic *murr.*]

myr·tle (mûrt'l) *n.* **1.** Any of several evergreen shrubs or trees of the genus *Myrtus;* especially, *M. communis,* an aromatic shrub native to the Mediterranean region and western Asia, having pink or white flowers and blue-black berries. **2.** Any of various other plants or shrubs, such as the **crape myrtle** and the **periwinkle** *(both of which see).* [Middle English *mirtille,* from Old French, from Medieval Latin *myrtillus,* diminutive of Latin *myrtus,* from Greek *murtos*†.]

myrtle warbler. A songbird, *Dendroica coronata,* of North America. The male is gray and black on top and white below, with yellow markings.

my·self (mī-sĕlf') *pron.* A specialized form of the first person singular pronoun. It is used: **1.** As a reflexive pronoun, forming the direct or indirect object of a verb or the object of a preposition: *hurt myself; give myself time; talk to myself.* **2.** For emphasis, after *I: I myself do.* **3.** As an emphasizing substitute: **a.** For *I,* in a compound subject. **b.** For *me,* in a compound object. See Usage note below. **c.** For *I,* in an absolute construction: *Myself in debt, I could offer no assistance.* **d.** *Archaic.* For *I,* as a simple subject: *"Myself have letters of the self-same tenure."* (Shakespeare). **4.** As an indication of one's real, normal, or healthy condition or identity: *I have not been myself.* [Middle English *miself,* alteration of *meself,* Old English *mē selfum* (dative), *mē selfne* (accusative) : *mē,* me (see **me-**[1] in Appendix*) + *selfum, selfne,* dative and accusative of *self,* SELF.]

Usage: The use of *myself* (for *me*) in compound objects, as in *He asked John and myself,* is condemned by 95 per cent of the Usage Panel (Gilbert Highet: "a prissy evasion of *me*"; Walter "Red" Smith: "the refuge of idiots taught early that *me* is a dirty word"). Also strongly condemned is the use of *myself* (for *I*) in subjects, as in *Mr. Jones and myself are undecided.*

my·so·phil·i·a (mī'sō-fĭl'ē-ə) *n.* A pathological interest in and attraction to excreta. [New Latin : Greek *musos,* uncleanness, defilement (see **meu-** in Appendix*) + -PHILIA.]

my·so·pho·bi·a (mī'sō-fō'bē-ə) *n.* A pathological fear of dirt or contamination. [New Latin : Greek *musos,* uncleanness, defilement (see **meu-** in Appendix*) + -PHOBIA.]

My·sore (mī-sôr', -sōr'). **1.** A state of the Republic of India, 74,122 square miles in area. Population, 19,399,000. Capital, Bangalore. **2.** A city in this state, about 80 miles southwest of Bangalore. Population, 254,000.

mys·ta·gogue (mĭs'tə-gôg', -gŏg') *n.* **1.** In Mediterranean mystery religions, one who prepared candidates for initiation into the mysteries. **2.** A teacher of religious mysteries; a hierophant. **3.** One who holds or spreads mystical doctrines. [Old French, from Latin *mystagogus,* from Greek *mustagōgos* : *mustēs,* an initiate (see **mystery**) + *agōgos,* leader, from *agein,* to lead (see **ag-** in Appendix*).] —**mys'ta·go'gy** (-gō'jē) *n.* —**mys'ta·gog'ic** (mĭs'tə-gŏj'ĭk) *adj.*

mys·te·ri·ous (mĭ-stîr'ē-əs) *adj.* **1.** Full of mystery; difficult to explain or account for; of obscure origin: *a mysterious light from nowhere.* **2.** Unknowable: *"The cold, mysterious presence of God was all around him."* (Louis Zara). **3.** Implying a mystery: *"poetically enveloped in a mysterious blue cloak"* (Dickens). **4.** Enigmatic in manner: *"She was not usually given to mysterious silences."* (Loretta Burrough). **5.** Struck with a sense of mystery. [Old French *mysterieux,* from *mystère,* mystery, from Latin *mystērium,* MYSTERY (riddle).] —**mys·te'ri·ous·ly** *adv.* —**mys·te'ri·ous·ness** *n.*

Synonyms: *mysterious, esoteric, occult, obscure, abstruse, enigmatic, inscrutable. Mysterious* applies to anything that arouses wonder by being difficult to understand or solve. *Esoteric* pertains to that which is understandable only to those with special knowledge or powers of perception, as in a religious discipline or a field of scholarship. *Occult* applies to what is so beyond human understanding that comprehension is possible only by supernatural means. *Obscure* pertains to that which is vaguely expressed or dimly defined, and *abstruse* to what has deep or hidden meaning, generally couched in difficult terminology. *Enigmatic* suggests the baffling quality of a riddle, with meaning hidden by a cryptic exterior. *Inscrutable* implies the impossibility of human understanding.

mys·ter·y[1] (mĭs'tər-ē) *n., pl.* **-ies.** **1.** Anything that arouses curiosity because it is unexplained, inexplicable, or secret: *"But I never ventured to inquire, and indeed rather cherished the mystery."* (Max Beerbohm). **2.** The quality or air of being unexplained, secret, or unknown: *"The very thorn trees that grew in the fields had about them an aspect of mystery."* (Arthur Machen). **3.** A piece of fiction dealing with a puzzling crime: *"The ideal mystery was one you would read if the end was missing."* (Raymond Chandler). **4.** The behavior of someone given to secrecy and intrigue: *"He professed to despise all mystery . . . either in a prince or a minister."* (Swift). **5.** *Theology.* A religious truth revealed through Christ to the elect: *"Unto you it is given to know the mystery of the kingdom of God."* (Mark 4:11). **6.** *Archaic.* Something having a symbolic significance: *"I will tell thee the mystery of the woman, and of the beast that carrieth her"* (Revelation 17:7). **7.** One of 15 incidents in the life of Christ, as commemorated in the 15 divisions of the rosary and regarded as having a mystical significance. **8.** A **mystery play** *(see).* **9.** *Plural.* **a.** Among some ancient Mediterranean peoples, any of certain cults and secret rites to which only initiates were admitted. **b.** The secrets of Freemasonry. [Middle English *misterie, mysterie,* from Latin *mystērium,* from Greek *mustērion,* "secret rites," from *mustēs,* one initiated into secret rites, from *mueîn,* to initiate, from *muein,* to close the eyes or mouth, hence to keep secret (as in religious initiation). See **mu-** in Appendix.*]

mys·ter·y[2] (mĭs'tər-ē) *n., pl.* **-ies.** *Archaic.* A trade or occupation: *"The invention of men has been sharpening and improving the mystery of murder."* (Burke). [Middle English *mysterie, misterie,* from Late Latin *misterium,* variant (by association with *mystērium,* secret rites, mystery) of Latin *ministerium,* service, work, occupation, from *minister,* servant. See **mei-**[2] in Appendix.*]

mystery play. A form of medieval drama developed from church liturgy and based on episodes in the life of Christ. Compare **miracle play.** [Old French *mistere, mystere,* from Latin *mystērium,* religious symbol, MYSTERY.]

mys·tic (mĭs'tĭk) *adj.* **1.** Of or pertaining to the religious mysteries of Greece and Rome or to other occult rites and practices. **2.** Mysteriously symbolic; inspiring a sense of mystery and wonder. **3.** Mystical. —*n.* One who practices or believes in mysticism or a specified form of mysticism. [Middle English *mistik,* from Latin *mysticus,* from Greek *mustikos,* from *mustēs,* an initiated person. See **mystery** (secret).]

mys·ti·cal (mĭs'tĭ-kəl) *adj.* **1.** Characteristic of mystics or of the nature of mysticism: *"It is no mystical intuition, but an analysable conception."* (Stanley Parry). **2.** Believing in or practicing mysticism. **3.** *Theology.* **a.** Of a nature or import that by virtue of its divinity surpasses understanding: *"The mystical vision of God cannot be passed on from father to son."* (Thomas Merton). **b.** Spiritually symbolic: *a mystical emblem of the Trinity.* —**mys'ti·cal·ly** *adv.* —**mys'ti·cal·ness** *n.*

mys·ti·cete (mĭs'tə-sēt') *n.* Any of several whales having symmetrical skulls, paired blowholes, and plates of whalebone instead of teeth. Also called "whalebone whale." [New Latin *mysticetus,* from Greek *mustikētos,* some kind of whale, supposedly a corruption of *ho mus to kētos,* "the mouse, the whale," i.e., "that whale which is called 'the mouse' " (the semantic development is obscure) : *mus,* mouse (see **mū-**[1] in Appendix*) + *kētos,* whale (see **cetacean**).] —**mys'ti·ce'tous** (mĭs'tə-sē'təs) *adj.*

mys·ti·cism (mĭs'tə-sĭz'əm) *n.* **1. a.** A spiritual discipline aiming at union with the divine through deep meditation or trancelike contemplation. **b.** The experience of such communion, as described by mystics. **2.** Any belief in the existence of realities beyond perceptual or intellectual apprehension but central to being and directly accessible by intuition. **3.** Confused and groundless speculation; superstitious self-delusion.

mys·ti·fi·ca·tion (mĭs'tə-fĭ-kā'shən) *n.* **1. a.** The act or an instance of making something obscure or mysterious. **b.** The fact or condition of being thus obscured: *"The mystification of metaphysical systems does not imply the demise of philosophy."* (I.L. Horowitz). **2.** The fact or condition of being mystified or bewildered; bafflement.

mys·ti·fy (mĭs'tə-fī') *tr.v.* **-fied, -fying, -fies.** **1.** To awe or perplex; bewilder. **2.** To make obscure or difficult to comprehend. —See Synonyms at **puzzle.** [French *mystifier,* irregularly from *mystère,* mystery, from Latin *mystērium,* MYSTERY.] —**mys'ti·fi'er** *n.* —**mys'ti·fy'ing·ly** *adv.*

mys·tique (mĭ-stēk') *n.* **1. a.** An attitude of mystical veneration conferring upon an occupation, a person, or a thing an awesome and mythical status; the special cult of anything: *the mystique of Eastern music.* **b.** The object of such veneration: *"For the beat generation sex is . . . a mystique."* (Charles Glicksberg). **2.** A mystical or philosophical conception used as a guide, especially for political action: *"The theory did not require a Hegelian mystique."* (M.A. Kaplan and N.deB. Katzenbach). **3.** Qualities or skills that set a person or thing apart and beyond the understanding of an outsider. [French, from adjective, "mystic," from Latin *mysticus,* MYSTIC.]

myth (mĭth) *n.* **1. a.** A traditional story originating in a preliterate society, dealing with supernatural beings, ancestors, or heroes that serve as primordial types in a primitive view of the world: *"myths bring the unknown into relation with the known"* (Cecil M. Bowra). **b.** A body of such stories told among a given people; a mythology: *in Norse myth.* **c.** All such stories collectively: *"For many writers, myth is the common denominator between poetry and religion"* (R. Wellek and A. Warren). **2.** Any real or fictional story, recurring theme, or character type that appeals to the consciousness of a people by embodying its cultural ideals or by giving expression to deep, commonly felt emotions: *the Oedipal myth; the myth of Horatio Alger.* **3.** One of the fictions or half-truths forming part of the ideology of a society: *the myth of Anglo-Saxon superiority.* **4.** Any fictitious or imaginary story, explanation, person, or thing: *"German artillery superiority on the Western Front was a myth."* (Leon Wolff). **5.** A notion based more on tradition or convenience than on fact; a received idea: *"Without such uncertainty we are left with a set of dogmas and myths."* (I.L. Horowitz). [New Latin *mythus,* from Late Latin *mythos,* tale, myth, from Greek *muthos*†.]

myth. mythological; mythology.

myth·i·cal (mĭth′ĭ-kəl) *adj.* Also **myth·ic. 1.** Having the nature of a myth. **2.** Existing only in myth: *the mythical unicorn.* **3.** Imaginary; fictitious; fancied. —**myth′i·cal·ly** *adv.*

myth·i·cize (mĭth′ə-sīz′) *tr.v.* **-cized, -cizing, -cizes. 1.** To turn (a person or event) into myth. **2.** To interpret as a myth or in terms of mythology.

my·thog·ra·pher (mĭ-thŏg′rə-fər) *n.* A recorder or narrator of myths. [Greek *muthographos : muthos,* MYTH + *-graphos,* -GRAPHER.]

my·thoi. Plural of **mythos.**

mythol. mythological; mythology.

myth·o·lo·gem (mĭth′ə-lŏ′jəm) *n.* A mythological motif, such as the hidden treasure, the walled garden, or the animal-man. [Greek *muthologēma,* mythical narrative, from *muthologein,* to narrate myths, from *muthologia,* MYTHOLOGY.]

myth·o·log·i·cal (mĭth′ə-lŏj′ĭ-kəl) *adj. Abbr.* **myth., mythol.** Also **myth·o·log·ic. 1.** Of, pertaining to, or celebrated in mythology. **2.** Fabulous; imaginary. **3.** Myth-making: *the mythological proclivities of children.* —**myth′o·log′i·cal·ly** *adv.*

my·thol·o·gist (mĭ-thŏl′ə-jĭst) *n.* A student of mythology.

my·thol·o·gize (mĭ-thŏl′ə-jīz′) *v.* **-gized, -gizing, -gizes.** —*tr.* To convert into myth; mythicize. —*intr.* **1.** To construct or relate a myth. **2.** To interpret or write about myths or mythology. —**my·thol′o·giz′er** *n.*

my·thol·o·gy (mĭ-thŏl′ə-jē) *n., pl.* **-gies.** *Abbr.* **myth., mythol. 1. a.** A collection of myths about the origin and history of a people and their deities, ancestors, and heroes. **b.** A body of myths concerning some individual, event, or institution: *"A new mythology, essential to the . . . American funeral rite, has grown up"* (Jessica Mitford). **2.** The field of scholarship dealing with the systematic collection and study of myths. [French *mythologie,* from Late Latin *mȳthologia,* from Greek *muthologia : muthos,* MYTH + *-logia,* -LOGY.]

myth·o·ma·ni·a (mĭth′ə-mā′nē-ə, -mān′yə) *n.* A compulsion to embroider the truth, exaggerate, or tell lies. [MYTH + -MANIA.] —**myth′o·ma′ni·ac′** (-mā′nē-ăk′) *n. & adj.*

myth·o·poe·ic (mĭth′ə-pē′ĭk) *adj.* Also **myth·o·pe·ic.** Productive of myths; myth-making. [From Greek *muthopoios,* mythmaker, from *muthopoiein,* to make a myth : *muthos,* MYTH + *poiein,* to make, create (see **kwei-²** in Appendix*).] —**myth′o·poe′ia** (-pē′ə), **myth′o·po·e′sis** (-pō-ē′sĭs) *n.*

my·thos (mī′thŏs′, mĭth′ŏs′) *n., pl.* **mythoi** (mī′thoi′, mĭth′oi′). **1.** Myth. **2.** Mythology. **3.** The pattern of basic values and historical experiences of a people, characteristically transmitted through the arts. **4.** A deliberately fostered cult: *"Sukarno . . . established a mythos in which towns were named for him, and his picture displayed everywhere."* (New York Times). [Greek *muthos,* MYTH.]

Myt·i·le·ne (mĭt′ə-lē′nē). **1.** A city of the Greek island of Lesbos in the eastern Aegean Sea. Population, 26,000. **2.** The island of Lesbos.

myx·e·de·ma, myx·oe·de·ma (mĭk′sə-dē′mə) *n.* A disease caused by decreased activity of the thyroid gland in adults, and characterized by dry skin, swellings around the lips and nose, mental deterioration, and a subnormal basal metabolic rate. See **cretinism.** [MYX(O)- + EDEMA.] —**myx′e·dem′a·tous** (-dĕm′ə-təs, -dē′mə-təs), **myx′e·dem′ic** (-dĕm′ĭk) *adj.*

myxo-, myx-. Indicates mucus or mucuslike material; for example, **myxomycete, myxoid.** [New Latin, from Greek *muxa,* mucus, slime. See **meug-²** in Appendix.*]

myx·o·cyte (mĭk′sə-sīt′) *n.* A large cell found in mucous tissue. [MYXO- + -CYTE.]

myx·oid (mĭk′soid′) *adj.* Containing mucus; mucoid. [MYX(O)- + -OID.]

myx·o·ma (mĭk-sō′mə) *n., pl.* **-mas** or **-mata** (-mə-tə). A benign tumor composed of connective tissue and mucous elements. [New Latin : MYX(O)- + -OMA.] —**myx·om′a·tous** (mĭk-sŏm′ə-təs, -sō′mə-təs) *adj.*

myx·o·ma·to·sis (mĭk-sō′mə-tō′sĭs) *n., pl.* **-ses** (-sēz′). **1.** *Pathology.* A condition characterized by the growth of many myxomas. **2.** A highly infectious, usually fatal, viral disease of rabbits characterized by many skin tumors similar to myxomas. [New Latin : MYXOMA + -OSIS.]

myx·o·my·cete (mĭk′sō-mī-sēt′, -mī′sēt′) *n. Botany.* A type of fungus, a **slime mold** (see). [New Latin *Myxomycetes* (class) : MYXO- + -MYCETE.] —**myx′o·my·ce′tous** (-mī-sē′təs) *adj.*

---

t tight/th thin, path/*th* this, bathe/ŭ cut/ûr urge/v valve/w with/y yes/z zebra, size/zh vision/ə about, item, edible, gallop, circus/ à *Fr.* ami/œ *Fr.* feu, *Ger.* schön/ü *Fr.* tu, *Ger.* über/KH *Ger.* ich, *Scot.* loch/N *Fr.* bon. ***Follows main vocabulary. †Of obscure origin.**

Myrmidon
Sixth-century B.C. vase
painting of Myrmidons *(left)*
battling Trojans for
the body of Achilles

Nn

Around 1000 B.C. the Phoenicians and other Semites of Syria and Palestine began to use a sign representing the consonant n, first in form (1), later in form (2). They named the sign nūn, meaning "fish." After 900 B.C. the Greeks borrowed the sign from the Phoenicians in the form (3), altering its name to nū, later reversing its orientation (4), and eventually making it symmetrical (5). The Greek forms passed via Etruscan to the Romans (6,7); they developed the Monumental Capital (8) that is the basis of our modern capital, printed (11) and written (12). The written Roman forms (6,7) underwent various medieval modifications, including the medieval Uncial (9) and Cursive (10), the bases of our modern small letter, printed (13) and written (14).

n, N (ĕn) *n.*, *pl.* **n's** or *rare* **ns, N's** or **Ns. 1.** The 14th letter of the modern English alphabet. See **alphabet. 2.** Any of the speech sounds represented by this letter.

n, N, n., N. *Note:* As an abbreviation or symbol, *n* may be a small or a capital letter, with or without a period. Established forms or those generally preferred precede the definition. When no form is given, all four forms are in general use in that sense. **1. N** Avogadro number. **2. n.** born (Latin *nātus*). **3. n, N** *Printing.* en. **4. N** *Chess.* knight. **5. n** nano-. **6. n.** *Commerce.* net. **7. n** neutron. **8. N** newton. **9. N** The symbol for the element nitrogen. **10. n, N.** noon. **11. n, N, n-** *Chemistry.* normal. **12. N.** Norse. **13. n** north; northern. **14. n.** note. **15. n.** noun. **16. N.** November. **17. n.** number. **18. n** *Mathematics.* The symbol for an indefinite number. **19.** The 14th in a series; 13th when *J* is omitted.

na (nä, nə) *adv. Chiefly Scottish.* Not; in no way; no. Often added to modal auxiliaries as a suffix: *canna, mauna.* [Middle English (northern) *na,* Old English *nā,* never, NO.]

Na The symbol for the element sodium (Latin *natrium*).

N.A. 1. Narcotics Anonymous. **2.** National Academician; National Academy. **3.** North America.

N.A.A. 1. National Aeronautic Association. **2.** National Automobile Association.

NAACP, N.A.A.C.P. National Association for the Advancement of Colored People.

nab (năb) *tr.v.* **nabbed, nabbing, nabs.** *Slang.* **1.** To catch in the act; arrest. **2.** To grab; snatch. [Variant of dialectal *nap,* to seize, probably from Scandinavian, akin to KIDNAP.]

Nab·a·tae·an (năb'ə-tē'ən) *n.* Also **Nab·a·te·an. 1.** One of a northwestern Arab people whose kingdom, centered on Petra, flourished from the fourth century B.C. to the first century A.D. **2.** The Aramaic dialect of this people. —**Nab'a·tae'an** *adj.*

na·bob (nā'bŏb') *n.* **1.** A governor in India under the Mogul Empire. **2.** In the 18th and 19th centuries, an Englishman who returned from India having acquired a fortune. **3.** A man of wealth and prominence. [Portuguese *nababo,* from Hindi *nawwāb,* NAWAB.] —**na'bob'er·y, na'bob'ism'** *n.*

Na·bo·kov (nä-bô'kôf), **Vladimir Vladimirovich.** Born 1899. Russian-born American novelist and poet.

Na·both (nā'bŏth'). A man of Jezreel whom Jezebel caused to be stoned to death so that Ahab could have his vineyard. I Kings 21.

na·celle (nə-sĕl') *n.* A separate streamlined enclosure on some kinds of aircraft for sheltering the crew or cargo or housing an engine. [French, "small boat," from Latin *naucella, nāvicella,* diminutive of *nāvis,* ship. See **nāu-²** in Appendix.*]

na·cre (nā'kər) *n.* **Mother-of-pearl** (*see*). [French, from Old Italian *naccara,* mother-of-pearl, from Arabic *naqqārah,* shell.]

na·cre·ous (nā'krē-əs) *adj.* **1.** Consisting of nacre. **2.** Like nacre; pearly.

Na·De·ne (nä-dā'nē) *n.* Also **Na·Dé·né.** A phylum of North American Indian languages that includes Athapascan, Haida, and Tlingit. [Coined by E. Sapir : Haida *na,* "to dwell," "house" + Athapascan *dene* (unattested), "people."]

na·dir (nā'dər, nā'dîr') *n.* **1.** A point on the celestial sphere diametrically opposite the zenith. **2.** The place or time of deepest depression; lowest point: *the nadir of misery.* [Middle English, from Old French, from Arabic *naẓīr as-samt,* opposite the zenith : *naẓīr,* opposite + *as-samt,* the ZENITH.]

nae (nā). *Scottish.* **1.** No. **2.** Not.

nae·vus. Variant of **nevus.**

nag¹ (năg) *v.* **nagged, nagging, nags.** —*tr.* **1.** To pester or annoy by constant scolding, complaining, or urging. **2.** To torment with anxiety, discomfort, or doubt: *nagged by worries.* —*intr.* **1.** To scold, complain, or find fault constantly. Often followed by *at.* **2.** To be a continuing source of discomfort, anxiety, or annoyance. Often followed by *at: The half-remembered quotation nagged at his mind.* —See Synonyms at **scold.** —*n.* A person, especially a woman, who nags. [British (chiefly Northern) dialectal *nag, naeg,* to bite, worry at, nag, from Old Norse *gnaga,* to bite. See **ghen-** in Appendix.*] —**nag'ger** *n.* —**nag'ging·ly** *adv.*

nag² (năg) *n.* **1.** Any horse; especially: **a.** An old or worn-out horse. **b.** *Slang.* A racehorse, regarded with contempt. **2.** *Archaic.* A small saddle horse or pony. [Middle English *nagge,* from Middle Dutch *negghe,* horse, probably from an imitative Germanic root *hnajj-, gnajj-, knajj-,* "to neigh," also the source of NEIGH.]

Na·ga·land (nä'gə-lănd'). A state of the Republic of India, 6,236 square miles in area, in the northeast adjoining Burma. Capital, Kohima. Population, 369,000.

na·ga·na (nə-gä'nə) *n.* Also **n'ga·na.** An often fatal disease of African livestock transmitted by the bite of the tsetse or other flies. Also called "tsetse disease." [Zulu *u-nakane.*]

Na·ga·o·ka (nä'gä-ō'kä). A city in north-central Honshu, Japan, in an oil-producing region. Population, 151,000.

Na·ga·sa·ki (nä'gə-sä'kē). A seaport of Japan, located on western Kyushu Island, target of a U.S. atomic bomb dropped on August 9, 1945. Population, 404,000.

Na·gor·no-Ka·ra·bakh Autonomous Region (nə-gôr'nō-kär-ə-bäk'). A division, 1,700 square miles in area, of the Azerbaijan S.S.R. Population, 145,000. Capital, Stepanakert.

Na·go·ya (nä-goi'ä). A seaport and major industrial center of Japan, located in south-central Honshu Island on Ise Bay. Population, 1,907,000.

Nag·pur (näg'pŏŏr'). A city of India, in Maharashtra State, about 420 miles northeast of Bombay. Population, 644,000.

Nagy (nŏj), **Imre.** 1896–1958. Premier of Hungary (1953–55 and 1956); executed.

Na·ha (nä'hä). Formerly **Na·wa** (nä'wä). A seaport of the Ryukyu Islands, located on the west coast of Okinawa Island. Population, 251,000.

Na·hua (nä'wä) *n., pl.* **Nahua** or **-huas.** Nahuatl.

Na·hua·tl (nä'wät'l) *n., pl.* **Nahuatl** or **-tls. 1.** A group of Mexican and Central American Indian tribes, including the Aztecs. **2.** A member of any of these tribes. **3.** The Uto-Aztec language of the Nahuatl. [Spanish, from Nahuatl *Nahuatl,* singular of *Nahua,* the Nahuatl people.]

Na·huel Hua·pí (nä-wĕl' wä-pē'). A lake occupying about 300 square miles in southwestern Argentina near the border with Chile.

Na·hum¹ (nā'həm, nā'əm). A Hebrew prophet of the seventh century B.C. who predicted the fall of Nineveh.

naiad
Sixteenth-century bas-relief by Jean Goujon on the Fountain of the Innocents, Paris, France

ă pat/ā pay/âr care/ä father/b bib/ch church/d deed/ĕ pet/ē be/f fife/g gag/h hat/hw which/ĭ pit/ī pie/îr pier/j judge/k kick/l lid, needle/m mum/n no, sudden/ng thing/ŏ pot/ō toe/ô paw, for/oi noise/ou out/ŏŏ took/ōō boot/p pop/r roar/s sauce/sh ship, dish/

Na·hum² (nā′həm, nā′əm) *n.* The book of the Old Testament containing the prophecies of Nahum.
nai·ad (nā′əd, nā′ăd′, nī′-) *n., pl.* **-ades** (-ə-dēz′) or **-ads.** **1.** *Greek Mythology.* One of the nymphs living in and presiding over brooks, springs, and fountains. **2.** The aquatic nymph of certain insects, such as the mayfly. **3.** A freshwater mussel of the family Unionidae. **4.** An aquatic plant of the genus *Naias.* [Greek *Naias* (stem *Naiad-*). See **snā-** in Appendix.*]
na·if, na·ïf. Variants of **naive.**
nail (nāl) *n.* **1.** A slim, pointed piece of metal hammered into wood or other materials as a fastener. **2. a.** A fingernail or toenail. **b.** A claw or talon. **3.** Anything resembling a nail in shape, sharpness, or use. **4.** A former measure of length for cloth, equal to 2¼ inches. **—hard as nails. 1.** Cold; harsh; pitiless. **2.** In rugged physical condition; tough. **—hit the nail on the head.** To express the sense of something exactly and concisely. *—tr.v.* **nailed, nailing, nails. 1.** To fasten, join, or attach with or as if with nails. **2.** To cover, enclose, or shut by fastening with nails. Often used with *up: nail up a window.* **3.** To keep fixed, motionless, or intent: *Fear nailed him to his seat; eyes nailed to the stage.* **4.** To secure or make sure of, especially by prompt action or concentrated effort; clinch. Often used with *down: nail down the facts.* **5.** *Informal.* To stop and seize; catch. **6.** *Informal.* To detect and expose: *nail a lie.* **7.** *Informal.* To strike or bring down, especially with something shot or hurled: *nail a bird in flight.* **8.** *Baseball.* To put out (a base runner). [Middle English *nail,* Old English *nægl.* See **nogh-** in Appendix.*] **—nail′er** *n.*
nail file. A small, flat file used for shaping the fingernails.
nail fold. A keratinous material overlapping the base of a fingernail or toenail as a circular fold; cuticle.
nail polish. A clear or colored cosmetic lacquer applied to the fingernails or toenails.
nail scissors. Small scissors with short, curved blades for trimming and shaping fingernails or toenails.
nain·sook (nān′so͝ok) *n.* A soft, light cotton material, often with a woven stripe. [Hindi *nainsukh,* "pleasure to the eye" : *nain,* eye, from Sanskrit *nayana,* "leading," hence eye, from *nayati,* he leads (see **nei-²** in Appendix*) + *sukh,* pleasure, from Sanskrit *sukha*†.]
Nairn (nârn). **1.** Also **Nairn·shire** (nârn′shîr, -shər). A county, 163 square miles in area, in northern Scotland. Population, 8,000. **2.** The county seat of this county. Population, 5,000.
Nai·ro·bi (nī-rō′bē). The capital of Kenya, in the south-central part of the country. Population, 267,000.
na·ive, na·ïve (nä-ēv′) *adj.* Also **na·if, na·ïf** (nä-ēf′). **1. a.** Lacking worldliness and sophistication; artless; unaffected. **b.** Simple and credulous as a child; ingenuous. **2.** Lacking critical ability or analytical insight; not subtle or learned: *"This extravagance of metaphors, with its naïve bombast"* (H.L. Mencken). *—n.* Also **na·if, na·ïf.** A naive person. [French, feminine of *naïf,* from Old French, ingenuous, natural, from Latin *nātīvus,* native, from *nāscī,* to be born. See **gene-** in Appendix.*] **—na·ive′ly** *adv.* **—na·ive′ness** *n.*
Synonyms: *naive, simple, innocent, ingenuous, unsophisticated, natural, unaffected, guileless, artless.* These words signify lack of artifice and affectation. *Naive* generally implies lack of perception, or intuitive judgment, that is the basis of sound behavior in a practical world. *Simple* stresses utter lack of deviousness or deceit as well; it may imply a favorable quality or an unfavorable one, such as lack of good sense. *Innocent* primarily signifies freedom from guilt or sin; applied to an adult, it too may imply lack of practical wisdom. *Ingenuous* denotes childlike simplicity and directness; it connotes lack of ability to mask one's feelings, without implying a desire to dissemble. *Unsophisticated* specifically indicates absence of worldly wisdom; it is not as strong as the foregoing words in its implication of innate simplicity or innocence. *Natural* stresses spontaneity, the result of freedom from self-consciousness or other inhibitions—the state of "being oneself." *Unaffected* likewise signifies merely lack of pretense, without implying simplicity, naiveté, or even sophistication. *Guileless* signifies absence of deceit. *Artless* also stresses absence of deceit, but implies a detached quality of a person either actually or seemingly unconcerned about, or unaware of, the reaction of others.
na·ive·té, na·ïve·té (nä′ēv-tā′) *n.* Also **na·ive·ty,** (nä-ēv′ə-tē), **na·ïve·ty** *pl.* **-ties. 1.** The quality of being naive; natural simplicity or artlessness; ingenuousness. **2.** A naive statement or action. [French, ingenuousness, from *naïf,* NAIVE.]
Najd. Variant of **Nejd.**
na·ked (nā′kĭd) *adj.* **1.** Without clothing or covering on the body; nude. **2.** Without covering; especially, without the usual covering: *a naked sword.* **3.** Devoid of vegetation, trees, or foliage: *"Beneath them the earth was naked of grass"* (William Styron). **4.** Without addition, concealment, disguise, or embellishment: *the naked facts.* **5.** Stripped or bare of something specified; destitute. Often used with *of: "When the Lord of All things made himself Naked of glory for His mortal change."* (Tennyson). **6.** Exposed to harm; defenseless; vulnerable: *"naked to mine enemies"* (Shakespeare). **7.** *Botany.* **a.** Not encased in ovaries. Said of seeds. **b.** Unprotected by scales. Said of buds. **c.** Lacking a perianth. Said of flowers. **d.** Without leaves or pubescence. Said of branches or stalks. **8.** Lacking protective covering such as scales, fur, feathers, shell, or the like. **9.** *Law.* Unsupported or uncorroborated by authority, evidence, or proof. [Middle English *naked,* Old English *nacod.* See **nogw-** in Appendix.*] **—na′ked·ly** *adv.* **—na′ked·ness** *n.*
naked eye. The eye unassisted by an optical instrument.
Na·khi·che·van Autonomous Soviet Socialist Republic (nä′-kə-chə-vän′). An administrative division, 2,120 square miles in area, of the Azerbaijan S.S.R., separated from it by Soviet Armenia. Population, 178,000. Capital, Nakhichevan.
Na·khod·ka (nə-KHôt′kə). A city and ice-free port of the Soviet Union, constructed after 1945 in southeastern Siberia, southeast of Vladivostok. Population, 64,000.
Nal·chik (näl′chĭk). The capital of the Kabardin-Balkar A.S.S.R., 320 miles southeast of Rostov. Population, 106,000.
N.A.M. National Association of Manufacturers.
Na·ma (nä′mä). Also **Na·ma·qua** (nə-mä′kwə) *n.* **1.** A Hottentot people inhabiting Namaqualand. **2.** A Hottentot dialect.
Na·ma·qua·land (nə-mä′kwə-lănd′). Also **Na·ma·land** (nä′mä-lănd′). A region of southwestern Africa divided by the Orange River into Great Namaqualand in South-West Africa and Little Namaqualand in the Republic of South Africa.
nam·by-pam·by (năm′bē-păm′bē) *adj.* **1.** Weakly sentimental; insipidly affected. **2.** Lacking vigor or decisiveness; spineless. *—n., pl.* **namby-pambies. 1.** Insipid, mawkish language or style. **2.** A namby-pamby person. [From *Namby-Pamby,* a satire on the sentimental pastorals of *Ambrose* Philips (1675?–1749), by Henry Carey (died 1743).]
name (nām) *n.* **1.** A word or words by which any entity is designated and distinguished from others. **2.** A word or words used to describe or evaluate, often disparagingly: *Names will never hurt me.* **3.** Verbal representation or repute as opposed to effective reality: *a democracy in name, a police state in fact.* **4. a.** General reputation: *a bad name.* **b.** A distinguished reputation; renown. **5.** *Informal.* A famous or outstanding person: *a big name in state politics.* **—in the name of. 1.** In behalf of; for the sake of. **2.** By the authority of. **—to one's name.** Belonging to one: *not a book to his name.* *—tr.v.* **named, naming, names. 1.** To attach an appellation to. **2.** To identify by name; call by the right name: *name the 50 states.* **3.** To mention, specify, or cite by name. **4.** To call by some epithet: *He named them all cowards.* **5.** To nominate or appoint to some duty, office, or honor. **6.** To specify or fix: *name the day.* *—adj. Informal.* Well-known by a name: *name brands.* [Middle English *name,* Old English *nama.* See **nomen-** in Appendix.*] **—nam′a·ble, name′a·ble** *adj.*
Synonyms: *name, designation, denomination, title, appellation, nickname, sobriquet, cognomen, moniker. Name* is the general term among these related words. A *designation* is a name given expressly to classify according to distinguishing characteristics. A *denomination* is also a categorizing name and is applied to persons or things, often religious groups or monetary units, having close relationship. A *title,* applied to persons, indicates specific rank or position, and generally connotes distinction and respect; applied to things, such as literary or musical works, it is a form of proper name. An *appellation* is a name, other than a proper one, that describes or characterizes, generally in pictorial terms, and that gains currency more through use than through a formal act of designation; "Great Emancipator" is thus an appellation for Lincoln. A *nickname* is an appellation with informal, sometimes humorous, overtones, such as "Honest Abe." A *sobriquet* is an especially humorous or picturesque nickname. *Cognomen* (in its informal sense) and *moniker* (a slang word) are rather loosely employed as the equivalent of proper name or, more often, of nickname.
name day. 1. The feast day of the saint after whom one is named. **2.** The day on which one is baptized.
name·less (nām′lĭs) *adj.* **1.** Having or bearing no name: *nameless stars.* **2.** Unknown by name; obscure: *the nameless dead.* **3.** Not designated by name; anonymous: *a nameless benefactor.* **4.** Inexpressible; indescribable: *nameless horror.* **—name′less·ly** *adv.* **—name′less·ness** *n.*
name·ly (nām′lē) *adv.* That is to say; to wit; specifically.
name·sake (nām′sāk′) *n.* A person or thing named after another. [From *for the name's sake.*]
Nam·hoi (näm′hoi′). Formerly **Fat·shan** (făt′shän′). A city of central Kwangtung Province, China. Population, 123,000.
Nam·po. See **Chinnampo.**
Nam Tso (näm′ tsô′). *Mongolian* **Teng·ri Nor** (tĕng′rē nôr′). A saltwater lake about 700 square miles in area, lying north of Lhasa in eastern Tibet, at an altitude of over 15,000 feet.
Nan (nän). A river rising in northeastern Thailand and flowing 350 miles south to join the Ping River and form the Chao Phraya.
nan·a (năn′ə) *n.* **1.** A nurse or nursemaid. **2.** A grandmother. [From baby talk. See **nana** in Appendix.*]
Na·nak (nä′nək). 1469–1538. Called "Guru." Indian religious leader; founder of Sikhism and compiler of its sacred texts.
Nan·chang (nän′chäng′). A port city, the capital of Kiangsi Province, China. Population, 520,000.
Nan·chung (nän′cho͞ong′). A city of China, on the Kialing River in Szechwan Province. Population, 206,000.
Nan·cy¹ (năn′sē). A feminine given name. [Variant of *Nanny,* pet form of ANN.]
Nan·cy² (năn′sē; *French* näN-sē′). A city of France, about 175 miles east of Paris. Population, 129,000.
Nan·da De·vi (nŭn′dä dā′vē). A Himalayan mountain rising to 25,645 feet in northern Uttar Pradesh, Republic of India.
nan·din (năn′dĭn) *n.* An evergreen Asiatic shrub, *Nandina domestica,* having compound leaves and small white flowers that grow in a branching cluster and are followed by bright-red berries. [New Latin *Nandina* (genus name), from Japanese *nanten,* "southern sky," from Chinese (Mandarin) *nan² t'ien¹* : *nan²,* south, southern + *t'ien¹,* sky.]
Nan·ga Par·bat (nŭng′gə pûr′bət). A Himalayan peak rising to 26,660 feet in northwestern Kashmir.

nail

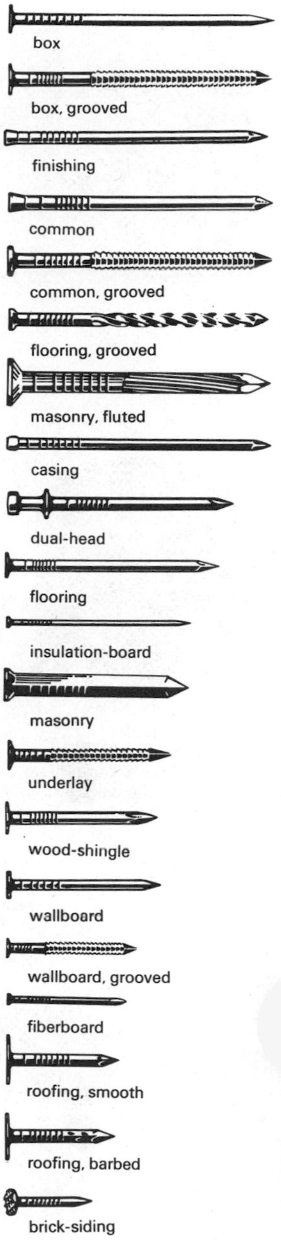
box
box, grooved
finishing
common
common, grooved
flooring, grooved
masonry, fluted
casing
dual-head
flooring
insulation-board
masonry
underlay
wood-shingle
wallboard
wallboard, grooved
fiberboard
roofing, smooth
roofing, barbed
brick-siding

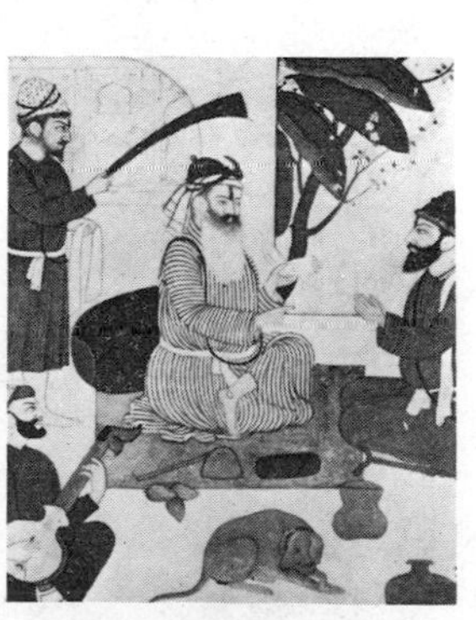

Nanak
The Guru receiving a visitor, an illustration from *The Great Humanist Guru Nanak*

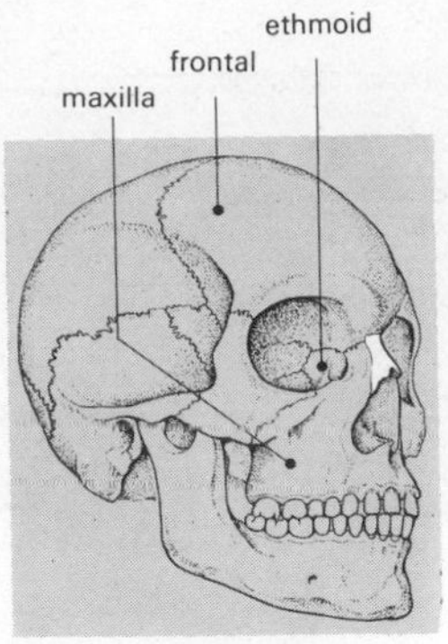
ethmoid
frontal
maxilla

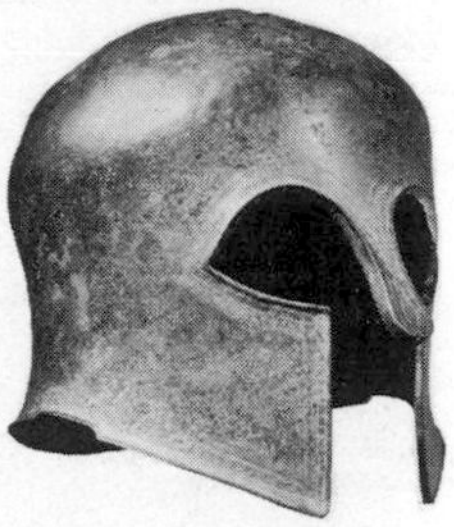

nasal
Above: Nasal bone
Below: Bronze Corinthian helmet, about 600 B.C.

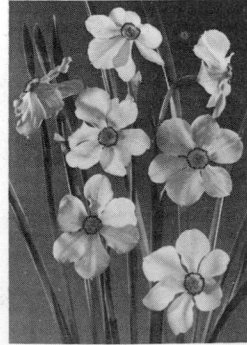

narcissus
Narcissus poetica

nan·keen (năn-kēn′) *n.* Also **nan·kin** (năn-kēn′, -kĭn′). **1.** A sturdy yellow or buff cotton cloth. **2.** *Capital* **N.** A kind of Chinese porcelain with a blue-and-white pattern. [Originally imported from NANKING.]

Nan·king (năn′kĭng′; *Chinese* nän′jĭng′). An industrial city and textile center the capital of Kiangsu Province, China, on the south bank of the Yangtze River. Population, 1,419,000. [Chinese (Mandarin) *nan² ching¹*, "southern capital" : *nan²*, south + *ching¹*, capital.]

Nan Ling (nän′ lĭng′). Also **Nan Shan** (nän′ shän′). A mountain range in southern China, forming an irregular boundary between Kwangsi-Chuang Autonomous Region and Kwangtung Province to the south and Hunan Province to the north. [Chinese (Mandarin) *nan² ling³* : *nan²*, south + *ling³*, mountain.]

Nan·ning (nän′nĭng′). Formerly **Yung·ning** (yŏŏng′nĭng′). A city in south-central Kwangsi Province, China. Population, 260,000. [Chinese (Mandarin) *nan² ning²* : *nan²*, south + *ning²*, peace.]

nan·ny (năn′ē) *n., pl.* **-nies.** A children's nurse. [From baby talk *nana.* See **nana** in Appendix.*]

nan·ny·ber·ry (năn′ē-bĕr′ē) *n., pl.* **-ries.** A shrub, the **sheepberry** *(see).*

nanny goat *pl.* **nanny goats.** A female goat. [From *Nanny,* pet form for ANN.]

nano–. *Abbr.* **n** Indicates: **1.** Extreme smallness; for example, **nanoplankton. 2.** One-billionth of (a specified unit); for example, **nanosecond.** [Latin *nānus,* dwarf, from Greek *nan(n)os.* See **nana** in Appendix.*]

na·no·plank·ton (nā′nə-plăngk′tən, năn′ə-) *n.* Also **nan·no·plank·ton** (năn′ə-plăngk′tən). Aquatic animal and plant organisms of microscopic size comprising the smallest of the **plankton** *(see).* [NANO- + PLANKTON.]

na·no·sec·ond (năn′ə-sĕk′ənd, nā′nə-) *n.* One-billionth (10^{-9}) of a second. [NANO- + SECOND.]

Nan·sei Sho·to. The Japanese name for the **Ryukyu Islands.**

Nan·sen (nän′sən, năn′-), **Fridt·jof.** 1861–1930. Norwegian Arctic explorer, statesman, and scientist.

Nan·sen passport (nän′sən, năn′-). A passport issued after World War I by the League of Nations to individuals who were stateless. [Invented by the League's High Commissioner for Refugees, Fridtjof NANSEN.]

Nan Shan (nän′ shän′). **1.** A complex of mountain ranges in northwestern China, forming the boundary between Kansu and Tsinghai provinces. **2.** See **Nan Ling.** [Chinese (Mandarin) *nan² shan¹* : *nan²*, south + *shan¹*, mountain.]

Nantes (nănts; *French* näNt). An inland port and industrial city of western France, on the Loire River. Population, 240,000.

Nantes, Edict of. A decree issued in 1598 by Henry IV of France, granting restricted religious and civil liberties to Huguenots; revoked in 1685 by Louis XIV.

Nan·tuck·et (năn-tŭk′ĭt). **1.** An island of Massachusetts, about 46 square miles in area, in the Atlantic Ocean 25 miles south of Cape Cod. **2.** The main town on this island.

Nan·tung (nän′tŏŏng′). Formerly **Tung·chow** (tŏŏng′jō′). A city and port of China, on the Yangtze River in southeastern Kiangsu Province. Population, 260,000.

Naoi·se (nē′sē). *Irish Mythology.* The husband of **Deirdre** *(see).*

Na·o·mi (nā-ō′mē). The mother-in-law of Ruth. Ruth 1:1–4.

nap¹ (năp) *n.* A brief sleep, often during a period other than one's regular sleeping hours. —*intr.v.* **napped, napping, naps. 1.** To doze or sleep for a brief period. **2.** To be unaware of imminent danger or trouble. [Middle English *nappen,* to doze, Old English *hnappian.* See **ken-²** in Appendix.*]

nap² (năp) *n.* A dense, soft or fuzzy surface on certain textiles or leathers, usually formed by raising fibers from the underlying material. Compare **pile.** —*tr.v.* **napped, napping, naps.** To form or raise a nap on (fabric or leather). [Middle English *noppe,* from Middle Dutch *noppe.* See **ken-²** in Appendix.*]

NAP Airport code for Naples, Italy.

na·palm (nā′päm′) *n.* **1.** An aluminum soap of various fatty acids that when mixed with gasoline makes a firm jelly used in flame throwers and incendiary bombs. **2.** The jelly so used in flame throwers and bombs. **3.** A similarly incendiary mixture of polystyrene, benzene, and gasoline. Also called "napalm-B." [*Na(phthenate),* salt of naphthenic acid, from NAPHTHENE + PALM(ITATE).]

nape (nāp) *n.* The back of the neck. [Middle English, probably akin to Old Frisian *(hals)knap*†, nape.]

na·per·y (nā′pə-rē) *n.* Household linen; especially, table linen. [Middle English *naperie,* from Old French *nap(p)erie,* from *nap(p)e,* tablecloth, from Latin *mappa,* napkin, towel. See **mappa** in Appendix.*]

Naph·ta·li¹ (năf′tə-lī′). A son of Jacob. Genesis 30:7, 8.

Naph·ta·li² (năf′tə-lī′) *n.* A tribe of Israel descended from Naphtali. Numbers 1:15, 43.

naph·tha (năf′thə, năp′-) *n.* **1.** A colorless flammable liquid, obtained from crude petroleum and used as a solvent and cleaning fluid, and as a raw material for gasoline. **2.** Any of several volatile hydrocarbon liquids derived from coal tar and other materials and used as solvents. **3.** An obsolete name for petroleum. [Greek *naphtha*†.]

naph·tha·lene (năf′thə-lēn′, năp′-) *n.* Also **naph·tha·line, naph·tha·lin** (năf′thə-lĭn, năp′-). A white crystalline compound, $C_{10}H_8$, derived from coal tar or petroleum, and used to manufacture dyes, moth repellents, explosives, and solvents. Also called "tar camphor." [NAPHTH(A) + AL(COHOL) + -ENE.]

naph·thene (năf′thēn′, năp′-) *n.* Any of several cycloparaffin hydrocarbons having the general formula C_nH_{2n}, found in various petroleums. [NAPHTH(A) + -ENE.]

naph·thol (năf′thôl′, -thōl′, năp′-) *n.* Also **naph·tol** (năf′tôl′, -tōl′, năp′-). An organic compound, $C_{10}H_7OH$, occurring in two isomeric forms: **a.** *alpha-naphthol,* colorless or yellow prisms or powder, used in dyes, organic synthesis, and perfumes. **b.** *beta-naphthol,* white lustrous leaflets or powder, used in dyes, insecticides, and in the manufacture of rubber. [NAPHTH(ALENE) + -OL (hydroxyl group).]

Na·pi·er (nā′pē-ər), **John.** 1550–1617. Scottish mathematician; inventor of logarithms.

Na·pier·i·an logarithm (nə-pîr′ē-ən, nā-). Also **Na·per·i·an logarithm.** *Symbol* **ln** *Mathematics.* A logarithm to the base *e* (=2.71828...). For example, $\ln 10 = \log_e 10 = 2.30258$. Also called "natural logarithm." [Invented by John NAPIER.]

na·pi·form (nā′pə-fôrm′) *adj.* Shaped like a turnip. Said of a root. [Latin *nāpus,* turnip (probably of Mediterranean origin) + -FORM.]

nap·kin (năp′kĭn) *n.* **1.** A piece of fabric, such as cotton or linen, or a similar piece of soft, absorbent paper, used at table to protect one's clothes or wipe one's lips and fingers. **2.** Any similar cloth or towel. **3.** *Chiefly British.* A diaper. **4.** A **sanitary napkin** *(see).* [Middle English *nappekin,* diminutive of *nappe,* tablecloth, from Old French, from Latin *mappa,* napkin, towel. See **mappa** in Appendix.*]

Na·ples (nā′pəlz). *Italian* **Na·po·li** (nä′pō-lē). The capital of Campania Region, Italy, a seaport in the southwest. Population, 1,221,000.

Na·po (nä′pō). A river rising in central Ecuador and flowing 550 miles southeast to join the Amazon.

na·po·le·on (nə-pō′lē-ən, -pōl′yən) *n.* **1.** A rectangular piece of pastry, iced on top, with crisp, flaky layers filled with custard cream. **2.** A former 20-franc gold coin of France. **3. a.** A card game in which the players bid for the right to name the trump. **b.** A bid in this game, whereby a player contracts to take all five tricks of one hand. [After NAPOLEON I.]

Na·po·le·on I (nə-pō′lē-ən, -pōl′yən). Surname, Bonaparte. 1769–1821. Emperor of the French (1804–15).

Na·po·le·on II (nə-pō′lē-ən, -pōl′yən). Full name, François Charles Joseph Bo·na·parte (bō′nə-pärt′). 1811–1832. Unrecognized emperor of the French and king of Rome; son of Napoleon I and Marie Louise.

Na·po·le·on III (nə-pō′lē-ən, -pōl′yən). Full name, Charles Louis Napoleon Bo·na·parte (bō′nə-pärt′). Known as Louis Napoleon. 1808–1873. President of the Second Republic of France (1848–52); emperor of Second Empire of France (1852–70); nephew of Napoleon I.

Na·po·le·on·ic (nə-pō′lē-ŏn′ĭk) *adj.* Pertaining to or characteristic of Napoleon I or his era.

nappe (năp) *n.* **1.** A sheet of water flowing over a dam or similar structure. **2.** *Geology.* **a.** A recumbent anticline or fold of strata. **b.** A mass of rock moved from its original position by an anticline. **3.** *Geometry.* Either of the two parts into which a cone is divided by the vertex. [From French *nappe (d'eau),* sheet (of water), from Old French *nappe,* tablecloth, from Latin *mappa,* napkin, towel. See **mappa** in Appendix.*]

nap·py¹ (năp′ē) *adj.* **-pier, -piest.** Having a nap; shaggy; fuzzy.

nap·py² (năp′ē) *n., pl.* **-pies.** A round, shallow cooking or serving dish with a flat bottom and sloping sides. [Probably from British dialectal *nappie,* diminutive of *nap,* wooden bowl, small kettle, Middle English *nap,* Old English *hnæpp.* See **hanaper.**]

Na·ra (nä′rä). A city and former capital of Japan, on southern Honshu Island. Population, 116,000.

Nar·ba·da (nər-bŭd′ə). A river rising in central India and flowing 800 miles west to the Gulf of Cambay.

nar·ce·ine (när′sē-ēn′, -ən) *n.* Also **nar·ce·in** (när′sē-ən). A white crystalline narcotic, $C_{23}H_{27}O_8N \cdot 3H_2O$, obtained from opium. [French *narcéine* : Greek *narkē,* numbness (see **sner-²** in Appendix*) + -INE.]

nar·cis·sism (när′sə-sĭz′əm) *n.* Also **nar·cism** (när′sĭz′əm). **1.** Excessive admiration of oneself. **2.** *Psychoanalysis.* An arresting of development at, or a regression to, the infantile stage of development in which one's own body is the object of erotic interest. [After NARCISSUS.] —**nar′cis·sist** (när′sə-sĭst) *n.* —**nar′cis·sis′tic** (när′sə-sĭs′tĭk) *adj.*

nar·cis·sus (när-sĭs′əs) *n., pl.* **-suses** or **-cissi** (-sĭs′ī′, -sĭs′ē). **1.** Any of several widely cultivated plants of the genus *Narcissus,* having narrow, grasslike leaves, and usually white or yellow flowers characterized by a cup-shaped or trumpet-shaped central crown. See **daffodil, jonquil, Chinese sacred lily. 2.** Moderate to strong yellow. See **color.** [Latin, from Greek *narkissos,* probably of Mediterranean origin.]

Nar·cis·sus (när-sĭs′əs). *Greek Mythology.* A youth who, having spurned the love of Echo, pined away in love for his own image in a pool of water and was transformed into the flower that bears his name.

narco–. Indicates: **1.** Numbness, sluggishness, or stupor; for example, **narcolepsy. 2.** A narcotic drug; for example, **narcotine.** [Greek *narko-,* from *narkoun,* to benumb, from *narkē,* numbness. See **sner-²** in Appendix.*]

nar·co·a·nal·y·sis (när′kō-ə-năl′ə-sĭs) *n.* Psychoanalysis conducted while the patient is in a drug-induced drowsy state.

nar·co·lep·sy (när′kə-lĕp′sē) *n. Pathology.* A condition characterized by sudden and uncontrollable attacks of deep sleep. [NARCO- + -LEPSY.] —**nar′co·lep′tic** *adj.*

nar·co·sis (när-kō′sĭs) *n.* **1.** Deep unconsciousness produced by a drug. Also called "narcotism." **2.** *Biology.* Immobility in an organism, caused by chemicals such as carbon dioxide. [Greek *narkōsis,* a numbing, from *narkoun,* to make numb, from *narkē,* numbness (see **sner-²** in Appendix*).]

nar·co·syn·the·sis (när′kō-sĭn′thə-sĭs) *n.* Narcoanalysis di-

ă pat/ā pay/âr care/ä father/b bib/ch church/d deed/ĕ pet/ē be/f fife/g gag/h hat/hw which/ĭ pit/ī pie/îr pier/j judge/k kick/l lid, needle/m mum/n no, sudden/ng thing/ŏ pot/ō toe/ô paw, for/oi noise/ou out/ŏŏ took/ōō boot/p pop/r roar/s sauce/sh ship, dish/

rected toward making the patient recall suppressed memories and emotional traumas for later interpretation.

nar·cot·ic (när-kŏt′ĭk) *n.* **1.** Any drug that dulls the senses, induces sleep, and with prolonged use becomes addictive. **2.** Something that numbs, soothes, or induces a dreamlike or insensitive state. —*adj.* **1.** Inducing sleep or stupor. **2.** Of or pertaining to narcotics, their effects, or their use. **3.** Of or pertaining to one addicted to a narcotic drug. [Middle English *narkotike,* from Old French *narcotique* (originally an adjective), from Medieval Latin *narcōticus,* from Greek *narkōtikos,* numbing, narcotic, from *narkoun,* to make numb, from *narkē,* numbness. See **sner-**[2] in Appendix.*] —**nar·cot′i·cal·ly** *adv.*

nar·co·tine (när′kə-tēn′, -tən) *n.* An alkaloid, $C_{22}H_{23}NO_7$, obtained from opium and used to relieve coughing, fever and spasms. [French : *narcotique,* NARCOT(IC) + -INE.]

nar·co·tism (när′kə-tĭz′əm) *n.* **1.** Addiction to narcotics such as opium, heroin, or morphine. **2.** A drugged state, **narcosis** *(see).* [French *narcotisme,* from *narcotique,* NARCOTIC.]

nar·co·tize (när′kə-tīz′) *tr.v.* **-tized, -tizing, -tizes. 1.** To place under the influence of a narcotic. **2.** To lull or induce to sleep. **3.** To dull; deaden. —**nar′co·ti·za′tion** *n.*

nard (närd) *n.* **1.** A plant, **spikenard** *(see).* **2.** A balm made from spikenard. **3.** Any of several plants of the genus *Valeriana,* or related plants, whose aromatic roots have been used in medicine. [Middle English *narde,* from Old French, from Latin *nardus,* from Greek *nardos,* probably ultimately from Sanskrit *naladaf*†, Indian spikenard.]

nar·es (nâr′ēz) *pl.n. Singular* **-is** (-ĭs). The openings in the nasal cavities of vertebrates; nostrils. [Latin *nārēs,* plural of *nāris,* nostril. See **nas-** in Appendix.*]

Na·rew (nä′rĕf′). *Russian* **Na·rev** (nə-ryôf′). A river rising near the Polish-Russian frontier and flowing 275 miles to join the Bug River.

nar·ghi·le (när′gə-lĕ, -lē′) *n.* Also **nar·gi·le, nar·gi·leh.** An Oriental tobacco pipe in which smoke is drawn through a container of water by a flexible tube. [French *narguilé,* from Persian *nārgīleh,* a pipe (whose bowl was originally made of coconut shell), from *nārgīl,* coconut, from Sanskrit *nārikela*†, coconut.]

nar·i·al (nâr′ē-əl) *adj.* Also **nar·ic** (nâr′ĭk), **nar·ine** (nâr′ĭn, -īn′). Of or pertaining to the nares, or nostrils.

nark (närk) *n. British Slang.* An informer, especially to the police. —*intr.v.* **narked, narking, narks.** *British Slang.* To be an informer. [Old thieves' slang, borrowed from Gypsy *nak,* nose, from Prakrit *nakka.* See **nas-** in Appendix.*]

Nar·ra·gan·set (năr′ə-găn′sĭt) *n., pl.* **Narraganset** or **-sets.** Also **Nar·ra·gan·sett** *pl.* **Narragansett** or **-setts. 1.** A tribe of Algonquian-speaking Indians that formerly inhabited the area of Rhode Island. **2.** A member of this tribe. **3.** The Algonquian language of this tribe. **4.** A small, sturdy saddle horse of a breed developed in Rhode Island. [Corruption of Narraganset *Nanhigganeuck*†.] —**Nar′ra·gan′set** *adj.*

Nar·ra·gan·sett Bay (năr′ə-găn′sĭt). An inlet of the Atlantic Ocean extending northward about 30 miles from southeastern Rhode Island.

nar·rate (năr′āt′, nă-rāt′) *v.* **-rated, -rating, -rates.** —*tr.* To give an oral or written account of; tell (a story). —*intr.* To give an account or description; especially, to supply a running commentary for a motion picture or other performance. [Latin *narrāre,* from *gnārus,* knowing. See **gnō-** in Appendix.*] —**nar′ra′tor** (năr′ā′tər, nă-rā′tər, năr′ə-tər), **nar′rat′er** *n.*

nar·ra·tion (nă-rā′shən) *n.* **1. a.** The act or process of narrating. **b.** An instance of this. **2.** Something narrated; a narrative.

nar·ra·tive (năr′ə-tĭv) *n.* **1.** A story or description of actual or fictional events; narrated account. **2.** The act, technique, or process of narrating. —*adj.* **1.** Consisting of or characterized by the telling of a story: *narrative poetry.* **2.** Of or pertaining to narration: *narrative skill.* —**nar′ra·tive·ly** *adv.*

nar·row (năr′ō) *adj.* **-rower, -rowest. 1.** Of small or limited width, especially in comparison with length. **2.** Limited in area or scope; lacking space or room; cramped. **3.** Lacking flexibility; rigid in adherence to an idea or way: *"A strange effect of narrow principles and short views!"* (Swift). **4.** Straitened; meager; pinched: *narrow circumstances.* **5.** Barely sufficient or successful; precarious: *a narrow margin of victory.* **6.** Painstakingly thorough or attentive: *a narrow scrutiny.* **7.** *Regional.* Miserly; stingy. **8.** *Phonetics.* **Tense** *(see).* —*v.* **narrowed, -rowing, -rows.** —*tr.* **1.** To make narrow or narrower; reduce in width or extent. **2.** To limit or restrict. Often followed by *down: He narrowed down the possibilities.* —*intr.* To become narrower; contract. —*n.* **1.** A narrow part, such as a narrow pass through mountains or the narrow part of a valley. **2. a.** *Plural.* A narrow body of water connecting two larger ones. **b.** A narrow part of a river or ocean current. [Middle English *nearwe, narow,* Old English *nearu.* See **sner-**[2] in Appendix.*] —**nar′row·ly** *adv.* —**nar′row·ness** *n.*

narrow gauge. Also **narrow gage. 1.** A distance between the rails of a railroad track that is less than the standard width of 56½ inches. **2.** A narrow-gauge locomotive, car, or railway.

nar·row-gauge (năr′ō-gāj′) *adj.* Also **nar·row-gage, nar·row-gauged** (-gājd′), **nar·row-gaged. 1. a.** Having a width between the rails of less than the standard 56½ inches. Said of railroad track. **b.** Intended for or used on a railroad so constructed. **2.** *Informal.* Narrow; limited; petty.

nar·row-mind·ed (năr′ō-mīn′dĭd) *adj.* Lacking breadth of view, tolerance, or sympathy; bigoted; prejudiced. —**nar′row-mind′ed·ly** *adv.* —**nar′row-mind′ed·ness** *n.*

Nar·rows, The (năr′ōz). A strait in New York State, 0.8 miles wide at its narrowest point, between Brooklyn and Staten Island, and connecting Upper and Lower New York bays.

nar·thex (när′thĕks′) *n. Architecture.* **1.** A portico or lobby of an early Christian or Byzantine church or basilica, originally separated from the nave by a railing or screen. **2.** Any church entrance hall leading to the nave. [Medieval Greek *narthēx,* "enclosure," originally "casket," "box" (made in ancient times of hollow stems of giant fennel), from Greek, *narthēx,* giant fennel, from Sanskrit *narda*†.]

Nar·vik (när′vĭk). A port of northern Norway. Population, 14,000.

nar·whal (när′wəl) *n.* Also **nar·wal, nar·whale** (när′hwāl′). An arctic aquatic mammal, *Monodon monoceros,* having a spotted pelt and (in the male) a spiral tusk several feet long. It is hunted for ivory and oil. [Norwegian or Danish *narhval,* from Old Norse *nāhvalr,* "corpse-whale" (so called because with its whitish color it resembles a floating corpse) : *nār,* corpse (see **nāu-**[1] in Appendix*) + *hvalr,* whale (see **skwalo-** in Appendix*).]

nar·y (nâr′ē) *adj. Regional.* Not one; no. Usually followed by *a* or *an.* [From *ne'er a,* "never a."]

NAS Airport code for Nassau, Bahamas.

NASA (năs′ə) National Aeronautics and Space Administration.

na·sal (nā′zəl) *adj.* **1.** Of or pertaining to the nose. **2.** *Phonetics.* Formed by lowering the soft palate so that most of the air is exhaled through the nose rather than the mouth, as in sounding *m, n,* and *ng.* **3.** Characterized by or resembling sounds so formed: *a nasal whine.* —*n.* **1.** *Phonetics.* A nasal sound. **2.** A nasal part or bone. **3.** The nosepiece of a helmet. [French, from New Latin *nāsālis,* from Latin *nāsus,* nose. See **nas-** in Appendix.*] —**na·sal′i·ty** (nā-zăl′ə-tē) *n.* —**na′sal·ly** *adv.*

nasal index. The ratio of the width to the height of the nose, multiplied by 100. It is used in anthropological measurements.

na·sal·ize (nā′zə-līz′) *v.* **-ized, -izing, -izes.** —*tr.* To render nasal. —*intr.* To produce nasal sounds. —**na′sal·i·za′tion** *n.*

Nas·by, Petroleum V. Pen name of David Ross **Locke** *(see).*

nas·cent (năs′ənt, nā′sənt) *adj.* Coming into existence; in the process of emerging: *"the moral shock of our nascent imperialism"* (Richard Hofstadter). [Latin *nāscēns,* present participle of *nāscī,* to be born. See **genə-** in Appendix.*] —**nas′cence** *n.*

nase·ber·ry (nāz′bĕr′ē, -bə-rē) *n., pl.* **-ries.** A tropical tree, the **sapodilla** *(see),* or its fruit. [From Spanish *néspera* (influenced by BERRY), from Latin *mespila,* MEDLAR.]

Nase·by (nāz′bē). A village in Northamptonshire, England, site of a decisive Parliamentarian victory (1645) in the Civil War.

Nash (năsh), **Ogden.** Born 1902. American humorous poet.

Nashe (năsh), **Thomas.** Also **Nash.** 1567–1601. English author of satirical pamphlets, plays, and fiction.

Nash·u·a (năsh′o͞o-ə). An industrial city in south-central New Hampshire, on the Merrimack River. Population, 39,000.

Nash·ville (năsh′vĭl′). The capital of Tennessee, on the Cumberland River. Population, 171,000.

naso–. Indicates nose; for example, **nasofrontal.** [New Latin, from Latin *nāsus,* nose. See **nas-** in Appendix.*]

na·so·fron·tal (nā′zō-frŭn′təl) *adj.* Of or pertaining to the nasal and frontal bones.

na·so·phar·ynx (nā′zō-făr′ĭngks) *n., pl.* **-pharynges** (-fə-rĭn′jēz) or **-ynxes.** The portion of the pharynx directly behind the nasal cavity and above the soft palate. —**na′so·pha·ryn′ge·al** (-fə-rĭn′jē-əl, -jəl, -făr′ən-jē′əl) *adj.*

Nas·sau (năs′ô′; *German* nä′sou′ *for sense 2*). **1.** The capital of the Bahama Islands, on the northeastern coast of New Providence Island. Population, 82,000. **2.** A former duchy of Germany, now incorporated in the West German state of Hesse.

Nas·ser (nä′sər, năs′ər), **Gamal Abdel.** Born 1918. Prime Minister of Egypt (1954–58); president of the United Arab Republic since 1958.

Nas·ser, Lake (năs′ər). A reservoir formed by the Aswan High Dam extending from southern Egypt into northern Sudan.

Nast (năst), **Thomas.** 1840–1902. German-born American political cartoonist and illustrator.

nas·tic (năs′tĭk) *adj.* Of, pertaining to, or characterized by a tendency in plants to grow or change according to internal cell pressures, as distinguished from growth due to environmental influences. [From Greek *nastos,* pressed down, from *nassein*†, to press.]

–nastic. Indicates nastic movement toward or by; for example, **epinastic.**

na·stur·tium (nə-stûr′shəm, nă-) *n.* **1.** Any of various plants of the genus *Tropaeolum,* having flowers with five broad petals that are usually yellow, orange, or red. Their pungent leaves and seeds are sometimes used as seasoning. **2.** Brilliant orange yellow. See **color.** [Latin *nāsturtium,* a kind of cress, originally *nāsitortium* (unattested), "nose-pain" (so called because cress plants such as mustard when eaten cause burning sensations in the nose) : *nāsus,* nose (see **nas-** in Appendix*) + *tort-,* past stem of *torquēre,* to twist, torture (see **terkw-** in Appendix*).]

nas·ty (năs′tē) *adj.* **-tier, -tiest. 1.** Disgusting to see, smell, or touch; filthy; foul. **2.** Morally offensive; indecent. **3.** Malicious; spiteful; mean: *"Will he say nasty things at my funeral?"* (Ezra Pound). **4.** Causing discomfort or trouble; unpleasant; annoying: *nasty weather.* **5.** Painful and dangerous; grave: *a nasty accident.* —See Synonyms at **dirty.** [Middle English, *nasty, naxty,* probably akin to Dutch *nestig,* earlier *nistich,* possibly originally meaning "fouled like a dirty bird's nest," from *nest,* nest. See **nizdo-** in Appendix.*] —**nas′ti·ly** *adv.* —**nas′ti·ness** *n.*

–nasty. Indicates a specified kind of nastic response or change; for example, **epinasty.** [From NASTIC.]

nat. 1. national. 2. native. 3. natural.

na·tal (nāt′l) *adj.* **1.** Of or relating to birth; accompanying birth: *natal injuries.* **2.** Of or pertaining to the time or place of one's

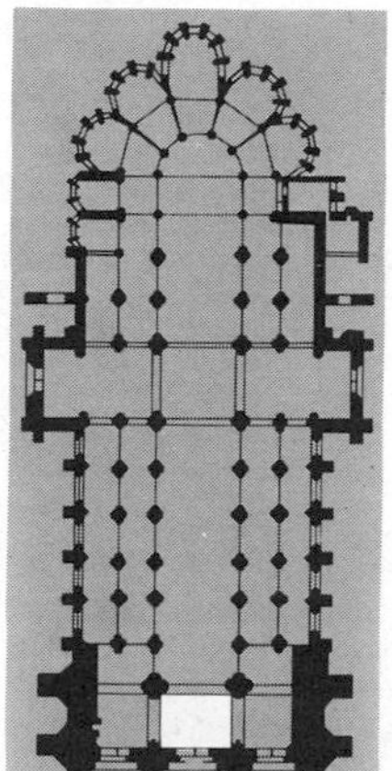

narthex
Plan of
Troyes Cathedral, France

birth. [Middle English, from Latin *nātālis*, from *nāscī* (past participle *nātus*), to be born. See **gene-** in Appendix.*]

Na·tal (nə-tăl′, -täl′). **1.** A province of the Republic of South Africa, occupying 35,284 square miles in the eastern part of the country. Population, 2,980,000. Capital, Pietermaritzburg. **2.** A city and port of northeastern Brazil. Population, 162,000.

Natal brown. Grayish brown. See **color.**

na·tal·i·ty (nā-tăl′ə-tē, nə-) *n., pl.* **-ties. Birth rate** *(see).*

Natal plum. A South African shrub, *Carissa grandiflora,* having forked spines, white flowers, and an edible scarlet berry. Also called "amatungula." [From NATAL, South Africa.]

na·tant (nā′tənt) *adj.* Swimming or floating. [Latin *natāns,* from *natāre,* to swim. See **snā-** in Appendix.*]

na·ta·tion (nā-tā′shən, nă-) *n.* The action or art of swimming. [Latin *natātiō,* from *natāre,* to swim. See **snā-** in Appendix.*]

na·ta·to·ri·al (nā′tə-tôr′ē-əl, -tōr′ē-əl, năt′ə-) *adj.* Also **na·ta·to·ry** (nā′tə-tôr′ē, -tōr′ē, năt′ə-). Of, pertaining to, or adapted for swimming. [Late Latin *natātōrius,* from Latin *natāre,* to swim. See **snā-** in Appendix.*]

na·ta·to·ri·um (nā′tə-tôr′ē-əm, -tōr′ē-əm, năt′ə-) *n., pl.* **-toriums** or **-toria** (-tôr′ē-ə, -tōr′ē-ə). An indoor swimming pool. [Late Latin *natātōrium,* from *natāre,* to swim. See **snā-** in Appendix.*]

Natch·ez[1] (năch′ĭz) *n., pl.* **Natchez. 1.** A tribe of Muskhogean-speaking Indians, formerly living in the area of Mississippi. **2.** A member of this tribe. **3.** The Muskhogean language of this tribe. [French, from the name of the chief town of the tribe.] **—Natch′ez** *adj.*

Natch·ez[2] (năch′ĭz). A Mississippi River port in southwestern Mississippi. Population, 24,000.

Natch·i·toches (năk′ə-tŏsh′). The oldest city in Louisiana, founded in 1714. Population, 14,000.

na·tes (nā′tēz′) *pl.n.* The **buttocks** *(see).* [Latin *natēs,* plural of *natis,* buttock. See **nōt-** in Appendix.*]

Na·than[1] (nā′thən). A masculine given name. [Hebrew *nāthān,* "he gave."]

Na·than[2] (nā′thən). A prophet during the reigns of David and Solomon. II Samuel 12:1–15.

Na·than·ael (nə-thăn′yəl). One of the 12 Apostles, usually known as **Bartholomew.**

Na·than·iel, Na·than·ael (nə-thăn′yəl). A masculine given name. [Middle English, from Late Latin, from Greek *Nathaniēl,* from Hebrew *nəthan'ēl,* "God has given."]

nathe·less (nāth′lĭs) *adv.* Also **nath·less** (năth′lĭs). *Archaic.* Nevertheless; notwithstanding. [Middle English *nathles,* Old English *nā thē lǣs,* "not less by that" : *nā,* NO + *thē,* by that, instrumental case of *sē,* that (see **to-** in Appendix*) + *lǣs,* LESS.]

Na·tick (nā′tĭk) *n.* A dialect based on English and the language of the Massachuset tribe spoken in the village of Natick, near the present Natick, Massachusetts. [Origin unknown.]

na·tion (nā′shən) *n.* **1.** A people, usually the inhabitants of a specific territory, who share common customs, origins, history, and frequently language or related languages. **2.** An aggregation of people organized under a single government; a country. **3.** The government of a sovereign state: *The Western nations have reacted favorably to the proposal.* **4. a.** A federation or tribe, especially one composed of North American Indians. **b.** The territory occupied by such a federation or tribe. **—the nation.** The entire people of a country, as distinct from any of the classes composing it: *"By subduing disparate lesser groups the nation has . . . broadened the capacity for individual liberty."* (Arthur S. Miller). **—the nations. 1.** In Biblical use, the gentile or heathen peoples: *"And the Lord shall scatter you among the nations."* (Deuteronomy 4:27). **2.** The population of the earth; the peoples. [Middle English *nacioun,* from Old French *nacion,* from Latin *nātiō,* "race," "breed," from *nāscī* (past participle *nātus*), to be born. See **gene-** in Appendix.*]

Synonyms: *nation, state, commonwealth, country, land, people, race, folk. Nation* primarily signifies a political body rather than a physical territory—the citizens united under one independent government, without close regard for their origins; secondarily it denotes institutional ties, a community of economic and cultural interests. *State* even more specifically indicates political (governmental) organization, generally on a sovereign basis and pertaining to a well-defined area. *Commonwealth* is also used in a variety of political senses; to a much lesser degree it retains an earlier sense of union based on mutual interests. *Country,* in strict usage, is a geographical term signifying the territory of one nation, but it is often used in the extended sense of *nation. Land,* specifically, is a somewhat less precise geographical term for an area inhabited by one people, but not necessarily a single political unit. *People,* in this context, signifies a group united over a long period by common cultural and social ties, although not necessarily by racial and national bonds. *Race* refers to those recognizable physical traits, stemming from common ancestry, that succeeding generations have in common. *Folk,* somewhat narrower than *people,* has specific reference to distinctive cultural characteristics of long standing.

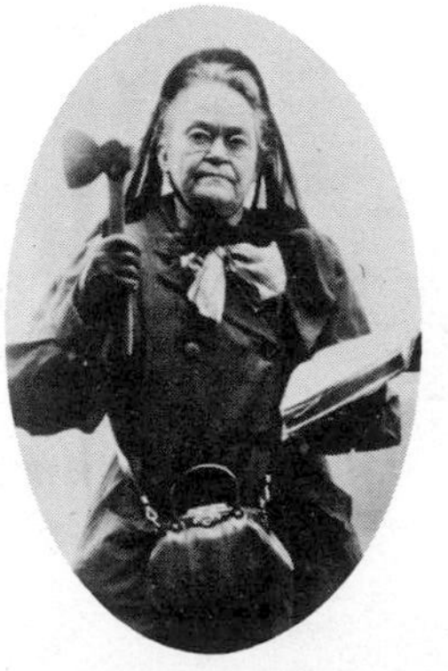

Carry Nation
With hatchet she used to smash bottles and furnishings in saloons

Na·tion (nā′shən), **Carry Amelia Moore.** Often misspelled "Carrie." 1846–1911. American reformer; temperance leader.

na·tion·al (năsh′ən-əl, năsh′nəl) *adj. Abbr.* **nat., natl. 1.** Of, pertaining to, or belonging to a nation as an organized whole. **2.** Of or relating to nationality: *the national question.* **3.** Characteristic of or peculiar to the people of a nation: *a national trait.* **4.** Big or important enough to have significance for a whole nation: *a national figure.* **5.** Of or maintained by the government of a nation: *a national park.* **6.** In the interest of one's own nation: *The foreign aid program was in fact strictly national in motivation.* **7.** Devoted to one's own nation or its interests; patriotic. *—n.* **1.** A citizen of a particular nation. **2.** *Usually plural.* A contest or tournament involving participants from all parts of a nation. **—na′tion·al·ly** *adv.*

national bank. 1. In the United States, one in a system of Federally chartered, privately owned banks, each required by law to be an investing member of its district Federal Reserve Bank and to be insured by the Federal Deposit Insurance Corporation. **2.** A bank associated with national finances and usually owned or controlled by a government.

national debt. The total financial obligations of a national government.

National Guard. *Abbr.* **NG, N.G.** The military reserve units controlled by each state of the United States, consisting of the Army National Guard and the Air National Guard.

National Guard of the United States. Members or units of the National Guard that are considered components of the U.S. Army or Air Force when called to active service.

national income. The total net value of all goods and services produced within a nation over a specified period of time, usually a year, and representing the sum of wages, profits, rents, interest, and pension payments to residents of the nation. Compare **gross national product.**

na·tion·al·ism (năsh′ən-əl-ĭz′əm, năsh′nəl-) *n.* **1.** Devotion to the interests of a particular nation. **2.** The belief that nations would benefit from acting independently rather than collectively, emphasizing national rather than international goals. **3.** In countries under foreign political or economic domination, aspirations for national independence. **—na′tion·al·ist** *adj. & n.* **—na′tion·al·is′tic** *adj.* **—na′tion·al·is′ti·cal·ly** *adv.*

Nationalist Chi·na (chī′nə). The unofficial name for the Republic of China. [After the *Chinese Nationalist Party (Kuomintang),* the ruling party.]

na·tion·al·i·ty (năsh′ə-năl′ə-tē) *n., pl.* **-ties. 1.** The status of belonging to a particular nation by origin, birth, or naturalization. **2.** A people having common origins or traditions and constituting or being considered to constitute a nation. **3.** Existence as a politically autonomous entity; the status of a nation. **4.** National character.

na·tion·al·ize (năsh′ən-əl-īz′, năsh′nəl-) *tr.v.* **-ized, -izing, -izes 1.** To convert (a sector of industry, agriculture, commerce, or public service, together with associated means of production) from private to governmental ownership and control. **2.** To make national in character. **3.** To accept as a citizen or national. **—na′tion·al·i·za′tion** *n.*

National League. One of the major professional leagues in baseball. See **major league.**

national monument. A natural landmark or a structure or site of historic interest set aside by a national government and maintained for enjoyment or study by the public.

national park. A tract of land declared public property by a national government with a view to its preservation and development for purposes of recreation and culture.

National Road. A highway, the **Cumberland Road** *(see).*

National Socialism. Nazism *(see).*

na·tion·hood (nā′shən-ho͝od′) *n.* The state of being a nation.

Nation of Islam. An organization of American Negroes who follow the religious practices of Islam and propose segregation of Negroes and whites, with a view to the establishment of a new black nation. Members are often called "Black Muslims."

na·tion·wide (nā′shən-wīd′) *adj.* Throughout a whole nation.

na·tive (nā′tĭv) *adj. Abbr.* **nat. 1.** Belonging to one by nature; inborn; innate: *native ability.* **2.** Being such by birth or origin: *a native Englishman.* **3.** One's own because of the place or circumstances of one's birth: *our native land; one's native language.* **4.** Originating, growing, or produced in a certain place; indigenous as opposed to exotic or foreign: *native products.* **5.** Belonging to or characteristic of the original inhabitants of a particular place, especially those of primitive culture. **6.** Occurring in nature pure or uncombined with other substances. Said of minerals or metals: *native copper.* **7.** In a natural state; unaffected by artificial influences: *native beauty.* **8.** *Archaic.* Closely related, as by birth or race. *—n. Abbr.* **nat. 1.** One born in or connected with a place by birth. **2.** One of the original inhabitants or lifelong residents of a place, as distinguished from immigrants or visitors. **3.** One belonging to a people of primitive culture originally occupying a country, as distinguished from visitors or invaders. **4.** Something, especially an animal or a plant, that originated in a particular place. [Middle English *natif,* from Old French, from Latin *nātīvus,* born, native, from *nāscī* (past participle *nātus*), to be born. See **gene-** in Appendix.*] **—na′tive·ly** *adv.* **—na′tive·ness** *n.*

Synonyms: *native, indigenous, endemic, aboriginal. Native,* said of people and cultural products, indicates birth or immediate origin in a specified place without eliminating the possibility of foreign origin through an earlier generation or historical period: *a native American. Indigenous* goes further in eliminating introduction from outside. *Indigenous* is used in this strict sense in the life sciences, but *native* is also commonly applied by biologists in the same sense. *Endemic,* said of plant life and diseases, emphasizes restriction to a limited area in which an organism especially thrives. *Aboriginal,* applied principally to people, describes the earliest-known inhabitants of a place.

na·tive-born (nā′tĭv-bôrn′) *adj.* Belonging to a place by birth.

Native States. The former semi-independent states of India. See **Indian States.**

na·tiv·ism (nā′tĭv-ĭz′əm) *n.* **1.** *U.S. History.* A 19th-century political program favoring the interests of native inhabitants over those of immigrants. **2.** *Philosophy.* The doctrine that the mind produces ideas that are not derived from external sources; the doctrine of innate ideas. **3.** The re-establishment or per-

ă pat/ā pay/âr care/ä father/b bib/ch church/d deed/ĕ pet/ē be/f fife/g gag/h hat/hw which/ĭ pit/ī pie/îr pier/j judge/k kick/l lid, needle/m mum/n no, sudden/ng thing/ŏ pot/ō toe/ô paw, for/oi noise/ou out/o͝o took/o͞o boot/p pop/r roar/s sauce/sh ship, dish/

petuation of native cultural traits, especially in opposition to acculturation. —**na′tiv·ist** *n.* —**na′tiv·is′tic** *adj.*

na·tiv·i·ty (nə-tĭv′ə-tē, nā-) *n., pl.* **-ties.** **1.** Birth, especially the place, conditions, or circumstances of one's birth. **2.** *Capital* **N.** **a.** The birth of Jesus. **b.** A representation, such as a painting, of this. **c.** Christmas. **3.** *Astrology.* A horoscope for the time of one's birth. [Middle English *nativite*, from Old French, from Latin *nātīvitās*, from *nātīvus*, born, NATIVE.]

natl. national.

NATO (nā′tō) North Atlantic Treaty Organization.

na·tro·lite (nā′trə-līt′) *n.* A colorless to white zeolite with composition $Na_2(Al_2Si_3O_{10})\cdot 2H_2O$. [German *Natrolith* : NATRO(N) + -LITE.]

na·tron (nā′trŏn′, -trən) *n.* A mineral of hydrous sodium carbonate, $Na_2CO_3\cdot 10H_2O$, often found crystallized with other salts. [French, from Spanish *natrón*, from Arabic *naṭrūn*, from Greek *nitron*, niter, soda. See **nitron** in Appendix.*]

NATS (năts) Naval Air Transport Service.

nat·ty (năt′ē) *adj.* **-tier, -tiest.** *Informal.* Neat, trim, and smart; spruce; dapper: *"He was very natty in his yachting cap, striped jacket, and white flannels."* (T.K. Brown III). [Perhaps variant of obsolete *netty*, from Middle English *net*, trim, neat, from Old French *net*, NEAT (tidy).]

nat·u·ral (năch′ər-əl, năch′rəl) *adj. Abbr.* **nat.** **1.** Present in or produced by nature; not artificial or man-made. **2.** Pertaining to or concerning nature: *natural science.* **3.** Pertaining to or produced solely by nature or the expected order of things: *a natural death; natural causes.* **4. a.** Pertaining to or resulting from inherent nature; not acquired: *"The love of power . . . and the admiration of it . . . are both natural to man."* (Christopher Morris). **b.** Distinguished by innate qualities or aptitudes: *a natural leader.* **5.** Free from affectation or artificiality; spontaneous. **6.** Not altered, treated, or disguised: *natural coloring.* **7.** Consonant with particular circumstances; expected and accepted: *"In Willie's mind marriage remained the natural and logical sequel to love."* (Duff Cooper). **8.** Established by moral certainty or conviction: *natural rights.* **9.** In a primitive, uncivilized, or unregenerate state. **10.** Illegitimate. Said of offspring. **11.** *Mathematics.* Of or pertaining to positive integers. **12.** *Music.* **a.** Not sharped or flatted. **b.** Having no sharps or flats. —See Synonyms at **naive, normal, sincere.** —*n.* **1.** *Informal.* One seeming to have the qualifications necessary for success: *a natural for the job.* **2.** *Music.* **a.** The sign (♮) placed before a note to cancel a preceding sharp or flat. **b.** A note so affected. **3.** Yellowish gray to pale orange yellow. See **color.** **4.** In certain card and dice games, a combination that wins immediately. [Middle English, from Old French, from Latin *nātūrālis*, from *nātūra*, NATURE.] —**nat′u·ral·ness** *n.*

natural childbirth. Childbirth regarded and performed as a natural process involving little pain or stress, and requiring preparatory training and medical supervision but no anesthesia or surgical aid.

natural gas. A mixture of hydrocarbon gases occurring with petroleum deposits, principally methane together with varying quantities of ethane, propane, butane, and other gases. It is used as a fuel and in the manufacture of organic compounds.

natural gender. *Grammar.* Gender based upon actual sex or absence of sex of the referent of a noun. Compare **common gender, grammatical gender.**

natural history. The study of natural objects and organisms, their origins, evolution, interrelationships, and description.

nat·u·ral·ism (năch′ər-ə-lĭz′əm, năch′rə-) *n.* **1.** Conformity to nature; factual or realistic representation, especially in art and literature. **2.** *Philosophy.* The system of thought holding that all phenomena can be explained in terms of natural causes and laws, without attributing moral, spiritual, or supernatural significance to them. **3.** *Theology.* The doctrine that all religious truths are derived from nature and natural causes and not from revelation. **4.** Conduct or thought prompted by natural desires or instincts.

nat·u·ral·ist (năch′ər-ə-lĭst, năch′rə-) *n.* **1.** One versed in natural history, especially in zoology or botany. **2.** One who believes in and follows the tenets of naturalism.

nat·u·ral·is·tic (năch′ər-ə-lĭs′tĭk, năch′rə-) *adj.* **1.** Imitating or producing the effect or appearance of nature. **2.** Of, pertaining to, or in accordance with the doctrines of naturalism.

nat·u·ral·ize (năch′ər-ə-līz′, năch′rə-) *v.* **-ized, -izing, -izes.** —*tr.* **1.** To grant full citizenship to (one of foreign birth). **2.** To adopt (something foreign, such as a word or custom) into general use. **3.** To adapt or acclimate (a plant or animal) to life in a new environment. **4.** To cause to conform to nature; make natural or lifelike. —*intr.* **1.** To become naturalized or acclimated; adapt. **2.** To study nature. —**nat′u·ral·i·za′tion** *n.*

natural logarithm. A **Napierian logarithm** *(see).*

nat·u·ral·ly (năch′ər-ə-lē, năch′rə-) *adv.* **1.** In a natural manner. **2.** By nature; inherently. **3.** Without a doubt; surely; of course.

natural number. *Mathematics.* One of the set of positive whole numbers; a positive integer. See **number.**

natural philosophy. The study of nature and the physical universe. Historically applied to studies that led to the modern science of physics.

natural resource. *Usually plural.* A material source of wealth that occurs in a natural state, such as forests or minerals.

natural science. A science, such as biology, chemistry, or physics, based chiefly on objective quantitative hypotheses.

natural selection. **a.** The principle that individuals possessing characteristics advantageous for survival in a specific environment constitute an increasing proportion of their species in that environment with each succeeding generation. **b.** The natural phenomenon of such a selective increase leading to new species. See **Darwinism.**

natural theology. A theology holding that knowledge of God may be acquired without recourse to revelation.

natural virtues. The **cardinal virtues** *(see).*

na·ture (nā′chər) *n.* **1.** The intrinsic characteristics and qualities of a person or thing. **2.** The order, disposition, and essence of all entities composing the physical universe. **3.** The physical world, usually the outdoors, including all living things. **4.** Natural scenery. **5.** *Often capital* **N.** The forces or processes of the physical world, generally personified as a female being. **6.** The primitive state of existence, untouched and uninfluenced by civilization or artificiality. **7.** *Theology.* Man's natural state, as distinguished from the state of grace. **8.** Kind; type: *or something of that nature.* **9.** The aggregate of a person's instincts, penchants, and preferences: *"She was only strong and sweet and in her nature when she was really deep in trouble"* (Gertrude Stein). **10. a.** A particular kind of individual character or disposition; temperament: *"In spite of her small vanities, Margaret had a sweet and pious nature"* (Louisa May Alcott). **b.** A person or thing characterized by some particular disposition: *"Strange natures made a brotherhood of ill."* (Shelley). **11.** The natural or real aspect of a person, place, or thing. **12.** Reality, as distinguished from the imaginary or marvelous. **13.** *Archaic.* Normal instincts or affections. **14.** The processes and functions of the body. Often used euphemistically in the phrase *the call of nature.* —See Synonyms at **disposition, type.** —**against nature.** Profoundly wrong or unnatural: *"the taking fish in spawning-time may be said to be against nature"* (Walton). —**by nature.** Because of natural qualities; inherently. —**in** (or **of**) **the nature of.** Belonging to the type or category of. [Middle English, from Old French, from Latin *nātūra*, nature, "birth," from *nāscī* (past participle *nātus*), to be born. See **gene-** in Appendix.*] —**na′tured** *adj.*

nature study. The observation and study of plants, animals, and natural phenomena, usually nontechnical and informal.

na·tur·op·a·thy (nā′chə-rŏp′ə-thē) *n.* A system of therapy that relies exclusively on natural remedies, such as sunlight supplemented with diet and massage, to treat the sick. [From NATURE + -PATHY.] —**na′tur·o·path′** (nā′chər-ə-păth′, nə-chŏŏr′ə-) *n.* —**na·tur′o·path′ic** (nə-chŏŏr′ə-păth′ĭk) *adj.*

naught (nôt) *n.* Also **nought.** **1.** Nothing. **2.** A cipher; zero; the figure 0. —*adj.* Also **nought.** *Rare.* Worthless; of no value. —*adv.* Also **nought.** *Rare.* Not in the least. [Middle English *nauht*, Old English *nāwiht* : *nā*, NO + *wiht*, creature, thing (see **wekti-** in Appendix*).]

naugh·ty (nô′tē) *adj.* **-tier, -tiest.** **1.** Disobedient; mischievous; perverse. Usually said of a child or a child's misdeeds. **2.** Indecent or suggestive of indecency. Now used as a term of playful or mild censure: *a naughty wink.* **3.** *Archaic.* Wicked; evil: *"a good deed in a naughty world"* (Shakespeare). [Middle English *nauhty*, from *nauht*, "worthless," NAUGHT.] —**naugh′ti·ly** *adv.* —**naugh′ti·ness** *n.*

nau·pli·us (nô′plē-əs) *n., pl.* **-plii** (-plē-ī′). *Zoology.* The microscopic, free-swimming first stage of the larva of certain crustaceans. [Latin, from Greek *nauplios*, sailor, perhaps variant of *nautilos*, sailor, NAUTILUS.]

Na·u·ru (nä-ōō′rōō). Formerly **Pleasant Island.** An island, eight square miles in area, in the Pacific Ocean west of the Gilbert Islands. It is a United Nations Trust Territory administered by Australia.

nau·se·a (nô′zē-ə, -zhə, -sē-ə, -shə) *n.* **1.** A stomach disturbance characterized by a feeling of the need to vomit. **2.** Strong aversion; repugnance; disgust. [Latin, from Greek *nausia*, seasickness, from *naus*, ship. See **nāu-²** in Appendix.*]

nau·se·ate (nô′zē-āt′, -zhē-āt′, -sē-āt′, -shē-āt′) *v.* **-ated, -ating, -ates.** —*tr.* **1.** To cause to feel nausea; make queasy. **2.** To cause to feel loathing or disgust. —*intr.* To feel nausea or queasiness; be queasy. [Latin *nauseāre*, from *nausea*, NAUSEA.] —**nau′se·a′tion** *n.*

nau·se·ated (nô′zē-ā′tĭd) *adj.* Suffering from nausea.

nau·seous (nô′shəs, nô′zē-əs) *adj.* **1.** Causing nausea; sickening. **2.** Intellectually repulsive: *"What proper person can be partial / To all those nauseous epigrams of Martial?"* (Byron). **3.** Nauseated. See Usage note. —**nau′seous·ly** *adv.*

Usage: Employment of *nauseous* in the sense of *nauseated* (experiencing nausea) is considered unacceptable by 88 per cent of the Usage Panel.

Nau·sic·a·a (nô-sĭk′ē-ə, -ā-ə, nou-). In the *Odyssey*, a maiden who befriended the stranded Odysseus.

naut. nautical.

nautch (nôch) *n.* A dance form of northern India for a single girl dancer accompanied by several musicians and sometimes by a singer. [Hindi *nāc*, from Prakrit *nacca*, dance, from Sanskrit *nṛtya*, from *nṛtyati*, he dances. See **sner-²** in Appendix.*] —**nautch** *adj.*

nau·ti·cal (nô′tĭ-kəl) *adj. Abbr.* **naut.** Of, pertaining to, or characteristic of ships, shipping, seamen, or navigation. [From Latin *nauticus*, from Greek *nautikos*, from *nautēs*, seaman, from *naus*, ship. See **nāu-²** in Appendix.*] —**nau′ti·cal·ly** *adv.*

Synonyms: *nautical, naval. Nautical* is a general term pertaining to sailors, ships, and navigation. *Naval*, once synonymous with *nautical*, now pertains specifically to the personnel and ships of a navy, or military sea force.

nautical mile. *Abbr.* **nm, n.m.** A unit of length used in sea and air navigation, based on the length of one minute of arc of a great circle; especially, an international and U.S. unit equal to 1,852 meters, or about 6,076 feet. See **measurement.**

nau·ti·loid (nô′tə-loid′) *n.* A mollusk of the subclass Nau-

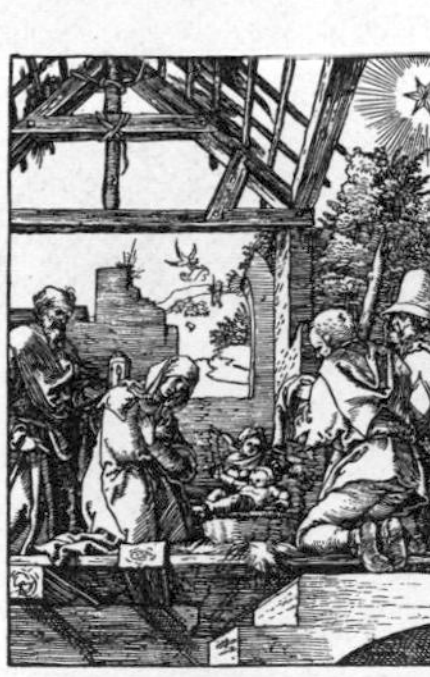

Nativity
Woodcut made in 1511
by Albrecht Dürer

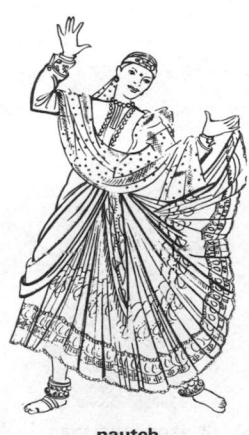

nautch
Nautch dancing girl

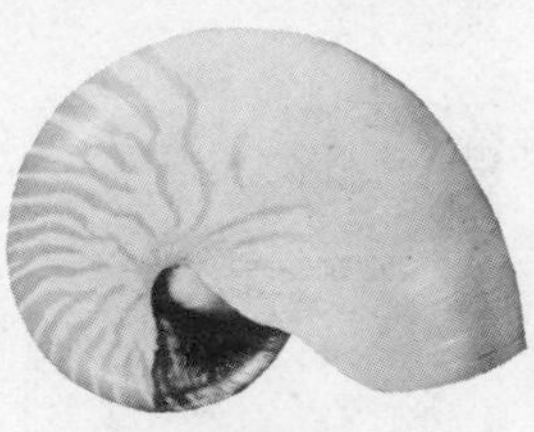
nautilus
Nautilus pompilius

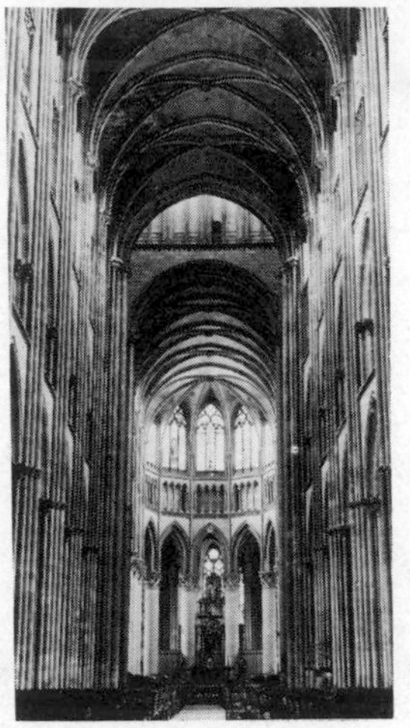
nave[1]
Cathedral of Rouen

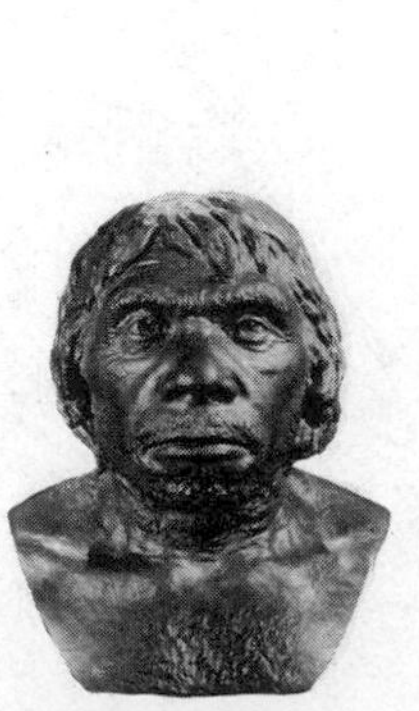
Neanderthal man
Probable appearance reconstructed from a study of skeletal remains

tiloidea, which includes the nautiluses and numerous extinct species known only as fossils. —*adj.* Of or belonging to the Nautiloidea. [From New Latin *Nautiloidea* : NAUTIL(US) + *-oidea,* from Latin *-oidēs,* -OID.]

nau·ti·lus (nô′tə-ləs) *n., pl.* **-luses** or **-li** (-lī′). **1.** Any mollusk of the genus *Nautilus,* found in the Indian and Pacific oceans, and having a spiral shell with a series of air-filled chambers. **2.** The **chambered nautilus** *(see).* [Latin, from Greek *nautilos,* sailor, from *naus,* ship. See **nāu-**[2] in Appendix.*]

Nau·ti·lus (nô′tə-ləs) *n.* A U.S. atomic-powered submarine, the first to make a submerged transit under the Arctic icecap and the North Pole (1958).

nav. **1.** naval. **2.** navigable. **3.** navigation.

Nav·a·ho (năv′ə-hō′, nä′və-) *n., pl.* **Navaho, -hos** or **-hoes.** Also **Nav·a·jo** (năv′ə-hō′, nä′və-). **1.** A group of Athapascan-speaking Indians occupying an extensive reservation in parts of New Mexico, Arizona, and Utah. **2.** A member of this group. **3.** The Athapascan language of this group. [Spanish *(Apache de) Navajo,* "(Apache of) Navaho," from Tewa (Tanoan language) *Navahu,* "great planted fields," the name of a Tewa Pueblo. "Apaches of Navaho" refers to the Apache living near this pueblo (i.e., the modern Navaho) as opposed to the other Apache (i.e., the modern Apache).] —**Nav′a·ho′** *adj.*

Nav·a·jo Mountain (năv′ə-hō′, nä′və-). An isolated 10,416-foot peak in southern Utah.

na·val (nā′vəl) *adj. Abbr.* **nav. 1.** Of or pertaining to the equipment, installations, personnel, or customs of a navy. **2.** Having a navy: *a great naval power.* —See Synonyms at **nautical.** [Latin *nāvālis,* from *nāvis,* ship. See **nāu-**[2] in Appendix.*]

naval base. A shore and port installation having equipment for the maintenance, repair, and servicing of naval vessels.

naval officer. 1. An officer in a navy. **2.** An official of the U.S. Treasury Department associated with the customs house in a major port.

naval stores. 1. Repositories of all goods, except armaments, needed by naval operations. **2.** Products such as turpentine or pitch, originally used to calk the seams of wooden ships.

nav·ar (năv′är′) *n.* A method of air navigation in which traffic in a pilot's vicinity is observed by ground radar and relayed to the pilot's radarscope. [NAV(IGATIONAL) + (RAD)AR.]

Nav·a·ri·no (năv′ə-rē′nō; *Spanish* nä′vä-rē′nō *for sense 1*). **1.** A Chilean island, 955 square miles in area, south of Tierra del Fuego. **2.** A former name for **Pylos.**

Na·varre (nə-vär′). *Spanish* **Na·var·ra** (nä-vär′rä). **1.** A former kingdom extending from Spain into France. **2.** A province of Spain, 4,024 square miles in area, lying on the western French-Spanish border. Population, 402,000. Capital, Pamplona. —**Na′var·rese′** (nä′və-rēz′, -rēs′, năv′ə-) *adj.* & *n.*

nave[1] (nāv) *n.* The central part of a church, extending from the narthex to the chancel and flanked by aisles. [Medieval Latin *nāvis,* "ship" (from the metaphor of the church as a ship), from Latin. See **nāu-**[2] in Appendix.*]

nave[2] (nāv) *n. Archaic.* The hub of a wheel. [Middle English *nave,* Old English *nafu.* See **nobh-** in Appendix.*]

na·vel (nā′vəl) *n.* **1.** The mark on the abdomen of mammals, where the umbilical cord was attached during gestation; the umbilicus. **2.** A central point; middle. [Middle English *navel,* Old English *nafela.* See **nobh-** in Appendix.*]

navel orange. A sweet, usually seedless orange having at its apex a navellike formation enclosing an underdeveloped fruit.

na·vel·wort (nā′vəl-wûrt′) *n.* **1.** A plant, **pennywort** *(see).* **2.** Any plant of the genus *Omphalodes,* having one-sided clusters of usually blue flowers. [From the navellike depression on its leaves.]

na·vic·u·lar (nə-vĭk′yə-lər) *n.* Also **na·vic·u·la·re** (nə-vĭk′yə-lâr′ē, -lä′rē). **1.** A comma-shaped bone of the wrist. **2.** The concave bone in front of the anklebone on the instep of the foot. Also called "scaphoid." —*adj.* Shaped like a boat. [Late Latin *nāviculāris,* "boat-shaped," from Latin *nāvicula,* boat, diminutive of *nāvis,* ship. See **nāu-**[2] in Appendix.*]

nav·i·ga·ble (năv′ə-gə-bəl) *adj. Abbr.* **nav. 1.** Sufficiently deep or wide to provide passage for (all or specified) vessels. **2.** Capable of being steered. Said of vessels or aircraft. —**nav′i·ga·bil′i·ty, nav′i·ga·ble·ness** *n.* —**nav′i·ga·bly** *adv.*

nav·i·gate (năv′ə-gāt′) *v.* **-gated, -gating, -gates.** —*tr.* **1.** To plan, record, and control the course and position of (a ship or aircraft). **2.** To follow a planned course on, across, or through: *navigate a stream.* —*intr.* **1.** To control the course of a ship or aircraft. **2.** To voyage over water in a boat or ship; sail. **3.** *Informal.* To direct oneself toward some destination. [Latin *nāvigāre,* to manage a ship : *nāvis,* ship (see **nāu-**[2] in Appendix*) + *agere,* to drive, conduct (see **ag-** in Appendix*).]

nav·i·ga·tion (năv′ə-gā′shən) *n. Abbr.* **nav. 1.** The theory and practice of navigating, especially the charting of a course for a ship or aircraft. **2.** Travel or traffic by vessels; especially, commercial shipping. —**nav′i·ga′tion·al** *adj.*

nav·i·ga·tor (năv′ə-gā′tər) *n.* **1.** One who navigates, especially: **a.** One who explores by ship. **b.** A crew member who plots the course of a ship or aircraft. **2.** A device that directs the course of an aircraft or missile.

nav·vy (năv′ē) *n., pl.* **-vies.** *British.* A laborer, especially one employed in construction or excavation projects. [Slang shortening of NAVIGATOR (in an obsolete, and originally humorous, sense of a laborer employed in building the navigation canals of England in the 18th and 19th centuries).]

na·vy (nā′vē) *n., pl.* **-vies. 1.** All of a nation's warships. **2.** *Often capital* **N.** A nation's entire military organization for sea warfare and defense, including vessels, personnel, and shore establishments. **3.** *Rare.* A group of ships; a fleet. **4. Navy blue** *(see).* [Middle English *navie,* from Old French, from Vulgar Latin *nāvia* (unattested), fleet, from Latin *nāvis,* ship. See **nāu-**[2] in Appendix.*]

navy bean. Any of several varieties of the **kidney bean** *(see),* cultivated for their nutritious white seeds. Also called "pea bean." [Formerly a standard provision of the U.S. Navy.]

navy blue. Dark grayish blue. Also "navy." See **color.** [From the color of the British naval uniform.] —**na′vy-blue′** *adj.*

Navy Cross. A decoration in the form of a bronze cross awarded by the U.S. Navy for exceptional heroism in action.

navy gray. Dark gray. See **color.**

navy yard. A dockyard, owned by the government, for the construction, repair, equipping, or docking of naval ships.

Na·wa. See **Naha.**

na·wab (nə-wôb′) *n.* A governor or ruler in India under the Mogul empire. [Hindi *nawwāb,* from Arabic *nuwwāb,* originally plural of *na'ib,* governor.]

Nax·os (năk′sŏs′, -səs). The largest island, 169 square miles in area, of the Cyclades in the Aegean Sea.

nay (nā) *adv.* **1.** No. Now archaic except in recording or expressing a vote. **2.** And moreover. Used to introduce a more precise or emphatic expression than the one first made: *He was ill-favored, nay, hideous.* —*n.* **1.** A denial or refusal. **2.** A negative or dissenting vote or voter. —**say (someone) nay.** To deny, refuse, or prohibit (someone). [Middle English *nay, nei,* from Old Norse *nei* : *ne,* not (see **ne-** in Appendix*) + *ei,* ever (see **aiw-** in Appendix*).]

na·ya pai·sa (nə-yä′ pī-sä′) *pl.* **naye paise** (nə-yā′ pī-sā′). A monetary unit of India, the **piasa** *(see).* [Hindi *nayā paisā,* "new pice" : *nayā,* new, from Sanskrit *nāvya, nava* (see **newo-** in Appendix*) + *paisā,* PICE.]

Na·ya·rit (nä′yä-rēt′). A state of Mexico, 10,547 square miles in area, centrally situated on the Pacific Coast. Population, 427,000. Capital, Tepic.

Naz·a·rene (năz′ə-rēn′, năz′ə-rēn′) *n.* **1. a.** A native or inhabitant of Nazareth. **b.** Jesus. Used with *the.* **2.** A member of a sect of early Christians of Jewish origin who retained many of the prescribed Jewish observances. **3.** A member of an American Protestant denomination, the Church of the Nazarene, that follows many of the doctrines of early Methodism. —*adj.* Of or pertaining to Nazareth or Nazarenes. [Middle English *Nazaren,* from Late Latin *Nazarēnus,* from Greek *Nazarēnos,* from *Nazarat,* NAZARETH.]

Naz·a·reth (năz′ə-rĭth). A town in northern Israel, site of the town of Jesus' childhood. Population, 25,000.

Naze, The (nāz). **1.** A cape of southern Norway. Also called "Lindesnes." **2.** Headlands on the coast of Essex, England.

Na·zi (nät′sē, năt′-) *n., pl.* **-zis. 1.** A member of the National Socialist German Workers' Party, founded in Germany in 1919 and brought to power in 1933 under Adolf Hitler. **2.** *Often small* **n.** An adherent or advocate of policies characteristic of this party; a fascist. —*adj.* Of, relating to, controlled by, or typical of Nazis. [German, phonetic shortening of *National-sozialist,* National Socialist.]

Na·zism (nät′sĭz′əm, năt′-) *n.* Also **Na·zi·ism** (nät′sē-ĭz′əm, năt′-). The ideology and practice of the Nazis; especially, the policy of state control of the economy, racist nationalism, and national expansion. Also called "National Socialism."

Nb The symbol for the element niobium.

NB Nebraska (with Zip Code).

n.b. nota bene.

N.B. 1. New Brunswick. **2.** nota bene.

NBA, N.B.A. 1. National Basketball Association. **2.** National Boxing Association.

NbE north by east.

NBO Airport code for Nairobi, Kenya.

NBS National Bureau of Standards.

NbW north by west.

NC 1. North Carolina (with Zip Code). **2.** Nurse Corps.

N.C. North Carolina.

NCAA, N.C.A.A. National Collegiate Athletic Association.

NCO, N.C.O. noncommissioned officer.

Nd The symbol for the element neodymium.

ND North Dakota (with Zip Code).

N.D. North Dakota (unofficial).

N. Dak. North Dakota.

NDH Airport code for New Delhi, India.

Ndo·la (ĕn-dō′lə). A city of north-central Zambia, near the Congolese (Kinshasa) border. Population, 73,000.

Ne The symbol for the element neon.

NE northeast.

N.E. New England.

NEA, N.E.A. National Education Association.

Neagh, Lough (lŏKH nā′). The largest lake of the United Kingdom, occupying 153 square miles in Northern Ireland.

Neal. Variant of **Neil.**

Ne·an·der·thal (nē-ăn′dər-thôl′, -tôl′, nā-än′dər-täl′) *n.* **1.** A Neanderthal man. **2.** *Slang.* A crude, boorish, or old-fashioned person. —*adj.* **1.** Of or pertaining to Neanderthal man. **2.** *Slang.* Crude or old-fashioned: *a Neanderthal mentality.*

Neanderthal man. An extinct species or race of man, *Homo neanderthalensis,* living during the late Pleistocene age in the Old World, and associated with Middle Paleolithic tools. [Identified in 1856 from remains found in the *Neanderthal,* a valley near Düsseldorf, West Germany.]

ne·an·throp·ic (nē′ən-thrŏp′ĭk) *adj. Anthropology.* Of or pertaining to members of the extant species *Homo sapiens,* as compared with other, now extinct species of *Homo.* Compare **paleoanthropic.** [NE(O)- + ANTHROP(O)- + -IC.]

ă pat/ā pay/âr care/ä father/b bib/ch church/d deed/ĕ pet/ē be/f fife/g gag/h hat/hw which/ĭ pit/ī pie/îr pier/j judge/k kick/l lid, needle/m mum/n no, sudden/ng thing/ŏ pot/ō toe/ô paw, for/oi noise/ou out/ŏŏ took/ōō boot/p pop/r roar/s sauce/sh ship, dish/

Ne·a·pol·i·tan (nē′ə-pŏl′ə-tən) *adj.* Of, belonging to, or characteristic of Naples. —*n.* A native or resident of Naples.

Neapolitan ice cream. Ice cream in brick form, with layers of different colors and flavors.

neap tide (nēp). A tide of lowest range, occurring when the sun and moon are in quadrature. Compare **spring tide.** [Middle English *neep,* Old English *nēpflōd,* neap (tide). See **ken-²** in Appendix.*]

near (nîr) *adv.* **nearer, nearest. 1.** To, at, or within a short distance or interval in space or time: *Come near the fire.* **2.** Almost; nearly: *near exhausted by the heat.* **3.** With or in a close relationship. —*adj.* **nearer, nearest. 1.** Close in time, space, position, or degree: *near neighbors; near equals.* See Usage note below. **2.** Closely related by kinship or association; intimate: *near and dear friends.* **3.** Accomplished or missed by a small margin; close; narrow: *near escape.* **4.** Closely corresponding to or resembling an original: *a near likeness.* **5. a.** Closer of two or more. **b.** On the left side of a vehicle or draft team. **6.** Short and direct: *the near route to town.* **7.** *Archaic.* Strictly economical; stingy; parsimonious: *"Mr. Barkis was an excellent husband, she said, though still a little near"* (Dickens). —*prep.* Close to; within a short distance or time of. —*v.* **neared, nearing, nears.** —*tr.* To come close or closer to. —*intr.* To draw near or nearer. [Middle English *nere,* Old English *nēar,* comparative adverb of *nēah,* "near." See **nēwh-iz** in Appendix.*] —**near′ness** *n.*

Usage: The adjectives *near* and *close* both denote proximity in time or space, but *close* is preferable when the desired sense is that of immediate proximity. See Usage note at **next.**

near·by (nîr′bī′) *adj.* Located a short distance away; close at hand; adjacent. —*adv.* Also **near by.** Not far away.

Ne·arc·tic (nē-ärk′tĭk, -är′tĭk) *adj.* Of or designating the zoogeographic region that includes the arctic and temperate areas of North America and also includes Greenland. Compare **Palearctic.** [NE(O)- + ARCTIC.]

Near East. 1. A region including the countries of the eastern Mediterranean, the Arabian Peninsula, and, sometimes, northeastern Africa. **2.** Formerly, the Balkan Peninsula.

near·ly (nîr′lē) *adv.* **1.** Almost but not quite. **2.** Closely; intimately: *a matter nearly affecting our interests.*

near·sight·ed (nîr′sī′tĭd) *adj.* **1.** Afflicted with **myopia** *(see).* **2.** Shortsighted. —**near′sight′ed·ly** *adv.* —**near′sight′ed·ness** *n.*

neat¹ (nēt) *adj.* **1.** In good order or clean condition; tidy. **2.** Orderly and precise in appearance or procedure; not careless or messy. **3.** Skillfully executed; deft; adroit: *a neat turn of phrase.* **4.** Simple and smoothly consistent: *"Though many things fitted her theories, I never believed them. They were too neat"* (John Updike). **5.** Not diluted or mixed with other substances. Said of liquors. **6.** Obtained after all deductions; net: *neat profit.* **7.** *Slang.* Stylish; appealing: *Man, that hot rod is neat!* [Old French *net,* from Latin *nitidus,* elegant, shiny, from *nitēre,* to shine. See **nei-¹** in Appendix.*] —**neat′ly** *adv.* —**neat′ness** *n.*

Synonyms: *neat, tidy, trim. Neat* primarily denotes simplicity, close attention to detail, and cleanliness. *Tidy* emphasizes precise arrangement and consequent good order. *Trim* stresses especially pleasing or smart appearance, resulting from neatness, tidiness, sense of proportion, and deftness of design.

neat² (nēt) *n., pl.* **neat.** *Archaic.* A domestic bovine animal. [Middle English *nete,* Old English *nēat.* See **neud-** in Appendix.*]

neath, 'neath (nēth) *prep. Poetic.* Beneath.

neat·herd (nēt′hûrd′) *n. Archaic.* A cowherd.

neat's-foot oil (nēts′fo͝ot′). A light, yellow oil obtained from the feet and shinbones of cattle, used chiefly to dress leather.

neb (nĕb) *n. Chiefly Scottish.* **1. a.** A beak of a bird. **b.** A nose or snout. **2.** A projecting part, especially a nib. [Middle English *neb(b),* Old English *neb(b).* See **nabja-** in Appendix.*]

NEbE northeast by east.

Ne·bi·im (nĕb′ē-ēm′; *Hebrew* nĕ-vē′ēm′) *pl.n.* The second section of the Hebrew Scriptures, or Old Testament; the Prophets. See **prophet.** [Hebrew *nəbhī'īm,* plural of *nābhī,* prophet.]

NEbN northeast by north.

Nebr. Nebraska.

Ne·bras·ka (nə-brăs′kə). *Abbr.* **Nebr.** A Midwestern state of the United States, 77,237 square miles in area. It joined the Union in 1867. Population, 1,411,000. Capital, Lincoln. See map at **United States of America.** [Osage *nibthacka, nibraska,* "flat water."] —**Ne·bras′kan** *adj.* & *n.*

Neb·u·chad·nez·zar II (nĕb′ə-kəd-nĕz′ər, nĕb′yo͞o-). Also **Neb·u·chad·rez·zar** (nĕb′ə-kəd-rĕz′ər, nĕb′yo͞o-). King of Babylon (605–562 B.C.); destroyed Jerusalem and carried the Jews into Babylonian Captivity.

neb·u·la (nĕb′yə-lə) *n., pl.* **-lae** (-lē′, -lī′) or **-las. 1.** *Astronomy.* **a.** Any diffuse mass of interstellar dust, gas, or both, visible as luminous patches or areas of darkness depending on the way the mass absorbs or reflects incident radiation. **b.** Such a mass that absorbs ultraviolet radiation from stars and re-emits it as visible light. Also called "emission nebula." **c.** Such a mass that absorbs all incident radiation without re-emission. Also called "absorption nebula." **d.** Such a mass that reflects visible radiation. Also called "reflection nebula." **e.** A **galactic nebula** *(see).* **2.** *Pathology.* **a.** A cloudy spot on the cornea. **b.** Cloudiness in the urine. **3.** *Medicine.* A liquid medication applied by spraying. [New Latin, from Latin, cloud. See **nebh-** in Appendix.*] —**neb′u·lar** *adj.*

nebular hypothesis. A theory of the origin of the solar system, according to which a rotating nebula cooled and contracted, throwing off rings of matter that contracted into the planets and their moons, while the great mass of the condensing nebula became the sun. Compare **planetesimal hypothesis.**

neb·u·lize (nĕb′yə-līz′) *tr.v.* **-lized, -lizing, -lizes. 1.** To convert (a liquid) to a fine spray; atomize. **2.** To treat with a medicated spray. [From NEBULA.] —**neb′u·li·za′tion** *n.* —**neb′u·liz′er** *n.*

neb·u·los·i·ty (nĕb′yə-lŏs′ə-tē) *n., pl.* **-ties. 1.** The quality or condition of being nebulous. **2.** A nebula or a mass of material constituting a nebula.

neb·u·lous (nĕb′yə-ləs) *adj.* Also *rare* **neb·u·lose** (-lōs′). **1.** Cloudy, misty, or hazy. **2.** Lacking definite form or limits; unclearly identified or established; vague: *"that nebulous area known as 'off-Broadway'"* (Leo Lemon). **3.** Of or characteristic of a nebula. [Latin *nebulōsus,* from *nebula,* cloud, NEBULA.] —**neb′u·lous·ly** *adv.* —**neb′u·lous·ness** *n.*

nec·es·sar·i·ly (nĕs′ə-sĕr′ə-lē) *adv.* **1.** As dictated by necessity: *"Men are necessarily born in a family-society, at least"* (Hume). **2.** As a necessary result; inevitably.

nec·es·sar·y (nĕs′ə-sĕr′ē) *adj.* **1.** Needed for the continuing existence or functioning of something; essential; indispensable: *Oxygen is necessary to most living organisms.* **2.** Needed to achieve a certain result or effect; requisite: *the necessary tools.* **3.** Following unavoidably from conditions, circumstances, or premises; inevitable: *the necessary results of overindulgence.* **4.** Required by obligation, compulsion, or convention: *making the necessary apologies.* —*n., pl.* **necessaries. 1.** *Often plural.* That which is needed; especially, money or provisions: *the necessaries for the trip.* **2.** *Plural. Law.* Whatever is needed for the maintenance of a dependent, in keeping with his economic and social status. **3.** *Regional.* A privy. [Middle English *necessarie,* from Latin *necessārius,* extension of *necesse,* necessary. See **ked-** in Appendix.*]

Synonyms: *necessary, essential, vital, indispensable, requisite, required, prerequisite, necessitous, needy, needful. Necessary* denotes that which fills an urgent need, but not invariably an all-compelling need. The stronger *essential* and *vital* are applied to that without which something, by its nature, cannot exist, or without which it cannot exist or continue in normal condition or form. *Indispensable* even more specifically denotes that which cannot be sacrificed; frequently it is applied to part of a whole. *Requisite* and *required* are more specific and less powerful terms; they usually signify a need that complements other needs and is imposed externally rather than by the nature of the subject itself. *Prerequisite* adds the dimension of need that must be met beforehand; it specifies a prior condition that determines whether something desired is to follow. *Necessitous* and *needy* signify want in the subjective sense of privation, and are applied to persons in a condition of great want. *Needful* expresses want much less urgently than any of the foregoing.

ne·ces·si·tar·i·an·ism (nə-sĕs′ə-târ′ē-ə-nĭz′əm) *n.* Also **nec·es·sar·i·an·ism** (nĕs′ə-sâr′ē-ə-nĭz′əm). The doctrine that events are inevitably determined by preceding causes. —**ne·ces′si·tar′i·an** *adj.* & *n.*

ne·ces·si·tate (nə-sĕs′ə-tāt′) *tr.v.* **-tated, -tating, -tates. 1.** To make necessary or unavoidable: *The emergency necessitated a change in plans.* **2.** To require or compel (someone). Used chiefly in the passive. —See Synonyms at **force.** [Medieval Latin *necessitāre,* from Latin *necessitās,* NECESSITY.] —**ne·ces′si·ta′tion** *n.* —**ne·ces′si·ta′tive** *adj.*

ne·ces·si·tous (nə-sĕs′ə-təs) *adj.* Needy; destitute; indigent. See Synonyms at **necessary.** [French *nécessiteux,* from Old French *necessite,* NECESSITY.] —**ne·ces′si·tous·ly** *adv.*

ne·ces·si·ty (nə-sĕs′ə-tē) *n., pl.* **-ties. 1.** Something needed for the existence, effectiveness, or success of something; a requirement. **2.** Something that must inevitably exist or occur: **a.** That which is dictated by invariable physical laws or strict social requirements. **b.** That which is dictated by constraining circumstances: *"the brutal necessities of war"* (Joseph Frank). **3.** The state or fact of being required or unavoidable. **4.** Pressing or urgent need, such as that arising from poverty, misfortune, or emergency. —See Synonyms at **need.** —**of necessity.** As an inevitable consequence; necessarily. [Middle English *necessite,* from Old French, from Latin *necessitās,* from *necesse,* NECESSARY.]

Nech·es (nĕch′ĭz). A river rising in eastern Texas and flowing 280 miles southeast and south to Sabine Lake.

neck (nĕk) *n.* **1.** The part of the body joining the head to the trunk. **2. a.** The part of a garment around or near the neck of the wearer. **b.** The neckline of a dress or blouse. **3.** *Anatomy.* Any relatively narrow portion of a structure, as of a bone or organ, that joins its parts. **4.** The part of a tooth between the crown and the root. **5.** Any relatively narrow elongation, projection, or connecting part: *a neck of land; the neck of a flask.* **6.** *Music.* The narrow part along which the strings of a stringed instrument extend to the pegs. **7.** *Architecture.* The narrow, upper part of a column, just below the capital. **8.** *Geology.* Solidified lava filling the vent of an extinct volcano. **9.** The siphon of a bivalve mollusk, such as a clam. **10. a.** The length of the head and neck of a horse: *winning a race by a neck.* **b.** *Slang.* Any narrow margin by which a competition is won or lost. —**break one's neck.** *Slang.* To make a great effort to accomplish something. —**get it in the neck.** *Slang.* To undergo severe punishment, rebuke, or penalty. —**neck and neck.** Even in a race or contest. —**neck of the woods.** *Informal.* An area or neighborhood. —**save one's neck.** *Slang.* To get out of a situation that threatens one's life or security. —**stick one's neck out.** *Slang.* To act boldly, despite the risk of criticism, trouble, or danger. —*v.* **necked, necking, necks.** —*intr. Slang.* To make love by kissing and caressing. —*tr.* **1.** *Slang.* To make love to by kissing and caressing. **2.** To strangle or decapitate (a fowl).

nebula
The Great Nebula in Orion

t tight/th thin, path/*th* this, bathe/ŭ cut/ûr urge/v valve/w with/y yes/z zebra, size/zh vision/ə about, item, edible, gallop, circus/ à *Fr.* ami/œ *Fr.* feu, *Ger.* schön/ü *Fr.* tu, *Ger.* über/KH *Ger.* ich, *Scot.* loch/N *Fr.* bon. ***Follows main vocabulary. †Of obscure origin.**

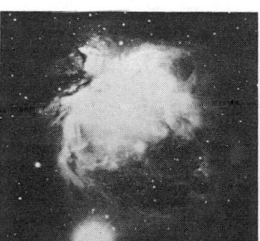

[Middle English *necke*, Old English *hnecca*. See **ken-**[5] in Appendix.*]

Neck·ar (nĕk′ər; *German* nĕk′är′). A river rising in the Black Forest in southern West Germany, flowing north and west 246 miles to join the Rhine at Mannheim.

Neck·er (nĕk′ər; *French* nĕ-kâr′), **Jacques**. 1732–1804. Swiss-born French progressive minister of finance under Louis XVI.

neck·er·chief (nĕk′ər-chĭf) *n.* A kerchief worn around the neck.

neck·ing (nĕk′ĭng) *n. Architecture.* A molding or moldings between the upper part of the shaft of a column and the projecting part of the capital.

neck·lace (nĕk′lĭs) *n.* An ornament, such as a string of beads or a flexible metal chain or band, worn around the neck.

neck·line (nĕk′līn′) *n.* The line formed by the edge of a garment at or near the neck.

neck·piece (nĕk′pēs′) *n.* A scarf, often of fur.

neck·tie (nĕk′tī′) *n.* A long, narrow band of fabric worn around the neck and tied in a knot or bow close to the throat, usually with the ends left hanging down the shirt front.

neck·wear (nĕk′wâr′) *n.* Articles of dress worn around the neck, such as neckties, scarfs, and collars.

necro–, necr–. Indicates: **1.** Death or the dead; for example, **necrology**. **2.** A dead body or dead tissue; for example, **necrobiosis**, **necropsy**. [New Latin, from Greek *nekros*, corpse. See **nek-**[1] in Appendix.*]

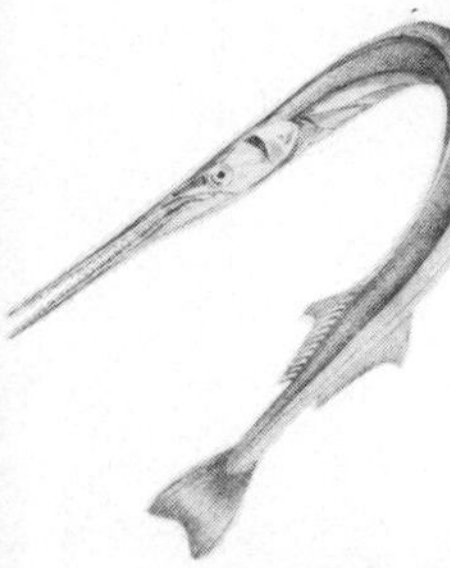

needlefish
Strongylura marina
Atlantic needlefish

nec·ro·bi·o·sis (nĕk′rō-bī-ō′sĭs) *n.* The natural degeneration and death of cells and tissues, as opposed to death from injury or disease and distinguished from death of the entire organism. Compare **gangrene**, **necrosis**. [New Latin : NECRO- + -BIOSIS.] —**nec′ro·bi·ot′ic** (-bī-ŏt′ĭk) *adj.*

ne·crol·o·gy (nə-krŏl′ə-jē, nĕ-) *n., pl.* **-gies**. **1.** A list or record of people who have died, especially in the recent past. **2.** An obituary. [New Latin *necrologium* : NECRO- + -LOGY.] —**nec′ro·log′ic** (nĕk′rə-lŏj′ĭk), **nec′ro·log′i·cal** *adj.* —**ne·crol′o·gist** *n.*

nec·ro·man·cy (nĕk′rə-măn′sē) *n.* **1.** The art that professes to conjure up the spirits of the dead and commune with them in order to predict the future. **2.** Black magic; sorcery. **3.** Magical qualities: *"the necromancy of female gracefulness"* (Poe). See Synonyms at **magic**. [Confusion of two words: **a.** Late Latin *necromantia*, from Greek *nekromanteia*, divination by corpses : NECRO- + -MANCY; **b.** Middle English *nigromancie*, from Old French, from Medieval Latin *nigromantia*, black magic : *niger*, black (see **niger-** in Appendix*) + -MANCY.] —**nec′ro·man′cer** *n.* —**nec′ro·man′tic** *adj.*

ne·croph·a·gous (nə-krŏf′ə-gəs, nĕ-) *adj.* Feeding on carrion or corpses. [Greek *nekrophagos* : NECRO- + -PHAGOUS.]

nec·ro·phile (nĕk′rə-fīl′) *n.* Also **nec·ro·phil** (-fĭl′), **nec·ro·phil·i·ac** (nĕk′rə-fĭl′ē-ăk). One suffering from necrophilia.

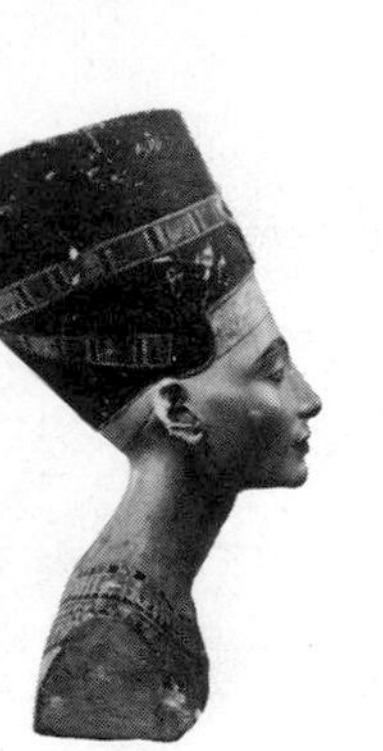

Nefertiti

nec·ro·phil·i·a (nĕk′rə-fĭl′ē-ə) *n.* Also **ne·croph·i·lism** (nə-krŏf′ə-lĭz′əm, nĕ-). An abnormal, often erotic attraction to dead bodies. [New Latin : NECRO- + -PHILIA.] —**nec′ro·phil′ic** *adj.*

nec·ro·pho·bi·a (nĕk′rə-fō′bē-ə) *n.* **1.** A morbid fear of death. **2.** A morbid horror of corpses. [New Latin : NECRO- + -PHOBIA.] —**nec′ro·pho′bic** *adj.*

ne·crop·o·lis (nə-krŏp′ə-lĭs, nĕ-) *n., pl.* **-lises** or **-leis** (-lās′). A cemetery; especially, a large and elaborate one belonging to an ancient city. [Greek *nekropolis* : NECRO- + *polis*, city (see **pelə-**[2] in Appendix*).]

nec·rop·sy (nĕk′rŏp′sē) *n., pl.* **-sies**. Also **ne·cros·co·py** (nə-krŏs′kə-pē, nĕ-) *pl.* **-pies**. A post-mortem examination; an **autopsy** *(see)*. [NECR(O)- + -OPSY.]

ne·crose (nĕ-krōs′, nĕk′rōs′) *v.* **-crosed, -crosing, -croses**. Also **nec·ro·tize** (nĕk′rə-tīz′), **-tized, -tizing, -tizes**. —*intr.* To be affected with necrosis. —*tr.* To affect with necrosis. [Back-formation from NECROSIS.]

ne·cro·sis (nə-krō′sĭs, nĕ-) *n., pl.* **-ses** (-sēz′). The pathologic death of living tissue in a plant or animal. Compare **necrobiosis**. [Late Latin *necrōsis*, from Greek *nekrōsis*, mortification, from *nekroun*, to mortify, from *nekros*, corpse. See **nek-**[1] in Appendix.*] —**ne·crot′ic** (-krŏt′ĭk) *adj.*

nec·tar (nĕk′tər) *n.* **1.** *Greek & Roman Mythology.* The drink of the gods. Compare **ambrosia**. **2.** Any delicious or invigorating drink. **3. a.** The undiluted juice of a fruit. **b.** A rich blend of fruit juices. **4.** A sweet liquid secreted by flowers of various plants and gathered by bees for making honey. [Latin, from Greek *nektar*. See **nek-**[1] in Appendix.*] —**nec′tar·ous** *adj.*

nec·tar·ine (nĕk′tə-rēn′) *n.* A variety of peach of ancient origin, having a smooth, waxy skin. [Short for *nectarine peach*, from obsolete *nectarine*, "sweet as nectar," from NECTAR.]

nec·ta·ry (nĕk′tə-rē) *n., pl.* **-ries**. **1.** *Botany.* **a.** A glandlike organ, usually at the base of a flower, that secretes nectar. **b.** The part of a flower in which such an organ is contained. **2.** *Entomology.* An obsolete term for **siphuncle** *(see)*. [New Latin *nectarium*, from NECTAR.] —**nec·tar′i·al** (nĕk-târ′ē-əl) *adj.*

NED, N.E.D. New English Dictionary (Oxford).

Ne·der·land. The Dutch name for **Netherlands**.

nectarine

née (nā) *adj.* Also **nee**. Born. Used when identifying a married woman by her maiden name. [French, feminine past participle of *naître*, to be born, from Latin *nāscī* (past participle *nātus*). See **genə-** in Appendix.*]

Usage: *Née* is followed solely by a family name, the only name a person has at birth: *Mrs. Mary Parks, née Case.* Not: *Mrs. Mary Parks, née Mary Case.*

need (nēd) *n.* **1.** A condition or situation in which something necessary or desirable is required or wanted: *crops in need of water.* **2.** A wish for something that is lacking or desired: *a need for affection.* **3.** Necessity; obligation: *There is no need for you to go.* **4.** Something required or wanted; a requisite: *Our needs are modest.* **5.** A condition of poverty or misfortune: *He is in dire need.* —See Synonyms below. —*v.* **needed, needing, needs**. Used as an uninflected auxiliary followed by an infinitive without *to*, or as an inflected auxiliary followed by an infinitive with *to*, meaning "to be under the necessity of, be obliged, or have to": *He need not come. He needs to study.* See Usage note below. —*tr.* To have need of; require; want urgently. —*intr.* **1.** To be in need or want. **2.** *Rare.* To be necessary. —See Synonyms at **lack**. [Middle English *nede*, Old English *nēd, nēod*, necessity, distress. See **nāu-**[1] in Appendix.*]

Synonyms: *need, necessity, exigency, requisite. Need,* as a noun, is the most general of the words compared here and the least strong in signifying urgency. *Necessity* greatly intensifies urgency to the point of denying that the particular need can be ignored. *Exigency* (usually plural in this sense) stresses great urgency brought about by particular conditions or circumstances, often those of an emergency. *Requisite* specifies need closely associated with attainment of a given goal; like *exigency*, but unlike the other terms, it connotes need imposed by external requirements rather than by inner compulsion.

Usage: *Need,* when used as an auxiliary, is often followed by an infinitive with *to: I need to rest. He needs to study.* In negative statements and in questions employing *need* as an auxiliary, the infinitive construction that follows may or may not employ *to: You need not go. Need we go?* But: *You do not need to go. Do we need to go?* In such constructions, *to* is always used when the infinitive follows the inflected forms *needs* and *needed.* In negative statements and in questions, *need* as an auxiliary is not inflected in the third person singular, present tense (as it is in positive statements): *He need not come. Need it have happened?*

need·ful (nēd′fəl) *adj.* **1.** Necessary; required. **2.** *Rare.* In want; needy. —See Synonyms at **necessary**. —*n.* Whatever is needed, especially money. —**need′ful·ly** *adv.* —**need′ful·ness** *n.*

need·i·ness (nē′dē-nĭs) *n.* The state of being in need; poverty.

nee·dle (nēd′l) *n.* **1.** A small, slender sewing implement, now usually of polished steel, pointed at one end, and having an eye at the other through which a length of thread is passed and held. **2.** Any of various implements similar in appearance and use: **a.** A short, sharp instrument with an eye near the pointed end, used in sewing machines. **b.** A slender, pointed rod used in knitting. **c.** A similar implement, usually shorter, and with a hook at one end, used in crocheting. **3.** A small, pointed stylus used to transmit vibrations from the grooves of a phonograph record. **4. a.** Any slender pointer or indicator on a dial, scale, or similar part of a mechanical device. **b.** A **magnetic needle** *(see)*. **5.** A **hypodermic needle** *(see)*. **6.** A stiff, narrow leaf, such as those of conifers. **7.** Any fine, sharp projection, such as a spine of a sea urchin or a crystal. **8.** A sharp, pointed instrument used in engraving. —**give (someone) the needle**. *Informal.* To goad or provoke so as to rouse to action; prod. —*v.* **needled, -dling, -dles**. —*tr.* **1.** To prick, pierce, or stitch with or as if with a needle. **2.** *Informal.* To goad, provoke, or tease. **3.** *Slang.* To increase the alcoholic content of (a beverage, such as beer). —*intr.* **1.** To sew or do similar work with a needle. **2.** To crystallize into fine, pointed spicules. [Middle English *nedle*, Old English *nǣdl*. See **snē-**[1] in Appendix.*]

nee·dle·fish (nēd′l-fĭsh′) *n., pl.* **-fish** or **-fishes**. **1.** Any of several marine fishes of the family Belonidae, having slender bodies and narrow jaws. **2.** Any of various fishes with projecting jaws, such as the **pipefish** *(see)*.

nee·dle·point (nēd′l-point′) *n.* **1.** Decorative needlework on canvas, usually in a diagonal stitch covering the entire surface of the material. See **gros point**, **petit point**. **2.** A type of lace worked on paper patterns with a needle, as distinguished from bobbin lace. Also called "point lace." —**nee′dle·point′** *adj.*

need·less (nēd′lĭs) *adj.* Not needed or wished for; unnecessary. —**need′less·ly** *adv.* —**need′less·ness** *n.*

needle valve. A valve having a slender point fitting into a conical seat, for accurately regulating the flow of a liquid or gas.

nee·dle·wom·an (nēd′l-wo͝om′ən) *n., pl.* **-women** (-wĭm′ĭn). A woman who does needlework, especially a seamstress.

nee·dle·work (nēd′l-wûrk′) *n.* Work done with a needle, such as sewing or embroidery. —**nee′dle·work′er** *n.*

need·n't (nēd′ənt). Contraction of *need not.*

needs (nēdz) *adv.* Of necessity; necessarily. Used following *must* and preceding a simple infinitive: *He must needs go;* or preceding *must*, with an infinitive understood: *"She shall go, if needs must."* (Robert Browning). [Middle English *nedes*, Old English *nēdes*, "of need," genitive of *nēd*, NEED.]

need·y (nē′dē) *adj.* **-ier, -iest**. Being in need; impoverished. See Synonyms at **necessary**.

ne'er (nâr). *Poetic.* Contraction of **never**.

ne'er-do-well (nâr′do͞o-wĕl′) *n.* An irresponsible person who never succeeds in any enterprise. —**ne'er′-do-well′** *adj.*

ne·far·i·ous (nĭ-fâr′ē-əs) *adj.* Evil; infamous: *a nefarious plot.* [Latin *nefārius*, from *nefās*, sin : *ne-*, not (see **ne** in Appendix*) + *fās*, divine law, right (see **dhē-**[1] in Appendix*).] —**ne·far′i·ous·ly** *adv.* —**ne·far′i·ous·ness** *n.*

Nef·er·ti·ti (nĕf′ər-tē′tē). Also **Nef·er·ti·it** (nĕf′ər-tē′ĭt), **Nof·re·te·te** (nŏf′rə-tē′tē). Queen of Egypt in the early 14th century B.C.; wife of Akhenaton.

neg. negative.

ne·gate (nĭ-gāt′) *tr.v.* **-gated, -gating, -gates**. **1.** To render ineffective or invalid; nullify: *"There could be no negation if there were no preceding affirmation to be negated."* (Paul Tillich). **2.** To rule out; deny. —See Synonyms at **nullify**, **neutralize**. [Latin *negāre*, to deny. See **ne** in Appendix.*]

ne·ga·tion (nĭ-gā′shən) *n.* **1.** The act or process of negating. **2.** A denial, contradiction, or negative statement. **3.** The opposite or absence of something regarded as actual, positive, or

ă pat/ā pay/âr care/ä father/b bib/ch church/d deed/ĕ pet/ē be/f fife/g gag/h hat/hw which/ĭ pit/ī pie/îr pier/j judge/k kick/l lid, needle/m mum/n no, sudden/ng thing/ŏ pot/ō toe/ô paw, for/oi noise/ou out/o͝o took/o͞o boot/p pop/r roar/s sauce/sh ship, dish/

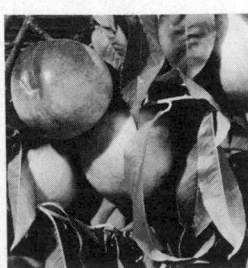

affirmative: *"Death is nothing more than the negation of life."* (Fielding). **4.** A condition characterized by the absence of that which is positive or affirmative: *"but a change from order and truth to disorder and negation"* (Stanley Parry).

neg·a·tive (nĕg′ə-tĭv) *adj. Abbr.* **neg. 1.** Expressing, containing, or consisting of a negation, refusal, or denial: *a negative answer.* **2.** Lacking the quality of being positive or affirmative: *negative ideas.* **3.** Indicating opposition or resistance: *a negative response to an advertising campaign.* **4.** Tending to oppose or disagree with that which is considered positive or constructive. **5.** *Medicine.* Not indicative of the presence of microorganisms, disease, or a specific condition. **6.** *Logic.* Denying agreement between the subject and its predicate. Said of a proposition. **7.** *Mathematics.* Pertaining to or denoting: **a.** A quantity less than zero. **b.** The sign (−). **c.** A quantity to be subtracted from another. **d.** A quantity, number, angle, velocity, or direction, in a sense opposite to another of the same magnitude indicated or understood to be positive. **8.** *Physics.* Pertaining to or denoting: **a.** Electric charge of the same sign as that of an electron, designated by the symbol (−). **b.** Any body having an excess of electrons. **9.** *Chemistry.* Pertaining to or denoting an ion, the anion, that is attracted to a positive electrode. **10.** *Biology.* Indicating resistance to, opposition to, or motion away from a stimulus: *a negative tropism.* Compare **positive.** —*n.* **1.** A statement or act indicating or expressing a contradiction, denial, or refusal. **2.** A thing or concept considered to be the counterpart of something positive. **3.** *Grammar.* A word or part of a word, such as *no, not,* or *non-,* that indicates negation. **4.** The side contradicting or opposing the opinion upheld by the affirmative side in a debate or argument. **5. a.** An image in which the light areas of the object rendered appear dark and the dark areas appear light. **b.** A film, plate, or other photographic material containing such an image. **6.** *Mathematics.* A negative quantity. **7.** *Rare.* The right to veto something. —**in the negative. 1.** In a sense or manner indicating a refusal or denial: *answer in the negative.* **2.** On the side opposed to the affirmative: *argue in the negative.* —*adv.* No. Used in the armed forces and in telecommunications. —*tr.v.* **negatived, -tiving, -tives. 1.** To refuse to approve; veto. **2.** To deny; contradict. **3.** To demonstrate to be false. **4.** To counteract or neutralize. [Late Latin *negātīvus,* from Latin *negāre,* to NEGATE.] —**neg′a·tive·ly** *adv.* —**neg′a·tive·ness, neg′a·tiv′i·ty** *n.*

Usage: The form of double negative now considered clearly nonstandard is that which employs two negatives in a single statement, usually a brief construction: *He didn't say nothing. We aren't going, neither.* In modern usage this is considered as illiteracy or dialect, and as such is to be avoided. Formerly such constructions were common even in written English as a form of intensified negation, and they still survive in literary works. An example is Hamlet's advice to the players: *"Be not too tame neither, but let your own discretion be your tutor."* Two other constructions employing more than one negative are generally accepted at present, however. One of these employs *not* before an adjective having a negative sense: *a not infrequent visitor; a not uncommon experience.* These form conditional, or weak, positives, whose meanings express a shade of distinction not contained in the forthrightly positive *frequent* and *common.* The other construction employs a second, reinforcing negative as a reminder of the prevailing negative sense. This type is often found in long sentences in which emphasis of the negative is sought: *He would not surrender, not even in the face of impossible odds.* This is approved by 71 per cent of the Usage Panel.

negative feedback. Feedback that reduces the output of a system, for example, the action of heat on a thermostat to limit the output of a furnace. See **feedback.**

neg·a·tiv·ism (nĕg′ə-tĭv-ĭz′əm) *n.* **1.** An attitude or system of thought, such as skepticism, formed by questioning or denying traditional beliefs. **2.** Behavior characterized by stubborn and unfounded resistance to suggestions, orders, or instructions of others. —**neg′a·tiv·ist** *n.* & *adj.* —**neg′a·tiv·is′tic** *adj.*

neg·a·tron (nĕg′ə-trŏn′) *n.* An obsolete name for the electron. [NEGA(TIVE) + (ELEC)TRON.]

Neg·ev (nĕg′ĕv′). Also **Neg·eb** (nĕg′ĕb′). A triangular desert region, about 4,700 square miles in area, in southern Israel.

ne·glect (nĭ-glĕkt′) *tr.v.* **-glected, -glecting, -glects. 1.** To ignore or pay no attention to; disregard: *They neglected his warning.* **2.** To fail to care for or give proper attention to: *She neglected her appearance.* **3.** To fail to do or carry out through carelessness or oversight: *He neglected to make his point.* —*n.* **1. a.** The act of neglecting something. **b.** An instance of this. **2.** The state of being neglected. **3.** Habitual lack of care. [Latin *negligere, neglegere* (past participial stem *neglect-*), "not to choose," "not to heed" : *neg-,* not (see **ne** in Appendix*) + *legere,* to choose (see **leg-** in Appendix*).] —**ne·glect′er, ne·glec′tor** *n.*

ne·glect·ful (nĭ-glĕkt′fəl) *adj.* Characterized by neglect; careless; heedless. Often followed by *of: neglectful of responsibilities.* —**ne·glect′ful·ly** *adv.* —**ne·glect′ful·ness** *n.*

neg·li·gee (nĕg′lĭ-zhā′) *n.* Also **neg·li·gée, neg·li·gé. 1.** A woman's loose dressing gown, often of soft, delicate fabric. **2.** Any informal or incomplete attire. [French, "casual," "neglected," from *négliger,* to neglect, from Latin *negligere,* NEGLECT.]

neg·li·gence (nĕg′lĭ-jəns) *n.* **1.** The state or quality of being negligent. **2.** Any negligent act or failure to act. **3.** *Law.* The omission or neglect of any reasonable precaution, care, or action.

neg·li·gent (nĕg′lĭ-jənt) *adj.* **1.** Habitually guilty of neglect; lacking in due care or concern. **2.** Extremely careless. [Middle English, from Old French, from Latin *negligens,* present participle of *negligere,* to NEGLECT.] —**neg′li·gent·ly** *adv.*

neg·li·gi·ble (nĕg′lĭ-jə-bəl) *adj.* Not worth considering; trifling: *a negligible amount.* [From Latin *negligere,* to NEGLECT.] —**neg′li·gi·bil′i·ty, neg′li·gi·ble·ness** *n.* —**neg′li·gi·bly** *adv.*

ne·go·tia·ble (nĭ-gō′shə-bəl, -shē-ə-bəl) *adj.* **1.** Capable of being negotiated. **2.** Capable of being legally transferred from one person to another, either by delivery or by delivery and endorsement: *a negotiable document.* —**ne·go′tia·bil′i·ty** *n.*

ne·go·ti·ant (nĭ-gō′shē-ənt, -shənt) *n.* One who negotiates.

ne·go·ti·ate (nĭ-gō′shē-āt′) *v.* **-ated, -ating, -ates.** —*intr.* To treat with another or others in order to come to terms or reach an agreement: *"It is difficult to negotiate where neither will trust."* (Samuel Johnson). —*tr.* **1.** To arrange or settle by conferring or discussing: *negotiate a union contract.* **2.** *Finance.* **a.** To transfer title to or ownership of (notes, funds, documents, or similar property) to another person or party in return for value received. **b.** To sell or discount. **3.** To succeed in passing over, accomplishing, or coping with: *negotiate a sharp curve.* [Latin *negōtiārī,* to transact business, from *negōtium,* business, "lack of leisure" : *neg-,* not (see **ne** in Appendix*) + *ōtium*†, leisure (see **otiose**).] —**ne·go′ti·a′tor** *n.*

Usage: In the sense of "to succeed in passing over," "accomplishing," or "coping with," only 46 per cent of the Usage Panel approve of *negotiate* in written usage.

ne·go·ti·a·tion (nĭ-gō′shē-ā′shən) *n.* The act or procedure of negotiating.

Ne·gress (nē′grĭs) *n.* A female Negro. Now often considered offensive.

Ne·gril·lo (nĭ-grĭl′ō, -grē′yō) *n., pl.* **-los** or **-loes.** One of a group of Negroid peoples of Africa, including the Bushmen and the Pygmies, who are short in stature. Also called "Negrito." [Spanish, diminutive of *negro,* NEGRO.]

Ne·gri Sem·bi·lan (nə-grē′ səm-bē′lən). A state of Malaysia, 2,580 square miles in area, situated in the southwestern part of the Malay Peninsula. Population, 466,000. Capital, Seremban.

Ne·grit·ic (nĭ-grĭt′ĭk) *adj.* Of, pertaining to, or characteristic of Negroes or Negritos.

Ne·gri·to (nĭ-grē′tō) *n., pl.* **-tos** or **-toes. 1.** A **Negrillo** *(see).* **2.** One of various groups of Negroid people of short stature inhabiting parts of Malaysia, the Philippines, and southeastern Asia. [Spanish, diminutive of *negro,* NEGRO.]

ne·gri·tude (nē′grə-to͞od′, -tyo͞od′) *n.* An aesthetic and ideological concept affirming the independent validity of Negro culture. [French *négritude* (coined by Léopold Senghor), from *nègre,* Negro, from Spanish *negro,* NEGRO.]

Ne·gro (nē′grō) *n., pl.* **-groes. 1.** A member of the Negroid ethnic division of the human species, especially one of various peoples of central and southern Africa. **2.** A descendant of these or other Negroid peoples. See **Negroid.** —*adj.* **1.** Of, pertaining to, denoting, or characteristic of a Negro or Negroes. **2. Negroid** *(see).* [Spanish and Portuguese *negro,* a Negro, "black," from Latin *niger,* black. See **niger** in Appendix.*]

Ne·groid (nē′groid′) *adj.* **1.** *Anthropology.* Of, pertaining to, or designating a major ethnic division of the human species whose members are characterized by brown to black pigmentation, and often by tightly curled hair, broad nose, and thick lips. This division includes the Negro and other peoples, such as the **Negrito, Andamanese,** and **Melanesian** *(all of which see).* **2.** Of or characteristic of Negroes. —*n.* A member of the Negroid ethnic division of the human species. [NEGR(O)- + -OID.]

ne·gro·phile (nē′grə-fīl′) *n.* *Often capital* **N.** One friendly to Negroes and their interests.

ne·gro·pho·bi·a (nē′grə-fō′bē-ə) *n.* *Often capital* **N.** Intense aversion to or fear of Negroes. —**ne′gro·phobe′** *n.*

Ne·gros (nā′grōs). An island (4,905 square miles) of the Republic of the Philippines. It is one of the Visayan group lying south of Panay, in the Sulu Sea. Population, 1,850,000.

ne·gus (nē′gəs) *n.* A beverage made of wine, hot water, lemon juice, sugar, and nutmeg. [Invented by Colonel Francis *Negus* (died 1732), English soldier.]

Ne·gus (nē′gəs) *n.* The title of the emperor of Ethiopia. [Amharic *negūs,* from Ethiopian *nĕgūsā,* "king of kings."]

Neh. Nehemiah.

Ne·he·mi·ah[1] (nē′hə-mī′ə). A Jewish leader and governor of Judea during the Babylonian Captivity (fifth century B.C.).

Ne·he·mi·ah[2] (nē′hə-mī′ə) *n. Abbr.* **Neh.** A book of the Old Testament describing the moral, political, and religious reforms of Nehemiah, and the rebuilding of Jerusalem under his leadership. Also called "Esdras."

Neh·ru (nā′ro͞o), **Jawaharlal.** 1889–1964. Indian nationalist leader; first prime minister (1947–64).

neigh (nā) *v.* **neighed, neighing, neighs.** —*intr.* **1.** To utter the cry of a horse. **2.** To utter a sound similar to a horse's cry. —*tr.* To utter with a sound like the neigh of a horse. —*n.* The cry of a horse. [Middle English *neien,* Old English *hnǣgan,* from an imitative Germanic root, *hnajj-, gnajj-, knajj-,* also the source of NAG (horse).]

neigh·bor (nā′bər) *n.* Also *chiefly British* **neigh·bour. 1.** One who lives near or next to another. **2.** A person or thing adjacent to or located near another. **3.** A human being like oneself; a fellow man. —*adj.* Living or situated near another. —*v.* **neighbored, -boring, -bors.** Also *chiefly British* **neigh·bour.** —*tr.* To lie close to; border upon; adjoin. —*intr.* To live or be situated close by. [Middle English *neigh(e)bor,* Old English *nēahgebūr* : *nēah,* near (see **nēwh-iz** in Appendix*) + *gebūr,* dweller (see **bheu-** in Appendix*).]

neigh·bor·hood (nā′bər-ho͝od′) *n.* **1.** A district considered in regard to its inhabitants or distinctive characteristics: *a fashionable neighborhood.* **2.** The people who live in a particular vicinity: *The noise disturbed the entire neighborhood.* **3.** *Informal.*

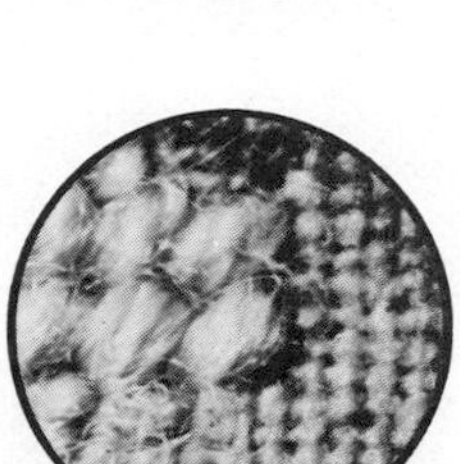

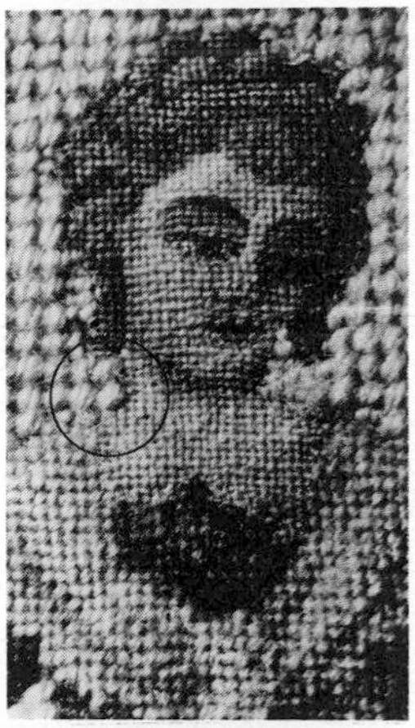

needlepoint
Circled area shown in detail on top

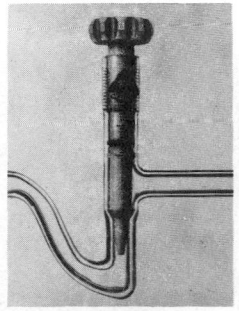

needle valve

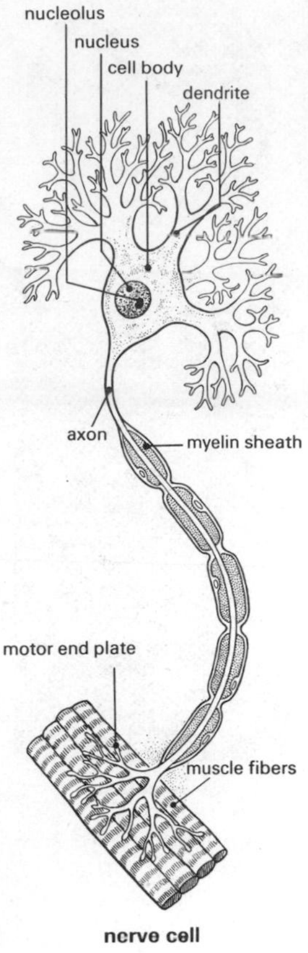
nucleolus
nucleus
cell body
dendrite
axon
myelin sheath
motor end plate
muscle fibers

nerve cell

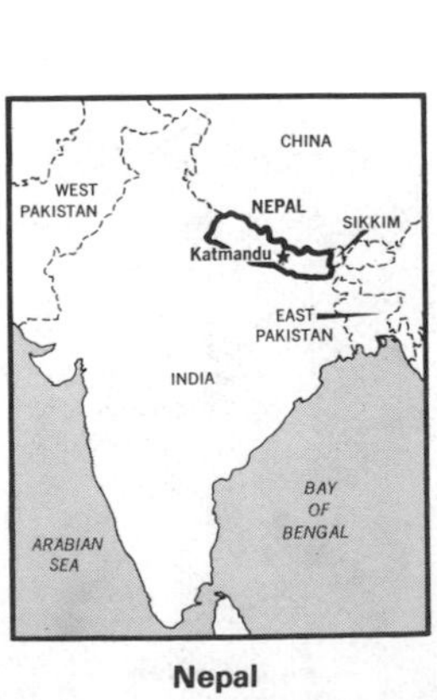
CHINA
WEST PAKISTAN
NEPAL
SIKKIM
Katmandu
EAST PAKISTAN
INDIA
BAY OF BENGAL
ARABIAN SEA

Nepal

Approximate amount or range: *in the neighborhood of ten million dollars.*

neighborhood of a point. *Mathematics.* The set of points surrounding a specified point, each of which is at a distance from the specified point less than an arbitrary bound.

neigh·bor·ing (nā′bər-ĭng) *adj.* Living or situated close by.

neigh·bor·ly (nā′bər-lē) *adj.* Appropriate to, characteristic of, or showing the feelings of a friendly neighbor. —**neigh′bor·li·ness** *n.*

Neil, Neal (nēl). A masculine given name. [Middle English *Neel, Nele,* from Old English *Nel* and Norman French *Nele,* both from Old Norse *Njal,* from Old Irish *Níall,* (genitive *Néill).* See **nei-**[1] in Appendix.*]

Neil·son (nēl′sən), **William Allan.** 1869–1946. Scottish-born American educator, author, and lexicographer.

Neis·se (nī′sə). *Polish* **Ny·sa** (nĭs′ə). A river rising in northern Czechoslovakia and flowing 140 miles north into the Oder, forming the boundary between Poland and East Germany.

nei·ther (nē′*th*ər, nī′-) *adj.* Not either; not one or the other: *Neither shoe fits comfortably.* —*pron.* Not either one; not the one nor the other: *Neither of them fits.* —*conj.* **1.** Not either; not in either case. Used with the correlative conjunction *nor: Neither we nor they want it.* **2.** Nor yet; nor: *"They toil not, neither do they spin."* (Matthew 6:28). —*adv. Nonstandard.* In any case; either. Forms a double negative when used for *either* following a negative statement. See Usage note at **negative.** [Middle English *neither, nauther,* Old English *nāhwæther, nōhwæther* : *nā,* no, not (see **na**) + *hwæther,* which of two (see **kwo-** in Appendix*).]

Usage: *Neither* as an adjective or pronoun is limited to two. When more than two are involved, *none* is proper: *Painting, drawing, and sculpture are his major interests, but he is expert in none* (not *neither*) *of them.* In correct usage, *neither* takes a singular verb: *Neither book was available. Neither of the houses is finished.* Accompanying possessive pronouns or pronominal adjectives that appear in such constructions must agree in number with the verb: *Neither man is likely to reveal his* (not *their*) *identity.* As a conjunction, *neither* is always followed by *nor* (not *or*) in constructions signifying negation with regard to two or more elements: *Neither prayer nor curses brought relief.* However, when the element introduced by *nor* contains two or more closely related components that, taken together, may be construed as one, *or* is properly used to join them: *Neither a professional counselor nor the boy's mother or father was able to help.* When all the elements within a *neither . . . nor* construction are singular, the verb is always singular: *Neither he nor she was told.* When the elements are all plural, the verb is plural: *Neither diagrams nor written instructions were provided.* When the elements differ in point of number, the verb agrees in number with the elements to which it is nearer: *Neither my father nor my uncles were included. Neither one's parents nor a total stranger is likely to be in sympathy with such tactics.* When the nearer element is a personal pronoun, the verb agrees with it: *Neither Tom nor I know. Neither I nor he knows.* When possessive pronouns or pronominal adjectives appear in such constructions, they must agree in number with the verb: *Neither Harriet nor Janet has her* (not *their*) *work in order.* When the *neither . . . nor* construction comes after a verb to which both elements of the construction apply, *neither* is properly placed immediately after the verb: *It specified neither time nor place* (not *It neither specified time nor place*). See Usage note at **nor.**

Nejd (nĕjd). Also **Najd** (năjd). A province of Saudi Arabia, about 450,000 square miles in area. Population, 1,500,000. Capital, Riyadh.

nek·ton (nĕk′tən, -tŏn′) *n.* The total population of marine animal organisms that swim independently of currents, ranging in size from microscopic organisms to whales. [German, from Greek *nēkton,* "swimming thing," neuter of *nēktos,* swimming, from *nēkhein,* to swim. See **snā-** in Appendix.*] —**nek·ton′ic** (nĕk-tŏn′ĭk) *adj.*

nel·son (nĕl′sən) *n. Wrestling.* One of a variety of holds in which the user places an arm under the opponent's arm and applies pressure with the palm of the hand against the opponent's neck. See also **full nelson, half nelson.** [Origin unknown.]

Nel·son (nĕl′sən), **Horatio.** Viscount Nelson. 1758–1805. British admiral; hero of the Battle of Trafalgar, in which he died.

Nel·son River (nĕl′sən). A river rising in northern Manitoba, Canada, and flowing north and east 400 miles to Hudson Bay.

ne·lum·bo (nə-lŭm′bō) *n., pl.* **-bos.** An aquatic plant of the genus *Nelumbo,* having large, variously colored flowers. See **lotus, water chinquapin.** [New Latin, from Singhalese *nelumbu,* lotus, probably of Dravidian origin.]

Ne·man (nĕm′ən). *German* **Me·mel** (mā′məl); *Polish* **Nie·men** (nyĕ′mĕn′); *Lithuanian* **Ne·mu·nas** (nyĕ′mo͝o-näs′). A river rising in central Byelorussia and flowing 597 miles west and northwest to the Baltic Sea.

nemato–. Indicates threadlike form; for example, **nematocyst.** [New Latin, from Greek *nēma* (stem *nēmat-*), thread. See **snē-**[1] in Appendix.*]

nem·a·to·cyst (nĕm′ə-tō-sĭst′, nĭ-măt′ə-) *n. Zoology.* A stinging organ in various coelenterates, such as jellyfish, which when stimulated ejects a coiled tube that chemically paralyzes its victim. [NEMATO- + CYST.] —**nem′a·to·cys′tic** *adj.*

nem·a·tode (nĕm′ə-tōd′) *n.* Any worm of the phylum Nematoda, having unsegmented, threadlike bodies, many of which, as the hookworm, are parasitic. Also called "roundworm." [New Latin *Nematoda,* "the threadlike ones" : NEMAT(O)- + -ODE (like).]

Nem·bu·tal (nĕm′byə-tôl′) *n.* A trademark for the drug **pentobarbital sodium** *(see).* [N(A) (sodium) + E(THYL) + M(ETHYL) + BU(TYL) + (BARBI)TAL.]

ne·mer·te·an (nĭ-mûr′tē-ən) *adj.* Also **ne·mer·ti·an, nem·er·tine** (nĕm′ər-tīn′), **nem·er·tin·e·an** (nĕm′ər-tĭn′ē-ən). Of, pertaining to, or belonging to the phylum Nemertea, consisting chiefly of marine worms having soft, cylindrical or flattened bodies, usually brightly colored. —*n.* A worm of this phylum. Also called "ribbon worm." [New Latin *Nemertea,* "the Nemertes group," from *Nemertēs,* name of one of the genuses in the group, from Greek *Nēmertēs,* name of a Nereid.]

nem·e·sis (nĕm′ə-sĭs) *n., pl.* **-ses** (-sēz′). **1.** An inflicter of retribution; avenger. **2.** One that inflicts relentless vengeance or destruction. **3.** An unbeatable rival, as in sports: *The team met its nemesis.* **4.** Retributive justice in its execution or outcome: *invite nemesis.* **5.** An unavoidable result. [From NEMESIS.]

Nem·e·sis (nĕm′ə-sĭs). *Greek Mythology.* The goddess of retributive justice or vengeance. [Greek, "retribution," from *nemein,* to allot. See **nem**[2] in Appendix.*]

Ne·mu·nas. The Lithuanian name for the **Neman** River.

ne·ne (nā′nā) *n.* A goose, *Branta sandvicensis,* of the Hawaiian Islands, now very rare. It is the state bird of Hawaii. [Hawaiian *nēnē.*]

neo–, Neo–. Indicates: **1.** A new or recent form, development, or type; for example, **neologism, neomycin. 2.** A recent formation, modification, or abnormal change; for example, **neoplasm. 3.** The most recent subdivision of a series of periods; for example, **Neocene.** ***Note:*** Many compounds other than those entered here may be formed with *neo-.* In forming compounds, *neo-* is normally joined to the following word without space or hyphen: *neocolonialism.* However, if the second element begins with a capital letter, it is separated with a hyphen and the *N* of *Neo-* is also capitalized: *Neo-Platonism.* (The *N* may be capitalized in other words too: *Neolithic.*) If the second element begins with *o,* it is separated by a hyphen: *neo-orthodoxy.* [Greek, from *neos,* new. See **newo-** in Appendix.*]

ne·o·ars·phen·a·mine (nē′ō-ärs-fĕn′ə-mēn′) *n. Medicine.* A yellow powder, $C_{13}H_{13}As_2N_2NaO_4S$, containing arsenic, used chiefly in the treatment of syphilis and yaws.

Ne·o·cene (nē′ə-sēn′) *n.* A division of the Tertiary period comprising the Miocene and Pliocene. Not in current technical use. [NEO- + -CENE.] —**Ne′o·cene′** *adj.*

ne·o·clas·si·cism (nē′ō-klăs′ə-sĭz′əm) *n.* **1.** A revival of classical aesthetics and forms in art, music, and literature. **2.** *Often capital* **N.** Such a revival during the 17th and 18th centuries in Europe. —**ne′o·clas′sic, ne′o·clas′si·cal** *adj.*

ne·o·col·on·i·al·ism (nē′ō-kə-lō′nē-əl-ĭz′əm) *n.* Control of former colonies by colonial powers, especially by economic means: *"By neocolonialism we mean the practice of granting a sort of independence with the concealed intention of making the liberated country a client-state."* (Alex Quaison-Sackey). —**ne′o·col·on′i·al·ist** *adj.*

Ne·o-Dar·win·ism (nē′ō-där′wĭn-ĭz′əm) *n.* The theory that the evolutionary development of plants and animals is principally determined by **natural selection** *(see),* and that acquired characteristics cannot be inherited. Compare **Neo-Lamarckism.** —**Ne′o-Dar·win′i·an** (-där-wĭn′ē-ən) *adj.* & *n.*

ne·o·dym·i·um (nē′ō-dĭm′ē-əm) *n. Symbol* **Nd** A bright, silvery, rare-earth metal element, found in the minerals monazite and bastnaesite, and used for coloring glass and for doping some glass lasers. Atomic number 60, atomic weight 144.24, melting point 1,024°C, boiling point 3,027°C, specific gravity 6.80 or 7.004 (depending on allotropic form), valence 3. See **element.** [New Latin : NEO- + (DI)DYMIUM.]

Ne·o·gae·a (nē′ə-jē′ə) *n.* Also **Ne·o·ge·a.** A region that is coextensive with the Neotropical region and is considered one of the primary zoogeographic realms. See **Neotropical.** [New Latin : NEO- + Greek *gaia,* earth (see **gē** in Appendix*).] —**Ne′o·gae′an** *adj.*

ne·o·gen·e·sis (nē′ō-jĕn′ə-sĭs) *n. Medicine.* The regeneration of tissue.

ne·o·im·pres·sion·ism (nē′ō-ĭm-prĕsh′ən-ĭz′əm) *n.* Also **ne·o-im·pres·sion·ism, Ne·o-Im·pres·sion·ism.** A movement in 19th-century painting led by Georges Seurat. Its works are strict and formal in composition and meticulous in their execution, which is characterized by the juxtaposition of dots of primary colors to achieve brighter secondary colors, the mixture of pure tones being left for the eye itself to complete. Compare **pointillism.** —**ne′o·im·pres′sion·ist** *n.* & *adj.*

Ne·o-La·marck·ism (nē′ō-lə-mär′kĭz′əm) *n.* The theory that acquired characteristics can be inherited, but that natural selection is also a valid evolutionary principle. Compare **Neo-Darwinism.** —**Ne′o-La·marck′i·an** *adj.* & *n.*

Ne·o·lith·ic (nē′ə-lĭth′ĭk) *adj. Archaeology.* Of or denoting the cultural period beginning around 10,000 B.C. in the Middle East and later elsewhere, and characterized by the invention of farming and the making of technically advanced stone implements. —*n. Archaeology.* The Neolithic Age. Preceded by *the.* [NEO- + -LITHIC.]

ne·ol·o·gism (nē-ŏl′ə-jĭz′əm) *n.* **1. a.** A newly coined word, phrase, or expression, or a new meaning for an old word. **b.** The use of new words, phrases, or expressions or of new meanings for old words. **c.** A meaningless word or phrase coined or used by a psychotic. **2.** A new doctrine, especially in theology. [French *néologisme* : NEO- + LOG(O)- + -ISM.] —**ne·ol′o·gist** *n.* —**ne·ol′o·gis′tic, ne·ol′o·gis′ti·cal** *adj.*

ne·ol·o·gy (nē-ŏl′ə-jē) *n., pl.* **-gies.** Neologism or an instance of it. [French *néologie* : NEO- + -LOGY.] —**ne′o·log′i·cal** (nē′ə-lŏj′ĭ-kəl) *adj.* —**ne′o·log′i·cal·ly** *adv.*

ne·o·morph (nē′ə-môrf′) *n.* A biological structure that has not evolved from a similar structure in an ancestor. [NEO- + -MORPH.] —**ne′o·morph′ic** *adj.*

ne·o·my·cin (nē′ō-mī′sĭn) *n.* An antibiotic drug consisting of a group of organic complexes produced by the metabolism of bacteria. [NEO- + -MYCIN.]

ne·on (nē′ŏn′) *n. Symbol* **Ne** A rare, inert, gaseous element occurring in the atmosphere to the extent of 18 parts per million, and obtained by fractional distillation of liquid air. It is colorless but glows reddish-orange in an electric discharge and is used in display and television tubes. Atomic number 10, atomic weight 20.183, melting point −248.67°C, boiling point −245.95°C, valence 0. See **element**. ["The new (gas)," from Greek, neuter of *neos*, new. See **newo-** in Appendix.*]

ne·o·nate (nē′ə-nāt′) *n.* A newborn child. [New Latin *neonātus* : NEO- + Latin *nātus*, born, from *nascī*, to be born (see **genə-** in Appendix*).] —**ne′o·na′tal** (nē′ō-nāt′l) *adj.*

neon tetra. A small, tropical American freshwater fish, *Hyphessobrycon innesi*, having blue and red markings. [NEON (from the luminous blue band on its body) + TETRA.]

ne·o·or·tho·dox·y (nē′ō-ôr′thə-dŏk′sē) *n.* A Protestant movement of the 20th century that aims to revive adherence to certain older theological doctrines. —**ne′o-or′tho·dox′** *adj.*

ne·o·phyte (nē′ə-fīt′) *n.* **1.** A recent convert. **2. a.** A newly ordained Roman Catholic priest. **b.** A novice of a religious order. **3.** A beginner; novice; tyro. [Late Latin *neophytus*, from New Testament Greek *neophutos*, "newly planted" : NEO- + *phutos*, "grown," from *phuein*, to bring forth, produce (see **bheu-** in Appendix*).]

ne·o·plasm (nē′ə-plăz′əm) *n.* An abnormal new growth of tissue in animals or plants; tumor. [NEO- + -PLASM.]

Ne·o·Pla·to·nism (nē′ō-plāt′n-ĭz′əm) *n.* Also **Ne·o·pla·to·nism.** **1.** A philosophical and religious system developed at Alexandria in the third century A.D., based on the doctrines of Plato and other Greek philosophers, and combined with elements of Oriental mysticism and some Judaic and Christian concepts. **2.** A revival of this system, as in the Middle Ages and Renaissance. —**Ne′o-Pla·ton′ic** (-plə-tŏn′ĭk) *adj.* —**Ne′o-Pla′to·nist** *n.*

ne·o·prene (nē′ə-prēn′) *n.* A synthetic rubber produced by polymerization of chloroprene and used in weather-resistant products, adhesives, shoe soles, paints, and rocket fuels. [NEO- + PR(OPYL) + -ENE.]

Ne·o·Scho·las·ti·cism (nē′ō-skə-lăs′tə-sĭz′əm) *n.* A movement to revive the Scholasticism of Aquinas by infusing it with modern concepts. —**Ne′o-Scho·las′tic** *adj.*

ne·o·ter·ic (nē′ə-tĕr′ĭk) *adj.* Of recent origin; new; modern. —*n.* A modern, especially an author. [Late Latin *neōtericus*, from Greek *neōterikos*, "youthful," modern, from *neōteros*, younger, comparative of *neos*, new. See **newo-** in Appendix.*]

Ne·o·trop·i·cal (nē′ō-trŏp′ĭ-kəl) *n.* Of or designating the zoogeographic region stretching southward from the tropic of Cancer and including southern Mexico, Central and South America, and the West Indies.

Ne·o·zo·ic (nē′ə-zō′ĭk) *adj.* Of, pertaining to, or designating the geological period from the end of the Mesozoic era to the present. [NEO- + -ZOIC.]

N.E.P. New Economic Policy.

Ne·pal (nə-pôl′, -päl′). *Abbr.* **Nep.** A kingdom, 54,000 square miles in area, in the Himalayas between India and Tibet. Population, 9,500,000. Capital, Katmandu.

Nep·al·ese (nĕp′əl-ēz′) *n., pl.* **Nepalese. 1.** A native or resident of Nepal. **2.** The central Indic language of Nepal. —*adj.* Of, pertaining to, or designating Nepal, its inhabitants, its language, or its culture.

ne·pen·the (nĭ-pĕn′thē) *n.* **1.** A drug, perhaps opium, mentioned in the *Odyssey* as a remedy for grief. **2.** Anything that induces oblivion of sorrow or eases pain. [Greek *nēpenthes (pharmakon)*, "grief-banishing (drug)" : *nē-*, not (see **ne** in Appendix*) + *penthos*, grief (see **kwenth-** in Appendix*).] —**ne·pen′the·an** (nĭ-pĕn′thē-ən) *adj.*

neph·e·line (nĕf′ə-lēn′, -lĭn) *n.* A mineral of sodium- or potassium-aluminum silicate, occurring worldwide in igneous rocks, and used in the manufacture of ceramics and enamels. Also called "nephelite." [French *néphéline*, from Greek *nephelē*, cloud (because it becomes cloudy when placed in nitric acid). See **nebh-** in Appendix.*]

neph·e·lin·ite (nĕf′ə-lĭn-īt′) *n.* An igneous rock consisting chiefly of pyroxene and nepheline.

neph·e·lom·e·ter (nĕf′ə-lŏm′ə-tər) *n.* Any apparatus used to measure the size and concentration of particles in a liquid by analysis of light transmitted through or reflected by the liquid. [Greek *nephelē*, cloud (see **nebh-** in Appendix*) + -METER.] —**neph′e·lo·met′ric** (-lō-mĕt′rĭk) *adj.* —**neph′e·lom′e·try** *n.*

neph·ew (nĕf′yōō; *chiefly British* nĕv′yōō) *n.* **1.** The son of one's brother or sister, or of one's brother-in-law or sister-in-law. **2.** A son of a celibate ecclesiastic. [Middle English *neveu*, nephew, grandson, from Old French *neveu*, from Latin *nepōs*, nephew, grandson. See **nepōt-** in Appendix.*]

ne·phol·o·gy (nĕ-fŏl′ə-jē) *n.* The science of clouds. [Greek *nephos*, cloud (see **nebh-** in Appendix*) + -LOGY.] —**neph′o·log′i·cal** (nĕf′ə-lŏj′ĭ-kəl) *adj.*

ne·phrec·to·my (nə-frĕk′tə-mē) *n., pl.* **-mies.** The surgical removal of a kidney. [NEPHR(O)- + -ECTOMY.]

ne·phrid·i·um (nə-frĭd′ē-əm) *n., pl.* **-ia** (-ē-ə). **1.** An excretory organ in many invertebrates. **2.** The excretory organ of a vertebrate embryo, from which the kidney develops. [New Latin : NEPHR(O)- + -IDIUM.] —**ne·phrid′i·al** *adj.*

neph·rite (nĕf′rīt′) *n.* A white to dark green variety of jade, chiefly a metasilicate of iron, calcium, and magnesium. [German *Nephrit*, "kidney mineral" (from its once supposed power to cure kidney diseases) : NEPHR(O)- + -ITE.]

ne·phrit·ic (nə-frĭt′ĭk) *adj.* **1.** Pertaining to the kidneys. **2.** *Pathology.* Of, pertaining to, or affected with nephritis.

ne·phri·tis (nə-frī′tĭs) *n. Pathology.* Any of various acute or chronic inflammations of the kidneys. Also called "Bright's disease" when chronic. [Late Latin, from Greek : NEPHR(O)- + -ITIS.]

nephro-, nephr-. Indicates the kidney; for example, **nephrogenous, nephrite.** [Greek, from *nephros*, kidney. See **negwhro-** in Appendix.*]

ne·phrog·e·nous (nə-frŏj′ə-nəs) *adj.* Also **neph·ro·gen·ic** (nĕf′rə-jĕn′ĭk). **1.** Originating in the kidney. **2.** Having the capacity to generate new kidney tissue. [NEPHRO- + -GENOUS.]

ne·phro·sis (nə-frō′sĭs) *n.* Any disease of the kidneys, especially when marked by degenerative lesions of the renal tubules, as opposed to the inflammation characteristic of nephritis. [New Latin : NEPHR(O)- + -OSIS.] —**ne·phrot′ic** (nə-frŏt′ĭk) *adj.*

ne·phrot·o·my (nə-frŏt′ə-mē) *n., pl.* **-mies.** Surgical incision into the kidney. [New Latin *nephrotomia* : NEPHRO- + -TOMY.]

ne plus ul·tra (nē plŭs ŭl′trə; nā plōōs ōōl′trä). The extreme or utmost point; especially, the point of highest achievement. [Latin, "(sail) no more beyond (this point)," a warning to mariners allegedly inscribed on the Pillars of Hercules.]

nep·o·tism (nĕp′ə-tĭz′əm) *n.* Favoritism shown or patronage granted by persons in high office to relatives or close friends. [French *népotisme*, from Italian *nepotismo*, "favoring of 'nephews' (by 16th-century prelates)," from *nepote*, nephew, from Latin *nepōs*. See **nepōt-** in Appendix.*] —**ne·pot′ic** (nə-pŏt′ĭk) *adj.* —**nep′o·tist** *n.* —**nep′o·tis′tic, nep′o·tis′ti·cal** *adj.*

Nep·tune¹ (nĕp′tōōn′, -tyōōn′). *Roman Mythology.* The god of the sea, corresponding to the Greek Poseidon. [Latin *Neptūnus*†.]

Nep·tune² (nĕp′tōōn′, -tyōōn′) *n. Poetic.* The ocean or sea.

Nep·tune³ (nĕp′tōōn′, -tyōōn′) *n.* The eighth planet from the sun, having a sidereal period of revolution around the sun of 164.8 years at a mean distance of 2.8 billion (2.8×10^9) miles, a mean radius of 14,000 miles, and a density 17.2 times that of earth. See **solar system.** —**Nep·tu′ni·an** *adj.*

nep·tu·ni·um (nĕp-tōō′nē-əm, -tyōō′nē-əm) *n. Symbol* **Np** A silvery, metallic, naturally radioactive element, atomic number 93, the first of the transuranium elements, having thirteen isotopes with mass numbers from 231 to 241 and half-lives ranging from 7.3 minutes to 2.2 million years. It is found in trace quantities in uranium ores and is produced synthetically by nuclear reactions. See **element.** [After *Neptune* (planet), since neptunium follows uranium in the periodic table, as Neptune is the next planet after Uranus.]

Ne·re·id¹ (nîr′ē-ĭd). *Greek Mythology.* A daughter of Nereus; a sea nymph. [Greek *Nēreis*, from *Nēreus*, NEREUS.]

Ne·re·id² (nîr′ē-ĭd) *n.* The smaller of the two satellites of the planet Neptune. [From NEREID (nymph); the Nereids were attendants on Poseidon (Neptune).]

ne·re·is (nîr′ē-ĭs) *n., pl.* **nereides** (nə-rē′ə-dēz′). Any of several marine worms of the genus *Nereis*, having a long, flat, segmented body and a pair of paddles on each segment. Also called "clamworm." [New Latin, from Latin *Nēreis*, NEREID.]

Ne·re·us (nîr′ē-əs, nîr′ōōs′). *Greek Mythology.* A sea god, father of the Nereids. [Greek *Nēreus*. See **nēr-** in Appendix.*]

ne·rit·ic (nə-rĭt′ĭk) *adj.* Pertaining to the waters and deposits of a shoreline. See **continental shelf.** [Probably from Latin *nērīta*, sea snail, from Greek *nēritēs*, from *Nēreus*, NEREUS.]

Ne·ro (nîr′ō), **Claudius Caesar Drusus Germanicus.** Original name, Lucius Domitius Ahenobarbus. A.D. 37–68. Roman emperor (A.D. 54–68).

ner·o·li (nĕr′ə-lē) *n.* An essential oil distilled from orange flowers and used in perfumery. Also called "neroli oil," "orange flower oil." [French; it was introduced into France in about 1680 by Anna Maria de la Trémoille, princess of *Neroli.*]

Ne·ro·ni·an (nĭ-rō′nē-ən) *adj.* **1.** Displaying a disposition to cruelty, tyranny, or depravity comparable to that of the emperor Nero. **2.** Of or pertaining to Nero or his times.

ner·vate (nûr′vāt′) *adj. Botany.* Having veins. Said of leaves.

ner·va·tion (nûr-vā′shən) *n.* A pattern of veins or nerves, **venation** *(see).*

nerve (nûrv) *n.* **1.** Any of the bundles of fibers interconnecting the central nervous system and the organs or parts of the body, capable of transmitting both sensory stimuli and motor impulses from one part of the body to another. **2.** A tendon or muscle. Now rare except in the expression *to strain every nerve.* **3.** The source from which feeling, energy, or dynamic action emanates. **4.** *Usually plural.* The nervous system regarded as the source of patience, endurance, courage, sensitivity, or the like. **5. a.** Forcefulness; stamina. **b.** Strong will; firm self-control; courage. **c.** *Informal.* Brazenness; effrontery: *He has a nerve, trying to corner the market.* **6.** *Plural.* Neurological manifestations, such as involuntary trembling, agitation, or hysteria: *an attack of nerves.* **7.** *Entomology.* A vein in an insect's wing. **8.** *Botany.* The midrib and larger veins in a leaf. —See Synonyms at **temerity.** —**get on one's nerves.** To exasperate or irritate. —*tr.v.* **nerved, nerving, nerves.** To give strength or courage to. [Latin *nervus*, sinew, nerve. See **snēu-** in Appendix.*]

nerve cell. Any of the cells of nerve tissue consisting of a nucleated portion, and cytoplasmic extensions, the cell body, the dendrites and axons. Also called "neuron."

nerve center. 1. A group of nerve cells that perform a specific function. **2.** A source or focus of power or control.

nerve fiber. A threadlike process that is part of a nerve; an axon or dendrite.

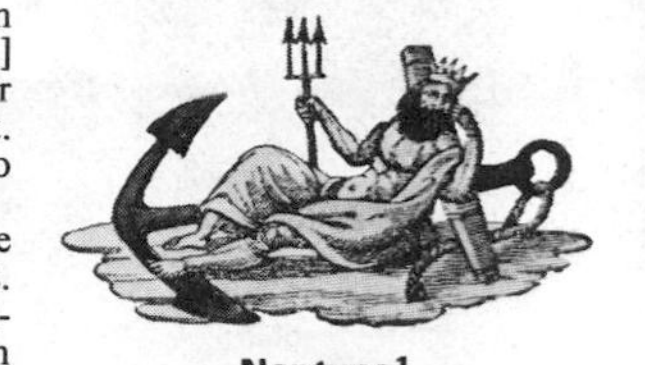

Neptune¹
Nineteenth-century illustration showing the god with his trident

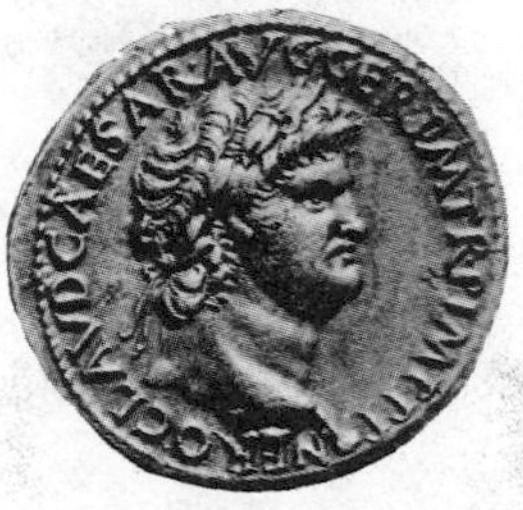

Nero
Portrait on a Roman coin

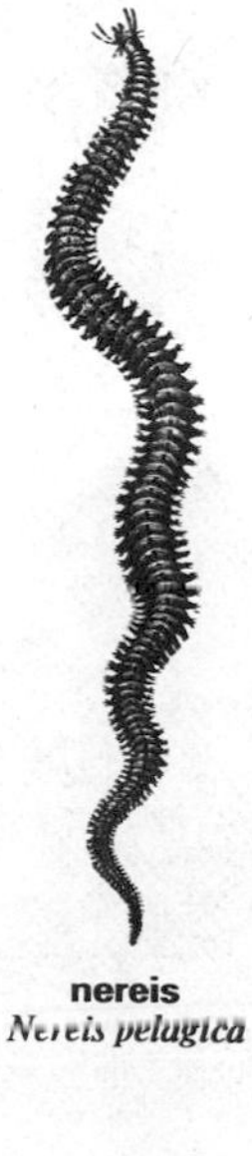

nereis
Nereis pelagica

nest

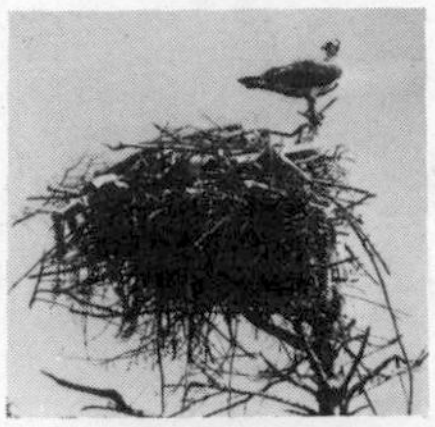

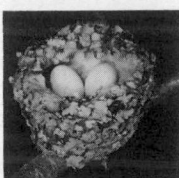

osprey on its nest

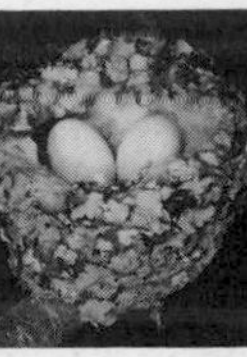

hummingbird's nest and eggs

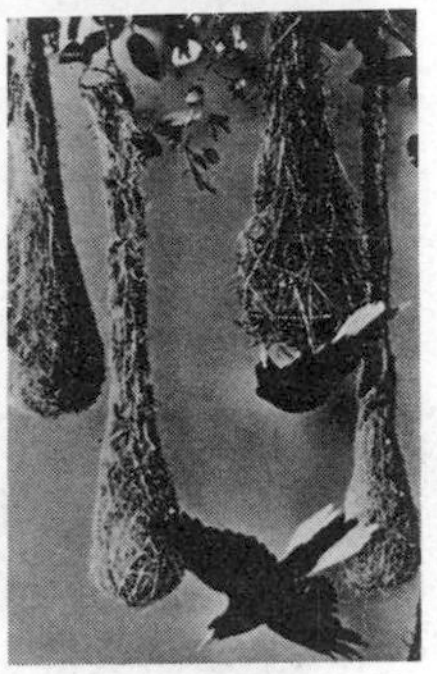

hanging nest of a cacique

netsuke

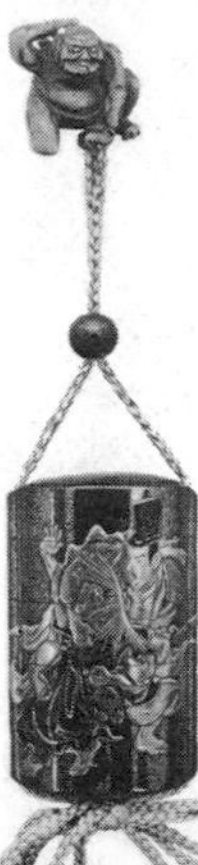

lacquer case suspended from netsuke

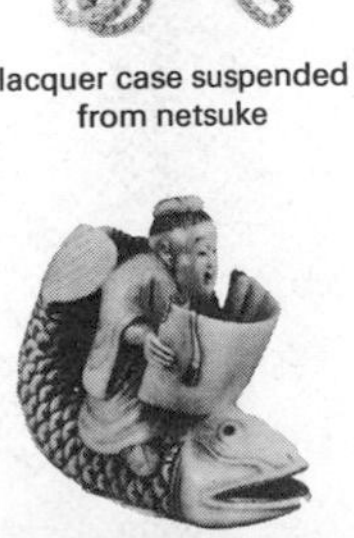

ivory netsuke with Buddhist sage riding carp

nerve impulse. The wavelike progression of chemical and electrical disturbance along a stimulated nerve fiber.

nerve·less (nûrv′lĭs) *adj.* **1.** Lacking strength or energy; listless; inert. **2.** Undisturbed by danger or upsetting circumstances; self-controlled. —**nerve′less·ly** *adv.* —**nerve′less·ness** *n.*

nerve-rack·ing (nûrv′răk′ĭng) *adj.* Also **nerve-wrack·ing.** Intensely distressing or irritating to the nerves.

nerv·ine (nûr′vēn′) *adj.* **1.** Affecting the nerves; especially, calming nervous excitement. **2.** Of or pertaining to the nerves. —*n.* A tonic for nervous disorders.

nerv·ous (nûr′vəs) *adj.* **1.** Having nerves easily affected; high-strung; excitable; jittery. **2.** Spirited in style, feeling, or thought: *a nervous, vibrant prose.* **3.** Strung with nerves; containing many delicate nerves. **4. a.** Of or relating to the nerves or nervous system. **b.** Stemming from or affecting the nerves or nervous system: *a nervous disorder.* **5.** *Rare.* Strong; vigorous: *"The nervous, rocky West"* (Emerson). **6.** Uneasy; fearful, anxious: *nervous about staying home alone.* [Middle English, from Latin *nervōsus,* from *nervus,* sinew, NERVE.] —**ner′vous·ly** *adv.* —**ner′vous·ness** *n.*

nervous breakdown. 1. Neurasthenia *(see).* **2.** Any severe or incapacitating emotional disorder. Not in technical use.

nervous exhaustion. Neurasthenia *(see).* Not in technical use.

nervous prostration. Neurasthenia *(see).* Not in technical use.

nervous system. *Anatomy.* A coordinating mechanism in all multicellular animals, except sponges, that regulates internal body functions and responses to external stimuli. In vertebrates it consists of the brain, spinal cord, nerves, ganglia, and parts of receptor and effector organs. See **autonomic nervous system, central nervous system, peripheral nervous system.**

ner·vure (nûr′vyo͝or) *n.* **1.** *Botany.* One of the vascular ridges that form the framework of a leaf. **2.** *Entomology.* One of the thickened ribs of tissue that form the framework of an insect's wing. [French, from Latin *nervus,* NERVE.]

nerv·y (nûr′vē) *adj.* **-ier, -iest. 1.** *Informal.* Impudently confident; brazen; rude. **2.** *Archaic.* Full of muscular force; sinewy. **3.** Showing or requiring fortitude, energy, or endurance. **4.** *Chiefly British.* Having bad nerves; jumpy; nervous.

nes·cience (nĕsh′əns, nĕsh′ē-əns, nĕs′ē-əns) *n.* **1.** Absence of knowledge or awareness; ignorance. **2.** Agnosticism. [Late Latin *nescientia,* from *nesciens,* ignorant, from *nescīre,* to be ignorant : *ne-,* not (see **ne** in Appendix*) + *scīre,* to know (see **skei-** in Appendix*).] —**nes′cient** *adj.* & *n.*

–ness. Indicates: **1.** State, quality, or condition of being; for example, **quietness. 2.** An instance or example of a state, quality, or condition; for example, **kindness.** [Middle English, from Old English *-ness, -niss,* of Germanic origin.]

Ness, Loch (lôKH nĕs′). A lake, about 24 miles long and one mile wide, in northern Scotland, noted for persistent, unconfirmed reports of a monster inhabiting it.

Nes·sel·rode (nĕs′əl-rōd′) *n.* A mixture, often rum-flavored, of chestnuts, preserved oranges, cherries, and dried fruits, used in puddings, ice cream, or pies. [Invented by the chef of Count Karl von *Nesselrode* (1780–1862), Russian diplomat.]

nest (nĕst) *n.* **1. a.** The structure made by a bird for holding its eggs and young. **b.** The structure or place in which fishes or insects deposit eggs or shelter their young. **c.** Any place where young are reared; a lair. **d.** A number of insects, birds, or other animals occupying such a place; a swarm, brood, or colony: *a nest of hornets.* **2.** A place affording snug seclusion or lodging. **3. a.** A place or environment favoring rapid growth or development of something bad or dangerous; a haunt: *a nest of robbers.* **b.** The persons occupying or frequenting such a place. **4.** A set of objects, such as small tables, of graduated size, that can be stacked together, each fitting within the immediately larger. **5.** A group of weapons in a prepared position: *a nest of missiles.* —*v.* **nested, nesting, nests.** —*intr.* **1.** To build or occupy a nest. **2.** To hunt for birds' nests, especially in order to collect the eggs. —*tr.* To place in or as if in a nest. [Middle English *nest,* Old English *nest.* See **nizdo-** in Appendix.*]

nested interval. *Mathematics.* An interval in a sequence of intervals, each lying within its predecessor.

nested set. *Mathematics.* A set in a collection of sets, each of which either contains or is contained by any other set in the collection.

nest egg. 1. An artificial or natural egg placed in a nest to induce a bird to lay. **2.** A sum of money put by as a reserve.

nest·er (nĕs′tər) *n. Western U.S.* A squatter, farmer, or homesteader who settles in cattle-grazing territory.

nes·tle (nĕs′əl) *v.* **-tled, -tling, -tles.** —*intr.* **1. a.** To settle snugly and comfortably: *The kittens nestled lazily among the cushions.* **b.** To lie half-sheltered or settled comfortably: *The cottage nestled in the wood.* **2.** To draw or press close, especially in an affectionate manner: *She nestled up to him.* **3.** *Rare.* To nest. —*tr.* To rest, snuggle, or press contentedly. [Middle English *nestlen,* Old English *nestlian,* to make a nest. See **nizdo-** in Appendix.*] —**nes′tler** *n.*

nest·ling (nĕst′lĭng) *n.* **1.** A bird too young and frail to leave its nest. **2.** A young child.

Nes·tor[1] (nĕs′tər, -tôr′). In the Homeric poems, a hero celebrated for his age and for the wisdom of his counsel.

Nes·tor[2] (nĕs′tər, -tôr′) *n. Sometimes small* **n.** A venerable and wise old man.

Nes·to·ri·an (nĕ-stôr′ē-ən) *adj.* Designating a church of the East that adheres to the doctrines of Nestorius, a fifth-century Patriarch of Constantinople, asserting that Christ had two distinct natures, divine and human, and that the Virgin Mary should not be called the Mother of God. —*n.* A member of this church. —**Nes·to′ri·an·ism′** *n.*

net[1] (nĕt) *n.* **1.** An openwork fabric with the threads woven, knotted, or twisted together at regular intervals, forming meshes of varying sizes. **2.** Something made of net: **a.** A device for capturing birds, fish, butterflies, or other animals. **b.** A **mosquito net** *(see).* **c.** A mesh for holding the hair in place. **3.** *Sports.* **a.** A barrier of meshwork cord or rope strung between two posts to divide the playing area in half. **b.** A ball that is hit into such a net. Also called "net ball." **c.** *Often plural.* A goal in ice hockey. **4.** A meshed network of lines, figures, or fibers. **5.** A situation or circumstance that entraps. —*tr.v.* **netted, netting, nets. 1.** To catch or entangle in or as if in a net. **2.** To cover, protect, or surround with or as if with a net. **3.** To hit (a ball) into a net. **4.** To make into a net. [Middle English *net,* Old English *net(t).* See **ned-** in Appendix*.]

net[2] (nĕt) *adj.* **1.** *Abbr.* **n.** Remaining after all necessary deductions have been made or all losses accounted for: *net profit; net weight.* **2.** Ultimate; final: *net result; net conclusion.* —*n. Abbr.* **n.** Total gain; the net amount, as of profit, income, price, or weight. —*tr.v.* **netted, netting, nets.** To bring in as profit: *"the primaries had netted some 134 delegate votes"* (Theodore H. White). [Middle English *net,* neat, clear, plain, from Old French *net,* neat, elegant, from Latin *nitidus,* bright, clear, good-looking, from *nitēre,* to shine. See **nei-**[1] in Appendix.*]

neth·er (nĕth′ər) *adj.* Located beneath or below. [Middle English *nether,* Old English *nithera,* lower, under, from *nither,* down, downward. See **ni** in Appendix.*]

Neth·er·lands, the (nĕth′ər-ləndz). *Dutch* **Ne·der·land** (nā′dər-länt′). Officially, Kingdom of the Netherlands. A country of western Europe, north of Belgium, between West Germany and the North Sea. It has a land and water area of 13,433 square miles. Population, 12,212,000. Constitutional capital, Amsterdam; de facto capital, The Hague. Also called "Holland."

Netherlands Antilles. Formerly **Dutch West In·dies** (ĭn′dēz). An autonomous territory of the Netherlands, consisting of six islands, with a total area of about 400 square miles, in the West Indies. Population, 204,000. Capital, Willemstad, on Curaçao.

Netherlands East Indies. *Abbr.* **Neth. Ind.** The former name for **Indonesia.**

Netherlands Guiana. *Abbr.* **Neth. Gu.** A former name for **Surinam.**

Netherlands New Guinea. A former name for **West Irian.**

Netherlands Timor. The former name for Indonesian Timor. See **Timor.**

neth·er·most (nĕth′ər-mōst′) *adj.* Farthest down; deepest.

neth·er·ward (nĕth′ər-wərd) *adv.* Also **neth·er·wards** (nĕth′ər-wərdz). In a downward direction.

nether world. 1. The world of the dead; Hades. **2.** Hell. **3.** A place or human situation like hell: *"in this black-white nether world, nobody judged the customers"* (Malcolm X).

net knot. Part of a cell nucleus, a **karyosome** *(see).*

ne·top (nē′tŏp′) *n.* Friend; companion. A greeting used by the American colonists when addressing an Indian. [Narraganset *nétop* or Natick *neetomp,* "my friend," from Proto-Algonquian *niitaapeewa* (unattested), "my fellow man."]

net·su·ke (nĕt′so͞o-kā′) *n.* A small Japanese toggle, usually decorated with inlays or carving, used to fasten a purse or other article to a kimono sash. [Japanese.]

net·ting (nĕt′ĭng) *n.* **1.** An openwork fabric; net; network. **2.** The process of making a net. **3.** Fishing with a net.

net·tle (nĕt′l) *n.* **1.** Any plant of the genus *Urtica,* having toothed leaves covered with hairs that secrete a stinging fluid that affects the skin on contact. **2.** Any of various other stinging or prickly plants. —*tr.v.* **nettled, -tling, -tles. 1.** To sting with or as if with a nettle. **2.** To irritate; vex. [Middle English *nettle,* Old English *netle, netel(e).* See **ned-** in Appendix.*]

nettle rash. A rash caused by a nettle; **urticaria** *(see).*

net ton. A short **ton** *(see).*

net·work (nĕt′wûrk′) *n.* **1.** An openwork fabric or other structure in which rope, thread, wires, or other materials cross at regular intervals. **2.** Anything resembling a net in concept or form, as by being dispersed in intersecting lines of communication: *espionage network; network of railways.* **3.** A chain of interconnected radio or television broadcasting stations. **4.** A group or system of electric components and connecting circuitry designed to function in a specific manner.

Neuf·châ·tel (no͞o′shə-tĕl′; *French* nœ-shä-tĕl′) *n.* A soft, white cheese made from skimmed or whole milk or cream. [Made at *Neufchâtel,* town in Bray, northern France.]

Neu·mann (noi′män′), **John von.** 1903–1957. Hungarian-born American mathematician; formulated the game theory.

Neu-Meck·len·burg. The former name for **New Ireland.**

neumes, neums (no͞omz, nyo͞omz) *pl.n.* The signs used in the notation of plainsong during the Middle Ages, surviving today in transcriptions of Gregorian chant. [Middle English, musical phrase sung to a single syllable, from Old French, from Medieval Latin *neuma, neupma,* from Greek *pneuma,* breath. See **pneu-** in Appendix.*] —**neu·mat′ic** (no͞o-măt′ĭk, nyo͞o-) *adj.*

Ne·u·quén (nā′o͞o-kān′). **1.** A river rising in west-central Argentina and flowing east 375 miles to join the Limay and form the Río Negro. **2.** A territory of western Argentina, 36,429 square miles in area, adjoining Chile. Population, 126,000.

neur. neurological; neurology.

neu·ral (no͝or′əl, nyo͝or′-) *adj.* **1.** Of or pertaining to the nerves: *a neural cavity.* **2.** Of, pertaining to, or located on the same side of the body as the spinal cord; dorsal. [NEUR(O)- + -AL.]

neu·ral·gia (no͞o-răl′jə, nyo͞o-) *n.* Paroxysmal pain along a nerve. [New Latin : NEUR(O)- + -ALGIA.] —**neu·ral′gic** *adj.*

neu·ras·the·ni·a (no͝or′əs-thē′nē-ə, nyo͝or′-) *n.* A condition marked by fatigue, loss of energy and memory, and feelings of inadequacy, once thought to result from exhaustion of the nervous system. Now rare in scientific use. Also called "nervous breakdown," "nervous exhaustion," "nervous prostration." [NEUR(O)- + ASTHENIA.] —**neu'ras·then'ic** (no͝or'əs-thĕn'ĭk, nyo͝or'-) *adj.* —**neu'ras·then'i·cal·ly** *adv.*

neu·rax·on (no͞o-răk'sŏn', nyo͞o-) *n.* A part of a nerve cell, the **axon** *(see).* [New Latin : NEUR(O)- + AXON.]

neu·rec·to·my (no͞o-rĕk'tə-mē, nyo͞o-) *n., pl.* **-mies.** Surgical removal of a nerve or part of a nerve. [NEUR(O)- + -ECTOMY.]

neu·ri·lem·ma (no͝or'ə-lĕm'ə, nyo͝or'-) *n.* Also **neu·ri·lem·a, neu·ro·lem·ma.** The outer covering of a nerve fiber. [New Latin : NEUR(O)- + Greek *eilēma,* veil, covering, from *eilein,* to wind. See **wel-³** in Appendix.*] —**neu'ri·lem'mal, neu'ri·lem·mat'ic** (-lĕ-măt'ĭk), **neu'ri·lem'ma·tous** (-lĕm'ə-təs) *adj.*

neu·ri·tis (no͞o-rī'tĭs, nyo͞o-) *n.* Inflammation of a nerve, causing pain, loss of reflexes, and muscular atrophy. [New Latin : NEUR(O)- + -ITIS.] —**neu·rit'ic** (no͞o-rĭt'ĭk, nyo͞o-) *adj.*

neuro-, neur-. Indicates nerve or nervous system; for example, **neuroblast, neurectomy.** [New Latin, from Greek *neuron,* tendon, nerve. See **snēu-** in Appendix.*]

neu·ro·blast (no͝or'ə-blăst', nyo͝or'-) *n.* An embryonic cell from which a nerve cell develops. [NEURO- + -BLAST.]

neu·ro·cyte (no͝or'ə-sīt', nyo͝or'-) *n.* Any nerve cell and its processes. [NEURO- + -CYTE.]

neu·rog·li·a (no͞o-rŏg'lē-ə, nyo͞o-) *n.* The network of branched cells and fibers that supports the tissue of the central nervous system. [New Latin : NEURO- + Medieval Greek *glia,* "glue," tissue. See **gel-¹** in Appendix.*]

neurol. neurological; neurology.

neu·rol·o·gist (no͞o-rŏl'ə-jĭst, nyo͞o-) *n.* A specialist in the diagnosis and treatment of disorders of the nervous system.

neu·rol·o·gy (no͞o-rŏl'ə-jē, nyo͞o-) *n. Abbr.* **neur., neurol.** The medical science of the nervous system and its disorders. [New Latin *neurologia* : NEURO- + -LOGY.] —**neu'ro·log'i·cal** (no͝or'ə-lŏj'ĭ-kəl, nyo͝or'-) *adj.*

neu·ro·ma (no͞o-rō'mə, nyo͞o-) *n., pl.* **-mata** (-mə-tə). A tumor made of nerve tissue. [New Latin : NEUR(O)- + -OMA.]

neu·ron (no͝or'ŏn', nyo͝or'-) *n.* Also **neu·rone** (no͝or'ōn', nyo͝or'-). A **nerve cell** *(see)* with all its processes. [Greek *neuron,* sinew, nerve. See **snēu-** in Appendix.*] —**neu·ron'ic** (no͞o-rŏn'ĭk, nyo͞o-) *adj.* —**neu·ron'i·cal·ly** *adv.*

neu·ro·path (no͝or'ə-păth', nyo͝or'-) *n.* One suffering from or having a hereditary tendency toward nervous disorders or neurosis. [NEURO- + -PATH.] —**neu'ro·path'ic, neu'ro·path'i·cal** *adj.* —**neu'ro·path'i·cal·ly** *adv.*

neu·ro·pa·thol·o·gy (no͝or'ō-pə-thŏl'ə-jē, nyo͝or'-) *n.* The medical study of diseases of the nervous system. —**neu'ro·path'o·log'ic** (-păth'ə-lŏj'ĭk), **neu'ro·path'o·log'i·cal** *adj.* —**neu'ro·pa·thol'o·gist** *n.*

neu·rop·a·thy (no͞o-rŏp'ə-thē, nyo͞o-) *n.* Disease or abnormality of the nervous system. [NEURO- + -PATHY.]

neu·ro·psy·chi·a·try (no͝or'ō-sī-kī'ə-trē, nyo͝or'-) *n. Abbr.* **NP** The integrated medical study of both neurological and psychiatric disorders. —**neu'ro·psy'chi·at'ric** (-sī-kē-ăt'rĭk) *adj.* —**neu'ro·psy·chi'a·trist** *n.*

neu·rop·ter·an (no͞o-rŏp'tər-ən, nyo͞o-) *n.* Any insect of the order Neuroptera, having four net-veined wings, such as the **ant lion, dobson fly,** or **lacewing** *(all of which see).* —*adj.* Of or belonging to the Neuroptera. [New Latin *Neuroptera,* "nerve-winged" : NEURO- + -PTER.] —**neu·rop'ter·ous** *adj.*

neu·ro·sis (no͞o-rō'sĭs, nyo͞o-) *n., pl.* **-ses** (-sēz'). Any of various functional disorders of the mind or emotions, without obvious organic lesion or change, and involving anxiety, phobia, or other abnormal behavior symptoms. Also called "psychoneurosis." Compare **psychosis.** [New Latin : NEUR(O)- + -OSIS.]

neu·ro·sur·ger·y (no͝or'ō-sûr'jər-ē, nyo͝or'-) *n.* Surgery of any part of the nervous system. —**neu'ro·sur'geon** *n.* —**neu'ro·sur'gi·cal** *adj.*

neu·rot·ic (no͞o-rŏt'ĭk, nyo͞o-) *adj.* **1.** Derived from or pertaining to a neurosis; nervous: *a neurotic disorder.* **2.** Of, pertaining to, or afflicted with neurosis: *neurotic symptoms; a neurotic patient.* —*n.* A person suffering from a neurosis. —**neu·rot'i·cal·ly** *adv.*

neu·rot·o·my (no͞o-rŏt'ə-mē, nyo͞o-) *n., pl.* **-mies.** The surgical cutting or stretching of a nerve, usually to relieve pain. [NEURO- + -TOMY.]

Neus·tri·a (no͞os'trē-ə, nyo͞os'-). The western part of the Frankish Merovingian kingdom, comprising what is now northern France, formed in A.D. 561.

neut. **1.** neuter. **2.** neutral.

neu·ter (no͞o'tər, nyo͞o'-) *adj. Abbr.* **neut.** **1.** *Grammar.* **a.** Neither masculine nor feminine in gender. **b.** Neither active nor passive; indicating state rather than action. Said of verbs. **2. a.** *Biology.* Having no sexual organs. **b.** *Botany.* Having no pistils or stamens; asexual. **c.** *Zoology.* Sexually undeveloped. **3.** Taking no side; neutral. —*n.* **1.** *Grammar.* **a.** The neuter gender. **b.** A neuter word. **2. a.** A castrated animal. **b.** A sexually undeveloped or imperfectly developed female insect; worker. **c.** A plant without stamens or pistils. **3.** A neutral person. [Middle English *neutre,* from Old French, from Latin *neuter,* neither : *ne-,* not (see **ne** in Appendix*) + *uter,* either of two (see **kwo-** in Appendix*).]

neu·tral (no͞o'trəl, nyo͞o'-) *adj. Abbr.* **neut.** **1.** Not inclining toward or actively taking either side in a matter under dispute. **2.** Belonging to neither side nor party: *on neutral ground.* **3.** Occupying a middle position; not one thing or the other; indifferent. **4.** Of no sex; sexless; neuter. **5.** *Chemistry.* **a.** Of or pertaining to a compound that is neither acidic nor alkaline. **b.** Of or pertaining to a solution in which the concentrations of positive and negative ions are equal. **6.** *Physics.* **a.** Of or pertaining to a particle, object, or system that has neither positive nor negative electric charge. **b.** Of or pertaining to a particle, object, or system that has a net electric charge of zero. **7.** Of or pertaining to the state of a mechanical system in which gears are not engaged for transmission of power. **8. Achromatic** *(see).* **9.** Pronounced with the tongue in a relaxed, middle position, as the *a* in *around.* —*n.* **1.** One who takes no side in a dispute or competition. **2.** A neutral nation. **3.** An achromatic color: *decorated in neutrals.* **4.** *Machinery.* The position of gears in a power system when power cannot be transmitted: *The car is in neutral.* [Latin *neutrālis,* neuter (grammatically), from *neuter,* NEUTER.] —**neu'tral·ly** *adv.*

neu·tral·ism (no͞o'trə-lĭz'əm, nyo͞o'-) *n.* A political attitude of nonalignment or noninvolvement with conflicting alliances.

neu·tral·i·ty (no͞o-trăl'ə-tē, nyo͞o-) *n.* The quality or state of being neutral; especially, a state of impartiality in disputes and nonparticipation in war.

neu·tral·i·za·tion (no͞o'trə-lə-zā'shən, nyo͞o'-) *n.* **1.** The act of neutralizing. **2.** *Chemistry.* A reaction between an acid and a base that yields a salt and water.

neu·tral·ize (no͞o'trə-līz', nyo͞o'-) *tr.v.* **-ized, -izing, -izes.** **1.** To make neutral. **2.** To make ineffective; counterbalance and bring to nothing. **3.** To prohibit warfare in (an area) by signed agreement. **4.** *Chemistry.* **a.** To make (a solution) chemically neutral. **b.** To cause (an acid or base) to undergo neutralization. **5.** *Medicine.* To counteract the effect of (a drug or toxin). —**neu'tral·iz'er** *n.*

Synonyms: *neutralize, negate, nullify, counteract. Neutralize,* in nonscientific usage, is employed to indicate a state of ineffectiveness, inaction, or inoperativeness. *Negate* and *nullify* imply finality rather than a stalemate; often they also imply loss incurred through the rendering of something useless or valueless. *Counteract* is frequently used when the contending forces are thought of as desirable and undesirable; it suggests positive action to correct or set right.

neutral spirits. Ethyl alcohol distilled at or above 190 proof and used frequently in alcoholic beverage blends.

neu·tri·no (no͞o-trē'nō, nyo͞o-) *n., pl.* **-nos.** *Symbol* ν *Physics.* Either of two massless, electrically neutral, stable subatomic particles in the lepton family: *"Neutrinos zip through the earth as if it wasn't there . . . .The great problem with studying neutrinos is catching them in the first place."* (Leon Lederman). See **particle.** [Italian, diminutive of *neutrone,* neutron, from English NEUTRON.]

neu·tron (no͞o'trŏn', nyo͞o'-) *n. Symbol* **n** *Physics.* An electrically neutral subatomic particle in the baryon family, having a mass 1,839 times that of the electron, stable when bound in an atomic nucleus and having a mean lifetime of approximately 16.6 minutes as a free particle. It and the proton combine to form nearly the entire mass of atomic nuclei and in numbers characteristic of each nuclear species: *"these strange effects were due to a neutral particle . . . the neutron postulated by Rutherford in 1920 had at last revealed itself"* (Sir James Chadwick). See **particle.** [NEUTR(AL) + -ON.]

neutron star. A celestial body hypothesized to occur in a terminal stage of stellar evolution, consisting of a superdense mass essentially of neutrons, and having a powerful gravitational attraction from which only neutrinos and high-energy photons could escape, thus rendering the body invisible.

neu·tro·phil (no͞o'trə-fĭl', nyo͞o'-) *adj.* Also **neu·tro·phile** (no͞o'trə-fīl', nyo͞o'-), **neu·tro·phil·ic** (no͞o'trə-fĭl'ĭk, nyo͞o'-). Easily stained by neutral dyes. Said of such cells as leucocytes. [NEUTR(AL) + -PHIL(E).] —**neu'tro·phil'** *n.*

Nev. Nevada.

Ne·va (nē'və; *Russian* nyĕ-vä'). A navigable river of the Soviet Union, flowing about 40 miles west from Lake Ladoga to the Gulf of Finland. Part of its delta forms the site of Leningrad.

Ne·vad·a (nə-văd'ə, -vä'də). *Abbr.* **Nev.** A Mountain state, 110,540 square miles in area, in the western United States. It was admitted to the Union in 1864. Population, 285,000. Capital, Carson City. See map at **United States of America.** [After the SIERRA NEVADA.] —**Ne·vad'an** *adj.* & *n.*

né·vé (nā-vā') *n.* **1.** The upper part of a glacier, where the snow turns into ice. **2.** A field of snow at the head of a glacier. **3.** The granular snow typically found in such a field. [French dialectal (Valais), from Latin *nix* (stem *niv-*), snow. See **sneigwh-** in Appendix.*]

nev·er (nĕv'ər) *adv.* **1. a.** Not ever; on no occasion: *never better.* **b.** At no time whatsoever. Used emphatically: *Do such a thing? Never!* **2.** Not at all; in no way: *Never fear.* [Middle English *never,* Old English *nǣfre* : *ne,* not (see **ne** in Appendix*) + *ǣfre,* ever (see **aiw-** in Appendix*).]

nev·er·more (nĕv'ər-môr', -mōr') *adv.* Never again.

nev·er·the·less (nĕv'ər-*th*ə-lĕs') *adv.* None the less; however. See Synonyms at **but.**

Nev·ins (nĕv'ĭnz), **Allan.** Born 1890. American historian.

Ne·vis (nē'vĭs). An island, 52 square miles in area, in the Caribbean Sea, 3 miles from St. Kitts. Population, 13,000.

Nev·ski, Alexander. See **Alexander Nevski.**

ne·vus (nē'vəs) *n., pl.* **-vi** (-vī'). Also **nae·vus.** Any congenital growth or mark on the skin, such as a birthmark. [Latin *naevus.* See **genə-** in Appendix.*] —**ne'void** (nē'void') *adj.*

new (no͞o, nyo͞o) *adj.* **newer, newest.** **1.** Of recent origin; having existed only a short time; lately made, produced, or grown: *a new movie.* **2. a.** Not yet old; fresh; recent. **b.** Used for the first time; not secondhand. **3.** Recognized or experienced lately for the first time, although existing before; recently become known: *a new galaxy.* **4.** Freshly introduced; unfamiliar; unaccustomed. Used with *to* or *at: I'm new at it.* **5.** Begun afresh;

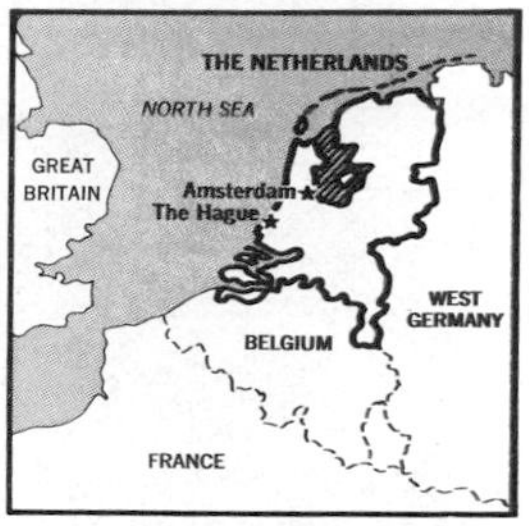

the Netherlands

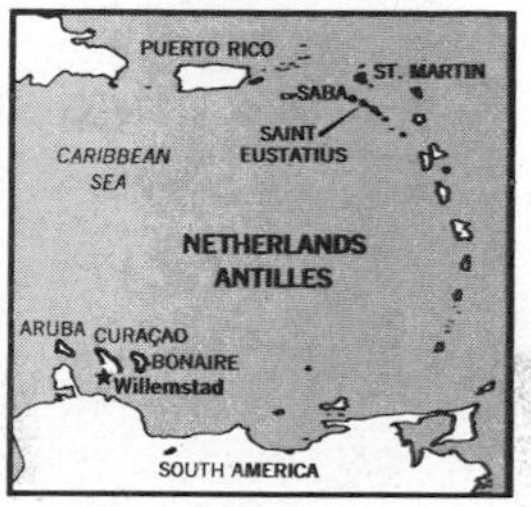

Netherlands Antilles

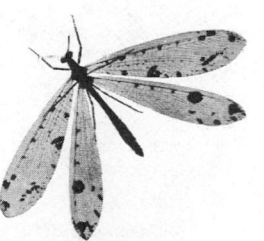

neuropteran
Adult ant lion

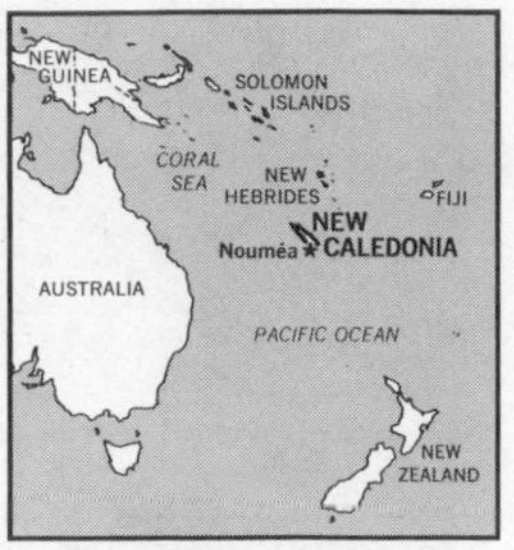

New Caledonia

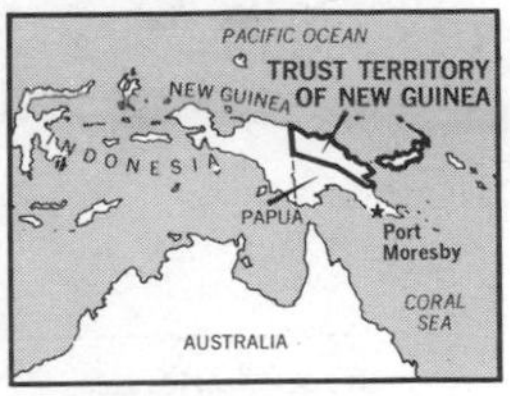

Trust Territory of New Guinea

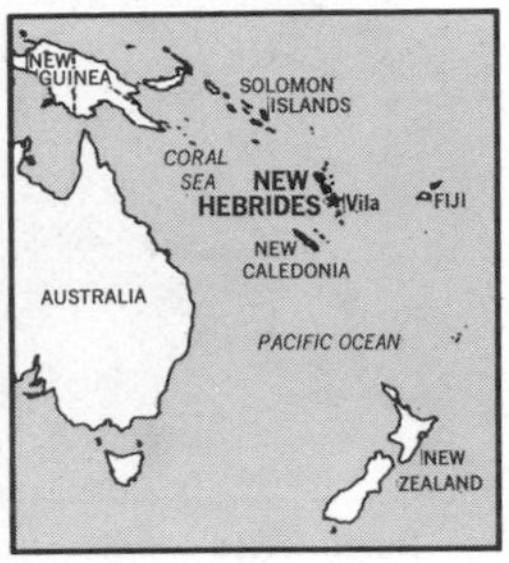

New Hebrides

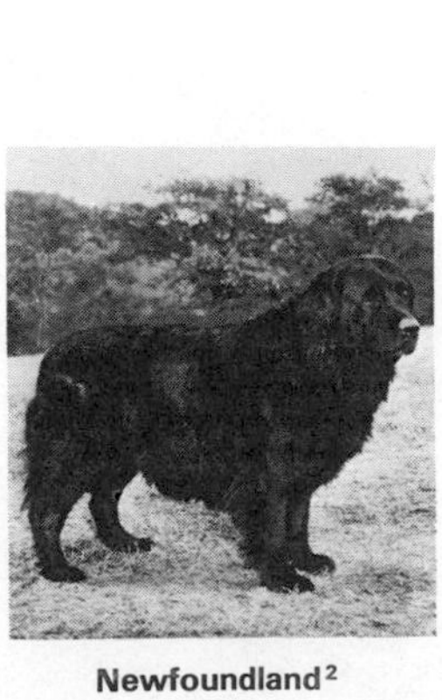
Newfoundland[2]

started in repetition: *the new moon.* **6. a.** Newly entered into a state, position, or experience: *a new convert.* **b.** Changed for the better; refreshed; rejuvenated: *A nap made a new man of him.* **7.** Different and distinct from what was before: *a new boy friend.* **8. a.** Modern; current; fashionable: *a new dance.* **b.** In the most recent form, period, or development of something: *New Latin.* —*n.* That which is new. —*adv.* Freshly; recently: *the smell of new-cut grass.* [Middle English *newe,* Old English *nēowe, nīwe.* See **newo-** in Appendix.*] —**new′ness** *n.*

Synonyms: *new, novel, original. New* is a broad, general term having reference to both time and condition. *Novel,* which emphasizes condition, is applied to that which is both new and strikingly unusual: *His symphony is not only new* (chronologically), *but novel in its treatment of folk songs. Original* also emphasizes state rather than time, and is said of that which is the first of its kind.

New Am·ster·dam (ăm′stər-dăm′). The capital of New Netherland, founded on Manhattan Island in 1625, and renamed New York after its capture by the English in 1664.

New·ark (no͞o′ərk, nyo͞o′-; *also* -ärk′ *for sense 1*). **1.** A city in northern Delaware, near the site of the Revolutionary Battle of Cooch's Bridge. Population, 11,000. **2.** The largest city in New Jersey, nine miles west of Lower Manhattan at the mouth of the Passaic River. Population, 405,000.

New·ark Bay (no͞o′ərk, nyo͞o′-). A bay extending six miles into northeastern New Jersey north of Staten Island, New York.

New Bed·ford (bĕd′fərd). A port and industrial city of Massachusetts, 50 miles south of Boston. Population, 102,000.

new·born (no͞o′bôrn′, nyo͞o′-) *adj.* **1.** Just born; very recently born: *a newborn baby.* **2.** Born anew: *newborn courage.*

New Brit·ain (brĭt′n). **1.** A city of central Connecticut, about eight miles southwest of Hartford. Population, 82,000. **2.** The largest island (14,600 square miles) of the Bismarck Archipelago, Trust Territory of New Guinea. Population, 122,000. Principal city, Rabaul.

New Bruns·wick (brŭnz′wĭk). *Abbr.* **N.B.** A Maritime Province of Canada, about 28,000 square miles in area. It was admitted to the Confederation in 1867. Population, 623,000. Capital, Fredericton. See map at **Canada.**

New·burg (no͞o′bûrg′, nyo͞o′-) *adj.* Also **New·burgh. 1.** Designating a sauce used for seafood, made of cream, egg yolks, butter, wine, and usually nutmeg. **2.** Cooked or served in this sauce: *lobster à la Newburg.* [Alteration of *Wenburg,* name of patron for whom sauce was created.]

New Cal·e·do·ni·a (kăl′ə-dō′nē-ə, -dōn′yə). *French* **Nou·velle Ca·lé·do·nie** (no͞o-vĕl′ kȧ-lā-dô-nē′). **1.** An island, 8,548 square miles in area, in the southwestern Pacific Ocean about 800 miles east of Australia. Population, 87,000. **2.** A French Overseas Territory consisting of this island and several smaller island dependencies nearby. Capital, Nouméa.

New·cas·tle (no͞o′kăs′əl, -käs′əl, nyo͞o′-). A port and the second-largest city of New South Wales, Australia, on the Tasman Sea coast, north of Sydney. Population, 219,000.

New·cas·tle-up·on-Tyne (no͞o′kăs′əl-ə-pŏn′tīn′, no͞o′käs′əl-, nyo͞o′-). Also **New·cas·tle.** A coal-mining center, the capital of Northumberland, England. Population, 257,000. —**carry coals to Newcastle.** To supply something already abundant.

New·chwang. The former name for **Yingkow.**

new·com·er (no͞o′kŭm′ər, nyo͞o′-) *n.* One who has lately come to a place or situation.

New Deal. 1. The programs and policies for economic recovery and reform, relief, and social security, introduced during the 1930's by President Franklin D. Roosevelt and his administration. **2.** The period between 1933 and 1940 during which these programs and policies were developed.

New Dealer. A supporter of the New Deal.

New Del·hi (dĕl′ē). The capital of the Republic of India, constructed in the early 20th century just south of Delhi (or Old Delhi), on the west bank of the Jumna River.

New Economic Policy. *Abbr.* **N.E.P.** The program in the U.S.S.R. between 1921 and 1928 whereby concessions were made to capitalism in small industry, retail trade, and agriculture.

new·el (no͞o′əl, nyo͞o′-) *n.* **1.** The vertical support at the center of a winding staircase. **2.** Any of the posts supporting a handrail at the bottom or at the landings of a staircase. Also called "newel post." [Middle English *nowell,* from Old French *nouel,* "kernel," newel, from Latin *nucālis,* nut-shaped, from *nux,* nut. See **ken-**[5] in Appendix.*]

New Eng·land (ĭng′glənd). *Abbr.* **N.E.** The northeastern United States, comprising the states of Maine, New Hampshire, Vermont, Massachusetts, Connecticut, and Rhode Island. Population, 10,905,000. —**New Englander.**

New England aster. A wild aster, *Aster novae-angliae,* of northeastern North America, having deep-purple flowers.

New England clam chowder. A kind of **clam chowder** *(see).*

Newf. Newfoundland.

new·fan·gled (no͞o′făng′gəld, nyo͞o′-) *adj.* **1.** Excessively or needlessly novel: *newfangled ideas.* **2.** Excessively fond of novelty and new things; modish. [Middle English *newe fangled,* alteration of *newefangel,* fond of new things : NEW + *-fangel,* from Old English *fangol* (unattested), "ready to seize," from *fangen,* past participle of *fōn,* to seize (see **pag-** in Appendix*).]

New·found·land[1] (no͞o′fən-lənd, -lănd′, nyo͞o′-, no͞o-found′lənd, nyo͞o-). *Abbr.* **Newf., N.F., Nfld. 1.** An island, 42,734 square miles in area, off the southeastern coast of Canada, separated from the mainland by the Strait of Belle Isle, the Gulf of St. Lawrence, and Cabot Strait. **2.** A province of Canada, consisting of this island and Labrador, with an area of 152,734 square miles. Population, 498,000. Capital, St. John's. See map at **Canada.**

New·found·land[2] (no͞o′fən-lənd, nyo͞o′-) *n.* A large breed of dog, growing to 28 inches at the shoulder, with a broad head and square muzzle, a powerful body, and a dense, usually black coat. [Believed bred in NEWFOUNDLAND, Canada.]

New France. The French territory in North America, which developed from 16th-century settlements on the St. Lawrence River to include much of southeastern Canada, the Great Lakes region, and the Mississippi valley. All of it except St. Pierre and Miquelon was surrendered to England and Spain by 1763.

New·gate (no͞o′gāt′, -gĭt, nyo͞o′-). A famous prison in London, demolished in 1902.

New Geor·gia (jôr′jə). **1.** An island group, with a land area of about 2,000 square miles, in the Solomon Islands in the southwestern Pacific Ocean. **2.** The principal island of this group.

New Gra·na·da (grə-nä′də). **1.** A former viceroyalty of Spain in northwestern South America, consisting of present-day Colombia, Panama, Ecuador, and Venezuela. **2.** A republic (1819–30) consisting of present-day Colombia and Panama.

New Greek. *Abbr.* **NGr, NGr., N.Gr. Modern Greek** *(see).*

New Guin·ea (gĭn′ē). An island, the second-largest in the world (304,000 square miles), lying in the Pacific Ocean north of Australia, and divided politically between West Irian, Papua, and the Trust Territory of New Guinea.

New Guin·ea, Trust Territory of (gĭn′ē). A trust territory of Australia consisting of northeastern New Guinea, the Bismarck Archipelago, and Bougainville in the Solomons. Population, 1,539,000. Administrative center, Port Moresby in Papua.

New Hamp·shire (hămp′shər, hăm′shər, -shîr′). *Abbr.* **N.H.** A New England state of the United States, 9,304 square miles in area, with a short coastline on the Atlantic. It joined the Union in 1788 as one of the original 13 states. Population, 607,000. Capital, Concord. See map at **United States of America.**

New Har·mo·ny (här′mə-nē). A village of southwestern Indiana on the Wabash River, the site of the utopian community (1825–28) founded by Robert Owen.

New Ha·ven (hā′vən). A port and industrial city of Connecticut with a harbor on Long Island Sound; seat of Yale University. Population, 152,000.

New Heb·ri·des (hĕb′rə-dēz′). *Abbr.* **N. Heb.** A group of islands, 5,700 square miles in area, in the Pacific Ocean east of Australia, constituting a condominium of the United Kingdom and France. Population, 66,000. Capital, Vila.

New High German. *Abbr.* **NHG, NHG., N.H.G. German** *(see).*

New Ire·land (īr′lənd). Formerly **Neu-Meck·len·burg** (noi-mĕk′lən-bo͝orKH′). An island, 3,340 square miles in area, of the Bismarck Archipelago. Population, 42,000.

New Jer·sey (jûr′zē). *Abbr.* **N.J.** A Middle Atlantic state of the United States, 7,836 square miles in area, with almost its entire eastern border on the Atlantic Ocean. It joined the Union in 1787 as one of the original 13 states. Population, 6,067,000. Capital, Trenton. See map at **United States of America.** —**New Jerseyite.**

New Latin. *Abbr.* **NL, NL., N.L.** The form of Latin in use, especially in scientific nomenclature, since the beginning of the Renaissance.

New Lon·don (lŭn′dən). A city and naval base in southeastern Connecticut on Long Island Sound. Population, 34,000.

new·ly (no͞o′lē, nyo͞o′-) *adv.* **1.** Lately; recently: *newly baked bread.* **2.** Once more; anew: *The apartment was newly painted.* **3.** In a new or different way: *an old idea newly phrased.*

new·ly·wed (no͞o′lē-wĕd′, nyo͞o′-) *n.* Also **new·ly·wed.** A person recently married.

New M. New Mexico (unofficial).

New·man (no͞o′mən, nyo͞o′-), **John Henry.** 1801–1890. English theologian; Anglican leader and later Roman Catholic cardinal.

New Mex·i·co (mĕk′sĭ-kō′). *Abbr.* **N. Mex.** A southwestern Mountain state of the United States, 121,511 square miles in area, bordering on Mexico at its southwestern corner. It was admitted to the Union in 1912. Population, 1,029,000. Capital, Santa Fe. See map at **United States of America.** —**New Mexican** *adj.*

new moon. 1. The phase of the moon occurring when it passes between the earth and the sun and is invisible, or visible only as a narrow crescent at sunset. **2.** The crescent moon.

New Neth·er·land (nĕth′ər-lənd). The early Dutch colony comprising several settlements along the Hudson and lower Delaware rivers. By 1664 the English had incorporated it into Delaware, New Jersey, and New York.

New Or·le·ans (ôr′lē-ənz, ôr′lənz, ôr-lēnz′). A city and river port of Louisiana, on the Mississippi about 110 miles up from the Gulf of Mexico. It is the site of a battle (January 1815) in which the Americans defeated the British. Population, 951,000.

New·port (no͞o′pôrt′, -pōrt′, nyo͞o′-). **1.** A resort city and port in southeastern Rhode Island, at the entrance to Narragansett Bay. Population, 47,000. **2.** The county seat of Monmouthshire, Wales, near the Severn estuary. Population, 107,000.

New·port News (no͞o′pôrt′ no͞oz, -pōrt, nyo͞oz). A harbor and city in southeastern Virginia. Population, 114,000.

Newport pink. A plant, the **sweet William** *(see).*

New Prov·i·dence Island (prŏv′ə-dəns). An island of the British West Indies, 20 miles long and 6 miles wide. Population, 81,000. Site of Nassau, capital of the Bahamas.

New Que·bec (kwĭ-bĕk′). A sparsely populated area of eastern Canada, occupying about 300,000 square miles between Hudson Bay and Labrador, north of the Eastmain River.

news (no͞oz, nyo͞oz) *n.* Plural in form, used with a singular verb. **1.** Recent events and happenings, especially those that are

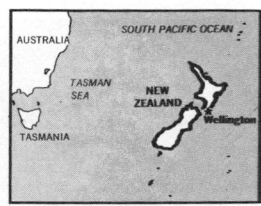

New Zealand

unusual or notable. **2. a.** Information about recent events of general interest, especially as reported by newspapers, periodicals, radio, or television. **b.** A presentation or broadcast of such information. **c.** A newspaper. **3.** New information about anything previously unknown.

news agency. An organization that provides news coverage to subscribers. Also called "press agency," "press association."

news·boy (nōōz′boi′, nyōōz′-) *n.* A boy who sells newspapers.

news·cast (nōōz′kăst′, -käst′, nyōōz′-) *n.* A radio or television broadcast of events in the news, often with commentary. [NEWS + (BROAD)CAST.]

New Siberian Islands. An island group of the Yakutsk A.S.S.R., in the Arctic Ocean off the northern coast of Siberia.

news·let·ter (nōōz′lĕt′ər, nyōōz′-) *n.* A printed periodical report devoted to news for a special-interest group.

news·man (nōōz′măn′, -mən, nyōōz′-) *n., pl.* **-men** (-mĕn′, -min). **1.** A person who reports or edits news, especially for a newspaper. **2.** One who sells or delivers newspapers.

New South Wales. *Abbr.* **N.S.W.** A state of Australia, occupying 309,433 square miles in the southeast. Population, 4,193,000. Capital, Sydney.

New Spain. The former Spanish possessions governed from Mexico City, including islands in the West Indies, Central America north of Panama, Mexico, the southwestern United States, and the Philippine Islands.

news·pa·per (nōōz′pā′pər, nyōōz′-) *n.* A typically daily or weekly publication containing news and opinion of current events, feature articles, and usually advertising.

news·pa·per·man (nōōz′pā′pər-măn′, nyōōz′-) *n., pl.* **-men** (-mĕn′). One who owns or is employed on a newspaper.

news·print (nōōz′prĭnt′, nyōōz′-) *n.* Inexpensive paper made from wood pulp, used chiefly for printing newspapers.

news·reel (nōōz′rēl′, nyōōz′-) *n.* A short motion picture that presents current events.

news·stand (nōōz′stănd′, nyōōz′-) *n.* An open booth or shop at which newspapers are sold.

New Style. *Abbr.* **N.S.** The current method of reckoning the months and days of the year, according to the Gregorian calendar, as distinct from the former style of reckoning according to the Julian calendar. See **calendar.**

New Sweden. An early Swedish colony (1638–55) in North America, extending roughly from the site of present-day Trenton, New Jersey, south to the mouth of the Delaware River.

news·y (nōō′zē, nyōō′-) *adj.* **-ier, -iest.** *Informal.* Full of news; informative. **—***n., pl.* **newsies.** *Informal.* A newsboy.

newt (nōōt, nyōōt) *n.* Any of several small, semiaquatic salamanders of the genus *Triturus* and related genera. [Middle English, from the phrase *a newt(e)*, originally *an ewt(e)* : *an* (indefinite article) + *ewt(e)*, *evete*, EFT.]

New Territories. The portion of Hong Kong colony leased by Great Britain from China in 1898 for 99 years; an area of 359 square miles including most of the colony's islands and the greater part of its mainland north of Kowloon.

New Test. New Testament.

New Testament. *Abbr.* **NT, N.T., New Test.** The Gospels, Acts, Pauline and other Epistles, and the Book of Revelation, which together have been viewed by Christians as forming the record of the new dispensation belonging to the Church, as distinct from the Old Testament dispensation shared with Judaism. [Translation of Latin *Novum Testāmentum*, translation of Greek *Kainē Diathēkē*, "new dispensation, covenant, or testament," in Christ's words, "This is my blood of the new testament, which is shed for many" (Mark 14:24), to which Saint Paul alludes as a mystery distinct from the "reading of the old testament" (II Corinthians 3:14), a distinction later used by the Church Fathers to differentiate the Christian covenant from Hebrew Scripture.]

new·ton (nōōt′n, nyōōt′n) *n. Abbr.* **N** *Physics.* In the meter-kilogram-second system, the unit of force required to accelerate a mass of one kilogram one meter per second per second. It is equal to 100,000 dynes. See **measurement.** [After Sir Isaac NEWTON.]

New·ton (nōōt′n, nyōōt′n). A city and suburb of Boston, in eastern Massachusetts. Population, 92,000.

New·ton (nōōt′n, nyōōt′n), Sir **Isaac.** 1642–1727. English mathematician, scientist, and philosopher; major work included the theories of universal gravitation, terrestrial mechanics, and color, and the invention of differential calculus.

New·to·ni·an (nōō-tō′nē-ən, nyōō-) *adj.* Pertaining to or in accordance with the work of Newton, especially that in mechanics and gravitation: *Newtonian physics; a Newtonian explanation.*

New World. The Western Hemisphere; North and South America and adjacent islands.

new year. 1. The year about to begin or just begun. **2.** *Capital* **N,** *capital* **Y.** The first day or days of the calendar year: *Happy New Year!* **3.** Rosh Hashanah *(see).*

New Year's Day. The first day of the year, as reckoned according to the Gregorian calendar; January 1.

New Year's Eve. The eve of New Year's Day; December 31.

New Year's gift. A plant, **winter aconite** *(see).*

New York (yôrk). *Abbr.* **N.Y. 1.** A Middle Atlantic state of the United States, 49,576 square miles in area (including inland waterways and part of Lake Erie), extending from the Canadian border in the north to the Atlantic Ocean in the southeast. It was admitted to the Union in 1788 as one of the 13 original states. Population, 16,782,000. Capital, Albany. See map at **United States of America. 2.** The largest city and leading seaport of the United States, in southeastern New York State at

the mouth of the Hudson River. It comprises the boroughs of Manhattan, the Bronx, Queens, Brooklyn, and Richmond. Population, 7,782,000. Also called "City of New York," "New York City." **—New Yorker.**

New York aster. A wild aster, *Aster novi-belgi,* of eastern North America, with pointed leaves and bluish-violet flowers.

New York Bay. An inlet of the Atlantic Ocean in southeast New York State. It is divided into Upper New York Bay and Lower New York Bay, which are connected by The Narrows.

New York State Barge Canal. A system of inland waterways in New York State totaling 525 miles. It connects the Hudson River with Lakes Erie and Ontario, and, via Lake Champlain, with the St. Lawrence River. See **Erie Canal.**

New Zea·land (zē′lənd). *Abbr.* **N.Z.** An independent member of the Commonwealth of Nations, 103,416 square miles in area, in the Pacific Ocean about 1,200 miles southeast of Australia. It comprises North Island, South Island, and several smaller adjacent islands. Population, 2,640,000. Capital, Wellington. **—New Zealander.**

next (nĕkst) *adj.* **1.** Nearest in space; adjacent: *the next room.* **2.** Coming directly after in time or sequence; immediately succeeding: *next Monday; the next President.* **—***adv.* **1.** In the time, order, or place immediately following. **2.** On the first subsequent occasion: *when next I write.* **—***prep.* Close to; nearest: *next my heart.* [Middle English *nexte,* Old English *nēahst, nēhst,* superlative of *nēah,* near. See **nēhw-iz** in Appendix.*]

Usage: *Next* and *nearest* are sometimes interchangeable, but not always. *Next* always indicates direct succession in a series. *Nearest,* which does not imply a sequence, is employed more generally to indicate close proximity, as in time, space, or kinship.

next door. To or in the adjacent house or building. **—next′-door′** *adj.*

next friend. *Law.* One who is admitted to court to sue as the representative of a minor or other person under legal disability.

next of kin. 1. The person or persons most nearly related to one by blood. **2.** *Law.* **a.** The closest relative of a deceased person. **b.** Those relatives entitled to the estate of a deceased person in accordance with the statutes of distribution.

nex·us (nĕk′səs) *n., pl.* **nexus** or **-uses. 1.** The bond, link, or tie existing between members of a group or series; a means of connection between things. **2.** A connected series or group. [Latin, from *nectere* (past participle *nexus*), to bind, connect. See **ned-** in Appendix.*]

Ney (nā), **Michel.** 1769–1815. Marshal of France; served in the armies of the First Republic and of the Empire; proscribed and executed after Waterloo.

Nez Perce (nĕz′ pûrs′). *pl.* **Nez Perce** or **Nez Perces** (pûr′sĭz). **1.** A tribe of Sahaptin-speaking Indians, formerly occupying much of the Pacific Northwest. **2.** A member of this tribe. **3.** The language of this tribe. [Canadian French *Nez Percé,* either translation of Salish *Chopunnish,* "Nez Perce," or from the pierced nose sign whereby the tribe was designated in Salishan sign language, presumably with reference to the custom of wearing ornamental seashells on pierced noses.]

N.F. 1. National Formulary. **2.** Newfoundland. **3.** Norman French.

NFL National Football League.

Nfld. Newfoundland.

NG, N.G. National Guard.

Nga·mi, Lake (ong-gä′mē). A lake in northern Botswana covering 200 square miles, discovered in 1849 by David Livingstone.

n′ga·na. Variant of **nagana.**

NGr, NGr., N. Gr. New Greek.

ngwee (ong-gwā′) *n.* A coin equal to 1/100 of the new unit kwacha of Zambia. See table of exchange rates at **currency.**

NH New Hampshire (with Zip Code).

N.H. New Hampshire.

N. Heb. New Hebrides.

NHG, NHG., N.H.G. New High German.

NHI *British.* National Health Insurance.

NHL National Hockey League.

Ni The symbol for the element nickel.

ni·a·cin (nī′ə-sĭn) *n.* One of the B vitamins, **nicotinic acid** *(see).* [NI(COTINIC) AC(ID) + -IN.]

Ni·ag·a·ra Falls (nī-ăg′rə, -ăg′ər-ə). **1.** An industrial and resort city of western New York State. Population, 102,000. **2.** An industrial and resort city of Ontario, Canada. Population, 22,000. **3.** The waterfalls of the Niagara River between these cities, consisting of two main falls, the Canadian or Horseshoe Falls (about 160 feet high and 2,500 feet wide), and the American Falls (about 167 feet high and 1,000 feet wide).

Niagara green. Pale green to light bluish green. See **color.**

Niagara River. A river flowing 34 miles north from Lake Erie to Lake Ontario, forming part of the boundary between western New York State and Ontario, Canada.

Nia·mey (nyä-mā′). The capital of Niger, on the Niger River in the southwestern part of the country. Population, 30,000.

nib (nĭb) *n.* **1. a.** The point of a quill pen, especially when sharpened. **b.** A penpoint designed to be inserted into a penholder. **2.** A beak or bill, as of a bird; neb. **3.** Any small, sharp, projecting part. [Possibly a survival of Old English *nibba* (attested only in a place name), "bird's beak." See **nabja-** in Appendix.*]

nib·ble (nĭb′əl) *v.* **-bled, -bling, -bles.** *—tr.* **1.** To bite at gently and repeatedly. **2. a.** To eat with small, quick bites, in the manner of a mouse or other small creature. **b.** To eat in small morsels: *nibble a cracker. —intr.* **1.** To bite or hesitant bites: *The fish nibbled at the bait. —n.* **1.** A small quantity, especially of food; a bite; morsel. **2.** An act or instance of

newel
Seventeenth-century
carved English staircase

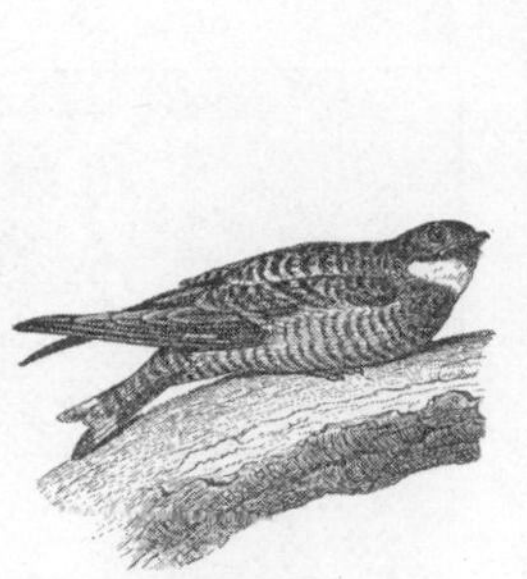

nighthawk
Chordeiles minor

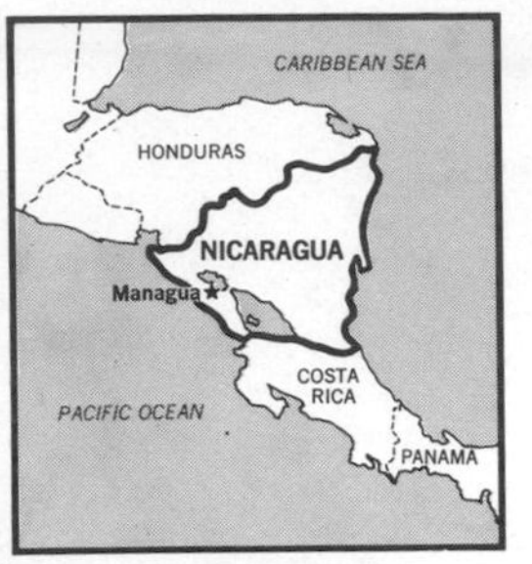

Nicaragua

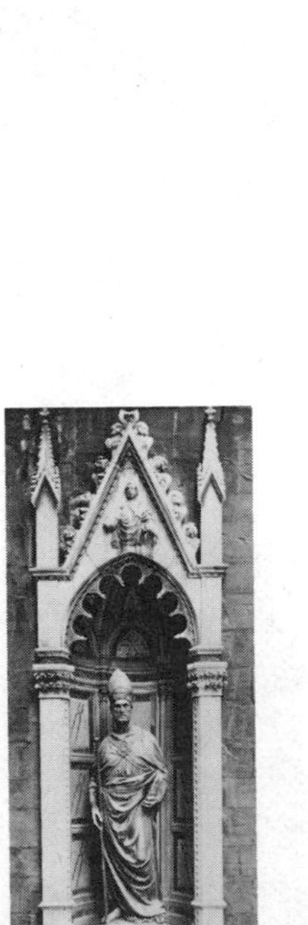

niche
Niche with Donatello statue of Saint Eligio

nibbling. [Probably from Low German *nibbeln, knibbeln,* to gnaw, nibble. See **ken-²** in Appendix.*]

Ni·be·lung (nē′bə-lo͝ong′) *n., pl.* **-lungs** or **-lungen** (-lo͝ong′ən). *Germanic Mythology.* **1.** Any of a race of subterranean dwarfs who possessed a hoard of riches and a magic ring, taken from them by Siegfried. **2.** Any of the followers of Siegfried. **3.** Any of the Burgundian kings in the *Nibelungenlied.* [German, from Middle High German *Nibelungen,* probably corresponding to a tribal name *Nebulones,* possibly from Old High German *nĕbul,* mist. See **nebh-** in Appendix.*]

Ni·be·lung·en·lied (nē′bə-lo͝ong′ən-lēt′) *n.* A Middle High German epic poem written in the early 13th century by an unknown author, based on the legends of Siegfried and of the Burgundian kings.

nib·lick (nĭb′lĭk) *n.* A golf club, a **nine iron** *(see).* [Origin unknown.]

Nic·a·ra·gua (nĭk′ə-ră′gwə). *Abbr.* **Nicar.** The largest republic (57,143 square miles) in Central America, situated south of Honduras, and having long coastlines on both the Pacific Ocean and the Caribbean Sea. Population, 1,593,000. Capital, Managua. —**Nic′a·ra′guan** *adj.* & *n.*

Nicaragua, Lake. The largest lake (3,100 square miles) of Central America, located in southern Nicaragua.

nic·co·lite (nĭk′ə-līt′) *n.* A nickel ore, essentially nickel arsenide, NiAs, found in America and Europe. [New Latin *niccolum,* nickel, probably from Swedish *nickel,* NICKEL + -ITE.]

nice (nīs) *adj.* **nicer, nicest. 1.** Pleasing to the senses; attractive; appealing: *a nice dress.* **2.** Kind; considerate; well-mannered: *a nice person.* **3.** Morally upright; virtuous: *a nice girl, careful of her reputation.* **4.** Showing refinement or delicacy; proper; seemly: *a nice way of putting it.* **5.** Difficult to please; fastidious; exacting: *"Good company requires only birth, education, and manners, and with regard to education is not very nice."* (Jane Austen). **6. a.** Showing or requiring sensitive critical discernment; subtle: *a nice distinction.* **b.** Done with precision and skill; deft: *a nice bit of craftsmanship.* **7.** *Obsolete.* **a.** Wanton; profligate. **b.** Affectedly modest; coy. **c.** Silly. [Middle English, foolish, wanton, shy, from Old French, silly, from Latin *nescius,* ignorant, from *nescīre,* to be ignorant : *ne-,* not (see **ne** in Appendix*) + *scīre,* to know (see **skei-** in Appendix*).] —**nice′ness** *n.*

Nice (nēs). A seaport and leading resort city of the French Riviera. Population, 293,000.

nice·ly (nīs′lē) *adv.* **1.** In a pleasing manner: *She curtsies nicely.* **2.** With precision; exactly: *"The American Legislatures are nicely balanced."* (Samuel Adams). **3.** Satisfactorily; acceptably. See Usage note.

Usage: *Nicely* is frequently used in the rather general sense of satisfactorily or quite acceptably: *This will serve nicely.* In written usage, 68 per cent of the Usage Panel approve such a sense.

Ni·cene Creed (nī′sēn′). **1.** A formal statement of the tenets of Christian faith, and chiefly of the doctrine of the Trinity, set forth by the Council of Nicaea in A.D. 325. **2.** Any of several modifications of this statement, now used in the services of the Roman Catholic Church, the Eastern Orthodox Church, and certain Protestant churches.

ni·ce·ty (nī′sə-tē) *n., pl.* **-ties. 1.** The quality of showing or requiring careful and precise treatment; delicacy; subtlety: *the nicety of a diplomatic exchange.* **2.** Delicacy of character or feeling; scrupulousness; fastidiousness. **3.** *Often plural.* A subtle point, detail, or distinction: *He left the niceties of composition to his copy editor.* **4.** *Often plural.* An elegant or refined characteristic or feature; amenity: *niceties of dress.* —**to a nicety.** With the utmost care and precision; exactly. [Middle English *nicete,* nicety, foolishness, from Old French *nicete,* foolishness, from *nice,* silly, NICE.]

niche (nĭch) *n.* **1.** A recess in a wall for holding a statue or other ornament. **2.** Any steep, shallow recess or concavity, as in a rock or hill. **3.** A situation or activity specially suited to a person's abilities or character. **4.** *Ecology.* **a.** The set of functional relationships of an organism or population to the environment it occupies. **b.** The area within a habitat occupied by an organism. —*tr.v.* **niched, niching, niches.** To place in a niche. [French, from Old French *niche,* "nest," from *nichier,* to nest, from Vulgar Latin *nīdicāre* (unattested), from Latin *nīdus,* nest. See **nizdo-** in Appendix.*]

Nich·o·las (nĭk′ə-ləs). A masculine given name. [Middle English *Nicholas,* Old English *Nicolas,* from Medieval Latin *Nicolaus,* from Greek *Nikolaos* : *nikē,* victory (see **nikē** in Appendix*) + *laos*†, the people.]

Nich·o·las II (nĭk′ə-ləs). Russian, Nikolai Aleksandrovich. 1868–1918. Czar of Russia; succeeded Alexander III (1894); abdicated (1917); executed with his family at Ekaterinburg.

Nich·o·las (nĭk′ə-ləs), **Saint.** Often identified with Santa Claus. Fourth-century bishop of Myra, Asia Minor.

Nich·o·las of Cu·sa (nĭk′ə-ləs əv kyo͞o′zə). 1401–1464. German cardinal; philosopher and mathematician.

nick (nĭk) *n.* A shallow notch, cut, or indentation on a surface: *nicks in the table; razor nicks on one's face.* —**in the nick of time.** Just at the critical moment. —*tr.v.* **nicked, nicking, nicks. 1.** To cut a nick or notch in. **2.** To cut short; check: *He nicked his impulse.* **3.** *Slang.* To cheat or defraud; especially, to overcharge. [Middle English *nyke,* variant of *nocke,* NOCK.]

nick·el (nĭk′əl) *n.* **1.** *Symbol* **Ni** A silvery, hard, ductile, ferromagnetic metallic element. It is used in alloys, in corrosion-resistant surfaces and batteries, and for electroplating. Atomic number 28, atomic weight 58.71, melting point 1,453°C, boiling point 2,732°C, specific gravity 8.902, principal valence 2. See **element. 2.** A U.S. coin worth five cents, made of a nickel and copper alloy. [Swedish *nickel,* shortened from *kopparnickel,* from German *Kupfernickel,* "copper-demon," an old mining term for the ore (niccolite) from which nickel was first extracted, so called because it appeared to contain copper but did not : *Kupfer,* copper, from Old High German *kupfar,* from Late Latin *cuprum, cyprum,* COPPER + *nickel,* demon, dwarf, from *Nickel,* familiar form of the name *Nikolaus,* NICHOLAS (probably by association with *Nix,* sprite, NIX).]

nick·el·ic (nĭ-kĕl′ĭk) *adj.* **1.** Of or containing nickel. **2.** Of or containing trivalent nickel, Ni^{3+}.

nick·el·if·er·ous (nĭk′ə-lĭf′ər-əs) *adj.* Bearing or containing nickel. Said of ores.

nick·el·o·de·on (nĭk′ə-lō′dē-ən) *n.* **1.** In the early 20th century, a movie house charging an admission price of five cents. **2.** A juke box or player piano. [NICKEL + (MEL)ODEON.]

nick·el·ous (nĭk′ə-ləs) *adj.* **1.** Of or containing nickel. **2.** Of or containing bivalent nickel, Ni^{2+}.

nick·el-plate (nĭk′əl-plāt′) *tr.v.* **-plated, -plating, -plates.** To deposit a thin, even layer of nickel on (a surface of metal or other conducting material), as by the electrolysis of a solution containing nickel. —**nickel plate.**

nickel silver. A silvery, hard, corrosion-resistant, malleable alloy of copper, zinc, and nickel, used in tableware, and as a structural material for hospital and restaurant equipment. Also formerly called "German silver."

nick·nack. Variant of **knickknack.**

nick·name (nĭk′nām′) *n.* **1.** A descriptive appellation added to or replacing the actual name of a person, place, or thing. **2.** A familiar or shortened form of a proper name. —See Synonyms at **name.** —*tr.v.* **nicknamed, -naming, -names. 1.** To give a nickname to; call by a nickname. **2.** To call by an incorrect name; misname. [Middle English *a nekename,* originally *an ekename,* an additional name : *eke,* an addition, Old English *ēaca* (see **aug-¹** in Appendix*) + NAME.]

Nic·o·bar Islands (nĭk′ə-bär′). An island group in the Bay of Bengal constituting, with the Andaman Islands, a territory of the Republic of India. Population, 15,000.

Nic·o·de·mus (nĭk′ə-dē′məs). A Pharisee and member of the Sanhedrin who defended Christ when he was denounced by other Pharisees.

Ni·co·let (nĭk′ə-lā′; *French* nē-kô-lĕ′), **Jean.** 1598–1642. French explorer of Lake Michigan region.

Ni·colle (nē-kôl′), **Charles Jean Henri.** 1866–1936. French physician; ascertained carrier of typhus.

Ni·col·let (nĭk′ə-lā′; *French* nē-kô-lĕ′), **Joseph Nicholas.** 1786–1843. French mathematician and astronomer; explored and mapped the upper Mississippi and Missouri rivers.

Nic·o·si·a (nĭk′ə-sē′ə). The capital of Cyprus, located in the north-central part of the island. Population, 103,000.

ni·co·ti·an·a (nĭ-kō′shē-ăn′ə, -ä′nə, -ā′nə) *n.* Any of various flowering tobacco plants of the genus *Nicotiana,* native to the Americas. [New Latin *herba nicotiana,* "herb of Nicot," after Jean *Nicot,* French ambassador at Lisbon, who, in 1560, sent some tobacco to Catherine de Médicis.]

nic·o·tine (nĭk′ə-tēn′) *n.* A poisonous alkaloid, $C_5H_4NC_4H_7N$-CH_3, derived from the tobacco plant, used in medicine and as an insecticide. [French, earlier *nicotiane,* from NICOTIANA.]

nic·o·tin·ic (nĭk′ə-tĭn′ĭk) *adj.* **1.** Of or pertaining to nicotine. **2.** Of or pertaining to nicotinic acid.

nicotinic acid. A member of the vitamin B complex, C_5H_4NC-OOH, occurring in living cells as an essential substance for growth and synthesized for use in treating pellagra. Also called "niacin." [Often obtained by the oxidation of NICOTINE.]

nic·o·tin·ism (nĭk′ə-tē-ĭz′əm) *n.* Nicotine poisoning.

Nic·the·roy. The former name for **Niterói.**

nic·ti·tate (nĭk′tə-tāt′) *intr.v.* **-tated, -tating, -tates.** Also **nic·tate** (nĭk′tāt′). To wink. [Latin *nictitāre,* frequentative of *nictāre,* to wink. See **kneigwh-** in Appendix.*] —**nic′ti·ta′tion** *n.*

nictitating membrane. Also **nictating membrane.** An inner eyelid in birds, reptiles, and some mammals that helps to keep the eye clean.

Ni·da·ros. A former name for **Trondheim.**

nid·der·ing (nĭd′ər-ĭng) *n. Rare.* A cowardly person; wretch. —*adj.* Base; cowardly; vile. [Earlier *nidering,* 16th-century misreading of Middle English *nithing,* Old English *nīthing,* wretch, coward, villain, from Old Norse *nīdhingr,* from *nīdh,* scorn. See **nei-¹** in Appendix.*]

nide (nīd) *n.* A nest or brood of pheasants. [Latin *nīdus,* nest. See **nizdo-** in Appendix.*]

nid·i·fy (nĭd′ə-fī′) *intr.v.* **-fied, -fying, -fies.** Also **nid·i·fi·cate** (nĭd′ə-fĭ-kāt′) **-cated, -cating, -cates.** To make a nest. [Latin *nīdificāre* : *nīdus,* nest (see **nizdo-** in Appendix*) + *facere,* to make (see **dhē-¹** in Appendix*).] —**nid′i·fi·cant** (-kənt) *adj.* —**nid′i·fi·ca′tion** *n.*

ni·dus (nī′dəs) *n., pl.* **-duses** or **-di** (-dī′). **1.** A nest; especially one for the eggs of insects or spiders. **2.** A cavity where spores develop. **3.** *Pathology.* The seat of bacterial growth in a living organism. [Latin *nīdus,* nest. See **nizdo-** in Appendix.*]

Nie·buhr (nē′bo͝or′), **Reinhold.** Born 1892. American Protestant theologian, educator, and author.

niece (nēs) *n.* **1.** A daughter of one's brother or brother-in-law, or sister or sister-in-law. **2.** The daughter of a celibate ecclesiastic. [Middle English *nece,* from Norman French, from Old French *niece,* from Vulgar Latin *neptia* (unattested), from Latin *neptis,* granddaughter, niece. See **nepōt-** in Appendix.*]

ni·el·lo (nē-ĕl′ō) *n., pl.* **-elli** (-ĕl′ē) or **-los. 1.** Any of several black metallic alloys of sulfur with copper, silver, or lead, used to fill an incised design on the surface of another metal. **2.** A surface or object decorated with niello. **3.** The art or process of

ă pat/ā pay/âr care/ä father/b bib/ch church/d deed/ĕ pet/ē be/f fife/g gag/h hat/hw which/ĭ pit/ī pie/îr pier/j judge/k kick/l lid, needle/m mum/n no, sudden/ng thing/ŏ pot/ō toe/ô paw, for/oi noise/ou out/o͝o took/o͞o boot/p pop/r roar/s sauce/sh ship, dish/

ornamenting metal surfaces with niello. —*tr.v.* **nielloed, -loing, -los.** To decorate or inlay with niello. [Italian, from Medieval Latin *nigellum,* from Latin *nigellus,* blackish, diminutive of *niger,* black. See **niger** in Appendix.*] —**ni·el′list** *n.*

Nie·men. The Polish name for the **Neman** River.

Nie·mey·er (nē′mī′ər), **Oscar.** Born 1907. Brazilian architect.

Nie·möl·ler (nē′mœl′ər), **Martin.** Born 1892. German Protestant leader; member of anti-Hitler opposition.

Nier·stein·er (nîr′shtī′nər) *n.* A kind of white Rhine wine. [Made at *Nierstein,* city in central West Germany.]

Nie·tzsche (nē′chə, -chē), **Friedrich Wilhelm.** 1844–1900. German philosopher, poet, and critic.

Nie·tzsche·an·ism (nē′chē-ə-nĭz′əm) *n.* Also **Nie·tzsche·ism** (nē′chē-ĭz′əm). **1.** The philosophy of Nietzsche, based upon a distinction between thought and emotion, and emphasizing the value of intense emotion in art and life. **2.** Nietzsche's doctrine of the superman. —**Nie′tzsche·an** *adj.* & *n.*

Nif·l·heim (nĭv′əl-hām′) *n.* Also **Nif·el·heim.** *Norse Mythology.* The realm of the dead. [Old Norse *niflheimr,* "home of mist" : *nifl,* mist (see **nebh-** in Appendix*) + *heimr,* home (see **kei-**[1] in Appendix*).]

nif·ty (nĭf′tē) *adj.* **-tier, -tiest.** *Slang.* Stylish; pleasing. Used as a term of admiration. —*n., pl.* **nifties.** *Slang.* Something regarded as nifty, such as a pun. [Possibly from MAGNIFICENT.]

Nig. Nigeria.

Ni·gel (nī′jəl). A masculine given name. [Middle English *Nigelle,* from Medieval Latin *Nigellus,* alteration (by influence of *nigellus,* "little black one") of Old Norse *Njal,* NEIL.]

Ni·ger (nī′jər). **1.** A republic, 449,400 square miles in area, in west-central Africa. Formerly part of French West Africa, it has been independent since 1960. Population, 3,100,000. Capital, Niamey. **2.** The third-longest river in Africa, rising near the Sierra Leone-Guinea border and flowing 2,600 miles northeast and then southeast to the Gulf of Guinea.

Ni·ger-Con·go (nī′jər-kŏng′gō) *n.* A family of West and Central African languages, including Mande, Gur, and Kwa. [NIGER (river) + CONGO (river).]

Ni·ge·ri·a (nī-jîr′ē-ə). *Abbr.* **Nig.** A federal republic in Africa, 372,674 square miles in area, on the Gulf of Guinea. Formerly a British colony, it has been independent since 1960. Population, 55,654,000. Capital, Lagos. —**Ni·ge′ri·an** *adj.* & *n.*

Niger seed. The seed of the African plant **ramtil** *(see),* used as birdseed. [Probably first found near the NIGER River.]

nig·gard (nĭg′ərd) *n.* A stingy, grasping person; miser. —*adj.* Parsimonious; niggardly. [Middle English *nigart, niggard,* earlier *nigon,* from *nig,* a miser, from Scandinavian, akin to Swedish dialectal *nygg,* from Old Norse *hnöggr,* miserly. See **ken-**[2] in Appendix.*]

nig·gard·ly (nĭg′ərd-lē) *adj.* **1.** Unwilling to part with anything; stingy: *"Nature has been rather niggardly with Japan in mineral resources."* (Edwin Reischauer). **2.** Meager; insufficient. —See Synonyms at **stingy.** —**nig′gard·li·ness** *n.* —**nig′gard·ly** *adv.*

nig·ger (nĭg′ər) *n. Vulgar.* A Negro or member of any dark-skinned people. An offensive term used derogatorily. [Earlier English dialectal *neeger, neger,* from French *nègre,* from Spanish *negro,* NEGRO.]

nig·gle (nĭg′əl) *intr.v.* **-gled, -gling, -gles.** **1.** To be preoccupied with trifles; worry over petty details; fret. **2.** To keep finding fault; complain trivially; carp. [Probably from Scandinavian and akin to NIGGARD.] —**nig′gler** *n.*

nig·gling (nĭg′lĭng) *adj.* **1.** Excessively concerned with details; fussy. **2.** Persistently nagging; petty. **3.** Showing or requiring close attention to details; exacting: *niggling paperwork.* —*n.* Work or behavior characterized by too much attention to detail. —**nig′gling·ly** *adv.*

nigh (nī) *adj.* **nigher, nighest** or **next.** *Archaic* & *Regional.* **1.** Close at hand; near. **2.** Short; direct. **3.** Mean and stingy. —*adv. Archaic* & *Regional.* **1.** Near in time or location: *Night is drawing nigh.* **2.** Nearly; almost. Used with *on* or *onto: nigh onto two hours.* —*prep. Archaic* & *Regional.* Not far from; near to. —*v.* **nighed, nighing, nighs.** *Archaic* & *Regional.* —*tr.* To come near to; approach. —*intr.* To draw near. [Middle English *neigh,* Old English *nēah.* See **nehw-iz** in Appendix.*]

night (nīt) *n.* **1.** The period between sunset and sunrise; especially, the hours of darkness. **2.** The period between dusk and midnight of a given day: *Tuesday night.* **3.** Darkness: *vanished into the night.* **4.** Any time or condition of gloom, obscurity, ignorance, or sorrow: *"In a real dark night of the soul it is always three o'clock in the morning."* (F. Scott Fitzgerald). [Middle English *niht, night,* Old English *niht, neaht.* See **nekwt-** in Appendix.*] —**night** *adj.*

night blindness. Poor vision in the dark, **nyctalopia** *(see).* —**night′-blind′** *adj.*

night-bloom·ing cereus (nīt′blōō′mĭng). Any of several flowering cacti having large, fragrant flowers that open at night.

night·cap (nīt′kăp′) *n.* **1.** A cloth head-covering worn especially in bed. **2.** *Informal.* A drink, usually of liquor, taken just before bedtime. **3.** *Sports Slang.* The last event in a day's competition; especially, the final game in a baseball double-header.

night·clothes (nīt′klōz′, -klōthz′) *pl.n.* Clothes worn in bed.

night·club (nīt′klŭb′) *n.* An establishment that stays open late at night and provides food, drink, and entertainment.

night crawler. Any earthworm that emerges from the ground at night. Also called "nightwalker."

night·dress (nīt′drĕs′) *n.* **1.** A nightgown. **2.** Nightclothes.

night·fall (nīt′fôl′) *n.* The approach of darkness; close of day.

night·gown (nīt′goun′) *n.* **1.** A loose gown, often long, worn to bed by women and children. **2.** A man's nightshirt.

night·hawk (nīt′hôk′) *n.* **1.** Any of several mainly nocturnal birds of the genus *Chordeiles,* having buff to black mottled feathers; especially, *C. minor,* of North America. Also called "bullbat," "mosquito hawk." **2.** A related European bird, the **nightjar** *(see).* **3.** *Informal.* One who stays up and works or prowls about at night; night owl.

night heron. Any of several nocturnal herons of the genus *Nycticorax;* especially, the black-crowned heron, *N. nycticorax.*

night·in·gale (nīt′n-gāl′, nī′tĭng-) *n.* **1.** A European songbird, *Luscinia megarhynchos,* with brownish plumage, noted for its nocturnal song. **2.** Any of various nocturnal songbirds. [Middle English *nihtyngale,* Old English *nihtegale,* "night-singer" : *niht,* NIGHT + *galan,* to sing (see **ghel-**[1] in Appendix*).]

Night·in·gale (nīt′n-gāl′, nī′tĭng-), **Florence.** 1820–1910. British nursing pioneer and hospital reformer.

night·jar (nīt′jär′) *n.* Any of various nocturnal birds of the family Caprimulgidae; especially, the common European nightjar, *Caprimulgus europaeus.* Sometimes called "nighthawk." [NIGHT + JAR (make a harsh sound).]

night jasmine. **1.** A shrub, *Nyctanthes arbortristis,* cultivated for its small, white, fragrant flowers. **2.** A West Indian shrub, *Cestrum nocturnum,* having small, greenish-white flowers that are very fragrant at night.

night latch. A spring lock that may be opened from the inside by turning a knob, but from the outside only with a key.

night letter. A telegram sent at night at a reduced rate.

night·long (nīt′lông′, -lŏng′) *adj.* Lasting through the whole night. —*adv.* Through the night; all night.

night·ly (nīt′lē) *adj.* **1.** Of or occurring during the night; nocturnal: *nightly prowlings.* **2.** Happening or done every night: *nightly rounds.* —*adv.* On every night: *He visited her nightly.*

night·mare (nīt′mâr′) *n.* **1.** A dream arousing feelings of intense, inescapable fear, horror, and distress. **2.** An event or condition that evokes feelings of horror, anguish, or intense distress: *the nightmare of urban loneliness.* **3.** A demon or spirit thought to plague sleeping people. —*adj.* Like something in a nightmare; appalling: *"We waited in suspense that made the seconds pass with nightmare slowness."* (Bram Stoker). [Middle English *nihtmare,* female incubus : NIGHT + *mare,* incubus, Old English *mare, mære,* goblin (see **mer-**[2] in Appendix*).]

night owl. A person who habitually stays up late at night.

night·rid·er (nīt′rī′dər) *n.* Any of a band of mounted and usually masked men who engaged in nocturnal terrorism for revenge or intimidation in the southern United States.

nights (nīts) *adv.* At night: *He works nights.* [Middle English *nightes,* Old English *nihtes,* adverbial genitive of *niht,* NIGHT.]

night-scent·ed stock (nīt′sĕn′tĭd). A plant, **evening stock** *(see).*

night school. A school that holds classes in the evening.

night·shade (nīt′shād′) *n.* Any of several plants of the genus *Solanum,* many of them having a poisonous juice; especially, the **deadly nightshade** and the **bittersweet** *(both of which see).* See **belladonna.** [Middle English *nighteschede,* Old English *nihtscada* : probably NIGHT + SHADE (since it was used in folk medicine as a soporific).]

night·shirt (nīt′shûrt′) *n.* A long shirt worn as nightclothes.

night soil. Human excrement collected for use as fertilizer.

night·spot (nīt′spŏt′) *n. Informal.* A night club.

night·stick (nīt′stĭk′) *n.* A club carried by a policeman.

night table. A small table or stand placed at a bedside.

night terror. A sudden awakening with terror, dread, and alarm, usually occurring in children.

night·tide (nīt′tīd′) *n. Chiefly Poetic.* Nighttime.

night·time (nīt′tīm′) *n.* The time between sunset and sunrise.

night·walk·er (nīt′wô′kər) *n.* **1.** One who walks the streets at night. **2.** An earthworm, the **night crawler** *(see).*

night watch. **1.** A guard or watch kept during the night, as on a ship or encampment. **2.** A person who keeps watch at night. **3.** One of the periods of a watch kept at night.

night watchman. One who acts as guard during the night.

night·y (nī′tē) *n., pl.* **-ies.** *Informal.* A nightgown.

ni·gres·cence (nī-grĕs′əns) *n.* **1.** The process of becoming black or dark. **2.** Blackness or darkness of hair, eyes, or skin. [From adjective *nigrescent,* from Latin *nigrescens,* from *nigrescere,* to become black, from *niger,* black. See **niger** in Appendix.*] —**ni·gres′cent** *adj.*

nig·ri·fy (nĭg′rə-fī′) *tr.v.* **-fied, -fying, -fies.** To make black; blacken. [Late Latin *nigrificāre* : *niger,* black (see **niger** in Appendix*) + *facere,* to make (see **dhē-**[1] in Appendix*).]

nig·ri·tude (nĭg′rə-tōōd′, -tyōōd′) *n.* Blackness. [Late Latin *nigritūdō,* from *niger,* black. See **niger** in Appendix.*]

ni·gro·sin blue (nī′grə-sĭn). Grayish purplish blue. See **color.** [From NIGROSINE.]

ni·gro·sine (nī′grə-sēn′, -sĭn) *n.* Any of a class of dyes, varying from blue to black, used in the manufacture of inks and for dyeing wood and textiles. [Latin *niger,* black (see **niger** in Appendix*) + -OS(E) + -INE.]

nigrosin violet. Dark purple. See **color.** [From NIGROSINE.]

ni·hil (nī′hĭl, nĭ′hĭl) *n.* **1.** Nothing. **2.** A thing of no value. [Latin, shortened from *nihilum,* nothing. See **ne** in Appendix.*]

ni·hil·ism (nī′əl-ĭz′əm, nĭ′hĭl-, nē′-) *n.* **1.** *Metaphysics.* A doctrine that nothing exists, is knowable, or can be communicated. **2.** *Ethics.* Rejection of all distinctions in moral value, constituting a willingness to refute all previous theories of morality. **3.** The belief that destruction of existing political or social institutions is necessary to ensure future improvement; extreme radicalism. **4.** A doctrine among the Russian intelligentsia of the 1860's and 1870's, denying all authority in favor of individualism and advocating terrorism. [From Latin *nihil,* nothing. See **ne** in Appendix.*] —**ni′hil·ist** *n.* —**ni′hil·is′tic** *adj.*

ni·hil·i·ty (nī-hĭl′ə-tē, nĭ-) *n.* Nonexistence; nothingness.

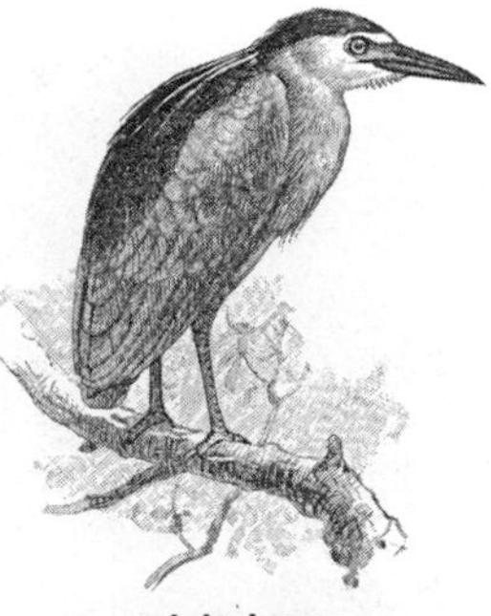

night heron
Nycticorax nycticorax
Black-crowned
night heron

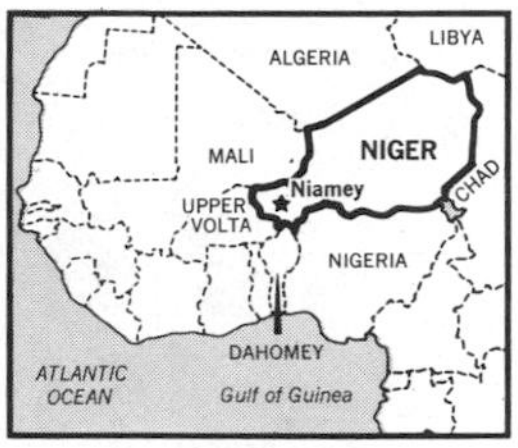

Niger

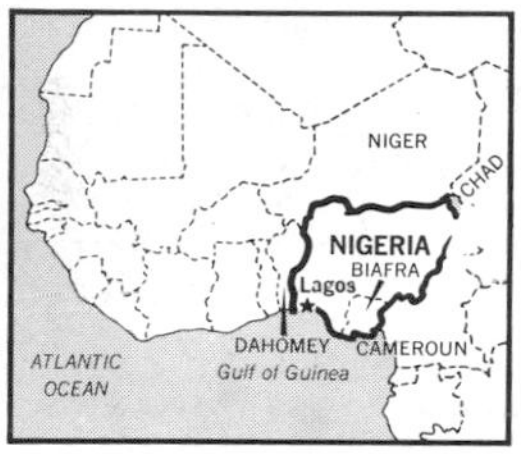

Nigeria

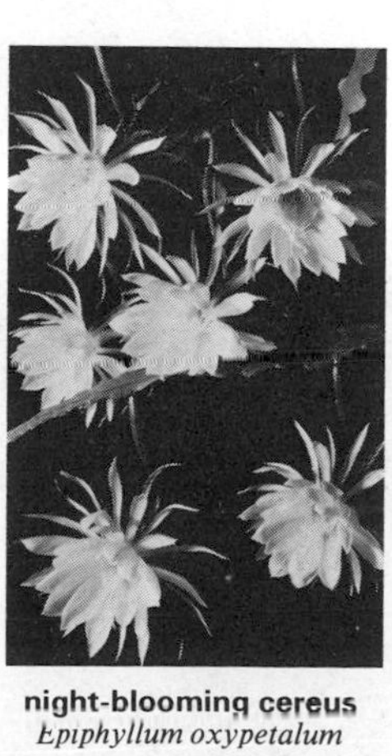

night-blooming cereus
Epiphyllum oxypetalum

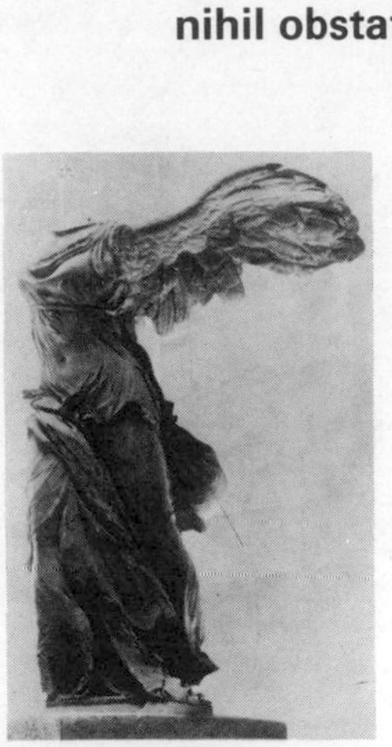

Nike
Second-century B.C.
Greek statue,
"Nike of Samothrace"

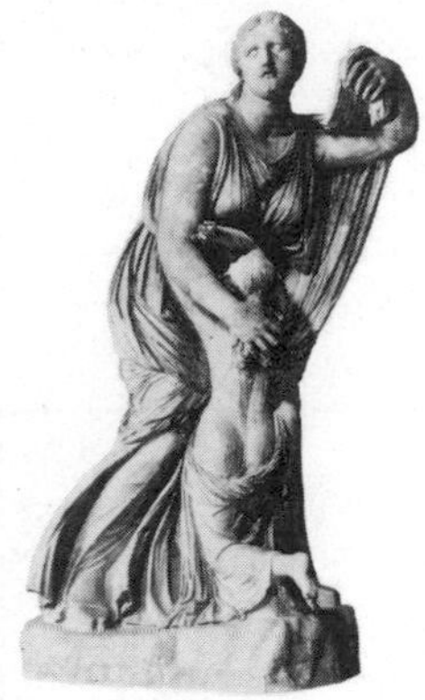

Niobe
Roman copy of a Greek statue
of Niobe with a daughter

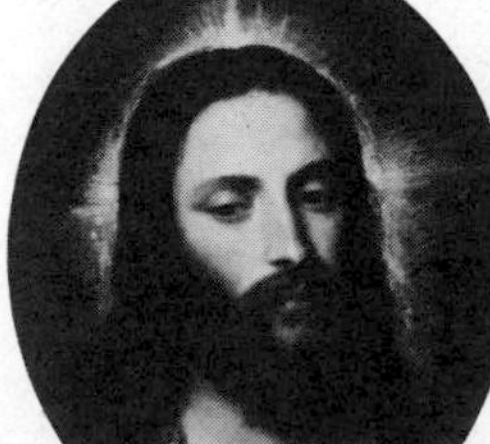

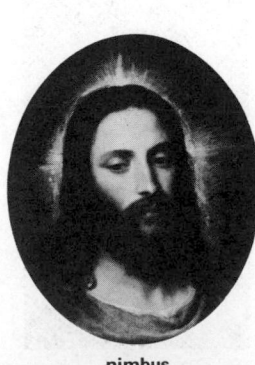

nimbus
Nimbus glowing around
the head of Christ
in a painting by Titian

[French *nihilité*, from Old French, from Medieval Latin *nihilitās*, from *nihil*, nothing. See **ne** in Appendix.*]

ni·hil ob·stat (nī′hĭl ŏb′stăt′, nī′hĭl). **1.** An attestation by a Roman Catholic censor that a book contains nothing damaging to faith or morals. **2.** Official approval, especially of an artistic work. [Latin, "nothing hinders."]

Ni·hon (nē′hŏn′). The official Japanese name for **Japan**. [Japanese, "Land of the Rising Sun" : *ni*, the sun, from Ancient Chinese *ńiet* (unattested) + Japanese *hon*, source, origin. See also **Japan, Nippon.**]

Ni·i·ga·ta (nē′ē-gä′tä). A city and seaport on the western coast of Honshu, Japan. Population, 345,000.

Ni·jin·sky (nə-jĭn′skē, -zhĭn′skē), **Vaslav.** 1890–1950. Russian ballet dancer and choreographer.

Nij·me·gen (nī′mā′gən). A city and port on the Waal River in the Netherlands. Population, 130,000.

Ni·ke (nī′kē). The Greek goddess of victory. [Greek. See **nikē** in Appendix.*]

Nik·ko (nēk′kō). A resort town and center for both Shinto and Buddhist pilgrims in central Honshu, Japan. Population, 33,000. [Japanese *Nikkō*, "sunlight" : *ni-*, *nichi*, the sun, from Ancient Chinese *ńiet* (unattested) + *kō*, light, from Ancient Chinese *kwâng* (unattested).]

Nikko fir. An evergreen tree, *Abies homolepis*, native to Japan, having needles about one inch long, and erect, purplish cones.

Ni·ko·la·ev (nĭk′ə-lä′yəf). Also **Ni·ko·la·yev.** Formerly, Vernoleninsk. A port in the Ukraine, at the mouth of the Bug River, 70 miles northeast of Odessa. Population, 280,000.

nil (nĭl) *n.* Nothing; naught. [Latin, contraction of NIHIL.]

Nile (nīl). A river in eastern Africa, the longest on the continent (3,405 miles). It emerges from Lake Victoria as the Victoria Nile and then from Lake Albert as the Albert Nile, continuing to Sudan as the Bahr el Jebel as far as Lake No and as the White Nile to Khartoum. It is joined by the Blue Nile from western Ethiopia, continuing as the Nile proper to its delta on the Mediterranean. [Latin *Nīlus*, from Greek *Neilos*, probably from Egyptian *nwy*, "water," river.]

Nile blue. Light bluish green. See **color.**

Nile green. Moderate yellow green to vivid pale green. See **color.**

nill (nĭl) *v.* **nilled, nilling, nills.** *Obsolete.* —*tr.* Not to will; not to wish. —*intr.* To be unwilling. [Middle English *nilen*, Old English *nyllan* : *ne*, not (see **ne** in Appendix*) + *wyllan*, to wish (see **wel-**² in Appendix*).]

Ni·lo-Ham·ite (nī′lō-hăm′īt′) *n.* One of a group of Negroid peoples of eastern Africa. [NILO(TIC) + HAMITE.]

Ni·lo-Ham·it·ic (nī′lō-hă-mĭt′ĭk). See **Chari-Nile.**

Ni·lo-Sa·har·an (nī′lō-sə-hâr′ən) *n.* A large language family of Africa, found from Chad and the Sudan down to Kenya and Tanzania. —**Ni′lo-Sa·har′an** *adj.*

Ni·lot·ic (nī-lŏt′ĭk) *adj.* **1.** Belonging to the Nile or the Nile Valley. **2.** Pertaining to or characteristic of a Negroid group of peoples in eastern Africa. [Latin *Nīlōticus*, from Greek *Neilōtikos*, from *Neilos*, the NILE.]

nim (nĭm) *v.* **nimmed, nimming, nims.** *Archaic.* —*tr.* **1.** To take. **2.** To steal; filch; pilfer. —*intr.* To steal. [Middle English *nimen*, Old English *niman*. See **nem-**² in Appendix.*]

nim·ble (nĭm′bəl) *adj.* **-bler, -blest.** **1.** Quick and agile in movement or action; deft: *nimble fingers.* **2. a.** Quick and deft at devising; cleverly alert; acute: *"Like a nimble dialectician, the political novelist must be able to handle several ideas at once"* (Irving Howe). **b.** Cleverly contrived: *a nimble trick.* —See Synonyms at **dexterous.** [Middle English *nemel*, *nym(b)yl*, agile, Old English *næmel*, quick to seize or understand, quick-witted, and *numol*, seizing. See **nem-**² in Appendix.*] —**nim′ble·ness** *n.* —**nim′bly** *adv.*

Synonyms: *nimble, agile, quick, brisk, facile, spry, sprightly, chipper. Nimble* is applied to both mental capacity (*nimble wit*) and physical ability; in each case it indicates lightness, speed, and adroitness. *Agile* primarily applies to physical dexterity. *Quick*, in this context applicable to both physical and mental capacity, connotes readiness born more of alertness than of innate ability. *Brisk* may indicate either animated physical movement or, applied to nouns that do not themselves have the sense of movement, that which is conducive to such activity: *a brisk climate. Facile*, used in describing physical and mental activity and speech, befits ease bordering on effortlessness; sometimes it has the disparaging implications of superficiality, cursoriness, or glibness. *Spry* usually pertains to physical alacrity in elderly persons. *Sprightly* and *chipper* are said of one showing animation of spirit.

nim·bo·stra·tus (nĭm′bō-strā′təs, -străt′əs) *n. Abbr.* **Ns** A low, gray cloud, often dark, that precipitates rain, snow, or sleet. Formerly called "nimbus." [From NIMB(US) + STRATUS.]

nim·bus (nĭm′bəs) *n., pl.* **-bi** (bī′) or **-buses.** **1.** *Classical Iconography.* A cloudy luminescence enveloping a deity when on earth. **2.** *Christian Iconography.* Any of various devices symbolizing sanctity, usually a radiance or a bright circle, appearing behind or above the heads of saints and of the Deity. **3.** A favorable or splendid aura about someone or something. **4.** Formerly, a rain cloud, **nimbostratus** *(see).* [Latin *nimbus*, heavy rain, rain cloud. See **nebh-** in Appendix.*]

Nîmes (nēm). An industrial and resort city of southeastern France, noted for its Roman arena and other ruins. Population, 100,000.

ni·mi·e·ty (nĭ-mī′ə-tē) *n.* Excess; redundancy. [Late Latin *nimietās*, from Latin *nimius*, excessive, from *nimis*, excessively. See **ne** in Appendix.*]

nim·i·ny-pim·i·ny (nĭm′ə-nē-pĭm′ə-nē) *adj.* Affectedly delicate or refined; mincing. [Perhaps variant of NAMBY-PAMBY.]

Nim·itz (nĭm′ĭts), **Chester William.** 1885–1966. American admiral of the fleet; commander of Pacific fleet in World War II.

Nim·rod¹ (nĭm′rŏd′). A mighty hunter and king; Noah's great-grandson. Genesis 10:8–10.

Nim·rod² (nĭm′rŏd′) *n.* Also **nim·rod.** A hunter.

Nim·rud (nĭm-ro͝od′). The site of the ruins of **Kalakh** *(see).*

Ni·ña (nē′nyə, nē′nə). One of the three ships of Columbus on his first voyage to the New World.

nin·com·poop (nĭn′kəm-po͞op′, nĭng′-) *n.* A fool; simpleton; blockhead; dolt. [Origin unknown.] —**nin′com·poop′er·y** *n.*

nine (nīn) *n.* **1.** The cardinal number written 9 or in Roman numerals IX. See **number.** **2. a.** A playing card marked with nine pips. **b.** Any set of nine persons or things; specifically, a baseball team. —**The Nine.** The nine Muses. —**(up) to the nines.** To the highest degree; to perfection: *"in walked Marcel Proust, dressed to the nines"* (Frank Budgen). [Middle English *ni(gh)en*, *nyne*, Old English *nigon*. See **newn** in Appendix.*] —**nine** *adj.* & *pron.*

nine·bark (nīn′bärk′) *n.* A shrub, *Physocarpus opulifolius*, of eastern North America, having peeling or shredding bark and clusters of small, white flowers. Also called "opulaster." [From the many layers in its bark.]

nine days' wonder. Something that creates brief sensation.

nine·fold (nīn′fōld′) *adj.* **1.** Having nine parts. **2.** Nine times as many or as much. —**nine′fold′** *adv.*

nine iron. *Golf.* An iron-headed club with a face slanted at a greater angle than any other iron. Also called "niblick."

nine·pin (nīn′pĭn′) *n.* **1.** A wooden pin used in the game of ninepins. **2.** *Plural.* A bowling game in which nine wooden pins are the target. Used with a singular verb.

nine·teen (nīn′tēn′) *n.* The cardinal number written 19 or in Roman numerals XIX. See **number.** [Middle English *nynetene*, Old English *nigontīne* : *nigon*, NINE + -TEEN.] —**nine′teen′** *adj.* & *pron.*

nine·teenth (nīn′tēnth′) *n.* **1.** The ordinal number nineteen in a series. Also written 19th. **2.** One of nineteen equal parts. See **number.** —**nine′teenth′** *adj.* & *adv.*

nineteenth hole. *Slang.* A place, such as the locker room or club bar, where golfers gather after a game for relaxation.

nine·ti·eth (nīn′tē-ĭth) *n.* **1.** The ordinal number ninety in a series. Also written 90th. **2.** One of ninety equal parts. See **number.** —**nine′ti·eth** *adj.* & *adv.*

nine·ty (nīn′tē) *n., pl.* **-ties.** The cardinal number written 90 or in Roman numerals XC or LXXXX. See **number.** [Middle English *nynety*, from Old English *nigontig* : *nigon*, NINE + *-tig*, -TY (ten).] —**nine′ty** *adj.* & *pron.*

nine·ty-day wonder (nīn′tē-dā′). *Slang.* An officer commissioned in the armed services after a short training period.

Nin·e·veh (nĭn′ə-və). A capital of Assyria, the ruins of which are located on the Tigris River, opposite Mosul.

Ning·po (nĭng′pō′). A city in Chekiang Province, China, about 90 miles southeast of Hangchow. Population, 280,000.

Ning·sia (nĭng′shyä′). **1.** A former province of China, now part of Inner Mongolia. **2.** The capital of this province, called **Yinchwan** since 1945.

Ning·sia Hui Autonomous Region (nĭng′shyä′wā′). A territory of China, 30,039 square miles in area, situated in the north along the western course of the Yellow (Huang) River and bounded on the north by Inner Mongolia. Population, 1,810,000.

nin·ny (nĭn′ē) *n., pl.* **-nies.** A fool; simpleton. [From INNOCENT (simple, foolish), on analogy with *Ninny*, familiar form for the given name *Innocent.*]

ni·non (nē′nŏn′; *French* nē-nôN′) *n.* A sheer fabric of silk, rayon, or nylon made in a variety of tight, smooth weaves or open lacy patterns. [Probably from French *Ninon*, a nickname for *Anne*, ANNE.]

ninth (nīnth) *n.* **1.** The ordinal number nine in a series. Also written 9th. **2.** One of nine equal parts. See **number.** **3.** *Music.* **a.** A harmonic or melodic interval of an octave and a second. **b.** The tone at the upper limit of such an interval. **c.** A chord consisting of a root with its third, seventh, and ninth. [Middle English *nynthe*, Old English *nigotha*, from *nigon*, NINE.] —**ninth** *adj.* & *adv.*

Ni·nus (nī′nəs). The legendary founder of Nineveh and husband of Semiramis.

Ni·o·be (nī′ō-bē). *Greek Mythology.* The daughter of Tantalus; turned to stone while bewailing the loss of her children.

ni·o·bi·um (nī-ō′bē-əm) *n. Symbol* **Nb** A silvery, soft, ductile, metallic element. It occurs chiefly in columbite-tantalite, and is used in steel alloys, arc welding, and superconductivity research. Atomic number 41, atomic weight 92.906, melting point 2,468°C, boiling point 4,927°C, specific gravity 8.57, valences 2, 3, 5. Formerly called "columbium." See **element.** [New Latin, after NIOBE (because obtained from tantalite, which is named after Tantalus, father of Niobe).]

Ni·o·brar·a River (nī′ə-brâr′ə). A river rising in eastern Wyoming and flowing 431 miles east to the Missouri River in northeastern Nebraska.

nip¹ (nĭp) *v.* **nipped, nipping, nips.** —*tr.* **1. a.** To catch, pinch, or press between two surfaces or points, such as the fingers. **b.** To give a small, sharp bite to. Used of animals. **2.** To remove or sever by pinching, biting, or snipping. Usually used with *off.* **3.** To sting, as cold. **4.** To check in growth or cut off the development of: *Strong measures were taken to nip the conspiracy.* **5.** *Slang.* **a.** To snatch up hastily. **b.** To steal. —*intr. British Slang.* To go or move quickly and nimbly. Used with *along, away, off, out,* or *up.* —*n.* **1.** The act of catching, pressing, or pinching between two surfaces; a bite or pinch. **2. a.** A pinch or snip that cuts off or removes a part: *He gave a nip to each corner.* **b.** The small piece removed in this manner. **3.** A small bit of anything: *out for a nip of air.* **4.** *Western Canadian.* A hamburger. **5. a.** A sharp, stinging quality, as of frosty air. **b.** Severely sharp cold or frost. **6.** A cutting or stinging remark; a taunt or bitter sarcasm. **7.** A pungent or sharp flavor; tang: *the nip of Mexican cooking.* **—nip and tuck.** Very close; closely contested; neck and neck. [Middle English *nippen, nipen,* probably from Old Norse *hnippa.* See **ken-**[2] in Appendix.*]

nip[2] (nĭp) *n.* A small dose or sip of liquor: *a nip from the bottle.* *—v.* **nipped, nipping, nips.** *—tr.* To drink (alcoholic liquor) in small doses: *He had been nipping brandy.* *—intr.* To take a nip or nips of alcoholic liquor: *He nips all day.* [Short for *nipperkin,* probably from Dutch *nippertje,* a dram, from *nippen,* to sip. See **ken-**[2] in Appendix.*] **—nip′per** *n.*

Nip (nĭp) *n. Slang.* A Japanese person. An offensive term used derogatorily. [Short for *Nipponese,* from NIPPON.] **—Nip** *adj.*

ni·pa (nē′pə) *n.* **1.** A large palm, *Nipa frutescens,* of the Philippines and Australia, having long leaves much used for thatching. Also called "nipa palm." **2.** An alcoholic beverage made from the sap of this palm. [New Latin, from Malay *nipah.*]

Nip·i·gon, Lake (nĭp′ĭ-gŏn′). A lake, 1,870 square miles in area, in southwestern Ontario, Canada, north of Lake Superior.

Nip·is·sing, Lake (nĭp′ə-sĭng). A lake, 330 square miles in area, in southeastern Ontario, Canada, east of Lake Huron.

nip·per (nĭp′ər) *n.* **1.** One that nips. **2.** *Often plural.* Any of various devices for squeezing or snipping, such as pliers or pincers. **3. a.** The large claw of a crustacean. **b.** An incisor tooth of a horse. **c.** Any of various crabs, shrimps, and prawns. **4.** *Plural.* Handcuffs. **5.** *Chiefly British.* A boy.

nip·ping (nĭp′ĭng) *adj.* **1.** Sharp and biting, as the cold. **2.** Sarcastic. **—nip′ping·ly** *adv.*

nip·ple (nĭp′əl) *n.* **1.** The small conical protuberance near the center of the mammary gland containing the outlets of the milk ducts. **2. a.** The rubber cap on a nursing bottle. **b.** A pacifier for an infant. **3.** Any of various devices resembling or functioning like a nipple: **a.** A regulated opening for discharging a liquid, as in a small stopcock. **b.** A pipe coupling threaded on both ends. **c.** A short extension of pipe to which a nozzle can be attached. **4.** Any natural or geographic body or projection resembling a nipple, such as a mountain crest. [From earlier *neble, nible,* diminutives of *neb, nib,* a point, beak, NEB.]

nip·ple·wort (nĭp′əl-wûrt′) *n.* A plant, *Lapsana communis,* having a milky juice and small, yellow flower heads. [Formerly used in folk medicine to cure breast tumors.]

Nip·pon (nĭ-pŏn′; *Japanese* nēp′pōn′). A Japanese name for **Japan.** [Short for *Nippon-koku,* "land of the origin of the sun" : *ni, nichi,* the sun + *pon* (also *hon*), origin + *koku,* land; respectively from Ancient Chinese *ńiet puən kuok* (now *jih*[4] *pen*[3] *kuo*[2]).] **—Nip′pon·ese′** (nĭp′ə-nēz′, -nēs′) *adj. & n.*

nip·py (nĭp′ē) *adj.* **-pier, -piest. 1.** Sharp or biting; nipping. **2.** *British Informal.* Active; vigorous; sharp; quick. **—nip′pi·ly** *adv.* **—nip′pi·ness** *n.*

nir·va·na (nîr-vä′nə, nər-) *n.* **1.** *Often capital* **N. a.** *Buddhism.* The state of absolute blessedness, characterized by release from the cycle of reincarnations and attained through the extinction of the self. **b.** *Hinduism.* A similar state in which reunion with Brahma is attained through the suppression of individual existence. **2.** Freedom from the pain and care of the external world; bliss. [Sanskrit *nirvāna,* "extinction (of individual existence)," from *nirvā,* to be extinguished, be blown out : *nir-, nis-*†, out + *vāti,* he blows (see **wē** in Appendix*).]

Niš, Nish (nĭsh). Former name, **Nis·sa** (nĭs′ä). A city in southern Serbia, Yugoslavia. Population, 85,000.

Ni·san (nĭs′ən; *Hebrew* nē-sän′) *n.* Also **Nis·san.** In the Hebrew calendar, the seventh month of the civil year and the first of the religious year. At one time called "Abib." See **calendar.** [Hebrew *Nīsān,* from Akkadian *Nissanu,* "the first month."]

Ni·sei (nē-sā′, nē′sā′) *n., pl.* **Nisei** or **-seis.** One born in America of immigrant Japanese parents. Compare **Issei, Kibei, Sansei.** [Japanese, "second generation" : *ni,* two, second + *sei,* generation; respectively from Ancient Chinese *ńźi śyäi.*]

Ni·shi·no·mi·ya (nē′shē-nō′mē-yä′). A city and sake-brewing center on southwestern Honshu, Japan. Population, 210,000.

ni·si (nī′sī′) *adj. Law.* Unless. Used as a modifier after such words as *decree, order,* or *rule* to indicate that it shall take effect at a specified date unless cause is shown for modification or nullification. [Latin *nisi,* unless, if not : *ni-,* from *ne-,* not (see **ne** in Appendix*) + *sī,* if (see **swo-** in Appendix*).]

ni·si pri·us (nī′sī′ prī′əs). *Law.* **1.** The court in which a civil action is tried before a judge and jury, as distinguished from an appellate court: *court of nisi prius.* **2.** The trial of a civil action before such a court: *cause of nisi prius.* [Middle English, from Medieval Latin, "unless before" (originally the first two words of a writ ordering a sheriff to provide a jury at the Westminster court on a fixed day, *unless* the judges of assize come to the county *before* this day).]

Nis·sen hut (nĭs′ən). A prefabricated building of corrugated steel in the shape of half a cylinder, used as a military shelter. [Designed by Lieut. Col. Peter N. Nissen (1871–1930), British mining engineer.]

ni·sus (nī′səs) *n., pl.* **nisus.** Effort; endeavor; exertion; impulse. [Latin *nīsus,* from the past participle of *nītī,* to strive, endeavor. See **kneigwh-** in Appendix.*]

nit (nĭt) *n.* **1.** The egg of a parasitic insect, such as that of a louse. **2.** The young insect. [Middle English *nite,* Old English *hnitu,* louse egg. See **knid-** in Appendix.*] **—nit′ty** *adj.*

ni·ter (nī′tər) *n.* Also *chiefly British* **ni·tre.** A white, gray, or colorless mineral of potassium nitrate, KNO_3, used in making gunpowder. Also called "saltpeter." [Middle English *nitre,* from Old French, from Latin *nitrum,* from Greek *nitron,* natron. See **nitron** in Appendix.*]

Ni·te·rói (nē′tĕ-roi′). Former name, **Nic·the·roy** (nē′tĕ-roi′). The capital of Rio de Janeiro State, Brazil, situated on Guanabara Bay opposite Rio de Janeiro. Population, 245,000.

nit-pick (nĭt′pĭk′) *intr.v.* **-picked, -picking, -picks.** *Informal.* To be concerned with insignificant details.

ni·trate (nī′trāt′, -trĭt) *n.* **1.** The radical NO_3^- or any compound containing it, as a salt or ester of nitric acid. **2.** Fertilizer consisting of sodium nitrate or potassium nitrate. *—tr.v.* **nitrated, -trating, -trates.** To treat with nitric acid or with a nitrate, usually to change an organic compound into a nitrate. [French : NITR(O)- + -ATE.] **—ni·tra′tion** (nī-trā′shən) *n.*

ni·tric (nī′trĭk) *adj.* Of, derived from, or containing nitrogen, especially in a valence state higher than that in a comparable nitrous compound. [French *nitrique* : NITR(O)- + -IC.]

nitric acid. A transparent, colorless to yellowish, fuming, corrosive liquid, HNO_3, a highly reactive oxidizing agent, used in the production of fertilizers, explosives, and rocket fuels, and in a wide variety of industrial metallurgical processes. Formerly called "aqua fortis."

nitric oxide. A colorless, poisonous gas, NO, produced as an intermediate during the manufacture of nitric acid from ammonia or atmospheric nitrogen.

ni·tride (nī′trīd′) *n.* A compound containing nitrogen with another, more electropositive element. [NITR(O)- + -IDE.]

ni·trid·ing (nī′trī′dĭng) *n. Metallurgy.* The casehardening of a ferrous alloy, such as steel, by heating it in ammonia.

ni·tri·fy (nī′trə-fī′) *tr.v.* **-fied, -fying, -fies. 1.** To oxidize into nitric acid, nitrous acid, or any nitrate or nitrite, as by the action of nitrobacteria. **2.** To treat or combine with nitrogen or compounds containing nitrogen. [French *nitrifier* : NITR(O)- + -FY.] **—ni′tri·fi·ca′tion** *n.* **—ni′tri·fi′er** *n.*

ni·trile (nī′trəl) *n.* Also **ni·tril.** Any compound containing trivalent nitrogen, N^{-3}, in a cyanogen group. [NITR(O)- + -ILE.]

ni·trite (nī′trīt′) *n.* Any salt or ester of nitrous acid. [NITR(O)- + -ITE.]

nitro–, nitr–. Indicates a compound containing the univalent group NO_2; for example, **nitrobenzene** ($C_6H_5NO_2$), **nitride.** [New Latin, from Latin *nitrum,* natron, from Greek *nitron.* See **nitron** in Appendix.*]

ni·tro·bac·te·ri·a (nī′trō-băk-tîr′ē-ə) *pl.n.* Soil bacteria that produce nitrification.

ni·tro·ben·zene (nī′trō-bĕn′zēn′, -bĕn-zēn′) *n.* A poisonous organic compound, $C_6H_5NO_2$, either bright-yellow crystals or an oily liquid, having the odor of almonds, and used in the manufacture of aniline, insulating compounds, and polishes.

ni·tro·cel·lu·lose (nī′trō-sĕl′yə-lōs′) *n.* A pulpy or cottonlike polymer derived from cellulose treated with sulfuric and nitric acids, and used in the manufacture of explosives, collodion, plastics, and solid monopropellants. Also called "cellulose nitrate," "guncotton."

ni·tro·chlo·ro·form (nī′trō-klôr′ə-fôrm′, -klōr′ə-fôrm′) *n.* A poison gas, **chloropicrin** *(see).*

ni·tro·gen (nī′trə-jən) *n. Symbol* **N** A nonmetallic element constituting nearly four-fifths of the air by volume, occurring as a colorless, odorless, almost inert diatomic gas, N_2, in various minerals and in all proteins. It is used in a wide variety of important manufactures, including ammonia, nitric acid, TNT, and fertilizers. Atomic number 7, atomic weight 14.0067, melting point −209.86°C, boiling point −195°C, valence 3, 5. See **element.** [French *nitrogène* : NITR(O)- + -GEN.] **—ni·trog′e·nous** (nī-trŏj′ə-nəs) *adj.*

nitrogen balance. The difference between the amounts of nitrogen taken into and lost by the body or the soil.

nitrogen cycle. 1. The continuous cyclic progression of chemical reactions in which atmospheric nitrogen is compounded, dissolved in rain, deposited in the soil, assimilated and metabolized by bacteria and plants, and returned to the atmosphere by organic decomposition. **2. Carbon-nitrogen cycle** *(see).*

nitrogen dioxide. A mildly poisonous brown gas, NO_2, often found in smog and automobile exhaust fumes, and synthesized for use as a nitrating agent, catalyst, and oxidizing agent.

nitrogen fixation. 1. The conversion of atmospheric nitrogen into nitrogenous compounds by natural agencies or by various industrial processes. **2.** The conversion by certain algae and soil bacteria of inorganic nitrogen compounds into organic compounds assimilable by plants. **—ni′tro·gen-fix′ing** *adj.*

ni·trog·en·ize (nī-trŏj′ə-nīz′, nī′trə-jə-nīz′) *tr.v.* **-izing, -izes, -ized.** To combine or treat with nitrogen.

ni·tro·glyc·er·in (nī′trō-glĭs′ər-ĭn) *n.* Also **ni·tro·glyc·er·ine.** A thick, pale-yellow liquid, $CH_2NO_3CHNO_3CH_2NO_3$, explosive on concussion or exposure to sudden heat. It is used in the production of dynamite and blasting gelatin, and as a vasodilator in medicine. Also called "trinitroglycerin."

ni·tro·hy·dro·chlo·ric acid (nī′trō-hī′drə-klôr′ĭk, -klōr′ĭk). A mixture of acids, **aqua regia** *(see).*

ni·tro·meth·ane (nī′trō-mĕth′ān′) *n.* An oily, colorless liquid, CH_3NO_2, used in making dyes and resins, in organic synthesis, and as a rocket propellant.

ni·tro·par·af·fin (nī′trō-păr′ə-fĭn) *n.* Any of a group of organic compounds formed by replacing one or more of the hydrogen atoms of a paraffin hydrocarbon with the nitro group, NO_2^-, as in nitromethane, CH_3NO_2.

ni·tro·starch (nī′trō-stärch′) *n.* A highly explosive orange-colored powder, $C_{12}H_{12}(NO_2)_8O_{10}$, derived from starch, and used for demolition.

nipper

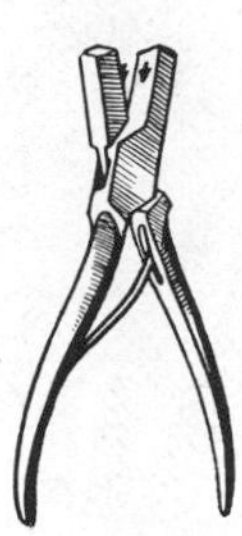

ticket

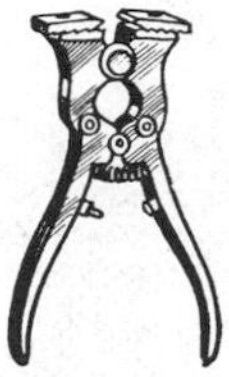

tile

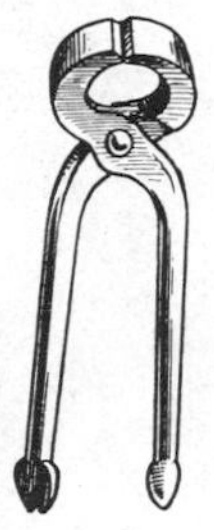

combination end

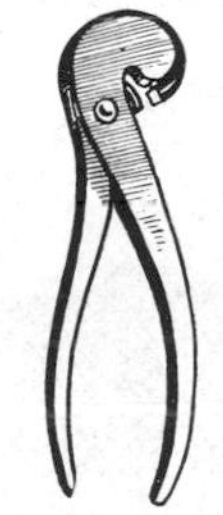

wire

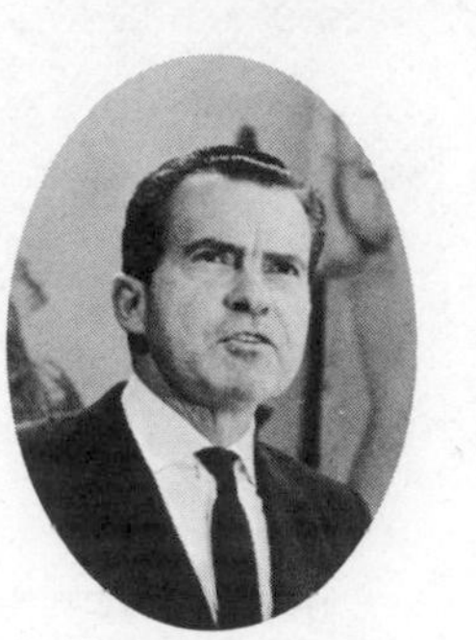

Richard M. Nixon

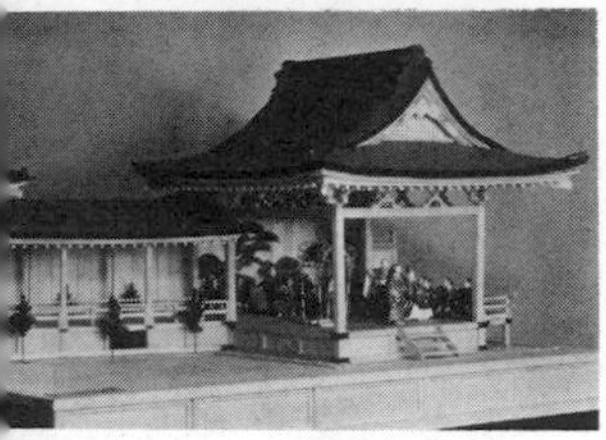

no[3]
Model of a no stage

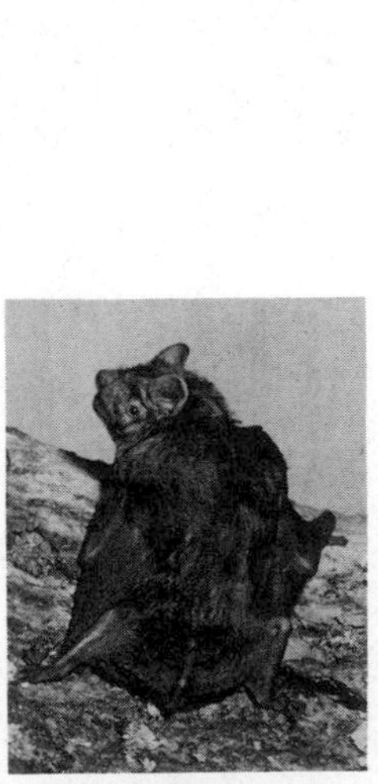

noctule
Nyctalus noctula

ni·trous (nī′trəs) *adj.* Of, derived from, or containing nitrogen, especially in a valence state lower than that in a comparable nitric compound. [New Latin *nitrosus,* from Latin *nitrōsus,* full of natron, from *nitrum,* natron, from Greek *nitron.* See **nitron** in Appendix.*]

nitrous acid. An unstable inorganic acid, HNO_2, existing in solution only.

nitrous oxide. A colorless, sweet inorganic gas, N_2O, used as a mild anesthetic. Also called "laughing gas."

nits-and-lice (nĭts′ənd-līs′) *n.* Used with a singular or plural verb. A plant, *Hypericum drummondii,* of the central United States, having narrow leaves and yellow flowers.

nit·ty-grit·ty (nĭt′ē-grĭt′ē) *n. Slang.* The hard core of a matter; the harsh truth: *Let's get down to the nitty-gritty.* [Probably based on a reduplication of *grit* in various connotations.]

nit·wit (nĭt′wĭt′) *n. Informal.* A stupid or silly person. [Originally slang : perhaps NIT + WIT.]

Ni·u·e (nē-ōō′ā). An island dependency of New Zealand, 100 square miles in area, in the south-central Pacific, east of Tonga. Population, 5,000. Also called "Savage Island."

ni·val (nī′vəl) *adj.* Of or growing in or under snow. [Latin *nivālis,* from *nix* (stem *niv-*), snow. See **sneigwh-** in Appendix.*]

niv·e·ous (nĭv′ē-əs) *adj.* Like snow; snowy. [Latin *niveus,* from *nix* (stem *niv-*), snow. See **sneigwh-** in Appendix.*]

Ni·ver·nais (nē′vĕr-nĕ′). A former province of central France.

nix[1] (nĭks) *n. Germanic Mythology.* A water sprite, usually in human form or half-human and half-fish. [German *Nix,* from Middle High German *nickes,* from Old High German *nihhus.* See **neigw-** in Appendix.*]

nix[2] (nĭks) *n. Slang.* Nothing. —*adv. Slang.* No. —*interj. Slang.* Stop! Watch out! —*tr.v.* **nixed, nixing, nixes.** *Slang.* To forbid; veto; deny. [German, from *nichts,* nothing, from Middle High German *nihtes, nihtes niht,* "(nothing) of nothing," from genitive of *niht,* nothing, from Old High German *niwiht,* nothing : *ni, ne,* no (see **ne** in Appendix*) + *wiht,* thing, man (see **wekti-** in Appendix*).]

nix·ie (nĭk′sē) *n., pl.* **-ies.** Also **nix·y.** *Slang.* A misaddressed piece of mail. [From NIX (no).]

Nix·on (nĭk′sən), **Richard Milhous.** Born 1913. Thirty-seventh President of the United States (from 1969).

ni·zam (nĭ-zäm′, -zăm′, nī-) *n., pl.* **nizam.** A Turkish soldier. [Turkish, from Arabic *niẓām,* government, NIZAM.]

Ni·zam (nĭ-zäm′, -zăm′, nī-) *n.* The title of the former rulers of Hyderabad, India. [Hindi *nizām(-al-mulk),* "governor (of the empire)," from Arabic *niẓām,* government.]

Nizh·ni Nov·go·rod. The former name for **Gorkiy.**

Nizh·ni Ta·gil (nĭzh′nē tə-gĭl′). A city of the Soviet Union, in the east-central Ural Mountains. Population, 370,000.

NJ New Jersey (with Zip Code).

N.J. New Jersey.

Nkru·mah (əng-krōō′mə), **Kwame.** Born 1909. Premier of the Gold Coast (1952–60), first president of Ghana (1960–66).

NKVD, N.K.V.D. People's Commissariat for Internal Affairs (Russian *Narodniy Kommisariat Vnutrĕnnikh Dĕl*), a former administrative branch of the Soviet government functioning as a successor organization to the **Cheka** and corresponding in broad outline to the later **KGB** *(both of which see).*

NL, NL., N.L. New Latin.

NLRB, N.L.R.B. National Labor Relations Board.

nm 1. nautical mile. **2.** nuclear magneton.

NM New Mexico (with Zip Code).

n.m. nautical mile.

N.M. New Mexico (unofficial).

N. Mex. New Mexico.

NNE north-northeast.

NNW north-northwest.

no[1] (nō) *adv.* **1.** Not so; opposed to "yes." Used in expressing refusal, denial, or disagreement. **2.** Not at all; not by any degree. Used with the comparative: *no better; no more.* **3.** Not: *whether or no.* —*n., pl.* **noes. 1.** A negative response; a denial or refusal: *The proposal produced only noes.* **2.** A negative vote or voter. [Middle English *no, na,* Old English *nā* : *ne,* no (see **ne** in Appendix*) + *ā,* ever (see **aiw-** in Appendix*).]

no[2] (nō) *adj.* **1.** Not any; not one; not a: *No cookies are left.* **2.** Not at all; not close to being: *He is no child.* [Middle English *no, na,* Old English *nā,* reduced form of *nān,* NONE.]

no[3] (nō) *n., pl.* **no.** Also **noh** *pl.* **noh.** *Often capital* **N.** The classical drama of Japan with music and dance performed in a highly stylized manner by elaborately dressed actors on an almost bare stage. [Japanese *nō,* "talent," "ability," from Chinese *neng*[2].]

No The symbol for the element nobelium.

No, Lake (nō). A lake, about 40 square miles in area, in south-central Sudan, the source of the White Nile.

no., No. 1. north; northern. **2.** number.

no-ac·count (nō′ə-kount′) *adj.* Also **no-count** (nō′kount′). *Regional.* Worthless; good-for-nothing: *a no-account fellow.* —**no′-ac·count′** *n.*

No·a·chi·an (nō-ā′kē-ən) *adj.* Also **No·ach·ic** (-ăk′ĭk, -ā′kĭk), **No·ach·i·cal** (-ăk′ĭ-kəl, -ā′kĭ-kəl). **1.** Of or relating to Noah or his time: *Noachian flood.* **2.** Antiquated or long obsolete.

No·ah (nō′ə). The patriarch chosen by God to build the ark in which he, his family, and many animals were saved from the Flood. Genesis 5–9. [Hebrew *Nōah,* "rest."]

nob[1] (nŏb) *n. Slang.* The head. [Slang variant of KNOB.]

nob[2] (nŏb) *n. Slang.* A person of wealth or social standing. [Origin uncertain.] —**nob′by** *adj.*

nob·ble (nŏb′əl) *tr.v.* **-bled, -bling, -bles.** *British Slang.* **1.** To disable (a racehorse), especially by drugging. **2.** To win over, outdo, or get the better of (a person) by devious means. **3.** To filch or steal. [Origin obscure.] —**nob′bler** *n.*

No·bel (nō-bĕl′), **Alfred Bernhard.** 1833–1896. Swedish chemist and inventor; his will provided for the Nobel Prizes.

no·bel·i·um (nō-bĕl′ē-əm) *n.* Symbol **No** A radioactive transuranium element in the actinide series, artificially produced in trace amounts. Atomic number 102, isotopic masses 252, 253, 254, 255, 256, half-lives 4.5, 95, 75, 180, 8 seconds. See **element.** [Discovered at the *Nobel* Institute at Stockholm.]

Nobel Prize. Any of the prizes awarded annually by the Nobel Foundation for outstanding achievements in the fields of literature, medicine, chemistry, and physics, and for the promotion of world peace.

Nob Hill. A fashionable part of San Francisco, California.

no·bil·i·ar·y (nō-bĭl′ē-ĕr′ē, -bĭl′yər-ē) *adj.* Of or pertaining to the nobility. [French *nobiliaire,* from Latin *nōbilis,* NOBLE.]

no·bil·i·ty (nō-bĭl′ə-tē) *n., pl.* **-ties. 1. a.** The class comprising nobles: *"The old English nobility of office made way for the Norman nobility of faith and landed wealth."* (Winston Churchill). **b.** The state of being a noble. **2.** The state or quality of being exalted in character or being morally noble: *"nobility is to be found less in men's creations than in their aspirations"* (G.G. Coulton). [Middle English *nobilite,* from Old French, from Latin *nōbilitās,* from *nōbilis,* NOBLE.]

no·ble (nō′bəl) *adj.* **-bler, -blest. 1.** Possessing hereditary rank in a political system or social class usually derived directly or indirectly from a feudalistic stage of a country's development. **2. a.** Lofty and exalted in character. **b.** Proceeding from such a character; showing greatness and magnanimity: *a noble deed.* **3.** Grand, stately, and magnificent in appearance: *"a mighty Spanish chestnut, bare now of leaves, but in summer a noble tree"* (Richard Jefferies). **4.** Designating an especially corrosion-resistant metal, such as gold. **5.** *Chemistry.* Inactive or inert. —*n.* **1.** A person of high birth, rank, or title; a nobleman. **2.** A former English gold coin worth six shillings and eight pence, or ten shillings. [Middle English, from Old French, from Latin *nōbilis,* knowable, known, famous, noble. See **gnō-** in Appendix.*] —**no′ble·ness** *n.* —**no′bly** *adv.*

no·ble·man (nō′bəl-mən) *n., pl.* **-men** (-mĭn). A man of noble rank.

no·blesse (nō-blĕs′) *n.* **1.** Noble birth or condition. **2.** The nobility; the aristocracy. [Middle English *noblesce, noblesse,* from Old French *noblesse,* from *noble,* NOBLE.]

no·blesse o·blige (nō-blĕs′ ō-blēzh′). Benevolent and honorable behavior considered to be the responsibility of persons of high birth or rank. [French, "nobility obligates."]

no·ble·wom·an (nō′bəl-wŏŏm′ən) *n., pl.* **-women** (-wĭm′ĭn). A woman of noble rank.

no·bod·y (nō′bŏd′ē, -bə-dē) *pron.* No person; no one: *Nobody told him what to do.* See Usage note at **no one.** —*n., pl.* **nobodies.** A person of no importance, influence, or social position. [Middle English *no body* : NO (adjective) + BODY.]

no·cent (nō′sənt) *adj. Rare.* **1.** Causing injury; harmful. **2.** Guilty. [Middle English, from Latin *nocēns,* from the present participle of *nocēre,* to harm. See **nek-**[1] in Appendix.*]

nock (nŏk) *n.* **1.** The groove at either end of a bow for holding the bowstring. **2.** The notch in the end of an arrow that fits on the bowstring. —*tr.v.* **nocked, nocking, nocks. 1.** To put a notch in (a bow or arrow). **2.** To fit (an arrow) to a bowstring. [Middle English *nocke, nokke,* from Middle Dutch *nocke.* See **ken-**[5] in Appendix.*]

no-count. *Regional.* Variant of **no-account.**

noc·tam·bu·lism (nŏk-tăm′byə-lĭz′əm) *n.* Also **noc·tam·bu·la·tion** (nŏk-tăm′byə-lā′shən). Sleep walking, **somnambulism** *(see).* [From noctambulation : NOCT(I)- + AMBULATION.] —**noc·tam′bu·list** *n.*

nocti–, noct–. Indicates night; for example, **noctilucent, noctambulism.** [New Latin, from Latin *nox* (stem *noct-*), night. See **nekwt-** in Appendix.*]

noc·ti·lu·ca (nŏk′tə-lōō′kə) *n., pl.* **-cae** (-sē′). Any of various plantlike, bioluminescent marine organisms of the genus *Noctiluca* which, when grouped in large numbers, make the seas phosphorescent. [New Latin, from Latin *noctilūca,* moon, lantern : NOCTI- + *lūcere,* to shine (see **leuk-** in Appendix*).]

noc·ti·lu·cent (nŏk′tə-lōō′sənt) *adj.* Luminous at night. Said especially of certain high clouds. [NOCTI- + LUCENT.]

noc·tu·id (nŏk′chōō-ĭd) *n.* Any night-flying moth of the family Noctuidae, the larvae of which are destructive pests. —*adj.* Of or pertaining to these moths. [New Latin *Noctuidae* (family name) : *Noctua,* generic name, from Latin *noctua,* night owl (see **nekwt-** in Appendix*) + -IDAE.]

noc·tule (nŏk′chōōl′) *n.* Any large, reddish-brown, insectivorous bat of the genus *Nyctalus,* found in Eurasia, Indonesia, and the Philippines. [French, from Italian *nottola,* from Late Latin *noctula,* diminutive of Latin *noctua,* night owl. See **nekwt-** in Appendix.*]

noc·turn (nŏk′tûrn′) *n.* Any of the three canonical divisions of the office of **matins** *(see).* [Middle English *nocturne,* from Old French, from Medieval Latin *nocturna,* from the feminine of Latin *nocturnus,* NOCTURNAL.]

noc·tur·nal (nŏk-tûr′nəl) *adj.* **1.** Of, suitable to, or occurring at night. **2.** *Botany.* Having flowers that open during the night. **3.** *Zoology.* Active by night, as certain animals. [Late Latin *nocturnālis,* from Latin *nocturnus,* of night, at night, from *nox* (stem *noct-*), night. See **nekwt-** in Appendix.*] —**noc′tur·nal′i·ty** (-năl′ə-tē) *n.* —**noc·tur′nal·ly** *adv.*

noc·turne (nŏk′tûrn′) *n.* **1.** A painting of a night scene. **2.** *Music.* A romantic composition intended to embody sentiments appropriate to the evening or night; a pensive melody; reverie. [French, "nocturnal," from Latin *nocturnus,* NOCTURNAL.]

ă pat/ā pay/âr care/ä father/b **bib**/ch **church**/d **deed**/ĕ pet/ē be/f **fife**/g **gag**/h **hat**/hw **which**/ĭ pit/ī pie/îr pier/j **judge**/k **kick**/l **lid,** need**le**/m **mum**/n **no,** sudd**en**/ng **thing**/ŏ pot/ō toe/ô paw, for/oi noise/ou out/ŏŏ took/ōō boot/p **pop**/r **roar**/s **sauce**/sh **ship,** di**sh**/

noc·u·ous (nŏk′yo͞o-əs) *adj. Rare.* Harmful; noxious; poisonous. [Latin *nocuus,* from *nocēre,* to harm. See **nek-¹** in Appendix.*] **—noc′u·ous·ly** *adv.* **—noc′u·ous·ness** *n.*

nod (nŏd) *v.* **nodded, nodding, nods.** *—intr.* **1.** To lower and raise the head in a gesture of agreement or acknowledgment. **2.** To let the head fall forward when sleepy; doze momentarily. **3.** To be careless or momentarily inattentive as if sleepy; to lapse. **4.** To sway, droop, or bend, as trees or flowers in the wind. *—tr.* **1.** To lower and raise (the head) in agreement or acknowledgment. **2.** To express (greeting, approval) by lowering and raising the head: *He nodded his agreement.* **3.** To summon, guide, send, or the like by nodding the head: *He nodded her into the room.* *—n.* **1.** A forward or up-and-down inclination of the head, usually expressive of affirmation or drowsiness. **2.** The nodding motion of anything. **—give** (or **get**) **the nod.** *Informal.* **1.** To give (or receive) approval, assent, or the like. **2.** *Boxing.* To give (or receive) the decision: *The challenger got the nod from the judges.* [Middle English *nodden,* perhaps of Low German origin, akin to Middle High German *notten.* See **ken-²** in Appendix.*] **—nod′der** *n.*

Nod, Land of. See **Land of Nod.**

nodding pogonia. A North American orchid, *Triphora trianthophora,* having pink or white flowers. Also "three birds."

nodding trillium. A North American woodland plant, *Trillium cernuum,* having nodding white or pink flowers.

nod·dle¹ (nŏd′l) *n.* The head. Used humorously: *not an idea in his noddle.* [Middle English *nodle*†, back of the head.]

nod·dle² (nŏd′l) *v.* **-dled, -dling, -dles.** *—intr.* To nod frequently. *—tr.* To nod (the head) lightly. [Frequentative of NOD (verb).]

nod·dy (nŏd′ē) *n., pl.* **-dies. 1.** A dunce or fool; simpleton. **2.** Any tern of the genus *Anous,* that is found in tropical waters and is dark brown with a white head. [From obsolete adjective *noddy,* foolish, "sleepy," "drowsy," probably from NOD (verb). The tern is so named because it is fearless of man and therefore seems stupid.]

node (nōd) *n.* **1.** A knob, knot, protuberance, or swelling: *a lymph node.* **2.** *Botany.* The often enlarged point on a stem where a leaf, bud, or other organ diverges from the stem to which it is attached; a joint. **3.** *Physics.* A point or region of minimum or zero amplitude in a periodic system. **4.** *Mathematics.* The point at which a continuous curve crosses itself; the **crunode** *(see).* **5.** *Astronomy.* **a.** Either of two diametrically opposite points at which the orbit of a planet intersects the ecliptic. **b.** Either of two points at which the orbit of a satellite intersects the orbital plane of a planet. [Latin *nōdus,* a knob, knot. See **ned-** in Appendix.*] **—nod′al** *adj.*

no·di·cal (nō′dĭ-kəl, nŏd′ĭ-) *adj. Astronomy.* Of or pertaining to a node or nodes.

nod·ule (nŏj′o͞ol) *n.* **1.** A small, knotlike protuberance; a node. **2.** *Anatomy.* A localized swelling. **3.** *Botany.* A small, knoblike outgrowth, such as those found on the roots of most leguminous plants. **4.** A small lump of a mineral or mineral mixture. [Latin *nōdulus,* diminutive of *nōdus,* a knob, NODE.] **—nod′u·lar** (nŏj′o͞o-lər), **nod′u·lose′** (nŏj′o͞o-lōs′), **nod′u·lous** (-ləs) *adj.*

no·dus (nō′dəs) *n., pl.* **-di** (-dī′). A knotty situation, problem, or point; a complication. [Latin *nōdus,* "knot," NODE.]

No·ël (nō-ĕl′) *n.* **1.** Christmas. **2.** *Small* **n.** A Christmas carol. [French, from Old French *no(u)el, nael,* from Latin *nātālis (dies),* "birth(day of Christ)," from *nātālis,* of birth, from *nāscī* (past participle *nātus*), to be born. See **genə-** in Appendix.*]

no·e·sis (nō-ē′sĭs) *n.* **1.** *Psychology.* The cognitive process; cognition. **2.** *Philosophy.* The highest knowledge, as of universal forms. [Greek *noēsis,* intelligence, understanding, from *noein,* to perceive, from *nous,* the mind. See **nous** in Appendix.*]

no·et·ic (nō-ĕt′ĭk) *adj.* **1.** Of, relating to, originating in, or apprehended by the intellect. **2.** Of cognition or rational thought that is apprehended by intellect alone. [Greek *noētikos,* from *noēsis,* NOESIS.]

Nof·re·te·te. See **Nefertiti.**

nog¹ (nŏg) *n.* A wooden block built into a masonry wall to hold nails that support joinery structures. [Origin unknown.]

nog² (nŏg) *n.* **Eggnog** *(see).* [Origin unknown.]

nog·gin (nŏg′ĭn) *n.* **1.** A small mug or cup. **2.** A unit of liquid measure equal to one-quarter of a pint. **3.** *Slang.* The head. [Origin unknown.]

No·gu·chi (nō-go͞o′chē), **Hideyo.** 1876–1928. Japanese-born American bacteriologist; investigated syphilis and yellow fever.

No·gu·chi (nō-go͞o′chē), **Isamu.** Born 1904. American architectural sculptor.

noh. Variant of **no** (Japanese drama).

no-hit (nō′hĭt′) *adj. Baseball.* Of or relating to a game in which one pitcher allows his opponents no hits and no runs.

no-hit·ter (nō′hĭt′ər) *n. Baseball.* A no-hit game.

no·how (nō′hou′) *adv. Nonstandard.* In no way; not at all.

noil (noil) *n.* A short fiber combed from the long fibers during the preparation of textile yarns. [Old French *noel,* "small knot (of wool)," from Medieval Latin *nōdellus,* diminutive of Latin *nōdus,* a knob, knot. See **ned-** in Appendix.*]

noise (noiz) *n.* **1.** A sound of any kind, especially when loud, confused, indistinct, or disagreeable. **2.** An outcry or clamor: *the noise of the mob.* **3.** General interest or commotion; a stir: *"Kitty Fisher, the notorious beauty, who made so much noise in her own day"* (Henry B. Wheatley). **4.** *Physics.* Any disturbance, especially a random and persistent disturbance, that obscures or reduces the clarity or quality of a signal. *—v.* **noised, noising, noises.** *—tr.* To spread the rumor, or report of. Usually used with *about* or *abroad.* *—intr.* **1.** To talk much or volubly. **2.** To be noisy; make noise. [Middle English, from Old French *noise, noyse,* from Latin *nausea,* seasickness (with extended senses in popular use, e.g., "unpleasant situation," "noisy confusion"), from Greek *nausia,* from *naus,* a ship. See **nāu-²** in Appendix.*]

Synonyms: *noise, din, racket, uproar, pandemonium, hullabaloo, hubbub, clamor, babel. Noise* is the most general and least forceful of these words. Both *din,* associated with prolonged, ear-splitting sound, and *racket,* which is more general and somewhat less emphatic, are subjective terms that indicate strong discomfort on the part of the user. *Uproar, pandemonium,* and the somewhat weaker *hullabaloo* all strongly imply uncontrolled commotion together with loud, confused sound. *Hubbub* also emphasizes physical movement and resultant confusing sound, but not necessarily disorder; the term is often applied to commercial activity conducted with great intensity. *Clamor* stresses intense and prolonged sound designed to express a purpose, such as protest, and only secondarily implies movement. *Babel* is concerned expressly with vocal sound, not primarily with volume but with the confusion resulting from diversity of language and from simultaneous utterance.

noise·less (noiz′lĭs) *adj.* Creating no noise; silent; quiet. See Synonyms at **still.** **—noise′less·ly** *adv.* **—noise′less·ness** *n.*

noise·mak·er (noiz′mā′kər) *n.* One that makes noise; especially, a device used to celebrate. **—noise′mak′ing** *n.* & *adj.*

noi·some (noi′səm) *adj.* **1.** Offensive to the point of arousing disgust; foul and filthy: *a noisome odor.* **2.** Harmful or dangerous: *"that noisome gulf which gaping lies / Between the jaws of hellish jealousy!"* (Philip Sidney). [Middle English *noyesum* : *(a)noy,* vexation, annoyance, from *anoien,* ANNOY + -SOME.] **—noi′some·ly** *adv.* **—noi′some·ness** *n.*

nois·y (noi′zē) *adj.* **-ier, -iest. 1.** Making a loud noise. **2.** Characterized by noise. **—nois′i·ly** *adv.* **—nois′i·ness** *n.*

no·li-me-tan·ge·re (nō′lē-mē-tăn′jə-rē) *n. Latin.* **1.** A warning or prohibition against meddling, touching, or interfering. **2.** A picture representing Christ appearing to Mary Magdalene after the Resurrection. **3.** Any disfiguring skin ulceration, a **lupus** *(see).* [Latin, "do not touch me," Christ's warning to Mary Magdalene (Vulgate, John 20:17).]

nol·le pros·e·qui (nŏl′ē prŏs′ə-kwī′). *Abbr.* **nol. pros.** *Law.* A declaration that the plaintiff in a civil case or the prosecutor in a criminal case will drop prosecution of all or part of a suit or indictment. [Latin, "to be unwilling to pursue."]

no·lo con·ten·de·re (nō′lō kən-tĕn′də-rē). *Law.* A plea made by the defendant in a criminal action, equivalent to an admission of guilt and subjecting him to punishment but leaving open the possibility for him to deny the alleged facts in other proceedings. [Latin, "I do not wish to contend."]

nol-pros (nŏl′prŏs′) *tr.v.* **-prossed, -prossing, -prosses.** *Law.* To drop prosecution of by entering a **nolle prosequi** *(see)* on the court records.

nol. pros. nolle prosequi.

nom. nominative.

no·ma (nō′mə) *n.* A severe, often gangrenous inflammation of the mouth, occurring especially in a young child after a debilitating disease. [Latin *nomē,* "eating ulcer," from Greek *nomē,* spreading ulcer, "a feeding," "a pasturage." See **nem-²** in Appendix.*]

no·mad (nō′măd′) *n.* **1.** One of a group of pastoral people having no fixed abode and usually moving from place to place in a search for food and water. **2.** One who has no permanent domicile; a wanderer. *—adj.* Nomadic; wandering. [Old French *nomade,* from Latin *nomas* (stem *nomad-*), from Greek *nomas,* one that wanders about for pasture. See **nem-²** in Appendix.*] **—no′mad′ism′** (nō′măd′ĭz′əm) *n.*

no·mad·ic (nō-măd′ĭk) *adj.* Also **no·mad·i·cal** (-ĭ-kəl). Leading the life of a nomad; wandering; roving. **—no·mad′i·cal·ly** *adv.*

no man's land. 1. An unclaimed or unowned piece of land; a wasteland. **2.** Land under dispute by two opposing parties; especially, the field of battle between two opposing entrenched armies. **3.** Any area into which a man does not venture because of fear or uncertainty; a realm of danger or ambiguity.

nom·arch (nŏm′ärk′) *n.* The governor of a nome or nomarchy. [Greek *nomarkhēs, nomarkhos* : NOME + -ARCH.]

nom·ar·chy (nŏm′är′kē) *n., pl.* **-chies.** One of the provinces of modern Greece. Also called "nome."

nom·bril (nŏm′brəl) *n. Heraldry.* The point on an escutcheon between the fess point and the base point. [Old French *nombril,* "navel," probably alteration of *l'ombril,* the navel : *le,* the + *ombril,* navel, from Vulgar Latin *umbilīculus* (unattested), diminutive of Latin *umbilicus,* navel. See **nobh-** in Appendix.*]

nom de guerre (nŏm′ də gâr′; *French* nôN də gĕr′). **1.** A pseudonym formerly assumed by a French soldier upon entering military service. **2.** Any fictitious name taken for a particular course of action. [French, "war name."]

nom de plume (nŏm′ də plo͞om′; *French* nôN də plüm′). A pseudonym adopted by a writer. [French, "pen name."]

nome (nōm) *n.* **1.** A province or department in ancient Egypt. **2. Nomarchy** *(see).* [Greek *nomos,* division, district. See **nem-²** in Appendix.*]

Nome (nōm). The westernmost city of the continental United States, on Seward Peninsula in Alaska. Population, 2,000.

no·men·cla·tor (nō′mən-klā′tər) *n.* One who assigns names, as in scientific classification. [Latin *nōmenclātor,* "name-caller," a slave who accompanied his master to tell him the names of people he met : *nōmen,* name (see **nomen-** in Appendix*) + *-clātor,* caller, from *calāre,* to call (see **kel-³** in Appendix*).]

no·men·cla·ture (nō′mən-klā′chər, nō-mĕn′klə-chər) *n.* A system of names; systematic naming in any art or science. [Latin *nōmenclātūra,* from *nōmenclātor,* NOMENCLATOR.]

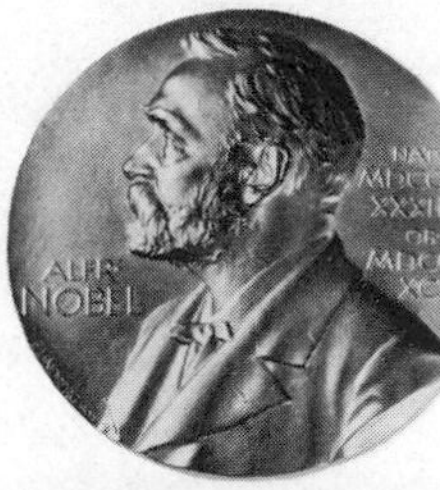

Alfred Bernhard Nobel
Portrait on the Prize medal

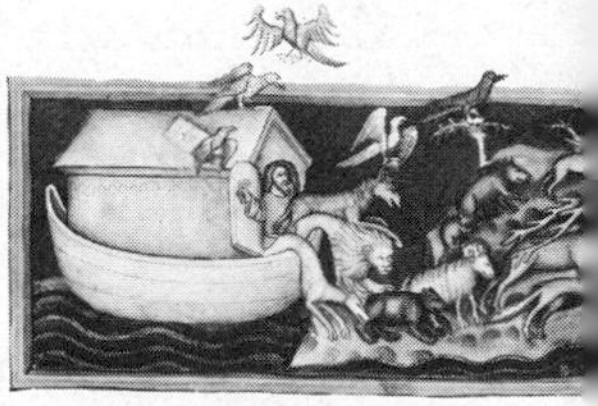

Noah
Late 14th-century Bavarian illustration of Noah's ark

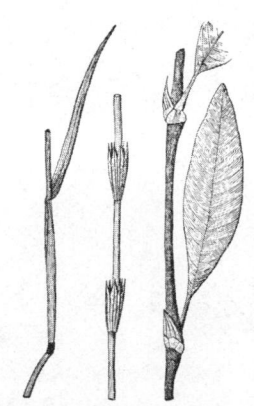

rye grass
horsetail
buckwheat

node

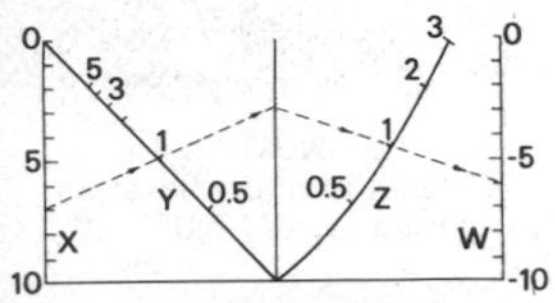

nomograph
Combination straight-line and curved-scale nomograph for equation $xy + wz = z^2$ Dashed line graphically determines that $w = -6$ when $x = 7, y = 1$, and $z = 1$.

nom·i·nal (nŏm′ə-nəl) *adj.* **1. a.** Of, like, pertaining to, or consisting of a name or names. **b.** Bearing a person's name: *nominal shares.* **2.** Existing in name only; not real or actual; theoretical; so-called: *"seduced by fashion, and blindly accepting nominal pleasures, I lost real ones"* (Lord Chesterfield). **3.** Minimal in comparison to the real value: *a nominal sum.* **4.** *Grammar.* Of, like, or pertaining to a noun or nouns; substantive. [Latin *nōminālis,* from *nōmen* (stem *nōmin-*), name. See **nomen-** in Appendix.*] —**nom′i·nal·ly** *adv.*

Usage: Applied to amounts, *nominal* and *low* are not interchangeable. *Low* is nonspecific. *Nominal* pertains only to that which is so low in relation to value that it is a mere token.

nom·i·nal·ism (nŏm′ə-nəl-ĭz′əm) *n. Philosophy.* The doctrine that abstract concepts, general terms, or universals have no objective reference but exist only as names. Compare **realism.** —**nom′i·nal·ist** *adj. & n.* —**nom′i·nal·is′tic** *adj.*

nominal value. The stated, par, or book value of a share of stock, as opposed to the actual or market value.

nom·i·nate (nŏm′ə-nāt′) *tr.v.* **-nated, -nating, -nates. 1.** To propose by name as a candidate. **2.** To designate or appoint to some office, responsibility, or honor. —*adj.* (nŏm′ə-nĭt). Having a particular or special name. [Latin *nōmināre,* to name, from *nōmen* (stem *nōmin-*), name. See **nomen-** in Appendix.*] —**nom′i·na′tor** (-nā′tər) *n.*

nom·i·na·tion (nŏm′ə-nā′shən) *n.* **1.** The act of appointing a person to office. **2.** The submission of a name for candidacy or for appointment. **3.** The state of being nominated.

nom·i·na·tive (nŏm′ə-nā′tĭv *for senses 1 and 2;* nŏm′ə-nə-tĭv, nŏm′nə-tĭv *for sense 3*) *adj. Abbr.* **nom. 1. a.** Appointed to office. **b.** Nominated as candidate to office. **2.** Having or bearing a person's name: *nominative shares.* **3.** *Grammar.* Of or designating the case of the subject of a finite verb (as *We* in *We awoke at dawn*) and of words identified with the subject, such as a predicate nominative (as *men* in *These are the men*). —*n.* (nŏm′ə-nə-tĭv, nom′nə-tĭv). *Abbr.* **nom.** The nominative case or a word in that case. [Noun; Middle English *nominatif (case),* from Old French *(cas) nominatif,* from Latin *nōminātīvus (cāsus),* from *nōmināre,* to NOMINATE.]

nom·i·nee (nŏm′ə-nē′) *n.* One who is nominated to an office or for candidacy. [NOMIN(ATE) + -EE.]

nomo–. Indicates law, usage, or custom; for example, **nomograph.** [Greek *nomos,* usage, law. See **nem-²** in Appendix.*]

nom·o·graph (nŏm′ə-grăf′, -gräf′, nō′mə-) *n.* **1.** A graph consisting of three coplanar curves, usually parallel straight lines, each graduated for a different variable so that a straight line cutting all three curves intersects the related values of each variable. **2.** Any chart representing numerical relationships. Also called "alignment chart," "nomogram." ["A diagram representing mathematical laws" : NOMO- + -GRAPH.] —**no·mog′ra·phy** (nō-mŏg′rə-fē) *n.*

–nomy. Indicates the systematization of knowledge about, or laws governing, a specified field; for example, **astronomy.** [From Latin *-nomia,* from Greek; either from agent nouns or adjectives in *-nomos,* from *nemein,* to distribute, manage, or from *nomos,* law. See **nem-²** in Appendix.*]

non–. Indicates not. ***Note:*** Many compounds other than those entered here may be formed with *non-.* In forming compounds, *non-* is normally joined with the following element without space or hyphen: *nonnutritive.* However, if the second element begins with a capital letter, it is separated with a hyphen: *non-French.* [Middle English *non-, nown-,* from Old French *non-,* from Latin *nōn,* not. See **ne** in Appendix.*]

Usage: *Non-* is generally restricted in meaning to simple negation; it adds the sense of *not* and implies nothing further. It is usually less forceful than the following prefixes used in negation: *un-, in-, il-, im-, ir-,* and *a-.* Unlike *non-,* these generally either emphasize negation strongly or add a sense in direct opposition to that of the words to which they are joined. *Non-American* specifies only a limitation; *un-American* implies active opposition. *Nonreligious* and *nonhuman* are not directly opposed to *religious* and *human* in the sense that *irreligious* and *inhuman* are.

nona–. Indicates ninth or nine; for example, **nonagon.** [From Latin *nōnus,* ninth. See **newn̥** in Appendix.*]

non·age (nŏn′ĭj, nō′nĭj) *n.* **1.** The period during which one is legally underage; legal minority. **2.** A stage of immaturity: *"the bravest achievements were always accomplished in the nonage of a nation"* (Thomas Paine). [Middle English, from Old French : NON- + *age, aage,* AGE.]

non·a·ge·nar·i·an (nŏn′ə-jə-nâr′ē-ən, nō′nə-) *adj.* **1.** Being ninety years old or between ninety and one hundred years old. **2.** Of or like someone of this age. —*n.* A person of ninety or between ninety and one hundred years of age. [From Latin *nōnāgēnārius,* from *nōnāgēnī,* ninety each, from *nōnāginta,* ninety : *novem,* nine (see **newn̥** in Appendix*) + *-gintā,* ten times (see **dekm̥** in Appendix*).]

non·a·gon (nŏn′ə-gŏn′, nō′nə-) *n.* A polygon having nine sides. [NONA- + -GON.]

non·a·no·ic acid (nŏn′ə-nō′ĭk). A chemical, **pelargonic acid** *(see).* [From *nonane,* a paraffin : NONA- + -ANE (because it is the ninth in the methane series).]

non·ap·pear·ance (nŏn′ə-pîr′əns) *n.* Failure to appear, especially in courts of law, as witness or accessory in a suit.

nonce (nŏns) *n.* The present or particular time or occasion. Used in the expression *for the nonce: "her tendency to discover a touch of sadness had for the nonce disappeared"* (Theodore Dreiser). [Middle English *for the nones, for the nanes,* originally *for then anes,* "for the one (purpose or occasion)" : FOR + *then,* dative singular neuter of THE + *anes,* ONCE.]

nonce word. A word invented and used for a particular occasion, or for the nonce; for example, the word *mileconsuming* in *"the wagon beginning to fall into its slow and mileconsuming clatter"* (William Faulkner).

non·cha·lance (nŏn′shə-läns′) *n.* Debonair lack of concern: *"The contemptuous nonchalance of her trailed hand irritated him"* (Elizabeth Bowen). See Synonyms at **equanimity.**

non·cha·lant (nŏn′shə-länt′) *adj.* Appearing casually unconcerned; indifferent. See Synonyms at **cool.** [French, from Old French, from *nonchaloir,* to be unconcerned : NON- + *chaloir,* to be interested or concerned, from Latin *calēre,* to be warm (see **kel-¹** in Appendix*).] —**non′cha·lant′ly** *adv.*

non·com (nŏn′kŏm′) *n.* A noncommissioned officer.

non·com·bat·ant (nŏn′kəm-băt′ənt, -kŏm′bə-tənt) *n.* **1.** A person connected with the armed forces whose duties are other than fighting, such as a chaplain. **2.** A civilian in wartime.

non·com·mis·sioned officer (nŏn′kə-mĭsh′ənd). *Abbr.* **NCO, N.C.O.** An enlisted member of the armed forces appointed to a rank conferring leadership over other men. Compare **commissioned officer, warrant officer.**

non·com·mit·tal (nŏn′kə-mĭt′l) *adj.* Refusing commitment to any particular course of action or opinion; revealing no preference or purpose: *"his face was the color of a freshly baked pork pie and as noncommittal"* (Thomas Pynchon). See Synonyms at **silent.** —**non′com·mit′tal·ly** *adv.*

non·com·pli·ance (nŏn′kəm-plī′əns) *n.* Failure or refusal to comply with something. —**non′com·pli′ant** *adj. & n.*

non com·pos men·tis (nŏn kŏm′pəs mĕn′tĭs). *Law.* Not of sound mind and hence not legally responsible. [Latin, "not having control of the mind."]

non·con·duc·tor (nŏn′kən-dŭk′tər) *n.* A substance that conducts little or no electricity or heat. —**non′con·duct′ing** *adj.*

non·con·form·ist (nŏn′kən-fôr′mĭst) *n.* One who refuses to be bound by the accepted rules, beliefs, or practices of a group. —**non′con·form′i·ty** *n.*

non·co·op·er·a·tion (nŏn′kō-ŏp′ə-rā′shən) *n.* **1.** Failure or refusal to cooperate. **2.** Resistance to government through civil disobedience or refusal to perform civil duties, such as paying taxes. —**non′co·op′er·a′tion·ist** *n.* —**non′co·op′er·a·tive** (-ŏp′ər-ə-tĭv, -ŏp′ə-rā′tĭv) *adj.* —**non′co·op′er·a′tor** (-tər) *n.*

non·de·nom·i·na·tion·al (nŏn′dĭ-nŏm′ə-nā′shən-əl) *adj.* Not restricted to or associated with a religious denomination.

non·de·script (nŏn′dĭ-skrĭpt′) *adj.* Lacking in distinctive qualities; without any individual character or form: *"This expression gave temporary meaning to a set of features otherwise nondescript"* (Katherine Anne Porter). —*n.* A person or thing with no outstanding or distinguishing features. [NON- + Latin *dēscriptus,* past participle of *dēscribere,* DESCRIBE.]

non·dis·junc·tion (nŏn′dĭs-jŭngk′shən) *n. Biology.* The failure of paired chromosomes to separate during mitosis.

non·dis·tinc·tive (nŏn′dĭs-tĭngk′tĭv) *adj.* **1.** Not distinctive. **2.** *Linguistics.* Not helping to distinguish meaning: *The vowel sound in the words "hit" and "slip" is nondistinctive.*

none (nŭn) *pron.* **1.** No one; not one; nobody: *None dared to do it.* **2.** Not any; no persons or things of a specified group: *Of all my classmates, none survived the war.* **3.** No part; not any; nothing: *none of my business; none of his concern.* —*adj.* Not one; no. Used before vowels: *There is none other available.* —*adv.* In no way; to no extent; not at all: *He is none too happy.* [Middle English *nan, none,* Old English *nān* : *ne,* no (see **ne** in Appendix*) + *ān,* one (see **oino-** in Appendix*).]

Usage: *None* (pronoun) may take a singular verb or a plural one, according to 68 per cent of the Usage Panel. They specify a singular verb when *none* can logically be construed as singular (when *not one* or *no one* can be substituted for *none*): *None of us is wholly blameless.* A singular verb should also be used when *none* precedes a singular noun: *None of the laundry was really clean.* A plural verb should be used when *none* applies to more than one (when *no persons, not any of a group of persons or things* can be substituted for *none*): *None are more wretched than victims of natural disasters.* When *none* can be logically construed as either singular or plural, either a singular or plural verb is possible: *None of these books is* (or *are*) *really helpful.* In every case the verb and related personal pronouns and pronominal adjectives must agree in number: *none has his* (or *none have theirs*). According to 28 per cent of the Panel, *none* must always take a singular verb. See Usage note at **neither.**

non·ef·fec·tive (nŏn′ĭ-fĕk′tĭv) *adj.* **1.** Not effective. **2.** Not fit for regular duty in military service. —*n.* A member of one of the armed services who is not fit for regular duty, as from illness or injury.

non·e·go (nŏn-ē′gō) *n., pl.* **-gos.** All that is not part of the ego or the conscious self. [Translation of German *Nicht-ich.*]

non·en·ti·ty (nŏn-ĕn′tə-tē) *n., pl.* **-ties. 1.** Nonexistence. **2.** Something that does not exist, or that exists only in the imagination. **3.** A totally insignificant person or thing.

nones (nōnz) *pl.n.* **1.** In the ancient Roman calendar, the ninth day before the ides of a month; the seventh of March, May, July, and October, and the fifth day of the other months. **2.** *Ecclesiastical.* **a.** The fifth of the seven **canonical hours** *(see).* **b.** The time of day set aside for this prayer, usually the ninth hour after sunrise. [In sense 1, Middle English *nonys, nonas,* from Old French *nones,* from Latin *nōnae,* feminine plural of *nōnus,* ninth. See **newn̥** in Appendix.* In sense 2, plural of *none,* from Old French *none,* from Late Latin *nōna (hōra),* the ninth hour, from the feminine of Latin *nōnus,* ninth.]

none·such (nŭn′sŭch′) *n.* Also **non·such. 1.** A person or thing without equal: *a nonesuch among athletes.* **2.** A plant, the **black medic** *(see).* [NONE + SUCH.] —**none′such′** *adj.*

none·the·less (nŭn′thə-lĕs′) *adv.* Nevertheless; however.
non-Eu·clid·e·an (nŏn′yo͞o-klĭd′ē-ən) *adj.* Designating any of several modern geometries that are not based on the postulates of Euclid, used especially in mathematical physics to describe spaces different from that of common experience.
non·ex·ist·ence (nŏn′ĭg-zĭs′təns) *n.* **1.** The condition of not existing. **2.** A thing that does not exist. **—non′ex·ist′ent** *adj.*
non·fea·sance (nŏn-fē′zəns) *n. Law.* Failure to perform some act that is either an official duty or a legal requirement. Compare **malfeasance, misfeasance.** [NON- + obsolete *feasance,* a doing, from Old French *faisance* (see **malfeasance**).]
non·fer·rous (nŏn-fĕr′əs) *adj.* **1.** Not composed of or containing iron. **2.** Of or pertaining to metals other than iron.
non·fic·tion (nŏn-fĭk′shən) *n.* Prose works other than fiction. **—non·fic′tion·al** *adj.*
no·nil·lion (nō-nĭl′yən) *n.* **1.** The cardinal number represented by the figure 1 followed by 30 zeros; usually written 10^{30}. Called in British usage "quintillion." **2.** In Great Britain, the cardinal number represented by the figure 1 followed by 54 zeros; usually written 10^{54}. See **number.** [French, from Old French, "the ninth power of a million" : *non-,* nine, ninth + *(m)ilion, (m)illion,* (M)ILLION.] **—no·nil′lion** *adj.*
no·nil·lionth (nō-nĭl′yənth) *n.* The ordinal number nonillion in a series. See **number.** **—no·nil′lionth** *adj.*
non·in·duc·tive (nŏn′ĭn-dŭk′tĭv) *adj.* Having low inductance.
non·in·ter·ven·tion (nŏn′ĭn-tər-vĕn′shən) *n.* Failure or refusal to interfere or intervene in the affairs of another, especially in international affairs. **—non′in·ter·ven′tion·ist** *n.* & *adj.*
non·join·der (nŏn-join′dər) *n. Law.* The omission of a party, plaintiff, defendant, or cause of action that should have been included as a necessary part of an action or suit.
non·ju·ror (nŏn-jo͝or′ər, -jo͝or′ôr′) *n.* **1.** One who refuses to take an oath, as of allegiance. **2.** *Capital* **N.** An Anglican clergyman who refused to swear allegiance to William and Mary in 1689.
non·met·al (nŏn-mĕt′l) *n. Chemistry.* Any of a number of elements, such as oxygen or sulfur, that generally occur as negatively charged ions or radicals, form oxides that produce acids, and are poor conductors of heat and of electricity when solid.
non·me·tal·lic (nŏn′mə-tăl′ĭk) *adj.* **1.** Not of metal. **2.** *Chemistry.* Of or pertaining to a nonmetal.
non·mor·al (nŏn-môr′əl, -mŏr′əl) *adj.* Unrelated to morals or to ethical considerations; neither moral nor immoral; amoral.
Non·ni (nŭn′nē′). A river of Manchuria, China, rising in the north and flowing 740 miles south to join the Sungari River.
non·ob·jec·tive (nŏn′əb-jĕk′tĭv) *adj.* Designating a style of graphic art that does not represent objects.
non ob·stan·te (nŏn ŏb-stăn′tē, nōn ōb-stän′tā). *Abbr.* **non obs., non obst.** *Latin.* Notwithstanding.
non·pa·reil (nŏn′pə-rĕl′) *adj.* Without rival; matchless; peerless; unequaled. *—n.* **1.** A person or thing that is unmatched or unequaled; a paragon or nonesuch. **2.** A bird, the **painted bunting** *(see).* **3.** *Printing.* **a.** A size of type between minion and agate; 6-point type. **b.** A 6-point slug. **4.** A small, flat chocolate drop covered with white pellets of sugar. [Middle English *nonparaille,* from Old French *nonpareil* : NON- + *pareil,* equal, like, from Vulgar Latin *pariculus* (unattested), diminutive of Latin *pār,* equal (see **perə-** in Appendix*).]
non·par·tic·i·pat·ing (nŏn′pär-tĭs′ə-pā′tĭng) *adj.* **1.** Not participating. **2.** *Insurance.* Not giving the right to participate in the profits of a company. **—non′par·tic′i·pat′or** (-pā′tər) *n.*
non·par·ti·san (nŏn-pär′tə-zən) *adj.* Also **non·par·ti·zan. 1.** Not partisan. **2.** Not influenced by, affiliated with, or supporting the interests or policies of any one political party.
non·plus (nŏn plŭs′) *n.* A state of perplexity or bafflement prohibiting action, speech, or thought. Used chiefly in the expressions *at* or *to a nonplus: never at a nonplus; reduced to a perfect nonplus.* *—tr.v.* **nonplused, -plusing, -pluses.** Also *chiefly British* **-plussed, -plussing, -plusses.** To perplex; put at a loss; baffle: *"being completely nonplussed and confounded about the stranger, I . . . was as much afraid of him as . . . the devil himself"* (Melville). [Latin *nōn plūs,* "no more (can be said)" : *nōn,* not (see **ne** in Appendix*) + *plūs,* more (see **pel-**[8] in Appendix*).]
non pos·su·mus (nŏn pŏs′ə-məs, nōn pōs′o͞o-mo͞os′). *Latin.* We cannot.
non·pro·duc·tive (nŏn′prə-dŭk′tĭv) *adj.* **1.** Not productive. Said of that part of the labor force that does not directly produce goods, such as clerical personnel. **2.** Not yielding what was expected; unproductive. **—non′pro·duc′tive·ly** *adv.*
non·prof·it (nŏn-prŏf′ĭt) *adj.* Not seeking profit.
non·pros (nŏn′prŏs′) *tr.v.* **-prossed, -prossing, -prosses.** *Law.* To enter a judgment of non prosequitur against (a plaintiff).
non pro·se·qui·tur (nŏn prō-sĕk′wĭ-to͝or′). *Abbr.* **non pros.** *Law.* The judgment entered against a plaintiff who fails to appear in court to prosecute his suit. [Latin, "he does not prosecute."]
non·rep·re·sen·ta·tion·al (nŏn′rĕp-rĭ-zĕn-tā′shən-əl) *adj.* Not representational; especially in art, not depicting objects as they are recognized in nature; nonobjective. **—non′rep·re·sen·ta′tion·al·ism′** *n.*
non·re·sis·tant (nŏn′rĭ-zĭs′tənt) *adj.* **1.** Not resistant; submissively obedient. **2.** Unable to resist illness or infection. *—n.* **1.** One who believes in complete obedience to authority, even though unjust or arbitrary. **2.** One who will not resort to force, even to defend himself against violence. **—non′re·sis′tance** *n.*
non·re·stric·tive (nŏn′rĭ-strĭk′tĭv) *adj.* **1.** Not restrictive. **2.** *Grammar.* Denoting a word, clause, or phrase that is descriptive of but not essential to the denotation of the sentence element it modifies; the omission of a nonrestrictive word or word group does not change the basic meaning. In the sentence *Mary, who has brown hair, is two years younger than Helen,* the nonrestrictive clause *who has brown hair* may be omitted. Compare **restrictive.**
non·rig·id (nŏn-rĭj′ĭd) *adj.* **1.** Not rigid. **2.** Designating a lighter-than-air aircraft that holds its shape by gas pressure.
non·sched·uled (nŏn-skĕj′o͞old) *adj.* **1.** Operating without fixed published flying schedules. Said of certain airlines. **2.** Not according to a schedule or plan: *a nonscheduled stop at Boston.*
non·sec·tar·i·an (nŏn′sĕk-târ′ē-ən) *adj.* Not limited to or associated with any particular religious denomination.
non·sense (nŏn′sĕns′, -səns) *n.* **1.** Something that does not make or have sense; especially, behavior or language that is meaningless or absurd. **2.** Extravagant foolishness or frivolity. **3.** Things of little or no importance or usefulness; trifles: *ribbons, laces, and other nonsense.* [NON- (not) + SENSE.] **—non·sen′si·cal** (nŏn-sĕn′sĭ-kəl) *adj.* **—non·sen′si·cal·ly** *adv.*
non se·qui·tur (nŏn sĕk′wĭ-to͝or′). *Abbr.* **non seq. 1.** *Logic.* An inference or conclusion that does not follow from established premises or evidence. **2.** A statement to which no answer seems appropriate or reasonable. [Latin, "it does not follow."]
non·sked (nŏn′skĕd′) *n.* An airline without regular published flight schedules. [Shortened form of NONSCHEDULED.] **—non′sked′** *adj.*
non·skid (nŏn′skĭd′) *adj.* Having a striated tread or surface designed to prevent or inhibit skidding.
non·stan·dard (nŏn-stăn′dərd) *adj.* **1.** Varying from or not adhering to the standard. **2.** *Linguistics.* Of or pertaining to usages or varieties of a language that do not conform to those approved by educated native users of the language.
non·stop (nŏn′stŏp′) *adj.* Making or having made no stops: *a nonstop flight.* **—non′stop′** *adv.*
non·stri·at·ed (nŏn-strī′ā′tĭd) *adj.* Having no striations. Said chiefly of certain muscle fibers.
non·such. Variant of **nonesuch.**
non·suit (nŏn-so͞ot′) *n. Law.* A judgment given against a plaintiff when he fails to prosecute his case or to introduce sufficient evidence. *—tr.v.* **nonsuited, -suiting, -suits.** To dismiss the lawsuit of. [Middle English, from Norman French *no(u)nsuyte* : NON- + Old French *suite, sieute,* SUIT.]
non·sup·port (nŏn′sə-pôrt′, -pōrt′) *n. Law.* Failure to provide for the maintenance of one's legal dependents.
non trop·po (nōn trô′pō). *Music.* Moderately. Used to modify a direction: *adagio non troppo.* [Italian, "not too much."]
non-U (nŏn′yo͞o′) *adj. British Informal.* Not belonging or appropriate to upper-class custom, especially in language habits. Compare **U.**
non·un·ion[1] (nŏn-yo͞on′yən) *n. Medicine.* Failure of a bone fracture to heal.
non·un·ion[2] (nŏn-yo͞on′yən) *adj.* **1. a.** Not belonging to a labor union. **b.** Not unionized: *a nonunion shop.* **2.** Not manufactured or serviced by union labor.
non·u·ple (nŏn′yə-pəl) *adj.* **1.** Consisting of nine members; having nine parts or elements; ninefold. **2.** Multiplied by nine. *—n.* A number or total that is nine times as great as another. [Old French *nonuple* : *non-,* nine + *-ple,* -fold, from Latin *-plus* (see **pel-**[3] in Appendix*).]
non·vi·a·ble (nŏn-vī′ə-bəl) *adj.* **1.** Not capable of living or developing: *a nonviable fetus.* **2.** Not workable or practicable.
non·vi·o·lence (nŏn-vī′ə-ləns) *n.* Lack of violence; specifically, a social philosophy based on the rejection of violent means to gain objectives. **—non·vi′o·lent** *adj.* **—non·vi′o·lent·ly** *adv.*
non·white (nŏn-hwīt′) *n.* A person not of the white race. **—non·white′** *adj.*
noo·dle[1] (no͞od′l) *n.* **1.** *Slang.* The head. **2.** A fool; simpleton. [Possibly blend of NODDLE (head) and NOODLE (food).]
noo·dle[2] (no͞od′l) *n.* A thin strip of food paste, usually made of flour and eggs. [German *Nudel*†.]
noo·dle[3] (no͞od′l) *intr.v.* **-dled, -dling, -dles.** To improvise music idly or tentatively. [Origin uncertain.]
nook (no͝ok) *n.* **1.** A corner, especially in a room. **2.** A quiet, narrow, or secluded spot; a recess. [Middle English *noke, nok,* perhaps from Scandinavian, akin to Norwegian (dialectal) *nok,* hook. See **ken-**[5] in Appendix.*]
nook·y (no͝ok′ē) *n. Vulgar Slang.* Woman regarded as a sexual object. [Origin obscure.]
noon (no͞on) *n.* **1.** *Abbr.* **n., N., 12 M. a.** Twelve o'clock in the daytime; midday. **b.** The time or the point in the sun's path when it is on the local meridian. **2.** The highest point or zenith; the best or brightest part. **3.** The midpoint: *the noon of night.* [Middle English *none, noon,* midday, the hour of the nones (originally at 3 P.M.), Old English *nōn,* "the ninth hour (after sunrise)," from Late Latin *nōna (hōra),* from the feminine of Latin *nōnus,* ninth. See **newŋ** in Appendix.*] **—noon** *adj.*
noon·day (no͞on′dā′) *n.* Noon. **—noon′day′** *adj.*
no one. Also **no-one** (nō′wŭn′). No person; nobody.
Usage: *No one* and *nobody* (in the sense of *no one, no person*) invariably take singular verbs. Related personal pronouns and pronominal adjectives must also be singular, as in: *No one* (or *nobody) has his* (not *their) work finished.*
noon·tide (no͞on′tīd′) *n.* Noon. [Middle English *nonetyde,* Old English *nōntīd* : *nōn,* NOON + *tīd,* TIDE (time).] **—noon′tide′** *adj.*
noon·time (no͞on′tīm′) *n.* Noon. **—noon′time′** *adj.*
noose (no͞os) *n.* **1.** A loop formed by a running knot in a rope or cord, as in a lasso. **2.** A snare or trap. *—tr.v.* **noosed, noosing, nooses. 1.** To capture or to hold by or as if by a noose. **2.** To make a noose of or in (cord, rope, or the like). [Middle English *nose,* from Old French *nos, nous,* from Latin *nōdus,* a knot. See **ned-** in Appendix.*]
Noot·ka (no͞ot′kə, no͝ot′-) *n.* **1.** A tribe of Wakashan-speaking North American Indians living on Vancouver Island, British

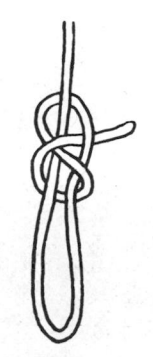

noose
Figure-eight noose

Columbia, and Cape Flattery, northwestern Washington. **2.** A member of this tribe. **3.** The Wakashan language of this tribe. —**Noot′ka** *adj.*

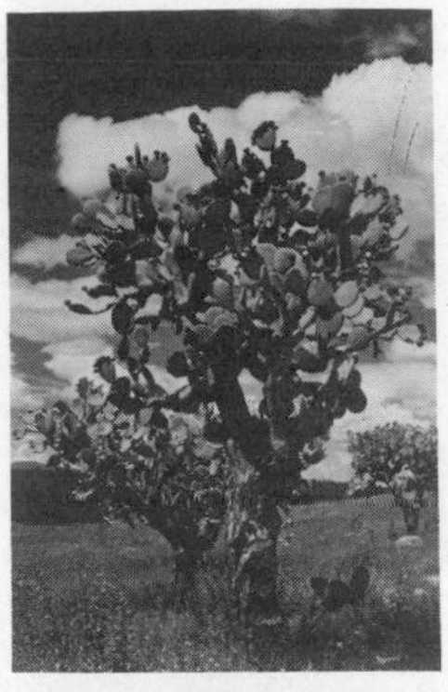

nopal
Opuntia lindheimeri

Nootka cypress. A tall evergreen tree, *Chamaecyparis nootkatensis,* of the northwestern coast of North America. Also called "Alaska cedar," "Sitka cypress," "yellow cypress." [First discovered at NOOTKA SOUND.]

Nootka Sound. An inlet of the Pacific Ocean in British Columbia, Canada.

no·pal (nō′pəl, nō-päl′, -păl′) *n.* **1.** Any cactus of the genus *Nopalea,* found chiefly in Mexico; especially, *N. coccinellifera,* which is also called "cochineal plant." **2.** A species of prickly pear, *Opuntia lindheimeri,* having yellow or red flowers and purple fruit. [Spanish, from Nahuatl *nopalli.*]

no-par (nō′pär′) *adj.* Without face value; having no par value. Said of stock certificates.

nope (nōp) *adv. Slang.* No. [Alteration of NO (adverb).]

nor[1] (nôr; *unstressed* nər) *conj.* And not; or not; likewise not; not either. Used: **a.** As a correlative to give continuing negative force: *He never worked nor offered to help.* **b.** For rhetorical effect following a clause that is affirmative: *The day was bright, nor were there clouds above.* **c.** Archaically in place of *neither,* as the first correlative of a negative pair: *Nor gray his beard, nor shambling his gait.* [Middle English *nor,* contraction of *nother, nauther,* NEITHER.]

Usage: *Nor* (not *or*) invariably follows *neither* in constructions involving continuing negation: *He is neither able nor willing to go.* Likewise *nor* must always be used to indicate continuing negation involving independent clauses: *He has no experience in chemistry, nor does the subject interest him.* But in constructions such as the following, *or* may be substituted for *nor* to indicate continuing negation: *He has no experience or interest in chemistry. He will not permit the change, or even consider it.* This substitution, common in modern usage, is possible only when it is clear that the negative sense, stated once, is felt in the succeeding element or elements without restatement. See Usage note at **neither.**

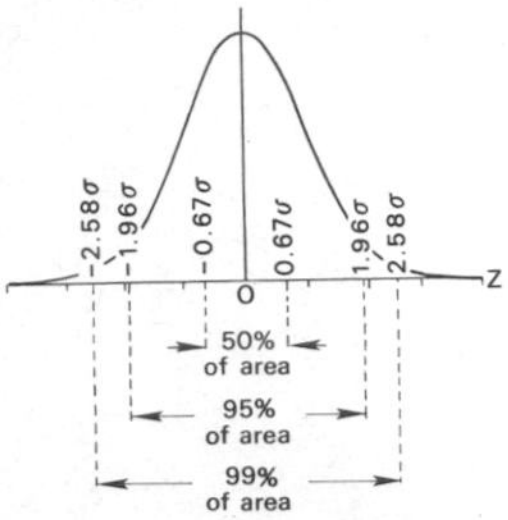

normal distribution
Frequency curve of the normal distribution.
σ is the standard deviation

nor[2] (nôr) *conj. Regional.* Than. [Middle English *nor*†.]

nor-. *Chemistry.* Indicates an unaltered parent compound; for example, **norepinephrine.** [From NORMAL.]

Nor. **1.** Norman. **2.** north. **3.** Norway; Norwegian.

No·ra (nôr′ə, nōr′ə). A feminine given name. [Irish, shortened form of HONORA.]

nor·a·dren·a·lin (nôr′ə-drĕn′ə-lĭn) *n.* A hormone, **norepinephrine** *(see).* [NOR- + ADRENALIN.]

Nor·den·skjöld (nōō′dən-shœld′), Baron **Nils Adolf Erik.** 1832–1901. Finnish-born Swedish explorer and geologist; first to navigate the Northeast Passage around Europe and Asia (1878–80).

Nor·den·skjöld Sea. A former name for the **Laptev Sea.**

Nor·dic (nôr′dĭk) *adj. Anthropology.* Of, pertaining, or belonging to a subdivision of the Caucasoid ethnic group most predominant in Scandinavia. The typical Nordic person is tall, long-headed, blond, and has blue eyes. —*n.* One of the Nordic people. [French *nordique,* from Old French *nord,* north, from Old English *north.* See **ner-**[1] in Appendix.*]

Nord·kyn, Cape (nôr′kün′). A cape, the northernmost point of the European mainland, off Norway, on the Barents Sea.

Nord·mann fir (nôrd′mən). A widely planted evergreen tree, *Abies nordmanniana,* having reddish-brown, erect cones. [Discovered by A. von *Nordmann* (died 1866), Russian botanist.]

Nore, The (nôr, nōr). A sand island in the Thames River, England, considered to divide the river and estuary.

nor′east·er. *Nautical.* Variant of **northeaster.**

nor·ep·i·neph·rine (nôr′ĕp-ə-nĕf′rĭn, -rēn′) *n.* A hormone, $(OH)_2C_6H_3 \cdot CHOH \cdot CH_2 \cdot NH_2$, formed naturally in the body's sympathetic nerve endings. It is a vasoconstrictor. Also called "noradrenalin." [NOR- + EPINEPHRINE.]

Nor·folk (nôr′fək). **1.** *Abbr.* **Norf.** A county of England, 2,035 square miles in area, on the North Sea north of Suffolk. Population, 561,000. County seat, Norwich. **2.** A seaport, naval base, and industrial city of southeastern Virginia, on the southern edge of Hampton Roads. Population, 306,000. [Middle English *Northfolk,* Old English *Northfolc,* "northern people" (i.e., within East Anglia) : NORTH + FOLK.]

Norfolk Island pine. An evergreen tree, *Araucaria excelsa,* native to Norfolk Island in the South Pacific. It is a popular house plant.

Norfolk jacket. A single-breasted men's jacket with a belt, a pocket on each side, and two box pleats in front and back. [Formerly worn for duck hunting in *Norfolk,* England.]

Nor·ge. The Norwegian name for **Norway.**

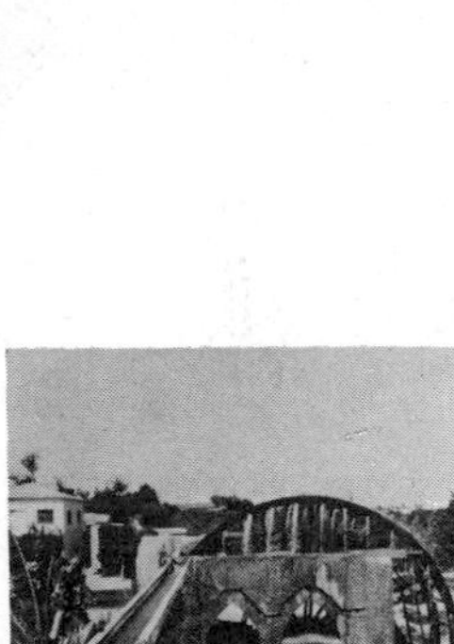

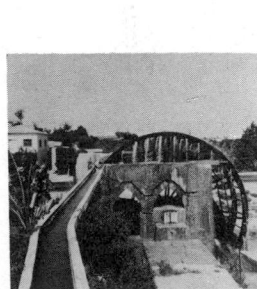

noria
Noria and *(left)* irrigation canal in southeastern Spain

no·ri·a (nôr′ē-ə, nōr′-) *n.* A water wheel with buckets attached to its rim that are used to raise water from a stream, especially for transferral to an irrigation trough. [Spanish, from Arabic *nā'ūrah,* "creaking device," from *na'ara,* to grunt, creak.]

No·rilsk (nŏ-rēlsk′). The largest city of northern Siberia. Population, 124,000.

nor·ite (nôr′īt′) *n.* A mineral, **gabbro** *(see).* [Norwegian *norit,* "Norwegian rock," from *Norge,* Norway, from Old Norse *Norvegr, Noregr,* NORWAY.] —**nor·it′ic** (nô-rĭt′ĭk) *adj.*

Nor·land (nôr′lənd) *n.* Also **nor·land.** *Poetic.* Northland.

norm (nôrm) *n.* **1.** A standard, model, or pattern regarded as typical for a specific group. **2.** *Mathematics.* **a.** A **mode** *(see).* **b.** An average. **c.** The length of a vector. [Latin *norma,* carpenter's square, pattern. See **gnō-** in Appendix.*]

norm. normal.

Nor·ma[1] (nôr′mə). A feminine given name. [Perhaps from Latin *norma,* a square, pattern. See **gnō-** in Appendix.*]

Nor·ma[2] (nôr′mə) *n.* A constellation in the Southern Hemisphere within the Milky Way near Lupus and Ara.

nor·mal (nôr′məl) *adj.* **1.** Conforming, adhering to, or constituting a usual or typical pattern, level, or type; usual; typical: *"Almost all normal people want to be rich without great effort"* (F. Scott Fitzgerald). **2.** *Abbr.* **norm.** *Biology.* **a.** Not affected, immunized, or changed by experimentation. **b.** Functioning or occurring in a natural way. **3.** *Chemistry.* **a.** *Abbr.* **n, N** Describing a solution having one gram equivalent weight of solute per liter of solution. **b.** *Abbr.* **n-** Describing an aliphatic hydrocarbon having a straight and unbranched chain of carbon atoms. **4.** *Abbr.* **norm.** *Mathematics.* Being perpendicular; at right angles. See **normal** (noun). **5.** *Abbr.* **norm.** *Psychology.* Average in intelligence, ability, emotional traits, or personality. —*n. Abbr.* **norm.** **1.** Anything that is normal; the standard. **2.** The usual or expected state, form, amount, or degree. **3. a.** Correspondence to a norm. **b.** An average. **4.** *Geometry.* A perpendicular, especially a perpendicular to a line tangent to a plane curve or to a plane tangent to a space curve. [Late Latin *normālis,* from Latin, made according to the carpenter's square, rectangular, from *norma,* carpenter's square, precept. See **gnō-** in Appendix.*] —**nor′mal·ly** *adv.*

Synonyms: *normal, regular, standard, natural, typical.* Nontechnically, all these words suggest group characteristics. *Normal* stresses adherence to an established level or pattern that is associated with well-being, although based on group tendencies rather than on an arbitrary ideal. *Regular* and *standard* indicate unvarying conformity to a pattern in a narrower, impersonal sense. *Natural* emphasizes harmony between something (such as an act or an emotion) and the essence of the individual or object considered as a representative of a group. *Typical* stresses adherence to those qualities considered collectively and impersonally that identify a group.

nor·mal·cy (nôr′məl-sē) *n.* Normality.

Usage: *Normalcy* is widely employed in standard usage. It is disapproved by some, however, as a needless alternative to *normality,* coined outside the normal pattern of the language. It is unacceptable in writing to 59 per cent of the Usage Panel.

normal distribution. *Statistics.* A theoretical frequency distribution for a set of variable data, usually represented by a bell-shaped curve symmetrical about the mean. Also called "Gaussian distribution."

nor·mal·i·ty (nôr-măl′ə-tē) *n.* The state or fact of being normal. See Usage note at **normalcy.**

nor·mal·ize (nôr′mə-līz′) *tr.v.* **-ized, -izing, -izes.** **1.** To make normal; cause to conform to a standard or norm: *The two governments normalized their relations.* **2.** *Metallurgy.* To remove strains and reduce coarse crystalline structures by applying heat. —**nor′mal·i·za′tion** *n.* —**nor′mal·iz′er** *n.*

normal pentane. A **pentane** *(see).*

normal school. A school that trains teachers, chiefly for the elementary grades. [Translation of French *école normale,* originally the name of a school founded as a model for other teacher-training schools, from Late Latin *normālis,* NORMAL.]

Nor·man[1] (nôr′mən). A masculine given name. [Middle English *Norman,* Old English *Northman,* "man living in or coming from the North" : *north,* NORTH + *mann,* MAN.]

Nor·man[2] (nôr′mən) *n. Abbr.* **Nor.** **1.** One of a Scandinavian people who conquered Normandy in the tenth century. **2.** One of the people of Normandy who conquered England in 1066. **3.** A native or inhabitant of Normandy. **4.** A language, **Norman French** *(see).* —*adj.* **1.** Of or pertaining to Normandy, the Normans, their culture, or their language. **2.** *Architecture.* Designating a variety of Romanesque architecture that was introduced from Normandy into England before the Norman Conquest and flourished until about 1200. [Middle English *Norman,* from Norman French, variant of Old French *Normant,* from Old Norse *Northmathr* (stem *Northmann-*), Northman, Scandinavian : *northr,* north (see **ner-**[1] in Appendix*) + *mathr* (stem *mann-*), man (see **man-**[1] in Appendix*).]

Norman Conquest. The conquest of England by the Normans under William the Conqueror beginning in 1066.

Nor·man·dy (nôr′mən-dē). *French* **Nor·man·die** (nôr-mäN-dē′). A region of northwestern France on the English Channel.

Norman French. *Abbr.* **N.F.** **1.** The dialect of Old French used in medieval Normandy and England. **2.** The form of this dialect used in English court and legal circles from the Norman Conquest until the 15th century, still surviving in some legal formulas. Also called "Anglo-French," "Anglo-Norman."

nor·ma·tive (nôr′mə-tĭv) *adj.* **1.** Based upon or prescribing a norm, especially one regarded as a standard of usage in speech and writing: *normative grammar.* **2.** Relating to, implying, or establishing a norm or standard: *normative laws.* [French *normatif,* from *norme,* a norm, from Latin *norma,* carpenter's square, NORM.] —**nor′ma·tive·ly** *adv.* —**nor′ma·tive·ness** *n.*

nor·mo·blast (nôr′mō-blăst′) *n.* An immature red blood cell, characterized by abundant hemoglobin and a small nucleus. [NORM + -BLAST.]

Norn[1] (nôrn) *n., pl.* **Nornir** (nôr′nîr′) or **Norns.** *Norse Mythology.* One of the Fates, Skuld (the Future), Verdaude (the Present), and Urd (the Past). [Old Norse. See **sner-**[1] in Appendix.*]

Norn[2] (nôrn) *n.* An extinct Norse dialect spoken in Orkney and Shetland. [Old Norse *Norrœnn,* Norse, from *nordhr,* north. See **ner-**[1] in Appendix.*] —**Norn** *adj.*

nor·nic·o·tine (nôr-nĭk′ə-tēn′) *n.* A colorless liquid alkaloid, $C_9H_{12}N_2$, extracted from tobacco and used as a plant insecticide. [NOR- + NICOTINE.]

No·ro·dom Si·ha·nouk, Prince. See **Sihanouk.**

Nor·ris (nôr′ĭs, nŏr′-), **Frank.** Full name, Benjamin Franklin

Norris. 1870–1902. American author of novels of social protest.

Norse (nôrs) *adj. Abbr.* **N.** **1.** Of or pertaining to ancient Scandinavia, its people, or their language. **2. a.** Of or pertaining to West Scandinavia (Norway, Iceland, and the Faroe Islands) or the languages of its inhabitants. **b.** Of or pertaining to Norway, its people, or their language. —*n., pl.* **Norse.** *Abbr.* **N.** **1.** *Plural.* Preceded by *the.* **a.** The people of Scandinavia; the Scandinavians. **b.** The people of West Scandinavia; the West Scandinavians; especially, the Norwegians. **c.** The ancient Norwegians. **2.** The Scandinavian or North Germanic branch of Germanic languages; especially, Norwegian. **3.** Any of the West Scandinavian languages or dialects. [Dutch *noors,* a Norwegian, variant of *noords,* northern, from *noord,* north, from Middle Dutch *nort.* See **ner-¹** in Appendix.*]

Norse·man (nôrs′mən) *n., pl.* **-men** (-mĭn). Any of the ancient Scandinavians.

north (nôrth) *n. Abbr.* **n, N, n., N., no., No., Nor.** **1. a.** The direction along a meridian to the left of an observer facing in the direction of the earth's rotation; the direction to the left of sunrise. **b.** The cardinal point on the mariner's compass, located at 0 degrees. See **compass card.** **2.** Any area or region lying in this direction. **3.** *Often capital* **N. a.** The northern or arctic part of the earth. **b.** The northern part of any country or region. **4.** *Poetic.* The north wind. —**the North.** In the United States, the states lying north of Maryland, the Ohio River, and Missouri, and including those that fought for the Union against the Confederacy (or the South) in the Civil War. —*adj.* **1.** To, toward, of, facing, or in the north. **2.** Coming from or originating in the north, as a wind. **3.** *Capital* **N.** Officially designating the northern part of a country, continent, or other geographical area: *North Korea.* —*adv.* In, from, or toward the north. [Middle English *north,* Old English *north.* See **ner-¹** in Appendix.*]

North (nôrth), **Frederick.** Lord North. 1732–1792. British statesman; prime minister under George III (1770–82).

North (nôrth), Sir **Thomas.** 1535?–1601? English translator.

North America. *Abbr.* **N.A.** The northern continent of the Western Hemisphere with a total area, including adjacent islands, of 9,385,000 square miles. It extends from the Colombia-Panama border in the south through Central America, the United States (except Hawaii), Canada, and the Arctic Archipelago to the northern tip of Greenland. —**North American.**

North·amp·ton (nôr-thămp′tən, nôrth-hămp′-). A city and the county seat of Northamptonshire. Population, 121,000.

North·amp·ton·shire (nôr-thămp′tən-shîr′, -shər, nôrth-hămp′-). Also **North·amp·ton.** *Abbr.* **Northants.** A county, 994 square miles in area, in central England. Population, 398,000. County seat, Northampton.

North Atlantic Current. An ocean current or drift formed southeast of Newfoundland, Canada, by the junction of the Gulf Stream and the Labrador Current, and flowing generally northeast across the Atlantic.

North Atlantic Treaty Organization. Also **NATO** (nā′tō). An alliance for military and naval defense established April 4, 1949, by 15 countries located on or near the Atlantic Ocean. The original membership was: Belgium, Canada, Denmark, France (withdrew in 1966), Greece, Iceland, Italy, Luxembourg, the Netherlands, Norway, Portugal, Turkey, the United Kingdom, the United States, and West Germany.

North Bor·ne·o. Former name of **Sabah** *(see).*

north·bound (nôrth′bound′) *adj.* Going toward the north.

North Bra·bant (brə-bănt′ -bänt′). A province of the Netherlands, 1,965 square miles in area, located in the southern part of the kingdom. Population, 1,639,000. Capital, 's Hertogenbosch.

north by east. *Abbr.* **NbE** The direction, or point on the mariner's compass, halfway between due north and north-northeast. It is 11 degrees 15 minutes east of due north. See **compass card.**

north by west. *Abbr.* **NbW** The direction, or point on the mariner's compass, halfway between due north and north-northwest. It is 11 degrees 15 minutes west of due north. See **compass card.**

North Canadian. A river rising in northeastern New Mexico and flowing 760 miles to the Canadian River.

North Cape. **1.** A point on an island in the Arctic Sea off northern Norway, popularly held to be the northernmost part of Europe. Compare Cape **Nordkyn.** **2.** A cape on northern North Island, New Zealand.

North Car·o·li·na (kăr′ə-lī′nə). *Abbr.* **N.C.** A Southern state of the United States, 52,712 square miles in area, with its entire eastern boundary on the Atlantic Ocean. It was admitted to the Union in 1789 as one of the original 13 states. Population, 4,556,000. Capital, Raleigh. See map at **United States of America.** —**North Car′o·lin′i·an** (-lĭn′ē-ən).

North Channel. The strait between Northern Ireland and Scotland.

North·cliffe (nôrth′klĭf′), **Viscount.** Title of A.C.W. Harmsworth. 1865–1922. Irish born British newspaper proprietor.

North Da·ko·ta (də-kō′tə). *Abbr.* **N. Dak.** A Middle Western state of the United States, 70,665 square miles in area, on the Canadian border. It was admitted to the Union in 1889. Population, 632,000. Capital, Bismarck. See map at **United States of America.** —**North Dakotan.**

north·east (nôrth-ēst′; *Nautical* nôr-ēst′) *n. Abbr.* **NE** **1.** The direction, or point on the mariner's compass, halfway between north and east. It is 45 degrees east of due north. See **compass card.** **2.** Any area or region lying in this direction. —**the Northeast.** In the United States, the area including New England, New York, and sometimes Pennsylvania and New Jersey. —*adj.* **1.** Situated toward, facing, or in the northeast. **2.** Coming from or originating in the northeast, as a wind. —*adv.* In, from, or toward the northeast. —**north·east′ern** *adj.*

northeast by east. *Abbr.* **NEbE** The direction, or point on the mariner's compass, halfway between northeast and east-northeast. It is 56 degrees 15 minutes east of due north. See **compass card.**

northeast by north. *Abbr.* **NEbN** The direction, or point on the mariner's compass, halfway between northeast and north-northeast. It is 33 degrees 45 minutes east of due north. See **compass card.**

north·east·er (nôrth-ē′stər; *Nautical* nôr-ē′stər) *n.* Also **nor′-east·er** (nôr-ē′stər). A storm or gale from the northeast.

north·east·er·ly (nôrth-ē′stər-lē; *Nautical* nôr-ē′stər-lē) *adj.* **1.** Toward or in the northeast. **2.** From the northeast. —**north·east′er·ly** *adv.*

north·east·ward (nôrth-ēst′wərd; *Nautical* nôr-ēst′wərd) *adv.* Also **north·east·wards.** Toward the northeast. —*adj.* Situated toward or facing the northeast. —*n.* **1.** A direction or point toward the northeast. **2.** A region or part situated in or toward the northeast. —**north·east′ward·ly** *adj.* & *adv.*

north·er (nôr′*th*ər) *n.* A sudden, cold gale from the north, especially around the Gulf of Mexico.

north·er·ly (nôr′*th*ər-lē) *adj.* **1.** Situated toward the north. **2.** From the north. Said of wind. —*n., pl.* **northerlies.** A storm or wind from the north. —**north′er·ly** *adv.*

north·ern (nôr′*th*ərn) *adj. Abbr.* **n, n., no., N, N., No.** **1.** Situated toward, in, or facing the north. **2.** Coming from the north. Said of wind. **3.** Growing in the north. **4.** *Often capital* **N.** Of, pertaining to, or characteristic of northern regions or the North. **5.** *Astronomy.* North of the celestial equator. [Middle English *northerne,* Old English *northerne.* See **ner-¹** in Appendix.*]

Northern Cross. A constellation, **Cygnus** *(see).*

Northern Crown. The constellation **Corona Borealis** *(see).*

north·ern·er (nôr′*th*ər-nər) *n.* **1.** A native or inhabitant of the north. **2.** *Often capital* **N.** A native or inhabitant of the northeastern United States.

Northern Hemisphere. The half of the earth north of the equator.

Northern Ire·land (īr′lənd). A component of the United Kingdom, 5,238 square miles in area, in the northeastern part of the island of Ireland. Population, 1,458,000. Capital, Belfast.

northern lights. The **aurora borealis** *(see).*

north·ern·most (nôr′*th*ərn-mōst′) *adj.* Farthest north.

Northern Ni·ge·ri·a (nī-jîr′ē-ə). The largest administrative division, 281,872 square miles in area, of the Federation of Nigeria, occupying the northern and central parts of the country. Population, 29,778,000. Capital, Kano.

Northern Rho·de·sia. The former name for **Zambia.**

Northern Spor·a·des. See **Sporades.**

Northern Spy. A large, yellowish-red, late-ripening apple.

Northern Territory. A territory of Australia, occupying 523,620 square miles in the north-central region of the continent. Population, 52,000. Capital, Darwin.

North Germanic. A branch of the Germanic group of languages, which includes Danish, Faroese, Icelandic, Norwegian, and Swedish. See **Germanic.**

North Hol·land (hŏl′ənd). A province of the Netherlands, 1,016 square miles in area, on the North Sea. Population, 2,163,000. Capital, Haarlem.

north·ing (nôr′thĭng, -*th*ĭng) *n. Navigation.* **1.** The difference in latitude between two positions as a result of a movement to the north. **2.** Progress toward the north.

North Island. The smaller, 44,280 square miles in area, of the two principal islands of New Zealand. Population, 1,855,000.

North Italic. The northern division of the Italic group of languages, little attested except for Umbrian.

North Ko·re·a (kô-rē′ə, kō-). The unofficial name for the People's Democratic Republic of Korea. See **Korea.**

north·land (nôrth′lănd′, -lənd) *n.* **1.** *Often capital* **N.** A region in the north, such as the northern part of the earth or of a country. **2.** *Capital* **N.** Scandinavia. —**north′land′er** *n.*

North Little Rock. A city and industrial center of Arkansas, on the Arkansas River opposite Little Rock. Population, 58,000.

North·man (nôrth′mən) *n., pl.* **-men.** (-mĭn). A Norseman.

north-north·east (nôrth′nôrth-ēst′; *Nautical* nôr′nôr-ēst′) *n. Abbr.* **NNE** The direction, or point on the mariner's compass, halfway between due north and northeast. It is 22 degrees 30 minutes east of due north. See **compass card.** —*adj.* Situated toward, facing, or in this direction. —*adv.* In, from, or toward this direction.

north-north·west (nôrth′nôrth-wĕst′; *Nautical* nôr′nôr-wĕst′) *n. Abbr.* **NNW** The direction, or point on the mariner's compass, halfway between due north and northwest. It is 22 degrees 30 minutes west of due north. See **compass card.** —*adj.* Situated toward, facing, or in this direction. —*adv.* In, from, or toward this direction.

North Os·se·tian Autonomous Soviet Socialist Republic (ŏ-sē′shən). An administrative division, 3,088 square miles in area, of the southwestern Russian S.F.S.R. Population, 504,000. Capital, Ordzhonikidze. Also called "North Ossetia."

North Platte River (plăt). A river rising in northern Colorado and flowing 680 miles to join the South Platte River in southwestern Nebraska, where the two rivers become the Platte.

North Pole. **1.** The northern end of the earth's axis of rotation. **2.** The celestial zenith of this terrestrial point, slightly more than 1 degree from Polaris, the North Star. **3.** *Small* **n,** *small* **p.** The north-seeking **magnetic pole** *(see)* of a magnet.

North Rhine-West·pha·lia (rīn′wŏst fāl′yə, -fā′lē-ə). A state of

t tight/th thin, path/*th* this, bathe/ŭ cut/ûr urge/v valve/w with/y yes/z zebra, size/zh vision/ə about, item, edible, gallop, circus/ à *Fr.* ami/œ *Fr.* feu, *Ger.* schön/ü *Fr.* tu, *Ger.* über/KH *Ger.* ich, *Scot.* loch/N *Fr.* bon. *Follows main vocabulary. †Of obscure origin.

frontal sinuses   sphenoid sinus

Eustachian tube

pharyngeal tonsil

nose

nose cone
Modified nose cone of
a Gemini space vehicle

Norway

West Germany, 13,157 square miles in area, in the northwestern section of the Federal Republic. Population, 16,554,000. Capital, Düsseldorf.

North Rid·ing (rī′dǐng). An administrative division, 2,127 square miles in area, of Yorkshire, England. Population, 564,000.

North River. That part of the Hudson River estuary separating New Jersey and New York City.

Nor·throp (nôr′thrəp), **John Howard.** Born 1891. American biochemist; synthesized enzymes.

North Sas·katch·e·wan (săs-kăch′ə-wän,-wən). A river of Canada, rising in the Rockies and flowing 760 miles to the South Saskatchewan River in central Saskatchewan.

North Sea. A part of the Atlantic Ocean bordered by Belgium, the Netherlands, West Germany, Denmark, and Norway on the east and Britain on the west.

North Star. The polar star, Polaris (see).

North·um·ber·land (nôr-thŭm′bər-lənd). Abbr. **Northum.**, **Northumb.** A county of England, occupying 2,019 square miles in the north, bordering on Scotland. Population, 821,000. Capital, Newcastle-upon-Tyne.

North·um·ber·land Strait (nôr-thŭm′bər-lənd). A 200-mile-long strait between Prince Edward Island and New Brunswick and Nova Scotia.

North·um·bri·a (nôr-thŭm′brē-ə). An Anglo-Saxon kingdom of Britain, extending northward from the Humber to the Forth. [Latinized form of Old English Northhymbre, (dwellers) north of the Humber : NORTH + Hymbre, Humbre, the HUMBER.]

North·um·bri·an (nôr-thŭm′brē-ən) adj. **1.** Of or pertaining to Northumbria or its Old English dialect. **2.** Of or pertaining to Northumberland. —n. **1.** A native of Northumbria or Northumberland. **2.** The Old English dialect of Northumbria.

North Vietnam. The unofficial name for the Democratic Republic of Vietnam. See **Vietnam.**

north·ward (nôrth′wərd; Nautical nôr′thərd) adv. Also **northwards** (-wərdz; Nautical -thərdz). Toward the north. —adj. Situated toward, facing, or in the north. —n. **1.** A direction or point toward the north. **2.** A region situated in or toward the north. —**north′ward·ly** adj. & adv.

north·west (nôrth-wěst′; Nautical nôr-wěst′) n. Abbr. **NW** **1.** The direction, or point on the mariner's compass, halfway between north and west. It is 45 degrees west of due north. See **compass card. 2.** Any area or region lying in this direction. —**the Northwest. 1.** Formerly, the area west of the Mississippi and generally north of the Missouri. **2.** The present states of Washington, Oregon, and Idaho. —adj. **1.** To, toward, of, facing, or in the northwest. **2.** Coming from or originating in the northwest, as a wind. —adv. In, from, or toward the northwest. —**north·west′ern** adj.

northwest by north. Abbr. **NWbN** The direction, or point on the mariner's compass, halfway between northwest and north-northwest. It is 33 degrees 45 minutes west of due north. See **compass card.**

northwest by west. Abbr. **NWbW** The direction, or point on the mariner's compass, halfway between northwest and west-northwest. It is 56 degrees 15 minutes west of due north. See **compass card.**

north·west·er·ly (nôrth-wěs′tər-lē; Nautical nôr-wěs′tər-lē) adj. **1.** Toward or in the northwest. **2.** From the northwest. —**north·west′er·ly** adv.

Northwest Passage. The water route from the Atlantic to the Pacific through the Arctic Archipelago of Canada and north of Alaska, the search for which during 400 years was a major force in the exploration of North America. It was first navigated in 1903–06.

Northwest Semitic. A subgroup of the Semitic family of languages, comprising Canaanite and Aramaic.

Northwest Territories. Abbr. **N.W.T.** A territorial and political division of Canada, 1,304,903 square miles in area, that includes the Arctic Archipelago, the islands in Hudson Bay, and the mainland north of the Canadian provinces and east of the Yukon Territory. Population, 23,000. Capital, Yellowknife.

Northwest Territory. U.S. History. A region of 248,000 square miles extending from the Ohio and Mississippi rivers to the Great Lakes, awarded to the United States in 1783 by the Treaty of Paris, and organized by the U.S. Congress in 1787. It included the present states of Illinois, Indiana, Michigan, Ohio, Wisconsin, and part of Minnesota.

north·west·ward (nôrth-wěst′wərd; Nautical nôr-wěst′ərd) adv. Also **north·west·wards** (-wərdz; Nautical -thərdz). Toward the northwest. —adj. Situated toward, facing, or in the northwest. —n. **1.** A direction or point toward the northwest. **2.** A region or part situated in or toward the northwest. —**north·west′ward·ly** adj. & adv.

Nor·ton Sound (nôrt′n). An inlet of the Bering Sea, about 130 miles long and 90 miles wide, in western Alaska along the southern shore of the Seward Peninsula.

Norw. Norway; Norwegian.

Nor·walk (nôr′wôk). **1.** A city of California, southeast of Los Angeles. Population, 89,000. **2.** A city of Connecticut, on Long Island Sound. Population, 68,000.

Nor·way (nôr′wā). Norwegian **Nor·ge** (nôr′gə). Abbr. **Nor.**, **Norw.** A kingdom of northern Europe, about 125,000 square miles in area, situated on the Scandinavian Peninsula. Population, 3,708,000. Capital, Oslo. [Middle English Norwei, Old English Norweg, from Old Norse Norvegr, "northern region" : northr, north (see **ner-**[1] in Appendix*) + vegr, "way," (in place names) region (see **wegh-** in Appendix*).]

Norway maple. A tall Eurasian tree, Acer platanoides, widely used in North America as a shade tree. [First cultivated in NORWAY.]

Norway pine. A tree, the red pine (see). [Assumed to be first found at Norway, town in Maine.]

Norway rat. The common brown rat, Rattus norvegicus, highly destructive and found worldwide, especially in populated areas.

Norway spruce. A tall evergreen tree, Picea abies, of northern regions, growing to 150 feet in height and having long, dark-green needles.

Nor·we·gian (nôr-wē′jən) n. Abbr. **Nor.**, **Norw. 1.** A native or inhabitant of Norway. **2.** The North Germanic language of the Norwegians. [From Medieval Latin Norwegia, Norway, from Old Norse Norvegr, NORWAY.] —**Nor·we′gian** adj.

Norwegian elkhound. See **elkhound.**

Norwegian Sea. The part of the Arctic Ocean between Greenland and Norway.

Nor·wich (nôr′ĭj, -ĭch for sense 1; nôr′wĭch for sense 2). **1.** The county seat of Norfolk, England, in the east-central part of the county. Population, 119,000. **2.** A city of Connecticut, in the southeast at the head of the Thames River. Population, 39,000. [Middle English Norwich, Old English Northwīc, "northern village" : north, NORTH + wīc, WICK (village).]

nos., Nos. numbers.

nose (nōz) n. **1.** In man and other primates, the part of the face bearing the nostrils and containing the organ of smell and the beginning of the respiratory tract. **2.** In many other animals, a similar feature or organ in the face, muzzle, snout, or front end. **3. a.** The sense of smell: a dog with a good nose. **b.** The ability to sense or discover, as if by smell: a nose for a good story. **4.** Informal. The nose as a symbol of prying: Keep your nose out of my business. **5.** Anything that resembles a nose because of shape or position, such as the forward part of an aircraft. —**by a nose.** In horse racing, by the length of a horse's nose, considered as a narrow margin of victory. —**follow one's nose. 1.** To go straight ahead. **2.** To be guided by instinct. —**lead by the nose.** To control (someone) completely, often humiliatingly, without his perceiving it. —**look down one's nose at.** Informal. To treat haughtily. —**on the nose.** Slang. **1.** Designating a bet on a horse to win. **2.** Exactly; precisely. —**pay through the nose.** Informal. To pay an exorbitant price. —**turn up one's nose at.** To treat with contempt. —v. nosed, nosing, noses. —tr. **1.** To find out by or as if by smell. **2.** To touch or examine with the nose; nuzzle. **3.** To steer (a vehicle or one's way) with care to avoid collision. —intr. **1.** To smell or sniff. **2.** Informal. To pry curiously or in a meddlesome way. Followed by around, about, or into. **3.** To push forward with ponderous caution, as a ship. —**nose out.** To defeat by a very narrow margin. —**nose over.** To turn over on the nose, as an airplane crashing while taxiing or landing. [Middle English nose, Old English nosu. See **nas-** in Appendix.*]

nose·bag (nōz′băg′) n. A feedbag (see).

nose·band (nōz′bănd′) n. The part of a bridle or halter that passes over the animal's nose. Also called "nosepiece."

nose·bleed (nōz′blēd′) n. A nasal hemorrhage; bleeding from the nose. Also called "epistaxis."

nose cone. The forwardmost and usually separable section of a rocket or guided missile, shaped to offer minimum aerodynamic resistance and often bearing a protective cladding against heat.

nose dive. 1. A sudden plunge of an aircraft, nose toward the earth. **2.** Any sudden, swift, downward plunge.

nose-dive (nōz′dīv′) intr.v. -dived or -dove (-dōv′), -diving, -dives. To perform a nose dive.

no-see-um (nō-sē′əm) n. An insect, the punkie (see).

nose·gay (nōz′gā′) n. A small bunch of flowers. [Middle English : NOSE + gay, toy, ornament, from GAY (adjective).]

nose·piece (nōz′pēs′) n. **1.** A piece of armor forming part of a helmet and serving as a guard for the nose. **2.** The part of a pair of eyeglasses that fits across the nose. **3.** Part of a bridle, a noseband (see). **4.** The part of a microscope, often rotatable, to which one or more objective lenses are attached.

nosh (nŏsh) n. Informal. A tidbit; snack. —intr.v. noshed, noshing, noshes. Informal. To eat snacks between meals. [Shortened from Yiddish nosherai, tidbits, from Old High German (h)nascōn, to gnaw, nibble. See **ken-**[2] in Appendix.*]

no-show (nō′shō′) n. Slang. A traveler who reserves a place, especially on an airplane, but neither claims nor cancels the reservation before the time of departure.

nos·ing (nō′zǐng) n. **1.** The horizontally projecting edge of a stair tread. **2.** A shield covering this edge. **3.** A projecting edge of a molding.

noso-. Indicates disease; for example, nosology. [Greek, from nosos†, a disease.]

no·sog·ra·phy (nō-sŏg′rə-fē) n. The systematization and description of diseases. [New Latin nosographia : NOSO- + -GRAPHY.] —**no·sog′ra·pher** n. —**no′so·graph′ic** (nō′sə-grăf′ĭk, nŏs′ə-), no′so·graph′i·cal adj.

no·sol·o·gy (nō-sŏl′ə-jē) n. **1.** The branch of medicine that deals with the classification of diseases. **2.** A classification of diseases. [New Latin nosologia : NOSO- + -LOGY.] —**no′so·log′i·cal** (nō′sə-lŏj′ĭ-kəl, nŏs′ə-) adj. —**no′so·log′i·cal·ly** adv. —**no·sol′o·gist** n.

nos·tal·gi·a (nŏ-stăl′jə, nə-) n. **1.** A longing for things, persons, or situations that are not present: "a vague nostalgia for ancient aesthetic battles only dimly defined through the mists of memory" (Andrew Sarris). **2.** Homesickness. [New Latin (translation of German Heimweh, homesickness) : Greek nostos, a return (see **nes-**[1] in Appendix*) + -ALGIA.] —**nos·tal′gic** adj.

nos·toc (nŏs′tŏk′) n. Any freshwater algae of the genus Nostoc, forming colonies of blue-green cells embedded in a jelly. [New Latin; coined by Paracelsus as a name for algae that he believed were derived from starlight.]

Nos·tra·da·mus (nŏs′trə-dä′məs, nŏs′trə-dā′məs). Latinized form of the name of Michel de Nostre-Dame or Nostredame. 1503–1566. French astrologer and physician; author of a collection of prophecies (1555).

nos·tril (nŏs′trəl) *n.* Either of the external openings of the nose. [Middle English *nostrill,* Old English *nosthyrl* : *nosu,* NOSE + *thyrl, thyrel,* hole (see **ter-³** in Appendix*).]

nos·trum (nŏs′trəm) *n.* **1.** A medicine, the ingredients of which are kept secret; especially, a quack remedy. **2.** A pet scheme for the solution of some problem. [New Latin *nostrum,* "our own" (i.e., invented and made by the seller), from Latin, neuter of *noster,* ours. See **nes-²** in Appendix.*]

nos·y, nos·ey (nō′zē) *adj.* **-ier, -iest.** *Informal.* Prying; inquisitive. See Synonyms at **curious.** [From NOSE.] —**nos′i·ly** *adv.* —**nos′i·ness** *n.*

not (nŏt) *adv.* In no way; to no degree. Used to express negation, denial, refusal, prohibition: *I will not go. You may not have any.* In informal speech and writing, *not* is often contracted and suffixed to auxiliary verbs, for example, *aren't.* See Usage notes at **negative, only.** [Middle English *not,* reduced form of *nought,* nothing, not, Old English *nōwiht, nāwiht* : *nō, nā,* no (see **na**) + *wiht,* a man, thing (see **wekti-** in Appendix*).]

no·ta be·ne (nō′tə bĕn′ē, nō′tä bā′nā). *Abbr.* **n.b., N.B.** *Latin.* Note well.

no·ta·bil·i·ty (nō′tə-bĭl′ə-tē) *n., pl.* **-ties. 1.** The state or quality of being notable. **2.** A notable or prominent person.

no·ta·ble (nō′tə-bəl; *also* nŏt′ə-bəl *for sense 2*) *adj.* **1.** Worthy of notice; remarkable; striking: *notable beauty.* **2.** *Archaic & Regional.* Diligent, especially in housework. —See Synonyms at **noted.** —*n.* **1.** A person of note or distinction. **2.** *Often capital* **N.** *French History.* One of a council of prominent persons, before the Revolution, called into assembly by the king to deliberate at times of emergency. [Middle English, from Old French, from Latin *notābilis,* from *notāre,* to note, from *nota,* a NOTE.] —**no′ta·ble·ness** *n.* —**no′ta·bly** *adv.*

no·tar·i·al (nō-târ′ē-əl) *adj.* **1.** Of or pertaining to a notary. **2.** Executed or drawn up by a notary. —**no·tar′i·al·ly** *adv.*

no·ta·rize (nō′tə-rīz′) *tr.v.* **-rized, -rizing, -rizes.** To authenticate or attest to as a notary. [From NOTARY.] —**no′ta·ri·za′tion** *n.*

no·ta·ry (nō′tə-rē) *n., pl.* **-ries. 1.** *Obsolete.* A stenographer. **2.** A **notary public** *(see).* [Middle English *notarie,* "clerk," from Latin *notārius,* "stenographer," from *notārius,* cipher, shorthand character, from *nota,* mark, NOTE.]

notary public *pl.* **notaries public.** *Abbr.* **N.P.** A public officer authorized by law to certify documents, take affidavits, and administer oaths.

no·ta·tion (nō-tā′shən) *n.* **1.** A system of figures or symbols used in specialized fields to represent numbers, quantities, or other facts or values: *musical notation.* **2.** The act or process of using such a system. **3.** A jotting or annotation; a note: *a notation in the margin.* [Latin *notātiō,* from *notāre,* to note, from *nota,* a NOTE.] —**no·ta′tion·al** *adj.*

notch (nŏch) *n.* **1.** A V-shaped cut, especially one used for keeping count. **2.** A narrow pass between mountains. **3.** *Informal.* A level or degree: *He is a notch better than his brother.* —*tr.v.* **notched, notching, notches. 1.** To cut a notch or notches in. **2.** To record by, or as if by, making notches: *notched the score on a stick.* [From *a notch,* originally *an otch,* from Old French *o(s)che,* from *o(s)chier,* to notch, from Latin *absecāre,* to cut off : *ab-,* off + *secāre,* to cut (see **sek-** in Appendix*).]

note (nōt) *n. Abbr.* **n. 1.** *Often plural.* A brief record of something, written down to aid the memory. **2.** A brief written communication. **3.** A formal written diplomatic or official communication. **4.** A commentary to or explanation of a passage in a text, printed in the margin, at the foot of the page, or at the end of the text. **5. a.** A piece of paper currency. **b.** A certificate issued by a government or a bank and sometimes negotiable as money. **c.** A **promissory note** *(see).* **6.** *Music.* **a.** A tone of definite pitch. **b.** The symbol of such a tone in musical notation, indicating the pitch by its position on the staff and the duration by its shape. **c.** A key of a piano or similar instrument. **7. a.** The musical call of a bird. **b.** Any expressive vocal sound, such as the sound, cry, or call of an animal. **8.** A tone, sign, or suggestion that reveals a quality, or by which something may be known; a mark: *a note of gaiety.* **9.** Importance or consequence: *Nothing of note happened.* **10.** Notice or observation: *He took note of what had happened.* **11.** *Poetic.* A song, melody, or tune. —See Synonyms at **sign.** —**compare notes.** To exchange ideas, views, or opinions. —**strike the right note.** To say or do what is suitable. —*tr.v.* **noted, noting, notes. 1.** To observe carefully; notice; perceive. **2.** To write down; make a note of. **3.** To show; indicate. **4.** To make particular mention of; remark. —See Synonyms at **see.** [Middle English *note,* from Old French, from Latin *nota,* mark, sign, cipher, shorthand character. See **gnō-** in Appendix.*] —**not′er** *n.*

note·book (nōt′bo͝ok′) *n.* A book of blank pages for notes.

not·ed (nō′tĭd) *adj.* Distinguished by reputation; notable; eminent: *a noted author.* —**not′ed·ly** *adv.* —**not′ed·ness** *n.*

Synonyms: *noted, notable, noteworthy, notorious.* Applied to persons, *noted* emphasizes actual celebrity without stressing worthiness. *Notable* and *noteworthy* stress worthiness more strongly than celebrity. *Notorious* is usually unfavorable, implying disreputable celebrity.

note of hand. A **promissory note** *(see).*

note·wor·thy (nōt′wûr′thē) *adj.* Deserving recognition; worthy of notice; remarkable: *a noteworthy young talent.* See Synonyms at **noted.** —**note′wor′thi·ly** *adv.* —**note′wor′thi·ness** *n.*

noth·ing (nŭth′ĭng) *n.* **1.** No thing; not anything. **2.** No significant or notable thing: *There is nothing on television tonight.* **3.** No part; no portion: *Nothing remains of its former glory.* **4.** Insignificance; obscurity: *rising from nothing.* **5.** A person or thing of no consequence or significance. **6.** Absence of anything perceptible; nonexistence: *The sound faded into nothing.* **7. a.** That which has no quantitative value; naught; zero: *Nothing plus nothing equals nothing.* **b.** That which has no qualitative value or positive effect: *amount to nothing.* **8.** A trivial word or remark: *sweet nothings.* —**know** (or **not know**) **from nothing.** *Slang.* To be completely ignorant. —**nothing but.** Only; no more than; no other than. —**nothing doing.** *Informal.* **1.** Certainly not. Used as an emphatic refusal. **2.** Nothing of interest happening; not a thing going on. —**nothing like. 1.** Not at all like: *She's nothing like her sister.* **2.** Not nearly: *The blizzard here was nothing like as heavy as it was up North.* —*adj. Slang.* Insignificant or small; trifling: *a nothing part in a play.* —*adv.* In no way or degree; not at all: *It nothing avails to plead for quarter where you have given none.* [Middle English *nathing, nothing,* Old English *nāthing, nān thing* : *nān,* NONE + *thing,* THING.]

Usage: *Nothing,* used as the subject, always takes a singular verb, even when *nothing* is separated from the verb by a qualifying phrase or clause introduced by *but, except,* or the like, and containing a plural noun or pronoun; for example, *Nothing except your fears stands* (not *stand*) *in your path. Nothing but roses meets* (not *meet*) *the eye.* See Usage note at **negative.**

noth·ing·ness (nŭth′ĭng-nĭs) *n.* **1.** The condition or quality of being nothing; nonexistence. **2.** Empty or featureless space; void. **3.** Lack of consequence; insignificance. **4.** Something inconsequential or insignificant.

no·tice (nō′tĭs) *n.* **1.** The act of observing or regarding with the senses; perception; attention; heed: *That detail escaped my notice.* **2.** Heed or attention to another person or thing; especially, respectful attention or consideration: *grateful for his notice.* **3.** A formal written announcement, published or displayed for all to see: *a notice of sale.* **4.** A formal announcement of purpose, especially of intention to withdraw from an agreement or leave a job: *give two weeks' notice.* **5.** A printed critical review of a play, book, or other cultural work. **6.** Any announcement, information, or indication of some present or coming event. —*tr.v.* **noticed, -ticing, -tices. 1.** To observe; perceive; be aware of: *He did not notice the man in the doorway.* **2.** To consider; take note of; mark: *notice the discrepancy.* **3.** To comment on; mention in passing: *He began his speech by noticing the size of the audience.* **4.** To treat with courteous attention. —See Synonyms at **see.** [Middle English *notyce,* from Old French *notice,* from Latin *nōtitia,* knowledge, acquaintance, from *nōtus,* known, from the past participle of *nōscere,* to get acquainted with. See **gnō-** in Appendix.*]

no·tice·a·ble (nō′tĭs-ə-bəl) *adj.* **1.** Readily observed or detected; evident. **2.** Worth noticing; significant. —See Synonyms at **perceptible.** —**no′tice·a·bly** *adv.*

no·ti·fi·ca·tion (nō′tə-fĭ-kā′shən) *n.* **1.** The act or an instance of notifying. **2.** The sign, letter, or other form by which notice is given.

no·ti·fy (nō′tə-fī′) *tr.v.* **-fied, -fying, -fies. 1.** To give notice to (someone); inform. **2.** *Chiefly British.* To give notice or information of (something); make known; proclaim. [Middle English *notifien,* from Old French *notifier,* from Latin *nōtificāre,* to make known : *nōtus,* known, from *nōscere,* to get acquainted with (see **gnō-** in Appendix*) + *facere,* to make (see **dhē-¹** in Appendix*).] —**no′ti·fi′er** *n.*

no·tion (nō′shən) *n.* **1.** A general impression or feeling. **2.** A view; conception; theory *"I subscribe to the notion that education is an active process instead of an exercise in absorption."* (Paul P. Mok). **3.** Intention or inclination: *"Men's notion was, not for abolishing punishments, but for making laws just"* (Carlyle). **4.** *Plural.* Small items of household and clothing use, such as needles, buttons, thread, and ribbons. —See Synonyms at **idea.** [Latin *nōtiō,* "a becoming acquainted," from *nōscere* (past participle *nōtus*), to get acquainted. See **gnō-** in Appendix.*]

no·tion·al (nō′shən-əl) *adj.* **1.** Of, containing, or being a notion or notions; speculative or imaginary rather than factual. **2.** *Linguistics.* **a.** Conveying an idea of a thing or action; having full lexical meaning, as distinguished from relational meaning: *"Did"* is notional in *"we did the work"* and relational in *"we did not agree."* **b.** Conveying an idea directly to the mind; nonsymbolic; presentive. —**no′tion·al·ly** *adv.*

noto–, not–. Indicates south or southern; for example, **notornis, Notogaea.** [New Latin, from Greek *notos,* south, south wind. See **snā-** in Appendix.*]

no·to·chord (nō′tə-kôrd′) *n.* **1.** A flexible rodlike structure in some lower vertebrates that provides dorsal support; the primitive backbone. **2.** A similar structure in embryos of higher vertebrates, from which the spine develops. [Greek *nōtos,* back (see **nōt-** in Appendix*) + CHORD (cord).]

No·to·gae·a, No·to·ge·a (nō′tə-jē′ə) *n.* A zoogeographic region that includes Australia, New Zealand, and the southwestern Pacific islands. [New Latin, "south realm" : NOTO- + Greek *gaia,* land, earth (see **gē** in Appendix*).] —**No′to·gae′al, No′to·gae′an** *adj.*

no·to·ri·e·ty (nō′tə-rī′ə-tē) *n.* The quality or condition of being notorious. See Synonyms at **fame.**

no·to·ri·ous (nō-tôr′ē-əs, -tōr′ē-əs) *adj.* **1.** Known widely and regarded unfavorably; infamous: *"The deterioration in quality of her ships' companies was notorious"* (Alfred Thayer Mahan).

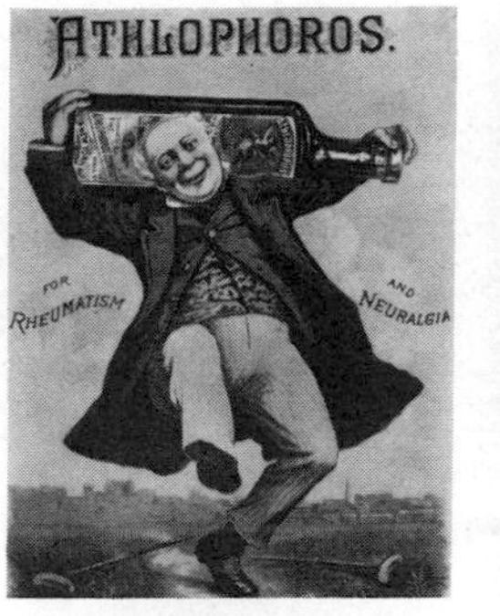
ATHLOPHOROS.
FOR RHEUMATISM
AND NEURALGIA

nostrum
Nineteenth-century poster

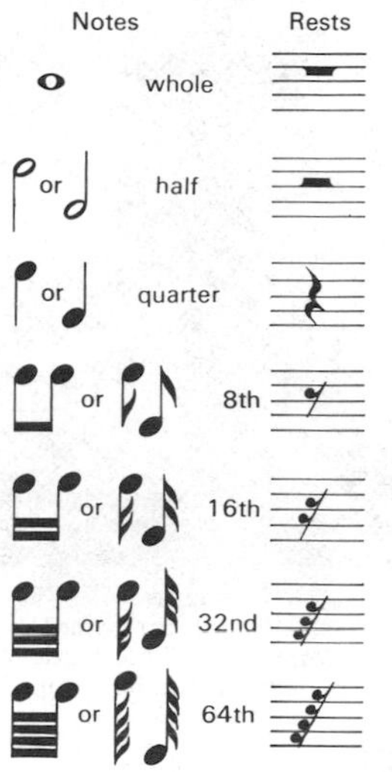
Notes
Rests
whole
or
half
or
quarter
or
8th
or
16th
or
32nd
or
64th

note

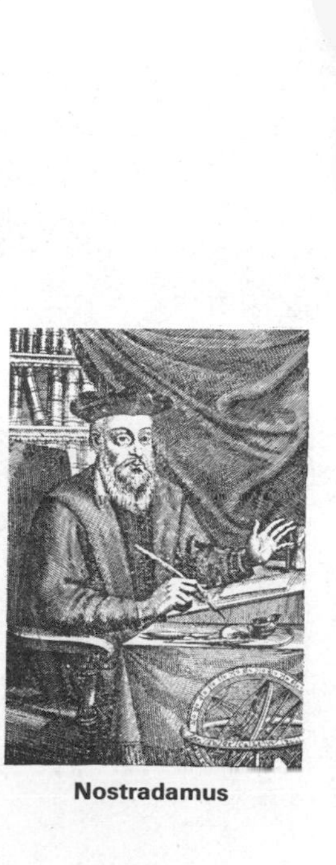

Nostradamus

t tight/th thin, path/*th* this, bathe/ŭ cut/ûr urge/v valve/w with/y yes/z zebra, size/zh vision/ə about, item, edible, gallop, circus/ à *Fr.* ami/œ *Fr.* feu, *Ger.* schön/ü *Fr.* tu, *Ger.* über/KH *Ger.* ich, *Scot.* loch/N *Fr.* bon. ***Follows main vocabulary. †Of obscure origin.**

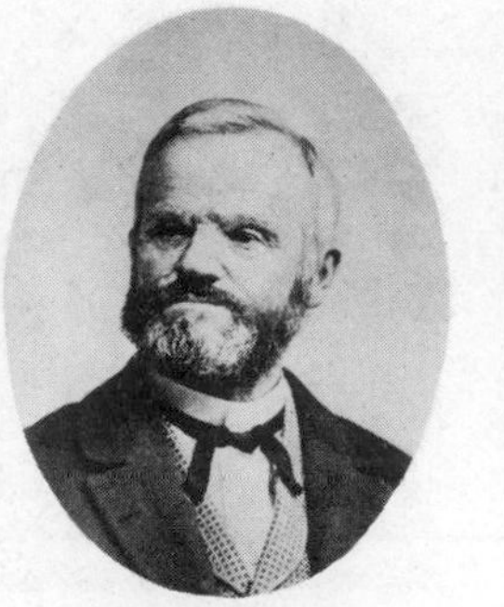

John Humphrey Noyes

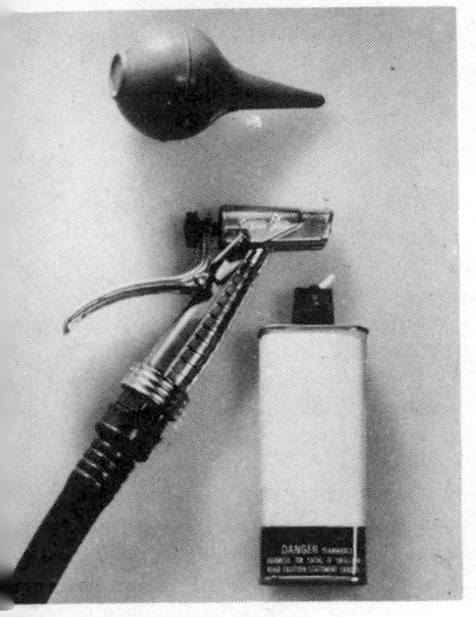

nozzle
Top: Rubber ear syringe
Center: Metal hose nozzle
Bottom: Lighter-fluid can, plastic nozzle at top

2. Generally known and discussed: *notorious facts.* —See Synonyms at **noted.** [Medieval Latin *nōtōrius,* from Late Latin, causing to be known, from *nōtus,* known, from the past participle of *nōscere,* to get acquainted. See **gnō-** in Appendix.*] —**no·to′ri·ous·ly** *adv.* —**no·to′ri·ous·ness** *n.*

no·tor·nis (nō-tôr′nĭs) *n.* Any flightless bird, now rare, of the genus *Notornis,* found in New Zealand. See **takahe.** [New Latin, "bird of the south" (i.e., New Zealand) : NOT(O)- + Greek *ornis,* bird (see **er-²** in Appendix*).]

no-trump (nō′trŭmp′) *n.* **1.** In bridge and other card games, a declaration to play a hand without a trump suit. **2.** A hand played without a trump suit. —**no′-trump′** *adj.*

Not·ta·way (nŏt′ə-wā′). A river rising in southwestern Quebec and flowing about 400 miles generally northwest to James Bay.

Not·ting·ham (nŏt′ĭng-əm). **1.** Also **Nottinghamshire** (nŏt′ĭng-əm-shîr′, shər). A county occupying 843 square miles in central England. Population, 903,000. **2.** The county seat of this county, a lace and textile center on the Trent River. Population, 311,000.

not·tur·no (nə-tŏŏr′nō, nō-) *n., pl.* **-ni** (-nē). **1.** *Music.* A nocturne. **2.** An 18th-century musical composition for a small instrumental ensemble, generally in sonata form and resembling a serenade. [Italian, night piece, nocturnal, from Latin *nocturnus,* from *nox,* night. See **nekwt-** in Appendix.*]

not·with·stand·ing (nŏt′wĭth-stăn′dĭng, nŏt′wĭth-) *prep.* In spite of; regardless of hindrance by: *He left notwithstanding his father's opposition.* —*adv.* All the same; nevertheless: *We proceeded, notwithstanding.* —*conj.* In spite of the fact that; although. [Middle English *notwithstonding* : NOT + present participle of *withstonden,* to WITHSTAND.]

Synonyms: *notwithstanding, despite, in spite of. Notwithstanding* is the weakest of three terms used to indicate opposition of varying intensity to contrary forces or circumstances. *Despite* is used when the opposition is relatively stronger and *in spite of* when the forces are resisted most actively and vigorously.

Nouak·chott (nwäk′shŏt′). The capital of Mauritania, located in the west about 3 miles inland. Population, 13,000.

nou·gat (nōō′gət) *n.* A confection made from a sweet sugar or honey paste into which pistachios and almonds are mixed. [French *nougat,* from Provençal, from Old Provençal *nogat,* confection of nuts, from Vulgar Latin *nucātum* (unattested), from Latin *nux* (stem *nuc-*), nut. See **ken-⁵** in Appendix.*]

nought. Variant of **naught.**

Nou·mé·a (nōō-mā′ə). The capital of New Caledonia, on the southwestern coast. Population, 35,000.

nou·me·non (nōō′mə-nŏn′) *n., pl.* **-na** (-nə). *Philosophy.* **1.** An object of purely intellectual intuition, as opposed to an object of sensuous perception. **2.** A thing-in-itself, independent of sensuous or intellectual perception of it. Compare **phenomenon.** [German *Noumenon,* from Greek *noumenon,* concept, thought, from *nouein,* to think, apprehend, from *nous,* mind. See **nous** in Appendix.*] —**nou′me·nal** *adj.* —**nou′me·nal·ism′** *n.* —**nou′me·nal·ist** *n.* —**nou′me·nal·ly** *adv.*

noun (noun) *n. Abbr.* **n.** **1.** A word used to denote or name a person, place, thing, quality, or act. **2. a.** The part of speech of a word that is the subject or object of a verb, object of a preposition, or an appositive. **b.** Any word, phrase, or clause used in this way. [Middle English *nowne,* from Norman French *noun,* a name, noun, from Old French *non, nom,* from Latin *nōmen,* name. See **nomen-** in Appendix.*] —**noun, noun′al** *adj.* —**noun′al·ly** *adv.*

Usage: Many nouns are used as attributive adjectives to qualify other nouns; for example, *life* in *life insurance* and *music* in *music critic.* Modern usage has broadened this practice to include nouns not previously so employed. Common examples of such extended usage are the following combinations: *health reasons* (as in *resigned for health reasons*), which is accepted by only 29 per cent of the Usage Panel; *disaster proportions,* accepted by 57 per cent; *beatnik-type beards,* accepted by 63 per cent; and *sex-education courses,* accepted by 87 per cent. This extended use of nouns as adjectives has the guarded approval of many Panel members as a means of conciseness. But many warn against uncouth constructions like *health reasons,* and against lengthy combinations that are overloaded and cumbersome (*mass media education level*).

nour·ish (nûr′ĭsh) *tr.v.* **-ished, -ishing, -ishes.** **1.** To provide with food or other substances necessary for life and growth. **2.** To foster the development of; promote and sustain: *"Athens was an imperial city, nourished by the tribute of subjects."* (V. Gordon Childe). [Middle English *nurishen, norishen,* from Old French *norrir* (stem *norriss-*), from Latin *nūtrīre,* to feed. See **sneu-** in Appendix.*] —**nour′ish·a·ble** *adj.* —**nour′ish·er** *n.*

nour·ish·ment (nûr′ĭsh-mənt) *n.* **1. a.** The act of nourishing. **b.** The state of being nourished. **2.** That which supports life and growth in a living organism; food; sustenance. **3.** That which promotes the development or vitality of something.

nous (nōōs) *n. Philosophy.* Mind; reason; specifically, the principle of divine reason. [Greek. See **nous** in Appendix.*]

nou·veau riche (nōō-vō rēsh′) *pl.* **nouveaux riches** (nōō-vō rēsh′). One who has lately become rich. Usually used disparagingly to imply ostentation. [French, "new rich."]

Nov. November.

no·va (nō′və) *n., pl.* **-vae** (-vē) or **-vas.** *Astronomy.* A variable star that suddenly increases in brightness to several times its normal magnitude, and returns to its original appearance in a few weeks to several months or years. Compare **supernova.** [New Latin *(stella) nova,* "new (star)," from Latin *novus,* new. See **newo-** in Appendix.*]

no·vac·u·lite (nō-văk′yə-līt′) *n.* A very hard, dense, even-textured, silica-bearing rock used in whetstones. [Latin *novācula,* razor (see **kes-¹** in Appendix*) + -ITE.]

No·va Go·a (nō′və gō′ə). The capital of the former Portuguese colony of Goa, on the western coast of India. Population, 79,500.

No·va Lis·bo·a (nô′və lēzh-vō′ə). Formerly **Huam·bo** (wäm′bō). A city of west-central Angola, designated a future capital of the province. Population, 39,000.

No·va Sco·tia (nō′və skō′shə). *Abbr.* **N.S.** A maritime province and peninsula of southeastern Canada, 21,743 square miles in area. Population, 763,000. Capital, Halifax. See map at **Canada.** —**Nova Scotian.**

no·va·tion (nō-vā′shən) *n. Law.* The substitution of a new obligation for an old one; specifically, transference of a debt. [Late Latin *novātiō,* a making new, from Latin *novāre,* to make new, from *novus,* new. See **newo-** in Appendix.*]

No·va·ya Zem·lya (nô′və-yə zĕm-lyä′). **1.** A Soviet archipelago with a land area of 35,000 square miles, lying between the Barents and Kara seas. **2.** Its two main islands.

nov·el¹ (nŏv′əl) *n.* **1.** A fictional prose narrative of considerable length, typically having a plot that is unfolded by the actions, speech, and thoughts of the characters: "Uncle Tom's Cabin *is a very bad novel"* (James Baldwin). **2.** The literary genre represented by this form of narrative. Used with *the: "The novel . . . is a perpetual quest for reality"* (Lionel Trilling). [Italian *(storia) novella,* a short tale, "new story," from feminine of *novello,* new, from Latin *novellus,* NOVEL.]

nov·el² (nŏv′əl) *adj.* Strikingly new, unusual, or different. See Synonyms at **new.** [Middle English *novel,* from Old French, from Latin *novellus,* from *novus,* new. See **newo-** in Appendix.*] —**nov′el·ly** *adv.*

nov·el·ette (nŏv′ə-lĕt′) *n.* A short novel.

nov·el·ist (nŏv′ə-lĭst) *n.* A writer of novels.

nov·el·is·tic (nŏv′ə-lĭs′tĭk) *adj.* Of, relating to, or characteristic of novels. —**nov′el·is′ti·cal·ly** *adv.*

no·vel·la (nō-vĕl′ə) *n., pl.* **-las** or **-le** (-vĕl′ē). **1.** A short prose tale of the type developed by Boccaccio, characterized by epigrammatic terseness and point. **2.** A short novel. [Italian. See **novel** (narrative).]

Nov·els (nŏv′əlz) *pl.n. Roman Law.* Amendments made by the Emperor Justinian and his successors to the Code of Justinian. [New Latin *novella,* singular of Late Latin *novellae (constitūtiōnēs),* "new (statutes)," from Latin *novellus,* new, from *novus,* new. See **newo-** in Appendix.*]

nov·el·ty (nŏv′əl-tē) *n., pl.* **-ties.** **1.** The quality of being novel; newness; originality. **2.** Something that is novel; a new or unusual thing; an innovation. **3.** *Plural.* Small mass-produced articles, as toys or trinkets. [Middle English *noveltee,* from Old French *novelte,* from *novel,* new, NOVEL.]

No·vem·ber (nō-vĕm′bər) *n. Abbr.* **Nov., N.** The 11th month of the Gregorian calendar. November has 30 days. See **calendar.** [Middle English *Novembre,* from Old French, from Latin *November,* for *Novembris (mēnsis),* the ninth (month) (of the Roman calendar), from *novem,* nine. See **newn̥** in Appendix.*]

no·ve·na (nō-vē′nə) *n., pl.* **-nas** or **-nae** (-nē). *Roman Catholic Church.* A recitation of prayers and devotions for nine consecutive days. [Medieval Latin *novēna,* from Latin *novēnus,* nine each, from *novem,* nine. See **newn** in Appendix.*]

no·ver·cal (nō-vûr′kəl) *adj.* Of, pertaining to, or characteristic of a stepmother. [Latin *novercālis,* from *noverca,* a stepmother. See **newo-** in Appendix.*]

Nov·go·rod (nŏv′gə-rŏd′). An ancient city of the Soviet Union in the northwest, about 115 miles south of Leningrad. Population, 61,000.

nov·ice (nŏv′ĭs) *n.* **1.** A person new to any field or activity; beginner. **2.** A person who has entered a religious order, but who is on probation before taking final vows. Compare **postulant.** [Middle English *novyce,* from Old French *novice,* from Medieval Latin *novīcius,* from Latin *novīcius,* extension of *novus,* new. See **newo-** in Appendix.*]

No·vi Sad (nō′vē säd′). A city of Yugoslavia, on the Danube about 45 miles northwest of Belgrade. Population, 111,000.

no·vi·ti·ate (nō-vĭsh′ē-ĭt, -āt′) *n.* Also **no·vi·ci·ate.** **1.** *Ecclesiastical.* **a.** The period of time served by a novice. **b.** A place where novices live. **c.** A novice. **2.** The state or time of being a beginner. **3.** A beginner. [French *noviciat,* from Medieval Latin *novīciātus,* from *novīcius,* NOVICE.]

No·vo·cain (nō′və-kān′) *n.* A trademark for the anesthetic **procaine hydrochloride** *(see).* [German *Novokain* : Latin *novus,* new (see **newo-** in Appendix*) + German *Kokain,* COCAINE.]

No·vo Kuz·netsk (nō′vō kŏŏz-nĕtsk′). Formerly **Sta·linsk** (stä′-lĭnsk). A major Soviet iron and steel center in south-central Siberia. Population, 475,000.

No·vo·ros·siisk (nō′vō-rŏ-sēsk′). A seaport of the southeastern Soviet Union, on the Black Sea. Population, 115,000.

No·vo·si·birsk (nō′vō-sĭ-bîrsk′). A city in south-central Siberia, on the Ob River. Population, 1,029,000.

no·vus or·do se·clo·rum (nō′vəs ôr′dō sĕ-klōr′əm). *Latin.* A new order of the ages. It is the motto on the U.S. Great Seal.

now (nou) *adv.* **1.** At the present time. **2.** At once; immediately: *Stop that now.* **3.** In the immediate past; very recently. Often preceded by *just: He left just now.* **4.** In the immediate future; very soon. Often preceded by *just: They are going just now.* **5.** At this point in the narrative or series of events; then: *The ship was now badly listing to port.* **6.** Nowadays: *Now women rarely wear long skirts.* **7.** In these circumstances; as things are: *Now we won't be able to stay.* —*conj.* Since; seeing that. Often followed by *that: Now that we have eaten, let's go.* —*n.* The present time or moment: *Now is the time to act.* —**now and**

again (or **then**). Occasionally. [Middle English *nu, now,* Old English *nū*. See **nu-** in Appendix.*]

Usage: *Now* is often used as an emphatic expletive, as in cases of command, remonstrance, or entreaty: *Come now, don't cry.*

now·a·days (nou'ə-dāz') *adv.* In these days; during the present time. [Middle English *now a dayes,* "on this day" : NOW + *a dayes,* Old English *on dæges* (adverbial genitive) : ON + DAY.]

no·way (nō'wā') *adv.* Also **no·ways** (nō'wāz'). Nowise.

no·where (nō'hwâr') *adv.* Also *nonstandard* **no·wheres** (-hwârz'). In, to, or at no place; not anywhere. **—get nowhere.** *Informal.* To accomplish nothing; fail utterly to make progress. *—n.* No place; a nonexistent or insignificant place.

no·whith·er (nō'hwĭth'ər) *adv.* In no definite direction.

no·wise (nō'wīz') *adv.* In no way, manner or degree; not at all. [Middle English *nawyse* : NO + WISE (way).]

nox·ious (nŏk'shəs) *adj.* Injurious or harmful to health or morals. [Latin *noxius,* from *noxa,* injury, damage. See **nek-**[1] in Appendix.*] **—nox·ious·ly** *adv.* **—nox'ious·ness** *n.*

Noyes (noiz), **Alfred.** 1880–1958. English poet and critic.

Noyes (noiz), **John Humphrey.** 1811–1886. American reformer; founder (1848) of the experimental Oneida Community in New York State.

Noy·on (nwà-yôɴ'). A town of northern France, site of the coronations of Charlemagne (768) and of Hugh Capet (987). Population, 9,000.

noz·zle (nŏz'əl) *n.* **1.** A projecting, often regulated, spout through which gas or liquid is discharged, such as the end of a hose, the nose of a pair of bellows, or the spout of a teapot. **2.** *Slang.* The nose. [Earlier *nosel, nosle,* diminutive of NOSE.]

Np The symbol for the element neptunium.

NP neuropsychiatric; neuropsychiatry.

N.P. notary public.

NPN, N.P.N. nonprotein nitrogen.

n.p.t. normal pressure and temperature.

NRA, N.R.A. National Recovery Administration.

n.s. **1.** new series. **2.** not specified.

N.S. **1.** New Style. **2.** Nova Scotia.

NSA National Shipping Authority.

NSC National Security Council.

NSF National Science Foundation.

n.s.f., N.S.F. not sufficient funds.

N.S.P.C.A. National Society for the Prevention of Cruelty to Animals.

N.S.W. New South Wales.

NT, N.T. New Testament.

nth (ĕnth) *adj.* **1.** Pertaining to an indefinitely large ordinal number: *ten to the nth power.* **2.** Infinitely or indefinitely large or small; most extreme; utmost: *exaggerated to the nth degree.*

n.t.p., N.T.P. normal temperature and pressure.

nu (no͞o, nyo͞o) *n.* The thirteenth letter of the Greek alphabet (Ν, ν), corresponding to the English *N, n.* See **alphabet.** [Greek *nu,* from a Phoenician word meaning "fish," from a Semitic root *nyn* meaning "to increase" or, possibly, "to endure."]

nu·ance (no͞o-äns', nyo͞o-, no͞o'äns', nyo͞o'-) *n.* A subtle or slight variation, as in meaning, color, or quality; a gradation: *"I seem to grasp at certain moments the nuance that divides bad from worse."* (Samuel Beckett). [French *nuance,* from Old French, from *nuer,* to show shades of color (as in clouds), from *nue,* cloud, from Vulgar Latin *nūbe* (unattested), from Latin *nūbēs.* See **sneudh-** in Appendix.*]

nub (nŭb) *n.* **1.** A protuberance or knob. **2.** A small lump or piece. **3.** *Informal.* The gist or point: *the nub of a story.* [Variant of *knub,* from Middle Low German *knubbe,* knot on a tree, variant of *knobbe,* KNOB.]

Nu·ba (no͞o'bə, nyo͞o'-) *n., pl.* **Nuba.** **1.** A Nubian. **2.** A member of any of several Negroid tribes of southern Sudan. **3.** The language spoken by the Nuba people.

nub·bin (nŭb'ĭn) *n.* **1.** A small, stunted ear of corn. **2.** Anything stunted or imperfectly developed. [Diminutive of NUB.]

nub·ble (nŭb'əl) *n.* A small protuberance or lump. [Diminutive of NUB.] **—nub'bly** *adj.*

Nu·bi·a (no͞o'bē-ə, nyo͞o'-). A desert region and ancient kingdom in the Nile valley of southern Egypt and northern Sudan.

Nu·bi·an (no͞o'bē-ən, nyo͞o'-) *n.* **1.** A native or inhabitant of Nubia. **2.** Any of the languages of Nubia. **—Nu'bi·an** *adj.*

Nubian Desert. A desert in northeastern Sudan, extending east of the Nile to the Red Sea.

nu·bile (no͞o'bĭl, -bīl', nyo͞o'-) *adj.* Ready for marriage; of a marriageable age. Said of women, often with a suggestion of sexuality: *"she yet continued to burrow into my heart as a young and nubile houri"* (Kenneth Tynan). [French *nubile,* from Latin *nūbilis,* marriageable, from *nūbere,* to take a husband. See **sneubh-** in Appendix.*] **—nu·bil'i·ty** (no͞o-bĭl'ə-tē, nyo͞o-) *n.*

nu·cel·lus (no͞o-sĕl'əs, nyo͞o-) *n., pl.* **-celli** (-sĕl'ī'). *Botany.* The center of the rudimentary seed of a plant, containing the embryo sac. Also called "nucleus." [New Latin, irregularly from Latin *nucella,* diminutive of *nux* (stem *nuc-*), nut. See **ken-**[5] in Appendix.*] **—nu·cel'lar** *adj.*

nu·cha (no͞o'kə, nyo͞o'-) *n.* The nape of the neck. [Middle English *nucha, nuca,* from Medieval Latin *nucha,* from Arabic *nukhā'*, spinal marrow.] **—nu'chal** *adj.*

nu·cle·ar (no͞o'klē-ər, nyo͞o'-) *adj.* **1.** *Biology.* Of, pertaining to, or forming a nucleus: *a nuclear membrane.* **2.** *Physics.* Of or concerning atomic nuclei: *nuclear physics.* **3.** Using or derived from the energy of atomic nuclei; atomic: *nuclear power plants.* **4.** Of, involving, or possessing atomic or hydrogen bombs: *nuclear war; nuclear nations.* [From NUCLEUS.]

nuclear emulsion. *Physics.* Any of several photographic emulsions used to detect and visually display the paths of charged subatomic particles, especially of charged cosmic ray particles.

nuclear energy. *Physics.* The energy released by a nuclear reaction, especially by fission, fusion, or radioactive decay.

nuclear fission. *Physics.* **Fission** *(see).*

nuclear fusion. *Physics.* **Fusion** *(see).*

nuclear magneton. *Physics. Abbr.* **nm** A unit of the magnetic moment of the nucleon. See **magneton.**

nuclear physics. The scientific study of the forces, reactions, and internal structures of atomic nuclei.

nuclear reaction. *Physics.* A reaction that alters the energy, composition, or structure of an atomic nucleus.

nuclear reactor. Any of several devices in which a **chain reaction** *(see)* is initiated and controlled, with the consequent production of heat, typically used for power generation, and of neutrons and fission products, used for a variety of experimental and medical purposes. Also called "atomic pile," "atomic reactor," "chain-reacting pile," "pile," "reactor."

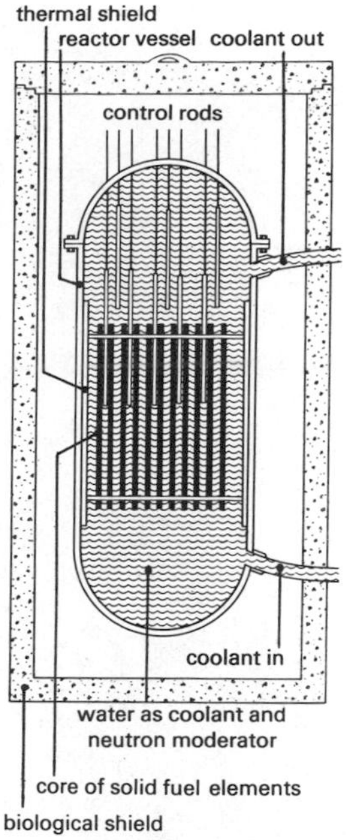

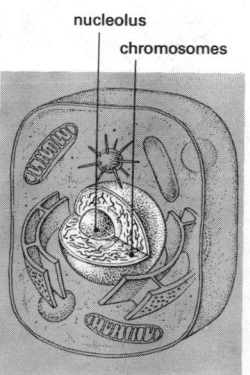

thermal shield
reactor vessel
coolant out
control rods
coolant in
water as coolant and neutron moderator
core of solid fuel elements
biological shield

nuclear reactor

nu·cle·ase (no͞o'klē-ās', -āz', nyo͞o'-) *n.* Any of several enzymes that hydrolize nucleic acids. [NUCLE(O)- + -ASE.]

nu·cle·ate (no͞o'klē-ĭt, nyo͞o'-) *adj.* Having a nucleus or nuclei. *—v.* (no͞o'klē-āt', nyo͞o'-) **nucleated, -ating, -ates.** *—tr.* **1.** To bring together into a nucleus. **2.** To act as a nucleus for. *—intr.* To form a nucleus. [NUCLE(US) + -ATE.] **—nu'cle·a'tion** *n.* **—nu'cle·a'tor** (-ā'tər) *n.*

nu·cle·i. Plural of **nucleus.**

nu·cle·ic acid (no͞o-klē'ĭk, nyo͞o-). Any member of either of two groups of complex compounds found in all living cells, and composed of purines, pyrimidines, carbohydrates, and phosphoric acid. See **deoxyribonucleic acid, ribonucleic acid.** [From NUCLE(O)- + -IC (because found in nucleoproteins).]

nucleo-, nucle-. Indicates: **1.** Nucleus; for example, **nucleon, mononucleosis.** **2.** Nucleic acid; for example, **nucleoprotein, nucleoside.** [From NUCLEUS.]

nu·cle·o·late (no͞o'klē-ə-lāt', nyo͞o'-) *adj.* Also **nu·cle·o·lat·ed** (no͞o'klē-ə-lā'tĭd, nyo͞o'-). Having a nucleolus or nucleoli. [NUCLEOL(US) + -ATE.]

nu·cle·o·lus (no͞o-klē'ə-ləs, nyo͞o-, -klē-ō'ləs) *n., pl.* **-li** (-lī'). Also **nu·cle·ole** (no͞o'klē-ōl', nyo͞o'-). *Biology.* **1.** A small, usually round body composed of protein and ribonucleic acid in the nucleus of a cell. Also called "plasmosome." **2.** Any discrete, cellular particle resembling a nucleolus, other than a chromosome. See **endosome.** [New Latin, from Latin, diminutive of *nucleus,* a kernel, NUCLEUS.] **—nu·cle'o·lar** (-lər) *adj.*

nu·cle·on (no͞o'klē-ŏn', nyo͞o'-) *n.* A proton or a neutron, especially as part of an atomic nucleus. See **particle.** [NUCLE(O)- + -ON.] **—nu'cle·on'ic** *adj.*

nu·cle·on·ics (no͞o'klē-ŏn'ĭks, nyo͞o'-) *n.* Plural in form, used with a singular verb. The technology of nuclear energy. [From NUCLEON.]

nucleon number. *Physics.* **Mass number** *(see).*

nu·cle·o·plasm (no͞o'klē-ə-plăz'əm, nyo͞o'-) *n.* The protoplasm of a cell nucleus. Also called "karyoplasm." [NUCLEO- + -PLASM.] **—nu'cle·o·plas'mic, nu'cle·o·plas·ma'tic** (-plăz-măt'ĭk) *adj.*

nu·cle·o·pro·tein (no͞o'klē-ō-prō'tēn', -prō'tē-ĭn, nyo͞o'-) *n.* Any of a group of substances found in all living cells and viruses, and composed of a protein and a nucleic acid.

nu·cle·o·side (no͞o'klē-ə-sīd', nyo͞o'-) *n.* Any compound made of a sugar and a purine or pyrimidine base, especially one obtained by hydrolysis of a nucleic acid, such as adenosine. [NUCLE(O) + -OS(E) + -IDE.]

nu·cle·o·tide (no͞o'klē-ə-tīd', nyo͞o'-) *n.* Any of various organic compounds consisting of a nucleoside combined with phosphoric acid. [From NUCLEO- + -IDE.]

nu·cle·us (no͞o'klē-əs, nyo͞o'-) *n., pl.* **-clei** (-klē-ī') or *rare* **-uses.** **1.** A central thing or part around which other things are grouped; core: *the nucleus of a city.* **2.** Anything regarded as a basis for future development and growth; a kernel; a beginning: *"For Lenin the Party as it already existed was the . . . nucleus of rule"* (Bertram D. Wolfe). **3.** *Biology.* A complex, usually spherical, protoplasmic body within a living cell that contains the cell's hereditary material and that controls its metabolism, growth, and reproduction. **4.** *Botany.* **a.** The **nucellus** *(see).* **b.** The central kernel of a nut or seed. **c.** The central point of a starch granule. **5.** *Anatomy.* A group of nerve cells or localized mass of gray matter in the brain, where nerve fibers interconnect. **6.** *Physics.* The positively charged central region of an atom, composed of protons and neutrons, and containing almost all of the mass of the atom. See **atomic number, mass number.** **7.** *Chemistry.* A group of atoms chemically bound in a structure resistant to alteration in chemical reactions. **8.** *Astronomy.* **a.** The central portion of the head of a comet. **b.** The central or brightest part of a nebula or of a galaxy. **9.** *Meteorology.* A particle upon which water vapor molecules accumulate in free air to form a droplet or ice crystal. [Latin, "a nut," "kernel," from *nux* (stem *nuc-*), a nut. See **ken-**[5] in Appendix.*]

nucleolus
chromosomes

nucleus

nu·clide (no͞o'klīd', nyo͞o'-) *n. Physics.* Any atomic nucleus specified by its atomic number, atomic mass, and energy state. Compare **isotope.** [NUCLE(O)- + -IDE.] **—nu·clid'ic** (no͞o-klĭd'ĭk, nyo͞o-) *adj.*

nude (no͞od, nyo͞od) *adj.* **1.** Without clothing; naked. **2.** *Law.* Lacking any of various legal requisites, such as evidence or consideration: *a nude contract.* *—n.* **1.** The nude human figure or a representation of it. **2.** Nude state: *in the nude.* [Latin *nūdus,* nude, bare. See **nogw-** in Appendix.*] **—nude'ly** *adv.* **—nude'ness** *n.*

nudge (nŭj) *tr.v.* **nudged, nudging, nudges.** To push against gently, especially in order to gain attention or give a signal. *—n.* A gentle push. [Probably from a Scandinavian word

akin to Norwegian dialectal *nugga, nyggja*†, to push, rub.]

nudi-. Indicates nakedness or bareness; for example, **nudibranch, nudicaul.** [From Latin *nūdus,* NUDE.]

nu·di·branch (no͞o′də-brăngk′, nyo͞o′-) *n.* Any mollusk of the order Nudibranchia, **sea slug** *(see).* [New Latin *Nudibranchia,* "ones having naked gills" : NUDI- + BRANCHIA.] —**nu′di·bran′chi·ate** (-brăng′kē-ĭt), **nu′di·bran′chi·an** (-brăng′kē-ən) *adj.* & *n.*

nu·di·caul (no͞o′də-kôl′, nyo͞o′-) *adj.* Also **nu·di·cau·lous** (no͞o′də-kô′ləs, nyo͞o′-). *Botany.* Having no leaves on the stem. [NUDI- + Latin *caulis,* stalk, stem (see **kau-l-** in Appendix*).]

nud·ism (no͞o′dĭz′əm, nyo͞o′-) *n.* The doctrine or practice of living in the nude. —**nud′ist** *adj.* & *n.*

nu·di·ty (no͞o′də-tē, nyo͞o′-) *n., pl.* **-ties.** **1.** The quality or state of being nude; bareness; nakedness. **2.** A nude figure as represented in painting or sculpture.

nud·nik (no͝od′nĭk) *n.* Also **nud·nick.** *Slang.* A boring or bothersome person; pest. [Yiddish, from Polish *nudny,* tedious, tiresome, from *nudu,* boredom. See **nāu-**[1] in Appendix.*]

Nu·e·ces River (no͞o-ā′səs, nyo͞o-). A river of southwestern Texas, flowing 315 miles south and southeast to the Gulf of Mexico, near Corpus Christi.

Nue·vo La·re·do (nwā′vō lä-rā′*thō*). A border city in eastern Mexico. Population, 112,000.

Nue·vo Le·ón (nwā′vō lā-ōn′). A northeastern state of Mexico, 25,134 square miles in area. Population, 1,211,000. Capital, Monterrey.

nu·ga·to·ry (no͞o′gə-tôr′ē, -tōr′ē, nyo͞o′-) *adj.* **1.** Of no value; worthless; trifling: *a nugatory point.* **2.** Having no power; invalid; inoperative: *a nugatory statute.* [Latin *nūgātōrius,* trifling, from *nūgārī,* to jest, trifle, from *nūgae*†, jokes.]

nug·get (nŭg′ĭt) *n.* **1.** A small lump, especially one of natural gold. **2.** A small but valuable portion or unit: *nuggets of information.* [Southwestern English dialectal *nugget,* lump, diminutive of *nug*†, protuberance, lump.]

nui·sance (no͞o′səns, nyo͞o′-) *n.* **1.** A source of inconvenience, annoyance, or vexation; bother. **2.** *Law.* A use of property or course of conduct that interferes with the legal rights of others by causing damage, annoyance, or inconvenience. [Middle English *nusaunce,* injury, harmful thing, from Old French *nuisance,* from *nuire* (stem **nuis-**), to harm, injure, from Latin *nocēre.* See **nek-**[1] in Appendix.*]

nuisance tax. A tax levied on separate purchases.

Nu·ku·a·lo·fa (no͞o′ko͞o-ə-lô′fə). The capital of Tonga, situated on Tongatabu Island. Population, 9,000.

Nu·ku Hi·va (no͞o′ko͞o hē′və). The largest (186 square miles) of the Marquesas Islands.

Nu·kus (no͞o-ko͞os′). The capital of the Kara-Kalpak A.S.S.R. in southwestern Uzbek. Population, 51,000.

null (nŭl) *adj.* **1.** Having no legal force; invalid. Often used in the phrase *null and void.* **2. a.** Of no consequence, effect, or value; insignificant. **b.** Lacking distinctive personality; colorless: *a null face.* **3.** Amounting to nothing; lacking; absent; nonexistent. **4.** *Mathematics.* Of or pertaining to a set having no members or to zero magnitude. —*n.* **1.** Zero. **2.** An instrumental reading of zero. [Old French *nul,* "none," from Latin *nūllus* : *ne,* not (see **ne** in Appendix*) + *ūllus,* any (see **oino-** in Appendix*).]

nul·lah (nŭl′ə) *n.* **1.** A ravine or gully. **2.** A watercourse. [Hindi *nālā,* rivulet, ravine, probably from Dravidian.]

nul·li·fi·ca·tion (nŭl′ə-fĭ-kā′shən) *n.* **1.** The action of nullifying. **2.** The refusal or failure of a U.S. state to recognize or enforce Federal laws within its boundaries: *"Where powers are assumed which have not been delegated, a nullification of the act is the rightful remedy."* (Jefferson). —**nul′li·fi·ca′tion·ist** *n.*

nul·li·fi·er (nŭl′ə-fī′ər) *n.* **1.** One that nullifies. **2.** A partisan of nullification, especially by a U.S. state.

nul·li·fy (nŭl′ə-fī′) *tr.v.* **-fied, -fying, -fies.** **1.** To deprive of legal force; annul; make void: *The court nullified the contract.* **2.** To make ineffective or useless: *"Thus content was he to be nullified, that the Lord might be magnified!"* (Cotton Mather). See Synonyms at **neutralize.** [Late Latin *nūllificāre,* to make light of, despise : *nūllus,* none, NULL + *facere,* to make (see **dhē-**[1] in Appendix*).]

Synonyms: *nullify, negate, abolish, annul, void, invalidate, abrogate, cancel, repeal, revoke, rescind. Nullify* and *negate,* as compared here, both indicate reduction to ineffectiveness. *Abolish* goes further and stresses complete removal. *Annul* and *void* are general terms indicating deprivation of effectiveness or validity. *Invalidate* is also applied to action that destroys effectiveness or validity, but it is narrower in that it implies a specific cause; a contract may be invalidated by faulty execution or by lack of fulfillment of a single term. *Abrogate,* applied to treaties or other formal agreements, stresses executive action that terminates. *Cancel* has the same force as the preceding term, but is applied to more commonplace agreements, such as contracts, leases, and deeds. *Repeal* is usually confined to a legislative act that terminates existing legislation. *Revoke* and *rescind* involve the taking back by executive action of a previous grant of privilege or power.

nul·li·ty (nŭl′ə-tē) *n., pl.* **-ties.** **1.** The state or quality of being null: *the nullity of third parties in a two-party system.* **2.** *Law.* **a.** The fact of being null and void. **b.** An act having no legal validity. **3.** A nonentity.

num. **1.** number. **2.** numeral.

Num. Numbers.

Nu·ma·zu (no͞o-mä′zo͞o). A seaport of Japan, in south-central Honshu. Population, 155,000.

numb (nŭm) *adj.* **number, numbest.** **1.** Insensible, as from excessive chill; benumbed: *toes numb with cold.* **2.** Stunned or paralyzed, as from shock or strong emotion: *"There remained a numb speculation as to why this question should make him angry."* (James Baldwin). **3.** Insensitive or inept. **4.** Resembling or of the nature of loss of sensation: *a numb feeling.* —*v.* **numbed, numbing, numbs.** —*tr.* To make numb; deaden. —*intr.* To become numb. [Middle English *nome(n),* originally "seized with palsy, paralyzed," past participle of *nimen,* to take, seize, Old English *niman.* See **nem-**[2] in Appendix.*] —**numb′ly** *adv.* —**numb′ness** *n.*

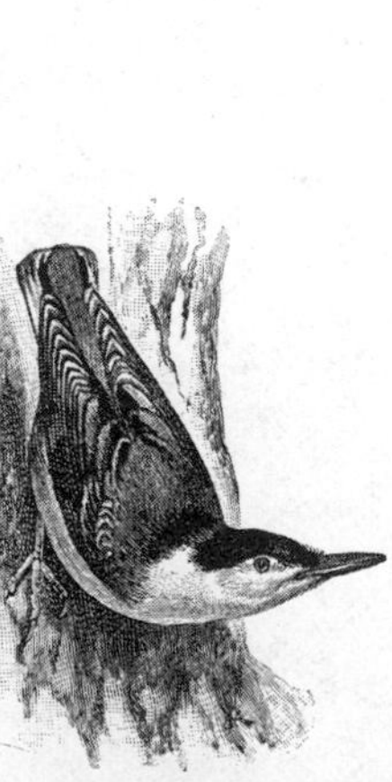

nuthatch
Sitta carolinensis
White-breasted nuthatch

num·ber (nŭm′bər) *n. Abbr.* **n., no., No., num.** *Symbol* # **1.** *Mathematics.* **a.** A member of the set of positive integers; one of a series of symbols of unique meaning in a fixed order which may be derived by counting. See also **cardinal number, ordinal number. b.** A member of any of the further sets of mathematical objects that may be derived from the positive integers by mathematical induction. See **induction.** Thus, given the positive integers and zero, the operation of addition makes it possible to define the negative integers (those which added to the positive integers produce zero). The integers together with the fractions (of the form m/n, where m and n are integers and n is not zero) form the set of *rational numbers.* The rational numbers together with the *irrational numbers* (those not expressible as quotients of integers) form the set of *real numbers.* Numbers of the form $a + bi$, where a and b are real numbers and $i^2 = -1$, form the set of *complex numbers,* which is the broadest set commonly used in mathematics. See also **transfinite number. 2.** *Plural.* The study or processes of arithmetic. **3.** A numeral or series of numerals assigned to or designating a specific person or thing: *a telephone number.* **4.** A specific quantity composed of equal units: *The number of apples in the bowl is ten.* See Usage note below. **5.** Quantity of units or individuals: *The crowd was small in number.* **6.** *Plural.* A large quantity or collection; multitude: *Numbers of people visited the fair.* **7.** One item in a group or series considered to be in numerical order. **8.** One of the separate offerings in a program of music. **9.** *Informal.* A person or thing singled out for some notable characteristic. **10.** *Usually plural.* Strength or superiority based on quantity: *The South had leaders, the North numbers.* **11.** *Grammar.* The indication, as by inflection, of the singularity or plurality of a linguistic form. **12. a.** *Plural.* Metrical periods or feet; verses: *the melodious numbers of our old poets.* **b.** Measured rhythm in verse. **13.** *Plural.* Musical periods or measures. **14.** *Plural.* A lottery, **policy** *(see).* —**a number of.** A considerable, indefinite quantity of. See Usage note below. —**any number of.** A large, indefinite quantity of; numerous. —**by the numbers. 1.** *Military.* Step by step, as consecutive numbers are called out. **2.** *Slang.* In a mechanical or excessively regulated manner. —**get** (or **have**) **someone's number.** To determine (or know) someone's real character or motives. —**without** (or **beyond**) **number.** In quantity too great to be counted. —*v.* **numbered, -bering, -bers.** —*tr.* **1.** To total in number or amount; add up to. **2.** To count or determine the number or amount of. **3.** To include in a group or category: *He was numbered among the lost.* **4.** To mention one by one; enumerate. **5.** To assign a number to. **6.** To limit or restrict in number: *The days of his life are numbered.* —*intr.* **1.** To count or call off numbers: *numbering to ten.* **2.** To constitute a group or number: *The applicants numbered in the thousands.* [Middle English *n(o)umbre,* from Old French *nombre,* from Latin *numerus.* See **nem-**[2] in Appendix.*] —**num′ber·er** *n.*

Usage: *Number,* when preceded by *the,* takes a singular verb: *The number of unskilled workers is small.* When preceded by *a,* it takes a plural verb: *A number of the workers are unskilled.*

num·ber·less (nŭm′bər-lĭs) *adj.* **1.** Innumerable; countless. **2.** Having no number. See Synonyms at **infinite.**

number one. *Informal.* **1.** Oneself: *He thinks only of number one.* **2.** The first or most important. —**num′ber-one′** *adj.*

Num·bers (nŭm′bərz) *n.* Plural in form, used with a singular verb. *Abbr.* **Num.** The fourth book of the Old Testament, containing the two censuses of the Israelites after the Exodus.

numbers game. A lottery, **policy** *(see).*

numb·fish (nŭm′fĭsh′) *n., pl.* **-fish** or **-fishes.** A fish, the **electric ray** *(see).*

numb·skull. Variant of **numskull.**

nu·men (no͞o′mən, nyo͞o′-) *n., pl.* **numina** (no͞o′mə-nə, nyo͞o′-). **1.** The presiding divinity or spirit (of a place). **2.** The spirit believed by animists to inhabit certain natural objects. **3.** Creative energy regarded as a genius or demon dwelling within one. [Latin *nūmen,* "a nod," hence "command," divine power, deity. See **neu-**[2] in Appendix.*]

nu·mer·a·ble (no͞o′mər-ə-bəl, nyo͞o′-) *adj.* Capable of being counted; consisting of a finite collection of distinct units. [Latin *numerābilis,* from *numerāre,* NUMERATE.]

nu·mer·al (no͞o′mər-əl, nyo͞o′-) *n. Abbr.* **num. 1.** A symbol, such as a letter, figure, or word used alone or in a group to denote a number. See **Arabic numeral, Roman numeral. 2.** *Plural.* The numbers indicating the year of a graduating class in a school or college, usually shown as only the last two figures, as in "class of '34." —*adj.* Of, pertaining to, or expressing numbers. [Old French *numeral,* from Latin *numerālis,* from Latin *numerus,* NUMBER.] —**nu′mer·al·ly** *adv.*

nu·mer·ar·y (no͞o′mə-rĕr′ē, nyo͞o′-) *adj.* Of or pertaining to a number or numbers. [Medieval Latin *numerārius,* from Latin *numerus,* NUMBER.]

nu·mer·ate (no͞o′mə-rāt′, nyo͞o′-) *tr.v.* **-ated, -ating, -ates. 1.** To enumerate; number; reckon. **2.** To read (numerals). [Latin *numerāre,* to number, count, from *numerus,* NUMBER.]

nu·mer·a·tion (no͞o′mə-rā′shən, nyo͞o′-) *n.* **1.** The act or process of counting by means of reading, writing, or naming numbers.

ă pat/ā pay/âr care/ä father/b bib/ch church/d deed/ĕ pet/ē be/f fife/g gag/h hat/hw which/ĭ pit/ī pie/îr pier/j judge/k kick/l lid, needle/m mum/n no, sudden/ng thing/ŏ pot/ō toe/ô paw, for/oi noise/ou out/o͝o took/o͞o boot/p pop/r roar/s sauce/sh ship, dish/

2. A system of numbering or of reading numbers.

nu·mer·a·tor (no͞o′mə-rā′tər, nyo͞o′-) *n.* **1.** *Mathematics.* **a.** The expression written above the line in a common fraction. Compare **denominator. b.** An expression to be divided by another; the dividend. **2.** One that numbers; an enumerator.

nu·mer·i·cal (no͞o-mĕr′ĭ-kəl, nyo͞o-) *adj.* Also **nu·mer·ic** (no͞o-mĕr′ĭk, nyo͞o-). **1.** Of or pertaining to a number or series of numbers: *numerical order.* **2.** Denoting number or a number: *a numerical symbol.* **3.** Expressed in or counted by numbers: *numerical strength.* **4.** Represented by a number or numbers rather than by letter or symbol: *a numerical grade.* [From Medieval Latin *numericus,* from Latin *numerus,* a NUMBER.] **—nu·mer′i·cal·ly** *adv.*

numerical value. *Mathematics.* The absolute value of a number, regardless of sign: *The numerical values of −9 and +9 are equal.*

nu·mer·ol·o·gy (no͞o′mə-rŏl′ə-jē, nyo͞o′-) *n.* The study of the occult meanings of numbers and of their supposed influence on human life. [Latin *numerus,* NUMBER + -LOGY.] **—nu′mer·o·log′i·cal** (no͞o′mər-ə-lŏj′ĭ-kəl, nyo͞o′-) *adj.* **—nu′mer·ol′o·gist** *n.*

nu·mer·ous (no͞o′mər-əs, nyo͞o′-) *adj.* **1.** Consisting of many persons or things: *a numerous collection.* **2.** Many: *numerous books.* [Old French *numereux,* from Latin *numerōsus,* from *numerus,* NUMBER.] **—nu′mer·ous·ly** *adv.* **—nu′mer·ous·ness** *n.*

Nu·mid·i·a (no͞o-mĭd′ē-ə, nyo͞o-). An ancient kingdom and Roman province of northern Africa. **—Nu·mid′i·an** *adj.* & *n.*

nu·mi·nous (no͞o′mə-nəs, nyo͞o′-) *adj.* **1.** Of or pertaining to a **numen** *(see).* **2.** Spiritually elevated: *"the strange numinous sense of presentness . . . like a spell"* (William G. Polland). *—n.* The presence or revelation of the numen. Used with *the.* [From Latin *nūmen* (stem *nūmin-*), NUMEN.]

numis., numism. numismatic; numismatics.

nu·mis·mat·ics (no͞o′mĭz-măt′ĭks, no͞o′mĭs-, nyo͞o′-) *n.* Plural in form, used with singular verb. *Abbr.* **numis., numism.** The study and collection of money and medals. Also called "numismatology." [From *numismatic* (adjective), from French *numismatique,* from Latin *numisma,* a coin, from Greek *nomisma,* usage, current coin, from *nomizein,* to have in use, from *nomos,* custom. See **nem-²** in Appendix.*] **—nu′mis·mat′ic** *adj.* **—nu·mis′ma·tist** (no͞o-mĭz′mə-tĭst, no͞o-mĭs′-, nyo͞o-) *n.*

num·mu·lar (nŭm′yə-lər) *adj.* Shaped like a coin; circular. [French *nummulaire,* from Latin *nummulus,* diminutive of *nummus,* a coin, "currency," probably from Greek *nomimos,* customary, legal, from *nomos,* custom. See **nem-²** in Appendix.*]

num·mu·lite (nŭm′yə-līt′) *n.* Any protozoan of the family Nummulitidae, chiefly marine, tiny, mostly extinct, and characterized by a coin-shaped shell. [New Latin *Nummulites* (genus name) : Latin *nummulus,* coin (see **nummular**) + *-ites,* -ITE.] **—num′mu·lit′ic** (nŭm′yə-lĭt′ĭk) *adj.*

num·skull (nŭm′skŭl′) *n.* Also **numb·skull.** A stupid person; blockhead. [NUMB + SKULL.]

nun¹ (nŭn) *n.* **1.** A woman who belongs to a religious order devoted to religious service or meditation, usually under vows of poverty, chastity, and obedience, as in the Roman, Anglican, and Orthodox Churches. **2.** Any of various birds, especially one of a breed of pigeons. [Middle English *nunne, nun, nonne,* from Old English *nunne* and Old French *nonne,* both from Medieval Latin *nonna,* nun (originally a respectful form of address to old women). See **nana** in Appendix.*]

nun² (no͞on, no͝on) *n.* **1.** The 14th letter of the Hebrew alphabet. See **alphabet. 2.** The 25th letter of the Arabic alphabet. **3.** The consonant sound represented by either of these letters. [Hebrew and Arabic *nūn,* akin to NU.]

Nunc Di·mit·tis (no͝ongk′ dĭ-mĭt′ĭs, no͞ongk′). **1.** The canticle of Simeon, beginning *"Nunc dimittis servum tuum"* ("Now lettest thou thy servant depart"). Luke 2:29–32. **2.** *Small* **n,** *small* **d.** Permission to depart; a dismissal.

nun·ci·a·ture (nŭn′sē-ə-cho͝or′, no͝on′-) *n.* The office or term of a nuncio. [Italian *nunciatura,* from *nuncio,* NUNCIO.]

nun·ci·o (nŭn′sē-ō′, no͝on′-) *n., pl.* **-os.** An ambassador from the pope. [Italian, from Latin *nūntius,* messenger. See **neu-¹** in Appendix.*]

nun·cle (nŭng′kəl) *n. Archaic.* An uncle. [From *an uncle.*]

nun·cu·pa·tive (nŭng′kyə-pā′tĭv, nŭng-kyo͞o′pə-tĭv) *adj. Law.* Designating a will delivered orally to witnesses rather than written. [Medieval Latin *nūncupātīvus,* from Latin *nūncupāre,* to call by name, name one's heirs : *nōmen,* name (see **nomen-** in Appendix*) + *capere,* to take (see **kap-** in Appendix*).]

Nu·ni·vak (no͞o′nə-văk′). An island 56 miles long and 40 miles wide, in the Bering Sea off the southwestern coast of Alaska.

nun·ner·y (nŭn′ə-rē) *n., pl.* **-ies.** A community of nuns or the buildings in which they live.

nup·tial (nŭp′shəl, -chəl) *adj.* **1.** Of or pertaining to marriage or the wedding ceremony. **2.** *Entomology.* Of or at the time of mating. *—n. Usually plural.* A wedding ceremony. See Synonyms at **marriage.** [Latin *nuptiālis,* from *nuptiae,* wedding, from *nūbere* (past participle *nuptus*), to take a husband (see **sneubh-** in Appendix*).] **—nup′tial·ly** *adv.*

Nu·rem·berg (no͝or′əm-bûrg′, nyo͝or′-), *German* **Nürn·berg** (nürn′bĕrk′). A city of north central Bavaria, West Germany. Population, 469,000.

Nu·re·yev (no͞o-rā′ĕf), **Rudolf (Hametovich).** Born 1938. Russian ballet dancer and choreographer; emigrated (1961); permanent guest artist with the British Royal Ballet.

Nu·ri·stan (no͝or′ĭ-stăn′). A district of Afghanistan, on the southern slopes of the Hindu Kush.

nurse (nûrs) *n.* **1.** A person trained to care for the sick or disabled under the supervision of a physician. See **registered nurse. 2.** A **practical nurse** *(see).* **3.** A woman employed to take care of another's children; nursemaid. **4.** A woman employed to suckle children other than her own; a wet nurse. **5.** That which fosters some quality or condition: *"Town life is the nurse of civilization."* (C.L.R. James). **6.** *Entomology.* A worker ant or bee that cares for the young in the insect colony. *—v.* **nursed, nursing, nurses.** *—tr.* **1.** To feed at the breast; suckle. **2.** To care for or tend (a child). **3.** To care for or tend (an invalid). **4.** To try to cure or treat: *to nurse a cough.* **5.** To take special care of; foster; cultivate: *He nursed his business through the depression.* **6.** To bear privately in the mind: *nursing a grudge.* **7.** To hold or clasp carefully; fondle: *He nursed his bruised knee between his hands.* **8.** To drink (usually an alcoholic drink) slowly. *—intr.* **1.** To take nourishment from the breast; suckle. **2.** To serve as a nurse. [Middle English *norse, nurse,* from Old French *norrice,* from Late Latin *nūtrīcia,* from *nūtrīcius,* adjective of *nūtrix,* a nurse. See **sneu-** in Appendix.*] **—nurs′er** *n.*

nurse·maid (nûrs′mād′) *n.* Also **nurs·er·y·maid** (nûr′sər-ē-mād′, nûrs′rē-). A girl or woman employed to take care of children.

nurs·er·y (nûr′sə-rē, nûrs′rē) *n., pl.* **-ies. 1.** A room or area set apart for the use of children. **2.** A **nursery school** *(see).* **3.** A place where plants are grown for sale, transplanting, or experimentation. **4.** Any place in which something is produced or developed. [Middle English *norserie,* from *norse,* NURSE.]

nurs·er·y·man (nûr′sə-rē-mən, nûrs′rē-) *n., pl.* **-men** (-mĭn). One who owns or works in a nursery for plants.

nursery rhyme. A short, rhymed poem or tale for children.

nursery school. A school for children who are not old enough to attend kindergarten. Also called "nursery."

nursing home. A hospital for convalescent or aged people.

nurs·ling (nûrs′lĭng) *n.* Also **nurse·ling. 1.** A nursing infant or young animal. **2.** A carefully nurtured person or thing.

nur·ture (nûr′chər) *n.* **1.** Anything that nourishes; sustenance; food. **2.** The act of promoting development or growth; upbringing; rearing. **3.** *Biology.* The sum of environmental influences and conditions acting upon an organism. *—tr.v.* **nurtured, -turing, -tures. 1.** To nourish. **2.** To educate or train. [Middle English *norture, nurture,* from Old French *nour(e)ture,* from Late Latin *nūtrītūra,* a feeding, suckling, from Latin *nūtrīre,* to feed, suckle. See **sneu-** in Appendix.*] **—nur′tur·er** *n.*

Nu·sa Teng·ga·ra (no͞o′sə tĕng-gä′rə). Formerly, **Lesser Sun·da Islands** (so͞on′dä). A province and island chain of Indonesia, 28,241 square miles in area, extending from Bali to Timor.

nut (nŭt) *n.* **1. a.** A hard-shelled, solid-textured, one-celled fruit that does not split open, such as an acorn or a hazelnut. **b.** Any seed borne in a fruit having a hard shell, such as the peanut or almond. **c.** The kernel of any of these. **2.** *Informal.* Any difficult person, endeavor, or problem. Usually in the phrase: *hard nut to crack.* **3.** *Slang.* An eccentric, fanciful, or deranged person. **4.** *Slang.* The head. **5.** *Plural. Vulgar Slang.* The testicles. **6. a.** A ridge of wood at the top of the finger board or neck of stringed instruments, over which the strings pass. **b.** A device at the lower end of the bow of a violin or similar instrument, used for adjusting the hairs. **7.** A small block of metal or wood having a central, threaded hole, designed to fit around and secure a bolt or screw. **8.** *Informal.* The amount of money invested in a theatrical production, or the cost of running it until a profit can be made. *—intr.v.* **nutted, nutting, nuts.** To gather or hunt for nuts. [Middle English *note, nute,* Old English *hnutu.* See **ken-⁵** in Appendix.*] **—nut′ter** *n.*

nu·ta·tion (no͞o-tā′shən, nyo͞o-) *n.* **1.** A nodding of the head. **2.** *Astronomy.* A small periodic motion of the celestial pole of the earth with respect to the pole of the ecliptic. **3.** *Botany.* A slight curving or circular movement in the stem of a plant, caused by irregular growth rates of different parts. [Latin *nūtātiō,* from *nūtāre,* frequentative of *nuere* (unattested), to nod. See **neu-²** in Appendix.*] **—nu·ta′tion·al** *adj.*

nut·crack·er (nŭt′krăk′ər) *n.* **1.** An implement, typically consisting of two levers, used to crack nuts. **2. a.** A bird, *Nucifraga caryocatactes,* of northern Eurasia. **b.** A bird, *N. columbianus,* of western North America. **c.** A bird, the **nuthatch** *(see).*

nut·gall (nŭt′gôl′) *n.* A small, nut-shaped parasitic growth on a tree, especially on an oak. Also called "gallnut." See **gall.**

nut·hatch (nŭt′hăch′) *n.* Any of several small birds of the family Sittidae, having long, sharp bills, and noted for their insectlike ability to maneuver on tree trunks and branches. Also called "nutcracker." [Middle English *notehache, nuthak,* "nut hatchet" (named from its habit of wedging nuts in bark and hacking them open) : *nute,* NUT + *hache,* ax, hatchet, from Old French, from Medieval Latin *hapia* (see **skep-¹** in Appendix*).]

nut·let (nŭt′lĭt) *n.* **1.** A small nut. **2.** The stone or pit in certain fruits, such as the peach or cherry.

nut·meat (nŭt′mēt′) *n.* The edible kernel of a nut.

nut·meg (nŭt′mĕg′) *n.* **1.** An evergreen tree, *Myristica fragrans,* native to the East Indies and cultivated elsewhere in the tropics. **2.** The hard, aromatic seed of this tree, much used as a spice when grated or ground. See **mace. 3.** Grayish to moderate brown. See **color.** [Middle English *notemugge, nutemuge,* from Old French *nois muscade,* from Vulgar Latin *nuce muscāta* (unattested), "musky nut" : Latin *nux,* nut (see **ken-⁵** in Appendix*) + *muscus,* MUSK.] **—nut′meg′** *adj.*

Nutmeg State. A nickname for Connecticut. [Originally *Wooden Nutmeg* State, from the reputed skill of the Connecticut traders at such deceptions as the selling of wooden nutmegs.]

nut pick. A small, sharp-pointed tool used for digging the meat from nuts.

nut pine. A tree, the **piñon** *(see).*

nu·tri·a (no͞o′trē-ə, nyo͞o′-) *n.* **1.** A rodent, the **coypu** *(see).* **2.** The fur of the coypu, often dyed to resemble beaver. **3.** Olive gray. See **color.** [Spanish *nutr(i)a,* nasalized variant of *lutra,* otter, from Latin *lutra.* See **wed-¹** in Appendix.*] **—nu′tri·a** *adj.*

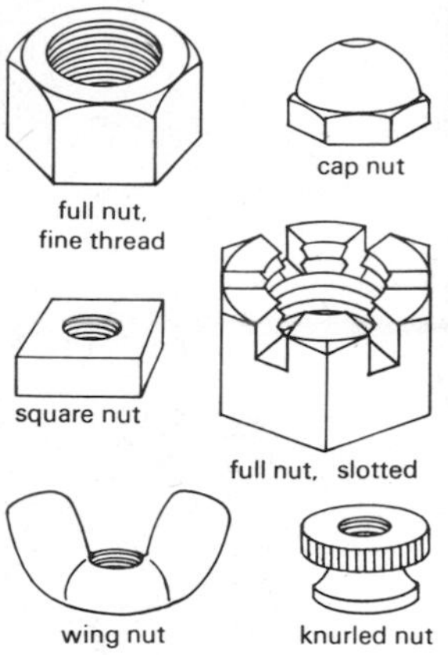

nut

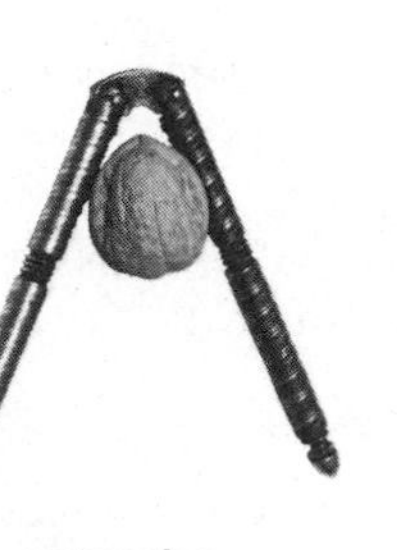

nutcracker
Metal nutcracker with walnut in position to be cracked open

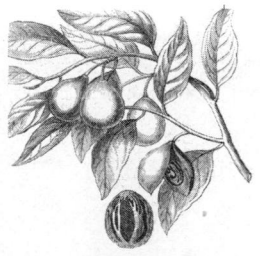

nutmeg
Branch with seeds

nu·tri·ent (nōō′trē-ənt, nyōō′-) *n.* Something that nourishes; especially, a nourishing ingredient in a food. —*adj.* Having nutritive value, as certain body fluids. [Latin *nūtriēns,* present participle of *nūtrīre,* to feed, nourish. See sneu- in Appendix.*]

nu·tri·ment (nōō′trə-mənt, nyōō′-) *n.* **1.** Anything that nourishes; food. **2.** Anything that aids growth or development. [Latin *nūtrīmentum,* from *nūtrīre,* to feed, nourish. See sneu- in Appendix.*] —**nu′tri·men′tal** (nōō′trə-měn′təl, nyōō′-) *adj.*

nu·tri·tion (nōō-trĭsh′ən, nyōō-) *n.* The process of nourishing or being nourished; especially, the interrelated steps by which a living organism assimilates food and uses it for growth and for replacement of tissues. [Old French, from Late Latin *nūtrītiō,* from Latin *nūtrīre,* to feed, nourish. See sneu- in Appendix.*] —**nu·tri′tion·al** *adj.* —**nu·tri′tion·al·ly** *adv.*

nu·tri·tion·ist (nōō-trĭsh′ən-ĭst, nyōō-) *n.* A person who specializes in the study of nutrition.

nu·tri·tious (nōō-trĭsh′əs, nyōō-) *adj.* Aiding the growth and development of a living organism; nourishing. [Latin *nūtrītius,* from *nūtrix,* a nurse. See sneu- in Appendix.*] —**nu·tri′tious·ly** *adv.* —**nu·tri′tious·ness** *n.*

nu·tri·tive (nōō′trə-tĭv, nyōō′-) *adj.* Promoting nutrition; nourishing. [Middle English *nutritif,* from Old French, from Late Latin *nūtrītivus,* from Latin *nūtrīre,* to feed, nourish. See sneu- in Appendix.*] —**nu′tri·tive·ly** *adv.*

nuts (nŭts) *adj. Slang.* **1.** Crazy; insane. **2.** Extremely enthusiastic: *He's nuts about opera.* —*interj. Slang.* Used as an exclamation of contempt, disappointment, or emphatic refusal. [From NUT (in various senses).]

nut·shell (nŭt′shĕl′) *n.* The shell enclosing the meat of a nut. —**in a nutshell.** In concise or brief form; epitomized.

nut·ty (nŭt′ē) *adj.* -tier, -tiest. **1.** Containing or producing many nuts. **2.** Having a flavor like that of nuts. **3.** *Informal.* Crazy. —**nut′ti·ly** *adv.* —**nut′ti·ness** *n.*

nux vom·i·ca (nŭks′ vŏm′ĭ-kə). **1.** A tree, *Strychnos nux-vomica,* native to southeastern Asia, having poisonous seeds that are the source of strychnine, brucine, and the medical preparation nux vomica. **2.** *Pharmacology.* A bitter tonic. [Medieval Latin, "emetic nut" : Latin *nux,* nut (see ken-⁵ in Appendix*) + *vomica,* from Latin *vomere,* to VOMIT.]

nuz·zle (nŭz′əl) *v.* -zled, -zling, -zles. —*tr.* **1.** To rub or push against gently with the nose or snout. **2.** To uproot with the snout. —*intr.* **1.** To make rubbing or pressing motions with the nose or snout. **2.** To nestle or cuddle together. [Earlier *nousle,* Middle English *noselen,* from *nose,* NOSE.]

NV Nevada (with Zip Code).

NW northwest.

NWbN northwest by north.

NWbW northwest by west.

n.wt. net weight.

N.W.T. Northwest Territories.

NY New York (with Zip Code).

N.Y. New York.

Nyan·ja (nyän′jə) *n.* A Bantu language of Malawi.

Ny·as·a, Lake (nī-ăs′ə). A lake in southeastern Africa, 11,000 square miles in area and about 380 miles long, between Tanzania, Mozambique, and Malawi.

Ny·as·a·land. The former name of **Malawi.**

N.Y.C. New York City.

nyc·ta·lo·pi·a (nĭk′tə-lō′pē-ə) *n.* Vision that is normal in daylight but abnormally weak when the light is dim. Also called "moon blindness," "night blindness." Compare **hemeralopia.** [Late Latin *nyctalōpia,* from Latin *nyctalops,* night-blind, from Greek *nuktalōps* : *nux* (stem *nukt-*), night (see nekwt- in Appendix*) + *alaos†,* blind + *ōps,* eye (see okw- in Appendix*).] —**nyc′ta·lo′pic** (-lō′pĭk, -lŏp′ĭk) *adj.*

nyc·tit·ro·pism (nĭk-tĭt′rə-pĭz′əm) *n. Botany.* The tendency of the leaves of some plants to change their position at nightfall. [Greek *nux* (stem *nukt-*), night (see nekwt- in Appendix*) + -TROPISM.] —**nyc′ti·tro′pic** (nĭk′tĭ-trō′pĭk, -trŏp′ĭk) *adj.*

ny·lon (nī′lŏn′) *n.* **1.** Any of a family of high-strength, resilient, synthetic materials, the long-chain molecule of which contains the recurring amide group CONH. **2.** Cloth or yarn made from nylon. **3.** *Plural.* Stockings made of nylon. [Coined by the inventors, E. I. duPont de Nemours & Co., Inc.]

nymph (nĭmf) *n.* **1.** *Greek & Roman Mythology.* Any of numerous female nature spirits, inhabiting and animistically representing features of nature. **2.** *Poetic.* A beautiful woman. **3.** *Entomology.* One of the young of any insect that undergoes metamorphosis. Also called "nympha." Compare **pupa.** [Middle English *nimphe,* from Latin *nympha,* nymph, pupa, from Greek *numphē,* nymph, bride. See sneubh- in Appendix.*] —**nymph′al, nym·phe′an** (nĭm-fē′ən) *adj.*

nym·pha (nĭm′fə) *n., pl.* -phae (-fē). **1.** *Entomology.* A nymph *(see).* **2.** *Plural. Anatomy.* The **labia minora** *(see).* [New Latin, from Latin, NYMPH.]

nym·pha·lid (nĭm′fə-lĭd) *n.* Any of various medium to large butterflies of the family Nymphalidae, found worldwide, and often brilliantly colored. See **mourning cloak, fritillary.** [New Latin *Nymphalidae* (family) : *Nymphalis* (genus), from Latin *nymphālis,* "nymphal," from *nympha,* NYMPH + -IDAE.]

nym·phet (nĭm-fĕt′, nĭm′fĭt) *n.* **1.** A young nymph. **2.** A pubescent girl regarded as sexually desirable. [Old French *nymphette,* from *nymphe,* NYMPH.]

nym·pho (nĭm′fō) *n., pl.* -phos. *Slang.* A nymphomaniac.

nym·pho·lep·sy (nĭm′fə-lĕp′sē) *n., pl.* -sies. **1.** A frenzy induced by having seen nymphs. **2.** An obsession for something unattainable. [From NYMPHOLEPT.]

nym·pho·lept (nĭm′fə-lĕpt′) *n.* One in a state of nympholepsy. [Greek *numpholēptos,* "caught by nymphs," raptured : *numphē,* NYMPH + *lēptos,* seized (see slagw- in Appendix*).] —**nym′pho·lept′, nym′pho·lep′tic** *adj.*

nym·pho·ma·ni·a (nĭm′fə-mā′nē-ə, -mān′yə) *n.* Abnormally strong and uncontrollable sexual desire in women. [New Latin : Latin *nympha,* NYMPH + -MANIA.]

nym·pho·ma·ni·ac (nĭm′fə-mā′nē-ăk′) *n.* A woman suffering from nymphomania. —**nym′pho·ma′ni·ac′, nym·pho·ma·ni′a·cal** (nĭm′fō-mə-nī′ə-kəl) *adj.*

NYP not yet published.

Ny·sa. The Polish name for the **Neisse** River.

Ny·sa Klodz·ka. The Polish name for the **Glatzer Neisse** River.

NYSE New York Stock Exchange.

nys·tag·mus (nī-stăg′məs) *n. Pathology.* A spasmodic, involuntary motion of the eyeball. [New Latin, from Greek *nustagmos,* drowsiness, from *nustazein,* to be sleepy. See sneudh- in Appendix.*] —**nys·tag′mic** *adj.*

N.Z. New Zealand.

ă pat/ā pay/âr care/ä father/b bib/ch church/d deed/ĕ pet/ē be/f fife/g gag/h hat/hw which/ĭ pit/ī pie/îr pier/j judge/k kick/l lid, needle/m mum/n no, sudden/ng thing/ŏ pot/ō toe/ô paw, for/oi noise/ou out/ōō took/ōō boot/p pop/r roar/s sauce/sh ship, dish/

nux vomica

nymph
Archaic relief
showing nymphs

Oo

1	2	3	4	5	6	7	8	9	10	11
Phoenician		Greek		Roman		Medieval				Modern

Around 1000 B.C. *the Phoenicians and other Semites of Syria and Palestine began to use a sign in the form of a circle (1), a sign smaller in size than all other signs in their writing. They gave it the name* ᶜayin, *meaning "eye," and used it for an emphatic laryngeal consonant,* ᶜ, *which is not found in English or in any other Indo-European language. After 900* B.C. *the Greeks borrowed the sign from the Phoenicians, first retaining its small size (2), then gradually enlarging it to the size of the other letters of their alphabet (3). Since the Greeks had no use in their language for the Semitic consonant sound* ᶜ, *they used the sign to represent the vowel* o. *They also changed the name of the sign from* ᶜayin, *first simply to* o, *and then to* omikron, *meaning "short* o," *in order to distinguish it from* ōmega, *"long* ō," *which they introduced and placed at the end of their alphabet. The Greek sign* omikron *passed via Etruscan to the Romans, who used it for both short and long* o *and gradually gave it an oval shape (4,5). The Roman forms passed to our modern capital, printed (8) and written (9). The medieval Uncial (6) and Cursive (7) are the bases of our modern small letter, printed (10) and written (11).*

o, O (ō) *n., pl.* **o's,** *or rare* **os, O's** or **Os. 1.** The 15th letter of the modern English alphabet. See **alphabet. 2.** Any of the speech sounds represented by this letter. **3.** A zero: *a phone number with three O's.* **4.** Anything shaped like the letter **O**; a circle.

o, O, o., O. *Note:* As an abbreviation or symbol, *o* may be a small or a capital letter, with or without a period. Established forms or those generally preferred precede the definition. When no form is given, all four forms are in general use in that sense. **1. O, O.** ocean. **2. o., O.** octavo. **3. O.** October (unofficial). **4. O.** Ohio (unofficial). **5. O, O.** old. **6. O, O.** order. **7. O** The symbol for the element oxygen. **8. o.** pint (Latin *octarius*). **9. O** A human blood type of the **ABO** group. See **ABO. 10.** The 15th in a series; 14th when *J* is omitted.

O (ō). Used before the substantive in direct address, especially, as in poetry or prayer, to express earnestness or solemnity: *O my people, what have I done unto thee?* (Micah 6:3). See Usage note below. —*interj. Rare.* Variant of **oh.**

Usage: O and *oh* have separate functions. Except for infrequent use as a variant of *oh, O* is confined to direct address, in prayer and invocation, in literary and religious contexts (*O God on high! O mighty ocean!*), and to the exclamations *O dear!* and *O my!* In such use it is always dependent on the words that follow it; it is always capitalized and never followed directly by punctuation. The interjection *oh* is more independent. It can stand alone or as part of a sentence, to express strong emotions or merely a reflective pause: *Oh! What a horse!* or *Oh, I see.* It is only capitalized when it is the first word of a sentence, and is followed directly by a comma or, when the emphasis is strong, by an exclamation point.

o' (ə, ō) *prep.* A reduced form of the preposition *of.* Used especially in the phrase *o'clock,* but also found in such terms as *will-o'-the-wisp, man-o'-war,* and in numerous dialects.

O'. Indicates a descendant of. Used in some Irish surnames, such as *O'Connor, O'Malley, O'Reilly.* [Irish ō, grandson, descendant, from Old Irish *aue.* See **awo-** in Appendix.*]

oaf (ōf) *n., pl.* **oafs. 1.** A stupid or clumsy person. **2.** *Obsolete.* A deformed child supposedly substituted for a human one by elves; changeling. [Earlier *ouph, aufe,* elf, goblin, from Old Norse *alfr.* See **albho-** in Appendix.*] —**oaf'ish** *adj.* —**oaf'ish·ly** *adv.* —**oaf'ish·ness** *n.*

O·a·hu (ō-ä'hōō). An island of Hawaii, 589 square miles in area. Site of the state capital, Honolulu. Population, 500,000.

oak (ōk) *n.* **1.** Any of various deciduous or evergreen trees or shrubs of the genus *Quercus,* bearing acorns as fruit. **2.** The durable wood of any of these trees. **3.** Any of various trees or shrubs resembling the oak in some feature, such as the **poison oak** (*see*). **4.** Something made of oak wood. **5.** Any of various brown shades resembling oak wood. [Middle English *ok, ook,* Old English *āc,* from Germanic *aik-* (unattested).] —**oak** *adj.*

oak apple. A harmless gall on oak trees, caused by the larva of a type of wasp. Also called "oak gall."

oak·en (ō'kən) *adj.* Of oak.

Oak·land (ōk'lənd). A city of western California on San Francisco Bay opposite San Francisco. Population, 368,000.

oak leaf cluster. A decoration of bronze or silver oak leaves and acorns, awarded to holders of various U.S. military medals in recognition of acts entitling them to a second decoration with the same medal.

Oak·ley (ōk'lē), **Annie.** Original name, Phoebe Anne Oakley Mozee. 1860–1926. American sharpshooter and vaudevillian.

Oak Park. A residential city in northeastern Illinois, just west of Chicago. Population, 61,000.

Oak Ridge. A city in eastern Tennessee, at the site originally occupied in 1943 by a unit of the Manhattan District to produce materials for atomic bombs. Population, 27,000.

oa·kum (ō'kəm) *n.* Loose hemp or jute fiber, sometimes treated with tar, creosote, or asphalt. It is used for caulking seams in wooden ships and packing pipe joints. [Middle English *okum,* Old English *ācumba,* "off-combings" : *ā-,* off, away (see **e** in Appendix*) + *-cumba,* from *cemban,* to comb (see **gembh-** in Appendix*).]

oak wilt. A disease of oak trees caused by a fungus, *Chalara quercina,* and often resulting in wilting and dropping of leaves.

OAPC, O.A.P.C. Office of Alien Property Custodian.

oar (ôr, ōr) *n.* **1.** A long, thin pole, usually wooden, with a blade at one end, used to row and, occasionally, to steer a boat. **2.** A person using an oar; rower. —**put one's oar in.** To intrude impertinently; meddle. —**rest on one's oars.** To stop trying or working; take a rest. —*v.* **oared, oaring, oars.** —*tr.* **1.** To propel with or as if with oars. **2.** To traverse with or as if with oars: *an hour to oar the strait.* —*intr.* To move forward by or as if by rowing. [Middle English *oor, or,* Old English *ār,* from Common Germanic *airo* (unattested).] —**oared** *adj.*

oar·fish (ôr'fĭsh', ōr'-) *n., pl.* **oarfish** or **-fishes.** A marine fish, *Regalecus glesne,* having a slender body up to 30 feet long, a dorsal fin extending the entire body length, and red-tipped rays above the head.

oar·lock (ôr'lŏk', ōr'-) *n.* A device used as a fulcrum to hold an oar in place while rowing, usually a U-shaped metal hoop on a swivel in the gunwale. Also *chiefly British* "rowlock."

oars·man (ôrz'mən, ōrz'-) *n., pl.* **-men** (-mĭn). A person who rows, especially an expert in rowing; a rower. [*Oar's,* possessive of OAR + MAN.]

OAS Organization of American States.

o·a·sis (ō-ā'sĭs) *n., pl.* **-ses** (-sēz'). **1.** A fertile or green spot in a desert or waste, made so by the presence of water. **2.** A small place preserved from surrounding unpleasantness: *"I am lost in love with this room . . . it's an oasis of hiding"* (J.P. Donleavy). [Late Latin *oasis,* from Greek, from an Egyptian word akin to Coptic *ouahe,* oasis, "dwelling area."]

oast (ōst) *n.* A kiln for drying hops or malt, or for drying and curing tobacco. [Middle English *ost,* Old English *āst.* See **aidh-** in Appendix.*]

oat (ōt) *n.* **1.** *Usually plural.* Any of several grasses of the genus *Avena;* especially, *A. sativa,* widely cultivated for its edible seeds. **2.** *Usually plural.* The seeds of this plant, used as food

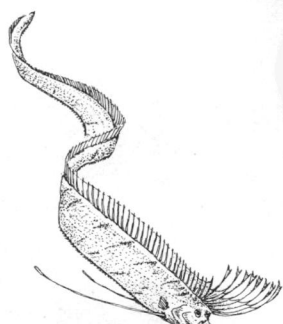

oarfish

oak
Quercus alba
White oak

---

t tight/th thin, path/*th* this, bathe/ŭ cut/ûr urge/v valve/w with/y yes/z zebra, size/zh vision/ə about, item, edible, gallop, circus/ à *Fr.* ami/œ *Fr.* feu, *Ger.* schön/ü *Fr.* tu, *Ger.* über/ᴋʜ *Ger.* ich, *Scot.* loch/ɴ *Fr.* bon. *Follows main vocabulary. †Of obscure origin.

and fodder. **3.** *Archaic.* A shepherd's musical pipe made of an oat straw. **—feel one's oats.** *Informal.* **1.** To be gay or frisky. **2.** To feel self-satisfied and important, or to act in a way suggesting this. **—sow one's wild oats.** To indulge in the adventures and excesses of youth. [Middle English *ote,* Old English *āte.* See **oid-** in Appendix.*]

oat·cake (ōt′kāk′) *n.* A flattened cake of baked oatmeal.

oat·en (ōt′n) *adj.* Of, made of, or containing oats, oatmeal, or oat straw: *oaten fodder.*

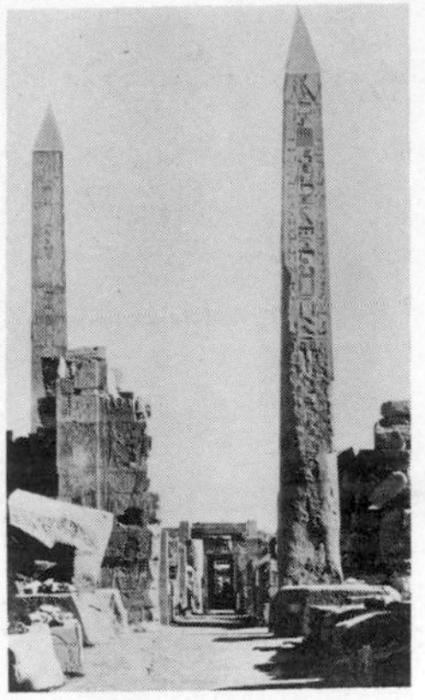

obelisk
Obelisks at the Temple of Karnak, built about 1500 B.C.

oat grass. 1. Any grass of the genus *Arrhenatherum,* common in meadows. **2.** Any of several oatlike grasses.

oath (ōth) *n., pl.* **oaths** (ōthz, ōths). **1.** A formal declaration or promise to fulfill a pledge, often calling upon God or some other sacred object as witness. **2.** The words or formula of such a declaration or promise. **3.** That which is promised or declared. **4.** An irreverent or blasphemous use of the name of God or anything held sacred. **5.** Any imprecation. [Middle English *ooth,* Old English *āth.* See **oito-** in Appendix.*]

oat·meal (ōt′mēl′) *n.* **1.** Meal made from oats; rolled oats; ground oats. **2.** A porridge made from rolled or ground oats.

Oa·xa·ca (wä-hä′kä). Officially, Oaxaca de Juárez. **1.** A state of Mexico, 36,375 square miles in area, in the south on the Pacific coast. Population, 1,833,000. **2.** The capital of this state. Population, 72,000.

Ob (ŏb, ôb; *Russian* ôp′y′). A river of the Soviet Union, in western Siberia, flowing 2,113 miles first northwest and then north to the Kara Sea.

ob–. Indicates inverse shape or attachment: for example, **obcordate, obovate.** [In borrowed Latin compounds, *ob-* becomes *o-* before *m,* as in *omit, oc-* before *c,* as in *occlude, of-* before *f,* as in *offend, op-* before *p. Ob-* indicates: 1. To, toward, as in **offer, obvert.** 2. Directed toward in a negative way, against, in opposition to, as in **oppose, obstacle.** 3. Opposite to, before, on, in front of, as in **obsess, obstetric.** 4. On account of, for, as in **obsecrate.** 5. In a certain direction, down, down upon, over, in back of, as in **occasion, omit.** 6. Out of, away from, as in **obliterate.** 7. Intensified action, as in **obdurate, obtain.** Latin *ob-,* from the preposition *ob,* to, toward, in front of, on account of, against. See **epi** in Appendix.*]

ob. 1. obiit. **2.** incidentally (Latin *obiter*). **3.** oboe. **4.** obstetric.

Obad. Obadiah (Old Testament).

O·ba·di·ah[1] (ō′bə-dī′ə). A Hebrew prophet of the sixth century B.C.

O·ba·di·ah[2] (ō′bə-dī′ə) *n. Abbr.* **Obad.** The book in the Old Testament written by Obadiah. Also, in the Douay Bible, "Abdias."

ob·bli·ga·to (ŏb′lə-gä′tō) *adj.* Also **ob·li·ga·to.** *Music.* Not to be left out; indispensable. Said of an accompaniment that is an integral part of a piece. *—n., pl.* **obbligatos** or **-ti** (-tē). Also **ob·li·ga·to.** *Music.* An obbligato musical accompaniment. Compare **ad libitum.** [Italian, past participle of *obbligare,* to obligate, from Latin *obligāre,* OBLIGE.]

ob·cor·date (ŏb-kôr′dāt′) *adj. Botany.* Heart-shaped, with the tapering end at the point of attachment: *an obcordate leaf.* [OB- + CORDATE.]

ob·du·ra·cy (ŏb′dyŏŏ-rə-sē, ŏb′dŏŏ-) *n.* The state or quality of being obdurate.

ob·du·rate (ŏb′dyŏŏ-rĭt, ŏb′dŏŏ-) *adj.* **1.** Hardened against good or moral influence; stubbornly impenitent: *"obdurate conscience of the old sinner"* (Scott). **2.** Hardened against feeling; unyielding; hardhearted: *"the convention . . . for love poetry: the poet is in love with some obdurate mistress"* (Northrop Frye). **3.** Not giving in to persuasion; intractable: *"the lyric mood today was obdurate, and not to be persuaded"* (Ronald Firbank). —See Synonyms at **inflexible.** [Middle English *obdurat,* from Latin *obdūrātus,* past participle of *obdūrāre,* to harden : *ob* (intensive) + *dūrāre,* to harden, from *dūrus,* hard (see **deru-** in Appendix*).] **—ob′du·rate·ly** *adv.* **—ob′du·rate·ness** *n.*

O.B.E. 1. Officer (of the Order) of the British Empire. **2.** Order of the British Empire.

o·be·ah (ō′bē-ə) *n.* Also **o·bi** (ō′bē). **1.** A form of religious belief, probably of African origin, involving witchcraft or sorcery. It is practiced in some parts of the West Indies and nearby tropical America. **2.** A fetish or object used in the practice of obeah. [Of West African origin.]

o·be·di·ence (ō-bē′dē-əns) *n.* **1. a.** The quality or condition of being obedient. **b.** The act of obeying. **2.** A sphere of ecclesiastical authority. **3.** A group of persons under such authority.

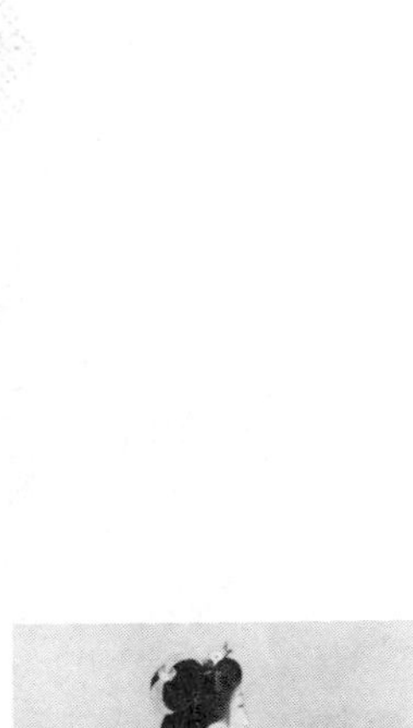

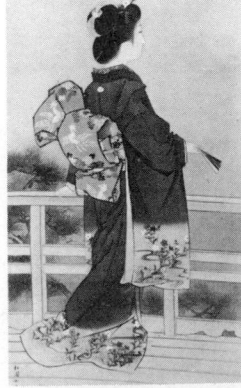

obi[1]
Painting from the Meiji era showing a type of obi worn by unmarried girls

o·be·di·ent (ō-bē′dē-ənt) *adj.* Obeying or carrying out a request, command, or the like; submissive to control; dutiful. [Middle English, from Old French, from Latin *oboediēns,* present participle of *oboedīre,* OBEY.] **—o·be′di·ent·ly** *adv.*

Synonyms: *obedient, compliant, acquiescent, submissive, docile, amenable, obsequious, servile, tractable, dutiful. Obedient,* said of persons and animals, refers to acceptance of authority in general; its implications, if any, are favorable. *Compliant* and *acquiescent* suggest innate disposition of persons to yield to authority without protest. This sense is intensified in *submissive* and *docile;* the latter, also applicable to animals, specifies capacity for being taught. *Amenable* pertains to congenial acceptance of authority in a more positive sense; besides agreeableness, it sometimes also indicates accountability and responsibility. *Obsequious* and *servile* refer to slavish, truckling obedience in persons. *Tractable* applies to persons, animals, and things with the capacity for being handled or led; *dutiful* signifies a scrupulous sense of responsibility, an interest or reliability in carrying out what is specifically assigned or required.

o·bei·sance (ō-bā′səns, ō-bē′-) *n.* **1.** A gesture or movement of the body expressing reverence or respect, such as a bow or curtsy: *"The mute drew back with another profound obeisance."* (H. Rider Haggard). **2.** An attitude associated with this gesture, as deference or homage: *"a humble obeisance to life's uncertainties"* (Loren Eiseley). [Middle English *obeisaunce,* from Old French *obeissance,* from *obeissant,* present participle of *obeir,* to OBEY.] **—o·bei′sant** *adj.*

ob·e·lisk (ŏb′ə-lĭsk) *n.* **1.** A tall, four-sided shaft of stone, usually tapering and monolithic, that rises to a pyramidal point. **2.** *Printing.* The dagger sign (†), used especially as a reference mark, as in this Dictionary it refers to an etymological footnote indicating that the word or form so marked is of obscure origin. In this sense, also called "obelus," "dagger." [Old French *obelisque,* from Latin *obeliscus,* from Greek *obeliskos,* diminutive of *obelos,* spit, OBELUS.] **—ob′e·lis′cal** (-lĭs′kəl) *adj.* **—ob′e·lis′koid′** (-lĭs′koid′) *adj.*

ob·e·lize (ŏb′ə-līz′) *tr.v.* **-lized, -lizing, -lizes.** To mark or annotate with an obelus. [Greek *obelizein,* from *obelos,* OBELUS.]

ob·e·lus (ŏb′ə-ləs) *n., pl.* **-li** (-lī′). **1.** A mark (— or ÷) used in ancient manuscripts to indicate a doubtful or spurious passage. **2.** *Printing.* An **obelisk** *(see).* [Late Latin *obelus,* from Greek *obelos*†, spit, obelisk, obelus.]

O·ber·hau·sen (ō′bər-hou′zən). A city and steel-producing center in the Ruhr district of West Germany, in North Rhine-Westphalia northwest of Essen. Population, 260,000.

O·ber·land (ō′bər-lănd′; *German* ō′bər-länt′). The Bernese Alps, the Alpine range lying north of the upper Rhône valley in south-central Switzerland.

O·ber·on (ō′bə-rŏn′, -rən). *Medieval Folklore.* The king of the fairies, husband of Titania. [French, from Old French *Auberon,* of Frankish origin, akin to Old High German *Alberich.* See **albho-** in Appendix.*]

o·bese (ō-bēs′) *adj.* Extremely fat; corpulent. See Synonyms at **fat.** [Latin *obēsus,* "grown fat by eating," from past participle of *obedere,* to eat away : *ob,* away + *edere,* to eat (see **ed-** in Appendix*).] **—o·be′si·ty** (ō-bē′sə-tē), **o·bese′ness** *n.*

o·bey (ō-bā′) *v.* **obeyed, obeying, obeys.** *—tr.* **1.** To carry out or fulfill the command, order, or instruction of. **2.** To carry out or comply with (a command, order, or request). *—intr.* To behave obediently. [Middle English *obeien,* from Old French *obeir,* from Latin *oboedīre,* "to listen to" : *ob,* to, toward + *audīre,* to hear (see **aw-**[2] in Appendix*).] **—o·bey′er** *n.*

ob·fus·cate (ŏb′fə-skāt′, ŏb-fŭs′kāt′) *tr.v.* **-cated, -cating, -cates. 1.** To render indistinct or dim; darken: *The fog obfuscated the shore.* **2.** To confuse or becloud: *His emotions obfuscated his judgment.* [Late Latin *obfuscāre,* to darken : *ob* (intensive) + Latin *fuscāre,* to darken, from *fuscus,* dark (see **dheu-**[1] in Appendix*).] **—ob′fus·ca′tion** *n.*

o·bi[1] (ō′bē) *n.* A wide sash fastened in the back with a large flat bow, worn by women in Japan as a part of the traditional dress. [Japanese, "belt," "band," "sash."]

o·bi[2]. Variant of **obeah.**

O·bi Islands (ō′bē). A cluster of islands of the northern and central Moluccas, Indonesia, between Sulawesi and West Irian.

o·bi·it (ō′bē-ĭt). *Abbr.* **ob.** *Latin.* He (or she) died.

o·bit (ō′bĭt, ō-bĭt′) *n. Informal.* An obituary.

o·bi·ter dic·tum (ō′bĭ-tər dĭk′təm) *pl.* **obiter dicta** (dĭk′tə). **1.** *Law.* An opinion voiced by a judge that has only incidental bearing on the case in question and is therefore not binding. **2.** Any incidental remark or observation; a passing comment. [Latin, "a statement in passing."]

o·bit·u·ar·y (ō-bĭch′ōō-ĕr′ē) *n., pl.* **-ies.** *Abbr.* **obit.** A notice of a death, usually with a brief biography of the deceased. [Medieval Latin *obituārius,* (report) of death, from Latin *obitus,* death, from the past participle of *obīre,* to fall, to die : *ob,* down + *ire,* to go (see **ei-**[1] in Appendix*).] **—o·bit′u·ar′y** *adj.*

obj. 1. *Grammar.* object; objective. **2.** objection.

ob·ject[1] (əb-jĕkt′) *v.* **-jected, -jecting, -jects.** *—intr.* **1.** To present a dissenting or opposing argument; raise an objection. Usually followed by *to: object to the testimony of a witness.* **2.** To feel adverse to or express disapproval of something. Usually followed by *to: object to modern materialism.* *—tr.* To put forward in, or as a reason for, opposition; offer as criticism: *They objected that discipline was lacking.* [Middle English *objecten,* from Latin *objicere, obicere* (past participle *objectus*), to throw against, oppose : *ob,* toward + *jacere,* to throw (see **yē-** in Appendix*).] **—ob·jec′tor** (əb-jĕk′tər) *n.*

Synonyms: *object, protest, kick, complain, dissent, demur, remonstrate, expostulate, boggle. Object* is a general term for denoting expression of opposition; the following terms have this basic sense, together with specific implications. *Protest* suggests strong opposition forthrightly expressed; *kick,* used informally, stresses the same implications even more forcefully. *Complain* applies to opposition usually stemming from a sense of personal injury or wrong. *Dissent* often implies formal expression of opposition, along with finality of judgment not inherent in the other terms. *Demur* is applicable to more tentative opposition or expression of doubt that may delay ultimate decision or action pending reconsideration. *Remonstrate* specifies objection in the form of argument or pleading; *expostulate,* objection in the form of earnest reasoning. *Boggle* pertains to opposition in the sense of hesitancy or shying away caused by fear or scruples.

ob·ject[2] (ŏb′jĭkt, -jĕkt′) *n.* **1.** Anything perceptible by one or more of the senses, especially something that can be seen and felt; a material thing. **2.** *Philosophy.* Anything intelligible or perceptible by the mind. **3.** A person or thing serving as a focus of attention, curiosity, discussion, feeling, thought, or action: *an object of contempt.* **4.** The purpose, aim, or goal of a specific action or effort: *the object of the game.* **5.** *Abbr.* **obj.** *Grammar.* **a.** A noun or substantive that receives or is affected by the

action of a verb within a sentence. See Usage note below. **b.** A noun or substantive following and governed by a preposition. In *on the street,* the noun *street* is the object of the preposition *on.* —See Synonyms at **intention.** —**no object.** *Informal.* Not an obstacle or hindrance: *Cost is no object.* [Middle English, from Latin *objectus,* "something thrown before or presented to (the mind)," from the past participle of *obicere,* to throw before or against, OBJECT (verb).]

Usage: Nouns, noun clauses, and pronouns all function as objects (grammatical sense). In the following example, *what she said* is a noun clause used as a direct object: *I did not understand what she said.* The following pronouns (all in the objective case) regularly function as objects: *me, him, her, us, them,* and *whom.* In addition, the uninflected pronouns *you, it, which,* and *that* are employed as objects, although not restricted to that use.

object glass. A lens in an optical instrument, an **objective** *(see).*

ob·jec·ti·fy (əb-jĕk′tə-fī′) *tr.v.* **-fied, -fying, -fies.** To present (something) as an object; impart reality to; externalize or make objective. [From OBJECT (noun).] —**ob·jec′ti·fi·ca′tion** *n.*

ob·jec·tion (əb-jĕk′shən) *n. Abbr.* **obj. 1.** An act of objecting. **2.** A statement or other expression offered or presented in opposition; an adverse contention. **3.** A ground, reason, or cause for expressing opposition or disagreement.

ob·jec·tion·a·ble (əb-jĕk′shən-ə-bəl) *adj.* Arousing disapproval; offensive; unpleasant: *an objectionable odor.* —**ob·jec′tion·a·bil′i·ty** *n.* —**ob·jec′tion·a·bly** *adv.*

ob·jec·tive (əb-jĕk′tĭv) *adj.* **1.** Of or having to do with a material object as distinguished from a mental concept, idea, or belief. Compare **subjective. 2.** Having actual existence or reality. **3. a.** Uninfluenced by emotion, surmise, or personal prejudice. **b.** Based on observable phenomena; presented factually: *an objective appraisal.* **4.** *Medicine.* Indicating a symptom or condition perceived as a sign of disease by someone other than the person afflicted. **5.** *Grammar.* **a.** Denoting the case of a noun or pronoun serving as the object of the verb. **b.** Pertaining to a noun or pronoun used in such a case. See Usage note at **object** (noun). **6.** Serving as a goal; being the object of a course of action: *an objective point.* —See Synonyms at **fair.** —*n.* **1.** Anything that actually exists, as distinguished from something thought or felt to exist. **2.** Something worked toward or striven for; a goal. **3.** *Abbr.* **obj.** *Grammar.* **a.** The objective case. **b.** A noun or pronoun in the objective case. **4.** *Optics.* **a.** The lens or lens system in a microscope or telescope that is closest to the object. **b.** A lens or lens system in a camera or projector that forms the image of the object. Also called "object glass," "object lens." —See Synonyms at **intention.** [Medieval Latin *objectīvus,* from Latin *objectus,* an OBJECT.] —**ob·jec′tive·ly** *adv.* —**ob·jec′tive·ness** *n.*

objective complement. *Grammar.* A noun, adjective, or pronoun serving as a complement to a verb and qualifying its direct object. In *they elected him governor, governor* is an objective complement.

ob·jec·tiv·ism (ŏb-jĕk′tĭv-ĭz′əm) *n.* **1.** *Philosophy.* Any one of several doctrines holding that all reality is objective and external to the mind, and that knowledge is reliably based on observed objects and events. Compare **solipsism. 2.** *Art & Literature.* An emphasis on objective themes or subjects. —**ob·jec′tiv·ist** *n.* —**ob·jec′tiv·is′tic** *adj.*

ob·jec·tiv·i·ty (ŏb′jĕk-tĭv′ə-tē) *n.* **1.** The state, condition, or quality of being objective. **2.** External or material reality.

object lens. A lens in an optical instrument, an **objective** *(see).*

object lesson. 1. A lesson taught by using a material object or objects. **2.** An illustration of a moral or principle.

ob·jet d'art (ôb-zhĕ där′) *pl.* **objets d'art** (ôb-zhĕ där′). An object valued for its artistry. [French, "object of art."]

ob·jur·gate (ŏb′jər-gāt′, ŏb-jûr′gāt′) *tr.v.* **-gated, -gating, -gates.** To scold or rebuke sharply; berate. [Latin *objurgāre,* "to bring a lawsuit against," chide : *ob,* against + *jurgāre,* "to bring a lawsuit," rebuke : *jūs* (stem *jūr-*), law (see **yewo-**[1] in Appendix*) + *agere,* to act, perform (see **ag-** in Appendix*).] —**ob′jur·ga′tion** *n.* —**ob·jur′ga·to′ri·ly** (ŏb-jûr′gə-tôr′ə-lē, -tōr′ə-lē) *adv.* —**ob·jur′ga·to′ry** (-tôr′ē, -tōr′ē) *adj.*

obl. 1. oblique. **2.** oblong.

ob·lan·ce·o·late (ŏb-lăn′sē-ə-lāt′) *adj. Botany.* Broader and rounded at the apex, and tapering at the base: *an oblanceolate leaf.* [OB- + LANCEOLATE.]

o·blast (ô′bləst, ô′bläst′) *n.* In the Soviet Union, a territorial administrative division within some of the Union's republics. [Russian *oblast′,* from Old Church Slavonic : *ob-,* on (see **epi** in Appendix*) + *vlast′,* administration (see **wal-** in Appendix*).]

ob·late[1] (ŏb′lāt′, ŏb-lāt′) *adj.* **1.** Having the shape of a spheroid; spheroidal. **2.** Having an equatorial diameter greater than the distance between poles; compressed along or flattened at the poles: *The earth is an oblate solid.* Compare **prolate.** [New Latin *oblatus,* "carried toward," stretched, from Latin *oblātus* (past participle of *obferre,* to bring to, offer) : *ob,* to, toward + *-lātus,* "carried" (see **tel-**[1] in Appendix*).] —**ob′late·ly** *adv.* —**ob·late′ness** *n.*

ob·late[2] (ŏb′lāt′) *n.* **1.** A lay person dedicated to a religious life. **2.** *Capital* **O.** *Roman Catholic Church.* A member of one of various religious communities for men or women. [Medieval Latin *oblātus,* "one offered (to God)," from Latin, past participle of *offerre,* to offer. See **oblate** (adjective).] —**ob′late′** *adj.*

ob·la·tion (ŏb-lā′shən) *n.* **1.** The act of offering something, such as worship or thanksgiving, to a deity. **2.** *Capital* **O. a.** The act of offering the bread and wine of the Eucharist. **b.** That which is offered, especially the bread and wine of the Eucharist. **3.** Any charitable offering or gift. [Middle English *oblacioun,* from Old French *oblation,* from Medieval Latin *oblātiō,* from *oblātus,* OBLATE (noun).] —**ob·la′tion·al, ob′la·to′ry** (ŏb′lə-tôr′ē, -tōr′ē) *adj.*

ob·li·gate (ŏb′lə-gāt′) *tr.v.* **-gated, -gating, -gates.** To bind, compel, or constrain by a legal or moral tie. See Synonyms at **force.** See Usage note at **oblige.** —*adj.* (ŏb′lə-gĭt, -gāt′). **1.** *Biology.* Able to survive in only one environment. Said of certain parasites. Also "obligatory." Compare **facultative. 2.** Absolutely indispensable; essential. **3.** *Obsolete.* Bound or constrained; obliged. [Latin *obligāre,* to OBLIGE.] —**ob′li·ga·ble** (ŏb′lĭ-gə-bəl) *adj.* —**ob′li·ga′tor** (-gā′tər) *n.*

ob·li·ga·tion (ŏb′lə-gā′shən) *n.* **1.** The act of binding oneself by a social, legal, or moral tie. **2. a.** A duty, contract, promise, or any other social, moral, or legal requirement that compels one to follow or avoid a certain course of action. **b.** A course of action imposed by law, society, or conscience by which one is bound or restricted. **3.** The constraining power of a law, promise, contract, or sense of duty. **4.** *Law.* **a.** A legal agreement stipulating a specified payment or action, especially if the agreement also specifies the penalty for failure to comply. **b.** The document containing the terms of such an agreement. **5. a.** Something owed as payment or in return for a special service or favor. **b.** The service or favor for which one is indebted to another. **6.** The state, fact, or condition of being indebted to another for a special service or favor received.

Synonyms: *obligation, responsibility, duty.* Each of these terms involves constraint in conduct or choice of course. *Obligation* applies to a specific instance of constraint in which the constraining factors are immediate and objectively defined (as by terms of a contract or treaty). *Responsibility* lacks the implication of a single instance and immediate constraint; in a more general way, it stresses that for which one is accountable. *Duty* involves continuing constraint deriving from moral or ethical considerations.

ob·li·ga·to. *Music.* Variant of **obbligato.**

o·blig·a·to·ry (ə-blĭg′ə-tôr′ē, -tōr′ē, ŏb′lĭ-gə-) *adj.* **1.** Legally or morally constraining; binding. **2.** Imposing or recording an obligation: *a bill obligatory.* **3.** Of the nature of an obligation; compulsory: *Attendance is obligatory.* **4.** *Biology.* Restricted to one mode of life, **obligate** *(see).* —**o·blig′a·to′ri·ly** *adv.*

o·blige (ə-blīj′) *v.* **obliged, obliging, obliges.** —*tr.* **1.** To cause to do or refrain from doing something; constrain by physical, legal, social, or moral means: *"Elizabeth Bennet had been obliged, by the scarcity of gentlemen, to sit down for two dances"* (Jane Austen). **2.** To make indebted or grateful. Used with *to: They were obliged to him for his hospitality.* **3.** To gratify the wishes of; do a service or favor for: *He obliged us by arriving early.* —*intr.* To do a service or favor; perform a courtesy: *The pianist will oblige with an encore.* —See Synonyms at **force.** [Middle English *obligen,* from Old French *obliger,* from Latin *obligāre,* to tie to : *ob,* to, + *ligāre,* to bind (see **leig-**[1] in Appendix*).] —**o·blig′er** *n.*

Usage: In the sense of rendering a service or kindness, *oblige, favor,* and *accommodate* are frequently interchangeable. *Oblige* and the somewhat more forceful *favor* generally apply to gratuitous service. *Accommodate* can be used in that sense, but is applicable also to business dealings, such as to services provided by banks, hospitals, hotels, and the like. *Oblige* and *obligate* are interchangeable in the sense of genuine constraint, but not in instances involving a sense of gratitude for a service or favor. A person is *obliged* (not *obligated*) when he feels a debt of gratitude and nothing more; he is *obligated* (or *obliged*) when under direct compulsion to follow a given course.

ob·li·gee (ŏb′lə-jē′) *n.* **1.** A person who is under obligation to another. **2.** *Law.* A person to whom another is bound by contract or legal agreement. Compare **obligor.**

o·blig·ing (ə-blī′jĭng) *adj.* Ready to do favors for others; accommodating; helpful; considerate. See Synonyms at **amiable.** —**o·blig′ing·ly** *adv.* —**o·blig′ing·ness** *n.*

ob·li·gor (ŏb′lə-gôr′) *n. Law.* A person who binds himself to another by contract or legal agreement. Compare **obligee.**

o·blique (ō-blēk′, ə-; *Military* ō-blīk′, ə-) *adj. Abbr.* **obl. 1. a.** Having a slanting or sloping direction, course, or position; inclined. **b.** *Geometry.* Designating lines or planes that are neither parallel nor perpendicular. **2.** Indirect or evasive in execution, meaning, or expression; not straightforward. **3.** Devious, misleading, or dishonest: *oblique answers.* **4.** Not direct in descent; collateral. **5.** *Botany.* Having sides of unequal length or form: *an oblique leaf.* **6.** *Grammar.* Designating any noun case except the nominative or the vocative. **7.** *Rhetoric.* **Indirect** *(see).* —*n.* **1.** An oblique thing, such as a line, direction, or muscle. **2.** *Nautical.* The act of changing course by less than 90 degrees. —*adv. Military.* At an angle of 45 degrees: *Right oblique, march!* [Middle English *oblike,* from Latin *oblīquus*†.] —**o·blique′ly** *adv.* —**o·blique′ness** *n.*

oblique angle. An angle that is not a right angle; an acute or obtuse angle. —**o·blique′-an′gled** *adj.*

oblique triangle. A triangle having no right angle.

o·bliq·ui·ty (ō-blĭk′wə-tē, ə-blĭk′-) *n., pl.* **-ties. 1.** The state, quality, or condition of being oblique. **2. a.** A deviation from a vertical or horizontal line, plane, position, or direction. **b.** The angle or extent of such a deviation. **3. a.** A mental deviation or aberration. **b.** Immoral conduct. [Middle English *obliquitee,* from Old French *obliquite,* from Latin *oblīquitas,* from *oblīquus,* OBLIQUE.] —**o·bliq′ui·tous** *adj.*

o·blit·er·ate (ə-blĭt′ə-rāt′) *tr.v.* **-ated, -ating, -ates. 1.** To do away with completely; destroy so as to leave no trace: *"The automobile has tended to obliterate the difference between rural and urban life"* (Walter Prescott Webb). **2.** To wipe out, rub off, or erase (writing or other markings). —See Synonyms at

t tight/th thin, path/*th* this, bathe/ŭ cut/ûr urge/v valve/w with/y yes/z zebra, size/zh vision/ə about, item, edible, gallop, circus/ à *Fr.* ami/œ *Fr.* feu, *Ger.* schön/ü *Fr.* tu, *Ger.* über/KH *Ger.* ich, *Scot.* loch/N *Fr.* bon. ***Follows main vocabulary. †Of obscure origin.**

abolish. [Latin *obliterāre*, "to strike out words," erase : *ob*, away from + *littera*, letter (see **deph-** in Appendix*).] —**o·blit′er·a′tion** *n.* —**o·blit′er·a′tive** (ə-blĭt′ə-rā′tĭv, -ər-ə-tĭv) *adj.* —**o·blit′er·a′tor** (-ə-rā′tər) *n.*

o·bliv·i·on (ə-blĭv′ē-ən) *n.* **1.** The state or condition of being completely forgotten. **2.** Forgetfulness or an instance of forgetting or overlooking. **3.** An official forgetting of offenses, or remission of punishment for them. [Middle English, from Old French, from Latin *oblīviō*, from *oblīviscī*, to forget. See **legwh-** in Appendix.*]

o·bliv·i·ous (ə-blĭv′ē-əs) *adj.* **1.** Lacking all memory of something; forgetful. **2.** Unaware or unmindful. —See Synonyms at **forgetful.** —**o·bliv′i·ous·ly** *adv.* —**o·bliv′i·ous·ness** *n.*

Usage: The broad, general sense *not conscious of* or *not aware of* is accepted by 70 per cent of the Usage Panel; the remainder restrict *oblivious* to *forgetful of that which one has known at some time in the past*, and to the secondary senses pertaining to forgetfulness and oblivion. Both *of* and *to* are acceptable to 53 per cent of the Panel as prepositions following *oblivious;* the remainder accept only *of.*

ob·long (ŏb′lông′, -lŏng′) *adj. Abbr.* **obl. 1.** Having a long dimension, especially having one of two perpendicular dimensions, as length or width, greater than the other; elongated. **2.** Having the shape of or resembling a rectangle or an ellipse. **3.** *Botany.* Having a somewhat elongated form with approximately parallel sides: *an oblong leaf.* —*n.* An object or figure, such as a rectangle, with an elongated shape. [Middle English *oblonge*, from Latin *oblongus* : *ob* (intensive) + *longus*, long (see **del-**[1] in Appendix*).]

ob·lo·quy (ŏb′lə-kwē) *n., pl.* **-quies. 1.** Abusively detractive language or utterance; calumny: *"I have had enough obloquy for one lifetime."* (Anthony Eden). **2.** Ill repute or discredit suffered by one subjected to such abuse: *"he felt that he could not live, under such a weight of obloquy"* (Trollope). —See Synonyms at **disgrace.** [Middle English *obloqui*, from Late Latin *obloquium*, from Latin *obloquī*, to speak against, contradict : *ob*, against + *loquī*, to speak (see **tolkw-** in Appendix*).]

ob·nox·ious (ŏb-nŏk′shəs, əb-) *adj.* **1.** Highly disagreeable or offensive; odious. **2.** *Obsolete.* Exposed to harm, injury, or evil of any kind: *"The town . . . now lies obnoxious to its foes."* (Bunyan). **3.** *Obsolete.* Deserving of or liable to censure or punishment; reprehensible. —See Synonyms at **hateful, offensive.** [Latin *obnoxiōsus*, injurious, from *obnoxius*, subject to harm : *ob*, to + *noxa*, a hurt (see **nek-**[1] in Appendix*).] —**ob·nox′ious·ly** *adv.* —**ob·nox′ious·ness** *n.*

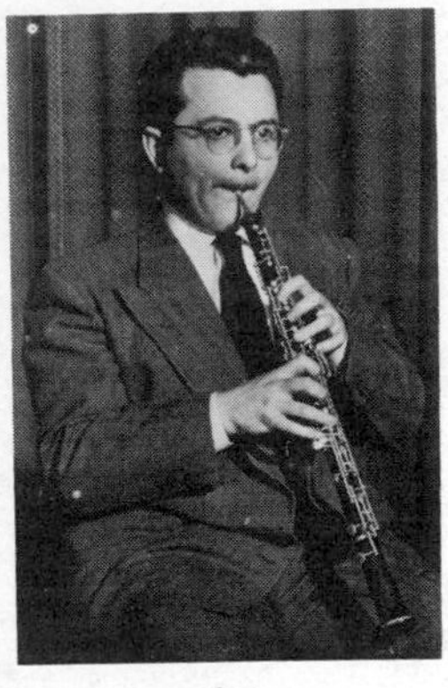

oboe

o·boe (ō′bō) *n. Abbr.* **ob. 1.** A slender woodwind musical instrument with a conical bore and a double-reed mouthpiece. It has a range of three octaves, and a penetrating, poignant sound. **2.** A reed stop in an organ that produces a similar sound. [Italian, from French *hautbois*, HAUTBOY.] —**o′bo·ist** *n.*

ob·o·lus (ŏb′ə-ləs) *n., pl.* **-li** (-lī′). Also **ob·ol** (ŏb′əl) *pl.* **-ols. 1.** A silver coin or unit of weight of ancient Greece equal to one-sixth of a drachma. **2. a.** Any of various coins, mostly of small value, circulated in medieval Europe. **b.** Any small coin. [Latin, from Greek *obolos*, variant of *obelos*, a spit, nail (nails were used in early times as money). See **obelus.**]

ob·o·vate (ŏb-ō′vāt′) *adj. Botany.* Egg-shaped, with the narrow end attached to the stalk: *an obovate leaf.* [OB- + OVATE.]

ob·o·void (ŏb-ō′void′) *adj. Botany.* Egg-shaped, with the narrow end attached to the stem: *an obovoid fruit.* [OB- + OVOID.]

O·bre·gón (ō′vrā-gôn′), **Álvaro.** 1880–1928. President of Mexico (1920–24); re-elected (1928) but assassinated.

obs. 1. obscure. **2.** observation. **3.** observatory. **4.** obsolete. **5.** obstetric; obstetrician; obstetrics.

Obs. observatory.

ob·scene (ŏb-sēn′, əb-) *adj.* **1.** Offensive to accepted standards of decency or modesty. **2.** Inciting lustful feelings; indecent; lewd. **3.** Offensive or repulsive to the senses; loathsome: *"In rags obscene decreed to roam."* (Pope). —See Synonyms at **coarse.** [Old French, from Latin *obscēnus, obscaenus*†, ill-boding, inauspicious, repulsive.] —**ob·scene′ly** *adv.* —**ob·scene′ness** *n.*

ob·scen·i·ty (ŏb-sĕn′ə-tē, əb-) *n., pl.* **-ties. 1.** The character or quality of being obscene. **2.** Indecency, lewdness, or offensiveness in behavior, expression, or appearance. **3.** Something obscene, such as a word, act, or expression.

ob·scur·ant (ŏb-skyŏŏr′ənt, əb-) *n.* **1.** One who opposes intellectual advancement and political reform; an enemy of rationalism. **2.** *German History.* An enemy of the Enlightenment in the 18th century. —*adj.* Characteristic of an obscurant. [Latin *obscūrāns*, present participle of *obscūrāre*, to darken, from *obscūrus*, dark, OBSCURE.]

ob·scur·ant·ism (ŏb-skyŏŏr′ən-tĭz′əm, əb-, ŏb′skyŏŏ-răn′tĭz′əm) *n.* The principles or practice of obscurants; opposition to the diffusion of enlightenment. —**ob·scur′ant·ist** *n.* & *adj.*

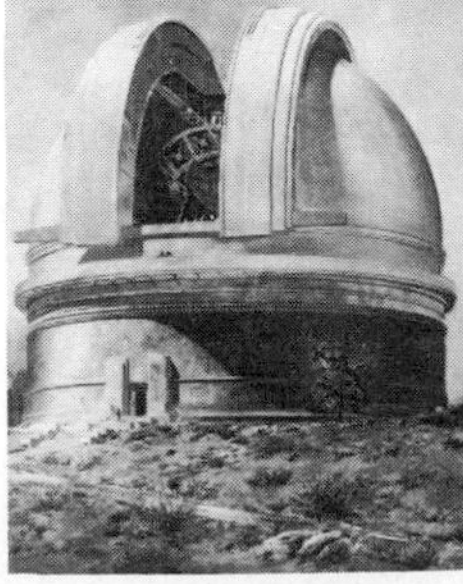

observatory
Dome housing the telescope at Mount Palomar Observatory in southern California

ob·scure (ŏb-skyŏŏr′, əb-) *adj.* **-scurer, -scurest.** *Abbr.* **obs. 1.** Partially or altogether deficient in light; dark; gloomy. **2. a.** Of somber hue; dark. **b.** Dingy; dull. **3. a.** So faintly perceptible as to lack clear delineation; indistinct. **b.** Indistinctly heard; faint. **c.** *Phonetics.* Having the mid-central unstressed sound represented by the schwa (ə). **4.** Out-of-sight; hidden: *an obscure retreat.* **5.** Inconspicuous; unnoticed: *the obscure beginnings of mighty things.* **6.** Of undistinguished or humble descent, station, or reputation. **7.** Imperfectly known or understood: *the obscure workings of nature.* **8.** Not clearly understood or expressed; vague; cryptic; difficult: *an obscure text.* **9.** *Archaic.* Belonging to or inhabiting darkness: *"The obscure bird clamored the livelong night."* (Shakespeare). —See Synonyms at **ambiguous, dark, mysterious.** —*tr.v.* **obscured, -scuring, -scures. 1.** To darken. **2.** To lessen the glory of; overshadow: *"That faith no agony shall obscure in me."* (Shelley). **3.** *Phonetics.* To reduce (a vowel) to the mid-central unstressed sound represented by the schwa (ə). **4.** To conceal from view; hide. **5.** To obstruct; hinder. **6.** To render unintelligible. —*n. Poetic.* Darkness; obscurity. [Middle English, from Old French *obscur*, from Latin *obscūrus*. See **skeu-**[1] in Appendix.*] —**ob·scure′ly** *adv.* —**ob·scure′ness** *n.*

ob·scu·ri·ty (ŏb-skyŏŏr′ə-tē, əb-) *n., pl.* **-ties. 1.** Deficiency or absence of light; darkness: *"We wait for light, but behold obscurity."* (Isaiah 59:9). **2. a.** The condition of being unknown: *from obscurity to fame.* **b.** An unknown person. **3. a.** The condition or quality of being imperfectly known or of being difficult to understand. **b.** An instance of this: *The origin of the race is lost in obscurity.* [Old French *obscurite*, from Latin *obscūritās*, from *obscūrus*, OBSCURE.]

ob·se·crate (ŏb′sə-krāt′) *tr.v.* **-crated, -crating, -crates.** *Rare.* To beg for (something); entreat solemnly. [Latin *obsecrāre*, "to entreat in the name of something sacred" : *ob*, for the sake of + *sacer*, sacred (see **sak-** in Appendix*).] —**ob′se·cra′tion** *n.*

ob·se·qui·ous (ŏb-sē′kwē-əs, əb-) *adj.* **1.** Full of servile compliance; fawning: *"the undertaker's obsequious grimaces"* (Theodore Roethke). **2.** *Archaic.* Submissive and obedient; dutiful. —See Synonyms at **obedient.** [Middle English, from Latin *obsequiōsus*, from *obsequium*, compliance, from *obsequī*, to comply with : *ob*, to + *sequī*, to follow (see **sekw-**[1] in Appendix*).] —**ob·se′qui·ous·ly** *adv.* —**ob·se′qui·ous·ness** *n.*

ob·se·quy (ŏb′sə-kwē) *n., pl.* **-quies.** *Usually plural.* A funeral rite or ceremony. [Middle English *obseque*, from Old French, from Medieval Latin *obsequiae* (influenced by *exequiae*, exequy), from Latin *obsequia*, plural of *obsequium*, compliance, service. See **obsequious.**]

ob·serv·a·ble (əb-zûr′və-bəl) *adj.* **1.** Capable of being observed; noticeable; discernible: *observable improvement.* **2.** Deserving or worthy of notice or mention; noteworthy. **3.** Requiring or deserving special notice or observance: *an observable religious holiday.* —*n. Physics.* A physical property, such as weight or temperature, that can be observed or measured directly, as distinguished from a quantity, such as work or entropy, that must be derived from observed quantities. —**ob·serv′a·ble·ness** *n.* —**ob·serv′a·bly** *adv.*

ob·ser·vance (əb-zûr′vəns) *n.* **1.** The act or practice of observing or complying with a law, custom, command, or other prescribed duty. **2.** The act or custom of keeping or celebrating a holiday or other ritual occasion. **3.** A customary rite or ceremony. **4.** The action of watching; observation: *"Consider how much intellect was needed in the architect, and how much observance of nature."* (Ruskin). **5.** *Roman Catholic Church.* **a.** The rule governing a religious order. **b.** The order itself or the house of such an order. **6.** *Archaic.* Respectful attention: *"He compassed her with sweet observances and worship."* (Tennyson).

ob·ser·vant (əb-zûr′vənt) *adj.* **1.** Quick to perceive or apprehend; alert: *an observant traveler.* **2.** Diligent in observing a law, custom, duty, or principle. Usually followed by *of: observant of family customs.* [French, from Latin *observāns*, present participle of *observāre*, OBSERVE.] —**ob·ser′vant·ly** *adv.*

Ob·ser·van·tine (əb-zûr′vən-tēn′, -tĭn) *n.* Also **Ob·ser·vant** (əb-zûr′vənt). *Roman Catholic Church.* A member of a former branch of the Franciscan Order claiming strict adherence to the rule of Saint Francis, especially to the vow of poverty.

ob·ser·va·tion (ŏb′zər-vā′shən) *n. Abbr.* **obs. 1.** The act or faculty of paying attention or noticing; the fact of being observed; notice. **2.** The act of noting a phenomenon, often with instruments, and recording it for scientific or other purposes. **3.** The result or record of such notation: *a meteorological observation.* **4.** A comment or remark. **5.** *Archaic.* That which is acquired from or based on observing, such as a conclusion or rule. **6.** Observance. [Old French, from Latin *observātiō*, from *observāre*, to OBSERVE.] —**ob′ser·va′tion·al** *adj.* —**ob′ser·va′tion·al·ly** *adv.*

ob·ser·va·to·ry (əb-zûr′və-tôr′ē, -tōr′ē) *n., pl.* **-ries.** *Abbr.* **Obs., obs. 1.** A building designed and equipped for making observations of astronomical, meteorological, or other natural phenomena. **2.** A structure overlooking an extensive view. [French *observatoire*, from Old French *observer*, to OBSERVE (influenced by CONSERVATORY).]

ob·serve (əb-zûrv′) *v.* **-served, -serving, -serves.** —*tr.* **1.** To perceive; notice; see. **2.** To watch attentively: *observe a child's behavior.* **3.** To make a systematic or scientific observation of (a natural or other phenomenon): *observe the moon's orbit.* **4.** To say by way of comment or remark. **5.** To adhere to or abide by (a law, duty, custom, decision, or the like): *observe the terms of a contract.* **6.** To keep or pay tribute to (a holiday, custom, rite, or the like) by celebration, solemnity, or other procedure: *observe an anniversary.* —See Synonyms below. —*intr.* **1.** To take notice. **2.** To say something; make a comment or remark. Often followed by *on* or *upon.* **3.** To watch or be present without participating actively: *He was invited to the conference to observe.* —See Synonyms at **see.** [Middle English *observen*, from Old French *observer*, from Latin *observāre*, to pay attention to, look to : *ob*, to + *servāre*, to keep, watch, pay attention (see **ser-**[1] in Appendix*).] —**ob·serv′ing·ly** *adv.*

Synonyms: *observe, keep, celebrate, solemnize, commemorate.* These are compared in the sense of heeding, marking, or complying with rules, customs, ceremonials, holidays, and the like. *Observe* stresses respectful adherence (to law or tradition, for example), often in the form of compliance with prescribed rites. *Keep* may be used broadly, in opposition to breaking or violating (a promise or the Sabbath, for example), or it may imply rigid adherence. *Celebrate* stresses observance in the form of demonstrations or other group activity; it generally suggests festivity, but can also be applied to religious rites. *Solemnize* is restricted to functions, especially religious ones, characterized by dignity and gravity. *Commemorate* refers to the marking, in the present, of a past event; almost always it implies reverential activity.

ob·serv·er (əb-zûr′vər) *n.* **1.** One who observes. **2.** A delegate sent to observe and report on the proceedings of an assembly or meeting, but not to vote or otherwise participate. **3.** *Military.* **a.** An aircraft crew member who makes observations. **b.** A soldier watching and reporting from an observation post. **4.** *Physics.* One whose observations are made in or referred to a completely specified frame of reference.

ob·sess (əb-sĕs′, ŏb-) *tr.v.* **-sessed, -sessing, -sesses.** To harass or beset like an evil spirit; haunt as a fixed idea. [Latin *obsidēre* (past participle *obsessus*), to sit down before, besiege, beset : *ob*, on + *sedēre*, to sit (see **sed-**[1] in Appendix*).] **—ob·ses′sive** *adj.*

ob·ses·sion (əb-sĕsh′ən, ŏb-) *n.* **1.** *Archaic.* The state of being beset or actuated by the devil or an evil spirit. **2. a.** Compulsive preoccupation with a fixed idea or unwanted feeling or emotion, often with symptoms of anxiety. **b.** A compulsive, often unreasonable, idea or emotion causing such preoccupation. **3.** The act of obsessing. **—ob·ses′sion·al** *adj.*

ob·sid·i·an (ŏb-sĭd′ē-ən) *n.* An acid-resistant, lustrous volcanic glass, usually black or banded and displaying curved, shiny surfaces when fractured. [Latin *obsidiānus*, manuscript error for *obsiānus*, from *Obsius*, mentioned by Pliny as a discoverer of a stone similar to obsidian.]

ob·so·les·cent (ŏb′sə-lĕs′ənt) *adj.* In the process of passing out of use or usefulness; becoming obsolete. See Synonyms at **old.** [Latin *obsolēscēns*, present participle of *obsolēscere*, to grow old, from *obsolēre* (unattested), to be old or in disuse. See **obsolete.**] **—ob′so·les′cence** *n.* **—ob′so·les′cent·ly** *adv.*

ob·so·lete (ŏb′sə-lēt′, ŏb′sə-lēt′) *adj.* **1.** *Abbr.* **obs.** No longer in use or in fashion: *an obsolete word.* **2.** No longer used or useful, because of outmoded design or construction, or because of hard wear: *an obsolete locomotive.* **3.** *Biology.* Increasingly vestigial or disappearing in each succeeding generation. Said of plant or animal characteristics or organs. —See Synonyms at **old.** [Latin *obsolētus*, from *obsolēre* (unattested), to be old or in disuse : *ob*, away from + *solēre*†, to use, be accustomed. See also **insolent.**] **—ob′so·lete′ly** *adv.* **—ob′so·lete′ness** *n.* **—ob′so·let′ism′** *n.*

ob·sta·cle (ŏb′stə-kəl) *n.* One that opposes, stands in the way of, or holds up progress toward some goal. [Middle English, from Old French, from Latin *obstāculum*, from *obstāre*, to hinder : *ob*, against + *stāre*, to stand (see **stā-** in Appendix*).]

Synonyms: *obstacle, obstruction, bar, barrier, block, impediment, hindrance, encumbrance, snag.* These nouns have in common the sense of preventing action or slowing progress. *Obstacle* applies broadly to that which must be removed, circumvented, or surmounted, and usually to that which can be so handled. *Obstruction* more strongly suggests physical interference with passage. *Bar* and *barrier* stress difficulty of passage to the point of implying prohibition, exclusion, or confinement; *block* suggests equally strong opposition of more temporary duration. *Impediment* emphasizes interference with normal function, but not cessation of function. *Hindrance* also, and less strongly, implies mere delay. *Encumbrance* is applicable to that which weighs down, and *snag* to that which provides unforeseen and usually transitory opposition.

obstet. obstetric; obstetrics.

ob·stet·ric (ŏb-stĕt′rĭk, əb-) *adj.* Also **ob·stet·ri·cal** (ŏb-stĕt′rĭ-kəl, əb-). *Abbr.* **ob., obs., obstet.** Of or pertaining to the profession of obstetrics or to the care of women during and after pregnancy. [Latin *obstetrīcius*, from *obstetrīx*, midwife, "she who is present," from *obstāre*, to stand before : *ob*, before + *stāre*, to stand (see **stā-** in Appendix*).] **—ob·stet′ri·cal·ly** *adv.*

ob·ste·tri·cian (ŏb′stə-trĭsh′ən) *n.* *Abbr.* **obs.** A physician specializing in obstetrics.

ob·stet·rics (ŏb-stĕt′rĭks, əb-) *n.* Plural in form, used with a singular or plural verb. *Abbr.* **ob., obs., obstet.** The branch of medicine concerned with the care of women during pregnancy, childbirth, and the recuperative period following delivery.

ob·sti·na·cy (ŏb′stə-nə-sē) *n., pl.* **-cies.** **1.** The state or quality of being obstinate. **2.** An act or instance of stubbornness.

ob·sti·nate (ŏb′stə-nĭt) *adj.* **1.** Stubbornly adhering to an attitude, opinion, or course of action; resistant to argument or entreaty; inflexible; obdurate. **2.** Difficult to manage, control, or subdue; refractory. **3.** Difficult to alleviate or cure: *an obstinate headache.* [Middle English *obstinat*, from Latin *obstinātus*, past participle of *obstināre*, to persist. See **stā-** in Appendix.*] **—ob′sti·nate·ly** *adv.* **—ob′sti·nate·ness** *n.*

Synonyms: *obstinate, stubborn, headstrong, stiff-necked, bullheaded, pigheaded, mulish, dogged, pertinacious. Obstinate* applies specifically to unreasonable rigidity in the face of external stimulus, such as persuasion or attack. *Stubborn* pertains to innate unyieldingness of persons, animals, and things; it does not imply a specific instance of provocation. *Headstrong*, said of persons, pertains to inflexibility combined with reckless willfulness; more than the other terms, it implies action along with resistance. *Stiff-necked* applies to extreme inflexibility in persons, combined with arrogance. *Bullheaded* is said of obstinacy viewed as foolish or irrational; *pigheaded*, of obstinacy as blindly stupid; and *mulish*, of human stubbornness on the level of a beast. *Dogged*, applied to persons and their attributes, emphasizes perseverance in the face of odds, but not necessarily in the sense of contrariness. *Pertinacious*, said of persons, stresses tenacity of purpose viewed as perverse.

ob·strep·er·ous (ŏb-strĕp′ər-əs, əb-) *adj.* Noisily defiant; unruly; boisterous; unmanageable. [Latin *obstreperus*, from *obstrepere*, to make noise against : *ob*, against + *strepere*, to make noise (see **strep-** in Appendix*).] **—ob·strep′er·ous·ly** *adv.* **—ob·strep′er·ous·ness** *n.*

ob·struct (əb-strŭkt′, ŏb-) *tr.v.* **-structed, -structing, -structs.** **1.** To block or fill (a passage) with obstacles; make impassable. **2.** To interfere with, impede, or retard. **3.** To get in the way of so as to hide from view. —See Synonyms at **hinder.** [Latin *obstruere* (past participle *obstructus*) : *ob*, against + *struere*, to pile up (see **ster-**[2] in Appendix*).] **—ob·struct′er, ob·struc′tor** (-strŭk′tər) *n.* **—ob·struc′tive** *adj.*

ob·struc·tion (əb-strŭk′shən, ŏb-) *n.* **1.** One that gets in the way; an obstacle. **2.** An act or instance of impeding or obstructing. **3.** The causing of delay, or an attempt to cause a delay in the conduct of business, especially in a legislative body. —See Synonyms at **obstacle.**

ob·struc·tion·ist (əb-strŭk′shən-ĭst, ŏb-) *n.* One who systematically obstructs or interrupts progress; especially, one who impedes the passage of legislation by various means, as by filibuster. —*adj.* Systematically obstructing legislative proceedings. **—ob·struc′tion·ism′** *n.*

ob·tain (əb-tān′, ŏb-) *v.* **-tained, -taining, -tains.** —*tr.* **1.** To succeed in gaining possession of (something) as the result of planning or endeavor; get or acquire. **2.** *Archaic.* To reach or arrive at: *"obtain the age of manhood"* (Scott). —*intr.* **1.** To be established, accepted, or customary: *Certain formal customs still obtain today.* **2.** *Archaic.* To win the victory; prevail; succeed: *"This, though it failed at present, yet afterwards obtained."* (Swift). [Middle English *obteinen*, from Old French *obtenir*, from Latin *obtinēre*, attain : *ob* (intensive) + *tenēre*, to hold (see **ten-** in Appendix*).] **—ob·tain′a·ble** *adj.* **—ob·tain′er** *n.*

ob·tect (ŏb-tĕkt′) *adj.* Also **ob·tect·ed** (ŏb-tĕk′tĭd). *Entomology.* Enclosed or covered by a hardened secretion. Said especially of pupae having wings, antennae, and legs so enclosed and sealed against the body surface by such a covering. [Latin *obtectus*, past participle of *obtegere*, to cover up, conceal : *ob*, down upon, over + *tegere*, to cover (see **steg-**[1] in Appendix*).]

ob·test (ŏb-tĕst′) *v.* **-tested, -testing, -tests.** —*tr.* To supplicate; entreat. —*intr.* To protest. [Old French *obtester*, from Latin *obtestārī*, to call as a witness to, entreat : *ob*, to + *testārī*, to call as a witness, from *testis*, witness (see **trei-** in Appendix*).] **—ob′tes·ta′tion** (ŏb′tĕs-tā′shən) *n.*

ob·trude (ŏb-trōōd′, əb-) *v.* **-truded, -truding, -trudes.** —*tr.* **1.** To force (oneself or one's ideas) upon others with undue insistence or without invitation: *"I wish not to obtrude any constraints or restraints upon you."* (Lincoln). **2.** To thrust out; push forward; eject. —*intr.* To force oneself upon others or upon their attention. See Synonyms at **intrude.** [Latin *obtrūdere* : *ob*, against + *trūdere*, to thrust (see **treud-** in Appendix*).] **—ob·trud′er** *n.* **—ob·tru′sion** (ŏb trōō′zhən, əb-) *n.*

ob·tru·sive (ŏb-trōō′sĭv, -zĭv, əb-) *adj.* **1.** Projecting; protruding: *an obtrusive rock formation.* **2.** Tending to push self-assertively forward; brash; intrusive: *the obtrusive behavior of a spoiled child.* **3.** Undesirably noticeable; unattractively showy. [From Latin *obtrūs-*, past participle stem of *obtrūdere*, OBTRUDE.] **—ob·tru′sive·ly** *adv.* **—ob·tru′sive·ness** *n.*

ob·tund (ŏb-tŭnd′) *tr.v.* **-tunded, -tunding, -tunds.** To dull or deaden; make less intense. [Middle English *obtunden*, from Latin *obtundere*, to strike against, blunt : *ob*, against + *tundere*, to beat (see **steu-** in Appendix*).] **—ob·tund′ent** *adj.* & *n.*

ob·tu·rate (ŏb′tyə-rāt′, ŏb′tə-) *tr.v.* **-rated, -rating, -rates.** **1.** To close by obstructing or stopping up. **2.** To seal (a gun breech) in order to prevent gas from escaping on firing. [Latin *obturāre*†.] **—ob′tu·ra′tion** *n.*

ob·tu·ra·tor (ŏb′tyə-rā′tər, ŏb′tə-) *n.* **1. a.** Any organic structure, such as the soft palate, that closes an opening in the body. **b.** A prosthetic device serving the same purpose. **2.** A device for sealing a gun breech to prevent gas from escaping on firing.

ob·tuse (ŏb-tōōs′, -tyōōs′, əb-) *adj.* **1. a.** Not sharp, pointed, or acute in form; blunt. **b.** Not acute or intense; indistinctly perceived; dull: *an obtuse pain.* **2.** *Botany.* Having a blunt or rounded tip: *an obtuse leaf.* **3.** Lacking astuteness or discernment; slow to apprehend or perceive. —See Synonyms at **dull, stupid.** [Latin *obtūsus*, past participle of *obtundere*, to blunt, OBTUND.] **—ob·tuse′ly** *adv.* **—ob·tuse′ness** *n.*

obtuse angle. An angle greater than 90 degrees and less than 180 degrees.

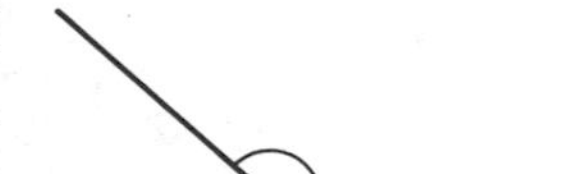

obtuse angle

ob·verse (ŏb-vûrs′, ŏb′vûrs′) *adj.* **1.** Facing or turned toward the observer: *the obverse side of a statue.* **2.** *Botany.* Having a narrower base than top, as certain leaves; inverse. **3.** Serving as a counterpart or complement. —*n.* (ŏb′vûrs′, ŏb-vûrs′). **1.** The side of a coin, medal, badge, or the like that bears the principal stamp or design and, on U.S. coins, the date. Compare **verso.** **2.** A counterpart or complement. **3.** *Logic.* The counterpart of a proposition obtained by exchanging the affirmative for the negative quality of the whole proposition and then negating the predicate. The obverse of *every act is predictable* is *no act is unpredictable.* [Latin *obversus*, past participle of *obvertere*, to turn toward, OBVERT.] **—ob·verse′ly** *adv.*

ob·ver·sion (ŏb-vûr′zhən, -shən) *n.* **1.** The process of or condition resulting from obverting. **2.** *Logic.* Inference of the obverse of a proposition.

ob·vert (ŏb-vûrt′) *tr.v.* **-verted, -verting, -verts.** **1.** To turn so as to present another side or aspect to view. **2.** *Logic.* To subject to obversion. [Latin *obvertere*, to turn toward : *ob*, toward + *vertere*, to turn (see **wer-**[3] in Appendix*).]

ob·vi·ate (ŏb′vē-āt′) *tr.v.* **-ated, -ating, -ates.** To prevent or dispose of effectively; anticipate so as to render unnecessary. See Synonyms at **prevent.** [Late Latin *obviāre,* "to meet in the way," prevent, from Latin *obviam,* in the way. See **obvious.**] —**ob′vi·a′tion** *n.* —**ob′vi·a′tor** (-ā′tər) *n.*

ob·vi·ous (ŏb′vē-əs) *adj.* **1.** Easily perceived or understood; quite apparent. **2.** Easily seen through; lacking subtlety. **3.** *Archaic.* Standing in the way or in front. —See Synonyms at **evident.** [Latin *obvius,* from *obviam,* in the way : *ob,* against + *viam,* accusative of *via,* way (see **wei-²** in Appendix*).] —**ob′vi·ous·ly** *adv.* —**ob′vi·ous·ness** *n.*

ob·vo·lute (ŏb′və-lo͞ot′, ŏb′və-lo͞ot′) *adj. Botany.* Folded together with overlapping edges. Said of leaves and petals in a bud. [Latin *obvolutus,* past participle of *obvolvere,* to wrap around, surround : *ob,* over + *volvere,* to roll, wrap (see **wel-³** in Appendix*).] —**ob′vo·lu′tion** *n.* —**ob′vo·lu′tive** *adj.*

OC **1.** Office of Censorship. **2.** Officer Commanding.

oc., Oc. ocean.

o.c. in the work cited (Latin *opere citato*).

O.C. **1.** Office of Censorship. **2.** Officer Commanding. **3.** Old Catholic.

o/c overcharge.

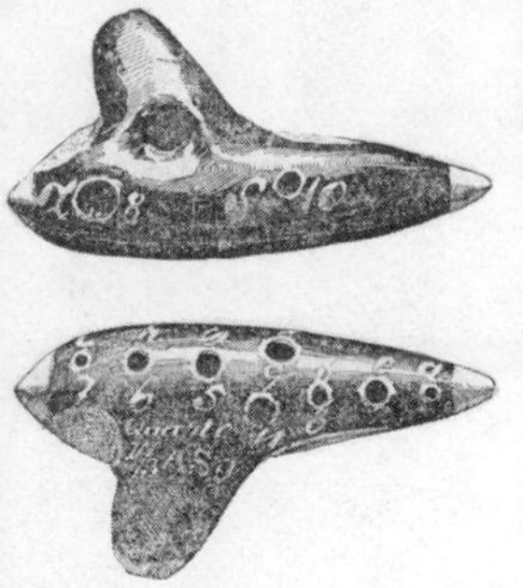

ocarina

oc·a·ri·na (ŏk′ə-rē′nə) *n. Music.* A small terra-cotta or plastic wind instrument with a mouthpiece, finger holes, and an elongated ovoid shape. Also called "sweet potato." [Italian, "little goose," diminutive of *oca,* goose, from Vulgar Latin *avica* (unattested), from Latin *avicula,* diminutive of *avis,* bird. See **awi-** in Appendix.*]

OCAS Organization of Central American States.

O'Ca·sey (ō-kā′sē), **Sean.** 1880–1964. Irish dramatist and autobiographer; lived in self-exile in England after 1926.

occ. **1.** occident; occidental. **2.** occupation.

Oc·cam, William of. See **Ockham.**

occas. occasional; occasionally.

oc·ca·sion (ə-kā′zhən) *n.* **1. a.** An event or happening. **b.** The time at which an event or happening occurs. **2.** A significant or extraordinary event or happening. **3.** An appropriate or favorable time; opportunity. **4.** That which brings on or precipitates an action or event; immediate cause. **5.** Ground; reason. See Usage note below. **6.** Requirement; need; necessity: *"He must buy what he has little occasion for"* (Sterne). **7.** *Plural. Archaic.* Personal requirements or necessities. **8.** *Plural. Archaic.* Personal affairs or business matters. —See Synonyms at **cause, opportunity.** —**by occasion of.** Because of; by reason of. —**on occasion.** From time to time; now and then. —*tr.v.* **occasioned, -sioning, -sions.** To provide occasion for. [Middle English *occasioun,* from Old French *occasion,* from Latin *occāsiō,* "a falling down, happening," from *occidere* (past participle *occāsus*), to fall down : *ob,* down + *cadere,* to fall (see **kad-** in Appendix*).]

Usage: In the sense of reason or ground, *occasion* is followed by *for* (and noun or gerund) or *to* (and infinitive): *An occasion for rejoicing gave us no occasion to object.* In the sense of opportunity, *to* is customary: *took the occasion to ask.* In the sense of time of occurrence, *of* is used: *on the occasion of your visit.*

oc·ca·sion·al (ə-kā′zhən-əl) *adj. Abbr.* **occas. 1.** Coming irregularly; occurring from time to time. **2.** Occurring on or created for a special occasion: *occasional verse.* **3.** Designed not as part of a set but for use as the occasion requires: *an occasional chair or two for unexpected guests.* —See Synonyms at **periodic.**

oc·ca·sion·al·ly (ə-kā′zhən-əl-ē) *adv. Abbr.* **occas.** Now and then; from time to time; sometimes.

oc·ci·dent (ŏk′sə-dənt, -dĕnt′) *n. Abbr.* **occ. 1.** The west; western lands or regions. **2.** *Capital* **O.** The countries of Europe and the Western Hemisphere. Compare **Orient.** [Middle English, from Old French, from Latin *occidēns,* "quarter of the setting sun," west, from present participle of *occidere,* to fall down, set (of the sun). See **occasion.**]

oc·ci·den·tal (ŏk′sə-dĕn′təl) *adj. Abbr.* **occ.** *Often capital* **O.** Of or pertaining to the countries of the Occident, their peoples, or their culture; western. —*n. Usually capital* **O.** A native or inhabitant of a western country.

oc·ci·den·tal·ize (ŏk′sə-dĕn′təl-īz′) *tr.v.* **-ized, -izing, -izes.** *Often capital* **O.** To make occidental in character, outlook, or way of life. —**oc′ci·den′tal·i·za′tion** *n.*

oc·cip·i·tal (ŏk-sĭp′ə-təl) *adj.* Of or pertaining to the occiput or to the occipital bone: *an occipital fracture.* —*n.* The occipital bone. [Old French, from Medieval Latin *occipitālis,* from Latin *occiput* (stem *occipit-*), OCCIPUT.]

occipital bone. A curved, trapezoidal, compound bone that forms the lower posterior part of the skull.

oc·ci·put (ŏk′sə-pŭt′, -pət) *n., pl.* **occipita** (ŏk-sĭp′ə-tə) or **-puts.** The back of the skull, especially the occipital area. [Latin : *ob,* in back of + *caput,* head (see **kaput** in Appendix*).]

oc·clude (ə-klo͞od′) *v.* **-cluded, -cluding, -cludes.** —*tr.* **1.** To cause to become closed; obstruct: *occlude a larynx.* **2.** To prevent the passage of; shut in, out, or off: *occlude light.* **3.** *Chemistry.* To absorb or adsorb (a substance) in great quantity. **4.** *Meteorology.* To force (air) upward from the earth's surface, as when a cold front overtakes and undercuts a warm front. **5.** *Dentistry.* To bring together (the upper and lower teeth) in proper alignment for chewing. —*intr. Dentistry.* To close so that the cusps fit together. Used of the teeth of the upper and lower jaws. [Latin *occlūdere* : *ob* (intensive) + *claudere,* to close (see **klēu-** in Appendix*).] —**oc·clud′ent** *adj.*

occluded front. *Meteorology.* The air front established when a cold front occludes a warm front. Also called "occlusion."

oc·clu·sion (ə-klo͞o′zhən) *n.* **1. a.** The process of occluding. **b.** That which occludes or blocks. **2.** *Meteorology.* **a.** The process of occluding air masses. **b.** An **occluded front** *(see).* **3.** *Dentistry.* The fit of the teeth when brought together. **4.** *Phonetics.* **a.** The closing of the breath passage in a stop. **b.** The blocking of the mouth passage in a nasal consonant.

oc·clu·sive (ə-klo͞o′sĭv, -zĭv) *adj.* Occluding or tending to occlude. —*n. Phonetics.* **1.** A closing of the breath passage; a stop. **2.** A nasal consonant.

oc·cult (ə-kŭlt′, ŏ-kŭlt′, ŏk′ŭlt′) *adj.* **1.** Of, pertaining to, dealing with, or knowledgeable in supernatural influences, agencies, or phenomena. **2.** Beyond the realm of human comprehension; mysterious; inscrutable. **3.** Available only to the initiate; not divulged; secret: *occult lore.* **4.** *Rare.* Hidden from view; concealed. —See Synonyms at **mysterious.** —*n.* Occult practices or techniques. Usually preceded by *the: a student of the occult.* —*v.* (ə-kŭlt′, ŏ-kŭlt′) **occulted, -culting, -cults.** —*tr.* **1.** To conceal or cause to disappear from view. **2.** *Astronomy.* To conceal by occultation: *The moon occulted Mars.* —*intr.* To become concealed or extinguished at regular intervals: *a lighthouse beacon that occults every 45 seconds.* [Latin *occultus,* past participle of *occulere,* to conceal (see **kel-⁴** in Appendix*).] —**oc·cult′ly** *adv.* —**oc·cult′ness** *n.*

oc·cul·ta·tion (ŏk′ŭl-tā′shən) *n.* **1.** *Astronomy.* **a.** The passage of a celestial body across a line between an observer and another celestial object, as when the moon moves between earth and sun in a solar eclipse. **b.** The progressive blocking of light, radio waves, or other radiation from a celestial source during such a passage. **c.** An observational technique for determining the position or radiant structure of a celestial source so occulted: *a lunar occultation of a quasar.* **2.** The act of occulting or the state of being occulted. [Middle English *occultacion,* concealment, from Latin *occultātiō,* from *occultāre,* frequentative of *occulere,* to conceal. See **occult.**]

oc·cult·ism (ə-kŭl′tĭz′əm, ŏ-kŭl′-, ŏk′ŭl-tĭz′əm) *n.* **1.** The study of the supernatural. **2.** A belief in occult powers and the possibility of bringing them under human control. —**oc·cult′ist** *n.*

oc·cu·pan·cy (ŏk′yə-pən-sē) *n., pl.* **-cies. 1. a.** The act of taking or holding possession; the act of occupying. **b.** The condition of being occupied. **2.** The period during which one owns, rents, or uses certain premises or land. **3.** The state of being an occupant or tenant. **4.** *Law.* The taking possession of previously unowned property with the intent of obtaining the right to own it.

oc·cu·pant (ŏk′yə-pənt) *n.* **1.** One who holds a position or place. **2.** One who has certain legal rights to or control over the premises he occupies; a tenant or owner. **3.** *Law.* One who is the first to take possession of something previously unowned. [Old French, from the present participle of *occuper,* OCCUPY.]

oc·cu·pa·tion (ŏk′yə-pā′shən) *n. Abbr.* **occ. 1. a.** An activity that serves as one's regular source of livelihood; profession; vocation. **b.** An activity engaged in especially as a means of passing time. **2. a.** The act or process of holding or possessing a place. **b.** The state of being held or possessed. **3. a.** The invasion, conquest, and control of a nation or territory by a foreign military force. **b.** The military government exercising such control. [Middle English *occupacioun,* from Old French *occupation,* from Latin *occupātiō,* from *occupāre,* OCCUPY.]

oc·cu·pa·tion·al (ŏk′yə-pā′shən-əl) *adj.* Of, pertaining to, or caused by engagement in a particular occupation: *occupational disease.* —**oc′cu·pa′tion·al·ly** *adv.*

occupational therapy. Therapy in which the principal element is some form of productive or creative activity.

oc·cu·py (ŏk′yə-pī′) *tr.v.* **-pied, -pying, -pies. 1.** To seize possession of and maintain control over (a place or region) by military conquest. **2.** To fill up; take (time or space): *a lecture that occupied three hours.* **3.** To dwell or reside in; be a tenant of. **4.** To hold or fill (an office or position). **5.** To engage, employ, or busy (oneself): *occupied himself with a mystery story for the rest of the hour.* [Middle English *occupien,* from Old French *occuper,* from Latin *occupāre,* to seize : *ob* (intensive) + *capere,* to take (see **kap-** in Appendix*).] —**oc′cu·pi′er** *n.*

oc·cur (ə-kûr′) *intr.v.* **-curred, -curring, -curs. 1.** To take place; come about. See Usage note below. **2.** To be found to exist or appear: *Heavy rains occur during a summer monsoon.* **3.** To come to mind; suggest itself: *The idea never occurred to me.* —See Synonyms at **happen.** [Latin *occurrere,* to run to meet : *ob,* toward + *currere,* to run (see **kers-²** in Appendix*).]

Usage: *Occur* is preferred usage when the action is spontaneous, accidental, or unforeseen: *The collision occurred at a highway intersection.* When the action is prearranged, *take place* is preferable: *The wedding will take place in two days.*

oc·cur·rence (ə-kûr′əns) *n.* **1.** An act or instance of occurring. **2.** Something that takes place; an incident. —**oc·cur′rent** *adj.*

Synonyms: *occurrence, happening, event, incident, episode, circumstance. Occurrence* and *happening* pertain, without implication, to anything that takes place. *Event* denotes a notable occurrence, usually considered as the result of antecedent happenings. *Incident* may apply to any minor occurrence or, in a special sense, to that part of an event that takes on sharp identity and momentary significance: *a border incident* (considered as part of a diplomatic event). *Episode* denotes a progression of occurrences that has independent character and significance within a larger sequence. *Circumstance,* in this context, denotes a detail of an event that, in combination with others of its kind, explains or interprets the nature of the event.

OCD Office of Civil Defense.

o·cean (ō′shən) *n.* **1.** *Abbr.* **O, O., oc., Oc.** The entire body of salt water that covers about 72 per cent of the earth's surface. **2.** *Often capital* **O.** *Abbr.* **O, O., oc., Oc.** Any of the principal divisions of this body of water, including the Atlantic, Pacific, and Indian oceans, their southern extensions in Antarctica, and

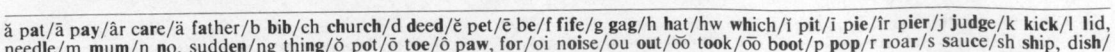

the Arctic Ocean. **3.** Any great expanse or amount: *oceans of money.* **4.** In classical mythology, the sea encircling the earth. [Middle English *occean*, from Old French, from Latin *ōceanus*, from Greek *ōkeanos*, OCEANUS.]

o·cean·ar·i·um (ō'shə-nâr'ē-əm) *n., pl.* **-iums** or **-ia** (-ē-ə). A large aquarium for the study or display of marine life.

O·ce·an·i·a (ō'shē-ăn'ē-ə, -ā'nē-ə). Also **O·ce·an·i·ca** (ō'shē-ăn'ĭ-kə). The islands of the central, western, and southern Pacific Ocean, customarily including Australia and New Zealand. **—O'ce·an'i·an** *adj.* & *n.*

o·ce·an·ic (ō'shē-ăn'ĭk) *adj.* **1.** Of or pertaining to the ocean. **2.** Produced by or living in an ocean, especially in the open sea rather than in shallow coastal waters. **3.** Like an ocean in expanse; wide; vast; huge.

O·ce·an·ic (ō'shē-ăn'ĭk) *adj.* **1.** Pertaining to a subfamily of the Austronesian language family, comprising Melanesian and Polynesian. **2.** Pertaining to the cultures of the peoples speaking languages in this subfamily. **—O'ce·an'ic** *n.*

O·ce·a·nid (ō-sē'ə-nĭd) *pl.* **Oceanides** (ō'sē-ăn'ə-dēz'). *Greek Mythology.* Any of the ocean nymphs held to be the daughters of Oceanus and Tethys. [Greek *ōkeanis* (stem *ōkeanid-*), from *Ōkeanos*, OCEANUS.]

oceanog. oceanography.

o·cean·og·ra·phy (ō'shə-nŏg'rə-fē) *n. Abbr.* **oceanog.** The exploration and scientific study of the ocean and its phenomena. [OCEAN + -GRAPHY.] **—o'cean·og'ra·pher** *n.* **—o'cean·o·graph'ic** (ō'shən-ə-grăf'ĭk), **o'cean·o·graph'i·cal** *adj.*

ocean sunfish. A marine fish, *Mola mola*, with a large globular body, found in warm seas. Also called "globefish."

O·ce·a·nus (ō-sē'ə-nəs). *Greek Mythology.* A Titan, the god of the outer sea encircling the earth; father of the Oceanides and of the river gods.

oc·el·lat·ed (ŏs'ə-lā'tĭd, ō'sə-, ō-sĕl'ā'tĭd) *adj.* Also **oc·el·late** (ŏs'ə-lāt', ō'sə-, ō-sĕl'āt'). **1.** Having an ocellus or ocelli. **2.** Resembling an ocellus. **3.** Having spots. [Latin *ocellātus*, having little eyes, from *ocellus*, little eye, OCELLUS.] **—oc'el·la'tion** *n.*

o·cel·lus (ō-sĕl'əs) *n., pl.* **ocelli** (ō-sĕl'ī'). **1.** A small simple eye, found in many invertebrates. **2.** A marking that resembles an eye. [New Latin, from Latin, diminutive of *oculus*, eye. See **okw-** in Appendix.*] **—o·cel'lar** (ō-sĕl'ər) *adj.*

oc·e·lot (ŏs'ə-lŏt', ō'sə-) *n.* A brush- and forest-dwelling cat, *Felis pardalis*, of the southwestern United States and Central and South America, having a tawny-grayish or yellow coat with black spots. [French, from Nahuatl *ocelotl*.]

o·cher (ō'kər) *n.* Also **o·chre.** **1.** Any of several earthy mineral oxides of iron mingled with varying amounts of clay and sand, occurring in yellow, brown, or red, and used either untreated or processed for color intensification as pigments. **2.** Moderate orange yellow, from moderate or deep orange to moderate or strong yellow. See **color.** —*tr.v.* **ochered, ochering, ochers.** Also **o·chre, ochred, ochring, ochres.** To color or mark with ocher. [Middle English *oker*, from Old French *ocre*, from Latin *ōchra*, from Greek *ōkhra*, from *ōkhros*†, yellow, pale yellow.] **—o'cher·ous** (ō'kər-əs), **o'cher·y** (ō'krē) *adj.*

och·loc·ra·cy (ŏk-lŏk'rə-sē) *n., pl.* **-cies.** Government by the masses; mob rule. [Old French *ochlocratie*, from Greek *okhlokratia* : *okhlos*, mob (see **wegh-** in Appendix*) + *-kratia*, -CRACY.] **—och'lo·crat'** (ŏk'lə-krăt') *n.* **—och'lo·crat'ic, och'lo·crat'i·cal** *adj.* **—och'lo·crat'i·cal·ly** *adv.*

och·lo·pho·bi·a (ŏk'lə-fō'bē-ə) *n.* Abnormal dread of crowds. [New Latin : Greek *okhlos*, crowd (see **wegh-** in Appendix*) + -PHOBIA.]

-ock. Indicates smallness; for example, **hillock.** [Middle English *-oc*, Old English *-oc*, *-uc*.]

Ock·ham (ŏk'əm), **William of.** Also **Oc·cam.** English philosopher of the early 14th century.

o'clock (ə-klŏk') *adv.* **1.** Of or according to the clock: *three o'clock.* **2.** According to an imaginary clock dial with the observer at the center and 12 o'clock considered as straight ahead in horizontal position or straight up in vertical position. Used to indicate relative position: *enemy planes at 10 o'clock.* [Reduced from *of the clock*.]

Oc·mul·gee National Monument (ōk-mŭl'gē). An area occupying 683 acres in central Georgia, reserved to protect its Indian mounds.

O'Con·nell (ō-kŏn'əl), **Daniel.** 1775–1847. Irish lawyer, orator, and statesman; liberator of the Irish Roman Catholics.

O'Con·nor (ō-kŏn'ər), **Frank.** Pen name of Michael O'Donovan. 1903–1966. Irish author of short stories.

O'Con·nor (ō-kŏn'ər), **Thomas Power.** Called "Tay Pay." 1848–1929. Irish journalist and political figure.

o·co·ti·llo (ō'kə-tē'yō) *n., pl.* **-llos.** A cactuslike tree, *Fouquieria splendens*, of Mexico and the southwestern United States, having clusters of scarlet tubular flowers. Also called "candlewood." [Mexican Spanish, diminutive of *ocote*, a Mexican pine, from Nahuatl *ocotl*, torch.]

oc·re·a (ŏk'rē-ə) *n., pl.* **-reae** (-rē-ē'). *Botany.* A sheath composed of one or more stipules, enclosing the leafstalks of certain plants. [Latin *ocrea*†, greave, legging.]

OCS Officer Candidate School.

oct. octavo.

Oct. October.

oc·tad (ŏk'tăd') *n.* A group or sequence of eight. [Greek *oktas* (stem *oktad-*), number eight, from *oktō*, eight. See **oktō** in Appendix.*] **—oc·tad'ic** *adj.*

oc·ta·gon (ŏk'tə-gŏn') *n.* A polygon with eight sides and angles. [Latin *octagōnum*, from Greek *oktagōnon*, from neuter of *oktagōnos*, having eight angles : OCTO- + -GON.]

oc·tag·o·nal (ŏk-tăg'ə-nəl) *adj.* Having eight sides and eight angles. **—oc·tag'o·nal·ly** *adv.*

oc·ta·he·dral (ŏk'tə-hē'drəl) *adj.* Having eight plane surfaces.

oc·ta·he·drite (ŏk'tə-hē'drīt') *n.* A mineral, **anatase** (*see*). [French *octaédrite*, from *octaèdre*, octahedron (with reference to its octahedral crystals), from Greek *oktaedron*, OCTAHEDRON.]

oc·ta·he·dron (ŏk'tə-hē'drən) *n., pl.* **-drons** or **-dra** (-drə). A polyhedron with eight plane surfaces. [Greek *oktaedron* : OCTO- + -HEDRON.]

oc·tam·er·ous (ŏk-tăm'ər-əs) *adj.* Also **oc·tom·er·ous** (ŏk-tŏm'ər-əs). *Biology.* Having organs or organic parts arranged in groups of eight. [Greek *oktamerēs* : OCTO- + -MEROUS.] **—oc·tam'er·ism'** (ŏk-tăm'ə-rĭz'əm) *n.*

oc·tam·e·ter (ŏk-tăm'ə-tər) *adj.* Having eight measures or metrical feet to a line of verse. —*n.* A verse having eight measures or metrical feet to each line. [Late Latin, from Late Greek *oktametros* : OCTO- + *metron*, METER.]

oc·tane (ŏk'tān') *n.* **1.** Any of various isomeric paraffin hydrocarbons with the formula C_8H_{18}. **2.** A colorless, inflammable hydrocarbon, $CH_3(CH_2)_6CH_3$, found in petroleum, and used as a solvent. **3.** Octane number. [OCT(O)- + -ANE.]

octane number. A numerical measure of the antiknock properties of motor fuel, based on the percentage by volume of iso-octane in a standard reference fuel. For example, a motor fuel that produces the same degree of knocking as a standard reference fuel containing 80% iso-octane has an octane number of 80. Also called "octane rating." Compare **cetane number.**

Oc·tans (ŏk'tănz') *n.* The constellation that includes the south celestial pole. Also called "Octant." [New Latin, from Latin *octāns*, half-quadrant. See **octant.**]

oc·tant (ŏk'tənt) *n.* **1.** One-eighth of a circle: **a.** A 45° arc. **b.** The area enclosed by two radii at a 45° angle and the intersected arc. **2.** An instrument based on the principle of the sextant, but employing only a 45° angle, used as an aid in navigation. **3.** *Astronomy.* The position of a celestial body when it is separated from another by a 45° angle. **4.** Any one of eight parts into which three-dimensional space is divided by three, usually perpendicular, coordinate planes. **5.** *Capital* **O.** Octans. [Latin *octans*, half-quadrant, from *octō*, eight. See **oktō** in Appendix.*] **—oc·tan'tal** (ŏk-tăn'təl) *adj.*

oc·tave (ŏk'tĭv, -tāv') *n.* **1.** *Music.* **a.** The interval of eight diatonic degrees between two tones, one of which has twice as many vibrations per second as the other. **b.** A tone that is eight full tones above or below another given tone. **c.** Two tones, eight diatonic degrees apart, sounded together, or the consonance that results. **d.** A series of tones included within this interval, or the keys of an instrument that produce such a series. **e.** An organ stop that produces tones an octave above those usually produced by the keys played. **2.** *Ecclesiastical.* **a.** The eighth day after a feast day, counting the feast day as one. **b.** The entire period between a feast day and the eighth day following it. **3.** Any group or series of eight. **4.** *Prosody.* **a.** A stanza of eight lines. **b.** An **octet** (*see*). **5.** *Fencing.* A rotating parry. —*adj.* **1.** Composed of eight elements or parts. **2.** *Music.* Producing tones one octave higher, as an organ stop. [Middle English, the eighth day (after a festival), from Medieval Latin *octāva (diēs)*, from Latin, feminine of *octāvus*, eighth, from *octō*, eight. See **oktō** in Appendix.*] **—oc·ta'val** (ŏk-tā'vəl, ŏk'tə-vəl) *adj.*

Oc·ta·vi·an. See **Augustus.**

oc·ta·vo (ŏk-tā'vō, -tä'vō) *n., pl.* **-vos.** *Abbr.* **o., O., oct.** **1.** The page size (from 5 × 8 inches to 6 × 9½ inches) of a book composed of printer's sheets folded into eight leaves, originally printed on one side of each sheet. **2.** A book composed of pages of this size. Also called "eightvo." Also written *8vo*, *8°*. [Latin *(in) octāvō*, "in eighth," ablative of *octāvus*, eighth. See **octave.**] **—oc·ta'vo** *adj.*

oc·ten·ni·al (ŏk-tĕn'ē-əl) *adj.* **1.** Happening or recurring every eight years. **2.** Lasting eight years. [From Late Latin *octennium*, period of eight years : OCT(O)- + Latin *annus*, a year (see **at-** in Appendix*).] **—oc·ten'ni·al·ly** *adv.*

oc·tet (ŏk-tĕt') *n.* Also **oc·tette.** **1.** A musical composition written for eight voices or eight instruments. **2.** A group of eight singers or eight instrumentalists. **3.** Any group of eight. **4.** *Prosody.* The first eight lines of an Italian sonnet. In this sense, also called "octave," "octonary." Compare **sestet.** [Italian *ottetto* (influenced by *duet*), from *otto*, eight, from Latin *octō*. See **oktō** in Appendix.*]

oc·til·lion (ŏk-tĭl'yən) *n.* **1.** The cardinal number represented by the figure 1 followed by 27 zeros; usually written 10^{27}. **2.** In Great Britain, the cardinal number represented by the figure 1 followed by 48 zeros; usually written 10^{48}. See **number.** [French : OCT(O)- + (M)ILLION.]

oc·til·lionth (ŏk-tĭl'yənth) *n.* The ordinal number octillion in a series. See **number.** **—oc·til'lionth** *adj.*

octo-, oct-. Indicates eight parts or elements; for example, **octopus, octameter, octane.** [Latin *octō-*, from *octō*, eight; Greek *okta-*, from *oktō*, eight. See **oktō** in Appendix.*]

Oc·to·ber (ŏk-tō'bər) *n. Abbr.* **Oct.** **1.** The tenth month of the Gregorian calendar. October has 31 days. See **calendar.** **2.** *British.* Ale brewed in this month. [Middle English *octobre*, from Old French, from Latin *Octōber*, "eighth month," from *octō*, eight. See **oktō** in Appendix.*]

October Revolution. A part of the **Russian Revolution** (*see*).

oc·to·dec·i·mo (ŏk'tə-dĕs'ə-mō') *n., pl.* **-mos.** **1.** The page size (4 × 6½ inches) of a book composed of printer's sheets folded into 18 leaves or 36 pages. **2.** A book composed of pages of this size. Also called "eighteenmo." Also written *18mo*, *18°*. [Latin *octōdecimō*, ablative of *octodecimus*, eighteenth, from *oc-*

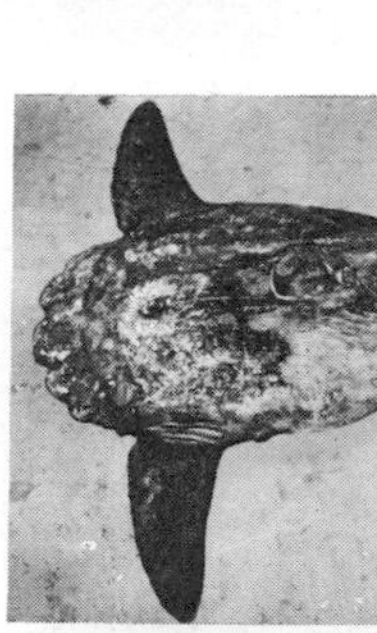

ocean sunfish

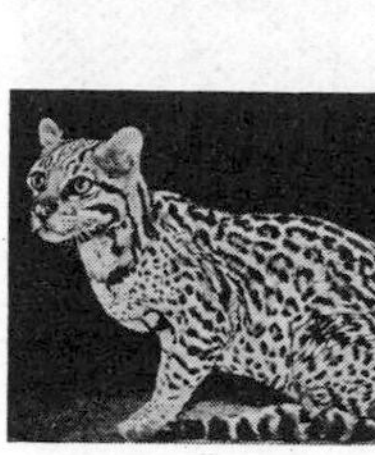

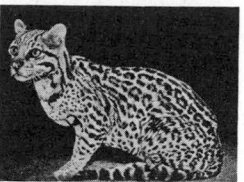

ocelot

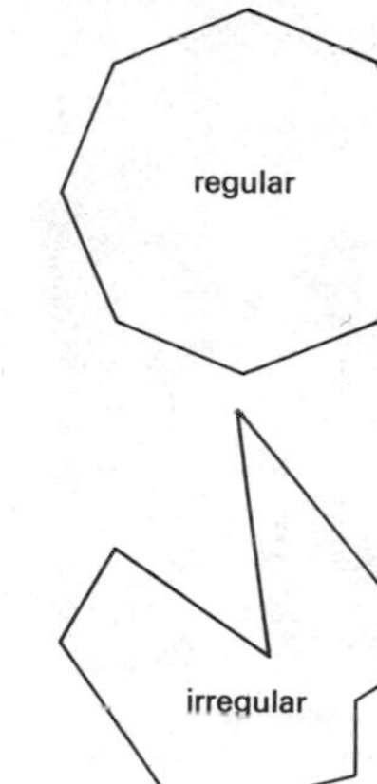
regular
irregular

octagon

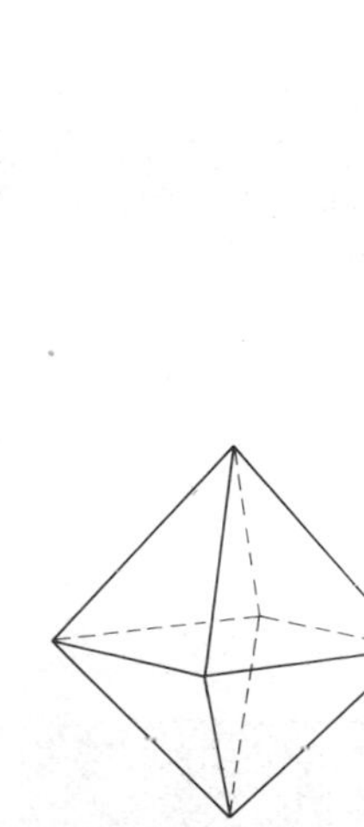

octahedron

tōdecim, eighteen: OCTO- + *decem,* ten (see **dekm** in Appendix*).] —**oc'to·dec'i·mo** *adj.*

oc·to·ge·nar·i·an (ŏk'tə-jə-nâr'ē-ən) *adj.* Also **oc·tog·e·nar·y** (ŏk-tŏj'ə-nĕr'ē). Being between eighty and ninety years of age. —*n.* Also **oc·tog·e·nar·y** *pl.* **-ies.** A person between eighty and ninety years of age. [From Latin *octōgēnārius,* containing eighty, from *octōgēnī,* eighty each, from *octōgintā,* eighty : *octō,* OCTO- + *-ginta,* "ten times" (see **dekm** in Appendix*).]

oc·tom·er·ous. Variant of **octamerous.**

oc·to·nar·y (ŏk'tə-nĕr'ē) *adj.* **1.** Of or pertaining to the number eight. **2.** Consisting of eight members or of groups containing eight. —*n., pl.* **octonaries. 1.** *Prosody.* An **octet** *(see).* **2.** A group or set of eight. [Latin *octōnārius,* containing eight, from *octōnī,* eight at a time, from *octō,* eight. See **oktō** in Appendix.*]

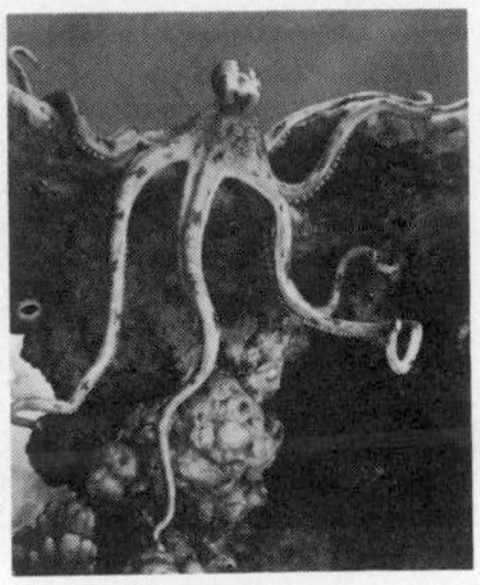

octopus
Octopus maculosa

oc·to·ploid (ŏk'tə-ploid') *adj. Genetics.* Having eight haploid sets of chromosomes in a body cell. [OCTO- + -PLOID.]

oc·to·pod (ŏk'tə-pŏd') *n.* Any mollusk of the order Octopoda, such as an octopus, having eight arms. [New Latin *Octopoda,* from Greek *oktōpoda,* neuter plural of *oktōpous* (stem *oktōpod-*), OCTOPUS.]

oc·to·pus (ŏk'tə-pəs) *n., pl.* **-puses** or **octopodes** (ŏk-tŏp'ə-dēz') or **octopi** (ŏk'tə-pī'). **1.** Any of numerous carnivorous, nocturnal, marine mollusks of the genus *Octopus,* or related genera, found worldwide. It has a rounded, saclike body, eight tentacles, each bearing two rows of suckers, a large distinct head, and a strong beaklike mouth. Also called "devilfish." Compare **squid. 2.** Any powerful and far-reaching organization, such as a large corporation. [New Latin, from Greek *oktōpous,* eight-footed: OCTO- + *pous,* foot (see **ped-**[1] in Appendix*).]

oc·to·roon (ŏk'tə-ro͞on') *n.* The offspring of a white person and a quadroon; one who is one-eighth Negro. [OCTO- + (QUAD)ROON.]

oc·to·syl·la·ble (ŏk'tə-sĭl'ə-bəl) *n.* **1.** Also **oc·to·syl·lab·ic** (ŏk'-tō-sĭ-lăb'ĭk). *Prosody.* **a.** A line of verse containing eight syllables. **b.** A verse with eight syllables in each line. **2.** A word of eight syllables. [Late Latin *octosyllabus,* having eight syllables : OCTO- + *syllaba,* SYLLABLE.] —**oc'to·syl·lab'ic** *adj.*

oc·troi (ŏk'troi'; *French* ôk-trwà') *n., pl.* **-trois** (-troiz'; *French* ôk-trwà'). A local tax levied on certain items brought into some European cities. [French, from Old French, a tax which a city is authorized to levy, from *octroyer,* to grant as a privilege, authorize, from Gallo-Roman *auctōricāre* (unattested), to authorize, from Latin *auctor,* author, originator, from *augēre,* to originate, increase (see **aug-**[1] in Appendix*).]

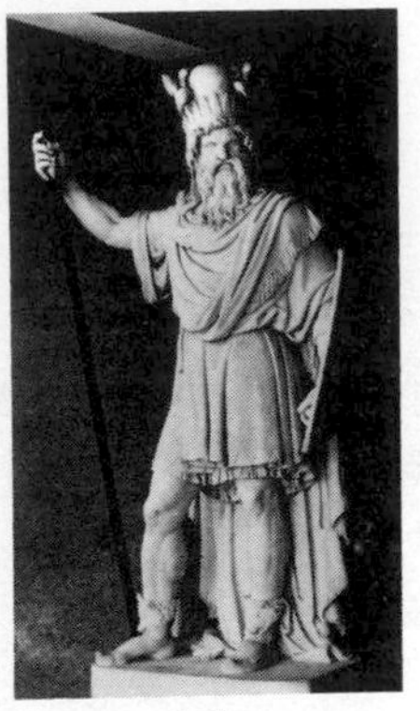

Odin
Nineteenth-century statue by Swedish sculptor Bengt Fogelberg

oc·tu·ple (ŏk'to͞o-pəl, ŏk'tyo͞o-, ŏk-to͞o'pəl, ŏk-tyo͞o'-) *adj.* **1.** Having eight parts, members, or copies. **2.** Multiplied by eight; eightfold. —*n.* A quantity eight times as great as another. —*tr.v.* **octupled, -pling, -ples.** To multiply by eight. [Latin *octuplus* : OCTO- + *-plus,* -fold (see **pel-**[3] in Appendix*).]

oc·u·lar (ŏk'yə-lər) *adj.* **1.** Of or pertaining to the eye: *ocular exercises.* **2.** Of or pertaining to the sense of sight: *an ocular aberration.* **3.** Seen by the eye; visual: *ocular proof.* —*n.* The eyepiece of an optical instrument. [Late Latin *oculāris,* of the eyes, from Latin *oculus,* eye. See **okw-** in Appendix.*]

oc·u·list (ŏk'yə-lĭst) *n.* **1.** A physician who treats diseases of the eyes; an ophthalmologist. **2.** An optometrist. [French *oculiste,* from Latin *oculus,* eye. See **okw-** in Appendix.*]

Usage: The following terms are sometimes confused. *Oculist* and *ophthalmologist* denote a physician who specializes in diseases of the eye, *ophthalmologist* being the preferred term among professionals. *Optometrist* applies more narrowly to one skilled in testing the eyes and prescribing corrective lenses. *Optician* is one who makes or sells optical goods.

oc·u·lo·mo·tor (ŏk'yə-lō-mō'tər) *adj.* **1.** Pertaining to movements of the eyeball. **2.** Pertaining to the oculomotor nerve. [Latin *oculus,* eye (see **okw-** in Appendix*) + MOTOR.]

oculomotor nerve. *Anatomy.* Either of the two cranial nerves that control the muscles of the eyeballs.

Od, Odd (ŏd) *interj. Archaic.* God. Used in oaths.

o.d. 1. olive drab. **2.** on demand.

O.D. 1. Doctor of Optometry. **2.** officer of the day. **3.** overdraft. **4.** overdrawn.

o·da·lisque (ō'də-lĭsk') *n.* Also **o·da·lisk.** A female slave or concubine in a harem. [French *odalisque,* from Turkish *ōdalik,* chambermaid : *ōdah,* room + *-lık,* noun suffix.]

odd (ŏd) *adj.* **odder, oddest. 1. a.** Strange, unusual, or peculiar. **b.** Queer or eccentric in conduct. **2.** In excess of what is usual, regular, approximated, or expected. **3. a.** Being one of an incomplete pair or set: *an odd shoe.* **b.** Remaining after others are paired or grouped: *odd man at the dinner party.* **4.** *Mathematics.* Designating an integer not divisible by two: *1, 3, and 5 are odd numbers.* Compare **even.** —See Synonyms at **strange.** —*n.* **1.** Anything odd. **2.** *Golf.* **a.** In the United States, a score one stroke higher than the score of one's opponent. **b.** In Great Britain, a handicap of one stroke given to a player as odds, or an advantage of one stroke taken away from a player's score as odds. [Middle English *odde,* from Old Norse *oddi,* triangle, point, third, odd number. See **ozdo-** in Appendix.*] —**odd'ly** *adv.* —**odd'ness** *n.*

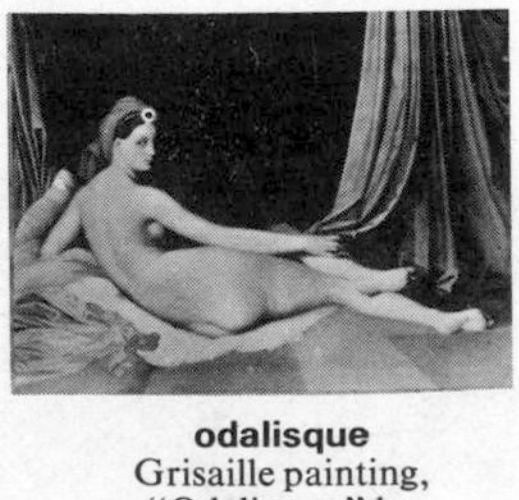

odalisque
Grisaille painting, "Odalisque," by Jean Auguste Ingres

Usage: *Odd,* used to indicate an indefinite amount in excess of a specified round number, should be preceded by a hyphen in cases where ambiguity might result otherwise: *70-odd persons. Odd* in this sense is used with round numbers.

odd·ball (ŏd'bôl') *n. Informal.* A person marked by eccentric behavior or way of thinking. —**odd'ball'** *adj.*

Odd Fellow. A member of the Independent Order of Odd Fellows, a fraternal and benevolent secret society.

odd·ish (ŏd'ĭsh) *adj.* Somewhat odd; rather peculiar.

odd·i·ty (ŏd'ə-tē) *n., pl.* **-ties. 1.** A person or thing that is odd. **2.** An odd quality, trait, or characteristic; an eccentricity. **3.** The state or quality of being odd; strangeness.

odd·ment (ŏd'mənt) *n.* **1.** *Usually plural.* Something left over; a fragment, scrap, or remnant. **2.** An oddity.

odd-pin·nate (ŏd'pĭn'āt') *adj. Botany.* Pinnate with a single, unpaired leaflet at the end of the leafstalk.

odds (ŏdz) *pl.n.* Sometimes used with a singular verb. **1.** A certain number of points given beforehand to a weaker side in a contest to equalize the chances of all participants. **2.** A ratio expressing the probability of an event or outcome. Used especially of sports contests: *The odds on the champion winning are three to two.* **3.** A ratio expressing the amount by which the stake of one bettor differs from that of his opposing bettor: *He gave odds of ten to one, which I couldn't pass up.* **4.** The likelihood of one thing occurring, rather than another, in any contest or issue of indefinite outcome: *The odds are that he will get the nomination on the first ballot.* —**at odds.** In disagreement; in conflict. [Plural of ODD.]

odds and ends. Miscellaneous items, remnants, or pieces.

Odd's bod·i·kins. Variant of **Od's bodkins.**

ode (ōd) *n.* **1.** In classical literature, a poem intended to be sung by a chorus at a public festival or as part of a drama. **2.** A lengthy lyrical poem, usually rhymed, often addressed to some praised object, person, or quality, and characterized by exalted style. See **Horatian ode, Pindaric ode.** [French, from Old French, from Late Latin *ōda, ōdē,* from Greek *ōidē, aoidē,* song. See **wed-**[2] in Appendix.*] —**od'ic** (ō'dĭk) *adj.*

-ode[1]. Indicates a way or path; for example, **electrode, cathode.** [Greek *-odos,* from *hodos,* a way. See **sed-**[2] in Appendix.*]

-ode[2]. Indicates resemblance or characteristic nature; for example, **nematode.** [Greek *-ōdēs,* from *eidos,* form, shape. See **weid-** in Appendix.*]

O·den·se (ō'*th*ən-sə). A city and industrial center of Denmark, the birthplace of Hans Christian Andersen. Population, 111,000.

O·der (ō'dər). *Polish* and *Czechoslovakian* **O·dra** (ô'drä). A river rising in north-central Czechoslovakia and flowing north 563 miles through Poland and East Germany to the Baltic Sea.

O·des·sa (ō-dĕs'ə). **1.** An industrial city of the Ukrainian Soviet Socialist Republic on the Black Sea near the mouth of the Dniester River. Population, 735,000. **2.** A city in west-central Texas. Population, 80,000.

o·de·um (ō-dē'əm, ō'dē-əm) *n., pl.* **odea** (ō-dē'ə, ō'dē-ə). Also **o·de·on** (ō-dē'ŏn') *pl.* **-ons. 1.** A small building of ancient Greece and Rome used for public performances of music and poetry. **2.** A contemporary theater or concert hall. [Latin *ōdēum,* from Greek *ōideion,* from *ōidē,* song, ODE.]

O·din (ō'dĭn). *Norse Mythology.* The supreme deity and creator of the cosmos and man; the god of wisdom, war, art, culture, and the dead, often identified with the Teutonic god Woden. [Old Norse *Ódhinn.* See **wāt-** in Appendix.*]

o·di·ous (ō'dē-əs) *adj.* Exciting hatred or repugnance; abhorrent; offensive. See Synonyms at **hateful.** [Middle English, from Old French, from Latin *odiōsus,* from *odium,* ODIUM.] —**o'di·ous·ly** *adv.* —**o'di·ous·ness** *n.*

o·di·um (ō'dē-əm) *n.* **1.** The state or quality of being odious. **2.** Strong dislike; contempt or aversion. **3.** The disgrace resulting from hateful conduct. —See Synonyms at **disgrace.** [Latin, hatred, from *ōdī,* I hate. See **od-**[2] in Appendix.*]

O·do·a·cer (ō'dō-ā'sər). Also **O·do·va·car, O·do·va·kar** (ō'dō-vā'kər). A.D. 434?–493. Germanic leader of the insurrection that caused the fall of the Western Roman Empire (476).

o·do·graph (ō'də-grăf', -gräf') *n.* **1.** A device for recording speed and distance traveled on foot. **2.** An instrument for recording the distance and course traveled by a vehicle. [Greek *hodos,* road, journey (see **sed-**[2] in Appendix*) + -GRAPH.]

o·dom·e·ter (ō-dŏm'ə-tər) *n.* An instrument that indicates distance traveled by a vehicle. [French *odomètre,* modification of Greek *hodometron* : *hodos,* road, journey (see **sed-**[2] in Appendix*) + *metron,* measure, METER.] —**o·dom'e·try** *n.*

-odon. Indicates an animal having a certain kind of teeth; for example, **mastodon.** [New Latin, from Greek *odōn,* tooth. See **dent-** in Appendix.*]

-odont. Indicates a tooth or teeth of a specified type; for example, **acrodont.** [From Greek *odōn* (stem *odont-*), tooth. See **dent-** in Appendix.*]

odonto-. Indicates tooth or teeth; for example, **odontoblast, odontology.** [Greek, from *odōn* (stem *odont-*), tooth. See **dent-** in Appendix.*]

o·don·to·blast (ō-dŏn'tə-blăst') *n.* A tooth cell in the outer surface of dental pulp that produces dentine. [ODONTO- + -BLAST.] —**o·don'to·blas'tic** *adj.*

o·don·toid (ō-dŏn'toid') *adj.* **1.** Resembling a tooth. **2.** Of or pertaining to the **odontoid process** *(see).* [Greek *odontoeidēs* : ODONT(O)- + -OID.]

odontoid process. *Anatomy.* A small, toothlike projection from the second vertebra of the neck, around which the first vertebra rotates.

o·don·tol·o·gy (ō'dŏn-tŏl'ə-jē) *n.* The study of the anatomy, growth, and diseases of the teeth. [French *odontologie* : ODONTO- + -LOGY.] —**o·don'to·log'i·cal** (ō-dŏn'tə-lŏj'ĭ-kəl) *adj.* —**o·don'to·log'i·cal·ly** *adv.* —**o'don·tol'o·gist** *n.*

o·don·to·phore (ō-dŏn'tə-fôr', -fōr') *n.* A protrusile structure at the base of the mouth of most mollusks, supporting the radula. [ODONTO- + -PHORE.] —**o'don·toph'o·ral** (ō'dŏn-tŏf'ər-əl), **o'don·toph'o·rine** (-tŏf'ə-rīn', -rĭn), **o'don·toph'o·rous** *adj.*

o·dor (ō'dər) *n.* Also *chiefly British* **o·dour. 1.** The property or

ă pat/ā pay/âr care/ä father/b bib/ch church/d deed/ĕ pet/ē be/f fife/g gag/h hat/hw which/ĭ pit/ī pie/îr pier/j judge/k kick/l lid, needle/m mum/n no, sudden/ng thing/ŏ pot/ō toe/ô paw, for/oi noise/ou out/o͝o took/o͞o boot/p pop/r roar/s sauce/sh ship, dish/

quality of a thing that affects, stimulates, or is perceived by the sense of smell; a scent. **2.** Any sensation, stimulation, or perception of the sense of smell; a smell. **3.** A strong, pervasive quality: *an odor of sadness at dusk.* **4.** Esteem; repute: *a doctrine that is not currently in good odor.* —See Synonyms at **smell.** [Middle English *odour,* from Old French, from Latin *odor.* See **od-¹** in Appendix.*] —**o'dored** *adj.*

o·dor·if·er·ous (ō'də-rĭf'ər-əs) *adj.* Having or giving off an odor. [Latin *odōrifer* : *odor,* ODOR + -FER.] —**o'dor·if'er·ous·ly** *adv.* —**o'dor·if'er·ous·ness** *n.*

o·dor·im·e·ter (ō'də-rĭm'ə-tər) *n.* Also **o·dor·om·e·ter** (ō'də-rŏm'ə-tər). An instrument for measuring the intensity of odors.

o·dor·less (ō'dər-lĭs) *adj.* Having no odor: *an odorless gas.*

o·dor·ous (ō'dər-əs) *adj.* Having a distinctive odor, usually, but not necessarily, an unpleasant odor. —**o'dor·ous·ly** *adv.* —**o'dor·ous·ness** *n.*

O·do·va·car, O·do·va·kar. See **Odoacer.**

Od's bod·kins (ŏdz bŏd'kĭnz) *interj.* Also **Odd's bod·i·kins** (bŏd'ĭ-kĭnz). *Archaic.* Used as an oath. [Euphemism for *"(by) God's body."*]

O·dys·seus (ō-dĭs'yo͞os', ō-dĭs'ē-əs). Latin name, **U·lys·ses** (yo͞o-lĭs'ēz). *Greek Mythology.* The cunning king of Ithaca, a leader of the Greeks in the Trojan War, whose return home after the war was for ten years frustrated by the enmity of Poseidon.

od·ys·sey (ŏd'ə-sē) *n.* An extended adventurous wandering. [After ODYSSEY.]

Od·ys·sey (ŏd'ə-sē). The second epic of Homer, recounting the wanderings and adventures of Odysseus after the fall of Troy and his eventual return home. [French *Odyssée,* from Latin *Odyssēa,* from Greek *Odusseia,* from *Odusseus,* ODYSSEUS.] —**Od'ys·sey'an** (ŏd'ə-sē'ən) *adj.*

Oe oersted.

OE, OE., O.E. Old English.

oec·u·men·i·cal. Variant of **ecumenical.**

OED, O.E.D. Oxford English Dictionary.

oe·de·ma. Variant of **edema.**

oed·i·pal (ĕd'ə-pəl, ē'də-) *adj.* Also **oed·i·pe·an** (ĕd'ə-pē'ən, ē'də-). *Sometimes capital* **O.** Of, relating to, or characteristic of the Oedipus complex.

Oed·i·pus (ĕd'ə-pəs, ē'də-). *Greek Mythology.* A son of Laius and Jocasta, who was abandoned at birth and who unwittingly killed his father and married his mother; subject of two plays by Sophocles.

Oedipus complex. *Psychoanalysis.* Libidinal feelings in a child, especially a male child, for the parent of the opposite sex, usually accompanied by hostility to the parent of the same sex, generally manifesting itself first between ages three and five. Compare **Electra complex.**

OEEC Organization for European Economic Cooperation.

oe·nol·o·gy (ē-nŏl'ə-jē) *n.* Also **oi·nol·o·gy** (oi-nŏl'ə-jē), **e·nol·o·gy** (ē-nŏl'ə-jē). The study of wines. [Greek *oinos,* wine (see **vinum** in Appendix*) + -LOGY.] —**oe'no·log'i·cal** (ē'nə-lŏj'ĭ-kəl) *adj.* —**oe·nol'o·gist** *n.*

oe·no·mel (ē'nə-mĕl') *n.* **1.** A beverage of ancient Greece, consisting of wine and honey. **2.** *Poetic.* A source of strength and sweetness. [Greek *oinomeli* : *oinos,* wine (see **vinum** in Appendix*) + *meli,* honey (see **melit-** in Appendix*).]

OEO Office of Economic Opportunity.

OEP Office of Emergency Planning.

o'er. *Poetic.* Variant of **over.**

oer·sted (ûr'stĕd') *n. Abbr.* **Oe** The centimeter-gram-second electromagnetic unit of magnetic intensity, equal to the magnetic intensity one centimeter from a unit magnetic pole. [After Hans Christian *Oersted* (1777–1851), Danish physicist.]

oe·soph·a·gus. Variant of **esophagus.**

oes·tro·gen. Variant of **estrogen.**

oes·trus. Variant of **estrus.**

oeu·vre (œ'vr') *n., pl.* **oeuvres** (œ'vr'). *French.* **1.** A work of art. **2.** The sum of an artist's work.

of (ŭv; *unstressed* əv) *prep.* **1.** Derived or coming from; originating at or from: *William of Orange; men of the north.* **2.** Caused by; resulting from: *his death of tuberculosis.* **3.** Away from; at a distance from: *a mile east of here.* **4.** So as to be separated or relieved from: *robbed of his dignity, cured of distemper.* **5.** From the total or group comprising: *give of one's time; two of his friends; most of the cases.* **6.** Composed or made from: *a dress of silk.* **7.** Associated with or adhering to: *a man of your religion.* **8.** Belonging or connected to: *the rungs of a ladder.* **9.** Possessing; having: *a man of honor.* **10.** Containing or carrying: *a basket of groceries.* **11.** Specified as; named or called: *a depth of ten feet; the Garden of Eden.* **12.** Centering upon (some object); directed toward: *a love of horses.* **13.** Produced by; issuing from: *the novels of Ernest Hemingway; products of the vine.* **14.** Characterized or identified by: *a year of famine.* **15.** Concerning; with reference to; about: *think highly of his proposals; speak of it later.* **16.** Set aside for; taken up by: *a day of rest.* **17.** Before; until. Used in telling time: *five minutes of two.* **18.** During or on (a specified time): *of recent years.* **19.** *Rare.* By: *beloved of his family.* [Middle English *of,* Old English *of* (preposition and adverb). See **apo** in Appendix.*]

Usage: In constructions indicating possession, *of* may be followed by either an uninflected noun *(crew of the ship; friend of my father)* or by a noun or pronoun in the possessive case *(friend of my father's; uncle of his).*

o·fay (ō'fā') *n. Negro Slang.* A white person. Used derogatorily. [Possibly Pig Latin, from English FOE.]

off (ôf, ŏf) *adv.* **1.** At or to a distance from a nearer place; so as to be away: *drive off.* **2.** Distant or away in space or time: *The state line is a mile off. The party is a week off.* **3.** So as to be no longer on, attached, or connected: *The electricity was cut off.* **4.** So as to be no longer continuing, operating, or functioning: *turn off the radio.* **5.** So as to be completely removed, finished, or eliminated: *write off a report; kill off the mice.* **6.** So as to be smaller, fewer, or less: *Sales dropped off.* **7.** So as to be away from work or duty: *They took a day off.* —**off and on.** Intermittently: *He slept off and on.* —**off with.** Remove. Used as an imperative interjection: *Off with his head! Off with all of you!* —*adj.* **1.** Distant or removed; remote; farther: *the off side of the barn.* **2.** Not on, attached, or connected: *with his shoes off.* **3.** Not continuing, operating, or functioning: *The oven is off.* **4.** No longer existing or effective; canceled: *The wedding is off.* **5.** Fewer, smaller, or less: *Production was off this year.* **6.** Not up to standard; below a normal or satisfactory level: *Your pitching is off today.* **7.** In (a specified) circumstance or condition: *You are better off staying home.* **8.** Inconsistent with accuracy or truth; in error: *My guess was slightly off.* **9.** Started on the way; going: *They saw us off at the pier.* **10.** Absent or away from work or duty: *He's off every Tuesday.* **11.** On the right side of a vehicle or draft team: *The off horse is lame.* **12.** *Nautical.* Seaward; farthest from the shore. **13.** *Cricket.* Designating or toward the side of the field facing the batsman. —*prep.* **1.** So as to be removed or distant from (a position of rest or support): *The bird hopped off the branch.* **2.** Away or relieved from: *off duty.* **3. a.** By consuming: *living off locusts and honey.* **b.** With the means provided by: *living off his pension.* **4.** Extending or branching out from: *an artery off the heart.* **5.** Deviating from; not up to the standard of: *off his game.* **6.** Abstaining from: *He went off narcotics.* **7.** Seaward of: *a mile off Sandy Hook.* [Middle English *of, off,* of, off, from Old English *of.* See **apo-** in Appendix.*]

Usage: Particularly in written usage, *off* should not be followed by *of* or *from: He stepped off* (not *off of* or *off from*) *the platform.* Nor should *off* be used for *from* to indicate a source in such phrases as: *I got a loan from* (not *off*) *him.*

off. office; officer; official.

of·fal (ô'fəl, ŏf'əl) *n.* **1.** Waste parts, especially of a butchered animal. **2.** Refuse; rubbish. [Middle English *offal, ofall,* from Middle Dutch *afval,* "that which falls off," giblets, refuse : *af,* off (see **apo-** in Appendix*) + *vallen,* to fall (see **phol-** in Appendix*).]

Of·fa·ly (ô'fə-lē, ŏf'ə-). A county of the Republic of Ireland, 771 square miles in area. Population, 52,000. Capital, Tullamore.

off·beat (ôf'bēt', ŏf'-) *n.* An unaccented beat in a musical measure. —*adj.* (ôf'bēt', ŏf'-). *Slang.* Not conforming to an ordinary type or pattern; unconventional.

off-Broad·way (ôf'brôd'wā', ŏf'-) *adj.* **1.** Designating or pertaining to theatrical activity, often experimental and low-cost, presented in theaters outside the Broadway entertainment district of New York City. **2.** Located outside of the Broadway entertainment district. —*n.* Theatrical productions presented outside the Broadway entertainment district. Compare **Broadway.**

off·cast (ôf'kăst', -käst', ŏf'-) *adj.* Rejected; discarded.

off chance. A remote or slight chance.

off-col·or (ôf'kŭl'ər, ŏf'-) *adj.* **1.** Varying from the usual, expected, or required color. **2.** Improper; in bad taste: *an off-color joke.* **3.** *Chiefly British.* Not in good health or spirits.

Of·fen·bach (ôf'ən-bäкн'). Also **Of·fen·bach am Main** (äm mīn'). An industrial city of West Germany, on the opposite bank of the Main River from Frankfurt. Population, 117,300.

Of·fen·bach (ô'fən-bäk', ŏf'ən-; *French* ô-fĕn-bȧk'), **Jacques.** Original surname, Levy. 1819–1880. German-born French composer of operettas.

of·fend (ə-fĕnd') *v.* **-fended, -fending, -fends.** —*tr.* **1.** To create or excite anger, resentment, or annoyance in; hurt the feelings of; affront: *Her brusqueness offends many people.* **2.** To be displeasing or disagreeable to: *Onions offend his sense of smell.* **3.** *Obsolete.* **a.** To transgress; violate: *"He hath offended the law"* (Shakespeare). **b.** To cause to sin: *"If thy right eye offend thee, pluck it out."* (Matthew 5:29). —*intr.* **1.** To cause displeasure: *Bad manners may offend.* **2.** To violate a moral or divine law; to sin. [Middle English *offenden,* from Old French *offendre,* from Latin *offendere,* to strike against. See **gwhen-¹** in Appendix.*]

Synonyms: *offend, insult, affront, outrage. Offend* is the least specific of these verbs denoting the act of giving displeasure; it often makes no implication regarding intent. *Insult* applies to a deliberate act calculated to cause humiliation; *affront* adds to this a stress on openness of attack, a sense of an insult to one's face. *Outrage,* stronger still, emphasizes that which causes extreme resentment by flagrantly violating one's standards of right and decency.

of·fense (ə-fĕns' *for senses 1, 2, 3;* ŏf'ĕns' *for senses 4, 5*) *n.* Also *chiefly British* **of·fence.** **1.** The act of offending or causing anger, resentment, displeasure, or the like. **2. a.** Any violation or infraction of a moral or social code; a transgression or sin. **b.** A transgression of law; a crime. **3.** Something that offends. **4.** The act of attacking or assaulting. **5.** An athletic team in possession of the ball or puck. —**give offense.** To cause anger, displeasure, or resentment. —**take offense.** To become angered, displeased, or resentful; feel hurt. [Middle English, from Old French, from Latin *offensa,* from the feminine past participle of *offendere,* OFFEND.]

Synonyms: *offense, crime, sin, error.* These terms are related in denoting infraction of a code. *Offense* is broadly applicable to any such infraction. *Crime* applies to transgression of law,

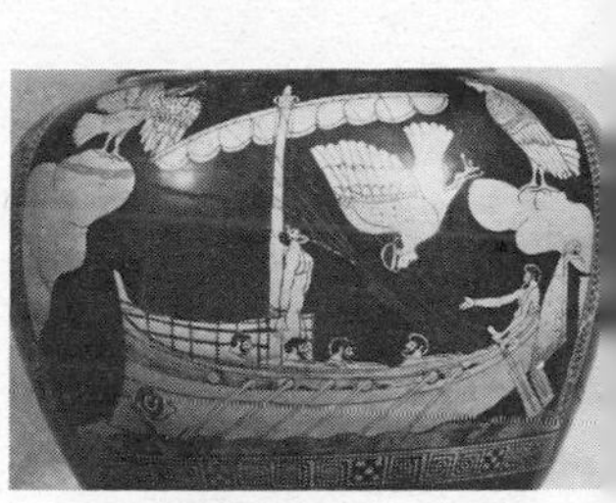

Odysseus
Greek vase painting of Odysseus tied to his ship's mast while listening to the songs of the sirens

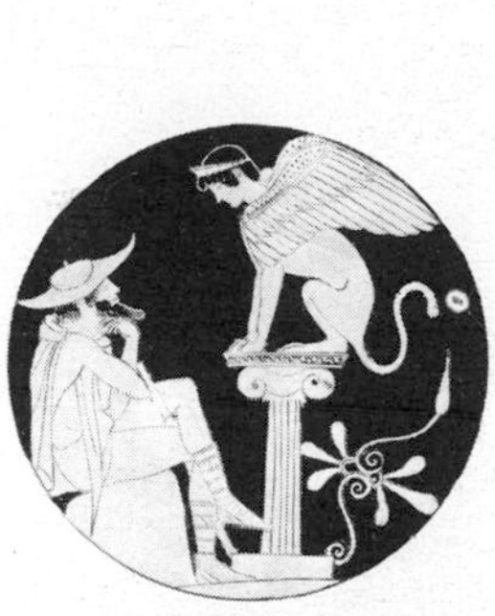

Oedipus
Greek vase painting of Oedipus answering the riddle of the Sphinx

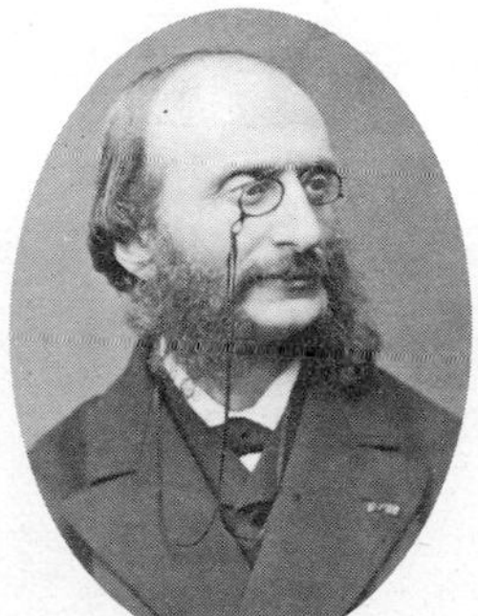

Jacques Offenbach

generally to a serious violation, which, like its punishment, is defined by law. *Sin* pertains less specifically to serious violation of moral law. *Error,* like *offense,* is nonspecific as to magnitude and code; it differs from all of the others by stressing lack of knowledge or bad judgment rather than willful violation.

of·fen·sive (ə-fĕn′sĭv) *adj.* **1.** Disagreeable to the senses: *an offensive odor.* **2.** Causing anger, displeasure, or resentment; giving offense; affronting. **3.** Of, pertaining to, or characteristic of an attack; aggressive. —See Synonyms at **hateful.** —*n.* **1.** An attitude of attack. Often used with *the.* **2.** An attack; assault. —**of·fen′sive·ly** *adv.* —**of·fen′sive·ness** *n.*

Synonyms: *offensive, insulting, forward, obnoxious.* These adjectives describe unpleasant effects to the senses or feelings. *Offensive* generally applies to sight, smell, or sound or to the intellect or feelings. While *insulting* can apply to an action, particularly a gesture, it most commonly refers to a verbal offense. *Forward* implies a breach in propriety or etiquette, and is applied to persons as the approximate equivalent of the informal "pushy." *Obnoxious* emphasizes an extremely unpleasant quality.

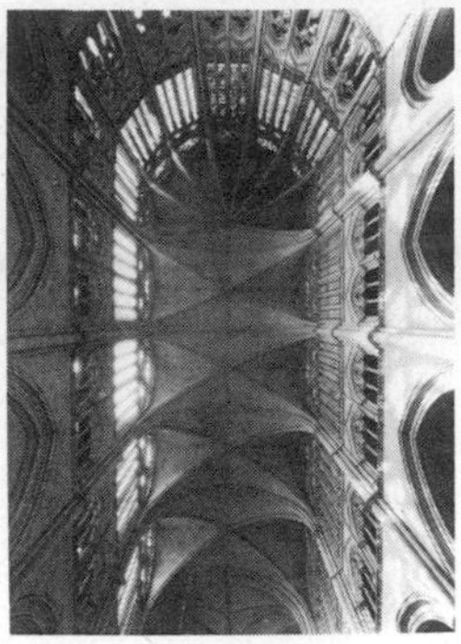

ogive
Vaults in the ceiling of the cathedral in Amiens, France

of·fer (ô′fər, ŏf′ər) *v.* **-fered, -fering, -fers.** —*tr.* **1.** To present for acceptance or rejection; proffer: *"Jake bought everything the newsboys offered him."* (Willa Cather). **2.** To put forward for consideration; propose: *offer an opinion.* **3.** To present for sale. **4.** To propose as payment; to bid. **5.** To present as an act of worship. Often followed by *up: offer up prayers.* **6.** To exhibit readiness or desire to do; volunteer: *The gentleman offered to escort her.* **7.** To exhibit an intention; attempt: *"ready to shoot me if I should offer to stir"* (Swift). **8.** To try to inflict upon: *"He was not afraid of their offering him any harm."* (Melville). **9.** To provide; furnish; afford. **10.** To produce or introduce on the stage; present in exhibition: *The repertory group is offering two new plays this season.* —*intr.* **1.** To present an offering in worship or devotion. **2.** To make an offer or proposal; especially, to make an offer of marriage. **3.** To present itself; appear; arise: *"This plan was dropped, because of its risk, and because a better offered."* (T.E. Lawrence). —*n.* **1.** The act of offering: *an offer of assistance.* **2.** Something offered, such as a suggestion, proposal, bid, or recommendation. **3.** *Law.* A proposal which, if accepted, constitutes a legally binding contract. **4.** The condition of being offered, especially for sale: *thousands of bushels of wheat on offer.* **5. a.** An attempt; a try: *"imperfect offers and essays"* (Bacon). **b.** A show of intention. [Middle English *offeren, offren,* partly (in the sense "to sacrifice") from Old English *offrian,* and partly (in other senses) from Old French *offrir;* both from Latin *offerre* : *ob,* to + *ferre,* to bring, carry (see **bher-¹** in Appendix*).] —**of′fer·er, of′fer·or** (-ər) *n.*

Synonyms: *offer, proffer, tender, present. Offer* is the basic, general term among this group. *Proffer,* used in polite discourse, is somewhat more emphatic through its implication of voluntary action motivated by courtesy or generosity. *Tender,* in business or legal usage, may stress formality *(tender one's resignation),* or it may apply specifically to discharge of an obligation *(tender payment);* in more general usage it emphasizes formality and observance of amenities *(tender one's respects). Present* stresses both formality and overt show.

of·fer·ing (ô′fər-ĭng, ŏf′ər-) *n.* **1.** The act of making an offer. **2.** Something that is offered. **3.** A presentation made to God or a deity as an act of religious worship or sacrifice; an oblation. **4.** A contribution or gift, especially one made at a religious service. [Middle English *offring,* Old English *offrung,* from *offrian,* to sacrifice, OFFER.]

of·fer·to·ry (ô′fər-tôr′ē, -tōr′ē, ŏf′ər-) *n., pl.* **-ries. 1.** *Often capital* **O. a.** One of the principal parts of the Eucharistic liturgy at which bread and wine are offered to God by the celebrant. **b.** A musical setting of the Offertory. **2.** A collection of offerings of the congregation. [Old French *offertoire,* from Medieval Latin *offertōrium,* from Latin *offerre,* OFFER.]

off·hand (ôf′hănd′, ŏf′-) *adv.* Without preparation or forethought; impromptu; extemporaneously. —*adj.* Also **off·hand·ed** (-hănd′ĭd). Said or done offhand. —See Synonyms at **extemporaneous.** —**off′hand′ed·ly** *adv.* —**off′hand′ed·ness** *n.*

of·fice (ô′fĭs, ŏf′ĭs) *n. Abbr.* **off. 1. a.** A place, such as a building, room, or suite, in which services, clerical work, professional duties, or the like are carried out. **b.** The administrative personnel, executives, or entire staff working in such a place. **2.** A duty or function assigned to or assumed by someone: *"the maternal office was supplied by my aunt"* (Gibbon). **3.** A position of authority, duty, or trust given to a person, as in a government, corporation, or other organization: *the office of vice president.* **4. a.** Any of the branches of the Federal government of the United States ranking just below the departments. **b.** A major executive division of the British national government, often headed by a cabinet minister. **5.** A public position: *seek office.* **6.** *Plural. Chiefly British.* The parts of a house, such as the laundry and kitchen, in which the servants carry out household work, and often including outbuildings such as the barn. **7.** *Often plural.* An act performed for another, usually beneficial; a favor: *"The projected duel . . . was halted by the offices of friends on both sides."* (Katherine Anne Porter). **8.** *Ecclesiastical.* A ceremony, rite, or service, usually prescribed by liturgy: **a.** *Roman Catholic Church.* The canonical hours. **b.** *Anglican Church.* Morning and Evening Prayer or the Holy Communion. **c.** Any ceremony, rite, or service for a special purpose; especially, a rite for the dead. [Middle English, from Old French, from Latin *officium,* performance of duty. See **dhē-¹** in Appendix.*]

of·fice·hold·er (ô′fĭs-hōl′dər, ŏf′ĭs-) *n.* One who holds a public office.

of·fi·cer (ô′fĭ-sər, ŏf′ĭ-) *n. Abbr.* **off. 1.** One who holds an office of authority or trust in a corporation, government, or other institution; especially, one who acts in a managerial capacity for a private corporation: *bank officers.* **2.** One holding a commission in the armed forces. **3.** A man licensed in the merchant marine as master, mate, chief engineer, or assistant engineer. **4.** A policeman or constable. **5.** A rank above the lowest rank in some honorary societies. [Middle English, Old French *officier,* from Medieval Latin *officiārius,* "officeholder," from Latin *officium,* OFFICE.]

officer of the day. *Abbr.* **O.D.** A military officer who for a given day assumes responsibility for security, order, and the performance of the guard.

officer of the deck. *Abbr.* **O.O.D.** A naval officer assigned to represent the commanding officer of a vessel or installation for a specified period, during which he is superior to all officers below the executive officer.

of·fi·cial (ə-fĭsh′əl) *adj. Abbr.* **off. 1.** Of or pertaining to an office or post of authority: *official duties.* **2.** Authorized by a proper authority; authoritative: *official permission.* **3.** Holding office or serving in some public capacity; authorized to perform some special duty: *an official representative.* **4.** Characteristic of or befitting a person of authority: *official behavior.* **5.** Formal or ceremonious: *an official banquet.* **6.** *Pharmacology.* Authorized by or contained in the U.S. Pharmacopoeia or National Formulary. —*n. Abbr.* **off.** One who holds an office or position; especially, one who acts in a subordinate capacity for a corporation, governmental agency, or other institution. [Middle English, an authority, from Old French, from Late Latin *officiālis,* functionary, official, from Latin, of an office or duty, from *officium,* OFFICE.] —**of·fi′cial·ly** *adv.* —**of·fi′cial·dom** *n.*

of·fi·cial·ese (ə-fĭsh′ə-lēz′, -lēs′) *n.* Language characteristic of official documents or statements, often considered obscure, pretentiously wordy, or formal in style.

of·fi·cial·ism (ə-fĭsh′ə-lĭz′əm) *n.* Rigid adherence to official regulations, forms, and procedures.

of·fi·ci·ant (ə-fĭsh′ē-ənt) *n.* One who officiates at a religious service or ceremony; celebrant.

of·fi·ci·ar·y (ə-fĭsh′ē-ĕr′ē) *n., pl.* **-ies. 1.** A body of officials or officers. **2.** *Rare.* An official or officer. —*adj.* **1.** Attached to or resulting from an office held. Said of a title. **2.** Having a title resulting from the holding of an office. Said of a dignitary.

of·fi·ci·ate (ə-fĭsh′ē-āt′) *intr.v.* **-ated, -ating, -ates. 1.** To perform the duties and functions of an office or position of authority. **2.** To serve as a priest or minister at a religious service. **3.** To serve as referee or umpire in any of various sports. [Medieval Latin *officiāre,* to conduct a religious service, from Latin *officium,* OFFICE (in Late Latin, also "religious service").] —**of·fi′ci·a′tion** *n.* —**of·fi′ci·a′tor** (-ā′tər) *n.*

of·fic·i·nal (ə-fĭs′ə-nəl) *adj.* **1.** Designating a drug available without prescription. Compare **magistral. 2.** Designating a plant used in medicine. —*n.* An officinal drug. [Medieval Latin *officinālis,* "used or kept in a workshop" (especially a medical laboratory), from Latin *officīna,* workshop, reduction of *opificina,* workshop, from *opifex,* workman : *opus,* work (see **op-¹** in Appendix*) + *facere,* to do (see **dhē-¹** in Appendix*).]

of·fi·cious (ə-fĭsh′əs) *adj.* **1.** Excessively forward in offering one's services or advice to others. **2.** *Obsolete.* Eager to render services or help others. **3.** *Diplomacy.* Of a casual nature; not official; unauthorized. [Latin *officiōsus,* from *officium,* duty, service, OFFICE.] —**of·fi′cious·ly** *adv.* —**of·fi′cious·ness** *n.*

off·ing (ô′fĭng, ŏf′ĭng) *n.* **1.** The part of the sea that is distant yet visible from the shore: *"In the offing the sea and sky were welded together without a joint."* (Conrad). **2.** A position at a distance from the shore. **3.** The near or immediate future. Used in the phrase *in the offing.* [From OFF.]

off·ish (ô′fĭsh, ŏf′ĭsh) *adj.* Inclined to be distant and reserved in manner; aloof. —**off′ish·ly** *adv.* —**off′ish·ness** *n.*

off-load (ôf′lōd′, ŏf′-) *tr.v.* **-loaded, -loading, -loads. 1.** *Aerospace.* To launch (a guided missile or rocket) with propellant tanks less than fully loaded, for altering the center of gravity of the vehicle. **2.** To unload (a vehicle, especially an airplane).

off·print (ôf′prĭnt′, ŏf′-) *n.* A reproduction or excerpt of a printed article that was originally contained in a larger publication. —*tr.v.* **offprinted, -printing, -prints.** To reproduce or reprint (an excerpt). [Translation of German *Abdruck.*]

off·scour·ing (ôf′skour′ĭng, ŏf′-) *n.* **1.** *Usually plural.* That which is scoured off; refuse. **2.** A social outcast or misfit.

off·set (ôf′sĕt′, ŏf′-) *n.* **1.** Something that balances, counteracts, or compensates. **2.** Something deriving or originating but set off from something else. **3.** *Architecture.* A ledge or recess in a wall, formed by a reduction in thickness above; setoff. **4.** *Botany.* A shoot that develops laterally at the base of a plant, often rooting to form a new plant. **5.** *Geology.* A spur of a range of mountains or hills. **6.** *Technology.* A bend in a pipe or bar to allow it to pass around an obstruction. **7.** *Mining.* A crosscut or drift from a main level. **8.** *Surveying.* A short distance measured perpendicularly from the main line, used to help in calculating the area of an irregular plot. **9.** A descendant of a race or family; offshoot. **10.** *Printing.* **a.** Offset printing *(see).* **b.** The unintentional or faulty transfer of ink not yet dry from a printed sheet to any surface, such as the next sheet, that is laid over it. —*v.* (ôf′sĕt′, ŏf′-) **offset, -setting, -sets.** —*tr.* **1.** To counterbalance, counteract, or compensate for. **2.** *Printing.* **a.** To print by offset. **b.** To smear with an offset. **3.** To make or form an offset in (a wall, bar, or pipe). —*intr.* To develop as an offset. —**off′set′** *adj.*

offset printing. Planographic printing by indirect image transfer, as: **a.** Printing from photo-mechanical plates. Also called "photo-offset." **b.** Printing from paper mats. Also known by the trademark "Multilith."

off·shoot (ôf′sho͞ot′, ŏf′-) *n.* **1.** Something that branches out or derives its existence or origin from a particular source. **2.** A branch, descendant, or member of a family or social group. **3.** A lateral shoot from the main stem of a plant.

off·shore (ôf′shôr′, -shōr′, ŏf′-) *adj.* **1.** Moving or directed away from the shore: *an offshore wind.* **2.** Located or occurring at a distance from the shore: *an offshore mooring.* —*adv.* **1.** Away from the shore: *The storm moved offshore.* **2.** At a distance from the shore: *a boat moored offshore.*

off·side (ôf′sīd′, ŏf′-) *adj.* Also **off side. 1.** In front of the ball before the play has properly begun. Said of a player, team, or play in football. **2.** Illegally ahead of the ball or puck in an attacking zone. Said of a player, team, or play in various games.

off·spring (ôf′spring′, ŏf′-) *n., pl.* **offspring** or *rare* **-springs. 1.** The progeny of a person, animal, or plant. **2.** A result; outcome; product. [Middle English *ofspring,* Old English *ofspring* : *of,* OFF + *springan,* to SPRING.]

off-stage (ôf′stāj′, ŏf′-) *adj.* Located or occurring in the area of a stage not visible to the audience. —*adv.* Away from the area of a stage visible to the audience.

off-the-rec·ord (ôf′*th*ə-rĕk′ərd, ŏf′-) *adj.* Not intended for publication; not to be repeated. —**off′-the-rec′ord** *adv.*

off-track (ôf′trăk′, ŏf′-) *adj.* Of or pertaining to gambling on horse races that is conducted away from a racetrack.

off-white (ôf′hwīt′, ŏf′-) *n.* Grayish or yellowish white. See **color.** —**off′-white′** *adj.*

O.F.M. Order of Friars Minor.

O.F.S. Orange Free State.

oft (ôft, ŏft) *adv. Poetic.* Often. Sometimes used in compounds: *oft-repeated.* [Middle English *oft,* Old English *oft.* See **op-¹** in Appendix.*]

of·ten (ô′fən, ŏf′ən) *adv.* Frequently; repeatedly; many times. —*adj. Archaic.* Repeated; frequent. [Middle English *oftin, often,* variants (before vowels and *h*) of *ofte,* from *oft,* OFT.]

of·ten·times (ô′fən-tīmz′, ŏf′ən-) *adv.* Also **oft·times** (ôf′tīmz′, ŏf′). Frequently; repeatedly.

OG, O.G. 1. officer of the guard. **2.** *Philately.* original gum.

O·ga·sa·wa·ra Ji·ma. The Japanese name for **Bonin Islands.**

Og·bo·mo·sho (ŏg′bō-mō′shō). A city in western Nigeria, about 50 miles north of Ibadan. Population, 320,000.

Og·den (ŏg′dən). An industrial city in northern Utah, 33 miles north of Salt Lake City. Population, 70,000.

Og·den (ŏg′dən), **C(harles) K(ay).** 1889–1957. English psychologist; inventor of Basic English.

o·gee (ō′jē′) *n. Architecture.* **1.** A double curve with the shape of an elongated S. **2.** A molding having in profile an S-shaped curve. **3.** An arch of two of these curves meeting at a point. In this sense, also called "ogee arch." [Alteration of OGIVE.]

og·ham, o·gam (ŏg′əm, ō′əm) *n.* **1. a.** An alphabet used for writing Irish from the fourth or fifth century A.D. to the early seventh century. **b.** A character of this alphabet. **2. a.** An inscription in the ogham alphabet. **b.** A stone inscribed in the ogham alphabet. [Irish *ogham,* from Old Irish *ogom,* said to be after its mythical inventor *Ogma*†.]

o·give (ō′jīv′) *n.* **1.** *Statistics.* **a.** The graphic representation of a frequency distribution, in which every ordinate represents the sum of frequencies in preceding intervals. **b.** A frequency distribution. **2.** *Architecture.* **a.** A diagonal rib of a Gothic vault. **b.** A pointed arch. Also called "ogive curve." [French, from Old French *augive*†.] —**o·gi′val** (ō-jī′vəl) *adj.*

O·gla·la (ō-glä′lə) *n., pl.* **Oglala** or **-las.** Also **O·ga·la·la** (ō′gə-lä′lə). **1.** A tribe of Siouan-speaking North American Indians of the Teton Dakota group, inhabiting the area west of the Missouri River in South Dakota. **2.** A member of this tribe. **3.** The language of this tribe. [Tribal name *Oglála*†.]

o·gle (ō′gəl, ô′-) *v.* **ogled, ogling, ogles.** —*tr.* **1.** To stare at. **2.** To stare at impertinently, flirtatiously, or amorously. —*intr.* To stare in an impertinent or amorous manner. —See Synonyms at **gaze.** —*n.* An impertinent or flirtatious stare. [Probably from Low German *oegeln,* frequentative of *oegen,* to eye, from *oog,* eye. See **okw-** in Appendix.*] —**o′gler** *n.*

O·gle·thorpe (ō′gəl-thôrp′), **James Edward.** 1696–1785. English philanthropist and army officer; founder (1733) and administrator of the American colony of Georgia.

OGPU (ŏg′po͞o, gā′ pā′ o͞o′ *from the last three Russian initials*). Also **O.G.P.U.** Unified Government Political Administration (Russian *Objedinionnoje Gosudarstvennoje Politicheskoje Upravlenie*), a former security branch of the Soviet government functioning as a successor organization to the **Cheka** and corresponding in broad outline to the later **KGB** *(both of which see).*

o·gre (ō′gər) *n.* **1.** A fabled, man-eating giant or monster. **2.** Anyone who is especially cruel, brutish, or hideous. [French, probably from Latin *Orcus,* ORCUS (god of the underworld).] —**o′gre·ish** (ō′gər-ĭsh) *adj.*

o·gress (ō′grĭs) *n.* A female ogre.

oh (ō) *interj.* Also *rare* **O.** Used to express strong emotion, such as surprise, fear, anger, or pain. —*n., pl.* **oh's** or **ohs.** The exclamation *oh* or any occurrence of it. See Usage note at **O.** [Middle English *o* (expressive formation). The spelling *oh* is not older than 1548.]

OH Ohio (with Zip Code).

O'Har·a (ō-hăr′ə), **John (Henry).** Born 1905. American writer.

O. Hen·ry. Pen name of William Sydney **Porter** *(see).*

O'Hig·gins (ō-hĭg′ĭnz; *Spanish* ō-ē′gēns), **Bernardo.** Called "Liberator of Chile." 1778–1842. Chilean general and revolutionary leader; dictator (1817–23); deposed.

O·hi·o (ō-hī′ō). A Middle Western and leading industrial state of the United States, 41,222 square miles in area, bounded on the south by the Ohio River and on the north by Lake Erie. It was admitted to the Union in 1803. Population, 9,706,000. Capital, Columbus. See map at **United States of America.** [Iroquois *ohíyo,* "grand river."] —**O·hi′o·an** *n. & adj.*

Ohio buckeye. A tree, *Aesculus glabra,* of the central United States, having compound leaves and yellowish-green flowers.

O·hi·o River (ō-hī′ō). A river formed by the Allegheny and Monongahela rivers at Pittsburgh, Pennsylvania, and flowing 980 miles west and southwest to the Mississippi River at Cairo, Illinois.

ohm (ōm) *n. Symbol* Ω A unit of electrical resistance equal to that of a conductor in which a current of one ampere is produced by a potential of one volt across its terminals. See **measurement.** [After Georg Simon *Ohm* (1787–1854), German physicist.]

ohm·age (ō′mĭj) *n. Electricity.* Resistance expressed in ohms.

ohm·me·ter (ōm′mē′tər) *n. Electricity.* An instrument for direct measurement of the resistance of a conductor in ohms.

OHMS, O.H.M.S. On His (or Her) Majesty's Service.

o·ho (ō-hō′) *interj.* Used especially to express surprise or mock astonishment. [Middle English (expressive formation), perhaps combination of OH and HO.]

O·hře (ôr′zhě). *German* **E·ger** (ā′gər). A river of western Bohemia, Czechoslovakia, flowing for 193 miles along the foot of the Ore Mountains into the Elbe.

-oic. Indicates the presence of a carboxyl group or a derivative of it; for example, **decanoic acid.** [Lengthening of -IC (denoting acids).]

-oid. Indicates likeness, resemblance, or similarity to; for example, **anthropoid, crystalloid, planetoid.** [Latin *-oidēs,* from Greek *-oeidēs,* of or having the shape or nature of, from *eidos,* form, shape. See **weid-** in Appendix.*]

oil (oil) *n.* **1.** Any of numerous mineral, vegetable, and synthetic substances and animal and vegetable fats, that are generally slippery, combustible, viscous, liquid or liquefiable at room temperatures, soluble in various organic solvents, such as ether, but not in water, and used in a great variety of products, especially lubricants and fuels. **2. a.** Petroleum. **b.** A petroleum derivative, such as a machine oil or lubricant. **3.** Any substance with an oily consistency. **4.** An **oil color** *(see).* **5.** An **oil painting** *(see).* **6.** *Informal.* Insincere flattery. —**strike oil. 1.** To discover oil by drilling in the ground for it. **2.** To gain sudden wealth. —*v.* **oiled, oiling, oils.** —*tr.* **1.** To lubricate, supply, cover, or polish with oil. **2.** *Informal.* To bribe. **3.** *Informal.* To flatter. —*intr.* **1.** To load up with or take on fuel oil. **2.** To become oil by melting. [Middle English *oli, oil(e),* (olive) oil, from Old French, from Latin *oleum,* from Greek *elaion,* from *elaia,* olive. See **elaia** in Appendix.*] —**oil** *adj.*

oil beetle. Any of various insects of the subfamily Meloinae, that, when disturbed, exude an oily yellow substance.

oil·bird (oil′bûrd′) *n.* A bird, the **guacharo** *(see).*

oil burner. 1. A heating unit, furnace, or boiler that burns fuel oil. **2.** A device for spraying fine droplets of oil into such a heating unit prior to ignition.

oil cake. The solid residue left after certain oily seeds, such as cottonseed and linseed, have been pressed free of their oil. It is used after grinding as cattle feed or fertilizer.

oil·can (oil′kăn′) *n.* A can for applying lubricating oil.

oil·cloth (oil′klôth′, -klŏth′) *n.* A fabric treated with clay, oil, and pigments to make it waterproof. It is used as a cover for tables or shelving.

oil color. A color consisting of pigment ground in oil, usually linseed, used in oil painting.

oil·er (oi′lər) *n.* **1.** One that oils machinery and engines. **2.** An oil tanker. **3.** An oilcan. **4.** A well that produces oil. **5.** A ship that burns oil. **6.** *Informal.* An oilskin garment.

oil field. An area with reserves of recoverable petroleum, especially one with several oil-producing wells.

oil gland. 1. Any gland that secretes oil. **2.** *Ornithology.* The **uropygial gland** *(see).*

oil of turpentine. Refined turpentine.

oil of vitriol. *Chemistry.* **Sulfuric acid** *(see).*

oil paint. Any paint in which the vehicle is a drying oil.

oil painting. 1. A painting done in oil colors. **2.** The art or practice of painting with oil colors.

oil palm. 1. A tall palm tree, *Elaeis guineensis,* native to tropical Africa, having nutlike fruits that yield a commercially valuable oil. **2.** Any of several other palms yielding oil.

oil pan. The bottom of the crankcase in an internal-combustion engine, serving as an oil reservoir.

oil·pa·per (oil′pā′pər) *n.* Paper that is soaked in oil to make it transparent and water-resistant.

Oil Rivers. The large delta region of the Niger River in southern Nigeria, formed by the several channels that flow into the Gulf of Guinea; formerly a British protectorate (1890–93).

oil sand. *Geology.* **1.** Any stratum or rock formation containing oil. **2.** A stratum of porous sandstone from which petroleum can be extracted through drilled wells.

oil shale. *Geology.* A black or dark-brown shale containing hydrocarbons that yield petroleum by distillation.

oil·skin (oil′skĭn′) *n.* **1.** Cloth treated with oil so that it is waterproof. **2.** A garment made of this material.

oil slick. A thin film of oil on water.

oil·stone (oil′stōn′) *n.* A smooth whetstone lubricated with oil, used for fine sharpening.

oil well. A hole dug or drilled in the earth, from which petroleum flows or is pumped.

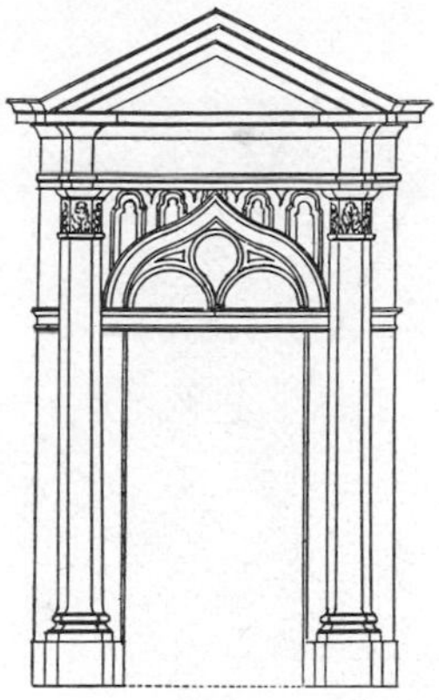

ogee
Gothic ogee in the framework of a classical doorway

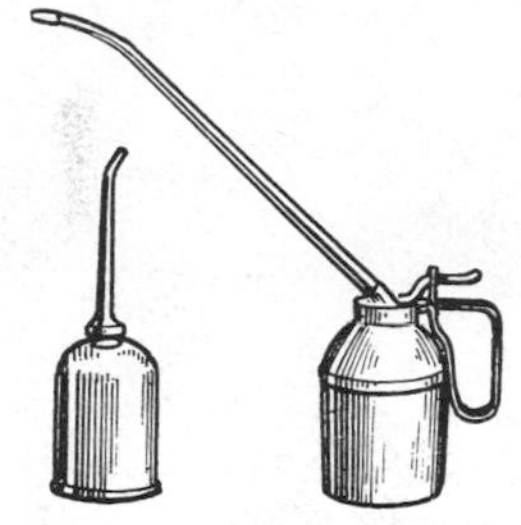

oilcan
Left: Bench oilcan
Right: Direct-pump oilcan

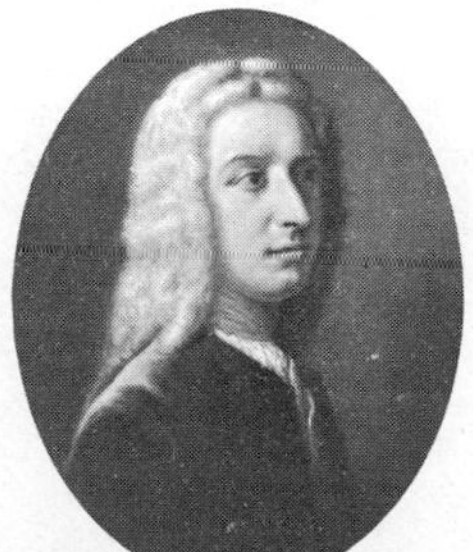

James Edward Oglethorpe

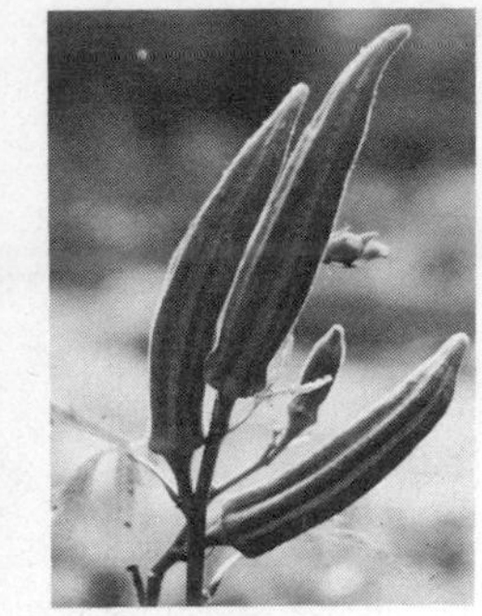

okra
Okra pods

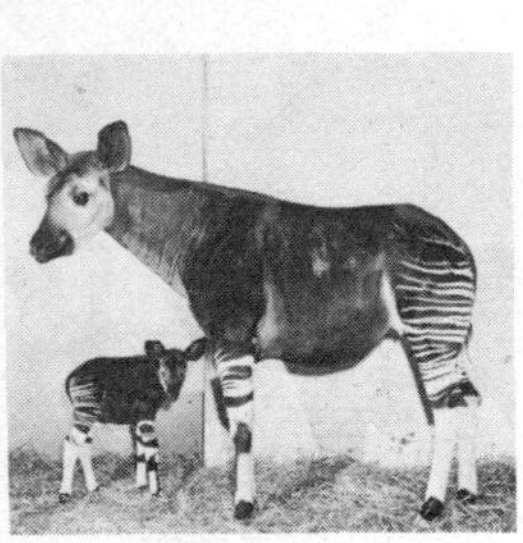

okapi

oil·y (oi′lē) *adj.* **-ier, -iest. 1.** Of or pertaining to oil. **2.** Impregnated or smeared with oil; greasy. **3.** Excessively suave in action or behavior; unctuous. **—oil′i·ly** *adv.* **—oil′i·ness** *n.*

oi·nol·o·gy. Variant of **oenology.**

oint·ment (oint′mənt) *n.* Any of numerous highly viscous or semisolid substances used on the skin as a cosmetic, an emollient, or a medicament; an unguent; a salve. [Middle English, variant (influenced by obsolete *oint,* to anoint) of *oinement,* from Old French *oignement,* from Vulgar Latin *unguimentum* (unattested), from Latin *unguentum,* from *unguens,* present participle of *unguere,* to anoint. See **ongw-** in Appendix.*]

Oir·each·tas (ĕr′əKH-thəs) *n.* The legislature of the Republic of Ireland, consisting of the Dail Eireann (the representative assembly) and the Seanad Eireann (the senate). [Irish, "assembly," "conference," from Old Irish *airech,* nobleman, free man. See **aryo-** in Appendix.*]

Oise (wäz). A river of France formed in the northeast, near the Belgian border, by the confluence of two streams, and flowing 186 miles southwest to the Seine, 15 miles northwest of Paris.

O·i·ta (ô′ē-tä′). A city and seaport in northeastern Kyushu, Japan. Population, 228,000.

O·jib·wa (ō-jĭb′wā′, -wə) *n., pl.* **Ojibwa** or **-was.** Also **O·jib·way** (ō-jĭb′wā′) *pl.* **Ojibway** or **-ways. 1.** A tribe of Algonquian-speaking North American Indians inhabiting regions of the United States and Canada around Lake Superior. **2.** A member of this tribe. **3.** The Algonquian language spoken by this tribe. Also called "Chippewa," "Chippeway." [Ojibwa *Očipwee,* name of a 17th-century Ojibwa band.]

O·jos del Sa·la·do (ō′hōz thĕl sä-lä′thō). A mountain in the Andes, on the border of Chile and Argentina. It is the second-highest elevation in the New World, rising to 22,539 feet.

OK Oklahoma (with Zip Code).

O.K., OK, o·kay (ō-kā′) *n., pl.* **O.K.'s** or **OK's** or **okays.** Also *rare* **o·keh.** *Informal.* Approval; endorsement; agreement. *—tr.v.* **O.K.'d** or **OK'd** or **okayed, O.K.'ing** or **OK'ing** or **okaying, O.K.'s** or **OK's** or **okays.** To approve or endorse by signing with an O.K.; agree to. *—interj.* All correct; all right. Used to express approval or agreement. [Probably popularized by a slogan of the O.K. Club, the Democratic party's political club of 1840; for *Old Kinderhook,* the nickname of President Martin Van Buren, who was born at *Kinderhook,* New York; but previously attested in the 1830's as a modish slang abbreviation of favorable but uncertain meaning, possibly connected with another such abbreviation, *D.K.,* for "don't know."] **—O.K.** *adj.* & *adv.*

Usage: *O.K.* (or *OK*) is especially appropriate to business correspondence and informal speech and writing, and usually inappropriate to expressly formal usage. In the following examples of general written usage, distinguished from the aforementioned, *O.K.* is termed most acceptable by the Usage Panel when employed as a noun (*his O.K. is considered a formality,* acceptable to 57 per cent) or as a verb (*to O.K. an arrangement,* acceptable to 42 per cent). As a predicate adjective (*all is not O.K. in their relationship*), it is acceptable to only 23 per cent, and as an adverb (*the radio was working O.K.*) to only 20 per cent. Many Panel members term *O.K.* acceptable in speech generally, however.

O·ka (ō-kä′). **1.** A river rising in southwestern Russian S.F.S.R. and flowing 920 miles northeast to the Volga at Gorki. **2.** A river rising in the south-central Soviet Union, in Asia, and flowing 530 miles northeast to join the Angara River.

O·ka·nog·an River (ō′kə-nŏg′ən). A river rising in southern British Columbia, Canada, and flowing 300 miles south to the Columbia River in north-central Washington, United States.

o·ka·pi (ō-kä′pē) *n., pl.* **okapi** or **-pis.** A ruminant forest mammal, *Okapia johnstoni,* related to the giraffe, but smaller and having a short neck, found in the Congo region in Africa. [Native Central African name.]

O·ka·ya·ma (ô′kä-yä′mä). A seaport and textile manufacturing city of Japan, situated on the Inland Sea on southwestern Honshu. Population, 301,000.

O·ka·za·ki (ô′kä-zä′kē). A city of central Honshu, Japan. Population, 194,000.

OKC Airport code for Oklahoma City, Oklahoma.

O·kee·cho·bee, Lake (ō′kē-chō′bē). A lake in south-central Florida, over 700 square miles in area, with access to the Atlantic Ocean via the Okeechobee Waterway.

O·kee·cho·bee Waterway (ō′kē-chō′bē). A water route across Florida from the Atlantic Ocean to the Gulf of Mexico through Lake Okeechobee. Also called "Cross-Florida Waterway."

O'Keeffe (ō-kēf′), **Georgia.** Born 1887. American painter.

O·ke·fe·no·kee Swamp (ō′kə-fə-nō′kē). Also **O·ke·fi·no·kee Swamp.** A swamp occupying about 700 square miles in northeastern Florida and southeastern Georgia.

o·keh. *Rare.* Variant of **O.K.**

O'Kel·ly (ō-kĕl′ē), **Seán Thomas.** 1883–1966. Irish political leader and journalist; a founder of Sinn Fein; president of Ireland (1945–59).

O·ken (ō′kən), **Lorenz.** Original name, Ockenfuss. 1779–1851. German naturalist, biologist, and mystical philosopher.

O·khotsk, Sea of (ō-kŏtsk′). An arm of the Pacific Ocean covering over 550,000 square miles, between the Soviet Union's Kamchatka Peninsula and Kurile Islands on the east and Sakhalin Island on the west, with Hokkaido, Japan, forming its southern boundary.

O·kie (ō′kē) *n.* *Informal.* An impoverished migrant farm worker; especially, one from Oklahoma forced to leave his farm during the depression of the 1930's. Used disparagingly. [From OKLAHOMA.]

O·ki·na·wa (ō′kĭ-nä′wə). The largest (794 square miles) of the Ryukyu Islands, off the southern tip of Japan; the scene of heavy combat in World War II. Population, 759,000. [Japanese, "rope on the sea" (from the chainlike position of the Ryukyu Islands) : *oki,* the open sea + *nawa,* a rope.]

O·kla·ho·ma (ō′klə-hō′mə). *Abbr.* **Okla.** A southwestern state of the United States, 69,920 square miles in area, bounded on the south by Texas and the north by Kansas. It was admitted to the Union in 1907. Population, 2,328,000. Capital, Oklahoma City. See map at **United States of America.** [Choctaw *okla homma,* "red people."] **—O′kla·ho′man** *adj.* & *n.*

O·kla·ho·ma City (ō′klə-hō′mə). The capital and largest city of Oklahoma, located in the center of the state. Population, 324,000.

O·ko·vang·go (ō′kō-văng′gō). *Portuguese* **Cu·ban·go** (kōō-văNng′gōō). A river rising in central Angola, southwestern Africa, and flowing 1,000 miles south and east to the marshlands of the Okovanggo Basin in Botswana.

o·kra (ō′krə) *n.* **1.** A tall tropical and semitropical plant, *Hibiscus esculentus,* having edible, mucilaginous green pods. **2.** The edible pods of this plant, used in soups and as a vegetable. **3.** A dish prepared with okra, **gumbo** *(see).* [West African native name *nkruma.*]

-ol[1]. *Chemistry.* Indicates alcohol or phenol; for example, **glycerol, naphthol.** [From ALCOHOL.]

-ol[2]. Variant of **-ole.**

O·laf I (ō′ləf). Also **O·lav** (ō′läv, ō′läf). Called "Olaf Tryggvesson." A.D. 969?–1000. King of Norway (995–1000); hero of many legends.

O·laf II (ō′ləf). Also **O·lav** (ō′läv, ō′läf). Also called "Saint Olaf." A.D. 995?–1030. King (1015–28) and patron saint of Norway; canonized in 1164.

O·laf V (ō′ləf). Also **O·lav** (ō′läv, ō′läf). Original name, Alexander Edward Christian Frederik of Glücksburg. Born 1903 in England. King of Norway from 1957.

Ö·land (œ′länd′). An island, 519 square miles in area, in the Baltic Sea off the coast of Sweden. Population, 6,000.

Ol·bers (ôl′bərs), **Heinrich Wilhelm Matthaus.** 1758–1840. German physician and astronomer; discovered many comets and asteroids.

old (ōld) *adj.* **older** or **elder** (ĕl′dər), **oldest** or **eldest** (ĕl′dĭst). **1.** Having lived or existed for a relatively long time; far advanced in years or life, either actually or relatively: *a feeble old man.* See Usage note at **elder. 2.** Made long ago; in existence for many years; not new: *an old book.* **3.** Of or pertaining to a long life or to persons who have had a long life: *a ripe old age.* **4.** Having or exhibiting the physical characteristics of advanced life or an aged person: *She had an old face for her years.* **5.** Having or exhibiting the wisdom of age; mature; sensible: *That child is old for her years.* **6.** Having a specified age: *She was twelve years old.* **7. a.** Belonging to a remote or former period in history; ancient: *old manuscripts.* **b.** Belonging to or being of an earlier time: *his old classmates.* **8.** *Usually capital* **O.** *Abbr.* **O, O.** Being the earlier or earliest of two or more related objects, stages, versions, or periods: *the Old Testament; Old High German.* **9.** *Geology.* **a.** Having become slower in flow and less vigorous in action. Said of rivers. **b.** Having become simpler in form and of lower relief. Said of land forms. **10.** Worn or dilapidated through age or use; worn-out: *an old coat.* **11.** Known through long acquaintance or use; long familiar: *an old friend.* **12.** Dear or cherished through long acquaintance. Used as a term of affection or cordiality: *good old Harry.* **13.** Skilled or able through long experience; practiced: *He was an old hand at shipbuilding.* **14.** *Informal.* Fine; excellent; great: *We had a high old time.* *—n.* **1.** Former times; yore: *in days of old.* **2.** An individual of a specified age. Used in combination: *a five-year-old.* [Middle English *old, ald,* Old English *eald, ald.* See **al-**[3] in Appendix.*] **—old′ness** *n.*

Synonyms: *old, elderly, aged, venerable, superannuated.* These terms are compared in their application to persons. *Old,* though ostensibly general, often stresses advanced years strongly. *Elderly* specifies the period past late middle age without necessarily implying marked decline. *Aged* emphasizes advanced years, and often suggests infirmity. *Venerable* suggests dignity and qualities, associated with age, that are worthy of great respect. *Superannuated,* in contrast, applies narrowly to the state of being pensioned or retired, or, more generally, to one figuratively discarded or outmoded. *Olden, ancient, archaic, obsolete, obsolescent, antique, antiquated,* and *old-fashioned* are terms that are applied principally to inanimate objects and historical associations. *Old* is the general term. *Olden* connotes a bygone age, often with some nostalgia. *Ancient* pertains to the distant past, and usually to what no longer exists. *Archaic* similarly specifies a very early, often primitive, period, but does not always imply the fact of being discarded; archaic language, though not in general use, is preserved for historical value and limited application. *Obsolete* indicates merely the fact of having passed from use, and *obsolescent* the state of becoming obsolete. *Antique* may indicate association with the ancient past; more often it characterizes that which is valued for its membership in a class of things from the more recent past. *Antiquated,* in contrast, indicates that which is discarded as now out-of-date or discredited. *Old-fashioned* pertains more generally to something from the recent past that is no longer in vogue or general use; it does not invariably imply low regard or the fact of having been discarded.

Old Bai·ley (bā′lē). The chief criminal court of England, located in London on the site of the original Old Bailey, which was replaced in 1903 by the present structure.

ă pat/ā pay/âr care/ä father/b bib/ch church/d deed/ĕ pet/ē be/f fife/g gag/h hat/hw which/ĭ pit/ī pie/îr pier/j judge/k kick/l lid, needle/m mum/n no, sudden/ng thing/ŏ pot/ō toe/ô paw, for/oi noise/ou out/ŏŏ took/ōō boot/p pop/r roar/s sauce/sh ship, dish/

Old Bald·y (bôl'dē). A mountain peak, 14,125 feet high, of the Sangre de Cristo Mountains of southern Colorado.

old boy. *British.* A graduate of a boys' public school.

Old Breton. Breton from the middle of the 9th century to the beginning of the 12th.

Old Bulgarian. Old Church Slavonic (see).

Old Catalan. Catalan before the middle of the 16th century.

Old Catholic. *Abbr.* **O.C.** A member of an independent religious organization formed by a group of German Roman Catholics who refused to accept the doctrine of papal infallibility proclaimed by the Vatican Council in 1870.

Old Church Slavonic. The literary language of the oldest Slavic manuscripts (10th or early 11th century). Sometimes called "Old Bulgarian."

Old Cornish. Cornish from the 9th century to the 14th.

old country. The native country of an immigrant.

Old Danish. Danish from the beginning of the 12th century to the end of the 14th.

Old Delhi. See **Delhi**.

Old Dominion. A nickname for the state of Virginia.

Old Dutch. Dutch from the beginning of the 12th century to the middle of the 13th.

old·en (ōl'dən) *adj.* *Archaic & Poetic.* Old; ancient: *in olden times.* —See Synonyms at **old.** [Middle English, from *old*, OLD.]

Ol·den·burg (ōl'dən-bûrg'; *German* ôl'dən-bŏŏrk'). **1.** A former state in northwestern Germany. **2.** A city in northwestern West Germany, on the Hunte River. Population, 127,000.

Old English. *Abbr.* **OE, OE., O.E. 1.** English from the beginning of the 8th century to the middle of the 12th. Also called "Anglo-Saxon." **2.** *Printing.* **Black letter** (see).

Old English sheepdog. A sturdy dog of a breed derived from Scottish and Russian ancestors, having a thick, shaggy, bluishgray and white coat that hangs over the eyes.

old fashioned. A cocktail made of whiskey, bitters, sugar, and fruit.

old-fash·ioned (ōld'făsh'ənd) *adj.* **1.** Of a style or method formerly in vogue; outdated; antiquated. **2.** Attached to or favoring methods, ideas, or customs of an earlier time: *an old-fashioned girl.* —See Synonyms at **old.**

old fogy. Also **old fogey.** One who is tiresomely conservative or old-fashioned. [Probably from obsolete Scottish *old fogey*†, an old and invalid soldier.] —**old'fo'gy·ish, old'fo'gey·ish** (ōld'-fō'gē-ĭsh) *adj.*

Old French. French from the 9th century to the early 16th.

Old Frisian. Frisian from the beginning of the 13th century to the end of the 15th.

Old Glory. A nickname for the flag of the United States.

old gold. Dark yellow, from light olive or olive brown to deep or strong yellow. See **color.** —**old'-gold'** *adj.*

old guard. 1. *Capital* **O,** *capital* **G.** The imperial guard of Napoleon I. **2.** A group of defenders of an existing or formerly existing cause or principle. **3.** The conservative, often reactionary element of a given class, society, or political group. [Translation of French *Vieille Garde.*]

Old·ham (ōl'dəm). A city in Lancashire, England, six miles northeast of Manchester. Population, 121,000.

old hat. *Informal.* Behind the times; obsolete; old-fashioned.

Old High German. High German from the middle of the 9th century to the end of the 11th.

Old Icelandic. Icelandic from the middle of the 12th century to the middle of the 16th. Also called "Old Norse."

Old Iranian. Iranian before the Christian era, the principal attested forms being Avestan and Old Persian.

Old Irish. Irish from 725 A.D. to the mid-tenth century.

Old I·ron·sides (īr'ən-sīdz') *n.* The frigate **Constitution** (see).

Old Italian. Italian before the middle of the 16th century.

old lady. *Slang.* **1.** One's mother. **2.** One's wife.

Old Latin. Latin from first texts (sixth century B.C.) through the second century B.C. Also called "Archaic Latin."

old-line (ōld'līn') *adj.* **1.** Adhering to conservative or reactionary principles. **2.** Long established; traditional.

Old Low Franconian. The extinct Low German language of Franconia that existed from the beginning of the 10th century to the middle of the 13th.

Old Low German. Low German from the middle of the 9th century to the middle of the 13th. Also called "Old Saxon."

old maid. 1. *Informal.* A woman who is not married, especially an older woman; a spinster. **2.** *Informal.* A primly fastidious person. **3.** A child's card game. —**old'-maid'ish** *adj.*

old man. 1. *Slang.* **a.** One's father. **b.** One's husband. **c.** A man in authority. **2.** A plant, the **southernwood** (see).

old-man-and-wom·an (ōld'măn'ənd-wŏŏm'ən) *n.* A plant, the **houseleek** (see).

old-man cactus. A treelike cactus, *Cephalocereus senilis,* having tufts of long, white hair on the tips of its branches.

old-man's-beard (ōld'mănz'bîrd') *n.* Any of various plants having parts suggestive of a beard, such as **virgin's bower** and **Spanish moss** (both of which see).

old master. 1. A distinguished European artist of the period from around 1500 to the early 1700's; especially, one of the great painters of this period. **2.** A work created by an old master.

old moon. A phase of the waning moon; the last quarter.

Old Nick. The devil; Satan.

Old Norse. *Abbr.* **ON, O.N. 1.** The North Germanic language from which the modern Scandinavian languages are descended. **2.** This language as represented in either of two national literatures: **a. Old Icelandic** (see). **b. Old Norwegian** (see).

Old North French. The northern dialect of Old French.

Old Norwegian. Norwegian from the middle of the 12th century to the end of the 14th. Also called "Old Norse."

Old Persian. An ancient form of Persian, recorded in cuneiform inscriptions dating from the sixth to the fifth century B.C.

Old Pretender. James Francis Edward **Stuart** (see).

Old Provençal. Provençal before mid-16th century.

Old Prussian. The Baltic language of the original Prussians, that became extinct in the 18th century.

old rose. Dark pink to grayish or moderate red. See **color.** —**old'-rose'** *adj.*

Old Russian. The language of medieval Slavic texts which show definite features, from the middle of the 11th century to the end of the 16th.

Olds (ōldz), **Ransom Eli.** 1864–1950. American automotive pioneer and industrialist; manufacturer of the Oldsmobile.

Old Saxon. Old Low German (see).

old school. Any group committed to traditional ideas or practices. —**old'-school'** *adj.*

old-school tie. 1. A necktie that has the colors of an English public school. **2.** The upper-middle-class solidarity and system of mutual assistance attributed to graduates of the English public schools. **3.** A narrow, clannish attitude among members of a snobbishly aloof group.

Old Slavic. The language of those Slavic texts of the 11th, 12th, and 13th centuries which are not generally considered to be part of the canonical Old Church Slavonic corpus, but which are rather in one or another recension of Old Church Slavonic.

Old Spanish. Spanish before the middle of the 16th century.

old squaw. A marine duck, *Clangula hyemalis,* that is black with a white breast and is found in Arctic and North Temperate regions. Also called "oldwife."

old·ster (ōld'stər) *n.* *Informal.* An old or elderly person.

Old Stone Age. See **Paleolithic**.

old style. 1. A style of printing type originating in the 18th century and characterized by slight contrast between light and heavy strokes and by slanting serifs. **2.** *Capital* **O,** *capital* **S.** *Abbr.* **O.S.** The old method of reckoning dates according to the Julian calendar. See **calendar**.

Old Swedish. Swedish from the early 13th century to the late 14th.

Old Testament. *Abbr.* **Old Test., OT, O.T. 1.** The first of the two main divisions of the Christian Bible, containing the Hebrew Scriptures. Compare **Hebrew Scriptures. 2.** The covenant of God with Israel as distinguished in Christianity from the dispensation of Christ constituting the New Testament. [Middle English, translation of Late Latin *Vetus Testāmentum,* translation of Greek *Palaia Diathēkē,* "Old Testament," a designation for the Hebrew Scriptures which the primitive Church based on the Pauline distinction between the mystery of the new covenant and the "reading of the old testament (covenant)." II Corinthians 3:14.]

old-time (ōld'tīm') *adj.* Of or pertaining to a time in the past.

old-tim·er (ōld'tī'mər) *n.* *Informal.* **1.** One who has been a resident, member, employee, or the like for a long time. **2.** Something that is very old or antiquated.

Old Turkic. Turkic from the seventh century A.D. to the tenth century, attested in documents from various places in Central Asia, divided into two principal dialects, Turkut and Old Uighur.

Old Uighur. See **Old Turkic.**

Ol·du·vai (ōl'də-wā', -vā', -vī'). A gorge in northern Tanzania, 150 miles west of Mount Kilimanjaro, in which is located a site containing remains of **paranthropus** (see).

Old Welsh. Welsh before the 12th century.

old·wife (ōld'wīf') *n., pl.* **-wives** (-wīvz'). **1.** A duck, the **old squaw** (see). **2.** Any of several fishes, such as the **alewife** and the **menhaden** (both of which see). [Origins uncertain.]

old wives' tale. A bit of superstitious folklore.

Old World. The Eastern Hemisphere, including Eurasia and Africa, with special reference to Europe.

old-world (ōld'wûrld') *adj.* **1.** Antique; old-fashioned; quaint. **2.** Often *capital* **O,** *capital* **W.** Native or pertaining to the Eastern Hemisphere, or Old World.

o·lé (ō-lā') *interj.* Used to express excited approval. —*n.* A cry of olé. [Spanish.]

–ole[1], **–ol.** *Chemistry.* **1.** Indicates a compound, usually heterocyclic, having a five-membered ring; for example, **pyrrole. 2.** Indicates a compound not containing hydroxyl, especially an ether; for example, **eucalyptol.** [Latin *oleum,* oil, olive oil, from Greek *elaion,* from *elaia,* olive. See **elaia** in Appendix.*]

–ole[2]. Indicates small, little; for example, **petiole.** [Latin *-olus, -ola, -olum,* diminutive suffixes.]

o·le·ag·i·nous (ō'lē-ăj'ə-nəs) *adj.* **1.** Of or pertaining to oil. **2.** Oily; unctuous. [Latin *oleāginus,* belonging to the olive tree, from *olea,* olive, from Greek *elaia.* See **elaia** in Appendix.*] —**o'le·ag'i·nous·ly** *adv.* —**o'le·ag'i·nous·ness** *n.*

o·le·an·der (ō'lē-ăn'dər, ō'lē·ăn'dər) *n.* Any poisonous evergreen shrub of the genus *Nerium,* found in warm climates, especially *N. oleander,* having fragrant white, rose, or purple flowers. Also called "rosebay." [Medieval Latin, alteration of *arodandrum, lorandrum,* perhaps from a Vulgar Latin deformation of Latin *rhododendron,* RHODODENDRON.]

o·le·as·ter (ō'lē-ăs'tər) *n.* A small Eurasian tree, *Elaeagnus angustifolia,* having oblong silvery leaves, fragrant greenish flowers, and olivelike fruit. Also called "Russian olive." [Latin, wild olive tree: *olea,* olive tree, olive, from Greek *elaia* (see **elaia** in Appendix*) + *-aster,* diminutive suffix.]

o·le·ate (ō'lē-āt') *n.* An ester or salt of oleic acid. [French *oléate:* OLE(O)- + -ATE.]

Old English sheepdog

oleander
Nerium oleander

olive

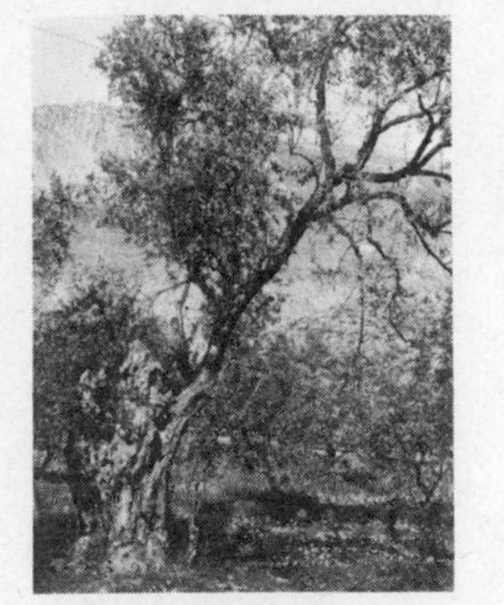

olive tree

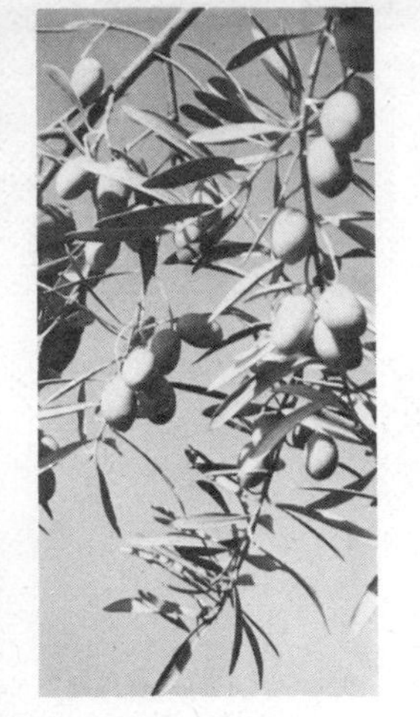

section of branch
with leaves and fruit

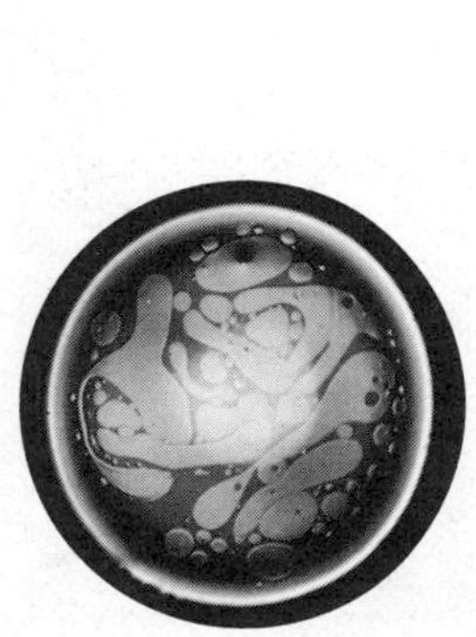

oleograph
Dispersion pattern of a drop of oil on a water surface

o·lec·ra·non (ō-lĕk′rə-nŏn′, ō′lə-krā′nŏn′) *n.* The large point on the upper end of the ulna that projects behind the elbow joint and forms the point of the elbow. Informally called "crazy bone." [New Latin, from Greek *ōlekranon*, "elbow-tip" : *ōlenē*, elbow (see **el-**[1] in Appendix*) + *kranion*, head, skull (see **ker-**[1] in Appendix*).] —**o·lec′ra·nal** (ō-lĕk′rə-nəl, ō′lə-krā′nəl), **o′le·cra′ni·al, o′le·cra′ni·an** *adj.*

o·le·fin (ō′lə-fĭn) *n.* Also **o·le·fine** (ō′lə-fĭn, -fēn′). Any of a class of unsaturated hydrocarbons, such as ethylene, having the general formula C_nH_{2n} and characterized by relatively great chemical activity. Also called "alkene." [French *(gaz) oléfiant*, "oil forming (gas)," ethylene (which forms an oily liquid with chlorine) : OLE(O)- + *-fiant*, making, from *-fier*, -FY + -IN.] —**o′le·fin′ic** (-fĭn′ĭk) *adj.*

o·le·ic (ō-lē′ĭk) *adj. Chemistry.* Of, pertaining to, or derived from oil. [OLE(O)- + -IC.]

oleic acid. An oily liquid, $CH_3(CH_2)_7CH{:}CH(CH_2)_7COOH$, occurring in animal and vegetable oils.

o·le·in (ō′lē-ĭn) *n.* Also **o·le·ine** (ō′lē-ĭn, -ēn′). A yellow oily liquid, $(C_{17}H_{33}COO)_3C_3H_5$, occurring naturally in most fats and oils, including olive oil, of which it is the major constituent. It is used as a textile lubricant. [French *oléine* : OLE(O)- + -IN.]

O·lek·ma (ō-lĕk′mə). A river rising in the southeastern Soviet Union and flowing 700 miles north to join the Lena River.

O·le·nek (ŏl′ən-yôk′). A river rising in north-central Soviet Union and flowing 1,325 miles east and northeast into the Laptev Sea, a branch of the Arctic Ocean.

oleo-, ole-. Indicates oil or pertaining to oil; for example, **oleoresin, oleomargarine, oleic.** [French *olé-, oléo-*, from Latin *oleo-*, from *oleum*, (olive) oil, from Greek *elaion*, from *elaia*, olive. See **elaia** in Appendix.*]

o·le·o·graph (ō′lē-ə-grăf′, -gräf′) *n.* **1.** A chromolithograph printed in imitation of an oil painting. **2.** The lacelike pattern formed by a drop of oil on the surface of water. [OLEO- + -GRAPH.] —**o′le·og′ra·pher** (ō′lē-ŏg′rə-fər) *n.* —**o′le·o·graph′ic** *adj.* —**o′le·og′ra·phy** *n.*

o·le·o·mar·ga·rine (ō′lē-ō-mär′jə-rĭn, -gə-rĭn, -rēn′) *n.* Also **o·le·o·mar·ga·rin** (ō′lē-ō-mär′jə-rĭn). **Margarine** *(see).* Also called "oleo." [French *oléomargarine* : OLEO- + MARGARINE.]

o·le·o·res·in (ō′lē-ō-rĕz′ən) *n.* **1.** A naturally occurring mixture of an oil and resin, such as the exudate from pine trees. **2.** An oil-resin mixture extracted from plants, such as capsicum. [OLEO- + RESIN.] —**o′le·o·res′in·ous** (-rĕz′ən-əs) *adj.*

o·le·um (ō′lē-əm) *n., pl.* **-lea** (-lē-ə) or **-ums.** A corrosive solution of sulfur trioxide in sulfuric acid. [Latin, OIL.]

ol·fac·tion (ŏl-făk′shən, ōl-) *n.* **1.** The sense of smell. **2.** The action of smelling. [From Latin *olfacere*, to smell. See **olfactory.**]

ol·fac·to·ry (ŏl-făk′tər-ē, -trē, ōl-) *adj.* Of or contributing to the sense of smell: *olfactory organ.* [Latin *olfactōrius*, from *olfacere*, to smell : *olēre*, to smell (see **od-**[1] in Appendix*) + *facere*, to make (see **dhē-**[1] in Appendix*).]

olfactory nerve. Either of two bundles of nerve fibers, one on each side of the nasal cavity, that conduct chemical indications of smell.

Ol·ga (ŏl′gə, ōl′-). A feminine given name. [Russian, from Old Norse *Helga*, "holy." See **kailo-** in Appendix.*]

o·lib·a·num (ō-lĭb′ə-nəm) *n.* A gum resin, **frankincense** *(see).* [Middle English, from Medieval Latin, from Arabic *al-lubān*, "the frankincense," probably from Greek *libanos*, of Semitic origin, akin to Hebrew *lĕbōriā*, incense.]

Ol·i·fants (ŏl′ə-fənts). A river rising in northeastern South Africa and flowing 350 miles generally northeast to join the Limpopo River in western Mozambique.

ol·i·garch (ŏl′ə-gärk′) *n.* A member of an oligarchy. [Greek *oligarkhēs* : OLIG(O)- + *-arkhēs*, -ARCH.]

ol·i·gar·chy (ŏl′ə-gär′kē) *n., pl.* **-chies.** **1. a.** Government by the few, especially by a small faction of persons or families. **b.** Those making up such a faction. **2.** A state governed by oligarchy: *"Greek oligarchies were based on . . . the notion that their members were superior to other men."* (C.M. Bowra). —**ol′i·gar′chic, ol′i·gar′chi·cal, ol′i·gar′chal** *adj.*

oligo-. Indicates few; for example, **oligopoly, oligocythemia.** [Greek, from *oligos*, few, little. See **leig-**[2] in Appendix.*]

Ol·i·go·cene (ŏl′ĭ-gō-sēn′) *adj.* Of or designating the geologic time and deposits of the epoch in the Tertiary period of the Cenozoic era that extended from the Eocene to the Miocene. See **geology.** —*n.* **1.** The Oligocene epoch. Preceded by *the.* **2.** The deposits of this epoch. [OLIGO- + -CENE.]

ol·i·go·chaete (ŏl′ĭ-gō-kēt′) *n.* Any of various worms of the class Oligochaeta, including the earthworms. [New Latin *Oligochaeta* : OLIGO- + CHAETA.] —**ol′i·go·chae′tous** *adj.*

ol·i·go·clase (ŏl′ĭ-gō-klās′, -klāz′) *n.* A mineral, **plagioclase** *(see).* [German *Oligoklas* : OLIGO- + -CLASE.]

ol·i·go·cy·the·mi·a (ŏl′ĭ-gō-sī-thē′mē-ə) *n.* Also **ol·i·go·cy·thae·mi·a.** Deficiency of the cellular elements of the blood, causing a form of anemia. [New Latin : OLIGO- + CYT(O)- + -(H)EMIA.]

ol·i·go·gene (ŏl′ĭ-gō-jēn′) *n. Genetics.* A gene that determines major qualitative hereditary characteristics. Also called "major gene." Compare **polygene.** —**ol′i·go·gen′ic** (-jĕn′ĭk) *adj.*

ol·i·go·phre·ni·a (ŏl′ĭ-gō-frē′nē-ə) *n.* Arrested mental development, **mental deficiency** *(see).* [New Latin : OLIGO- + -PHRENIA.] —**ol′i·go·phren′ic** (-frĕn′ĭk) *adj.*

ol·i·gop·o·ly (ŏl′ĭ-gŏp′ə-lē) *n., pl.* **-lies.** *Economics.* A market condition in which sellers are so few that the actions of any one of them will materially affect price and hence have a measurable impact upon competitors: *"Profits above normal may persist in oligopoly"* (Melville Ullmer). Compare **monopoly.** [OLIGO- + (MONO)POLY.] —**ol′i·gop′o·lis′tic** (-gŏp′ə-lĭs′tĭk) *adj.*

ol·i·gop·so·ny (ŏl′ĭ-gŏp′sə-nē) *n., pl.* **-nies.** *Economics.* A market condition in which purchasers are so few that the actions of any one of them can materially affect price and hence the costs that competitors must pay. Compare **monopsony.** [OLIG(O)- + (MON)OPSONY.] —**ol′i·gop′so·nis′tic** (-gŏp′sə-nĭs′tĭk) *adj.*

o·li·o (ō′lē-ō′) *n., pl.* **-os.** **1.** A heavily spiced stew of meat, vegetables, and chickpeas. **2. a.** Any mixture or medley; a hodgepodge. **b.** A collection of various artistic or literary works or musical pieces; miscellany. **3.** Vaudeville or musical entertainment presented between the acts of a burlesque or minstrel show. [Modification of Spanish *olla*, pot, OLLA.]

ol·i·va·ceous (ŏl′ə-vā′shəs) *adj.* Olive-green. [OLIV(E) + -ACEOUS.]

ol·i·var·y (ŏl′ə-vĕr′ē) *adj.* **1.** Shaped like an olive. **2.** *Anatomy.* Of, pertaining to, or designating one of the two oval bodies of nervous tissue (olivary bodies) found on either side of the medulla oblongata. [Latin *olīvārius*, from *olīva*, OLIVE.]

ol·ive (ŏl′ĭv) *n.* **1.** An Old World semitropical evergreen tree, *Olea europaea*, having an edible fruit, yellow flowers, and leathery leaves. **2.** The small ovoid fruit of this tree, an important food from the earliest historical times and a source of oil. **3.** Yellow green of low to medium lightness and low to moderate saturation. See **color.** [Middle English, from Old French, from Latin *olīva*, from Greek *elaia*. See **elaia** in Appendix.*] —**ol′ive** *adj.*

olive branch. **1.** A branch of an olive tree regarded as an emblem of peace. **2.** An offer of peace.

olive drab. *Abbr.* **o.d.** **1.** Grayish olive to dark olive brown or olive gray. See **color.** **2.** Cloth of this color. **3.** *Also plural.* A uniform made from such cloth. —**ol′ive-drab′** *adj.*

olive green. Green yellow hue of low to medium lightness and low to moderate saturation. See **color.** —**ol′ive-green′** *adj.*

o·liv·e·nite (ō-lĭv′ə-nīt′) *n.* A basic arsenate of copper, $Cu_2(AsO_4)(OH)$, brown, olive green, or gray in color, found in copper deposits. [German *Olivenit* : OLIVE + -ITE.]

olive oil. Oil pressed from olives, used in salad dressings, for cooking, as an ingredient of soaps, and as an emollient.

Ol·i·ver (ŏl′ĭ-vər). A masculine given name. [Middle English, from Old French *Olivier*, alteration (influenced by *olivier*, olive tree) of a Germanic compound corresponding to Old English *Ælfhere*, "elf army" : *ælf*, elf (see **albho-** in Appendix*) + *here*, army (see **koro-** in Appendix*).]

Olives, Mount of. Also **Ol·i·vet** (ŏl′ə-vĕt′). A hill east of Jerusalem, in Jordan, mentioned in the Old and New Testaments.

O·liv·i·er (ō-lĭv′ē-ā′), Sir **Laurence (Kerr).** Born 1907. English actor and director.

ol·i·vine (ŏl′ə-vēn′, ŏl′ə-vēn′) *n.* **1.** A mineral silicate of iron and magnesium, principally Fe_2SiO_4 and Mg_2SiO_4, found in igneous and metamorphic rocks and used as a structural material in refractories and in cements. Also called "chrysolite." **2.** A transparent green variety valued as a gem. Also called "peridot." [German *Olivin*, chrysolite : OLIVE (because of its color) + -IN.]

o·lla (ŏl′ə; *Spanish* ô′lyä, ô′yä) *n.* **1.** An earthenware pot or jar with a wide mouth. **2.** An olla podrida. [Spanish, from Old Spanish, from Latin *olla*, variant of *aulla*, jar, pot. See **aukwh-** in Appendix.*]

o·lla po·dri·da (ŏl′ə pə-drē′də; *Spanish* ô′lyä pō-*thrē′thä*, ô′yä). **1.** A stew of highly seasoned meat and vegetables. **2.** Any assorted mixture or miscellany. [Spanish, "rotten pot" : OLLA + *podrida*, rotten, from Latin *putridus*, from *putrēre*, to rot, from *puter*, decaying, rotten (see **pu-**[2] in Appendix*).]

Olm·sted (ŏm′stĕd′, -stĭd), **Frederick Law.** 1822–1903. American landscape architect; a designer of Central Park (New York City).

ol·o·gy (ŏl′ə-jē) *n., pl.* **-gies.** *Informal.* Any of various studies or concepts designated by terms ending in *-logy* and thereby regarded as generically related: *"such names as amphibology, parisology, and other ologies"* (Evan Esar).

Olt (ôlt). A river rising in central Rumania and flowing 348 miles south to the Danube.

O·lym·pi·a (ō-lĭm′pē-ə). **1.** The capital of the state of Washington, at the southern end of Puget Sound. Population, 18,000. **2.** A plain of Elis in the northwestern Peloponnesus, where the Olympic games of antiquity were held.

O·lym·pi·ad (ō-lĭm′pē-ăd′) *n.* **1.** The interval of four years between celebrations of the Olympic games, by which the ancient Greeks reckoned dates. **2.** A celebration of the modern Olympic games. [Middle English *Olympiade*, from Latin *Olympias*, from Greek *Olumpias*, from *Olumpia*, OLYMPIA.]

O·lym·pi·an (ō-lĭm′pē-ən) *adj.* **1.** Of or pertaining to the greater gods of the ancient Greek pantheon, whose abode was Olympus. **2. a.** Majestic in manner. **b.** Superior to mundane affairs. **3.** Of or pertaining to the Olympic games. —*n.* **1.** One of the 12 major gods inhabiting Olympus. **2.** A contestant in the ancient Olympic games.

O·lym·pic (ō-lĭm′pĭk) *adj.* Of or belonging to the games held at Olympia or the modern international revival of them.

Olympic games. **1.** In ancient Greece, a Pan-Hellenic festival of athletic games and contests of choral poetry and dance, first celebrated in 776 B.C., and held every four years until A.D. 393 on the plain of Olympia in honor of the Olympian Zeus. Also called "Olympian games." **2.** A modern international revival of athletic contests patterned after these ancient games and held every four years. In this sense, also called "Olympics."

Olympic Peninsula. A peninsula of northwestern Washington, between the Pacific Ocean and Puget Sound.

O·lym·pus (ō-lĭm′pəs). **1.** The highest mountain in Greece (9,750 feet), the fabled abode of the greater deities of the

ancient pantheon, lying about ten miles inland from the Aegean Sea, between Thessaly and Macedonia. **2.** A mountain, 7,954 feet high, on the Olympic Peninsula, Washington.
Om (ôm). A river of the Soviet Union, rising in western Siberia, and flowing 450 miles west to join the Irtish River at Omsk.
OM. ostmark.
-oma. Indicates tumor; for example, **fibroma, myoma.** [New Latin, from Greek *-ōma,* abstract nominal ending formed from *-o-* stem verbs.]
OMA Airport code for Omaha, Nebraska.
O·ma·ha[1] (ō′mə-hô′, -hä′) *n., pl.* **Omaha** or **-has. 1.** A tribe of Siouan-speaking Indians of northeastern Nebraska. **2.** A member of this tribe. [Dhegiha (Siouan) *umãhã,* "upstream."] **—O′ma·ha′** *adj.*
O·ma·ha[2] (ō′mə-hô′, -hä′). An industrial city in eastern Nebraska, on the Missouri River. Population, 302,000. [From OMAHA (tribe).]
Omaha Beach. Code word for a beach on the Normandy coast where units of the American forces landed, June 6, 1944.
O·man (ō-män′). An Arab sultanate under British protection, at the easternmost tip of the Arabian peninsula. Population, 750,000. Capital, Muscat. Also called "Muscat and Oman."
Oman, Gulf of. An inlet of the Arabian Sea extending 340 miles toward the Persian Gulf, between Oman and Iran.
O·mar Khay·yám (ō′mär′ kī-yäm′, kī-yăm′, ō′mər). A.D. 1050?–1123? Persian poet, mathematician, and astronomer; author of the *Rubáiyát.*
o·ma·sum (ō-mā′səm) *n., pl.* **-sa** (-sə). The third stomach of a ruminant animal, located between the **abomasum** and the **reticulum** *(both of which see).* Also called "manyplies," "psalterium." [Latin *omāsum,* pouch, bullock's tripe, probably from Gaulish.]
-omat. Indicates automated operation, chiefly in names of retail establishments using coin-operated devices; for example, **laundromat.** [From AUTOMAT.]
om·bre (ŏm′bər) *n.* Also **om·ber, hom·bre** (hŏm′bər). A card game played by three players with forty cards, that was popular in Europe during the 17th and 18th centuries. [Spanish *hombre,* "man" (name given to the player who attempts to win the pool), from Latin *homo.* See **dhghem-** in Appendix.*]
om·buds·man (ŏm′bŭdz-mən) *n., pl.* **-men** (-mĭn). A government official, especially in Scandinavian countries, who investigates citizens' complaints against the government or its functionaries. [Norwegian, from Old Norse *umbodhsmadhr,* "administration-man, king's representative" : *um,* about (see **ambhi-** in Appendix*) + *bodh,* command (see **bheudh-** in Appendix*) + *madhr,* (rarely) *mannr,* man (see **man-**[1] in Appendix*).]
Om·dur·man (ŏm′do͝or-män′). A city in northeast-central Sudan, on the White Nile opposite Khartoum; nearby in 1898, Anglo-Egyptian forces defeated the Khalifa. Population, 167,000.
-ome. *Botany.* Indicates mass, body, or group; for example, **biome, phyllome.** [From -OMA.]
OME Airport code for Nome, Alaska.
o·me·ga (ō-mĕg′ə, ō-mē′gə, ō-mā′-) *n.* **1.** The 24th and final letter in the Greek alphabet, written Ω, ω. Transliterated in English as long *o.* See **alphabet. 2.** The ending; the last of anything: *"I am Alpha and Omega, the beginning and the ending"* (Revelation 1:8). **3.** *Symbol* Ω^- *Physics.* A subatomic particle in the baryon family, having a mass 3,276 times that of the electron, a negative electric charge, and a mean lifetime of 1.5×10^{-10} second. Also called "omega minus." See **particle.** [Greek *ō mega,* "large *ō*" : *ō* + *mega,* neuter of *megas,* large, great (see **meg-** in Appendix*).]
om·e·let (ŏm′lĭt, ŏm′ə-lĭt) *n.* Also **om·e·lette.** A dish consisting of beaten eggs cooked and folded, often around a filling. See **French omelet, Western omelet.** [French *omelette,* from Old French *amelette,* "thin plate," alteration of *alumette,* variant of *alumelle,* from *lemelle,* from Latin *lāmella,* thin metal plate, diminutive of *lāmina,* plate, layer. See **stel-**[2] in Appendix.*]
o·men (ō′mən) *n.* **1.** Any phenomenon supposed to portend good or evil; a prophetic sign: *"Many tribes . . . considered the call of the barking deer to be an omen of ill luck."* (Osa Johnson). **2.** Prognostication; portent: *birds of ill omen.* —*tr.v.* **omened, omening, omens.** To be an omen of; portend; presage. [Latin *ōmen.* See **ō-** in Appendix.*]
o·men·tum (ō-mĕn′təm) *n., pl.* **-ta** (-tə). *Anatomy.* One of two pairs of peritoneal folds. The greater omentum, consisting of a double fold of peritoneum, passes from the stomach to the transverse colon; the lesser omentum is doubled to join the lesser curve of the stomach and duodenum to the liver. [Latin *ōmentum*†.] **—o·men′tal** *adj.*
o·mer (ō′mər) *n.* An ancient Hebrew dry measure roughly equal to 3.7 quarts. [Hebrew *'ōmer,* "a measure."]
om·i·cron (ŏm′ə-krŏn′, ō′mə-) *n.* The 15th letter in the Greek alphabet, written O, o. Transliterated in English as *O, o.* See **alphabet.** [Greek *o mikron,* "small o" : *o* + *mikron,* neuter of *mikros,* small (see **smē-** in Appendix*).]
om·i·nous (ŏm′ə-nəs) *adj.* **1.** Being or pertaining to an evil omen; portentous; foreboding: *"The Mountain standing ominous and alone had looked taller than it was."* (J.R.R. Tolkien). **2.** Menacing; threatening: *"The growl outside turned more ominous."* (Thomas Pynchon). [Latin *ōminōsus,* from *ōmen* (stem *ōmin-*), OMEN.] **—om′i·nous·ly** *adv.* **—om′i·nous·ness** *n.*
o·mis·si·ble (ō-mĭs′ə-bəl) *adj.* Capable of or fit for omission. [From Latin *omittere* (past participle *omissus-*), OMIT.]
o·mis·sion (ō-mĭsh′ən) *n.* **1.** The act or an instance of omitting: *"We do not have TV, and because of this curious omission we are looked upon as eccentrics, possibly radicals."* (E.B. White). **2.** The state of being omitted. **3.** Something that is omitted or neglected. [Middle English *omissioun,* from Late Latin *omissiō,* from Latin *omittere* (past participle *omissus-*), OMIT.]
o·mis·sive (ō-mĭs′ĭv) *adj.* Characterized by omission.
o·mit (ō-mĭt′) *tr.v.* **omitted, omitting, omits. 1.** To leave out; fail to include: *"Omit needless words."* (William Strunk, Jr.). **2. a.** To pass over; neglect: *"He swore he would never omit any opportunity . . . of showing her the sincerity of his affection"* (Fielding). **b.** To neglect, forbear, or fail (to do): *"Emily omitted to wash, since there seemed such a hurry"* (Richard Hughes). [Middle English *omitten,* from Latin *omittere* : *ob,* away + *mittere,* to send (see **smeit-** in Appendix*).]
om·ma·tid·i·um (ŏm′ə-tĭd′ē-əm) *n., pl.* **-ia** (-ē-ə). *Zoology.* One of the elements, resembling a single simplified eye, that make up the compound eye of arthropods. [New Latin, "small eye" : Greek *omma* (stem *ommat-*), eye (see **okw-** in Appendix*) + -IDIUM.] **—om′ma·tid′i·al** *adj.*
om·mat·o·phore (ō-măt′ə-fôr′, -fōr′) *n. Zoology.* A movable stalk ending with an eye, such as found in snails. [Greek *omma* (stem *ommat-*), eye (see **okw-** in Appendix*) + -PHORE.] **—om′ma·toph′o·rous** (ŏm′ə-tŏf′ər-əs) *adj.*
Om·mi·ad. Variant of **Umayyad.**
omni-. Indicates all; for example, **omnidirectional, omnirange.** [Latin, from *omnis,* all. See **op-**[1] in Appendix.*]
om·ni·bus (ŏm′nĭ-bŭs′) *n., pl.* **-buses. 1.** A **bus** *(see).* **2.** A printed anthology of the works of one author or of writings on related subjects. —*adj.* Including many things or classes; covering many things or situations at once: *an omnibus law.* [French *(voiture) omnibus* "(vehicle) for all," and Latin *omnibus* "for all," dative plural of *omnis,* all. See **op-**[1] in Appendix.*]
om·ni·di·rec·tion·al (ŏm′nē-dĭ-rĕk′shən-əl, -dī-rĕk′shən-əl) *adj.* Capable of transmitting or receiving (signals) in all directions.
om·ni·far·i·ous (ŏm′nə-fâr′ē-əs) *adj.* Of all kinds: *omnifarious knowledge.* [Late Latin *omnifarius* : OMNI- + *fārius,* "-doing" (see **dhē-**[1] in Appendix*).] **—om′ni·far′i·ous·ness** *n.*
om·nip·o·tent (ŏm-nĭp′ə-tənt) *adj.* Having unlimited or universal power, authority, or force; all-powerful: *"The Marxist God is the omnipotent if impersonal force of dialectical materialism."* (Crane Brinton). —*n. Capital* **O.** God. Used with *the.* [Middle English, from Old French, from Latin *omnipotēns* : OMNI- + *potēns,* POTENT.] **—om·nip′o·tence, om·nip′o·ten·cy** *n.* **—om·nip′o·tent·ly** *adv.*
om·ni·pres·ence (ŏm′nĭ-prĕz′əns) *n.* The fact of being present everywhere. [Medieval Latin *omnipraesentia,* from *omnipraesēns* : OMNI- + *praesēns,* PRESENT.] **—om′ni·pres′ent** *adj.*
om·ni·range (ŏm′nĭ-rānj′, ŏm′nē-) *n.* A radio network that provides complete bearing information for aircraft. Also called "omnidirectional radio range."
om·nis·cient (ŏm-nĭsh′ənt) *adj.* Having total knowledge; knowing everything: *"The idea of the sage who is omniscient from birth"* (H.G. Creel). —*n. Capital* **O.** God. Used with *the.* [Medieval Latin *omnisciēns* : OMNI- + *sciēns,* present participle of *scīre,* to know (see **skei-** in Appendix*).] **—om·nis′cience, om·nis′cien·cy** *n.* **—om·nis′cient·ly** *adv.*
om·ni·um-gath·er·um (ŏm′nē-əm-găth′ər-əm) *n.* A miscellaneous collection; hodgepodge. [Mock Latin formation : Latin *omnium,* of all, genitive plural of *omnis,* all (see **op-**[1] in Appendix*) + GATHER.]
om·ni·vore (ŏm′nə-vôr′, -vōr′) *n.* An omnivorous animal. [From Latin *omnivorus,* OMNIVOROUS.]
om·niv·o·rous (ŏm-nĭv′ər-əs) *adj.* **1.** *Zoology.* Eating both animal and vegetable substances. **2.** Eating all kinds of food: *"The rat, like men, has become practically omnivorous—it eats anything that lets it."* (Hans Zinsser). **3.** Taking in everything available, as with the mind: *an omnivorous reader.* [Latin *omnivorus* : OMNI- + *-vorus,* -VOROUS.] **—om·niv′o·rous·ly** *adv.* **—om·niv′o·rous·ness** *n.*
O·mo·lon (ŏm′ə-lôn′). A river of the Soviet Union rising in the northeast and flowing 600 miles northwest to join the Kolyma River near its mouth on the Siberian Sea.
om·pha·los (ŏm′fə-lŏs′, -ləs) *n., pl.* **-li** (-lī′). **1.** *Anatomy.* The navel. **2.** A center. [Greek. See **nobh-** in Appendix.*]
Omsk (ômsk). The capital of the Omsk Region in the west-central Soviet Union, on the Irtish River. Population, 721,000.
O·mu·ta (ō′mo͞o-tä′). A seaport city of Japan, on Shimabara Bay in northwestern Kyushu Island. Population, 221,000.
on (ŏn, ôn) *prep.* **1.** Used to indicate: **a.** Position upon and above the surface of; position in contact with and supported by the surface of: *The vase is on the table.* **b.** Contact with any surface, regardless of position: *a picture on the wall.* **c.** Location at or along: *a house on the beach.* **d.** Proximity: *a town on the border.* **e.** Attachment to or suspension from: *beads on a string.* **2.** Used to indicate: **a.** Motion or direction toward a position: *He threw the books on the floor.* **b.** Motion toward, against, or onto: *jump on the table; the march on Washington.* See Usage note below. **3.** Used to indicate: **a** Occurrence during: *on July third.* **b.** The occasion of what is stated: *On entering the room, she saw him.* **c.** The exact moment or point of: *every hour on the hour.* **4.** Used to indicate: **a.** The object affected by actual, perceptible action: *The spotlight fell on the actress.* **b.** The agent or agency performing a specified action: *He cut his foot on the broken glass.* **c.** The object affected by a figurative action: *Have pity on them.* **d.** The object of an action directed, tending, or moving against it: *an attack on the fortress.* **e.** Something used to perform a stated action: *talk on the telephone.* **5.** Used to indicate an originating or sustaining source or agency: *live on bread and water; make a profit on gambling.* **6.** Used to indicate: **a.** The state, condition, or process of: *on leave; on fire.* **b.** The

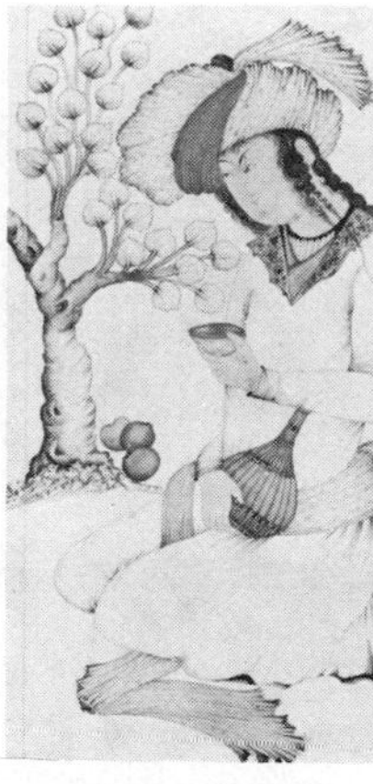

Omar Khayyám
Represented in an early 16th-century Persian miniature

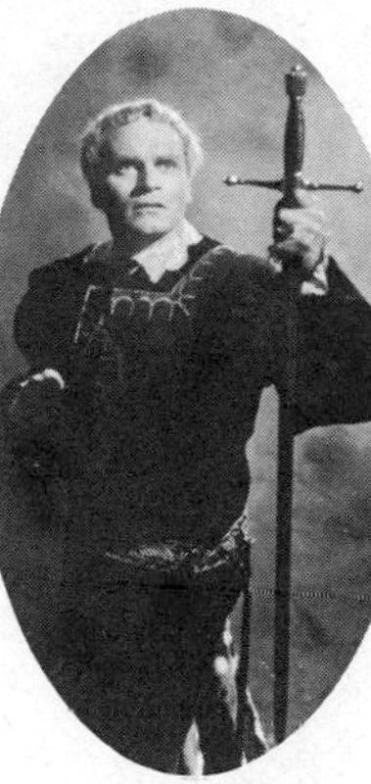

Laurence Olivier
In the role of Hamlet

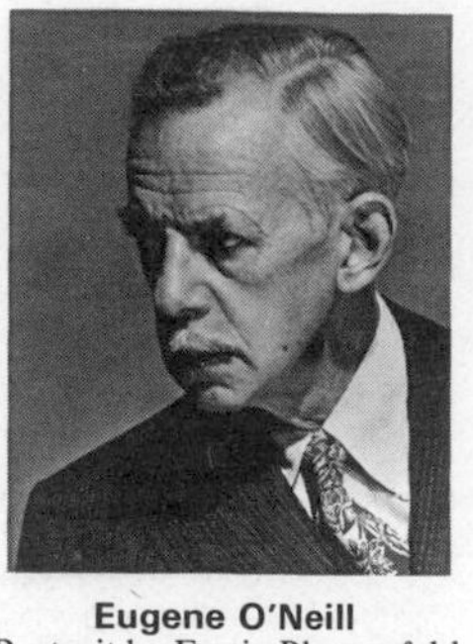

Eugene O'Neill
Portrait by Erwin Blumenfeld

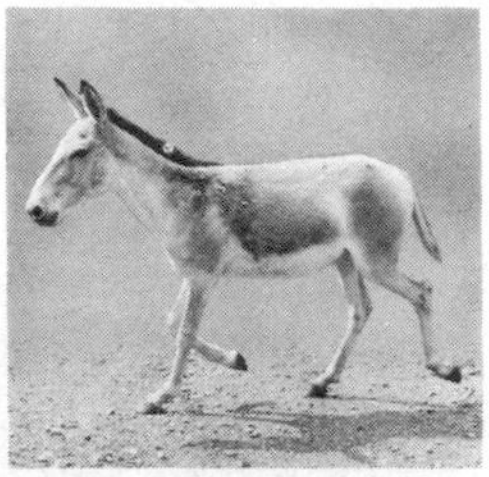

onager

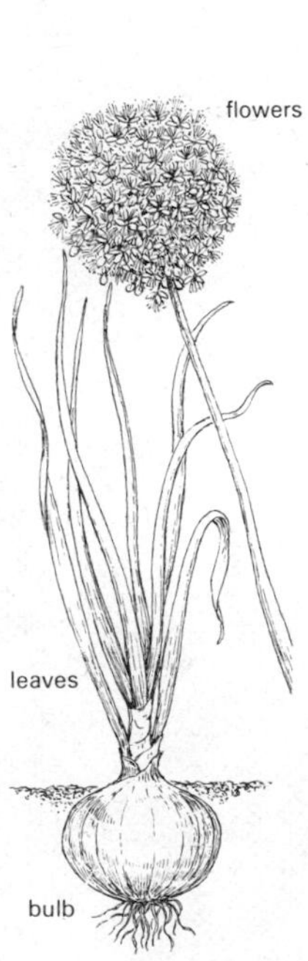

onion

purpose of: *travel on business.* **c.** A means of conveyance: *ride on a train.* **d.** Availability by means of: *beer on tap; a nurse on call.* **e.** Association with: *a doctor on the hospital staff.* **f.** The ground or basis for: *I refused it on principle.* **g.** Addition or repetition: *error on error.* **7.** Concerning; about: *a book on astronomy.* **8.** In one's possession; with: *I haven't a cent on me.* **9.** At the expense of: *drinks on the house.* —*adv.* **1.** In or into a position of being attached to or covering something: *Put your clothes on.* **2.** In or into a position or condition of being supported by or in contact with (an unstated object or surface implied by context): *Put the coffee on.* **3.** In the direction of: *He looked on while the ship docked.* **4. a.** Toward or at a point lying ahead in space or time; forward: *The army moved on to the next town.* **b.** At or to a more distant point in time or space: *I'll do it later on.* **5.** In a continuous course: *He worked on quietly.* **6. a.** In or into performance or operation: *Turn on the radio.* **b.** In progress or action; in a state of activity: *The show is on.* **7.** In or at the present position: *stay on; hang on.* **8.** In a condition of being scheduled for or decided upon: *There is a party on tonight.* —**and so on.** And like the preceding; and so forth. —**on and off.** Intermittently. —**on and on.** Without stopping; continuously. —**to be on to.** *Informal.* To be aware of or have information on. See Usage note below. [Middle English *on,* preposition and adverb, Old English *on, an.* See **an**[1] in Appendix.*]

Usage: To indicate motion to a position, the prepositions *on* and *onto* are frequently used interchangeably, though *onto* more strongly conveys movement toward: *jumped on the table; jumped onto the table.* In constructions where *on* is an adverb and *to* a preposition, they must not be joined as one word: *move on to* (not *onto*) *new subjects, hold on to* (not *onto*) *our gains.* In such cases *on* may be considered part of the verb. The distinction between *on* and *upon* is that *on* stresses a position of rest *(a book lay on the table)* and *upon* emphasizes movement *(he jumped upon the table).* But *on* and *upon* are often interchangeable in such typical examples. When *up* functions adverbially and *on* as a preposition, the words are not joined: *Climb up on the roof.* (Again *up* is, in effect, part of the verb; it stresses elevation, whereas *upon* would indicate mere contact.)

ON, O.N. Old Norse.

-on. Indicates: subatomic particle, unit, or quantum; for example, **electron, photon.** [From (I)ON.]

on·a·ger (ŏn'ə-jər) *n., pl.* **-gers.** **1.** A wild ass, *Equus hemionus onager,* of central Asia. **2.** An ancient and medieval stone-propelling siege engine. [Middle English, from Latin *onager,* from Greek *onagros* : *onos,* ass (see **asinus** in Appendix*) + *agros,* field (see **agro-** in Appendix*).]

o·nan·ism (ō'nə-nĭz'əm) *n.* **1.** Male masturbation. **2.** Coitus interruptus. [After *Onan,* son of Judah (Genesis 38:9).] —**o'nan·ist** *n.* —**o'nan·is'tic** *adj.*

O·ña·te (ō-nyä'tā), **Juan de.** 1549?–1624? Spanish explorer and conquistador; first governor of New Mexico.

once (wŭns) *adv.* **1.** One time only: *once a day.* **2.** One time in the past; formerly: *"Let not the land once proud of him insult him now"* (Whittier). **3.** At any time; ever: *Once known, never forgotten.* —**once and for all.** Finally; conclusively. —**once in a while.** Now and then; occasionally. —**once upon a time.** At an indefinite time in the past. —*n.* A single occurrence; one time: *You can go this once.* —**all at once.** **1.** All at the same time. **2.** Suddenly. —**at once.** **1.** All together; simultaneously. **2.** Without delay; immediately. —*conj.* As soon as; if ever; when: *Once he goes, we can clean up.* —*adj.* Having been formerly; former: *the once capital of the nation.* [Middle English *ones, anes,* adverbial genitive of *on, an,* one, Old English *ān.* See **oino-** in Appendix.*]

once-o·ver (wŭns'ō'vər) *n. Informal.* A quick but comprehensive survey or performance. Often preceded by *the.*

on·col·o·gy (ŏn-kŏl'ə-jē) *n.* The scientific study of tumors. [Greek *onkos,* mass, tumor (see **nek-**[2] in Appendix*) + -LOGY.]

on·com·ing (ŏn'kŭm'ĭng, ôn'-) *adj.* Coming nearer; approaching: *the oncoming storm.* —*n.* An approach; advance.

one (wŭn) *adj.* **1.** Being a single entity, unit, object, or being; single; individual. **2.** Characterized by unity; of a single kind or nature; undivided: *with one accord.* **3.** Designating a person or thing that is contrasted with another or others: *from one end to the other.* **4.** Designating a particular but indefinite thing or time: *He will come one day.* **5.** Designating a certain person, especially a person not previously known or mentioned. **6.** A or an. Used informally as a substitute for the indefinite article for emphasis: *That is one fine dog.* **7.** Single in kind; alike or the same. —*n.* **1.** The cardinal number written 1 or roman numeral I. See **number.** **2.** A single person or thing; unit. —*pron.* **1.** A certain person or thing; someone or something. **2.** Any person or thing; anyone or anything. **3.** A single person or thing among persons or things already known or mentioned: *one of the Elizabethans.* —**all one.** Of equal importance; all the same. —**at one.** In accord or unity. —**one and all.** Everyone. —**one another.** Each other. Used to describe a reciprocal relation or action. See Usage note at **another.** —**one by one.** Individually and in succession. [Middle English *an, on,* Old English *ān.* See **oino-** in Appendix.*]

Usage: In the construction *One in every ten men was found deficient,* the verb must be singular, in proper agreement with the subject *one.* Although some grammarians have sought to make a case for plural verbs in such sentences (using *ten men* or the like as justification), 92 per cent of the Usage Panel accept only a singular verb. The following common examples employing *one of* also involve problems in number: *one of those men who are constantly complaining about their wives; one of the most costly defeats that have been inflicted.* According to 58 per cent of the Panel, only the plural verbs *are* and *have* are possible (since the respective subjects, *who* and *that,* properly refer to *men* and *defeats,* not to *one*). The remainder also accept singular verbs in such examples, if the writer or speaker wishes to emphasize the sense inherent in *one.* Whatever the choice of verb, accompanying elements must agree in number. Thus, in the first example: *who are complaining about their wives* or *who is complaining about his wife.*

-one. Indicates: **1.** An oxygen-containing or ketone compound; for example, **acetone.** **2.** A chemical compound containing oxygen, especially in a carbonyl or similar group; for example, **lactone.** [From Greek *-ōnē,* feminine patronymic suffix.]

one-base hit (wŭn'bās'). *Baseball.* A base hit by which a batter can reach first base safely. Also called "single," "one-bagger."

O·ne·ga, Lake (ō-nĕg'ə). The second-largest lake in Europe (3,764 square miles), in the northwestern Soviet Union.

one-horse (wŭn'hôrs') *adj.* **1.** Drawn by or using only one horse: *a one-horse carriage.* **2.** Contemptibly small or insignificant: *a one-horse town.*

O·nei·da[1] (ō-nī'də). A city in central New York State; site of an experiment in communal living (1848–81). Population, 12,000.

O·nei·da[2] (ō-nī'də) *n., pl.* **Oneida** or **-das.** **1.** One of the five tribes belonging to the league of the Iroquois. **2.** A member of this tribe. **3.** The Iroquoian language of this tribe. [Iroquois *onẽyóte',* "standing stone."]

O'Neill (ō-nēl'), **Eugene (Gladstone).** 1888–1953. American dramatist.

o·nei·ro·man·cy (ō-nī'rə-măn'sē) *n.* Divination by dreams. [Greek *oneiros,* dream (see **oner-** in Appendix*) + -MANCY.] —**o·nei'ro·man'cer** *n.*

one·ness (wŭn'nĭs) *n.* **1.** The quality or state of being one; singleness: *the infinite oneness of God.* **2.** Singularity; uniqueness. **3.** Undividedness; wholeness. **4.** Identity of character (of several things): *the disagreeable oneness of roadside landscapes.* **5.** Unison; agreement: *oneness of mind and purpose.*

one-night stand (wŭn'nīt'). **1.** A performance by a traveling musical or dramatic performer or group in one place on one night only. **2.** The place at which such a performance is given.

on·er·ous (ŏn'ər-əs, ō'nər-) *adj.* **1.** Troublesome or oppressive; burdensome. **2.** *Law.* Entailing obligations that exceed any advantage to the possessor, as a contract. —See Synonyms at **burdensome.** [Middle English, from Old French *onereus,* from Latin *onerōsus,* from *onus* (stem *oner-*), burden. See **enos-** in Appendix.*] —**on'er·ous·ly** *adv.* —**on'er·ous·ness** *n.*

one·self (wŭn-sĕlf') *pron.* Also **one's self** (wŭn sĕlf', wŭnz sĕlf'). A specialized form of the third person singular pronoun **one.** It is used: **1.** As a reflexive pronoun, forming the direct or indirect object of a verb or the object of a preposition: *forget oneself; faith in oneself.* **2.** For emphasis, after *one: One must take a certain amount of initiative oneself.* **3.** For emphasis, in place of *one,* in various constructions: *Oneself is to blame in certain situations.* **4.** As an indication of one's real, normal, or healthy condition or identity: *come to oneself.*

one-sid·ed (wŭn'sī'dĭd) *adj.* **1.** Favoring one side or group; partial; biased: *a one-sided view.* **2.** Larger or more developed on one side: *a one-sided pattern.* **3.** Existing or occurring on one side only. —**one'-sid'ed·ly** *adv.* —**one'-sid'ed·ness** *n.*

one-step (wŭn'stĕp') *n.* A ballroom dance consisting of a series of unbroken rapid steps in $\frac{2}{4}$ time. —*intr.v.* **one-stepped, -stepping, -steps.** To dance the one-step.

one-time (wŭn'tīm') *adj.* Also **one·time.** At or in some past time; former: *a one-time boxing champion.*

one-to-one (wŭn'tə-wŭn') *adj.* **1. a.** Allowing the pairing of each member of a class uniquely with a member of another class. **b.** *Mathematics.* Pertaining to a correspondence that assigns to each member of one set a unique member of another set. **2.** Characterized by proportional amounts on both sides.

one-track (wŭn'trăk') *adj.* Obsessively limited to a single idea or purpose: *a one-track mind.*

one-up·man·ship (wŭn-ŭp'mən-shĭp') *n. Informal.* The technique of keeping one step ahead of a competitor.

one-way (wŭn'wā') *adj.* **1.** Moving, or permitting movement, in one direction only: *a one-way street.* **2.** Providing for travel in one direction only: *a one-way ticket.*

on·go·ing (ŏn'gō-ĭng, ôn'-) *adj.* Progressing or evolving.

ONI Office of Naval Intelligence.

on·ion (ŭn'yən) *n.* **1.** A bulbous plant, *Allium cepa,* cultivated worldwide as a vegetable. **2.** The rounded, edible bulb of the onion plant, composed of tight, concentric layers, and having a pungent odor and taste. See **chive, garlic, leek, shallot.** [Middle English *unyon, oyn(y)oun,* from Old French *oignon,* from Latin *uniō,* a dialectal word for a kind of onion, possibly from *ūniō,* oneness, unity, from *ūnus,* one (possibly referring to the perfect concentric unity of the layers of an onion in contrast to the polymerism of, e.g., garlic). See **oino-** in Appendix.*]

On·ions (ŭn'yənz), **Charles Talbut.** 1873–1965. English lexicographer; an editor of the *Oxford English Dictionary* and author of the *Oxford Dictionary of English Etymology.*

on·ion·skin (ŭn'yən-skĭn') *n.* A thin, strong, translucent paper.

on-line (ŏn'līn', ôn'-) *adj.* Under the control of a central computer, as in a manufacturing process or experiment.

on·look·er (ŏn'lo͝ok'ər, ôn'-) *n.* One who looks on; spectator. —**on·look·ing** (ŏn'lo͝ok'ĭng, ôn'-) *adj.* & *n.*

on·ly (ōn'lē) *adj.* **1.** Alone in kind or class; sole. **2.** Standing alone by reason of superiority or excellence. —*adv.* **1.** Without anyone or anything else; alone: *Only three survived.* **2. a.** No more than; at least; just: *If you would only come home.* **b.** Merely: *I only work here.* See Usage note below. **3.** Exclusively; solely: *I work only here.* See Usage note below. **—only too.** Eagerly; readily: *only too glad to help.* —*conj.* But; except (that): *"Spend all I have, only give me so much of your time in exchange"* (Shakespeare). [Middle English *only,* Old English *ānlīc* : *ān,* ONE + *-līc,* -LY.]

Usage: When used as an adverb, *only* should be placed with care to prevent ambiguity. Generally this means having *only* adjoin the word or group of words it actually limits, such as *dollar* in *He has only a dollar* (less precisely, *He only has a dollar*). The Usage Panel specifies precise placement in the following examples: *He arrived only an hour ago* (not *only arrived*). *Dictators respect only force* (not *only respect*). *Real cooperation is possible only when there is mutual respect* (not *is only possible when*). Particular care should be taken in placing *not only* in examples such as these: *He recognizes not only the legal commitment but also the moral issue* (not *He not only recognizes*). *It is not only possible but profitable* (not *It not only is*). *Only,* as a conjunction, is not appropriate to written usage, as the equivalent of *but* or *were it not that* (followed by a restraining condition): *They would have come, only the automobile broke down.* This typical example is unacceptable in writing to 85 per cent of the Usage Panel.

on·o·mas·tic (ŏn′ə-măs′tĭk) *adj.* Of or pertaining to a name or names. [Greek *onomastikos,* from *onomazein,* to name, from *onoma,* a name. See **nomen-** in Appendix.*]

on·o·mas·tics (ŏn′ə-măs′tĭks) *n.* Plural in form, used with a singular verb. The study of the origins of names.

on·o·mat·o·poe·ia (ŏn′ə-măt′ə-pē′ə) *n. Abbr.* **onomat. 1.** The formation of a word that sounds like its referent, as *buzz, crack, cuckoo.* **2.** A word so formed. **3.** Use of such words. [Late Latin, from Greek *onomatopoiia,* from *onomatopoiein,* to coin names : *onoma* (stem *onomat-*), name (see **nomen-** in Appendix*) + *poiein,* to make (see **kwei-²** in Appendix*).] **—on′o·mat′o·poe′ic** (-pē′ĭk), **on′o·mat′o·po·et′ic** (-pō-ĕt′ĭk) *adj.* **—on′o·mat′o·po·et′i·cal·ly** *adv.*

On·on·da·ga (ŏn′ən-dô′gə, -dä′gə) *n., pl.* **Onondaga** or **-gas. 1.** A tribe of Iroquoian-speaking Indians, formerly inhabiting upper New York state and Ontario. **2.** A member of this tribe. [Iroquois *onōtáge′,* name of their chief village, "on the top of the hill."] **—On′on·da′gan** *adj.*

ONR Office of Naval Research.

on·rush (ŏn′rŭsh′, ôn′-) *n.* **1.** A forward rush or flow: *the onrush of events.* **2.** An assault. **—on′rush′ing** *adj.*

on·set (ŏn′sĕt′, ôn′-) *n.* **1.** An onslaught; assault. **2.** A beginning; start: *the onset of a cold.*

on·shore (ŏn′shôr′, -shōr′, ôn′-) *adj.* **1.** Toward the shore: *an onshore gale.* **2.** Located or operating on the shore: *an onshore patrol.* —*adv.* Toward the shore: *The wind shifted onshore.*

on·slaught (ŏn′slôt′, ôn′-) *n.* A violent attack. [Earlier *anslaight,* from Dutch *aanslag* (influenced by obsolete English *slaught,* slaughter), from Middle Dutch *aenslag* : *aan,* on (see **an¹** in Appendix*) + *slag,* a striking (see **slak-** in Appendix*).]

On·tar·i·o (ŏn-târ′ē-ō′). *Abbr.* **Ont.** A province of Canada, 363,282 square miles in area, between Hudson Bay to the north and the Great Lakes to the south. Population, 6,731,000. Capital, Toronto. See map at **Canada. —On·tar′i·an** *adj.* & *n.*

On·tar·i·o, Lake (ŏn-târ′ē-ō′). The smallest and easternmost of the Great Lakes, 7,540 square miles in area, between southeastern Ontario, Canada, and northwestern New York. [Huron *ōtarīyo,* "great lake."]

on·to (ŏn′to͞o′, ôn′-, ŏn′tə, ôn′-) *prep.* Also **on to. 1.** On top of; to a position on; upon: *The dog jumped onto the chair.* —See Usage note at **on. 2.** *Informal.* Aware or cognizant of; informed about: *I'm onto your schemes.* [ON + TO.]

onto-. Indicates being or existence; for example, **ontogeny.** [Late Greek, from *ōn* (stem *ont-*), present participle of *einai,* to be. See **es-** in Appendix.*]

on·tog·e·ny (ŏn-tŏj′ə-nē) *n., pl.* **-nies.** The course of development of an individual organism. Compare **phylogeny.** [ONTO- + -GENY.] **—on′to·ge·net′ic** (ŏn′tō-jə-nĕt′ĭk) *adj.*

on·tol·o·gy (ŏn-tŏl′ə-jē) *n.* The branch of philosophy that deals with being. [New Latin *ontologia* : ONTO- + -LOGY.] **—on′to·log′i·cal** (ŏn′tə-lŏj′ĭ-kəl) *adj.* **—on′to·log′i·cal·ly** *adv.*

o·nus (ō′nəs) *n.* **1.** Anything that is burdensome, especially a disagreeable responsibility or necessity. **2.** A stigma or blame. [Latin *onus,* burden. See **enos-** in Appendix.*]

on·ward (ŏn′wərd, ôn′-) *adv.* Also **on·wards** (-wərdz). In a direction or toward a position that is ahead in space or time; forward. —*adj.* Moving or tending forward.

-onym. Indicates word or name; for example, **acronym, tautonym.** [Latin *-onymum,* from Greek *-onumon,* from *onuma, onoma,* name. See **nomen-** in Appendix.*]

-onymy. Indicates a set of names or the study of a kind of names; for example, **toponymy.** [Greek *-ōnumia,* from *-ōnumos,* having a (specific) name, from *onuma, onoma,* name. See **nomen-** in Appendix.*]

on·yx (ŏn′ĭks) *n.* A kind of chalcedony that occurs in bands of different colors. It is used as a gemstone, especially in cameos and intaglios. [Middle English *onix,* from Old French, from Latin *onyx,* from Greek *onux,* claw, fingernail, hence onyx (which sometimes has a vein of white on a pink background, like the lunula in a fingernail). See **nogh-** in Appendix.*]

oo-. Indicates egg or ovum; for example, **oogenesis, oology.** [Greek *ōio-,* from *ōion,* egg. See **awi-** in Appendix.*]

o·o·cyte (ō′ə-sīt′) *n.* **1.** A cell, derived from an oogonium, that undergoes meiosis and produces an ovum. **2.** A female gamete in certain protozoa. [OO- + -CYTE.]

O.O.D. officer of the deck.

oo·dles (o͞od′əlz) *pl.n. Informal.* A great amount; a lot. [Perhaps alteration of *huddles,* plural of HUDDLE.]

o·o·ga·mete (ō′ə-găm′ēt′, -gə-mēt′) *n.* A female gamete of sporozoans.

o·og·a·mous (ō-ŏg′ə-məs) *adj.* **1.** Characterized by small male gametes and large, less mobile female gametes. **2.** Pertaining to reproduction by oogamy.

o·og·a·my (ō-ŏg′ə-mē) *n., pl.* **-mies.** The fertilization of oogamous gametes. [OO- + -GAMY.]

o·o·gen·e·sis (ō′ə-jĕn′ə-sĭs) *n. Biology.* The enlargement and meiotic division of an oogonium that produces an ovum. [New Latin : OO- + -GENESIS.]

o·o·go·ni·um (ō′ə-gō′nē-əm) *n., pl.* **-nia** (-nē-ə) or **-ums. 1.** *Biology.* One of the cells that form the bulk of ovarian tissue. **2.** *Botany.* A female reproductive structure in certain fungi, containing oospores. [New Latin : OO- + -GONIUM.]

o·o·lite (ō′ə-līt′) *n.* Also **o·o·lith** (ō′ə-lĭth′). **1.** A small, round, calcareous grain found, for example, in limestones and dolomites. **2.** Rock, usually limestone, composed of such grains. [New Latin *oolites* (translation of German *Rogenstein,* "roe stone") : OO- + -LITE.] **—o′o·lit′ic** (ō′ə-lĭt′ĭk) *adj.*

o·ol·o·gy (ō-ŏl′ə-jē) *n.* The branch of ornithology that deals with birds' eggs. [OO- + -LOGY.] **—o′o·log′ic** (ō′ə-lŏj′ĭk), **o′o·log′i·cal** *adj.* **—o′o·log′i·cal·ly** *adv.* **—o·ol′o·gist** *n.*

oo·long (o͞o′lông′, -lŏng′) *n.* A dark Chinese tea that is partly fermented before drying. Compare **black tea.** [Mandarin Chinese *wu¹ lung²,* "black dragon" : *wu¹,* black + *lung²,* dragon.]

oo·mi·ak. Variant of **umiak.**

oomph (o͝omf) *n. Slang.* **1.** Irrepressible enthusiasm; spirited vigor. **2.** Sex appeal. [Expressive.]

o·o·pho·rec·to·my (ō′ə-fə-rĕk′tə-mē) *n., pl.* **-mies.** The surgical removal of one or both ovaries. [OOPHOR(E) + -ECTOMY.]

o·o·pho·ri·tis (ō′ə-fə-rī′tĭs) *n.* Ovarian inflammation. Also called "ovaritis." [New Latin : OOPHOR(E) + -ITIS.]

o·o·phyte (ō′ə-fīt′) *n. Botany.* The stage in plants undergoing metagenesis during which the sexual organs are developed. [OO- + -PHYTE.] **—o′o·phyt′ic** (ō′ə-fĭt′ĭk) *adj.*

o·o·sperm (ō′ə-spûrm′) *n. Biology.* A fertilized ovum. [OO- + SPERM.]

o·o·sphere (ō′ə-sfîr′) *n. Botany.* A nonmotile female gamete or egg, formed in an oogonium and ready for fertilization. [OO- + -SPHERE.]

o·o·spore (ō′ə-spôr′, -spōr′) *n. Botany.* A thick-walled spore, developed from a fertilized oosphere or by parthenogenesis. **—o′o·spor′ic** (ō′ə-spôr′ĭk, -spŏr′ĭk), **o·os′po·rous** (ō-ŏs′pər-əs, ō′ə-spôr′əs, -spōr′əs) *adj.*

o·o·the·ca (ō′ə-thē′kə) *n., pl.* **-cae** (-sē). *Zoology.* The capsule or egg case of certain insects and mollusks. [New Latin : OO- + THECA.] **—o′o·the′cal** *adj.*

o·o·tid (ō′ə-tĭd′) *n. Biology.* One of the four sections into which a mature ovum divides. [OO- + (SPERMA)TID.]

ooze¹ (o͞oz) *v.* **oozed, oozing, oozes.** —*intr.* **1.** To flow or leak out slowly, as through small openings. **2.** To disappear or ebb slowly: *His courage oozed away.* **3.** To progress slowly but steadily: *"The first three acts . . . oozed patiently but heavily on."* (Byron). **4.** To emit or exude moisture. —*tr.* **1.** To give off; exude. **2.** To emit or radiate in pervasive abundance: *"The English have had a tendency to ooze prettiness."* (Bernard Berenson). —*n.* **1.** The act of oozing; a gradual flow or leak. **2.** Something that oozes. **3.** An infusion of vegetable matter, as from oak bark, used in tanning. [Middle English *wosen,* from *wose,* juice, Old English *wōs.* See **wes-²** in Appendix.*]

ooze² (o͞oz) *n.* **1.** Soft, thin mud. **2.** The layer of mudlike sediment covering the floor of oceans and lakes, composed chiefly of remains of microscopic sea animals. **3.** Muddy ground; bog. [Middle English *wose,* Old English *wāse.* See **weis-¹** in Appendix.*]

ooz·y¹ (o͞o′zē) *adj.* **-ier, -iest.** Slowly leaking; oozing; dripping: *an oozy package of ice cream.* **—ooz′i·ness** *n.*

ooz·y² (o͞o′zē) *adj.* **-ier, -iest.** Of, resembling, or containing ooze: *an oozy riverbed.* **—ooz′i·ly** *adv.* **—ooz′i·ness** *n.*

op out of print.

OP out of print.

op. 1. operation. **2.** opposite. **3.** opus. **4.** out of print.

Op. 1. operation. **2.** opus. **3.** out of print.

o.p. out of print.

O.P. Order of Preachers.

o·pac·i·ty (ō-păs′ə-tē) *n., pl.* **-ties. 1.** The quality or state of being opaque. **2.** Something that is opaque. **3.** Obscurity; impenetrability. [French *opacité,* from Latin *opācitās,* from *opācus,* OPAQUE.]

o·pah (ō′pə) *n.* A large, vividly colored marine fish, *Lampris regius,* found in all oceans and having edible red flesh. Also called "moonfish." [West African. Compare Ibo *úbà.*]

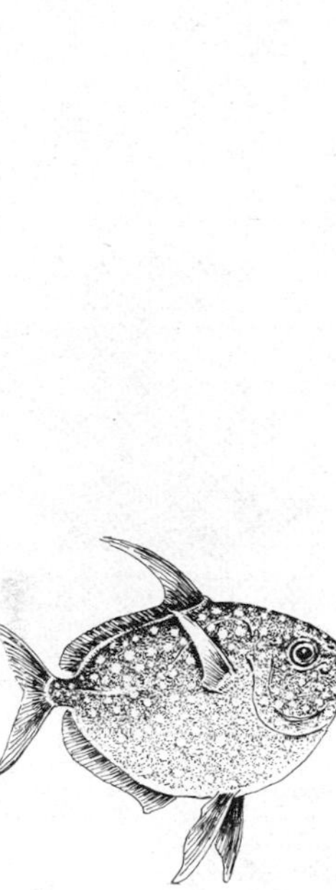

opah

o·pal (ō′pəl) *n.* A translucent mineral of hydrated silicon dioxide, often used as a gem. Also called "girasol." See **fire opal.** [Latin *opalus,* from Greek *opallios,* from Sanskrit *úpala,* (precious) stone, from *úpara,* lower, comparative of *úpa,* under. See **upo** in Appendix.*] **—o′pal·ine′** (ō′pə-lĭn′, -lēn′) *adj.*

o·pal·esce (ō′pə-lĕs′) *intr.v.* **-esced, -escing, -esces.** To emit or show an iridescent shimmer of colors. [Back-formation from OPALESCENCE.]

o·pal·es·cence (ō′pə-lĕs′əns) *n.* The quality or state of exhibiting a milky iridescence like that of an opal. [OPAL + -ESCENCE.] **—o′pal·es′cent** *adj.*

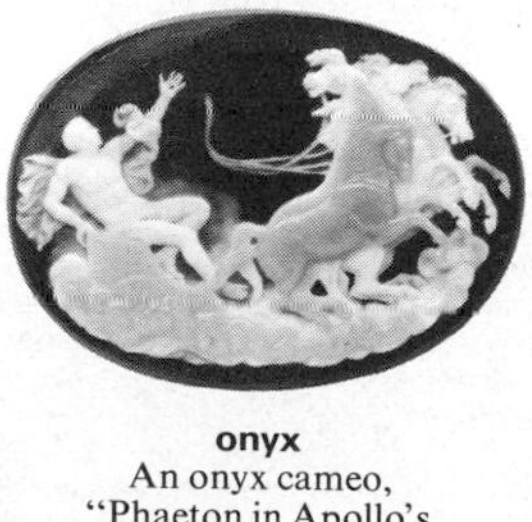

onyx
An onyx cameo, "Phaeton in Apollo's Chariot," by Adolph David

o·paque (ō-pāk′) *adj.* **1. a.** Impenetrable by light; neither transparent nor translucent. **b.** Not reflecting light; without luster; dull: *an opaque finish.* **2.** Impenetrable by a form of radiant energy other than visible light: *a chemical solution opaque to x* *rays.* **3. a.** Obtuse; dense: *"this thick skinned, seemingly opaque . . . almost stupid man"* (Carlyle). **b.** Obscure or unintelligible: *"The opaque allusion . . . accomplishes nothing."* (Marianne Moore). —See Synonyms at **dark.** —*n.* Something that is opaque; especially, an opaque pigment used to darken parts of a photographic print or negative. [Partly from Middle English *opake,* partly from Old French *opaque,* both from Latin *opācus*†, dark.] —**o·paque′ly** *adv.* —**o·paque′ness** *n.*

op. cit. In the work cited (Latin *opere citato*).

o·pen (ō′pən) *adj.* Also *poetic* **ope** (ōp). **1. a.** Affording unobstructed entrance and exit; not shut or closed. **b.** Affording unobstructed passage or view; spacious and unenclosed. **2.** Having no protecting or concealing cover; exposed. **3.** Not sealed, tied, or folded: *an open package.* **4.** Having interspersed gaps, spaces, or intervals: *open columns.* **5. a.** Accessible to all; unrestricted: *open meeting.* **b.** Unhampered by restrictions. **6. a.** Susceptible; inviting. **b.** Unprotected; vulnerable: *open to attack.* **7. a.** Available; obtainable: *The job is still open.* **b.** Available for use; active: *an open account.* **8.** Ready to transact business; operating. **9.** Unengaged; unoccupied: *an hour open for emergency cases.* **10. a.** Characterized by lack of pretense; candid; undissembling: *an open nature.* **b.** Free of prejudice; receptive to new ideas and arguments: *an open mind.* **11.** Widely spaced or leaded. Said of printed matter. **12.** *Music.* **a.** Not stopped by a finger. Said of a string or hole of an instrument. **b.** Produced by an unstopped string or hole, or without the use of slides, valves, or keys: *an open note on a trumpet.* **c.** Played without a mute: *an open wind instrument.* **13.** *Phonetics.* **a.** Articulated with the tongue in a low position: *The vowel sound in the word "far" is open.* **b.** Ending in a vowel or diphthong: *an open syllable.* **14.** Designating a method of punctuation in which commas and other pause marks are used sparingly. —See Synonyms at **frank.** —*v.* **opened, opening, opens.** —*tr.* **1.** To cause to become open; release from a closed or fastened position. **2.** To remove obstructions from; clear. **3.** To make or force an opening in: *open an old wound.* **4.** To form spaces or gaps between; spread out: *soldiers opening ranks.* **5. a.** To remove the cover or lid from; expose. **b.** To remove the wrapping from; unseal; undo. **6.** To unfold so that the inner parts are displayed; spread out: *a newspaper opened to the sports page.* **7. a.** To begin; initiate; commence: *open a meeting.* **b.** To commence the operation of; start business in. **8.** To permit the use of; make available. **9.** To make more responsive or understanding. **10.** To reveal the secrets of; to bare. **11.** *Law.* To recall (an order or judgment) for a re-examination of its merits. —*intr.* **1.** To become open or unfastened. **2.** To draw apart; separate: *The wound opened under pressure.* **3.** To spread apart; unfold. **4.** To come into view; become revealed: *The plain opened before us.* **5.** To become receptive or understanding. **6. a.** To begin; commence. **b.** To begin business or operation. **c.** To give the first public performance. **7.** To give access or view. Usually followed by *on* or *onto.* —**open up.** *Informal.* To speak or act freely and unrestrainedly. —*n.* **1. a.** An unobstructed area of land or water; an opening or clearing. **b.** The outdoors. Used with *the.* **2.** An undisguised or unconcealed state. Used with *the.* **3.** A tournament or contest in which both professional and amateur players may participate. [Middle English *open,* Old English *open.* See **upo** in Appendix.*] —**o′pen·ly** *adv.* —**o′pen·ness** *n.*

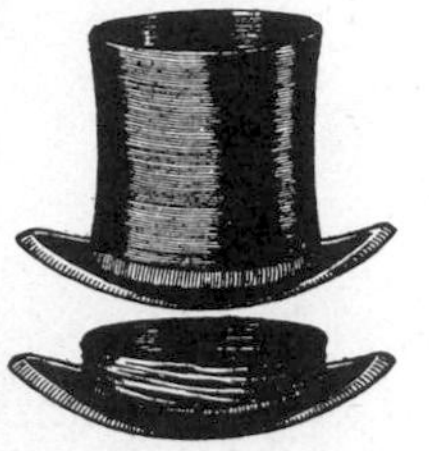

opera hat
Above: Hat as worn
Below: Hat collapsed

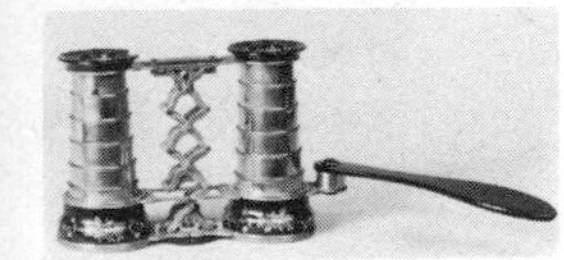

opera glass
French bronze, gilt, and tortoiseshell opera glasses made about 1840

o·pen-air (ō′pən-âr′) *adj.* Occurring, done, or existing out-of-doors: *an open-air concert.*

o·pen-and-shut (ō′pən-ən-shŭt′) *adj.* Presenting no difficulties; easily settled: *an open-and-shut case.*

open chain. *Chemistry.* A linear arrangement of atoms that is the basic form of various carbon and silicon compounds.

open city. A city that is declared demilitarized during a war, thus, under international law, gaining immunity from attack.

open door. 1. An unhindered opportunity for progress; free access. **2.** Admission to all on equal terms. **3.** A policy whereby a nation opens its foreign and internal trade to nationals of all other nations on equal terms. —**o′pen-door′** *adj.*

o·pen-end (ō′pən-ĕnd′) *adj.* **1.** Having no definite limit of duration or amount: *an open-end contract.* **2.** Permitting the borrowing of additional funds under existing terms: *an open-end mortgage.*

open-end investment company. A **mutual fund** *(see).*

o·pen·er (ō′pən-ər) *n.* **1.** One that opens; especially, a device used to cut open cans or pry up bottle caps. **2.** *Card Games.* **a.** The player who starts the betting in a gambling game such as poker. **b.** *Plural.* Cards of sufficient value for the holder to open the betting legally in such games. **3.** The first act in a theatrical variety show. **4.** The first game in a series.

o·pen-eyed (ō′pən-īd′) *adj.* **1.** Having the eyes wide open as in surprise. **2.** Watchful and alert.

o·pen-faced (ō′pən-fāst′) *adj.* **1.** Having an undisguised or sincere face or expression. **2.** Designating a sandwich having one side uncovered.

o·pen·hand·ed (ō′pən-hăn′dĭd) *adj.* Giving freely; generous. —**o′pen·hand′ed·ly** *adv.* —**o′pen·hand′ed·ness** *n.*

o·pen-heart (ō′pən-härt′) *adj.* Of, pertaining to, or designating surgery or surgical procedures in which the heart is open while its normal functions in the circulatory system are assumed by external apparatus.

o·pen·heart·ed (ō′pən-här′tĭd) *adj.* **1.** Revealing thoughts and intentions freely; frank; candid. **2.** Especially kindly and generous. —**o′pen·heart′ed·ly** *adv.* —**o′pen·heart′ed·ness** *n.*

o·pen-hearth (ō′pən-härth′) *adj.* **1.** Designating a reverberatory furnace used in the production of high-quality steel. **2.** Describing steel produced in such a furnace.

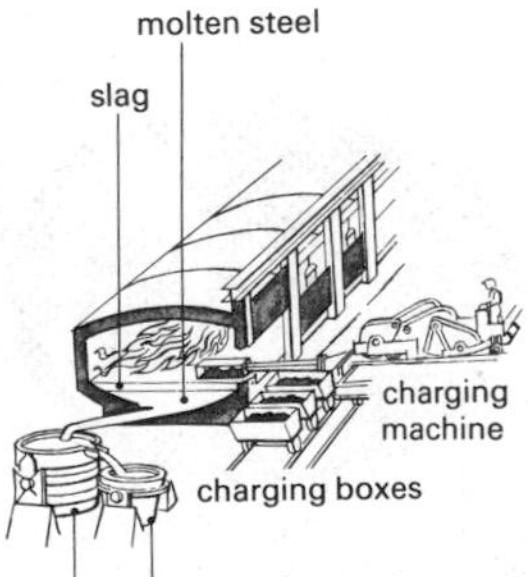
molten steel
slag
charging machine
charging boxes
slag ladle
steel ladle

open-hearth
Open-hearth furnace

open house. 1. A social event in which hospitality is extended to all. **2.** A public occasion in which a school, business organization, or other institution is open for visiting and inspection.

o·pen·ing (ō′pən-ĭng) *n.* **1.** The act of becoming open or being made to open. **2.** An open space serving as a passage or gap. **3.** A hole or aperture. **4.** The first period or stage. **5.** The first occasion for something, as a play. **6.** A specific pattern or series of beginning moves in certain games, especially chess. **7.** A favorable opportunity or chance. **8.** An unfilled job or position; vacancy. —See Synonyms at **opportunity.**

open letter. A letter on a subject of general interest, addressed to an individual but intended for general readership.

o·pen-mind·ed (ō′pən-mīn′dĭd) *adj.* Having a mind receptive to new ideas or to reason; free from prejudice or bias. —**o′pen-mind′ed·ly** *adv.* —**o′pen-mind′ed·ness** *n.*

o·pen-mouthed (ō′pən-mou*th*d′, -moutht′) *adj.* Having an open mouth, especially gaping in astonishment.

open season. 1. A period when hunting is permitted for a specified game animal. **2.** *Informal.* A situation in which criticism is unconstrained: *After the exposé, it was open season on (for) government officials.*

open ses·a·me (sĕs′ə-mē). A seemingly unfailing means of gaining admittance or attaining success. [From the magical formula used by Ali Baba in the *Arabian Nights* to open the door of the robbers' cave.]

open shop. 1. A business establishment or factory in which workers are employed without regard to union membership. Compare **union shop. 2.** A nonunion establishment which does not knowingly employ union members.

open stock. 1. A form of merchandising in which replacements for articles sold in sets are carried at all times. **2.** Such articles collectively.

o·pen·work (ō′pən-wûrk′) *n.* Ornamental or structural work containing numerous openings, usually in set patterns.

op·er·a[1] (ŏp′rə, ŏp′ər-ə) *n.* **1.** A form of theatrical presentation in which a dramatic performance is set to music. See **grand opera, music drama, opera buffa, opéra comique, operetta. 2.** A work of this kind. **3.** A theater designed primarily for operas. [Italian, from Latin *opera,* work. See **op-**[1] in Appendix.*]

o·pe·ra[2]. Alternate plural of **opus.**

op·er·a·ble (ŏp′ər-ə-bəl, ŏp′rə-) *adj.* **1.** Capable of being used or operated: *an outmoded but operable motor.* **2.** Capable of being put into practice; practicable: *an operable plan.* **3.** Capable of being treated by surgical operation: *an operable stage of cancer.* —**op′er·a·bil′i·ty** *n.*

o·pe·ra buf·fa (ŏp′rə bo͞o′fə, ŏp′ər-ə; *Italian* ô′pä-rä bo͞of′fä). Also *French* **o·pé·ra bouffe** (ô-pā-rȧ bo͞of′). A comic opera, especially one of the 18th century. [Italian : OPERA + *buffa,* feminine of *buffo,* comic, BUFFO.]

o·pé·ra co·mique (ŏp′rə kŏ-mēk′, ŏp′ər-ə; *French* ô-pā-rȧ kô-mēk′). Opera that, in addition to musical solos and ensembles, has dialogue that is spoken rather than sung. [French, "comic opera."]

opera glass. *Often plural.* A small, low-powered binocular for use especially at a theatrical performance.

opera hat. A collapsible top hat.

opera house. A theater designed chiefly for operas.

op·er·and (ŏp′ər-ənd) *n.* A quantity on which a mathematical operation is performed.

op·er·ant (ŏp′ər-ənt) *adj.* **1.** Operating to produce effects; effective. **2.** *Psychology.* Characterizing a response or behavior elicited by an environment rather than by a specific stimulus and identified by its consequences in the environment. —*n.* **1.** One that operates. **2.** *Psychology.* An element of operant behavior. [Latin *operāns,* present participle of *operārī,* to OPERATE.]

op·er·ate (ŏp′ə-rāt′) *v.* **-ated, -ating, -ates.** —*intr.* **1.** To function effectively; work. **2.** To bring about a desired or proper effect. **3.** To perform surgery. **4.** To carry on a military or naval action or campaign. —*tr.* **1.** To run or control the functioning of: *operate a machine.* **2.** To conduct the affairs of; manage: *operate a business.* **3.** To perform surgery upon. **4.** To bring about or effect. [Latin *operārī,* to work, labor, from *opus* (stem *oper-*), a work. See **op-**[1] in Appendix.*]

op·er·at·ic (ŏp′ə-răt′ĭk) *adj.* **1.** Of, related to, or typical of the opera: *an operatic aria.* **2.** Histrionic or implausible in a way considered characteristic of grand opera: *"realistic not operatic conspiracy"* (Oscar Wilde). [From OPERA (influenced by DRAMATIC).] —**op′er·at′i·cal·ly** *adv.*

op·er·at·ics (ŏp′ə-răt′ĭks) *n.* Plural in form, used with a singular or plural verb. Histrionics.

op·er·a·tion (ŏp′ə-rā′shən) *n. Abbr.* **op., Op. 1.** The act, process, or way of operating. **2.** The state of being operative or functioning: *in operation.* **3.** A process or series of acts performed to effect a certain purpose or result: *"The operation of shaving, dressing, and coffee-imbibing was soon performed."* (Dickens). **4.** A process or method of productive activity. **5.** *Medicine.* Any procedure for remedying an injury, ailment, or dysfunction in a living body, especially one performed with instruments. **6.** *Mathematics.* A process or action, such as addition, substitution, transposition, or differentiation, performed in a specified sequence and in accordance with specific rules of procedure. **7.** A military or naval action, campaign, or project. [Middle English *operacioun,* from Old French *operation,* from Latin *operātiō,* from *operārī,* OPERATE.]

op·er·a·tion·al (ŏp′ə-rā′shən-əl) *adj.* **1.** Of or pertaining to an operation or a series of operations. **2.** Of, for, or engaged in military operations. **3.** Serviced and declared fit for proper functioning: *an operational aircraft.* —**op′er·a′tion·al·ly** *adv.*

op·er·a·tion·al·ism (ŏp′ə-rā′shən-əl-ĭz′əm) *n. Philosophy.* The

ă pat/ā pay/âr care/ä father/b bib/ch church/d deed/ĕ pet/ē be/f fife/g gag/h hat/hw which/ĭ pit/ī pie/îr pier/j judge/k kick/l lid, needle/m mum/n no, sudden/ng thing/ŏ pot/ō toe/ô paw, for/oi noise/ou out/o͝o took/o͞o boot/p pop/r roar/s sauce/sh ship, dish/

doctrine that the meanings of concepts are derived from or given by specific operations. —**op'er·a'tion·al·ist** *n.*

operations research. Mathematical or scientific analysis of the systematic efficiency and performance of manpower, machinery, equipment, and policies used in a governmental, military, or commercial operation.

op·er·a·tive (ŏp′ər-ə-tĭv, ŏp′rə-, ŏp′ə-rā′tĭv) *adj.* **1.** Exerting influence or force: *"a lively operative desire for the good of others"* (John Woolman). **2.** Functioning effectively; efficient. **3.** Being in force, in effect, or in operation. **4.** Engaged in, concerned with, or related to physical or mechanical activity. **5.** Of, pertaining to, or resulting from a surgical operation. —*n.* **1.** A skilled worker, especially in industry. **2. a.** A secret or trusted agent. **b.** A private detective. —**op'er·a·tive·ly** *adv.*

op·er·a·tor (ŏp′ə-rā′tər) *n.* **1.** A person who operates a mechanical device: *a telephone operator.* **2.** The owner or director of a business or industrial concern. **3.** A dealer in stocks or commodities. **4.** A symbol, such as a plus sign, that represents a mathematical operation. **5.** *Informal.* A shrewd and sometimes unscrupulous person who gets what he wants by devious means.

o·per·cu·late (ō-pûr′kyə-lĭt) *adj.* Also **o·per·cu·lat·ed** (ō-pûr′kyə-lā′tĭd). Having an operculum.

o·per·cu·lum (ō-pûr′kyə-ləm) *n., pl.* **-la** (-lə) or **-lums. 1.** *Biology.* A lid or flap covering an aperture, such as the gill cover in some fishes or the horny shell cover in snails or other mollusks. **2.** *Anatomy.* Any flap or lid, such as the layer of tissue over an erupting tooth. [Latin, a lid, cover, diminutive formation from *operīre,* to cover. See **wer-**[5] in Appendix.*] —**o·per'cu·lar** *adj.* —**o·per'cu·lar·ly** *adv.*

op·e·ret·ta (ŏp′ə-rĕt′ə) *n.* A theatrical production that has many of the musical elements of opera, but is lighter and more popular in subject and style, and contains spoken dialogue. Also called "light opera." See Synonyms at **musical comedy.** [Italian, diminutive of OPERA.]

op·er·on (ŏp′ə-rŏn′) *n. Genetics.* A cluster of genes in physical proximity to one another, together with a distant gene that regulates the cluster's production of a set of different but functionally related enzymes. [From OPERATE.]

op·er·ose (ŏp′ə-rōs′) *adj.* **1.** Involving great labor; laborious: *"What an operose business it is to establish a government absolutely new."* (Burke). **2.** Industrious; diligent. [Latin *operōsus,* from *opus* (stem *oper-*), work. See **op-**[1] in Appendix.*] —**op'er·ose'ly** *adv.* —**op'er·ose'ness** *n.*

oph·i·cleide (ŏf′ə-klīd′, ō′fə-) *n.* A former musical wind instrument consisting of a long, tapering brass tube bent double and having keys. [French *ophicléide* : Greek *ophis,* snake (see **ophidian**) + *kleis* (stem *kleid-*), key (see **klēu-** in Appendix*).]

o·phid·i·an (ō-fĭd′ē-ən) *adj.* Of or pertaining to limbless reptiles, or snakes; snakelike. —*n.* Any member of the suborder Ophidia or Serpentes; a snake; serpent. [New Latin *Ophidia,* from Greek *ophis,* snake. See **angwhi-** in Appendix.*]

oph·i·ol·o·gy (ŏf′ē-ŏl′ə-jē, ō′fē-) *n.* A branch of herpetology dealing with snakes. [Greek *ophis,* snake (see **ophidian**) + -LOGY.] —**oph'i·o·log'i·cal** (ə-lŏj′ĭ-kəl) *adj.* —**oph'i·ol'o·gist** *n.*

O·phir (ō′fər). A land rich in gold. I Kings 10:11.

oph·ite (ŏf′īt′, o′fīt′) *n.* **1.** A mottled-green rock composed of diabase. **2.** Any of various green rocks, such as serpentine. [Latin *ophītes,* from Greek *ophitēs,* serpentine (stone), from *ophis,* serpent. See **angwhi-** in Appendix.*]

o·phit·ic (ŏ-fĭt′ĭk, ō-fĭt′-) *adj. Mineralogy.* **1.** Of or pertaining to ophite. **2.** Having a texture composed of plagioclase crystals in a matrix of pyroxene crystals.

Oph·i·u·chus (ŏf′ē-yo͞o′kəs, ō′fē-) *n.* A constellation in the equatorial region near Hercules and Scorpius. [Latin *Ophiūchus,* from Greek *ophioukhos,* "serpent-holder" : *ophis,* snake (see **angwhi-** in Appendix*) + *ekhein,* to hold (see **segh-** in Appendix*).]

ophthal. ophthalmologist; ophthalmology.

oph·thal·mia (ŏf-thăl′mē-ə, ŏp-thăl′-) *n.* Also **oph·thal·mi·tis** (ŏf′thăl-mī′tĭs, ŏp′-). Inflammation of the eye, especially of the conjunctiva. [Middle English *obtalmia,* from Late Latin *ophthalmia,* from Greek, from *ophthalmos,* eye. See **okw-** in Appendix.*]

oph·thal·mic (ŏf-thăl′mĭk, ŏp-thăl′-) *adj.* **1.** Of or pertaining to the eye or eyes; ocular. **2.** Having ophthalmia. [Greek *ophthalmikos,* from *ophthalmos,* eye. See **okw-** in Appendix.*]

ophthalmo-. Indicates the eye or eyeball; for example, **ophthalmoscope, ophthalmology.** [Greek, from *ophthalmos,* eye. See **okw-** in Appendix.*]

oph·thal·mol·o·gist (ŏf′thăl-mŏl′ə-jĭst, ŏf′thəl-, ŏp′-) *n. Abbr.* **ophthal.** A physician specializing in the treatment of diseases of the eye. See Usage note at **oculist.**

oph·thal·mol·o·gy (ŏf′thăl-mŏl′ə-jē, ŏf′thəl-, ŏp′-) *n. Abbr.* **ophthal.** The medical specialty encompassing the anatomy, functions, pathology, and treatment of the eye. [OPHTHALMO- + -LOGY.] —**oph·thal'mo·log'ic** (-thăl′mə-lŏj′ĭk), **oph·thal'mo·log'i·cal** *adj.* —**oph·thal'mo·log'i·cal·ly** *adv.*

oph·thal·mom·e·ter (ŏf′thăl-mŏm′ə-tər, ŏf′thəl-, ŏp′-) *n.* An optical instrument for measuring astigmatism. [OPHTHALMO- + -METER.] —**oph·thal'mo·met'ric** (ŏf-thăl′mə-mĕt′rĭk, ŏp-thăl′-), **oph·thal'mo·met'ri·cal** *adj.*

oph·thal·mo·scope (ŏf-thăl′mə-skōp′, ŏp-thăl′-) *n.* An instrument consisting essentially of a mirror with a central hole through which the eye is examined. [OPHTHALMO- + -SCOPE.] —**oph·thal'mo·scop'ic** (-skŏp′ĭk), **oph·thal'mo·scop'i·cal** *adj.* —**oph'thal·mos'co·py** (ŏf′thăl-mŏs′kə-pē, ŏp′thăl-) *n.*

-opia. Indicates a specific visual condition or defect; for example, **diplopia, senopia.** [Greek *-opia,* from *ōps,* eye. See **okw-** in Appendix.*]

o·pi·ate (ō′pē-ĭt, -āt′) *n.* **1.** Any of various sedative narcotics containing opium or one of more of its derivatives. **2.** Any sedative or narcotic drug. **3.** Anything that relaxes or that induces sleep or torpor: *"here all opiates to grief . . . were in vain"* (C.B. Brown). —*adj.* (ō′pē-ĭt, -āt′). **1.** Consisting of or containing opium. **2.** Causing or producing sleep or sedation. —*tr.v.* (ō′pē-āt′) **opiated, -ating, -ates. 1.** To subject to the action of an opiate. **2.** To dull or deaden as if with a narcotic drug. [Medieval Latin *opiātum,* an opiate, from *opiātus,* treated with opium, soporific, from Latin *opium,* OPIUM.]

o·pine (ō-pīn′) *tr.v.* **opined, opining, opines.** To hold or state as an opinion; think: *"They were, he opined, mere imitations of Arthur Symons."* (Stanislaus Joyce). [Old French *opiner,* from Latin *opīnārī,* to think. See **op-**[2] in Appendix.*]

o·pin·ion (ə-pĭn′yən) *n.* **1.** A belief or conclusion held with confidence, but not substantiated by positive knowledge or proof. **2.** An evaluation or judgment based on special knowledge and given by an expert: *a legal opinion.* **3.** A judgment or estimation of the worth or value of a person or thing: *In my opinion, he is a fool.* **4.** The common, usual, or prevailing feeling or sentiment: *public opinion.* **5.** *Law.* A formal statement by a judge or jury of the legal reasons and principles for the conclusions of the court. [Middle English, from Old French, from Latin *opīniō,* from *opīnārī,* to think. See **op-**[2] in Appendix.*]

Synonyms: *opinion, view, sentiment, feeling, impression, inclination, belief, conviction, persuasion, judgment. Opinion* is applicable to any conclusion to which one adheres without ruling out the possibility of debate. *View* differs principally in that it stresses individuality of outlook as a determinant of the conclusion. *Sentiment* and especially *feeling* stress the role of emotion as a determinant. *Impression* and *inclination,* in this context, denote tentative conclusions. *Belief* pertains to a conclusion, not necessarily derived first-hand, to which one subscribes strongly. *Conviction* denotes belief that excludes doubt and that proceeds usually from weight of evidence. *Persuasion* applies to strong belief, but does not necessarily suggest an intellectual basis. *Judgment,* strictly, is opinion based on reasoning and evaluation rather than emotion or will.

o·pin·ion·at·ed (ə-pĭn′yə-nā′tĭd) *adj.* Holding stubbornly and often unreasonably to one's own opinions. —**o·pin'ion·at'ed·ly** *adv.* —**o·pin'ion·at'ed·ness** *n.*

o·pin·ion·a·tive (ə-pĭn′yə-nā′tĭv) *adj.* **1.** Pertaining to or of the nature of an opinion; based on opinion. **2.** Opinionated. —**o·pin'ion·a'tive·ly** *adv.*

op·is·thog·na·thous (ŏp′ĭs-thŏg′nə-thəs) *adj.* Having receding jaws. [Greek *opisthen,* behind (see **epi** in Appendix*) + -GNATHOUS.] —**op'is·thog'na·thism'** *n.*

o·pi·um (ō′pē-əm) *n.* **1.** A bitter yellowish-brown drug prepared from the dried juice of unripe pods of the opium poppy, containing alkaloids such as morphine, narcotine, codeine, and papaverine, and used as an anesthetic. Habitual use induces strong addiction; excessive use is fatal. **2.** Something that numbs or stupefies. [Middle English, from Latin, from Greek *opion,* poppy juice, opium, diminutive of *opos,* juice. See **swekwo-** in Appendix.*]

opium poppy. A plant, *Papaver somniferum,* originally of Asia Minor, having grayish-green leaves and variously colored flowers. The juice of its unripe pods is the original source of opium.

O·por·to (ō-pôr′tō, ō-pōr′tō). *Portuguese* **Pôr·to** (pōr′to͞o). An industrial city and seaport of Portugal, on the Douro River. Population, 303,000.

o·pos·sum (ə-pŏs′əm, pŏs′əm) *n., pl.* **opossum** or **-sums.** Also **pos·sum** (pŏs′əm). **1.** Any of various nocturnal, arboreal marsupials of the family Didelphidae, especially *Didelphis marsupialis,* of the Western Hemisphere. **2.** Any of several Australian marsupials of the family Phalangeridae, some of which have valuable fur. [Algonquian (Powhatan) *aposoum,* from Proto-Algonquian *waap-a'themwa* (unattested), "white beast."]

opp. opposite.

Op·pen·heim·er (ŏp′ən-hī′mər), **J. Robert.** 1904–1967. American theoretical physicist; scientific leader of the **Manhattan District** *(see).*

op·po·nent (ə-pō′nənt) *n.* One that opposes another or others in a battle, contest, controversy, or debate. —*adj.* **1.** Acting against an antagonist or an opposing force: *opponent armies.* **2.** Opposite. [Latin *oppōnēns,* present participle of *oppōnere,* OPPOSE.] —**op·po'nen·cy** *n.*

Synonyms: *opponent, adversary, antagonist, competitor, rival.* These nouns all describe persons engaged in contests or struggles. *Opponent,* somewhat impersonal, means one who takes a contrary position. *Adversary* suggests a more formidable opponent and can imply animosity, while an *antagonist* is an actively hostile opponent. *Competitor,* a milder word, suggests a person trying to outdo one or more opponents, as in sports or business. *Rival* most frequently implies a single, more personal opponent. Rivals are opponents competing for an objective.

op·por·tune (ŏp′ər-to͞on′, -tyo͞on′) *adj.* **1.** Suited or right for a particular purpose: *an opportune meeting.* **2.** Occurring at a time that is fitting or advantageous: *Wait for the opportune moment.* [Middle English, from Old French *opportun,* from Latin *opportūnus,* seasonable, (originally of wind) "blowing toward the harbor" : *ob,* to + *portus,* harbor (see **per-**[2] in Appendix*).] —**op'por·tune'ly** *adv.* —**op'por·tune'ness** *n.*

op·por·tun·ist (ŏp′ər-to͞o′nĭst, -tyo͞o′nĭst) *n.* A person who takes advantage of any opportunity to achieve an end, usually with little or no regard for moral principles. [French *opportuniste,* from *opportunisme,* from Italian *opportunismo,* from *opportuno,* opportune, from Latin *opportūnus,* OPPORTUNE.] —**op'por·tun'ism'** *n.* —**op'por·tun·is'tic** *adj.*

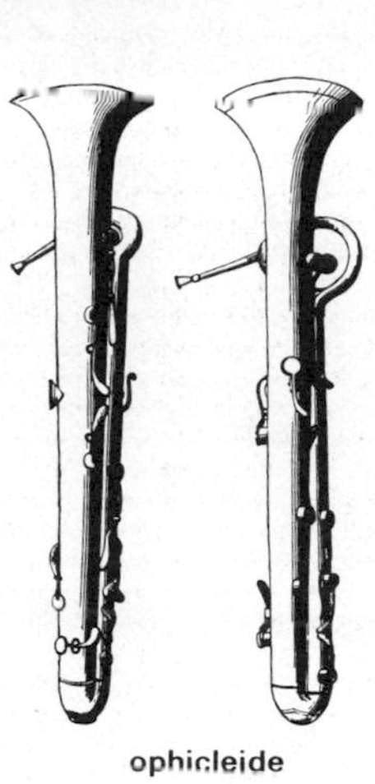

ophicleide

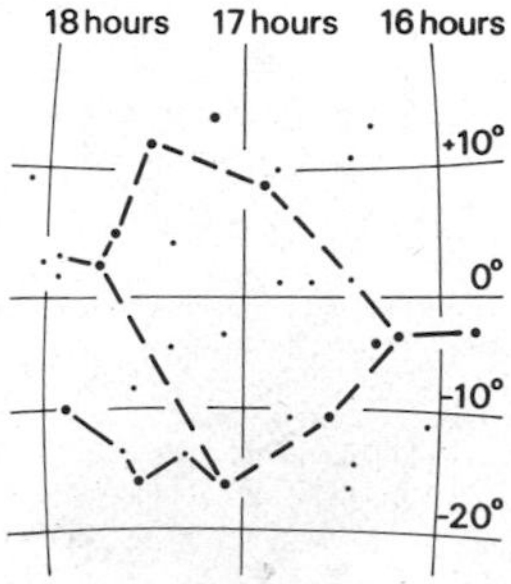

Ophiuchus

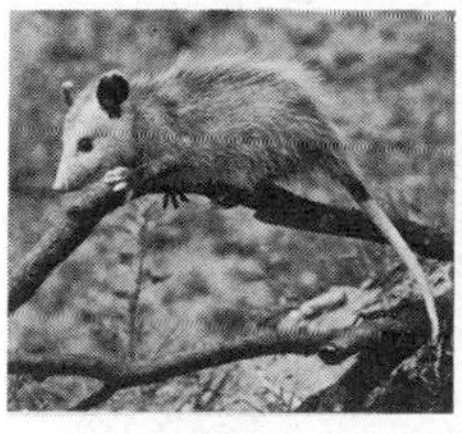

opossum
Didelphis marsupialis

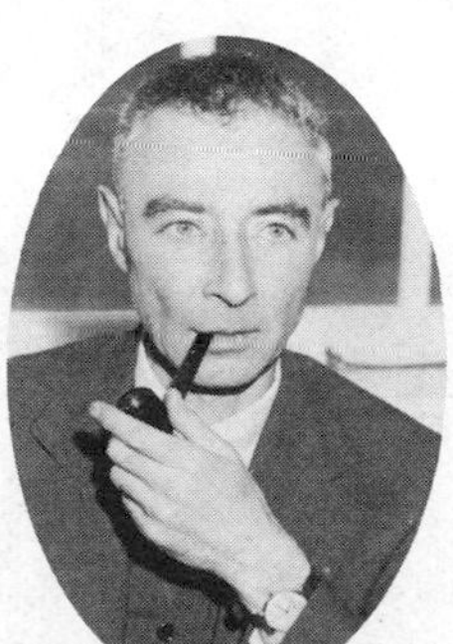

J. Robert Oppenheimer

op·por·tu·ni·ty (ŏp′ər-to͞o′nə-tē, -tyo͞o′nə-tē) *n., pl.* **-ties.** A favorable or advantageous combination of circumstances; suitable occasion or time. [Middle English *opportunite*, from Old French, from Latin *opportūnitās*, from *opportūnus*, OPPORTUNE.]
Synonyms: *opportunity, occasion, opening, chance, break.* All these nouns refer to a favorable time or circumstance. An *opportunity* is the right moment to take action toward a definite goal. *Occasion*, weaker than *opportunity*, suggests the proper time for action: *The victory was the occasion for celebrating.* An *opening* is either an unexpected or awaited opportunity to embark on a new career or to launch an enterprise. *Chance* implies luck or accident in the arrival of an opportunity. *Break*, an informal word, adds to *chance* the idea that adverse circumstances have unexpectedly become favorable.
Usage: *Opportunity* is often followed by *for, of,* or *to,* as in *opportunity for* (or *of*) *writing, opportunity to write.*

op·pos·a·ble (ə-pō′zə-bəl) *adj.* **1.** Capable of being opposed. **2.** Capable of being placed opposite or in opposition to something: *The thumb is an opposable digit.* —**op·pos′a·bil′i·ty** *n.*

op·pose (ə-pōz′) *v.* **-posed, -posing, -poses.** —*tr.* **1.** To be in contention or conflict with; combat; resist: *oppose the enemy force.* **2.** To be against; be hostile to: *oppose new ideas.* **3.** To place in opposition, or be in opposition to; contrast or counterbalance by antithesis. **4.** To move so as to be opposite something else; place in contraposition. —*intr.* To act or be in opposition to something. [French *opposer*, from Old French, from Latin *oppōnere* (past participial stem *opposit-*), to set against : *ob*, against + *pōnere*, to put (see **apo-** in Appendix*).] —**op·pos′er** *n.*
Synonyms: *oppose, resist, withstand, combat, contest.* Acting against someone or something is implied by all these verbs. *Oppose* simply states disagreement and does not suggest the method of opposition. *Resist* and *withstand* primarily imply taking action against an opposing force. *Resist* often suggests a struggle within oneself: *resist temptation. Withstand* implies successful resistance: *withstand a shock; withstand a siege. Combat* implies physical action: *combat an enemy; combat a disease. Contest* more aptly applies to an intellectual or legal struggle and emphasizes protest: *contest a will; contest an election.*

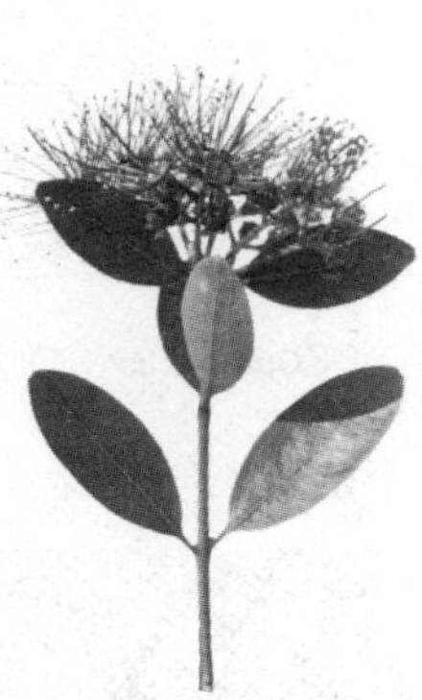

opposite
Opposite leaves of an ironwood of the genus *Metrosideros*

op·po·site (ŏp′ə-zĭt) *adj. Abbr.* **op., opp. 1.** Placed or located directly across from something else or from each other; lying in corresponding positions from an intervening space or object: *opposite sides of a building.* **2.** Facing the other way; moving or tending away from each other: *opposite directions.* **3.** Contrary or antithetical in nature or tendency; diametrically opposed; altogether different. **4.** *Botany.* Growing in pairs on either side of a stem. Said especially of leaves. Compare **alternate.** —*n.* **1.** A person or thing that is opposite or contrary to another. See Usage note below. **2.** *Archaic.* An opponent or antagonist. —*adv.* In an opposite position or positions: *They sat opposite at the table.* —*prep.* **1.** Across from or facing: *Park your car opposite the bank.* **2.** In a complementary dramatic role to: *She played opposite him.* [Middle English, from Old French, from Latin *oppositus*, from the past participle of *oppōnere*, OPPOSE.] —**op′po·site·ly** *adv.* —**op′po·site·ness** *n.*
Synonyms: *opposite, contrary, antithetical, contradictory.* These adjectives have the common meaning of being irreconcilably set apart. When two things have a definite relationship and yet differ to the extent of revealing marked contrast, they are *opposite: opposite sides of the street; opposite points of view. Contrary* stresses extreme divergence and may imply stubbornness. *Antithetical* emphasizes sharp, diametrical opposition, usually intellectual. *Contradictory* implies denial of one view by another.
Usage: *Opposite*, as a noun, may be followed by *of*, as in *The opposite of right is wrong.* As an adjective it may be followed by *to* or *from*, as in *This is opposite to* (or *from*) *my belief.* It is never followed by *than.*

opposite number. A person who holds a position in an organization which corresponds to that of a person in another organization.

op·po·si·tion (ŏp′ə-zĭsh′ən) *n.* **1.** The act or condition of opposing or of being in conflict; resistance or antagonism. **2. a.** A position or location opposite to or facing another. **b.** Placement in such a position or location. **3.** That which is or serves as an obstacle. **4.** *Often capital* **O.** A political party or organized group opposed to the group, party, or government in power. **5.** *Astronomy.* **a.** A geometric configuration in which the earth lies on a straight line between the sun and a planet. **b.** The position of the exterior planet in this configuration. **6.** *Logic.* The relation existing between two propositions having an identical subject and predicate but differing in quantity, quality, or both. **7.** *Linguistics.* Contrast between two phonemes or other elements of a language that have a relationship such that the contrast is significant. [Middle English *opposicioun* (only in the astronomical sense), from Old French *opposition*, from Medieval Latin *oppositiō*, from Latin, act of opposing, from *oppōnere* (past participial stem *opposit-*), OPPOSE.] —**op′po·si′tion·al** *adj.* —**ŏp′po·si′tion·ist** *n.*

op·press (ə-prĕs′) *tr.v.* **-pressed, -pressing, -presses. 1.** To subjugate or persecute by unjust or tyrannical use of force or authority. **2.** To weigh heavily upon, especially so as to depress the mind or spirits: *"a hideous dizziness oppressed me at the mere idea"* (Poe). **3.** *Obsolete.* To overwhelm or crush. [Middle English *oppressen*, from Old French *oppresser*, from Medieval Latin *oppressāre*, frequentative of Latin *opprimere* (past participle *oppressus*), to press against : *ob*, against + *premere*, to press (see **per-**[6] in Appendix*).] —**op·pres′sor** (ə-prĕs′ər) *n.*

op·pres·sion (ə-prĕsh′ən) *n.* **1.** The act of oppressing, or the state of being oppressed. **2.** That which oppresses or burdens. **3.** A feeling of being heavily weighed down, either mentally or physically; depression; weariness.

op·pres·sive (ə-prĕs′ĭv) *adj.* **1.** Difficult to bear; harsh; tyrannical. **2.** Causing a state of physical or mental distress: *an oppressive afternoon.* —See Synonyms at **burdensome.** [Medieval Latin *oppressīvus*, from Latin *opprimere*, OPPRESS.] —**op·pres′sive·ly** *adv.* —**op·pres′sive·ness** *n.*

op·pro·bri·ous (ə-prō′brē-əs) *adj.* **1.** Expressing or carrying a sense of disgrace or contemptuous scorn: *opprobrious epithets.* **2.** Shameful; infamous. [Middle English, from Old French *opprobreus*, from Late Latin *opprobriōsus*, from Latin *opprobrium*, OPPROBRIUM.] —**op·pro′bri·ous·ly** *adv.*

op·pro·bri·um (ə-prō′brē-əm) *n.* **1.** Disgrace inherent in or arising from shameful conduct; ignominy. **2.** Scornful reproach or contempt: *a term of opprobrium.* **3.** A cause of shame or disgrace. —See Synonyms at **disgrace.** [Latin, "a reproach against," dishonor : *ob*, against + *probrum*, reproach, infamy (see **bher-**[1] in Appendix*).]

op·pugn (ə-pyo͞on′) *tr.v.* **-pugned, -pugning, -pugns.** To oppose, contradict, or call into question. [Middle English *oppugnen*, from Latin *oppugnāre*, to fight against : *ob*, against + *pugnāre*, to fight (see **peuk-** in Appendix*).] —**op·pugn′er** *n.*

op·sin (ŏp′sən) *n.* The protein constituent of **rhodopsin** *(see).*

-opsis. Indicates view, appearance, or resemblance; for example, **coreopsis.** [Greek, from *opsis*, sight, appearance. See **okw-** in Appendix.*]

op·son·ic (ŏp-sŏn′ĭk) *adj.* Of, pertaining to, or having the effect of opsonin. [OPSON(IN) + -IC.]

op·son·i·fy (ŏp-sŏn′ə-fī′) *tr.v.* **-fied, -fying, -fies.** To make (bacteria) susceptible to phagocytosis by opsonic action; opsonize. [OPSON(IN) + -FY.] —**op·son′i·fi·ca′tion** *n.*

op·so·nin (ŏp′sə-nĭn) *n.* A substance naturally present in the blood that renders bacteria susceptible to phagocytosis. [From Latin *opsōnium*, relish (opsonin being a "relish" enabling the body to "digest" bacteria), indirectly from Greek *opsōnein*, to buy food or delicacies, from *opson*†, relish, delicacy.]

op·so·nize (ŏp′sə-nīz′) *tr.v.* **-nized, -nizing, -nizes. 1.** To form opsonins in. **2.** To opsonify. [From OPSONIN.]

-opsy. Indicates an examination; for example, **biopsy.** [New Latin *-opsia*, condition of the eyes, examination, from Greek, from *opsis*, sight, appearance. See **okw-** in Appendix.*]

opt (ŏpt) *intr.v.* **opted, opting, opts.** To make a choice or decision. [French *opter*, from Latin *optāre*. See **op-**[2] in Appendix.*]

opt. 1. optative. **2.** optical; optician; optics. **3.** optimum. **4.** optional.

op·ta·tive (ŏp′tə-tĭv) *adj.* **1.** Expressing a wish or choice. **2.** *Abbr.* **opt.** *Grammar.* **a.** Denoting a mood of verbs in some languages, such as Greek, used to express a wish. **b.** Designating a statement using a verb in the subjunctive mood to indicate a wish or desire; for example, *Had I the means, I would do it.* —*n. Abbr.* **opt.** *Grammar.* **1.** The optative mood. **2.** A verb or expression in this mood. [Middle English, from Old French *optatif*, from Late Latin *optātīvus*, from Latin *optāre*, to choose, wish. See **op-**[2] in Appendix.*] —**op′ta·tive·ly** *adv.*

op·tic (ŏp′tĭk) *adj.* **1.** Of or pertaining to the eye or to vision. **2.** Of or pertaining to the science of optics. —*n.* **1.** An eye. Not in technical use. **2.** Any of the components of an optical instrument. [Old French *optique*, from Medieval Latin *opticus*, from Greek *optikos*, from *optos*, visible. See **okw-** in Appendix.*]

op·ti·cal (ŏp′tĭ-kəl) *adj. Abbr.* **opt. 1.** Of or pertaining to sight: *an optical illusion.* **2.** Designed to assist sight: *optical instruments.* **3.** Of or pertaining to optics. —**op′ti·cal·ly** *adv.*

optical activity. *Chemistry.* A property of a substance that enables it to rotate the plane of incident polarized light.

optical fiber. A flexible optically transparent fiber, as of glass or plastic, through which light can be transmitted by successive internal reflections.

optical maser. *Physics.* A laser, especially one that produces visible radiation.

optic axis. *Crystallography.* An optical path through a crystal along which a ray of light can pass without undergoing double refraction.

op·ti·cian (ŏp-tĭsh′ən) *n. Abbr.* **opt. 1.** One who makes lenses and eyeglasses. **2.** One who sells lenses, eyeglasses, and other optical instruments. —See Usage note at **oculist.** [French *opticien*, from Medieval Latin *optica*, OPTICS.]

optic nerve. Either of two sensory nerves that connect the retinas of the eyes with the brain.

op·tics (ŏp′tĭks) *n.* Plural in form, used with a singular verb. *Abbr.* **opt.** *Physics.* The scientific study of light and vision, chiefly of the generation, propagation, and detection of electromagnetic radiation having wavelengths greater than x rays and shorter than microwaves. [Medieval Latin *optica*, from Greek *optika*, neuter plural of *optikos*, OPTIC.]

op·ti·mism (ŏp′tə-mĭz′əm) *n.* **1.** A tendency or disposition to expect the best possible outcome, or to dwell upon the most hopeful aspects of a situation: *"The incurable optimism of childhood"* (Frank O'Connor). **2.** *Philosophy.* **a.** The doctrine, asserted by Leibnitz, that our world is the best of all possible worlds. **b.** The belief that the universe is improving and that good will ultimately triumph over evil. [French *optimisme*, from Latin *optimum*, best, OPTIMUM.]

op·ti·mist (ŏp′tə-mĭst) *n.* **1.** One who habitually or in a particular case expects a favorable outcome. **2.** A believer in philosophical optimism. —**op′ti·mis′tic** *adj.* —**op′ti·mis′ti·cal·ly** *adv.*

op·ti·mize (ŏp′tə-mīz′) *tr.v.* **-mized, -mizing, -mizes.** To make the most effective use of.

op·ti·mum (ŏp′tə-məm) *n., pl.* **-ma** (-mə) or **-mums.** *Abbr.* **opt.** The best or most favorable condition, degree, or amount for a particular situation. —*adj.* Most favorable or advantageous; best. [Latin, from neuter of *optimus,* best. See **op-**[1] in Appendix.*] —**op′ti·mal** *adj.* —**op′ti·mal·ly** *adv.*

op·tion (ŏp′shən) *n.* **1.** The act of choosing; choice. **2.** The power or right of choosing; freedom to choose. **3. a.** The exclusive right, usually obtained for a fee, to buy or sell property within a specified time and at a specified price. **b.** By contract, the privilege of demanding a specified fulfillment during a specified future time. **c.** A right to buy or sell specific securities at a specified price within a specified time. **d.** A clause in an insurance policy permitting the policyholder to specify the manner in which payments are to be made or credited to him. **4.** Something chosen or available as a choice. —See Synonyms at **choice.** [French, from Latin *optiō,* choice. See **op-**[2] in Appendix.*]

op·tion·al (ŏp′shən-əl) *adj. Abbr.* **opt.** Left to choice; not compulsory or automatic. —**op′tion·al·ly** *adv.*

option play. *Football.* An offensive play in which either a back or the fullback has the choice of running with the ball or throwing a forward pass.

op·tom·e·trist (ŏp-tŏm′ə-trĭst) *n.* One who specializes in optometry. See Usage note at **oculist.**

op·tom·e·try (ŏp-tŏm′ə-trē) *n.* The profession of examining, measuring, and treating certain visual defects by means of corrective lenses or other methods that do not require license as a physician. [Greek *optos,* visible (see **okw-** in Appendix*) + -METRY.] —**op′to·met′ric** (ŏp′tə-mĕt′rĭk), **op′to·met′ri·cal** *adj.*

op·u·las·ter (ŏp′yə-lăs′tər) *n.* A shrub, the **ninebark** *(see).* [Origin unknown.]

op·u·lent (ŏp′yə-lənt) *adj.* **1.** Having or characterized by great wealth; rich; affluent. **2. a.** Abundant; plentiful; luxuriant; profuse; lavish. **b.** Characterized by fullness and vitality. [Latin *opulentus.* See **op-**[1] in Appendix.*] —**op′u·lent·ly** *adv.* —**op′u·lence, op′u·len·cy** *n.*

o·pun·ti·a (ō-pŭn′shē-ə, -shə) *n.* **1.** Any of various cacti of the genus *Opuntia.* **2.** A **prickly pear** *(see).* [New Latin, from Latin, an herb, after *Opus* (stem *Opunt-*), ancient city of Locris, Greece, where it grew abundantly.]

o·pus (ō′pəs) *n., pl.* **opera** (ō′pər-ə, ŏp′ər-ə) or **opuses.** *Often capital* **O.** *Abbr.* **op., Op.** A creative work; especially, a musical composition. Used with a number to designate the order of a composer's works. [Latin, work. See **op-**[1] in Appendix.*]

o·pus·cule (ō-pŭs′kyōōl) *n.* A small and minor work. [French, from Latin *opusculum,* diminutive of *opus,* work, OPUS.]

o·quas·sa (ō-kwăs′ə, ō-kwä′sə) *n., pl.* **oquassa** or **-sas.** A freshwater fish, *Salvelinus oquassa,* found in the Rangeley Lakes in Maine. [After *Oquassa,* one of the Rangeley Lakes.]

or[1] (ôr; *unstressed* ər) *conj.* Used to indicate: **1. a.** An alternative, usually only before the last term of a series: *hot or cold; this, that, or the other.* **b.** The second of two alternatives, the first being preceded by *either* or *whether: Your answer is either ingenious or wrong. She didn't know whether to laugh or cry.* **c.** *Archaic.* The first of two alternatives, with the force of *either* or *whether: "Tell me where is fancy bred/ Or in the heart or in the head?"* (Shakespeare). **2.** A synonymous or equivalent expression: *acrophobia, or fear of great heights.* **3.** Uncertainty or indefiniteness: *two or three.* [Middle English *or,* contraction of *other,* alteration (influenced by EITHER, WHETHER) of Old English *oththe,* from Common Germanic.]

Usage: When all of the elements connected by *or* are singular, the verb they govern must be singular: *Tom or Jack is coming. Beer or ale or wine is included in the charge.* When the elements are all plural, the verb is plural. When the elements do not agree in number, or when one or more of the elements is a personal pronoun, the verb is governed by the element to which it is nearer: *Tom or his brothers are going. Cold symptoms or headache is the usual first sign. He or we are likely to be asked.* See Usage notes at **either, neither, nor.**

or[2] (ôr) *conj. Archaic.* Before. Followed by *ever* or *ere: "I doubt he will be dead or ere I come."* (Shakespeare). —*prep. Archaic.* Before. [Middle English *ar, or,* Old English *ār,* early, before, from Old Norse. See **ayer** in Appendix.*]

or[3] (ôr) *n. Heraldry.* Gold, represented in engraving by a white field sprinkled with small dots. —*adj.* Of gold. Used after the noun: *a bezant or.* [Old French, from Latin *aurum.* See **aurum** in Appendix.*]

-or[1]. Indicates the person or thing performing the action expressed by the root verb; for example, **percolator, investor.** [Middle English *-our, -or,* from Old French *-eor, -eur,* partly from Latin *-or,* and partly from Latin *-ātor* (past participial stem *-āt-* + *-or*).]

-or[2]. Also *British* **-our.** Used to form nouns indicating a state, quality, or activity; for example, **behavior.** [Middle English *-or, -our,* from Old French *-eur,* from Latin *-or,* abstract suffix.]

OR Oregon (with Zip Code).

Or. Oregon (unofficial).

o·ra. Plural of **os** (mouth).

or·ach (ôr′ĭch, ŏr′-) *n.* Also **or·ache** (ôr′ĭch, ŏr′-). Any of various plants of the genus *Atriplex;* especially, *A. hortensis,* whose edible leaves resemble spinach. [Middle English *arage, orage,* from Old French *arrache,* modification of Vulgar Latin *atrapica* (unattested), variant of Latin *atriplex,* from Greek *atraphaxus*†.]

or·a·cle (ôr′ə-kəl, ŏr′-) *n.* **1.** A shrine consecrated to the worship and consultation of a prophetic god, such as that of Apollo at Delphi. **2.** The priest or other transmitter of prophecies at such a shrine. **3.** A prophecy made known at such a shrine, often in the form of an enigmatic statement or allegory. **4.** Any person or agency considered to be a source of wise counsel or prophetic opinions; an infallible authority or judge. **5.** *Theology.* A command or revelation from God. **6.** In the Old Testament, the sanctuary of the Temple. I Kings 6:16, 19–23. [Middle English, from Old French, from Latin *ōrāculum,* from *ōrāre,* to speak. See **ōr-** in Appendix.*]

o·rac·u·lar (ô-răk′yə-lər, ō-răk′-) *adj.* **1.** Of, pertaining to, or being an oracle. **2.** Resembling or characteristic of an oracle: **a.** Solemnly prophetic: *an oracular warning.* **b.** Brief and enigmatic; mysterious: *a gloomy child, given to oracular remarks.* [From Latin *ōrāculum,* ORACLE.] —**o·rac′u·lar·ly** *adv.*

O·ra·dea (ô-rä′dyä). A city in northwestern Rumania. Population, 112,000.

o·ral (ôr′əl, ōr′-) *adj.* **1.** Spoken, rather than written. See Usage note at **verbal.** **2.** Of or pertaining to the mouth: *oral hygiene.* **3.** Used in or taken through the mouth: *an oral thermometer; oral vaccine.* **4.** Consisting of or using speech: *oral instruction.* **5.** Designating a speech sound emitted through the mouth only, with the nasal passages closed. **6.** *Psychology.* Of, pertaining to, or denoting the first stage of psychosexual development of the infant, when sexual gratification is derived chiefly from stimulation of the mouth parts. —*n. Often plural.* A school or college examination in which questions and answers are spoken rather than written. [From Latin *ōs* (stem *ōr-*), the mouth. See **ōs-** in Appendix.*] —**o′ral·ly** *adv.*

oral contraceptive. *Medicine.* Any of various hormone compounds in pill form, used in specific sequence to prevent ovulation and conception. Informally called "the Pill."

O·ran (ō-răn′, ō-rän′). A city and Mediterranean seaport in northwestern Algeria. Population, 93,000.

or·ange (ôr′ĭnj, ŏr′-) *n.* **1.** Any of several evergreen trees of the genus *Citrus,* cultivated in tropical and subtropical regions, and having fragrant white flowers and round fruit with a yellowish-red rind and a sectioned, pulpy interior; especially, *C. sinensis,* the sweet orange, and *C. aurantium,* the Seville or sour orange. **2.** The fruit of these trees, having a sweetish, acid juice. **3.** Any of several plants or trees resembling the orange in some respect, such as the **Osage orange** and the **mock orange** *(both of which see).* **4.** Any of a group of colors between red and yellow in hue, of medium lightness and moderate saturation. See **color.** [Middle English, from Old French *orenge, orange,* from Arabic *nāranj,* from Persian *nārang,* from Sanskrit *nāranga*†, orange, orange tree.] —**or′ange** *adj.*

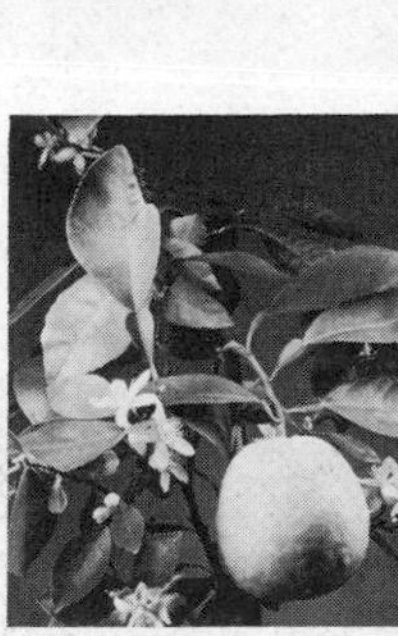

orange
Citrus aurantium

Or·ange (ôr′ĭnj). Also **Or·ange-Nas·sau** (-năs′ô). Name of a princely European family who have been rulers of the Netherlands since 1815.

or·ange·ade (ôr′ĭn-jād′, ŏr′-) *n.* A beverage of orange juice, sugar, and water. [French : ORANGE + -ADE.]

orange flower oil. An essential oil, **neroli** *(see).*

Orange Free State. *Afrikaans* **O·ran·je Vry·staat** (ô-rän′yə frü′stät′). Formerly **Orange River Colony.** *Abbr.* **O.F.S.** A province of the Republic of South Africa, 49,647 square miles in area, lying between the Orange River and the Vaal River. Population, 1,386,000. Capital, Bloemfontein.

orange hawkweed. A plant, *Hieracium aurantiacum,* native to Europe, having hairy leaves and clusters of orange-red flowers. Also called "devil's paintbrush."

Or·ange·man (ôr′ĭnj-mən, ŏr′-) *n., pl.* **-men** (-mĭn). **1.** A member of a Protestant secret society founded in Northern Ireland in 1795. **2.** Any Protestant Irishman. [After William, Prince of *Orange* (King William III of England).]

orange milkweed. **Butterfly weed** *(see).*

orange pekoe. **1.** A grade of black tea consisting of the end buds and their surrounding leaves. **2.** A grade of black tea consisting of small leaves obtained by screening. **3.** A grade of black tea consisting of the first two full leaves of the shoot.

Orange River. A river rising in Lesotho, southern Africa, and flowing 1,300 miles westward across South Africa to the Atlantic Ocean.

or·ange·ry (ôr′ĭnj-rē, ŏr′-) *n., pl.* **-ries.** A place where orange trees are cultivated, usually an enclosure or greenhouse. [French *orangerie,* from *orange,* from Old French, ORANGE.]

orange stick. A stick of orangewood, used in manicuring.

or·ange·wood (ôr′ĭnj-wŏŏd′, ŏr′-) *n.* The fine-grained wood of the orange tree, used in fine woodwork.

o·rang-u·tan (ō-răng′ə-tăn′, ə-răng′-) *n.* Also **o·rang-u·tan, o·rang-ou·tan, o·rang-u·tang** (ō-răng′ə-tăng′, ə-răng′-). An arboreal anthropoid ape, *Pongo pygmaeus,* of Borneo and Sumatra, having a shaggy reddish-brown coat, very long arms, and no tail. [Malay *orang hutan* : *ōrang,* man + *hūtan,* forest.]

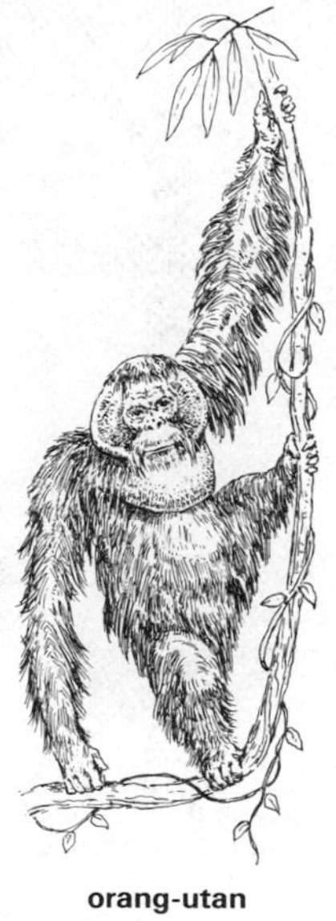

orang-utan

o·rate (ô-rāt′, ō-rāt′, ôr′āt′, ōr′āt′) *intr.v.* **orated, orating, orates.** To speak publicly in a pompous, oratorical manner: *"The Democrats orated and snarled"* (Eric F. Goldman). [Back-formation from ORATION.]

o·ra·tion (ô-rā′shən, ō-rā′-) *n.* **1.** A formal address or speech, especially one given on some special occasion such as a civic holiday, academic celebration, or funeral: *"the subject of my oration will be, Hail to Civil Law, and Death and Damnation to Military Domination"* (Conrad Richter). **2.** An address, written out and memorized, as for school or college speech contests. **3.** Any highflown speech. [Latin *ōrātiō,* from *ōrāre,* to speak. See **ōr-** in Appendix.*]

or·a·tor (ôr′ə-tər, ŏr′-) *n.* **1.** A person who delivers an oration. **2.** A person skilled in the art of public address. [Middle English *oratour,* from Old French *orateur,* from Latin *ōrātor,* from *ōrāre,* to speak. See **ōr-** in Appendix.*] —**or′a·tor·ship′** *n.*

or·a·tor·i·cal (ôr′ə-tôr′ĭ-kəl, ŏr′ə-tŏr′-) *adj.* Of or pertaining to an orator, or to oratory. —**or′a·tor′i·cal·ly** *adv.*

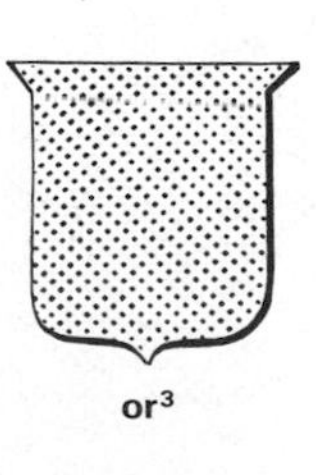

or[3]

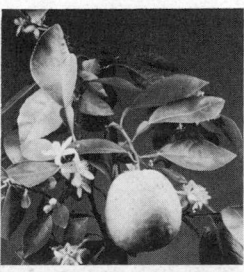

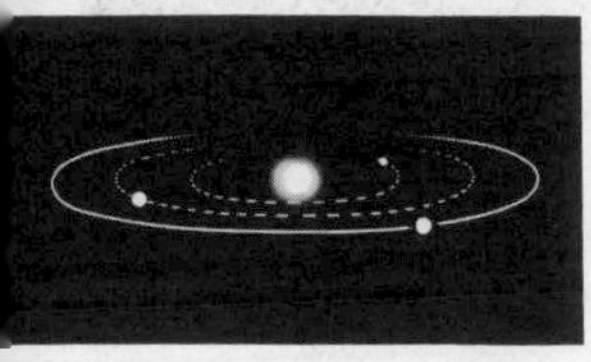

orbit
The orbits of Mercury, Venus, and Earth around the Sun, represented as if seen 100 million miles from Earth

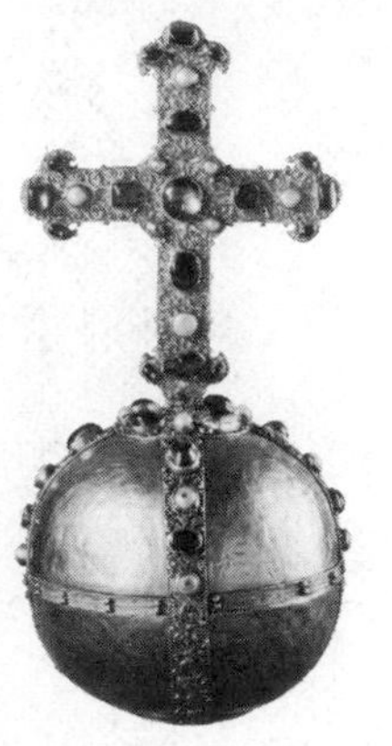

orb
Late 12th-century orb, part of the treasure of the Holy Roman Emperors

or·a·to·ri·o (ôr′ə-tôr′ē-ō′, -tōr′ē-ō′, ŏr′-) *n., pl.* **-os.** A musical composition for voices and orchestra, telling a sacred story. [Italian, from *Oratorio,* the Oratory of St. Philip Neri at Rome, where famous musical services were held in the 16th century, from Late Latin *ōrātōrium,* ORATORY (chapel).]

or·a·to·ry[1] (ôr′ə-tôr′ē, -tōr′ē, ŏr′-) *n.* **1.** The art of public speaking; rhetoric. **2.** Rhetorical style or skill, or an instance of it, especially as vain rhetoric: *"The demand for the cession of Canada had become largely a matter of Congressional oratory"* (W.L. Morton). [Old French *(art) oratoire,* from Latin *(ars) ōrātōria,* (the art) of public speaking, from *ōrātōrius,* of an orator, oratorical, from *ōrātor,* ORATOR.]

or·a·to·ry[2] (ôr′ə-tôr′ē, -tōr′ē, ŏr′-) *n., pl.* **-ries.** A place for prayer, such as a small private chapel. [Middle English *oratorie,* from Late Latin *ōrātōrium (templum),* (place) of prayer, from *ōrātōrius,* of praying, from Latin *ōrāre,* to pray, speak. See **ōr-** in Appendix.*]

orb (ôrb) *n.* **1. a.** A sphere. **b.** A compass of endeavor, influence, or activity; sphere; province: *"It* [Christianity] *has put the whole orb of reason into shade."* (Thomas Paine). **2. a.** A heavenly body. **b.** *Archaic.* The earth. **3.** One of a series of concentric transparent spheres revolving about the earth, postulated by medieval astronomers as support for the stars and planets. **4.** A jeweled globe surmounted by a cross, part of the regalia of a sovereign. **5.** An eye: *"These dark orbs shall no more treat with light"* (Milton). **6.** *Archaic.* A circle or an object of circular form. **7.** The orbit of a planet or satellite: *"Instruct the planets in what orbs to run."* (Pope). *—v.* **orbed, orbing, orbs.** *—tr.* **1.** To shape into a circle or sphere. **2.** *Archaic.* To encircle; enclose. *—intr.* To move in an orbit. [Old French *orbe,* from Latin *orbis*†, orb, disk.]

or·bic·u·lar (ôr-bĭk′yə-lər) *adj.* **1.** Orb-shaped; circular or spherical. **2.** *Botany.* Circular and flat, as a leaf. **3.** Rounded out; complete: *"The household ruin was thus full and orbicular."* (De Quincey). [Middle English *orbiculer,* from Old French *orbiculaire,* from Late Latin *orbiculāris,* from Latin *orbiculus,* diminutive of *orbis,* ORB.] **—or·bic′u·lar′i·ty** (ôr-bĭk′yə-lăr′ə-tē) *n.* **—or·bic′u·lar·ly** *adv.*

or·bic·u·late (ôr-bĭk′yə-lĭt, -lāt′) *adj.* Also **or·bic·u·lat·ed** (-lā′tĭd). Orbicular. [Latin *orbiculātus,* from *orbiculus,* diminutive of *orbis,* ORB.] **—or·bic′u·late·ly** *adv.*

or·bit (ôr′bĭt) *n.* **1.** The path of a celestial body or man-made satellite as it revolves around another body. **2.** The path of any body in a field of force surrounding another body; for example, the movement of an atomic electron in relation to a nucleus. **3. a.** A range of activity, experience, or knowledge: *one's social orbit.* **b.** A range of control or influence: *"What magnetism drew these quaking ruined creatures into his orbit?"* (Malcolm Lowry). **4.** Either of two bony cavities in the skull containing an eye and its external structures; eye socket. *—v.* **orbited, -biting, -bits.** *—tr.* **1.** To put into or cause to move in an orbit: *The first man-made satellite was orbited in 1957.* **2.** To revolve around (a center of attraction): *The moon orbits the earth. The designer orbited the fashion world.* *—intr.* To revolve or move in orbit. [Latin *orbita,* from *orbitus,* circular, from *orbis,* ORB.] **—or′bit·al** *adj.* **—or′bit·al·ly** *adv.*

orbital decay. The effect of atmospheric drag on an earth-orbiting satellite, causing eventual re-entry.

orbital velocity. The minimum velocity required to place a satellite in orbit about a celestial body.

orc (ôrk) *n.* A sea animal, the **grampus** *(see).* [Old French *orque,* from Latin *orca,* whale, probably from Greek *oruga,* accusative of *orux,* a pickax, hence (from its horn), narwhal, from *orussein,* to dig. See **ruk-**[2] in Appendix.*]

or·chard (ôr′chərd) *n.* **1.** An area of land devoted to the cultivation of fruit or nut trees. **2.** The trees cultivated in such an area. [Middle English *orchard,* Old English *ortceard, ortgeard* : Latin *hortus,* a garden (see **gher-**[2] in Appendix*) + Old English *geard,* yard (see **gher-**[2] in Appendix*).]

orchard grass. An Old World grass, *Dactylis glomerata,* widely planted in pastures.

or·ches·tra (ôr′kĭ-strə, ôr′kĕs′trə) *n. Abbr.* **orch. 1. a.** A large group of musicians who play together on various musical instruments, usually including strings, woodwinds, brass instruments, and percussion instruments. **b.** The instruments played by such a group of musicians. **2.** In theaters and concert halls, the area where the musicians sit, immediately in front of and below the stage. Also called "orchestra pit." **3. a.** The front section of seats nearest the orchestra pit in a theater. **b.** The entire main floor of a theater. Also called "parquet." **4.** In ancient Greek theaters, a semicircular space in front of the stage on which the chorus danced. [Latin *orchēstra,* from Greek *orkhēstra,* from *orkheisthai,* to dance. See **er-**[1] in Appendix.*] **—or·ches′tral** (ôr-kĕs′trəl) *adj.* **—or·ches′tral·ly** *adv.*

or·ches·trate (ôr′kĭ-strāt′) *tr.v.* **-trated, -trating, -trates. 1.** To compose or arrange (music) for performance by an orchestra. **2.** To arrange, put together, or organize so as to achieve a desired or effective combination. [French *orchestrer,* from *orchestre,* orchestra, from Latin *orchēstra,* ORCHESTRA.]

or·ches·tra·tion (ôr′kĭ-strā′shən) *n. Abbr.* **orch. 1.** A musical composition that has been orchestrated. **2.** Arrangement of music for performance by an orchestra.

or·ches·tri·on (ôr-kĕs′trē-ən) *n.* Also **or·ches·tri·na** (ôr′kĭ-strē′nə). A large mechanical musical instrument, resembling a barrel organ and producing sound in imitation of an orchestra. [ORCHESTR(A) + (MELOD)ION.]

or·chid (ôr′kĭd) *n.* **1.** Any of numerous epiphytic or terrestrial plants of the family Orchidaceae, found worldwide, but chiefly in the tropics, and often having brightly colored flowers of irregular and unusual shapes. **2.** The flower of one of these plants, especially one cultivated for ornament or personal adornment. **3.** Pale to light purple, from grayish to purplish pink to strong reddish purple. See **color.** [Latin *orchis* (stem *orchid-*), from Greek *orkhis,* testicle, hence (from the shape of its root) orchid. See **orghi-** in Appendix.*]

or·chi·da·ceous (ôr′kĭ-dā′shəs) *adj.* **1.** Of, relating to, or characteristic of the orchid family of plants. **2.** Suggesting ostentatious luxury; showy. [From New Latin *Orchidaceae* (family); *orchis,* ORCHID + -ACEOUS.]

orchid tree. 1. A small tree, *Bauhinia variegata,* native to southeastern Asia, and having showy lavender or purple flowers. **2.** A tree, *Amherstia nobilis,* of India, having compound leaves and a great profusion of large, yellow-spotted, scarlet flowers.

or·chil (ôr′kĭl, -chĭl) *n.* Also **ar·chil** (är′-). **1.** Any of several lichens, chiefly of the genera *Roccella* and *Lecanora,* from which a dye is obtained. **2.** The reddish dyestuff obtained from these lichens. [Middle English *orchell,* from Old French *orchel, orseille,* from Catalan *orxella, orcella,* from Spanish (Mozarabic) *orchella,* perhaps from Arabic.]

or·chis (ôr′kĭs) *n.* Any orchid of the genus *Orchis,* having magenta, white, or magenta-spotted flowers. [New Latin *Orchis,* from Latin, ORCHID.]

Or·cus (ôr′kəs). *Roman Mythology.* **1.** The world of the dead; Hades. **2.** The underworld god Pluto. [Latin *Orcus*†.]

ORD Airport code for O'Hare Field, Chicago, Illinois.

ord. 1. order. **2.** ordinal. **3.** ordinance. **4.** ordnance.

or·dain (ôr-dān′) *tr.v.* **-dained, -daining, -dains. 1. a.** To invest with ministerial or priestly authority; confer holy orders upon. **b.** To authorize as a rabbi. **2. a.** To order by virtue of superior authority. **b.** To decree as part of the order of nature or of the universe: *"From this hour I ordain myself loos'd of limits and imaginary lines."* (Walt Whitman). **3.** To prearrange unalterably; predestine: *by fate ordained.* [Middle English *ordeinen,* from Norman French *ordeiner,* from Late Latin *ōrdināre,* from Latin, to arrange in order, from *ōrdō* (stem *ōrdin-*), order. See **ar-** in Appendix.*] **—or·dain′er** *n.* **—or·dain′ment** *n.*

or·deal (ôr-dēl′) *n.* **1. a.** A severely difficult or painful experience that tests character or endurance. **b.** A trying experience: *"what he was undergoing was not a romantic adventure, but an unpleasant ordeal"* (A.A. Milne). **2.** A former method of legal trial in which the accused was subjected to physically painful or dangerous tests by way of determining guilt or innocence, the result being regarded as a divine judgment. [Middle English *ordal,* Old English *ordāl, ordēl.* See **dail-** in Appendix.*]

ordeal bark. The poisonous bark of an African tree, *Erythrophloeum guineense.* [From its use in trials by ordeal.]

ordeal bean. The **Calabar bean** *(see).*

ordeal tree. The **upas tree** *(see).*

or·der (ôr′dər) *n. Abbr.* **ord., O, O. 1.** A condition of logical or comprehensible arrangement among the separate elements of a group. **2. a.** A condition of methodical or prescribed arrangement among component parts, such that proper functioning or appearance is achieved. **b.** The state, condition, or disposition of a thing: *"There was at Wilton no state, no grand order"* (Boswell). **3. a.** The existing structures of a given society and the relations thereby defined among individuals and classes comprising it: *"Every revolution exaggerates the evils of the old order."* (C. Wright Mills). **b.** The condition in which these structures and relations are maintained and preserved by the rule of law and the police power of the state: *Order was restored after the riot.* **4.** A sequence or arrangement of successive things. **5.** The established sequence; customary procedure: *the order of worship.* **6.** A command or direction. **7.** *Military.* **a.** A command given by a superior officer requiring execution of a task or other obedience. **b.** *Plural.* Formal written instructions, usually issued by the Department of Defense, to report for duty at a specified time and place: *He received his orders to fly to Japan.* **8. a.** A commission or instruction to buy, sell, or supply something. **b.** That which is supplied, bought, or sold. **9.** A portion of food requested by a customer at a restaurant. **10.** *Law.* Any direction or command delivered by a court and entered into the court record, but not included in the final judgment or verdict. **11.** *Ecclesiastical.* **a.** Any of several grades of the Christian ministry: *the order of priesthood.* **b.** *Plural.* The office and rank of an ordained minister or priest. **c.** *Plural.* **Holy orders** *(see).* **12.** Any of the nine grades or choirs of angels. See **angel. 13.** *Abbr.* **O, O.** A monastic institution: *the Order of St. Benedict.* **14.** An organization of people united by some common fraternal bond or social aim: *the Benevolent and Protective Order of Elks.* **15. a.** A group of persons upon whom a government or sovereign has formally conferred honor for unusual service or merit, entitling such persons to wear a special insignia: *the Order of the Garter.* **b.** The insignia worn by such persons. **16.** *Usually plural.* A social class: *higher orders; lower orders.* **17.** Degree of quality or importance; distinction; rank: *poetry of a high order.* **18.** *Architecture.* **a.** Any of several specific styles of classical architecture characterized by the type of column employed, such as **Composite order, Corinthian order, Doric order, Ionic order, Tuscan order** *(all of which see).* **b.** A specific style of architecture: *a cathedral of the Gothic order.* **19.** *Biology.* A taxonomic category of plants and animals ranking above the family and below the class. See **taxonomy. 20.** *Mathematics.* **a.** An indicated number of successive differentiations to be performed. **b.** The number of elements in a finite group. **c.** The number of rows or columns in a determinant or matrix. Compare **degree. 21.** Approximate size or magnitude: *equipment costing on the order of a million dollars.* **—call to order. 1.** To request to be quiet and attentive. **2.** To begin a meeting. —In order that. So that. **in order to**. For the purpose of; so that; in order that. —**in short order**. Quickly; with no delay. —**on order**. Requested but not yet delivered. —**on the order of**. Similar to; like; resembling. —**out of order**. 1. Not working; broken. 2. Not according to rule or general procedure: *The objection is out of order.* —**to order**. According to the buyer's specifications. —*v.* **ordered, -dering, -ders.** —*tr.* 1. To issue a command or instruction to. 2. To give a command or instruction that (something) be done: *The judge ordered a recount of the ballots.* 3. To give an order for; request to be supplied with (something). 4. To put in a methodical and systematic arrangement. 5. To ordain: *He was ordered priest.* —*intr.* To give an order or orders; request that something be done or supplied: *Order now, before prices go up.* —See Synonyms at **command.** —**order arms.** *Military.* 1. To bring a rifle vertically against the right side of the body with the butt touching the ground. 2. The command to move the rifle to this position. [Middle English *ordre,* from Old French *ordre,* earlier *ord(e)ne,* from Latin *ōrdō* (stem *ōrdin-*). See **ar-** in Appendix.*] —**or'der·er** *n.*

or·der·ly (ôr′dər-lē) *adj.* 1. Having a methodical and systematic arrangement; tidy: *an orderly arrangement.* 2. Without violence or disruption; peaceful: *an orderly transition of governments.* 3. *Military.* Of or pertaining to the transmission of military orders. —*n., pl.* **orderlies.** 1. A male attendant in a hospital. 2. *Military.* A soldier assigned to attend upon a superior officer and carry orders or messages: *"Everybody dismounted, orderlies surged up to lead away the horses."* (Winston Churchill). —*adv.* Systematically; regularly. —**or'der·li·ness** *n.*

Synonyms: **orderly, methodical, systematic.** These mean procedural in manner or nature and imply neatness or efficiency. *Orderly* means correctly conducted, properly arranged, or peaceable, and is used particularly where disorder is considered possible: *orderly evacuation of the school. Methodical* means scrupulous in execution and planned or paced in a logical way, often slowly. Its emphasis on a set procedure may suggest plodding rigidity: *methodical study habits; a performance too methodical for romantic music. Systematic* is more impersonal and suggests efficiency, thoroughness, and precision. Often it also implies activity of rather broad scope: *systematic check of each candidate's campaign expenditures.*

order of magnitude. *Physics.* 1. An estimate of size or magnitude expressed as a power of ten: *The earth's mass is of the order of magnitude of 10^{22} tons; that of the sun 10^{27} tons.* 2. A range of values between a designated lower value and an upper value ten times as large: *The masses of the earth and the sun differ by five orders of magnitude.*

or·di·nal (ôrd′n-əl) *adj. Abbr.* **ord.** 1. Being of a specified position in a numbered series: *an ordinal rank of seventh.* 2. Pertaining to a biological order. —*n.* 1. An **ordinal number** (*see*). 2. *Ecclesiastical.* **a.** A book of instructions for daily services. **b.** A book of forms for ordination. [Late Latin *ōrdinālis,* from Latin *ōrdō* (stem *ōrdin-*), order. See **ar-** in Appendix.*]

ordinal number. A number indicating position in a series or order. The ordinal numbers are first (1st), second (2nd), third (3rd), etc. See **number.** Compare **cardinal number.**

or·di·nance (ôrd′n-əns) *n. Abbr.* **ord.** 1. An authoritative command or order. 2. A custom or practice established by long usage. 3. A religious rite; especially, Holy Communion. 4. A statute or regulation, especially as enacted by a city government. [Middle English *ordinaunce,* from Old French *ordenance,* "the art of arranging," from Medieval Latin *ōrdinantia,* from Latin *ōrdināns,* present participle of *ōrdināre,* to put in order, from *ōrdō,* order. See **ar-** in Appendix.*]

or·di·nar·i·ly (ôrd′n-ĕr′ə-lē, ôrd′n-ĕr′-) *adv.* 1. As a general rule; usually. 2. In the regular or usual manner: *ordinarily dressed.* 3. To the usual extent or degree: *ordinarily large profits.*

or·di·nar·y (ôrd′n-ĕr′ē) *adj.* 1. Commonly encountered; usual: *"a man to be sought for on great emergencies, but ill adapted for ordinary services"* (Trollope). 2. *Mathematics.* Designating a differential equation containing no more than two variables and derivatives of one with respect to the other. 3. Occurring regularly or periodically; normal. 4. Average in rank or merit; of no exceptional degree or quality; commonplace. 5. Having immediate rather than delegated jurisdiction, as a judge. —See Synonyms at **common.** —*n., pl.* **ordinaries.** 1. A person, object, or situation that is common, normal, or average. 2. *Law.* A judge or other official with immediate rather than delegated jurisdiction. 3. In some states of the United States, the judge of a probate court. 4. *Usually capital* **O.** *Ecclesiastical.* **a.** The part of the Mass that remains unchanged from day to day. Compare **proper.** **b.** A division of the Roman Breviary containing the unchangeable parts of the office other than the Psalms. **c.** A cleric, such as the residential bishop of a diocese, with ordinary jurisdiction in the external forum over a specified territory. 5. *Heraldry.* One of the simplest and commonest charges, such as the bend and the cross. —**out of the ordinary.** Extraordinary or exceptional; unusual; abnormal. [Middle English *ordinarie,* from Latin *ōrdinārius,* from *ōrdō* (stem *ōrdin-*), order. See **ar-** in Appendix.*] —**or'di·nar'i·ness** *n.*

ordinary seaman. *Abbr.* **O.S.** A seaman of the lowest grade in the merchant marine. Compare **able-bodied seaman.**

or·di·nate (ôrd′n-ĭt, -āt′) *adj.* Arranged in regular rows, as spots on an insect's wings. —*n. Symbol* **y** *Mathematics.* The plane Cartesian coordinate representing the distance from a specified point to the *x*-axis, measured parallel to the *y*-axis. [Latin *ōrdināre,* to arrange in order, from *ōrdō* (stem *ōrdin-*), order. See **ar-** in Appendix.*]

or·di·na·tion (ôrd′n-ā′shən) *n.* 1. *Ecclesiastical.* **a.** The cere-

mony during which a person is admitted to the ministry of a church. **b.** The admission itself. 2. Any proper arrangement.

ordn. ordnance.

ord·nance (ôrd′nəns) *n. Abbr.* **ord., ordn.** 1. Military weapons collectively, along with ammunition and the equipment to keep them in good repair. 2. Heavy guns; artillery. [Middle English *ordinaunce,* ORDINANCE.]

Ordnance Corps. A branch of the U.S. Army that designs, develops, procures, stores, maintains, and issues weapons.

or·do (ôr′dō) *n., pl.* **-dines** (-də-nēz′). *Roman Catholic Church.* An annual calendar containing instructions for the Mass and office to be celebrated on each day of the year. [Medieval Latin *ōrdō,* from Latin, order. See **ar-** in Appendix.*]

or·don·nance (ôr′də-nāns′) *n.* 1. The arrangement of elements in a literary or artistic composition, or architectural plan. 2. *French History.* **a.** Under the monarchy, a royal decree or body of laws on a specific subject. **b.** An order of a criminal court. [French, variant (influenced by *ordonner,* to order) of Old French *ordenance,* ORDINANCE.]

Or·do·vi·cian (ôr′də-vĭsh′ən) *adj. Geology.* Of, pertaining to, or designating the geologic time, system of rocks, and sedimentary deposits of the second period of the Paleozoic era, characterized by the appearance of primitive fishes. See **geology.** —*n. Geology.* The Ordovician period. Preceded by *the.* [After the *Ordovices,* an ancient Celtic tribe of North Wales, by analogy with SILURIAN.]

or·dure (ôr′jər, ôr′dyōōr) *n.* 1. Excrement; dung. 2. Something morally offensive; filth. [Middle English, from Old French, from *ord,* dirty, "disgusting," from Latin *horridus,* horrid, from *horrēre,* to shudder. See **ghers-** in Appendix.*]

Or·dzho·ni·kid·ze (ôr′jŏn-ə-kĭd′zə). Formerly **Dzau·dzhi·kau** (dzou-jē′kou′). A city of the Soviet Union and the capital of the North Ossetian A.S.S.R., in the south in the Caucasus mountains. Population, 202,000.

ore (ôr, ōr) *n.* A mineral or aggregate of minerals from which a valuable constituent, especially a metal, can be profitably mined or extracted. [Middle English *oor, or,* Old English *ār,* brass (in sense influenced by Old English *ora,* unwrought metal, ore). See **ayos-** in Appendix.*]

ö·re (œ′rə) *n., pl.* **öre.** A coin equal to ¹/₁₀₀ of the krona of Sweden and the krone of Denmark and Norway. See table of exchange rates at **currency.** [Danish and Norwegian *øre* and Swedish *öre,* from Latin *aureus,* gold coin, from *aurum,* gold. See **aurum** in Appendix.*]

Ore. Oregon (unofficial).

o·re·ad (ôr′ē-ăd′, ōr′-) *n. Greek Mythology.* A mountain nymph. [From Greek *Oreias* (stem *Oreiad-*), from *oreios,* of a mountain, from *oros,* mountain. See **oro-.**]

Ö·re·bro (œ′rə-brōō′). A city in south-central Sweden, on the western shore of Lake Hjälmaren. Population, 265,000.

Oreg. Oregon.

o·reg·a·no (ə-rĕg′ə-nō′, ô-rĕg′-) *n.* An herb seasoning made from the dried leaves of a species of marjoram, *Origanum vulgare.* [American Spanish *orégano,* from Spanish, marjoram, from Latin *origanum,* from Greek *origanon,* oregano, marjoram (probably from some North African language).]

Or·e·gon (ôr′ə-gən, -gŏn′, ōr′-). *Abbr.* **Oreg.** A Pacific northwestern state of the United States, 96,981 square miles in area, with a 300-mile coastline on the Pacific Ocean. It was admitted to the Union in 1859. Population, 1,769,000. Capital, Salem. See map at **United States of America.** —**Or'e·go'ni·an** (ôr′ə-gō′nē-ən, ōr′-) *adj. & n.*

Oregon Country. In the early 19th century, a region of northwestern North America comprising present-day Washington, Oregon, Idaho, western parts of Montana and Wyoming, and most of British Columbia, Canada.

Oregon fir. The **Douglas fir** (*see*).

Oregon grape. An evergreen shrub, *Mahonia aquifolium,* of northwestern North America, having fragrant yellow flowers and small, edible, bluish berries.

Oregon maple. A tree, *Acer macrophyllum,* of the Pacific coast of North America, having very large, lobed leaves.

Oregon myrtle. A tree, the **California laurel** (*see*).

Oregon pine. The wood of the **Douglas fir** (*see*).

Oregon Trail. The main route to the Oregon Country for settlers in the 1840's. It stretched over 2,000 miles from Independence, Missouri, to Astoria, Oregon, at the mouth of the Columbia River.

o·re·ide. Variant of **oroide.**

O·rel (ô-rĕl′; *Russian* ô-ryôl′). A city of the Russian S.F.S.R., on the Oka River in the southwest. Population, 183,000.

Ore Mountains. See **Erzgebirge.**

O·ren·burg. The former name for **Chkalov.**

O·res·tes (ô-rĕs′tēz) *n. Greek Mythology.* The son of Agamemnon and Clytemnestra, who, with his sister Electra, avenged his father's death by slaying his mother and Aegisthus.

Ö·re·sund (œ′rə-sŭn′). A strait between southern Sweden and eastern Denmark, connecting the Baltic Sea with the Kattegat.

ORF. Airport code for Norfolk, Virginia.

Orff (ôrf), **Carl.** Born 1895. German composer.

or·fray. Variant of **orphrey.**

org. 1. organic. 2. organization; organized.

or·gan (ôr′gən) *n.* 1. A musical instrument consisting of a keyboard and a number of pipes supplied with wind by means of bellows. Also called "pipe organ." 2. Any of various other instruments resembling the organ either in mechanism or sound, such as the electronic organ. 3. *Biology.* A differentiated part of an organism, adapted for a specific function. 4. Euphemism for penis. 5. An institution or medium through which or

Oregon grape

organ

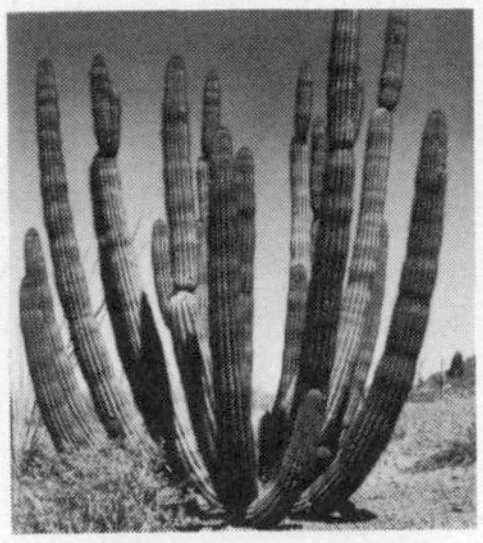

organ-pipe cactus

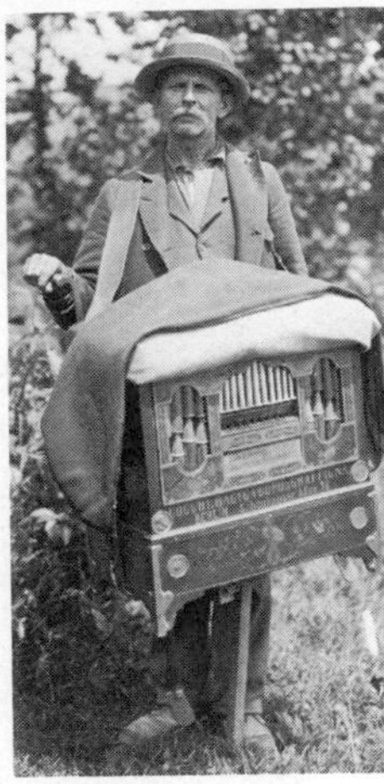

organ grinder

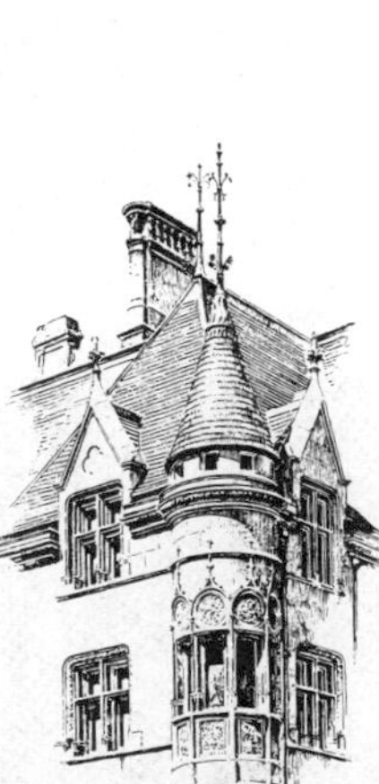

oriel
Sketch showing oriel on late 19th-century house designed by Richard Morris Hunt

by means of which some action is performed. **6.** An instrument or vehicle of communication; especially, a periodical publication issued by a political party, business firm, or other group. [Middle English, from Old French *organe*, from Late Latin *organum*, church organ, from Latin, implement, instrument, from Greek *organon*. See **werg-**[1] in Appendix.*]

or·ga·na. 1. Alternate plural of **organon. 2.** Alternate plural of **organum.**

or·gan·dy (ôr′gən-dē) *n., pl.* **-dies.** Also **or·gan·die.** A transparent crisp fabric of cotton or silk, used for trim, curtains, and for light apparel. [French *organdi*, possibly akin to *organsin*, ORGANZINE.]

or·gan·elle (ôr′gə-nĕl′) *n. Biology.* A specialized part of a cell that resembles and functions as an organ. [New Latin *organella*, diminutive of Latin *organum*, ORGAN.]

organ grinder. A street musician who plays a hurdy-gurdy.

or·gan·ic (ôr-găn′ĭk) *adj. Abbr.* **org. 1.** Of, pertaining to, or affecting an organ of the body. **2.** Of, pertaining to, or derived from living organisms. **3.** Having properties associated with living organisms. **4.** Likened to an organism in organization or development: *"he saw society as an organic whole, with the health of one part vitally necessary to the health of all the others"* (Richard B. Sewall). **5. a.** Of or constituting the essential part of something; constitutional; substantive. **b.** *Law.* Designating or pertaining to the fundamental laws and precepts of a government or organization. **6.** *Chemistry.* Of or designating carbon compounds. [Old French *organique*, from Late Latin *organicus*, from Greek *organikos*, serving as an instrument, from *organon*, implement, ORGAN.] **—or·gan′i·cal·ly** *adv.*

organic chemistry. The chemistry of carbon compounds.

organic gardening. A system of gardening that uses fertilizers and mulches consisting only of animal or vegetable matter.

or·gan·i·cism (ôr-găn′ə-sĭz′əm) *n.* **1.** The theory that all disease is associated with structural alterations of organs. **2.** The theory that the total organization of an organism, rather than the functioning of individual organs, is the principal or exclusive determinant of every life process. **3.** The concept that society is analogous to a biological organism. **—or·gan′i·cist** *n.*

or·gan·ism (ôr′gə-nĭz′əm) *n.* **1.** Any living individual; any plant or animal. **2.** Any system regarded as analogous to a living body: *the social organism.* [ORGAN + -ISM.] **—or′gan·is′mal** (ôr′gə-nĭz′məl), **or′gan·is′mic** *adj.*

or·gan·ist (ôr′gə-nĭst) *n.* One who plays the organ.

or·gan·i·za·tion (ôr′gə-nə-zā′shən) *n. Abbr.* **org. 1.** The act of organizing or the process of being organized. **2.** The state or manner of being organized: *a high degree of organization.* **3.** Something that has been organized or made into an ordered whole. **4.** Something comprising elements with varied functions that contribute to the whole and to collective functions; an organism. **5.** A number of persons or groups having specific responsibilities and united for some purpose or work. **—or′gan·i·za′tion·al** *adj.* **—or′gan·i·za′tion·al·ly** *adv.*

Organization of American States. *Abbr.* **OAS** An association formed (1948) by the 21 American republics to promote mutual cooperation.

or·gan·ize (ôr′gə-nīz′) *v.* **-ized, -izing, -izes.** *—tr.* **1.** To pull or put together into an orderly, functional, structured whole. **2. a.** To arrange or systematize: *organize one's thoughts before speaking.* **b.** To arrange in a desired pattern; provide with an organic structure: *"The painting is organized about a young reaper enjoying his noonday rest."* (William Carlos Williams). **3.** To arrange systematically for harmonious or united action: *organize a strike.* **4.** To establish as an organization: *organize a club.* **5. a.** To cause (employees) to form or join a labor union. **b.** To induce the employees of (a business or industry) to form or join a union: *organize a department store.* *—intr.* **1.** To develop into or assume an organic structure. **2.** To join or form a labor union or other group. [Middle English *organysen*, from Old French *organiser*, from Medieval Latin *organizāre*, from Latin *organum*, instrument, ORGAN.] **—or′gan·iz′er** *n.*

organo–. Indicates organ or organic; for example, **organology.** [Middle English, from Medieval Latin *organum*, organ of the body, from Latin, implement, ORGAN.]

or·gan·o·gen·e·sis (ôr′gə-nō-jĕn′ə-sĭs, ôr-găn′ə-) *n., pl.* **-ses** (-sēz′). The origin and development of biological organs. [New Latin : ORGANO- + -GENESIS.] **—or′gan·o·ge·net′ic** (-jə-nĕt′ĭk) *adj.* **—or′gan·o·ge·net′i·cal·ly** *adv.*

or·gan·og·ra·phy (ôr′gə-nŏg′rə-fē) *n.* The scientific description of the organs of animals and plants. [ORGANO- + -GRAPHY.] **—or′gan·o·graph′ic** (ôr′gə-nō-grăf′ĭk, ôr-găn′ə-), **or′gan·o·graph′i·cal** *adj.*

or·gan·o·lep·tic (ôr′gə-nō-lĕp′tĭk, ôr-găn′ə-) *adj.* Pertaining to or perceived by a sensory organ. [French *organoleptique* : ORGANO- + Greek *lēptikos*, receptive, from *lēptos*, to be apprehended (by the senses), from *lambanein*, to take, seize, apprehend (see **slagw-** in Appendix*).] **—or′gan·o·lep′ti·cal·ly** *adv.*

or·gan·ol·o·gy (ôr′gə-nŏl′ə-jē) *n.* The study of plant and animal organs and their functions. [ORGANO- + -LOGY.] **—or′gan·o·log′ic** (ôr′gə-nə-lŏj′ĭk, ôr-găn′ə-), **or′gan·o·log′i·cal** *adj.*

or·ga·non (ôr′gə-nŏn′) *n., pl.* **-na** (-nə) or **-nons.** Also **or·ga·num** (-nəm). *Philosophy.* A set of logical requirements for scientific demonstration. [Greek, tool. See **werg-**[1] in Appendix.*]

or·gan·o·ther·a·py (ôr′gə-nō-thĕr′ə-pē, ôr-găn′ō-) *n.* The treatment of disease with animal organs or extracts such as insulin and thyroxin. **—or′gan·o·ther′a·peu′tic** (-thĕr′ə-pyōō′tĭk) *adj.*

or·gan·ot·ro·pism (ôr′gə-nŏt′rə-pĭz′əm) *n.* Also **or·gan·ot·ro·py** (ôr′gə-nŏt′rə-pē). *Medicine.* The attraction of certain chemical compounds or microorganisms to specific tissues or organs of the body. [ORGANO- + -TROPISM.] **—or′gan·o·trop′ic** (ôr′gə-nō-trŏp′ĭk, ôr-găn′ō-) *adj.* **—or′gan·o·trop′i·cal·ly** *adv.*

or·gan-pipe cactus (ôr′gən-pīp′). A tall cactus, *Pachycereus marginatus*, of Mexico and the southwestern United States.

organ point. *Music.* **Pedal point** *(see).*

or·ga·num[1] (ôr′gə-nəm) *n., pl.* **-na** (-nə) or **-nums.** Any of several types of vocal polyphonic music, in two, three, or four parts, of the 9th to the early 13th century. [Medieval Latin, from Late Latin, ORGAN.]

or·ga·num[2]. Variant of **organon.**

or·gan·za (ôr-găn′zə) *n.* A sheer, stiff fabric of silk or synthetic material used for trimming, neckwear, or evening dresses. [Possibly akin to ORGANZINE.]

or·gan·zine (ôr′gən-zēn′) *n.* A raw-silk thread, usually used as a warp thread. [French *organsin*, from Italian *organzino*, probably after *Urgandi*, Urgench, an ancient city in western Uzbek S.S.R.]

or·gasm (ôr′găz′əm) *n.* **1.** The climax of sexual excitement, marked normally by ejaculation of semen by the male and by the release of tumescence in erectile organs of both sexes. **2.** Any intense excitement. [French *orgasme*, from Greek *orgasmos*, from *organ*, to swell (with lust), be excited. See **werg-**[2] in Appendix.*] **—or·gas′mic** (ôr-găz′mĭk), **or·gas′tic** *adj.*

or·geat (ôr′zhä′) *n.* A sweet flavoring of orange and almond used in cocktails and food. [French, from Old French, from Old Provençal *orjat*, from *orge*, barley, from Latin *hordeum*. See **ghers-** in Appendix.*]

or·gi·as·tic (ôr′jē-ăs′tĭk) *adj.* Of, pertaining to, or characteristic of an orgy. [Greek *orgiastikos*, from *orgiazein*, to hold secret rites, from *orgia*, secret rites. See **orgy.**]

or·gy (ôr′jē) *n., pl.* **-gies. 1.** *Often plural.* A secret rite in the cults of Demeter, Dionysus, or other Greek or Mediterranean deities, typically involving frenzied singing, dancing, drinking, and sexual activity. **2.** A revel involving unrestrained indulgence, especially sexual excesses. **3.** Excessive indulgence in any activity: *an orgy of reading.* [Originally in the plural *orgies*, from Old French, from Latin *orgia*, from Greek. See **werg-**[1] in Appendix.*]

or·i·bi (ôr′ə-bē, ŏr′-) *n., pl.* **oribi** or **-bis.** A small, brownish African antelope, *Ourebia ourebia.* [Afrikaans, said to be from a Hottentot word meaning "antelope."]

o·ri·el (ôr′ē-əl, ōr′-) *n.* A projecting bay window, supported from below with corbels or brackets. [Middle English *oriole*, *oriel*, from Old French *oriol*, from Medieval Latin *oriolum*†, upper chamber.]

o·ri·ent (ôr′ē-ənt, -ĕnt′, ōr′-) *n.* **1.** The east; eastern regions. **2.** *Capital* **O. a.** The countries of Asia, especially of eastern Asia. Compare **Occident. b.** In ancient times, the lands and regions east of the Mediterranean. **3. a.** The luster characteristic of a pearl of high quality. **b.** A pearl having this luster. *—adj.* **1.** *Poetic.* Eastern; oriental. **2.** Having exceptional quality and luster. Said of pearls and gems. **3.** *Archaic.* Rising; ascending: *"The orient moon of Islam"* (Shelley). *—v.* (ôr′ē-ĕnt′, ōr′-) **oriented, -enting, -ents.** Also **or·i·en·tate** (-ən-tāt′), **-tated, -tating, -tates.** *—tr.* **1.** To locate or place in a particular relation to the points of the compass: *orient the swimming pool north and south.* **2.** To cause to face the east; locate or place so as to face the east. **3.** To align or position with respect to a reference system. **4.** To discover the bearings of. Often used reflexively: *He oriented himself by finding a familiar landmark.* **5.** To cause to become familiar with or adjusted to facts, principles, or a situation. *—intr.* **1.** To turn toward the east. **2.** To become adjusted or aligned. [Middle English, from Old French, from Latin *oriēns*, rising, rising sun, east, from *orīrī*, to rise. See **er-**[1] in Appendix.*]

o·ri·en·tal (ôr′ē-ĕn′təl, ōr′-) *adj.* **1.** Eastern. **2.** *Usually capital* **O.** Pertaining to the countries or regions of the Orient or to their peoples, languages, or culture. **3.** *Capital* **O.** *Ecology.* Of or designating the zoographic region that includes tropical Asia and the adjacent islands of the Malay Archipelago. **4.** Lustrous and valuable. Said of gems, especially pearls. **5.** Pertaining to or designating precious varieties of corundum: *an oriental ruby.* *—n. Usually capital* **O.** An inhabitant of the Orient; especially, a native of an Oriental country or tribe. **—o′ri·en′tal·ly** *adv.*

O·ri·en·tal·ism (ôr′ē-ĕn′təl-ĭz′əm, ōr′-) *n.* Also **o·ri·en·tal·ism. 1.** A quality, mannerism, or custom peculiar to or characteristic of the Orient. **2.** Scholarly knowledge of eastern cultures, languages, and peoples. **—O′ri·en′tal·ist** *n.*

O·ri·en·tal·ize (ôr′ē-ĕn′təl-īz′, ōr′-) *v.* **-ized, -izing, -izes.** Also **o·ri·en·tal·ize.** *—tr.* To give an Oriental character or appearance to. *—intr.* To become Oriental; appear Oriental.

Oriental poppy. A plant, *Papaver orientale*, native to the Mediterranean region, and widely cultivated for its brilliant scarlet and black flowers.

Oriental rug. Any of numerous kinds of rug made by hand in the Orient.

o·ri·en·ta·tion (ôr′ē-ĕn-tā′shən, ôr′ē-ən-, ōr′-) *n.* **1.** The act of orienting or the state of being oriented. **2.** Location or position relative to the points of the compass. **3.** *Architecture.* The location of a church so that its longitudinal axis is from west to east and its main altar at the eastern end. **4.** The line or direction followed in the course of a trend, movement, or development. **5.** An adjustment or adaptation to a new environment, situation, custom, or set of ideas. **6.** *Psychology.* Individual awareness of the objective world in its relation to the self. **7.** Introductory instruction concerning a new situation.

O·ri·en·te (ō′rē-ĕn′tā). The easternmost province of Cuba, 14,132 square miles in area, where Fidel Castro organized the overthrow of Fulgencio Batista (1959). Population, 2,444,000. Capital, Santiago de Cuba.

ă pat/ā pay/âr care/ä father/b bib/ch church/d deed/ĕ pet/ē be/f fife/g gag/h hat/hw which/ĭ pit/ī pie/îr pier/j judge/k kick/l lid, needle/m mum/n no, sudden/ng thing/ŏ pot/ō toe/ô paw, for/oi noise/ou out/ŏŏ took/ōō boot/p pop/r roar/s sauce/sh ship, dish/

or·i·fice (ôr′ə-fĭs, ŏr′-) *n.* A mouth or vent; an aperture of a cavity. [Old French, from Late Latin *ōrificium* : Latin *ōs* (stem *ōr-*), mouth (see **ōs-** in Appendix*) + *facere,* to make (see **dhē-**[1] in Appendix*).]

or·i·flamme (ôr′ə-flăm′, ŏr′-) *n.* Also **aur·i·flamme.** **1.** The red or orange-red flag of the Abbey of St. Denis, France, used as a standard by the early kings of France. **2.** Any inspiring standard or symbol. [Middle English *oriflamble,* from Old French *oriflambe,* from Medieval Latin *auriflamma* : Latin *aurum,* gold (see **aurum** in Appendix*) + *flamma,* FLAME.]

orig. original; originally.

o·ri·ga·mi (ôr′ĭ-gä′mē) *n.* **1.** The art or process, originating in Japan, of folding paper into flower, bird, or other shapes. **2.** A decorative object made in this way. Compare **kirigami.** [Japanese : *ori,* a folding + *-gami,* from *kami,* paper.]

Or·i·gen (ôr′ə-jən, ŏr′-). A.D. 185?–254? Christian teacher and theologian, born in Alexandria.

or·i·gin (ôr′ə-jĭn, ŏr′-) *n.* **1.** That from which anything derives its existence; a source or cause. **2.** Parentage; ancestry; derivation: *"We cannot escape our origins, however hard we try."* (James Baldwin). **3.** A coming into being. **4.** *Anatomy.* The point of attachment of a muscle. **5.** *Mathematics.* The point of intersection of coordinate axes, as in the **Cartesian coordinate system** *(see).* [Middle English *origyne,* from Latin *origō* (stem *origin-*), from *orīrī,* to rise. See **er-**[1] in Appendix.*]

Synonyms: *origin, inception, source, root.* These nouns relate to beginnings. *Origin,* applicable to persons as well as things, indicates the often remote place and time when something began. *Inception,* more specific, marks the actual start of an action or process. *Source,* also more specific, stresses the place from which something is derived or comes into being. It may also denote a person or printed work considered as a giver of information. *Root* usually refers to beginnings in the sense of fundamental cause or basic reason for something of consequence.

o·rig·i·nal (ə-rĭj′ən-əl) *adj. Abbr.* **orig. 1.** Of or pertaining to the beginning of something; initial; first. **2.** Fresh and unusual; not copied; new: *"some verses written by a famous painter which were original and not conventional"* (Emerson). **3.** Able to produce new things; able to think of and present new ideas; creative; inventive. **4.** Designating that from which a copy, reproduction, or translation is made. —See Synonyms at **new.** —*n. Abbr.* **orig. 1.** The primary form of anything from which varieties arise: *Later models retained many features of the original.* **2.** An authentic work of art, literature, or the like, as distinguished from a copy or reproduction. **3.** One that is the model for an artistic or literary work. **4.** A peculiar, especially an eccentric person. [Middle English, from Old French, from Latin *originālis,* from *origō,* ORIGIN.]

o·rig·i·nal·i·ty (ə-rĭj′ə-năl′ə-tē) *n., pl.* **-ties. 1.** The quality of being original. **2.** The capacity to act or think independently. **3.** Something original.

o·rig·i·nal·ly (ə-rĭj′ən-əl-ē) *adv. Abbr.* **orig. 1.** With reference to origin. **2.** At first. **3.** In a highly distinctive manner.

original sin. *Theology.* **1.** The tendency to evil inherent in human beings as a result of Adam's first act of disobedience. **2.** *Roman Catholic Church.* The state of deprivation from grace resulting from Adam's sinful disobedience.

o·rig·i·nate (ə-rĭj′ə-nāt′) *v.* **-nated, -nating, -nates.** —*tr.* To bring into being; create; invent. —*intr.* To come into being; start; spring. —**o·rig′i·na′tion** *n.* —**o·rig′i·na′tor** (-nā′tər) *n.* —**o·rig′i·na′tive** *adj.* —**o·rig′i·na′tive·ly** *adv.*

o·ri·na·sal (ôr′ĭ-nā′zəl, ŏr′-) *adj. Phonetics.* Pronounced with both nasal and oral passages open. —*n. Phonetics.* A sound, such as a French nasal vowel, pronounced in this way. [Latin *ōs* (stem *ōr-*), mouth (see **ōs-** in Appendix*) + NASAL.]

O·ri·no·co (ôr′ə-nō′kō, ōr′-). A river rising in southeastern Venezuela and flowing 1,500 miles first west, then north, and then east to the Atlantic Ocean.

o·ri·ole (ôr′ē-ōl′, ōr′-) *n.* **1.** Any of various Old World birds of the family Oriolidae, of which the males are characteristically bright-yellow and black. **2.** Any of various New World birds of the family Icteridae, of which the males are black and orange or yellow. See **Baltimore oriole.** [French *oriol,* from Old French, from Medieval Latin *oriolus,* "golden (bird)," variant of Latin *aureolus,* diminutive of *aureus,* golden, from *aurum,* gold. See **aurum** in Appendix.*]

O·ri·on[1] (ō-rī′ən). *Greek Mythology.* A giant hunter, pursuer of the Pleiades and lover of Eos, killed by Artemis.

O·ri·on[2] (ō-rī′ən) *n.* A constellation in the celestial equator near Gemini and Taurus, containing the stars Betelgeuse and Rigel.

or·i·son (ôr′ə-sən, -zən, ŏr′-) *n.* A prayer. [Middle English, from Old French, from Latin *ōrātiō,* ORATION.]

O·ris·sa (ō-rĭs′ə, ô-rĭs′ə). A state in eastern Republic of India, 60,136 square miles in area, north of Madras, on the Bay of Bengal. Population, 17,549,000. Capital, Bhubaneswar.

O·ri·ya (ô-rē′yə) *n.* An Indic language, spoken chiefly in Orissa, Republic of India.

O·ri·za·ba, Pi·co de (pē′kō thā ō′rē-sä′vä). *Aztec* **Ci·tlal·te·petl** (sē′tläl-tā′pĕt′l). An 18,700-foot volcanic peak, the highest elevation in Mexico, in central Veracruz State.

Or·khon (ôr′kŏn′). A river rising in central Mongolia and flowing 450 miles northeast to join the Selenga River.

Ork·ney Islands (ôrk′nē). Also **Ork·neys** (ôrk′nēz). *Abbr.* **Ork.** A cluster of islands, 376 square miles in area, off the northeastern coast of Scotland, of which they constitute a county. Population, 18,000. Capital, Kirkwall.

Or·lan·do (ôr-lăn′dō). A city and winter resort in central Florida. Population, 88,000.

Or·lan·do (ôr-län′dō), **Vittorio Emanuele.** 1860–1952. Prime Minister of Italy (1917–19).

Or·le·an·ist (ôr′lē-ə-nĭst) *n.* A supporter of the Orléans branch of the French royal family, descended from the Duke of Orléans, younger brother of Louis XIV.

Or·lé·ans (ôr-lā-äN′). A city in north-central France, on the Loire River south of Paris. Population, 84,000.

Or·lon (ôr′lŏn′) *n.* A trademark for a synthetic acrylic fiber that is used alone or with other fibers in a variety of fabrics.

or·lop (ôr′lŏp′) *n. Nautical.* The lowest deck of a ship, especially a warship. Also called "orlop deck." [Middle English *overlop,* deck of a single-decker covering the hold, from Middle Low German *overlōp,* "a leaping over" : *over,* over (see **uper** in Appendix*) + *lōpen,* to leap (see **klou-** in Appendix*).]

Or·ly (ôr-lē′). A suburb of southeastern Paris, site of the chief airport of Paris. Population, 18,000.

Or·mazd (ôr′məzd). Also **Or·muzd.** The chief deity of Zoroastrianism, the creator of the world, the source of light, and the embodiment of good. Also called "Ahura Mazda." Compare **Ahriman.** [Persian *Ormazd,* from Avestan *Ahura-Mazda,* "wise spirit" : *ahura,* spirit (see **ansu-** in Appendix*) + *mazdā,* wise (see **mendh-** in Appendix*).]

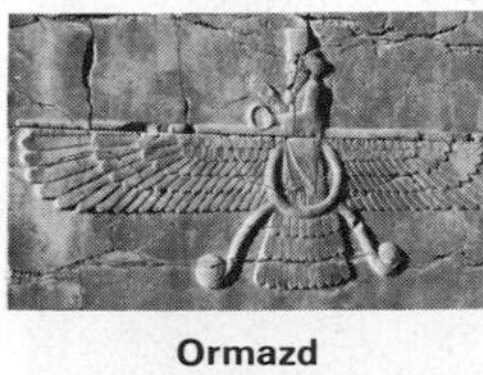

Ormazd
Relief of the symbol of the deity on the eastern doorway of the main council hall at Persepolis, Iran

or·mer (ôr′mər) *n. British.* An abalone shell; especially, the shell of an edible species, *Haliotis tuberculata,* found chiefly in the Channel Islands. [Channel Islands French, from French *ormier,* short for *oreille-de-mer,* "sea-ear," from Latin *auris maris* : *auris,* ear (see **ous-** in Appendix*) + *maris,* genitive of *mare,* sea (see **mori** in Appendix*).]

or·mo·lu (ôr′mə-lo͞o′) *n.* **1.** Any of several copper and tin or zinc alloys resembling gold in appearance and used to decorate furniture, moldings, architectural ornamentations, and jewelry. Also called "mosaic gold." **2.** An imitation of gold. [French *or moulu,* "ground gold" : *or,* gold, from Latin *aurum* (see **aurum** in Appendix*) + *moulu,* past participle of *moudre,* to grind, from Latin *molere* (see **melə-** in Appendix*).]

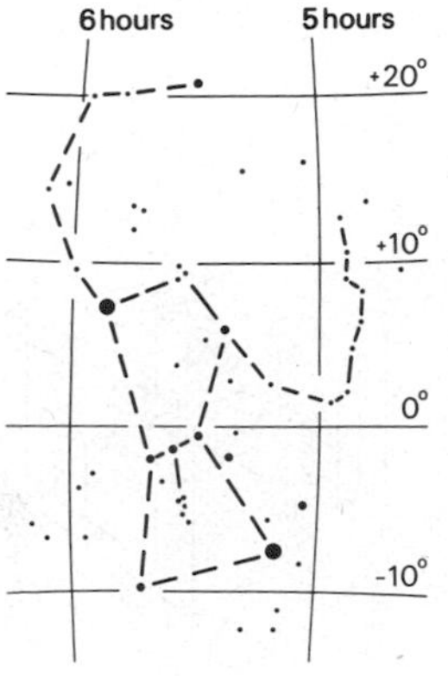

Orion[2]

Or·muz. Variant of **Hormuz.**

or·na·ment (ôr′nə-mənt) *n.* **1.** Anything that decorates or adorns; an embellishment. **2.** Decorations or adornments collectively. **3.** A person considered as a source of pride, honor, or credit because of character, personality, talent, or skill: *He is an ornament to his profession.* **4.** *Music.* A group of notes that embellishes a melody. —*tr.v.* (ôr′nə-mĕnt′) **ornamented, -menting, -ments. 1.** To furnish with ornaments. **2.** To be an ornament to. [Middle English, from Old French *ornement,* from Latin *ōrnāmentum,* from *ōrnāre,* to adorn. See **ar-** in Appendix.*] —**or′na·ment′er** *n.*

or·na·men·tal (ôr′nə-mĕn′təl) *adj.* Of, pertaining to, or serving as an ornament: *"A handsome boy and not only ornamental but useful"* (Carl Sandburg). —*n.* Something that is ornamental; especially, a plant grown for its beauty. —**or′na·men′tal·ly** *adv.*

or·na·men·ta·tion (ôr′nə-mĕn-tā′shən) *n.* **1. a.** The act, process, or result of ornamenting. **b.** The state of being ornamented. **2.** That which ornaments. **3.** Ornaments collectively.

or·nate (ôr-nāt′) *adj.* **1.** Elaborately and heavily ornamented; excessively decorated. **2.** Flashy, showy, or florid in style or manner; flowery: *"Its style was ornate, and many of its opinions outrageous."* (Kenneth Tynan). [Middle English *ornat,* from Latin *ōrnātus,* past participle of *ōrnāre,* to adorn. See **ar-** in Appendix.*] —**or·nate′ly** *adv.* —**or·nate′ness** *n.*

Synonyms: *ornate, florid, flamboyant, lavish, gaudy, showy, ostentatious.* These adjectives indicate colorful and often excessive display in words, actions, or aspects. *Ornate* pertains to what is lavishly decorated, and can apply in that sense to use of words: *an ornate style. Florid* stresses excesses of adornment in design, writing, or speech. *Flamboyant* strongly implies vivid color, boldness of design, or personal behavior marked by boldness and dash: *flamboyant gestures; a flamboyant speech. Lavish* emphasizes opulent display or very generous action: *a lavish dinner party; a lavish donor. Gaudy* implies vulgarity or poor taste in color or style in general. *Showy,* a weaker word, describes a flashy display which is usually in poor taste. *Ostentatious* always implies a deliberate effort to attract attention or to outdo another by means of display.

or·ner·y (ôr′nə-rē) *adj.* **-ier, -iest.** Having an ugly disposition; specifically, stubborn and mean-spirited. [Variant of ORDINARY.] —**or′ner·i·ness** *n.*

ornith. ornithological; ornithology.

or·nith·ic (ôr-nĭth′ĭk) *adj.* Of, relating to, or characteristic of birds. [Greek *ornithikos* : ORNITH(O)- + *-ikos,* -IC.]

ornitho–, ornith–. Indicates bird or birds; for example, **ornithology.** [New Latin, from Greek, from *ornis* (stem *ornith-*), bird. See **er-**[2] in Appendix.*]

or·ni·thol·o·gy (ôr′nə-thŏl′ə-jē) *n. Abbr.* **ornith., ornithol.** The scientific study of birds as a branch of zoology. [New Latin *ornithologia* : ORNITHO- + -LOGY.] —**or′ni·tho·log′i·cal** (ôr′nĭ-thə-lŏj′ĭ-kəl), **or′ni·tho·log′ic** *adj.* —**or′ni·tho·log′i·cal·ly** *adv.* —**or′ni·thol′o·gist** *n.*

or·ni·thop·ter (ôr′nə-thŏp′tər) *n.* A theoretical aircraft held aloft and propelled by wing movements. [ORNITHO- + -PTER.]

or·ni·tho·sis (ôr′nə-thō′sĭs) *n.* A contagious virus disease resembling psittacosis, that infects domestic fowl and other birds, and is transmissible to man. [New Latin : ORNITH(O)- + -OSIS.] —**or′ni·thot′ic** (-thŏt′ĭk) *adj.*

oro–. Indicates mountain; for example, **orology.** [From Greek *oros,* mountain†.]

o·rog·e·ny (ô-rŏj′ə-nē) *n.* Also **or·o·gen·e·sis** (ôr′ə-jĕn′ə-sĭs, ŏr′-). The process of mountain building, especially by folding and faulting of the earth's crust. [ORO- + -GENY.] —**or′o·gen′ic** (ôr′ə-jĕn′ĭk, ŏr′-) *adj.* —**or′o·gen′i·cal·ly** *adv.*

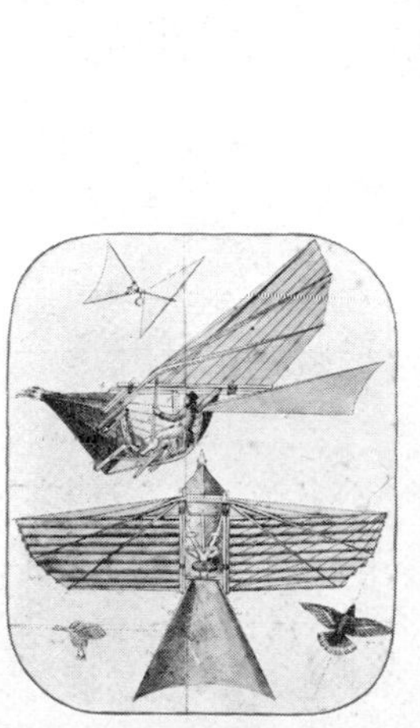

ornithopter
Drawing made by Thomas Walker in 1810

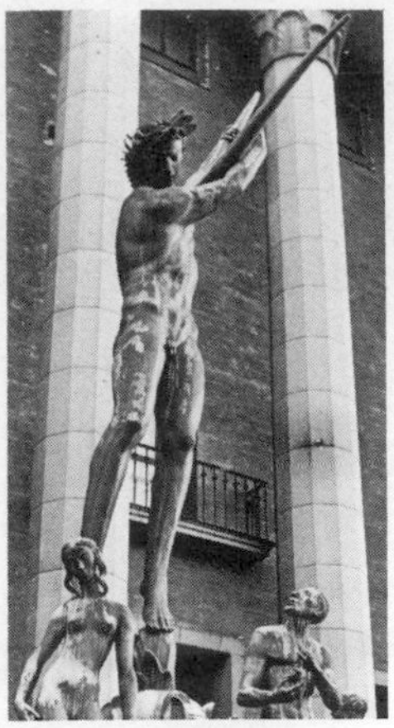

Orpheus
Statue by Swedish sculptor Carl Milles

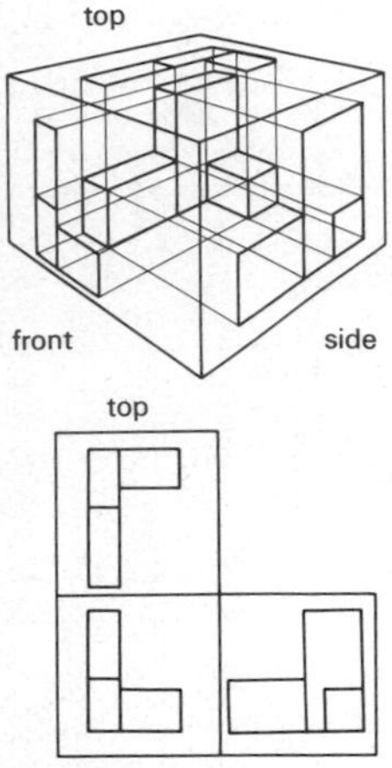
top
front
side
top
front
side

orthogonal projection

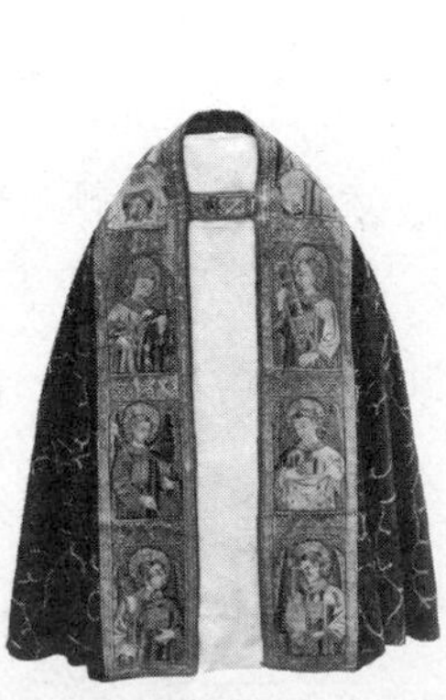

orphrey
Fifteenth-century Spanish cope with silk-embroidered orphrey

o·rog·ra·phy (ô-rŏg′rə-fē) *n.* The study of the physical geography of mountains and mountain ranges. [ORO- + -GRAPHY.] —**or′o·graph′ic** (ôr′ə-grăf′ĭk, ōr′-), **or′o·graph′i·cal** *adj.* —**or′o·graph′i·cal·ly** *adv.*

o·ro·ide (ôr′ō-īd′, ōr′-) *n.* Also **o·re·ide** (ôr′ē-īd′, ōr′-). An inexpensive alloy of copper, zinc, and tin, used in imitation gold jewelry. [French *oréide* : *or,* gold, from Latin *aurum,* gold (see **aurum** in Appendix*) + *-éide,* -OID.]

o·rol·o·gy (ô-rŏl′ə-jē) *n.* The study of mountains. [ORO- + -LOGY.] —**o′ro·log′i·cal** (ôr′ə-lŏj′ĭ-kəl, ōr′-) *adj.* —**o′ro·log′i·cal·ly** *adv.* —**o·rol′o·gist** *n.*

O·ron·tes (ô-rŏn′tēz). A river rising in northwestern Lebanon and flowing 250 miles north through Syria, and southwest through Turkey to the Mediterranean Sea.

o·ro·tund (ôr′ə-tŭnd′, ōr′-) *adj.* **1.** Full in sound; sonorous: *orotund tones.* **2.** Pompous and bombastic: *orotund talk.* [Latin *ōre rotundō,* "with round mouth" : *ōs* (stem *ōr-*), mouth (see **ōs-** in Appendix*) + *rotundus,* rounded, ROTUND.] —**o′ro·tun′di·ty** (ôr′ə-tŭn′də-tē, ōr′-) *n.*

O·roz·co (ō-rōs′kō), **José Clemente.** 1883–1949. Mexican painter and lithographer.

or·phan (ôr′fən) *n.* A child whose parents are dead; sometimes, a child who has lost one parent by death. —*adj.* **1.** Being an orphan. **2.** For orphans: *an orphan home.* —*tr.v.* **orphaned, -phaning, -phans.** To deprive (a child) of one or both parents. [Late Latin *orphanus,* from Greek *orphanos,* orphaned. See **orbh-** in Appendix.*] —**or′phan·hood′** *n.*

or·phan·age (ôr′fə-nĭj) *n.* **1.** A public institution for the care and protection of orphans and abandoned children. **2.** The state or condition of being an orphan.

Or·phe·us (ôr′fē-əs, -fyo͞os′). The legendary Thracian poet and musician to whom the establishment of the Orphic mysteries was ascribed. —**Or·phe′an** (ôr-fē′ən, ôr′fē-ən) *adj.*

Or·phic (ôr′fĭk) *adj.* **1.** Of or ascribed to Orpheus: *the Orphic poems; Orphic mysteries.* **2.** Of, pertaining to, or characteristic of the dogmas, mysteries, and philosophical principles set forth in the poems ascribed to Orpheus. **3.** Capable of casting a charm or spell as Orpheus did by his singing. **4.** *Sometimes small* **o.** Mystic or occult in nature; esoteric. [Latin *Orphicus,* from Greek *Orphikos,* from ORPHEUS.] —**Or′phi·cal·ly** *adv.*

Or·phism (ôr′fĭz′əm) *n.* An ancient Greek mystery religion arising in the sixth century B.C. from a synthesis of pre-Hellenic beliefs with the Thracian cult of Dionysus Zagreus and soon becoming mingled with the Eleusinian mysteries and the doctrines of Pythagoras, but continuing to influence later antiquity through the Orphic poems and kindred teachings incorporated by Neo-Platonic thought. [French *orphisme,* from *Orphée,* Orpheus, from Greek *Orpheus,* ORPHEUS.] —**Or′phist** *n.*

or·phrey (ôr′frē) *n., pl.* **-phreys.** Also **or·fray** (ôr′frā′). **1.** A band of elaborate embroidery decorating the front of certain ecclesiastical vestments. **2.** Any elaborate embroidery, especially when made of gold. [Middle English *orfrey, orphreis* (taken as plural), from Old French *orfreis,* from Medieval Latin *aurifrigium* : Latin *aurum,* gold (see **aurum** in Appendix*) + *Phrygium,* neuter of *Phrygius,* PHRYGIAN.]

or·pi·ment (ôr′pə-mənt) *n.* Arsenic trisulfide, As_2S_3, a lemon-yellow pigment, used in tanning and in linoleum manufacture. [Middle English, from Old French, from Latin *auripigmentum* : *aurum,* gold (see **aurum** in Appendix*) + *pigmentum,* PIGMENT.]

or·pine (ôr′pĭn) *n.* Any of several plants of the genus *Sedum;* especially, *S. telephium,* native to Eurasia, having clusters of reddish-purple flowers. Also called "live-forever." [Middle English *orpin,* from Old French *orpine,* short for *orpiment,* ORPIMENT, probably after the yellow flowers of one species.]

Or·ping·ton[1] (ôr′pĭng-tən). A former administrative division of London, England, now part of **Bromley** *(see).*

Or·ping·ton[2] (ôr′pĭng-tən) *n.* A breed of domestic fowls having a large body, a single comb, and unfeathered legs. [From *Orpington,* Kent, England, where the breed originated.]

or·re·ry (ôr′ə-rē, ŏr′-) *n., pl.* **-ries.** A mechanical model of the solar system. [After Charles Boyle (1676–1731), fourth Earl of *Orrery,* for whom one was made.]

or·ris (ôr′ĭs, ŏr′-) *n.* **1.** Any of several species of iris having a fragrant rootstock; especially, *Iris florentina.* **2.** Orrisroot. [Variant of IRIS.]

or·ris·root (ôr′ĭs-ro͞ot′, -ro͝ot′, ŏr′-) *n.* The fragrant rootstock of the orris, used in perfumes and cosmetics.

Orsk (ôrsk). A city of the Soviet Union, in the southern Ural Mountains, on the Ural River. Population, 210,000.

ort (ôrt) *n. Usually plural. Archaic.* **1.** A small scrap or leaving of food after a meal is completed. **2.** A scrap; bit. [Middle English, probably from Middle Dutch *orte,* contraction of *oor aete,* leftover, "out eat" : *oor-,* out (see **ud-** in Appendix*) + *eten,* to eat (see **ed-** in Appendix*).]

orth. orthopedic; orthopedics.

or·thi·con (ôr′thĭ-kŏn′) *n.* A television camera pickup tube that uses a low-velocity electron beam to scan a photoactive mosaic. Also called "image orthicon." [ORTH(O)- + ICON(OSCOPE).]

or·tho (ôr′thō) *adj.* **1.** *Chemistry.* **a.** Designating the most fully hydrated form of an acid or of its salts. **b.** Of, pertaining to, or designating adjacent carbon positions in a benzene ring. **2.** *Physics.* Designating diatomic molecules in which the nuclei have the same spin directions. [From ORTHO-.]

ortho-, orth-. Indicates: **1.** Straight or upright; for example, **orthotropic. 2.** *Mathematics.* Perpendicular to or at right angles; for example, **orthorhombic. 3.** Correct or standard; for example, **orthography. 4.** *Medicine.* Correction of maladjustments or deformities; for example, **orthopedics.** [Middle English, from Old French, from Latin, from Greek, from *orthos,* straight, correct, right, upright. See **werdh-** in Appendix.*]

or·tho·cen·ter (ôr′thō-sĕn′tər) *n.* The point of intersection of the three altitudes of a triangle.

or·tho·ce·phal·ic (ôr′thō-sə-făl′ĭk) *adj.* Also **or·tho·ceph·a·lous** (ôr′thō-sĕf′ə-ləs). Having a ratio of skull height to skull length between 0.70 and 0.75. [ORTHO- + -CEPHALIC.] —**or′tho·ceph′a·ly′** (-sĕf′ə-lē) *n.*

or·tho·chro·mat·ic (ôr′thō-krō-măt′ĭk) *adj.* **1.** Of, having, or reproducing the colors of nature accurately. **2.** Of or pertaining to a film, plate, or emulsion that renders all colors, except red, in tones of gray approximating the relative brilliance of these colors. —**or′tho·chro′ma·tism′** (-krō′mə-tĭz′əm) *n.*

or·tho·clase (ôr′thə-klās′, -klāz′) *n.* A **feldspar** *(see),* essentially potassium aluminum silicate, $KAlSi_3O_8$, characterized by a monoclinic crystalline structure and found in igneous or granitic rock. Also called "potash feldspar." [German *Orthoklas* : ORTHO- + -CLASE.]

or·tho·clas·tic (ôr′thə-klăs′tĭk) *adj. Geology.* Having right-angled cleavage. [German *orthklastisch* : ORTHO- + CLASTIC.]

or·tho·don·tia (ôr′thə-dŏn′shə) *n.* The dental specialty and practice of correcting abnormally aligned or positioned teeth. Also called "orthodontics." [ORTHO- + Greek *odous,* tooth (see **-odont**).] —**or′tho·don′tic** *adj.* —**or′tho·don′tist** *n.*

or·tho·dox (ôr′thə-dŏks′) *adj.* **1.** Adhering to the accepted or traditional and established faith, especially in religion. Compare **heterodox. 2.** Adhering to the Christian faith as expressed in the early Christian ecumenical creeds. **3.** Adhering to a commonly accepted, customary, or traditional practice or belief. **4.** *Capital* **O. a.** Of, pertaining to, or designating any of the churches of the Eastern Orthodox Church. **b.** Of, pertaining to, or denoting Orthodox Judaism. [Old French *orthodoxe,* from Late Latin *orthodoxus,* from Greek *orthodoxos,* having the right opinion : ORTHO- + *doxa,* opinion, from *dokein,* to think, seem (see **dek-**[1] in Appendix*).] —**or′tho·dox′ly** *adv.*

Orthodox Church. The **Eastern Orthodox Church** *(see).*

Orthodox Judaism. The branch of the Jewish faith that adheres to the Mosaic Law as interpreted in the Talmud, and considers it binding in modern as well as ancient times. Compare **Conservative Judaism, Reform Judaism.**

or·tho·dox·y (ôr′thə-dŏk′sē) *n., pl.* **-ies. 1.** The quality or state of being orthodox. **2.** Orthodox practice, custom, or belief.

or·tho·e·py (ôr-thō′ə-pē, ôr′thō-ĕp′ē) *n.* **1.** The study of the pronunciation of words. **2.** The customary pronunciation of words. [New Latin *orthoepia,* from Greek *orthoepeia* : ORTHO- + *epos,* word (see **wekw-** in Appendix*).] —**or′tho·ep′ic** (ôr′thō-ĕp′ĭk), **or′tho·ep′i·cal** *adj.* —**or·tho′e·pist** *n.*

or·tho·gen·e·sis (ôr′thō-jĕn′ə-sĭs) *n.* **1.** *Biology.* The theory that evolutionary change is predetermined by the constitution of germ plasm and independent of external factors. **2.** *Sociology.* The theory that all cultures pass through sequential periods in the same order. [New Latin : ORTHO- + -GENESIS.] —**or′tho·ge·net′ic** (-jə-nĕt′ĭk) *adj.* —**or′tho·ge·net′i·cal·ly** *adv.*

or·tho·gen·ic (ôr′thō-jĕn′ĭk) *adj. Psychiatry.* Pertaining to the correction or treatment of mental and emotional abnormalities in children. [ORTHO- + -GENIC.]

or·thog·na·thous (ôr-thŏg′nə-thəs) *adj.* Also **or·thog·nath·ic** (ŏr′thŏg-năth′ĭk). Having the lower jaw aligned with the upper so that it does not protrude or recede. [ORTHO- + -GNATHOUS.] —**or·thog′na·thism′, or·thog′na·thy** *n.*

or·thog·o·nal (ôr-thŏg′ə-nəl) *adj. Mathematics.* Pertaining to or composed of right angles. [Greek *orthogōnios* : ORTHO- + *gōnia,* angle (see **genu-**[1] in Appendix*).] —**or·thog′o·nal·ly** *adv.*

orthogonal projection. The two-dimensional graphic representation of an object formed by the perpendicular intersections of lines drawn from points on the object to a plane of projection. Also called "orthographic projection."

or·tho·graph·ic (ôr′thə-grăf′ĭk) *adj.* Also **or·tho·graph·i·cal** (ôr′thə-grăf′ĭ-kəl). **1.** Of or pertaining to orthography. **2.** Spelled correctly. **3.** *Mathematics.* Having perpendicular lines. —**or′tho·graph′i·cal·ly** *adv.*

or·thog·ra·phy (ôr-thŏg′rə-fē) *n., pl.* **-phies. 1.** The art or study of correct spelling according to established usage. **2.** The aspect of language study concerned with letters and their sequences in words. **3.** Any method of representing the sounds of language by literal symbols. [Middle English *ortografie,* from Old French, from Latin *orthographia,* from Greek : ORTHO- + -GRAPHY.] —**or·thog′ra·pher, or·thog′ra·phist** *n.*

or·tho·pe·dics (ôr′thə-pē′dĭks) *n.* Also **or·tho·pae·dics.** Plural in form, used with a singular verb. *Abbr.* **orth.** The surgical or manipulative treatment of disorders of the skeletal system and associated motor organs. [From French *orthopédie* : ORTHO- + Greek *paideia,* education, from *pais* (stem *paid-*), child (see **pǒu-** in Appendix*).] —**or′tho·pe′dic** *adj.* —**or′tho·pe′di·cal·ly** *adv.* —**or′tho·pe′dist** *n.*

or·tho·psy·chi·a·try (ôr′thō-sĭ-kī′ə-trē, -sī-kī′ə-trē) *n.* The psychiatric study and treatment of incipient and borderline mental disorders, especially their development in the young. —**or′tho·psy′chi·at′ric** (-sī′kē-ăt′rĭk), **or′tho·psy′chi·at′ri·cal** *adj.* —**or′tho·psy·chi′a·trist** *n.*

or·thop·ter·an (ôr-thŏp′tər-ən) *n.* Also **or·thop·ter·on** (ôr-thŏp′tə-rŏn′, -tər-ən). Any insect of the order Orthoptera, characterized by membranous, folded hind wings covered by leathery, narrow fore wings, and including the locusts, cockroaches, crickets, and grasshoppers. [New Latin *Orthoptera* (order), "straight-wings" : ORTHO- + *-ptera,* from *-pterus,* -PTEROUS.] —**or·thop′ter·an, or·thop′ter·ous, or·thop′ter·al** *adj.*

or·tho·rhom·bic (ôr′thō-rŏm′bĭk) *adj.* Of or pertaining to a crystalline structure of three mutually perpendicular axes of different length. Also "rhombic."

or·tho·scope (ôr′thə-skōp′) *n.* An instrument for examining the eye through a layer of water that compensates for the curvature of the cornea. [ORTHO- + -SCOPE.]
or·tho·scop·ic (ôr′thə-skŏp′ĭk) *adj.* **1.** Having normal vision. **2.** Pertaining to the use of the orthoscope.
or·thos·ti·chous (ôr-thŏs′tĭ-kəs) *adj. Biology.* Characterized by parallel arrangement in a vertical row. [ORTHO- + Greek *stikhos,* a row (see **steigh-** in Appendix*).] —**or·thos′ti·chy** *n.*
or·tho·trop·ic (ôr′thə-trŏp′ĭk) *adj.* Tending to grow or form along a vertical axis. [ORTHO- + -TROPIC.] —**or′tho·trop′i·cal·ly** *adv.* —**or·thot′ro·pism′** (ôr-thŏt′rə-pĭz′əm) *n.*
or·thot·ro·pous (ôr-thŏt′rə-pəs) *adj. Botany.* Growing straight, so that the micropyle is at the side opposite the stalk. Said of an ovule. [ORTHO- + -TROPOUS.]
Ort·ler (ôrt′lər). **1.** A mountain range of the Alps in northern Italy. **2.** The highest elevation of this range (12,800 feet).
or·to·lan (ôr′tə-lən) *n.* **1.** A small, brownish bird, *Emberiza hortulana,* of the Old World, eaten as a delicacy. **2.** Loosely, any of several New World birds, such as the bobolink and the sora. [French, from Provençal, gardener, from Latin *hortulānus,* from *hortulus,* diminutive of *hortus,* garden. See **gher-**[2] in Appendix.*]
Or·vie·to (ôr-vyâ′tō). A historic town in east-central Italy, on the Tiber 60 miles north of Rome. Population, 10,000.
Or·well (ôr′wĕl′, -wəl), **George.** Pen name of Eric Blair. 1903–1950. English novelist, essayist, and political satirist.
-ory[1]. Indicates a place for or something used as (with reference to the first element); for example, **conservatory, reformatory, observatory.** [Middle English *-orie,* from Norman French *-orie* or Old French *-orie, -oire,* from Latin *-ōrium, -ōria,* from *-ōrius,* adjective suffix.]
-ory[2]. Indicates characterization by, possession of the nature of, or tendency toward; for example, **compensatory.** [Middle English *-orie,* from Old French *-oire, -orie,* from Latin *-ōrius,* adjective suffix.]
o·ryx (ôr′ĭks, ōr′-, ŏr′-) *n., pl.* **oryxes** or **oryx.** Any of several antelopes of the genus *Oryx,* of Africa and southwestern Asia, having long, straight or arching horns. [Latin, from Greek *orux,* pickax, spike, hence (from the sharp horns) gazelle, perhaps from *orussein,* to dig. See **ruk-**[2] in Appendix.*]
os[1] (ŏs) *n., pl.* **ora** (ôr′ə, ōr′ə). *Anatomy.* A mouth or opening. [Latin *ōs* (stem *ōr-*), mouth. See **ōs-** in Appendix.*]
os[2] (ŏs) *n., pl.* **ossa** (ŏs′ə). *Anatomy.* A bone. [Latin *os* (stem *oss-*), bone. See **osth-** in Appendix.*]
os[3] (ōs) *n., pl.* **osar** (ō′sär′). *Geology.* An **esker** *(see).* [Swedish *ås,* ridge, from Old Norse *āss.* See **omeso-** in Appendix.*]
Os The symbol for the element osmium.
o.s., o/s out of stock.
O.S. **1.** Old Series. **2.** Old Style. **3.** ordinary seaman.
OSA, O.S.A. Order of St. Augustine.
O·sage (ō′sāj′, ō-sāj′) *n., pl.* **Osage** or **Osages. 1.** A tribe of Siouan-speaking North American Indians, formerly inhabiting the region between the Missouri and Arkansas rivers. **2.** A member of this tribe. **3.** The Siouan language of this tribe. [French, from Osage *Wazházhe,* tribal name.] —**O′sage′** *adj.*
Osage orange. A tree, *Maclura pomifera,* native to midwestern North America, bearing inedible, orangelike fruit.
Osage River. A river of eastern Kansas, flowing east 500 miles to join the Missouri River in central Missouri.
O·sa·ka (ō-sä′kə). An industrial metropolis, seaport, and the second-largest city of Japan, situated on southwestern Honshu Island. Population, 3,119,000.
O·sa·wat·o·mie (ō′sə-wŏt′ə-mē, ŏs′ə-). A town in eastern Kansas, site of an Underground Railroad station and of antislavery action by John Brown in 1855. Population, 5,000.
OSB, O.S.B. Order of St. Benedict.
Os·can (ŏs′kən) *n.* **1.** One of an ancient people of Campania. **2.** The Italic language of this people. —*adj.* Of or pertaining to the Oscans or their language.
Os·car[1] (ŏs′kər). A masculine given name. [Revival of Old English *Ōsgar* : *ōs,* a god (see **ansu-** in Appendix*) + *gār,* a spear (see **ghei-**[1] in Appendix*).]
Os·car[2] (ŏs′kər) *n.* One of the golden statuettes awarded annually by the Academy of Motion Picture Arts and Sciences for achievement in motion pictures. [Origin uncertain.]
Os·ce·o·la (ŏs′ē-ō′lə). 1804?–1838. American Indian leader; war leader of the Seminoles.
os·cil·late (ŏs′ə-lāt′) *intr.v.* **-lated, -lating, -lates. 1.** To swing back and forth with a steady uninterrupted rhythm. **2.** To waver between two or more thoughts or courses of action; vacillate. **3.** *Physics.* To vary between alternate extremes, usually with a definable period. —See Synonyms at **swing.** [Latin *ōscillāre,* from *ōscillum,* a swing, originally a mask of Bacchus hung from a tree in a vineyard to swing in the wind (as a charm), diminutive of *ōs,* face, mouth. See **ōs-** in Appendix.*] —**os′cil·la′tor** *n.* —**os′cil·la·to′ry** (ŏs′ə-lə-tôr′ē, -tōr′ē) *adj.*
os·cil·la·tion (ŏs′ə-lā′shən) *n.* **1.** The state or act of oscillating. **2.** A single oscillatory cycle.
os·cil·lo·gram (ŏ-sĭl′ə-grăm′, ə-sĭl′-) *n.* **1.** The graph traced by an oscillograph. **2.** An instantaneous oscilloscope trace or photograph. [OSCILLO(GRAPH) + -GRAM.]
os·cil·lo·graph (ŏ-sĭl′ə-grăf′, -gräf′) *n.* A device that records oscillations as a continuous graph of corresponding variation in an electric current. [French *oscillographe* : OSCILL(ATION) + -GRAPH.] —**os′cil·log′ra·phy** (ŏs′ə-lŏg′rə-fē) *n.*
os·cil·lo·scope (ŏ-sĭl′ə-skōp′, ə-sĭl′-) *n.* An electronic instrument that produces an instantaneous visual display or trace of electron motion on the screen of a cathode-ray tube corresponding to some external oscillatory motion. [OSCILL(ATION) + -SCOPE.] —**os·cil′lo·scop′ic** (-skŏp′ĭk) *adj.*
os·cine (ŏs′īn′) *adj.* Of or pertaining to the Oscines, a large suborder of the passerine birds that includes most songbirds. [New Latin *Oscines,* from Latin *oscinēs,* plural of *oscen,* a singing bird used for augury. See **kan-** in Appendix.*] —**os′cine′** *n.*
os·ci·tan·cy (ŏs′ə-tən-sē) *n., pl.* **-cies.** Also **os·ci·tance** (ŏs′ə-təns). **1.** The act of yawning. **2.** The state of being drowsy or inattentive; dullness. [From Latin *ōscitāns,* present participle of *ōscitāre,* to gape : *ōs,* mouth (see **ōs-** in Appendix*) + *citāre,* to move (see **kei-**[3] in Appendix*).] —**os′ci·tant** *adj.*
Os·co-Um·bri·an (ŏs′kō-ŭm′brē-ən) *n.* A subdivision of the Italic languages, consisting of Oscan and Umbrian.
os·cu·lant (ŏs′kyə-lənt) *adj.* **1.** *Biology.* Intermediate in characteristics between two similar or related taxonomic groups. **2.** Closely adhering or joined; embracing. [Latin *ōsculāns,* present participle of *ōsculārī,* OSCULATE.]
os·cu·late (ŏs′kyə-lāt′) *v.* **-lated, -lating, -lates.** —*tr.* To kiss. —*intr. Biology.* To have characteristics intermediate between those of two similar or related taxonomic groups. [Latin *ōsculārī,* from *ōsculum,* kiss, OSCULUM.]
os·cu·la·tion (ŏs′kyə-lā′shən) *n.* **1. a.** The act of kissing. **b.** A kiss. **2.** *Mathematics.* A point where two branches of a curve have a common tangent and extend in both directions of the tangent. —**os′cu·la·to′ry** (ŏs′kyə-lə-tôr′ē, -tōr′ē) *adj.*
os·cu·lum (ŏs′kyə-ləm) *n., pl.* **-la** (-lə). Also **os·cule** (ŏs′kyo͞ol′). *Zoology.* An opening in a sponge for expelling water. [New Latin, from Latin *ōsculum,* little mouth, kiss, diminutive of *ōs,* mouth. See **ōs-** in Appendix.*] —**os′cu·lar** *adj.*
-ose[1]. Indicates possession of or similarity to; for example, **grandiose.** [Middle English, from Latin *-ōsus.* See **-ous.**]
-ose[2]. *Chemistry.* Indicates: **1.** A carbohydrate; for example, **fructose, lactose. 2.** A product of protein hydrolysis; for example, **proteose.** [From GLUCOSE.]
Ö·sel. The Swedish name for **Saaremaa.**
OSF, O.S.F. Order of St. Francis.
Osh·a·wa (ŏsh′ə-wə, -wä′, -wô′). A city in southeastern Ontario, Canada, on Lake Ontario. Population, 50,000.
Osh·kosh (ŏsh′kŏsh′). A city and summer resort in eastern Wisconsin, on Lake Winnebago. Population, 45,000. [From the name of an Algonquin chief, from Algonquian *oskas,* "his claw."]
o·sier (ō′zhər) *n.* **1.** Any of several willows having long, rodlike twigs used in basketry; especially, *Salix viminalis* and *S. purpurea,* both native to Eurasia. **2.** A twig of such a willow. **3.** Any of various similar trees. [Middle English, from Old French, from Medieval Latin *auseria*†, willow bed.]
O·si·ris (ō-sī′rĭs). The ancient Egyptian god whose annual death and resurrection personified the self-renewing vitality and fertility of nature.
-osis. Indicates: **1.** A condition or process; for example, **metamorphosis, osmosis. 2.** A diseased or abnormal condition; for example, **tuberculosis, neurosis. 3.** An increase or formation of; for example, **sclerosis, leukocytosis.** [Middle English, from Latin, from Greek *-ōsis,* abstract noun suffix formed from *o*-stem verbs.]
OSL Airport code for Oslo, Norway.
Os·ler (ŏs′lər, ŏz′lər), Sir **William.** 1849–1919. Canadian physician and professor of medicine; taught in Canada, the United States, and Great Britain.
Os·lo (ŏz′lō, ŏs′lō). Formerly **Chris·ti·an·i·a** (krĭs′chē-ăn′ē-ə, -ä′nē-ə, krĭs′tē-). The capital and principal industrial and shipping city of Norway, in the southeast, at the northern end of Oslo Fjord, an inlet of the Skagerrak. Population, 483,000.
Os·man I (ŏs-män′). Also **Oth·man** (ŏth-män′). 1259–1326. Emir (1299–1326) and founder of the Ottoman Empire.
Os·man·li (ŏz-măn′lē, ŏs-) *n., pl.* **-lis. 1.** An Ottoman Turk. **2. Ottoman Turkish** *(see).* —*adj.* Ottoman. [Turkish : *Osman,* Osman I + *-li,* adjectival suffix.]
os·mat·ic (ŏz-măt′ĭk) *adj.* Also **os·mic** (ŏz′mĭk). Having or characterized by a sense of smell. [Greek *osmē,* odor (see **od-**[1] in Appendix*) + -ATE + -IC.]
os·mic[1] (ŏz′mĭk) *adj.* Of, pertaining to, or containing osmium in a compound with a valence higher than that in a comparable osmous compound. [From OSMIUM.]
os·mic[2]. Variant of **osmatic.**
os·mi·rid·i·um (ŏz′mə-rĭd′ē-əm) *n.* A natural alloy of osmium and iridium with small inclusions of platinum, rhodium, and other metals, used in needles and wearing points. Also called "iridosmine." [German : OSM(IUM)- + IRIDIUM.]
os·mi·um (ŏz′mē-əm) *n. Symbol* **Os** A bluish-white, hard, metallic element, found in small amounts in osmiridium, nickel, and platinum ores. It is used as a platinum hardener, in making pen points, phonograph needles, and instrument pivots, and also as a catalyst in cortisone synthesis. Atomic number 76, atomic weight 190.2, melting point 3,000° C, boiling point 5,000° C, specific gravity 22.57, valences 2, 3, 4, 8. See **element.** [New Latin, from Greek *osmē,* odor (from the odor of osmium tetroxide). See **od-**[1] in Appendix.*]
os·mose (ŏz′mōs′, ŏs′-) *v.* **-mosed, -mosing, -moses.** —*intr.* To undergo or diffuse by osmosis. —*tr.* To subject to osmosis. [From OSMOSIS, taken to be the common element of exosmose and endosmose, obsolete forms of EXOSMOSIS and ENDOSMOSIS.]
os·mo·sis (ŏz-mō′sĭs, ŏs-) *n.* **1.** The diffusion of fluid through a semipermeable membrane until there is an equal concentration of fluid on either side of the membrane. **2.** The tendency of fluids to diffuse in such a manner. **3.** Any gradual, often unconscious, process of assimilation or absorption that resembles this diffusion: *to learn a language by osmosis.* [Earlier *osmose,* from Greek *ōsmos,* action of pushing, from *ōthein* to

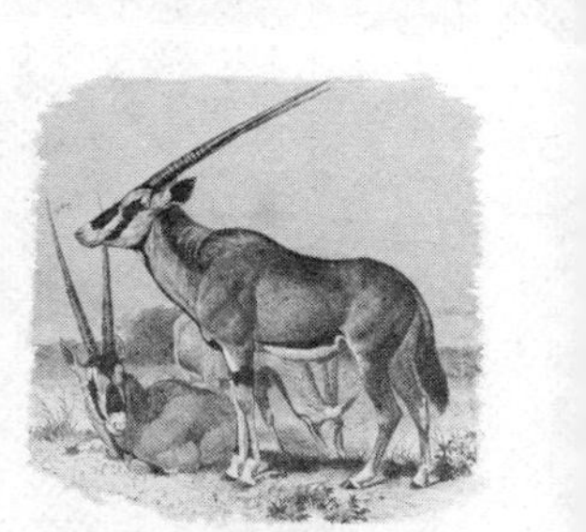

oryx
Oryx beisa

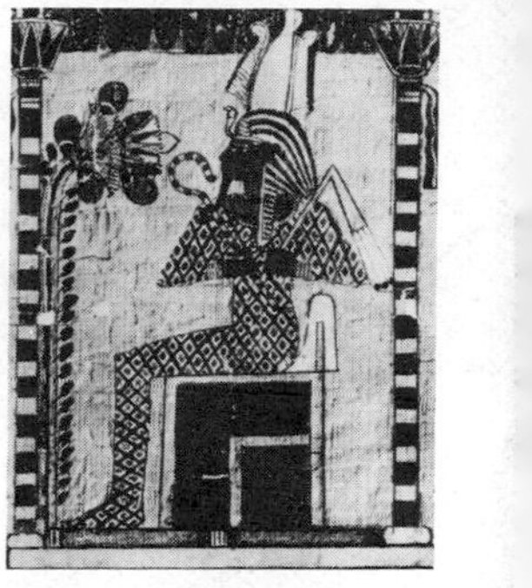

Osiris
Papyrus showing the god seated and swathed in mummy wrappings

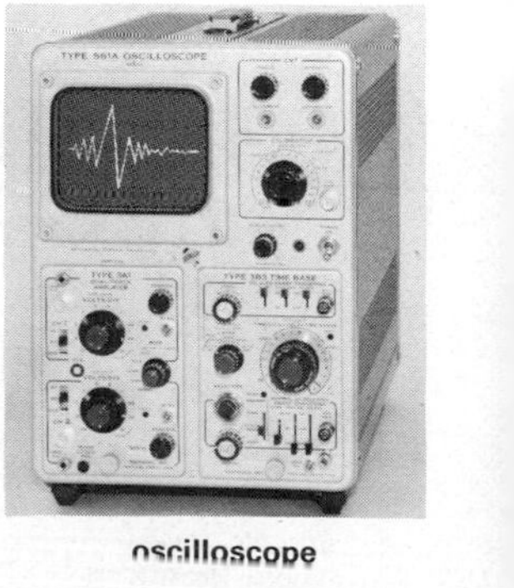

oscilloscope

push. See **wedh-**[1] in Appendix.*] —**os·mot'ic** (ŏz-mŏt'ĭk, ŏs-) *adj.* —**os·mot'i·cal·ly** *adv.*

os·mous (ŏz'məs) *adj.* Also **os·mi·ous** (ŏz'mē-əs). Of, pertaining to, or containing osmium in a compound with a valence lower than that in a comparable osmic compound.

os·mun·da (ŏz-mŭn'də) *n.* Also **os·mund** (ŏz'mənd). Any fern of the genus *Osmunda,* having erect, compound fronds, and, in some species, fibrous roots used as a potting medium for cultivated plants. [Middle English, from Old French *osmunde*†.]

Os·na·brück (ŏz'nə-brŏŏk'; *German* ôs'nä-brük'). An industrial city of West Germany, 30 miles northeast of Münster. Population, 142,000.

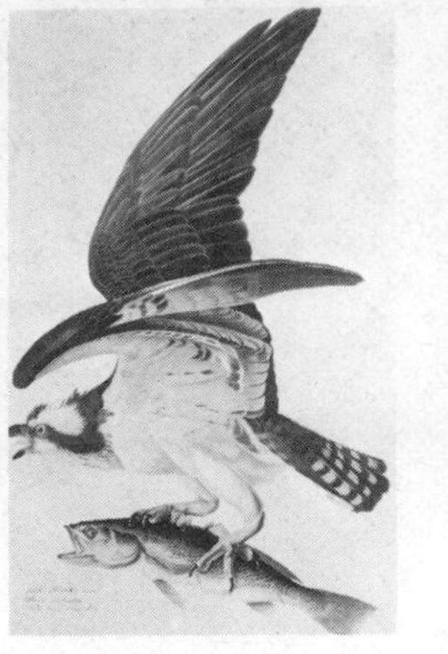

osprey
Painting of a male osprey by John James Audubon

os·na·burg (ŏz'nə-bûrg') *n.* A heavy, coarse cotton fabric, used for grain sacks, upholstery, and draperies. [After *Osnaburg,* variant of OSNABRÜCK.]

os·prey (ŏs'prē, -prā') *n., pl.* **-preys. 1.** A fish-eating hawk, *Pandion haliaetus,* having plumage that is dark on the back and white below. Also called "fish hawk," "ossifrage." **2.** A plume formerly used to trim women's hats. [Middle English *ospray,* probably from Old French *ospreit* (unattested), from Vulgar Latin *avispreda* (unattested), from Latin *avis praedae,* "bird of prey" : *avis,* bird, (see **awi-** in Appendix*) + *praeda,* prey (see **ghend-** in Appendix*). The Old French form and denotation are influenced by Old French *osfraie,* from Latin *ossifraga,* OSSIFRAGE.]

os·sa. Plural of **os** (bone).

Os·sa (ŏs'ə). A mountain peak (6,489 feet) in east-central Greece, near the Aegean Sea. In Greek mythology, the Titans piled Ossa on Mount Olympus and Mount Pelion on Ossa in a futile attempt to reach heaven.

os·se·in (ŏs'ē-ĭn) *n.* The residue of bone after acid dissolution, used in gelatin and glue. [OSSE(OUS) + -IN.]

os·se·ous (ŏs'ē-əs) *adj.* Composed of, containing, or resembling bone; bony. [Latin *osseus,* from *os,* bone. See **osth-** in Appendix.*] —**os'se·ous·ly** *adv.*

Os·set (ŏs'ĭt, ŏ-sĕt') *n.* Also **Os·sete** (ŏs'ēt', ŏ-sēt'). One of a people of Iranian origin living in Ossetia. —**Os·set'ic** *adj.*

Os·se·tia (ŏ-sē'shə). A region in the Soviet Union, between the Black and Caspian seas, divided into North Ossetia and South Ossetia by the Caucasus mountains. —**Os·se'tian** *adj.* & *n.*

os·si·a (ō-sē'ə) *conj. Music.* Or else. Used as a direction to the performer to designate an alternative section or passage. [Italian, from *o sia,* "or let it be."]

Os·sian (ŏsh'ən, ŏs'ē-ən). A legendary Gaelic hero and bard of the third century A.D. James Macpherson's purported translations from Ossian (1760–63) had wide literary influence.

os·si·cle (ŏs'ĭ-kəl) *n. Anatomy.* A small bone; especially, one of the three bones of the inner ear. [Latin *ossiculum,* diminutive of *os,* bone. See **osth-** in Appendix.*] —**os·sic'u·lar** (ŏ-sĭk'yə-lər), **os·sic'u·late** (-lĭt) *adj.*

os·si·fi·ca·tion (ŏs'ə-fĭ-kā'shən) *n.* **1.** The natural process of bone formation. **2. a.** The abnormal hardening or calcification of soft tissue into a bonelike material. **b.** A mass or deposit of such material. **3.** The process of becoming or state of being set in a rigidly conventional pattern, as of behavior, habits, beliefs, or the like. —**os·sif'i·ca·to'ry** (ŏ-sĭf'ĭ-kə-tôr'ē, -tōr'ē) *adj.*

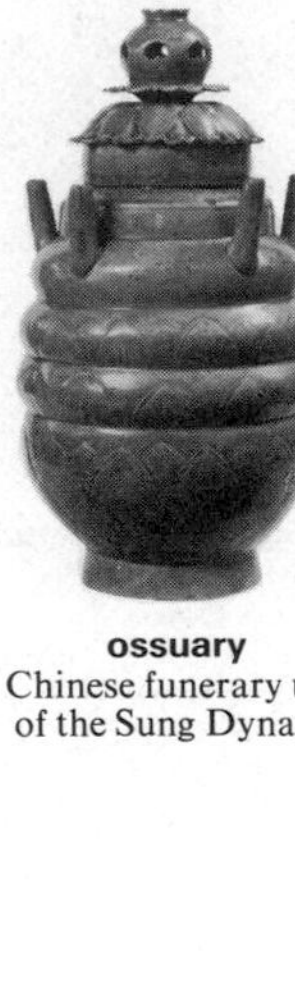

ossuary
Chinese funerary urn of the Sung Dynasty

os·si·frage (ŏs'ə-frĭj, -frāj') *n.* Either of two hawks, the **osprey** or the **lammergeier** *(both of which see).* [Latin *(avis) ossifraga,* "bone-breaking (bird)," lammergeier (which is said to drop its prey from a height to break the bones), from *ossifragus,* bone-breaking : *os* (stem *oss-*), bone (see **osth-** in Appendix*) + *frangere,* to break (see **bhreg-** in Appendix*).]

os·si·fy (ŏs'ə-fī') *v.* **-fied, -fying, -fies.** —*intr.* **1.** To change into bone; become bony. **2.** To become set in a rigidly conventional pattern. —*tr.* **1.** To make or form bone in or of; convert (a membrane or cartilage, for example) into bone. **2.** To mold into a rigidly conventional pattern. [Latin *os,* (stem *oss-*), bone (see **osth-** in Appendix*) + -FY.] —**os·sif'ic** (ŏ-sĭf'ĭk) *adj.*

os·su·ar·y (ŏsh'ōō-ĕr'ē, ŏs'yōō-) *n., pl.* **-ies.** A container or receptacle, such as an urn or vault, for holding the bones of the dead. [Late Latin *ossuārium,* from Latin, neuter of *ossuārius,* of bones, from *ossu,* variant of *os* (stem *oss-*), bone. See **osth-** in Appendix.*]

os·te·al (ŏs'tē-əl) *adj.* **1.** Bony; osseous. **2.** Pertaining to bone or to the skeleton. [OSTE(O)- + -AL.]

os·te·i·tis (ŏs'tē-ī'tĭs) *n.* Inflammation of bone or bony tissue. [New Latin : OSTE(O)- + -ITIS.]

Ost·end (ŏ-stĕnd', ŏs'tĕnd'). A seaport in northwestern Belgium, on the North Sea. Population, 57,000.

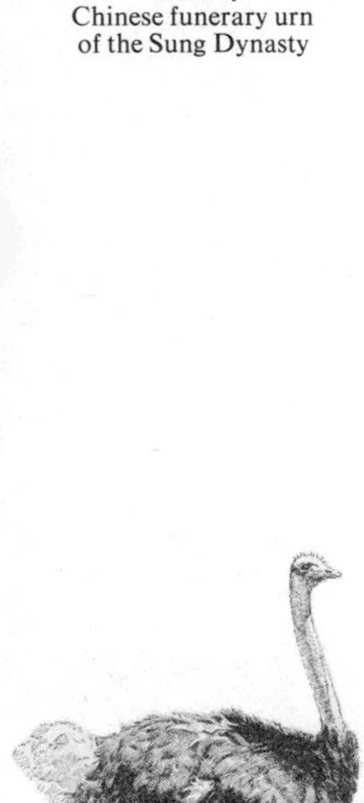

ostrich
Struthio camelus
A male of the species

os·ten·si·ble (ŏ-stĕn'sə-bəl) *adj.* Given or appearing as such; seeming; professed: *His ostensible purpose was charity, his real goal popularity.* [French, from Medieval Latin *ostensibilis,* from Latin *ostendere,* to show : *ob,* before + *tendere,* to stretch (see **ten-** in Appendix*).] —**os·ten'si·bly** *adv.*

os·ten·sive (ŏ-stĕn'sĭv) *adj.* **1. a.** Ostensible; apparent. **b.** Showing; revealing; betokening. **2.** Obviously or manifestly demonstrative. [Late Latin *ostensīvus,* from Latin *ostensus,* past participle of *ostendere,* to show. See **ostensible.**] —**os·ten'sive·ly** *adv.*

os·ten·so·ri·um (ŏs'tən-sôr'ē-əm, -sōr'ē-əm) *n., pl.* **-soria** (-sôr'ē-ə, -sōr'ē-ə). Also **os·ten·so·ry** (ŏ-stĕn'sə-rē) *pl.* **-ries.** *Roman Catholic Church.* A receptacle in which the Host is exposed for adoration; monstrance. [Medieval Latin *ostensōrium,* from Latin *ostendere,* to show. See **ostensible.**]

os·ten·ta·tion (ŏs'tĕn-tā'shən, ŏs'tən-) *n.* **1.** Pretentious display meant to impress others; boastful showiness. **2.** *Archaic.* An act of showing; exhibition. [Middle English *ostentacioun,* from Old French *ostentation,* from Latin *ostentātiō,* from *ostentāre,* frequentative of *ostendere,* to show. See **ostensible.**]

os·ten·ta·tious (ŏs'tĕn-tā'shəs, ŏs'tən-) *adj.* Characterized by or given to ostentation; showy; pretentious. See Synonyms at **ornate.** —**os'ten·ta'tious·ly** *adv.*

osteo-, oste-. Indicates bone or bones; for example, **osteomyelitis, osteoid.** [Greek, from *osteon,* bone. See **osth-** in Appendix.*]

osteo. osteopath; osteopathy.

os·te·o·ar·thri·tis (ŏs'tē-ō-är-thrī'tĭs) *n.* Degenerative joint disease.

os·te·o·blast (ŏs'tē-ə-blăst') *n.* A cell from which bone develops. [OSTEO- + -BLAST.] —**os'te·o·blas'tic** *adj.*

os·te·oc·la·sis (ŏs'tē-ŏk'lə-sĭs) *n.* **1.** Surgical fracture of a bone, performed to correct a deformity. **2.** The process of dissolution and resorption of bony tissue in the regeneration of bone. [New Latin : OSTEO- + Greek *klasis,* breakage (see **-clase**).]

os·te·o·clast (ŏs'tē-ə-klăst') *n.* **1.** An instrument used in surgical osteoclasis. **2.** A large multinuclear cell that resorbs bony tissue in osteoclasis. [OSTEO- + -CLAST.] —**os'te·o·clas'tic** *adj.*

os·te·o·cra·ni·um (ŏs'tē-ō-krā'nē-əm) *n.* The ossified embryonic cranium, as distinguished from the **chondrocranium** *(see).* [New Latin : OSTEO- + CRANIUM.] —**os'te·o·cra'ni·al** *adj.*

os·te·oid (ŏs'tē-oid') *adj.* Resembling bone. —*n.* The bone matrix, especially before calcification. [OSTE(O)- + -OID.]

os·te·ol·o·gy (ŏs'tē-ŏl'ə-jē) *n.* **1.** The anatomical study of bones. **2.** The bone structure or system of an animal. [Greek *osteologia* : OSTEO- + -LOGY.] —**os'te·o·log'i·cal** (ŏs'tē-ə-lŏj'ĭ-kəl) *adj.* —**os'te·ol'o·gist** *n.*

os·te·o·ma (ŏs'tē-ō'mə) *n., pl.* **-mas** or **-mata** (-mə-tə). A benign bony tumor, especially one in the skull. [OSTE(O)- + -OMA.]

os·te·o·ma·la·cia (ŏs'tē-ō-mə-lā'shə, -shē-ə) *n.* Softening of the bones because of a deficiency of vitamin D or of calcium and phosphorus. [New Latin : OSTEO- + *malacia,* softness, from Greek *malakia,* from *malakos,* soft (see **mel-**[1] in Appendix*).]

os·te·o·my·e·li·tis (ŏs'tē-ō-mī'ə-lī'tĭs) *n.* Inflammation of the bone marrow. [New Latin : OSTEO- + MYELITIS.]

os·te·o·path (ŏs'tē-ə-păth') *n.* Also **os·te·op·a·thist** (ŏs'tē-ŏp'ə-thĭst). *Abbr.* **osteo.** One who practices osteopathy.

os·te·op·a·thy (ŏs'tē-ŏp'ə-thē) *n. Abbr.* **osteo.** A medical therapy that emphasizes manipulative techniques for correcting somatic abnormalities thought to cause disease and inhibit recovery. [OSTEO- + -PATHY.] —**os'te·o·path'ic** (ŏs'tē-ə-păth'ĭk) *adj.* —**os'te·o·path'i·cal·ly** *adv.*

os·te·o·phyte (ŏs'tē-ə-fīt') *n.* A small abnormal bony outgrowth. [OSTEO- + -PHYTE.] —**os'te·o·phyt'ic** (-fĭt'ĭk) *adj.*

os·te·o·plas·tic (ŏs'tē-ə-plăs'tĭk) *adj.* **1.** *Surgery.* Of or pertaining to osteoplasty. **2.** *Physiology.* Pertaining to or functioning in bone formation.

os·te·o·plas·ty (ŏs'tē-ə-plăs'tē) *n., pl.* **-ties.** The surgical repair or alteration of bone. [OSTEO- + -PLASTY.]

os·te·ot·o·my (ŏs'tē-ŏt'ə-mē) *n., pl.* **-mies.** The surgical division or sectioning of bone. [OSTEO- + -TOMY.] —**os'te·ot'o·mist** *n.*

Ö·ster·reich. The German name for **Austria.**

Os·ti·a (ŏs'tē-ə; *Italian* ôs'tyä). A town of east-central Italy, at the mouth of the Tiber east of ancient Ostia, the port of Rome.

Os·ti·ak. Variant of **Ostyak.**

os·ti·ar·y (ŏs'tē-ĕr'ē) *n., pl.* **-ies. 1.** *Roman Catholic Church.* One who is ordained in the lowest of the minor orders. **2.** A doorkeeper at a church. [Latin *ōstiārius,* doorkeeper, from *ōstium,* an opening, from *ōs,* mouth. See **ōs-** in Appendix.*]

os·ti·na·to (ŏs'tĭ-nä'tō) *n., pl.* **-tos.** *Music.* A short melody or phrase that is constantly repeated in the same pitch. [Italian, "stubborn," from Latin *obstinātus,* OBSTINATE.]

os·ti·ole (ŏs'tē-ōl') *n. Biology.* A small opening or pore. [Latin *ōstiolum,* diminutive of *ōstium,* OSTIUM.] —**os'ti·o'lar** *adj.*

os·ti·um (ŏs'tē-əm) *n., pl.* **-tia** (-tē-ə). *Biology.* A small opening; an ostiole. [Latin *ōstium,* river mouth, opening, from *ōs,* mouth. See **ōs-** in Appendix.*]

os·tler. Variant of **hostler.**

ost·mark (ôst'märk', ŏst'-) *n. Abbr.* **OM. 1.** The basic monetary unit of East Germany, equal to 100 pfennigs. See table of exchange rates at **currency. 2.** A coin worth one ostmark. [German *Ostmark,* "east Mark" : *Ost,* east, from Old High German *ōstan* (see **awes-** in Appendix*) + *Mark,* MARK (money).]

Ost·preus·sen. The German name for **East Prussia.**

os·tra·cism (ŏs'trə-sĭz'əm) *n.* **1.** Banishment or exclusion from a group; disgrace. **2.** In Athens and other cities of ancient Greece, the temporary banishment by popular vote of a citizen considered dangerous to the state. **3.** The act of ostracizing. **4.** The state or condition of being ostracized. [French *ostracisme,* from Greek *ostrakismos,* from *ostrakizein,* OSTRACIZE.]

os·tra·cize (ŏs'trə-sīz') *tr.v.* **-cized, -cizing, -cizes. 1.** To banish or exclude from a group; shut out; shun. **2.** To banish by ostracism, as in ancient Greece. [Greek *ostrakizein,* from *ostrakon,* shell, shard (from the shard with which the Athenian citizen voted for ostracism). See **osth-** in Appendix.*]

os·tra·cod (ŏs'trə-kŏd') *n.* Any of various minute, chiefly freshwater crustaceans of the order Ostracoda, having a bivalve carapace. [New Latin *ostracoda,* from Greek *ostrakōdēs,* testaceous, from *ostrakon,* shell. See **osth-** in Appendix.*]

O·stra·va (ô'strə-və). Formerly **Mo·rav·ská Ostrava** (mō'räv-skä). A city of north-central Czechoslovakia. Population, 259,000.

os·trich (ŏs'trĭch, ôs'-) *n., pl.* **-triches** or **ostrich. 1.** Any of several large, flightless African birds of the genus *Struthio,* characterized by long, bare necks and legs, two-toed feet, and plumage used for decoration and brushes. **2.** A similar bird, the **rhea** *(see).* **3.** One who is thought to emulate the ostrich's alleged habit of burying its head in the sand to escape from disagreeable situations. [Middle English *ostriche,* from Old

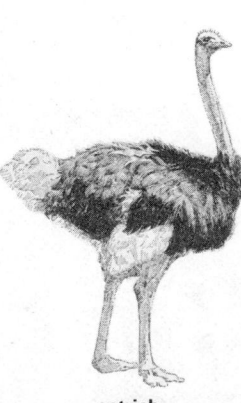

French *ostrusce,* from Vulgar Latin *avistrūthius* (unattested) : Latin *avis,* bird (see **awi-** in Appendix*) + Late Latin *strūthiō,* ostrich, from Greek *struthiōn* (see **struthious**).]

ostrich fern. A fern, *Matteuccia Struthiopteris* of northern temperate regions, having long, plumelike fronds.

Os·tro·goth (ŏs′trə-gŏth′) *n.* One of a tribe of eastern Goths that conquered and ruled Italy from A.D. 493 to 555. [Late Latin *Ostrogothis* : *ostro-,* eastward (see **awes-** in Appendix*) + *Gothus,* GOTH.] **—Os′tro·goth′ic** *adj.*

Ost·wald (ôst′vält′), **(Friedrick) Wilhelm.** 1853–1932. Russian-born German physical chemist; pioneered in catalysis.

Os·ty·ak (ŏs′tē-ăk′) *n.* Also **Os·ti·ak.** **1.** One of a Finno-Ugric people inhabiting western Siberia. **2.** The Ugric language spoken by this people. [Russian, from Ostyak *āsyakh,* dwellers on the Ob River, from *Ās,* the Ob River, USSR.]

OSU, O.S.U. Order of St. Ursula.

Os·wald (ŏz′wôld′). A masculine given name. [Middle English *Oswald,* Old English *Ōsweald* : *ōs,* god (see **ansu-** in Appendix*) + *weald,* power (see **wel-**[3] in Appendix*).]

Os·wald (ŏz′wôld′), **Lee Harvey.** 1939–1963. American who was declared by the Warren Commission the assassin of President John F. Kennedy (November 22, 1963).

Os·we·go tea (ŏs-wē′gō). An aromatic plant, *Monarda didyma,* of North America, having clusters of fragrant scarlet flowers. Also called "bee balm."

Oś·wię·cim (ôsh-vyĕɴ′tsēm). *German* **Ausch·witz** (oush′vĭts). A city in southern Poland and the site of a German extermination camp during World War II. Population, 57,000.

OT, O.T. Old Testament.

O·ta·hei·te. The former name for **Tahiti.**

Otaheite orange. A widely cultivated house plant, *Citrus taitensis,* resembling a miniature orange tree, and having lemon-shaped, insipid fruit. Also called "Tahiti orange."

O·ta·ru (ō-tä′rōō). A city and seaport of Japan on Ishikari Bay on the west coast of Hokkaido. Population, 207,000.

OTC, O.T.C. **1.** Officer in Tactical Command. **2.** Officer's Training Corps.

oth·er (ŭth′ər) *adj.* **1.** Being or designating the remaining one of two or more: *the other ear.* **b.** Being or designating the remaining ones of several. Used before a plural noun: *His other books are still in storage.* **2.** Different from that or those implied or specified: *Any other man would tell the truth. Call me some other time.* **3.** Of a different character or quality. Used with *than: His personality is other than meets the eye.* See Usage note below. **4.** Of a different time or era either future or past: *other centuries; other generations.* **5.** Additional; extra: *I have no other shoes.* **6.** Opposite; contrary; reverse: *other side.* **7.** Alternate; second: *every other day.* **—the other day** (or **night, evening,** or the like). Not long ago; recently. **—***n.* **1. a.** The remaining one of two or more: *One took a taxi, and the other walked home.* **b.** *Plural.* The remaining ones of several: *After his departure the others resumed the discussion.* **2. a.** A different person or thing: *Each cold wave came after the other.* **b.** An additional person or thing: *How many others will come later?* **—***pron.* **1.** A different or another person or thing: *something or other.* **2.** *Plural.* People aside from oneself: *"Others may indeed talk."* (Anthony Berkeley). **—***adv.* Otherwise; differently; in another way: *She performed other than perfectly.* See Usage note below. [Middle English *other,* Old English *ōther.* See **an**[2] in Appendix.*]

Usage: *Other than* is employed both adjectively and adverbially to express difference or opposition: *books other than fiction; perform other* (or *otherwise*) *than perfectly.* It should not be used as the equivalent of *apart from* or *aside from* in the following: *He said nothing more, apart* (or *aside*) *from noting a minor change* (not *other than to note*). *There is a slight inflammation, but apart from that* (or *otherwise*) *his progress is good* (not *other than that*). —See Usage note at **each other.**

oth·er·wise (ŭth′ər-wīz′) *adv.* **1.** In another way; differently: *She thought otherwise.* **2.** Under other circumstances: *Otherwise I might have helped.* **3.** In other respects: *an otherwise logical mind.* **—***adj.* **1.** Other than supposed; different: *The evidence is otherwise.* **2.** Other: *be otherwise than happy.* See Usage note at **other.** [Middle English *otherwise,* Old English *(on) ōthre wīsan,* (in) another manner : *ōther,* OTHER + *wīse,* way, -WISE.]

oth·er·world·ly (ŭth′ər-wûrld′lē) *adj.* **1.** Of, pertaining to, or characteristic of another world, especially a mystical or transcendental world. **2.** Devoted to the world of the mind; concerned with intellectual or imaginative things. **—oth′er·world′li·ness** *n.*

Oth·man[1]. *Poetic.* Variant of **Ottoman.**

Oth·man[2]. See **Osman I.**

o·tic (ō′tĭk) *adj.* Of, pertaining to, or located near the ear; auricular. [Greek *ōtikos,* from *ous* (stem *ōt-*), ear. See **ous-** in Appendix.*]

-otic. Indicates: **1.** Affected with or by; for example, **sclerotic.** **2.** Producing or causing; for example, **narcotic.** **3.** Having a specific disease; for example, **epizootic.** [Old French *-otique* and Latin *-ōticus,* from Greek *-ōtikos,* adjectival suffix formed from *-o-*stem verbs and *-ōt-*stem nouns.]

o·ti·ose (ō′shē-ōs′, ō′tē-) *adj.* **1.** Having a lazy nature; indolent. **2.** Of no use; ineffective; futile. [Latin *ōtiōsus,* from *ōtium*†, leisure. See also **negotiate.**] **—o′ti·ose′ly** *adv.* **—o′ti·os′i·ty** (-ŏs′ə-tē) *n.*

O·tis (ō′tĭs), **James.** 1725–1783. American revolutionary leader and pamphleteer.

o·ti·tis (ō-tī′tĭs) *n.* Inflammation of the ear. [New Latin : OT(O)- + -ITIS.] **—o·tit′ic** (ō-tĭt′ĭk) *adj.*

oto-, ot-. Indicates the ear; for example, **otology.** [New Latin, from Greek *ous* (stem *ōt-*), ear. See **ous-** in Appendix.*]

o·to·cyst (ō′tə-sĭst′) *n.* **1.** The auditory capsule in a vertebrate embryo. **2.** An organ of balance; a **statocyst** *(see).* **—o′to·cys′tic** (ō′tə-sĭs′tĭk) *adj.*

O·toe (ō′tō) *n., pl.* **Otoe** or **Otoes.** Also **O·to** *pl.* **Oto** or **Otos.** **1.** A member of a tribe of North American Indians that once inhabited Nebraska. **2.** A member of this tribe. **3.** The Siouan language of this tribe. [Possibly from Iowa-Otoe *wat′ota,* "lechers" (referring to a historical or legendary incident of seduction).] **—O′toe** *adj.*

otol. otology.

o·to·lar·yn·gol·o·gy (ō′tō-lăr′ĭng-gŏl′ə-jē) *n.* The branch of medicine that combines treatment of the ear, nose, and throat. [OTO- + LARYNGO- + -LOGY.] **—o′to·lar·yn′go·log′i·cal** (ō′tō-lə-rĭng′gə-lŏj′ĭ-kəl) *adj.* **—o′to·lar′yn·gol′o·gist** *n.*

o·to·lith (ō′tə-lĭth′) *n.* One of many minute calcareous particles found in the inner ear of certain vertebrates and in the statocysts of many invertebrates. Also called "ear stone." [French *otolithe* : OTO- + -LITH.]

o·tol·o·gy (ō-tŏl′ə-jē) *n. Abbr.* **otol.** The anatomy, physiology, and pathology of the ear. **—o′to·log′i·cal** (ō′tə-lŏj′ĭ-kəl) *adj.* **—o·tol′o·gist** *n.* [OTO- + -LOGY.]

O·tran·to, Strait of (ō-trän′tō). A strait between Italy and Albania, connecting the Adriatic and Ionian seas.

OTS, O.T.S. Officer's Training School.

ot·tar. Variant of **attar.**

ot·ta·va (ō-tä′və; *Italian* ôt-tä′vä) *adv. Music.* At an octave higher or lower than indicated. Used as a musical direction.

ot·ta·va ri·ma (ō-tä′və rē′mə; *Italian* ôt-tä′vä rē′mä). A stanza perfected by Ariosto and Tasso, consisting of eight lines of eleven syllables each in iambic pentameter and having a rhyme pattern *abababcc.* [Italian, "eighth rhyme."]

Ot·ta·wa[1] (ŏt′ə-wə, -wä′, -wô′) *n.* **1.** A group of Algonquian-speaking Indians, originally inhabiting the region of the Ottawa River in Ontario, Canada. **2.** A member of this group. **3.** The Ojibwa dialect of this group. [From the *Ottawa* River, from Algonquian *otaawaa.*]

Ot·ta·wa[2] (ŏt′ə-wə, -wä′, -wô′). **1.** The capital of Canada, on the Ottawa River, at the southeastern tip of Ontario near the U.S. border. Population, 281,000. **2.** A river of Canada, rising in southeastern Ontario and flowing 628 miles, south and southeast, to join the St. Lawrence at Montreal.

ot·ter (ŏt′ər) *n., pl.* **otter** or **-ters.** **1.** Any of various aquatic, carnivorous mammals of the genus *Lutra* and allied genera, having webbed feet and dense, dark-brown fur. **2.** The fur of any of these animals. [Middle English *oter,* Old English *otor.* See **wed-**[1] in Appendix.*]

ot·to. Variant of **attar.**

Ot·to I (ŏt′ō). Called "Otto the Great." A.D. 912–973. King of Germany (936–73); first Holy Roman Emperor (962–73).

Ot·to (ŏt′ō), **Nikolaus August.** 1832–1891. German automotive inventor and manufacturer.

ot·to·man (ŏt′ə-mən) *n., pl.* **-mans.** **1. a.** An upholstered sofa or divan without arms or a back. **b.** An upholstered low seat or cushioned footstool. **2.** A heavy silk or rayon fabric with a corded texture, usually used for coats and trimmings. [French *ottomane,* from feminine of OTTOMAN.]

Ot·to·man (ŏt′ə-mən) *n., pl.* **-mans.** *Poetic.* **Oth·man** (ŏth′mən, ŏth-man′). A Turk; especially, one belonging to the tribe or family of **Osman I** *(see).* **—***adj.* **1.** Of or pertaining to the Turks; Turkish. **2.** Of or pertaining to the Turkish Empire and dynasty founded by Osman I. [French, from Medieval Latin *Ottomānus,* from Arabic *Othmānī,* Turkish, from Turkish *Osman,* Osman I. See **Osmanli.**]

Ottoman Empire. The Turkish Empire (1299–1919) in southwestern Asia, northeastern Africa, and southeastern Europe. Capital, Constantinople. Also called "Turkish Empire."

Ottoman Turkish. The form of Turkish used by the Ottoman Turks. Also called "Osmanli."

Ot·way (ŏt′wā′), **Thomas.** 1652–1685. English dramatist.

oua·ba·in (wä-bā′ĭn) *n.* A white poisonous glucoside, $C_{29}H_{44}O_{12} \cdot 8H_2O$, extracted from the seeds of the African trees *Strophanthus gratus* and *Acokanthera ouabaio,* and used as a heart stimulant, and by some African tribes as a dart poison. [French *ouaba(io),* from Somali *wabayo.*]

Ouach·i·ta (wŏsh′ə-tô′, wôsh′-). Also **Wash·i·ta.** A river rising in southwestern Arkansas and flowing about 600 miles east and southeast to join the Red River in Louisiana.

Oua·ga·dou·gou (wä′gə-dōō′gōō). The capital of Upper Volta, in the center of the country. Population, 51,000.

ou·bli·ette (ōō′blē-ĕt′) *n.* A dungeon with a trap door in the ceiling as its only means of entrance or exit. [French, from *oublier,* to forget, from Old French *oblider,* from Vulgar Latin *oblītāre* (unattested), from Latin *oblīvīscī* (past participle *oblītus*), to forget. See **legwh-** in Appendix.*]

ouch[1] (ouch) *interj.* Used to express sudden pain or displeasure. [Expressive.]

ouch[2] (ouch) *n. Archaic.* **1.** A setting for a precious stone. **2.** A brooch or ornament set with jewels. [Middle English *ouche,* from the phrase *an ouche,* mistaken division of *a nouche,* from Old French *nouche,* brooch, from Germanic. See **ned-** in Appendix.*]

oud (ōōd) *n.* A musical instrument of northern Africa and southwest Asia resembling a lute. [Arabic *'ūd,* "wood."]

Oudh (oud). A region and former kingdom, 24,071 square miles in area, in central Uttar Pradesh State, Republic of India.

ought[1] (ôt) *v.* Used as an auxiliary verb followed by an infinitive with *to.* Indicates: **1.** Obligation or duty: *You ought to work harder than that.* **2.** Expediency or prudence: *You ought to wear a raincoat.* **3.** Desirability: *You ought to have been there; it was*

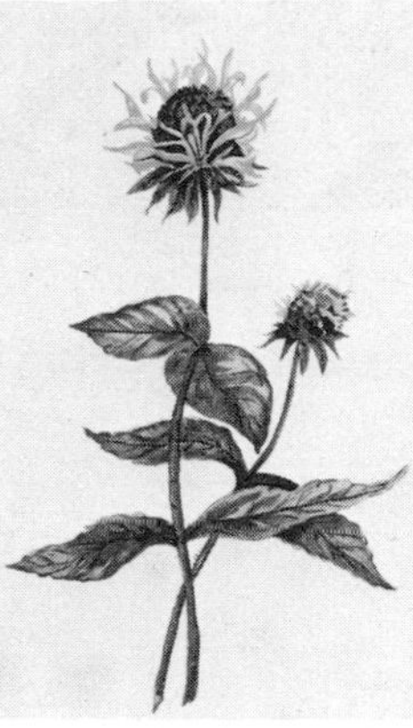

Oswego tea

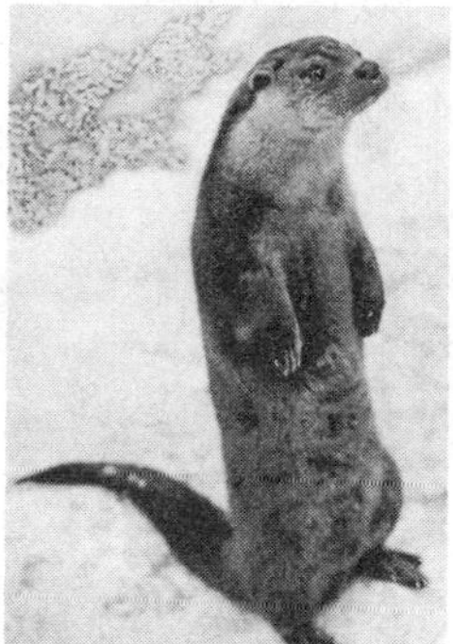

otter
Lutra canadensis
River otter

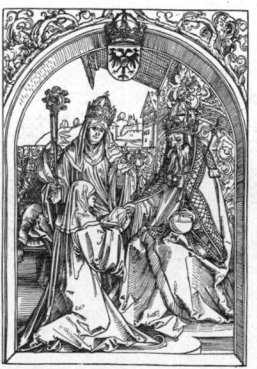

Otto I
Sixteenth-century woodcut of the emperor receiving the works of Roswitha, Benedictine nun and poetess

t tight/th thin, path/*th* this, bathe/ŭ cut/ûr urge/v valve/w with/y yes/z zebra, size/zh vision/ə about, item, edible, gallop, circus/ à *Fr.* ami/œ *Fr.* feu, *Ger.* schön/ü *Fr.* tu, *Ger.* über/KH *Ger.* ich, *Scot.* loch/N *Fr.* bon. ***Follows main vocabulary.** †**Of obscure origin.**

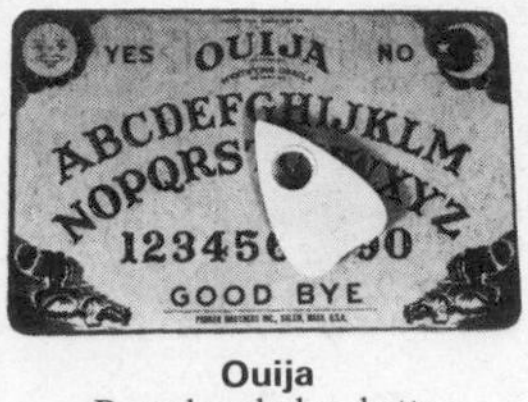

Ouija
Board and planchette

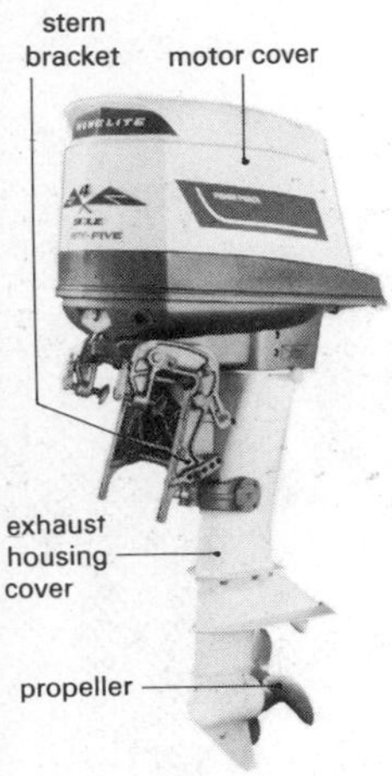

outboard motor

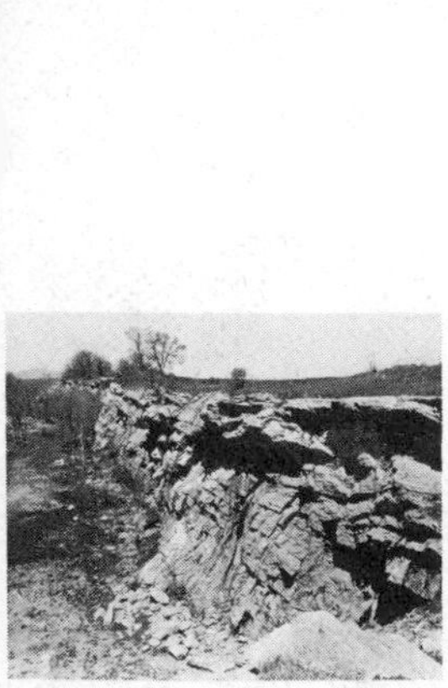

outcrop
Natural exposure of rock enlarged by quarrying

great fun. **4.** Probability or likelihood: *She ought to finish by next week.* [Middle English *aghten, oughten,* to be obliged to, owe, from *aghte, oughte,* possessed, owned, Old English *āhte,* first and third singular past indicative of *āgan,* to possess. See **eik-** in Appendix.*]

Usage: Sometimes the infinitive following *ought* is omitted if it is understood from the context: *Should we begin soon? We ought to. Ought,* used without *to,* is improper in such combinations as. *He ought and can come* (properly *can and ought to*); *He ought and could have come* (properly *could and ought to have*). *Ought* is not inflected. With a present infinitive, it expresses present time: *He ought to go.* Past time is indicated by the perfect infinitive: *He ought to have gone.* Negation is accomplished by using *not* immediately after *ought: ought not to have gone.* Auxiliary verbs such as *did, had, should,* and *could* are never used with *ought.* Thus, *He ought to write* (not *had ought*); *He ought not to complain* (not *hadn't ought* or *shouldn't ought*).

ought². Variant of **aught**.

ought³. *Obsolete.* Alternate past participle of **owe**.

Oui·ja (wē′jə, -jē) *n.* A trademark for a board with the alphabet and other symbols on it, and a planchette that is thought, when touched with the fingers, to move in such a way as to spell out spiritualistic and telepathic messages on the board. [French *oui,* yes + German *ja,* yes.]

ounce¹ (ouns) *n. Abbr.* **oz** **1. a.** A unit of weight in the U.S. Customary System, an avoirdupois unit equal to 16 drams or 437.5 grains. There are 16 ounces to the pound. **b.** A unit of apothecary weight, equal to 480 grains or 1.097 avoirdupois ounces. **2. a.** A unit of volume or capacity in the U.S. Customary System, used in liquid measure, equal to 8 fluid drams or 1.804 cubic inches. There are 16 ounces to the pint. **b.** A unit of volume or capacity in the British Imperial System, used in dry and liquid measure, equal to 1.734 cubic inches. The ounce, as a unit of liquid measure in both the U.S. and British Systems, is also called "fluid ounce." See **measurement**. **3.** A tiny bit. [Middle English *unce,* from Old French, from Latin *uncia,* a twelfth, ounce, from *ūnus,* unit, one. See **oino-** in Appendix.*]

ounce² (ouns) *n.* The **snow leopard** *(see).* [Middle English *once,* from Old French, variant of *lonce* (the *l* being taken as the definite article), from Latin *lynx* (stem *lync-*), lynx, from Greek *lunx.* See **leuk-** in Appendix.*]

our (our) *adj.* The possessive form of the pronoun *we.* Used attributively to indicate possession, agency, or reception: *our children; pursuing our aims; receiving our first setback.* [Middle English *ure, oure,* Old English *ūre.* See **nes-²** in Appendix.*]

Our Lady. The Virgin Mary.

ours (ourz). Possessive pronoun, absolute form of *our.* **1.** Belonging to us; our own. Used predicatively: *The house is ours.* **2.** The one or ones that belong to us. Used substantively: *Ours is the best.* **—of ours.** Belonging to us: *friends of ours.* [Middle English *ures, oures,* from *ure, oure,* OUR.]

our·self (our-sĕlf′, är-) *pron.* Myself or ourselves collectively. A form corresponding to *ourselves,* but used only in regal or formal proclamations or editorial comments with the formal *we,* construed as singular.

our·selves (our-sĕlvz′, är-) *pron.* A form of the first person plural pronoun. It is used: **1.** As a reflexive direct or indirect object, or the object of a preposition: *We injured ourselves.* **2.** For emphasis, with *we: We ourselves are excluded from the contract.* **3.** As an indication of our normal, customary, or healthy condition: *We have not been ourselves since he left.*

-ous. Indicates: **1.** Possessing, having, or full of; for example, **odorous, joyous**. **2.** *Chemistry.* Occurring with a valence that is lower than that in a comparable *-ic* system; for example, **ferrous, osmous**. Compare **-ic**. [Middle English, from Old French *-os, -us, -eus, -eux,* from Latin *-ōsus, -us,* adjectival suffixes.]

Ouse (o͞oz). **1.** Also **Great Ouse**. A river rising in Northamptonshire, England, and flowing 160 miles to The Wash. **2.** A river rising in Yorkshire, England, and flowing 57 miles southeast to join the Trent, with which it forms the Humber.

ou·sel. Variant of **ouzel**.

oust (oust) *tr.v.* **ousted, ousting, ousts.** To eject from a position or place; force out: *"the American Revolution, which ousted the English"* (Virginia S. Eifert). See Synonyms at **eject**. [Norman French *ouster,* from Latin *obstāre,* to hinder : *ob,* off, against + *stāre,* to stand (see **stā-** in Appendix*).]

oust·er (ous′tər) *n.* **1. a.** The act of ousting. **b.** The state of being ousted. **2.** One who ousts. **3.** *Law.* The act of forcing one out of possession or occupancy of material property to which he is entitled; illegal or wrongful dispossession. [Norman French, substantive use of the infinitive *ouster,* to OUST.]

out (out) *adv.* **1.** Away or forth from inside: *go out of the office.* **2.** Away from the center or middle: *The troops fanned out.* **3.** Away from a normal or usual place: *stepped out for a minute.* See Usage note below. **4.** From inside a building or shelter into the open air; outside: *The boy went out to play.* **5.** From within a container or source: *drain the water out.* **6.** To exhaustion or depletion: *The supplies have run out.* See Usage note below. **7.** Into extinction or imperceptibility: *The fire has gone out.* **8.** To a finish or conclusion: *Play the game out.* **9.** Into being or evident existence: *The new car models have come out.* **10.** Into view: *The moon came out.* See Usage note below. **11.** Without inhibition; boldly: *Speak out.* **12.** Into possession of another or others; into distribution: *giving out free passes.* **13.** Into disuse or an unfashionable status: *Knee-length hems have gone out.* See Usage note below. **14.** *Baseball.* So as to be retired, or counted as an out: *He grounded out to the shortstop.* **—out of.** **1.** From among: *one out of thousands.* **2.** Past the boundaries, limits, or usual position of: *The eagle soared out of sight.* **3.** *Informal.* With headquarters in: *He works out of the branch office.* **4.** From: *made out of wood.* **5.** Because of; owing to: *He did it out of malice.* **6.** Born of; foaled by. *—adj.* **1.** Exterior; external: *On the out surface of a ship's hull.* **2.** Unable to be used; in disrepair: *The road is out beyond this point.* **3.** *Informal.* Without an amount (of money) possessed previously: *I am out ten dollars.* **4.** Not available for use or consideration: *A taxi is out, because we haven't the money.* **5.** Bare or threadbare: *a jacket, out at the elbow.* **—out from under.** *Informal.* Relieved from danger or distress: *He's finally out from under financially.* *—prep.* **1.** Through; forth from: *He fell out the window.* **2.** Beyond or outside of: *Out this door is the garage.* *—n.* **1.** A person or thing that is out; especially, one who is out of power. **2.** A means of escape: *The window was my only out.* **3.** *Baseball.* **a.** Any play in which a batter or base runner is retired. **b.** The player retired in such a play. **4.** *Tennis.* A serve or return that falls out of bounds. **5.** *Printing.* A word or other part of a manuscript omitted from the printed copy. **—on the outs.** *Informal.* Not on friendly terms; disagreeing. *—v.* **outed, outing, outs.** *—intr.* To be disclosed or revealed; come out: *Truth will out.* *—tr.* **1.** To put (a person or thing) out. **2.** *British Slang.* To knock unconscious. [Middle English *out,* Old English *ūt.* See **ud-** in Appendix.*]

Usage: In addition to the adjectival senses defined above, **out** is used in its adverbial senses as a predicate adjective with the verb *be.* For example, the definitions given for the adverb may be used adjectivally as follows: *He was out when I phoned* (sense 3); *The oil supply was out* (sense 6); *The sun may be out later* (sense 10); *Shoulder pads are out this year* (sense 13).

out-. Indicates: **1.** To a surpassing or superior degree; for example, **outwork, outplay, outshoot**. **2.** Located outside or externally; for example, **outboard, outhouse**. ***Note:*** Many compounds other than those entered here may be formed with *out-*. In forming compounds, *out-* is normally joined with the following element without space or hyphen: **outlive**. However, in formations (usually nonce words) in which the second element begins with a capital, the hyphen is used: *"Father Guarini's caprices out-Borromini even Borromini himself"* (William Wilson). Also, the separate word *out* appears in a few phrases that are hyphenated. Those entered here are: **out-and-out, out-group, out-of-date, out-of-door** and **out-of-doors**, and **out-of-the-way**. *Out* may also be used separately as an adjective, as in *out sister.*

out·age (out′ĭj) *n.* **1.** A quantity or portion of something lacking after delivery or storage. **2.** A temporary suspension of operation, especially of electric power. [OUT + -AGE.]

out-and-out (out′n-out′) *adj.* Complete; unconditional; thoroughgoing: *an out-and-out liar.*

out·back (out′băk′) *adv.* Out to or in the back country of Australia or New Zealand: *going outback.* *—n.* (out′băk′). The hinterland of a given country, usually Australia or New Zealand. Often used attributively: *outback life.* **—out′back′er** *n.*

out·bid (out-bĭd′) *tr.v.* **-bid, -bidden** (bĭd′n), or **-bid, -bidding, -bids.** To bid higher than: *He outbid his rivals at the auction.*

out·board (out′bôrd′, -bōrd′) *adj.* **1.** *Nautical.* **a.** Situated outside the hull of a vessel. **b.** Being away from the center line of the hull of a ship. **2.** *Aviation.* Situated toward or nearer the end of a wing. **—out′board′** *adv.*

outboard motor. A detachable engine mounted on the stern of a boat, or on outboard brackets.

out·bound (out′bound′) *adj.* Outward bound; headed away.

out·break (out′brāk′) *n.* A sudden eruption: *"an outbreak of strikes, violent agitation, and arrests"* (Samuel Chew).

out·breed (out′brēd′) *tr.v.* **-bred** (-brĕd′), **-breeding, -breeds.** To subject to outbreeding.

out·breed·ing (out′brē′dĭng) *n.* **1.** The breeding of distantly related or unrelated stocks of animals. **2.** *Anthropology.* The mating of persons from different groups, often as a consequence of taboos against marriage within the group.

out·build·ing (out′bĭl′dĭng) *n.* A building separate from but associated with a main building.

out·burst (out′bûrst′) *n.* A sudden, violent outpouring; an energetic display, as of activity or passion: *an outburst of hatred.*

out·cast (out′kăst′, -käst′) *n.* One that has been excluded from a society or system. **—out′cast′** *adj.*

out·caste (out′kăst′, -käst′) *n.* A native of India who has been expelled from or has abandoned his caste.

out·class (out-klăs′, -kläs′) *tr.v.* **-classed, -classing, -classes.** To surpass decisively, so as to appear of a higher class.

out·come (out′kŭm′) *n.* A natural result; consequence. See Synonyms at **effect**.

out·crop (out′krŏp′) *n. Geology.* A portion of bedrock or other stratum protruding through the soil level. *—intr.v.* (out-krŏp′) **outcropped, -cropping, -crops.** *Geology.* To protrude above the soil, as rock formations.

out·cross (out′krôs′, -krŏs′) *tr.v.* **-crossed, -crossing, -crosses.** To breed (animals) that belong to different strains of the same breed. *—n.* **1.** The process of outcrossing. **2.** An offspring produced by outcrossing.

out·cry (out′krī′) *n., pl.* **-cries.** **1.** A loud cry or clamor. **2.** A strong protest or objection: *public outcry over the price rise.*

out·curve (out′kûrv′) *n. Baseball.* A pitched ball that curves away from the batter.

out·date (out-dāt′) *tr.v.* **-dated, -dating, -dates.** To replace or make obsolete, antiquated, or old-fashioned.

out·dis·tance (out-dĭs′təns) *tr.v.* **-tanced, -tancing, -tances.** **1.** To outrun, especially in a long-distance race. **2.** To surpass by a wide margin, especially through superior skill or endurance: *completely outdistanced by younger salesmen.*

ă pat/ā pay/âr care/ä father/b bib/ch church/d deed/ĕ pet/ē be/f fife/g gag/h hat/hw which/ĭ pit/ī pie/îr pier/j judge/k kick/l lid, needle/m mum/n no, sudden/ng thing/ŏ pot/ō toe/ô paw, for/oi noise/ou out/o͝o took/o͞o boot/p pop/r roar/s sauce/sh ship, dish/

out·do (out-do͞o′) *tr.v.* **-did** (-dĭd′), **-done** (-dŭn′), **-doing, -does** (-dŭz′). To exceed in performance. See Synonyms at **excel.**
out·door (out′dôr′, -dōr′) *adj.* Also **out-of-door** (out′əv-dôr′, -dōr′). Located in, done in, or suited to the open air.
out·doors (out-dôrz′, -dōrz′) *adv.* Also **out-of-doors** (out′əv-dôrz′, -dōrz′). In or into the open; outside of a house or shelter: *walking outdoors for fresh air.* —*n.* Also **out-of-doors.** The open air; the area away from human habitation.
out·er (out′ər) *adj.* **1.** Located on the outside; external. **2.** Farther from the center or middle.
Outer Heb·ri·des. See **Hebrides.**
Outer Mon·go·li·a. See **Mongolian People's Republic.**
out·er·most (out′ər-mōst′) *adj.* Most distant from the center or inside; farthest out; outmost.
outer space. Any region of space beyond limits determined with reference to the boundaries of a celestial body or system. Not in technical use.
out·face (out-fās′) *tr.v.* **-faced, -facing, -faces. 1.** To overcome with a bold or self-assured look; stare down. **2.** To defy; resist.
out·fall (out′fôl′) *n.* The place where a sewer, drain, or stream discharges.
out·field (out′fēld′) *n.* **1.** The grass-covered playing area extending outward from a baseball diamond, divided into right, center, and left field. Compare **infield. 2.** The members of a baseball team playing in the outfield. —**out′field′er** *n.*
out·fit (out′fĭt′) *n.* **1.** A set of tools or equipment for a specialized purpose: *a mountain-climber's outfit; a welder's outfit.* **2.** A set of clothing: *appear at the dance in an elegant outfit.* **3.** *Informal.* An association of persons, especially a military unit or a business organization. **4.** The act of equipping. —*tr.v.* **outfitted, -fitting, -fits.** To provide with an outfit: *This store outfits skiers.* See Synonyms at **furnish.** —**out′fit′ter** *n.*
out·flank (out-flăngk′) *tr.v.* **-flanked, -flanking, -flanks. 1.** To maneuver around and behind the flank of (an opposing force). **2.** To gain a tactical advantage over.
out·flow (out′flō′) *n.* **1.** The act of flowing out. **2.** Something that flows out. **3.** The amount flowing out.
out·fox (out-fŏks′) *tr.v.* **-foxed, -foxing, -foxes.** To get the better of by cunning; outsmart.
out·gas (out′găs′) *tr.v.* **-gassed, -gassing, -gasses.** *Technology.* To remove embedded gas from (a solid) by heating.
out·gen·er·al (out-jĕn′ər-əl, -jĕn′rəl) *tr.v.* **-aled, -aling, -als.** To surpass in leadership.
out·go (out-gō′) *tr.v.* **-went** (-wĕnt′), **-gone** (-gôn′, -gŏn′), **-going, -goes** (-gōz′). To exceed; surpass. —*n.* (out′gō′) *pl.* **outgoes.** Something that goes out, especially expenditure or cost. **2.** The act of going out.
out·go·ing (out′gō′ĭng) *adj.* **1.** Departing; going out; *an outgoing steamship.* **2.** To be taken out: *an outgoing order of coffee.* **3.** Friendly; sociable; extroverted.
out·group (out′gro͞op′) *n.* A group of people not belonging to or excluded from an **in-group** *(see).*
out·grow (out-grō′) *tr.v.* **-grew** (-gro͞o′), **-grown** (-grōn′), **-growing, -grows. 1.** To grow too large for: *He outgrew his new suit.* **2.** To lose or discard in the course of maturation: *He outgrew his former idealism.* **3.** To surpass in growth: *He had outgrown his father by the time he was eighteen.*
out·growth (out′grōth′) *n.* **1.** That which grows out of something; an offshoot: *an outgrowth of new shoots on a branch.* **2.** A result or consequence: *Inflation is an outgrowth of war.*
out·guess (out-gĕs′) *tr.v.* **-guessed, -guessing, -guesses. 1.** To anticipate correctly the actions of. **2.** To gain the advantage over by cleverness or forethought; outwit.
out·haul (out′hôl′) *n. Nautical.* A rope used to extend a sail along a spar or boom.
out·house (out′hous′) *n.* A toilet housed in a small structure.
out·ing (ou′tĭng) *n.* **1.** An excursion or pleasure trip, often including a picnic. **2.** A walk outdoors; an airing.
outing flannel. A soft, lightweight cotton fabric, usually with a short nap on both sides.
out·land (out′lănd′, -lənd) *n.* **1.** A foreign land. **2.** *Plural.* The outlying areas of a country; the provinces. [Middle English *outland,* Old English *ūtland* : *ūt,* OUT + land, LAND.] —**out′land′** *adj.* —**out′land′er** *n.*
out·land·ish (out-lăn′dĭsh) *adj.* **1.** Strikingly foreign; unfamiliar. **2.** *Archaic.* Of foreign origin; not native. **3.** Geographically remote from the familiar world. **4.** Conspicuously unconventional; bizarre; absurd. —See Synonyms at **strange.** [Middle English *outlandish,* Old English *ūtlandisc* : OUTLAND + -ISH.] —**out·land′ish·ly** *adv.* —**out·land′ish·ness** *n.*
out·last (out-lăst′, -läst′) *tr.v.* **-lasted, -lasting, -lasts.** To endure or live longer than. See Synonyms at **outlive.**
out·law (out′lô′) *n.* **1.** A habitual criminal. **2.** A person excluded from normal legal protection and rights. **3.** A wild or vicious animal. —*tr.v.* **outlawed, -lawing, -laws. 1.** To declare illegal. **2.** To ban. **3.** To deprive of the protection of the law. [Middle English *outlawe, outlage,* Old English *ūtlaga,* from Old Norse *ūtlagi,* from *ūtlagr,* outlawed : *ūt,* out (see **ud-** in Appendix*) + *lög,* law (see **legh-**[1] in Appendix*).]
out·law·ry (out′lô′rē) *n., pl.* **-ries. 1.** The act or process of outlawing. **2.** The state of being outlawed. **3.** Defiance of the law. [Middle English *outlagerie,* from Norman French *utlagerie,* from Middle English *outlage,* an OUTLAW.]
out·lay (out′lā′) *n.* **1.** The spending or disbursing of money: *"a few pennies had survived his weekly outlay on comics"* (Alan Sillitoe). **2.** The amount spent. —See Synonyms at **price.** —*tr.v.* (out-lā′) **outlaid** (-lād′), **-laying, -lays.** To expend (money).
out·let (out′lĕt′, -lĭt) *n.* **1.** A passage for escape or exit; vent. **2. a.** A means of releasing energies, drives, desires, or the like; emotional gratification: *"There is now scarcely any outlet for energy in this country except business."* (John Stuart Mill). **b.** A means of achieving self-expression. **3. a.** A commercial market for goods or services. **b.** A store that sells the goods of a particular manufacturer or wholesaler. **4.** *Electricity.* A receptacle, especially one mounted in a wall, that is connected to a power supply and equipped with a socket for a plug.
out·li·er (out′lī′ər) *n.* **1.** A portion of anything that exists or lies apart from the main body or system to which it belongs. **2.** One whose domicile lies at some appreciable remove from his place of business. **3.** *Geology.* A portion of stratified rock separated from a main formation by erosion. **4.** In U.S. frontier regions of the 19th century, a bushwhacker or marauder who lived out in the woods.
out·line (out′līn′) *n.* **1. a.** A line described in the plane of vision by the outer boundary of any object or figure. **b.** *Plural.* Contours delineating such a figure; lineaments. **c.** Contour; shape. **2.** A style of drawing in which objects are delineated in contours without shading. **3. a.** A general description or schematic summary. **b.** An abstract. **c.** A schematic synopsis of a written work. **d.** A preliminary draft or plan. **4.** *Plural.* The salient characteristics or general principles of a given subject; gist: *They agreed as to the grand outlines, but quibbled over particulars.* —See Synonyms at **form.** —*tr.v.* **outlined, -lining, -lines. 1.** To draw the outline of. **2.** To display or accentuate the outline of. **3.** To give the main points of; summarize.
out·live (out-lĭv′) *tr.v.* **-lived, -living, -lives. 1.** To live longer than; outlast. **2.** To live through; survive.
Synonyms: *outlive, outlast, survive.* These verbs all mean to exist longer than another person or thing. *Outlive* often implies the capacity for endurance in competition: *outlive one's enemies.* Sometimes it refers to going beyond a certain time: *He outlived his usefulness. Outlast* can often be used interchangeably with *outlive,* but it more commonly applies to things, stressing duration, rather than to persons. When applied to persons, *outlast* suggests endurance. *Survive* may be used with reference merely to living longer than another: *He is survived by his wife.* However, *survive* has the more common meaning of remaining alive after a dangerous event: *He survived the auto accident.*
out·look (out′lo͝ok′) *n.* **1.** The act of looking out. **2. a.** A place where something can be viewed. **b.** The view seen from such a place. **3.** A point of view or attitude. **4.** The probable result; expectation. —See Synonyms at **prospect.**
out·ly·ing (out′lī′ĭng) *adj.* Comparatively distant or remote from a center or middle.
out·mod·ed (out-mō′dĭd) *adj.* **1.** Not in fashion. **2.** No longer usable or practical; obsolete: *"an unpardonable reversion to an outmoded imperialism."* (W.L. Morton).
out·most (out′mōst′) *adj.* Farthest out; outermost.
out-of-date (out′əv-dāt′) *adj.* Outmoded; old-fashioned.
out-of-door. Variant of **outdoor.**
out-of-doors. Variant of **outdoors.**
out-of-the-way (out′əv-*thə*-wā′) *adj.* **1.** Distant; remote; secluded. **2.** Out of the ordinary; unusual.
out·pa·tient (out′pā′shənt) *n.* A patient who receives treatment at a hospital or clinic without being hospitalized.
out·play (out-plā′) *tr.v.* **-played, -playing, -plays.** To surpass (one's opponent) in playing some game.
out·post (out′pōst′) *n.* **1.** A detachment of troops stationed at a distance from a main unit of forces. **2.** The station occupied by such troops. **3.** Any outlying settlement.
out·pour (out-pôr′, -pōr′) *tr.v.* **-poured, -pouring, -pours.** To pour out. —*n.* (out′pôr′, -pōr′). A rapid outflow; an outpouring. —**out·pour′er** *n.*
out·pour·ing (out′pôr′ĭng, -pōr′ĭng) *n.* **1.** The act of pouring out: *"He cannot give himself fully in an outpouring of love unless someone else is there"* (Walter J. Ong). **2. a.** Something that pours out or is poured out; an outflow: *an outpouring of lava.* **b.** An outburst or effusion, especially of passionate or otherwise exaggerated utterance.
out·put (out′po͝ot′) *n.* **1.** The act of producing; production. **2.** The amount of something produced or manufactured during a given span of time. **3.** *Technology.* **a.** The energy, power, or work produced by a system. **b.** The information produced by a computer from a specific input.
out·rage (out′rāj′) *n.* **1.** An act of extreme violence or viciousness. **2.** Any act grossly offensive to decency, morality, or good taste. **3.** A severe insult or offense to one's integrity or pride: *"I have only had insults and outrage from her."* (Thackeray). **4.** A feeling of resentful anger. —*tr.v.* **outraged, -raging, -rages. 1.** To commit an outrage upon. **2.** To rape. **3.** To produce anger or resentment in: *Incompetence outraged him.* —See Synonyms at **offend.** [Middle English, excess, from Old French, "excess," atrocity, from *outre,* beyond. See **outré.**]
out·ra·geous (out-rā′jəs) *adj.* **1. a.** Being an outrage; grossly offensive; heinous. **b.** Disgraceful; shameful: *"I thought it was outrageous that our small temple still had some empty seats."* (Malcolm X). **2.** Having no regard for morality. **3.** Violent or unrestrained in temperament or behavior. **4.** Extravagant; immoderate; extreme: *She spends an outrageous amount on clothes.* —**out·ra′geous·ly** *adv.* —**out·ra′geous·ness** *n.*
Synonyms: *outrageous, flagrant, infamous, monstrous.* These adjectives describe behavior grossly offensive or revolting to society, and are often used interchangeably. *Outrageous* applies to any action, or result of an action, so distasteful or appalling as to be shocking or intolerable: *an outrageous remark; an outrageous price. Flagrant* adds to outrageous the idea of defiance of recognized authority: *a flagrant violation of the law. Infamous* has a personal sense, suggesting scandalous, odious,

t tight/th thin, path/*th* this, bathe/ŭ cut/ûr urge/v valve/w with/y yes/z zebra, size/zh vision/ə about, item, edible, gallop, circus/ à *Fr.* ami/œ *Fr.* feu, *Ger.* schön/ü *Fr.* tu, *Ger.* über/KH *Ger.* ich, *Scot.* loch/N *Fr.* bon. *Follows main vocabulary. †Of obscure origin.

or treasonable actions. *Monstrous* describes actions so outrageous as to be inhuman: *Kidnaping is a monstrous act.*

outrance. See **à outrance.**

ou·tré (o͞o-trā′) *adj.* Deviating from what is usual or proper; eccentric. [French, past participle of *outrer,* to pass beyond, go to excess, from *outre,* beyond, from Old French, from Latin *ultrā,* beyond, further. See **al-¹** in Appendix.*]

out·reach (out-rēch′) *v.* **-reached, -reaching, -reaches.** —*tr.* **1.** To reach or go beyond; surpass. **2.** To extend (something) outward. —*intr.* To reach out. —*n.* (out′rēch′). **1.** An act of reaching out. **2.** The extent of reach.

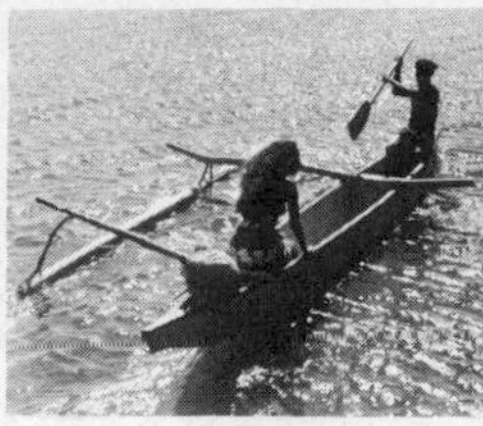

outrigger
Tahitian canoe equipped with an outrigger

out·ride¹ (out-rīd′) *tr.v.* **-rode** (-rōd′), **-ridden** (-rĭd′n), **-riding, -rides.** To ride faster, farther, or better than; outstrip.

out·ride² (out′rīd′) *n. Prosody.* An unstressed syllable or cluster of syllables within a given metrical unit that is omitted from the scansion pattern in sprung rhythm. [Coined by Gerard Manley Hopkins.]

out·rid·er (out′rī′dər) *n.* **1.** A mounted attendant who rides in front of or beside a carriage. **2.** Any guide or escort.

out·rig·ger (out′rĭg′ər) *n.* **1. a.** In seagoing canoes of the South Pacific and Indian oceans and in derivative craft, a float attached to laterally projecting spars so as to ride parallel to the length of the craft on either side as a means of preventing it from capsizing. **b.** Any vessel fitted with such a float. **2.** Any projecting frame extending laterally beyond the main structure of a vessel, vehicle, aircraft, or machine, to stabilize the structure or to support an extending part.

out·right (out′rīt′, -rīt′) *adv.* **1.** Without reservation or qualification; openly. **2.** Entirely; utterly; wholly. **3.** Without delay; straightway: *kill outright.* —*adj.* (out′rīt′). **1.** Without reservation; unqualified: *an outright gift.* **2. a.** Complete; total: *the outright cost.* **b.** Thoroughgoing; out-and-out: *outright viciousness.* **3.** Directed straight on; moving straight onward: *"an even, outright, but imperceptible speed"* (R.L. Stevenson).

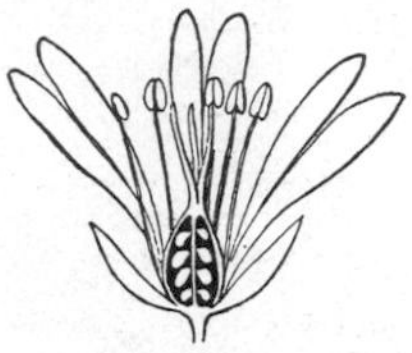

ovary
Longitudinal section of a chickweed-flower ovary, showing the ovules

out·run (out-rŭn′) *tr.v.* **-ran** (-răn′), **-run, -running, -runs. 1.** To run faster than. **2.** To escape from: *outrun one's creditors.* **3.** To go beyond or exceed (some limit): *"man's ingenuity has outrun his intelligence"* (Joseph Wood Krutch).

out·sell (out-sĕl′) *tr.v.* **-sold** (-sōld′), **-selling, -sells. 1.** To surpass in amount sold. **2.** To outdo in selling.

out·set (out′sĕt′) *n.* Beginning; start; commencement.

out·shine (out-shīn′) *v.* **-shone** (-shōn′, -shŏn′), **-shining, -shines.** —*tr.* **1.** To shine brighter than. **2.** To surpass in beauty or obvious excellence. —*intr.* To shine forth.

out·shoot (out-sho͞ot′) *v.* **-shot** (-shŏt′), **-shooting, -shoots.** —*tr.* **1.** To shoot better than. **2.** To extend beyond. —*intr.* To protrude or project. —*n.* (out′sho͞ot′). **1.** A protuberance, projection, or outgrowth. **2.** A flowing or gushing forth.

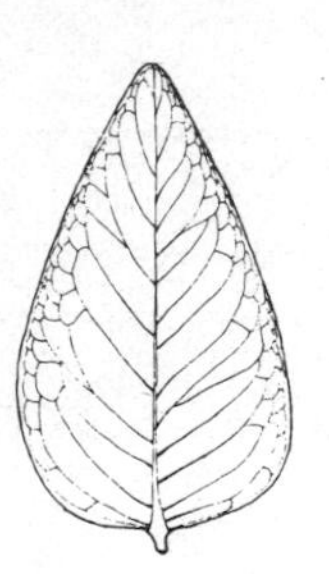

ovate
An ovate leaf

out·side (out-sīd′, out′sīd′) *n.* **1.** The part or parts that face out; outer surface; exterior. **2. a.** The part or side of an object that is presented to the viewer; external aspect. **b.** The superficial or obvious aspect of something. **3.** The space beyond a boundary or limit. —**at the outside.** At the utmost limit; at the most: *We'll be leaving in ten days at the outside.* —*adj.* **1.** Acting, occurring, originating, or existing at a place beyond certain limits; outer; foreign: *outside assistance.* **2.** Of, restricted to, or situated on the outside of an enclosure or boundary; external: *outside environs; an outside door lock.* **3.** Extreme; uttermost: *The cost exceeded even my outside estimate.* **4.** Slight; slim: *an outside possibility.* —*adv.* On or into the outside; outdoors: *Let's go outside for some fresh air.* —*prep.* **1.** On or to the outer side of. **2.** Beyond the limits of. **3.** With the exception of; except: *no information outside the figures given.* —**outside of.** Outside: *"His objects of interest outside of his special work"* (O.W. Holmes). See Usage note.

Usage: *Outside* (preposition) is preferable to *outside of,* applied either to physical extent *(outside the house)* or, figuratively, to scope *(outside my authority).* In such construction in writing, *outside of* is unacceptable to 84 per cent of the Usage Panel.

out·sid·er (out-sī′dər) *n.* **1. a.** A person who is excluded from some particular party, association, or set. **b.** One who is isolated or detached from the activities or concerns of the community in which he lives. **2.** A contestant in a race, especially a horse race, given little chance of winning; a long shot.

out·size (out′sīz′) *n.* **1.** An unusual size; especially, a very large size. **2.** An outsize garment. —**out′size′, out′sized′** *adj.*

out·skirts (out′skûrts′) *pl.n.* The parts or regions remote from a central district; peripheral areas: *"The train began to pick up speed on the outskirts of the city."* (William Styron).

out·smart (out-smärt′) *tr.v.* **-smarted, -smarting, -smarts.** To gain the advantage over by cunning; outwit.

out·speak (out-spēk′) *v.* **-spoke** (-spōk′), **-spoken** (-spō′kən), **-speaking, -speaks.** —*tr.* **1.** To outdo in speech; speak better or more cogently than. **2.** To say candidly and frankly. —*intr.* To speak out.

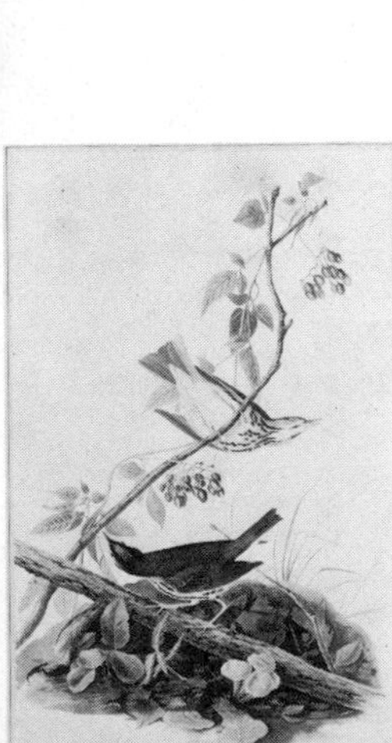

ovenbird
Painting by John James Audubon

out·spo·ken (out-spō′kən) *adj.* **1.** Spoken without reserve; candid. **2.** Frank and unsparing in speech. —See Synonyms at **frank.** —**out·spo′ken·ly** *adv.* —**out·spo′ken·ness** *n.*

out·spread (out-sprĕd′) *v.* **-spread, -spreading, -spreads.** —*intr.* To spread out; stretch. —*tr.* To cause to spread out. —*n.* (out′sprĕd′). The act of spreading out. —*adj.* (out-sprĕd′). Spread out; extended.

out·stand (out-stănd′) *intr.v.* **-stood** (-sto͝od′), **-standing, -stands. 1.** To stand out plainly; be outstanding. **2.** *Nautical.* To set sail; put out to sea.

out·stand·ing (out′stăn′dĭng, out-stăn′dĭng) *adj.* **1.** Standing out; projecting upward or outward. **2.** Standing out among others of its kind; prominent; salient. **3.** Superior to others of its kind; distinguished; excellent. **4.** Still in existence; not settled or resolved: *outstanding debts; a long outstanding problem.*

out·stare (out-stâr′) *tr.v.* **-stared, -staring, -stares.** To stare out of countenance; face down; outface.

out·sta·tion (out′stā′shən) *n.* A remote station or post.

out·stay (out-stā′) *tr.v.* **-stayed, -staying, -stays.** To stay longer than; overstay.

out·stretch (out-strĕch′) *tr.v.* **-stretched, -stretching, -stretches. 1.** To stretch out; extend. **2.** To stretch beyond.

out·strip (out-strĭp′) *tr.v.* **-stripped, -stripping, -strips. 1.** To leave behind; outrun. **2.** To exceed; surpass: *"Material development outstripped human development."* (Edith Hamilton). —See Synonyms at **excel.**

out·stroke (out′strōk′) *n.* An outward stroke; especially, the stroke of an engine piston moving toward the crankshaft. Compare **instroke.**

out·turn (out′tûrn′) *n.* A total amount produced during a given period; output.

out·ward (out′wərd) *adj.* **1.** Of, pertaining to, or moving toward the outside or exterior; outer. **2.** Pertaining to the physical self, as distinguished from the mind or spirit: *The ascetics have no interest in the outward man.* **3.** Easily perceptible, especially to sight; evident: *His outward manner remained composed.* **4.** Purely external; superficial. —*adv.* Also **out·wards** (-wərdz). **1.** Toward the outside; away from a central point. **2.** On the outside; externally. **3.** Obviously; apparently. —*n.* **1.** The outside; exterior. **2.** Outward appearance. **3.** The material or external world. [Middle English *outward,* Old English *ūtanweard* : *ūtan,* outside, from *ūt,* OUT + *-weard,* -WARD.] —**out′ward·ly** *adv.* —**out′ward·ness** *n.*

out·wear (out-wâr′) *tr.v.* **-wore** (-wôr′, -wōr′), **-worn** (-wôrn′, -wōrn′), **-wearing, -wears. 1.** To wear out; exhaust by using. **2.** To last longer than; outlast. **3.** To outgrow or outlive: *ethics outworn by a changing people.*

out·weigh (out-wā′) *tr.v.* **-weighed, -weighing, -weighs. 1.** To weigh more than. **2.** To be more significant than: *"Johnson's fear of the Deity outweighed his love."* (George Sherburn).

out·wit (out-wĭt′) *tr.v.* **-witted, -witting, -wits. 1.** To surpass in cleverness or cunning; to fool. **2.** *Archaic.* To surpass in intelligence. —See Synonyms at **deceive.**

out·work¹ (out-wûrk′) *tr.v.* **-worked** or **-wrought** (-rôt′), **-working, -works. 1.** To work better or faster than. **2.** To work out to a finish; complete.

out·work² (out′wûrk′) *n. Military.* A trench or fortification beyond the main defenses.

ou·zel (o͞o′zəl) *n.* Also **ou·sel. 1.** Any of various European birds of the genus *Turdus.* **2.** The **water ouzel** *(see).* [Middle English *ousel,* Old English *ōsle.* See **ames-** in Appendix.*]

ou·zo (o͞o′zō) *n., pl.* **-zos.** An aniseed-flavored Greek liqueur. [Modern Greek *ouzon*†.]

o·va. Plural of **ovum.**

o·val (ō′vəl) *adj.* **1.** Resembling an egg in shape. **2.** Resembling an ellipse in shape; ellipsoidal or elliptical. —*n.* **1.** An oval form or figure. **2.** An oval track, as for horse racing or athletic events. [Medieval Latin *ōvālis,* from Latin *ōvum,* egg. See **awi-** in Appendix.*] —**o′val·ly** *adv.* —**o′val·ness** *n.*

o·var·i·ec·to·my (ō-vâr′ē-ĕk′tə-mē) *n., pl.* **-mies.** Surgical excision of an ovary. [OVAR(Y) + -ECTOMY.]

o·var·i·ot·o·my (ō-vâr′ē-ŏt′ə-mē) *n., pl.* **-mies. 1.** Ovariectomy. **2.** Surgical incision into an ovary. [New Latin *ovariotomia* : OVAR(Y) + *-tomia,* -TOMY.]

o·va·ri·tis (ō′və-rī′tĭs) *n. Pathology.* **Oophoritis** *(see).* [New Latin : OVAR(Y) + -ITIS.]

o·va·ry (ō′və-rē) *n., pl.* **-ries. 1.** *Zoology.* One of a pair of female reproductive glands that produce ova. **2.** *Botany.* The part of a pistil containing the ovules. [New Latin *ovarium,* from Latin *ōvum,* egg. See **awi-** in Appendix.*] —**o·var′i·an** (ō-vâr′ē-ən), **o·var′i·al** *adj.*

o·vate (ō′vāt′) *adj.* **1.** Oval; egg-shaped. **2.** *Botany.* Broad and rounded at the base and tapering toward the end: *an ovate leaf.* [Latin *ōvātus,* egg-shaped, from *ōvum,* egg. See **awi-** in Appendix.*] —**o′vate′ly** *adv.*

o·va·tion (ō-vā′shən) *n.* **1.** An ancient Roman victory ceremony of somewhat less importance than a triumph. **2.** A show of public homage or welcome. **3.** Enthusiastic and prolonged applause. [Latin *ovātiō,* from *ovāre,* to rejoice, from imitative base *eu-.*]

ov·en (ŭv′ən) *n.* A chamber or enclosed compartment, as in a stove, equipped to heat objects placed within. [Middle English *oven,* Old English *ofen.* See **aukwh-** in Appendix.*]

ov·en·bird (ŭv′ən-bûrd′) *n.* **1.** A thrushlike North American warbler, *Seiurus aurocapillus,* having a shrill call, and characteristically building a domed nest on the ground. **2.** Any of various South American birds of the family Furnariidae, often building similar nests. [From its oven-shaped nests.]

o·ver (ō′vər) *prep.* Also *poetic* **o'er** (ōr, ôr). **1.** In or at a position above or higher than: *a sign over the door.* **2.** Above and across from one end or side to the other: *a jump over the fence.* **3.** On the other side of: *a village over the border.* **4.** Upon the surface of: *a coat of varnish over the woodwork.* **5.** Covering various parts of; through the extent of: *a tour over the nation.* **6.** So as to cover or close: *a sliding rock over a cave entrance.* **7.** Up to or higher than the level or height of: *water over one's head.* **8.** Through the period or duration of: *records maintained over two years.* **9.** Until or beyond the end of: *stay over the holidays.* **10.** More than, in degree, quantity, or extent: *over ten miles.* See Usage note below. **11.** In preference to: *respected over all others.* **12.** In a position to rule or control: *preside over the meeting.* **13.** Upon; directed toward: *his influence over children.* **14.** While occupied with, engaged in, or partaking of: *a chat*

ă pat/ā pay/âr care/ä father/b bib/ch church/d deed/ĕ pet/ē be/f fife/g gag/h hat/hw which/ĭ pit/ī pie/îr pier/j judge/k kick/l lid, needle/m mum/n no, sudden/ng thing/ŏ pot/ō toe/ô paw, for/oi noise/ou out/o͝o took/o͞o boot/p pop/r roar/s sauce/sh ship, dish/

over coffee. **15.** With reference to; concerning: *an argument over methods.* **—over and above.** In addition to; besides. *—adv.* Also *poetic* **o'er.** **1.** Above the top or surface. **2. a.** Across to another or opposite side. **b.** Across the edge or brim of: *The coffee spilled over.* **3. a.** Across a distance in a particular direction or at a location: *over in Europe.* **b.** To another specified place or position: *Move your chair over toward the fire.* **4.** Throughout an entire area or region: *wander all over.* **5.** To a different opinion or allegiance: *win someone over.* **6.** To a different person, condition, or title: *sign over land.* **7.** So as to be completely enclosed or covered: *The river froze over.* **8.** Completely through, from beginning to end: *Think the problem over.* **9. a.** From an upright position: *The book fell over.* **b.** From an upward position to an inverted or reversed position: *turn the book over.* **10.** Another time; again: *Count your cards over.* **11.** In repetition: *ten times over.* **12.** In addition or excess; in surplus: *three pennies left over.* **13.** Beyond or until a specified time: *stay a day over.* **—over against.** As opposed to; contrasted with. *—adj.* **1.** Completely finished; done; past: *The war is over.* **2.** Having gone across or to the other side. **3. a.** Upper; higher. **b.** External; outer. **4.** In excess or addition; in surplus: *His estimate was fifty dollars over.* *—n.* **1.** Something remaining or extra. **2.** *Cricket.* A series of six balls bowled from one end of the pitch. *—tr.v.* **overed, overing, overs.** *Rare.* To go or pass over. *—interj.* Used in radio conversations to mark the end of a transmission by one speaker. [Middle English *over,* Old English *ofer.* See **uper** in Appendix.*]

Usage: *Over* (preposition), in the sense of *more than (over ten dollars),* is acceptable in writing to 63 per cent of the Usage Panel. A clearly incongruous use of *over* occurs in comparisons involving reduction: *Sales are down 10 per cent over last year's figure* (properly *down . . . from*).

over–. Indicates: **1.** Superiority of rank or power; for example, **overseer.** **2.** Location above or across a specified position; for example, **overhead.** **3.** Passage beyond or above a limit or boundary; for example, **overshoot.** **4.** Movement or transferal to a lower or inferior position; for example, **overturn, overwhelm.** **5.** Quantity in excess of what is normal or desirable; for example, **overheat.** ***Note:*** Many compounds other than those entered here may be formed with *over-*. In forming compounds, *over-* is joined with the following element without space or a hyphen: **overrule.** [Middle English *over-,* Old English *ofer-,* from *ofer,* OVER.]

o·ver·a·bun·dance (ō′vər-ə-bŭn′dəns) *n.* Prodigally lavish abundance; excessive profusion. **—o′ver·a·bun′dant** *adj.*

o·ver·a·chieve (ō′vər-ə-chēv′) *intr.v.* **-achieved, -achieving, -achieves.** To perform better than expected. **—o′ver·a·chiev′er** *n.* **—o′ver·a·chieve′ment** *n.*

o·ver·act (ō′vər-ăkt′) *v.* **-acted, -acting, -acts.** *—tr.* To act (a part) with unnecessary exaggeration. *—intr.* To exaggerate a part; overplay.

o·ver·age¹ (ō′vər-ĭj) *n. Commerce.* **1.** An amount, as of money or goods, actually on hand that exceeds the listed amount in records or books of account. **2.** Rent payments, usually a percentage of tenant sales, in excess of a fixed base rental in retail leases. [OVER + -AGE.]

o·ver·age² (ō′vər-āj′) *adj.* Beyond the proper or required age.

o·ver·all (ō′vər-ôl′) *adj.* Also **o·ver-all.** **1.** From one end to the other. **2.** Including everything; comprehensive. *—n. British.* A loose-fitting protective outer garment; smock.

o·ver·alls (ō′vər-ôlz′) *pl.n.* Loose-fitting, coarse trousers with a bib front and shoulder straps, often worn over regular clothing as protection from dirt and wear.

o·ver·arch (ō′vər-ärch′) *tr.v.* **-arched, -arching, -arches.** To form an arch over.

o·ver·arm (ō′vər-ärm′) *adj. Sports.* Executed with the arm raised above the shoulder: *an overarm throw.*

o·ver·awe (ō′vər-ô′) *tr.v.* **-awed, -awing, -awes.** To subdue by inspiring awe; overcome with awe: *"But I have always been very easily overawed by a schoolmaster."* (Samuel Butler).

o·ver·bal·ance (ō′vər-băl′əns) *v.* **-anced, -ancing, -ances.** *—tr.* **1.** To have greater weight or importance than. **2.** To throw off balance. *—intr.* To lose one's balance. *—n.* (ō′vər-băl′əns). Something that overbalances; an excess of weight or quantity.

o·ver·bear (ō′vər-bâr′) *v.* **-bore** (-bôr′), **-borne** (bôrn′), **-bearing, -bears.** *—tr.* **1.** To crush or press down upon with physical force. **2.** To prevail over, as if by superior weight or force; dominate. *—intr.* To bear too much fruit or offspring.

o·ver·bear·ing (ō′vər-bâr′ĭng) *adj.* **1.** Overwhelming in power or significance; predominant. **2.** Domineering in manner; arrogant: *"the overbearing character and insulting manners of the English people"* (Jawaharlal Nehru). —See Synonyms at **dictatorial.** **—o′ver·bear′ing·ly** *adv.*

o·ver·bid (ō′vər-bĭd′) *v.* **-bid, -bidden** (-bĭd′n), or **-bid, -bidding, -bids.** *—tr.* To outbid (a person) for something. *—intr.* To bid higher than the actual value of something. *—n.* (ō′vər-bĭd′). A bid that is higher than another bid.

o·ver·bite (ō′vər-bīt′) *n. Dentistry.* Malocclusion in which the front upper incisor and canine teeth project over the lower.

o·ver·blow (ō′vər-blō′) *tr.v.* **-blew** (-blo͞o′), **-blown** (-blōn′), **-blowing, -blows.** To blow (a wind instrument) so as to produce an overtone instead of a fundamental tone.

o·ver·blown (ō′vər-blōn′) *adj.* **1.** Blown down or over. **2.** Blown up with conceit. **3.** Past the stage of full bloom.

o·ver·board (ō′vər-bôrd′, -bōrd′) *adv.* Over the side of a boat or ship. **—go overboard.** *Informal.* To show wild enthusiasm.

o·ver·build (ō′vər-bĭld′) *tr.v.* **-built, -building, -builds.** **1.** To build over or on top of. **2.** To build more buildings in (an area) than necessary. **3.** To build with excessive size or elaboration.

o·ver·bur·den (ō′vər-bûrd′n) *tr.v.* **-dened, -dening, -dens.** **1.** To burden with too much weight. **2.** To burden with too much work, care, or responsibility. *—n.* (ō′vər-bûrd′n). **1.** *Geology.* **a.** Material overlying a useful mineral deposit. **b.** Sedimentary rock covering older crystalline layers. **2.** *Archaeology.* A sterile stratum overlying a stratum bearing traces of the culture being studied.

o·ver·buy (ō′vər-bī′) *v.* **-bought** (-bôt′), **-buying, -buys.** *—tr.* **1.** To buy in excessive amounts. **2.** *Finance.* To buy (stock) on margin in excess of one's ability to provide further security if prices drop. *—intr.* To buy goods beyond one's means.

o·ver·call (ō′vər-kôl′) *tr.v.* **-called, -calling, -calls.** **1.** To overbid. **2.** *Bridge.* To bid higher than (one's opponent) when one's partner has not bid. *—n.* (ō′vər-kôl′). **1.** An overbid. **2.** *Bridge.* An instance of overcalling.

o·ver·cap·i·tal·ize (ō′vər-kăp′ə-təl-īz′) *tr.v.* **-ized, -izing, -izes.** **1.** To provide an excess amount of capital for (a business enterprise). **2.** To estimate the value of (property) too highly. **3.** To place an unlawfully or unreasonably high value on the nominal capital of (a corporation). **—o′ver·cap′i·tal·i·za′tion** *n.*

o·ver·cast (ō′vər-kăst′, -käst′, ō′vər-kăst′, -käst′) *adj.* **1.** Covered or obscured, as with clouds or mist. **2.** Gloomy; dark; melancholy. **3.** Sewn with long, overlying stitches in order to prevent raveling, as the edges of fabric. *—n.* (ō′vər-kăst′, -käst′). **1.** A covering, as of mist or clouds. **2.** *Mining.* An arch or support for a passage over another passage. **3.** A fishing cast falling beyond the point intended. **4.** An overcast stitch or seam. In this sense, also called "overcasting." *—tr.v.* (ō′vər-kăst′, -käst′, ō′vər-kăst′, -käst′) **overcasted, -casting, -casts.** **1.** To make cloudy or gloomy. **2.** In fishing, to cast beyond (the intended point). **3.** To sew with an overcast stitch.

o·ver·charge (ō′vər-chärj′) *tr.v.* **-charged, -charging, -charges.** **1.** To charge (a person) too high a price for something. **2.** To fill too full; overload. **3.** To exaggerate. *—n.* (ō′vər-chärj′). **1.** *Abbr.* **o/c** An excessive charge or price. **2.** A load or burden that is too full or heavy.

o·ver·cloud (ō′vər-kloud′) *v.* **-clouded, -clouding, -clouds.** *—tr.* **1.** To cover with clouds. **2.** To make dark and gloomy. *—intr.* To become cloudy.

o·ver·coat (ō′vər-kōt′) *n.* A heavy coat worn over the ordinary clothing in cold weather.

o·ver·come (ō′vər-kŭm′) *v.* **-came** (-kām′), **-come, -coming, -comes.** *—tr.* **1.** To defeat in competition or conflict; conquer. **2.** To surmount; prevail over: *overcome the obstacles of poverty.* **3.** To overpower, as with emotion; affect deeply. *—intr.* To surmount opposition; be victorious. —See Synonyms at **defeat.** [Middle English *overcomen,* Old English *ofercuman* : *ofer,* OVER + *cuman,* to COME.]

o·ver·com·pen·sate (ō′vər-kŏm′pən-sāt′) *v.* **-sated, -sating, -sates.** *—intr.* **1.** To make a greater effort than required to achieve compensation. **2.** To engage in overcompensation. *—tr.* To compensate excessively. **—o′ver·com·pen′sa·to′ry** (-kəm-pĕn′sə-tôr′ē, -tōr′ē) *adj.*

o·ver·com·pen·sa·tion (ō′vər-kŏm′pən-sā′shən) *n.* The exertion of effort in excess of that needed to compensate for a physical or psychological characteristic or defect.

o·ver·crop (ō′vər-krŏp′) *tr.v.* **-cropped, -cropping, -crops.** To exhaust the fertility of (land) by overcultivation.

o·ver·de·vel·op (ō′vər-dĭ-vĕl′əp) *tr.v.* **-oped, -oping, -ops.** **1.** To develop to excess: *muscles overdeveloped by weightlifting.* **2.** *Photography.* To process (a plate or film) too long or in too concentrated a solution. **—o′ver·de·vel′op·ment** *n.*

o·ver·do (ō′vər-do͞o′) *tr.v.* **-did** (-dĭd′), **-done** (-dŭn′), **-doing, -does** (-dŭz′). **1.** To do, use, or stress to excess; carry too far: *"Kierkegaard's point was that Luther overdid this subjective . . . side of life"* (Erik Erikson). **2.** To wear out the strength of; overtax. **3.** To cook too much or too long.

o·ver·dose (ō′vər-dōs′) *tr.v.* **-dosed, -dosing, -doses.** To give too large a dose to. *—n.* (ō′vər-dōs′). An excessive dose.

o·ver·draft (ō′vər-drăft′, -dräft′) *n.* Also **o·ver·draught** (for sense 2 only). **1. a.** The act of overdrawing an account. **b.** *Abbr.* **O.D.** The amount overdrawn. **2. a.** A current of air made to pass over the ignited fuel in a furnace. **b.** A series of flues in a brick kiln designed to force air down from the top. **c.** The air so forced.

o·ver·draw (ō′vər-drô′) *tr.v.* **-drew** (-dro͞o′), **-drawn** (-drôn′), **-drawing, -draws.** **1.** To draw against (an account) in excess of credit. **2.** To pull back too far: *overdraw a bow.* **3.** To spoil the effect of by exaggeration in telling or describing.

o·ver·dress (ō′vər-drĕs′) *intr.v.* **-dressed** or **-drest, -dressing, -dresses.** To dress in a more formal or elaborate manner than is desirable in a given situation. *—n.* A skirted garment, such as a pinafore, worn over other outer clothing.

o·ver·drive (ō′vər-drīv′) *n.* A gearing mechanism of an automotive engine that reduces the power output required to maintain driving speed in a specific range by increasing the ratio of drive shaft to engine speed. *—tr.v.* (ō′vər-drīv′) **over-drove** (-drōv′), **-driven** (-drĭv′ən), **-driving, -drives.** **1.** To drive (a vehicle) too far or too long. **2.** To push (oneself) too far; overwork.

o·ver·due (ō′vər-do͞o′, -dyo͞o′) *adj.* **1.** Being unpaid after becoming due. **2.** Past due; expected or required but not come: *"Such an invention has been overdue for about fifty years"* (Arthur C. Clarke). —See Synonyms at **tardy.**

o·ver·es·ti·mate (ō′vər-ĕs′tə-māt′) *tr.v.* **-mated, -mating, -mates.** **1.** To estimate too highly. **2.** To esteem too greatly. **—o′ver·es′ti·mate** (-ĕs′tə-mĭt) *n.* **—o′ver·es′ti·ma′tion** *n.*

o·ver·ex·ert (ō′vər-ĭg-zûrt′) *tr.v.* **-erted, -erting, -erts.** To exert too much; overtax: *We took care not to overexert ourselves before the main activities.* **—o′ver·ex·er′tion** *n.*

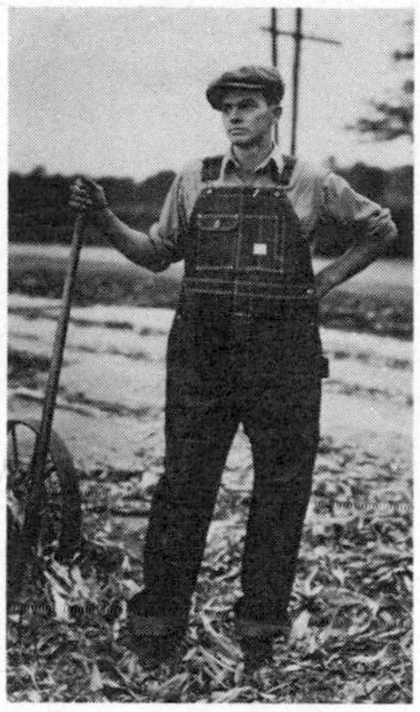

overalls
Farm worker in overalls

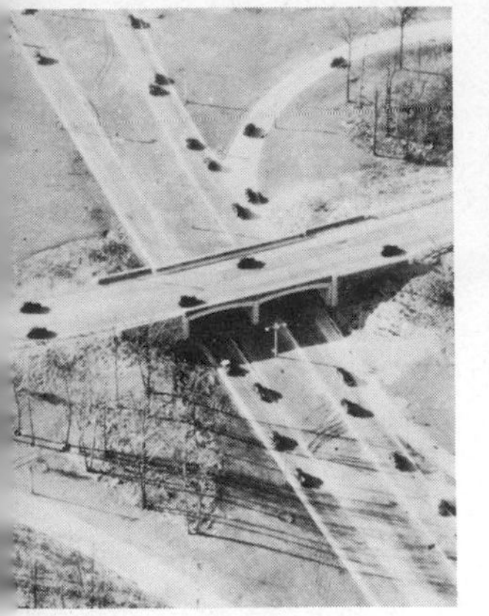
overpass

o·ver·ex·pose (ō′vər-ĭk-spōz′) *tr.v.* **-posed, -posing, -poses.** **1.** To expose too long or too much. **2.** *Photography.* To expose (a film or plate) too long or with too much light. **—o′ver·ex·po′sure** *n.*
o·ver·ex·tend (ō′vər-ĭk-stĕnd′) *tr.v.* **-tended, -tending, -tends.** To expand or disperse (one's defenses, for example) beyond a safe or reasonable limit. **—o′ver·ex·ten′sion** *n.*
o·ver·fill (ō′vər-fĭl′) *tr.v.* **-filled, -filling, -fills.** To fill to overflowing.
o·ver·flow (ō′vər-flō′) *v.* **-flowed, -flowing, -flows.** *—intr.* **1.** To flow or run over the top, brim, or banks. **2.** To be filled beyond capacity, as a container or waterway. **3.** To have a boundless supply; be superabundant: *overflowing with gratitude.* *—tr.* **1.** To flow over the top, brim, or banks of. **2.** To spread or cover over; flood. **3.** To cause to fill beyond capacity. *—n.* (ō′vər-flō′). **1.** The act of overflowing. **2.** That which flows over; an excess of capacity. **3.** An outlet or vent through which excess liquid may escape.
o·ver·gar·ment (ō′vər-gär′mənt) *n.* An outer garment.
o·ver·glaze (ō′vər-glāz′) *n.* An outer coat of glaze on a piece of pottery. *—tr.v.* (ō′vər-glāz′, ō′vər-glāz′), **overglazed, -glazing, -glazes.** To apply an overglaze to.
o·ver·grow (ō′vər-grō′, ō′vər-grō′) *v.* **-grew** (-grōō′), **-grown, -growing, -grows.** *—tr.* **1.** To spread over with growth. **2.** To grow too large for. *—intr.* To grow beyond normal size.
o·ver·growth (ō′vər-grōth′) *n.* **1.** A growth over or upon something. **2.** Excessively abundant or luxuriant growth.
o·ver·hand (ō′vər-hănd′) *adj.* Also **o·ver·hand·ed** (ō′vər-hăn′-dĭd). **1.** Thrown, struck, or executed with the hand above the level of the shoulder. **2.** Sewn with stitches drawing two edges together, with each stitch passing over the seam formed by the edges. *—adv.* In an overhand manner. *—n.* **1.** An overhand throw, stroke, or delivery. **2.** An overhand stitch or seam. *—tr.v.* **overhanded, -handing, -hands.** To sew with an overhand seam or stitches.
overhand knot. A knot formed by making a loop in a piece of cord and pulling the end through it. Also called "single knot."
o·ver·hang (ō′vər-hăng′) *v.* **-hung** (-hŭng′), **-hanging, -hangs.** *—tr.* **1.** To project or extend beyond. **2.** To threaten or menace; loom over. **3.** To ornament with hangings. *—intr.* To hang or project over something. *—n.* (ō′vər-hăng′). **1.** A projecting part of something, as an architectural structure or rock formation. **2.** The amount of projection: *an overhang of six inches.*
o·ver·haul (ō′vər-hôl′, ō′vər-hôl′) *tr.v.* **-hauled, -hauling, -hauls.** **1. a.** To examine or go over carefully for needed repairs. **b.** To dismantle in order to make repairs. **c.** *Nautical.* To slacken (a line) or to release and separate the blocks of (a tackle). **2.** To make all needed repairs on; fix; renovate. **3.** To catch up with; overtake. *—n.* (ō′vər-hôl′). A repair job; renovation.
o·ver·head (ō′vər-hĕd′) *adj.* **1.** Located or functioning above the level of the head: *an overhead light.* **2.** Of or pertaining to the operating expenses of a business concern. *—n.* (ō′vər-hĕd′). **1.** The operating expenses of a business, including the costs of rent, utilities, interior decoration, and taxes, and excluding labor and materials. **2.** The top surface in an enclosed space of a ship. **3.** Something located above head height, as a light fixture. *—adv.* (ō′vər-hĕd′). Over or above the level of the head: *look overhead.*
o·ver·hear (ō′vər-hîr′) *tr.v.* **-heard** (-hûrd′), **-hearing, -hears.** To hear (something spoken or someone speaking) without being addressed by the speaker. **—o′ver·hear′er** *n.*
o·ver·heat (ō′vər-hēt′) *v.* **-heated, -heating, -heats.** *—tr.* **1.** To heat too hot. **2.** To cause to become hot or excited: *overheated by a sharp exchange of insults.* *—intr.* To become overheated.
O·ver·ijs·sel (ō′vər-ī′səl). A province of the Netherlands, 1,318 square miles in area, in the northeastern part of the country. Population, 861,000. Capital, Zwolle.
o·ver·in·dulge (ō′vər-ĭn-dŭlj′) *v.* **-dulged, -dulging, -dulges.** *—tr.* To indulge excessively; gratify too much or unwisely. *—intr.* To indulge in something to excess. **—o′ver·in·dul′gence** *n.* **—o′ver·in·dul′gent** *adj.* **—o′ver·in·dul′gent·ly** *adv.*
o·ver·joyed (ō′vər-joid′) *adj.* Filled with joy; delighted.
o·ver·kill (ō′vər-kĭl′) *n.* Nuclear destructive capacity exceeding the amount needed to destroy an enemy.
o·ver·lad·en (ō′vər-lād′n) *adj.* Overloaded; overburdened.
o·ver·land (ō′vər-lănd′, -lənd) *adj.* Proceeding over or traversing land: *an overland journey.* *—adv.* By way of land.
o·ver·lap (ō′vər-lăp′) *v.* **-lapped, -lapping, -laps.** *—tr.* **1.** To lie or extend over and cover part of. **2.** To have an area or range in common with; coincide partly with. *—intr.* **1.** To lie over and partly cover something. **2.** To coincide partly: *Their duties overlap.* *—n.* (ō′vər-lăp′). **1.** A part or portion that overlaps or is overlapped. **2.** An instance of overlapping.
o·ver·lay (ō′vər-lā′) *tr.v.* **-laid, -laying, -lays.** **1.** To lay or spread over or upon. **2. a.** To cover or decorate the surface of. Followed by *with: overlay wood with silver.* **b.** To embellish superficially: *a simple tune overlaid with ornate harmonies.* **3.** *Printing.* To put an overlay upon. *—n.* (ō′vər-lā′). **1.** Something that is laid over or covers something else. **2.** A layer of decoration, such as gold leaf or wood veneer, applied to a surface. **3.** *Printing.* A piece of paper used on a press tympan to vary the pressure that produces light and dark tones. **4.** A transparent sheet containing graphic matter, such as labels or colored areas, placed on illustrative matter to be incorporated into it.
Usage: *Overlay* (verb) and *overlie* are both transitive and agree in basic sense. But *overlay* applies principally to the act of superimposing, as a carpenter *overlays* plywood with veneer, or a writer *overlays* a simple story with a cryptic style. The plywood and the story are thus *overlaid. Overlie* pertains to the act of lying over or resting upon something, as sand *overlies* bedrock (which is thus *overlain*).
o·ver·leap (ō′vər-lēp′) *tr.v.* **-leaped** or **-leapt** (-lĕpt′), **-leaping, -leaps.** **1.** To leap across or over. **2.** To pass over; omit; ignore: *The report overleaps all but the most essential points.* **—overleap oneself.** To miss one's mark by leaping too far.
o·ver·lie (ō′vər-lī′) *tr.v.* **-lay, -lain, -laying, -lies.** **1.** To lie over or upon. See Usage note at **overlay. 2.** To smother by lying upon (an infant or other newborn creature).
o·ver·load (ō′vər-lōd′) *tr.v.* **-loaded, -loading, -loads.** To load too heavily. *—n.* (ō′vər-lōd′). An excessive load.
o·ver·long (ō′vər-lông′, -lŏng′) *adj.* Excessively long. **—o′ver·long′** *adv.*
o·ver·look (ō′vər-lo͝ok′) *tr.v.* **-looked, -looking, -looks.** **1.** To look over or at from a higher place. **2.** To rise above, especially so as to afford a view over: *The tower overlooks the sea.* **3.** To fail to notice or consider; miss. **4.** To ignore deliberately or indulgently; disregard. **5.** To look over; examine. **6.** To watch over; supervise; oversee. **7.** To cast a spell with an evil eye. *—n.* (ō′vər-lo͝ok′). **1.** An elevated place that affords an extensive view. **2.** An act or instance of overlooking something.
o·ver·lord (ō′vər-lôrd′) *n.* **1.** A lord having power or supremacy over another or other lords. **2.** One who is in a position of supremacy or domination over others. **—o′ver·lord′ship** *n.*
o·ver·ly (ō′vər-lē) *adv.* To an excessive degree; too: *"To my eye it seems not to be overly peopled."* (James Fenimore Cooper).
Usage: *Overly* is acceptable in writing to 60 per cent of the Usage Panel. But its sense is expressed more concisely, and just as properly, by the many adjectives and adverbs formed with *over-*, such as *overcautious* (for *overly cautious*), *overfast.*
o·ver·man (ō′vər-mən, -măn′ *for sense 1;* ō′vər-măn′ *for sense 2*) *n., pl.* **-men** (-mĭn, -mĕn). **1.** A man having authority over others; especially, an overseer or foreman. **2.** The Nietzschean superman. *—tr.v.* (ō′vər-măn′), **overmanned, -manning, -mans.** To provide with more men than are needed.
o·ver·mas·ter (ō′vər-măs′tər, -mäs′tər) *tr.v.* **-tered, -tering, -ters.** To overpower; overcome.
o·ver·match (ō′vər-măch′) *tr.v.* **-matched, -matching, -matches.** **1.** To be more than the match of; exceed. **2.** To match with a superior opponent. *—n.* (ō′vər-măch′). A contest in which one opponent is distinctly superior.
o·ver·much (ō′vər-mŭch′) *adj.* Too much; excessive. *—adv.* In too great a degree. *—n.* (ō′vər-mŭch′, ō′vər-mŭch′). An excessive amount.
o·ver·night (ō′vər-nīt′) *adj.* **1.** Lasting for, extending over, or remaining during a night: *an overnight journey.* **2.** For use over a single night or for a short journey. *—adv.* (ō′vər-nīt′). **1.** During or for the length of the night. **2.** On the preceding night or evening. **3.** In or as if in the course of one night; suddenly: *The situation changed overnight.*
o·ver·pass (ō′vər-păs′, -päs′) *n.* A passage, roadway, or bridge that crosses above another roadway or thoroughfare. *—tr.v.* (ō′vər-păs′, -päs′), **overpassed** or **-past, -passing, -passes.** **1.** To pass over or across; traverse. **2.** To go beyond; exceed; surpass. **3.** To overlook; disregard.
o·ver·pay (ō′vər-pā′) *v.* **-paid, -paying, -pays.** *—tr.* **1.** To pay (someone) too much. **2.** To pay an amount in excess of (a sum due). *—intr.* To pay too much. **—o′ver·pay′ment** *n.*
o·ver·per·suade (ō′vər-pər-swād′) *tr.v.* **-suaded, -suading, -suades.** To persuade (someone) contrary to inclination. **—o′ver·per·sua′sion** *n.*
o·ver·play (ō′vər-plā′) *tr.v.* **-played, -playing, -plays.** **1.** To play (a dramatic role) in an exaggerated manner; overact. **2.** To overestimate the strength of (one's holding or position) and thus contribute to one's own defeat. Used chiefly in the phrase *overplay one's hand.* **3.** To hit (a golf ball) beyond the green.
o·ver·plus (ō′vər-plŭs′) *n.* An amount in excess of need.
o·ver·pow·er (ō′vər-pou′ər) *tr.v.* **-ered, -ering, -ers.** **1.** To overcome or vanquish by superior force; subdue. **2.** To affect so strongly as to make helpless or ineffective; overwhelm. **3.** To furnish with excessive mechanical power.
o·ver·pow·er·ing (ō′vər-pou′ər-ĭng) *adj.* So strong as to overpower; overwhelming. **—o′ver·pow′er·ing·ly** *adv.*
o·ver·price (ō′vər-prīs′) *tr.v.* **-priced, -pricing, -prices.** To put too high a price on.
o·ver·print (ō′vər-prĭnt′) *tr.v.* **-printed, -printing, -prints.** To imprint over something already printed; especially, to print over (printed images) with another color. *—n.* (ō′vər-prĭnt′). **1.** A mark or impression made by overprinting. **2. a.** A mark or words printed over a postage stamp to note a change in use or a special occasion. **b.** A stamp so marked.
o·ver·pro·duce (ō′vər-prə-do͞os′, -dyo͞os′) *tr.v.* **-duced, -ducing, -duces.** To produce too much of. **—o′ver·pro·duc′tion** (ō′vər-prə-dŭk′shən) *n.*
o·ver·proof (ō′vər-pro͞of′) *adj.* Containing a greater proportion of alcohol than proof spirit; especially, containing more than 50% alcohol by volume.
o·ver·rate (ō′vər-rāt′) *tr.v.* **-rated, -rating, -rates.** To rate too highly; overestimate the merits of.
o·ver·reach (ō′vər-rēch′) *v.* **-reached, -reaching, -reaches.** *—tr.* **1.** To reach or extend over or beyond. **2.** To miss by reaching too far or attempting too much: *overreach a goal.* **3.** To defeat (oneself) by going too far, doing or trying to gain too much, or by being too cunning. **4.** To get the better of; trick; outwit. *—intr.* **1.** To reach or go too far. **2.** To outwit others; cheat. **3.** To strike the front part of a hind foot against the rear or side part of a forefoot or foreleg on the same side of the body. **—o′ver·reach′er** *n.*

o·ver·ride (ō′vər-rīd′) *tr.v.* **-rode** (-rōd′), **-ridden** (-rĭd′n), **-riding, -rides. 1.** To ride across. **2.** To trample upon. **3.** To ride (a horse) too hard. **4.** To prevail over; conquer: *"If it be possible that mercy shall override vengeance"* (John Michael Ray). **5.** To declare null and void; set aside. —*n.* (ō′vər-rīd′). A sales commission collected by an executive, in addition to the commission received by the salesman. Also "overrider."

o·ver·ripe (ō′vər-rīp′) *adj.* **1.** More than ripe; too ripe. **2.** Jaded; decadent. —**o′ver·ripe′ness** *n.*

o·ver·rule (ō′vər-ro͞ol′) *tr.v.* **-ruled, -ruling, -rules. 1. a.** To disallow the arguments of or rule against (a person), especially by virtue of higher authority. **b.** To decide or rule against (an argument, action, or the like). **c.** To declare null and void; invalidate; reverse. **2.** To dominate by strong influence; prevail over so as to change the opinion or course of action; influence.

o·ver·run (ō′vər-rŭn′) *v.* **-ran, -run, -running, -runs.** —*tr.* **1.** To attack and defeat conclusively; crush: *"A large party of screeching warriors had overrun our company."* (James D. Horan). **2.** To spread or swarm over destructively: *"The Western part had been overrun by barbarians . . . and had ceased to exist."* (W. Montgomery Watt). **3.** To spread swiftly throughout: *The new fashion overran the country.* **4.** To overflow: *The river overran its banks.* **5.** To run or extend beyond: *His speech has overrun the time limit.* **6.** *Archaic.* To run faster than; pass in running; outrun. **7.** *Printing.* **a.** To rearrange or move (set type or pictures) from one column, line, or page to another. **b.** To print (a job order) in a quantity larger than that ordered. —*intr.* **1.** To run over; overflow. **2.** To go or extend beyond the normal or desired limit. —*n.* (ō′vər-rŭn′). **1.** An instance or act of overrunning. **2.** The amount of overrunning or the extent to which something overruns. **3.** The printing of a job order in a quantity larger than that ordered by the customer.

o·ver·score (ō′vər-skôr′, -skōr′) *tr.v.* **-scored, -scoring, -scores.** To cross out by drawing a line or lines over or through.

o·ver·seas (ō′vər-sēz′, ō′vər-sēz′) *adv.* Also *rare* **o·ver·sea.** Beyond the sea; abroad. —*adj.* Also *rare* **o·ver·sea.** Of, pertaining to, originating in, or situated in areas across the sea.

overseas cap. A **garrison cap** *(see).*

o·ver·see (ō′vər-sē′) *tr.v.* **-saw** (-sô), **-seen, -seeing, -sees. 1.** To watch over and direct; supervise. **2.** *Archaic.* To scrutinize; inspect. —See Synonyms at **conduct.**

o·ver·se·er (ō′vər-sē′ər) *n.* **1.** One who keeps watch over and directs the work of others, especially laborers. **2.** A supervisor or superintendent.

o·ver·sell (ō′vər-sĕl′) *tr.v.* **-sold** (-sōld′), **-selling, -sells. 1.** To contract to sell more of (a stock or commodity) than can be delivered within the terms of a contract. **2.** To be too aggressive in attempting to sell something to (someone). **3.** To present with excessive or unwarranted enthusiasm.

o·ver·set (ō′vər-sĕt′) *v.* **-set, -setting, -sets.** —*tr.* **1.** To tip or push over; overturn. **2.** To throw into a confused or disturbed state; upset. **3.** *Printing.* To set too much for a given space. —*intr.* **1.** To fall over; overturn; upset. **2.** *Printing.* To set too much printed matter for a given space. —*n.* (ō′vər-sĕt′). **1.** An upset. **2.** *Printing.* An excess of set type.

o·ver·sew (ō′vər-sō′, ō′vər-sō′) *tr.v.* **-sewed, -sewn** or **-sewed, -sewing, -sews.** To sew with overhand stitches.

o·ver·sexed (ō′vər-sĕkst′) *adj.* Obsessed with sex.

o·ver·shad·ow (ō′vər-shăd′ō) *tr.v.* **-owed, -owing, -ows. 1.** To cast a shadow over. **2.** To make insignificant by comparison; dominate: *"overshadowing, in power if not in dignity, the nobility, and even the Crown itself."* (Winston Churchill).

o·ver·shoe (ō′vər-sho͞o′) *n.* An article of footwear worn over shoes as protection from water, snow, or cold.

o·ver·shoot (ō′vər-sho͞ot′) *v.* **-shot** (-shŏt′), **-shooting, -shoots.** —*tr.* **1.** To shoot or pass over or beyond. **2.** To miss by or as if by shooting, hitting, or propelling something too far. **3.** To fly beyond or past a specific location: *The plane overshot the runway.* **4.** To go beyond; exceed. —*intr.* To shoot or go too far.

o·ver·shot (ō′vər-shŏt′) *adj.* **1.** Having an upper part projecting beyond the lower: *an overshot jaw.* **2.** Designating a water wheel or mill in which the millstream hits the wheel at the top of its circumference.

o·ver·sight (ō′vər-sīt′) *n.* **1.** An unintentional omission or mistake. **2.** Watchful care or management; supervision. —See Synonyms at **error.**

o·ver·sim·pli·fy (ō′vər-sĭm′plə-fī′) *tr.v.* **-fied, -fying, -fies.** To distort by presenting in too simple a form. —**o′ver·sim′pli·fi·ca′tion** *n.*

o·ver·size (ō′vər-sīz′) *adj.* Also **o·ver·sized** (ō′vər-sīzd′). Larger than usual or necessary in size. —*n.* (ō′vər-sīz′). **1.** An unusually large size. **2.** An article made in an unusually large size.

o·ver·skirt (ō′vər-skûrt′) *n.* An outer skirt, especially a shorter one worn draped over another skirt.

o·ver·sleep (ō′vər-slēp′) *v.* **-slept** (-slĕpt′), **-sleeping, -sleeps.** —*intr.* To sleep beyond one's usual time for waking. —*tr.* **1.** To permit to sleep too long. **2.** To sleep beyond the time for.

o·ver·soul (ō′vər-soul′) *n.* In New England transcendentalism, a spiritual essence or vital force in the universe, in which all souls participate, and which therefore transcends individual consciousness.

o·ver·spend (ō′vər-spĕnd′) *v.* **-spent** (-spĕnt′), **-spending, -spends.** —*intr.* To spend more than is prudent or necessary. —*tr.* **1.** To spend in excess of: *overspend one's income.* **2.** To exhaust. Used chiefly in the past participle: *overspent with toil.*

o·ver·state (ō′vər-stāt′) *tr.v.* **-stated, -stating, -states.** To state in exaggerated terms. —**o′ver·state′ment** *n.*

o·ver·stay (ō′vər-stā′) *tr.v.* **-stayed, -staying, -stays.** To stay beyond the set limits or expected duration of: *He overstayed his welcome.*

o·ver·step (ō′vər-stĕp′) *tr.v.* **-stepped, -stepping, -steps.** To go beyond (a limit or bound): *overstep the bounds of taste.*

o·ver·stock (ō′vər-stŏk′) *tr.v.* **-stocked, -stocking, -stocks. 1.** To supply with too much of (a commodity). **2.** To stock too much of (a commodity). —*n.* (ō′vər-stŏk′). An excessive supply.

o·ver·stuff (ō′vər-stŭf′) *tr.v.* **-stuffed, -stuffing, -stuffs. 1.** To stuff too much into. **2.** To upholster overall and thickly.

o·ver·sub·scribe (ō′vər-səb-skrīb′) *tr.v.* **-scribed, -scribing, -scribes.** To subscribe for (something) in excess of available supply or accommodation: *The opera season was oversubscribed.* —**o′ver·sub·scrip′tion** (-səb-skrĭp′shən) *n.*

o·ver·sup·ply (ō′vər-sə-plī′) *n., pl.* **-plies.** A supply in excess of what is required. —*tr.v.* (ō′vər-sə-plī′) **oversupplied, -plying, -plies.** To supply in excess.

o·vert (ō-vûrt′, ō′vûrt′) *adj.* Open and observable; not concealed or hidden: *"These tendencies . . . are often revealed in less overt or dramatic forms."* (Erich Fromm). [Middle English, from Old French, from the past participle of *ovrir,* to open, from Vulgar Latin *operīre* (unattested), from Latin *aperīre.* See **wer-**[5] in Appendix.*] —**o·vert′ly** *adv.*

o·ver·take (ō′vər-tāk′) *tr.v.* **-took** (-to͝ok) **-taken, -taking, -takes. 1.** To catch up with; draw even or level with: *"Go, Gratiano, run and overtake him."* (Shakespeare). **2.** To pass after catching up with. **3.** To come upon unexpectedly; take by surprise.

o·ver·tax (ō′vər-tăks′) *tr.v.* **-taxed, -taxing, -taxes. 1.** To impose an excessive tax or taxes on. **2.** To subject to an excessive burden or strain. —**o′ver·tax·a′tion** *n.*

o·ver-the-count·er (ō′vər-*thə*-koun′tər) *adj.* **1.** Not listed or available on an officially recognized stock exchange but traded in direct negotiation between buyers and sellers. Said of stocks and securities. **2.** Capable of being sold legally without a prescription. Said of drugs or medicines.

o·ver·throw (ō′vər-thrō′) *tr.v.* **-threw** (-thro͞o) **-thrown, -throwing, -throws. 1.** To throw over; overturn. **2.** To bring about the downfall or destruction of, especially by force or concerted action: *a plot to overthrow the government.* **3.** To throw something over and beyond (an intended mark), especially a baseball over and beyond (a base). —*n.* (ō′vər-thrō′). **1.** An instance of overthrowing. **2.** Downfall; destruction. **3.** *Baseball.* The throwing of a ball over and beyond a base.

o·ver·time (ō′vər-tīm′) *n.* **1.** Time beyond an established limit, such as: **a.** Working hours in addition to those of the regular schedule. **b.** A period of playing time added after the expiration of the set time limit of an athletic contest: *The game went into overtime.* **2.** Payment for additional work done outside of regular working hours. —*adv.* Beyond the established time limit, especially that of the normal working day: *The staff worked overtime.* —*adj.* **1.** Of or for overtime: *overtime pay.* **2.** Beyond the permitted or allotted time: *overtime parking.* —*tr.v.* (ō′vər-tīm′) **overtimed, -timing, -times.** To exceed the desired timing for: *overtime a photographic exposure.*

o·ver·tone (ō′vər-tōn′) *n.* **1.** *Music & Acoustics.* A **harmonic** *(see).* **2.** *Often plural.* An implication: *praise with overtones of envy.* [Translation of German *Oberton.*]

o·ver·top (ō′vər-tŏp′) *tr.v.* **-topped, -topping, -tops. 1.** To extend or rise over or beyond the top of; tower above. **2.** To be superior to; surpass in importance; override: *"religion overtopped the common affairs of life"* (Albert C. Baugh).

o·ver·trick (ō′vər-trĭk′) *n. Card Games.* A trick won in excess of contract or game.

o·ver·trump (ō′vər-trŭmp′, ō′vər-trŭmp′) *v.* **-trumped, -trumping, -trumps.** *Card Games.* —*tr.* To trump with a higher trump card than any played on the same trick. —*intr.* To play a trump higher than one previously played on a trick.

o·ver·ture (ō′vər-cho͝or′) *n.* **1.** *Music.* **a.** An instrumental composition intended especially as an introduction to an opera, oratorio, or other extended musical work. **b.** A similar orchestral work, such as one written as introductory music to a play, or as a concert piece. **2.** Any introductory section or part, as of a poem. **3.** An act, offer, or proposal that indicates readiness to undertake a course of action or to open a relationship: *"I wanted revenge for her snub of my flirting overture."* (John Updike). **4.** *Presbyterian Church.* **a.** The submitting of a proposal by the highest church court to the presbyteries for their judgment on it preceding formal decision by the court. **b.** A proposal thus submitted. —*tr.v.* **overtured, -turing, -tures. 1.** To present as an overture or proposal. **2.** To present or offer an overture to. **3.** To introduce with an overture or prelude. [Middle English, from Old French, from Vulgar Latin *opertūra* (unattested), from Latin *apertūra,* an opening, from *aperīre* (past participle *apertus*), to open. See **wer-**[5] in Appendix.*]

o·ver·turn (ō′vər-tûrn′) *v.* **-turned, -turning, -turns.** —*tr.* **1.** To cause to turn over or capsize; upset. **2.** To overthrow; defeat. —*intr.* To turn over or capsize; become upset. —*n.* (ō′vər-tûrn′). **1.** The act or process of overturning. **2.** The state of being overturned. **3.** **Turnover** *(see).*

o·ver·use (ō′vər-yo͞oz′) *tr.v.* **-used, -using, -uses.** To use to excess. —*n.* (ō′vər-yo͞os′). Excessive use.

o·ver·val·ue (ō′vər-văl′yo͞o) *tr.v.* **-ued, -uing, -ues.** To set too high a value on.

o·ver·view (ō′vər-vyo͞o′) *n.* A broad, comprehensive view; survey or inspection.

o·ver·ween·ing (ō′vər-wē′nĭng) *adj.* **1.** Presumptuously arrogant; overbearing: *"it was an affront to his overweening vanity that you should disagree with him."* (Maugham). **2.** Excessive; immoderate: *"whose expression of benevolence concealed overweening ambition"* (S.J. Perelman)

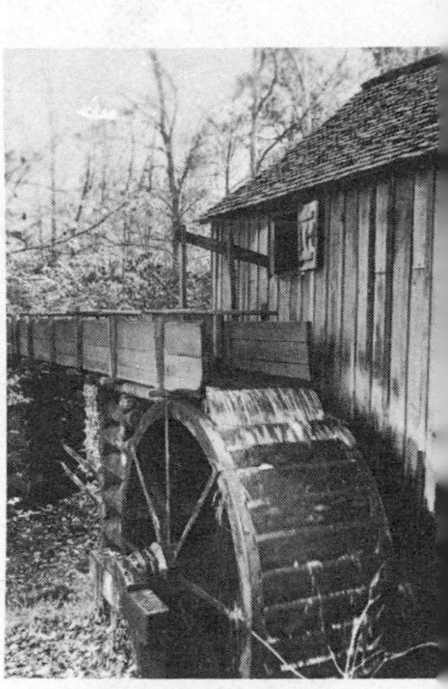

overshot

t tight/th thin, path/*th* this, bathe/ŭ cut/ûr urge/v valve/w with/y yes/z zebra, size/zh vision/ə about, item, edible, gallop, circus/ à *Fr.* ami/œ *Fr.* feu, *Ger.* schön/ü *Fr.* tu, *Ger.* über/KH *Ger.* ich, *Scot.* loch/N *Fr.* bon. ***Follows main vocabulary.** †**Of obscure origin.**

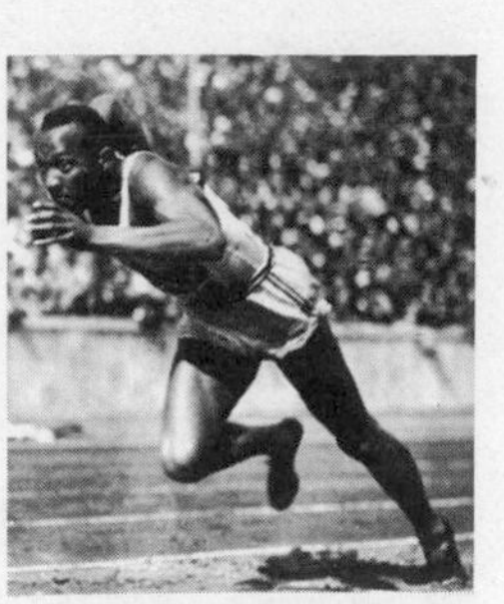
Jesse Owens
Setting 20.7-second record for 200-meter race at 1936 Olympics in Berlin

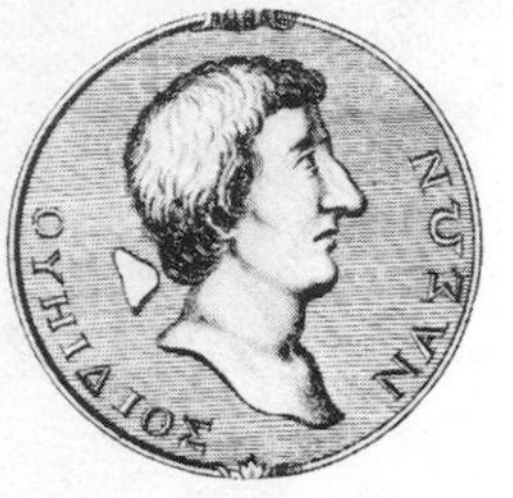
Ovid
Late 17th-century engraving

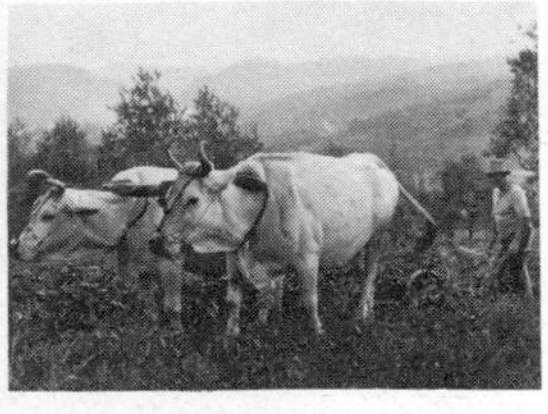
ox
Oxen pulling plow

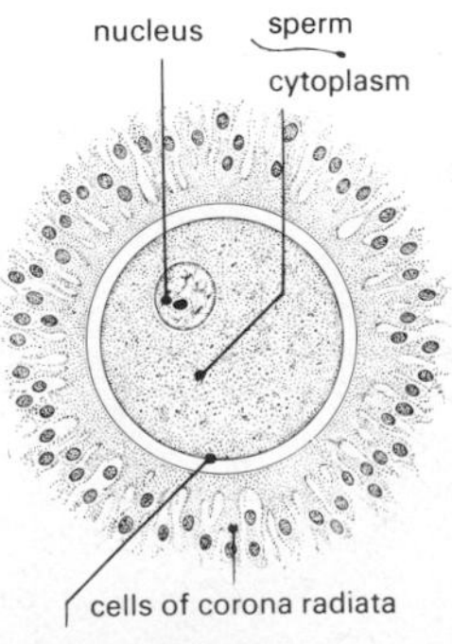
nucleus
sperm
cytoplasm
cells of corona radiata
vitelline membrane
ovum
Human ovum, enlarged 126 diameters

o·ver·weigh (ō′vər-wā′) *tr.v.* **-weighed, -weighing, -weighs. 1.** To have more weight than; outweigh; overbalance. **2.** To weigh down excessively; overburden.

o·ver·weight (ō′vər-wāt′) *adj.* Weighing more than is normal, necessary, or allowed. —*n.* (ō′vər-wāt′). **1.** More weight than is normal, necessary, or allowed; excess of weight. **2.** Greater weight or importance; preponderance. —*tr.v.* (ō′vər-wāt′) **overweighted, -weighting, -weights. 1.** To weigh down too heavily; overload. **2.** To give too much emphasis, importance, or consideration to.

o·ver·whelm (ō′vər-hwĕlm′) *tr.v.* **-whelmed, -whelming, -whelms. 1.** To surge over and submerge; engulf: *waves overwhelming the rocky shoreline.* **2.** To overcome completely, either physically or emotionally; overpower: *"Fredrigo was overwhelmed with excitement by her visit"* (Wayne C. Booth). **3.** To turn over; upset; overthrow. [Middle English *overwhelmen* : OVER- + *whelmen,* to WHELM.]

o·ver·whelm·ing (ō′vər-hwĕl′mĭng) *adj.* Overpowering in effect or strength: *overwhelming news; an overwhelming majority.* —**o′ver·whelm′ing·ly** *adv.*

o·ver·work (ō′vər-wûrk′) *v.* **-worked** or *archaic* **-wrought** (-rôt′), **-working, -works.** —*tr.* **1.** To force to work too hard or too long. **2.** To use or rework too often or to excess: *overwork a metaphor.* —*intr.* To work too long or too hard. —*n.* (ō′vər-wûrk′). Excess work; especially, work done on overtime.

o·ver·write (ō′vər-rīt′) *v.* **-wrote** (-rōt′), **-written, -writing, -writes.** —*tr.* **1.** To write (something) over other writing. **2.** To write about in an excessively flowery, mannered, or prolix style. —*intr.* To write at unnecessarily great length.

o·ver·wrought (ō′vər-rôt′). *Archaic.* Alternate past participle of **overwork.** —*adj.* **1.** Excessively nervous or excited; agitated; strained: *"The Queen was so overwrought that she became physically ill."* (Philip Magnus). **2.** Extremely elaborate or ornate; overdone: *an overwrought prose style.*

ovi–, ovo–. Indicates egg or ovum; for example, **oviduct, ovoviviparous.** [Latin *ōvi-, ōvo-,* from *ōvum,* egg. See **awi-** in Appendix.*]

o·vi·bos (ō′və-bŏs′) *n.* The **musk ox** *(see).* [New Latin : Latin *ovis,* sheep (see **owi-** in Appendix*) + *bōs,* ox (see **gwou-** in Appendix*).]

o·vi·ci·dal (ō′və-sīd′l) *adj.* Capable of killing eggs. [OVI- + -CID(E) + -AL.] —**o′vi·cide′** (ō′və-sīd′) *n.*

Ov·id (ŏv′ĭd). Latin, Publius Ovidius Naso. 43 B.C.–A.D. 17? Roman poet.

o·vi·duct (ō′və-dŭkt′) *n. Zoology.* A tube through which ova travel from an ovary. In mammals it is called a **Fallopian tube** *(see).* [New Latin *oviductus* : OVI- + DUCT.] —**o′vi·duc′tal** *adj.*

O·vie·do (ō-vyā′*th*ō). An industrial city in northwestern Spain. Population, 134,000.

o·vif·er·ous (ō-vĭf′ər-əs) *adj.* Bearing or producing ova. [OVI- + -FEROUS.]

o·vi·form (ō′və-fôrm′) *adj.* Egg-shaped. [OVI- + -FORM.]

o·vine (ō′vīn′) *adj.* Designating sheep; sheeplike. —*n.* An ovine animal. [Late Latin *ovīnus,* from Latin *ovis,* sheep. See **owi-** in Appendix.*]

o·vip·a·rous (ō-vĭp′ər-əs) *adj.* Producing eggs that hatch outside the body. Compare **ovoviviparous, viviparous.** [Latin *ōviparus* : OVI- + -PAROUS.] —**o·vip′a·rous·ly** *adv.* —**o′vi·par′i·ty** (ō′və-păr′ə-tē) *n.*

o·vi·pos·it (ō′və-pŏz′ĭt) *intr.v.* **-ited, -iting, -its.** *Entomology.* To lay eggs, especially with an ovipositor. —**o′vi·po·si′tion** (ō′və-pə-zĭsh′ən) *n.*

o·vi·pos·i·tor (ō′və-pŏz′ə-tər) *n. Entomology.* A tubular structure, sometimes extending outside the abdomen, with which many insects lay eggs.

o·vi·sac (ō′və-săk′) *n. Biology.* An egg-containing capsule, such as an **ootheca** or a **Graafian follicle** *(both of which see).*

ovo–. Variant of **ovi-.**

o·void (ō′void′) *adj.* Also **o·voi·dal** (ō-void′l). Egg-shaped. —*n.* Something egg-shaped. [French *ovoide* : OV(I)- + -OID.]

o·vo·lo (ō′və-lō′) *n., pl.* **-li** (-lī′). *Architecture.* A rounded convex molding, often a quarter section of a circle or ellipse. Also called "thumb." [Italian, diminutive of *ovo,* egg, from Latin *ōvum.* See **awi-** in Appendix.*]

o·vo·tes·tis (ō′vō-tĕs′tĭs) *n., pl.* **-tes** (-tēz′). *Zoology.* The hermaphroditic reproductive gland of some gastropods. [New Latin : OVO- + TESTIS.]

o·vo·vi·vip·a·rous (ō′vō-vī-vĭp′ər-əs) *adj.* Producing eggs that hatch within the female's body, as some fishes and reptiles. Compare **viviparous, oviparous.** [New Latin *ovoviviparus* : OVO- + *viviparus,* VIVIPAROUS.] —**o′vo·vi′vi·par′i·ty** (-vī′və-păr′ə-tē), **o′vo·vi·vip′a·rous·ly** *adv.* —**o′vo·vi·vip′a·rous·ness** *n.*

o·vu·late (ō′vyə-lāt′) *intr.v.* **-lated, -lating, -lates.** *Biology.* **1.** To produce ova. **2.** To discharge ova. [From New Latin *ovulum,* OVULE.] —**o′vu·la′tion** *n.*

o·vule (ō′vyo͞ol) *n.* **1.** *Zoology.* An immature ovum. **2.** *Botany.* A minute structure which after fertilization becomes a plant seed. [French, from New Latin *ovulum,* diminutive of Latin *ōvum,* egg. See **awi-** in Appendix.*] —**o′vu·lar** (ō′vyə-lər), **o′vu·lar′y** (ō′vyə-lĕr′ē) *adj.*

o·vum (ō′vəm) *n., pl.* **ova** (ō′və). The female reproductive cell of animals; an egg. [New Latin, from Latin *ōvum, egg.* See **awi-** in Appendix.*]

owe (ō) *v.* **owed** or *obsolete* **ought** (ôt), **owing, owes.** —*tr.* **1.** To be indebted to the amount of; have to pay or repay: *He owes me five dollars.* **2.** To be morally obligated to; have an obligation to render or offer: *I owe him an apology.* **3.** To be in debt to. **4. a.** To be indebted or obliged for: *"whether England owes more to the Roman Catholic religion or the Reformation"* (Macaulay). **b.** To be indebted to for being the cause of: *He owes his success to his father.* **5.** To bear (a certain feeling) toward a person: *He owes them a grudge.* **6.** *Obsolete.* To own; have. —*intr.* To be in debt: *He owes for everything he has.* [Middle English *owen,* possess, to owe, Old English *āgan,* to possess. See **eik-** in Appendix.*]

Ow·en (ō′ĭn). A masculine given name. [Welsh *Owein,* from Gaulish *Esugenios* (unattested), from Greek *eugenios,* "wellborn." See **Eugene.**]

Ow·en (ō′ĭn), Sir **Richard.** 1804–1892. British zoologist and philosopher.

Ow·en (ō′ĭn), **Robert.** 1771–1858. British industrialist and reformer; with his son, **Robert Dale** (1801–1877), he established the community of New Harmony, Indiana (1825).

Ow·en Falls (ō′ĭn). Former falls of the Nile River, north of Lake Victoria, that became submerged when the Owen Falls Dam was built.

Ow·ens (ō′ĭnz), **Jesse.** Original name, John Cleveland or J.C. Owens. Born 1913. American athlete; hero of the 1936 Olympic games at Berlin.

Ow·en Stan·ley Range (ō′ĭn stăn′lē). A mountain range, 600 miles long, in southeastern Papua, New Guinea. Highest elevation, Mount Victoria (13,240 feet).

OWI, O.W.I. Office of War Information.

ow·ing (ō′ĭng) *adj.* Still to be paid; due; owed. —**owing to.** Because of; on account of.

owl (oul) *n.* **1.** Any of various often nocturnal birds of prey of the order Strigiformes, having hooked and feathered talons, large heads with short, hooked beaks, and eyes set in a frontal facial plane. **2.** Any of a breed of domestic pigeons resembling owls. [Middle English *owle,* Old English *ūle.* See **ul-** in Appendix.*]

owl·et (ou′lĭt) *n.* **1.** A young owl. **2.** The **little owl** *(see).*

owl·ish (ou′lĭsh) *adj.* Resembling an owl. —**owl′ish·ly** *adv.* —**owl′ish·ness** *n.*

owl's claws. Used with a singular and plural verb. A plant, *Helenium hoopesii,* of western North America, having large yellow flower heads.

owl's-clo·ver (oulz′klō′vər). Any of various New World plants of the genus *Orthocarpus,* having spikes of red or purple flowers. [After the flowers of some species that resemble owl's faces.]

own (ōn) *adj.* Of or belonging to oneself or itself; individual; particular. Used to intensify the fact of possession and usually preceded by a possessive pronoun: *My own book.* Sometimes used to indicate oneself as the sole agent of the action expressed by the verb: *He made his own bed.* —*n.* That which belongs to one: *It is my own.* —**come into one's own. 1.** To obtain possession of what belongs to one. **2.** To obtain rightful recognition. —**hold one's own.** To maintain one's place in spite of attack or criticism. —**of one's own.** Belonging completely to oneself. —**on one's own.** Completely independent; responsible for oneself. —*v.* **owned, owning, owns.** —*tr.* **1.** To have or possess: *He owns the store.* **2.** To acknowledge or admit: *"I own myself a debtor to the world for two items."* (Sterne). —*intr.* To confess. Used with *to: He owned to being annoyed.* —See Synonyms at **acknowledge.** —**own up.** To confess fully and openly. [Middle English *owen,* Old English *āgen.* See **eik-** in Appendix.*] —**own′er** *n.*

own·er·ship (ō′nər-shĭp′) *n.* **1.** The state or fact of being an owner. **2.** Legal right to the possession of a thing; proprietorship; dominion.

ox (ŏks) *n., pl.* **oxen** (ŏk′sən). **1.** An adult castrated bull of the genus *Bos.* **2.** A bovine mammal. [Middle English *ox,* Old English *oxa.* See **wegw-** in Appendix.*]

Ox. Oxford.

oxa–, ox–. *Chemistry.* Indicates the presence of oxygen atoms, especially when replacing carbon; for example, **oxalic acid.**

ox·a·late (ŏk′sə-lāt′) *n.* Any salt or ester of oxalic acid. —*tr.v.* **oxalated, -lating, -lates.** To treat (a specimen) with an oxalate or oxalic acid. [French : *oxalique,* OXALIC ACID + -ATE.]

oxalic acid. A poisonous, crystalline organic acid, HOOCCOOH·$2H_2O$, used as a cleansing agent for automobile radiators and for metals in general, as a laundry bleach, and in textile finishing and cleaning. [French *oxalique,* from Latin *oxalis,* wood sorrel, OXALIS.]

ox·a·lis (ŏk′sə-lĭs, ŏk-săl′ĭs) *n.* Any plant of the genus *Oxalis,* having pink, yellow, or white flowers. Many species are also called "wood sorrel." [New Latin, from Latin, from Greek, from *oxus,* "sharp," sour. See **ak-** in Appendix.*]

ox·blood red (ŏks′blŭd′). Dark or deep red to medium reddish brown. See **color.**

ox·bow (ŏks′bō′) *n.* **1.** A U-shaped piece of wood that fits under and around the neck of an ox, with its upper ends attached to the bar of the yoke. **2.** A U-shaped bend in a river. **3.** The land within such a bend of a river.

Ox·en·stier·na (o͝ok′sən-shĕr′nə, ŏk′sən-), Count **Axel Gustafsson.** Also **Ox·en·stjer·na, Ox·en·stiern** (ŏk′sən-stîrn′). 1583–1654. Swedish statesman.

ox·eye (ŏks′ī′) *n.* **1.** Any of various Eurasian plants of the genus *Buphthalmum,* having daisylike flowers with yellow rays and dark centers. **2.** Any of various North American plants of the genus *Heliopsis,* having similar flowers. **3.** A round or oval dormer window. [Middle English.]

oxeye daisy. See **daisy.**

Oxf. 1. Oxford. **2.** Oxfordshire.

ox·ford (ŏks′fərd) *n.* **1.** A stout, low shoe that laces over the instep. **2.** A cotton cloth of a tight basket weave, used primarily for men's shirts. [After OXFORD, England.]

Ox·ford (ŏks′fərd). *Abbr.* **Ox., Oxf.** **1.** The county seat of Oxfordshire, England, on the Thames (locally called "Isis"), 52 miles northwest of London; site of Oxford University. Population, 109,000. **2. Oxfordshire** *(see).* [Middle English *Oxeneford,* Old English *Ox(e)naford* : *oxena,* genitive plural of *oxa,* OX + FORD.] —**Ox·o′ni·an** *adj.*

oxford gray. Dark gray. See **color.**

Oxford movement. A movement within the Church of England that originated at Oxford University in 1833. It sought to link the Anglican Church more closely to the Roman Catholic Church. Compare **Tractarianism.**

Ox·ford·shire (ŏks′fərd-shîr′, -shər). Also **Ox·ford.** *Abbr.* **Oxf., Oxon.** A county occupying 749 square miles in south-central England. Population, 309,000. County seat, Oxford.

ox·heart (ŏks′härt′) *n.* A variety of cultivated cherry having sweet, juicy fruit.

ox·i·dant (ŏk′sə-dənt) *n.* A chemical reagent that oxidizes.

ox·i·dase (ŏk′sə-dās′, -dāz′) *n.* Any of various plant or animal enzymes that act as oxidants. [OXID(ATION) + -ASE.] —**ox′i·da′sic** (ŏk′sə-dā′sĭk, -zĭk) *adj.*

ox·i·da·tion (ŏk′sə-dā′shən) *n.* **1.** The combination of a substance with oxygen. **2.** A reaction in which the atoms in an element lose electrons and its valence is correspondingly increased. Compare **reduction.** [French, from *oxyder,* to oxidize.] —**ox·i·da·tive** (ŏk′sə-dā′tĭv) *adj.* —**ox′i·da′tive·ly** *adv.*

ox·i·da·tion-re·duc·tion (ŏk′sə-dā′shən-rĭ-dŭk′shən) *n.* A chemical reaction in which an atom or molecule loses electrons to another atom or molecule. Also called "redox."

oxidative phos·pho·ryl·a·tion (fŏs′fə-rə-lā′shən). *Biochemistry.* A vital process of intracellular respiration, occurring within the mitochondria of the cell, and responsible for most **adenosine triphosphate** *(see)* formation.

ox·ide (ŏk′sīd′) *n.* A binary compound of an element or radical with oxygen. [French, from *oxygène,* OXYGEN.] —**ox·id′ic** (ŏk-sĭd′ĭk) *adj.*

ox·i·dize (ŏk′sə-dīz′) *v.* **-dized, -dizing, -dizes.** *Chemistry.* —*tr.* **1.** To combine with oxygen; make into an oxide. **2.** To increase the positive charge or valence of (an element) by removing electrons. **3.** To coat with oxide. —*intr.* To become oxidized. [From OXIDE.] —**ox′i·diz′a·ble** *adj.* —**ox′i·di·za′tion** *n.*

ox·i·diz·er (ŏk′sə-dī′zər) *n.* Any substance that oxidizes or induces another substance to oxidize; an oxidizing agent.

ox·lip (ŏks′lĭp′) *n.* A Eurasian primrose, *Primula elatior,* having clusters of yellow flowers. [Old English *oxanslyppe* : *oxan,* genitive of *oxa,* OX + *slyppe, slypa,* sticky substance, dung (see **sleubh-** in Appendix*).]

Oxon. Oxfordshire.

Ox·o·ni·an (ŏk-sō′nē-ən) *adj.* Of, pertaining to, or characteristic of Oxford or Oxford University. —*n.* **1.** A native or inhabitant of Oxford. **2.** A student or graduate of Oxford University. [From Medieval Latin *Oxōnia,* Oxford, from Old English *Ox(e)naford,* OXFORD.]

ox·o·phen·ar·sine hydrochloride (ŏk′sō-fĕn-är′sēn′). A drug, $C_6H_3AsO(OH)NH_2HCl$, formerly used in treating syphilis. [*Oxophenarsine* : OX(YGEN)- + PHEN(O)- + ARSINE.]

ox·peck·er (ŏks′pĕk′ər) *n.* Either of two African birds, *Buphagus africanus* or *B. erythrorhyncus,* that feed upon ticks on the hides of large wild or domestic animals.

ox·tail (ŏks′tāl′) *n.* The tail of an ox, especially used in soup.

Ox·us River. The ancient name for the **Amu Darya.**

oxy–¹. Indicates something sharp; for example, **oxycephaly.** [From Greek *oxus,* sharp. See **ak-** in Appendix.*]

oxy–². *Chemistry.* Indicates: **1.** The presence of combined or added oxygen; for example, **oxyhemoglobin. 2.** Oxygen used in some combination; for example, **oxysulfide.** [From OXYGEN.]

ox·y·a·cet·y·lene (ŏk′sē-ə-sĕt′l-ĭn, -ə-sĕt′l-ēn′) *adj.* Containing a mixture of acetylene and oxygen, as commonly used in metal welding and cutting torches.

ox·y·ceph·a·ly (ŏk′sē-sĕf′ə-lē) *n.* A congenital cephalic abnormality in which the skull assumes a conical shape. [OXY- (sharp) + *-cephaly,* from -CEPHALIC.] —**ox′y·ce·phal′ic** (-sə-făl′ĭk), **ox′y·ceph′a·lous** *adj.*

ox·y·gen (ŏk′sĭ-jən) *n. Symbol* **O** A colorless, odorless, tasteless gaseous element constituting 21 per cent of the atmosphere by volume from which the pure liquid form is obtained by fractional distillation. It combines with most elements, is essential for plant and animal respiration, and is required for nearly all combustion and combustive processes. Atomic number 8, atomic weight 15.9994, melting point −218.4°C, boiling point −183.0°C, gas density at 0°C 1.429 grams per liter, valence 2. See **element.** [French *oxygène,* "acid-former" : OXY- (sharp, here, "acid") + -GEN.] —**ox′y·gen′ic** (ŏk′sĭ-jĕn′ĭk), **ox·yg′e·nous** (ŏk-sĭj′ə-nəs) *adj.* —**ox′y·gen′i·cal·ly** *adv.*

ox·y·gen·ate (ŏk′sĭ-jə-nāt′) *tr.v.* **-ated, -ating, -ates.** Also **ox·y·gen·ize** (-nīz′), **-ized, -izing, -izes.** To treat, combine, or infuse with oxygen. —**ox′y·gen·a′tion** *n.*

oxygen mask. A masklike device covering the mouth and nose through which oxygen is supplied from a tank or other source.

oxygen tent. A canopy placed over the head and shoulders of a patient to provide oxygen therapy.

ox·y·he·mo·glo·bin (ŏk′sē-hē′mə-glō′bĭn, -hĕm′ə-glō′bĭn) *n.* A bright-red chemical complex of hemoglobin and oxygen, that transports oxygen from the lungs to the tissues via the blood.

ox·y·hy·dro·gen blowpipe (ŏk′sē-hī′drə-jən). A torch that burns a mixture of hydrogen and oxygen for welding.

ox·y·mo·ron (ŏk′sē-môr′ŏn′, -mōr′ŏn′) *n., pl.* **-mora** (-môr′ə, -mōr′ə). A rhetorical figure in which an epigrammatic effect is created by the conjunction of incongruous or contradictory terms; for example, "a mournful optimist." [Greek *oxumoron,* a clever remark, more pointedly witty for seeming absurd or foolish, neuter of *oxumōros,* "sharp-foolish" : OXY- (sharp) + *mōros,* stupid, foolish (see **mōuro-** in Appendix*).]

Ox·y·rhyn·chus (ŏk′sē-rĭng′kəs). An ancient city of Middle Kingdom of Egypt, on the site of which exceptional quantities of Greco-Roman papyri were recovered during the 19th century. [Greek *Oxurhunkhos,* "the sharp-snouted," Greek name of the city's tutelary deity, a fish that devoured the phallus of the dismembered Osiris : OXY- (sharp) + *rhunkhos,* snout (see **srenk-** in Appendix*).]

ox·y·sul·fide (ŏk′sē-sŭl′fīd′) *n. Chemistry.* A compound consisting of sulfur and oxygen, combined with a metal or positive radical, in which part of the sulfur has been replaced by oxygen.

ox·y·tet·ra·cy·cline (ŏk′sē-tĕt′rə-sī′klĭn, -sī′klēn′) *n.* An antibiotic, $C_{22}H_{24}N_2O_9 \cdot 2H_2O$, derived from the mold *Streptomyces rimosus,* and used to treat bacterial infection in man and animals. A trademark is "Terramycin."

ox·y·to·cic (ŏk′sĭ-tō′sĭk) *n.* Any drug that hastens the process of childbirth, especially by inducing contraction of the uterine muscle. [OXY- (sharp) + Greek *tokos,* childbirth, from *tiktein,* to bear (see **tek-¹** in Appendix*) + -IC.] —**ox′y·to′cic** *adj.*

ox·y·to·cin (ŏk′sĭ-tō′sĭn) *n.* An oxytocic pituitary hormone.

ox·y·tone (ŏk′sĭ-tōn′) *adj.* **1.** Designating a Greek word that has an acute accent on its last syllable. **2.** Designating a word that has a heavy stress accent on its last syllable. —*n.* A word having the stress or the acute accent on the last syllable. [Greek *oxutonos* : OXY- (sharp) + *tonos,* TONE.]

oyer and ter·mi·ner (oi′ər; tûr′mə-nər). *Law.* **1.** A hearing or trial. **2.** In the United States, a designation occasionally used for a high criminal court. **3.** In Great Britain: **a.** A commission to a judge by which he is empowered to hear and rule on a criminal case at the assizes. **b.** The court in which such a hearing is held. [Middle English, from Norman French *oyer et terminer,* "to hear and determine" : *oyer,* to hear (see **oyez**) + *terminer,* to determine, from Latin *termināre,* TERMINATE.]

o·yez (ō′yĕs′, ō′yĕz′, ō′yā′) *interj.* Also **o·yes** (ō′yĕs′). Used three times in succession to introduce the opening of a court of law. —*n.* Also **o·yes** *pl.* **oyesses** (ō′yĕs′ĭz). The cry "oyez": "*Fame with her loud'st Oyes cries 'This is he!'*" (Shakespeare). [Middle English *oyes!* from Norman French *oyez!,* hear ye!, imperative plural of *oyer,* variant of Old French *oïr,* to hear, from Latin *audīre.* See **aw-²** in Appendix.*]

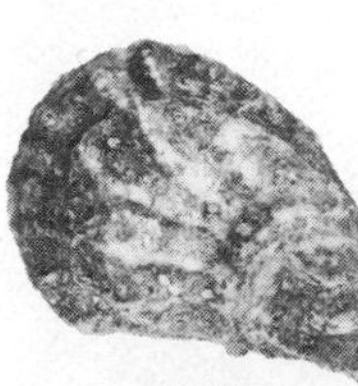
oyster
Ostrea virginica

oys·ter (oi′stər) *n.* **1.** Any of several edible bivalve mollusks of the genus *Ostrea,* chiefly of shallow marine waters, having an irregularly shaped shell. **2.** Any of various similar or related bivalve mollusks, such as the **pearl oyster** *(see).* **3.** A bit of muscle, regarded as a delicacy, found in the hollow of the pelvic bone of a fowl. **4. a.** Any special delicacy. **b.** Anything from which benefits may be extracted. **5.** *Slang.* A close-mouthed person. —*intr.v.* **oystered, -tering, -ters.** To gather, dredge for, or raise oysters. [Middle English *oistre,* from Old French, from Latin *ostrea,* from Greek *ostreon.* See **osth-** in Appendix.*]

oyster bed. A place where oysters breed or are raised.

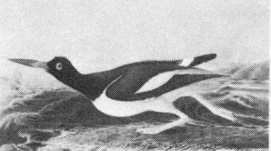

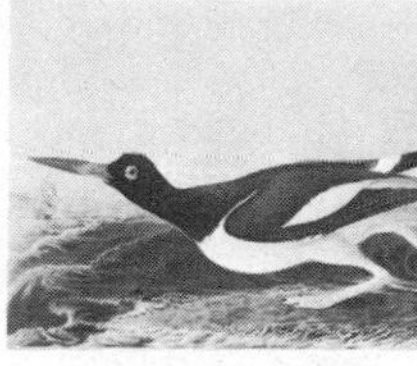
oystercatcher
Haematopus pallatus
Painting by
John James Audubon

oys·ter·catch·er (oi′stər-kăch′ər) *n.* Any of several shore birds of the genus *Haematopus,* having black and white plumage and a long orange-red bill.

oyster crab. A small crab, *Pinnotheres ostreum,* that lives inside the shells of living oysters.

oyster cracker. A small, dry soda cracker.

oys·ter·man (oi′stər-mən) *n., pl.* **-men** (-mĭn). **1.** One who cultivates or sells oysters. **2.** An oyster-dredging vessel.

oyster plant. A vegetable, **salsify** *(see).*

oyster white. Pale yellowish green to light gray. See **color.**

oz ounce.

oz ap apothecaries' ounce.

O·zark Mountains (ō′zärk). A range of low mountains (1,500 to 2,500 feet) spreading over an area of 60,000 square miles in southwestern Missouri, northwestern Arkansas, and eastern Oklahoma. Also called "Ozark Plateau," "Ozarks."

oz av, oz avdp avoirdupois ounce.

o·zo·ce·rite (ō′zō-sîr′īt′) *n.* Also **o·zo·ke·rite** (ō′zō-kîr′īt′). A yellow-brown to black or green mineral hydrocarbon wax, used in making electrical insulation, lubricants, and inks. Also called "mineral wax." [German *Ozokerit* : Greek *ozein,* to smell (see **od-¹** in Appendix*) + *kēros,* wax (see **kēr-** in Appendix*) + -ITE.]

o·zone (ō′zōn′) *n.* **1.** A blue, gaseous allotrope of oxygen, O_3, derived or formed naturally from diatomic oxygen by electric discharge or exposure to ultraviolet radiation. It is an unstable, powerfully bleaching, poisonous, oxidizing agent, with a pungent, irritating odor, used to purify and deodorize air, to sterilize water, and as a bleach. **2.** *Informal.* Fresh, pure air. [German *Ozon,* from Greek *ozōn,* present participle of *ozein,* to smell, reek. See **od-¹** in Appendix.*] —**o·zo′nic** (ō-zō′nĭk, ō-zŏn′ĭk), **o′zon′ous** (ō′zō′nəs) *adj.*

o·zo·nide (ō′zō-nīd′) *n.* **1.** Any of various often explosive chemicals formed by attachment of ozone to the double bond of an unsaturated compound and used in analytical chemistry to locate such bonds.

o·zo·nize (ō′zō-nīz′) *tr.v.* **-nized, -nizing, -nizes. 1.** To treat or impregnate with ozone. **2.** To convert (oxygen) to ozone. —**o′zon·iz′er** *n.*

o·zo·no·sphere (ō-zō′nə-sfîr′) *n.* A region of the upper atmosphere, between ten and twenty miles in altitude, containing a relatively high concentration of ozone that absorbs solar ultraviolet radiation in a wavelength range not screened by other atmospheric components. [OZON(E) + -SPHERE.] —**o·zo′no·spher′ic** (ō-zō′nə-sfîr′ĭk, -sfĕr′ĭk), **o·zo′no·spher′i·cal** *adj.*

oz t troy ounce.

Pp

1 Phoenician **2** ... **3 4** Greek **5 6 7** ... **8 9 10** Roman ... **11 12** Medieval **13 14 15 16** Modern

Around 1000 B.C. *the Phoenicians and other Semites of Syria and Palestine began to use a sign representing the consonant* p, *in a rounded or angular form (1,2). They named the sign* pē, *meaning "mouth." After 900 B.C. the Greeks borrowed the sign from the Phoenicians in a vertical rounded form (3). They later enlarged the curve (4) and reversed the orientation (5), then gave the sign a rectangular form (6) and eventually made it symmetrical (7). They also changed its name to* pi. *The Greek form (5) passed via Etruscan to the Romans (8). They closed the curve into a loop (9) and developed the Monumental Capital (10) that is the basis of our modern capital, printed (13) and written (14). The written Roman form (9) gave rise to various medieval forms, such as the Uncial (11) and Cursive (12), which are the bases of our modern small letter, printed (15) and written (16).*

p, P (pē) *n., pl.* **p's** or *rare* **ps, P's** or **Ps. 1.** The 16th letter of the modern English alphabet. See **alphabet. 2.** Any of the speech sounds represented by the letter P.

p, P, p., P. *Note:* As an abbreviation or symbol, *p* may be a small or a capital letter, with or without a period. Established forms or those generally preferred precede the definition. When no form is given, all four forms are in general use in that sense. **1.** p *Physics.* momentum. **2.** p. page. **3.** P *Physics.* parity. **4.** p. part. **5.** p. participle. **6.** P *Chess.* pawn. **7.** p. penny. **8.** p. per. **9.** p. peseta. **10.** p. peso. **11.** P The symbol for the element phosphorus. **12.** p, p. *Music.* piano (a direction). **13.** p *Physics.* pico-. **14.** p. pint. **15.** p. pipe. **16.** p. pole. **17.** p. population. **18.** p., P. president. **19.** P *Physics.* pressure. **20.** P. priest. **21.** p, P. prince. **22.** p. pro. **23.** p proton. **24.** p. purl. **25.** P The medieval Roman numeral for 400. **26.** The 16th in a series; 15th when *J* is omitted.

P₁ *Genetics.* The parental generation.

pa (pä) *n. Informal.* Papa; father. [Short for PAPA.]

Pa The symbol for the element protactinium.

PA 1. Pennsylvania (with Zip Code). **2.** public-address system.

Pa. Pennsylvania.

p.a. per annum.

P.A. 1. power of attorney. **2.** press agent. **3.** prosecuting attorney.

P/A power of attorney.

pab·u·lum (păb′yə-ləm) *n., pl.* **-lums. 1.** Any substance that gives nourishment; food. **2.** Insipid intellectual nourishment. [Latin *pābulum*, food, fodder. See **pap-²** in Appendix.*]

pac (păk) *n.* Also **pack.** A type of moccasin or soft shoe designed to be worn inside a boot. [Delaware *paku*.]

Pac. Pacific.

pa·ca (pä′kə, păk′ə) *n.* A nocturnal tropical American rodent of the genus *Cuniculus*, having a short tail and blackish or brown fur. [Portuguese and Spanish, from Tupi *páca*.]

pace¹ (pās) *n.* **1.** A step made in walking; a stride. **2.** The distance spanned by a step or stride; specifically: **a.** A unit of length equal to 30 inches. **b.** *U.S. Army.* Thirty inches at quick time or 36 inches at double time. In full, "regulation pace." **c.** Five Roman feet or 58.1 English inches, measured from the point at which the heel of one foot is raised to the point at which it is set down again after an intervening step by the other foot. In full, "Roman pace." **d.** The modern version of the Roman pace, measuring five English feet. In full, "geometric pace." **3. a.** The rate of speed at which a person, animal, or group walks or runs. **b.** The rate of speed at which any activity or movement proceeds. **4.** A manner of walking or running: *He set out at a jaunty pace.* **5.** A gait of a horse in which both feet on one side leave and return to the ground together. Also called

"rack." —**put one through one's paces.** To test one's abilities; demand a demonstration of one's skills. —**set the pace. 1.** To go at a speed that other competitors attempt to match or surpass. **2.** To behave or perform in a way that others try to emulate. —*v.* **paced, pacing, paces.** —*tr.* **1.** To walk or stride back and forth across. **2.** To measure by counting the number of steps needed to cover a distance. **3.** To set or regulate the rate of speed for. **4.** To train (a horse) in a particular gait, especially the pace. —*intr.* **1.** To walk with long, deliberate steps. **2.** To go at the pace. Used of a horse or rider. [Middle English *pas*, from Old French, from Latin *passus*, a step, "a stretch of the leg," from *pandere* (past participle *passus*), to stretch. See **pet-²** in Appendix.*]

pa·ce² (pā′sē) *prep.* With the permission of; with deference to. Used to express polite, or ironically polite, disagreement: *I have not, pace my detractors, entered into any "deals."* [Latin *pāce*, ablative of *pāx*, peace. See **pag-** in Appendix.*] —**pa′ce** *adv.*

pace·mak·er (pās′mā′kər) *n.* **1.** One who sets the pace in a race; pacer. **2.** A leader in any field: *This fashion house is the pacemaker.* **3. a.** *Physiology.* A mass of specialized muscle fibers of the heart that regulate the heartbeat. **b.** *Medicine.* Any of several usually miniaturized and surgically implanted electronic devices used to regulate, or to aid in the regulation of, the heartbeat. **4.** *Biochemistry.* A substance that regulates a series of related reactions. —**pace′mak′ing** *n. & adj.*

pac·er (pā′sər) *n.* **1.** A horse trained to pace. **2.** A pacemaker.

pace·set·ter (pās′sĕt′ər) *n.* A pacemaker. —**pace′set′ting** *adj.*

pa·cha. Variant of **pasha.**

pa·chi·si (pə-chē′zē) *n.* **1.** An ancient game of India similar to backgammon but using cowry shells instead of dice. **2.** **Parcheesi** (*see*). [Hindi *pacīsī*, from *pacīs*, twenty-five (twenty-five is the highest throw) : Sanskrit *pañca*, five (see **penkwe** in Appendix*) + *vimsati*, twenty (see **wīkṃtī** in Appendix*).]

pach·ou·li. Variant of **patchouli.**

Pa·chu·ca (pä-chōō′kä). Officially **Pa·chu·ca de So·to** (*th*ä sō′tō). The capital and a silver-mining center of Hidalgo State, Mexico, 50 miles northeast of Mexico City. Population, 69,000.

pa·chu·co (pə-chōō′kō) *n., pl.* **-cos.** One of a gang of Mexican-American youths. [Mexican Spanish.]

pach·y·derm (păk′ĭ-dûrm′) *n.* Any of various large, thick-skinned, hoofed mammals, such as the elephant, rhinoceros, or hippopotamus. [French *pachyderme*, from Greek *pakhudermos*, thick-skinned : *pakhus*, thick (see **bhengh-** in Appendix*) + *derma*, skin, -DERM.] —**pach′y·der′ma·tous** (-dûr′mə-təs), **pach′y·der′mous** (-dûr′məs) *adj.*

pach·y·san·dra (păk′ĭ-săn′drə) *n.* Any of several plants of the genus *Pachysandra*; especially, *P. terminalis*, native to Japan, having evergreen leaves and inconspicuous white flowers. This species is frequently cultivated as a ground cover, and is also called "Japanese spurge." [New Latin, "with thick stamens" : Greek *pakhus*, thick (see **bhengh-** in Appendix*) + New Latin *-andra*, from -ANDROUS.]

Pacif. Pacific.

pa·cif·ic (pə-sĭf′ĭk) *adj.* Also **pa·cif·i·cal** (-ĭ-kəl). **1.** Tending to diminish or put an end to conflict; appeasing; calming. **2.** Of a peaceful nature; tranquil; serene: *"Great clouds along pacific skies"* (Rupert Brooke). [Old French *pacifique*, from Latin *pācificus* : *pāx* (stem *pāc-*), peace (see **pag-** in Appendix*) + *-ficus*, -FIC.] —**pa·cif′i·cal·ly** *adv.*

Pa·cif·ic (pə-sĭf′ĭk) *n. Abbr.* **Pac., Pacif.** The Pacific Ocean. —*adj. Abbr.* **Pac., Pacif.** Of or in the Pacific Ocean.

pa·cif·i·cate (pə-sĭf′ĭ-kāt′) *tr.v.* **-cated, -cating, -cates.** To make calm; pacify. [Latin *pācificāre*, to PACIFY.] —**pac′i·fi·ca′tion**

paca
Cuniculus paca

pachysandra
Pachysandra terminalis

ă pat/ā pay/âr care/ä father/b **b**i**b**/ch **ch**ur**ch**/d **d**ee**d**/ĕ pet/ē be/f **f**i**f**e/g **g**a**g**/h **h**at/hw **wh**ich/ĭ pit/ī pie/îr pier/j **j**u**dg**e/k **k**i**ck**/l **l**i**d**, needle/m **m**u**m**/n **n**o, sudde**n**/ng thi**ng**/ŏ pot/ō toe/ô paw, for/oi noise/ou out/ōō took/ōō boot/p **p**o**p**/r **r**oar/s **s**au**ce**/sh **sh**ip, di**sh**/

(păs′ə-fĭ-kā′shən), —**pa·cif′i·ca′tor** (pə-sĭf′ĭ-kā′tər) n. —**pa·cif′-i·ca·to′ry** (pə-sĭf′ĭ-kə-tôr′ē, -tōr′ē) adj.

Pacific Islands, Trust Territory of the. A United Nations strategic trust territory in the Pacific Ocean administered by the United States. It comprises some 2,000 islands in the Caroline, Mariana, and Marshall islands. Population, 91,000.

Pacific Ocean. The earth's largest body of water (70,000,000 square miles), extending from the Arctic to the Antarctic and from the Americas to Asia and Australia.

Pacific Standard Time. Abbr. **PST, P.S.T.** One of the four standard time zones of North America, operative from longitude 120 degrees to 140 degrees, with wide local variations in boundary. Also called "Pacific Time." See **standard time.**

pac·i·fi·er (păs′ə-fī′ər) n. **1.** One that pacifies. **2.** A rubber or plastic nipple or teething ring for a baby to suck or chew on.

pac·i·fism (păs′ə-fĭz′əm) n. **1.** The belief that disputes between nations should and can be settled peacefully. **2. a.** Opposition to war or violence as a means of resolving disputes. **b.** Such opposition demonstrated by refusal to participate in military action. [French pacificisme, from pacifique, pacific, from Old French, PACIFIC.] —**pac′i·fist** n. & adj. —**pac′i·fis′tic** adj.

pac·i·fy (păs′ə-fī′) tr.v. **-fied, -fying, -fies. 1.** To ease the anger or agitation of; restore calm to; appease: "Pearl . . . began to cry for a red rose, and would not be pacified." (Hawthorne). **2.** To establish peace in; end war, fighting, or violence in: Troops were dispatched to pacify the frontier. [Middle English pacifien, from Old French pacifier, from Latin pācificāre : pax (stem pāc-), peace (see **pag-** in Appendix*) + facere, to make (see **dhē-¹** in Appendix*).]

Synonyms: pacify, placate, mollify, conciliate, appease, quiet. These words all suggest leading someone hostile or demanding to moderation, accord, or satisfaction. Pacify applies broadly to any alleviation of hostility by diplomatic means. Placate more strongly suggests gratification of demands, and usually implies that the person so gratified is difficult to please. Mollify stresses mitigation of hostile feeling by soothing. Conciliate usually pertains to winning over by reasoning, and may imply a more lasting solution than the other terms. Appease (more strongly than placate) stresses overt gratification of a claim, often to the point of surrender of principle, and often implies that the claim is unworthy. Quiet is general, in this context, but often is used to indicate response to urgent demands.

pack¹ (păk) n. Abbr. **pk. 1. a.** A collection of items tied up or wrapped; bundle. **b.** A container made to be carried on the back of a person or an animal. **2.** The amount of something, such as a food, that is processed and packaged at one time or in one season. **3.** A small package containing a standard number of identical or similar items: a pack of matches. **4. a.** A complete set of related items: a pack of cards. **b.** A large amount; heap. **5. a.** A group of animals, such as dogs or wolves, that run and hunt together. **b.** A gang or band of people: a pack of hoodlums. **6.** A mass of large pieces of floating ice driven together. **7.** Medicine. **a.** The swathing of a patient in hot, cold, wet, or dry sheets or blankets. **b.** The sheets or blankets so used. **c.** A material, such as gauze, therapeutically inserted into a body cavity or wound. **8.** A folded cloth filled with crushed ice and applied to sore or swollen parts of the body. Also called "ice pack." **9.** A cosmetic paste applied to the skin and allowed to dry. —See Synonyms at **flock.** —v. **packed, packing, packs.** —tr. **1.** To fold, roll, or combine into a bundle; wrap up. **2. a.** To put into a receptacle for transporting or storing: pack one's belongings. **b.** To fill up with items: pack one's trunk. **3.** To process and put into containers in order to preserve, transport, or sell. **4. a.** To bring together (persons or things) closely; crowd together. **b.** To fill up tight; cram. **5.** Medicine. To wrap (a patient) in a pack. **6.** To wrap tightly for protection or to prevent leakage: pack a valve stem. **7.** To press together; compact firmly: clay and straw packed into bricks. **8.** Informal. To have available for action: pack a pistol; pack a hard punch. **9.** To send peremptorily. Used with off or away: They packed him off to camp. **10.** To rig (a voting panel) to be fraudulently favorable: pack the jury. —intr. **1.** To place one's belongings in boxes or luggage for transporting or storing. **2.** To be susceptible of compact storage: Dishes pack more easily than glasses. **3.** To become compacted; form lumps or masses: Rain caused the loose dirt to pack. **4.** To depart abruptly. Sometimes used with off or away. —**send packing.** To dismiss (someone) abruptly. —adj. Used in or suitable for packing. [Middle English pak, pack, akin to Middle Low German and Middle Dutch pak†.] —**pack′a·ble** adj.

pack² (păk). Variant of **pac.**

pack·age (păk′ĭj) n. Abbr. **pkg., pkge. 1.** A wrapped or boxed object; a parcel or bundle containing one or more objects. **2.** A container in which something is packed for storage or transporting. **3.** A proposition or offer made up of several items, each of which must be accepted. Used especially in the phrase package deal. —tr.v. **packaged, -aging, -ages.** To place in a package or make a package of. [Probably from Dutch pakkage, from pak, pack, from Middle Dutch, pak, PACK.]

package store. A store that sells sealed bottles of alcoholic beverages for consumption away from its premises.

pack·ag·ing (păk′ĭj-ĭng) n. The act, process, industry, art, or style of packing.

pack·er (păk′ər) n. One that packs; especially, one whose occupation is the processing and packing of wholesale goods, usually meat products.

pack·et (păk′ĭt) n. **1.** Abbr. **pkt.** A small package or bundle. **2.** Slang. A sizable sum of money. **3.** A boat, usually a coastal or river steamer, that plies a regular route, carrying passengers,

freight, and mail. [Old French paquet, from pacquer, to pack, from pakke, pack, from Middle Dutch pak, PACK.]

pack ice. Floating ice driven together into a single mass.

pack·ing (păk′ĭng) n. **1.** The act or process of one that packs; especially, the processing and packaging of food products. **2.** A material used to prevent leakage or seepage, as around a pipe joint. **3.** The application of a medical pack.

packing fraction. Physics. The quotient of the algebraic difference between the isotopic mass and the mass number of a nuclide, divided by its mass number, often interpreted as a measure of stability. For most nuclides, a negative or small positive value indicates relatively high stability. [From the presumed manner in which neutrons and protons are packed in the atomic nucleus.]

pack rat. 1. Any of various small North American rodents of the genus Neotoma, that collect in their nests a great variety of small objects. Also called "trade rat," "wood rat." **2.** Western U.S. Slang. A petty thief. **3.** Slang. An eccentric collector of miscellaneous objects.

pack·sack (păk′săk′) n. A canvas or leather traveling bag designed to be carried strapped to the shoulders.

pack·sad·dle (păk′săd′l) n. A saddle for a pack animal on which loads can be secured.

pack·thread (păk′thrĕd′) n. A strong two-ply or three-ply twine for sewing or tying packages or bundles.

pack train. A line of animals, such as horses or mules, loaded with supplies for an expedition.

pact (păkt) n. **1.** A formal agreement, as between nations; treaty. **2.** A compact; bargain. [Middle English, from Old French, from Latin pactum, from pacisci (past participle pactus), to agree. See **pag-** in Appendix*]

pad¹ (păd) n. **1.** A thin, cushionlike mass of soft material used as filling or for protection against jarring, scraping, or other injury. **2.** A flexible saddle made without a frame. **3.** An ink-soaked cushion used to ink a rubber stamp. **4.** A number of sheets of paper of the same size stacked one on top of the other and glued together at one end; tablet. **5.** The broad, floating leaf of an aquatic plant, such as the water lily. **6. a.** The cushionlike flesh on the underpart of the toes and feet of many animals. **b.** The foot of such an animal. **7.** The fleshy underside of the end of a finger or toe: the pad of one's thumb. **8.** A launch pad (see). **9.** Slang. **a.** One's apartment or room. **b.** One's bed. —tr.v. **padded, padding, pads. 1.** To line or stuff with soft material. **2.** To lengthen (something written or spoken) with extraneous material. [Akin to Flemish pad, and probably to Lithuanian pādas, "sole of the foot," possibly from some pre-Germanic, non-Indo-European language.]

pad² (păd) v. **padded, padding, pads.** —intr. **1.** To go about on foot. **2.** To move or walk about almost inaudibly: "But Doris, towelled from the bath, enters padding on broad feet." (T.S. Eliot). —tr. To go along (a route) on foot: padding the long road into town. —n. **1.** A muffled sound resembling that of soft footsteps. **2.** A horse with a plodding gait. [Probably from Middle Dutch paden, to walk along a path, from pad, path, road. See **ped-¹** in Appendix*]

Pa·dang (pä′däng′). A city and seaport of Indonesia, on the western coast of the island of Sumatra. Population, 144,000.

pa·dauk (pə-dôk′) n. Also **pa·douk** (pə-dōōk′). **1.** Any of various tropical trees of the genus Pterocarpus, having reddish wood with a mottled or striped grain. **2.** The wood of any of these trees, used for decorative cabinetwork. See **amboyna.** [Native Burmese name.]

pad·ding (păd′ĭng) n. **1.** The act of stuffing, filling, or lining something. **2.** Any soft material used to make a pad. **3.** Matter added to a speech or written work to make it longer.

Pad·ding·ton (păd′ĭng-tən). A former administrative division of London, England, now part of **Westminster** (see).

pad·dle¹ (păd′l) n. **1.** A wooden implement having a blade at one end, or sometimes at both ends, used without an oarlock to propel a canoe or small boat. **2.** Any of various implements resembling this: **a.** An iron tool for stirring molten ore in a furnace. **b.** A tool with a shovellike blade used to mix materials in glassmaking. **c.** A pallet with which to mix and shape clay. **d.** A narrow board used to beat clothes in hand-laundering. **e.** A flattened board used to administer physical punishment. **f.** A light wooden racket used in playing table tennis. **3.** A board of a paddle wheel. **4.** A flipper or flattened appendage of certain animals. **5.** The act of paddling. —v. **paddled, -dling, -dles.** —intr. **1.** To propel a watercraft with a paddle. **2.** To row slowly and gently. **3.** To move through water by means of repeated short strokes of the limbs. —tr. **1.** To propel (a watercraft) with a paddle or paddles. **2.** To convey in a watercraft propelled by paddles. **3.** To beat with a paddle; especially, to punish by spanking. **4.** To stir or shape (material) with a paddle. [Middle English padell†.] —**pad′dler** n.

pad·dle² (păd′l) intr.v. **-dled, -dling, -dles. 1.** To dabble about in shallow water; splash gently with the hands or feet. **2.** To move with a waddling motion; toddle. [Origin uncertain.]

paddle boat. A steamship propelled through the water by paddle wheels on each side or by one paddle wheel astern.

pad·dle·fish (păd′l-fĭsh′) n., pl. **paddlefish** or **-fishes.** A large fish, Polyodon spathula, of the Mississippi River basin, having a long, paddle-shaped snout. Also called "spoonbill."

paddle wheel. A steam-driven wheel with boards or paddles affixed around its circumference, used to propel a ship.

pad·dling (păd′lĭng, păd′l-ĭng) n. **1.** The act of moving a boat by means of a paddle. **2.** A spanking with a paddle.

pad·dock¹ (păd′ək) n. **1.** A fenced area, usually near a stable, used chiefly for grazing horses. **2.** An enclosure at a racetrack

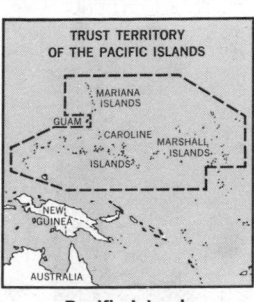

TRUST TERRITORY OF THE PACIFIC ISLANDS

MARIANA ISLANDS · GUAM · CAROLINE ISLANDS · MARSHALL ISLANDS · NEW GUINEA · AUSTRALIA

Pacific Islands

paddlefish

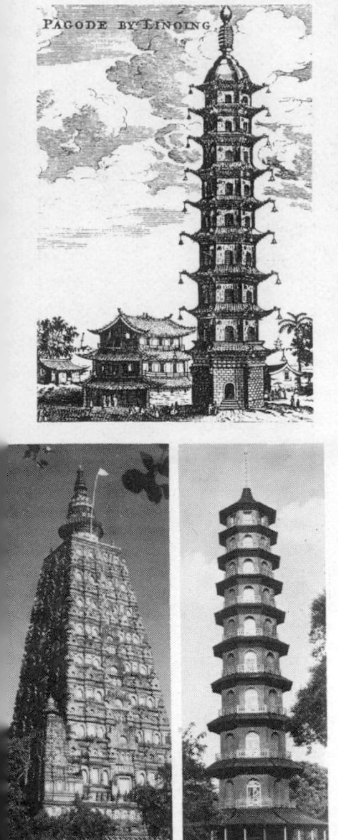
pagoda
Left: Bodh Gaya Hindu temple, Bihar, India
Top: Engraving of Chinese Buddhist temple
Right: Imitation of Chinese pagoda in Kew Gardens, England

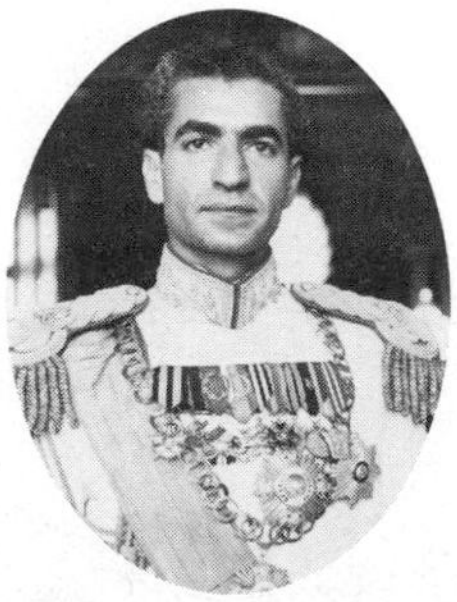
Mohammed Riza Pahlavi

where the horses are assembled, saddled, and paraded before each race. **3.** *Australian.* Any piece of fenced-in land. —*tr.v.* **paddocked, -docking, -docks.** To confine in a paddock. [Variant of dialectal *parrock,* Middle English *parrok,* Old English *pearroc,* from West Germanic *parruk* (unattested), perhaps from Medieval Latin *parricus*†. See also **park.**]

pad·dock² (păd′ək) *n. Archaic.* A frog or toad: *"Heaving up my either hand/Cold as paddocks though they be"* (Herrick). [Middle English *paddok,* from *pad, pade,* toad, probably from Old Norse *padda*†, toad.]

pad·dy (păd′ē) *n., pl.* **-dies.** **1.** Rice, especially in the husk, whether gathered or still in the field. **2.** A specially irrigated or flooded field where rice is grown. [Malay *padi.*]

Pad·dy (păd′ē) *n. Slang.* An Irishman. [Pet name for PATRICK.]

paddy wagon. *Slang.* A police van for taking suspects into custody. [From PADDY.]

Pa·de·rew·ski (păd′ə-rĕf′skē, pä′də-), **Ignace Jan.** 1860–1941. Polish concert pianist and statesman; prime minister (1919).

Pa·di·shah (pä′dĭ-shä′) *n.* **1.** A title of the shah of Iran. **2.** A former title of the sultan of Turkey. [Persian *pādshāh,* from Middle Persian *pātakh-shāh* : Old Persian *pati,* master (see **poti-** in Appendix*) + *shāh,* SHAH.]

pad·lock (păd′lŏk′) *n.* A detachable lock with a U-shaped bar hinged at one end, designed to be passed through the staple of a hasp or a link in a chain, and then snapped shut. —*tr.v.* **padlocked, -locking, -locks.** To lock up with or as if with a padlock. [Middle English *padlok* : *pad*†, padlock + *lok,* LOCK.]

pa·douk. Variant of **padauk.**

pa·dre (pä′drā, -drē) *n.* **1.** Father. Used as a title of address for a priest in Italy, Spain, Portugal, and Latin America. **2.** *Informal.* A military chaplain. **3.** *Chiefly British Informal.* A parson. [Spanish and Italian, father, from Latin *pater* (stem *patr-*). See **peter** in Appendix.*]

pa·dro·ne (pə-drō′nē, -nā; *Italian* pä-drō′nā) *n., pl.* **-nes** (-nēz, -nāz) or *Italian* **padroni** (pä-drō′nē). **1.** A master. **2.** An owner or manager, especially of an inn; proprietor. **3.** A man who exploitatively employs or finds work for Italian immigrants in America. [Italian, from Latin *patrōnus,* protector, PATRON.] —**pa·dro′nism′** (pə-drō′nĭz′əm) *n.*

Pad·u·a (păj′ōō-ə, păd′yōō-ə). *Italian* **Pa·do·va** (pä′dō-vä). An industrial city and cultural center in northeastern Italy, 22 miles west of Venice. Population, 211,000.

pad·u·a·soy (păj′ōō-ə-soi′) *n.* **1.** A rich, heavy silk fabric with a corded effect. **2.** A hanging or garment made of this fabric. [Variant (taken as obsolete *Padua say,* serge of Padua) of French *pou-de-soie,* from earlier *poult-de-soie*†.]

Pa·dus. The ancient name for the **Po.**

pae·an (pē′ən) *n.* Also **pe·an. 1.** A song of joyful praise or exultation. **2.** Any fervent expression of joy or praise: *"The art . . . was a paean to paganism."* (Will Durant). **3.** An ancient Greek hymn of thanksgiving to a god, especially to Apollo. [Latin *paeān,* from Greek *paian, paiōn,* war cry, hymn of praise to Apollo, from *Paiōn*†, title of Apollo as physician of the gods, ultimately from a cultic cry.]

paedo–. Variant of **pedo-.**

pae·do·gen·e·sis (pē′dō-jĕn′ə-sĭs) *n.* Reproduction of young during the larval or preadult stage, occurring chiefly in insects. [PAEDO- + GENESIS.] —**pae′do·ge·net′ic** (-jə-nĕt′ĭk) *adj.*

pa·e·lla (pä-ā′lyä, -ā′yä) *n.* A saffron-flavored Spanish dish made with varying combinations of rice, vegetables, meat, chicken, and seafood. [Catalan, "frying pan," from Old French *paelle,* from Latin *patella,* diminutive of *patina,* pan, from Greek *patanē,* dish. See **pet-²** in Appendix.*]

pae·on (pē′ən, -ŏn′) *n. Greek & Latin Prosody.* A metrical foot having one long syllable and three short syllables occurring in random order. [Latin *paeōn,* from Greek *paiōn,* PAEAN.]

Paes·tum (pĕs′təm). *Italian* **Pe·sto** (pĕs′tō). An ancient city in southwestern Italy, originally a colony of Sybaris, famous for its temples.

pa·gan (pā′gən) *n.* **1.** A person who is not a Christian, Moslem, or Jew; heathen. **2.** One who has no religion. **3.** Formerly, any non-Christian. —*adj.* **1.** Not Christian, Moslem, or Jewish. **2.** Not religious; heathen. [Middle English, from Late Latin *pāgānus,* civilian (i.e., not a "soldier of Christ"), from Latin *pāgānus,* country-dweller, from *pāgus,* village, country. See **pag-** in Appendix.*] —**pa′gan·dom** (-dəm) *n.* —**pa′gan·ish** *adj.* —**pa′gan·ism′** *n.*

Pa·ga·ni·ni (păg′ə-nē′nē, pä′gə-; *Italian* pä′gä-nē′nē), **Nicolò.** 1782–1840. Italian violinist and composer.

pa·gan·ize (pā′gə-nīz′) *v.* **-ized, -izing, -izes.** —*tr.* To make pagan. —*intr.* To become pagan. —**pa′gan·i·za′tion** *n.*

page¹ (pāj) *n.* **1.** In chivalry, a boy attending a knight, as the first stage of training for knighthood. **2.** A youth in ceremonial employment or attendance at court. **3. a.** A boy employed to run errands, carry messages, or act as a guide, as in a hotel, theater, or club. Also called "page boy." **b.** A boy similarly employed in Congress or another legislature. **5.** A boy who bears the bride's train at a wedding. —*tr.v.* **paged, paging, pages. 1.** To summon or call (a person) by name. **2.** To attend as a page. [Middle English, from Old French, from Italian *paggio,* probably from Greek *paidion,* child, diminutive of *pais* (stem *paid-*), child, boy. See **pōu-** in Appendix.*]

page² (pāj) *n. Abbr.* **p.,** *pl.* **pp. 1.** One side of a leaf of a book, letter, newspaper, manuscript, or the like. Often used of the entire leaf: *tearing out a page.* **2.** The writing or printing on one side of a leaf. **3.** *Printing.* The type set for printing a page. **4.** A noteworthy or memorable event: *a new page in history.* **5.** *Plural.* A source or record of knowledge: *in the pages of science.* —*v.* **paged, paging, pages.** —*tr.* To number the pages of; paginate. —*intr.* To turn pages. Usually followed by *through.* [Old French, from Latin *pāgina,* page. See **pag-** in Appendix.*]

pag·eant (păj′ənt) *n.* **1.** An elaborate public dramatic presentation, usually depicting some historical or traditional event. **2.** *Archaic.* **a.** A scene of a medieval mystery play. **b.** A portable platform on which mystery plays were presented. **3.** A spectacular procession or celebration. **4.** Colorful display; pageantry. **5.** Showy display; pomp. [Middle English *pagyn,* from Medieval Latin *pāgina,* scene of a play, from Latin, PAGE.]

pag·eant·ry (păj′ən-trē) *n., pl.* **-ries. 1.** Pageants and their presentation. **2.** Grand display; pomp. **3.** Empty pomp or show; flashy display.

pag·i·nal (păj′ən-əl) *adj.* **1.** Of, pertaining to, or consisting of pages. **2.** Page-for-page: *paginal facsimile.* [Late Latin *pāginālis,* from Latin *pāgina,* PAGE.]

pag·i·nate (păj′ə-nāt′) *tr.v.* **-nated, -nating, -nates.** To number the pages of; page. Compare **foliate.** [From Latin *pāgina,* PAGE.]

pag·i·na·tion (păj′ə-nā′shən) *n.* **1.** The system with which pages are numbered. **2.** The arrangement and number of pages in a book, as noted in a catalogue or bibliography.

pa·go·da (pə-gō′də) *n.* **1.** A religious building of the Far East, typically: **a.** An ornate pyramidal Hindu temple. **b.** A many-storied Buddhist tower, erected as a memorial or shrine. **2.** A structure, as a garden pavilion, built in imitation of this. [Portuguese *pagode,* from Dravidian, probably from Sanskrit *bhagavati,* feminine of *bhagavat,* blessed, perhaps from *bhaga,* good fortune. See **bhag-¹** in Appendix.*]

Pa·go Pa·go (päng′gō päng′gō, päng′ō päng′ō). Also **Pa·go·pa·go.** Formerly **Pan·go Pan·go.** The capital of American Samoa, a port on the southern coast of Tutuila Island.

pah (pä) *interj.* An exclamation of disgust or irritation. [Expressive formation.]

Pa·hang (pə-hăng′). **1.** A river rising at the Tembeling River in southeastern Malay Peninsula and flowing 285 miles southeast to the China Sea. **2.** A constituent state of Malaysia occupying 13,820 square miles on the southeastern coast of the Malay Peninsula. Population, 387,368. Capital, Kuala Lipis.

pah·la·vi (pä′lə-vē′) *n., pl.* **-vis.** A gold coin formerly in use in Iran, equal to 100 rials. [Persian *pahlawī,* after Mohammed Riza PAHLAVI.]

Pah·la·vi (pä′lə-vē′) *n.* Also **Peh·le·vi** (pā′lə-vē′). A southwestern dialect of Middle Persian. [Persian *pahlawī,* from *Pahlaw,* from Middle Persian, from Old Persian *Parthava,* PARTHIA.]

Pah·la·vi (pä′lə-vē′), **Mohammed Riza.** Also **Pah·le·vi** (pä′lə-vē′). Born 1919. Shah of Iran (since 1941).

Pai. See **Pei Ho.**

paid. Past tense and past participle of **pay.**

pail (pāl) *n.* **1.** A watertight cylindrical vessel, open at the top and fitted with a handle; bucket. **2.** The amount contained in such a vessel. [Middle English *payle,* Old English *pægel,* small measure, from Medieval Latin *pagella,* a measure, from Latin, diminutive of *pagina,* page. See **pag-** in Appendix.*]

pail·lasse (păl-yăs′, păl′yăs′) *n.* Also **pal·liasse.** A thin mattress filled with straw, sawdust, or the like. [French, from *paille,* straw, from Latin *palea,* chaff, straw. See **pel-¹** in Appendix.*]

pail·lette (pä-yĕt′, pă-, pă-lĕt′) *n.* **1.** A small piece of metal or foil, used in enamel painting. **2.** A spangle used to ornament a dress or costume. [French, diminutive of *paille,* straw. See **paillasse.**]

pain (pān) *n.* **1.** An unpleasant sensation, occurring in varying degrees of severity as a consequence of injury, disease, or emotional disorder. **2.** Suffering or distress. **3.** *Plural.* The pangs of childbirth. **4.** *Plural.* Great care or effort: *take pains with one's work.* **5.** *Informal.* A nuisance. —**on** (or **upon** or **under**) **pain of.** Subject to the penalty of (some specified punishment, as death). —*v.* **pained, paining, pains.** —*tr.* To hurt or injure; cause pain to. —*intr.* To be the cause of pain. [Middle English *paine,* from Old French *peine,* from Latin *poena,* penalty, from Greek *poinē,* penalty. See **kwei-¹** in Appendix.*]

Paine (pān), **Thomas.** 1737–1809. British-born political leader and theoretician in the American Revolution; active in French Revolutionary politics.

pain·ful (pān′fəl) *adj.* **1.** Causing pain; hurtful. **2.** Full of pain; distressing; hurting. **3.** Requiring care and labor; irksome: *a painful task.* **4.** *Archaic.* Painstaking. —**pain′ful·ly** *adv.*

pain·kill·er (pān′kĭl′ər) *n.* Something, such as a drug, that relieves pain. —**pain′kill′ing** *adj.*

pain·less (pān′lĭs) *adj.* Free from complication or pain: *a painless operation.* —**pain′less·ly** *adv.* —**pain′less·ness** *n.*

pain principle. *Psychoanalysis.* The unconscious tendency to seek death or forgetfulness; the desire for pain or destruction.

pains·tak·ing (pānz′tā′kĭng) *adj.* Taking great pains; careful. —*n.* The taking of pains; extremely careful and diligent work or effort. —**pains′tak′ing·ly** *adv.*

paint (pānt) *n.* **1. a.** A liquid mixture, usually of a solid pigment in a liquid vehicle, used as a decorative or protective coating. **b.** The thin dry film formed by such a mixture applied to a surface. **c.** The solid pigment before it is mixed with a vehicle. **2. a.** A cosmetic, especially one that colors, as rouge. **b. Grease paint** *(see).* **3.** A **pinto** *(see).* —*v.* **painted, painting, paints.** —*tr.* **1.** To make (a picture) with paints. **2. a.** To represent in a picture with paints. **b.** To depict vividly in words. **3.** To coat or decorate with paint: *paint a house.* **4.** To apply cosmetics to. **5.** To apply medicine to; swab: *paint a wound.* —*intr.* **1.** To practice the art of painting pictures. **2.** To cover something with paint. **3.** To apply cosmetics to oneself: *"let her paint an inch thick, to this favor she must come"* (Shakespeare). **4.** To serve as a surface to be coated with paint: *These nonporous surfaces paint badly with a brush and should be sprayed.* —**paint the town red.** *Slang.* To go on a bout of uproarious carousal. [From Middle English *peynten,* to paint, from Old French *peindre* (past participle *peint*), from Latin *pingere.* See **peig-**[1] in Appendix.*]

paint·brush (pānt′brŭsh′) *n.* A brush for applying paint.

paint·ed (pān′tĭd) *adj.* **1.** Represented in paint. **2. a.** Covered or adorned with paint. **b.** Brightly colored; variegated; gaudy. **3.** Excessively or improperly made up with cosmetics. **4.** Having no reality; artificial; false; pretended: *painted expressions.*

painted bunting. A small bird, *Passerina ciris,* of the southern United States, having brilliant multicolored plumage. Also called "nonpareil."

painted cup. A plant, the **Indian paintbrush** *(see).*

Painted Desert. A colorful, eroded plateau area in east-central Arizona, east of the Little Colorado River.

painted lady. A widely distributed butterfly, *Vanessa cardui,* having brown, black, and orange markings. Also called "cosmopolite," "thistle butterfly."

paint·er[1] (pān′tər) *n.* A person who paints, either as an artist or as a workman.

pain·ter[2] (pān′tər) *n. Nautical.* A rope attached to the bow of a boat, used for tying up. [Middle English *paynter,* perhaps from Old French *pentoir,* clothesline, from *pendre,* to hang, from Latin *pendēre.* See **spen-** in Appendix.*]

pain·ter[3] (pān′tər) *n. Regional.* A mountain lion or lynx. [Variant of PANTHER.]

paint·er·ly (pān′tər-lē) *adj.* **1.** Of, pertaining to, or characteristic of a painter; artistic. **2. a.** Having qualities unique to the art of painting as distinguished from other visual arts. **b.** Designating a style of painting marked by openness of form, with shapes distinguished by variations of color, rather than by outline or contour: *the painterly style of Titian.* Compare **linear.**

painter's colic. Chronic intestinal pains and constipation caused by lead poisoning. Also called "lead colic." [So called because often caused by exposure to lead-base paint.]

paint·ing (pān′tĭng) *n.* **1.** The process, art, or occupation of coating surfaces with paint, for either a utilitarian or an artistic effect. **2.** A picture or design in paint.

pair (pâr) *n., pl.* **pairs** or *informal* **pair.** See Usage note below. *Abbr.* **pr. 1.** Two corresponding persons or items, similar in form or function and matched or associated: *a pair of shoes.* **2.** One object composed of two joined, similar parts, dependent upon each other: *a pair of pliers.* **3. a.** Two persons joined together in marriage or engagement. **b.** Two persons having something in common and considered together: *a pair of hunters.* **c.** Two mated animals. **d.** Two animals joined together in work. **4.** Two playing cards of the same denomination. **5.** *Government.* Two members of a deliberative body with opposing opinions on a given issue who agree to abstain from voting on the issue, thereby offsetting each other. **6.** *Chemistry.* An **electron pair** *(see).* —See Synonyms at **couple.** —*v.* **paired, pairing, pairs.** —*tr.* **1.** To arrange in sets of two; to couple. **2.** To join in a pair; mate. Sometimes followed by *off.* **3.** To provide a partner for. —*intr.* **1.** To form a pair or pairs. Often followed by *off.* **2.** To join in marriage; to mate. [Middle English *paire,* from Old French, from Latin *paria,* equal things, from the neuter plural of *pār,* equal. See **pera** in Appendix.*]

Usage: *Pair,* as a noun, can be followed by a singular or plural verb. The singular is always used when *pair* emphasizes oneness or unity of components: *This pair (of shoes) is not on sale.* A plural verb is used when the members are considered as individuals: *The pair are working more harmoniously now.* After a numeral other than *one, pairs* is the customary form in a construction such as *She bought six pairs* (not *pair*) *of stockings.*

pair production. *Physics.* The simultaneous creation of a positron and electron from a high-energy gamma ray in a very strong electric field, especially in that of an atomic nucleus.

pai·sa (pī′sä) *n., pl.* **paise** (pī-sā′) (for sense 1) or **paisas** (pī′säz) (for sense 2). **1.** A coin equal to 1/100 of the rupee of India. Also called "naya paisa." **2.** A coin equal to 1/100 of the rupee of Pakistan. See table of exchange rates at **currency.** [Hindi *paisā,* PICE.]

pai·sa·no (pī-zä′nō) *n., pl.* **-nos.** Also **pai·san** (pī-zän′). **1.** Countryman; compatriot. **2.** *Slang.* Friend; buddy; pal. [Spanish, from French *paysan,* from Old French *païsant,* PEASANT.]

pais·ley (pāz′lē) *adj.* **1.** Made of a soft wool fabric with a woven or printed colorful, swirled pattern of abstract, curved shapes, ultimately derived from the palmette motif of Persian rugs. **2.** Marked with such a pattern. —*n., pl.* **paisleys.** A shawl or other article of clothing made of paisley fabric. [Originally popular in shawls made in PAISLEY.]

Pais·ley (pāz′lē). The county seat of Renfrew, Scotland, on the Clyde, west of Glasgow. Population, 96,000.

Pai·ute (pī′yo͞ot′, pī-yo͞ot′) *n., pl.* **Paiute** or **-utes.** Also **Pi·ute. 1.** Either of two distinct North American Indian peoples, the Northern Paiute and the Southern Paiute, belonging to the Shoshonean subfamily of the Uto-Aztecan language family. They formerly lived in the southwestern United States. **2.** A member of either of these peoples. **3.** The language of either of these peoples. —**Pai′ute′** *adj.*

pa·ja·mas (pə-jä′məz, -jăm′əz) *pl.n.* Also *chiefly British* **py·ja·mas** (pə-jä′məz, -jăm′əz). Sometimes **pa·ja·ma. 1.** A loose-fitting garment consisting of trousers and a jacket, for sleeping or lounging. **2.** Loose-fitting trousers worn in the Orient by both sexes. [Hindi *pāejāma* : Persian *pāi,* leg, foot, from Middle Persian (see **ped-**[1] in Appendix*) + *jāmah*†, garment.]

pak choi (bäk′ choi′). A Chinese plant, *Brassica chinensis,* that is similar to the common cabbage and is used as a vegetable. [Cantonese *paak ts'oi,* corresponding to Mandarin Chinese *pai^{2}ts'ai^4,* "white vegetable" : *pai^2,* white + *ts'ai,* vegetable.]

Pak·i·stan (păk′ĭ-stăn′, pä′kĭ-stän′). Officially, Islamic Republic of Pakistan. A republic situated in southern Asia and consisting of two provinces, East and West Pakistan, separated by over 900 miles of territory of the Republic of India. Population, 93,721,000. Capital, Islamabad. —**Pak′i·stan′i** *adj.* & *n.*

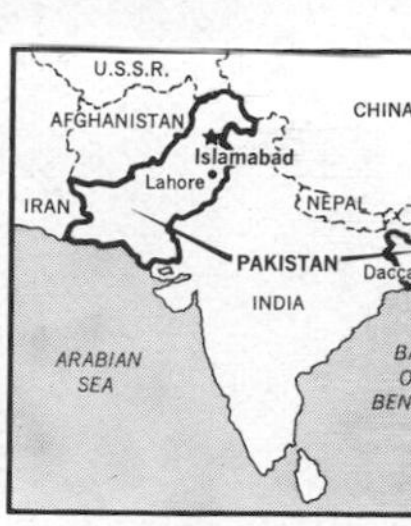

Pakistan

pal (păl) *n. Informal.* A friend; chum. —*intr.v.* **palled, palling, pals.** *Informal.* To associate as pals: *palling around together.* [Romany (English) *pal, phal,* from *phrall* (continental), from Sanskrit *bhrātar-,* brother. See **bhrāter-** in Appendix.*]

Pal. Palestine.

pal·ace (păl′ĭs) *n.* **1.** The official residence of a royal person. **2.** The official residence of a high dignitary, as a bishop or archbishop. **3. a.** Any large or splendid residence. **b.** A stately public building. **4.** Any large, often gaudy and ornate building used for entertainment, exhibitions, and the like. [Middle English *palais,* from Old French, from Latin *palātium,* from *Palātium,* the PALATINE Hill (where the palaces of the emperors were built).]

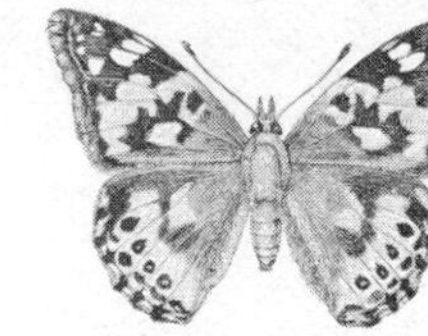
painted lady

pal·a·din (păl′ə-dĭn) *n.* **1.** Any of the 12 peers of Charlemagne's court. **2.** A paragon of chivalry; heroic champion. [French, from Italian *paladino,* from Latin *palātīnus,* PALATINE.]

pa·laes·tra. Variant of **palestra.**

pal·an·quin (păl′ən-kēn′) *n.* Also **pal·an·keen.** An east Asian covered litter, carried on poles on the shoulders of two or four men. [Portuguese *palanquim,* from Javanese *pĕlangki,* from Sanskrit *palyanka, paryanka,* bed : *pari,* around (see **per**[1] in Appendix*) + *añcati,* he bends (see **ank-** in Appendix*).]

pal·at·a·ble (păl′ĭt-ə-bəl) *adj.* **1.** Acceptable to the taste; sufficiently agreeable in flavor to be eaten. **2.** Acceptable to the mind or sensibilities; agreeable: *a palatable solution to the problem.* [From PALATE.] —**pal′at·a·bil′i·ty, pal′at·a·ble·ness** *n.*

pal·a·tal (păl′ə-təl) *adj.* **1.** Of or pertaining to the palate. **2.** *Phonetics.* **a.** Produced with the front of the tongue against the hard palate, as the *y* in *young.* **b.** Produced with the blade of the tongue near the hard palate, as the *ch* in *chin.* **c.** Produced with the back of the tongue against the soft palate, as the *c* in *cat.* —*n.* A palatal sound. —**pal′a·tal·ly** *adv.*

pal·a·tal·ize (păl′ə-təl-īz′) *tr.v.* **-ized, -izing, -izes.** *Phonetics.* To pronounce with a palatal quality; specifically, to alter (a nonpalatal sound) to a palatal sound, as (yo͞or) to (zhər) in the pronunciation of *pleasure.* —**pal′a·tal·i·za′tion** *n.*

pal·ate (păl′ĭt) *n.* **1.** The roof of the mouth in vertebrates having a complete or partial separation of the mouth cavity and nasal passage, consisting of a bony front, the *hard palate,* backed by the fleshy *soft palate.* **2.** A similar part, as in a lipped flower. **3.** The sense of taste: *delicacies pleasing to the palate.* [Middle English, from Latin *palātum,* perhaps from Etruscan.]

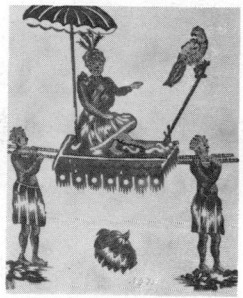

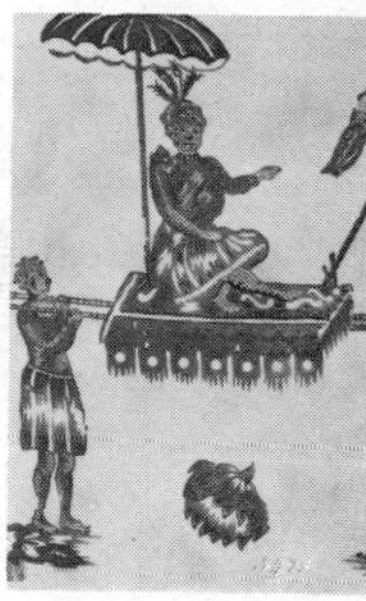
palanquin
Late 18th-century French textile design

pa·la·tial (pə-lā′shəl) *adj.* **1.** Of or suitable for a palace: *the palatial gardens.* **2.** Of the nature of a palace; spacious and ornate. [From Latin *palātium,* PALACE.] —**pa·la′tial·ly** *adv.*

pa·lat·i·nate (pə-lăt′n-āt′, -ĭt) *n.* **1.** The office or powers of a palatine. **2.** The territory of a palatine, especially: **a.** The **Palatinate** *(see).* **b.** Any of the English counties palatine (Durham, Lancaster, Chester, and Ely), whose lords had royal powers. **c.** Any of the American palatine colonies (Maine, Maryland, and Carolina), whose proprietors had royal prerogatives. [Medieval Latin *palātīnātus,* from *palātīnus,* a PALATINE.]

Pa·lat·i·nate, the (pə-lăt′n-āt′, -ĭt). *German* **Pfalz** (pfälts). A state of the Holy Roman Empire, ruled by a count palatine (the Elector Palatine), consisting of two territories, the Lower Palatinate (now in the state of Rhineland-Palatinate), and the Upper Palatinate (now in Bavaria).

pal·a·tine[1] (păl′ə-tīn′) *n.* **1. a.** A soldier of the palace guard of the Roman emperors formed in the time of Diocletian. **b.** A soldier of a major division of the Roman army formed in the time of Constantine. **2. a.** A title of various administrative officials of the late Roman and Byzantine empires. **b.** A Frankish **Mayor of the Palace** *(see).* **3.** A count delegated with royal powers, as: **a.** An imperial minister or emissary in the Carolingian Empire. **b.** A minor imperial official in the late Holy Roman Empire. **c.** The Elector Palatine, ruler of the **Palatinate** *(see).* **d.** The lord of an English palatinate. **4.** The senior proprietor of a colonial American palatinate. —*adj.* **1.** Belonging to or fit for a palace. **2.** Of or designating a palatine or palatinate. [Latin *palātīnus,* from *palātium,* a PALACE.]

pal·a·tine[2] (păl′ə-tēn′) *n.* A fur cape and hood worn by women. [French; introduced about 1676 by Anne de Gonzague, Princess *Palatine.*]

pal·a·tine[3] (păl′ə-tīn′) *adj.* **1.** Of or pertaining to the palate. **2.** Designating either of the two bones that make up the hard palate. —*n.* Either of these bones.

Pal·a·tine[1] (păl′ə-tīn′) *adj.* Of or pertaining to the Palatinate. —*n.* A native or resident of the Palatinate.

Pal·a·tine[2] (păl′ə-tīn′). The chief of the seven hills of Rome. —*adj.* Designating this hill or situated on it.

Pa·lau (pä-lou′). Formerly **Pe·lew** (pə-lo͞o′). **1.** A group of about 100 small islands within the Caroline Islands. Population, 11,000. **2.** See **Ba·bel·thu·ap.**

pa·lav·er (pə-lăv′ər, -lä′vər) *n.* **1. a.** Idle chatter. **b.** Talk intended to charm or beguile. **2.** *Obsolete.* A parley between European explorers and representatives of local populations, especially in Africa. —*v.* **palavered, -ering, -ers.** —*tr.* To flatter or cajole. —*intr.* To chatter idly. [Portuguese *palavra,* word, speech, from Late Latin *parabola,* speech, PARABLE.]

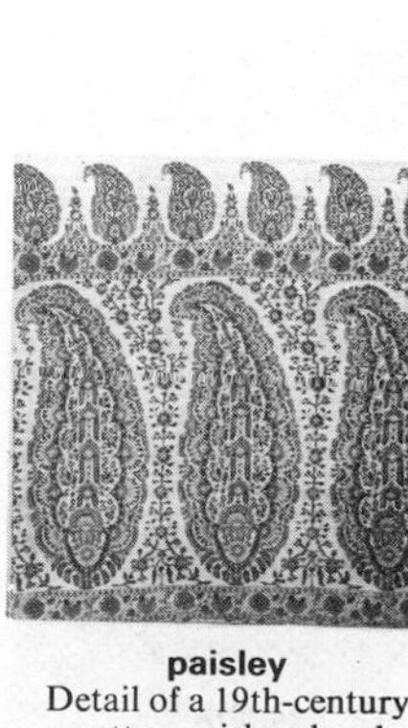
paisley
Detail of a 19th-century cotton paisley shawl

Pa·la·wan (pä-lä′wän). A long, narrow island in the southwestern Philippines, 4,550 square miles in area.

pale[1] (pāl) *n.* **1.** A stake or pointed stick; picket. **2.** *Archaic.* A fence enclosing an area. **3.** The area enclosed by a fence or boundary. **4.** *Heraldry.* A wide vertical band in the center of the escutcheon. —**the Pale.** Also **the English Pale, the Irish Pale.** The medieval dominions of the English in Ireland. —**beyond the pale.** Irrevocably unacceptable or unreasonable. —*tr.v.* **paled, paling, pales.** To enclose with pales; fence in. [Middle English, pointed stake, boundary, from Old French *pal,* stake, from Latin *pālus.* See **pag-** in Appendix.*]

pale[2] (pāl) *adj.* **paler, palest. 1.** Whitish in complexion; pallid; wan. **2.** Of a low intensity of color; light. **3.** Of a color, having high lightness and low saturation. Compare **deep.** See **color. 4.** Of a low intensity of light; dim; faint. **5.** Feeble; weak; inferior. —*v.* **paled, paling, pales.** —*tr.* To cause to turn pale. —*intr.* **1.** To become pale; blanch. **2.** To decrease in relative importance; be outshone; diminish. [Middle English, from Old French, from Latin *pallidus,* from *pallēre,* to be pale. See **pel-**[2] in Appendix.*] —**pale′ly** *adv.* —**pale′ness** *n.*

pa·le·a (pā′lē-ə) *n., pl.* **-leae** (-lē-ē′). *Botany.* A small, chafflike bract enclosing the flower of a grass spikelet. [New Latin, from Latin, chaff. See **pel-**[1] in Appendix.*]

Pa·le·arc·tic (pā′lē-ärk′tĭk, -är′tĭk) *adj.* Of or designating the zoogeographic region that includes Europe, the northwestern coast of Africa, and Asia north of the Himalayas. Compare **Nearctic.** [PALE(O)- + ARCTIC.]

pa·le·eth·nol·o·gy (pā′lē-ĕth-nŏl′ə-jē) *n.* Also **pa·le·ëth·nol·o·gy.** The ethnology of early man. [PALE(O)- + ETHNOLOGY.] —**pa′le·eth′no·log′ic** (-ĕth′nə-lŏj′ĭk), **pa′le·eth′no·log′i·cal** *adj.* —**pa′le·eth·nol′o·gist** *n.*

pale·face (pāl′fās′) *n.* A white person. A term held to be first used by North American Indians.

Pa·lem·bang (pä′lĕm-bäng′). A trade center and river port of southeastern Sumatra, Indonesia. Population, 283,000.

paleo–, pale–. Also *chiefly British* **palaeo-.** Indicates ancient or prehistoric; for example, **paleography, pale-ethnology.** [Greek *palaio-,* from *palaios,* ancient, from *palai,* long ago. See **kwel-**[2] in Appendix.*]

pa·le·o·an·throp·ic (pā′lē-ō-ăn-thrŏp′ĭk) *adj. Anthropology.* Of or pertaining to extinct members of the genus *Homo* that preceded *H. sapiens.* Compare **neanthropic.**

pa·le·o·an·thro·pol·o·gy (pā′lē-ō-ăn′thrə-pŏl′ə-jē) *n.* The study of manlike creatures more primitive than *Homo sapiens.* —**pa′le·o·an′thro·po·log′ic** (-ăn′thrə-pə-lŏj′ĭk), **pa′le·o·an′thro·po·log′i·cal** *adj.* —**pa′le·o·an′thro·pol′o·gist** *n.*

pa·le·o·bot·a·ny (pā′lē-ō-bŏt′n-ē) *n. Abbr.* **paleobot.** The study of plant fossils and ancient vegetation. —**pa′le·o·bo·tan′ic** (-bə-tăn′ĭk), **pa′le·o·bo·tan′i·cal** *adj.* —**pa′le·o·bot′a·nist** *n.*

Palladian[2]
The Basilica in Vicenza, Italy, renovated by Palladio

Pa·le·o·cene (pā′lē-ə-sēn′) *adj. Geology.* Of, belonging to, or designating the geologic time, rock series, and sedimentary deposits of the first epoch of the Tertiary period, preceding the Eocene and characterized by the appearance of placental mammals. See **geology.** —*n. Geology.* **1.** The Paleocene epoch. Preceded by *the.* **2.** The deposits of this epoch. Preceded by *the.* [PALEO- + -CENE.]

pa·le·og·ra·phy (pā′lē-ŏg′rə-fē) *n. Abbr.* **paleog. 1.** The study and scholarly interpretation of ancient written documents. Compare **epigraphy. 2.** The documents so studied. —**pa′le·og′ra·pher** *n.* —**pa′le·o·graph′ic** (-ə-grăf′ĭk), **pa′le·o·graph′i·cal** *adj.*

pa·le·o·lith (pā′lē-ə-lĭth′) *n.* A stone implement of the Paleolithic period. [PALEO- + -LITH.]

Pa·le·o·lith·ic (pā′lē-ə-lĭth′ĭk) *adj. Archaeology.* Of, belonging to, or designating the cultural period beginning with the earliest chipped stone tools, about 750,000 years ago, until the beginning of the Mesolithic, about 15,000 years ago. —*n. Archaeology.* The Paleolithic Age. Preceded by *the.*

pa·le·on·tol·o·gy (pā′lē-ŏn-tŏl′ə-jē) *n. Abbr.* **paleontol. 1.** The study of fossils and ancient life forms. **2.** Paleozoology. [PALE(O)- + ONTO- + -LOGY.] —**pa′le·on′to·log′ic** (-ŏn′tə-lŏj′ĭk), **pa′le·on′to·log′i·cal** *adj.* —**pa′le·on·tol′o·gist** *n.*

Pa·le·o·zo·ic (pā′lē-ə-zō′ĭk) *adj. Geology.* Of, belonging to, or designating the era of geologic time that includes the Cambrian, Ordovician, Silurian, Devonian, Mississippian, Pennsylvanian, and Permian periods, and is characterized by the appearance of marine invertebrates, primitive fishes, land plants, and primitive reptiles. See **geology.** —*n. Geology.* The Paleozoic era. Preceded by *the.* [PALEO- + -ZOIC.]

pa·le·o·zo·ol·o·gy (pā′lē-ō-zō-ŏl′ə-jē) *n.* The study of animal fossils and ancient animal life. —**pa′le·o·zo′o·log′i·cal** (-zō′ə-lŏj′ĭ-kəl) *adj.* —**pa′le·o·zo·ol′o·gist** *n.*

Pa·ler·mo (pä-lĕr′mō). The capital of Sicily, a seaport on the northwestern coast. Population, 623,000.

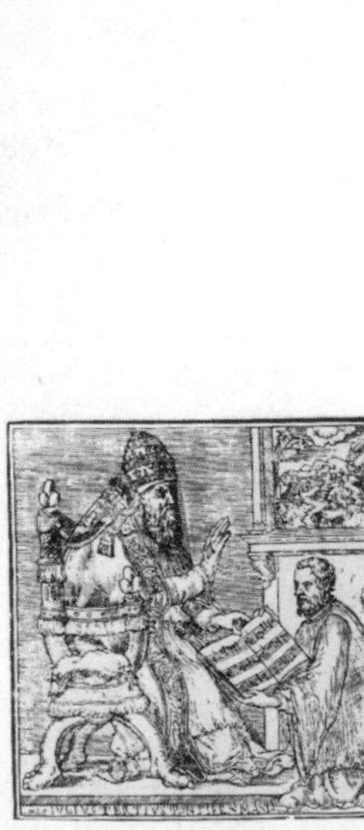

Palestrina
The composer shown with Pope Julius III on the frontispiece of Palestrina's first book of Masses, 1554

Pal·es·tine (păl′ĭ-stīn′). *Abbr.* **Pal.** Biblical name **Ca·naan** (kā′nən). **1.** The land between the Mediterranean Sea and the Jordan River that was occupied by the Hebrews in the second millennium B.C., and was the scene of most of the events described in the Bible. **2.** This country, formerly a province of the Ottoman Empire, subsequently a British mandated territory, divided between Israel, Jordan, and Egypt in 1948. In 1967, the Egyptian and Jordanian sections were occupied by Israel. Also called "the Holy Land." [Latin *Palaestīna,* from Greek *Palaistinē,* from Hebrew *Pelēsheth.*] —**Pal′es·tin′i·an** (păl′ĭ-stĭn′ē-ən) *n.*

pa·les·tra (pə-lĕs′trə) *n., pl.* **-trae** (-trē) or **-tras.** Also **pa·laes·tra.** In ancient Greece, a public place for training and practice in wrestling and other athletics. [Latin *palaestra,* from Greek *palaistra,* from *palaiein*†, to wrestle.] —**pa·les′tral** *adj.*

Pa·le·stri·na (păl′ĭ-strē′nə; *Italian* pä′lā-strē′nä), **Giovanni Pierluigi da.** 1526?–1594. Italian composer of motets, hymns, and Masses.

pal·ette (păl′ĭt) *n.* **1.** A board, typically with a hole for the thumb, upon which an artist mixes colors. **2.** The range of colors used in a particular painting or class of paintings, or by a particular artist: *a limited palette.* [French, from Old French, flat board, diminutive of *pale,* shovel, from Latin *pāla,* spade, shovel. See **pag-** in Appendix.*]

palette knife. A knife with a thin, flexible blade, used by artists for mixing, scraping, or applying paint.

pal·frey (pôl′frē) *n., pl.* **-freys.** *Archaic.* A woman's saddle horse. [Middle English, from Old French *palefrei,* from Medieval Latin *palafrēdus,* from Late Latin *paraverēdus,* extra post horse : Greek *para,* beside (see **per**[1] in Appendix*) + Latin *verēdus,* post horse (see **reidh-** in Appendix*).]

Pa·li (pä′lē) *n.* An ancient Indic language, surviving in the scriptures and liturgics of Hinayana Buddhism. [Sanskrit *pāli,* a row, canon, from Dravidian.]

pal·i·kar (păl′ĭ-kär′) *n.* A Greek soldier in the struggle for Greece's independence from Turkey (1821–28). [Modern Greek *palikari,* youth, from Late Greek *pallikarion,* page, diminutive of Greek *pallēx*†, a youth.]

pal·imp·sest (păl′ĭmp-sĕst′) *n.* A written document, typically on vellum or parchment, that has been written upon several times, often with remnants of earlier, imperfectly erased writing still visible, remnants of this kind being a major source for the recovery of lost literary works of classical antiquity. [Latin *palimpsēstus,* from Greek *palimpsēstos,* rubbed again : *palin,* again (see **kwel-**[1] in Appendix*) + *-psēstos,* "scraped," from *psēn,* to rub, scrape (see **bhes-**[1] in Appendix*).]

pal·in·drome (păl′ĭn-drōm′) *n.* A word, phrase, verse, or sentence which reads the same backward or forward, as *A man, a plan, a canal, Panama!* [Greek *palindromos,* running back again : *palin,* again (see **kwel-**[1] in Appendix*) + *dromos,* a running (see **der-**[1] in Appendix*).] —**pal′in·drom′ic** (păl′ĭn-drŏm′ĭk, -drō′mĭk) *adj.*

pal·ing (pā′lĭng) *n.* **1.** One of a row of upright, pointed sticks forming a fence; a pale; picket. **2.** Pointed sticks used in making fences; pales. **3.** A fence made of pales or pickets.

pal·in·gen·e·sis (păl′ĭn-jĕn′ə-sĭs) *n., pl.* **-ses** (-sēz′). **1.** The doctrine of transmigration of souls; metempsychosis. **2.** *Biology.* The repetition by a single organism of various stages in the evolution of its species during embryonic development. [Greek *palin,* again (see **kwel-**[1] in Appendix*) + GENESIS.] —**pal′in·ge·net′ic** (-jə-nĕt′ĭk) *adj.* —**pal′in·ge·net′i·cal·ly** *adv.*

pal·i·node (păl′ə-nōd′) *n.* **1.** A poem in which the poet retracts something said in a previous poem. **2.** Any formal statement of retraction. [Late Latin *palinōdia,* from Greek *palinōidia* : *palin,* again (see **kwel-**[1] in Appendix*) + *ōidē,* song (see **ode**).]

pal·i·sade (păl′ə-săd′) *n.* **1.** A fence of pales forming a defense barrier or fortification. **2.** One of the pales of such a fence. **3.** *Plural.* A line of lofty, steep cliffs, usually along a river. —*tr.v.* **palisaded, -sading, -sades.** To equip or fortify with a palisade. [French *palissade,* from Provençal *palissada,* from *palissa,* a pale, from Vulgar Latin *pālicea* (unattested), from Latin *pālus.* See **pag-** in Appendix.*]

Pal·i·sades (păl′ə-sādz′), **the.** A row of cliffs in northeastern New Jersey, along the west bank of the Hudson River.

Palk Strait (pôk, pôlk). The strait, 40 miles wide, between India and Ceylon.

pall[1] (pôl) *n.* **1.** A cover for a coffin, bier, or tomb, often made of black, purple, or white velvet. **2.** A coffin, especially one being borne to a grave or tomb. **3. a.** Any covering that darkens or obscures: *a pall of smoke over the city.* **b.** A gloomy effect or atmosphere: *Defeats cast a pall over the troops.* **4.** *Ecclesiastical.* **a.** A linen cloth, or a square of cardboard faced with cloth, used to cover the chalice. **b.** A vestment, the **pallium** *(see).* **c.** *Archaic.* An altar covering. —*tr.v.* **palled, palling, palls.** To cover with a pall. [Middle English *pal,* Old English *pæll,* from Latin *pallium,* a cover, cloak, PALLIUM.]

pall[2] (pôl) *v.* **palled, palling, palls.** —*intr.* **1.** To become insipid, boring, or wearisome. **2.** To have a dulling, wearisome, or unpleasant effect. **3.** To become cloyed or satiated. —*tr.* **1.** To cloy; satiate. **2.** To make vapid or wearisome. [Middle English *pallen,* short for *appallen,* APPALL.]

Pal·la·di·an[1] (pə-lā′dē-ən) *adj.* **1.** Of, pertaining to, or characteristic of Athena, the Greek goddess of wisdom. **2.** Of, pertaining to, or characterized by wisdom or study. [From Latin *Palladius,* of Pallas, from Greek *Palladios,* from *Pallas* (stem *Pallad-*), goddess of wisdom, PALLAS (ATHENA).]

Pal·la·di·an[2] (pə-lā′dē-ən) *adj.* **1.** In or designating the Renaissance architectural style of Andrea Palladio. **2.** In or designating a mid-18th-century architectural style derived from that of Palladio, especially in Britain.

pal·lad·ic (pə-lăd′ĭk, -lā′dĭk) *adj. Chemistry.* Of or designating compounds containing trivalent or tetravalent palladium.

Pal·la·dio (päl-lä′dyō), **Andrea.** 1518–1580. Italian architect.

pal·la·di·um[1] (pə-lā′dē-əm) *n. Symbol* **Pd** A soft, ductile, steel-white, tarnish-resistant, metallic element occurring naturally with platinum, especially in gold, nickel, and copper ores. It is used as a catalyst in hydrogenation process, as a purification filter for hydrogen, and is alloyed for use in electric contacts, jewelry, nonmagnetic watch parts, and surgical instruments. Atomic number 46, atomic weight 106.4, melting point 1,552°C, boiling point 2,927°C, specific gravity 12.02 (20°C), valence 2, 3, 4. See **element.** [New Latin, from the asteroid PALLAS, discovered at the same time as the element.]

pal·la·di·um[2] (pə-lā′dē-əm) *n., pl.* **-dia** (-dē-ə) or **-ums. 1.** A sacred object having the power to preserve a city or state

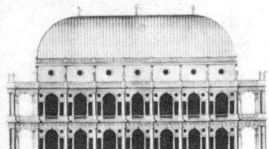

ă pat/ā pay/âr care/ä father/b bib/ch church/d deed/ĕ pet/ē be/f fife/g gag/h hat/hw which/ĭ pit/ī pie/îr pier/j judge/k kick/l lid, needle/m mum/n no, sudden/ng thing/ŏ pot/ō toe/ô paw, for/oi noise/ou out/ŏŏ took/ōō boot/p pop/r roar/s sauce/sh ship, dish/

possessing it. **2.** A safeguard, especially one viewed as a guarantee of the integrity of social institutions: *the Bill of Rights, palladium of American civil liberties.* [Latin, from Greek *Palladion,* the fabled statue of Pallas Athena that assured the safety of Troy as long as it remained within the city, from *Pallas* (stem *Pallad-*), PALLAS (ATHENA).]

pal·la·dous (pə-lā′dəs, păl′ə-dəs) *adj. Chemistry.* Of, pertaining to, or containing palladium, especially bivalent palladium.

Pal·las (păl′əs) *n.* The second-largest asteroid of the solar system, approximately 300 miles in diameter. [Discovered by Peter S. *Pallas* (died 1811), German naturalist.]

Pallas Athena, Pallas Athene. The goddess **Athena** *(see).*

pall·bear·er (pôl′bâr′ər) *n.* One of the persons who carry or attend the coffin at a funeral. [Originally, one who held up the corners of the pall covering the coffin.]

pal·let[1] (păl′ĭt) *n.* **1.** A machine part that converts reciprocating motion to rotary motion, or vice versa, as a click or pawl for controlling the motion of a ratchet wheel in a watch escapement. **2.** The lip or projection of a pawl for engaging the teeth on a ratchet wheel. **3.** A wooden, paddlelike potter's tool for mixing and shaping clay. **4.** A tool used for printing or gilding letters on book bindings or taking up and applying gold leaf. **5.** A portable platform for storing or moving cargo or freight. **6.** A painter's palette. [Old French *palette,* diminutive of *pale,* blade, shovel. See **palette.**]

pal·let[2] (păl′ĭt) *n.* A narrow, hard bed or straw-filled mattress: *"A narrow bed, I mean one just wide enough to contain you, a pallet shall we say"* (Samuel Beckett). [Middle English *pailet,* from Norman French *paillete,* bundle of straw, from *paille,* straw, from Latin *palea,* chaff. See **pel-**[1] in Appendix.*]

pal·lette (pă-lĕt′) *n.* A plate that protects the armpit on a suit of armor. [Variant of PALETTE (in the sense of a thin board).]

pal·liasse. Variant of **paillasse.**

pal·li·ate (păl′ē-āt′) *tr.v.* **-ated, -ating, -ates. 1.** To make (an offense or crime) seem less serious; extenuate; excuse. **2.** To make less severe, without curing; reduce the pain or intensity of; mitigate; alleviate: *"They have endeavored to heighten the advantages, or palliate the evils of those forms."* (James Madison). [Late Latin *palliāre,* to cloak, from Latin *pallium,* cloak, PALLIUM.] **—pal′li·a′tion** *n.*

pal·li·a·tive (păl′ē-ā′tĭv, -ē-ə-tĭv) *adj.* Tending or serving to palliate. *—n.* Something that palliates. **—pal′li·a′tive·ly** *adv.*

pal·lid (păl′ĭd) *adj.* **1.** Having an abnormally pale or wan complexion: *the pallid face of an invalid.* **2.** Lacking intensity of hue or luminousness: *"She opened her left hand, color of the pallid stone on which she lay."* (Ross Lockridge, Jr.). **3.** Lacking in radiance or vitality; dull; lackluster; lifeless: *"Consider . . . how pallid, and faint and dilute a thing, all the honors of this world are."* (Donne). [Latin *pallidus,* from *pallēre,* to be pale. See **pel-**[2] in Appendix.*] **—pal′lid·ly** *adv.* **—pal′lid·ness** *n.*

pal·li·um (păl′ē-əm) *n., pl.* **-ums** or **-lia** (-lē-ə). **1.** A cloak worn by the Romans. **2.** A vestment worn by the pope, and conferred by him on archbishops and sometimes on bishops. Also called "pall." **3.** *Zoology.* An outer layer or covering, such as the mantle of a mollusk or the cerebral cortex. [Latin *pallium*†.]

pall-mall (pĕl′mĕl′, păl′măl′, pôl′môl′) *n.* **1.** A 17th-century game in which a boxwood ball was struck with a mallet to drive it through an iron ring suspended at the end of an alley. **2.** The alley in which this game was played. [Obsolete French *palle maille,* from Italian *pallamaglio* : *palla, balla,* ball, from Middle High German *balle* (see **bhel-**[2] in Appendix*) + *maglio,* mallet, from Latin *malleus* (see **melə-** in Appendix*).]

Pall Mall (pĕl′mĕl′). A street in London, noted for its clubs.

pal·lor (păl′ər) *n.* Extreme or unnatural paleness: *"The winter's sun on his face revealed a hospital pallor."* (Nelson Algren). [Latin, from *pallēre,* to be pale. See **pel-**[2] in Appendix.*]

palm[1] (päm) *n.* **1.** The inner surface of the hand, extending from the wrist to the base of the fingers. **2.** The similar part of the forefoot of a quadruped. **3. a.** A unit of length equal to either the width or the length of the hand. **b.** Three inches. **4.** The part of a glove or mitten that covers the palm of the hand. **5.** A metal shield worn by sailmakers over the palm of the hand and used to force a needle through heavy canvas. **6.** The blade of an oar or paddle. **7.** The flattened part of the antlers of certain animals, such as the moose. **—cross one's palm.** To pay, tip, or bribe. **—grease the palm of.** To bribe. **—have an itching palm.** To have a craving for money. *—tr.v.* **palmed, palming, palms. 1.** To conceal (something) in the palm of the hand, as in cheating at dice or cards or in a sleight-of-hand trick. **2.** To pick up furtively. **—palm off.** To dispose of or pass off by deception. [Middle English *paume,* from Old French, from Latin *palma,* palm of the hand, palm tree. See **pelə-**[1] in Appendix.*]

palm[2] (päm) *n.* **1.** Any of various chiefly tropical evergreen trees or shrubs of the family Palmaceae, characteristically having unbranched trunks with a crown of large pinnate or palmate leaves. **2.** A leaf or frond of a palm tree, carried as an emblem of victory, success, or joy. **3.** Triumph; victory. **4.** A small metallic representation of a palm leaf added to a military decoration that has been awarded a second time. **—bear** (or **carry off**) **the palm.** To win the prize in a given contest; be the victor. [Middle English *palme,* Old English *palm,* from Latin *palma,* PALM, hence (from the resemblance of its leaves to the outspread human hand) palm tree.]

Pal·ma (päl′mä). **1.** Also **Pal·ma de Ma·llor·ca** (päl′mä *th*ā mä-yôr′kä). The capital and principal port of the Balearic Islands, on Majorca, of which it is also the capital. Population, 162,000. **2.** See **La Palma.**

pal·mar (păl′mər, päl′-, pä′mər) *adj.* Of, pertaining to, or corresponding to the palm of the hand or an animal's paw: *palmar folds.* [New Latin *palmaris,* from Latin *palma,* PALM (hand).]

pal·ma·ry (păl′mə-rē, päl′-, pä′mə-) *adj.* Worthy of the palm; outstanding; superior. [Latin *palmārius,* deserving of the palm of victory, from *palma,* PALM (tree).]

Pal·mas, Las. See **Las Palmas.**

pal·mate (păl′māt′, päl′-, pä′māt′) *adj.* Also **pal·mat·ed** (păl′-mā′tĭd, päl′-, pä′mā′-). **1.** Resembling a hand with the fingers extended: *palmate antlers; palmate coral.* **2.** *Botany.* Having leaflets or lobes radiating or diverging from one point: *a palmate leaf.* **3.** *Zoology.* Having webbed toes, as the feet of many water birds. [Latin *palmātus,* from *palma,* PALM (hand).] **—pal′mate′ly** *adv.*

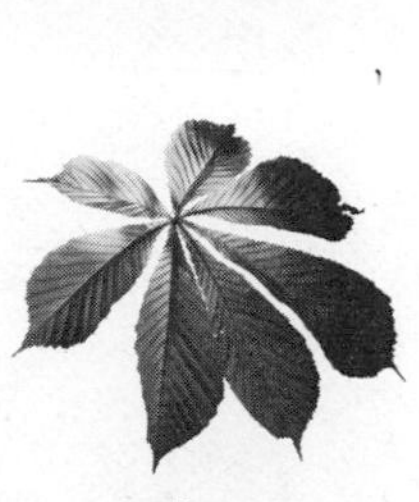

palmate
Palmate compound leaf of horse chestnut

pal·ma·tion (păl-mā′shən, päl-, pä-mā′-) *n.* **1.** The state of being palmate. **2. a.** A palmate structure or form. **b.** A division or part of a palmate structure.

Palm Beach[1]. A winter resort town in southeastern Florida, on the Atlantic Ocean. Population, 6,000.

Palm Beach[2]. A trademark for a lightweight fabric made by various combinations of animal or man-made fibers, used for summer apparel.

palm civet. Any of several arboreal mammals of the family Viverridae, of Africa and Asia, having long tails and gray or brown fur. Also called "palm cat."

palm·er (pä′mər) *n.* In medieval Europe, a pilgrim who carried a palm branch as a token of having visited the Holy Land. [Middle English *palmere,* from Medieval Latin *palmārius,* from Latin *palma,* PALM (frond).]

Palm·er (pä′mər), **Daniel David.** 1845–1913. Canadian-born American founder of chiropractic.

Palm·er Archipelago (pä′mər). Former name **Antarctic Archipelago.** A group of small islands in the Antarctic Ocean, between the southern tip of South America and Antarctica, north of the Antarctic Peninsula. They are part of the Falkland Islands Dependencies.

Palm·er Land (pä′mər). The southern part of the Antarctic Peninsula.

Palm·er Peninsula. A former name for the **Antarctic Peninsula.**

Palm·er·ston (pä′mər-stən), **Third Viscount.** Title of Henry John Temple. 1784–1865. Prime Minister of Great Britain (1855–58, 1859–65).

palm·er·worm (pä′mər-wûrm′) *n.* Any of several caterpillars that injure fruit trees by feeding upon their leaves; especially, the small green caterpillar of a North American moth, *Dichomeris ligulella.* [PALMER + WORM.]

pal·mette (păl-mĕt′) *n.* A stylized palm leaf used as a decorative element, notably in Persian rugs and in classical moldings, reliefs, frescoes, and vase paintings. [French, diminutive of *palme,* palm, from Latin *palma,* PALM.]

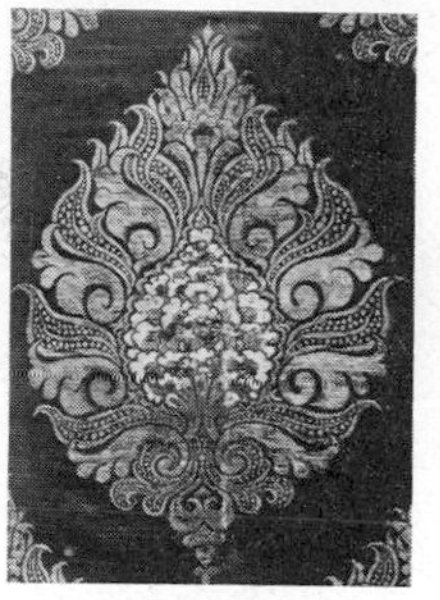

palmette
Detail of a 17th-century silk brocade from Asia Minor

pal·met·to (păl-mĕt′ō) *n., pl.* **-tos** or **-toes.** Any of several small, mostly tropical palms having fan-shaped leaves; especially, *Sabal palmetto,* of the southeastern United States. This species is also called "cabbage palmetto." [Spanish *palmito,* diminutive of *palma,* palm, from Latin, PALM.]

Palmetto State. The nickname for South Carolina.

palm·ist (pä′mĭst) *n.* Also **palm·is·ter** (pä′mĭ-stər). One who practices palmistry. [Back-formation from PALMISTRY.]

palm·is·try (pä′mĭ-strē) *n.* The practice or art of telling fortunes from the lines, marks, and patterns on the palms of the hands; chiromancy. [Middle English *pawmestrie* : *paume,* PALM + an obscure element not corresponding to *-ist* + *-ry.*]

pal·mi·tate (păl′mə-tāt′, päl′mə-, pä′mə-) *n. Chemistry.* An ester or salt of palmitic acid. [PALMIT(IN) + -ATE.]

pal·mit·ic acid (păl-mĭt′ĭk, päl-, pä-mĭt′-). A common fatty acid, $CH_3(CH_2)_{14}COOH$, occurring in many natural oils and fats, and used in making soaps. [From PALMITIN.]

pal·mi·tin (păl′mə-tĭn, päl′-, pä′mə-) *n.* The glyceryl ester, $C_3H_5(OC_{16}H_{31}O)_3$, of palmitic acid, found in palm oil and animal fats, and used to manufacture soap. Also called "tripalmitin." [French *palmitine,* perhaps from *palmite,* pith of the palm tree, from *palme,* palm, from Latin *palma,* PALM.]

palm oil. 1. A yellowish fatty oil obtained from the crushed nuts of the West African palm, *Elaeis guineensis,* and used to manufacture soaps, chocolates, cosmetics, and candles. **2.** A reddish-yellow fatty oil with a butterlike consistency obtained from the fermented pulp of this palm and used as a lubricant and in the manufacture of soaps and candles.

palm sugar. Sugar made from the sap of various palm trees.

Palm Sunday. The Sunday before Easter, commemorating Christ's entry into Jerusalem, when palm fronds were strewn before Him.

palm·y (pä′mē) *adj.* **-ier, -iest. 1.** Of or pertaining to palm trees. **2.** Covered with palm trees. **3.** Prosperous; flourishing.

pal·my·ra (păl-mī′rə) *n.* A tall palm, *Borassus flabellifera,* of tropical Asia, having large, fanlike leaves. Also called "palmyra palm." [Variant of earlier *palmeira,* from Portuguese, palm tree, from *palma,* palm, from Latin, PALM.]

Pal·my·ra (păl-mī′rə). Biblical name **Tad·mor** (tăd′môr′). An ancient city of Syria, northeast of Damascus, on the northern edge of the Syrian Desert.

Pal·o Al·to (păl′ō ăl′tō). **1.** A city of western California, near the southern end of San Francisco Bay. Population, 52,000. **2.** A battlefield near Brownsville, in southern Texas, where the first engagement of the Mexican War was fought (1846).

Pal·o·mar, Mount (păl′ə-mär′). A mountain, 6,126 feet high, in extreme southwestern California, the site of the Mount Palomar Observatory.

pal·o·mi·no (păl′ə-mē′nō) *n., pl.* **-nos.** A type of horse having a golden or tan coat and a white or cream-colored mane and

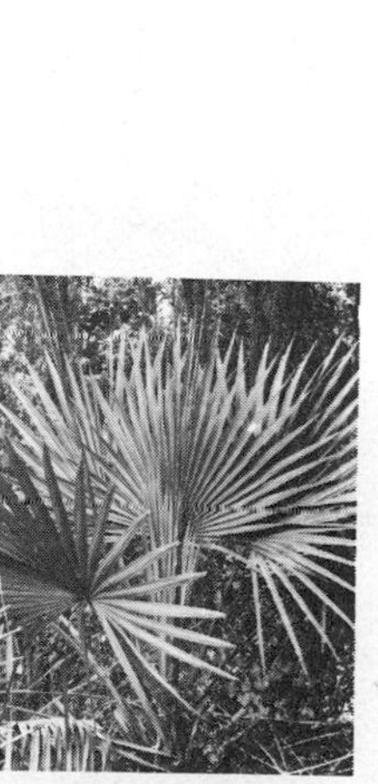

palmetto
Sabal minor

t tight/th thin, path/*th* this, bathe/ŭ cut/ûr urge/v valve/w with/y yes/z zebra, size/zh vision/ə about, item, edible, gallop, circus/ à *Fr.* ami/œ *Fr.* feu, *Ger.* schön/ü *Fr.* tu, *Ger.* über/KH *Ger.* ich, *Scot.* loch/N *Fr.* bon. ***Follows main vocabulary.** **†Of obscure origin.**

tail. [American Spanish, from Spanish, dove-colored, from Latin *palumbīnus*, pertaining to ring doves, from *palumbes*, ring dove. See **pel-²** in Appendix.*]

pa·loo·ka (pə-lo͞o′kə) *n. Sports Slang.* An incompetent or easily defeated player, especially a prize fighter. [Coined by Jack Conway (1886–1928), American journalist.]

Pa·lou (pə-lō′), **Francisco.** 1722?–1789? Spanish Franciscan missionary; explored from Mexico to San Francisco Bay.

pa·lo·ver·de (păl′ō-vûr′dē, -vûrd′) *n.* **1.** A spiny, nearly leafless shrub, *Cercidium torreyanum*, of southwestern North America, having showy yellow flowers. **2.** Any of several similar or related shrubs. [Mexican Spanish, "green tree" : Spanish *palo*, lumber, tree, from Latin *pālus*, stake (see **pag-** in Appendix*) + *verde*, green, from Latin *viridis* (see **virēre** in Appendix*).]

palp (pălp) *n. Zoology.* An elongated sensory organ, usually near the mouth, in invertebrate organisms such as mollusks, crustaceans, and insects. Also called "palpus." [French *palpe*, from Latin *palpus*, a touching. See **pōl-** in Appendix.*]

pal·pa·ble (păl′pə-bəl) *adj.* **1.** Capable of being handled, touched, or felt; tangible: *"Anger rushed out in a palpable wave through his arms and legs."* (Herman Wouk). **2.** Easily perceived; obvious. **3.** *Medicine.* Perceptible by palpation: *a palpable tumor.* —See Synonyms at **perceptible.** [Middle English, from Late Latin *palpābilis*, from Latin *palpāre*, to touch. See **pōl-** in Appendix.*] —**pal′pa·bil′i·ty** *n.* —**pal′pa·bly** *adv.*

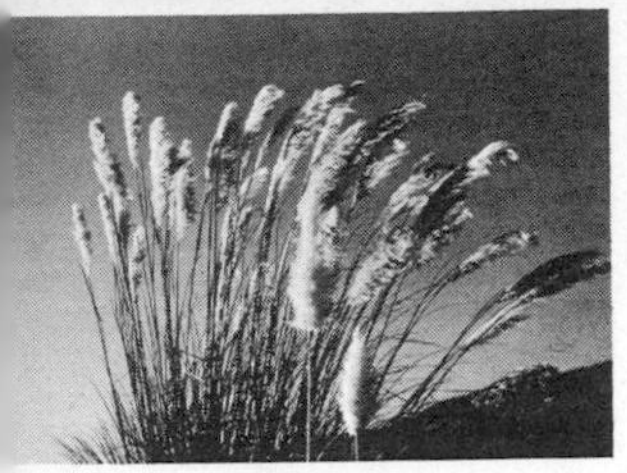

pampas grass

pal·pate¹ (păl′pāt′) *tr.v.* **-pated, -pating, -pates.** *Medicine.* To examine or explore by touching (an organ or area of the body) as a diagnostic aid. [Latin *palpāre*, to touch. See **pōl-** in Appendix.*] —**pal·pa′tion** *n.* —**pal′pa′tor** (păl′pā′tər) *n.*

pal·pate² (păl′pāt′) *adj. Zoology.* Having a palp or palps.

pal·pe·bral (păl′pə-brəl, păl-pē′brəl, -pĕb′rəl) *adj.* Of or relating to the eyelids. [Late Latin *palpebrālis*, from Latin *palpebra*, eyelid. See **pōl-** in Appendix.*]

pal·pi·tant (păl′pə-tənt) *adj.* Palpitating; trembling; quivering. [Latin *palpitāns*, present participle of *palpitāre*, to PALPITATE.]

pal·pi·tate (păl′pə-tāt′) *intr.v.* **-tated, -tating, -tates.** **1.** To shake; quiver; flutter. **2.** To beat more quickly than normal; throb. Used especially of the heart. —See Synonyms at **pulsate.** [Latin *palpitāre*, to palpitate, frequentative of *palpāre*, to touch. See **pōl-** in Appendix.*] —**pal′pi·tat′ing·ly** *adv.*

pal·pi·ta·tion (păl′pə-tā′shən) *n.* **1.** A trembling or shaking. **2.** Irregular, rapid beating or pulsation of the heart.

pal·pus (păl′pəs) *n., pl.* **-pi** (-pī′). *Zoology.* A **palp** *(see).*

pals·grave (pôlz′grāv′) *n.* A count palatine, especially one of the Counts Palatine of the Rhine or Electors Palatine. See the **Palatinate.** [Dutch *paltsgrave*, from Middle Dutch : *palts*, palatine, ultimately from Vulgar Latin *palāntius* (unattested), variant of *palātīnus*, PALATINE + *grave*, count, from Middle Dutch (see **gravo-** in Appendix*).]

pal·sied (pôl′zēd) *adj.* **1.** *Medicine.* Afflicted with palsy. **2.** Trembling; shaking.

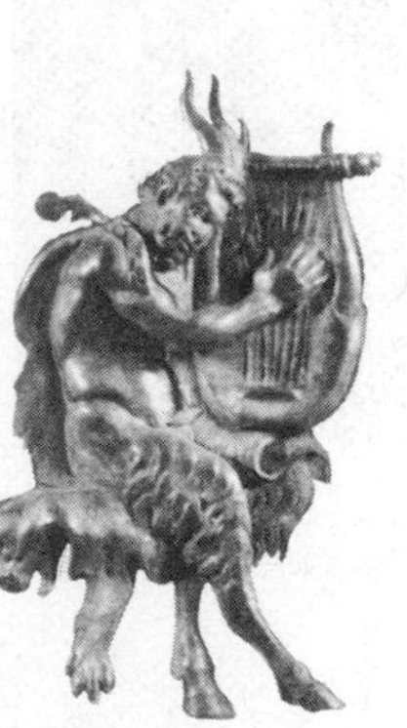

Pan
Roman silver plaque of Pan playing lyre

pal·sy (pôl′zē) *n., pl.* **-sies.** **1.** Paralysis. **2.** A condition marked by loss of power to feel or to control movement in any part of the body. **3. a.** A weakening or debilitating influence. **b.** An enfeebled condition or debilitated state thought to result from such an influence. **4.** A fit of some strong emotion marked by an inability to act: *"Flaherty dithered in a little palsy of indignation."* (Anthony Burgess). —*tr.v.* **palsied, -sying, -sies.** **1. a.** To paralyze. **b.** To deprive of strength: *"The step was palsied now, that had been foremost in the charge."* (Hawthorne). **2.** To make helpless, as with fear. [Middle English *palesie*, from Old French *paralisie*, from Latin *paralysis*, PARALYSIS.]

pal·ter (pôl′tər) *intr.v.* **-tered, -tering, -ters.** **1.** To talk or act insincerely; use trickery; equivocate. **2.** To be capricious; trifle. **3.** To quibble, especially in bargaining. [Origin unknown.]

pal·try (pôl′trē) *adj.* **-trier, -triest.** **1.** Petty; trifling; insignificant. **2.** Worthless; contemptible. —See Synonyms at **trivial.** [Dialectal English *paltry*, feeble, from *palt*, *pelt*†, rags, rubbish.] —**pal′tri·ly** *adv.*

pa·lu·dal (pə-lo͝od′l, păl′yə-dəl) *adj.* Of or pertaining to a swamp; marshy. [From Latin *palūs* (stem *palūd-*), marsh. See **pel-⁸** in Appendix.*]

pal·u·dism (păl′yə-dĭz′əm) *n.* A disease, **malaria** *(see).* [From Latin *palūs* (stem *palūd-*), marsh. See **pel-⁸** in Appendix.*]

pal·y (pā′lē) *adj. Archaic.* Pale.

pal·y·nol·o·gy (păl′ə-nŏl′ə-jē) *n.* The scientific study of spores and pollen. [From Greek *palunein*, to sprinkle (see **pel-¹** in Appendix*) + -LOGY.]

pam (păm) *n. Card Games.* The jack of clubs and highest trump in certain variations of **loo** *(see).* [Gamblers' slang, from Greek *pamphilos*, "loved by all" : *pan*, all, PAN- + *philos*, beloved (see **bhilo-** in Appendix*).]

pam. pamphlet.

Pam·e·la (păm′ə-lə). A feminine given name. [Coined by Sir Philip Sidney in *Arcadia* (1590).]

Pa·mirs, the (pə-mîrz′). Also **Pa·mir** (pə-mîr′). A mountain region of central Asia, chiefly in Tadzhik S.S.R., bordering on Afghanistan, Kashmir, and China. Highest elevation is Mount Kungur (25,325 feet) in western China.

Pam·li·co Sound (păm′lĭ-kō′). An inlet of the Atlantic Ocean, 80 miles long, between the eastern coast of North Carolina and its chain of offshore islands.

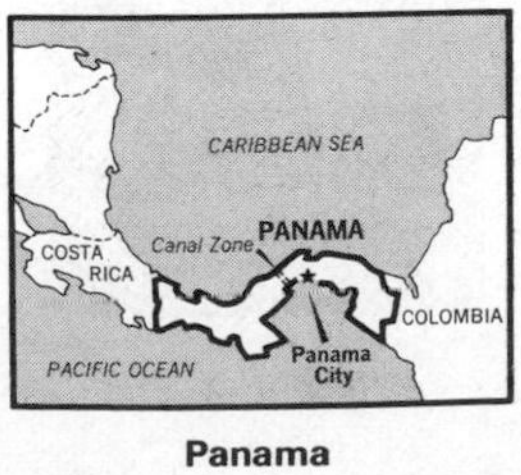

Panama

pam·pas (păm′pəz) *pl.n.* Singular **-pa** (-pə). A nearly treeless grassland area of South America, chiefly in central Argentina and Uruguay between the Andes and the Atlantic. [Plural of American Spanish *pampa*, from Aymara and Quechua, plain.]

pam·pas grass (păm′pəs). A tall grass, *Cortaderia argentea*, of southern South America, having silvery plumes.

pam·pe·an (păm′pē-ən, păm-pē′ən) *adj.* Of or pertaining to the pampas or the Indian people who inhabit them. —*n. Capital* **P.** An Indian of the pampas.

pam·per (păm′pər) *tr.v.* **-pered, -pering, -pers.** **1.** To treat with excessive indulgence; cater to; coddle. **2.** *Archaic.* To indulge with rich food; glut. [Middle English *pamperen*, of Low German origin, akin to Flemish *pamperen*. See **pap-²** in Appendix.*] —**pam′per·er** *n.*

Synonyms: *pamper, indulge, humor, spoil, coddle, baby.* These all mean to cater excessively to another's (or one's own) desires or feelings, typically those of a child and more pejoratively those of an adult. To *pamper* is to be overattentive to somebody's physical comforts. *Indulge* is applied principally to instincts or appetites, sometimes without very strong condemnation. *Humor* usually implies short-term submission to another's mood or idiosyncrasies as a means to an end. *Spoil* usually implies a long-term oversolicitude that badly affects a person's character. *Coddle* points to overprotecting, serving, or favoring somebody. *Baby* suggests bestowing on someone the indulgence and attention appropriate to an infant, and is always unfavorable.

pam·pe·ro (păm-pâr′ō, päm-) *n., pl.* **-ros.** A strong, cold, southwest wind that blows across the pampas. [American Spanish, "pampean," from *pampa*, PAMPAS.]

pam·phlet (păm′flĭt) *n. Abbr.* **pam., pamph., pph.** **1.** An unbound printed work, usually with a paper cover. **2.** A short essay or treatise, usually on a current topic, published without a binding. [Middle English *pamflet*, from *Pamflet*, familiar name of *Pamphilus*, a popular short amatory Latin poem of the 12th century.] —**pam′phlet·ar′y** (păm′flə-tĕr′ē) *adj.*

pam·phlet·eer (păm′flə-tîr′) *n.* A writer of pamphlets or other short works taking a partisan stand on an issue. —*intr.v.* **pamphleteered, -eering, -eers.** To write and publish pamphlets.

Pam·phy·li·a (păm-fĭl′ē-ə). An ancient region of southern Asia Minor that became a Roman province.

Pam·phyl·i·an (păm-fĭl′ē-ən) *n.* The Ancient Greek dialect of Pamphylia, belonging to Arcado-Cyprian.

Pam·plo·na (päm-plō′nä). Also **Pam·pe·lu·na** (päm′pā-lo͞o′nä). The capital of Navarre Province in northern Spain, southeast of San Sebastián. Population, 115,000.

pan¹ (păn) *n.* **1.** A shallow, wide, open container, usually of metal and without a lid, used for holding liquids, cooking, and other domestic purposes. **2.** Any vessel similar in form: **a.** An open, metal dish used to separate gold or other metal from gravel, earth, or other waste, by washing. **b.** Either of the receptacles on a balance or pair of scales. **c.** A vessel used for boiling and evaporating liquids. **3. a.** A basin or depression in the earth, often containing mud or water. **b.** A natural or artificial basin used to obtain salt by evaporating brine. **4.** A piece of drift ice that has broken off a larger floe. **5.** In flintlocks, the small cavity in the lock used to hold powder. **6.** *Slang.* The face. —*v.* **panned, panning, pans.** —*tr.* **1.** To wash (gravel, sand, or other sediments) in a pan for precious metal. **2.** To cook (food) in a pan. **3.** *Informal.* To criticize harshly. —*intr.* **1.** To wash gravel, sand, or other sediments in a pan. **2.** To yield gold as a result of washing in a pan. —**pan out.** *Informal.* To turn out well; be successful: *"if I don't pan out as an actor I can still go back to school"* (Saul Bellow). [Middle English *panne*, Old English *panne*, from West Germanic *panna* (unattested), perhaps from Latin *patina*, from Greek *patanē*, pan, dish. See **pet-²** in Appendix.*]

pan² (pän) *n.* **1.** The leaf of the betel tree. **2.** A preparation of this leaf with betel nuts and lime, used for chewing in the Orient. [Hindi *pān*, from Sanskrit *parṇá*, feather, leaf. See **per-²** in Appendix.*]

pan³ (păn) *v.* **panned, panning, pans.** —*intr.* To move a motion-picture or television camera to follow a moving object or create a panoramic effect. —*tr.* To move (a camera) in such a manner. [Short for PANORAMA.]

Pan (păn). *Greek Mythology.* The god of woods, fields, and flocks, having a human torso with goat's legs, horns, and ears.

pan-. Indicates: **1.** All; for example, **panacea, panorama.** **2.** *Capital* **P. a.** Of, involving, comprising, or applying to all. Usually followed by a hyphen; for example, **Pan-American.** **b.** The aspiration for the political union of a specified group: **Pan-Germanism.** [Greek, from *pas* (neuter *pan*, oblique stem *pant-*), all. See **keu-³** in Appendix.*]

Pan. Panama.

pan·a·ce·a (păn′ə-sē′ə) *n.* A remedy for all diseases, evils, or difficulties; cure-all: *"Here was a panacea . . . for all human woes; here was the secret of happiness."* (De Quincey). [Latin *panacēa*, from Greek *panakeia*, from *panakēs*, all-healing : PAN- + *akos*, cure (see **yēk-** in Appendix*).] —**pan′a·ce′an** *adj.*

pa·nache (pə-năsh′, -näsh′) *n.* **1.** A bunch of feathers or a plume, especially on a helmet. **2.** Dash; swagger; verve: *"There was a grandeur and panache—and impatience of all constraint—about everything he did."* (Arland Ussher). [French, from Italian *pennachio*, from Late Latin *pinnāculum*, diminutive of Latin *pinna*, feather. See **pet-¹** in Appendix.*]

pa·na·da (pə-nä′də) *n.* A paste or gruel of bread crumbs, toast, or flour combined with milk, stock, or water, used for soups, for binding forcemeats, or for thickening sauces. [Spanish, from *pan*, bread, from Latin *pānis*, bread. See **pā-** in Appendix.*]

Pan·a·ma (păn′ə-mä′). *Spanish* **Pa·na·má** (pä′nä-mä′). *Abbr.* **Pan.** **1.** A republic of Central America, 28,575 square miles in area, on the Isthmus of Panama. Population, 1,076,000. **2.** The capital of this republic, at the Pacific terminus of the Panama Canal. Population, 273,000. Also called "Panama City." —**Pan′a·ma′ni·an** (păn′ə-mā′nē-ən) *adj. & n.*

Pan·a·ma, Isthmus of (păn′ə-mä′). Formerly Isthmus of **Dar·i·én** (dâr′ē-ĕn′, dâr′ē-ĕn′). A 420-mile-long isthmus (narrowest point, 31 miles) connecting North and South America and separating the Pacific Ocean from the Caribbean Sea.
Pan·a·ma Canal (păn′ə-mä). A ship canal, 51 miles long, across the Isthmus of Panama, connecting the Caribbean Sea with the Pacific Ocean.
Pan·a·ma Canal Zone. See **Canal Zone.**
Panama hat. A natural-colored, hand-plaited hat made from leaves of the jipijapa plant of South and Central America.
Pan-A·mer·i·can (păn′ə-mĕr′ə-kən) *adj.* Of or pertaining to North, South, and Central America collectively.
Pan·a·mint Mountains (păn′ə-mĭnt). A range in southeastern California, west of Death Valley. Highest elevation, Telescope Peak (11,045 feet).
pan·a·tel·a (păn′ə-tĕl′ə) *n.* Also **pan·a·tel·la, pan·e·tel·a, pan·e·tel·la.** A long, slender cigar. [Spanish, from American Spanish, a long thin biscuit, from Italian *panatella,* from *panata,* panada, from *pane,* bread, from Latin *pānis.* See **pā-** in Appendix.*]
Pa·nay (pə-nī′). An island, 4,446 square miles in area, of the Visayan Islands, Republic of the Philippines, situated between Mindoro and Negros islands. Principal town, Iloilo.
pan-broil (păn′broil′) *tr.v.* **-broiled, -broiling, -broils.** To cook over direct heat in an uncovered, usually ungreased skillet.
pan·cake (păn′kāk′) *n.* **1.** A thin cake made of batter, poured on a hot, greased skillet and cooked on both sides until brown. Also called "griddle cake," "flannel cake," "flapjack." **2.** A face-powder cosmetic pressed into a flat cake. Also called "pancake make-up." —*v.* **pancaked, -caking, -cakes.** *Aviation.* —*intr.* To make a pancake landing. —*tr.* To cause (an airplane) to make a pancake landing.
pancake landing. *Aviation.* An irregular or emergency landing in which an aircraft drops flat to the ground from a low altitude.
pan·chax (păn′chăks′) *n.* Any of various small, brightly colored Old World tropical fishes of the genus *Aplocheilus* and related genera, often kept in home aquariums. [New Latin *Panchax*†, former generic name.]
Pan·chen La·ma (pän′chən lä′mə). One of Tibet's two grand lamas, the other being the Dalai Lama. See **Lamaism.** [From the Tibetan title *Pan-chen-rin-po-che,* "great jewel (among the) scholars."]
pan·chro·mat·ic (păn′krō-măt′ĭk) *adj. Photography.* Sensitive to all colors: *panchromatic film.* —**pan·chro′ma·tism′** (păn-krō′mə-tĭz′əm) *n.*
pan·cre·as (păng′krē-əs, păn′-) *n. Anatomy.* A long, soft, irregularly shaped gland lying behind the stomach. It secretes pancreatic juice into the duodenum and, in the islands of Langerhans, produces insulin which is taken up by the bloodstream. [Greek *pankreas,* "all-flesh," pancreas : PAN- + *kreas,* flesh (see **kreu-**[1] in Appendix*).] —**pan′cre·at′ic** (-ăt′ĭk) *adj.*
pancreatic juice. A clear, alkaline secretion of the pancreas containing enzymes that aid in the digestion of proteins, carbohydrates, and fats.
pan·cre·a·tin (păng′krē-ə-tĭn, păn′-, păn-krē′ə-tĭn) *n.* A mixture of enzymes extracted from the pancreases of cattle or hogs and used as a digestive aid.
pan·da (păn′də) *n.* **1.** A carnivorous, bearlike mammal, *Ailuropoda melanoleuca,* of the mountains of China and Tibet, having woolly fur with distinctive black and white markings. Also called "giant panda." **2.** A small, raccoonlike mammal, *Ailurus fulgens,* of northeastern Asia, having reddish fur and a long, ringed tail. Also called "lesser panda." [French, perhaps from a native Nepalese word.]
pan·da·nus (păn-dā′nəs, -dăn′əs) *n.* Any of various palmlike trees and shrubs of the genus *Pandanus,* of southeastern Asia, having large prop roots and a crown of narrow leaves that yield a fiber used in weaving mats and similar articles. Also called "screw pine." [New Latin, from Malay *pandan.*] —**pan′da·na′ceous** (păn′də-nā′shəs) *adj.*
Pan·da·rus (păn′də-rəs). Also **Pan·dar** (păn′dər). **1.** In the *Iliad,* the leader of the Lycians, slain by Diomedes. **2.** In medieval romance, the procurer of Cressida for Troilus.
Pan·de·an pipes (păn-dē′ən). A **panpipe** *(see).*
pan·dect (păn′dĕkt′) *n.* **1.** A comprehensive digest or complete treatise. **2.** *Plural.* Any complete body of laws; a legal code. **3.** *Plural. Capital* **P.** A digest of Roman civil law, compiled for the emperor Justinian in the sixth century A.D., and part of the **Corpus Juris Civilis** *(see).* Also called "the Digest." [Late Latin *Pandectēs,* the Corpus Juris Civilis, from Latin, book containing everything, from Greek *pandektēs,* all-receiving : PAN- + *dektēs,* receiver, from *dekheisthai,* to receive (see **dek-**[1] in Appendix*).]
pan·dem·ic (păn-dĕm′ĭk) *adj.* **1.** Widespread; general; universal. **2.** *Medicine.* Epidemic over an especially wide geographic area. —*n.* A pandemic disease. [From Late Latin *pandemus,* from Greek *pandēmos,* of all the people : PAN- + *dēmos,* people (see **dā-** in Appendix*).]
pan·de·mo·ni·um (păn′də-mō′nē-əm) *n.* Also **pan·dae·mo·ni·um. 1.** Any place characterized by uproar and noise: *"The whole lobby was a perfect pandemonium, and the din was terrific."* (Jerome K. Jerome). **2.** Wild uproar or noise. —See Synonyms at **noise.** [From *Pandæmonium,* capital of Hell in Milton's *Paradise Lost* : PAN- + Greek *daimōn,* demon, spirit, deity (see **dā-** in Appendix*).] —**pan′de·mo′ni·ac′** (păn′də-mō′nē-ăk′) *adj.*
pan·der (păn′dər) *n.* Also **pan·der·er** (păn′dər-ər). **1.** A go-between or liaison in sexual intrigues; pimp; procurer. **2.** One who caters to the lower tastes and desires of others or exploits their weaknesses. —*v.* **pandered, -dering, -ders.** —*tr.* To act as a pander for. —*intr.* To act as a pander. Used with *to.* [From *Pandare,* character in Chaucer's *Troilus and Criseyde,* who procures Criseyde's love for Troilus; name taken from *Pandaro* (in Boccaccio's *Filostrata*), *Pandarus* (in the *Aeneid*), *Pandaros* (in the *Iliad*).] —**pan′der·ism′** *n.*
Pan·dit (pŭn′dĭt), **Vijaya Lakshmi.** Born 1900. Indian diplomat and political figure; sister of Jawaharlal Nehru.
Pan·do·ra (păn-dôr′ə, -dōr′ə). *Greek Mythology.* The first woman, bestowed upon mankind as a punishment for Prometheus' theft of fire. Entrusted with a box containing all the ills that could plague mankind, she opened it.
pan·dore (păn′dôr′, -dōr′) *n.* An ancient musical instrument; a **bandore** *(see).* [Greek *pandoura,* three-stringed lute. See **pandoura** in Appendix.*]
pan·dow·dy (păn-dou′dē) *n., pl.* **-dies.** Sliced apples baked with sugar and spices in a deep dish, with a thick top crust. Sometimes called "apple pandowdy." [Origin unknown.]
pan·du·rate (păn-dŏŏr′ĭt, -dyŏŏr′ĭt) *n.* Also **pan·du·ri·form** (păn-dŏŏr′ə-fôrm′, -dyŏŏr′ə-fôrm′). *Botany.* Resembling a violin in shape. Said of leaves. [New Latin *panduratus,* from Late Latin *pandūra,* three-stringed lute, PANDORE.]
pane (pān) *n.* **1.** One of the divisions of a window or door, filled with glass. **2.** The glass used in such a division. **3.** A panel of a door, wall, or other surface. **4.** One of the flat surfaces or facets of an object, such as a bolt, having many sides. [Middle English *pane, pan,* piece of cloth, section, from Old French *pan,* from Latin *pannus,* rag. See **pan-** in Appendix.*]
pan·e·gyr·ic (păn′ə-jĭr′ĭk, -jī′rĭk) *n.* **1.** A formal eulogistic composition intended as a public compliment. **2.** Elaborate praise or laudation; an encomium. [French *panégyrique,* from Latin *panēgyricus,* from Greek *(logos) panēgurikos,* "(speech) for a public festival," from *panēguris,* general assembly, public festival : PAN- + *aguris, agora,* assembly (see **ger-**[1] in Appendix*).] —**pan′e·gyr′i·cal** *adj.* —**pan′e·gyr′i·cal·ly** *adv.*
pan·e·gyr·ist (păn′ə-jĭr′ĭst, -jī′rĭst) *n.* One who writes or delivers panegyrics; a eulogist.
pan·e·gy·rize (păn′ə-jə-rīz′) *v.* **-rized, -rizing, -rizes.** —*tr.* To eulogize. —*intr.* To compose, deliver, or indulge in panegyrics.
pan·el (păn′əl) *n.* **1.** A flat, usually rectangular piece forming a part of a surface in which it is set, and being raised, recessed, or framed. **2.** The space or section in a fence or railing between two posts. **3.** A vertical section of fabric; gore. **4. a.** A thin wooden board, used as a surface for oil painting. **b.** A painting on such a board. **5. a.** A board having switches to control parts of an electric device. **b.** An **instrument panel** *(see).* **6.** A section of a telephone switchboard. **7. a.** The complete list of persons summoned for jury duty. **b.** Those persons selected from the list to compose a jury. **c.** A jury. **8. a.** A group of people gathered to plan or discuss an issue, judge a contest, or act as a team on a radio or television quiz program. **b.** A discussion by such a group. —*tr.v.* **paneled, -eling, -els.** Also *chiefly British* **-elled, -elling. 1.** To cover or furnish with panels. **2.** To decorate with panels. **3.** To separate into panels. **4.** To select or impanel (a jury). [Middle English, from Old French, piece of parchment on which names of a jury were written, from Vulgar Latin *panellus* (unattested), diminutive of Latin *pannus,* rag, cloth. See **pan-** in Appendix.*]
pan·el·ing (păn′əl-ĭng) *n.* A section of panels or paneled wall.
pan·el·ist (păn′əl-ĭst) *n.* A member of a panel.
panel truck. A small delivery truck with a fully enclosed body.
pan·e·tel·a, pan·e·tel·la. Variants of **panatela.**
pan·et·to·ne (păn′ə-tō′nē; *Italian* pä′nāt-tō′nā) *n., pl.* **-nes** or *Italian* **-ni** (-nē). A festive Italian yeast cake, made with candied fruit peels and raisins. [Italian, from *panetto,* diminutive of *pane,* bread. See **panatela.**]
pan fish. Any fish small enough to be fried whole in a pan.
pan-fry (păn′frī′) *tr.v.* **-fried, -frying, -fries.** To fry in a frying pan or skillet with a small amount of shortening. —**pan′-fried′** *adj.*
pang (păng) *n.* **1.** A sudden, sharp spasm of pain. **2.** A sudden, sharp feeling of emotional distress. [Origin unknown.]
pan·gen·e·sis (păn-jĕn′ə-sĭs) *n. Biology.* The discredited hypothesis that every somatic cell generates self-representative hereditary materials that enter the bloodstream and eventually coalesce in reproductive cells, making possible the inheritance of acquired characteristics. [PAN- + -GENESIS.] —**pan′ge·net′ic** (păn′jə-nĕt′ĭk) *adj.* —**pan′ge·net′i·cal·ly** *adv.*
Pan-Ger·man·ism (păn′jûr′mə-nĭz′əm) *n.* A political movement advocating the union of all German-speaking peoples and their native territories into a single German state. [French *Pangermanisme* (translation of German *Alldeutschtum*) : PAN- + *Germanisme,* Germanism.] —**Pan′-Ger′man·ist** *n.*
pan·go·lin (păng-gō′lĭn) *n.* Any of several long-tailed, scale-covered mammals of the genus *Manis,* of tropical Africa and Asia, having a long snout and a sticky tongue with which it catches and cats ants. Also called "scaly anteater." [Malay *pĕngguling,* from *guling,* to roll.]
Pan·go Pan·go. The former name for **Pago Pago.**
pan·han·dle[1] (păn′hăn′dl) *intr.v.* **-dled, -dling, -dles.** *Informal.* To beg, especially on the streets. [Origin obscure.] —**pan′han′dler** *n.*
pan·han·dle[2] (păn′hăn′dl) *n.* **1.** The handle of a pan. **2.** *Often capital* **P.** A narrow strip of territory projecting from a larger, broader area to which it belongs in such a way that its borders as drawn on a map appear to outline the handle of a pan.
Pan-Hel·len·ic (păn′hə-lĕn′ĭk) *adj.* Also **Pan·hel·len·ic. 1.** Of or pertaining to Greek peoples or a movement to unify them. **2.** Of or pertaining to Greek-letter fraternities and sororities.

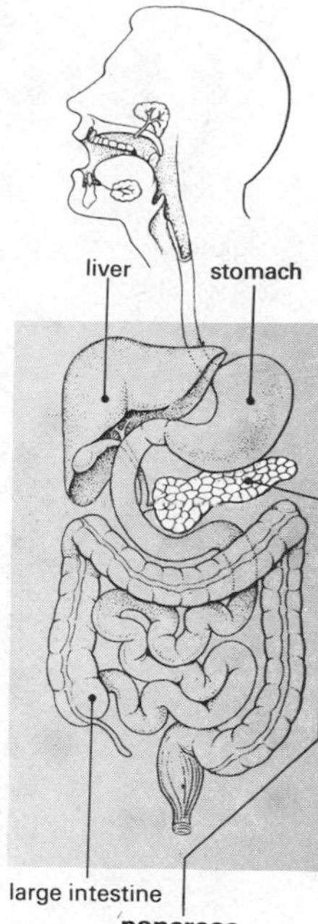

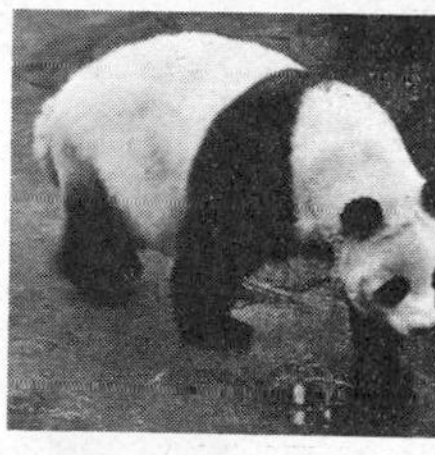

panda
Ailuropoda melanoleuca
Giant panda

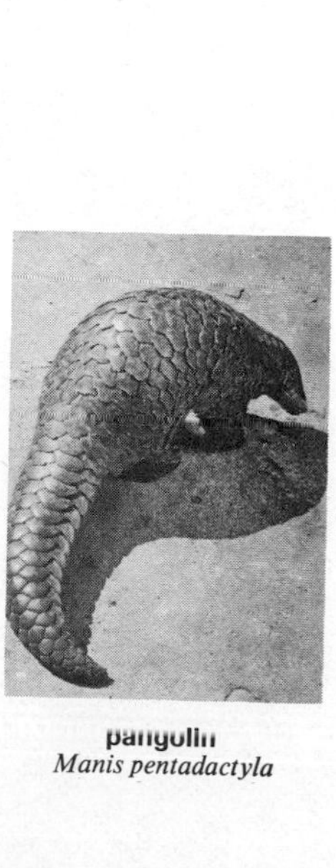

pangolin
Manis pentadactyla

panicle

panther
Panthera pardus
Black color phase

pantile
Detail of a pantiled roof

pan·ic (păn′ĭk) *n.* A sudden, overpowering terror, often affecting many people at once. See Synonyms at **fear.** —*adj.* **1.** Of, pertaining to, or resulting from such terror. **2.** *Usually capital* **P.** Of or pertaining to Pan. —*v.* **panicked, -icking, -ics.** —*tr.* To affect with panic. —*intr.* To be affected with panic. —See Synonyms at **frighten.** [Originally adjectival, from French *panique,* from Greek *panikos,* of Pan (who would arouse terror in lonely places), from *Pan,* PAN.] —**pan′ick·y** *adj.*

panic button. *Slang.* An imaginary device said to be pushed when one is overexcited in the face of a supposed emergency.

panic grass. Any of numerous grasses of the genus *Panicum,* many of which are grown for grain and fodder. [Middle English *panyk,* from Latin *panicum†.*]

pan·i·cle (păn′ĭ-kəl) *n. Botany.* A flower cluster that is loosely and irregularly branched. [Latin *panicula,* diminutive of *panus,* tuft, from Greek *pēnos,* web. See **pan-** in Appendix.*] —**pan′i·cled** *adj.*

pan·ic-strick·en (păn′ĭk-strĭk′ən) *adj.* Also **pan·ic-struck** (păn′ĭk-strŭk′). Overcome by panic; terrified.

pa·nic·u·late (pə-nĭk′yə-lĭt, -lāt′) *adj.* Also **pa·nic·u·lat·ed** (pə-nĭk′yə-lā′tĭd). *Botany.* Growing or arranged in a panicle. [New Latin *paniculatus,* from Latin *panicula,* PANICLE.] —**pa·nic′u·late·ly** *adv.*

Pan·ja·bi. Variant of **Punjabi.**

pan·jan·drum (păn-jăn′drəm) *n.* A muckamuck: *"Once an editor of ladies' magazines and now a panjandrum of the publishing business."* (Nat Hentoff). [From the *Grand Panjandrum,* character in a nonsense story by Samuel Foote (1720–1777), English playwright.]

Pank·hurst (păngk′hûrst′), **Emmeline Goulden.** 1858–1928. British feminist leader.

Pan·mun·jom (păn′mŏon′jŏm′). A village of western South Korea, southeast of Kaesong, and the site of armistice talks leading to the end of the Korean War.

panne (păn) *n.* A special finish for velvet and satin that produces a high luster. [French, from Old French, fur lining, from Latin *penna, pinna,* feather. See **pet-¹** in Appendix.*]

pan·nier (păn′yər, păn′ē-ər) *n.* **1.** A large wicker basket: **a.** One of a pair of baskets carried on either side of a pack animal. **b.** A basket carried on a person's back. **2. a.** A framework of wire, bone, or other material formerly used to expand a woman's skirt at the hips. **b.** A skirt or overskirt puffed out at the hips. [Middle English *panier,* from Old French, from Latin *panarium,* breadbasket, from *panis,* bread. See **pa-** in Appendix.*] —**pan′niered** *adj.*

pan·ni·kin (păn′ĭ-kĭn) *n. British.* A small saucepan or metal cup. [Diminutive of PAN.]

Pan·no·ni·a (pə-nō′nē-ə) *n.* A Roman province in central Europe occupying parts of modern Hungary and Yugoslavia.

pa·no·cha (pə-nō′chə) *n.* Also **pa·no·che** (pə-nō′chē). **1.** A coarse grade of Mexican sugar. **2.** A type of candy, penuche *(see).* [Mexican Spanish, diminutive of Spanish *pan,* bread, from Latin *panis.* See **pa-** in Appendix.*]

pan·o·ply (păn′ə-plē) *n., pl.* **-plies. 1.** The complete arms and armor of a warrior. **2.** Any magnificent, shining array that covers or protects. [Greek *panoplia,* full suit of armor of a hoplite : PAN- + *hoplon†,* weapon.]

pan·op·tic (păn-ŏp′tĭk) *adj.* Also **pan·op·ti·cal** (păn-ŏp′tĭ-kəl). Including everything visible in one view. [From Greek *panoptēs,* all-seeing : PAN- + *optos,* visible (see **okw-** in Appendix*).]

pan·o·ram·a (păn′ə-răm′ə, -rä′mə) *n.* **1.** An unlimited view of all visible objects over a wide area. **2.** A comprehensive picture of a chain of events or a specific subject: *a panorama of ancient history.* **3.** A picture or series of pictures representing a continuous scene, exhibited a part at a time by being unrolled and passed before the spectator. [PAN- + Greek *horama,* sight, from *horan,* to see (see **wer-⁴** in Appendix*).] —**pan′o·ram′ic** *adj.* —**pan′o·ram′i·cal·ly** *adv.*

pan·pipe (păn′pīp′) *n. Sometimes capital* **P.** *Often plural.* A primitive wind instrument consisting of a series of pipes or reeds of graduated length bound together, and played by blowing across the top open ends. Also called "mouth organ," "Pandean pipes," "Pan's pipes," "syrinx." [PAN + PIPE.]

pan·sy (păn′zē) *n., pl.* **-sies. 1.** A garden plant hybridized from *Viola tricolor hortensis,* having rounded, velvety petals of various colors. **2.** Deep to strong violet. See **color. 3.** *Slang.* A male homosexual. Used as a term of contempt. [Fanciful formation from French *pensée,* "thought," from the feminine past participle of *penser,* to think, from Old French, from Latin *pendere,* to weigh. See **spen-** in Appendix.*] —**pant′ing·ly** *adv.*

pant (pănt) *v.* **panted, panting, pants.** —*intr.* **1.** To breathe rapidly in short gasps, as after exertion. **2.** To give off or emit (smoke, steam, or the like) in loud puffs. **3.** To pulsate rapidly; throb. **4.** To yearn with frantic exhaustion: *"my spirit began to burn and pant"* (R.D. Blackmore). —*tr.* To utter hurriedly or breathlessly. —*n.* **1.** The act of panting. **2.** A short, labored breath; gasp. **3.** A short, loud puff, as of steam from an engine. **4.** A throb; pulsation. [Middle English *panten,* from Old French *pantaisier,* from Vulgar Latin *phantasiare* (unattested), to fantasize, have nightmares, gasp with horror, from Latin *phantasia,* an apparition, fantasy, from Greek, from *phantazein,* to make visible, from *phainein,* to show. See **bhā-¹** in Appendix.*] —**pant′ing·ly** *adv.*

pansy

pan·ta·lets (păn′tə-lĕts′) *pl.n.* Also **pan·ta·lettes. 1.** Long underdrawers, trimmed with ruffles extending below the skirt, worn by women in the mid-19th century. **2.** Frills to be attached to the legs of underdrawers. [From PANTALOON.]

pan·ta·loon (păn′tə-lōon′) *n.* **1.** *Plural.* **a.** Formerly, men's tight trousers extending from waist to ankle. **b.** Later, any kind of trousers. **2.** *Capital* **P.** A character in the commedia dell'arte, portrayed as a foolish old man with slippers and tight trousers. **3.** A stock character, the butt of a clown's jokes in modern pantomime. [French *Pantalon,* from Old Italian *Pantalone,* originally a nickname for a Venetian, from *Pantaleone,* a saint once popular in Venice.]

pan·tech·ni·con (păn-tĕk′nĭ-kŏn′, -kən) *n. British.* **1.** A storage warehouse, especially for furniture. **2.** A large truck, especially a furniture van. [Originally the name of a 19th-century bazaar in London where artistic things were sold : PAN- + Greek *tekhnikon,* neuter of *tekhnikos,* artistic, from *tekhnē,* art, skill (see **teks-** in Appendix).]

Pan·tel·le·ri·a (păn′tāl-lā-rē′ä). An Italian island, 32 square miles in area, 70 miles southwest of Sicily.

pan·the·ism (păn′thē-ĭz′əm) *n.* **1.** The doctrine identifying the Deity with the various forces and workings of nature. **2.** Belief in and worship of all gods. Compare **deism, theism.** —**pan′the·ist** *n.* —**pan′the·is′tic, pan′the·is′ti·cal** *adj.*

pan·the·on (păn′thē-ŏn′, -ən) *n.* **1.** *Capital* **P.** A circular temple in Rome, completed in 27 B.C., and dedicated to all the gods. **2.** Any temple dedicated to all gods. **3.** All the gods of a people. **4.** A public building commemorating and dedicated to the great persons of a nation. [Middle English *Panteon,* the Pantheon, from Latin *Pantheon,* from Greek *pantheion* : PAN- + *theos,* god (see **dhēs-** in Appendix*).]

pan·ther (păn′thər) *n.* **1.** The leopard, *Panthera pardus,* especially in its black, unspotted form. **2.** Any of several similar or related animals, such as the **mountain lion** *(see).* [Middle English *panter,* from Old French *pantere,* from Latin *panthēra,* from Greek *panthēr†.*]

pan·tie (păn′tē) *n.* Also **pant·y** *pl.* **-ies.** *Informal.* A pair of women's or children's underpants. Usually used in the plural. [From PANTS.]

pan·tile (păn′tīl′) *n.* An S-curved roofing tile, laid so the down curve of one tile overlaps the up curve of the next one. [PAN + TILE (i.e., "dish-tile," from the concave shape).]

pan·tof·fle (păn-tŏf′əl, -tō′fəl, -tōo′fəl, păn′tə-fəl) *n.* Also **pan·to·fle.** A slipper. [Middle English *pantufle,* from Old French *pantoufle,* from Old Italian *pantofola,* possibly from Medieval Greek *pantophellos,* "all cork" (of which medieval slippers were made) : *pas* (stem *pant-*), PAN- + *phellos†,* cork, cork oak.]

pan·to·graph (păn′tə-grăf′, -gräf′) *n.* **1.** An instrument for copying a plane figure to any desired scale. It consists of styluses for tracing and copying, mounted on four jointed rods in the form of a parallelogram with extended sides. **2.** Any similarly linked framework, such as a power-collecting trolley on an electric locomotive or an extensible telephone arm. [French *pantographe* : *panto-,* variant of PAN- + -GRAPH.] —**pan′to·graph′ic, pan′to·graph′i·cal** *adj.* —**pan′to·graph′i·cal·ly** *adv.* —**pan·tog′ra·phy** (păn-tŏg′rə-fē) *n.*

pan·to·mime (păn′tə-mīm′) *n.* **1. a.** A genre of theatrical performance invented in Rome in the reign of Augustus, in which one actor played all the parts in dumb show, with music and singing in the background. **b.** The actor in this genre. **c.** Any of various revivals or derivatives of this genre. **2.** *British.* A genre of musical plays for children, usually based on fairy stories, having specific conventions, especially farcical, deriving from the commedia dell'arte. **3.** Acting that consists mostly of gesture, as in grand opera. **4.** Dumb show used for expressive communication. Also called "mime." —*v.* **pantomimed, -miming, -mimes.** —*tr.* To represent by pantomime. —*intr.* To express oneself in pantomime. [Latin *pantomīmus,* "the complete mime" : Greek *pas* (stem *pant-*), PAN- + *mimos,* MIME.] —**pan′to·mim′ic** (păn′tə-mĭm′ĭk), **pan′to·mim′i·cal** *adj.* —**pan′to·mim′ist** (păn′tə-mī′mĭst) *n.*

pan·to·then·ic acid (păn′tə-thĕn′ĭk). A component of the vitamin B complex, $C_9H_{17}NO_5$, common in liver but found in all living tissue. [From Greek *pantothen,* from all sides, from *pan,* all. See **pan-**.]

pan·toum (păn-tōom′) *n.* A verse form consisting of quatrains in which the second and fourth lines are repeated as the first and third lines of the following quatrain, and in which the final line of the poem repeats the opening line. [French, from Malay *pantūn.*]

pan·try (păn′trē) *n., pl.* **-tries.** A small room or closet, usually off a kitchen, where food, china, silver, linens, and the like are stored. [Middle English *pantrie,* from Old French *paneterie,* bread closet, from *panetier,* servant in charge of the bread, from *pan,* bread, from Latin *panis.* See **pa-** in Appendix.*]

pants (pănts) *pl.n.* **1.** A pair of trousers. **2.** A pair of underpants. [Short for *pantaloons,* plural of PANTALOON.]

pant·y. Variant of **pantie.**

pant·y·waist (păn′tē-wāst′) *n.* **1.** Formerly, a child's undergarment consisting of a shirt and pants buttoned together at the waist. **2.** *Slang.* A weak, effeminate man.

Pan·za, Sancho. See **Sancho Panza.**

pan·zer (păn′zər; German pän′tsər) *adj.* **1.** Protected by armor; armored. **2.** Using or equipped with armored or mechanized units: *a panzer division.* —*n.* *Capital* **P.** An armored tank. [German *Panzer,* armor, from Middle High German *Panzier,* from Old French *pancier,* body-armor, from *panse,* body, from Vulgar Latin *pantica* (unattested), variant of Latin *pantex,* PAUNCH.]

Pao·ki (pou′kē′). A commercial and industrial city of north-central China, on the Wei River. Population, 180,000.

Pao·ting (bou′dĭng′). Formerly **Tsing·yuan** (chĭng′yōo-än′). A city in northeastern China, about 90 miles southwest of Tientsin. Population, 250,000.

Pao·tow (bou′tō′). Also **Pao·tou.** An industrial city of northern China, in central Inner Mongolia. Population, 490,000.

pap[1] (păp) *n.* **1.** *Archaic.* A teat or nipple. **2.** Something resembling a nipple. [Middle English *pappe* (imitative). See **pap-**[1] in Appendix.*]

pap[2] (păp) *n.* **1.** Soft or semiliquid food, as for infants. **2.** Something lacking real value or substance and considered to be unsuitable for the minds of adults. **3.** *Slang.* Money and favors obtained as political patronage: *"uncouth, self-seeking politicians primarily interested in patronage, privilege, and pap"* (Fiorello LaGuardia). [Middle English *pape*, probably from Latin *pappa*, baby talk for food. See **pap-**[2] in Appendix.*]

pa·pa (pä′pə, pə-pä′) *n.* Father. Used especially by children. [French, from Old French *papa*. See **papa** in Appendix.*]

pa·pa·cy (pā′pə-sē) *n., pl.* **-cies.** **1.** The office and jurisdiction of a pope. **2.** The period of time during which a pope is in office. **3.** *Capital* **P.** The system of church government headed by the pope. [Middle English *papacie*, from Medieval Latin *pāpātia*, from Late Latin *pāpa*, POPE.]

pa·pa·in (pə-pā′ĭn, -pī′ən) *n.* An enzyme capable of digesting protein, obtained from the unripe fruit of the papaya and used as a meat tenderizer, and in medicine as a protein digestant. [From PAPAYA.]

pa·pal (pā′pəl) *adj.* **1.** Of, pertaining to, or issued by the pope: *a papal bull.* **2.** Of or pertaining to the papacy: *papal succession.* **3.** Of or pertaining to the Roman Catholic Church. [Middle English, from Old French, from Medieval Latin *pāpālis*, from Late Latin *pāpa*, POPE.] **—pa′pal·ly** *adv.*

Pa·pal States (pā′pəl). The territories in central Italy ruled by the popes until 1870. Also called "States of the Church."

Pa·pa·ni·co·laou's test (pä′pə-nē′kə-louz′). *Medicine.* A **Pap test** *(see).*

pa·pav·er·ine (pə-păv′ə-rēn′, -rĭn) *n.* Also **pa·pav·er·in** (pə-păv′ə-rĭn). A nonaddictive opium derivative, $C_{20}H_{21}NO_4$, used medicinally as an antispasmodic. [From New Latin *Papaver* (genus name), from Latin *papāver*, POPPY.]

pa·paw (pô′pô′) *n.* Also **paw·paw.** **1.** A tree, *Asimina triloba*, of central North America, having small, fleshy, edible fruit. **2.** The fruit of this tree. Also called "custard apple." [Probably from Spanish *papaya*, PAPAYA.]

pa·pa·ya (pə-pä′yə) *n.* **1.** An evergreen tropical American tree, *Carica papaya*, bearing large, yellow, edible fruit. **2.** The fruit of this tree. [Spanish, from Cariban.]

Pa·pe·e·te (pä′pā-ā′tā, pə-pē′tē). The capital of French Polynesia, on the northwestern coast of Tahiti. Population, 20,000.

pa·per (pā′pər) *n.* **1.** A thin sheet material made of cellulose pulp, derived mainly from wood, rags, and certain grasses, processed into flexible leaves or rolls by deposit from an aqueous suspension, and used chiefly for writing, printing, drawing, wrapping, and covering walls. **2.** A single sheet or leaf of this material. **3.** One or more sheets of this material, bearing writing or printing, as: **a.** An official document. **b.** An essay, treatise, or scholarly dissertation. **c.** An examination, report, theme, or other written academic assignment. **d.** A newspaper. **4.** *Plural.* A collection of letters, diaries, and other writings, especially those produced by one person: *the Madison papers.* **5.** *Plural.* Documents establishing the identity of the bearer. **6.** *Plural.* **Ship's papers** *(see).* **7.** A negotiable note, such as a bill, check, or letter of credit; a commercial paper. **8.** *Slang.* **a.** A free pass to a theater. **b.** The audience admitted with free passes. **—on paper.** **1.** In writing or print. **2.** In theory, as distinguished from actual performance or fact: *a good team on paper, but the members really don't play well together.* *—tr.v.* **papered, -pering, -pers.** **1.** To wrap or cover in paper. **2.** To supply with paper. **3.** To cover with wallpaper. **4.** *Slang.* To issue free passes for (a theater, for example). *—adj.* **1.** Made of paper. **2.** Resembling paper in thinness or flimsiness. **3.** Existing only in printed or written form; planned but not realized; theoretical: *paper profits.* [Middle English *papir*, from Old French *papier*, from Latin *papȳrus*, paper, from Greek *papuros*, PAPYRUS.] **—pa′per·er** *n.* **—pa′per·y** *adj.*

pa·per·back (pā′pər-băk′) *n.* A book having a flexible paper binding. **—pa′per·back′, pa′per·backed′** *adj.*

paper birch. A North American birch tree, *Betula papyrifera*, having paperlike white bark used to make baskets, toy canoes, and other articles. Also called "canoe birch," "white birch."

pa·per·board (pā′pər-bôrd′, -bōrd′) *n.* Cardboard; pasteboard.

pa·per·bound (pā′pər-bound′) *adj.* Bound in paper; paperback.

pa·per·hang·er (pā′pər-hăng′ər) *n.* A person whose occupation is covering or decorating walls with wallpaper; paperer. **—pa′per·hang′ing** *n.*

pa·per·knife (pā′pər-nīf′) *n., pl.* **-knives** (-nīvz′). A thin, dull knife used for opening sealed envelopes, slitting uncut pages of books, and creasing paper.

paper mulberry. A shade tree, *Broussonetia papyrifera*, native to Asia, having bark that can be processed into a paperlike fabric. See **tapa.**

paper nautilus. A marine mollusk, *Argonauta argo*, having a paper-thin spiral shell. Also called "argonaut."

paper wasp. Any wasp, such as a hornet, that builds paperlike nests.

pa·per·weight (pā′pər-wāt′) *n.* A small heavy object made of glass, metal, or the like and often decorative, placed on top of loose papers to keep them in place.

pa·per·work (pā′pər-wûrk′) *n.* Also **paper work.** Work involving the handling of reports, letters, forms, and the like.

pap·e·terie (păp′ə-trē; *French* pȧp-trē′) *n.* A box used to hold paper and other writing materials. [French, stationery box, from *papier*, paper, from Old French, PAPER.]

pa·pier-mâ·ché (pā′pər-mə-shā′; *French* pȧ-pyā′mä-shā′) *n.* A material made from paper pulp or shreds of paper mixed with glue or paste, that can be molded into various shapes when wet and that becomes hard and suitable for painting and varnishing when dry. [French, "chewed paper" : *papier*, paper, from Old French, PAPER + past participle of *mâcher*, to chew, from Old French, from Late Latin *masticāre*, to MASTICATE.] **—pa′pier-mâ·ché** *adj.*

pa·pil·la (pə-pĭl′ə) *n., pl.* **-pillae** (-pĭl′ē). *Biology.* Any small, nipplelike projection, such as a protuberance on the top of the tongue, at the root of a hair, or at the base of a developing tooth. [New Latin, from Latin, nipple, diminutive of *papula*, pimple. See **pap-**[1] in Appendix.*] **—pap′il·lar′y** (păp′ə-lĕr′ē, pə-pĭl′ə-rē) *adj.* **—pap′il·late′** (păp′ə-lāt′, pə-pĭl′ĭt) *adj.* **—pap·il·lose** (păp′ə-lōs′, pə-pĭl′ōs′) *adj.*

pap·il·lo·ma (păp′ə-lō′mə) *n., pl.* **-mata** (-mə-tə) or **-mas.** A small, benign epithelial tumor in the breast, intestine, mucous membrane, or skin, seen as an overgrowth of cells on a core of smooth connective tissue. [PAPILL(A) + -OMA.]

pap·il·lon (păp′ə-lŏn′; *French* pȧ-pē-yôɴ′) *n.* A toy spaniel of a breed originating in Europe, having long, fringed ears and a plumed tail. [French, "butterfly" (from the shape of its ears), from Latin *pāpiliō*†.]

pap·il·lote (păp′ə-lōt′; *French* pȧ-pē-yôt′) *n.* **1.** A frilled paper cover used to decorate the bone end of a cooked chop or cutlet. **2.** Oiled parchment in which certain foods are baked. [French, from *papillon*, butterfly. See **papillon.**]

pa·pist (pā′pĭst) *n.* A Roman Catholic. Usually used disparagingly. [French *papiste*, from *pape*, pope, from Late Latin *pāpa*, POPE.] **—pa·pis′ti·cal** *adj.* **—pa′pi·stry** *n.*

pa·poose (pă-po͞os′, pə-) *n.* Also **pap·poose.** A North American Indian infant or young child. [Algonquian *papoos.*]

pa·poose-root (pă-po͞os′ro͞ot′, -ro͝ot′) *n.* A plant, the **blue cohosh** *(see).*

pap·pus (păp′əs) *n., pl.* **pap·pi** (păp′ī′). A tuft of bristles, or a similar structure, surmounting the **achene** *(see)* of certain plants, such as dandelions and thistles. [Latin, from Greek *pappos*, grandfather, hence pappus (compare **old man's beard**). See **papa** in Appendix.*] **—pap′pose′** (păp′ōs′), **pap′pous** (păp′əs) *adj.*

pap·py[1] (păp′ē) *adj.* **-pier, -piest.** Of or like pap; mushy; pulpy.

pap·py[2] (păp′ē) *n., pl.* **-pies.** Father. [Diminutive of PAPA.]

pa·pri·ka (pă-prē′kə, pə-, păp′rĭ-kə) *n.* **1.** A mild, powdered seasoning made from sweet red peppers. **2.** Dark to deep or vivid reddish orange. See **color.** [Hungarian, from Serbian, from *papar*, pepper, from Greek *peperi*, PEPPER.]

Pap. Ter. Territory of Papua.

Pap test (păp). A test in which a smear of a bodily secretion, especially from the cervix or vagina, is immediately fixed and examined for exfoliated cells to detect cancer in an early stage or to evaluate hormonal condition. Also called "Pap smear," "Papanicolaou's test." [Invented by George *Papanicolaou* (1883–1962), American scientist.]

Pap·u·a, Territory of (păp′yo͞o-ə). *Abbr.* **Pap. Ter.** Formerly **British New Guin·ea** (gĭn′ē). A trust territory of the United Nations, 90,600 square miles in area, administered by Australia and comprising the southeastern section of New Guinea. Population, 562,000. Capital, Port Moresby.

Pap·u·a and New Guin·ea, Territory of (păp′yo͞o-ə; gĭn′ē). The eastern half of New Guinea, 183,000 square miles in area, comprising the Territory of Papua, the Trust Territory of New Guinea, and adjacent islands, and administered by Australia. Population, 1,101,000. Capital, Port Moresby.

Pap·u·an (păp′yo͞o-ən) *n.* **1.** A native or inhabitant of New Guinea. **2.** A member of a subgroup of an Oceanic Negroid people of Melanesia. **3.** Any of numerous languages of New Guinea.

pap·ule (păp′yo͞ol) *n.* Also **pap·u·la** (păp′yə-lə) *pl.* **-lae** (-lē). *Pathology.* A small, inflammatory, congested spot on the skin; pimple. [Latin *papula*, pimple. See **pap-**[1] in Appendix.*] **—pap′u·lar** (-yə-lər), **pap′u·lif′er·ous** (-yə-lĭf′ər-əs) *adj.*

pa·py·rus (pə-pī′rəs) *n., pl.* **-ruses** or **-ri** (-rī′). **1.** A tall aquatic sedge, *Cyperus papyrus*, of southern Europe and northern Africa. **2.** A kind of paper made from the pith or the stems of this plant, used in antiquity as a writing material. **3.** A document written on this paper: *the Oxyrhynchus papyri.* [Middle English *papirus*, paper, from Latin *papȳrus*, from Greek *papuros*†. See also **paper.**]

par (pär) *n.* **1.** An accepted average; normal standard: *up to par.* **2.** An equality of status, level, or value; equal footing: *on a par.* **3.** *Finance.* **a.** The established face value of a monetary unit expressed in terms of a monetary unit of another country using the same metal standard. **b.** A condition of equality between the face value of a stock, bond, or other negotiable instrument and its current market value: *sell at par.* **4.** *Golf.* The number of strokes considered necessary to complete a hole or course in expert play. *—adj.* **1.** Equal to the standard; normal. **2.** *Finance.* Of or pertaining to face value. [Latin *par*, equal. See **perə-** in Appendix.*]

PAR Airport code for Paris, France.

par. **1.** paragraph. **2.** parallel. **3.** parenthesis. **4.** parish.

par·a[1] (păr′ə) *adj. Chemistry.* Of, pertaining to, or designating positions in a benzene ring separated by two carbon atoms. **2.** *Physics.* Designating a diatomic molecule in which the nuclei have opposite spin directions. [From PARA- (isomeric to).]

pa·ra[2] (pä-rä′, pä′rä) *n.* A monetary unit equal to $1/100$ of the dinar of Yugoslavia. See table of exchange rates at **currency.** [Serbo-Croatian, from Turkish, from Persian *parāh*, "piece"†.]

Pa·rá (pə-rä′). **1.** A state of northern Brazil, 170,750 square

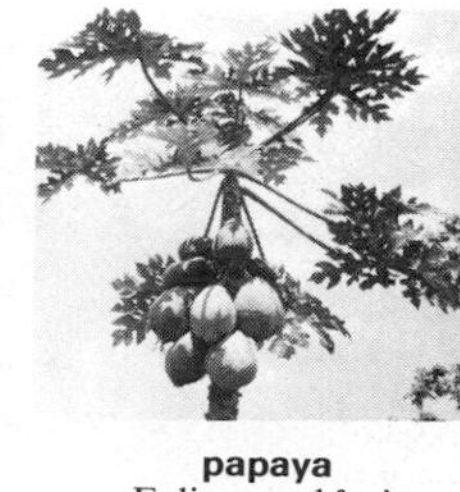

papaya
Foliage and fruit

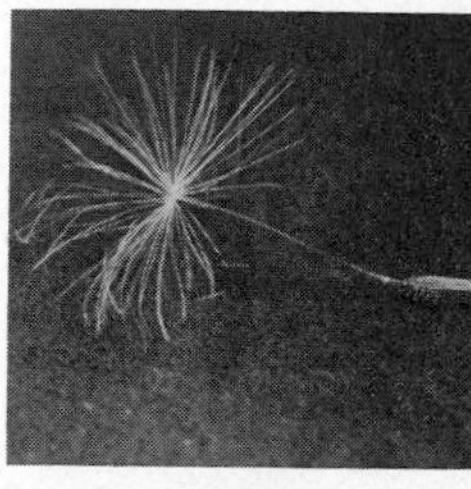

pappus
Pappus of dandelion, with achene

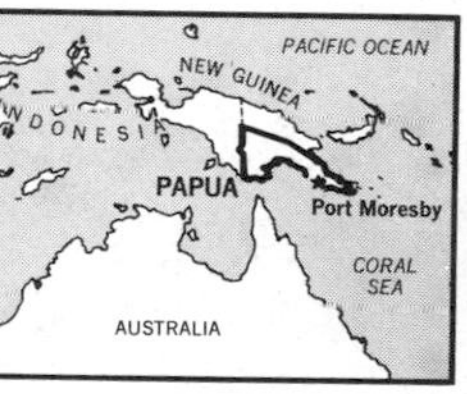

Papua

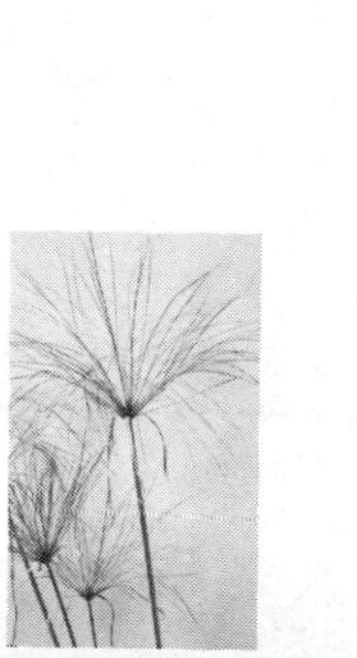

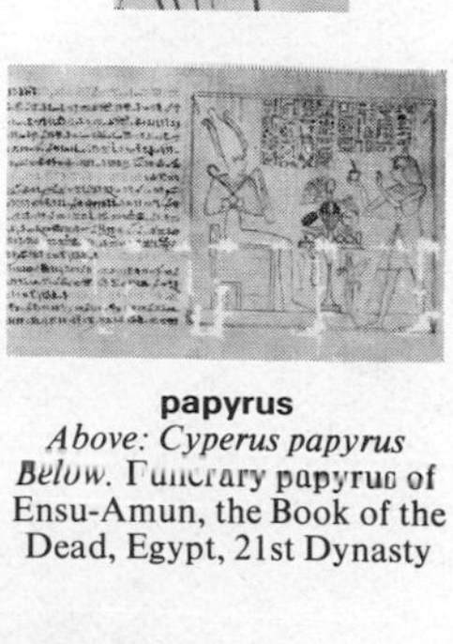

papyrus
Above: Cyperus papyrus
Below. Funerary papyrus of Ensu-Amun, the Book of the Dead, Egypt, 21st Dynasty

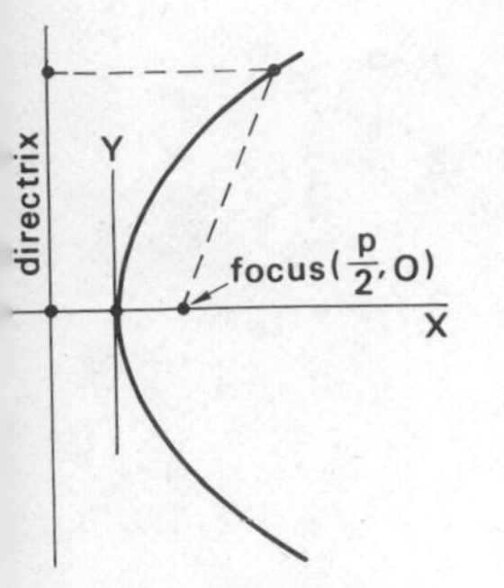

parabola
Dashed lines, from focus and directrix to any point on parabola, are equal. Equation of parabola is $y^2 = 2px$

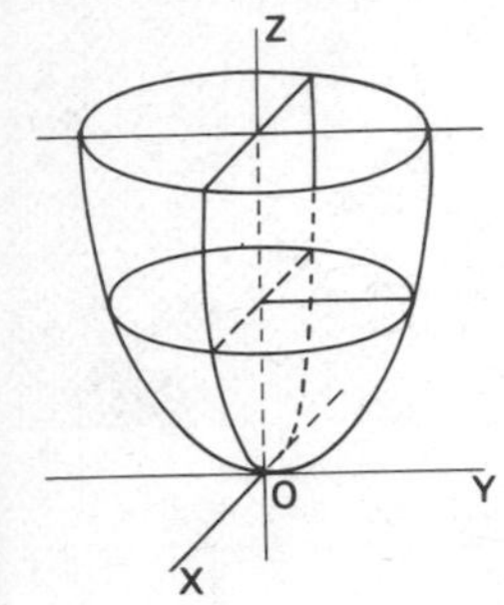

paraboloid
Equation of paraboloid shown is $\frac{x^2}{a^2} + \frac{y^2}{b^2} = 2cz$, where *a*, *b*, and *c* are constants

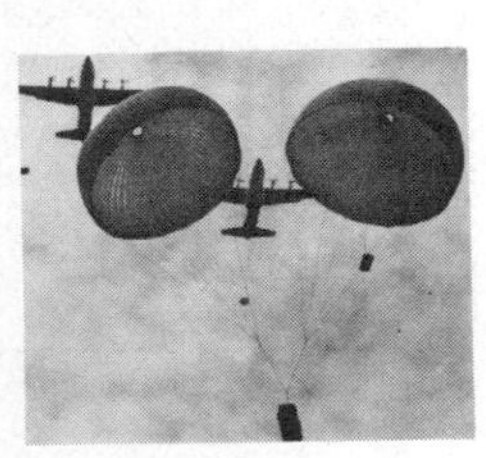

parachute

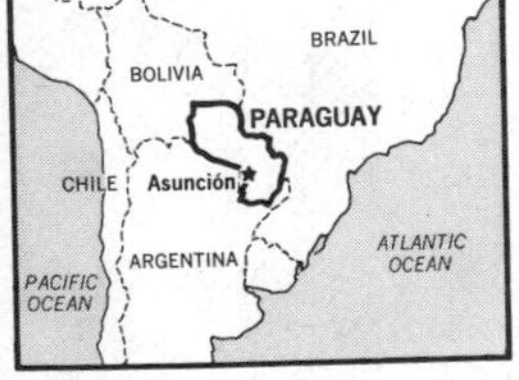

Paraguay

miles in area. Population, 1,551,000. Capital, Belém. **2.** The navigable eastern distributary of the Amazon River delta, flowing 200 miles northeast to the Atlantic Ocean.

para–¹, par–. Indicates: **1.** Alongside; for example, **paragenesis.** **2.** Near or beside; for example, **parathyroid gland.** **3.** Beyond; for example, **paranormal.** **4.** Incorrectly; for example, **paresthesia.** **5.** Resembling or similar to; for example, **parablast, paratyphoid fever.** **6.** Subsidiary to; for example **paramorph.** **7.** Isomeric to or polymeric to; for example, **paraldehyde.** [In borrowed Greek compounds, *para-* indicates: 1. Beside, to the side of, alongside, as in **paradigm, Paraclete.** 2. Beyond, as in **paradox.** 3. Wrongly, harmfully, unfavorably, as in **paralysis.** 4. Among, as in **parallax.** *Para-* is the preverbal form of the preposition *para,* beside, for. See **per¹** in Appendix.*]

para–². Indicates parachute; for example, **paratroops.** [From PARACHUTE.]

Para. Paraguay.

par·a·bi·o·sis (păr'ə-bī-ō'sĭs) *n. Biology.* The natural or artificial fusion of two organisms, as in the development of Siamese twins or the experimental joining of animals for research. —**par'a·bi·ot'ic** (-bī-ŏt'ĭk) *adj.* —**par'a·bi·ot'i·cal·ly** *adv.*

par·a·blast (păr'ə-blăst') *n. Embryology.* The food yolk of a meroblastic egg. [PARA- (resembling) + -BLAST.] —**par'a·blas'tic** *adj.*

par·a·ble (păr'ə-bəl) *n.* A simple story illustrating a moral or religious lesson. [Middle English, from Old French *parabole,* from Late Latin *parabola,* from Greek *parabolē,* juxtaposition, comparison, parable, from *paraballein,* to set beside : *para,* beside + *ballein,* to throw (see **gwel-¹** in Appendix*).]

pa·rab·o·la (pə-răb'ə-lə) *n. Geometry.* A plane curve formed by: **a.** A conic section taken parallel to an element of the intersected cone. **b.** The locus of points equidistant from a fixed line and a fixed point not on the line. [New Latin, from Greek *parabolē,* juxtaposition, parallelism (see **parable**); refers to the parallelism of the plane section containing the parabola and an element in the conical surface.]

par·a·bol·ic (păr'ə-bŏl'ĭk) *adj.* Also **par·a·bol·i·cal** (-ĭ-kəl). **1.** Of or like a parable. **2.** Of or having the form of a parabola. —**par'a·bol'i·cal·ly** *adv.*

pa·rab·o·loid (pə-răb'ə-loid') *n. Geometry.* A surface having parabolic sections parallel to a single coordinate axis, such as a paraboloid of revolution. [PARABOL(A) + -OID.] —**pa·rab'o·loi'dal** (pə-răb'ə-loid'l) *adj.*

paraboloid of revolution. *Geometry.* An elliptic paraboloid formed by revolving a parabola about its own axis.

Par·a·cel·sus (păr'ə-sĕl'səs), **Philippus Aureolus.** Original name, Theophrastus Bombastus von Hohenheim. 1493–1541. Swiss alchemist and physician; wrote on medicine.

par·a·chute (păr'ə-shōōt') *n.* **1.** An apparatus used to retard free fall from an aircraft, consisting of a hemispherical canopy attached by conically arrayed cords to a harness and worn or stored folded until deployed in descent. **2.** Any of various similar unpowered devices for retarding free-speeding or free-falling motion. **3.** A membranous, winglike extension between the limbs of flying squirrels and certain lizards; a patagium. —*v.* **parachuted, -chuting, -chutes.** —*tr.* To drop (supplies, for example) by means of a parachute. —*intr.* To descend by means of a parachute. [French : *para-,* "protecting against," "preventing," extracted from *parasol,* PARASOL + *chute,* fall, CHUTE.] —**par'a·chut'ist** *n.*

Par·a·clete (păr'ə-klēt') *n.* The Holy Ghost. [Middle English *Paraclit,* from Old French *Paraclet,* from Late Latin *Paraclētus,* from Greek *Paraklētos,* "the Comforter," advocate, "one called to help," from *parakalein,* to call to help : *para,* to the side of + *kalein,* to call (see **kel-³** in Appendix*).]

pa·rade (pə-rād') *n.* **1. a.** A public procession on some festive or ceremonial occasion. **b.** The occasion or action of making such a procession. **c.** The event itself, or the persons involved: *the Easter parade.* **d.** An assembly or congregation, as of strollers. **2. a.** A ceremonial review of troops. **b.** The troops taking part in such a review. **c.** The place of assembly for a review of troops. In this sense, also called "parade ground." **3.** A succession: *the parade of fads and styles.* **4.** A movement deriving momentum and strength from the increasing popularity of its approach to some political issue; bandwagon. **5.** An ostentatious show; a pompous display: *make a parade of humanitarian zeal.* **6.** A public square or promenade. —*v.* **paraded, -rading, -rades.** —*tr.* **1.** *Military.* To assemble (troops) for a formal display or review. **2.** To march or walk through or around. **3.** To exhibit ostentatiously; flaunt. —*intr.* **1.** *Military.* To assemble for a formal review. **2.** To take part in a parade. **3.** To promenade in a public place. —See Synonyms at **show.** [French, from Italian *parata,* from Vulgar Latin *parāta* (unattested), "a making ready," from Latin *parāre,* to prepare. See **per-⁴** in Appendix.*] —**pa·rad'er** *n.*

parade rest. *Military.* **1.** A formal position of alert rest in which soldiers assume a prescribed stance without talking or moving. **2.** The command to assume this position.

par·a·digm (păr'ə-dĭm', -dīm') *n.* **1.** A list of all the inflectional forms of a word taken as an illustrative example of the conjugation or declension to which it belongs. **2.** Any example or model. [Late Latin *paradīgma,* from Greek *paradeigma,* model, from *paradeiknunai,* to compare, exhibit : *para,* alongside + *deiknunai,* to show (see **deik-** in Appendix*).] —**par'a·dig·mat'ic** (păr'ə-dĭg-măt'ĭk) *adj.*

par·a·dise (păr'ə-dīs', -dīz') *n.* **1.** *Often capital* **P.** The Garden of Eden. **2.** *Theology.* **a.** Heaven, the abode of righteous souls after death. **b.** An intermediate resting place for righteous souls awaiting the Resurrection. **3.** Any place of ideal beauty or loveliness. **4.** A state of delight. [Middle English *paradis,* from Old French, from Late Latin *paradīsus,* from Greek *paradeisos,* garden, park, paradise, from Avestan *pairi-daēza,* circumvallation, walled-in park : *pairi,* around (see **per¹** in Appendix*) + *daēza,* wall (see **dheigh-** in Appendix*).] —**par'a·di·si'a·cal** (păr'ə-dĭ-sī'ə-kəl, -zī'ə-kəl), **par'a·di·sa'i·cal** (-dĭ-sā'ĭ-kəl, -zā'ĭ-kəl) *adj.* —**par'a·di·si'a·cal·ly, par'a·di·sa'i·cal·ly** *adv.*

par·a·dox (păr'ə-dŏks') *n., pl.* **-doxes.** **1.** A seemingly contradictory statement that may nonetheless be true. **2.** A person, situation, or action exhibiting inexplicable or contradictory aspects. **3.** An assertion that is essentially self-contradictory, although based on a valid deduction from acceptable premises. **4.** A statement contrary to received opinion. [Latin *paradoxum,* from Greek *paradoxon,* from *paradoxos,* incredible, conflicting with expectation : *para,* beyond + *doxa,* opinion, from *dokein,* to think (see **dek-¹** in Appendix*).] —**par'a·dox'i·cal** *adj.* —**par'a·dox'i·cal·ly** *adv.* —**par'a·dox'i·cal·ness** *n.*

par·a·drop (păr'ə-drŏp') *n. Military.* The delivery of supplies to a place by parachute. —*tr.v.* **paradropped, -dropping, -drops.** To deliver (something) by parachute.

par·aes·the·sia. Variant of **paresthesia.**

par·af·fin (păr'ə-fĭn) *n.* **1.** *Chemistry.* A waxy, white or colorless, solid hydrocarbon mixture used to make candles, wax paper, lubricants, and sealing materials. Also called "paraffin wax." **2.** *Chemistry.* Any member of the **paraffin series** *(see).* **3.** *British.* **Kerosene** *(see).* —*tr.v.* **paraffined, -fining, -fins.** To saturate, treat, or coat with paraffin. [German *Paraffin* : Latin *parum,* too little (see **pau-** in Appendix*) + *affinis,* neighboring (see **affinity**); from its lack of affinity to other materials.] —**par'af·fin'ic** *adj.*

paraffin series. *Chemistry.* A homologous group of saturated aliphatic hydrocarbons having the general formula C_nH_{2n+2}, the simplest and most abundant of which is methane. Also called "methane series," "alkane series."

par·a·form·al·de·hyde (păr'ə-fôr-măl'də-hīd') *n.* A white solid polymer of formaldehyde, $(HCHO)_n$, where *n* is at least 6, used as a disinfectant, a fumigant, and a fungicide.

par·a·gen·e·sis (păr'ə-jĕn'ə-sĭs) *n.* Also **par·a·ge·ne·sia** (păr'ə-jə-nē'zhə, -zhē-ə). *Geology.* The successive order in which a formation of associated minerals is generated. [PARA- (alongside) + -GENESIS.] —**par'a·ge·net'ic** (-jə-nĕt'ĭk) *adj.*

par·a·gon (păr'ə-gŏn', -gən) *n.* **1.** A model or pattern of excellence or perfection of a kind; peerless example: *the paragon of virtue.* **2. a.** An unflawed diamond weighing at least 100 carats. **b.** A very large spherical pearl. **3.** *Printing.* A type size of 20 points. [Obsolete French, from Italian *paragone,* comparison, touchstone, from Medieval Greek *parakonē,* whetstone, from Greek *parakonan,* to sharpen against, to compare : *para,* alongside + *akonan,* to sharpen, from *akonē,* whetstone, from *akē,* point (see **ak-** in Appendix*).]

par·a·graph (păr'ə-grăf', -gräf') *n. Abbr.* **par.** **1.** A distinct division of a written work or composition that expresses some thought or point relevant to the whole but is complete in itself, and may consist of a single sentence or several sentences. **2.** A mark (¶) used to indicate where a new paragraph should begin or to serve as a reference mark. **3.** A brief article, notice, or announcement, as in a newspaper. —*tr.v.* **paragraphed, -graphing, -graphs.** *Abbr.* **par.** To divide or arrange in paragraphs. [Medieval Latin *paragraphus,* sign marking a new section of writing, from Greek *paragraphos,* line to mark exchange in dialogue, from *paragraphein,* to write beside : *para,* beside + *graphein,* to write (see **gerebh-** in Appendix*).] —**par'a·graph'ic, par'a·graph'i·cal** *adj.*

Par·a·guay (păr'ə-gwī', -gwā'; *Spanish* pä'rä-gwī'). **1.** *Abbr.* **Para.** A republic of central South America, 157,000 square miles in area. Population, 1,817,000. Capital, Asunción. **2.** A river rising in southwestern Brazil and flowing 1,500 miles south to join the Paraná in southwestern Paraguay. —**Par'a·guay'an** (păr'ə-gwī'ən, -gwā'ən) *adj.* & *n.*

Paraguay tea. A tree, **maté** *(see),* or the beverage made from its leaves.

Pa·ra·í·ba (pä'rä-ē'bä). Formerly **Pa·ra·hi·ba, Pa·ra·hy·ba.** **1.** A state of northeastern Brazil, 21,700 square miles in area. Population, 2,177,000. Capital, João Pessoa. **2.** Also **Paraíba do Nor·te** (dōō nôr'tē). A river rising in northeastern Brazil and flowing 240 miles northeast to the Atlantic Ocean. **3.** Also **Paraíba do Sul** (dōō sōōl'). A river rising in southeastern Brazil and flowing 660 miles northeast to the Atlantic.

par·a·keet (păr'ə-kēt') *n.* Also **par·ra·keet, par·a·quet** (-kĕt'), **par·o·quet, par·ro·ket, par·ro·quet** (-kĕt'). Any of various small parrots, usually having long, tapering tails. [Old French *paroquet,* possibly a pet form of *Pierre,* from Latin *Petrus,* PETER.]

par·al·de·hyde (pă-răl'də-hīd') *n.* A colorless aromatic liquid polymer, $C_6H_{12}O_3$, of acetaldehyde, used as a solvent and as a sedative. [PAR(A)- + (ACET)ALDEHYDE.]

par·al·lax (păr'ə-lăks') *n.* An apparent change in the direction of an object, caused by a change in observational position that provides a new line of sight. [French *parallaxe,* from Greek *parallaxis,* change of position, parallax, from *parallassein,* to change : *para,* among + *allassein,* to exchange, from *allos,* other (see **al-¹** in Appendix*).] —**par'al·lac'tic** (păr'ə-lăk'tĭk) *adj.*

par·al·lel (păr'ə-lĕl') *adj. Abbr.* **par.** **1.** Being an equal distance apart at every point. **2.** *Geometry.* **a.** Designating two or more straight coplanar lines that do not intersect. Compare **skew.** **b.** Designating two or more planes that do not intersect. **c.** Designating a line and a plane that do not intersect. **d.** Designating curves or surfaces everywhere equidistant. **3. a.** Having com-

parable parts, analogous aspects, or readily recognized similarities. **b.** Having the same tendency or direction. **4.** *Grammar.* Containing or characterized by corresponding syntactical forms or constructions. **5.** *Music.* Moving consistently by the same intervals. Said of two or more melodies. **6.** *Electricity.* Designating a circuit or part of a circuit connected in parallel. —*adv.* In a parallel relationship or manner. —*n. Abbr.* **par. 1.** A surface or line that is equidistant from another. **2.** *Geometry.* One of a set of parallel geometric figures, usually lines. **3. a.** Anything that closely resembles or is analogous to something else. **b.** A comparison indicating likeness or analogy. See Usage note below. **4.** The condition of being parallel; near similarity or exact agreement in particulars. **5.** *Geography.* Any of the imaginary lines representing degrees of latitude, encircling the earth parallel to the plane of the equator. **6.** *Printing.* A sign indicating material referred to in a note or reference. **7.** *Electricity.* A configuration of two or more two-terminal components connected between two points in a circuit with one terminal of each connected to one of the two points. Used chiefly in the phrase *in parallel.* —*tr.v.* **paralleled, -leling, -lels.** Also *chiefly British* **-lelled, -lelling. 1.** To make or place parallel to. **2.** To be or extend parallel to. **3.** To be similar or analogous to. **4.** To be or provide an equal or match for. **5.** To show to be analogous; compare or liken. [Latin *parallēlus,* from Greek *parallēlos : para,* beside + *allēlon,* of one another, from *allos,* other (see **al-¹** in Appendix*).]
Usage: As an adjective, *parallel* is followed by *to* (when it takes a preposition). As a noun in the figurative senses of likeness or comparison, it can be followed by *between* or *with.*

par·al·lel·e·ped (păr′ə-lĕl′ə-pī′pĭd, -pĭp′ĭd) *n.* Also **par·al·lel·o·pi·ped.** A solid with six faces, each a parallelogram. [Greek *parallēlepipedon : parallēlos,* PARALLEL + *epipedon,* plane surface, from *epipedos,* level : *epi,* on + *pedon,* ground (see **ped-¹** in Appendix*).]

par·al·lel·ism (păr′ə-lĕl-ĭz′əm) *n.* **1.** The state or position of being parallel; a parallel relationship. **2.** Likeness, correspondence, or similarity in aspect, course, or tendency. **3.** *Grammar.* **a.** The use of corresponding syntactical forms. **b.** An instance of this. **4.** *Philosophy.* The doctrine that to every mental change there corresponds a concomitant, but causally unconnected, physical alteration.

par·al·lel·o·gram (păr′ə-lĕl′ə-grăm) *n.* A four-sided plane figure with opposite sides parallel. [Late Latin *parallēlogrammum,* from Greek *parallēlogrammon,* from *parallēlogrammos,* bounded by parallel lines : *parallēlos,* PARALLEL + *grammē,* line (see **gerebh-** in Appendix*).]

pa·ral·o·gism (pə-răl′ə-jĭz′əm) *n. Logic.* Fallacious or illogical reasoning; especially, a faulty argument of whose fallacy the reasoner is not aware. [French *paralogisme,* from Late Latin *paralogismus,* from Greek *paralogismos,* from *paralogos,* unexpected, beyond calculation : *para,* beyond + *logos,* word (see **leg-¹** in Appendix*).] —**pa·ral′o·gist** *n.* —**pa·ral′o·gis′tic** *adj.*

pa·ral·y·sis (pə-răl′ĭ-sĭs) *n., pl.* **-ses** (-sēz′). **1.** Loss or impairment of the ability to move or have sensation in a bodily part as a result of injury to or disease of its nerve supply. **2.** Partial or complete inability to move or function; stoppage or impairment of activity. [Latin, from Greek *paralusis,* from *paraluein,* to loosen, disable : *para,* "unfavorably" + *luein,* to release (see **leu-¹** in Appendix*).] —**par′a·lyt′ic** (păr′ə-lĭt′ĭk) *adj. & n.*

paralysis ag·i·tans (ăj′ə-tănz′). Parkinson's disease *(see).* [New Latin, "shaking palsy."]

par·a·lyze (păr′ə-līz′) *tr.v.* **-lyzed, -lyzing, -lyzes. 1.** To affect with paralysis; cause to be paralytic. **2.** To make (as by emotion or fear) helpless or unable to move. **3.** To impair the progress or functioning of; make inoperative or powerless. [French *paralyser,* from *paralysie,* paralysis, from Latin *paralysis,* PARALYSIS.] —**par′a·ly·za′tion** *n.* —**par′a·lyz′er** *n.*

par·a·mag·net (păr′ə-măg′nĭt) *n.* A paramagnetic substance.

par·a·mag·net·ic (păr′ə-măg-nĕt′ĭk) *adj. Physics.* Pertaining to or denoting a substance in which an induced magnetic field is in the same direction as, and greater in strength than, the magnetizing field, but much weaker than in ferromagnetic materials. —**par′a·mag′net·ism′** (-nə-tĭz′əm) *n.*

Par·a·mar·i·bo (păr′ə-măr′ə-bō′) *n.* The capital and principal seaport of Surinam, on the Atlantic Ocean at the mouth of the Suriname River. Population, 123,000.

par·a·mat·ta (păr′ə-măt′ə) *n.* Also **par·ra·mat·ta.** A soft, light, dress fabric woven with a cotton warp and a silk or wool filling. [First made in *Parramatta,* Australia.]

par·a·me·ci·um (păr′ə-mē′shē-əm, -sē-əm) *n., pl.* **-cia** (-shē-ə, -sē-ə) or **-ums.** Any of various ciliate protozoans of the genus *Paramecium,* usually oval and having an oral groove for feeding. [New Latin, from Greek *paramēkēs,* oblong : *para,* alongside + *mēkos,* length (see **māk-** in Appendix*).]

par·a·ment (păr′ə-mənt) *n., pl.* **-ments** or **paramenta** (păr′ə-mĕn′tə). *Usually plural.* Ecclesiastical vestments or hangings. [Middle English, from Medieval Latin *paramentum,* from *parāre,* to decorate, prepare. See **per-⁴** in Appendix.*]

pa·ram·e·ter (pə-răm′ə-tər) *n.* A variable or an arbitrary constant appearing in a mathematical expression, each value of which restricts or determines the specific form of the expression. [New Latin : PARA- (alongside) + -METER.] —**par′a·met′ric** (păr′ə-mĕt′rĭk) *adj.*

par·am·ne·si·a (păr′ăm-nē′zhə) *n. Psychiatry.* A distortion of memory in which fantasy and experience are confused. [PAR(A)- (resembling) + AMNESIA.]

pa·ra·mo (pä′rə-mō′, păr′ə-) *n., pl.* **-mos.** A high, treeless plain of tropical South America. [American Spanish, from Spanish *paramo†,* wasteland.]

par·a·morph (păr′ə-môrf′) *n.* A mineral crystal formed or affected by paramorphism. [PARA- (subsidiary to) + -MORPH.]

par·a·mor·phine (păr′ə-môr′fēn′) *n.* A drug, thebaine *(see).*

par·a·mor·phism (păr′ə-môr′fĭz′əm) *n.* Structural alteration of a mineral without change of chemical composition. Also called "metastasis." —**par′a·mor′phic, par′a·mor′phous** *adj.*

par·a·mount (păr′ə-mount′) *adj.* **1.** Of chief concern or importance; primary; foremost. **2.** Supreme in rank, power, or authority. —See Synonyms at **dominant.** —*n.* A person of the highest power or authority; supreme ruler. [Norman French *paramont,* "superior" (used of feudal overlordship) : Old French *par,* by, from Latin *per* (see **per¹** in Appendix*) + *amont,* above : *a,* to, from Latin *ad* (see **ad-¹** in Appendix*) + *mont,* mountain, from Latin *mōns* (stem *mont-)* (see **men-²** in Appendix*).] —**par′a·mount·cy** *n.* —**par′a·mount·ly** *adv.*

par·a·mour (păr′ə-mŏŏr′) *n.* **1.** A lover, of either sex, especially in an adulterous relationship. **2.** *Archaic.* A sweetheart. [Middle English, originally an adverb, "by way of love," from Old French *par amour : par,* by, from Latin *per* (see **per¹** in Appendix*) + *amour,* love, from Latin *amor,* from *amāre,* to love (see **amma** in Appendix*).]

Pa·ra·ná (păr′ə-nä′; *Portuguese and Spanish* pä′rä-nä′). **1.** A river rising in east-central Brazil and flowing 2,040 miles south to the Río de la Plata in northeastern Argentina. **2.** A state of southern Brazil, about 78,000 square miles in area. Population, 6,024,000. Capital, Curitiba. **3.** A city in eastern Argentina, on the Paraná River. Population, 76,000.

Pa·ra·na·í·ba (pä′rä-nä-ē′bä). A river rising in eastern Brazil and flowing 530 miles south and southwest to join with the Rio Grande and form the Paraná River.

pa·rang (pä′räng′) *n.* A short, heavy, straight-edged knife used in Malaysia and Indonesia as a tool and weapon. [Malay.]

par·a·noi·a (păr′ə-noi′ə) *n.* A nondegenerative, limited, usually chronic psychosis characterized by delusions of persecution or of grandeur, strenuously defended by the afflicted with apparent logic and reason. [New Latin, from Greek, madness, from *paranoos,* demented : *para,* beyond + *nous,* mind (see **nous** in Appendix*).]

par·a·noi·ac (păr′ə-noi′ăk′, -noi′ĭk) *n.* One who is afflicted with paranoia. —*adj.* Of, pertaining to, or resembling paranoia.

par·a·noid (păr′ə-noid′) *adj.* **1.** Pertaining to, characteristic of, or afflicted with paranoia. **2.** Suggestive of paranoia; showing unreasonable distrust, suspicion, or an exaggerated sense of one's own importance. —*n.* One afflicted with paranoia; a paranoiac.

par·a·nor·mal (păr′ə-nôr′məl) *adj.* Not within the range of normal experience or scientifically explainable phenomena.

par·an·thro·pus (păr′ən-thrō′pəs, pă-răn′thrə-pəs) *n., pl.* **-puses.** One of a genus, *Paranthropus,* of extinct anthropoid apes, known from remains found in Olduvai Gorge, Tanzania. [New Latin : PAR(A)- (resembling) + Greek *anthrōpos,* man (see **ner-²** in Appendix*).]

par·a·pet (păr′ə-pĭt, -pĕt′) *n.* **1.** A low, protective wall or railing along the edge of a roof, balcony, or similar structure. **2.** An earthen or stone embankment protecting soldiers from enemy fire. —See Synonyms at **bulwark.** [French, from Italian *parapetto,* chest-high wall : *para-,* "protecting," as in *parasole,* PARASOL + *petto,* chest, from Latin *pectus* (see **peg-** in Appendix*).] —**par′a·pet′ed** (păr′ə-pĕt′ĭd) *adj.*

par·aph (păr′əf, pə-răf′) *n.* A flourish made after or below a signature, originally to prevent forgery. [French *parafe, paraphe,* from Old French *paraffe,* from Medieval Latin *paraphus,* from *paragraphus,* PARAGRAPH.]

par·a·pher·na·lia (păr′ə-fər-nāl′yə, -fə-nāl′yə) *n.* Sometimes used with a plural verb. **1.** Personal belongings. **2.** The articles used in some activity; equipment; gear. **3.** *Common Law.* A married woman's personal property exclusive of her dowry. [Medieval Latin *paraphernālia* (in sense 3), from Greek *parapherna : para,* beyond + *phernē,* dowry (see **bher-¹** in Appendix*).]

par·a·phrase (păr′ə-frāz′) *n.* **1.** A restatement of a text or passage in another form or other words, often to clarify meaning. Compare **metaphrase. 2.** The making of paraphrases, often used as a teaching device. —*v.* **paraphrased, -phrasing, -phrases.** —*tr.* To express in or restate as a paraphrase. —*intr.* To compose a paraphrase. [French, from Latin *paraphrasis,* from Greek, from *paraphrazein,* to paraphrase : *para,* alongside + *phrazein,* to show (see **phrazein** in Appendix*).] —**par′a·phras′er** *n.*

par·a·phras·tic (păr′ə-frăs′tĭk) *adj.* Also **par·a·phras·ti·cal** (-tĭ-kəl). Of the nature of a paraphrase; restating accurately and clearly. —**par′a·phras′ti·cal·ly** *adv.*

pa·raph·y·sis (pə-răf′ə-sĭs) *n., pl.* **-ses** (-sēz′). One of the sterile filaments accompanying the spore-carrying or sexual organs of certain fungi or other cryptogamous plants. [PARA- (subsidiary to) + Greek *phusis,* nature (see **physic**).]

par·a·ple·gi·a (păr′ə-plē′jē-ə, -jə) *n.* Complete paralysis of the lower half of the body, including both legs, caused by injury to or disease of the spinal cord. [New Latin, from Greek *paraplēgia,* a stroke on one side, from *paraplēssein,* to strike on one side : *para,* beside + *plēssein,* to strike (see **plāk-²** in Appendix*).] —**par′a·ple′gic** (-plē′jĭk) *adj. & n.*

par·a·psy·chol·o·gy (păr′ə-sī-kŏl′ə-jē) *n.* The study of phenomena such as telepathy, clairvoyance, and psychokinesis that are not explainable by known natural laws.

par·a·quet (păr′ə-kĕt′) *n.* Variant of **parakeet.**

Pa·rá rubber (pə-rä′, păr′ə). Rubber obtained from various tropical South American trees of the genus *Hevea,* especially *H. brasiliensis.* [From PARÁ.]

parallelogram

parapet

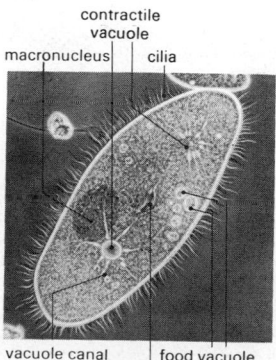

contractile vacuole
macronucleus | cilia
vacuole canal | food vacuole
gullet opening

paramecium
Enlarged 600 times

ă pat/ā pay/âr care/ä father/b bib/ch church/d deed/ĕ pet/ē be/f fife/g gag/h hat/hw which/ĭ pit/ī pie/îr pier/j judge/k kick/l lid, needle/m mum/n no, sudden/ng thing/ŏ pot/ō toe/ô paw, for/oi noise/ou out/ŏŏ took/ōō boot/p pop/r roar/s sauce/sh ship, dish/t tight/th thin, path/th this, bathe/ŭ cut/ûr urge/v valve/w with/y yes/z zebra, size/zh vision/ə about, item, edible, gallop, circus/ à *Fr.* ami/œ *Fr.* feu, *Ger.* schön/ü *Fr.* tu, *Ger.* über/KH *Ger.* ich, *Scot.* loch/N *Fr.* bon. *Follows main vocabulary. †Of obscure origin.

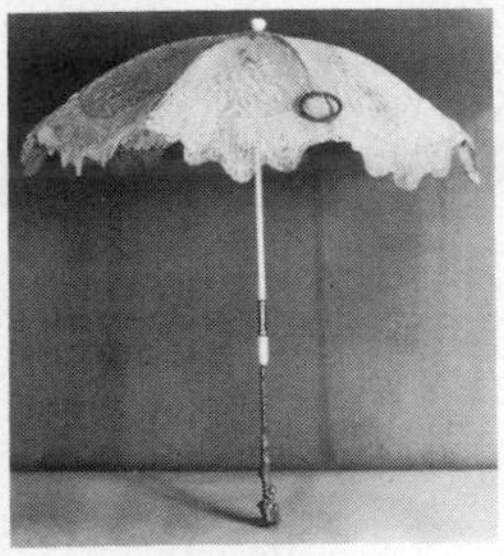

parasol

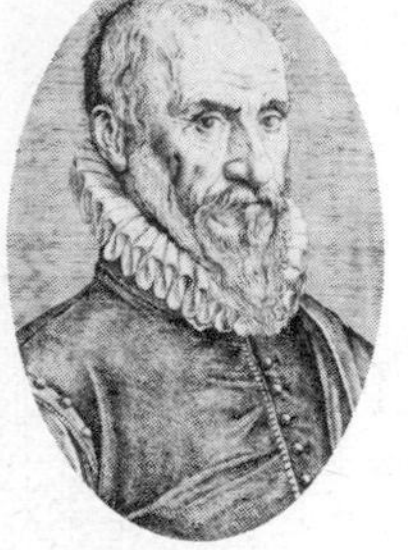

Ambroise Paré

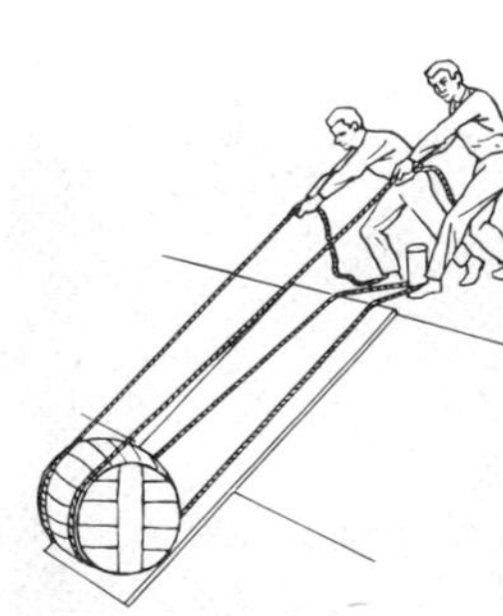

parbuckle

par·a·sang (păr′ə-săng′) *n.* An ancient Persian unit of distance, usually estimated at 3½ miles. [Latin *parasanga,* from Greek *parasangēs,* from Iranian, akin to Persian *farsang*†.]

par·a·se·le·ne (păr′ə-sĭ-lē′nē) *n., pl.* **-nae** (-nē). A luminous spot on a lunar halo. Also called "mock moon," "moon dog." [New Latin : PARA- (resembling) + Greek *selēnē,* moon (see **selenium**).] —**par′a·se·le′nic** (-lē′nĭk, -lĕn′ĭk) *adj.*

Par·a·shu·ra·ma (păr′ə-shōō-rä′mə). *Hinduism.* The sixth incarnation of Vishnu; destroyed the Kshatriyas. Also called "Rama."

par·a·site (păr′ə-sīt′) *n.* **1.** *Biology.* Any organism that grows, feeds, and is sheltered on or in a different organism while contributing nothing to the survival of its host. **2.** A person who habitually takes advantage of the generosity of others without making any useful return. **3.** A professional dinner guest, especially in ancient Greece. [Old French, from Latin *parasītus,* from Greek *parasitos,* originally "fellow guest," later "parasite" : *para,* beside + *sitos,* grain, food (see **sitology**).]

par·a·sit·ic (păr′ə-sĭt′ĭk) *adj.* Also **par·a·sit·i·cal** (-ĭ-kəl). **1.** Of, pertaining to, or characteristic of a parasite. **2.** Caused by a parasite, as certain diseases. —**par′a·sit′i·cal·ly** *adv.*

par·a·sit·i·cide (păr′ə-sĭt′ə-sīd′) *n.* An agent or preparation used to destroy parasites. —*adj.* Destructive to parasites. [From PARASIT(E) + -CIDE.] —**par′a·sit′i·ci′dal** (-sīd′l), **par′a·sit′i·cid′ic** (-sĭd′ĭk) *adj.* —**par′a·sit′i·ci′dal·ly** *adv.*

par·a·sit·ism (păr′ə-sīt-ĭz′əm) *n.* **1.** The characteristic behavior or mode of existence of a parasite. **2.** A diseased condition resulting from parasitic infestation.

par·a·sit·ize (păr′ə-sĭ-tīz′, -sī-tīz′) *tr.v.* **-ized, -izing, -izes.** To live on (a host) as a parasite.

par·a·si·tol·o·gy (păr′ə-sī-tŏl′ə-jē, -sĭ-tŏl′ə-jē) *n.* The scientific study of parasitism. [From PARASIT(E) + -LOGY.] —**par′a·si′to·log′i·cal** (-sī′tə-lŏj′ĭ-kəl) *adj.* —**par′a·si·tol′o·gist** *n.*

par·a·sol (păr′ə-sôl′, -sŏl′) *n.* A light, usually small umbrella carried, especially by women, as protection from the sun. [French, from Old French, from Old Italian *parasole* : *parare,* to shield, from Latin *parāre,* to prepare (see **per-**[4] in Appendix*) + *sole,* sun, from Latin *sōl* (see **sāwel-** in Appendix*).]

par·a·sym·pa·thet·ic nervous system (păr′ə-sĭm′pə-thĕt′ĭk). *Anatomy.* The part of the autonomic nervous system originating in the central and back parts of the brain and in the lower part of the spinal cord that, in general, inhibits or opposes the physiological effects of the sympathetic nervous system, as in tending to stimulate digestive secretions, slowing the heart, and dilating blood vessels. Also called "craniosacral system."

par·a·syn·the·sis (păr′ə-sĭn′thə-sĭs) *n. Grammar.* The formation of words by a combination of compounding and adding an affix, as in *downhearted,* formed from *down* plus *heart* plus *-ed,* not *down* plus *hearted.* —**par′a·syn·thet′ic** (-sĭn-thĕt′ĭk) *adj.*

par·a·tax·is (păr′ə-tăk′sĭs) *n.* The coordination of grammatical elements such as phrases or clauses, without the use of coordinating elements such as conjunctions, as *It was cold; the snows came.* Compare **asyndeton, hypotaxis.** [Greek, from *paratassein,* to arrange side by side : *para,* beside + *tassein,* to arrange (see **tāg-** in Appendix*).] —**par′a·tac′tic** (-tăk′tĭk), **par′a·tac′ti·cal** *adj.* —**par′a·tac′ti·cal·ly** *adv.*

par·a·thi·on (păr′ə-thī′ŏn′) *n.* A highly poisonous yellowish liquid agricultural insecticide, $(C_2H_5O)_2P(S)OC_6H_4NO_2$. [PARA- + *thio(phosphate)* + -ON.]

par·a·thy·roid gland (păr′ə-thī′roid). Any of four small kidney-shaped glands that lie in pairs near the lateral lobes of the thyroid gland and secrete a hormone necessary for calcium and phosphorus metabolism.

par·a·troop (păr′ə-trōōp′) *adj.* Of or pertaining to paratroops: *a paratroop landing.*

par·a·troop·er (păr′ə-trōō′pər) *n.* A member of the paratroops.

par·a·troops (păr′ə-trōōps′) *pl.n.* Infantry, trained and equipped to parachute. [PARA- (parachute) + TROOPS.]

par·a·ty·phoid fever (păr′ə-tī′foid′). An acute intestinal disease, similar to typhoid fever but less severe and caused by any of three bacteria of the genus *Salmonella.*

par·a·vane (păr′ə-vān′) *n. Naval.* A device equipped with sharp teeth and towed alongside a ship to cut the mooring cables of submerged mines. [PARA- (alongside) + VANE.]

par a·vi·on (pär ȧ-vyôɴ′). *French.* By airplane. Used as a label or notation on letters or articles sent by air mail.

par·boil (pär′boil′) *tr.v.* **-boiled, -boiling, -boils.** **1.** To cook partially by boiling for a brief period. **2.** To subject to intense, often uncomfortable heat. [Middle English *parboilen,* "to boil thoroughly," later (by influence of PART) to parboil, from Old French *parbo(u)illir,* from Late Latin *perbullīre* : Latin *per,* thoroughly + *bullīre,* to boil (see **beu-**[1] in Appendix*).]

par·buck·le (pär′bŭk′əl) *n.* **1.** A rope sling for rolling cylindrical objects up or down an inclined plane. **2.** A sling for raising or lowering an object vertically. —*tr.v.* **parbuckled, -ling, -les.** To raise or lower with a parbuckle. [Earlier *parbunkle*†.]

Par·cae (pär′sē, pär′kī′) *pl.n. Roman Mythology.* The three **Fates** *(see).* [Latin. See **per-**[4] in Appendix.*]

par·cel (pär′səl) *n.* **1.** Something wrapped up or packaged; bundle; package. **2.** A portion or plot of land, usually a division of a larger area. **3.** A quantity of merchandise offered for sale. **4.** A group or company; pack; bunch: *a parcel of idiots.* **5.** A distinct, often essential part of something. Used chiefly in the expression *part and parcel.* —*tr.v.* **parceled, -celing, -cels.** Also *chiefly British* **-celled, -celling.** **1.** To divide into portions or allotments and distribute. Usually followed by *out.* **2.** To make into a parcel or parcels; wrap; package. **3.** *Nautical.* To wind protective strips of canvas around (rope). [Middle English *parcelle,* from Old French, from Vulgar Latin *particella* (unattested), from Latin *particula,* portion, particle, diminutive of *pars* (stem *part-*), part. See **perə-** in Appendix.*]

parcel post. *Abbr.* **p.p., P.P.** The branch of the postal service that handles and delivers parcels sent through the mail.

par·ce·nar·y (pär′sə-nĕr′ē) *n., pl.* **-ies.** *Law.* **Coparcenary** *(see).* [Norman French *parcenarie,* from Old French *parçonerie,* from *parçonier,* partner, PARCENER.]

par·ce·ner (pär′sə-nər) *n. Law.* A **coparcener** *(see).* [Norman French, from Old French *parçonier,* partner, from Vulgar Latin *partiōnārius* (unattested), from Latin *partītiō,* partition, from *partīre,* to divide, from *pars* (stem *part-*), part. See **perə-** in Appendix.*]

parch (pärch) *v.* **parched, parching, parches.** —*tr.* **1.** To make very dry, especially by the action of heat. **2.** To make thirsty. **3.** To dry or roast (corn, peas, or the like) by exposing to heat. —*intr.* **1.** To become very dry. **2.** To become thirsty. —See Synonyms at **burn.** [Middle English *parchen*†.]

Par·chee·si (pär-chē′zē) *n.* A trademark for a board game based on the ancient game of **pachisi** *(see).* [From PACHISI.]

parch·ment (pärch′mənt) *n.* **1.** The skin of a sheep or goat, prepared for writing or painting upon. **2.** A written text or drawing on a sheet of this material. **3.** Paper made in imitation of this material. [Middle English *perchement, parchemin,* from Old French *parchemin, parcamin,* from Vulgar Latin *particamīnum* (unattested), blend of Latin *Parthica (pellis),* "Parthian (leather)," and *pergamīna,* parchment, from Greek *pergamēnē,* from *Pergamēnos,* of Pergamun, from *Pergamon,* PERGAMUM (where it was first used as a substitute for papyrus).]

pard (pärd) *n. Archaic.* A leopard or other large cat. [Middle English *parde,* from Old French, from Latin *pardus,* from Greek *pardos,* from an Oriental source. See also **leopard.**]

par·don (pärd′n) *tr.v.* **-doned, -doning, -dons.** **1.** To release (a person) from punishment; forgive. **2.** To pass over (an offense) without punishment. **3.** To make courteous allowance for; to excuse. —*n.* **1.** The act of forgiving. **2.** *Law.* **a.** The exemption of a convicted person from the penalties of an offense or crime by the power of the executor of the laws. **b.** The official document or warrant declaring such an exemption. **3.** *Roman Catholic Church.* An indulgence. [Middle English *pardonen,* from Old French *pardoner,* to give, pardon, from Late Latin *perdōnāre,* to give wholeheartedly : *per,* thoroughly + *dōnāre,* to give, from *dōnum,* gift (see **dō-** in Appendix*).] —**par′don·a·ble** *adj.* —**par′don·a·bly** *adv.*

par·don·er (pärd′n-ər) *n.* **1.** One who pardons. **2.** A medieval ecclesiastic authorized to raise money for religious works by granting papal indulgences to contributors.

pare (pâr) *tr.v.* **pared, paring, pares.** **1.** To remove the outer covering or skin of by peeling with a knife or similar instrument. **2.** To remove by or as if by cutting, clipping, or shaving. Used with *off* or *away: paring off lemon rind.* **3.** To whittle away. [Middle English *paren,* from Old French *parer,* to prepare, from Latin *parāre.* See **per-**[4] in Appendix.*]

Pa·ré (pȧ-rā′), **Ambroise.** 1517?–1590. French surgeon; introduced the technique of ligature of arteries.

par·e·gor·ic (păr′ə-gôr′ĭk, -gŏr′ĭk) *n.* Camphorated tincture of opium, taken internally for the relief of diarrhea and intestinal pain. [Late Latin *parēgoricus,* from Greek *parēgorikos,* from *parēgoros,* encouraging, soothing, addressing : *para,* beside, alongside + *agora,* assembly (see **ger-**[1] in Appendix*).]

paren. parenthesis.

pa·ren·chy·ma (pə-rĕng′kə-mə) *n.* **1.** *Anatomy.* The tissue characteristic of an organ, as distinguished from connective tissue. **2.** *Botany.* Tissue composed of soft, unspecialized, thin-walled cells. [New Latin, from Greek *parenkhuma,* visceral flesh, from *parenkhein,* to pour in beside (from the belief that the tissues of the organs were poured in by their blood vessels) : *para,* beside + *en,* in (see **en** in Appendix*) + *khein,* to pour (see **gheu-** in Appendix*).] —**pa·ren′chy·mal, par′en·chym′a·tous** (păr′ĕn-kĭm′ə-təs) *adj.* —**par′en·chym′a·tous·ly** *adv.*

par·ent (pâr′ənt) *n.* **1.** A father or mother. **2.** A forefather; ancestor; progenitor. **3.** Any organism that produces or generates another. **4.** A guardian; protector. **5.** The source or cause of something; origin. [Middle English, from Old French, from Latin *parēns,* from the present participle of *parere,* to give birth. See **per-**[4] in Appendix.*] —**par′ent·hood′** *n.*

par·ent·age (pâr′ən-tĭj) *n.* **1.** Descent or derivation from parents or ancestors; lineage; origin. **2.** Derivation from a source; origin or cause. **3.** The state or relationship of being a parent.

pa·ren·tal (pə-rĕnt′l) *adj.* **1.** Of, pertaining to, or characteristic of a parent. **2.** *Genetics.* Designating the generation from which a genetic experiment begins. —**pa·ren′tal·ly** *adv.*

par·en·ter·al (pă-rĕn′tər-əl) *adj.* **1.** Located outside the alimentary canal. **2.** Taken into the body or administered in a manner other than through the digestive tract, as by intravenous or intramuscular injection. [PAR(A)- + ENTER(O)- + -AL.]

pa·ren·the·sis (pə-rĕn′thə-sĭs) *n., pl.* **-ses** (-sēz′). *Abbr.* **par., paren.** **1.** Either or both of the upright curved lines, (), used to mark off explanatory or qualifying remarks in writing or printing. **2.** *Mathematics.* Such a mark used as one of a pair to enclose a sum, product, or other expression considered or treated as a collective entity in a mathematical operation. **3. a.** A qualifying or amplifying phrase occurring within a sentence in such a way as to form an interpolation independent of the surrounding syntactical structure. **b.** A comment departing from the theme of discourse; digression. **4.** An interruption of continuity; interval; interlude. [Late Latin, from Greek, "a putting in beside," from *parentithenai,* to insert : *para,* beside + *en,* in (see **en** in Appendix*) + *tithenai,* to put (see **dhē-**[1] in Appendix*).]

par·en·thet·i·cal (păr′ən-thĕt′ĭ-kəl) *adj.* Also **par·en·thet·ic** (-thĕt′ĭk). **1.** Contained, or as if contained, in parentheses; qualifying or explanatory: *a parenthetical remark.* **2.** Using or containing parentheses. —**par′en·thet′i·cal·ly** *adv.*

pa·re·sis (pə-rē′sĭs, păr′ə-sĭs) *n. Pathology.* **1.** Slight or partial paralysis. **2. General paresis** *(see).* [New Latin, from Greek, act of letting go, from *parienai,* to loose, let fall : *para,* beside + *hienai,* to throw (see **yē-** in Appendix*).] —**pa·ret′ic** (-rĕt′ĭk) *n.* & *adj.* —**pa·ret′i·cal·ly** *adv.*

par·es·the·sia (păr′ĭs-thē′zhə) *n.* Also **par·aes·the·sia.** *Pathology.* Abnormal or impaired skin sensation, such as burning, prickling, itching, or tingling. [New Latin : PAR(A)- (incorrectly) + ESTHESIA.] —**par′es·thet′ic** (-thĕt′ĭk) *adj.*

Pa·re·to (pä-rā′tō), **Vilfredo.** 1848–1923. Italian sociologist and economist.

pa·re·u (pä′rā-o͞o′) *n.* A rectangular piece of cloth worn in Polynesia as a wraparound skirt or loincloth. [Tahitian.]

pa·re·ve (pä′rə-və) *adj.* Also **par·ve** (pär′və). *Judaism.* Designating or pertaining to foods that are prepared without meat, milk, or their derivatives, and that therefore may be eaten with meat or dairy dishes. [Yiddish *parev*†.]

par ex·cel·lence (pär ĕk-sə-läns′). Regarded as the highest degree or epitome of something; pre-eminently: *the discreet friend par excellence.* [French *par excellence,* "by (way of) pre-eminence."]

par·fait (pär-fā′) *n.* **1.** A dessert made of cream, eggs, sugar, and flavoring frozen together and served in a tall glass. **2.** A dessert made of several layers of different flavors of ice cream or ices, variously garnished and served in a tall glass. [French, from *parfait,* perfect, from Latin *perfectus,* PERFECT.]

par·fleche (pär′flĕsh′, pär-flĕsh′) *n.* **1.** Rawhide soaked in lye and water to remove the hair and dried on a stretcher. **2.** An article, such as a shield, made of this rawhide. [Canadian French : *parer,* to protect, from Latin *parāre,* to prepare (see **per-**[4] in Appendix*) + *flèche,* arrow, from Old French *fleche,* from Frankish *fliugika* (unattested) (see **pleu-** in Appendix*).]

par·get (pär′jĭt) *n.* **1.** Plaster, roughcast, or any similar mixture used to coat walls or line chimneys. **2.** Ornamental plasterwork. **3.** A cement mixture used to waterproof outer walls. —*tr.v.* **pargeted, -geting, -gets.** Also *chiefly British* **-getted, -getting.** To cover or adorn with parget. [Middle English *pargetten,* from Old French *parjeter,* to throw onto a surface : *par,* onto, from Latin *per* (see **per**[1] in Appendix*) + *jeter,* to throw, from Latin *jactāre,* frequentative of *jacere,* to throw (see **yē-** in Appendix*).] —**par′get·ing** *n.*

par·he·lic circle (pär-hē′lĭk). *Meteorology.* A luminous halo visible at the height of the sun and parallel to the horizon, caused by the sun's rays reflecting off atmospheric ice crystals. Also called "parhelic ring." See **anthelion.**

par·he·li·on (pär-hē′lē-ən, -hēl′yən) *n., pl.* **-helia** (-hē′lē-ə, -hēl′yə). *Meteorology.* A bright spot sometimes appearing to either side of the sun, often on a luminous ring or halo. Also called "mock sun," "sundog." [Latin *parēlion,* from Greek : *para,* beside, beyond + *hēlios,* sun (see **sāwel-** in Appendix*).] —**par·he′lic, par′he·li′a·cal** *adj.*

Pa·ri·a, Gulf of (pä′rē-ə). An arm of the Atlantic Ocean off the northeastern coast of Venezuela.

pa·ri·ah (pə-rī′ə) *n.* **1.** A member of a low caste of agricultural and domestic workers in southern India and Burma. **2.** A social outcast. [Tamil *paraiyan,* drummer, from *parai,* drum (the pariahs having been originally a caste of drummers), probably from *parāi,* to tell.]

Par·i·an (pâr′ē-ən) *adj.* **1.** Of or pertaining to Paros. **2.** Of or resembling the white marble mined in Paros. —*n.* **1.** A native or inhabitant of Paros. **2.** A fine unglazed porcelain.

Pa·ri·cu·tín (pä-rē-ko͞o-tēn′). Also **Pa·rí·cu·tin** (pä-rē′ko͞o-tēn). A volcano about 9,100 feet above sea level, in Michoacán State, southwestern Mexico. It first erupted in February 1943.

pa·ri·es (pâr′ē-ez′) *n., pl.* **parietes** (pə-rī′ə-tēz′). *Biology. Usually plural.* The wall of an organ. [New Latin, from Latin *pariēs*†, wall of a room.]

pa·ri·e·tal (pə-rī′ə-təl) *adj.* **1.** *Biology.* Pertaining to or forming the wall of a hollow structure. **2.** *Anatomy.* Of or relating to either of the parietal bones. **3.** *Botany.* Attached to the ovary wall. Said of the ovules or placenta in certain plants. **4.** Dwelling within, or having authority within, the walls or buildings of a college. [French *pariétal,* from Late Latin *parietālis,* from Latin *pariēs* (stem *pariet-*), PARIES.]

parietal bone. *Anatomy.* Either of two large, irregularly quadrilateral bones, between the frontal and occipital bones, that together form the sides and top of the skull.

parietal lobe. *Anatomy.* The division of each hemisphere of the brain that lies beneath each parietal bone.

par·i·mu·tu·el (păr′ĭ-myo͞o′cho͞o-əl) *n., pl.* **pari-mutuels** (for both senses) or **paris-mutuels** (păr′ĭ-myo͞o′cho͞o-əlz) (for sense 1 only). **1.** A system of betting on races whereby the winners divide the total amount bet, after deducting management expenses, in proportion to the sums they have wagered individually. **2.** The machine that records bets placed under this system. [French *pari mutuel,* mutual stake : *pari,* wager, from Old French *parier,* to make equal, from Vulgar Latin *pariāre* (unattested), from Latin *pār,* equal (see **perə-** in Appendix*) + *mutuel,* MUTUAL.]

pa·ri pas·su (păr′ē păs′o͞o, pä′rē päs′o͞o). *Latin.* With equal pace, speed, or progress; side by side: *proceed pari passu.*

Par·is[1] (păr′ĭs). *Greek Mythology.* The prince of Troy whose abduction of Helen provoked the Trojan War.

Par·is[2] (păr′ĭs; *French* pà-rē′). The capital and principal city of France, in the northwest on the Seine. Population, 2,790,000; metropolitan area, 7,369,000. [French, from Old French, from Gallo-Roman *(Lūtētia) Parīsiōrum,* "(swamps) of the Parisii" (the Gaulish tribe whose capital was on the Île de la Cité, then marshy).] —**Pa·ri′sian** (pə-rĭzh′ən, -rē′zhən) *adj.* & *n.*

Paris, Treaty of. **1.** A treaty (1763) between Great Britain, France, and Spain that ended the French and Indian War. **2.** A treaty (1783) between Great Britain and the United States that ended the American Revolution. **3.** A treaty (1898) between the United States and Spain that ended the Spanish-American War.

Paris daisy. A plant, the **marguerite** *(see).*

Paris green. A poisonous emerald-green powder, $(CuO)_3 \cdot As_2O_3 \cdot Cu(C_2H_3O_2)_2$, used as a pigment, insecticide, and wood preservative. [After PARIS, where it was once made.]

par·ish (păr′ĭsh) *n. Abbr.* **par.** **1.** In the Anglican, Roman Catholic, and some other churches, an administrative part of a diocese that has its own church. **2.** In Great Britain, a political division of a county for local civil government, usually corresponding to the ecclesiastical parish. **3.** A civil district in Louisiana, corresponding to a county in other states. **4.** Members of a parish; the community of parishioners. [Middle English *paroche, parisshe,* from Old French *paroisse,* from Late Latin *parochia,* from Late Greek *paroikia,* from *paroikos,* Christian, from Greek, "neighbor," "sojourner," "stranger" : *para,* near, beside + *oikos,* house (see **weik-**[1] in Appendix*).]

pa·rish·ion·er (pə-rĭsh′ən-ər) *n.* A member of a parish. [Middle English *parisshoner,* perhaps from Old French *paroissien,* from *paroisse,* PARISH.]

par·i·ty[1] (păr′ə-tē) *n., pl.* **-ties.** **1.** Equality, as in amount, status, or value. **2.** Equivalence, correspondence, or resemblance. **3.** The equivalent in value of a sum of money expressed in terms of a different currency, at a fixed, official rate of exchange. **4.** Equality of prices of goods or securities in two different markets. **5.** A level for farm-product prices, maintained by governmental support and intended to give farmers the same purchasing power they had during a chosen base period. **6.** *Mathematics.* The comparative odd-even relationship between two integers. If both are odd, or even, they are said to have the same parity; if one is odd and one even, they have different parity. **7.** *Symbol* **P** *Physics.* **a.** An intrinsic symmetry property of subatomic particles that is characterized by the behavior of the wave function of such particles under reflection through the origin of spatial coordinates. **b.** A quantum number, either +1 (even) or −1 (odd), that mathematically describes this property. [Latin *paritās,* from *pār,* equal. See **perə-** in Appendix.*]

par·i·ty[2] (păr′ə-tē) *n. Medicine.* **1.** The condition of having borne offspring. **2.** The number of children borne by one woman. [From -PAR(OUS) + -ITY.]

park (pärk) *n. Abbr.* **pk.** **1.** A tract of land set aside for public use, as: **a.** An expanse of enclosed grounds for recreational use within or adjoining a town. **b.** A landscaped city square. **c.** A tract of land kept in its natural state. **2.** A stadium or enclosed playing field: *ball park.* **3.** A country estate, especially when including extensive gardens, woods, pastures, and game preserves. **4.** *Military.* **a.** An area where vehicles and artillery are stored and serviced. **b.** The materiel kept in such an area. —*v.* **parked, parking, parks.** —*tr.* **1.** To put or leave (a vehicle) for a time in a certain location. **2.** *Informal.* To place, put, set, or leave (something) somewhere. **3.** *Military.* To assemble (artillery or other equipment) in order. —*intr.* To park a vehicle. [Middle English, from Old French *parc,* enclosure, from Medieval Latin *parricus*†. See **paddock.**]

Park (pärk), **Mungo.** 1771–1806. Scottish explorer in Africa.

par·ka (pär′kə) *n.* **1.** A hooded fur jacket worn as an outer garment by Eskimos. **2.** A similar garment of warm cloth, worn for sports or outdoor work. [Aleutian, skin, from Russian, pelt of a reindeer, from Samoyed.]

Par·ker (pär′kər), **Charles Christopher ("Bird").** 1920–1955. American jazz saxophonist and composer.

Par·ker (pär′kər), **Dorothy (Rothschild).** 1893–1967. American writer.

Par·ker (pär′kər), **Theodore.** 1810–1860. American Unitarian clergyman and abolitionist leader.

Parker House roll. A yeast-leavened roll, shaped by folding a flat round of dough in half. [Introduced by the *Parker House,* a hotel in Boston, Massachusetts.]

Par·kers·burg (pär′kərz-bûrg). A city of West Virginia, a river port in the northwest on the Ohio. Population, 45,000.

parking lot. An area for parking motor vehicles.

parking meter. A coin-operated device to regulate car parking.

parking orbit. *Aerospace.* A temporary orbit for spacecraft.

Par·kin·son·ism (pär′kĭn-sə-nĭz′əm) *n.* A chronic neurological condition marked by muscular rigidity, tremor, and impaired motor control. [From PARKINSON'S DISEASE.]

Par·kin·son's disease (pär′kĭn-sənz). A progressive nervous disease of the later years, characterized by muscular tremor, slowing of movement, partial facial paralysis, peculiarity of gait and posture, and weakness. Also called "paralysis agitans," "shaking palsy." [Described by James *Parkinson* (1755–1824), English surgeon.]

Park·man (pärk′mən), **Francis.** 1823–1893. American historian and author.

Park Range. A range of the Rocky Mountains in northwestern Colorado and south-central Wyoming, west of the North Platte River. Highest elevation, Mount Lincoln (14,284 feet).

park·way (pärk′wā′) *n.* A broad landscaped highway, often divided by planted median strips.

parl. parliamentary.

Parl. Parliament.

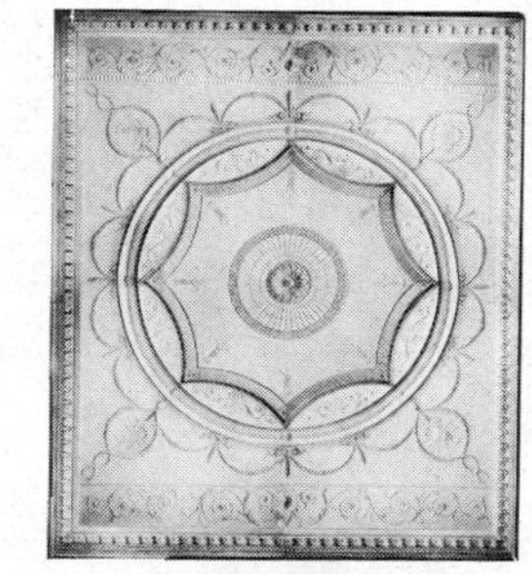

parget
Ceiling of tapestry room at Croome Court, near Worcester, England

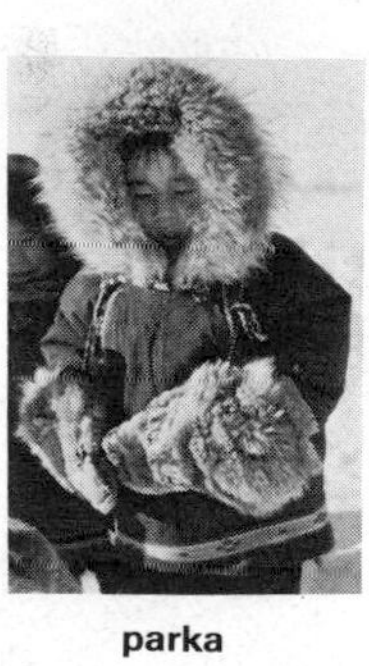

parka

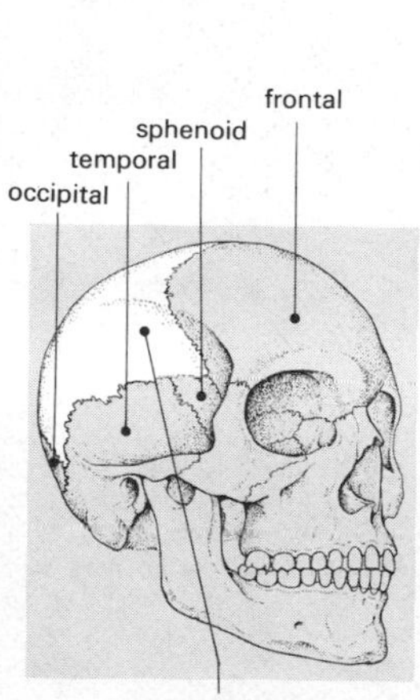

parietal bone

par·lance (pär′ləns) *n.* **1.** Particular manner of speaking; language, style, or idiom: *legal parlance.* **2.** *Archaic.* Conversation, especially a parley or debate. [Old French, from *parler,* to speak, from Medieval Latin *parabolāre,* to PARLEY.]

par·lan·do (pär-län′dō) *adj.* Also **par·lan·te** (pär-län′tā). To be sung in a style suggestive of speech. Used as a musical direction. [Italian, from *parlare,* to speak, from Medieval Latin *parabolāre,* to PARLEY.] —**par·lan′do** *adv.*

par·lay (pär′lā, -lē) *tr.v.* **-layed, -laying, -lays. 1.** To bet (an original wager and its winnings) on a subsequent event, as a race or contest. **2.** To maneuver (an asset) to great advantage: *She parlayed her physical attributes into a film career.* —*n.* A bet comprising the sum of an original wager plus its winnings, or a series of bets made in such a manner. [French *paroli,* from Italian (Neapolitan), plural of *parolo,* a set of dice, from *paro,* a pair, from Latin *pār,* equal. See **perə-** in Appendix.*]

par·ley (pär′lē) *n., pl.* **-leys.** Also *obsolete* **parle** (pärl). A discussion or conference especially between enemies over terms of truce or other matters. —*intr.v.* **parleyed, -leying, -leys.** To discuss, confer, or debate, as with an enemy or over a disagreement. [French *parlée,* from the past participle of *parler,* to talk, from Old French, from Medieval Latin *parabolāre,* from Late Latin *parabola,* discourse, PARABLE.]

par·lia·ment (pär′lə-mənt) *n.* **1.** A national representative body having supreme legislative powers within the state. **2.** *Capital* **P.** *Abbr.* **Parl.** The legislative body of various countries, especially that of the United Kingdom, made up of the House of Lords and the House of Commons. [Middle English, from Old French *parlement,* from *parler,* to talk. See **parley.**]

par·lia·men·tar·i·an (pär′lə-mĕn-târ′ē-ən) *n.* **1.** One who is expert in parliamentary procedures, rules, or debate. **2.** *Capital* **P.** A supporter of the Long Parliament during the English Civil War and the Commonwealth; a Roundhead. —*adj.* Of or pertaining to the Long Parliament or to the Roundheads.

par·lia·men·ta·ry (pär′lə-mĕn′tə-rē, -mĕn′trē) *adj. Abbr.* **parl. 1.** Of, pertaining to, or like a parliament. **2.** Proceeding from, passed, or decreed by parliament. **3.** In accordance with the rules and customs of a parliament. **4.** Having a parliament.

parliamentary law. A body of rules governing procedure in legislative and deliberative assemblies.

par·lor (pär′lər) *n.* Also *chiefly British* **par·lour. 1.** A room in a private home set apart for the entertainment of visitors. **2.** A small lounge or sitting room affording limited privacy at an inn, tavern, or the like. **3.** A room equipped and furnished for some special function or business: *beauty parlor.* [Middle English *parlour,* from Old French *parleur,* room used for conversation, from *parler,* to talk. See **parley.**]

parlor car. A railroad car for day travel fitted with individual reserved seats. Also called "chair car."

par·lous (pär′ləs) *adj. Archaic.* **1.** Perilous; dangerous. **2.** *Obsolete.* Dangerously cunning. [Middle English, variant of *perilous,* from *peril,* PERIL.] —**par′lous·ly** *adv.*

Par·ma (pär′mə; *Italian* pär′mä). **1.** A city in northern Italy, northwest of Reggio. Population, 119,000. **2.** A city of northeastern Ohio and suburb of Cleveland. Population, 97,000.

Parma violet. A variety of violet, *Viola odorata sempervirens,* cultivated for its fragrant lavender flowers.

Par·me·san (pär′mə-zăn′, -zăn′, -zən) *n.* A hard, dry Italian cheese made from skim milk and usually served grated as a garnish. —*adj.* Of or from Parma.

Par·na·í·ba (pär′nä-ē′bä). Formerly **Par·na·hi·ba, Par·na·hy·ba.** A river rising in northeastern Brazil and flowing about 750 miles northeast to the Atlantic Ocean.

Par·nas·si·an[1] (pär-năs′ē-ən) *adj.* Of, pertaining to, or symbolically associated with Mount Parnassus or with poetry.

Par·nas·si·an[2] (pär-năs′ē-ən) *n.* A member of a school of late 19th-century French poets whose work is characterized by detachment and emphasis on metrical form. [*Le Parnasse contemporain,* first published in 1866, was the name of the group's first collection of poems.] —**Par·nas′si·an** *adj.*

Par·nas·sus, Mount (pär-năs′əs). Modern name **Liá·kou·ra** (lyä′ko͝o-rä′). A peak, about 8,060 feet high, in southern Greece, north of the Gulf of Corinth; sacred in Greek mythology to Apollo and the Muses.

Par·nell (pär-nĕl′, pär′nəl), **Charles Stewart.** 1846–1891. Irish nationalist hero.

pa·ro·chi·al (pə-rō′kē-əl) *adj.* **1.** Of, pertaining to, supported by, or located in a parish. **2.** Restricted to a narrow scope; provincial: *parochial attitudes.* [Middle English *parochiel,* from Old French *parochial,* from Late Latin *parochiālis,* from *parochia,* PARISH.] —**pa·ro′chi·al·ly** *adv.* —**pa·ro′chi·al·ism′** *n.* —**pa·ro′chi·al·ist** *n.*

parochial school. A school supported by a church parish.

par·o·dy (păr′ə-dē) *n., pl.* **-dies. 1.** A literary or artistic work that broadly mimics an author's characteristic style and holds it up to ridicule. **2.** A performance so bad as to be equivalent to intentional mockery; travesty: *The trial was a parody of justice.* —See Synonyms at **caricature.** —*tr.v.* **parodied, -dying, -dies.** To make a parody of. See Synonyms at **imitate.** [Latin *parōdia,* from Greek *parōidia,* "mock-song," burlesque poem : *para,* beside, subsidiary to, "quasi-" + *ōidē,* song (see **wed-**[2] in Appendix*).] —**pa·rod′ic** (pə-rŏd′ĭk), **pa·rod′i·cal** *adj.* —**par′o·dist** *n.*

pa·rol (pə-rōl′) *n. Law.* An oral utterance; word of mouth. Used in the phrase *by parol.* —*adj. Law.* Given by word of mouth. Compare **documentary.** [French *parole,* "word," from Old French, from Vulgar Latin *paraula* (unattested), variant of Late Latin *parabola,* discourse, PARABLE.]

pa·role (pə-rōl′) *n.* **1.** *Law.* **a.** The release of a prisoner before his term has expired on condition of continued good behavior. **b.** The duration of such conditional release. **2.** A password used by a military officer of the day or an officer on guard. **3.** Word of honor; a promise. —*tr.v.* **paroled, -roling, -roles.** To release (a prisoner) on parole. [French, word of honor, "word," PAROL.]

pa·rol·ee (pə-rō′lē′) *n.* One who is released on parole.

par·o·no·ma·sia (păr′ə-nō-mā′zhə, -zhē-ə) *n.* Word play; especially, a **pun** *(see).* [Latin, from Greek, from *paronomazein,* to call by a different name, to name besides : *para,* besides + *onomazein,* to name, from *onoma,* name (see **nomen-** in Appendix*).] —**par′o·no·mas′tic** (-măs′tĭk), **par′o·no·ma′sial** *adj.* —**par′o·no·mas′ti·cal·ly** *adv.*

par·o·nym (păr′ə-nĭm′) *n.* A paronymous word. [Greek *parōnumon,* from *parōnumos,* PARONYMOUS.] —**par′o·nym′ic** *adj.*

pa·ron·y·mous (pə-rŏn′ə-məs) *adj.* Allied by derivation from the same root; having the same stem; conjugate; for example, *beautiful* and *beauteous.* [Greek *parōnumos,* derivative : *para,* beside + *onuma, onoma,* name (see **nomen-** in Appendix*).]

par·o·quet. Variant of **parakeet.**

Par·os (pâr′ŏs′). A Greek island, 81 square miles in area, one of the Cyclades, six miles west of Naxos.

pa·rot·id gland (pə-rŏt′ĭd). Either of the largest of the paired salivary glands, located below and in front of each ear. Also "parotid." [From Greek *parōtis,* "(tumor) near the ear" : *para,* beside + *ōt-,* stem of *ous,* ear (see **ous-** in Appendix*).]

par·o·ti·tis (păr′ə-tī′tĭs) *n.* Also **pa·rot·i·di·tis** (pə-rŏt′ĭ-dī′tĭs). Inflammation of the parotid glands, as in mumps. —**par′o·tit′ic** (-tĭt′ĭk) *adj.*

-parous. Indicates giving birth to or bearing; for example, **multiparous.** [Latin *-parus,* from *parere,* to give birth to. See **per-**[4] in Appendix.*]

par·ox·ysm (păr′ək-sĭz′əm) *n.* **1.** A sudden outburst of emotion or action: *a paroxysm of laughter.* **2.** *Pathology.* **a.** A crisis in or recurrent intensification of a disease. **b.** A spasm or fit; convulsion. [French *paroxysme,* from Greek *paroxusmos,* irritation, exasperation, paroxysm, from *paroxunein,* to stimulate, irritate : *para* (intensifier), beside + *oxunein,* to sharpen, goad, from *oxus,* sharp (see **ak-** in Appendix*).] —**par′ox·ys′mal** (păr′ək-sĭz′məl) *adj.* —**par′ox·ys′mal·ly** *adv.*

par·ox·y·tone (pă-rŏk′sĭ-tōn′) *adj.* Having an acute accent on the penultimate syllable. Said of certain words in Greek and certain Romance languages, such as French and Portuguese. —*n.* A paroxytone word. [Greek *paroxutonos* : *para,* beside + *oxutonos,* OXYTONE.]

par·quet (pär-kā′) *n.* **1. a.** The part of the main floor of a theater between the orchestra pit and the parquet circle. **b.** The entire main floor of a theater, **orchestra** *(see).* **2.** A floor of parquetry. —*tr.v.* **parqueted** (-kād′), **-queting** (-kā′ĭng), **-quets** (-kāz′). **1.** To furnish (a room) with a floor of parquetry. **2.** To make (a floor) of parquetry. —*adj.* Made of parquetry. [French, from Old French, small enclosure, diminutive of *parc,* enclosure, PARK.]

parquet circle. The section of an orchestra, or parquet, in a theater that lies under a rear balcony. Also called "parterre."

par·quet·ry (pär′kĭ-trē) *n., pl.* **-ries.** Wood, often of contrasting colors, worked into an inlaid mosaic, used especially for floors. [French *parqueterie,* from *parquet,* theater floor, PARQUET.]

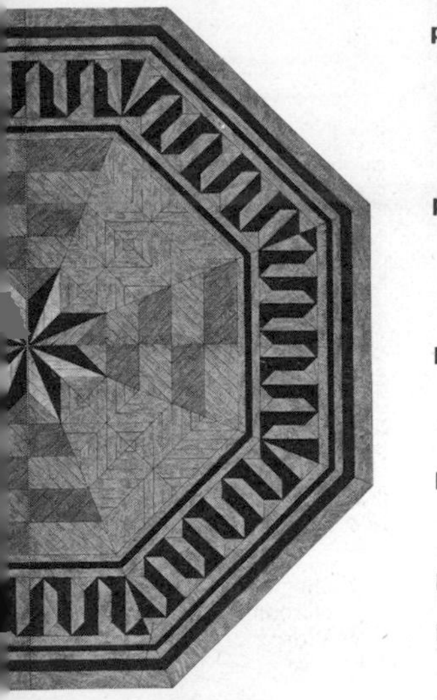

parquetry
Section of a 19th-century French floor of parquetry

parr (pär) *n., pl.* **parr** or **parrs. 1.** A young salmon during the first two years of its life when it lives in fresh water. **2.** The young of various other fishes. [Origin unknown.]

Parr (pär), **Catherine.** 1512–1548. Queen of England; sixth and last wife of Henry VIII.

par·ra·keet. Variant of **parakeet.**

par·ra·mat·ta. Variant of **paramatta.**

par·rel (păr′əl) *n.* Also **par·ral.** *Nautical.* A sliding loop of rope or chain to which a running yard or gaff is fastened, permitting movement of the yard up and down the mast. [Middle English *perell,* from *parail,* equipment, short for *appareil,* APPAREL.]

par·ri·cide (păr′ə-sīd′) *n.* **1.** One who murders his father or mother or other near relative. **2.** The act of committing such a murder. **3.** *Rare.* One who murders someone to whom he owes reverence. [Latin *parricīda* (the perpetrator) and *parricīdium* (the crime) : *parri-*†, "kin" + -CIDE.] —**par·ri·cid′al** (păr′ə-sīd′l) *adj.* —**par′ri·cid′al·ly** *adv.*

Par·rish (păr′ĭsh), **Maxfield.** 1870–1966. American painter.

par·ro·ket, par·ro·quet. Variants of **parakeet.**

par·rot (păr′ət) *n.* **1.** Any of numerous tropical and semitropical birds of the order Psittaciformes, characterized by short, hooked bills, brightly colored plumage, and, in some species, the ability to mimic human speech or other sounds. **2.** One who mindlessly imitates words or actions of another. —*tr.v.* **parroted, -roting, -rots.** To repeat or imitate without meaning or understanding. [Dialectal French *perrot,* from Old French *perroquet,* variant of *paroquet,* PARAKEET.] —**par′rot·er** *n.*

parrot fever. A virus disease, **psittacosis** *(see).*

par·rot·fish (păr′ət-fĭsh′) *n., pl.* **parrotfish** or **-fishes.** Any of various brightly colored tropical marine fishes of the family Scaridae, having jaws resembling a parrot's beak.

par·ry (păr′ē) *v.* **-ried, -rying, -ries.** —*tr.* **1.** To deflect or ward off (a fencing thrust, for example). **2.** To avoid, evade, or turn aside: *He skillfully parried her questions.* —*intr.* To deflect or ward off a blow. —*n., pl.* **parries. 1.** The act of deflecting or warding off a blow, especially in fencing. **2.** An evasive answer or action; an evasion. [From French *Parez,* "Parry!" (fencing expression), imperative of *parer,* to defend, parry, from Italian *parare,* from Latin *parāre,* to prepare. See **per-**[4] in Appendix.*]

Par·ry (păr′ē), Sir **William Edward.** 1790–1855. British naval officer and explorer of the Arctic.

Par·ry Islands (păr′ē). A group of islands north of Viscount Melville Sound, in the Arctic Ocean, off the northern coast of Northwest Territories, Canada.

parse (pärs) *v.* **parsed, parsing, parses.** —*tr.* **1.** To break (a sentence) down into its component parts of speech with an explanation of the form, function, and syntactical relationship of each part. **2.** To describe (a word) by stating its part of speech, form, and syntactical relationships in a sentence. —*intr.* To admit of being parsed: *His sentences do not parse easily.* [From Latin *pars,* part (in phrase *pars ōrātiōnis,* part of speech). See **perə-** in Appendix.*] —**pars′er** *n.*

par·sec (pär′sĕk′) *n.* A unit of astronomical length based on the distance from earth at which stellar parallax is one second of arc and equal to 3.258 light years or 1.918×10^{13} miles. [PAR(ALLAX) + SEC(OND).]

Par·see (pär′sē′, pär-sē′) *n.* Also **Par·si.** A member of a Zoroastrian religious sect in India, descended from Persians. [Persian *Pārsī,* a Persian, from *Pārs,* Persia, from Old Persian *Pārsa,* PERSIA.] —**Par′see′ism′** *n.*

par·si·mo·ni·ous (pär′sə-mō′nē-əs) *adj.* Marked by parsimony. See Synonyms at **stingy.** —**par′si·mo′ni·ous·ly** *adv.* —**par′si·mo′ni·ous·ness** *n.*

par·si·mo·ny (pär′sə-mō′nē) *n.* **1.** Unusual or excessive frugality; extreme economy; stinginess. **2.** Economy or simplicity of assumptions in logical formulation. [Middle English *parcimony,* from Latin *parsimōnia,* from *parcere*† (past participle *parsus*), to spare.]

pars·ley (pär′slē) *n.* A cultivated herb, *Petroselinum crispum,* having much-divided, curled leaves that are used as a garnish and for seasoning. [Middle English *persely, peresil,* from Old English *petersilie* and Old French *persil, perresil,* both from Late Latin *petrosīlium,* from Latin *petroselīnum,* from Greek *petroselinon,* rock parsley : *petra,* rock (see **petra** in Appendix*) + *selinon,* parsley, CELERY.]

pars·nip (pär′snĭp) *n.* **1.** A strong-scented plant, *Pastinaca sativa,* cultivated for its long, white, edible root. **2.** The root of this plant. [Middle English *pasnepe* (influenced by *nepe,* turnip), from Old French *pasnaie,* from Latin *pastināca,* parsnip, carrot, from *pastinum*†, a kind of two-pronged dibble.]

par·son (pär′sən) *n.* **1.** *Anglican Church.* A clergyman with full control of a parish under ecclesiastical law. **2.** Any clergyman in the Christian Reformed tradition. [Middle English *persone,* parish priest, from Old French, person, parson, from Medieval Latin *persōna (ecclēsiae),* "PERSON (of the church)."]

par·son·age (pär′sən-ĭj) *n.* The official residence of a parson, as provided by his church.

parson's nose. A part of a fowl, a **pope's nose** *(see).*

part (pärt) *n. Abbr.* **p., pt. 1.** A portion, division, or segment of a whole; piece. **2.** Any of several equal portions or fractions into which a whole may be divided. **3.** *Mathematics.* An aliquot part. **4. a.** An organ, member, or other division of an animal or plant. **b.** *Plural.* The external genitals. **5.** A component that can be separated from a system: *a machine part.* **6.** A role. **7.** One's proper or expected share in responsibility or obligation; duty. **8.** *Usually plural.* Individual endowment or ability; talent: *"Though his parts were not brilliant, he made up for his lack of talent by meritorious industry."* (Thackeray). **9.** *Usually plural.* A region, land, or territory: *foreign parts.* **10.** The line where the hair on the head is parted. **11.** *Music.* **a.** One of the melodic lines in concerted music or in harmony. **b.** The individual score for it. —**for one's part.** So far as one is concerned. —**for the most part.** To the greater extent; generally; mostly. —**in good part.** With good grace; without taking offense: *to take a joke in good part.* —**in part.** To some extent; partly. —**part and parcel.** A basic part or essential function. Used as an emphatic expression. —**take part.** To join in; participate. Usually followed by *in: He took part in the celebration.* —**take someone's part.** To side with someone in a disagreement; support: *He took her part in the argument.* —*v.* **parted, parting, parts.** —*tr.* **1.** To divide or break (something) into separate pieces. **2.** To break up or end (a relationship) by separating. Used chiefly in the expression *to part company.* **3.** To separate by or as if by coming between; put or keep apart. **4.** To comb (the hair) away from a dividing line on the scalp. **5.** *Archaic.* To divide into shares or portions. —*intr.* **1.** To divide or break; come apart: *The curtain parted in the middle.* **2.** To go away from one another; separate: *They parted as friends.* **3.** To separate into ways going in different directions: *The road parts in the forest.* **4.** To leave; depart. Usually followed by *from.* **5.** To die. Used euphemistically. —See Synonyms at **separate.** —**part with.** To give up; relinquish. —*adv.* Partially; in part: *part yellow, part green.* —*adj. Abbr.* **p., pt.** Not full or complete; partial: *a part owner.* [Middle English, from Old French, from Latin *pars* (stem *part-*). See **perə-** in Appendix.*]

part. 1. participle. **2.** particular.

par·take (pär-tāk′) *v.* **-took** (-to͝ok′), **-taken, -taking, -takes.** *intr.* **1.** To take part or have a share; participate. Followed by *in: partake in the festivities.* **2.** To take or be given part or portion. Usually followed by *of: "Rawdon Crawley, who came dutifully to partake of his aunt's chicken"* (Thackeray). **3.** To have some quality or characteristic; show evidence. Followed by *of: a nature that partook of the ferocity of the lion.* —*tr.* To take or have part of; share. —See Synonyms at **share.** [Backformation from partaker, from *part taker.*] —**par·tak′er** *n.*

part·ed (pär′tĭd) *adj.* **1.** Separated or divided into parts; cleft. **2.** Kept apart; separated. **3.** *Botany.* Cleft almost to the base, so as to have distinct divisions or lobes. **4.** *Archaic.* Deceased.

par·terre (pär-târ′) *n.* **1.** A section of a theater, **parquet circle** *(see).* **2.** A flower garden having the beds and paths arranged to form a pattern. [French, from Old French, from *par terre,* on the ground : *par,* on, from Latin *per* (see **per**[1] in Appendix*) + *terre,* ground, from Latin *terra* (see **ters-** in Appendix*).]

par·the·no·car·py (pär′thə-nō-kär′pē) *n. Botany.* The production of fruit without fertilization. [Greek *parthenos,* virgin (see **gwhen-**[2] in Appendix*) + *-carpy,* from CARPOUS.]

par·the·no·gen·e·sis (pär′thə-nō-jĕn′ə-sĭs) *n. Biology.* Reproduction of organisms without conjunction of gametes of opposite sexes. [New Latin : Greek *parthenos,* virgin (see **gwhen-**[2] in Appendix*) + -GENESIS.] —**par′the·no·ge·net′ic** (-jə-nĕt′ĭk) *adj.* —**par′the·no·ge·net′i·cal·ly** *adv.*

Par·thi·a (pär′thē-ə). An ancient country in western Asia, roughly corresponding to northeastern Iran.

Par·thi·an (pär′thē-ən) *adj.* **1.** Of or pertaining to Parthia, its inhabitants, or their culture. **2.** Delivered in or as if in retreat, in simulation of the Parthian archers who shot at the enemy while feigning flight: *"a Parthian volley of expletives from Uncle Billy"* (Bret Harte). —*n.* A native or inhabitant of Parthia.

par·tial (pär′shəl) *adj.* **1.** Of, pertaining to, or affecting only part; not total; incomplete. **2.** Favoring one person or side over another or others; biased; prejudiced: *"The character of Hannibal, as drawn by Livy, is esteemed partial"* (Hume). **3.** Having a particular liking for someone or something; especially fond. Usually followed by *to.* **4.** *Mathematics.* Of, designating, or pertaining to operations or sequences of operations, such as differentiation and integration, when applied to only one of several variables at a time. —*n.* **1.** *Music & Acoustics.* A **harmonic** *(see).* **2.** *Mathematics.* A partial derivative. [Middle English *parcial,* from Old French *partial,* from Late Latin *partiālis,* from Latin *pars* (stem *part-*), PART.] —**par′tial·ness** *n.*

partial derivative. *Mathematics.* The derivative with respect to a single variable of a function of two or more variables, regarding other variables as constants.

partial differential equation. *Mathematics.* A **differential equation** *(see)* containing at least one partial derivative.

partial differentiation. *Mathematics.* Differentiation with respect to a single variable in a function of several variables, regarding other variables as constants.

partial fraction. *Mathematics.* One of a set of fractions having an algebraic sum equal to a specified fraction.

par·ti·al·i·ty (pär′shē-ăl′ə-tē, pär-shăl′-) *n., pl.* **-ties. 1.** The state or condition of being partial. **2.** Favorable prejudice or bias. **3.** A special fondness; predilection: *"an almost feminine partiality for old china"* (Lamb).

par·tial·ly (pär′shə-lē) *adv.* **1.** In part; to a certain degree; partly. See Usage note at **partly. 2.** *Obsolete.* **a.** In a prejudiced or biased manner. **b.** With special favor or fondness toward something or someone; with partiality.

partial tone. *Music & Acoustics.* A **harmonic** *(see).*

par·ti·ble (pär′tə-bəl) *adj.* Capable of being parted, divided, or separated; divisible. [Late Latin *partībilis,* from Latin *partīrī,* to divide, from *pars* (stem *part-*), PART.]

par·tic·i·pant (pär-tĭs′ə-pənt) *n.* One who participates or takes part in something. —*adj.* Participating; taking part.

par·tic·i·pate (pär-tĭs′ə-pāt′) *v.* **-pated, -pating, -pates.** —*intr.* To take part; join or share with others. Usually followed by *in.* —*tr. Rare.* To share in; partake of. —See Synonyms at **share.** [Latin *participāre,* from *particeps,* a partaker : *pars* (stem *part-*), PART + *-ceps,* "-taking" (see **kap-** in Appendix*).] —**par·tic′i·pance** *n.* —**par·tic′i·pa′tor** (-pā′tər) *n.*

par·tic·i·pa·tion (pär-tĭs′ə-pā′shən) *n.* **1.** The act of participating: *participation in a game.* **2.** A taking part or sharing: *each investor's participation in the profits.*

par·ti·cip·i·al (pär′tə-sĭp′ē-əl) *adj.* Of, pertaining to, consisting of, or formed with a participle. [Latin *participiālis,* from *participium,* PARTICIPLE.] —**par′ti·cip′i·al·ly** *adv.*

par·ti·ci·ple (pär′tə-sĭp′əl) *n. Abbr.* **p., part.** *Grammar.* A nominal form of a verb that is used with an auxiliary verb to indicate certain tenses, and that can also function independently as an adjective. In the expressions *a glowing coal* and *a beaten dog, glowing* and *beaten* are participles. See **dangling participle, past participle, present participle.** [Middle English, from Old French *participle, participe,* from Latin *participium,* from *particeps,* partaker (translation of Greek *metokhē*). See **participate.**]

Usage: When a participle acts as a modifier, there should be no ambiguity or illogicality about the element it modifies. Special care should be taken to avoid the dangling participle, one that is wrongly attached to (and seemingly modifies) a noun, pronoun, or other substantive, and thus produces an absurdity. For example, *Turning the corner, the view was much changed* (properly *Turning the corner, he discovered that the view,* since *turning* cannot modify *view*). *His discharge, after serving the company for 20 years, was a shock to him* (properly *His discharge, coming after he had served*). A few participial constructions are exempt from this rule, even though they seem loosely and illogically attached. Included are such stock expressions as *speaking of, strictly speaking, generally speaking, judging by, allowing for,* and similar constructions employing *considering, concerning, granting,* and *failing.* Typical examples, all acceptable to substantial majorities of the Usage Panel, are: *Judging by his programs, the conductor is not adventurous. Strictly speaking, the work is not a concerto.* Here the participles are considered as having the force of adverbs, conjunctions, or prepositions. Also grammatically acceptable to the Panel are participles in absolute constructions: *Everything considered, the performance was satisfactory. The program being over* (or *The program over*), *we went home.* (Note that there is no comma between *program* and *being.*) The gerund (verbal noun ending, like the present participle, in *-ing*) and not the participle is the

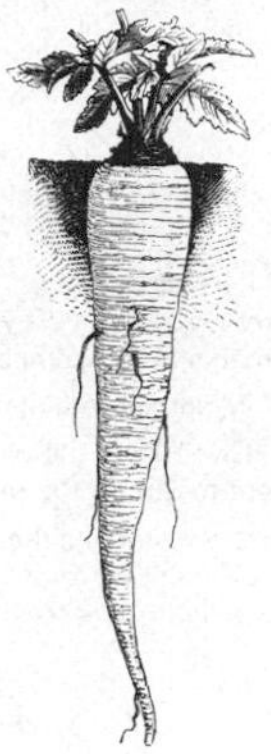

parsnip

SUBATOMIC PARTICLES

Family Name	Particle Name	Particle Symbol*	Anti-particle Symbol	Mass**	Particle's Electric Charge†	Average Lifetime‡ (sec)
	photon	γ	(γ)	0	0	stable
lepton	electron's neutrino	ν_e	$\bar{\nu}_e$	0	0	stable
	muon's neutrino	ν_μ	$\bar{\nu}_\mu$	0	0	stable
	electron	e^-	e^+	1	−1	stable
	muon	μ^-	μ^+	207	−1	2.2×10^{-6}
meson	pion	π^0	π^0	264	0	0.9×10^{-16}
		π^+	π^-	273	+1	2.6×10^{-8}
	kaon	K^+	K^-	966	+1	1.2×10^{-8}
		K^0	$\bar{K}^0$	975	0	0.9×10^{-10} or 5.7×10^{-8}
baryon	***nucleon***					
	proton	p	$\bar{p}$	1,836	+1	stable
	neutron	n	$\bar{n}$	1,839	0	$1.0 \times 10^{+3}$
	hyperon					
	lambda	Λ	$\bar{\Lambda}$	2,183	0	2.5×10^{-10}
	sigma	Σ^+	$\bar{\Sigma}^-$	2,328	+1	0.8×10^{-10}
		Σ^0	$\bar{\Sigma}^0$	2,333	0	$< 1.0 \times 10^{-14}$
		Σ^-	$\bar{\Sigma}^+$	2,343	−1	1.7×10^{-10}
	xi	Ξ^0	$\bar{\Xi}^0$	2,572	0	3.0×10^{-10}
		Ξ^-	$\bar{\Xi}^-$	2,585	−1	1.7×10^{-10}
	omega	Ω^-	Ω^+	3,276	−1	1.5×10^{-10}

*Particle symbols are frequently written without superscripts indicating charge; antiparticles are commonly identified by a bar over the particle symbol, but variations using parentheses, or no distinguishing marks at all, are also widely used.

**Approximate masses expressed in terms of the electron's mass.

†Given in terms of the electron's charge, and for particles only; antiparticles have the opposite charge or are neutral if the particle is neutral.

‡Stable means the particle lasts an indefinitely long time and has no known decay mode; the neutral kaon is a composite of two particles, the average lifetime of each of which is given; when bound in a nucleus, the neutron is stable.

form strongly recommended by the Usage Panel in constructions such as *Father objected to my going.* Here *going* is the gerund, and it is properly preceded by the possessive *my.* The alternative, always to be avoided when the possessive plus gerund is possible, would be *Father objected to me going.* Sometimes the possessive is awkward: *His absence prevented anything's being accomplished.* In such cases it is advisable to rephrase: *prevented the accomplishment of anything.*

par·ti·cle (pär′tĭ-kəl) *n.* **1.** A very small piece or part; speck. **2.** A very small amount, trace, or degree: *not a particle of doubt.* **3.** *Physics.* **a.** A body whose spatial extent and internal motion and structure, if any, are irrelevant in a specific problem. **b.** An **elementary particle** *(see).* **4.** *Grammar.* **a.** One of a class of forms, such as prepositions or conjunctions, consisting of a single word that has no inflection. **b.** A suffix or prefix, such as *-ness* or *in-.* **5.** A small division or section of something written, such as a clause of a document. **6.** *Roman Catholic Church.* **a.** A small piece of a consecrated Host. **b.** One of the smaller, individual Hosts. [Middle English, from Latin *particula,* diminutive of *pars* (stem *part-*), PART.]

particle accelerator. *Physics.* An **accelerator** *(see).*

par·ti·col·ored (pär′tē-kŭl′ərd) *adj.* Having different parts or sections colored differently; pied. [From Middle English *party,* parti-colored, from Old French *parti,* striped, from the past participle of *partir,* to divide, from Latin *partīre,* from *pars* (stem *part-*), PART.]

par·tic·u·lar (pər-tĭk′yə-lər) *adj. Abbr.* **part. 1.** Of, belonging to, or associated with a single person, group, thing, or category; not general or universal. **2.** Separate and distinct from others; specific. **3.** Worthy of note; exceptional; special. **4.** Especially or excessively attentive to or concerned with details or niceties; fussy. **5.** *Logic.* Encompassing some, but not all, of a class or group; restricted. Said of a proposition. *Some snakes are venomous* is a particular proposition. Compare **universal. 6.** *Mathematics.* Designating a solution of a differential equation, as distinguished from the general representation of the set of all solutions. —*n.* **1.** An individual item, fact, or detail: *correct in every particular.* **2.** *Usually plural.* Items or details of information or news: *"Thus, Sir, we have acquainted you with the particulars of our discovery made this present voyage"* (Arthur Barlowe). **3.** *Often plural.* A separate case or individual instance: *"What particulars were ambushed behind these generalizations?"* (Aldous Huxley). **4.** *Logic.* A particular proposition. —**in particular.** Particularly; especially. [Middle English *particuler,* concerned with details, from Old French, from Late Latin *particulāris,* from Latin *particula,* detail, PARTICLE.]

par·tic·u·lar·ism (pər-tĭk′yə-lə-rĭz′əm) *n.* **1.** Exclusive adherence to or interest in one's own group, party, sect, or nation. **2.** *Government.* A policy of allowing each state in a nation or federation to act independently. **3.** *Theology.* The belief that a particular individual is elected to salvation and grace by God's free choice, rather than by God's foreseeing the individual's response. —**par·tic′u·lar·ist** *n.* —**par·tic′u·lar·is′tic** *adj.*

par·tic·u·lar·i·ty (pər-tĭk′yə-lăr′ə-tē) *n., pl.* **-ties. 1.** The quality or state of being particular rather than general. **2.** Exactitude of detail, especially in description. **3.** Attention to or concern with details; fastidiousness. **4.** A specific point or detail; a particular. **5.** An individual characteristic; peculiarity.

par·tic·u·lar·ize (pər-tĭk′yə-lə-rīz′) *v.* **-ized, -izing, -izes.** —*tr.* **1.** To state or enumerate in detail; itemize. **2.** To mention or treat individually; specify: *"It is needless to particularize the number of the vehicle."* (Thackeray). —*intr.* To give particulars. —**par·tic′u·lar·i·za′tion** *n.* —**par·tic′u·lar·iz′er** *n.*

par·tic·u·lar·ly (pər-tĭk′yə-lər-lē) *adv.* **1.** To a great degree; especially. **2.** With particular reference or emphasis; specifically. **3.** In a particular manner; severally; individually: *"Everyone has a moment in history which belongs particularly to him."* (John Knowles). **4.** With regard to particulars; in detail.

par·tic·u·late (pər-tĭk′yə-lĭt, -lāt′) *adj.* Of, pertaining to, or formed of separate particles.

part·ing (pär′tĭng) *n.* **1.** The act or process of separating or dividing. **2.** A division or separation: *the parting of the ways.* **3.** A departure or leave-taking. **4.** The act or time of dying. Used euphemistically. —*adj.* **1.** Pertaining to, done, given, or said on departing or separating: *a parting gift.* **2.** Going away; leaving; departing: *"The curfew tolls the knell of parting day."* (Gray). **3.** Dividing; separating.

par·ti·san¹ (pär′tə-zən) *n.* **1.** A militant supporter of a party, cause, faction, person, or idea: *"I avow myself the partisan of truth alone"* (William Harvey). **2.** A member of a detached, often unofficially organized body of fighters who attack or harass an enemy within occupied territory; guerrilla. —*adj.* **1.** Of, pertaining to, or characteristic of a partisan or partisans. **2.** Devoted to, or biased in support of, a single party or cause: *partisan politics.* [French, from Italian (Tuscan) *partigiano,* from *parte,* part, party, from Latin *pars* (stem *part-*), PART.] —**par′ti·san·ship′** *n.*

par·ti·san² (pär′tə-zən) *n.* Also **par·ti·zan.** A weapon having a long shaft surmounted by a blade with broad, horizontally projecting cutting edges, used chiefly in the 16th and 17th centuries. [Obsolete French *partizane,* from obsolete Italian *partesana,* weapon used by a strong supporter, variant of (Tuscan) *partigiano,* PARTISAN (supporter).]

par·ti·ta (pär-tē′tə) *n. Music.* A set of related instrumental pieces, as a series of variations or a suite. [Italian, from the feminine past participle of *partire,* to divide, from Latin *partīre,* from *pars* (stem *part-*), PART.]

par·tite (pär′tīt′) *adj.* Divided into parts. [Latin *partītus,* past participle of *partīre,* to divide, from *pars* (stem *part-*), PART.]

par·ti·tion (pär-tĭsh′ən) *n.* **1. a.** The act or process of dividing something into parts. **b.** The state of being so divided. **2.** Something that separates, such as a partial wall dividing a larger area. **3.** A part or section into which something has been divided. **4.** *Mathematics.* **a.** An expression of a positive integer as a sum of positive integers. **b.** The decomposition of a set into a family of mutually exclusive sets. **5.** *Logic.* The analysis of a class into its component parts. —*tr.v.* **partitioned, -tioning, -tions. 1.** To divide into parts, pieces, or sections. **2.** To divide or separate by means of a partition. Often followed by *off: partition off an alcove.* [Middle English *particioun,* from Old French *partition,* from Latin *partītiō,* from *partīre,* to divide, from *pars* (stem *part-*), PART.] —**par·ti′tion·ment** *n.*

par·ti·tive (pär′tə-tĭv) *adj.* **1.** Serving to divide something into parts. **2.** *Grammar.* Indicating a part as distinct from a whole. In the sentence *She drank some of the coffee, some of the coffee* is a partitive construction. —*n. Grammar.* **1.** A partitive word, such as *many* or *less.* **2.** A partitive construction or case. [Medieval Latin *partītīvus,* from Latin, from *partīre,* to divide, from *pars* (stem *part-*), PART.] —**par′ti·tive·ly** *adv.*

part·let (pärt′lĭt) *n.* A woman's garment worn especially in the 16th century, consisting of a covering for the neck and shoulders, and having a band or ruffle at the neck. [Middle English *patelet,* from Old French *patelete,* band of cloth, diminutive of *patte,* paw, band. See **patten.**]

part·ly (pärt′lē) *adv.* In part; in some degree; not completely.

Usage: *Partly* and *partially* are not invariably interchangeable. *Partly,* which has the wider application, is the choice when stress is laid on the part (in contrast to the whole), when the reference is to physical things, and when the sense is equivalent to *in part, to some extent: partly to blame; a partly finished building. Partially* is especially applicable to conditions or states in the sense of *to a certain degree;* as the equivalent of *incompletely,* it indirectly stresses the whole: *partially dependent.*

part·ner (pärt′nər) *n.* A person associated with another or others in some activity of common interest, especially: **a.** A member of a business partnership. **b.** A spouse. **c.** Either of two persons dancing together. **d.** One of a pair or a team in a game or sport, such as bridge or tennis. —*tr.v.* **partnered, -nering, -ners. 1.** To make a partner of. **2.** To bring together as partners. **3.** To be the partner of. [Middle English *partener,* variant of *parcener,* from Norman French, PARCENER.]

Synonyms: *partner, colleague, ally, confederate, accomplice, associate.* These all denote one who cooperates in a venture, occupation, or challenge. *Partner* implies a relationship, frequently between two people, in which each has equal status and a certain independence but also implicit or formal obligations to the other or others. A *colleague* is any coworker in a given occupation, usually a profession. An *ally* is one who, out of a common cause, has taken one's side and can ostensibly be relied upon, at least temporarily. *Confederate* and *accomplice* are both derogatory, usually applied to alleged criminals and suggesting guilt by willful association. *Confederate* is the more general,

ă pat/ā pay/âr care/ä father/b bib/ch church/d deed/ĕ pet/ē be/f fife/g gag/h hat/hw which/ĭ pit/ī pie/îr pier/j judge/k kick/l lid, needle/m mum/n no, sudden/ng thing/ŏ pot/ō toe/ô paw, for/oi noise/ou out/o͝o took/o͞o boot/p pop/r roar/s sauce/sh ship, dish/

signifying any collaborator in a suspicious relationship or venture. An *accomplice* is more specifically somebody who assists another in a single crime. An *associate* is broadly anybody who works in the same place (as distinct from the same field) as another, usually in direct contact with him.

part·ner·ship (pärt'nər-shĭp') *n.* **1.** The state of being a partner; an association of partners. **2.** A contract entered into by two or more persons in which each agrees to furnish a part of the capital and labor for a business enterprise, and by which each shares in some fixed proportion in profits and losses.

part of speech. 1. One of a group of traditional classifications of words according to their functions in context. They are **noun, pronoun, verb, adjective, adverb, preposition, conjunction,** and **interjection** (*all of which see*). Sometimes an **article** (*see*) is considered a ninth classification. **2.** A word considered as a member of such a class.

par·tridge (pär'trĭj) *n., pl.* **-tridges** or **partridge. 1.** Any of several plump-bodied Old World game birds, especially of the genera *Perdix* and *Alectoris.* **2.** Any of several similar or related birds, such as the **ruffed grouse** or the **bobwhite** (*both of which see*). [Middle English *partrich,* from Old French *perdriz,* from Latin *perdix,* from Greek. See **perd-** in Appendix.*]

par·tridge·ber·ry (pär'trĭj-bĕr'ē) *n., pl.* **-ries.** A creeping, woody, evergreen plant, *Mitchella repens,* of eastern North America, having small white flowers and scarlet berries. Also called "twinberry."

partridge pea. A plant, *Cassia fasciculata,* of eastern and central North America, having yellow flowers.

part song. A song with two or more voice parts.

part-time (pärt'tīm') *adj.* For or during less than the customary time: *a part-time job.* —**part'-time'** *adv.* —**part'-tim'er** *n.*

par·tu·ri·ent (pär-tyŏŏr'ē-ənt, pär-tŏŏr'-) *adj.* **1.** About to bring forth young; being in labor. **2.** Of or pertaining to giving birth. **3.** About to produce or come forth with something, such as an idea or discovery. [Latin *parturiēns,* present participle of *parturīre,* to be in labor, from *parere* (future participle *parturus*), to bear. See **per-4** in Appendix.*] —**par·tu'ri·en·cy** *n.*

par·tu·ri·tion (pär'tyŏŏ-rĭsh'ən, pär'chŏŏ-, pär'tŏŏ-) *n.* The act of giving birth; childbirth. [Late Latin *parturītiō,* from Latin *parturīre,* to be in labor. See **parturient.**]

par·ty (pär'tē) *n., pl.* **-ties. 1. a.** A group of persons gathered together for pleasure: *cocktail party.* **b.** A group of persons gathered together to participate in some activity: *a sailing party.* **2.** A permanent political group organized to promote and support its principles and candidates for public office. **3.** *Law.* A person or group involved in a legal proceeding. **4.** A participant or accessory. **5.** *Informal.* A person: *He's an amusing old party.* [Middle English *partie,* part, party, from Old French, from the feminine past participle of *partir,* to divide, from Latin *partīre* (stem *part-*), PART.] —**par'ty** *adj.*

party line. 1. A telephone circuit connecting two or more subscribers with the exchange. **2.** The official policies and principles of a political party to which loyal members are expected to adhere. —**par'ty-line'** *adj.*

par·ty-poop·er (pär'tē-pōō'pər) *n. Slang.* One who declines to participate enthusiastically in the recreation of a group.

party wall. *Law.* A wall built on the boundary line of adjoining properties and shared by two owners or tenants.

pa·rure (pə-rŏŏr') *n.* A set of matched jewelry or other ornaments. [French, adornment, from Old French, from *parer,* to prepare, adorn, from Latin *parāre.* See **per-4** in Appendix.*]

par value. The value imprinted on a stock certificate or bond which provides the basis for bond interest, preferred stock dividend, or share of equity capital; face value.

par·ve. *Judaism.* Variant of **pareve.**

par·ve·nu (pär'və-nōō', -nyōō') *n.* A person who has suddenly risen above his social and economic class without the background or qualifications for his new status. [French, from past participle of *parvenir,* to arrive, from Latin *parvenīre,* to come through : *per,* through (see **per1** in Appendix*) + *venīre,* to come (see **gwā-** in Appendix*).] —**par've·nu'** *adj.*

par·vis (pär'vĭs) *n.* **1.** An enclosed courtyard or space in front of a palace or church. **2.** A portico or colonnade in front of a church. [Middle English *parvys,* from Old French *parvis,* from Late Latin *paradīsus,* enclosed garden, PARADISE.]

pas (pä) *n., pl.* **pas** (pä). **1.** *Ballet.* **a.** A dance step or series of steps. **b.** A dance. **2.** The right to go before; precedence. [French, from Latin *passus,* step, from the past participle of *pandere,* to stretch out. See **pet-2** in Appendix.*]

Pas·a·de·na (păs'ə-dē'nə). **1.** A residential city in southwestern California, eight miles northeast of Los Angeles. Population, 116,000. **2.** An industrial city in southeastern Texas, just east of Houston. Population, 59,000.

Pa·say. The former name for **Rizal.**

Pas·cal (păs-kăl'), **Blaise.** 1623–1662. French philosopher and mathematician.

pas·cal celery (păs'kəl). Also **Pas·cal celery.** Any of several types of commercially grown celery having green, unblanched stalks. [Origin uncertain.]

pas·chal (păs'kəl) *adj.* Of or pertaining to the Passover or to Easter. [Middle English *paskal,* from Old French *pascal,* from Late Latin *paschālis,* from *pascha,* Passover, Easter, from Late Greek *paska,* from Hebrew *pesah,* PESACH.]

paschal lamb. 1. A lamb eaten at the feast of the Passover. **2.** *Capital* **P,** *capital* **L.** Christ.

pas de deux (pä də dœ') *pl.* **pas de deux.** A ballet figure or dance for two persons. [French, "step for two."]

passe (pä'sä) *n.* A presentation and movement of the cape by the matador to attract, receive, and direct the charge of the bull.

Also called "pass." [Spanish, "a passing," "pass," from *pasar,* to pass, from Vulgar Latin *passāre.* See **pass.**]

pa·sha (pä'shə, păsh'ə; Turkish pä-shä') *n.* Also **pa·cha.** A former title of honor placed after the name of Turkish military and civil officials. Also called "bashaw." [Turkish *paşa.*]

Pash·to (pŭsh'tō) *n.* An Iranian language that is a major language of Afghanistan. Also called "Pushtu," "Afghan."

Pa·siph·a·ë (pə-sĭf'ə-ē'). *Greek Mythology.* The wife of Minos and mother, by a white bull, of the Minotaur.

pasque-flow·er (păsk'flou'ər) *n.* Any of several plants of the genus *Anemone,* having large blue, purple, or white flowers and conspicuously plumed fruit. *A. patens,* of western North America, is also called "prairie smoke." [From earlier *passeflower* (influenced by Old French *pasque,* Easter), from Old French *passefleur : passer,* to PASS (surpass) + *fleur, flor,* FLOWER.]

pas·qui·nade (păs'kwə-nād') *n.* A lampoon posted in a public place. —*tr.v.* **pasquinaded, -ading, -ades.** To ridicule with a pasquinade. [French, from Italian *pasquinata,* from *Pasquino,* nickname of an ancient statue in Rome on which lampoons were posted in the 16th century.] —**pas'qui·nad'er** *n.*

pass (păs, päs) *v.* **passed, passing, passes.** —*intr.* **1.** To move on or ahead; proceed. **2.** To run; extend: *The river passes through our land.* **3.** To gain passage despite obstacles: *pass through difficult years.* **4.** To catch up with and move past another vehicle: *The sports car passed on the right.* See Usage note below. **5.** To move past in time; elapse: *The days passed quickly.* **6.** To be transferred from one to another; circulate: *The wine passed around the table.* **7.** To be communicated or exchanged between persons: *Loud words passed.* **8.** To be transferred or conveyed to another by will, deed, or the like: *The title passed to the older son.* **9.** To undergo transition from one condition, form, quality, or characteristic to another: *Daylight passed into darkness.* **10.** To come to an end; be terminated: *His anger passed suddenly.* **11.** To cease to exist; die. Often used with *on.* **12.** To happen; take place: *What passed during the morning?* **13.** To be allowed to happen without notice or challenge: *Let their rude remarks pass.* **14.** To undergo an examination or trial with favorable results. **15.** To be accepted as something different. Used with *as* or *for:* "*would have his Noise and Laughter pass for Wit*" (William Wycherly). **16.** To be approved or adopted: *The motion to adjourn passed.* **17.** *Law.* **a.** To sit in judicial or legal investigation. Used with *on* or *upon: A jury passed on that issue.* **b.** To pronounce an opinion, judgment, or sentence. Used with *on* or *upon.* **c.** To sit in adjudication. Used with *between.* **18.** To throw a ball to a teammate. **19.** *Fencing.* To thrust or lunge. **20.** *Card Games.* To let one's turn to play or bid go by. —*tr.* **1.** To go by without stopping; leave behind. See Usage note below. **2. a.** *Rare.* To go by without paying attention to; let go unmentioned. **b.** To fail to pay (a dividend). **3.** To go beyond; exceed: *The returns passed all expectations.* **4.** To go across; go through: *pass enemy lines.* **5. a.** To undergo (a trial or examination) with favorable results: *He passed every test.* **b.** To cause or allow to go through a trial, test, examination, or the like successfully: *The instructor passed all the candidates.* **6. a.** To cause to move: *He passed his hand over the fabric.* **b.** To cause to move into a certain position: *pass a cable around a cylinder.* **c.** To cause to move as part of a process: *pass liquid through a filter.* **7.** To cause to go by: *pass foot soldiers in review.* **8.** To allow to go by or elapse; spend: *He passed his winter in Vermont.* **9. a.** To cause to be transferred from one to another; circulate: *They passed the news quickly.* **b.** To hand over to someone else: *pass the bread.* **c.** To circulate fraudulently: *pass counterfeit money.* **d.** *Law.* To transfer title or ownership of. **10.** *Sports.* **a.** To throw (a ball) to a teammate. **b.** *Baseball.* To walk (a batter) intentionally. **11.** To cross over; issue from: *No secrets pass her lips.* **12.** To discharge; void (bodily waste). **13. a.** To approve; adopt: *The legislature passed the bill.* **b.** To be sanctioned, ratified, or approved by: *The bill passed the House of Representatives.* **14.** To pronounce; utter: *pass judgment.* **15.** To go past without noticing. Used with *by: He passed them by without even a nod.* —**bring to pass.** To cause to happen. —**come to pass.** To happen. —**pass away. 1.** To go away in time; end; terminate. **2.** To die. **3.** To spend or while away (time). —**pass for.** To be accepted as being something one is not. —**pass off. 1.** To offer, sell, or put into circulation (an imitation of something) as genuine. —**pass out. 1.** To distribute. **2.** *Informal.* To faint. —**pass over.** To leave out; overlook; disregard. —**pass up.** *Informal.* To reject; let go by: *pass up an opportunity.* —*n.* **1.** The act of passing; passage. **2.** A way through or on which one can move or travel, especially a narrow gap between mountain peaks. **3. a.** A permit, ticket, or authorization to come and go at will. **b.** A free ticket entitling one to transportation or admission. **c.** Written leave of absence from military duty. **4.** A sweep or run by an aircraft over an area or target. **5.** A condition or situation, often critical in nature; predicament. **6.** A sexual invitation or overture. **7.** A motion of the hand or the waving of a wand for magic. **8. a.** A throw of a ball between teammates. **b.** *Fencing.* A lunge or thrust. **c.** *Baseball.* An intentional walk. **9.** *Card Games.* A refusal to bid, draw, bet, or play. **10.** A winning throw of the dice in the game of craps. **11.** *Bullfighting.* A cape maneuver, *pase* (*see*). —**a pretty pass.** A bad or difficult situation. —See Synonyms at **way.** [Middle English *passen,* to proceed, from Old French *passer,* from Vulgar Latin *passāre* (unattested), from Latin *passus,* step, pace, stride, from the past participle of *pandere,* to stretch out. See **pet-2** in Appendix.*] —**pass'less** *adj.*

Usage: Pass, as a verb, can be applied to two persons or objects going in the same direction or on courses that intersect. In

partridge
Perdix perdix

Blaise Pascal

the first case it has the transitive sense of *overtake;* in the second, that of *meet* (transitive or intransitive). When the direction is important to an understanding of the context, as in a report of a collision of automobiles, an elaboration of *pass* is necessary. The past tense and past participle are now *passed: He passed* (or *has passed*). But *past* is the adjective, adverb, and preposition: *a past time; walk past; past the crisis.*

pass. 1. passage. 2. passenger. 3. passive.

pass·a·ble (păs′ə-bəl, päs′-) *adj.* 1. Capable of being passed, traversed, or crossed, as a road or stream. 2. Acceptable for general circulation: *passable currency.* 3. Satisfactory but not outstanding. —**pass′a·ble·ness** *n.* —**pass′a·bly** *adv.*

pas·sa·ca·glia (pä′sə-käl′yə, păs′ə-kăl′yə) *n.* A 17th- and 18th-century musical form consisting of continuous variations on a ground bass in slow triple meter. Compare **chaconne**. [Italian, from Spanish *passacalle* : *pasar,* to pass, from (unattested) Vulgar Latin *passāre* (see **pass**) + *calle,* street, from Latin *callis*†, path.]

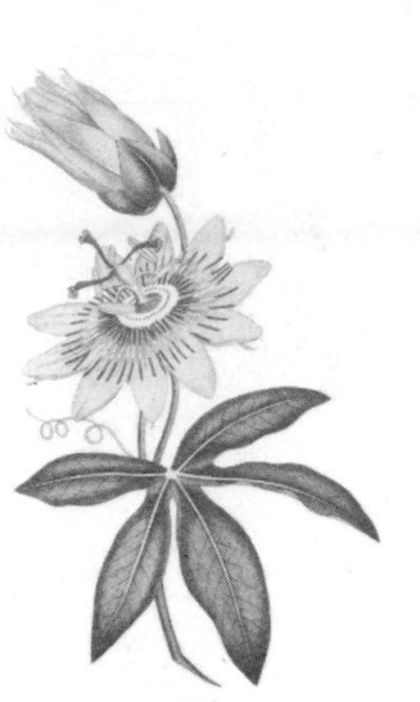

passionflower
Passiflora caerulea

pas·sage (păs′ĭj) *n. Abbr.* **pass.** 1. The act or process of passing: **a.** A movement from one place to another; a going by, through, over, or across; transit. **b.** The process of elapsing. **c.** The process of passing from one state, condition, or stage to another; transition. **d.** *Obsolete.* Death. **e.** The enactment into law of a legislative measure. 2. A journey, especially one by air or water. 3. **a.** The right to travel on something, especially a ship: *to book a passage.* **b.** The price paid for this. 4. The right, permission, or power to come and go freely. 5. **a.** A path, channel, or duct through, over, or along which something may pass: *the nasal passages.* **b.** A corridor. 6. An occurrence between two persons: **a.** An exchange of words, arguments, or vows. **b.** An exchange of blows: *passage at arms.* 7. A segment of a literary work: *a celebrated passage from Gibbon.* 8. *Music.* A segment of a composition. 9. *Medicine.* An emptying of the bowels. —See Synonyms at **way**. [Middle English, from Old French, from *passer,* to PASS.]

pas·sage·way (păs′ĭj-wā′) *n.* A corridor.

Pas·sa·ic (pə-sā′ĭk). 1. An industrial city in northeastern New Jersey, on the Passaic River. Population, 54,000. 2. A river rising in north-central New Jersey and flowing about 100 miles generally east and south to Newark Bay.

Pas·sa·ma·quod·dy (păs′ə-mə-kwŏd′ē) *n., pl.* **Passamaquoddy** or **-dies**. 1. A tribe of Algonquian-speaking North American Indians, formerly inhabiting Maine and New Brunswick, Canada. 2. A member of this tribe. 3. The language of this tribe, closely akin to Malecite.

Pas·sa·ma·quod·dy Bay (păs′ə-mə-kwŏd′ē). An arm of the Bay of Fundy between New Brunswick, Canada, and Maine.

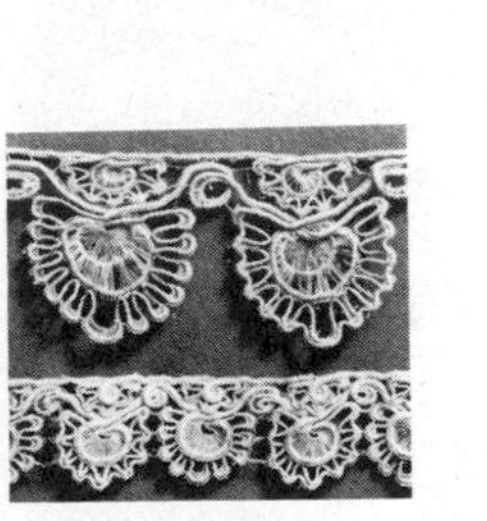

passementerie
Silk-and-gilt tinsel passementerie made in 18th-century Italy

pas·sant (păs′ənt) *adj. Heraldry.* Designating a beast facing and walking toward the viewer's right with one front leg raised. [Middle English, from Old French, from the present participle of *passer,* to PASS.]

pass·book (păs′bo͝ok′, päs′-) *n. Abbr.* **P.B.** 1. A **bankbook** *(see).* 2. A book in which a merchant records credit sales.

pas·sé (pă-sā′) *adj.* 1. Out-of-date; no longer current or in fashion. 2. Past the prime; faded; aged. [French, past participle of *passer,* to pass, from Old French, to PASS.]

passed ball. A baseball pitch missed by the catcher, even though it passes reasonably close to him, and allowing a base runner to advance a base. Compare **wild pitch**.

pas·sel (păs′əl) *n. Regional.* A large quantity or number: *They had a whole passel of children.* [Variant of PARCEL.]

passe·men·terie (păs-mĕn′trē) *n.* Ornamental trimming for a garment, such as braid, lace, or metallic beads. [French, from *passement,* trimming, from *passer,* from Old French, to PASS.]

pas·sen·ger (păs′ən-jər) *n. Abbr.* **pass.** 1. A person who travels in a train, airplane, ship, bus, or other conveyance, without participating in its operation. 2. A wayfarer or traveler. [Middle English *passyngere, passager,* from Old French *passager,* from adjective, passing, from *passage,* PASSAGE.]

passenger pigeon. An extinct migratory bird, *Ectopistes migratorius,* abundant in North America until the latter part of the 19th century.

passe par·tout (păs pär-to͞o′). 1. Something enabling one to pass or go everywhere; especially, a master key. 2. **a.** A mounting for a picture in which colored tape forms the frame. **b.** The tape so used. 3. A mat used in mounting a picture. [French, "pass everywhere."]

pas·ser-by (păs′ər-bī′, päs′-) *n., pl.* **passers-by**. Also **pas·ser·by** *pl.* **passersby**. A person who passes by, often by chance.

pas·ser·ine (păs′ə-rīn′) *adj.* Pertaining to or designating birds of the order Passeriformes, which includes perching birds and songbirds such as the jays, blackbirds, finches, warblers, and sparrows. More than half of all known birds belong to this order. —*n.* A bird of the order Passeriformes. [Latin *passerīnus,* from *passer*†, sparrow.]

pas seul (pä sœl′). A dance or ballet figure performed by one person. [French, "step by oneself."]

pas·si·ble (păs′ə-bəl) *adj.* Capable of suffering; sensitive. [Middle English, from Old French, from Medieval Latin *passibilis,* from Latin *patī* (past participle *passus*), to suffer. See **pēi-** in Appendix.*] —**pas′si·bil′i·ty** *n.*

pas·sim (păs′ĭm) *adv.* Throughout; frequently. Used in textual annotation to indicate that the word or passage occurs frequently in the work cited. [Latin *passim,* here and there, everywhere, scattered about, adverbial formation from *pandere,* to spread out, scatter. See **pet-²** in Appendix.*]

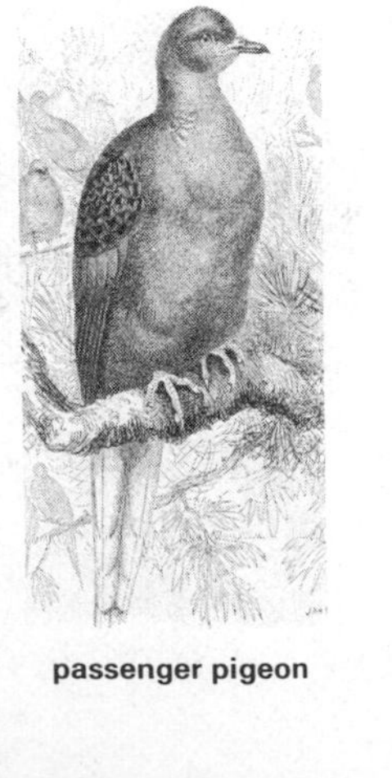

passenger pigeon

pass·ing (păs′ĭng, päs′-) *adj.* 1. Of brief duration; transitory: *a passing fancy.* 2. Cursory; superficial; casual: *a passing glance.* 3. Allowing one to pass an examination, test, course of study, or the like; satisfactory: *a passing mark on the test.* 4. *Archaic.* Very; great; surpassing: *" 'Tis a passing shame."* (Shakespeare). —*adv. Archaic.* Very; surpassingly: *"A man he was to all the country dear / And passing rich with forty pounds a year."* (Goldsmith). —*n.* 1. The act of one that passes or the fact of having passed. 2. A place where or a means by which one can pass. 3. Death. —**in passing.** While going by; incidentally.

passing bell. A **death bell** *(see).*

passing note. *Music.* A note that is not part of a particular chord but is placed between two chords to provide a smooth transition from one to the other. Also called "passing tone."

pas·sion (păsh′ən) *n.* 1. Any powerful emotion or appetite, such as love, joy, hatred, anger, or greed. 2. **a.** Ardent adoring love. **b.** Strong sexual desire; lust. **c.** The object of such love or desire. 3. **a.** Boundless enthusiasm: *"I was seized very early with a passion for literature, which has been the ruling passion of my life"* (Hume). **b.** The object of such enthusiasm. 4. An abandoned display of emotion, especially of anger. 5. *Archaic.* Passivity. 6. *Archaic.* Martyrdom. 7. *Capital* **P.** **a.** The sufferings of Christ in the period following the Last Supper and including the Crucifixion. **b.** A narrative of this (as in one of the Gospels), or a musical setting or serial pictorial representation of it. [Middle English, from Old French, from Late Latin *passiō* (translation of Greek *pathos*), suffering, from Latin *patī* (past participle *passus*), to suffer. See **pēi-** in Appendix.*] —**pas′sion·less** *adj.*

Synonyms: *passion, fervor, enthusiasm, zeal, ardor.* These all denote strong feeling, either sustained or passing, for or about something or somebody. *Passion* is a deep, overwhelming feeling or emotion. When directed toward a person, it usually connotes love as well as sexual desire, although it can also refer to hostile emotions such as anger and hatred. Used lightly, it suggests an avid interest, as in a hobby: *a passion for gardening. Fervor* is a highly intense, sustained emotional state, frequently (like *passion*) with a potential loss of control implied: *he fought with fervor.* Quite different is *enthusiasm,* which reflects excitement and responsiveness to more specific or concrete things. *Zeal,* sometimes reflecting strong, forceful devotion to a specific cause, expresses a driving attraction to something which grows out of motivation or attitude: *zeal for the project. Ardor* can be for a cause but commonly connotes a warm, rapturous feeling directed toward persons.

pas·sion·al (păsh′ən-əl) *adj. Rare.* Of or pertaining to passion. —*n.* A book of the sufferings of saints and martyrs.

pas·sion·ate (păsh′ən-ĭt) *adj.* 1. Capable of or having intense feelings; excitable. 2. Wrathful by temperament; choleric. 3. Amorous; lustful. 4. Showing or expressing strong emotion; ardent: *a passionate speech against injustice.* 5. Arising from or marked by passion: *a passionate rage.* —**pas′sion·ate·ly** *adv.*

pas·sion·flow·er (păsh′ən-flou′ər) *n.* Any of various chiefly tropical American vines of the genus *Passiflora,* usually having large, showy flowers. Some species bear edible fruit. See **granadilla, maypop**. [From the imagined resemblance of its parts to the instruments of the Passion.]

passion fruit. The edible fruit of the passionflower.

Passion play. A play representing the Passion of Christ.

Passion Sunday. The second Sunday before Easter.

Pas·sion·tide (păsh′ən-tīd′) *n.* The fortnight between Passion Sunday and Easter.

Passion Week. The week between Passion Sunday and Palm Sunday.

pas·sive (păs′ĭv) *adj.* 1. Receiving or subjected to an action without responding or initiating an action in return. 2. Accepting without objection or resistance; submissive; compliant. 3. Not participating, acting, or operating; inert. 4. *Finance.* Designating certain bonds or shares that do not bear interest. 5. *Abbr.* **pass.** *Grammar.* Denoting a verb form or voice used to indicate that the grammatical subject is the object of the action or the effect of the verb. For example, in the sentence *They were impressed by his manner, were impressed* is in the passive voice. Compare **active**. —See Synonyms at **inactive**. —*n. Abbr.* **pass.** *Grammar.* 1. The passive voice. 2. A verb or construction in this voice. [Middle English, from Latin *passīvus,* capable of suffering, from *patī* (past participle *passus*), to suffer. See **pēi-** in Appendix.*] —**pas′sive·ly** *adv.* —**pas′sive·ness** *n.*

passive resistance. Resistance to authority or law by nonviolent methods, such as refusal to comply, peaceful demonstrations, or fasting. —**passive resister.**

pas·siv·ism (păs′ĭv-ĭz′əm) *n.* Passive character, quality, or behavior. —**pas′siv·ist** *n.*

pas·siv·i·ty (pă-sĭv′ə-tē) *n.* The condition or quality of being passive; inactivity; quiescence.

pass·key (păs′kē′, päs′-) *n.* Any of various kinds of keys, such as a **master key, skeleton key,** or **latchkey** *(all of which see).*

Pass·o·ver (păs′ō′vər, päs′-) *n.* A Jewish festival beginning on the 14th of Nisan and traditionally celebrated for eight days. It commemorates the escape of the Jews from Egypt. Exodus 12. Also called "Pesach," "Pesah." See **Seder**. [From the phrase *pass over,* translation of Hebrew *pesaḥ,* PESACH.]

pass·port (păs′pôrt′, -pōrt′, päs′-) *n.* 1. An official governmental document that certifies the identity and citizenship of an individual and grants him permission to travel abroad. 2. A permit issued by a foreign country allowing one to transport goods or to travel through that country. 3. An official document issued to a ship, especially a neutral merchant ship in time of war, authorizing it to leave port, or to enter certain waters freely. 4. Anything that enables one to be admitted or accepted: *His wit was his passport.* [French *passeport,* safe-conduct, permission to pass through a port : *passer,* to pass,

ă pat/ā pay/âr care/ä father/b bib/ch church/d deed/ĕ pet/ē be/f fife/g gag/h hat/hw which/ĭ pit/ī pie/îr pier/j judge/k kick/l lid, needle/m mum/n no, sudden/ng thing/ŏ pot/ō toe/ô paw, for/oi noise/ou out/o͝o took/o͞o boot/p pop/r roar/s sauce/sh ship, dish/

from Old French, to PASS + *port,* port, from Old French, PORT (harbor).]

pass·word (păs′wûrd′, päs′-) *n.* A secret word or phrase which indicates that the speaker is to be admitted.

past (păst, päst) *adj.* **1.** No longer current; gone by; over: *His youth is past.* **2.** Having existed or occurred in, or belonging to, an earlier time; bygone: *past events; past centuries.* **3. a.** Earlier than the present time; ago: *forty years past.* **b.** Just gone by or elapsed: *in the past month.* **4.** Having served formerly in some official capacity: *a past vice president.* **5.** *Grammar.* Of, pertaining to, or denoting a verb tense or form used to express an action or condition prior to the time it is expressed. —*n.* **1.** The time before the present. Used with *the.* **2. a.** Former background, career, experiences, and activities: *a man with a distinguished past.* **b.** A former period of someone's life kept secret: *a man with a past.* **3.** *Grammar.* **a.** The past tense. **b.** A verb form in the past tense. —*adv.* So as to pass by or go beyond: *He waved as he walked past.* —*prep.* **1.** Beyond in time; later than; after: *It is past midnight.* **2.** Beyond in position: *the lake past the meadow.* **3.** Beyond the power, scope, extent, or influence of: *The problem is past understanding.* **4.** Beyond the number or amount of: *The child couldn't count past 20.* [Middle English, *passed, past,* from the past participle of *passen,* to PASS.]

pas·ta (päs′tə) *n.* **1.** Paste or dough made of flour and water, used dried, as in macaroni, or fresh, as in ravioli. **2.** A prepared dish of pasta. [Italian, from Late Latin, PASTE.]

Pas·ta·za (päs-tä′sä). A river rising in central Ecuador and flowing 400 miles south to join the Marañón in Peru.

paste[1] (pāst) *n.* **1.** A smooth viscous adhesive, such as flour and water or starch and water, used to join light materials, such as paper and cloth. **2.** Any similar soft, smooth, thick mixture. **3.** A smooth dough of water, flour, and butter or other shortening, used in making pastry. **4.** A food that has been pounded until it is reduced to a smooth, creamy mass: *anchovy paste.* **5.** A sweet, doughy candy or confection. **6.** Moistened clay used in making porcelain or pottery. **7. a.** A hard, brilliant glass used in making artificial gems. **b.** A gem made of this glass. In this sense, also called "strass." —*tr.v.* **pasted, pasting, pastes. 1.** To cause to adhere by applying paste. **2.** To cover with something to which paste has been applied: *He pasted the wall with burlap.* [Middle English, from Old French, from Late Latin *pasta,* dough, paste, from Greek *pastē,* barley porridge, from *pastos,* sprinkled, from *passein,* to sprinkle. See **kwēt-** in Appendix.*]

paste[2] (pāst) *tr.v.* **pasted, pasting, pastes.** *Slang.* To punch. —*n.* *Slang.* A hard blow. [Alteration of BASTE (to beat).]

paste·board (pāst′bôrd′, -bōrd′) *n.* **1.** A thin, firm board made of sheets of paper pasted together or of pressed paper pulp, used especially to make book covers. **2. a.** A ticket. **b.** A playing card. **c.** A visiting card. —*adj.* **1.** Made of pasteboard. **2.** Unsubstantial; fake.

pas·tel (pă-stĕl′) *n.* **1. a.** A dried paste made of ground and mixed pigment, chalk, water, and gum, used to make crayons. **b.** A crayon of this material. Also called "pastille." **2.** A picture or sketch drawn with this type of crayon. **3.** The art or process of drawing with such crayons. **4.** A soft, delicate hue, a light tint. **5.** A sketchy or brief prose work. [French, from Italian *pastello,* from Late Latin *pastellus,* woad dye, crayon, diminutive of *pasta,* PASTE (referring to the paste made by decoction of woad twigs).] —**pas·tel′** *adj.* —**pas·tel′ist, pas·tel′list** *n.*

pas·tern (păs′tərn) *n.* The part of a horse's foot between the fetlock and hoof. [Middle English *pastron,* a horse's hobble, hence the part of the leg to which it is attached, from Old French *pasturon,* variant of *pasture,* a hobble, from Late Latin *pāstōria,* a sheep's hobble, from *pāstor,* shepherd, PASTOR.]

Pas·ter·nak (păs′tər-năk′), **Boris Leonidovich.** 1890–1960. Soviet poet, novelist, and translator.

paste-up (pāst′ŭp′) *n.* **1.** Any composition of light, flat objects pasted on a sheet of paper or other backing; a collage. **2.** *Printing.* A **mechanical** *(see).*

Pas·teur (pă-stûr′), **Louis.** 1822–1895. French chemist; made discoveries in immunology and microbiology.

pas·teur·i·za·tion (păs′chər-ə-zā′shən, păs′tər-) *n.* The process of destroying most disease-producing microorganisms and limiting fermentation in milk, beer, and other liquids by partial or complete sterilization. [Invented by Louis PASTEUR.]

pas·teur·ize (păs′chə-rīz′, păs′tə-) *tr.v.* **-ized, -izing, -izes.** To subject (a liquid) to pasteurization. —**pas′teur·iz′er** *n.*

Pasteur treatment. A rabies treatment in which the growth of antibodies is stimulated during the incubation of the disease by increasingly strong inoculations of the attenuated rabies virus. [After Louis PASTEUR.]

pas·tic·cio (pă-stē′chō, -chē-ō; *Italian* päs-tēt′chō) *n., pl.* **-ci** (-chē). A work, especially of music, produced by borrowing fragments or motifs from various sources; potpourri. [Italian, "pasty," "hodgepodge," from Medieval Latin *pasticius,* pasty, from Late Latin *pasta,* PASTE.]

pas·tiche (pă-stēsh′, pä-) *n.* **1.** A dramatic, literary, or musical piece openly imitating the previous work of another artist, often with satirical intent. **2.** A hodgepodge of borrowed elements from various sources; pasticcio. [French, from Italian *pasticcio,* PASTICCIO.]

pas·tille (pă-stēl′) *n.* Also **pas·til** (păs′tĭl). **1.** A small medicated or flavored tablet; lozenge; troche. **2.** A tablet containing aromatic substances, burned to fumigate or deodorize the air. **3.** Paste for crayons, **pastel** *(see).* **4.** A crayon, **pastel** *(see).* [French, from Latin *pāstillus,* little loaf, roll, diminutive of *pānis,* bread. See **pā-** in Appendix.*]

pas·time (păs′tīm′, päs′-) *n.* An activity that occupies one's time pleasantly; something that interests, amuses, or diverts.

pas·ti·na (pă-stē′nə) *n.* Tiny pieces of macaroni, usually cooked in soups or used as baby food. [Italian, diminutive of *pasta,* pasta, from Late Latin, PASTE.]

past·i·ness (pā′stē-nĭs) *n.* A pasty quality or appearance.

past master. *Abbr.* **P.M. 1.** One who has formerly held the position of master in an organization such as a lodge or club. **2.** A person thoroughly experienced and skilled in a particular craft.

Pas·to (päs′tō). **1.** A city in the gold-mining region of southwestern Colombia. Population, 113,000. **2.** A volcano rising to 13,990 feet near this city.

pas·tor (păs′tər, päs′-) *n.* **1.** A Christian minister in his capacity of having spiritual charge over a congregation or other group. **2.** *Rare.* A shepherd. [Middle English *pastour,* from Old French, from Latin *pāstor,* shepherd, from *pāscere* (past participle *pāstus*), to graze, feed. See **pā-** in Appendix.* Sense 1 arises from a recurrent Biblical metaphor, seen in Psalms 23:1, John 10:11 and 21:15.]

pas·tor·al (păs′tər-əl, päs′-) *adj.* **1.** Of or pertaining to shepherds, herdsmen, and others directly involved in animal husbandry. **2. a.** Of or pertaining to the country or country life; rural. **b.** Having the qualities of idealized country life, such as charming simplicity and a leisurely, carefree pace. **3.** Of or designating an artistic work that portrays country life in this way. **4.** Of or pertaining to a pastor or his duties. —See Synonyms at **rural.** —*n.* **1.** A literary or other artistic work that portrays rural life, usually in an idealized manner. **2.** *Music.* A pastorale. [Middle English, from Latin *pāstōrālis,* from *pāstor,* shepherd, PASTOR.] —**pas′tor·al·ism′** *n.* —**pas′tor·al·ist** *n.* —**pas′tor·al·ly** *adv.*

pas·to·rale (păs′tə-räl′, -răl′, päs′-; *Italian* päs′tō-ra′lā) *n., pl.* **-rali** (-rä′lē) or **-les.** *Music.* **1.** An opera or other vocal composition based on a rural theme or subject. **2.** An instrumental composition with a tender melody in a moderately slow rhythm, suggestive of idyllic rural life. Also called "pastoral." [Italian, from *pastorale,* pastoral, from Latin *pāstōrālis,* PASTORAL.]

pas·tor·ate (păs′tər-ĭt, päs′-) *n.* **1.** The office, rank, or jurisdiction of a pastor. **2.** A pastor's term of office with one congregation. **3.** A body of pastors.

pas·to·ri·um (pă-stôr′ē-əm, -stōr′ē-əm, pä-) *n., pl.* **-ums.** *Southern U.S.* The residence of a pastor; a parsonage.

past participle. *Abbr.* **pp., p.p., P.P.** A verb form indicating past or completed action or time. It is used as a verbal adjective in phrases such as *finished work, baked beans,* and with auxiliaries to form the passive voice or perfect and pluperfect tenses in constructions such as *The work was finished* and *She had baked the beans.* Also called "perfect participle."

past perfect. A verb tense, the **pluperfect** *(see).*

pas·tra·mi (pə-strä′mē) *n.* A highly seasoned smoked cut of beef, usually from the breast or shoulder. [Yiddish, from Rumanian *pastramă,* from *pāstra*†, to preserve.]

pas·try (pās′trē) *n., pl.* **-tries. 1.** A baked paste of flour, water, and shortening, used for the crusts of pies, tarts, and the like. **2.** Baked foods, such as pies, tarts, or turnovers, made with this paste. [From PASTE.]

past tense. A verb tense used to express an action or condition that occured in or during the past. For example, in *While she was sewing, he read aloud, was sewing* and *read* are in the past tense.

pas·tur·age (păs′chər-ĭj, päs′-) *n.* **1.** The grass or other vegetation eaten by grazing animals. **2. a.** Land covered with such grass or vegetation. **b.** The right to graze cattle on such land. **3.** The business of grazing cattle.

pas·ture (păs′chər, päs′-) *n.* **1.** Grass or other vegetation eaten as food by grazing animals. **2.** Ground on which such vegetation grows. —*v.* **pastured, -turing, -tures.** —*tr.* **1.** To herd (animals) into a pasture to graze. **2.** To provide (animals) with pasturage. Used of land. —*intr.* To graze in a pasture. [Middle English, from Old French, from Late Latin *pāstūra,* from Latin *pāscere* (past participle *pāstus*), to pasture, feed. See **pā-** in Appendix.*] —**pas′tur·a·ble** *adj.* —**pas′tur·er** *n.*

past·y[1] (pā′stē) *adj.* **-ier, -iest. 1.** Resembling paste in color or consistency. **2.** Pale and lifeless-looking.

pas·ty[2] (păs′tē, päs′-) *n., pl.* **-ties.** *Chiefly British.* A pie with a filling of seasoned meat or fish. [Middle English *pastee,* from Old French *paste,* from noun, dough, PASTE.]

past·y[3] (pā′stē) *n., pl.* **-ies.** A patch used by striptease performers to conceal the nipple. [From PASTE (to stick).]

PA system. A **public-address system** *(see).*

pat[1] (păt) *v.* **patted, patting, pats.** —*tr.* **1. a.** To tap gently with the open hand or with something flat. **b.** To stroke lightly as a gesture of affection. **2.** To mold by tapping gently with the hands or a flat implement. —*intr.* **1.** To run or walk with a tapping sound. **2.** To hit something or against something gently or lightly. —*n.* **1.** A light stroke or tap. **2.** The sound made by such a stroke or tap, or by light footsteps. **3.** A small mass of something, shaped by or as if by patting: *a pat of butter.* [Middle English *patte* (probably imitative).]

pat[2] (păt) *adj.* **1.** Timely; opportune; fitting: *a pat answer.* **2.** Needing no change; exactly right. —*adv. Informal.* **1.** Without changing position; steadfastly. **2.** Perfectly; precisely; aptly. —**have down pat.** *Informal.* To know and understand completely. —**stand pat.** *Informal.* **1.** To refuse to change one's position or opinion. **2.** To decline to draw more cards to a poker hand. [Probably "with a hitting stroke," from PAT (to tap).] —**pat′ly** *adv.* —**pat′ness** *n.*

pat. patent.

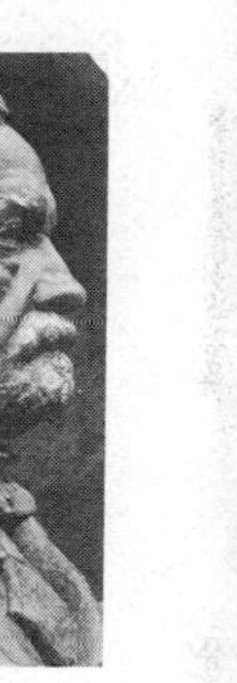

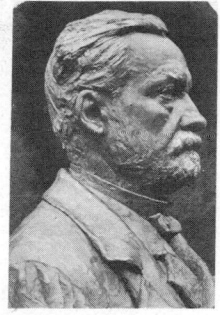

Louis Pasteur

t tight/th thin, path/*th* this, bathe/ŭ cut/ûr urge/v valve/w with/y yes/z zebra, size/zh vision/ə about, item, edible, gallop, circus/ à *Fr.* ami/œ *Fr.* feu, *Ger.* schön/ü *Fr.* tu, *Ger.* über/KH *Ger.* ich, *Scot.* loch/N *Fr.* bon. *Follows main vocabulary. †Of obscure origin.

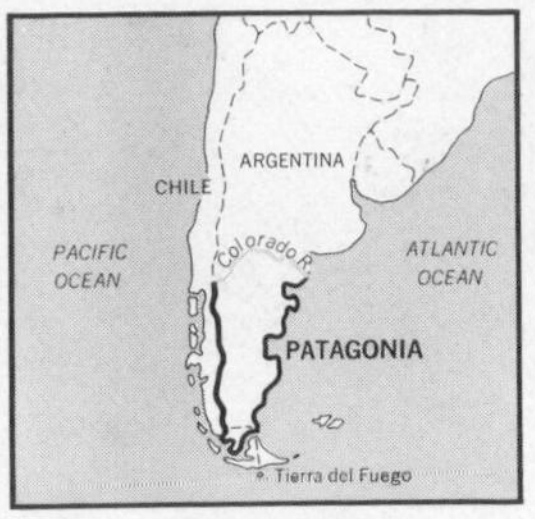

Patagonia

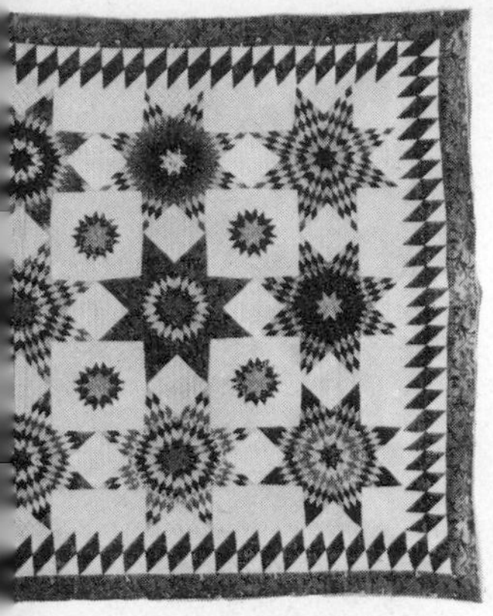

patchwork
Early 19th-century American coverlet of embroidered and quilted patchwork

pa·ta·gi·um (pə-tā′jē-əm) *n., pl.* **-gia** (-jē-ə). *Zoology.* **1.** A thin membrane extending between the fore and hind limb to form a wing or winglike extension, as in bats and flying squirrels. **2.** An expandable, membranous fold of skin between the wing and body of a bird. [New Latin, from Latin, gold edging on a woman's tunic, from Greek *patageion* (unattested), "clattering gold braid," from *patagos*, a clatter (imitative).]

Pat·a·go·ni·a (păt′ə-gō′nē-ə, -gōn′yə). A region in southern South America, about 311,000 square miles in area, extending from the Strait of Magellan north to the Limay and Río Negro rivers in Argentina, and from the Andes east to the Atlantic Ocean. —**Pat′a·go′ni·an** *adj.* & *n.*

patch (păch) *n.* **1.** A small piece of material affixed to another, larger piece to conceal or reinforce a weakened or worn area. **2. a.** Any small piece of cloth used for patchwork. **b.** *Military.* A small cloth badge affixed to a sleeve to indicate the unit to which one belongs. **3.** A dressing or bandage applied to protect a wound or sore. **4.** A small pad or shield of cloth worn over an injured eye. **5.** A **beauty spot** *(see)*. **6. a.** A small piece of land. **b.** The produce grown on such a piece of land: *a patch of beans.* **7.** A small part or section of a surface that differs from or contrasts with the whole: *The flowers made white patches against the grass.* **8.** A small piece or part of anything: *"that little patch of blue which prisoners call the sky"* (Oscar Wilde). —*tr.v.* **patched, patching, patches. 1.** To put a patch or patches on. **2. a.** To make by sewing scraps of material together: *patch a quilt.* **b.** To make by piecing various elements together, especially hastily: *They patched together a treaty.* **3.** To mend, repair, or put together, especially hastily, clumsily, or poorly: *patching old costumes for the tour.* —**patch up.** To settle; make up: *They patched up their quarrel.* [Middle English *pacche*, perhaps variant of *peche*, from Old French *pece, pieche*, PIECE.] —**patch′a·ble** *adj.* —**patch′er** *n.*

patch·ou·li (păch′o͝o-lē, pə-cho͞o′lē) *n., pl.* **-lis.** Also **patch·ou·ly** *pl.* **-lies, pach·ou·li** *pl.* **-lis. 1.** Any of several Asiatic trees of the genus *Pogostemon*, especially *P. patchouly* and *P. cablin*, having leaves that yield a fragrant oil used in the manufacture of perfumes. **2.** A perfume made from this oil. [Tamil *paccilai* : *paccu*, green + *ilai*, leaf.]

patch test. A test for allergic sensitivity made by applying a suspected allergen to the skin by a small surgical pad.

patch·work (păch′wûrk′) *n.* **1.** Needlework consisting of varicolored patches of material sewed together, as in a quilt. **2.** A collection of miscellaneous or incongruous parts; jumble.

patch·y (păch′ē) *adj.* **-ier, -iest. 1.** Made up of or marked by patches: *a patchy pair of trousers.* **2.** Uneven in quality or performance: *patchy work.* —**patch′i·ly** *adv.* —**patch′i·ness** *n.*

patd. patented.

pate (pāt) *n.* **1.** The head; especially, the top of the head: *a bald pate.* **2.** The brains; intellect. Usually used disparagingly. [Middle English *pate*†.]

pâte (pät) *n.* Paste used in making porcelain and pottery. [French, patty, paste, from Old French *paste*, PASTE.]

pâ·té (pä-tā′) *n.* **1.** A meat paste; especially, pâté de foie gras. **2.** A small pastry filled with meat or fish. [French *paté(e)*, from Old French *pasté(e)*, from *paste*, PASTE.]

pâ·té de foie gras (pä-tā′ də fwä grä′). A paste made from goose liver, usually with truffles. [French, "pâté of fat liver."]

pa·tel·la (pə-tĕl′ə) *n., pl.* **-tellae** (-tĕl′ē). **1. a.** A flat, triangular bone located at the front of the knee joint. Also called "kneecap." **b.** Any dish-shaped anatomical formation. **2.** An ancient Roman pan or dish. [Latin, diminutive of *patina*, plate. See **paten.**] —**pa·tel′lar, pa·tel′late** (pə-tĕl′ĭt, -āt′) *adj.*

pa·tel·li·form (pə-tĕl′ə-fôrm′) *adj.* Shaped like a pan, dish, or cup: *the patelliform shell of the limpet.* [New Latin *patelliformis* : PATELL(A) + -FORM.]

pat·en (păt′n) *n.* Also **pat·in, pat·ine** (păt′n). **1.** A plate used to hold the Eucharistic bread. **2.** Any plate. **3.** A thin disk of metal. Also called "patina." [Middle English *paten, pat(e)yn*, from Old French *patene*, from Latin *patina*, dish, pan, from Greek *patanē*. See **pet-**[2] in Appendix.*]

pa·ten·cy (pāt′n-sē) *n.* The state or quality of being obvious.

pat·ent (păt′ənt) *n. Abbr.* **pat. 1. a.** A grant made by a government to an inventor, assuring him the sole right to make, use, and sell his invention for a certain period of time. **b.** The official instrument conveying such a grant, **letters patent** *(see)*. **2.** Something that is protected by such a grant. **3. a.** A grant made by a government to an individual, conveying to him fee-simple title to public lands. **b.** The official document of such a grant. **c.** The land so granted. **4.** Any exclusive right or title. —*adj.* (păt′ənt *for senses 1,3,4,6;* pāt′ənt *for senses 2,5*). **1.** Open to general inspection; unsealed. Used chiefly in the phrase *letters patent.* **2.** Obvious; plain: *"Her profession of sorrow . . . though its insincerity was patent."* (John Updike). **3.** *Abbr.* **pat.** Protected by a patent. **4.** *Abbr.* **pat.** Of, pertaining to, or dealing in patents: *patent law.* **5.** *Biology.* Spreading open; expanded. **6.** Of high quality. Said of flour. —*tr.v.* (păt′ənt). **patented, -enting, -ents.** *Abbr.* **pat. 1.** To obtain a patent on. **2.** To grant a patent to. [As noun, Middle English *(letters) patente*, letters patent, from Old French *(lettres) patentes*, from Medieval Latin *(litterae) patentes*, "open letter or document," from *patentes*, feminine plural of *patēns*, open, from the present participle of *patēre*, to be open. See **pet-**[2] in Appendix.*] —**pat′ent·a·bil′i·ty** *n.* —**pat′ent·a·ble** *adj.*

pat·ent·ee (păt′n-tē′) *n.* One who has been granted a patent.

patent leather. 1. Black leather finished to a hard, glossy surface. **2.** Any of several synthetic materials having a similar appearance. [Made by a once-patented process.]

patent log. *Nautical.* A **screw log** *(see)*.

pat·ent·ly (pāt′ənt-lē) *adv.* In a patent manner; obviously; clearly; plainly.

patent medicine. A drug or other medical preparation that is protected by a patent and can be bought without a prescription.

Patent Office. A bureau of the U.S. Department of Commerce in which claims for patents are studied and patents are issued and recorded.

pat·en·tor (păt′n-tər, păt′n-tôr′) *n.* One that grants a patent.

patent right. The right granted by a patent; especially, the right to have exclusive manufacture and sale of an invention.

pa·ter (pā′tər) *n. Obsolete British.* Father. [Latin. See **pəter** in Appendix.*]

Pa·ter (pā′tər), **Walter Horatio.** 1839–1894. English essayist, novelist, and critic.

pa·ter·fa·mil·i·as (pā′tər-fə-mĭl′ē-əs, pä′tər-) *n., pl.* **patresfamilias** (pā′trēz-fə-mĭl′ē-əs, pä′trēz-). The father of a family in his capacity of head of the household. [Latin : *pater*, father (see **pater**) + *familiās*, archaic genitive of *familia*, FAMILY.]

pa·ter·nal (pə-tûr′nəl) *adj.* **1.** Of, pertaining to, or characteristic of a father; fatherly. **2.** Received or inherited from a father. **3.** Of or pertaining to the father's side of a family. [Medieval Latin *paternālis*, from Latin *paternus*, fatherly, from *pater*, father. See **pəter** in Appendix.*] —**pa·ter′nal·ly** *adv.*

pa·ter·nal·ism (pə-tûr′nəl-ĭz′əm) *n.* A policy or practice of treating or governing people in a fatherly manner, especially by providing for their needs without giving them responsibility. —**pa·ter′nal·is′tic** (-ĭs′tĭk) *adj.* —**pa·ter′nal·is′ti·cal·ly** *adv.*

pa·ter·ni·ty (pə-tûr′nə-tē) *n.* **1.** The fact or condition of being a father; fatherhood. **2.** Descent on a father's side; paternal descent. **3.** Authorship; origin. [Old French *paternite*, from Late Latin *paternitās*, from Latin *paternus*, fatherly, PATERNAL.]

pa·ter·nos·ter (pā′tər-nŏs′tər, păt′ər-) *n.* **1.** *Often capital* **P.** Also **Pater Noster.** The **Lord's Prayer** *(see)*. **2.** One of the large beads on a rosary, on which the Lord's Prayer is said. **3.** A sequence of words spoken as a prayer or as a magic formula. **4.** A weighted fishing line having several jointed attachments for hooks connected by beadlike swivels. [Latin *pater noster*, "our father," first two words in the prayer : *pater*, father (see **pater**) + *noster*, our (see **nes-**[2] in Appendix*).]

Pat·er·son (păt′ər-sən). An industrial city in northeastern New Jersey, on the Passaic River. Population, 144,000.

path (păth, päth) *n., pl.* **paths** (păthz, päthz, păths, päths). **1.** A trodden track or way. **2.** Any road, way, or track. **3.** The route or course along which something moves: *the path of a hurricane.* **4.** A course of action or conduct: *the path of righteousness.* —See Synonyms at **way.** [Middle English *path*, Old English *pæth*. See **pent-** in Appendix.*]

path. pathological; pathology.

Pa·than (pə-tän′) *n.* An Afghan; especially, one of Indo-Iranian stock and Moslem religion. [Hindi *Paṭhan*, from Afghan *Pĕṣtana*, plural of *Pĕṣtūn*, an Afghan, from *Paštó*, the Afghan language, PASHTO.]

pa·thet·ic (pə-thĕt′ĭk) *adj.* Also **pa·thet·i·cal** (pə-thĕt′ĭ-kəl). **1.** Of, pertaining to, expressing, or arousing pity, sympathy, or tenderness; full of pathos: *"Johnson's vigorous and pathetic enumeration of the miseries of a literary life."* (Macaulay). **2.** Distressing and inadequate: *"Her little harmless magic was the pathetic effort of a child to kill a dragon."* (Melville D. Post). —See Synonyms at **moving.** [French *pathétique*, from Late Latin *patheticus*, from Greek *pathētikos*, from *pathētos*, liable to suffer, from *pathos*, passion, suffering. See **kwenth-** in Appendix.*] —**pa·thet′i·cal·ly** *adv.*

Synonyms: *pathetic, pitiful, regrettable, lamentable.* These describe a person or an unfortunate condition that inspires profound concern and, often, either sympathy or rather mild scorn. *Pathetic* and *pitiful* apply expressly to what is rendered helpless through misfortune, to what is abject or cast down, and in some contexts to what is hopelessly inadequate. Often they express genuine compassion; where ineptitude or inadequacy is stressed, the terms usually suggest contempt. *Regrettable* applies to whatever offers ground for regret or apprehension, without necessarily implying sympathy or scorn. Similarly, *lamentable*, a much stronger term, suggests only extreme concern for what is gravely unfortunate.

pathetic fallacy. The attribution of human emotions or characteristics to things; for example, "It's a naive domestic Burgundy but I think you'll be amazed at its presumption." (James Thurber).

path·find·er (păth′fīn′dər, päth′-) *n.* One who discovers a way through or into unexplored regions.

patho–. Indicates disease or suffering; for example, **pathogenesis.** [New Latin, from Greek, from *pathos*, emotion, suffering. See **kwenth-** in Appendix.*]

path·o·gen (păth′ə-jən) *n.* Also **path·o·gene** (păth′ə-jēn′). Any agent that causes disease, especially a microorganism such as a bacterium or fungus. [PATHO- + -GEN.]

path·o·gen·e·sis (păth′ə-jĕn′ə-sĭs) *n.* Also **pa·thog·e·ny** (pă-thŏj′ə-nē). The development of a diseased or morbid condition. [New Latin : PATHO- + -GENESIS.]

path·o·gen·ic (păth′ə-jĕn′ĭk) *adj.* Also **path·o·ge·net·ic** (păth′ō-jə-nĕt′ĭk). Capable of causing disease: *pathogenic bacteria.*

pathol. pathological; pathology.

path·o·log·i·cal (păth′ə-lŏj′ĭ-kəl) *adj.* Also **path·o·log·ic** (păth′ə-lŏj′ĭk). *Abbr.* **path., pathol. 1.** Of or pertaining to pathology. **2.** Pertaining to or caused by disease. **3.** Disordered in behavior: *a pathological liar.* —**path′o·log′i·cal·ly** *adv.*

pa·thol·o·gy (pă-thŏl′ə-jē) *n., pl.* **-gies.** *Abbr.* **path., pathol. 1.** The scientific study of the nature of disease, its causes, processes, development, and consequences. **2.** The anatomic or functional manifestations of disease. [New Latin *pathologia* and Old French *pathologie,* from Greek *pathologia,* study of passions : PATHO- + -LOGY.] —**pa·thol'o·gist** *n.*

pa·thos (pā'thŏs', -thôs') *n.* **1.** A quality in something or someone that arouses feelings of pity, sympathy, tenderness, or sorrow in another: *"The flock of birds flying south had a terrible pathos for her, as if they were orphaned in space."* (Mary McCarthy). **2.** A feeling of sympathy or pity. **3.** In aesthetics, the transient, emotional or subjective elements in a work of art, as distinguished from the ideal or objective. [Greek, passion, suffering. See **kwenth-** in Appendix.*]

path·way (păth'wā', päth'-) *n.* A path.

-pathy. Indicates: **1.** Feeling; perception; for example, **telepathy.** **2.** *Medicine.* **a.** Disease; a diseased condition; for example, **neuropathy.** **b.** A system of treating disease; for example, **homeopathy.** [Latin *-pathia,* from Greek *-patheia,* from *pathos,* passion, suffering. See **kwenth-** in Appendix.*]

Pa·ti·a·la (pŭt'ē-ä'lə). **1.** A former princely state of northwestern India. **2.** A city, formerly the capital of this state, about 125 miles northwest of New Delhi. Population, 144,000.

pa·tience (pā'shəns) *n.* **1.** The capacity of calm endurance: *"This is the story of what a woman's patience can endure."* (Wilkie Collins). **2.** Tolerant understanding: *"Have patience with me, and I will pay thee all."* (Matthew 18:29). **3.** *Chiefly British.* A game of solitaire.

Synonyms: *patience, resignation, forbearance.* These all denote tolerance of something or somebody over a period of time, generally without complaint though not necessarily without annoyance. *Patience* is any admirable endurance of a trying situation or person, usually through a passiveness which comes out of understanding. *Resignation,* on the other hand, implies a feeling of failure with an attitude of seeing something through out of despair or necessity: *his resignation to defeat. Forbearance* denotes restraint, usually in the face of considerable provocation: *forbearance to one's enemies.*

pa·tient (pā'shənt) *adj.* **1.** Capable of bearing affliction with calmness: *"My uncle Toby was a man patient of injuries."* (Sterne). **2.** Tolerant; understanding. **3.** Persevering; constant: *a patient worker.* **4.** Capable of bearing delay and waiting for the right moment. —*n.* One under medical treatment. [Middle English *pacient,* from Old French *patient,* from Latin *patiēns,* from the present participle of *patī,* to suffer. See **pēi-** in Appendix.*] —**pa'tient·ly** *adv.*

pat·in. Variant of **paten.**

pat·i·na¹ (păt'ə-nə) *n., pl.* **-nae** (-nē'). A **paten** *(see).* [Medieval Latin, from Latin, a shallow dish, pan. See **paten.**]

pat·i·na² (păt'ə-nə) *n.* Also **pa·tine** (pă-tēn'). **1.** A thin layer of corrosion, usually brown or green, that appears on copper or copper alloys, such as bronze, as a result of natural or artificial oxidation. Compare **verdigris.** **2.** The sheen produced by age and use on any antique surface. [Italian, originally, "a mixture prepared in a bowl and used to coat calfskins," from Latin *patina,* shallow dish, plate. See **paten.**]

pa·tine (pă-tēn') *tr.v.* **-tined, -tining, -tines.** To coat with a patina. —*n.* **1.** Variant of **paten.** **2.** Variant of **patina** (layer). [French *patine,* from Old French *patene,* from Latin *patina,* paten, PATINA.]

pat·i·o (păt'ē-ō', pä'tē-ō') *n., pl.* **-os.** **1.** An inner, roofless courtyard. **2.** A space for dining or recreation, adjacent to a house or apartment. [Spanish, from Old Spanish *patio*†, untilled land, courtyard.]

pa·tis·se·rie (pä-tēs-rē') *n.* A bakery specializing in French pastry. [French *pâtisserie,* from Old French, "pastry," from *pâtissier,* pastry cook, from *pastitz* (unattested), pasty, from Vulgar Latin *pastīcium* (unattested), from Late Latin *pasta,* dough, PASTE.]

Pat·mos (păt'məs). One of the Dodecanese Islands, 13 square miles in area.

Pat·na (pŭt'nə). The capital of Bihar State, India, on the river Ganges. Population, 364,000.

pat·ois (păt'wä'; *French* pȧ-twä') *n., pl.* **patois** (păt'wäz'; *French* pȧ-twä'). **1.** Any subliterate regional French dialect. **2. a.** Any regional dialect. **b.** Illiterate or nonstandard speech. **3.** The special jargon of a group; cant. —See Synonyms at **dialect.** [French, from Old French, possibly from *patte,* paw (expressing clumsiness or rusticity). See **patten.**]

Pa·tos, La·go·a dos. See **Lagoa dos Patos.**

Pa·tras (pə-trăs', păt'rəs). *Greek* **Pa·trai** (pä'trā). The capital of Achaea, Greece, a seaport on the Gulf of Patras in northwestern Peloponnesus. Population, 95,000.

Pa·tras, Gulf of (pə-trăs', păt'rəs). An inlet of the Ionian Sea in western Greece, north of the Peloponnesus. Also called "Gulf of Calydon."

pat·res·fa·mil·i·as. Plural of **paterfamilias.**

patri-. Indicates father; for example, **patriclinous.** [From Latin *pater,* father, and Greek *patēr,* father. See **pəter** in Appendix.*]

pa·tri·arch (pā'trē-ärk') *n.* **1.** The paternal leader of a family or tribe. **2.** In the Old Testament: **a.** Any of the antediluvian progenitors of the human race, from Adam to Noah. **b.** Abraham, Isaac, Jacob, or any of Jacob's 12 sons, the eponymous progenitors of the 12 tribes of Israel: *"and Jacob begat the twelve patriarchs"* (Acts 7:8). **3.** A title dating from the sixth century A.D. for the bishops of Rome, Constantinople, Jerusalem, Antioch, and Alexandria. **4.** *Roman Catholic Church.* **a.** A bishop who holds the highest episcopal rank after the pope. **b.** The title of the bishops of Constantinople, Antioch, Jerusalem, and Alexandria. **5.** *Eastern Orthodox Church.* **a.** The bishop of Alexandria, Antioch, Constantinople, Jerusalem, Moscow, Serbia, or Rumania. **b.** The bishop of Constantinople, leader of the Greek Orthodox Church. Also called "ecumenical patriarch." **6.** The head of the Coptic, Armenian, Syrian Jacobite, or Nestorian churches. **7.** The head of the Sanhedrin in Syrian Palestine from about 180 B.C. to A.D. 429. **8.** *Mormon Church.* A high dignitary of the priesthood, empowered to invoke blessings. Also called "evangelist." **9.** Someone regarded as the founder or original head of an enterprise, organization, or tradition. **10.** A very old and venerable man; an elder. **11.** The most venerable specimen in a group: *patriarch of the herd.* [Middle English *patriarke,* from Old French *patriarche,* from Late Latin *patriarcha,* from Greek *patriarkhēs* : *patria,* lineage, family, from *patēr,* father (see **pəter** in Appendix*) + -ARCH.]

pa·tri·ar·chal (pā'trē-är'kəl) *adj.* Also **pa·tri·ar·chic** (-kĭk). **1.** Pertaining to or characteristic of a patriarch; venerable; dignified. **2.** Of or pertaining to a patriarchy: *a patriarchal social system.* **3.** Ruled by a patriarch: *a patriarchal see.* —**pa'tri·ar'chal·ly** *adv.* —**pa'tri·ar'chal·ism'** *n.*

patriarchal cross. A Latin cross having two horizontal bars, of which the upper is the shorter.

pa·tri·ar·chate (pā'trē-är'kĭt, -kāt') *n.* **1.** The territory, rule, or rank of a patriarch. **2.** A patriarchy.

pa·tri·ar·chy (pā'tre-är'kē) *n., pl.* **-chies.** **1.** A system of social organization in which descent and succession are traced through the male line. **2.** The rule of a tribe or family by men.

Pa·tri·cia (pə-trĭsh'ə, -trē'shə). A feminine given name. [Latin, feminine of *patricius,* PATRICK.]

pa·tri·cian (pə-trĭsh'ən) *n.* **1.** A member of one of the noble families of the Roman Republic, which before the 3rd century B.C. had exclusive rights to the Senate and the magistracies. **2.** A dignity or title conferred by the Byzantine emperors. **3.** A member of the hereditary ruling class in the medieval free cities of Italy and Germany. **4.** A member of an aristocracy. **5.** A person of notably superior upbringing, manners, and tastes. [Middle English *patricion,* from Old French *patricien,* from Latin *patricius,* (nobleman) of senatorial rank, from *patres,* "fathers," senators, from *pater,* father. See **pəter** in Appendix.*] —**pa·tri'cian** *adj.* —**pa·tri'cian·ly** *adv.*

pa·tri·ci·ate (pə-trĭsh'ē-ĭt, -āt') *n.* **1.** The rank of patrician. **2.** Patricians as a class; nobility; aristocracy. [Latin *patriciātus,* from *patricius,* PATRICIAN.]

pat·ri·cide (păt'rə-sīd') *n.* **1.** The act of murdering one's father. **2.** One who murders his father. [Late Latin *patricīdium* (crime) and Latin *patricīda* (killer) : PATRI- + -CIDE.] —**pat'ri·cid'al** (păt'rə-sīd'l) *adj.*

Pat·rick (păt'rĭk). A masculine given name. [Middle English, after Saint Patrick, from Latin *patricius,* PATRICIAN.]

Pat·rick (păt'rĭk), **Saint.** A.D. 389?–461? The patron saint and apostle of Ireland.

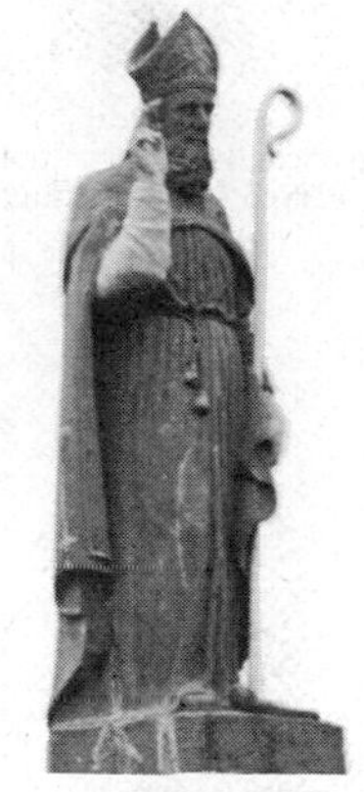

Saint Patrick
Statue in the graveyard on the Hill of Tara, County Meath, Ireland

pat·ri·cli·nous (păt'rə-klī'nəs) *adj.* Also **pat·ro·cli·nous.** Derived from the male line. [PATRI- + *-clinous,* from Greek *-klinēs,* leaning, from *klinein,* to lean (see **klei-** in Appendix*).]

pat·ri·lin·e·al (păt'rə-lĭn'ē-əl) *adj.* Relating to, based on, or tracing descent through the male line.

pat·ri·lo·cal (păt'rə-lō'kəl) *adj.* Pertaining to the home territory of a husband's family or tribe in primitive societies.

pat·ri·mo·ny (păt'rə-mō'nē) *n., pl.* **-nies.** **1.** An inheritance from a father or other ancestor. **2.** Legacy; heritage. **3.** An endowment or estate belonging to a church. [Middle English *patrimoine,* from Old French, from Latin *patrimōnium,* from *pater,* father. See **pəter** in Appendix.*] —**pat'ri·mo'ni·al** (păt'rə-mō'nē-əl) *adj.* —**pat'ri·mo'ni·al·ly** *adv.*

pa·tri·ot (pā'trē-ət, -ŏt') *n.* A person who loves, supports, and defends his country. [Old French *patriote,* compatriot, from Late Latin *patriōta,* from Greek *patriōtēs,* from *patris,* fatherland, from *patēr,* father. See **pəter** in Appendix.*] —**pa'tri·ot'ic** (pā'trē-ŏt'ĭk) *adj.* —**pa'tri·ot'i·cal·ly** *adv.* —**pa'tri·ot·ism'** (pā'trē-ə-tĭz'əm) *n.*

Patriots' Day. April 19, the anniversary of the battles of Lexington and Concord in 1775, celebrated as a legal holiday in Maine and Massachusetts.

pa·tris·tic (pə-trĭs'tĭk) *adj.* Also **pa·tris·ti·cal** (-tĭ-kəl). Of or relating to the fathers of the early Christian church or to their writings. [PATR(I)- + -IST + -IC.] —**pa·tris'ti·cal·ly** *adv.*

Pa·tro·clus (pə-trō'kləs). *Greek Mythology.* A Greek warrior, the friend of Achilles.

pa·trol (pə-trōl') *n.* **1.** The action of moving about an area for purposes of observation or security. **2.** A person or group of persons who carry out such an action. **3. a.** A military unit sent out on a reconnaissance mission. **b.** One or more vehicles, boats, ships, or aircraft assigned to guard or reconnoiter a given area. **4.** A group of eight Boy Scouts, a division of a troop. —*v.* **patrolled, -trolling, -trols.** —*tr.* To engage in a patrol of. —*intr.* To engage in a patrol. [French *patrouiller,* from Old French *patouiller,* to paw or paddle around in mud: *patte,* paw (see **patten**) + *-ouiller,* imitative verb suffix.] —**pa·trol'ler** *n.*

patrol car. A **squad car** *(see).*

pa·trol·man (pə-trōl'mən) *n., pl.* **-men** (-mĭn). A policeman or guard who patrols an assigned area.

patrol torpedo boat. A **PT boat** *(see).*

patrol wagon. A police truck used to convey prisoners.

pa·tron (pā'trən) *n.* **1.** Anyone who supports, protects, or champions; benefactor: *a patron of the arts.* **2.** A regular customer. [Middle English *patroun,* from Old French *patron,* from Medieval Latin *patrōnus,* patron, patron saint, from Latin, defender, advocate, from *pater,* father. See **pəter** in Appendix.*] —**pa'tron·al** (pā'trən-əl) *adj.*

pa·tron·age (pā'trə-nĭj, păt'rə-) *n.* **1.** Support, encouragement,

or championship from a patron. **2.** A patronizing manner. **3.** The trade given to a commercial establishment by its customers. **4.** Customers or patrons collectively; clientele. **5.** The power or action of distributing governmental or political positions. **6.** The positions so distributed.

pa·tron·ess (pā′trə-nĭs) *n.* A female patron.

pa·tron·ize (pā′trə-nīz′, păt′rə-) *tr.v.* **-ized, -izing, -izes. 1.** To act as a patron to; support. **2.** To go to regularly as a customer. **3.** To treat in an offensively condescending manner. **—pa′tron·iz′er** *n.* **—pa′tron·iz′ing·ly** *adv.*

patron saint. The guardian saint of any nation, place, craft, activity, class, or person.

pat·ro·nym·ic (păt′rə-nĭm′ĭk) *n.* A name received from a paternal ancestor; especially, one formed by a prefix or suffix, as in *Johnson,* the son of John, or *Fitzgerald,* the son of Gerald. [Late Latin *patronymicum,* from *patrōnymicus,* "derived from the name of a father," from Greek *patrōnumikos,* from *patrōnumia,* patronymic : PATR(I)- + *onuma,* name (see **nomen-** in Appendix*).] **—pat′ro·nym′ic** *adj.* **—pat′ro·nym′i·cal·ly** *adv.*

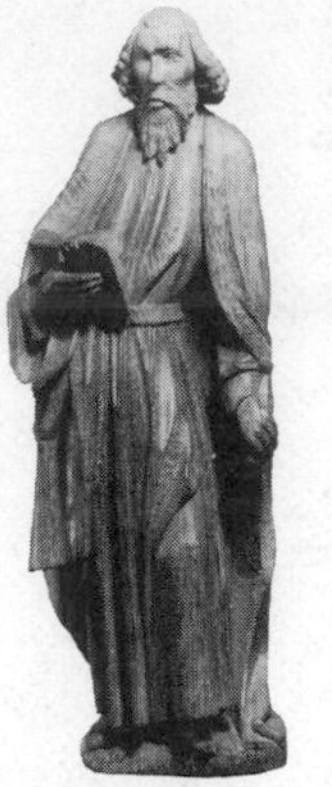

Saint Paul
Fourteenth-century French carved wooden statue

pa·troon (pə-trōōn′) *n.* A member of the Dutch West India Company who on condition of planting 50 settlers within the New Netherlands was granted proprietary and manorial rights to 16 miles of frontage on the Hudson River, with all the land behind. [Dutch, from French *patron,* patron, from Old French, PATRON.]

pat·sy (păt′sē) *n., pl.* **-sies.** *Slang.* A person who is cheated, victimized, or made the butt of a joke. [Origin unknown.]

pat·ten (păt′n) *n.* A wooden sandal, shoe, or clog. [Middle English *patin,* from Old French *patin,* from *patte,* a paw, hoof, from (unattested) Vulgar Latin *patta*†.]

pat·ter[1] (păt′ər) *v.* **-tered, -tering, -ters.** *—intr.* **1.** To make a quick succession of light, soft taps: *Rain pattered on the roof.* **2.** To move with quick, light, softly audible steps. *—tr.* To cause to patter. *—n.* A succession of quick, light, tapping sounds. [Frequentative of PAT (tap lightly).]

pat·ter[2] (păt′ər) *v.* **-tered, -tering, -ters.** *—intr.* **1.** To chatter glibly and rapidly. **2.** To mumble prayers in a mechanical manner. *—tr.* To utter in a glib, rapid, or mechanical manner. *—n.* **1.** The jargon of a particular group; cant; patois. **2.** Glib, rapid-fire speech, as of an auctioneer, salesman, or comedian. **3.** Meaningless talk; chatter. [Middle English *patren, patern,* from Latin *pater(noster),* PATER(NOSTER), from the mechanical recitation of the prayer.] **—pat′ter·er** *n.*

pat·tern (păt′ərn) *n.* **1. a.** An archetype. **b.** An ideal worthy of imitation: *a pattern of womanly virtues.* **2.** A plan, diagram, or model to be followed in making things: *dress pattern.* **3.** A representative sample; specimen. **4. a.** Any artistic or decorative design: *a paisley pattern.* **b.** A design of natural or accidental origin: *"the crystalline pattern of new ice on a country pool"* (William Carlos Williams). **5.** A composite of traits or features characteristic of an individual: *behavioral patterns.* **6.** Form and style in an artistic work or body of artistic works. **7. a.** The configuration of identically aimed rifle shots upon a target. **b.** The distribution and spread of shot from a shotgun. **8.** Enough material to make a complete garment. *—tr.v.* **patterned, -terning, -terns. 1.** To make, mold, or design by following a pattern. Usually used with *on, upon,* or *after.* **2.** To cover or ornament with a design or pattern. [Alteration of Middle English *patron,* from Old French, from Medieval Latin *patrōnus,* patron, (hence) "something to be imitated," pattern. See **patron.**]

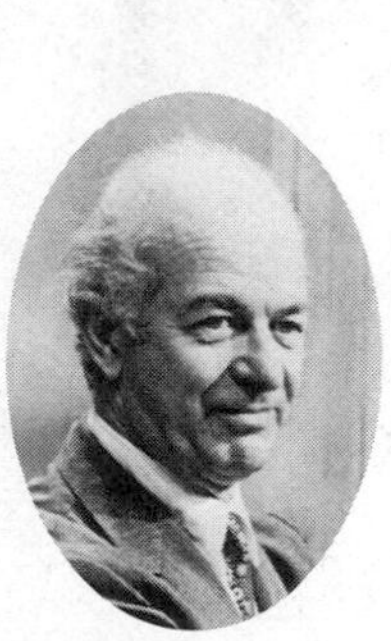

Linus Carl Pauling

Pat·ton (păt′n), **George Smith.** 1885–1945. American general; commander of the Seventh and Third Armies in World War II.

pat·ty (păt′ē) *n., pl.* **-ties. 1.** A small, oval, flattened cake of chopped or minced food. **2.** A small pie. [French *pâté,* small pie, from Old French *paste,* from *paste,* PASTE.]

pat·ty·pan squash (păt′ē-păn′). The **cymling** *(see).*

patty shell. A shell of baked puff pastry made to be filled with creamed meat, seafood, vegetables, or fruit.

pat·u·lous (păch′ōō-ləs) *adj.* Also **pat·u·lent** (păch′ōō-lənt). *Botany.* Spreading or expanded: *patulous branches.* [Latin *patulus,* from *patēre,* to be open. See **pet-**[2] in Appendix.*] **—pat′u·lous·ly** *adv.* **—pat′u·lous·ness** *n.*

P.A.U. Pan American Union.

pau·ci·ty (pô′sə-tē) *n.* **1.** Smallness of number; fewness. **2.** Smallness of quantity; scarcity; dearth. [Middle English *paucite,* from Old French, from Latin *paucitās,* from *paucus,* little, few. See **pòu-** in Appendix.*]

Paul (pôl). A masculine given name. [Latin *Paulus,* Roman surname, from *paulus,* small. See **pòu-** in Appendix.*]

Paul III (pôl). Original name, Alessandro Farnese. 1468–1549. Pope (1534–49); convened the Council of Trent.

Paul VI (pôl). Original name, Giovanni Battista Montini. Born 1897. Pope since 1963.

Paul (pôl), **Saint.** A.D. 5?–67? Originally called "Saul of Tarsus." The Apostle to the Gentiles; life and doctrines are set forth in the Acts of the Apostles and his epistles.

Pau·li (pou′lē), **Wolfgang.** 1900–1958. Austrian-born American physicist; discovered the exclusion principle.

Paul·ine (pô′līn′) *adj.* Of or pertaining to Saint Paul, his writings, or his teachings and the theological doctrines derived from them. **—Paul′in·ism′** (pô′lə-nĭz′əm) *n.* **—Paul′in·ist** *n.*

Paul·ing (pô′lĭng), **Linus Carl.** Born 1901. American chemist; awarded the Nobel Prize in chemistry (1954) and the Nobel Peace Prize (1962).

Paul·ist (pô′lĭst) *n.* A priest belonging to the Roman Catholic Missionary Society of Saint Paul the Apostle.

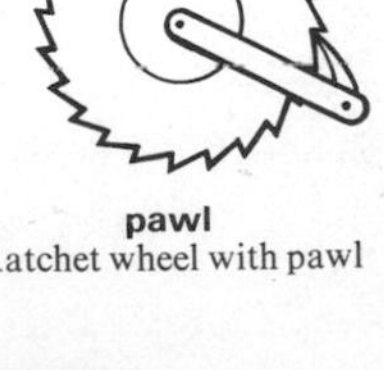

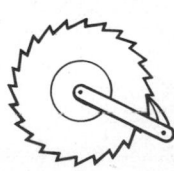

pawl
Ratchet wheel with pawl

pau·low·ni·a (pô-lō′nē-ə) *n.* Any of several trees of the genus *Paulownia,* native to the Orient, having large, heart-shaped leaves and clusters of purplish or white flowers. [New Latin, after Anna *Paulovna* (died 1865), Russian princess.]

paunch (pônch, pänch) *n.* **1.** The belly; especially, a potbelly: *"His hands clasped themselves over his capacious paunch."* (Virginia Woolf). **2.** A ruminant's first stomach, the **rumen** *(see).* [Middle English *paunche,* from Norman French, from Old French *pance,* from Latin *pantex*† (stem *pantic-*).] **—paunch′i·ness** *n.* **—paunch′y** *adj.*

pau·per (pô′pər) *n.* **1.** One who is extremely poor. **2.** One living on public charity. *—tr.v.* **paupered, -pering, -pers.** To pauperize. [Latin, poor. See **pòu-** in Appendix.*]

pau·per·ism (pô′pə-rĭz′əm) *n.* **1.** The quality or state of being a pauper. **2.** Paupers collectively.

pau·per·ize (pô′pə-rīz′) *tr.v.* **-ized, -izing, -izes.** To make a pauper of; impoverish. **—pau′per·i·za′tion** *n.*

Pau·sa·ni·as (pô-sā′nē-əs). Greek geographer and historian of the second century A.D.

pause (pôz) *intr.v.* **paused, pausing, pauses. 1.** To cease or suspend an action for a time: *She paused to listen.* **2.** To linger; tarry: *pausing for a while at the café.* **3.** To hesitate: *He paused before accepting the task.* *—n.* **1.** A hiatus in action or activity; temporary respite. **2.** A delay or suspended reaction, as from uncertainty; hesitation: *After a pause, the audience burst into cheers.* **3.** A break, stop, or rest for a calculated purpose or effect: *a pause to let the words sink in.* **4. a.** *Music.* A sign indicating that a note or rest is to be held. **b.** *Prosody.* A measured break or rest; caesura. **5.** A reason for hesitation. Usually in the phrase *give one pause.* [Middle English, a pause, from Old French, from Latin *pausa,* from Greek *pausis,* a stopping, from *pauein,* to stop. See **pauein** in Appendix.*]

pa·van (pə-văn′, -văn′, păv′ən) *n.* Also **pa·vane** (pə-văn′, -văn′), **pav·in** (păv′ən). **1.** A slow, stately court dance of the 16th century. **2.** Music for this dance. [Old French *pavane,* from Old Spanish *pavana,* from Old Italian *(danza) pavanna,* "(dance) of Padua," dialectal variant of *padovana,* feminine of *padovano,* of Padua, from *Padova,* PADUA.]

pave (pāv) *tr.v.* **paved, paving, paves. 1.** To cover with any hard, smooth surface that will bear travel. **2.** To cover uniformly, as if with pavement. **3.** To be or compose the pavement of. **—pave the way.** To make progress or development easier: *experiments that paved the way for future research.* [Middle English *paven,* from Old French *paver,* from Latin *pavīre,* to strike, stamp. See **peuə-**[2] in Appendix.*] **—pav′er** *n.*

pa·vé (pă-vā′) *n.* A setting of precious stones placed together so closely that no metal shows: *a brooch in pavé.* [French, from Old French, from the past participle of *paver,* PAVE.]

pave·ment (pāv′mənt) *n.* **1.** A hard, paved surface, especially of a public area or thoroughfare. **2.** The material of which such a surface is made. **3.** *Chiefly British.* A sidewalk: *"Duke Street, famous as the first street in which a pavement was laid down for walkers"* (Henry B. Wheatley).

pav·id (păv′ĭd) *adj.* Fearful; frightened; timid. [Latin *pavidus,* from *pavēre,* to fear. See **peuə-**[2] in Appendix.*]

pa·vil·ion (pə-vĭl′yən) *n.* **1.** An ornate tent, especially of the kinds used in chivalry in medieval Europe. **2. a.** A temporary, ornamental, and often open structure, used at parks or fairs for amusement or shelter. **b.** A summerhouse. **3.** A building or other structure connected to a larger building; annex. **4.** One of a group of related buildings forming a complex, as of a hospital. **5.** The surface of a brilliant-cut gem that slants outward from girdle to culet. *—tr.v.* **pavilioned, -ioning, -ions.** To shelter in or as if in a pavilion. [Middle English *pavilon,* from Old French *paveillon,* from Latin *pāpiliō*† (stem *pāpiliōn-*), butterfly, tent (from its resemblance to a butterfly's wings).]

pav·ing (pā′vĭng) *n.* **1.** The laying of pavement. **2.** A pavement. **3.** Material used for pavement.

pav·ior (pāv′yər) *n.* Also *chiefly British* **pav·iour. 1.** One that puts down paving. **2.** Material or tools used for paving. [Middle English *pavier,* from *paven,* PAVE.]

pav·is (păv′ĭs) *n.* Also **pav·ise.** A medieval shield large enough to cover the whole body. [Middle English, from Old French *pavais,* from Old Italian *pavese,* "of Pavia," from *Pavia,* a city in northwestern Italy, where pavises were first made.]

Pav·lov (păv′lôf′, păv′lŏv′), **Ivan Petrovich.** 1849–1936. Russian physiologist; worked on conditioned reflexes.

Pav·lo·va (păv-lō′və, păv-; *Russian* pä′vlə-və), **Anna.** 1885–1931. Russian classical ballerina.

Pa·vo (pā′vō) *n.* A constellation in the Southern Hemisphere near Apus and Indus. [Latin *pāvō,* peacock (probably imitative), obscurely related to Greek *taōs,* a peacock. See also **peacock.**]

pav·o·nine (păv′ə-nīn′) *adj.* **1.** Of or like a peacock. **2.** Resembling a peacock's tail in color, design, or iridescence. [Latin *pāvōnīnus,* from *pāvō,* peacock. See **peacock.**]

paw (pô) *n.* **1.** The nailed or clawed foot of an animal. **2.** *Informal.* A human hand, especially a large, clumsy one: *"Lennie dabbled his big paw in the water."* (Steinbeck). *—v.* **pawed, pawing, paws.** *—tr.* **1.** To strike with the paw or paws. **2.** To strike or scrape with a beating motion: *"His black charger pawed the straw"* (Thackeray). **3.** To handle clumsily, rudely, or with too much familiarity; caress awkwardly. *—intr.* **1.** To scrape the ground with the forefeet. **2.** To make clumsy, grasping motions with the hands: *"a hand pawing about the door"* (Hardy). [Middle English *pawe, powe,* from Old French *poue,* from Germanic *pauta* (unattested).] **—paw′er** *n.*

pawl (pôl) *n.* A hinged or pivoted device adapted to fit into a notch of a ratchet wheel to impart forward or prevent backward motion. Also called "detent." [Dutch *pal,* possibly from Latin *pālus,* stake. See **pag-** in Appendix.*]

pawn[1] (pôn) *n.* **1.** Something given as security for a loan; pledge; guaranty. **2.** The condition of being held as a pledge against the payment of a loan: *jewels at pawn.* **3.** A person serving as security; hostage. **4.** The act of pawning. —*tr.v.* **pawned, pawning, pawns.** **1.** To give or deposit as security for the payment of money borrowed. **2.** To risk; hazard; stake: *pawn one's honor.* [Middle English *paun,* from Old French *pan,* probably from *pan,* a piece of cloth, pane, from Latin *pannus,* from the frequent use of a garment as security. See **pan-** in Appendix.*] —**pawn'a·ble** *adj.* —**pawn'age** *n.* —**pawn'er, pawn'or** (pô'nər, -nôr') *n.*

pawn[2] (pôn) *n.* **1.** *Abbr.* **P** A chessman of lowest value, enabled to move forward one square at a time (or two squares for the first move) and capture on a one-space diagonal forward move. **2.** A person or entity composed of persons used to further the purposes of another: *"Mexico is not a major pawn in the struggle between Russia and the United States."* (Howard F. Kline). [Middle English *poun, pawne,* from Old French *poon, peon,* from Medieval Latin *pedō* (stem *pedōn-*), a foot soldier, from Late Latin, "one who has wide feet," from Latin *pēs* (stem *ped-*), foot. See **ped-**[1] in Appendix.*]

pawn·bro·ker (pôn'brō'kər) *n.* One who lends money at interest in exchange for personal property left with him as security. —**pawn'bro'king** *n.*

Paw·nee (pô-nē') *n., pl.* **Pawnee** or **-nees.** **1.** A confederation of four North American Plains Indian tribes of Caddoan linguistic stock in the region of Kansas and Nebraska, now living on a reservation in Oklahoma. **2.** A member of this confederation. **3.** The language of this confederation.

pawn·shop (pôn'shŏp') *n.* The business establishment or shop of a pawnbroker.

pawn ticket. A receipt for goods pawned.

paw·paw. Variant of **papaw.**

Paw·tuck·et (pô-tŭk'ĭt). A manufacturing city in northeastern Rhode Island four miles north of Providence. Population, 78,000.

pay[1] (pā) *v.* **paid, paying, pays.** —*tr.* **1.** To remunerate or recompense for goods or services rendered. **2.** To give (money) in exchange for goods or services. **3.** To give the indicated amount of; discharge (a debt or obligation): *pay taxes.* **4.** To gain revenge for or upon; requite; punish. Often used with *back* or *off: I paid him back for his insults.* **5.** To yield as recompense or return: *This job pays little.* **6.** To bear the cost of: *He paid my way through school.* **7.** To afford an advantage to; profit: *It paid him to be generous.* **8.** To give or bestow: *pay compliments.* **9.** To make (a visit or call). —*intr.* **1.** To make payment. **2.** To discharge a debt or obligation. **3.** To be profitable or worthwhile. —**pay down.** To pay as the first of a series of installment payments at the time of a purchase. —**pay one's way.** To contribute one's own share; pay for oneself. —**pay out.** **1.** To expend or hand out (money, for example). **2.** *Past* **payed out.** *Nautical.* To let out (a line or cable) by slackening. —**pay up.** To pay the full amount demanded. —*adj.* **1.** Of, pertaining to, giving, or receiving payments: *pay boarder.* **2.** Requiring payment to operate: *pay telephone.* **3.** Yielding valuable metal in mining: *pay streak.* —*n.* **1.** The act of paying or state of being paid. **2.** Money given in return for work done; salary; wages; hire. **3. a.** Recompense or reward: *His thanks were pay enough.* **b.** Retribution or punishment. **4.** Paid employment: *the men in our pay.* **5.** A person considered with regard to his credit or willingness to pay. [Middle English *payen,* from Old French *paier,* from Medieval Latin *pācāre,* to satisfy, pay, from Latin, to pacify, from *pāx,* peace. See **pag-** in Appendix.*]

pay[2] (pā) *tr.v.* **payed** or **paid, paying, pays.** *Nautical.* To coat or cover (seams of a ship, for example) with waterproof materials such as tar or asphalt. [Old French *peier,* from Latin *picāre,* to pitch, to tar, from *pix* (stem *pic-*), pitch. See **pik-** in Appendix.*]

pay·a·ble (pā'ə-bəl) *adj.* **1.** Requiring payment on a certain date; due. **2.** That can or may be paid. **3.** Capable of producing profit: *a payable business venture.* —**pay'a·bly** *adv.*

pay·day (pā'dā') *n.* The day on which wages are paid.

pay dirt. **1.** Earth, ore, or gravel with a rich enough metal content to make mining profitable. **2.** *Slang.* Anything that is useful or profitable.

P.A.Y.E. **1.** pay as you earn. **2.** pay as you enter.

payed. *Nautical.* Past tense and past participle of **pay** (to coat).

pay·ee (pā-ē') *n.* A person to whom money is paid.

pay·er (pā'ər) *n.* **1.** A person who pays. **2.** A person named responsible for paying a bill or note.

pay·load (pā'lōd') *n.* **1.** The revenue-producing part of a cargo. **2.** *Aerospace.* **a.** The passengers, mail, and cargo in an aircraft. **b.** The warhead of a missile. **c.** In rockets and satellites, the data-collecting and transmitting equipment. **d.** In manned spacecraft, the personnel, life-support systems, and equipment necessary to accomplish missions.

pay·mas·ter (pā'măs'tər, -mäs'tər) *n. Abbr.* **pm.** A person in charge of paying wages and salaries.

pay·ment (pā'mənt) *n. Abbr.* **payt., pt.** **1.** The act of paying or state of being paid. **2.** That which is paid; compensation; recompense. **3.** One's due, reward, or punishment; requital.

pay·nim (pā'nĭm) *n. Archaic.* **1.** A pagan or heathen; any non-Christian, especially a Moslem. **2.** The pagan world. [Middle English *painim,* from Old French *paienime,* from Late Latin *pāgānismus,* heathendom, from *pāgānus,* PAGAN.]

pay off. **1. a.** To pay the full amount owed on (a debt). **b.** To get revenge for or on; requite. **2.** To pay the wages due to (an employee) and discharge. **3.** *Informal.* To bribe. **4.** To give full return; be profitable: *The effort pays off in the long run.* **5.** *Nautical.* To turn or cause to turn (a vessel) to leeward.

pay·off (pā'ôf', -ŏf') *n.* **1. a.** Full payment of a salary or wages. **b.** The time of payment. **2.** *Informal.* Final settlement or reckoning; the climax of a narrative or of a sequence of events. **3.** Final retribution or revenge. **4.** *Informal.* A bribe. **5.** *Mathematics.* In game theory, the amount gained or lost by a player.

pay·o·la (pā-ō'lə) *n. Slang.* **1.** Bribery, especially the bribing of disc jockeys to promote records. **2.** Such a bribe. [PAY + (VICTR)OLA, originally of record payoffs.]

pay·roll (pā'rōl') *n.* Also **pay roll.** **1.** A list of employees receiving wages, with the amounts due to each. **2.** The total sum of money to be paid out to employees at a given time.

pay station. A coin-operated telephone for public use.

payt. payment.

Pb The symbol for the element lead (Latin *plumbum*).

P.B. **1.** passbook. **2.** prayer book.

P.B.I. protein-bound iodine.

PBX, P.B.X. private branch exchange.

p.c. **1.** after meals (Latin *post cibum*). **2.** per cent. **3.** petty cash. **4.** post card.

P.C. **1.** Past Commander. **2.** Police Constable. **3.** Post Commander. **4.** Privy Council.

p/c, P/C **1.** petty cash. **2.** prices current.

pct. per cent.

Pd The symbol for the element palladium.

pd. paid.

p.d. per diem.

P.D. **1.** per diem. **2.** Police Department.

Pd.B. Bachelor of Pedagogy.

Pd.D. Doctor of Pedagogy.

Pd.M. Master of Pedagogy.

PDX Airport code for Portland, Oregon.

pe (pā) *n.* The 17th letter of the Hebrew alphabet. See **alphabet.** [Hebrew *peh,* "mouth."]

pea (pē) *n.* **1.** A climbing annual vine, *Pisum sativum,* grown in all temperate zones, and having compound leaves, small white flowers, and edible seeds in a green, elongated pod. **2.** One of the rounded green seeds of the pea, used as a vegetable. **3.** *Plural.* The unopened pods of the pea plant. **4.** Any of several plants of the genus *Lathyrus,* such as the **sweet pea** or the **beach pea** *(both of which see).* See also **chickpea, cowpea.** [Taken as singular of earlier *pease,* from Middle English *pese,* Old English *pise,* from Late Latin *pīsa,* from Latin, plural of *pīsum,* pea, from Greek *pison*†, a pea.]

pea bean. The **navy bean** *(see).*

Pea·bod·y (pē'bŏd'ē, -bəd-ē), **Elizabeth Palmer.** 1804–1894. American educator; established first U.S. kindergarten.

peabody bird. The **white-throated sparrow** *(see).* [Probably imitative of its song.]

peace (pēs) *n.* **1.** The absence of war or other hostilities. **2.** An agreement or treaty to end hostilities: *the Peace of Westphalia.* **3.** Freedom from quarrels and disagreement; harmonious relations: *They made peace with each other.* **4.** Public security; law and order: *disturbing the peace.* **5.** Inner contentment; calm; serenity: *peace of mind.* —**at peace.** **1.** In a state of tranquillity; serene. **2.** Free from strife. —**hold** (or **keep**) **one's peace.** To be silent. —**keep the peace.** To maintain or observe law and order. [Middle English *pes, pais,* from Old French, from Latin *pāx* (stem *pāc-*). See **pag-** in Appendix.*]

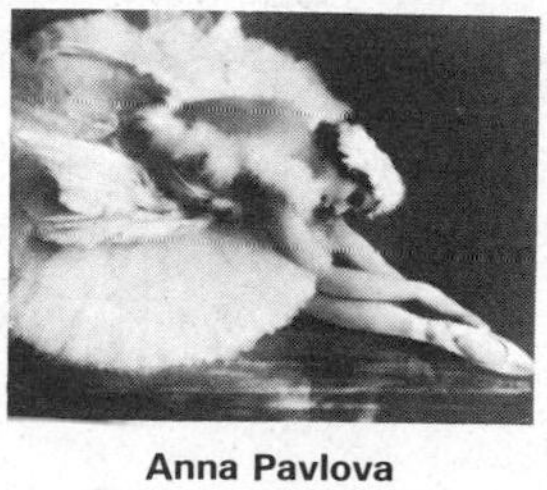
Anna Pavlova
In a 1911 performance of *The Dying Swan*

peace·a·ble (pē'sə-bəl) *adj.* **1.** Inclined or disposed to peace; promoting calm: *They met in a peaceable spirit.* **2.** Peaceful; undisturbed. —**peace'a·ble·ness** *n.* —**peace'a·bly** *adv.*

Peace Corps. A Federal government organization, set up in 1961, that trains and sends American volunteers abroad to work with people of developing countries on projects for technological, agricultural, and educational improvement.

peace·ful (pēs'fəl) *adj.* **1.** Undisturbed by strife, turmoil, or disagreement; tranquil. **2.** Opposed to strife; peaceable. **3.** Of or characteristic of a condition of peace. —See Synonyms at **calm.** —**peace'ful·ly** *adv.* —**peace'ful·ness** *n.*

peace·mak·er (pēs'mā'kər) *n.* **1.** One who makes peace, especially by settling the disputes of others. **2.** A revolver, especially the 1873 Colt model, used by law officers on the U.S. frontier. —**peace'mak'ing** *n.* & *adj.*

peace offering. **1.** Any offering made to an adversary in the interests of peace or reconciliation. **2.** An offering made to God in thanksgiving, especially a sacrificial offering as prescribed by Levitical law. Leviticus 3:2–6.

peace officer. A law officer, such as a sheriff, responsible for maintaining civil peace.

peace pipe. The **calumet** *(see).*

Peace River. A river rising in east-central British Columbia, Canada, and flowing 1,065 miles east and northeast to join the Slave River in northeastern Alberta.

peace·time (pēs'tīm') *n.* A time of absence of war. —**peace'time'** *adj.*

peach[1] (pēch) *n.* **1.** A small tree, *Prunus persica,* native to China but widely cultivated throughout the temperate zones, having pink flowers and edible fruit. **2.** The soft, juicy, single-seeded fruit of this tree, having yellow flesh and downy, red-tinted, yellow skin. **3.** Light moderate to strong yellowish pink to light orange. See **color.** **4.** *Slang.* Any especially admirable or pleasing person or thing. [Middle English *peche,* from Old French, from Late Latin *persica,* from Latin, plural of *persicum (mālum),* "Persian (apple)," from *Persicus,* PERSIAN.]

peach[2] (pēch) *v.* **peached, peaching, peaches.** —*intr. Slang.* To inform on someone; turn informer. —*tr. Obsolete.* To inform against: *"Make Mercury confess and peach / those thieves which he himself did teach."* (Samuel Butler). [Middle English *pechen,* variant of *impechen,* IMPEACH.]

peach[1]

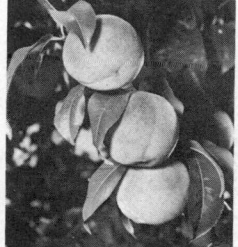

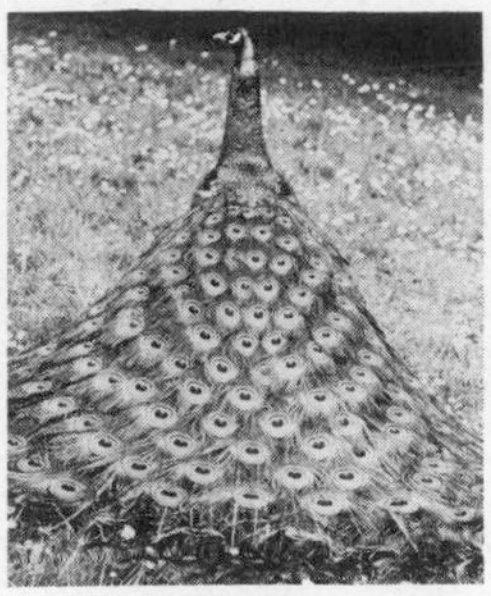

peacock

peach·blow (pēch′blō′) *n.* A purplish-pink monochrome glaze used on Chinese porcelain. Also called "peachbloom."

peach·y (pē′chē) *adj.* **-ier, -iest. 1.** Like a peach, especially in color or texture. **2.** *Slang.* Splendid; fine: *"Won't it be peachy if we win the game?"* (Tom Lehrer). **—peach′i·ness** *n.*

pea·cock (pē′kŏk′) *n.* **1.** The male **peafowl** *(see),* distinguished by its crested head, brilliant blue or green feathers, and long tail feathers that are marked with eyelike, iridescent spots, and that can be spread in a fanlike form. **2.** A vain person given to self-display; a dandy. *—intr.v.* **peacocked, -cocking, -cocks.** To strut about like a peacock; exhibit oneself vainly. [Middle English *pecok, pocok* : Old English *pēa, pāwa,* peafowl, from Latin *pāvō,* peacock, obscurely related to Greek *taōs*†, peacock + *cok,* COCK.] **—pea′cock′ish, pea′cock′y** *adj.*

Pea·cock (pē′kŏk′), **Thomas Love.** 1785–1866. English author.

peacock blue. Moderate to dark or strong greenish blue. See **color. —pea′cock′-blue′** *adj.*

pea·fowl (pē′foul′) *n., pl.* **peafowl** or **-fowls.** Either of two large pheasants, *Pavo cristatus,* of India and Ceylon, or *P. muticus,* of southeastern Asia. See **peacock.** [PEA(COCK) + FOWL.]

peag (pēg) *n.* Also **peage.** North American Indian money, **wampum** *(see).* [Narraganset *wampompeag,* WAMPUM.]

pea green. Moderate, strong, or brilliant yellow green to moderate yellowish green. See **color. —pea′-green′** *adj.*

pea·hen (pē′hĕn′) *n.* The female **peafowl** *(see).*

pea jacket. A short, warm, double-breasted coat of heavy wool, worn by sailors. [Probably from Dutch *pijjekker* : *pij,* a kind of coarse cloth, from Middle Dutch *pīe*† + *jekker,* a jacket, from Old French *jaque,* short garment originally worn by French peasants or *jaques* (see **jack**).]

peak[1] (pēk) *n. Abbr.* **pk. 1.** A tapering, projecting point; pointed extremity: *peak of a cap; peak of a roof.* **2. a.** The pointed summit of a mountain. **b.** The mountain itself: *Pikes Peak.* **3. a.** The point of a beard. **b.** A **widow's peak** *(see).* **4.** The point of greatest development, value, or intensity; height; maximum: *"It was the peak of summer in the Berkshires."* (Saul Bellow). **5.** *Physics.* The highest value attained by a varying quantity: *a current peak.* **6.** *Nautical.* **a.** The narrow portion of a ship's hull at the bow or stern. **b.** The upper after corner of a fore-and-aft sail. **c.** The outermost end of a gaff. —See Synonyms at **summit.** *—v.* **peaked, peaking, peaks.** *—tr.* **1.** *Nautical.* To raise (a gaff) above the horizontal. **2.** To bring to a peak, head, or maximum. *—intr.* **1.** To be formed into a peak or peaks: *Beat the egg whites until they peak.* **2.** To achieve a maximum of development, value, or intensity. *—adj.* Approaching or constituting the maximum: *peak efficiency.* [Probably alteration of PIKE (summit).]

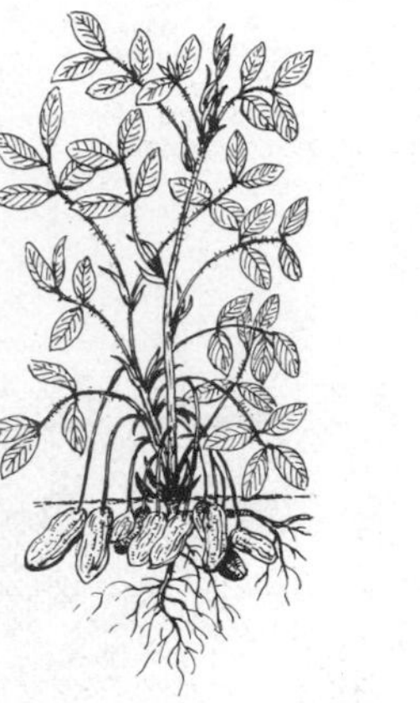

peanut

peak[2] (pēk) *intr.v.* **peaked, peaking, peaks.** To become sickly, emaciated, or pale. [Original sense, to fall, perhaps variant of *peck,* to pitch forward, variant of PITCH.]

Peak District. A moorland area in the southern part of the Pennine Chain, England.

peaked[1] (pēkt, pē′kĭd) *adj.* Ending in a peak; pointed.

peak·ed[2] (pē′kĭd) *adj.* Having a sickly, pale, or emaciated appearance; drawn.

peal (pēl) *n.* **1.** A ringing of a set of bells; especially, a change or set of changes, rung on bells. **2.** A set of bells tuned to each other; chime; carillon. **3.** A loud burst of noise or series of noises, as of bells or thunder. *—v.* **pealed, pealing, peals.** *—intr.* To sound in a peal; ring: *The bells pealed out.* *—tr.* To utter loudly and sonorously: *"I heard the watchman peal the sliding season"* (Tennyson). [Middle English *pele,* summons to church by bell, short for *appel,* an appeal, from *appelen,* to APPEAL.]

Peale (pēl). Family of American painters, including **Charles Willson Peale,** 1741–1827; his brother **James,** 1749–1831; and Charles' sons **Raphael,** 1774–1825; **Rembrandt,** 1778–1860; and **Titian Ramsay,** 1799–1885.

pe·an. Variant of **paean.**

Pe·a·no (pā-ä′nō), **Giuseppe.** 1858–1932. Italian mathematician and linguist.

pea·nut (pē′nŭt′) *n.* **1.** A vine, *Arachis hypogaea,* native to tropical America and widely cultivated in semitropical regions. It has yellow flowers on stalks that bend over so that the seed pods ripen underground. **2.** The edible, nutlike, oily seed of this vine, used for food and as a source of oil. Also called "goober," "groundnut." **3.** *Slang.* A small or insignificant person. **4.** *Plural. Slang.* A very small amount of money; trifling sum: *" 'Polish sausage is going for peanuts in Cracow' "* (Joseph Heller). [PEA + NUT.]

peanut brittle. A hard candy containing peanuts.

peanut butter. A paste made from roasted ground peanuts.

peanut oil. The oil pressed from peanuts, used for cooking, in soaps, and as a pharmaceutical vehicle.

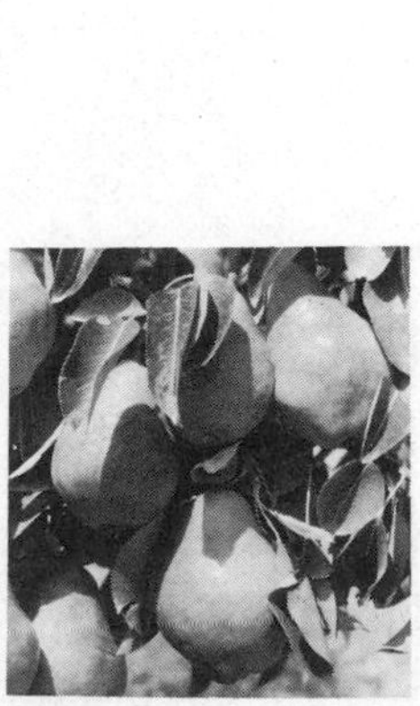

pear

pear (pâr) *n.* **1.** A widely cultivated tree, *Pyrus communis,* having glossy leaves, white flowers, and edible fruit. **2.** The fruit of this tree, spherical at the base and tapering toward the top. [Middle English *pere,* Old English *peru, pere,* from Latin *pirus,* pear tree, *pirum,* pear, akin to Greek *apios,* pear tree, probably from Mediterranean.]

pear haw. A shrub or small tree, *Crataegus uniflora,* of southeastern North America, having white flowers and small, orange-red, pear-shaped fruit. Also called "black thorn."

pearl[1] (pûrl) *n.* **1.** A smooth, lustrous, variously colored deposit, chiefly calcium carbonate, formed around a grain of sand or other foreign matter in the shells of certain mollusks and valued as a gem. **2.** Mother-of-pearl; nacre. **3.** A person or object likened to a pearl in beauty or value. **4.** *Printing.* A type size, 5 points. **5.** A yellowish white. See **color.** *—v.* **pearled, pearling, pearls.** *—tr.* **1.** To decorate or cover with or as with pearls. **2.** To make into the shape or color of pearls. *—intr.* **1.** To dive or fish for pearls or pearl-bearing mollusks. **2.** To form beads resembling pearls. *—adj.* **1.** Made of or containing pearl. **2.** Having the shape or color of pearls. [Middle English *perle,* from Old French, from Vulgar Latin *per(nu)la* (unattested), diminutive of Latin *perna,* ham, sea-mussel (from its ham-shaped peduncle). See **persnā** in Appendix.*]

pearl[2]**.** Variant of **purl.**

pearl ash *Chemistry.* **Potassium carbonate** *(see).*

pearl danio. A slender freshwater tropical fish, *Brachydanio albolineatus,* having silvery scales. It is popular as an aquarium fish. [New Latin *Danio*†, order name.]

pearl diver. A person who dives in search of mollusks containing pearls.

pearl·er (pûr′lər) *n.* **1.** A pearl diver. **2.** A boat engaged in seeking or trading pearls.

pearl gray. Light gray, from yellowish to light bluish gray. See **color. —pearl′-gray′** *adj.*

Pearl Harbor. An inlet on the southern coast of Oahu Island, Hawaii, with a narrow entrance to the Pacific. It is the site of the U.S. naval base attacked by Japan on December 7, 1941.

pearl·ite (pûr′līt′) *n.* **1.** A mixture of ferrite and cementite forming distinct layers or bands in slowly cooled carbon steels. **2.** Variant of **perlite.** [French *perlite,* from *perle,* a soft gelatinous capsule, from Old French, PEARL + -ITE.]

pearl millet. A tropical grass, *Pennisetum glaucum,* having long, dense flowering spikes and whitish seeds that are used as food in the Old World.

pearl oyster. Any of several bivalve marine mollusks of the genus *Pinctada* and related genera, of tropical waters. *P. margaritifera* is a major commercial source of pearls.

Pearl River. 1. A river rising in east-central Mississippi and flowing 490 miles southwest and south into the Gulf of Mexico. **2.** See **Chu Kiang.**

pearl·y (pûr′lē) *adj.* **-ier, -iest. 1.** Resembling pearls: *pearly teeth.* **2.** Covered or decorated with pearls or mother-of-pearl.

pearly everlasting. A plant, *Anaphalis margaritaceae,* having woolly, gray-green foliage and whitish, long-lasting flowers.

pearly nautilus. The **chambered nautilus** *(see).*

pear·main (pâr′mān′) *n.* An old variety of red-skinned apple. [Middle English *parmayn,* a kind of pear, from Old French *parmain,* from Vulgar Latin *parmānus* (unattested), of PARMA.]

pear oil. A solvent, **amyl acetate** *(see).*

Pear·son (pîr′sən), **Lester Bowles.** Born 1897. Prime Minister of Canada (1963–68).

Pea·ry (pîr′ē), **Robert Edwin.** 1856–1920. American naval officer and Arctic explorer; reached the North Pole (1909).

Pea·ry Land (pîr′ē). A rugged peninsula of northern Greenland extending into the Arctic Ocean.

peas·ant (pĕz′ənt) *n.* **1.** A member of the class comprising small farmers and tenants, sharecroppers, and laborers on the land where these constitute the main labor force in agriculture. **2.** A countryman; rustic. **3.** An uncouth, crude, or ill-bred person; a boor. [Middle English *paissaunt,* from Old French *païsant,* from *païs,* country, from Medieval Latin *pāgēnsis,* "inhabitant of a district," rustic, peasant, from Latin *pāgus,* a district, canton, the country. See **pag-** in Appendix.*]

peas·ant·ry (pĕz′ən-trē) *n.* **1.** The social class constituted by peasants. **2. a.** The condition or rank of a peasant. **b.** Conduct or manners thought to be characteristic of peasants.

pease (pēz) *n., pl.* **pease** or **peasen** (pē′zən). *Obsolete.* A pea.

pease·cod (pēz′kŏd′) *n.* Also **peas·cod.** *Obsolete.* The pod of the pea. [Middle English *pesecod* : *pese,* PEA + COD.]

pea·shoot·er (pē′sho͞o′tər) *n.* A toy consisting of a small tube through which dried peas or other pellets are blown at a target.

pea soup. 1. A purée or soup made of dried peas. **2.** *Slang.* Dense fog.

peat (pēt) *n.* Partially carbonized vegetable matter, usually mosses, found in bogs, and used as fertilizer and fuel. [Middle English *pete,* from Medieval Latin *peta,* probably from Celtic, akin to Medieval Latin *pecia, petia,* PIECE.] **—peat′y** *adj.*

peat bog. A bog or swamp where peat has accumulated.

peat moss. 1. Any moss of the genus *Sphagnum,* growing in very wet places. **2.** The partly carbonized remains of such mosses, used as a mulch and plant food.

pea·vey (pē′vē) *n., pl.* **-veys.** Also **pea·vy** *pl.* **-vies.** A wooden lever with a metal point and a hinged hook near the end, used by lumbermen to handle logs. Also called "cant hook." [After Joseph *Peavey,* American blacksmith, to whom its invention (about 1870) has been attributed.]

peb·ble (pĕb′əl) *n.* **1.** A small stone eroded smooth. **2. a.** Clear, colorless quartz; rock crystal. **b.** A lens made of such quartz. **3.** A crinkled surface, as on leather or paper. *—tr.v.* **pebbled, -bling, -bles. 1.** To pave or pelt with pebbles. **2.** To impart an irregularly rough, grainy surface to (leather or paper). [Middle English *pibbil, puble,* Old English *papol(stān)* : *papol-,* pebble (probably imitative) + *stān,* STONE.] **—peb′bly** *adj.*

pe·can (pĭ-kän′, -kăn′) *n.* **1.** A tree, *Carya illinoensis,* of the southern United States, having deeply furrowed bark and edible nuts. **2.** The smooth, thin-shelled, oval nut of the pecan. [Earlier *paccan,* from Algonquian, akin to Ojibwa *pagân,* hard-shell nut, Abnaki *pagann,* Cree *pakan.*]

pec·ca·ble (pĕk′ə-bəl) *adj.* Liable to sin. [Old French, from Latin *peccāre,* to sin. See **peccant.**] **—pec′ca·bil′i·ty** *n.*

pec·ca·dil·lo (pĕk′ə-dĭl′ō) *n., pl.* **-loes** or **-los.** A small sin or fault. [Spanish *pecadillo,* diminutive of *pecado,* sin, from Latin *peccātum,* from *peccāre,* to sin. See **peccant.**]

pec·cant (pĕk′ənt) *adj.* **1.** Sinful; guilty. **2.** Violating a rule or accepted practice; erring; faulty. [Latin *peccāns*, present participle of *peccāre*, to sin, stumble. See **ped-**[1] in Appendix.*] —**pec′can·cy** *n.* —**pec′cant·ly** *adv.*

pec·ca·ry (pĕk′ə-rē) *n., pl.* **-ries.** Either of two piglike, hoofed mammals, *Tayassu tajacu* or *T. pecari*, of southern North America, Central America, and South America, having dense, long, dark bristles. [Spanish *pecari*, from Cariban *pakira*.]

pec·ca·vi (pĕ-kā′vī, -kä′vē) *n., pl.* **-vis.** A confession of sin. [Latin, "I have sinned."]

Pe·cho·ra (pə-chôr′ə). A river of the Soviet Union, rising in the northern Ural Mountains and flowing over a winding course of about 1,100 miles into Pechora Bay of the Barents Sea.

peck[1] (pĕk) *v.* **pecked, pecking, pecks.** —*tr.* **1.** To strike with a beak or some sharp-pointed instrument. **2.** To make (a hole, for example) by striking repeatedly with the beak or a pointed instrument. **3.** To grasp and pick up with the beak: *The bird pecked insects from the log.* **4.** *Informal.* To kiss briefly and casually: *He pecked her on the cheek.* —*intr.* **1.** To make strokes with the beak or something pointed like a beak: *the noise of birds pecking outside.* **2.** To eat in small, sparing bits; nibble. Used with *at*: *pecking at her food.* **3.** To criticize repeatedly; nag; carp. Used with *at.* —*n.* **1.** A stroke or light blow with the beak or a prick. **2.** A mark or hole made by such a stroke. **3.** *Slang.* A light, quick kiss. [Middle English *pecken*, probably variant of *piken*, PIKE (to prick).]

peck[2] (pĕk) *n. Abbr.* **pk., pk 1. a.** A unit of volume or capacity in the U.S. System, used in dry measure, equal to 8 quarts or 537.605 cubic inches. **b.** A unit of volume or capacity in the British Imperial System, used in dry and liquid measure, equal to 554.84 cubic inches. See **measurement. 2.** A container holding or measuring this amount. **3.** *Informal.* A great deal: *a peck of troubles.* [Middle English, from Norman French *pek*†.]

peck·er (pĕk′ər) *n.* **1.** A person who or a thing that pecks. **2.** *Vulgar.* The penis. **3.** *British Slang.* Courage; mettle; pluck.

pecking order. 1. A hierarchy within flocks of poultry, according to which each member submits to pecking and domination by the stronger or more aggressive members, and has the privilege of pecking and dominating the weaker members. **2.** Any supposedly similar hierarchy in a human group. [Translation of German *Hackordnung*.]

Peck·sniff·i·an (pĕk-snĭf′ē-ən) *adj.* Addicted to fatuous and hypocritical talk of benevolence and other kindly virtues. [After Seth *Pecksniff*, a character in Dickens' novel *Martin Chuzzlewit* (1844).]

Pe·cos Bill (pā′kōs bĭl). The archetypal cowboy of American legend whose feats included digging the Rio Grande.

Pe·cos River (pā′kəs). A river rising in the Sangre de Christo Mountains in north-central New Mexico and flowing 735 miles southeast to the Rio Grande.

Pécs (pāch). *German* **Fünf·kir·chen** (fünf′kĭr′KHən). A city in the coal-mining region of southern Hungary, west of the Danube and north of the Drava rivers. Population, 125,000.

pec·tase (pĕk′tās′, -tāz′) *n.* An enzyme found in certain fruits that catalyzes the conversion of pectins to pectic acids. [PECT(IN) + -ASE.]

pec·tate (pĕk′tāt′) *n.* A salt or ester of pectic acid. [PECT(IC ACID) + -ATE.]

pec·ten (pĕk′tən) *n., pl.* **-tines** (-tə-nēz′). *Zoology.* **1.** Any body structure or organ resembling a comb, such as the ridged part of the eyelid of reptiles and birds. **2.** A scallop of the genus *Pecten.* [New Latin, from Latin, comb. See **pek-**[2] in Appendix.*]

pec·tic acid (pĕk′tĭk). *Chemistry.* Any of several colloidal substances, essentially complex organic acids, derived from pectin. [French *pectique*. See **pectin.**]

pec·tin (pĕk′tĭn) *n.* Any of a group of complex colloidal substances of high molecular weight found in ripe fruits, such as apples, and used to gel various foods, drugs, and cosmetics. [French *pectine*, from *pectique*, from Greek *pēktikos*, coagulating, from *pēktos*, coagulated, from *pēgnunai*, to coagulate. See **pag-** in Appendix.*] —**pec′tic, pec′tin·ous** *adj.*

pec·tin·ase (pĕk′tə-nās′, -nāz′) *n.* A plant enzyme that catalyzes the hydrolysis of pectin.

pec·ti·nate (pĕk′tə-nāt′) *adj.* Also **pec·ti·nat·ed** (-nā′tĭd). Having teeth like a comb; comblike. [Latin *pecten* (stem *pectin-*), comb, PECTEN + -ATE.] —**pec′ti·na′tion** *n.*

pec·to·ral (pĕk′tər-əl) *adj.* **1.** *Anatomy.* Pertaining to the breast or chest: *a pectoral muscle.* **2.** *Medicine.* Useful in diseases of the chest. **3.** Worn on the chest or breast: *a pectoral cross.* —*n.* **1.** A chest muscle or organ. **2.** A pectoral fin. **3.** A medicine for chest diseases. **4.** An ornament or decoration worn on the chest. [Middle English, something worn on the chest, from Old French, of or worn on the chest, from Latin *pectorālis*, from *pectus* (stem *pector-*), breast. See **peg-** in Appendix.*]

pectoral fin. Either of the anterior pair of fins attached to the pectoral girdle of fishes.

pectoral girdle. *Zoology.* A skeletal structure in vertebrates, attached to and supporting the forelimbs or fins. Also called "pectoral arch," and, chiefly in man, "shoulder girdle."

pectoral sandpiper. A New World sandpiper, *Erolia melanotos*, having brownish streaks on the upper part of the breast. Also called "grass snipe."

pec·u·late (pĕk′yə-lāt′) *v.* **-lated, -lating, -lates.** —*tr.* To embezzle or take for one's own use. —*intr.* To steal money or goods entrusted to one. [Latin *peculārī*, to embezzle, from *pecūlium*, "wealth in cattle," private property. See **peku-** in Appendix.*] —**pec′u·la′tion** *n.* —**pec′u·la′tor** (lā′tər) *n.*

pe·cu·liar (pĭ-kyōōl′yər) *adj.* **1.** Unusual or eccentric; strange; queer; odd: *His actions are most peculiar.* **2.** Standing apart from others; calling for special consideration or attention; distinct and particular: *"the experience of Stalinism remains a problem of peculiar complexity"* (Robert Warshow). **3. a.** Exclusive; unique: *the peculiar attributes of beauty.* **b.** Belonging distinctively or especially to one person, group, or kind: *"talking in the manner peculiar, probably limited, to former college roommates"* (J.D. Salinger). —See Synonyms at **characteristic, strange.** —*n.* **1.** Some privilege or property that belongs exclusively to one. **2.** *British.* A church or parish under the jurisdiction of a diocese different from that in which it lies. [Middle English *peculier*, from Latin *pecūliāris*, individual, peculiar, of private property, from *pecūlium*, "wealth in cattle," private property. See **peku-** in Appendix.*] —**pe·cu′liar·ly** *adv.*

pe·cu·li·ar·i·ty (pĭ-kyōō′lē-ăr′ə-tē) *n., pl.* **-ties. 1.** The quality or state of being peculiar. **2. a.** A notable or distinctive feature or characteristic: *"the diphthongal peculiarities that betray Americans to the twittering English"* (John Updike). **b.** An eccentricity; idiosyncrasy; quirk.

pe·cu·ni·ar·y (pĭ-kyōō′nē-ĕr′ē) *adj.* **1.** Consisting of or pertaining to money: *a pecuniary loss; pecuniary motives.* **2.** Requiring the payment of money: *a pecuniary offense.* —See Synonyms at **financial.** [Latin *pecūniārius*, from *pecūnia*, "wealth in cattle," property, money. See **peku-** in Appendix.*]

-ped, -pede. Indicates foot or feet; for example, **biped, centipede.** [Latin *pēs* (stem *ped-*), foot. See **ped-**[1] in Appendix.*]

ped·a·gog·ic (pĕd′ə-gŏj′ĭk, -gō′jĭk). Also **ped·a·gog·i·cal** (-ĭ-kəl, -gō′jĭ-kəl) *adj.* **1.** Of, pertaining to, or characteristic of teaching: *"Judge Milford's pedagogical scheme was to let the children read whatever they pleased."* (Sinclair Lewis). **2.** Characterized by pedantic formality. —**ped′a·gog′i·cal·ly** *adv.*

ped·a·gog·ics (pĕd′ə-gŏj′ĭks, -gō′jĭks) *n.* Plural in form, used with a singular verb. The art of teaching; education; pedagogy.

ped·a·gogue (pĕd′ə-gŏg′, -gôg′) *n.* **1.** A schoolteacher; educator. **2.** One who instructs in a pedantic or dogmatic manner. [Middle English *pedagoge*, from Old French *pedagogue*, from Latin *paedagōgus*, from Greek *paidagōgos*, teacher, trainer (of boys) : *paid-*, PEDO- + *agōgos*, leader, from *agein*, to lead (see **ag-** in Appendix*).] —**ped′a·gogu′ish** *adj.*

ped·a·go·gy (pĕd′ə-gō′jē, -gŏj′ē) *n.* **1.** The art or profession of teaching. **2.** Preparatory training or instruction.

ped·al (pĕd′l) *n.* **1.** A lever operated by the foot on various musical instruments, such as the piano, organ, or harp. **2.** A **pedal point** *(see).* **3.** A lever worked by the foot in a machine, such as a bicycle or sewing machine; treadle. —*adj.* **1.** Of or pertaining to a foot or footlike part: *the pedal extremities.* **2.** *Music.* Of or pertaining to a pedal. —*v.* **pedaled, -aling, -als.** Also *chiefly British* **-alled, -alling.** —*intr.* **1.** To use or operate a pedal or pedals. **2.** To ride a bicycle. —*tr.* To operate the pedals of. [French *pédale*, from Italian *pedale*, (organ) pedal, from Latin *pedālis*, of the foot, from *pēs*, foot. See **ped-**[1] in Appendix.*]

pe·dal·fer (pĭ-dăl′fər) *n. Geology.* Soil rich in alumina and iron and deficient in carbonates, characteristic of humid, high-temperature regions with forest cover. [PED(O)- (soil) + AL(UM) + Latin *ferrum*, iron (see **ferrum** in Appendix*).]

pedal point. *Music.* A note, usually in the bass and on the tonic or the dominant, sustained through harmonic changes in the other parts. Also called "organ point," "pedal."

ped·ant (pĕd′ənt) *n.* **1.** One who pays undue attention to book learning and formal rules without having an understanding or experience of practical affairs; a doctrinaire. **2.** One who exhibits his learning or scholarship ostentatiously: *"a pedant, who reads only to be called learned"* (Lord Chatham). **3.** *Archaic.* A schoolmaster; pedagogue. [Old French, from Italian *pedante*, probably from Latin *paedagōgāns*, present participle of *paedagōgāre*, to instruct, from *paedagōgus*, PEDAGOGUE.] —**pe·dan′tic** (pə-dăn′tĭk), **pe·dan′ti·cal** *adj.* —**pe·dan′ti·cal·ly** *adv.*

ped·ant·ry (pĕd′n-trē) *n., pl.* **-ries. 1.** Pedantic attention to detail or rules. **2. a.** The habit of mind or manner characteristic of a pedant. **b.** An instance of pedantic behavior.

ped·ate (pĕd′āt′) *adj.* **1.** *Zoology.* Having feet. **2.** Resembling or functioning as a foot or feet: *pedate appendages.* **3.** *Botany.* Having radiating lobes or divisions, with the lateral lobes cleft or divided: *a pedate leaf.* [Latin *pedātus*, from *pēs* (stem *ped-*), foot. See **ped-**[1] in Appendix.*]

ped·dle (pĕd′l) *v.* **-dled, -dling, -dles.** —*tr.* **1.** To travel about selling (wares): *peddling goods from door to door.* **2.** To sell or dispense, especially in small quantities. —*intr.* **1.** To travel about selling wares. **2.** To occupy oneself with trifles. [Back-formation from PEDDLER.]

ped·dler (pĕd′lər) *n.* Also **ped·lar, ped·ler.** One who peddles for a living; a hawker. [Middle English *pedlere*, probably altered from *peddere*, from *pedde*†, covered basket.] —**ped′dler·y** *n.*

ped·er·ast (pĕd′ə-răst′) *n.* A man who practices pederasty. [Greek *paiderastēs*, "a lover of boys" : *paid-*, PEDO- + *erastēs*, lover, from *erasthai*, to love, akin to *erōs*, love, EROS.]

ped·er·as·ty (pĕd′ə-răs′tē) *n.* Sexual relations between a man and a boy. —**ped′er·as′tic** *adj.* —**ped′er·as′ti·cal·ly** *adv.*

pe·des. Plural of **pes.**

ped·es·tal (pĕd′ə-stəl) *n.* **1.** An architectural support or base, as for a column or statue. **2.** Any support or foundation. **3.** A position of high regard or adoration. —*tr.v.* **pedestaled, -taling, -tals.** Also *chiefly British* **-talled, -talling.** To place on or provide with a pedestal. [Old French *piedestal*, from Old Italian *piedestallo*, from *pie di stallo*, "foot of a stall" : *pie*, foot, from Latin *pēs* (see **ped-**[1] in Appendix*) + *di*, of, from Latin *dē* (see **de-** in Appendix*) + *stallo*, stall, from Germanic (see **stel-**[1] in Appendix*).]

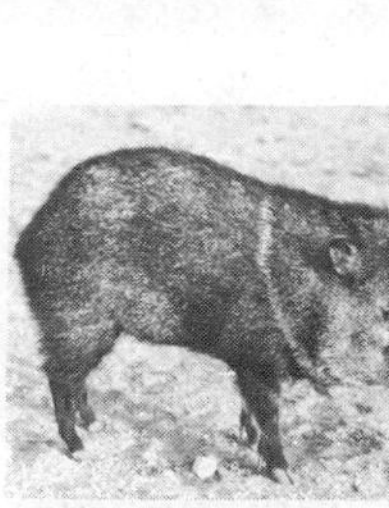

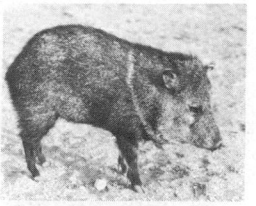

peccary
Tayassu tajacu
Collared peccary

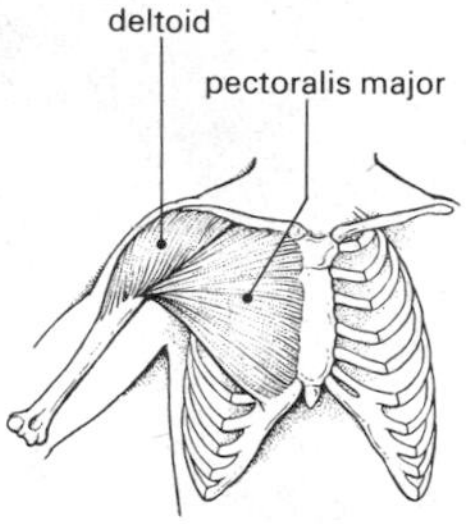

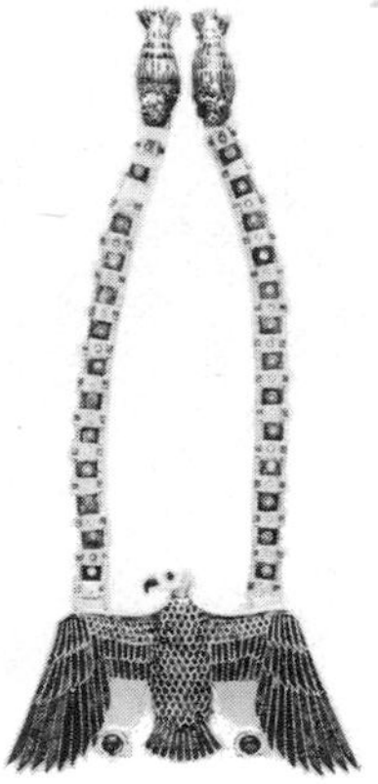

pectoral
Above: Chest muscle
Below: Egyptian pectoral from the tomb of Tutankhamen

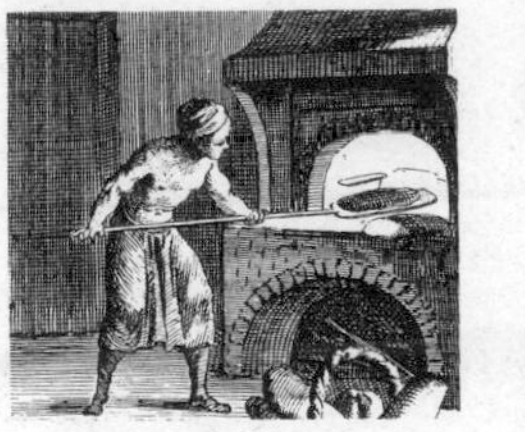
peel[2]
Eighteenth-century engraving of a baker's peel

pe·des·tri·an (pə-dĕs′trē-ən) *n.* A person traveling on foot; a walker, especially on city streets. —*adj.* **1.** Of or pertaining to pedestrians: *pedestrian traffic.* **2.** Going or performed on foot: *a pedestrian journey.* **3.** Commonplace; undistinguished; ordinary. [From Latin *pedester,* going on foot, hence prosaic, from *pedes,* one who goes on foot, from *pēs* (stem *ped-*), a foot. See **ped-**[1] in Appendix.*] —**pe·des′tri·an·ism′** *n.*

pedi–. Indicates foot; for example, **pediform.** [Latin, from *pēs* (stem *ped-*), foot. See **ped-**[1] in Appendix.*]

pe·di·a·tri·cian (pē′dē-ə-trĭsh′ən) *n.* Also **pe·di·at·rist** (pē′dē-ăt′rĭst). A physician who specializes in pediatrics.

pe·di·at·rics (pē′dē-ăt′rĭks) *n.* Plural in form, usually used with a singular verb. The branch of medicine that deals with the care of infants and children and the treatment of their diseases. [PED(O)- + -IATRICS.] —**pe′di·at′ric** *adj.*

ped·i·cel (pĕd′ə-səl, -sĕl′) *n.* Also **ped·i·cle** (pĕd′ĭ-kəl). **1.** A small stalk, part, or organ, especially one serving as a support. **2.** *Botany.* **a.** Any of several small stalks bearing a single flower in an inflorescence. **b.** A support for a fern sporangium or moss capsule. [New Latin *pedicellus,* diminutive of Latin *pedĭculus,* little foot, pedicel, from *pēs,* a foot. See **ped-**[1] in Appendix.*] —**ped′i·cel′lar** (pĕd′ə-sĕl′ər) *adj.*

ped·i·cel·late (pĕd′ə-sĕl′ĭt, -āt′) *adj.* Having or supported by a pedicel.

pe·dic·u·lar (pə-dĭk′yə-lər) *adj.* Of, pertaining to, or caused by lice. [Latin *pediculāris,* from *pedĭculus,* louse, diminutive of *pedis,* louse. See **pezd-** in Appendix.*]

pe·dic·u·late (pə-dĭk′yə-lĭt, -lāt′) *adj.* Of or pertaining to marine fishes of the order Pediculati (or Lophiiformes), which includes the anglerfishes. —*n.* A fish of this order. [New Latin *Pediculati,* "little-footed ones" (from the shape of their pectoral fins), from Latin *pedĭculus,* little foot. See **pedicel.**]

pe·dic·u·lo·sis (pə-dĭk′yə-lō′sĭs) *n.* Infestation with lice; lousiness. [New Latin : Latin *pedĭculus,* louse (see **pedicular**) + -OSIS.] —**pe·dic′u·lous** (pə-dĭk′yə-ləs) *adj.*

ped·i·cure (pĕd′ĭ-kyŏŏr′) *n.* **1. a.** Podiatry. **b.** A podiatrist. **2. a.** Cosmetic care of the feet and toenails. **b.** A single cosmetic treatment of the feet and toenails. —*tr.v.* **pedicured, -curing, -cures.** To give a pedicure to. [French *pédicure* : PEDI- + Latin *cūrāre,* to take care of, from *cūra,* care (see **cūra** in Appendix*).] —**ped′i·cur′ist** *n.*

ped·i·form (pĕd′ə-fôrm′) *adj.* Shaped like a foot. [French *pédiforme* : PEDI- + -FORM.]

ped·i·gree (pĕd′ə-grē′) *n.* **1.** A line of ancestors; ancestry; lineage: *"Every form in literature has a pedigree."* (Northrop Frye). **2.** A list of ancestors; family tree. **3.** The recorded descent of a purebred animal. [Middle English *pedegru,* from Old French *pie de grue,* "crane's foot," from the three-line, claw-shaped mark formerly used to show the succession in a pedigree : *pie,* foot, from Latin *pēs* (see **ped-**[1] in Appendix*) + *de,* of, from Latin *dē* (see **de-** in Appendix*) + *grue,* crane, from Latin *grūs* (see **ger-**[4] in Appendix*).] —**ped′i·greed′** *adj.*

ped·i·ment (pĕd′ə-mənt) *n.* **1.** A wide, low-pitched gable surmounting the facade of a building in the Grecian style. **2.** A similar or derivative element used widely in architecture and decoration. [Variant of earlier *perement,* probably variant (influenced by PEDI-) of PYRAMID.] —**ped′i·men′tal** (pĕd′ə-mĕnt′l) *adj.* —**ped′i·ment′ed** *adj.*

ped·lar, ped·ler. Variants of **peddler.**

pedo–[1], **ped–.** Indicates soil; for example, **pedalfer, pedocal.** [Greek *pedon,* earth, soil. See **ped-**[1] in Appendix.*]

pedo–[2], **ped–, paed–, paedo–.** Indicates child; for example, **pediatrics, pedodontia.** [Greek *paido-,* from *pais,* child. See **pōu-** in Appendix.*]

ped·o·cal (pĕd′ə-kăl′) *n. Geology.* A lime-rich soil of cool, semiarid and arid regions. [PEDO- (soil) + Latin *calx,* lime, limestone, from Greek *khalix,* pebble, small stone (see **calcium**).] —**ped′o·cal′ic** *adj.*

pe·do·don·tia (pē′də-dŏn′shə, -shē-ə) *n.* The dentistry of children's teeth. [PED(O)- (child) + -ODONT + -IA.] —**pe′do·don′tist** (-dŏn′tĭst) *n.*

pe·dol·o·gy[1] (pē-dŏl′ə-jē) *n.* The study of the behavior and development of children. [PEDO- (child) + -LOGY.] —**pe′do·log′ic** (pē′də-lŏj′ĭk), **pe′do·log′i·cal** *adj.* —**pe′do·log′i·cal·ly** *adv.* —**pe·dol′o·gist** *n.*

pe·dol·o·gy[2] (pĭ-dŏl′ə-jē, pĕ-dŏl′-) *n.* The scientific study of soils, their origins, characteristics, and uses. Compare **agrology.** [PEDO- (soil) + -LOGY.] —**ped′o·log′ic** (pĕd′ə-lŏj′ĭk), **ped′o·log′i·cal** *adj.* —**ped′o·log′i·cal·ly** *adv.* —**pe·dol′o·gist** *n.*

pe·dom·e·ter (pĭ-dŏm′ə-tər) *n.* An instrument that gauges the approximate distance traveled on foot by registering the number of steps taken. [French *pédomètre* : *pedo-,* variant of PEDI- + -METER.]

pe·dun·cle (pĭ-dŭng′kəl, pē′dŭng′kəl) *n.* **1.** *Botany.* The main stalk of an inflorescence, or a stalk or stem bearing a solitary flower. **2.** *Zoology.* A stalklike structure in invertebrate animals. **3.** *Anatomy.* A stalklike bundle of fibers, especially of nerve fibers, connecting different parts of the central nervous system. [New Latin *pedunculus,* diminutive of Latin *pēs* (stem *ped-*), a foot. See **ped-**[1] in Appendix.*] —**pe·dun′cu·lar** *adj.*

pe·dun·cu·late (pĭ-dŭng′kyə-lĭt, -lāt′) *adj.* Also **pe·dun·cu·lat·ed** (-lā′tĭd). Having or supported on a peduncle.

pee[1] (pē) *n.* The letter *p.*

pee[2] (pē) *intr.v.* **peed, peeing, pees.** *Vulgar.* To urinate. —*n. Vulgar.* **1.** Urine. **2.** An act of urination. [Originally, a children's euphemism for PISS (from the first letter), akin to French *pipi.*]

Pee·bles (pē′bəlz). **1.** Also **Pee·bles·shire** (pē′bəl-shîr, -shər). A county in southeastern Scotland. Population, 14,000. Also called "Tweeddale." **2.** A burgh and the capital of this county, on the Tweed River.

Pee Dee (pē′ dē′). A river flowing 233 miles southeast from south-central North Carolina to Winyah Bay in northeastern South Carolina.

peek (pēk) *intr.v.* **peeked, peeking, peeks.** **1.** To glance quickly. **2.** To look or peer furtively, as from a place of concealment. —*n.* A furtive or brief look. [Middle English *piken* (expressive formation).]

peek·a·boo (pēk′ə-bōō′) *n.* A game for amusing a child, in which one repeatedly covers and exposes one's face, exclaiming "peekaboo!" [Akin to Dutch *kiekeboe,* English *peep-bo.*]

peel[1] (pēl) *n.* The skin or rind of certain fruits, such as the orange or banana. —*v.* **peeled, peeling, peels.** —*tr.* **1.** To strip or cut away the skin, rind, or bark from; pare. **2.** To strip away; pull off (an outer covering). —*intr.* **1.** To lose or shed skin, bark, or other covering. **2.** To come off in thin strips or pieces, as bark, skin, or paint. **3.** *Slang.* To remove one's clothes; undress. —**peel off.** To leave flight formation in order to land or make a dive. Used of an aircraft. [Middle English *pelen,* from Old French *peler,* to peel, remove hair from, from Latin *pilāre,* to plunder, "pile up (booty)," from *pīla,* "pile," PILLAR.]

peel[2] (pēl) *n.* **1.** A long-handled, shovellike tool used by bakers to move bread or pastries into and out of an oven. **2.** A T-shaped pole, used by printers for hanging freshly printed sheets of paper to dry. [Middle English *pele,* from Old French, shovel, from Latin *pāla,* spade. See **pag-** in Appendix.*]

peel[3] (pēl) *n.* One of a class of fortified houses or towers constructed in the borderland of Scotland and England in the 16th century. [Middle English *pel(e),* castle, small tower, (originally) palisade, from Norman French, from Latin *pālus,* stake. See **pag-** in Appendix.*]

Peel (pēl). A river rising in western Yukon Territory, Canada, and flowing 365 miles northeast to join the Mackenzie River in the Northwest Territories.

Peel (pēl), Sir **Robert.** 1788–1850. Prime Minister of Great Britain (1834–35 and 1841–46).

peel·er[1] (pē′lər) *n.* **1.** A person or device that peels; especially, a kitchen implement for peeling the rind or skin from a fruit or vegetable. **2.** *Slang.* A stripteaser.

peel·er[2] (pē′lər) *n. Obsolete British Slang.* A policeman. [After Sir Robert PEEL who as Secretary for Ireland instituted the Irish constabulary (1817) and who later as Home Secretary organized the Metropolitan Police Force (1828).]

peel·ing (pē′lĭng) *n.* A piece or strip that has been peeled off, such as skin, bark, or rind.

peen (pēn) *n.* The end of a hammerhead opposite the flat striking surface, often wedge-shaped or ball-shaped and used for chipping, indenting, and metalworking. —*tr.v.* **peened, peening, peens.** To hammer, bend, or shape with a peen. [Akin to Norwegian *penn* and Swedish *pen*†.]

peep[1] (pēp) *intr.v.* **peeped, peeping, peeps.** **1.** To utter short, soft, high-pitched sounds, like those of a baby bird; cheep. **2.** To speak in a hesitant, thin, high-pitched voice. —*n.* **1.** A weak, shrill sound or utterance, like that of a young bird. **2.** Any slight sound or utterance: *I don't want to hear a peep out of you.* **3.** Any of various small North American sandpipers. [Middle English *pepen* (imitative).]

peep[2] (pēp) *v.* **peeped, peeping, peeps.** —*intr.* **1.** To peek furtively; steal a quick glance: *"He peeped at me from time to time across a nose as sharp as a quill."* (Kenneth Tynan). **2.** To peer through a small aperture or from behind something: *"She stretched herself up on tiptoe, and peeped over the edge of the mushroom."* (Lewis Carroll). **3.** To become visible gradually, as though emerging from a hiding place: *At dawn the sun peeped over the horizon.* —*tr.* To cause to emerge or become partly visible. —*n.* **1.** A quick or furtive look; glance. **2.** A first glimpse or first appearance: *the peep of dawn.* [Middle English *pepen,* alteration of *piken,* PEEK.]

peep·er[1] (pē′pər) *n.* A creature that peeps, especially a frog.

peep·er[2] (pē′pər) *n.* **1.** Someone who looks furtively. **2.** *Slang.* An eye.

peep·hole (pēp′hōl′) *n.* A small hole or crevice through which one may peep.

peeping Tom. One who derives pleasure from pruriently and secretly spying on others; voyeur. [From *Peeping Tom* of Coventry, a tailor who was the sole person to peep at the naked Lady Godiva (and was struck blind).]

peep·show (pēp′shō′) *n.* Also **peep show.** An exhibition of pictures or objects viewed through a small hole or magnifying glass. Also called "raree show."

peep sight. A rear sight of a firearm consisting of an adjustable eyepiece with a small opening through which the front sight and the target are aligned.

pee·pul (pē′pəl) *n.* Also **pi·pal** (pē′pəl). A fig tree, *Ficus religiosa,* of India, regarded as sacred by Buddhists. Also called "bo tree." [Hindi *pīpal,* from Sanskrit *pippala.* See **pippalī** in Appendix.*]

peer[1] (pîr) *intr.v.* **peered, peering, peers.** **1.** To look intently, searchingly, or with difficulty: *"We peered at each other in the dull light."* (William Golding). **2.** To be partially visible; show: *The moon peered from behind a cloud.* —See Synonyms at **gaze.** [Perhaps contraction of APPEAR.]

peer[2] (pîr) *n.* **1.** A person who has equal standing with another, as in rank, class, or age. **2.** *Archaic.* A companion; fellow. **3. a.** A nobleman. **b.** A member of the British peerage; a duke, marquis, earl, viscount, or baron. **4.** One of the Twelve Peers of France; a designation originally, in the *chansons de geste,* of the chosen companions of Charlemagne, and subsequently for 12 feudal magnates (6 prelates and 6 temporal lords) of the Kingdom. [Middle English *peer(e)*, from Old French *per*, equal, one's equal, (hence) nobleman, from Latin *pār*, equal. See **pere-** in Appendix.*]

peer·age (pîr′ĭj) *n.* **1.** The rank or title of a peer. **2.** The body of peers. **3.** A book listing peers and their families.

peer·ess (pîr′ĭs) *n.* **1.** The wife or widow of a peer. **2.** A woman who holds a peerage by descent or appointment.

peer·less (pîr′lĭs) *adj.* Without peer; unmatched. —**peer′less·ly** *adv.* —**peer′less·ness** *n.*

peet·weet (pēt′wēt′) *n.* A bird, the **spotted sandpiper** *(see)*. [Imitative of its cry.]

peeve (pēv) *tr.v.* **peeved, peeving, peeves.** To annoy or make resentful; vex. See Synonyms at **annoy.** —*n.* **1.** A vexation; grievance: *a pet peeve.* **2.** A resentful mood: *be in a peeve.* [Back-formation from PEEVISH.]

pee·vish (pē′vĭsh) *adj.* **1.** Querulous; discontented; fretful: *"how peevish a patient was the . . . old lady; how angry; how sleepless"* (Thackeray). **2.** Ill-tempered. **3.** Contrary; fractious. [Middle English *pevish*, perhaps altered from French *pervers*, PERVERSE.] —**pee′vish·ly** *adv.* —**pee′vish·ness** *n.*

pee·wee (pē′wē) *n.* **1.** *Informal.* Any relatively or unusually small person or thing. **2.** Variant of **pewee.** [Whimsical formation on WEE.] —**pee′wee** *adj.*

peg (pĕg) *n.* **1.** A small cylindrical or tapered pin, as of wood, used to fasten things, such as floor boards, or to plug a hole, such as the vent of a barrel. **2.** A similar pin forming a projection that may be used as a support or as a boundary marker. **3.** One of the pins of a stringed musical instrument that are turned to tighten or slacken the strings so as to regulate their pitch. **4.** An implement fitted with a pointed prong or claw for tearing or catching. **5.** A degree or notch, especially in estimation. **6.** *Chiefly British.* A shot of liquor. **7.** A pretext or occasion for: *a peg to hang one's grievances upon.* **8.** *Baseball.* A low and fast throw of the ball to a baseman to retire a runner. **9.** *Informal.* A wooden leg. —**take one down a peg.** To reduce the pride of; to humble. —*v.* **pegged, pegging, pegs.** —*tr.* **1. a.** To put or insert a peg into. **b.** To provide (a barrel) with a vent and peg. **c.** To pierce or strike with or as with a peg. **2.** To designate or mark by means of pegs: *pegging the score in a cribbage game.* **3.** *Finance.* To stabilize or fix prices, as of securities or stocks, so they fluctuate very little or not at all. **4.** To aim and throw (a missile, as a stone or a ball) at or to a person or target. **5.** *Baseball.* **a.** To throw (the ball) fast and low to a baseman so as to retire a runner. **b.** To retire (a runner) in this manner. —*intr.* To work steadily; hammer away; persist. Often followed by *away: "The only thing to do is . . . to keep pegging steadily away until the luck turns."* (T. Roosevelt). [Middle English *pegge*, probably from Middle Dutch. See **bak-** in Appendix.*]

Peg·a·sus¹ (pĕg′ə-səs). *Greek Mythology.* The winged steed that caused Hippocrene, the fountain of the Muses on Helicon, to well forth with a stroke of his hoof.

Peg·a·sus² (pĕg′ə-səs). A constellation in the Northern Hemisphere near Aquarius and Andromeda.

Peg·gy (pĕg′ē). A feminine given name. [Variant of *Meggy, Meg*, pet forms for MARGARET.]

peg leg. *Informal.* An artificial leg.

peg·ma·tite (pĕg′mə-tīt′) *n.* *Mineralogy.* A coarse-grained igneous rock, largely granite, sometimes rich in rare elements such as uranium, tungsten, and tantalum. [French : Greek *pēgma* (stem *pēgmat-*), framework, from *pēgnunai*, to fasten (see **pag-** in Appendix*) + -ITE.] —**peg′ma·tit′ic** (-tĭt′ĭk) *adj.*

Pe·gu (pĕ-gōō′). **1.** A river rising in Lower Burma and flowing 150 miles south to join the Rangoon River. **2.** A sacred Buddhist city in Lower Burma. Population, 47,000.

Peh·le·vi. Variant of **Pahlavi.**

P.E.I. Prince Edward Island.

pei·gnoir (pān-wär′, pĕn-) *n.* A woman's loose-fitting dressing gown. [French, "garment worn while combing the hair," from Old French *peigner*, to comb the hair, from Latin *pectināre*, from *pecten* (stem *pectin-*), comb. See **pek-²** in Appendix.*]

Pei Ho, Pei-Ho (bī′ hō′). Also **Pai** (bī). A river rising in northeastern China and flowing 350 miles southeast into the Gulf of Po Hai, east of Tientsin. [Chinese (Mandarin) *pei³ ho²*, "northern river" : *pei³*, north + *ho²*, river.]

Pei·pus (pī′pəs). *Estonian* **Peip·si** (pāp′sē); *Russian* **Chud·sko·ye O·ze·ro** (chōōt′skə-yə ô′zĭ-rə). A lake, 1,357 square miles in area, in northwestern Soviet Russia and eastern Estonia, with an outlet, the Narova River, to the Gulf of Finland.

Peirce (pûrs), **Charles Sanders.** 1839–1914. American philosopher, physicist, and mathematician; founder of pragmatism.

Pei·sis·tra·tus. See **Pisistratus.**

pej·o·ra·tion (pĕj′ə-rā′shən, pē′jə-) *n.* **1.** The process or condition of worsening or degenerating. **2.** *Linguistics.* The process by which the semantic status of a word changes for the worse, over a period of time. For example, *egregious*, which formerly meant "distinguished or remarkable," has come to mean "conspicuously bad or flagrant." Compare **melioration.** [Medieval Latin *pējōrātiō*, from Late Latin *pējōrāre*, to become or make worse, from Latin *pējor*, worse. See **ped-¹** in Appendix.*]

pe·jor·a·tive (pĭ-jôr′ə-tĭv, -jŏr′ə-tĭv, pĕj′ə-rā′tĭv, pē′jə-) *adj.* Tending to make or become worse; disparaging; downgrading. —*n.* A pejorative word. —**pe·jor′a·tive·ly** *adv.*

pek·an (pĕk′ən) *n.* A mammal, the **fisher** *(see)*. [Canadian French *pékan*, of Algonquian origin, akin to Abnaki *pékané*.]

pe·kin (pē′kĭn′) *n.* **1.** A striped or figured silk fabric. **2.** *Capital* **P.** A large white duck of an Oriental breed, widely raised in the United States for food. [French *pékin*, from *Pékin*, PEKING.]

Pe·king (pē′kĭng′). Formerly **Pei·ping** (bā′pĭng′). The capital of China, south of the Great Wall in the northeastern part of the country. Population, 5,420,000. [Chinese *pei³ ching¹*, "northern capital" : *pei³*, north + *ching¹*, capital.]

Pe·king·ese (pē′kĭng-ēz′, -ēs′ *for senses 1, 2;* pē′kə-nēz′, -nēs′ *for sense 3*) *n., pl.* **Pekingese.** Also **Pe·kin·ese** (pē′kə-nēz′, -nēs′). **1.** A resident or native of Peking, China. **2.** The Chinese dialect of Peking. **3.** A toy dog of a breed developed in China, having a flat nose, a long-haired coat, and short, bowed forelegs. —**Pe′king·ese′** *adj.*

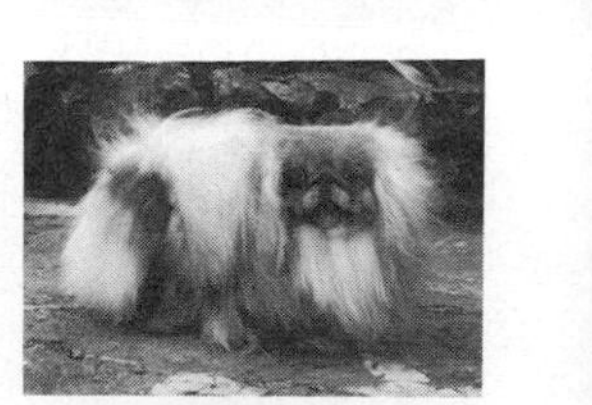
Pekingese

Peking man. An extinct hominid primate of the genus *Sinanthropus*, known from fossil remains of the Pleistocene epoch. [The remains were found at Choukoutien, near *Peking*.]

pe·koe (pē′kō, pĕk′ō) *n.* A grade of black tea consisting of the leaves around the buds. [Chinese (Amoy) *peh ho* : *peh* (Mandarin *pai²*) white + *ho* (Mandarin *hao²*) down.]

pel·age (pĕl′ĭj) *n.* The coat of a mammal, consisting of hair, fur, wool, or other soft covering, as distinct from bare skin. [French, from Old French *pel, poil*, hair, from Latin *pilus*. See **pilo-** in Appendix.*]

Pe·la·gi·an Islands (pə-lā′jē-ən, -jən). Also **Pe·la·gie Islands** (pā-lä′jä). Three Italian islands in the Mediterranean Sea between Malta and Tunisia.

Pe·la·gi·an·ism (pə-lā′jē-ə-nĭz′əm) *n.* The theological doctrine propounded by Pelagius, a British or Irish monk, and condemned as heresy by the Roman Catholic Church in A.D. 416. Included in its tenets were denial of original sin and affirmation of man's ability to be righteous by the exercise of free will. —**Pe·la′gi·an** *adj.* & *n.*

pe·lag·ic (pə-lăj′ĭk) *adj.* Of, pertaining to, or living in open oceans or seas rather than waters adjacent to land or inland waters: *"I had a net overboard to catch pelagic animals."* (Darwin). See **plankton, nekton.** [Latin *pelagicus*, from Greek *pelagikos*, from *pelagos*, sea. See **plāk-¹** in Appendix.*]

pel·ar·gon·ic acid (pĕl′är-gŏn′ĭk, -gō′nĭk). A colorless or yellow oil, $CH_3(CH_2)_7COOH$, used as a gasoline additive and in the manufacture of lacquers, plastics, and pharmaceuticals. Also called "nonanoic acid." [Obtained from the leaves of PELARGONIUM.]

pel·ar·go·ni·um (pĕl′är-gō′nē-əm) *n.* Any of various plants and shrubs of the genus *Pelargonium*, which includes the geraniums. [New Latin, from Greek *pelargos*, a stork (from the long, beak-shaped capsules of the plants). See **pel-²** in Appendix.*]

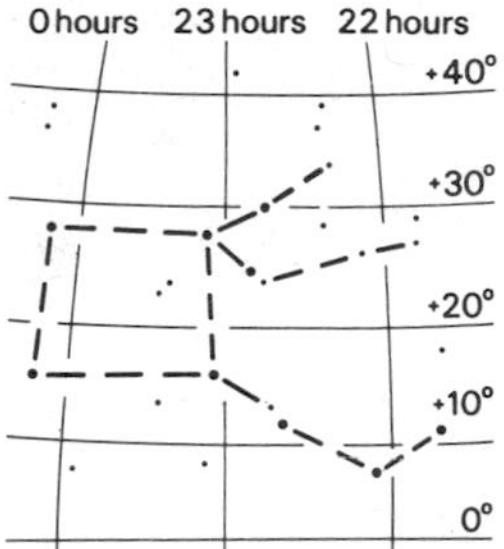

Pegasus²

Pe·las·gi·an (pə-lăz′jē-ən) *n.* One of a people living in the region of the Aegean Sea before the coming of the Greeks. [Greek *Pelasgoi*, native name of unknown origin probably reshaped by folk etymology as if to mean "sea people," from *pelagos*, sea.] —**Pe·las′gi·an, Pe·las′gic** (pə-lăz′jĭk) *adj.*

Pe·lée, Mount (pə-lā′). A volcanic mountain peak, 4,428 feet high, on northern Martinique. It erupted in 1902, causing the death of more than 30,000 people.

pel·er·ine (pĕl′ə-rēn′, pĕl′ər-ĭn) *n.* A woman's cape, usually short, with points in front. [French *pèlerine*, from the feminine of *pèlerin*, a pilgrim, from Late Latin *pelegrīnus*, PILGRIM.]

Pe·lew. Former name for the **Palau.**

pelf (pĕlf) *n.* Wealth or riches, especially when dishonestly acquired: *"Penniless paupers have become the possessors of uncounted pelf."* (Ross Lockridge, Jr.). [Middle English, booty, property, from Old French *pelfre*. See **pilfer.**]

pel·i·can (pĕl′ĭ-kən) *n.* Any of various large, web-footed birds of the genus *Pelecanus*, of tropical and warm regions, having under the lower bill a large pouch used for catching and holding fish. [Middle English *pelican*, Old English *pellican*, from Late Latin *pelicānus*, from Greek *pelekan, pelekinos*, from *pelekus*, an ax (probably from the shape of its bill), akin to Sanskrit *parasu*, an ax, probably of Mesopotamian origin.]

Pe·li·on (pē′lē-ən). A mountain peak, 5,250 feet high, in northeastern Greece. See **Ossa.**

pe·lisse (pə-lēs′) *n.* **1.** A long cloak or outer robe, usually of fur or with a fur lining. **2.** A woman's loose, light cloak, often with openings for the arms. [French, from Medieval Latin *pellicia*, leather garment, cloak, from Latin *pellicius*, made of skin, from *pellis*, skin. See **pel-⁴** in Appendix.*]

pe·lite (pē′līt′) *n.* Any rock composed of fine fragments, as of clay, quartz particles, or rock flour. [Greek *pēlos*†, clay + -ITE.] —**pe·lit′ic** (pĭ-lĭt′ĭk) *adj.*

pel·lag·ra (pə-lăg′rə, -lā′grə, -lä′grə) *n.* A chronic disease caused by niacin deficiency, and characterized by skin eruptions, digestive and nervous disturbances, and eventual mental deterioration. [Italian : *pelle*, skin, from Latin *pellis* (see **pel-⁴** in Appendix*) + *agra*, seizure (see **ag-** in Appendix*).] —**pel·lag′rous** *adj.*

pel·lag·rin (pə-lăg′rĭn, -lā′grĭn, -lä′grĭn) *n.* A person afflicted with pellagra. [From PELLAGRA.]

pel·let (pĕl′ĭt) *n.* **1.** A small, solid or densely packed ball or mass, as of bread, wax, or medicine. **2.** A bullet or piece of small shot. **3.** A stone ball, used as a catapult missile or as a primitive cannonball. —*tr.v.* **pelleted, -leting, -lets.** **1.** To make or form into pellets. **2.** To strike with pellets. [Middle English *pelet*, from Old French *pelote*, from Vulgar Latin *pilotta* (unattested), diminutive of Latin *pila*, ball, PILL.]

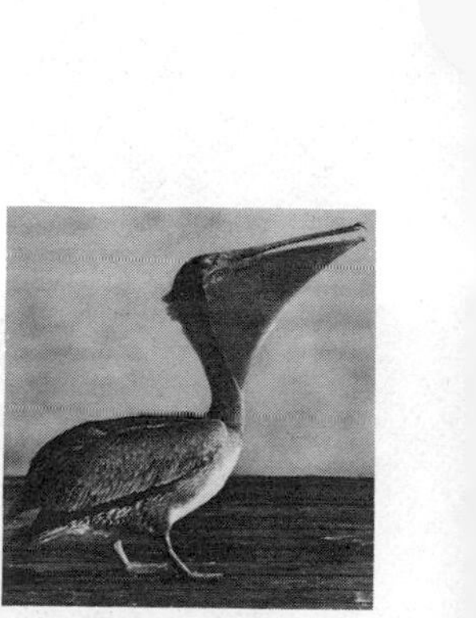
pelican
Pelecanus occidentalis
Brown pelican

Pel·le·tier (pĕl-tyā′), **Pierre Joseph.** 1788–1842. French chemist; isolated chlorophyll, quinine, and other substances.

pel·li·cle (pĕl′ĭ-kəl) *n.* A thin skin or film, such as an organic membrane or a liquid film. [Old French *pellicule*, from Medieval Latin *pellicula*, from Latin, diminutive of *pellis*, skin. See **pel-⁴** in Appendix.*] —**pel·lic′u·lar** (pə-lĭk′yə-lər) *adj.*

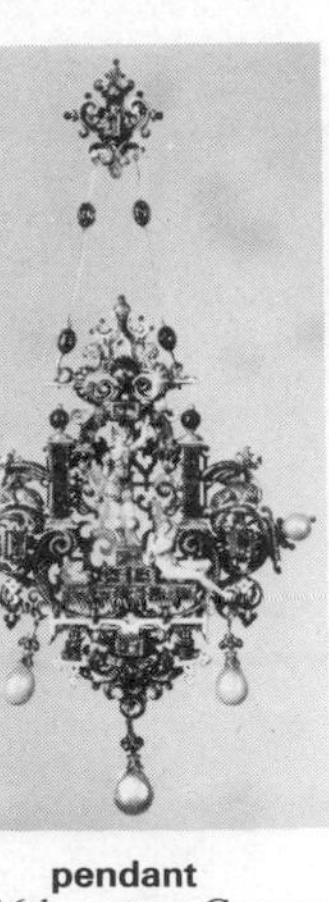

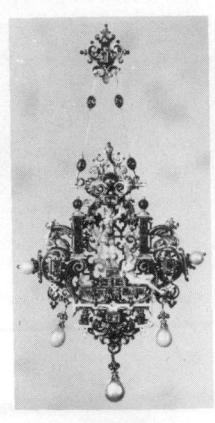

pendant
Late 16th-century German pendant of enameled gold with jewels and figures

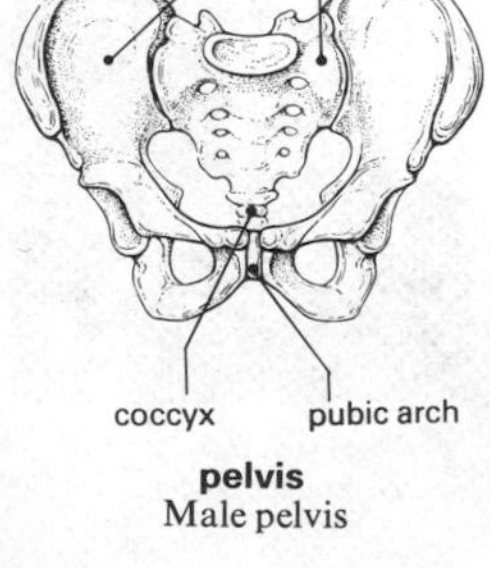

pelvis
Male pelvis

pel·li·to·ry (pĕl′ə-tôr′ē, -tōr′ē) *n., pl.* **-ries.** **1.** Any of various plants of the genus *Parietaria,* having long, narrow leaves with hairy tufts at the base. **2.** A small plant, *Anacyclus pyrethrum,* of the Mediterranean region, containing a volatile oil once used for the relief of toothache and facial neuralgia. [Sense 2, altered from earlier *peletyr,* Middle English *peletre, peretre,* from Latin *pyrethrum,* PYRETHRUM. Sense 1, altered from Middle English *peritorie, paritorie,* from Old French *paritaire,* from Late Latin *parietāria (herba),* "herb of the wall," from *parietārius,* belonging to walls, from Latin *pariēs* (stem *pariet-*), wall. See **paries.**]

pell-mell (pĕl′mĕl′) *adv.* Also **pell·mell.** **1.** In a jumbled, confused manner; helter-skelter. **2.** In frantic, disorderly haste; headlong. [French *pêle-mêle,* from Old French *pesle mesle, mesle mesle,* reduplications of *mesle,* imperative of *mesler,* to mix, from Vulgar Latin *misculāre* (unattested), from Latin *miscēre.* See **meik-** in Appendix.*] —**pell′-mell′** *adj.* & *n.*

pel·lu·cid (pə-lo͞o′sĭd) *adj.* **1.** Admitting the maximum passage of light; transparent; translucent. **2.** Transparently clear in style or meaning: *pellucid prose.* [Latin *pellūcidus,* from *pellūcēre, perlūcēre,* to shine through : *per,* through + *lūcēre,* to shine (see **leuk-** in Appendix*).] —**pel·lu·cid′i·ty** (pĕl′yo͞o-sĭd′ə-tē), **pel·lu′cid·ness** *n.* —**pel·lu′cid·ly** *adv.*

Pel·ly River (pĕl′ē). A river rising in the Mackenzie Mountains in east-central Yukon Territory, Canada, and flowing west 330 miles to join the Lewes River and form the Yukon River.

Peloponnesian War. A war between Athens and Sparta with their allies (431–404 B.C.) that was won by Sparta.

Pel·o·pon·ne·sus (pĕl′ə-pə-nē′səs). Also **Pel·o·pon·ne·sos** (-nē′səs, -sôs), **Pel·o·pon·nese** (-nēz′, -nēs′). Medieval name, **Mo·re·a** (mô-rē′ə, mō-). A peninsula, about 8,400 square miles in area, lying south of the Gulf of Corinth, and forming the southern part of Greece. It is one of the ten divisions of modern Greece. [Latin *Peloponnēsus,* from Greek *Peloponnēsos,* "isle of Pelops" : PELOPS + *nēsos,* island (see **snā-** in Appendix*).] —**Pel′o·pon·ne′sian** *adj.* & *n.*

Pe·lops (pē′lŏps′). *Greek Mythology.* The son of Tantalus and father of Atreus. [Latin, from Greek, "dark-faced" : *pelios,* dark (see **pel-**[2] in Appendix*) + *ops,* eye, face (see **okw-** in Appendix*).]

pe·lo·ri·a (pə-lôr′ē-ə, -lōr′ē-ə) *n. Botany.* Unusual regularity in the form of a flower that is normally irregular. [New Latin, from Greek *pelōros,* monstrous, from *pelōr,* monster, prodigy. See **kwer-**[1] in Appendix.*] —**pe·lor′ic** (pə-lôr′ĭk, -lŏr′ĭk) *adj.*

pe·lo·rus (pə-lôr′əs, -lōr′əs) *n., pl.* **-ruses.** A fixed compass card on which bearings relative to the ship's heading are taken. [Possibly after *Pelorus,* pilot of Hannibal.]

pe·lo·ta (pə-lō′tə) *n.* **1.** The game of **jai alai** *(see).* **2.** The ball used in the game of jai alai. [Spanish, "ball," from Old French *pelote,* PELLET.]

Pe·lo·tas (pə-lō′täs). A city and seaport on Lagoa dos Patos in southeastern Brazil. Population, 120,000.

pelt[1] (pĕlt) *n.* **1. a.** The skin of an animal with the fur or hair still on it. **b.** A stripped animal skin ready for tanning. **2.** An animal hide used as a garment. **3.** The human skin; hide. [Middle English, perhaps back-formation from PELTRY.]

pelt[2] (pĕlt) *v.* **pelted, pelting, pelts.** —*tr.* **1.** To strike or assail repeatedly with or as with blows or missiles; throw things at; bombard. **2.** To cast, hurl, or throw (missiles). **3.** To strike repeatedly: *"Your laughter pelts my skin with small delicious blows."* (Edna St. Vincent Millay). —*intr.* **1.** To beat or strike heavily and repeatedly. **2.** To move at a vigorous gait. —*n.* **1.** A sharp blow; whack. **2.** A rapid pace; speed. Used chiefly in the phrase *at full pelt.* [Middle English *pelten,* perhaps from Latin *pultāre.* See **pel-**[6] in Appendix.*] —**pelt′er** *n.*

pel·tate (pĕl′tāt′) *adj. Botany.* Having the leaf stalk attached near the center of the surface, rather than at or near the margin: *the peltate leaf of the nasturtium.* [New Latin *peltatus,* "having a shield," from Latin *pelta,* small light shield, from Greek *peltē.* See **pel-**[4] in Appendix.*] —**pel′tate′ly** *adv.*

pelt·ing (pĕl′tĭng) *adj. Archaic.* Paltry; petty; contemptible: *"A set of pelting wretches"* (Shelley). [Akin to PALTRY.]

pel·try (pĕl′trē) *n.* Undressed pelts collectively. [Middle English, from Old French *peleterie,* from *peletier,* furrier, from *pel,* skin, from Latin *pellis.* See **pel-**[4] in Appendix.*]

pel·vic (pĕl′vĭk) *adj.* Of, in, near, or pertaining to the pelvis: *a pelvic artery.*

pelvic fin. Either of a pair of lateral hind fins of fishes, attached to the pelvic girdle. Also called "ventral fin."

pelvic girdle. The skeletal structure of bone or cartilage by which the hind limbs or analogous parts are supported and joined to the vertebral column. Also called "pelvic arch."

pel·vis (pĕl′vĭs) *n., pl.* **-vises** or **-ves** (-vēz′). *Anatomy.* **1.** A basin-shaped skeletal structure, composed of the innominate bones on the sides, the pubis in front, and the sacrum and coccyx behind, that rests on the lower limbs and supports the spinal column. **2.** The hollow funnel in the outlet of the kidney, into which urine is discharged before entering the ureter. In this sense, also called "renal pelvis." [New Latin, from Latin *pēlvis,* basin. See **pel-**[7] in Appendix.*]

Pemb. Pembrokeshire.

Pem·ba (pĕm′bə). An island of Tanzania, 380 square miles in area, in the Indian Ocean. Population, 134,000.

Pem·broke (pĕm′bro͝ok). Also **Pem·broke·shire** (-shîr, -shər). *Abbr.* **Pemb** A county in southwestern Wales, 614 square miles in area. Population, 94,000. County seat, Pembroke.

pem·mi·can (pĕm′ĭ-kən) *n.* Also **pem·i·can.** **1.** A food prepared by North American Indians from lean, dried strips of meat pounded into paste, mixed with fat and berries, and pressed into small cakes. **2.** A similar food made chiefly from beef, dried fruit, and suet, used as emergency rations. [Cree *pimikân,* from *pimii,* grease, fat.]

pem·phi·gus (pĕm′fĭ-gəs, pĕm-fī′gəs) *n.* Any of several acute or chronic skin diseases characterized by groups of itching blisters. [New Latin, from Greek *pemphix* (stem *pemphig-*), breath, drop, pustule, of imitative origin.]

pen[1] (pĕn) *n.* **1.** An instrument for writing or drawing with ink: **a.** Formerly, one made from a large quill with the nib split and sharpened. **b.** A tapering metal device with a split point, fitted to a metal, plastic, or wooden holder. It may be dipped in ink or supplied by a reservoir within the holder. **c.** A penholder and its pen together. See **ball-point pen, fountain pen.** **2.** The instrument of authorship viewed as the writer's weapon or instrument, or as the practice of writing. **3.** A writer or author: *a hired pen.* **4.** A style of writing: *a witty pen.* **5.** *Plural.* Pinions. **6.** *Zoology.* The chitinous internal shell of a squid. —*tr.v.* **penned, penning, pens.** To write or compose with a pen. [Middle English *penne,* from Old French, feather, pen, from Latin *penna,* feather (in Late Latin, also "pen"). See **pet-**[1] in Appendix.*] —**pen′ner** *n.*

pen[2] (pĕn) *n.* **1.** A fenced enclosure for animals. **2.** The animals kept in such an enclosure. **3.** Any of various other enclosures, such as a **bullpen** or a **playpen** *(both of which see).* **4.** A repair dock for submarines. —*tr.v.* **penned** or **pent** (pĕnt), **penning, pens.** To confine in or as if in a pen. [Middle English *pen,* Old English *penn.* See **bend-** in Appendix.*]

pen[3] (pĕn) *n.* A female swan. [Origin unknown.]

pen[4] (pĕn) *n. Slang.* Penitentiary. [Short for PENITENTIARY.]

pen., Pen. peninsula.

pe·nal (pē′nəl) *adj.* **1.** Of or pertaining to punishment, especially for breaking the law. **2.** Subject to punishment; legally punishable: *a penal offense.* **3.** Prescribing or enumerating punishments or penalties for offenses: *penal laws.* **4.** Serving as or constituting a means or place of punishment: *penal servitude.* [Middle English, from Old French, from Latin *poenālis,* from *poena,* penalty. See **kwei-**[1] in Appendix.*] —**pe′nal·ly** *adv.*

Pe·ña·la·ra (pā′nyä-lä′rä). The highest elevation (7,972 feet) of the Sierra de Guadarrama, in central Spain.

penal code. The body of laws relating to crimes and offenses and the penalties for their commission.

pe·nal·ize (pē′nəl-īz′, pĕn′əl-) *tr.v.* **-ized, -izing, -izes.** **1.** To subject to a penalty, especially for infringement of a law or official regulation. **2.** To impose a handicap on; place at a disadvantage. **3.** To make punishable by a penalty. —See Synonyms at **punish.** —**pe′nal·i·za′tion** *n.*

pen·al·ty (pĕn′əl-tē) *n., pl.* **-ties.** **1.** A punishment established by law or authority for a crime or offense. **2.** Something, especially a sum of money, required as a forfeit for an offense. **3.** The disadvantage or painful consequences resulting from an action or condition. **4.** *Sports.* A punishment, handicap, or loss of advantage imposed on a team or competitor for infraction of a rule. **5.** *Often plural.* In contract bridge, points scored by the opponents when the declarer fails to make his bid. [Norman French *penalte* (unattested), from Medieval Latin *poenālitās,* from Latin *poenālis,* PENAL.]

pen·ance (pĕn′əns) *n.* **1.** An act of self-mortification or devotion performed by way of demonstrating contrition for sin. **2.** *Ecclesiastical.* **a.** A sacrament that includes contrition, confession to a priest, acceptance of punishment, and absolution. **b.** The punishment so imposed. **3.** A feeling of sorrow for wrongdoing or sin prompting one to a firm purpose of amendment. —**do penance.** To show repentance by undergoing imposed or voluntary punishment. —*tr.v.* **penanced, -ancing, -ances.** *Rare.* To impose penance upon. [Middle English *penaunce,* from Old French *penance,* from Latin *paenitentia,* penitence, from *paenitēns,* PENITENT.]

Pe·nang (pē-năng′). **1.** An island, 110 square miles in area, off the western coast of the Malay Peninsula. **2.** A state of Malaysia, about 400 square miles in area, including Penang Island and part of the nearby mainland. Population, 697,000. **3.** Formerly **George Town.** The capital of this state, a port city on Penang Island. Population, 235,000.

pe·na·tes (pə-nā′tēz, -nä′tēz) *pl.n.* The Roman gods of the household, tutelary deities of the home and of the state, whose cult was closely connected and often identified with that of the **lares** *(see).* [Latin *Penātēs,* household gods, akin to *penus*†, the interior of a house (compare **penetrate**).]

pence (pĕns). *British.* Alternate plural of **penny.** Used especially in combination; for example, **twopence.**

pen·cel (pĕn′səl) *n.* Also **pen·sil.** A narrow flag, streamer, or pennon, especially one carried at the top of a lance or spear. [Middle English, from Norman French, contracted from Old French *penoncel,* diminutive of *penon,* PENNON.]

pen·chant (pĕn′chənt) *n.* A strong inclination; a definite and continued liking. [French, from the present participle of *pencher,* to incline, from Vulgar Latin *pendicāre* (unattested), from Latin *pendēre,* to hang. See **spen-** in Appendix.*]

pen·cil (pĕn′səl) *n.* **1.** A narrow, generally cylindrical implement for writing, drawing, or marking, consisting of a thin rod of graphite, crayon, or similar substance encased in wood or held in a plastic or metal mechanical device. **2.** Something shaped or used like a pencil; especially, a narrow medicated or cosmetic stick: *a styptic pencil; an eyebrow pencil.* **3. a.** *Archaic.* An artist's brush, especially a fine one. **b.** An artist's style or technique in drawing or delineating. **c.** Descriptive skill. **4.** A cluster of rays, especially light rays, radiating from or converging on a single point. **5.** *Mathematics.* A one-parameter family of three-dimensional or plane figures, such as all straight

ă pat/ā pay/âr care/ä father/b bib/ch church/d deed/ĕ pet/ē be/f fife/g gag/h hat/hw which/ĭ pit/ī pie/îr pier/j judge/k kick/l lid, needle/m mum/n no, sudden/ng thing/ŏ pot/ō toe/ô paw, for/oi noise/ou out/o͝o took/o͞o boot/p pop/r roar/s sauce/sh ship, dish/

lines in a plane that pass through a fixed point. —*tr.v.* **penciled, -ciling, -cils.** Also *chiefly British* **-cilled, -cilling. 1.** To write or produce by using a pencil. **2.** To mark or color with or as if with a pencil. [Middle English *pensel, pencel,* from Old French *pincel,* from Vulgar Latin *pēnicellus* (unattested), from Latin *pēnicillus,* a brush, pencil, "small tail," diminutive of *pēnis,* tail. See **pes-** in Appendix.*] —**pen'cil·er** *n.*

pen·dant (pĕn'dənt) *n.* Also **pen·dent. 1.** Something suspended from something else; especially, an ornament or piece of jewelry attached to a necklace or bracelet. **2.** A hanging lamp or chandelier. **3.** A sculptured ornament suspended from a vaulted Gothic roof or ceiling. **4. a.** One of a matched pair; a parallel or companion piece. **b.** An additional thing or part that supplements or complements another; complement. —*adj.* Variant of **pendent.** [Middle English *pendaunt,* from Old French *pendant,* from the present participle of *pendre,* to hang, from Vulgar Latin *pendere* (unattested), to hang, variant of Latin *pendēre,* to hang. See **spen-** in Appendix.*]

pen·dent (pĕn'dənt) *adj.* Also **pen·dant. 1.** Hanging down; dangling; suspended. **2.** Projecting; jutting; overhanging. **3.** Awaiting settlement; undecided; pending. —*n.* Variant of **pendant.** [Middle English *penda(u)nt,* from Old French *pendant,* hanging. See **pendant.**] —**pen'dent·ly** *adv.*

pen·den·tive (pĕn-dĕn'tĭv) *n. Architecture.* An overhanging, triangular section of vaulting between the rim of a dome and each adjacent pair of the arches that support it. [French *pendentif,* "overhanging feature," from Latin *pendēns,* present participle of *pendēre,* to hang. See **spen-** in Appendix.*]

Pen·der·gast (pĕn'dər-găst'), **Thomas Joseph.** 1870–1945. American political figure; Democratic party boss of Kansas City and the state of Missouri (1916–39).

pend·ing (pĕn'dĭng) *adj.* **1.** Not yet decided or settled; awaiting conclusion or confirmation. **2.** Impending; imminent: *"She was very much aware that a climax was pending."* (Dreiser). —*prep.* **1.** While in process of; during. **2.** While awaiting; until. [Anglicized form of French *pendant,* from Old French, "hanging" (after Latin *pendēns,* hanging, pending). See **pendant.**]

Pend O·reille Lake (pŏn'də-rā'). A lake occupying about 125 square miles in northern Idaho.

pen·drag·on (pĕn-drăg'ən) *n.* The title of the supreme war leader of the post-Roman Celts of southern Britain. [Middle English, from Welsh : *pen,* chief, head, from Common Celtic *gwenno-* (unattested) + *dragon,* standard, from Latin *dracō,* cohort's standard, DRAGON.] —**pen·drag'on·ship'** *n.*

pen·du·lar (pĕn'jo͝o-lər, pĕn'dyə-) *adj.* Of or resembling the motion of a pendulum; swinging back and forth.

pen·du·lous (pĕn'jo͝o-ləs, pĕn'dyə-) *adj.* **1.** Hanging loosely; suspended so as to swing or sway. **2.** Wavering; undecided. [Latin *pendulus,* from *pendēre,* to hang. See **spen-** in Appendix.*] —**pen'du·lous·ly** *adv.* —**pen'du·lous·ness** *n.*

pen·du·lum (pĕn'jo͝o-ləm, pĕn'dyə-, pĕn'də-) *n.* **1. a.** A mass suspended from a fixed low-friction support at the end of a relatively light thread so that it is free to swing in a vertical plane under the influence of gravitational force only. Also called "simple pendulum." **b.** Any of several related, freely swinging configurations differing in mass distribution, suspension, and possible modes of motion. **2.** Any such object used to regulate the movement of various devices, especially clocks. **3.** Something that swings back and forth from one course, opinion, or condition to another: *the pendulum of public opinion.* [New Latin, from Latin, neuter of *pendulus,* PENDULOUS.]

Pe·nel·o·pe[1] (pə-nĕl'ə-pē). A feminine given name. [Latin *Pēnelopē,* from Greek *Pēnelopeia*†.]

Pe·nel·o·pe[2] (pə-nĕl'ə-pē). In the *Odyssey,* the wife of Odysseus and mother of Telemachus, celebrated for her constancy.

Pe·nel·o·pe[3] (pə-nĕl'ə-pē) *n.* A chaste wife.

pe·ne·plain (pē'nə-plān') *n.* Also **pe·ne·plane.** *Geology.* A nearly flat land surface representing an advanced stage of erosion. [Latin *paene, pēne,* almost (see **penult**) + PLAIN.]

pe·nes. Alternate plural of **penis.**

pen·e·tra·ble (pĕn'ə-trə-bəl) *adj.* Capable of being penetrated: *"The moon made the night extraordinarily penetrable."* (Henry James). [Latin *penetrābilis,* from *penetrāre,* PENETRATE.] —**pen'e·tra·bil'i·ty** *n.* —**pen'e·tra·bly** *adv.*

pen·e·tra·li·a (pĕn'ə-trā'lē-ə) *pl.n.* **1.** The innermost parts of a building; especially, the sanctuary of a temple. **2.** Innermost or hidden parts; recesses: *the penetralia of the soul.* [Latin *penetrālia,* plural of *penetrāle,* innermost part, from *penetrālis,* inner, interior, from *penetrāre,* PENETRATE.]

pen·e·trance (pĕn'ə-trəns) *n. Genetics.* The degree or frequency with which a gene manifests its effect. [From PENETRANT.]

pen·e·trant (pĕn'ə-trənt) *adj.* Penetrating; piercing. —*n.* Something that penetrates or is capable of penetrating. [Latin *penetrāns,* present participle of *penetrāre,* PENETRATE.]

pen·e·trate (pĕn'ə-trāt') *v.* **-trated, -trating, -trates.** —*tr.* **1.** To enter or force a way into; pierce. **2. a.** To enter into and permeate. **b.** To cause to be permeated or diffused; steep. **3.** To grasp the inner significance of; understand: *"with eyes that penetrated his point of view"* (Elizabeth Bowen). **4.** To see through. **5.** To affect deeply, as by piercing the consciousness or emotions. —*intr.* **1.** To pierce or enter into something; make a way in or through something; get in or through: *"Beyond the bonds of their own self their senses cannot penetrate."* (Blake). **2.** To gain admittance or access. **3.** To gain insight (into something). [Latin *penetrāre,* from *penitus,* deeply, from *penus*†, the interior of a house.]

pen·e·trat·ing (pĕn'ə-trā'tĭng) *adj.* **1.** Able or seeming to penetrate: *a penetrating wind.* **2.** Keenly perceptive or understanding: *penetrating insight.* —**pen'e·trat'ing·ly** *adv.*

pen·e·tra·tion (pĕn'ə-trā'shən) *n.* **1.** The act or process of piercing or penetrating something. **2.** The power or ability to penetrate. **3.** The depth reached by a projectile after hitting its target. **4.** The capacity or action of understanding; insight.

pen·e·tra·tive (pĕn'ə-trā'tĭv) *adj.* Capable of penetrating; tending to penetrate; piercing.

pen·e·trom·e·ter (pĕn'ə-trŏm'ə-tər) *n.* Also **pen·e·tram·e·ter** (pĕn'ə-trăm'ə-tər). **1.** A device for measuring the penetrating power of x rays. **2.** A device for measuring the penetrability of semisolids.

Penge (pĕnj). A former administrative division of London, England, now part of **Bromley** *(see).*

Peng·hu. The Chinese name for the **Pescadores.**

Peng·pu (pŭng'po͞o'). A city and rail-river transshipment port on the Hwai River in eastern China. Population, 330,000.

pen·guin (pĕn'gwĭn, pĕng'gwĭn) *n.* **1.** Any of various flightless marine birds of the family Spheniscidae, of cool regions of the Southern Hemisphere. They have scalelike, barbless feathers, flipperlike wings, and webbed feet. See **Adélie penguin, emperor penguin. 2.** *Obsolete.* The great auk. [Perhaps from Welsh *pen gwyn* : *pen,* head (see **pendragon**) + *gwyn,* white (see **weid-** in Appendix*).]

-penia. Indicates lack or deficiency; for example, **leukopenia.** [New Latin, from Greek *penia,* poverty, lack. See **spon** in Appendix.*]

pen·i·cil·late (pĕn'ə-sĭl'ĭt, -āt') *adj.* Having or resembling a tuft or brush of fine hairs, as those on caterpillars and certain grasses. [Latin *pēnicillus,* brush, PENCIL + -ATE.] —**pen'i·cil'late·ly** *adv.* —**pen·i·cil·la'tion** (pĕn'ə-sĭ-lā'shən) *n.*

pen·i·cil·lin (pĕn'ə-sĭl'ĭn) *n.* Any of several isomeric antibiotic compounds obtained from penicillin molds, especially *Penicillium notatum* and *P. chrysogenum,* or produced biosynthetically, and used to prevent or treat a wide variety of diseases and infections. [From New Latin *penicillium,* PENICILLIUM.]

pen·i·cil·li·um (pĕn'ə-sĭl'ē-əm) *n., pl.* **-ums** or **-cillia** (-sĭl'ē-ə). Any of various molds of the genus *Penicillium,* having a characteristic blue-green color, and producing tufts of fine filaments. They grow on decaying fruits and ripening cheese, and are used in the production of penicillin and in making cheese. [New Latin, from Latin *pēnicillus,* brush, PENCIL.]

pen·in·su·la (pə-nĭn'syə-lə, -sə-lə) *n. Abbr.* **pen., Pen.** A long projection of land into water, connected with the mainland by an isthmus. Compare **cape.** [Latin *pēninsula* : *pēne,* almost (see **penult**) + *īnsula,* an island (see **isle**).] —**pen·in'su·lar** *adj.*

Peninsula, the. 1. The peninsula comprising Spain and Portugal, **Iberia** *(see).* **2.** The area between the York and James rivers in southeastern Virginia.

pe·nis (pē'nĭs) *n., pl.* **-nises** or **-nes** (-nēz'). *Anatomy.* **1.** The male organ of copulation in higher vertebrates, and usually of urinary excretion in mammals. **2.** Any of various copulatory organs in males of lower animals. [Latin *pēnis,* tail, penis. See **pes-** in Appendix.*]

pen·i·tent (pĕn'ə-tənt) *adj.* Feeling or expressing remorse for one's misdeeds or sins. —*n.* **1.** One who is penitent. **2.** A person performing penance under the direction of a confessor. [Middle English, from Old French, from Latin *paenitēns,* present participle of *paenitēre*†, to repent.] —**pen'i·tence** *n.* —**pen'i·tent·ly** *adv.*

pen·i·ten·tial (pĕn'ə-tĕn'shəl) *adj.* **1.** Of, pertaining to, or expressing penitence. **2.** Pertaining to or of the nature of penance. —*n.* **1.** A book or set of church rules concerning the sacrament of penance. **2.** A penitent. —**pen'i·ten'tial·ly** *adv.*

pen·i·ten·tia·ry (pĕn'ə-tĕn'shə-rē) *n., pl.* **-ries. 1.** A prison for those convicted of major crimes. **2.** *Roman Catholic Church.* **a.** A tribunal of the Roman Curia, presided over by a cardinal designated in this office as the Grand Penitentiary, having jurisdiction in matters relating to penance, dispensations, and papal absolutions. **b.** In cathedrals or churches having a chapter of canons, a canon whose special function is the administration of the sacrament of penance. —*adj.* **1.** Of or for the purpose of penance; penitential. **2.** Pertaining to or used for punishment or reform of criminals or wrongdoers. **3.** Resulting in or punishable by imprisonment in a penitentiary: *a penitentiary offense.* [Middle English *penitenciary,* penance officer, from Medieval Latin *penitentiārius,* from Latin *paenitentia,* repentance, from *paenitēns,* PENITENT.]

Pen·ki (bŭn'chē'). A coal-mining city in Manchuria, northeastern China. Population, 449,000.

pen·knife (pĕn'nīf') *n., pl.* **-knives** (-nīvz'). A small pocketknife, originally used to make or sharpen quill pens.

pen·man (pĕn'mən) *n., pl.* **-men** (-mĭn). **1.** A copyist; scribe. **2.** An expert in penmanship. **3.** An author; writer.

pen·man·ship (pĕn'mən-shĭp') *n.* The art, skill, style, or manner of handwriting; calligraphy. Also called "chirography."

Penn (pĕn), **William.** 1644–1718. English Quaker leader; appointed proprietor of Pennsylvania (1681).

Penn. Pennsylvania (unofficial).

pen·na (pĕn'ə) *n., pl.* **pennae** (pĕn'ē). *Ornithology.* Any of the larger feathers forming the visible plumage of a bird, as distinguished from the down feathers. [Latin, feather. See **pet-**[1] in Appendix.*] —**pen·na'ceous** (pĕ-nā'shəs) *adj.*

Penna. Pennsylvania (unofficial).

pen name. Also **pen·name** (pĕn'nām'). A literary pseudonym.

pen·nant (pĕn'ənt) *n.* **1.** *Nautical.* A long, narrow, relatively small flag, often triangular, used for signaling or for identification. **2.** Any similar flag, such as one used as an emblem or one awarded to the winner of a contest. **3.** The championship in certain sports. [Blend of PENDANT and PENNON.]

pen·nate (pĕn'āt') *adj.* Also **pen·nat·ed** (pĕn'ā'tĭd). Feathered

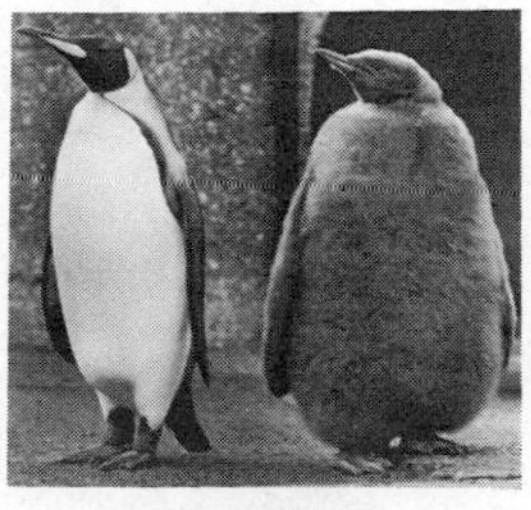

penguin
Aptenodytes patagonica
Adult *(left)* and young bird

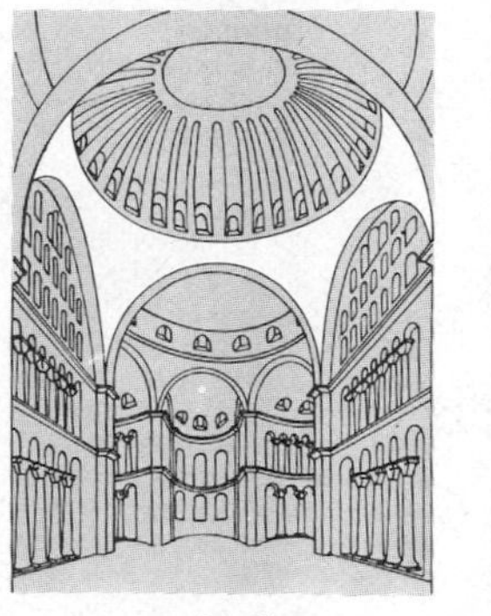

pendentive

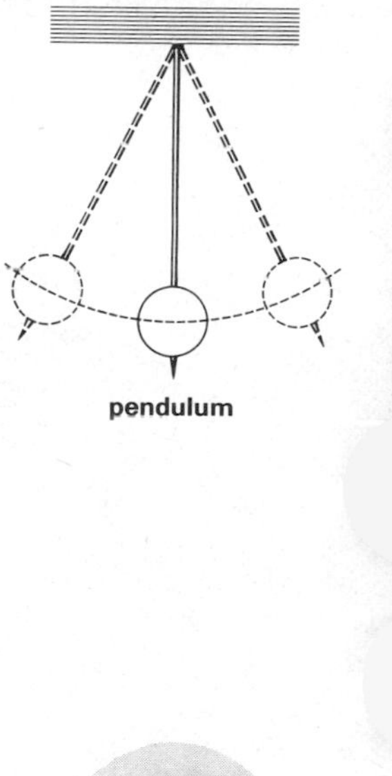

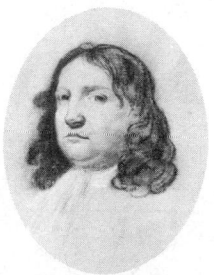

pendulum

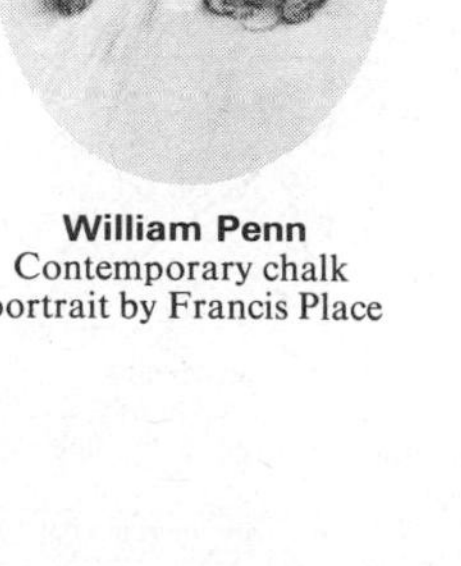

William Penn
Contemporary chalk portrait by Francis Place

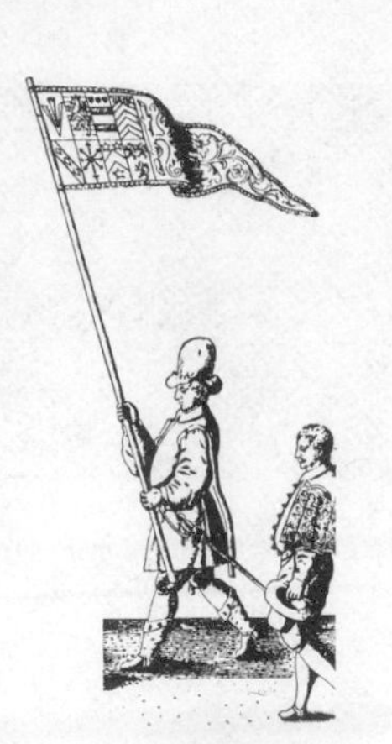

pennon
Pennon of Sir Philip Sidney carried at his funeral procession

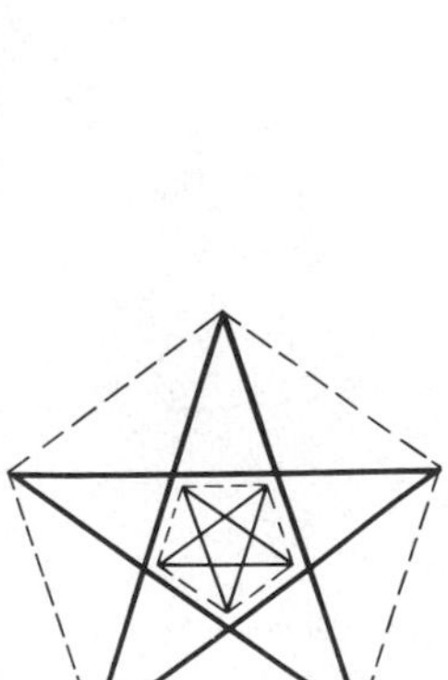

pentacle

or winged; pinnate. [Latin *pennātus*, winged, from *penna*, feather, wing. See **pet-**[1] in Appendix.*]

Pen·nell (pĕn′əl), **Joseph.** 1860–1926. American etcher and illustrator.

pen·ni (pĕn′ē) *n., pl.* **-nis** or **pennia** (pĕn′ē-ə). A coin equal to 1/100 of the markka of Finland. See table of exchange rates at **currency.** [Finnish, perhaps from Middle Low German *pennige*, from West Germanic *panninga* (unattested). See also **penny, pfennig.**]

pen·ni·less (pĕn′ē-lĭs, pĕn′ə-lĭs) *adj.* Entirely without money; very poor. **—pen′ni·less·ly** *adv.* **—pen′ni·less·ness** *n.*

Pen·nine Alps (pĕn′īn′). A mountain range of the Alps, in southwest Switzerland on the Italian border. Highest elevation, Monte Rosa (15,203 feet).

Pen·nine Chain (pĕn′īn′). A range of hills extending from southern Scotland to the Trent River in central England. Highest elevation, Cross Fell (2,930 feet).

pen·non (pĕn′ən) *n.* **1.** A long, narrow banner or streamer borne upon a lance. **2.** Any banner, flag, or pennant. **3.** *Poetic.* A pinion; wing. [Middle English, from Old French *penon*, augmentative of *penne*, feather, wing, from Latin *penna.* See **pet-**[1] in Appendix.*] **—pen′noned** *adj.*

pen·non·cel (pĕn′ən-sĕl′) *n.* Also **pen·on·cel, pen·non·celle.** A small pennon, flag, or streamer borne upon a lance. [Middle English *penoncelle*, from Old French *penoncel*, diminutive of *penon*, PENNON.]

Penn·syl·va·nia (pĕn′səl-vān′yə, -vā′nē-ə). Officially, the Commonwealth of Pennsylvania. *Abbr.* **Pa.** A Middle Atlantic state of the eastern United States, 45,333 square miles in area, with the Delaware River forming its eastern boundary. It was admitted to the Union in 1787 as one of the 13 original states. Population, 11,459,000. Capital, Harrisburg. See map at **United States of America.**

Pennsylvania Dutch. 1. The descendants of German and Swiss immigrants who settled in Pennsylvania in the 17th and 18th centuries. **2.** German as spoken by this group. Also called "Pennsylvania German."

Penn·syl·va·nian (pĕn′səl-vān′yən, -vā′nē-ən) *adj.* **1.** Of or pertaining to the state of Pennsylvania. **2.** *Geology.* Of, belonging to, or designating the geologic time, system of rocks, and sedimentary deposits of the sixth period of the Paleozoic era, characterized by the development of coal-bearing rock formations. In Europe, called "Upper Carboniferous." See **geology.** *—n.* **1.** A native or inhabitant of Pennsylvania. **2.** *Geology.* The Pennsylvanian period. Preceded by *the.*

pen·ny (pĕn′ē) *n., pl.* **-nies** or **pence** (pĕns) (for senses 2,3). **1.** *Abbr.* **p.** A coin of the United States and Canada, the **cent** *(see).* **2.** *Abbr.* **d.** A coin equal to 1/240 of the pound of the United Kingdom. After 1971, it will equal 1/100 of the pound. **3.** *Abbr.* **d.** A coin equal to 1/240 of the pound of Gambia, the Republic of Ireland, Jamaica, Malawi, Malta, Nigeria, Rhodesia, and of various dependent territories of the United Kingdom, such as Bermuda. See table of exchange rates at **currency. 4.** Any of various other coins of small denomination. **5.** A sum of money. **—a pretty penny.** *Informal.* A relatively large sum of money. [Middle English *penny*, Old English *penig, penning*, from West Germanic *panninga* (unattested), probably from Latin *pannus*, a cloth (pieces of cloth were in barbarian Europe used as a medium of exchange). See **pan-** in Appendix.*]

penny ante. 1. A poker game in which the highest bet is limited to a penny or some other small sum. **2.** *Informal.* Any business transaction on a small scale. **—pen′ny-an′te** *adj.*

pen·ny·cress (pĕn′ē-krĕs′) *n.* Any of several plants of the genus *Thlaspi*, native to Europe, and characteristically having small, winged seed pods; especially, *T. arvense*, which grows as a weed throughout North America. [Perhaps variant of *penny grass*, from its round, flat pods.]

penny pincher. *Informal.* A person who is very stingy with money. **—pen′ny-pinch′ing** *adj.* & *n.*

pen·ny·roy·al (pĕn′ē-roi′əl) *n.* **1.** A Eurasian plant, *Mentha pulegium*, having hairy leaves and small lilac-blue flowers. It yields a useful aromatic oil. **2.** An aromatic plant, *Hedeoma pulegioides*, of eastern North America, having a similar appearance and uses. In this sense also called "mock pennyroyal." [Variant of Middle English *puliol real*, from Norman French : Old French *poliol*, pennyroyal, from Latin *pūlegium*†, fleabane + *real, roial*, ROYAL.]

pen·ny·weight (pĕn′ē-wāt′) *n. Abbr.* **dwt., pwt.** A unit of troy weight equal to 24 grains, 1/20 of a troy ounce or approximately 1.555 grams.

pen·ny·wort (pĕn′ē-wûrt′, -wôrt) *n.* Any of several plants having rounded leaves suggestive of pennies, such as: **a.** A North American plant, *Obolaria virginica*, having fleshy leaves and small white or purplish flowers. **b.** A Eurasian plant, *Cotyledon umbilicus*, having thick, rounded leaves and yellowish-green flowers. This species is also called "navelwort."

pen·ny·worth (pĕn′ē-wûrth′) *n.* **1.** As much as a penny will buy. **2.** A small amount; modicum. **3.** A bargain.

Pe·nob·scot (pə-nŏb′skət, -skŏt′) *n., pl.* **Penobscot** or **-scots. 1.** A tribe of Algonquian-speaking North American Indians who were part of the Algonquin federation and formerly inhabited central Maine. **2.** A member of this tribe. **3.** The Algonquian language of this tribe. **—Pe·nob′scot** *adj.*

Pe·nob·scot River (pə-nŏb′skət, -skŏt′). A river rising in north-central Maine and flowing 100 miles south to Penobscot Bay, an inlet of the Atlantic in southeastern Maine.

pe·nol·o·gy (pē-nŏl′ə-jē) *n.* Also **poe·nol·o·gy.** The theory and practice of prison management and criminal rehabilitation. [Latin *poena*, penalty, from Greek *poinē* (see **kwei-**[1] in Appendix*) + -LOGY.] **—pe′no·log′i·cal** (pē′nə-lŏj′ĭ-kəl) *adj.* **—pe′no·log′i·cal·ly** *adv.* **—pe·nol′o·gist** *n.*

pen·on·cel, pen·non·celle. Variants of **pennoncel.**

Pen·sa·co·la (pĕn′sə-kō′lə). The site of a U.S. naval air station on Pensacola Bay in northwestern Florida.

pen·sil. Variant of **pencel.**

pen·sile (pĕn′sīl′) *adj.* **1.** Hanging down loosely; suspended: *the pensile nest of the Baltimore oriole.* **2.** Building a hanging nest. Said of birds. [Latin *pēnsilis*, from *pendēre* (past participle *pēnsus*), to hang. See **spen-** in Appendix.*] **—pen′sile′ness, pen·sil′i·ty** (pĕn-sĭl′ə-tē) *n.*

pen·sion[1] (pĕn′shən) *n.* A sum of money paid regularly as a retirement benefit or by way of patronage. *—tr.v.* **pensioned, -sioning, -sions. 1.** To grant a pension to. **2.** To retire or dismiss with a pension. Usually used with *off.* [Middle English *pensioun*, from Old French *pension*, from Medieval Latin *pēnsiō*, from Latin, payment, from *pendere* (past participle *pēnsus*), to weigh, pay. See **spen-** in Appendix.*]

pen·sion[2] (pän′syôn; *French* pän-syôN′) *n.* A boarding house or small hotel in Europe. **—en pension** (äN′ päN-syôN′, än′ pän′-syôn). *Chiefly British.* **1.** Designating the system of hotel charges at a fixed rate per day or a longer period, inclusive of meals: *en pension terms.* **2.** At such a rate or under such a system: *living en pension.* [French, boarding house, boarding school, originally "payment for the board and education of a child," extended use of Old French *pension*, payment, PENSION (grant).]

pen·sion·ar·y (pĕn′shə-nĕr′ē) *adj.* **1.** Constituting a pension. **2.** Mercenary; venal. *—n., pl.* **pensionaries. 1.** A pensioner. **2.** One who is venally dependent on another; a hireling.

pen·sion·er (pĕn′shən-ər) *n.* **1.** One who receives a pension. **2.** One who is dependent on the bounty of another. **3.** *Obsolete.* A pensionary.

pen·sive (pĕn′sĭv) *adj.* **1.** Engaged in deep thoughtfulness. **2.** Suggesting or expressing deep, often melancholy thoughtfulness. [Middle English *pensif*, from Old French, from *penser*, to think, from Latin *pēnsāre*, frequentative of *pendere* (past participle *pēnsus*), to weigh. See **spen-** in Appendix.*] **—pen′sive·ly** *adv.* **—pen′sive·ness** *n.*

Synonyms: *pensive, contemplative, reflective, meditative.* These describe the quality or nature of being mentally or spiritually preoccupied, usually in a quiet way but one which is or would be apparent to other people. One is *pensive* when one is silently thinking in a serious way about some matter or problem, frequently despite oneself. It can be in a rational (if troubled) way, but it more often has a wistful, dreamy, or sad sense. *Contemplative* implies a slow, directed consideration of a lofty object of thought, or physical object, with conscious intent of better understanding or of spiritual or aesthetic enrichment: *a contemplative attitude toward nature. Reflective* expresses a more analytical deliberation about past experience or about something which has just happened, often as a process of second thought or reappraisal of a particular occurrence. *Meditative* means to be consciously intent or reflective in a spiritual sense. It differs from contemplative in that the object of one's thought is usually inward, as a self-examination, rather than outward.

pen·ste·mon (pĕn-stē′mən, pĕn′stĭ-mən) *n.* Also **pent·ste·mon.** Any plant of the genus *Penstemon*, which includes the beardtongues. [New Latin : PENT(A)- + Greek *stēmōn*, thread, here taken as "stamen" (see **stā-** in Appendix*).]

pen·stock (pĕn′stŏk′) *n.* **1.** A sluice or gate used to control a flow of water. **2.** A pipe or conduit used to carry water to a water wheel or turbine. [PEN (enclosure) + STOCK.]

pent (pĕnt). Alternate past tense and past participle of **pen.** *—adj.* Penned or shut up; closely confined: *"the love in the heart long pent, now loose, now at last tumultuously bursting"* (Walt Whitman).

penta-, pent-. Indicates five; for example, **pentameter, pentangular.** [Greek, from *pente*, five. See **penkwe** in Appendix.*]

pen·ta·chlo·ro·phe·nol (pĕn′tə-klôr′ə-fē′nōl′, -klōr′ə-fē′nōl′, -nôl′) *n.* A compound, C_6Cl_5OH, used in solution as a fungicide and wood preservative. [PENTA- + CHLORO- + PHENOL.]

pen·ta·cle (pĕn′tə-kəl) *n.* A five-pointed star formed by five straight lines connecting the vertices of a pentagon and enclosing another pentagon in the completed figure. Also called "pentagram." [Medieval Latin *pentaculum* (unattested) : Greek *penta-*, PENTA- + *-culum*, diminutive suffix.]

pen·tad (pĕn′tăd′) *n.* **1.** The number five. **2.** A group of five members. **3.** A five-year period. [Greek *pentas* (stem *pentad-*), from *pente*, five. See **penkwe** in Appendix.*]

pen·ta·dac·tyl (pĕn′tə-dăk′təl) *adj.* Also **pen·ta·dac·ty·late** (-tə-lĭt, -lāt′). Having five fingers or toes on each hand or foot. [Latin *pentadactylus*, from Greek *pentadaktulos* : PENTA- + *daktulos*, finger, DACTYL.]

pen·ta·gon (pĕn′tə-gŏn′) *n.* A polygon having five sides and five interior angles. [Latin *pentagōnum*, from Greek *pentagōnon* : PENTA- + -GON.] **—pen·tag′o·nal** (pĕn-tăg′ə-nəl) *adj.* **—pen·tag′o·nal·ly** *adv.*

Pentagon, the. 1. A five-sided building in Arlington, Virginia, containing the Department of Defense and the offices of the various branches of the U.S. Armed Forces. **2.** The Department of Defense itself; the U.S. military command.

pen·ta·he·dron (pĕn′tə-hē′drən) *n., pl.* **-drons** or **-dra** (-drə). A solid having five plane faces. [New Latin : PENTA- + -HEDRON.] **—pen′ta·he′dral** (-hē′drəl) *adj.*

pen·tam·er·ous (pĕn-tăm′ər-əs) *adj.* **1.** Having five similar parts. **2.** *Botany.* Having flower parts, such as petals, sepals, and stamens, in sets of five. Also written *5-merous.* [New Latin *pentamerus* : PENTA- + -MEROUS.] **—pen·tam′er·ism′** *n.*

ă pat/ā pay/âr care/ä father/b bib/ch church/d deed/ĕ pet/ē be/f fife/g gag/h hat/hw which/ĭ pit/ī pie/îr pier/j judge/k kick/l lid, needle/m mum/n no, sudden/ng thing/ŏ pot/ō toe/ô paw, for/oi noise/ou out/ŏŏ took/ōō boot/p pop/r roar/s sauce/sh ship, dish/

pen·tam·e·ter (pĕn-tăm'ə-tər) *n.* **1.** A line of verse composed of five metrical feet. **2.** English verse composed in iambic pentameter; heroic verse. **3.** In Greek and Latin prosody, a form of dactylic verse that constitutes a hexameter with the second halves of the third and sixth feet syncopated and alternates with the hexameters in elegiacs as the latter half of each elegiac couplet. [Old French *pentametre*, from Greek *pentametros* : PENTA- + -METER.]

pen·tane (pĕn'tān') *n.* Any of three isomeric hydrocarbons, C₅H₁₂, of the methane series: **a.** *Normal pentane.* A colorless flammable liquid used as an anesthetic, a general solvent, and in the manufacture of artificial ice. **b.** *Isopentane.* A colorless flammable liquid used as a solvent and in the manufacture of polystyrene foam. **c.** *Neopentane.* A colorless gas used in the manufacture of synthetic rubber. [PENT(A)- + -ANE.]

pen·tan·gu·lar (pĕn-tăng'gyə-lər) *adj.* Having five angles.

pen·ta·quine (pĕn'tə-kwēn', -kwĭn) *n.* Also **pen·ta·quin** (-kwĭn). A drug used with quinine in the treatment of malaria. [PENTA- + QUIN(OLINE).]

pen·tar·chy (pĕn'tär'kē) *n., pl.* **-chies. 1.** Government by five rulers. **2.** A body of five rulers governing jointly. **3.** An association or federation of five governments, each ruled by a different leader. [Greek *pentarkhia* : PENTA- + -ARCHY.] —**pen·tar'chi·cal** (pĕn-tär'kĭ-kəl) *adj.*

pen·ta·stich (pĕn'tə-stĭk') *n.* A poem or stanza containing five lines. [Late Greek *pentastikhos*, of five verses : PENTA- + *stikhos*, -STICH.]

Pen·ta·teuch (pĕn'tə-tōōk', -tyōōk') *n.* The first five books of the Bible: Genesis, Exodus, Leviticus, Numbers, and Deuteronomy. [Late Latin *Pentateuchus*, from Greek *Pentateukhos* : PENTA- + *teukhos*, a tool, case for papyrus rolls, scroll (see **dheugh-** in Appendix*).] —**Pen'ta·teuch'al** *adj.*

pen·tath·lon (pĕn-tăth'lən, -lŏn') *n.* An athletic contest consisting of five events for each participant. Originating in the ancient Olympics, it was revived in the modern Olympics as a series of track and field events. It now consists of running, horseback riding, swimming, fencing, and pistol shooting. [Greek : PENT(A)- + *athlon*, contest (see **athlete**).]

pen·ta·ton·ic scale (pĕn'tə-tŏn'ĭk). Any of various five-tone musical scales, especially one composed of the first, second, third, fifth, and sixth tones of a diatonic scale.

pen·ta·va·lent (pĕn'tə-vā'lənt) *adj. Chemistry.* Having a valence of 5.

Pen·te·cost (pĕn'tĭ-kôst', -kŏst') *n.* **1.** A festival of the Christian Church occurring on the seventh Sunday after Easter, to celebrate the descent of the Holy Ghost upon the disciples. Also called "Whitsunday." **2.** A Jewish festival, Shavuoth *(see).* [Middle English *Pentecost*, Old English *Pentecosten*, from Late Latin *Pentēcostē*, from Greek *pentēkostē* (*hēmera*), the fiftieth day (after the Resurrection), Pentecost, from *pentēkostos*, fiftieth, from *pentēkonta*, fifty : *pente*, five (see **penkwe** in Appendix*) + *-konta*, "ten times" (see **dekm** in Appendix*).]

Pen·te·cos·tal (pĕn'tĭ-kôs'təl, -kŏs'təl) *adj.* **1.** Of, pertaining to, or occurring at Pentecost. **2.** Of, pertaining to, or designating any of various Christian religious congregations that seek to be filled with the Holy Ghost, in emulation of the disciples at Pentecost. —**Pen'te·cos'tal** *n.* —**Pen'te·cos'tal·ism'** *n.*

pent·house (pĕnt'hous') *n.* **1. a.** An apartment or dwelling situated on the roof of a building. **b.** A residence, often with a terrace, comprising the top floor of an apartment house. **c.** A structure housing machinery on the roof of a building. **2.** A shed or sloping roof attached to the side of a building. [Alteration of Middle English *pentis*, from Old French *appentis*, from Medieval Latin *appenticium, appendicium*, appendage, from Latin *appendix*, from *appendēre*, to append, attach : *ad*, on + *pendēre*, to suspend, hang (see **spen-** in Appendix*).]

Pent·land Firth (pĕnt'lənd). A channel between northeastern Scotland and the Orkney Islands.

pent·land·ite (pĕnt'lən-dīt') *n.* The principal ore of nickel, a light-brown nickel iron sulfide. [French; discovered by Joseph B. *Pentland* (died 1873), Irish scientist.]

pen·to·bar·bi·tal sodium (pĕn'tə-bär'bĭ-tôl'). A white crystalline or powdery barbiturate, C₁₁H₁₇N₂O₃Na, used as a sedative. [From PENT(A)- + BARBITAL.]

pen·to·san (pĕn'tə-săn') *n.* Any of a group of complex carbohydrates found with cellulose in many woody plants and yielding pentoses on hydrolysis. [PENTOS(E) + -AN.]

pen·tose (pĕn'tōs', -tōz') *n.* A sugar having five carbon atoms per molecule. [PENT(A)- + -OSE.]

Pen·to·thal Sodium (pĕn'tə-thôl'). A trademark for a drug, thiopental sodium *(see).*

pent·ox·ide (pĕnt-ŏk'sīd') *n.* An oxide having five atoms of oxygen in the molecule. [PENT(A)- + OXIDE.]

pent·ste·mon. Variant of **penstemon.**

pent·up (pĕnt'ŭp') *adj.* Not given expression; repressed: *pent-up emotions.*

pen·tyl (pĕn'təl) *n. Chemistry.* **Amyl** *(see).* [PENT(A)- + -YL.]

pen·tyl·ene·tet·ra·zol (pĕn'tə-lēn'tĕt'rə-zōl', -zŏl') *n.* A drug, C₆H₁₀N₄, used as a stimulant of the central nervous system. [PENT(A)- + (METH)YLENE + TETR(A)- + AZ(O)- + -OL.]

pe·nu·che (pə-nōō'chē) *n.* Also **pe·nu·chi.** A fudgelike confection of brown sugar, water or milk, and chopped nuts. Also called "panocha." [Mexican Spanish *panocha*, diminutive of Spanish *pan*, bread, from Latin *pānis.* See **pā-** in Appendix*.]

pe·nuch·le, pe·nuck·le. Variants of **pinochle.**

pe·nult (pē'nŭlt', pĭ-nŭlt') *n.* Also **pe·nul·ti·ma** (pĭ-nŭl'tə-mə). The next to the last syllable in a word. [Latin *paenultimus*, last but one : *paene, pēne†*, almost + *ultimus*, farthest away, last, from *uls*, beyond (see **al-¹** in Appendix*).]

pe·nul·ti·mate (pĭ-nŭl'tə-mĭt) *adj.* **1.** Next to last. **2.** Of or pertaining to the penult of a word: *penultimate stress.* —*n.* The next to the last. [From Latin *paenultimus*, PENULT.]

pe·num·bra (pĭ-nŭm'brə) *n., pl.* **-brae** (-brē) or **-bras. 1.** A partial shadow between regions of complete shadow and complete illumination. **2.** *Astronomy.* The partly darkened fringe around a sunspot. **3.** An outlying, surrounding region; periphery; fringe: "*Around the core area of Mayan civilization lay a penumbra of other societies*" (William H. McNeill). [New Latin : Latin *paene, pēne*, almost (see **penult**) + UMBRA.] —**pe·num'bral, pe·num'brous** *adj.*

pe·nu·ri·ous (pə-nŏŏr'ē-əs, -nyŏŏr'ē-əs) *adj.* **1.** Miserly; stingy. **2.** Yielding little; barren: *a penurious land.* **3.** Poverty-stricken; needy. [Medieval Latin *pēnūriōsus*, from *pēnūria*, PENURY.] —**pe·nu'ri·ous·ly** *adv.* —**pe·nu'ri·ous·ness** *n.*

pen·u·ry (pĕn'yə-rē) *n.* **1.** Extreme want or poverty; destitution. **2.** Extreme dearth; barrenness; insufficiency. [Middle English, from Latin *paenūria, pēnūria†*, want, scarcity.]

Pe·nu·ti·an (pə-nōō'tē-ən, -shən) *n.* A family or phylum of North American Indian languages of Pacific coastal areas from California through British Columbia.

Pen·za (pĕn'zə) *n.* A shipping center in the east-central Soviet Union, on the Sura River. Population, 315,000.

Pen·zhi·na (pĕn'zhĭ-nə). **1.** A bay of the Sea of Okhotsk extending 185 miles into northeastern Siberia. **2.** A river flowing 446 miles from the Kolyma mountains to this bay.

pe·on (pē'ŏn', pē'ən; *Spanish* pā-ŏn' *for sense 1; British* pyōōn *for sense 2*) *n., pl.* **peons** or **peones** (pā-ō'nĕz; *Spanish* pā-ō'nās). **1. a.** An unskilled laborer or farm worker of Latin America or the southwestern United States. **b.** Such a worker bound in servitude to a landlord creditor. **2.** A native Indian or Ceylonese messenger, servant, or foot soldier. **3.** Any menial worker; a drudge. [Spanish *peon*, Portuguese *peão* and French *pion*, all from Medieval Latin *pedo* (stem *pedōn-*), a foot soldier, from Latin, one who has broad feet, from *pēs* (stem *ped-*), a foot. See **ped-¹** in Appendix*.]

pe·on·age (pē'ə-nĭj) *n.* Also **pe·on·ism** (-nĭz'əm). **1.** The condition of being a peon. **2.** A system by which debtors are bound in servitude to their creditors until the debts are paid.

pe·o·ny (pē'ə-nē) *n., pl.* **-nies.** Any of various garden plants of the genus *Paeonia*, having large pink, red, white, or creamy flowers. [Middle English *pione*, Old English *peonie*, from Latin *peōnia*, from Greek *paiōniā*, supposedly discovered by *Paiōn*, physician (of the gods). See **paean.**]

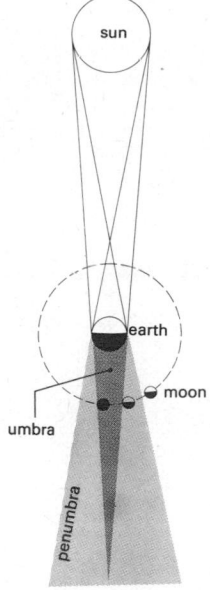

penumbra

peo·ple (pē'pəl) *n., pl.* **people** or **peoples** (for senses 1, 2). **1.** A body of persons living in the same country under one national government; nationality. **2.** A body of persons sharing a common religion, culture, language, or inherited condition of life. **3.** Persons with regard to their residence, class, profession, or group. **4.** The mass of ordinary persons; the populace. Usually preceded by *the*: "*and what the people but a herd confus'd,/A miscellaneous rabble*" (Milton). **5.** The citizens of a nation, state, or other political unit; electorate. See Usage note below. **6.** Persons subordinate to or loyal to a ruler, superior, or employer. **7.** Family, relatives, or ancestors. **8.** Members of the community; persons in general. **9.** Human beings considered as distinct from lower animals or inanimate things. **10.** A race or kind of beings distinct from human beings: *the little people.* —See Synonyms at **nation.** —*tr.v.* peopled, -pling, -ples. To furnish with a population; populate. [Middle English *peple, poeple*, from Old French *pueple, pople*, from Latin *populus.* See **populus** in Appendix*.] —**peo'pler** *n.*

Usage: The possessive form is usually *people's* (*the people's rights*), but *peoples'* is the possessive of the plural form *peoples* (*the Semitic peoples' interests*). *People* (not *persons*) is the proper term when referring to a large group of individuals collectively and indefinitely: *People can be pushed only so far. Persons* is applicable to a specific and relatively small number: *Ten persons were killed.* But *people* is also acceptable in this example. *The people* and *the public* are sometimes interchangeable, but only *the people* has the political sense of an electorate.

peony
Paeonia albiflora

people's front. A political coalition, **popular front** *(see).*

People's party. The **Populist party** *(see).*

People's Republic of China. The official name for **China** *(see).*

Pe·o·ri·a (pē-ôr'ē-ə, -ōr'ē-ə). A city in north-central Illinois, on the Illinois River, 67 miles north of Springfield. Population, 103,000.

pep (pĕp) *n. Informal.* Energy; high spirits; vim. —*tr.v.* **pepped, pepping, peps.** *Informal.* To bring energy or liveliness to; invigorate. Usually followed by *up.* [Short for PEPPER.] —**pep'py** *adj.* —**pep'pi·ness** *n.*

Pep·in the Short (pĕp'ĭn). A.D. 714?–768. King of the Franks (751–768); son of Charles Martel and father of Charlemagne.

pep·los (pĕp'ləs, -lŏs') *n., pl.* **-loses.** Also **pep·lus** (pĕp'ləs). A loose outer robe worn by women in ancient Greece. Also called "peplum." [Greek *peplos†.*]

pep·lum (pĕp'ləm) *n., pl.* **-lums. 1.** A short overskirt or ruffle attached at the waistline. **2.** A **peplos** *(see).* [Latin, from *peplus, peplos*, from Greek *peplos*, PEPLOS.]

pe·po (pē'pō) *n., pl.* **-pos.** The fruit of any of various related plants, such as the cucumber, squash, pumpkin, and melon, having a hard rind, fleshy pulp, and numerous seeds. [Latin, melon, from Greek *pepōn.* See **pekw-** in Appendix*.]

pep·per (pĕp'ər) *n.* **1.** A woody vine, *Piper nigrum*, of the East Indies, having small, berrylike fruit. **2.** The dried, blackish fruit of this plant, used as a pungent condiment. When ground whole, it is called *black pepper*, and with the shell removed, *white pepper.* **3.** Any of several other plants of the genus *Piper*, such as cubeb, betel, and kava. **4.** Any of several varieties of a

peplum

ă pat/ā pay/âr care/ä father/b bib/ch church/d deed/ĕ pet/ē be/f fife/g gag/h hat/hw which/ĭ pit/ī pie/îr pier/j judge/k kick/l lid, needle/m mum/n no, sudden/ng thing/ŏ pot/ō toe/ô paw, for/oi noise/ou out/ōō took/ōō boot/p pop/r roar/s sauce/sh ship, dish/t tight/th thin, path/th this, bathe/ŭ cut/ûr urge/v valve/w with/y yes/z zebra, size/zh vision/ə about, item, edible, gallop, circus/ à *Fr.* ami/œ *Fr.* feu, *Ger.* schön/ü *Fr.* tu, *Ger.* über/кн *Ger.* ich, *Scot.* loch/N *Fr.* bon. *Follows main vocabulary. †Of obscure origin.

woody plant, *Capsicum frutescens* (or *C. annuum*), of tropical origin. **5.** The podlike fruit of any of these plants, varying in size, shape, and degree of pungency. The milder types include the **bell pepper** and **pimiento** *(both of which see)*, and the more pungent types include the **cherry pepper** *(see)*. **6.** Any of various condiments made from the more pungent varieties of *C. frutescens*, such as **cayenne pepper** and **chili** *(both of which see)*. In this sense, also called "hot pepper." —*tr.v.* **peppered, -pering, pers. 1.** To season or sprinkle with pepper. **2.** To sprinkle liberally; dot. **3.** To pelt or shower with small missiles. **4.** To make lively and vivid with wit or invective, as a speech or article. [Middle English *peper*, Old English *pipor*, from Latin *piper*, from Greek *peperi*, from Sanskrit *pippalī*, berry. See **pippalī** in Appendix.*]

pep·per-and-salt (pĕp′ər-ən-sôlt′) *adj.* Having a close mixture of black and white. Said of hair or fabrics: *"a pepper-and-salt matted beard hung almost into his lap"* (Conrad).

pep·per·box (pĕp′ər-bŏks′) *n.* A container with small holes in the top for sprinkling ground pepper. Also called "pepper pot."

pep·per·bush (pĕp′ər-bo͝osh′) *n.* See **sweet pepperbush.**

pep·per·corn (pĕp′ər-kôrn′) *n.* **1.** A dried berry of the pepper vine *Piper nigrum*. **2.** Any small or insignificant thing.

pep·per·grass (pĕp′ər-grăs′, -gräs′) *n.* Any of several plants of the genus *Lepidium;* especially, *L. virginicum*, having small white flowers and pungent seeds. Also called "pepperwort."

pep·per·idge (pĕp′ər-ĭj) *n.* A tree, the **sour gum** *(see)*. [Origin unknown.]

pepper mill. A utensil for grinding peppercorns.

pep·per·mint (pĕp′ər-mĭnt′) *n.* **1.** A plant, *Mentha piperita*, having small purple or white flowers and downy leaves that yield a pungent oil. **2.** The oil from this plant, or a preparation made from it, used as flavoring. **3.** A candy or lozenge with this flavoring. [PEPPER + MINT.]

peppermint camphor. A chemical, **menthol** *(see)*.

pepper pot. 1. A soup made with vegetables and tripe or other meat, seasoned with pepper, and often containing dumplings. Also called "Philadelphia pepper pot." **2.** A thick West Indian stew of meat or fish, vegetables, and regional condiments. **3.** A **pepperbox** *(see)*.

pep·per·root (pĕp′ər-ro͞ot′, -ro͝ot′) *n.* Any of several plants of the genus *Dentaria*, such as the **crinkleroot** *(see)*.

pepper tree. Any of several trees of the genus *Schinus;* especially, *S. molle*, native to South America, having compound leaves and yellowish-white flowers. This species is also called "mastic tree."

pep·per·wort (pĕp′ər-wûrt′, -wôrt) *n.* **1.** Any of various aquatic or marsh plants of the genus *Marsilea*, having floating leaves rising from long runners. **2.** A plant, **peppergrass** *(see)*.

pep·per·y (pĕp′ə-rē) *adj.* **1.** Of, like, or containing pepper; sharp or pungent in flavor. **2.** Vigorously sharp-tempered in disposition and manner: *a peppery old general.* **3.** Sharp and stinging in style or content; vivid; fiery: *a peppery speech.* —**pep′per·i·ness** *n.*

pep pill. *Slang.* Any tablet or capsule containing an ingredient that stimulates the central nervous system; especially, one of the amphetamines.

pep·sin (pĕp′sĭn) *n.* Also **pep·sine** (pĕp′sĭn). **1.** A digestive enzyme found in gastric juice that catalyzes the breakdown of protein to peptides. **2.** A substance containing this enzyme, obtained from the stomachs of hogs and used as a digestive aid. [German *Pepsin*, from Greek *pepsis*, digestion, from *peptein*, to digest, cook. See **pekw-** in Appendix.*]

pep·sin·o·gen (pĕp-sĭn′ə-jən) *n.* An inert substance found in the cells of the gastric mucosa that is converted to pepsin during digestion by the action of hydrochloric acid. [PEPSIN + -GEN.]

pep talk. A speech of exhortation delivered by a leader, as to his team or staff.

pep·tic (pĕp′tĭk) *adj.* **1. a.** Of, pertaining to, or assisting digestion: *peptic secretion.* **b.** Induced by or associated with the action of digestive secretions: *peptic ulcer.* **2.** Of, pertaining to, or involving pepsin. **3.** Capable of digesting. —*n.* A digestive agent. [Latin *pepticus*, from Greek *peptikos*, from *peptein*, to digest. See **pekw-** in Appendix.*]

pep·ti·dase (pĕp′tĭ-dās′, -dāz′) *n.* An enzyme that hydrolyzes peptides, releasing amino acids. [PEPTID(E) + -ASE.]

pep·tide (pĕp′tīd′) *n.* Also **pep·tid** (pĕp′tĭd). Any of various natural or synthetic compounds containing two or more amino acids linked by the carboxyl group of one amino acid and the amino group of another. [PEPT(ONE) + -IDE.]

peptide bond. The chemical bond between the organic acid groups and amine groups of neighboring amino acids, constituting the primary linkage of all protein structures.

pep·tize (pĕp′tīz′) *tr.v.* **-tized, -tizing, -tizes. 1.** To increase the dispersion of (a colloidal solution). **2.** To liquefy (a colloidal gel) to form a sol. [Greek *peptein*, to digest (see **peptic**) + -IZE.] —**pep′ti·za′tion** *n.*

pep·tone (pĕp′tōn′) *n.* Any of various protein compounds obtained by acid or enzyme hydrolysis of natural protein and used as nutrients and culture media. [German *Pepton*, from Greek *pepton*, from *peptein*, to digest, cook. See **pekw-** in Appendix.*] —**pep·ton′ic** (pĕp-tŏn′ĭk) *adj.*

pep·to·nize (pĕp′tə-nīz′) *tr.v.* **-nized, -nizing, -nizes. 1.** To convert (protein) into a peptone. **2.** To dissolve (food) by means of a proteolytic enzyme. **3.** To combine with peptone. —**pep′to·ni·za′tion** *n.*

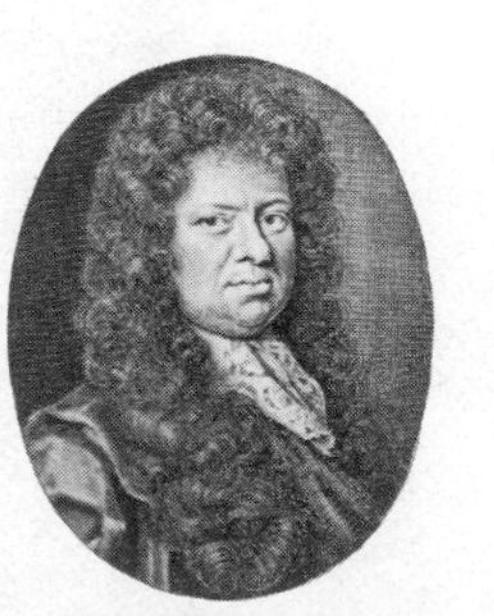

Samuel Pepys

Pepys (pēps), **Samuel.** 1633–1703. English diarist and secretary of the admiralty.

Pe·quot (pē′kwŏt′) *n., pl.* **Pequot** or **-quots. 1.** A tribe of Algonquian-speaking Indians formerly living in southern New England. **2.** A member of this tribe. **3.** The Algonquian language of this tribe. [Probably modification of Narraganset *paquatanog*, destroyers.] —**Pe′quot** *adj.*

per (pûr) *prep. Abbr.* **p. 1.** Through; by means of: *per bearer.* Used in business. **2.** To, for, or by each; for every: *40 cents per gallon.* **3.** According to; by the: *per instructions.* [Latin. See **per¹** in Appendix.*]

per–. *Chemistry.* Indicates: **1.** A compound that includes an element in its highest oxidation state; for example, **perchloric acid. 2.** A compound that includes the peroxy group in its structure; for example, **hydrogen peroxide. 3.** A complete substitution or addition in an organic compound; for example, **perchloroethylene.** [Latin, from preposition *per*, through, by, away. See **per¹** in Appendix.* In borrowed Latin compounds, *per-* indicates: 1. Through, as in **percolate.** 2. Throughout, to the end, as in **perennial, perorate.** 3. Thoroughly, completely, as in **perfect, perceive.** 4. Away, as in **perdition, peregrine.** 5. Destruction, as in **perfidy, perjure.** 6. Intensified action, as in **perfervid, perform.**]

per. 1. period. **2.** person.

per·ac·id (pûr′ăs′ĭd) *n.* **1.** Any acid containing the peroxy group. **2.** An inorganic acid, such as perchloric acid, containing the largest proportion of oxygen in a series of related acids.

per·ad·ven·ture (pûr′əd-vĕn′chər, pĕr′-) *adv. Archaic.* Perhaps; perchance; it may be. —*n.* Chance or uncertainty; doubt; question: *The proposed budget decreed beyond peradventure a tax increase.* [Middle English *per aventure* : Old French *per*, by, from Latin *per*, PER + *aventure*, ADVENTURE.]

Pe·rak (pā′răk′, -räk′; *Malay* pĕr′ä). A state of Malaysia, 7,980 square miles in area, on the Strait of Malacca. Population, 1,508,000. Capital, Ipoh.

per·am·bu·late (pə-răm′byə-lāt′) *v.* **-lated, -lating, -lates.** —*tr.* To traverse, especially in order to inspect: *perambulate the boundaries of the site.* —*intr.* To walk about; roam; stroll. [Latin *perambulāre* : *per-*, through + *ambulāre*, to walk, AMBULATE.] —**per·am′bu·la·to′ry** (pə-răm′byə-lə-tôr′ē, -tōr′ē) *adj.* —**per·am′bu·la′tion** *n.*

per·am·bu·la·tor (pə-răm′byə-lā′tər) *n. Chiefly British.* A baby carriage. Also called "pram."

per an·num (ăn′əm). *Abbr.* **p.a., per an., per ann.** *Latin.* By the year; annually.

per·bo·rate (pər-bôr′āt′, -bōr′āt′) *n.* A salt containing the radical BO_3, formed from a borate and hydrogen peroxide.

per·cale (pər-kāl′) *n.* An opaque cotton fabric used to make sheets and clothing. [French, from Persian *pargālah*†.]

per·ca·line (pûr′kə-lēn′) *n.* A glazed fine cotton fabric used for dress goods, shirting, and linings. [French, from PERCALE.]

per cap·i·ta (kăp′ə-tə). **1.** Per person: *income per capita.* **2.** Equally to each heir. [Latin, "by heads."]

per·ceive (pər-sēv′) *tr.v.* **-ceived, -ceiving, -ceives. 1.** To become aware of directly through any of the senses; especially, to see or hear. **2.** To take notice of; observe; detect. **3.** To become aware of in one's mind; achieve understanding of; apprehend. —See Synonyms at **see.** [Middle English *perceiven*, from Old French *perceivre*, from Latin *percipere*, "to seize wholly," "see all the way through" : *per-*, thoroughly + *capere*, to seize (see **kap-** in Appendix*).] —**per·ceiv′a·ble** *adj.* —**per·ceiv′a·bly** *adv.*

per cent. Also **per·cent** (pər-sĕnt′). *Abbr.* **p.c., pct.** *Symbol* % Per hundred; for or out of each hundred. Used to indicate that the preceding number is a percentage: *One quarter of ten is 25 per cent. Sixty per cent of the members approved.* [Short for Latin *per centum*, by the hundred : *per*, by + *centum*, hundred (see **dekm̥** in Appendix*).]

Usage: *Per cent* and *percentage* are both used to express quantity with relation to a whole. *Per cent* is employed only specifically and always with a number or numeral. *Percentage* is never preceded by such a figure, but should be qualified by a general term to indicate size (since *percentage* does not necessarily imply smallness). The number of the noun that follows *per cent* or *percentage*, or is understood to follow them, governs the choice of verb: *Forty per cent of his estate is in securities. A large percentage of the patients are children.*

per·cent·age (pər-sĕn′tĭj) *n.* **1.** A fraction or ratio with 100 fixed and understood as the denominator. It is formed by multiplying a decimal equivalent of a fraction by 100. For example, 0.98 equals a percentage of 98. **2.** A proportion or share in relation to the whole. **3.** An amount, such as an allowance, duty, or commission, that varies in proportion to a larger sum, such as total sales: *work for a percentage.* **4.** *Informal.* Advantage; gain: *There is no percentage in work without pay.* —See Usage note at **per cent.**

per·cen·tile (pər-sĕn′tīl′) *n. Statistics.* A number that corresponds to one of 100 equal divisions of the range of a statistic in a given sample and characterizes a contained value of the statistic as not exceeded by a specified percentage of all the values in the sample. For example, a score higher than 97 per cent of those attained on an examination is said to be in the ninety-seventh percentile. [From PER CENT.]

per cen·tum (sĕn′təm). Per cent.

per·cept (pûr′sĕpt′) *n.* **1.** The object of perception. **2.** An impression in the mind of something perceived by the senses, viewed as the basic component in the formation of concepts. [Back-formation from PERCEPTION.]

per·cep·ti·ble (pər-sĕp′tə-bəl) *adj.* Capable of being perceived; discernible by the senses or mind. —**per·cep′ti·bil′i·ty** *n.* —**per·cep′ti·bly** *adv.*

Synonyms: *perceptible, palpable, appreciable, noticeable, discernible.* These are used to convey the sense of being real, apprehensible, or discriminable. *Perceptible* basically means perceivable, but differs in more often being used of comparisons themselves: *a perceptible difference. Palpable* means tangible or readily ascertainable. It is sometimes used for emphasis: *a palpable case of indigestion. Appreciable* means considerable in a quantitative sense and suggests the admitted possibility of apprehending what is in question: *an appreciable quantity. Noticeable* has the broad sense of visible or remarkable (in its weaker literal meaning), describing something which is adequately revealed or observable to anybody: *a noticeable tremor in his voice. Discernible,* like *perceptible* and *noticeable,* need not be visual in connotation. It means only apparent through scrutiny: *a discernible symptom.*

per·cep·tion (pər-sĕp′shən) *n.* **1.** The process, act, or faculty of perceiving. **2.** The effect or product of perceiving. **3.** Any insight, intuition, or knowledge gained by perceiving. [Latin *perceptiō,* from *percipere* (past participle *perceptus*), PERCEIVE.] —**per·cep′tion·al** *adj.*

per·cep·tive (pər-sĕp′tĭv) *adj.* **1.** Of or pertaining to perception: *perceptive faculties.* **2. a.** Having the ability to perceive; keen in discernment; knowing. **b.** Marked by discernment and understanding; sensitive. —**per·cep′tive·ly** *adv.* —**per′cep·tiv′i·ty** (pûr′sĕp-tĭv′ə-tē) *n.*

per·cep·tu·al (pər-sĕp′cho͞o-əl) *adj.* Of, based on, or involving perception. —**per·cep′tu·al·ly** *adv.*

perch[1] (pûrch) *n.* **1.** A rod or branch serving as a roost for a bird. **2.** A place for resting or sitting. **3.** A pole used in acrobatics. **4.** *Chiefly British.* **a.** A unit of length, the **rod** *(see).* **b.** One square rod of land. **5.** A unit of cubic measure used in stonework, usually 16.5 feet (one rod) by one foot by 1.5 feet, or 24.75 cubic feet. **6.** A frame on which cloth is laid for examination of quality. —*v.* **perched, perching, perches.** —*intr.* **1.** To alight or rest on a perch; roost. **2.** To stand, sit, or rest on some elevated place or position: *The child perched on the window sill.* —*tr.* **1.** To place on or as on a perch: *"The long thin nose near the end of which a pair of spectacles was perched"* (George Orwell). **2.** To lay (cloth) on a perch in order to examine it. [Middle English *perche,* from Old French, from Latin *pertica,* stick, from Italic root **pert-** (unattested), pole.]

perch[2] (pûrch) *n., pl.* **perch** or **perches. 1.** Any of various fresh-water fishes of the genus *Perca,* especially either of two edible species, *P. flavescens,* of North America, and *P. fluviatilis,* of Europe. **2.** Any of various related or similar fishes, such as the **pike perch** *(see).* [Middle English *perche,* from Old French, from Latin *perca,* from Greek *perkē.* See **perk-[1]** in Appendix.*]

per·chance (pər-chăns′, -chäns′) *adv.* Perhaps; possibly. [Middle English *perchaunce,* from Old French *per chance, par chance* : *per, par,* by, from Latin *per* + CHANCE.]

Per·che·ron (pûr′chə-rŏn′, pûr′shə-) *n.* A large draft horse of a breed developed in France, having a dark, often dappled coat. [French, from *Percheron,* a native of *le Perche,* district south of Normandy.]

perch·ing (pûr′chĭng) *adj. Ornithology.* Having feet especially adapted for grasping a perch.

per·chlo·rate (pər-klôr′āt′, -klōr′āt′) *n.* An ester or a salt of perchloric acid.

per·chlo·ric acid (pər-klôr′ĭk, -klōr′ĭk). A clear, colorless liquid, $HClO_4$, explosively unstable under some conditions. It is a powerful oxidant and is used as a catalyst and in explosives.

per·chlo·ride (pər-klôr′īd′, -klōr′īd′) *n.* Also **per·chlo·rid** (-klôr′-ĭd, -klōr′ĭd). A chloride having more chlorine than other chlorides of the same element.

per·chlor·o·eth·yl·ene (pər-klôr′ō-ĕth′ə-lēn′, pər-klōr′-) *n.* A colorless, nonflammable organic solvent, $Cl_2C{:}CCl_2$, used in dry-cleaning solutions and to dissolve a variety of waxes, tars, rubbers, and gums. [PER- + CHLORO- + ETHYLENE.]

per·cip·i·ent (pər-sĭp′ē-ənt) *adj.* Having the power of perceiving; especially, perceiving keenly and readily. —*n.* One that perceives. [Latin *percipiēns,* present participle of *percipere,* PERCEIVE.] —**per·cip′i·ence, per·cip′i·en·cy** *n.*

per·coid (pûr′koid′) *adj.* Also **per·coi·de·an** (pər′koi′dē-ən). Of or pertaining to the Percoidea, a large suborder of fishes that includes the perches, sunfishes, groupers, and grunts. —*n.* Also **per·coi·de·an.** Any fish of this group. [New Latin *Percoidea* : Latin *perca,* PERCH (fish) + -OID.]

per·co·late (pûr′kə-lāt′) *v.* **-lated, -lating, -lates.** —*tr.* **1.** To cause (liquid, powder, or small particles) to pass through a porous substance or small holes; filter; sift. **2.** To pass or ooze through: *Water percolated the sand.* **3.** To make (coffee) in a percolator. —*intr.* **1.** To drain or seep through a porous substance or filter. **2.** *Informal.* To become lively or active. —*n.* (pûr′kə-lĭt, -lāt′). A liquid that has been percolated. [Latin *percōlāre* : *per-,* through + *cōlāre,* to filter, strain, from *cōlum,* sieve (see **kagh-** in Appendix*).] —**per′co·la′tion** *n.*

per·co·la·tor (pûr′kə-lā′tər) *n.* A type of coffeepot in which boiling water is forced repeatedly up through a center tube to filter through a basket of ground coffee.

per con·tra (pər kŏn′trə, pĕr kōn′trä). *Latin.* On the contrary.

per·cur·rent (pər-kûr′ənt) *adj. Botany.* Designating a midrib of a leaf that extends from base to apex. [Latin *percurrens,* present participle of *percurrere,* to run through : *per-,* through + *currere,* to run (see **kers-[2]** in Appendix*).]

per·cuss (pər-kŭs′) *tr.v.* **-cussed, -cussing, -cusses.** To strike or tap firmly, as in medical percussion: *percuss a patient's chest.* [Latin *percutere* (past participle *percussus*), to strike hard : *per-* (intensive) + *quatere,* to strike (see **kwēt-** in Appendix*).]

per·cus·sion (pər-kŭsh′ən) *n.* **1.** The striking together of two bodies, especially when noise is produced. **2.** The sound, vibration, or shock caused by such a striking together. **3.** The act of detonating a percussion cap in a firearm. **4.** A method of medical diagnosis in which various areas of the body, especially the chest, back, and abdomen, are tapped to determine by resonance the condition of internal organs. **5.** Musical percussion instruments collectively. [Latin *percussiō,* from *percutere,* PERCUSS.]

percussion cap. A thin metal cap containing gunpowder or some other detonator that explodes on being struck.

percussion figure. The pattern of cracks formed in a crystalline mineral when struck. Also called "strike figure."

percussion instrument. A musical instrument in which sound is produced by striking, as a drum, xylophone, or piano.

per·cus·sion·ist (pər-kŭsh′ən-ĭst) *n.* One who plays percussion instruments.

per·cus·sive (pər-kŭs′ĭv) *adj.* Of, pertaining to, or marked by percussion. —**per·cus′sive·ly** *adv.* —**per·cus′sive·ness** *n.*

per·cu·ta·ne·ous (pûr′kyo͞o-tā′nē-əs) *adj. Medicine.* Passed, done, or effected through or by means of the skin. [PER- + CUTANEOUS.] —**per′cu·ta′ne·ous·ly** *adv.*

Per·cy (pûr′sē), **Thomas.** 1729–1811. English antiquary.

Per·di·do (pər-dē′dō). A river rising in southern Alabama and flowing 60 miles south to Perdido Bay, an arm of the Gulf of Mexico, forming part of the Alabama-Florida boundary.

per di·em (dē′əm, dī′əm). *Abbr.* **p.d., P.D. 1.** Per day. **2.** An allowance for daily expenses. **3.** Reckoned on a daily basis: *per diem costs.* [Latin, "by the day."]

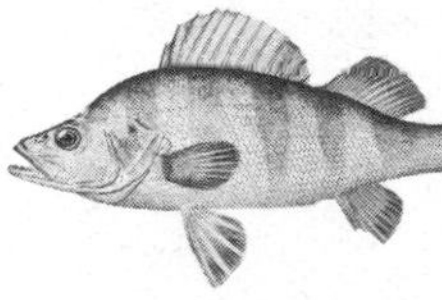

perch[2]
Perca flavescens

per·di·tion (pər-dĭsh′ən) *n.* **1. a.** The loss of the soul; eternal damnation: *"but perdition be my lot if I do more"* (Charles Brockden Brown). **b.** Hell: *"To bottomless perdition, there to dwell"* (Milton). **2.** *Archaic.* Utter loss or ruin. [Middle English *perdicioun,* from Late Latin *perditiō,* from Latin *perdere* (past participle *perditus*), to throw away, destroy, lose : *per-,* away + *dare,* to give (see **dō-** in Appendix*).]

per·du, per·due (pər-do͞o′, -dyo͞o′) *n. Obsolete.* A soldier sent on a dangerous mission. [Old French, "lost," from the past participle of *perdre,* to lose, from Latin *perdere.* See **perdition.**]

per·du·ra·ble (pər-do͝or′ə-bəl, -dyo͝or′ə-bəl) *adj.* Extremely durable; permanent. [Middle English, from Old French, from Late Latin *perdūrābilis,* from Latin *perdūrāre,* "to last throughout," endure : *per-,* throughout + *dūrāre,* to last (see **deu-[4]** in Appendix*).] —**per·du′ra·bil′i·ty** *n.* —**per·du′ra·bly** *adv.*

per·e·gri·nate (pĕr′ə-grə-nāt′) *v.* **-nated, -nating, -nates.** —*intr.* To journey or travel from place to place. —*tr.* To travel through or over. [Latin *peregrīnārī,* to travel in foreign lands, from *peregrīnus,* foreigner. See **peregrine.**] —**per′e·gri·na′tor** (-nā′tər) *n.* —**per′e·gri·na′tion** *n.*

per·e·grine (pĕr′ə-grĭn, -grēn′) *adj.* **1.** Foreign; alien. **2.** Roving or wandering; migratory. —*n.* The peregrine falcon. [Medieval Latin *peregrīnus,* from Latin, a foreigner, stranger, from *pereger,* being abroad : *per-,* away + *ager,* land, field (see **agro-** in Appendix*).]

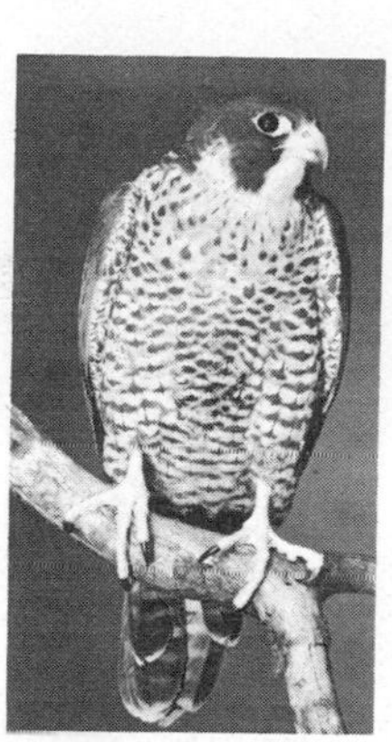

peregrine falcon

peregrine falcon. A widely distributed bird of prey, *Falco peregrinus,* having gray and white plumage, formerly much used in falconry. In America, usually called "duck hawk." [Middle English, translation of Medieval Latin *falco peregrinus,* "pilgrim falcon;" so named because young peregrines were caught in passage ("pilgrimage") from their breeding place, rather than taken from the nest as were EYAS falcons.]

pe·rei·ra bark (pə-râr′ə). The bark of a South American tree, *Geissospermum vellosii,* the source of a substance formerly used in the treatment of malaria. [After Jonathan *Pereira* (1804–1853), English pharmacologist.]

Per·el·man (pĕr′əl-mən), **S(idney) J(oseph).** Born 1904. American humorist, feuilletonist, and playwright.

per·emp·to·ry (pə-rĕmp′tə-rē) *adj.* **1.** *Law.* Precluding further debate or action: *a peremptory decree.* **2.** Not admitting denial; imperative: *"Her scruples gave way to his peremptory commands."* (Fielding). **3.** Having the nature of or expressing a command; urgent: *"A bell began to toll with a peremptory clang."* (Hardy). **4.** Offensively self-assured; dictatorial; imperious: *a peremptory manner.* [Late Latin *peremptōrius,* "precluding debate," decisive, from *perimere* (past participle *peremptus*), to take away completely : *per-,* completely + *emere,* to obtain (see **em-** in Appendix*).] —**per·emp′to·ri·ly** *adv.* —**per·emp′to·ri·ness** *n.*

per·en·ni·al (pə-rĕn′ē-əl) *adj.* **1.** Lasting or active through the year or through many years: *the perennial snowcaps of the Alps.* **2. a.** Lasting an indefinitely long time; everlasting; perpetual: *perennial happiness.* **b.** Appearing again and again; continually recurring: *"Milton felt the impact of modernity which is perennial in every generation."* (John Crowe Ransom). **3.** *Botany.* Having a life span of more than two years. Compare **annual, biennial.** —See Synonyms at **continual.** —*n. Botany.* A perennial plant. [From Latin *perennis* : *per-,* throughout + *annus,* year (see **at-** in Appendix*).] —**per·en′ni·al·ly** *adv.*

Per·etz (pĕr′ĕts), **Isaac Loeb.** Original name, Yitzchok Leibush Perez. 1852–1915. Polish writer, primarily in Yiddish.

perf. 1. perfect. **2.** perforated.

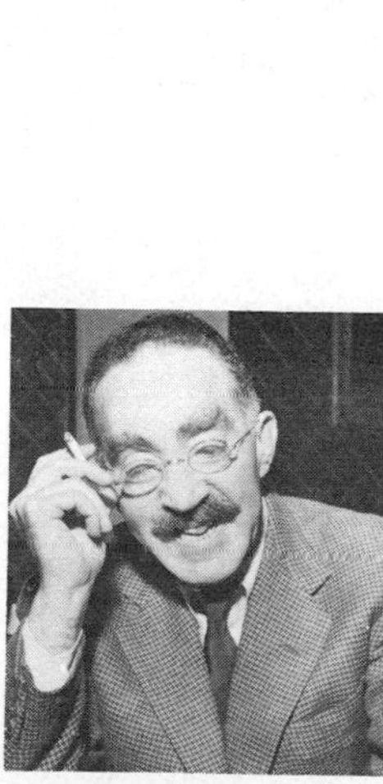

S.J. Perelman

per·fect (pûr′fĭkt) *adj. Abbr.* **perf. 1.** Lacking nothing essential to the whole; complete of its nature or kind. **2.** In a state of undiminished or highest excellence; without defect; flawless: *a perfect specimen.* **3.** Completely skilled or talented in a certain field or area: *a perfect artist.* **4.** Completely reproducing or corresponding to a type or original; accurate; exact: *a perfect reproduction of a painting.* **5.** Complete; thorough; utter: *a perfect fool.* **6.** Pure; undiluted; unmixed: *perfect red.* **7.** Excellent and delightful in all respects: *a perfect day.* **8.** *Botany.* Having both stamens and pistils in the same flower; monoclinous. **9.** *Grammar.* Of, pertaining to, or constituting a verb form expressing action completed prior to a fixed point of refer-

ence in time. English verbs have three perfect tenses: the present (or simple) perfect, the pluperfect (or past perfect), and the future perfect. **10.** *Mathematics.* Of, pertaining to, or constituting a number or quantity equal to an integral power of another number or quantity: *4, 9, and 16 are perfect squares.* **11.** *Music.* **a.** Designating the three basic intervals of the octave, fourth, and fifth. **b.** Designating a cadence in which the final chord has its root in both bass and soprano. —*n. Abbr.* **perf.** *Grammar.* **1.** The perfect tense. **2.** A verb or verb form in this tense. —*tr.v.* (pər-fĕkt′) **perfected, -fecting, -fects.** To bring to perfection or completion: *"The telegraph was perfected and applied to news reporting."* (Daniel J. Boorstin). [Middle English *perfit, parfit,* from Old French *parfit,* from Latin *perfectus,* finished, complete, excellent, from the past participle of *perficere,* to complete : *per-,* completely + *facere,* to do (see **dhē-**[1] in Appendix*).] —**per·fect′er** *n.* —**per′fect·ness** *n.*

Usage: In absolute senses, *perfect* and *perfectly* cannot correctly be used in the comparative and superlative. However, when used in senses that only approach the absolute or that simply denote excellence, the comparative and superlative are standard.

per·fect·i·ble (pər-fĕk′tə-bəl) *adj.* Capable of becoming or being made perfect. —**per·fect′i·bil′i·ty** *n.*

per·fec·tion (pər-fĕk′shən) *n.* **1.** The state, quality, or condition of being perfect. **2.** The process or act of perfecting: *The perfection of the invention took years.* **3.** A person or thing that perfectly embodies something: *Her pastry is a perfection of the culinary art.* **4.** An instance or quality of excellence.

per·fec·tion·ism (pər-fĕk′shə-nĭz′əm) *n.* **1.** A belief that moral or spiritual perfection can be achieved by man in this life. **2.** A propensity for setting extremely high standards and being displeased with anything less. —**per·fec′tion·ist** *n.*

per·fec·tive (pər-fĕk′tĭv) *adj.* **1.** Tending toward perfection. **2.** *Grammar.* Of or designating a verb in the perfective aspect. —*n. Grammar.* **1.** The perfective aspect. **2.** A verb in the perfective aspect. —**per·fec′tive·ly** *adv.* —**per·fec′tive·ness, per′fec·tiv′i·ty** (pûr′fĕk-tĭv′ə-tē) *n.*

perfective aspect. An aspect of verbs that expresses a completed action as distinct from a continuing or not necessarily completed action. See **aspect.**

per·fect·ly (pûr′fĭkt-lē) *adv.* **1.** In a perfect manner or to a perfect degree. **2.** Completely; fully; wholly: *perfectly black.*

Usage: In writing, *perfectly* is sometimes objected to when it is used as a mere intensive denoting *quite, altogether,* or *just,* as in *perfectly good, perfectly dreadful.* But it is widely used by educated speakers in this sense.

per·fec·to (pər-fĕk′tō) *n., pl.* **-tos.** A cigar of standard length, thick in the center and tapering at each end. [Spanish, perfect, from Latin *perfectus,* PERFECT.]

perfect participle. The **past participle** *(see).*

perfect pitch. **Absolute pitch** *(see).*

perfect rhyme. **1.** The commonest English rhyme, having identity in sound for the last accented vowel and any final consonants or syllables but with variation in the preceding consonant, for example, *great, late; rider, beside her; dutiful, unbeautiful.* Also called "full rhyme," "true rhyme." **2.** A rhyme of two words pronounced identically but differing in meaning, for example, *right, rite.*

perfect square. An integer that is the square of an integer.

perfect year. In the Hebrew calendar, a year having 355 days or a leap year having 385 days. See **calendar.**

per·fer·vid (pər-fûr′vĭd) *adj.* Impassioned; zealous; extremely or extravagantly eager. [New Latin *perfervidus* : *per-* (intensifier) + Latin *fervidus,* FERVID.] —**per·fer′vid·ly** *adv.* —**per·fer′vid·ness** *n.*

per·fi·dy (pûr′fə-dē) *n., pl.* **-dies.** Deliberate breach of faith; calculated violation of trust; treachery: *"By the perfidy of her leaders, France has disgraced the tone of lenient council."* (Burke). [Latin *perfidia,* from *perfidus,* treacherous : *per-* (destruction) + *fidēs,* faith (see **bheidh-** in Appendix*).] —**per·fid′i·ous** (pər-fĭd′ē-əs) *adj.* —**per·fid′i·ous·ly** *adv.*

per·fo·li·ate (pər-fō′lē-ĭt) *adj. Botany.* Designating a leaf that completely clasps the stem and is apparently pierced by it. [New Latin *perfoliatus,* "pierced through the leaf" : Latin *per-,* through + *foliātus,* "leaved," FOLIATE.] —**per·fo′li·a′tion** *n.*

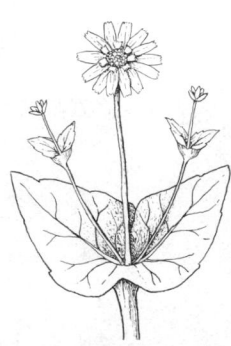

perfoliate
Perfoliate leaf of cup plant, *Silphium perfoliatum*

per·fo·rate (pûr′fə-rāt′) *tr.v.* **-rated, -rating, -rates.** **1.** To pierce, punch, or bore a hole or holes in; penetrate. **2.** To pierce or stamp with rows of holes, such as those between postage stamps, to allow easy separation. —*adj.* (pûr′fə-rĭt, -rāt′) Perforated. [Latin *perforāre* : *per-,* through + *forāre,* to bore (see **bher-**[2] in Appendix*).] —**per′fo·ra·ble** (pûr′fər-ə-bəl) *adj.* —**per′fo·ra′tive, per′fo·ra·to′ry** (pûr′fər-ə-tôr′ē, -tōr′ē) *adj.* —**per′fo·ra′tor** (-rā′tər) *n.*

per·fo·ra·ted (pûr′fə-rā′tĭd) *adj. Abbr.* **perf.** Having a perforation or perforations.

per·fo·ra·tion (pûr′fə-rā′shən) *n.* **1.** The act of perforating, or state of being perforated. **2.** A hole or series of holes punched or bored through something; specifically, a hole in a series, separating sections in a sheet or roll. Compare **roulette.**

per·force (pər-fôrs′, -fōrs′) *adv.* By necessity; willy-nilly: *"there is no whiskey either at tavern or store, and the people are perforce sober!"* (Anne Langton). [Middle English *par force,* from Old French : *par,* by, from Latin *per* + FORCE.]

per·form (pər-fôrm′) *v.* **-formed, -forming, -forms.** —*tr.* **1.** To begin and carry through to completion; do: *perform an appendectomy.* **2.** To take action in accordance with the requirements of; fulfill (a promise or duty, for example). **3. a.** To enact (a feat or role) before an audience. **b.** To give a public presentation of. —*intr.* **1.** To carry on; function. **2.** To fulfill an obligation or requirement; accomplish something as promised or expected. **3.** To portray a role or demonstrate some skill before an audience. **4.** To present a dramatic or musical work or other entertainment before an audience. [Middle English *performen,* from Norman French *parformer,* variant of Old French *parfornir* : *par-* (intensifier), from Latin *per-* + *fornir,* FURNISH.] —**per·form′a·ble** *adj.* —**per·form′er** *n.*

Synonyms: *perform, execute, accomplish, achieve, effect, fulfill, discharge, render.* These synonyms for *do* stress the action, effort, or completion of a prescribed or significant deed or task. *Perform* stresses the skill or care involved in carrying something out by established procedures. It can also mean, as with machines, to function routinely. *Execute* implies doing a planned task with efficiency, precision, or finality: *execute the maneuver. Accomplish* connotes completion of a job or feat which reflects a person's impressive talents. *Achieve* places more weight on the effort, significance, or difficulty involved. *Effect* suggests practical carrying out of something, often collectively or impersonally: *A new policy was effected.* To *fulfill* means to live up to the expectations or demands of somebody or some challenge: *fulfill one's obligation.* To *discharge* a duty is to complete it from a purely mechanical standpoint: *Your duties must be correctly discharged. Render* refers less to doing a task than to the effect of one's action: *render a service.*

per·form·ance (pər-fôr′məns) *n.* **1.** The act of performing, or the state of being performed. **2.** The act or style of performing a work or role before an audience. **3.** The way in which someone or something functions. **4.** A presentation, especially a theatrical one, before an audience. **5.** Something performed; an accomplishment; a deed.

per·fume (pûr′fyo͞om′, pər-fyo͞om′) *n.* **1.** A volatile liquid, distilled from flowers or prepared synthetically, that emits and diffuses a fragrant odor. **2.** Any pleasing, agreeable scent or odor. —See Synonyms at **smell.** —*tr.v.* (pər-fyo͞om′) **perfumed, -fuming, -fumes.** To impregnate with fragrance; impart a pleasant odor to. [Old French *parfum,* probably from Old Italian *parfumare,* to smoke through : *par-,* through, from Latin *per-* + *fumare,* to smoke, from Latin *fūmāre,* from *fūmus,* smoke (see **dheu-**[1] in Appendix*).]

per·fum·er (pər-fyo͞o′mər) *n.* A maker or seller of perfumes.

per·fum·er·y (pər-fyo͞o′mə-rē) *n., pl.* **-ies.** **1.** Perfumes in general. **2.** An establishment that specializes in making or selling perfume. **3.** The art of making perfume.

per·func·to·ry (pər-fŭngk′tə-rē) *adj.* Done or acting routinely and with little interest or care. [Late Latin *perfunctōrius,* from Latin *perfungī* (past participle *perfunctus*), "to get through with" : *per-,* completely + *fungī,* to perform (see **bheug-**[2] in Appendix*).] —**per·func′to·ri·ly** *adv.* —**per·func′to·ri·ness** *n.*

per·fuse (pər-fyo͞oz′) *tr.v.* **-fused, -fusing, -fuses.** **1.** To coat, suffuse, or permeate with liquid, color, or light. **2.** To pour or diffuse (a liquid) over or through something. [Latin *perfundere* (past participle *perfusus*), to pour over or through : *per-,* through + *fundere,* to pour (see **gheu-** in Appendix*).] —**per·fu′sive** (pər-fyo͞o′sĭv, -zĭv) *adj.*

per·fu·sion (pər-fyo͞o′zhən) *n. Medicine.* The injection of fluid into an artery in order to reach tissues.

Per·ga·mum (pûr′gə-məm). Also **Per·ga·mon** (pûr′gə-mŏn′), **Per·ga·mos** (pûr′gə-məs, -mŏs′), **Per·ga·mus** (pûr′gə-məs). A Greek city in western Asia Minor, on the site of modern Bergama, that became the center of a Hellenistic kingdom in the Attalid dynasty. —**Per′ga·mene′** (pûr′gə-mēn′) *adj.*

per·go·la (pûr′gə-lə) *n.* An arbor or passageway with a roof of trelliswork on which climbing plants are trained to grow. [Italian, from Latin *pergula.* See **perg-**[1] in Appendix.*]

Per·go·le·si (pĕr′gō-lā′zē), **Giovanni Battista.** 1710–1736. Italian composer of operas and sacred music.

per·haps (pər-hăps′) *adv.* Maybe; possibly. [PER (by) + plural of HAP (chance).]

Pe·ri (pā′rē), **Jacopo.** 1561–1633. Italian composer.

peri-. Indicates: **1.** About, around, encircling, or enclosing; for example, **periotic, periscope.** **2.** Close at hand, adjacent, or near; for example, **perihelion.** [Latin, from Greek, from *peri,* about, near, around. See **per**[1] in Appendix.*]

per·i·anth (pĕr′ē-ănth′) *n. Botany.* The outer envelope of a flower, consisting of the calyx and corolla, or of one of these if the other is absent. [French *périanthe,* from New Latin *perianthium* : PERI- + ANTH(O)- + -IUM.]

per·i·apt (pĕr′ē-ăpt′) *n.* An amulet or charm worn as protection against mischief and disease. [Old French *periapte,* from Greek *periapton,* from *periaptos,* appended, from *periaptein,* to hang or fasten around : *peri-,* around + *haptein,* to fasten (see **synapse**).]

per·i·car·di·tis (pĕr′ə-kär-dī′tĭs) *n.* Inflammation of the pericardium. [New Latin : PERICARD(IUM) + -ITIS.]

per·i·car·di·um (pĕr′ə-kär′dē-əm) *n., pl.* **-dia** (-dē-ə). The membranous sac enclosing the heart. [New Latin, from Greek *perikardion,* from *perikardios,* around the heart : *peri-,* around + *kardia,* heart (see **kerd-**[1] in Appendix*).] —**per′i·car′di·al, per′i·car′di·ac′** *adj.*

per·i·carp (pĕr′ə-kärp′) *n. Botany.* The wall of a ripened ovary or fruit. Also called "seed vessel." [New Latin *pericarpium,* from Greek *perikarpion,* pod, shell : *peri-,* around + -CARP.] —**per′i·car′pi·al** (-kär′pē-əl) *adj.*

per·i·chon·dri·um (pĕr′ə-kŏn′drē-əm) *n., pl.* **-dria** (-drē-ə). *Anatomy.* The fibrous membrane covering the surface of cartilage except at joint endings. [New Latin : PERI- + CHONDR(O)- + -IUM.] —**per′i·chon′dri·al** *adj.*

per·i·clase (pĕr′ə-klās′, -klāz′) *n.* A mineral form of magnesium oxide, MgO, usually occurring in isomeric crystals or grains.

[German *Periklas*, from New Latin *periclasia*, "perfect cleavage (of the crystals)" : PERI- (around, hence above others, exceedingly) + -CLASE.]

Per·i·cles (pĕr′ə-klēz′). 495?–429 B.C. Athenian statesman, orator, and general. —**Per·i·cle′an** (pər′ə-klē′ən) *adj.*

per·i·cline (pĕr′ə-klīn′) *n. Mineralogy.* A variety of albite occurring as elongated white crystals. [From Greek *periklinēs*, sloping on all sides : *peri-*, around, on all sides + *klinein*, to slope, lean (see **klei-** in Appendix*).]

per·i·cra·ni·um (pĕr′ə-krā′nē-əm) *n., pl.* **-nia** (-nē-ə). *Anatomy.* The external **periosteum** *(see)* that covers the outer surface of the skull. [New Latin, from Greek *perikranion*, from *perikranios*, around the skull : *peri-*, around + *kranion*, CRANIUM.] —**per′i·cra′ni·al** *adj.*

per·i·cy·cle (pĕr′ə-sī′kəl) *n. Botany.* The growing layer of parenchyma cells and fibers between the endodermis and the conducting tissue in plant roots and stems. [French *péricycle*, from Greek *perikuklos*, spherical : *peri-*, around + *kuklos*, CYCLE.] —**per′i·cy′clic** (-sī′klĭk) *adj.*

per·i·derm (pĕr′ə-dûrm′) *n. Botany.* An outer layer of tissue of plant roots and stems, consisting of the bark and the layer of growing tissue beneath the bark. [New Latin *peridermis* : PERI- + -DERM.] —**per′i·der′mal** (-dûr′məl), **per′i·der′mic** *adj.*

pe·rid·i·um (pə-rĭd′ē-əm) *n., pl.* **-ia** (-ē-ə). The covering of the spore-bearing organ in many fungi. [New Latin, from Greek *pēridion*, diminutive of *pēra*†, leather bag.] —**pe·rid′i·al** *adj.*

per·i·dot (pĕr′ə-dŏt′, -dō′) *n.* A clear green variety of **olivine** *(see).* [French *péridot*, from Old French *peritot*†.] —**per′i·dot′ic** (pĕr′ə-dŏt′ĭk, -dō′tĭk) *adj.*

per·i·do·tite (pĕr′ə-dō′tīt′, pə-rĭd′ə-tīt′) *n.* Any of a group of igneous rocks having a granitelike texture and composed mainly of olivine and various pyroxenes and amphiboles. [French *péridotite*, from *péridot*, PERIDOT.]

per·i·gee (pĕr′ə-jē) *n.* The point nearest the earth in the orbit of the moon or a satellite. Compare **apogee**. [French *périgée*, from New Latin *perigeum*, from Greek *perigeion*, from *perigeios*, near the earth : *peri-*, near + *gē*, the earth (see **gē** in Appendix*).] —**per′i·ge′al** (pĕr′ə-jē′əl), **per′i·ge′an** *adj.*

pe·rig·y·nous (pə-rĭj′ə-nəs) *adj. Botany.* **1.** Having sepals, petals, and stamens around the edge of a cuplike receptacle containing the ovary. **2.** Designating flower parts arranged in this way: *perigynous stamens.* [New Latin *perigynus* : PERI- + -GYNOUS.] —**pe·rig′y·ny** (pə-rĭj′ə-nē) *n.*

per·i·he·li·on (pĕr′ə-hē′lē-ən, -hēl′yən) *n., pl.* **-helia** (-hē′lē-ə, -hēl′yə). The point nearest the sun in the orbit of a planet or other body. Compare **aphelion**. [New Latin : PERI- + Greek *hēlios*, sun (see **sāwel-** in Appendix*).]

per·il (pĕr′əl) *n.* **1.** A condition of imminent danger; exposure to the risk of harm or loss. **2.** Something that endangers; serious risk. —See Synonyms at **danger**. —*tr.v.* **periled, -iling, -ils.** Also *chiefly British* **-illed, -illing.** To expose to danger or the chance of injury; imperil. [Middle English, from Old French, from Latin *periculum*, trial, danger. See **per-**[5] in Appendix.*] —**per′il·ous** *adj.* —**per′il·ous·ly** *adv.*

pe·rim·e·ter (pə-rĭm′ə-tər) *n.* **1. a.** *Mathematics.* A closed curve bounding a plane area. **b.** The length of such a boundary. **2.** *Military.* A fortified strip or boundary protecting a position. [French *périmètre*, from Latin *perimetros*, from Greek : *peri-*, around + -METER.] —**per′i·met′ric** (pĕr′ə-mĕt′rĭk), **per′i·met′ri·cal** *adj.* —**per′i·met′ri·cal·ly** *adv.*

per·i·morph (pĕr′ə-môrf′) *n.* A mineral that encloses a different mineral. Compare **endomorph**. [PERI- + -MORPH.] —**per′i·mor′phic, per′i·mor′phous** *adj.* —**per′i·mor′phism′** *n.*

per·i·my·si·um (pĕr′ə-mĭzh′ē-əm, -mĭz′ē-əm) *n., pl.* **-mysia** (-mĭzh′ē-ə, -mĭz′ē-ə). A sheath of connective tissue enveloping bundles of muscle fibers. [New Latin : PERI- + Greek *mus*, muscle (see **mū-**[1] in Appendix*) + -IUM.]

per·i·neph·ri·um (pĕr′ə-nĕf′rē-əm) *n., pl.* **-ria** (-rē-ə). The connective and fatty tissue surrounding the kidney. [New Latin, from Greek *perinephros*, fat around the kidney : *peri-*, around + *nephros*, kidney (see **negwhro-** in Appendix*).] —**per′i·neph′ral, per′i·neph′ri·al, per′i·neph′ric** *adj.*

per·i·ne·um (pĕr′ə-nē′əm) *n., pl.* **-nea** (-nē′ə). **1.** The portion of the body in the pelvis occupied by urogenital passages and the rectum, bounded in front by the pubic arch, in the back by the coccyx, and laterally by part of the hipbone. **2.** The region between the scrotum and the anus in males, and between the posterior vulva junction and the anus in females. [New Latin, from Late Latin *perinaion*, from Greek : *peri-*, around + *inan*†, to excrete.] —**per′i·ne′al** *adj.*

per·i·neu·ri·um (pĕr′ə-no͝or′ē-əm, -nyo͝or′ē-əm) *n., pl.* **-neuria** (-no͝or′ē-ə, -nyo͝or′ē-ə). A sheath of connective tissue enclosing a primary bundle of nerve fibers. [New Latin : PERI- + NEUR(O)- + -IUM.] —**per′i·neu′ri·al** *adj.*

pe·ri·od (pîr′ē-əd) *n. Abbr.* **per. 1.** An interval of time characterized by the occurrence of certain conditions or events. **2.** An interval of time characterized by the prevalence of a specified culture, ideology, or technology: *artifacts of the pre-Columbian period.* **3.** A unit of geologic time, longer than an epoch and shorter than an era. **4.** An interval regarded as a distinct evolutionary or developmental phase; stage: *Picasso's blue period.* **5.** Any of various arbitrary temporal units, especially: **a.** Any of the divisions of the academic day. **b.** A division of the playing time of a game. **6.** *Physics & Astronomy.* The time interval between two successive occurrences of any recurrent event; cycle. **7.** An instance or occurrence of menstruation. **8.** A point or portion of time at which something is ended; completion; conclusion. **9.** The full pause at the end of a spoken sentence. **10.** A punctuation mark (.) indicating a full stop, placed at the end of declarative sentences and other statements thought to be complete, and after many abbreviations. See Usage note at **ellipsis**. **11.** *Rhetoric.* In formal literary composition, a sentence of several carefully balanced clauses. **12.** A metrical unit of Greek verse consisting of two or more cola. **13.** *Music.* A group of two or more phrases within a composition, made up of eight or sixteen measures and terminating with a cadence. **14.** *Mathematics.* **a.** The least interval in the range of the independent variable of a periodic function of a real variable in which all possible values of the dependent variable are assumed. **b.** A group of digits separated by commas in a written number. **c.** The number of digits that repeat in a repeating decimal. For example, $1/7$ = 0.142857142857 . . . has a six-digit period. —*adj.* Of or representing a certain historical age or time: *a period piece.* [Middle English *paryode*, from Old French *periode*, from Late Latin *periodus*, period of time, from Latin, sentence, from Greek *periodos*, circuit, rhetorical period : *peri-*, around + *hodos*, way (see **sed-**[2] in Appendix*).]

Synonyms: *period, time, epoch, era, age, term.* These are general words for an imprecise portion of time, usually of actual or seemingly long duration. A *period* can be a roughly specified interval or it can objectively denote a time historically: *an endless waiting period; the Romantic period. Time*, used here in its concrete rather than conceptual sense, often implies a period with certain diversities or possibilities as seen from a more personal vantage: *those times were the best. Time* can also be used loosely for a period of not precisely defined limits: *it was a time of sorrow. Epoch* is a formal word for more precise historical emphasis, implying usually that the given period is one of change and is seen as but one among many. More colorful is *era*, which conjures up associations of a notable flavor or way of life over a long and important span of time. *Age* accents the great duration of a period with a salient characteristic, seen from a distant or at least hypothetical perspective. Used of geological and historical periods, an *age* can cover centuries but it is often used hyperbolically: *ages ago.* A *term* is a formally delimited period, usually relating to particular institutions: *his term of imprisonment; his term of office.*

pe·ri·od·ic (pîr′ē-ŏd′ĭk) *adj.* **1.** Having periods or repeated cycles. **2.** Happening or appearing at regular intervals. **3.** Taking place now and then; intermittent. [French *périodique*, from Latin *periodicus*, from Greek *periodikos*, from *periodos*, PERIOD.] —**pe′ri·od′i·cal·ly** *adv.*

Synonyms: *periodic, sporadic, intermittent, occasional, fitful.* These specify recurrence over a period of time. Something is *periodic* which occurs at intervals that are, if not regular, at least generally predictable. *Sporadic* emphasizes the irregularity of what recurs, as well as its unpredictability. *Intermittent* describes anything which comes and goes, usually infrequently but somewhat expectedly, and stresses the pauses or interruptions rather than the occurrences. It usually implies recurrence within understood limits, and may hint at a significant pattern: *intermittent periods of rationality.* What is *occasional* happens at random, usually infrequently, and is generally not considered very important or disruptive. Something is *fitful* which comes abruptly, at odd times, and does not last long.

per·i·od·ic acid (pûr′ī-ŏd′ĭk). A white, crystalline inorganic acid, $H_5IO_4 \cdot 2H_2O$, used as an oxidizer. [PER- + IODIC.]

pe·ri·od·i·cal (pîr′ē-ŏd′ĭ-kəl) *adj.* **1.** Periodic. **2. a.** Published at regular intervals of more than one day. **b.** Of or pertaining to a publication issued at such intervals. —*n.* A publication issued at regular intervals of more than one day.

pe·ri·o·dic·i·ty (pîr′ē-ə-dĭs′ə-tē) *n.* The quality of being periodic; recurrence at regular intervals.

periodic law. *Chemistry.* The principle that the properties of the elements recur periodically with increasing atomic number.

periodic table. *Chemistry.* A tabular arrangement of the elements according to their atomic number. See **element**.

per·i·o·don·tal (pĕr′ē-ō-dŏnt′l) *adj. Dentistry.* Of or designating tissue and structures surrounding and supporting the teeth. [PERI- + ODONT(O)- + -AL.]

per·i·o·don·tics (pĕr′ē-ō-dŏn′tĭks) *n.* Plural in form, used with a singular verb. Also **per·i·o·don·tia** (-shə). The dental specialty of periodontal disease. [From New Latin *periodontium*, periodontal tissue : PERI- + ODONT(O)- + -IUM.] —**per′i·o·don′tic, per′i·o·don′ti·cal** *adj.* —**per′i·o·don′tist** *n.*

per·i·os·te·um (pĕr′ē-ŏs′tē-əm) *n., pl.* **-tea** (-tē-ə). A fibrous membrane covering all bones, except at points of articulation. [New Latin, from Late Latin *periosteon*, from Greek, from *periosteos*, around the bones : *peri-*, around + *osteon*, bone (see **osth-** in Appendix*).] —**per′i·os′te·al, per′i·os′te·ous** *adj.*

per·i·os·ti·tis (pĕr′ē-ŏs-tī′tĭs) *n.* Inflammation of the periosteum. —**per′i·os·tit′ic** (-tĭt′ĭk) *adj.*

per·i·o·tic (pĕr′ē-ō′tĭk) *adj.* **1.** Situated around the ear. **2.** Of or designating the bones immediately around the inner ear. [PERI- + OTIC.]

per·i·pa·tet·ic (pĕr′ə-pə-tĕt′ĭk) *adj.* **1.** Walking about from place to place; traveling on foot: *"A baggy figure, equally pathetic / When sedentary and when peripatetic."* (Robert Frost). **2.** Carried on while walking or moving from place to place. —*n.* One who walks from place to place; an itinerant. [From PERIPATETIC.]

Per·i·pa·tet·ic (pĕr′ə-pə-tĕt′ĭk) *adj.* Of or pertaining to the philosophy or methods of teaching of Aristotle, who conducted discussions while walking about in the Lyceum of ancient Athens. —*n.* **1.** A member of Aristotle's school. **2.** A follower of the philosophy of Aristotle; an Aristotelian. [Old French *peripatetique*, from Latin *peripatēticus*, from Greek *peripatē-*

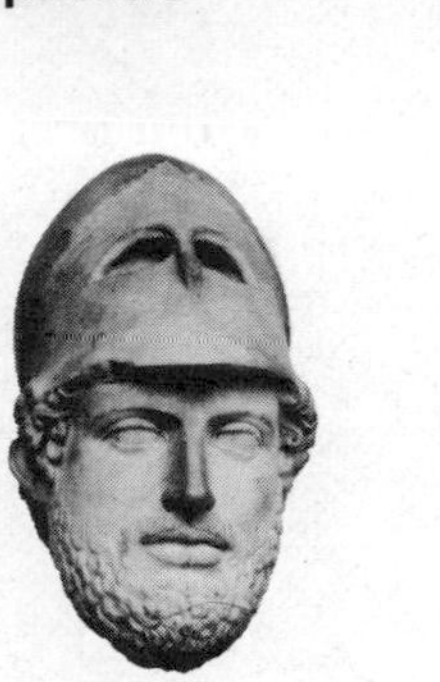

Pericles

t tight/th thin, path/*th* this, bathe/ŭ cut/ûr urge/v valve/w with/y yes/z zebra, size/zh vision/ə about, item, edible, gallop, circus/ à *Fr.* ami/œ *Fr.* feu, *Ger.* schön/ü *Fr.* tu, *Ger.* über/KH *Ger.* ich, *Scot.* loch/N *Fr.* bon. *Follows main vocabulary. †Of obscure origin.

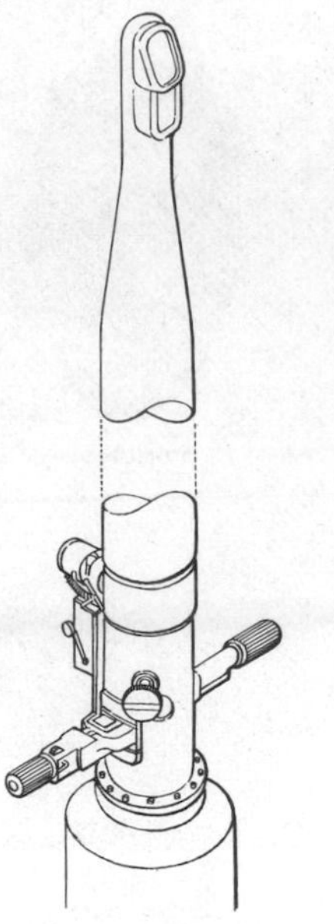

periscope
Periscope of a submarine
Above: Optical head that projects above the water
Below: Directional control and eyepiece inside the ship

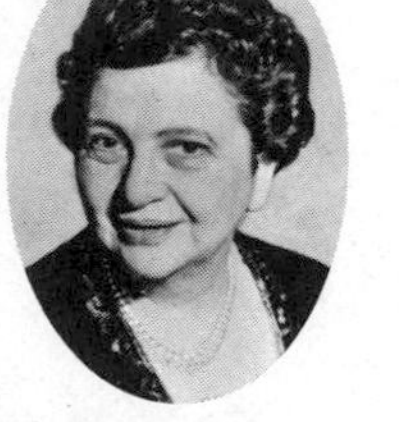

Frances Perkins

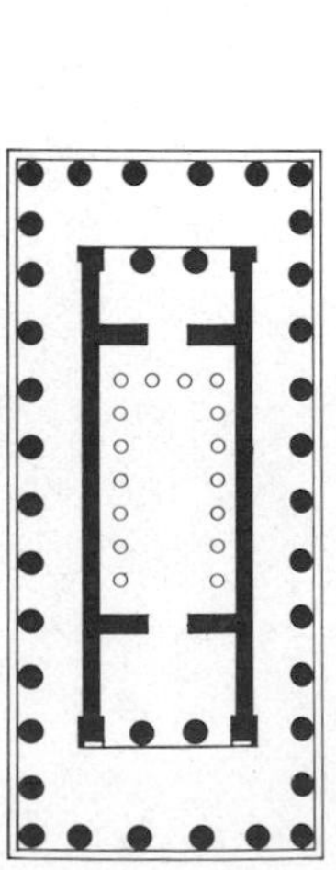

peristyle

tikos, from *peripatein,* to walk about while teaching : *peri-,* around + *patein,* to tread, walk (see **pent-** in Appendix*).]

per·i·pe·te·ia (pĕr′ə-pə-tē′ə, -tī′ə) *n.* Also **per·i·pe·ti·a, pe·rip·e·ty** (pə-rĭp′ə-tē). An abrupt or unexpected change in a course of events or situation, especially in a literary work. [Greek, from *peripiptein,* to change suddenly, "fall around" : *peri-,* around + *piptein,* to fall (see **pet-¹** in Appendix*).]

pe·riph·er·al (pə-rĭf′ər-əl) *adj.* Also **per·i·pher·ic** (pĕr′ə-fĕr′ĭk), **per·i·pher·i·cal.** Pertaining to, located on, or comprising the periphery. —**pe·riph′er·al·ly** *adv.*

peripheral nervous system. The part of the nervous system comprising the cranial nerves, the spinal nerves, and the sympathetic nervous system.

pe·riph·er·y (pə-rĭf′ə-rē) *n., pl.* **-ies. 1. a.** The outermost part or region within a precise boundary. **b.** The region or area immediately beyond a precise boundary. **c.** A zone constituting an imprecise boundary. **2.** *Mathematics.* **a.** A **perimeter** *(see).* **b.** The surface of a solid. **3.** *Anatomy.* A region in which nerves end. [Middle English *peripherie,* from Late Latin *peripheria,* from Greek *periphereia,* from *peripherēs,* carrying around, from *peripherein,* to carry around : *peri-,* around + *pherein,* to carry (see **bher-¹** in Appendix*).]

pe·riph·ra·sis (pə-rĭf′rə-sĭs) *n., pl.* **-ses** (-sēz′). Also **per·i·phrase** (pĕr′ə-frāz′). **1.** The use of circumlocution. **2.** A circumlocution. [Latin, from Greek, from *periphrazein,* to express in a roundabout way : *peri-,* around + *phrazein,* to show, say (see **phrazein** in Appendix*).]

per·i·phras·tic (pĕr′ə-frăs′tĭk) *adj.* **1.** Of the nature of or characterized by periphrasis. **2.** *Grammar.* Constructed by using an auxiliary word rather than an inflected form; for example, the phrases *the word of his father* and *his father did say* are periphrastic, while *his father's word* and *his father said* are inflected. —**per′i·phras′ti·cal·ly** *adv.*

pe·rip·ter·al (pə-rĭp′tər-əl) *adj. Architecture.* Built with a row of columns on all sides. —*n.* A structure with such rows of columns. [Latin *peripteros,* from Greek, "flying around" : *peri-,* around + *pteron,* wing (see **pet-¹** in Appendix*).]

pe·rique (pə-rēk′) *n.* A strongly flavored, black tobacco grown in Louisiana and used in various blends. [Louisianian French, said to be after *Périque,* nickname of *Pierre* Chenet, planter who introduced tobacco-growing in Louisiana.]

per·i·sarc (pĕr′ə-särk′) *n. Zoology.* A horny external covering that encloses the polyp colonies of certain hydrozoans. [PERI- + Greek *sarx,* flesh (see **twerk-** in Appendix*).] —**per′i·sar′cal, per′i·sar′cous** *adj.*

per·i·scope (pĕr′ə-skōp′) *n.* Any of various optical instruments that contain reflecting elements, such as mirrors and prisms, to permit observation from a position displaced from a direct line of sight. [PERI- + -SCOPE.] —**per′i·scop′ic** (pĕr′ə-skŏp′ĭk), **per′i·scop′i·cal** *adj.*

per·ish (pĕr′ĭsh) *intr.v.* **-ished, -ishing, -ishes. 1.** To die, especially in a violent or untimely manner. **2.** To pass from existence; disappear gradually. [Middle English *perisshen,* from Old French *perir* (present stem *periss-*), from Latin *perīre,* to pass away : *per-,* away + *īre,* to go (see **ei-¹** in Appendix*).]

per·ish·a·ble (pĕr′ĭsh-ə-bəl) *adj.* Liable to perish, decay, or spoil; easily injured or destroyed. —*n. Usually plural.* Something, especially foodstuff, apt to decay or spoil. —**per′ish·a·bil′i·ty, per′ish·a·ble·ness** *n.* —**per′ish·a·bly** *adv.*

pe·ris·so·dac·tyl (pə-rĭs′ō-dăk′təl) *adj.* Also **pe·ris·so·dac·tyle** (pə-rĭs′ō-dăk′təl, -tīl′). *Zoology.* **1.** Having an odd number of toes. **2.** Of or pertaining to certain hoofed mammals, such as horses and rhinoceroses, of the order Perissodactyla, that have an odd number of toes. —*n. Zoology.* A hoofed mammal of this order. [Greek *perissodaktulos* : *perissos,* excessive, uneven, from *peri-,* beyond (see **per¹** in Appendix*) + *daktulos,* DACTYL.] —**pe·ris′so·dac′ty·lous** (-dăk′tə-ləs) *adj.*

per·i·stal·sis (pĕr′ə-stôl′sĭs, -stăl′sĭs) *n., pl.* **-ses** (-sēz′). Wavelike muscular contractions that propel contained matter along tubular organs, as in the alimentary canal. [New Latin, from *peristalticus,* of peristalsis, from Greek *peristaltikos,* compressing around, from *peristellein,* to wrap around : *peri-,* around + *stellein,* to place, set (see **stel-¹** in Appendix*).] —**per′i·stal′tic** (-stôl′tĭk, -stăl′tĭk) *adj.*

per·i·stome (pĕr′ə-stōm′) *n.* **1.** *Botany.* A circular row of toothlike appendages surrounding the mouth of a moss capsule. **2.** *Zoology.* The area around the mouth in certain invertebrates. [New Latin *peristoma* : PERI- + -STOME.] —**per′i·sto′mal** (-stō′məl), **per′i·sto′mi·al** (-stō′mē-əl) *adj.*

per·i·style (pĕr′ə-stīl′) *n. Architecture.* **1.** A series of columns surrounding a temple or other structure, or enclosing a court. **2.** A court enclosed by such columns. [French *péristyle,* from Latin *peristȳlum,* from Greek *peristulon,* from *peristulos,* surrounded by columns : *peri-,* around + *stulos,* pillar (see **stā-** in Appendix*).] —**per′i·sty′lar** (-stī′lər) *adj.*

per·i·the·ci·um (pĕr′ə-thē′shē-əm, -sē-əm) *n., pl.* **-cia** (-shē-ə, -sē-ə). *Botany.* A small fruiting body in certain fungi, containing ascospores. [New Latin : PERI- + Greek *thēkion,* diminutive of *thēkē,* a case, chest (see **dhē-¹** in Appendix*).]

per·i·to·ne·um (pĕr′ə-tə-nē′əm) *n., pl.* **-nea** (-nē′ə). Also **per·i·to·nae·um.** The membrane lining the walls of the abdominal cavity and enclosing the viscera. [Late Latin *peritonēum,* from Greek *peritonaion,* neuter of *peritonaios,* stretched across, from *peritonos,* stretched around or over : *peri-,* around + *tenein,* to stretch (see **ten-** in Appendix*).] —**per′i·to·ne′al** *adj.*

per·i·to·ni·tis (pĕr′ə-tə-nī′tĭs) *n.* Inflammation of the peritoneum. [New Latin : PERITON(EUM) + -ITIS.]

pe·rit·ri·cha (pə-rĭt′rĭ-kə) *pl.n. Singular* **peritrich** (pĕr′ə-trĭk′). Bell-shaped or tubular microorganisms of the order Peritrichida, characterized by a wide oral opening surrounded by cilia. [New Latin : PERI- + Greek *thrix* (stem *trikh-*), hair (see **thrix** in Appendix*).] —**pe·rit′ri·chous** (-kəs) *adj.*

per·i·wig (pĕr′ĭ-wĭg′) *n.* A wig or peruke. [Earlier *perwyke,* from Old French *perruque,* PERUKE.]

per·i·win·kle¹ (pĕr′ĭ-wĭng′kəl) *n.* **1.** Any of several small, edible marine snails, especially of the genus *Littorina,* having thick, cone-shaped, whorled shells. **2.** The shell of any of these snails. Also called "winkle." [Middle English *periwinkle* (unattested), probably altered from Old English *pīnewincle* : Latin *pīna,* a mussel, from Greek *pinē,* from Mediterranean + Old English *-wincel,* snail shell (see **weng-** in Appendix*).]

per·i·win·kle² (pĕr′ĭ-wĭng′kəl) *n.* Any of several trailing, evergreen plants of the genus *Vinca;* especially, *V. minor,* having glossy, dark-green leaves and blue flowers. Also called "myrtle," "creeping myrtle." [Variant (influenced by PERIWINKLE, snail) of Middle English *pervenke,* from Old French *pervenche,* from Latin *pervinca,* shortening of *vincapervinca*†.]

per·jure (pûr′jər) *tr.v.* **-jured, -juring, -jures.** To render (oneself) guilty of perjury by deliberately testifying falsely under oath. [Middle English *perjuren,* from Old French *perjurer,* from Latin *perjūrāre* : *per-* (destruction) + *jūrāre,* to swear (see **yewo-¹** in Appendix*).] —**per′jur·er** *n.*

per·ju·ry (pûr′jə-rē) *n., pl.* **-ries. 1.** *Law.* The deliberate, willful giving of false, misleading, or incomplete testimony on a relevant matter, by a witness under oath in a criminal proceeding, whether given in a court or by affidavit. **2.** Any violation of an oath or promise. [Middle English *perjurie,* from Norman French *parjurie,* from Latin *perjūrium,* from *perjūrus,* perjured, from *perjūrāre,* PERJURE.] —**per·ju′ri·ous** (pər-jŏŏr′ē-əs) *adj.* —**per·ju′ri·ous·ly** *adv.*

perk (pûrk) *v.* **perked, perking, perks.** —*intr.* **1.** To stick up or jut out jauntily, as a dog's ears. **2.** To carry oneself in a lively and jaunty manner; rise up spiritedly. **3.** To regain one's animation or good spirits. Followed by *up.* —*tr.* **1.** To raise smartly and quickly. Often used with *up.* **2.** To make vigorous and lively again; cheer. Often used with *up: The good news perked him up.* **3.** To make (oneself) trim and spruce in appearance. Often used with *up.* —*adj.* Perky. [Middle English *perken,* perhaps from Norman French *perquer,* to perch, from *perque,* rod, from Latin *pertica.* See **perch** (roost).]

Per·kin (pûr′kən), Sir **William Henry.** 1838–1907. British chemist: discovered first synthetic dye and synthetic perfume.

Per·kins (pûr′kənz), **Frances.** 1882–1965. American social worker; first woman cabinet member as Secretary of Labor (1933–45).

perk·y (pûr′kē) *adj.* **-ier, -iest.** Cheerful and brisk; animated; jaunty. —**perk′i·ly** *adv.* —**perk′i·ness** *n.*

Per·lis (pûr′lĭs). The smallest (310 square miles) state of Malaysia, in the northwest on the Thai frontier and the Andaman Sea. Population, 109,102. Capital, Kangar.

per·lite (pûr′līt′) *n.* Also **pearl·ite.** A natural volcanic glass similar to obsidian but having distinctive concentric cracks and a relatively high water content. In a fluffy heat-expanded form it is used as a lightweight aggregate in plaster and concrete and in thermal and acoustic insulation. [French, from Old French *perle,* PEARL.] —**per·lit′ic** (pər-lĭt′ĭk) *adj.*

Perm (pĕrm). Formerly **Mo·lo·tov** (môl′ə-tôf′, mō′lə-). A city of the Soviet Union, on the Kama River west of the central Ural Mountains. Population, 764,000.

perm. permanent.

per·ma·frost (pûr′mə-frôst′, -frŏst′) *n.* Permanently frozen subsoil continuous in underlying polar regions and occurring locally in perennially frigid areas. [PERMA(NENT) + FROST.]

Perm·al·loy (pûr′mə-loi′, pûrm′ăl′oi′) *n.* A trademark for any of several alloys of nickel and iron, often with small amounts of other elements, having exceptionally high magnetic permeability. [PERM(EABLE) + ALLOY.]

per·ma·nence (pûr′mə-nəns) *n.* The condition or quality of being permanent.

per·ma·nen·cy (pûr′mə-nən-sē) *n., pl.* **-cies. 1.** Permanence. **2.** Someone or something permanent.

per·ma·nent (pûr′mə-nənt) *adj. Abbr.* **perm. 1.** Fixed and changeless; lasting or meant to last indefinitely. **2.** Not expected to change in status, condition, or place: *permanent address; permanent secretary to the president.* —*n.* **1.** A **permanent wave** *(see).* **2.** A long-lasting hair setting. [Middle English, from Old French, from Latin *permanēns,* present participle of *permanēre,* to remain throughout : *per-,* throughout + *manēre,* to remain (see **men-³** in Appendix*).] —**per′ma·nent·ly** *adv.*

permanent magnet. A material that retains induced magnetic properties after it is removed from a magnetic field.

permanent wave. 1. Artificial waves in the hair produced by applying chemicals to it while wet, winding it on curlers, and drying with heat. **2.** The process used in making these waves. **3.** A preparation used in this process. Compare **cold wave.** Also called "permanent."

per·man·ga·nate (pər-măn′gə-nāt′) *n.* Any of the salts of permanganic acid, all of which are strong oxidizing agents. [PERMANGAN(IC ACID) + -ATE.]

per·man·gan·ic acid (pûr′măn-găn′ĭk). An unstable inorganic acid, $HMnO_4$, existing as a strongly oxidizing, purple aqueous solution. [PER- + MANGANIC.]

per·me·a·bil·i·ty (pûr′mē-ə-bĭl′ə-tē) *n.* **1.** The property or condition of being permeable. **2.** *Physics.* **Magnetic permeability** *(see).* **3.** The rate of diffusion of a pressurized gas through a porous material.

per·me·a·ble (pûr′mē-ə-bəl) *adj.* Capable of being permeated.

[Late Latin *permeābilis,* from Latin *permeāre,* PERMEATE.] —**per′me·a·bly** *adv.*

per·me·ance (pûr′mē-əns) *n.* A measure of the ability of a magnetic circuit to conduct magnetic flux; the reciprocal of **reluctance** *(see).* [From Latin *permeāns,* present participle of *permeāre,* PERMEATE.]

per·me·ate (pûr′mē-āt′) *v.* **-ated, -ating, -ates.** —*tr.* **1.** To spread or flow throughout; pervade. **2.** To pass through the openings or interstices of: *liquid permeating a membrane.* —*intr.* To spread; penetrate; diffuse. [Latin *permeāre* : *per-,* through + *meāre,* to go, pass (see **mei-**[1] in Appendix*).] —**per′me·ant** (pûr′mē-ənt), **per′me·a′tive** *adj.* —**per′me·a′tion** *n.*

Per·mi·an (pûr′mē-ən, pĕr′-) *adj.* Of, belonging to, or designating the geologic time, system of rocks, and sedimentary deposits of the seventh and last period of the Paleozoic era. See **geology.** —*n. Geology.* The Permian period. Preceded by *the.* [After *Perm,* former Russian province, where the rock strata were first identified.]

per mill. Also **per mil.** By the thousand; per thousand. [PER + MILL (thousandth).]

per·mil·lage (pər-mĭl′ĭj) *n.* Rate per thousand.

per·mis·si·ble (pər-mĭs′ə-bəl) *adj.* That can be permitted; allowable. —**per·mis′si·bil′i·ty** *n.* —**per·mis′si·bly** *adv.*

per·mis·sion (pər-mĭsh′ən) *n.* **1.** The act of permitting. **2.** Consent, especially formal consent; leave; authorization. [Middle English, from Old French, from Latin *permissiō,* from *permittere* (past participle *permissus*), PERMIT.]

per·mis·sive (pər-mĭs′ĭv) *adj.* **1.** Granting permission; allowing. **2.** Not forbidden; permitted; allowed. **3.** Lenient; tolerant. **4.** Permitting discretion, as distinct from prescriptive. —**per·mis′sive·ly** *adv.* —**per·mis′sive·ness** *n.*

per·mit (pər-mĭt′) *v.* **-mitted, -mitting, -mits.** —*tr.* **1.** To allow (something); consent to; tolerate. See Usage note below. **2.** To give consent; authorize. **3.** To afford opportunity to. —*intr.* To afford opportunity; allow. —See Synonyms at **allow.** —*n.* (pûr′mĭt, pər-mĭt′). **1.** Permission, especially in written form. **2.** A document or certificate giving permission to do something; license; warrant. [Latin *permittere* : *per-,* through + *mittere,* to let go, send (see **smeit-** in Appendix*).] —**per·mit′ter** *n.*

Usage: *Permit of* is sometimes used for the transitive verb *permit* (to allow, to admit), as in *the wording permits of two interpretations.*

per·mit·tiv·i·ty (pûr′mĭ-tĭv′ə-tē) *n., pl.* **-ies.** *Physics.* The ratio of electric flux density produced by an electric field in a medium to that produced in a vacuum by the same field. Also called "relative permittivity," "dielectric constant." [From PERMIT.]

per·mu·ta·tion (pûr′myōō-tā′shən) *n.* **1.** A complete change; transformation. **2.** The act of altering a given set of objects in a group. **3.** *Mathematics.* An ordered arrangement of all or some of the elements of a set. —**per′mu·ta′tion·al** *adj.*

per·mute (pər-myōōt′) *tr.v.* **-muted, -muting, -mutes.** **1.** To change the order of. **2.** *Mathematics.* To subject to permutation. [Middle English *permuten,* from Old French *permuter,* from Latin *permūtāre* : *per-,* completely + *mūtāre,* to change (see **mei-**[1] in Appendix*).] —**per·mut′a·ble** *adj.*

Per·nam·bu·co (pûr′nəm-bōō′kō). A state in northeastern Brazil, 38,315 square miles in area. Population, 4,136,000. Capital, Recife.

per·ni·cious (pər-nĭsh′əs) *adj.* **1. a.** Tending to cause death or serious injury; deadly. **b.** Causing great harm; destructive; ruinous. **2.** Causing moral injury; evil: *a pernicious philosophy.* [Latin *perniciōsus,* from *perniciēs,* destruction : *per-,* completely + *nex* (stem *nec-*), death, violence (see **nek-**[1] in Appendix*).] —**per·ni′cious·ly** *adv.* —**per·ni′cious·ness** *n.*

pernicious anemia. A severe anemia associated with failure to absorb vitamin B_{12} and characterized by the presence of abnormally large red blood cells, gastrointestinal disturbances, and lesions of the spinal cord.

per·nick·e·ty. Variant of **persnickety.**

Pe·rón (pā-rōn′), **Juan Domingo.** Born 1895. President of Argentina (1946–55).

per·o·ne·al (pĕr′ə-nē′əl) *adj. Anatomy.* Of or pertaining to the fibula or to the outer portion of the leg. [From New Latin *peroneus,* of the fibula, from *perone,* fibula, from Greek *peronē,* "pin, buckle." See **per-**[2] in Appendix.*]

per·o·rate (pĕr′ə-rāt′) *intr.v.* **-rated, -rating, -rates.** **1.** To conclude a speech with a formal recapitulation. **2.** To speak at great length, often in a grandiloquent manner; declaim. [Latin *perōrāre,* to harangue at length : *per-,* thoroughly, to the end + *ōrāre,* to speak (see **ōr-** in Appendix*).] —**per′o·ra′tion** *n.*

per·ox·i·dase (pə-rŏk′sə-dās′, -dāz′) *n.* An enzyme found in most plant cells and some animal cells that catalyzes peroxide oxidation reactions. [PEROXID(E) + -ASE.]

per·ox·ide (pə-rŏk′sīd′) *n.* Also **per·ox·id** (pə-rŏk′sĭd). *Chemistry.* **1. Hydrogen peroxide** *(see).* **2.** Any compound containing oxygen that yields hydrogen peroxide with an acid, such as sodium peroxide, Na_2O_2. —*tr.v.* **peroxided, -iding, -ides.** **1.** To treat with peroxide. **2.** To bleach (hair) with hydrogen peroxide. [PER- + OXIDE.] —**per·ox′ide′** *adj.*

per·pend[1] (pər-pĕnd′) *v.* **-pended, -pending, -pends.** *Archaic.* —*tr.* To wonder about; ponder. —*intr.* To wonder; reflect. [Latin *perpendere,* to consider carefully : *per-,* thoroughly + *pendere,* to consider, weigh (see **spen-** in Appendix*).]

per·pend[2] (pûr′pənd, pär′-) *n.* Also **per·pent** (pûr′pənt, pär′-). *Architecture.* A large stone extending through the thickness of a wall and finished on both ends. [Middle English *perpend,* from Old French *perpain,* perhaps from Vulgar Latin *perpetānus* (unattested), from Latin *perpes,* uninterrupted. See **perpetual.**]

per·pen·dic·u·lar (pûr′pən-dĭk′yə-lər) *adj.* **1.** *Mathematics.* Intersecting at or forming right angles. **2.** At right angles to the horizontal; vertical. **3.** *Often capital* **P.** Designating a style of English Gothic architecture of the 14th and 15th centuries, characterized by emphasis of the vertical element. —See Synonyms at **vertical.** —*n.* **1.** A line or plane perpendicular to a given line or plane. **2.** A perpendicular position. **3.** A device, such as a plumb line, used in marking the vertical from a given point. **4.** A vertical or nearly vertical line or plane. [Middle English *perpendiculer,* from Old French, from Latin *perpendiculārius,* from *perpendiculum,* plumb line : *per-,* thoroughly + *pendēre,* to hang (see **spen-** in Appendix*) + *-culum,* instrumental suffix.] —**per′pen·dic′u·lar′i·ty** (-lăr′ə-tē) *n.*

per·pe·trate (pûr′pə-trāt′) *tr.v.* **-trated, -trating, -trates.** **1.** To be guilty of; commit: *perpetrate a crime.* **2.** To carry out; perform: *perpetrate a practical joke.* [Latin *perpetrāre,* to accomplish : *per-,* completely + *patrāre,* to do, bring about, "perform in the capacity of a father," from *pater,* father (see **pəter** in Appendix*).] —**per′pe·tra′tion** *n.* —**per′pe·tra′tor** (-trā′tər) *n.*

per·pet·u·al (pər-pĕch′ōō-əl) *adj.* **1.** Lasting for eternity: *the perpetual fires of hell.* **2.** Lasting for an indefinitely long duration: *"It was a hard rain, a perpetual rain."* (Ray Bradbury). **3.** Instituted to be in effect or have tenure for an unlimited duration: *a treaty of perpetual friendship. "Joseph Smiggers, esq., Perpetual Vice-President—Member Pickwick Club"* (Dickens). **4.** Ceaselessly repeated or continuing without interruption: *perpetual nagging.* **5.** *Horticulture.* Flowering throughout the growing season. —See Synonyms at **continual.** [Middle English *perpetuel,* from Old French, from Latin *perpetuālis,* from *perpetuus,* continuous, permanent, from *perpes* (stem *perpet-*), throughout, uninterrupted : *per-,* thoroughly + *petere,* to go toward (see **pet-**[1] in Appendix*).] —**per·pet′u·al·ly** *adv.* —**per·pet′u·al·ness** *n.*

perpetual calendar. A chart or mechanical device that indicates the day of the week corresponding to any given date over a period of many years.

perpetual motion. The hypothetical continuous operation of an isolated mechanical device or other closed system without a sustaining energy source.

per·pet·u·ate (pər-pĕch′ōō-āt′) *tr.v.* **-ated, -ating, -ates.** **1.** To make perpetual. **2.** To prolong the existence of; cause to be remembered for a long time: *"Parents perpetuate their lives in their posterity."* (Anne Bradstreet). [Latin *perpetuāre,* from *perpetuus,* PERPETUAL.] —**per·pet′u·a′tion, per·pet′u·ance** *n.* —**per·pet′u·a′tor** (-ā′tər) *n.*

per·pe·tu·i·ty (pûr′pə-tōō′ə-tē, -tyōō′ə-tē) *n., pl.* **-ties.** **1.** The quality, state, or condition of being perpetual: *"The perpetuity of the Church was an article of faith."* (Morris L. West). **2.** Time without end; eternity. **3.** *Law.* **a.** The condition of an estate that is limited so as to be inalienable either perpetually or longer than the period determined by law. **b.** An estate so limited. **4.** *Finance.* An annuity payable indefinitely.

per·plex (pər-plĕks′) *tr.v.* **-plexed, -plexing, -plexes.** **1.** To confuse or puzzle; bewilder. **2.** To make confusedly intricate: *"the complication of narrow streets which perplex that portion of the city"* (Hawthorne). —See Synonyms at **puzzle.** [From obsolete adjective *perplex,* involved, perplexed, from Latin *perplexus,* intricate : *per-,* thoroughly + *plectere* (past participle *plexus*), to weave, entwine (see **plek-** in Appendix*).]

per·plexed (pər-plĕkst′) *adj.* **1.** Puzzled; bewildered; confused. **2.** Complicated; involved. —**per·plex′ed·ly** (pər-plĕk′sĭd-lē) *adv.*

per·plex·i·ty (pər-plĕk′sə-tē) *n., pl.* **-ties.** **1.** The state or condition of being perplexed or puzzled: *"'My father!' he cried, in strange perplexity."* (Emily Brontë). **2.** The state or condition of being intricate or complicated: *"I remain impressed by the perplexity of life in twentieth-century America."* (Daniel J. Boorstin). **3.** Something that perplexes.

per·qui·site (pûr′kwə-zĭt) *n.* **1.** A payment or profit received in addition to a regular wage or salary; especially, a benefit expected as one's due. **2.** A tip; gratuity. **3.** Something claimed as an exclusive right: *"Politics was the perquisite of the upper class."* (Richard B. Sewall). —See Synonyms at **right.** [Middle English, from Medieval Latin *perquīsītum,* acquisition, perquisite, from the past participle of Latin *perquīrere,* to search for : *per-,* thoroughly + *quaerere,* to seek (see **quaerere** in Appendix*).]

Per·rault (pə-rō′, pĕ-), **Charles.** 1628–1703. French poet; author of many of the Mother Goose stories.

Per·rin (pĕ-răN′), **Jean Baptiste.** 1870–1942. French physicist; worked on theory of the discontinuous structure of matter.

per·ry (pĕr′ē) *n., pl.* **-ries.** A fermented beverage, similar to cider, made from pears. [Middle English *pereye,* from Old French *pere,* from Vulgar Latin *pirātum* (unattested), from Latin *pirum,* PEAR.]

Per·ry (pĕr′ē), **Matthew Calbraith.** 1794–1858. American naval officer; opened Japan to American commerce (1853–54); brother of O.H. Perry.

Per·ry (pĕr′ē), **Oliver Hazard.** 1785–1819. American naval officer; victor at Battle of Lake Erie (September 10, 1813).

Pers. Persia; Persian.

per se (sā′, sē′). In or by itself; intrinsically. [Latin *per sē* : *per,* by, PER + *sē* (accusative), self (see **seu-**[2] in Appendix*).]

per·se·cute (pûr′sə-kyōōt′) *tr.v.* **-cuted, -cuting, -cutes.** **1.** To oppress or harass with ill-treatment. **2.** To annoy persistently; bother. [Old French *persecuter,* from Latin *persequī* (past participle *persecūtus*), to pursue : *per-,* throughout, to the end + *sequī,* to follow (see **sekw-**[1] in Appendix*).] —**per′se·cu′tive, per′se·cu·to′ry** (pûr′sə-kyōō-tôr′ē, -tōr′ē, pûr′sə-kyōō′tə-rē) *adj.* —**per′se·cu′tor** (-kyōō′tər) *n.*

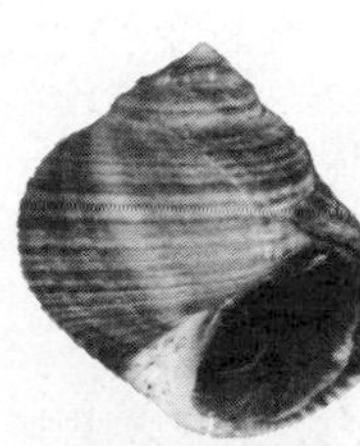

periwinkle[1]
Littorina littorea

periwinkle[2]
Vinca rosea

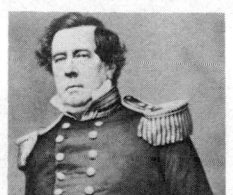

Matthew Calbraith Perry

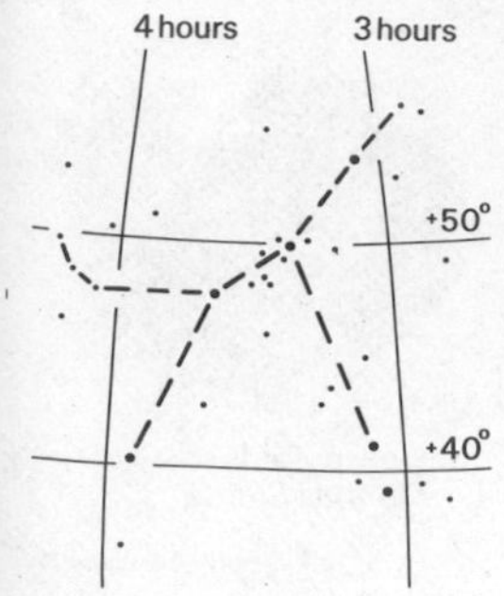

Perseus[2]

per·se·cu·tion (pûr′sə-kyo͞o′shən) *n.* **1.** The act or practice of persecuting. **2.** The state or condition of being persecuted. —**per′se·cu′tion·al** *adj.*

Per·se·id (pûr′sē-ĭd) *n., pl.* **-ids** or **Perseides** (pər-sē′ə-dēz′). *Astronomy.* One of a shower of meteors that appears to originate in the vicinity of the constellation Perseus during the second week of August. [New Latin *Perseïdes,* plural of *Perseis,* daughter of PERSEUS.]

Per·seph·o·ne (pər-sĕf′ə-nē). *Greek Mythology.* The wife of Pluto and queen of the underworld; identified with Proserpina.

Per·sep·o·lis (pər-sĕp′ə-lĭs). A ruined capital of ancient Persia, about 30 miles northeast of Shiraz.

Per·se·us[1] (pûr′sē-əs, -so͞os′). *Greek Mythology.* The son of Zeus and Danae who slew Medusa and rescued Andromeda.

Per·se·us[2] (pûr′sē-əs, -so͞os′). A constellation in the Northern Hemisphere near Andromeda and Auriga.

per·se·ver·ance (pûr′sə-vîr′əns) *n.* **1.** The holding to a course of action, belief, or purpose without giving way; steadfastness: *"Great works are performed, not by strength, but perseverance."* (Samuel Johnson). **2.** *Theology.* The Calvinistic doctrine that those who have been chosen by God will continue in a state of grace to the end and will finally be saved.

Synonyms: *perseverance, persistence, tenacity, steadfastness.* Each of these conveys a sense of endurance in the pursuit of a desired end. *Perseverance,* which is favorable, suggests continuing strength or patience in dealing with something arduous. It particularly implies withstanding difficulty or resistance. *Persistence* is usually but not always unfavorable. It implies dogged resolve in dealing with others and hence often a willful insistence which is unreasonable or annoying: *her suitor's persistence. Tenacity* means tough, aggressive persistence, and accents will power. Whereas *perseverance* and *persistence* largely apply to striving for a goal, *tenacity* basically denotes holding on to something: *his tenacity in defending his position. Steadfastness* is moral in connotation and implies unswerving adherence to principles, usually in the face of opposition.

per·sev·er·a·tion (pər-sĕv′ə-rā′shən) *n. Psychology.* Continued or repetitive activity or actions: **a.** The uncontrollable repetition of a word, phrase, or gesture. **b.** The spontaneous recurrence of a thought, image, phrase, or tune in the mind.

per·se·vere (pûr′sə-vîr′) *intr.v.* **-vered, -vering, -veres.** To persist in or remain constant to a purpose, idea, or task in the face of obstacles or discouragement. [Middle English *perseveren,* from Old French *perseverer,* from Latin *persevērāre,* from *persevērus,* very serious : *per-* (intensifier) + *sevērus,* serious, severe (see **wēros** in Appendix*).] —**per′se·ver′ing·ly** *adv.*

Per·shing (pûr′shĭng), **John Joseph.** Called "Black Jack." 1860–1948. American General of the Armies; commander in chief of the A.E.F. in World War I.

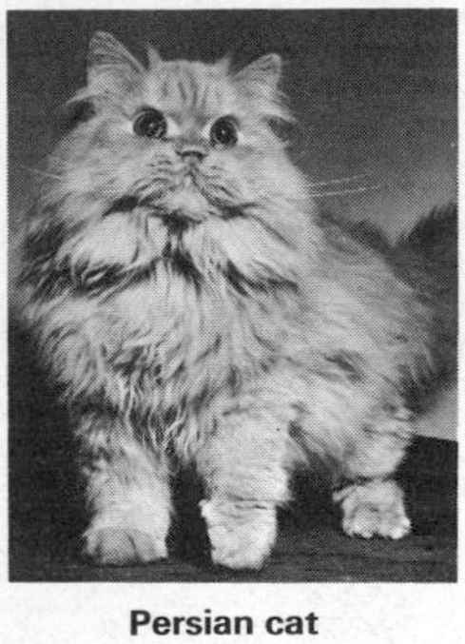

Persian cat

Per·sia (pûr′zhə). *Abbr.* **Pers.** An ancient country in southwestern Asia; officially renamed Iran in 1935.

Per·sian (pûr′zhən) *adj. Abbr.* **Pers.** Of or pertaining to Persia or Iran, its people, language, or culture. —*n.* **1.** A native or inhabitant of ancient Persia or modern Iran. **2.** The Iranian language of the Persians in any of its several historical forms, Old Persian, Avestan, Pahlavi, Middle Persian, and modern Persian.

Persian cat. A type of domestic cat having long silky fur.

Persian Empire. The empire founded by Cyrus the Great (sixth century B.C.), who expanded the small kingdom of Anshan, at the head of the Persian Gulf, from the Mediterranean Sea to the Indus River and from the Caucasus to the Indian Ocean. It was conquered by Alexander the Great (334–331 B.C.).

Persian Gulf. An inlet of the Arabian Sea, 550 miles long, between the Arabian Peninsula and Iran.

Persian lamb. **1.** The lamb of the karakul sheep of Asia. **2.** The glossy, tightly curled fur obtained from such a lamb, usually when it is three or four days old. Compare **broadtail.**

Persian melon. A melon, *Cucumis melo inodorus,* having a light-colored, unridged rind and orange-colored flesh.

Persian walnut. The **English walnut** *(see).*

per·si·flage (pûr′sə-fläzh′) *n.* **1.** Light, bantering style in writing or speaking. **2.** Idle, good-natured banter. [French, from *persifler,* to banter : *per-* (intensive), from Latin + *siffler,* to whistle, hiss, boo, from Vulgar Latin *sīfilāre* (unattested), from Latin *sībilāre* (see **swei-**[1] in Appendix*).]

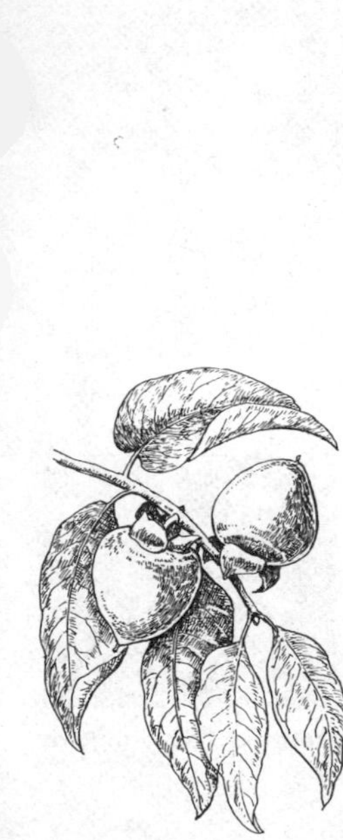

persimmon
Diospyros kaki

per·sim·mon (pər-sĭm′ən) *n.* **1.** Any of various chiefly tropical trees of the genus *Diospyros,* having hard wood and orange-red fruit that is edible only when completely ripe. **2.** The fruit of any of these trees. [Of Algonquian origin; akin to Cree *pasiminan,* dried fruit, Delaware *pasĭmĕnan.*]

Per·sis. The ancient name for **Fars.**

per·sist (pər-sĭst′, -zĭst′) *intr.v.* **-sisted, -sisting, -sists.** **1.** To be obstinately repetitious, insistent, or tenacious in some activity. **2.** To hold firmly and steadfastly to some purpose, state, or undertaking, despite obstacles, warnings, or setbacks: *"that my wife should persist to the very last in this obstinate humour of hers"* (Sterne). **3.** To continue in existence; last: *"The tragic conflict . . . persists through most of the poem."* (Paul Goodman). [Latin *persistere* : *per-* (intensive) + *sistere,* to stand firm (see **stā-** in Appendix*).]

per·sist·ence (pər-sĭs′təns, -zĭs′təns) *n.* Also **per·sis·ten·cy** (-tən-sē). **1.** The act of persisting. **2.** The quality of being persistent; perseverance; tenacity. **3.** The continuance of an effect after the cause is removed: *persistence of vision.* —See Synonyms at **perseverance.**

per·sist·ent (pər-sĭs′tənt, -zĭs′tənt) *adj.* **1.** Refusing to give up or let go; persevering obstinately. **2.** Insistently repetitive or continuous: *a persistent ringing of the phone.* **3.** Enduring: *"Beyond our infatuations, . . . our persistent self"* (George Eliot). **4.** *Botany.* Lasting past maturity without falling off, as certain leaves or flowers. **5.** *Zoology.* Retained permanently, rather than disappearing in an early stage of development: *the persistent gills of fishes.* —**per·sist′ent·ly** *adv.*

per·snick·e·ty (pər-snĭk′ə-tē) *adj.* Also **per·nick·e·ty** (pər-nĭk′ə-tē). *Informal.* **1.** Fastidious; exacting. **2.** Requiring strict attention to detail. [Originally *pernickety,* perhaps whimsical variant of PARTICULAR.] —**per·snick′e·ti·ness** *n.*

per·son (pûr′sən) *n. Abbr.* **per.** **1.** A living human being, especially as distinguished from an animal or thing. **2.** The composite of characteristics that make up an individual personality. **3.** An individual of some specified character: *"My name is George Nathaniel Curzon, / I am a most superior person."* (Anonymous). **4.** The living body of a human being: *"But if government be taken away, the property and persons of men are insecure."* (Macaulay). **5.** Guise; character: *"Well, in her person, I say I will not have you."* (Shakespeare). **6.** Physique and general appearance. **7.** *Law.* A human being or organization with legal rights and duties. **8.** *Theology.* The separate individualities of the Father, Son, and Holy Spirit, as distinguished from the essence of the Godhead that unites them. **9.** *Grammar.* **a.** Any of three groups of pronoun forms with corresponding verb inflections that distinguish between the speaker (first person), the individual addressed (second person), and the individual or thing spoken of (third person). **b.** Any of the different forms or inflections expressing these distinctions. —**in person.** Physically present. [Middle English *persone, person,* from Old French *persone,* from Latin *persōna,* mask (especially one worn by an actor), hence the character played by an actor, probably from Etruscan *phersu,* mask.]

Usage: In constructions involving *person* (meaning *individual*), accompanying pronouns and pronominal adjectives of reference are singular: *If a person has talent, he* (not *they*) *will show it in his* (not *their*) *work.* See Usage note at **people.**

per·so·na (pər-sō′nə, -nä′) *n., pl.* **-nae** (-nē) (for sense 1) or **-nas** (for sense 2). **1.** *Usually plural.* A character in a dramatic or literary work. **2.** *Psychology.* The role that a person assumes in order to display his conscious intentions to himself and to others. [Latin *persōna,* mask, PERSON.]

per·son·a·ble (pûr′sən-ə-bəl) *adj.* Pleasing in appearance or personality; attractive; comely. —**per′son·a·ble·ness** *n.*

per·son·age (pûr′sən-ĭj) *n.* **1.** A character in a literary work. **2. a.** A person. **b.** A person of distinction. [Middle English, from Old French, from *persone,* PERSON.]

per·so·na gra·ta (pər-sō′nə grä′tə, grăt′ə) *pl.* **personae gratae** (pər-sō′nē grä′tē, grăt′ē) or **persona grata.** A person who is acceptable; especially, a diplomat who is fully acceptable to a foreign government. [Latin, "an acceptable person."]

per·son·al (pûr′sən-əl) *adj.* **1.** Of or pertaining to a particular person; private; one's own: *personal affairs.* **2. a.** Done, made, or performed in person: *a personal appearance.* **b.** Done to or for or directed toward a particular person: *a personal favor.* **3.** Concerning a particular individual and his intimate affairs, interests, or activities; intimate: *I have something personal to tell you.* **4. a.** Aimed pointedly at the most intimate aspects of a person, especially in a critical or hostile manner: *an uncalled-for, highly personal remark.* **b.** Tending to make remarks, or be unduly questioning, about another's affairs: *He always becomes personal in an argument.* **5.** Of or pertaining to the body or physical being: *personal cleanliness.* **6.** Pertaining to or having the nature of a person or self-conscious being: *a personal God.* **7.** *Law.* Pertaining to a person's movable property: *personal effects.* Compare **real.** **8.** *Grammar.* Indicating grammatical person. —*n.* A personal item or notice in a newspaper.

personal equation. The characteristics of a person as they tend to cause variation in observation, judgment, and reasoning.

per·son·al·ism (pûr′sən-əl-ĭz′əm) *n.* **1.** The quality of being characterized by purely personal modes of expression or behavior; idiosyncrasy. **2.** *Philosophy.* **a.** Any of various trends of subjective idealism regarding personality as the key to the interpretation of reality. **b.** A doctrine formulated during the 1930's by Emmanuel Mounier as a synthesis of Christianity and socialism. —**per′son·al·ist** *n.* & *adj.* —**per′son·al·is′tic** *adj.*

per·son·al·i·ty (pûr′sən-ăl′ə-tē) *n., pl.* **-ties.** **1.** The state or quality of being a person. **2. a.** The dynamic character, self, or psyche that constitutes and animates the individual person and makes his experience of life unique. **b.** A person as the embodiment of distinctive traits of mind and behavior. **3.** The pattern of collective character, behavioral, temperamental, emotional, and mental traits of an individual. **4.** Distinctive qualities of an individual; especially, those distinguishing personal characteristics that make one socially appealing: *"It's not what you say, it's how you say it—because personality always wins the day."* (Arthur Miller). **5.** A person of prominence or notoriety: *personalities in the news.* See Usage note below. **6.** The characteristics of a place or situation that give it a distinctive character. —See Synonyms at **disposition.** [Middle English *personalite,* from Old French, from Late Latin *persōnālitās,* from Latin *persōnālis,* personal, from *persōna,* PERSON.]

Usage: *Personality,* for *celebrity* or *notable (a television personality),* is widely used in speech and journalism. In more formal writing, however, it is considered acceptable by only 43 per cent of the Usage Panel.

per·son·al·ize (pûr′sən-əl-īz′) *tr.v.* **-ized, -izing, -izes.** **1.** To take (a remark or characterization) personally. **2.** To personify. **3.** To have printed, engraved, or monogrammed with one's name or initials: *personalized stationery.*

per·son·al·ly (pûr′sən-əl-ē) *adv.* **1.** In person; without the intervention of another: *I thanked him personally.* **2.** As far as oneself is concerned: *Personally, I don't mind going to the theater.* **3.** As a person: *I admire his skill but dislike him personally.* **4.** In a personal manner: *Don't take his disparaging remarks personally.*

personal pronoun. A pronoun denoting speaker, person spoken to, or person or thing spoken about. The personal pronouns in the subject form in current English are: *I, we, you, he, she, it, they.*

personal property. *Law.* Temporary or movable property as distinguished from real property.

per·son·al·ty (pûr′sən-əl-tē) *n., pl.* **-ties.** *Law.* Personal property; chattels. [Norman French *personalte,* from Late Latin *persōnālitās,* PERSONALITY.]

per·so·na non gra·ta (pər-sō′nə nŏn grä′tə, grăt′ə) *pl.* **personae non gratae** (pər-sō′nē nŏn grä′tē, grăt′ē) or **persona non grata.** *Abbr.* **p.n.g.** A person who is not acceptable or welcome; especially, a diplomat who is not fully acceptable to a foreign government. [Latin, "unacceptable person."]

per·son·ate[1] (pûr′sən-āt′) *tr.v.* **-ated, -ating, -ates. 1.** To impersonate (a character); play the role or portray the part of. **2.** To endow with personal qualities; personify. **3.** *Law.* To assume the identity of with intent to deceive. [From PERSON.] **—per′son·a′tion** *n.* **—per′son·a′tive** *adj.* **—per′son·a′tor** (-ā′tər) *n.*

per·son·ate[2] (pûr′sən-ĭt) *adj. Botany.* Two-lipped, with the base closed by a prominent palate. Said of a corolla. [Latin *persōnātus,* masked, from *persōna,* mask, PERSON.]

per·son·i·fi·ca·tion (pər-sŏn′ə-fĭ-kā′shən) *n.* **1.** The act of personifying or something that personifies. **2.** A rhetorical figure of speech in which inanimate objects or abstractions are endowed with human qualities or are represented as possessing human form, as in *Hunger sat shivering on the road* or *Flowers danced about the lawn.* **3.** The artistic representation of an abstract quality or idea as a person. **4.** A person or thing typifying a certain quality or idea that is outstanding; an embodiment; exemplification: *"He's invisible, a walking personification of the Negative."* (Ralph Ellison).

per·son·i·fy (pər-sŏn′ə-fī′) *tr.v.* **-fied, -fying, -fies. 1.** To think of or represent (an inanimate object or abstraction) as having personality or the qualities, thoughts, or movements of a living being. **2.** To represent (an object or abstraction) by a human figure. **3.** To represent (an abstract quality or idea): *This character personifies evil.* **4.** To be the embodiment or perfect example of: *"Stalin now personified bolshevism in the eyes of the world."* (A.J.P. Taylor). [French *personnifier,* from *personne,* person, from Old French *persone,* PERSON.] **—per·son′i·fi′er** *n.*

per·son·nel (pûr′sən-ĕl′) *n.* **1.** The body of persons employed by or active in an organization, business, or service. **2.** An administrative division of an organization concerned with this body of persons. [French, from Old French *personal,* personal, from Late Latin *persōnālis,* from Latin *persōna,* mask, PERSON.]

Usage: *Personnel* may take either a singular or plural verb. When it is construed as a unit, use a singular verb; when as a collection of individuals, a plural verb. But the term should not be applied to specific members, as in *six personnel of the armed forces testified.*

per·spec·tive (pər-spĕk′tĭv) *n.* **1.** Any of various techniques for representing three-dimensional objects and depth relationships on a two-dimensional surface. *Linear perspective* renders depth by using actual or suggested lines that intersect in the background to delimit relative size from background to foreground. *Aerial* or *atmospheric perspective* renders depth by changes of form, size, tone, and color with recession of objects from the picture plane. **2.** Any picture in perspective. **3.** A view or vista. **4.** The appearance of objects in depth as perceived by normal binocular vision. **5.** The relationship of aspects of a subject to each other and to a whole: *a perspective of history.* **6.** Subjective evaluation of relative significance; point of view. [Middle English, from Medieval Latin *perspectiva,* optics, from Late Latin *perspectīvus,* of a view, from Latin *perspicere* (past participle *perspectus*), to see through or into, inspect : *per-* (intensive) + *specere,* to look (see **spek-** in Appendix*).] **—per·spec′tive** *adj.* **—per·spec′tive·ly** *adv.*

per·spi·ca·cious (pûr′spĭ-kā′shəs) *adj.* Acutely discerning, perceptive, or understanding. [From Latin *perspicāx,* clear-sighted, from *perspicere,* to see through. See **perspective.**] **—per′spi·ca′cious·ly** *adv.* **—per′spi·ca′cious·ness** *n.*

per·spi·cac·i·ty (pûr′spĭ-kăs′ə-tē) *n.* Acuteness of perception, discernment, or understanding: *"It was a marvellous effort of perspicacity to discover I did not love her."* (Emily Brontë).

per·spi·cu·i·ty (pûr′spĭ-kyōō′ə-tē) *n.* **1.** The quality of being perspicuous: *"He was at pains to insist on the perspicuity of what he wrote."* (Lionel Trilling). **2.** Perspicacity.

per·spic·u·ous (pər-spĭk′yōō-əs) *adj.* Clearly expressed or presented; easy to understand; lucid. [Latin *perspicuus,* from *perspicere,* to see through. See **perspective.**] **—per·spic′u·ous·ly** *adv.* **—per·spic′u·ous·ness** *n.*

per·spi·ra·tion (pûr′spə-rā′shən) *n.* **1.** The saline moisture excreted through the pores of the skin by the sweat glands; sweat. **2.** The act or process of perspiring. **—per·spir′a·to′ry** (pər-spīr′ə-tôr′ē, -tōr′ē, pûr′spə-rə-) *adj.*

per·spire (pər-spīr′) *v.* **-spired, -spiring, -spires.** *—intr.* To excrete perspiration through the pores of the skin. *—tr.* To expel through external pores; exude. [French *perspirer,* from Old French, from Latin *perspīrāre,* breathe through : *per-,* through + *spīrāre,* to blow, breathe (see **spirāre** in Appendix*).]

per·suade (pər-swād′) *tr.v.* **-suaded, -suading, -suades. 1. a.** To cause (someone) to do something by means of argument, reasoning, or entreaty. **b.** To win over (someone) to a course of action by reasoning or inducement. Often used with *into: "Catherine would not be persuaded into tranquillity."* (Emily Brontë). **2.** To make (someone) believe something; convince: *"to make children fit to live in a society by persuading them to learn and accept its codes"* (Alan W. Watts). See Usage note at **convince.** [Latin *persuādēre* : *per-* (intensive) + *suādēre,* to persuade, urge (see **swād-** in Appendix*).] **—per·suad′a·ble** *adj.* **—per·suad′er** *n.*

Synonyms: *persuade, induce, prevail on, convince.* Frequently interchangeable, these are compared as they relate to influencing successfully another's thinking toward a decision or in a direction in accord with one's own will. *Persuade* means to resolve, change, or form another's feelings or opinion, in any effective but reputable manner. One can be persuaded by reasoning, by personal forcefulness, or even impersonally by circumstances or an event. *Induce* implies a more significant but subtle—if not deceptive—form of persuasion, often by promise of reward, where the focus is on the success of the effort: *If I could only induce you to stay.* To *prevail on* (or *upon*) suggests persuasion which is an imposition. One *prevails on* somebody who resists or who is indifferent, so that a reluctant submission rather than genuine agreement is often implied. *Convince* means to persuade one decisively of a truth or necessity.

per·sua·si·ble (pər-swā′zə-bəl, -sə-bəl) *adj.* That can be persuaded; persuadable. **—per·sua′si·bil′i·ty, per·sua′si·ble·ness** *n.*

per·sua·sion (pər-swā′zhən) *n.* **1.** The act of persuading or the state of being persuaded: *"The persuasion of a democracy to big changes is at best a slow process."* (Harold J. Laski). **2.** The ability or power to persuade. **3.** A strong conviction or belief. **4.** A body of religious beliefs; religion: *worshipers of various persuasions.* **5.** A faction; sect; party. —See Synonyms at **opinion.** [Latin *persuāsiō,* from *persuādēre,* to PERSUADE.]

per·sua·sive (pər-swā′sĭv, -zĭv) *adj.* Tending or having the power to persuade: *a persuasive argument.* **—per·sua′sive·ly** *adv.* **—per·sua′sive·ness** *n.*

pert (pûrt) *adj.* **perter, pertest. 1.** Impudently bold; saucy. **2.** High-spirited; vivacious: *a pert old lady.* **3.** Jaunty: *a pert little hat.* [Middle English, short for Old French *apert,* straightforward, open, from Latin *aperire* (past participle *apertus*), to open. See **wer-**[5] in Appendix.*] **—pert′ly** *adv.* **—pert′ness** *n.*

pert. pertaining.

per·tain (pər-tān′) *intr.v.* **-tained, -taining, -tains. 1.** To have reference; relate: *evidence pertaining to the accident.* **2.** To belong as an adjunct or accessory: *the farm and all the lands which pertain to it.* **3.** To be fitting or suitable. [Middle English *partenen,* from Old French *partenir,* from Latin *pertinēre,* to relate to, to reach to : *per-,* to, thoroughly + *tenēre,* to hold (see **ten-** in Appendix*).]

Perth (pûrth). **1.** The capital of Western Australia, on the Swan River. Population, 465,000. **2. a.** Also **Perth·shire** (pûrth′shîr′, -shər). A county in central Scotland. Population, 127,000. **b.** The capital of this county. Population, 26,000.

per·ti·na·cious (pûr′tə-nā′shəs) *adj.* **1.** Holding firmly or tenaciously to some purpose, belief, or opinion. **2.** Stubbornly or perversely persistent. —See Synonyms at **obstinate.** [From Latin *pertināx* : *per-,* thoroughly, completely + *tenāx,* tenacious, from *tenēre,* to hold (see **ten-** in Appendix*).] **—per′ti·na′cious·ly** *adv.* **—per′ti·na′cious·ness** *n.*

per·ti·nac·i·ty (pûr′tə-năs′ə-tē) *n.* The quality or state of being pertinacious.

per·ti·nent (pûr′tə-nənt) *adj.* Of, relating to, or connected with a specific matter; apposite: *a pertinent fact.* See Synonyms at **relevant.** [Middle English, from Old French, from Latin *pertinēns,* present participle of *pertinēre,* to reach, concern, belong, PERTAIN.] **—per′ti·nence, per′ti·nen·cy** *n.* **—per′ti·nent·ly** *adv.*

per·turb (pər-tûrb′) *tr.v.* **-turbed, -turbing, -turbs. 1.** To disturb greatly; make uneasy or anxious; upset. **2.** To throw into great confusion. **3.** *Physics.* To cause perturbation, as of an electronic or celestial orbit. [Middle English *perturben,* from Old French *perturber,* from Latin *perturbāre* : *per-* (intensifier), thoroughly + *turbāre,* to throw into disorder, from *turba,* confusion, probably from Greek *turbē,* disorder (see **twer-**[1] in Appendix*).]

per·tur·ba·tion (pûr′tər-bā′shən) *n.* **1. a.** The act of perturbing. **b.** The state or condition of being perturbed; agitation. **2.** Variation in a designated orbit, as of an electron or planet, resulting from the influence of one or more external bodies.

per·tus·sis (pər-tŭs′ĭs) *n.* A disease, **whooping cough** *(see).* [New Latin : Latin *per-* (intensive) + *tussis,* a cough, TUSSIS.] **—per·tus′sal** *adj.*

Pe·ru (pə-rōō′). A republic in western South America, 482,257 square miles in area, with a coastline on the Pacific. Population, 10,365,000. Capital, Lima.

Pe·ru·gia (pā-rōō′jä). A city in central Italy, 85 miles north of Rome. Population, 119,000.

Pe·ru·gia, Lake of. See Lake **Trasimeno.**

Pe·ru·gi·no, Il (pā′rōō-jē′nō). Original name, Pietro Vannucci. 1446–1523. Italian painter; master of Raphael.

pe·ruke (pə-rōōk′) *n.* A wig, especially one worn by men in the 17th and 18th centuries; periwig. [French *perruque,* from Italian *parrucca, perrucca*†, head of hair, wig.]

pe·rus·al (pə-rōō′zəl) *n.* The action of perusing: *"Her natural good sense was improved by the perusal of the best books."* (Gibbon).

pe·ruse (pə-rōōz′) *tr.v.* **-rused, -rusing, -ruses.** To read or examine, especially with great care. [Middle English *perusen,* to use up : Latin *per-,* completely, thoroughly + Middle English *usen,* to USE.] **—pe·rus′a·ble** *adj.* **—pe·rus′er** *n.*

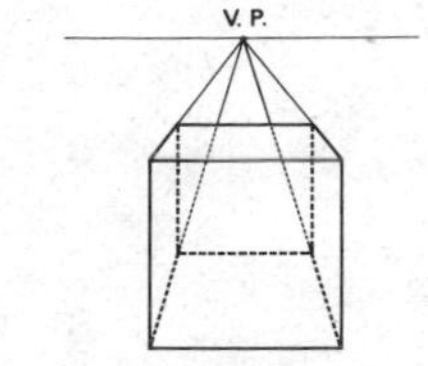

perspective referred to one vanishing point (V.P.)

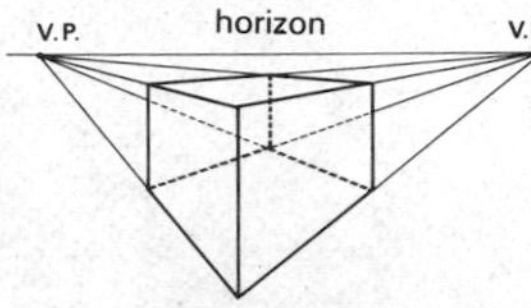

perspective referred to two vanishing points (V.P.)

perspective
Two representations of the same cube

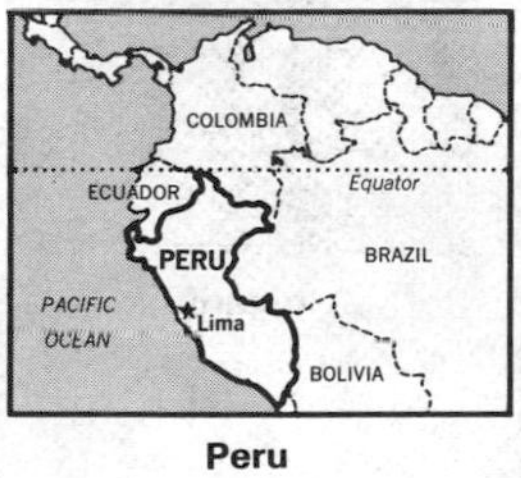

Peru

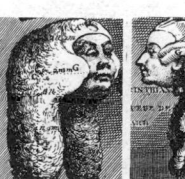

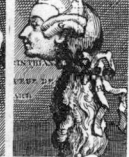

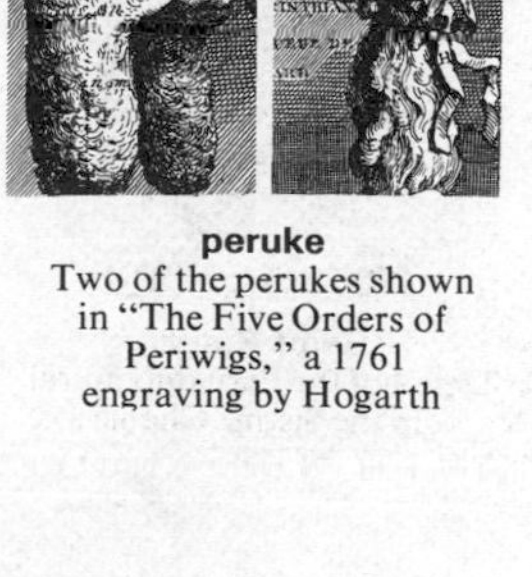
peruke
Two of the perukes shown in "The Five Orders of Periwigs," a 1761 engraving by Hogarth

Per·utz (pĕr′əts), **Max Ferdinand.** Born 1914. Austrian-born British biochemist; worked on the structure of hemoglobin.

Pe·ru·vi·an (pə-ro͞o′vē-ən) *adj.* Of or pertaining to Peru, its inhabitants, or their culture. —*n.* A native or inhabitant of Peru.

Peruvian bark. A medicinal bark, **cinchona** *(see).*

Pe·ruz·zi (pā-ro͞ot′tsē), **Baldassare.** 1481–1536. Italian architect and painter

per·vade (pər-vād′) *tr.v.* **-vaded, -vading, -vades.** To spread through; be present throughout; permeate: *"A marvellous stillness pervaded the world."* (Conrad). [Latin *pervādere* : *per-*, through + *vādere*, to go (see **wādh-** in Appendix*).] —**per·vad′er** *n.* —**per·va′sion** (pər-vā′zhən) *n.*

per·va·sive (pər-vā′sĭv, -zĭv) *adj.* Having the quality or tendency to pervade or permeate. [From Latin *pervāsus*, past participle of *pervādere*, to PERVADE.] —**per·va′sive·ly** *adv.* —**per·va′sive·ness** *n.*

per·verse (pər-vûrs′) *adj.* **1.** Directed away from what is right or good; perverted. **2.** Obstinately persisting in an error or fault; wrongly self-willed or stubborn. **3. a.** Marked by a disposition to oppose and contradict. **b.** Characterized by or arising from such a disposition. **4.** Cranky; peevish. —See Synonyms at **contrary.** [Middle English *pervers*, from Old French, from Latin *pervertere* (past participle *perversus*), to PERVERT.] —**per·verse′ly** *adv.* —**per·verse′ness** *n.*

per·ver·sion (pər-vûr′zhən, -shən) *n.* **1.** The act of perverting or the state of being perverted. **2.** A sexual practice or act considered deviant. —**per·ver′sive** (pər-vûr′sĭv, -zĭv) *adj.*

per·ver·si·ty (pər-vûr′sə-tē) *n., pl.* **-ties. 1.** The quality or state of being perverse. **2.** An instance of being perverse.

per·vert (pər-vûrt′) *tr.v.* **-verted, -verting, -verts. 1.** To cause to turn from what is considered morally right; corrupt: *"We forbid bad men to pervert society."* (John Stuart Mill). **2.** To bring to a worse condition; debase; vitiate: *"Luxury . . . while she polishes perverts the taste."* (Cowper). **3.** To employ wrongly or incorrectly; misuse. **4.** To interpret incorrectly; misconstrue. —*n.* (pûr′vûrt′). One who practices sexual perversion. [Middle English *perverten*, from Old French *pervertir*, from Latin *pervertere*, to turn the wrong way, turn around : *per-*, completely + *vertere*, to turn (see **wer-**[3] in Appendix*).] —**per·vert′er** *n.* —**per·vert′i·ble** *adj.*

per·vert·ed (pər-vûr′tĭd) *adj.* **1.** Deviating greatly from what is considered right and correct: *a perverted idea of justice.* **2.** Of, pertaining to, or practicing sexual perversion. **3.** Misinterpreted; misconstrued: *a perverted translation of an epic poem.* —**per·vert′ed·ly** *adv.*

per·vi·ous (pûr′vē-əs) *adj.* **1.** Open to passage or entrance; permeable. **2.** Open to arguments, ideas, or change. [Latin *pervius* : *per-*, through + *via*, way, road (see **wei-**[2] in Appendix*).] —**per′vi·ous·ly** *adv.* —**per′vi·ous·ness** *n.*

pes (pās) *n., pl.* **pedes** (pĕd′ās′). *Biology.* A foot or footlike part; especially, the foot of a four-footed vertebrate. [New Latin, from Latin *pēs*, foot. See **ped-**[1] in Appendix.*]

Pe·sach (pā′säкн′) *n.* Also **Pe·sah. Passover** *(see).* [Hebrew *pesaḥ*, a passing over, from *pāsaḥ*, to pass over.]

pe·sade (pə-säd′, -zäd′) *n. Horsemanship.* The act or position of a horse when rearing on its hind legs with its forelegs in the air. [French, variant of obsolete *posade*, from Old French, from Old Italian *posata*, "a pause," from *posare*, to pause, from Late Latin *pausāre*, from Latin *pausa*, PAUSE.]

Pes·ca·do·res (pĕs′kə-dôr′ēz, -dôr′ĭs). *Chinese* **Peng·hu** (pŭng′-ho͞o′). A group of islands in Formosa Strait between Taiwan and the Chinese mainland. Population, 80,000.

Pe·sca·ra (pā-skä′rä). An industrial seaport in southeastern Italy, on the Adriatic Sea. Population, 100,000.

pe·se·ta (pə-sā′tə; *Spanish* pĕ-sĕ′tä) *n. Abbr.* **p., pta. 1.** The basic monetary unit of Spain, equal to 100 centimos. See table of exchange rates at **currency. 2.** A coin worth one peseta. [Spanish, diminutive of PESO.]

pe·se·wa (pā-sā′wä) *n., pl.* **pesewa** or **pesewas.** A monetary unit equal to 1/100 of the cedi of Ghana. See table of exchange rates at **currency.**

Pe·sha·war (pə-shä′wər). A city, nine miles southeast of the entrance to the Khyber Pass, in northern West Pakistan. Population, 219,000.

pes·ky (pĕs′kē) *adj.* **-kier, -kiest.** *Informal.* Troublesome; annoying: *a pesky mosquito.* [Probably irregularly from PEST.] —**pes′ki·ly** *adv.* —**pes′ki·ness** *n.*

pe·so (pā′sō) *n., pl.* **-sos.** *Abbr.* **p. 1. a.** The basic monetary unit of Argentina, Bolivia, Colombia, Cuba, the Dominican Republic, Mexico, and the Republic of the Philippines, equal to 100 centavos. **b.** The basic monetary unit of Uruguay, equal to 100 centesimos. See table of exchange rates at **currency. 2.** A coin or note worth one peso. [Spanish, "weight," from Latin *pēnsum*, from *pendere* (past participle *pēnsus*), to weigh. See **spen-** in Appendix.*]

pes·sa·ry (pĕs′ə-rē) *n., pl.* **-ries.** *Medicine.* **1.** Any of various contraceptive or supportive devices placed and worn in the vagina. **2.** A medicated vaginal suppository. [Middle English *pessarie*, from Medieval Latin *pessārium*, from Late Latin *pessum*, *pessus*, from Greek *pessos*, pessary, oval stone for games, possibly from Aramaic *pīsā*, *pissā*, a stone, tablet.]

pes·si·mism (pĕs′ə-mĭz′əm) *n.* **1.** A tendency to take the gloomiest possible view of a situation. **2.** The doctrine or belief that this is the worst of all possible worlds and that all things ultimately tend toward evil. **3.** The doctrine or belief that the evil in the world outweighs the good. [French *pessimisme*, from Latin *pessimus*, worst. See **ped-**[1] in Appendix.*] —**pes′si·mist** *n.* —**pes′si·mis′tic** *adj.* —**pes′si·mis′ti·cal·ly** *adv.*

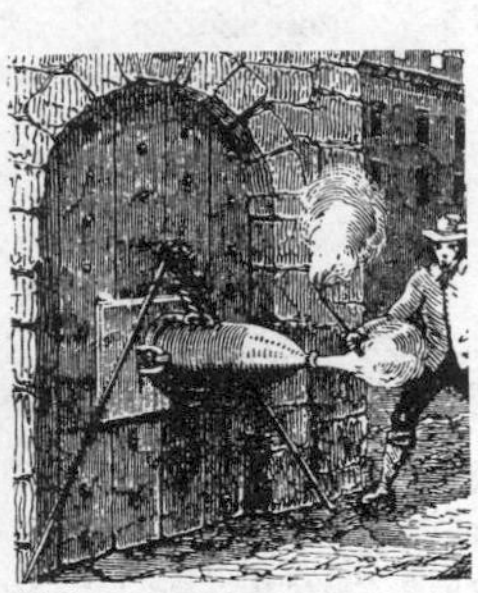

petard

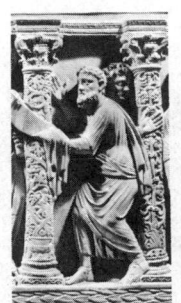

Saint Peter
Detail of the Perugino mural in the Sistine Chapel

pest (pĕst) *n.* **1.** An annoying person or thing; nuisance. **2.** An injurious plant or animal, especially one harmful to man. **3.** *Rare.* A pestilence. [French *peste*, from Latin *pestis*†.]

pes·ter (pĕs′tər) *tr.v.* **-tered, -tering, -ters.** To harass with petty annoyances; bother. See Synonyms at **harass.** [Probably from Old French *empestrer*, to tie up (an animal), impede, from Vulgar Latin *impastōriāre* (unattested) : *in*, on, in + *pastōria* (unattested), the tying up of an animal, from Late Latin *pāstūra*, PASTURE.] —**pes′ter·er** *n.*

pest house. Formerly, a hospital for patients suffering from plague or other infectious disease.

pes·ti·cide (pĕs′tə-sīd′) *n.* Any chemical that is used to kill pests, especially insects and rodents. [From PEST + -CIDE.]

pes·tif·er·ous (pĕs-tĭf′ər-əs) *adj.* **1.** Producing or breeding infectious disease. **2.** Infected with or contaminated by an epidemic disease. **3.** Morally evil or deadly; pernicious. **4.** *Informal.* Bothersome; annoying. [Middle English, from Latin *pestiferus* : *pestis*, PEST + -FEROUS.] —**pes·tif′er·ous·ly** *adv.*

pes·ti·lence (pĕs′tə-ləns) *n.* **1.** Any usually fatal epidemic disease, especially bubonic plague. **2.** An epidemic of such a disease. **3.** A pernicious, evil influence or agent.

pes·ti·lent (pĕs′tə-lənt) *adj.* Also **pes·ti·len·tial** (pĕs′tə-lĕn′shəl). **1.** Tending to cause death; deadly; fatal. **2.** Likely to cause an epidemic disease. **3.** Infected or contaminated with a contagious disease. **4.** Morally, socially, or politically noxious: *"a pestilent fellow, and a mover of sedition among all the Jews throughout the world"* (Acts 24:5). [Middle English, from Latin *pestilēns*, from *pestis*, plague, PEST.]

pes·tle (pĕs′əl, pĕs′təl) *n.* **1.** A club-shaped hand tool for grinding or mashing substances in a mortar. **2.** A large bar moved vertically to stamp or pound, as in a press or mill. —*v.* **pestled, -tling, -tles.** —*tr.* To pound, grind, or mash with a pestle. —*intr.* To use a pestle. [Middle English *pestel*, from Old French, from Latin *pistillum*. See **peis-**[1] in Appendix.*]

pet[1] (pĕt) *n.* **1.** An animal kept for amusement or companionship. **2.** Any object of the affections. **3.** A person especially loved or indulged; a favorite: *teacher's pet.* —*adj.* **1.** Kept as a pet: *a pet cat.* **2.** Especially cherished or indulged; favorite: *a pet daughter; a pet aversion.* —*v.* **petted, petting, pets.** —*tr.* To stroke or caress gently; pat. —*intr. Informal.* To make love by fondling and caressing. [Origin uncertain.] —**pet′ter** *n.*

pet[2] (pĕt) *n.* A fit of bad temper or pique. —*intr.v.* **petted, petting, pets.** To be sulky and peevish. [Origin uncertain.]

pet. petroleum.

Pé·tain (pā-tăɴ′), **Henri Philippe.** 1856–1951. Marshal of France and premier of unoccupied (Vichy) France (1940–44).

pet·al (pĕt′l) *n. Botany.* A separate, often brightly colored segment of a corolla. Compare **sepal.** [New Latin *petalum*, from Greek *petalon*, leaf. See **pet-**[2] in Appendix.*] —**pet′aled, pet′alled** *adj.*

-petal. Indicates a moving toward or seeking; for example, **centripetal.** [From New Latin *-petus*, from Latin *petere*, to seek. See **pet-**[1] in Appendix.*]

pet·al·if·er·ous (pĕt′l-ĭf′ər-əs) *adj.* Bearing petals. [From PETAL + -FEROUS.]

pet·al·ine (pĕt′l-ĭn, -īn′) *adj.* Of or resembling a petal.

pet·al·oid (pĕt′l-oid′) *adj.* Resembling a petal; petallike.

pet·al·ous (pĕt′l-əs) *adj.* Having petals; petaled.

pe·tard (pĭ-tärd′) *n.* **1.** A small bell-shaped bomb used to breach a gate or wall. **2.** A firecracker. —**hoist with one's own petard.** Injured by one's own cleverness. [French *pétard*, from *péter*, to break wind, from *pet*, a fart, from Latin *pēditum*, from *pēdere*, to break wind. See **pezd-** in Appendix.*]

pet·cock (pĕt′kŏk′) *n.* Also **pet cock.** A small valve or faucet used to drain or reduce pressure from pipes, radiators, and boilers. [Perhaps PET(TY) + COCK.]

pe·te·chi·a (pə-tē′kē-ə, -tĕk′ē-ə) *n., pl.* **-chiae** (-kē-ē′). A small spot on a body surface, such as the skin or mucous membrane, caused by a minute hemorrhage and often seen in typhus. [New Latin, from Italian *petecchia*†, skin spot.] —**pe·te′chi·al** *adj.* —**pe·te′chi·ate** (-ĭt) *adj.*

pe·ter (pē′tər) *intr.v.* **-tered, -tering, -ters. 1.** To diminish gradually. Usually used with *out.* **2.** To become exhausted. Used with *out: all petered out.* [U.S. mining slang, *peter*†.]

Pe·ter[1] (pē′tər). A masculine given name. [Middle English, from Latin *Petrus*, from Greek *Petros*, St. PETER.]

Pe·ter[2] (pē′tər). Either of the two books of the New Testament attributed to Saint Peter.

Pe·ter I (pē′tər). Called "Peter the Great." 1672–1725. Czar of Russia (1682–1725); established capital at St. Petersburg.

Pe·ter (pē′tər), **Saint.** Original name, Simon. Called "Simon Peter." Died A.D. 67? The chief of the Apostles; traditionally regarded as first bishop of Rome. [Greek *petros*, stone, rock, translation of Aramaic *Kēphā*, symbolic name conferred upon the Apostle by Christ: *"thou art Peter, and upon this rock I will build my church"* (Matthew 16:18). See **petra** in Appendix.*]

Pe·ters·burg (pē′tərz-bûrg′). A city in southeastern Virginia, on the Appomattox River, 23 miles south of Richmond; scene of Civil War battles (1864–65). Population, 37,000.

Peter's pence. Also **Peter pence. 1.** A tax of one penny per household paid in medieval England to the Papal See. **2.** An annual voluntary contribution made by Roman Catholics toward the expenses of the Holy See. Also called "hearth money," "Peter's penny," "Peter penny." [From St. PETER, as symbolizing the papacy.]

Peter the Hermit. Called "Peter of Amiens." 1050?–1115? French monk; preacher of the first Crusade.

pet·i·o·lar (pĕt′ē-ō′lər) *adj. Biology.* Of, pertaining to, or growing on a petiole.

ă pat/ā pay/âr care/ä father/b bib/ch church/d deed/ĕ pet/ē be/f fife/g gag/h hat/hw which/ĭ pit/ī pie/îr pier/j judge/k kick/l lid, needle/m mum/n no, sudden/ng thing/ŏ pot/ō toe/ô paw, for/oi noise/ou out/o͝o took/o͞o boot/p pop/r roar/s sauce/sh ship, dish/

pet·i·o·late (pĕt′ē-ə-lāt′, pĕt′ē-ō′lĭt) *adj. Biology.* Having a petiole.

pet·i·ole (pĕt′ē-ōl′) *n.* **1.** *Botany.* The stalk by which a leaf is attached to a stem; a leafstalk. **2.** *Zoology.* The slender, stalklike connection between the thorax and abdomen in certain insects. [New Latin *petiolus,* from Late Latin *petiolus, peciolus,* small foot, fruit stalk, irregularly from Latin *pediculus,* diminutive of *pēs* (stem *ped-*), foot. See **ped-**[1] in Appendix.*]

pet·i·o·lule (pĕt′ē-ō-lo͞ol′, pĕt′ē-ŏl′yo͞ol) *n. Botany.* The stalk of a leaflet in a compound leaf. [New Latin *petiolulus,* diminutive of *petiolus,* PETIOLE.]

pet·it (pĕt′ē) *adj.* Also **pet·ty.** *Law.* Lesser; minor. [Middle English, from Old French *petit*†, "small," possibly from Gallo-Roman (unattested) *pittitto-* (expressive).]

pe·tit bour·geois (pĕt′ē bo͝or-zhwä′; *French* pə-tē′ bo͝or-zhwä′). Also **pet·ty bour·geois.** A member of the petty bourgeoisie. —**pe′tit-bour′geois** *adj.*

pe·tite (pə-tēt′) *adj.* Small, slender, and trim. Said of a girl or woman. See Synonyms at **small.** [French, feminine of PETIT.]

pe·tite bour·geoi·sie (pə-tēt′ bo͝or′zhwä-zē′). *French.* The **petty bourgeoisie** *(see).*

pet·it four (pĕt′ē fôr′, fōr′; *French* pə-tē′ fo͞or′) *pl.* **petits fours** or **petit fours** (pĕt′ē fôrz′, fōrz′; *French* pə-tē′ fo͞or′). A small, rich tea cake, frosted and decorated.

pe·ti·tion (pə-tĭsh′ən) *n.* **1.** A solemn supplication or request to a superior authority; an entreaty. **2.** A formal written document requesting a right or a benefit from a person or group in authority. **3.** *Law.* **a.** A formal written application requesting a court for a specific judicial action: *a petition for appeal.* **b.** That which is asked for in any such request. —*v.* **petitioned, -tioning, -tions.** —*tr.* **1.** To address a petition to. **2.** To ask for by petition; request formally. —*intr.* To make an entreaty. Often followed by *for: petition for retrial.* [Middle English *peticioun,* from Old French *petition,* from Latin *petītiō,* attack, solicitation, from *petere* (past participle *petītus*), to seek, demand. See **pet-**[1] in Appendix.*] —**pe·ti′tion·ar′y** (pə-tĭsh′ə-nĕr′ē) *adj.* —**pe·ti′tion·er** *n.*

pe·ti·ti·o prin·ci·pi·i (pə-tĭsh′ē-ō′ prĭn-sĭp′ē-ē′). *Logic.* The fallacy of assuming in the premise of an argument that which one wishes to prove in the conclusion; begging the question. [Medieval Latin, "postulation of the beginning" : *petītiō,* PETITION + *principium,* beginning, from *princeps,* chief, PRINCE.]

pet·it juror (pĕt′ē). Also **pet·ty juror.** A member of a petit jury.

pet·it jury (pĕt′ē). Also **pet·ty jury.** A jury of 12 persons that sits at civil and criminal trials. Also called "trial jury." Compare **grand jury.**

pet·it larceny (pĕt′ē). Also **pet·ty larceny.** The theft of objects whose value is below a certain arbitrary standard. Compare **grand larceny.**

pe·tit mal (pə-tē′ mäl′, măl′). *Pathology.* A form of epilepsy characterized by frequent but transient lapses of consciousness and only rare spasms or falling. Compare **grand mal.** [French, "small illness" : PETIT + *mal,* illness, from Old French, from adverb, badly, from Latin *malē,* from *malus,* bad (see **mel-**[5] in Appendix*).]

pet·it point (pĕt′ē point′). **1.** A small stitch used in needlepoint. **2.** Needlepoint done with such a stitch. [French, "small point."]

petr. petrology.

Pe·tra (pē′trə). The ancient capital of Edom, in southwestern Jordan, famous for its Hellenistic tombs carved in rock.

Pe·trarch (pē′trärk′). Italian name, Francesco Petrarca. 1304–1374. Italian humanist poet.

Pe·trar·chan sonnet (pĭ-trär′kən). A sonnet form of Italian origin comprising an octave with the rhyme pattern *abbaabba,* and a sestet of various rhyme patterns such as *cdccdc* or *cdecde.*

pet·rel (pĕt′rəl) *n.* Any of various sea birds of the order Procellariiformes, especially the **storm petrel** *(see).* Also called "Mother Carey's chicken." [Variant of earlier *pitteral*†.]

Pe·tri dish (pē′trē). A shallow dish with a loose-fitting cover, used especially to culture microorganisms for research. [After Julius R. *Petri* (died 1921), German bacteriologist.]

Pe·trie (pē′trē), Sir **(William Matthew) Flinders.** 1853–1942. British Egyptologist.

pet·ri·fac·tion (pĕt′rə-făk′shən) *n.* Also **pet·ri·fi·ca·tion** (-fĭ-kā′shən). **1.** The process of petrifying; the conversion of organic matter into stone or a stony substance. **2.** The state of being petrified, as by fear. [From PETRIFY (by analogy with, for example, STUPEFACTION).]

Petrified Forest National Monument. An area occupying 133 square miles in the Painted Desert of eastern Arizona, reserved for the protection of its petrified trees.

pet·ri·fy (pĕt′rə-fī′) *v.* **-fied, -fying, -fies.** —*tr.* **1.** To convert (wood or other organic matter) into a stony replica by structural impregnation with dissolved minerals. **2.** To cause to become stiff or stonelike; deaden. **3.** To stun or paralyze with terror; daze: *petrified by fear.* —*intr.* To become stony, especially by mineral replacement of organic matter. [Old French *petrifier* : Latin *petra,* stone, from Greek (see **petra** in Appendix*) + *facere,* to make (see **dhē-**[1] in Appendix*).]

Pe·trine (pē′trīn′) *adj.* Of or pertaining to Saint Peter.

petro–. Indicates: **1.** Rock or stone; for example, **petrology. 2.** Petroleum; for example, **petrochemistry.** [From Greek *petros,* stone and *petra,* rock. See **petra** in Appendix.*]

pet·ro·chem·i·cal (pĕt′rō-kĕm′ĭ-kəl) *n.* Any chemical derived from petroleum or natural gas. —**pet′ro·chem′i·cal** *adj.*

pet·ro·chem·is·try (pĕt′rō-kĕm′ĭ-strē) *n.* The chemistry of petroleum and its derivatives.

petrog. petrography.

pet·ro·glyph (pĕt′rə-glĭf′) *n. Archaeology.* A carving or line drawing on rock. [PETRO- + GLYPH.] —**pet′ro·glyph′ic** *adj.*

Pet·ro·grad. A former name for **Leningrad.**

pe·trog·ra·phy (pə-trŏg′rə-fē) *n. Abbr.* **petrog.** The description and classification of rocks. [PETRO- + -GRAPHY.] —**pe·trog′ra·pher** *n.* —**pet′ro·graph′ic** (pĕt′rə-grăf′ĭk), **pet′ro·graph′i·cal** *adj.* —**pet′ro·graph′i·cal·ly** *adv.*

pet·rol (pĕt′rəl) *n. Chiefly British.* Gasoline. [French *pétrole* (in the phrase *essence de pétrole,* gasoline), from Old French *petrole,* from Medieval Latin *petroleum,* PETROLEUM.]

petrol. petrology.

pet·ro·la·tum (pĕt′rə-lā′təm, -lä′təm) *n.* A colorless-to-amber gelatinous semisolid, obtained from petroleum, consisting of various methane and olefin hydrocarbons, and used in lubricants and medicinal ointments. Also called "petroleum jelly." [New Latin, from Medieval Latin *petroleum,* PETROLEUM.]

pe·tro·le·um (pə-trō′lē-əm) *n. Abbr.* **pet.** A natural, yellow-to-black, thick, flammable liquid hydrocarbon mixture found principally beneath the earth's surface and processed for fractions including natural gas, gasoline, naphtha, kerosene, fuel and lubricating oils, paraffin wax, asphalt, and a wide variety of derivative products. Also called "crude oil." [Medieval Latin : PETRO- + *oleum,* oil (see **elaia** in Appendix*).]

pe·trol·ic (pə-trŏl′ĭk) *adj.* Derived from petroleum.

pe·trol·o·gy (pə-trŏl′ə-jē) *n. Abbr.* **petr., petrol.** The study of the origin, composition, structure, and alteration of rocks. [PETRO- + -LOGY.] —**pet′ro·log′ic** (pĕt′rə-lŏj′ĭk), **pet′ro·log′i·cal** *adj.* —**pet′ro·log′i·cal·ly** *adv.* —**pe·trol′o·gist** *n.*

Pe·tro·ni·us (pə-trō′nē-əs), **Gaius.** Called "Petronius Arbiter." Roman courtier and wit of the first century A.D.; putative author of the *Satyricon,* a novel surviving only in fragments.

Pet·ro·pav·lovsk (pĕt′rə-päv′lôfsk′). A city of the Soviet Union, in northern Kazakhstan. Population, 158,000.

pe·tro·sal (pə-trō′səl) *adj.* Also **pet·rous** (pĕt′rəs). *Anatomy.* Pertaining to or located near the portion of the temporal bone that surrounds the inner ear. [From Latin *petrōsus,* PETROUS.]

pet·rous (pĕt′rəs) *adj.* **1.** Of, pertaining to, or resembling rock; stony; hard. **2.** *Anatomy.* Variant of **petrosal.** [Latin *petrōsus,* rocky, from *petra,* rock, from Greek. See **petra** in Appendix.*]

Pe·trovsk. The former name for **Makhachkala.**

Pet·ro·za·vodsk (pĕt′rə-zä-vôtsk′). *Finnish* **Pet·ro·skoi** (pĕt′rə-skoi′). The capital of the Karelian A.S.S.R., on the western shore of Lake Onega in the northwestern Soviet Union. Population, 157,000.

pe·tsai (bā′tsī′, bī′-) *n.* A plant, **Chinese cabbage** *(see).* [Central Chinese pronunciation of Mandarin Chinese *pai*[2] *ts'ai*[4] : *pai*[2], white + *ts'ai*[4], vegetable.]

pet·ti·coat (pĕt′ē-kōt′) *n.* **1.** A skirt, especially a woman's slip or underskirt. **2.** Something resembling this, such as a decorative hanging. **3.** *Slang.* A woman or girl. —*adj.* **1.** Female; feminine. **2.** Of or by women: *a petticoat government.* [Middle English *petycote* : *pety,* small, PETTY + *cote,* COAT.]

petticoat narcissus. A small daffodil, *Narcissus bulbocodium,* native to the Mediterranean region, having yellow or white flowers. Also called "hoop-petticoat narcissus." [From its bell-shaped flowers, resembling a hoop petticoat.]

pet·ti·fog (pĕt′ē-fŏg′, -fôg′) *intr.v.* **-fogged, -fogging, -fogs.** To act like a pettifogger. [Back-formation from PETTIFOGGER.]

pet·ti·fog·ger (pĕt′ē-fŏg′ər, -fôg′ər) *n.* A petty, quibbling, unscrupulous lawyer. [PETTY + an obscure second element.]

pet·tish (pĕt′ĭsh) *adj.* Ill-tempered; peevish; petulant. [Probably from PET (ill temper).] —**pet′tish·ly** *adv.* —**pet′tish·ness** *n.*

pet·ty (pĕt′ē) *adj.* **-tier, -tiest. 1.** Small, trivial, or insignificant in quantity or quality: *petty grievances.* **2.** Of contemptibly narrow mind or views: *a petty outlook.* **3.** *Informal.* Spiteful; mean. **4.** Of subordinate or inferior rank. **5.** *Law.* Variant of **petit.** —See Synonyms at **trivial.** [Middle English *pety,* small, variant of *petit,* PETIT.] —**pet′ti·ly** *adv.* —**pet′ti·ness** *n.*

petty bourgeois. Variant of **petit bourgeois.**

petty bour·geoi·sie (bo͝or′zhwä-zē′). The class of small businessmen, tradesmen, and professional people. Also *French* "petite bourgeoisie."

petty cash. *Abbr.* **p.c., p/c, P/C** A small fund of money for incidental expenses, as in an office.

petty juror. Variant of **petit juror.**

petty jury. Variant of **petit jury.**

petty larceny. Variant of **petit larceny.**

petty officer. *Abbr.* **P.O., p.o.** A naval noncommissioned officer.

pet·u·lant (pĕch′o͞o-lənt) *adj.* Unreasonably irritable or ill-tempered; peevish. [Old French *petulant,* saucy, from Latin *petulāns,* present participle of *petulāre* (unattested), to jab at, frequentative of *petere,* to attack. See **pet-**[1] in Appendix.*] —**pet′u·lance, pet′u·lan·cy** *n.* —**pet′u·lant·ly** *adv.*

pe·tu·nia (pə-to͞on′yə, -tyo͞on′yə) *n.* **1.** Any of various widely cultivated plants of the genus *Petunia,* native to South America, having funnel-shaped flowers in colors from white to purple. **2.** Moderate to dark purple. See **color.** [New Latin, from obsolete French *petun,* tobacco, from Tupi *petyn, petyma.*]

pe·tun·tze, pe·tun·tse (pə-to͞on′tsĕ) *n.* A variety of feldspar sometimes mixed with kaolin in Chinese porcelain. [Chinese (Central China) *pe*[2]*tun*[1] *tzŭ*[0] : *pe*[2] (Mandarin *pai*[2]), white + *tun*[1] *tzŭ*[0], mound of earth : *tun*[1], heap, mound + *tzŭ*[0], noun enclitic.]

pew (pyo͞o) *n.* A bench for the congregation in a church. [Middle English *pewe, puwe,* from Old French *puie,* raised seat, balcony, from Latin *podia,* plural of *podium,* podium, balcony, from Greek *podion,* small foot, base, diminutive of *pous* (stem *pod-*), foot. See **ped-**[1] in Appendix.*]

pe·wee (pē′wē) *n.* Also **pee·wee.** Any of various small, olive

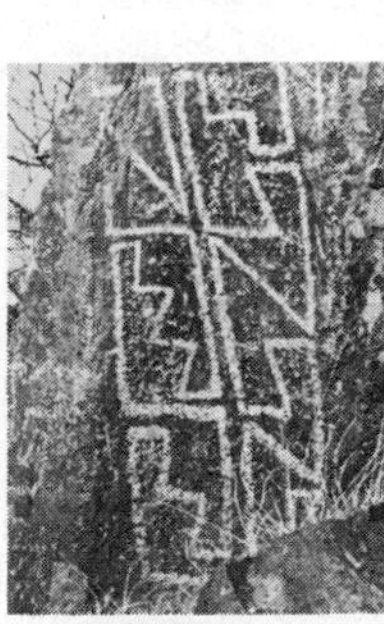

petroglyph
Rock with Indian petroglyphs near Three Rivers, southern New Mexico

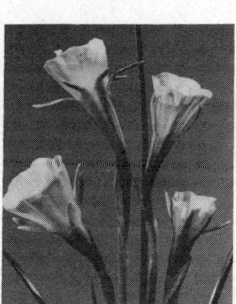

petticoat narcissus

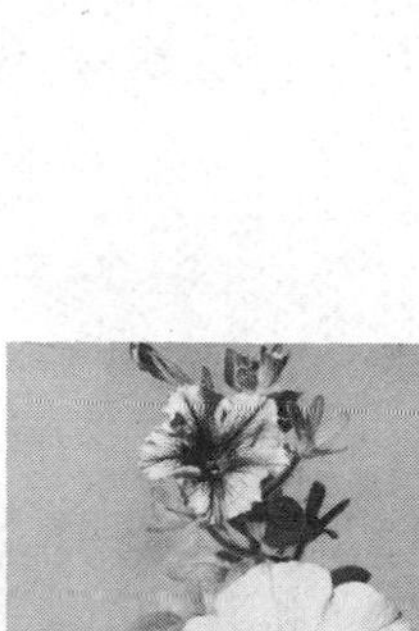

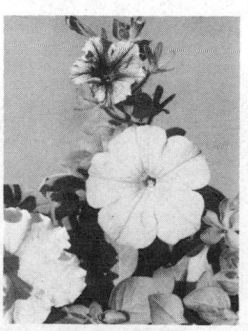

petunia
Petunia hybrida

brown North American woodland birds of the genus *Contopus.* [Imitative of the bird's cry.]
pe·wit (pē′wĭt′, pyōō′ĭt) *n.* A bird, the **lapwing** *(see).* [Imitative of the bird's cry.]
pew·ter (pyōō′tər) *n.* **1.** Any of numerous silver-gray alloys of tin with various amounts of antimony, copper, and lead, formerly used widely for fine kitchen utensils and tableware. **2.** Pewter articles collectively. *—adj.* Made of pewter. [Middle English *pewtre,* from Old French *peutre, peautre,* variant of *peltre,* tin, from (unattested) Vulgar Latin *peltrum*†.]
pe·yo·te (pā-ō′tē) *n.* Also **pe·yo·tl** (pā-ōt′l). **1.** A cactus, **mescal** *(see).* **2.** A hallucinatory drug derived from the tubercles of this cactus. [Mexican Spanish, from Nahuatl.]
pf. **1.** pfennig. **2.** preferred.
Pfalz. The German name for the **Palatinate.**
Pfc, Pfc. private first class.
pfen·nig (fĕn′ĭg) *n., pl.* **-nigs** or **pfennige** (fĕn′ĭ-gə). *Abbr.* **pf., pfg.** A coin equal to 1/100 of the Deutsche mark of West Germany and the ostmark of East Germany. See table of exchange rates at **currency.** [German *Pfennig,* from Old High German *pfenning,* from West Germanic *panninga* (unattested). See also **penny, penni.**]
pfg. pfennig.
Pg. Portugal; Portuguese.
P.G. **1.** paying guest. **2.** postgraduate.
PGA Professional Golfers' Association.
pH *Chemistry.* A measure of the acidity or alkalinity of a solution, numerically equal to 7 for neutral solutions, increasing with increasing alkalinity and decreasing with increasing acidity. [P(OTENTIAL OF) H(YDROGEN).]
PH Purple Heart.
ph. phase.
P.H. Purple Heart.
PHA Public Housing Administration.

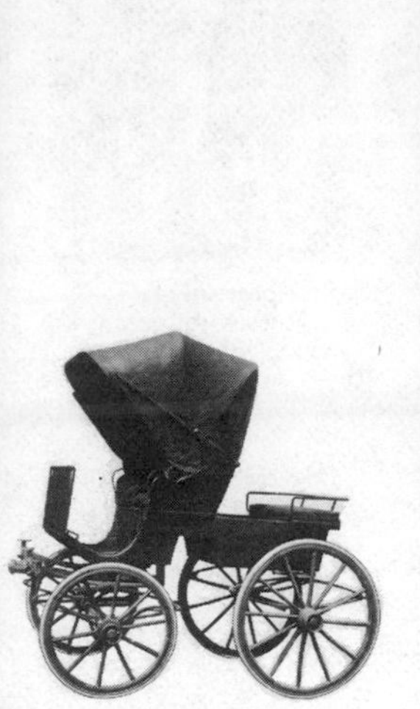
phaeton

pha·e·ton (fā′ə-tən) *n.* A light, open, four-wheeled carriage, usually drawn by a pair of horses. [French *phaéton,* after *Phaéton,* French form of *Phaethon,* son of Helios who attempted to drive the chariot of the sun.]
phage (fāj) *n.* A **bacteriophage** *(see).*
-phage. Indicates something that eats or destroys; for example, **bacteriophage.** [Greek *-phagos,* from *phagein,* to eat. See **bhag-¹** in Appendix.*]
phago-. Indicates eating or destroying; for example, **phagocyte.** [Greek, from *phagein,* to eat. See **bhag-¹** in Appendix.*]
phag·o·cyte (făg′ə-sīt′) *n. Physiology.* A cell such as a leukocyte that engulfs and digests cells, microorganisms, or other foreign bodies in the bloodstream and tissues. [PHAGO- + -CYTE.] **—phag′o·cyt′ic** (făg′ə-sĭt′ĭk) *adj.*

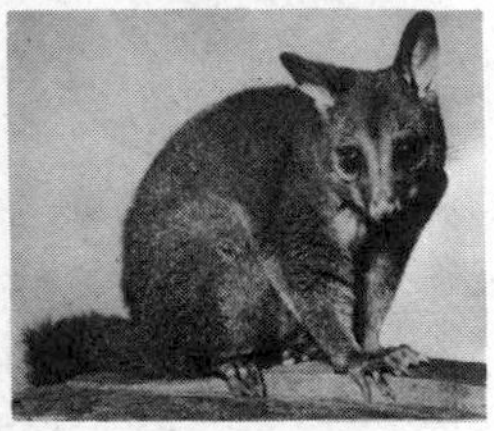
phalanger
Trichosurus vulpecula

phag·o·cy·to·sis (făg′ə-sī-tō′sĭs) *n. Physiology.* The envelopment and digestion of bacteria or other foreign bodies by phagocytes. [New Latin : PHAGOCYT(E) + -OSIS.]
phag·o·ma·ni·a (făg′ə-mā′nē-ə, -mān′yə) *n.* A morbid compulsion to eat. [New Latin : PHAGO- + -MANIA.]
phag·o·pho·bi·a (făg′ə-fō′bē-ə) *n.* A morbid fear of eating. [New Latin : PHAGO- + -PHOBIA.]
-phagous. Indicates eating or tending to eat; for example, **phyllophagous.** [Latin *-phagus,* from Greek *-phagos,* eating, from *phagein,* to eat. See **bhag-¹** in Appendix.*]
-phagy, -phagia. Indicates an eating or consumption; for example, **cytophagy, dysphagia.** [Greek *-phagia,* from *phagein,* to eat. See **bhag-¹** in Appendix.*]
pha·lange (fā′lănj′, fə-lănj′) *n. Anatomy.* A **phalanx** *(see).* [French, from New Latin *phalanx* (stem *phalang-*), PHALANX.]
pha·lan·ge·al (fə-lăn′jē-əl, fā-) *adj.* Also **pha·lan·gal** (fə-lăng′gəl, fā-), **pha·lan·ge·an** (fə-lăn′jē-ən, fā-). *Anatomy.* Of or pertaining to a phalanx.
pha·lan·ger (fə-lăn′jər) *n.* Any of various small, arboreal marsupials of the family Phalangeridae, of Australia and adjacent islands, having a long tail and dense, woolly fur. [New Latin, from PHALANX, "toe bone" (with reference to the peculiar structure of the second and third toes of its hind feet).]
phal·an·ster·y (făl′ən-stĕr′ē, fə-lăn′stə-rē) *n., pl.* **-ies.** **1.** A community of the followers of Charles **Fourier** *(see).* Also called "phalanx." **2.** The buildings of such a community. [French *Phalanstère* : *phalange,* phalanx, from New Latin *phalanx,* PHALANX + *monastère,* monastery, from Late Latin *monastērium,* MONASTERY.] **—phal′an·ste′ri·an** (făl′ən-stîr′ē-ən) *n.* & *adj.* **—phal′an·ste′ri·an·ism′** *n.*

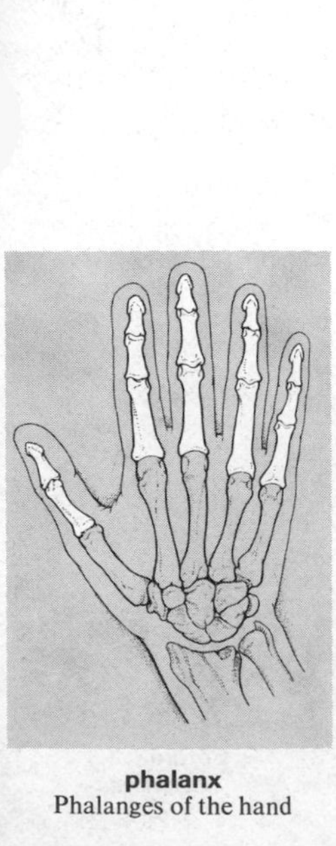
phalanx
Phalanges of the hand

pha·lanx (fā′lăngks′; *British* făl′ăngks′) *n., pl.* **-lanxes** or **phalanges** (fə-lăn′jēz, fā-) (only form for sense 4). **1.** A formation of infantry carrying overlapping shields and long spears, developed by Philip II of Macedonia and used by Alexander the Great. **2.** Any close-knit or compact body of people: *"formed a solid phalanx in defence of the Constitution and Protestant religion"* (G.M. Trevelyan). **3.** A **phalanstery** *(see).* **4.** *Anatomy.* Any bone of a finger or toe. Also called "phalange." [Latin, from Greek, wooden beam, finger bone, line of battle. See **bhelg-** in Appendix.*]
phal·a·rope (făl′ə-rōp′) *n.* Any of several wading birds of the family Phalaropodidae, having lobed toes that enable them to swim. [French, from New Latin *phalaropus* : Greek *phalaris,* coot (which has a white patch on the head), from *phalaros,* having a white spot (see **bhel-¹** in Appendix*) + *-pus,* from Greek *pous,* foot (see **ped-¹** in Appendix*).]
phal·lic (făl′ĭk) *adj.* **1.** Of, pertaining to, or resembling a phallus. **2.** Of or pertaining to the cult of the phallus as an embodiment of generative power: *phallic worship.* [Greek *phallikos,* from *phallos,* PHALLUS.]
phal·lus (făl′əs) *n., pl.* **phalli** (făl′ī′) or **-luses.** **1.** *Anatomy.* **a.** The penis. **b.** The sexually undifferentiated tissue in the embryo that becomes the penis or clitoris. **2.** A representation of the penis and testes as an embodiment of generative power. **3.** *Psychoanalysis.* The immature penis considered as the libidinal object of infantile sexuality. [Late Latin *phallus,* penis, from Greek *phallos.* See **bhel-²** in Appendix.*]
-phane. Indicates resemblance or similarity to (a specified material); for example, **cellophane.** [Greek *-phanēs,* appearing, shining, from *phainesthai,* to appear. See **bhā-¹** in Appendix.*]
phan·er·o·gam (făn′ər-ə-găm′) *n. Botany.* A plant that produces flowers and true seeds. Compare **cryptogam.** [New Latin *phanerogamus,* "one having visible reproductive parts" : Greek *phaneros,* visible, from *phainein,* to show (see **bhā-¹** in Appendix*) + -GAMOUS.] **—phan′er·o·gam′ic, phan′er·og′a·mous** (făn′ə-rŏg′ə-məs) *adj.*
phan·tasm (făn′tăz′əm) *n.* Also **phan·tas·ma** (făn′tăz′mə) *pl.* **-mata** (-mə-tə). **1.** Something apparently seen but having no physical reality; a phantom. **2.** An illusory mental image. **3.** In Platonic philosophy, objective reality as perceived and distorted by the five senses. [Middle English *fantasme,* from Old French, from Latin *phantasma,* apparition, specter, from Greek, from *phantazein,* to make visible, from *phainein,* to show. See **bhā-¹** in Appendix.*] **—phan·tas′mal** (făn-tăz′məl), **phan·tas′mic** (făn-tăz′mĭk) *adj.*
phan·tas·ma·go·ri·a (făn-tăz′mə-gôr′ē-ə, -gōr′ē-ə) *n.* Also **phan·tas·ma·go·ry** (făn-tăz′mə-gôr′ē, -gōr′ē). **1.** A fantastic sequence of haphazardly associative imagery, as seen in dreams or fever. **2.** Such imagery as represented in art. [Originally, the name of an early 19th-century magic-lantern show producing optical illusions, from PHANTASM + an obscure second element.] **—phan·tas′ma·gor′ic, phan·tas′ma·gor′i·cal** *adj.*
phan·ta·sy. Variant of **fantasy.**
phan·tom (făn′təm) *n.* Also **fan·tom.** **1.** Something apparently seen, heard, or sensed, but having no physical reality; ghost; specter. **2.** An image that appears only in the mind. *—adj.* Also **fan·tom.** Unreal; ghostlike. [Middle English *fantosme, fantome,* from Old French, from Latin *phantasma,* PHANTASM.]
phar., Phar. pharmaceutical; pharmacist; pharmacopoeia; pharmacy.
Phar·aoh (fâr′ō, fā′rō) *n.* Also **phar·aoh.** **1.** A king of ancient Egypt. **2.** A tyrant. [Late Latin *Pharaō,* from Greek *Pharaō,* transcription of Hebrew *Par'ōh,* from an Egyptian word meaning "great house."] **—Phar′a·on′ic** (fâr′ā-ŏn′ĭk) *adj.*
pharaoh ant. A very small, reddish ant, *Monomorium pharaonis,* that infests human dwellings.
Phar.B. Bachelor of Pharmacy (Latin *Pharmaciae Baccalaureus*).
Phar.D. Doctor of Pharmacy (Latin *Pharmaciae Doctor*).
phar·i·sa·ic (făr′ə-sā′ĭk) *adj.* Also **phar·i·sa·i·cal** (făr′ə-sā′ĭ-kəl). **1.** *Capital* **P.** Of, relating to, or characteristic of the Pharisees. **2.** Hypocritically self-righteous and condemnatory: *"and pharisaical Dissemblers feign devotion"* (Donne). **—phar′i·sa′i·cal·ly** *adv.* **—phar′i·sa′i·cal·ness** *n.*
Phar·i·sa·ism (făr′ə-sā-ĭz′əm) *n.* Also **phar·i·see·ism** (făr′ə-sē-ĭz′əm). **1.** *Capital* **P.** The doctrines and practices of the Pharisees. **2.** Hypocritical observance of the letter of religious or moral law without regard for the spirit; sanctimoniousness.
phar·i·see (făr′ə-sē) *n.* **1.** *Capital* **P.** A member of an ancient Jewish sect that emphasized strict interpretation and observance of the Mosaic law in both its oral and written form. Compare **Sadducee.** **2.** A hypocritically self-righteous person. [Middle English *pharise,* Old English *farise,* from Late Latin *pharisaeus,* from Greek *pharisaios,* from Aramaic *perīshayyā,* plural of *perīsh,* "separated."]
pharm., Pharm. pharmaceutical; pharmacist; pharmacopoeia; pharmacy.
Phar.M. Master of Pharmacy (Latin *Pharmaciae Magister*).
phar·ma·ceu·ti·cal (fär′mə-sōō′tĭ-kəl) *adj.* Also **phar·ma·ceu·tic** (-tĭk), **phar·ma·cal** (fär′mə-kəl). *Abbr.* **phar., Phar., pharm., Pharm.** Of or pertaining to pharmacy or pharmacists. *—n.* Also **phar·ma·ceu·tic.** *Abbr.* **phar., Phar., pharm., Pharm.** A pharmaceutical product or preparation. [From Late Latin *pharmaceuticus,* from Greek *pharmakeutikos,* from *pharmakeutēs,* druggist, from *pharmakeuein,* to give drugs, from *pharmakon,* drug. See **pharmaco-.**] **—phar′ma·ceu′ti·cal·ly** *adv.*
phar·ma·ceu·tics (fär′mə-sōō′tĭks) *n.* Plural in form, used with a singular verb. The science of preparing and dispensing drugs.
phar·ma·cist (fär′mə-sĭst) *n.* Also **phar·ma·ceu·tist** (fär′mə-sōō′tĭst). *Abbr.* **phar., Phar., pharm., Pharm.** A person trained in pharmacy; druggist.
pharmaco-. Indicates drugs; for example, **pharmacology.** [From Greek *pharmakon*†, drug, poison, potion.]
phar·ma·co·dy·nam·ics (fär′mə-kō′dī-năm′ĭks) *n.* Plural in form, used with a singular verb. The study of drug action on living organisms. **—phar′ma·co′dy·nam′ic** *adj.*
phar·ma·cog·no·sy (fär′mə-kŏg′nə-sē) *n.* The branch of pharmacology dealing with crude natural drugs. [PHARMACO- + Greek *-gnōsia,* knowledge, from -GNOSIS.] **—phar′ma·cog′no·sist** *n.* **—phar′ma·cog·nos′tic** (-kŏg-nŏs′tĭk) *adj.*
phar·ma·col·o·gy (fär′mə-kŏl′ə-jē) *n.* The science of drugs, including their composition, uses, and effects. [PHARMACO- + -LOGY.] **—phar′ma·co·log′ic** (-kə-lŏj′ĭk), **phar′ma·co·log′i·cal** *adj.* **—phar′ma·co·log′i·cal·ly** *adv.* **—phar′ma·col′o·gist** *n.*
phar·ma·co·poe·ia (fär′mə-kə-pē′ə) *n., pl.* **-ias.** *Abbr.* **phar., Phar., pharm., Pharm.** **1.** A book containing an official list of medicinal drugs together with articles on their preparation and use. **2.** A collection or stock of drugs. [New Latin, from Greek *pharmakopoiia,* preparation of drugs, from *pharmakopoios,* preparing drugs : PHARMACO- + *-poios,* "making,"

from *poiein*, to make (see **kwei-**[2] in Appendix*).] —**phar′ma·co·poe′ial** (-pē′əl) *adj.* —**phar′ma·co·poe′ist** (-pē′ĭst) *n.*

phar·ma·cy (fär′mə-sē) *n.*, *pl.* **-cies.** *Abbr.* **phar., Phar., pharm., Pharm. 1.** The art of preparing and dispensing drugs. **2.** A place where drugs are sold; drugstore. [Middle English *farmacie*, from Old French, from Late Latin *pharmacia*, from Greek *pharmakeia*, from *pharmakon*, drug. See **pharmaco-**.]

pha·ros (fâr′ŏs′) *n.* A lighthouse. [From PHAROS.]

Pha·ros (fâr′ŏs′). A former island in the bay of Alexandria, celebrated in antiquity for its lighthouse.

Phar·sa·la (fär′sə-lə). A town in northeastern Greece; site of Caesar's victory over Pompey (48 B.C.).

pha·ryn·ge·al (fə-rĭn′jē-əl, -jəl, făr′ĭn-jē′əl) *adj.* Also **pha·ryn·gal** (fə-rĭng′gəl). Of, pertaining to, located in, or coming from the pharynx: *pharyngeal speech sounds.* —*n.* Also **pha·ryn·gal.** A speech sound produced in the pharynx. [From New Latin *pharyngeus*, from *pharynx*, PHARYNX.]

phar·yn·gi·tis (făr′ĭn-jī′tĭs) *n.* Inflammation of the pharynx. [New Latin : PHARYNG(O)- + -ITIS.]

pharyngo-, pharyng-. Indicates pharynx; for example, **pharyngoscope, pharyngitis.** [New Latin, from Greek *pharungo-*, from *pharunx*, PHARYNX.]

phar·yn·gol·o·gy (făr′ĭn-gŏl′ə-jē) *n.* The medical study of the pharynx and its diseases. [PHARYNGO- + -LOGY.]

pha·ryn·go·scope (fə-rĭng′gə-skōp′) *n.* An instrument used in examining the pharynx. [PHARYNGO- + -SCOPE.] —**phar′yn·gos′co·py** (făr′ĭn-gŏs′kə-pē) *n.*

phar·yn·got·o·my (făr′ĭn-gŏt′ə-mē) *n.*, *pl.* **-mies.** A surgical incision of the pharynx. [PHARYNGO- + -TOMY.]

phar·ynx (făr′ĭngks) *n.*, *pl.* **pharynges** (fə-rĭn′jēz) or **pharynxes.** The section of the digestive tract that extends from the nasal cavities to the larynx, there becoming continuous with the esophagus. [New Latin, from Greek *pharunx*, throat, pharynx. See **bher-**[2] in Appendix.*]

phase (fāz) *n. Abbr.* **ph. 1.** One of a sequence of distinct apparent forms. **2.** A distinct stage of development: *"The American occupation of Japan fell into three successive phases"* (Edwin Reischauer). **3.** A temporary manner, attitude, or pattern of behavior: *a passing phase.* **4.** *Astronomy.* One of the cyclically recurring apparent forms of the moon or a planet. **5.** *Physics.* **a.** A particular stage in a periodic process or phenomenon. **b.** The fraction of a complete cycle elapsed as measured from a specified reference point and often expressed as an angle. **6.** *Chemistry.* A discrete homogeneous part of a material system that is mechanically separable from the rest, as is ice from water. **7.** *Biology.* A characteristic form or appearance that occurs in a cycle or that distinguishes some individuals of a group. —**in phase.** *Physics.* Reaching corresponding phases at the same time, as two waves. —*tr.v.* **phased, phasing, phases.** To plan or carry out systematically by phases. —**phase in.** To introduce by one stage at a time. —**phase out.** To eliminate by one stage at a time. [Back-formation from phases (plural), from New Latin *phasis*, from Greek, appearance, phase of the moon, from *phainein*, to show. See **bhā-**[1] in Appendix.*] —**pha′sic** (fā′zĭk) *adj.*

Synonyms: *phase, aspect, facet, angle, side, stage.* These terms refer to various particular or possible views or levels of a process, consideration, or object. The visual astronomical meaning of *phase* has more and more given way to a sequential one, though the word still connotes change in an object itself rather than in viewpoint. A *phase*, in scientific or organizational usage, is often a stage or period of development. In everyday life, it refers to a temporary attitude or manner: *going through a new phase.* An *aspect* is a single area of interest from a chosen vantage point, usually as a matter for study, judgment, or emotional reaction: *a neglected aspect of medicine.* A *facet* is in this context usually one of several theoretical or practical aspects of a situation or problem: *the unexpected facets of a new concept; many facets of the welfare state. Angle* more informally expresses a deliberate limitation of perspective, with emphasis on the observer's own view of the object under consideration: *a loser from any angle. Side* is used in discussion and argumentation of an issue over which opinion has been divided into two contradictory points of view: *You've got to look at this side of it. Stage* is similar to *phase* and always denotes a point or interval of time, change, or achievement.

phase contrast microscope. A microscope that renders differences in the phase of light transmitted or reflected by a specimen as variations in contrast. Also called "phase microscope."

phase modulation. *Telecommunications.* Variation of the phase of a carrier wave by an amount proportional to the amplitude of a modulating signal.

phase rule. A rule stating that the number of degrees of freedom in a material system at equilibrium is equal to the number of components minus the number of phases plus the constant 2. For example, the system of water vapor, water, and ice has zero degrees of freedom, since three phases of one component coexist.

-phasia. Indicates a specified speech disorder; for example, **dysphasia.** [New Latin, from Greek, speech, from *phasis*, utterance, from *phanai*, to say, speak. See **bhā-**[2] in Appendix.*]

Ph.B. Bachelor of Philosophy (Latin *Philosophiae Baccalaureus*).

Ph.C. Pharmaceutical Chemist.

Ph.D. Doctor of Philosophy (Latin *Philosophiae Doctor*).

pheas·ant (fĕz′ənt) *n.*, *pl.* **-ants** or **pheasant. 1.** Any of various birds of the family Phasianidae, native to the Old World, characteristically having long tails and, in the males of many species, brilliantly colored plumage. **2.** Any of various similar birds, such as the **ruffed grouse** *(see).* [Middle English *fesaunt*, *fesant*, from Old French *fesan*, *faisan*, from Latin *phasiānus*, from Greek *phasianos*, "the Phasian (bird)," of the Phasis River in the Caucasus, from *Phāsis*, the Phasis River.]

phel·lo·derm (fĕl′ə-dûrm′) *n.* The soft, green cortex tissue that forms on the inner side of the phellogen of some trees. [Greek *phellos*, cork (see **bhel-**[2] in Appendix*) + -DERM.] —**phel′lo·der′mal** *adj.*

phel·lo·gen (fĕl′ə-jən) *n.* A tissue in woody plants, from which cork and phelloderm develop. Also called "cork cambium." [Greek *phellos*, cork (see **bhel-**[2] in Appendix*) + -GEN.] —**phel′lo·ge·net′ic** (fĕl′ə-jə-nĕt′ĭk), **phel′lo·gen′ic** *adj.*

phe·nac·e·tin (fə-năs′ə-tĭn) *n.* Also **phe·nac·e·tine.** An analgesic drug, **acetophenetidin** *(see).* [PHEN(O)- + ACET(O)- + -IN.]

phen·a·cite (fĕn′ə-sīt′) *n.* A natural beryllium silicate, Be_2SiO_4, occurring as vitreous crystals sometimes used as gems. [From Greek *phenax*†, an impostor (from its resemblance to quartz).]

phe·nan·threne (fə-năn′thrēn′) *n.* A colorless crystalline compound, $C_{14}H_{10}$, obtained by fractional distillation of coal-tar oils and used in dyes, drugs, and explosives. [PHEN(O)- + ANTHR(AC)ENE.]

phen·ar·sa·zine chloride (fĭ-när′sə-zēn′). A highly poisonous yellow crystalline compound, $C_{12}H_9AsClN$, used as a poison gas and sometimes with tear gas. Also called "diphenylaminechloroarsine." [From PHEN(O)- + ARS(ENIC) + AZINE.]

phen·a·zine (fĕn′ə-zēn′) *n.* Also **phen·a·zin** (fĕn′ə-zĭn). A yellow crystalline compound, $C_6H_4N_2C_6H_4$, used in the manufacture of dyes. [PHEN(O)- + AZINE.]

pheno-, phen-. *Chemistry.* Indicates: **1.** Showing or displaying; for example, **phenocryst. 2.** A compound derived from, containing, or related to benzene; for example, **phenol, phenothiazine.** [From Greek *phainein*, to show. See **bhā-**[1] in Appendix.* Sense 2 is from French *(acide) phénique*, an early name for phenol, from Greek *phainein* (so named because it was originally extracted from illuminating gas).]

phe·no·bar·bi·tal (fē′nō-bär′bə-tôl′) *n.* A white, shiny, crystalline compound, $C_{12}H_{12}N_2O_3$, used in medicine as a sedative and hypnotic. [PHENO- + BARBITAL.]

phe·no·cop·y (fē′nə-kŏp′ē) *n. Genetics.* **1.** An environmentally induced phenotypic variation that closely resembles a genetically determined character. **2.** A characteristic or organism existing as such a variation. [PHENO(TYPE) + COPY.]

phe·no·cryst (fē′nə-krĭst′) *n. Mineralogy.* A conspicuous, usually large, crystal embedded in porphyritic igneous rock. [PHENO- + CRYST(AL).] —**phe′no·crys′tic** *adj.*

phe·nol (fē′nōl′, -nôl′) *n. Chemistry.* **1.** A caustic, poisonous, white, crystalline compound, C_6H_5OH, derived from benzene and used in various resins, plastics, disinfectants, and pharmaceuticals. Also called "carbolic acid." **2.** Any of a class of aromatic organic compounds having at least one hydroxyl group attached directly to the benzene ring. [PHEN(O)- + -OL.]

phe·no·lic (fĭ-nō′lĭk, -nôl′ĭk) *adj. Chemistry.* Of, pertaining to, containing, or derived from phenol.

phenolic resin. Any of various synthetic thermosetting resins, obtained by the reaction of phenols with simple aldehydes and used to make molded products and as coatings and adhesives.

phe·nol·o·gy (fĭ-nŏl′ə-jē) *n.* The study of periodic biological phenomena, such as flowering, breeding, and migration, especially as related to climate. [PHENO(MENON) + -LOGY.] —**phe′no·log′i·cal** (fē′nə-lŏj′ĭ-kəl) *adj.* —**phe·nol′o·gist** *n.*

phe·nol·phthal·ein (fē′nōl-thăl′ēn′, -thăl′ē-ĭn, -thā′lēn′, -thā′lē-ĭn) *n.* A pale-yellow crystalline powder, $(C_6H_4OH)_2C_2O_2C_6H_4$, used as an acid-base indicator, in making dyes, and as a cathartic. [PHENOL + PHTHALEIN.]

phe·nom·e·nal (fĭ-nŏm′ə-nəl) *adj.* **1.** Of, pertaining to, or constituting a phenomenon or phenomena. **2.** Extraordinary; outstanding; remarkable: *a phenomenal feat of memory.* **3.** *Philosophy.* Known or derived through the senses, rather than through the mind. —**phe·nom′e·nal·ly** *adv.*

phe·nom·e·nal·ism (fĭ-nŏm′ə-nəl-ĭz′əm) *n. Philosophy.* The doctrine, set forth by Hume and his successors, that percepts and concepts actually present in the mind constitute the sole object of knowledge, the objects of perception themselves, their origin outside the mind, or the nature of the mind itself remaining forever beyond inquiry. —**phe·nom′e·nal·ist** *n.* —**phe·nom′e·nal·is′tic** *adj.* —**phe·nom′e·nal·is′ti·cal·ly** *adv.*

phe·nom·e·nol·o·gy (fĭ-nŏm′ə-nŏl′ə-jē) *n.* **1.** The study of all possible appearances in human experience, during which considerations of objective reality and of purely subjective response are temporarily left out of account. **2.** A philosophical movement based on phenomenology, originated by Edmund Husserl about 1905. [German *Phänomenologie* : PHENOMENO(N) + -LOGY.] —**phe·nom′e·no·log′i·cal** (fĭ-nŏm′ə-nə-lŏj′ĭ-kəl) *adj.* —**phe·nom′e·no·log′i·cal·ly** *adv.* —**phe·nom′e·nol′o·gist** *n.*

phe·nom·e·non (fĭ-nŏm′ə-nŏn′) *n.*, *pl.* **-na** (-nə) or **-nons** (for sense 2). **1.** Any occurrence or fact that is directly perceptible by the senses. **2. a.** An unusual, significant, or unaccountable fact or occurrence; a marvel. **b.** A person outstanding for some extreme quality or achievement; paragon: *"I thought Mr. Barkis a phenomenon of respectability."* (Dickens). **3.** *Philosophy.* That which appears real to the senses, regardless of whether its underlying existence is proved or its nature understood. Compare **noumenon. 4.** *Physics.* An observable event. [Late Latin *phaenomenon*, from Greek *phainomenon*, from *phainomenos*, present participle of *phainesthai*, to appear, from *phainein*, to show. See **bhā-**[1] in Appendix.*]

phe·no·thi·a·zine (fē′nō-thī′ə-zēn′) *n.* A greenish organic compound, $C_{12}H_9NS$, used in insecticides, livestock anthelmintics, and dyes. [PHENO- + THIAZINE.]

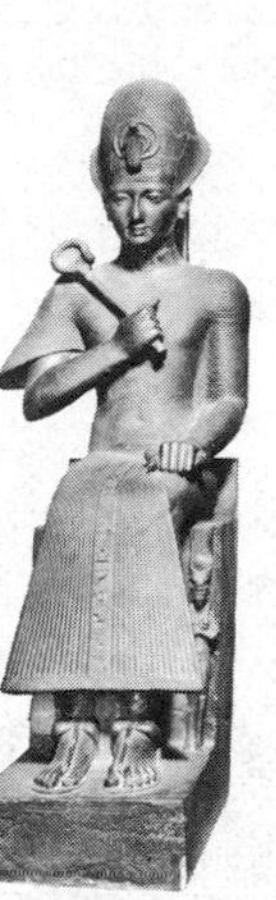

Pharaoh
Statue of Rameses II represented in heroic proportions with his knee-high wife at his side

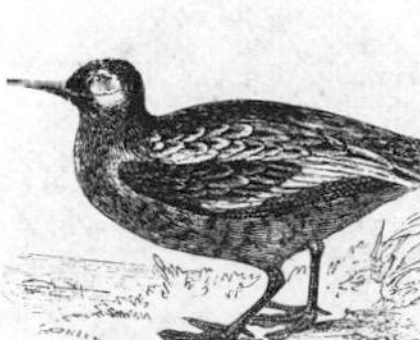

phalarope
Phalaropus fulicarius

phe·no·type (fē′nə-tīp′) *n. Genetics.* **1.** The environmentally and genetically determined observable appearance of an organism, especially as considered with respect to all possible genetically influenced expressions of one specific character. Compare **genotype**. **2.** An individual or group of organisms exhibiting a particular phenotype. [German *Phänotypus* : PHENO- + TYPE.] —**phe′no·typ′ic** (-tĭp′ĭk), **phe′no·typ′i·cal** *adj.* —**phe′no·typ′i·cal·ly** *adv.*

phen·yl (fĕn′əl, fē′nəl) *n.* The organic radical C_6H_5, derived from benzene by the removal of one hydrogen atom. [PHEN(O)- + -YL.] —**phe·nyl′ic** (fĭ-nĭl′ĭk) *adj.*

phen·yl·al·a·nine (fĕn′əl-ăl′ə-nēn′, fē′nəl-) *n. Biochemistry.* A natural amino acid, $C_6H_5CH_2CH(NH_2)COOH$, that occurs as a constituent of many proteins and is extracted for use as a dietary supplement. [PHENYL + ALANINE.]

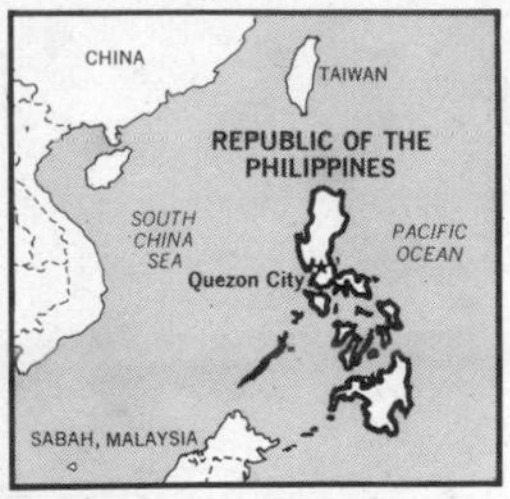

Republic of the Philippines

phen·yl·ene (fĕn′əl-ēn′, fē′nəl-) *n.* An organic radical, C_6H_4, derived from benzene by removal of two hydrogen atoms.

phew (fyo͞o) *interj.* Used to express relief, fatigue, surprise, or disgust. [Expressive formation.]

Ph.G. graduate in pharmacy.

phi (fī) *n.* The 21st letter in the Greek alphabet, written Φ, φ. Transliterated in English as *ph.* See **alphabet**. [Medieval Greek, from Greek *phei.*]

phi·al (fī′əl) *n.* A small bottle, a **vial** *(see).* [Middle English *fiole,* from Old French, from Old Provençal *fiola,* from Latin *phiala,* vessel, saucer, from Greek *phialē*†, broad vessel.]

Phi Be·ta Kap·pa (fī′ bā′tə kăp′ə). An honorary fraternity of college students and graduates whose members are chosen on the basis of high academic standing. It is the oldest fraternity in America (founded 1776). [From the initials of the Greek phrase *philosophia biou kubernētēs,* "philosophy the guide of life" (motto of the society).]

Phid·i·as (fĭd′ē-əs). Athenian sculptor of the fifth century B.C.

phil. philosopher; philosophical; philosophy.

Phil. **1.** Philippians (New Testament). **2.** Philippine.

Phil·a·del·phi·a (fĭl′ə-dĕl′fē-ə). **1.** *Abbr.* **Phila.** A city in southeastern Pennsylvania, at the junction of the Delaware and Schuylkill rivers. Population, 2,003,000. **2.** An ancient city and Hellenic commercial center in Lydia, Asia Minor, the site of which is near the modern Turkish town of Alaşehir. **3.** The ancient name for **Amman,** Jordan. [Greek, "brotherly love" : PHIL(O)- + *adelphos,* brother (see **gwelbh-** in Appendix*).] —**Phil′a·del′phi·an** *adj.* & *n.*

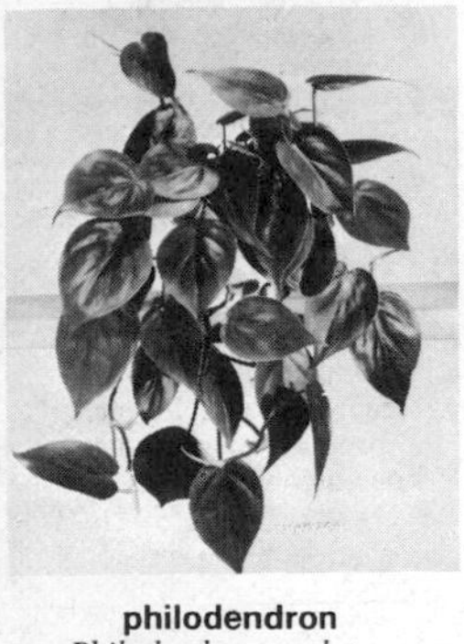

philodendron
Philodendron cordatum

Philadelphia lawyer. A lawyer of great ingenuity in the discovery and manipulation of subtle legalisms.

Philadelphia pepper pot. A soup, **pepper pot** *(see).*

phi·lan·der (fĭ-lăn′dər) *intr.v.* **-dered, -dering, -ders.** To engage in love affairs frivolously or casually; flirt. [From *Philander,* a traditional literary name for a lover, mistakenly adopted from Greek *philandros,* "loving men," "loving one's husband" : PHIL(O)- + *anēr* (stem *andr-*), man (see **ner-²** in Appendix*).] —**phi·lan′der·er** *n.*

phi·lan·thro·py (fĭ-lăn′thrə-pē) *n., pl.* **-pies.** **1.** The effort or inclination to increase the well-being of mankind, as by charitable aid or donations. **2.** Love of mankind in general. **3.** An action or institution designed to promote human welfare. [Late Latin *philanthrōpia,* from Greek *philanthrōpia,* humanity, from *philanthrōpos,* "lover of mankind" : PHIL(O)- + *anthrōpos,* mankind (see **ner-²** in Appendix*).] —**phil′an·throp′ic** (fĭl′ən-thrŏp′ĭk), **phil′an·throp′i·cal** *adj.* —**phi·lan′thro·pist** *n.*

phi·lat·e·ly (fĭ-lăt′l-ē) *n.* The collection and study of postage stamps, postmarks, and related materials; stamp collecting. [French *philatélie* : PHILO- + Greek *atelēs,* tax-free (here used as a rendering of the old postmark *franc de port,* "carriage-free"; see **frank**) : A- (without) + *telos,* charge (see **tel-¹** in Appendix*).] —**phil′a·tel′ic** (fĭl′ə-tĕl′ĭk), **phil′a·tel′i·cal** *adj.* —**phil′a·tel′i·cal·ly** *adv.* —**phi·lat′e·list** *n.*

-phile, -phil. Indicates one having love or strong affinity or preference for; for example, **Anglophile.** [French *-phile* or New Latin *-philus,* from Greek *-philos,* from *philos,* beloved, dear, loving. See **bhilo-** in Appendix.*]

Philem. Philemon (New Testament).

Phi·le·mon¹ (fĭ-lē′mən, fī-). A friend and convert of Saint Paul.

Phi·le·mon² (fĭ-lē′mən, fī-). *Abbr.* **Philem.** A book of the New Testament, a short epistle to Philemon by Saint Paul.

phil·har·mon·ic (fĭl′här-mŏn′ĭk, fĭl′ər-) *adj.* **1.** Devoted to or appreciative of music. **2.** Pertaining to a symphony orchestra. —*n.* Also **Phil·har·mon·ic.** A symphony orchestra or the group that supports it. [French *philharmonique,* from Italian *filarmonico* : *fil-,* loving, from Greek *philo-,* PHILO- + *armonico,* harmonic, from Latin *harmonicus* (see **harmonica**).]

phil·hel·lene (fĭl-hĕl′ēn′) *n.* Also **Phil·hel·lene, phil·hel·len·ist** (fĭl-hĕl′ən-ĭst). One who admires Greece or the Greeks. [Greek *philellēn* : PHIL(O)- + *Hellēn,* HELLENE.] —**phil′hel·len′ic** (fĭl′hĕ-lĕn′ĭk) *adj.* —**phil·hel′len·ism′** *n.*

Phil. I. Philippine Islands.

-philia. Indicates: **1.** Tendency toward; for example, **hemophilia.** **2.** Abnormal attraction to; for example, **necrophilia.** [New Latin, from Greek *philia,* friendship, from *philos,* loving. See **bhilo-** in Appendix.*]

-philic. Variant of **-philous.**

Philip II of Macedonia

Phil·ip¹ (fĭl′ĭp). Also **Phil·lip.** A masculine given name. [Middle English *Phelyp,* from Latin *Philippus,* from Greek *Philippos,* "lover of horses" : PHILO- + *hippos,* horse (see **ekwo-** in Appendix*).]

Phil·ip² (fĭl′ĭp). Duke of Edinburgh. Born 1921. Husband of Elizabeth II of Great Britain.

Phil·ip II¹ (fĭl′ĭp). 382–336 B.C. King of Macedonia (359–336 B.C.); father of Alexander the Great.

Phil·ip II² (fĭl′ĭp). Called "Philip Augustus." 1165–1223. King of France (1180–1223); strengthened monarchy.

Phil·ip II³ (fĭl′ĭp). 1527–1598. King of Spain (1556–98); son of Charles V; launched the Armada against England (1588).

Phil·ip IV (fĭl′ĭp). Called "the Fair." 1268–1314. King of France (1285–1314); convened first States-General; established Avignon as the Papal See.

Phil·ip (fĭl′ĭp), **King.** American Indian name **Met·a·com·et** (mĕt′ə-kŏm′ĭt). Died 1676. Sachem of the Wampanoag; son of Massasoit; waged King Philip's War (1675–76) against the New England colonists.

Phil·ip (fĭl′ĭp), **Saint¹.** One of the Apostles; said to have spread the Gospel in Asia Minor. Matthew 10:3; Acts 1:13.

Phil·ip (fĭl′ĭp), **Saint².** Called "the Evangelist." Christian leader of the first century A.D.

Phi·lip·pi (fĭ-lĭp′ī′). An ancient town in north-central Macedonia, Greece, near the Aegean Sea; the scene of the defeat of Brutus and Cassius by Antony and Octavian (42 B.C.).

Phi·lip·pi·ans (fĭ-lĭp′ē-ənz) *n.* Plural in form, used with a singular verb. *Abbr.* **Phil.** A book of the New Testament, the epistle of Saint Paul to the Christians of Philippi.

Phi·lip·pic (fĭ-lĭp′ĭk) *n.* **1.** Any of the orations of Demosthenes against Philip of Macedonia in the fourth century B.C. **2.** Any of the orations of Cicero against Antony in 44 B.C. **3.** *Small* **p.** Any verbal denunciation characterized by invective.

Phil·ip·pine Islands (fĭl′ə-pēn′). *Abbr.* **P.I., Phil. I., Phil. Is.** A group of about 7,000 islands in the western Pacific Ocean, southeast of China, constituting the Republic of the Philippines. —**Phil′ip·pine′** *adj.*

Philippine mahogany. Any of various Philippine hardwood trees of the genus *Shorea* and related genera.

Phil·ip·pines, Republic of the (fĭl′ə-pēnz′, fĭl′ə-pēnz′). A republic, 114,830 square miles in area, consisting of the Philippine Islands. Population, 27,088,000. Capital, Quezon City. [Spanish *(Las Islas) Filipinas,* the Philippine Islands, from *Felipe,* King Philip II of Spain.]

Philippine Sea. A large area of the western Pacific Ocean, east of the Philippine Islands, extending northwest to Formosa.

Phil. Is. Philippine Islands.

Phi·lis·ti·a (fĭ-lĭs′tē-ə). An ancient country on the southwestern coast of Palestine.

Phi·lis·tine (fĭ-lĭs′tĭn, -tēn′, fĭl′ĭ-stēn′) *n.* **1.** One of the people of ancient Philistia. **2.** A smug, ignorant, especially middle-class person who is held to be indifferent or antagonistic to artistic and cultural values. —*adj.* **1.** Of or pertaining to the ancient Philistines. **2.** *Sometimes small* **p.** Boorish; barbarous: *"Interpretation amounts to the philistine refusal to leave the work of art alone."* (Susan Sontag). [Middle English, from Late Latin *Philistīnus,* from Late Greek *Philistinos,* from Hebrew *Pelishtī,* Philistia, from *pelesheth,* "land of the Philistines."]

Phi·lis·tin·ism (fĭ-lĭs′tə-nĭz′əm, -tē-nĭz′əm, fĭl′ĭ-stē-nĭz′əm) *n.* Also **phi·lis·tin·ism.** Smug conventionalism: *"the contrast between intellect and philistinism"* (Richard Hofstadter).

Phil·lip. Variant of **Philip.**

Phillips Screw. A trademark for a screw with two perpendicular grooves in its head, used with a matching screwdriver.

Phi·lo (fī′lō). Known as Philo Judaeus. 30 B.C.–45 A.D. Hellenizing Jewish philosopher of Alexandria.

philo-. Indicates love; for example, **philology.** [New Latin, from Greek, from *philos,* loving. See **bhilo-** in Appendix.*]

phil·o·den·dron (fĭl′ə-dĕn′drən) *n., pl.* **-drons** or **-dra** (-drə). Any of various climbing tropical American plants of the genus *Philodendron,* many of which are cultivated as house plants. [New Latin, from Greek, from *philodendros,* "tree-loving" : PHILO- + *dendron,* tree (see **deru-** in Appendix*).]

phi·lol·o·gy (fĭ-lŏl′ə-jē) *n. Abbr.* **philol.** **1.** **Historical linguistics** *(see).* **2.** *Archaic.* Literary study or classical scholarship. [French *philologie,* from Old French, from Latin *philologia,* love of learning, from Greek, from *philologos,* loving reason or learning : PHILO- + *logos,* word, reason (see **-logy**).] —**phil′o·log′ic** (fĭl′ə-lŏj′ĭk), **phil′o·log′i·cal** *adj.* —**phil′o·log′i·cal·ly** *adv.* —**phi·lol′o·gist, phi·lol′o·ger** *n.*

phil·o·mel (fĭl′ə-mĕl′) *n.* Also **phil·o·me·la** (fĭl′ə-mā′lə, -mē′lə). *Poetic.* A nightingale. [From PHILOMELA.]

Phil·o·me·la (fĭl′ə-mā′lə, -mē′lə). *Greek Mythology.* A princess of Athens who, after being raped and having her tongue cut out by Tereus, was turned into either a swallow or a nightingale.

phil·o·pro·gen·i·tive (fĭl′ō-prō-jĕn′ə-tĭv) *adj.* **1.** Producing many offspring; prolific. **2.** Loving one's own offspring or children in general. **3.** Of or pertaining to love of children. —**phil′o·pro·gen′i·tive·ly** *adv.* —**phil′o·pro·gen′i·tive·ness** *n.*

philos. philosopher; philosophical; philosophy.

phil·o·sophe (fĭl′ə-sŏf′; *French* fē-lô-zôf′) *n.* Any of the leading philosophical, political, and social writers of the French Enlightenment. [French, a philosopher, from Old French, PHILOSOPHER.]

phi·los·o·pher (fĭ-lŏs′ə-fər) *n.* **1.** *Abbr.* **phil., philos.** A student of or specialist in philosophy. **2.** A person who lives and thinks according to a particular philosophy. **3.** A person who is calm and rational under any circumstances. **4.** *Archaic.* An alchemist. [Middle English *philosophre,* from Old French *philosophe,* from Latin *philosophus,* from Greek *philosophos* "loving wisdom" : PHILO- + *sophos,* wise (see **sophist**).]

philosophers' stone. Also **philosopher's stone.** **1.** In alchemy: **a.** The substance held to have the power of transmuting baser metals into gold. **b.** The **elixir** *(see).* **c.** The mystical substance serving as catalyst in the redemption of man and of the universe. **2.** Anything, as a principle or idea, thought capable of effecting spiritual or other regeneration.

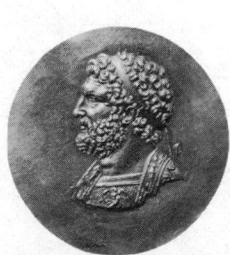

phil·o·soph·i·cal (fĭl'ə-sŏf'ĭ-kəl) *adj.* Also **phil·o·soph·ic** (-ĭk). *Abbr.* **phil., philos.** **1.** Of, pertaining to, or based on a system of philosophy. **2.** Characterizing a philosopher; enlightened; wise; serene; thoughtful. —**phil'o·soph'i·cal·ly** *adv.*

phi·los·o·phize (fĭ-lŏs'ə-fīz') *intr.v.* **-phized, -phizing, -phizes.** To speculate in a philosophical manner. —**phi·los'o·phiz'er** *n.*

phi·los·o·phy (fĭ-lŏs'ə-fē) *n., pl.* **-phies.** *Abbr.* **phil., philos.** **1. a.** Love and pursuit of wisdom by intellectual means and moral self-discipline. **b.** The investigation of causes and laws underlying reality. **c.** Any system of philosophical inquiry or demonstration. **2.** Inquiry into the nature of things based on logical reasoning rather than empirical methods. **3.** The critique and analysis of fundamental beliefs as they come to be conceptualized and formulated. **4.** The synthesis of all learning. **5.** In archaic and historical use, the investigation of natural phenomena and its systematization in theory and experiment, as in alchemy, astrology, or astronomy: *hermetic philosophy; natural philosophy.* **6.** All learning except technical precepts and practical arts. **7.** All the disciplines presented in university curriculums of science and the liberal arts, except medicine, law, and theology: *Doctor of Philosophy.* **8.** The science comprising logic, ethics, aesthetics, metaphysics, and epistemology. **9.** Any system of motivating concepts or principles: *the philosophy of a culture.* **10.** A basic theory; a viewpoint: *an original philosophy of advertising.* **11.** The system of values by which one lives. **12.** The calmness, equanimity, and detachment thought to befit a philosopher. [Middle English *philosophie*, from Old French, from Latin *philosophia*, from Greek, from *philosophos*, "loving wisdom." See **philosopher.**]

–philous, –philic. Indicates a love of or fondness for something; for example, **photophilous, lyophilic.** [From Greek *philos*, beloved, dear, loving. See **bhilo-** in Appendix.*]

phil·ter (fĭl'tər) *n.* Also **phil·tre.** **1.** A love potion. **2.** Any magic potion or charm. —*tr.v.* **philtered, -tering, -ters.** Also **philtre, -tred, -tring, -tres.** To enchant with or as with a philter. [Old French *philtre*, potion, from Latin *philtrum*, from Greek *philtron*, "love charm," from *philein*, to love, from *philos*, beloved, dear, loving. See **bhilo-** in Appendix.*]

phiz (fĭz) *n. Archaic Slang.* A face or facial expression. [Alteration and shortening of PHYSIOGNOMY.]

PHL Airport code for International Airport, Philadelphia.

phle·bi·tis (flĭ-bī'tĭs) *n. Pathology.* Inflammation of a vein. [PHLEB(O)- + -ITIS.] —**phle·bit'ic** (-bĭt'ĭk) *adj.*

phlebo-, phleb-. Indicates a vein; for example, **phlebotomy, phlebitis.** [Greek, from *phleps*† (stem *phleb-*), blood vessel, vein.]

phle·bot·o·mize (flĭ-bŏt'ə-mīz') *tr.v.* **-mized, -mizing, -mizes.** *Medicine.* To perform a phlebotomy on.

phle·bot·o·my (flĭ-bŏt'ə-mē) *n., pl.* **-mies.** *Medicine.* The therapeutic practice of opening a vein to draw blood. Also called "venesection." [Middle English *flebotomye*, from Old French *flebotomie*, from Late Latin *phlebotomia*, from Greek *phlebotomia*, "blood-letting" : PHLEBO- + -TOMY.] —**phleb'o·tom'ic** (flĕb'ə-tŏm'ĭk), **phleb'o·tom'i·cal** *adj.* —**phle·bot'o·mist** *n.*

Phleg·e·thon (flĕg'ə-thŏn'). *Greek Mythology.* A river of fire, one of the six rivers of Hades. [Greek, from *phlegethein*, to blaze, from *phlegein*, to burn. See **bhel-¹** in Appendix.*]

phlegm (flĕm) *n.* **1.** *Physiology.* Stringy, thick mucus secreted by the respiratory mucosa. **2.** One of the four humors of ancient physiology. **3.** Sluggishness of temperament. **4.** Calm self-possession; equanimity. [Middle English *fleume*, from Old French, from Late Latin *phlegma*, body moisture, from Greek, flame, inflammation, phlegm, from *phlegein*, to burn. See **bhel-¹** in Appendix.*] —**phlegm'y** (flĕm'ē) *adj.*

phleg·mat·ic (flĕg-măt'ĭk) *adj.* Also **phleg·mat·i·cal** (flĕg-măt'ĭ-kəl). **1.** Of or pertaining to phlegm; phlegmy. **2.** Having or suggesting a calm, sluggish temperament; unemotional. [Middle English *flaumatike*, from Old French *flaumatique*, from Late Latin *phlegmaticus*, like phlegm, from Greek *phlegmatikos*, having phlegm, from *phlegma* (stem *phlegmat-*), PHLEGM.]

phlo·em (flō'ĕm') *n. Botany.* The food-conducting tissue of vascular plants, consisting of sieve tubes and other cellular material. Compare **xylem.** [German *Phloem*, from Greek *phloios, phloos,* bark. See **bhleu-** in Appendix.*]

phlo·gis·tic (flō-jĭs'tĭk) *adj.* **1.** Of or pertaining to phlogiston. **2.** *Medicine.* Of or pertaining to inflammation or fever.

phlo·gis·ton (flō-jĭs'tŏn', -tən) *n.* A hypothetical substance formerly thought to be a volatile constituent of all combustible substances released as flame in combustion. [New Latin, from Greek, from *phlogistos*, "inflammable," from *phlogizein*, to set on fire, from *phlox* (stem *phlog-*), flame, from *phlegein*, to burn. See **bhel-¹** in Appendix.*]

phlog·o·pite (flŏg'ə-pīt') *n.* A yellow to dark-brown mica, KMg₃AlSi₃O₁₀(OH)₂, used in insulation. [German *Phlogopit*, from Greek *phlogōpos*, "fiery-looking" : *phlox* (stem *phlog-*), flame (see **phlogiston**) + *ōps*, eye (see **okw-** in Appendix.*).]

phlox (flŏks) *n., pl.* **phlox** or **phloxes.** Any plant of the genus *Phlox*, chiefly of North America, having lance-shaped leaves and clusters of white, red, or purple flowers. [New Latin, from Latin, a flower, from Greek, wallflower, flame, from *phlegein*, to burn. See **bhel-¹** in Appendix.*]

phlyc·te·na (flĭk-tē'nə) *n., pl.* **-nae** (-nē). Also **phlyc·tae·na.** *Medicine.* A small blister; vesicle. [New Latin, from Greek *phluktaina*, blister, from *phluein, phluzein*, to boil over. See **bhleu-** in Appendix.*]

Ph.M. Master of Philosophy (Latin *Philosophiae Magister*).

Phnom Penh (pə-nôm' pĕn'). Also **Pnom-Penh.** The capital and largest city of Cambodia, on the Mekong River in the south-central part of the country. Population, 403,000.

–phobe. Indicates one who fears or is averse to something; for example, **xenophobe.** [Greek *-phobos*, fearing, from *phobos*, fear, flight. See **bhegw-** in Appendix.*]

pho·bi·a (fō'bē-ə) *n.* **1.** A persistent, abnormal, or illogical fear of a specific thing or situation. **2.** Any strong fear, dislike, or aversion. [New Latin, from Late Latin *-phobia*, -PHOBIA.] —**pho'bic** (fō'bĭk) *adj.*

–phobia. Indicates persistent, illogical, abnormal, or intense fear; for example, **hypnophobia.** [New Latin, from Late Latin, from Greek, from *phobos*, fear, flight. See **bhegw-** in Appendix.*]

Pho·bos (fō'bŏs', fŏb'ŏs') *n. Astronomy.* The smaller and inner of the two satellites of the planet Mars.

Pho·cae·a (fō-sē'ə). An ancient Ionian city, on the Aegean Sea, on the western coast of Asia Minor.

Pho·cis (fō'sĭs). An ancient country of central Greece, north of the Gulf of Corinth.

phoe·be (fē'bē) *n.* Any of several small dull-colored North American birds of the genus *Sayornis*. [Imitative (influenced by the name PHOEBE).]

Phoe·be¹ (fē'bē). A feminine given name.

Phoe·be² (fē'bē). *Greek Mythology.* The goddess Artemis. [Greek *Phoibē*, from *phoibos*, shining. See **bheigw-** in Appendix.*]

Phoe·be³ (fē'bē) *n.* **1.** *Poetic.* The moon. **2.** *Astronomy.* The ninth satellite of Saturn. [From PHOEBE (Artemis).]

Phoe·bus¹ (fē'bəs). *Greek Mythology.* Apollo, the god of the sun. [Greek *phoibos*, radiant. See **Phoebe.**]

Phoe·bus² (fē'bəs) *n. Poetic.* The sun. [From PHOEBUS.]

Phoe·ni·cia (fĭ-nĭsh'ə, -nē'shə). An ancient maritime country consisting of a group of city-states of Syria, extending from the Mediterranean Sea eastward to the Lebanon Mountains.

Phoe·ni·cian (fĭ-nĭsh'ən, -nē'shən) *n.* **1.** A native, inhabitant, or subject of ancient Phoenicia. **2.** The Northwest Semitic language of ancient Phoenicia. [Middle English *Phenicien*, from Old French, from Latin *Phoenicius*, from Greek *phoinix*, PHOENIX, also a Phoenician (the nature of the association is uncertain).] —**Phoe·ni'cian** *adj.*

phoe·nix (fē'nĭks) *n.* Also **phe·nix.** **1.** *Egyptian Mythology.* A bird that consumed itself by fire after 500 years, and rose renewed from its ashes. **2.** A person or thing of unsurpassed excellence or beauty; paragon. [Middle English *fenix*, from Old French, from Latin *phoenix*, from Greek *phoinix*, perhaps from Egyptian *bynw*, phoenix.]

Phoe·nix¹ (fē'nĭks) *n. Astronomy.* A constellation in the Southern Hemisphere near Tucana and Sculptor.

Phoe·nix² (fē'nĭks). The capital and largest city of Arizona, in the south-central part of the state. Population, 439,000.

phon. phonetic; phonetics; phonology.

pho·nate (fō'nāt') *v.* **-nated, -nating, -nates.** —*intr.* To utter speech sounds; vocalize. —*tr.* To utter (a sound). [PHON(O)- + -ATE.] —**pho'na'tion** (fō'nā'shən) *n.*

phone¹ (fōn) *n. Linguistics.* Any individual speech sound. [From Greek *phōnē*, sound, voice. See **bhā-²** in Appendix.*]

phone² (fōn) *n. Informal.* A telephone. —*v.* **phoned, phoning, phones.** *Informal.* —*intr.* To telephone. —*tr.* **1.** To telephone (someone). **2.** To impart (information or news, for example) by telephone. [Short for TELEPHONE.]

–phone. Indicates a sound or sound-emitting device; for example, **radiophone.** [From Greek *phōnē*, sound, voice. See **bhā-²** in Appendix.*]

pho·neme (fō'nēm') *n. Linguistics.* One of the set of the smallest units of speech that distinguish one utterance or word from another in a given language. The *m* of *mat* and the *b* of *bat* are two English phonemes. [French *phonème*, from Greek *phōnēma*, an utterance, from *phōnein*, to sound, speak, from *phōnē*, sound, voice. See **bhā-²** in Appendix.*]

pho·ne·mic (fə-nē'mĭk, fō-) *adj.* Also **pho·ne·mat·ic** (fō'nĭ-măt'ĭk). **1.** Of or pertaining to phonemes. **2.** Of or pertaining to phonemics. **3.** Serving to distinguish phonemes or distinctive features. —**pho·ne'mi·cal·ly** *adv.*

pho·ne·mics (fə-nē'mĭks, fō-) *n.* Plural in form, used with a singular verb. *Linguistics.* The study and establishment of the phonemes of a language. —**pho·ne'mi·cist** (-mə-sĭst) *n.*

phonet. phonetic; phonetics.

pho·net·ic (fə-nĕt'ĭk) *adj.* *Abbr.* **phon., phonet.** **1.** Of or pertaining to phonetics. **2.** Representing the sounds of speech with a set of distinct symbols, each denoting a single sound: *phonetic spelling.* [Greek *phōnētikos*, from *phōnein*, to sound, speak, from *phōnē*, sound, voice. See **bhā-²** in Appendix.*] —**pho·net'i·cal·ly** *adv.*

phonetic alphabet. **1.** A standardized set of symbols used in phonetic transcription. See **International Phonetic Alphabet.** **2.** *Telecommunications.* Any of various systems of code words for identifying letters in voice communication.

pho·ne·ti·cian (fō'nə-tĭsh'ən) *n.* Also **pho·net·i·cist** (fə-nĕt'ə-sĭst), **pho·ne·tist** (fō'nə-tĭst). An expert in phonetics.

pho·net·ics (fə-nĕt'ĭks) *n.* Plural in form, used with a singular verb. *Abbr.* **phon., phonet. 1.** The branch of linguistics dealing with the study of the sounds of speech, their production, combination, description, and representation by written symbols. **2.** The system of sounds of a particular language.

pho·ney. Variant of **phony.**

phon·ic (fŏn'ĭk) *adj.* Of, pertaining to, or having the nature of sound, especially speech sound. [PHON(O)- + -IC.] —**phon'i·cal·ly** *adv.*

phon·ics (fŏn'ĭks) *n.* Plural in form, used with a singular verb. **1.** The study or science of sound; acoustics. **2.** The use of elementary phonetics in the teaching of reading.

phlox
Phlox paniculata

---

t tight/th thin, path/*th* this, bathe/ŭ cut/ûr urge/v valve/w with/y yes/z zebra, size/zh vision/ə about, item, edible, gallop, circus/ à *Fr.* ami/œ *Fr.* feu, *Ger.* schön/ü *Fr.* tu, *Ger.* über/KH *Ger.* ich, *Scot.* loch/N *Fr.* bon. *Follows main vocabulary. †Of obscure origin.

phono-, phon-. Indicates sound or voice; for example, **phonograph.** [Greek *phōnē*, sound, voice. See bhā-² in Appendix.*]

pho·no·gram (fō'nə-grăm') *n.* A character or symbol, as in a phonetic alphabet, representing a word or phoneme in speech. [PHONO- + -GRAM.] —**pho'no·gram'ic, pho'no·gram'mic** *adj.* —**pho'no·gram'i·cal·ly, pho'no·gram'mi·cal·ly** *adv*

pho·no·graph (fō'nə-grăf', -gräf') *n.* A machine that reproduces sound from a disc. [PHONO- + -GRAPH.] —**pho'no·graph'ic** *adj.* —**pho'no·graph'i·cal·ly** *adv.*

pho·nog·ra·phy (fə-nŏg'rə-fē, fō-) *n.* **1.** The science or practice of transcribing speech by means of symbols representing elements of sound; phonetic transcription. **2.** Any system of shorthand based on phonetic transcription. [PHONO- + -GRAPHY.] —**pho·nog'ra·pher, pho·nog'ra·phist** *n.*

pho·no·lite (fō'nə-līt') *n.* A volcanic rock composed principally of orthoclase and nepheline. Also called "clinkstone." [French, from German *Phonolith* : PHONO- + -LITH (it clinks when struck).] —**pho·no·lit'ic** (fō'nə-lĭt'ĭk) *adj.*

pho·nol·o·gy (fə-nŏl'ə-jē, fō-) *n. Abbr.* **phon., phonol.** The science of speech sounds, including phonetics and phonemics. [PHONO- + -LOGY.] —**pho·no·log'ic** (fō'nə-lŏj'ĭk), **pho'no·log'i·cal** *adj.* —**pho'no·log'i·cal·ly** *adv.* —**pho·nol'o·gist** *n.*

pho·non (fō'nŏn') *n. Physics.* The quantum of acoustic or vibrational energy, considered a discrete particle and used especially in mathematical models to calculate thermal and vibrational properties of solids. [PHON(O)- + -ON.]

pho·no·re·cep·tion (fō'nō-rĭ-sĕp'shən) *n.* Perception of or response to sound waves. —**pho'no·re·cep'tor** (-tər) *n.*

pho·no·scope (fō'nə-skōp') *n.* A device that produces a visible display of the mechanical properties of a sounding body, especially of musical instruments. [PHONO- + -SCOPE.]

pho·no·type (fō'nə-tīp') *n.* **1.** A phonetic symbol used in printing. **2.** Text printed in phonetic symbols. —**pho'no·typ'ic** (fō'nə-tĭp'ĭk), **pho'no·typ'i·cal** *adj.* —**pho'no·typ'i·cal·ly** *adv.*

pho·no·typ·y (fō'nə-tī'pē) *n.* The practice of transcribing speech sounds by means of phonetic symbols. —**pho'no·typ'ist** *n.*

pho·ny (fō'nē) *adj.* **-nier, -niest.** Also **pho·ney.** *Informal.* Not genuine or real; spurious; fake: "*The very air seemed colored with phony folklore.*" (Vladimir Nabokov). —*n., pl.* **phonies.** Also **pho·ney,** *pl.* **-neys.** *Informal.* **1.** Something not genuine; a fake. **2.** A spurious person; impostor; hypocrite. [Origin unknown.] —**pho'ni·ly** *adv.* —**pho'ni·ness** *n.*

-phony. Indicates sound of a specified kind; for example, **telephony.** [Greek *-phōnia,* from *phōnē,* sound. See bhā-² in Appendix.*]

phoo·ey (foo'ē) *interj.* Used as an exclamation of disappointment or contempt. [From *phoo,* variant of PHEW.]

-phore. Indicates a bearer or producer of; for example, **semaphore.** [From Greek *-phoros,* bearing, from *pherein,* to bear. See bher-¹ in Appendix.*]

-phoresis. Indicates transmission; for example, **electrophoresis.** [Greek *phorēsis,* a bearing, from *phorein,* frequentative of *pherein,* to bear. See bher-¹ in Appendix.*]

-phorous. Indicates bearing or producing; for example, **gonophorous.** [Greek *-phoros,* from *pherein,* to bear. See bher-¹ in Appendix.*]

phos-. Indicates the presence of light; for example, **phosgene.** [Greek *phōs,* light. See bhā-¹ in Appendix.*]

phos·gene (fŏs'jēn', fŏz'-) *n.* A colorless volatile liquid or gas, COCl₂, used as a poison gas and in making glass, dyes, resins, and plastics. Also called "carbonyl chloride." [PHOS- (from the former method of obtaining the compound by exposure to sunlight) + -gene, variant of -GEN.]

phos·pha·tase (fŏs'fə-tās', -tāz') *n.* Any of numerous enzymes that catalyze the hydrolysis of esters to phosphoric acid and are distinguished by activity in carbohydrate and nucleotide metabolism and in bone formation. [PHOSPHAT(E) + -ASE.]

phos·phate (fŏs'fāt') *n.* **1.** *Chemistry.* Any salt or ester of phosphoric acid containing mainly pentavalent phosphorus and oxygen. **2.** A fertilizer containing phosphorus compounds. **3.** A carbonated beverage of water, flavoring, and a small amount of phosphoric acid. [French *phosphat,* from *phosphore,* phosphorous, from New Latin *phosphorus,* PHOSPHORUS.] —**phos·phat'ic** (fŏs·făt'ĭk) *adj.*

phosphate rock. Any of various sedimentary rocks composed largely of apatite, and used as fertilizer and as a source of phosphorous compounds.

phos·pha·tide (fŏs'fə-tīd') *n.* Any of a group of lipid compounds, such as lecithin and cephalin, composed mainly of glycerol and phosphoric acid, and found in great abundance in plant and animal tissues with stored fats. Also called "phospholipid." [PHOSPHAT(E) + -IDE.]

phos·pha·tize (fŏs'fə-tīz') *tr.v.* **-tized, -tizing, -tizes. 1.** To change into a phosphate or phosphates. **2.** To treat with phosphate or phosphoric acid. —**phos'pha·ti·za'tion** *n.*

phos·pha·tu·ri·a (fŏs'fə-tŏŏr'ē-ə, -tyŏŏr'ē-ə) *n.* A condition in which excessive phosphates are discharged in the urine. [New Latin : PHOSPHAT(E) + -URIA.] —**phos'pha·tu'ric** *adj.*

phos·phene (fŏs'fēn') *n.* A luminous visual sensation experienced when the eyeball is pressed. [PHOS- + Greek *phainein,* to show (see bhā-¹ in Appendix*).]

phos·phide (fŏs'fīd') *n.* Also **phos·phid** (fŏs'fĭd). A compound of phosphorus and a more electropositive element. [PHOSPH(O)- + -IDE.]

phos·phine (fŏs'fēn') *n.* Also **phos·phin** (fŏs'fĭn). **1.** A colorless, spontaneously flammable poisonous gas, PH₃, having a garlic-like odor and used as a doping agent for solid-state components. **2.** A synthetic yellow dye. [PHOSPH(O)- + -INE.]

phos·phite (fŏs'fīt') *n.* Any salt of phosphorous acid.

phospho-. Indicates the presence of phosphorus; for example, **phosphocreatine.** [French, from *phosphore,* phosphorus, from New Latin *phosphorus,* PHOSPHORUS.]

phos·pho·cre·a·tine (fŏs'fō-krē'ə-tēn') *n.* Also **phos·pho·cre·a·tin** (fŏs'fō-krē'ə-tĭn). An organic compound, C₄H₁₀N₃O₅, capable of providing physiologic energy as in muscular contraction. [PHOSPHO- + CREATINE.]

phos·pho·ni·um (fŏs-fō'nē-əm) *n.* A univalent radical, PH₄, derived from phosphine. [PHOSPH(O)- + (AMM)ONIUM.]

phos·pho·pro·tein (fŏs'fō-prō'tēn', -prō'tē-ĭn) *n.* Any of a group of proteins, such as casein, containing chemically bound phosphoric acid.

phos·phor (fŏs'fər, -fôr') *n.* **1.** Any substance that can be stimulated to emit light by incident radiation. **2.** Something exhibiting phosphorescence. [French *phosphore,* from New Latin *phosphorus,* PHOSPHORUS.]

phosphor bronze. A hard, strong, corrosion-resistant bronze containing up to 0.5 per cent phosphorus and used in electric switches, springs, and chains.

phos·pho·resce (fŏs'fə-rĕs') *intr.v.* **-resced, -rescing, -resces.** To persist in emitting light, unaccompanied by sensible heat or combustion, after exposure to and removal of a source of radiation. [Probably a back-formation from phosphorescent : PHOSPHOR + -ESCENT.]

phos·pho·res·cence (fŏs'fə-rĕs'əns) *n.* **1.** Persistent emission of light following exposure to and removal of incident radiation. **2.** Organically generated light emission; bioluminescence: "*He saw the phosphorescence of the Gulf weed in the water.*" (Hemingway). [From PHOSPHOR.] —**phos'pho·res'cent** *adj.* —**phos'pho·res'cent·ly** *adv.*

phos·phor·ic (fŏs-fôr'ĭk, -fŏr'ĭk) *adj.* Of, pertaining to, or containing phosphorus, especially in a valence state higher than that of a comparable phosphorous compound.

phosphoric acid. A clear colorless liquid, H₃PO₄, used in fertilizers, soaps and detergents, food flavoring, pharmaceuticals, and animal feed.

phos·pho·rism (fŏs'fə-rĭz'əm) *n.* Chronic phosphorus poisoning from ingestion or inhalation. [PHOSPHOR(US) + -ISM.]

phos·pho·rite (fŏs'fə-rīt') *n.* **1.** A fibrous variety of **apatite** (see). **2.** A concretionary mass of rock consisting predominantly of calcium phosphate. [PHOSPHOR(US) + -ITE.]

phos·pho·rous (fŏs'fər-əs, fŏs-fôr'əs, fŏs-fōr'əs) *adj.* Of, pertaining to, or containing phosphorus, especially with valence 3.

phosphorous acid. *Chemistry.* A white or yellowish hygroscopic crystalline solid, H₃PO₃, used as a reducing agent and to produce phosphite salts.

phos·pho·rus (fŏs'fər-əs) *n.* **1.** *Symbol* **P** A highly reactive, poisonous, nonmetallic element occurring naturally in phosphates, especially apatite, and existing in three allotropic forms, white (sometimes yellow), red, and black. It is an essential constituent of protoplasm and, depending on the allotropic form, is used in safety matches, pyrotechnics, incendiary shells, fertilizers, glass, and steel. Atomic number 15, atomic weight 30.9738, melting point (white) 44.1°C, boiling point 280°C, specific gravity (white) 1.82, valences 3, 5. See **element. 2.** Any phosphorescent substance. [New Latin, from Greek *phosphoros,* "light-bearing" (so named from the fact that white phosphorus is phosphorescent in air) : PHOS- + -PHOROUS.]

phos·phor·yl·ase (fŏs'fər-ə-lās', -lāz') *n. Biochemistry.* An enzyme that catalyzes the production of phosphates from glycogen. [PHOSPHOR(US) + -YL + -ASE.]

phos·phor·yl·ate (fŏs'fər-ə-lāt') *tr.v.* **-ated, -ating, -ates.** To change (an organic substance) into an organic phosphate. [PHOSPHOR(US) + -YL + -ATE.]

phot (fōt, fŏt) *n. Physics.* A unit of illumination equal to one **lumen** (see) per square centimeter. [Greek *phōs* (stem *phōt-*), light. See bhā-¹ in Appendix.*]

pho·tic (fō'tĭk) *adj.* **1.** Of or pertaining to light. **2.** *Biology.* Pertaining to the production of light by organisms. **3.** Pertaining to or designating the upper zone or region of a body of water, into which sunlight penetrates. [PHOT(O)- + -IC.]

pho·to (fō'tō) *n., pl.* **-tos.** *Informal.* A photograph.

photo-, phot-. Indicates: **1.** Light; for example, **photosynthesis, photic. 2.** Photographic; for example, **photomontage.** [Greek *phōs* (stem *phōt-*), light. See bhā-¹ in Appendix.*]

pho·to·ac·tive (fō'tō-ăk'tĭv) *adj.* **1.** Capable of responding to light photoelectrically. **2.** Capable of responding to light by chemical reaction. —**pho'to·ac·tiv'i·ty** *n.*

pho·to·au·to·troph·ic (fō'tō-ô'tə-trŏf'ĭk, -trō'fĭk) *adj. Biology.* Capable of using light as a source of energy in the synthesis of food from inorganic materials.

pho·to·bi·ot·ic (fō'tō-bī-ŏt'ĭk) *adj. Biology.* Depending on light for the continuance of life and growth.

pho·to·cell (fō'tō-sĕl') *n. Electronics.* A photoelectric cell (see).

pho·to·chem·is·try (fō'tō-kĕm'ĭs-trē) *n.* The chemistry of the interactions of radiant energy and chemical systems. —**pho'to·chem'i·cal** *adj.*

pho·to·com·pose (fō'tō-kəm-pōz') *tr.v.* **-posed, -posing, -poses.** To prepare (written matter) for printing by photocomposition. Also "photoset." —**pho'to·com·pos'er** *n.*

pho·to·com·po·si·tion (fō'tō-kŏm'pə-zĭsh'ən) *n.* The preparation of manuscript for printing by the projection of images of type characters on photographic film, which is then used to make printing plates. Also called "phototypesetting."

pho·to·con·duc·tiv·i·ty (fō'tō-kŏn'dŭk-tĭv'ə-tē) *n. Physics.* Electrical conductivity affected by illumination. —**pho'to·con·duc'tive** (-kən-dŭk'tĭv) *adj.* —**pho'to·con·duc'tion** *n.*

pho·to·cop·i·er (fō'tō-kŏp'ē-ər) *n.* A device for photographically reproducing written, printed, or graphic material.

pho·to·cop·y (fō′tō-kŏp′ē) *tr.v.* **-copied, -copying, -copies.** To make a photographic reproduction of (printed, written, or graphic material). Also "photoduplicate." —*n., pl.* **photocopies.** A photographic reproduction. Also "photoduplicate."

pho·to·cur·rent (fō′tō-kûr′ənt) *n. Physics.* An electric current produced by illumination of a photoelectric material.

pho·to·dis·in·te·gra·tion (fō′tō-dĭs-ĭn′tə-grā′shən) *n. Physics.* Nuclear disintegration or transformation caused by absorption of high-energy radiation, as of gamma rays.

pho·to·dra·ma (fō′tə-drä′mə, -drăm′ə) *n.* A **photoplay** *(see).*

pho·to·du·pli·cate (fō′tō-dōō′plĭ-kāt′, -dyōō′plĭ-kāt′) *tr.v.* **-cated, -cating, -cates.** To **photocopy** *(see).* —**pho′to·du′pli·cate** (-kĭt) *n.* —**pho′to·du′pli·ca′tion** *n.*

pho·to·dy·nam·ic (fō′tō-dī-năm′ĭk) *adj.* Producing or increasing in organisms a toxic reaction to light.

pho·to·e·lec·tric (fō′tō-ĭ-lĕk′trĭk) *adj.* Also **pho·to·e·lec·tri·cal** (fō′tō-ĭ-lĕk′trĭ-kəl). Of or pertaining to electric effects, especially increased electrical conduction, caused by illumination. —**pho′to·e·lec′tri·cal·ly** *adv.*

photoelectric cell. An electronic device having an electrical output that varies in response to incident radiation, especially to visible light. Also called "photocell," "electric eye."

photoelectric effect. *Physics.* The ejection of electrons from a substance by incident electromagnetic radiation, especially by visible light.

pho·to·e·lec·tron (fō′tō-ĭ-lĕk′trŏn′) *n. Physics.* An electron released or ejected from a substance by the photoelectric effect.

pho·to·e·mis·sion (fō′tō-ĭ-mĭsh′ən) *n. Physics.* The emission of photoelectrons, especially from metallic surfaces.

pho·to·en·grave (fō′tō-ĕn-grāv′) *tr.v.* **-graved, -graving, -graves.** To reproduce by photoengraving. —**pho′to·en·grav′er** *n.*

pho·to·en·grav·ing (fō′tō-ĕn-grā′vĭng) *n.* **1.** The process of reproducing graphic material by transferring the image photomechanically to a plate or other surface in etched relief for printing. **2.** A plate prepared by this method. **3.** A reproduction made by this method.

photo finish. 1. A race in which the leading contestants cross the finish line so close together that the winner must be determined by a photograph taken at the moment of crossing. **2.** *Informal.* Any extremely close competition.

pho·to·flash (fō′tō-flăsh′) *n. Photography.* A **flash bulb** *(see).*

pho·to·flood (fō′tō-flŭd′) *n. Photography.* A reusable electric lamp that produces a bright continuous light for photographic illumination. Also called "photoflood lamp."

pho·to·fluor·og·ra·phy (fō′tō-flōō-rŏg′rə-fē) *n. Medicine.* The photography of fluoroscopic images. [PHOTO- + FLUORO- + -GRAPHY.] —**pho′to·fluor·o·graph′ic** (-flŏŏr′ə-grăf′ĭk) *adj.*

photog. photograph; photographer; photography.

pho·to·gel·a·tin process (fō′tō-jĕl′ə-tĭn). *Photography.* **Collotype** *(see).*

pho·to·gene (fō′tə-jēn′) *n. Physiology.* A retinal **afterimage** *(see).* [PHOTO- + *-gene,* variant of -GEN.]

pho·to·gen·ic (fō′tə-jĕn′ĭk) *adj.* **1.** Attractive as a subject for photography. **2.** *Biology.* Producing or emitting light; phosphorescent. **3.** *Rare.* Caused or produced by light. [PHOTO- + -GENIC.] —**pho′to·gen′i·cal·ly** *adv.*

pho·to·gram (fō′tə-grăm′) *n. Photography.* **1.** A shadowy image produced without a camera by placing an object in contact with film or photosensitive paper and exposing to light. **2.** A photograph. [PHOTO- + -GRAM.]

pho·to·gram·me·try (fō′tə-grăm′ə-trē) *n.* **1.** The process of making maps or scale drawings by aerial or other photography. **2.** The process of making precise measurements by the use of photography. [PHOTOGRAM + -METRY.] **pho′to·gram·met′ric** (-grə-mĕt′rĭk) *adj.*

pho·to·graph (fō′tə-grăf′, -gräf′) *n. Abbr.* **photog.** An image, especially a positive print, recorded by a camera and reproduced on a photosensitive surface. —*v.* **photographed, -graphing, -graphs.** —*tr.* To take a photograph of. —*intr.* **1.** To practice photography. **2.** To be the subject for photographs: *She photographs well.* [PHOTO- + -GRAPH.]

pho·tog·ra·pher (fə-tŏg′rə-fər) *Abbr.* **photog.** A person who takes photographs, especially as a profession.

pho·to·graph·ic (fō′tə-grăf′ĭk) *adj.* Also **pho·to·graph·i·cal** (fō′tə-grăf′ĭ-kəl). **1.** Of, pertaining to, or consisting of photography or a photograph. **2.** Used in photography: *a photographic lens.* **3.** Resembling a photograph; especially, representing or simulating something with great accuracy and fidelity of detail. **4.** Capable of forming accurate and lasting impressions: *a photographic memory.* —**pho′to·graph′i·cal·ly** *adv.*

pho·tog·ra·phy (fə-tŏg′rə-fē) *n. Abbr.* **photog. 1.** The process of rendering optical images on photosensitive surfaces. **2.** The art, practice, or occupation of taking and printing photographs. **3.** A body of photographs. [PHOTO- + -GRAPHY.]

pho·to·gra·vure (fō′tə-grə-vyŏŏr′) *n.* The process of printing from an intaglio plate, etched according to a photographic image. [PHOTO- + GRAVURE.]

pho·to·he·li·o·graph (fō′tō-hē′lē-ə-grăf′, -gräf′) *n.* A telescope equipped to photograph the sun.

pho·to·jour·nal·ism (fō′tō-jûr′nəl-ĭz′əm) *n.* Journalism making primary use of photographs. —**pho′to·jour′nal·ist** *n.*

pho·to·ki·ne·sis (fō′tō-kĭ-nē′sĭs, -kī-nē′sĭs) *n. Biology.* Movement as a response to light. [PHOTO- + -KINESIS.] —**pho′to·ki·net′ic** (-nĕt′ĭk) *adj.*

pho·to·lith·o·graph (fō′tə-lĭth′ə-grăf′, -gräf′) *tr.v.* **-graphed, -graphing, -graphs.** To reproduce by means of photolithography. —*n.* A picture made by photolithography. Also shortened to "photolith." [PHOTO- + LITHOGRAPH.] —**pho·to·li·thog′ra·pher** (fō′tō-lĭ-thŏg′rə-fər) *n.*

pho·to·li·thog·ra·phy (fō′tō-lĭ-thŏg′rə-fē) *n.* A planographic printing process using plates made according to a photographic image. Also shortened to "photolith." —**pho′to·lith′o·graph′ic** (fō′tə-lĭth′ə-grăf′ĭk) *adj.*

pho·tol·y·sis (fō-tŏl′ə-sĭs) *n.* Chemical decomposition induced by light or other radiant energy. [New Latin : PHOTO- + -LYSIS.] —**pho′to·lyt′ic** (fō′tə-lĭt′ĭk) *adj.*

photom. photometry.

pho·to·map (fō′tə-măp′) *n.* A map made by superimposing orienting data on an aerial photograph.

pho·to·me·chan·i·cal (fō′tō-mĭ-kăn′ĭ-kəl) *adj.* Of, pertaining to, or designating any of various methods by which plates are prepared for printing by means of photography. —**pho′to·me·chan′i·cal·ly** *adv.*

pho·tom·e·ter (fō-tŏm′ə-tər) *n.* An instrument for measuring a property of light, especially luminous intensity or flux. [PHOTO- + -METER.]

pho·tom·e·try (fō-tŏm′ə-trē) *n. Abbr.* **photom.** *Physics.* The measurement of the properties of light, especially of luminous intensity. [PHOTO- + -METRY.] —**pho′to·met′ric** (fō′tə-mĕt′rĭk), **pho′to·met′ri·cal** *adj.* —**pho·tom′e·trist** *n.*

pho·to·mi·cro·graph (fō′tō-mī′krə-grăf′, -gräf′) *n.* A photograph made through a microscope. Compare **microphotograph.** —*tr.v.* **photomicrographed, -graphing, -graphs.** To make (a photograph) through a microscope. —**pho′to·mi·crog′ra·pher** (-mī-krŏg′rə-fər) *n.* —**pho′to·mi′cro·graph′ic** *adj.* —**pho′to·mi·crog′ra·phy** *n.*

pho·to·mon·tage (fō′tō-mŏn-täzh′, -môn-täzh′) *n.* **1.** The technique of making a picture by assembling pieces of photographs, often in combination with other types of graphic material. **2.** The composite picture produced by this technique.

pho·ton (fō′tŏn′) *n. Physics.* The quantum of electromagnetic energy, generally regarded as a discrete **particle** *(see)* having zero mass, no electric charge, and an indefinitely long lifetime. [PHOT(O)- + -ON.] —**pho′ton′ic** *adj.*

Pho·ton (fō′tŏn′) *n. Printing.* A trademark for certain related machines for photographically composing matter for printing.

pho·to·nu·cle·ar (fō′tō-nōō′klē-ər, -nyōō′klē-ər) *adj. Physics.* Designating a nuclear reaction induced by photons.

pho·to·off·set (fō′tō-ôf′sĕt′, -ŏf′sĕt′) *n.* **Offset printing** *(see).*

pho·to·pe·ri·od (fō′tō-pîr′ē-əd) *n. Biology.* The relative exposure of an organism to daylight as a proportion of the total day, considered especially with regard to the effect on growth and functioning. —**pho′to·pe′ri·od′ic** (-pîr′ē-ŏd′ĭk), **pho′to·pe′ri·od′i·cal** *adj.* —**pho′to·pe′ri·od·ism′** *n.*

pho·toph·i·lous (fō-tŏf′ə-ləs) *adj.* Also **pho·to·phil·ic** (fō′tə-fĭl′ĭk). *Biology.* Growing or functioning best in strong light. [PHOTO- + -PHILOUS.] —**pho·toph′i·ly** *n.*

pho·to·pho·bi·a (fō′tə-fō′bē-ə) *n.* Abnormal intolerance of light. [PHOTO- + -PHOBIA.] —**pho′to·pho′bic** (-fō′bĭk) *adj.*

pho·to·pi·a (fō-tō′pē-ə) *n.* Adaptation of the eyes to light; daylight vision. [New Latin : PHOT(O)- + -OPIA.] —**pho·to′pic** (fō-tō′pĭk, -tŏp′ĭk) *adj.*

pho·to·play (fō′tō-plā′) *n.* A play filmed or arranged for filming as a motion picture. Also called "photodrama."

pho·to·re·cep·tion (fō′tō-rĭ-sĕp′shən) *n.* The detection or perception of visible light; vision; sight. —**pho′to·re·cep′tive** *adj.*

pho·to·re·cep·tor (fō′tō-rĭ-sĕp′tər) *n.* A photoreceptive nerve.

pho·to·re·con·nais·sance (fō′tō-rĭ-kŏn′ə-səns, -zəns) *n. Military.* Photographic aerial reconnaissance.

pho·to·sen·si·tive (fō′tō-sĕn′sə-tĭv) *adj.* Sensitive to light. —**pho′to·sen′si·tiv′i·ty** *n.*

pho·to·sen·si·ti·za·tion (fō′tō-sĕn′sə-tə-zā′shən) *n.* **1.** The act or process of photosensitizing something. **2.** *Medicine.* Hypersensitivity of the skin to sunlight or ultraviolet radiation, caused by ingestion of endocrine products, fluorescent dyes, or small amounts of heavy metals, and resulting in skin eruptions.

pho·to·sen·si·tize (fō′tō-sĕn′sə-tīz′) *tr.v.* **-tized, -tizing, -tizes.** To make (an organism or substance) sensitive to light.

pho·to·set (fō′tō-sĕt′) *tr.v.* **-set, -setting, -sets.** *Printing.* To **photocompose** *(see).*

pho·to·sphere (fō′tə-sfîr′) *n.* The surface of a star, especially of the sun. —**pho′to·spher′ic** (fō′tə-sfîr′ĭk, -sfĕr′ĭk) *adj.*

Pho·to·stat (fō′tə-stăt′) *n.* **1.** A trademark for a device used to make quick, direct-reading negative or positive copies of written, printed, or graphic material. **2.** *Sometimes small* **p.** A copy made by Photostat. —*v.* **Photostated, -stating, -stats.** Also **-statted, -statting.** *Sometimes small* **p.** —*tr.* To make a copy of by Photostat. —*intr.* To make a copy by Photostat. [PHOTO- + -STAT.] —**Pho′to·stat′er** *n.* —**Pho′to·stat′ic** *adj.*

pho·to·syn·the·sis (fō′tō-sĭn′thə-sĭs) *n.* The process by which chlorophyll-containing cells in green plants convert incident light to chemical energy and synthesize organic compounds from inorganic compounds, especially carbohydrates from carbon dioxide and water, with the simultaneous release of oxygen. —**pho′to·syn·thet′ic** (-sĭn-thĕt′ĭk) *adj.* —**pho′to·syn·thet′i·cal·ly** *adv.*

pho·to·syn·the·size (fō′tō-sĭn′thə-sīz′) *v.* **-sized, -sizing, -sizes.** —*tr.* To synthesize by the process of photosynthesis. —*intr.* To perform the process of photosynthesis.

pho·to·tax·is (fō′tō-tăk′sĭs) *n.* Also **pho·to·tax·y** (fō′tō-tăk′sē). *Biology.* The movement of an organism in response to a source of light. [PHOTO- + -TAXIS.] —**pho′to·tac′tic** (-tăk′tĭk) *adj.*

pho·to·tel·e·graph (fō′tō-tĕl′ə-grăf′, -gräf′) *tr.v.* **-graphed, -graphing, -graphs.** To transmit (printed or other graphic material) by **facsimile** *(see).* —**pho′to·te·leg′ra·phy** (-tə-lĕg′rə-fē) *n.* —**pho′to·tel′e·graph′ic, pho′to·tel′e·graph′i·cal** *adj.* —**pho′to·tel′e·graph′i·cal·ly** *adv.*

pho·to·ther·a·py (fō′tō-thĕr′ə-pē) *n.* The treatment of disease,

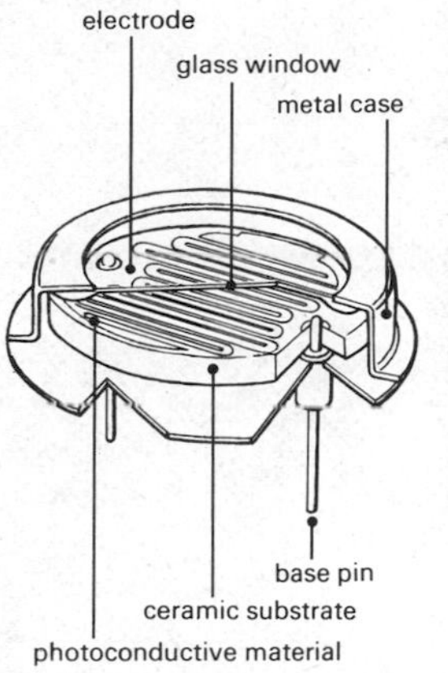
electrode
glass window
metal case
base pin
ceramic substrate
photoconductive material

photoelectric cell

especially certain skin conditions, with light, including infrared and ultraviolet radiation. Also called "phototherapeutics."

pho·tot·o·nus (fō-tŏt′ə-nəs) *n. Biology.* Sensitivity to light. [PHOTO- + TONUS.] —**pho′to·ton′ic** (fō′tə-tŏn′ĭk) *adj.*

pho·to·tran·sis·tor (fō′tō-trăn-zĭs′tər, -sĭs′tər) *n. Electronics.* A transistor having highly photosensitive electrical characteristics.

pho·tot·ro·pism (fō-tŏt′rə-pĭz′əm) *n.* Also **pho·tot·ro·py** (fō-tŏt′rə-pē). *Biology.* Growth or movement in response to a source of light. [PHOTO- + -TROPISM.] —**pho′to·trop′ic** (fō′tə-trŏp′ĭk) *adj.* —**pho′to·trop′i·cal·ly** *adv.*

pho·to·tube (fō′tō-to͞ob′, -tyo͞ob′) *n. Electronics.* An electron tube with a photosensitive cathode.

pho·to·type·set·ter (fō′tō-tīp′sĕt′ər) *n.* Any of various machines used in photocomposition.

pho·to·type·set·ting (fō′tō-tīp′sĕt′ĭng) *n. Printing.* **Photocomposition** *(see).*

pho·to·ty·pog·ra·phy (fō′tō-tī-pŏg′rə-fē) *n.* Photomechanical printing that resembles metal typography. —**pho′to·ty′po·graph′ic** (-tī′pə-grăf′ĭk), **pho′to·ty′po·graph′i·cal** *adj.* —**pho′to·ty′po·graph′i·cal·ly** *adv.*

pho·to·vol·ta·ic (fō′tō-vŏl-tā′ĭk, -vōl-tā′ĭk) *adj. Electronics.* Capable of producing a voltage when exposed to radiant energy, especially light.

pho·to·zin·co·graph (fō′tō-zĭng′kə-grăf′, -gräf′) *tr.v.* **-graphed, -graphing, -graphs.** To make (prints) by photozincography. —*n.* A print produced by photozincography.

pho·to·zin·cog·ra·phy (fō′tō-zĭng-kŏg′rə-fē) *n.* A photoengraving process in which sensitized zinc plates are used.

phr. phrase.

phrase (frāz) *n. Abbr.* **phr. 1.** Any sequence of words intended to have meaning. **2.** A brief, apt, and cogent expression, such as *behind the iron curtain.* **3.** A word or group of words read or spoken as a unit and separated by pauses or other junctures. **4.** *Grammar.* Two or more words in sequence that form a syntactic unit or group of syntactic units, less completely predicated than a sentence. **5.** *Dance.* A series of movements forming a unit in a choreographic pattern. **6.** *Music.* A segment of a composition, usually consisting of four or eight measures. —*v.* **phrased, phrasing, phrases.** —*tr.* **1.** To express orally or in writing: *He phrased several opinions.* **2.** To pace or mark off (something read aloud or spoken) by pauses. **3.** *Music.* **a.** To divide (a passage) into phrases. **b.** To combine (notes) in a phrase. —*intr.* To make or render phrases: *The reader phrased monotonously.* [Latin *phrasis,* from Greek, speech, style of speech, from *phrazein,* to show, explain. See **phrazein** in Appendix.*] —**phras′al** *adj.* —**phras′al·ly** *adv.*

phra·se·o·gram (frā′zē-ə-grăm′) *n.* A symbol, such as one used in shorthand, that denotes a particular phrase.

phra·se·o·graph (frā′zē-ə-grăf′, -gräf′) *n.* A phrase having a phraseogram. —**phra′se·o·graph′ic** *adj.*

phra·se·ol·o·gist (frā′zē-ŏl′ə-jĭst) *n.* A maker of phrases.

phra·se·ol·o·gy (frā′zē-ŏl′ə-jē) *n., pl.* **-gies. 1.** The way in which words and phrases are used in speech or writing; style. **2.** A set of expressions used by a particular person or group: *nautical phraseology.* [New Latin *phraseologia* : *phrasis,* PHRASE + -LOGY.] —**phra′se·o·log′i·cal** (frā′zē-ə-lŏj′ĭ-kəl) *adj.*

phras·ing (frā′zĭng) *n.* **1.** The act of making phrases. **2.** The manner in which an expression is phrased; wording. **3.** *Music.* The manner in which a phrase is rendered or interpreted.

phra·try (frā′trē) *n., pl.* **-tries. 1.** A kinship group constituting an intermediate division in the primitive structure of the Hellenic tribe or phyle, consisting of several patrilinear clans, and surviving in classical times as a territorial subdivision in the political and military organization of the Athenian state. **2.** *Anthropology.* An exogamous subdivision of the tribe, comprising two or more related clans. [Greek *phratria,* from *phratēr,* fellow clan member. See **bhrāter-** in Appendix.*] —**phra′tric** *adj.*

phre·at·ic (frē-ăt′ĭk) *adj. Geology.* Of or pertaining to **ground water** *(see).* [From Greek *phrear* (stem *phreat-*), a well. See **bhreu-²** in Appendix.*]

phren. phrenology.

phre·net·ic, phre·net·i·cal. Variants of **frenetic.**

-phrenia. Indicates mental disorder; for example, **schizophrenia.** [From Greek *phrēn,* mind. See **gwhren-** in Appendix.*]

phren·ic (frĕn′ĭk, frē′nĭk) *adj.* **1.** Of or pertaining to the mind. **2.** *Anatomy.* Of or pertaining to the diaphragm: *the phrenic nerve.* [New Latin *phrenicus* : PHREN(O)- + -IC.]

phre·ni·tis (frĭ-nī′tĭs) *n. Pathology.* **1.** Inflammation of the diaphragm. **2.** Frenzy; delirium. [Late Latin *phrenītis,* from Greek *phrenitis* : *phrēn,* diaphragm, mind (see **gwhren-** in Appendix*) + -ITIS.] —**phre·nit′ic** (-nĭt′ĭk) *adj.*

phreno-, phren-. Indicates: **1.** The mind; for example, **phrenology. 2.** The diaphragm; for example, **phrenic.** [From Greek *phrēn,* diaphragm, mind. See **gwhren-** in Appendix.*]

phre·nol·o·gy (frĭ-nŏl′ə-jē) *n. Abbr.* **phren., phrenol.** The practice of studying character and mental capacity from the conformation of the skull. [PHRENO- + -LOGY.] —**phren′o·log′ic** (frĕn′ə-lŏj′ĭk, frē′nə-), **phren′o·log′i·cal** *adj.* —**phre·nol′o·gist** *n.*

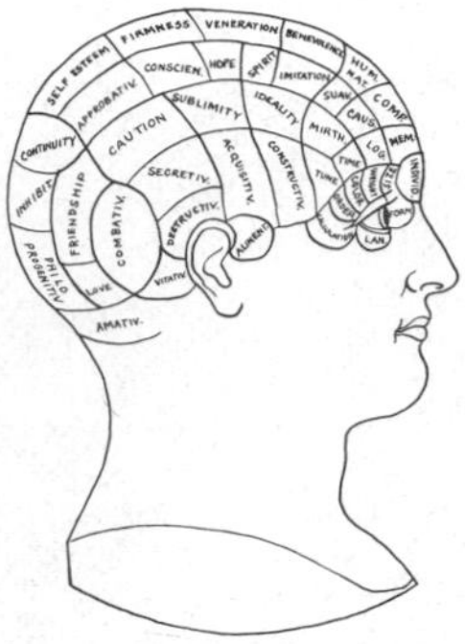

phrenology
Diagram showing location on the human head of brain segments believed to control various characteristics

phren·sy. Variant of **frenzy.**

Phryg·i·a (frĭj′ē-ə). An ancient country of west-central Asia Minor, settled in the 13th century B.C.

Phryg·i·an (frĭj′ē-ən) *adj.* Of or pertaining to Phrygia or its people, language, and culture. —*n.* **1.** A native or inhabitant of Phrygia. **2.** The Indo-European language of the Phrygians.

Phrygian cap. A soft cap with a forward-curving peak, represented in ancient Greek art as part of the attire worn by Phrygians. Compare **liberty cap.**

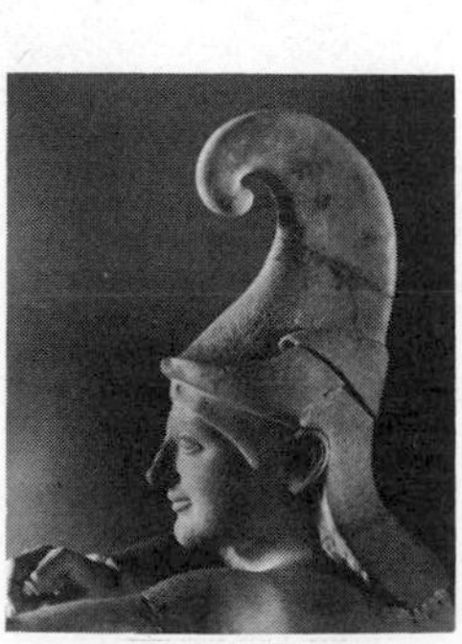

Phrygian cap
Head of a statue in the temple at Aegina, Greece

PHS Public Health Service.

phthal·ein (thăl′ēn′, thăl′ē-ĭn, thā′lēn′, thā′lē-ĭn) *n.* Also **phthal·eine.** Any of a group of chemical compounds formed by a combination of phthalic anhydride with a phenol, from which certain synthetic dyes are derived. [PHTHAL(IC) + -EIN.]

phthal·ic (thăl′ĭk, thā′lĭk) *adj. Chemistry.* **1.** Of, pertaining to, or derived from naphthalene. **2.** Pertaining to phthalic acid. [Short for *naphthalic* : NAPHTH(A) + AL(COHOL) + -IC.]

phthalic acid. A colorless, crystalline organic acid, $C_6H_4(COOH)_2$, prepared from naphthalene and used in the synthesis of dyes, perfumes, and other organic compounds.

phthalic anhydride. A white, crystalline compound, $C_6H_4(CO)_2O$, prepared by oxidizing naphthalene and used in the manufacture of phthaleins and other dyes, resins, plasticizers, and insecticides.

phthal·in (thăl′ĭn, thā′lĭn) *n.* Any of various colorless compounds derived from the reduction of phthaleins.

phthal·o·cy·a·nine (thăl′ō-sī′ə-nēn′, thā′lō-) *n.* Any of several stable, light fast, blue or green organic pigments derived from the basic compound $(C_6H_4C_2N)_4N_4$, and used in enamels, printing inks, linoleum, and plastics. [PHTHAL(IC) + CYANINE.]

phthi·ri·a·sis (thĭ-rī′ə-sĭs, thī-) *n. Pathology.* Infestation with lice; pediculosis. [Latin *phthiriasis,* from Greek *phtheiriasis* : *phtheir,* louse (see **gzwher-** in Appendix*) + -IASIS.]

phthis·ic (tĭz′ĭk) *n. Pathology.* **1.** Variant of **phthisis. 2.** Archaic name for asthma. [Sense 2, from Middle English *ptisike,* from Old French *tisique,* from Latin *phthisicus,* from Greek *phthisikos,* consumptive, from *phthisis,* PHTHISIS.] —**phthis′ic, phthis′i·cal** *adj.*

phthi·sis (thī′sĭs) *n.* Also **phthis·ic** (tĭz′ĭk). *Pathology.* **1.** Tuberculosis of the lungs; pulmonary tuberculosis. **2.** Wasting away or emaciation and atrophy of the body or part of the body. [Latin, from Greek, from *phthinein, phthien,* to decay, waste away. See **gzwhei-** in Appendix.*]

Phu·mi·phol A·dul·det. See **Rama IX.**

PHX Airport code for Phoenix, Arizona.

phyco-. Indicates seaweed; for example, **phycology.** [From Greek *phukos*†, seaweed.]

phy·col·o·gy (fī-kŏl′ə-jē) *n.* The branch of botany concerned with the study of seaweeds and algae. [PHYCO- + -LOGY.] —**phy·co·log′i·cal** (fī′kə-lŏj′ĭ-kəl) *adj.* —**phy·col′o·gist** *n.*

phy·co·my·cete (fī′kō-mī′sēt′, -mī-sēt′) *n. Botany.* Any of various fungi that resemble algae, including certain molds and mildews. [New Latin *phycomycetes* : PHYCO- + -MYCETE.] —**phy′co·my·ce′tous** *adj.*

phy·la. Plural of **phylum.**

phy·lac·ter·y (fĭ-lăk′tə-rē) *n., pl.* **-ies. 1.** *Judaism.* Either of two small leather boxes, each containing strips of parchment inscribed with quotations from the Hebrew Scriptures. One is strapped to the forehead and the other to the left arm by observant Jewish men during morning worship, except on Sabbath and holidays. **2.** *Archaic.* **a.** An amulet **b.** A reminder. [Middle English *filakterie,* from Late Latin *phylactērium,* from Greek *phulaktērion,* safeguard, from *phulaktēr,* guard, from *phulax* (stem *phulak-*), guard. See **phulax** in Appendix.*]

phy·lax·is (fĭ-lăk′sĭs) *n.* Inhibiting of infection by the body. [Greek *phulaxis,* "a guarding," from *phulassein,* to guard. See **phulax** in Appendix.*] —**phy·lac′tic** (-lăk′tĭk) *adj.*

phy·le (fī′lē) *n., pl.* **-lae** (-lē′). A large citizens' organization, based on kinship, constituting the largest political subdivision of an ancient Greek city-state. [Greek *phulē,* tribe. See **bheu-** in Appendix.*] —**phy′lic** *adj.*

phy·let·ic (fī-lĕt′ĭk) *adj. Biology.* Of or pertaining to phylogeny or phylogenetic development. [From New Latin *phylesis,* a genus development, from Greek *phulon,* tribe, class, race. See **bheu-** in Appendix.*] —**phy·let′i·cal·ly** *adv.*

-phyll. Indicates leaf; for example, **chlorophyll.** [From Greek *phullon,* leaf. See **phyllo-.**]

Phyl·lis (fĭl′ĭs). A feminine given name. [Greek *Phullis,* from *phullon,* leaf, foliage. See **bhel-³** in Appendix.*]

phyl·lite (fĭl′īt′) *n.* A green, gray, or red metamorphic rock, similar to slate but often having a wavy surface and a distinctive micaceous luster. [PHYLL(O)- + -ITE.]

phyllo-, phyll-. Indicates leaf; for example, **phylloclade.** [New Latin, from Greek *phullon,* leaf. See **bhel-³** in Appendix.*]

phyl·lo·clade (fĭl′ə-klād′) *n.* Also **phyl·lo·clad** (-klăd′). *Botany.* A flattened branch or stem that performs the functions of a leaf, as in some cacti. [New Latin *phyllocladium* : PHYLLO- + Greek *klados,* a branch (see **kel-²** in Appendix*).]

phyl·lode (fĭl′ōd′) *n. Botany.* Also **phyl·lo·di·um** (fĭ-lō′dē-əm) *pl.* **-dia** (-dē-ə). A flattened leafstalk that serves as a leaf. [New Latin *phyllodium,* from Greek *phullōdēs,* like a leaf : PHYLL(O)- + -ODE (like).] —**phyl·lo′di·al** *adj.*

phyl·loid (fĭl′oid′) *adj. Botany.* Resembling a leaf; leaflike. [New Latin *phylloides* : PHYLL(O)- + -OID.]

phyl·lome (fĭl′ōm′) *n. Botany.* A leaf, or a plant structure that functions as a leaf. [PHYLL(O)- + -OME.] —**phyl·lom′ic** (fĭ-lŏm′ĭk, -lō′mĭk) *adj.*

phyl·loph·a·gous (fĭ-lŏf′ə-gəs) *adj. Zoology.* Feeding on leaves. [PHYLLO- + -PHAGOUS.]

phyl·lo·pod (fĭl′ə-pŏd′) *n.* Any of various crustaceans of the order Phyllopoda, having swimming and respiratory appendages that resemble leaves. —*adj.* Also **phyl·lop′o·dous** (fĭ-lŏp′ə-dəs). **1.** Possessing leaflike feet. **2.** Of or relating to the phyllopods. [New Latin *phyllopoda,* "leaf-footed" : PHYLLO- + -POD.] —**phyl·lop′o·dan** (fĭ-lŏp′ə-dən) *adj.* & *n.*

phyl·lo·tax·y (fĭl′ə-tăk′sē) *n.* Also **phyl·lo·tax·is** (fĭl′ə-tăk′sĭs). *Botany.* **1.** The arrangement of leaves on a stem. **2.** The principles governing leaf arrangement. [New Latin : PHYLLO- + -TAXIS.] —**phyl′lo·tac′tic** (-tăk′tĭk), **phyl′lo·tac′ti·cal** *adj.*

ă pat/ā pay/âr care/ä father/b bib/ch church/d deed/ĕ pet/ē be/f fife/g gag/h hat/hw which/ĭ pit/ī pie/îr pier/j judge/k kick/l lid, needle/m mum/n no, sudden/ng thing/ŏ pot/ō toe/ô paw, for/oi noise/ou out/o͝o took/o͞o boot/p pop/r roar/s sauce/sh ship, dish/

-phyllous. Indicates a specified kind or number of leaves; for example, **heterophyllous.** [New Latin *-phyllus,* from Greek *phullon,* leaf. See **bhel-**[3] in Appendix.*]

phyl·lox·e·ra (fĭl′ŏk-sîr′ə, fĭ-lŏk′sər-ə) *n., pl.* **-rae** (-rē′). Any of several small insects of the genus *Phylloxera;* especially, *P. vitifoliae,* a widely distributed species very destructive to grape crops. [New Latin : PHYLLO- + Greek *xēros,* dry (see **ksero-** in Appendix*).] —**phyl′lox·e′ran** *adj. & n.*

phy·log·e·ny (fī-lŏj′ə-nē) *n., pl.* **-nies.** Also **phy·lo·gen·e·sis** (fī′lō-jĕn′ə-sĭs) *pl.* **-ses** (-sēz′). **1.** The evolutionary development of any species of plant or animal. Compare **ontogeny. 2.** The historical development of a tribe or racial group. [From Greek *phulē,* tribe, clan, and *phulon,* tribe, race (see **bheu-** in Appendix*) + -GENY.] —**phy′lo·ge·net′ic** (fī′lō-jə-nĕt′ĭk), **phy′lo·gen′ic** *adj.* —**phy′lo·ge·net′i·cal·ly** *adv.*

phy·lum (fī′ləm) *n., pl.* **-la** (-lə). **1.** *Biology.* A taxonomic division of the animal kingdom or, less commonly, the plant kingdom, next above a class in size. **2.** *Linguistics.* A large division of genetically related families of languages or linguistic stocks. [New Latin, from Greek *phulon,* tribe, class, race. See **bheu-** in Appendix.*]

phys. 1. physical. **2.** physician. **3.** physicist; physics. **4.** physiological; physiology.

phys·i·at·rics (fĭz′ē-ăt′rĭks) *n.* Plural in form, used with a singular verb. *Medicine.* **Physical therapy** *(see).* [PHYS(IO)- + -IATRICS.]

phys·i·at·rist (fĭz′ē-ăt′rĭst) *n.* A physician who specializes in physical medicine or physical therapy.

phys·i·at·ry (fĭz′ē-ăt′rē) *n. Medicine.* **Physical therapy** *(see).* [PHYS(IO)- + -IATRY.]

phys·ic (fĭz′ĭk) *n.* **1.** Any medicine or drug. **2.** A cathartic. **3.** *Archaic.* The profession of medicine: *"ignorant fellows, quacking and tampering in physic, and inviting people to come to them for remedies"* (Defoe). **4.** *Obsolete.* Physics. —*tr.v.* **physicked, -icking, -ics. 1.** *Archaic.* To treat with or as if with medicine. **2.** To act upon as a cathartic. [Middle English *fisike,* from Old French *fisique,* from Latin *physica,* natural medicine or science, physics, from Greek *phusikē,* from *phusikos,* natural, from *phusis,* nature, from *phuein,* to bring forth, make grow. See **bheu-** in Appendix.*]

phys·i·cal (fĭz′ĭ-kəl) *adj. Abbr.* **phys. 1.** Of or pertaining to the body, as distinguished from the mind or spirit; bodily; corporeal: *physical strength.* **2.** Of or pertaining to material things: *physical environment.* **3.** Of or pertaining to matter and energy or the sciences dealing with them, especially physics. —*n.* A **physical examination** *(see).* [Middle English *phisycal,* from Medieval Latin *physicālis,* medicinal, from Latin *physica,* natural medicine. See **physic.**] —**phys′i·cal·ly** *adv.*

physical anthropology. The science of human evolutionary biology, racial variation, and classification. Also called "somatology." Compare **cultural anthropology.**

physical chemistry. The scientific analysis of the properties and behavior of chemical systems primarily by physical theory and technique as, for example, the thermodynamic analysis of macroscopic chemical phenomena.

physical education. Education in the care and development of the human body, stressing athletics and including hygiene.

physical examination. A medical examination to detect illness or dysfunction and, especially, to determine physical fitness for a specified activity or service. Also called "physical."

physical geography. The study of the structure and phenomena of the earth's surface, especially in its current aspects, including land formation, climate, currents, and distribution of flora and fauna. Also called "physiography."

phys·i·cal·ism (fĭz′ĭ-kə-lĭz′əm) *n. Philosophy.* The doctrine that all phenomena can be described in spatiotemporal terms and consequently that any descriptive scientific statement can in principle be reduced to an empirically verifiable physical statement. —**phys′i·cal·is′tic** *adj.* —**phys′i·cal·ist** *n.*

physical medicine. The branch of medicine that diagnoses and treats disease by essentially physical means, including manipulation, massage, and exercise, often with mechanical devices, and the application of heat, cold, electricity, radiation, and water. Compare **physical therapy.**

physical science. Any of the sciences, such as physics, chemistry, astronomy, and geology, that analyzes the nature and properties of energy and nonliving matter.

physical therapy. *Abbr.* **P.T.** The treatment of disease and injury by mechanical means such as exercise, heat, light, and massage. Also called "physiatry," "physiotherapy," "physiatrics." Compare **physical medicine.**

phy·si·cian (fĭ-zĭsh′ən) *n. Abbr.* **phys. 1.** A person licensed to practice medicine; medical doctor. **2.** Any person who heals or exerts a healing influence. [Middle English *fisicien,* from Old French, from *fisique,* medicine, PHYSIC.]

phy·si·cian·ly (fĭ-zĭsh′ən-lē) *adj.* Suitable to or characteristic of a physician.

phys·i·cist (fĭz′ə-sĭst) *n. Abbr.* **phys.** A scientist who specializes in physics: *"As we cannot use* physician *for a cultivator of* physics, *I have called him a* physicist." (William Whewell).

phys·ics (fĭz′ĭks) *n.* Plural in form, used with a singular verb. *Abbr.* **phys. 1.** The science of matter and energy and of interactions between the two, grouped in traditional fields such as acoustics, optics, mechanics, thermodynamics, and electromagnetism, as well as in modern extensions including atomic and nuclear physics, cryogenics, solid-state physics, particle physics, and plasma physics. **2.** Physical properties, interactions, processes, or laws: *the physics of supersonic flight.* **3.** *Archaic.* The study of the natural or material world and phenomena; natural philosophy. [Plural of PHYSIC (translation of Latin plural *physica,* natural science).]

physio-, phys-. Indicates: **1.** Natural or nature; for example, **physiography. 2.** Physical; for example, **physiatry, physiotherapy.** [Greek *phusio-,* from *phusis,* nature, from *phuein,* to make grow. See **bheu-** in Appendix.*]

phys·i·og·no·my (fĭz′ē-ŏg′nə-mē, -ŏn′ə-mē) *n., pl.* **-mies. 1. a.** The art of judging human character from facial features. **b.** Divination based on facial features. **2. a.** Facial features, especially when regarded as revealing character. **b.** Aspect and character of an inanimate or abstract entity: *the physiognomy of New England.* [Learned respelling of Middle English *fysnamye, phisnomye,* from Old French *phizonomie,* from Medieval Latin *physionomia,* from Late Greek *phusiognōmia,* short for Greek *phusiognōmonia* : PHYSIO- + *gnōmōn,* "judge," "interpreter" (see **gnō-** in Appendix*).] —**phys′i·og·nom′ic** (fĭz′ē-ŏg-nŏm′ĭk, fĭz′ē-ə-nŏm′ĭk), **phys′i·og·nom′i·cal** *adj.* —**phys′i·og·nom′i·cal·ly** *adv.* —**phys′i·og′no·mist** *n.*

phys·i·og·ra·phy (fĭz′ē-ŏg′rə-fē) *n.* Physical geography. [PHYSIO- + -GRAPHY.] —**phys′i·og′ra·pher** *n.* —**phys′i·o·graph′ic** (fĭz′ē-ə-grăf′ĭk), **phys′i·o·graph′i·cal** *adj.* —**phys′i·o·graph′i·cal·ly** *adv.*

physiol. physiological; physiology.

phys·i·o·log·i·cal (fĭz′ē-ə-lŏj′ĭ-kəl) *adj.* Also **phys·i·o·log·ic** (-ĭk). *Abbr.* **phys., physiol. 1.** Of or pertaining to physiology. **2.** In accord with or characteristic of the normal functioning of a living organism. —**phys′i·o·log′i·cal·ly** *adv.*

phys·i·ol·o·gy (fĭz′ē-ŏl′ə-jē) *n. Abbr.* **phys., physiol. 1.** The biological science of essential and characteristic life processes, activities, and functions. **2.** All the vital processes of an organism. [Latin *physiologia,* from Greek *phusiologia,* study of nature : PHYSIO- + -LOGY.] —**phys′i·ol′o·gist** *n.*

phys·i·o·ther·a·py (fĭz′ē-ō-thĕr′ə-pē) *n. Medicine.* **Physical therapy** *(see).* —**phys′i·o·ther′a·peu′tic** (-thĕr′ə-pyōō′tĭk) *adj.*

phy·sique (fĭ-zēk′) *n.* The body, considered with reference to its proportions, muscular development, and appearance: *"Leamas was a short man with . . . the physique of a swimmer."* (John LeCarré). [French, from adjective, "physical," from Latin *physicus,* natural, from Greek *phusikos,* from *phusis,* nature, from *phuein,* to make grow. See **bheu-** in Appendix.*]

phy·so·stig·mine (fī′sō-stĭg′mēn′) *n.* Also **phy·so·stig·min** (fī′sō-stĭg′mĭn). A colorless or pink poisonous crystalline compound, $C_{15}H_{21}N_3O_2$, extracted from the Calabar bean, and used in a variety of medicines. Also called "eserine." [From New Latin *Physostigma* (genus of the Calabar bean) : Greek *phusa,* bellows, bladder (see **pu-**[1] in Appendix*) + STIGMA.]

phy·sos·to·mous (fī-sŏs′tə-məs) *adj. Zoology.* Having a connecting tube between the air bladder and a part of the alimentary canal, as in certain fishes. [Greek *phusa,* bellows, bladder (see **pu-**[1] in Appendix*) + -STOME + -OUS.]

-phyte. *Botany.* Indicates a plant with a specified character or habitat; for example, **thallophyte.** [Greek *phuton,* plant, from *phuein,* to make grow. See **bheu-** in Appendix.*]

Phy·tin (fī′tĭn) *n.* A trademark for a nutrient material derived from various seeds, used as a dietary supplement to supply inositol. [PHYT(O)- + -IN.]

phyto-, phyt-. Indicates plant or plant life; for example, **phytogenesis.** [New Latin, from Greek *phuto-,* from *phuton,* plant, from *phuein,* to make grow. See **bheu-** in Appendix.*]

phy·to·gen·e·sis (fī′tō-jĕn′ə-sĭs) *n.* Also **phy·tog·e·ny** (fī-tŏj′ə-nē). The origin and evolutionary development of plants. [PHYTO- + -GENESIS.] —**phy′to·ge·net′ic** (-jə-nĕt′ĭk), **phy′to·ge·net′i·cal** *adj.* —**phy′to·ge·net′i·cal·ly** *adv.*

phy·to·gen·ic (fī′tō-jĕn′ĭk) *adj.* Also **phy·tog·e·nous** (fī-tŏj′ə-nəs). Having a plant origin, as coal. [PHYTO- + -GENIC.]

phy·to·ge·og·ra·phy (fī′tō-jē-ŏg′rə-fē) *n.* The study of the distribution of plants. —**phy′to·ge·og′ra·pher** *n.* —**phy′to·ge′o·graph′i·cal** (-jē′ə-grăf′ĭ-kəl), **phy′to·ge′o·graph′ic** *adj.*

phy·tog·ra·phy (fī-tŏg′rə-fē) *n.* The science of plant description; descriptive botany. [PHYTO- + -GRAPHY.]

phy·to·hor·mone (fī′tō-hôr′mōn′) *n.* A hormone produced by a plant; especially, one that affects plant growth.

phy·to·lite (fī′tə-līt′) *n.* Also **phy·to·lith** (fī′tə-lĭth′). A fossil plant. [PHYTO- + -LITE.]

phy·tol·o·gy (fī-tŏl′ə-jē) *n. Rare.* The study of plants; botany. [New Latin *phytologia* : PHYTO- + -LOGY.] —**phy′to·log′ic** (fī′tə-lŏj′ĭk), **phy′to·log′i·cal** *adj.*

phy·ton (fī′tŏn′) *n.* A unit of plant structure; especially, the smallest part of a plant that, when cut off, is able to grow. [New Latin, from Greek *phuton,* plant, from *phuein,* to make grow. See **bheu-** in Appendix.*] —**phy·ton′ic** *adj.*

phy·to·pa·thol·o·gy (fī′tō-pə-thŏl′ə-jē) *n.* The science of plant diseases. —**phy′to·path′o·log′ic** (-păth′ə-lŏj′ĭk), **phy′to·path′o·log′i·cal** *adj.* —**phy′to·pa·thol′o·gist** *n.*

phy·toph·a·gous (fī-tŏf′ə-gəs) *adj.* Feeding on plants, including shrubs and trees. Said especially of certain insects. [PHYTO- + -PHAGOUS.] —**phy·toph′a·gy** (-jē) *n.*

phy·to·plank·ton (fī′tō-plăngk′tən) *n.* Minute, floating aquatic plants. —**phy′to·plank·ton′ic** (-plăngk-tŏn′ĭk) *adj.*

phy·to·so·ci·ol·o·gy (fī′tō-sō′sē-ŏl′ə-jē, -sō′shē-ŏl′ə-jē) *n.* The branch of ecology that deals with the characteristics, relationships, and distribution of associated plants. —**phy′to·so′ci·o·log′i·cal** (-sō′sē-ə-lŏj′ĭ-kəl, -sō′shē-ə-lŏj′ĭ-kəl) *adj.* —**phy′to·so′ci·o·log′i·cal·ly** *adv.* —**phy′to·so′ci·ol′o·gist** *n.*

phy·to·tox·ic (fī′tō-tŏk′sĭk) *adj.* Poisonous to plants. —**phy′to·tox·ic′i·ty** (-tŏk-sĭs′ə-tē) *n.*

pi[1] (pī) *n., pl.* **pis. 1.** The 16th letter in the Greek alphabet, written Π, π, and transliterated in English as *P, p.* See **alphabet. 2.** *Symbol* π *Mathematics.* A transcendental number, approxi-

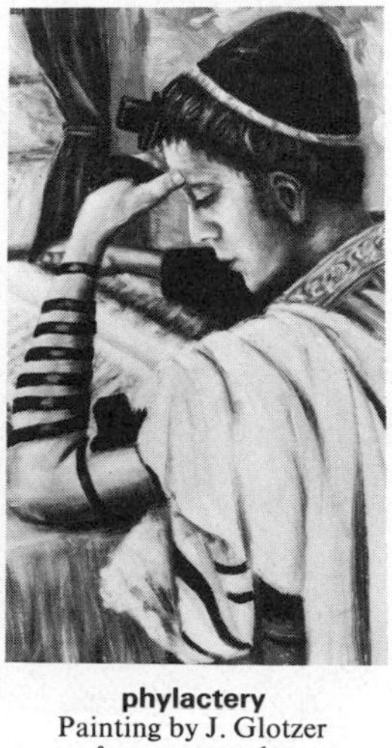

phylactery
Painting by J. Glotzer of a young student wearing phylacteries

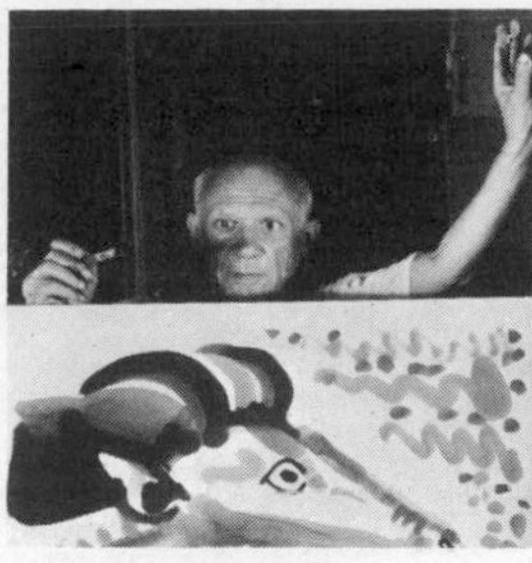

Picasso
On the set of the film
The Mystery of Picasso

mately 3.14159, representing the ratio of the circumference to the diameter of a circle and appearing as a constant in a wide range of mathematical problems. [The letter is from Medieval Greek, from Greek *pei,* from Semitic, akin to Hebrew *peh,* PE. The mathematical sense is from the first letter of Greek *periphireia,* PERIPHERY, and *perimetros,* PERIMETER.]

pi[2] (pī) *n., pl.* **pis.** Also **pie. 1.** *Printing.* Any amount of type that has been jumbled or thrown together at random. **2.** Any jumble or disorder: *An army without ranks will go to pi.* —*v.* **pied, piing, pies.** Also **pie, pied, pieing, pies.** *Printing.* —*tr.* To jumble or mix up (type). —*intr.* To become jumbled: *5-point type has a way of piing by itself.* [Possibly from PIE (church almanac), in association with PICA and Latin *pīca,* PIE (magpie).]

P.I. Philippine Islands.

pi·a (pī′ə, pē′ə) *n. Anatomy.* The **pia mater** *(see).* —**pi′al** *adj.*

PIA Airport code for Peoria, Illinois.

Pia·cen·za (pyä-chĕn′tsä). A town in northern Italy, on the Po River, 40 miles southeast of Milan. Population, 79,000.

pi·ac·u·lar (pī-ăk′yə-lər) *adj.* **1.** Making expiation or atonement for a sacrilege: *piacular sacrifice.* **2.** Requiring expiation; wicked; blameworthy. [Latin *piāculāris,* from *piāculum,* sin offering, propitiatory sacrifice, from *piāre,* to appease, atone for, from *pius,* pious. See **pius** in Appendix.*]

piaffe (pyăf) *intr.v.* **piaffed, piaffing, piaffes.** *Horsemanship.* To perform the piaffer. [French *piaffer,* to strut (expressive).]

piaf·fer (pyăf′ər) *n. Horsemanship.* A movement in which a horse trots in place with high action of the legs. [French, from *piaffer,* to strut, PIAFFE.]

pi·a ma·ter (pī′ə mā′tər, pē′ə mä′tər). *Anatomy.* The fine vascular membrane that envelops the brain and spinal cord under the arachnoid membrane and the dura mater. Also called "pia." [Medieval Latin (translation of Arabic *al′umm raqīqah,* "tender mother").]

pi·an·ism (pē-ăn′ĭz′əm, pē′ə-nĭz′əm) *n.* The technique or execution of piano playing.

pi·a·nis·si·mo (pē′ə-nĭs′ə-mō′) *adv. Abbr.* **pp, pp.** *Music.* Very softly or quietly. Used as a direction. —*n., pl.* **pianissimos.** *Music.* A very quietly played part of a composition. [Italian, superlative of PIANO (softly).] —**pi′a·nis′si·mo′** *adj.*

pi·an·ist (pē-ăn′ĭst, pē′ə-nĭst) *n.* One who plays the piano.

pi·a·nis·tic (pē′ə-nĭs′tĭk) *adj.* **1.** Of or pertaining to the piano. **2.** Well-adapted to the piano. —**pi′a·nis′ti·cal·ly** *adv.*

pi·a·nis·tics (pē′ə-nĭs′tĭks) *n.* Plural in form, sometimes used with a singular verb. **1.** The art or principles of piano playing. **2.** A show of virtuosity in playing the piano.

pi·an·o[1] (pē-ăn′ō) *n., pl.* **-os.** A musical instrument with a manual keyboard actuating hammers that strike wire strings, producing sounds that may be softened or sustained by means of pedals. [Italian, short for PIANOFORTE.]

pi·a·no[2] (pē-ä′nō) *adv. Abbr.* **p, p.** *Music.* Softly; quietly. Used as a direction. —*n., pl.* **pianos.** *Music.* A passage to be played softly. [Italian, from Late Latin *plānus,* smooth, from Latin, even, level, flat. See **pelə-**[1] in Appendix.*] —**pi·a′no** *adj.*

pi·an·o·for·te (pē-ăn′ō-fôr′tā, -fôr′tē, -fôrt′) *n.* A piano. [Italian, from *piano e forte,* soft and loud : PIANO (softly) + *forte,* strong, from Latin *fortis* (see **bhergh-**[2] in Appendix*).]

pi·as·sa·va (pē′ə-sä′və) *n.* Also **pi·as·sa·ba** (pē′ə-sä′bə). **1.** Either of two South American palm trees, *Attalea funifera* or *Leopoldina piassaba,* from which a strong, coarse fiber is obtained. **2.** The fiber of these trees, used for making ropes, brushes, and brooms. [Portuguese *piassaba,* from Tupi *piaçaba.*]

pi·as·ter (pē-ăs′tər, -ä′stər) *n.* Also **pi·as·tre. 1.** The basic monetary unit of South Vietnam, equal to 100 cents. **2.** A coin equal to $1/100$ of the pound of Lebanon, Libya, Sudan, Syria, Turkey, and the United Arab Republic. See table of exchange rates at **currency. 3.** Formerly, a Spanish dollar; a piece of eight. [French *piastre,* from Italian *piastra,* thin metal plate, from Latin *emplastra, emplastrum,* PLASTER.]

Piau·í (pyou-ē′). A state in northeastern Brazil, 94,819 square miles in area, bounded on the east by the Parnaíba River and having a short coastline on the Atlantic Ocean. Population, 1,263,000. Capital, Teresina.

pi·az·za (pē-ăz′ə, -äz′ə; *Italian* pyät′tsä) *n., pl.* **-zas** (for all senses) or *Italian* **piazze** (pyät′tsā) (for sense 1). **1.** A public square in an Italian town. **2.** *British.* A roofed and arcaded passageway; colonnade. **3.** A verandah; porch. [Italian, from Latin *platea,* broad street, courtyard, from Greek *plateia,* from *platus,* broad, flat. See **plat-** in Appendix.*]

Piaz·zi (pyät′tsē), **Giuseppi.** 1746–1826. Italian monk and astronomer; discoverer of the first asteroid (Ceres).

pi·broch (pē′brŏKH′) *n.* A series of variations on a traditional dirge or martial theme for the highland bagpipe. [Scottish Gaelic *piobaireachd,* pipe music, from *piobair,* piper, from *píob,* pipe. See **pipp-** in Appendix.*]

pi·ca[1] (pī′kə) *n.* **1.** A printer's unit of type size, equal to 12 points or about $1/6$ inch. **2.** An equivalent unit of composition measurement used in determining the dimensions of lines, illustrations, or printed pages. [Probably from Medieval Latin *pīca,* PIE (church almanac).]

pi·ca[2] (pī′kə) *n.* A craving for unnatural food, as seen in hysteria and pregnancy. [New Latin, from Latin *pīca,* magpie (from its omnivorous nature). See **speik-** in Appendix.*]

pic·a·dor (pĭk′ə-dôr′; *Spanish* pē′kä-thôr′) *n., pl.* **-dors** or *Spanish* **picadores** (pē′kä-thō′räs). A horseman in a bullfight who lances the bull's neck muscles so that it will tend to keep its head low for the subsequent stages. [Spanish, from *picar,* to prick, pierce. See **picaro.**]

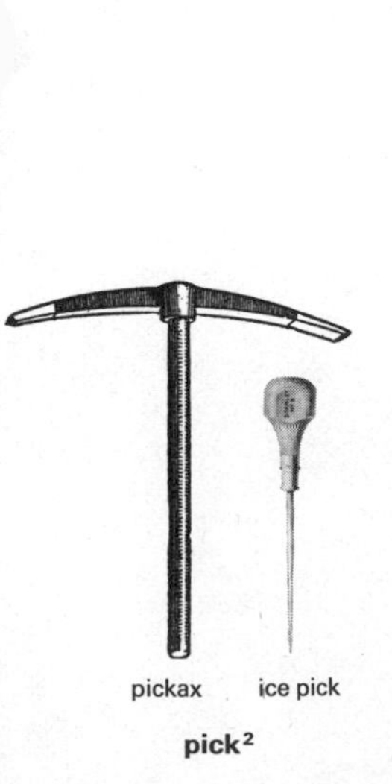

pickax ice pick

pick[2]

pic·a·ra (pĭk′ə-rä′; *Spanish* pē′kä-rä) *n., pl.* **-ras** (-räz′; *Spanish* -räs). A female picaro; an adventuress.

Pic·ar·dy (pĭk′ər-dē). A region and former province in northern France, extending from the English Channel to the Belgian border. —**Pic′ard** (pĭk′ərd) *n. & adj.*

pic·a·resque (pĭk′ə-rĕsk′, pē′kə-) *adj.* **1.** Of or involving clever rogues or adventurers. **2.** Of, belonging to, or characteristic of the picaresque novel, a genre in which the rogue-hero and his escapades are depicted with broad realism and satire. [French, from Spanish *picaresco,* from *picaro,* rogue, PICARO.]

pic·a·ro (pĭk′ə-rō′; *Spanish* pē′kä-rō) *n., pl.* **-ros** (-rōz′; *Spanish* -rōs). An adventurer; a social parasite; rogue. [Spanish, "rogue," from *picar,* to wound lightly, "to prick," from Vulgar Latin *piccāre* (unattested), to pick, from *piccus* (unattested), woodpecker, from Latin *pīcus.* See **speik-** in Appendix.*]

pic·a·roon (pĭk′ə-ro͞on′) *n.* **1. a.** A pirate. **b.** A picaro. **2.** A pirate ship. —*intr.v.* **picarooned, -rooning, -roons.** To act as a pirate. [Spanish *picarón,* augmentative of *picaro,* PICARO.]

Pi·cas·so (pĭ-kä′sō, pē-), **Pablo.** Born 1881. Spanish painter and sculptor, resident in France; founder of cubism.

pic·a·yune (pĭk′ē-yo͞on′) *adj.* **1.** Of little value or importance; paltry. **2.** Petty; mean. —See Synonyms at **trivial.** —*n.* **1.** A Spanish-American half-real piece formerly used in parts of the southern United States. **2.** A five-cent piece. **3.** Something of very small value; a trifle: *not worth a picayune.* [French *picaillon,* small copper coin, from Provençal *picaioun*†.]

Pic·ca·dil·ly (pĭk′ə-dĭl′ē). A well-known thoroughfare in London, running from the Haymarket to Hyde Park Corner.

pic·ca·lil·li (pĭk′ə-lĭl′ē) *n., pl.* **-lis.** A pickled relish made of various chopped vegetables. [Perhaps blend of PICKLE and CHILI.]

Pic·card (pē-kär′), **Auguste.** 1884–1962. Swiss physicist, author, and inventor; with his brother **Jean Félix** (1884–1963) he explored the stratosphere; with his son **Jacques Ernst** (born 1922) he invented the bathyscaph and explored ocean depths.

pic·co·lo[1] (pĭk′ə-lō′) *n., pl.* **-los.** A small flute pitched an octave above a regular flute. [Shortened from *piccolo flute,* from PICCOLO (adjective).]

pic·co·lo[2] (pĭk′ə-lō′) *adj.* Designating a musical instrument considerably smaller than the usual size: *piccolo trumpet; piccolo concertina.* [Italian *piccolo*†, small.]

Pic de Né·thou. French name for **Pico de Aneto.**

pice (pīs) *n., pl.* **pice.** A coin equal to $1/100$ of the rupee of Nepal. See table of exchange rates at **currency.** [Hindi *paisā,* perhaps from *pā′ī,* a quarter, PIE (coin).]

pi·ce·ous (pĭ′sē-əs) *adj.* **1.** Of or pertaining to pitch. **2.** Glossy-black in color. [Latin *piceus,* from *pix* (stem *pic-*), pitch. See **pik-** in Appendix.*]

pich·i·ci·e·go (pĭch′ə-sē-ā′gō) *n.* Also **pich·i·ci·a·go** (-ä′gō, -ā′gō) *pl.* **-gos. 1.** A small armadillo, *Chlamyphorus truncatus,* of Argentina, having pale-pink armor and soft, silky white hair. **2.** A similar South American armadillo, *Burmeisteria retusa,* having yellow-brown armor and whitish hair. [Perhaps from Allentiac.]

pick[1] (pĭk) *v.* **picked, picking, picks.** —*tr.* **1.** To select from a group: *The best swimmer was picked.* **2. a.** To select or cull. **b.** To gather in; harvest: *They were picking cotton.* **c.** To gather the harvest from: *We picked the whole field in one day.* **3. a.** To remove the outer covering of; pluck: *pick a chicken clean of feathers.* **b.** To tear off bit by bit: *pick meat from the bones.* **4.** To remove extraneous matter from (the teeth). **5.** To poke and pull at with the fingers. **6.** To break up, separate, or detach by means of a sharp, pointed instrument. **7.** To pierce or make (a hole) with a sharp instrument. **8.** To seek and discover (a flaw): *He picked holes in their argument.* **9.** To take up (food) with the beak; peck: *The parrot picked its seed.* **10.** To steal the contents of: *My pocket has been picked.* **11.** To open (a lock) without the use of the key. **12.** To make (one's way) carefully: *"picked her way as daintily through the mud holes as a lady in a satin dress"* (Margaret Mitchell). **13.** To provoke: *pick a fight.* **14. a.** To pluck (the strings) of a musical instrument. **b.** To play (a tune) by plucking strings: *He picked a tune on his guitar.* —*intr.* **1.** To decide with care or forethought: *pick and choose.* **2.** To work with a pick. **3.** To find fault or make petty criticisms: carp: *He's always picking about something.* **4.** To be harvested or gathered: *The ripe apples picked easily.* —See Synonyms at **choose.** —**pick apart. 1.** To separate into pieces by picking: *He picked apart an old quilt.* **2.** To refute or find flaws in by close examination: *The lawyer picked apart his testimony.* —**pick at. 1.** To pluck or pull at with the fingers. **2.** To eat sparingly or without appetite: *He picked at his meal.* **3.** *Informal.* To nag: *She picks at him day and night.* —**pick off.** To shoot after singling out: *I picked the ducks off one by one.* —**pick on.** To tease or bully. —**pick out. 1.** To choose or select. **2.** To discern from the surroundings; distinguish. **3.** To play (music) slowly by ear: *He managed to pick out the tune.* —**pick over.** To sort out or examine item by item. —*n.* **1.** The act of picking, especially with a pointed instrument. **2.** The act of selecting or choosing; choice. **3.** That which is selected as the most desirable; the best or choicest part: *the pick of the crop.* **4.** The amount or quantity of a crop that is picked by hand. [Middle English *piken,* to pierce, probably from Old French *piquer,* to prick, pick, from Vulgar Latin *piccāre* (unattested), to prick, pierce. See **picaro.**] —**pick′er** *n.*

pick[2] (pĭk) *n.* **1.** A tool for breaking hard surfaces, consisting of a curved bar sharpened at both ends and fitted to a long handle. **2.** Anything used for picking, as an ice pick, a toothpick, or a picklock. **3.** *Music.* A **plectrum** *(see).* [Middle English *pik,* probably a variant of PIKE (pole).]

pick[3] (pĭk) *n.* **1.** A weft thread in weaving. **2.** A passage or throw of the shuttle in a loom. —*tr.v.* **picked, picking, picks.** **1.** To throw (a shuttle) across the loom. **2.** *Archaic.* To cast; pitch: *"as high as I could pick my lance"* (Shakespeare). [Middle English *pykken,* to throw (a shuttle), to cast, variant of *picchen,* to PITCH.]

pick·a·back. Variant of **piggyback.**

pick·a·nin·ny (pĭk′ə-nĭn′ē) *n., pl.* **-nies.** A small Negro child. Used condescendingly. [A diminutive (used by West Indian slaves) of Portuguese *pequeno,* little, or Spanish *pequeño,* possibly from *pico,* a point, from *picar,* to prick. See **picador.**]

pick·ax, pick·axe (pĭk′ăks′) *n.* A pick, especially with one end of the head pointed and the other end with a chisel edge for cutting through roots. —*v.* **pickaxed, -axing, -axes.** —*intr.* To use a pickax. —*tr.* To use a pickax on. [Alteration (influenced by AX) of Middle English *pikois, pikeis,* pickax, from Old French *picois,* from *pic,* pickax, perhaps from *piquer,* to prick. See **picket.**]

picked (pĭkt) *adj.* **1.** Chosen by careful selection. **2.** Cleaned by picking out damaged or undesirable parts. **3.** Gathered; plucked; harvested. **4.** Worked upon with a pick. **5.** In tailoring, ornamented with a hand-worked line of short running stitches along the edges.

pick·er·el (pĭk′ər-əl, pĭk′rəl) *n., pl.* **pickerel** or **-els.** **1.** Any of several North American freshwater game and food fishes of the genus *Esox,* especially *E. niger* and *E. vermiculatus.* **2.** Any of various similar or related fishes, such as the **walleye** *(see).* **3.** *British.* A young pike. [Middle English *pikerel,* diminutive of *pik, pike,* PIKE (fish).]

pick·er·el·weed (pĭk′ər-əl-wēd′, pĭk′rəl-) *n.* A plant, *Pontederia cordata,* growing in freshwater shallows of North America, and having heart-shaped leaves and spikes of violet-blue flowers.

pick·et (pĭk′ĭt) *n.* **1.** A pointed stake driven into the ground to support a fence, secure a tent, tether animals, mark points in surveying or, when pointed at the top, serve as a defense. **2.** *Military.* A detachment of one or more soldiers advanced or held in readiness to give warning of enemy approach. **3. a.** A person or persons stationed outside a place of employment, usually during a strike, to express grievance or protest and discourage entry by nonstriking employees or customers. **b.** A person or persons present outside any building to protest. —*v.* **picketed, -eting, -ets.** —*tr.* **1.** To enclose, secure, tether, mark out, or fortify with pickets. **2.** *Military.* **a.** To post as a picket. **b.** To guard with a picket. **3.** To post a picket or pickets during a strike or demonstration. —*intr.* To act or serve as a picket. [French *piquet,* from Old French, from *piquer,* to prick, pierce, from Vulgar Latin *piccāre* (unattested), from *piccus* (unattested), woodpecker, from Latin *pīcus.* See **speik-** in Appendix.*] —**pick′et·er** *n.*

picket fence. A fence of pointed, upright pickets.

picket line. A line or procession of people picketing a place of business or otherwise staging a public protest.

Pick·ett (pĭk′ĭt), **George Edward.** 1825–1875. American army officer; Confederate major general in the Civil War.

Pick·ford (pĭk′fərd), **Mary.** Original name, Gladys Smith. Born 1893. Canadian-born American motion-picture actress.

pick·ing (pĭk′ĭng) *n.* **1.** The act of someone or something that picks. **2.** *Plural.* Something that is or may be picked. **3.** *Usually plural.* **a.** Leftovers. **b.** A share of spoils.

pick·le (pĭk′əl) *n.* **1.** Any edible product, such as a cucumber, that has been preserved and flavored in a solution of brine or vinegar. **2.** A solution of brine or vinegar, often spiced, for preserving and flavoring food. **3.** An acid or other chemical solution used as a bath to remove scale and oxides from the surface of metals before plating or finishing. **4.** *Informal.* A troublesome, embarrassing, or difficult situation. —*tr.v.* **pickled, -ling, -les.** **1.** To preserve or flavor in a solution of brine or vinegar. **2.** To treat (metal) in a chemical bath. [Middle English *pekille,* probably from Middle Dutch *pekel,* possibly after William *Beukelz* (died 1397), Dutch fisherman credited with the invention of the pickling process.]

pick·led (pĭk′əld) *adj.* **1.** Preserved in or treated with pickle. **2.** *Slang.* Drunk.

pick·lock (pĭk′lŏk′) *n.* **1.** A person who picks locks; especially, a thief. **2.** An instrument for picking a lock.

pick-me-up (pĭk′mē-ŭp′) *n. Informal.* A drink, often an alcoholic beverage, taken as a stimulant or hangover cure.

pick·pock·et (pĭk′pŏk′ĭt) *n.* One who steals from pockets.

pick up. **1.** To take up (something) by hand: *pick up a suitcase.* **2.** To take on (passengers, freight, survivors, hitchhikers, or the like). **3.** *Informal.* To fetch or acquire by the way: *She picked up her new dress and a quick lunch at noon.* **4.** To succeed in bringing by chance or intent within sight or hearing. **5.** To accelerate: *pick up speed.* **6.** *Slang.* To take into custody: *The coast guard picked up five smugglers.* **7.** *Slang.* To make casual acquaintance with, usually in anticipation of sexual relations. **8.** *Informal.* To improve in condition or activity: *Sales will pick up next fall.*

pick·up (pĭk′ŭp′) *n.* **1. a.** The action or process of picking up: *the pickup and delivery of farm produce.* **b.** *Sports.* The act of striking or fielding a ball after it has touched the ground: *a good pickup and throw from third base.* **c.** Capacity for acceleration: *a sports car with good pickup.* **d.** *Informal.* An improvement in condition or activity: *a pickup in sales.* **e.** *Slang.* An arrest. **2.** One that is picked up; especially: **a.** Passengers or freight: *Taxi drivers expect good tips from airport pickups.* **b.** *Accounting.* A balance brought forward. **c.** *Journalism.* Previous copy to which succeeding copy is added. **d.** *Music.* The unstressed note or notes introductory to a phrase or composition. **e.** *Informal.* A hitchhiker. **f.** *Slang.* A stranger with whom casual acquaintance is made, usually in anticipation of sexual relations. **3.** One that picks up; especially: **a.** A **pickup truck** *(see).* **b.** The rotary rake on machinery such as a harvester that picks up windrowed hay or straw. **4.** *Electronics.* **a.** A device that converts the oscillations of a phonograph needle into electrical impulses for subsequent conversion into sound. **b.** The tone arm of a record player. See also **crystal pickup, magnetic pickup.** **5.** *Radio & Television.* **a.** The reception of light or sound waves for conversion to electrical impulses. **b.** The apparatus used for such reception. **c.** A telecast originating outside of a studio. **d.** The apparatus for transmitting a broadcast from some outside place to the broadcasting station.

pickup truck. A light truck with an open body and low sides.

pick·y (pĭk′ē) *adj.* **-ier, -iest.** *Informal.* Excessively meticulous.

pic·nic (pĭk′nĭk) *n.* **1.** A meal eaten outdoors on an excursion. **2.** *Slang.* An easy task or pleasant experience. —*intr.v.* **picnicked, -nicking, -nics.** To go on or participate in a picnic. [French *piquenique,* probably a reduplication (influenced by obsolete French *nique,* a trifle) of *piquer,* to pick, peck, from Old French. See **picket.**] —**pic′nick·er** *n.*

pico-. *Symbol* **p** Indicates one trillionth, 10^{-12}; for example, *picosecond,* one-trillionth of a second. [Spanish *pico,* small quantity, peak, from *picar,* to prick. See **picaro.**]

Pi·co Bo·lí·var (pē′kō bō-lē′vär). The highest mountain in Venezuela, rising to 16,411 feet in the Cordillera de Mérida, south of Lake Maracaibo. Also called "La Columna."

Pi·co de A·ne·to (pē′kō *th*ā ä-nā′tō). *French* **Pic de Né·thou** (pēk də nā-to͞o′). The highest peak of the Pyrenees (11,168 feet), in northeastern Spain, just south of the French border.

Pi·co del·la Mi·ran·do·la (pē′kō dĕl′lä mē-rän′dō-lä), Count **Giovanni.** 1463–1494. Italian humanist scholar.

Pi·co Duar·te (pē′kō dwär′tā). Former name, **Pi·co Tru·ji·llo** (tro͞o-hē′yō). The highest mountain of the Dominican Republic (10,115 feet) and of the West Indies.

pic·o·line (pĭk′ə-lēn′, pī′kə-) *n.* Any of three isomeric liquid methylpyridine bases, C_6H_7N, derived from coal tar, horse urine, and bone oil and used as an industrial solvent. [Latin *pix* (stem *pic-*), pitch (see **pik-** in Appendix*) + -OL + -INE.]

pi·cot (pē′kō, pē-kō′) *n.* A small embroidered loop forming an ornamental edging on some ribbon and lace. —*tr.v.* **picoted** (pē′kōd, pē-kōd′), **-coting** (pē′kō-ĭng, pē-kō′ĭng), **-cots** (pē′kōz, pē-kōz′). To trim with edging. [French, "small point," from Old French, from *pic,* peak, point, prick, from *piquer,* to prick. See **picket.**]

pic·o·tee (pĭk′ə-tē′) *n.* A type of carnation having pale petals bordered by a darker color. [French *picoté,* furnished with points, from *picoter,* to mark with points or pricks, from PICOT.]

pic·quet. Variant of **piquet.**

pic·rate (pĭk′rāt′) *n.* A salt or ester of picric acid. [PICR(O)- + -ATE.]

pic·ric acid (pĭk′rĭk). A poisonous, explosive yellow crystalline solid, $C_6H_2(NO_2)_3OH$, used in explosives, dyes, and antiseptics. Also called "trinitrophenol."

picro-. Indicates something bitter; for example, **picrotoxin.** [Greek *pikro-,* from *pikros,* bitter. See **peig-**[1] in Appendix.*]

pic·ro·tox·in (pĭk′rə-tŏk′sĭn) *n.* A bitter powder, $C_{30}H_{34}O_{13}$, used as a stimulant and antidote for barbiturate poisoning.

Pict (pĭkt) *n.* One of the ancient people of North Britain, who were absorbed by the invading Scots between the sixth and ninth centuries A.D. [Middle English, from Latin *Pictī* (plural), probably a reshaping of the indigenous name by folk etymology, as if to mean "the painted (i.e., tattooed) people."]

Pict·ish (pĭk′tĭsh) *adj.* Of or pertaining to the Picts or their language. —*n.* The language of the Picts, known chiefly from place names, probably representing an aboriginal pre-Indo-European language mixed with a Brythonic form of Celtic closely akin to Gaulish that was introduced by invasion around the sixth century B.C.

pic·to·gram (pĭk′tə-grăm′) *n.* Any pictorial representation of numerical data or relationships. [PICTO(GRAPH) + -GRAM.]

pic·to·graph (pĭk′tə-grăf′, -gräf′) *n.* **1.** A picture representing a word or idea; hieroglyph. **2.** A record in hieroglyphic symbols. [Latin *pictus,* past participle of *pingere,* to paint (see **peig-**[1] in Appendix*) + -GRAPH.] —**pic′to·graph′ic** *adj.* —**pic′to·graph′i·cal·ly** *adv.* —**pic·tog′ra·phy** (pĭk-tŏg′rə-fē) *n.*

Pic·tor (pĭk′tər) *n.* A constellation in the Southern Hemisphere near Columba and Dorado. [Latin, painter, from *pingere* (past participle *pictus*), to paint. See **peig-**[1] in Appendix.*]

pic·to·ri·al (pĭk-tôr′ē-əl, -tōr′ē-əl) *adj.* **1.** Pertaining to, characterized by, or composed of pictures. **2.** Represented as if in a picture: *pictorial prose.* **3.** Illustrated by pictures. —*n.* An illustrated periodical. [From Late Latin *pictōrius,* from Latin *pictor,* painter. See **Pictor.**] —**pic·to′ri·al·ly** *adv.*

pic·ture (pĭk′chər) *n.* **1.** A visual representation or image painted, drawn, photographed, or otherwise rendered on a flat surface. **2.** Any visible image, especially one on a flat surface: *the picture reflected in the lake.* **3.** A vivid or realistic verbal description: *a Shakespearean picture of guilt.* **4.** A person or object that bears a striking resemblance to another: *She's the picture of her mother.* **5.** A person, object, or scene that typifies or embodies an emotion, state of mind, or mood: *"Edna's face was a blank picture of bewilderment."* (Kate Chopin). **6.** The chief circumstances of an event or time; situation: *"With the accession of John, the picture changed considerably."* (Samuel E. Thorne). **7.** A motion picture. **8.** A **tableau vivant** *(see).* —*tr.v.* **pictured, -turing, -tures.** **1.** To make a visible representation or picture of. **2.** To form a mental image of; visualize: *"My toes curled on the deck, as I pictured their laughter."* (Mary Renault). **3.** To describe vividly in words; make a verbal picture of: *He*

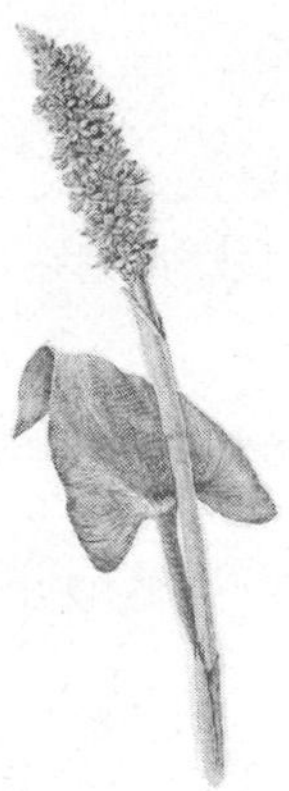

pickerelweed

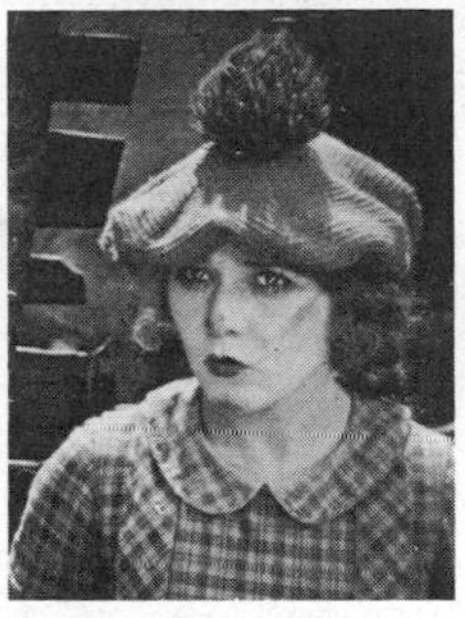

Mary Pickford
In the role of
Little Annie Rooney

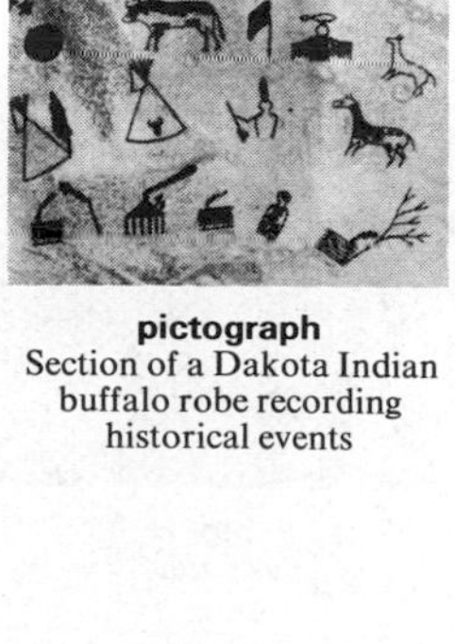

pictograph
Section of a Dakota Indian buffalo robe recording historical events

pictured her heroism in glowing language. [Middle English, from Latin *pictūra,* from *pingere* (past participle *pictus*), to paint. See **peig-¹** in Appendix.*]

pic·tur·esque (pĭk′chə-rĕsk′) *adj.* **1.** Of or suggesting a picture; suitable for a picture: *"the picturesque craggy shores which make the entrance to Japan so memorable"* (Pearl Buck). **2.** Striking or interesting in an unusual way; irregularly or quaintly attractive; charming: *"courtiers of all sorts about him . . . because such adjuncts are picturesque"* (Hilaire Belloc). **3.** Strikingly expressive or vivid: *picturesque language.* [Alteration (influenced by PICTURE) of French *pittoresque,* from Italian *pittoresco,* from *pittore,* painter, from Latin *pictor,* from *pingere* (past participle *pictus*), to paint. See **peig-¹** in Appendix.*] —**pic′tur·esque′ly** *adv.* —**pic′tur·esque′ness** *n.*

pic·ul (pĭk′əl) *n.* Any of various units of weight used in the Far East; especially, a Chinese unit equal to 133.33 pounds. [Malay *pikul,* a man's load.]

pid·dle (pĭd′l) *v.* **-dled, -dling, -dles.** —*tr.* To use triflingly; squander. Usually used with *away: piddle away one's time.* —*intr.* **1.** To spend time aimlessly; diddle. **2.** *Informal.* To urinate. [Akin to Low German *piddeln*†.]

pid·dling (pĭd′lĭng) *adj.* Beneath consideration; trifling; trivial.

pid·dock (pĭd′ək) *n.* Any of various marine bivalve mollusks of the family Pholadidae, capable of boring into wood, rock, and other materials. [Origin unknown.]

pidg·in (pĭj′ən) *n.* A simplified form of speech, usually a mixture of two or more languages, that has a rudimentary grammar and vocabulary and is used for communication between groups speaking different languages. Compare **creolized language.** [From PIDGIN ENGLISH.] —**pidg′in** *adj.*

Pidgin English. Also **pidgin English.** A pidgin based on English and used as a trade language in Far Eastern ports. [A pidgin corruption of *business English.*]

pie¹ (pī) *n.* **1.** A baked food composed of a shell of pastry that is filled with fruit, meat, cheese, or other ingredients, and usually covered with a pastry crust. **2.** A layer cake having cream, custard, or jelly filling. [Middle English *pie*†.]

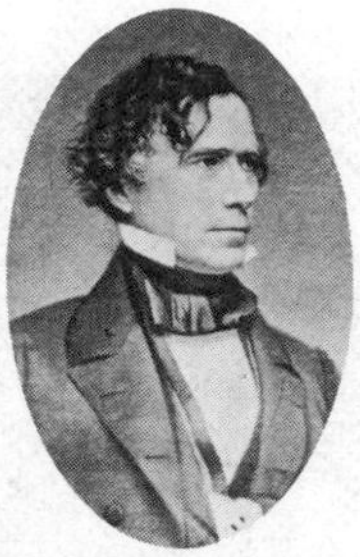

Franklin Pierce

pie² (pī) *n.* A bird, the **magpie** *(see).* [Middle English, from Old French, from Latin *pīca.* See **speik-** in Appendix.*]

pie³ (pī) *n.* A former monetary unit of India and Pakistan. [Hindi *pā'ī,* from Sanskrit *pādikā,* quarter, from *pāda,* foot, leg, quarter. See **ped-¹** in Appendix.*]

pie⁴ (pī) *n.* An almanac of services used in the English church before the Reformation. [Medieval Latin *pīca,* almanac, PICA.]

pie⁵. *Printing.* Variant of **pi.**

pie·bald (pī′bôld′) *adj.* Spotted or patched, especially in black and white: *a piebald horse.* —*n.* A piebald animal, especially a horse. [PIE (magpie) + BALD.]

piece (pēs) *n.* **1.** A thing considered as a unit or element of a larger quantity or class; portion: *a piece of string.* **2.** A portion or part that has been separated from a whole: *a piece of cake.* **3.** An object that is one member of a group or class: *a piece of furniture.* **4.** An artistic, musical, or literary work or composition: *"They are lively and well-plotted pieces, both in prose"* (Tucker Brooke). **5.** An instance; specimen: *a piece of folly.* **6.** One's fully expressed opinion; one's mind: *speak one's piece.* **7.** A coin or counter: *a ten-cent piece.* **8.** In various board games, one of the counters or men used in playing. **9.** *Chess.* Any of the figures other than a pawn. **10.** A firearm, especially a rifle: *"Here upon this island I killed with my piece a gray hare."* (John Davis). **11.** *Chiefly Regional.* A short or manageable distance: *"there was farm country down the road on the right a piece"* (James Agee). **12.** *Vulgar Slang.* A woman regarded as the object of coitus. —**a piece of one's mind.** *Informal.* Frank criticism or censure. —**go to pieces. 1.** To break into small pieces; fall apart. **2.** *Informal.* To lose mental and emotional self-control; break down. —**of a piece.** Belonging to the same kind or class. —*tr.v.* **pieced, piecing, pieces. 1.** To mend by adding a piece to. **2.** To join or unite the pieces of: *He pieced together the vase.* [Middle English *pece, piece,* from Old French *pece,* from Medieval Latin *pecia, petia,* from Gaulish *pettia*† (unattested).]

pièce de ré·sis·tance (pyĕs də rā-zē-stäɴs′). *French.* **1.** The principal dish of a meal. **2.** An outstanding accomplishment.

piece goods. Fabrics made and sold in standard lengths. Also called "yard goods."

piece·meal (pēs′mēl′) *adv.* **1.** Piece by piece; gradually: *articles acquired piecemeal.* **2.** In pieces; apart. —*adj.* Accomplished or made piece by piece. [Middle English *pecemele* : *pece,* PIECE + *-mele,* by a certain measure, Old English *mǣlum,* dative plural of *mǣl,* a point of time. See **meal.**]

piece of eight. An obsolete Spanish silver coin.

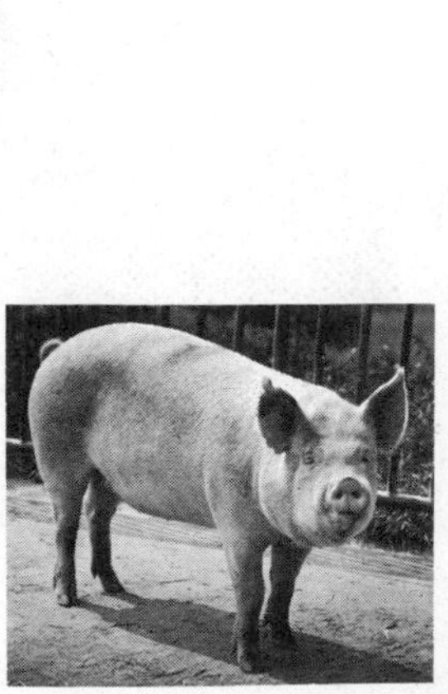

pig
Sus scrofa

piece·work (pēs′wûrk′) *n.* Work paid for according to the number of products turned out. —**piece′work′er** *n.*

pie chart. A circular chart having radii dividing the circle into sectors proportional in angle and area to the relative size of the quantities represented. [From PIE (pastry).]

pied (pīd) *adj.* Patchy in color; splotched; piebald: *"There grew pied wind-flowers and violets."* (Shelley). [Middle English, from PIE (magpie), from its piebald coloring.]

pied-à-terre (pyā-dà-târ′) *n., pl.* **pieds-à-terre.** *French.* A secondary or temporary lodging: *They live in the country but have a small pied-à-terre in the city.* [French, "foot to the ground."]

pied·mont (pēd′mŏnt′) *adj. Geology.* Formed or lying at the foot of a mountain or mountain range: *a piedmont plain.* —*n.* *Geology.* A piedmont area or region. [French, from Italian *piémonte,* from *Piémonte,* PIEDMONT.]

Pied·mont (pēd′mŏnt′). **1.** A region of northwestern Italy, 11,335 square miles in area, bordered on the west by France, on the north by Switzerland, and on the east by Lombardy. **2.** The low platform in the eastern United States extending eastward from the Appalachian and Blue Ridge mountains to the Fall Line, and northward from Alabama to New Jersey. [Italian *Piémonte,* "foothill (country)" : *pié,* syncopated form of *piede,* foot, from Latin *pēs* (see **ped-¹** in Appendix*) + *monte,* mountain, from Latin *mōns* (see **men-²** in Appendix*).]

Pied Piper of Ham·e·lin (hăm′ə-lĭn). *German Legend.* A piper who rid the town of Hamelin of its rats by piping. When refused due payment, he led away the children of the town.

pie·plant (pī′plănt′, -plänt′) *n.* A plant, **rhubarb** *(see).* [From its use in pies.]

pier (pîr) *n.* **1. a.** A platform extending from a shore over water and supported by piles or pillars, used to secure, protect, and provide access to ships or boats. **b.** Such a structure used predominantly for entertainment. **2.** A supporting structure at the junction of connecting spans of a bridge. **3.** *Architecture.* Any of various vertical supporting structures, especially: **a.** A pillar, rectangular in cross section, supporting an arch or roof. **b.** The portion of a wall between windows. **c.** A reinforcing structure that projects from a wall; buttress. [Middle English *per, pere,* from Norman French *pere, piere,* from Old French *puiere,* "something serving as a support," from *puie,* support, from *puier,* to support, from Vulgar Latin *podiāre* (unattested), to support, from Latin *podium,* raised platform, PODIUM.]

pierce (pîrs) *tr.v.* **pierced, piercing, pierces. 1.** To cut or pass through with or as with a sharp instrument; stab; penetrate. **2.** To make a hole or opening in; perforate. **3.** To make a way through: *The path pierced the wilderness.* **4.** To sound sharply through: *His shout pierced the din.* **5.** To succeed in discerning or understanding: *He pierced the heart of the mystery.* **6.** To affect penetratingly; move deeply; transfix: *pierced by anguish.* —*intr.* To penetrate into or through something: *The rocket pierced through space.* [Middle English *percen,* from Old French *percer, percier,* from Vulgar Latin *pertūsiāre* (unattested), from Latin *pertundere* (past participle *pertūsus*), to pierce through : *per,* through + *tundere,* to thrust (see **steu-** in Appendix*).] —**pierc′er** *n.* —**pierc′ing·ly** *adv.*

Pierce (pîrs), **Franklin.** 1804–1869. Fourteenth President of the United States (1853–57).

Pierce (pîrs), **John Robinson.** Born 1910. American electrical engineer; pioneer in communications satellites.

Pi·e·ri·an Spring (pī-îr′ē-ən). **1.** *Greek Mythology.* A spring in Macedonia, sacred to the Muses. **2.** A source of inspiration.

Pie·ro del·la Fran·ce·sca (pyâ′rō dĕl′lä frän-chās′kä). 1420?–1492. Italian painter; a leader of the Umbrian school.

Pie·ro di Co·si·mo (pyâ′rō dē kô′zē-mō). 1462–1521. Italian painter of the Florentine school.

Pierre (pîr). The capital of South Dakota, in the center of the state on the Missouri River. Population, 10,000.

Pier·rot (pē′ə-rō′; *French* pyĕ-rō′) *n.* A character in French pantomime, dressed in a floppy white outfit. [French, diminutive of *Pierre,* from Latin *Petrus,* PETER.]

pie·tà (pyā-tä′) *n.* Also **Pie·tà.** A painting or sculpture of the Virgin Mary holding and mourning over the dead body of Jesus. [Italian, "pity," from Latin *pietās,* PIETY.]

Pie·ter·mar·itz·burg (pē′tər-măr′ĭts-bûrg′). The capital of Natal Province, Republic of South Africa, about 50 miles north of Durban. Population, 129,000.

pi·e·tism (pī′ə-tĭz′əm) *n.* **1.** Piety. **2.** Affected or exaggerated piety. **3.** *Capital* **P.** A reform movement in the German Lutheran Church during the 17th and 18th centuries, which strove to renew the devotional ideal in the Protestant religion. [German *Pietismus,* from Latin *pietās,* PIETY.] —**pi′e·tist** *n.* —**pi′e·tis′tic, pi′e·tis′ti·cal** *adj.* —**pi′e·tis′ti·cal·ly** *adv.*

pi·e·ty (pī′ə-tē) *n., pl.* **-ties. 1.** Religious devotion and reverence to God. **2.** Devotion and reverence to parents and family. **3.** A pious act or thought. **4.** The state or quality of being pious. [French *pieté,* from Latin *pietās,* from *pius,* PIOUS.]

piezo–. Indicates pressure; for example, **piezometer.** [From Greek *piezein,* to squeeze, press. See **sed-¹** in Appendix.*]

pi·e·zo·e·lec·tric·i·ty (pī-ē′zō-ə-lĕk′trĭs′ə-tē, pē-ā′zō-) *n. Physics.* The generation of electricity or of electric polarity in dielectric crystals subjected to mechanical stress, and, conversely, the generation of stress in such crystals subjected to an applied voltage. Also called "piezoelectric effect." —**pi·e′zo·e·lec′tric, pi·e′zo·e·lec′tri·cal** *adj.* —**pi·e′zo·e·lec′tri·cal·ly** *adv.*

pi·e·zom·e·ter (pī′ə-zŏm′ə-tər, pē′ə-) *n.* Any instrument for measuring pressure, especially high pressure. [PIEZO- + -METER.] —**pi·e′zo·met′ric** (pī-ē′zə-mĕt′rĭk, pē-ā′zə-), **pi′e·zo·met′ri·cal** *adj.* —**pi′e·zom′e·try** *n.*

pif·fle (pĭf′əl) *intr.v.* **-fled, -fling, -fles.** To talk or act in a feeble or futile way. —*n.* Foolish or futile talk or ideas; nonsense. [Origin uncertain.]

pig (pĭg) *n.* **1.** Any of several mammals of the family Suidae, having short legs, cloven hoofs, bristly hair, and a cartilaginous snout used for digging; especially, the domesticated hog, *Sus scrofa,* when young or of comparatively small size. **2.** The edible parts of a pig. **3.** *Informal.* A person regarded as being piglike, greedy, or gross. **4.** The **guinea pig** *(see).* **5. a.** An oblong block of metal, chiefly iron or lead, poured from a smelting furnace. **b.** A mold in which such metal is cast. **c. Pig iron** *(see).* —*intr.v.* **pigged, pigging, pigs.** To give birth to pigs; farrow. —**pig it.** To live in a piglike fashion. [Middle English *pigge,* probably from Old English *picga*† (unattested).]

pig bed. A bed of sand in which pigs of iron are cast.

pig·boat (pĭg′bōt′) *n. Slang.* A submarine.

pi·geon (pĭj′ən) *n.* **1.** Any of various birds of the widely distributed family Columbidae, characteristically having deep-chested bodies, small heads, and short legs; especially *Columba livia* or any of its domesticated varieties. This species is also called "rock dove." **2.** *Slang.* One who is easily swindled; a dupe. [Middle English *pijon,* from Old French, young bird, pigeon, from Latin *pīpiō,* squab, young chirping bird, from *pīpīre,* to chirp. See **pipp-** in Appendix.*]

pigeon breast. A human chest deformity, **chicken breast** *(see).* —**pi'geon-breast'ed** *adj.*

pigeon hawk. A small falcon, *Falco columbarius.* Also called "merlin."

pi·geon·hole (pĭj'ən-hōl') *n.* **1.** The small hole or holes for nesting, in a pigeon loft. **2.** A small compartment or recess, as in a desk, for holding papers; cubbyhole. —*tr.v.* **pigeonholed, -holing, -holes. 1.** To place or file in a pigeonhole. **2.** To classify mentally; categorize. **3.** To put aside and ignore; shelve.

pigeon pea. 1. A tropical shrub, *Cajanus indicus,* having showy orange-yellow flowers. **2.** The edible brown seed of this shrub.

pi·geon-toed (pĭj'ən-tōd') *adj.* Having the toes turned inward.

pi·geon·wing (pĭj'ən-wĭng') *n.* A dance step performed by jumping and clapping the feet together. [Probably a translation of French *ailes de pigeon,* a ballet term for a leap in which the dancer's legs imitate the motion of a bird's wings.]

pig·fish (pĭg'fĭsh') *n., pl.* **pigfish** or **fishes.** A marine fish, *Orthopristis chrysopterus,* of Atlantic waters along the U.S. coast. Also called "hogfish." [It grunts like a pig.]

pig·ger·y (pĭg'ə-rē) *n., pl.* **-ies.** A place where pigs are kept.

pig·gin (pĭg'ĭn) *n.* A small wooden bucket with one stave projecting above the rim for use as a handle. Also called "pipkin." [Origin unknown.]

pig·gish (pĭg'ĭsh) *adj.* Like a pig; greedy; dirty. —**pig'gish·ly** *adv.* —**pig'gish·ness** *n.*

pig·gy (pĭg'ē) *n., pl.* **-gies.** A little pig.

pig·gy·back (pĭg'ē-băk') *adv.* Also **pick·a·back** (pĭk'ə-băk'). **1.** On the shoulders or back: *ride piggyback.* **2.** By a method of transportation in which truck trailers are carried on trains, or cars on specially designed trucks. [Alteration of PICKABACK.] —**pig'gy·back'** *adj.*

piggy bank. A child's coin bank shaped like a pig.

pig·head·ed (pĭg'hĕd'ĭd) *adj.* Stubborn. See Synonyms at **obstinate.** —**pig'head'ed·ly** *adv.* —**pig'head'ed·ness** *n.*

pig iron. Crude iron cast in blocks or pigs. Also called "pig."

pig Latin. A coded jargon in which the initial consonant of each word is transposed to the end of that word with *-ay* (ā) added to form a new syllable, as *igpay atinlay* for *pig Latin.*

pig·let (pĭg'lĭt) *n.* A young pig.

pig·ment (pĭg'mənt) *n.* **1.** Any substance or matter used as coloring. **2.** Dry coloring matter, usually an insoluble powder to be mixed with water, oil, or another base to produce paint and similar products. **3.** *Biology.* A substance, such as chlorophyll or hemoglobin, that produces a characteristic color in plant or animal tissue. —*tr.v.* **pigmented, -menting, -ments.** To color with pigment. [Latin *pigmentum,* from *pingere,* to paint. See **peig-**[1] in Appendix.*] —**pig'men·tar'y** (pĭg'mən-tĕr'ē) *adj.*

pig·men·ta·tion (pĭg'mən-tā'shən) *n. Biology.* **1.** Coloration of tissues by pigment. **2.** Deposition of pigment by cells.

pigment cell. A **chromatophore** *(see).*

pig·my. Variant of **pygmy.**

Pig·my. Variant of **Pygmy.**

pig·nut (pĭg'nŭt') *n.* **1.** Either of two trees, *Carya glabra* or *C. ovalis,* of the eastern United States, bearing nuts with somewhat bitter kernels. **2.** The nut of either of these trees. **3.** A plant, the **earthnut** *(see),* or its tuberous root.

pig·pen (pĭg'pĕn') *n.* **1.** A pen for pigs. **2.** A dirty place.

pig·skin (pĭg'skĭn') *n.* **1.** The skin of a pig. **2.** Leather made from this. **3.** *Informal.* **a.** A football. **b.** A saddle.

pigs·ney (pĭgz'nē) *n. Obsolete.* **1.** A darling. **2.** An eye. [Middle English *piggesnye,* "pig's eye" (probably originally baby talk) : *pigge,* PIG + *nye,* variant of EYE (from *an eye*).]

pig·sty (pĭg'stī') *n., pl.* **-sties.** A shelter where pigs are kept.

pig·tail (pĭg'tāl') *n.* **1.** A plait of braided hair that hangs down the back. **2.** A twisted roll of tobacco. —**pig'tailed'** *adj.*

pig·weed (pĭg'wēd') *n.* **1.** A common wild plant, *Chenopodium album,* having leaves with a mealy surface and small green flowers. Also called "lamb's quarters." **2.** A coarse weed, *Amaranthus retroflexus,* having hairy leaves and spikes of green flowers. Also called "redroot."

pi·ka (pē'kə) *n.* Any of several small, tailless, harelike mammals of the genus *Ochotona,* of the mountains of North America and Eurasia. Also called "cony." [Tungus (East Siberia) *piika.*]

pike[1] (pīk) *n.* A long spear formerly used by infantry. —*tr.v.* **piked, piking, pikes.** To pierce with a pike. [Old French *pique,* from *piquer,* to prick, pierce, pique, from Vulgar Latin *piccāre* (unattested), probably from Latin *pīcus,* woodpecker. See **speik-** in Appendix.*]

pike[2] (pīk) *n., pl.* **pike** or **pikes. 1.** A freshwater game and food fish, *Esox lucius,* of the Northern Hemisphere, having a long snout and attaining a length of over four feet. **2.** Any of various similar or related fishes. [Middle English, perhaps from PIKE (spike).]

pike[3] (pīk) *n.* **1.** A turnpike. **2. a.** A tollgate on a turnpike. **b.** The toll paid. —*intr.v.* **piked, piking, pikes.** To move quickly. Often used with *along.* [Short for TURNPIKE.]

pike[4] (pīk) *n. Chiefly British.* A hill with a pointed summit. [Middle English, akin to Norwegian dialectal *pīk*†.]

pike[5] (pīk) *n.* Any spike or sharp point, such as the tip of a spear. [Middle English *pike,* Old English *pīc*†.]

Pike (pīk), **Zebulon Montgomery.** 1779–1813. American army officer and explorer of the West and Southwest.

pike perch. Any of various fishes related to the perches and resembling the pike, such as the **walleye** *(see).*

pik·er (pī'kər) *n. Slang.* A stingy, petty person, especially one who gambles cautiously. [Origin uncertain.]

Pikes Peak (pīks' pēk'). Also **Pike's Peak.** A mountain peak, 14,110 feet high, in central Colorado in the Rocky Mountains.

pike·staff (pīk'stăf', -stäf') *n., pl.* **-staves** (-stāvz'). **1.** The shaft of a pike. **2.** A walking stick tipped with a metal spike. [PIKE (point) + STAFF.]

pi·laf, pi·laff (pĭ-läf', pē-) *n.* Also **pi·lau** (pĭ-lô', pē-), **pi·law.** A steamed rice dish with meat, shellfish, or vegetables in a seasoned broth. [Turkish *pilāw,* from Persian *pilāw,* from Osmanli *pilav*†, "rice porridge."]

pi·lar (pī'lər) *adj.* Of, pertaining to, or covered with hair. [New Latin *pilaris,* from Latin *pilus,* a hair. See **pilo-** in Appendix.*]

pi·las·ter (pĭ-lăs'tər) *n. Architecture.* A rectangular column with a capital and base, set into a wall as an ornamental motif. [Old French *pilastre,* from Italian *pilastro,* from Medieval Latin *pilastrum,* from Latin *pīla,* PILLAR.]

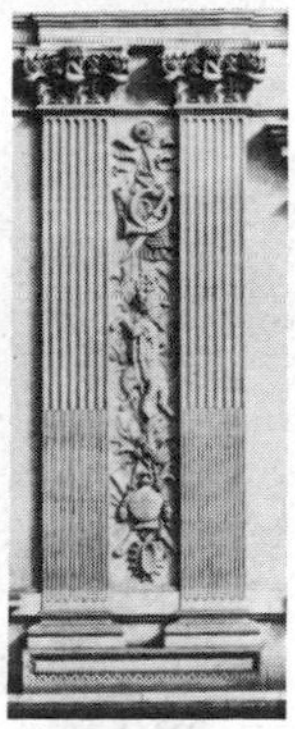
pilaster

Pi·late (pī'lĭt), **Pontius.** Roman official, procurator of Judea (A.D. 26?–36?); assumed to have authorized the execution of Jesus.

pil·chard (pĭl'chərd) *n.* Any of various small marine fishes related to the herrings; especially a commercially important edible species, *Sardina pilchardus,* of European waters. [Earlier *pylcher*†.]

Pil·co·ma·yo (pēl'kō-mä'yō). A river rising in central Bolivia and flowing 1,000 miles along the boundary between Argentina and Paraguay to the Paraguay River at Asunción, Paraguay.

pile[1] (pīl) *n.* **1.** A quantity of objects stacked or thrown together in a heap. **2.** *Informal.* A large accumulation or quantity: *a pile of trouble.* **3.** *Slang.* A large sum of money; fortune. **4.** A funeral pyre. **5.** A very large building or complex of buildings. **6.** *Physics.* A **nuclear reactor** *(see).* **7.** *Electricity.* **Voltaic pile** *(see).* —*v.* **piled, piling, piles.** —*tr.* **1.** To set or stack in a pile or heap. **2.** To load with a pile: *He piled the table with books.* —*intr.* **1.** To form a heap or pile. **2.** To move in a disorderly mass or group. Used with *in, on, off,* or *out: pile out of a car.* —**pile up.** To accumulate. [Middle English, from Old French, heap, heap of stone, from Latin *pīla,* PILLAR.]

pile[2] (pīl) *n.* **1.** A heavy beam of timber, concrete, or steel, driven into the earth as a foundation or support for a structure. **2.** *Heraldry.* A wedge-shaped charge pointing downward. —*tr.v.* **piled, piling, piles. 1.** To drive piles into. **2.** To support with piles. [Middle English *pile,* pointed shaft, stake, Old English *pīl,* from West Germanic *pīla* (unattested), from Latin *pīlum,* heavy javelin, pestle. See **peis-** in Appendix.*]

pile[3] (pīl) *n.* **1.** Cut or uncut loops of yarn forming the surface of certain fabrics, such as velvet, plush, and carpeting. Compare **nap. 2.** The surface so formed. **3.** Soft, fine hair, fur, or wool. [Middle English, from Norman French *pyle,* from Latin *pilus,* hair. See **pilo-** in Appendix.*] —**piled** *adj.*

pi·le·at·ed (pī'lē-ā'tĭd, pĭl'ē-) *adj.* Also **pi·le·ate** (pī'lē-ĭt, pĭl'ē-). **1.** *Botany.* Having a pileus. **2.** *Ornithology.* Having a crest. [From Latin *pīleātus,* wearing a pileus, from *pīleus,* PILEUS.]

pileated woodpecker. A large North American woodpecker, *Dryocopus pileatus,* having black and white plumage and a bright red crest.

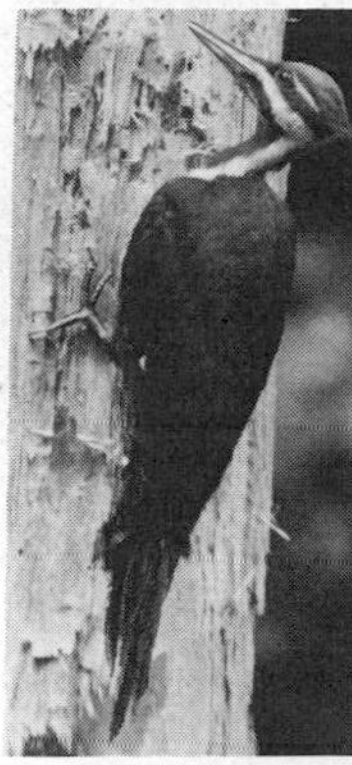
pileated woodpecker

pile driver. A machine that drives piles by raising a weight between guideposts and dropping it on the head of the pile.

piles (pīlz) *pl.n.* **Hemorrhoids** *(see).* [Plural of *pile,* from Latin *pila,* ball. See **pill.**]

pi·le·um (pī'lē-əm, pĭl'ē-) *n., pl.* **pilea** (pī'lē-ə, pĭl'ē-). *Ornithology.* The top of a bird's head, extending from the base of the bill to the nape. [New Latin, from Latin *pīleus,* felt cap, PILEUS.]

pi·le·us (pī'lē-əs, pĭl'ē-) *n., pl.* **pilei** (pī'lē-ī', pĭl'ē-ī'). **1.** *Botany.* The umbrellalike cap of a stalked, fleshy fungus, such as a mushroom. **2.** A round, brimless skullcap worn in ancient Rome. [New Latin, from Latin *pīleus, pilleus,* felt cap. See **pilo-** in Appendix.*]

pile·wort (pīl'wûrt', -wôrt) *n.* Any of several plants reputed to be effective in treating piles, such as the **lesser celandine** and the **fireweed** *(both of which see).*

pil·fer (pĭl'fər) *v.* **-fered, -fering, -fers.** —*tr.* To steal (a small amount or item); filch. —*intr.* To steal or filch. —See Synonyms at **rob.** [Old French *pelfrer,* to rob, despoil, from *pelfre*†, booty.] —**pil'fer·age** (pĭl'fər-ĭj) *n.* —**pil'fer·er** *n.*

pil·grim (pĭl'grĭm, -grəm) *n.* **1.** A religious devotee who journeys to a shrine or sacred place. **2.** One who embarks on a quest for some end conceived as sacred. **3.** Any traveler. **4.** *Capital* **P.** One of the English Puritans who founded the colony of Plymouth in New England (1620). [Middle English *pelegrim,* from Old French *peligrin,* from Late Latin *pelegrīnus,* alteration of Latin *peregrīnus,* PEREGRINE.]

pil·grim·age (pĭl'grə-mĭj) *n.* **1.** A journey to a sacred place or shrine. **2.** Any long journey or search, especially one of exalted purpose or moral significance. —*intr v* **pilgrimaged, -aging, -ages.** To go on a pilgrimage.

pika
Ochotona princeps

pil·ing (pī'lĭng) *n.* **1.** The act of driving piles. **2.** Piles collectively. **3.** A structure composed of piles.

Pil·i·pi·no (pĭl'ə-pē'nō) *n.* The national language of the Philippines, based primarily on Tagalog, and having many Spanish and local dialectal elements. [Tagalog, from *pilipino,* Filipino, from Philippine Spanish, FILIPINO.]

pill[1] (pĭl) *n.* **1.** A small pellet or tablet of medicine, often coated, taken by swallowing whole or chewing. **2.** *Usually capital* **P.** *Informal.* An oral contraceptive. Preceded by *the.* **3.** *Slang.* Something resembling a pill, as a baseball. **4.** Anything dis-

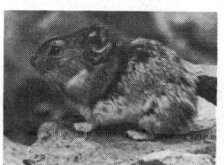

tasteful or unpleasant, but necessary. **5.** *Slang.* An insipid or ill-natured person. —*v.* **pilled, pilling, pills.** —*tr.* **1.** To dose with pills. **2.** To make into pills. **3.** *Slang.* To blackball. —*intr.* To form small balls resembling pills: *a sweater that pills.* [Latin *pilula,* diminutive of *pila*†, ball.]

pill[2] (pĭl) *v.* **pilled, pilling, pills.** —*tr. Archaic.* To pillage (people or a place). —*intr. Archaic.* To pillage. [Middle English *pillen,* from Old French *piller,* to plunder (see **pillage**).]

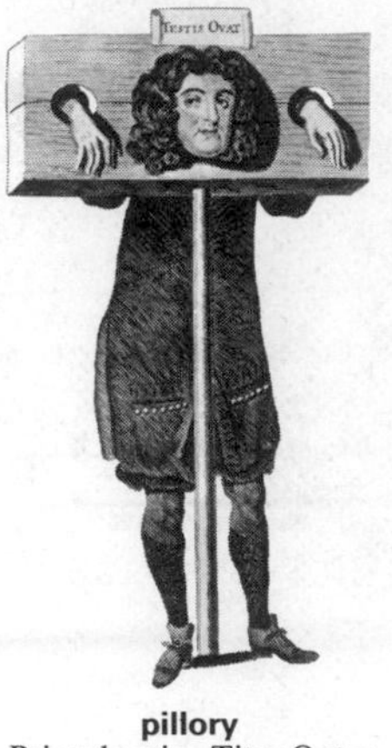

pillory
Print showing Titus Oates confined in a pillory

pil·lage (pĭl′ĭj) *v.* **-laged, -laging, -lages.** —*tr.* **1.** To rob of goods by violent seizure; plunder. **2.** To take as spoils. —*intr.* To take spoils by robbery and violence. —*n.* **1.** The act of pillaging. **2.** Something pillaged; spoils. [Middle English, from Old French, from *piller,* to tear up, maltreat, plunder, from *pille,* dialectal variant of *peille,* rag, cloth, probably from Latin *pilleus,* felt cap. See **pilo-** in Appendix.*] —**pil′lag·er** *n.*

pil·lar (pĭl′ər) *n.* **1.** A slender, freestanding, vertical support; column. **2.** Any similar structure used for decoration. **3.** One who occupies a central or responsible position: *a pillar of the state.* —**from pillar to post.** From one resource to another; hither and thither. —*tr.v.* **pillared, -laring, -lars.** To support or decorate with a pillar or pillars. [Middle English *piler, piller,* from Old French *pilier,* from Vulgar Latin *pīlāre* (unattested), extension of Latin *pīla*†, pillar.]

Pillars of Hercules. The headlands, Gibraltar and Jebel Musa, at the eastern end of the Strait of Gibraltar.

pill·box (pĭl′bŏks′) *n.* **1.** A small box for pills. **2.** A woman's small, round hat. **3.** A roofed concrete emplacement for a machine gun or other weapon.

pill bug. Any of various small, terrestrial crustaceans of the genus *Armadillidium* or related genera, having convex, segmented bodies capable of being curled into a ball.

pil·lion (pĭl′yən) *n.* A pad or cushion for an extra rider behind the saddle on a horse or motorcycle. [Scottish Gaelic *pillean,* diminutive of *peall,* covering, cushion, from Latin *pellis,* skin, hide. See **pel-**[4] in Appendix.*]

pil·lo·ry (pĭl′ə-rē) *n., pl.* **-ries.** A wooden framework on a post, with holes for the head and hands, in which offenders were formerly locked to be exposed to public scorn as punishment. —*tr.v.* **pilloried, -rying, -ries.** **1.** To put in a pillory as punishment. **2.** To expose to ridicule and abuse. [Middle English, from Old French *pilori,* from Medieval Latin *pilōrium,* probably from Latin *pīla,* PILLAR.]

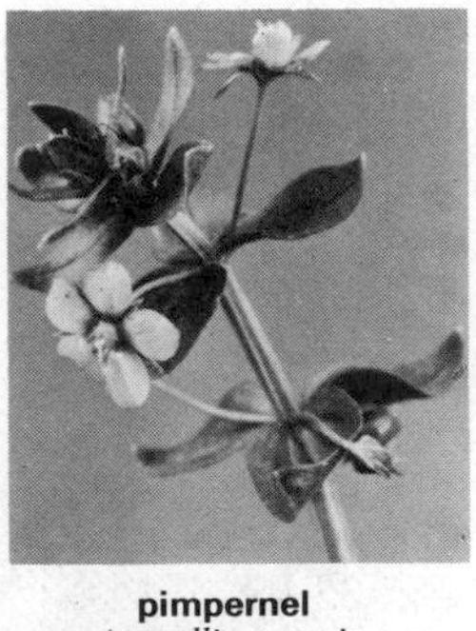

pimpernel
Anagallis arvensis
Scarlet pimpernel

pil·low (pĭl′ō) *n.* **1.** A cloth case, stuffed with something soft, such as down, feathers, or foam rubber, and used to cushion the head during sleep. **2.** A decorative cushion. **3.** The pad on which bobbin lace is made. —*v.* **pillowed, -lowing, -lows.** —*tr.* **1.** To rest (one's head) on or as if on a pillow. **2.** To act as a pillow for: *Grass pillows my head.* —*intr.* To rest on or as if on a pillow. [Middle English *pilwe,* Old English *pyle, pylu,* from Latin *pulvīnus*†, pillow.] —**pil′low·y** *adj.*

pillow block. *Machinery.* A block that encloses and supports a journal or shaft; bearing.

pil·low·case (pĭl′ō-kās′) *n.* A removable covering for a pillow, usually of cotton or linen. Also called "pillow slip."

pillow lace. Bobbin lace *(see).*

pi·lo·car·pine (pī′lō-kär′pēn′) *n.* A poisonous colorless or yellow compound, $C_{11}H_{16}N_2O_2$, obtained from the leaves of the jaborandi tree and used to induce sweating. [From New Latin *Pilocarpus,* genus of the jaborandi : Greek *pilos,* felt (see **pilo-** in Appendix*) + -CARPOUS.]

pi·lose (pī′lōs′) *adj.* Covered with fine, soft hair. [Latin *pilōsus,* from *pilus,* a hair. See **pilo-** in Appendix.*]

pi·lot (pī′lət) *n.* **1.** One who operates or is licensed to operate an aircraft in flight. **2. a.** One who, though not belonging to a ship's company, is licensed to have conduct of her into and out of port or through dangerous waters. **b.** The helmsman of a ship. **3.** One who guides or directs a course of action for others. **4.** The part of a tool, device, or machine that leads or guides the whole: *a pilot parachute.* **5.** A **pilot light** *(see).* **6.** A **cowcatcher** *(see).* **7.** A television program produced as a prototype of a series being considered for adoption by a network. —*tr.v.* **piloted, -loting, -lots.** **1.** To serve as the pilot of. **2.** To steer, or control the course of. —*adj.* **1.** Serving as a tentative model for future experiment or development: *a pilot project.* **2.** Serving or leading as guide. [French *pilote,* from Italian *pilota,* alteration of obsolete *pedota,* from Medieval Greek *pēdōtēs* (unattested), from Greek *pēda,* plural of *pēdon,* rudder, steering oar. See **ped-**[1] in Appendix.*]

pi·lot·age (pī′lə-tĭj) *n.* **1.** *Nautical.* **a.** The technique or act of piloting. **b.** The fee paid to a pilot. **2.** *Aviation.* Navigation by visual identification of landmarks.

pilot balloon. A small balloon used to determine wind velocity.

pilot bread. Hardtack *(see).*

pilot burner. **1.** A small service burner, as in a boiler system, kept lighted to ignite main fires. **2.** A **pilot light** *(see).*

pilot cell. A storage battery cell tested to determine the condition of the entire battery.

pilot engine. A locomotive sent ahead of a train to check the track for safety and clearance.

pilot fish. A marine fish, *Naucrates ductor,* that often swims in company with larger fishes, especially sharks.

pi·lot·house (pī′lət-hous′) *n.* An enclosed area on the deck or bridge of a vessel from which the vessel is controlled when under way. Also called "wheel house."

pi·lot·ing (pī′lə-tĭng) *n.* **1.** The occupation or service of a pilot. **2.** *Nautical.* Coastal navigation by reference to landmarks, buoys, soundings, and the like. See **celestial navigation.**

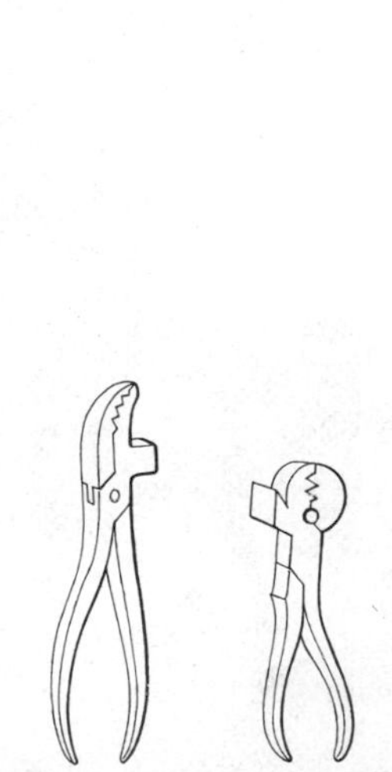

saddler's pincers shoe pincers
pincers

pilot lamp. A small electric lamp wired to light in response to specified conditions in an electric circuit.

pilot light. **1.** A small jet of gas that is kept burning in order to ignite a gas burner, as in a stove. Also called "pilot," "pilot burner." **2.** A **pilot lamp** *(see).*

pilot whale. Any of several small, dark-colored whales of the genus *Globicephala.* Also called "blackfish."

Pil·sen. The German name for **Plzeň.**

Pil·sud·ski (pĭl-so͞ot′skē), **Józef.** 1867–1935. Polish army officer and Socialist leader; virtual dictator (1920–21, 1926–35).

Pilt·down man (pĭlt′doun′). A chimerical early genus and species of man, *Eoanthropus dawsoni,* postulated from bones allegedly found in an early Pleistocene gravel bed between 1909 and 1915 and proved in 1953 to have been a forgery based on the artificial modification and juxtaposition of the cranium of a man and the mandible of an ape. [From the site near *Piltdown* Common, Sussex, England, identified by Charles Dawson (died 1916), English lawyer and amateur paleontologist.]

pil·ule (pĭl′yo͞ol) *n.* A pill, especially a little pill. [French, from Latin *pilula,* diminutive of *pila,* ball. See PILL.] —**pil′u·lar** (pĭl′yə-lər) *adj.*

Pi·ma (pē′mə) *n., pl.* **Pima** or **-mas.** **1.** A tribe of North American Indians of the Uto-Aztecan language family living in southern Arizona and northern Mexico. **2.** A member of this tribe. **3.** The language of this tribe. —**Pi′man** *adj.*

pi·ma cotton (pē′mə) *n.* A very strong high-grade cotton of medium staple developed from selected Egyptian cottons in the southwestern United States. Also called "pima." [Developed in *Pima* County, Arizona.]

pi·men·to (pĭ-mĕn′tō) *n., pl.* **-tos.** **1.** A tree, the **allspice** *(see),* or its berries. **2.** The **pimiento** *(see).* [Spanish *pimienta,* pepper, allspice, from Late Latin *pigmenta,* plural of *pigmentum,* plant juice, PIGMENT.]

pi mes·on (mĕz′ŏn′, mē′zŏn′, mĕs′ŏn′, mē′sŏn′). *Physics.* A subatomic particle, the **pion** *(see).*

pi·mien·to (pĭ-mĕn′tō, -myĕn′tō) *n., pl.* **-tos.** Also **pi·men·to.** A garden pepper, *Capsicum anuum,* or its mild, ripe, red fruit, used in salads, cookery, and as stuffing for green olives. [Spanish, from *pimienta,* pepper, allspice, PIMENTO.]

pimp (pĭmp) *n.* A procurer; pander. —*intr.v.* **pimped, pimping, pimps.** To serve as a pimp. [Origin obscure.]

pim·per·nel (pĭm′pər-nĕl′, -nəl) *n.* Any plant of the genus *Anagallis,* especially the scarlet pimpernel, *A. arvensis,* whose red, purple, or white flowers close in bad weather. Also called "poor man's weatherglass." [Middle English *pympernele,* from Old French *pimpernelle,* from Vulgar Latin *piperīnella* (unattested), from Latin *piper,* PEPPER.]

pim·ple (pĭm′pəl) *n.* A small swelling of the skin, sometimes containing pus; a papule or pustule. [Middle English *pinple*†.] —**pim′pled, pim′ply** *adj.*

pin (pĭn) *n.* **1.** A short, straight, stiff piece of wire with a blunt head and a sharp point, used especially for fastening. **2.** Anything resembling a pin in shape or use, as a hairpin or safety pin. **3.** An ornament fastened to the clothing by means of a clasp. **4.** Something of little or no value: *"I would not care a pin."* (Shakespeare). **5.** A slender, cylindrical piece of wood or metal for holding or fastening parts together, or serving as a support for suspending one thing from another, as: **a.** A thin rod for securing the ends of fractured bones. **b.** A peg for fixing the crown to the root of a tooth. **c.** A cotter pin. **6.** *Nautical.* **a.** A **belaying pin** *(see).* **b.** A **thole pin** *(see).* **7.** *Music.* One of the pegs securing the strings and regulating their tension on a stringed instrument. **8.** The part of a key stem entering a lock. **9.** A **rolling pin** *(see).* **10.** One of the wooden clubs at which the ball is aimed in bowling. **11.** *Golf.* The pole bearing a pennant to mark a hole. **12.** *Plural. Informal.* The legs: *spry for his age, and steady on his pins.* —*tr.v.* **pinned, pinning, pins.** **1.** To fasten or secure with or as if with a pin or pins. **2. a.** To transfix. **b.** To place in a position of trusting dependence. Used with *on* or *to: He pinned his faith on an absurdity.* **3. a.** To win a fall from in wrestling. **b.** To hold fast; immobilize: *He was pinned under the wreckage.* **4.** To oblige (someone) to make a definite response or commitment. Often used with *down: He's hard to pin down on money matters.* **5.** To give (a girl) a fraternity pin in token of attachment. **6.** To attribute (a wrongdoing or crime). Used with *on: The murder was pinned on the wrong man.* —*adj.* Having a grain suggestive of the heads of pins. [Middle English *pin,* peg, Old English *pinn,* probably from Latin *pinna,* quill. See **pet-**[1] in Appendix.*]

pi·ña cloth (pēn′yə). A soft, sheer fabric made from the fibers of pineapple leaves. [Spanish *piña,* pineapple, pinecone, from Latin *pīnea,* from *pīnus,* PINE.]

pin·a·fore (pĭn′ə-fôr′, -fōr′) *n.* A sleeveless garment like an apron, worn especially by small girls as a dress or overdress. [PIN (verb) + AFORE.]

pi·nas·ter (pī-năs′tər) *n.* A pine tree, *Pinus pinaster,* native to the Mediterranean region, having a characteristic pyramidal form. [Latin *pīnaster,* a wild pine : *pīnus,* PINE + *-aster,* suffix denoting partial resemblance.]

pin·ball (pĭn′bôl′) *n.* A game played on a device (a pinball machine) in which the player operates a plunger to shoot a ball down a slanted surface having obstacles and targets.

pince-nez (păns′nā′, pĭns′-) *n., pl.* **pince-nez** (-nāz′, -nā′). Eyeglasses that are clipped to the bridge of the nose. [French, "pinch-nose" : *pincer,* to pinch, from Old French *pincier,* PINCH + *nez,* nose, from Latin *nāsus* (see **nas-** in Appendix*).]

pin·cer (pĭn′sər) *n.* Anything resembling one of the grasping parts of pincers.

pin·cers (pĭn′sərz) *n.* Also **pin·chers** (pĭn′chərz). Plural in form, sometimes used with a singular verb. **1.** A grasping tool having a pair of jaws and handles pivoted together to work in opposition. Also called "pair of pincers." **2.** The articulated, prehensile claws of certain arthropods, such as the lobster. **3.** A military maneuver in which the enemy is attacked from two flanks and the front. Also called "pincers movement," "pincer movement." [Middle English *pynsour*, a pincer, from Old French *pinceour* (unattested), from *pincier*, to PINCH.]

pinch (pĭnch) *v.* **pinched, pinching, pinches.** —*tr.* **1.** To squeeze between the thumb and a finger, the jaws of a tool, or other edges. **2.** To squeeze or bind (a part of the body) in such a way as to cause discomfort or pain: *The shoes pinch my toes.* **3.** To nip, wither, or shrivel: *buds pinched by the frost; her face all pinched with grief.* **4.** To straiten: *"A year and a half of the blockade has pinched Germany."* (William L. Shirer). **5.** *Slang.* To steal: *"He cannot pinch the painful soldiers pay, and shear him out his share"* (George Gascoigne). **6.** *Slang.* To arrest. **7.** To move by means of a pinch bar. **8.** *Nautical.* To head (a boat) very close into the wind. —*intr.* **1.** To press, squeeze, or bind painfully: *This collar pinches.* **2.** To be miserly. **3.** To drag an oar at the end of a stroke. —**pinch pennies.** To be thrifty or miserly. —*n.* **1.** The act of pinching. **2.** An amount of something that can be held between thumb and forefinger: *a pinch of rosemary.* **3.** A painful, difficult, or straitened circumstance: *to feel the pinch.* **4.** Any emergency situation: *"Once people guessed you would fail them at the pinch, they took care you should not live to do it."* (Mary Renault). **5.** *Informal.* A theft or robbery. **6.** *Slang.* An arrest. [Middle English *pinchen*, to pinch, prick, from Old North French *pinchier* (unattested), variant of Old French *pincier*, from Gallo-Roman *pints-, pits-* (unattested), a point (expressive).]

pinch bar. A crowbar with a pointed projection at one end.

pinch·beck (pĭnch′bĕk′) *n.* **1.** An alloy of zinc and copper used as imitation gold. **2.** A cheap imitation. —*adj.* **1.** Made of pinchbeck. **2.** Imitation; spurious. [Invented by Christopher *Pinchbeck* (1670?–1732), English watchmaker.]

pinch·cock (pĭnch′kŏk′) *n.* A clamp used to regulate or close a flexible tube, especially in laboratory apparatus.

pinch effect. *Physics.* The radial constriction of a **plasma** *(see),* caused by the interaction of its internal electric currents and its self-generated magnetic field.

pinch-hit (pĭnch′hĭt′) *intr.v.* **-hit, -hitting, -hits. 1.** *Baseball.* To bat in place of a player scheduled to bat, especially when a hit is badly needed. **2.** *Informal.* To substitute for another in an emergency. [From PINCH (emergency).] —**pinch hitter.**

Pinck·ney (pĭnk′nē). A family of colonial leaders in South Carolina, including **Charles Cotesworth** (1746–1825), his brother, **Thomas** (1750–1828), and his cousin, **Charles** (1757–1824).

pin clover. A plant, the **alfilaria** *(see).*

pin curl. A coiled strand of hair, usually damp, secured with a bobby pin or clip and combed into a wave or curl when dry.

pin·cush·ion (pĭn′koosh′ən) *n.* A small, firm cushion in which pins are stuck when not in use.

Pin·dar (pĭn′dər). 522?–443 B.C. Greek lyric poet.

Pin·dar·ic (pĭn-dăr′ĭk) *adj.* **1.** Pertaining to or characteristic of the poetic **style** of Pindar. **2.** Of or characteristic of a Pindaric ode. —*n.* A Pindaric ode.

Pindaric ode. 1. An ode in the form developed by Pindar, consisting of a series of triads formed by the strophe, antistrophe, and epode. **2.** An adaptation of this form, with irregular stanzas and rhyme schemes, especially as practiced by English poets of the 17th and 18th centuries.

pine¹ (pīn) *n.* **1.** Any of various evergreen trees of the genus *Pinus,* having needle-shaped leaves in clusters and bearing cones. Many are valued for shade and ornament and for their wood and resinous sap, which yields turpentine and pine tar. **2.** Loosely, any coniferous tree, especially of the family Pinaceae, such as the cedar, spruce, or fir. **3.** The wood of any of these trees. [Middle English *pine,* from Old English *pīn* and Old French *pin,* from Latin *pīnus.* See **peye-** in Appendix.*]

pine² (pīn) *v.* **pined, pining, pines.** —*intr.* **1.** To suffer intense longing or yearning. Usually used with *for: "I entreat you to tell him I am pining for a valentine."* (Emily Dickinson). **2.** To wither or waste away from longing or grief. Usually used with *away.* —*tr. Archaic.* To grieve or mourn for. —See Synonyms at **yearn.** —*n. Archaic.* Intense longing or grief. [Middle English *pinen,* Old English *pīnian,* from *pīne* (unattested), torture, anguish, from Latin *poena,* penalty, from Greek *poinē,* payment, punishment. See **kwei-¹** in Appendix.*]

pin·e·al (pĭn′ē-əl, pīn′-) *adj.* **1.** Having the form of a pine cone. **2.** Pertaining to the pineal body. [French *pinéal,* from Latin *pīnea,* pine cone, from *pīneus,* of the pine, from *pīnus,* PINE.]

pineal body. A small, rudimentary glandular body of uncertain function, in the brain at the roof of the third ventricle. Also called "pineal eye," "pineal gland," "pineal organ."

pine·ap·ple (pīn′ăp-əl) *n.* **1.** A tropical American plant, *Ananas comosus,* having large, swordlike leaves and a large, fleshy, edible fruit consisting of the flowers fused into a compound whole with a terminal tuft of leaves. **2.** The fruit of this plant. **3.** *Slang.* A small hand grenade. [Originally "pine cone" (from the structural resemblance of this fruit to that of a pine cone), Middle English *pinappel* : PINE + APPLE.]

pineapple weed. A North American plant, *Matricaria matricarioides,* having greenish-yellow, rayless flower heads and an odor of pineapple when crushed.

pine·drops (pīn′drŏps′) *n.* Plural in form, sometimes used with a singular verb. A purplish-brown, leafless, parasitic plant, *Pterospora andromedea,* having reddish or white flowers.

pine mouse. Any of various voles of the genus *Pitymys,* especially, *P. pinetorum,* a tiny forest animal of eastern North America. Also called "pine vole."

pi·nene (pī′nēn′) *n.* Either of two isomeric terpene liquids, $C_{10}H_{16}$, that are the main constituents of oil or spirits of turpentine. [PINE + -ENE.]

pine needle. The needle-shaped leaf of a pine tree.

pine nut. The edible seed of certain pines, such as the piñon.

Pi·ne·ro (pĭ-nîr′ō), Sir **Arthur Wing.** 1855–1934. English playwright; author of farces and social melodramas.

pin·er·y (pī′nə-rē) *n., pl.* **-ies. 1.** A hothouse or plantation for growing pineapples. **2.** A forest of pine trees.

Pines, Isle of. Spanish **Is·la de Pi·nos** (ēs′lä dä pē′nōs). An island, 1,182 square miles in area, in the Caribbean Sea off the southern coast of western Cuba.

pine·sap (pīn′săp′) *n.* A fleshy white or reddish plant, *Monotropa hypopithys,* growing as a saprophyte or parasite on tree roots.

pine siskin. A North American finch, *Spinus pinus,* having streaked, brownish plumage. Also called "pine finch."

pine tar. A viscous or semisolid brown to black substance produced by the destructive distillation of pine wood and used in roofing compositions, paints and varnishes, expectorants, and as an antiseptic.

pine-tree shilling (pīn′trē′). A silver coin bearing the stamp of a pine tree, minted in Massachusetts from 1652 to about 1684.

Pine Tree State. The nickname for Maine.

pi·ne·tum (pī-nē′təm) *n., pl.* **-ta** (-tə). An area planted with pine trees or related conifers, especially for botanical study. [Latin *pīnētum,* pine-wood, from *pīnus,* PINE.]

pine warbler. A small, yellow-breasted songbird, *Dendroica pinus,* of eastern North America.

pin·ey. Variant of **piny.**

pin·feath·er (pĭn′fĕth′ər) *n. Ornithology.* A growing feather still enclosed in its horny sheath; especially, one just emerging through the skin.

pin·fish (pĭn′fĭsh′) *n., pl.* **pinfish** or **-fishes.** A small, spiny-finned fish, *Lagodon rhomboides,* of the waters off the southeastern coast of the United States. Also called "sailor's-choice."

pin·fold (pĭn′fōld′) *n.* A pound for stray animals. —*tr.v.* **-folded, -folding, -folds.** To confine in or as in a pinfold. [Middle English *pyn(de)fold,* Old English *pundfald* : *pund-,* POUND (enclosure) + *fald,* FOLD.]

ping (pĭng) *n.* A brief, high-pitched sound, such as that made by a bullet striking metal. —*intr.v.* **pinged, pinging, pings.** To produce a ping. [Imitative.]

Ping (pĭng). A river of Thailand, rising in the northwest and flowing about 350 miles southeast to its confluence with the Nan River, with which it forms the Chao Phraya River.

Ping-Pong (pĭng′pông′, -pŏng′) *n.* A trademark for table-tennis equipment. Often applied to the game of table tennis.

pin·head (pĭn′hĕd′) *n.* **1.** The head of a pin. **2.** Anything small, trifling, or insignificant. **3.** *Slang.* A stupid person. —**pin·head·ed** *adj.*

pin·hole (pĭn′hōl′) *n.* A tiny puncture made by or as if by a pin.

pin·ion¹ (pĭn′yən) *n.* **1.** A bird's wing. **2.** The outer rear edge of a bird's wing, containing the primary feathers. **3.** A primary feather of a bird. —*tr.v.* **pinioned, -ioning, -ions. 1. a.** To remove or bind the wing feathers of (a bird) to prevent flight. **b.** To cut or bind (the wings of a bird). **2.** To restrain or immobilize (a person) by binding the arms. **3.** To fix in one place; make fast: *"he jabbed out harpoon fashion with his fork to pinion a biscuit"* (Stephen Crane). [Middle English *pynyon,* from Old French *pignon,* from Vulgar Latin *pinniō* (unattested), augmentative of Latin *pinna, penna,* a feather, wing. See **pot¹** in Appendix.*]

pin·ion² (pĭn′yən) *n.* A small cogwheel that engages or is engaged by a larger cogwheel or a rack. [French *pignon,* from Old French *p(e)ignon,* from *peigne,* a comb, from Latin *pecten.* See **pek-²** in Appendix.*]

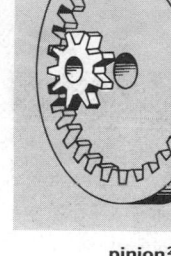

pinion²

pin·ite (pĭn′īt′, pē′nīt′) *n.* A hydrous, usually amorphous mineral silicate of aluminum and potassium. [German *Pinit;* found at *Pini,* mine in Saxony.]

pink¹ (pĭngk) *n.* **1.** Any of various plants of the genus *Dianthus,* often cultivated for their fragrant flowers. **2.** Any of various plants of other genera, such as the **wild pink** and the **moss pink** *(both of which see).* **3.** A flower of any of these plants. **4.** The highest degree of excellence or perfection: *He is in the pink of health.* **5.** Any of a group of colors reddish in hue, of medium to high lightness, and low to moderate saturation. See **color.** **6.** *Plural.* Light-brown trousers formerly worn as part of the winter semidress uniform by U.S. Army officers. **7.** *Slang.* A person regarded as sympathetic with or influenced by Communist doctrine. Used contemptuously. Also called "pinko." —*adj.* **pinker, pinkest. 1.** Pink in color. **2.** *British.* Designating the scarlet coat worn by fox-hunting men. **3.** *Slang.* Sympathetic with or influenced by Communist doctrine. Used contemptuously. [Possibly short for *pink eye,* "small eye" (from the shape of the flower), from obsolete Dutch *pinck oog(en),* "small eye(s)," (also) conjunctivitis : *pin(c)k†,* the little finger + *oog,* eye (see **okw-** in Appendix*).] —**pink′ness** *n.*

pink² (pĭngk) *tr.v.* **pinked, pinking, pinks. 1.** To stab lightly with a pointed weapon; prick: *"it was as if Nixon were wielding a club while Kennedy pinked him with a rapier"* (Theodore H. White). **2.** To decorate with a perforated pattern. **3.** To cut with pinking shears. [Middle English *pynken,* probably of Low German origin, akin to Low German *pinken†,* to peck.]

pink³ (pĭngk) *n.* Also **pink·ie** (pĭng′kē), **pink·y.** *Nautical.* A sailing vessel with a narrow stern. [Middle English *pynk,* from Middle Dutch *pin(c)ke†.*]

Pink·er·ton (pĭng′kər-tən), **Allan.** 1819–1884. Scottish-born American detective; Civil War intelligence agent.

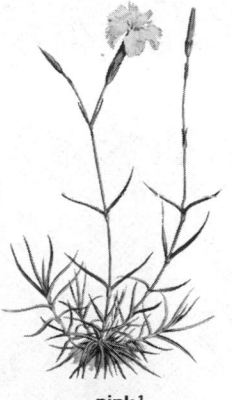

pink¹
Dianthus petraeus

---

pink·eye (pĭngk'ī') *n.* Also **pink eye.** Acute contagious conjunctivitis, characterized by inflamed eyelids and eyeballs. [Partial translation of obsolete Dutch *pinck oog(en),* "small eye(s)." See **pink** (color).]

Pin·kiang. The Chinese name for **Harbin.**

pink·ie (pĭng'kē) *n.* Also **pink·y** *pl.* **-ies.** *Informal.* The fifth or little finger. [Dutch *pinkje,* diminutive of *pink,* little finger, from obsolete *pin(c)k*†. See also **pink** (color).]

pinking shears. Sewing scissors with notched or serrated blades. They are used to finish edges of cloth with a scalloped or zigzag pattern, for decoration or to prevent raveling.

pink·ish (pĭng'kĭsh) *adj.* Somewhat pink. —**pink'ish·ness** *n.*

pink lady. A cocktail of gin, brandy, lemon or lime juice, egg white, and grenadine, shaken with cracked ice and strained.

pink·o (pĭng'kō) *n., pl.* **-os.** *Slang.* A political **pink** *(see).*

pink root. A disease of onions and related plants caused by a fungus, *Pyrenochaeta terrestris,* resulting in small plants with shriveled pink roots.

pink·root (pĭngk'ro͝ot', -ro͞ot') *n.* A plant, *Spigelia marilandica,* of eastern North America, having red and yellow flowers. Its root was once used as a vermifuge. Also called "wormgrass."

Pink·ster (pĭngk'stər) *n.* Also **Pinx·ter.** *Regional.* Whitsunday or Whitsuntide. [Dutch, from Middle Dutch *pinxter, pinxten,* from Gothic *paintekuste,* from Greek *pentēkostē,* PENTECOST.]

pinkster flower. Also **pinxter flower.** A North American shrub, *Rhododendron nudiflorum,* having fragrant pink flowers that bloom before the leaves appear. [It blooms at Whitsun.]

pink·y[1]. Variant of **pinkie** (finger).

pink·y[2]. *Nautical.* Variant of **pink.**

pin money. Money for incidental expenses given especially by a husband to his wife for her personal expenses.

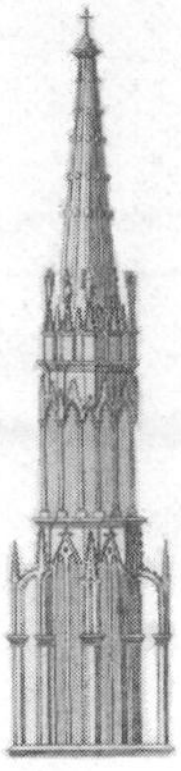

pinnacle

pin·na (pĭn'ə) *n., pl.* **pinnae** (pĭn'ē) or **-nas.** **1.** *Botany.* Any of the leaflets of a pinnate leaf. **2.** *Zoology.* A feather, wing, fin, or similar appendage. **3.** *Anatomy.* The external part of the ear; auricle. [Latin *pinna, penna,* wing, feather. See **pet-**[1] in Appendix.*] —**pin'nal** *adj.*

pin·nace (pĭn'ĭs) *n. Nautical.* **1.** A small sailing boat formerly used as a tender for merchant and war vessels. **2.** Any small ship or ship's boat. [French *pinace,* from Old Spanish *pinaza* or Italian *pinaccia,* from (unattested) Vulgar Latin *pīnācea (nāvis),* "(ship) of pine-wood," from Latin *pīnus,* pine tree. See **peye-** in Appendix.*]

pin·na·cle (pĭn'ə-kəl) *n.* **1.** *Architecture.* A small turret or spire on a roof or buttress. **2.** Any tall, pointed formation, such as a mountain peak. **3.** The highest point; summit; acme: *the pinnacle of achievement.* —See Synonyms at **summit.** —*tr.v.* **pinnacled, -cling, -cles.** **1.** To furnish with a pinnacle. **2.** To place on or as on a pinnacle. [Middle English *pin(n)acle,* from Old French, from Late Latin *pinnāculum,* "little wing," from Latin *pinna,* a feather, wing. See **pet-**[1] in Appendix.*]

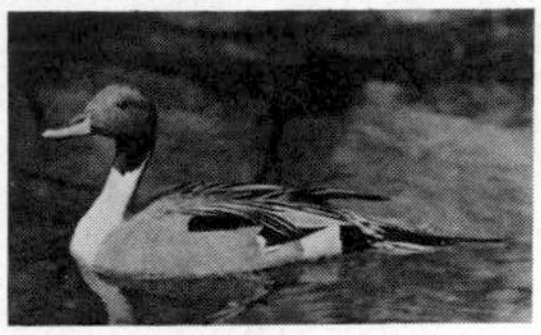

pintail

pin·nate (pĭn'āt') *adj.* Also **pin·nat·ed** (pĭn'ā'tĭd). **1.** Resembling a feather; pennate. **2.** *Botany.* Having leaflets, lobes, or divisions in a featherlike arrangement on each side of a common axis, as many compound leaves do. [Latin *pinnātus,* feathered, from *pinna,* feather. See **pet-**[1] in Appendix.*] —**pin'nate'ly** *adv.*

pinnati–. *Botany.* Indicates resemblance to a feather; for example, **pinnatifid.** [From Latin *pinnātus,* feathered, from *pinna, penna,* feather. See **pet-**[1] in Appendix.*]

pin·nat·i·fid (pĭ-năt'ə-fĭd) *adj. Botany.* Having pinnately cleft lobes or divisions. Said of certain leaves. [PINNATI- + -FID.] —**pin·nat'i·fid·ly** *adv.*

pin·nat·i·sect (pĭ-năt'ə-sĕkt') *adj. Botany.* Divided nearly to the midrib. Said of certain leaves. [PINNATI- + -SECT.]

pin·ni·ped (pĭn'ə-pĕd') *adj. Zoology.* Of or belonging to the Pinnipedia, an order of aquatic mammals that includes the seals, walruses, and similar animals having finlike flippers as organs of locomotion. —*n.* A mammal belonging to this order. [Latin *pinna,* a feather, wing, PINNA + -PED.]

pin·nule (pĭn'yo͞ol) *n.* Also **pin·nu·la** (pĭn'yə-lə) *pl.* **-lae** (-lē'). **1.** *Botany.* Any of the leaflets of a pinnately compound leaf. **2.** *Zoology.* A featherlike or plumelike organ or part, such as a small fin, or one of the appendages of a crinoid. [New Latin *pinnula,* from Latin, diminutive of *pinna, penna,* feather, wing, fin. See **pet-**[1] in Appendix.*] —**pin'nu·lar** (pĭn'yə-lər) *adj.*

pin oak. A tree, *Quercus palustris,* of eastern North America, having horizontal or drooping branches and sharply lobed leaves. [Because the stumps of its dead branches appear like pins stuck into the tree.]

pi·noch·le (pē'nŭk'əl, -nŏk'əl) *n.* Also **pi·noc·le, pe·nuch·le, pe·nuck·le.** **1.** A game of cards for two to four persons, played with a special deck of 48 cards, with points being scored by taking tricks and forming certain combinations. **2.** The combination of the queen of spades and jack of diamonds in this game. [Earlier *binuochle,* perhaps from Swiss German *binokel,* from Swiss French *binocle,* extended use of French *binocle,* pince-nez, binocular, from New Latin *binoculus,* the two eyes : BIN- + Latin *oculus,* eye (see **okw-** in Appendix*).]

pi·no·le (pĭ-nō'lē) *n.* Meal of ground corn or wheat and mesquite beans. [American Spanish, from Nahuatl *pinolli.*]

pi·ñon (pĭn'yŏn', -yən) *n., pl.* **piñons** or **piñones** (pĭn-yō'nēz). Also **pin·yon.** Any of several pine trees bearing edible, nutlike seeds; especially, *Pinus cembroides edulis,* of the western United States and Mexico. Also called "nut pine." [American Spanish, from Spanish, pine nut, pine cone, augmentative of *piña,* from Latin *pīnea,* from the feminine of *pīneus,* of the pine tree, from *pīnus,* pine. See **peye-** in Appendix.*]

piñon jay. Also **pinyon jay.** A small, dull-blue, uncrested jay, *Gymnorhinus cyanocephala,* of western North America. [It feeds on piñon nuts.]

pin·point (pĭn'point') *n.* **1.** An extremely small thing; particle; bit: *a pinpoint of light.* **2.** A tiny or insignificant spot: *the pinpoint of ground upon which we stand.* **3.** *Military.* **a.** A point on a map designating a strictly defined target. **b.** A precisely identified and limited target. —*tr.v.* **pinpointed, -pointing, -points.** **1.** To pierce with or as if with a pin; punctuate: *The ship's running lights pinpointed the dark.* **2.** To locate and identify precisely: *Our radar pinpointed the attacking planes.* **3.** *Military.* To take precise aim at: *pinpoint a target.* —*adj.* **1.** Characterized by meticulous precision: *He spots flaws with pinpoint accuracy.* **2.** Minuscule: *Pinpoint creatures swarmed on the leaf.*

pin·prick (pĭn'prĭk') *n.* **1.** A slight puncture made by a pin. **2.** An insignificant wound. **3.** A minor annoyance. —*v.* **pinpricked, -pricking, -pricks.** —*tr.* To puncture with a pin. —*intr.* To make a slight puncture with a pin.

pins and needles. A tingling felt in a part of the body that has been numbed from lack of circulation. —**on pins and needles.** In a state of anxiety or tense anticipation.

pin·scher (pĭn'shər) *n.* See **Doberman pinscher.**

pin·set·ter (pĭn'sĕt'ər) *n.* A person or device employed to set up pins in a bowling alley.

pin·stripe (pĭn'strīp') *n.* **1.** A thin stripe on a fabric. **2.** A kind of fabric with thin stripes, often used for men's suits.

pint (pīnt) *n. Abbr.* **p., pt., o.** **1. a.** A unit of volume or capacity in the U.S. Customary System, used in liquid measure, equal to 16 fluid ounces or 28.875 cubic inches. **b.** A unit of volume or capacity in the U.S. Customary System, used in dry measure, equal to ½ quart or 33.6 cubic inches. **c.** A unit of volume or capacity in the British Imperial System, used in dry and liquid measure, equal to 34.678 cubic inches. See **measurement.** **2.** A container with such a capacity or the amount of a substance that can be contained in it. [Middle English *pinte,* from Old French, probably from Medieval Latin *pincta,* "painted mark (on a measuring container)," from Vulgar Latin *pinctus* (unattested), painted. See **pinto.**]

pin·ta (pĭn'tə; *Spanish* pēn'tä) *n.* A contagious skin disease prevalent in tropical America, caused by spirochete microorganisms, and characterized by extreme thickening and spotty discoloration of the skin. [American Spanish, from Spanish, painted mark, from the feminine of Vulgar Latin *pinctus* (unattested), painted. See **pinto.**]

Pin·ta (pĭn'tə; *Spanish* pēn'tä) *n.* One of the three ships commanded by Columbus on his first voyage to America.

pin·ta·do (pĭn-tä'dō) *n., pl.* **-dos** or **-does.** Also **pin·ta·da** (pĭn-tä'də). A fish, the **cero** *(see).* [Portuguese, "painted," "spotted" (from its brown spots), from *pintar,* to paint, from Vulgar Latin *pinctāre* (unattested), from *pinctus,* painted. See **pinto.**]

pin·tail (pĭn'tāl') *n., pl.* **-tails** or **pintail.** A duck, *Anas acuta,* of the Northern Hemisphere, having gray, brown, and white plumage and a sharply pointed tail.

pin·ta·no (pĭn-tä'nō) *n., pl.* **-nos** or **pintano.** A dark-banded fish, *Abudefduf marginatus,* of southern Atlantic waters. Also called "cow pilot." [American Spanish *pintano*†.]

pin·tle (pĭnt'l) *n.* An upright pin or bolt used as a pivot; specifically: **a.** *Nautical.* The pin on which a rudder turns. **b.** The pin on a gun carriage. [Middle English *pintel,* "penis," Old English *pintel.* See **bend-** in Appendix.*]

pin·to (pĭn'tō) *n., pl.* **-tos** or **-toes.** Any horse with irregular spots or markings. Also called "paint." —*adj.* Irregularly marked; piebald. [American Spanish, from obsolete Spanish, "painted," "spotted," from Vulgar Latin *pinctus* (unattested), variant of Latin *pictus,* past participle of Latin *pingere,* to paint. See **peig-** in Appendix.*]

pinto bean. A form of the common string bean that has mottled seeds and is grown chiefly in the southwestern United States.

pint·size (pīnt'sīz') *adj.* Also **pint·sized** (-sīzd'). *Informal.* Of small dimensions; diminutive.

Pin·tu·ric·chio (pēn'to͞o-rēk'kyō). Original name, Bernardino Betti. 1454–1513. Italian painter of the Umbrian school.

pin·up (pĭn'ŭp') *n.* **1.** A picture to be pinned up on a wall, especially a sexually attractive photograph of a girl or movie star. **2.** A girl considered a suitable model for such a picture. —*adj.* **1.** Pertaining to or suitable for a pinup: *pinup calendar; pinup girl.* **2.** Designed to be attached to a wall: *pinup lamp.*

pin·wale (pĭn'wāl') *n.* A corduroy made with narrow ribs or wales. —*adj.* Of, pertaining to, or designating such a fabric.

pin·weed (pĭn'wēd') *n.* Any of various plants of the genus *Lechea,* having narrow leaves and numerous small flowers.

pin·wheel (pĭn'hwēl') *n.* **1.** A toy consisting of vanes of colored paper or plastic pinned to the end of a stick in such a way that they turn when blown upon. **2.** A firework that forms a rotating wheel of colored flames. **3.** A wheel with a circle of pins at right angles to its face, used as a tripping device.

pin·work (pĭn'wûrk') *n.* The fine stitches raised in needlepoint lace from the surface of a motif.

pin·worm (pĭn'wûrm') *n.* A small nematode worm, *Enterobius vermicularis,* that infects the human intestines and rectum, especially in children. Also called "threadworm."

pin·wrench (pĭn'rĕnch') *n.* Also **pin wrench.** A wrench having a projection designed to fit a hole in the object to be turned.

pinx·it (pĭngk'sĭt) *n. Abbr.* **pinx., pxt.** *Latin.* He painted (this). Formerly used as part of the painter's signature.

Pinx·ter. Variant of **Pinkster.**

pinxter flower. Variant of **pinkster flower.**

pin·y (pī'nē) *adj.* **-ier, -iest.** Also **pine·y.** Resembling, characteristic of, consisting of, or covered with pines.

pin·yon. Variant of **piñon.**

pinyon jay. Variant of **piñon jay.**

Pin·zón (pēn-*thôn′*), **Martín Alonso.** 1440?–1493. Spanish navigator. He and his brother, **Vicente Yáñez** (1460?–1542?), sailed with Christopher Columbus on his first voyage as captains of *Pinta* and *Niña*.

pi·o·let (pē′ə-lā′) *n.* A kind of ice ax. [French, diminutive of French dialectal *piola,* small ax, ultimately from Old Provençal *apcha, apia,* ax, from Germanic, akin to Old High German *hāppa,* sickle. See **skep-**[1] in Appendix.*]

pi·on (pī′ŏn′) *n. Symbol* π *Physics.* Either of two subatomic particles in the meson family: **a.** *pi zero,* having a mass 264 times that of the electron, zero electric charge, and a mean lifetime of 0.9×10^{-16} second. **b.** *pi plus,* having a mass 273 times that of the electron, a positive electric charge, and a mean lifetime of 2.6×10^{-8} second. Also called "pi meson." See **particle.** [Shortened from PI MESON.]

pi·o·neer (pī′ə-nîr′) *n.* **1.** One who ventures into unknown or unclaimed territory to settle. **2.** An innovator in any field: *a pioneer in aviation.* **3.** A military engineer employed in the construction and fortification of positions and the maintenance of communication lines. **4.** *Ecology.* An animal or plant species that establishes itself in a previously barren environment. —*adj.* **1.** Of the nature of a pioneer; trailblazing; innovating: *a pioneer chemist.* **2.** Of or relating to early settlers or their time: *the pioneer spirit.* —*v.* **pioneered, -neering, -neers.** —*tr.* **1. a.** To explore or open up (a region): *Our icebreakers pioneered the Arctic Ocean.* **b.** To settle: *The taiga is still being pioneered.* **2.** To innovate or participate in the development of: *men who pioneered the submarine.* —*intr.* To act as a pioneer. [Old French *pionier,* originally "a foot soldier sent out to clear the way," from *pion, peon,* foot soldier, from Medieval Latin *pedō,* extended use of Late Latin *pedō,* one with large feet, (later) pedestrian, from Latin *pēs* (stem *ped-*), foot. See **ped-**[1] in Appendix.*]

pi·os·i·ty (pī-ŏs′ə-tē) *n., pl.* **-ties.** Ostentatious piousness; exaggerated devoutness.

pi·ous (pī′əs) *adj.* **1.** Having or exhibiting reverence and earnest compliance in the observance of religion; devout. **2. a.** Marked by conspicuous devoutness: *a pious and holy observation.* **b.** Marked by false devoutness; solemnly hypocritical: *a pious fraud.* **3.** Devotional: *pious readings.* Compare **secular. 4.** Professing or exhibiting a strict, traditional sense of virtue and morality; high-minded: *"The pious instructions of my parents were often fresh in my mind"* (John Woolman). **5.** Commendable; worthy: *a pious attempt.* **6.** *Archaic.* Having filial reverence; dutiful. —See Synonyms at **religious.** [Latin *pius.* See **pius** in Appendix.*] —**pi′ous·ly** *adv.* —**pi′ous·ness** *n.*

Pioz·zi (pyôt′tsē), **Hester Lynch.** Previously, Mrs. Thrale. 1741–1821. English writer; friend of Samuel Johnson.

pip[1] (pĭp) *n.* **1.** The small seed of a fruit, such as an apple or orange. **2.** *Informal.* Something remarkable of its kind: *a pip of a plan.* [Shortened from PIPPIN.]

pip[2] (pĭp) *tr.v.* **pipped, pipping, pips.** *British Slang.* **1.** To strike with a gunshot; hit. **2.** To blackball. [Perhaps from PIP (dot on dice, hence, "small ball").]

pip[3] (pĭp) *n.* **1.** A dot indicating a unit of numerical value on dice or dominoes. **2.** *Horticulture.* A rootstock of certain flowering plants, especially the lily of the valley. **3.** *Informal.* A shoulder insignia of officers in the British Army. **4.** A radar signal. [Earlier *peepe*†.]

pip[4] (pĭp) *v.* **pipped, pipping, pips.** —*tr.* To break through (an eggshell) in hatching. —*intr.* To peep or chirp, as a chick or young bird does. —*n.* A short, high-pitched radio signal. [Variant of PEEP (peek) and PEEP (cheep).]

pip[5] (pĭp) *n.* **1. a.** A disease of birds, characterized by a thick mucous discharge that forms a crust in the mouth and throat. **b.** The crust symptomatic of this disease. **2.** *Slang.* Any minor or imaginary human ailment. Preceded by *the: She gives me the pip.* [Middle English *pippe,* from Middle Dutch, phlegm, mucus, from West Germanic *pipit* (unattested), probably from Vulgar Latin *pīppita,* (earlier) *pītīta* (both unattested), alterations of Latin *pītuīta,* phlegm. See **peyə-** in Appendix.*]

pip·age (pī′pĭj) *n.* Also **pipe·age. 1.** The transmission of liquids through pipes. **2.** The charge for such transmission. **3.** Pipes; piping.

pi·pal. Variant of **peepul.**

pipe (pīp) *n.* **1. a.** Any hollow cylinder or tubular conveyance for a fluid or gas. **b.** A section or piece of such a tube. **2. a.** An instrument for smoking, consisting of a tube of wood or clay with a mouthpiece at one end and a small bowl at the other. **b.** Sufficient tobacco or other substance to fill the bowl of a smoking pipe; pipeful. **3. a.** *Biology.* A tubular part or organ. **b.** *Plural. Informal.* The human respiratory system. **4.** *Abbr.* **p. a.** A wine cask having a capacity of 126 gallons. **b.** This volume as a unit of liquid measure. **5.** *Abbr.* **p.** *Music.* **a.** A tubular wind instrument, such as a flute. **b.** Any of the tubes in an organ. **c.** *Plural.* A small wind instrument, consisting of tubes of different lengths bound together: *pipes of Pan.* **d.** *Plural.* A bagpipe. **6.** The sound of the voice, especially as used in singing or acting: *"His pipe clear and harmonious"* (Lamb). **7.** A birdcall: *"The earliest pipe of half-awaken'd birds"* (Tennyson). **8.** *Nautical.* A kind of whistle used for signaling crewmen: *a boatswain's pipe.* **9.** *Mining.* **a.** A vertical, cylindrical vein of ore. **b.** One of the vertical veins of eruptive origin in which diamonds are found in South Africa. **10.** *Geology.* An eruptive passageway opening into the crater of a volcano. **11.** *Metallurgy.* A cone-shaped cavity in a steel ingot, formed during cooling by escaping gases. **12.** *Slang.* An easy task; especially, an easy course in school. —*v.* **piped, piping, pipes.** —*tr.* **1.** To convey (liquid or gas) by means of pipes. **2.** To provide or connect with pipes. **3. a.** To play (a tune) on a pipe or pipes: *"Piper, pipe that song again."* (Blake). **b.** To lead by playing on pipes. **4.** *Nautical.* To call (the crew) by sounding the boatswain's pipe. **5.** To utter in a shrill, reedy tone. **6.** To furnish (a garment or fabric) with piping. —*intr.* **1.** To play on a pipe. **2.** To speak shrilly; make a shrill sound. **3.** To chirp or whistle, as a bird does. **4.** *Nautical.* To signal the crew with a boatswain's pipe. **5.** *Metallurgy.* To develop conical cavities. —**pipe down.** *Slang.* To stop talking; be quiet. —**pipe up.** To speak up in a small, shrill voice. [Middle English *pipe,* Old English *pīpe,* from Common Germanic *pīpa* (unattested), from Common Romance *pīpa* (unattested), from Latin *pīpāre,* to chirp. See **pipp-** in Appendix.*]

pipe clay. A fine white clay used in making tobacco pipes and pottery, in calico printing, and in whitening leather.

pipe cleaner. A pliant, tufted rod used for cleaning the stem of a tobacco pipe.

pipe dream. A wishful, fantastic notion or hope. [From the fantasies induced by opium.]

pipe·fish (pīp′fĭsh′) *n., pl.* **pipefish** or **-fishes.** Any of various slim, elongated marine or freshwater fishes of the family Syngnathidae, characterized by a tubelike snout and an external covering of bony plates. Also called "needlefish."

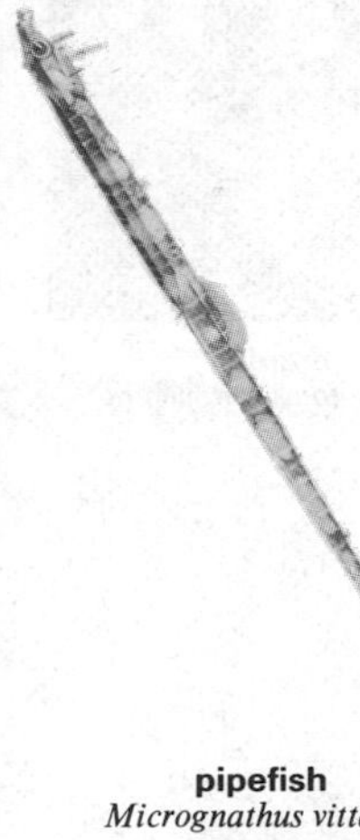

pipefish
Micrognathus vittatus

pipe·fit·ting (pīp′fĭt′ĭng) *n.* **1. a.** The act or work of joining pipes together. **b.** A branch of the plumbing trade that deals specifically with the installation and repair of piping systems. **2.** A section of pipe used to join two or more pipes together.

pipe·ful (pīp′fo͝ol′) *n.* Sufficient tobacco to fill a pipe.

pipe·line (pīp′līn′) *n.* **1.** A conduit of pipe for the conveyance of water or petroleum products. **2.** A channel by which information of a generally secret or confidential nature is transmitted. **3.** A line of communication or route of supply: *a new pipeline for medical supplies.* —*tr.v.* **pipelined, -lining, -lines. 1.** To convey by means of a pipeline. **2.** To lay a pipeline through.

pipe organ. A musical instrument, **organ** *(see).*

pip·er (pī′pər) *n.* **1.** One who plays on a pipe. **2.** One who lays or installs piping. —**pay the piper.** To bear the consequences of a pleasurable indulgence.

pi·per·a·zine (pī-pĕr′ə-zēn′, pĭ-) *n.* A colorless crystalline compound, $C_4H_{10}N_2$, used to inhibit corrosion, in insecticides, and as an anthelmintic. [PIPER(INE) + AZ(O)- + -INE.]

pi·per·i·dine (pī-pĕr′ə-dēn′, pĭ-) *n.* A strongly basic, colorless liquid, $C_5H_{10}NH$, used in the manufacture of rubber and as a curing agent in epoxy resins. [PIPER(INE) + -IDE + -INE.]

pip·er·ine (pĭp′ə-rēn′) *n.* A crystalline solid, $C_{17}H_{19}NO_3$, extracted from black pepper, and used as flavoring and as an insecticide. [Latin *piper,* PEPPER + -INE.]

pi·per·o·nal (pī-pĕr′ə-năl′, pĭ-) *n.* A white powder, $C_8H_6O_3$, having a floral odor, used as flavoring and in perfume. Also called "heliotropin." [PIPER(INE) + -ON(E) + -AL.]

pipe·stone (pīp′stōn′) *n.* A heat-hardened compacted red clay used by American Indians for making tobacco pipes.

pi·pette (pī-pĕt′) *n.* Also **pi·pet.** *Chemistry.* Any of variously shaped glass tubes, open at both ends, usually calibrated, and used especially to transfer small volumes of liquid. [Old French, diminutive of *pipe,* PIPE.]

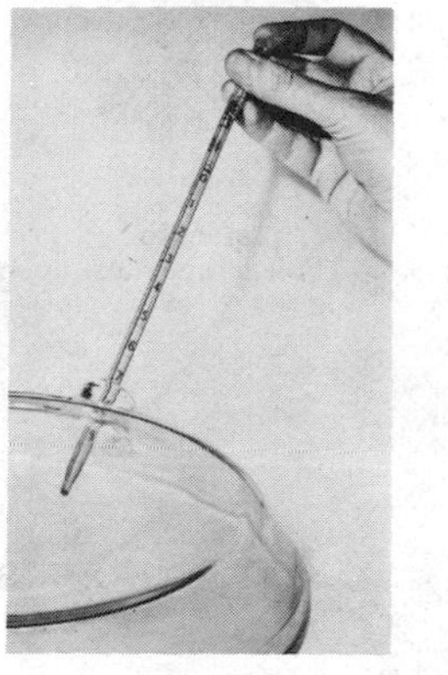

pipette

pipe vine. A woody vine, *Aristolochia durior,* of the eastern United States, having greenish, brown-mottled flowers shaped like a curved pipe. Also called "Dutchman's-pipe."

pipe wrench. A wrench with two serrated jaws, one adjustable, for gripping and turning pipe. Compare **Stillson wrench.**

pip·ing (pī′pĭng) *n.* **1.** A system of pipes, such as one used in plumbing. **2.** *Music.* **a.** The act of playing on a pipe. **b.** The music produced by a pipe. **3.** A shrill, high-pitched sound. **4.** A rounded strip of cloth used for trimming garments or furniture covers made of fabric. **5.** *Cooking.* A rounded ribbon of icing on a pastry. —*adj.* **1.** Playing on a pipe. **2.** Making a high-pitched sound with little resonance, as does a pipe: *"the high, piping notes of the flute don't seem to fit"* (Leonard Bernstein). —*adv.* With a sizzling sound: *piping hot.*

pip·it (pĭp′ĭt) *n.* Any of various widely distributed songbirds of the genus *Anthus,* characteristically having brownish upper plumage and a streaked breast. Also called "titlark." [Imitative of its note.]

pip·kin (pĭp′kĭn) *n.* **1.** A small earthenware or metal cooking pot. **2.** A piggin *(see).* [Probably PIPE (cask) + -KIN.]

pip·pin (pĭp′ĭn) *n.* **1.** Any of several varieties of apple. **2.** The seed of a fruit; pip. **3.** *Slang.* An admired person or thing. [Middle English *pepin, pipin,* seed, seedling apple, from Old French *pepin,* from Common Romance stem *pipp-* (suggestive of the small size of the seed).]

pip·sis·se·wa (pĭp-sĭs′ə-wô′) *n.* Any of several North American evergreen plants of the genus *Chimaphila;* especially, *C. umbellata,* having white or pinkish flowers. Also called "prince's-pine," "wintergreen." [Cree *pipisisikweu,* "it breaks it (i.e., a gallstone) into small pieces," from its use as a diuretic.]

pip-squeak (pĭp′skwēk′) *n.* A small or insignificant person. Often used contemptuously. [Originally an imitative name given to a small shell used by the Germans in World War I : PIP (dot) + SQUEAK.]

pi·quant (pē′kənt, -känt′, pē-känt′) *adj.* **1.** Pleasantly pungent in taste or odor; spicy. **2.** Pleasantly disturbing; appealingly provocative: *touched by the piquant faces of children.* **3.** *Archaic.* Causing hurt pride or feelings; stinging: *"never to make any piquant or angry answer"* (Erasmus Darwin). [Old French, present participle of *piquer,* to pierce, prick, PIQUE.] —**pi′quan·cy, pi′quant·ness** *n.* —**pi′quant·ly** *adv.*

pique (pēk) *n.* A feeling of resentment or vexation arising from wounded pride or vanity. —*tr.v.* **piqued, piquing, piques. 1.** To

cause to feel resentment or vexation; injure the feelings of: *"The Devil was piqued such sainthood to behold"* (Pope). **2.** To provoke; arouse; spur: *The portrait piqued my curiosity.* **3.** To pride (oneself). Used with *on* or *upon: They piqued themselves on their modish attire.* [Old French, "a pricking," from *piquer,* to pierce, prick, from Vulgar Latin *piccāre* (unattested), probably from Latin *pīcus,* woodpecker. See **speik-** in Appendix.*]

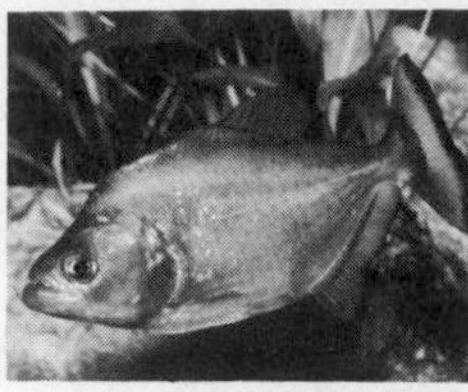

piranha
Serrasalmus spilopleura

pi·qué (pĭ-kā′, pē-) *n.* A tightly woven fabric with various patterns of wales, produced especially by a double warp. [French, "quilting," from *piquer,* to backstitch (as in quilting), to pierce, PIQUE.]

pi·quet (pĭ-kā′) *n.* Also **pic·quet.** A card game for two people, played with a deck from which all cards below the seven (aces being high) are omitted. [French, diminutive of *pic,* "a sting," a score of 30 points at cards, from *piquer,* to prick, PIQUE.]

pi·ra·cy (pī′rə-sē) *n., pl.* **-cies.** The act or practice of pirating.

Pi·rae·us (pī-rē′əs). The chief seaport of Greece, near Athens. Population, 185,000.

pi·ra·gua (pĭ-rä′gwə) *n.* **1.** A canoe made by hollowing out a tree trunk; a dugout. **2.** A flat-bottomed sailing boat with two masts. [Spanish, from Carib *piraguas.*]

Pi·ran·del·lo (pĭr′ən-dĕl′ō; *Italian* pē′rän-dĕl′lō), **Luigi.** 1867–1936. Italian playwright, poet, and novelist.

Pi·ra·ne·si (pē′rä-nā′zē), **Giambattista.** 1720–1778. Italian architect, decorative artist, and engraver.

pi·ra·nha (pĭ-rän′yə, -răn′yə) *n.* Also **pi·ra·ña.** Any of several tropical American freshwater fishes of the genus *Serrasalmus.* They are voraciously carnivorous and often attack and destroy living animals. Also called "caribe." [Portuguese, from Tupi, "toothed fish" : *pirá,* fish + *sainha,* tooth.]

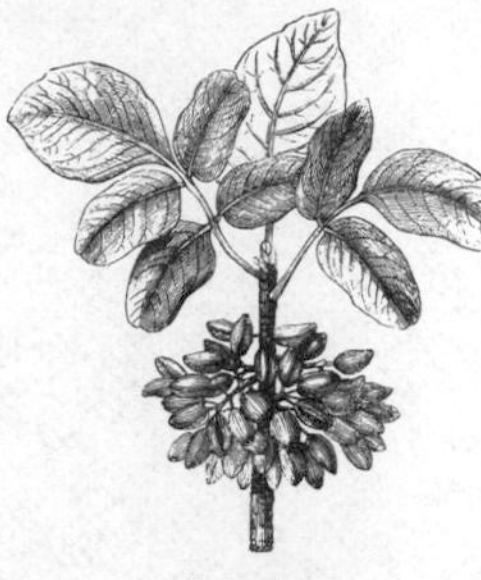

pistachio
Foliage and nuts

pi·ra·ru·cu (pĭ-rär′ə-kōō′) *n.* A fish, the **arapaima** *(see).* [Portuguese *pirarucú,* from Tupi *pirá-rucú,* "red fish" : *pirá,* fish + *(u)rucú,* red.]

pi·rate (pī′rĭt) *n.* **1.** One who robs at sea or plunders the land from the sea without commission from a sovereign nation. **2.** A ship used for this purpose. **3.** One who makes use of or reproduces the work, especially literary work, of another, without permission or illicitly. —*v.* **pirated, -rating, -rates.** —*tr.* **1.** To attack and rob (a ship at sea). **2.** To seize (goods) by piracy. **3.** To make use of or reproduce (another's work) illicitly. —*intr.* To act as a pirate; practice piracy. [Middle English, from Latin *pīrāta,* from Greek *peiratēs,* "attacker," from *peiran,* to attempt, attack, from *peira,* an attempt. See **per-**[5] in Appendix.*] —**pi·rat′ic** (pī-răt′ĭk), **pi·rat′i·cal** *adj.* —**pi·rat′i·cal·ly** *adv.*

pirate perch. A small North American freshwater fish, *Aphredoderus sayanus,* that is unusual because its anal opening is in the throat.

Pi·ri·ne·os. The Spanish name for the **Pyrenees.**

pi·rog (pĭ-rōg′) *n., pl.* **-rogen** (-rō′gən) or **-roghi** (-rō′gē) or **-rogi.** A large Russian pastry made of dough stuffed with various combinations of meat, fish, rice, eggs, and vegetables. [Russian, probably from *pir,* feast, party. See **poi-**[1] in Appendix.*]

pi·rogue (pĭ-rōg′) *n.* A canoe made from a hollowed tree trunk; piragua. [French, from Spanish *piragua,* PIRAGUA.]

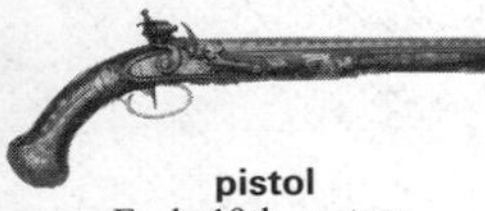

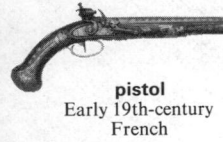

pistol
Early 19th-century French

pir·ou·ette (pĭr′ōō-ĕt′) *n. Ballet.* A full turn of the body on the tip of the toe or on the ball of the foot. —*intr.v.* **pirouetted, -etting, -ettes.** To execute a pirouette. [French, from Old French *pirouet*†, a spinning top.]

pi·rozh·ki (pĭ-rôzh′kē) *pl.n.* Also **pi·rosh·ki, pi·roj·ki.** *Singular* **pirozhok** (pĭr′ō-zhôk). Small Russian pastries made with various fillings. [Yiddish *pirozshke,* from Russian *pirozhki,* plural of *pirozhok,* small pocket of pastry, diminutive of PIROG.]

Pi·sa (pē′zə; *Italian* pē′zä). A city of Tuscany, Italy, on the Arno River; famous for leaning tower, the campanile of its cathedral. Population, 81,000.

pis al·ler (pē zà-lā′). *French.* The final recourse or expedient; last resort. [French, "worst to go."]

Pi·sa·no (pē-zä′nō), **Andrea.** Also Andrea da Pontedera. 1270?–1348. Italian sculptor; father of Nino Pisano.

Pi·sa·no (pē-zä′nō), **Antonio.** Called "Il Pisanello." 1397?–1455? Italian painter, graphic artist, and medalist.

Pi·sa·no (pē-zä′nō), **Giovanni.** 1245–1314. Italian sculptor, painter, and architect; son of Nicola Pisano.

Pi·sa·no (pē-zä′nō), **Nicola** or **Niccolò.** Also Nicola da Pisa. 1220–1284. Italian sculptor; father of Giovanni Pisano.

Pi·sa·no (pē-zä′nō), **Nino.** 1315?–1368? Italian sculptor, goldsmith, and architect; son of Andrea Pisano.

pis·ca·ry (pĭs′kə-rē) *n., pl.* **-ries. 1.** *Law. Rare.* The right to fish. Used in the phrase *common of piscary,* meaning the right to fish in waters belonging to another. **2.** A place in which to fish. [Middle English *piscarie,* from Medieval Latin *piscāria,* right to fish, from Latin, neuter plural of *piscārius,* of fish or fishing, from *piscis,* fish. See **pisk-** in Appendix.*]

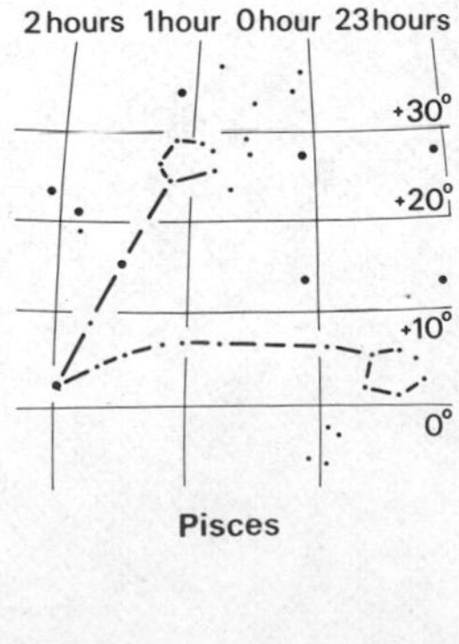
2hours
1hour
0hour
23hours
+30°
+20°
+10°
0°

Pisces

pis·ca·to·ri·al (pĭs′kə-tôr′ē-əl, -tōr′ē-əl) *adj.* Also **pis·ca·to·ry** (pĭs′kə-tôr′ē, -tōr′ē). **1.** Of or pertaining to fish, fishermen, or fishing. **2.** Involved in fishing. [Latin *piscātōrius,* of fish or fishing, from *piscātor,* fisherman, from *piscārī,* to fish, from *piscis,* fish. See **peisk-** in Appendix.*] —**pis′ca·to′ri·al·ly** *adv.*

Pi·sces (pī′sēz) *n.* **1.** A constellation in the equatorial region of the Northern Hemisphere near Aries and Pegasus. **2.** The 12th sign of the **zodiac** *(see).* Also called "the Fish," "the Fishes." [Middle English, from Medieval Latin, "the Fishes," from plural of Latin *piscis,* fish. See **peisk-** in Appendix.*]

pisci–. Indicates fish; for example, **pisciform.** [From Latin *piscis,* fish. See **peisk-** in Appendix.*]

pi·sci·cul·ture (pī′sĭ-kŭl′chər, pĭs′ĭ-) *n.* The breeding, hatching, and rearing of fish under controlled conditions. —**pi′sci·cul′tur·al** *adj.* —**pi′sci·cul′tur·ist** *n.*

pi·sci·form (pī′sĭ-fôrm′, pĭs′ĭ-) *adj.* Having the shape of a fish. [PISCI- + -FORM.]

pi·sci·na (pĭ-sī′nə, -sē′nə, -shē′nə) *n., pl.* **-nae** (-nē′). *Ecclesiastical.* A stone basin with a drain for carrying away the water used in ceremonial ablutions. Also called "sacrarium." [Medieval Latin, from Latin, fish tank, from *piscis,* fish. See **peisk-** in Appendix.*] —**pis′ci·nal** (pĭs′ə-nəl) *adj.*

pi·scine (pī′sēn′, pĭs′īn′) *adj.* Of, pertaining to, or typical of a fish or fishes. [Medieval Latin *piscīnus,* from *piscis,* fish. See **peisk-** in Appendix.*]

Pi·scis Aus·tri·nus (pī′sĭs ôs-trī′nəs) *n.* A constellation in the Southern Hemisphere near Aquarius and Grus. [New Latin, "(the) Southern Fish."]

pi·sciv·o·rous (pĭ-sĭv′ər-əs, pī-) *adj.* Habitually feeding on fish; fish-eating. [PISCI- + -VOROUS.]

Pis·gah, Mount (pĭz′gə). A mountain ridge east of the northern end of the Dead Sea, in Jordan. Highest elevation 2,644 feet.

pish (pĭsh) *interj.* Used to express disdain. [Expressive.]

Pish·pek. The former name for **Frunze.**

Pi·sid·i·a (pĭ-sĭd′ē-ə, pī-). An ancient region of southern Asia Minor that became a Roman province. —**Pi·sid′i·an** *adj.*

pi·si·form (pī′sə-fôrm′) *adj.* Suggestive of a pea in size or shape; pealike. —*n. Anatomy.* A small bone at the junction of the ulna and the wrist. [Latin *pīsum,* PEA + -FORM.]

Pi·sis·tra·tus (pī-sĭs′trə-təs, pī-). Also **Pei·sis·tra·tus** (pī-sĭs′trə-təs). 605?–527 B.C. Tyrant of Athens (560–527 B.C.).

pis·mire (pĭs′mīr′, pĭz′-) *n.* An ant. [Middle English *pissemyre,* from *pisse,* PISS (from the urinous smell of an anthill) + *mire,* ant, probably from Scandinavian, akin to Danish *myre,* ant (see **morwi-** in Appendix*).]

pis·mo clam (pĭz′mō). An edible marine clam, *Tivela stultorum,* of the southern Pacific coast of North America. [Found at *Pismo* Beach, California.]

pi·so·lite (pī′sə-līt′) *n. Geology.* A small round accretionary mass. [New Latin *pisolithus,* "pea stone" : Greek *pisos, pison,* PEA + -LITE.] —**pi′so·lit′ic** (pī′sə-lĭt′ĭk) *adj.*

piss (pĭs) *n. Vulgar.* **1.** Urine. **2.** An act of urinating. —*v.* **pissed, pissing, pisses.** *Vulgar.* —*intr.* To urinate. —*tr.* To discharge as, or with, urine. [Middle English *pissen,* to urinate, from Old French *pissier,* from Vulgar Latin (unattested) *pissiāre* (imitative).]

Pis·sar·ro (pĭ-sär′ō; *French* pē-sà-rō′), **Camille.** 1830–1903. French painter; a leader of the impressionists.

pis·soir (pē-swär′). *French.* A public urinal.

pis·ta·chi·o (pĭ-stăsh′ē-ō′, -stä′shē-ō′) *n., pl.* **-os.** Also **pis·tache** (pĭ-stăsh′). **1.** A tree, *Pistacia vera,* of the Mediterranean region and western Asia, bearing small hard-shelled nuts. **2.** The nut of this tree, having an edible, oily, green kernel. Also called "pistachio nut." **3.** The flavor of these nuts. [Italian *pistacchio,* from Latin *pistācium,* from Greek *pistakion,* pistachio nut, from *pistakē,* pistachio tree, from Persian *pistah*†.]

pistachio green. Moderate to light yellowish or yellow green. See **color.**

pis·ta·reen (pĭs′tə-rēn′) *n.* A small silver coin used in America and the West Indies during the 18th century. [Probably altered from Spanish *peseta,* PESETA.]

pis·til (pĭs′tĭl) *n. Botany.* The seed-bearing organ of a flower, including the stigma, style, and ovary. [French *pistil,* from Latin *pistillum,* pestle. See **peis-**[1] in Appendix.*]

pis·til·late (pĭs′tə-lāt′, -lĭt) *adj. Botany.* **1.** Having a pistil or pistils. **2.** Bearing pistils but no stamens: *pistillate flowers.*

pis·tol (pĭs′təl) *n.* A firearm designed to be held and fired with one hand. —*tr.v.* **pistoled, -toling, -tols.** Also *chiefly British* **-tolled, -tolling.** To shoot with a pistol. [French *pistole,* from German *Pistole,* from Czech *pišťala,* "pipe," akin to Russian *pischal,* shepherd's pipe (probably imitative).]

pis·tole (pĭ-stōl′) *n.* An obsolete gold coin, used in various European countries until the late 19th century. [French, variant of *pistolet,* "small pistol" (originally a name given in jest to Spanish coins which were smaller than French coins, as a pistol is smaller than a harquebus), from *pistole,* PISTOL.]

pis·to·leer (pĭs′tə-lĭr′) *n. Archaic.* One armed with a pistol.

pistol grip. 1. The grip of a pistol, shaped to fit the hand. **2.** A similar grip sometimes used on a rifle or other firearm. **3.** A grip used on certain tools, such as a saw, shaped to fit the hand.

pis·tol-whip (pĭs′təl-hwĭp′) *tr.v.* **-whipped, -whipping, -whips. 1.** To beat with a pistol barrel. **2.** To beat while threatening with a gun.

pis·ton (pĭs′tən) *n.* **1.** A solid cylinder or disk that fits snugly into a larger cylinder and moves back and forth under fluid pressure, as in a reciprocating engine, or displaces or compresses fluids, as in pumps and compressors. **2.** *Music.* A valve mechanism in brass instruments for altering pitch. [French, from Old French, from Old Italian *pistone, pestone,* a large pestle, from *pistare, pestare,* to pound, from Latin *pistāre,* frequentative of *pinsāre,* to pound. See **peis-**[1] in Appendix.*]

piston ring. An adjustable metal ring that fits around a piston and closes the gap between the piston and cylinder wall.

piston rod. A connecting rod that transmits power to or is powered by a piston.

pit[1] (pĭt) *n.* **1.** A relatively deep hole in the ground, either natural, as a pothole or sinkhole, or man-made, as a mine shaft. **2.** A trap consisting of a concealed hole in the ground; pitfall. **3.** Any hidden danger or unexpected trouble. **4. a.** An abysmal or despairing condition. **b.** Hell. **5.** An enclosed space, often one dug in the ground, in which animals, such as dogs or gamecocks, are placed for fighting. **6. a.** A natural depression in the surface of a body, organ, or part. **b.** A small indentation in the skin left by disease or injury; pockmark. **7. a.** The section

ă pat/ā pay/âr care/ä father/b bib/ch church/d deed/ĕ pet/ē be/f fife/g gag/h hat/hw which/ĭ pit/ī pie/îr pier/j judge/k kick/l lid, needle/m mum/n no, sudden/ng thing/ŏ pot/ō toe/ô paw, for/oi noise/ou out/ŏŏ took/ōō boot/p pop/r roar/s sauce/sh ship, dish/

directly in front of the stage of a theater, in which the musicians sit. **b.** *Chiefly British.* The area behind the stalls of a theater. **8.** The section of an exchange where trading in a specific commodity is carried on. **9.** *Botany.* A thin-walled spot or depression in the wall of some plant cells. —See Synonyms at **hole.** —*v.* **pitted, pitting, pits.** —*tr.* **1.** To make cavities, depressions, or scars in: *"the mountain was pitted with deep craters"* (Muriel Spark). **2.** To place in contest against another; set in direct opposition: *"a man pitted in conflict against the sea"* (D.H. Lawrence). —*intr.* To become marked with small pits. [Middle English *pitt,* Old English *pytt,* from West Germanic *putti* (unattested), from Latin *puteus,* a pit, well. See **peue-**[2] in Appendix.*]

pit[2] (pĭt) *n.* The single, central kernel of certain fruits, such as a peach or cherry; stone. —*tr.v.* **pitted, pitting, pits.** To extract pits from (fruit). [Dutch, from Middle Dutch *pit(te),* from West Germanic *pithan* (unattested), pit, pith. See also **pith.**]

PIT Airport code for Pittsburgh, Pennsylvania.

pi·ta (pē′tə) *n.* **1.** Any of several plants of the genus *Agave,* that yield a strong fiber. Also called "istle," "ixtle," "Tampico hemp." **2.** A species of pineapple, *Ananas magdalenae,* from whose leaves a fine, whitish fiber is obtained. **3.** The fiber of any of these plants, used in making cordage and paper. In this sense also called "pita fiber." [Spanish, from Quechua.]

pit·a·pat (pĭt′ə-păt′) *intr.v.* **-patted, -patting, -pats. 1.** To move with a series of quick, tapping steps. **2.** To make a repeated tapping sound. —*n.* A series of quick steps, taps, or beats. —*adv.* With a rapid tapping sound. [Imitative.]

Pit·cairn Island (pĭt′kârn′). A small (two square miles) British island in the South Pacific, between Easter Island and Tahiti, settled in 1790 by the mutineers from H.M.S. *Bounty.* Population, 91.

pitch[1] (pĭch) *n.* **1.** Any of various thick, dark, sticky substances obtained from the distillation residue of coal tar, wood tar, or petroleum, and used for waterproofing, roofing, caulking, and paving. **2.** Any of various natural bitumens, such as mineral pitch or asphalt, having similar uses. **3.** A resin derived from the sap of various coniferous trees, such as the pines. —*tr.v.* **pitched, pitching, pitches.** To smear or cover with or as if with pitch. [Middle English *pich,* Old English *pic,* from Latin *pix.* See **pik-** in Appendix.*]

pitch[2] (pĭch) *v.* **pitched, pitching, pitches.** —*tr.* **1.** To throw, usually in a specific, intended direction; hurl; toss: *"Ancestral pearls all pitched into a sty"* (Yeats). **2.** *Baseball.* **a.** To throw (the ball) from the mound to the batter. **b.** To play (a game, or part of one) in the position of pitcher. **3.** To put up or in position; establish: *pitching a tent.* **4.** To set firmly; implant; embed: *pitch stakes.* **5. a.** To fix the level of: *pitch one's expectations high.* **b.** To set the character and course of: *He pitched his speech to the party line.* **6.** To set at a specified pitch: *"Hummel's voice, though slight, was expertly pitched to pierce the noise of the shop."* (John Updike). **7.** *Card Games.* To lead (a card), thus establishing the trump suit. —*intr.* **1.** To throw or toss something, such as a ball, horseshoe, or bale. **2.** *Baseball.* To play in the position of pitcher. **3.** To plunge; fall, especially forward: *He pitched over the railing.* **4.** To stumble around; lurch. **5. a.** Of a vessel, to dip bow and stern alternately: *"the broad ferryboats pitching ponderously at anchor"* (Conrad). Compare **roll. b.** To buck, as a horse. **6.** To slope downward. **7.** To set up living quarters; encamp; settle. **8.** To come to a decision. Used with *on* or *upon: They pitched on his solution as the best.* —See Synonyms at **throw.** —**pitch in.** *Informal.* **1.** To set to work vigorously. **2.** To join forces with others; help; cooperate. —**pitch into.** *Informal.* To attack verbally or physically; assault. —*n.* **1.** An act or instance of pitching. **2.** *Baseball.* **a.** A throw of the ball by the pitcher for action by the batter. **b.** A ball so thrown: *The pitch was fouled off.* **3.** *Cricket.* The rectangular area between the wickets, 22 yards by 10 feet. **4.** *Nautical.* The alternate dip and rise of a ship's bow and stern. **5. a.** Any steep downward slant. **b.** The degree of such a slant. **6.** *Architecture.* **a.** The angle of a roof. **b.** The highest point of a structure: *the pitch of an arch.* **7.** A point or stage of development or intensity: *"the surges themselves in their utmost pitch of power"* (Ruskin). **8.** *Acoustics.* The subjective quality of a complex sound, dependent on frequency, loudness, and intensity, and often measured as the frequency of a pure tone of specified intensity judged equivalent to the complex sound by a normal ear. **9. a.** The relative position of a tone in a scale, as determined by its frequency. **b.** *Music.* Any of various standards that establish a frequency for each musical tone, used in the tuning of instruments. See **concert pitch, international pitch. 10.** *Machinery.* **a.** The distance traveled by a screw in a single revolution. **b.** The distance between two corresponding points on adjacent screw threads or gear teeth. **11.** The distance a propeller would travel in an ideal medium during one complete revolution, measured parallel to the shaft of the propeller. **12. a.** *Slang.* A set talk designed to persuade. **b.** The stand of a vender or hawker. **13.** A card game, **seven-up** *(see).* [Middle English *picchen,* to pierce, fix, set, throw, Old English *picc(e)an* (unattested), to prick, thrust, peculiar causative of *pician* (unattested), PICK (prick).]

pitch accent. *Linguistics.* **Tonic accent** *(see).*

pitch-black (pĭch′blăk′) *adj.* Extremely black; black as pitch.

pitch·blende (pĭch′blĕnd′) *n.* The principal ore of uranium, a brownish-black mineral of uraninite and uranium trioxide with small amounts of water and uranium decay products. [German *Pechblende* : *Pech,* pitch (from its black color), from Latin *pix* (see **pik-** in Appendix*) + BLENDE.]

pitch-dark (pĭch′därk′) *adj.* Extremely dark.

pitched battle. 1. A battle fought in close contact by troops whose formation and tactics have been carefully planned: *"The Texas border war was not a warfare of pitched battles . . . but of great distances, sudden incursions and rapid flight"* (Walter Prescott Webb). **2.** Any fierce combat or dispute. [From the past participle of PITCH (to put in position, array for battle).]

pitch·er[1] (pĭch′ər) *n.* **1.** One that pitches. **2.** *Baseball.* The player who throws the ball from the mound for action by the batter. **3.** *Golf.* An iron with a sharply inclined head.

pitch·er[2] (pĭch′ər) *n.* **1.** A vessel for liquids, with a handle and a lip or spout for pouring. **2.** *British Archaic.* A large earthenware vessel with two handles. **3.** *Botany.* A pitcherlike part such as the leaf of a pitcher plant. [Middle English *picher,* from Old French *pichier, bichier,* from Medieval Latin *bicārius,* goblet, from Greek *bikos,* possibly from Egyptian *bik,* oil vessel. See also **beaker.**]

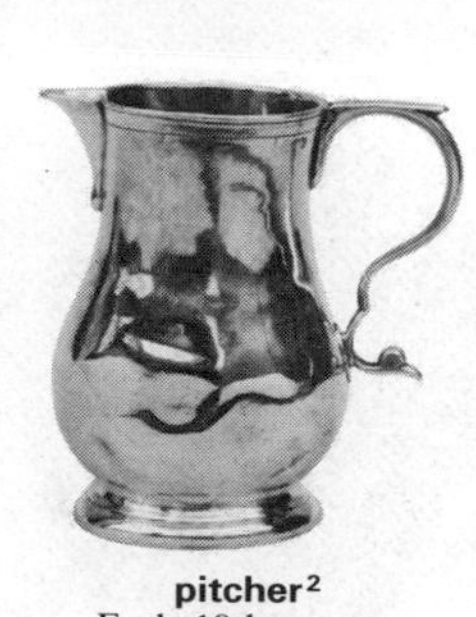

pitcher[2]
Early 18th-century American

Pitch·er (pĭch′ər), **Molly.** Original name, Mary Ludwig Hays McCauley. 1754–1832. American heroine of the Revolutionary War; carried water at the Battle of Monmouth (1778).

pitcher plant. Any of various insectivorous plants of the genera *Sarracenia, Nepenthes,* or *Darlingtonia,* having leaves modified to form pitcherlike organs that attract and trap insects.

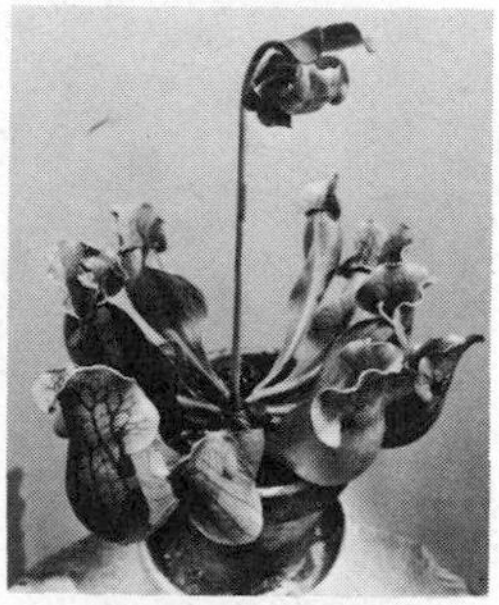

pitcher plant
Sarracenia purpurea

pitch·fork (pĭch′fôrk′) *n.* A large fork with sharp, widely spaced prongs for pitching hay and breaking ground. —*tr.v.* **pitchforked, -forking, -forks.** To lift or toss with a pitchfork. [Middle English *pychforke,* alteration of *pikforke* (through wrong association with *picchen,* to toss, PITCH) : PICK + FORK.]

pitch·man (pĭch′mən) *n., pl.* **-men** (-mĭn). A peddler or vender of small wares, especially one with a colorful sales talk.

pitch·out (pĭch′out′) *n.* **1.** *Baseball.* A pitch deliberately thrown high and away from the batter to make it easier for the catcher to throw out a base runner attempting to steal. **2.** *Football.* A lateral pass from the back receiving the snap from the center to another back behind the line of scrimmage.

pitch pine. Any of various American pine trees yielding pitch or turpentine, such as *Pinus rigida* or *P. echinata,* of eastern North America.

pitch pipe. *Music.* A small pipe that, when sounded, gives the standard pitch for a piece of music or for tuning an instrument.

pitch·stone (pĭch′stōn′) *n.* Any of various volcanic glasses distinguished by their pitchlike luster and relatively high water content. [Translation of German *Pechstein.*]

pitch·y (pĭch′ē) *adj.* **-ier, -iest. 1.** Full of pitch; covered or smeared with pitch. **2.** Resembling pitch; having the texture of pitch. **3.** Extremely dark; black. —**pitch′i·ness** *n.*

pit·e·ous (pĭt′ē-əs) *adj.* **1.** Exciting pity; pathetic. **2.** *Archaic.* Pitying; compassionate. [Middle English *piteus, pitous,* from Old French *piteus,* from *pite,* PITY.] —**pit′e·ous·ly** *adv.* —**pit′e·ous·ness** *n.*

pit·fall (pĭt′fôl′) *n.* **1.** A trap made by digging a hole in the ground and concealing its opening. **2.** Any danger or difficulty that is not easily anticipated or avoided.

pith (pĭth) *n.* **1.** *Botany.* The soft, spongelike substance in the center of stems and branches of most vascular plants. **2.** The essential or central part of anything; essence; gist. **3.** Force; strength; vigor. —*tr.v.* **pithed, pithing, piths. 1.** To remove the pith from (a plant stem). **2.** To sever or destroy the spinal cord of (a laboratory animal), usually by means of a needle inserted into the vertebral canal. **3.** To kill (cattle) by cutting the spinal cord. [Middle English *pithe,* Old English *pitha,* from West Germanic *pithan* (unattested). See also **pit** (stone of fruit).]

pith·e·can·thro·pus (pĭth′ĭ-kăn′thrə-pəs, -kăn-thrō′pəs) *n. Paleontology.* A member of a genus formerly designated *Pithecanthropus,* based on bone fragments found in Java and thought to indicate the existence of a primate between man and ape. It is now reclassified in the extinct species *Homo erectus.* Also called "Trinil man," "Java man." [New Latin : Greek *pithēkos*†, ape + -ANTHROPUS.]

pith helmet. A light sun hat made from dried pith; topi.

pith·y (pĭth′ē) *adj.* **-ier, -iest. 1.** Consisting of or resembling pith. **2.** Precisely meaningful; cogent and terse. —See Synonyms at **concise.** —**pith′i·ly** *adv.* —**pith′i·ness** *n.*

pit·i·a·ble (pĭt′ē-ə-bəl) *adj.* **1.** Arousing or deserving of pity or compassion; lamentable. **2.** Arousing disdainful pity; paltry; despicable. —**pit′i·a·ble·ness** *n.* —**pit′i·a·bly** *adv.*

pit·i·ful (pĭt′ĭ-fəl) *adj.* **1.** Arousing pity; pathetic. **2.** So inferior or insignificant as to be contemptible; mean; paltry. **3.** *Archaic.* Filled with pity or compassion. —See Synonyms at **pathetic.** —**pit′i·ful·ly** *adv.* —**pit′i·ful·ness** *n.*

pit·i·less (pĭt′ĭ-lĭs) *adj.* Having no pity; without mercy. See Synonyms at **cruel.** —**pit′i·less·ly** *adv.* —**pit′i·less·ness** *n.*

pit·man (pĭt′mən) *n., pl.* **-men** (-mĭn). A worker employed inside a pit in various industrial operations, as in a coal mine.

pi·ton (pē′tŏn′) *n.* A metal spike fitted at one end with an eye or ring through which to pass a rope, used in mountain climbing as a hold. [French, pointed mountain peak, from Old French, "nail," from Romance root *pitt-,* pointed thing.]

Pi·tot-stat·ic tube (pē′tō-stăt′ĭk, pē-tō′-). A device consisting of a Pitot tube and a static tube combined to simultaneously measure total and static pressure in a fluid stream. It can be used in aircraft to determine relative wind speed.

Pi·tot tube (pē′tō, pē-tō′). A device used to measure the total pressure of a fluid stream. It is essentially a tube attached to a manometer at one end and pointed upstream at the other. [Invented by Henri *Pitot* (1695–1771), French physicist.]

pit·saw (pĭt′sô′) *n.* Also **pit saw.** A large saw for cutting logs, hand-operated by two men, one of whom stands on the log and the other in a pit underneath.

Pitt (pĭt), **William**[1]. First Earl of Chatham. Called "the Elder."

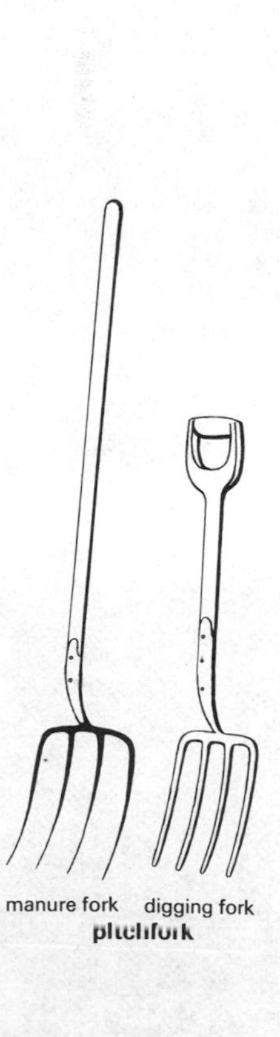

pitchfork

1708–1778. British statesman; leader of the government (1756–61, 1766–68); father of William Pitt the Younger.

Pitt (pĭt), **William**^{2}. 1759–1806. Called "the Younger." British statesman; prime minister (1783–1801 and 1804–06).

pit·tance (pĭt′ns) *n.* **1.** A meager allowance of money. **2.** A very small salary or remuneration. **3.** A small amount or portion of anything. [Middle English *pitaunce*, from Old French *pitance*, from Medieval Latin *pittantia*, from Vulgar Latin *pietantia* (unattested), pious donation, portion (of food) given to monastics, from *pietārī*, to be charitable, from Latin *pietās*, piety, from *pius*, pious. See **pius** in Appendix.*]

pit·ter-pat·ter (pĭt′ər-păt′ər) *n.* A rapid series of light, tapping sounds. **—pit′ter-pat′ter** *adv.* [Imitative.]

Pitts·burgh (pĭts′bûrg′). An industrial city in southwestern Pennsylvania where the confluence of the Allegheny and Monongahela rivers forms the Ohio. Population, 604,000.

Pitts·burg Landing (pĭts′bûrg′). A village in western Tennessee on the Tennessee River; site of the Battle of **Shiloh** *(see)*.

Pitts·field (pĭts′fēld′). A city of western Massachusetts, on the Housatonic River. Population, 58,000.

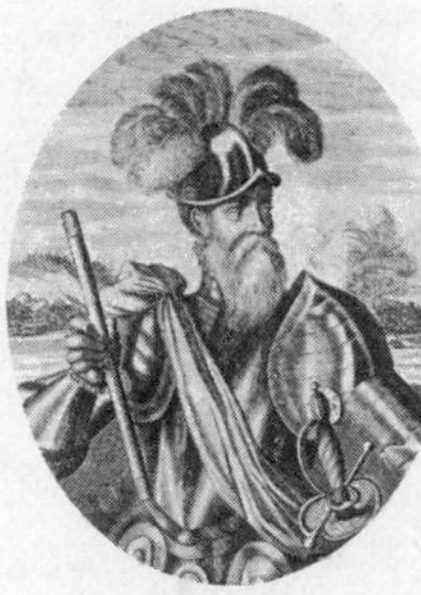

Francisco Pizarro

pi·tu·i·tar·y (pĭ-to͞o′ə-tĕr′ē, pĭ-tyo͞o′-) *n., pl.* **-ies. 1.** *Anatomy.* The pituitary gland. **2.** *Medicine.* An extract from the anterior or posterior lobes of the pituitary gland, prepared for therapeutic use. *—adj.* **1.** Of the pituitary gland. **2.** Of or designating a type of body structure characterized by obesity, enlarged bones and soft parts of arms, legs, and face, believed to be due to excessive secretion from the pituitary gland. **3.** Of or secreting phlegm or mucus; mucous. [Latin *pītuītārius*, from *pītuīta*, phlegm. See **peye-** in Appendix.*]

pituitary gland. *Anatomy.* A small, oval endocrine gland attached to the base of the vertebrate brain, the secretions of which control the other endocrine glands and influence growth, metabolism, and maturation. Also called "hypophysis," "pituitary body."

pi·tu·i·tous (pĭ-to͞o′ə-təs, pĭ-tyo͞o′-) *adj.* Containing, discharging, or resembling mucus. [Latin *pītuītōsus*, from *pītuīta*, phlegm, mucus. See **peye-** in Appendix.*]

pit viper. Any of various venomous snakes of the family Crotalidae, such as a copperhead or rattlesnake, characterized by a small pit on each side of the head.

pit·y (pĭt′ē) *n., pl.* **-ies. 1. a.** Sorrow or grief aroused by the misfortune of another; compassion for suffering. **b.** Concern or regret for one considered inferior or less favored; condescending sympathy. **2.** A regrettable or disagreeable fact or necessity. **—take pity on.** To attempt to alleviate the misfortune of. *—v.* **pitied, pitying, pities.** *—tr.* To feel pity for. *—intr.* To feel pity. [Middle English *pite*, from Old French *pit(i)e*, from Late Latin *pietās*, compassion, extended sense of Latin *pietās*, piety, from *pius*, pious. See **pius** in Appendix.*] **—pit′y·ing·ly** *adv.*

Synonyms: *pity, compassion, commiseration, sympathy, condolence, empathy.* These are words for grief or concern felt for someone in misfortune. *Pity* implies a disposition to help but little emotional sharing of the distress. *Compassion* always favorably connotes broad or profound feeling for the misfortunes of others and a desire to aid them. A more casual involvement is conveyed by *commiseration*, which signifies an expressed, sometimes superficial, solace. *Sympathy* is as broad as *pity* but connotes spontaneous emotion rather than considered attitude. *Condolence* expresses commiseration extended on specific occasions of loss common to all people, usually to relatives upon a death in their family. *Empathy*, with literary and psychological overtones, is a conscious involvement with a person's situation in the sense of vicarious identification.

pit·y·ri·a·sis (pĭt′ĭ-rī′ə-sĭs) *n.* Any of various skin diseases of man and animals, characterized by epidermal shedding of flaky scales. [Greek *pituriasis*, from *pituron*†, grain husk, dandruff.]

più (pyo͞o) *adv. Music.* More. Used in directions to performers, as in *più forte*, more loudly. [Italian, from Latin *plūs*, more. See **pel-**^{8} in Appendix.*]

Pi·us V (pī′əs). Original name, Michele Ghislieri. 1504–1572. Pope (1566–72); canonized (1712).

Pi·us IX (pī′əs). Original name, Giovanni Maria Mastai-Ferretti. 1792–1878. Pope (1846–78); proclaimed dogmas of Immaculate Conception and papal infallibility.

Pi·us X (pī′əs). Original name, Giuseppe Melchiorre Sarto. 1835–1914. Pope (1903–14); reformed church music and laws; canonized (1954).

Pi·us XI (pī′əs). Original name, Achille Ambrogio Damiano Ratti. 1857–1939. Pope (1922–39); signed Lateran Treaty (1929) with Mussolini, making Vatican City autonomous.

Pi·us XII (pī′əs). Original name, Eugenio Pacelli. 1876–1958. Pope (1939–58).

Pi·ute. Variant of **Paiute.**

piv·ot (pĭv′ət) *n.* **1.** A short rod or shaft about which a related part rotates or swings. **2.** A person or thing that chiefly determines the direction or effect of something; the essential component. **3.** The act of turning on or as if on a pivot. *—v.* **pivoted, -oting, -ots.** *—tr.* **1.** To mount on, attach by, or furnish with a pivot or pivots. **2.** To cause to turn on a pivot; especially, to place under the control of a determining factor: *"in Egypt the whole cycle of agriculture is pivoted round the inundation"* (V. Gordon Childe). *—intr.* To turn on or as if on a pivot; wheel: *"The plot . . . lacks direction, pivoting on Hamlet's incertitude"* (G. Wilson Knight). [French, from Old French, perhaps from Old Provençal *pua*, tooth of a comb, from Vulgar Latin *puga* (unattested), perhaps from Latin *pungere*, to prick. See **peuk-** in Appendix.*] **—piv′ot·al** *adj.* **—piv′ot·al·ly** *adv.*

pix^1 (pĭks) *pl.n. Slang.* Photographs or motion pictures.

pix^2. Variant of **pyx.**

pix·i·lat·ed (pĭk′sə-lā′tĭd) *adj.* **1.** Behaving as if led by pixies; bemused; whimsical; eccentric. **2.** *Slang.* Drunk. [From PIXY, arbitrarily after past participles such as TITILLATED.]

pix·y (pĭk′sē) *n., pl.* **-ies.** Also **pix·ie.** A fairylike or elfin creature. [Origin uncertain.]

Pi·zar·ro (pĭ-zär′ō; *Spanish* pē-*th*är′rō, -sär′rō), **Francisco.** 1470?–1541. Spanish explorer and conquistador.

Piz Ber·ni·na (pēts bĕr-nē′nä). The highest (13,304 feet) of the Rhaetian Alps, on the border between Italy and Switzerland.

pizz. *Music.* pizzicato.

piz·za (pēt′sə) *n.* An Italian baked dish consisting of a shallow pielike crust covered usually with a spiced mixture of tomatoes and cheese. [Italian, probably from Old Italian, a point. See **pizzicato.**]

piz·zazz (pĭ-zăz′) *n. Slang.* Flamboyance; zest; flair. [Expressive.]

piz·ze·ri·a (pēt′sə-rē′ə) *n. Italian.* A place where pizzas are made and sold.

piz·zi·ca·to (pĭt′sĭ-kä′tō) *adj. Abbr.* **pizz.** *Music.* Played by plucking rather than bowing the strings of an instrument. [Italian, past participle of *pizzicare*, to pluck, pinch, from *pizzare*, to prick, pinch, from Old Italian *pizza*, a point, from Gallo-Roman *pīnts-, pīts-* (unattested). See also **pinch.**] **—piz′zi·ca′to** *adv. & n.*

piz·zle (pĭz′əl) *n.* The penis of an animal. [Earlier *peezel*, from Low German *pēsel*, diminutive of Middle Low German *pēse*, sinew, penis, perhaps an early borrowing of Latin *pēniculus*, diminutive of *pēnis*, PENIS.]

Piz·zo Ro·ton·do (pēt′tsō rō-tōn′dō). The highest mountain (10,483 feet) in the Saint Gotthard range of the Lepontine Alps, in south-central Switzerland.

pk peck.

PK psychokinesis.

pk. **1.** pack. **2.** park. **3.** peak. **4.** peck.

pkg., pkge. package.

pkt. packet.

pl. **1.** place. **2.** plate. **3.** plural.

Pl. Place.

PL/1. A symbolic language designed for programming computers and having a structure closely analogous to English. [P(ROGRAM) L(ANGUAGE) (NUMBER) 1.]

plac·a·ble (plăk′ə-bəl, plā′kə-) *adj.* Easily calmed or pacified; tolerant: *"persons of a kind and placable disposition"* (Thackeray). [Middle English, agreeable, from Old French, placable, from Latin *plācābilis*, from *plācāre*, to calm, appease. See **plāk-**^{1} in Appendix.*] **—plac′a·bil′i·ty** *n.* **—plac′a·bly** *adv.*

plac·ard (plăk′ärd′, -ərd) *n.* **1.** A printed or written announcement for display in a public place; poster. **2.** A nameplate, as on the door of a house. *—tr.v.* **placarded, -arding, -ards. 1.** To announce or advertise (a message or product) on a placard. **2.** To post placards on or in. **3.** To display as a placard. [Middle English *placquart*, plate, breastplate, from Old French *plaquart*, from *plaquier*, to plaster, from Middle Dutch *placken*†, to patch, paste. See also **plaque.**] **—plac′ard′er** *n.*

pla·cate (plā′kāt′, plăk′āt′) *tr.v.* **-cated, -cating, -cates.** To allay the anger of, especially by yielding concessions; appease. See Synonyms at **pacify.** [Latin *plācāre*, to calm, appease. See **plāk-**^{1} in Appendix.*] **—pla′cat′er** *n.* **—pla·ca′tion** (plā-kā′shən) *n.* **—pla′ca·to′ry** (-tôr′ē, -tōr′ē), **pla′ca′tive** *adj.*

place (plās) *n.* **1.** A portion of space; an area with definite or indefinite boundaries. **2.** An area occupied by or set aside for someone or something: *"It was a place to play cards and a place to stay, on cold winter nights"* (Ivan Gold). **3.** A definite location, especially: **a.** A house, apartment, or other abode. **b.** A business establishment or office. **c.** A particular town or city. **4.** *Usually capital* **P.** *Abbr.* **Pl.** A public square or thoroughfare in a town. **5. a.** A space for one person to sit or stand, as a passenger or spectator. **b.** A setting for one person at a table. **6.** A position regarded as possessed by someone or something else; stead: *I was chosen in his place.* **7.** A particular point up to which one has read in a book: *I lost my place.* **8.** A position figuratively occupied by a thing, group, or activity in a larger complex; existing function; role. **9.** Proper or customary location or order: *Everything is in place.* **10.** A social station entailing a certain mode of behavior: *He overstepped his place.* **11.** Any high rank or office: *"By any means get wealth and place."* (Pope). **12.** A relative position in a series; standing: *fourth place.* **13.** *Abbr.* **pl.** *Arithmetic.* The position of a number in relation to other numbers in a series. **—go places.** *Informal.* To enjoy increasing success. **—take place.** To occur; happen. See Usage note at **occur.** *—v.* **placed, placing, places.** *—tr.* **1.** To put in some particular position; set: *"Place the ham over the vegetables, its fattiest side up"* (Julia Child). **2.** To put in a relation or order: *Place the words in alphabetical order.* **3.** To find a job or living quarters for (someone). **4.** To arrange for the publication or production of (a literary or dramatic work): *place a novel.* **5.** To appoint to a post: *He was placed in a key position by the president.* **6.** To rank (someone or something) in an order or sequence: *I'd place him second best.* **7.** To date or identify in some context: *I placed the artifacts as Paleolithic.* **8.** To recollect clearly the circumstances or context of: *I remember that face, but I can't place him now.* **9.** To make: *place a telephone call; place a bet.* **10.** To apply for; request formally: *place an order.* **11.** To invest (money): *place the interest with a broker.* **12.** To adjust (one's voice) for the best possible effects. *—intr. Sports.* **1.** To arrive among the first three finishers in a race. **2.** To finish in second place in a race. Compare **win, show.** [Middle English, space, locality, from Old French, from Latin *platea*, "broad street," space, from Greek *plateia* *(hodos),* from feminine of *platus,* broad. See **plat-** in Appendix.*]

Usage: *Place* (verb) always implies care and precision in bringing something to a desired position. When this sense of exactness is not appropriate, *put* is used as a more general term.

pla·ce·bo (plä-chā′bō *for sense 1;* plə-sē′bō *for senses 2 and 3*) *n., pl.* **-bos** or **-boes. 1.** *Roman Catholic Church.* The service or office of vespers for the dead. **2. a.** *Medicine.* A substance containing no medication and given merely to humor a patient. **b.** An inactive substance used as a control in an experiment. **3.** Anything lacking intrinsic remedial value, done or given to humor another. [Medieval Latin, from the first word of the first antiphon of the service, *Placēbo (Dominō in rēgiōne vivōrum),* "I shall please (the Lord in the land of the living)," from *placēre,* to please. See **plāk-**[1] in Appendix.*]

place hitter. *Baseball.* A batter who tends to place his hits into areas not covered by the opposing fielders.

place kick. *Football.* A kick, as for a field goal, for which the ball is held or propped up in a fixed position.

place mat. A decorative and protective mat for a single setting of dishes and silver at mealtime.

place·ment (plās′mənt) *n.* **1. a.** The act of placing or arranging. **b.** The state of being placed or arranged. **2.** The act or business of finding jobs, lodgings, or other positions for applicants. **3.** *Football.* **a.** The setting of the ball in position for a place kick. **b.** A place kick.

pla·cen·ta (plə-sĕn′tə) *n., pl.* **-tas** or **-tae** (-tē). **1.** *Anatomy.* A vascular, membranous organ that develops in female mammals during pregnancy, lining the uterine wall and partially enveloping the fetus, to which it is attached by the **umbilical cord** *(see).* Following birth, the placenta is expelled. **2.** An organ in certain other animals, including certain sharks and reptiles, with similar functions. **3.** *Botany.* **a.** The part of the ovary to which the ovules are attached. **b.** In nonflowering plants, the tissue that bears the spore cases. [From Latin, flat cake, from Greek *plakoenta,* accusative of *plakoeis, plakous,* flat, flat cake, from *plax,* flat surface. See **plāk-**[1] in Appendix.*] —**pla·cen′tal** *adj.*

plac·en·ta·tion (plăs′ən-tā′shən) *n.* **1.** *Zoology.* **a.** The process of formation of a placenta. **b.** The type or structure of a placenta. **2.** *Botany.* The way in which the placenta is arranged in or attached to the ovary.

Pla·cen·tia Bay (plə-sĕn′shə, -shē-ə). An inlet of the Atlantic Ocean, 75 miles long, in southeastern Newfoundland; site of the signing (1941) of the Atlantic Charter.

plac·er (plăs′ər) *n.* **1.** A glacial or alluvial deposit of sand or gravel containing eroded particles of valuable minerals. **2.** A place where such a deposit is washed to extract its mineral content. [Spanish, "shoal," from *plaza,* place, from Latin *platea,* "broad road," PLACE.]

placer mining. The obtaining of minerals from placers by washing or dredging. —**placer miner.**

plac·id (plăs′ĭd) *adj.* **1.** Having an undisturbed surface or aspect; outwardly calm or composed: *"Rosemary waited, placid but inwardly on fire"* (F. Scott Fitzgerald). **2.** Self-satisfied; complacent: *"the placid hum of business and the buzzing of placid businessmen"* (James Thurber). —See Synonyms at **calm.** [French, from Latin *placidus,* pleasing, gentle, from *placēre,* to please. See **plāk-**[1] in Appendix.*] —**pla·cid′i·ty** (plə-sĭd′ə-tē), **plac′id·ness** *n.* —**plac′id·ly** *adv.*

plack·et (plăk′ĭt) *n.* **1.** A slit in a dress, blouse, or skirt to make the garment easy to put on or take off. **2.** A pocket, especially in a woman's skirt. [Earlier *plackerd,* dress, petticoat, originally, "breastplate," variant of PLACARD.]

plac·oid (plăk′oid′) *adj. Zoology.* Platelike, as the hard, toothlike scales of sharks, skates, and rays are. [Greek *plax* (stem *plak-*), flat surface, plate (see **plāk-**[1] in Appendix*) + -OID.]

pla·gal (plā′gəl) *adj. Music.* **1.** Designating a medieval mode having a range from the fourth below to the fifth above its final tone. **2.** Designating a cadence with the subdominant chord immediately preceding the tonic chord. Compare **authentic.** [Medieval Latin *plagālis,* from *plaga,* plagal mode, from *plagius,* plagal, from Medieval Greek *plagios (ēkhos),* plagal (mode), from Greek *plagios,* placed sideways, oblique, from *plagos,* side. See **plāk-**[1] in Appendix.*]

pla·gia·rism (plā′jə-rĭz′əm) *n.* **1.** The act of plagiarizing. **2.** That which is plagiarized. [From PLAGIARY.] —**pla′gia·rist** *n.* —**pla′gia·ris′tic** *adj.*

pla·gia·rize (plā′jə-rīz′) *v.* **-rized, -rizing, -rizes.** —*tr.* **1.** To steal and use (the ideas or writings of another) as one's own. **2.** To appropriate passages or ideas from (another) and use them as one's own: *"I did hate to be accused of plagiarizing Bret Harte."* (Mark Twain). —*intr.* To take and use as one's own the writings or ideas of another. [From PLAGIARY.] —**pla′gia·riz′er** *n.*

pla·gia·ry (plā′jə-rē) *n., pl.* **-ries.** *Archaic.* **1.** Plagiarism. **2.** A plagiarist. [Originally "kidnaper," from Latin *plagiārius,* from *plagium,* kidnaping, from *plaga,* net. See **plāk-**[1] in Appendix.*]

plagio–. Indicates a slanting or inclining; for example, **plagiotropism.** [From Greek *plagios,* placed sideways, oblique, from *plagos,* side. See **plāk-**[1] in Appendix.*]

pla·gi·o·clase (plā′jē-ə-klās′, -klāz′, plăj′ē-) *n.* Any of a common rock-forming series of triclinic feldspars, consisting of mixtures of sodium and calcium aluminum silicates. Also called "oligoclase." [German *Plagioklas* : PLAGIO- + -CLASE.]

pla·gi·ot·ro·pism (plā′jē-ŏt′rə-pĭz′əm) *n. Biology.* Tendency to grow at an oblique or horizontal angle. Said chiefly of roots, stems, or branches. [PLAGIO- + -TROPISM.] —**pla′gi·o·trop′ic** (-ə-trŏp′ĭk) *adj.* —**pla′gi·o·trop′i·cal·ly** *adv.*

plague (plāg) *n.* **1.** A pestilence, affliction, or calamity, originally one of divine retribution: *"till the seven plagues of the seven angels were fulfilled"* (Revelation 15:8). **2.** A sudden influx, as of destructive or injurious insects: *a plague of locusts.* **3.** Any cause for annoyance; a nuisance: *"The blessed silence of the Sabbath saved one from the plague of social jabbering."* (George Santayana). **4.** A highly infectious, usually fatal, epidemic disease, especially the bubonic plague. —*tr.v.* **plagued, plaguing, plagues. 1.** To harass, pester, or annoy: *"What business have people to get children to plague their neighbors?"* (Smollett). **2.** To afflict with or as if with plague or any other evil: *"Runaway inflation further plagued the wage- or salary-earner."* (Edwin Reischauer). —See Synonyms at **harass.** [Middle English, a blow, calamity, malignant disease, from Old French, from Late Latin *plāga,* from Latin, a stroke, wound. See **plāk-**[2] in Appendix.*] —**plagu′er** *n.* —**plague′some** *adj.*

pla·guy (plā′gē) *adj.* Also **pla·guey.** *Informal.* Irritating; bothersome. —**pla′guey, pla′gui·ly** (-gə-lē) *adv.*

plaice (plās) *n., pl.* **plaice** or **plaices. 1.** An edible marine flatfish, *Pleuronectes platessa,* of western European waters. **2.** Any of related flatfishes, such as *Hippoglossoides platessoides* of North American Atlantic waters. [Middle English, from Old French *plaïs, plaïz,* from Late Latin *platessa,* "flatfish," ultimately from Greek *platus,* broad, flat. See **plat-** in Appendix.*]

plaid (plăd; *Scottish* plād) *n.* **1.** A rectangular woolen scarf of a checked or tartan pattern worn over one shoulder by Scottish Highlanders. **2.** Cloth with a tartan or checked pattern. **3.** A tartan or checked pattern. —*adj.* Having a tartan or checked pattern. [Scottish Gaelic *plaide*†.] —**plaid′ed** *adj.*

plain (plān) *adj.* **plainer, plainest. 1.** Free from obstructions; open to view; clear: *plain sight.* **2.** *Archaic.* Having no visible elevation or depression; flat; level. **3.** Easily understood; clearly evident; obvious to the mind: *make one's intent plain.* **4.** Uncomplicated; easily done; simple. **5.** Straightforward; frank; candid: *plain dealing.* **6.** Not mixed with other substances; pure: *plain water.* **7.** Common in rank or station; average; ordinary: *a plain man.* **8.** Not pretentious; unaffected; unsophisticated. **9.** Not rich; ordinary; simple: *plain food.* **10.** With little ornamentation or decoration: *a plain dress.* **11.** Not dyed, twilled, or patterned: *a plain fabric.* **12.** Not beautiful or handsome; unattractive: *a plain face.* **13.** Sheer; utter; unqualified: *plain terror.* —See Synonyms at **evident.** —*n.* **1.** An extensive, level, treeless land region, such as a valley floor or a plateau summit. **2.** *Capital* **P.** A popular name for the more moderate party of the French legislature during the French Revolution. —*adv.* In a clear or intelligible manner. [Middle English, from Old French, from Latin *plānus,* flat, clear. See **pelə-**[1] in Appendix.*] —**plain′ly** *adv.* —**plain′ness** *n.*

plain·chant (plān′chănt′, -chänt′) *n.* A form of medieval music, **plainsong** *(see).* [French, from Medieval Latin *cantus plānus,* PLAINSONG.]

plain·clothes man (plān′klōz′) *pl.* **plainclothes men.** Also **plain·clothes·man** (plān′klōz′mən) *pl.* **-men** (-mĭn). A member of a police force, especially a detective, who wears civilian clothes on duty.

plain-laid (plān′lād′) *adj.* Designating a rope made of three strands laid together with a right-hand twist.

Plain People. Members of the Mennonite, Amish, or Dunker sects, noted for their custom of wearing plain dress.

plain sailing. Easy progress over a direct course. [Alteration of *plane sailing* (navigation using PLANE angles).]

Plains Indian. A member of any of the tribes of North American Indians that once inhabited the Great Plains of the United States and Canada.

plains·man (plānz′mən) *n., pl.* **-men** (-mĭn). An inhabitant or settler of the prairie regions of the United States.

Plains of Abraham. A plain near Quebec, scene of a battle of the French and Indian War (1759) in which the British under Wolfe defeated the French under Montcalm.

plain·song (plān′sông′, -sŏng′) *n. Music.* **1. Gregorian chant** *(see).* **2.** The general designation for the various bodies of medieval liturgical music without strict meter and sung without accompaniment. Also called "plainchant." [Translation of Medieval Latin *cantus plānus.*]

plaint (plānt) *n.* **1.** A complaint. **2.** An utterance of grief or sorrow; lamentation. **3.** *Law.* A statement of grievance submitted to a court as a request for redress. [Middle English *pleinte, plaint,* from Old French *plainte,* from Latin *planctus,* past participle of *plangere,* to strike (one's breast), lament. See **plak-**[2] in Appendix.*]

plain·tiff (plān′tĭf) *n. Abbr.* **plf.** *Law.* The party that institutes a suit in a court. Compare **defendant.** [Middle English *plaintif,* from Old French, from adjective *plaintif,* PLAINTIVE.]

plain·tive (plān′tĭv) *adj.* Expressing sorrow; mournful; melancholy: *"a fragile, plaintive fluting of woodwind notes"* (J.R. Salamanca). [Middle English *pleintif,* from Old French *plaintif,* from *plainte,* lamentation, PLAINT.] —**plain′tive·ly** *adv.* —**plain′tive·ness** *n.*

plain weave. A weave in which the filling threads and the warp threads interlace alternately, forming a checkerboard pattern. Also called "taffeta weave."

plain weave

plait (plāt, plăt) *n.* **1.** A braid, especially of hair. **2.** A pleat. —*tr.v.* **plaited, plaiting, plaits. 1.** To braid. **2.** To pleat. **3.** To make by braiding or pleating. [Middle English, fold, crease, from Old French *pleit,* from Vulgar Latin *plic(i)tus* (unattested), from Latin *plicitus,* variant past participle of *plicāre,* to fold. See **plek-** in Appendix.*] —**plait′er** *n.*

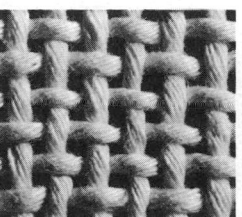

plan (plăn) *n.* **1.** Any detailed scheme, program, or method worked out beforehand for the accomplishment of an object: *a plan of attack.* **2.** A proposed or tentative project or goal: *Do you have any plans for the evening?* **3.** A systematic arrangement

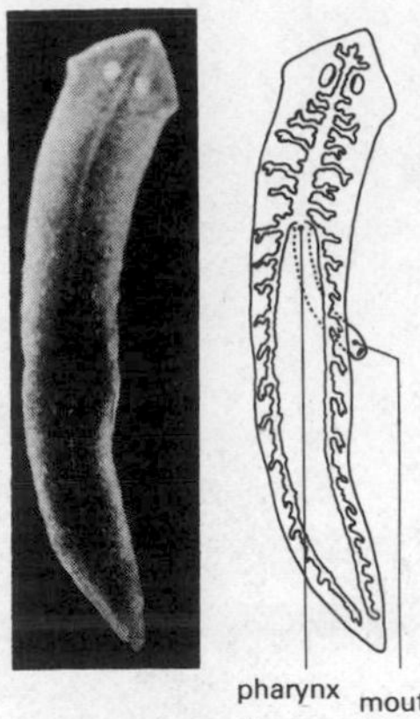
pharynx
mouth

planarian
Diagram *(right)* showing branched digestive tract

of details; an outline or sketch: *the plan of a story.* **4.** A drawing or diagram made to scale showing the structure or arrangement of something. **5.** In perspective rendering, one of several imaginary planes perpendicular to the line of vision between the viewer and the object being depicted. —*v.* **planned, planning, plans.** —*tr.* **1.** To formulate a scheme or program for the accomplishment or attainment of: *plan a campaign.* **2.** To have as a specific aim or purpose; intend: *They plan to go to the beach.* See Usage note below. **3.** To draw or make a graphic representation of. —*intr.* To make plans. [French, as "level ground," "plane," from Latin *plānum,* from *plānus,* flat (see **pelə-**[1] in Appendix*); as "ground plan," "map," altered from *plant* (in sense influenced by Italian *pianta,* ground plan or design), from *planter,* to plant, from Latin *plantāre,* "to drive in with the sole of the foot," from *planta,* sole of the foot. See **plant.**] —**plan′ner** *n.*

Usage: *Plan to* (as in *plan to go*) is preferable to *plan on* and gerund *(plan on going),* especially in written usage.

pla·nar (plā′nər) *adj.* **1.** Of, pertaining to, or situated in a plane. **2.** Flat: *a planar surface.* [Late Latin *plānāris,* from Latin *plānum,* level surface, from *plānus,* flat, PLAIN.] —**pla·nar′i·ty** (plə-nâr′ə-tē) *n.*

pla·nar·i·an (plə-nâr′ē-ən) *n.* Any of various flatworms of the order Tricladida, having broad, ciliated bodies and a three-branched digestive cavity. [From New Latin *Planaria* (genus), from Latin *plānus,* flat. See **pelə-**[1] in Appendix.*]

pla·na·tion (plā-nā′shən) *n.* Lateral mechanical erosion, as of a valley, by a running stream. [From PLANE (level surface).]

planch·et (plăn′chĭt) *n.* **1.** A flat disk of metal ready for stamping as a coin; a coin blank. **2.** A small disk of metal on which a radioactive substance is deposited for measurement of its activity. [Diminutive of *planch,* board, Middle English *plaunche,* from Old French *planche,* from Latin *planca.* See **plāk-**[1] in Appendix.*]

plan·chette (plăn-shĕt′) *n.* A small triangular board with a pointer supported by two casters and a vertical pencil which is said to spell out messages from the spirit world when the operator's fingers are placed lightly upon it. [French, diminutive of Old French *planche,* board. See **planchet.**]

Planck (plängk), **Max (Karl Ernst Ludwig).** 1858–1947. German physicist; formulated the quantum theory.

Planck's constant. *Symbol* $\hbar$ *Physics.* The constant of proportionality relating the quantum of energy that can be possessed by radiation to the frequency of that radiation. Its value is approximately 6.625×10^{-27} erg-sec. [After Max PLANCK.]

plane[1] (plān) *n.* **1.** *Geometry.* A surface containing all the straight lines connecting any two points on it. **2.** Any flat or level surface. **3.** A level of development, existence, or achievement. **4.** An airplane or hydroplane. **5.** *Aviation.* A supporting surface of an airplane; an airfoil or wing. —*adj.* **1.** *Geometry.* Designating a figure lying in a plane: *a plane curve.* **2.** Flat. —See Synonyms at **level.** [Latin *plānum,* a flat surface, from *plānus,* flat. See **pelə-**[1] in Appendix.*] —**plane′ness** *n.*

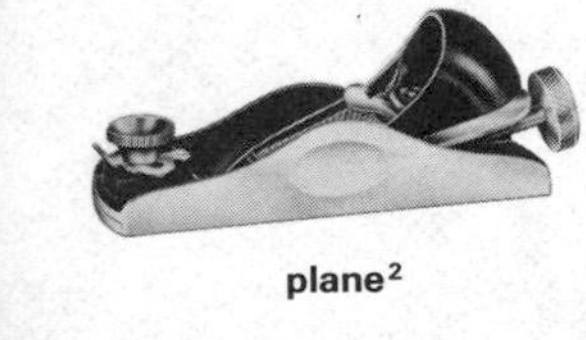

plane[2]

plane[2] (plān) *n.* **1.** A carpenter's tool with an adjustable blade for smoothing and leveling wood. **2.** A trowel-shaped tool for smoothing the surface of clay, sand, or plaster in a mold. —*v.* **planed, planing, planes.** —*tr.* **1.** To smooth or finish with or as with a plane. **2.** To remove with a plane. —*intr.* **1.** To undergo planing: *Poplar planes easily.* **2.** To act as a plane. [Middle English, from French *plane, plaine,* from Late Latin *plāna,* from *plānāre,* to plane, from *plānus,* level. See **pelə-**[1] in Appendix.*]

plane[3] (plān) *intr.v.* **planed, planing, planes. 1.** To rise partly out of the water, as a hydroplane does at high speeds. **2.** To soar or glide. **3.** To travel by airplane. [French *planer,* to soar (with wings stretched on a level), from *plan,* a level surface, from Latin *plānum,* from *plānus,* flat. See **pelə-**[1] in Appendix.*]

plane[4] (plān) *n.* The **plane tree** *(see).*

plane angle. An angle formed by two straight lines.

plane geometry. The geometry of planar figures.

plan·er (plā′nər) *n.* **1.** One that planes. **2.** A machine tool for smoothing and planing the surfaces of wood or metal. **3.** *Printing.* A smooth block of wood used to level a form of type.

pla·ner tree (plā′nər). A small swamp tree, *Planera aquatica,* of the southern United States, having small, rough, nutlike fruit. Also called "water elm." [After J.J. *Planer* (1743–1789), German botanist.]

plan·et (plăn′ət) *n.* **1.** A nonluminous celestial body illuminated by light from a star, such as the sun, around which it revolves. In the **solar system** *(see)* there are nine known major planets: Mercury, Venus, Earth, Mars, Jupiter, Saturn, Uranus, Neptune, and Pluto. **2.** In ancient astronomy, one of the seven celestial bodies (Mercury, Venus, the Moon, the Sun, Mars, Jupiter, and Saturn) visible to the naked eye and thought to revolve in the heavens about a fixed Earth and among fixed stars. **3.** *Astrology.* One of the seven revolving celestial bodies that in conjunction with the stars are supposed to influence human affairs and personalities. [Middle English *planete,* from Old French, from Late Latin *planēta,* from Greek *planēs, planētēs,* plural of *planētos,* wandering planet, from *planasthai,* to wander. See **pelə-**[1] in Appendix.*]

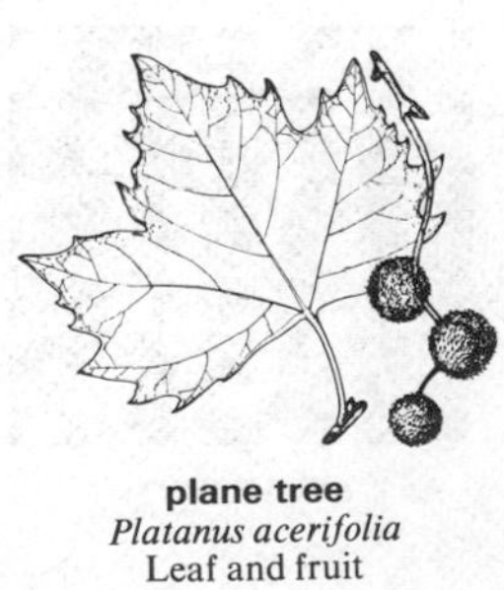

plane tree
Platanus acerifolia
Leaf and fruit

plane table. A portable surveying instrument consisting essentially of a drawing board and a ruler mounted on a tripod and used to sight and map topographical details.

plan·e·tar·i·um (plăn′ə-târ′ē-əm) *n., pl.* **-iums** or **-ia** (-ē-ə). **1.** An apparatus or model representing the solar system. **2.** A device for projecting images of celestial bodies in their courses, on the inner surface of a hemispherical dome. **3.** A building or room containing such a device, with seats for an audience. [PLANET + -ARIUM.]

plan·e·tar·y (plăn′ə-tĕr′ē) *adj.* **1.** Of, pertaining to, or resembling the physical or orbital characteristics of a planet or the planets. **2.** Terrestrial; mundane; earthly. **3.** Wandering; erratic: *planetary life.* **4.** *Machinery.* Denoting or pertaining to a **gear train** *(see),* consisting of a central gear with an internal ring gear and one or more pinions.

planetary nebula. Any of several objects in the Galaxy, each consisting of a hot, blue-white, central star surrounded by an envelope of expanding gas. See **Ring Nebula.**

plan·e·tes·i·mal (plăn′ə-tĕs′ə-məl, -tĕz′ə-məl) *n. Astronomy.* Any of innumerable small bodies thought to have orbited the sun during the formation of the planets. [PLANET + (INFINIT)-ESIMAL.] —**plan′e·tes′i·mal** *adj.*

planetesimal hypothesis. The hypothesis that the planets and satellites of the solar system were formed by gravitational aggregation of planetesimals. Compare **nebular hypothesis.**

plan·e·toid (plăn′ə-toid′) *n. Astronomy.* An **asteroid** *(see).* —**plan′e·toi′dal** *adj.*

plane tree. Any of several trees of the genus *Platanus,* having ball-shaped fruit clusters, and, usually, outer bark that flakes off in patches. Also called "plane." See **sycamore.** [*Plane,* from Middle English, from Old French, from Latin *platanus,* from Greek *platanos,* from *platus,* broad (from its broad leaves). See **plat-** in Appendix.*]

planet wheel. *Machinery.* One of the small gear wheels in an **epicyclic train** *(see).*

plan·gent (plăn′jənt) *adj.* **1.** Striking with a deep, reverberating sound, as waves against the shore. **2. a.** Loud and resounding, as the sound of bells. **b.** Expressing sadness; plaintive: *"From a doorway came the plangent sounds of a guitar."* (Malcolm Lowry). [Latin *plangens,* present participle of *plangere,* to strike (one's breast). See **plāk-**[2] in Appendix.*] —**plan′gen·cy** *n.* —**plan′gent·ly** *adv.*

plani–. Variant of **plano-.**

pla·nim·e·ter (plə-nĭm′ə-tər, plā-) *n.* An instrument that measures the area of a plane figure as a mechanically coupled pointer traverses the figure's perimeter. [French *planimètre* : PLANI- + -METER.] —**pla′ni·met′ric** (plā′nə-mĕt′rĭk), **pla′ni·met′ri·cal** *adj.* —**pla′ni·met′ri·cal·ly** *adv.* —**pla·nim′e·try** *n.*

plan·ish (plăn′ĭsh) *tr.v.* **-ished, -ishing, -ishes.** To flatten, smooth, toughen, or polish (metal) by rolling or hammering. [French *planir* (present stem *planiss-*), to make level, from *plan,* level, from Latin *plānus.* See **pelə-**[1] in Appendix.*]

pla·ni·sphere (plā′nə-sfîr′) *n.* **1.** A representation of a sphere or part of a sphere on a plane surface. **2.** *Astronomy.* A polar projection of the celestial sphere on a chart equipped with an adjustable overlay to show the stars visible at a particular time and place. [Middle English *planispherie,* from Medieval Latin *plānisphaerium* : PLANI- + -SPHERE.] —**pla′ni·spher′ic** (plā′nə-sfîr′ĭk, -sfĕr′ĭk), **pla′ni·spher′i·cal** *adj.*

plank (plăngk) *n.* **1. a.** A piece of lumber cut thicker than a board. **b.** Such pieces of lumber considered collectively; planking. **2.** A foundation; support. **3.** One of the articles of a political platform: *"Planks had been published by the subcommittees on farm policy, on education, on national defense."* (Theodore H. White). —*tr.v.* **planked, planking, planks. 1.** To furnish, lay, or cover with planks. **2.** To bake or broil and serve (fish or meat) on a plank. **3.** To put or set down emphatically or with force. **4.** *Informal.* To pay at once. Usually used with *down* or *out.* [Middle English *plank(e),* from Old North French *planke,* from Latin *planca.* See **plāk-**[1] in Appendix.*]

plank·ing (plăng′kĭng) *n.* **1.** The act of laying planks. **2.** Planks considered collectively. **3.** Something made of planks.

plank-sheer (plăngk′shîr′) *n.* A horizontal timber forming the outer edge of the upper deck of a wooden ship. Also called "covering board." [Altered (by association with PLANK and SHEER) from earlier *planshire,* Middle English *plancher,* from Old French *planchier,* from *planche,* plank, from Latin *planca.* See **plāk-**[1] in Appendix.*]

plank·ter (plăngk′tər) *n.* One of the minute organisms that collectively constitute plankton. [Greek *planktēr,* "wanderer," from *planktos,* wandering. See **plankton.**]

plank·ton (plăngk′tən) *n. Biology.* Plant and animal organisms, generally microscopic, that float or drift in great numbers in fresh or salt water. [German, from Greek, "wanderer," neuter of *planktos,* wandering, from *plazesthai,* to wander, drift. See **plāk-**[2] in Appendix.*] —**plank·ton′ic** (plăngk-tŏn′ĭk) *adj.*

plano–, plani–. Indicates flatness; for example, **planometer, planimeter.** [From Latin *plānus,* flat. See **pelə-**[1] in Appendix.*]

pla·no·con·cave (plā′nō-kŏn-kāv′, -kŏn′kāv′) *adj.* Flat or plane on one side and concave on the other.

pla·no·con·vex (plā′nō-kŏn-vĕks′, -kŏn′vĕks′) *adj.* Flat or plane on one side and convex on the other.

pla·no·graph (plā′nə-grăf′, -gräf′) *tr.v.* **-graphed, -graphing, -graphs.** To print by planography.

pla·nog·ra·phy (plə-nŏg′rə-fē, plā-) *n.* A process for printing from a smooth surface, as lithography or offset. [PLANO- + -GRAPHY.] —**pla′no·graph′ic** (plā′nə-grăf′ĭk) *adj.* —**pla′no·graph′i·cal·ly** *adv.*

pla·nom·e·ter (plə-nŏm′ə-tər, plā-) *n.* A flat metal plate for gauging the accuracy of a plane surface in precision metalworking; a surface plate. [PLANO- + -METER.] —**pla·nom′e·try** *n.*

plant (plănt, plänt) *n.* **1.** Any organism of the vegetable kingdom, characteristically having cellulose cell walls, growing by synthesis of inorganic substances, and lacking the power of locomotion. **2.** A plant having no permanent woody stem; an herb, as distinguished from a tree or shrub. ***Note:*** In this Dictionary, *plant* is used in this sense rather than the word *herb,* to avoid confusion with the medicinal and cookery senses of the latter term. **3.** The equipment, including machinery, tools, instruments, and fixtures, and the buildings containing them, necessary for any industrial or manufacturing operation; factory. **4.** The buildings, equipment, and fixtures of any institution. **5.** A seemingly trivial passage or line in a play or story that becomes important later. **6.** A person placed in an audience to encourage applause or contribute to the action of the play. **7.** A misleading piece of evidence placed so as to be discovered. **8.** *Slang.* A scheming trick; a swindle. —*tr.v.* **planted, planting, plants. 1.** To place or set (seeds, roots, cuttings, or young plants) in the ground to grow. **2. a.** To furnish or supply (a plot of land) with plants or seeds. **b.** To stock (water) with fish or spawn. **c.** To introduce (an animal) into an area. **3.** To fix or set firmly in position: *He planted both feet on the ground.* **4.** To establish or set up; to found: *plant a colony.* **5.** To implant (an idea, sentiment, or the like) in the mind; introduce and establish firmly: *"The right of revolution is planted in the heart of man."* (Clarence Darrow). **6.** *Slang.* **a.** To place or station (a person) for the purposes of observation, spying, informing, or the like: *Detectives were planted all over the store.* **b.** To place (something) for the purpose of deception: *plant false evidence.* **7.** *Informal.* To hide by burying. **8.** *Slang.* To deliver (a blow or punch). [Middle English *plante,* from Old French and Old English, from Latin *planta,* shoot, from *plantāre,* to plant, "drive in with the sole of the foot," from *planta,* sole of the foot. See **plat-** in Appendix.*] —**plant'a·ble** *adj.*

Plan·tag·e·net (plăn-tăj'ə-nĭt). Family name of the Angevin line of English sovereigns from Henry II (1154) through Richard III (1485). [Middle English, from Old French, "sprig of broom," nickname referring to the crest of the Angevins : Latin *planta,* sprig, PLANT + *gneista, genesta,* the broom plant (probably from Etruscan).]

plan·tain[1] (plăn'tən) *n.* Any of various plants of the genus *Plantago;* especially, *P. major,* a weed with broad leaves and a spike of small, greenish flowers. See **ribgrass.** [Middle English, from Old French, from Latin *plantāgō,* from *planta,* sole of the foot (from its broad leaves). See **plat-** in Appendix.*]

plan·tain[2] (plăn'tən) *n.* **1.** A large tropical plant, *Musa paradisiaca,* resembling the banana and bearing similar fruit. **2.** The fruit of this plant, used as a staple food in tropical regions. [Spanish *plantano,* plane tree, from Medieval Latin *plantanus,* variant of Latin *platanus,* PLANE TREE.]

plantain lily. Any of several plants of the genus *Hosta,* native to Asia, widely cultivated for their white, blue, or lilac flowers. Sometimes called "day lily."

plan·tar (plăn'tər, -tär') *adj.* Of, pertaining to, or occurring on the sole of the foot. [Latin *plantāris,* from *planta,* sole of the foot. See **plat-** in Appendix.*]

plan·ta·tion (plăn-tā'shən) *n.* **1.** An area under cultivation. **2.** A group of cultivated trees or plants. **3.** A large estate or farm on which crops such as cotton, tobacco, or sugar are grown and harvested, often by resident workers. **4.** A newly established colony or settlement.

plant·er (plăn'tər) *n.* **1. a.** One who plants. **b.** A machine or tool for planting or sowing seeds. **2.** The owner or manager of a plantation. **3.** An early settler or colonist. **4.** A decorative container for house plants.

planter's punch. A drink of rum with lemon or lime juice, sugar syrup, water or soda, bitters, and grenadine.

plan·ti·grade (plăn'tə-grād') *adj. Zoology.* Walking with the entire lower surface of the foot on the ground, as man and bears do. —*n.* A plantigrade animal. Compare **digitigrade.** [French, from New Latin *plantigradus* : Latin *planta,* sole of the foot (see **plat-** in Appendix*) + -GRADE.]

plant louse. An **aphid** *(see).*

plan·u·la (plăn'yə-lə) *n., pl.* **-lae** (-lē'). The free-swimming, ciliated larva of a coelenterate. [New Latin, from Latin, little plane (from the flatness of the larva), from *plānus,* flat, level. See **pelə-**[1] in Appendix.*] —**plan'u·lar** *adj.*

plaque (plăk) *n.* **1.** A flat plate, slab, or disk that is ornamented or engraved for mounting, as on a wall for decoration or on a monument for information. **2.** A small pin or brooch worn as an ornament or a badge of membership. **3.** *Pathology.* A small, disk-shaped formation or growth; patch. [French, from Old French, metal plate, coin, from Middle Dutch *placke,* from *placken*†, to patch, paste. See also **placard.**]

plash (plăsh) *n.* **1.** A light splash. **2.** The sound of such a splash. —*v.* **plashed, plashing, plashes.** —*tr.* To spatter (liquid) about; splash. —*intr.* To splash lightly. [Perhaps from Dutch *plassen,* from Middle Dutch *plasschen* (imitative).]

-plasia, -plasy. Indicates growth or change; for example, **hypoplasia, heteroplasy.** [New Latin, from Greek *plasis,* molding, from *plassein,* to mold. See **pelə-**[1] in Appendix.*]

plasm (plăz'əm) *n.* **1.** Genetic material, **germ plasm** *(see).* **2.** Variant of **plasma.**

-plasm. *Biology.* Indicates the material characteristically forming cells; for example, **protoplasm.** [From PLASMA.]

plas·ma (plăz'mə) *n.* Also **plasm** (plăz'əm). **1. a.** *Physiology.* The clear, yellowish fluid portion of blood, lymph, or intramuscular fluid in which cells are suspended. **b.** *Medicine.* Cell-free, sterilized **blood plasma** *(see),* used in transfusions. **2.** Protoplasm or cytoplasm. **3.** The fluid portion of milk from which the curd has been separated by coagulation; whey. **4.** *Physics.* An electrically neutral, highly ionized gas composed of ions, electrons, and neutral particles. [New Latin, extended use of Late Latin *plasma,* a form, mold, from Greek, from *plassein,* to mold. See **pelə-**[1] in Appendix.*] —**plas·mat'ic** (plăz-măt'ĭk), **plas'mic** *adj.*

plas·ma·gel (plăz'mə-jĕl') *n. Biology.* A jellylike state of cytoplasm, characteristically occurring in the periphery of the amoeba. [PLASMA + GEL.]

plas·ma·gene (plăz'mə-jēn') *n. Genetics.* A self-reproducing hereditary structure thought to exist in cytoplasm and function in a manner analogous to, but independent of, chromosomal genes. —**plas'ma·gen'ic** (plăz'mə-jē'nĭk, -jĕn'ĭk) *adj.*

plasma membrane. *Biology.* The semipermeable membrane that encloses the cytoplasm of a cell.

plas·ma·sol (plăz'mə-sôl', -sŏl', -sōl') *n. Biology.* A state of cytoplasm that is more liquid than **plasmagel** *(see).* [PLASMA + SOL (colloid).]

plas·min (plăz'mĭn) *n. Biochemistry.* A proteolytic enzyme in plasma that dissolves fibrin and other clotting factors in blood. [PLASM(O)- + -IN.]

plasmo-, plasm-. Indicates plasma or resemblance to plasma; for example, **plasmolysis, plasmin.** [From New Latin PLASMA.]

plas·mo·des·ma (plăz'mə-dĕz'mə) *n., pl.* **-mata** (-mə-tə). Also **plas·mo·des·mus** (plăz'mə-dĕz'məs), *pl.* **-mi** (-mī'), **plas·mo·desm** (plăz'mə-dĕz'əm). *Biology.* A strand of living cytoplasm connecting two cells that are otherwise functionally separate. [New Latin : PLASMO- + Greek *desma,* a band, bond, from *dein,* to bind (see **dē-** in Appendix*).]

plas·mo·di·um (plăz-mō'dē-əm) *n., pl.* **-dia** (-dē-ə). **1.** Any protozoan of the genus *Plasmodium,* which includes the parasites that cause malaria. **2.** A naked, multinucleate mass of protoplasm such as that characteristic of the vegetative phase of the slime molds. [New Latin : PLASMO- + -ODE + -IUM.]

plas·mol·y·sis (plăz-mŏl'ə-sĭs) *n. Biology.* Shrinkage or contraction of the protoplasm in a cell, especially a plant cell, caused by loss of water through osmosis. [PLASMO- + -LYSIS.] —**plas'mo·lyt'ic** (plăz'mə-lĭt'ĭk) *adj.* —**plas'mo·lyt'i·cal·ly** *adv.*

plas·mo·lyze (plăz'mə-līz') *v.* **-lyzed, -lyzing, -lyzes.** —*tr.* To subject to plasmolysis. —*intr.* To undergo plasmolysis. [From PLASMOLYSIS.]

plas·mo·some (plăz'mə-sōm') *n. Biology.* A **nucleolus** *(see).* [PLASMO- + -SOME.]

-plast. Indicates an organized unit of living matter; for example, **protoplast.** [From Greek *plastos,* molded, from *plassein,* to mold. See **pelə-**[1] in Appendix.*]

plas·ter (plăs'tər, pläs'-) *n.* **1.** A mixture of lime, sand, and water, sometimes with hair or other fiber added, that hardens to a smooth solid and is used for coating walls and ceilings. **2. Plaster of Paris** *(see).* **3.** A pastelike mixture applied to a part of the body for healing or cosmetic purposes. **4. Mustard plaster** *(see).* —*tr.v.* **plastered, -tering, -ters. 1.** To cover, coat, or repair with plaster. **2.** To cover by or as if by pasting; especially, to cover conspicuously or to excess: *"The face of the house was plastered with tea roses."* (Elizabeth Bowen). **3.** To apply a plaster to. **4.** To cause to adhere to another surface: *"His hair was plastered to his forehead."* (William Golding). **5.** To make smooth by applying a sticky substance. Used with *down: His hair is always plastered down and glossy.* [Middle English *plaster,* Old English *plaster,* from Medieval Latin *plastrum,* short for Latin *emplastrum,* from Greek *emplastron, emplaston,* salve, from *emplastos,* past participle of *emplassein,* to daub on, plaster : *em-, en,* in + *plassein,* to mold, plaster (see **pelə-**[1] in Appendix*).] —**plas'ter·er** *n.*

plas·ter·board (plăs'tər-bôrd', -bōrd', pläs'-) *n.* A thin, rigid board or sheet of layers of fiberboard or paper, bonded to a plaster core and used to cover walls and ceilings.

plaster cast. 1. A mold or cast of a piece of sculpture or other object made with plaster of Paris. **2.** *Surgery.* A **cast** *(see).*

plas·tered (plăs'tərd, pläs'-) *adj. Slang.* Drunk.

plas·ter·ing (plăs'tər-ĭng, pläs'-) *n.* **1.** The act of applying or working with plaster. **2.** A layer or coating of plaster.

plaster of Paris. Any of a group of gypsum cements, essentially hemihydrated calcium sulfate, $CaSo_4 \cdot \frac{1}{2}H_2O$, a white powder that forms a paste when mixed with water and hardens into a solid. It is used in making casts, molds, and sculpture. Also called "plaster." [Middle English; originally made in *Paris.*]

plas·tic (plăs'tĭk) *adj.* **1.** Capable of being shaped or formed; pliable: *"in the plastic clays of instinctive curiosity"* (William James). **2.** Pertaining to or dealing with shaping or modeling: *the plastic arts.* **3.** Giving form or shape to a substance. **4.** Easily influenced; impressionable. **5.** Having the qualities of a piece of sculpture; well-formed: *"the astonishing plastic beauty of the chorus girls"* (Frank Harris). **6.** Made of a plastic or plastics: *a plastic garden hose.* **7.** *Physics.* Capable of undergoing continuous deformation without rupture or relaxation. **8.** *Biology.* Capable of building tissue; formative. —See Synonyms at **flexible.** —*n.* Any of various complex organic compounds produced by polymerization. They can be molded, extruded, or cast into various shapes and films, or drawn into filaments used as textile fibers. [French *plastique,* from Latin *plasticus,* from Greek *plastikos,* fit for molding, from *plastos,* molded, from *plassein,* to mold. See **pelə-**[1] in Appendix.*] —**plas'ti·cal·ly** *adv.* —**plas·tic'i·ty** *n.*

-plastic. Indicates a forming or growing; for example, **cytoplastic.** [Greek *plastikos,* fit for molding, PLASTIC.]

plas·ti·cize (plăs'tə-sīz') *v.* **-cized, -cizing, -cizes.** —*tr.* To make plastic. —*intr.* To become plastic.

plas·ti·ciz·er (plăs'tə-sī'zər) *n.* Any of various substances added to plastics or other materials to keep them soft or pliable.

plastic surgery. Surgery to remodel, repair, or restore injured or defective tissue or body parts. —**plastic surgeon.**

plas·tid (plăs'tĭd) *n. Biology.* Any of several specialized cytoplasmic structures occurring in plant cells and in some plantlike organisms, and having various physiological functions. [German *Plastid,* from *Plastiden* (plural), from Greek *plastides,*

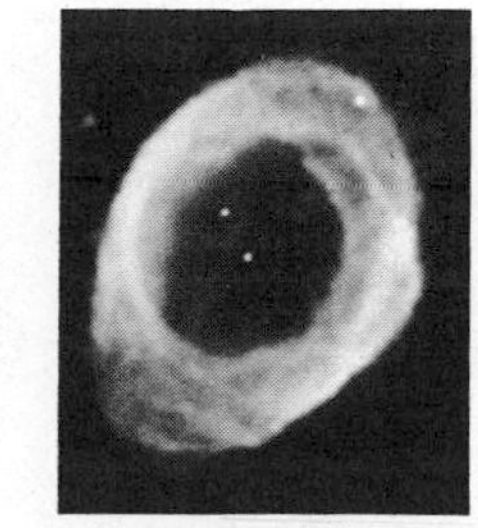

planetary nebula
The Ring Nebula in Lyra

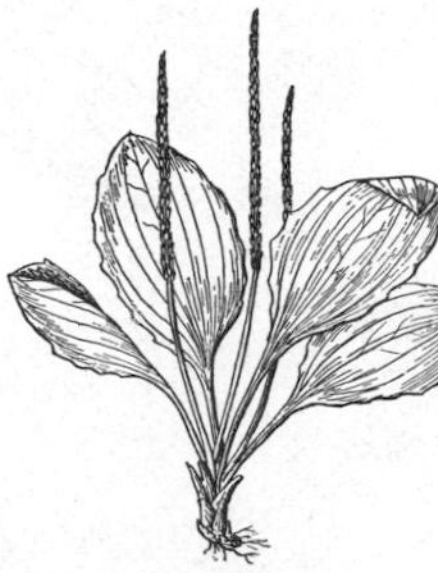

plantain[1]
Plantago major

feminine plural of *plastēs,* molder, sculptor, from *plastos,* molded, from *plassein,* to mold. See **pele-**[1] in Appendix.*] —**plas·tid′i·al** (plăs-tĭd′ē-əl) *adj.*

plas·to·mer (plăs′tə-mər) *n. Chemistry.* Any of various tough, hard polymers, such as **acrylate resin** *(see).* [Greek *plastos,* molded (see **plastic**) + (POLY)MER.]

plas·tron (plăs′trən) *n.* **1.** A breastplate worn under a coat of mail. **2.** A protective breastplate worn by fencers. **3.** A trimming on the front of a bodice. **4.** The front of a man's dress shirt. **5.** *Zoology.* The ventral surface of the shell of a turtle or tortoise. [Old French, from Old Italian *piastrone,* augmentative of *piastra,* "metal plate," from Latin *emplastra, emplastrum,* PLASTER.] —**plas′tral** (plăs′trəl) *adj.*

–plasty. Indicates plastic surgery; for example, **dermatoplasty.** [Greek *-plastia,* from *plastos,* molded, from *plassein,* to mold. See **pele-**[1] in Appendix.*]

–plasy. Variant of **–plasia.**

plat (plăt) *tr.v.* **platted, platting, plats.** To plait or braid. —*n.* A braid. [Middle English *platen,* variant of *plaiten,* to plait, from *plait,* PLAIT.]

plat. 1. platform. **2.** platoon.

Pla·ta, La. See **La Plata.**

Pla·ta, Rí·o de la. See **Río de la Plata.**

Pla·tae·a (plə-tē′ə). An ancient city of southeastern Boeotia in Greece, southwest of Thebes, the scene of a Greek victory over the Persians (479 B.C.). —**Pla·tae′an** *n.* & *adj.*

plate (plāt) *n.* **1.** A smooth, flat, relatively thin, rigid body of uniform thickness. **2. a.** A sheet of hammered, rolled, or cast metal. **b.** A very thin plated coat or layer of metal. **3. a.** A flat piece of metal forming part of a machine: *a boiler plate.* **b.** A flat piece of metal on which something is engraved. **4. a.** A thin piece of metal used for armor. **b.** Armor made of this. **5.** *Abbr.* **pl.** *Printing.* **a.** A sheet of metal, plastic, rubber, paperboard, or other material converted into a printing surface, such as an electrotype or stereotype. **b.** A print of a woodcut, lithograph, or other engraved material, especially when reproduced in a book. **c.** A full-page book illustration, often in color and printed on paper different from that used on the text pages. **6.** *Abbr.* **pl.** *Photography.* A light-sensitive sheet of glass or metal upon which an image can be recorded. **7.** *Dentistry.* A thin metallic or plastic support fitted to the gums to anchor artificial teeth. **8.** *Architecture.* In wood-frame construction, a horizontal member, capping the exterior wall studs, upon which the roof rafters rest. **9.** *Baseball.* Home base, usually a flat piece of heavy rubber. Also called "home plate." **10. a.** A shallow dish in which food is served or from which it is eaten. **b.** The contents of such a dish. **c.** A whole course served on such a dish. **11.** Food and service for one person at a meal: *dinner at a set price per plate.* **12.** Household articles covered with a precious metal, such as gold or silver. **13.** A dish passed among a congregation for the collection of offerings. **14.** *Sports.* **a.** A dish, cup, or other article of silver or gold offered as a prize. **b.** A contest, especially a horse race, offering such a prize. **15.** A thin cut of beef from the brisket. **16.** *Anatomy & Zoology.* **a.** A thin, flat layer or scale. **b.** A platelike part or organ. **17.** *Electronics.* **a.** Any electrode, as in a storage battery or capacitor. **b.** The anode in an electron tube. —*tr.v.* **plated, plating, plates. 1.** To coat or cover with a thin layer of metal. **2.** To armor. **3.** *Printing.* To make a stereotype or electrotype from. **4.** To give a glossy finish to (paper) by pressing between metal sheets or rollers. [Middle English, from Old French, from feminine of *plat,* flat, from Vulgar Latin *plattus* (unattested), from Greek *platus,* broad, flat. See **plat-** in Appendix.*]

pla·teau (plă-tō′) *n., pl.* **-teaus** or **-teaux** (-tōz′). **1.** An elevated and comparatively level expanse of land; tableland. **2.** A relatively stable or quiescent period or state; a leveling off: *a plateau of business activity.* [French, from Old French *platel,* a flat piece, from *plat,* flat, from Vulgar Latin *plattus* (unattested), from Greek *platus,* broad, flat. See **plat-** in Appendix.*]

plat·ed (plā′tĭd) *adj.* **1.** Coated with a thin layer of metal. Often used in combination: *goldplated.* **2.** Covered or furnished with plates or sheets of metal, as armor. **3.** Knitted with two kinds of yarn, one on the face and one on the back.

plate·ful (plāt′fo͝ol′) *n., pl.* **-fuls. 1.** The amount of food or other substance that a plate will hold. **2.** A generous portion of food.

plate glass. A strong rolled and polished glass containing few impurities and used for mirrors and large windows.

plate·let (plāt′lĭt) *n.* A protoplasmic disk, smaller than a red blood cell, found in the blood of vertebrates and thought to promote coagulation. [Diminutive of PLATE.]

plat·en (plăt′n) *n.* **1.** One of the two flat members of the printing unit of a printing press that serves to position the paper and hold it against the inked type. **2.** The roller on a typewriter against which the keys strike. [Earlier *plattin,* from Old French *platine,* from *plate,* PLATE.]

plate proof. A proof taken from the master printing plate.

plat·er (plā′tər) *n.* **1.** One that plates. **2.** *Slang.* An inferior racehorse.

plat·form (plăt′fôrm′) *n. Abbr.* **plat. 1.** Any floor or horizontal surface raised above the level of the adjacent area, such as a stage for public speaking or a landing alongside railroad tracks. **2.** A vestibule at the end of a railway car. **3.** A formal declaration of the principles on which a group, such as a political party, makes its appeal to the public. [Old French *plate-forme,* "flat form" : feminine of *plat,* flat (see **plateau**) + *forme,* FORM.]

platform balance. An equal-arm balance having two flat platforms above the beam and frequently using a sliding rider instead of weights.

platform car. A railroad car having no sides or roof; flatcar.

platform scale. An industrial weighing instrument consisting of a platform coupled to an automatic system of levers and adjustable weights, used to weigh large or heavy objects.

pla·ti·na (plə-tē′nə, plăt′ə-nə) *n. Rare.* Platinum, especially as found naturally. [Spanish, diminutive of *plata,* silver, plate, from Vulgar Latin *plattus* (unattested), flat. See **plateau.**]

plat·ing (plā′tĭng) *n.* **1.** A thin layer or coating of metal, such as gold or silver. **2.** A covering or layer of metal sheets or plates.

pla·tin·ic (plə-tĭn′ĭk) *adj. Chemistry.* Of, pertaining to, or containing platinum, especially with valence 4.

plat·i·nize (plăt′ə-nīz′) *tr.v.* **-nized, -nizing, -nizes.** To electroplate with platinum. [PLATIN(I)- + -IZE.]

platino–, platin–, platini–. Indicates the presence or characteristics of platinum; for example, **platinotype, platinoid.**

plat·i·noid (plăt′ə-noid′) *adj.* Like platinum. —*n.* **1.** An alloy of copper, nickel, tungsten, and zinc, formerly used in electric coils. **2.** Any metal resembling platinum chemically, especially osmium, iridium, or palladium. [PLATIN(O)- + -OID.]

plat·i·no·type (plăt′ə-nō-tīp′) *n.* **1.** A process formerly used for making photographic prints, using a finely precipitated platinum salt and an iron salt in the sensitizing solution to produce photographic prints in platinum black. **2.** A photographic print produced by this process. [PLATINO- + -TYPE.]

plat·i·nous (plăt′ə-nəs) *adj.* Of, pertaining to, or containing platinum, especially with valence 2.

plat·i·num (plăt′ə-nəm) *n.* **1.** *Symbol* **Pt** A silver-white metallic element occurring worldwide, usually mixed with other metals such as iridium, osmium, or nickel. It is ductile and malleable, does not oxidize in air, and is used in electrical components, jewelry, dentistry, electroplating, and as a catalyst. Atomic number 78, atomic weight 195.09, melting point 1769°C, boiling point 3827°C, specific gravity 21.45, valences 1, 2, 3, 4. See **element. 2.** Medium to light gray. See **color.** [New Latin, from Spanish *platina,* PLATINA.]

platinum black. A fine black powder of metallic platinum, used as a catalyst and as a gas absorbent.

platinum blond. 1. A very light silver-blond hair color. **2.** A person having hair of this color. See Usage note at **blond.**

plat·i·tude (plăt′ə-to͞od′, -tyo͞od′) *n.* **1.** A trite remark or statement. **2.** Lack of originality; triteness. —See Synonyms at **cliché.** [French, "flatness," from *plat,* flat, from Old French, from Vulgar Latin *plattus* (unattested), from Greek *platus,* broad, flat. See **plat-** in Appendix.*] —**plat′i·tu′di·nous** *adj.*

plat·i·tu·di·nize (plăt′ə-to͞od′n-īz′, plăt′ə-tyo͞od′-) *intr.v.* **-nized, -nizing, -nizes.** To use platitudes in speaking or writing.

Pla·to (plā′tō). Original name, Aristocles. 427?–347 B.C. Greek philosopher.

Pla·ton·ic (plə-tŏn′ĭk, plā-) *adj.* Also **Pla·ton·i·cal** (plə-tŏn′ĭ-kəl, plā-) (for sense 1). **1.** Of, pertaining to, or characteristic of Plato or his philosophy. **2.** *Often small* **p.** Transcending physical desire and tending toward the purely spiritual or ideal: *platonic love.* **3.** *Sometimes small* **p.** Speculative or theoretical. —**Pla·ton′i·cal·ly** *adv.*

Pla·to·nism (plāt′n-ĭz′əm) *n.* The philosophy of Plato, especially insofar as it asserts the ideal forms as an absolute and eternal reality of which the phenomena of the world are an imperfect and transitory reflection. —**Pla′to·nist** *n.*

pla·toon (plə-to͞on′) *n. Abbr.* **plat. 1.** A subdivision of a military company divided into squads or sections and usually commanded by a lieutenant. **2.** A body of persons working together. **3.** *Football.* A group of players within a team used for offense or defense. [French *peloton,* "little ball," group of soldiers, from Old French *pelote,* from Vulgar Latin *pilotta* (unattested), diminutive of Latin *pila,* ball. See **pill.**]

platoon sergeant. *U.S. Army.* The senior noncommissioned officer in a platoon or comparable unit.

Platt·deutsch (plät′doich′) *n.* The Low German vernacular of northern Germany. [German, from Dutch *platduits* : *plat,* flat, low, clear, from Middle Dutch, from Old French, flat (see **platitude**) + *Duitsch,* German, from Middle Dutch *duutsch* (see **teutā-** in Appendix*).]

Platte (plăt). A river formed by the confluence of the North Platte and South Platte rivers in southwestern Nebraska. It flows 310 miles east to the Missouri below Omaha, Nebraska.

Plat·ten·see. The German name for Lake **Balaton.**

plat·ter (plăt′ər) *n.* **1.** A large, shallow dish or plate, used especially for serving food. **2.** A meal or course served on such a dish. **3.** *Slang.* A phonograph record. [Middle English *plater,* from Norman French, from Old French *plate,* PLATE.]

Platts·burgh (plăts′bûrg′). Also **Platts·burg.** A city in northeastern New York, on Lake Champlain. It was the site of a U.S. naval victory in the War of 1812. Population, 21,000.

plat·y[1] (plā′tē) *adj.* **-ier, -iest.** Designating soil or minerals occuring in flaky layers.

plat·y[2] (plăt′ē) *n., pl.* **platys** or **platies.** Any of several small freshwater fish of the genus *Xiphophorus,* of southern North America; especially, *X. maculatus,* a colorful aquarium fish. Also called "platyfish." [From New Latin *Platypoecilus,* "flat and colorful" (Greek *poikilos,* variegated), from Greek *platus,* broad, flat. See **plat-** in Appendix.*]

platy–. Indicates flatness; for example, **platyhelminth.** [From Greek *platus,* broad, flat. See **plat-** in Appendix.*]

plat·y·hel·minth (plăt′ĭ-hĕl′mĭnth) *n. Zoology.* Any of various parasitic and nonparasitic worms of the phylum Platyhelminthes, such as a tapeworm or a planarian, characteristically having a flattened body. Also called "flatworm." [PLATY- + Greek *helmis* (stem *helminth-*), parasitic worm (see **wel-**[3] in Appendix*).] —**plat′y·hel·min′thic** *adj.*

ă pat/ā pay/âr care/ä father/b bib/ch church/d deed/ĕ pet/ē be/f fife/g gag/h hat/hw which/ĭ pit/ī pie/îr pier/j judge/k kick/l lid, needle/m mum/n no, sudden/ng thing/ŏ pot/ō toe/ô paw, for/oi noise/ou out/o͝o took/o͞o boot/p pop/r roar/s sauce/sh ship, dish/

plat·y·pus (plăt′ĭ-pəs) *n., pl.* **-puses.** A semiaquatic, egg-laying mammal, *Ornithorhynchus anatinus,* of Australia and Tasmania, having a broad, flat tail, webbed feet, and a snout resembling a duck's bill. Also called "duckbill," "duck-billed platypus." [New Latin, from Greek *platupous,* "flat-footed" : PLATY- + *pous,* foot (see **ped-¹** in Appendix*).]

plat·yr·rhine (plăt′ĭ-rīn′) *adj.* Also **plat·yr·rhin·i·an** (plăt′ĭ-rĭn′ē-ən). **1.** *Anthropology.* Having a broad, flat nose. **2.** *Zoology.* Of or designating the New World monkeys, many of which are characterized by widely separated nostrils. —*n.* Also **plat·yr·rhin·i·an.** A platyrrhine person or monkey. [New Latin *Platyrrhina,* "flat-nosed ones," from *platyrrhinus,* flat-nosed, from Greek *platurrhis, platurrhinos* : PLATY- + Greek *rhis* (stem *rhin-*), nose (see **rhino-**).]

plau·dit (plô′dĭt) *n.* An enthusiastic expression of approbation or praise. Usually used in the plural. [Originally "an appeal for applause," from Latin *plaudite,* "applaud ye!" from *plaudere,* to applaud. See **explode.**]

plau·si·ble (plô′zə-bəl) *adj.* **1.** Seemingly or apparently valid, likely, or acceptable: *a plausible excuse.* **2.** Giving a deceptive impression of truth, acceptability, or reliability; specious. [Originally "deserving applause," (hence) acceptable, from Latin *plausibilis,* from *plaudere* (past participle *plausus*), to applaud, acclaim. See **explode.**] —**plau′si·bil′i·ty, plau′si·ble·ness** *n.* —**plau′si·bly** *adv.*

plau·sive (plô′zĭv, -sĭv) *adj.* **1.** Showing or expressing praise or approbation; applauding. **2.** *Obsolete.* Plausible. [From Latin *plaudere,* to applaud. See **plausible.**]

Plau·tus (plô′təs), **Titus Maccius.** 254?–184 B.C. Roman comic playwright.

play (plā) *v.* **played, playing, plays.** —*intr.* **1.** To occupy oneself in amusement, sport, or other recreation. **2. a.** To take part in a game. **b.** To participate in a betting game; to gamble. **3.** To act in jest or sport. **4.** To deal or behave carelessly or indifferently; toy; trifle. Usually followed by *with.* **5.** To make love in a sportive or playful way. **6.** To act or behave in a specified way. Usually followed by an adjective: *play fair.* **7.** To act or perform, especially in a dramatic production. **8.** To perform on a musical instrument. **9.** To emit sound or be sounded in performance: *The band is playing.* **10.** To be performed, as in a theater or on television: Othello *is playing next week.* **11.** To move or seem to move quickly, lightly, or irregularly: *The breeze played on the water.* **12.** To function or operate uninterruptedly; especially, to discharge a steady stream: *The fountains played in the courtyard.* **13.** To move or operate freely within a bounded space, as machine parts do. —*tr.* **1. a.** To perform or act (a role or part) in a dramatic performance. **b.** To assume the role of; act as: *play the villain.* **2.** To put on or perform (a drama or other theatrical work) on or as if on the stage. **3.** To put on or produce a theatrical performance in (a given place): *They played Boston last week.* **4.** To pretend to be; mimic the activities of: *The boys played cowboy.* **5.** To participate in (a game or sport). **6.** To compete against in a game or sport. **7. a.** To occupy or work at (a position) in a game: *He plays first base.* **b.** To employ (a player) in a game or position: *play Russell at first base.* **c.** To use or move (a card, piece, or ball) in a game or sport: *play the queen of hearts.* **8.** To perform or put into effect, especially as a jest or deception: *play a joke on someone.* **9.** To use or manipulate, especially for one's own interests: *He played his two opponents against each other.* **10. a.** To bet or wager. **b.** To make a wager on. **11. a.** To perform on (a musical instrument): *play the guitar.* **b.** To perform (music) on an instrument or instruments. **12.** To cause (a record or phonograph, for example) to emit recorded sounds. **13.** To discharge, set off, or cause to operate in or as if in a continuous stream: *play a hose on a fire.* **14.** To cause to move rapidly, lightly, or irregularly: *play lights over the dance floor.* **15.** *Angling.* To exhaust (a hooked fish) by allowing it to pull on the line. —**play along.** *Informal.* To agree to participate in or cooperate with an activity or plan. —**play at. 1.** To participate in; engage in. **2.** To do or take part in half-heartedly. —**play down.** To minimize the importance of; make little of: *play down one's failings.* —**play down to.** To simplify one's manner or meaning for, especially to win support or favor. —**play into the hands of.** To act or behave so as to give an advantage to (an opponent). —**play on** (or **upon**). To take advantage of (another's attitudes or feelings) for one's own interests: *He played on her sympathies.* —**play out. 1.** To do or play until completed; finish. **2.** To use up; exhaust. —**play up.** *Informal.* To emphasize or publicize: *play up one's conquests.* —**play up to.** *Informal.* **1.** To support (another actor) in a performance. **2.** To curry favor with. —*n.* **1. a.** A literary work written for performance on the stage; drama. **b.** The performance of such a work. **2.** Activity engaged in for enjoyment or recreation. **3.** Fun or jesting: *It was done in play.* **4. a.** The act of carrying on or engaging in a game or sport. **b.** The manner or way of playing a game or sport. **5.** A manner or method of dealing with people generally: *fair play.* **6.** A move or action in a game: *It's your play.* **7.** Participation in betting; gambling. **8.** *Sports.* The condition of a ball, puck, or similar object in active or legitimate use or motion. Used in the phrases *in play* and *out of play.* **9.** Action, motion, or use: *the play of the imagination.* **10.** Quick, often irregular movement or action, especially of light or color: *the play of color on iridescent feathers.* **11.** Movement or space for movement, as of mechanical parts. —**make a play for.** *Informal.* To attempt to attract or obtain by using art, wiles, or skill. [As verb, Middle English *playen,* from Old English *plegan;* as noun, Middle English *pley, play,* Old English *plega.* See **plegan** in Appendix.*] —**play′a·ble** *adj.*

pla·ya (plī′ə) *n.* **1.** The beach or bank of a river. **2.** A nearly level area at the bottom of a desert basin, sometimes temporarily covered with water. [Spanish, "shore," from Medieval Latin *plagia,* from Greek, sides, neuter plural of *plagios,* placed sideways, from *plagos,* side. See **plāk-¹** in Appendix.*]

play-act (plā′ăkt′) *intr.v.* **-acted, -acting, -acts. 1.** To play a role in a dramatic performance. **2.** To play a pretended role; make believe. **3.** To behave in an overdramatic or artificial manner.

play back. A replaying, as of a tape recording.

play·back (plā′băk′) *n.* **1.** The act or process of replaying a newly made record or tape. **2.** A method of or apparatus for reproducing sound recordings.

play·bill (plā′bĭl′) *n.* **1.** A program for a theatrical performance. **2.** A poster announcing a theatrical performance.

play·boy (plā′boi′) *n.* A wealthy, carefree man devoted to the pleasures of nightclubs, sports, and female company.

play-by-play (plā′bī-plā′) *adj.* Consisting of a detailed running commentary or account, as of the action of a sports event.

play·er (plā′ər) *n.* **1.** One who participates in a game or sport. **2.** One who performs in theatrical roles; actor. **3.** One who plays a musical instrument. **4.** The mechanism actuating a player piano. **5.** A phonograph. **6.** A gambler. **7.** A trifler.

player piano. A mechanically operated piano that uses a perforated paper roll to actuate the keys.

play·fel·low (plā′fĕl′ō) *n.* A companion in play; playmate.

play·ful (plā′fəl) *adj.* **1.** Full of fun and good spirits; frolicsome; sportive: *a playful kitten.* **2.** Humorous; jesting: *"He meant to be conversationally playful but his voice had no tone."* (Saul Bellow). —**play′ful·ly** *adv.* —**play′ful·ness** *n.*

Synonyms: *playful, mischievous, impish, waggish, frivolous.* Lighthearted or heedless behavior or remarks are implied by these adjectives. *Playful,* the most general, suggests high spirits, gaiety, and humor in action or speech. *Mischievous* and *impish* often imply harm, usually unintentional, in addition to playfulness, and *impish* also suggests boldness and mockery: *mischievous rumor; impish grin. Waggish* stresses jocularity and good humor, and may imply indelicacy though not offensiveness. *Frivolous* refers to silly, superficial behavior or attitudes.

play·go·er (plā′gō′ər) *n.* One who attends the theater.

play·ground (plā′ground′) *n.* **1.** An outdoor area set aside for recreation and play; especially, one containing seesaws, swings, and the like. **2.** A field or sphere of unrestricted activity: *"Foreign affairs had been T.R.'s personal playground during his Presidency."* (John Dos Passos).

play·house (plā′hous′) *n.* **1.** A theater. **2.** A small house for children to play in. **3.** A child's toy house; doll house.

playing card. A card marked with its rank and suit belonging to any of several decks used in playing various games.

playing field. A field for games such as cricket and soccer.

play·mate (plā′māt′) *n.* A companion in play or recreation.

play off. *Sports.* **1.** To establish the winner of (a tie) by playing an additional game or series of games. **2.** To participate or meet in a play-off.

play-off (plā′ôf′, -ŏf′) *n. Sports.* **1.** A final game or series of games played to break a tie. **2.** A series of games played to determine a championship.

play·pen (plā′pĕn′) *n.* A portable enclosure in which a baby or young child can be left to play.

play·room (plā′ro͞om′, -ro͝om′) *n.* A room designed or set aside for recreation or playing.

play·thing (plā′thĭng′) *n.* **1.** Something to play with; a toy. **2.** One treated as a toy: *a plaything of fate.*

play·wright (plā′rīt′) *n.* One who writes plays; dramatist.

pla·za (plä′zə, plăz′ə) *n.* **1.** A public square or similar open area in a town or city. **2.** A broad paved area for automobiles, such as: **a.** The widened roadway forming the approach to a group of tollbooths on a highway. **b.** A parking or servicing area next to a highway. [Spanish, from Vulgar Latin *plattea* (unattested), variant of Latin *platea,* broad street, courtyard, from Greek *plateia (hodos),* from the feminine of *platus,* broad, flat. See **plat-** in Appendix.*]

plea (plē) *n.* **1.** An appeal or entreaty: *a plea for leniency.* **2.** An excuse; pretext: *"Necessity, the tyrant's plea"* (Milton). **3.** *Law.* **a.** An allegation offered in pleading a case. **b.** In common law, a defendant's establishment of an allegation of fact in answer to the declaration made by the plaintiff. Compare **demurrer. c.** In criminal law, the answer of the accused to a charge or indictment. **d.** In equity law, a special answer depending upon or demonstrating one or more reasons why a suit should be delayed, dismissed, or barred. **e.** An action or suit. [Middle English *plai(d), plee,* a lawsuit, pleading, from Norman French *plai, ple,* variants of Old French *plaid,* legal action, agreement, decree, from Medieval Latin *placitum,* from Latin, "something agreeable," opinion, decision, from the neuter of *placitus,* pleasing, agreeable, from the past participle of *placēre,* to please. See **plāk-¹** in Appendix.*]

pleach (plēch, plăch) *tr.v.* **pleached, pleaching, pleaches.** To plait or interlace (branches or twigs, for example), especially in making a hedge or an arbor. [Middle English *plechen,* from Old North French *plechier,* from Latin *plectere* (past participle *plexus*), to weave, plait. See **plek-** in Appendix.*]

pleached (plēcht, plăcht) *adj.* Bordered or shaded with interlaced branches or vines: *a pleached walk.*

plead (plēd) *v.* **pleaded** or **pled** (plĕd), **pleading, pleads.** —*intr.* **1.** To appeal earnestly; implore; beg. **2.** To argue or offer persuasive reasons for or against something. **3.** To furnish or provide an argument or appeal: *His misfortunes plead for him.* **4.** *Law.* **a.** To put forward a plea of a specific nature in a court of law: *plead guilty.* See Usage note below. **b.** To file an answer

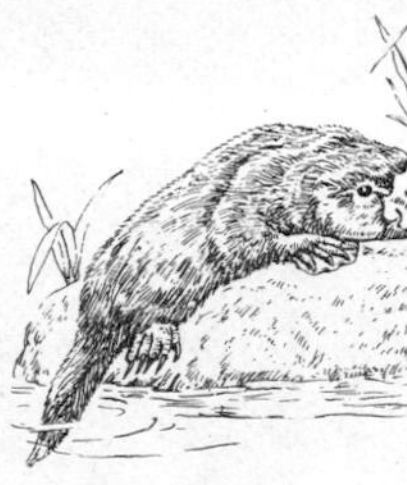

platypus

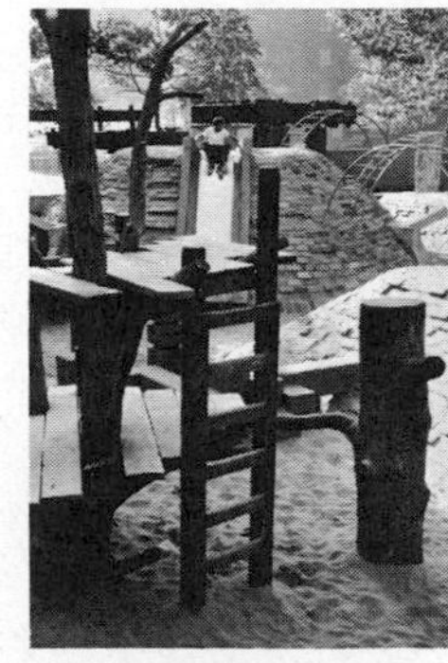

playground
Riis Plaza playground in New York City

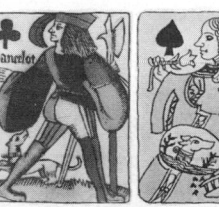

playing card
Left: Eighteenth-century French
Right: Fifteenth-century Provencal

or pleading on behalf of a defendant or as part of the prosecution in a law action. **c.** To address a court as a lawyer or advocate. *—tr.* **1.** To assert or urge as defense, vindication, or excuse; submit as a plea: *plead illness.* **2.** To present as an answer to a charge, indictment, or declaration made against one. **3.** To argue or present (a case) in a court or similar tribunal, or to an authorized person. —See Synonyms at **urge.** [Middle English *pleden, playden,* from Old French *plaidier,* from Medieval Latin *placitāre,* from *placitum,* legal action, PLEA.] **—plead'a·ble** *adj.* **—plead'er** *n.*

Usage: In strict legal usage, one is said to *plead guilty* or *plead not guilty,* but not to *plead innocent.* In nonlegal contexts, however, *plead innocent* is well established.

plead·ing (plē'dĭng) *n.* **1. a.** The act of entreating or making a plea. **b.** A plea or entreaty thus made. **2.** *Law.* **a.** The act or procedure of one who acts as an advocate in a law court. **b.** The act or technique of drawing up or presenting pleas in legal cases. **c.** A formal statement, generally written, propounding the cause of action or the defense of a legal case. **d.** *Plural.* The consecutive statements, allegations, and counter allegations made in turn by plaintiff and defendant, or prosecutor and accused, until a single issue is reached upon which the trial may be held. **—plead'ing·ly** *adv.*

pleas·ance (plĕz'əns) *n.* **1.** A secluded garden or landscaped area. **2.** *Archaic.* Pleasure or a source of pleasure. [Old French *(maison de) plaisance,* "(house of) pleasure," from *plaisant,* PLEASANT.]

pleas·ant (plĕz'ənt) *adj.* **1.** Giving or affording pleasure or enjoyment; agreeable. **2.** Pleasing in manner, appearance, or other personal qualities. **3.** Fair and comfortable: *pleasant weather.* **4.** Merry; lively. —See Synonyms at **amiable.** [Middle English *plesaunt,* from Old French *plaisant,* from the present participle of *plaisir,* to please, from Latin *placēre.* See **plāk-¹** in Appendix.*] **—pleas'ant·ly** *adv.* **—pleas'ant·ness** *n.*

Pleasant Island. The former name for **Nauru.**

pleas·ant·ry (plĕz'ən-trē) *n., pl.* **-ries. 1.** A jesting, entertaining, or humorous remark or action. **2.** Pleasingly humorous style or manner in conversation or social situations. [Old French *plaisanterie,* from *plaisant,* PLEASANT.]

please (plēz) *v.* **pleased, pleasing, pleases.** *—tr.* **1.** To give enjoyment, pleasure, or satisfaction to; make glad or contented. **2.** To be the will or desire of. Used impersonally with *it: May it please the court to admit this gun as evidence.* **3.** To be willing to; be so obliging as to. Used in the imperative to introduce or indicate a politely intended request, or as an exclamation expressing an earnest wish or protest. *—intr.* **1.** To give satisfaction or pleasure; be agreeable. **2.** To have the will or desire; wish: *Do whatever you please.* **—if you please. 1.** If it is your will, desire, or pleasure. **2.** If you can believe or imagine it. Used as an ironical expression of indignation or surprise. [Middle English *plaisen, plesen,* from Old French *plaisir,* from Latin *placēre.* See **plāk-¹** in Appendix.*]

pleas·ing (plē'zĭng) *adj.* Giving pleasure or enjoyment; agreeable; gratifying. **—pleas'ing·ly** *adv.* **—pleas'ing·ness** *n.*

pleas·ur·a·ble (plĕzh'ər-ə-bəl) *adj.* Agreeable; gratifying. **—pleas'ur·a·ble·ness** *n.* **—pleas'ur·a·bly** *adv.*

pleas·ure (plĕzh'ər) *n.* **1.** An enjoyable sensation or emotion; satisfaction; delight. **2.** A source of enjoyment, gratification, or delight: *"My chief pleasure at the time was conversation."* (Susan Sontag). **3.** Amusement, diversion, or worldly enjoyment: *"Pleasure . . . is a safer guide than either right or duty."* (Samuel Butler). **4.** Sensual gratification or indulgence. **5.** One's preference, wish, or choice: *What is your pleasure?* *—v.* **pleasured, -uring, -ures.** *—tr.* To give pleasure or enjoyment to; please; gratify. *—intr.* **1.** To take pleasure; delight. Often used with *in.* **2.** *Informal.* To go in search of pleasure or enjoyment. [Middle English *plesure,* (earlier) *plesir,* from Old French *plaisir,* substantive use of *plaisir,* to PLEASE.]

Synonyms: *pleasure, enjoyment, delight, joy.* These terms denote, with varying force, a state of happiness or personal satisfaction. *Pleasure* is the least forceful. Sometimes, though not invariably, it suggests superficial and transitory emotion resulting from the conscious pursuit of happiness, and sometimes it is merely a form in polite address: *the pleasure of announcing your appointment. Enjoyment* is relatively stronger in its implication of sustained happiness. *Delight* suggests keen, intense, often transitory emotion. *Joy,* also a strong term, implies a more sustained state, and is often associated with sharing, self-realization, and high-mindedness in general.

pleasure principle. *Psychoanalysis.* The tendency to seek immediate gratification of instinctual needs, and to reduce pain. [Translation of German *Lustprinzip.*]

pleat (plēt) *n.* A fold in cloth or other material, made by doubling the material upon itself and then pressing or stitching into place; plait. *—tr.v.* **pleated, pleating, pleats.** To press or arrange in pleats; plait. [Earlier *plete,* variant of PLAIT.]

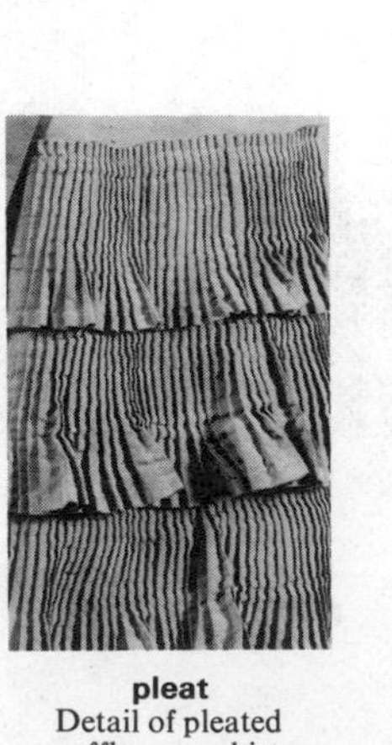

pleat
Detail of pleated ruffles on a skirt

pleat·er (plē'tər) *n.* A sewing-machine attachment that pleats.

pleb (plĕb) *n.* **1.** A commoner; plebeian. **2.** A freshman; plebe. [Short for PLEBEIAN.]

plebe (plēb) *n.* **1.** A freshman at the U.S. Military or Naval Academy. **2.** *Obsolete.* Plebs. [French *plèbe,* "a common," from Latin *plēbs,* common people. See **pel-⁸** in Appendix.*]

ple·be·ian (plĭ-bē'ən) *adj.* **1.** Of or pertaining to the Roman plebs. **2.** Of, belonging to, or characteristic of commoners. **3.** Crude; vulgar; low: *plebeian tastes.* *—n.* **1.** One of the Roman plebs. **2.** A member of the lower classes. **3.** Someone who is vulgar or coarse. [Latin *plēbēius,* from *plēbs,* common people. See **pel-⁸** in Appendix.*] **—ple·be'ian·ism** *n.*

pleb·i·scite (plĕb'ə-sīt', -sĭt) *n.* **1.** A direct vote in which the entire people is invited to accept or refuse the measure, program, or government of the man or party initiating the consultation. **2.** A consultation whereby a population exercises the right of national self-determination. [French *plébiscite,* from Latin *plēbiscītum,* people's decree : *plēbi,* genitive of *plēbs,* common people (see **pel-⁸** in Appendix*) + *scītum,* decree, from *sciscere* (past participle *scītus*), to approve, decree, "to seek to know," from *scīre,* to know (see **skei-** in Appendix*).]

plebs (plĕbz) *n., pl.* **plebes** (plē'bēz'). **1.** The common people of ancient Rome. **2.** The common people; the populace. [Latin *plēbs.* See **pel-⁸** in Appendix.*]

plec·tog·nath (plĕk'tŏg-năth') *n.* Any of various tropical marine fishes of the order Tetraodontiformes (or Plectognathi), which includes the triggerfishes, puffers, trunkfishes, and others. [New Latin *Plectognathi,* "ones having twisted jaws" (from their ankylosed jaws) : Greek *plektos,* past participle of *plekein,* to weave, twist (see **plek-** in Appendix*) + *-gnathi,* plural of *-gnathus,* -GNATHOUS.] **—plec'tog·nath'** *adj.*

plec·trum (plĕk'trəm) *n., pl.* **-trums** or **-tra** (-trə). Also **plec·tron** (plĕk'trŏn'). A small, thin, flexible piece of metal, plastic, bone, or other material, used to pluck the strings of certain musical instruments, such as the guitar or lute. Also called "pick." [Latin, from Greek *plēktron,* from *plēssein* (stem *plek-*), to strike (see **plāk-²** in Appendix*) + *-tron,* instrumental suffix.]

pled. Alternate past tense and past participle of **plead.**

pledge (plĕj) *n.* **1.** A formal promise to do something, as the performance of an obligation or duty, or to refrain from doing something. **2. a.** Something given or held as security to guarantee payment of a debt or fulfillment of an obligation. **b.** The condition of something thus given or held: *put an article in pledge.* **3.** *Law.* **a.** A delivery of goods or personal property as security for a debt or obligation. **b.** The contract by which such delivery is made. **4.** A token or sign: *"Fair pledges of a fruitful tree"* (Herrick: "Blossoms"). **5.** A person who has been accepted for membership in a fraternity or similar organization, and has promised to join, but has not yet been initiated. **6.** The act of drinking to someone; a toast. **—take the pledge.** To make a solemn vow to abstain from drinking alcoholic liquor. *—v.* **pledged, pledging, pledges.** *—tr.* **1.** To offer or guarantee by a solemn promise. **2.** To bind or secure by or as if by a pledge. **3.** To deposit as security; pawn. **4.** To drink a toast to. **5. a.** To promise to join (a fraternity or similar organization). **b.** To accept as a prospective member of such an organization. *—intr.* **1.** To make a solemn promise. **2.** To drink a toast to someone: *"Drink to me only with thine eyes, and I will pledge with mine."* (Jonson). —See Synonyms at **devote.** [Middle English *pleg(g)e,* from Old French *plege,* from Late Latin *plebium,* from *plebere* (unattested), to pledge, probably from Frankish *plegan* (unattested), to guarantee (influenced by Latin *praebēre,* to offer). See **plegan** in Appendix.*]

pledg·ee (plĕj-ē') *n.* **1.** A person to whom something is pledged. **2.** A person with whom something is deposited as a pledge.

pledg·er (plĕj'ər) *n.* One who makes or gives a pledge.

pledg·or (plĕj'ər, plĕj-ôr') *n.* Also **pledge·or.** *Law.* A person who deposits property as a pledge.

-plegia. *Medicine.* Indicates a form of paralysis; for example, **paraplegia.** [New Latin, from Greek *plēgē,* a stroke, blow, from *plēssein* (stem *plēg-*), to strike. See **plāk-²** in Appendix.*]

Ple·iad¹ (plē'əd) *n., pl.* **Pleiades** (plē'ə-dēz'). Also *French* **Plé·iade** (plā-yȧd'). Also **ple·iad.** A group of seven illustrious persons. [French *Pléiade,* the name adopted by Ronsard (1556) to designate himself and his six most eminent companions among the poets of the "brigade," in allusion to a group of Alexandrian poets named after the PLEIADES.]

Plei·ad² (plē'əd). Also **Plei·ade.** One of the **Pleiades** *(see).*

Plei·ad³ (plē'əd). Also **Plei·ade.** *Astronomy.* One of the stars in **Pleiades** *(see).*

Plei·a·des¹ (plē'ə-dēz'). *Greek Mythology.* The seven daughters of Atlas (Maia, Electra, Celaeno, Taygeta, Merope, Alcyone, and Sterope), who were metamorphosed as stars.

Plei·a·des² (plē'ə-dēz') *pl.n. Astronomy.* An open star cluster in the constellation Taurus, consisting of several hundred stars, of which six are visible to the naked eye.

plei·ot·ro·pism (plī-ŏt'rə-pĭz'əm) *n.* Also **plei·ot·ro·py** (plī-ŏt'rə-pē). *Genetics.* The control or determination of more than one characteristic or function by a single gene. [Greek *ple(i)ōn,* more (see **pel-⁸** in Appendix*) + -TROPISM.] **—plei'o·trop'ic** (plī'ə-trŏp'ĭk) *adj.* **—plei'o·trop'i·cal·ly** *adv.*

Pleis·to·cene (plī'stə-sēn') *adj. Geology.* Of, belonging to, or designating the geologic time, rock series, and sedimentary deposits of the earlier of the two epochs of the Quaternary period, characterized by the alternate appearance and recession of northern glaciation and the appearance of the progenitors of man. See **geology.** *—n. Geology.* The Pleistocene epoch or system of deposits. Preceded by *the.* [Greek *pleistos,* most (see **pel-⁸** in Appendix*) + -CENE.]

ple·na·ry (plē'nə-rē, plĕn'ə-) *adj.* **1.** Complete in all aspects or essentials; full; absolute: *a diplomat with plenary powers.* **2.** Fully attended by all qualified members: *a plenary session of the council.* [Late Latin *plēnārius,* from Latin *plēnus,* full. See **pel-⁸** in Appendix.*] **—ple'na·ri·ly** *adv.* **—ple'na·ri·ness** *n.*

plenary indulgence. *Roman Catholic Church.* An indulgence that remits the full temporal punishment incurred by a sinner.

plen·i·po·ten·ti·ar·y (plĕn'ē-pə-tĕn'shē-ĕr'ē, -shə-rē) *adj.* Invested with or conferring full powers. *—n., pl.* **-ies.** A diplomatic agent, such as an ambassador or minister, fully authorized to represent his government. [Medieval Latin *plēnipotentiārius,* from Late Latin *plēnipotens* : Latin *plēnus,* full (see **pel-⁸** in Appendix*) + *potens,* POTENT.]

ă pat/ā pay/âr care/ä father/b bib/ch church/d deed/ĕ pet/ē be/f fife/g gag/h hat/hw which/ĭ pit/ī pie/îr pier/j judge/k kick/l lid, needle/m mum/n no, sudden/ng thing/ŏ pot/ō toe/ô paw, for/oi noise/ou out/ŏŏ took/ōō boot/p pop/r roar/s sauce/sh ship, dish/

plen·i·tude (plĕn′ə-to͞od′, -tyo͞od′) *n.* **1.** Abundance; copiousness. **2.** The condition of being full, ample, or complete. [Middle English, fullness, from Old French, from Latin *plēnitūdō*, from *plēnus*, full. See **pel-**[8] in Appendix.*]

plen·te·ous (plĕn′tē-əs) *adj.* **1.** Abundant; copious. **2.** Producing or yielding in abundance. [Middle English *plenti(v)ous*, from Old French *plentiveus*, from *plentif*, abundant, from *plente(t)*, PLENTY.] **—plen′te·ous·ly** *adv.* **—plen′te·ous·ness** *n.*

plen·ti·ful (plĕn′tĭ-fəl) *adj.* **1.** Existing in great quantity or ample supply. **2.** Providing or producing an abundance: *a plentiful harvest.* **—plen′ti·ful·ly** *adv.* **—plen′ti·ful·ness** *n.*

plen·ty (plĕn′tē) *n.* **1.** A full or completely adequate amount or supply; as much as one could want; sufficiency. **2.** A large quantity or amount; abundance: *goods in plenty.* **3.** A condition of general abundance or prosperity: *"fruitful regions gladdened by plenty and lulled by peace!"* (Samuel Johnson). *—adj.* Plentiful; abundant. Always used predicatively. *—adv. Informal.* Sufficiently; very: *It's plenty hot.* [Middle English *plen-t(i)e, plentet*, from Old French *plente(t)*, from Latin *plēnitās*, from *plēnus*, full. See **pel-**[8] in Appendix.*]

Plenty, Bay of. An inlet of the South Pacific Ocean in the northern part of North Island, New Zealand.

ple·num (plē′nəm, plĕn′əm) *n., pl.* **-nums** or **plena** (plē′nə, plĕn′ə). **1.** In the philosophy of the Stoics, the whole of space regarded as being filled with matter. **2.** An enclosure in which air or other gas is at a pressure greater than that outside the enclosure. **3.** An assembly or meeting with all members present. **4.** Fullness. [Latin, neuter of *plēnus*, full. See **pel-**[8] in Appendix.*] **—ple′num** *adj.*

pleo–. Indicates more; for example, **pleomorphism.** [Greek *pleiōn, pleōn*, more. See **pel-**[8] in Appendix.*]

ple·och·ro·ism (plē-ŏk′rō-ĭz′əm) *n.* The property possessed by some crystals of exhibiting different colors, especially three different colors, when viewed along different axes. Compare **dichroism.** [PLEO- + -CHRO(OUS) + -ISM.] **—ple′o·chro′ic** (plē′ə-krō′ĭk) *adj.*

ple·o·mor·phism (plē′ə-môr′fĭz′əm) *n.* **1.** *Chemistry.* Crystallization in two or more forms, **polymorphism** *(see).* **2.** *Biology.* The occurrence of two or more structural forms during a life cycle, especially of certain plants. [PLEO- + -MORPH + -ISM.] **—ple′o·mor′phic** *adj.*

ple·o·nasm (plē′ə-năz′əm) *n.* **1.** The use of more words than are required to express an idea; redundancy. **2.** An instance of this. **3.** A superfluous word or phrase. [Late Latin *pleonasmus*, from Greek *pleonasmos*, "superabundance," from *pleonazein*, to be more than enough, from *ple(i)ōn*, more. See **pel-**[8] in Appendix.*] **—ple′o·nas′tic** *adj.* **—ple′o·nas′ti·cal·ly** *adv.*

ple·o·pod (plē′ə-pŏd′) *n. Zoology.* An appendage of crustaceans, a **swimmeret** *(see).* [PLEO- + -POD.]

ple·si·o·sau·rus (plē′sē-ə-sôr′əs, plē′zē-) *n., pl.* **-sauri** (-sôr′ī′). Also **ple·si·o·saur** (plē′sē-ə-sôr′, plē′zē-). *Paleontology.* A large marine reptile of the extinct suborder Plesiosauria, common in Europe and North America during the Mesozoic era. [Greek *plēsios*, near (see **pel-**[8] in Appendix*) + -SAURUS.]

ples·sim·e·ter. Variant of **pleximeter.**

ples·sor. *Medicine.* Variant of **plexor.**

pleth·o·ra (plĕth′ər-ə) *n.* **1.** Superabundance; excess. **2.** An excess of blood in the circulatory system or in one organ or area. [Medieval Latin *plēthōra*, from Greek *plēthōra, plēthōrē*, fullness, from *plēthein*, to be full. See **pel-**[8] in Appendix.*]

ple·thor·ic (plĕ-thôr′ĭk, -thŏr′ĭk, plĕth′ə-rĭk) *adj.* **1. a.** Excessive in quantity; superabundant: *"This successful industry of England, with its plethoric wealth"* (Carlyle). **b.** Excessive in style; overburdened; turgid: *plethoric prose.* **2.** Characterized by an overabundance of blood. **—ple·thor′i·cal·ly** *adv.*

pleu·ra (plo͝or′ə) *n., pl.* **pleurae** (plo͝or′ē). *Anatomy.* Either of two membranous sacs, each of which lines one side of the thoracic cavity and envelops the contiguous lung, reducing the friction of respiratory movements to a minimum. [Medieval Latin, from Greek *pleura*†, side, rib.] **—pleu′ral** *adj.*

pleu·ri·sy (plo͝or′ə-sē) *n. Pathology.* Inflammation of the pleura, often characterized when acute by exudation into the pleural cavity and production of adhesions that may become permanent or, if infected, result in empyema. [Middle English *pleresye, pluresy*, from Old French *pleuresie*, from Medieval Latin *pleuresis*, variant of Late Latin *pleurisis*, for Latin *pleurītis*, from Greek *pleuritis*, from *pleura*, side, rib. See **pleura.**] **—pleu·rit′ic** (plo͝o-rĭt′ĭk) *adj.*

pleurisy root. A plant, **butterfly weed** *(see).* [From the use of the root as a remedy for pleurisy.]

pleuro–. Indicates: **1.** The side; for example, **pleurodont.** **2.** The pleura; for example, **pleuropneumonia.** [New Latin, from Greek *pleura*, side, rib. See **pleura.**]

pleu·ro·dont (plo͝or′ə-dŏnt′) *adj. Zoology.* **1.** Having the teeth attached by their sides to the inner side of the jaw, as in some lizards. **2.** Attached in this way: *pleurodont teeth.* *—n.* A lizard with pleurodont teeth. [PLEUR(O)- + -ODONT.]

pleu·ron (plo͝or′ŏn) *n., pl.* **pleura** (plo͝or′ə). *Zoology.* An external, lateral part of the body segments of arthropods. [New Latin, from Greek *pleuron, pleura*, rib, side. See **pleura.**]

pleu·ro·pneu·mo·nia (plo͝or′ō-no͞o-mōn′yə, -nyo͞o-mōn′yə) *n. Pathology.* Pneumonia aggravated by pleurisy.

pleu·rot·o·my (plo͞o-rŏt′ə-mē) *n., pl.* **-mies.** Surgical incision of the pleura. [PLEURO- + -TOMY.]

pleus·ton (plo͞o′stən, -stŏn′) *n.* Plants that float upon the surface of bodies of fresh water. [Greek *pleusis*, sailing, from *plein*, to sail (see **pleu-** in Appendix*) + (PLANK)TON.] **—pleus·ton′ic** (plo͞o-stŏn′ĭk) *adj.*

Ple·ven (plĕv′ən). Also **Plev·na** (plĕv′nə). A city in north-central Bulgaria, taken from the Turks in 1877 after a siege of 143 days. Population, 80,000.

plex·i·form (plĕk′sə-fôrm′) *adj.* Similar to or having the form of a plexus; complicated in structure. [PLEX(US) + -FORM.]

Plex·i·glas (plĕk′sĭ-glăs′, -gläs′) *n.* A trademark for a light, permanently transparent, weather-resistant thermoplastic.

plex·im·e·ter (plĕk-sĭm′ə-tər) *n.* Also **ples·sim·e·ter** (plĕ-sĭm′ə-tər). *Medicine.* A small, thin plate held against the body and struck with a **plexor** *(see).* [PLEX(OR) + -METER.] **—plex′i·met′ric** (plĕk′sə-mĕt′rĭk) *adj.* **—plex·im′e·try** *n.*

plex·or (plĕk′sər) *n.* Also **ples·sor** (plĕs′ər). *Medicine.* A small, rubber-headed hammer used in diagnosis by **percussion** *(see).* [From Greek *plexis*, stroke, from *plēssein*, to strike. See **plāk-**[2] in Appendix.*]

plex·us (plĕk′səs) *n., pl.* **plexus** or **-uses.** **1.** *Anatomy.* A structure in the form of a network, especially of nerves, blood vessels, or lymphatics: *the solar plexus.* **2.** Any interlacing of parts; network. [New Latin, from Latin, network, from *plexus*, past participle of *plectere*, to plait. See **plek-** in Appendix.*]

plf. plaintiff.

pli·a·ble (plī′ə-bəl) *adj.* **1.** Easily bent or shaped; flexible **2. a.** Receptive to change; adaptable. **b.** Easily influenced, persuaded, or swayed; tractable. —See Synonyms at **flexible.** **—pli′a·bil′i·ty, pli′a·ble·ness** *n.* **—pli′a·bly** *adv.*

pli·an·cy (plī′ən-sē) *n.* The quality or condition of being pliant or flexible.

pli·ant (plī′ənt) *adj.* **1.** Easily bent or flexed; supple; limber. **2.** Easily altered or modified to fit conditions; adaptable. **3.** Yielding readily to influence or domination; docile; compliant. —See Synonyms at **flexible.** [Middle English *plyante*, from Old French *pliant*, present participle of *plier*, to bend, fold, from Latin *plicāre*, to fold. See **plek-** in Appendix.*] **—pli′ant·ly** *adv.* **—pli′ant·ness** *n.*

pli·ca (plī′kə) *n., pl.* **plicae** (plī′sē′). **1.** *Zoology.* A fold or ridge as of skin, membrane, or shell. **2.** *Pathology.* A matted and encrusted state of the hair, resulting from uncleanliness and vermin. [Medieval Latin, a fold, plait, from Latin *plicāre*, to fold. See **plek-** in Appendix.*] **—pli′cal** (plī′kəl) *adj.*

pli·cate (plī′kat′) *adj.* Also **pli·cat·ed** (plī′kā′tĭd). Arranged in folds like those of a fan; pleated. [Latin *plicātus*, past participle of *plicāre*, to fold. See **plek-** in Appendix.*] **—pli′cate′ly** *adv.* **—pli′cate′ness** *n.*

pli·ca·tion (plī-kā′shən) *n.* Also **plic·a·ture** (plĭk′ə-cho͝or′). **1. a.** The act or process of folding. **b.** The state of being folded. **2.** A fold.

pli·er (plī′ər) *n.* One who plies (a trade).

pli·ers (plī′ərz) *pl.n.* Any of variously shaped tools having a pair of pivoted jaws, used for holding, bending, or cutting.

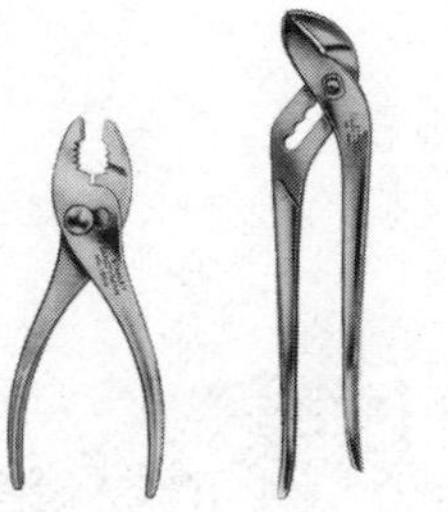
slip-joint
pump-type

pliers

plight[1] (plīt) *n.* A condition or situation of difficulty or adversity: *"Paul arrived . . . in sorry plight . . . nervously shaken and half blind."* (C.H. Dodd). See Synonyms at **predicament.** [Middle English *plit*, from Norman French, variant of Old French *pleit, ploit*, "a fold," from Vulgar Latin *plicitum* (unattested), from Latin *plicitus*, past participle of *plicāre*, to fold. See **plek-** in Appendix.*]

plight[2] (plīt) *tr.v.* **plighted, plighting, plights.** **1.** To promise or bind by a solemn pledge; especially, to betroth. **2.** To give or pledge (one's word or oath, for example). **—plight one's troth.** **1.** To become engaged to marry. **2.** To give one's solemn oath. *—n.* A solemn pledge, as of faith; engagement. [Middle English *plighten*, Old English *plihtan*, to imperil, compromise, from *pliht*, peril. See **plegan** in Appendix.*] **—plight′er** *n.*

plim·soll (plĭm′səl, -sôl′) *n.* Also **plim·sol, plim·sole** (plĭm′sōl′). *British.* A rubber-soled cloth shoe; sneaker. [Probably because its mudguard resembles a PLIMSOLL MARK.]

Plimsoll mark. One of a set of lines on the hull of a merchant ship to indicate the depth to which it may be legally loaded under specified conditions. Also called "load line," "Plimsoll line." [After Samuel *Plimsoll* (1824–1898), English Member of Parliament who caused it to be adopted.]

plinth (plĭnth) *n. Architecture.* **1.** A block or slab upon which a pedestal, column, or statue is placed. **2.** The base block at the intersection of the horizontal baseboard and vertical trim around an opening. **3.** A continuous course of stones supporting a wall. Also called "plinth course." **4.** A square base as of a vase. [French *plinthe*, from Latin *plinthus*, from Greek *plinthos*†, brick, square stone block.]

Plin·y[1] (plĭn′ē). Latin, Gaius Plinius Secundus. Called "the Elder." A.D. 23–79. Roman scholar; author of the *Historia Naturalis;* uncle of Pliny the Younger.

Plin·y[2] (plĭn′ē). Latin, Gaius Plinius Caecilius Secundus. Called "the Younger." A.D. 62–113. Roman consul and orator; author of the *Letters;* nephew of Pliny the Elder.

Pli·o·cene (plī′ə-sēn′) *adj. Geology.* Of, belonging to, or designating the geologic time, rock series, and sedimentary deposits of the last of the five epochs of the Tertiary period, characterized by the appearance of distinctly modern plants and animals. See **geology.** *—n. Geology.* The Pliocene epoch or system of deposits. Preceded by *the.* [Literally "more recent" : Greek *pleiōn*, more (see **pel-**[8] in Appendix*) + -CENE.] **—Pli′o·cen′ic** (plī′ə-sĕn′ĭk, -sē′nĭk) *adj.*

Pli·o·film (plī′ə-fĭlm′) *n.* A trademark for a pliant, transparent rubber compound used for raincoats, umbrellas, and other waterproof items. [PLI(ABLE) + FILM.]

plis·sé (plĭ-sā′) *n.* Also **plis·se.** **1.** A puckered texture of cloth created by treating fabric with a caustic soda. **2.** Fabric having such a texture. [French, "creased," "crumpled," from Old French *plisser*, to fold, pleat, from *pli*, a fold, from *plier*, to bend, fold, from Latin *plicāre*. See **plek-** in Appendix.*]

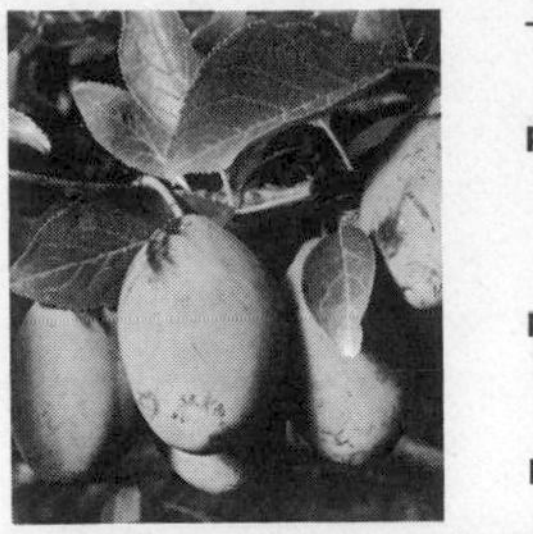

plum[1]

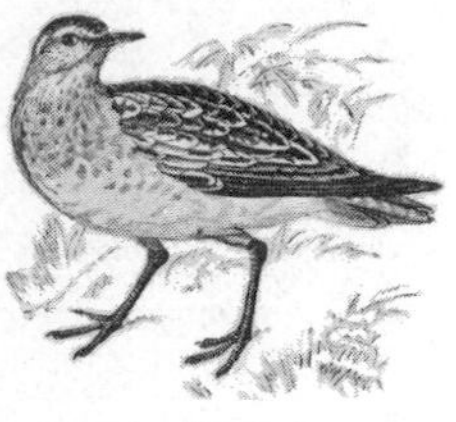

plover
Pluvialis apricaria
In winter plumage

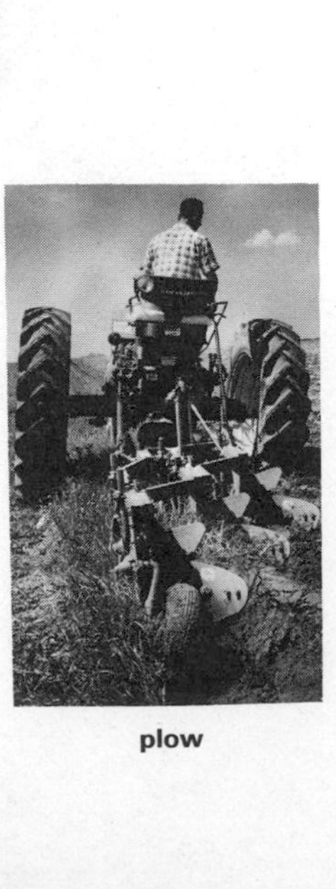

plow

plod (plŏd) *v.* **plodded, plodding, plods.** —*intr.* **1.** To move or walk heavily or laboriously; trudge: *"donkeys that plodded wearily in a circle round a gin"* (D.H. Lawrence). **2.** To work or act perseveringly or monotonously; drudge. Used with *at, on,* or *upon.* —*tr.* To trudge heavily and slowly along or over. —*n.* **1.** The act of moving or walking heavily and slowly. **2.** The sound made by a heavy step. [Imitative.] —**plod′ding·ly** *adv.*

plod·der (plŏd′ər) *n.* One who works or moves laboriously.

Plo·eș·ti (plô-yĕsht′). A city of south-central Rumania, northwest of Bucharest. Population, 134,000.

-ploid. *Biology.* Indicates a specific multiple of a set of chromosomes; for example, **polyploid.** [Greek *-ploos,* -fold (see **pel-**[3] in Appendix*) + -OID.]

plop (plŏp) *v.* **plopped, plopping, plops.** —*intr.* **1.** To fall with a sound like that of an object falling into water without splashing. **2.** To drop or sink heavily: *plop into a chair.* —*tr.* To drop or move so as to make such a sound. —*n.* A plopping sound or movement. [Imitative.] —**plop** *adv.*

plo·sion (plō′zhən) *n. Phonetics.* **1.** The articulation of a plosive sound. **2.** The sudden release of breath in the articulation of a plosive. Also called "explosion." Compare **implosion.** [From EXPLOSION.]

plo·sive (plō′sĭv, -zĭv) *adj. Phonetics.* Designating a speech sound whose articulation requires, at some stage, the complete closure of the oral passage, as in the sound of (p) in *top* or (d) in *adorn.* —*n. Phonetics.* A plosive speech sound. Also called "explosive." [French, from *explosif,* EXPLOSIVE.]

plot (plŏt) *n.* **1. a.** A small piece of ground, generally used for a specific purpose. **b.** A measured area of land; lot. **2.** A ground plan, as for a building; chart; diagram. **3.** The series of events consisting of an outline of the action of a narrative or drama. **4.** A secret plan to accomplish a hostile or illegal purpose; scheme. —See Synonyms at **conspiracy.** —*v.* **plotted, plotting, plots.** —*tr.* **1.** To represent graphically, as on a chart: *plot a ship's course.* **2.** To form a plot for; prearrange secretly or deviously: *plot an assassination.* **3.** To conceive and arrange the action and incidents of: *"I began plotting novels at about the time I learned to read."* (James Baldwin). **4.** *Mathematics.* **a.** To locate (points or other figures) on a graph by means of coordinates. **b.** To draw (a curve) connecting points on a graph. —*intr.* To devise secretly; conspire. [In the sense of "a piece of ground" (and hence the extended senses "plan," "diagram"), Middle English *plot(te),* Old English *plot*†. In the sense of "secret plan," from *complot,* from Old French *complote*†.] —**plot′ter** *n.*

Plo·ti·nus (plō-tī′nəs). A.D. 205?–270? Egyptian-born Roman Neo-Platonist philosopher.

plough. *Chiefly British.* Variant of **plow.**

Plov·div (plôv′dĭf). The principal city of southern Bulgaria, on the Maritsa River. Population, 206,000.

plov·er (plŭv′ər, plō′vər) *n., pl.* **-ers** or **plover. 1.** Any of various widely distributed wading birds of the family Charadriidae, having rounded bodies, short tails, and short bills. **2.** Any of various similar or related birds. [Middle English, from Old French *plover, plovier,* from Vulgar Latin *pluviārius, ploviārius* (unattested), "rain-bird" (reason for naming obscure), from Latin *pluvia,* rain, from feminine of *pluvius,* rainy, from *pluere,* to rain. See **pleu-** in Appendix.*]

plow (plou) *n.* Also *chiefly British* **plough. 1.** A farm implement consisting of a heavy blade at the end of a beam, usually hitched to a draft team or motor vehicle, and used for breaking up soil and cutting furrows in preparation for sowing **2.** Any implement of similar function, as a snowplow. **3.** *Capital* **P.** *Astronomy.* The **Big Dipper** *(see).* —*v.* **plowed, plowing, plows.** Also *chiefly British* **plough.** —*tr.* **1.** To break and turn over (earth) with a plow. **2. a.** To form (a furrow, for example) with a plow. **b.** To make or form with driving force: *plowed his way through the crowd.* **3.** To make furrows or indentations in. **4.** To cut through (water): *plow the high seas.* —*intr.* **1.** To break and turn up earth with a plow. **2.** To admit of being plowed: *Rocky earth plows poorly.* **3.** To move or progress in the manner of a plow. Usually used with *through.* **4.** To proceed laboriously; plod. —**plow back.** To reinvest (earnings or profits) in one's business. —**plow into.** *Informal.* **1.** To strike with force. **2.** To undertake (a task, for example) with eagerness and vigor. [Middle English *plou, plogh,* Old English *plōg, plōh,* plowland, probably from late Germanic *plogaz, plogwaz* (unattested), of non-Indo-European origin.] —**plow′er** *n.*

plow·boy (plou′boi′) *n.* **1.** A boy who leads or guides a team of animals in plowing. **2.** A country boy.

plow·head (plou′hĕd′) *n.* The metal shackle at the leading end of the beam of a plow, used to attach the plow to a tractor or draft animal; the clevis of a plow.

plow·land (plou′lănd′) *n.* **1.** In medieval England, a unit of land area roughly equivalent to the area capable of being plowed by a team of eight oxen in a single year. **2.** Land under cultivation or suitable for cultivation.

plow·man (plou′mən) *n., pl.* **-men** (-mĭn). **1.** A person who plows. **2.** A farmer or rustic.

plow·share (plou′shâr′) *n.* The cutting blade of a plow; a share.

ploy (ploi) *n.* A stratagem or artifice, as in a conversation or game, to obtain an advantage over one's opponent. [Scottish, business, trick, escapade, short for EMPLOY (noun).]

plu. plural.

pluck (plŭk) *v.* **plucked, plucking, plucks.** —*tr.* **1.** To detach by grasping and pulling abruptly with the fingers; pick: *pluck a flower.* **2.** To pull out the hair or feathers of: *pluck a chicken.* **3.** To give an abrupt pull to; tug at: *pluck a sleeve.* **4.** *Music.* To sound (the strings of an instrument) by pulling and releasing them with the fingers or a plectrum. **5.** *Slang.* To rob or swindle. —*intr.* To give an abrupt pull; tug. —*n.* **1.** The act of plucking; a tug; snatch. **2.** Resourceful courage and daring in the face of difficulties; spirit. **3.** The heart, liver, windpipe, and lungs of a slaughtered animal. [Middle English *plukken,* Old English *pluccian,* from West Germanic *plukkōn* (unattested), from Vulgar Latin *piluccāre* (unattested), to remove the hair, pluck, irregularly from *pilus,* hair. See **pilo-** in Appendix.*] —**pluck′er** *n.*

pluck·y (plŭk′ē) *adj.* **-ier, -iest.** Having or showing courage or spirited resourcefulness in trying circumstances. See Synonyms at **brave.** —**pluck′i·ly** *adv.* —**pluck′i·ness** *n.*

plug (plŭg) *n.* **1.** An object, such as a cork or wad of cloth, used to stop a hole or gap. **2.** *Electricity.* **a.** A fitting, commonly with two metal prongs for insertion in a fixed socket, used to connect an appliance to a power supply. **b.** A **spark plug** *(see).* **3.** A **fireplug** *(see).* **4. a.** A flat cake of pressed or twisted tobacco. **b.** A portion of chewing tobacco. **5.** *Geology.* A mass of igneous rock filling the opening, or vent, of a volcano. **6.** *Informal.* A favorable public mention of a commercial product, business, or the like, especially when spoken over television or radio. **7.** *Slang.* Anything inferior, useless, or defective; especially, an old, worn-out horse. **8.** *Slang.* A gunshot or bullet: *a plug in the back.* **9.** *Slang.* A **plug hat** *(see).* —*v.* **plugged, plugging, plugs.** —*tr.* **1.** To fill (a hole) tightly with or as with a plug or stopper; stop up. **2.** To use as a plug: *plugged a cork in a bottle.* **3.** To connect (an electrical appliance) to a socket. Used with *in.* **4.** *Slang.* **a.** To hit with a bullet; shoot. **b.** To hit with the fist; punch. **5.** *Informal.* **a.** To make favorable public mention of (a product or business). **b.** To publicize (a song, for example) by constant repetition. —*intr.* **1.** To function by being connected to an electrical outlet. Used with *in.* **2.** *Informal.* To work doggedly and persistently at some activity: *"You may plug along fifty years before you get anywhere."* (Saul Bellow). **3.** *Informal.* To work for a particular cause or person: *plug for a promotion.* **4.** *Slang.* To fire bullets. [Middle Dutch *plugge,* akin to Middle Low German *pluck,* Old High German *pfloc,* Swedish *plugg* (possibly imitative).] —**plug′ger** *n.*

plug hat. *Slang.* A man's high silk hat. Also called "plug." [Probably because the head fits into it like a plug.]

plug-ug·ly (plŭg′ŭg′lē) *n., pl.* **-lies.** *Slang.* A gangster or ruffian. [After the *plug-ugly* gangs in 19th-century New York, whose members wore PLUG HAT(S).]

plum[1] (plŭm) *n.* **1.** Any of several shrubs or small trees of the genus *Prunus,* bearing smooth-skinned, fleshy, edible fruit with a single hard-shelled seed. **2.** The fruit of any of these trees. **3. a.** Any of several trees bearing plumlike fruit. **b.** The fruit of such a tree. **4.** A raisin, when added to a pudding or cake. **5.** A **sugarplum** *(see).* **6.** Dark purple to deep reddish purple. See **color. 7.** Something especially desirable, as a good position. [Middle English *plum(me), plowme,* Old English *plūme,* from West Germanic, from Latin *prūnum.* See **prune.**]

plum[2]. *Informal.* Variant of **plumb.**

plum·age (plo͞o′mĭj) *n.* **1.** The feathers of a bird. **2.** Feathers used ornamentally. **3.** Elaborate dress; finery. [Middle English, from Old French, from *plume,* PLUME.]

plu·mate (plo͞o′māt′) *adj.* Resembling a plume or feather. [Latin *plūmātus,* feathered, from *plūma,* a feather. See **pleus-** in Appendix.*]

plumb (plŭm) *n.* **1.** A weight suspended from the end of a line, used to determine water depth. **2.** Such a device used to establish a true vertical. —**out of** (or **off**) **plumb.** Not vertical. —*adj.* Also **plum** (for sense 2). **1.** Exactly vertical. **2.** *Informal.* Utter; absolute; sheer: *a plumb fool.* —See Synonyms at **vertical.** —*adv.* Also **plum** (for sense 2). **1.** In a vertical or perpendicular line. **2.** *Informal.* Utterly; completely; entirely: *plumb tired.* —*v.* **plumbed, plumbing, plumbs.** —*tr.* **1.** To test the alignment or angle of with a plumb. **2.** To straighten or make perpendicular. Usually used with *up.* **3.** To determine the depth of; sound. **4.** To examine closely; probe into: *"shallow ideas are plumbed and discarded"* (Gilbert Highet). **5.** To seal with lead. —*intr.* To work as a plumber. [Middle English *plumbe, plombe,* from Old French *plombe,* from Latin *plumbum,* lead. See **plumbum** in Appendix.*] —**plumb′a·ble** *adj.*

plum·ba·go (plŭm-bā′gō) *n., pl.* **-gos. 1.** Graphite. **2.** Any plant of the genus *Plumbago,* a **leadwort** *(see).* [Latin *plumbāgō,* lead ore, leadwort, from *plumbum,* lead. See **plumbum** in Appendix.*]

plumb bob. A usually conical piece of metal attached to the end of a plumb line. Also called "plummet."

plumb·er (plŭm′ər) *n.* A workman who installs and repairs pipes and plumbing. [Middle English *plummer,* from Old French *plommier,* from Late Latin *plumbārius,* lead worker, from Latin *plumbum,* lead. See **plumbum** in Appendix.*]

plumber's helper. A device having a large suction cup at the end of a handle, used to clear drains.

plumber's snake. A plumber's tool, a **snake** *(see).*

plumb·er·y (plŭm′ə-rē) *n., pl.* **-ies. 1.** A plumber's workshop or place of business. **2.** A plumber's work; plumbing.

plumb·ing (plŭm′ĭng) *n.* **1.** The pipes, fixtures, and other apparatus of a water, gas, or sewage system. **2.** The work or trade of a plumber. **3.** The act of using a plumb line.

plum·bism (plŭm′bĭz′əm) *n.* Chronic lead poisoning. [From Latin *plumbum,* lead. See **plumbum** in Appendix.*]

plumb line. 1. A line from which a weight is suspended to determine verticality or depth. **2.** A line regarded as directed exactly toward the earth's center of gravity.

plumb rule. A narrow strip of wood with a plumb line and bob attached, used to test verticality, as of walls.

plum duff. A flour pudding with raisins or currants, boiled in a cloth bag.
plume (plo͞om) *n.* **1.** A feather, especially one that is large and ornamental. **2.** A large feather or cluster of feathers worn as an ornament or symbol of rank, as on a helmet. **3.** A token of honor or achievement. **4.** A featherlike structure, form, or object: *a plume of smoke.* —*tr.v.* **plumed, pluming, plumes.** **1.** To decorate, cover, or supply with or as with plumes. **2.** To smooth (its feathers); preen. Said of a bird. **3.** To pride or congratulate (oneself). Used with *on* or *upon.* [Middle English, from Old French, from Latin *plūma.* See **pleus-** in Appendix.*]
plume·let (plo͞om′lĭt) *n.* A small plume.
plum·met (plŭm′ĭt) *n.* **1.** A **plumb bob** *(see).* **2.** Anything that weighs down or oppresses. —*intr.v.* **plummeted, -meting, -mets.** To drop straight down; plunge. [Middle English *plomet,* from Old French *plombet,* ball of lead, diminutive of *plomb,* lead, from Latin *plumbum.* See **plumbum** in Appendix.*]
plu·mose (plo͞o′mōs′) *adj.* **1.** Having plumes or feathers; feathered. **2.** Resembling a feather or plume; feathery. [Latin *plūmōsus,* from *plūma,* a feather. See **pleus-** in Appendix.*] —**plu′mose′ly** *adv.* —**plu·mos′i·ty** (plo͞o-mŏs′ə-tē) *n.*
plump[1] (plŭmp) *adj.* **plumper, plumpest.** **1.** Well-rounded and full in form; chubby. **2.** Abundant; ample: *a plump reward.* —See Synonyms at **fat.** —*v.* **plumped, plumping, plumps.** —*tr.* To make chubby or well-rounded. Often used with *up* or *out: plump up a pillow.* —*intr.* To become rounded or chubby. Often used with *up* or *out.* [Middle Low German *plomp, plump,* thick, blunt, dull, probably akin to *plumpen,* to PLUMP.] —**plump′ly** *adv.* —**plump′ness** *n.*
plump[2] (plŭmp) *v.* **plumped, plumping, plumps.** —*intr.* **1.** To drop abruptly or heavily: *plump into a chair.* **2.** To come or go abruptly or hurriedly. Used with *in* or *out.* **3.** To give full support or praise. Used with *for.* —*tr.* To drop or throw down heavily or abruptly: *plump an ice cube into a glass.* —*n.* **1.** A heavy or abrupt fall or collision. **2.** The sound of this. —*adj.* Blunt; direct. —*adv.* **1.** With a heavy or abrupt impact. **2.** Straight down. **3.** Without qualification; bluntly. [Middle Low German *plumpen,* to fall or plunge into water (probably imitative).]
plum pudding. A rich boiled or steamed pudding made with flour, suet, raisins, currants, citron, and spices.
plum tomato. A form of the **cherry tomato** *(see),* having somewhat oblong fruit.
plu·mule (plo͞om′yo͞ol) *n.* **1.** *Ornithology.* A down feather. **2.** *Botany.* The rudimentary bud of a plant embryo. [Latin *plūmula,* diminutive of *plūma,* feather. See **pleus-** in Appendix.*]
plum·y (plo͞o′mē) *adj.* **1.** Consisting of or covered with feathers. **2.** Resembling a feather or plume.
plun·der (plŭn′dər) *v.* **-dered, -dering, -ders.** —*tr.* **1.** To rob of goods by force, especially in time of war; pillage; loot. **2.** To seize wrongfully or by force; steal. —*intr.* To take booty; rob; pillage. —See Synonyms at **rob.** —*n.* **1.** Property stolen by fraud or force; booty. **2.** The act or practice of plundering. [Middle Dutch *plunderen* or Frisian *plunderje,* "to rob (of household goods)," akin to Middle Dutch *plunde, plunne*†, household goods, clothes.] —**plun′der·a·ble** *adj.* —**plun′der·er** *n.* —**plun′der·ous** *adj.*
plun·der·age (plŭn′dər-ĭj) *n.* **1.** Robbery. **2.** *Maritime Law.* **a.** The embezzling of goods on board a ship. **b.** The goods so acquired.
plunge (plŭnj) *v.* **plunged, plunging, plunges.** —*tr.* **1.** To thrust or throw forcefully into a substance or place: *"Plunge the lobsters head first into a large pot of boiling salted water"* (Craig Claiborne). **2.** To cast suddenly or violently into a given state or situation: *"the street was plunged in cool shadow"* (Richard Wright). —*intr.* **1.** To throw oneself into a substance or place. **2.** To throw oneself earnestly or wholeheartedly into a given state or activity. **3.** To enter violently or speedily. **4.** To descend steeply; fall precipitously, as a road or cliff. **5.** To move forward and downward violently. **6.** *Informal.* To speculate or gamble extravagantly. —*n.* **1.** An act or instance of plunging. **2. a.** A place or area for diving or plunging, as a swimming pool. **b.** A swim; dip. [Middle English *plungen, plongen,* from Old French *plonger, plongier,* from Vulgar Latin *plumbicāre* (unattested), to sound with a plumb, from Latin *plumbum,* lead. See **plumbum** in Appendix.*]
plung·er (plŭn′jər) *n.* **1.** One that plunges. **2.** *Machinery.* A part that operates with a repeated thrusting or plunging movement, such as a piston. **3.** A device consisting of a rubber suction cup attached to the end of a stick, used to clean out clogged drains and pipes.
plunk (plŭngk) *v.* **plunked, plunking, plunks.** *Informal.* —*tr.* **1.** To strum or pluck (the strings of a musical instrument). **2.** To throw or place heavily or abruptly. Used with *down: plunk one's money down.* —*intr.* **1.** To emit a hollow, twanging sound. **2.** To drop or fall abruptly or heavily; plump. —*n. Informal.* **1.** A short, hollow, twanging sound. **2.** A heavy blow or stroke. —*adv. Informal.* **1.** With a short, hollow thud. **2.** Exactly; precisely: *The dart landed plunk in the center of the target.* [Imitative.] —**plunk′er** *n.*
plu·per·fect (plo͞o-pûr′fĭkt) *adj. Abbr.* **plup., plupf.** *Grammar.* Of or designating a verb tense used to express action completed prior to a specified or implied past time. —*n.* **1.** The pluperfect tense, formed in English with the past participle of a verb and one or more auxiliaries; for example, in the sentence *He had been gone an hour when we arrived, had been gone* is in the pluperfect. **2.** A verb or form in this tense. Also called "past perfect." [New Latin *plūsperfectum,* contracted from Latin *(tempus praeteritum) plūs quam perfectum,* "(past tense) more than perfect" (translation of Greek *khronos hupersuntelikos*) : Latin *plūs,* more (see **pel-**[8] in Appendix*) + *quam,* than + *perfectus,* PERFECT (tense).]
plu·ral (plo͝or′əl) *adj. Abbr.* **pl., plu., plur.** **1.** Of or composed of more than one member, set, or kind. **2.** Of or relating to a grammatical form that designates more than one of the things specified. Compare **dual, singular.** —*n. Grammar.* **1.** The plural number or form. **2.** A word or term in this form. —See Usage note below. [Middle English *plurel, plural,* from Old French *plurel,* from Latin *plūrālis,* from *plūs* (stem *plūr-*), more. See **pel-**[8] in Appendix.*] —**plu′ral·ly** *adv.*
Usage: Terms made up of single letters or numbers, or groups of letters or numbers, are made plural by the addition of *'s* or *s,* as *two R's* (or *Rs*), *two 6's* (or *6s*), *GI's* (or *GIs*), *the 1930's* (or *1930s*). The *'s* form is usually used for lower-case letters: *two t's.* Plurals of surnames of one syllable ending in *s* are formed by adding *es: Joneses.* Plurals of given names ending in *y* preceded by a consonant are formed by adding *s: the three Marys.*
plu·ral·ism (plo͝or′ə-lĭz′əm) *n.* **1.** The condition of being plural. **2.** A condition of society in which numerous distinct ethnic, religious, or cultural groups coexist within one nation. **3.** The holding by one person of more than one position or office, especially two or more ecclesiastical benefices, at the same time. **4.** *Philosophy.* **a.** The doctrine that reality is composed of many ultimate substances. **b.** The belief that no single explanatory system or view of reality can account for all the phenomena of life. Compare **monism, dualism.**
plu·ral·ist (plo͝or′ə-lĭst) *n.* **1.** A person who holds more than one office, especially two or more ecclesiastical benefices, at the same time. **2.** One who adheres to philosophical pluralism. —**plu′ral·is′tic** *adj.*
plu·ral·i·ty (plo͝o-răl′ə-tē) *n., pl.* **-ties.** *Abbr.* **plur.** **1.** The state or fact of being plural. **2.** A large number or amount; multitude: *"man burst forth with a plurality of tools and art"* (Edmund Carpenter). **3.** *Ecclesiastical.* **a.** Pluralism. **b.** The offices or benefices held by a pluralist. **4. a.** In a contest of more than two alternatives, the number of votes cast for the winning alternative, if this number is not more than one half of the total votes cast. **b.** The number by which the vote of a winning candidate exceeds that of his closest opponent. Compare **majority.** **5.** The larger or greater part of anything.
plu·ral·ize (plo͝or′ə-līz′) *v.* **-ized, -izing, -izes.** —*tr.* **1.** To make plural. **2.** To express in the plural. —*intr.* **1.** To become plural. **2.** To hold more than one position or ecclesiastical benefice at one time. —**plu′ral·i·za′tion** *n.*
plus (plŭs) *prep.* **1.** Added to. See Usage note below. **2.** Increased by; along with: *earnings plus dividends.* —*adj.* **1. a.** Involving or pertaining to addition. **b.** Positive, as on a scale. **2.** Added or extra: *a plus benefit.* **3.** *Informal.* Increased to a further degree: *personality plus.* **4.** Slightly more than: *a grade of C plus.* **5.** *Electricity.* Positive. —*n.* **1.** The plus sign (+). **2.** A positive quantity. **3.** A favorable factor: *The clear weather was a plus for the golf tournament.* [Latin *plūs,* more. See **pel-**[8] in Appendix.*]
Usage: *Plus,* as a preposition, does not have the conjunctive force of *and.* Consequently, a verb that follows it may be singular or plural, depending on the number of the subject: *Two* (construed as singular) *plus two equals four. Their strength* (singular) *plus their spirit makes them formidable. Our resources* (plural) *plus our determination have saved the day.*
plus fours. Loose knickerbockers bagging below the knees, worn for sports.
plush (plŭsh) *n.* A fabric of silk, rayon, cotton, or other material, having a thick, deep pile. —*adj.* **1.** Made of or covered with plush. **2.** *Informal.* Luxurious. [Old French *p(e)luche,* from *peluch(i)er,* to pluck, from Vulgar Latin *pilūccāre* (unattested), "to remove the hair," irregularly from *pilus,* hair. See **pilo-** in Appendix.*] —**plush′ly** *adv.*
plush·y (plŭsh′ē) *adj.* **-ier, -iest.** **1.** Resembling plush in texture. **2.** *Informal.* Ostentatiously luxurious: *a plushy office.* —**plush′i·ly** *adv.* —**plush′i·ness** *n.*
plus sign. *Mathematics.* The symbol (+), as in *2 + 2 = 4,* used to indicate addition or a positive quantity. Compare **minus sign.**
Plu·tarch (plo͞o′tärk′). A.D. 46?–120? Greek biographer and philosopher; author of the *Parallel Lives.*
Plu·to[1] (plo͞o′tō). *Roman Mythology.* The god of the dead and the ruler of the underworld, identified with the Greek god Hades. [Latin, from Greek *Ploutōn,* "the rich one," from *ploutos,* wealth. See **pleu-** in Appendix.*]
Plu·to[2] (plo͞o′tō) *n. Astronomy.* The ninth and farthest planet from the sun, having a sidereal period of revolution about the sun of 248.4 years, 2.8 billion miles distant at perihelion and 4.6 billion miles at aphelion, and a diameter approximately half that of the earth. See **solar system.** [After PLUTO (god).]
plu·toc·ra·cy (plo͞o-tŏk′rə-sē) *n., pl.* **-cies.** **1.** Government by the wealthy. **2.** A wealthy class that controls a government. **3.** A government or state in which the wealthy rule. [Greek *ploutokratia* : *ploutos,* wealth (see **pleu** in Appendix*) + -CRACY.]
plu·to·crat (plo͞o′tə-krăt′) *n.* **1.** A member of a governing wealthy class. **2.** Anyone having political influence or control because of wealth. [From PLUTOCRACY.]
plu·to·crat·ic (plo͞o′tə-krăt′ĭk) *adj.* Also **plu·to·crat·i·cal** (-ĭ-kəl). Of, pertaining to, or resembling a plutocrat or plutocracy. —**plu′to·crat′i·cal·ly** *adv.*
plu·ton (plo͞o′tŏn′) *n.* Igneous rock formed beneath the surface of the earth by consolidation of magma. [Probably back-formation from PLUTONIC.]
Plu·to·ni·an (plo͞o-tō′nē-ən) *adj.* Also **Plu·ton·ic** (-tŏn′ĭk). **1.** Of

t tight/th thin, path/*th* this, bathe/ŭ cut/ûr urge/v valve/w with/y yes/z zebra, size/zh vision/ə about, item, edible, gallop, circus/ à *Fr.* ami/œ *Fr.* feu, *Ger.* schön/ü *Fr.* tu, *Ger.* über/KH *Ger.* ich, *Scot.* loch/N *Fr.* bon. *Follows main vocabulary. †Of obscure origin.

or pertaining to Pluto or the underworld. **2.** Of or pertaining to the planet Pluto.

plu·ton·ic (plo͞o-tŏn′ĭk) *adj. Geology.* Of deep igneous or magmatic origin: *plutonic water.* [From PLUTO (referring to the infernal regions).]

plu·to·ni·um (plo͞o-tō′nē-əm) *n. Symbol* **Pu** A naturally radioactive, silvery, metallic transuranium element, occurring in uranium ores and produced artificially by neutron bombardment of uranium, having fifteen isotopes with masses ranging from 232 to 246 and half-lives from 20 minutes to 76 million years. It is a radiological poison, specifically absorbed by bone marrow, and is used, especially the highly fissionable isotope Pu239, as a reactor fuel and in nuclear weapons. Atomic number 94, melting point 639.5°C, boiling point 3,235°C, specific gravity 19.8, valence 3, 4, 5, 6. See **element.** [Discovered shortly after NEPTUNIUM, and named by analogy after the planet PLUTO (beyond the planet Neptune).]

plu·vi·al (plo͞o′vē-əl) *adj.* Also **plu·vi·an** (-ən). **1.** Of or pertaining to rain; rainy. **2.** *Geology.* Caused by rain. [Latin *pluviālis,* from *pluvia,* rain, from *pluvius,* rainy, from *pluvere,* to rain. See **pleu-** in Appendix.*]

pluvio–. Indicates rain; for example, **pluviometer.** [From Latin *pluvia,* rain. See **pluvial.**]

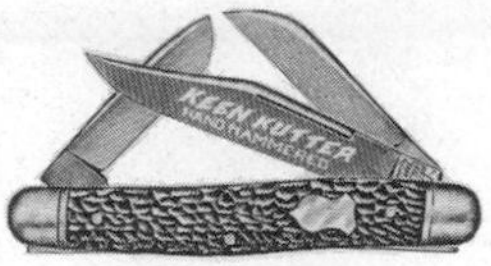

pocketknife

plu·vi·om·e·ter (plo͞o′vē-ŏm′ə-tər) *n.* A device for measuring rainfall, a **rain gauge** *(see).* [French *pluviomètre* : PLUVIO- + -METER.] —**plu′vi·o·met′ric** (plo͞o′vē-ə-mĕt′rĭk), **plu′vi·o·met′ri·cal** *adj.* —**plu′vi·o·met′ri·cal·ly** *adv.* —**plu′vi·om′e·try** *n.*

plu·vi·ous (plo͞o′vē-əs) *adj.* Also **plu·vi·ose** (plo͞o′vē-ōs′). Characterized by heavy rainfall; rainy. [Middle English *pluvyous,* from Latin *pluviōsus,* from *pluvia,* rain, from *pluvius,* rainy, from *pluvere,* to rain. See **pleu-** in Appendix.*] —**plu′vi·os′i·ty** (plo͞o′vē-ŏs′ə-tē) *n.*

ply¹ (plī) *tr.v.* **plied, plying, plies. 1.** To join together, as by molding or twisting. **2.** To double over (cloth, for example). —*n., pl.* **plies. 1.** A layer, as of doubled-over cloth or of paperboard. **2.** One of the sheets of wood glued together to form plywood. **3.** One of the strands twisted together to make yarn, rope, or thread. Used in combination to indicate a specified number of strands, twists, or folds: *three-ply.* **4.** A bias; inclination. [Middle English *plien,* from Old French *plier,* from Latin *plicāre,* to fold. See **plek-** in Appendix.*]

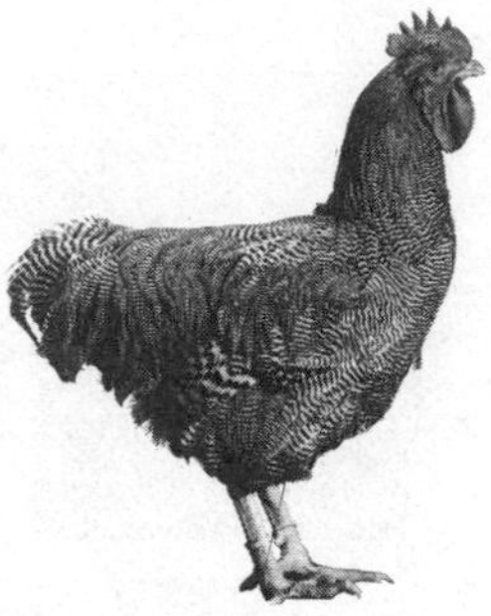

Plymouth Rock

ply² (plī) *v.* **plied, plying, plies.** —*tr.* **1.** To use diligently as a tool or weapon; wield: *He plies an ax with the assurance of a lumberjack.* **2.** To engage in (a trade, for example); practice diligently. **3.** To traverse or sail over regularly: *Trading ships plied the routes between coastal ports.* **4.** To continue supplying or offering to: *plying her guests with food.* **5.** To assail vigorously. —*intr.* **1.** To traverse a route or course regularly: *The boat plies between the islands on a weekly schedule.* **2.** To perform or work diligently or regularly: *He plied at the weaver's trade.* **3.** *Nautical.* To work against the wind by a zigzag course; to tack. [Middle English *(ap)plien,* to employ, APPLY.]

Plym·outh (plĭm′əth). **1.** A city of Devonshire, England, on the English Channel. Population, 213,000. **2.** A town in southeastern Massachusetts on Plymouth Bay, where the Pilgrims from the *Mayflower* landed, December 21, 1620. Population, 6,000.

Plymouth Colony. A New England settlement established in December 1620 by the Pilgrims. It became part of the Massachusetts Bay colony in 1691.

Plymouth Rock. 1. A boulder on the coast of Massachusetts, traditionally regarded as the landing place of the Pilgrims. **2.** An American breed of fowl raised for both meat and eggs.

ply·wood (plī′wo͝od′) *n.* A structural material made of layers of wood glued tightly together, usually with the grains of adjoining layers at right angles to each other. [PLY (layer) + WOOD.]

Pl·zeň (pŭl′zĕn′y′). *German* **Pil·sen** (pĭl′zən). The regional capital of western Bohemia, Czechoslovakia, in a valley about 52 miles southwest of Prague. Population, 139,000.

Pm The symbol for the element promethium.

PM postmaster.

pm. 1. paymaster. **2.** premium.

p.m. 1. post meridiem (*usually small capitals* P.M.). **2.** postmortem. **3.** post-mortem examination.

P.M. 1. past master. **2.** postmaster. **3.** post meridiem (*usually small capitals* P.M.). **4.** post-mortem examination. **5.** prime minister. **6.** provost marshal.

P.M.G. postmaster general.

p.n., P/N promissory note.

pneum. pneumatic; pneumatics.

pneu·ma (no͞o′mə, nyo͞o′-) *n.* The soul or vital spirit. [Greek *pneuma,* blast of wind, breath, divine inspiration, spirit. See **pneu-** in Appendix.*]

pneu·mat·ic (no͞o-măt′ĭk, nyo͞o-) *adj.* Also **pneu·mat·i·cal** (-ĭ-kəl). *Abbr.* **pneum. 1.** Of or pertaining to air or other gases. **2.** Of or pertaining to pneumatics. **3.** Run by or using compressed air: *a pneumatic drill.* **4.** Filled with air, especially compressed air: *a pneumatic tire.* **5.** *Zoology.* Having air cavities, as the bones of certain birds. **6.** Having or pertaining to a shapely, ample bust: *"Uncorseted, her friendly bust/Gives promise of pneumatic bliss."* (T.S. Eliot). **7.** Of or pertaining to the pneuma; spiritual. [French *pneumatique,* from Latin *pneumaticus,* from Greek *pneumatikos,* from *pneuma* (stem *pneumat-*), wind, spirit. See **pneu-** in Appendix.*] —**pneu·mat′i·cal·ly** *adv.* —**pneu′ma·tic′i·ty** (no͞o′mə-tĭs′ə-tē, nyo͞o′-) *n.*

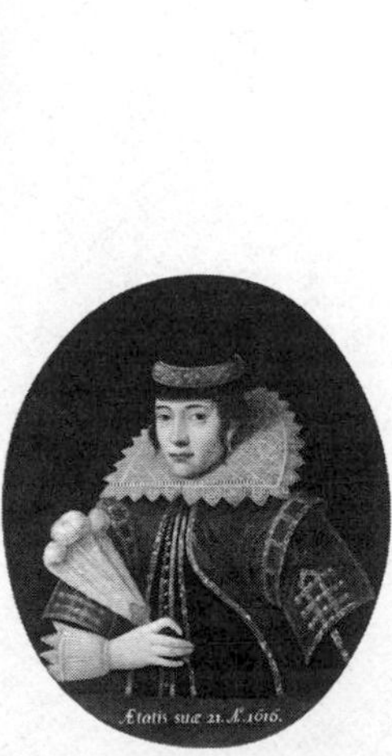

Pocahontas
Contemporary portrait by an unknown artist

pneu·mat·ics (no͞o-măt′ĭks, nyo͞o-) *n.* Plural in form, used with a singular verb. *Abbr.* **pneum.** The study of the mechanical properties of air and other gases. Now rarely used.

pneumato–. Indicates: **1.** Air; for example, **pneumatophore. 2.** Breath or breathing; for example, **pneumatometer. 3.** Spirit or spirits; for example, **pneumatology.** [From Greek *pneuma* (stem *pneumat-*), blast of wind, breath, spirit. See **pneu-** in Appendix.*]

pneu·mat·o·graph. Variant of **pneumograph.**

pneu·ma·tol·o·gy (no͞o′mə-tŏl′ə-jē, nyo͞o′-) *n.* **1.** The doctrine or study of spiritual beings and phenomena; especially, the belief in spirits intervening between man and God. **2.** The Christian doctrine of the Holy Ghost. [New Latin *pneumatologia,* PNEUMATO- + -LOGY.] —**pneu′ma·to·log′ic** (no͞o′mə-tə-lŏj′ĭk, nyo͞o′-), **pneu′ma·to·log′i·cal** *adj.* —**pneu′ma·tol′o·gist** *n.*

pneu·ma·tom·e·ter (no͞o′mə-tŏm′ə-tər, nyo͞o′-) *n.* A device for measuring the pressure of inspiration or expiration in the lungs. [PNEUMATO- + -METER.] —**pneu′ma·tom′e·try** *n.*

pneu·mat·o·phore (no͞o-măt′ə-fôr′, -fōr′, nyo͞o-) *n.* **1.** *Zoology.* A gas-filled sac serving as a float in certain colonial organisms, such as the Portuguese man-of-war. **2.** *Botany.* A specialized respiratory root structure in certain aquatic plants. [PNEUMATO- + -PHORE.]

pneumo–. Indicates the lung or respiratory organs; for example, **pneumograph.** [From Greek *pneuma,* wind, breath, spirit. See **pneu-** in Appendix.*]

pneu·mo·ba·cil·lus (no͞o′mō-bə-sĭl′əs, nyo͞o′-) *n., pl.* **-cilli** (sĭl′ī′). A bacterium, *Klebsiella pneumoniae,* associated with respiratory infections, especially pneumonia.

pneu·mo·coc·cus (no͞o′mə-kŏk′əs, nyo͞o′-) *n., pl.* **-cocci** (-kŏk′-sī′, kŏk′ī′). A bacterium, *Diplococcus pneumoniae,* that causes pneumonia. —**pneu′mo·coc′cal** (-kŏk′əl) *adj.*

pneu·mo·co·ni·o·sis (no͞o′mō-kō′nē-ō′sĭs, nyo͞o′-) *n.* A lung disease caused by long-continued inhalation of mineral or metallic dusts. [New Latin : PNEUMO- + Greek *konia, konis,* dust (see **keni-** in Appendix*) + -OSIS.]

pneu·mo·gas·tric (no͞o′mō-găs′trĭk, nyo͞o′-) *adj.* **1.** Of or involving the lungs and the stomach. **2.** Relating to the vagus nerve.

pneumogastric nerve. *Anatomy.* The **vagus** *(see).*

pneu·mo·graph (no͞o′mə-grăf′, -gräf′, nyo͞o′-) *n.* Also **pneu·mat·o·graph** (no͞o-măt′ə-grăf′, -gräf′, nyo͞o-). A device for recording chest movements during respiration. [PNEUMO- + -GRAPH.] —**pneu′mo·graph′ic** *adj.*

pneu·mo·nec·to·my (no͞o′mə-nĕk′tə-mē, nyo͞o′-) *n., pl.* **-mies.** Also **pneu·mec·to·my** (no͞o-mĕk′tə-mē, nyo͞o-). Surgical removal of lung tissue. [Greek *pneumōn,* lung (see **pneumonic**) + -ECTOMY.]

pneu·mo·nia (no͞o-mōn′yə, nyo͞o-) *n.* An acute or chronic disease marked by inflammation of the lungs, and caused by viruses, bacteria, and physical and chemical agents. [New Latin, from Greek *pneumonia,* alteration (by association with *pneuma,* breath) of *pleumonia,* disease of the lungs, from *pleumōn,* lung. See **pleu-** in Appendix.*]

pneu·mon·ic (no͞o-mŏn′ĭk, nyo͞o-) *adj.* **1.** Pertaining to, affected by, or similar to pneumonia. **2.** Of, affecting, or pertaining to the lungs; pulmonary. [New Latin *pneumonicus,* from Greek *pneumonikos,* of the lungs, from *pneumōn,* alteration of *pleumōn,* lung. See **pleu-** in Appendix.*]

pneu·mo·tho·rax (no͞o′mō-thôr′ăks′, -thōr′ăks′, nyo͞o′-) *n.* Accumulation of air or gas in the pleural cavity, occurring as a result of disease or injury, or sometimes induced to collapse the lung in the treatment of tuberculosis and other lung diseases.

p.n.g. persona non grata.

Pnom-Penh. See **Phnom Penh.**

po *Baseball.* putout.

Po The symbol for the element polonium.

Po (pō). Ancient name **Pa·dus** (pā′dəs). A river rising on the slope of Mount Viso in northwestern Italy and flowing 418 miles to the Adriatic Sea southwest of Venice.

p.o. 1. petty officer. **2.** post office. **3.** *Baseball.* putout.

P.O. 1. Personnel Officer. **2.** petty officer. **3.** postal order. **4.** post office.

poach¹ (pōch) *tr.v.* **poached, poaching, poaches.** To cook in a boiling or simmering liquid: *fish poached in wine.* [Middle English *pochen,* to cook (eggs out of the shells) in boiling water, from Old French *poch(i)er (des œufs),* "to put (egg yolks) in pockets" (i.e., bags formed by the whites), from *poche,* pocket, from Frankish *pokka* (unattested). See **beu-¹** in Appendix.*]

poach² (pōch) *v.* **poached, poaching, poaches.** —*intr.* **1.** To trespass on another's property in order to take fish or game. **2.** To take fish or game in a forbidden area. **3.** To become muddy or broken up from being trampled. Said of land. **4.** To sink into soft earth when walking. —*tr.* **1.** To trespass on (another's property) for fishing or hunting. **2.** To take (fish or game) illegally. **3.** To make (land) muddy or broken up by trampling. [Old French *poch(i)er,* to trample, poach into, probably from Middle High German *puchen, buchen,* to strike, thrust, akin to Middle Dutch *poken,* to POKE.]

poach·er¹ (pō′chər) *n.* A vessel or dish designed for the poaching of food, as eggs or fish.

poach·er² (pō′chər) *n.* **1.** A person who hunts or fishes illegally on the property of another. **2.** Any of various marine fishes of the family Agonidae, chiefly of northern Pacific waters, having an external covering of bony plates.

Po·be·da Peak (pō-bā′dä). The highest mountain (24,406 feet) in the Tien Shan range, on the border between the Kirghiz S.S.R. and China.

Po·ca·hon·tas (pō′kə-hŏn′təs). Original name, Matoaka. 1595?–1617. American Indian princess; daughter of Powhatan; allegedly saved life of Captain John Smith; married (1614) John Rolfe.

Po·ca·tel·lo (pō′kə-tĕl′ō, -tĕl′ə). A city and railroad and communications center in southeastern Idaho. Population, 29,000.

ă pat/ā pay/âr care/ä father/b bib/ch church/d deed/ĕ pet/ē be/f fife/g gag/h hat/hw which/ĭ pit/ī pie/îr pier/j judge/k kick/l lid, needle/m mum/n no, sudden/ng thing/ŏ pot/ō toe/ô paw, for/oi noise/ou out/o͝o took/o͞o boot/p pop/r roar/s sauce/sh ship, dish/

po·chard (pō′chərd) *n.* Any of various ducks of the genera *Aythya* and *Netta;* especially, *A. ferina,* of Europe, having gray and black plumage and a reddish head. [Origin uncertain.]
pock (pŏk) *n.* **1.** A pustule caused by smallpox or a similar eruptive disease. **2.** A mark or scar left in the skin by such a pustule; pockmark. [Middle English *pokke,* Old English *pocc.* See **beu-**[1] in Appendix.*]
pock·et (pŏk′ĭt) *n.* **1. a.** A small, flat pouch sewed into a garment and used to carry small articles. **b.** A piece of material sewed onto the outside of a garment with the top edge open. **2.** A small sack or bag. **3.** Any receptacle, cavity, or opening. **4.** Supply of money; financial means. **5.** *Mining.* **a.** A small cavity in the earth containing ore. **b.** A small body or accumulation of ore. **6.** One of the pouchlike receptacles at the corners and sides of a billiard or pool table. **7.** *Racing.* A position in which a contestant has no room to pass a group of contestants immediately to his front or side. **8.** A small, isolated or protected area or group. **9.** An **air pocket** *(see).* **10.** A bin for storing ore, grain, or other materials. —See Synonyms at **hole.** —*adj.* **1.** Suitable for or capable of being carried in one's pocket: *pocket money; a pocket edition.* **2.** Tiny; miniature. —*tr.v.* **pocketed, -eting, -ets. 1.** To place in or as if in one's pocket. **2.** To take possession of for oneself, especially dishonestly. **3.** To accept or tolerate (an insult, for example). **4.** To suppress or conceal: *He pocketed his pride.* **5.** To prevent (a bill) from becoming law by delaying its signing until the adjournment of the legislature. See **pocket veto. 6.** To hem in (a competitor) in a race. **7.** To hit (a ball) into a pocket of a pool or billiard table. [Middle English *poket,* from Old North French *poket(e),* diminutive of *poke, poque,* bag, variant of Old French *poche,* pocket, from Frankish *pokka* (unattested). See **beu-**[1] in Appendix.*] —**pock′et·a·ble** *adj.* —**pock′et·er** *n.*
pocket billiards. The game of **pool** *(see).*
pock·et·book (pŏk′ĭt-bo͝ok′) *n.* **1.** A pocket-sized folder or case used to hold money and papers; wallet; billfold. **2.** A bag used by women to carry money, papers, and other small articles; purse. **3.** Supply of money; financial resources. **4.** A pocket-sized, usually paperbound book.
pocket borough. A borough in England, prior to the Parliamentary reform of 1832, whose representation was controlled by a single person or family.
pock·et·ful (pŏk′ĭt-fo͝ol′) *n., pl.* **-fuls** or **pocketsful.** As much as a pocket will hold.
pocket gopher. See **gopher.**
pock·et·knife (pŏk′ĭt-nīf′) *n., pl.* **-knives** (-nīvz′). A small knife with a blade or blades folding into the handle.
pocket money. Money for incidental or minor expenses.
pocket mouse. Any of various small, North American burrowing rodents of the genus *Perognathus,* having fur-lined external cheek pouches.
pocket veto. 1. The President's indirect veto of a bill presented to him within ten days of Congressional adjournment, by his retaining the bill unsigned until Congress adjourns. **2.** A similar action exercised by a state governor or other chief executive.
pock·mark (pŏk′märk′) *n.* A pitlike scar left on the skin by smallpox or another eruptive disease. —**pock′marked′** *adj.*
pock·y (pŏk′ē) *adj.* **-ier, -iest. 1.** Pertaining to, resembling, or having pocks. **2.** Pertaining to, having, or resembling syphilis.
po·co (pō′kō) *adv. Music.* Somewhat; a little. Used as a direction: *poco adagio.* [Italian, little, from Latin *paucus,* little, few. See **pou-** in Appendix.*]
po·co a po·co (pō′kō ä pō′kō). *Music.* Gradually; little by little. Used as a direction: *poco a poco diminuendo.*
po·co·cu·ran·te (pō′kō-ko͞o-răn′tē, -rän′tē) *adj.* Indifferent; unconcerned; apathetic. —*n.* One who does not care; an unconcerned person. [Italian : POCO + *curante,* caring, from Latin *cūrans,* present participle of *cūrāre,* to care for, from *cūra,* care. See **cūra** in Appendix.*] —**po′co·cu·ran′tism′** *n.*
po·co·sin (pə-kō′sən) *n. Chiefly Southeastern U.S.* A swamp in an upland coastal region. [Algonquian (Delaware) *pâkwesen,* "shallow place" : *pâkw-,* shallow + *-sen,* place-name suffix.]
pod[1] (pŏd) *n.* **1.** *Botany.* **a.** A dehiscent seed vessel or fruit of a leguminous plant, such as the pea. **b.** A fruit that contains several seeds, and that usually dries and splits open. **2.** A podlike protective covering. **3.** *Aviation.* A streamlined housing that encloses engines, machine guns, or fuel, carried externally on aircraft. —*v.* **podded, podding, pods.** —*intr.* **1.** To bear or produce pods. **2.** To expand or swell like a pod. —*tr.* To remove (seeds) from a pod. [Probably altered from COD (through assimilation of *peasecod* into *peasepod*).]
pod[2] (pŏd) *n.* A school of seals or whales. See Synonyms at **flock.** [Origin unknown.]
pod[3] (pŏd) *n.* **1.** The lengthwise groove in certain boring tools, such as augers. **2.** The socket for holding the bit in a boring tool. [Origin unknown.]
-pod, -pode. Indicates a specified kind or number of feet; for example, **pseudopod.** [New Latin *-podius, -poda,* from Greek *pous* (stem *pod-*), foot. See **ped-**[1] in Appendix.*]
po·dag·ra (pə-dăg′rə) *n. Pathology.* Gout, especially of the great toe. [Middle English, from Latin, from Greek, "trap for the feet," foot disease, gout : *pous* (stem *pod-*), foot (see **ped-**[1] in Appendix*) + *agra, agrē,* hunting, seizure (see **ag-** in Appendix*).] —**po·dag′ral, po·dag′ric** *adj.*
po·des·ta (pō-dĕs′tə; *Italian* pô′dĕ-stä′) *n.* **1.** A governor appointed by Frederick Barbarossa to rule over one or more of the Lombard cities. **2.** The chief magistrate or officer in any of the republics of medieval Italy. **3.** Under the Fascist regime, the chief magistrate or mayor in any of the Italian communes except Rome and Naples. **4.** A subordinate magistrate or judge in some modern Italian towns. [Italian *podestà, potestà,* from Latin *potestātem,* from neuter of *potestās,* power, magistrate, from *potis,* able. See **poti-** in Appendix.*]
Pod·go·ri·ca, Pod·go·ri·tsa. Former names for **Titograd.**
po·di·a·try (pə-dī′ə-trē) *n.* The study and treatment of foot ailments. Also called "chiropody." [Greek *pous* (stem *pod-*), foot (see **ped-**[1] in Appendix*) + -IATRY.] —**po·di′a·trist** *n.*
po·di·um (pō′dē-əm) *n., pl.* **-dia** (-dē-ə) or **-ums. 1.** An elevated platform for an orchestra conductor, lecturer, or the like; dais. **2.** *Architecture.* A low wall serving as foundation. **3.** A wall circling the arena of an ancient amphitheater. **4.** *Biology.* Any structure resembling or functioning as a foot. [Latin, raised platform, balcony, from Greek *podion,* "small foot," base, from *pous* (stem *pod-*), foot. See **ped-**[1] in Appendix.*]
-podium. Indicates a part that resembles a foot; for example, **monopodium.** [New Latin, from Greek *podion,* "small foot," from *pous,* foot. See **ped-**[1] in Appendix.*]
Po·dolsk (pə-dôlsk′). An industrial town in the western Soviet Union, about 25 miles south of Moscow. Population, 157,000.
pod·o·phyl·lin (pŏd′ə-fĭl′ĭn) *n.* A bitter-tasting resin obtained from the dried root of the **May apple** *(see),* and used as a cathartic. [New Latin *podophyllum,* genus of herbs including May apple, "(plant with) footlike leaves" : Greek *pous* (stem *pod-*), foot (see **ped-**[1] in Appendix*) + *phullon,* a leaf (see **bhol**[3] in Appendix*) + -IN.]
-podous. Indicates possession of feet or footlike parts of a specified kind or number; for example, **gastropodous, decapodous.** [-POD + -OUS.]
Po·dunk (pō′dŭngk′) *n. Slang.* Any small, isolated, and unimportant town. [After *Podunk,* locality in Connecticut or town in Massachusetts.]
pod·zol (pŏd′zôl′) *n.* Also **pod·sol** (-sôl′). A leached soil formed mainly in cool, humid climates. [Russian, "ash ground" : *pod,* bottom, ground (see **ped-**[1] in Appendix*) + *zola,* ashes (see **ghel-**[2] in Appendix*).] —**pod·zol′ic** *adj.*
pod·zol·i·za·tion (pŏd′zô-lə-zā′shən) *n.* Also **pod·sol·i·za·tion** (pŏd′sô-). **1.** The process by which soils are depleted of bases and become acidic. **2.** The development of a podzol.
P.O.E. port of entry.
Poe (pō), **Edgar Allan.** 1809–1849. American short-story writer, poet, and journalist.
po·em (pō′əm, -ĭm) *n.* **1.** A composition designed to convey a vivid and imaginative sense of experience, characterized by the use of condensed language, chosen for its sound and suggestive power as well as its meaning, and by the use of such literary techniques as structured meter, natural cadences, rhyme, or metaphor. **2.** Any composition in verse rather than in prose. **3.** Any literary composition written with an intensity or beauty of language more characteristic of poetry than of prose: *a prose poem.* **4.** Any creation, object, or experience thought to embody the lyrical beauty or structural perfection characteristic of poetry. [Old French *poeme,* from Latin *poēma,* from Greek *poiēma, poēma,* "created thing," work, poem, from *poiein,* to make, create. See **kwei-**[2] in Appendix.*]
poe·nol·o·gy. Variant of **penology.**
po·e·sy (pō′ə-zē, -sē) *n., pl.* **-sies.** *Archaic.* **1.** Poetry. **2.** The art or practice of composing poems. **3.** The inspiration involved in composing poetry. [Middle English *poesie,* from Old French, from Common Romance *poēsia* (unattested), variant of Latin *poēsis,* from Greek *po(i)ēsis,* "a making," "creation," poetry, from *poiein,* to make, create. See **kwei-**[2] in Appendix.*]
po·et (pō′ĭt) *n.* **1.** A writer of poems. **2.** One who is especially gifted in the perception and expression of the beautiful or lyrical. [Middle English *poete,* from Old French, from Latin *poēta,* from Greek *poiētēs,* "maker," poet, from *poiein,* to make, create. See **kwei-**[2] in Appendix.*]
Synonyms: *poet, bard, versifier, rhymer, rhymester, poetaster.* These nouns denote persons who write in verse. *Poet* is the most inclusive, but usually identifies one who composes verse of considerable merit; sometimes the term is applied to anyone gifted in artistic expression. *Bard,* in its original meaning, denoted a Celtic poet who composed and sang verses dealing with legendary events. Now the term can apply to any poet, but especially to a lyric poet. *Versifier, rhymer,* and *rhymester,* all lesser terms than *poet,* now refer principally to minor writers in verse. *Poetaster,* the lowest of these terms, applies to a verse writer of little or no merit.
poet. poetic; poetical; poetry.
po·et·as·ter (pō′ĭt-ăs′tər) *n.* An inferior poet. See Synonyms at **poet.** [New Latin : Latin *poēt(a),* POET + -ASTER.]
po·et·ess (pō′ĭ-tĭs) *n.* A female poet.
po·et·ic (pō-ĕt′ĭk) *adj.* Also **po·et·i·cal** (-ĭ-kəl). *Abbr.* **poet. 1.** Of or pertaining to poetry: *poetic works.* **2.** Having a quality or style characteristic of poetry: *poetic diction.* **3.** Suitable as a subject for poetry: *a poetic love affair.* **4.** Of, pertaining to, or befitting a poet: *poetic insight.* **5.** Characterized by romantic imagery: *"Turner's vision of the rainbow . . . was poetic, and he knew it."* (Lawrence Gowing). [Middle English *poetical* and Old French *poetique,* from Latin *poēticus,* from Greek *poiētikos,* inventive, ingenious, from *poiētēs,* "maker," POET.]
po·et·i·cal (pō-ĕt′ĭ-kəl) *adj.* **1.** Poetic. **2.** Fancifully depicted or embellished; idealized. —**po·et′i·cal·ly** *adv.*
po·et·i·cism (pō-ĕt′ə-sĭz′əm) *n.* A poetic term or expression that has become no longer vivid or evocative.
po·et·i·cize (pō-ĕt′ə-sīz′) *v.* **-cized, -cizing, -cizes.** —*tr.* To put into poetry; make poetic. —*intr.* To speak or write poetically.
poetic justice. An outcome whereby a person receives his just deserts in a manner peculiarly or ironically appropriate.
poetic license. The liberty taken, especially by an artist or

pod[1]

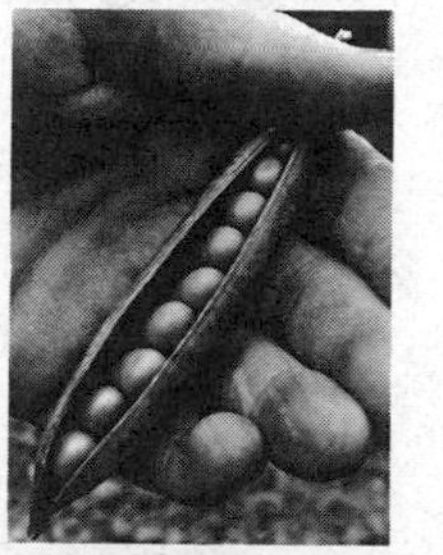

pea pod

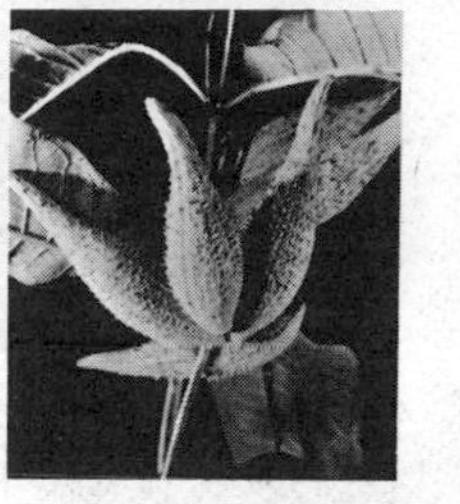

milkweed pods

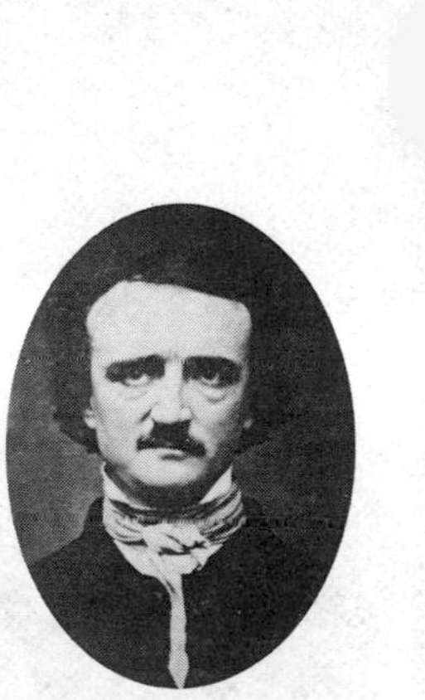

Edgar Allan Poe

writer, in deviating from conventional form or fact to achieve a desired effect.

po·et·ics (pō-ĕt′ĭks) *n.* Plural in form, used with a singular verb. **1.** Literary criticism that deals with the nature, forms, and laws of poetry. **2.** A treatise on or study of poetry or aesthetics. **3.** Poetic utterances or feelings.

po·et·ize (pō′ĭ-tīz′) *v.* **-ized, -izing, -izes.** —*intr.* To write or express oneself in poetry. —*tr.* To give poetic expression to. —**po′et·iz′er** *n.*

poet laureate *pl.* **poets laureate** or **poet laureates. 1.** A poet appointed by the British sovereign to a lifetime position as chief poet of the kingdom. **2.** A poet acclaimed as the most excellent or most representative of a locality or group. **3.** Any poet honored for excellence.

po·et·ry (pō′ĭ-trē) *n.* **1.** *Abbr.* **poet.** The art or work of a poet. **2.** *Abbr.* **poet. a.** Poems regarded as forming a division of literature. **b.** The poetic works of a given author, group, nation, or kind. **3.** Any piece of literature written in meter; verse. **4.** Prose that resembles a poem in form, sound, or the like. **5.** The essence of or characteristic quality possessed by a poem or poems. **6.** The quality of a poem or poems, as possessed by an object, act, or experience: *the poetry of her dance movements.* [Middle English *poetrie,* from Old French, from Medieval Latin *poētria,* from Latin *poēta,* POET.]

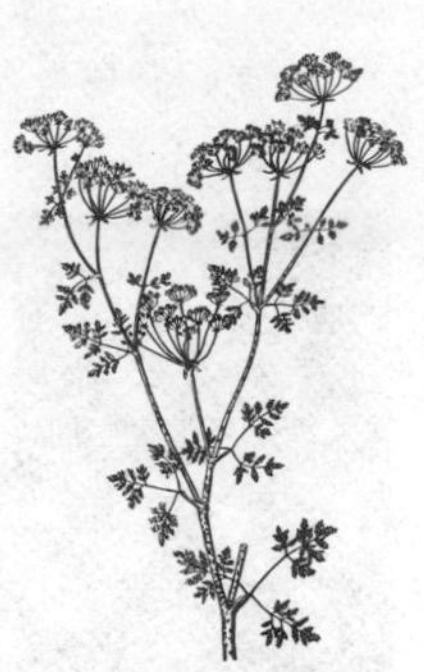

poison hemlock

po·go·ni·a (pə-gō′nē-ə, -gōn′yə) *n.* Any of various small terrestrial orchids of the genus *Pogonia,* of the North Temperate Zone, having pink or whitish flowers. [New Latin, "bearded plant" (from the yellow hair covering the lip of its flower), from Greek *pōgōn*†, beard.]

pog·o·nip (pŏg′ə-nĭp′) *n.* A dense fog of suspended ice particles, occurring especially in mountain valleys of the western United States. Also called "ice fog." [Shoshonean (Paiute), from *pagina-,* cloud, fog.]

po·go stick (pō′gō). A strong stick with footrests and a heavy spring set into the bottom end, propelled along the ground by hopping.

po·grom (pō′grəm, pō-grŏm′) *n.* An organized and often officially encouraged massacre or persecution of a minority group, especially one conducted against the Jews. [Russian, "like thunder," devastation : *po-,* like, from *po,* at, by, next to (see **apo-** in Appendix*) + *grom,* thunder (see **ghrem-** in Appendix*).]

po·gy (pō′gē, pŏg′ē) *n., pl.* **pogy** or **-gies.** A fish, the **menhaden** *(see).* [Probably shortened from Algonquian *pauhaugen.*]

Po Hai, Gulf of (bō′ hī′). Formerly Gulf of **Chih·li** (chē′lē′). An inlet of the Yellow Sea in northeastern China between Manchuria and Shantung.

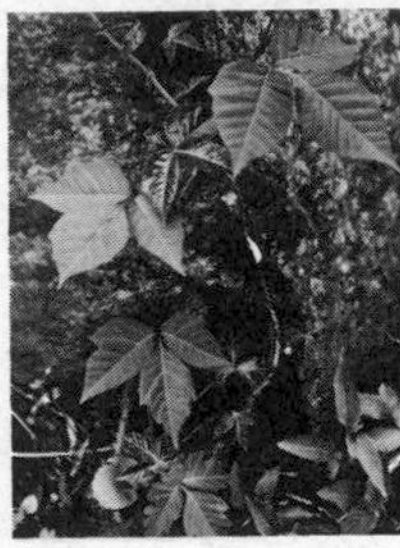

poison ivy

poi (poi, pō′ē) *n.* A Hawaiian food made from taro root cooked, pounded to a paste, and fermented. [Hawaiian.]

–poiesis. Indicates making, creating, or producing; for example, **hematopoiesis.** [From Greek *poiēsis,* a making, creation, from *poiein,* to make. See **kwei-²** in Appendix.*]

–poietic. Indicates productive or formative; for example, **hematopoietic.** [From Greek *poiētikos,* creative, productive, from *poiētēs,* maker, creator, from *poiein,* to make. See **kwei-²** in Appendix.*]

poign·ant (poin′yənt, poi′nənt) *adj.* **1. a.** Physically painful: *"Keen, poignant agonies seemed to shoot from his neck downward."* (Ambrose Bierce). **b.** Keenly distressing to the mind: *poignant anxiety.* **c.** Appealing to the emotions; affecting; touching: *poignant sentiment.* **2.** Piercing; incisive: *poignant criticism.* **3. a.** Neat, skillful, and to the point: *"Her illustrations were apposite and poignant."* (Lamb). **b.** Astute and pertinent; relevant: *poignant suggestions.* **4.** Agreeably intense or stimulating: *poignant delight.* **5. a.** *Archaic.* Sharp or sour to the taste; piquant. **b.** Sharp or pungent to the smell: *a poignant perfume.* —See Synonyms at **moving.** [Middle English *poynaunt, pugnaunt,* pointed, sharp, from Old French *puignant,* from Latin *pungens,* present participle of *pungere,* to prick, pierce. See **peuk-** in Appendix.*] —**poign′an·cy, poign′ance** *n.* —**poign′ant·ly** *adv.*

poi·ki·lo·therm (poi-kĭl′ə-thûrm′) *n. Zoology.* A poikilothermous organism, such as a fish or reptile. [Greek *poikilos,* various, variant (see **peig-¹** in Appendix*) + -THERM.]

poi·ki·lo·ther·mous (poi′kĭl-ə-thûr′məs) *adj.* Also **poi·ki·lo·ther·mal** (-məl). *Zoology.* Having a body temperature that varies with the external environment; cold-blooded. Compare **homoiothermous.**

poi·lu (pwä-lü′) *n. World War I Slang.* A French front-line soldier. [French, "hirsute," hence (slang) brave, pugnacious, from *poil,* hair, from Latin *pilus.* See **pilo-** in Appendix.*]

Poin·ca·ré (pwăN-kä-rā′), **Jules Henri.** 1854–1912. French mathematician and physicist.

poin·ci·an·a (poin′sē-ăn′ə, -ä′nə) *n.* **1.** Any of various tropical trees of the genus *Poinciana,* having large orange or red flowers. **2.** A related tree, the **royal poinciana** *(see).* [New Latin, after M. de Poinci, 17th-century governor of French Antilles.]

poin·set·ti·a (poin-sĕt′ē-ə) *n.* A tropical American shrub, *Euphorbia pulcherrima,* having showy, usually scarlet bracts beneath the small yellow flowers. [New Latin; discovered by J.R. Poinsett (1799–1851), U.S. minister to Mexico.]

pointer

point (point) *n. Abbr.* **pt. 1.** The sharp or tapered end of something: *the point of a knife.* **2.** Something that has a sharp or tapered end, as a knife or needle. **3.** A tapering extension of land projecting into water; promontory; cape. **4.** A mark formed by or as if by the sharp end of something. **5.** A mark or dot used in printing or writing. **6.** A mark used in punctuation; especially, a period. **7.** A **decimal point** *(see).* **8.** *Phonetics.* A diacritical mark, the **vowel point** *(see).* **9.** One of the protruding marks used in certain methods of writing and printing for the blind. **10.** *Geometry.* A dimensionless geometric object having no property but location. **11.** A position, place, or locality; spot: *a good point to begin.* **12.** A specified degree, condition, or limit in a scale, course, or the like. **13. a.** Any of the 32 equal divisions marked at the circumference of a mariner's compass card that indicate direction. **b.** The distance or interval of 11 degrees, 15 minutes between any two adjacent markings. **14.** Any distinct condition or degree: *the point of no return.* **15.** A specific moment in time. **16.** A crucial situation in a course of events. **17.** An important, essential, or primary factor. **18.** A purpose, goal, advantage, or reason. **19.** The major idea or essential part of a concept or narrative. **20.** A significant, outstanding, or effective idea, argument, or suggestion. **21.** A separate or individual item or element; detail. **22. a.** A striking or distinctive characteristic or quality. **b.** A quality or characteristic that is important or distinctive; especially, a standard characteristic used to judge an animal. **23.** A single unit, as in counting, rating, or measuring. **24.** *Education.* **a.** A unit of credit usually equal to one hour of class work per week during one semester. **b.** A numerical unit equal to a letter grade in grading academic achievement. **25.** A unit of scoring or counting in a game or sport. **26.** The stiff and attentive stance taken by a hunting dog. **27.** *Electricity.* **a.** An electrical contact, especially one in the distributor of an automobile engine. **b.** *British.* A socket or outlet. **28.** *Finance.* **a.** A unit equal to one dollar and used to quote or state the current prices of stocks, commodities, or the like. **b.** A unit equal to one percentage point used in reference to ownership. **29.** *Music.* A phrase, such as a fugue subject, in contrapuntal music. **30.** *Printing.* A unit of type size equal to 0.01384 inch, or approximately 1/72 of an inch. **31.** A jeweler's unit of mass equal to 2 milligrams or 0.01 carat. **32. a.** Needlepoint. **b.** Bobbin lace. **33.** *Railroading.* **a.** *British.* A movable rail, tapered at the end, such as that used in a switch. **b.** The vertex or tip of the angle created by the intersection of rails in a frog or switch. **34.** A ribbon or cord with a metal tag at the end, used to fasten clothing in the 16th and 17th centuries. —**in point.** Being considered: *a case in point.* —**in point of.** With reference to; in the matter of. —**stretch** (or **strain**) **a point. 1.** To make an exception. **2.** To exaggerate. —*v.* **pointed, pointing, points.** —*tr.* **1.** To direct or aim: *point a weapon.* **2.** To bring to notice. Usually used with *out: "To point out other people's errors was a duty that Mr. Bulstrode seldom shrank from"* (George Eliot). **3.** To indicate the position or direction of: *"Geoff pointed the way and they set off"* (Malcolm Lowry). **4.** To sharpen (a pencil, for example); provide with a point. **5.** To separate with a decimal point. Used with *off.* **6.** To mark with a point or period; punctuate. **7.** To mark (a consonant) with a vowel point. **8.** To give emphasis to (a remark, for example); to stress. Often used with *up.* **9.** To indicate the presence and position of (game) by standing immobile and directing the muzzle toward it. **10.** *Masonry.* To fill and finish the joints of (brickwork) with cement or mortar. —*intr.* **1.** To direct attention or indicate position with or as if with the finger. **2.** To turn the mind or thought in a particular direction. **3.** To be turned or faced in a given direction; to aim. **4.** To perform the action of a hunting dog scenting game and gazing toward it fixedly. **5.** *Nautical.* To sail close to the wind. [Middle English *poynt,* from Old French *point,* a prick, dot, small particle, and *pointe,* pointed end or tip, respectively from Latin *punctum* and Vulgar Latin *puncta* (unattested), from the neuter and feminine of *punctus,* past participle of *pungere,* to pierce, prick. See **peuk-** in Appendix.*]

Point Bar·row. See **Barrow, Point.**

point-blank (point′blăngk′) *adj.* **1.** Aimed straight at the mark or target; especially, aimed straight without allowing for the drop in a projectile's course. **2. a.** So close to a target that a weapon may be aimed directly at it: *pointblank range.* **b.** Close enough so that missing the target is unlikely or impossible: *a pointblank shot.* **3.** Straightforward; blunt: *a pointblank accusation.* —*adv.* **1.** With a straight aim; directly; straight: *The policeman fired pointblank.* **2.** Without hesitation, deliberation, or equivocation: *answer pointblank.* [Probably from Old French *de pointe en blanc,* "(straight) from the aiming into the target," i.e., from close enough range to ensure a flat trajectory.]

Point de Galle. The former name for **Galle.**

point-de·vice (point′dĭ-vīs′) *adj. Archaic.* Scrupulously correct or neat; precise. [Middle English *at point devis,* probably from Norman French *à point devis* (unattested), "arranged to (the) point" : *à point,* to point, to perfection + *devis,* "divided," arranged, from Latin *divisus,* past participle of *dīvidere,* to divide (see **weidh-** in Appendix*).] —**point′-de·vice′** *adv.*

point·ed (poin′tĭd) *adj.* **1.** Having an end coming to a point. **2.** Sharp; piercing; cutting; appropriate: *a pointed question.* **3.** Obviously directed at or making reference to a particular person: *a pointed comment.* **4.** Clearly evident or conspicuous; emphasized; marked: *a pointed lack of interest.* **5.** Characterized by the use of a pointed crown, as in Gothic architecture: *a pointed arch.* —**point′ed·ly** *adv.* —**point′ed·ness** *n.*

point·er (poin′tər) *n.* **1.** One that sharpens, directs, indicates, or points. **2.** A scale indicator on a watch, balance, or other measuring instrument. **3.** A long, tapered stick for indicating objects on a chart, blackboard, or the like. **4.** One of a breed of hunting dogs having a short-haired coat that is usually white with black or brownish spots. **5.** A suggestion; hint; piece of advice.

poin·til·lism (pwăn′tl-ĭz′əm) *n.* A postimpressionist school of

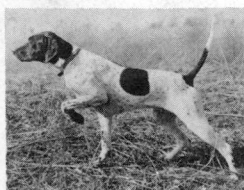

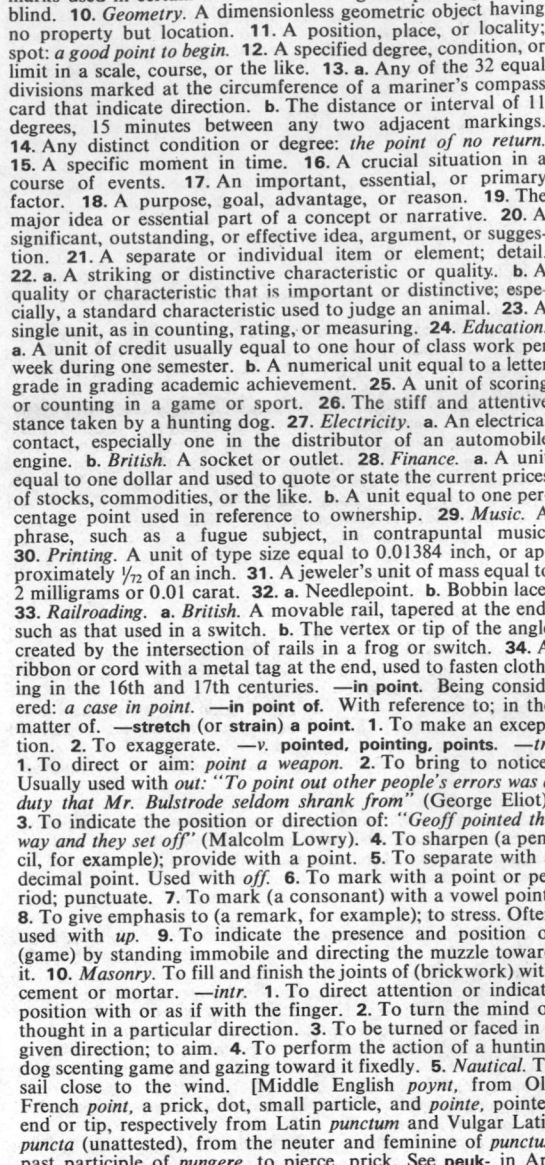

ă pat/ā pay/âr care/ä father/b bib/ch church/d deed/ĕ pet/ē be/f fife/g gag/h hat/hw which/ĭ pit/ī pie/îr pier/j judge/k kick/l lid, needle/m mum/n no, sudden/ng thing/ŏ pot/ō toe/ô paw, for/oi noise/ou out/ŏŏ took/ōō boot/p pop/r roar/s sauce/sh ship, dish/

painting exemplified by Seurat and his followers in late 19th-century France and characterized by the application of paint in small dots and brush strokes so as to create an effect of blending and luminosity. Compare **neoimpressionism.** [French *pointillisme,* from *pointiller,* to paint small dots, from *pointille,* small point or dot, from Italian *puntiglio,* diminutive of *punto,* point, dot, from Latin *punctum,* from the neuter past participle of *pungere,* to pierce, prick. See **peuk-** in Appendix.*] **—poin′til·list** *n.* & *adj.* **—poin′til·lis′tic** *adj.*

Point Ju·dith (jo͞o′dĭth). A cape in south-central Rhode Island on the western side of the entrance to Narragansett Bay.

point lace. A type of handmade lace, **needlepoint** *(see).* **—point′-laced′** *adj.*

point·less (point′lĭs) *adj.* **1.** Meaningless; irrelevant. **2.** Ineffectual. **—point′less·ly** *adv.* **—point′less·ness** *n.*

point of honor. A matter that affects one's honor or reputation.

point of order. A question as to whether that which is being discussed is in order or allowed by the rules.

point of view. **1.** The position from which something is observed or considered; standpoint. **2.** One's manner of viewing things; attitude.

point system. **1.** *Printing.* A system of measurement by the **point** *(see).* **2.** Any system of printing or writing for the blind that uses an alphabet of raised symbols or dots that correspond to letters, such as Braille. **3.** A system of evaluating and averaging a student's academic achievement by using numerical units or points that are equivalent to letter grades.

poise[1] (poiz) *v.* **poised, poising, poises.** *—tr.* To carry or hold in equilibrium; balance. *—intr.* To be balanced or held in suspension; hover: *poise on the brink.* *—n.* **1.** The state or condition of being balanced or held in equilibrium; stability; balance: *"He always kept his poise/to the top branches, climbing carefully"* (Robert Frost). **2.** Freedom from affectation or embarrassment; dignity of manner; assurance; composure: *"This gives him a built-in poise, since it deprives him of the chance to say anything asinine."* (Tom Wolfe). **3.** The bearing or deportment of the head or body; mien. **4.** A state or condition of hovering or being suspended. [Middle English *poisen, peisen,* to weigh, from Old French *poiser, peser,* from Vulgar Latin *pēsāre* (unattested), variant of Latin *pensāre,* frequentative of *pendere,* to weigh, ponder. See **spen-** in Appendix.*]

poise[2] (poiz) *n.* A centimeter-gram-second unit of dynamic viscosity equal to one dyne-second per square centimeter. [French, after Jean Louis Marie *Poiseuille* (1799–1869), French physician.]

poi·son (poi′zən) *n.* **1.** Any substance that causes injury, illness, or death, especially by chemical means. **2.** Anything that is destructive or fatal. **3.** *Chemistry.* A substance that inhibits or retards a chemical reaction. *—tr.v.* **poisoned, -soning, -sons.** **1.** To give poison to; kill or harm with poison. **2.** To put poison on or into. **3.** To make poisonous; envenom. **4.** *Chemistry.* To inhibit or retard (a chemical reaction). *—adj.* Poisonous. [Middle English *poysoun,* potion, poisonous drink, from Old French *poison,* from Latin *pōtiō,* from *pōtāre,* to drink. See **poi-[1]** in Appendix.*] **—poi′son·er** *n.*

poison gas. Any lethal or crippling vapor used in warfare.

poison hemlock. A poisonous plant, *Conium maculatum,* native to Eurasia but naturalized in North America, having compound leaves and umbels of small, white flowers.

poison ivy. A North American shrub or vine, *Rhus radicans,* having leaflets in groups of three, small green flowers, and whitish berries, causing a rash on contact. Sometimes called "poison oak."

poison oak. **1.** Either of two shrubs, *Rhus toxicodendron* of the southeastern United States, or *R. diversiloba* of western North America, related to poison ivy and causing a similar rash. **2.** Loosely, poison ivy.

poi·son·ous (poi′zən-əs) *adj.* **1.** Capable of harming or killing by or as if by poison; broadly, toxic or venomous. **2.** Containing a poison. **3.** Marked by apparent ill will or enmity; full of malice: *a poisonous glance.* **—poi′son·ous·ly** *adv.* **—poi′son·ous·ness** *n.*

poison sumac. A swamp shrub, *Rhus vernix,* of the southeastern United States, having compound leaves and greenish-white berries, and causing an itching rash on contact with the skin. Sometimes called "poison dogwood," "poison elder."

Pois·son distribution (pwä-sôN′). *Statistics.* A probability distribution used to describe the occurrence of unlikely events in a large number of independent repeated trials. [After Siméon Denis *Poisson* (1781–1840), French mathematician.]

Poi·tiers (pwä-tyā′). A city of west-central France, about 65 miles south of Tours. Population, 60,000.

Poi·tou (pwä-to͞o′). A region and former province of west-central France.

poke[1] (pōk) *v.* **poked, poking, pokes.** *—tr.* **1.** To push or jab, as with a finger or arm; prod. **2.** To make (a hole or pathway, for example) by or as if by prodding, thrusting, or poking: *He poked his way to the front of the crowd.* **3.** To push; thrust: *A seal poked its head out of the water.* **4.** To stir (a fire) by prodding the wood or coal with a poker or stick. Often used with *up.* **5.** To strike; punch. *—intr.* **1.** To make thrusts or jabs with a stick, poker, or the like. **2.** To pry or meddle; intrude: *poking into another's business.* **3.** To search or look curiously in a desultory manner: *"lonely old grubber, poking around the meats in the refrigerator"* (Allen Ginsberg). **4.** To live or proceed in a slow or lazy manner; dawdle; putter. **5.** To thrust forward; appear: *His head poked from under the blankets.* **—poke fun at.** To ridicule in a mischievous manner; tease. *—n.* **1.** A push, thrust, or jab. **2.** A punch or blow with the fist. **3.** A person who moves slowly or aimlessly; dawdler. [Middle English *poken,* from Middle Dutch and Middle Low German *poken,* to strike, thrust (probably imitative).]

poke[2] (pōk) *n.* **1.** A large bonnet having a projecting brim at the front. Also called "poke bonnet." **2.** The brim of such a bonnet. [From POKE (to thrust).]

poke[3] (pōk) *n. Chiefly Regional.* A sack or bag. [Middle English, from Old North French *poque,* variant of Old French *poche,* pocket, from Frankish *pokka* (unattested), bag. See **beu-[1]** in Appendix.*]

poke[4] (pōk) *n.* A plant, **pokeweed** *(see).* [Short for earlier *pocan,* from Algonquian (Virginian) *pakon,* "bloody," from *pak,* blood.]

poke·ber·ry (pōk′bĕr′ē) *n., pl.* **-ries.** **1.** The blackish-red berry of the pokeweed. **2.** The plant itself, **pokeweed** *(see).*

pok·er[1] (pō′kər) *n.* One that pokes; specifically, a metal rod used to stir a fire.

pok·er[2] (pō′kər) *n.* Any of various card games played by two or more players who bet on the value of their hands. [Origin obscure.]

poker face. A face lacking any interpretable expression, as that of an expert poker player. **—pok′er-faced′** (pō′kər-fāst′) *adj.*

poke·weed (pōk′wēd′) *n.* A tall North American plant, *Phytolacca americana,* having small white flowers, blackish-red berries, and a poisonous root. The young shoots are sometimes eaten as greens. Also called "poke," "pokeberry," "pokeroot," "inkberry." [POKE (bag) + WEED.]

po·key (pō′kē) *n., pl.* **-keys.** Also **po·ky** *pl.* **-kies.** *Slang.* Jail; prison. *—adj.* Variant of **poky.** [From POKY.]

pok·y (pō′kē) *adj.* **-ier, -iest.** Also **poke·y.** *Informal.* **1.** Dawdling; dull; slow. **2.** Frumpish; shabby. Said of dress. **3.** Small and cramped: *a poky apartment.* *—n.* Variant of **pokey.** [From POKE, to thrust, (hence, slang) to confine.]

pol. political; politician; politics.

Pol. Poland; Polish.

Po·la. The Italian name for **Pula.**

Po·lack (pō′lŏk′, -lăk′) *n.* **1.** *Obsolete.* A native of Poland; a Pole. **2.** *Slang.* A person of Polish descent or birth. An offensive term used derogatorily. [Polish *Polak,* from *pol-,* field. See **pele-[1]** in Appendix.*] **—Po′lack′** *adj.*

Po·land (pō′lənd). *Polish* **Pol·ska** (pôl′skä). *Abbr.* **Pol.** Officially, Polish People's Republic. A republic, 120,000 square miles in area, in central Europe, on the Baltic Sea. Population, 31,340,000. Capital, Warsaw. [Polish *Polanie,* "dwellers of the field" (i.e., Poland) : *pol-,* field (see **pele-[1]** in Appendix*) + *-anie,* suffix denoting "inhabitants."]

Poland China. A large black-and-white pig of a breed developed in North America.

po·lar (pō′lər) *adj.* **1. a.** Of, pertaining to, or designating a pole. **b.** Measured from or referred to a pole or poles: *polar distance; polar diameter.* **2.** Pertaining to, connected with, or located near the North Pole or South Pole. **3.** Occupying or characterized by opposite extremes. **4.** Serving as a guide, such as a polestar or a pole of the earth. **5.** Central or pivotal. [New Latin *polāris,* from Latin *polus,* POLE.]

polar angle. The angle formed by the polar axis and the radius vector in a polar coordinate system.

polar axis. The fixed reference axis from which the polar angle is measured in a polar coordinate system.

polar bear. A large, white-furred bear, *Thalarctos maritimus,* of Arctic regions.

polar body. *Genetics.* A minute cell produced and ultimately discarded in the development of an oocyte, containing little or no cytoplasm but having one of the nuclei derived from the first or second meiotic division.

polar cap. **1. a.** A high-altitude icecap. **b.** The polar regions of ice. **2.** *Astronomy.* Any differentiated polar region of a planet.

polar circle. *Geography.* Either the **Arctic Circle** or **Antarctic Circle** *(both of which see).*

polar coordinate. Either of two coordinates, the radius vector or the polar angle, that together specify the position of any point in a plane.

po·lar·im·e·ter (pō′lə-rĭm′ə-tər) *n.* An instrument used to measure the rotation of the plane of polarization of polarized light, or the degree of polarization of light passing through an optical structure or sample. **—po′lar·i·met′ric** (pō′lər-ə-mĕt′rĭk) *adj.* **—po′lar·im′e·try** *n.*

Po·lar·is (pō-lăr′ĭs, -lâr′ĭs) *n.* **1.** A star of the second magnitude, at the end of the handle of the Little Dipper and almost at the north celestial pole. Also called "North Star," "polar star," "polestar." **2.** A U.S. Navy intermediate range surface-to-surface ballistic missile. [New Latin *(Stella) Polāris,* polar (star).]

po·lar·i·scope (pō-lăr′ə-skōp′, pō-lâr′-) *n.* An instrument for ascertaining, measuring, or exhibiting the properties of polarized light, or for studying the interactions of polarized light with optically transparent media.

po·lar·i·ty (pō-lăr′ə-tē, pō-lâr′-) *n., pl.* **-ties.** **1.** Intrinsic polar separation, alignment, or orientation, especially of a physical property: *magnetic polarity; ionic polarity.* **2.** The possession or manifestation of two opposing attributes, tendencies, or principles: *political polarity.* **3.** An indicated polar extreme: *an electric terminal with positive polarity.*

po·lar·i·za·tion (pō′lər-ə-zā′shən, -ī-zā′shən) *n.* **1.** The production or condition of polarity, as: **a.** *Optics.* The uniform and nonrandom elliptical, circular, or linear variation of a wave characteristic, especially of vibrational orientation, in light or other radiation. **b.** *Physics & Chemistry.* The partial or complete polar separation of positive and negative electric charge in

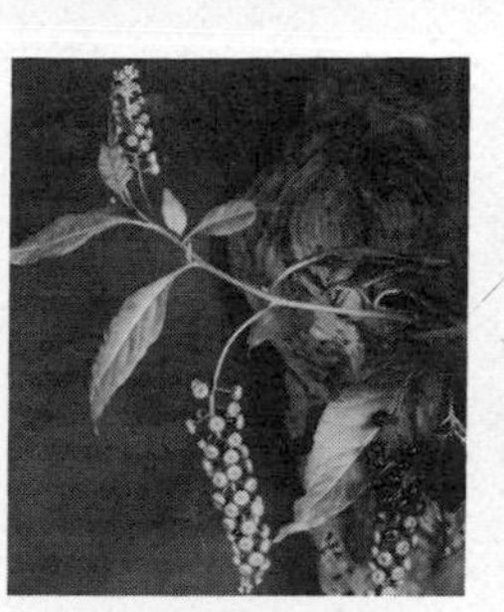

pokeweed
Foliage and berries

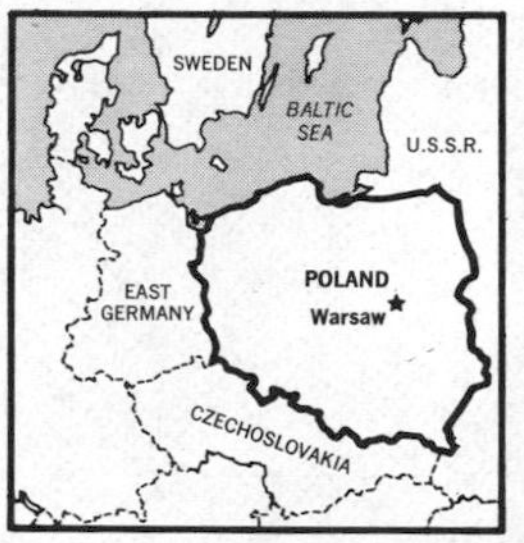

Poland

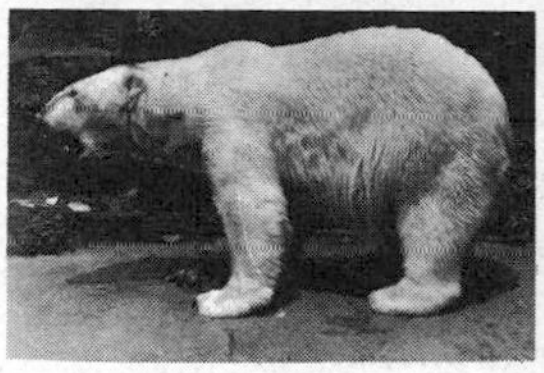

polar bear

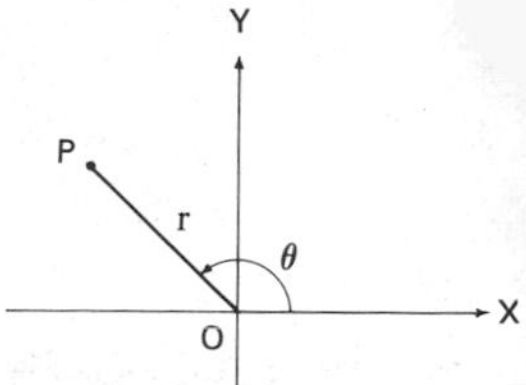

polar coordinate
r. Radius vector
θ. Polar angle
P. A point in the X-Y plane
O. Origin or pole

a nuclear, atomic, molecular, or chemical system. **2.** A concentration, as of groups, forces, or interests, about two conflicting or contrasting positions.

po·lar·ize (pō′lə-rīz′) *v.* **-ized, -izing, -izes.** —*tr.* **1.** To induce polarization in; impart polarity to. **2.** To cause to concentrate about two conflicting or contrasting positions. —*intr.* To acquire polarity. —**po′lar·iz′a·ble** *adj.* —**po′lar·iz′er** *n.*

po·lar·og·ra·phy (pō′lə-rŏg′rə-fē) *n.* An electrochemical method of quantitative or qualitative analysis based on the relationship between an increasing current passing through the solution being analyzed and the increasing voltage used to produce the current. [From POLAR(IZATION) + -GRAPHY.] —**po·lar′o·graph′ic** (pō-lăr′ə-grăf′ĭk) *adj.* —**po·lar′o·graph′i·cal·ly** *adv.*

Po·lar·oid (pō′lə-roid) *n.* A trademark for a specially treated, transparent plastic capable of polarizing light passing through it, used in glare-reducing optical devices.

Polar Regions. The land and water areas surrounding the North and South poles.

polar star. A star, **Polaris** *(see).*

pol·der (pōl′dər) *n.* An area of low-lying land, especially in the Netherlands, that has been reclaimed from a body of water and is protected by dikes. [Middle Dutch *polre, polder*†.]

pole[1] (pōl) *n. Abbr.* **p. 1.** Either axial extremity of any axis through a sphere. **2.** Either of the regions contiguous to the extremities of the earth's rotational axis, the **North Pole** or the **South Pole** *(both of which see).* **3.** *Physics.* A **magnetic pole** *(see).* **4.** *Electricity.* Either of two oppositely charged terminals, as in an electric cell or battery. **5.** *Astronomy.* A **celestial pole** *(see).* **6.** *Biology.* A structurally or physiologically distinct region at either axial extremity of a nucleus, cell, or organism. **7.** Either of two antithetical ideas, propensities, forces, or positions. **8.** Any fixed point of reference. **9.** *Geometry.* The origin in a polar coordinate system; the polar angle vertex. [Middle English, from Latin *polus,* Greek *polos,* axis of the sphere, firmament. See **kwel-**[1] in Appendix.*]

pole[2] (pōl) *n.* **1.** A long, relatively slender, and generally rounded piece of wood or other material. **2.** The long, tapering, wooden shaft extending up from the front axle of a vehicle to the collars of the animals drawing it; a tongue. **3. a.** *Abbr.* **p.** A unit of length, a **rod** *(see).* **b.** A unit of area equal to a square rod (30¼ square yards). **4.** *Nautical.* A small or light spar. —*v.* **poled, poling, poles.** —*tr.* **1.** To propel with a pole. **2.** To support (plants) with a pole. **3.** To strike, poke, or stir with a pole. —*intr.* **1.** To propel a boat, raft, or the like with a pole. **2.** To use ski poles to gain speed. [Middle English *po(o)le,* Old English *pāl,* from Common Germanic, from Latin *pālus,* stake. See **pag-** in Appendix.*]

Pole (pōl) *n.* A native or inhabitant of Poland.

pole·ax, pole·axe (pōl′ăks′) *n.* **1.** A battle-ax used in the Middle Ages and consisting of an ax, or an ax, hammer, and pick combination, with a long shaft. **2.** An ax having a hammer face opposite the blade, used to slaughter cattle. —*tr.v.* **pole·axed, -axing, -axes.** To strike or fell with or as if with a poleax. [Middle English *pollax* : POLL (head) + AX.]

pole bean. Any of various cultivated climbing beans trained to grow on poles or supports.

pole·cat (pōl′kăt′) *n.* **1.** A carnivorous mammal, *Mustela putorius,* of Eurasia and northern Africa, having dark-brown or black fur. **2.** Any of several similar or related animals, especially the **skunk** *(see).* [Middle English *polcat* : *pol-*† (meaning unknown) + CAT.]

pole horse. A horse harnessed to the pole, or tongue, of a vehicle. Also called "poler."

pole jump. *Sports.* A **pole vault** *(see).*

po·lem·ic (pə-lĕm′ĭk) *n.* **1.** A controversy or argument, especially one that is a refutation of or an attack upon a specified opinion, doctrine, or the like. **2.** *Plural.* **a.** The art or practice of argumentation or controversy. **b.** The practice of theological controversy to refute errors of doctrine. Usually used with a singular verb. **3.** A person engaged in or inclined to controversy, argument, or refutation. —*adj.* Also **po·lem·i·cal** (pə-lĕm′ĭ-kəl). Of or pertaining to a controversy, argument, or refutation. [Medieval Latin *polemicus,* controversialist, from Greek *polemikos,* of war, hostile, opposed, from *polemos*†, war.] —**po·lem′i·cal·ly** *adv.*

po·lem·i·cist (pə-lĕm′ə-sĭst) *n.* Also **pol·e·mist** (pŏl′ə-mĭst, pə-lĕm′ĭst). A person skilled or involved in polemics.

pol·er (pō′lər) *n.* **1.** One that propels, supports, conveys, or strikes with a pole. **2.** A **pole horse** *(see).*

pole·star (pōl′stär′) *n.* **1.** The star **Polaris** *(see).* **2.** A guiding principle.

pole vault. *Sports.* A field event in which the contestant jumps or vaults over a high crossbar with the aid of a long pole. Also called "pole jump."

pole-vault (pōl′vôlt′) *intr.v.* **-vaulted, -vaulting, -vaults.** *Sports.* To perform or complete a pole vault. —**pole′-vault′er** *n.*

po·lice (pə-lēs′) *n., pl.* **police. 1.** The regulation and control of the affairs of a community, especially with respect to the maintenance of order, law, health, morals, safety, and other matters affecting general welfare. **2. a.** The governmental department charged with this, now chiefly the department established to maintain order, enforce the law, and prevent and detect crime. **b.** The official civil force, or body of persons, established and maintained for this purpose; police force. **c.** The members of such a force; policemen. Used with a plural verb. **3. a.** Any group of persons resembling the police force of a community in organization or function: *campus police.* **b.** The members of such a group. **4.** *U.S. Army.* The cleaning of a camp or other military area: *Police of battalion headquarters must be completed.* **5.** The soldiers assigned to a specified maintenance duty: *kitchen police.* —*tr.v.* **policed, -licing, -lices. 1.** To regulate, control, or keep in order with or as with police. **2.** To make (a military area) neat in appearance. [Originally "policy," "government organization," from French, from Late Latin *polītia,* administration of the commonwealth, from Latin *polītia,* the state, from Greek *politeia,* polity, citizenship, from *politēs,* citizen, from *polis,* city. See **pele-**[2] in Appendix.*]

police court. An inferior court having the power to prosecute minor criminal offenses and to hold for trial persons charged with more serious offenses.

police dog. A dog trained to aid the police; especially, the **German shepherd** *(see).*

police force. A body of persons trained in methods of law enforcement and crime prevention and detection, and given authority to maintain the peace, safety, and order of the community.

po·lice·man (pə-lēs′mən) *n., pl.* **-men** (-mĭn). A member of a police force.

police power. The inherent authority of a government to impose restrictions on private rights for the sake of public welfare, order, and security.

police reporter. A newspaper reporter whose assignment is to obtain and cover news in a local police department.

police state. A country or other political unit in which the government exercises rigid and repressive controls over the social, economic, and political life, especially by means of a secret police force.

police station. The headquarters of a unit of a police force where those under arrest are first charged.

po·lice·wom·an (pə-lēs′wo͝om′ən) *n., pl.* **-women** (-wĭm′ĭn). A female member of a police force.

pol·i·clin·ic (pŏl′ē-klĭn′ĭk) *n.* The department of a hospital that treats outpatients. [German *Poliklinik,* originally "clinic instruction held at a patient's house in town (as opposed to that held in the hospital)" : Greek *polis,* city (see **pele-**[2] in Appendix*) + *klinikē,* CLINIC (instruction).]

pol·i·cy[1] (pŏl′ə-sē) *n., pl.* **-cies. 1.** Any plan or course of action adopted by a government, political party, business organization, or the like, designed to influence and determine decisions, actions, and other matters: *American foreign policy; the company's personnel policy.* **2. a.** A course of action, guiding principle, or procedure considered to be expedient, prudent, or advantageous: *Honesty is the best policy.* **b.** Prudence, shrewdness, or sagacity in practical matters. [Middle English *policye,* polity, commonwealth, policy, from Old French *policie,* from Latin *polītia,* state, from Greek *politeia,* citizenship, from *politēs,* citizen, from *polis,* city. See **pele-**[2] in Appendix.*]

pol·i·cy[2] (pŏl′ə-sē) *n., pl.* **-cies. 1.** A written contract or certificate of insurance. **2.** A form of gambling in which bets are made on unpredictable numbers, such as the U.S. Treasury balance or various pari-mutuel totals. Also called "numbers," "numbers game," "policy racket." [Old French *police,* from Italian *polizza,* from Medieval Latin *apodixa,* from Latin *apodīxis,* from Greek *apodeixis,* "a showing or making known," proof, from *apodeiknunai,* to show off, display, make known : *apo,* off, from + *deiknunai,* to show (see **deik-** in Appendix*).]

pol·i·cy·hold·er (pŏl′ə-sē-hōl′dər) *n.* A person who holds an insurance contract or policy.

Po·li·llo Islands (pō-lē′yō). A group of about 21 islands and islets of the Republic of the Philippines, off the eastern coast of Luzon Island. Largest island, Polillo (234 square miles).

po·li·o (pō′lē-ō′) *n.* Poliomyelitis.

po·li·o·my·e·li·tis (pō′lē-ō-mī′ə-lī′tĭs) *n.* An infectious viral disease occurring mainly in children and in its acute forms attacking the central nervous system and producing paralysis, muscular atrophy, and often deformity. Also called "infantile paralysis." [Greek *polios,* gray (see **pel-**[2] in Appendix*) + MYELITIS.]

po·lis (pō′lĭs) *n., pl.* **-leis** (-lās′). A city-state of ancient Greece. [Greek *polis,* city. See **pele-**[2] in Appendix.*]

pol·ish (pŏl′ĭsh) *v.* **-ished, -ishing, -ishes.** —*tr.* **1.** To make smooth and shiny by abrasion or chemical action. **2.** To free from coarseness; make elegant; refine. **3.** To remove flaws from; perfect or complete: *polish one's piano technique.* —*intr.* **1.** To become smooth or shiny by or as if by rubbing. **2.** To become perfect or refined. —**polish off.** *Informal.* **1.** To complete or finish quickly: *polish off a meal.* **2.** To eliminate or dispose of: *He polished off his enemies.* —**polish up.** To improve: *polish up the lyrics.* —*n.* **1.** Smoothness or shininess of surface or finish. **2.** A substance containing chemical agents or abrasive particles and applied to smooth or shine a surface. **3.** The act or process of polishing. **4.** Elegance of style or manners; refinement. [Middle English *polisshen,* from Old French *polir* (present stem *poliss-*), from Latin *polīre.* See **pel-**[6] in Appendix.*] —**pol′ish·er** *n.*

Po·lish (pō′lĭsh) *adj. Abbr.* **Pol.** Of or pertaining to Poland, its inhabitants, or their language or culture. —*n. Abbr.* **Pol.** The West Slavic language that is the major language of Poland. [From POLE.]

Polish Corridor. A strip of territory about 120 miles long and 60 miles wide, separating East Prussia from the rest of Germany; awarded to Poland in the Treaty of Versailles.

pol·ished (pŏl′ĭsht) *adj.* **1. a.** Made shiny and smooth. **b.** Naturally shiny and smooth. **2.** Refined; polite; cultured. **3.** Having no imperfections or errors; flawless.

polit. political; politics.

pol·it·bu·ro (pŏl′ĭt-byo͝or′ō, pə-lĭt′-) *n.* The chief political and

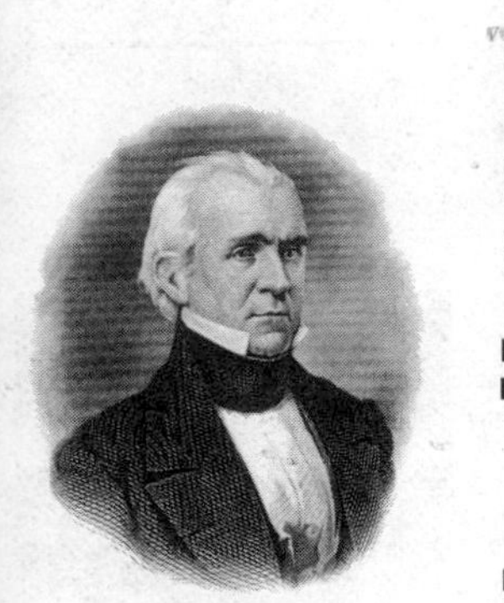

James K. Polk

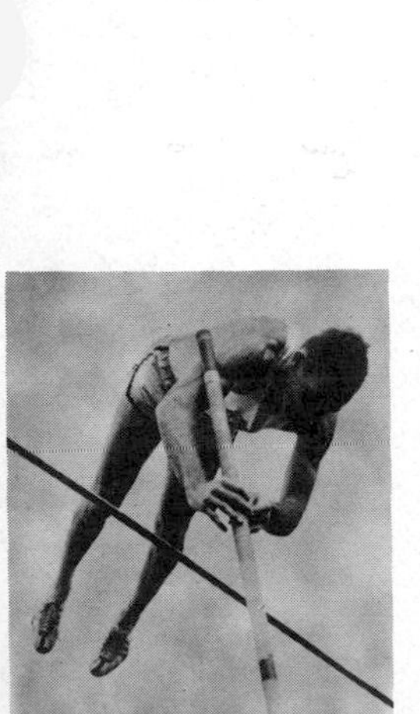

pole vault
U.S. pole-vaulter John Pennel in a July 1963 meet in Hanover, West Germany

ă pat/ā pay/âr care/ä father/b bib/ch church/d deed/ĕ pet/ē be/f fife/g gag/h hat/hw which/ĭ pit/ī pie/îr pier/j judge/k kick/l lid, needle/m mum/n no, sudden/ng thing/ŏ pot/ō toe/ô paw, for/oi noise/ou out/o͝o took/o͞o boot/p pop/r roar/s sauce/sh ship, dish/

executive committee of a Communist party. [From Russian *Polit(icheskoe) Buro,* political bureau.]
po·lite (pə-līt′) *adj.* **-liter, -litest.** **1.** Marked by consideration for others, correct manners, or tact; courteous. **2.** Refined; elegant; cultivated: *polite society.* [Middle English *polyt,* polished, smoothed, from Latin *polītus,* past participle of Latin *polīre,* to POLISH.] **—po·lite′ly** *adv.* **—po·lite′ness** *n.*
Synonyms: *polite, civil, courteous, genteel.* These all describe social behavior as being proper or commendatory. *Polite* means duly respectful or indulgent with other people according to social norms. *Civil,* suggesting only the barest agreeability or tact in manners, means friendly in a reserved, correct sense. *Courteous* is similar to *polite* but implies a more voluntary, generous consideration which is of a helpful nature. *Genteel* refers to the quality of good taste or propriety in a cultured person. It can suggest fine sensibilities and respectability but now usually suggests overrefinement to the point of artificiality.
pol·i·tesse (pŏl′ĭ-tĕs′; *French* pô-lē-tĕs′) *n.* Courteous formality; politeness. [French, from Italian *politezza, pulitezza,* cleanliness, from *pulito,* "polished," clean, from Latin *polītus,* past participle of *polīre,* to POLISH.]
Po·li·tian (pə-lĭsh′ən). Original name, Angelo Ambrogini. Also called Poliziano. 1454–1494. Florentine humanist poet.
pol·i·tic (pŏl′ə-tĭk) *adj.* **1.** Artful; ingenious, shrewd: *a politic senator.* **2.** Using, displaying, or proceeding from policy; wise; prudent; judicious: *a politic decision.* **3.** Crafty; unscrupulous; cunning. —See Synonyms at **suave.** [Middle English *polytyk,* "political," pursuing a policy, prudent, from Old French *politique,* from Latin *polīticus,* from Greek *politikos,* of a citizen, from *politēs,* citizen, from *polis,* city. See **pelə-**[2] in Appendix.*] **—pol′i·tic·ly** *adv.*
po·lit·i·cal (pə-lĭt′ĭ-kəl) *adj. Abbr.* **pol., polit.** **1.** Of, pertaining to, or dealing with the study, structure, or affairs of government, politics, or the state. **2.** Having a definite or organized policy or structure of government. **3.** Characteristic of or resembling politics, political parties, or politicians. **—po·lit′i·cal·ly** *adv.*
political economy. The science of economics.
political science. The study of the processes, principles, and structure of government and of political institutions; politics.
pol·i·ti·cian (pŏl′ə-tĭsh′ən) *n. Abbr.* **pol.** **1. a.** One who is actively involved in politics, especially party politics. **b.** One who holds or seeks a political office. **2.** One who is interested in personal or partisan gain and other selfish interests: *"Mothers may still want their favorite sons to grow up to be President, but . . . they do not want them to become politicians in the process."* (John F. Kennedy). **3.** One skilled or experienced in the science or administration of government. —Compare **statesman.**
po·lit·i·cize (pə-lĭt′ə-sīz′) *v.* **-cized, -cizing, -cizes.** *—intr.* To engage in or discuss politics. *—tr.* To make political.
pol·i·tick (pŏl′ə-tĭk) *intr.v.* **-ticked, -ticking, -ticks.** To engage in or talk politics.
po·lit·i·co (pə-lĭt′ĭ-kō′) *n., pl.* **-cos.** A politician. [Italian and Spanish, "political," from Latin *polīticus,* POLITIC.]
pol·i·tics (pŏl′ə-tĭks) *n.* Plural in form, usually used with a singular verb. See Usage note below. *Abbr.* **pol., polit.** **1.** The art or science of political government, political science. **2.** The policies, goals, or affairs of a government or of the groups or parties within it. **3. a.** The conducting of or engaging in political affairs, often professionally. **b.** The business, activities, or profession of a person so involved. **4.** The methods or tactics involved in managing a state or government. **5.** Partisan or factional intrigue within a given group: *office politics.* **6.** Opinions or principles dealing with political subjects. Used with a plural verb: *His politics are conservative.*
Usage: *Politics,* now usually construed as singular, takes a singular verb especially when the term is considered in a collective sense as a science, art, or profession, and when it is linked to a predicate noun that is singular: *Politics is a funny game.* The word is construed as plural principally when it denotes the opinions, principles, or activities of one or more individuals: *My politics are my own concern.*
pol·i·ty (pŏl′ə-tē) *n., pl.* **-ties.** **1.** The form of government of a nation, state, church, or organization. **2.** Any organized society, such as a nation, having one specific form of government: *"His alien philosophy found no roots in the American polity."* (New York Times). [Old French *politie,* from Latin *polītia,* from Greek *politeia,* government, constitution, from *politēs,* citizen, from *polis,* city. See **pelə-**[2] in Appendix.*]
Polk (pōk), **James Knox.** 1795–1849. Eleventh President of the United States (1845–49).
pol·ka (pōl′kə, pō′kə) *n.* **1.** A lively round dance, originating in Bohemia, performed by couples in duple meter. **2.** Music for this dance. *—intr.v.* **polkaed, -kaing, -kas.** To dance the polka. [French and German, from Czech, from Polish *polka,* Polish woman : *pol-,* field, name of region identified with Poland (see **pelə-**[1] in Appendix*) + *-ka,* feminine suffix.]
pol·ka dot (pō′kə). **1.** One of a number of dots or round spots forming a pattern on cloth. **2.** A pattern or fabric with such dots. [Perhaps a respelling of *poke a dot.*]
poll (pōl) *n.* **1.** The casting and registering of votes in an election. **2.** The number of votes cast or recorded. **3.** *Usually plural.* The place where votes are cast and registered. **4.** A tax required for voting, a **poll tax** *(see).* **5.** A list or record of persons, especially for taxing or voting purposes. **6.** A canvassing of a selected sample group of persons to analyze public opinion on a particular question. **7.** The head, especially the top of the head where hair grows. **8.** The blunt or broad end of a hammer, ax, or other similar tool. *—v.* **polled, polling, polls.** *—tr.* **1.** To receive (a given number of votes). **2.** To register (someone), especially for voting or taxing purposes. **3.** To receive or record the votes of. **4.** To draw forth (voters) to the polls. **5.** To cast (a vote or ballot). **6.** To canvass or question (a sample group of persons) to survey public opinion. **7.** To cut off or trim (hair, horns, or wool, for example); clip. **8.** To trim or cut off the hair, wool, branches, or horns of; shear: *poll sheep.* *—intr.* To vote at the polls or in an election. [Middle English *pol, polle,* head (whence the Modern English senses of "counting by heads," "registering of votes"), of Low German origin, akin to Middle Low German *polle*†.] **—poll′er** *n.*
pol·lack. Variant of **pollock.**
pol·lard (pŏl′ərd) *n.* **1.** A tree whose top branches have been cut back to the trunk so that it may produce a dense growth of new shoots. **2.** An animal, such as an ox, goat, or sheep, that no longer has its horns. *—tr.v.* **pollarded, -larding, -lards.** To convert or change into a pollard. [From POLL.]
polled (pōld) *adj.* Having no horns; hornless.
pol·len (pŏl′ən) *n. Botany.* The fine, powderlike material produced by the anthers of flowering plants, and functioning as the male element in fertilization. [New Latin, from Latin, flour, dust. See **pel-**[1] in Appendix.*]
pollen count. The average number of pollen grains, usually of ragweed, in a cubic yard or other standard volume of air over a 24-hour period at a specified time and place, used to estimate the possible severity of hay-fever attacks.
pollen tube. *Botany.* The slender tube that is emitted by a grain of pollen, and that penetrates an ovule and fertilizes it.
pol·lex (pŏl′ĕks′) *n., pl.* **pollices** (pŏl′ə-sēz′). The innermost forelimb digit; thumb. [Latin, thumb. See **pol-** in Appendix.*] **—pol′li·cal** *adj.*
pollin-, pollini-. Indicates pollen; for example, **pollinosis, polliniferous.** [From New Latin *pollen* (stem *pollin-*), POLLEN.]
pol·li·nate (pŏl′ə-nāt′) *tr.v.* **-nated, -nating, -nates.** Also **pol·len·ate.** *Botany.* To convey or transfer pollen from an anther to a stigma of (a plant or flower) in the process of fertilization. Also "pollinize." [From New Latin *pollen* (stem *pollin-*), POLLEN.] **—pol′li·na′tion** *n.* **—pol′li·na′tor** (-nā′tər) *n.*
pol·lin·ic (pŏ-lĭn′ĭk) *adj. Botany.* Of or pertaining to pollen.
pol·li·nif·er·ous (pŏl′ə-nĭf′ər-əs) *adj.* Also **pol·len·if·er·ous.** **1.** Producing or yielding pollen. **2.** Adapted for carrying pollen. [POLLINI- + -FEROUS.]
pol·lin·i·um (pŏ-lĭn′ē-əm) *n., pl.* **-ia** (-ē-ə). *Botany.* A mass of agglutinated pollen grains, found in the flowers of most orchids and milkweeds. [New Latin : POLLIN- + -IUM.]
pol·li·nize (pŏl′ə-nīz′) *tr.v.* **-nized, -nizing, -nizes.** *Botany.* To pollinate. **—pol′li·ni·za′tion** *n.*
pol·li·no·sis (pŏl′ə-nō′sĭs) *n.* Also **pol·len·o·sis.** *Pathology.* Allergic reaction to pollen, as in disorders such as hay fever or asthma. [New Latin : POLLIN- + -OSIS.]
pol·li·wog (pŏl′ē-wŏg′, -wôg′) *n.* Also **pol·ly·wog.** An immature frog or toad, a **tadpole** *(see).* [Middle English *polwygle* : *pol, polle,* POLL (head) + *wiglen, wigelen,* to WIGGLE.]
pol·lock (pŏl′ək) *n., pl.* **pollock** or **-locks.** Also **pol·lack.** A marine food fish, *Pollachius virens,* of northern Atlantic waters. [Scottish *podlok*†.]
Pol·lock (pŏl′ək), **Jackson.** 1912–1956. American artist; a leader of the abstract expressionist school.
poll·ster (pōl′stər) *n.* A practitioner of opinion polls.
poll tax. A tax levied on persons rather than on property, often as a requirement for voting. Also called "poll."
pol·lut·ant (pə-lo͞ot′nt) *n.* Anything that pollutes; especially, any gaseous, chemical, or organic waste that contaminates air, soil, or water.
pol·lute (pə-lo͞ot′) *tr.v.* **-luted, -luting, -lutes.** **1.** To render morally impure; corrupt. **2.** To make ceremonially impure; profane; desecrate: *"Churches and altars were polluted by atrocious murders."* (Gibbon). **3.** To dirty; contaminate. [Middle English *polluten,* from Latin *polluere.* See **leu-**[2] in Appendix.*] **—pol·lut′er** *n.*
pol·lu·tion (pə-lo͞o′shən) *n.* **1.** The act or process of polluting or the state of being polluted. **2.** The contamination of soil, water, or the atmosphere by the discharge of noxious substances.
Pol·lux[1] (pŏl′əks). *Greek Mythology.* One of the twin sons of Zeus and Leda. See **Castor and Pollux.**
Pol·lux[2] (pŏl′əks) *n. Astronomy.* A bright star in the constellation Gemini. [After the mythical twin POLLUX.]
Pol·ly[1] (pŏl′ē). A feminine given name. [Variant of MOLLY, pet form for MARY.]
Pol·ly[2] (pŏl′ē) *n.* A common nickname for a parrot.
Pol·ly·an·na (pŏl′ē-ăn′ə) *n.* A foolishly or blindly optimistic person. [After the title character in *Pollyanna* (1913), novel by Eleanor Porter (1868–1920).]
po·lo (pō′lō) *n.* **1.** A game of Oriental origin played by two teams of three or four players on horseback, equipped with long-handled mallets for driving a small wooden ball through the opponents' goal. **2.** Any similar game, such as water polo. [From Balti *polo,* "ball," akin to Tibetan *bo-lo.*] **—po′lo·ist** *n.*
Po·lo (pō′lō), **Marco.** 1254?–1324? Venetian traveler to the court of Kublai Khan.
polo coat. A kind of loose-fitting, tailored overcoat, made from camel's hair or a similar material.
pol·o·naise (pŏl′ə-nāz′, pō′lə-) *n.* **1.** A stately, marchlike Polish dance in triple time, consisting primarily of a promenade of couples. **2.** Music for or in the style of this dance. **3.** A woman's dress of the 18th century, having a fitted bodice and draped cutaway skirt, worn over an elaborate underskirt. [French, from the feminine of *polonais,* Polish, from Medieval

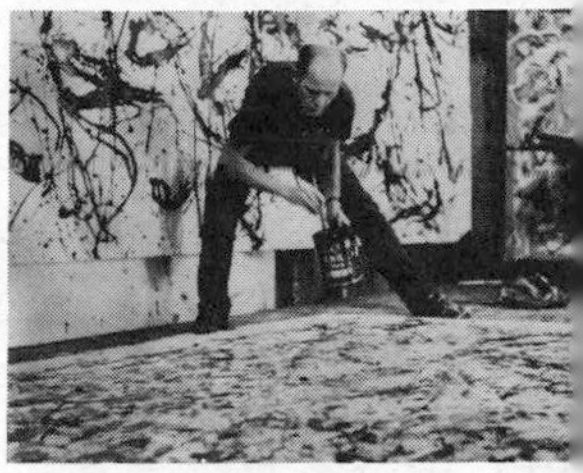

Jackson Pollock
At work on one of his large canvases

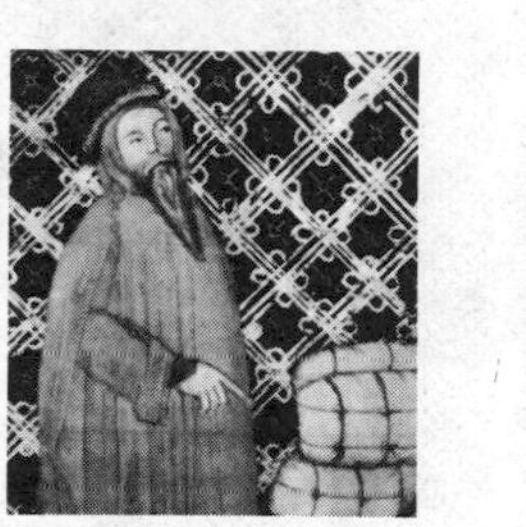

Marco Polo
Portrait in a 15th-century Spanish manuscript

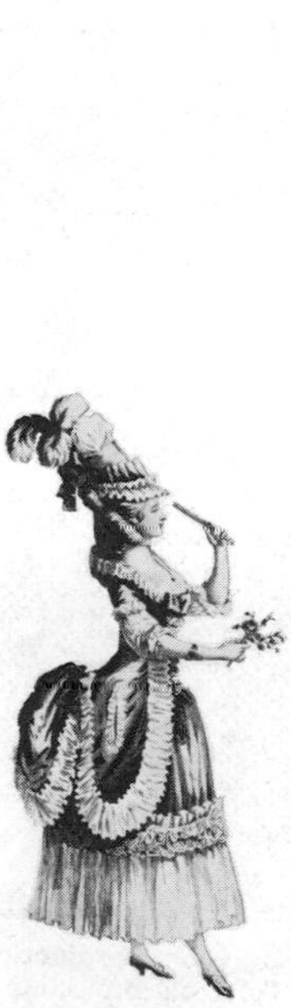

polonaise

Latin *Polōnia,* Poland, from Polish *Polanie,* "field-dwellers," POLAND.]

po·lo·ni·um (pə-lō'nē-əm) *n. Symbol* **Po** A naturally radioactive metallic element, occurring in minute quantities as a product of radium disintegration and produced by bombarding bismuth or lead with neutrons. It has 27 isotopes ranging in mass number from 192 to 218, of which Po 210, with a half-life of 138.39 days, is the most readily available. Atomic number 84, melting point 254°C, boiling point 962°C, specific gravity 9.32, valence 2, 4, 6. See **element.** [From Latin *Polōnia,* Poland (see **polonaise**), native country of its discoverers, the Curies.]

polo shirt. A pullover sport shirt of knitted cotton, usually having short sleeves and a buttoned collar.

Pol·ska. The Polish name for **Poland.**

Pol·ta·va (pəl-tä'və). A city in east-central Ukraine, about 90 miles southwest of Kharkov. Population, 170,000.

pol·ter·geist (pōl'tər-gīst') *n.* A ghost that manifests itself by noises and rappings. [German *Poltergeist* : *poltern,* to make noises, rattle, knock, from Middle High German *boldern, buldern* (see **bhel-**[4] in Appendix*) + German *Geist,* ghost, from Old High German *geist* (see **gheis-** in Appendix*).]

Pol·tor·atsk. The former name for **Ashkhabad.**

pol·troon (pŏl-trōōn') *n. Archaic.* A base coward. [Old French *po(u)ltron,* from Old Italian *poltrone,* "foal" from *poltro,* from Vulgar Latin *pulliter* (unattested), from Latin *pullus,* young animal. See **pōu-** in Appendix.*] —**pol·troon'er·y** *n.*

poly–. Indicates: **1.** More than one, many, or much; for example, **polygamy. 2.** More than usual; abnormal or excessive; for example, **polydipsia.** [From Greek *polus,* much, many. See **pel-**[8] in Appendix.*]

pol·y·am·ide (pŏl'ē-ăm'īd') *n. Chemistry.* A polymer containing repeated amide groups, as in various kinds of nylon.

pol·y·an·drous (pŏl'ē-ăn'drəs) *adj.* **1.** Pertaining to or practicing polyandry. **2.** *Botany.* Having an indefinite number of stamens. [Greek *poluandros.* See **polyandry.**]

pol·y·an·dry (pŏl'ē-ăn'drē) *n.* **1.** The state or practice of having more than one husband at a single time. **2.** *Botany.* The condition of being polyandrous. [Greek *poluandria,* from *poluandros* : POLY- + -ANDROUS.]

pol·y·an·thus (pŏl'ē-ăn'thəs) *n., pl.* **-thuses.** Any of a group of hybrid garden primroses having clusters of variously colored flowers. [New Latin, from Greek *poluanthos,* "having many flowers" : POLY- + -ANTHOUS.]

polyanthus narcissus. A bulbous plant, *Narcissus tazetta,* native to Eurasia, having clusters of fragrant white or yellow flowers.

pol·y·a·tom·ic (pŏl'ē-ə-tŏm'ĭk) *adj. Physics.* Having three or more atoms as constituents. Said especially of molecules.

pol·y·ba·sic (pŏl'ē-bā'sĭk) *adj. Chemistry.* **Polyprotic** *(see).*

pol·y·ba·site (pŏl'ē-bā'sīt') *n.* A black mineral with a metallic luster, containing silver, copper, antimony, and sulfur, essentially $(Ag, Cu)_{16}Sb_2S_{11}$, often found in veins of silver. [German *Polybasit* : POLY- + BAS(IS) + -ITE.]

Po·lyb·i·us (pə-lĭb'ē-əs). 205?–125? B.C. Greek historian.

Pol·y·carp (pŏl'ē-karp'), **Saint.** A.D. 69?–155? Christian martyr, bishop of Smyrna, and one of the Apostolic Fathers.

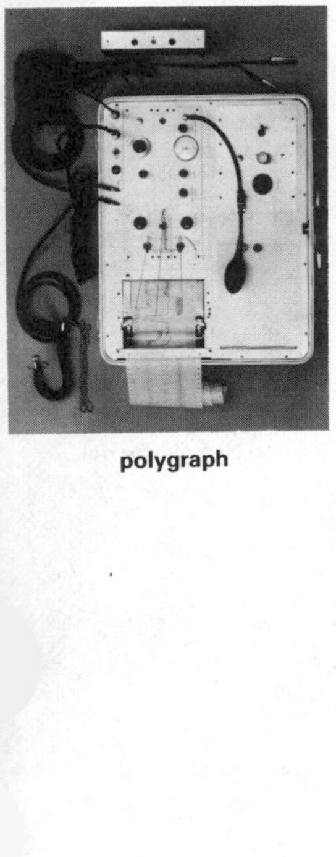

polygraph

pol·y·car·pel·lar·y (pŏl'ē-kär'pə-lĕr'ē) *adj. Botany.* Having or consisting of many carpels. [POLY- + CARPEL + -ARY.]

pol·y·car·pous (pŏl'ē-kär'pəs) *adj.* Also **po·ly·car·pic** (-pĭk). *Botany.* Having fruit with two or more carpels. [POLY- + -CARPOUS.] —**pol'y·car'py** *n.*

pol·y·chaete (pŏl'ĭ-kēt') *n.* Also **pol·y·chete.** Any of various marine worms of the class Polychaeta, having paired, flattened, bristle-tipped organs of locomotion. [New Latin *Polychaeta,* from Greek *polukhaitēs,* with much hair : POLY + *khaitē,* long hair, CHAETA.] —**pol'y·chaete, pol'y·chae'tous** *adj.*

pol·y·chro·mat·ic (pŏl'ē-krō-măt'ĭk) *adj.* Also **pol·y·chro·mic** (-krō'mĭk), **pol·y·chro·mous** (-krō'məs). Having many colors or manifesting changes of color.

pol·y·chro·mat·o·phil·i·a (pŏl'ē-krō-măt'ə-fĭl'ē-ə) *n.* Also **pol·y·chro·mo·phil·i·a** (-krō'mə-fĭl'ē-ə). *Medicine.* Susceptibility to staining with more than one type of dye, as seen in diseased red blood cells. [POLY- + CHROMATO- + -PHILIA.] —**pol'y·chro·mat'o·phil'ic** *adj.*

pol·y·chrome (pŏl'ē-krōm') *adj.* **1.** Having many or various colors; polychromatic. **2.** Made or decorated in many or various colors. —*n.* An object having or decorated in many colors. [Greek *polukhrōmos* : POLY- + -CHROME.]

pol·y·chro·my (pŏl'ē-krō'mē) *n.* The art of employing many colors in decoration, especially in architecture and statuary.

pol·y·clin·ic (pŏl'ē-klĭn'ĭk) *n.* A clinic or hospital that treats all types of diseases and injuries.

Pol·y·cli·tus (pŏl'ĭ-klī'təs). Greek sculptor and architect of the fifth century B.C.

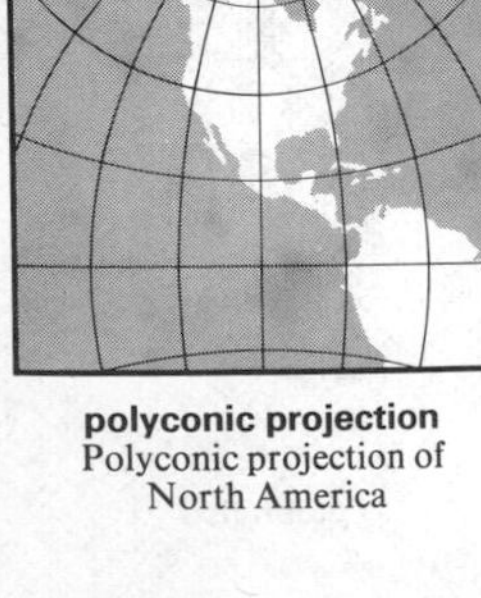

polyconic projection
Polyconic projection of North America

pol·y·con·ic projection (pŏl'ē-kŏn'ĭk). *Geography.* A conic map projection having distances between meridians along every parallel equal to those distances on a globe. The central geographic meridian is a straight line and the others are curved, while the parallels are arcs of circles.

pol·y·cot·y·le·don (pŏl'ē-kŏt'l-ēd'n) *n.* Also **pol·y·cot** (pŏl'ē-kŏt'). *Botany.* A plant having several cotyledons. —**pol'y·cot'y·le'don·ous** *adj.*

pol·y·cy·the·mi·a (pŏl'ē-sī-thē'mē-ə) *n. Pathology.* A condition marked by an abnormally large number of red cells in the blood. [POLY- + CYT(O)- + -HEMIA.]

pol·y·dac·tyl (pŏl'ē-dăk'təl) *adj.* Also **pol·y·dac·ty·lous** (-tə-ləs). Having more than the normal number of fingers or toes. —*n.* A polydactyl person or animal. [Greek *poludaktulos* : POLY- + DACTYL.] —**pol'y·dac'tyl·ism, pol'y·dac'ty·ly** *n.*

pol·y·dem·ic (pŏl'ē-dĕm'ĭk) *adj. Ecology.* Occurring in or inhabiting two or more regions. [POLY- + (EN)DEMIC.]

pol·y·dip·si·a (pŏl'ē-dĭp'sē-ə) *n.* Excessive or abnormal thirst. [New Latin : POLY- + Greek *dipsa,* thirst (see **dipsas**).] —**pol'y·dip'sic** *adj.*

pol·y·em·bry·o·ny (pŏl'ē-ĕm'brē-ə-nē, -ĕm-brī'ə-nē) *n. Biology.* The development of more than one embryo from a single egg or ovule. [From POLY- + EMBRYO(N) + -Y.] —**pol'y·em'bry·on'ic** (-ĕm'brē-ŏn'ĭk) *adj.*

pol·y·es·ter (pŏl'ē-ĕs'tər) *n. Chemistry.* Any of numerous synthetic resins, produced chiefly by reaction of dibasic acids with dihydric alcohols. Reinforced polyester resins are light, strong, and weather-resistant, and are used in boat hulls, swimming pools, waterproof fibers, adhesives, and molded parts. [POLY(MER) + ESTER.] —**pol'y·es'ter·i·fi·ca'tion** *n.*

pol·y·eth·yl·ene (pŏl'ē-ĕth'ə-lēn') *n.* Also *chiefly British* **pol·y·thene** (pŏl'ə-thēn'). *Chemistry.* A polymerized ethylene resin, used especially in the form of films and sheets for packaging, or molded for a wide variety of containers, kitchenware, and tubing. [POLY(MER) + ETHYLENE.]

po·lyg·a·la (pə-lĭg'ə-lə) *n.* Any plant of the genus *Polygala,* a **milkwort** *(see).* [New Latin *Polygala,* from Latin, from Greek *polugalon* : POLY- + *gala,* milk (see **melg-** in Appendix*).]

po·lyg·a·mist (pə-lĭg'ə-mĭst) *n.* One who practices polygamy.

po·lyg·a·mous (pə-lĭg'ə-məs) *adj.* **1.** Of, relating to, engaged in, or characterized by polygamy. **2.** *Botany.* **a.** Having both hermaphroditic and unisexual flowers on the same plant. **b.** Having either hermaphroditic or unisexual flowers on different plants of the same species. [Greek *polugamos* : POLY- + -GAMOUS.] —**po·lyg'a·mous·ly** *adv.*

po·lyg·a·my (pə-lĭg'ə-mē) *n.* The state or practice of having more than one wife, husband, or mate at a single time. [Old French *polygamie,* from Late Latin *polygamia,* from Greek *polugamia* : POLY- + -GAMY.]

pol·y·gene (pŏl'ē-jēn') *n.* One of a set of cooperating genes, each producing a small quantitative effect. Also called "quantitative gene." Compare **oligogene.**

pol·y·gen·e·sis (pŏl'ē-jĕn'ə-sĭs) *n.* The derivation of a species or type from more than one ancestor. Compare **monogenesis.** [New Latin : POLY- + -GENESIS.] —**pol'y·gen'e·sist** *n.* —**pol'y·ge·net'ic** (pŏl'ē-jə-nĕt'ĭk), **pol'y·gen'ic** (-jĕn'ĭk), **po·lyg'e·nous** (pə-lĭj'ə-nəs) *adj.*

pol·y·glot (pŏl'ē-glŏt') *adj.* Speaking, writing, written in, or composed of several languages. —*n.* **1.** A person with a reading, writing, or speaking knowledge of several languages. **2.** A book, especially a Bible, containing several versions of the same text in different languages. **3.** A mixture or confusion of languages. [French *polyglotte,* from Greek *poluglōttos* : POLY- + *glōtta, glōssa,* tongue (see **glōgh-** in Appendix*).] —**pol'y·glot'ism, pol'y·glot'tism** *n.*

pol·y·gon (pŏl'ē-gŏn') *n. Geometry.* A closed plane figure bounded by three or more line segments. [Late Latin *polygōnum,* from Greek *polugōnon,* from *polugōnos,* "having many angles" : POLY- + -GON.] —**po·lyg'o·nal** (pə-lĭg'ə-nəl) *adj.* —**po·lyg'o·nal·ly** *adv.*

po·lyg·o·num (pə-lĭg'ə-nəm) *n.* Any of numerous plants of the widely distributed genus *Polygonum,* characterized by stems with knotlike joints. [New Latin, from Greek *polugonon,* knotgrass : POLY- + *gonu,* knee (see **genu-**[1] in Appendix*).]

pol·y·graph (pŏl'ē-grăf', -gräf') *n.* An instrument that simultaneously records changes in such physiological processes as heartbeat, blood pressure, and respiration, and is sometimes used in lie detection. [Greek *polugraphos,* "writing a lot" : POLY- + -GRAPH.] —**pol'y·graph'ic** *adj.*

po·lyg·y·ny (pə-lĭj'ə-nē) *n.* The condition or practice of having more than one wife or female mate at a single time. [POLY- + Greek *gunē,* woman (see **gwen-** in Appendix*).] —**po·lyg'y·nous** *adj.*

pol·y·he·dral angle (pŏl'ē-hē'drəl). *Geometry.* The configuration formed by three or more planes having intersections that form a common vertex. Compare **solid angle.**

pol·y·he·dron (pŏl'ē-hē'drən) *n., pl.* **-drons** or **-dra** (-drə). *Geometry.* A solid bounded by polygons. [New Latin, from Greek *poluedron,* neuter of *poluedros,* having many sides or seats : POLY- + -HEDRON.] —**pol'y·he'dral** *adj.*

pol·y·his·tor (pŏl'ē-hĭs'tər) *n.* A polymath. [From Greek *poluistōr* : POLY- + *histōr,* learned (see **weid-** in Appendix*).] —**pol'y·his·tor'ic** (-hĭs-tôr'ĭk, -tŏr'ĭk) *adj.*

pol·y·hy·dric (pŏl'ē-hī'drĭk) *adj. Chemistry.* Containing at least two hydroxyl groups. [POLY- + HYDRIC.]

Pol·y·hym·ni·a (pŏl'ē-hĭm'nē-ə). Also **Po·lym·ni·a** (pə-lĭm'nē-ə). *Greek Mythology.* The Muse of singing, rhetoric, and mime. [Latin, from Greek *Polumnia,* from *polumnos,* abounding in songs : POLY- + *humnos,* HYMN.]

pol·y·mas·ti·gote (pŏl'ē-măs'tə-gōt') *adj. Zoology.* Having a tuftlike arrangement of flagella. [POLY- + Greek *mastix*† (stem *mastig-*), whip + -ATE.]

pol·y·math (pŏl'ē-măth') *n.* A person of great or varied learning. [Greek *polumathēs* : POLY- + *math-,* stem of *manthanein,* to learn (see **mendh-** in Appendix*).] —**pol'y·math', pol'y·math'ic** *adj.*

pol·y·mer (pŏl'ə-mər) *n. Chemistry.* Any of numerous natural and synthetic compounds of usually high molecular weight consisting of up to millions of repeated linked units, each a relatively light and simple molecule. [From POLYMERIC.]

pol·y·mer·ic (pŏl'ə-mĕr'ĭk) *adj. Chemistry.* Of, pertaining to, or consisting of a polymer. [From Greek *polumerēs,* having many parts : POLY- + -MEROUS.] —**pol'y·mer'i·cal·ly** *adv.* —**po·lym'er·ism** (pə-lĭm'ə-rĭz'əm, pŏl'ə-mə-) *n.*

ă pat/ā pay/âr care/ä father/b bib/ch church/d deed/ĕ pet/ē be/f fife/g gag/h hat/hw which/ĭ pit/ī pie/îr pier/j judge/k kick/l lid, needle/m mum/n no, sudden/ng thing/ŏ pot/ō toe/ô paw, for/oi noise/ou out/ŏŏ took/ōō boot/p pop/r roar/s sauce/sh ship, dish/

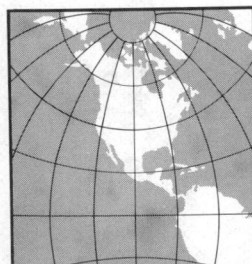

po·lym·er·i·za·tion (pə-lĭm′ər-ə-zā′shən, pŏl′ə-mər-) *n. Chemistry.* 1. The uniting of two or more monomers to form a polymer. 2. Any chemical process that effects such a union.

pol·y·mer·ize (pŏl′ə-mə-rīz′, pə-lĭm′ə-) *v.* **-ized, -izing, -izes.** *Chemistry.* —*tr.* To subject to polymerization. —*intr.* To undergo polymerization.

po·lym·er·ous (pə-lĭm′ər-əs) *adj. Biology.* Consisting of numerous parts. [POLY- + -MEROUS.]

pol·y·morph (pŏl′ē-môrf′) *n.* 1. *Biology.* An organism characterized by polymorphism. 2. *Chemistry.* A specific crystalline form of a compound that can crystallize in different forms. [From *polymorphous*, having many forms, from Greek *polumorphos* : POLY- + -MORPHOUS.]

pol·y·mor·phism (pŏl′ē-môr′fĭz′əm) *n.* 1. *Biology.* The occurrence of different forms, stages, or color types in individual organisms or in organisms of the same species. 2. *Chemistry.* Crystallization of a compound in at least two distinct forms. —**pol′y·mor′phic, pol′y·mor′phous** *adj.*

pol·y·myx·in (pŏl′ē-mĭk′sĭn) *n. Medicine.* Any of various mainly toxic antibiotics derived from strains of the soil bacterium *Bacillus polymixa.* [New Latin (*Bacillus*) *polymixa* : POLY- + MYX(O)- + -IN.]

Pol·y·ne·sia (pŏl′ə-nē′zhə, -shə). One of the three major divisions of Oceania, a scattered group of islands of the eastern and southeastern Pacific Ocean, extending from New Zealand north to Hawaii and east to Easter Island. [New Latin : POLY- + -nesia, from Greek *nēsos*, island (see **sna-** in Appendix*).]

Pol·y·ne·sian (pŏl′ə-nē′zhən, -shən) *adj.* Of or pertaining to Polynesia, its inhabitants, culture, or languages. —*n.* 1. One of the brown-skinned natives of Polynesia, including the Hawaiians, Maoris, Samoans, and Tahitians. 2. A language of the subfamily of Austronesian languages spoken in Polynesia.

pol·y·no·mi·al (pŏl′ē-nō′mē-əl) *adj.* Of, pertaining to, or consisting of more than two names or terms. —*n.* 1. *Biology.* A taxonomic designation consisting of more than two terms. 2. *Mathematics.* **a.** An algebraic function of two or more summed terms, each term consisting of a constant multiplier and one or more variables raised, in general, to integral powers. For example, the general form of a polynomial of degree *n* in a single real variable *x* is $a_0x^n + a_1x^{n-1} + \cdots + a_{n-1}x + a_n$ where $a_0, a_1, \cdots, a_n$ are real numbers with $a_0 \neq 0$ and *n* is a positive integer. **b.** Any mathematical expression of two or more terms. Also called "multinomial." [POLY- + (BI)NOMIAL.]

po·lyn·ya (pŏl′ən-yä′) *n.* A large area of open water surrounded by sea ice. [Russian *polyn'ya*, from *polyĭ*, open. See **pele-**¹ in Appendix.*]

pol·yp (pŏl′ĭp) *n.* 1. *Zoology.* A coelenterate having a cylindrical body and an oral opening usually surrounded by tentacles, as a hydra or coral. 2. *Pathology.* A growth protruding from the mucous lining of an organ, such as the nose. In this sense, also called "polypus." [French *polype*, octopus, from Latin *polypus*, from Greek *polupous*, "many-footed" : POLY- + *pous*, foot (see **ped-**¹ in Appendix*).] —**pol′yp·oid** *adj.*

pol·y·par·y (pŏl′ə-pĕr′ē) *n.,* pl. **-ies.** Also **pol·y·par·i·um** (pŏl′ə-pâr′ē-əm) pl. **-ia** (-ē-ə). *Zoology.* The common framework and base of a polyp colony, especially of coral. [From POLYP.]

pol·y·pep·tide (pŏl′ē-pĕp′tīd′) *n. Biochemistry.* A **peptide** (*see*) containing between 10 and 100 amino acids.

pol·y·pet·al·ous (pŏl′ē-pĕt′l-əs) *adj. Botany.* Having distinctly separate petals: *a polypetalous corolla.*

pol·y·pha·gi·a (pŏl′ē-fā′jē-ə, -jə) *n.* An excessive or pathological desire to eat. [New Latin, from Greek *poluphagia*, from *poluphagos*, eating much, POLYPHAGOUS.] —**pol′y·pha′gi·an** *adj.*

po·lyph·a·gous (pə-lĭf′ə-gəs) *adj. Zoology.* Feeding on or utilizing a variety of foods. [Greek *poluphagos*, eating much : POLY- + -PHAGOUS.]

Pol·y·phe·mus (pŏl′ə-fē′məs). *Greek Mythology.* The Cyclops who confined Odysseus and his companions in a cave until Odysseus blinded him and escaped.

pol·y·phe·mus moth (pŏl′ə-fē′məs). A large North American moth, *Antheraea polyphemus,* having an eyelike spot on each hind wing. [New Latin, after POLYPHEMUS.]

pol·y·phone (pŏl′ē-fōn′) *n. Phonetics.* A written character or combination of characters having two or more phonetic values, such as the *a.* [POLY- + -PHONE.]

pol·y·phon·ic (pŏl′ē-fŏn′ĭk) *adj. Music.* Of, pertaining to, or characteristic of polyphony. —**pol′y·phon′i·cal·ly** *adv.*

po·lyph·o·ny (pə-lĭf′ə-nē) *n.,* pl. **-nies.** 1. The simultaneous combination of two or more independent melodic parts, especially when in close harmonic relationship; counterpoint. Compare **homophony, monophony.** 2. The representation of two or more sounds by one written character, such as the *c* in *cake* and *certain.* [Greek *poluphōnia*, variety of tones, from *poluphōnos*, having many tones : POLY- + *phōnē*, sound, PHONE.] —**po·lyph′o·nous** *adj.* —**po·lyph′o·nous·ly** *adv.*

pol·y·phy·let·ic (pŏl′ē-fī-lĕt′ĭk) *adj. Biology.* Pertaining to or characterized by development from more than one ancestral type. [POLY- + PHYLETIC.] —**pol′y·phy·let′i·cal·ly** *adv.*

pol·y·ploid (pŏl′ē-ploid′) *adj. Genetics.* Having more than twice the normal haploid chromosome number. —*n. Genetics.* An organism with more than two sets of chromosomes. [POLY- + -PLOID.] —**pol′y·ploi′dic** *adj.*

pol·yp·ne·a (pŏl′ĭp-nē′ə) *n.* Very rapid breathing; panting. [New Latin : POLY- + Greek *pnoia*, breathing, from *pnein*, to breathe (see **pneu-** in Appendix*).] —**pol′yp·ne′ic** (-nē′ĭk) *adj.*

pol·y·pod (pŏl′ē-pŏd′) *adj.* Also **po·lyp·o·dous** (pə-lĭp′ə-dəs). Having numerous feet. [Greek *polypous* (stem *polypod-*), "many-footed" : POLY- + *pous*, foot (see **ped-**¹ in Appendix*).]

pol·y·po·dy (pŏl′ē-pō′dē) *n.,* pl. **-dies.** Any of various ferns of

the widely distributed genus *Polypodium,* having simple or compound fronds and creeping rootstocks. [Middle English *polypodie,* from Latin *polypodium,* from Greek *polupodion,* diminutive of *polupous,* POLYPOD.]

pol·y·pore (pŏl′ē-pôr′, -pōr′) *n.* A pore fungus (*see*).

pol·y·pro·tic (pŏl′ē-prō′tĭk) *adj. Chemistry.* Designating an acid with two or more replaceable hydrogen atoms in each molecule. Also called "polybasic." [POLY- + PROT(ON) + -IC.]

pol·yp·tych (pŏl′ĭp-tĭk′) *n.* A decorated altarpiece or panel having three or more hinged sections which can be folded together. [From Greek *poluptukhos,* having many folds : POLY- + *ptukhē,* a fold, from *ptussein†,* to fold.]

pol·y·pus (pŏl′ə-pəs) *n.,* pl. **-pi** (-pī′) or **-puses.** *Pathology.* A polyp (*see*). [Latin, POLYP.]

pol·y·sac·cha·ride (pŏl′ē-săk′ə-rīd′) *n.* Also **pol·y·sac·cha·rid** (pŏl′ē-săk′ə-rĭd), **pol·y·sac·cha·rose** (pŏl′ē-săk′ə-rōs′, -rōz′). A group of nine or more monosaccharides joined by glycosidic bonds, such as starch and cellulose.

pol·y·sep·al·ous (pŏl′ē-sĕp′ə-ləs) *adj. Botany.* Having distinctly separated sepals.

pol·y·so·mic (pŏl′ē-sō′mĭk) *adj. Genetics.* Having an excess number of one or more chromosomes. [POLY- + (CHROMO)-SOM(E) + -IC.]

pol·y·sper·my (pŏl′ē-spûr′mē) *n.* The entry of several sperms into an ovum during fertilization. —**pol′y·sper′mic** *adj.*

po·lys·ti·chous (pə-lĭs′tĭ-kəs) *adj.* Arranged in two or more series or rows. [POLY- + -STICHOUS.]

pol·y·sty·rene (pŏl′ē-stī′rēn′) *n.* A hard, rigid, dimensionally stable, clear thermoplastic polymer that is easily colored and molded for a wide variety of applications as a structural material. It is an excellent thermal and electrical insulator, and in the form of an expanded foam is extremely buoyant. [POLY- + STYRENE.]

pol·y·sul·fide (pŏl′ē-sŭl′fīd′) *n. Chemistry.* A sulfide compound containing at least two sulfur atoms per molecule.

pol·y·syl·lab·ic (pŏl′ē-sĭ-lăb′ĭk) *adj.* 1. Having more than three syllables. 2. Characterized by words having more than three syllables. —**pol′y·syl·lab′i·cal·ly** *adv.*

pol·y·syl·la·ble (pŏl′ē-sĭl′ə-bəl) *n.* A word of more than three syllables. [Medieval Latin *polysyllaba,* feminine of *polysyllabus,* polysyllabic, from Greek *polusullabos* : POLY- + *sullabē,* SYLLABLE.] —**pol′y·syl·lab′i·cism, pol′y·syl′la·bism** *n.*

pol·y·syn·de·ton (pŏl′ē-sĭn′də-tŏn′) *n.* The repetition of connectives or conjunctions in close succession for rhetorical effect, as in the phrase *here and there and everywhere.* [Late Greek *polusundeton,* from *polusundetos,*· using many connectives : Greek, POLY- + *sundetos,* bound together (see **syndetic**).]

pol·y·syn·thet·ic (pŏl′ē-sĭn-thĕt′ĭk) *adj. Linguistics.* Designating a language, such as Eskimo, in which many of the elements of a sentence or phrase are combined into one utterance and do not exist separately. Also called "holophrastic," "incorporating." Compare **synthetic.**

pol·y·tech·nic (pŏl′ē-tĕk′nĭk) *adj.* Pertaining to or dealing with many arts or sciences. —*n.* A school specializing in the teaching of industrial arts and applied sciences. [French *polytechnique,* from Greek *polutekhnos,* skilled in many arts : POLY- + *tekhē,* art (see **teks-** in Appendix*).]

pol·y·tet·ra·fluor·o·eth·y·lene (pŏl′ē-tĕt′rə-floôr′ō-ĕth′ə-lēn′) *n.* A waxy, opaque-white, thermoplastic resin, $(C_2F_4)_n$, thermally stable, resistant to acids, alkalies, and oxidizing agents, and having an extremely low coefficient of friction. It is used as a low-friction coating, especially for cooking vessels, and for chemical-resistant gaskets, seals, and hoses. A trademark is "Teflon." [POLY- + TETRA- + FLUORO- + ETHYLENE.]

pol·y·the·ism (pŏl′ē-thē-ĭz′əm) *n.* The worship of or belief in more than one god. [French *polythéisme,* from Greek *polutheos,* believing in many gods : POLY- + *theos,* god (see **dhēs-** in Appendix*).] —**pol′y·the′ist** *n.* —**pol′y·the·is′tic** *adj.*

pol·y·thene. *Chiefly British.* Variant of **polyethylene.**

po·lyt·o·cous (pə-lĭt′ə-kəs) *adj. Biology.* Producing many offspring or ova at a single time. [Greek *polutokos,* bearing numerous offspring : POLY- + *tokos,* offspring, from *tiktein,* to beget (see **tek-**¹ in Appendix*).]

pol·y·to·nal·i·ty (pŏl′ē-tō-năl′ə-tē) *n. Music.* Simultaneity of two or more tonalities in a composition. —**pol′y·ton′al** (-tō′nəl) *adj.* —**pol′y·ton′al·ly** *adv.*

pol·y·troph·ic (pŏl′ē-trŏf′ĭk, -trō′fĭk) *adj.* 1. *Biology.* Subsisting on various types of organic material. 2. *Pathology.* Characterized by or relating to excessive nutrition. [From Greek *polytrophos,* well-fed : POLY- + *trephein,* to feed (see **threph-** in Appendix*).]

pol·y·typ·ic (pŏl′ē-tĭp′ĭk) *adj.* Also **pol·y·typ·i·cal** (-ĭ-kəl). Existing in, having, or involving many different forms or types.

pol·y·un·sat·u·rat·ed (pŏl′ē-ŭn-săch′ə-rā′tĭd) *adj. Chemistry.* Pertaining to long-chain carbon compounds, especially fats, having many unsaturated bonds.

pol·y·u·re·thane (pŏl′ē-yŏŏr′ə-thān′) *n.* Also **pol·y·ur·e·than** (-thăn′). Any of various thermoplastic or thermosetting resins, widely varying in flexibility, used in tough chemical-resistant coatings and in adhesives, foams, and electrical insulation.

pol·y·u·ri·a (pŏl′ē-yŏŏr′ē-ə) *n. Pathology.* Excessive passage of urine, as in diabetes. [POLY- + -URIA.] —**pol′y·u′ric** *adj.*

pol·y·va·lent (pŏl′ē-vā′lənt) *adj.* 1. *Microbiology.* Containing, sensitive to, or interacting with more than one kind of antigen, antibody, toxin, or microorganism. 2. *Chemistry.* **a.** Having more than one valence. **b.** Having a valence of 3 or higher. In this sense, also "multivalent." [POLY- + *valent,* from VALENCE.] —**pol′y·va′lence, pol′y·va′len·cy** *n.*

pol·y·vi·nyl (pŏl′ē-vī′nəl) *adj.* Designating any of a group of

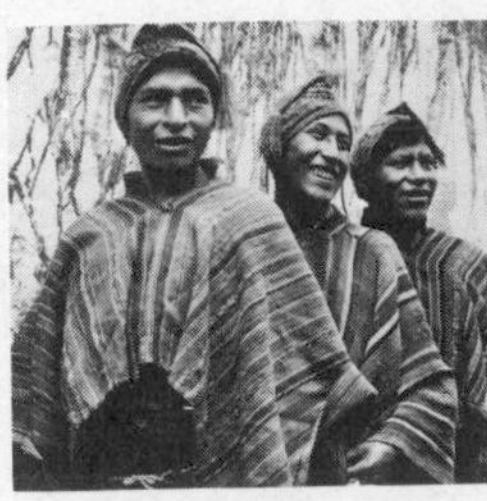

poncho
Peruvian Quechua Indians

pomegranate

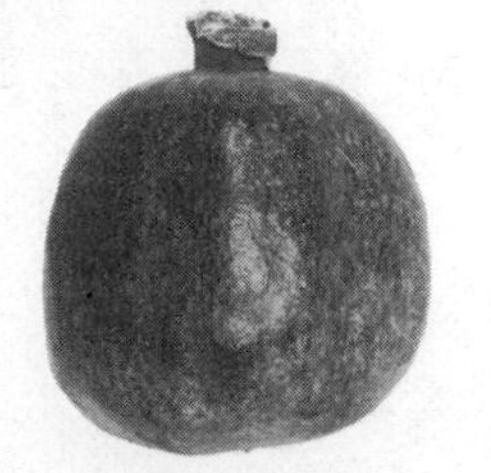

fruit

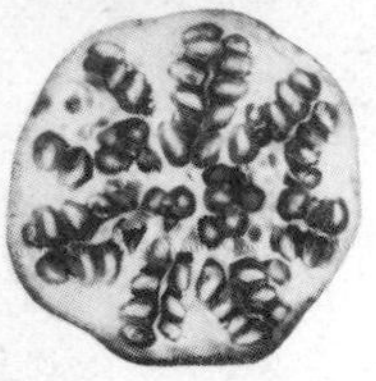

transverse section

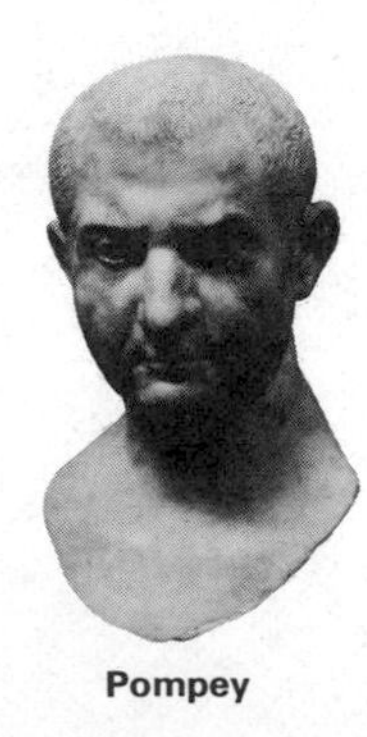

Pompey

polymerized thermoplastic vinyls, such as polyvinyl chloride.
polyvinyl chloride. A common thermoplastic resin, used in a wide variety of manufactured products, including rainwear, garden hoses, phonograph records, and floor tiles.
pol·y·zo·an (pŏl′ē-zō′ən) *n. Zoology.* A **bryozoan** *(see).* [From New Latin *Polyzoa* : POLY- + -ZOA.] —**pol′y·zo′an** *adj.*
pol·y·zo·ar·i·um (pŏl′ē-zō-âr′ē-əm) *n., pl.* **-ia** (-ē-ə). Also **pol·y·zo·a·ry** (-zō′ə-rē) *pl.* **-ries.** *Zoology.* A bryozoan colony or its supporting skeletal structure. [POLY- + -ZO(A) + -ARIUM.]
pol·y·zo·ic (pŏl′ē-zō′ĭk) *adj. Biology.* **1.** Forming or consisting of a colony of zooids. **2.** Containing numerous sporozoites. [POLY- + -ZOIC.]
pom·ace (pŭm′ĭs) *n.* **1.** The pulpy refuse remaining after the juice has been pressed from apples or other fruit. **2.** Any similar pulpy material, such as that remaining after the extraction of oil from nuts, seeds, or fish. [Medieval Latin *pōmācium,* cider, from Latin *pōmum,* apple. See **pōmum** in Appendix.*]
pomace fly. An insect, the **fruit fly** *(see).*
po·ma·ceous (pō-mā′shəs) *adj.* **1.** Of, pertaining to, or characteristic of apples. **2.** Of, pertaining to, or bearing pomes. [New Latin *pomaceus* : Latin *pōmum,* apple (see **pomace**) + -ACEOUS.]
po·made (pə-măd′, -mäd′, pō-) *n.* A perfumed ointment applied to the hair. —*tr.v.* **pomaded, -mading, -mades.** To anoint with pomade. [French *pommade,* from Italian *pomata,* hair ointment originally apple-scented, from *pomo,* apple, from Latin *pōmum.* See **pōmum** in Appendix.*]
po·man·der (pō′măn′dər, pō-măn′-) *n.* **1.** An apple-shaped mixture of aromatic substances, formerly worn as a protection against odor and infection. **2.** A case or box for holding this mixture. [Middle English, variant of Old French *pome d'embre,* from Medieval Latin *pōmum de ambra,* "apple" or "ball of amber" : *pōmum,* apple, POME + *de,* of + *ambra,* AMBER.]
pome (pōm) *n. Botany.* A fleshy fruit having seeds but no stone, such as the apple, pear, or quince. [Middle English, from Old French *pomme, pome,* apple, from Vulgar Latin *pōma* (unattested), from Latin *pōmum.* See **pōmum** in Appendix.*]
pome·gran·ate (pŏm′grăn′ĭt, pŭm′-) *n.* **1.** A semitropical shrub or small tree, *Punica granatum,* native to Asia, and widely cultivated for its edible fruit. **2.** The fruit of this tree, having a tough, reddish rind, and containing many seeds enclosed in a juicy red pulp with a mildly acid flavor. [Middle English *poumgarnei, pomegranard,* from Old French *pome grenate* : *pome,* apple, POME + *grenate,* having many seeds, from Latin *grānātus,* from *grānum,* grain (see **grə-no-** in Appendix*).]
pom·e·lo (pŏm′ə-lō′) *n., pl.* **-los.** The **grapefruit** *(see).* [Variant of POMPELMOUS.]
Pom·er·a·ni·a (pŏm′ə-rā′nē-ə, -rān′yə). *German* **Pom·mern** (pôm′ərn). *Polish* **Po·mo·rze** (pô-mô′zhĕ). A historic region of north-central Europe, extending along the south coast of the Baltic Sea from Stralsund to the Vistula River, now divided between Poland and East Germany.
Pom·er·a·ni·an (pŏm′ə-rā′nē-ən, -rān′yən) *adj.* Of or relating to Pomerania or its people. —*n.* **1.** A native of Pomerania. **2.** One of a breed of small dogs having long, silky hair.
po·mi·cul·ture (pō′mĭ-kŭl′chər) *n.* The cultivation of fruit. [Latin *pōmum,* fruit, POME + CULTURE.]
po·mif·er·ous (pō-mĭf′ər-əs) *adj. Botany.* Bearing pomes. [Latin *pōmifer,* fruit-bearing : *pōmum,* fruit, POME + -FER.]
pom·mel (pŭm′əl, pŏm′-) *n.* **1.** A knob on the hilt of a sword or other weapon. **2.** The upper front part of a saddle; saddlebow. —*tr.v.* **pommeled, -meling, -mels.** Also *chiefly British* **-melled, -melling.** To beat; pummel. [Middle English *pomel,* from Old French, from Vulgar Latin *pōmellum* (unattested), rounded knob, diminutive of Latin *pōmum,* fruit, apple, POME.]
po·mol·o·gy (pō-mŏl′ə-jē) *n.* The scientific study and cultivation of fruit. [New Latin *pomologia* : Latin *pōmum,* fruit, POME + -LOGY.] —**po′mo·log′i·cal** (pō′mə-lŏj′ĭ-kəl) *adj.* —**po′mo·log′i·cal·ly** *adv.* —**po·mol′o·gist** *n.*
Po·mo·na (pə-mō′nə). **1.** A city in California, 25 miles east of Los Angeles. Population, 67,000. **2.** The largest of the Orkney Islands, 190 square miles in area. Also called "Mainland."
pomp (pŏmp) *n.* **1.** Dignified or magnificent display; splendor. **2.** Vain or ostentatious display. [Middle English, from Old French *pompe,* from Latin *pompa,* from Greek *pompē,* "a sending," solemn procession, from *pempein*†, to send.]
pom·pa·dour (pŏm′pə-dôr′, -dōr′) *n.* **1.** A woman's hair style formed by sweeping the hair straight up from the forehead. **2.** A man's hair style with the hair brushed up from the forehead. [Invented by the Marquise de POMPADOUR.]
Pom·pa·dour (pŏm′pə-dôr′, -dōr′; *French* pôɴ-pà-dōōr′), **Marquise de.** Original name, Jeanne Antoinette Poisson. 1721–1764. Mistress of Louis XV of France.
pom·pa·no (pŏm′pə-nō′, pŭm′-) *n., pl.* **pompano** or **-nos.** **1.** Any of several marine food fishes of the genus *Trachinotus;* especially, *T. carolinus,* of tropical and temperate Atlantic waters. **2.** Any of several other fishes, such as *Palometa simillima,* a butterfish of American Pacific coast waters. [Spanish *pámpano*†, name of a stromateoid fish.]
Pompeian red. Grayish to moderate red. See **color.**
Pom·pe·ii (pŏm-pā′, -pā′ē). An ancient city of Campania, 14 miles southeast of Naples, destroyed by an eruption of Mount Vesuvius in A.D. 79. —**Pom·pe′ian** *adj.* & *n.*
pom·pel·mous (pŏm′pəl-mōōs′) *n.* A tree, the **shaddock** *(see),* or its fruit. [Dutch *pompelmoes*†.]
Pom·pey (pŏm′pē). Latin name, Gnaeus Pompeius Magnus. Called "The Great." 106–48 B.C. Roman statesman and general; member of the First Triumvirate; rival of Caesar.
pom-pom (pŏm′pŏm′) *n.* **1.** In World War I, a variety of large machine gun using one-pound shells. **2.** In World War II, an automatic, rapid-fire, antiaircraft cannon. [Imitative.]
pom·pon (pŏm′pŏn′) *n.* Also **pom·pom** (-pŏm′). **1.** A tuft or ball of wool, feathers, or other material worn as decoration, especially on a hat. **2.** A small, buttonlike flower of some chrysanthemums and dahlias. [French *pompon*†.]
pom·pous (pŏm′pəs) *adj.* **1.** Characterized by an exaggerated show of dignity or self-importance; pretentious. **2.** Bombastic or self-important in speech or manner. **3.** Characterized by pomp or stately display; ceremonious. [Middle English, from Old French *pompeux,* from Late Latin *pompōsus,* from Latin *pompa,* POMP.] —**pom·pos′i·ty** (pŏm-pŏs′ə-tē) *n.* —**pom′pous·ly** *adv.* —**pom′pous·ness** *n.*
Po·na·pe (pō′nə-pā′). An island, 134 square miles in area, of the eastern Caroline Islands in the western Pacific Ocean. Population, 19,000.
Pon·ce (pôn′sā). A seaport in Puerto Rico, 45 miles southwest of San Juan. Population, 146,000.
Ponce de Le·ón (pŏns′ də lē′ən; *Spanish* pôn′thā *thā* lā-ôn′), **Juan.** 1460?–1521. Spanish explorer; conqueror and governor (1510–12) of Puerto Rico; discovered Florida (1513).
pon·cho (pŏn′chō) *n., pl.* **-chos.** **1.** A blanketlike cloak having a hole in the center for the head, worn originally in South America. **2.** A similar garment used as a raincoat. [American Spanish, from Araucanian *pontho,* woolen fabric.]
pond (pŏnd) *n.* A still body of water, smaller than a lake, often of artificial construction. [Middle English *ponde, pounde,* enclosure, Old English *pund-.* See **bend-** in Appendix.*]
pon·der (pŏn′dər) *v.* **-dered, -dering, -ders.** —*tr.* To weigh mentally; consider carefully. —*intr.* To meditate; deliberate; reflect. [Middle English *ponderen,* from Old French *ponderer,* from Latin *ponderāre,* to weigh, ponder, from *pondus* (stem *ponder-*), weight. See **spen-** in Appendix.*] —**pon′der·er** *n.*
Synonyms: *ponder, consider, deliberate, ruminate.* These mean to think deeply about something, usually in terms of its outcome or significance. *Ponder* suggests painstaking care and thoroughness. *Consider* is less subjective and suggests orderly evaluation. *Deliberate* can apply to the thought of a single person, but more often is used with reference to several persons engaged in seeking a decision. *Ruminate* designates a slow but less orderly process.
pon·der·a·ble (pŏn′dər-ə-bəl) *adj.* Capable of being weighed or assessed; appreciable. —**pon′der·a·bil′i·ty** *n.*
pon·der·o·sa pine (pŏn′də-rō′sə). A tall timber tree, *Pinus ponderosa,* of western North America, having long, dark-green needles. Also called "yellow pine." [New Latin *Pinus ponderosa* : Latin *ponderōsus,* PONDEROUS + *pīnus,* PINE.]
pon·der·ous (pŏn′dər-əs) *adj.* **1.** Having great weight; massive; huge. **2.** Graceless or unwieldy from weight. **3.** Lacking fluency; labored; dull: *a ponderous speech.* —See Synonyms at **heavy.** [Middle English, from Old French *pondereux,* from Latin *ponderōsus,* from *pondus* (stem *ponder-*), weight. See **spen-** in Appendix.*] —**pon′der·ous·ly** *adv.* —**pon′der·os′i·ty** (pŏn′də-rŏs′ə-tē), **pon′der·ous·ness** *n.*
Pon·di·cher·ry (pŏn′dĭ-chĕr′ē, -shĕr′ē). Also **Pon·di·ché·ry** (pôɴ-dē-shā-rē′). A city in Madras State, India, on the Bay of Bengal, about 90 miles southwest of Madras, that was until 1954 the chief French settlement in India. Population, 40,000.
pond lily. The **water lily** *(see).*
pond scum. Any of various freshwater algae that form a usually greenish scum on the surface of stagnant water.
pond·weed (pŏnd′wēd′) *n.* Any of various submerged or floating aquatic plants of the genus *Potamogeton.*
pone (pōn) *n.* **Corn pone** *(see).* [Of Algonquian origin, akin to Delaware *āpân,* baked, Passamaquoddy *ābân.*]
pon·gee (pŏn-jē′, pŏn′jē) *n.* A soft, thin cloth of Chinese or Indian silk with a knotty weave. [Mandarin Chinese *pen^{3}chi^{1},* "(made by) one's own loom" : *pen^{3},* own + *chi^{1},* loom.]
pon·iard (pŏn′yərd) *n.* A dagger. —*tr.v.* **poniarded, -iarding, -iards.** To stab with a poniard. [French *poignard,* from *poing,* fist, from Old French, from Latin *pugnus.* See **peuk-** in Appendix.*]
pons (pŏnz) *n., pl.* **pontes** (pŏn′tēz). *Anatomy.* **1.** Any slender tissue joining two parts of an organ. **2.** The **pons varolii** *(see).* [Latin *pōns,* bridge. See **pent-** in Appendix.*]
pons as·i·no·rum (pŏnz′ ăs′ə-nôr′əm, -nōr′əm). **1.** The proposition of the first book of Euclid, stating that the angles opposite the equal sides of an isosceles triangle are equal. **2.** A problem difficult for beginners. [Latin, "asses' bridge" : *pōns,* PONS + *asinōrum,* genitive plural of *asinus,* ASS.]
pons va·ro·li·i (pŏnz′ və-rō′lē-ī′). A band of nerve fibers in the brain connecting the medulla oblongata and the mesencephalon below the cerebellum. Also called "pons." [New Latin, "bridge of Varoli," after Constanzo *Varoli* (1542–1575), Italian surgeon and anatomist.]
Pon·ta Del·ga·da (pŏn′tə dĕl-gä′də). The capital of the Azores, on the southwestern coast of São Miguel Island. Population, 22,000.
Pont·char·train, Lake (pŏn′chər-trān′). A shallow lake, 600 square miles in area, in southeastern Louisiana.
Pon·ti·ac[1] (pŏn′tē-ăk′). Died 1769. American Indian chief of the Ottawa.
Pon·ti·ac[2] (pŏn′tē-ăk′). An automobile-manufacturing city in southeastern Michigan. Population, 82,000.
Pon·tic (pŏn′tĭk) *adj.* Of or pertaining to the Black Sea region. [Latin *Ponticus,* from Greek *Pontikos,* from *Pontos,* PONTUS.]
pon·ti·fex (pŏn′tə-fĕks′) *n., pl.* **pontifices** (pŏn-tĭf′ə-sēz′). In ancient Rome, a member of the Pontifical College, the highest college of priests, headed by the Pontifex Maximus. [Latin,

probably from Etruscan, reshaped by folk etymology as if to mean "bridge-maker."]

pon·tiff (pŏn′tĭf) *n.* **1. a.** The pope. **b.** A bishop. **2.** A pontifex. [French *pontif,* from Latin *pontifex,* PONTIFEX.]

pon·tif·i·cal (pŏn-tĭf′ĭ-kəl) *adj.* **1.** Pertaining to, characteristic of, or suitable for a pope or bishop. **2.** Having the dignity, pomp, or authority of a pontiff. **3.** Pompously authoritative. —*n.* **1.** *Plural.* The vestments and insignia of a pontiff. **2.** A book of ceremonies and rites for a bishop. [Latin *pontificālis,* from *pontifex,* PONTIFEX.] —**pon·tif′i·cal·ly** *adv.*

Pontifical Mass. *Ecclesiastical.* A celebration of the Eucharist performed by a bishop in all Roman Catholic churches, many Anglican churches, and some Lutheran churches.

pon·tif·i·cate (pŏn-tĭf′ĭ-kĭt, -kāt′) *n.* The office or term of office of a pontiff. —*intr.v.* (pŏn-tĭf′ĭ-kāt′). **pontificated, -cating, -cates. 1.** To administer the office of a pontiff. **2.** To speak or behave with pompous authority. [Latin *pontificātus,* from *pontifex,* PONTIFEX.]

pon·til (pŏn′tĭl) *n.* A glassmaker's tool, a **punty** *(see).* [French, perhaps from Italian *puntello,* diminutive of *punto,* point, from Latin *punctum,* from the neuter past participle of *pungere,* to prick. See **peuk-** in Appendix.*]

pon·tine (pŏn′tīn′) *adj.* **1.** Of or pertaining to bridges. **2.** *Anatomy.* Of or pertaining to the **pons varolii** *(see).* [From Latin *pōns* (stem *pont-*), bridge. See **pent-** in Appendix.*]

Pon·tius. See **Pilate.**

Pont l'É·vêque (pŏnt′ lə-vĕk′; *French* pôN lā-vĕk′). A French cheese that is mild and soft-centered and is made of whole milk. [After *Pont L'Évêque,* town in northern France.]

pon·to·nier (pŏn′tə-nîr′) *n. Military.* One in charge of pontoons or engaged in the construction of pontoon bridges. [French *pontonnier,* from *ponton,* PONTOON.]

pon·toon (pŏn-to͞on′) *n.* **1. a.** A flat-bottomed boat or other structure used to support a floating bridge. **b.** A floating structure serving as a dock. **2.** A float on a seaplane. [French *ponton,* floating bridge, from Old French, from Latin *pontō,* boat bridge, from *pōns,* bridge. See **pent-** in Appendix.*]

pontoon bridge. A temporary floating bridge using pontoons for support. Also called "bateau bridge."

Pon·tus (pŏn′təs). An ancient region in northeastern Asia Minor along the southern shore of the Black Sea. [Latin, from Greek *Pontos,* the Black Sea. See **pent-** in Appendix.*]

po·ny (pō′nē) *n., pl.* **-nies. 1.** A horse of any of several small breeds, usually not over 14 hands high. **2.** *Informal.* A racehorse. **3.** Something small for its kind. **4.** *Informal.* A word-for-word translation or a synopsis of a text used by students, often illicitly, as an aid to understanding the original. Also called "trot," *chiefly British* "crib." **5.** *British Slang.* The sum of 25 pounds. —*v.* **ponied, -nying, -nies.** *Slang.* —*tr.* To prepare (lessons) with a pony. —*intr.* To prepare lessons with a pony. —**pony up.** *Slang.* To pay money owed or due. [Earlier *powny,* probably from obsolete French *poulenet,* diminutive of *poulain,* from Late Latin *pullāmen,* from Latin *pullus,* foal. See **pōu-** in Appendix.*]

pony express. A system of mail transportation by relays of ponies; specifically, the system in operation from St. Joseph, Missouri, to Sacramento, California (1860–61).

po·ny·tail (pō′nē-tāl′) *n.* A woman's hair style in which the hair is clasped in the back so as to hang down like a pony's tail.

pooch (po͞och) *n. Slang.* A dog. [Origin unknown.]

pood (po͞od) *n.* A Russian weight equivalent to slightly over 36 pounds avoirdupois. [Russian *pud,* from Old Norse *pund,* pound, from Old English, POUND.]

poo·dle (po͞od′l) *n.* Any of a breed of dogs originally developed in Europe as hunting dogs, having thick, curly hair, and ranging in size from the fairly large standard poodle to the very small toy poodle. [German *Pudel(hund),* "poodle (dog)," probably from Low German, perhaps "splashing dog" (because the poodle was originally trained as a water dog), akin to Old English *pudd,* ditch. See **puddle.**]

pooh (po͞o) *interj.* Used to express disdain. [Expressive formation.]

Pooh-Bah (po͞o′bä′) *n.* A pompous, ostentatious official, especially one who, holding many offices, fulfills none of them. [After a character, the Lord-High-Everything-Else, in W.S. Gilbert's *Mikado* (1885).]

pooh-pooh (po͞o′po͞o′) *tr.v.* **-poohed, -poohing, -poohs.** *Informal.* To express contempt or disdain for; make light of. [Reduplication of POOH.]

pool[1] (po͞ol) *n.* **1.** A small body of still water; small pond. **2.** A puddle of any liquid. **3.** A deep place in a river or stream. **4.** A **swimming pool** *(see).* [Middle English *pool,* Old English *pōl,* from West Germanic *pōla-, pōl-* (unattested).]

pool[2] (po͞ol) *n.* **1.** In certain gambling games, the total amount staked by all players. **2.** Any grouping of resources for the common advantage of the participants: *a car pool.* **3.** *Finance.* **a.** A mutual fund established by a group of stockholders for speculating in or manipulating prices of securities. **b.** The persons or parties participating in such a combination. **4.** An agreement between competing business concerns to establish controls over production, market, and prices for common profit. **5.** *Fencing.* A match in which each member of a team fences successively with each member of an opposing team. **6.** Any of several games played on a six-pocket billiard table usually with 15 object balls and a cue ball. Also called "pocket billiards." Compare **billiards.** —See Synonyms at **monopoly.** —*v.* **pooled, pooling, pools.** —*tr.* To combine (money, funds, or interests) into a common stock for mutual benefit. —*intr.* To join or form a pool. [French *poule,* stakes, target (as in *jeu de la poule,* "game of the hen"), hen, from Late Latin *pullus,* hen, from Latin, young of an animal. See **pōu-** in Appendix.*]

Poole (po͞ol). A municipal borough in Dorsetshire, southwestern England, on the English Channel. Population, 213,000.

pool·room (po͞ol′ro͞om′, -ro͝om′) *n.* A commercial establishment or room for the playing of pool or billiards.

pool table. A six-pocket billiard table on which pool is played.

poon (po͞on) *n.* Any of several trees of the genus *Calophyllum,* of southern Asia, having light, hard wood used for masts and spars. [Singhalese *pūna,* probably from Tamil *punnai.*]

Poo·na (po͞o′nə). A city in Maharashtra State, Republic of India, 75 miles southeast of Bombay. Population, 598,000.

poop[1] (po͞op) *n. Nautical.* **1.** The stern superstructure of a ship. **2.** The **poop deck** *(see).* —*tr.v.* **pooped, pooping, poops.** *Nautical.* To break over the stern of (a ship). Used of waves. [Old French *poupe,* from Latin *puppis*†.]

poop[2] (po͞op) *tr.v.* **pooped, pooping, poops.** *Slang.* To cause to become fatigued or exhausted; tire. —**poop out.** To quit because of exhaustion: *poop out of the race.* [Origin unknown.]

poop[3] (po͞op) *n. Slang.* Inside information. [Origin unknown.]

poop deck. *Nautical.* The aftermost deck of a ship.

poor (po͝or) *adj.* **poorer, poorest. 1. a.** Having little or no wealth and few or no possessions; poverty-stricken. **b.** *Law.* Dependent on charity or public funds; destitute. **c.** Wanting in financial or other resources: *an area poor in timber and coal.* **2. a.** Lacking in mental or moral quality: *"A poor spirit is poorer than a poor purse."* (Cyril Tourneur). **b.** Inferior; inadequate; inefficient: *"'It's a poor sort of memory that only works backwards,' the Queen remarked."* (Lewis Carroll). **3. a.** Lacking desirable elements or constituents: *Poor soil makes poor pasture and poor milk.* **b.** Undernourished; lean. **4. a.** Lacking in value; trivial: *"An atheist's laugh's a poor exchange / For Deity offended."* (Burns). **b.** Lacking in quantity: *poor attendance.* **5. a.** Humble: *in my poor opinion.* **b.** Pitiable: *a poor fool.* [Middle English *povere, poure,* from Old French *povre,* from Latin *pauper.* See **pōu-** in Appendix.*] —**poor′ness** *n.*

Synonyms: *poor, indigent, impoverished, destitute.* These describe a person without income. *Poor* is the most general and means, broadly, lacking money or means for an adequate existence. One who is *poor* is usually characteristically or continually so. *Indigent* more specifically refers to one in straitened circumstances but not in total adversity. Like *poor,* it sometimes denotes a social class. *Impoverished* means abjectly poor, usually conspicuously so. The strongest of these words is *destitute,* which suggests poverty due to misfortune and particularly implies urgent need.

poor box. A box, especially in a church, for collecting alms.

poor farm. A farm that houses, supports, and employs paupers at public expense.

poor·house (po͝or′hous′) *n.* An establishment maintained at public expense as a place for the internment of paupers.

poo·ri (po͝or′ē) *n.* Also **pu·ri.** A light, flat wheat cake of Pakistan and northern India, usually fried in deep fat. [Hindi *puri,* from Sanskrit *puraḥ,* cake. See **pel-**[6] in Appendix.*]

poor law. A law or system of laws providing for public relief and support of the poor.

poor·ly (po͝or′lē) *adv.* In a poor manner. —*adj. Regional.* In poor health; ailing; ill. Used predicatively: *feeling poorly.*

poor man's weatherglass. A plant, the scarlet pimpernel. See **pimpernel.**

poor Robin's plantain. A plant, the **rattlesnake weed** *(see).*

poor white. A member of a drastically exploited, often expropriated and pauperized class of white farmers and laborers, especially in the American South. Often used disparagingly.

pop[1] (pŏp) *v.* **popped, popping, pops.** —*intr.* **1.** To make a short, sharp, explosive sound. **2.** To burst open with such a sound. **3.** To move quickly or unexpectedly; appear abruptly. **4.** To open wide suddenly so as to protrude from the sockets: *"The janitor's eyes popped with interest and amazement."* (Chester Hines). **5.** *Baseball.* To hit a short high fly ball that can be caught by an infielder. **6.** To shoot a pistol or other firearm. —*tr.* **1.** To cause to make a sharp bursting sound: *"I could hear soda bottles being popped open in the kitchen."* (Philip Roth). **2.** To cause to explode with such a sound. **3.** To put or thrust suddenly or unexpectedly: *"Amber, popping a crisp plump shrimp into her mouth"* (Kathleen Winsor). **4.** To fire (a pistol or other firearm). **5.** To fire at; shoot. —**pop off.** *Informal.* **1.** To leave abruptly or hurriedly. **2.** To speak in a burst of vehement anger. —**pop the question.** *Informal.* To propose marriage. —*n.* **1.** A sudden sharp, explosive sound. **2.** A shot with a firearm. **3.** A nonalcoholic, flavored, carbonated beverage. —*adv.* **1.** With a popping sound. **2.** Abruptly or unexpectedly. [Middle English *poppen* (imitative).]

pop[2] (pŏp) *n.* Father. Used as a familiar term of address. [Short for *poppa,* variant of PAPA.]

pop[3] (pŏp) *adj. Informal.* **1.** Of, pertaining to, or specializing in popular music: *a pop singer.* **2.** Suggestive of **pop art** *(see).* [Short for POPULAR.]

pop. **1.** popular. **2.** population.

pop art. A form of art that depicts objects of everyday life and adapts techniques of commercial art, such as comic strips.

pop·corn (pŏp′kôrn′) *n.* **1.** A variety of corn, *Zea mays everta,* having hard kernels that burst to form white, irregularly shaped puffs when heated. **2.** The edible, popped kernels of popcorn. [Contraction of *popped corn.*]

popcorn flower. Any of several plants of the genus *Plagiobothrys,* of northwestern North America, having clusters of small white flowers.

pope (pōp) *n.* **1.** *Often capital* **P.** The bishop of Rome and head

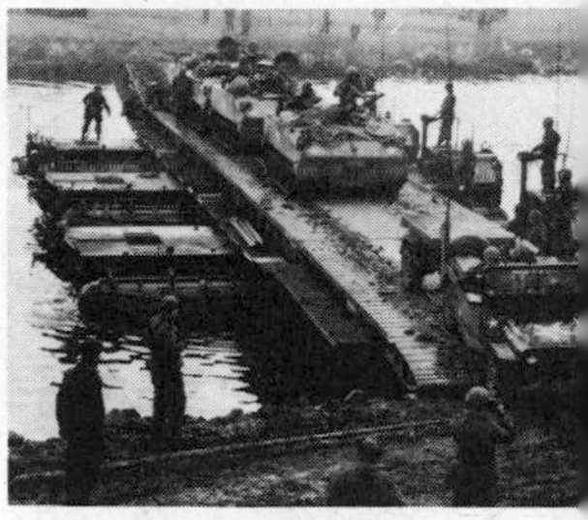

pontoon bridge

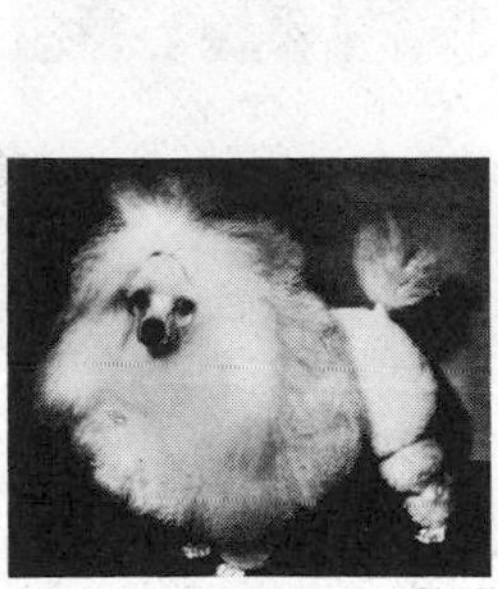

poodle
Clipped and trimmed toy poodle

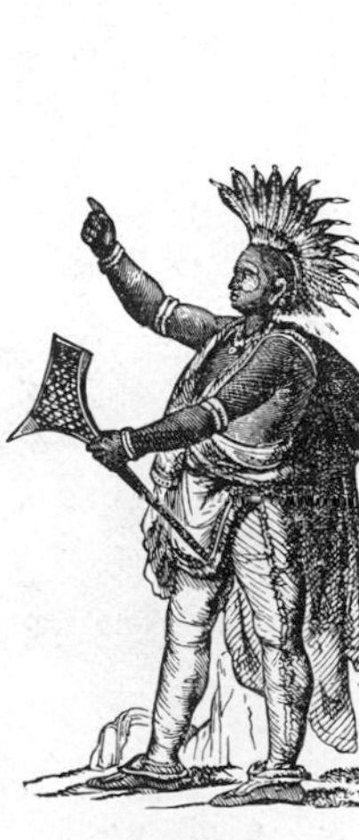

Pontiac[1]

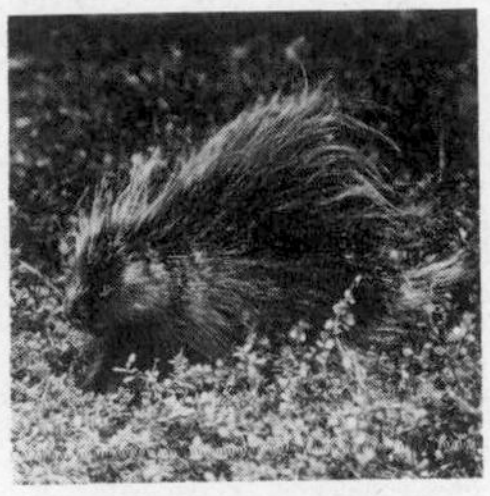

porcupine
Erethizon dorsatum

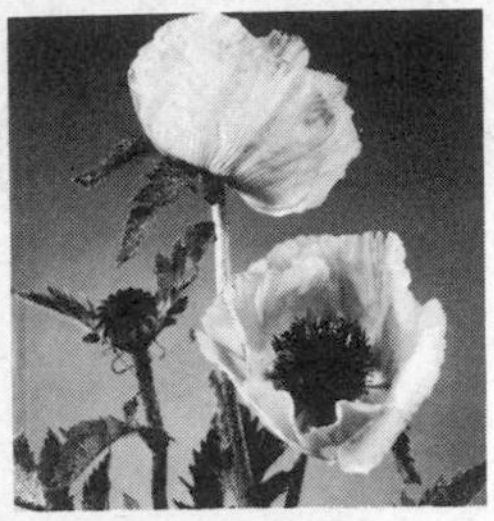

poppy
Papaver orientale

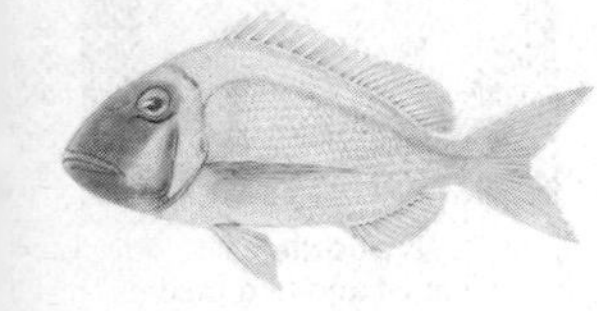

porgy
Calamus bajonado

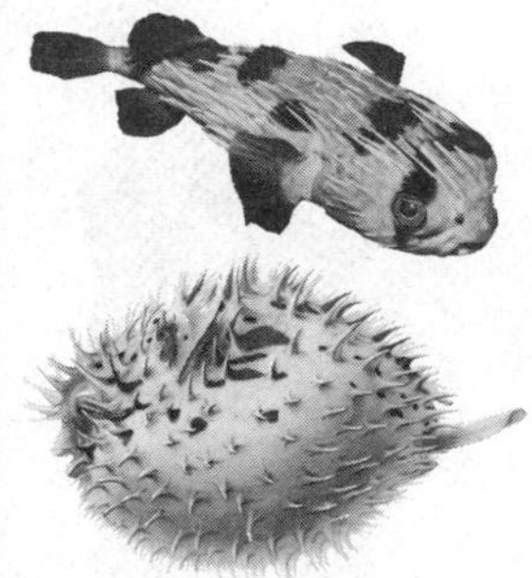

porcupine fish
Shown inflated below

of the Roman Catholic Church, acting (by apostolic succession from Saint Peter) as vicar of Christ on earth. **2.** *Eastern Orthodox Church.* A priest. **3.** Any figure considered to have unquestioned authority: *the pope of surrealism.* [Middle English *pope,* Old English *pāpa,* from Late Latin *pāpa,* from Greek *pappas,* title of bishops, papa. See **papa** in Appendix.*]

Pope (pōp), **Alexander.** 1688–1744. English poet and satirist.

pope·dom (pōp′dəm) *n.* The office, jurisdiction, or tenure of a pope; papacy.

pop·er·y (pō′pə-rē) *n.* The doctrines, practices, and rituals of the Roman Catholic Church. Used disparagingly.

pope's nose. The rump of a cooked fowl. Also called "parson's nose."

pop-eyed (pŏp′īd′) *adj.* **1.** Having bulging eyes. **2.** Amazed; astonished: *popeyed with wonder.*

pop fly. *Baseball.* A short high fly ball.

pop·gun (pŏp′gŭn′) *n.* A toy gun that operates by compressed air, firing corks or pellets with a popping noise.

pop·in·jay (pŏp′ĭn-jā′) *n.* **1.** A vain, supercilious person; fop. **2.** *Obsolete.* A parrot. [Middle English *papejay, papengay,* parrot, from Old French *papegai,* from Arabic *babaghā.*]

pop·ish (pō′pĭsh) *adj.* Of or pertaining to the popes or the Roman Catholic Church. Used disparagingly. —**pop′ish·ly** *adv.* —**pop′ish·ness** *n.*

pop·lar (pŏp′lər) *n.* **1.** Any of several fast-growing deciduous trees of the genus *Populus.* See **aspen, cottonwood, Lombardy poplar. 2.** The wood of these trees. **3.** Loosely, the **tulip tree** *(see).* [Middle English *poplere,* from Old French *poplier,* earlier *pople,* from Latin *pōpulus.* See **pteleyā** in Appendix.*]

Pop·lar (pŏp′lər). A former administrative division of London, England, now part of **Tower Hamlets** *(see).*

pop·lin (pŏp′lĭn) *n.* A ribbed fabric of silk, rayon, wool, or cotton, used in making clothing and upholstery. [Obsolete French *papeline,* from Italian *papalina,* feminine of *papalino,* papal, from Medieval Latin *papalis,* from Late Latin *papa,* POPE (the fabric was first made at the papal town of Avignon).]

pop·lit·e·al (pŏp-lĭt′ē-əl, pŏp′lĭ-tē′əl) *adj.* Of or pertaining to the part of the leg behind the knee joint. [New Latin *popliteus,* from Latin *poples*† (stem *poplit-*), the ham of the knee.]

Po·po·ca·té·petl (pō′pō-kăt′ə-pĕt′l, -kə-tā′pĕt′l). A dormant volcano in Mexico, in Puebla State, 43 miles southeast of Mexico City. Its summit is 17,887 feet high.

Po·pov (pə-pôf′), **Aleksandr Stepanovich.** 1859–1905. Russian physicist; used first antenna in experiments on radio waves.

pop·o·ver (pŏp′ō′vər) *n.* A very light, puffy, hollow muffin made with eggs, milk, and flour. [So called because it pops up over the rim of the baking tin.]

pop·per (pŏp′ər) *n.* **1.** One that pops. **2.** A container or pan for making popcorn.

pop·pet (pŏp′ĭt) *n.* **1.** A **poppet valve** *(see).* **2.** *Nautical.* **a.** A small wooden strip on the gunwale of a boat that forms or supports the oarlocks. **b.** One of the beams of a launching cradle supporting a ship's hull. **3.** *Chiefly British.* A darling. [Middle English *popet,* child, doll, PUPPET.]

poppet valve. An intake or exhaust valve, operated by springs and cams, that plugs and unplugs its opening by axial motion.

pop·ple[1] (pŏp′əl) *intr.v.* **-pled, -pling, -ples.** To move in a tossing, bubbling, or rippling manner, as choppy water. —*n.* **1.** Choppy water. **2.** The sound made by boiling liquid. [Middle English *poplen,* from Middle Dutch *popelen*†.]

pop·ple[2] (pŏp′əl) *n. Informal.* A poplar. [Middle English *popul,* Old English *popul,* from Latin *pōpulus,* POPLAR.]

pop·py (pŏp′ē) *n., pl.* **-pies. 1.** Any of numerous plants of the genus *Papaver,* of temperate regions, having showy red, orange, or white flowers, and a milky white juice. See **opium poppy. 2.** Any of several similar or related plants, such as the **California poppy** *(see).* **3.** The narcotic extracted from the opium poppy. **4.** Vivid red to reddish orange. See **color.** [Middle English *popi,* Old English *popig, popaeg,* altered from Vulgar Latin *papāvum* (unattested), variant of Latin *papāver*†.]

pop·py·cock (pŏp′ē-kŏk′) *n.* Senseless talk; humbug. [Dutch dialect *pappekak,* "soft dung" : *pap,* soft food, pap, from Middle Dutch *pappe,* probably from Latin *pappa,* father, food (see **pap-**[2] in Appendix*) + *kak,* dung, from *kakken,* to defecate, from Latin *cacāre* (see **kakka-** in Appendix*).]

pop·u·lace (pŏp′yə-lĭs) *n.* **1.** The common people; masses: *"The populace cannot understand the bureaucracy: it can only worship the national idols."* (G.B. Shaw). **2.** A population. [French, from Italian *popolaccio,* rabble, from *popolo,* the people, from Latin *populus.* See **populus** in Appendix.*]

pop·u·lar (pŏp′yə-lər) *adj. Abbr.* **pop. 1.** Widely liked or appreciated. **2.** Liked by friends, associates, or acquaintances; sought after for company. **3.** Of, representing, or carried on by the common people or the people at large: *"The Reformation was a popular uprising."* (A.N. Whitehead). **4.** Fit for or reflecting the taste and intelligence of the people at large. **5.** Accepted by or prevalent among the people in general: *a popular misunderstanding.* **6.** Suited to or within the means of ordinary people: *popular prices.* **7.** Originating among the people: *popular legend.* [Latin *populāris,* of the people, from *populus,* people. See **populus** in Appendix.*] —**pop′u·lar·ly** *adv.*

popular front. A political coalition of a kind formed in European countries during the 1930's, as an alliance of democratic and revolutionary parties having common interests in the struggle against reaction and fascism. Also called "people's front."

pop·u·lar·i·ty (pŏp′yə-lăr′ə-tē) *n.* The quality or state of being popular; especially, the state of being widely admired, accepted, or sought after.

pop·u·lar·ize (pŏp′yə-lə-rīz′) *tr.v.* **-ized, -izing, -izes.** To make popular; especially, to cause to become readily intelligible to the layman. —**pop′u·lar·i·za′tion** *n.* —**pop′u·lar·iz′er** *n.*

pop·u·late (pŏp′yə-lāt′) *tr.v.* **-lated, -lating, -lates. 1.** To supply with inhabitants, as by colonization; to people. **2.** To inhabit or become inhabitants of. [Medieval Latin *populāre,* to people, from Latin *populus,* people. See **populus** in Appendix.*]

pop·u·la·tion (pŏp′yə-lā′shən) *n. Abbr.* **p., pop. 1. a.** All of the people inhabiting a specified area. **b.** The total number of such people. **2.** The total number of inhabitants of a particular race, class, or group in a specified area. **3.** The act or process of furnishing with inhabitants. **4.** *Ecology.* All the organisms that constitute a specific group or occur in a specified habitat. **5.** *Statistics.* The entire set of individuals, items, or scores from which a sample is drawn. [Late Latin *populātiō,* from Latin *populus,* people. See **populus** in Appendix.*]

population inversion. *Physics.* A condition in which the usual or unexcited energy distribution of atoms in laser material is inverted, making stimulated emission and laser action possible.

Pop·u·list (pŏp′yə-lĭst) *n.* A member or supporter of the Populist Party. —*adj.* Of or pertaining to the Populist Party. —**Pop′u·lism** *n.*

Populist Party. An American political party, formed to represent agrarian interests in the Presidential election of 1892. It advocated increased currency issue, free coinage of gold and silver, public ownership of railroads, and a graduated federal income tax. Also called "People's Party."

pop·u·lous (pŏp′yə-ləs) *adj.* Containing many people or inhabitants; thickly settled or populated. [Middle English *populus,* from Latin *populōsus,* from *populus,* people. See **population.**] —**pop′u·lous·ly** *adv.* —**pop′u·lous·ness** *n.*

p.o.r. pay on return.

por·bea·gle (pôr′bē′gəl) *n.* A shark, *Lamna nasus,* of temperate Atlantic waters. [Cornish *porghbugel*†.]

por·ce·lain (pôrs′lĭn, pōrs′-, pôr′sə-lĭn, pōr′sə-) *n.* **1.** A hard, white, translucent ceramic made by firing a pure clay and glazing with variously colored fusible materials; china. **2.** An object made of this material. [French *porcelaine,* from Old French *pourcelaine,* from Italian *porcellana,* "of a sow," hence cowry shell, hence porcelain (from the resemblance of the shell to the vulva of a sow), from *porcella,* diminutive of *porca,* sow, from Latin, feminine of *porcus,* swine. See **porko-** in Appendix.*] —**por′ce·la′ne·ous** (pôr′sə-lā′nē-əs, pōr′-) *adj.*

porcelain enamel. A silicate glass fired on metal. Also called "vitreous enamel."

porch (pôrch, pōrch) *n.* **1.** A covered platform, usually having a separate roof, at an entrance to a house. **2.** An open or enclosed gallery or room attached to the outside of a building; verandah. **3.** *Obsolete.* A portico or covered walk. —**the Porch.** Zeno's Stoic school of philosophy, so named for the portico in Athens where he instructed his disciples. [Middle English *porche,* from Old French, from Latin *porticus,* PORTICO.]

por·cine (pōr′sīn′) *adj.* **1.** Of or pertaining to swine or pigs. **2.** Resembling a pig; piglike: *"a bald porcine old man"* (Vladimir Nabokov). [Latin *porcīnus,* from *porcus,* pig. See **porko-** in Appendix.*]

por·cu·pine (pôr′kyə-pīn′) *n.* Any of various rodents, including members of the Old World genus *Hystrix,* the New World genus *Erethizon,* and related genera, characteristically covered with long, sharp quills or spines. [Middle English *porkepin,* from Old French *porc espin,* "spiny pig," from Vulgar Latin *porcospīnus* (unattested) : Latin *porcus,* pig (see **porko-** in Appendix*) + *spina,* thorn (see **spei-** in Appendix*).]

porcupine fish. A spiny tropical marine fish, *Diodon hystrix,* capable of inflating itself when attacked.

porcupine grass. Any grass of the genus *Stipa,* of western North America, having stiff, pointed bristles.

pore[1] (pôr, pōr) *intr.v.* **pored, poring, pores. 1.** To gaze steadily or earnestly. **2.** To read or study carefully and attentively: *"With long poring, he is grown almost into a book."* (Lamb). **3.** To meditate deeply; ponder. [Middle English *pouren*†.]

pore[2] (pôr, pōr) *n.* **1.** A minute orifice, such as one in the skin of an animal, serving as an outlet for perspiration, or in a plant leaf or stem, serving as a means of absorption and transpiration. **2.** Any minute surface opening or passageway, as in a rock. [Middle English, from Old French, from Latin *porus,* from Greek *poros,* passage. See **per-**[2] in Appendix.*]

pore fungus. A fungus having a crustlike fruiting body with a pitted or porous surface. Also called "polypore."

por·gy (pôr′gē) *n., pl.* **-gies** or **porgy. 1.** Any of various deep-bodied marine fishes of the family Sparidae. **2.** Any of several similar or related fishes. [Variant of *pargo,* from Spanish, from Latin *p(h)agrus,* sea bream, from Greek *phagros,* sea bream, whetstone. See **bhag-**[2] in Appendix.*]

po·rif·er·an (pə-rĭf′ər-ən) *n.* Any animal of the phylum Porifera; a sponge. [From New Latin *Porifera,* neuter plural of *porifer,* bearing pores : Latin *porus,* PORE + -FER.] —**po·rif′er·al, po·rif′er·an** *adj.*

po·rif·er·ous (pə-rĭf′ər-əs) *adj.* **1.** Having pores. **2.** *Zoology.* Of or relating to the phylum Porifera, which includes the sponges. [From PORE + -FEROUS.]

pork (pôrk, pōrk) *n.* **1.** The flesh of a pig or hog used as food. **2.** *Slang.* Government funds, appointments, or other favors acquired by a representative for his constituency as political patronage. [Middle English, from Old French *porc,* pig, from Latin *porcus.* See **porko-** in Appendix.*]

pork barrel. *Slang.* A government project or appropriation benefiting a specific locale and a legislator's constituents.

pork·er (pôr′kər, pōr′-) *n.* A fattened young pig.

pork·pie (pôrk′pī′, pōrk′-) *n.* Also **pork pie. 1.** A thick-crusted pie filled with chopped pork. **2.** A man's hat having a low, flat crown and a snap brim.

por·nog·ra·phy (pôr-nŏg′rə-fē) *n.* Written, graphic, or other forms of communication intended to excite lascivious feelings. [From Greek *pornographos,* writing about prostitutes : *pornē,* harlot, prostitute (see **per-⁷** in Appendix*) + -GRAPH.] —**por·nog′ra·pher** *n.* —**por′no·graph′ic** (pôr′nə-grăf′ĭk) *adj.*

po·ros·i·ty (pə-rŏs′ə-tē, pō-) *n., pl.* **-ties. 1.** The state or property of being porous. **2.** A structure or part that is porous. [Medieval Latin *porōsitās,* from *porōsus,* POROUS.]

po·rous (pôr′əs, pōr′-) *adj.* **1.** Having or full of pores. **2.** Admitting the passage of gas or liquid through pores or interstices. [Middle English, from Medieval Latin *porōsus,* from Latin *porus,* PORE.] —**po′rous·ly** *adv.* —**po′rous·ness** *n.*

por·phy·rin (pôr′fə-rĭn) *n. Biochemistry.* Any of various nitrogen-containing organic compounds occurring universally in protoplasm and providing the foundation structure for hemoglobin, chlorophyll, and certain enzymes. [From Greek *porphura,* PURPLE (from its color).]

por·phy·rit·ic (pôr′fə-rĭt′ĭk) *adj.* Also **por·phy·rit·i·cal** (-ĭ-kəl). *Mineralogy.* **1.** Of or containing porphyry. **2.** Containing relatively large isolated crystals in a mass of fine texture.

por·phy·roid (pôr′fə-roid′) *n. Geology.* Metamorphic rock having porphyritic texture. [PORPHYR(Y) + -OID.]

por·phy·ry (pôr′fə-rē) *n., pl.* **-ries.** *Geology.* Rock containing relatively large conspicuous crystals, especially feldspar, in a fine-grained igneous matrix. [Middle English *porfurie,* red or purple stone, from Medieval Latin *porphyrium,* from Latin *porphyrītēs,* purple-colored stone, from Greek *porphuritēs,* from *porphura,* PURPLE.]

por·poise (pôr′pəs) *n., pl.* **-poises** or **porpoise. 1.** Any of several gregarious aquatic mammals of the genus *Phocaena* and related genera, of oceanic waters, characteristically having a blunt snout and a triangular dorsal fin. **2.** Broadly, any of several related mammals, such as the **dolphin** *(see).* [Middle English *porpoys,* from Old French *porpois,* from Vulgar Latin *porcopiscis* (unattested) : Latin *porcus,* a pig (see **porko-** in Appendix*) + *piscis,* fish (see **peisk-** in Appendix*).]

por·ridge (pôr′ĭj, pŏr′-) *n.* **1.** Boiled oatmeal, usually eaten with milk at breakfast. **2.** *Obsolete.* Thick soup. [Variant (influenced by Middle English *porray,* a pottage) of POTTAGE.]

por·rin·ger (pôr′ĭn-jər, pŏr′-) *n.* A shallow cup or bowl with a handle. [Alteration of *pottinger,* Middle English *potinger, poteger,* from Old French *potager,* from *potage,* POTTAGE.]

port¹ (pôrt, pōrt) *n. Abbr.* **pt. 1. a.** A town having a harbor for ships taking on or discharging cargoes. **b.** A place on a waterway that provides a harbor for a nearby city. **c.** The harbor or waterfront district of a city. **2.** A place of anchorage or shelter; haven. **3.** A **port of entry** *(see).* [Middle English *port,* from Old English *port* and Old French *port,* both from Latin *portus,* house door, port. See **per-²** in Appendix.*]

port² (pôrt, pōrt) *n.* The left-hand side of a ship or aircraft facing forward. Also *obsolete* "larboard." Compare **starboard.** —*adj.* Of, pertaining to, or on the port. —*tr.v.* **ported, porting, ports.** To turn or shift (the helm of a vessel) to the left. [Origin uncertain.]

port³ (pôrt, pōrt) *n.* **1.** *Nautical.* **a.** A porthole. **b.** A covering for this. **2.** An opening, as in a cylinder or valve face, for the passage of steam or fluid. **3.** *Scottish.* A gateway or portal, as to a town. [Middle English, opening, from Old French *porte,* gate, door, from Latin *porta.* See **per-²** in Appendix.*]

port⁴ (pôrt, pōrt) *n.* **1.** A rich sweet fortified wine of Portugal. **2.** Any of various similar wines produced in other countries. [Short for *O Porto (wine),* after OPORTO (Portuguese *o porto,* "the port").]

port⁵ (pôrt, pōrt) *tr.v.* **ported, porting, ports.** *Military.* To carry (a rifle, sword, or other weapon) diagonally across the body, with the muzzle or blade near the left shoulder. —*n.* **1.** *Military.* The position of a rifle or other weapon when ported. **2.** The manner in which a person carries himself; bearing. [Middle English, "a bearing," from Old French, from *porter,* to bear, from Latin *portāre.* See **per-²** in Appendix.*]

Port. Portugal; Portuguese.

port·a·ble (pôr′tə-bəl, pōr′-) *adj.* **1.** Capable of being carried. **2.** Easily carried or moved. **3.** *Archaic.* Endurable; supportable; bearable. —*n.* Something that is portable, such as a light typewriter. [Middle English, from Old French, from Late Latin *portābilis,* from Latin *portāre,* to carry. See **per-²** in Appendix.*] —**port′a·bil′i·ty, port′a·ble·ness** *n.* —**port′a·bly** *adv.*

port·age (pôr′tĭj, pōr′-, pôr-täzh′) *n.* **1.** The carrying of boats and supplies overland between two waterways. **2.** A track or route by which this is done. —*v.* **portaged, -aging, -ages.** —*tr.* To transport by portage; pack: *"they had illegally portaged back to Canada a small fortune in beaver skins"* (Irving Stone). —*intr.* To make a portage. [Middle English, from Old French, from Medieval Latin *portāgium,* from Latin *portāre,* to carry. See **per-²** in Appendix.*]

por·tal (pôrt′l, pōrt′l) *n.* **1.** A doorway, entrance, or gate; especially, one that is large and imposing: *"Stepping through a portal, between giant oaken doors"* (J.P. Donleavy). **2.** Any entrance or means of entrance: *a portal of knowledge.* **3.** A blood vessel, the **portal vein** *(see).* —*adj.* Of or pertaining to the portal vein. [Middle English, from Old French, from Medieval Latin *portāle,* a city gate, porch, from *portālis,* of a gate, from Latin *porta,* a gate. See **per-²** in Appendix.*]

por·tal-to-por·tal (pôrt′l-tə-pôrt′l, pōrt′l-) *adj.* Of or based on the time spent by a worker on the employer's property, from the moment of arrival to that of departure: *portal-to-portal pay.*

portal vein. *Anatomy.* A vein that conducts blood from the digestive organs, spleen, pancreas, and gall bladder to the liver. Also called "portal."

por·ta·men·to (pôr′tə-mĕn′tō, pōr′-) *n., pl.* **-ti** (-tē). A smooth, uninterrupted glide in passing from one tone to another, especially with the voice or a bowed stringed instrument. [Italian, "a carrying," from *portare,* to carry, from Latin *portāre.* See **per-²** in Appendix.*]

Port Ar·thur (är′thər). **1.** A city and entry port on Sabine Lake, in southeastern Texas, 18 miles south of Beaumont. Population, 67,000. **2.** The former name for **Lüshun. 3.** A port of Ontario, Canada, on Lake Superior. Population, 45,000.

por·ta·tive (pôr′tə-tĭv, pōr′-) *adj.* **1.** Portable. **2.** Capable of carrying. [Middle English *portatif,* from Old French, from Latin *portāre,* to carry. See **per-²** in Appendix.*]

Port-au-Prince (pôrt′ō-prĭns′, pōrt′-; *French* pôr-tō-prăɴs′). The capital of Haiti, on the southeastern shore of the Gulf of Gonaïves. Population, 250,000.

port·cul·lis (pôrt-kŭl′ĭs, pōrt-) *n.* A sliding grille of iron or wood suspended in the gateway of a fortified place in such a way that it can be quickly lowered in case of attack. [Middle English *porculis, port colice,* from Old French *porte coleïce* : *porte,* gate, from Latin *porta* (see **per-²** in Appendix*) + *coleïce,* feminine of *couleïs,* sliding, from *couler,* to slide, from Latin *colāre,* to strain, from *cōlum,* sieve (see **kagh-** in Appendix*).]

Port du Sa·lut. Variant of **Port Salut.**

Porte (pôrt, pōrt) *n.* The government of the Ottoman Empire. [French *(la Sublime) Porte,* "(the High) Gate" (translation of Turkish *Bab-i Ali,* "the high house"), from Old French *porte,* gate, PORT.]

porte-co·chère, porte-co·chere (pôrt′kō-shâr′, pōrt′-) *n.* **1.** A carriage entrance leading into the courtyard of a town house. **2.** A porch roof projecting over a driveway at the entrance to a building, providing shelter for those getting in and out of vehicles. [French *porte cochère,* "coach-door" : Old French *porte,* gate, PORT + *cochère,* for coaches, from *coche,* COACH.]

Port E·liz·a·beth (ĭ-lĭz′ə-bəth, ē-). A seaport and city of the Republic of South Africa, in the southeastern Cape of Good Hope Province, on the Indian Ocean. Population, 291,000.

por·tend (pôr-tĕnd′, pōr-) *tr.v.* **-tended, -tending, -tends.** To serve as an omen or warning of; presage: *"tumults and rumours of tumult far and near; portending, on all sides, that a new Civil War is at hand"* (Carlyle). See Synonyms at **foretell.** [Middle English *portenden,* from Latin *portendere.* See **ten-** in Appendix.*]

por·tent (pôr′tĕnt′, pōr′-) *n.* **1.** An indication of something momentous or calamitous about to occur; an omen: *"the Beat Generation was a portent, the first wind of a new storm"* (Jack Newfield). **2.** Prophetic or threatening significance: *a vision of dire portent.* **3.** Something amazing or marvelous; a prodigy. [Latin *portentum,* from *portendere,* to PORTEND.]

por·ten·tous (pôr-tĕn′təs, pōr-) *adj.* **1.** Of the nature of or constituting a portent; foreboding; ominous: *"the present aspect of society is portentous of great change"* (Edward Bellamy). **2.** Full of unspecifiable significance; exciting wonder and awe; prodigious: *"Such a portentous and mysterious monster roused all my curiosity."* (Melville). **3.** Marked by pompousness; pretentiously weighty. —**por·ten′tous·ly** *adv.* —**por·ten′tous·ness** *n.*

por·ter¹ (pôr′tər, pōr′-) *n.* **1.** A person employed to carry travelers' luggage. **2.** A railroad employee who waits on passengers in a sleeping car or parlor car. [Middle English *portour,* from Old French *porteur,* from Late Latin *portātor,* from Latin *portāre,* to carry. See **per-²** in Appendix.*]

por·ter² (pôr′tər, pōr′-) *n. Chiefly British.* A gatekeeper; doorman. [Middle English, from Old French *portier,* from Late Latin *portārius,* from Latin *porta,* a gate. See **per-²** in Appendix.*]

por·ter³ (pôr′tər, pōr′-) *n.* A dark beer resembling light stout, made from malt browned or charred by drying at a high temperature. [Shortened from *porter's beer* or *porter's ale* (originally associated with *porters* (carriers) and low laborers in general).]

Por·ter (pôr′tər, pōr′-), **Cole.** 1893–1964. American musical-comedy composer and lyricist.

Por·ter (pôr′tər, pōr′-), **Katherine Anne.** Born 1890. American author of short stories and novels.

Por·ter (pôr′tər, pōr′-), **William Sydney.** Pen name, O. Henry. 1862–1910. American author of short stories.

por·ter·age (pôr′tər-ĭj, pōr′-) *n.* **1.** The carrying of parcels or goods as done by porters. **2.** The charge for this.

por·ter·ess. Variant of **portress.**

por·ter·house (pôr′tər-hous′, pōr′-) *n.* **1.** In 19th-century America, an alehouse or chophouse. **2.** A cut of beef taken from the thick end of the short loin, having a T-bone and a sizable piece of tenderloin. Also called "porterhouse steak."

port·fo·li·o (pôrt-fō′lē-ō′, pōrt-) *n., pl.* **-os. 1. a.** A portable case for holding loose sheets of paper, drawings, maps, and the like. **b.** Such a case containing the official documents of a ministry. **2.** The office or post of a cabinet member or minister of state. **3.** An itemized list of the investments, securities, and commercial paper owned by a bank, investment organization, or other investor. [Italian *portafoglio* : *portare,* to carry, from Latin *portāre* (see **per-²** in Appendix*) + *foglio,* leaf, sheet, from Latin *folium* (see **bhel-³** in Appendix*).]

Port Har·court (här′kərt, -kôrt′, -kōrt′). A city in southern Nigeria, on the Niger Delta. Population, 180,000.

port·hole (pôrt′hōl′, pōrt′-) *n.* **1.** A small, usually circular window in a ship's side. **2.** An embrasure.

por·ti·co (pôr′tĭ-kō′, pōr′-) *n., pl.* **-coes** or **-cos.** A porch or walkway with a roof supported by columns, often leading to the

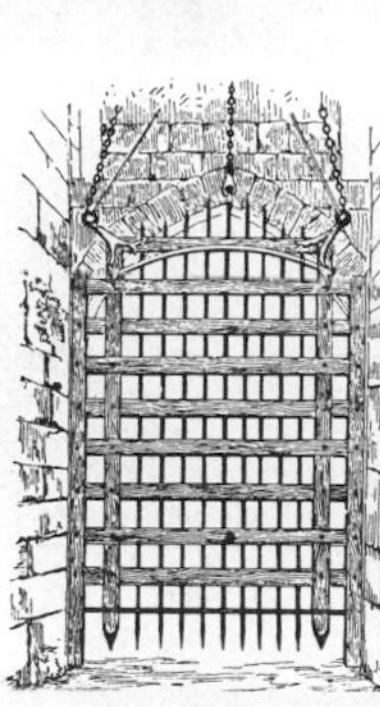

portcullis

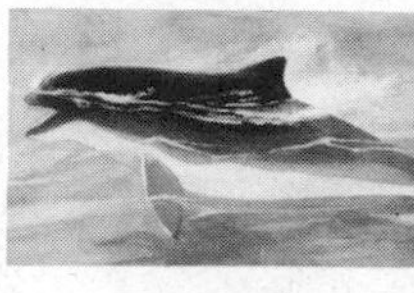

porpoise
Phocaena phocoena
Harbor porpoise

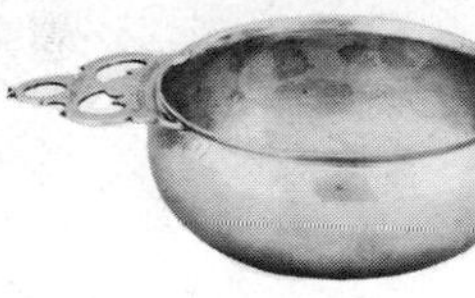

porringer
Eighteenth-century American

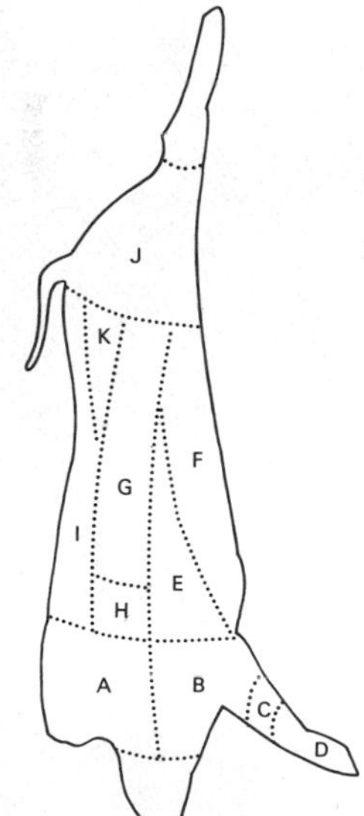

pork
A. Boston butt
B. Picnic ham
C. Hock
D. Foot
E. Spareribs
F. Bacon
G. Center loin
H. Rib chops
I. Fatback for salt pork
J. Ham
K. Tenderloin

t tight/th thin, path/*th* this, bathe/ŭ cut/ûr urge/v valve/w with/y yes/z zebra, size/zh vision/ə about, item, edible, gallop, circus/ à *Fr.* ami/œ *Fr.* feu, *Ger.* schön/ü *Fr.* tu, *Ger.* über/KH *Ger.* ich, *Scot.* loch/N *Fr.* bon. *Follows main vocabulary. †Of obscure origin.

entrance of a building. [Italian, from Latin *porticus,* porch, from *porta,* a gate. See **per-**[2] in Appendix.*] **—por′ti·coed′** *adj.*

por·tière, por·tiere (pôr-tyâr′, pōr-) *n.* A heavy curtain hung across a doorway. [French *portière,* from *porte,* door, from Old French, gate, PORT.]

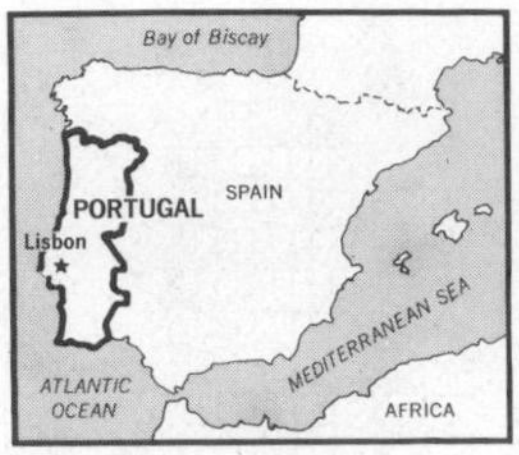

Portugal

por·tion (pôr′shən, pōr′-) *n.* **1.** A section or quantity within a larger thing; a part of a whole: *"Important portions of the surface are green."* (Isaac Asimov). **2.** A part separated from a whole. **3.** A part that is allotted to a person or group, such as: **a.** The amount of food, or the amount of a specific dish, served to one person at a meal; helping. **b.** The part of an estate received by an heir. **4.** A woman's dowry. **5.** The part of human destiny allotted to a person or group; one's lot or fate: *"all liars will have their portion in the lake burning with fire and brimstone"* (Charlotte Brontë). *—tr.v.* **portioned, -tioning, -tions. 1.** To divide into parts or shares for distribution; parcel. Usually used with *out.* **2.** To provide with a share, inheritance, or dowry. [Middle English, from Old French, from Latin *portiō.* See **pere-** in Appendix.*] **—por′tion·a·ble** *adj.* **—por′tion·er** *n.* **—por′tion·less** *adj.*

Port·land (pôrt′lənd, pōrt′-). **1.** A seaport city in southwestern Maine, on Casco Bay. Population, 73,000. **2.** An industrial city and river port in northwestern Oregon on the Willamette River, 12 miles southeast of its confluence with the Columbia River at Vancouver, Washington. Population, 380,000.

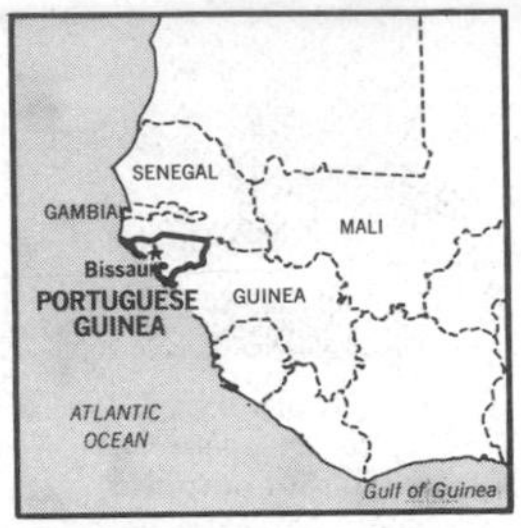

Portuguese Guinea

Portland cement. A hydraulic cement made by heating a mixture of limestone and clay, containing oxides of calcium, aluminum, iron, and silicon, in a kiln and pulverizing the resultant clinker. [The concrete resembles *Portland stone,* limestone quarried at *Portland,* England.]

Port Lou·is (lo͞o′ĭs, lo͞o′ē, lo͞o-ē′). The capital city and principal seaport of Mauritius. Population, 128,000.

port·ly (pôrt′lē, pōrt′-) *adj.* **-lier, -liest. 1.** Comfortably stout; corpulent. **2.** *Archaic.* Stately; majestic; imposing. —See Synonyms at **fat.** [From PORT (bearing).] **—port′li·ness** *n.*

Port Lyau·tey (lyō-tā′). A river port in northwestern Morocco, about 30 miles northeast of Rabat. Population, 87,000.

port·man·teau (pôrt-măn′tō, pōrt-, pôrt′măn-tō′, pōrt′-) *n., pl.* **-teaus** or **-teaux** (-tōz). *Chiefly British.* A large leather suitcase that opens into two hinged compartments. [French *portemanteau,* from Old French, "coat-carrier" : *porter,* to carry, from Latin *portāre* (see **per-**[2] in Appendix*) + MANTEAU.]

portmanteau word. A word formed by merging the sounds and meanings of two different words; for example, *slithy,* from *lithe* and *slimy; chortle,* from *chuckle* and *snort;* a blend. ["You see, it's like a *portmanteau* . . . there are two meanings packed up in one word." (Lewis Carroll).]

Port Mores·by (môrz′bē, mōrz′-). The capital of the Territory of Papua and New Guinea, on the southeastern coast of New Guinea. Population, 30,000.

Pôr·to. The Portuguese name for **Oporto.**

Pôr·to A·le·gre (pôr′to͞o ä-lĕg′rē). The capital of the state of Rio Grande do Sul, at the northern end of Lagôa dos Patos in extreme southern Brazil. Population, 641,000.

port of call. A port where ships dock in the course of voyages to load or unload cargo, obtain supplies, or undergo repairs.

port of entry. *Abbr.* **P.O.E.** A place where travelers or goods may enter or leave a country under official supervision.

Port-of-Spain (pôrt′əv-spān′, pōrt′-). Also **Port of Spain.** The capital city and principal port of Trinidad and Tobago, on the northwest coast of Trinidad. Population, 94,000.

Por·to·lá (pôr-tō-lä′), **Gaspar de.** 1723?–1784? Spanish army officer and explorer; governor of the Californias (1767–70).

Por·to-No·vo (pôr′tō-nō′vō). The capital of Dahomey. Population, 65,000.

Por·to Ri·co. The former name for **Puerto Rico.**

por·trait (pôr′trĭt, -trāt′, pōr′-) *n.* **1.** A painting, photograph, or other likeness of a person, especially one showing the face. **2.** A verbal picture or description, especially of a person. **3.** Any close likeness of one thing to another: *"Every man's work . . . is always a portrait of himself."* (Samuel Butler). [French, from Old French, from the past participle of *portraire,* PORTRAY.]

por·trait·ist (pôr′trə-tĭst, pōr-) *n.* A person who makes portraits, especially a painter or photographer.

por·trai·ture (pôr′trĭ-cho͝or′, pōr′-) *n.* **1.** The practice or art of making portraits. **2.** A portrait. **3.** Portraits collectively.

por·tray (pôr-trā′, pōr-) *tr.v.* **-trayed, -traying, -trays. 1.** To depict or represent pictorially; make a picture of. **2.** To depict or describe in words. **3.** To represent dramatically, as on the stage. [Middle English *portraien,* from Old French *portraire,* from Latin *prōtrahere,* to draw forth, reveal (in Medieval Latin, also "to portray") : *prō,* forth + *trahere,* to draw (see **tragh-** in Appendix*).] **—por·tray′a·ble** *adj.* **—por·tray′er** *n.*

por·tray·al (pôr-trā′əl, pōr-) *n.* **1.** The act or process of depicting or portraying. **2.** A representation or description.

por·tress (pôr′trĭs, pōr′-) *n.* Also **por·ter·ess** (pôr′trĭs, -tər-ĭs, pōr′-). A female doorkeeper or porter, especially in a convent.

Port Roy·al (roi′əl). A town and former capital of Jamaica, at the entrance of Kingston Harbor.

Port Sa·id (sä-ēd′). A city and principal port of Egypt, at the Mediterranean end of the Suez Canal. Population, 244,000.

Port Sa·lut (sə-lo͞ot′, -lo͞o′). Also **Port du Sa·lut** (pôr′dü sà-lo͞o′). A semihard fermented French cheese, made originally by Trappist monks.

Ports·mouth (pôrts′məth, pōrts′-). **1.** A city of southeastern Hampshire, England, on the English Channel 65 miles southwest of London; the chief home port of the Royal Navy. Population, 216,000. **2.** A city in southeastern Virginia, on the Elizabeth River opposite Norfolk. Population, 115,000. **3.** A city and seaport of New Hampshire, in the southeast on the Atlantic. Population, 27,000.

Por·tu·gal (pôr′chə-gəl, pōr′-; *Portuguese* pôr′to͞o-gäl′). *Abbr.* **Pg., Port.** Ancient name **Lu·si·ta·nia** (lo͞o′sə-tā′nē-ə). A republic of southwestern Europe, occupying 34,216 square miles in the western part of the Iberian Peninsula, and including Madeira and the Azores. Population, 8,889,000. Capital, Lisbon. [Portuguese, earlier *Portucal,* from Medieval Latin *Portus Cale,* the port of Cale, on the Douro, from Latin *portus,* PORT (harbor).]

Por·tu·guese (pôr′chə-gēz′, -gēs′, pōr′-; pôr′chə-gēz′, -gēs′, pōr′-) *adj. Abbr.* **Pg., Port.** Of or pertaining to Portugal, its people, or their language. *—n., pl.* **Portuguese.** *Abbr.* **Pg., Port. 1.** A native or inhabitant of Portugal. **2.** The Romance language of Portugal and Brazil.

Portuguese East Africa. The former name for **Mozambique.**

Portuguese Guin·ea (gĭn′ē). An overseas province of Portugal (14,000 square miles), on the west coast of Africa between Guinea and Senegal. Population, 549,000. Capital, Bissau.

Portuguese man-of-war. A complex colonial organism of the genus *Physalia,* of warm seas, having a bluish, bladderlike float from which are suspended numerous long stinging tentacles capable of inflicting severe injury.

Portuguese Ti·mor (tē′môr′, tē-môr′). An overseas territory of Portugal, comprising the eastern part of the island of Timor, Oe-Cusse, in the northwest, and several offshore islands (7,387 square miles). Population, 517,000. Capital, Dili.

Portuguese West Af·ri·ca. See **Angola.**

por·tu·lac·a (pôr′chə-lăk′ə, pōr′-) *n.* Any plant of the genus *Portulaca,* having fleshy stems and leaves; especially, *P. grandiflora,* cultivated for its showy flowers that open only in sunlight. This species is also called "rose moss." [New Latin, from Latin *portulāca,* purslane, from *portula,* diminutive of *porta,* gate, from the gatelike covering on its capsule. See **per-**[2] in Appendix.*]

pos. 1. position. **2.** positive.

pose[1] (pōz) *v.* **posed, posing, poses.** *—intr.* **1.** To assume or hold a particular position or posture, as in sitting for a portrait. **2.** To affect a particular mental attitude. **3.** To represent oneself in a given character or as other than what one is: *"America was posing as the champion of legitimacy and order."* (Henry Adams). *—tr.* **1.** To place (a model, for example) in a specific position. **2.** To propound or assert: *"Today, man is posing for himself new problems"* (L. and M. Milne). *—n.* **1.** A bodily attitude or position, especially one assumed for an artist or photographer. **2.** An affected attitude of mind or body: *"Your cynicism is simply a pose."* (Oscar Wilde). —See Synonyms at **affectation.** [Middle English *posen,* from Old French *poser,* from Late Latin *pausāre,* to cease, which in Vulgar Latin took over the meaning of Latin *pōnere,* to place (past participle *positus*), from Latin *pausa,* a pause, from Greek *pausis,* from *pauein,* to pause. See **pauein** in Appendix.*]

pose[2] (pōz) *tr.v.* **posed, posing, poses.** To puzzle or confuse with a difficult question or problem. [Short for *appose,* Middle English *apposen, opposen,* to confront with objections, from Old French *opposer,* to OPPOSE.]

Po·sei·don (pō-sī′dən) *n. Greek Mythology.* The god of the waters, earthquakes, and horses; brother of Zeus; identified with the Roman god Neptune. [Latin, from Greek *Poseidōn*†.]

Po·sen. The German name for **Poznań.**

pos·er[1] (pō′zər) *n.* One who poses.

pos·er[2] (pō′zər) *n.* A baffling question or problem.

po·seur (pō-zœr′) *n.* A person who affects a particular attitude, character, or manner to impress others. [French, from Old French *poser,* POSE.]

posh (pŏsh) *adj. Informal.* Smart and fashionable; exclusive. [Possibly an acronym for "port (side) out, starboard home," with reference to accommodations on the shady and hence expensive side of ships plying between England and India.]

pos·it (pŏz′ĭt) *tr.v.* **-ited, -iting, -its. 1.** To place in position. **2.** To put forward as a fact or truth; to postulate. —See Synonyms at **presume.** [Latin *pōnere* (past participle *positus*), to place. See **position.**]

po·si·tion (pə-zĭsh′ən) *n. Abbr.* **pos. 1.** A place or location. **2.** The right or appropriate place: *The guns were in position.* **3. a.** The way in which something is placed. **b.** The arrangement of bodily parts; posture: *a standing position.* **4.** A mental posture; point of view: *the government's position on foreign aid.* **5.** A situation or state relative to circumstances: *in a difficult position.* **6.** Social standing or status; rank. **7.** A post of employment; job. **8.** *Sports.* The area for which a particular player is responsible. **9. a.** The act or process of positing. **b.** The principle or proposition posited. *—tr.v.* **positioned, -tioning, -tions.** To place in proper position. [Old French, from Latin *positiō,* from *pōnere* (past participle *positus*), to place. See **apo-** in Appendix.*] **—po·si′tion·al** *adj.* **—po·si′tion·er** *n.*

pos·i·tive (pŏz′ə-tĭv) *adj. Abbr.* **pos. 1.** Characterized by or displaying certainty, acceptance, or affirmation: *a positive answer.* **2.** Measured or moving in a direction of increase, progress, or forward motion. **3.** Explicitly or openly expressed or laid down: *a positive demand.* **4.** Admitting of no doubt; irrefutable. **5. a.** Determined or settled in opinion or assertion; confident: *a positive manner.* **b.** Overconfident; dogmatic. **6.** Formally or arbitrarily determined; prescribed. **7.** Concerned with practical rather than theoretical matters. **8.** Composed of or characterized by the presence of particular qualities or attributes; real. **9.** *Philosophy.* Of or pertaining to positivism. **10.** Without relation to or comparison with anything else; absolute. **11.** *Informal.* Used as an intensifier: *She is a positive angel.* **12.** *Mathematics.* Pertaining to or designating: **a.** A quantity greater than zero. **b.** The sign (+). **c.** A quantity, number, angle, or direction opposite to another designated as negative. **13.** *Physics.* Pertaining to or designating electric charge of a sign opposite to that of an electron. **14.** *Medicine.* Indicating the presence of a particular disease, condition, or organism: *a positive Wassermann test.* **15.** *Biology.* Indicating or characterized by response or motion toward the source of a stimulus: *positive tropism.* Compare **negative.** **16.** *Photography.* Having the areas of light and dark in their original and normal relationship, as in a print made from a negative. **17.** *Grammar.* Of, pertaining to, or denoting the simple uncompared degree of an adjective or adverb, as opposed to either the comparative or superlative. **18.** *Machinery.* Driven by or generating power directly through intermediate parts having little or no play: *positive drive.* —*n.* **1.** That which is positive. **2.** *Philosophy.* That which is perceptible to the senses. **3.** *Mathematics.* A quantity greater than zero. **4.** *Physics.* A positive electric charge. **5.** *Photography.* An image in which the lights and darks appear as they do in nature. **6.** *Grammar.* **a.** The uncompared degree of an adjective or adverb. **b.** A word in this degree. [Middle English, from Old French *positif,* from Latin *positīvus,* arbitrarily laid down, dogmatic, from *pōnere* (past participle *positus*), to place. See **apo-** in Appendix.*] —**pos'i·tive·ly** *adv.* —**pos'i·tive·ness** *n.*

pos·i·tiv·ism (pŏz'ə-tĭv-ĭz'əm) *n.* **1. a.** A philosophical doctrine contending that sense perceptions are the only admissible basis of human knowledge and precise thought. **b.** The application of this doctrine in logic, epistemology, and ethics. Compare **logical positivism.** **2.** The system of Auguste **Comte** *(see),* designed to supersede theology and metaphysics, and depending on a hierarchy of the sciences, beginning with mathematics and culminating in sociology. **3.** Dogmatic certainty, as in speculation and argument. —**pos'i·tiv·ist** *n.* —**pos'i·tiv·is'tic** *adj.*

pos·i·tron (pŏz'ə-trŏn') *n.* *Symbol* e^+ The **antiparticle** *(see)* of the electron. See also **particle.** [POSI(TIVE) + (ELEC)TRON.]

pos·i·tron·i·um (pŏz'ə-trō'nē-əm) *n.* *Physics.* A short-lived association of an electron and a positron bound together in a configuration resembling the hydrogen atom. [From POSITRON.]

poss. **1.** possession. **2.** possessive. **3.** possible; possibly.

pos·se (pŏs'ē) *n.* **1.** A **posse comitatus** *(see).* **2.** Any body of men armed with legal authority. —**in posse.** *Law.* Possible, potential. [Short for Medieval Latin *posse comitātūs,* POSSE COMITATUS.]

posse com·i·ta·tus (kŏm'ə-tā'təs). A body of men that a sheriff or other peace officer is empowered to summon to aid in maintaining peace. [Medieval Latin *posse comitātūs,* "force of the county" : *posse,* power, from Latin, to be able, have power (see **potent**) + *comitātūs,* genitive of *comitātus,* COUNTY.]

pos·sess (pə-zĕs') *tr.v.* **-sessed, -sessing, -sesses.** **1.** To have as property; to own. **2.** To have as a quality, characteristic, or other attribute. **3.** To acquire mastery of or have knowledge of: *possess valuable data.* **4.** To gain or exert influence or control over; dominate: *Fury possessed him.* **5.** To control or maintain (one's nature) in a particular state or condition: *He possessed his temper despite the insult.* **6.** To cause to own, hold, or master something, such as property or knowledge. Used with *of.* See Usage note at **possessed.** **7.** To cause to be influenced or controlled, as by an idea or emotion. Used with *with.* See Usage note at **possessed.** **8.** To have sexual intercourse with. **9.** *Obsolete.* To gain or seize. [Middle English *possessen,* from Old French *possesser,* from Latin *possidēre* (past participle *possessus*), "to sit as master," take possession of : *posse,* to be able (see **poti-** in Appendix*) + *sidere,* to sit down (see **sed-**[1] in Appendix*), and from Latin *possidēre* (past participle *possessus*), to own, possess : *posse,* to be able + *sedēre,* to sit (see **sed-**[1] in Appendix*).] —**pos·ses'sor** *n.*

pos·sessed (pə-zĕst') *adj.* **1.** Owning or having. **2.** Controlled by or as if by a spirit or other force; obsessed. See Usage note below. **3.** Calm; collected: *be possessed in time of trial.*

Usage: *Possessed* is often followed by the prepositions *of, by,* or *with.* Mere possession of a thing or attribute is indicated by *of: possessed of property; possessed of a sharp tongue.* When the term indicates obsession or lack of self-control, *by* and *with* are more often used: *possessed by* (or *with*) *an urge to kill.*

pos·ses·sion (pə-zĕsh'ən) *n.* **1.** The act or fact of possessing. **2.** The state of being possessed. **3.** *Abbr.* **poss.** That which is owned or possessed. **4.** *Plural.* Wealth or property. **5.** *Abbr.* **poss.** *Law.* Actual holding or occupancy with, or without, rightful ownership. **6.** Any territory subject to foreign control. **7.** Self-control. **8.** The state of being dominated by, or as if by, evil spirits or by an obsession. —See Synonyms at **asset.**

pos·ses·sive (pə-zĕs'ĭv) *adj. Abbr.* **poss.** **1.** Of or pertaining to ownership or possession. **2.** Having or manifesting a desire to control or dominate: *a possessive mother.* **3.** *Grammar.* Of, pertaining to, or designating a noun or pronoun case that expresses belonging or other similar relation. See Usage note below. —*n. Abbr.* **poss.** *Grammar.* **1.** The possessive case. **2.** A possessive form or construction. See Usage note below. —**pos·ses'sive·ly** *adv.* —**pos·ses'sive·ness** *n.*

Usage: Possessive forms are made in English in the following ways: 1. By adding an apostrophe *s* (*'s*): a. To the singular of most nouns, proper names, and irregular plurals, as in *the boy's chair, Bill's car, the men's hats.* b. To monosyllabic singular nouns and proper names ending in a sibilant, as in *the boss's car, Marx's philosophy.* 2. By adding an apostrophe (') alone: a. To regular plurals, as in *the girls' dresses, the ladies' furs.* b. To certain expressions with *sake,* as in *for appearance' sake, for goodness' sake.* c. To plurals of proper nouns, as in *the Joneses' house.* d. To proper nouns when a sibilant occurs before the last syllable, as in *Moses' law, Xerxes' palace.* e. To ancient or classical names, as in *Achilles' heel.* Usage varies, however, when a singular noun or a proper name ending in a sibilant has two or more syllables. In these cases, both forms may occur, but many prefer to use the apostrophe alone, as in *Dickens'* or *Dickens's* and *witness'* or *witness's.*

possessive adjective. *Grammar.* A pronominal adjective expressing possession. In the sentences *This is my duty* and *It is their fate,* the possessive adjectives are *my* and *their.*

possessive pronoun. *Grammar.* One of several pronouns denoting possession and capable of substituting for noun phrases. They are: *mine, his, hers, its, ours, yours, theirs, whose.*

pos·ses·so·ry (pə-zĕs'ə-rē) *adj.* **1.** Of, pertaining to, or having possession. **2.** *Law.* Depending on or arising from possession: *possessory interest.*

pos·set (pŏs'ĭt) *n.* A spiced drink of hot sweetened milk curdled with wine or ale. [Middle English *poshet, possot*†.]

pos·si·bil·i·ty (pŏs'ə-bĭl'ə-tē) *n., pl.* **-ties.** **1.** The fact or state of being possible. **2.** Something possible. **3.** Someone capable of succeeding or being chosen: *Wilson was an outside possibility for the nomination.* **4.** *Plural.* Capacity for favorable development; potential: *"The possibilities of modern technology were first in practice realised in England"* (A.N. Whitehead).

pos·si·ble (pŏs'ə-bəl) *adj. Abbr.* **poss.** **1.** Capable of happening, existing, or being true without contradicting proven facts, laws, or circumstances. **2.** Capable of occurring or being done without offense to character, nature, or custom. **3.** Capable of favorable development; potential: *a possible site for the new capital.* **4.** That may or may not occur; of uncertain likelihood. [Middle English, from Old French, from Latin *possibilis,* from *posse,* to be able. See **poti-** in Appendix.*] —**pos'si·bly** *adv.*

Synonyms: *possible, practical, workable, practicable, feasible, viable.* These refer to the likelihood that, or ease with which, something can be done. *Possible* indicates that something is realizable as an end. It can imply either a moderate degree of probability or the barest chance within the limits of circumstances: *admittedly possible; not at all possible. Practical* emphasizes the prudence, efficiency, or economy of an act, solution, or agent: *a practical way to do it; a practical person. Workable* is used of proposed ideas or plans, the success of which is likely if properly managed: *a workable production schedule. Practicable,* meaning fitted for actual use or application, is often used to describe projects where an initial forecast is important: *hardly practicable at this time.* Something is *feasible* if it is clearly possible and applicable; the word often connotes closer scrutiny and more guarded approval than *workable* or *practicable. Viable,* in current usage, has come to denote likelihood of continued effectiveness or success; it tends to be used comparatively: *a more viable method of negotiating a settlement.*

pos·sum. Variant of **opossum.** —**play possum.** To pretend to be dead, asleep, or unaware in order to deceive an opponent.

possum haw. **1.** A holly, *Ilex decidua,* of the southeastern United States, having bright-red fruit. **2.** A shrub, *Viburnum nudum,* of the eastern United States, having white flowers and bluish-black fruit.

post[1] (pōst) *n.* **1.** A stake of wood or other material set upright into the ground to serve as a marker or support. **2.** Anything resembling this. **3.** The starting gate at a racetrack. —*tr.v.* **posted, posting, posts.** **1. a.** To fasten up (an announcement) in a place of public view. **b.** To cover (a wall, for example) with posters; to placard. **2.** To announce by or as by posters: *post banns.* **3.** To denounce publicly: *post a man as a thief.* **4.** To publish (a name) on a list. [Middle English *post,* Old English *post,* from West Germanic *posta* (unattested), from Latin *postis.* See **stā-** in Appendix.*]

post[2] (pōst) *n.* **1. a.** A military base where troops are stationed. **b.** The grounds and buildings of a military base. **2.** A local organization of military veterans. **3.** *British Military.* Either of two bugle calls, *first post* or *last post,* sounded in the evening as a signal to retire to quarters. **4.** An assigned position or station, as of a guard or sentry. **5.** A position of employment; especially, an appointed public office. **6.** A place to which anyone is assigned for duty. **7.** A trading post. —*tr.v.* **posted, posting, posts.** **1.** To assign to a specific position or station: *post a sentry.* **2.** To appoint to a naval or military command. **3.** To put forward; present: *post bail.* [French *poste,* from Old Italian *posto,* from Vulgar Latin *postum* (unattested), contraction of Latin *positum,* neuter past participle of *pōnere,* to place. See **apo-** in Appendix.*]

post[3] (pōst) *n.* **1. a.** One of a series of relay stations along a fixed route, furnishing fresh riders and horses for the delivery of mail on horseback. **b.** A rider on such a mail route; courier. **2.** *British.* **a.** A governmental system for transporting and delivering the mail. **b.** A post office. **3. a.** A delivery of mail. **b.** The mail delivered. —*v.* **posted, posting, posts.** —*intr.* **1.** To travel in stages or relays. **2.** To travel quickly; speed or hasten. **3.** To bob up and down in the saddle in rhythm with a horse's trotting gait. —*tr.* **1.** To send by mail in a system of relays on horseback. **2.** To mail (a letter). **3.** To inform of the latest news. **4.** *Bookkeeping.* **a.** To transfer (an item or items) to a ledger. **b.** To make the necessary entries in (a ledger). —*adv.* **1.** By post horse. **2.** By mail. **3.** With great speed; rapidly. [French *poste,* from Italian *posta,* from Vulgar Latin *posta* (unattested), contraction of Latin *posita,* feminine past participle of *pōnere,* to place. See **post** (military).]

Post (pōst), **Emily (Price).** 1873–1960. American journalist and writer on etiquette.

post-. Indicates: **1.** After in time; later; subsequent to; for example, **postdate, postgraduate.** **2.** After in position; behind; posterior to; for example, **postfix, postaxial.** ***Note.*** Many com-

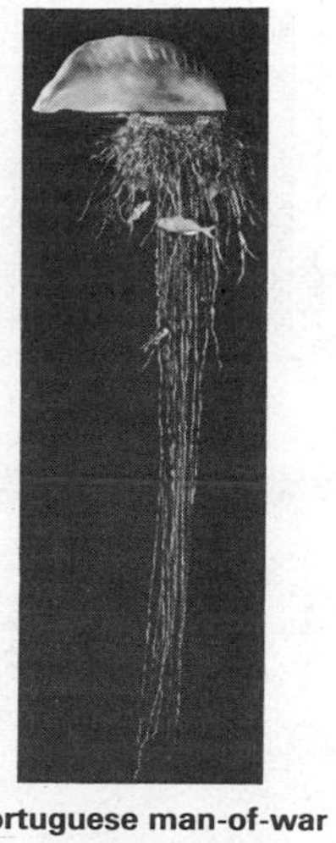

Portuguese man-of-war

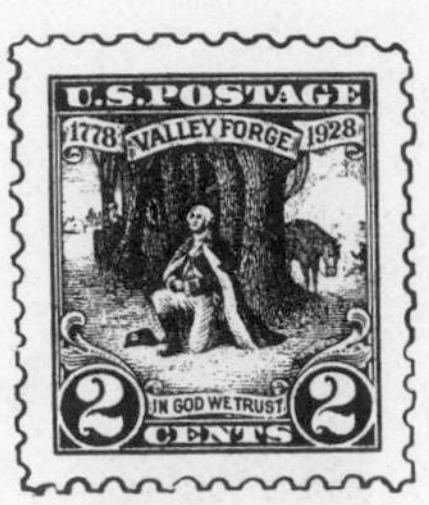

postage stamp
U.S. two-cent stamp issued in 1928 to commemorate Washington's winter at Valley Forge

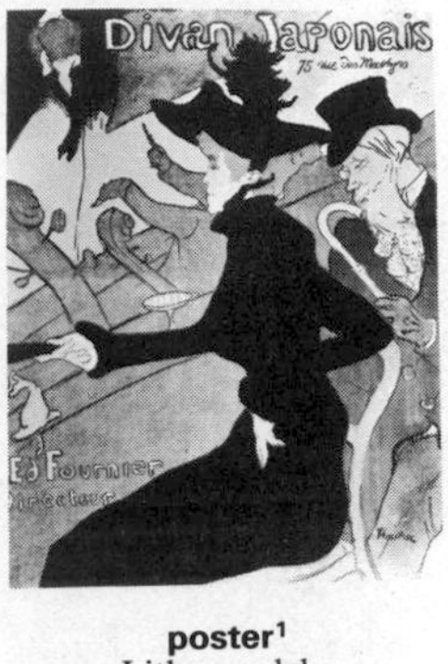

poster¹
Lithograph by Toulouse-Lautrec (1892)

pounds other than those entered here may be formed with *post-*. In forming compounds, *post-* is normally joined with the following element without space or hyphen: *posttraumatic*. However, if the second element begins with a capital letter, it is separated with a hyphen: *post-Victorian*. Compounds made up of the Latin word *post* and another Latin form are hyphenated. Those entered here are **post-bellum, post-mortem,** and **post-obit.** [Latin, from *post*, behind, after. See **apo-** in Appendix.*]

post·age (pōs′tĭj) *n.* The charge for mailing an item.

postage meter. A machine used in bulk mailing to print the correct amount of postage on each piece of mail.

postage stamp. A small engraved usually adhesive label issued by a government and sold in various denominations to be affixed to items of mail as evidence of the payment of postage.

post·al (pōs′tl) *adj.* Of or pertaining to the post office or mail service. —*n.* A **postal card** *(see)*. —**post′al·ly** *adv.*

postal card. A card printed with a postage stamp, issued by a government and sold by a governmental agency, for sending messages at low rates. Also called "postal," "post card."

post·ax·i·al (pōst-ăk′sē-əl) *adj. Anatomy.* Located behind an axis of the body, especially posterior to the fibula of the leg or the ulna of the arm.

post-bel·lum (pōst-bĕl′əm) *adj.* Happening after a war, especially the American Civil War. [Latin *post*, after + *bellum*, war (see **duellum** in Appendix*).]

post·box (pōst′bŏks′) *n.* Also **post box.** A mailbox.

post card. Also **post·card.** *Abbr.* **p.c.** **1.** An unofficial card, usually bearing a picture on one side, with space for an address, postage stamp, and short message. **2.** A **postal card** *(see)*.

post·ca·va (pōst-kä′və, -kā′və) *n. Anatomy.* The inferior **vena cava** *(see)*. —**post·ca′val** *adj.*

post chaise. A closed, four-wheeled, horse-drawn carriage, formerly used to transport mail and passengers. Also called "chaise." [POST (mail) + CHAISE.]

post·date (pōst-dāt′) *tr.v.* **-dated, -dating, -dates.** **1.** To put a date on (a check, letter, or document) that is later than the actual date. **2.** To occur later than; follow in time.

post·di·lu·vi·an (pōst′dĭ-lōō′vē-ən) *adj.* Also **post·di·lu·vi·al** (-əl). Existing or occurring after the Biblical Flood. —*n.* A person or thing living after the Biblical Flood.

post·doc·tor·al (pōst-dŏk′tər-əl) *adj.* Of, pertaining to, or engaged in academic study beyond the level of a doctor's degree.

post·er¹ (pō′stər) *n.* **1.** A large printed placard, bill, or announcement, often illustrated, posted to advertise or publicize something. **2.** One who posts bills or notices.

post·er² (pō′stər) *n. Archaic.* One who traveled post.

poste res·tante (pōst′ rĕ-stänt′). A notation written on a letter indicating that the letter should be held at the post office until claimed by the addressee. [French, "remaining mail" : *poste*, POST (mail) + *restante*, from *rester*, to REST.]

pos·te·ri·or (pŏ-stîr′ē-ər, pō-) *adj.* **1.** Located behind a part or toward the rear of a structure. **2.** *Anatomy.* Pertaining to the caudal end of the body in an animal or the dorsal side in man. **3.** *Botany.* Next to or nearest the main stem or axis. **4.** Coming after in order; following. **5.** Following in time; later; subsequent. —*n.* The buttocks. Sometimes used in the plural. [Latin, comparative of *posterus*, coming after, next, from *post*, after. See **apo-** in Appendix.*] —**pos·te′ri·or·ly** *adv.*

pos·te·ri·or·i·ty (pŏ-stîr′ē-ôr′ə-tē, -ŏr′ə-tē, pō-) *n.* The condition of being posterior in location or time.

pos·ter·i·ty (pŏ-stĕr′ə-tē) *n.* **1.** Future generations. **2.** All of a person's descendants. [Middle English *posterite*, from Old French *posterite*, from Latin *posteritās*, from *posterus*, next. See **posterior.**]

pos·tern (pō′stərn, pŏs′tərn) *n.* A small rear gate, especially one in a fort or castle. —*adj.* Situated in back or at the side. [Middle English *posterne*, from Old French, variant of *posterle*, from Late Latin *posterula*, diminutive of *postera*, back door, from the feminine of *posterus*, coming after. See **posterior.**]

poster paint. Opaque water-color paint in bright colors.

Post Exchange, post exchange. *Abbr.* **PX** A store or set of stores on a military base for the sale of tax-free merchandise and services to military personnel and their families.

post·ex·il·i·an (pōst′ĕg-zĭl′ē-ən, -zĭl′yən, -ĕk-sĭl′ē-ən, -ĕk-sĭl′yən) *adj.* Also **post·ex·il·ic** (-ĕg-zĭl′ĭk, -ĕk-sĭl′ĭk). Of or pertaining to the period of Jewish history following the Babylonian captivity (after 586 B.C.).

post·fix (pōst-fĭks′) *tr.v.* **-fixed, -fixing, -fixes.** To suffix. —*n.* (pōst′fĭks′). A suffix. —**post·fix′al, post·fix′i·al** *adj.*

post·gla·cial (pōst-glā′shəl) *adj. Geology.* Pertaining to or occurring during the time following a glacial period.

post·grad·u·ate (pōst-grăj′ōō-ĭt, -āt′) *adj. Abbr.* **P.G.** Of, pertaining to, or pursuing advanced study beyond the level of a bachelor's degree. —*n.* A person engaged in such study.

post·haste (pōst′hāst′) *adv.* With great speed; hastily; rapidly. —*n. Archaic.* Great speed; rapidity. [Originally *post, haste*, a direction on letters : POST (courier) + HASTE (imperative).]

post·hu·mous (pŏs′chōō-məs) *adj.* **1.** Occurring or continuing after one's death: *a posthumous award.* **2.** Published after the author's death: *a posthumous book.* **3.** Born after the death of the father; *a posthumous child.* [Latin *posthumus*, alteration (influenced by *humus*, earth, and taken as "after burial") of *postumus*, superlative of *posterus*, coming after, next. See **posterior.**] —**post′hu·mous·ly** *adv.* —**post′hu·mous·ness** *n.*

post·hyp·not·ic suggestion (pōst′hĭp-nŏt′ĭk). A suggestion made to a hypnotized person specifying an action to be performed in a subsequent waking state.

pos·tiche (pô-stēsh′, pŏ-) *adj.* **1.** Added superfluously or inappropriately. **2.** Artificial; false. —*n.* **1.** Something false; a sham. **2.** A small hairpiece. [French, from Italian *posticcio*, fake, counterfeit, from *posto*, added, placed, from Latin *positus*, past participle of *pōnere*, to place. See **apo-** in Appendix.*]

pos·til·ion (pō-stĭl′yən, pŏ-) *n.* Also **pos·til·lion.** One who rides the near horse of the leaders to guide the horses drawing a coach. [French *postillon*, from Italian *postiglione*, from *posta*, POST (mail).]

post·im·pres·sion·ism (pōst′ĭm-prĕsh′ə-nĭz′əm) *n.* A school of painting in France in the late 19th century, exemplified by a group including Cézanne and Matisse, who rejected the objective naturalism of impressionism and used form and color in ways more expressive of their own conception of the subject. —**post′im·pres′sion·ist** *n.* & *adj.* —**post′im·pres′sion·is′tic** *adj.*

post·lude (pōst′lōōd′) *n.* **1. a.** An organ voluntary played at the end of a church service. **b.** A concluding piece of music. **2.** A final chapter or phase. [POST- + (PRE)LUDE.]

post·man (pōst′mən) *n., pl.* **-men** (-mĭn). A **mailman** *(see)*.

post·mark (pōst′märk′) *n.* An official mark printed over the stamp on a piece of mail; especially, one that cancels the stamp and records the date and place of mailing. —*tr.v.* **postmarked, -marking, -marks.** To stamp with a postmark.

post·mas·ter (pōst′măs′tər, -mäs′tər) *n. Abbr.* **PM, P.M.** A government official in charge of the operations of a local post office. —**post′mas′ter·ship′** *n.*

postmaster general *pl.* **postmasters general.** *Abbr.* **P.M.G.** The executive head of a national postal service.

post·me·rid·i·an (pōst′mə-rĭd′ē-ən) *adj.* Of, pertaining to, or taking place in the afternoon. [Latin *postmerīdiānus* : *post*, after + *merīdiānus*, MERIDIAN.]

post me·rid·i·em (pōst′ mə-rĭd′ē-əm). *Abbr. Usually small capitals* P.M. Also **P.M., p.m.** After noon. Used chiefly in the abbreviated form to specify the hour: *10:30* P.M. [Latin *post merīdiem*, after midday : *post*, after + *merīdiem*, accusative of *merīdiēs*, midday, noon (see **meridian**).]

post·mil·le·nar·i·an (pōst′mĭl-ə-nâr′ē-ən) *adj.* Of or pertaining to postmillennialism. —*n.* A person who believes in postmillennialism. Compare **premillenarian.**

post·mil·len·ni·al (pōst′mə-lĕn′ē-əl) *adj.* Also **post·mil·len·ni·an.** Happening or existing after the millennium.

post·mil·len·ni·al·ism (pōst′mə-lĕn′ē-ə-lĭz′əm) *n.* The doctrine that Christ's second coming will follow the millennium. Also called "postmillenarianism." Compare **premillennialism.** —**post′mil·len′ni·al·ist** *n.*

post-mor·tem (pōst-môr′təm) *adj. Abbr.* **p.m.** **1.** Occurring or done after death. **2.** Of or pertaining to a post-mortem examination. —*n.* **1.** A post-mortem examination, especially an **autopsy** *(see)*. **2.** *Informal.* An analysis or review of some completed event. [Latin *post mortem*, after death : *post*, after (see **apo-** in Appendix*) + *mortem*, accusative of *mors*, death (see **mer-²** in Appendix*).]

post·na·sal (pōst-nā′zəl) *adj.* Posterior to the nose.

postnasal drip. The chronic secretion of mucus from the posterior nasal cavities, resulting in congestion and coughing.

post·na·tal (pōst-nāt′l) *adj.* Of or occurring during the period immediately after birth. —**post·na′tal·ly** *adv.*

post·nup·tial (pōst-nŭp′shəl, -chəl) *adj.* Happening after marriage. —**post·nup′tial·ly** *adv.*

post-o·bit (pōst-ō′bĭt, -ŏb′ĭt) *adj.* Also **post·o·bit·u·ar·y** (pōst′ō-bĭch′ōō-ĕr′ē). Happening or taking effect after a person's death. —*n.* A bond given by a borrower promising to repay the debt after the death of a specified person from whose estate he expects to inherit. Also called "post-obit bond." [Latin *post obitum*, after death : *post*, after + *obitum*, accusative of *obitus*, death (see **obituary**).]

post office. *Abbr.* **p.o., P.O.** **1.** The public department responsible for the transportation and delivery of the mails. **2.** Any local office where mail is received, sorted, and delivered, and stamps and other postal matter are sold.

post·op·er·a·tive (pōst-ŏp′ər-ə-tĭv, -ŏp′rə-tĭv, -ŏp′ə-rā′tĭv) *adj.* Happening or done after surgery. —**post·op′er·a·tive·ly** *adv.*

post·or·bi·tal (pōst-ôr′bĭ-təl) *adj. Anatomy.* Located behind the eye socket: *a postorbital bone.*

post·paid (pōst′pād′) *adj. Abbr.* **p.p., P.P., ppd.** With the postage paid in advance.

post·par·tum (pōst-pär′təm) *adj.* Of or occurring in the period shortly after childbirth. [Latin *post partum*, after birth : *post*, after + *partum*, accusative of *partus*, a bringing forth, from the past participle of *parere*, to bear (see **per-⁴** in Appendix*).]

post·pone (pōst-pōn′, pōs-pōn′) *tr.v.* **-poned, -poning, -pones.** **1.** To delay until a future time; put off. **2.** To place after in importance; subordinate. [Latin *postpōnere*, to place after : *post*, after + *pōnere*, to put, place (see **apo-** in Appendix*).] —**post·pon′a·ble** *adj.* —**post·pone′ment** *n.* —**post·pon′er** *n.*

post·po·si·tion (pōst′pə-zĭsh′ən) *n. Grammar.* **1.** The placing of a word or suffixed element after the word to which it is grammatically related. **2.** A word or element so placed, as a preposition placed after its object. In the forms *what for?* and *homeward, for* and *-ward* are postpositions. [French, from Old French *postposer*, to place after, from Latin *postpōnere*, POSTPONE.] —**post′po·si′tion·al** *adj.* —**post′po·si′tion·al·ly** *adv.*

post·pos·i·tive (pōst-pŏz′ə-tĭv) *adj. Grammar.* Placed after or suffixed to another word. —*n. Grammar.* An appended or suffixed word or word element; a postposition. [Late Latin *postpositīvus*, from Latin *postpōnere* (past participle *postpositus*), to place after, POSTPONE.] —**post·pos′i·tive·ly** *adv.*

post·pran·di·al (pōst-prăn′dē-əl) *adj.* Also **post·pran·di·al.** Following any meal, especially dinner.

post·script (pōst′skrĭpt′, pōs′skrĭpt′) *n. Abbr.* **p.s., P.S.** **1.** A message appended at the end of a letter after the writer's signature. **2.** Additional information appended to a book, article, or the like. [Latin *postscriptum*, from *postscrībere* (past participle *postscriptus*), to write after : *post*, after + *scrībere*, to write (see **skeri-** in Appendix*).]

post·trau·mat·ic (pōst′trou-măt′ĭk, -trô-măt′ĭk) *adj.* Following injury or resulting from it: *posttraumatic amnesia.*

pos·tu·lant (pŏs′cho͝o-lənt) *n.* **1.** A person submitting a request or application; petitioner. **2.** A candidate for admission into a religious order. Compare **novice.** [French, from Latin *postulāns*, present participle of *postulāre*, to demand, POSTULATE.] —**pos′tu·lan·cy, pos′tu·lant·ship′** *n.*

pos·tu·late (pŏs′cho͝o-lāt′) *tr.v.* **-lated, -lating, -lates. 1.** To make claim for; demand. **2.** To assume the truth or reality of with no proof, especially as a basis of an argument: " '*We can see individuals, but we can't see providence; we have to postulate it.*' " (Aldous Huxley). **3.** To assume as a premise or axiom; take for granted. —See Synonyms at **presume.** —*n.* (pŏs′cho͝o-lĭt, -lāt′). **1.** Something assumed without proof as being self-evident or generally accepted, especially when used as a basis for an argument: "*The sheer audacity of his postulate that women belong to the same species as men*" (S.J. Perelman). **2.** A fundamental element; basic principle. **3.** *Geometry.* An axiom. **4.** A requirement; prerequisite. [Latin *postulāre*, to request, demand. See **perk-**[2] in Appendix.*] —**pos′tu·la′tion** *n.*

pos·tu·la·tor (pŏs′cho͝o-lā′tər) *n.* **1.** One who postulates. **2.** *Roman Catholic Church.* A church official who presents a plea for canonization or beatification.

pos·ture (pŏs′chər) *n.* **1.** A position or attitude of the body or of bodily parts: *a sitting posture.* **2.** A characteristic way of bearing one's body, especially the trunk and head; carriage: *learning good posture.* **3.** A bodily position assumed by an artist's model. **4.** The present condition or tendency of something: *the military posture of a nation.* **5.** A frame of mind affecting one's thoughts or behavior; overall attitude: "*a posture of defenseless womanhood*" (Ross Lockridge, Jr.). —*v.* **postured, -turing, -tures.** —*intr.* To assume an exaggerated or unnatural pose or mental attitude; attitudinize. —*tr.* To put in a posture; pose. [French, from Italian *postura*, from Latin *positūra*, position, from *pōnere* (past participle *positus*), to place. See **apo-** in Appendix.*] —**pos′tur·al** *adj.* —**pos′tur·er, pos′tur·ist** *n.*

post·vo·cal·ic (pōst′vō-kăl′ĭk) *adj. Linguistics.* Designating a consonant or consonantal sound directly following a vowel.

post·war (pōst′wôr′) *adj.* Occurring after a particular war.

po·sy (pō′zē) *n., pl.* **-sies. 1.** A flower or bunch of flowers; nosegay. **2.** *Archaic.* A brief verse or sentimental phrase, especially when inscribed on a trinket. [Variant of POESY.]

pot (pŏt) *n.* **1. a.** A round, fairly deep cooking vessel with a handle. **b.** Such a vessel and its contents: *a pot of soup.* **c.** The amount that such a vessel will hold; potful. **2. a.** A large drinking cup; tankard. **b.** A drink of liquor contained in such a cup. **3.** An artistic or decorative ceramic vessel of any size or shape. **4.** A flowerpot. **5.** Something resembling a round cooking vessel in appearance or function, as a chimney pot or chamber pot. **6.** A trap for fish, crustaceans, or eels, consisting of a wicker or wire basket. **7.** *Card Games.* **a.** The total amount staked by all the players in one hand. **b.** The area on a card table where stakes are placed. **8.** *Informal.* A common fund to which the members of a group contribute and upon which they draw for certain stated purposes. **9.** *Informal.* A pot shot. **10.** *Slang.* **Marijuana** *(see).* —**go to pot.** *Informal.* To deteriorate. —*v.* **potted, potting, pots.** —*tr.* **1.** To place or plant in a pot: *pot a plant.* **2.** To preserve (food) in a pot. **3.** To cook in a pot. **4.** To shoot (game) for food rather than for sport. **5.** *Informal.* To shoot with a pot shot. **6.** *Informal.* To win or capture; to bag. —*intr. Informal.* To take a pot shot. [Middle English *pot*, Old English *pott*, from Vulgar Latin *pottus* (attested only in Late Latin). See **pott-** in Appendix.*]

pot. potential.

po·ta·ble (pō′tə-bəl) *adj.* Fit to drink. —*n. Plural.* Drinkables. [French, from Late Latin *pōtābilis*, from Latin *pōtāre*, to drink. See **pōi-**[1] in Appendix.*] —**po′ta·bil′i·ty, po′ta·ble·ness** *n.*

pot·ash (pŏt′ăsh′) *n.* **1. Potassium carbonate** *(see).* **2. Potassium hydroxide** *(see).* **3.** Any of several compounds containing potassium, especially soluble compounds, such as potassium oxide, potassium chloride, and various potassium sulfates, used chiefly in fertilizers. [Singular of earlier *pot ashes* (translation of obsolete Dutch *potasschen*) : POT + plural of ASH (so called because first obtained by evaporating the lye of wood ashes in iron pots).]

potash feldspar. A mineral, **orthoclase** *(see).*

potash muriate. *Chemistry.* **Potassium chloride** *(see).*

po·tas·si·um (pə-tăs′ē-əm) *n. Symbol* **K** A soft, silver-white, light, highly or explosively reactive metallic element obtained by electrolysis of its common hydroxide and found in, or converted to, a wide variety of salts used especially in fertilizers and soaps. Atomic number 19, atomic weight 39.102, melting point 63.65°C, boiling point 774°C, specific gravity 0.862, valence 1. See **element.** [New Latin, from *potassa*, potassium monoxide, from English POTASH.] —**po·tas′sic** *adj.*

potassium bitartrate. A white crystalline solid or powder, $KHC_4H_4O_6$, used in baking powder, in the tinning of metals, and as a component of laxatives. Also called "cream of tartar."

potassium bromide. A white crystalline solid or powder, KBr, used as a sedative, in photographic emulsion, and in spectroscopy. Also called "bromide."

potassium carbonate. A transparent, white, deliquescent, granular powder, K_2CO_3, used in making glass, pigments, ceramics, and soaps. Also called "pearl ash," "potash."

potassium chlorate. A poisonous crystalline compound, $KClO_3$, used as an oxidizing agent, bleach, and disinfectant, and in making explosives, matches, and fireworks.

potassium chloride. A colorless crystalline solid or powder, KCl, used widely in fertilizers and in the preparation of most potassium compounds. Also called "potassium muriate," "potash muriate."

potassium cyanide. An extremely poisonous white compound, KCN, used in the extraction of gold and silver from ores, electroplating, photography, and as a fumigant and insecticide.

potassium dichromate. A bright yellowish-red crystalline compound, $K_2Cr_2O_7$, used as an oxidizing agent, and in pyrotechnics, explosives, and safety matches.

potassium hydroxide. A caustic deliquescent solid, KOH, used as a bleach and in the manufacture of liquid detergents and soaps, oxalic acid, matches, and many potassium compounds. Also called "caustic potash," "lye."

potassium nitrate. A transparent white crystalline compound, KNO_3, used to pickle meat and in the manufacture of pyrotechnics, explosives, matches, rocket propellants, and fertilizers. Also called "niter," "saltpeter."

potassium permanganate. A dark-purple crystalline compound, $KMnO_4$, used as an oxidizing agent, disinfectant, and in deodorizers and dyes. Also called "purple salt."

potassium sulfate. A colorless or white crystalline compound, K_2SO_4, used in medicine, glassmaking, fertilizers, and as a reagent in analytical chemistry.

po·ta·tion (pō-tā′shən) *n.* **1.** The act of drinking. **2.** A drink, especially of an alcoholic beverage. [Middle English *potacioun*, from Old French *potation*, from Latin *pōtātiō*, drinking, from *pōtāre*, to drink. See **pōi-**[1] in Appendix.*]

po·ta·to (pə-tā′tō) *n., pl.* **-toes. 1.** A plant, *Solanum tuberosum*, native to South America and widely cultivated for its starchy, edible tubers. **2.** A tuber of this plant. Also called "Irish potato," "white potato." See **sweet potato.** [Spanish *patata*, from Taino *batata*.]

potato beetle. A small yellow-and-black striped beetle, *Leptinotarsa decemlineata*, that is a major agricultural pest. Also called "Colorado potato beetle," "potato bug."

potato chip. A thin slice of potato fried in deep fat until crisp and then salted.

po·ta·to·ry (pō′tə-tôr′ē, -tōr′ē) *adj.* Of, pertaining to, or given to drinking. [Latin *pōtātōrius*, from *pōtāre*, to drink. See **pōi-**[1] in Appendix.*]

pot-au-feu (pô-tō-fœ′) *n.* A French soup in which meats and vegetables are simmered with rice or pasta and garnishings. [French, "pot on the fire" : *pot*, pot, from Old French (see **potage**) + *au*, on the + *feu*, fire, from Old French, from Latin *focus*, fireplace (see **fuel**).]

Pot·a·wat·o·mi (pŏt′ə-wŏt′ə-mē) *n., pl.* **Potawatomi** or **-mis. 1.** A tribe of Algonquian-speaking North American Indians inhabiting Michigan. **2.** A member of this tribe. **3.** The Algonquian language of this tribe.

pot·bel·ly (pŏt′bĕl′ē) *n., pl.* **-lies.** A protruding abdominal region. —**pot′bel′lied** *adj.*

potbelly stove. A short rounded stove in which wood or coal is burned. Also called "potbellied stove."

pot·boil·er (pŏt′boi′lər) *n.* A literary or artistic work of poor quality, produced as quickly as possible for profit.

pot·boy (pŏt′boi′) *n. Chiefly British.* A boy or man who works in an inn or a public house serving customers and doing chores.

pot cheese. Cottage cheese *(see).*

po·teen (pō-tēn′) *n.* Irish whiskey that is distilled unlawfully. [Irish Gaelic *poitín*, small pot, whiskey made in a private still, from *pota*, pot, ultimately from Vulgar Latin *pottus* (attested only in Late Latin), POT.]

Po·tëm·kin (pō-tĕm′kĭn; *Russian* pə-tyôm′kĭn). Prince **Grigori Aleksandrovich.** 1739–1791. Russian army officer, political figure, and favorite of Catherine the Great.

po·ten·cy (pōt′n-sē) *n., pl.* **-cies.** Also **po·tence** (pōt′ns). **1.** The quality or state of being potent. **2.** Inherent capacity for growth and development; potentiality. —See Synonyms at **strength.**

po·tent (pōt′nt) *adj.* **1.** Possessing inner or physical strength; powerful. **2.** Capable of commanding attention; able to convince: *potent arguments.* **3.** Having great control or authority: "*The police were potent only so long as they were feared.*" (Thomas Burke). **4.** Capable of causing strong physiological or chemical effects, as medicines or alcoholic beverages. **5.** Able to perform sexually. Said of a male. [Middle English (Scottish), from Latin *potēns*, present participle of Old Latin *potēre* (unattested) (superseded by *posse*), to be able, have power. See **poti-** in Appendix.*] —**po′tent·ly** *adv.* —**po′tent·ness** *n.*

po·ten·tate (pōt′n-tāt′) *n.* **1.** One who has the power and position to rule over others; monarch. **2.** One who dominates or leads any group or endeavor: *industrial potentate.* [Middle English *potentat*, from Old French, from Late Latin *potentātus*, from Latin, power, rule, from *potēns*, POTENT.]

po·ten·tial (pə-tĕn′shəl) *adj. Abbr.* **pot. 1.** Possible but not yet realized; capable of being but not yet in existence; latent: "*Every admirer is a potential enemy.*" (Cyril Connolly). **2.** *Grammar.* Denoting possibility, capability, or power; designating a verb form with auxiliaries such as *may* or *can;* for example, *It may snow.* —*n. Abbr.* **pot. 1.** The inherent ability or capacity for growth, development, or coming into being: "*Negroes . . . have a potential for political influence that has never been realized.*" (New York Times). **2.** Something possessing this capacity: "*A site may be a rundown slum in appearance today but have excellent potentials for the future.*" (Richard I. McCosh). **3.** *Grammar.* A potential verb form. **4.** *Physics.* The work required to

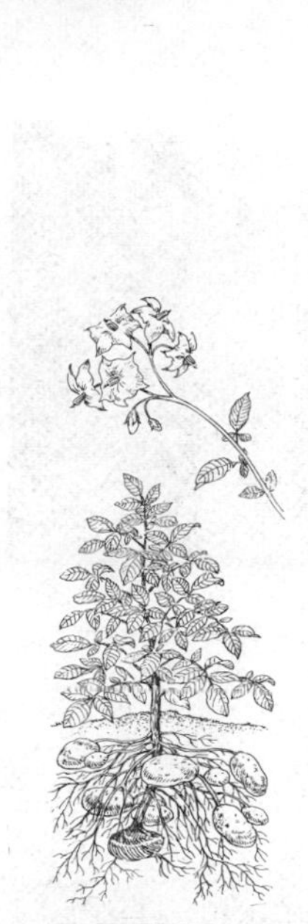

potato
Potato plant showing root system with tubers and *(above)* flowers

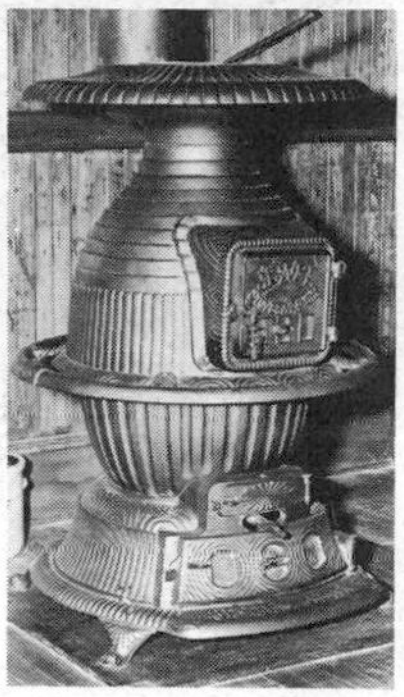

potbelly stove

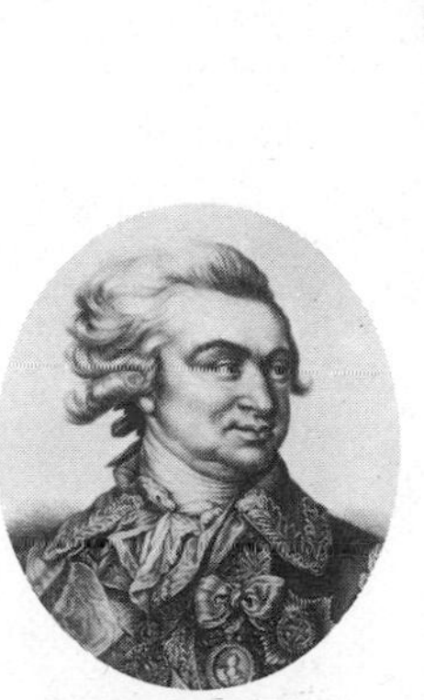

Prince Potëmkin

bring a unit electric charge, magnetic pole, or mass from an infinitely distant position to a designated point in a static electric, magnetic, or gravitational field, respectively. **5.** *Electricity.* The potential energy of a unit charge at any point in an electric circuit measured with respect to a specified reference point in the circuit or to ground; voltage. [Middle English *potencial,* from Old French, from Late Latin *potentiālis,* powerful, from *potentia,* latent power, from Latin, potency, from *potēns,* POTENT.] —**po·ten′tial·ly** *adv.*

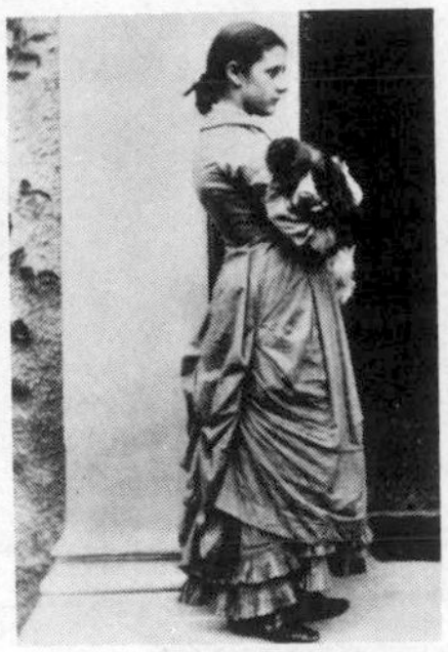

Beatrix Potter

potential energy. The energy of a particle or system of particles derived from position, rather than motion, with respect to a specified datum in a field of force. Compare **kinetic energy.**

po·ten·ti·al·i·ty (pə-tĕn′shē-ăl′ə-tē) *n., pl.* **-ties. 1.** Inherent capacity for growth, development, or coming into existence. **2.** Something possessing this capacity.

po·ten·til·la (pōt′n-tĭl′ə) *n.* Any of numerous plants or shrubs of the genus *Potentilla,* of the North Temperate Zone. See **cinquefoil.** [New Latin, from Medieval Latin, garden valerian, from Latin *potēns,* POTENT.]

po·ten·ti·om·e·ter (pə-tĕn′shē-ŏm′ə-tər) *n. Electricity.* **1.** An instrument for measuring an unknown voltage or potential difference by comparison to a standard voltage. **2.** Any three-terminal resistor with an adjustable center connection, widely used for volume control in radio and television receivers.

poth·er (pŏ*th*′ər) *n.* **1.** A commotion; disturbance. **2.** A state of nervous activity; fuss: *"What in particular had all that tragic pother been about?"* (Max Beerbohm). **3.** A cloud of smoke or dust that chokes or smothers. —*v.* **pothered, -ering, -ers.** —*tr.* To make confused; trouble; worry. —*intr.* To take too much concern with trifles; fuss. [Origin unknown.]

pot·herb (pŏt′ûrb′, -hûrb′) *n.* Any plant whose leaves, stems, or flowers are cooked and eaten or used as seasoning.

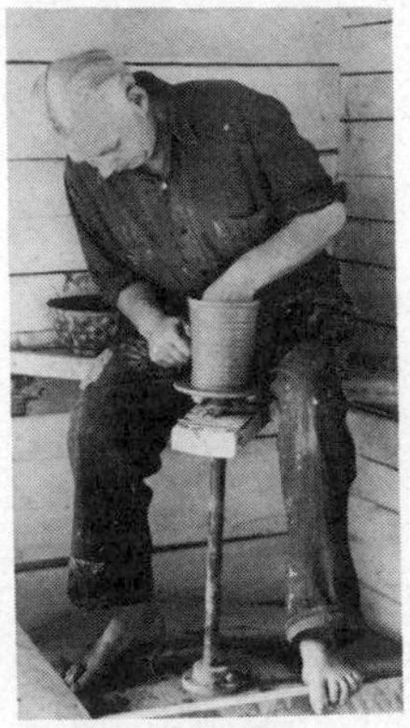

potter's wheel

pot·hole (pŏt′hōl′) *n.* **1.** A deep hole or pit, especially in a road surface. **2.** A deep, round hole worn in rock by whirling loose stones in strong rapids or waterfalls. **3.** *Western U.S.* A place filled with mud or quicksand that is a hazard to cattle.

pot·hook (pŏt′ho͝ok′) *n.* **1.** A bent or hooked piece of iron for hanging a pot or kettle over a fire. **2.** A curved iron rod with a hooked end used for lifting hot pots, irons, or stove lids. **3.** A curved, S-shaped mark made by children learning to write. **4.** *Usually plural.* **a.** Illegible handwriting or aimless scribbling. **b.** *Informal.* Stenographic writing.

pot·house (pŏt′hous′) *n. British.* A tavern.

pot·hunt·er (pŏt′hŭn′tər) *n.* **1.** One who hunts game for food, ignoring the rules of sport. **2.** One who participates in contests simply to win prizes. —**pot′hunt′ing** *adj.* & *n.*

po·tiche (pô-tēsh′) *n.* A vase or jar with a round or polygonal body tapering at the neck and having a removable cover. [French, from *pot,* pot, from Old French, from Vulgar Latin *pottus* (attested only in Late Latin). See **pott-** in Appendix.*]

po·tion (pō′shən) *n.* A liquid dose, especially of medicinal, magic, or poisonous content. [Middle English *pocioun,* from Old French *potion,* from Latin *pōtiō,* from *pōtāre* (alternate past participle *pōtus*), to drink. See **pōi-**[1] in Appendix.*]

Pot·i·phar (pŏt′ə-fər). Pharaoh's chief officer, who purchased Joseph as a slave. Genesis 39:1–20.

pot·latch (pŏt′lăch′) *n.* A ceremonial feast among Indians living on the Pacific coast of Washington, British Columbia, and Alaska, at the end of which the host gives valuable material goods to the guests who belong to other kin groups or destroys property to show that he can afford to do so. [Chinook, from Nootka *patshatl,* giving, gift.]

pot·luck (pŏt′lŭk′) *n.* Whatever food happens to be available for a meal, especially when offered to a guest.

pot marigold. A plant, *Calendula officinalis,* often grown for its showy yellow or orange flowers, the dried florets of which were formerly used for seasoning.

pot marjoram. Marjoram *(see).*

Po·to·mac (pə-tō′mək). A river flowing 287 miles from northwestern Maryland first northeast, then east, and then southeast, to Chesapeake Bay.

Po·to·sí (pō′tō-sē′). A city and departmental capital in south-central Bolivia, situated at an elevation of 13,600 feet. Population, 57,000.

pot·pie (pŏt′pī′) *n.* **1.** A mixture of meat or poultry and vegetables covered with a pastry crust and baked in a deep dish. **2.** A meat or poultry stew with dumplings.

pot·pour·ri (pō′po͞o-rē′) *n., pl.* **-ris. 1.** A combination of various incongruous elements. **2.** A miscellaneous anthology or collection. **3.** A mixture of dried flower petals and spices, kept in a jar and used to scent the air. [French *pot pourri* (translation of Spanish *olla podrida,* OLLA PODRIDA) : *pot,* pot, from Old French (see **pottage**) + *pourri,* rotten, from the past participle of *pourrir,* to rot, from Vulgar Latin *putrīre* (unattested), variant of Latin *putrēre, putrēscere,* from *puter,* rotten (see **pu-**[2] in Appendix*).]

pot roast. A cut of beef that is browned and then cooked until tender, often with vegetables, in a covered pot.

Pots·dam (pŏts′dăm′; *German* pôts′däm′). The capital of Brandenburg, East Germany, on the Havel River, 17 miles southwest of Berlin. Population, 110,000.

pot·sherd (pŏt′shûrd′) *n.* Also **pot·shard** (-shärd′). A fragment of broken pottery, especially one found in an archaeological excavation. Also called "shard," "sherd." [Middle English *pot-schoord* : POT + *schoord,* variant of SHARD.]

pot shot. 1. A shot aimed to kill, without regard for sporting rules. **2. a.** A random shot. **b.** A shot fired at an animal or person within easy range. [From the idea that pot shots are fired by a hunter who kills game only for his pot.]

pot·stone (pŏt′stōn′) *n.* An impure variety of steatite once used to make cooking vessels.

pot·tage (pŏt′ĭj) *n.* **1.** A thick soup or stew of vegetables and sometimes meat. **2.** *Archaic.* Porridge. [Middle English *potage,* from Old French, from Vulgar Latin *pottus* (attested only in Late Latin). See **pott-** in Appendix.*]

pot·ted (pŏt′ĭd) *adj.* **1. a.** Placed in a pot. **b.** Grown in a pot, as a plant. **2.** Preserved in a pot, can, or jar. **3.** *Slang.* Intoxicated.

pot·ter[1] (pŏt′ər) *n.* A person who makes earthenware pots, dishes, or other vessels. [Middle English *pottere,* Old English *pottere,* from *pott,* POT.]

pot·ter[2]. *Chiefly British.* Variant of **putter.**

Pot·ter (pŏt′ər), **Beatrix.** 1866–1943. English author and illustrator; creator of Peter Rabbit.

potter's clay. A clay suitable for making pottery or for modeling and low in iron content. Also called "potter's earth."

potter's field. A place for the burial of indigent or unknown persons. [From "the potter's field" mentioned in Matthew 27:7.]

potter's wheel. A device composed of a revolving, treadle-operated horizontal disk upon which clay is shaped manually.

potter wasp. Any of various wasps of the genus *Eumenes,* characteristically building pot-shaped nests of clay. Also called "mud wasp."

pot·ter·y (pŏt′ə-rē) *n., pl.* **-ies. 1.** Ware, such as vases, pots, bowls, or plates, shaped from moist clay and hardened by heat. **2.** The craft or occupation of a potter. **3.** The establishment in which this craft is pursued. [Old French *poterie,* from *potier,* potter, probably from *pot,* a pot. See **pottage.**]

pot·tle (pŏt′l) *n.* **1.** A pot or drinking vessel with a two-quart capacity. **2.** The liquid contained in such a vessel. **3.** An old liquid measure equal to about two quarts. [Middle English *potel,* from Old French, from *pot,* pot. See **pottage.**]

pot·to (pŏt′ō) *n., pl.* **-tos.** Any of several small African primates of the genera *Perodicticus* and *Arctocebus,* having woolly fur, and hands and feet adapted for grasping. [Of Niger-Congo origin, akin to Wolof *pata,* a tailless monkey, Twi *a*^{1}*pɔ*^{3}*sɔ̂w*^{3}, a fierce, monkeylike animal.]

Pott's disease (pŏts). Partial destruction of the bones of the vertebrae, usually caused by a tuberculous infection and often producing deformity and curvature of the spine. [After Percival *Pott* (1714–1788), British surgeon.]

pot·ty[1] (pŏt′ē) *adj.* **-tier, -tiest.** *British Informal.* **1.** Of little importance; trivial. **2.** Slightly intoxicated. **3.** Somewhat silly or crazy; addlebrained. [Probably from the phrase *to go to pot,* to deteriorate, and from POT (liquor).]

pot·ty[2] (pŏt′ē) *n., pl.* **-ties.** A small pot for use as a toilet by an infant or young child.

pouch (pouch) *n.* **1.** A small flexible receptacle; bag. **2.** A small bag of leather or other relatively nonporous material for carrying loose pipe tobacco in one's pocket. **3.** *Archaic.* A purse for small coins. **4.** A leather bag for carrying powder or small-arms ammunition. **5.** A mailbag, especially one for diplomatic dispatches. **6.** Anything resembling a bag in shape: *He had pouches under his eyes.* **7.** *Zoology.* A saclike structure, such as the cheek pockets of the gopher, or the external abdominal pocket in which marsupials carry their young. **8.** *Scottish.* A pocket. —*v.* **pouched, pouching, pouches.** —*tr.* **1.** To place in or as in a pouch; pocket: *He pouched all the money.* **2.** To cause to resemble a pouch in shape. **3.** To swallow. Used of certain birds or fishes. —*intr.* To assume the form of a pouch or pouchlike cavity. [Middle English *pouche,* from Old French *po(u)che,* from Frankish *pokka* (unattested). See **beu-**[1] in Appendix.*] —**pouch′y** *adj.*

pouf (po͞of) *n.* **1.** A woman's hair style popular in the 18th century, characterized by high rolled puffs. **2.** Any part of a dress or other garment gathered into a puff. **3.** A rounded ottoman. [French (imitative).]

Pough·keep·sie (pə-kĭp′sē, pō-). A city of southeastern New York, on the Hudson River, 65 miles north of New York City. It was the state capital (1777–97). Population, 38,000.

pou·lard (po͞o-lärd′) *n.* Also **pou·larde.** A young hen that has been spayed for fattening. Compare **capon.** [French *poularde,* from Old French *pollarde,* from *polle, poule,* hen, from Vulgar Latin *pulla* (unattested), from Latin *pullus,* young of an animal. See **pōu-** in Appendix.*]

Pou·lenc (po͞o-lăɴk′), **Francis.** 1899–1963. French composer.

poult (pōlt) *n.* A young fowl, especially a turkey. [Middle English *pult,* short for *polet, poulet,* pullet, from Old French *poulet,* diminutive of *poule,* hen, chicken. See **poulard.**]

poul·ter·er (pōl′tər-ər) *n. Chiefly British.* A poultry dealer. [Earlier *pulterer,* from Middle English *pulter,* poulterer, from Old French *pouletier,* from *poulet,* POULT.]

poul·tice (pōl′tĭs) *n.* A moist, soft mass of bread, meal, clay, or other adhesive substance, usually heated, spread on cloth, and applied to warm, moisten, or stimulate an aching or inflamed part of the body. Also called "cataplasm." —*tr.v.* **poulticed, -ticing, -tices.** To apply a poultice to. [Earlier *pultes* (taken as singular), from Medieval Latin *pultēs,* pulp, thick paste, from Latin, plural of *puls* (stem *pult-*), pap, possibly from Greek *poltos,* porridge. See **pel-**[1] in Appendix.*]

poul·try (pōl′trē) *n.* Domestic fowls, such as chickens, turkeys, ducks, or geese, raised for flesh or eggs. [Middle English *pultrie,* from Old French *pouleterie,* from *pouletier,* POULTERER.]

pounce[1] (pouns) *v.* **pounced, pouncing, pounces.** —*intr.* **1.** To spring or swoop with intent to seize someone or something. Used with *on, upon,* or *at.* **2.** To attack suddenly and unexpectedly. —*tr. Rare.* To seize with or as if with talons. —*n.*

1. The act of pouncing. **2.** The talon or claw of a bird of prey. [Middle English, talon, claw (hence verb, to seize), probably variant of *punson,* pointed tool, from Old French *poinçon.* See **pounce** (to ornament).] —**pounc'er** *n.*

pounce² (pouns) *n.* **1.** A fine powder formerly used to size the porous surfaces of paper and parchment and prepare them to receive writing. **2.** A fine powder, such as pulverized charcoal, dusted over a stencil to transfer a design to an underlying surface. —*tr.v.* **pounced, pouncing, pounces. 1.** To sprinkle, smooth, or treat with pounce. **2.** To transfer (a stenciled design) with pounce. [French *ponce,* from Vulgar Latin *pōmex* (unattested), variant of Latin *pūmex,* pumice. See **spoimo-** in Appendix.*] —**pounc'er** *n.*

pounce³ (pouns) *tr.v.* **pounced, pouncing, pounces.** To ornament (metal, for example) by perforating from the back with a pointed implement. [Middle English *pounsen,* variant of *pounsonen,* from Old French *poinçonner,* to prick, stamp, from *poinçon,* pointed tool, from Vulgar Latin *punctiō* (unattested), from *punctiāre* (unattested), to prick, from Latin *pungere* (past participle *punctus*). See **peuk-** in Appendix.*]

pounce box. A small box with a perforated top, formerly used to sprinkle sand or pounce on writing paper to dry the ink.

poun·cet box (poun'sĭt). A small perfume box with a perforated top. [Probably altered from POUNCE BOX.]

pound¹ (pound) *n., pl.* **pound** or **pounds. 1.** *Abbr.* **lb. a.** A unit of weight equal to 16 ounces or 7,000 grains. Also called "avoirdupois pound." **b.** A unit of apothecary weight, equal to 5,760 grains or 0.823 avoirdupois pound. See **measurement. 2.** A unit of weight differing in various countries and times. **3.** A British unit of force equal to the weight of a standard one-pound mass where the local acceleration of gravity is 32.174 feet per second. **4.** *Symbol* £ **a.** The basic monetary unit of the United Kingdom, originally equal to 20 shillings or 240 pence, but after 1971 equal to 100 new pence. Also called "pound sterling." **b.** The basic monetary unit of Gambia, Republic of Ireland, Jamaica, Malawi, Malta, Nigeria, Rhodesia, and of various dependent territories of the United Kingdom, such as Bermuda, equal to 20 shillings or 240 pence. See table of exchange rates at **currency. 5. a.** The basic monetary unit of Lebanon, Libya, Sudan, Syria, Turkey, and the United Arab Republic, equal to 100 piasters. **b.** The basic monetary unit of Cyprus, equal to 1,000 mils. **c.** The basic monetary unit of Israel, equal to 100 agorot. See table of exchange rates at **currency. 6.** *Historical.* A monetary unit of Scotland before the Union, usually worth a small fraction of the pound sterling. Also called "pound scots." **7.** A coin or note worth one pound. [Middle English *po(u)nd,* Old English *pund,* from Latin *pondō.* See **spen-** in Appendix.*]

pound² (pound) *v.* **pounded, pounding, pounds.** —*tr.* **1.** To strike or hammer with a heavy blow or blows. **2.** To drive (something) in or out with repeated blows; hammer. **3.** To beat to a powder or pulp; pulverize or crush. **4.** To instill by persistent and emphatic repetition: *pound knowledge into their heads.* —*intr.* **1.** To strike vigorous, repeated blows. Often used with *on* or *at: He pounded on the table.* **2.** To move along heavily and noisily: *with pounding footsteps.* **3.** To pulsate rapidly and heavily: *Her heart pounded.* **4.** To work or move laboriously: *a ship pounding through heavy seas.* —*n.* **1.** A heavy blow. **2.** The sound of a heavy blow; a thump. **3.** The act of pounding. [Alteration (with unhistorical *d*) of earlier *p(o)unne,* Middle English *pounen,* Old English *pūnian*†.]

pound³ (pound) *n.* **1.** A public enclosure for the confinement of stray dogs or livestock. **2.** A place in which impounded property is held until redeemed. **3.** An enclosure in which animals or fish are trapped or kept. **4.** A place of confinement for lawbreakers. —*tr.v.* **pounded, pounding, pounds.** To confine in or as if in a pound; impound. [Middle English *pound,* Old English *pund-.* See **bend-** in Appendix.*]

Pound (pound), **Ezra (Loomis).** Born 1885. American poet and critic.

pound·age¹ (poun'dĭj) *n.* **1.** A tax or commission based on value per pound (sterling). **2.** A rate or charge based on weight in pounds. **3.** Weight measured in pounds.

pound·age² (poun'dĭj) *n.* **1.** The confinement of animals in a pound. **2.** A fee charged for the redemption of impounded animals or other property.

pound·al (pound'l) *n. Abbr.* **pdl.** A unit of force in the foot-pound-second system of measurement, equal to the force required to accelerate a standard one-pound mass one foot per second per second. [POUND (QUINT)AL.]

pound cake. A rich cake containing eggs and originally made with a pound each of flour, butter, and sugar.

pound of flesh. A debt harshly insisted upon. [From Antonio's debt to Shylock in Shakespeare's *Merchant of Venice.*]

pour (pôr, pōr) *v.* **poured, pouring, pours.** —*tr.* **1.** To make (a liquid or granular solid) stream or flow. **2.** To send forth, produce, express, or utter copiously, as if in a stream or flood. —*intr.* **1.** To stream or flow continuously or profusely. **2.** To rain hard or heavily. **3.** To go forth or stream in large numbers or quantity: *The army poured into enemy territory.* —*n.* A pouring or flowing forth; especially, a downpour of rain. [Middle English *pouren*†.] —**pour'er** *n.*

pour·boire (po͝or-bwär') *n.* Money given as a gratuity; a tip. [French, "for drinking."]

pour·par·ler (po͝or'pär-lā') *n.* Conversation or discussion preliminary to negotiation. [French, "for speaking."]

pour point. The lowest temperature at which an oil or other liquid will pour when cooled under given conditions.

pousse-ca·fé (po͞os'kä-fā') *n.* **1.** A drink consisting of several liqueurs of different densities, poured to form differently colored layers. **2.** A brandy or liqueur served after dinner with coffee. [French, "coffee pusher" : *pousse,* a push (see **poussette**) + *café,* coffee, from Italian *caffè,* COFFEE.]

pous·sette (po͞o-sĕt') *n.* A country-dance figure in which a couple or couples join hands and swing around the floor. [French, from *pousse,* a push, from *pousser,* to push, from Old French, from Latin *pulsāre,* frequentative of *pellere,* to push, beat. See **pel-⁶** in Appendix.*]

Pous·sin (po͞o-săN'), **Nicolas.** 1594–1665. French painter of neoclassic landscapes and historical scenes.

pout¹ (pout) *v.* **pouted, pouting, pouts.** —*intr.* **1.** To protrude the lips in an expression of displeasure or sulkiness. **2.** To show displeasure or disappointment; sulk. **3.** To project or protrude: *Her lips pouted in expectation of a kiss.* —*tr.* **1.** To push out or protrude (as of the lips). **2.** To utter or express with a pout. —*n.* **1.** A protrusion of the lips, especially as an expression of sullen discontent. **2.** *Sometimes plural.* A fit of petulant sulkiness. [Middle English *pouten,* perhaps from Old English *pūtian* (unattested), to swell, be inflated. See **beu-¹** in Appendix.*]

pout² (pout) *n., pl.* **pout** or **pouts.** Any of various freshwater or marine fishes, especially an **eelpout** *(see).* [Middle English *poute* (unattested), Old English *-pūte* (as in *aele-pūte,* eelpout). See **beu-¹** in Appendix.*]

pout·er (pou'tər) *n.* One of a breed of pigeons capable of distending the crop until the breast becomes puffed out.

pov·er·ty (pŏv'ər-tē) *n.* **1.** The state or condition of being poor; lack of the means of providing material needs or comforts. **2.** Lack of something necessary or desirable; insufficiency; paucity: *a poverty of talent.* **3.** Deficiency in amount; scantiness: *the poverty of his vocabulary.* **4.** Unproductiveness; infertility: *the poverty of the soil.* [Middle English *poverte,* from Old French, from Latin *paupertās,* from *pauper,* poor. See **pôu-** in Appendix.*]

poverty grass. Any of several North American grasses that grow in poor or sandy soil.

POW, P.O.W. prisoner of war.

pow·der (pou'dər) *n.* **1.** A substance consisting of ground, pulverized, or otherwise finely dispersed solid particles. **2.** Any of various preparations in this form, as certain cosmetics and medicines. **3. a.** An explosive mixture, **gunpowder** *(see).* **b.** Any of various similar explosive substances. —**take a powder.** *Slang.* To make a quick departure; run away. —*v.* **powdered, -dering, -ders.** —*tr.* **1.** To reduce to powder; pulverize. **2.** To dust or cover with or as if with powder; apply powder to. —*intr.* **1.** To become pulverized; turn to powder. **2.** To use powder as a cosmetic. [Middle English *poudre,* from Old French, from Latin *pulvis* (stem *pulver-*). See **pel-¹** in Appendix.*] —**pow'der·er** *n.*

Pow·der (pou'dər). A river rising in northern Wyoming and flowing 375 miles northeast to join the Yellowstone in eastern Montana.

powder blue. Moderate to pale blue or purplish blue. See **color.** [The color of powdered smalt.] —**pow'der-blue'** *adj.*

powder flask. A small flask or similar receptacle formerly used for carrying gunpowder.

powder horn. A container consisting of an animal's horn capped at the open end, formerly used to carry gunpowder.

powder keg. 1. A barrel for holding gunpowder or other explosives. **2.** A potentially explosive thing or situation.

powder metallurgy. The technology of powdered metals, especially the production and utilization of metallic powders for massive materials and shaped objects.

powder puff. A soft pad for applying powder to the skin.

powder room. A lavatory for women.

pow·der·y (pou'də-rē) *adj.* **1.** Composed of or similar to powder. **2.** Dusted or covered with or as if with powder. **3.** Easily made into powder; friable.

powdery mildew. Any of various plant diseases caused by fungi and resulting in a white, powdery growth appearing mostly on the upper surface of leaves.

Pow·ell (pou'əl), **Cecil Frank.** Born 1903. British physicist.

pow·er (pou'ər) *n. Abbr.* **pwr. 1.** The ability or capacity to act or perform effectively. **2.** *Often plural.* A specific capacity, faculty, or aptitude: *his powers of concentration.* **3.** Strength or force exerted or capable of being exerted; might. **4.** The ability or official capacity to exercise control; authority. **5.** A person, group, or nation having great influence or control over others. **6.** The might of a nation, political organization, or similar group. **7.** Forcefulness; effectiveness. **8.** *Regional.* A large number or amount. **9.** *Physics.* The rate at which work is done, mathematically expressed as the first derivative of work with respect to time and commonly measured in units such as the watt and horsepower. **10.** *Electricity.* **a.** The product of applied potential difference and current in a direct-current circuit. **b.** The product of the effective values of the voltage and current with the cosine of the phase angle between current and voltage in an alternating-current circuit. **11.** *Mathematics.* **a.** An **exponent** *(see).* **b.** The number of elements in a finite set. **12.** *Optics.* A measure of the **magnification** *(see)* of an optical instrument, as a microscope or telescope. **13.** *Plural. Theology.* The sixth group of angels in the hierarchical order of nine. See **angel. 14.** *Archaic.* An armed force. —See Synonyms at **strength.** —*tr.v.* **powered, -ering, -ers.** To supply with power, especially mechanical power. [Middle English *pouer,* from Old French *poeir, povoir,* from *poeir,* to be able, from Old Latin *potēre* (unattested) (superseded by *posse*). See **poti-** in Appendix.*]

pow·er·boat (pou'ər-bōt') *n.* A **motorboat** *(see).*

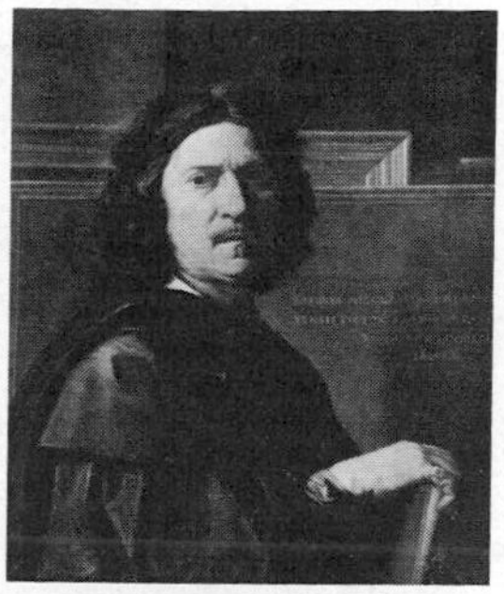

Nicolas Poussin
A self-portrait

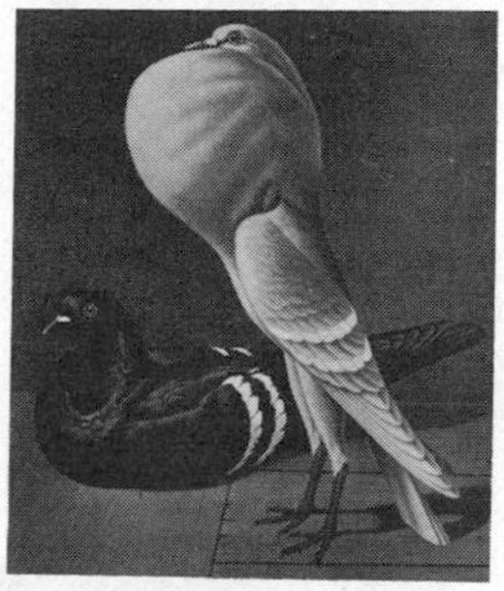

pouter

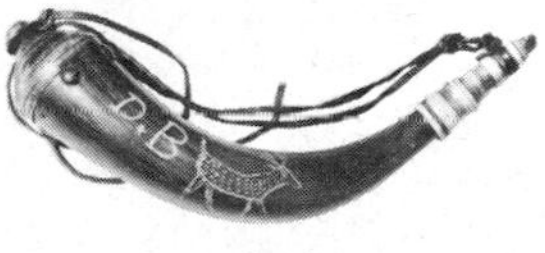

powder horn
Daniel Boone's powder horn

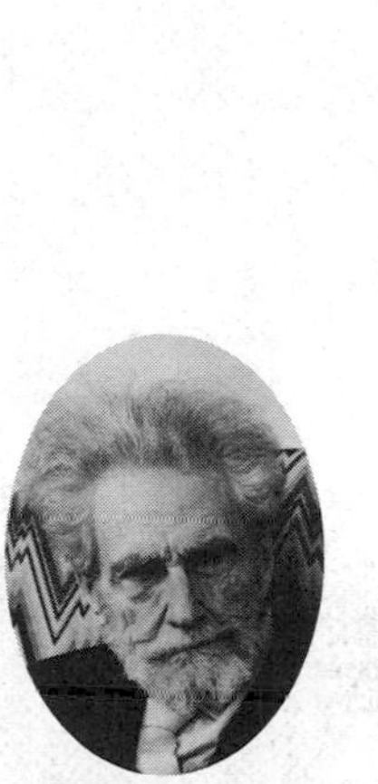

Ezra Pound

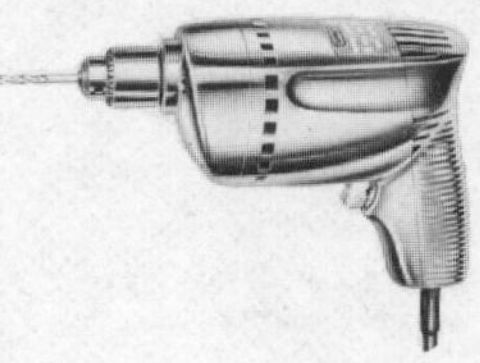

power drill

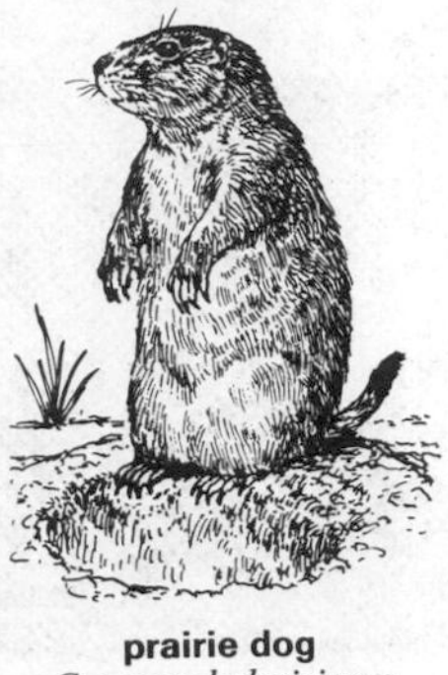

prairie dog
Cynomys ludovicianus

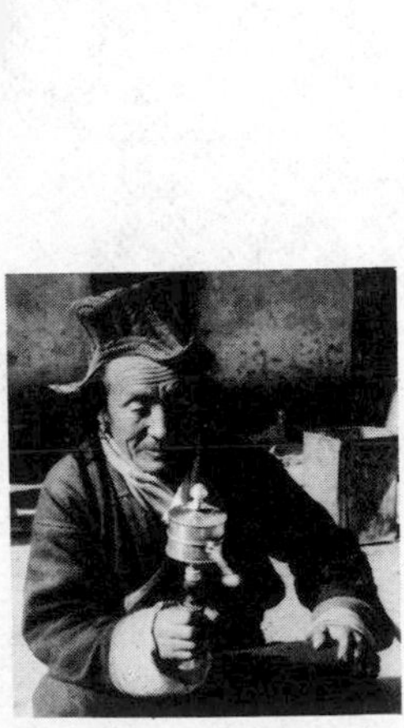

prayer wheel

power dive. A downward plunge of an aircraft accelerated by both gravity and engine power.
pow·er-dive (pou′ər-dīv′) *v.* **-dived** or **-dove** (-dōv′), **-diving, -dives.** —*intr.* To execute a power dive. —*tr.* To cause to execute a power dive.
power drill. **1.** A portable electric drill. **2.** A large drilling machine having a vertical, motorized drill set in a table stand.
pow·er·ful (pou′ər-fəl) *adj.* **1.** Having or capable of exerting power. **2.** Effective or potent, as medicine. **3.** *Regional.* Great: *It did a powerful lot of good.* —*adv. Regional.* Very: *It was powerful hot.* —**pow′er·ful·ly** *adv.* —**pow′er·ful·ness** *n.*
pow·er·house (pou′ər-hous′) *n.* **1.** A station for the generating of electricity. **2.** One who possesses great force or energy.
pow·er·less (pou′ər-lĭs) *adj.* **1.** Lacking strength or power; helpless; ineffectual. **2.** Lacking legal or other authority. —**pow′er·less·ly** *adv.* —**pow′er·less·ness** *n.*
power of appointment. *Law.* Authority granted to one person by another to succeed to property upon the death of the latter.
power of attorney. *Abbr.* **P/A, P.A.** *Law.* A legal instrument authorizing one to act as another's attorney or agent.
power pack. *Electronics.* A usually compact, portable device that converts supply current to direct or alternating current as required by specific equipment.
power plant. **1.** All the equipment, including structural members, that constitutes a unit power source: *the power plant of a truck.* **2.** A complex of structures, machinery, and associated equipment for generating power, especially electric power.
power play. **1.** *Sports.* An offensive maneuver in a team game in which a massive concentration of players is applied in a certain area. **2.** A strategic action or maneuver, as in politics, diplomacy, business, or warfare based on the use, or threatened use, of power as a means of coercion.
power politics. International diplomacy in which each nation uses or threatens to use military or economic power to further its own interests. [Translation of German *Machtpolitik.*]
power series. *Mathematics.* A sum of successively higher integral powers of a variable or combination of variables, each multiplied by a constant coefficient.
power shovel. A large, usually mobile machine having a boom, a dipper stick, and a bucket for excavating.
Pow·ha·tan[1] (pou′ə-tăn′). 1550?–1618. American Indian chief; father of Pocahontas.
Pow·ha·tan[2] (pou′ə-tăn′) *n., pl.* **Powhatan** or **-tans.** **1.** One of the Algonquian-speaking tribes of North American Indians, formerly inhabiting eastern Virginia. They comprised a confederacy known as the Powhatan Confederacy. **2.** A member of one of these tribes. **3.** An Algonquian language of these tribes.
pow·wow (pou′wou′) *n.* **1.** Among some North American Indians, a medicine man. **2.** A North American Indian ceremony in which incantations and dancing are used to invoke divine aid in hunting, in battle, or against disease. **3.** A conference or meeting with or of North American Indians. **4.** *Informal.* Any conference or gathering. —*intr.v.* **powwowed, -wowing, -wows.** To hold a conference or powwow. [From Algonquian, akin to Narraganset *powwaw.*]
pox (pŏks) *n.* **1.** Any disease characterized by purulent skin eruptions, such as chicken pox or smallpox. **2.** Syphilis. **3.** *Archaic.* Misfortune and calamity. [Alteration of pocks, plural of POCK (mark).]
Po·yang, Lake (pō′yäng′). The second-largest lake in China, occupying 1,070 square miles in northern Kiangsi Province.
Poz·nań (pôz′nän′y′). *German* **Po·sen** (pō′zən). An industrial city, cultural center, and provincial capital on the Warta River in west-central Poland. Population, 434,000.
Po·zsony. The Hungarian name for **Bratislava.**
poz·zuo·la·na (pŏt′swə-lä′nə) *n.* Also **poz·zo·la·na** (pŏt′sə-lä′nə). **1.** A siliceous volcanic ash used to produce hydraulic cement. **2.** Any of various artificially produced substances resembling this ash. [Italian *pozzolana,* "of Pozzuoli," town near Vesuvius, Italy.] —**poz′zuo·la′nic** *adj.*
pp *Music.* pianissimo.
pp. **1.** pages. **2.** past participle. **3.** *Music.* pianissimo.
p.p., P.P. **1.** parcel post. **2.** parish priest. **3.** past participle. **4.** postpaid.
ppd. **1.** postpaid. **2.** prepaid.
pph. pamphlet.
P.P.S. additional postscript (Latin *post postscriptum*).
p.q. previous question.
P.Q. Province of Quebec.
Pr The symbol for the element praseodymium.
PR **1.** public relations. **2.** Puerto Rico (with Zip Code).
pr. **1.** pair. **2.** present. **3.** price. **4.** printing. **5.** pronoun.
Pr. **1.** priest. **2.** prince. **3.** Provençal.
P.R. **1.** proportional representation. **2.** public relations. **3.** Puerto Rico.
praam (präm) *n.* Also **pram.** **1.** A flat-bottomed boat used especially in the Baltic as a barge. **2.** *Chiefly British.* A small dinghy having a flat, snub-nosed bow. [Dutch, from Middle Dutch *praem,* from Czech *prám,* from Old Church Slavonic *pramŭ.* See **per**[1] in Appendix.*]
prac·ti·ca·ble (prăk′tĭ-kə-bəl) *adj.* **1.** Capable of being effected, done, or executed; feasible. **2.** Capable of being used for a specified purpose: *a practicable way of entry.* —See Synonyms at **possible.** [French *practicable,* from *pratiquer,* to PRACTICE.] —**prac′ti·ca·bil′i·ty** *n.* —**prac′ti·ca·bly** *adv.*
prac·ti·cal (prăk′tĭ-kəl) *adj.* **1.** Of, relating to, governed by, or acquired through practice or action, rather than theory, speculation, or ideals. **2.** Manifested in or involving practice. **3.** Actually engaged in some work or occupation. **4.** Capable of being used or put into effect. **5.** Designed to serve a purpose without elaboration: *practical low-heeled shoes.* **6.** Concerned with the production or operation of something useful: *Woodworking is a practical art.* **7.** Level-headed, efficient, and unspeculative. **8.** Being actually so in almost every respect; virtual: *a practical disaster.* See Usage note at **practically.** —See Synonyms at **possible.** [From Late Latin *practicus,* practical, from Greek *praktikos,* from *praktos,* to be done, from *prattein, prassein,* to practice. See **prāk-** in Appendix.*] —**prac′ti·cal′i·ty** (prăk′tĭ-kăl′ə-tē), **prac′ti·cal·ness** *n.*
practical joke. A mischievous trick played on a person especially to cause him to feel embarrassment or indignity.
prac·ti·cal·ly (prăk′tĭk-lē) *adj.* **1.** In a way that is practical. **2.** In every important respect; virtually. **3.** Almost. See Usage note.

Usage: *Virtually,* not *practically,* is the more precise term for expressing the sense of *to all intents* or *in effect.* Only 51 per cent of the Usage Panel accept an example in which *practically extinct* is applied to a family whose sole surviving members are two aged sisters. Even less precise is *practically* as a synonym for *nearly* or *almost: He had practically finished his meal when I arrived* (acceptable to only 46 per cent). More objectionable by far is *practically* applied to something in glaring opposition to actual fact; for example, to say that the losing candidate in a closely contested election *practically won.*

practical nurse. A professional nurse who is not a nursing-school graduate. Compare **registered nurse.**
prac·tice (prăk′tĭs) *v.* **-ticed, -ticing, -tices.** Also *chiefly British* **prac·tise.** —*tr.* **1.** To do or perform habitually or customarily; make a habit of. **2.** To exercise or perform repeatedly in order to acquire or polish a skill: *practice a dance step.* **3.** To give lessons or repeated instructions to; drill: *to practice students in handwriting.* **4.** To work at, especially as a profession: *practice law.* **5.** To carry out in action; observe: *practice one's religion.* **6.** *Obsolete.* To plot (something evil). —*intr.* **1.** To do or perform something habitually or repeatedly. **2.** To do something repeatedly in order to acquire or polish a skill. **3.** To work at a profession. **4.** *Obsolete.* To intrigue or plot. Used with *against* or *with.* —*n.* Also **prac·tise.** **1.** A habitual or customary action or way of doing something: *make a practice of being punctual.* **2. a.** Repeated performance of an activity in order to learn or perfect a skill. **b.** *Archaic.* The skill so learned or perfected. **c.** The condition of being skilled through repeated exercise: *He is out of practice at golf.* **3.** The act or process of doing something; performance. **4.** The exercise of an occupation or profession. **5.** The business of a professional person. **6.** *Plural.* Habitual actions or acts that are objectionable, questionable, or unacceptable. **7.** The methods of procedure used in a court of law. **8.** *Archaic.* **a.** The act of tricking. **b.** A stratagem; trick. —See Synonyms at **habit.** [Middle English *practisen,* from Old French *practiser, pratiquer,* from Medieval Latin *practicāre,* from Late Latin *practicus,* PRACTICAL.] —**prac′tic·er** *n.*
prac·ticed (prăk′tĭst) *adj.* **1.** Proficient; skilled; expert. **2.** Acquired or brought to perfection by practice.
prac·ti·tion·er (prăk-tĭsh′ən-ər) *n.* **1.** One who practices an occupation, profession, or technique: *"Turner became the most successful practitioner of landscape painting in England."* (Monroe Wheeler). **2.** *Christian Science.* A person engaged in the public ministry of spiritual healing. [From earlier *practician,* from obsolete French *practicien,* from *pra(c)tique,* practice, from Late Latin *practicus,* PRACTICAL.]
prae·di·al (prē′dē-əl) *adj.* Also **pre·di·al.** **1.** Pertaining to land or its products. **2.** Attached to or arising from land or landed property: *praedial serfs.* [Medieval Latin *praediālis,* of an estate, from Latin *praedium,* estate, from *praes,* surety. See **wadh-** in Appendix.*]
prae·fect. Variant of **prefect.**
prae·lect. Variant of **prelect.**
prae·mu·ni·re (prē′myōō-nī′rē) *n. English History.* **1.** The offense of appealing to or obeying a foreign court or authority, thus challenging the supremacy of the Crown. **2.** The writ charging this offense. **3.** The penalty for this offense. [Middle English, from Medieval Latin *praemūnire (facias),* "(that you cause) to warn" (words in the writ), from Latin *praemūnīre,* to fortify (meaning influenced by *praemonēre,* to forewarn) : *prae,* before + *mūnīre,* to fortify (see **mei-**[3] in Appendix*).]
prae·no·men (prē-nō′mən) *n., pl.* **-nomina** (-nŏm′ə-nə, -nō′mə-nə) or **-nomens.** Any first or given name. [Latin *praenōmen* : *prae,* before + *nōmen,* name (see **nomen-** in Appendix*).] —**prae·nom′i·nal** (-nŏm′ə-nəl) *adj.*
prae·tor (prē′tər) *n.* A high elected magistrate of the Roman Republic, ranking below the consuls and functioning for one year as a high judge and for the next year as the chief administrator of a province. [Latin *praetor,* "leader," "chief," from *praeīre,* to go before : *prae-,* in front of + *īre,* to go (see **ei-**[1] in Appendix*).] —**prae′tor·ship** *n.*
prae·to·ri·an (prē-tôr′ē-ən, -tōr′ē-ən) *adj.* **1.** Of or pertaining to the praetorship. **2.** *Capital* **P.** Of, pertaining to, or characteristic of the Praetorian Guard. —*n.* **1.** An ex-praetor. **2.** *Capital* **P.** A member of the Praetorian Guard or of a group having comparable position and power.
Praetorian Guard. **1.** The elite guard of the Roman emperors, usually numbering about 5,000 men, whose notoriously venal allegiance on many occasions determined the imperial succession. **2.** A member of this guard. [Originally the bodyguard of a praetor under the Roman Republic.]
prag·mat·ic (prăg-măt′ĭk) *adj.* **1. a.** Dealing with facts or actual occurrences; practical. **b.** Active rather than contemplative.

2. Pertaining to the study of events and historical phenomena with emphasis on their practical outcome. 3. Of or pertaining to pragmatism. —*n.* 1. A **pragmatic sanction** *(see).* 2. A meddler; busybody. [Latin *pragmaticus,* skilled in affairs, from Greek *pragmatikos,* from *pragma* (stem *pragmat-*), deed, affair, from *prattein,* to do. See **prāk-** in Appendix.*] —**prag·mat′i·cal** *adj.* —**prag·mat′i·cal·ly** *adv.*

prag·mat·ics (prăg-măt′ĭks) *n.* Plural in form, usually used with a singular verb. The branch of semiotics concerned with the relations between signs or expressions and their users.

pragmatic sanction. An edict issued by a sovereign that becomes part of the fundamental law of the land.

prag·ma·tism (prăg′mə-tĭz′əm) *n.* 1. *Philosophy.* The theory, developed by Charles S. Peirce and William James, that the meaning of a proposition or course of action lies in its observable consequences, and that the sum of these consequences constitutes its meaning. 2. A method or tendency in the conduct of political affairs characterized by the rejection of theory and precedent, and by the use of practical means and expedients. —**prag′ma·tist** *n.* —**prag′ma·tis′tic** *adj.*

Prague (präg). *Czech* **Pra·ha** (prä′hä); *German* **Prag** (präKH). The capital and largest city of Czechoslovakia, on the Vltava River in central Bohemia. Population, 1,021,000.

prai·rie (prâr′ē) *n.* An extensive area of flat or rolling grassland; especially, the plain of central North America. [French, from Old French *praerie,* from Vulgar Latin *prātāria* (unattested), from Latin *prātum*†, meadow.]

prairie breaker. A plow that cuts a wide furrow and turns the earth completely over.

prairie chicken. Either of two birds, *Tympanuchus cupido* or *T. pallidicinctus,* of western North America, having deep-chested bodies and mottled brownish plumage.

prairie dog. Any of several burrowing rodents of the genus *Cynomys,* of west-central North America. They have yellowish fur, a barklike call, and live in large communities.

prairie oyster. 1. *Slang.* A raw egg immersed in liquid and swallowed whole, especially as a palliative for a hangover. 2. *U.S. Regional & Canadian.* The testis of a calf, cooked and served as food.

Prairie Provinces. Manitoba, Saskatchewan, and Alberta.

prairie schooner. A canvas-covered wagon, similar to but lighter than the **Conestoga wagon** *(see),* used by pioneers crossing the North American prairies.

prairie smoke. 1. A North American plant, *Geum triflorum,* having plumed seed clusters. 2. A species of **pasqueflower** *(see).*

prairie state. Any of the states in the Midwestern and Western U.S. prairie regions.

Prairie State. The nickname for Illinois.

prairie turnip. A plant, the **breadroot** *(see).*

praise (prāz) *n.* 1. An expression of warm approval or admiration; strong commendation. 2. The extolling of a deity, ruler, or hero. 3. *Archaic.* A reason for praise; merit. —*tr.v.* **praised, praising, praises.** 1. To express warm approval of or admiration for; commend; applaud. 2. To extol or exalt; worship. [Middle English *preisen,* from Old French *presier,* to prize, praise, from Late Latin *pretiāre,* from Latin *pretium,* price. See **per**[1] in Appendix.*] —**prais′er** *n.*

Synonyms: *praise, acclaim, commend, extol, laud.* These are words for expressing highest approval of somebody or something and often imply public accord for such favor. *Praise* means to express one's esteem of a person for his virtues or accomplishment, though one can also praise things or ideas. To *acclaim* somebody is collectively to praise or pronounce him or something he has done worthy of honor, but it is often used literally to mean actual applause or cheering. *Commend* suggests approval accorded by higher quarters in a judicious manner, often for a particular service rendered in the interests of society. *Extol* suggests resounding praise in a lofty style. It means to proclaim excellence, often repeatedly or excessively. *Laud* expresses respectful tribute given formally and decisively, usually for a particular deed.

praise·wor·thy (prāz′wûr′*th*ē) *adj.* Meriting praise; highly commendable. —**praise′wor′thi·ly** *adv.* —**praise′wor′thi·ness** *n.*

Pra·krit (prä′krĭt) *n.* 1. Any of the vernacular languages of India, as opposed to the literary language, **Sanskrit** *(see).* 2. Any of the various ancient Indic languages on which the modern vernaculars are based. [Sanskrit *prākṛta,* natural, vulgar, vernacular : *pra-,* before (see **per**[1] in Appendix*) + *kṛta,* made, from *kṛ,* to make (see **kwer-**[1] in Appendix*).] —**Pra·krit′ic** *adj.*

pra·line (prä′lēn, prā′-) *n.* A crisp confection made of nut kernels stirred in boiling sugar syrup until brown. [French, invented by the cook of César de Choiseul, Count du Plessis-Praslin, French field marshal (1598–1675).]

prall·tril·ler (präl′trĭl-ər) *n. Music.* A mordent using the auxiliary note above the principal note. Also called "inverted mordent." [German *Pralltriller,* "elastic trill" : *prallen,* to rebound (akin to Middle High German *prellen*†) + *triller,* trill, from Italian *trillo,* TRILL.]

pram[1] (prăm) *n. Chiefly British.* A **perambulator** *(see).*

pram[2]. Variant of **praam.**

prance (prăns, präns) *v.* **pranced, prancing, prances.** —*intr.* 1. a. To spring forward on the hind legs. Used of a horse. b. To move with a succession of such springs or bounds. 2. To ride a horse that moves in this way. 3. To walk or move about in a lively manner; to caper; strut. —*tr.* To cause (a horse) to prance. —*n.* An act of prancing; caper. [Middle English *prauncen*†.] —**pranc′er** *n.* —**pranc′ing·ly** *adv.*

pran·di·al (prăn′dē-əl) *adj.* Of or relating to a meal, especially dinner. [From Latin *prandium,* late breakfast. See **ed-** in Appendix.*] —**pran′di·al·ly** *adv.*

prank[1] (prăngk) *n.* A mischievous trick; practical joke. [Origin unknown.]

prank[2] (prăngk) *v.* **pranked, pranking, pranks.** —*tr.* To decorate or dress ostentatiously or gaudily. —*intr.* To make an ostentatious display. [Akin to Dutch *pronken*†, to strut.]

prank·ster (prăngk′stər) *n.* One who plays tricks or pranks.

pra·se·o·dym·i·um (prā′zē-ō-dĭm′ē-əm, prā′sē-) *n. Symbol* **Pr** A soft, silvery, malleable, ductile rare-earth element that develops a characteristic green tarnish in air. It occurs naturally with other rare earths in monazite and is used to color glass yellow, as a core material for carbon arcs, and in metallic alloys. Atomic number 59, atomic weight 140.907, melting point 935°C, boiling point 3,127°C, specific gravity 6.8, valence 3, 4. See **element.** [New Latin, contraction of *praseodidymium* : Greek *prasios,* leek-green, from *prason,* leek, probably from Mediterranean + DIDYMIUM.]

prat (prăt) *n. Vulgar.* The buttocks. [Probably imitative of the sound of spanking.]

prate (prāt) *v.* **prated, prating, prates.** —*intr.* To talk idly and at great length; chatter. —*tr.* To utter idly or to little purpose. —*n.* Empty, foolish, or trivial talk. [Middle English *praten,* akin to Middle Dutch and Middle Low German *praten*†.] —**prat′er** *n.* —**prat′ing·ly** *adv.*

prat·fall (prăt′fôl′) *n.* A fall on the buttocks. [PRAT + FALL.]

prat·in·cole (prăt′ĭng-kōl′, prā′tĭn-) *n.* Any of several Old World birds of the genus *Glareola,* having brown and black plumage, long, pointed wings, and a forked tail. [New Latin *pratincola,* "meadow-dweller" : Latin *prātum,* meadow (see **prairie**) + *incola,* inhabitant (see **kwel-**[1] in Appendix*).]

pra·tique (pră-tēk′, prăt′ĭk; *French* prà-tēk′) *n. Nautical.* Clearance granted to a ship to proceed into port after compliance with quarantine or health regulations. [French, PRACTICE.]

Pratt (prăt), **Francis Ashbury.** 1827–1902. American inventor; developed precision tooling and standard gauge for firearms.

prat·tle (prăt′l) *v.* **-tled, -tling, -tles.** —*intr.* To talk idly or meaninglessly; babble. —*tr.* To utter in a childish or silly way. —*n.* Childish or meaningless sounds; babble. [Frequentative of PRATE (akin to Low German *prateln*).] —**prat′tler** *n.*

prawn (prôn) *n.* Any of various edible crustaceans of the genus *Palaemonetes* and related genera, closely related to and resembling the shrimps. —*intr.v.* **prawned, prawning, prawns.** To fish for prawns. [Middle English *prayne*†.] —**prawn′er** *n.*

prax·i·ol·o·gy, prax·e·ol·o·gy (prăk′sē-ŏl′ə-jē) *n.* The study of human conduct. [From PRAXIS + -LOGY.]

prax·is (prăk′sĭs) *n., pl.* **-es.** 1. Practical application or exercise of a branch of learning. 2. Habitual or established practice; custom. [Medieval Latin, from Greek, doing, action, from *prattein, prassein,* to do. See **prāk-** in Appendix.*]

Prax·it·e·les (prăk-sĭt′l-ēz′). Greek sculptor of the fourth century B.C. —**Prax·it′e·le′an** *adj.*

pray (prā) *v.* **prayed, praying, prays.** —*intr.* 1. To utter or address a prayer to a deity or other object of worship. 2. To make a fervent request; plead; beg. —*tr.* 1. To say a prayer or prayers to. 2. To ask (someone) imploringly; beseech. Often used to introduce an entreaty or question: *Pray, be careful.* 3. To make a devout or earnest request for: *I pray your indulgence.* 4. To move or bring by prayer or entreaty. [Middle English *preyen,* from Old French *preier,* from Latin *precārī,* to entreat, from *prex* (stem *prec-*), prayer. See **perk-**[2] in Appendix.*]

pray·er[1] (prā′ər) *n.* One who prays.

prayer[2] (prâr) *n.* 1. A reverent petition made to a deity or other object of worship. 2. The act of making such a petition. 3. Any act of communion with God, such as a confession, praise, or thanksgiving. 4. A specially worded form used in addressing God. 5. *Often plural.* A religious service in which praying predominates. 6. Any fervent request. 7. The thing so requested: *His safe arrival was their prayer.* 8. *Law.* a. The request of a complainant, as stated in a bill in equity, that the court grant the aid or relief solicited. b. The section of the bill that contains this request. [Middle English *preyere,* from Old French *preiere,* from Medieval Latin *precāria,* written petition, prayer, from Latin, feminine of *precārius,* obtained by entreaty, from *precārī,* to entreat, PRAY.]

prayer beads. A string of beads for keeping count of the prayers one is saying; rosary.

prayer book. 1. A book containing prayers and other forms of worship. 2. *Usually capital* **P,** *capital* **B.** *Abbr.* **P.B.** The Book of Common Prayer.

prayer·ful (prâr′fəl) *adj.* Inclined to pray frequently; devout. —**prayer′ful·ly** *adv.* —**prayer′ful·ness** *n.*

prayer meeting. An evangelical service, especially one held on a weekday evening, in which the laity participate by singing, praying, or testifying.

prayer wheel. A cylinder inscribed with or containing written prayers and revolved on an axis, used especially by the Buddhists of Tibet.

praying mantis. A green or brownish predatory insect, *Mantis religiosa,* that, while at rest, folds its front legs as if in prayer.

pre-. Indicates: 1. An earlier or prior time; for example, **prearrange, pre-Columbian.** 2. Preliminary or preparatory work or activity; for example, **preschool.** 3. A location in front or anterior; for example, **preaxial.** ***Note:*** Many compounds other than those entered here may be formed with *pre-*. In forming compounds, *pre-* is normally joined with the following element without space or hyphen: *prearrange.* However, if the second element begins with a capital letter, it is separated with a hy-

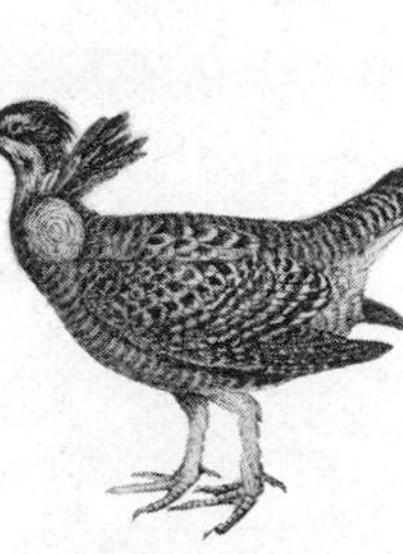

prairie chicken
Tympanuchus cupido

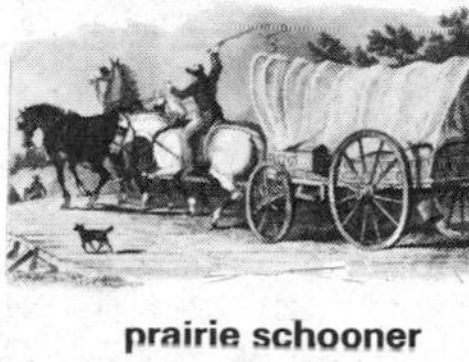

prairie schooner

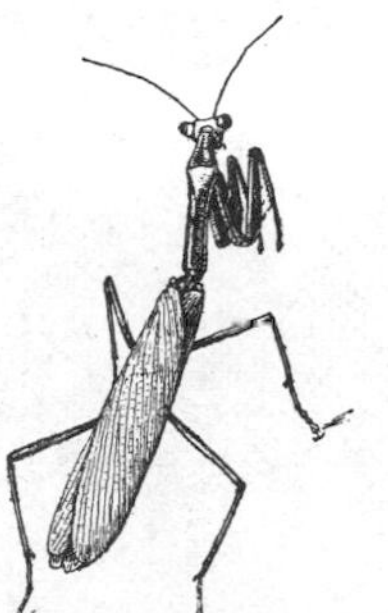

praying mantis

phen: *pre-Raphaelite.* It is preferable to use a hyphen if the second element begins with *e: pre-eminent;* however, such compounds are frequently and acceptably written without space or hyphen. In nonce compounds—formed for a single use—it is often desirable to hyphenate for clarity: *pre-precook.* The hyphen should also be used when the formation of a compound produces a series of three or more vowels that are difficult to read: *pre-aerify.* [Middle English, from Old French, from Latin *prae-*, from *prae,* before, in front. See **per**[1] in Appendix.* In Latin compounds, *prae-* indicates: 1. Before in time, as in **prescient.** 2. Before in position, in front, as in **premorse.** 3. Before in degree or importance, superior, exceeding, as in **preponderate.** 4. Intensifying action, as in **prepotent.**]

preach (prēch) *v.* **preached, preaching, preaches.** —*tr.* **1.** To expound upon in writing or speech; especially, to urge acceptance of or compliance with (specified religious or moral principles). **2.** To deliver (a sermon, lengthy advice, or the like). —*intr.* **1.** To deliver a sermon. **2.** To give religious or moral instruction, especially in a drawn-out, tiresome manner. [Middle English *prechen,* from Old French *prechier,* from Late Latin *praedīcāre,* from Latin, to proclaim : *prae,* before + *dicāre,* to say (see **deik-** in Appendix*).]

preach·er (prē′chər) *n.* **1.** A Protestant clergyman; minister. **2.** One who preaches.

preach·i·fy (prē′chə-fī′) *intr.v.* **-fied, -fying, -fies.** *Informal.* To preach tediously and didactically. —**preach′i·fi·ca′tion** *n.*

preach·ment (prēch′mənt) *n.* **1.** The act of preaching. **2.** A tiresome or unwelcome moral lecture; tedious sermonizing.

preach·y (prē′chē) *adj.* **-ier, -iest.** Inclined to preach.

pre·ad·o·les·cence (prē′ăd-ə-lĕs′əns) *n.* The period between childhood and adolescence, often designated as between the ages of ten and twelve. —**pre′ad·o·les′cent** *n.* & *adj.*

pre·am·ble (prē′ăm′bəl) *n.* **1.** A preliminary statement; especially, the introduction to a formal document, explaining its purpose. **2.** An introductory occurrence or fact; preliminary. [Middle English, from Old French *preambule,* from Medieval Latin *praeambulum,* from Late Latin *praeambulus,* walking in front : *prae,* in front + *ambulāre,* to walk (see **al-**[2] in Appendix*).] —**pre·am′bu·lar′y** *adj.*

pre·am·pli·fi·er (prē-ăm′plə-fī′ər) *n.* An electronic circuit or device that detects and sufficiently amplifies weak signals, especially from a radio receiver, for subsequent amplification stages. Informally shortened to "preamp."

pre·ar·range (prē′ə-rānj′) *tr.v.* **-ranged, -ranging, -ranges.** To arrange in advance. —**pre′ar·range′ment** *n.*

pre·a·tom·ic (prē′ə-tŏm′ĭk) *adj.* Of or pertaining to the period preceding the use of atomic energy.

pre·ax·i·al (prē-ăk′sē-əl) *adj.* Anatomically positioned in front of a body axis. —**pre·ax′i·al·ly** *adv.*

preb·end (prĕb′ənd) *n.* **1.** A clergyman's stipend, drawn from a special endowment belonging to his cathedral or church. **2.** The property or tithe providing the endowment for such a stipend. **3.** The clergyman who receives such a stipend; a prebendary. [Middle English *prebende,* from Old French, from Medieval Latin *praebenda,* from Late Latin, from Latin, "things to be given," from *praebēre,* to grant : *prae,* forth + *habēre,* to hold, offer (see **ghabh-** in Appendix*).] —**pre·ben′dal** *adj.*

preb·en·dar·y (prĕb′ən-dĕr′ē) *n., pl.* **-ies.** **1.** A clergyman who receives a prebend. **2.** *Anglican Church.* A clergyman holding the honorary title of prebend without a stipend.

prec. preceding.

Pre·cam·bri·an (prē-kăm′brē-ən) *adj.* Of, belonging to, or designating the oldest and largest division of geologic time, preceding the Cambrian, often subdivided into the Archeozoic and Proterozoic eras, and characterized by the appearance of primitive forms of life. See **geology.** —*n.* The Precambrian era. Preceded by *the.*

pre·can·cel (prē-kăn′səl) *tr.v.* **-celed** or **-celled, -celing** or **-celling, -cels.** To cancel a postage stamp before mailing. —*n.* A precanceled stamp or envelope.

pre·car·i·ous (prĭ-kâr′ē-əs) *adj.* **1.** Dangerously lacking in security or stability. **2.** Subject to chance or unknown conditions: *"his kingdom was still precarious; the Danes far from subdued"* (Christopher Brooke). **3.** Based upon uncertain or unproved premises. **4.** *Archaic.* Dependent on the will or favor of another. [From Latin *precārius,* dependent on prayer, from *precārī,* to entreat, from *prex* (stem *prec-*), entreaty, prayer. See **perk-**[2] in Appendix.*] —**pre·car′i·ous·ly** *adv.*

prec·a·to·ry (prĕk′ə-tôr′ē, -tōr′ē) *adj.* Also **prec·a·tive** (-tĭv). Relating to or expressing entreaty or supplication. [From Late Latin *precātōrius,* from *precārī,* to entreat. See **precarious.**]

pre·cau·tion (prĭ-kô′shən) *n.* **1.** An action taken in advance to protect against possible failure or danger; a safeguard. **2.** Caution practiced in advance; forethought; circumspection. [French *précaution,* from Late Latin *praecautiō,* from Latin *praecavēre,* to guard against before : *prae,* before + *cavēre,* to guard against (see **keu-**[1] in Appendix*).]

pre·cau·tion·ar·y (prĭ-kô′shə-nĕr′ē) *adj.* Also **pre·cau·tion·al.** **1.** Of or constituting a precaution. **2.** Advising or exercising precaution.

pre·cau·tious (prĭ-kô′shəs) *adj.* Exercising precaution. —**pre·cau′tious·ly** *adv.* —**pre·cau′tious·ness** *n.*

pre·cede (prĭ-sēd′) *v.* **-ceded, -ceding, -cedes.** —*tr.* **1.** To come before in time; exist or occur prior to. **2.** To come before in order or rank; surpass; outrank. **3.** To be in a position in front of; go in advance of. **4.** To preface; introduce: *precede a speech with an anecdote.* —*intr.* To exist or go before. [Middle English *preceden,* from Old French *preceder,* from Latin *praecēdere* : *prae,* before + *cēdere,* to go (see **ked-**[1] in Appendix*).]

pre·ced·ence (prĭ-sēd′əns, prĕs′ə-dəns) *n.* Also **pre·ced·en·cy** (prĭ-sēd′ən-sē, prĕs′ə-dən-). **1.** The act, state, or right of preceding; priority. **2.** A ceremonial order of rank observed on formal occasions: *"My wife and I . . . seated ourselves, she below me in the precedence of the pew"* (Pepys).
Usage: *Precedence* is followed by *of* or *over,* when it takes a preposition. A person, thing, or event is said to have, or take, *precedence of* (or *over*) another.

prec·e·dent (prĕs′ə-dənt) *n.* **1. a.** An act or instance that may be used as an example in dealing with subsequent similar cases. **b.** *Law.* A judicial decision that may be used as a standard in subsequent similar cases. **2.** Convention or custom: *"Governor Houston violated all precedent by delivering his inaugural address directly to the people"* (John F. Kennedy). —*adj.* (prĭ-sēd′ənt). Preceding; prior. See Usage note below. [Middle English, from Old French, from Latin *praecēdēns,* present participle of *praecēdere,* PRECEDE.] —**pre·ced′ent·ly** *adv.*
Usage: *Precedent* (noun) may be followed by *for* or *of: no precedent for the ruling; the precedent of limiting oneself to two terms. Precedent* (adjective) is used attributively or followed by *to: a precedent remark; a statement precedent to mine.*

prec·e·den·tial (prĕs′ə-dĕn′shəl) *adj.* **1.** Of or pertaining to a precedent. **2.** Having precedence.

pre·ced·ing (prĭ-sē′dĭng) *adj. Abbr.* **prec.** Existing or coming before in time, place, rank, or sequence; previous.

pre·cen·sor (prē-sĕn′sər) *tr.v.* **-sored, -soring, -sors.** To censor (a publication or film) prior to public release.

pre·cen·tor (prĭ-sĕn′tər) *n.* One who directs the singing of a church choir. [Late Latin, from Latin *praecinere,* to sing before : *prae,* before + *canere,* to sing (see **kan-** in Appendix*).] —**pre′cen·to′ri·al** (prē′sĕn-tôr′ē-əl, -tōr′ē-əl) *adj.*

pre·cept (prē′sĕpt′) *n.* **1.** A rule or principle imposing a particular standard of action or conduct. **2.** *Law.* A writ. [Middle English, from Latin *praeceptum,* from *praecipere* (past participle *praeceptus*), to take beforehand, warn, teach : *prae,* before + *capere,* to take (see **kap-** in Appendix*).]

pre·cep·tive (prĭ-sĕp′tĭv) *adj.* **1.** Of or expressing a precept. **2.** Giving precepts; didactic. —**pre·cep′tive·ly** *adv.*

pre·cep·tor (prĭ-sĕp′tər, prē′sĕp′tər) *n.* A teacher; instructor. [Middle English *preceptur,* from Latin *praeceptor,* teacher, from *praecipere,* to teach. See **precept.**] —**pre′cep·to′ri·al** (prē′sĕp-tôr′ē-əl, -tōr′ē-əl) *adj.* —**pre′cep·to′ri·al·ly** *adv.*

pre·cess (prĭ-sĕs′) *intr.v.* **-cessed, -cessing, -cesses.** *Physics & Astronomy.* To move in or be subjected to precession. [Back-formation from PRECESSION.]

pre·ces·sion (prĭ-sĕsh′ən) *n.* **1.** The act or state of preceding; precedence. **2.** *Physics.* A complex motion executed by a rotating body subjected to a torque tending to change its axis of rotation, characterized, for constant speed of rotation and constant magnitude of the applied torque, by a conical locus of the axis. **3.** *Astronomy.* Precession of the equinoxes. [New Latin *praecessio,* from Medieval Latin *praecessiō,* a going forward, from Latin *praecēdere* (past participle *praecessus*), PRECEDE.] —**pre·ces′sion·al** *adj.*

precession of the equinoxes. *Astronomy.* A slow westward shift of the equinoctial points along the plane of the ecliptic at a rate of 50.27 seconds of arc per year, resulting from precession of the earth's axis of rotation.

pre·cinct (prē′sĭngkt) *n.* **1. a.** A subdivision or district of a city patrolled by a unit of the police force. **b.** The police station in such a district. **2.** An election district of a city or town. **3.** *Often plural.* **a.** A place or enclosure marked off by definite limits. **b.** A boundary. **4.** *Plural.* Neighborhood; environs. **5.** *Plural.* A bounded area of thought or action; province: *"It was in these spacious precincts that Dryden's imagination was most at home"* (Mark Van Doren). [Middle English *precincte,* from Medieval Latin *praecinctum,* "enclosure," from Latin *praecingere* (past participle *praecinctus*), to gird about : *prae,* before, around + *cingere,* to gird (see **kenk-**[1] in Appendix*).]

pre·ci·os·i·ty (prĕsh′ē-ŏs′ə-tē) *n., pl.* **-ties.** Extreme meticulousness or overrefinement, as in language. [Middle English *preciousite,* from Old French *precieusite,* from Latin *pretiōsitās,* from *pretiōsus,* PRECIOUS.]

pre·cious (prĕsh′əs) *adj.* **1.** Of high cost or worth; valuable. **2.** Highly esteemed; cherished. **3.** Dear; beloved. **4.** Affectedly dainty or overrefined. **5.** *Informal.* Arrant; thoroughgoing. —See Synonyms at **costly.** —*n.* One who is precious; a darling. —*adv.* Very; extremely: *"he had precious little right to complain"* (James Agee). [Middle English, from Old French *precieus, precios,* from Latin *pretiōsus,* from *pretium,* price. See **per**[1] in Appendix.*] —**pre′cious·ly** *adv.* —**pre′cious·ness** *n.*

precious stone. Any of various minerals, such as diamond, ruby, or sapphire, valued for their rarity or appearance.

prec·i·pice (prĕs′ə-pĭs) *n.* **1.** An extremely steep or overhanging mass of rock, such as a crag or the face of a cliff. **2.** The edge of a dangerous situation. [Old French, from Latin *praecipitium,* from *praecipitāre,* to throw headlong. See **precipitate.**]

pre·cip·i·ta·ble (prĭ-sĭp′ə-tə-bəl) *adj.* Capable of being precipitated. [From PRECIPITATE.]

pre·cip·i·tance (prĭ-sĭp′ə-təns) *n.* Also **pre·cip·i·tan·cy** (-tən-sē) *pl.* **-cies.** The quality of being precipitant.

pre·cip·i·tant (prĭ-sĭp′ə-tənt) *adj.* **1.** Rushing or falling headlong. **2.** Impulsive in thought or action; rash. **3.** Abrupt or unexpected; sudden. See Usage note at **precipitate.** —*n.* Any substance that causes precipitation. [French *précipitant,* from Latin *praecipitāns,* present participle of *praecipitāre,* to throw headlong, PRECIPITATE.] —**pre·cip′i·tant·ly** *adv.*

pre·cip·i·tate (prĭ-sĭp′ə-tāt′) *v.* **-tated, -tating, -tates.** —*tr.* **1.** To throw from or as from a great height; hurl downward:

"the finest bridge in all Peru broke and precipitated five travelers into the gulf below" (Thornton Wilder). **2.** To cause to happen before anticipated or required. **3.** *Meteorology.* To cause (water vapor) to condense and fall as rain or snow. **4.** *Chemistry.* To chemically cause (a solid substance) to be separated from a solution. *—intr.* **1.** *Meteorology.* To condense and fall. **2.** *Chemistry.* To be chemically separated from a solution as a precipitate. **3.** To fall headlong. —See Synonyms at **speed.** *—adj.* (prĭ-sĭp′ə-tĭt, -tāt′). **1.** Speeding headlong; moving rapidly and heedlessly. **2.** Acting with excessive haste or impulse; lacking due deliberation. See Usage note below. **3.** Occurring suddenly or unexpectedly. Also loosely **precipitous.** —See Synonyms at **reckless.** *—n.* (prĭ-sĭp′ə-tāt′, -tĭt). *Chemistry.* A solid or solid phase chemically separated from a solution. [Latin *praecipitāre,* to throw headlong, from *praeceps,* headlong : *prae,* in front + *caput,* head (see **kaput** in Appendix*).] **—pre·cip′i·tate·ly** *adv.* **—pre·cip′i·tate·ness** *n.* **—pre·cip′i·ta′tive** *adj.* **—pre·cip′i·ta′tor** *n.*

Usage: *Precipitate* (adjective) and *precipitately* apply primarily to rash, overhasty human actions. *Precipitant* (adjective) and *precipitantly* are also used in the foregoing sense, with stress on rushing forward or falling headlong (literally or figuratively). *Precipitous* and *precipitously* are said primarily of physical steepness.

pre·cip·i·ta·tion (prĭ-sĭp′ə-tā′shən) *n.* **1.** A headlong fall or rush. **2.** Abrupt or impulsive haste. **3.** *Meteorology.* **a.** Water droplets or ice particles condensed from atmospheric water vapor and sufficiently massive to fall to the earth's surface; any form of rain or snow. **b.** The quantity of such precipitation falling in a specific area within a specific period. **4.** *Chemistry.* The production of a precipitate.

pre·cip·i·tin (prĭ-sĭp′ə-tĭn) *n.* *Biochemistry.* An antibody that reacts with an antigen to cause a precipitate. [PRECIPIT(ATE) + -IN.]

pre·cip·i·tous (prĭ-sĭp′ə-təs) *adj.* **1.** Like a precipice; extremely steep. **2.** Having several precipices. **3. Precipitate** *(see).* [French *précipiteux,* from Old French, from Latin *praecipitium,* PRECIPICE.] **—pre·cip′i·tous·ly** *adv.* **—pre·cip′i·tous·ness** *n.*

pré·cis (prā′sē, prā-sē′) *n., pl.* **précis** (prā′sēz, prā-sēz′). A concise summary of the essential facts or statements of a book, article, or other text; an abstract. *—tr.v.* **précised, -cising, -cises.** To make a précis of. [French *précis,* "precise," from Old French *precis,* PRECISE.]

pre·cise (prĭ-sīs′) *adj.* **1.** Clearly expressed or delineated; definite: *"outlines are not clear and concepts are not precise"* (Conrad M. Arensberg). **2.** Capable of, resulting from, or designating an action, performance, or process executed or successively repeated within close specified limits: *a precise measurement with precise instruments, yet completely inaccurate.* **3.** Exactly corresponding to what is indicated; correct: *the precise amount of seasoning.* **4.** Strictly distinguished from others; very: *at that precise moment.* **5.** Distinct and correct in sound or statement: *precise articulation.* **6.** Conforming strictly to rule or proper form: *"The setting up of this Maypole was a lamentable spectacle to the precise separatists that lived at New Plymouth."* (Thomas Morton). [Old French *precis,* from Latin *praecīsus,* shortened, from *praecīdere,* to cut off in front, shorten : *prae,* in front + *caedere,* to cut (see **skhai-** in Appendix*).] **—pre·cise′ly** *adv.* **—pre·cise′ness** *n.*

pre·ci·sian (prĭ-sĭzh′ən) *n.* **1.** A person who is strict and precise in adherence to established rules, forms, or standards. **2.** A person who is very strict about the forms of religious observance or moral behavior; especially, an English Puritan of the 16th or 17th century. [From PRECISE.] **—pre·ci′sian·ism** *n.*

pre·ci·sion (prĭ-sĭzh′ən) *n.* The state or quality of being precise. *—adj.* **1.** Used or intended for precise measurement: *a precision tool.* **2.** Made so as to vary minimally from a set standard: *precision components.* **3.** Of or characterized by precise action. [French *précision,* from Latin *praecīsiō,* act of cutting, from *praecīdere,* to cut off in front, abridge. See **precise.**] **—pre·ci′sion·ism** *n.*

pre·ci·sion·ist (prĭ-sĭzh′ə-nĭst) *n.* One who values precision.

pre·clin·i·cal (prē-klĭn′ĭ-kəl) *adj.* Occurring before the diagnosis of disease is possible.

pre·clude (prĭ-kloo͞d′) *tr.v.* **-cluded, -cluding, -cludes.** **1.** To make impossible or impracticable by previous action; prevent. **2.** To bar or prevent (a person) from something; debar. —See Synonyms at **prevent.** [Latin *praeclūdere* : *prae,* in front + *claudere,* to close (see **klēu-** in Appendix*).] **—pre·clu′sion** (-kloo͞′zhən) *n.* **—pre·clu′sive** (-kloo͞′sĭv, -zĭv) *adj.* **—pre·clu′sive·ly** *adv.*

pre·co·cial (prĭ-kō′shəl) *adj.* *Ornithology.* Of or characterizing birds that are covered with down and capable of moving about when first hatched. [From New Latin *praecoces,* precocial birds, from Latin *praecox,* PRECOCIOUS.]

pre·co·cious (prĭ-kō′shəs) *adj.* **1.** Characterized by unusually early development or maturity, especially in mental aptitude. **2.** Manifesting or characterized by premature or unusually early development. **3.** *Botany.* Blossoming before the leaves sprout. [From Latin *praecox,* "ripening before its time," from *praecoquere,* to cook or ripen before : *prae,* before + *coquere,* to cook, ripen (see **pekw-** in Appendix*).] **—pre·co′cious·ly** *adv.* **—pre·co′cious·ness, pre·coc′i·ty** (-kŏs′ə-tē) *n.*

pre·cog·ni·tion (prē′kŏg-nĭsh′ən) *n.* Knowledge of something in advance of its occurrence. [Late Latin *praecognitiō,* from Latin *praecognōscere* (past participle *praecognitus*), to know before : *prae,* before + *cognōscere,* to know (see **cognition**).] **—pre·cog′ni·tive** (prē-kŏg′nə-tĭv) *adj.*

pre-Co·lum·bi·an (prē′kə-lŭm′bē-ən) *adj.* Of, relating to, or originating in the Americas before the voyages of Columbus.

pre·con·ceive (prē′kən-sēv′) *tr.v.* **-ceived, -ceiving, -ceives.** To form an opinion or conception of (something) beforehand.

pre·con·cep·tion (prē′kən-sĕp′shən) *n.* **1.** An opinion or conception formed in advance of actual knowledge. **2.** A prejudice.

pre·con·cert (prē′kən-sûrt′) *tr.v.* **-certed, -certing, -certs.** To agree on or arrange in advance.

pre·con·di·tion (prē′kən-dĭsh′ən) *n.* A condition that must exist or be established before something can occur or be considered; prerequisite. *—tr.v.* **preconditioned, -tioning, -tions.** To condition, train, or accustom in advance.

pre·con·scious (prē-kŏn′shəs) *adj.* *Psychoanalysis.* Capable of being recalled although not present in the conscious mind. **—pre·con′scious·ly** *adv.*

pre·cook (prē-ko͝ok′) *tr.v.* **-cooked, -cooking, -cooks.** To cook in advance, or cook partially before final cooking.

pre·crit·i·cal (prē-krĭt′ĭ-kəl) *adj.* Prior to the occurrence of a critical condition.

pre·cur·sor (prĭ-kûr′sər, prē′kûr′sər) *n.* **1.** One that precedes and indicates or announces someone or something to come; forerunner; harbinger: *"the crafty smile, which was the precursor of the little joke"* (Hawthorne). **2.** One that precedes another; predecessor: *"The precursor of man had to pass through the stage of being a monkey."* (Julian Huxley). [Latin *praecursor,* from *praecurrere,* to run before : *prae,* before + *currere,* to run (see **kers-**[2] in Appendix*).]

pre·cur·so·ry (prĭ-kûr′sə-rē) *adj.* Also **pre·cur·sive** (-sĭv). **1.** Preceding in the manner of a precursor; preliminary; introductory. **2.** Suggesting or indicating something to follow; premonitory.

pred. predicate.

pre·da·cious, pre·da·ceous (prĭ-dā′shəs) *adj.* Living by seizing or taking prey; predatory. [From Latin *praedārī,* to plunder. See **predatory.**] **—pre·da′cious·ness, pre·dac′i·ty** (-dăs′ə-tē) *n.*

pre·date (prē-dāt′) *tr.v.* **-dated, -dating, -dates.** **1.** To mark or designate with an earlier date than the actual one. **2.** To precede in time; antedate.

pre·da·tion (prĭ-dā′shən) *n.* **1.** The act or practice of plundering or marauding. **2.** The capturing of prey as a means of maintaining life. [Latin *praedātiō,* from *praedārī,* to plunder. See **predatory.**]

pred·a·tor (prĕd′ə-tər, -tôr′) *n.* **1.** An animal that lives by preying upon others. **2.** One who habitually plunders. [Latin *praedātor,* from *praedārī,* to plunder. See **predatory.**]

pred·a·to·ry (prĕd′ə-tôr′ē, -tōr′ē) *adj.* **1.** Of, relating to, or characterized by plundering, pillaging, or marauding: *a predatory war.* **2.** Preying on other animals; predacious. **3.** Addicted to or characterized by a tendency to victimize or destroy others for one's own gain. [Latin *praedātōrius* from *praedārī,* to plunder, from *praeda,* booty. See **ghend-** in Appendix.*] **—pred′a·to′ri·ly** *adv.* **—pred′a·to′ri·ness** *n.*

pre·de·cease (prē′dĭ-sēs′) *tr.v.* **-ceased, -ceasing, -ceases.** To die before (some other person).

pred·e·ces·sor (prĕd′ə-sĕs′ər, prē′də-) *n.* **1.** One who precedes another in time, especially in an office or position. **2.** Something that has been succeeded by another. **3.** An ancestor or forefather. [Middle English *predecessour,* from Old French *predecesseur,* from Late Latin *praedecessor* : Latin *prae,* before + *dēcessor,* one who leaves, from *dēcessus,* past participle of *dēcēdere,* to die, go away : *dē,* away + *cēdere,* to go (see **ked-**[1] in Appendix*).]

pre·des·ti·nar·i·an (prē-dĕs′tə-nâr′ē-ən) *adj.* **1.** Of or pertaining to predestination. **2.** Believing in or based on the doctrine of predestination. *—n.* One who believes in the doctrine of predestination. **—pre·des′ti·nar′i·an·ism** *n.*

pre·des·ti·nate (prē-dĕs′tə-nāt′) *tr.v.* **-nated, -nating, -nates.** **1.** To destine or determine in advance; foreordain. **2.** *Theology.* To predestine. *—adj.* (prē-dĕs′tə-nĭt, -nāt′). Foreordained; predestined. [Middle English *predestinaten,* from Latin *praedestināre,* PREDESTINE.]

pre·des·ti·na·tion (prē-dĕs′tə-nā′shən) *n.* **1.** The act of predestining, or the condition of being predestined. **2.** *Theology.* **a.** The act whereby God is believed to have foreordained all things. **b.** The relegation of all souls to either salvation or damnation by this act. **c.** The doctrine that God has foreordained all things, especially the salvation of individual souls. **3.** Destiny; fate.

pre·des·tine (prē-dĕs′tĭn) *tr.v.* **-tined, -tining, -tines.** **1.** To fix upon, decide, or decree in advance; foreordain. **2.** *Theology.* To foreordain by divine will or decree; predestinate. [Middle English *predestinen,* from Old French *predestiner,* from Latin *praedestināre* : *prae,* before + *dēstināre,* to determine, DESTINE.]

pre·de·ter·mine (prē′dĭ-tûr′mĭn) *tr.v.* **-mined, -mining, -mines.** **1.** To determine, decide, or establish in advance: *"These factors predetermine to a large extent the outcome."* (Jessica Mitford). **2.** To influence or sway toward an action or opinion; give a tendency to beforehand; predispose; bias. [Late Latin *praedēterminare* : *prae,* before + *dēterminare,* DETERMINE.] **—pre′de·ter′mi·na′tion** *n.* **—pre′de·ter′mi·na′tive** (-tûr′mə-nā′tĭv, -nə-tĭv) *adj.* **—pre′de·ter′min·er** *n.*

pre·di·al. Variant of **praedial.**

pred·i·ca·ble (prĕd′ĭ-kə-bəl) *adj.* Capable of being stated or predicated. *—n.* **1.** Something that can be predicated; a quality or attribute. **2.** *Logic.* One of five general attributes of a class, *genus, species, property, difference,* and *accident,* designating the peculiar relation that a predicate bears to its subject, regardless of the quantity or quality of a proposition. [Medieval Latin *praedicābilis,* from Late Latin *praedicāre,* to proclaim, PREDICATE.] **—pred′i·ca·bil′i·ty, pred′i·ca·ble·ness** *n.*

pre·dic·a·ment (prĭ-dĭk′ə-mənt *for senses 1, 2,* prĕd′ĭ-kə-mənt *for sense 3) n.* **1.** A troublesome, embarrassing, or ludicrous situation. **2.** *Archaic.* A specific state or condition. **3.** *Logic.* A state or classification of existence, a **category** *(see).* [Middle English, from Late Latin *praedicāmentum* (translation of Greek *katēgoria,* category), something predicated, condition (especially an unpleasant one), from *praedicāre,* to proclaim, PREDICATE.] **—pre·dic′a·men′tal** *adj.* **—pre·dic′a·men′tal·ly** *adv.*

Synonyms: *predicament, plight, dilemma, quandary.* A *predicament* is a problematic situation seen in terms of a difficult decision and implies that one does not know what to do and is considering it rationally. A *plight* is a more serious pass, which may have been imposed on an individual with a course of action being less clear. *Dilemma* more abstractly denotes a problem which poses two alternatives, each of which must be carefully weighed. The term is sometimes loosely used of any problem. *Quandary,* somewhat more formal, suggests a complicated stalemate with numerous possibilities.

pred·i·cate (prĕd′ə-kāt′) *v.* **-cated, -cating, -cates.** *—tr.* **1.** To base or establish (a concept, statement, or action). Used with *on* or *upon: He predicates his argument on these facts.* See Usage note below. **2.** To state or affirm as an attribute or quality of something: *predicate perfectability of mankind.* **3.** To carry the connotation of; imply. **4.** *Logic.* To make (a term or expression) the predicate of a proposition. **5.** To proclaim; assert; declare. *—intr.* To make a statement or assertion. *—n.* (prĕd′ĭ-kĭt). *Abbr.* **pred. 1.** *Grammar.* The part of a sentence or clause that expresses something about the subject. It regularly consists of a verb and may include objects, modifiers, or complements of the verb. The predicates of the following simple sentences are enclosed in brackets: *The house [is white.] The man [hit the dog.]* Compare **attributive. 2.** *Logic.* Whatever is stated about the subject of a proposition. *—adj.* (prĕd′ĭ-kĭt). **1.** *Grammar.* Of or belonging to the predicate of a sentence or clause. **2.** Predicated; stated. [Late Latin *praedicāre,* to proclaim, Latin : *prae,* in front of, in public + *dicāre,* to say (see **deik-** in Appendix*).] **—pred′i·ca′tive** *adj.* **—pred′i·ca′tive·ly** *adv.*

Usage: *Predicate* (transitive verb) is now employed widely in the sense of *base upon* or *found* as a means of indicating dependence: *Success is predicated on continuing effort.* Though this sense is disputed by some lexicographers, the foregoing typical example is acceptable to 62 per cent of the Usage Panel.

predicate adjective. *Grammar.* An adjective that follows certain verbs and describes the subject of the verb. In the sentence *The man is good,* the predicate adjective is *good.*

predicate nominative. *Grammar.* A noun, or a pronoun in the subject form, that follows certain verbs, and is identified with the subject of the verb. In the sentences *It is I* and *He became president,* the predicate nominatives are *I* and *president.*

pred·i·ca·tion (prĕd′ĭ-kā′shən) *n.* **1.** The act or procedure of predicating; especially, a logical assertion or affirmation. **2.** Something predicated. **—pred′i·ca′tion·al** *adj.*

pred·i·ca·to·ry (prĕd′ĭ-kə-tôr′ē, -tōr′ē) *adj.* Of, pertaining to, or characteristic of preaching or a preacher. [Late Latin *praedicātōrius,* from *praedicāre,* to proclaim, PREDICATE.]

pre·dict (prĭ-dĭkt′) *v.* **-dicted, -dicting, -dicts.** *—tr.* To state, tell about, or make known in advance, especially on the basis of special knowledge; foretell: *predict the weather.* *—intr.* To foretell what will happen; prophesy. —See Synonyms at **foretell.** [Latin *praedīcere,* to foretell : *prae,* before + *dīcere,* to tell, say (see **deik-** in Appendix*).] **—pre·dict′a·bil′i·ty** *n.* **—pre·dict′a·ble** *adj.* **—pre·dict′a·bly** *adv.*

pre·dic·tion (prĭ-dĭk′shən) *n.* **1.** The act of foretelling or predicting. **2.** Something foretold or predicted; prophecy. **—pre·dic′tive** *adj.* **—pre·dic′tive·ly** *adv.* **—pre·dic′tive·ness** *n.*

pre·dic·tor (prĭ-dĭk′tər) *n.* One that predicts.

pre·di·gest (prē′dĭ-jĕst′, -dī-jĕst′) *tr.v.* **-gested, -gesting, -gests.** To subject to partial digestion. **—pre′di·ges′tion** *n.*

pre·di·lec·tion (prĕd′ə-lĕk′shən, prē′də-) *n.* A preference, often formed as the result of personal leanings or disposition, rather than from objective knowledge. [French *prédilection,* from Medieval Latin *praedīligere,* to prefer : Latin *prae,* before + *dīligere,* to love, choose (see **diligent**).]

pre·dis·pose (prē′dĭs-pōz′) *tr.v.* **-posed, -posing, -poses. 1.** To make (someone) inclined to something in advance; put into a certain frame of mind for: *His good manners predispose people to like him.* **2.** To make susceptible or liable. **3.** *Archaic.* To settle or dispose of in advance. **—pre′dis·pos′al** *n.*

pre·dis·po·si·tion (prē′dĭs-pə-zĭsh′ən) *n.* The state of being predisposed; tendency or inclination.

pre·dom·i·nance (prĭ-dŏm′ə-nəns) *n.* Also **pre·dom·i·nan·cy** (-nən-sē). The state or quality of being predominant; preponderance.

pre·dom·i·nant (prĭ-dŏm′ə-nənt) *adj.* **1.** Having greatest ascendancy, importance, influence, authority, or force. **2.** Most common or conspicuous; prevalent. —See Synonyms at **dominant.** [Old French, from Medieval Latin *praedominàns,* present participle of *praedominārī,* PREDOMINATE.] **—pre·dom′i·nant·ly** *adv.*

pre·dom·i·nate (prĭ-dŏm′ə-nāt′) *v.* **-nated, -nating, -nates.** *—intr.* **1.** To be of greater power, importance, or quantity; be most important or outstanding. **2.** To have authority, power, or controlling influence; prevail. Often used with *over.* *—tr.* *Rare.* To dominate or prevail over. [Latin *praedominārī;* to subdue beforehand : *prae,* before + *dominārī,* to DOMINATE.] **—pre·dom′i·nate·ly** (-nĭt-lē) *adv.* **—pre·dom′i·nat′ing·ly** *adv.* **—pre·dom′i·na′tion** *n.* **—pre·dom′i·na′tor** (-nā′tər) *n.*

pree·mie (prē′mē) *n.* Also **pre·mie.** *Informal.* An infant born prematurely. [Short for PREMATURE.]

pre·em·i·nent (prē-ĕm′ə-nənt) *adj.* Also **pre·em·i·nent, pre·ēm·i·nent.** Superior to or notable above all others; outstanding: *"Sublimity is the pre-eminent characteristic of the Paradise Lost."* (Emerson). See Synonyms at **dominant.** [Late Latin *praeēminēns,* from Latin, present participle of *praeēminēre,* to excel : *prae,* in front of + *ēminēre,* to stand out (see **eminent**).] **—pre·em′i·nence** *n.* **—pre·em′i·nent·ly** *adv.*

pre·empt (prē-ĕmpt′) *v.* **-empted, -empting, -empts.** Also **pre·empt, pre·ēmpt.** *—tr.* **1.** To gain possession of by prior right or opportunity; especially, to settle on (public land) so as to obtain the right to buy before others. **2.** To appropriate, seize, or act for oneself before others. *—intr.* *Bridge.* To make a pre-emptive bid. [Back-formation from PRE-EMPTION.] **—pre·emp′tor′** (-ĕmp′tôr′) *n.* **—pre·emp′to·ry** (-ĕmp′tə-rē) *adj.*

pre·emp·tion (prē-ĕmp′shən) *n.* Also **pre·emp·tion, pre·ēmp·tion. 1. a.** The right to purchase something, especially government-owned land, before others. **b.** A purchase made when such a right is granted. **2.** Acquisition or appropriation of something beforehand. [Medieval Latin *praeemptiō,* from *praeemere,* to buy beforehand : *prae,* before + *emere,* to buy (see **em-** in Appendix*).]

pre·emp·tive (prē-ĕmp′tĭv) *adj.* Also **pre·emp·tive, pre·ēmp·tive. 1.** Of, pertaining to, or characteristic of pre-emption. **2.** Having, or granted by, the right of pre-emption. **3.** *Bridge.* Designating or characteristic of a bid that is unnecessarily high, and is intended to prevent the opposing players from bidding. **—pre·emp′tive·ly** *adv.*

preen (prēn) *v.* **preened, preening, preens.** *—tr.* **1.** To smooth or clean (feathers) with the beak or bill. Used of a bird. **2.** To adorn or trim (oneself) carefully; primp. **3.** To take pride or satisfaction in (oneself). Used with *on: preening themselves on having won another victory.* *—intr.* To dress up; primp. [Middle English *preinen, proinen, prunen,* possibly from Old French *poroindre* (present stem *poroign-*), to anoint before : *por-,* from Latin *prō,* before + *oindre,* to anoint, from Latin *unguere* (see **ongw-** in Appendix*).] **—preen′er** *n.*

pre·es·tab·lish (prē′ə-stăb′lĭsh) *tr.v.* **-lished, -lishing, -lishes.** Also **pre·es·tab·lish, pre·ēs·tab·lish.** To establish beforehand.

pre·ex·il·ic (prē′ĕg-zĭl′ĭk, -ĕk-sĭl′ĭk) *adj.* Also **pre·ex·il·i·an** (prē′-ĕg-zĭl′ē-ən, -zĭl′yən, -ĕk-sĭl′ē-ən, -ĕk-sĭl′yən). Pertaining to the history of the Jewish people prior to their exile in Babylonia at the end of the sixth century B.C.

pre·ex·ist (prē′ĭg-zĭst′) *v.* **-isted, -isting, -ists.** Also **pre·ex·ist, pre·ēx·ist.** *—intr.* To exist before. *—tr.* To exist before (something): *dinosaurs that pre-existed mammals.* **—pre·ex·ist′ence** *n.* **—pre·ex·ist′ent** *adj.*

pref. 1. preface; prefatory. **2.** preference; preferred. **3.** prefix.

pre·fab (prē′făb′) *n.* A prefabricated part or structure.

pre·fab·ri·cate (prē-făb′rĭ-kāt′) *tr.v.* **-cated, -cating, -cates. 1.** To construct or manufacture in advance. **2.** To construct in standard sections that can be easily shipped and assembled. **—pre·fab′ri·ca′tion** *n.* **—pre·fab′ri·ca′tor** (-kā′tər) *n.*

pref·ace (prĕf′ĭs) *n. Abbr.* **pref. 1. a.** A statement or essay, usually by the author, introducing a book and explaining its scope, intention, or background. **b.** The introductory section of a speech. **2.** Anything introductory or preliminary. **3.** *Usually capital* **P.** A thanksgiving prayer ending with the Sanctus and introducing the canon of the Roman Catholic Mass. *—tr.v.* **prefaced, -acing, -aces. 1.** To introduce by or provide with a preliminary statement or essay. **2.** To serve as an introduction to. [Middle English, from Old French, from Medieval Latin *prefātia,* alteration of Latin *praefātiō,* a saying beforehand, from *praefārī,* to say beforehand : *prae,* before + *fārī,* to speak (see **bhā-**[2] in Appendix*).] **—pref′ac·er** *n.*

pref·a·to·ry (prĕf′ə-tôr′ē, -tōr′ē) *adj.* Also **pref·a·to·ri·al** (prĕf′ə-tôr′ē-əl, -tōr′ē-əl). *Abbr.* **pref.** Of the nature of, or serving as, an introductory statement or essay; preliminary. [From Latin *prefātiō,* PREFACE.] **—pref′a·to′ri·ly** *adv.*

pre·fect (prē′fĕkt′) *n.* Also **prae·fect. 1.** Any of several high military or civil officials, as magistrates or administrators of ancient Rome. **2.** Any high administrative official; especially, the chief of police of Paris. **3.** The dean in a Jesuit school. **4.** A student officer, especially in a private school. [Middle English, from Old French, from Latin *praefectus,* overseer, chief, from the past participle of *praeficere,* to place at the head of : *prae,* before + *facere,* to do (see **dhē-**[1] in Appendix*).]

prefect apostolic *pl.* **prefects apostolic.** A Roman Catholic priest with broad jurisdiction in a missionary territory.

pre·fec·ture (prē′fĕk′chər) *n.* **1.** The district, office, or authority of a prefect. **2.** The domicile or housing of a prefect. **—pre·fec′tur·al** *adj.*

pre·fer (prĭ-fûr′) *tr.v.* **-ferred, -ferring, -fers. 1.** To select in preference to another or others; value more highly; like better. **2.** *Law.* To give priority or precedence to (a creditor). **3.** *Law.* To file, prosecute, or offer for consideration or resolution before a magistrate, court, or other legal person or body: *He preferred charges against her for theft.* **4.** To promote: *"Joey was now preferred from the stable to attend on the lady."* (Fielding). [Middle English *preferren,* from Old French *preferer,* from Latin *praeferre,* to hold or set before : *prae,* before + *ferre,* to bear (see **bher-**[1] in Appendix*).] **—pre·fer′rer** *n.*

Usage: *Prefer* is usually followed by *to* (never by *than*) when the object of *prefer* is something other than an infinitive: *We prefer reading to television.* When an infinitive is the object, the usual construction is *rather than* (not merely *than*) plus infinitive (sometimes without *to*): *We prefer to read rather than watch television* (but not *prefer to read than watch*). In stricter usage this can be expressed: *prefer to read instead of watching* or *would rather read than watch.*

pref·er·a·ble (prĕf′ər-ə-bəl) *adj.* More desirable or worthy;

preferred. —pref·er·a·bil'i·ty, pref'er·a·ble·ness n. —pref'er·a·bly adv.

pref·er·ence (prĕf'ər-əns) n. Abbr. pref. 1. a. The selecting of someone or something over another or others. b. The right or chance to so choose: You may have your preference of any dress in the store. c. Someone or something so chosen. 2. The state of being better liked or more valued. 3. Law. a. The paying of one or more creditors by an insolvent debtor before, or to the exclusion of, other creditors. b. The right to be so paid. 4. The granting of precedence or advantage to one over all others, as to one country or group of countries in levying duties or in other matters of international trade. —See Synonyms at choice. [French préférence, from Medieval Latin praeferentia, from Latin praeferēns, present participle of praeferre, PREFER.]

pref·er·en·tial (prĕf'ə-rĕn'shəl) adj. 1. Of, having, providing, or obtaining advantage or preference: The sickest patients receive preferential treatment. 2. Manifesting or originating from partiality or preference: preferential tariff rates. —pref'er·en'tial·ism n. —pref'er·en'tial·ist n. —pref'er·en'tial·ly adv.

preferential shop. A union shop whose management gives priority or advantage to union members in hiring, promoting, or laying off.

preferential voting. A system of voting in which the voter indicates his choices in order of preference.

pre·fer·ment (prĭ-fûr'mənt) n. 1. The act of advancing to a higher position or office; promotion. 2. A position, appointment, or rank giving advancement. [Middle English preferrement, from preferren, PREFER.]

preferred stock. The portion of a corporation's stock having a priority or preference over the common stock in the distribution of dividends and assets.

pre·fig·u·ra·tion (prē-fĭg-yə-rā'shən) n. 1. The act of representing, suggesting, or imagining in advance; foreshadowing. 2. Something that prefigures. —pre·fig'ur·a·tive adj. —pre·fig'ur·a·tive·ly adv. —pre·fig'ur·a·tive·ness n.

pre·fig·ure (prē-fĭg'yər) tr.v. -ured, -uring, -ures. 1. To suggest, indicate, or represent by an antecedent form or model; presage; foreshadow: The art and theories of Cézanne prefigured the cubist school of art. 2. To imagine or picture to oneself in advance. [Middle English prefiguren, from Late Latin praefigūrāre, to shape beforehand : prae, before + figūrāre, to shape, from figūra, FIGURE.] —pre·fig'ure·ment n.

pre·fix (prē-fĭks'; also prē'fĭks' for sense 1) tr.v. -fixed, -fixing, -fixes. 1. To put or fix before. 2. Archaic. To settle or arrange in advance. —n. (prē'fĭks'). 1. Abbr. pref. Grammar. An affix put before a word, changing the meaning (as dis- in disbelieve) or modifying the meaning (as pre- in preheat). See combining form. 2. A title placed before a person's name. [New Latin praefixum, a prefix, from Latin praefigere (past participle praefixus), to fix before : prae, before + figere, to fix (see dhīgw- in Appendix*).] —pre'fix·al adj. —pre'fix'al·ly adv.

pre·flight (prē'flīt') adj. Preparing for or occurring prior to airplane flight.

pre·for·ma·tion (prē'fôr-mā'shən) n. 1. The act of shaping or forming in advance; prior formation. 2. A now invalidated biological theory that all parts of a future organism exist completely formed in the germ cell and develop only by increasing in size. —pre'for·ma'tion·ism n.

pre·fron·tal (prē-frŭnt'l) adj. Located in the forward part of the frontal lobe of the brain.

prefrontal lobotomy. An operation in which the white fibers connecting the prefrontal and frontal lobes of the brain to the thalamus are severed.

Pre·gl (prā'gəl), Fritz. 1869-1930. Austrian chemist; developed quantitative microanalysis.

preg·na·ble (prĕg'nə-bəl) adj. Vulnerable to seizure or capture, as a fort. [Earlier preignable, Middle English prenable, from Old French, from prendre, to take, capture, from Latin prehendere. See ghend- in Appendix*.] —preg'na·bil'i·ty n.

preg·nan·cy (prĕg'nən-sē) n., pl. -cies. 1. The condition of being pregnant. 2. The period during which a developing fetus is carried within the uterus.

preg·nant¹ (prĕg'nənt) adj. 1. Carrying a developing fetus within the uterus. 2. Creative; inventive. 3. Fraught with significance or implication: a pregnant silence. 4. a. Abounding; profuse. b. Overflowing; replete. c. Filled; charged; fraught: pregnant with fate. 5. Producing results; fruitful; momentous: a pregnant decision. [Middle English, from Latin praegnāns, variant of praegnās. See gene- in Appendix*.] —preg'nant·ly adv.

preg·nant² (prĕg'nənt) adj. Archaic. Convincing; cogent. Said of an argument, proof, or the like. [Middle English preignant, from Old French, present participle of preindre, to press, earlier priembre, from Latin premere. See per-⁶ in Appendix*.]

pre·heat (prē-hēt') tr.v. -heated, -heating, -heats. To heat beforehand: preheat the oven for 30 minutes.

pre·hen·sile (prĭ-hĕn'sĭl) adj. Adapted for seizing or holding, especially by wrapping around an object: a prehensile tail. [French préhensile, from Latin prehendere (past participle prehensus), to seize. See ghend- in Appendix*.] —pre'hen·sil'i·ty n.

pre·hen·sion (prĭ-hĕn'shən) n. 1. The act of grasping or seizing. 2. a. Apprehension by the senses. b. Understanding. [Latin prehensiō, from prehendere (past participle prehensus), to seize. See ghend- in Appendix*.]

pre·his·tor·ic (prē'hĭs·tôr'ĭk, -tŏr'ĭk) adj. Also pre·his·tor·i·cal (-ĭ-kəl). Abbr. prehist. Of, pertaining to, or belonging to the era before recorded history. —pre'his·tor'i·cal·ly adv.

pre·his·to·ry (prē-hĭs'tə-rē) n. The history of mankind in the period before written or recorded history, investigated by archaeology. —pre'his·to'ri·an n.

pre·ig·ni·tion (prē'ĭg-nĭsh'ən) n. The ignition of fuel, as in a gasoline engine, before maximum compression.

pre·judge (prē-jŭj') tr.v. -judged, -judging, -judges. To judge beforehand without possessing adequate evidence. [French préjuger, from Latin praejūdicāre : prae, before + jūdicāre, to judge, from jūdex, JUDGE.] —pre·judg'er n. —pre·judg'ment, pre·judge'ment n.

prej·u·dice (prĕj'ə-dĭs) n. 1. a. An adverse judgment or opinion formed beforehand or without knowledge or examination of the facts. b. A preconceived preference or idea; bias. 2. The act or state of holding unreasonable preconceived judgments or convictions. 3. Irrational suspicion or hatred of a particular group, race, or religion. 4. Detriment or injury caused to a person by the preconceived and unfavorable conviction of another or others. —in (or to) the prejudice of. To the harm or injury of. —without prejudice to. Law. Without injury to any right or claim. —tr.v. prejudiced, -dicing, -dices. 1. To cause (someone) to judge prematurely and irrationally; to bias. 2. To affect injuriously or detrimentally by some judgment or act. [Middle English, from Old French, from Latin praejūdicium : prae, before + jūdicium, judgment, from jūdex, JUDGE.]

prej·u·di·cial (prĕj'ə-dĭsh'əl) adj. Causing or of the nature of prejudice; detrimental. —prej'u·di'cial·ly adv.

prel·a·cy (prĕl'ə-sē) n., pl. -cies. 1. a. The office or station of a prelate. b. Prelates collectively. Also called "prelature." 2. Church government administrated by prelates. Often used disparagingly. In this sense, also called "prelatism."

prel·ate (prĕl'ĭt) n. A high-ranking clergyman, such as a bishop or an abbot. [Middle English prelat, from Old French, from Medieval Latin praelātus, from Latin (past participle of praeferre, to bear before, prefer) : prae, before + -lātus, "carried" (see tel-¹ in Appendix*).] —pre·lat'ic (prĭ-lăt'ĭk) adj.

prelate nul·li·us (nŏo'lē-əs). A Roman Catholic prelate, usually a titular bishop, who has jurisdiction over a territory not in a diocese but subject directly to the Holy See. [PRELATE + Latin nūllius, of nobody, from nūllus, NULL.]

pre·lect (prĭ-lĕkt') intr.v. -lected, -lecting, -lects. Also prae·lect. To lecture or discourse in public. [Latin praelegere (past participle praelectus) : prae, in front of, in public + legere, to read (see leg-¹ in Appendix*).] —pre·lec'tion n. —pre·lec'tor n.

pre·li·ba·tion (prē'lī-bā'shən) n. A foretaste. [Latin praelībātiō, from praelībāre, to taste beforehand : prae, before + lībāre, to taste (see lei-³ in Appendix*).]

pre·lim·i·nar·y (prĭ-lĭm'ə-nĕr'ē) adj. Abbr. prelim. Prior to or preparing for the main matter, action, or business; introductory; prefatory. —n., pl. preliminaries. Abbr. prelim. 1. Something antecedent or preparatory, as a statement or action. 2. a. An academic test or examination that is preparatory to one that is longer, more complex, or more important. b. Sports. Any event that precedes the main event of a particular program, especially in boxing or wrestling. Also informally called "prelim." 3. Plural. Printing. Matter that precedes the actual text of a book, such as the title pages, preface, or dedication. [French préliminaire, from Medieval Latin praelīmināris : prae, before + līmināris, of a threshold, from līmen, threshold, lintel (see limen).] —pre·lim'i·nar'i·ly adv.

pre·lit·er·ate (prē-lĭt'ər-ĭt) adj. Of or pertaining to any culture not having a written language.

prel·ude (prĕl'yŏod', prē'lŏod') n. 1. An introductory performance, event, or action preceding a more important one; a preliminary or preface. 2. Music. A piece or movement serving as an introduction to a musical composition: a. An independent piece of moderate length that precedes a fugue. b. The first or opening section of a suite (see). c. The overture to an opera or oratorio, or a similar piece played before one of the acts of an opera. d. A piece played before a church service; an introductory voluntary. e. A relatively short composition, in a free style, usually for piano or orchestra. —v. preluded, -luding, -ludes. —tr. 1. To serve as a prelude to. 2. To introduce with or as if with a prelude. —intr. 1. To serve as a prelude or introduction. 2. To provide a prelude to some later event. [Old French, from Medieval Latin praelūdium, from Latin praelūdere, to play beforehand : prae, before + lūdere, to play, from lūdus, game (see leid- in Appendix*).] —pre·lud'er (prĭ-lŏo'dər, prĕl'yə-) n. —pre·lu'di·al (prĭ-lŏo'dē-əl) adj.

pre·lu·sive (prĭ-lŏo'sĭv) adj. Also pre·lu·so·ry (-sə-rē). Serving as a prelude; introductory. —pre·lu'sive·ly adv.

prem. premium.

pre·ma·ture (prē'mə-chŏor', -tŏor', -tyŏor') adj. 1. Occurring, growing, or existing prior to the customary, correct, or assigned time; uncommonly or unexpectedly early: a premature end. 2. Too hurried or impulsive. 3. Born after a gestation period of less than the normal time: a premature baby. [Latin praemātūrus : prae, before + mātūrus, ripe, MATURE.] —pre'ma·ture'ly adv. —pre'ma·ture'ness, pre'ma·tu'ri·ty n.

pre·max·il·la (prē'măk-sĭl'ə) n., pl. -maxillae (-măk-sĭl'ē). Either of two bones located in front of and between the maxillary bones in the upper jaw of vertebrates. [New Latin : PRE- + MAXILLA.] —pre·max'il·lar'y (prē-măk'sĭ-lĕr'ē) adj.

pre·med (prē'mĕd') adj. Informal. Premedical. —n. Informal. A premedical student.

pre·med·i·cal (prē-mĕd'ĭ-kəl) adj. Preparing for, or pertaining to the studies that prepare for, the study of medicine.

pre·med·i·tate (prē-mĕd'ə-tāt') v. -tated, -tating, -tates. —tr. To plan, arrange, or plot (a deed or events) in advance. —intr. To meditate or deliberate beforehand. [Latin praemeditārī : prae, before + meditārī, MEDITATE.] —pre·med'i·ta'tive adj. —pre·med'i·ta'tor (-tər) n.

pre·med·i·tat·ed (prē-mĕd'ə-tā'tĭd) adj. Characterized by deliberate purpose, previous consideration, and some degree of planning. —**pre·med′i·tat′ed·ly** adv.

pre·med·i·ta·tion (prē-mĕd′ə-tā′shən) n. **1.** The act of speculating, arranging, or plotting in advance. **2.** Law. The contemplation and plotting of a crime in advance, showing intent to commit the crime.

pre·mie. Variant of **preemie.**

pre·mier (prē′mē-ər, prĭ-mîr′; chiefly British prĕm′yər) adj. **1.** First in status or importance; chief; supreme. **2.** First to occur or exist; earliest. —n. (prĭ-mîr′). **1.** A prime minister (see). **2.** The chief executive of a Canadian province. [Middle English premier, from Old French premier, first, chief, from Latin primārius, of the first rank, from primus, first. See per¹ in Appendix.*]

pre·mière (prĭ-mîr′; French prə-myâr′) n. **1.** The first public presentation of a movie, play, or other performance. **2.** The leading lady of a theatrical company. —v. premièred, -mièring, -mières. See Usage note below. —tr. To present the first public performance of. —intr. To have the first public presentation. —adj. Premier; paramount; outstanding. [French, feminine of premier,′ first, chief, PREMIER.]

Usage: Première, as a verb, is unacceptable to 86 per cent of the Usage Panel.

pre·mil·le·nar·i·an (prē′mĭl-ə-nâr′ē-ən) adj. Of or pertaining to premillennialism. —n. A person who believes in premillennialism. Compare **postmillenarian.**

pre·mil·len·ni·al (prē′mĭ-lĕn′ē-əl) adj. Of or happening before the millennium.

pre·mil·len·ni·al·ism (prē′mĭ-lĕn′ē-ə-lĭz′əm) n. The belief that Christ's second coming will immediately precede the millennium. Compare **postmillennialism.** —**pre′mil·len′ni·al·ist** n.

prem·ise (prĕm′ĭs) n. Also **prem·iss. 1. a.** A proposition upon which an argument is based or from which a conclusion is drawn. **b.** Logic. One of the first two propositions (major or minor) of a syllogism, from which the conclusion is drawn. **2.** Plural. Law. The preliminary or explanatory statements or facts of a document, as in an equity bill or deed. **3.** Plural. **a.** Land and the buildings upon it. **b.** A building or part of a building. —v. premised, -ising, -ises. —tr. **1.** To state in advance as introduction or explanation. **2.** To state or assume as a proposition in an argument. —intr. To make a premise. [Middle English premisse, from Old French, from Medieval Latin premissa (prōpositiō), "(proposition) put before," from Latin praemissus, past participle of praemittere, to send ahead : prae, before + mittere, to send (see smeit- in Appendix*).]

pre·mi·um (prē′mē-əm) n. Abbr. **pm., prem. 1.** A prize awarded for a particular act. **2.** Something offered free or at a reduced price as an inducement to buy. **3.** A sum of money or bonus paid in addition to a regular price, salary, or other amount. **4.** The amount paid, often in addition to the interest, to obtain a loan. **5.** The amount paid or payable, often in installments, for an insurance policy. **6.** The amount at which something is valued above its par or nominal value, as money or securities. **7.** Payment for training in a trade or profession. **8.** An unusual or high value: put a premium on honesty and hard work. See Synonyms at **bonus.** —**at a premium.** Above par; more valuable than usual. [Latin praemium, profit derived from booty, "that which is obtained before others" : prae, before + emere, to take (see em- in Appendix*).]

pre·mo·lar (prē-mō′lər) n. One of eight bicuspid teeth located in pairs on each side of the upper and lower jaws, behind the canines and in front of the molars. —**pre·mo′lar** adj.

pre·mo·ni·tion (prē′mə-nĭsh′ən, prĕm′ə-) n. **1.** A warning in advance; forewarning. **2.** A presentiment of the future; a foreboding. [Old French, from Late Latin praemonitiō, from Latin praemonēre, to warn beforehand : prae, before + monēre, to warn (see men-¹ in Appendix*).] —**pre·mon′i·to′ri·ly** (prē-mŏn′ə-tôr′ə-lē, -tōr′ə-lē) adv. —**pre·mon′i·to′ry** adj.

pre·morse (prĭ-môrs′) adj. Biology. Abruptly truncated, as though bitten or broken off. [Latin praemorsus, past participle of praemordēre, to bite off in front : prae, in front + mordēre, to bite (see mer-² in Appendix*).]

pre·mu·ni·tion (prē′myoō-nĭsh′ən) n. Relative immunity to severe infection as a result of inducing an active low-grade infection. [Latin praemūnitiō, fortification beforehand, from praemūnire, to fortify beforehand : prae, before + mūnire, to fortify (see mei-³ in Appendix*).] —**pre·mune′** adj.

pre·na·tal (prē-nāt′l) adj. Existing or taking place prior to birth; preceding birth. —**pre·na′tal·ly** adv.

pre·oc·cu·pan·cy (prē-ŏk′yə-pən-sē) n. **1.** The act or right of taking possession before others; preoccupation. **2.** The state of being preoccupied or engrossed.

pre·oc·cu·pa·tion (prē-ŏk′yə-pā′shən) n. **1.** The state of being preoccupied; absorption of the attention or intellect; engrossment. **2.** Something that preoccupies or engrosses the mind: "Nature was clearly their main preoccupation." (K.M. Sen). **3.** Possession or occupation in advance; preoccupancy.

pre·oc·cu·pied (prē-ŏk′yə-pīd′) adj. **1. a.** Absorbed in thought; engrossed. **b.** Excessively concerned with something; distracted. **2.** Formerly or already occupied. **3.** Already used and therefore unavailable for further use. Said of taxonomic names.

pre·oc·cu·py (prē-ŏk′yə-pī′) tr.v. -pied, -pying, -pies. **1.** To occupy completely the mind or attention of; engross. **2.** To occupy or take possession of in advance or before another. [Latin praeoccupāre : prae, before + occupāre, to OCCUPY.]

pre·op·er·a·tive (prē-ŏp′ər-ə-tĭv, -ŏp′ə-rā′tĭv) adj. Occurring prior to surgery. —**pre·op′er·a·tive·ly** adv.

pre·or·bit·al (prē-ôr′bĭ-təl) adj. Occurring prior to the establishing of an orbit, especially the orbital flight of a spacecraft.

pre·or·dain (prē′ôr-dān′) tr.v. -dained, -daining, -dains. To appoint, decree, or ordain in advance; foreordain. —**pre′or·di·na′tion** (-də-nā′shən) n.

prep (prĕp) adj. Informal. Preparatory: a prep course. —n. **1.** Informal. A preparatory school (see). **2.** British Slang. The preparing of lessons; homework. —intr.v. prepped, prepping, preps. Informal. **1.** To be enrolled in and attend a preparatory school. **2.** To study or train in preparation for something.

prep. 1. preparation; preparatory; prepare. **2.** preposition.

pre·pack·age (prē-păk′ĭj) tr.v. -aged, -aging, -ages. To wrap or package (products) before marketing them.

prep·a·ra·tion (prĕp′ə-rā′shən) n. Abbr. **prep. 1.** The act or process of preparing. **2.** The state of being made ready beforehand; readiness. **3.** Usually plural. Preliminary measures that serve to make ready for something: preparations for the wedding reception. **4.** A substance, such as a medicine, prepared for a particular purpose. **5.** Music. **a.** The anticipation of a dissonant tone by means of its introduction as a consonant tone in the preceding chord. **b.** The tone so used.

pre·par·a·tive (prĭ-păr′ə-tĭv, prĭ-pâr′-) adj. Serving or tending to prepare or make ready. —n. That which prepares for something following. —**pre·par′a·tive·ly** adv.

pre·par·a·tor (prĭ-păr′ə-tər, prĭ-pâr′-) n. A person who prepares specimens for scientific investigation or for display.

pre·par·a·to·ry (prĭ-păr′ə-tôr′ē, -tōr′ē, prĭ-pâr′-) adj. Abbr. **prep. 1.** Serving to make ready or prepare; preliminary; introductory. **2.** Occupied in or pertaining to preparation, especially for admission to college. —**preparatory to.** In preparing for. See Usage note. —**pre·par′a·to′ri·ly** adv.

Usage: Preparatory to, used adverbially, is restricted to situations involving preparation. The phrase is not the mere equivalent of before or prior to, although it is so used informally.

preparatory school. A secondary school, usually private, preparing students for college, or, in Britain, for public school. Also called informally "prep," "prep school."

pre·pare (prĭ-pâr′) v. -pared, -paring, -pares. —tr. **1.** To make ready beforehand for a specific purpose or for some event, occasion, or the like. **2.** To put together or make by combining various elements or ingredients; manufacture; compound. **3.** To fit out; equip: The troops were prepared for service in the Arctic. **4.** Music. To lead up to and soften (a dissonance or its impact) by means of preparation. —intr. To put things or oneself in readiness; get ready. [Middle English preparen, from Old French preparer, from Latin praeparāre, to prepare in advance : prae, before + parāre, to prepare (see per-⁴ in Appendix*).] —**pre·par′ed·ly** adv. —**pre·par′er** n.

pre·par·ed·ness (prĭ-pâr′id-nĭs) n. The state of being prepared; especially, military readiness for war.

pre·pay (prē-pā′) tr.v. -paid, -paying, -pays. To pay or pay for beforehand. —**pre·pay′ment** n.

pre·pense (prĭ-pĕns′) adj. Contemplated or arranged in advance; premeditated. Used chiefly in the phrase malice prepense. [Variant of obsolete prepensed, purpensed, from Middle English purpensen, think of in advance, from Old French pourpenser, to premeditate : pour, forth, before, from Latin prō- + penser, think, from Latin pensāre, frequentative of pendere, to weigh (see spen- in Appendix*).] —**pre·pense′ly** adv.

pre·pon·der·ance (prĭ-pŏn′dər-əns) n. Also **pre·pon·der·an·cy** (-ən-sē). Superiority in weight, quantity, power, importance, or the like.

pre·pon·der·ant (prĭ-pŏn′dər-ənt) adj. Having superior power, force, importance, or the like; predominant. See Synonyms at **dominant.** —**pre·pon′der·ant·ly** adv.

pre·pon·der·ate (prĭ-pŏn′də-rāt′) intr.v. -ated, -ating, -ates. **1.** To exceed something else in weight. **2.** To be greater in power, force, quantity, importance, or the like; predominate: "In balancing his faults with his perfections, the latter seemed rather to preponderate." (Fielding). **3.** Archaic. To be weighed down, as one end of a balance. [Latin praeponderāre : prae, in front of, exceeding + ponderāre, to weigh, from pondus (stem ponder-), weight (see spen- in Appendix*).] —**pre·pon′der·at′ing·ly** adv. —**pre·pon′der·a′tion** n.

prep·o·si·tion (prĕp′ə-zĭsh′ən) n. Abbr. **prep.** Grammar. **1.** In some languages, a word that indicates the relation of a substantive to a verb, an adjective, or another substantive. Some English prepositions are at, by, in, to, from, and with. **2.** Any word or construction of similar function, such as in regard to or concerning. [Middle English preposicioun, from Latin praepositiō (translation of Greek prothesis), from praepōnere (past participle praepositus), to place in front : prae, in front + pōnere, to place (see apo- in Appendix*).]

Usage: There is nothing inherently bad in ending a sentence with a preposition. Such placement may cause awkwardness by giving undue stress to the preposition: the arrogant manner he always spoke with; or it may provide a weak ending: He welcomed the invitation, for Maine was the state he hoped to spend most of his time in. But just as often the final position is the only natural one for the preposition: We have much to be thankful for. Where rearrangement would give an awkward or stilted effect, as in the example immediately preceding, the natural order should be kept.

prep·o·si·tion·al (prĕp′ə-zĭsh′ən-əl) adj. Relating to, composed of, or used as a preposition. —**prep′o·si′tion·al·ly** adv.

prepositional phrase. Grammar. A phrase consisting of a preposition and the noun it governs and having adjectival or adverbial value. In the examples a dress of wool and written in haste, the prepositional phrases are of wool (adjectival value) and in haste (adverbial value).

pre·pos·i·tive (prē-pŏz′ə-tĭv) adj. Grammar. Put before, prefixed. —*n. Grammar.* A word or particle put before another word. [Late Latin *praepositīvus,* from *praepōnere* (past participle *praepositus*), to place in front. See **preposition**.] —**pre·pos'i·tive·ly** *adv.*

pre·pos·sess (prē'pə-zĕs') *tr.v.* **-sessed, -sessing, -sesses. 1.** To preoccupy the mind of to the exclusion of other thoughts or feelings. **2.** To influence beforehand against or in favor of someone or something; prejudice; bias. **3.** To impress favorably in advance.

pre·pos·sess·ing (prē'pə-zĕs'ĭng) *adj.* **1.** Impressing favorably; pleasing. **2.** *Archaic.* Causing prejudice. —**pre'pos·sess'ing·ly** *adv.* —**pre'pos·sess'ing·ness** *n.*

pre·pos·ses·sion (prē'pə-zĕsh'ən) *n.* **1.** A preconception or prejudice. **2.** The state of being preoccupied with thoughts, opinions, or feelings.

pre·pos·ter·ous (prĭ-pŏs'tər-əs) *adj.* Contrary to nature, reason, or common sense; absurd. See Synonyms at **foolish**. [Latin *praeposterus,* "inverted," perverted, absurd : *prae-,* before + *posterus,* coming after, following, next, from *post,* after (see **apo-** in Appendix*).] —**pre·pos'ter·ous·ly** *adv.* —**pre·pos'ter·ous·ness** *n.*

pre·po·ten·cy (prĭ-pō'tən-sē) *n.* The state or condition of being prepotent; predominance.

pre·po·tent (prĭ-pō'tənt) *adj.* Also **pre·po·ten·tial** (prē'pə-tĕn'shəl). Greater in power, influence, or force; predominant. [Middle English, from Latin *praepotēns,* present participle of *praeposse,* to be very powerful : *prae-* (intensifier) + *posse,* to be able or powerful (see **poti-** in Appendix*).] —**pre·po'tent·ly** *adv.*

prep school. *Informal.* A **preparatory school** *(see).*

pre·puce (prē'pyōōs') *n.* **1.** The loose fold of skin that covers the glans of the penis. Also called "foreskin." **2.** A similar structure covering the glans of the clitoris. [Middle English, from Old French, from Latin *praepūtium.* See **pu-**[1] in Appendix.*] —**pre·pu'tial** (prĭ-pyōō'shəl) *adj.*

pre-Raph·a·el·ite (prē-răf'ē-ə-līt', prē-rā'fē-) *n.* A painter or writer belonging to or influenced by the pre-Raphaelite Brotherhood, a society founded in 1848 by Rossetti and others to advance the style and spirit of Italian painting before Raphael. —*adj.* Of, pertaining to, or characteristic of the pre-Raphaelites. —**pre-Raph'a·el·it'ism'** *n.*

pre·req·ui·site (prē-rĕk'wə-zĭt) *adj.* Required as a prior condition to something. See Synonyms at **necessary**. —*n.* That which is prerequisite.

Usage: The appropriate prepositions after this word are *to* (for the adjective) and *of* (for the noun).

pre·rog·a·tive (prĭ-rŏg'ə-tĭv) *n.* **1.** An exclusive right or privilege held by a person or group, especially a hereditary or official right. **2.** Any characteristically exclusive right or privilege. **3.** A natural gift or advantage making one superior. **4.** *Obsolete.* Priority or pre-eminence; superiority. —See Synonyms at **right**. —*adj.* Of, arising from, or exercising a prerogative. [Middle English, from Old French, from Latin *praerogātīva (centuria),* "(century) chosen to vote first," from *praerogātīvus,* asked to vote first, from *praerogāre,* to ask before others : *prae-,* before + *rogāre,* to ask (see **reg-**[1] in Appendix*).]

pres. 1. present (time). **2.** president.

Pres. President.

pres·age (prĕs'ĭj) *n.* **1.** An indication or warning of a future occurrence; omen; portent. **2.** A feeling or intuition of what is going to occur; presentiment; foreboding. **3.** Prophetic significance or meaning. **4.** *Rare.* A prediction. —*v.* **pre·sage** (prĭ-sāj') **-aged, -aging, -ages.** —*tr.* **1.** To indicate or warn of in advance; portend. **2.** To have a presentiment of. **3.** To foretell or predict. —*intr.* To make or utter a prediction. —See Synonyms at **foretell**. [Middle English, from Latin *praesāgium,* foreboding, from *praesāgīre,* to perceive beforehand : *prae-,* before + *sāgīre,* to perceive (see **sāg-** in Appendix*).] —**pre·sage'ful** (prĭ-sāj'fəl) *adj.*

pres·by·o·pi·a (prĕz'bē-ō'pē-ə, prĕs'-) *n.* The inability of the eye to focus sharply on nearby objects, resulting from hardening of the crystalline lens with advancing age. [New Latin : Greek *presbus,* old man (see **per**[1] in Appendix*) + -OPIA.] —**pres'by·op'ic** (-ŏp'ĭk) *adj.*

pres·by·ter (prĕz'bə-tər, prĕs'-) *n. Ecclesiastical.* **1.** In the early Christian church, an elder of the congregation. **2.** In various hierarchical churches, a priest. **3.** *Presbyterian Church.* **a.** A teaching elder. **b.** A ruling elder. [Late Latin, an elder, from Greek *presbuteros,* a priest, "older," comparative of *presbus,* old man. See **per**[1] in Appendix.*]

pres·byt·er·ate (prĕz-bĭt'ər-ĭt, -ə-rāt', prĕs-) *n.* **1.** The office of a presbyter. **2.** The body or order of presbyters.

pres·by·te·ri·al (prĕz'bə-tîr'ē-əl, prĕs'-) *adj.* Of or pertaining to a presbyter or the presbytery. —**pres'by·te'ri·al·ly** *adv.*

pres·by·te·ri·an (prĕz'bə-tîr'ē-ən, prĕs'-) *adj.* **1.** Of or pertaining to ecclesiastical government by presbyters. **2.** *Capital* **P.** Of or pertaining to a Presbyterian Church. —*n. Capital* **P.** A member or adherent of a Presbyterian Church. —**pres'by·te'ri·an·ism'** *n.*

Presbyterian Church. Any of various Protestant churches governed by presbyters and traditionally Calvinist in doctrine.

pres·by·ter·y (prĕz'bə-tĕr'ē, prĕs'-) *n., pl.* **-ies. 1.** *Presbyterian Church.* **a.** A court composed of the ministers and representative elders of a particular locality. **b.** The district represented by this court. **2.** Presbyters collectively. **3.** Government of a church by presbyters. **4.** The section of the church reserved for the clergy. **5.** *Roman Catholic Church.* The residence of a priest. [Middle English *presbytory,* from Late Latin *presbyterium,* a council of presbyters, from Greek *presbuterion,* from *presbuteros,* priest, PRESBYTER.]

pre·school (prē'skōōl') *adj.* Of or pertaining to a child of nursery-school age. —**pre·school'er** *n.*

pre·sci·ence (prē'shē-əns, prĕsh'ē-) *n.* Knowledge of actions or events before they occur; foreknowledge; foresight.

pre·sci·ent (prē'shē-ənt, prĕsh'ē-) *adj.* **1.** Of or pertaining to prescience. **2.** Possessing prescience. [Latin *praesciēns,* present participle of *praescīre,* to know beforehand : *prae-,* before + *scīre,* to know (see **skei-** in Appendix*).] —**pre'sci·ent·ly** *adv.*

pre·scind (prĭ-sĭnd') *v.* **-scinded, -scinding, -scinds.** —*tr.* To separate or divide in thought; consider individually. Used with *from.* —*intr.* To withdraw one's attention. Used with *from.* [Latin *praescindere,* to cut off in front : *prae-,* in front + *scindere,* to cut off (see **skei-** in Appendix*).]

Pres·cott (prĕs'kət), **William.** 1726–1795. Commander of the Continentals at Bunker Hill. Grandfather of William Hickling Prescott.

Pres·cott (prĕs'kət), **William Hickling.** 1796–1859. American historian of Spain and the Spanish conquests in the Americas. Grandson of William Prescott.

pre·scribe (prĭ-skrīb') *v.* **-scribed, -scribing, -scribes.** —*tr.* **1.** To set down as a rule or guide; ordain; enjoin. **2.** *Medicine.* To order or recommend the use of (a drug or other therapy). —*intr.* **1.** To establish rules, laws, or directions. **2.** *Medicine.* To order or recommend a remedy or treatment. **3.** *Law.* **a.** To assert a right or title to something on the grounds of prescription. **b.** To become invalidated or unenforceable by the process of prescription. [Middle English *prescriben,* to hold by right of prescription, from Medieval Latin *prescrībere,* to claim by such right, from Latin *praescrībere,* to write at the beginning, prescribe : *prae-,* before, in front + *scrībere,* to write (see **skeri-** in Appendix*).] —**pre·scrib'er** *n.*

pre·script (prē'skrĭpt') *n.* Something prescribed, especially a rule or regulation of conduct. —*adj.* (prē'skrĭpt, prĭ-skrĭpt'). Established as a rule; set down; prescribed. [Latin *praescriptum,* from *praescrībere* (past participle *praescriptus*), PRESCRIBE.]

pre·scrip·ti·ble (prĭ-skrĭp'tə-bəl) *adj.* Capable of, requiring, or derived from prescription. —**pre·scrip'ti·bil'i·ty** *n.*

pre·scrip·tion (prĭ-skrĭp'shən) *n.* **1. a.** The act of prescribing. **b.** That which is prescribed. **2.** *Medicine.* **a.** A written instruction by a physician for the preparation and administration of a medicine. **b.** A prescribed medicine. **c.** An ophthalmologist's or optometrist's written instruction for the grinding of corrective lenses. **3.** A formula directing the preparation of anything. **4.** *Law.* **a.** The process of acquiring title to property by reason of uninterrupted possession of specified duration. Also called "positive prescription." **b.** The limitation of time beyond which an action, debt, or crime is no longer valid or enforceable. Also called "negative prescription." [Middle English *prescripcion,* from Old French *prescription,* from Latin *praescriptiō,* a writing in front, from *praescrībere,* PRESCRIBE.]

pre·scrip·tive (prĭ-skrĭp'tĭv) *adj.* **1.** Sanctioned or authorized by long-standing custom or usage. **2.** Making or giving injunctions, directions, laws, or rules. **3.** *Law.* Acquired by or based upon uninterrupted possession. —**pre·scrip'tive·ly** *adv.*

pre·sell (prē'sĕl') *tr.v.* **-sold** (-sōld'), **-selling, -sells.** To promote (a product not yet on the market).

pres·ence (prĕz'əns) *n.* **1.** The state or fact of being present. **2.** Immediate proximity in time or space. **3. a.** The area immediately surrounding a great personage, especially a sovereign granting audience. **b.** A person who is present. **4.** A person's manner of carrying himself; bearing. **5.** A supernatural influence felt to be nearby. —See Synonyms at **bearing**.

presence of mind. Ability to think and act efficiently, especially in an emergency.

pres·ent[1] (prĕz'ənt) *n.* **1.** A moment or period in time perceptible as intermediate between past and future; now. **2.** *Abbr.* **pr., pres.** *Grammar.* **a.** The present tense. **b.** A verb form in the present tense. **3.** *Plural. Law.* The document or instrument in question: *be it known by these presents.* —*adj.* **1.** Being, pertaining to, or occurring at a moment or period in time considered as the present. **2.** Being at hand. **3.** *Obsolete.* Alert to circumstances; attentive. **4.** *Obsolete.* Readily available; immediate. **5.** *Abbr.* **pr., pres.** *Grammar.* Denoting a verb tense or form that expresses current time. [Middle English, from Old French, from Latin *praesēns,* present participle of *praeesse,* to be before one, be present : *prae-,* in front of + *esse,* to be (see **es-** in Appendix*).]

pre·sent[2] (prĭ-zĕnt') *tr.v.* **-sented, -senting, -sents. 1. a.** To introduce, especially with formal ceremony: *"This Brazilian king . . . was brought up to London and presented to King Henry VIII"* (Richard Hakluyt). **b.** To introduce (a girl) to society with conventional ceremony: *"she also was presented that year at the International Debutante Ball"* (New York Times). **2.** To bring before the public: *present a play.* **3. a.** To make a gift or award of: *present a medal.* **b.** To make a gift to; bestow formally: *present the college an endowment.* **4.** To offer to view; display: *present one's credentials.* **5.** To offer for consideration. **6.** To salute with or aim (a weapon). **7.** *Ecclesiastical.* To recommend (a clergyman) for a benefice. **8.** *Law.* **a.** To offer to a legislature or court for consideration. **b.** To bring a charge or indictment against. —See Synonyms at **offer**. —*n.* **pres·ent** (prĕz'ənt). Something presented; a gift. [Middle English *presenten,* from Old French *presenter,* from Latin *praesentāre,* from *praesēns,* PRESENT (adjective).] —**pre·sent'er** *n.*

pre·sent·a·ble (prĭ-zĕn'tə-bəl) *adj.* **1.** Capable of being given, displayed, or offered. **2.** Fit for introduction to others. —**pre·sent'a·bil'i·ty, pre·sent'a·ble·ness** *n.* —**pre·sent'a·bly** *adv.*

pres·en·ta·tion (prĕz'ən-tā'shən, prē'zən-) *n.* **1. a.** The act of presenting or offering for acceptance or approval. **b.** The state of being so presented. **2.** A performance, as of a drama. **3.** That which is presented, such as a gift. **4. a.** A formal introduction. **b.** A social debut. **5.** *Ecclesiastical.* The act or right of naming a clergyman to a benefice. **6.** The process of offering for consideration. **7.** *Medicine.* The position of the fetus in the uterus at birth, with respect to the mouth of the uterus. —**pres′en·ta′tion·al** *adj.*

pre·sent·a·tive (prĭ-zĕn′tə-tĭv) *adj.* **1.** Having the capacity or function of bringing an idea or image to mind. **2.** *Philosophy & Psychology.* **a.** Perceived or capable of being perceived directly rather than through association. **b.** Having the ability to so perceive. **3.** *Ecclesiastical.* Capable of naming or of being named to a benefice. —**pre·sent′a·tive·ness** *n.*

pres·ent-day (prĕz′ənt-dā′) *adj.* Current.

pres·en·tee (prĕz′ən-tē′) *n.* **1.** A person who is presented. **2.** A person to whom something is given.

pre·sen·tient (prē-sĕn′shənt, -shē-ənt) *adj.* Having a presentiment or presentiments. [Latin *praesentiēns,* present participle of *praesentīre,* to have a presentiment. See **presentiment.**]

pre·sen·ti·ment (prĭ-zĕn′tə-mənt) *n.* A sense of something about to occur; premonition. See Synonyms at **apprehension.** [Obsolete French, from Old French *presentir,* to have a presentiment, from Latin *praesentīre,* to perceive beforehand : *prae-,* before + *sentīre,* to perceive (see **sent-** in Appendix*).]

pres·ent·ly (prĕz′ənt-lē) *adv.* **1.** In a short time; soon; directly: *She will arrive presently.* **2.** At this time or period; now: *He is presently staying with us.* See Usage note below. **3.** *Obsolete.* At once; immediately. —See Synonyms at **immediately.**

Usage: In modern usage, *presently* is best restricted to *in a short time,* a sense approved by 73 per cent of the Usage Panel. However, 49 per cent accept the earlier sense of *at this time.*

pre·sent·ment (prĭ-zĕnt′mənt) *n.* **1.** The act of presenting; presentation. **2.** Something presented, such as a picture or exhibition. **3.** *Law.* **a.** The act of submitting or presenting a formal statement of a legal matter to a court or authorized person. **b.** The report written by a grand jury concerning an offense, based on the jury's own knowledge and observation. **4.** *Commerce.* The presenting of a bill or note for payment.

present participle. *Grammar.* A participle expressing present action, in English formed by the infinitive plus *-ing* and used: **1.** To express present action in relation to the time indicated by the finite verb in its clause. **2.** To form progressive tenses with modal auxiliaries. **3.** To function as a verbal adjective.

present perfect. *Grammar.* **1.** The verb tense expressing action completed at the present time. This tense is formed in English by combining the present tense of *have* with a past participle: *He has spoken.* **2.** A verb in this tense.

present tense. *Grammar.* The verb tense expressing action in the present time: *She sews.*

pre·serv·a·tive (prĭ-zûr′və-tĭv) *adj.* Tending to preserve or capable of preserving. —*n.* Something used to preserve; especially, a chemical used in foods to inhibit spoilage.

pre·serve (prĭ-zûrv′) *v.* **-served, -serving, -serves.** —*tr.* **1.** To protect from injury, peril, or other adversity; maintain in safety. **2.** To keep in perfect or unaltered condition; maintain in an unchanged form. **3.** To keep or maintain intact: *"the two women did what they could to preserve a decent dignity"* (Edith Wharton). **4.** To prepare (food) for future use as by canning or salting. **5.** To prevent (organic bodies) from decaying or spoiling. **6.** To keep or protect (game or fish) for one's private hunting or fishing. —*intr.* **1.** To treat fruit or other foods so as to prevent decay. **2.** To maintain a private area stocked with game or fish. —See Synonyms at **defend.** —*n.* **1.** Something that acts to preserve; a preservative. **2.** *Often plural.* Fruit cooked with sugar to protect against decay or fermentation; jam or confiture. **3.** An area maintained for the protection of wildlife or natural resources. **4.** Something considered restricted to the use of certain persons: *Ancient Greek is the preserve of scholars.* [Middle English *preserven,* from Old French *preserver,* from Medieval Latin *praeservāre,* "to guard beforehand" : Latin *prae-,* before + *servāre,* to keep, guard (see **ser-**[1] in Appendix*).] —**pre·serv′a·bil′i·ty** *n.* —**pre·serv′a·ble** *adj.* —**pres′er·va′tion** (prĕz′ər-vā′shən) *n.* —**pre·serv′er** *n.*

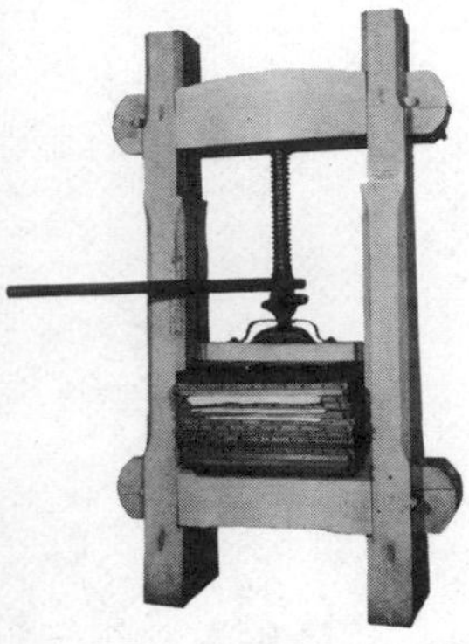

press[1]
Shaker laundry press

pre·shrunk (prē′shrŭngk′) *adj.* Also **pre-shrunk.** Shrunk during manufacture to minimize subsequent shrinkage.

pre·side (prĭ-zīd′) *intr.v.* **-sided, -siding, -sides.** **1.** To hold the position of authority; act as chairman or president. **2.** To possess or exercise authority or control. **3.** *Music.* To be the featured instrumental performer. [French *presider,* from Latin *praesidēre,* "to sit in front of," superintend : *prae-,* before + *sedēre,* to sit (see **sed-**[1] in Appendix*).] —**pre·sid′er** *n.*

pres·i·den·cy (prĕz′ə-dən-sē, -dĕn′sē) *n., pl.* **-cies.** **1.** The office, function, or term of a president. **2.** *Often capital* **P.** The office of president of a republic, especially of President of the United States. **3.** *Often capital* **P.** Any of the three original provinces (Bengal, Bombay, and Madras) of British India. **4.** *Mormon Church.* **a.** A governing body on a local level consisting of three men. **b.** *Often capital* **P.** The chief administrative body of the church.

pres·i·dent (prĕz′ə-dənt, -dĕnt′) *n. Abbr.* **p., P., pres., Pres.** **1.** One appointed or elected to preside over an organized body of people, as an assembly or meeting. **2.** *Often capital* **P.** The chief executive of a republic, especially of the United States. **3.** The chief officer of a branch of government, a corporation, a board of trustees, a university, or any similar body. [Middle English, from Old French, from Latin *praesidens,* present participle of *praesidēre,* PRESIDE.] —**pres′i·dent·ship′** *n.*

pres·i·dent-e·lect (prĕz′ə-dənt-ĭ-lĕkt′) *n.* A person who has been elected president but has not yet begun his term of office.

pres·i·den·tial (prĕz′ə-dĕn′shəl) *adj.* **1.** *Sometimes capital* **P.** Of or relating to a president or presidency: *A U.S. Presidential candidate.* **2.** Providing for a president elected independently of the legislature. —**pres′i·den′tial·ly** *adv.*

president pro tem·po·re (prō tĕm′pə-rē). Also *informal* **president pro tem** (prō tĕm′). The senator who presides over the Senate in the absence of the Vice President.

pre·sid·i·al (prĭ-sĭd′ē-əl) *adj.* Also **pre·sid·i·ar·y** (prĭ-sĭd′ē-ĕr′ē). Of, pertaining to, or possessing a presidio.

pre·si·di·o (prĭ-sē′dē-ō′, -sĭd′ē-ō′) *n., pl.* **-os.** A garrison; military post; especially, a fortress of the kind established in the Southwest by the Spanish to protect their holdings and missions. [Spanish, from Latin *praesidium,* garrison, fortification, from *praesidēre,* "to sit in front of," guard, PRESIDE.]

pre·sid·i·um (prĭ-sĭd′ē-əm) *n.* **1.** Any of various permanent executive committees in Communist countries having power to act for a larger governing body. **2.** *Capital* **P.** A committee of the Supreme Soviet, headed by the premier, and constituting the highest policy-making body of the Soviet Union. [Russian *prezidium,* from Latin *praesidium.* See **presidio.**]

pre·sig·ni·fy (prē-sĭg′nə-fī′) *tr.v.* **-fied, -fying, -fies.** To betoken or signify beforehand; prefigure; foreshadow.

press[1] (prĕs) *v.* **pressed, pressing, presses.** —*tr.* **1.** To exert steady weight or force against; bear down on. **2. a.** To squeeze the juice or other contents from. **b.** To extract (juice, for example) by squeezing or compressing. **3. a.** To make compact or reshape by applying steady force. **b.** To iron, as clothing. **4.** To clasp or embrace closely. **5.** To seek to influence as by insistent arguments; entreat insistently. **6.** To attempt to force to action; urge on; spur. **7.** To place in trying or constraining circumstances; distress; harass: *"pressed constantly by the hard daily compulsion of material wants"* (Matthew Arnold). **8.** To lay stress upon; emphasize. **9.** To advance or carry on vigorously: *"far from backing down, he pressed the attack"* (Justin Kaplan). **10.** To put forward importunately or insistently. —*intr.* **1.** To exert force or pressure. **2.** To weigh heavily, as on the mind. **3.** To advance eagerly; push forward. **4.** To require haste; be urgent. **5.** To iron clothes or other material. **6.** To assemble closely and in large numbers; crowd. **7.** To employ urgent persuasion or entreaty; ask earnestly or persistently. —See Synonyms at **urge.** —*n.* **1.** Any of various machines or devices that apply pressure. **2.** Any of various machines used for printing; a **printing press** *(see).* **3.** A place or establishment where matter is printed. **4.** The method, art, or business of printing. **5. a.** Printed matter as a whole, especially newspapers and periodicals. **b.** The people involved with such publications, as editors and reporters. **c.** The matter dealt with in such publications, as news and criticism. **6.** The act of gathering in large numbers or of pushing forward. **7.** A large gathering; throng: *"A great, slow-moving press of men and women in evening dress filled the vestibule"* (Frank Norris). **8. a.** The act of applying pressure. **b.** The state of being pressed. **9.** The haste or urgency of business or affairs. **10.** The set of proper creases in a garment or fabric, formed by ironing. **11.** An upright closet or case used for storing clothing, books, or other articles. [Middle English *pressen,* from Old French *presser,* from Latin *pressāre,* frequentative of *premere* (past participle *pressus*), to press. See **per-**[6] in Appendix.*]

press[2] (prĕs) *tr.v.* **pressed, pressing, presses.** **1.** To force into service in the army or navy; impress. **2.** To use in a manner different from the usual or intended. —*n.* **1.** Conscription or impressment into service, especially into the navy. **2.** An official warrant for impressing men. [Alteration (by association with PRESS, to apply pressure, compel) of earlier *prest,* to give press money to (recruits), from Middle English *prest,* press money, from Old French, "loan," from *prester,* to afford, lend, from Medieval Latin *praestāre,* from Latin, to place something at someone's disposal, furnish, from *praestō*†, at hand.]

press agent. *Abbr.* **P.A.** A person employed to arrange advertising and publicity for an actor, theater, business, or the like.

press agency. **News agency** *(see).*

press association. **News agency** *(see).*

press·board (prĕs′bôrd′, -bōrd′) *n.* **1.** A heavy glazed paper or pasteboard used to cover the platen or cylinder of a printing press. **2.** A small ironing board.

press box. A section for reporters, as in a stadium.

Press·burg. The German name for **Bratislava.**

press conference. An interview held for newsmen by a political figure or celebrity.

press·er (prĕs′ər) *n.* **1.** A person who presses clothes. **2.** Any of various devices that apply pressure to a product in manufacturing or canning.

press gang. Also **press-gang.** A company under an officer detailed to press men into military or naval service.

press·ing (prĕs′ĭng) *adj.* **1.** Demanding immediate attention; urgent: *a pressing need.* **2.** Importunate; insistent: *a pressing invitation.* —See Synonyms at **urgent.** —**press′ing·ly** *adv.*

press·man (prĕs′mən, -măn′) *n., pl.* **-men** (-mĭn, -mĕn′). **1.** A printing press operator. **2.** *British.* A newspaperman.

press·mark (prĕs′märk′) *n.* **1.** *Library Service.* A notation in or on a book indicating where it should be placed in a library. **2.** *Printing.* A notation or figure in the margin of a printed sheet indicating the press upon which it was printed.

press of sail. *Nautical.* The greatest amount of sail that a ship can carry safely. Also called "press of canvas."

pres·sor (prĕs′ôr′, -ər) *adj.* Causing an increase in blood pressure. [From Latin *premere* (stem *press-*), to PRESS.]

press release. An announcement of an event, performance, or other news or publicity item issued to the press.

press·room (prĕs′ro͞om′, -ro͝om′) *n.* The room in a printing or newspaper publishing establishment that contains the presses.
press·run (prĕs′rŭn′) *n.* The specific number of copies printed during a continuous operation of a printing press.
press secretary. A person who manages the public affairs and press conferences of a public figure.
pres·sure (prĕsh′ər) *n.* **1. a.** The act of pressing. **b.** The condition of being pressed. **2.** The application of continuous force by one body upon another that it is touching; compression. **3.** *Abbr.* **P** *Physics.* Force applied over a surface, measured as force per unit of area. **4.** A constraining influence upon the mind or will, as a moral force. **5.** Urgent claim or demand; harassment: *under the pressure of business.* **6.** A burdensome, distressing, or weighty condition; oppression, as of grief. **7.** *Obsolete.* A mark made by application of force or weight; impression. —*tr.v.* **pressured, -suring, -sures.** To force, as by overpowering influence or persuasion. [From Latin *pressūra,* from *premere,* to PRESS.]
pressure cabin. A pressurized section of an aircraft.
pressure cooker. An airtight metal pot that uses steam under pressure at high temperature to cook food quickly.
pressure gauge. 1. A device for measuring fluid pressure. **2.** A device for measuring the pressure of explosions.
pressure group. Any group that exerts pressure on legislators and public opinion to advance or protect its interests.
pressure suit. A garment that is worn in high-altitude aircraft or in spacecraft to compensate for low-pressure conditions. Compare **G-suit.**
pres·sur·ize (prĕsh′ə-rīz′) *tr.v.* **-ized, -izing, -izes. 1.** To maintain normal air pressure in (an enclosure, as an aircraft or submarine). **2.** To put (gas or liquid) under a greater than normal pressure. —**pres′sur·i·za′tion** *n.*
press·work (prĕs′wûrk′) *n.* **1.** The directing or running of a printing press. **2.** The matter printed by a printing press.
Pres·ter John (prĕs′tər jŏn′). A legendary medieval Christian priest and king thought to have reigned over a Christian kingdom in the Far East or in Ethiopia. [Middle English *prestre,* priest, from Old French, from Late Latin *presbyter.* See **priest.**]
pres·ti·dig·i·ta·tion (prĕs′tə-dĭj′ĭ-tā′shən) *n.* Manual skill and dexterity in the execution of tricks; sleight of hand. [French, from *prestidigitateur,* juggler, probably alteration (by association with *preste,* nimble, and Latin *digitus,* finger) of *prestigiateur,* from Latin *praestigiātor,* from *praestigiae,* juggler's tricks. See **prestige.**] —**pres′ti·dig′i·ta·tor** (-dĭj′ĭ-tā′tər) *n.*
pres·tige (prĕ-stēzh′, -stēj′) *n.* **1.** Prominence or influential status achieved through success, renown, or wealth. **2.** The power to command admiration in a group; coveted status: *His new position has much prestige.* —*adj.* Possessing or conferring prestige: *the prestige schools of the Ivy League.* [French, originally "illusion brought on by magic," phantasmagoria, from Latin *praestigiae,* "juggler's tricks," illusions, alteration of *praestrigiae* (unattested), "blindfold," tricks, from *praestringere,* to bind up, blind: *prae-,* before + *stringere,* to bind, tighten (see **streig-** in Appendix*).] —**pres·tig′ious** (prĕ-stĭj′əs, -stē′jəs) *adj.* —**pres·tig′ious·ly** *adv.* —**pres·tig′ious·ness** *n.*
pres·tis·si·mo (prĕ-stĭs′ə-mō′) *adv. Music.* At as fast a tempo as possible. Used as a direction. —*n. Music.* A section or passage to be played in this manner. [Italian, superlative of PRESTO.] —**pres·tis′si·mo′** *adj.*
pres·to (prĕs′tō) *adv.* **1.** *Music.* In rapid tempo. Used as a direction. **2.** Suddenly; at once. —*n. Music.* A section or passage to be played presto. [Italian, from Latin *praestus,* ready, from *praestō*†, at hand.] —**pres′to** *adj.*
Pres·ton (prĕs′tən). A county borough of Lancashire, in northwestern England east of Blackpool. Population, 109,000.
pre·sum·a·ble (prĭ-zo͞o′mə-bəl) *adj.* Capable of being presumed or taken for granted; reasonable as a supposition; probable. —**pre·sum′a·bly** *adv.*
pre·sume (prĭ-zo͞om′) *v.* **-sumed, -suming, -sumes.** —*tr.* **1.** To take for granted; assume to be true in the absence of proof to the contrary. **2.** To give reasonable evidence for assuming; appear to prove. **3.** To engage oneself in, without authority or permission; venture; dare. Often used with an infinitive. —*intr.* **1.** To act overconfidently; take liberties. **2.** To take unwarranted advantage of something. Used with *on* or *upon.* —See Synonyms at **conjecture.** [Middle English *presumen,* from Old French *presumer,* from Late Latin *praesūmere,* to venture, from Latin, "to take in advance," presuppose, foresee, assume : *prae-,* before + *sūmere,* to take (see **em-** in Appendix*).] —**pre·sum′ed·ly** (-zo͞o′mĭd-lē) *adv.* —**pre·sum′er** *n.*
Synonyms: *presume, presuppose, suppose, postulate, assume, posit.* These words signify the step of inferring certain things to be true as a probability, hypothesis, or convenience, sometimes without full justification. To *presume* something is to guess it as being reasonable or possible beforehand or without full knowledge, but it may imply an unwarranted conclusion and is often used in a questioning tone of voice: *I presume you're going?* It may indicate to take advantage of: *He presumed upon my good nature.* To *suppose* something is more hesitantly and objectively to subscribe to its likelihood, sometimes out of seeming disinterestedness. *Presuppose* implies a working or assumptive speculation about something based on some preceding evidence or condition. *Postulate* has a more exact, philosophical usage and means to assert or construe a hypothetical proposal formally and without proof: *He postulated a complete lie.* To *assume* something is to take it for granted without proof but sometimes on safe, if incomplete, grounds: *You can only assume so much.* To *posit* something is to affirm or present it flatly for consideration. It is close to *postulate* in meaning but is more decisive in spirit: *Posit a sound proof of the Devil's existence.*
pre·sump·tion (prĭ-zŭmp′shən) *n.* **1.** Behavior or language that is boldly arrogant or offensive; effrontery. **2.** The act of presuming or accepting as true. **3.** Acceptance or belief based on reasonable evidence; an assumption or supposition. **4.** A condition or basis for accepting or presuming. **5.** *Law.* An inference as to the truth of an allegation or proposition, based on probable reasoning, in the absence of, or prior to, actual proof or disproof. [Middle English *presumpcion,* from Old French, from Late Latin *praesumptiō,* audacity, from Latin, a taking for granted, assumption, from *praesūmere,* PRESUME.]
pre·sump·tive (prĭ-zŭmp′tĭv) *adj.* **1.** Providing a reasonable basis for belief or acceptance. **2.** Founded on probability or presumption: *an heir presumptive.* —**pre·sump′tive·ly** *adv.*
pre·sump·tu·ous (prĭ-zŭmp′cho͞o-əs) *adj.* **1.** Excessively forward or confident; arrogant: *"those presumptuous souls who wanted to walk on the pavements of Heaven"* (Thornton Wilder). **2.** *Obsolete.* Presumptive. [Middle English, from Old French *presumptueux,* from Late Latin *praesumptuōsus,* audacious, from *praesumptiō,* audacity, PRESUMPTION.] —**pre·sump′tu·ous·ly** *adv.* —**pre·sump′tu·ous·ness** *n.*
pre·sup·pose (prē′sə-pōz′) *tr.v.* **-posed, -posing, -poses. 1.** To assume or suppose in advance; take for granted. **2.** To require or involve necessarily as an antecedent condition: *"Thoreau's experiment actually presupposed all that complicated civilization which it theoretically abjured."* (James Russell Lowell). —See Synonyms at **presume.** [Middle English *presupposen,* from Old French *presupposer,* from Medieval Latin *praesuppōnere* : *prae-,* before + *suppōnere,* to SUPPOSE.] —**pre′sup·po·si′tion** (-sŭp-ə-zĭsh′ən) *n.*
pret. preterit.
pre·tend (prĭ-tĕnd′) *v.* **-tended, -tending, -tends.** —*tr.* **1.** To affect; feign: *"All princes pretend a regard to the rights of other princes"* (Hume). **2.** To claim or allege insincerely or falsely; profess: *"He had bursitis . . . but they pretended he was in perfect health."* (John O'Hara). **3.** To represent fictitiously in play; make believe. **4.** To take upon oneself; venture: *"Whether my bullets did any execution or not I cannot pretend to say."* (W.H. Hudson). —*intr.* **1.** To feign an action, character, or the like, as in play. **2.** To put forward a claim. Used with *to.* [Middle English *pretenden,* from Latin *praetendere,* "to stretch forth," hold out as a pretext, assert : *prae-,* before + *tendere,* to stretch (see **ten-** in Appendix*).]
Synonyms: *pretend, feign, dissemble, fake, simulate.* These all mean to assume falsely an identity, manner, or skill. *Pretend* is mild in force, implying no evil end, but it can suggest a vain or transparent attempt to fool others. *Feign* implies more strongly the false assumption of some condition so as to evade the responsibilities incurred by being sincere: *She feigned illness and left early. Dissemble* suggests artful deception in speech or manner to conceal one's true purposes or feelings. *Fake,* an informal term, suggests counterfeiting, proceeding as often from ineptitude as from deceitfulness. *Simulate* emphasizes misleading appearance rather than deceptive action, and implies the taking on of a false aspect that closely resembles reality.
pre·tend·ed (prĭ-tĕn′dĭd) *adj.* **1.** Reputed or asserted, alleged. **2.** False; untrue; feigned. —**pre·tend′ed·ly** *adv.*
pre·tend·er (prĭ-tĕn′dər) *n.* **1.** One who simulates, pretends, or alleges falsely; a hypocrite or dissembler. **2. a.** One who sets forth a claim. **b.** A claimant to a throne. **3.** *Capital* **P.** *British History.* James Edward **Stuart** *(see),* the Old Pretender, and Charles Edward **Stuart** *(see),* the Young Pretender.
pre·tense (prē′tĕns′, prĭ-tĕns′) *n.* Also *chiefly British* **pre·tence. 1.** The act of pretending; a false appearance or action intended to deceive. **2.** A false or studied show of something; an affectation. **3.** A false reason or excuse; pretext. **4.** Something imagined or pretended; a piece of make-believe. **5.** A mere show without reality; an outward appearance. Used with *at: "There was some pretence at local government."* (C.L.R. James). **6.** A right asserted with or without foundation; a claim. **7.** Ostentation; pretentiousness. [Middle English, from Norman French *pretensse,* from Medieval Latin *praetensa* (unattested), from Latin *praetendere,* to PRETEND.]
pre·ten·sion (prĭ-tĕn′shən) *n.* **1.** A specious allegation; a pretext. **2.** A claim to something, such as a privilege, right, or other position of distinction or importance. **3.** The advancing of a claim. **4.** Pretentiousness; ostentation; display.
pre·ten·tious (prĭ-tĕn′shəs) *adj.* **1.** Claiming or demanding a position of distinction or merit, especially when unjustified. **2.** Making an extravagant outer show; ostentatious. —**pre·ten′tious·ly** *adv.* —**pre·ten′tious·ness** *n.*
pret·er·it, pret·er·ite (prĕt′ər-ĭt) *adj. Abbr.* **pret., pt.** *Grammar.* Denoting the verb tense that expresses or describes a past or completed action or condition. —*n. Abbr.* **pret., pt.** *Grammar.* **1.** The verb form expressing or describing a past or completed action or condition; past tense. **2.** A verb in this form. [Middle English, past, past tense, from Old French, from Latin *praeteritus,* gone by, past, past participle of *praeterīre,* to go by, pass : *praeter,* beyond, comparative of *prae-,* before (see **per**[1] in Appendix*) + *īre,* to go (see **ei-**[1] in Appendix*).]
pret·er·i·tion (prĕt′ə-rĭsh′ən) *n.* **1.** The act of passing by, disregarding, or omitting. **2.** *Law.* The neglect of a testator to mention a legal heir or heirs in his will. **3.** *Theology.* The Calvinist doctrine that God neglected to designate those who would be damned, positively determining only the elect. [Late Latin *praeteritiō,* from Latin *praeterīre,* to go by, pass over. See **preterit.**]
pre·ter·i·tive (prĭ-tĕr′ə-tĭv) *adj. Grammar.* Limited to a past tense or past tenses. Said of certain verbs.

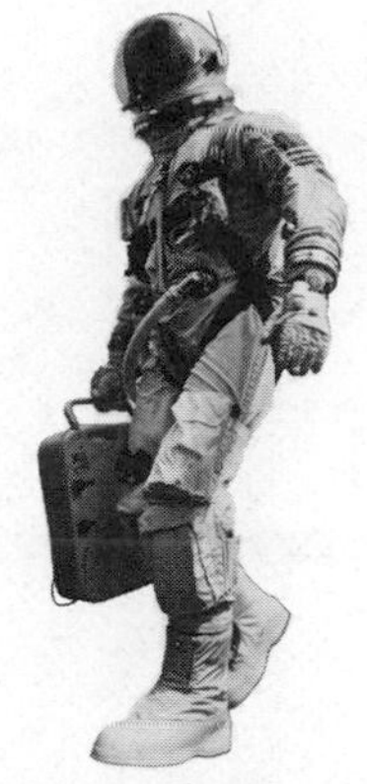

pressure suit
Astronaut John W. Young, July 1966

pre·ter·mit (prē′tər-mĭt′) *tr.v.* **-mitted, -mitting, -mits.** **1.** To disregard intentionally, or allow to pass unnoticed or unmentioned. **2.** To fail to do or include; omit; neglect. [Latin *praetermittere*, to let go by : *praeter*, beyond (see **preterit**) + *mittere*, to let go (see **smeit-** in Appendix*).] **—pre′ter·mis′sion** (-mĭsh′ən) *n.* **—pre′ter·mit′ter** *n.*

pre·ter·nat·u·ral (prē′tər-năch′ər-əl) *adj.* **1.** Out of or beyond the normal course of nature; differing from the natural; abnormal; exceptional: *"He bore a preternatural resemblance to his caricatures in the evening papers."* (Evelyn Waugh). **2.** Transcending the natural or material order, often connoting divinity; supernatural. [Medieval Latin *praeternātūrālis*, from Latin *praeter nātūram*, beyond nature : *praeter*, beyond (see **preterit**) + accusative of *nātūra*, NATURE.] **—pre′ter·nat′u·ral·ism** *n.* **—pre′ter·nat′u·ral·ly** *adv.* **—pre′ter·nat′u·ral·ness** *n.*

pre·test (prē′tĕst′) *n.* **1. a.** A test given to determine whether a class is sufficiently prepared for a new course. **b.** The condition of a sample prior to experimental modification. **2.** The advance testing of something, such as a questionnaire, product, or idea. *—v.* (prē-tĕst′) **pretested, -testing, -tests.** *—tr.* To subject to a pretest. *—intr.* To conduct a pretest.

pre·text (prē′tĕkst′) *n.* An ostensible or professed purpose; pretense; excuse. *—tr.v.* **pretexted, -texting, -texts.** To allege as an excuse: *"I shall pretext a catastrophe."* (Aldous Huxley). [Latin *praetextus*, outward show, pretense, from past participle of *praetexere*, to weave in front, cloak, disguise, pretend : *prae-*, before + *texere*, to weave (see **teks-** in Appendix*).]

Pre·to·ri·a (prĭ-tôr′ē-ə, -tōr′ē-ə). The administrative capital of the Republic of South Africa, in central Transvaal, 35 miles northeast of Johannesburg. Population, 423,000.

Pre·to·ri·us (prĭ-tôr′ē-əs, -tōr′ē-əs), **Marthinus Wessels.** 1819–1901. First president of the Republic of South Africa.

pret·ti·fy (prĭt′ĭ-fī′) *tr.v.* **-fied, -fying, -fies.** To make pretty. **—pret′ti·fi·ca′tion** *n.* **—pret′ti·fi′er** *n.*

pret·ty (prĭt′ē) *adj.* **-tier, -tiest.** **1.** Pleasing or attractive in a graceful or delicate way. **2.** Excellent; fine; good. Often used ironically: *"This is a pretty time to be coming to your sewing class, I must say."* (Lillian Hellman). **3.** *Archaic.* Elegant; fine. **4.** Effeminate; foppish. **5.** *Informal.* Considerable in size or extent: *a pretty fortune.* —See Synonyms at **beautiful.** *—adv.* **1.** To a fair degree; somewhat; moderately: *He is a pretty good student.* **2.** *Regional.* Prettily; pleasingly. **—sitting pretty.** *Informal.* In favorable circumstances; in a good position. *—n., pl.* **pretties.** One that is pleasing or pretty. *—tr.v.* **prettied, -tying, -ties.** *Informal.* To make pretty. Used with *up: pretty up the house.* [Middle English *prety, praty*, clever, skillfully made, fine, "pretty," Old English *prættig*, cunning, tricky, from *prætt*, trick, wile, craft, from West Germanic *pratt-*† (unattested).] **—pret′ti·ly** *adv.* **—pret′ti·ness** *n.*

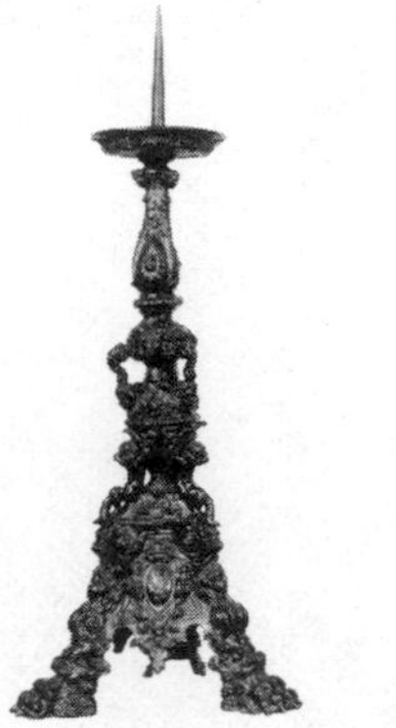

pricket
Sixteenth-century Venetian

pre·tu·ber·cu·lous (prē′tōō-bûr′kyə-ləs, -tyōō-bûr′kyə-ləs) *adj.* Pertaining to lesions of tuberculosis occurring before the actual development of the disease.

pret·zel (prĕt′səl) *n.* A glazed biscuit, salted on the outside, usually baked in the form of a loose knot or stick. [German *Pretzel, Brezel*, from Old High German *brezitella*, from Medieval Latin *brachiatellum* (unattested), diminutive of *brachītum* (unattested), "armlet," hence a ring-shaped cake, from Latin *bracchium*, arm, from Greek *brakhiōn*. See **mreghu-** in Appendix.*]

Preus·sen. The German name for **Prussia.**

pre·vail (prĭ-vāl′) *intr.v.* **-vailed, -vailing, -vails.** **1.** To be greater in strength or influence; to triumph or win a victory. Often used with *over* or *against.* **2.** To be or become effective; succeed; win out. **3.** To be most common or frequent; be predominant. **4.** To be in force, use, or effect; be current. **5.** To use persuasion or inducement successfully. Used with *on, upon,* or *with.* —See Synonyms at **persuade.** [Middle English *prevayllen*, from Latin *praevalēre*, to be more powerful : *prae-*, before, beyond + *valēre*, to be strong (see **wal-** in Appendix*).] **—pre·vail′er** *n.*

pre·vail·ing (prĭ-vā′lĭng) *adj.* **1.** Most frequent or common; predominant. **2.** Generally current; widespread; prevalent. **—pre·vail′ing·ly** *adv.* **—pre·vail′ing·ness** *n.*

Synonyms: *prevailing, prevalent, current, rife.* The widespread existence of some condition is implied by these adjectives. *Prevailing* implies predominance at a certain time: *prevailing opinion. Prevalent* suggests a condition that is merely widespread, with less emphasis on time. *Current* stresses the immediate present: *current trends.* It is often applied to things subject to frequent change. *Rife* emphasizes rapidity of multiplication.

prev·a·lent (prĕv′ə-lənt) *adj.* Widely or commonly occurring or existing; generally accepted or practiced. See Synonyms at **common, prevailing.** [Latin *praevalens*, present participle of *praevalēre*, to PREVAIL.] **—prev′a·lence** *n.* **—prev′a·lent·ly** *adv.*

pre·var·i·cate (prĭ-văr′ə-kāt′) *intr.v.* **-cated, -cating, -cates.** To stray from or evade the truth; equivocate: *"The curious thing about art-speech is that it prevaricates so terribly."* (D.H. Lawrence). [Latin *praevāricārī*, to walk crookedly, deviate from one's course or path of duty, collude : *prae-*, before, beyond + *vāricāre*, to straddle, from *vāricus*, straddling, from *vārus*, stretched, bent, knock-kneed (see **varus**).] **—pre·var′i·ca′tion** *n.* **—pre·var′i·ca′tor** (-kā′tər) *n.*

pre·ven·ience (prĭ-vēn′yəns) *n.* **1.** The act or state of being antecedent or prevenient. **2.** Attention to another's needs.

pre·ven·ient (prĭ-vēn′yənt) *adj.* **1.** Antecedent; previous; preceding. **2.** Expectant; anticipatory. [Latin *praeveniens*, present participle of *praevenīre*, to come before, precede, anticipate : *prae-*, before + *venīre*, to come (see **gwā-** in Appendix*).] **—pre·ven′ient·ly** *adv.*

pre·vent (prĭ-vĕnt′) *v.* **-vented, -venting, -vents.** *—tr.* **1.** To keep from happening, as by some prior action; avert; thwart. **2.** To keep (someone) from doing something; hinder; impede. Often used with *from.* **3.** *Obsolete.* To anticipate or counter in advance: *"Your goodness still prevents my wishes."* (Dryden). **4.** *Obsolete.* To come before; precede. *—intr.* To present an obstacle: *There will be a picnic, if nothing prevents.* [Middle English *preventen*, to anticipate, from Latin *praevenīre*, to come before, anticipate : *prae-*, before + *venīre*, to come (see **gwā-** in Appendix*).] **—pre·vent′a·bil′i·ty, pre·vent′i·bil′i·ty** *n.* **—pre·vent′a·ble, pre·vent′i·ble** *adj.* **—pre·vent′er** *n.*

Synonyms: *prevent, preclude, obviate, forestall.* These verbs refer to stopping or hindering an action or eliminating a situation or condition that could produce an action. *Prevent* strongly implies decisive counteraction to stop something from happening. *Preclude* makes an event or action impossible or largely ineffectual by removing the conditions for it, while *obviate* makes an event or action unnecessary in the same way. *Forestall* less forcefully implies anticipatory action to prevent or hinder an imminent happening, but not by eliminating the conditions for it.

Usage: *Prevent* is often followed by a gerund. A noun or pronoun preceding the gerund is in the possessive case: *We tried to prevent Jim's leaving* (not *Jim leaving*). Such examples can also be expressed: *We tried to prevent Jim from leaving. She prevented them from moving.*

pre·ven·tion (prĭ-vĕn′shən) *n.* **1.** The act of preventing. **2.** A hindrance; obstacle.

pre·ven·tive (prĭ-vĕn′tĭv) *adj.* Also **pre·ven·ta·tive** (-tə-tĭv). **1.** Designed or used to prevent or hinder; acting as an obstacle; precautionary. **2.** *Medicine.* Thwarting or warding off illness or disease; prophylactic. *—n.* Also **pre·ven·ta·tive.** **1.** Something that prevents; an obstacle. **2.** *Medicine.* Something used to ward off illness. **—pre·ven′tive·ly** *adv.* **—pre·ven′tive·ness** *n.*

pre·view (prē′vyōō′) *n.* Also **pre·vue.** **1.** An advance showing of a motion picture, an art exhibition, or some other event to an invited audience, prior to public presentation. **2.** Any advance viewing or exhibition, especially the presentation of several scenes advertising a forthcoming motion picture. *—tr.v.* **previewed, -viewing, -views.** Also **pre·vue, -vued, -vuing, -vues.** To view or exhibit in advance.

pre·vi·ous (prē′vē-əs) *adj.* **1.** Existing or occurring prior to something else in time or order; antecedent: *"The best public measures are seldom adopted from previous wisdom."* (Franklin). **2.** *Informal.* Premature; hasty. **—previous to.** Prior to; before. [Latin *praevius*, going before, leading the way : *prae-*, before + *via*, way (see **wei-**[2] in Appendix*).] **—pre′vi·ous·ly** *adv.* **—pre′vi·ous·ness** *n.*

previous question. *Abbr.* **p.q.** *Parliamentary Procedure.* The motion to take an immediate vote on the main question being considered or on any other questions so designated. Adopted by a two-thirds vote, this motion is often used to end debate. Compare **cloture.**

pre·vise (prē-vīz′) *tr.v.* **-vised, -vising, -vises.** **1.** To foresee. **2.** To notify in advance. [Latin *praevidēre* (stem *praevīs-*) : *prae-*, before + *vidēre*, to see (see **weid-** in Appendix*).] **—pre·vi′sion** (-vĭzh′ən) *n.* **—pre·vi′sor** (-vī′zər) *n.*

pre·vo·cal·ic (prē′vō-kăl′ĭk) *adj.* *Phonetics.* Preceding a vowel.

pre·vo·ca·tion·al (prē′vō-kā′shən-əl) *adj.* Of or pertaining to instruction given in preparation for vocational school.

pre·war (prē′wôr′) *adj.* Existing or occurring before a war.

prex·y (prĕk′sē) *n., pl.* **-ies.** *Slang.* A president, especially of a college or university. [Shortened variant of PRESIDENT.]

prey (prā) *n.* **1.** Any creature hunted or caught for food; quarry. **2.** A victim: *"To dumb Forgetfulness a prey"* (Gray). **3.** *Archaic.* Something taken by violence; booty: *"The rascal people, thirsting after prey"* (Shakespeare). *—intr.v.* **preyed, preying, preys.** **1.** To hunt, catch, or eat as prey: *Owls prey on mice.* **2.** To victimize or make a profit at someone's expense. **3.** To plunder or pillage. **4.** To exert a baneful or injurious effect: *Remorse preyed upon his mind.* [Middle English *preye*, from Old French *preie*, from Latin *praeda* "booty," prey. See **ghend-** in Appendix.*] **—prey′er** *n.*

PRG Airport code for Prague, Czechoslovakia.

Pri·am (prī′əm). *Greek Mythology.* King of Troy, the father of Paris and Hector, killed when his city fell to the Greeks.

pri·ap·ic (prī-ăp′ĭk, -ā′pĭk) *adj.* Also **pri·a·pe·an** (prī′ə-pē′ən). Phallic. [From PRIAPUS.]

pri·a·pism (prī′ə-pĭz′əm) *n.* Persistent, usually painful, erection of the penis, especially as a consequence of disease. [French *priapisme*, from Late Latin *priāpismus*, from Greek *priapismos*, from *priapizein*, "to act like Priapus," be lewd, from *Priapos*, PRIAPUS.]

pri·a·pus (prī-ā′pəs) *n.* **1.** *Capital* **P.** The Greco-Roman god of procreation, guardian of gardens and vineyards, and personification of the erect phallus. **2.** An image of the god Priapus, often used as a scarecrow in ancient gardens. **3.** A representation of the phallus. [Latin, from Greek *Priapos*†.]

Prib·i·lof Islands (prĭb′ə-lôf′). A group of islands in the Bering Sea, off the southwestern coast of Alaska. They are the breeding ground for most of the world's fur-bearing seals.

price (prīs) *n. Abbr.* **pr.** **1.** The sum of money or goods asked or given for something. **2.** The cost at which something is obtained. **3.** The cost of bribing someone: *Every man has his price.* **4.** A reward offered for the capture or killing of a person. **5.** Value or worth: *"She is a pearl / Whose price hath launched above a thousand ships."* (Shakespeare). *—tr.v.* **priced, pricing, prices.** **1.** To fix or establish a price for: *shoes priced at nine dollars.* **2.** To find out the price of: *spent the day pricing dresses.*

ă pat/ā pay/âr care/ä father/b bib/ch church/d deed/ĕ pet/ē be/f fife/g gag/h hat/hw which/ĭ pit/ī pie/îr pier/j judge/k kick/l lid, needle/m mum/n no, sudden/ng thing/ŏ pot/ō toe/ô paw, for/oi noise/ou out/ŏŏ took/ōō boot/p pop/r roar/s sauce/sh ship, dish/

—price out of the market. To charge so much for goods that people no longer buy them. [Middle English *pris,* price, value, praise, from Old French, from Latin *pretium,* price, value, reward. See **per¹** in Appendix.*]

Synonyms: *price, charge, cost, expense, expenditure, outlay, fee.* These nouns apply to money or other valuable consideration, such as labor and time, asked for or spent in payment for goods or services or for attainment of desired conditions. *Price* is the amount of money needed to purchase an object. *Charge* is the sum asked for the rendering of a service: *the charge for insuring the parcel. Cost,* a more inclusive term, generally applies to the total amount to be spent, including all *prices* and *charges. Expense* suggests cost in aggregate or in relation to a larger allocation of funds: *traveling expenses. Expenditure* usually refers to the total of money, time, or effort actually involved, sometimes with the suggestion of detailed accounting. *Outlay* refers to the act of spending money or to the total spent. *Fee* is used specifically in connection with professional services.

price index. A number relating prices of a group of commodities to their prices during an arbitrarily chosen base period.

price·less (prīs′lĭs) *adj.* **1.** Of inestimable worth; invaluable. **2.** Highly amusing, absurd, or odd. —See Synonyms at **costly.**

price tag. 1. A label attached to a piece of merchandise indicating its price. **2.** The cost of something: *a high price tag.*

prick (prĭk) *n.* **1. a.** The act of piercing or pricking. **b.** The sensation of being pierced or pricked. **2.** Any painful or stinging feeling or reflection: *prick of remorse.* **3.** A small mark or puncture made by a pointed object. **4.** A hare's track or footprint. **5.** A pointed object, as an ice pick, goad, thorn, or bee sting. **6.** *Vulgar.* **a.** The penis. **b.** An obnoxious person. —*v.* **pricked, pricking, pricks.** —*tr.* **1.** To puncture lightly. **2.** To sting with a mental or emotional pang. **3.** To incite; impel: *"My duty pricks me on"* (Shakespeare). **4.** To mark or delineate on a surface by means of small punctures: *prick a pattern.* **5.** *Nautical.* To measure with dividers on a chart. **6.** To pierce the quick of (a horse's hoof) while shoeing. **7.** To transplant (seedlings) preliminary to a final planting. Used chiefly with *out* or *off.* —*intr.* **1.** To pierce or puncture something. **2.** To feel a stinging or pricking sensation: *"When the blood creeps, and the nerves prick and tingle"* (Tennyson). **3.** *Archaic.* To ride at a gallop: *"A gentle knight was pricking on the plain"* (Spenser). **—prick up one's ears.** To listen with attentive interest. [Middle English *prik(ke),* Old English *prica,* pricked mark, puncture, from West Germanic *prikk-* (unattested).]

prick·er (prĭk′ər) *n.* **1.** A pricking tool. **2.** A prickle or thorn.

prick·et (prĭk′ĭt) *n.* **1. a.** A small point or spike for holding a candle upright. **b.** A candlestick having such a spike. **2.** A buck in his second year before his horns branch. [Middle English *priket,* from *prik,* PRICK.]

prick·le (prĭk′əl) *n.* **1.** A small, sharp point, spine, or thorn. **2.** A pricking or tingling sensation. —*v.* **prickled, -ling, -les.** —*tr.* **1.** To prick as with a thorn. **2.** To cause a tingling sensation in. —*intr.* **1.** To feel a tingling or pricking. **2.** To rise or stand up like prickles. [Middle English *prikle, prikel,* from Old English *pricel(s),* from West Germanic *prikkil-* (unattested), diminutive of *prikk-,* PRICK.]

prick·ly (prĭk′lē) *adj.* **-lier, -liest. 1.** Having prickles. **2.** Tingling; smarting. **3.** Bristling or irritable. **—prick′li·ness** *n.*

prickly ash. An aromatic shrub or small tree, *Zanthoxylum americanum,* of eastern North America, having prickly stems and feathery leaves. Also called "toothache tree."

prickly heat. A noncontagious skin disease, **miliaria** *(see).*

prickly pear. 1. Any of various cacti of the genus *Opuntia,* having bristly flattened or cylindrical joints, showy, usually yellow flowers, and ovoid, sometimes edible fruit. Some species are also called "cholla." **2.** The fruit of any of these plants.

prickly poppy. Any of various plants of the genus *Argemone,* chiefly of tropical America, having large yellow or white flowers and prickly leaves, stems and pods.

pride (prīd) *n.* **1.** A sense of one's own proper dignity or value; self-respect: *One should not be robbed of his pride.* **2.** Pleasure or satisfaction taken in one's work, achievements, or possessions. **3. a.** A cause or source of pride: *These men were their country's pride.* **b.** The most successful or thriving condition; prime; flower: *the flush and pride of youth.* **4. a.** An excessively high opinion of oneself; conceit; arrogance: *"Pride goeth before destruction"* (Proverbs 16:18). **b.** *Christian Theology.* The consideration or personification of this condition as the first of the seven cardinal sins. **5. a.** Mettle or spirit in horses. **b.** *Archaic.* The state of sexual desire or heat, especially in female animals; rut. **6.** A company of lions. —See Synonyms at **flock.** —*v.* **prided, priding, prides.** —*tr.* To esteem (oneself) for. Used with *on* or *upon: I pride myself on this garden.* —*intr.* To indulge in self-esteem; to glory: *"Those who pride in being scholars"* (Swift). [Middle English *pride, prude, prute,* Old English *prȳte, prȳde,* from *prūt, prūd,* PROUD.] **—pride′ful** *adj.* **—pride′ful·ly** *adv.* **—pride′ful·ness** *n.*

prie·dieu (prē-dyœ′) *n., pl.* **-dieus** or **-dieux** (-dyœz′). A low desk with space for a book above and with a foot piece below for kneeling in prayer. [French *prie-Dieu,* "pray God."]

pri·er (prī′ər) *n.* Also **pry·er.** One who pries.

priest (prēst) *n.* **1.** *Abbr.* **P., Pr.** In the Roman Catholic, Eastern Orthodox, Anglican, Armenian, and separated Catholic hierarchies, a member of the second grade of clergy ranking below a bishop but above a deacon and having authority to pronounce absolution and administer all sacraments save that of ordination. **2.** A minister in a non-Christian religion. **3.** One whose role is considered comparable to that of a priest: *"Ye sacred Muses . . . Whose Priest I am"* (Dryden). —*tr.v.* **priested, priesting, priests.** To ordain or admit to the priesthood. [Middle English *pre(e)st, preost,* from Old English *prēost,* from Vulgar Latin *prester* (unattested), contracted from Late Latin *presbyter,* from Greek *presbuteros,* "elder," comparative of *presbus,* old man. See **per¹** in Appendix.*]

priest·ess (prē′stĭs) *n.* A female priest.

priest·hood (prēst′ho͝od′) *n.* **1.** The character, office, or vocation of a priest. **2.** The clergy.

Priest·ley (prēst′lē), **Joseph.** 1733–1804. British chemist and clergyman; discoverer of oxygen; settled in America (1794).

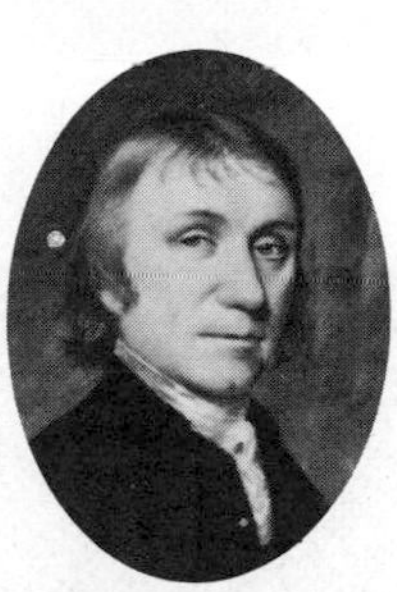

Joseph Priestley
Contemporary chalk portrait by Ellen Sharples

priest·ly (prēst′lē) *adj.* **-lier, -liest.** Of, pertaining to, or befitting a priest or priests. **—priest′li·ness** *n.*

prig (prĭg) *n.* **1.** A person regarded as overprecise, affectedly arrogant, smug, or narrow-minded. **2.** *Archaic.* A coxcomb: *"A cane is part of the dress of a prig"* (Steele). **3.** *British Slang.* A petty thief or pickpocket. —*tr.v.* **prigged, prigging, prigs.** *British Slang.* To steal or pilfer. [Origin obscure.] **—prig′ger·y** (-gə-rē) *n.* **—prig′gish** *adj.* **—prig′gish·ly** *adv.*

prim¹ (prĭm) *adj.* **primmer, primmest. 1.** Precise, neat, or proper to the point of affectation. **2.** Formal; trim. —*v.* **primmed, primming, prims.** —*tr.* To fix (the face or mouth) in a prim expression. —*intr.* To assume a prim expression. [Origin obscure.] **—prim′ly** *adv.* **—prim′ness** *n.*

prim² (prĭm) *n.* A shrub, the **privet** *(see).* [Origin unknown.]

prim. 1. primary. **2.** primitive.

pri·ma ballerina (prē′mə) *pl.* **prima ballerinas.** The leading female dancer in a ballet company. Compare **ballerina.**

pri·ma·cy (prī′mə-sē) *n., pl.* **-cies. 1.** The state or condition of being first or foremost. **2.** The office or province of an ecclesiastical primate.

pri·ma don·na (prē′mə dŏn′ə, prĭm′ə) *pl.* **prima donnas. 1.** The leading female soloist in an opera company. **2.** A temperamental and conceited performer. [Italian, "first lady."]

pri·ma fa·cie (prī′mə fā′shē, fā′shə). At first sight; before closer inspection. [Latin *prīmā faciē,* "on first appearance" : *prīmus,* first (see **per¹** in Appendix*) + *faciēs,* face, appearance (see **dhē-¹** in Appendix*).] **—pri′ma-fa′cie** *adj.*

prima-facie evidence. *Law.* Evidence that would, if uncontested, establish a fact or raise a presumption of a fact.

pri·mal (prī′məl) *adj.* **1.** Being first in time; original; archetypal: *"It hath the primal eldest curse upon't, a brother's murder"* (Shakespeare). **2.** Of first importance; primary. [Medieval Latin *prīmālis,* from Latin *prīmus,* first. See **per¹** in Appendix.*]

pri·ma·ri·ly (prī-mĕr′ə-lē, prī′mĕr′ə-lē) *adv.* **1.** At first; originally. **2.** Chiefly; principally.

pri·ma·ry (prī′mĕr′ē, -mə-rē) *adj. Abbr.* **prim. 1.** Occurring first in time or sequence; earliest; original: *primary source.* **2.** Primitive; unsophisticated; primal: *the primary instinct of motherhood.* **3.** Being or standing first in a list, series, or sequence. **4.** Being first or best in degree, quality, or importance. **5.** *Geology.* Of, pertaining to, or designating the earliest periods of geological development up to and including the Paleozoic era; Precambrian. **6.** Being a fundamental, or basic part of an organized whole: *primary element.* **7.** Immediate; direct: *primary effect.* **8.** Of or pertaining to the basic colors from which all other colors may be derived. See **primary color. 9.** *Linguistics.* **a.** Having a word root or other linguistic element as a basis that cannot be further analyzed or broken down. Used of the derivation of a word or word element. **b.** Referring to present or future time. Used as a collective designation for the various present and future tenses in Latin, Greek, and Sanskrit. **10.** *Electricity.* Of, pertaining to, or designating an inducting current, circuit, or coil. **11.** *Ornithology.* Of, pertaining to, or designating the main flight feathers projecting along the outer edge of a bird's wing. **12.** *Chemistry.* **a.** Pertaining to the replacement of one of several atoms or radicals in a compound by another atom or radical. **b.** Having a carbon atom attached solely to one other carbon atom in a molecule. —See Synonyms at **chief.** —*n., pl.* **primaries.** *Abbr.* **prim. 1. a.** One that is first in time, order, or sequence. **b.** One that is first or best in degree, quality, or importance. **c.** One that is fundamental, basic, or elemental. **2.** *Government.* **a.** A meeting of the registered voters of a political party for the purpose of nominating candidates and for choosing delegates to their party convention. **b.** A preliminary election in which the registered voters of a political party nominate candidates for office. **3.** A **primary color** *(see).* **4.** *Ornithology.* One of the main flight feathers projecting along the outer edge of a bird's wing. **5.** *Electronics.* An inducting current, circuit, or coil. **6.** *Astronomy.* A celestial body, especially a star, to which the orbit of a satellite, or secondary, is referred. **7.** A **cosmic ray** *(see).* [Latin *prīmārius,* of the first rank, chief, basic, from *prīmus,* first. See **per¹** in Appendix.*]

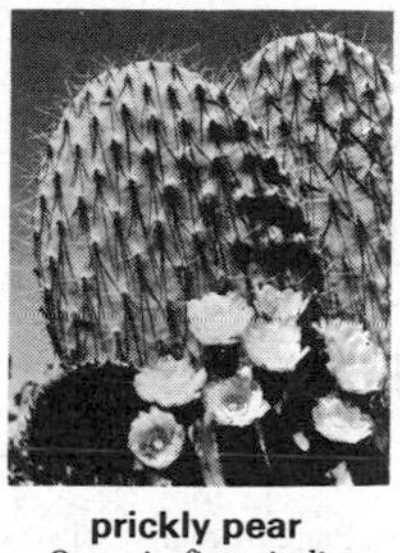

prickly pear
Opuntia ficus-indica

primary atypical pneumonia. A mild pneumonia, probably caused by a virus.

primary cell. A cell in which an irreversible chemical reaction generates electricity. Also called "galvanic cell," "voltaic cell." Compare **secondary cell.**

primary coil. An electrically conducting coil, as in a transformer, that carries an inducting current.

primary color. A color belonging to any three groups each of which is regarded as generating all colors. These groups are: **a.** *Additive, physiological,* or *light* primaries—red, green, and blue. Lights of red, green and blue wavelengths may be mixed to produce all colors. **b.** *Subtractive* or *colorant* primaries—magenta, yellow, and cyan. Substances that reflect light of one of these wavelengths and absorb (subtract) other wavelengths may be mixed to produce all colors. **c.** *Psychological* primaries—red, yellow, green, and blue, plus the achromatic pair black and white. All colors may be subjectively conceived as mixtures of these.

primary radiation. A **cosmic ray** *(see).*

primary school. A school usually comprising the first three or four grades of elementary school and sometimes kindergarten.

pri·mate (prī′mĭt, -māt′ *for sense 1;* prī′māt′ *for sense 2*) *n.* **1.** A bishop of highest rank in a province or country. **2.** Any member of the order Primates, which includes the monkeys, apes, and man. [Middle English *primat,* from Old French, from Medieval Latin *prīmās,* archbishop, from Latin "of the first rank," chief, leader, from *prīmus,* first. See **per**[1] in Appendix.*] **—pri·ma′tial** (prī-mā′shəl) *adj.*

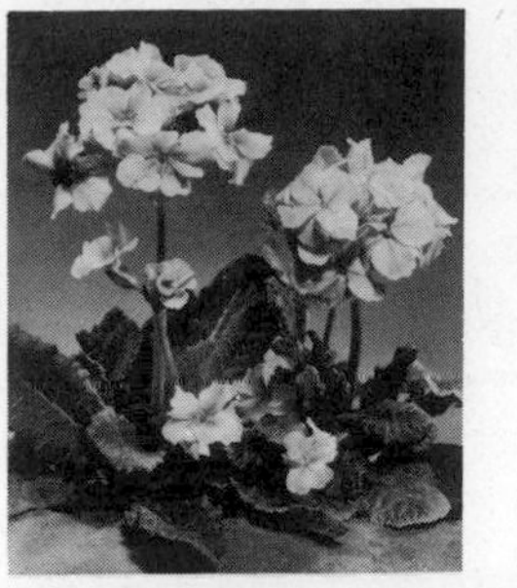

primrose
Primula polyantha

pri·ma·ve·ra (prē′mə-vĕr′ə) *n.* **1.** A tree, *Cybistax donnell-smithii,* of Central America, having yellow flowers and close-grained, light-colored wood. **2.** The wood of this tree, used in cabinetwork. In this sense, also called "white mahogany." [Spanish, "spring," from Late Latin *prīma vēra,* early spring, feminine of Latin *prīmum vēr* : *prīmum,* first part, from neuter of *prīmus,* first (see **per**[1] in Appendix*) + *vēr,* spring (see **wesr** in Appendix*).]

prime (prīm) *adj.* **1.** First in excellence, quality, or value: *prime television time.* **2.** First in degree or rank; chief: *"Have I not made you/The prime man of the state?"* (Shakespeare). **3.** First or early in time, order, or sequence. **4.** Of the highest U.S. Government grade of meat. **5.** *Mathematics.* Designating a **prime number** *(see).* —See Synonyms at **chief.** *—n.* **1.** The earliest hours of the day; dawn; morning. **2.** The first season of the year; spring: *"The teeming autumn, big with rich increase,/ Bearing the wanton burden of the prime."* (Shakespeare). **3.** The age of ideal physical perfection and intellectual vigor. **4.** The period or phase of ideal or peak condition. **5.** *Fencing.* The first position of thrust and parry. **6.** A mark (′) written above and to the right of a letter in order to distinguish it from the same letter already in use or to designate a related quantity or thing, as feet, minutes of angle, or minutes of time. **7.** *Ecclesiastical.* **a.** The second of the seven **canonical hours** *(see).* **b.** The time of day set aside for this prayer, usually about 6:00 A.M. **8.** *Mathematics.* A **prime number** *(see).* *—v.* **primed, priming, primes.** *—tr.* **1.** To make ready; prepare. **2.** To prepare (a gun or mine) for firing by inserting a charge of gunpowder or a primer. **3.** To prepare for operation, as by pouring water into a pump or gasoline into a carburetor. **4.** To prepare (a surface) for painting by covering with size, primer, or an undercoat. **5.** To prepare with information; coach. *—intr.* To prepare someone or something for future action or operation. [Middle English, from Old French, feminine of *prin,* from Latin *prīmus,* first (see **per**[1] in Appendix*); the ecclesiastical sense derives from Old English *prīm,* from Latin *prīma (hōra),* first (hour), from the feminine of *prīmus.*] **—prime′ly** *adv.* **—prime′ness** *n.*

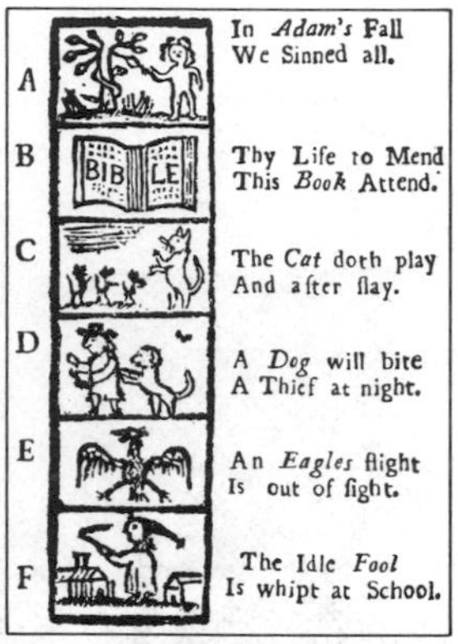

primer[1]
Page from an early edition of the *New England Primer*

prime cost. The expense of a produced commodity based on the cost of the labor and materials directly involved.

prime meridian. The zero meridian, (0°), from which longitude east and west is measured and which passes through Greenwich, England.

prime minister. *Abbr.* **P.M.** **1.** A chief minister appointed by a ruler. **2.** The head of the cabinet and often also the chief executive in various kinds of parliamentary democracy. **—prime ministership. —prime ministry.**

prime mover. **1.** The initial force that engages or moves a machine, as electricity, wind, or gravity. **2.** Anything regarded as the initial source of energy directed toward a goal: *Patriotism was the prime mover of the revolution.* **3.** Any machine or mechanism that converts natural energy into work. **4.** Any of various heavy-duty trucks or tractors. **5.** In Aristotelian philosophy, the self-moved being that causes all motion.

prime number. A number that has itself and unity as its only factors.

prim·er[1] (prĭm′ər) *n.* **1.** An elementary textbook. **2.** A book that covers the basic elements of any subject. [Middle English, from Norman French, from Medieval Latin *prīmārium (manuāle),* "basic handbook," from Latin *prīmārius,* basic, PRIMARY.]

prim·er[2] (prī′mər) *n.* **1.** A cap or tube containing a small amount of explosive used to detonate the main explosive charge of a firearm or mine. **2.** Someone or something that primes or causes to be primed. **3.** An undercoat of paint or size applied to prepare a surface, as for painting. [From PRIME (verb).]

pri·me·ro (prĭ-mâr′ō) *n.* A gambling card game, popular in Elizabethan England. [Alteration of Spanish *primera,* feminine of *primero,* "first," from Latin *prīmarius,* principal, from *prīmus,* first. See **per**[1] in Appendix.*]

pri·me·val (prī-mē′vəl) *adj.* Belonging to the first or earliest age or ages; original. [From Latin *prīmaevus,* in the first period of life : *prīmus,* first (see **per**[1] in Appendix*) + *aevum,* age (see **aiw-** in Appendix*).] **—pri·me′val·ly** *adv.*

prim·ing (prī′mĭng) *n.* **1.** The explosive used to ignite a charge. **2.** A preliminary coat of paint or size applied to a surface.

pri·mip·a·ra (prī-mĭp′ər-ə) *n., pl.* **-aras** or **-arae** (-ə-rē′). *Medicine.* **1.** A woman who is pregnant for the first time. **2.** A woman who has borne only one child. [Latin : *prīmus,* first (see **per**[1] in Appendix*) + *-para,* feminine of *-parus,* -PAROUS.] **—pri′mi·par′i·ty** (prī′mĭ-păr′ə-tē) *n.* **—pri·mip′a·rous** *adj.*

prim·i·tive (prĭm′ə-tĭv) *adj. Abbr.* **prim.** **1. a.** Of or pertaining to an earliest or original stage or state. **b.** Archetypal. **2.** Characterized by simplicity or crudity; unsophisticated: *primitive weapons.* **3.** Of or pertaining to early stages in the evolution of human culture: *primitive societies.* **4.** *Linguistics.* **a.** Serving as the basis for derived or inflected forms: *"Pick" is the primitive word from which "picket" is derived.* **b.** Being a protolanguage: *primitive Germanic.* **5.** *Mathematics.* Any form in geometry or algebra from which another form is derived. **6.** *Painting.* **a.** Having the style of an early or unsophisticated culture. **b.** Self-taught. **c.** Of or pertaining to late medieval European painters. **7.** *Geology.* Of or pertaining to rocks formed by the first solidification of the earth's crust. **8.** *Biology.* Occurring in or characteristic of an early stage of development or evolution. *—n.* **1.** A person belonging to a primitive society. **2.** Someone or something at a low or early stage of development. **3. a.** One belonging to an early stage in the development of a culture or artistic trend. **b.** An artist having or affecting a primitive style. **c.** A self-taught artist. **4.** *Linguistics.* A word or word element from which another word or inflected form of the word is derived. Compare **derivative.** [Middle English *primitif,* from Old French, from Latin *prīmitīvus,* first of its kind, from *prīmitus,* at first, in the first place, from *prīmus,* first. See **per**[1] in Appendix.*] **—prim′i·tive·ly** *adv.* **—prim′i·tive·ness, prim′i·tiv′i·ty** *n.*

prim·i·tiv·ism (prĭm′ə-tĭv-ĭz′əm) *n.* **1.** The state or quality of being primitive. **2.** A belief in primitive customs or ideas. **3.** The style of primitive painters. **4.** A belief that the acquisitions of civilization are evil or that the earliest period of human history was the best. **—prim′i·tiv·ist** *adj.* & *n.* **—prim′i·tiv·is′tic** *adj.*

pri·mo[1] (prē′mō, prī′-) *adv. Latin.* In the first place.

pri·mo[2] (prē′mō) *n., pl.* **-mi** (-mē). *Music.* The principal part in a duet or ensemble composition. [Italian, "first," from Latin *prīmus.* See **per**[1] in Appendix.*] **—pri′mo** *adj.*

pri·mo·gen·i·tor (prī′mō-jĕn′ə-tər) *n.* The earliest ancestor or forefather. [Medieval Latin : Latin *prīmus,* first (see **per**[1] in Appendix*) + GENITOR.]

pri·mo·gen·i·ture (prī′mō-jĕn′ə-cho͝or′) *n.* **1.** The state or condition of being the first-born or eldest child of the same parents. **2.** *Law.* The right of the eldest child, especially the eldest son, to inherit the entire estate of one or both of his parents. [Medieval Latin *prīmōgenitūra* : Latin *prīmus,* first (see **per**[1] in Appendix*) + *genitūra,* birth, from *gignere* (stem *genit-*), to beget (see **gena-** in Appendix*).] **—pri′mo·gen′i·tar′y** (-jĕn′ə-tĕr′ē), **pri′mo·gen′i·tal** *adj.*

pri·mor·di·al (prī-môr′dē-əl) *adj.* **1.** Being or happening first in sequence of time; original. **2.** Radical; fundamental: *play a primordial role.* **3.** *Biology.* Belonging to or characteristic of the earliest stage of development of an organism or part. *—n.* A basic principle. [Middle English, from Late Latin *prīmōrdiālis,* from Latin *prīmōrdium,* origin, from *prīmōrdius,* original : *prīmus,* first (see **per**[1] in Appendix*) + *ordīrī,* to begin a web (see **ar-** in Appendix*).] **—pri·mor′di·al·ly** *adv.*

pri·mor·di·um (prī-môr′dē-əm) *n., pl.* **-dia** (-dē-ə). An organ or part in its most rudimentary form or stage. [Latin, "origin." See **primordial.**]

primp (prĭmp) *v.* **primped, primping, primps.** *—tr.* To neaten (one's appearance) with considerable attention to detail. *—intr.* To preen. [Akin to PRIM.]

prim·rose (prĭm′rōz′) *n.* **1.** Any of various plants of the genus *Primula,* having tubular, variously colored flowers with five lobes. **2.** See **evening primrose.** [Middle English *primerose,* from Old French, from Medieval Latin *prīma rosa,* "first (or earliest) rose" (reason for naming obscure) : Latin *prīma,* feminine of *prīmus,* first (see **per**[1] in Appendix*) + *rosa,* ROSE.]

primrose path. A way of life of worldly ease or pleasure.

primrose yellow. Moderate or light yellow to light, brilliant, or vivid greenish-yellow. See **color.**

pri·mum mo·bi·le (prī′məm mō′bə-lē′; prē′məm mō′bĭ-lā′). **1.** In medieval astronomy, the tenth and outermost concentric sphere of the universe, thought to revolve around the earth from east to west in 24 hours and believed to cause the other nine spheres to revolve with it. **2.** A prime mover. [Medieval Latin, "first mover," a rendering of Arabic *al-muharrik al-awwal.*]

pri·mus (prī′məs) *n., pl.* **-muses.** The first in rank of the bishops of Scotland. [Medieval Latin *prīmus,* from Latin, first. See **per**[1] in Appendix.*]

pri·mus in·ter pa·res (prī′məs ĭn′tər pâr′ēz; prē′mo͝os ĭn′tər pä′rās′). *Latin.* The first among equals.

prin. **1.** principal. **2.** principle.

prince (prĭns) *n.* **1.** *Archaic.* A hereditary ruler; king. **2.** *Abbr.* **P., Pr.** The ruler of a principality. **3.** *Abbr.* **P., Pr.** A male member of a royal family other than the monarch. **4.** *Abbr.* **P., Pr.** A nobleman of varying status in different countries. **5.** An outstanding man in any group or class: *a merchant prince.* [Middle English, from Old French, from Latin *princeps,* first in rank, sovereign, ruler. See **per**[1] in Appendix.*]

Prince Albert. A man's long, double-breasted frock coat. [Popularized by Prince *Albert* Edward, later EDWARD VII.]

prince consort. The husband of a sovereign queen.

prince·dom (prĭns′dəm) *n.* **1.** The territory ruled by a prince; principality. **2.** The rank or status of a prince.

Prince Edward Island. *Abbr.* **P.E.I.** A Maritime Province of Canada, consisting of an island, 2,184 square miles in area, in the Gulf of St. Lawrence. Population, 108,000. Capital, Charlottetown. See map at **Canada.**

Prince Island. See **Principe Island.**

prince·ling (prĭns′lĭng) *n.* Also **prince·let** (prĭns′lət). A prince of minor status or importance.

prince·ly (prĭns′lē) *adj.* **-lier, -liest.** Of or befitting a prince; munificent. **—prince′li·ness** *n.* **—prince′ly** *adv.*

Prince of Wales. A title given to the eldest son of a British sovereign.

Prince of Wales Island. **1.** The largest island (1,500 square miles) of the Alexander Archipelago, off the extreme south-

ă pat/ā pay/âr care/ä father/b bib/ch church/d deed/ĕ pet/ē be/f fife/g gag/h hat/hw which/ĭ pit/ī pie/îr pier/j judge/k kick/l lid, needle/m mum/n no, sudden/ng thing/ŏ pot/ō toe/ô paw, for/oi noise/ou out/o͝o took/o͞o boot/p pop/r roar/s sauce/sh ship, dish/

eastern coast of Alaska. **2.** An island, about 13,000 square miles in area, of the Northwest Territories, Canada, in the Arctic Ocean between Victoria and Somerset islands.

prince regent. A prince who rules during the minority, absence, or incapacity of a sovereign.

prince royal. The eldest son of a sovereign.

prince's-feath·er (prĭn′sĭz-fĕth′ər) *n.* **1.** A tall plant, *Polygonum orientale,* having hairy stems and long spikes of pink or rose flowers. **2.** A plant, *Amaranthus hybridus hypochondriacus,* having reddish foliage and dense, brownish-red flower clusters.

prince's-pine (prĭn′sĭz-pīn′) *n.* A plant, the **pipsissewa** *(see).*

prin·cess (prĭn′sĭs, -sĕs′, prĭn-sĕs′) *n.* **1.** *Archaic.* A hereditary female ruler; queen. **2.** The female ruler of a principality. **3.** A female member of a royal family other than the monarch. **4.** A noblewoman of varying rank in different countries. **5.** The wife of a prince. **6.** Any woman thought of as having the status or qualities of a princess. —*adj.* Also **prin·cesse** (prĭn-sĕs′). Designed to hang in smooth, close-fitting, unbroken lines from shoulder to flared hem. [Middle English *princesse,* from Old French, from *prince,* PRINCE.]

princess royal. The eldest daughter of a sovereign.

Prince·ton (prĭns′tən). A city in west-central New Jersey, the site of Princeton University. Population, 12,000.

Prince William Sound. An arm of the Gulf of Alaska, east of the Kenai Peninsula of southern Alaska.

prin·ci·pal (prĭn′sə-pəl) *adj. Abbr.* **prin.** First, highest, or foremost in importance, rank, worth, or degree; chief. See Synonyms at **chief.** —*n. Abbr.* **prin. 1.** One who holds a position of presiding rank; especially, the head of an elementary school or high school. **2.** A main participant in a given situation. **3.** A person having a leading or starring role. **4.** *Finance.* **a.** The capital or main body of an estate or financial holding, as distinguished from the interest or revenue from it. **b.** A sum of money owed as a debt, upon which interest is calculated. **5.** *Law.* **a.** A person who empowers another to act as his representative. **b.** The person having prime responsibility for an obligation, as distinguished from one who acts as surety or as an endorser. **c.** One who commits or is an accomplice to a crime. **6.** The main truss or rafter that supports and gives form to a roof. [Middle English, from Old French, from Latin *principālis,* first, original, hence overseer, ruler, from *princeps,* first one in rank, chief, PRINCE.] —**prin′ci·pal·ly** *adv.*

Usage: *Principal* and *principle* are often confused, but have no sense in common. *Principal* is both an adjective *(leading, chief)* and a noun, pertaining most often to a person who is a leader or in charge, or, in finance, to capital. *Principle* is only a noun, pertaining to basic truths, rules of human conduct, and fundamental laws governing the operation of something.

principal focus. *Optics.* A **focal point** *(see).*

prin·ci·pal·i·ty (prĭn′sə-păl′ə-tē) *n., pl.* **-ties. 1.** A territory ruled by a prince or from which a prince derives his title. **2.** The position, authority, or jurisdiction of a prince; sovereignty. **3.** *Plural. Theology.* One of the nine orders of angels. See **angel.**

principal parts. In traditional grammars of inflected languages, the primary forms of a verb from which all other forms may be derived. In English, the principal parts are generally considered to be the present infinitive *(play, eat),* the past tense *(played, ate),* the past participle *(played, eaten),* and the present participle *(playing, eating).* ***Note:*** In this Dictionary, all inflected forms of verbs are given. For regular verbs, this includes, in addition to the principal parts, the third-person singular form *(plays, eats),* which is listed following the present participle.

Prin·ci·pe Island (prĭn′sə-pē′, -pā′; *Portuguese* prēɴn′sē-pə). Also **Prince Island.** A Portuguese island in the Gulf of Guinea north of the equator. It forms with São Tomé to the south the province of São Tomé e Principe.

prin·cip·i·um (prĭn-sĭp′ē-əm) *n., pl.* **-ia** (-ē-ə). A principle, especially one that is basic. [Latin, basis, origin. See **principle.**]

prin·ci·ple (prĭn′sə-pəl) *n. Abbr.* **prin. 1.** A basic truth, law, or assumption: *the principles of democracy.* **2. a.** A rule or standard, especially of good behavior: *a man of principle.* **b.** Moral or ethical standards or judgments collectively: *a decision based on principle rather than expediency.* **3.** A fixed or predetermined policy or mode of action: *acting on the principle of every man for himself.* **4.** A basic, or essential, quality or element determining intrinsic nature or characteristic behavior: *the principle of self-preservation natural to man.* **5.** A rule or law concerning the functioning of natural phenomena or mechanical processes: *the principle of jet propulsion.* **6.** A basic source. **7.** *Capital* **P.** *Christian Science.* God. —See Usage note at **principal.** [Middle English, origin, commencement, hence fundamental quality or truth, modification of Old French *principe,* from Latin *principium,* from *princeps,* first. See **per¹** in Appendix.*]

prin·ci·pled (prĭn′sə-pəld) *adj.* Motivated by or based on moral or ethical principles.

prink (prĭngk) *v.* **prinked, prinking, prinks.** —*tr.* To adorn (oneself) in a showy manner. —*intr.* To primp. [Probably alteration of PRANK (adorn).] —**prink′er** *n.*

print (prĭnt) *n.* **1.** A mark or impression made in or upon a surface by pressure: *the print of footsteps in the sand.* **2. a.** A device or implement, such as a stamp, die, or seal, used to press markings on or into a surface. **b.** Something formed or marked by such a device: *a print of butter.* **3. a.** Lettering or other impressions produced in ink from type by a printing press or other means. **b.** Matter, such as newsprint, so produced. **c.** The state or form of matter so produced. **4.** A design or picture transferred from an engraved plate, wood block, lithographic stone, or other medium. **5.** A photographic image transferred to paper or a similar surface, usually from a negative. **6. a.** A fabric or garment with a dyed pattern that has been pressed onto it, usually by engraved rollers. **b.** The pattern itself. —**in print. 1.** In printed or published form. **2.** Still offered for sale by the publisher: *books in print.* —**out of print.** No longer offered for sale by the publisher. —*v.* **printed, printing, prints.** —*tr.* **1.** To press (a mark or design, for example) onto or into a surface. **2.** To make an impression on or in (a surface) with a stamp, seal, die, or similar device. **3.** To press (a stamp or similar device) onto or into a surface to leave a marking. **4.** To produce by means of pressed type on a paper surface, with or as if with a printing press. **5.** To offer in printed form; publish. **6.** To write (something) in characters similar to those commonly used in print. **7.** To impress firmly in the mind or memory. **8.** To produce (a positive photograph) by passing light through a negative onto sensitized paper. —*intr.* **1.** To work as a printer. **2.** To write characters similar to those commonly used in print. **3.** To produce or receive an impression, marking, or image. [Middle English *pri(e)nte, pre(i)nte,* from Old French *preinte,* from the past participle of *preindre,* to press, from Latin *premere.* See **per-⁶** in Appendix.*]

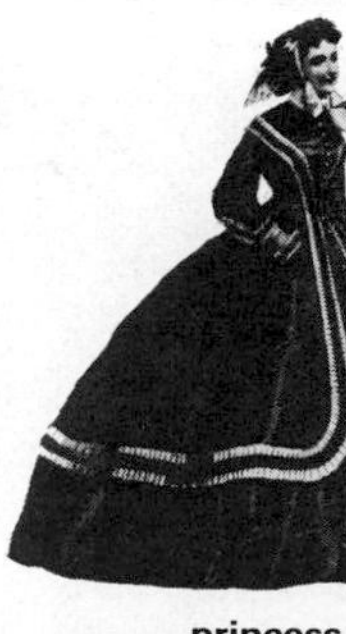

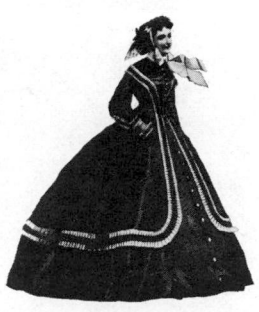

princess
Nineteenth-century French princess style

print. printing.

print·a·ble (prĭn′tə-bəl) *adj.* **1.** Capable of being printed or of producing a print. **2.** Regarded as fit for publication.

printed circuit. An electric circuit in which the conducting connections are formed by depositing a conducting metal, such as copper, in predetermined patterns on an insulating substrate, while other materials, especially semiconductors, are deposited to form various electronic components.

print·er (prĭn′tər) *n.* **1.** A person whose occupation is printing. **2.** One who or that which prints. **3.** The part of a computer that produces printed matter.

printer's devil. An apprentice in a printing establishment.

print·er·y (prĭn′tə-rē) *n., pl.* **-ies. 1.** A place where typographic printing is done. **2.** A factory where fabrics are printed.

print·ing (prĭn′tĭng) *n. Abbr.* **pr., print., ptg. 1.** The process, art, or business of producing printed material by means of inked type and a printing press or by similar means. **2. a.** The act of one that prints. **b.** Matter that is printed. **3.** All the copies of a book or other publication that are printed at one time. Compare **edition. 4.** Written characters not connected to one another and resembling those appearing in print.

printing office. An establishment where printed material is produced, especially an officially authorized one.

printing press. A machine that transfers lettering or images by contact with various forms of inked surface onto paper or similar material fed into it in various ways. See **flat-bed press, rotary press, web press.**

print out. To print as a computer function; produce print-out.

print-out (prĭnt′out′) *n.* The printed output of a computer.

pri·or¹ (prī′ər) *adj.* **1.** Preceding in time or order: *a prior commitment.* **2.** Preceding in importance or value: *a prior consideration.* [Latin. See **prior** (cleric).]

pri·or² (prī′ər) *n.* **1.** A monastic officer in charge of a priory, or ranking next under the abbot of an abbey. **2.** One of the ruling magistrates of the medieval Italian republic of Florence. [Middle English *pri(o)ur,* from Old English and Old French *prior,* both from Medieval Latin *prior,* from Late Latin, superior officer, administrator, from Latin, former, superior. See **per¹** in Appendix.*]

pri·or·ess (prī′ər-ĭs) *n.* A nun at the head of a priory or ranking next below an abbess in an abbey. [Middle English *prioresse,* from Old French, feminine of PRIOR.]

pri·or·i·ty (prī-ôr′ə-tē, -ŏr′ə-tē) *n., pl.* **-ties. 1.** Precedence, especially established by order of importance or urgency. **2. a.** An established right to precedence. **b.** An authoritative rating that establishes such precedence. **3.** A preceding or coming earlier in time. [Middle English *priorite,* from Old French, from Medieval Latin *priōritās,* from Latin *prior,* PRIOR.]

pri·or·y (prī′ə-rē) *n., pl.* **-ies.** A monastery or convent governed by a prior or prioress. [Middle English *priorie,* from Norman French, from Medieval Latin *priōria,* from PRIOR.]

Prip·et (prĭp′ĕt′, prē′pĕt′). *Polish* **Pry·peć** (prĭ′pĕch′). *Russian* **Pri·pyat** (prē′pyət). A river, 500 miles long, rising in the western Ukraine and flowing through a vast marshland, the *Pripet* (or *Pinsk) Marshes,* in the Ukraine and Byelorussia, to join the Dnieper north of Kiev.

Pris·cil·la (prĭ-sĭl′ə). A feminine given name. [Latin, diminutive of *Prisca,* feminine of the Roman cognomen *Priscus,* from *priscus,* ancient, old. See **per¹** in Appendix.*]

prise. Variant of **prize** (to pry).

prism (prĭz′əm) *n.* **1.** *Geometry.* A polyhedron having parallel, congruent polygons as bases and parallelograms as sides. **2.** *Optics.* A homogeneous transparent solid, usually with triangular bases and rectangular sides, used to produce or analyze a continuous spectrum. **3.** A cut-glass object, such as a pendant of a chandelier. **4.** A crystalline solid having three or more similar faces parallel to a single axis. [Late Latin *prisma,* from Greek, "a thing sawed," prism, from *priein*†, to saw.]

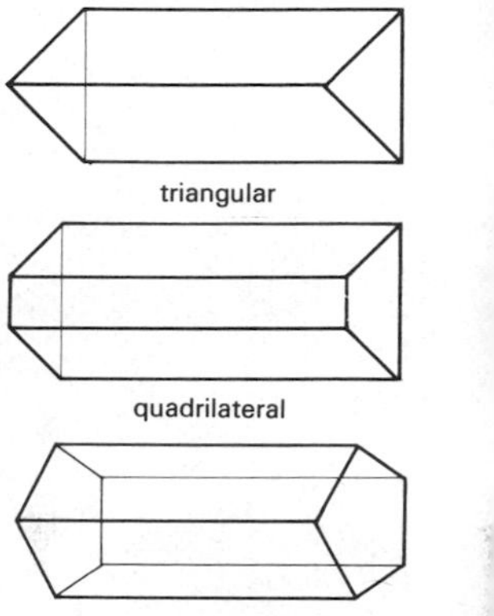

triangular

quadrilateral

pentagonal

prism
Geometric prisms

pris·mat·ic (prĭz-măt′ĭk) *adj.* Also **pris·mat·i·cal** (-ĭ-kəl). **1.** Of, pertaining to, or resembling a prism. **2.** Refracting light as a prism. **3.** Multicolored; iridescent. —**pris·mat′i·cal·ly** *adv.*

pris·ma·toid (prĭz′mə-toid′) *n. Geometry.* A polyhedron having all vertices lying in one of two parallel planes. [New Latin *prismatoides* : Greek *prisma* (stem *prismat-*), PRISM + -OID.] —**pris′ma·toi′dal** *adj.*

pris·moid (prĭz′moid′) *n.* A prismatoid having polygons with the same number of sides as bases, and faces that are parallelograms or trapezoids. [French *prismoïde* : *prisme,* prism, from Late Latin *prisma,* PRISM + -OID.] —**pris·moi′dal** *adj.*

pris·on (prĭz′ən) *n.* **1.** A place where persons convicted or accused of crimes are confined; a penitentiary or jail. **2.** Any place or condition of confinement or forcible restraint. **3.** Imprisonment. —*tr.v.* **prisoned, -oning, -ons.** To imprison. [Middle English *priso(u)n, prisun,* from Old French *prison,* "seizure, imprisonment," from Latin *pre(n)siō,* contraction from *prehensiō,* from *prehendere,* to seize. See **ghend-** in Appendix.*]

pris·on·er (prĭz′ə-nər, prĭz′nər) *n.* **1.** A person held in custody, captivity, or a condition of forcible restraint, especially while on trial or serving a prison sentence. **2.** One deprived of freedom of action or expression: *a prisoner of fate.*

prisoner of war. *Abbr.* **POW, P.O.W.** A person taken by or surrendering to enemy forces during wartime.

prisoner's base. A game in which two teams try to capture opposing players by tagging them and bringing them to a base.

prison fever. *Pathology.* **Typhus** *(see).* [So called because it formerly prevailed in prisons.]

pris·sy (prĭs′ē) *adj.* **-sier, -siest.** Finicky, fussy, and prudish: *"It's a prissy word invented by the clergy."* (J.D. Salinger). [Blend of PRIM and SISSY.] —**pris′si·ly** *adv.* —**pris′si·ness** *n.*

pris·tine (prĭs′tēn′, prĭ-stēn′) *adj.* **1.** Of, pertaining to, or typical of the earliest time or condition; primitive or original. **2.** Remaining in a pure state; uncorrupted. [Latin *pristinus,* original. See **per**[1] in Appendix.*]

prith·ee (prĭth′ē, prĭth′ē) *interj. Archaic.* Please; I pray thee. [Earlier *preythe,* from (I) *pray thee.*]

priv. private.

pri·va·cy (prī′və-sē) *n., pl.* **-cies. 1.** The condition of being secluded or isolated from the view of, or from contact with, others. **2.** Concealment; secrecy.

pri·vate (prī′vĭt) *adj. Abbr.* **priv., pvt. 1.** Secluded from the sight, presence, or intrusion of others: *a private bathroom.* **2.** Of or confined to one person; personal: *private opinions.* **3.** Not available for public use, control, or participation: *a private club.* **4.** Belonging to a particular person or persons, as opposed to the public or the government: *private property.* **5.** Not holding an official or public position: *"Othello himself is no mere private person; he is the general of the Republic."* (A.C. Bradley). **6.** Not public; intimate; secret: *"we were looking at the essence of some private tragedy"* (Doris Lessing). —*n.* **1. a.** *Abbr.* **Pvt.** An enlisted man ranking below private first class in the Army or Marine Corps. **b.** One having a similar rank in other armies or organizations. **2.** *Plural.* The genitals. —**in private.** Secretly; confidentially. [Middle English *privat,* from Latin *prīvātus,* not belonging to the state, not in public life, deprived of office, from the past participle of *prīvāre,* to deprive, release, from *prīvus,* single, individual, deprived of. See **per**[1] in Appendix.*] —**pri′vate·ly** *adv.* —**pri′vate·ness** *n.*

private detective. A privately employed detective as distinguished from one belonging to a public police force. Also called informally "private eye."

private enterprise. 1. Business activities unregulated by state ownership or control; privately owned business in general. **2.** A privately owned business enterprise, especially one operating under a system of free enterprise or laissez-faire capitalism.

pri·va·teer (prī′və-tîr′) *n.* **1.** A ship privately owned and manned but authorized by a government during wartime to attack and capture enemy vessels. **2.** The commander or one of the crew of such a ship. —*intr.v.* **privateered, -teering, -teers.** To sail as a privateer. [From PRIVATE (adjective) by analogy with *volunteer.*]

private first class. *Abbr.* **Pfc, Pfc.** An enlisted man ranking below corporal and above private in the Army or Marine Corps.

private law. The branch of law which deals with or affects the rights of, and the relations between, private individuals. Compare **public law.**

private member. *Chiefly British.* A member of Parliament who does not hold office in the government or in his party.

private parts. The genitals.

private school. A secondary or elementary school run and supported by private individuals or a corporation rather than by a government or public agency.

pri·va·tion (prī-vā′shən) *n.* **1. a.** Lack of the basic necessities or comforts of life. **b.** The condition resulting from such lack. **2.** An act, condition, or result of deprivation or loss. [Middle English *privacion,* from Old French *privation,* from Latin *prīvātiō,* from *prīvāre,* to deprive. See **private.**]

priv·a·tive (prĭv′ə-tĭv) *adj.* **1.** Causing deprivation, lack, or loss. **2.** *Grammar.* Altering the meaning of a term from positive to negative. —*n. Grammar.* A privative prefix or suffix, such as *a-, non-, un-,* or *-less: the alpha privative.* [Latin *prīvātīvus,* from *prīvāre,* to deprive. See **private.**] —**priv′a·tive·ly** *adv.*

priv·et (prĭv′ĭt) *n.* Either of two shrubs, *Ligustrum vulgare* or *L. ovalifolium,* having pointed leaves and clusters of white flowers. They are widely used for hedges. Also called "prim." **2.** Any of several similar or related plants. [Origin obscure.]

priv·i·lege (prĭv′ə-lĭj) *n.* **1. a.** A special advantage, immunity, permission, right, or benefit granted to or enjoyed by an individual, class, or caste. **b.** Such a right or advantage held as a prerogative of status or rank, and exercised to the exclusion or detriment of others. **2.** The principle of granting and maintaining privileges: *a society based on privilege.* **3.** *Finance.* Any option to buy or sell a stock, including **put, call, spread,** and **straddle** *(all of which see).* —See Synonyms at **right.** —*tr.v.* **privileged, -leging, -leges. 1.** To grant a privilege to. **2.** To free or exempt. Used with *from.* [Middle English, from Old French, from Latin *prīvilēgium,* law affecting an individual, prerogative : *prīvus,* single, individual (see **per**[1] in Appendix*) + *lēx* (stem *lēg-*), law (see **leg-** in Appendix*).]

priv·i·leged (prĭv′ə-lĭjd) *adj.* Enjoying a privilege or having privileges: *"None is privileged and no one shall escape disciplinary action."* (Kwame Nkrumah).

privileged communication. *Law.* **1.** A confidential communication that one cannot be made to divulge. **2.** A communication that is not subject to charges of slander or libel.

priv·i·ly (prĭv′ə-lē) *adv.* In a privy manner; privately; secretly.

priv·i·ty (prĭv′ə-tē) *n., pl.* **-ties. 1.** Knowledge of something private or secret shared between individuals, especially with the implication of approval or consent. **2.** *Law.* **a.** A relation between parties that is held to be sufficiently close and direct to support a legal claim on behalf of or against another person with whom this relation exists. **b.** A successive or mutual interest in or relationship to the same property. [Middle English *privete, privite,* a secret, privacy, from Old French, from Medieval Latin *prīvitās,* from Latin *prīvus,* single, private. See **per**[1] in Appendix.*]

priv·y (prĭv′ē) *adj.* **1.** Made a participant in knowledge of something private or secret. Used with *to: "If a man thinks at all . . . he must be privy to his own thoughts and desires."* (Sterne). **2.** Belonging or proper to a person (as the British sovereign) in his private rather than his official capacity. Now rare except in the designation of certain traditional appurtenances of the British monarchy, such as the **Privy Council** *(see).* **3.** *Archaic.* Concealed; secret. —*n., pl.* **privies. 1. a.** *Archaic.* A latrine. **b.** An outhouse. **2.** *Law.* One of the parties having an interest in the same matter. [Middle English *prive,* secret, private, acquainted with, from Old French *prive,* from Latin *prīvātus,* PRIVATE.]

Privy Council. *Abbr.* **P.C. 1.** A council of the British sovereign that until the 17th century was the supreme legislative body, that now consists of cabinet ministers ex officio and others appointed as a high honor, membership being for life, and that has no important function except through its Judicial Committee, which in certain cases acts as a supreme appellate court in the Commonwealth. **2.** A council of the Canadian sovereign that promulgates regulations under the authority of Acts of Parliament, consisting of cabinet ministers and the speaker of the house, appointment being for life. —**Privy Councillor.**

prix fixe (prē′ fēks′) *pl.* **prix fixes. 1.** A **table d'hôte** *(see).* **2.** The price at which a table d'hôte meal is offered. Compare **à la carte.** [French, "fixed price."]

prize[1] (prīz) *n.* **1.** Something offered or won as an award for achieving superiority or excellence in competition with others. **2.** Something offered for winning in a game of chance. **3.** Anything worth striving for or aspiring to. —See Synonyms at **bonus.** —*adj.* **1.** Offered or given as a prize: *a prize cup.* **2.** Given a prize, or likely to win a prize: *a prize cow.* **3.** Worthy of a prize; first-class. Often used ironically: *a prize blunder.* —*tr.v.* **prized, prizing, prizes. 1.** To value highly; to esteem, cherish, or treasure. **2.** To estimate the worth of; appraise; evaluate. —See Synonyms at **appreciate.** [Middle English *pris,* value, PRICE.]

prize[2] (prīz) *n.* **1.** Something seized by force or taken as booty; especially, an enemy ship and cargo captured at sea during wartime. **2.** The act of seizing; capture. [Middle English *pris(e),* from Old French *prise,* from Vulgar Latin *pre(n)sa* (unattested), "something seized," from the past participle of Latin *pre(he)ndere,* to seize. See **ghend-** in Appendix.*]

prize[3] (prīz) *tr.v.* **prized, prizing, prizes.** Also **prise** (prīz). To move or force with or as if with a lever; pry. —*n.* Also **prise. 1.** Leverage. **2.** *Regional.* Something used as a lever or for prying. [Middle English *prise,* a lever, specialized use of *prise,* PRIZE (seizure).]

prize fight. Also **prize·fight** (prīz′fīt′). A match fought between professional boxers for money. —**prize fighter.** —**prize′fight′er** *n.* —**prize fighting.** —**prize′fight′ing** *n.*

prize ring. 1. The platform enclosed by ropes in which contending boxers meet. **2.** Professional boxing. Preceded by *the.*

p.r.n. *Medicine.* as the situation demands (Latin *pro re nata*).

pro[1] (prō) *n., pl.* **pros.** *Abbr.* **p. 1.** An argument in favor of something; affirmative consideration or vote. Used chiefly in the expression *pros and cons.* **2.** One who supports a proposal or takes the affirmative side in debate. —*adv.* In favor of; affirmatively. —*adj.* Favoring; supporting. Compare **con.** [Middle English, from Latin *prō,* for. See **per**[1] in Appendix.*]

pro[2] (prō) *n., pl.* **pros.** *Informal.* **1.** A professional, especially in sports. **2.** An expert in any field (of endeavor). —*adj. Informal.* Professional: *pro football.* [Short for PROFESSIONAL.]

pro–[1]. Indicates: **1.** Favor or support; for example, **prorevolutionary. 2.** Acting as; for example, **properdin.** ***Note:*** Many compounds other than those entered here may be formed with *pro-.* In forming compounds, *pro-* is normally joined with the following element without space or hyphen: *profascist.* However, in sense 1, the second element frequently begins with a capital letter; in this case it is separated with a hyphen: *pro-American.* It is preferable to use the hyphen when the second element begins with *o* or when forming the compound brings together three or more vowels that would be confusing to read: *pro-aesthetic.* [In borrowed Latin compounds, *prō-* indicates: 1. Forward, forth, in public, as in **project, proclaim.** 2. Forward and downward, as in **profligate.** 3. Away, as in **prodigal.** 4. In front of, before, as in **prohibit.** 5. Anterior, before, in anticipation of, as in **provide.** 6. Onward, forward, as in **progress.** 7. Extending out, as in **prolong.** 8. Substituting for, acting as, as in **pronominal, proconsul.** 9. In behalf of, for, as in **prosit.** 10. Intensified action, as in **promiscuous.** Latin *prō-,* from *prō,* before, in front of, according to, for. See **per**[1] in Appendix.*]

ă pat/ā pay/âr care/ä father/b bib/ch church/d deed/ĕ pet/ē be/f fife/g gag/h hat/hw which/ĭ pit/ī pie/îr pier/j judge/k kick/l lid, needle/m mum/n no, sudden/ng thing/ŏ pot/ō toe/ô paw, for/oi noise/ou out/ŏŏ took/ōō boot/p pop/r roar/s sauce/sh ship, dish/

pro-². Indicates before in time or position, or forward; for example, **prophage, procarp, procephalic.** [From Greek *pro,* before, in front of, forward. See **per¹** in Appendix.*]

PRO, P.R.O. public relations officer.

pro., Pro. professional.

pro·a (prō′ə) *n.* A swift Malayan sailboat with a triangular sail and a single outrigger. [Earlier *parao, prau,* from Malay *pĕrāhū,* probably from Marathi *paḍāv.*]

prob. 1. probable; probably. **2.** problem.

prob·a·bi·lism (prŏb′ə-bə-lĭz′əm) *n.* **1.** *Philosophy.* The doctrine that probability is a sufficient basis for belief and action, since certainty in knowledge is unattainable. **2.** *Roman Catholic Church.* The doctrine that when there is doubt as to the moral rectitude of an action, the opinion which favors liberty may be followed, provided that it is solidly probable, even though the contrary may be equally, or even more, probable. —**prob′a·bi·list** *n.* —**prob′a·bi·lis′tic** *adj.*

prob·a·bil·i·ty (prŏb′ə-bĭl′ə-tē) *n., pl.* **-ties. 1.** The quality or condition of being probable; likelihood. **2.** A probable situation, condition, or event. **3.** *Mathematics.* A number expressing the likelihood of occurrence of a specific event, such as the ratio of the number of experimental results that would produce the event to the total number of results considered possible. —**in all probability.** Most probably; very likely.

prob·a·ble (prŏb′ə-bəl) *adj. Abbr.* **prob. 1.** Likely to happen or to be true. **2.** Relatively likely but not certain; plausible. **3.** *Theology.* Of or pertaining to moral opinions and actions for the lawfulness of which intrinsic reasons or extrinsic authority may be adduced; possible; provable. [Middle English, from Old French, from Latin *probābilis,* provable, laudable, from *probāre,* to approve, PROVE.]

probable cause. *Law.* Reasonable grounds for belief that an accused person is guilty as charged.

prob·a·bly (prŏb′ə-blē) *adv. Abbr.* **prob.** Most likely; in all probability; presumably.

pro·bang (prō′băng′) *n.* A long, slender, flexible rod having a tuft or sponge at the end, used to remove foreign bodies from the larynx or esophagus. [Alteration (influenced by PROBE) of earlier *provang,* probably from obsolete *provet,* a probing instrument, from French *éprouvette,* testing instrument, from Old French, from *e(s)prouver,* to test, try out, from Vulgar Latin *exprobāre* (unattested) : *ex-,* out + *probāre,* to test, PROVE.]

pro·bate (prō′bāt′) *adj.* Having to do with a probate court or its action. —*n.* **1.** Legal establishment of the validity of a will. **2.** The right to validate wills. —*tr.v.* **probated, -bating, -bates.** To establish the validity of (a will). [Middle English *probat,* from Latin *probātum,* something proved, from *probāre,* to examine, demonstrate as good, PROVE.]

probate court. A court limited to the jurisdiction of probating wills and administering estates.

pro·ba·tion (prō-bā′shən) *n.* **1.** A trial period in which a person's fitness for membership in a working or social group is tested. **2.** *Law.* The action of suspending the sentence of one convicted of a minor offense and granting him provisional freedom on the promise of good behavior. **3.** A trial period in which a student is permitted to redeem failing grades or bad conduct. **4.** The status of a person on probation. [Middle English *probacioun,* from Old French *probation,* from Latin *probātiō,* from *probāre,* to try, PROVE.] —**pro·ba′tion·al, pro·ba′tion·ar′y** *adj.* —**pro·ba′tion·al·ly** *adv.*

pro·ba·tion·er (prō-bā′shən-ər) *n.* A person on probation.

pro·ba·tive (prō′bə-tĭv) *adj.* Also **pro·ba·to·ry** (-tôr′ē, -tōr′ē). **1.** Serving to test, try, or prove. **2.** Furnishing evidence or proof. [Middle English *probatiffe,* from Latin *probātīvus,* of proof, from *probāre,* to try, PROVE.]

probe (prōb) *n.* **1.** Any object or device used to investigate an unknown configuration or condition. **2.** A slender, flexible instrument used to explore a wound or body cavity. **3.** The act of exploring or searching with the aid of such an instrument. **4.** An investigation into the nature of something; especially, an investigation of unlawful practices conducted by a legislative committee. —*v.* **probed, probing, probes.** —*tr.* **1.** To explore with a probe. **2.** To examine or investigate penetratingly; delve into. —*intr.* To conduct an exploratory investigation; search. [Medieval Latin *proba,* examination, from Late Latin, proof, test, from Latin *probāre,* to test, PROVE.] —**prob′er** *n.*

pro·bi·ty (prō′bə-tē) *n.* Complete and confirmed integrity; uprightness. See Synonyms at **honesty.** [Old French *probité,* from Latin *probitās,* goodness, honesty, from *probus,* good, honest, virtuous. See **per¹** in Appendix.*]

prob·lem (prŏb′ləm) *n. Abbr.* **prob. 1.** A question or situation that presents uncertainty, perplexity, or difficulty. **2.** A person who is difficult to deal with. **3.** A question put forward for consideration, discussion, or solution. —*adj.* **1.** Difficult to deal with or handle: *a problem child.* **2.** Dealing with a social or moral problem: *a problem play.* [Middle English *probleme,* from Old French, from Latin *problēma,* from Greek *problēma,* "thing thrown forward," projection, obstacle, problem, from *proballein,* to throw forward : *pro-,* forward + *ballein,* to throw (see **gwel-¹** in Appendix*).]

prob·lem·at·i·cal (prŏb′lə-măt′ĭ-kəl) *adj.* Also **prob·lem·at·ic** (-ĭk). **1.** Posing a problem; difficult to solve. **2.** Open to doubt; debatable: *"and if you ever get married, which seems to me extremely problematic"* (Oscar Wilde). —**prob′lem·at′i·cal·ly** *adv.*

pro·bos·cid·i·an (prō′bŏs-ĭd′ē-ən) *adj.* Also **pro·bos·ci·de·an** (prō-bŏs′ə-dē′ən, prō′bŏs-ĭd′ē-ən). Of or belonging to the Proboscidea, an order of mammals that is characterized by a trunk or proboscis and includes the elephant. —*n.* Any animal of this order.

pro·bos·cis (prō-bŏs′ĭs) *n., pl.* **-cises** or **proboscides** (prō-bŏs′ə-dēz′). **1.** A long, flexible snout or trunk, as of an elephant. **2.** A slender, tubular feeding and sucking structure of some insects and worms. **3.** A human nose, especially a prominent one. [Latin, from Greek *proboskis* : *pro-,* in front + *boskein,* to feed (see **gwou-** in Appendix*).]

proc. 1. proceedings. **2.** process.

pro·caine hydrochloride (prō′kān′). A white crystalline powder, $C_{13}H_{20}O_2N_2 \cdot HCl$, used as a local anesthetic in medicine and dentistry. A trademark is "Novocain." [PRO- (in place of) + (CO)CAIN.]

pro·cam·bi·um (prō-kăm′bē-əm) *n. Botany.* A layer of undifferentiated plant cells from which the vascular tissue is formed. [PRO- (before) + CAMBIUM.] —**pro·cam′bi·al** *adj.*

pro·carp (prō′kärp′) *n. Botany.* A specialized female sex organ in certain algae. [New Latin *procarpium* : PRO- (before) + -CARP.]

pro·ce·dur·al (prə-sē′jər-əl) *adj.* Of or concerning procedure, especially of a court of law or parliamentary body.

pro·ce·dure (prə-sē′jər) *n.* **1.** A manner of proceeding; way of performing or effecting something. **2.** An act composed of steps; course of action. **3.** A set of established forms or methods for conducting the affairs of a business, legislative body, or court of law. [French *procédure,* from Old French, from *proceder,* PROCEED.]

pro·ceed (prō-sēd′, prə-) *intr.v.* **-ceeded, -ceeding, -ceeds. 1.** To go forward or onward, especially after an interruption; continue. **2.** To undertake and carry on some action or process. **3.** To move on in an orderly manner. **4.** To issue forth; originate. **5.** To institute and conduct legal action. Used with *against.* [Middle English *proceden,* from Old French *proceder,* from Latin *prōcēdere* : *prō-,* forward + *cēdere,* to go (see **ked-¹** in Appendix*).] —**pro·ceed′er** *n.*

pro·ceed·ing (prō-sē′dĭng, prə-) *n.* **1.** A course of action; procedure. **2.** A continuing of an action. **3.** *Plural.* A sequence of events occurring at a particular place or occasion. **4.** *Plural. Abbr.* **proc.** A record of business carried on by a society or other organization; minutes. **5.** *Law.* **a.** *Plural.* Legal action; litigation. **b.** The instituting or conducting of litigation.

pro·ceeds (prō′sēdz′) *pl.n.* The amount of money derived from a commercial or fund-raising venture; profits; yield.

pro·ce·phal·ic (prō′sə-făl′ĭk) *adj.* Anatomically located on or near the front of the head. [PRO- (in front) + -CEPHALIC.]

proc·ess¹ (prŏs′ĕs′, prō′sĕs′) *n., pl.* **processes** (prŏs′ĕs′ĭz, prō′sĕs′-, prŏs′ə-sēz′, prō′sə-). *Abbr.* **proc. 1.** A system of operations in the production of something. **2.** A series of actions, changes, or functions that bring about an end or result. **3.** Course or passage of time. **4.** Ongoing movement; progression. **5.** *Law.* **a.** A summons or writ ordering a defendant to appear in court. **b.** The total amount of summonses or writs issued in a particular proceeding. **c.** The entire course of a judicial proceeding. **6.** *Biology.* A part extending or projecting from an organ or organism; an appendage. **7.** Any of various photomechanical or photoengraving methods. —*tr.v.* **processed, -cessing, -cesses. 1.** To put through the steps of a prescribed procedure. **2.** To prepare, treat, or convert by subjecting to some special process. **3.** *Law.* To serve with a summons or writ. **4.** To institute legal proceedings against; prosecute. —*adj. Abbr.* **proc. 1.** Prepared or converted by a special treatment: *process cheese.* **2.** Made by or used in photomechanical or photoengraving methods: *a process print.* [Middle English *proces(se),* from Old French *proces,* from Latin *prōcessus,* from the past participle of *prōcēdere,* to PROCEED.] —**proc′es′sor** (prŏs′ĕs′ər, prō′sĕs′-), **proc′es′ser** *n.*

pro·cess² (prə-sĕs′) *intr.v.* **-cessed, -cessing, -cesses.** To move along or go in or as if in a procession. [Back-formation from PROCESSION.]

pro·ces·sion (prə-sĕsh′ən) *n.* **1.** The act of proceeding, moving along, or issuing forth. **2. a.** A group of persons, vehicles, or objects moving along in an orderly and formal manner, usually in a long line. **b.** The movement of such a group. **3.** Any continuous and orderly course: *the procession of the seasons.* —*intr.v.* **processioned, -sioning, -sions.** To form or go in a procession. [Middle English, from Old French, from Late Latin *prōcessiō,* religious procession, from Latin, a marching forward, from *prōcēdere,* to PROCEED.]

pro·ces·sion·al (prə-sĕsh′ən-əl) *adj.* Of, pertaining to, or suitable for a procession. —*n.* **1.** A book containing the ritual observed during a religious procession. **2.** A hymn sung when the clergy enter a church at the beginning of the service. **3.** Any music intended to be played or sung during a procession. —**pro·ces′sion·al·ly** *adv.*

process printing. Printing from multiple, usually four, halftone images, each inked with a different color such that the composite impression will reproduce the colors of the original.

pro·cès-ver·bal (prō-sā′vĕr-bäl′) *n., pl.* **-baux** (-bō′). **1.** An official record of diplomatic negotiations. **2.** A detailed official record of legal or other proceedings. [French, from Old French, "verbal proceedings," originally referring to evidence delivered orally by illiterate subaltern police officers.]

pro·claim (prō-klām′, prə-) *tr.v.* **-claimed, -claiming, -claims. 1.** To announce officially and publicly; declare. **2.** To indicate unmistakably; make plain. **3.** To praise; extol. [Middle English *procla(y)men,* from Old French *proclamer,* from Latin *prōclāmāre* : *prō-,* forward, forth + *clāmāre,* to cry out (see **kel-³** in Appendix*).] —**pro·claim′er** *n.*

proc·la·ma·tion (prŏk′lə-mā′shən) *n.* **1.** The act of proclaiming. **2.** Something proclaimed; especially, an official public announcement.

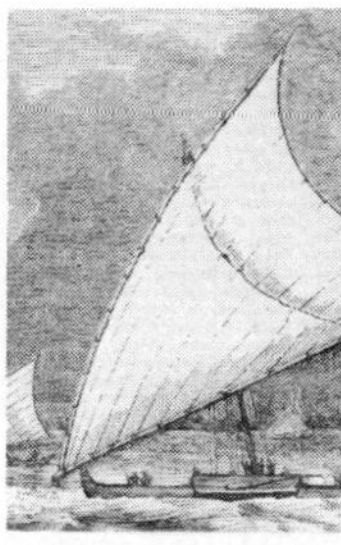

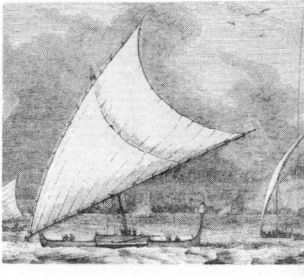

proa

t tight/th thin, path/*th* this, bathe/ŭ cut/ûr urge/v valve/w with/y yes/z zebra, size/zh vision/ə about, item, edible, gallop, circus/ à *Fr.* ami/œ *Fr.* feu, *Ger.* schön/ü *Fr.* tu, *Ger.* über/KH *Ger.* ich, *Scot.* loch/N *Fr.* bon. ***Follows main vocabulary. †Of obscure origin.**

pro·clit·ic (prō-klĭt′ĭk) *adj. Linguistics.* Forming an accentual unit with the following word and thus having no independent accent. Compare **enclitic.** —*n.* A proclitic word. [New Latin *procliticus,* formed by analogy with Late Latin *encliticus,* ENCLITIC : Greek *pro-,* forward + *klinein,* to lean (see **klei-** in Appendix*).]

pro·cliv·i·ty (prō-klĭv′ə-tē) *n., pl.* **-ties.** A natural propensity or inclination; predisposition. [Latin *prōclīvitās,* from *prōclīvus,* sloping forward : *prō-,* forward + *clīvus,* slope, hill (see **klei-** in Appendix*).]

pro·con·sul (prō-kŏn′səl) *n.* **1.** A Roman provincial governor of consular rank. **2.** A high administrator in one of the European colonial empires. [Middle English, from Latin, combined from *prō consule,* (one acting) for a consul : *prō-,* for + CONSUL.] —**pro·con′su·lar** (-sə-lər, -syə-lər) *adj.* —**pro·con′su·late** (-lĭt) *n.*

pro·cras·ti·nate (prō-krăs′tə-nāt′, prə-) *v.* **-nated, -nating, -nates.** —*intr.* To put off doing something until a future time. —*tr.* To postpone or delay needlessly. [Latin *prōcrāstināre,* "to put forward until tomorrow" : *prō-,* forward + *crāstinus,* of tomorrow, from *crās*†, tomorrow.] —**pro·cras′ti·na′tion** *n.* —**pro·cras′ti·na′tor** (-nā′tər) *n.*

pro·cre·ate (prō′krē-āt′) *v.* **-ated, -ating, -ates.** —*tr.* **1.** To beget (offspring). **2.** To produce or create; originate. —*intr.* To beget offspring; reproduce. [Latin *prōcreāre* : *prō-,* forward, forth + *creāre,* to create (see **ker-**[3] in Appendix*).] —**pro′cre·ant** *adj.* —**pro′cre·a′tion** *n.* —**pro′cre·a′tor** (-ā′tər) *n.*

pro·cre·a·tive (prō′krē-ā′tĭv) *adj.* **1.** Capable of reproducing; generative. **2.** Of or directed to procreation: *procreative instinct.*

pro·crus·te·an (prō-krŭs′tē-ən) *adj.* Also **Pro·crus·te·an.** Producing or designed to produce conformity by ruthless or arbitrary means. [After *Procrustes,* a fabulous Greek giant who stretched or shortened captives to fit one of his iron beds.]

procrustean bed. Also **Procrustean bed.** An arbitrary standard to which exact conformity is forced.

pro·cryp·tic (prō-krĭp′tĭk) *adj. Biology.* Having a pattern or coloration adapted for natural camouflage. [Probably PRO(TECT) + CRYPTIC.]

proc·tol·o·gy (prŏk-tŏl′ə-jē) *n.* The physiology and pathology of the rectum and anus. [Greek *prōktos,* anus (see **prōkto-** in Appendix*) + -LOGY.] —**proc′to·log′ic** (prŏk′tə-lŏj′ĭk), **proc′to·log′i·cal** *adj.* —**proc′to·log′i·cal·ly** *adv.* —**proc·tol′o·gist** *n.*

proc·tor (prŏk′tər) *n.* A dormitory and examination supervisor in a school. —*tr.v.* **proctored, -toring, -tors.** To serve as proctor at (an examination). [Middle English *proc(u)tour,* agent, deputy, contraction of *procuratour,* PROCURATOR.] —**proc·to′ri·al** (prŏk-tôr′ē-əl, -tōr′ē-əl) *adj.*

proc·to·scope (prŏk′tə-skōp′) *n.* An instrument for dilating and examining the rectum. [Greek *prōktos,* anus (see **prōkto-** in Appendix*) + -SCOPE.] —**proc′to·scop′ic** (prŏk′tə-skŏp′ĭk) *adj.* —**proc·tos′co·py** (prŏk-tŏs′kə-pē) *n.*

pro·cum·bent (prō-kŭm′bənt) *adj.* **1.** *Botany.* Trailing along the ground: *a procumbent vine.* **2.** Lying face down; prone. [Latin *prōcumbens,* present participle of *prōcumbere,* to fall forward, bend down : *prō-,* forward, down + *-cumbere,* to lie down (see **keu-**[2] in Appendix*).]

proc·u·ra·tor (prŏk′yə-rā′tər) *n.* **1.** An agent having power of attorney. **2.** An official of the Roman Empire acting as a financial agent of the emperor or as the administrator of a minor province. [Middle English *procuratour,* from Old French, from Latin *prōcūrātor,* from *prōcūrāre,* to take care of, PROCURE.] —**proc′u·ra·to′ri·al** (prŏk′yər-ə-tôr′ē-əl, -tōr′ē-əl), **proc′u·ra·to′ry** (prŏk′yər-ə-tôr′ē, -tōr′ē, prō-kyŏŏr′ə-, prə-) *adj.*

pro·cure (prō-kyŏŏr′, prə-) *v.* **-cured, -curing, -cures.** —*tr.* **1.** To obtain; acquire. **2.** To bring about; effect: *procure a solution.* **3.** To obtain (a woman) to serve as a prostitute. —*intr.* To work as a procurer of women. [Middle English *procuren,* to take care of, gain, obtain, from Old French *procurer,* from Late Latin *prōcūrāre,* to obtain, from Latin, to take care of, manage for someone else : *prō-,* for, on behalf of + *cūrāre,* to take care of (see **cūra** in Appendix*).] —**pro·cure′ment** *n.*

pro·cur·er (prō-kyŏŏr′ər, prə-) *n.* **1.** One who procures. **2.** A pander.

pro·cur·ess (prō-kyŏŏr′ĭs, prə-) *n.* A female procurer.

Pro·cy·on (prō′sē-ŏn′) *n.* A double star in the constellation Canis Minor. Also called "Dog Star." [Latin, from Greek *Prokuōn,* "before the dog star" : *pro-,* before + *kuōn,* dog (see **kwon-** in Appendix*).]

prod (prŏd) *tr.v.* **prodded, prodding, prods.** **1.** To jab or poke, as with a pointed instrument. **2.** To rouse to action; urge; goad. —*n.* **1.** Anything pointed used to prod; a goad. **2.** An incitement or stimulus. [Perhaps blend of POKE and *brod,* variant of BRAD.] —**prod′der** *n.*

prod. 1. produce. **2.** produced. **3.** product.

prod·i·gal (prŏd′ĭ-gəl) *adj.* **1.** Recklessly wasteful; extravagant. **2.** Profuse in giving; exceedingly abundant. **3.** Profuse; lavish: *prodigal praise.* —*n.* A person given to luxury or extravagance; a spendthrift or profligate. [Latin *prōdigus,* from *prōdigere,* to drive away, squander : *prōd-,* variant of *prō-,* forth, away + *agere,* to drive (see **ag-** in Appendix*).] —**prod′i·gal·ly** *adv.*

prod·i·gal·i·ty (prŏd′ĭ-găl′ə-tē) *n., pl.* **-ties.** **1.** Extravagant wastefulness. **2.** Profuse generosity. **3.** Extreme abundance; lavishness.

pro·di·gious (prə-dĭj′əs) *adj.* **1.** Impressively great in size, force, or extent; enormous. **2.** Extraordinary; marvelous. **3.** *Obsolete.* Portentous; ominous. [Latin *prōdigiōsus,* from *prōdigium,* omen, portent, PRODIGY.] —**pro·di′gious·ly** *adv.* —**pro·di′gious·ness** *n.*

prod·i·gy (prŏd′ə-jē) *n., pl.* **-gies.** **1.** A person with exceptional talents or powers: *a child prodigy.* **2.** An act or event so extraordinary or rare as to inspire wonder; a marvel. **3.** *Archaic.* An omen or portent. [Latin *prōdigium,* prophetic sign, marvel. See **ēg-** in Appendix*.]

pro·drome (prō′drōm′) *n., pl.* **-dromes** or **prodromata** (prō-drō′mə-tə). A symptom of the onset of a disease. [French, from Greek *prodromos,* precursor : *pro-,* forward + *dromos,* running (see **der-**[1] in Appendix*).] —**pro·dro′mal** (prō-drō′-məl), **pro·drom′ic** (prō-drŏm′ĭk) *adj.*

pro·duce (prə-dōōs′, -dyōōs′, prō-) *v.* **-duced, -ducing, -duces.** —*tr.* **1.** To bring forth; yield. **2.** To create by mental or physical effort. **3.** To manufacture. **4.** To cause to occur or exist; give rise to. **5.** To bring forward; exhibit. **6.** To sponsor and present to the public: *produce a play.* **7.** *Geometry.* To extend (an area or volume) or lengthen (a line). —*intr.* To make or yield the customary product or products. —*n.* (prŏd′ōōs, -yōōs, prō′dōōs, -dyōōs). *Abbr.* **prod.** Something produced; a product; especially, farm products collectively. [Latin *prōducere,* to lead or bring forth : *prō-,* forward + *dūcere,* to lead (see **deuk-** in Appendix*).] —**pro·duc′i·ble** *adj.*

pro·duc·er (prə-dōō′sər, -dyōō′sər, prō-) *n.* **1.** One that produces; specifically, a person or organization that grows or manufactures goods or services for sale. **2.** One who finances and supervises the production of a play or other public entertainment. **3.** A furnace that manufactures producer gas.

producer gas. A gas used as fuel, generated by passing air with steam over burning coke or coal, to yield a combustible mixture of nitrogen, carbon monoxide, and hydrogen. Also called "air gas."

producer goods, producers' goods. *Economics.* Goods, such as raw materials or tools, used to make consumer goods.

prod·uct (prŏd′əkt) *n. Abbr.* **prod.** **1.** Anything produced by human or mechanical effort or by a natural process. **2.** A direct result; consequence. **3.** *Chemistry.* A substance produced by a chemical change. **4.** *Mathematics.* **a.** The result obtained by performing multiplication. **b.** A **scalar product** *(see).* **c.** A **vector product** *(see).* [Latin *prōductum,* from the past participle of *prōdūcere,* to PRODUCE.]

pro·duc·tion (prə-dŭk′shən, prō-) *n.* **1.** The act or process of producing. **2.** The creation of value or wealth by producing goods and services. **3.** Something produced; a product. **4.** The total number of products; output. **5.** A public performance or showing of a play or other form of entertainment. —**pro·duc′tion·al** *adj.*

pro·duc·tive (prə-dŭk′tĭv, prō-) *adj.* **1.** Producing or capable of producing. **2.** Producing abundantly; fertile; prolific. **3.** Yielding favorable or useful results; constructive. **4.** *Economics.* Of or involved in the creation of goods and services to produce wealth or value. **5.** Resulting in. Used with *of: difficulties productive of dispute.* —**pro·duc′tive·ly** *adv.* —**pro′duc·tiv′i·ty** (prō′dŭk-tĭv′ə-tē, prŏd′ək-), **pro·duc′tive·ness** *n.*

pro·em (prō′ĕm′) *n.* A short introduction; preface. [Middle English *proheme,* from Old French *pro(h)eme,* from Latin *prooemium,* from Greek *prooimion* : *pro-,* before + *oimē,* song, lay, from *oimos,* way, path (see **sōi-** in Appendix*).] —**pro·e′mi·al** (prō-ē′mē-əl, prō-ĕm′ē-) *adj.*

pro·es·trus (prō-ĕs′trəs) *n.* The period of preparation for pregnancy that immediately precedes estrus in female mammals.

prof (prŏf) *n. Informal.* A professor.

prof., Prof. professor.

prof·a·na·tion (prŏf′ə-nā′shən) *n.* The act or an instance of profaning; desecration.

pro·fane (prō-fān′, prə-) *adj.* **1.** Showing contempt or irreverence toward God or sacred things; blasphemous. **2.** Nonreligious in subject matter, form, or use; secular: *sacred and profane music.* **3.** Not initiated into the mysteries of ritual. **4.** Vulgar; coarse. —*tr.v.* **profane, -faning, -fanes.** **1.** To treat with irreverence. **2.** To put to an improper, unworthy, or degrading use; abuse. [Middle English *prophane,* from Old French, from Medieval Latin *prophānus,* variant of Latin *profānus,* "before (i.e., outside) the temple," hence not sacred, secular, impious : *prō-,* before + *fānum,* temple (see **dhēs-** in Appendix*).] —**pro·fan′a·to′ry** (prō-făn′ə-tôr′ē, -tōr′ē, prə-) *adj.* —**pro·fane′ly** *adv.* —**pro·fane′ness** *n.* —**pro·fan′er** *n.*

Synonyms: *profane, blasphemous, sacrilegious.* The most common meaning of these adjectives refers to irreverence toward God or things held sacred. *Profane,* the most general, describes abusive disrespect of a sacred name by word or deed. *Blasphemous,* in careful usage, refers strictly to profane utterances about God. *Sacrilegious* usually implies extremely profane actions or desecration of sacred objects.

pro·fan·i·ty (prō-făn′ə-tē, prə-) *n., pl.* **-ties.** **1.** The condition or quality of being profane. **2. a.** Abusive, vulgar, or irreverent language. **b.** The use of such language.

pro·fess (prə-fĕs′, prō-) *v.* **-fessed, -fessing, -fesses.** —*tr.* **1.** To affirm openly; declare or claim: *"I profess both to learn and to teach anatomy, not from books but from dissections"* (William Harvey). **2.** To make a pretense of: *"He professed to despise everything that had happened since 1850"* (Louis Auchincloss). **3.** To claim skill in or knowledge of: *profess medicine.* **4.** To affirm belief in: *profess Catholicism.* **5.** To receive into a religious order. —*intr.* **1.** To make an open affirmation. **2.** To take the vows of a religious order. [Latin *prōfitērī* (past participle *prōfessus*), to declare publicly : *prō-,* forth, in public + *fatērī,* to acknowledge, confess (see **bhā-**[2] in Appendix*).] —**pro·fessed′** *adj.* —**pro·fess′ed·ly** *adv.*

pro·fes·sion (prə-fĕsh′ən) *n.* **1.** An occupation or vocation requiring training in the liberal arts or the sciences and advanced study in a specialized field. **2.** The body of qualified persons of one specific occupation or field. **3.** The act or an instance of professing; declaration; claim. **4.** An avowal of faith in a religion. [Middle English, vow made on entering a religious order, from Old French, from Latin *professiō*, declaration, confession, from *profitērī*, PROFESS.]

pro·fes·sion·al (prə-fĕsh′ən-əl) *adj.* **1.** Of, related to, engaged in, or suitable for a profession. **2.** Engaged in a specific activity as a source of livelihood. **3.** Performed by persons receiving pay. **4.** Having great skill or experience in a particular field or activity. —*n. Abbr.* **pro., Pro. 1.** A person following a profession. **2.** One who earns his livelihood as an athlete. **3.** One who has an assured competence in a particular field or occupation. —**pro·fes′sion·al·ly** *adv.*

pro·fes·sion·al·ism (prə-fĕsh′ən-ə-lĭz′əm) *n.* **1.** Professional status, methods, character, or standards. **2.** The use of professional players in organized athletics.

pro·fes·sor (prə-fĕs′ər) *n.* **1.** *Abbr.* **prof., Prof. a.** A teacher of the highest rank in an institution of higher learning. **b.** A teacher or instructor. **2.** One who professes. [Middle English *professour*, from Latin *professor*, from *profitērī*, PROFESS.] —**pro′fes·so′ri·al** *adj.* —**pro′fes·so′ri·al·ly** *adv.*

pro·fes·sor·ship (prə-fĕs′ər-shĭp′) *n.* The rank or office of a professor.

prof·fer (prŏf′ər) *tr.v.* **-fered, -fering, -fers.** To offer; to tender. See Synonyms at **offer.** —*n.* The act of proffering; an offer. [Middle English *profren*, from Old French *p(o)roffrir* : *por-*, from Latin *prō-*, forth + *offrir*, to offer, from Latin *offerre*, "to carry toward" : *ob-*, to, toward + *ferre*, to carry (see **bher-**[1] in Appendix*).] —**prof′fer·er** *n.*

pro·fi·cien·cy (prə-fĭsh′ən-sē) *n., pl.* **-cies.** The state or quality of being proficient; skill; competence.

pro·fi·cient (prə-fĭsh′ənt) *adj.* Performing in a given art, skill, or branch of learning with expert correctness and facility; adept. —*n.* An adept; expert. [Latin *prōficiens*, present participle of *prōficere*, to make progress. See **profit.**] —**pro·fi′cient·ly** *adv.*

Synonyms: *proficient, adept, skilled, skillful.* These adjectives describe varying degrees of ability. *Proficient* implies a high degree of competence through training. *Adept* suggests a natural aptitude, improved by practice. *Skilled* implies mastery of a craft or trade. *Skillful* adds to *skilled* the idea of natural dexterity or creativity in performance or achievement.

pro·file (prō′fīl′) *n.* **1. a.** A side view of an object or structure, especially of a human head. **b.** A representation of an object or structure seen from the side. **2.** An outline of any object. **3.** A biographical essay presenting the subject's most noteworthy characteristics and achievements. **4.** A graph or table representing numerically the extent to which a person or thing shows various tested characteristics: *an organizational profile.* —See Synonyms at **form.** —*tr.v.* **profiled, -filing, -files. 1.** To draw or shape a profile of. **2.** To write a profile of. [Italian *profilo*, from *profilāre*, to draw in outline : *prō-*, forward (from Latin) + *filāre*, to spin, draw a line, from Late Latin, to spin, from Latin *filum*, thread, string. See **gwhī-** in Appendix.*]

prof·it (prŏf′ĭt) *n.* **1.** An advantageous gain or return; benefit. **2.** The return received on a business undertaking after all operating expenses have been met. **3.** *Often plural.* **a.** The return received on an investment after all charges have been paid. **b.** The rate of increase in the net worth of a business enterprise in a given accounting period. **c.** Income received from investments or property. **d.** The amount received for a commodity or service in excess of the original cost. —*v.* **profited, -iting, -its.** —*intr.* **1.** To make a gain or profit. **2.** To be advantageous; benefit. —*tr.* To be beneficial to. [Middle English, from Old French, from Latin *prōfectus*, advance, progress, success, profit, from the past participle of *prōficere*, to go forward, make progress, accomplish, be advantageous : *prō-*, for + *facere*, to do, make. See **dhē-**[1] in Appendix.*] —**prof′it·a·bil′i·ty, prof′it·a·ble·ness** *n.* —**prof′it·a·ble** *adj.* —**prof′it·a·bly** *adv.*

profit and loss. An account showing net profit and loss over a given period. —**prof′it-and-loss′** *adj.*

prof·i·teer (prŏf′ə-tîr′) *n.* One who makes excessive profits on commodities in short supply. —*intr.v.* **profiteered, -teering, -teers.** To act as a profiteer.

profit sharing. A system by which employees receive a share of the profits of a business enterprise. —**prof′it-shar′ing** *adj.*

prof·li·gate (prŏf′lĭ-gĭt, -gāt′) *adj.* **1.** Given over to dissipation; dissolute. **2.** Recklessly wasteful; wildly extravagant. —*n.* A wastrel. [Latin *prōflīgātus*, from the past participle of *prōflīgāre*, to strike down, destroy, ruin : *prō-*, forward, down + *flīgere*, to strike. See **bhlīg-** in Appendix.*] —**prof′li·ga·cy** (-lĭ-gə-sē) *n.*

pro for·ma (prō fôr′mə). *Latin.* As a matter of, or according to, form.

pro·found (prə-found′, prō-) *adj.* **-er, -est. 1.** Situated at, extending to, or coming from a great depth; deep. **2.** Coming as if from the depths of one's being: *profound contempt.* **3.** Thoroughgoing; far-reaching. **4.** Penetrating beyond what is superficial or obvious. **5.** Unqualified; absolute; complete: *a profound silence.* [Middle English *profounde*, from Old French *profond, profund*, from Latin *profundus* : *prō-*, before + *fundus*, bottom (see **bhudh-** in Appendix*).] —**pro·found′ly** *adv.* —**pro·found′ness** *n.*

pro·fun·di·ty (prə-fŭn′də-tē, prō-) *n., pl.* **-ties. 1.** Great depth. **2.** Depth of intellect, feeling, or meaning. **3.** Something profound or abstruse. [Middle English *profundite*, from Old French, from Late Latin *profunditās*, from *profundus*, deep, PROFOUND.]

pro·fuse (prə-fyōōs′, prō-) *adj.* **1.** Plentiful; overflowing; copious. **2.** Giving or given freely and abundantly; extravagant. Usually used with *in: profuse in his compliments.* [Middle English, from Latin *prōfūsus*, from the past participle of *prōfundere*, to pour forth : *prō-*, forth + *fundere*, to pour (see **gheu-** in Appendix*).] —**pro·fuse′ly** *adv.* —**pro·fuse′ness** *n.*

pro·fu·sion (prə-fyōō′zhən, prō-) *n.* **1.** The state of being profuse; abundance. **2.** Lavish or unrestrained expense; extravagance. **3.** A profuse outpouring or display.

pro·gen·i·tor (prō-jĕn′ə-tər) *n.* **1.** A direct ancestor. **2.** An originator of a line of descent. [Middle English *progenitour*, from Old French *progeniteur*, from Latin *prōgenitor*, from *prōgenitus*, past participle of *prōgignere*, to beget : *prō-*, forth + *gignere*, to beget (see **gene-** in Appendix*).]

prog·e·ny (prŏj′ə-nē) *n., pl.* **-nies. 1.** Children or descendants; offspring. **2.** A result of creative effort; product. [Middle English *progenie*, from Old French, from Latin *prōgeniēs*, descent, descendants, from *prōgignere*, to beget. See **progenitor.**]

pro·ges·ta·tion·al (prō′jĕs-tā′shən-əl) *adj.* **1.** Preceding gestation. **2.** Preceding ovulation.

pro·ges·ter·one (prō-jĕs′tə-rōn′) *n.* A female hormone, $C_{21}H_{30}O_2$, secreted by the corpus luteum of the ovary prior to implantation of the fertilized ovum. [PRO- (acting for) + GES(TATION) + STER(OL) + -ONE.]

pro·glot·tid (prō-glŏt′ĭd) *n., pl.* **-tids.** Also **pro·glot·tis** (-ĭs) *pl.* **-tides** (-ə-dēz′). One of the segments of a tapeworm, containing both male and female reproductive organs. [New Latin *proglottis* (stem *proglottid-*), from Greek *proglōssis*, tip of the tongue (from its shape) : *pro-*, before + *glōssa, glōtta*, tongue (see **glōgh-** in Appendix*).] —**pro·glot′tic, pro′glot·ti·de′an** (prō′glŏt-ə-dē′ən, prō′glō-tĭd′ē-ən) *adj.*

prog·na·thous (prŏg′nə-thəs, prŏg-nā′-) *adj.* Also **prog·nath·ic** (prŏg-năth′ĭk). Having jaws that project forward to a considerable degree. [PRO- (in front, projecting) + -GNATHOUS.] —**prog′na·thism′** (prŏg′nə-thĭz′əm) *n.*

prog·no·sis (prŏg-nō′sĭs) *n., pl.* **-ses** (-sēz′). **1. a.** A prediction of the probable course and outcome of a disease. **b.** The likelihood of recovery from a disease. **2.** Any forecast or prediction. [Late Latin, from Greek *prognōsis*, from *progignōskein*, to foreknow, predict : *pro-*, before + *gignōskein*, to know (see **gnō-** in Appendix*).]

prog·nos·tic (prŏg-nŏs′tĭk) *adj.* **1.** Of, relating to, or acting as a prognosis. **2.** Predicting; foretelling. —*n.* **1.** A sign or omen of some future happening. **2.** A symptom indicating the future course of a disease. [Medieval Latin *prognōsticus*, from Greek *prognōstikos*, from *progignōskein*, to predict. See **prognosis.**]

prog·nos·ti·cate (prŏg-nŏs′tĭ-kāt′) *tr.v.* **-cated, -cating, -cates. 1.** To predict, using present indications as a guide. **2.** To foreshadow; portend. [Medieval Latin *prognōsticāre*, from *prognōsticus*, PROGNOSTIC.] —**prog·nos′ti·ca′tor** (-kā′tər) *n.* —**prog·nos′ti·ca′tion** (-nŏs′tĭ-kā′shən) *n.*

pro·gram (prō′grăm′, -grəm) *n.* Also *chiefly British* **pro·gramme. 1.** A listing of the order of events and other pertinent information for some public presentation. **2.** The presentation itself. **3.** A scheduled radio or television show. **4.** Any organized list of procedures; schedule. **5. a.** A procedure for solving a problem, including collection of data, processing, and presentation of results. **b.** Such a procedure coded for a computer. —*tr.v.* **programmed** or **-gramed, -gramming** or **-graming, -grams. 1.** To include or schedule in a program. **2.** To design or schedule programs. **3.** To provide (a computer) with a set of instructions for solving a problem. [French *programme*, from Late Latin *programma*, public notice, from Greek, from *prographein*, to set forth as a public notice : *pro-*, before + *graphein*, to write (see **gerebh-** in Appendix*).] —**pro′gram·mat′ic** (prō′grə-măt′ĭk) *adj.*

pro·gram·mer (prō′grăm′ər) *n.* Also **pro·gram·er.** One who prepares a computer program.

program music. Music embodying the episodes of a known story. Compare **absolute music.**

prog·ress (prŏg′rĕs′, -rəs; *chiefly British* prō′grĕs′) *n.* **1.** Movement toward a goal. **2.** Development; unfolding. **3.** Steady improvement, as of a society or civilization: *a believer in progress.* **4.** *Chiefly British.* A state journey made by a sovereign through his realm. —*intr.v.* **pro·gress** (prə-grĕs′), **-gressed, -gressing, -gresses. 1.** To advance; proceed. **2.** To advance toward a more desirable form. —See Synonyms at **advance.** [Middle English *progresse*, from Latin *prōgressus*, from past participle of *prōgredī*, to go forward : *prō-*, forward + *gradī*, to step, go (see **ghredh-** in Appendix*).]

pro·gres·sion (prə-grĕsh′ən) *n.* **1.** Progress. **2.** Advance. **3.** A sequence, as of events. **4.** *Mathematics.* A series of numbers or quantities, each derived from the one preceding by some consistent operation. See **arithmetic progression, geometric progression. 5.** *Music.* **a.** A succession of tones or chords. **b.** A series of repetitions of a phrase, each in a new position on the scale. —See Synonyms at **series.** —**pro·gres′sion·al** *adj.*

pro·gres·sive (prə-grĕs′ĭv) *adj.* **1.** Moving forward; ongoing; advancing. **2.** Proceeding in steps; continuing steadily by increments. **3.** Promoting or favoring political reform; liberal. **4.** *Capital* **P.** Of or belonging to a Progressive Party. **5.** Of, relating to, or influenced by a theory of education characterized by emphasis on the individual needs and capacities of each child and informality of curriculum. **6.** Of or denoting a tax system in which the rate of taxation increases as the taxable amount increases. **7.** *Pathology.* Continuously spreading or increasing in severity. **8.** Designating a verb form that expresses an action or condition in progress. —*n.* **1.** A person who favors or strives for reform in politics, education, or other fields. **2.** *Capital* **P.** One who belongs to a Progressive Party. **3.** A progressive verb form. —**pro·gres′sive·ly** *adv.* —**pro·gres′sive·ness** *n.*

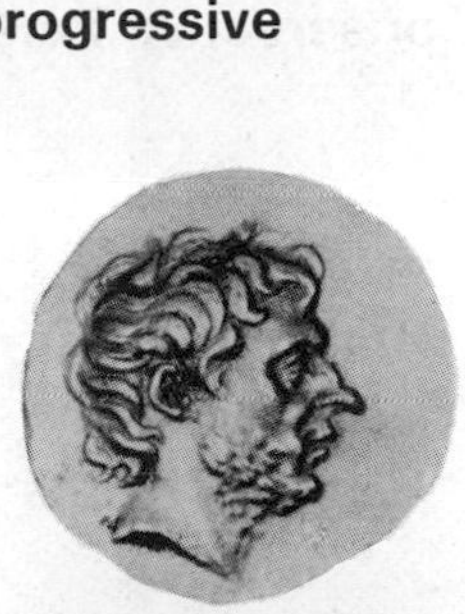

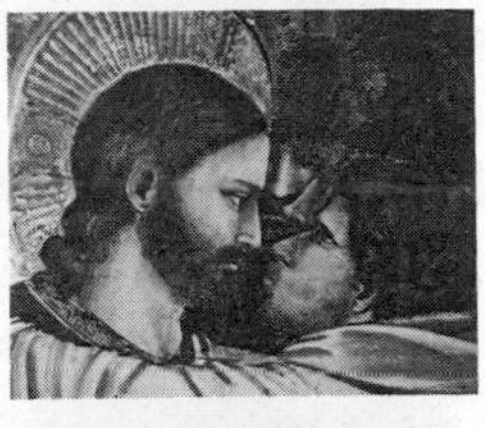

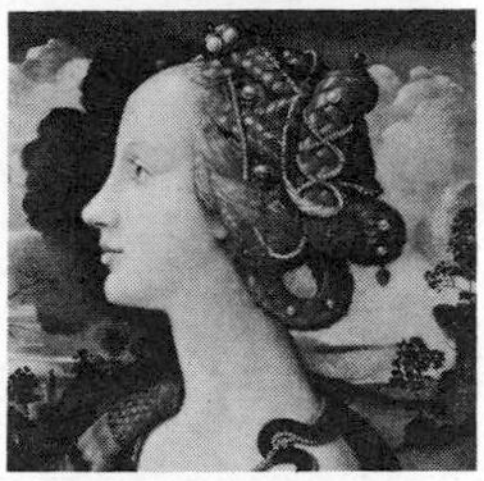

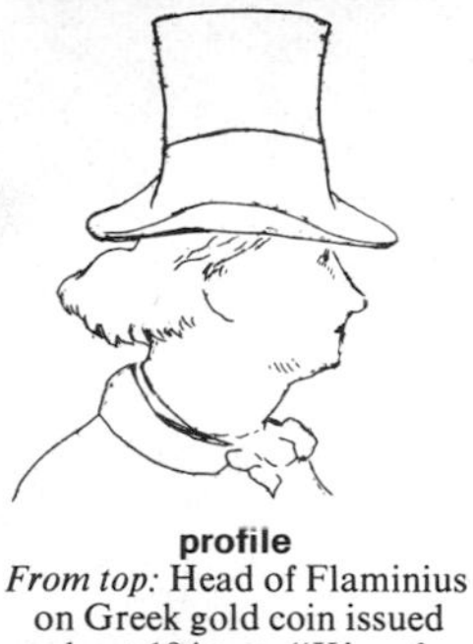

profile
From top: Head of Flaminius on Greek gold coin issued about 194 B.C.; "Kiss of Judas," by Giotto; "Simonetta," by Piero di Cosimo; portrait of Baudelaire by Edouard Manet

Pro·gres·sive-Con·ser·va·tive Party (prō-grĕs′ĭv-kən-sûr′və-tĭv). A leading Canadian political party.

Progressive Party. 1. An American political party organized under the leadership of Theodore Roosevelt in 1912. Also called "Bull Moose Party." **2.** A party with similar goals organized in 1924 and led by Robert M. La Follette. **3.** A party formed in 1948, originally led by Henry A. Wallace.

pro·gres·siv·ism (prə-grĕs′ĭ-vĭz′əm) *n.* The doctrines and practice of political or educational progressives.

pro·hib·it (prō-hĭb′ĭt) *tr.v.* **-ited, -iting, -its. 1.** To forbid by authority. **2.** To prevent or debar. [Middle English *prohibiten,* from Latin *prōhibēre,* to hold in front, hinder, hold back : *prō-,* in front + *habēre,* to hold (see **ghabh-** in Appendix*).]

pro·hi·bi·tion (prō′ə-bĭsh′ən) *n.* **1.** The act of prohibiting. **2.** A law, order, or decree that forbids something. **3. a.** The forbidding by law of the manufacture, transportation, sale, and possession of alcoholic beverages. **b.** *Capital* **P.** The period (1920–33) during which such a law was in force in the United States.

Prohibition Amendment. The **Eighteenth Amendment** *(see).*

pro·hi·bi·tion·ist (prō′ə-bĭsh′ən-ĭst) *n.* **1.** One in favor of outlawing the manufacture and sale of alcoholic beverages. **2.** *Often capital* **P.** A member of the Prohibition Party.

Prohibition Party. An American political party organized in 1869, advocating prohibition.

pro·hib·i·tive (prō-hĭb′ə-tĭv) *adj.* Also **pro·hib·i·to·ry** (-tôr′ē, -tōr′ē). **1.** Prohibiting; forbidding. **2.** Preventing or discouraging purchase or use. —**pro·hib′i·tive·ly** *adv.*

proj·ect (prŏj′ĕkt′, -ĭkt) *n.* **1.** A plan or proposal; scheme. **2.** An undertaking requiring concerted effort. **3.** A research undertaking. —*v.* **pro·ject** (prə-jĕkt′), **-jected, -jecting, -jects.** —*tr.* **1.** To thrust outward or forward. **2.** To throw forward; hurl; impel. **3.** To transport in one's imagination. **4.** To externalize and attribute (an emotion, for example) to someone or something else. **5.** To direct (one's voice) so as to be heard clearly at a distance. **6.** To form a plan or intention for. **7.** To cause (an image) to appear upon a surface. **8.** *Mathematics.* To produce a projection. —*intr.* **1.** To extend forward or out; protrude. **2.** To direct one's voice so as to be heard clearly at a distance. [Middle English *proiecte,* from Latin *prōjectum,* a projecting, projection, from the past participle of *prō(j)icere,* to throw forth : *prō-,* forth + *jacere,* to throw (see **yē-** in Appendix*).]

pro·jec·tile (prə-jĕk′təl, -tīl′) *n.* **1.** A fired, thrown, or otherwise projected object, such as a bullet, having no capacity for self-propulsion. **2.** A self-propelling missile, such as a rocket. —*adj.* **1.** Capable of being impelled or hurled forward. **2.** Driving forward; impelling. **3.** *Zoology.* Capable of being thrust outward; protrusile. [New Latin *prōjectilis,* from Latin *prō(j)icere,* to throw forth, PROJECT.]

pro·jec·tion (prə-jĕk′shən) *n.* **1.** The act of projecting. **2.** Something that thrusts outward; a protuberance. **3.** A plan for an anticipated course of action. **4. a.** The process of projecting a filmed image onto a screen or other viewing surface. **b.** The image so projected. **5.** The image of a geometric figure produced by a coordinate mapping. **6.** A system of intersecting lines, such as the grid of a map, on which part or all of the globe or the celestial sphere may be represented as a plane surface. **7.** *Psychology.* The naive or unconscious attribution of one's own feelings, attitudes, or desires to others.

pro·jec·tion·ist (prə-jĕk′shən-ĭst) *n.* **1.** One who operates a motion-picture projector. **2.** A map-maker.

pro·jec·tive (prə-jĕk′tĭv) *adj. Mathematics.* **1.** Pertaining to or made by projection. **2.** Extending outward; projecting. **3.** Designating a property of a geometric figure that does not vary when the figure undergoes projection. —**pro·jec′tive·ly** *adv.*

projective geometry. The study of geometric properties that are invariant under projection.

projective test. A psychological test in which a subject's responses to relatively unstructured standard stimuli, such as a series of cartoons, abstract patterns, or incomplete sentences, are analyzed for determinants of personality or sometimes cognition.

pro·jec·tor (prə-jĕk′tər) *n.* **1.** A machine for projecting an image onto a screen. **2.** A device for projecting a beam of light. **3.** One who devises plans or projects.

Pro·kof·iev (prə-kôf′yəf, -yĕf′), **Sergei Sergeevich.** 1891–1953. Soviet composer.

Pro·ko·pievsk (prə-kô′pyəfsk). Also **Pro·ko·pyevsk.** An industrial city and transportation center in southern Siberia, U.S.S.R. Population, 291,000.

pro·lac·tin (prō-lăk′tĭn) *n.* A pituitary hormone that stimulates the secretion of milk. [PRO- (forth) + LACT(O)- + -IN.]

pro·la·mine (prō′lə-mĭn, -mēn′, prō-lăm′ĭn, -ēn′) *n.* Also **pro·la·min** (prō′lə-mĭn, prō-lăm′ĭn). Any of a class of simple proteins found in wheat, rye, and other grains. [PROL(INE) + AM(MONIA) + -INE.]

pro·lan (prō′lăn′) *n.* The gonadotropic hormone in pregnant women's urine, used to indicate pregnancy. [German *Prolan,* from Latin *prōlēs,* offspring. See **al-³** in Appendix.*]

pro·lapse (prō-lăps′) *intr.v.* **-lapsed, -lapsing, -lapses.** *Medicine.* To fall or slip out of place. —*n.* (prō′lăps′, prō-lăps′). Also **pro·lap·sus** (prō-lăp′səs). *Medicine.* The falling down or slipping out of place of an organ or part, such as the uterus. [Late Latin *prōlapsus,* a falling, from Latin, past participle of *prōlābī,* to fall or slip down : *prō-,* forward, down + *lābī,* to fall, slip (see **leb-¹** in Appendix*).]

pro·late (prō′lāt′) *adj.* Designating the shape of a solid, especially of a spheroid, having its polar axis longer than its equatorial diameter; cigar-shaped. Compare **oblate.** [Latin *prōlātus,* stretched out (used as past participle of *prōferre,* to bring forward, stretch out) : *prō-,* forth + *-lātus,* "carried" (see **tel-¹** in Appendix*).] —**pro′late′ly** *adv.* —**pro′late′ness** *n.*

pro·leg (prō′lĕg′) *n.* One of the stubby limbs on the abdominal segments of caterpillars and some other insect larvae. [PRO- (for, serving as) + LEG.]

pro·le·gom·e·non (prō′lĭ-gŏm′ə-nŏn′, -nən) *n., pl.* **-na** (-nə). A critical introduction. [Greek, from the present participle passive of *prolegein,* to say beforehand : *pro-,* before + *legein,* to say (see **leg-** in Appendix*).] —**pro′le·gom′e·nous** *adj.*

pro·lep·sis (prō-lĕp′sĭs) *n., pl.* **-ses** (-sēz′). **1.** *Rhetoric.* The anticipation and answering of an objection or argument before one's opponent has put it forward. **2.** The use of a descriptive word in anticipation of the act or circumstances that would make it applicable. [Late Latin, rhetorical anticipation, from Greek *prolēpsis,* from *prolambanein,* to take beforehand, anticipate : *prō-,* before + *lambanein,* to take (see **slagw-** in Appendix*).] —**pro·lep′tic** (prō-lĕp′tĭk), **pro·lep′ti·cal** *adj.*

pro·le·tar·i·an (prō′lə-târ′ē-ən) *adj.* Of, pertaining to, or characteristic of the proletariat. —*n.* A member of the proletariat. [From Latin *prōlētārius,* Roman citizen of the lowest class (who serves the state only by producing offspring), from *prōlēs,* offspring. See **al-³** in Appendix.*] —**pro′le·tar′i·an·ism** *n.* —**pro′le·tar′i·an·ly** *adv.* —**pro′le·tar′i·an·ness** *n.*

pro·le·tar·i·at (prō′lə-târ′ē-ĭt) *n.* **1. a.** The class of industrial wage earners who, possessing neither capital nor production means, must earn their living from their labor power. **b.** The poorest class of working people. **2.** The nonpossessing class of ancient Rome constituting the lowest class of citizens. [French *prolétariat,* from Latin *prōlētārius,* PROLETARIAN.]

pro·lif·er·ate (prō-lĭf′ə-rāt′) *v.* **-ated, -ating, -ates.** —*intr.* **1.** To reproduce or produce new growth or parts rapidly and repeatedly: *proliferating cells.* **2.** To increase or spread at a rapid rate. —*tr.* To cause to grow or increase rapidly. [From French *prolifère,* proliferous, from Medieval Latin *prōlifer,* producing offspring, PROLIFEROUS.] —**pro·lif′er·a′tion** *n.* —**pro·lif′er·a′tive** *adj.*

pro·lif·er·ous (prō-lĭf′ər-əs) *adj.* **1.** *Biology.* Reproducing freely by means of buds and side branches. **2.** *Botany.* Freely producing buds or offshoots, sometimes from unusual places. [Medieval Latin *prōlifer,* producing offspring : Latin *prōlēs,* offspring (see **al-³** in Appendix*) + -FEROUS.]

pro·lif·ic (prō-lĭf′ĭk) *adj.* **1.** Producing offspring or fruit in great abundance; fertile. **2.** Producing abundant works or results. [French *prolifique,* from Medieval Latin *prōlificus,* from Latin *prōlēs,* offspring. See **al-³** in Appendix.*] —**pro·lif′i·cal·ly** *adv.*

pro·line (prō′lēn′) *n.* An amino acid, $C_5H_9O_2N$, found in many proteins. [German *Prolin* : P(YR)ROL(E) + -INE.]

pro·lix (prō-lĭks′, prō′lĭks) *adj.* **1.** Wordy and tedious. **2.** Tending to speak or write at great length. [Middle English, from Old French *prolixe,* from Latin *prōlixus,* "poured forth," extended, abundant. See **leikw-** in Appendix.*] —**pro·lix′i·ty** *n.* —**pro·lix′ly** *adv.*

pro·loc·u·tor (prō-lŏk′yə-tər) *n.* A presiding officer or chairman, especially of the lower house of a convocation in the Anglican Church. [Middle English, from Latin *prōlocūtor,* "one who speaks out," advocate, from *prōloquī,* to speak out, plead : *prō-,* forth + *loquī,* to speak (see **tolkw-** in Appendix*).]

pro·logue (prō′lôg′, -lŏg′) *n.* **1.** The lines introducing a discourse or play. **2.** An introductory act or event. [Middle English *prolog,* from Old French *prolog(u)e,* from Latin *prologus,* from Greek *prologos,* (speaker of) a prologue, introduction : *pro-,* before + *legein,* to speak (see **leg-** in Appendix*).]

pro·logu·ize (prō′lô-gīz′, -lŏg-īz′) *intr.v.* **-ized, -izing, -izes.** Also **pro·log·ize** (prō′lô-gīz′, -lŏg-īz′, prō′lə-jīz′). To write or deliver a prologue. —**pro′logu·iz′er** *n.*

pro·long (prə-lông′, -lŏng′) *tr.v.* **-longed, -longing, -longs.** Also **pro·lon·gate** (prə-lông′gāt′, -lŏng′gāt′), **-gated, -gating, -gates. 1.** To lengthen in duration; protract. **2.** To lengthen in extent. [Middle English *prolongen,* from Old French *prolonguer,* from Late Latin *prōlongāre* : Latin *prō-,* out, extending + *longus,* long (see **del-¹** in Appendix*).] —**pro′lon·ga′tion** *n.*

Synonyms: *prolong, protract, extend.* These verbs mean to lengthen in time or space. *Prolong* implies an increase in duration (time) beyond normal limits. *Protract* adds to *prolong* the idea of lengthening indefinitely or unnecessarily. *Extend* can refer to mere lengthening in time or space, or to increase in range or scope of activities or influence.

pro·lu·sion (prō-lo͞o′zhən) *n.* **1.** A preliminary exercise. **2.** An essay written as a preface to a more detailed work. [Latin *prōlūsiō,* from *prōlūdere* (past participle *prōlūsus*), to play or practice beforehand : *prō-,* before + *lūdere,* to play (see **leid-** in Appendix*).] —**pro·lu′so·ry** (-sə-rē) *adj.*

prom (prŏm) *n.* A ball or formal dance held for a high-school or college class. [Short for PROMENADE.]

prom. promontory.

prom·e·nade (prŏm′ə-nād′, -näd′) *n.* **1.** A leisurely walk, especially one taken in a public place as a social activity. **2.** A public place for such walking. **3. a.** A formal ball. **b.** A formal march by the guests at the opening of a ball. **4.** A march executed between the figures of a square dance. —*v.* **promenaded, -nading, -nades.** —*intr.* **1.** To go on a leisurely walk. **2.** To execute a promenade in square dancing. —*tr.* **1.** To take a promenade along or through. **2.** To take or display on or as if on a promenade. [French, from *se promener,* to take a walk, from Late Latin *prōmināre,* to drive forward : *prō-,* forward + *mināre,* to drive, from Latin *minārī,* to threaten, from *minae,* threats (see **men-²** in Appendix*).] —**prom′e·nad′er** *n.*

ă pat/ā pay/âr care/ä father/b bib/ch church/d deed/ĕ pet/ē be/f fife/g gag/h hat/hw which/ĭ pit/ī pie/îr pier/j judge/k kick/l lid, needle/m mum/n no, sudden/ng thing/ŏ pot/ō toe/ô paw, for/oi noise/ou out/o͝o took/o͞o boot/p pop/r roar/s sauce/sh ship, dish/

promenade deck. The upper deck or a section of the upper deck on a passenger ship where the passengers can promenade.

Pro·me·the·an (prə-mē′thē-ən) *adj.* **1.** Pertaining to or suggestive of Prometheus. **2.** Boldly creative; life-bringing. —*n.* One who is Promethean in manner or actions.

Pro·me·the·us (prə-mē′thē-əs, -thyo͞os′). *Greek Mythology.* A Titan who stole fire from Olympus and gave it to man.

pro·me·thi·um (prə-mē′thē-əm) *n. Symbol* **Pm** A radioactive rare-earth element prepared by fission of uranium or by neutron bombardment of neodymium, having 14 isotopes with mass numbers ranging from 141 to 154, and used as a source of beta rays. Atomic number 61, melting point 1,035°C, boiling point 2,730°C, valence 3. See **element.** [New Latin, after PROMETHEUS (referring to the fire of a nuclear furnace).]

prom·i·nence (prŏm′ə-nəns) *n.* Also **prom·i·nen·cy** (-nən-sē). **1.** The condition or quality of being prominent. **2.** Something that is prominent; a projection. **3.** *Astronomy.* A tonguelike cloud of flaming gas rising from the sun's surface, visible as part of the corona during a total solar eclipse.

prom·i·nent (prŏm′ə-nənt) *adj.* **1.** Projecting outward; protuberant. **2.** Immediately noticeable; conspicuous. **3.** Widely known; eminent. [Latin *prōminēns,* present participle of *prōminēre,* to jut out, project : *prō-,* forth + *-minēre,* to jut (see **men-**[2] in Appendix*).] —**prom′i·nent·ly** *adv.*

prom·is·cu·i·ty (prŏm′ĭ-skyo͞o′ə-tē, prō′mĭ-) *n., pl.* **-ties. 1.** The state or character of being promiscuous. **2.** Promiscuous sexual intercourse. **3.** An indiscriminate mixture; a hodgepodge.

pro·mis·cu·ous (prə-mĭs′kyo͞o-əs) *adj.* **1.** Consisting of diverse and unrelated parts or individuals; confused: *"throngs promiscuous strew the level green"* (Pope). **2.** Lacking standards of selection; indiscriminate. **3.** Indiscriminate in sexual relations. **4.** Casual; random. [Latin *prōmiscuus,* mixed : *prō-* (intensifier), thoroughly + *miscēre,* to mix (see **meik-** in Appendix*).] —**pro·mis′cu·ous·ly** *adv.* —**pro·mis′cu·ous·ness** *n.*

prom·ise (prŏm′ĭs) *n.* **1.** A declaration assuring that one will or will not do something; vow. **2.** Something promised. **3.** Indication of future excellence or success. —*v.* **promised, -mising, -mises.** —*tr.* **1.** To pledge or offer assurance. Followed by an infinitive or clause: *We promise to* (or *that we will*) *return.* **2.** To make a promise of. **3.** To afford a basis for expecting. —*intr.* **1.** To make a promise. **2.** To afford a basis for expectation. Often used with *well* or *fair.* [Middle English *promys(se),* from Latin *prōmissum,* from the neuter past participle of *prōmittere,* "to send forth," promise : *prō-,* forth + *mittere,* to let go, send (see **smeit-** in Appendix*).] —**prom′is·er** *n.*

Promised Land. 1. The land of Canaan, promised to Abraham and his descendants. Genesis 12:7. **2.** *Small* **p.** *small* **l.** Any place of anticipated happiness.

prom·is·ee (prŏm′ĭ-sē′) *n. Law.* An individual to whom a promise is made.

prom·is·ing (prŏm′ĭ-sĭng) *adj.* Likely to develop in a desirable manner. —**prom′is·ing·ly** *adv.*

prom·i·sor (prŏm′ĭ-sôr′) *n. Law.* An individual who makes a promise.

prom·is·so·ry (prŏm′ĭ-sôr′ē, -sōr′ē) *adj.* **1.** Containing, involving, or having the nature of a promise. **2.** Indicating how the provisions of an insurance contract will be carried out after it is signed. [Medieval Latin *prōmissōrius,* from Latin *prōmissor,* one who promises, from *prōmittere,* to PROMISE.]

promissory note. *Abbr.* **p.n., P/N** A written promise to pay or repay a specified sum of money at a stated time or on demand. Also called "note," "note of hand."

prom·on·to·ry (prŏm′ən-tôr′ē, -tōr′ē) *n., pl.* **-ries.** *Abbr.* **prom. 1.** A high ridge of land or rock jutting out into a sea or other expanse of water. **2.** *Anatomy.* A projecting bodily part. [Medieval Latin *prōmontōrium,* alteration of Latin *prōmunturium* : probably from *prō-,* forward + *mōns* (stem *mont-*), mountain (see **men-**[2] in Appendix*).]

pro·mote (prə-mōt′) *tr.v.* **-moted, -moting, -motes. 1. a.** To raise to a more important or responsible job or rank. **b.** To advance (a student) to the next higher grade. **2.** To contribute to the progress or growth of; to further. **3.** To urge the adoption of; to advocate. **4.** To attempt to sell or popularize by advertising or by securing financial support. —See Synonyms at **advance.** [Middle English *promoten,* from Latin *prōmovēre* (past participle *prōmōtus*), to move forward, advance : *prō-,* forward, onward + *movēre,* to move (see **mew-** in Appendix*).]

pro·mot·er (prə-mō′tər) *n.* **1.** An active supporter; advocate. **2.** A finance and publicity organizer, as of a boxing match.

pro·mo·tion (prə-mō′shən) *n.* **1.** The act of promoting. **2.** An advancement in rank or responsibility. **3.** Encouragement; furtherance. **4.** Advertising or other publicity. —**pro·mo′tion·al** *adj.* —**pro·mo′tion·al·ly** *adv.*

pro·mo·tive (prə-mō′tĭv) *adj.* Tending to promote. —**pro·mo′tive·ness** *n.*

prompt (prŏmpt) *adj.* **1.** On time; punctual. **2.** Done without delay. —*tr.v.* **prompted, prompting, prompts. 1.** To press into action; incite. **2.** To give rise to; inspire. **3.** To assist with a reminder; remind. **4.** *Theater.* To give a cue to. —*n.* **1. a.** The act of prompting or giving a cue. **b.** The information suggested; a reminder or cue. **2.** *Commerce.* **a.** A **prompt note** *(see).* **b.** The time limit stipulated in a prompt note. [Middle English, from Old French, from Latin *promptus,* "brought to light," "visible," hence, at hand, ready, prompt, from the past participle of *prōmere,* to bring forth, make manifest : *prō-,* forth + *emere,* to take (see **em-** in Appendix*).] —**prompt′ly** *adv.* —**promp′ti·tude′, prompt′ness** *n.*

prompt·book (prŏmpt′bo͝ok′) *n.* An annotated script used by a theater prompter.

prompt·er (prŏmp′tər) *n.* **1.** One who prompts. **2.** One who gives cues to actors.

prompt neutron. A neutron instantaneously emitted (within 10^{-8} second) in nuclear fission. Compare **delayed neutron.**

prompt note. A notice sent to the purchaser of goods reminding him of the amount due the seller and the date it is due. Also called "prompt."

prom·ul·gate (prŏm′əl-gāt′, prō-mŭl′gāt′) *tr.v.* **-gated, -gating, -gates. 1.** To make known (a decree, law, or doctrine) by public declaration; announce officially. **2.** To put (a law) into effect by formal public announcement. [Latin *prōmulgāre*†.] —**prom′ul·ga′tion** (prŏm′əl-gā′shən, prō′məl-) *n.* —**prom′ul·ga′tor** (prŏm′əl-gā′tər, prō-mŭl′-) *n.*

pron. 1. pronominal; pronoun. **2.** pronounced; pronunciation.

pro·nate (prō′nāt′) *tr.v.* **-nated, -nating, -nates.** To turn (the palm or inner surface of the hand or forelimb) downward or backward. [Late Latin *prōnāre,* to bend forward, bow, from Latin *prōnus,* PRONE.] —**pro·na′tion** *n.*

pro·na·tor (prō′nā′tər) *n., pl.* **pronatores** (prō′nə-tôr′ēz′, -tōr′ēz′). The forearm or forelimb muscle that effects pronation.

prone (prōn) *adj.* **1.** Lying with the front or face downward; prostrate. **2.** Tending: *prone to mischief.* [Middle English, from Latin *prōnus,* "bending" or "leaning forward." See **per**[1] in Appendix.*] —**prone′ly** *adv.* —**prone′ness** *n.*

Synonyms: *prone, supine, prostrate, recumbent.* The various positions assumed in the act of lying down are described by these adjectives. *Prone* always means lying face downward, the front of the body turned toward the surface it rests on. *Supine* also means lying down, but always on one's back. *Prostrate* can mean lying down in either position, and suggests a person's placing himself, being thrown, or collapsing into this position. *Recumbent* means lying down but emphasizes a position of comfort or rest.

pro·neph·ros (prō-nĕf′rəs, -rŏs′) *n.* A primitive kidney that disappears early in the embryonic development of higher vertebrates. Compare **mesonephros, metanephros.** [New Latin : Greek *pro-,* before + *nephros,* kidney (see **negwhro-** in Appendix*).] —**pro·neph′ric** (prō-nĕf′rĭk) *adj.*

prong (prông, prŏng) *n.* **1.** A sharply pointed part of a tool or instrument, such as a tine of a fork. **2.** Any sharply pointed projection. —*tr.v.* **pronged, pronging, prongs.** To pierce with a prong. [Middle English *pronge, prange,* forked instrument, akin to Middle Low German *prange,* pinching instrument, from Germanic *prang-* (unattested), pinch.]

prong·horn (prông′hôrn′, prŏng′-) *n., pl.* **-horns** or **pronghorn.** A small deer, *Antilocapra americana,* resembling an antelope and having small forked horns, found on western North American plains. Also called "pronghorn antelope."

pro·nom·i·nal (prō-nŏm′ə-nəl) *adj. Abbr.* **pron., pronom. 1.** Of, pertaining to, or functioning as a pronoun. **2.** Resembling a pronoun, as by specifying a person, place, or thing, while functioning primarily as another part of speech. *His* in *his choice* is a pronominal adjective. [Late Latin *prōnōminālis,* from Latin *prōnōmen,* PRONOUN.] —**pro·nom′i·nal·ly** *adv.*

pro·noun (prō′noun′) *n. Abbr.* **pron., pr.** One of a class of words that function as substitutes for nouns or noun phrases and denote persons or things asked for, previously specified, or understood from the context. [Middle English *pronom,* from Latin *prōnōmen* : *prō-,* in place of + *nōmen,* name (see **nomen-** in Appendix*).]

pro·nounce (prə-nouns′) *v.* **-nounced, -nouncing, -nounces.** —*tr.* **1.** To articulate (a word or speech sound). **2.** To transcribe (a word) in phonetic symbols. **3.** To state officially and formally; declare. **4.** To declare to be in a specified condition. —*intr.* **1.** To declare one's opinion or make a pronouncement. Used with *on.* **2.** To articulate words. [Middle English *pronuncen, pronouncen,* from Old French *prononcier,* from Latin *prōnuntiāre,* to speak in public, declare : *prō-,* forth, in public + *nuntiāre,* to declare, from *nuntius,* message, messenger (see **neu-**[1] in Appendix*).] —**pro·nounce′a·ble** *adj.* —**pro·nounc′er** *n.*

pro·nounced (prə-nounst′) *adj. Abbr.* **pron. 1.** Spoken; voiced. **2.** Distinct; strongly marked. —**pro·nounc′ed·ly** (prə-noun′sĭd-lē) *adv.* —**pro·nounc′ed·ness** *n.*

pro·nounce·ment (prə-nouns′mənt) *n.* **1.** A formal declaration. **2.** An authoritative statement.

pron·to (prŏn′tō) *adv. Informal.* Without delay; quickly. [Spanish, from Latin *promptus,* PROMPT.]

pro·nu·cle·us (prō-no͞o′klē-əs, -nyo͞o′klē-əs) *n., pl.* **-clei.** (-klē-ī′). The haploid nucleus of a sperm or egg prior to fusion of the nuclei in fertilization. —**pro·nu′cle·ar** *adj.*

pro·nun·cia·mien·to (prō-no͞on′thyä-myĕn′tō) *n., pl.* **-tos.** *Spanish.* **1.** An edict announcing a coup d'état. **2.** Any authoritarian pronouncement.

pro·nun·ci·a·tion (prə-nŭn′sē-ā′shən) *n. Abbr.* **pron. 1.** The act or manner of articulating speech. **2.** A phonetic transcription of a given word. —**pro·nun′ci·a′tion·al** *adj.*

proof (pro͞of) *n.* **1.** The evidence establishing the validity of a given assertion. **2.** Conclusive demonstration of something. **3.** The proving of something by experiment, test, or trial: *put one's beliefs to the proof.* **4.** *Archaic.* Proven impenetrability: *"I was clothed in Armour of proof."* (Bunyan). **5.** *Law.* The whole body of evidence that determines the verdict or judgment in a case. **6.** The validation of a proposition by application of specified rules, as of induction or deduction, to assumptions, axioms, and sequentially derived conclusions. **7.** The strength of a liquor with reference to **proof spirit** *(see).* **8.** *Printing.* A trial sheet of printed material that is checked against the original manuscript and on which corrections are made. Also called "proof sheet." **9.** *Engraving.* A trial impression of a plate,

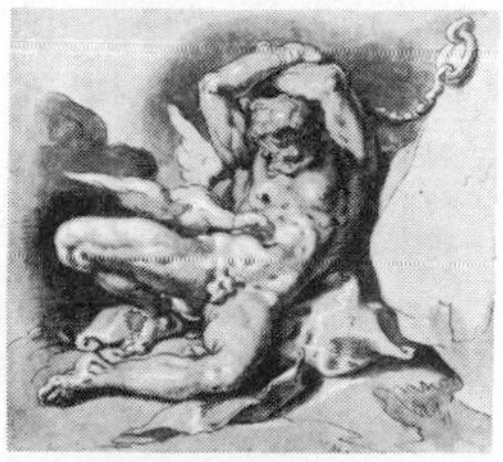

Prometheus
Pen-and-ink drawing
by Abraham Bloemaert

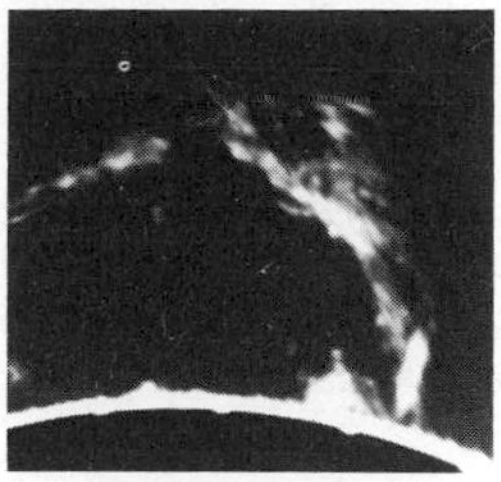

prominence
Solar prominence
estimated to be
205,000 miles high

PROOFREADERS' MARKS

Instruction	Mark in Margin	Mark in Type	Corrected Type
Delete	ℯ	the ~~good~~ word	the word
Insert indicated material	good	the word	the good word
Let it stand	stet	the ~~good~~ word	the good word
Make capital	cap	the word	the Word
Make lower case	lc	The Word	the Word
Set in small capitals	sc	See word.	See WORD.
Set in italic type	ital	The word is word.	The word is *word.*
Set in roman type	rom	the *word*	the word
Set in boldface type	bf	the entry word	the entry **word**
Set in lightface type	lf	the entry **word**	the entry word
Transpose	tr	the word good	the good word
Close up space	⌒	the wo rd	the word
Delete and close up space	⌒ℯ	the woord	the word
Spell out	sp	②words	two words
Insert: space	#	theword	the word
period	⊙	This is the word	This is the word.
comma	⌃	words words, words	words, words, words
hyphen	=/	word for word test	word-for-word test
colon	⊙	The following words	The following words:
semicolon	;	Scan the words skim the words.	Scan the words; skim the words.
apostrophe	⩗	Johns words	John's words
quotation marks	⩗/⩔/	the word word	the word "word"
parentheses	(/)/	The word word is in parentheses.	The word (word) is in parentheses.
brackets	[/]/	He read from the Word the Bible.	He read from the Word [the Bible].
en dash	⅟N	1964 1972	1964–1972
em dash	⅟M/⅟M/	The dictionary how often it is needed belongs in every home.	The dictionary—how often it is needed—belongs in every home.
superior type	⩡	2 = 4	$2^2 = 4$
inferior type	⩒	H₂O	H_2O
asterisk	⩡	word	word*
dagger	†	a word	a word†
double dagger	‡	words and words	words and words‡
section symbol	§	Book Reviews	§Book Reviews
virgule	/	either or	either/or
Start paragraph	¶	"Where is it?" "It's on the shelf."	"Where is it?" "It's on the shelf."
Run in	run in	The entry word is printed in boldface. The pronunciation follows.	The entry word is printed in boldface. The pronunciation follows.
Turn right side up	↻	the word	the word
Move left	⊏	⊏ the word	the word
Move right	⊐	the word	the word
Move up	⊓	the word	the word
Move down	⊔	the word	the word
Align	‖	the word the word the word	the word the word the word
Straighten line	=	the word	the word
Wrong font	wf	the word	the word
Broken type	✕	the word	the word

stone, or block taken at any of various stages of its execution. **10.** *Photography.* A trial print. —*adj.* **1.** Fully or successfully resistant; impervious. Used with *against: proof against fire.* **2.** Of standard alcoholic strength. **3.** Used in proving or making corrections. —*v.* **proofed, proofing, proofs.** —*tr.* **1.** To run off (a printed or engraved proof). **2.** To proofread (copy). —*intr.* To proofread. [Middle English *pre(o)ve, prof, prove,* from Old French *pre(o)ve,* from Late Latin *proba,* from Latin *probāre,* to test, PROVE.]

-proof. Indicates impervious to or able to resist or withstand; for example, **shockproof, waterproof, rustproof.** [From PROOF (adjective).]

proof-read (prōōf'rēd') *v.* **-read** (-rĕd'), **-reading, -reads.** —*tr.* To read (copy or a printer's proof) against the original manuscript for corrections. —*intr.* To correct a printer's proof while reading against the original manuscript. —**proof'read'er** *n.*

proof spirit. An alcohol-water mixture or a beverage containing a standard amount of alcohol, the U.S. standard being 100 proof, or 50 per cent, of ethyl alcohol by volume at 60°F.

prop¹ (prŏp) *n.* **1.** Anything used to shore something up. **2.** A person or thing serving as a support or stay. —*tr.v.* **propped, propping, props.** To keep from falling; support. [Middle English *proppe,* probably from Middle Dutch *proppe†,* vine-prop, stopper.]

prop² (prŏp) *n.* A stage property.

prop³ (prŏp) *n. Informal.* A propeller.

prop-. *Chemistry.* Indicates derivation from propionic acid; for example, **propane.** [From PROPIONIC (ACID).]

prop. **1.** proper; properly. **2.** property. **3.** proposition. **4.** proprietary; proprietor.

pro-pae-deu-tic (prō'pĭ-dōō'tĭk, -dyōō'tĭk) *adj.* Providing introductory instruction. —*n.* Preparatory instruction. [From Greek *propaideuein,* teach beforehand : *pro-,* before + *paideuein,* to rear or educate, from *pais* (stem *paid-*), child (see **pou-** in Appendix*).]

prop-a-ga-ble (prŏp'ə-gə-bəl) *adj.* Capable of being propagated.

prop-a-gan-da (prŏp'ə-găn'də) *n.* **1.** The systematic propagation of a given doctrine or of allegations reflecting its views and interests. **2.** Material disseminated by the proselytizers of a doctrine. [From PROPAGANDA.] —**prop'a-gan'dism'** *n.* —**prop'a-gan'dist** *n.* —**prop'a-gan-dis'tic** *adj.* —**prop'a-gan-dis'ti-cal-ly** *adv.*

Prop-a-gan-da (prŏp'ə-găn'də) *n.* The Congregation of the Roman Curia that has authority in the matter of preaching the gospel and of establishing the Church in non-Christian countries, and of administering Church missions in territories where there is no properly organized hierarchy. [Italian, short for the New Latin title *Sacra Congregatio de Propaganda Fide,* Sacred Congregation for Propagating the Faith, from Latin *prōpāgāndus,* gerundive of *prōpāgāre,* to PROPAGATE.]

prop-a-gan-dize (prŏp'ə-găn'dīz') *v.* **-dized, -dizing, -dizes.** —*tr.* **1.** To spread (a doctrine or opinion) by means of propaganda. **2.** To subject (a person or group of persons) to propaganda. —*intr.* To spread propaganda.

prop-a-gate (prŏp'ə-gāt') *v.* **-gated, -gating, -gates.** —*tr.* **1.** To cause (animals or plants) to multiply or breed. **2.** To breed (offspring). **3.** To transmit (characteristics) from one generation to another. **4.** To make known; publicize. **5.** *Physics.* To cause (a wave, for example) to move through a medium; transmit. —*intr.* **1.** *Physics.* To move through a medium. **2.** To breed or multiply. [Latin *prōpāgāre,* to propagate (plants) by means of slips, from *prōpāgō, prōpāgēs,* slip, shoot, offspring (see **pag-** in Appendix*).] —**prop'a-ga'tive** *adj.* —**prop'a-ga'tor** (-gā'tər) *n.*

prop-a-ga-tion (prŏp'ə-gā'shən) *n.* **1.** Increase or spread, as by natural reproduction. **2.** Dissemination, as of a belief: *propagation of the Gospel.* —**prop'a-ga'tion-al** *adj.*

pro-pane (prō'pān') *n.* A colorless gas, C_3H_8, found in natural gas and petroleum, and widely used as a fuel. [PROP- + -ANE.]

pro-par-ox-y-tone (prō'păr-ŏk'sĭ-tōn') *adj.* Having an acute accent on the antepenult in Classical Greek. —*n.* A proparoxytone word. [Greek *proparoxutonos* : *pro-,* before + PAROXYTONE.] —**pro'par-ox'y-ton'ic** (-ŏk'sĭ-tŏn'ĭk) *adj.*

pro-pel (prə-pĕl') *tr.v.* **-pelled, -pelling, -pels.** To cause to move or sustain in motion. [Middle English *propellen,* from Latin *prōpellere* : *prō-,* forward + *pellere,* to drive (see **pel-⁶** in Appendix*).]

pro-pel-lant (prə-pĕl'ənt) *n.* Also **pro-pel-lent.** Something that propels or provides thrust, as an explosive charge or a rocket fuel. —*adj.* Also **pro-pel-lent.** Serving to propel; propelling.

pro-pel-ler (prə-pĕl'ər) *n.* Also **pro-pel-lor.** Any of various related simple machines for propelling aircraft or boats, especially one having radiating blades mounted on a revolving power-driven shaft. Also called "screw," "screw propeller."

pro-pend (prō-pĕnd') *intr.v.* **-pended, -pending, -pends.** To have a propensity toward. [Latin *prōpendēre,* to hang forward or downward, be inclined or favorable : *prō-,* forward, down + *pendēre,* to hang (see **spen-** in Appendix*).]

pro-pene (prō'pēn') *n. Chemistry.* Propylene *(see).*

pro-pen-si-ty (prə-pĕn'sə-tē) *n., pl.* **-ties.** An innate inclination; tendency; bent. [From archaic *propense,* inclined, from Latin *prōpensus,* past participle of *prōpendēre,* to be inclined or favorable, PROPEND.]

prop-er (prŏp'ər) *adj. Abbr.* **prop. 1.** Suitable; fitting; appropriate: *the proper moment.* **2.** Out-and-out; thorough: *a proper whipping.* **3.** Worthy of the name: *take one's medicine like a proper man.* **4.** Meeting a requisite standard of competence or validity. **5. a.** Within the strict limitation of the term. Used

ă pat/ā pay/âr care/ä father/b bib/ch church/d deed/ĕ pet/ē be/f fife/g gag/h hat/hw which/ĭ pit/ī pie/îr pier/j judge/k kick/l lid, needle/m mum/n no, sudden/ng thing/ŏ pot/ō toe/ô paw, for/oi noise/ou out/ōō took/ōō boot/p pop/r roar/s sauce/sh ship, dish/

postpositively: *France proper.* **b.** Rigorously correct; exact. **6.** Characteristically belonging to the being or thing in question. Used postpositively with *to: an optical effect proper to fluids.* **7. a.** Seemly; decorous. **b.** Displaying exaggerated propriety or gentility. **8.** *Mathematics.* Designating a subset of a given set when the latter has at least one element not in the subset. —See Synonyms at **fit.** —*adv.* Thoroughly: *He got his ears pinned back good and proper.* —*n.* Also **Prop·er.** *Ecclesiastical.* **1.** The parts of the Mass that vary according to the particular day or feast. **2.** An office to be said on an appointed day or feast. Compare **ordinary.** [Middle English *propre,* one's own, distinctive, correct, proper, from Old French, from Latin *proprius,* one's own, personal, particular. See **per**[1] in Appendix.*] —**prop'er·ly** *adv.* —**prop'er·ness** *n.*

proper adjective. An adjective formed from a proper noun.

pro·per·din (prō-pûr'dĭn) *n.* A natural protein in human blood serum that helps provide immunity to infectious diseases. [Perhaps PRO- (acting as) + Latin *perdere,* "to give away," squander, hence, to destroy : *per-,* away, to destruction + *dare,* to give (see **dō-** in Appendix*) + -IN.]

proper fraction. 1. A numerical fraction in which the numerator is less than the denominator. **2.** A polynomial fraction in which the numerator is of lower degree than the denominator.

proper noun. A noun designating by name a being or thing without a limiting modifier. Also called "proper name."

prop·er·tied (prŏp'ər-tēd) *adj.* Owning land or securities as a principal source of revenue.

Pro·per·tius (prō-pûr'shəs, -shē-əs), **Sextus.** 50?–15? B.C. Roman elegiac poet.

prop·er·ty (prŏp'ər-tē) *n., pl.* **-ties.** *Abbr.* **prop. 1.** Ownership. **2.** A possession, or possessions collectively. **3.** Something tangible or intangible to which its owner has legal title. **4.** Any article, except costumes and scenery, used as part of a dramatic production. Also called "prop." **5. a.** A characteristic trait or peculiarity. **b.** A special capability or power; virtue. **c.** A quality serving to define or describe an object or substance. **d.** A characteristic attribute possessed by all members of a class. **e.** *Logic.* A predicable that is common and peculiar to the whole of a species and is necessarily predicated of its essence without being part of that essence. —See Synonyms at **asset, quality.** [Middle English *proprete,* from Old French *propr(i)ete,* from Latin *proprietās,* ownership, peculiarity, from *proprius,* own, particular, PROPER.]

pro·phage (prō'fāj') *n.* A noninfectious association between a bacterial virus and a bacterium, in which the viral chromosomes link with the bacterial chromosomes but do not cause disruption of the bacterial cell or promote replication of the virus itself. [PRO- (before) + -PHAGE.]

pro·phase (prō'fāz') *n.* The first stage in cell division by mitosis, during which chromosomes form from the chromatin of the nucleus. [PRO- (before) + PHASE.]

proph·e·cy (prŏf'ə-sē) *n., pl.* **-cies. 1.** A prediction. **2. a.** The inspired utterance of a prophet, viewed as a declaration of divine will. **b.** Such a revelation transmitted orally or in writing. [Middle English *propheci(e), prophesye,* from Old French *profecie, prophecie,* from Latin *prophētia,* from Greek *prophēteia,* from *prophētēs,* PROPHET.]

proph·e·sy (prŏf'ə-sī') *v.* **-sied, -sying, -sies.** —*tr.* **1.** To reveal by divine inspiration. **2.** To predict. **3.** To prefigure; foreshow. —*intr.* **1.** To reveal the will or message of God. **2.** To predict the future. **3.** To speak as a prophet. —See Synonyms at **foretell.** [Middle English *prophecien,* from Old French *prophecier,* from *prophecie,* PROPHECY.] —**proph'e·si'er** *n.*

proph·et (prŏf'ĭt) *n.* **1.** A person who speaks by divine inspiration or as the interpreter through whom a divinity expresses his will. **2.** A predictor or soothsayer. **3.** The chief spokesman of some movement or cause. —**the Prophet. 1.** *Islam.* Mohammed. **2.** *Mormon Church.* Joseph Smith. —**the Prophets.** The prophetic writings of the Hebrew Scriptures. [Middle English *prophet(e), profete,* from Old French, from Latin *prophēta,* from Greek *prophētēs,* "one who speaks beforehand," proclaimer, spokesman, or interpreter for the gods or oracles : *pro-,* before + *-phētēs,* "speaker," from *phanai,* to say (see **bhā-**[2] in Appendix*).]

proph·et·ess (prŏf'ĭ-tĭs) *n.* A female prophet.

pro·phet·ic (prə-fĕt'ĭk) *adj.* Also **pro·phet·i·cal** (-ĭ-kəl). **1.** Of or belonging to a prophet or prophecy. **2.** Of the nature of prophecy. —**pro·phet'i·cal·ly** *adv.* —**pro·phet'i·cal·ness** *n.*

pro·phy·lac·tic (prō'fə-lăk'tĭk, prŏf'ə-) *adj.* Acting to defend against or prevent something, especially disease; protective. —*n.* A prophylactic medicine, device, or measure; especially, a condom. [Greek *prophulaktikos,* from *prophulassein,* to stand on guard before (a place), take precautions against : *pro-,* before + *phulassein,* to guard, protect, from *phulax,* a guard (see **phulax** in Appendix*).] —**pro'phy·lac'ti·cal·ly** *adv.*

pro·phy·lax·is (prō'fə-lăk'sĭs, prŏf'ə-) *n., pl.* **-laxes** (-lăk'sēz'). The prevention of or protective treatment for disease. [New Latin, from Greek *prophulaktikos,* PROPHYLACTIC.]

pro·pin·qui·ty (prō-pĭng'kwə-tē) *n.* **1.** Nearness; proximity. **2.** Kinship. **3.** Similarity in nature. [Middle English *propinquite,* from Latin *propinquitās,* from *propinquus,* near. See **per**[1] in Appendix.*]

pro·pi·o·nate (prō'pē-ə-nāt') *n.* A salt or ester of propionic acid. [PROPION(IC ACID) + -ATE.]

pro·pi·on·ic acid (prō'pē-ŏn'ĭk) *n.* A fatty acid, $CH_3CH_2CO_2H$, prepared synthetically and widely used in a salt form as a mold inhibitor in bread. [From French *propionique* : Greek *pro-,* before, first (because this acid is first in order among the fatty acids) + *piōn,* fat (see **peyə-** in Appendix*) + -IC.]

pro·pi·ti·ate (prō-pĭsh'ē-āt') *tr.v.* **-ated, -ating, -ates.** To conciliate (an offended power); appease: *"Rain had to be prayed for and gods and priests propitiated."* (Lesley B. Simpson). [Latin *propitiāre,* from *propitius,* PROPITIOUS.] —**pro·pi'ti·a·ble** (prō-pĭsh'ē-ə-bəl, -pĭsh'ə-bəl) *adj.* —**pro·pi'ti·at'ing·ly** *adv.* —**pro·pi'ti·a'tive** *adj.* —**pro·pi'ti·a'tor** (-ā'tər) *n.*

pro·pi·ti·a·tion (prō-pĭsh'ē-ā'shən) *n.* **1.** The act of propitiating. **2.** Something that propitiates; especially, a conciliatory offering to a god.

pro·pi·ti·a·to·ry (prō-pĭsh'ē-ə-tôr'ē, -tōr'ē) *adj.* Of or offered in propitiation; conciliatory. —*n., pl.* **propitiatories.** In ancient Jewish ceremony, the **mercy seat** *(see).* —**pro·pi'ti·a·to'ri·ly** *adv.*

pro·pi·tious (prə-pĭsh'əs) *adj.* **1.** Presenting favorable circumstances; auspicious. **2.** Kindly; gracious. —See Synonyms at **favorable.** [Middle English *propycyous,* from Old French *propicius,* from Latin *propitius,* favorable, kind. See **pet-**[1] in Appendix.*] —**pro·pi'tious·ly** *adv.* —**pro·pi'tious·ness** *n.*

prop·o·lis (prŏp'ə-lĭs) *n.* A resinous substance collected from various plants by bees, and used together with beeswax in the construction of their hives. [Latin, from Greek, suburb, hence (unexplained sense development) bee glue : *pro-,* before, beyond + *polis,* city (see **pelə-**[2] in Appendix*).]

pro·po·nent (prə-pō'nənt) *n.* One who argues in support of something; an advocate. [Latin *prōpōnēns,* present participle of *prōpōnere,* to PROPOSE.]

Pro·pon·tis. The ancient name for the Sea of **Marmara.**

pro·por·tion (prə-pôr'shən, -pōr'shən) *n.* **1.** A part considered in relation to the whole. **2.** A relationship between things or parts of things with respect to comparative magnitude, quantity, or degree. **3.** A relationship between quantities, such that if one varies, another varies in a manner dependent on the first; ratio: *"we do not always find visible happiness in proportion to visible virtue"* (Samuel Johnson). **4.** Harmonious relation; balance; symmetry. **5.** *Usually plural.* Dimensions; size: *"Bourgeois meals reached such proportions that an intermission had to be introduced"* (Roger Shattuck). See Usage note below. **6.** *Mathematics.* A relation of equality between two ratios. Four quantities, *a, b, c, d,* are said to be in proportion if $a/b = c/d$. —*tr.v.* **proportioned, -tioning, -tions. 1.** To adjust so that proper relations between parts are attained. **2.** To form with symmetry. [Middle English *proporcioun,* from Old French *proportion,* from Latin *prōportiō* (translation of Greek *analogia,* analogy), from the phrase *prō portiōne,* "for (its or his) share," proportionally : *prō,* for + *portiō,* share, portion (see **perə-** in Appendix*).] —**pro·por'tion·a·ble** *adj.* —**pro·por'tion·a·bly** *adv.* —**pro·por'tion·er** *n.* —**pro·por'tion·ment** *n.*

Synonyms: *proportion, harmony, symmetry, balance.* These nouns are compared as they apply to aesthetic pleasure derived from proper arrangement. *Proportion* is the desirable, correct, or perfect relationship of parts within a whole. *Harmony* generally means the smooth and flowing joining of details. *Symmetry* and *balance* both imply an arrangement of parts and details on either side of a median line. They differ, however, in that *symmetry* emphasizes duplicate or mirror-image arrangement of parts, while *balance* emphasizes dissimilar or opposing parts that offset each other to make a harmonious whole.

Usage: *Proportions* (noun), used in the general sense of *size, extent,* or *dimension,* is acceptable to 65 per cent of the Usage Panel, although considered by some to be in disregard of the specialized senses of *proportion.*

pro·por·tion·al (prə-pôr'shən-əl, -pōr'shən-əl) *adj.* **1.** Forming a relationship with other parts or quantities; being in proportion. **2.** Properly related in size or other measurable characteristics. **3.** *Mathematics.* Having a constant ratio. —*n.* One of the quantities in a mathematical proportion. —**pro·por'tion·al'i·ty** (-shə-năl'ə-tē) *n.* —**pro·por'tion·al·ly** *adv.*

proportional representation. *Abbr.* **P.R.** Representation of all parties in a legislature in proportion to their popular vote.

pro·por·tion·ate (prə-pôr'shən-ĭt, prə-pōr'-) *adj.* Being in due proportion; proportional. —*tr.v.* (prə-pôr'shə-nāt', prə-pōr'-) **proportionated, -ating, -ates.** To make proportionate. —**pro·por'tion·ate·ly** (-ĭt-lē) *adv.* —**pro·por'tion·ate·ness** (-ĭt-nĭs) *n.*

pro·pos·al (prə-pō'zəl) *n.* **1.** The act of proposing. **2.** A plan or scheme that is proposed; suggestion. **3.** An offer of marriage.

pro·pose (prə-pōz') *v.* **-posed, -posing, -poses.** —*tr.* **1.** To put forward for consideration, discussion, or adoption; suggest: *propose new methods.* **2.** To present or nominate (a person) for a position, office, or membership. **3.** To offer (a toast to be drunk). **4.** To purpose; intend. —*intr.* To form or make a proposal, especially of marriage. [Middle English *proposen,* from Old French *proposer,* from Latin *prōpōnere* (past participle *prōpositus*), to put or set forth, declare, propound : *prō,* forward + *pōnere,* to place (see **apo-** in Appendix*).] —**pro·pos'er** *n.*

prop·o·si·tion (prŏp'ə-zĭsh'ən) *n. Abbr.* **prop. 1.** A plan or scheme suggested for acceptance. **2.** *Informal.* A matter requiring special handling: *a difficult proposition.* **3.** *Informal.* A dubious or immoral proposal. **4.** A subject for discussion or analysis. **5.** *Logic.* **a.** A statement in which the subject is affirmed or denied by the predicate. **b.** That which is expressed in a statement, as opposed to the way it is expressed. **c.** A statement containing only logical constants and having a fixed truth-value. —*tr.v.* **propositioned, -tioning, -tions.** *Informal.* To propose a private bargain to; especially, to make an offer of sexual intercourse to. [Middle English *proposicioun,* from Old French *proposition,* from Latin *prōpositiō,* from *prōpōnere,* PROPOSE.] —**prop'o·si'tion·al** *adj.* —**prop'o·si'tion·al·ly** *adv.*

propositional function. *Logic.* An expression having the form of a proposition, but containing undefined symbols for the sub-

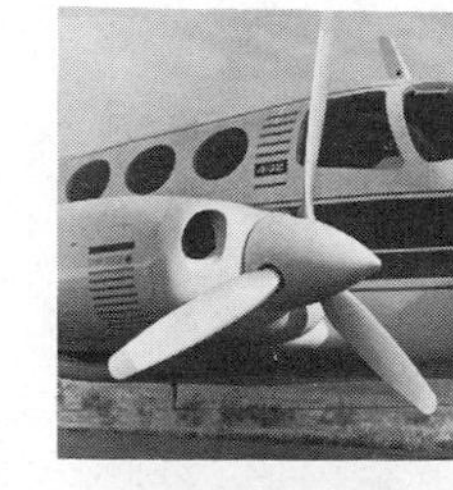

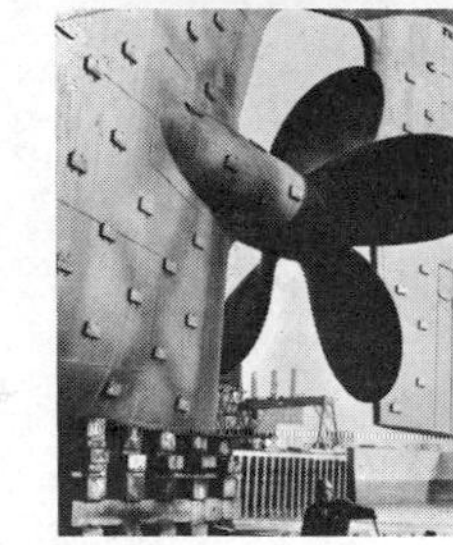

propeller
Above: Aircraft propeller
Below: Ship's propeller

stantive elements. It becomes a proposition when appropriate values are assigned to the symbols.

pro·pos·i·tus (prō-pŏz′ĭ-təs) *n., pl.* **-ti** (-tī′). **1.** *Law.* One from whom a line of descent is traced. **2.** The person immediately affected by an action. [New Latin, specialized use of the past participle of Latin *prōpōnere,* to place before, PROPOSE.]

pro·pound (prə-pound′) *tr.v.* To put forward for consideration; set forth; propose. [Alteration of earlier *propoune,* from Middle English (Scottish) *proponen,* from Latin *prōpōnere,* to PROPOSE.] **—pro·pound′er** *n.*

propr. proprietor.

pro·prae·tor (prō-prē′tər) *n.* A Roman official appointed, usually immediately after holding the praetorship, to be the chief administrator of a province. [Latin, from *prō praetōre,* (one acting) for a praetor : *prō,* for + PRAETOR.] **—pro′prae·to′ri·al** (prō′prĭ-tôr′ē-əl, -tōr′ē-əl), **pro′prae·to′ri·an** *adj.*

pro·pri·e·tar·y (prə-prī′ə-tĕr′ē) *adj. Abbr.* **prop., pty. 1.** Of or pertaining to a proprietor or to proprietors collectively. **2.** Exclusively owned; private. **3.** Befitting an owner: *a proprietary air.* **4.** Owned by a private individual or corporation under a trademark or patent. *—n., pl.* **proprietaries.** *Abbr.* **prop., pty. 1.** A proprietor. **2.** A group of proprietors. **3.** Ownership; proprietorship. **4.** *U.S. History.* The governor of a proprietary colony. **5.** A proprietary medicine. [Late Latin *proprietārius,* from Latin *proprietās,* property, PROPRIETY.] **—pro·pri′e·tar′i·ly** *adv.*

proprietary colony. Any of certain early North American colonies, such as Carolina and Pennsylvania, organized in the 17th century in territories granted by the Crown to one or more Lords Proprietary, who had full governing rights.

pro·pri·e·tor (prə-prī′ə-tər) *n. Abbr.* **prop., propr. 1.** A person who has legal title to something; an owner. **2.** The owner or owner-manager of a business or other institution. [Alteration of PROPRIETARY (noun).] **—pro·pri′e·to′ri·al** *adj.* **—pro·pri′e·to′ri·al·ly** *adv.* **—pro·pri′e·tor·ship′** *n.*

pro·pri·e·tress (prə-prī′ə-trĭs) *n.* A female proprietor.

pro·pri·e·ty (prə-prī′ə-tē) *n., pl.* **-ties. 1.** The quality of being proper; appropriateness. **2.** Conformity to prevailing customs and usages. —See Synonyms at **etiquette. —the proprieties.** The usages and customs of polite society: *"Like many professional libertines, Byron had a deep regard for the domestic proprieties"* (Peter Quennell). [Middle English *propriete,* ownership, one's own nature, idiosyncrasy, from Old French, from Latin *proprietās,* from *proprius,* PROPER.]

pro·pri·o·cep·tor (prō′prē-ə-sĕp′tər) *n.* A sensory receptor, chiefly in muscles, tendons, and joints, that responds to stimuli arising within the organism. [Latin *proprius,* one's own (see **per**[1] in Appendix*) + (RE)CEPTOR.] **—pro′pri·o·cep′tive** *adj.*

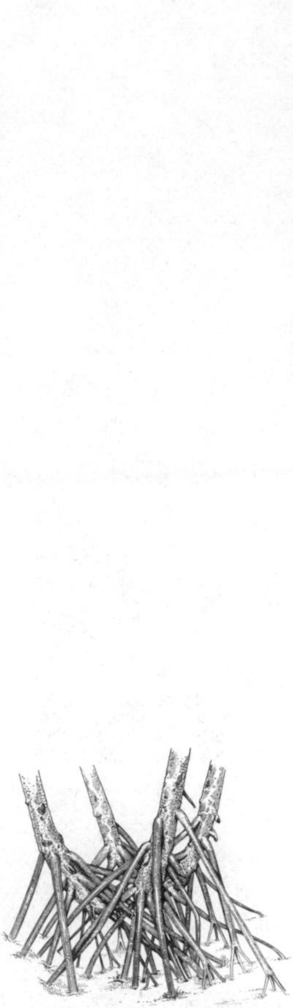

prop root
The prop-root system of a pandanus tree

prop root. A root growing from above ground into the soil and helping to support the plant stem, as in corn.

prop·to·sis (prŏp-tō′sĭs) *n., pl.* **-ses** (-sēz′). Forward displacement of an organ, such as the eyeball. [Late Latin, from Greek *proptōsis,* a falling forward, from *propiptein,* to fall forward : *pro-,* forward + *piptein,* to fall (see **pet-**[1] in Appendix*).]

pro·pul·sion (prə-pŭl′shən) *n.* **1.** The process of driving or propelling. **2.** A driving or propelling force. [Medieval Latin *prōpulsiō,* from Latin *prōpellere* (past participle *prōpulsus*), to drive forward, PROPEL.] **—pro·pul′sive, pro·pul′so·ry** *adj.*

pro·pyl (prō′pĭl) *n. Chemistry.* A univalent organic radical with composition C_3H_7, derived from propane. [PROP- + -YL.]

prop·y·lae·um (prŏp′ə-lē′əm) *n., pl.* **-laea** (-lē′ə). *Architecture.* An entrance or vestibule to a temple or group of buildings. Also called "propylon." [Latin, from Greek *propulaion* : *pro-,* before + *pulē,* gate (see **pulē** in Appendix*).]

propyl alcohol. A clear colorless liquid, $CH_3CH_2CH_2OH$, widely used as a solvent.

pro·pyl·ene (prō′pə-lēn′) *n.* A flammable gas, $CH_3CH{:}CH_2$, derived from petroleum hydrocarbon cracking and used in organic synthesis. Also called "propene." [PROPYL + -ENE.]

propylene glycol. A colorless viscous hygroscopic liquid, $CH_3CHOHCH_2OH$, used in antifreeze solutions, in hydraulic fluids, and as a solvent.

prop·y·lon (prŏp′ə-lŏn′) *n., pl.* **-la** (-lə). A **propylaeum** *(see).* [Greek *propulon,* gateway : *pro-,* in front of + *pulē,* gate (see **pulē** in Appendix*).]

pro ra·ta (prō rā′tə, răt′ə, rä′tə). In proportion. [Latin *pro rata (parte),* according to the calculated (share).]

pro·rate (prō-rāt′, prō′rāt′) *v.* **-rated, -rating, -rates.** *—tr.* To divide, distribute, or assess proportionately. *—intr.* To settle affairs on the basis of proportional distribution. [From PRO RATA.] **—pro·rat′a·ble** *adj.* **—pro·ra′tion** *n.*

pro·rogue (prō-rōg′) *tr.v.* **-rogued, -roguing, -rogues.** To discontinue a session of (a parliament or similar body). [Middle English *prorogen,* from Old French *prorog(u)er,* from Latin *prōrogāre,* "to ask publicly (for an extension of one's term of office)," prolong, defer : *prō-,* forward, in public + *rogāre,* to ask (see **reg-**[1] in Appendix*).] **—pro′ro·ga′tion** *n.*

pros-. Indicates: **1.** Near, to, or toward; for example, **prosenchyma. 2.** In front; for example, **prosencephalon.** [Greek, from *pros,* near, at, toward, to. See **per**[1] in Appendix.*]

pros. prosody.

pro·sa·ic (prō-zā′ĭk) *adj.* **1. a.** Of or like prose; not poetic. **b.** Matter-of-fact; straightforward. **2.** Lacking in imagination and spirit; dull; ordinary. [Late Latin *prōsaicus,* from Latin *prōsa,* PROSE.] **—pro·sa′i·cal·ly** *adv.* **—pro·sa′ic·ness** *n.*

pro·sa·ism (prō′zā-ĭz′əm) *n.* **1.** A quality or style that is prosaic. **2.** A prosaic expression, phrase, or word.

Pros. Atty. prosecuting attorney.

pro·sce·ni·um (prō-sē′nē-əm) *n., pl.* **-nia** (-nē-ə). **1.** In the modern theater, the area located between the curtain and the orchestra. **2.** In the ancient theater, the stage, located between the background and the orchestra. [Latin, from Greek *proskēnion* : *pro-,* before + *skēnē,* "tent," stage-building used as background (see **scene**).]

pro·scribe (prō-skrīb′) *tr.v.* **-scribed, -scribing, -scribes. 1.** To denounce or condemn. **2.** To prohibit; forbid. **3.** *Obsolete.* To publish the name of (a person) as outlawed. [Latin *prōscribere,* to publish in writing, proscribe : *prō-,* in front, publicly + *scrībere,* to write (see **skeri-** in Appendix*).] **—pro·scrib′er** *n.*

pro·scrip·tion (prō-skrĭp′shən) *n.* **1.** The act of proscribing; prohibition. **2.** The condition of being proscribed; outlawry. **—pro·scrip′tive** *adj.* **—pro·scrip′tive·ly** *adv.*

prose (prōz) *n.* **1.** Ordinary speech or writing, as distinguished from verse. **2.** Commonplace expression or quality. **3.** *Roman Catholic Church.* A hymn of irregular meter sung after the gradual. *—adj.* **1.** Written in prose. **2.** Commonplace; dry. *—v.* **prosed, prosing, proses.** *—tr.* To make into prose: *"By Jove I'll prose it."* (Burns). *—intr.* **1.** To write prose. **2.** To speak or write in a dull, tiresome style. [Middle English, from Old French, from Latin *prōsa (ōrātiō),* "straightforward discourse," from *prōsus, prorsus,* straightforward, direct, from *prōversus,* past participle of *prōvertere,* to turn forward : *prō-,* forward + *vertere,* to turn (see **wer-**[3] in Appendix*).]

pros·e·cute (prŏs′ə-kyōōt′) *v.* **-cuted, -cuting, -cutes.** *—tr.* **1.** To pursue or persist in so as to complete. **2.** To carry on; practice. **3. a.** To initiate legal or criminal court action against. **b.** To seek to obtain or enforce by legal action. *—intr.* **1.** To initiate and conduct legal proceedings. **2.** To act as prosecutor. [Middle English *prosecuten,* to follow, from Latin *prōsequī* (past participle *prōsecūtus*), to follow up or forward : *prō-,* forward + *sequī,* to follow (see **sekw-**[1] in Appendix*).]

prosecuting attorney. *Abbr.* **Pros. Atty., P.A.** An attorney empowered to prosecute cases on behalf of a government and the people.

pros·e·cu·tion (prŏs′ə-kyōō′shən) *n.* **1.** The act of prosecuting. **2.** The institution and conduct of a legal proceeding. **3.** A prosecuting attorney.

pros·e·cu·tor (prŏs′ə-kyōō′tər) *n.* **1.** One who prosecutes. **2.** One who initiates and carries out a legal action, especially criminal proceedings. **3.** A prosecuting attorney.

pros·e·lyte (prŏs′ə-līt′) *n.* A new convert to a religion or doctrine. *—v.* Variant of **proselytize.** [Middle English *proselite,* from Late Latin *prosēlytus,* from Greek *prosēlutos,* "one who comes to a place," stranger, religious convert. See **leudh-**[1] in Appendix.*] **—pros′e·lyt′er** *n.*

pros·e·lyt·ism (prŏs′ə-lə-tĭz′əm, -lĭt-ĭz′əm) *n.* **1.** The practice of proselytizing. **2.** The state of being a proselyte; conversion. **—pros′e·lyt′i·cal** (-lĭt′ĭ-kəl) *adj.* **—pros′e·lyt·ist** *n.*

pros·e·lyt·ize (prŏs′ə-lə-tīz′) *v.* **-ized, -izing, -izes.** Also **pros·e·lyte, -lyted, -lyting, -lytes.** *—intr.* To make proselytes. *—tr.* To convert from one belief or faith to another. **—pros′e·lyt·i·za′tion** *n.* **—pros′e·lyt·iz′er** *n.*

pros·en·ceph·a·lon (prŏs′ĕn′sĕf′ə-lŏn′) *n. Anatomy.* The **forebrain** *(see).* [New Latin : PROS- (before, in front) + ENCEPHALON.] **—pros′en′ce·phal′ic** (-sə-făl′ĭk) *adj.*

pros·en·chy·ma (prŏs-ĕng′kĭ-mə) *n. Botany.* Tissue consisting of elongated, unspecialized cells, occurring in most flowering plants. [New Latin : PROS- (near, toward) + (PAR)ENCHYMA.] **—pros′en·chym′a·tous** (-kĭm′ə-təs) *adj.*

Pros·er·pi·na (prō-sûr′pə-nə). Also **Pros·er·pi·ne** (prŏs′ər-pīn′, prō-sûr′pə-nē). *Roman Mythology.* The wife of Pluto and daughter of Ceres; the goddess of the underworld, corresponding to the Greek Persephone.

pro·sim·i·an (prō-sĭm′ē-ən) *adj.* Of or belonging to the Prosimii, a suborder of primates that includes the lemurs, lorises, and tarsiers. *—n.* A primate of this suborder. [From New Latin *Prosimii* : *pro-,* before + Latin *simia,* ape, from *simus,* snub-nosed, from Greek *simos* (see **simian**).]

pro·sit (prōst, prō′sĭt) *interj.* Your health! Used as a drinking toast. [German, from Latin, "may it be advantageous."]

pros·o·dist (prŏs′ə-dĭst) *n.* A specialist in prosody.

pros·o·dy (prŏs′ə-dē) *n. Abbr.* **pros. 1.** The study of the metrical structures of verse. **2.** A particular system of versification. [Middle English *prosodye,* from Latin *prosōdia,* tone or accent of a syllable, from Greek *prosōidia,* accompanied song, modulation of voice, pronunciation, diacritical mark : *pros-,* to, in addition to + *ōidē,* song, lay, ode (see **wed-**[2] in Appendix*).] **—pro·sod′ic** (prō-sŏd′ĭk) *adj.* **—pro·sod′i·cal·ly** *adv.*

pro·so·po·pe·ia (prō-sō′pə-pē′ə) *n.* Also **pro·so·po·poe·ia.** *Rhetoric.* **1.** The impersonation of an absent or imaginary speaker. **2.** Personification, as of abstractions or inanimate objects. [Latin *prosopopoiia,* from Greek *prosōpopoiia,* dramatization : *prosōpon,* face, mask, dramatic character : *pros,* toward + stem *op-,* to see (see **okw-** in Appendix*) + *poiein,* to make (see **kwei-**[2] in Appendix*).] **—pro′so·po·pe′ial** *adj.*

pros·pect (prŏs′pĕkt′) *n.* **1.** Something expected; possibility. **2.** *Plural.* Chances for success. **3. a.** A potential customer or purchaser. **b.** A candidate deemed likely to succeed. **4.** The direction in which an object, such as a building, faces; an outlook. **5.** That which is presented to the eye; a scene; view: *a pleasant prospect.* **6.** The act of surveying or examining. **7.** *Mining.* **a.** The location or probable location of a mineral deposit. **b.** An actual or probable deposit. **c.** The mineral yield obtained by working an ore. *—v.* **prospected, -pecting, -pects.** *—tr.* To search for or explore (a region) for gold or other mineral deposits. *—intr.* To explore for mineral deposits. [Middle English *prospecte,* from Latin *prōspectus,* distant view, vista, from the past participle of *prōspicere,* to look forward, foresee : *prō-*, forward + *specere*, to look (see **spek-** in Appendix*).]

Synonyms: *prospect, outlook, expectation.* These nouns refer to envisioning or predicting future conditions or personal chances or hopes. *Prospect* and *outlook* are projections of what the future has in store, good or bad. *Expectation* more strongly suggests anticipation of success or fulfillment.

pro·spec·tive (prə-spĕk′tĭv) *adj.* **1.** Looking forward in time; characterized by foresight. **2.** Being in prospect; looked forward to; expected. —**pro·spec′tive·ly** *adv.*

pros·pec·tor (prŏs′pĕk′tər) *n.* One who explores an area for natural deposits, such as gold or oil.

pro·spec·tus (prə-spĕk′təs) *n.* A formal summary of a proposed commercial, literary, or other venture. [Latin, PROSPECT.]

pros·per (prŏs′pər) *v.* **-pered, -pering, -pers.** —*intr.* To be fortunate or successful; thrive. —*tr. Archaic.* To cause to thrive. [Middle English *prosperen,* from Old French *prosperer,* from Latin *prosperāre,* to cause to succeed, make fortunate, from *prosperus,* fortunate. See **spēi-** in Appendix.*]

pros·per·i·ty (prŏs-pĕr′ə-tē) *n., pl.* **-ties.** The condition of being prosperous and having good fortune or financial success.

pros·per·ous (prŏs′pər-əs) *adj.* **1.** Having success; flourishing. **2.** Well-to-do; well-off. **3.** Propitious; favorable. —**pros′per·ous·ly** *adv.* —**pros′per·ous·ness** *n.*

pros·tate (prŏs′tāt′) *n.* A gland in male mammals composed of muscular and glandular tissue that surrounds the urethra at the bladder. Also called "prostate gland." [New Latin *prostata,* from Greek *prostatēs,* "stander before (the bladder)," from *proïstanai,* to cause to stand in front : *pro-,* in front + *histanai,* to cause to stand (see **stā-** in Appendix*).] —**pros′tate′, pro·stat′ic** (prō-stăt′ĭk) *adj.*

pros·ta·tec·to·my (prŏs′tə-tĕk′tə-mē) *n., pl.* **-mies.** The surgical removal of all or part of the prostate. [PROSTAT(E) + -ECTOMY.]

pros·ta·ti·tis (prŏs′tə-tī′tĭs) *n.* Inflammation of the prostate.

pros·the·sis (prŏs-thē′sĭs) *n., pl.* **-ses** (-sēz′). **1.** The artificial replacement of a limb, tooth, or other part of the body. **2.** An artificial device used in such replacement. [Late Latin, addition of a letter or syllable, from Greek, attachment, addition, from *prostithenai,* to put to, add : *pros-,* in addition + *tithenai,* to place, put (see **dhē-**[1] in Appendix*).] —**pros·thet′ic** (-thĕt′ĭk) *adj.* —**pros·thet′i·cal·ly** *adv.*

prosthetic group. A link other than an amino acid in a protein chain.

pros·thet·ics (prŏs-thĕt′ĭks) *n.* Plural in form, used with a singular verb. Prosthetic surgery. —**pros′the·tist** (-thə-tĭst) *n.*

pros·tho·don·tics (prŏs′thə-dŏn′tĭks) *n.* Plural in form, used with a singular verb. Also **pros·tho·don·ti·a** (-shē-ə). Prosthetic dentistry, especially the replacement of missing teeth by bridges and dentures. [From PROSTH(ESIS) + Greek *odons,* tooth (see **-odont**).] —**pros′tho·don′tist** *n.*

pros·ti·tute (prŏs′tə-to͞ot′, -tyo͞ot′) *n.* **1.** One who solicits and accepts payment for sexual intercourse. **2.** One who sells his abilities or name to an unworthy cause. —*tr.v.* **prostituted, -tuting, -tutes. 1.** To offer (oneself or another) for sexual hire. **2.** To sell (oneself or one's talents) to an unworthy cause. [Latin *prōstitūta,* from the past participle of *prōstituere,* to expose publicly, prostitute : *prō-,* forth, in public + *statuere,* to set, place, from *stare* (past participle *status*), to stand (see **stā-** in Appendix*).] —**pros′ti·tu′tor** (-tər) *n.*

pros·ti·tu·tion (prŏs′tə-to͞o′shən, -tyo͞o′shən) *n.* **1.** The act or practice of prostituting. **2.** The act of offering or devoting one's talents to an unworthy use or cause.

pros·trate (prŏs′trāt′) *tr.v.* **-trated, -trating, -trates. 1.** To make (oneself) bow or kneel down in humility or adoration. **2.** To throw down flat. **3.** To lay low; overcome. —*adj.* **1.** Lying face down, as in submission or adoration. **2.** Lying down full-length. **3.** Physically or emotionally exhausted; incapacitated. **4.** *Botany.* Growing flat along the ground. —See Synonyms at **prone.** [Middle English *prostrat* (adjective), from Latin *prōstrātus,* past participle of *prōsternere,* to throw down, prostrate : *prō-,* down before + *sternere,* to stretch out, cast down (see **ster-**[2] in Appendix*).] —**pros′tra′tor** (-trā′tər) *n.*

pros·tra·tion (prŏs-trā′shən) *n.* **1. a.** The act of prostrating oneself. **b.** The state of being prostrate. **2.** Total exhaustion.

pro·style (prō′stīl) *adj. Architecture.* Having a row of columns across the front only, as in some Greek temples. [Latin *prostylos,* from Greek *prostulos,* having pillars in front : *pro-,* in front + *stulos,* pillar (see **stā-** in Appendix*).]

pros·y (prō′zē) *adj.* **-ier, -iest. 1.** Matter-of-fact; dry; prosaic. **2.** Dull; commonplace. —**pros′i·ly** *adv.* —**pros′i·ness** *n.*

Prot. Protestant.

pro·tac·tin·i·um (prō′tăk-tĭn′ē-əm) *n. Symbol* **Pa** A rare radioactive element chemically similar to uranium, having 12 known isotopes, the most common of which is Pa 231 with a half-life of 32,480 years. Atomic number 91, melting point 1,230°C, specific gravity 15.37, valence 4 or 5. See **element.** [New Latin : PROT(O)- + ACTINIUM (because it disintegrates into actinium).]

pro·tag·o·nist (prō-tăg′ə-nĭst) *n.* **1.** The leading character in Greek drama or any other literary form. **2.** Any leading or principal figure. [Greek *prōtagōnistēs* : PROT(O)- + *agōnistēs,* actor, from *agōnizesthai,* to contend, from *agōnia,* a contest, from *agōn,* gathering, contest, from *agein,* to lead (see **ag-** in Appendix*).]

Usage: *Protagonist* inherently has the sense of leader. A phrase such as *chief protagonist* is redundant, and it is not proper to apply the plural *protagonists* when referring to a single literary work. *Protagonist* has the extended sense of *leader in a matter of importance,* but the term does not necessarily imply the sense of *partisan* or *champion* (in opposition to *antagonist*).

Pro·tag·o·ras (prō-tăg′ər-əs). 481?–411 B.C. Greek philosopher.

pro·ta·mine (prō′tə-mēn′, -mĭn) *n.* Also **pro·ta·min** (-mĭn). Any of the group of the simplest proteins that are highly basic, soluble in water, not coagulated by heat, and yield only amino acids, chiefly arginine, upon hydrolysis. [PROT(O)- + -AMINE.]

pro·ta·no·pi·a (prō′tə-nō′pē-ə) *n.* A form of colorblindness in which red and bluish-green stimuli are confused with neutral stimuli and with each other. [New Latin : PROT(O)- + AN- (without) + -OPIA.] —**pro′ta·nope′** (-nōp′) *n.*

prot·a·sis (prŏt′ə-sĭs) *n.* **1.** *Grammar.* A subordinate clause, especially in a conditional sentence. Compare **apodosis. 2.** The introductory part of a classical drama. [Late Latin, proposition, from Greek, "a stretching forward," proposition, premise, from *proteinein,* to stretch forward, offer, propose : *prō-,* before + *teinein,* to stretch (see **ten-** in Appendix*).]

pro·te·an (prō′tē-ən, prō-tē′-) *adj.* Readily taking on different shapes or forms; variable. [From PROTEUS.]

pro·te·ase (prō′tē-ās′) *n.* An enzyme that catalyzes the hydrolytic breakdown of proteins. [PROTE(IN) + -ASE.]

protec. protectorate.

pro·tect (prə-tĕkt′) *tr.v.* **-tected, -tecting, -tects. 1.** To keep from harm, attack, or injury; to guard. **2.** *Economics.* To help (domestic industry) with tariffs on imported goods. **3.** *Commerce.* To assure payment of (drafts or notes, for example) by setting aside funds. —See Synonyms at **defend.** [Latin *prōtegere* (past participle *prōtectus*), to cover in front, protect : *prō-,* in front + *tegere,* to cover (see **steg-**[1] in Appendix*).] —**pro·tect′ing·ly** *adv.*

pro·tec·tion (prə-tĕk′shən) *n.* **1.** The act of protecting. **2.** The condition of being protected. **3.** One that protects. **4.** A pass guaranteeing safe-conduct to travelers. **5.** *Economics.* A tariff system protecting domestic industries from foreign competition. **6.** Money extorted by racketeers in exchange for a promise of freedom from molestation. —**pro·tec′tion·al** *adj.*

pro·tec·tion·ism (prə-tĕk′shən-ĭz′əm) *n. Economics.* The theory and system of protection. —**pro·tec′tion·ist** *n.* & *adj.*

pro·tec·tive (prə-tĕk′tĭv) *adj.* Adapted or intended to afford protection. —*n.* Something that protects. —**pro·tec′tive·ly** *adv.* —**pro·tec′tive·ness** *n.*

pro·tec·tor (prə-tĕk′tər) *n.* Also **pro·tect·er. 1.** A person who protects; guardian. **2.** *English History.* A title given to one who ruled during the absence, minority, or illness of the monarch. —**pro·tec′tor·al** *adj.* —**pro·tec′tor·ship′** *n.*

pro·tec·tor·ate (prə-tĕk′tər-ĭt) *n. Abbr.* **protec. 1.** A relationship of protection and partial control assumed by a superior power over a dependent country or region. **2.** The protected country or region. **3.** *Capital* **P. a.** The government, office, or term of a protector. **b.** The government of England under Oliver Cromwell (1653–58) and his son Richard (1658–59).

pro·tec·to·ry (prə-tĕk′tə-rē) *n., pl.* **-ries.** An institution providing for the welfare of destitute children.

pro·té·gé (prō′tə-zhā′) *n. Feminine* **pro·té·gée.** One whose welfare, training, or career is promoted by an influential person. [French, from the past participle of *protéger,* to protect, from Latin *prōtegere,* PROTECT.]

pro·te·id (prō′tē-ĭd) *n. Obsolete.* Protein.

pro·tein (prō′tēn, -tē-ĭn) *n.* Any of a group of complex nitrogenous organic compounds of high molecular weight that contain amino acids as their basic structural units and that occur in all living matter and are essential for the growth and repair of animal tissue. [French *protéine,* "primary substance (to the body)," from Late Greek *proteios,* primary, from Greek *prōtos,* first. See **per**[1] in Appendix.*] —**pro′tein·a′ceous** (-tə-nā′shəs, -tī-nā-shəs), **pro·tein′ic, pro·tei′nous** *adj.*

pro·tein·ase (prō′tē-nās′, -tē-ĭ-nās′) *n.* A protease that hydrolyzes proteins into polypeptides.

pro·tein·ate (prō′tē-nāt′, -tē-ĭ-nāt′) *n.* A protein compound.

pro·tein-bound iodine (prō′tēn-bound′, prō′tē-ĭn-). *Abbr.* **P.B.I.** Iodine bound to the protein fraction of blood. It is a measure of circulating thyroid hormone used to determine basal metabolism.

pro·te·in·u·ri·a (prō′tē-nyo͝or′ē-ə, prō′tē-ĭ-) *n.* A condition of protein in the urine, commonly caused by kidney disease.

pro tem·po·re (prō tĕm′pə-rē). *Abbr.* **pro tem., p.t.** *Latin.* For the time being; temporarily.

proteo-. Indicates protein; for example, **proteolysis.**

pro·te·o·clas·tic (prō′tē-ō-klăs′tĭk) *adj.* Of, pertaining to, or causing proteolysis; proteolytic. [PROTEO- + -CLASTIC.]

pro·te·ol·y·sis (prō′tē-ŏl′ə-sĭs) *n.* The breaking down of proteins into simpler, soluble substances, as in digestion. [PROTEO- + -LYSIS.] —**pro′te·o·lyt′ic** (-ə-lĭt′ĭk) *adj.*

pro·te·ose (prō′tē-ōs′, -ōz′) *n.* Any of several water-soluble proteins produced during digestion. [PROTE(O)- + -OSE.]

Prot·er·o·zo·ic (prŏt′ər-ə-zō′ĭk, prō′tər-) *adj. Geology.* Of, belonging to, or designating the geologic time and deposits of the Precambrian era between the Archeozoic era and the Cambrian period of the Paleozoic era. See **geology.** —*n. Geology.* **1.** The Proterozoic era. Preceded by *the.* **2.** The deposits of this era. [Greek *proteros,* earlier, anterior (see **per**[1] in Appendix*) + -ZOIC.]

pro·test (prə-tĕst′, prō-tĕst′, prō′tĕst′) *v.* **-tested, -testing, -tests.** —*tr.* **1.** To object to, especially in a formal statement. **2.** To promise or affirm with earnest solemnity: *"He continually protested his profound respect"* (Frank Norris). **3.** *Law.* To declare (a bill) dishonored or refused. **4.** *Archaic.* To proclaim or make known: *"unrough youths that even now/Protest their first of*

t tight/th thin, path/*th* this, bathe/ŭ cut/ûr urge/v valve/w with/y yes/z zebra, size/zh vision/ə about, item, edible, gallop, circus/ à *Fr.* ami/œ *Fr.* feu, *Ger.* schön/ü *Fr.* tu, *Ger.* über/KH *Ger.* ich, *Scot.* loch/N *Fr.* bon. ***Follows main vocabulary.** †**Of obscure origin.**

manhood" (Shakespeare). —*intr.* **1.** To express strong objection. **2.** To make an earnest avowal or affirmation. —See Synonyms at **object.** —*n.* (prō′tĕst′). **1.** A formal declaration of disapproval or objection issued by a concerned party. **2.** Any individual or collective gesture or display of disapproval. **3.** *Law.* **a.** A formal statement drawn up by a notary for a creditor, declaring that the debtor has refused to accept or honor a bill. **b.** A formal declaration made by a taxpayer, stating that the tax demanded is illegal or excessive and reserving the right to contest it. [Middle English *protesten,* from Old French *protester,* from Latin *prōtestārī,* to declare in public, testify, protest : *prō-,* forth, in public + *testārī,* to be a witness, make a will, from *testis,* a witness, will (see **trei-** in Appendix*).] —**pro·test′er** *n.* —**pro·test′ing·ly** *adv.*

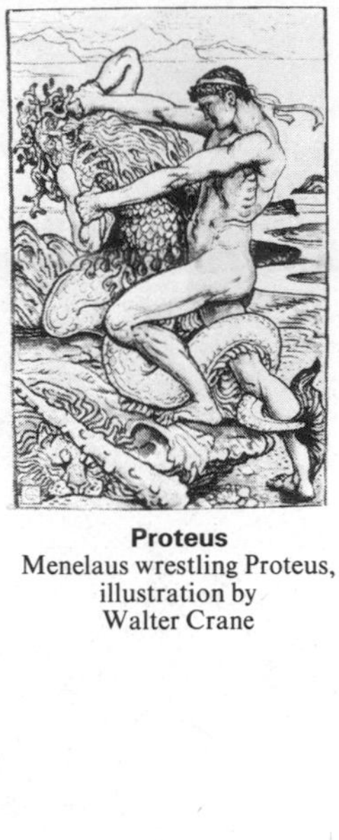

Proteus
Menelaus wrestling Proteus, illustration by Walter Crane

prot·es·tant (prŏt′ĭs-tənt, prə-tĕs′tənt) *n. Archaic.* One who makes a declaration or avowal.

Prot·es·tant (prŏt′ĭs-tənt) *n. Abbr.* **Prot. 1.** Any Christian belonging to a sect descending from those that seceded from the Church of Rome at the time of the Reformation. **2.** One of those who adhered to the doctrine of Luther and, in 1529, protested against the decree of the Diet of Spires commanding submission to the authority of Rome. —*adj.* Of or pertaining to Protestants or Protestantism. [From Latin *prōtestāns,* present participle of *prōtestārī,* to PROTEST.]

Protestant Episcopal Church. A church body in the United States originally associated with the Church of England, but since 1789 organized as a separate entity. Also called "Episcopal Church."

Prot·es·tant·ism (prŏt′ĭs-tənt-ĭz′əm) *n.* **1.** Adherence to a Protestant church. **2.** The religion and religious tendencies fostered by the Protestant movement. **3.** Protestants collectively.

prot·es·ta·tion (prŏt′ĭs-tā′shən, prō′tĭs-) *n.* **1.** An emphatic declaration. **2.** A strong or formal expression of dissent.

Pro·te·us (prō′tē-əs, -tyōōs). *Greek Mythology.* A sea god who could change his shape at will.

pro·tha·la·mi·on (prō′thə-lā′mē-ən, -ŏn′) *n., pl.* **-mia** (-mē-ə). A song in celebration of a wedding; epithalamium. [Coined by Edmund Spenser from PRO- (before) + Greek *epithalamion,* EPITHALAMIUM.]

pro·thal·lus (prō-thăl′əs) *n., pl.* **thalli** (-thăl′ī′). Also **pro·thal·li·um** (prō-thăl′ē-əm) *pl.* **-thallia** (-thăl′ē-ə). *Botany.* A small, flat mass of tissue produced by a germinating spore of ferns and some mosses and related plants. It bears sexual organs and eventually develops into a mature plant. [New Latin : Greek *pro-,* in front of, before + *thallos,* a shoot (see **dhal-** in Appendix*).] —**pro·thal′li·al** *adj.*

proth·e·sis (prŏth′ə-sĭs) *n., pl.* **-ses** (-sēz′). **1.** *Linguistics.* The addition of a phoneme at the beginning of a word to ease pronunciation or to form a new word. **2.** *Eastern Orthodox Church.* The preparation of the Eucharistic elements for consecration. [Greek, from *protithenai,* to put before : *pro-,* before + *tithenai,* to put, place (see **dhē-**[1] in Appendix*).] —**pro·thet′ic** (prŏ-thĕt′ĭk) *adj.* —**pro·thet′i·cal·ly** *adv.*

pro·thon·o·tar·y (prō-thŏn′ə-tĕr′ē, prō′thə-nō′tə-rē) *n., pl.* **-ies.** Also **pro·ton·o·tar·y** (-tŏn′ə-tĕr′ē, -tə-nō′tə-rē). **1.** The principal clerk in certain courts of law. **2.** *Roman Catholic Church.* One of a college of twelve ecclesiastics charged with the registry of important pontifical proceedings. **3.** *Archaic.* A chief scribe: *"Can I not sin but thou wilt be my private protonotary?"* (Herrick). [Middle English *prothonotarie,* from Late Latin *prōtonotārius* : PROTO- + *notārius,* "of shorthand," secretary, from *nota,* mark, shorthand character (see **gnō-** in Appendix*).] —**pro·thon′o·tar′i·al** (prō-thŏn′ə-târ′ē-əl, prō′thə-nō-târ′-) *adj.*

prothonotary warbler. A small bird, *Protonotaria citrea,* of southeastern North America, having a deep-yellow head and breast and grayish wings. [Probably from the bright-yellow robes worn by ecclesiastics at important meetings.]

pro·tho·rax (prō-thôr′ăks′, -thōr′ăks′) *n., pl.* **-axes** or **-thoraces** (-thôr′ə-sēz′, -thōr′ə-sēz′). The anterior division of the thorax of an insect, bearing the first pair of legs. [New Latin : PRO- (in front of, before) + THORAX.] —**pro′tho·rac′ic** (prō′thô-răs′ĭk, -thō-răs′ĭk) *adj.*

pro·throm·bin (prō-thrŏm′bĭn) *n.* A plasma protein that is converted into thrombin during blood coagulation.

pro·tist (prō′tĭst) *n. Biology.* Any of the unicellular organisms of the kingdom Protista, which includes protozoans, bacteria, some algae, and other forms not readily classified as either plants or animals. [New Latin *Protista,* "simplest organisms," from Greek *prōtista,* neuter plural of *prōtistos,* the very first, primal, from *prōtos,* first. See **per**[1] in Appendix.*] —**pro′tis·tol′o·gy** (-tĭs-tŏl′ə-jī) *n.*

pro·ti·um (prō′tē-əm, prō′shē-) *n.* The most abundant isotope of hydrogen, H^1, with atomic mass 1. [New Latin : PROT(O)- + -IUM.]

proto-, prot-. Indicates: **1.** The earliest form or the first in rank or time; for example, **protium, protoplast, prototype. 2.** *Capital* **P.** The earliest form of a language as reconstructed by comparative linguistics; for example, **Proto-Germanic. 3.** *Chemistry.* The member of a series that has the least amount of a specified element or radical; for example, **protoporphyrin.** [From Greek *prōtos,* first. See **per**[1] in Appendix.*]

Pro·to-Al·gon·qui·an (prō′tō-ăl-gŏng′kwē-ən, -kē-ən) *n.* The earliest reconstructed ancestor of the Algonquian languages.

pro·to·col (prō′tə-kôl′, -kōl′, -kŏl′) *n.* **1.** The forms of ceremony and etiquette observed by diplomats and heads of state. **2.** The first copy of a treaty or other document prior to its ratification. **3.** Any preliminary draft or record of a transaction. —See Synonyms at **etiquette.** —*intr.v.* **protocoled** or **-colled, -coling** or **-colling, -cols.** To form or issue protocols. [Earlier *prothocoll,* from Old French *prothocole,* from Medieval Latin *protocollum,* from Late Greek *prōtokollon,* first sheet glued to a papyrus roll, bearing a table of contents : PROTO- + Late Greek *kollema,* sheets of a papyrus glued together, from *kollan,* to glue together, from *kolla,* glue (see **kolei-** in Appendix*).] —**pro′to·col′ar** (prō′tə-kŏl′ər), **pro′to·col′a·ry, pro′to·col′ic** *adj.*

Pro·to-East·ern-Al·gon·qui·an (prō′tō-ē′stərn-ăl-gŏng′kwē-ən, -kē-ən) *n.* The earliest reconstructed ancestor of Eastern Algonquian.

Pro·to-Ger·man·ic (prō′tō-jûr-măn′ĭk) *n.* The prehistoric ancestor of the Germanic languages.

Pro·to-Greek (prō′tō-grēk′) *n.* Prehistoric Greek, after its separation from Indo-European and before its division into dialects.

pro·to·his·to·ry (prō′tō-hĭs′tə-rē, -hĭs′trē) *n.* The study of a culture just prior to its earliest recorded history. —**pro′to·his·tor′ic** (-hĭs-tôr′ĭk, -tŏr′ĭk) *adj.*

pro·to·hu·man (prō′tō-hyōō′mən) *adj.* Of or pertaining to several species of prehistoric primates resembling modern man but more primitive in development. —*n.* A protohuman primate.

Pro·to-In·do-Eur·o·pe·an (prō′tō-ĭn′dō-yŏŏr′ə-pē′ən) *n.* The earliest stage of Indo-European.

pro·to·lan·guage (prō′tō-lăng′gwĭj) *n. Linguistics.* A language that is the recorded or hypothetical ancestor of another language or group of languages. Compare **Ursprache.**

pro·to·lith·ic (prō′tə-lĭth′ĭk) *adj.* Of, pertaining to, or characteristic of the very beginning of the Stone Age; eolithic. [PROTO- + -LITHIC.]

pro·to·mar·tyr (prō′tō-mär′tər) *n.* The first martyr in a cause. Used especially of the first Christian martyr, Saint Stephen.

pro·to·mor·phic (prō′tə-môr′fĭk) *adj.* Primitive in structure or form. [PROTO- + -MORPHIC.]

pro·ton (prō′tŏn′) *n. Symbol* **p** *Physics.* A stable, positively charged subatomic particle in the baryon family having a mass 1,836 times that of the electron. See **neutron, particle.** [Greek *prōton,* neuter of *prōtos,* first. See **per**[1] in Appendix.*] —**pro·ton′ic** *adj.*

pro·to·ne·ma (prō′tə-nē′mə) *n., pl.* **-nemata** (-nē′mə-tə, -nĕm′ə-tə). *Botany.* A green, threadlike structure that arises on germination of a moss spore, and that eventually develops into a mature plant. [PROTO- + Greek *nēma,* thread (see **snē-**[1] in Appendix*).] —**pro′to·ne′mal** (-nē′məl), **pro′to·ne′ma·tal** (-nē′mə-təl, -nĕm′ə-təl) *adj.*

pro·ton·o·tar·y. Variant of **prothonotary.**

proton synchrotron. *Physics.* A ring-shaped **synchrotron** *(see)* that uses a frequency modulated accelerating voltage to accelerate protons to energies of several billion electron volts.

pro·to·path·ic (prō′tə-păth′ĭk) *adj.* Of or designating the cutaneous sensory reception of gross pressure, pain, heat, or cold. Compare **epicritic.** [From Medieval Greek *prōtopathēs,* affected first, from Greek *prōtopathein,* to feel or be affected first : PROTO- + *paskhein,* to feel, experience (see **kwenth-** in Appendix*).] —**pro·top′a·thy** (prō-tŏp′ə-thē) *n.*

pro·to·plasm (prō′tə-plăz′əm) *n.* A complex, jellylike colloidal substance conceived of as constituting the living matter of plant and animal cells, and performing the basic life functions. See **cytoplasm, nucleoplasm.** [German *Protoplasma* : PROTO- + -PLASM.] —**pro′to·plas′mic** (-plăz′mĭk), **pro′to·plas′mal, pro′to·plas·mat′ic** (-plăz-măt′ĭk) *adj.*

pro·to·plast (prō′tə-plăst′) *n.* **1.** *Rare.* That which is the first made or formed; prototype. **2.** *Biology.* The living material of a cell as distinguished from inert portions. [Old French *protoplaste,* from Late Latin *prōtoplastus,* "first formed," from Greek *prōtoplastos* : PROTO- + -PLAST.] —**pro′to·plas′tic** *adj.*

pro·to·por·phy·rin (prō′tō-pôr′fə-rĭn) *n.* A metal-free porphyrin, $C_{34}H_{34}N_4O_4$, derived from the hemin of blood.

Pro·to-Sem·it·ic (prō′tō-sə-mĭt′ĭk) *n.* The hypothetical common ancestor of the Asiatic (Eastern) branch of Hamito-Semitic, from which Arabic, Canaanite, Aramaic, Ethiopic, and Ugaritic are descended.

pro·to·stele (prō′tə-stēl′, prō′tə-stē′lē) *n. Botany.* A stele that lacks pith and has a solid core of xylem. —**pro′to·ste′lic** (prō′tə-stē′lĭk) *adj.*

pro·to·troph·ic (prō′tə-trŏf′ĭk, -trō′fĭk) *adj.* Obtaining nourishment by the assimilation of inorganic materials: *prototrophic bacteria.* [PROTO- + -TROPH(Y) + -IC.]

pro·to·type (prō′tə-tīp′) *n.* **1.** An original type, form, or instance that serves as a model on which later stages are based or judged. **2.** An early and typical example: *"Franklin is the real practical prototype of the American."* (D.H. Lawrence). **3.** *Biology.* A primitive or ancestral form or species. —See Synonyms at **ideal.** [French, from Greek *prōtotupon,* original form, archetype, from neuter of *prōtotupos,* "in the first form," original : PROTO- + -TYPE.] —**pro′to·typ′al** (prō′tə-tī′pəl), **pro′to·typ′ic** (-tĭp′ĭk), **pro′to·typ′i·cal** *adj.*

pro·to·zo·an (prō′tə-zō′ən) *n., pl.* **-zoans** or **-zoa** (-zō′ə). Also **pro·to·zo·on** (-ŏn′). Any of the single-celled, usually microscopic organisms of the phylum or subkingdom Protozoa, which includes the most primitive forms of animal life. [From New Latin *Protozoa* : PROTO- + -ZOA.] —**pro′to·zo′an, pro′to·zo′ic** (-zō′ĭk) *adj.*

pro·to·zo·ol·o·gy (prō′tō-zō-ŏl′ə-jē) *n.* The biological study of protozoans. —**pro′to·zo′o·log′i·cal** (-zō′ə-lŏj′ĭ-kəl) *adj.* —**pro′to·zo·ol′o·gist** *n.*

pro·tract (prō-trăkt′) *tr.v.* **-tracted, -tracting, -tracts. 1.** To draw out or lengthen in time; prolong. **2.** *Surveying.* To draw to scale by means of a scale and protractor; to plot. **3.** *Anatomy.* To extend or protrude. —See Synonyms at **prolong.** [Latin *prōtrahere* (past participle *prōtractus*), to drag out, lengthen : *prō-,*

ă pat/ā pay/âr care/ä father/b bib/ch church/d deed/ĕ pet/ē be/f fife/g gag/h hat/hw which/ĭ pit/ī pie/îr pier/j judge/k kick/l lid, needle/m mum/n no, sudden/ng thing/ŏ pot/ō toe/ô paw, for/oi noise/ou out/ŏŏ took/ōō boot/p pop/r roar/s sauce/sh ship, dish/

out, extending + *trahere*, to drag, pull (see **tragh-** in Appendix*).] —**pro·tract′ed·ly** *adv.* —**pro·tract′ed·ness** *n.* —**pro·trac′tive** *adj.*

pro·trac·tile (prō-trăk′tĭl) *adj.* Also **pro·tract·i·ble** (-tə-bəl). Capable of being protracted; extensible. —**pro′trac·til′i·ty** *n.*

pro·trac·tion (prō-trăk′shən) *n.* **1. a.** The act of protracting. **b.** The state of being protracted. **2.** *Prosody.* The irregular lengthening of a normally short syllable.

pro·trac·tor (prō-trăk′tər) *n.* **1.** A semicircular instrument for measuring and constructing angles. **2.** An adjustable pattern used by tailors. **3.** *Anatomy.* A muscle, an **extensor** *(see).*

pro·trude (prō-trōōd′) *v.* **-truded, -truding, -trudes.** —*tr.* To push or thrust outward. —*intr.* To jut out; project. [Latin *prōtrūdere* : *prō-*, forth + *trūdere*, to thrust (see **treud-** in Appendix*).] —**pro·trud′ent** *adj.*

pro·tru·sile (prō-trōō′sĭl, -sīl′) *adj.* Also **pro·tru·si·ble** (prō-trōō′sə-bəl). Capable of being thrust outward, as the tongue. [PRO-TRUS(ION) + -ILE.] —**pro′tru·sil′i·ty** (prō′trōō-sĭl′ə-tē) *n.*

pro·tru·sion (prō-trōō′zhən) *n.* **1. a.** The act of protruding. **b.** The state of being protruded. **2.** Something that protrudes.

pro·tru·sive (prō-trōō′sĭv, -zĭv) *adj.* **1.** Tending to protrude; protruding. **2.** Unduly or disagreeably conspicuous; obtrusive. —**pro·tru′sive·ly** *adv.* —**pro·tru′sive·ness** *n.*

pro·tu·ber·ance (prō-tōō′bər-əns, prō-tyōō′-) *n.* Also **pro·tu·ber·an·cy** *pl.* **-cies. 1.** That which protrudes; a bulge or knob. **2.** The condition of being protuberant.

pro·tu·ber·ant (prō-tōō′bər-ənt, prō-tyōō′-) *adj.* Swelling outward; bulging. [Late Latin *prōtūberāns*, present participle of *prōtūberāre*, to PROTUBERATE.] —**pro·tu′ber·ant·ly** *adv.*

pro·tu·ber·ate (prō-tōō′bə-rāt′, prō-tyōō′-) *intr.v.* **-ated, -ating, -ates.** To swell or bulge out. [Late Latin *prōtūberāre* : *prō-*, forth, outward + *tūber*, swelling, bump (see **tēue-** in Appendix*).] —**pro·tu′ber·a′tion** *n.*

proud (proud) *adj.* **prouder, proudest. 1.** Feeling pleasurable satisfaction over an attribute or act by which one's stature is measured: *proud of one's son; proud to serve one's country.* **2.** Occasioning pride; gratifying: *a proud moment.* **3.** Marked by exacting or constraining self-respect: *"a proud man who will not admit to himself that he is stooping"* (Edith Wharton). **4.** Having excessive self-esteem; haughty; arrogant. **5.** Of great dignity; honored: *a proud name.* **6.** Majestic; magnificent. **7.** Spirited. [Middle English *proud*, late Old English *prūt, prūd*, from Old French *prod, prud*, good, gallant, brave, from Late Latin *prōde*, advantageous, from Latin *prōdesse*, to be beneficial : *prōd-*, variant of *prō-*, for + *esse*, to be (see **es-** in Appendix*).] —**proud′ly** *adv.* —**proud′ness** *n.*

Synonyms: *proud, arrogant, haughty, disdainful, supercilious.* These adjectives imply self-esteem, most of them to the degree of belief in one's superiority over others. Although *proud* can suggest conceit or vanity, it more often implies justifiable satisfaction with oneself. *Arrogant* suggests one who demands more power or consideration than is rightly his. *Haughty* refers to a more consciously assumed manner, as of one who affects superiority by reason of birth or station. *Disdainful* emphasizes scorn or contempt. *Supercilious* combines the meanings of *haughty* and *disdainful* and adds the idea of aloofness.

proud flesh. *Pathology.* The swollen flesh around a healing wound due to granulation tissue. [Middle English *proud fleisch;* so called because of its swelling up.]

Prou·dhon (prōō-dôN′), **Pierre Joseph.** 1809–1865. French utopian socialist.

Proust (prōōst), **Joseph Louis.** 1754–1826. French chemist; established "Proust's law" of definite proportions.

Proust (prōōst), **Marcel.** 1871–1922. French novelist and critic.

prov. 1. province; provincial. **2.** provisional. **3.** provost.

Prov. 1. Provençal. **2.** Proverbs (Old Testament).

prove (prōōv) *v.* **proved, proved** or **proven** (prōō′vən), **proving, proves.** See Usage note below. —*tr.* **1.** To establish the truth or validity of by presentation of argument or evidence. **2.** *Law.* To establish the authenticity of (a will). **3.** To determine the quality of by testing; try out. **4.** *Mathematics.* **a.** To validate (a hypothesis or proposition) by a proof. **b.** To verify (the result of a calculation). **5.** *Printing.* To make a sample impression of (type). **6.** *Archaic.* To experience; undergo: *"And we will all the pleasures prove"* (Marlowe). —*intr.* To be shown to be; turn out: *"a very agreeable companion may . . . prove a very improper . . . friend"* (Lord Chesterfield). —See Synonyms at **confirm.** [Middle English *proven*, to put to test, prove, from Old French *prover*, from Latin *probāre*, to test, demonstrate as good, from *probus*, good, virtuous. See **per**[1] in Appendix.*] —**prov′a·bil′i·ty, prov′a·ble·ness** *n.* —**prov′a·ble** *adj.* —**prov′a·bly** *adv.* —**prov′er** *n.*

Usage: *Proved* is the preferred form as past participle: *It has proved satisfactory. He has proved his point.* The alternate *proven* is acceptable to only 27 per cent of the Usage Panel in such examples. But *proven* is the more widely employed form as an attributive adjective (used before a noun): *a proven record.* It is also used in the phrase *not proven.*

prov·en (prōō′vən) *adj.* Proved; verified. See Usage note at **prove.** —**prov′en·ly** *adv.*

prov·e·nance (prŏv′ə-nəns, -näns′) *n.* The place of origin; derivation. [French, from *provenant*, present participle of *provenir*, to come forth, originate, from Latin *prōvenīre* : *prō-*, forth + *venīre*, to come (see **gwā-** in Appendix*).]

Pro·ven·çal (prō′vən-säl′, prŏv′ən-; *French* prô-väN-sȧl′) *n.* *Abbr.* **Prov., Pr. 1.** A native or inhabitant of Provence, France. **2.** The Romance language of Provence, especially the literary language of the troubadours. —*adj.* Of or pertaining to Provence, its people, or their language.

Pro·vence (prô-väNs′). A region of southeastern France, on the Mediterranean between the Rhône and Italy.

prov·en·der (prŏv′ən-dər) *n.* **1.** Dry food, such as hay, used as food for livestock. **2.** *Informal.* Food or provisions. [Middle English *provendre*, from Old French *provend(r)e*, from Medieval Latin *prōbenda*, fodder, alteration of Late Latin *praebenda*, support, subsistence, pension, "things to be supplied," from *praebendus*, gerundive of *prae(hi)bēre*, to hold forth, supply : *prae-*, before + *habēre*, to hold (see **ghabh-** in Appendix*).]

pro·ve·nience (prə-vēn′yəns, -vē′nē-əns) *n.* A source or origin of something. [From Latin *prōveniēns*, present participle of *prōvenīre*, to come forth. See **provenance.**]

pro·ven·tric·u·lus (prō′vĕn-trĭk′yə-ləs) *n., pl.* **-li** (-lī′). *Zoology.* **1.** A division of the stomach anterior to the gizzard in birds. **2.** A similar digestive division in insects and some worms. [New Latin : PRO- (in front of) + Latin *ventriculus*, stomach, gizzard, VENTRICLE.] —**pro′ven·tric′u·lar** (-lər) *adj.*

prov·erb (prŏv′ûrb′) *n.* **1.** A short, pithy saying in frequent and widespread use, expressing a well-known truth or fact. **2.** A person or thing recognized as a typical example; one that is proverbial. —See Synonyms at **saying.** [Middle English *proverbe*, from Old French, from Latin *prōverbium*, "set of words put forth" : *prō-*, forth + *verbum*, word (see **wer-**[6] in Appendix*).]

pro·ver·bi·al (prə-vûr′bē-əl) *adj.* **1.** Of the nature of a proverb. **2.** Expressed in a proverb or proverbs. **3.** Widely referred to, as if the subject of a proverb; famous. —**pro·ver′bi·al·ly** *adv.*

Prov·erbs (prŏv′ûrbz′) *n.* Plural in form, used with a singular verb. *Abbr.* **Prov.** A book of the Old Testament.

pro·vide (prə-vīd′) *v.* **-vided, -viding, -vides.** —*tr.* **1.** To furnish; supply. **2.** To make ready; prepare. **3.** To make available; afford. **4.** To set down as a stipulation. —*intr.* **1.** To take measures in preparation. Used with *for* or *against.* **2.** To supply means of subsistence. Used with *for.* **3.** To make a stipulation or condition: *The Constitution provides for a bicameral legislature.* [Middle English *providen*, to foresee, make provision, from Latin *prōvidēre* : *prō-*, beforehand, in anticipation of + *vidēre*, to see (see **weid-** in Appendix*).] —**pro·vid′er** *n.*

pro·vid·ed (prə-vī′dĭd) *conj.* On the condition; if. Often followed by *that.*

Usage: *Provided* is preferable to *providing* in this sense. *Providing* is unacceptable in writing to 64 per cent of the Usage Panel. Both are applicable only when a requirement is explicitly set forth: *You may go, provided your work is done.* When a mere condition or possibility is expressed *if* is proper: *You may go, if you wish.*

prov·i·dence (prŏv′ə-dəns, -dĕns′) *n.* **1.** Care or preparation in advance; foresight. **2.** Prudent management; economy. **3.** The care, guardianship, and control exercised by a deity; divine direction: *"Some sought the key to history in the working of divine providence"* (William Ebenstein). **4.** *Capital* **P.** God.

Prov·i·dence (prŏv′ə-dəns, -dĕns′). The capital and largest city of Rhode Island, a port at the head of Narragansett Bay. Population, 187,000.

prov·i·dent (prŏv′ə-dənt, -dĕnt′) *adj.* **1.** Providing for future needs or events. **2.** Frugal; economical. [Middle English, from Latin *prōvidēns*, present participle of *prōvidēre*, to foresee, PROVIDE.] —**prov′i·dent·ly** *adv.*

prov·i·den·tial (prŏv′ə-dĕn′shəl) *adj.* **1.** Of or resulting from divine providence. **2.** Happening as if through divine intervention; fortunate; opportune. —**prov′i·den′tial·ly** *adv.*

pro·vid·ing (prə-vī′dĭng) *conj.* On the condition; provided. Followed by *that.* See Usage note at **provided.**

prov·ince (prŏv′ĭns) *n.* *Abbr.* **prov. 1.** Any of various lands outside Italy conquered by the Romans and administered by them as self-contained units. **2.** A territory governed as an administrative or political unit of a country or empire. **3.** *Ecclesiastical.* A division of territory under the jurisdiction of an archbishop. **4.** *Plural.* Areas of a country situated away from the capital or population center. Preceded by *the.* **5.** A comprehensive area of knowledge, activity, or interest: *"this type of writing was to be Gay's favored province"* (George Sherburn). **6.** The range of one's proper duties and functions; scope; jurisdiction. **7.** *Ecology.* A subdivision of a **region** *(see).* [Middle English *provynce*, from Old French *province*, from Latin *prōvincia*†.]

pro·vin·cial (prə-vĭn′shəl) *adj.* **1.** *Abbr.* **prov.** Of or pertaining to a province. **2.** Of or characteristic of people from the provinces; not fashionable or sophisticated: *"well-educated professional women . . . made me feel uncomfortably provincial"* (J.R. Salamanca). **3.** Limited in perspective; narrow and self-centered. —*n.* **1.** A native or inhabitant of the provinces. **2.** A person who has provincial ideas or habits. —**pro·vin′cial·ism′, pro·vin′ci·al′i·ty** *n.* —**pro·vin′cial·ly** *adv.*

proving ground. A place for testing new devices or theories.

pro·vi·sion (prə-vĭzh′ən) *n.* **1.** The act of supplying or fitting out. **2.** That which is provided. **3.** A preparatory measure. **4.** *Plural.* A stock of necessary supplies, especially food. **5.** A stipulation or qualification; especially, a clause in a document or agreement. —*tr.v.* **provisioned, -sioning, -sions.** To supply with provisions. [Middle English, foresight, precaution, from Old French, from Latin *prōvīsiō*, from *prōvīsus*, past participle of *prōvidēre*, to PROVIDE.] —**pro·vi′sion·er** *n.*

pro·vi·sion·al (prə-vĭzh′ən-əl) *adj.* Also **pro·vi·sion·ar·y** (-ə-nĕr′ē). *Abbr.* **prov.** Provided for the time being, pending permanent arrangements: *a provisional capital.* See Synonyms at **transient.** —**pro·vi′sion·al·ly** *adv.*

pro·vi·so (prə-vī′zō) *n., pl.* **-sos** or **-soes.** A clause in a document making a qualification, condition, or restriction. [Middle English, from Medieval Latin *prōvīsō (quod)*, provided

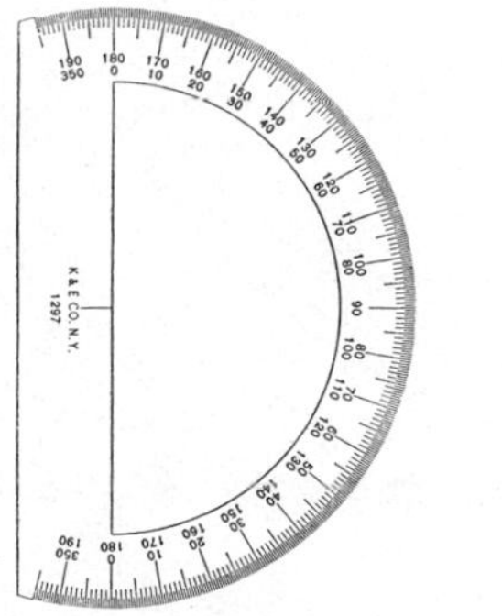

protractor

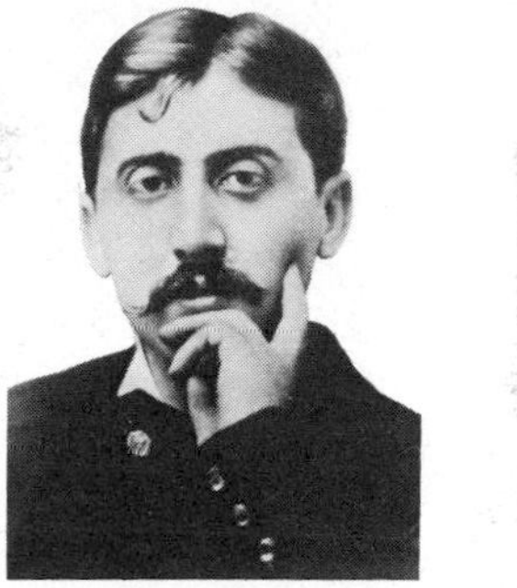

Marcel Proust

(that), from *prōvīsus*, past participle of *prōvidēre*, to PROVIDE.]
pro·vi·so·ry (prə-vī′zə-rē) *adj.* Depending on a proviso; conditional. —**pro·vi′so·ri·ly** *adv.*
pro·vi·ta·min (prō-vī′tə-mĭn) *n.* A substance converted to a vitamin within the body, as carotene into vitamin A.
Pro·vo (prō′vō′). A city of Utah, a summer resort in the north-central part of the state. Population, 36,000.
prov·o·ca·tion (prŏv′ə-kā′shən) *n.* **1.** The act of provoking or inciting. **2.** Something that provokes; a cause of irritation.
pro·voc·a·tive (prə-vŏk′ə-tĭv) *adj.* Tending to provoke; exciting; stimulating. —*n.* Something that provokes. —**pro·voc′a·tive·ly** *adv.* —**pro·voc′a·tive·ness** *n.*
pro·voke (prə-vōk′) *tr.v.* **-voked, -voking, -vokes. 1.** To incite to anger or resentment. **2.** To stir or incite to action; arouse. **3.** To bring on by inciting: *provoke a fight.* —See Synonyms at **annoy.** [Middle English *provoken*, from Old French *provoquer*, from Latin *prōvocāre*, to call forth, challenge : *prō-*, forth + *vocāre*, to call (see **wekw-** in Appendix*).] —**pro·vok′ing·ly** *adv.*
Synonyms: *provoke, incite, excite, stimulate, arouse, rouse, stir.* These verbs are compared in the sense of causing a person to take action or feel emotion. *Provoke*, the least explicit with respect to means, does little more than state the consequences produced: *He was provoked to anger. Incite* implies the urging on and directing of energies toward a certain course. *Excite* stresses, rather, a playing upon the emotions generally. The remaining terms suggest increasing degrees of emotional awakening. *Stimulate* and *arouse* connote immediate, often brief sensations, and *rouse* and *stir*, deeper, stronger responses.
pro·vost (prō′vōst′, prŏv′əst, prō′vəst) *n. Abbr.* **prov. 1.** The chief magistrate of certain Scottish cities. **2.** The chief officer of some colleges. **3.** The highest official in certain cathedrals or collegiate churches. [Middle English *provost*, from Old English *profost* and Old French *provost*, both from Medieval Latin *prōpositus, praepositus*, from Latin *praepositus*, "(one) placed before (others)," president, superintendent, from the past participle of *praepōnere*, to place before or over : *prae-*, before + *pōnere*, to place (see **apo-** in Appendix*).]
pro·vost court (prō′vō). A military court for the trial of minor offenses committed in occupied hostile territories.
pro·vost guard (prō′vō). A detail of soldiers on police duty under a provost marshal.
pro·vost marshal (prō′vō). *Abbr.* **P.M. 1.** *U.S. Army.* The head of military police. **2.** *U.S. Navy.* An officer responsible for the disposition of prisoners facing court-martial.
pro·vost sergeant (prō′vō). A noncommissioned officer who heads a detail of military police.
prow (prou) *n.* **1.** The forward part of a ship's hull; the bow. **2.** A similar projecting part, such as the forward end of a ski. [French *pro(u)e*, probably from dialectal Old Italian *prua*, from Latin *prōra*, from Greek *prōira*. See **per**[1] in Appendix.*]
prow·ess (prou′ĭs) *n.* **1.** Superior skill or ability. **2.** Superior strength, courage, or daring, especially in battle. [Middle English *prowesse*, from Old French *proesse*, from *prou*, variant of *prod, prud*, gallant, brave, PROUD.]
prowl (proul) *v.* **prowled, prowling, prowls.** —*tr.* To roam through stealthily, as in search of prey or plunder. —*intr.* To rove furtively or with predatory intent. —*n.* An act of prowling: *on the prowl.* [Middle English *prollen*†.] —**prowl′er** *n.*
prowl car. A **squad car** *(see).*
prox. proximo.
prox·i·mal (prŏk′sə-məl) *adj.* **1.** Nearest; proximate. **2.** *Biology.* Near the central part of the body or a point of attachment or origin: *the proximal end of a bone.* Compare **distal.** [From Latin *proximus*, nearest, next, PROXIMATE.] —**prox′i·mal·ly** *adv.*
prox·i·mate (prŏk′sə-mĭt) *adj.* **1.** Closely related in space, time, or order; nearest; next. **2.** Approximate. [Latin *proximātus*, past participle of *proximāre*, to come near, from *proximus*, nearest. See **per**[1] in Appendix.*] —**prox′i·mate·ly** *adv.*
prox·im·i·ty (prŏk-sĭm′ə-tē) *n.* The state, quality, or fact of being near or next; closeness. [Old French *proximite*, from Latin *proximitās*, from *proximus*, nearest. See **proximate.**]
proximity fuze. An electronic device for detonating a projectile as it approaches a target, used in antiaircraft shells.
prox·i·mo (prŏk′sə-mō′) *adv. Abbr.* **prox.** *Archaic.* Of or in the following month: *on the 15th proximo.* Compare **ultimo, instant.** [From Latin *proximō (mense)*, in the next (month), ablative of *proximus*, nearest, next. See **proximate.**]
prox·y (prŏk′sē) *n., pl.* **-ies. 1.** A person authorized to act for another; agent or substitute. **2.** The authority to act for another. **3.** The written authorization for such action. [Middle English *procusie, proxcy*, contractions of *procuracie*, from Norman French, from Medieval Latin *prōcūrātia*, from Latin *prōcūrātiō*, a caring for, from *prōcūrātus*, past participle of *prōcūrāre*, to take care of, PROCURE.]
prude (prōōd) *n.* A person, especially a woman, who is overconcerned with being or seeming to be proper, modest, or righteous. [French, short for Old French *pr(e)udefemme*, virtuous woman, "fine thing of a woman" : *preu*, virtuous, variant of *prod, prud* (see **proud**) + *de*, of + *femme*, woman.]
pru·dence (prōōd′əns) *n.* **1.** The state, quality, or fact of being prudent; discretion. **2.** Careful management; economy.
Synonyms: *prudence, discretion, circumspection.* These nouns are compared as they express caution and wisdom in the conduct of affairs. *Prudence*, the most comprehensive, implies not only caution but the capacity for judging in advance the probable results of one's actions. *Discretion* suggests prudence coupled with self-restraint and sound judgment. *Circumspection* adds to discretion the implication of wariness in one's actions out of consideration for social and moral consequences.
Pru·dence (prōōd′əns). A feminine given name. [Middle English, from Latin *prūdentia*, prudence, from *prūdēns*, PRUDENT.]
pru·dent (prōōd′ənt) *adj.* **1.** Wise in handling practical matters; exercising good judgment or common sense. **2.** Careful in regard to one's own interests; provident. **3.** Careful about one's conduct; circumspect; discreet. [Middle English, from Old French, from Latin *prūdēns*, foreseeing, wise, contraction of *prōvidēns*, PROVIDENT.] —**pru′dent·ly** *adv.*
pru·den·tial (prōō-dĕn′shəl) *adj.* **1.** Arising from or characterized by prudence. **2.** Exercising prudence, good judgment, or common sense. —**pru·den′tial·ly** *adv.*
prud·er·y (prōō′də-rē) *n., pl.* **-ies. 1.** The state or quality of being prudish; excessive regard for propriety, modesty, or morality. **2.** An instance of prudish behavior or talk. [French *pruderie*, from *prude*, PRUDE.]
prud·ish (prōō′dĭsh) *adj.* Marked by or exhibiting prudery. —**prud′ish·ly** *adv.* —**prud′ish·ness** *n.*
pru·i·nose (prōō′ə-nōs′) *adj. Botany.* Having a white, powdery covering or bloom. [Latin *pruīnōsus*, covered with frost, from *pruīna*, hoarfrost. See **preus-** in Appendix.*]
prune[1] (prōōn) *n.* **1.** The partially dried fruit of any of several varieties of the common plum, *Prunus domestica.* **2.** Any kind of plum that can be dried without spoiling. **3.** *Slang.* A crabbed or sour-natured person; spoilsport. [Middle English *prun(n)e*, from Old French *prune*, from Vulgar Latin *prūna* (unattested), from Latin, plural of *prūnum*, plum, akin to Greek *proumnon*, from an unknown source in Asia Minor.]
prune[2] (prōōn) *v.* **pruned, pruning, prunes.** —*tr.* **1.** To cut off or remove dead or living parts or branches of (a plant, shrub, or tree) to improve shape or growth. **2.** To remove or cut out as superfluous. **3.** To reduce; retrench: *prune the budget.* —*intr.* To remove branches or parts from a plant. [Middle English *prouynen*, from Old French *pro(o)ignier*, from Vulgar Latin *prōrotundiāre* (unattested), to cut round in front : Latin *prō-*, in front + *rotundus*, round (see **ret-** in Appendix*).] —**prun′er** *n.*
pru·nel·la (prōō-nĕl′ə) *n.* Also **pru·nel·lo** (-nĕl′ō). A strong, heavy fabric of worsted twill, used chiefly for shoe uppers, clerical robes, and academic gowns. [French *prunelle*, "sloe," (here perhaps) "sloe-colored stuff." See **prunelle.**]
pru·nelle (prōō-nĕl′) *n.* A brownish, sloe-flavored French liqueur. [French, "sloe," diminutive of *prune*, PRUNE.]
pru·ri·ent (prōōr′ē-ənt) *adj.* **1.** Obsessively interested in improper matters, especially of a sexual nature. **2.** Characterized by such an interest: *prurient thoughts.* **3.** Arousing or appealing to such an interest: *prurient literature.* [Latin *prūriēns*, present participle of *prūrīre*, to itch, yearn for, be lascivious. See **preus-** in Appendix.*] —**pru′ri·ence, pru′ri·en·cy** *n.* —**pru′ri·ent·ly** *adv.*
pru·ri·go (prōō-rī′gō) *n.* A chronic, inflammatory skin disease characterized by eruption and severe itching. [Latin, an itching, from *prūrīre*, to itch. See **preus-** in Appendix.*] —**pru·rig′i·nous** (-rĭj′ə-nəs) *adj.*
pru·ri·tus (prōō-rī′təs) *n. Pathology.* Severe itching, usually of undamaged skin. [Latin, from *prūrīre*, to itch. See **preus-** in Appendix.*] —**pru·rit′ic** (-rĭt′ĭk) *adj.*
Prus·sia (prŭsh′ə). *Abbr.* **Prus., Pruss.** A former German state in northern and central Germany, 113,545 square miles in area, formally dissolved (1947) and divided among East and West Germany, Poland, and the Soviet Union. [Medieval Latin, from *Prussi, Borussi*†, the Baltic Prussians.]
Prus·sian (prŭsh′ən) *adj.* **1.** *Abbr.* **Prus., Pruss.** Of or pertaining to Prussia, its people, or their language and culture. **2.** Like or suggestive of the Junkers and the military class of Prussia. —*n.* **1.** One of the western Balts anciently inhabiting the region between the Vistula and Neman. **2.** A Baltic inhabitant of Prussia. **3.** A German inhabitant of Prussia. **4.** A language, **Old Prussian** *(see).*
Prussian blue. 1. An insoluble, dark-blue pigment and dye, ferric ferrocyanide or one of its modifications. **2. Iron blue** *(see).* **3.** Moderate to strong blue or deep greenish blue. See **color.** [Discovered in Berlin (1704) by H. de Diesbach, a maker of artist's colors.] —**Prus′sian-blue′** *adj.*
Prussian Pom·er·a·ni·a (pŏm′ə-rā′nē-ə). A former province of Prussia. See **Pomerania.**
prus·si·ate (prŭs′ē-āt′) *n. Chemistry.* **1.** A ferrocyanide or ferricyanide. **2.** A salt of hydrocyanic acid; a cyanide. [French : from *(acide) prussique*, PRUSSIC (ACID) + -ATE.]
prus·sic acid (prŭs′ĭk). *Chemistry.* **Hydrocyanic acid** *(see).* [French *acide prussique*, because obtained from Prussian blue.]
Prut (prōōt). Also **Pruth** (prōōt). A river rising in the southwestern Soviet Union, flowing 530 miles to the Danube and forming the border between the Soviet Union and Rumania.
pry[1] (prī) *intr.v.* **pried, prying, pries.** To look or inquire closely, curiously, or inquisitively, often in a furtive manner; snoop. Often used with *into.* —*n., pl.* **pries. 1.** An act of prying. **2.** An excessively inquisitive person; a snoop. [Middle English *prien*, perhaps related to PEER.] —**pry′ing·ly** *adv.*
pry[2] (prī) *tr.v.* **pried, prying, pries. 1.** To raise, move, or force open with a lever. **2.** To obtain with effort or difficulty: *pry a confession out of a suspect.* —*n., pl.* **pries. 1.** Something used to apply leverage, such as a crowbar. **2.** Leverage. [Alteration of PRIZE (to force open), mistaken for a third person singular.]
pry·er. Variant of **prier.**
Pry·pec. The Polish name for **Pripet.**
Ps. Psalm; Psalms (Old Testament).
p.s. 1. passenger steamer. **2.** postscript.
P.S. 1. permanent secretary. **2.** Police Sergeant. **3.** postscript. **4.** public school.
Psa. Psalm; Psalms (Old Testament).
psalm (säm) *n.* **1.** A sacred song; hymn. **2.** *Usually capital* **P.**

Abbr. **Ps., Psa.** Any of the sacred songs or hymns collected in the Old Testament Book of Psalms. —*tr.v.* **psalmed, psalming, psalms.** To sing of or celebrate in psalms. [Middle English *(p)salm,* Old English *(p)sealm,* from Late Latin *psalmus,* from Greek *psalmos,* song sung to the harp, psalm (translation of Hebrew *mizmōr,* song, psalm), from *psallein,* to pluck, play the harp. See **pōl-** in Appendix.*]

psalm·ist (säʹmĭst) *n.* A writer or composer of psalms. —**the Psalmist.** King David, to whom many of the scriptural psalms are traditionally attributed.

psalm·o·dy (säʹmə-dē, sălʹmə-) *n., pl.* **-dies. 1.** The singing of psalms in divine worship. **2.** The composition or arranging of psalms for singing. **3.** A collection of psalms. [Middle English *psalmodie,* from Late Latin *psalmōdia,* from Late Greek, from Greek, singing to the harp : *psalmos,* PSALM + *ōidē,* song, ode (see **wed-**[2] in Appendix*).] —**psalmʹo·dist** *n.*

Psalms (sämz). *Abbr.* **Ps., Psa.** One of the books of the Old Testament, the Book of Psalms, containing 150 songs.

Psal·ter (sôlʹtər) *n.* Also **psal·ter.** A book containing the Book of Psalms or a particular version of, musical setting for, or selection from it. [Middle English *(p)salter, sauter,* from Old English *(p)saltere* and Old French *(p)sautier,* both from Late Latin *psaltērium,* early Christian transference of Greek *psaltērion,* psalm, song, PSALTERY.]

psal·te·ri·um (sôl-tîrʹē-əm) *n., pl.* **-teria** (-tîrʹē-ə). A division of the stomach of ruminants, the **omasum** *(see).* [New Latin, from Late Latin, PSALTER (when slit open its folds fall apart like the leaves of a book).] —**psal·teʹri·al** *adj.*

psal·ter·y (sôlʹtə-rē) *n., pl.* **-ies.** Also **psal·try** (sôlʹtrē). An ancient, stringed musical instrument played by plucking the strings with the fingers or a plectrum. [Middle English *(p)salterie, sautre,* from Old French *(p)salterie, sauter(i)e,* from Latin *psaltērium,* from Greek *psaltērion,* from *psallein,* to pluck, play upon a stringed instrument. See **pōl-** in Appendix.*]

pseud. pseudonym.

pseud·ax·is (sōō-dăkʹsĭs) *n. Botany.* A **sympodium** *(see).* [PSEUD(O)- + AXIS.]

pseud·e·pig·ra·pha (sōōʹdĭ-pĭgʹrə-fə) *pl.n.* **1.** Spurious writings; specifically, writings falsely attributed to Biblical characters or times. **2.** A body of Jewish religious texts written between 200 B.C. and A.D. 200 and spuriously ascribed to various prophets and kings of Hebrew Scriptures. [Greek, neuter plural of *pseudepigraphos,* falsely ascribed : PSEUDO- + *epigraphein,* to ascribe : *epi,* on, upon + *graphein,* to write (see **gerebh-** in Appendix*).] —**pseudʹe·pigʹra·phal, pseudʹep·i·graphʹic** (-dĕp-ə-grăfʹĭk), **pseudʹep·i·graphʹi·cal, pseudʹe·pigʹra·phous** *adj.* —**pseudʹe·pigʹra·phy** *n.*

pseu·do (sōōʹdō) *adj.* False or counterfeit; fake. [Middle English, from PSEUDO-.]

pseudo-, pseud-. Indicates: **1.** Inauthenticity; sham; for example, **pseudoscience. 2.** Deceptive similarity; for example, **pseudopodium.** ***Note:*** Many compounds other than those entered here may be formed with *pseudo-.* In forming compounds, *pseudo-* is normally joined with the following element without space or hyphen: *pseudoscience.* However, if the second element begins with a capital letter, it is separated with a hyphen: *pseudo-Americanism.* It is also preferable to use the hyphen if the second element begins with *o* or if forming the compound brings together three or more vowels that would be confusing to read. [Middle English, from Late Latin, from Greek *pseudēs,* false, from *pseudein*†, to lie.]

pseu·do·carp (sōōʹdə-kärpʹ) *n. Botany.* An **accessory fruit** *(see).* [PSEUDO- + -CARP.] —**pseuʹdo·carʹpous** *adj.*

pseu·do·morph (sōōʹdə-môrfʹ) *n.* **1.** A false, deceptive, or irregular form. **2.** *Mineralogy.* A mineral having the crystalline form of another mineral rather than that normally characteristic of its composition. [PSEUDO- + -MORPH.] —**pseuʹdo·morʹphism** *n.* —**pseuʹdo·morʹphic, pseuʹdo·morʹphous** *adj.*

pseu·do·nym (sōōʹdə-nĭmʹ) *n. Abbr.* **pseud.** A fictitious name assumed by an author; pen name. [French *pseudonyme,* from Greek *pseudōnumon,* neuter of *pseudōnumos* : PSEUD(O)- + -ONYM.] —**pseu·donʹy·mous** (sōō-dŏnʹə-məs) *adj.* —**pseu·donʹy·mous·ly** *adv.* —**pseuʹdo·nymʹi·ty** (sōōʹdə-nĭmʹə-tē), **pseu·donʹy·mous·ness** *n.*

pseu·do·po·di·um (sōōʹdə-pōʹdē-əm) *n., pl.* **-dia** (-dē-ə). Also **pseu·do·pod** (sōōʹdə-pŏdʹ). A temporary protrusion of the cytoplasm of a cell, serving, in organisms such as the amoeba, as a means of locomotion and of surrounding and ingesting food. [PSEUDO- + -PODIUM.] —**pseu·dopʹo·dal** (sōō-dŏpʹə-dəl), **pseuʹdo·poʹdi·al** *adj.*

pseu·do·sci·ence (sōōʹdō-sīʹəns) *n.* An unscientific or trivially scientific theory, methodology, or activity that appears to be or is presented as scientific. —**pseuʹdo·sciʹen·tifʹic** (-sīʹən-tĭfʹĭk) *adj.* —**pseuʹdo·sciʹen·tist** *n.*

psf, p.s.f. pounds per square foot.

pshaw (shô) *interj.* Used to indicate impatience, irritation, disapproval or disbelief.

psi (sī) *n.* The 23rd letter in the Greek alphabet written Ψ, ψ. Transliterated in English as *ps.* See **alphabet.** [Late Greek, from Greek *psei,* originally (in the alphabet used at Athens) written ΦΣ.]

psi, p.s.i. pounds per square inch.

psia, p.s.i.a. pounds per square inch absolute.

psig, p.s.i.g. pounds per square inch gauge.

psi·lom·e·lane (sī-lŏmʹə-lānʹ) *n.* A hard, black, hydrated oxide ore of manganese. [From Greek *psilos,* mere, bare (see **bhes-**[1] in Appendix*) + *melas* (stem *melan-*), black (see **mel-**[2] in Appendix*).]

psit·ta·cine (sĭtʹə-sīnʹ) *adj.* Of, pertaining to, or characteristic of parrots. [Latin *psittacīnus,* from *psittacus,* parrot, from Greek *psittakos*†.]

psit·ta·co·sis (sĭtʹə-kōʹsĭs) *n.* A virus disease of parrots and related birds, communicable to man, in whom it produces high fever and complications similar to pneumonia. Also called "parrot fever." [New Latin : Latin *psittacus,* parrot (see **psittacine**) + -OSIS.] —**psitʹta·cotʹic** (-kŏtʹĭk, -kōʹtĭk) *adj.*

Pskov (pskôf). A city of the western Soviet Union, 160 miles southwest of Leningrad. Population, 105,000.

pso·ri·a·sis (sə-rīʹə-sĭs) *n.* A chronic, noncontagious skin disease characterized by inflammation and white, scaly patches. [New Latin, from Greek *psōriasis,* from *psōrian,* to have the itch, from *psōra,* itch, from *psēn,* to rub, scratch. See **bhes-**[1] in Appendix.*] —**psoʹri·atʹic** (sôrʹē-ătʹĭk, sōrʹ-) *adj.*

PST, P.S.T. Pacific Standard Time.

psych (sīk) *n. Informal.* Psychology.

psych. psychological; psychologist; psychology.

psy·che (sīʹkē) *n.* **1.** The soul or spirit, as distinguished from the body. **2.** *Psychiatry.* The mind functioning as the center of thought, feeling, and behavior, and consciously or unconsciously adjusting and relating the body to its social and physical environment. [Latin, from Greek *psukhē,* breath, life, soul. See **bhes-**[2] in Appendix.*]

Psy·che (sīʹkē). *Classical Mythology.* A maiden loved by Eros and united with him after Aphrodite's jealousy was overcome; became the personification of the soul.

psych·e·del·ic (sīʹkə-dĕlʹĭk) *adj.* Of, pertaining to, or generating hallucinations, distortions of perception, and, occasionally, psychoticlike states. [From PSYCHE (mind) + Greek *dēlos,* clear, visible (see **deiw-** in Appendix*).]

psy·chi·a·trist (sĭ-kīʹə-trĭst, sī-) *n.* A licensed physician specially trained to practice psychiatry.

psy·chi·a·try (sĭ-kīʹə-trē, sī-) *n.* The medical study, diagnosis, treatment, and prevention of mental illness. [PSYCH(O)- + -IATRY.] —**psyʹchi·atʹric** (sīʹkē-ătʹrĭk), **psyʹchi·atʹri·cal** *adj.* —**psyʹchi·atʹri·cal·ly** *adv.*

psy·chic (sīʹkĭk) *adj.* Also **psy·chi·cal** (-kĭ-kəl). **1.** Of or pertaining to the human mind or psyche. **2. a.** Of or pertaining to extraordinary, especially extrasensory and nonphysical, mental processes, such as extrasensory perception and mental telepathy. **b.** Proceeding from, produced by, or responding to such processes. —*n.* **1.** An individual apparently responsive to psychic forces. **2.** A medium. [Greek *psukhikos,* from *psukhē,* soul, life, PSYCHE.] —**psyʹchi·cal·ly** *adv.*

psy·cho (sīʹkō) *n., pl.* **-chos.** *Slang.* A psychopath.

psycho-. Indicates the mind or mental processes; for example, **psychology.** [From Greek *psukhē,* breath, life, PSYCHE.]

psy·cho·a·nal·y·sis (sīʹkō-ə-nălʹə-sĭs) *n.* **1.** The analytic technique originated by Sigmund Freud that uses free association, dream interpretation, and analysis of resistance and transference to investigate mental processes. **2.** The theory of human psychology founded by Freud on the concepts of the unconscious, resistance, repression, sexuality, and the Oedipus complex. **3.** Any psychiatric therapy incorporating such an analytic technique in such a theoretical framework. —**psyʹcho·anʹa·lyst** (-ănʹə-lĭst) *n.* —**psyʹcho·anʹa·lytʹic** (-ănʹə-lĭtʹĭk), **psyʹcho·anʹa·lytʹi·cal** *adj.* —**psyʹcho·anʹa·lytʹi·cal·ly** *adv.*

psy·cho·an·a·lyze (sīʹkō-ănʹə-līzʹ) *tr.v.* **-lyzed, -lyzing, -lyzes.** To analyze and treat by psychoanalysis.

psy·cho·bi·ol·o·gy (sīʹkō-bī-ŏlʹə-jē) *n.* The study of interactions between mental and biological, especially physiological, processes. —**psyʹcho·biʹo·logʹi·cal** (-bīʹə-lŏjʹĭ-kəl), **psyʹcho·biʹo·logʹic** *adj.* —**psyʹcho·bi·olʹo·gist** *n.*

psy·cho·dra·ma (sīʹkō-drăʹmə, -drămʹə) *n.* **1.** A psychotherapeutic and analytic technique in which individuals are assigned roles to be spontaneously played within a dramatic context devised by a therapist. **2.** A performance so devised and enacted. —**psyʹcho·dra·matʹic** (-drə-mătʹĭk) *adj.*

psy·cho·dy·nam·ics (sīʹkō-dī-nămʹĭks) *n.* Plural in form, used with a singular verb. **1.** The interaction of various mental or emotional processes, especially when they are considered as constituents of a system of interrelated forces. **2.** Behavioral analysis in terms of motives or drives. —**psyʹcho·dy·namʹic** *adj.*

psy·cho·gen·e·sis (sīʹkō-jĕnʹə-sĭs) *n.* **1.** The generation and development of psychological processes, personality, or behavior. **2.** The psychological origin of a specific psychic process or event. —**psyʹcho·ge·netʹic** (-jə-nĕtʹĭk) *adj.* —**psyʹcho·ge·netʹi·cal·ly** *adv.*

psy·cho·gen·ic (sīʹkō-jĕnʹĭk) *adj.* Originating in the mind or in mental activities and conditions. [PSYCHO- + -GENIC.]

psy·chog·no·sis (sīʹkŏg-nōʹsĭs) *n. Psychiatry. Rare.* The diagnosis of psychic disorders. [PSYCHO- + -GNOSIS.] —**psyʹchog·nosʹtic** (-nŏsʹtĭk) *adj.*

psy·cho·ki·ne·sis (sīʹkō-kĭ-nēʹsĭs, -kī-nēʹsĭs) *n.* **1.** *Abbr.* **PK** *Parapsychology.* The production of motion, especially in inanimate and remote objects, by the exercise of psychic powers. **2.** *Psychiatry.* Uninhibited, maniacal motor response. [PSYCHO- + -KINESIS.]

psychol. psychological; psychologist; psychology.

psy·cho·log·i·cal (sīʹkə-lŏjʹĭ-kəl) *adj.* Also **psy·cho·log·ic.** *Abbr.* **psych., psychol. 1.** Of or pertaining to psychology. **2.** Of, pertaining to, or derived from the mind or emotions. **3.** Capable of influencing the mind or emotions. —**psyʹcho·logʹi·cal·ly** *adv.*

psychological moment. The time when the mental state of a person is most likely to produce the desired response.

psy·chol·o·gist (sī-kŏlʹə-jĭst) *n. Abbr.* **psych., psychol.** A person trained to perform psychological analysis, therapy, or research.

psy·chol·o·gize (sī-kŏlʹə-jīzʹ) *v.* **-gized, -gizing, -gizes.** —*tr.* To explain (behavior) psychologically. —*intr.* **1.** To investigate

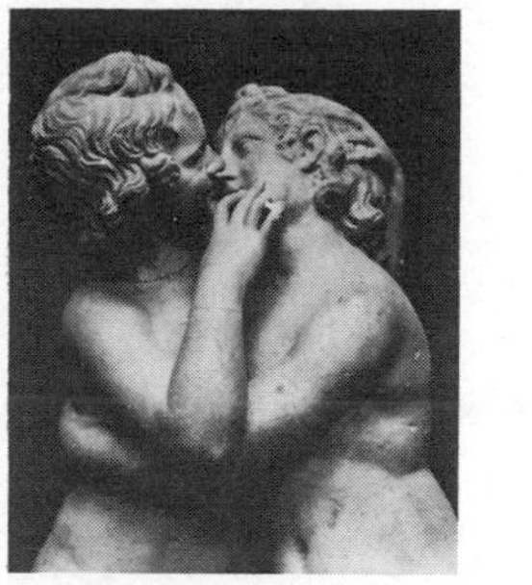

Psyche
Eros and Psyche

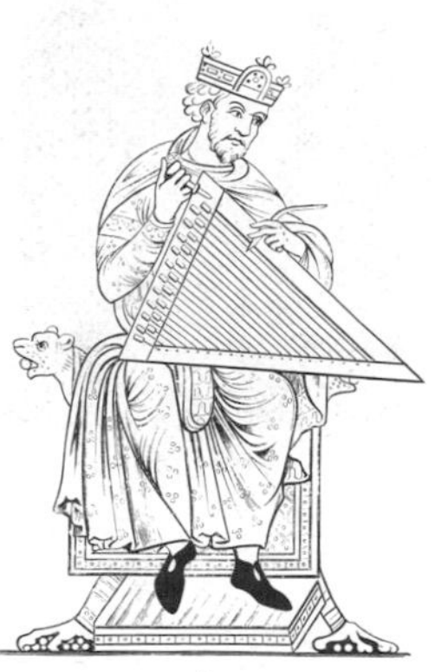

psaltery
Twelfth-century manuscript illustration of King David

t tight/th thin, path/*th* this, bathe/ŭ cut/ûr urge/v valve/w with/y yes/z zebra, size/zh vision/ə about, item, edible, gallop, circus/ à *Fr.* ami/œ *Fr.* feu, *Ger.* schön/ü *Fr.* tu, *Ger.* über/KH *Ger.* ich, *Scot.* loch/N *Fr.* bon. *Follows main vocabulary. †Of obscure origin.

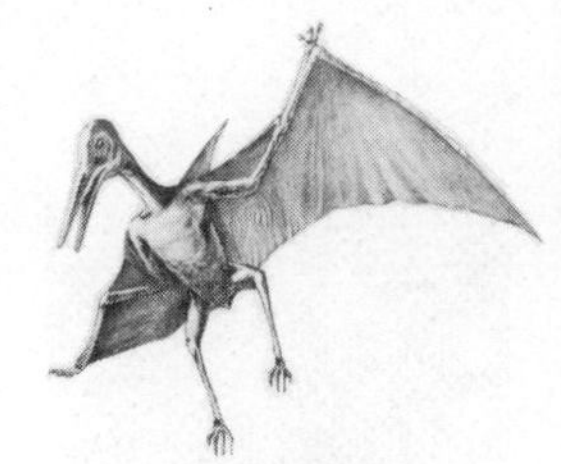

pterodactyl

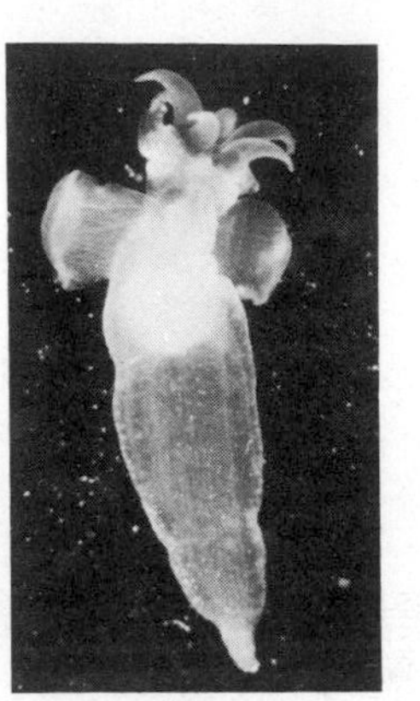

pteropod

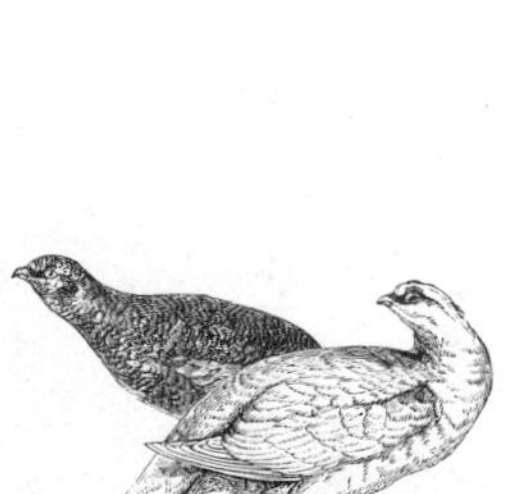

ptarmigan
Lagopus mutus

psychologically. **2.** To reason or speculate psychologically.
psy·chol·o·gy (sī-kŏl′ə-jē) *n., pl.* **-gies.** *Abbr.* **psych., psychol. 1.** The science of mental processes and behavior. **2.** The emotional and behavioral characteristics of an individual, group, or activity: *the psychology of war.* **3.** Subtle tactical action or argument: *He used poor psychology on his employer.* [New Latin *psychologia* : PSYCHO- + -LOGY.] —**psy·chol′o·gist** *n.*
psy·cho·met·rics (sī′kō-mĕt′rĭks) *n.* Plural in form, used with a singular verb. **1.** The measurement of psychological variables, such as intelligence, aptitude, and emotional disturbance. **2.** The mathematical, especially statistical, design of psychological tests and measures. —**psy′cho·met′ric, psy′cho·met′ri·cal** *adj.* —**psy′cho·met′ri·cal·ly** *adv.* —**psy·chom′e·tri′cian** (sī-kŏm′ə-trĭsh′ən), **psy·chom′e·trist** (sī-kŏm′ə-trĭst) *n.*
psy·cho·mo·tor (sī′kō-mō′tər) *adj. Psychology.* Of or pertaining to muscular activity associated with mental processes.
psy·cho·neu·ro·sis (sī′kō-nŏŏ-rō′sĭs, -nyŏŏ-rō′sĭs) *n., pl.* **-ses** (-sēz). *Psychiatry.* **Neurosis** (see). —**psy′cho·neu·rot′ic** (-nŏŏ-rŏt′ĭk, -nyŏŏ-rŏt′ĭk) *adj. & n.*
psy·cho·path (sī′kə-păth′) *n.* A person with a personality disorder, especially one manifested in aggressively antisocial behavior. [From PSYCHOPATHY.] —**psy′cho·path′ic** *adj.*
psy·cho·pa·thol·o·gy (sī′kō-pə-thŏl′ə-jē) *n.* The study of pathological mental conditions. —**psy′cho·path′o·log′i·cal** (-păth′ə-lŏj′ĭ-kəl), **psy′cho·path′o·log′ic** *adj.* —**psy′cho·pa·thol′o·gist** *n.*
psy·chop·a·thy (sī-kŏp′ə-thē) *n.* Mental disorder, especially when of unknown origin. [PSYCHO- + -PATHY.]
psy·cho·phys·ics (sī′kō-fĭz′ĭks) *n.* Plural in form, used with a singular verb. The psychological study of relationships between physical stimuli and sensory response. —**psy′cho·phys′i·cal** *adj.* —**psy′cho·phys′i·cal·ly** *adv.* —**psy′cho·phys′i·cist** (-fĭz′ə-sĭst) *n.*
psy·cho·phys·i·ol·o·gy (sī′kō-fĭz′ē-ŏl′ə-jē) *n.* The study of correlations between behavior and physiology. —**psy′cho·phys′i·o·log′i·cal** (-fĭz′ē-ə-lŏj′ĭ-kəl) *adj.* —**psy′cho·phys′i·o·log′i·cal·ly** *adv.*
psy·cho·sis (sī-kō′sĭs) *n., pl.* **-ses** (-sēz′). Any severe mental disorder, with or without organic damage, characterized by deterioration of normal intellectual and social functioning and by partial or complete withdrawal from reality. Compare **neurosis.** [New Latin : PSYCH(O)- + -OSIS.]
psy·cho·so·mat·ic (sī′kō-sō-măt′ĭk) *adj.* **1.** Of or pertaining to phenomena that are both physiological and psychological; somatic and psychic. **2.** Of or pertaining to a partially or wholly psychogenic disease or physiological disorder.
psy·cho·sur·ger·y (sī′kō-sûr′jə-rē) *n.* Brain surgery when used to treat mental disorders.
psy·cho·tech·nics (sī′kō-tĕk′nĭks) *n.* Plural in form, used with a singular verb. The practical or technological use of psychology, as in analysis of social or industrial problems. —**psy′cho·tech′ni·cal** *adj.* —**psy′cho·tech·ni′cian** (-tĕk-nĭsh′ən) *n.*
psy·cho·ther·a·py (sī′kō-thĕr′ə-pē) *n.* The psychological treatment of mental, emotional, and nervous disorders. —**psy′cho·ther′a·peu′tic** (-pyōō′tĭk) *adj.* —**psy′cho·ther′a·pist** *n.*
psy·chot·ic (sī-kŏt′ĭk) *n.* One afflicted with a psychosis. —*adj.* Of, pertaining to, or caused by psychosis. [From PSYCHOSIS.] —**psy·chot′i·cal·ly** *adv.*
psychro–. Indicates cold; for example, **psychrometer.** [From Greek *psukhros*†, cold.]
psy·chrom·e·ter (sī-krŏm′ə-tər) *n.* A hygrometer that uses the difference in readings between two thermometers, one having a wet bulb ventilated to cause evaporation and the other having a dry bulb, as a measure of atmospheric moisture. [PSYCHRO- + -METER.]
psy·chro·phil·ic (sī′krō-fĭl′ĭk) *adj. Biology.* Thriving at relatively low temperatures, usually at or below 15°C. Said of certain bacteria. [PSYCHRO- + -PHIL(E).]
psyl·la (sĭl′ə) *n.* Also **psyl·lid** (-ĭd). Any of various plant lice of the family Chermidae (or Psyllidae), especially *Psylla pyricola,* a pest that infests pear trees. [Greek *psulla,* flea. See **plou-** in Appendix.*]
Pt The symbol for the element platinum.
pt. 1. part. **2.** payment. **3.** pint. **4.** point. **5.** port. **6.** preterit.
p.t. pro tempore.
P.T. 1. Pacific Time. **2.** physical therapy. **3.** physical training. **4.** postal telegraph.
pta. peseta.
PTA, P.T.A. Parent-Teachers Association.
ptar·mi·gan (tär′mĭ-gən) *n., pl.* **ptarmigan** or **-gans.** Any bird of the genus *Lagopus,* of the arctic and subarctic regions of the Northern Hemisphere, having feathered feet and plumage that is brownish in summer and white in winter. [Alteration (by pseudo-learned association with Greek *pteron,* wing) of Scottish Gaelic *tarmachan,* diminutive of *tarmach*†.]
PT boat. A fast, maneuverable, lightly armed vessel used to torpedo enemy shipping. In full "patrol torpedo boat."
–pter. Indicates wings or winglike parts; for example, **ornithopter.** [New Latin *-ptera,* from Greek *-pteros,* -PTEROUS.]
pter·i·dol·o·gy (tĕr′ĭ-dŏl′ə-jē) *n.* The study of ferns. [Greek *pteris* (stem *pterid-*), fern, from *pteron,* feather (see **pet-**[1] in Appendix*) + -LOGY.] —**pter′i·do·log′i·cal** (tĕr′ĭ-də-lŏj′ĭ-kəl, tə-rĭd′ə-) *adj.* —**pter′i·dol′o·gist** *n.*
pte·rid·o·phyte (tə-rĭd′ə-fīt′, tĕr′ĭ-dō-) *n. Botany.* Any plant of the division Pteridophyta, including the ferns, club mosses, and horsetails. [New Latin *Pteridophyta* : Greek *pteris,* fern (see **pteridology**) + -PHYTE.] —**pte·rid′o·phyt′ic** (-fĭt′ĭk), **pter′i·doph′y·tous** (tĕr′ĭ-dŏf′ə-təs) *adj.*
ptero–. Indicates feather, wing, or winglike part; for example, **pterodactyl.** [From Greek *pteron,* feather, wing. See **pet-**[1] in Appendix.*]
pter·o·dac·tyl (tĕr′ə-dăk′tĭl) *n.* Any of various extinct flying reptiles of the family Pterodactylidae. See **pterosaur.** [New Latin *Pterodactylus,* "wing-finger" : PTERO- + DACTYL.]
pter·o·pod (tĕr′ə-pŏd′) *n.* Any of various small marine gastropod mollusks of the order Pteropoda, that swim with winglike expanded lobes of the foot. Also called "sea butterfly." [New Latin *Pteropoda,* "wing-footed ones," from Greek *pteropous,* wing-footed : PTERO- + *-pous,* -POD.] —**pter′o·pod′** *adj.*
pter·o·saur (tĕr′ə-sôr′) *n.* Any of various extinct flying reptiles of the order Pterosauria, including the pterodactyls, of the Jurassic and Cretaceous periods, characterized by wings consisting of a flap of skin supported by the very long fourth digit on each front leg. [New Latin *Pterosauria,* "winged lizards" : PTERO- + *-sauria,* plural of -SAURUS.]
–pterous. Indicates (a certain number or kind of) wings; for example, **dipterous.** [Greek *-pteros,* -winged, from *pteron,* feather, wing. See **pet-**[1] in Appendix.*]
pter·y·gold (tĕr′ə-goid′) *adj.* Also **pter·y·goi·dal** (tĕr′ə-goid′l), **pter·y·goi·de·an** (tĕr′ə-goi′dē-ən). *Anatomy.* Of or denoting either of two processes in the skull that are attached like wings to the body of the sphenoid bone. —*n. Anatomy.* Either of these processes. [Greek *pterugoeidēs* : *pterux,* wing, from *pteron,* feather, wing (see **pet-**[1] in Appendix*) + -OID.]
ptg. printing.
ptis·an (tĭz′ən, tĭ-zăn′) *n.* A slightly medicinal infusion, such as barley water. [Middle English *tisan,* peeled barley, barley water, from Old French, from Medieval Latin *tisana,* variant of Latin *ptisana,* from Greek *ptisanē,* from *ptissein,* to peel, crush. See **peis-** in Appendix.*]
Ptol·e·ma·ic (tŏl′ə-mā′ĭk) *adj.* **1.** Of or pertaining to the astronomer Ptolemy. **2.** Of or pertaining to the Ptolemies or to Egypt during their rule (323–30 B.C.).
Ptolemaic system. The astronomical system of Ptolemy, having the earth at the center of the universe, with the moon, planets, and the stars revolving about it.
Ptol·e·ma·ist (tŏl′ə-mā′ĭst) *n.* An adherent of or believer in the astronomical system of Ptolemy.
Ptol·e·my[1] (tŏl′ə-mē). Greek astronomer, mathematician, and geographer of second century A.D.; resident in Alexandria.
Ptol·e·my[2] (tŏl′ə-mē) *pl.* **-mies.** Any king of the dynasty that ruled in Egypt from 323 to 30 B.C.
Ptol·e·my I (tŏl′ə-mē). 367?–283 B.C. Macedonian general under Alexander the Great; founder of the Ptolemaic dynasty; king of Egypt 305–285 B.C.
pto·maine (tō′mān′, tō-mān′) *n.* Also **pto·main.** Any of various basic nitrogenous materials, some poisonous, produced by the putrefaction and decomposition of protein. [French *ptomaine,* from Italian *ptomaina,* from Greek *ptōma,* "fall, fallen body," corpse, from *piptein,* to fall. See **pet-**[1] in Appendix.*]
ptomaine poisoning. Food poisoning caused by bacteria or bacterial toxins.
pto·sis (tō′sĭs) *n.* Abnormal and permanent lowering of an organ; especially, drooping of the upper eyelid caused by muscle failure. [New Latin, from Greek *ptōsis,* fall, from *piptein,* to fall. See **pet-**[1] in Appendix.*] —**pto′tic** *adj.*
pty. proprietary.
pty·a·lin (tī′ə-lən) *n.* A salivary enzyme in man and some lower animals that hydrolyzes starch into maltose and various dextrins. [Greek *ptualon,* saliva, from *ptuein,* to spit (see **spyeu-** in Appendix*) + -IN.]
pty·a·lism (tī′ə-lĭz′əm) *n.* Excessive flow of saliva. [From Greek *ptualon,* saliva. See **ptyalin.**]
Pu The symbol for the element plutonium.
pub (pŭb) *n.* A tavern; inn; bar. [Short for PUBLIC HOUSE.]
pub. 1. public. **2.** publication. **3.** published; publisher.
pub-crawl (pŭb′krôl′) *intr.v.* **-crawled, -crawling, -crawls.** *Slang.* To make the rounds of a series of bars. —**pub crawler.**
pu·ber·ty (pyōō′bər-tē) *n.* **1.** The stage of maturation in which the individual becomes physiologically capable of sexual reproduction. **2.** The approach to maturity: *"mankind will not reach puberty for another hundred thousand years"* (René Dubos). [Middle English *puberte,* from Latin *pūbertās,* from *pūber,* adult. See **pūbes** in Appendix.*]
pu·ber·u·lent (pyōō-bĕr′yə-lənt, -bĕr′ə-lənt) *adj.* Also **pu·ber·u·lous** (-bĕr′yə-ləs, -bĕr′ə-ləs). *Biology.* Covered with minute hairs or very fine down; finely pubescent. [From Latin *pūber,* grown up, adult, (of plants) downy. See **pūbes** in Appendix.*]
pu·bes (pyōō′bēz′) *n. Anatomy.* **1.** The pubic region. **2.** The pubic hair. [Latin *pūbēs.* See **pūbes** in Appendix.*]
pu·bes·cence (pyōō-bĕs′əns) *n.* **1. a.** A covering of soft down or short hairs, as on certain plants and insects. **b.** The state of being pubescent. **2.** The attainment or onset of puberty.
pu·bes·cent (pyōō-bĕs′ənt) *adj.* **1.** Covered with short hairs or soft down. **2.** Reaching or having reached puberty. [French, from Latin *pūbēscens,* present participle of *pūbēscere,* to reach puberty, from *pūber,* adult. See **pūbes** in Appendix.*]
pu·bic (pyōō′bĭk) *adj.* Of or in the region of the lower part of the abdomen, the pubis, or the pubes. [From PUBES.]
pu·bis (pyōō′bĭs) *n., pl.* **-bes** (-bēz′). The forward portion of either of the hipbones, at the juncture forming the front arch of the pelvis. [New Latin *(os) pubis,* bone of the groin, from Latin *pūbis,* genitive of *pūbēs,* PUBES.]
publ. 1. publication. **2.** published; publisher.
pub·lic (pŭb′lĭk) *adj. Abbr.* **pub. 1.** Of, concerning, or affecting the community or the people: *the public good.* **2.** Maintained for or used by the people or community: *a public park.* **3.** Participated in or attended by the people or community: *public worship.* **4.** Connected with or acting on behalf of the people, community, or government, rather than private matters or

ă pat/ā pay/âr care/ä father/b bib/ch church/d deed/ĕ pet/ē be/f fife/g gag/h hat/hw which/ĭ pit/ī pie/îr pier/j judge/k kick/l lid, needle/m mum/n no, sudden/ng thing/ŏ pot/ō toe/ô paw, for/oi noise/ou out/ŏŏ took/ōō boot/p pop/r roar/s sauce/sh ship, dish/

interests: *public office.* **5.** Open to the knowledge or judgment of all; notorious: *a public scandal.* —*n. Abbr.* **pub. 1.** The community or the people as a whole. See Usage note at **people. 2.** A group of people sharing a common interest: *the reading public.* **3.** Admirers or followers, especially of a celebrity. [Middle English *publique, publyk,* from Old French *public, publique,* from Latin *pūblicus,* alteration of *poplicus,* from *populus,* people. See **populus** in Appendix.*] —**pub'lic·ness** *n.*

pub·lic-ad·dress system (pŭb'lĭk-ə-drĕs'). *Abbr.* **PA** An electronic amplification apparatus installed and used for broadcasting in public areas. Also called "PA system."

pub·li·can (pŭb'lĭ-kən) *n.* **1.** *Chiefly British.* The keeper of a public house; tavernkeeper. **2.** A collector of public taxes or tolls in the ancient Roman Empire. **3.** Any collector of taxes or tribute from the public. [Middle English, from Old French *publicain,* from Latin *pūblicānus,* contractor for public revenues, from *pūblicum,* public revenue, from *pūblicus,* PUBLIC.]

pub·li·ca·tion (pŭb'lĭ-kā'shən) *n. Abbr.* **pub., publ. 1.** The act or process of publishing printed matter. **2.** An issue of any printed material offered for sale or distribution. **3.** The communication of information to the public. [Middle English *publicatioun,* from Old French, from Late Latin *pūblicātiō,* from *pūblicāre,* to make public, from Latin *pūblicus,* PUBLIC.]

public defender. An attorney or staff of attorneys, usually publicly appointed, having responsibility for the legal defense of those unable to afford or obtain legal assistance.

public domain. 1. Land owned and controlled by the state or federal government. **2.** The status of publications, products, and processes that are not protected under patent or copyright.

Public Health Service. *Abbr.* **PHS** A branch of the U.S. Department of Health, Education, and Welfare under the jurisdiction of the Surgeon General.

public house. *Chiefly British.* An inn, tavern, bar, or similar place licensed to sell alcoholic beverages.

pub·li·cist (pŭb'lə-sĭst) *n.* A person who publicizes something or someone; especially, a press or publicity agent.

pub·lic·i·ty (pŭ-blĭs'ə-tē) *n.* **1.** Information that concerns a person, group, event, or product and is disseminated through various communications media to attract public notice. **2.** Public interest, notice, or notoriety achieved by the spreading of such information. **3.** The act, process, or occupation of disseminating information to gain public interest. **4.** The condition of being public. [French *publicité,* from *public,* PUBLIC.]

pub·li·cize (pŭb'lə-sīz') *tr.v.* **-cized, -cizing, -cizes.** To give publicity to; bring to public attention; advertise.

public law. 1. The branch of law dealing with the state or government and with its relationships with individuals or other governments. Compare **private law. 2.** A law affecting the public.

public library. A noncommercial library for the use of the general public, often supported by public funds.

pub·lic·ly (pŭb'lĭk-lē) *adv.* **1.** In a public manner; not privately; openly. **2.** By or with consent of the public.

public prosecutor. A government official who prosecutes criminal actions on behalf of the state or community.

public relations. *Abbr.* **PR, P.R. 1.** The methods and activities employed by an individual, organization, corporation, or government to promote a favorable relationship with the public. **2.** The degree of success obtained in achieving such a relationship. **3.** The staff employed to promote such a relationship. **4.** The art or science of establishing such a relationship: *a course in public relations.*

public school. 1. *Abbr.* **P.S.** In the United States, an elementary or secondary school supported by public funds and providing free education for children of the community or district. **2.** In Great Britain, a private boarding school for pupils of from thirteen to eighteen years of age for entry into a university or the public services.

public servant. A person who holds a government position by election or by appointment.

public service. 1. Employment within a governmental system, especially within the civil services. **2.** A service performed for the benefit of the public.

public-service corporation. A corporation providing utilities for the public.

public speaking. The art or process of making speeches before an audience. —**public speaker.**

pub·lic-spir·i·ted (pŭb'lĭk-spĭr'ĭ-tĭd) *adj.* Motivated by or showing active devotion to the good of the community; concerned for the public welfare. —**pub'lic-spir'it·ed·ness** *n.*

public utility. 1. A private business organization that is subject to governmental regulation because it provides an essential service or commodity, such as water, electricity, transportation, or communication, to the consuming public. **2.** *Usually plural. Finance.* Stock shares issued by such a company.

public works. Construction projects, such as highways or dams, financed by public funds and constructed by a government for the benefit or use of the general public.

pub·lish (pŭb'lĭsh) *v.* **-lished, -lishing, -lishes.** —*tr.* **1.** To prepare and issue (printed material) for public distribution or sale. **2.** To bring to the public attention; announce. —*intr.* **1.** To issue a publication. **2.** To be the author of a published work or works. [Middle English *publishen,* from Old French *publier* (stem *publiss-*), from Latin *pūblicāre,* to make public, from *pūblicus,* PUBLIC.] —**pub'lish·a·ble** *adj.*

pub·lish·er (pŭb'lĭsh-ər) *n. Abbr.* **pub., publ.** A person or company engaged in publishing printed material.

Puc·ci·ni (po͞ot-chē'nē), **Giacomo.** 1858–1924. Italian composer of operas.

puc·coon (pə-ko͞on') *n.* **1.** Any of several North American plants of the genus *Lithospermum,* yielding a red or yellow dye; especially, *L. canescens,* having orange flowers. Sometimes called "alkanet." **2.** Any of several other plants yielding a reddish dye, as the bloodroot. **3.** The dye from any of these plants. [Earlier *pocoon,* from Algonquian (Virginia).]

puce (pyo͞os) *n.* Deep red to dark grayish purple. See **color.** [French *(couleur) puce,* "flea (color)," from Latin *pūlex,* flea. See **plou-** in Appendix.*] —**puce** *adj.*

puck (pŭk) *n.* A hard rubber disk used in ice hockey as the playing and scoring medium instead of a ball. [From British dialectal *puck,* to strike, poke, variant of POKE.]

Puck (pŭk) *n. English Folklore.* A mischievous sprite. Also called "Robin Goodfellow." [Middle English *p(o)uke,* Old English *pūca*†.]

puck·a. Variant of **pukka.**

puck·er (pŭk'ər) *v.* **-ered, -ering, -ers.** —*tr.* To gather into small wrinkles or folds. —*intr.* To become contracted and wrinkled. —*n.* **1.** A wrinkle or wrinkled part, as in tightly stitched cloth. [Originally "to form a pocket," perhaps from POCKET.]

puck·ish (pŭk'ĭsh) *adj.* Mischievous; impish: *a puckish grin.* —**puck'ish·ly** *adv.*

pud·ding (po͝od'ĭng) *n.* **1. a.** A sweet dessert, usually containing flour or a cereal product, that has been boiled, steamed, or baked. **b.** Any mixture with a soft, puddinglike consistency. **2.** A sausagelike preparation made with minced meat or various other ingredients stuffed into a bag or skin and boiled. [Middle English, from Old French *boudin,* from Vulgar Latin *botellīnus* (unattested), diminutive of Latin *botulus,* sausage. See **gēu-** in Appendix.*]

pudding stone. A rock, a **conglomerate** *(see).*

pud·dle (pŭd'l) *n.* **1.** A small pool of usually dirty, stagnant water. **2.** A small pool of any liquid. **3.** A tempered paste of wet clay and sand used as waterproofing. —*v.* **puddled, -dling, -dles.** —*tr.* **1.** To make muddy. **2.** To work (clay or sand) into a thick, watertight paste. **3.** *Metallurgy.* To process (impure metal) by puddling. —*intr.* To splash or dabble in or as if in a puddle. [Middle English *podel, pothel,* diminutive of Old English *pudd*†, ditch. See also **poodle.**] —**pud'dly** *adj.*

pud·dler (pŭd'lər) *n.* One who puddles iron or clay.

pud·dling (pŭd'lĭng) *n.* **1.** *Metallurgy.* The purification of impure metal, especially pig iron, by agitation of a molten bath of the metal in an oxidizing atmosphere. **2.** Compaction of wet clay or a similar material to make a watertight paste.

pu·den·cy (pyo͞od'ən-sē) *n.* Modesty; shame; prudishness. [Late Latin *pudēntia,* shame, from Latin *pudēns,* present participle of *pudēre,* to feel shame. See **speud-** in Appendix.*]

pu·den·dum (pyo͞o-dĕn'dəm) *n., pl.* **-da** (-də). **1.** A woman's external genital organs; the vulva. **2.** *Plural.* The external genital organs of either sex. [New Latin, from Late Latin *pudenda,* from Latin *pudendus,* gerundive of *pudēre,* to be ashamed. See **pudency.**] —**pu·den'dal** *adj.*

pudg·y (pŭj'ē) *adj.* **-ier, -iest.** Short and fat; chubby: *pudgy fingers.* See Synonyms at **fat.** [Earlier *pudsy,* probably augmented from Scottish *pud,* belly, (hence) plump, healthy child, from Scottish Gaelic *poit,* ultimately from Vulgar Latin *pottus* (attested only in Late Latin). See **pott-** in Appendix.*]

Pue·bla (pwĕb'lä). **1.** A state in south-central Mexico, 13,124 square miles in area. Population, 2,095,000. **2.** In full, Puebla de Zaragoza. The capital of this state, one of the oldest cities in Mexico, founded about 1532. Population, 328,000.

pueb·lo (pwĕb'lō) *n., pl.* **-los. 1.** A community dwelling, up to five stories high, built of stone or adobe by Indian tribes of the southwestern United States. **2.** *Capital* **P.** A member of a tribe, such as the Hopi or Zuñi, inhabiting such dwellings. **3.** An Indian village of the southwestern United States. [Spanish, "people," "population," from Latin *populus,* people. See **populus** in Appendix.*]

Pueb·lo (pwĕb'lō). An industrial city and trade center in south-central Colorado. Population, 91,000.

pu·er·ile (pyo͞o'ər-ĭl, pyo͞or'ĭl, -īl', pwĕr'ĭl, -īl') *adj.* **1.** Belonging to childhood; juvenile. **2.** Immature; childish. [French *puéril,* from Latin *puerīlis,* from *puer,* child, boy. See **pōu-** in Appendix.*] —**pu'er·ile·ly** *adv.* —**pu'er·ile·ness** *n.*

pu·er·il·i·ty (pyo͞o'ə-rĭl'ə-tē, pyo͞o-rĭl'-, pwĕ-) *n., pl.* **-ties. 1.** The condition of being puerile; childishness. **2.** A childish action, idea, or utterance.

pu·er·per·al (pyo͞o-ûr'pər-əl) *adj. Medicine.* Connected with, resulting from, or following childbirth. [Latin *puerperus,* bearing young : *puer,* child (see **pōu-** in Appendix*) + -PAROUS.]

puerperal fever. Infection of the endometrium and of the bloodstream following childbirth. Also called "childbed fever."

pu·er·pe·ri·um (pyo͞o'ər-pîr'ē-əm) *n.* **1.** The state of a woman while bearing a child or immediately thereafter. **2.** The approximate six-week period from childbirth to return of normal uterine size. [Latin, childbirth, from *puerperus,* PUERPERAL.]

Puer·to Ri·co (pwĕr'tō rē'kō, pôr'-). *Abbr.* **P.R.** Formerly **Por·to Ri·co** (pôr'tə rē'kō). An island, about 3,435 square miles in area, in the eastern Greater Antilles. A U.S. territory since 1898, it became a self-governing Commonwealth in 1952. Population, 2,584,000. Capital, San Juan. —**Puerto Rican.**

puff (pŭf) *n.* **1. a.** A short, forceful exhalation of breath. **b.** A short, sudden gust of wind. **c.** A brief, sudden emission of air, vapor, or smoke. **d.** A short, sibilant sound produced by a puff. **2.** An amount of vapor, smoke, or similar material released in a puff. **3.** An act of drawing in and expelling the breath, as in smoking tobacco. **4.** A swelling or rounded protuberance. **5.** A light, inflated pastry, often filled with custard or cream. **6.** A light, soft pad for applying cosmetic powder. **7.** A soft roll of

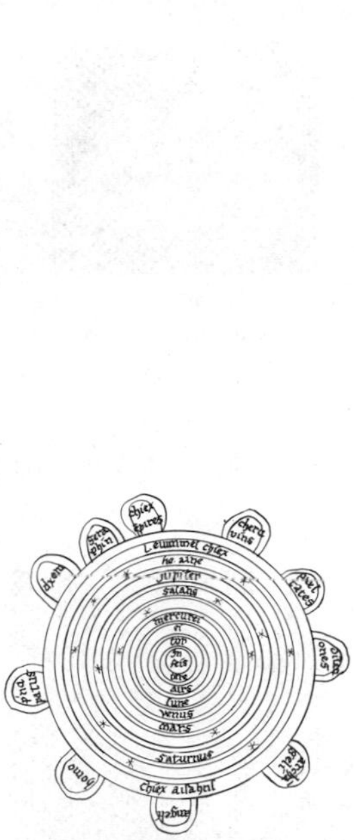

Ptolemaic system

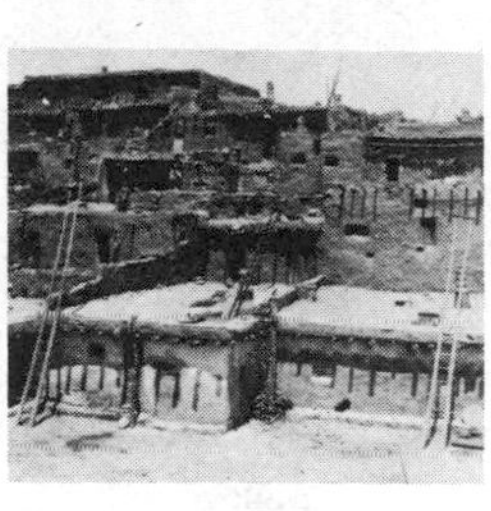

pueblo
Zuñi pueblo
in New Mexico

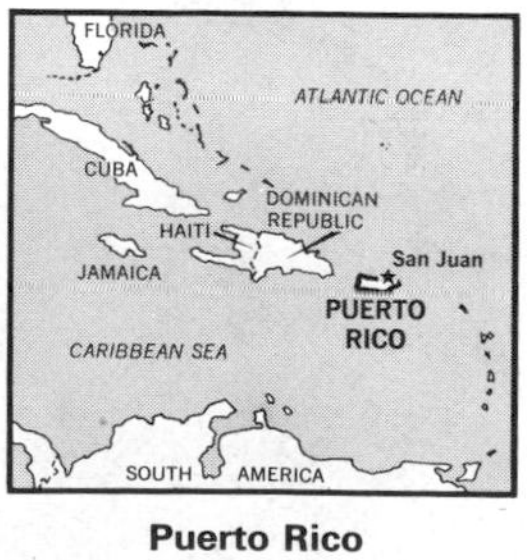

Puerto Rico

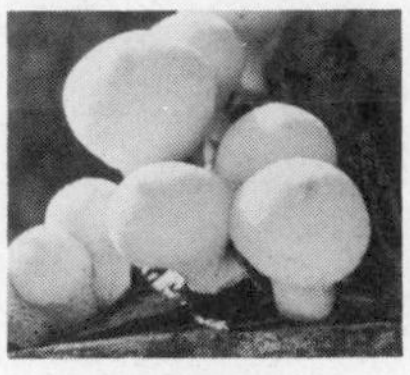

puffball
Genus *Lycoperdon*

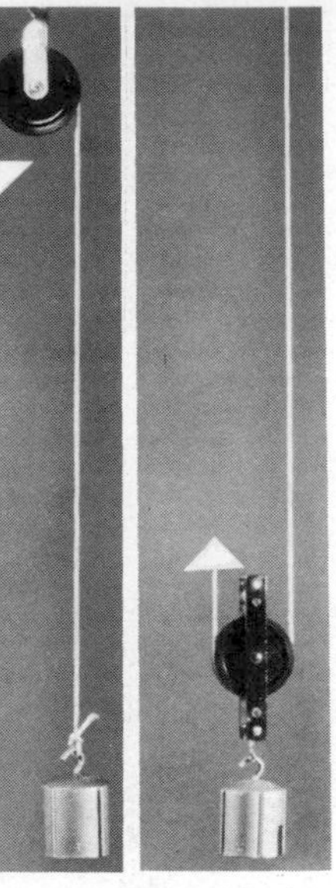

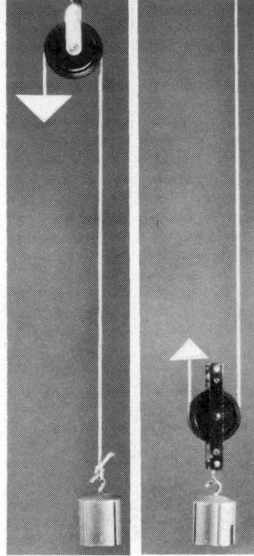

pulley
Left: Fixed pulley
Right: Movable pulley

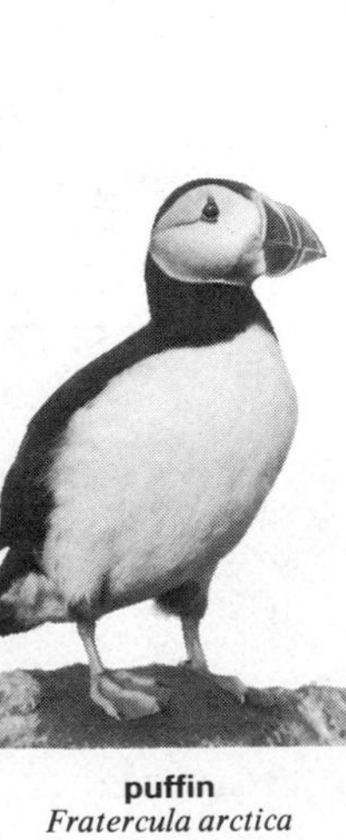

puffin
Fratercula arctica

hair forming part of a coiffure. **8.** A gathered and protruding portion of fabric. **9.** A light, padded bed covering. **10.** An approving or flattering recommendation. —*v.* **puffed, puffing, puffs.** —*intr.* **1.** To blow in puffs. **2.** To come forth in a puff or puffs. **3.** To breathe forcefully and rapidly. **4.** To emit puffs of smoke, vapor, or the like. **5.** To take puffs on a cigarette, pipe, or cigar. **6.** To swell or seem to swell, as with air or pride. Often used with *up* or *out.* —*tr.* **1.** To emit or give forth in a puff or puffs. **2.** To impel with puffs. **3.** To smoke (a cigar, for example). **4.** To inflate or distend. **5.** To fill with pride or conceit. **6.** To publicize with exaggerated praise. [Middle English *puffen,* Old English *pyffan.* See **beu-**[1] in Appendix.*] —**puff′i·ly** *adv.* —**puff′i·ness** *n.* —**puff′y** *adj.*

puff adder. 1. A venomous African viper, *Bitis arietans,* having crescent-shaped yellowish markings. **2.** The **hognose snake** *(see).* [Because it inflates its body when aroused.]

puff·ball (pŭf′bôl′) *n.* **1.** Any of various fungi of the genus *Lycoperdon* and related genera, having a ball-shaped fruiting body that, when broken open, releases the enclosed spores in puffs of dust. **2.** *Informal.* The rounded head of a dandelion that has gone to seed.

puff·er (pŭf′ər) *n.* **1.** One that puffs. **2.** Any of various marine fishes of the family Tetraodontidae, that are capable of swelling up. Also called "blowfish," "swellfish."

puf·fin (pŭf′ĭn) *n.* Any of several sea birds of the genera *Fratercula* and *Lunda,* of northern regions, characteristically having black and white plumage and a vertically flattened, brightly colored bill. [Middle English *poffo(u)n, pophyn*†.]

puff pastry. Dough that is rolled and folded in layers, and that expands in baking to form light, flaky pastry.

pug[1] (pŭg) *n.* **1.** A small dog of a breed originating in China, having a snub nose, wrinkled face, square body, short smooth hair, and a curled tail. **2.** A **pug nose** *(see).* [Origin obscure.]

pug[2] (pŭg) *n.* **1.** Clay ground and kneaded with water into a plastic consistency for forming bricks or pottery. **2.** A machine for grinding and mixing clay. —*tr.v.* **pugged, pugging, pugs. 1.** To work or knead (clay) with water. **2.** To fill in with clay or mortar. **3.** To cover or pack with clay, mortar, sawdust, or felt to soundproof. [Origin unknown.]

pug[3] (pŭg) *n.* A footprint, track, or trail, especially of an animal. [Hindi *pag,* probably from Sanskrit *padakaḥ,* foot, from *pada.* See **ped-**[1] in Appendix.*]

pug[4] (pŭg) *n. Slang.* A boxer. [Shortened from PUGILIST.]

Pu·get Sound (pyōō′jĭt). An inlet of the Pacific Ocean in northwestern Washington, extending about 100 miles south from Admiralty Inlet and Juan de Fuca Strait to Olympia.

pug·gree, pug·ree (pŭg′rē) *n.* Also **pug·ga·ree** (pŭg′ə-rē), **pug·a·ree.** A cloth band or scarf wrapped around the crown of a hat or sun helmet. [Hindi *pagṛī,* from Sanskrit *parikara,* akin to Arabic *pairikara,* turban.]

pu·gi·lism (pyōō′jə-lĭz′əm) *n.* The skill or practice of fighting with the fists; boxing. [From Latin *pugil,* fighter, from *pugnus,* fist. See **peuk-** in Appendix.*]

pu·gi·list (pyōō′jə-lĭst) *n.* One who fights with his fists; especially, a professional boxer. —**pu′gi·lis′tic** *adj.*

Pu·gli·a. The Italian name for **Apulia.**

pug·na·cious (pŭg-nā′shəs) *adj.* Eager to fight; having a quarrelsome disposition. See Synonyms at **belligerent.** [From Latin *pugnāx* (stem *pugnāc-*), fond of fighting, from *pugnāre,* to fight, from *pugnus,* fist. See **peuk-** in Appendix.*] —**pug·na′cious·ly** *adv.* —**pug·na′cious·ness** *n.* —**pug·nac′i·ty** (pŭg-năs′ə-tē) *n.*

pug nose. A short nose that is somewhat flattened and turned up at the end. [Probably from PUG (dog).] —**pug′-nosed′** *adj.*

puis·ne (pyōō′nē) *adj. Law.* Lower in rank; junior. —*n. Law.* One of lesser rank; especially, an associate judge. [Norman French *puisné,* from Old French, "born afterward." See **puny.**]

puis·sance (pwĭs′əns, pyōō′ə-səns, pyōō-ĭs′əns) *n.* Power; potency; might. See Synonyms at **strength.**

puis·sant (pwĭs′ənt, pyōō′ə-sənt, pyōō-ĭs′ənt) *adj.* Mighty; powerful; potent. [Middle English *puissaunt,* from Old French, from Gallo-Roman *possiantem* (unattested), from Latin *posse,* to be powerful. See **poti-** in Appendix.*] —**puis′sant·ly** *adv.*

puke (pyōōk) *v.* **puked, puking, pukes.** —*intr.* To vomit. —*tr.* To vomit (something) up. —*n.* **1.** Vomit. **2.** The act of vomiting. [Probably imitative.]

puk·ka (pŭk′ə) *adj.* Also **puck·a.** *Anglo-Indian.* **1.** Genuine; authentic. **2.** Superior; first-class. [Hindi *pakkā,* cooked, ripe, firm, from Sanskrit *pakva.* See **pekw-** in Appendix.*]

pul (pōōl) *n., pl.* **puls** or **pu·li** (pōō′lē). A coin of Afghanistan, equal to $\frac{1}{100}$ of the afghani. See table of exchange rates at **currency.** [Persian, from Turkish, possibly from Late Greek *phollis,* bellows, money bag, from Latin *follis.* See **bhel-**[2] in Appendix.*]

Pu·la (pōō′lä). *Italian* **Po·la** (pō′lä). A city in northwestern Yugoslavia on the tip of Istria. Population, 40,000.

Pu·las·ki (pōō-lăs′kē), **Casimir.** Original name, Kazimierz Pulaski. 1748?–1779. Polish general; commanded American troops in the Revolutionary War.

pul·chri·tude (pŭl′krĭ-tōōd′, -tyōōd′) *n.* Physical beauty and appeal. [Middle English *pulcritude,* from Latin *pulchritūdō,* from *pulcher*†, beautiful.]

pul·chri·tu·di·nous (pŭl′krĭ-tōōd′n-əs, -tyōōd′n-əs) *adj.* Having great physical beauty.

pule (pyōōl) *intr.v.* **puled, puling, pules.** To whine; whimper; fret. [Earlier *pewle, peule,* probably from French *piauler* (imitative).] —**pul′er** *n.*

pu·li[1] (pōōl′ē, pyōō′lē) *n., pl.* **-lis** or **pulik** (pōōl′ĕk, pyōō′lĕk). A long-haired sheep dog of a Hungarian breed. [Hungarian.]

pu·li[2]. Alternate plural of **pul.**

Pul·it·zer (pōōl′ĭt-sər, pyōō′lĭt-), **Joseph.** 1847–1911. Hungarian-born American journalist and newspaper publisher.

Pulitzer Prize. Any of several awards established by Joseph Pulitzer and conferred annually for accomplishment in various fields of American journalism, literature, and music.

pull (pōōl) *v.* **pulled, pulling, pulls.** —*tr.* **1.** To apply force to so as to cause or tend to cause motion toward the source of the force. **2.** To remove from a fixed position; extract: *pull teeth.* **3.** To tug at; jerk or tweak. **4.** To rip or tear; rend. **5.** To stretch (taffy, for example) repeatedly. **6.** To strain (a muscle, for example) injuriously. **7.** *Informal.* To attract; draw: *a performer who pulls large crowds.* **8.** *Informal.* To perform; bring about. Often used with *off.* **9.** *Slang.* To draw out (a knife or gun) in readiness for use. **10.** *Informal.* To use less than full force in delivering (a punch); soften. **11.** *Baseball.* To hit (a ball) in the direction one is facing when the swing is carried through. **12. a.** To operate (an oar) in rowing. **b.** To transport or propel by rowing. **c.** To be rowed by: *That boat pulls six oars.* **13.** To rein in (a horse) to keep it from winning a race. **14.** *Printing.* To produce (a print or impression) from type. —*intr.* **1.** To exert force in pulling something. **2.** To move: *The bus pulled away from the curb.* **3.** To drink or inhale deeply. **4.** To row a boat. —**pull for.** To work, hope, or cheer for the success of. —**pull (oneself) together.** To regain one's composure. —**pull through.** To come or bring successfully through trouble or illness. —**pull together.** To make a joint effort; cooperate. —*n.* **1.** The action or process of pulling. **2.** Force exerted in pulling, or required to overcome resistance in pulling. **3.** Any sustained effort: *a long pull across the mountains.* **4.** Something used for pulling, such as a knob on a drawer. **5.** A deep inhalation or draft, as on a cigar. **6.** *Slang.* A means of gaining special advantage; influence: *He has pull with the boss.* **7.** *Informal.* Ability to draw or attract; appeal: *a star with pull at the box office.* [Middle English *pullen,* to pull, pluck, Old English *pullian*†.] —**pull′er** *n.*

pull·back (pōōl′băk′) *n.* **1.** The act or process of pulling something back; especially, an orderly troop withdrawal. **2.** Any device for holding or drawing something back.

pul·let (pōōl′ĭt) *n.* A young hen, especially of the common domestic fowl, usually less than one year old. [Middle English *polet, pulet,* from Old French *poulet, pollet,* diminutive of *poul,* cock, *poule,* hen, from Latin *pullus,* young of an animal, chicken. See **pōu-** in Appendix.*]

pul·ley (pōōl′ē) *n., pl.* **-leys. 1.** A simple machine used to change the direction and point of application of a pulling force, especially for lifting weight, consisting essentially of a wheel with a grooved rim in which a pulled rope or chain is run. **2.** A wheel turned by or driving a belt. [Middle English *po(u)ley,* from Old French *po(u)lie,* from Vulgar Latin *polidium* (unattested), probably from Late Greek *polidion* (unattested), diminutive of Greek *polos,* pole, pivot. See **kwel-**[1] in Appendix.*]

Pull·man (pōōl′mən) *n.* A railroad parlor car or sleeping car. Also called "Pullman car." [Designed by George M. *Pullman* (1831–1897), American industrialist.]

pul·lo·rum disease (pə-lôr′əm, -lōr′əm). A severe contagious diarrhea of young poultry, caused by the bacterium *Salmonella pullorum.* [Latin *pullorum,* genitive plural of *pullus,* PULLET.]

pull out. To withdraw from a situation or commitment.

pull·out (pōōl′out′) *n.* **1.** A withdrawal, especially of troops. **2.** *Aviation.* The change from a dive into level flight. **3.** Something designed to be pulled out. —**pull′out′** *adj.*

pull over. To bring a vehicle to a stop at the curb or at the side of a road.

pull·o·ver (pōōl′ō′vər) *n.* A garment, such as a sweater, that must be put on by being drawn over the head. —**pull′o′ver** *adj.*

pul·lu·late (pŭl′yə-lāt′) *intr.v.* **-lated, -lating, -lates. 1.** To put forth sprouts; germinate. **2.** To breed rapidly or abundantly. **3.** To teem; swarm. [Latin *pullulāre,* to grow, sprout, from *pullulus,* "chicken," sprout, diminutive of *pullus,* PULLET.] —**pul′lu·la′tion** *n.* —**pul′lu·la′tive** *adj.*

pull up. 1. To bring or come to a halt. **2.** To move to a place or position ahead.

pull-up (pōōl′ŭp′) *n.* **1.** An exercise for strengthening the arms, performed by hanging by the hands from an overhead bar and pulling the body upward until the chin is even with or above the bar. **2.** *Aviation.* A short, quick climb from level flight.

pul·mo·nar·y (pōōl′mə-nĕr′ē, pŭl′-) *adj.* **1.** Of or pertaining to the lungs. **2.** Having lungs or lunglike organs. [Latin *pulmōnārius,* from *pulmō,* lung. See **pleu-** in Appendix.*]

pulmonary artery. An artery in which blood travels directly from the heart to the lungs.

pulmonary vein. One of four veins in which blood travels directly from the lungs to the heart.

pul·mo·nate (pōōl′mə-nāt′, pŭl′-) *adj.* **1.** Having lungs or lunglike organs. **2.** Relating to the Pulmonata, an order of gastropods including snails and slugs, in which the mantle cavity is modified to function as a lung. —*n.* A member of the Pulmonata. [Latin *pulmōnātus,* from *pulmō,* lung. See **pulmonary.**]

pul·mon·ic (pōōl-mŏn′ĭk, pŭl-) *adj.* Of or pertaining to the lungs; pulmonary.

pulp (pŭlp) *n.* **1.** A soft, moist, shapeless mass of matter. **2.** The soft, moist part of fruit. **3.** A mass of pressed vegetable matter; *apple pulp.* **4.** The soft pith forming the contents of the stem of a plant. **5.** A mixture of cellulose material, such as wood, paper, and rags, ground up and moistened to make paper. **6.** The soft inner structure of a tooth, consisting of nerve and blood vessels. **7.** *Mining.* A mixture of powdered ore and water. **8.** A magazine or book containing lurid subject matter and being characteristically printed on rough, unfinished paper.

Compare **slick.** —*v.* **pulped, pulping, pulps.** —*tr.* **1.** To reduce to pulp. **2.** To remove the pulp from. —*intr.* To become reduced to a pulpy consistency. [Latin *pulpa*†, solid flesh, pulp.] —**pulp'ous** (pŭl'pəs), **pulp'y** *adj.*

pul·pit (po͝ol'pĭt, pŭl'-) *n.* **1.** An elevated platform, lectern, or stand used in preaching or conducting a religious service. **2.** Any similar raised platform, such as one used by harpooners in a whaling boat. **3. a.** Clergymen collectively. Preceded by *the.* **b.** The ministry of preaching. [Middle English, from Latin *pulpitum*†, scaffold, platform.]

pulp·wood (pŭlp'wo͝od') *n.* Soft wood, such as spruce, aspen, or pine, used in making paper.

pul·que (po͞ol'kā', -kē', po͞ol'-) *n.* A fermented, milky beverage made in Mexico from various species of agave. [Mexican Spanish, obscurely from Nahuatl *poliuhqui, puliuhqui,* decomposed, spoiled.]

pul·sar (pŭl'sär') *n. Astronomy.* Any of several very short-period variable Galactic radio sources.

pul·sate (pŭl'sāt') *intr.v.* **-sated, -sating, -sates. 1.** To expand and contract rhythmically; throb. **2.** To quiver. [Latin *pulsāre,* frequentative of *pellere* (past participle *pulsus*), to push, beat, strike. See **pel-⁶** in Appendix.*] —**pul'sa'tive** *adj.*

Synonyms: pulsate, beat, palpitate, throb. These verbs refer to recurrent, rhythmical movement such as that involved in the action of the heart. *Pulsate,* which is largely technical in application, and *beat* imply regular and vigorous movement. *Beat* often also suggests rhythmical sound. *Palpitate* applies to excessively rapid movement, or pulsation; usually it also implies irregular movement, such as fluttering. *Throb* emphasizes both rapidity and strength of pulsation; the term is especially associated with physical or emotional stress.

pul·sa·tile (pŭl'sə-tĭl) *adj.* Pulsating; vibrating. [Medieval Latin *pulsātilis* from Latin *pulsāre,* PULSATE.]

pul·sa·tion (pŭl-sā'shən) *n.* **1.** The act of pulsating. **2.** A single beat, throb, or vibration.

pul·sa·tor (pŭl-sā'tər) *n.* A pulsating device or machine.

pul·sa·to·ry (pŭl'sə-tôr'ē, -tōr'ē) *adj.* Having rhythmical vibration or movement; pulsating.

pulse¹ (pŭls) *n.* **1.** *Physiology.* The rhythmical throbbing of arteries produced by the regular contractions of the heart. **2.** Any regular or rhythmical beating. **3.** Any single throb or beat. **4.** *Physics & Electronics.* A transient amplification or intensification of a characteristic of a system, especially of a wave characteristic, followed by return to equilibrium or steady state: *a signal pulse; beam pulse.* **5.** The perceptible emotions or sentiments of a group of people: *the pulse of the electorate.* —*intr.v.* **pulsed, pulsing, pulses.** To pulsate. [Middle English *pous, puls,* from Old French *pous, pols,* from Latin *pulsus,* beating, striking, from the past participle of *pellere,* to push, beat, strike. See **pel-⁶** in Appendix.*] —**pulse'less** *adj.*

pulse² (pŭls) *n.* **1.** The edible seeds of certain pod-bearing plants, such as peas and beans. **2.** A plant yielding such seeds. [Middle English *pols, puls,* from Old French *po(u)ls,* porridge, from Latin *puls,* pottage made of meal and pulse, possibly from Greek *poltos,* porridge. See **pel-¹** in Appendix.*]

pulse·jet (pŭls'jĕt') *n.* A jet engine in which air intake and combustion occur intermittently, producing rapid periodic bursts of thrusts.

pulse modulation. *Electronics.* Modulation by coded variation of the amplitude or other characteristic of wave pulses.

pul·sim·e·ter (pŭl-sĭm'ə-tər) *n.* Also **pul·som·e·ter** (-sŏm'ə-tər). *Medicine.* An instrument that measures the frequency or strength of the pulse. [From PULSE + -METER.]

pul·som·e·ter (pŭl-sŏm'ə-tər) *n.* **1.** A pump for raising water by the pulsed condensation of steam. Also called "vacuum pump." **2.** Variant of **pulsimeter.** [From PULSE + -METER.]

pul·ver·a·ble (pŭl'vər-ə-bəl) *adj.* Capable of being pulverized.

pul·ver·ize (pŭl'və-rīz') *v.* **-ized, -izing, -izes.** —*tr.* **1.** To pound, crush, or grind to a powder or dust. **2.** To demolish. —*intr.* To be ground or reduced to powder or dust. [Old French *pulveriser,* from Late Latin *pulverizāre,* from Latin *pulvis* (stem *pulver-*), dust. See **pel-¹** in Appendix.*] —**pul'ver·iz'a·ble** *adj.* —**pul'ver·i·za'tion** *n.* —**pul'ver·iz'er** *n.*

pul·ver·u·lent (pŭl-vĕr'yə-lənt) *adj.* **1.** Made of, covered with, or crumbling to fine powder or dust. **2.** Powdery; dusty; crumbly. [From Latin *pulverulentus,* dusty, from *pulvis,* dust. See **pulverize.**]

pul·vil·lus (pŭl-vĭl'əs) *n., pl.* **-villi** (-vĭl'ī'). One of the soft, cushionlike pads between the claws of an insect's foot. [Latin, diminutive of *pulvīnus,* cushion. See **pulvinus.**]

pul·vi·nate (pŭl'və-nāt') *adj.* Also **pul·vi·nat·ed. 1.** Cushion-shaped. **2.** *Botany.* Having a swelling at the base. Said of a leafstalk. [Latin *pulvīnātus,* from *pulvīnus,* PULVINUS.]

pul·vi·nus (pŭl-vī'nəs) *n., pl.* **-ni** (nī'). *Botany.* A swelling of the stem at the base of a leafstalk. [Latin *pulvīnus*†, cushion.]

pu·ma (pyo͞o'mə) *n.* The **mountain lion** *(see).* [Spanish, from Quechua.]

pum·ice (pŭm'ĭs) *n.* A porous, lightweight volcanic rock used in solid form as an abrasive and in powdered form as a polish and abrasive. Also called "pumice stone." —*tr.v.* **pumiced, -icing, -ices.** To clean, polish, or smooth with pumice. [Middle English *pomys,* from Old French *pomis,* from Latin *pūmex.* See **spoimo-** in Appendix.*] —**pu·mi'ceous** (pyo͞o-mĭsh'əs) *adj.* —**pum'ic·er** *n.*

pum·mel (pŭm'əl) *tr.v.* **-meled, -meling, -mels.** Also *chiefly British* **-melled, -melling.** To pommel. —*n.* A pommel.

pump¹ (pŭmp) *n.* A machine or device for transferring a liquid or gas from a source or container through tubes or pipes to another container or receiver. —*v.* **pumped, pumping, pumps.** —*tr.* **1.** To raise or cause to flow by means of a pump. **2.** To inflate with gas by means of a pump. Often used with *up.* **3.** To remove the water from. Often used with *out.* **4.** To cause to operate with the up-and-down motion of a pump handle. **5.** To propel, eject, or insert with or as with a pump. **6.** *Physics.* To supply (a laser) with sufficient energy to achieve population inversion. **7.** To question closely or persistently: *pump a witness.* —*intr.* **1.** To operate a pump. **2.** To raise or move gas or liquid with a pump. **3.** To move up and down in the manner of a pump handle. [Middle English *pumpe, pompe,* from Middle Low German *pumpe* or Middle Dutch *pompe,* probably from Spanish *bomba* (imitative).] —**pump'er** *n.*

pump² (pŭmp) *n.* A low-cut shoe without fastenings. [Origin unknown.]

pum·per·nick·el (pŭm'pər-nĭk'əl) *n.* A dark, sourish bread made from whole, coarsely ground rye. [German *Pumpernickel* : early New High German *Pumpern,* a fart (imitative) + *Nickel,* "devil," general pejorative (see **nickel**); so named from being hard to digest.]

pump·kin (pŭmp'kĭn, pŭm'-, pŭng'-) *n.* **1.** A coarse, trailing vine, *Cucurbita pepo,* widely cultivated for its fruit. **2.** The large, pulpy round fruit of this vine, having a thick, orange-yellow rind and numerous seeds. **3.** Either of two similar vines, *C. maxima* or *C. moschata,* bearing large, pumpkinlike squashes. **4.** Moderate to strong orange. See **color.** [Variant (influenced by -KIN) of earlier *pumpion, pompon,* from Old French *popon, pompon,* from Latin *pepō,* from Greek *pepōn,* a large melon (edible only when ripe), from *pepōn,* ripe, from *peptein,* to cook, ripen. See **pekw-** in Appendix.*]

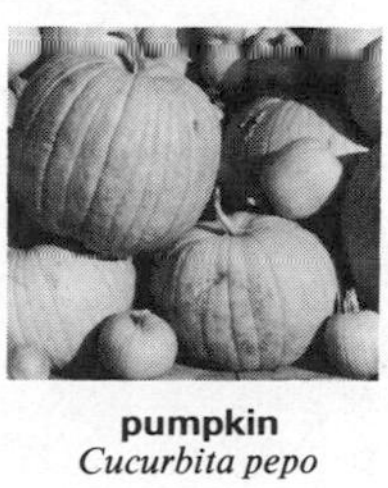

pumpkin
Cucurbita pepo

pump·kin·seed (pŭmp'kĭn-sēd', pŭm'-, pŭng'-) *n.* **1.** The seed of the pumpkin. **2.** A North American sunfish, *Lepomis gibbosus,* having brightly colored markings.

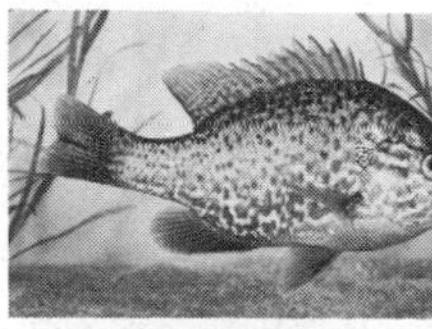

pumpkinseed

pun (pŭn) *n.* A play on words, sometimes on different senses of the same word and sometimes on the similar sense or sound of different words. Also called "paronomasia." —*intr.v.* **punned, punning, puns.** To make a pun. [Probably short for obsolete *pundigrion,* perhaps variant of Italian *puntiglio,* fine point, quibble, diminutive of *punto,* point, from Latin *punctum,* pricked hole, point, from *pungere,* to prick, pierce. See **peuk-** in Appendix.*] —**pun'ning·ly** *adv.*

Pu·na·kha (po͞o'nə-kə). Also **Pu·na·ka.** A former capital of Bhutan, 105 miles northeast of Darjeeling, Republic of India.

punch¹ (pŭnch) *n.* **1.** A tool for circular or other shaped piercing: *a leather punch.* **2.** A tool for forcing a pin, bolt, or rivet in or out of a hole. **3.** A tool for stamping a design on a surface. **4.** A **countersink** *(see).* —*v.* **punched, punching, punches.** —*tr.* To use a punch on; perforate; mark. —*intr.* To use a punch. [Short for PUNCHEON (punching tool).]

punch² (pŭnch) *tr.v.* **punched, punching, punches. 1.** To hit with a sharp blow of the fist. **2.** To poke or prod with a stick. **3.** *Western U.S.* To herd (cattle). —*n.* **1.** A blow with the fist. **2.** Vigor or drive. [Middle English *punchen,* probably variant of *pounsen,* POUNCE (to perforate).]

punch³ (pŭnch) *n.* A sweetened beverage of fruit juices, often spiced, usually with a wine or liquor base. [Perhaps from Hindi *pānch,* from Sanskrit *pañca,* five (originally prepared with five ingredients). See **penkwe** in Appendix.*]

Punch (pŭnch). The quarrelsome hook-nosed husband of Judy in the comic puppet show, *Punch and Judy.* —**pleased as Punch.** Highly pleased; gratified. [Short for PUNCHINELLO.]

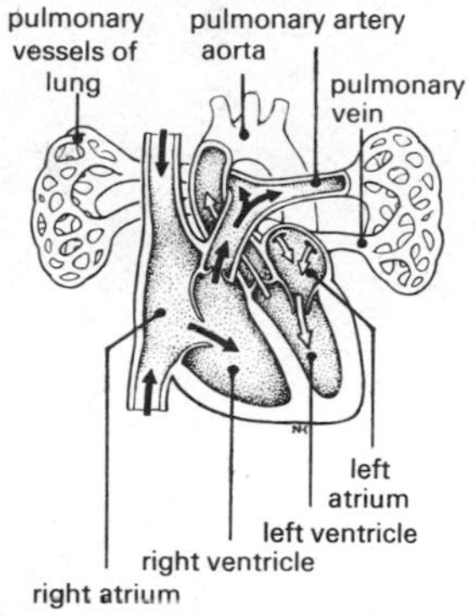

pulmonary vessels of lung
pulmonary artery
aorta
pulmonary vein
left atrium
left ventricle
right ventricle
right atrium

pulmonary
Pulmonary circulation

punch-drunk (pŭnch'drŭngk') *adj.* **1.** Suffering from the effects of repeated blows on the head. **2.** Acting in a dazed manner.

punched card. A card punched with holes or notches to represent letters and numbers or with a pattern of holes to represent related data, for use in a computer.

pun·cheon¹ (pŭn'chən) *n.* **1.** A short, wooden upright used in structural framing. **2.** A piece of broad, heavy timber, roughly dressed, with one face finished flat. **3.** A punching, perforating, or stamping tool, especially one used by a goldsmith. [Middle English *ponchon, pons(y)on,* a sharp tool, from Old French *po(i)nchon, poinçon,* from Vulgar Latin *punctiō* (unattested), from *punctiāre* (unattested), to pierce, prick, from Latin *pungere* (past participle *punctus*), to prick. See **peuk-** in Appendix.*]

pun·cheon² (pŭn'chən) *n.* **1.** A cask with a capacity of 84 U.S. gallons. **2.** This amount of liquid. [Old French *po(i)nçon, po(i)nchon*†.]

punch·er (pŭn'chər) *n.* **1.** One that punches. **2.** A cowboy; cowpuncher.

Pun·chi·nel·lo (pŭn'chə-nĕl'ō) *n., pl.* **-los** or **-loes. 1.** The short, fat character in an Italian puppet show and probable prototype of the English Punch. **2.** Someone thought to resemble this puppet. [Variant of earlier *policinello,* from Italian dialect (Neapolitan) *polecenella,* perhaps diminutive of *polecena,* young turkey cock (from the puppet's beaklike nose), from *pulcino,* chicken, from Late Latin *pullicenus,* diminutive of Latin *pullus,* PULLET.]

punching bag. A stuffed or inflated leather bag, usually suspended so that it can be punched with the fists for exercise.

punch line. The climax of a joke or humorous story.

punch press. A power press fitted with punches and dies for cutting, forming, or imprinting metal, plastic, or the like.

punch tape. Paper tape in which holes representing data to be processed by computer are punched.

punch·y (pŭn'chē) *adj.* **-ier, -iest.** Groggy or dazed from or as if from a punch or series of punches; punch-drunk.

punc·tate (pŭngk'tāt') *adj.* Also **punc·tat·ed** (-tā'tĭd). Having tiny spots, points, or depressions. [New Latin *punctatus,* from Latin *punctum,* pricked mark, POINT.] —**punc'ta'tion** *n.*

punc·til·i·o (pŭngk-tĭl'ē-ō') *n., pl.* **-os. 1.** A fine point of eti-

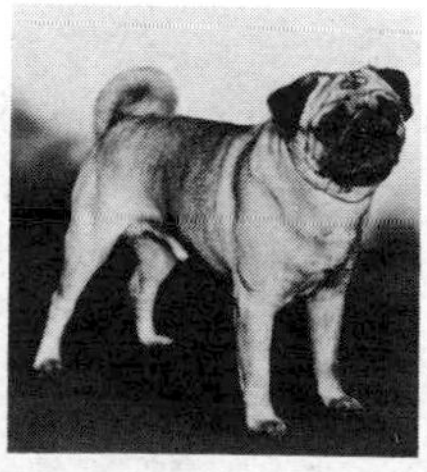

pug¹

quette. **2.** Precise observance of formalities. [Italian *punctiglio.* See **pun.**]

punc·til·i·ous (pŭngk-tĭl′ē-əs) *adj.* **1.** Attentive to the finer points of etiquette and formal conduct. **2.** Precise; scrupulous. —See Synonyms at **meticulous, upright.** —**punc·til′i·ous·ly** *adv.* —**punc·til′i·ous·ness** *n.*

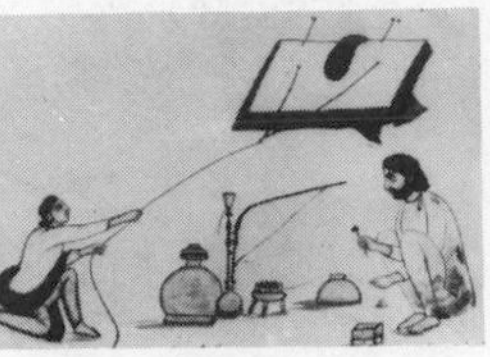

punka
Drawing of a servant operating a punka in a goldsmith's establishment

punc·tu·al (pŭngk′cho͞o-əl) *adj.* **1.** Acting or arriving exactly at the time appointed; prompt. **2.** Paid or accomplished at or by the appointed time. **3.** Precise; exact. **4.** Confined to or having the nature of a point in space. [Medieval Latin *punctuālis,* "to the point," from Latin *punctum,* pricked mark, POINT.] —**punc·tu·al′i·ty, punc′tu·al·ness** *n.* —**punc′tu·al·ly** *adv.*

punc·tu·ate (pŭngk′cho͞o-āt′) *v.* **-ated, -ating, -ates.** —*tr.* **1.** To provide (a text) with punctuation marks. **2.** To interrupt periodically: *"lectures punctuated by questions and discussions"* (Gilbert Highet). **3.** To stress; emphasize. —*intr.* To use punctuation. [Medieval Latin *punctuāre,* to mark with a point, punctuate, from Latin *punctum,* pricked mark, point, from the past participle of *pungere,* to prick, pierce. See **peuk-** in Appendix.*] —**punc′tu·a′tive** *adj.* —**punc′tu·a′tor** (-ā′tər) *n.*

punc·tu·a·tion (pŭngk′cho͞o-ā′shən) *n.* **1.** The use of standard marks and signs in writing and printing to separate words into sentences, clauses, and phrases in order to clarify meaning. **2.** The marks so used. **3.** An act or instance of punctuating.

punctuation mark. One of a set of marks or signs used to punctuate texts; for example, the comma (,) or the period (.).

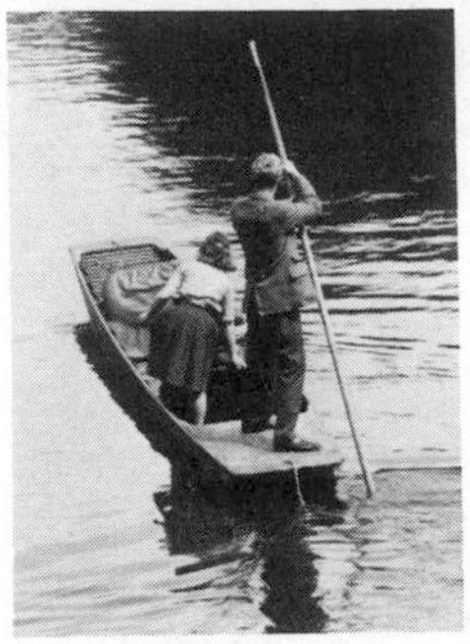

punt¹

punc·ture (pŭngk′chər) *v.* **-tured, -turing, -tures.** —*tr.* **1.** To pierce with a pointed object. **2.** To make (a hole) by piercing. **3.** To cause to collapse by piercing. **4.** To depreciate; deflate: *She punctured his ego.* —*intr.* To be pierced or punctured. —*n.* **1.** An act or instance of puncturing. **2.** A hole or depression made by a sharp object; especially, a hole in a pneumatic tire. [Latin *punctūra,* a pricking, puncture, from *pungere* (past participle *punctus*), to prick. See **peuk-** in Appendix.*] —**punc′tur·a·ble** *adj.*

puncture weed. A prostrate weed, *Tribulus terrestris,* native to Europe, bearing fruit with stout, divergent spines.

pun·dit (pŭn′dĭt) *n.* **1.** A Brahmanic scholar. **2.** A learned person. [Hindi *paṇḍit,* from Sanskrit *paṇḍita,* a learned man, from Dravidian (akin to Telegu *paṇḍa,* wisdom).]

pung (pŭng) *n. New England.* A low box sleigh drawn by one horse. [Shortened from *tom-pong, tow-pong,* of Algonquian origin, akin to TOBOGGAN.]

pun·gent (pŭn′jənt) *adj.* **1.** Affecting the organs of taste or smell with a sharp, acrid sensation. **2.** Penetrating; biting; caustic: *pungent satire.* **3.** Pointed. [Latin *pungēns,* present participle of *pungere,* to prick, sting. See **peuk-** in Appendix.*] —**pun′gen·cy** *n.* —**pun′gent·ly** *adv.*

Pu·nic (pyo͞o′nĭk) *adj.* **1.** Of or pertaining to ancient Carthage or its people. **2.** Having the character of treachery attributed to the Carthaginians by the Romans. —*n.* The West Semitic language of ancient Carthage, a dialect of Phoenician. [Latin *Pūnicus,* earlier *Poenicus,* from *Poenus,* a Carthaginian, from Greek *Phoinix,* Phoenician. See **phoenix.**]

Punic Wars. Three wars waged by Rome against Carthage (264–241 B.C., 218–201 B.C., and 149–146 B.C.) in which Rome finally defeated Carthage and annexed its territory.

pun·ish (pŭn′ĭsh) *tr.v.* **-ished, -ishing, -ishes.** **1.** To subject (someone) to penalty for a crime, fault, or misbehavior. **2.** To inflict a penalty on a criminal or wrongdoer for (an offense). **3.** To handle roughly; injure; hurt: *"the October wind / with frosty fingers punishes my hair"* (Dylan Thomas). **4.** *Informal.* To deplete (a stock or supply) heavily. —*intr.* To give punishment. [Middle English *punissen, punyschen,* from Old French *punir* (stem *puniss-*), from Latin *pūnīre, poenīre,* from *poena,* penalty, punishment, from Greek *poinē.* See **kwei-¹** in Appendix.*] —**pun′ish·er** *n.*

Synonyms: *punish, chastise, discipline, castigate, penalize.* These verbs refer to different ways of causing pain or loss to someone for wrong behavior. *Punish* usually means subjecting someone to loss of freedom or money or to physical pain for wrongdoing. *Chastise* usually refers to corporal punishment as a means of improving behavior. *Discipline* stresses punishment designed to control an offender and to eliminate or reform unacceptable conduct. *Castigate,* now always verbal, means to berate or censure, often in public. *Penalize,* weaker than *punish,* usually involves a demand for money or forfeiture of a privilege or gain because the rules of fair play or established conduct have been broken: *penalized for late payment of taxes.*

pun·ish·a·ble (pŭn′ĭsh-ə-bəl) *adj.* Liable to punishment.

pun·ish·ment (pŭn′ĭsh-mənt) *n.* **1. a.** An act of punishing. **b.** The condition of being punished. **2.** A penalty imposed for wrongdoing. **3.** *Informal.* Rough handling; mistreatment.

pu·ni·tive (pyo͞o′nə-tĭv) *adj.* Inflicting or aiming to inflict punishment; punishing. [French *punitif,* from Medieval Latin *pūnītīvus,* from Latin *pūnīre* (past participle *pūnītus*), PUNISH.] —**pu′ni·tive·ly** *adv.* —**pu′ni·tive·ness** *n.*

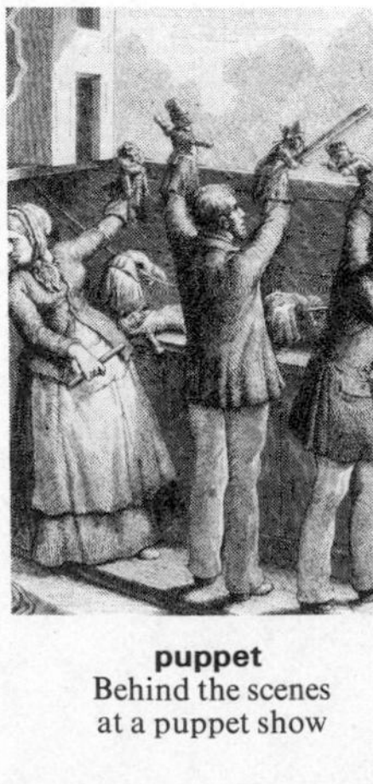

puppet
Behind the scenes at a puppet show

Pun·jab (pŭn-jäb′, -jăb′, pŭn′jäb′, -jăb′). **1.** A region and former province of India, occupying about 99,000 square miles in the northwest. See **West Punjab.** **2.** A former state of the Republic of India, divided in 1966 into the two states of Punjab and Hariana. **3.** A state of the Republic of India, occupying 19,425 square miles in the northwest. Population, 11,165,000. Capital, Chandigarh. [Persian *Pañjāb,* from Sanskrit *pañca āpah,* "five rivers" : *pañca,* five (see **penkwe** in Appendix*) + *āpah,* river (see **ap-²** in Appendix*).]

Pun·ja·bi (pŭn-jä′bē, -jăb′ē) *n.* Also **Pan·ja·bi** (pŭn-jä′bē, -jăb′ē) (for sense 2). **1.** A native of the Punjab. **2.** An Indic language spoken in the Punjab.

punk¹ (pŭngk) *n.* **1.** Dry, decayed wood, used as tinder. **2.** Any of various substances that smolder when ignited, used to light fireworks. **3.** Chinese incense. [Origin uncertain.]

punk² (pŭngk) *n.* **1.** *Slang.* **a.** An inexperienced or callow youth. **b.** A young tough. **c.** A passive homosexual; catamite. **2.** *Archaic.* A whore. —*adj. Slang.* **1.** Of poor quality; worthless. **2.** Weak in spirits or health. [Earlier *punck*†.]

pun·ka, pun·kah (pŭng′kə) *n.* A fan used especially in India, made of a palm frond or strip of cloth hung from the ceiling and moved by a servant. [Hindi *pankhā,* from Sanskrit *pakṣaka,* fan, from *pakṣa,* shoulder, wing. See **peg-** in Appendix.*]

punk·ie (pŭng′kē) *n., pl.* **-kies.** Also **punk·y** *pl.* **-kies, punk·ey** *pl.* **-keys.** Any of various tiny, winged, biting insects of the genus *Culicoides* and related genera. Also called "no-see-um." [From PUNK (tinder).]

pun·kin (pŭng′kĭn) *n. Regional.* A pumpkin.

pun·ster (pŭn′stər) *n.* A maker of puns.

punt¹ (pŭnt) *n.* An open, flat-bottomed boat with squared ends, propelled by a long pole and used in shallow waters. —*v.* **punted, punting, punts.** —*tr.* **1.** To propel (a boat) with a pole. **2.** To carry in a punt. —*intr.* To go in a punt. [Middle Low German *punte, punto,* ferryboat, from Latin *pontō,* floating bridge, pontoon, from *pōns,* bridge. See **pent-** in Appendix.*] —**punt′er** *n.*

punt² (pŭnt) *n. Football.* A kick in which the ball is dropped from the hands and kicked before it touches the ground. —*v.* **punted, punting, punts.** *Football.* —*tr.* To propel (a football) by means of a punt. —*intr.* To execute a punt. [Probably from English dialectal *bunt, punt*†, to push, kick.]

punt³ (pŭnt) *intr.v.* **punted, punting, punts.** **1.** In games such as roulette and the like, to lay a bet against the bank. **2.** To gamble. [French *ponter,* from *ponte,* bet against the banker, from Spanish *punto,* "point," "ace," from Latin *punctum,* pricked mark, point. See **punctuate.**] —**punt′er** *n.*

Pun·ta A·re·nas. The former name for **Magallanes.**

Pun·ta Gal·li·nas. The Spanish name for **Gallinas Point.**

pun·ty (pŭn′tē) *n., pl.* **-ties.** In glassmaking, an iron rod on which molten glass is handled. Also called "pontil." [Variant of PONTIL.]

pu·ny (pyo͞o′nē) *adj.* **-nier, -niest.** Of inferior size, strength, or significance; weak. [Old French *puisne,* "born afterward" : *puis,* afterward, from Vulgar Latin *postius* (unattested), comparative of Latin *post,* after (see **apo-** in Appendix*) + *ne,* born, from Latin *nātus,* past participle of *nāscī,* to be born (see **gena-** in Appendix*).] —**pu′ni·ly** *adv.* —**pu′ni·ness** *n.*

pup (pŭp) *n.* **1.** A young dog; puppy. **2.** The young of certain other animals, such as the seal. —*intr.v.* **pupped, pupping, pups.** To give birth to pups. [Back-formation from PUPPY.]

pu·pa (pyo͞o′pə) *n., pl.* **-pae** (-pē′) or **-pas.** The inactive stage in the metamorphosis of many insects, following the larval stage and preceding the adult form. Compare **nymph.** [New Latin *pupa,* from Latin *pūpa,* girl, doll, feminine of *pūpus,* boy. See **pap-¹** in Appendix.*] —**pu′pal** *adj.*

pu·pate (pyo͞o′pāt′) *intr.v.* **-pated, -pating, -pates.** To become a pupa. —**pu·pa′tion** (pyo͞o-pā′shən) *n.*

pu·pil¹ (pyo͞o′pəl) *n.* **1.** A student under the direct supervision of a teacher. **2.** *Law.* A minor under the supervision of a guardian. [Middle English *pupille,* orphan, ward, (hence) pupil, from Old French, from Latin *pūpillus,* diminutive of *pūpus,* boy. See **pap-¹** in Appendix.*]

pu·pil² (pyo͞o′pəl) *n.* The apparently black circular aperture in the center of the iris of the eye. [Middle English *pupilla* and Old French *pupille,* both from Latin *pūpilla,* "little orphan girl," pupil (by analogy with Greek *korē,* little girl, doll, pupil of the eye, originally a children's name referring to the miniature reflection of oneself seen by looking closely at another's eye), feminine of *pūpillus,* PUPIL.]

pu·pil·age (pyo͞o′pə-lĭj) *n.* Also **pu·pil·lage.** The state or period of being a pupil.

pu·pil·lar·y¹ (pyo͞o′pə-lĕr′ē) *adj.* Of or pertaining to a ward or a student.

pu·pil·lar·y² (pyo͞o′pə-lĕr′ē) *adj.* Also **pu·pi·lar·y.** Of or affecting the pupil of the eye.

pu·pip·a·rous (pyo͞o-pĭp′ər-əs) *adj.* Producing well-developed young that are ready to pupate, as certain parasitic flies do. [From PUPA + -PAROUS.]

pup·pet (pŭp′ĭt) *n.* **1.** A small figure of a person or animal, having jointed parts animated from above by strings or wires; marionette. **2.** A similar figure having a cloth body and hollow head, designed to be fitted over and manipulated by the hand. **3.** A toy representing a human figure; doll. **4.** One whose behavior is determined by the will of others. —*adj.* **1.** Of or pertaining to puppets. **2.** Sponsored and controlled by another or others while professing autonomy. [Middle English *popet, popette,* small child, doll, from Old French *poupette,* diminutive of *poupe* (unattested), doll, from Vulgar Latin *puppa* (unattested), doll, from Latin *pūpa,* girl, doll. See **pupa.**]

pup·pet·eer (pŭp′ĭ-tîr′) *n.* One who operates and entertains with puppets or marionettes.

pup·pet·ry (pŭp′ĭ-trē) *n., pl.* **-ries.** **1.** The art of making puppets and presenting puppet shows. **2.** The actions of puppets. **3.** Stilted or artificial dramatic performance.

Pup·pis (pŭp′ĭs) *n.* A constellation in the Southern Hemisphere near Canis Major and Pyxis. [Latin, "the ship," from *puppis,* POOP (stern).]

pup·py (pŭp′ē) *n., pl.* **-pies.** **1.** A young dog; pup. **2.** A conceited or inexperienced youth. [Middle English *popi,* from Old French *po(u)pee,* doll, toy, plaything, from Vulgar Latin *puppa* (unattested). See **puppet.**]

pup·py·ish (pŭp′ē-ĭsh) *adj.* Resembling or characteristic of a puppy.
puppy love. Adolescent love or infatuation.
pup tent. A **shelter tent** *(see).*
pur·blind (pûr′blīnd′) *adj.* **1.** Having poor vision; nearly or partly blind. **2.** Slow in understanding or discernment; dull. [Middle English *pur(e)blind,* originally "totally blind" : PURE (completely) + BLIND.] —**pur′blind′ly** *adv.* —**pur′blind′ness** *n.*
Pur·cell (pûr-sĕl′), **Edward Mills.** Born 1912. American physicist; worked on nuclear magnetic moments.
Pur·cell (pûr′səl), **Henry.** 1659–1695. English composer.
pur·chas·a·ble (pûr′chĭ-sə-bəl) *adj.* **1.** Capable of being bought. **2.** Capable of being bribed; venal. —**pur′chas·a·bil′i·ty** *n.*
pur·chase (pûr′chĭs) *tr.v.* **-chased, -chasing, -chases. 1.** To obtain in exchange for money or its equivalent; buy. **2.** To acquire by effort; earn. **3.** *Law.* To acquire (property) legally by means other than inheritance. **4.** To move or hold with a mechanical device, as a lever or wrench. —*n.* **1.** That which is bought. **2. a.** The act of buying. **b.** Acquisition through the payment of money or its equivalent. **3.** *Law.* The acquisition of property other than by inheritance. **4.** A grip applied manually or mechanically to move something or prevent it from slipping. **5.** A tackle, lever, or other device used to obtain mechanical advantage. **6.** A position, as of a lever or one's feet, affording means to move or secure a weight. **7.** Any means of increasing power, influence, or advantage. [Middle English *po(u)rchasen,* from Old French *po(u)rchacier, purchacier,* to pursue, seek to obtain : *po(u)r-,* for, from Latin *prō* (see **per**[1] in Appendix*) + *chacier,* to CHASE.] —**pur′chas·er** *n.*
purchasing power. 1. The ability of a person or group to purchase, generally measured by income. **2.** The value of a particular monetary unit in terms of the goods or services that can be purchased with it.
pur·dah (pûr′də) *n.* **1.** In India, a curtain used to screen women from men or strangers. **2.** The Hindu practice of secluding women. [Hindi *parda,* screen, veil, from Persian *pardah*†.]
pure (pyŏŏr) *adj.* **purer, purest. 1.** Having a homogeneous or uniform composition; not mixed: *pure oxygen.* **2.** Free from adulterants or impurities; full-strength: *pure chocolate.* **3.** Free from dirt, defilement, or pollution; clean. **4.** Free from foreign elements. **5.** Containing nothing inappropriate or extraneous. **6.** Complete; thorough; utter: *pure folly.* **7.** Without faults; perfect; sinless. **8.** Chaste; virgin. **9.** Of unmixed blood or ancestry. **10.** *Genetics.* Breeding true to parental type; homozygous. **11.** *Music.* Free from discordant qualities: *pure tones.* **12.** *Phonetics.* Articulated with a single unchanging speech sound; monophthongal: *a pure vowel.* **13.** Theoretical rather than applied: *pure science.* **14.** *Philosophy.* Free from empirical elements: *pure reason.* [Middle English *pur, pure,* from Old French *pur* (feminine *pure*), from Latin *pūrus,* clean. See **peue-**[1] in Appendix.*] —**pure′ness** *n.*
pure·bred (pyŏŏr′brĕd′) *adj.* Of a strain established through breeding many generations of unmixed stock. —*n.* (pyŏŏr′brĕd′). An animal so bred.
pu·rée (pyŏŏ-rā′, pyŏŏr′ā) *tr.v.* **puréed, -réeing, -rées.** To rub (food) through a strainer. —*n.* Food so prepared. [French, from Old French *purer,* to purify, strain, from Latin *pūrāre,* to purify, from *pūrus,* PURE.]
pure·ly (pyŏŏr′lē) *adv.* **1.** In a pure manner. **2.** Innocently; chastely. **3.** Totally; entirely: *purely by chance.*
pure temperament. *Music.* See **temperament.**
pur·fle (pûr′fəl) *tr.v.* **-fled, -fling, -fles.** To finish or decorate the border or edge of. —*n.* Also **pur·fling** (-flĭng). An ornamental border or edging. [Middle English *purfilen,* from Old French *porfiler,* to weave, from Vulgar Latin *prōfilāre* (unattested), to draw in outline : Latin *prō,* forth, out + *fīlum,* thread (see **gwhī-** in Appendix*).]
pur·ga·tion (pûr-gā′shən) *n.* The act of purging or purifying.
pur·ga·tive (pûr′gə-tĭv) *adj.* Tending to cleanse or purge; especially, tending to cause evacuation of the bowels. —*n.* A purgative agent or medicine; a cathartic.
pur·ga·to·ri·al (pûr′gə-tôr′ē-əl, -tōr′ē-əl) *adj.* **1.** Serving to purify of sin; expiatory. **2.** Of, pertaining to, or resembling purgatory.
pur·ga·to·ry (pûr′gə-tôr′ē, -tōr′ē) *n., pl.* **-ries. 1.** *Roman Catholic Church.* A state in which the souls of those who have died in grace must expiate their sins. **2.** Any place or condition of expiation, suffering, or remorse. —*adj.* Tending to cleanse or purge. [Middle English *purgatorie,* from Medieval Latin *purgātōrium,* from Late Latin *purgātōrius,* from Latin *purgāre,* to PURGE.]
purge (pûrj) *v.* **purged, purging, purges.** —*tr.* **1. a.** To free from impurities; purify. **b.** To remove (impurities and other elements) by or as if by cleansing: *"The calamity of his fall upon Lemnos purged all dross of arrogance from his heart."* (John Updike). **2.** To rid of sin, guilt, or defilement. **3.** *Law.* To clear (a person) of a charge or imputation. **4.** To rid (a nation, political party, or other group) of persons considered to be undesirable. **5.** *Medicine.* **a.** To cause evacuation of (the bowels). **b.** To induce evacuation of the bowels in (a patient). —*intr.* **1.** To become pure or clean. **2.** To undergo or cause an emptying of the bowels. —*n.* **1.** The act or process of purging. **2.** That which purges; especially, a medicinal purgative. [Middle English *purgen,* from Old French *purger,* from Latin *purgāre, pūrigāre* (unattested), to cleanse : *pūrus,* PURE + *agere,* to lead (see **ag-** in Appendix*).] —**purg′er** *n.*
pu·ri. Variant of **poori.**
pu·ri·fi·ca·tion (pyŏŏr′ə-fĭ-kā′shən) *n.* The act or process of cleansing or purifying.
pu·ri·fi·ca·tor (pyŏŏr′ə-fĭ-kā′tər) *n. Ecclesiastical.* A cloth used to clean the chalice after the celebration of the Eucharist.
pu·ri·fy (pyŏŏr′ə-fī′) *v.* **-fied, -fying, -fies.** —*tr.* **1.** To rid of impurities; cleanse. **2.** To rid of foreign or objectionable elements. **3.** To free from sin, guilt, or other defilement. —*intr.* To become clean or pure. [Middle English *purifien,* from Old French *purifier,* from Latin *pūrificāre,* to make pure : *pūrus,* PURE + *facere,* to make (see **dhē-**[1] in Appendix*).] —**pu·rif′i·ca·to′ry** (pyŏŏ-rĭf′ĭ-kə-tôr′ē, -tōr′ē) *adj.* —**pu′ri·fi′er** *n.*
Pu·rim (pŏŏr′ĭm; *Hebrew* pōō-rēm′) *n.* A Jewish holiday in the month of Adar, celebrating the deliverance of the Jews from massacre by Haman. Esther 9:20–22. [Hebrew *pūrīm,* plural of *pūr,* lot (from the lots cast by Haman to determine the day of destruction of the Jews), from Akkadian *pūru,* stone.]
pu·rine (pyŏŏr′ēn′) *n.* **1.** A colorless crystalline compound, $C_5H_4N_4$, used in organic synthesis and metabolism studies. **2.** Any of a group of naturally occurring organic compounds derived from or having molecular structures related to purine, including uric acid, adenine, guanine, and caffeine. [German *Purin* : blend of Latin *pūrus,* PURE + New Latin *uricus,* URIC-(ACID) (in which it is found) + -INE.]
pur·ism (pyŏŏr′ĭz′əm) *n.* Strict observance of or insistence upon traditional correctness, especially of language: *"By purism is to be understood a needless & irritating insistence on purity or correctness of speech."* (H.W. Fowler). [French *purisme,* from *pur,* PURE.]
pur·ist (pyŏŏr′ĭst) *n.* One who practices or urges strict correctness, especially in the use of words. —**pu·ris′tic** (pyŏŏ-rĭs′tĭk) *adj.* —**pu·ris′ti·cal·ly** *adv.*
Pu·ri·tan (pyŏŏr′ə-tən) *n.* **1.** A member of a group of English Protestants who, in the 16th and 17th centuries, advocated simplification of the ceremonies and creeds of the Church of England and strict religious discipline. **2.** *Small* **p.** One who lives in accordance with Protestant precepts; especially, one who regards luxury or pleasure as sinful. —*adj.* **1.** Of or pertaining to the Puritans or Puritanism. **2.** *Small* **p.** Characteristic of a puritan; puritanical: *"He had an intensely puritan nature to which all pleasure except that of the intellect was immoral."* (Irving Stone). [Formed (after Medieval Latin *Cathari,* "the pure ones," title assumed by a third-century sect of rigorist heretics) from Late Latin *pūritās,* purity, from *pūrus,* PURE.]
pu·ri·tan·i·cal (pyŏŏr′ə-tăn′ĭ-kəl) *adj.* **1.** Rigorous in religious observance; marked by stern morality. **2.** *Capital* **P.** Of, pertaining to, or characteristic of the Puritans. Used disparagingly. —See Synonyms at **religious.** —**pu′ri·tan′i·cal·ly** *adv.* —**pu′ri·tan′i·cal·ness** *n.*
Pu·ri·tan·ism (pyŏŏr′ə-tə-nĭz′əm) *n.* **1.** The practices and doctrines of the Puritans. **2.** *Small* **p.** Scrupulous moral rigor; especially, hostility to social pleasures and indulgences.
pu·ri·ty (pyŏŏr′ə-tē) *n.* **1.** The quality or condition of being pure. **2.** A quantitative assessment of homogeneity or uniformity. **3.** Freedom from sin or guilt; innocence; chastity. **4.** The absence in speech or writing of foreign words, slang, or other elements deemed inappropriate to good style. **5.** *Color Technology.* The proportion of a single-frequency spectral component in a mixture of achromatic and spectral colors. See **color.**
purl[1] (pûrl) *intr.v.* **purled, purling, purls.** To flow or ripple with a murmuring sound. —*n.* The sound made by rippling water. [Norwegian *purla*†.]
purl[2] (pûrl) *v.* **purled, purling, purls.** Also **pearl.** —*tr.* **1.** To knit with a purl stitch. **2.** To edge or finish with lace or embroidery. —*intr.* **1.** To do knitting with a purl stitch. **2.** To edge or finish with lace or embroidery. —*n.* Also **pearl.** *Abbr.* **p. 1.** The inversion of a knit stitch; a **purl stitch** *(see).* **2.** A decorative edging of lace or embroidery. **3.** Gold or silver wire used in embroidery. [Earlier *pyrle*†.]
Pur·ley (pûr′lē). A former administrative division of London, England, now part of **Croydon** *(see).*
pur·lieu (pûrl′yōō, pûr′lōō) *n.* **1.** Any outlying or neighboring area. **2.** *Plural.* Outskirts; environs. **3.** A place that one frequents. [Middle English *purlewe,* alteration of Norman French *puralée,* perambulation, from the past participle of Old French *poraler, puraler,* to traverse : *por,* through, from Latin *prō,* forth + *aler,* to go, probably from Vulgar Latin *amlāre* (unattested), from Latin *ambulāre,* to walk (see **al-**[2] in Appendix*).]
pur·lin (pûr′lĭn) *n.* Also **pur·line** (pûr′lĭn). One of several horizontal timbers supporting the rafters of a roof. [Middle English *purly(o)n*†.]
pur·loin (pər-loin′, pûr′loin′) *v.* **-loined, -loining, -loins.** —*tr.* To steal; filch. —*intr.* To commit theft. [Middle English *purloynen,* to remove, from Norman French *purloigner,* "to put far away" : Old French *pur-,* away, from Latin *prō-,* away + *loign,* far, from Latin *longē,* far, from *longus,* long (see **del-**[1] in Appendix*).] —**pur·loin′er** *n.*
purl stitch. An inverted knitting stitch, often alternated with the plain stitch to produce a ribbed effect. Also called "purl."
pur·ple (pûr′pəl) *n.* **1.** Any of a group of colors with a hue between that of violet and red. See **color. 2.** Cloth of this color, formerly worn as a symbol of royalty or high office. **3.** Imperial power; high rank. Used especially in the phrase *born to the purple.* **4.** The rank or office of a cardinal. **5.** The rank or office of a bishop. —*adj.* **1.** Of the color purple. **2.** Royal or imperial; regal. **3.** Elaborate and ornate: *purple prose.* —*v.* **purpled, -pling, -ples.** —*tr.* To make purple. —*intr.* To become purple. [Middle English *purpel, purpyl,* Old English *purple,* altered by dissimilation from *purpuran,* of purple, from *purpura,* purple cloth, from Latin, purple, from Greek *porphura,* shellfish yielding a purple dye, purple dye, from Semitic.]

pupa

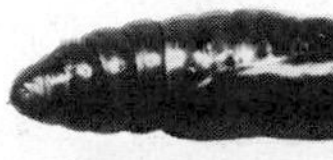

corn earworm

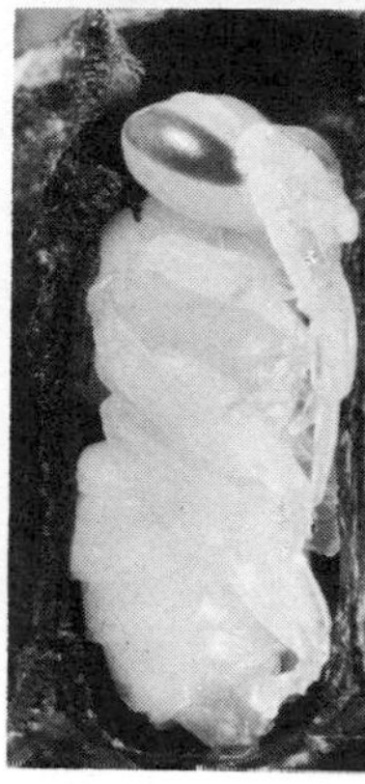

honeybee

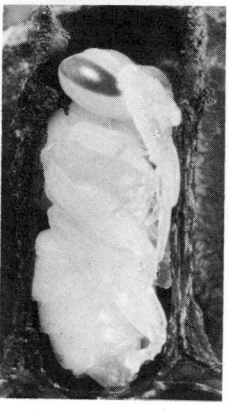

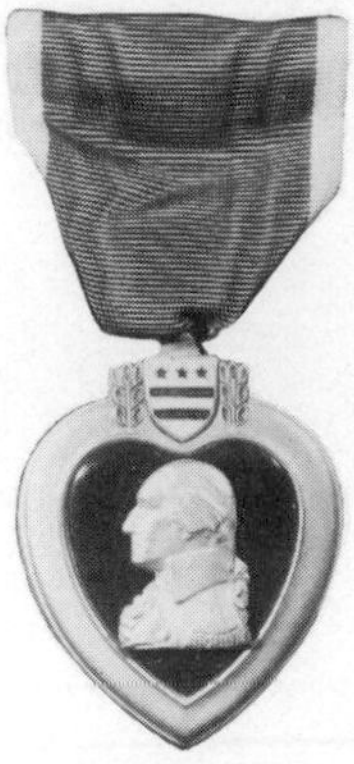
Purple Heart

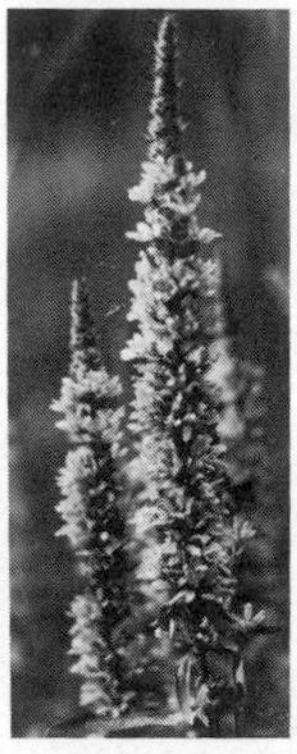
purple loosestrife

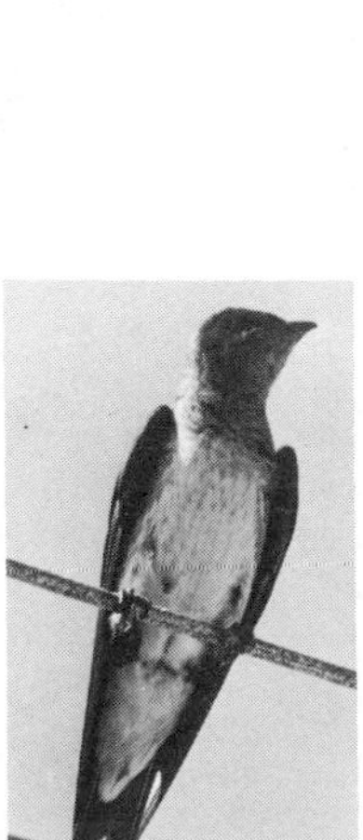
purple martin

Purple Heart. *Abbr.* **PH, P.H.** The U.S. Armed Forces medal of the Order of the Purple Heart, awarded to servicemen wounded in action.

pur·ple·heart (pûr′pəl-härt′) *n.* **1.** Any of several tropical American trees of the genus *Peltogyne,* valued for their decorative wood. **2.** The purple heartwood of any of these trees.

purple loosestrife. A marsh plant, *Lythrum salicaria,* having long spikes of purple flowers. Also called "long purples."

purple martin. A North American bird, *Progne subis,* related to the swallows, having a glossy, blue-black back, and, in the male, a dark breast.

purple salt. *Chemistry.* **Potassium permanganate** *(see).*

pur·plish (pûr′plĭsh) *adj.* Having a somewhat purple tint.

pur·port (pər-pôrt′, -pōrt′, pûr′pôrt′, -pōrt′) *tr.v.* **-ported, -porting, -ports. 1.** To contain the claim or profession (to be or do something). **2.** *Rare.* To have or give the appearance, often falsely, of being, professing, or intending. —See Synonyms at **mean.** —*n.* (pûr′pôrt′, -pōrt′). The apparent meaning or purpose; import; significance. See Synonyms at **meaning.** [Middle English *purporten,* to imply, from Old French *porporter,* to embody, contain, from Medieval Latin *prōportāre,* to carry forth : Latin *prō,* forth + *portāre,* to carry (see **per-²** in Appendix*).] —**pur·port′ed·ly** (pər-pôr′tĭd-lē, pər-pōr′-) *adv.*

pur·pose (pûr′pəs) *n.* **1.** The object toward which one strives or for which something exists; goal; aim. **2.** A result or effect that is intended or desired; intention. **3.** Determination; resolution. **4.** The matter at hand; point at issue. —See Synonyms at **intention.** —**on purpose.** Deliberately; intentionally. —*tr.v.* **purposed, -posing, -poses.** To intend or resolve to perform or accomplish: *"I was purposing to travel over the north this summer"* (Keats). [Middle English *porpos, purpos,* from Old French, from *porposer, purposer,* to design, intend, from Latin *prōpōnere* (past participle *prōpositus*), to put forward, PROPOSE.]

pur·pose·ful (pûr′pəs-fəl) *adj.* **1.** Having a purpose; intentional. **2.** Having or manifesting purpose; determined. —**pur′pose·ful·ly** *adv.* —**pur′pose·ful·ness** *n.*

pur·pose·less (pûr′pəs-lĭs) *adj.* Without any purpose; aimless; pointless. —**pur′pose·less·ly** *adv.* —**pur′pose·less·ness** *n.*

pur·pose·ly (pûr′pəs-lē) *adj.* With specific purpose; deliberately.

pur·pos·ive (pûr′pə-sĭv) *adj.* **1.** Having or serving a purpose. **2.** Purposeful as opposed to aimless or random: *purposive behavior.* —**pur′pos·ive·ly** *adv.* —**pur′pos·ive·ness** *n.*

purr (pûr) *n.* **1.** The softly vibrant sound made by a cat to express pleasure or contentment. **2.** Any similar sound. —*v.* **purred, purring, purrs.** —*intr.* To make or utter such a sound. —*tr.* To express by such a sound. [Imitative.]

purse (pûrs) *n.* **1.** A small bag or pouch for carrying money. **2.** A woman's pocketbook or handbag. **3.** Anything that resembles a bag or pouch. **4.** Available wealth or resources; money. **5.** A sum of money collected as a present or offered as a prize. —*tr.v.* **pursed, pursing, purses.** To gather or contract (the lips or brow) into wrinkles or folds; pucker. [Middle English *purs,* Old English *purs,* from Late Latin *bursa,* bag, oxhide, from Greek *bursa,* leather, hide. See **bursa** in Appendix.*]

purs·er (pûr′sər) *n.* The officer in charge of money matters on board a ship. [Middle English, from *purs,* PURSE.]

purse seine (sān). A fishing seine that is pursed or drawn into the shape of a bag to enclose the catch.

purs·lane (pûrs′lĭn, -lān′) *n.* A trailing weed, *Portulaca oleracea,* having small yellow flowers, reddish stems, and fleshy leaves that are sometimes used in salads. Also called "pussley." [Middle English *purcelan, purslane,* from Old French *porcelaine,* cowrie shell, from Late Latin *porcillāgo,* from Latin *porcil(l)āca, portulāca.* See **porko-** in Appendix.*]

pur·su·ance (pər-sōō′əns) *n.* The carrying out or putting into effect of something; pursuit; prosecution.

pur·su·ant (pər-sōō′ənt) *adj.* Proceeding from and comformable to; in accordance with. Used with *to.* —*adv.* Also **pur·su·ant·ly.** Accordingly; consequently. Often used with *to.* [Middle English *poursuiant,* from Old French, present participle of *poursuivre,* PURSUE.]

pur·sue (pər-sōō′) *v.* **-sued, -suing, -sues.** —*tr.* **1.** To follow in an effort to overtake or capture; chase. **2.** To strive to gain or accomplish. **3.** To proceed along the course of; follow. **4.** To carry further; advance. **5.** To be engaged in (a vocation, hobby, or the like). **6.** To harass; persecute. —*intr.* **1.** To chase; follow. **2.** To continue; carry on. [Middle English *pursuen,* from Norman French *pursuer,* from Old French *po(u)rsuivre, po(u)rsuir,* from Vulgar Latin *prōsequere* (unattested), from Latin *prōsequī* : *prō-,* forth, onward + *sequī,* to follow (see **sekw-¹** in Appendix*).] —**pur·su′a·ble** *adj.* —**pur·su′er** *n.*

pur·suit (pər-sōōt′) *n.* **1.** The act or an instance of chasing or pursuing. **2.** The act of striving: *the pursuit of success.* **3.** Any vocation, hobby, or the like. [Middle English *pursu(i)te,* from Old French *poursuite,* from *poursuivre,* PURSUE.]

pur·sui·vant (pûr′swĭ-vənt) *n.* **1.** In the British Colleges of Heralds, an officer ranking below a herald. **2.** *Archaic.* A follower or attendant. [Middle English *pursevant,* from Old French *pours(u)ivant,* follower, from the present participle of *poursuivre,* PURSUE.]

pur·te·nance (pûr′tn-əns) *n. Archaic.* An animal's viscera or inner organs, especially the heart, liver, and lungs. [Middle English *purtenaunce,* "appurtenance," "accessory," alteration of Old French *partenance,* pertinence, from PERTINENT.]

pu·ru·lence (pyŏŏr′ə-ləns, pyŏŏr′yə-) *n.* **1.** The condition of secreting or containing pus. **2.** Pus.

pu·ru·lent (pyŏŏr′ə-lənt, pyŏŏr′yə-) *adj.* Containing or secreting pus. [Latin *pūrulentus* : *pūs* (stem *pūr-*), pus (see **pu-²** in Appendix*) + -ULENT.] —**pu′ru·lent·ly** *adv.*

Pu·rus (pōō-rōōs′). A navigable river rising in the Andes Mountains in eastern Peru and flowing about 2,000 miles northeast to join the Amazon near Manaus, northwestern Brazil.

pur·vey (pər-vā′, pûr′vā′) *tr.v.* **-veyed, -veying, -veys.** To supply (food or information, for example); furnish. [Middle English *purveien, porveien,* from Old French *porveeir, porveioir,* from Latin *prōvidēre,* to foresee, PROVIDE.]

pur·vey·ance (pər-vā′əns) *n.* The act of procuring supplies.

pur·vey·or (pər-vā′ər) *n.* **1.** A person who furnishes provisions, especially food. **2.** A distributor; dispenser: *a purveyor of lies.*

pur·view (pûr′vyōō) *n.* **1.** The extent or range of function, power, or competence; scope. **2.** Range of vision, comprehension, or experience; outlook. **3.** *Law.* The body, scope, or limit of a statute. [Middle English *purveu, purvewe,* proviso, provisional clause, from Norman French *purveu,* "(it is) provided" (word used to introduce a proviso), from Old French *porveu,* past participle of *porveeir,* to provide, PURVEY.]

pus (pŭs) *n.* A viscous, yellowish-white fluid formed in infected tissue, consisting chiefly of leucocytes, cellular debris, and liquefied tissue elements. [Latin *pūs.* See **pu-²** in Appendix.*]

Pu·san (pōō′sän′). *Japanese* **Fu·san** (fōō′sän′). The principal port of South Korea, on Korea Strait at the extreme southeastern tip of the Korean Peninsula. Population, 1,391,000.

Pu·sey·ism (pyōō′zē-ĭz′əm, pyōō′sē-) *n.* A religious movement, **Tractarianism** *(see).* [After its leader, Edward B. *Pusey* (1800–1882), English theologian.] —**Pu′sey·ite′** (-īt′) *n.*

push (pŏŏsh) *v.* **pushed, pushing, pushes.** —*tr.* **1.** To exert force against (an object) to move it away. **2.** To move (an object) by exerting force in this manner; thrust; shove. **3.** To force (one's way): *He pushed through the crowd.* **4.** To promote; urge forward. **5.** To bear hard upon; press. **6.** To extend or enlarge: *push civilization past the frontier.* **7.** *Slang.* **a.** To promote or sell (a product). **b.** To sell (a narcotic) illegally. —*intr.* **1.** To exert outward force against something. **2.** To advance despite difficulty or opposition; press forward. **3.** To expend great or vigorous effort. —**push off.** *Informal.* To depart; set out. —**push on.** To proceed; continue. —*n.* **1.** The act of pushing; a thrust. **2.** A vigorous or insistent effort toward an end; drive. **3.** A provocation to action; a stimulus. **4.** *Informal.* Persevering energy; enterprise. [Middle English *posshen, pusshen,* from Old French *polser, poulser,* to push, beat, from Latin *pulsāre,* frequentative of *pellere* (past participle *pulsus*), to push, beat. See **pel-⁶** in Appendix.*]

push·ball (pŏŏsh′bôl′) *n.* **1.** A game in which two opposing teams attempt to push a heavy ball, six feet in diameter, across a goal. **2.** The ball used in this game.

push button. A small button that activates an electric circuit.

push-but·ton (pŏŏsh′bŭt′n) *adj.* Operated by or as if by push buttons: *push-button warfare.*

push·cart (pŏŏsh′kärt′) *n.* A light cart pushed by hand.

push·er (pŏŏsh′ər) *n.* **1.** Someone or something that pushes. **2.** *Slang.* A person who sells drugs illegally.

push·ing (pŏŏsh′ĭng) *adj.* **1.** Energetic; enterprising. **2.** Aggressive; forward; presuming. —**push′ing·ly** *adv.*

Push·kin (pŏŏsh′kĭn), **Aleksander Sergeyevich.** 1799–1837. Russian poet.

push·o·ver (pŏŏsh′ō′vər) *n.* **1.** Anything easily accomplished. **2.** A person or group easily defeated or taken advantage of.

push·pin (pŏŏsh′pĭn′) *n.* **1.** A tacklike pin with a large head that is easily inserted into a wall or board. **2.** A game played by children with pins.

push·rod (pŏŏsh′rŏd′) *n.* Also **push rod.** A rod moved by a cam to operate the valves in an internal-combustion engine.

Push·tu (pŭsh′tōō) *n.* An Iranian language, **Pashto** *(see).*

push·y (pŏŏsh′ē) *adj.* **-ier, -iest.** *Informal.* Disagreeably forward or aggressive. —**push′i·ly** *adv.* —**push′i·ness** *n.*

pu·sil·la·nim·i·ty (pyōō′sə-lə-nĭm′ə-tē) *n.* The state or quality of being pusillanimous; faint-hearted cowardice.

pu·sil·lan·i·mous (pyōō′sə-lăn′ə-məs) *adj.* Lacking manly courage; marked by cowardice; faint-hearted. [From Late Latin *pūsillanimis* : Latin *pūsillus,* very small, weak, from *pūsus,* boy (see **pōu-** in Appendix*) + *animus,* mind, soul (see **ane** in Appendix*).] —**pu′sil·lan′i·mous·ly** *adv.*

puss¹ (pŏŏs) *n. Informal.* **1.** A cat. **2.** A girl or young woman. Used affectionately. [Perhaps a survival of Old English *pusa, posa,* sack, bag, hence hypocoristic for anything soft, akin to Icelandic *pūss*†, sack, mare's vulva.]

puss² (pŏŏs) *n. Slang.* **1.** The mouth. **2.** The face. [Irish *bus,* lip, mouth, from Old Irish, lip. See **bu-** in Appendix.*]

puss·ley (pŭs′lē) *n.* Also **pus·ley.** A plant, **purslane** *(see).* [Variant of *pursley,* short for PURSLANE.]

puss·y¹ (pŏŏs′ē) *n., pl.* **-ies.** *Informal.* **1.** A cat. **2.** A fuzzy catkin, especially of the pussy willow. [See **puss** (cat).]

puss·y² (pŏŏs′ē) *n., pl.* **-ies.** *Vulgar Slang.* **1.** The female pudendum. **2.** A female regarded as a sexual object. [Perhaps from Swedish (dialectal) *pusa,* akin to Icelandic *pūss,* mare's vulva. See **puss** (cat).]

pus·sy³ (pŭs′ē) *adj.* **-sier, -siest.** Resembling or containing pus.

puss·y·foot (pŏŏs′ē-fŏŏt′) *intr.v.* **-footed, -footing, -foots. 1.** To move stealthily or cautiously. **2.** *Slang.* To act or proceed cautiously or timidly to avoid committing oneself.

pus·sy·toes (pŏŏs′ē-tōz′) *n.* Plural in form, used with a singular or plural verb. Any of several low-growing plants of the genus *Antennaria,* having leaves with whitish down, and clusters of small white flowers. [The cluster resembles a cat's paw.]

pussy willow. 1. A North American shrub or small tree, *Salix discolor,* having silky catkins. **2.** Any of several similar willows.

pus·tu·lant (pŭs′chōō-lənt, pŭs′tyə-) *adj.* Causing pustules to form. —*n.* An agent that produces pustules.

pus·tu·lar (pŭs′cho͝o-lər, pŭs′tyə-) *adj.* Of, pertaining to, or having pustules.
pus·tu·late (pŭs′cho͝o-lāt′, pŭs′tyə-) *v.* **-lated, -lating, -lates.** —*tr.* To cause (tissue) to form pustules. —*intr.* To form pustules. —*adj.* Covered with pustules or pustulelike blisters.
pus·tu·la·tion (pŭs′cho͝o-lā′shən, pŭs′tyə-) *n.* **1.** The formation or appearance of pustules. **2.** A pustule.
pus·tule (pŭs′cho͞ol, pŭs′tyo͞ol) *n.* **1.** A slight, inflamed elevation of the skin filled with pus. **2.** Any small swelling similar to a blister or pimple. [Middle English, from Old French, from Latin *pustula*, a blister. See **pu-**[1] in Appendix.*]
put (po͝ot) *v.* **put, putting, puts.** —*tr.* **1.** To place in a specified location; set. **2.** To cause to be in a specified condition: *put one's room in order.* **3.** To cause to undergo something; to subject. **4.** To assign; attribute: *put a false interpretation on events.* **5.** To estimate: *He put the time at five o'clock.* **6.** To impose or levy: *put a tax on cigarettes.* **7.** To bet; wager (a stake). **8.** To hurl with an overhand pushing motion: *put the shot.* **9.** To bring up for consideration or judgment: *The committee put the question.* **10.** To express; state: *putting it bluntly.* **11.** To render in a specified language or literary form: *put prose into verse.* **12.** To adapt: *lyrics put to music.* **13.** To urge or force to some action: *put an outlaw to flight.* **14.** To apply: *We must put our minds to it.* —*intr.* To proceed: *The ship put into the harbor.* —**put about.** *Nautical.* To change direction; go from one tack to another. —**put across.** To state so as to be understood or accepted. —**put aside** (or **away** or **by**). **1.** To save for later use; reserve. **2.** To abandon; discard. —**put forth. 1.** To grow: *The plant put forth leaves.* **2.** To exert; bring to bear. **3.** To offer for consideration. —**put in. 1.** *Nautical.* To enter a port or harbor. **2.** To insert; interject: *put in one's opinion.* **3.** To submit. **4.** *Informal.* To devote or contribute (time or money). —**put over.** *Informal.* To achieve (something). —**put through.** To carry to a successful termination. —**put upon.** To impose on; overburden. Used in the passive: *He was put upon by his friends.* —**put up with.** To endure patiently. —*n.* **1.** An act of putting the shot. **2.** *Finance.* An option to sell a stipulated amount of stock or securities within a specified time and at a fixed price. Compare **call, straddle.** —*adj. Informal.* Fixed; stationary: *stay put.* [Middle English *put(t)en* (unattested), Old English *pūtian*†, to push, thrust.]
pu·ta·men (pyo͞o-tā′mən) *n., pl.* **-tamina** (-tăm′ə-nə). *Botany.* A hard, shell-like covering, such as that enclosing the kernel of a peach. [New Latin, from Latin *putāmen*, clippings, prunings, shells, from *putāre*, to prune, cut. See **peue-**[2] in Appendix.*] —**pu·tam′i·nous** (pyo͞o-tăm′ə-nəs) *adj.*
pu·ta·tive (pyo͞o′tə-tĭv) *adj.* Generally regarded as such; supposed; reputed. [Middle English, from Old French *putatif*, from Late Latin *putātīvus*, from Latin *putāre*, to compute, consider. See **peue-**[2] in Appendix.*] —**pu′ta·tive·ly** *adv.*
put down. 1. To write down; record. **2.** To repress; defeat. **3.** *Slang.* To express rejection or criticism of.
put-down (po͝ot′doun′) *n. Slang.* A dismissal or rejection, especially in the form of a critical or slighting remark.
Put-in-Bay (po͝ot′ĭn-bā′). A bay in South Bass Island in western Lake Erie where, on September 10, 1813, Commodore Oliver Hazard Perry defeated a British fleet.
put·log (po͝ot′lôg′, -lŏg′, pŭt′-) *n.* One of the short pieces of lumber that support a scaffolding floor. [Earlier *putlock* : probably past participle of PUT + LOCK.]
Put·nam (pŭt′nəm), **Israel.** 1718–1790. American general in the French and Indian War and the Revolutionary War.
Put·nam (pŭt′nəm), **Rufus.** 1738–1824. American army officer in the Revolutionary War.
put off. 1. To delay or postpone. **2.** To discard; take off.
put·off (po͝ot′ôf′, -ŏf′) *n.* A pretext for inaction; an excuse.
put on. 1. To clothe oneself with; don. **2.** To apply or activate: *putting on the brake.* **3.** To present; perform: *put on a play.* **4.** To assume affectedly: *"'Don't put on the brogue, now.'"* (O'Neill). **5.** *Slang.* To tease or mock (someone).
put-on (po͝ot′ŏn′, -ôn′) *n. Slang.* An affected manner or behavior.
put out. 1. To extinguish: *put out a fire.* **2.** *Nautical.* To leave, as a port; depart: *the ship put out to sea.* **3.** To expel. **4.** To gouge out (an eye). **5.** To publish. **6.** To inconvenience. **7.** To confuse; disconcert. **8.** *Baseball.* To retire (a runner).
put·out (po͝ot′out′) *n. Abbr.* **po, p.o.** *Baseball.* A play in which a batter or base runner is retired.
put-put (pŭt′pŭt′) *n. Slang.* **1.** A small gasoline engine. **2.** A boat or vehicle operated by such an engine. [Imitative.]
pu·tre·fac·tion (pyo͞o′trə-făk′shən) *n.* **1.** The partial decomposition of organic matter by microorganisms, producing foul-smelling matter. **2.** Putrefied matter. **3.** The condition of being putrefied. [Middle English *putrefaccioun*, from Late Latin *putrefactiō*, from Latin *putrefacere*, PUTREFY.]
pu·tre·fac·tive (pyo͞o′trə-făk′tĭv) *adj.* **1.** Bringing about putrefaction. **2.** Of or pertaining to putrefaction.
pu·tre·fy (pyo͞o′trə-fī′) *v.* **-fied, -fying, -fies.** —*tr.* **1.** To decompose (something); cause to decay. **2.** To make gangrenous. —*intr.* **1.** To decompose. **2.** To become gangrenous. —See Synonyms at **decay.** [Middle English *putrefien*, from Old French *putrefier*, from Latin *putrefacere* : *puter*, rotten (see **pu-**[2] in Appendix*) + *facere*, to make (see **dhē-**[1] in Appendix*).]
pu·tres·cence (pyo͞o-trĕs′əns) *n.* **1.** Putrescent character or condition. **2.** Putrid matter.
pu·tres·cent (pyo͞o-trĕs′ənt) *adj.* **1.** Becoming putrid; putrefying. **2.** Of or pertaining to putrefaction. [Latin *putrēscens*, present participle of *putrēscere*, to grow rotten, inceptive of *putrēre*, to be rotten, from *puter*, rotten. See **pu-**[2] in Appendix.*]
pu·tres·ci·ble (pyo͞o-trĕs′ə-bəl) *adj.* Subject to putrefaction. [French, from Late Latin *putrēscibilis*, from Latin *putrēscere*, to grow rotten. See **putrescent.**]
pu·trid (pyo͞o′trĭd) *adj.* **1.** In a decomposed, foul-smelling state; rotten. **2.** Proceeding from, pertaining to, or displaying putrefaction. **3.** Corrupt; morally rotten. **4.** Extremely objectionable; vile. [Latin *putridus*, from *putrēre*, to be rotten. See **putrescent.**] —**pu·trid′i·ty, pu′trid·ness** *n.* —**pu′trid·ly** *adv.*
putsch (po͝och) *n.* Also **Putsch.** A suddenly effected attempt by a group to overthrow a government. See Synonyms at **rebellion.** [German, from Swiss German, a thrust (imitative).]
putt (pŭt) *n. Golf.* A light stroke made on the putting green in an effort to place the ball into the hole. —*v.* **putted, putting, putts.** *Golf.* —*tr.* To hit (the ball) with such a stroke on the green. —*intr.* To putt the ball. [Variant of PUT.]
put·tee (pŭ-tē′, pŭt′ē) *n.* Also **put·ty** (pŭt′ē) *pl.* **-ties. 1.** A strip of cloth wound spirally around the leg from ankle to knee. **2.** A gaiter covering the lower leg. [Hindi *paṭṭī*, from Sanskrit *paṭṭikā*, from *paṭṭaṭ*†, cloth band.]
put·ter[1] (pŭt′ər) *n. Golf.* **1.** A short, stiff-shafted club used for putting. **2.** A golfer who is putting.
put·ter[2] (pŭt′ər) *v.* **-tered, -tering, -ters.** Also *chiefly British* **pot·ter** (pŏt′ər). —*intr.* To occupy oneself in an aimless or desultory manner. —*tr.* To waste (especially time) in idling. Used with *away.* [Variant of dialectal *potter*, probably from *pote*, to push, kick, Middle English *poten*, Old English *potian*, akin to Middle Dutch *pōten*†, to put in the ground.] —**put′ter·er** *n.*
putting green. *Golf.* **1.** The area at the end of a fairway in which the hole is placed, having more closely mowed turf than the rest of the course. **2.** An area for practicing putting.
put·ty (pŭt′ē) *n., pl.* **-ties. 1.** A doughlike cement made by mixing whiting and linseed oil, used to fill holes in woodwork and secure panes of glass. **2.** Any substance with a similar consistency or function. **3.** A fine lime cement used as a finishing coat on plaster. **4.** Yellowish or light brownish gray to grayish yellow or light grayish brown. See **color.** —*tr.v.* **puttied, -tying, -ties.** To fill, cover, or secure with putty. [French *potée* from Old French, contents of a pot, a potful, from *pot*, a pot, from Middle Low German, from Vulgar Latin *pottus* (attested only in Late Latin). See **pott-** in Appendix.*]
put·ty·root (pŭt′ē-ro͞ot′, -ro͝ot′) *n.* A North American orchid, *Aplectrum hyemale*, bearing a single leaf and yellowish-brown or purplish flowers. Also called "Adam-and-Eve." [From the use of the sticky substance in its corm as a cement.]
Pu·tu·ma·yo (po͞o′to͞o-mä′yō). A river rising in southwestern Colombia and flowing about 980 miles southeast to the Amazon River in northwestern Brazil.
put up. 1. To erect; build. **2.** To preserve; can: *put up jam.* **3.** To nominate. **4.** To provide (funds) in advance. **5.** To provide lodgings for: *put someone up for the night.* **6.** To incite to some action: *put someone up to a prank.*
put-up (po͝ot′ŭp′) *adj. Informal.* Planned or prearranged secretly.
Puy-de-Dôme (pwē-də-dōm′). An extinct volcanic peak, 4,806 feet high, in the Auvergne Mountains of south-central France.
Pu-yi, Henry. See **Hsüan T'ung.**
puz·zle (pŭz′əl) *v.* **-zled, -zling, -zles.** —*tr.* **1.** To cause uncertainty and indecision in; perplex. **2.** To clarify or solve (something confusing) by reasoning or study. Used with *out: He puzzled out the significance of her statement.* —*intr.* **1.** To be perplexed. **2.** To ponder over a problem in an effort to solve or understand it. —*n.* **1.** Something that puzzles. **2.** A toy, game, or testing device that tests ingenuity. **3.** The condition of being perplexed; bewilderment. [Origin obscure.] —**puz′zler** *n.*
Synonyms: *puzzle, perplex, mystify, bewilder, confound, baffle.* These verbs refer to various degrees of mental challenge or confusion. *Puzzle* implies presenting an intricate, difficult, but solvable problem. *Perplex* stresses uncertainty or anxiety over reaching a decision or solution. To *mystify* is to puzzle by purposely obscuring or concealing facts. *Bewilder* emphasizes not only perplexity, but extreme confusion of the mind. *Confound* strongly implies astonishment. To *baffle* is to outwit or frustrate by puzzling.
puz·zle·ment (pŭz′əl-mənt) *n.* The state of being confused or baffled; perplexity.
PVD Airport code for Providence, Rhode Island.
pvt., Pvt. private.
PWA, P.W.A. Public Works Administration.
PWM Airport code for Portland, Maine.
pwr. power.
pwt. pennyweight.
PX post exchange; Post Exchange.
pxt. pinxit.
py·a (pē-ä′) *n.* A coin equal to $1/100$ of the kyat of Burma. See table of exchange rates at **currency.** [Burmese.]
pyc·nid·i·um (pĭk-nĭd′ē-əm) *n., pl.* **-ia** (-ē-ə). *Botany.* A rounded or flask-shaped asexual fruiting body containing spores that occurs in certain fungi. [New Latin : Greek *puknos*, thick (see **puk-**[1] in Appendix*) + *-idium*, Latin diminutive suffix, from Greek *-idion.*] —**pyc·nid′i·al** *adj.*
pyc·nom·e·ter (pĭk-nŏm′ə-tər) *n.* A standard vessel used in measuring the density or specific gravity of materials. [Greek *puknos*, thick, dense (see **puk-**[1] in Appendix*) + METER.]
py·e·li·tis (pī′ə-lī′tĭs) *n.* **Pyelonephritis** *(see).* [New Latin : Greek *puelos*, basin (see **pleu-** in Appendix*) + -ITIS.]
py·e·lo·ne·phri·tis (pī′ə-lō-nĭ-frī′tĭs) *n.* Inflammation of both the kidney and its pelvis. [New Latin : Greek *puelos*, basin (see **pyelitis**) + NEPHRITIS.]
py·e·mi·a (pī-ē′mē-ə) *n.* The presence of pus in the blood. [New Latin : PY(O)- + -EMIA.] —**py·e′mic** *adj.*

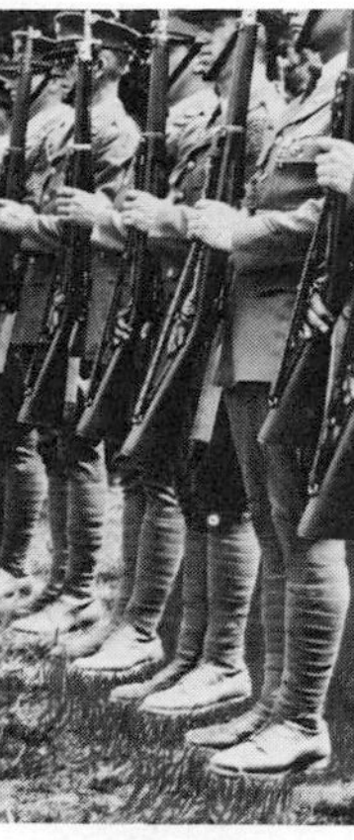
puttee

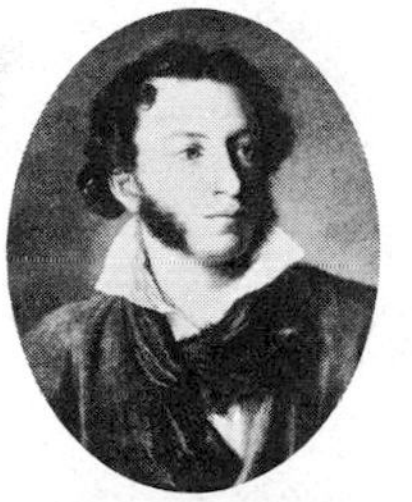
Aleksander Pushkin

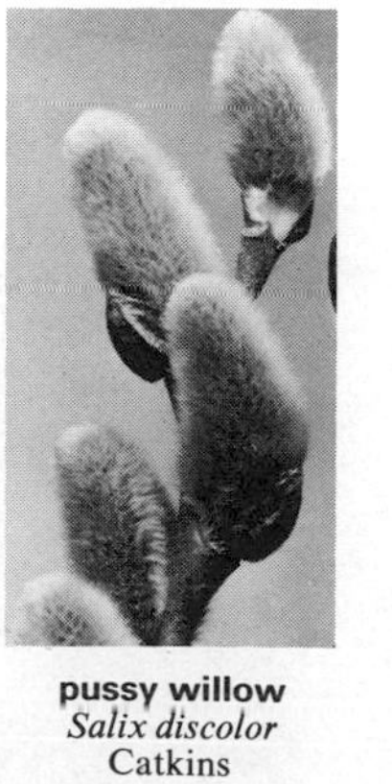
pussy willow
Salix discolor
Catkins

t tight/th thin, path/*th* this, bathe/ŭ cut/ûr urge/v valve/w with/y yes/z zebra, size/zh vision/ə about, item, edible, gallop, circus/ à *Fr.* ami/œ *Fr.* feu, *Ger.* schön/ü *Fr.* tu, *Ger.* über/KH *Ger.* ich, *Scot.* loch/N *Fr.* bon. ***Follows main vocabulary. †Of obscure origin.**

py·gid·i·um (pī-jĭd′ē-əm) *n., pl.* **-ia** (-ē-ə). The posterior body region of certain arthropods. [New Latin, from Greek *pugidion,* diminutive of *pugē*†, rump.] —**py·gid′i·al** *adj.*

Pyg·ma·lion (pĭg-māl′yən, -mā′lē-ən). *Greek Mythology.* A king of Cyprus who carved and then fell in love with a statue of a woman, which Aphrodite brought to life as Galatea.

pyg·moid (pĭg′moid′) *adj.* Resembling or characteristic of a Pygmy.

pyg·my (pĭg′mē) *n., pl.* **-mies.** Also **pig·my.** An individual of unusually small size or significance. —*adj.* Also **pig·my. 1.** Unusually or atypically small. **2.** Unimportant; trivial. [Middle English *pigmie,* from Latin *pygmaeus,* dwarfish, from Greek *pugmaios,* from *pugmē,* fist, the length from the elbow to the knuckles. See **peuk-** in Appendix.*]

Pyg·my (pĭg′mē) *n., pl.* **-mies.** Also **Pig·my. 1.** A member of any of several African and Asian peoples with a hereditary stature of from four to five feet. **2.** *Greek Mythology.* A member of a race of dwarfs. —*adj.* Of or pertaining to the Pygmies.

py·ja·mas. *Chiefly British.* Variant of **pajamas.**

pyk·nic (pĭk′nĭk) *adj. Anthropology.* Characterized by short, stocky, and powerful stature; endomorphic. [From Greek *puknos,* thick, dense. See **puk-**[1] in Appendix.*] —**pyk′nic** *n.*

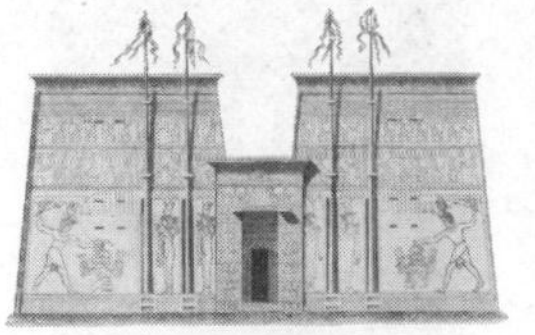

pylon
The temple of Apollinopolis Magna

py·lon (pī′lŏn′) *n.* **1.** A monumental gateway in the form of a pair of truncated pyramids serving as the entrance to an ancient Egyptian temple. **2.** Any large structure or structures marking an entrance or approach. **3.** *Aviation.* A tower marking a turning point in a race. **4.** A steel tower supporting high-tension wires. **5.** A temporary artificial leg. [Greek *pulōn,* gateway, from *pulē,* a gate. See **pulē** in Appendix.*]

py·lo·rus (pī-lôr′əs, -lōr′əs, pĭ-) *n.* The passage connecting the stomach and the duodenum. [Late Latin *pylōrus,* from Greek *pulōros,* "a gatekeeper" : *pulē,* a gate (see **pulē** in Appendix*) + *ouros,* watcher, from *horan,* to see (see **wer-**[4] in Appendix*).] —**py·lor′ic** (pī′lôr′ĭk, -lŏr′ĭk, pĭ-) *adj.*

Py·los (pī′lŏs′). A seaport in the southwestern Peloponnesus in southern Greece. Also formerly called "Navarino."

Pym (pĭm), **John.** 1584–1643. English statesman; Parliamentarian leader in the struggle against Charles I.

pyo–, py–. Indicates pus; for example, **pyorrhea, pyemia.** [From Greek *puon,* pus. See **pu-**[2] in Appendix.*]

py·o·der·ma (pī′ō-dûr′mə) *n.* Any pus-causing skin disease. [New Latin : PYO- + -DERMA.] —**py′o·der′mic** *adj.*

py·o·gen·e·sis (pī′ō-jĕn′ə-sĭs) *n. Pathology.* **Pyosis** *(see).* [PYO- + -GENESIS.] —**py′o·gen′ic** *adj.*

Pyong·yang (pyŭng′yäng′). The capital of North Korea, on the Taedong River east of Korea Bay. Population, 940,000.

py·or·rhe·a, py·or·rhoe·a (pī′ə-rē′ə) *n.* **1.** A discharge of pus. **2.** Inflammation of the gum and tooth sockets leading to loosening of the teeth. [New Latin : PYO- + -RRHEA.] —**py′or·rhe′al** *adj.*

py·o·sis (pī-ō′sĭs) *n.* The formation of pus. Also called "pyogenesis." [New Latin, from Greek *puōsis* : PY(O)- + -OSIS.]

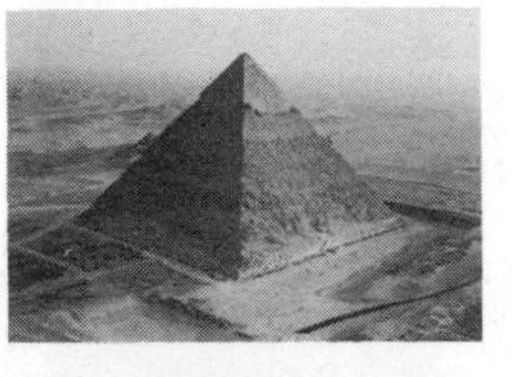

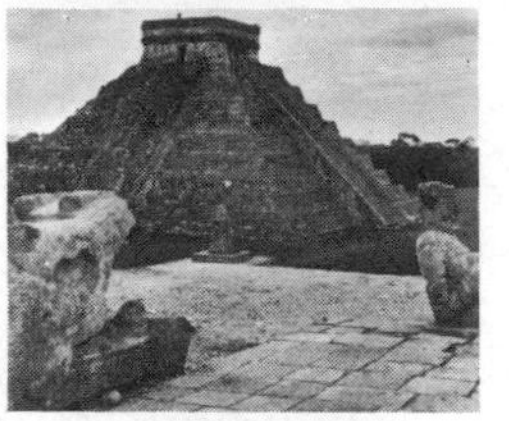

pyramid
Above: Egyptian
Below: Mayan

py·ra·can·tha (pī′rə-kăn′thə, pîr′ə-) *n.* A shrub of the genus *Pyracantha,* the **fire thorn** *(see).* [New Latin, from Greek *purakantha,* name of a shrub : PYR(O)- + Greek *akantha,* thorn, (see **ak-** in Appendix*).]

pyr·a·lid (pîr′ə-lĭd) *n.* Also **py·ral·i·did** (pĭ-răl′ə-dĭd). Any of various small or medium-sized moths of the large, widely distributed family Pyralididae. —*adj.* Of or belonging to the Pyralididae. [New Latin *pyralidae,* from *pyralis* (genus), from Greek *puralis* fabulous insect supposed to live in fire, from *pur,* fire. See **pūr-** in Appendix.*]

pyr·a·mid (pîr′ə-mĭd) *n.* **1.** *Geometry.* A polyhedron with a polygonal base and triangular faces meeting in a common vertex. **2.** Anything pyramidal in shape. **3.** A massive monument found especially in Egypt, having a rectangular base and four triangular faces culminating in a single apex, and serving as a tomb or temple. **4.** The transactions involved in pyramiding stock. —*v.* **pyramided, -miding, -mids.** —*tr.* **1.** To place or build in the shape of a pyramid. **2.** To build (an argument or thesis, for example) progressively from a basic general premise. **3.** To speculate in (stock) by making a series of buying and selling transactions in which paper profits are used as margin for buying more stock. —*intr.* **1.** To assume the shape of a pyramid. **2.** To increase rapidly and on a widening base. **3.** To pyramid stocks. [Latin *pyramis* (stem *pyramid-*), from Greek *puramis*†.]

py·ram·i·dal (pĭ-răm′ə-dəl) *adj.* Also **pyr·a·mid·ic** (pîr′ə-mĭd′ĭk), **pyr·a·mid·i·cal.** Of or having the shape of a pyramid. —**py·ram′i·dal·ly** *adv.*

py·rar·gy·rite (pī-rär′jə-rīt′, pĭ-) *n.* A deep red to black silver ore with composition Ag_3SbS_3. [German *Pyrargyrit* : PYR(O)- + Greek *arguros,* silver (see **arg-** in Appendix*) + -ITE.]

pyre (pīr) *n.* **1.** A heap of combustibles for burning a corpse as a funeral rite. **2.** Any pile of combustibles. [Latin *pyra,* from Greek *pura,* from *pur,* fire. See **pūr-** in Appendix.*]

py·rene (pī′rēn′, pī-rēn′) *n.* The stone of certain fruits. [New Latin *pyrena,* from Greek *purēn.* See **pūro-** in Appendix.*]

Pyr·e·nees (pîr′ə-nēz′). *Spanish* **Pi·ri·ne·os** (pē′rē-nā′ōs). The mountain range between France and Spain, extending for 260 miles between the Bay of Biscay and the Mediterranean. Highest elevation, Pico de Aneto (11,168 feet). —**Pyr′e·ne′an** *adj.*

py·re·noid (pī-rē′noid′, pîr′ə-) *n.* One of the protein granules of certain algae and similar plants in which starch is formed. [PYREN(E) (fruit stone; from shape of its nucleus) + -OID.]

py·re·thrin (pī-rē′thrĭn, -rĕth′rĭn) *n.* Either of two viscous liquid esters, $C_{21}H_{28}O_3$ or $C_{22}H_{28}O_5$, that are extracted from pyrethrum flowers and are used as insecticides. See **cinerin.** [French *pyréthrine* : PYRETHR(UM) + -IN.]

py·re·thrum (pī-rē′thrəm, -rĕth′rəm) *n.* **1.** Any of several Old World plants of the genus *Chrysanthemum* and related genera, such as *C. coccineum,* cultivated for its showy flowers. **2.** The dried flowers of *C. cinerariaefolium* or *C. coccineum,* used as an insecticide. [New Latin, from Latin, pellitory, from Greek *purethron,* feverfew, perhaps from *puretos,* fever. See **pyretic.**]

py·ret·ic (pī-rĕt′ĭk) *adj.* Characterized or affected by fever; feverish. [New Latin *pyreticus,* from Greek *puretikos,* from *puretos,* fever, from *pur,* fire. See **pūr-** in Appendix.*]

Py·rex (pī′rĕks′) *n.* A trademark for any of various types of heat-resistant and chemical-resistant glass.

py·rex·i·a (pī-rĕk′sē-ə) *n.* Fever. [New Latin, from Greek *purexis,* from *puressein,* to have a fever, from *puretos,* fever. See **pyretic.**] —**py·rex′i·al, py·rex′ic** *adj.*

pyr·he·li·om·e·ter (pīr′hē-lē-ŏm′ə-tər, pîr′-) *n.* Any of various devices that measure all or restricted components of incident solar radiation. [PYR(O)- + HELIO- + -METER.]

py·ric (pī′rĭk, pîr′ĭk) *adj.* Of, pertaining to, or resulting from burning. [French *pyrique* : PYR(O)- + -IC.]

pyr·i·dine (pîr′ə-dēn′) *n.* A flammable, colorless or yellowish liquid base, C_5H_5N, used to synthesize vitamins and drugs, as a solvent, and as a denaturant for alcohol. [PYR(O)- + -ID + -INE.] —**py·rid·ic** (pī-rĭd′ĭk) *adj.*

pyr·i·dox·ine (pîr′ə-dŏk′sēn′, -sĭn) *n.* Also **pyr·i·dox·in** (-sĭn). A pyridine derivative, $C_8H_{11}O_3N$, occurring in plant and animal tissues and active in various metabolic processes. Also called "vitamin B_6." [PYRID(INE) + OX- + -INE.]

pyr·i·form (pîr′ə-fôrm′) *adj.* Pear-shaped. [New Latin *pyriformis* : Medieval Latin *pyrum,* variant of Latin *pirum,* PEAR + -FORM.]

py·rim·i·dine (pī-rĭm′ə-dēn′, pĭ-) *n.* **1.** A liquid and crystalline organic base, $C_4H_4N_2$. **2.** Any of several basic compounds, such as uracil, having a molecular structure similar to pyrimidine and found in living matter as a nucleotide component. [German *Pyrimidin,* variant of PYRIDINE.]

py·rite (pī′rīt′) *n.* A yellow to brown, widely occurring mineral sulfide, FeS_2, used as an iron ore and to produce sulfur dioxide for sulfuric acid. Also called "fool's gold," "iron pyrites." [Latin *pyrītēs,* PYRITES.] —**py·rit′ic** (pī-rĭt′ĭk), **py·rit′i·cal** *adj.*

py·ri·tes (pī-rī′tēz, pə-) *n., pl.* **pyrites.** Any of various natural metallic sulfides, especially of iron. [Latin *pyrītēs,* flint, pyrite, from Greek *puritēs (lithos),* "fire (stone)," from *puritēs,* of fire, from *pur,* fire. See **pūr-** in Appendix.*]

pyro–. Indicates: **1.** Fire or heat; for example, **pyrotechnic. 2.** Resulting from or by the action of fire or heat; for example, **pyrography.** [From Greek *pur,* fire. See **pūr-** in Appendix.*]

pyro. pyrotechnics.

py·ro·cat·e·chol (pī′rō-kăt′ə-chôl′, -chōl′, -shôl′, -shōl′) *n.* A colorless, crystalline organic compound, $C_6H_4(OH)_2$, used as an antiseptic and photographic developer. [PYRO- + CATECH(U) + -OL.]

py·ro·cel·lu·lose (pī′rō-sĕl′yə-lōs′, -lōz′) *n.* A cellulose nitrate used as a component of smokeless powder.

py·ro·chem·i·cal (pī′rō-kĕm′ə-kəl) *adj.* Designating or pertaining to chemical activity at elevated temperatures. —**py′ro·chem′i·cal·ly** *adv.*

py·ro·clas·tic (pī′rō-klăs′tĭk) *adj.* Formed by rock fragmentation resulting from volcanic ejection. [PYRO- + -CLAST + -IC.]

py·ro·e·lec·tric (pī′rō-ə-lĕk′trĭk) *adj.* Exhibiting or pertaining to pyroelectricity. —*n.* A pyroelectric material.

py·ro·e·lec·tric·i·ty (pī′rō-ə-lĕk′trĭs′ə-tē) *n.* The generation of electric charge on a crystal by change of temperature.

py·ro·gal·lol (pī′rō-găl′ôl′, -ōl′) *n.* A white lustrous crystalline compound, $C_6H_3(OH)_3$, used as a photographic developer and to treat skin diseases. Also called "pyrogallic acid." [PYRO- + GALL(IC) + -OL (hydroxyl group).] —**py′ro·gal′lic** *adj.*

py·ro·gen (pī′rə-jən) *n.* A substance that produces fever. [PYRO- + -GEN.]

py·ro·gen·ic (pī′rō-jĕn′ĭk) *adj.* Also **py·rog·e·nous** (pī-rŏj′ə-nəs). **1.** Producing or produced by fever. **2.** Caused by or generating heat. **3.** *Geology.* **Igneous** *(see).*

py·rog·ra·phy (pī-rŏg′rə-fē) *n.* **1.** The art or process of producing designs on wood, leather, or other material by using heated tools or a fine flame. **2.** A design made by this process. [PYRO- + -GRAPHY.] —**py′ro·graph** (pī′rə-grăf′, -gräf′) *n.* —**py·rog′ra·pher** *n.* —**py′ro·graph′ic** *adj.*

py·ro·lig·ne·ous (pī′rō-lĭg′nē-əs) *adj.* Made by the destructive distillation of wood. [PYRO- + LIGNEOUS.]

pyroligneous acid. A reddish-brown wood distillate containing acetic acid, methyl alcohol, acetone, and a tarry residue. Also called "wood vinegar."

py·ro·lu·site (pī′rō-lo͞o′sīt′) *n.* A soft, black to dark gray ore of manganese, consisting essentially of manganese dioxide. [German *Pyrolusit* : PYRO- + Greek *lousis,* a washing, from *louein,* to wash (see **lou-** in Appendix*) + -ITE (it is used in purifying glass).]

py·rol·y·sis (pī-rŏl′ə-sĭs) *n.* Chemical change caused by heat. [PYRO- + -LYSIS.] —**py′ro·lyt′ic** (pī′rə-lĭt′ĭk) *adj.*

py·ro·lyze (pī′rə-līz′) *tr.v.* **-lyzed, -lyzing, -lyzes.** To subject (something) to pyrolysis. [PYRO- + -LYZE.]

py·ro·man·cy (pī′rə-măn′sē) *n.* Divination by fire or flames. [Middle English *piromance,* from Old French *pyromancie,* from Late Latin *pyromantīa,* from Greek *puromanteia* : PYRO- + -MANCY.] —**py′ro·man′tic** (pī′rə-măn′tĭk) *adj.*

py·ro·ma·ni·a (pī′rō-mā′nē-ə, -mān′yə) *n.* The uncontrollable impulse to start fires. [PYRO- + -MANIA.] —**py′ro·ma′ni·ac′** (-mā′nē-ăk′) *adj.* & *n.* —**py′ro·ma·ni′a·cal** (-mə-nī′ə-kəl) *adj.*

py·ro·met·al·lur·gy (pī′rō-mĕt′l-ûr′jē) *n.* Metallurgy that depends on the action of heat, as smelting.

ă pat/ā pay/âr care/ä father/b bib/ch church/d deed/ĕ pet/ē be/f fife/g gag/h hat/hw which/ĭ pit/ī pie/îr pier/j judge/k kick/l lid, needle/m mum/n no, sudden/ng thing/ŏ pot/ō toe/ô paw, for/oi noise/ou out/o͝o took/o͞o boot/p pop/r roar/s sauce/sh ship, dish/

py·rom·e·ter (pī-rŏm′ə-tər) *n.* An electrical thermometer for measuring high temperatures. [PYRO- + -METER.] —**py′ro·met′ric** (pī′rə-mĕt′rĭk), **py′ro·met′ri·cal** *adj.* —**py·rom′e·try** *n.*

py·ro·mor·phite (pī′rə-môr′fīt) *n.* A lead ore with composition $Pb_5(PO_4,AsO_4)_3Cl$, occurring in green, brown, or yellow crystals. [German *Pyromorphit* : PYRO- + MORPH(O)- + -ITE (its crystalline form occurs when it is heated).]

py·rope (pī′rōp′) *n.* A deep-red garnet, $Mg_3Al_2Si_3O_{12}$, used as a gem. [Middle English *pirope*, from Old French, from Latin *pyrōpus*, gold bronze, fiery garnet, from Greek *purōpos*, "fiery-eyed" : PYR(O)- + Greek *ōps*, eye (see **okw-** in Appendix*).]

py·ro·phor·ic (pī′rə-fôr′ĭk, -fŏr′ĭk) *adj.* **1.** Spontaneously igniting in air. **2.** Producing sparks by friction. [From Greek *purophoros*, "fire-bearing" : PYRO- + -PHOROUS.]

py·ro·phos·phor·ic acid (pī′rō-fŏs-fôr′ĭk, -fŏr′ĭk). A syrupy viscous liquid, $H_4P_2O_7$, used as a catalyst and in organic chemical manufacture. [PYRO- + PHOSPHORIC (it is made by heating a phosphoric acid).]

py·ro·phyl·lite (pī′rō-fĭl′īt′, pī-rŏf′ə-līt′) *n.* A silvery white or pale-green mineral aluminum silicate, $Al_2Si_4O_{10}(OH)_2$, occurring naturally in soft, compact masses. [German *Pyrophyllit* : PYRO- + PHYLL(O)- + -ITE (its foliations spread when heated).]

py·ro·sis (pī-rō′sĭs) *n.* Heartburn. [Greek *purōsis*, a burning, from *puroun*, to burn, from *pur*, fire. See **pūr-** in Appendix.*]

py·ro·stat (pī′rə-stăt, pîr′-) *n.* **1.** An automatic sensing device that activates an alarm or extinguisher in case of fire. **2.** A high-temperature thermostat. [PYRO- + -STAT.]

py·ro·sul·fate (pī′rə-sŭl′fāt, pîr′ə-) *n.* A salt of pyrosulfuric acid. [PYROSULF(URIC ACID) + -ATE (salt).]

py·ro·sul·fu·ric acid (pī′rō-sŭl-fyŏŏr′ĭk, -pîr′ō-). A heavy, oily, colorless to dark-brown liquid, $H_2S_2O_7$, produced by adding sulfur trioxide to concentrated sulfuric acid and used in petroleum refining and explosives. [PYRO- + SULFURIC.]

py·ro·tech·nic (pī′rə-tĕk′nĭk, pîr′ə-) *adj.* Also **py·ro·tech·ni·cal** (-nĭ-kəl). **1.** Of or pertaining to fireworks. **2.** Resembling fireworks; brilliant: *a pyrotechnic wit.* —**py′ro·tech′ni·cal·ly** *adv.*

py·ro·tech·nics (pī′rə-tĕk′nĭks, pîr′ə-) *n.* Also **py·ro·tech·ny** (-nē) (for sense 1). **1.** *Abbr.* **pyro., pyrotech.** The art of manufacturing or setting off fireworks. Used with a singular verb. **2.** A fireworks display. Used with a singular or plural verb. **3.** A brilliant display, as of rhetoric or wit, or of virtuosity in the performing arts. Used with a singular or plural verb. —**py′ro·tech′nist** *n.*

py·rox·ene (pī-rŏk′sēn′) *n.* Any of a group of crystalline mineral silicates common in igneous and metamorphic rocks and containing two metallic oxides, as of magnesium, iron, calcium, or sodium. [French *pyroxène*, "stranger to fire" (i.e., foreign substance in igneous rocks) : PYRO- + Greek *xenos*, stranger (see **xenos** in Appendix*).] —**py′rox·en′ic** (pī′rŏk-sĕn′ĭk) *adj.*

py·rox·e·nite (pī-rŏk′sə-nīt′) *n.* An igneous rock consisting chiefly of pyroxenes.

py·rox·y·lin (pī-rŏk′sə-lĭn) *n.* Also **py·rox·y·line** (-lēn′, -lĭn). A highly flammable nitrocellulose used in the manufacture of collodion, plastics, and lacquers. [PYRO- + XYL(O)- + -IN.]

pyr·rhic (pîr′ĭk) *n.* A Greek metrical foot composed of two short syllables. —*adj.* Of or characterized by pyrrhics. [Latin *(pēs) pyrrhichius*, pyrrhic (foot), from Greek *(pous) purrhikhios*, from *purrhikhē*, a war dance, from *Purrhikhos*, eponymous chorist.]

Pyr·rhic victory (pîr′ĭk). A victory won with staggering losses, such as that of Pyrrhus (319–272 B.C.), King of Epirus, over the Romans at Asculum in 279 B.C.

pyr·rho·tite (pîr′ə-tīt) *n.* Also **pyr·rho·tine** (-tīn). A naturally occurring brownish-bronze iron sulfide, FeS, characterized by weak magnetic properties and used as an iron ore and in the manufacture of sulfuric acid. Also called "magnetic pyrites." [German *Pyrrhotin*, from Greek *purrhotēs*, redness, from *purrhos*, fiery, red, from *pur*, fire. See **pūr-** in Appendix.*]

pyr·rhu·lox·i·a (pîr′ə-lŏk′sē-ə) *n.* A crested gray and red bird, *Pyrrhuloxia sinuata*, of the southwestern United States and Mexico, having a short, thick bill. [New Latin : *Pyrrhula*, finch, from Greek *purrhoulas*, red bird, from *purrhos*, red (see **pyrrole**) + *Loxia*, crossbill, from Greek *loxos*, oblique (see **loxodromic**).]

pyr·role (pī-rōl′, pîr′ōl′) *n.* A yellowish or brown liquid, C_4H_5N, having a characteristic odor similar to chloroform and used to manufacture a wide variety of drugs. [Greek *purrhos*, red, tawny, from *pur*, fire (see **pūr-** in Appendix*) + -OLE.] —**pyr·rol′ic** (pī-rōl′ĭk) *adj.*

py·ru·vic acid (pī-rōō′vĭk, pĭ-). A colorless liquid, CH_3CO-COOH, formed as a fundamental intermediate in protein and carbohydrate metabolism. [PYR(O)- + Latin *ūva*, grape (see **ōg-** in Appendix*).]

Py·thag·o·ras (pĭ-thăg′ər-əs). Greek philosopher of the sixth century B.C.

Pythagoras

Py·thag·o·re·an·ism (pĭ-thăg′ə-rē′ə-nĭz′əm) *n.* The syncretistic philosophy expounded by Pythagoras, chiefly distinguished by its description of reality in terms of arithmetical relationships. —**Py·thag′o·re′an** (pĭ-thăg′ə-rē′ən) *n. & adj.*

Pythagorean theorem. The theorem that the sum of the squares of the lengths of the sides of a right triangle is equal to the square of the length of the hypotenuse.

Pyth·e·as (pĭth′ē-əs). Greek navigator of Marseille (fourth century B.C.); explored the Atlantic coast of Europe.

Pyth·i·a (pĭth′ē-ə). The oracular priestess of Apollo at Delphi.

Pyth·i·an (pĭth′ē-ən) *adj.* **1.** Of or pertaining to Delphi, the temple of Apollo at Delphi, or its oracle. **2.** Of or pertaining to the Pythian games. [From Latin *Pythius*, from Greek *Puthios*, from *Puthō*, *Puthōn*, ancient name of Delphi, after the serpent PYTHON.] —**Pyth′ic** *adj.*

Pythian games. In ancient Greece, a pan-Hellenic festival of athletic tournaments held every four years at Delphi in honor of Apollo.

py·thon (pī′thŏn, -thən) *n.* **1.** Any of various large, nonvenomous Old World snakes of the family Pythonidae, that coil around and crush their prey. **2.** A soothsaying spirit or demon, or a person possessed by such a spirit. [After PYTHON.] —**py′tho·nine** (pī′thə-nīn′) *adj.*

Py·thon (pī′thŏn′, -thən). *Greek Mythology.* A dragon or serpent that was the tutelary demon of the oracular cult at Delphi until killed and expropriated by Apollo.

pyrotechnics

py·tho·ness (pī′thə-nĭs, pĭth′ə-) *n.* **1.** The priestess of Apollo at Delphi. **2.** A prophetess. [Middle English *phitonesse*, from Old French *phitonise, pithonise*, from Late Latin *pythōnissa*, from Greek *Puthōn*.]

py·thon·ic (pī-thŏn′ĭk) *adj.* **1.** Of, pertaining to, or resembling a python. **2.** Of or like an oracle; prophetic.

py·u·ri·a (pī-yŏŏr′ē-ə) *n.* The abnormal condition of pus in the urine. [New Latin : PY(O)- + -URIA.]

pyx (pĭks) *n.* Also **pix. 1.** *Ecclesiastical.* **a.** A container in which supplies of wafers for the Eucharist are kept. **b.** A container in which the Eucharist is carried to the sick. **2.** A chest in a mint in which specimen coins are placed to await assay. [Middle English *pyxe*, from Latin *pyxis*, box, from Greek *puxis*, box, PYXIS.]

pyx·id·i·um (pĭk-sĭd′ē-əm) *n., pl.* **-ia** (-ē-ə). *Botany.* A pyxis (see). [New Latin, from Greek *puxidion*, diminutive of *puxis*, PYXIS.]

pyx·ie (pĭk′sē) *n.* A creeping evergreen shrub, *Pyxidanthera barbulata*, native to pine barrens of the eastern United States, having small white or pinkish flowers. [Latin *Pyxidanthera* : PYXIS + ANTHER.]

pyx·is (pĭk′sĭs) *n., pl.* **pyxides** (pĭk′sə-dēz′). *Botany.* A seed capsule having a circular lid that falls off to release the seeds. Also called "pyxidium." [Greek *puxis*, box. See **puxos** in Appendix.*]

Pyx·is (pĭk′sĭs) *n.* A constellation in the Southern Hemisphere, near Antlia and Puppis. [New Latin *Pyxis (nautica)*, "the Mariner's Compass," from Greek *puxis*, box, PYXIS.]

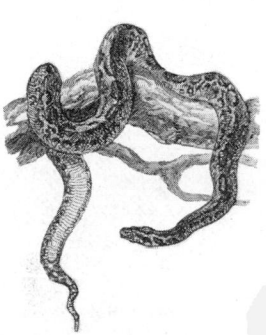

python
Python molurus
Indian python

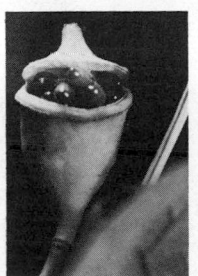

pyxis
Pyxis of twin-leaf

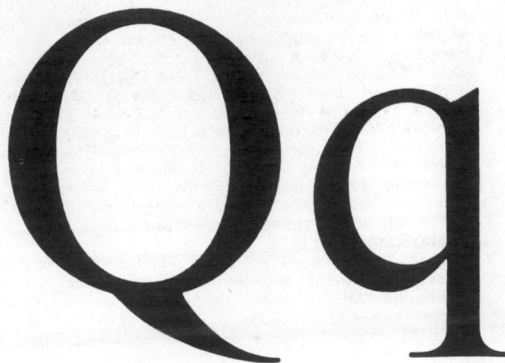

| 1 | 2 | 3 | 4 | 5 | 6 | 7 | 8 | 9 | 10 | 11 | 12 |
| Phoenician | | Greek | | | Roman | Medieval | | | Modern | | |

Around 1000 B.C. *the Phoenicians and other Semites of Syria and Palestine began to use a graphic sign in the form (1). They gave it the name* qōph, *meaning "monkey," and used it for an emphatic voiceless velar which is not found in English or in any other Indo-European language. After 900 B.C. the Greeks borrowed the sign from the Phoenicians (2), subsequently using a form in which the vertical did not cross the circle (3). They also changed its name to* qoppa. *Since the Greeks had no use in their language for the Semitic sound, they used the sign for the same sound* k *which they normally expressed with their sign* kappa; *and subsequently they dropped the sign from their alphabet as useless. The Greek form (3) passed via Etruscan to the Roman alphabet (4). The Romans gradually developed the habit of writing a curved tail in place of the vertical (5). They used the sign for a* k *sound before* u. *The Roman Monumental Capital (6) is the prototype of our modern capital, printed (9) and written (10). The written Roman form (5) developed into the late Roman and medieval Uncial (7) and Cursive (8), in which the tail changed into a long vertical line at the right. These are the bases of our modern small letter, printed (11) and written (12).*

q, Q (kyōō) *n., pl.* **q's** *or rare* **qs, Q's** *or* **Qs. 1.** The 17th letter of the modern English alphabet. See **alphabet. 2.** Any of the speech sounds represented by this letter.

q, Q, q., Q. Note: As an abbreviation or symbol, *q* may be a small or a capital letter, with or without a period. Established forms or those generally preferred precede the definition. When no form is given, all four forms are in general use in that sense. **1. q.** quart. **2. q.** quarter. **3. q.** quarterly. **4. q., Q.** *pl.* **Qq.** quarto. **5. Q** *Chess.* queen. **6. q.** query. **7. q.** question. **8. Q** quetzal. **9. q.** quintal. **10. q.** quire. **11.** The 17th in a series; 16th when *J* is omitted.

Qair·wan. See **Kairouan.**

Qan·da·har. See **Kandahar.**

Qa·tar (kä′tär′). A British-protected Arab sheikdom occupying 4,000 square miles on a peninsula in the Persian Gulf. Population, 60,000. Capital, Doha.

Qat·ta·ra Depression (kä-tä′rä). A depression occupying 7,500 square miles in the Libyan Desert in northern Egypt.

qb quarterback.

QB *Chess.* queen's bishop.

q.b. quarterback.

QBP *Chess.* queen's bishop's pawn.

Q.C. 1. quartermaster corps. **2.** Queen's Counsel.

Q.E.D. which was to be demonstrated or proved (Latin *quod erat demonstrandum*).

Q.E.F. which was to be done (Latin *quod erat faciendum*).

QKt *Chess.* queen's knight.

QKtP *Chess.* queen's knight's pawn.

ql. quintal.

qlty. quality.

QM, Q.M. quartermaster.

QMC, Q.M.C. quartermaster corps.

QMG, Q.M.G. Quartermaster General.

qn. question.

qoph (kôf) *n.* The 19th letter of the Hebrew alphabet. See **alphabet.** [Hebrew *qōph,* from a Northwest Semitic word meaning "eye of a needle."]

QP *Chess.* queen's pawn.

q. pl. as much as you please (Latin *quantum placet*).

qq. questions.

qq.v. which (things) see (New Latin *quae vide*).

QR *Chess.* queen's rook.

qr. 1. quarter. **2.** quarterly. **3.** quire.

QRP *Chess.* queen's rook's pawn.

q.s. as much as suffices (Latin *quantum sufficit*).

QSO *Astronomy.* quasi-stellar object.

QSRS *Astronomy.* quasi-stellar radio source.

qt quart.

qt. 1. quantity. **2.** quart.

q.t. *Slang.* Quiet; in secret. Used chiefly in the phrase *on the q.t.*

qto. quarto.

qty. quantity.

qu. 1. queen. **2.** query. **3.** question.

qua (kwā, kwä) *adv.* In the function or capacity of: "*But the war qua war could not shock us greatly.*" (Stanley Kauffman). [Latin *quā,* ablative singular feminine of *qui,* who. See **kwo-** in Appendix.*]

quack[1] (kwăk) *n.* The characteristic sound uttered by a duck. —*intr.v.* **quacked, quacking, quacks.** To utter a quack. [Imitative, like Dutch *kwaken* and German *quaken.*]

quack[2] (kwăk) *n.* **1.** An untrained person who pretends to have medical knowledge. **2.** A charlatan; mountebank. Also *archaic* "quacksalver." —See Synonyms at **impostor.** —*adj.* Pertaining to or characteristic of a quack. [Shortened from QUACK-SALVER.] —**quack′er·y** *n.*

quack grass. Couch grass (*see*). [Variant of QUITCH (or *quick*) GRASS.]

quack·sal·ver (kwăk′săl′vər) *n. Archaic.* A **quack** (*see*). [From early modern Dutch *quacksalver,* from Middle Dutch *quacsalven,* to cure with home remedies : *quac-,* unguent (see **gwĕbh-**[2] in Appendix*) + *salven,* to salve (see **selp-** in Appendix*).]

quad[1] (kwŏd) *n. Informal.* A **quadrangle** (*see*).

quad[2] (kwŏd) *n. Printing.* A type metal, **quadrat** (*see*).

quad[3] (kwŏd) *n.* Shortened form of **quadruplet.**

quad. 1. quadrangle. **2.** quadrant. **3.** quadrilateral.

quad·ran·gle (kwŏd′răng′gəl) *n. Abbr.* **quad. 1.** *Geometry.* A plane figure consisting of four points, no three of which are collinear, connected by straight lines. **2. a.** A rectangular area surrounded on all four sides by buildings. **b.** The buildings bordering this area. Also informally called "quad." **3.** The area of land shown on one atlas sheet charted by the United States Geological Survey. [Middle English, from Old French, from Late Latin *quadr(i)angulum,* from Latin, neuter of *quadr(i)angulus,* having four angles : QUADR(I)- + *angulus,* ANGLE.]

quad·rant (kwŏd′rənt) *n. Abbr.* **quad. 1.** *Geometry.* **a.** A circular arc subtending a central angle of 90 degrees; ¼ of the circumference of a circle. **b.** The plane area bounded by two perpendicular radii and the arc they subtend. **c.** Any of the four areas into which a plane is divided by the reference axes in a Cartesian coordinate system, designated *first, second, third,* and *fourth,* counting clockwise from the area in which both coordinates are positive. **2.** Anything, such as a machine part, that is shaped like a quarter circle. **3.** An early instrument for measuring altitudes, consisting of a 90-degree graduated arc with a movable radius for measuring angles. [Middle English, quarter of a day, from Latin *quadrāns,* fourth part, quarter. See **kwetwer-** in Appendix.*]

quad·rat (kwŏd′rət, -răt′) *n. Printing.* A piece of type metal lower than the raised typeface, and one en or more in width, used for filling spaces and blank lines. Also called "quad." [Middle English, a square geometrical instrument, variant of QUADRATE.]

quad·rate (kwŏd′rāt′, -rĭt) *n.* **1.** *Rare.* **a.** A square or cube. **b.** An approximately square or cubic area, space, or object. **2.** *Zoology.* A bone or cartilaginous structure of the skull, join-

quadrangle

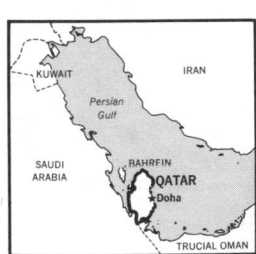

Qatar

ă pat/ā pay/âr care/ä father/b bib/ch church/d deed/ĕ pet/ē be/f fife/g gag/h hat/hw which/ĭ pit/ī pie/îr pier/j judge/k kick/l lid, needle/m mum/n no, sudden/ng thing/ŏ pot/ō toe/ô paw, for/oi noise/ou out/ŏŏ took/ōō boot/p pop/r roar/s sauce/sh ship, dish/

ing the upper and lower jaws in birds, fish, reptiles, and amphibians. —*adj.* **1.** Having four sides and four angles; square or rectangular. **2.** *Zoology.* Designating the quadrate bone or cartilage. —*v.* **quadrated, -rating, -rates.** —*intr.* To correspond; agree. —*tr.* To correspond to; conform to. [Middle English, square, from Latin *quadrātus,* past participle of *quadrāre,* to make square, from *quadrus,* a square. See **kwetwer-** in Appendix.*]

quad·rat·ic (kwŏ-drăt′ĭk) *adj.* Of, pertaining to, or containing mathematical quantities of the second degree or less. [From QUADRATE.] —**quad·rat′ic** *n.*

quadratic equation. An equation of the second degree, having the general form $ax^2 + bx + c = 0$, where *a, b,* and *c* are constants.

quadratic formula. The formula $x = [-b \pm \sqrt{(b^2 - 4ac)}]/2a$, used to compute the roots of a **quadratic equation** *(see).*

quad·rat·ics (kwŏ-drăt′ĭks) *n.* Plural in form, used with a singular verb. The algebra of quadratic equations.

quad·ra·ture (kwŏd′rə-chŏŏr′) *n.* **1.** The process of making something square. **2.** *Mathematics.* The process of constructing a square equal in area to a given surface. **3.** *Astronomy.* Any configuration in which the angular separation of two celestial bodies, as measured from a third, is 90 degrees.

quad·ren·ni·al (kwŏ-drĕn′ē-əl) *adj.* **1.** Happening once in four years. **2.** Lasting for four years. —*n.* An event occurring every four years.

quad·ren·ni·um (kwŏ-drĕn′ē-əm) *n., pl.* **-ums** or **quadrennia** (-drĕn′ē-ə). A period of four years. [Latin *quadr(i)ennium* : QUADR(I)- + *annus,* year (see **at-** in Appendix*).]

quadri-, quadr-. Indicates four; for example, **quadriceps, quadric.** [Latin. See **kwetwer-** in Appendix.*]

quad·ric (kwŏd′rĭk) *adj.* Of or pertaining to geometric surfaces that are defined by quadratic equations. [QUADR(I)- + -IC.]

quad·ri·cen·ten·ni·al (kwŏd′rĭ-sĕn-tĕn′ē-əl) *n.* A 400th anniversary. —**quad′ri·cen·ten′ni·al** *adj.*

quad·ri·ceps (kwŏd′rĭ-sĕps′) *n.* The large four-part extensor muscle at the front of the thigh. [New Latin : QUADRI- + (BI)CEPS.] —**quad′ri·cip′i·tal** (kwŏd′rĭ-sĭp′ə-təl) *adj.*

quad·ri·lat·er·al (kwŏd′rə-lăt′ər-əl) *n. Abbr.* **quad.** *Geometry.* A four-sided polygon. —*adj. Abbr.* **quad.** Having four sides.

qua·drille[1] (kwŏ-drĭl′, kwə-, kə-) *n.* **1.** A square dance of French origin composed of five figures and performed by four couples. **2.** Music for this dance in 6/8 and 2/4 time. [French, originally "one of the four divisions of an army, group of knights at a tournament," from Spanish *cuadrilla,* diminutive of *cuadra,* "square," from Latin *quadra.* See **kwetwer-** in Appendix.*]

qua·drille[2] (kwŏ-drĭl′, kwə-, kə-) *n.* A card game popular during the 18th century, played by four people with a deck of 40 cards. [French, perhaps from Spanish *cuartillo,* from *cuarto,* fourth, from Latin *quārtus.* See **kwetwer-** in Appendix.*]

quad·ril·lion (kwŏ-drĭl′yən) *n.* **1.** The cardinal number represented by 1 followed by 15 zeros; usually written 10^{15}. **2.** In British usage, the cardinal number represented by 1 followed by 24 zeros; usually written 10^{24}. See **number.** [French : QUADR(I)- + (M)ILLION.] —**quad·ril′lion** *adj.*

quad·ril·lionth (kwŏ-drĭl′yənth) *n.* The ordinal number quadrillion in a series. See **number.** —**quad·ril′lionth** *adj. & adv.*

quad·ri·par·tite (kwŏd′rə-pär′tīt′) *adj.* **1.** Consisting of or divided into four parts. **2.** Involving four participants.

quad·ri·va·lent (kwŏd′rə-vā′lənt) *adj. Chemistry.* **1.** Having four valences. **2.** *Rare.* Having a valence of four; tetravalent. —**quad′ri·va′lence, quad′ri·va′len·cy** *n.*

quad·riv·i·al (kwŏ-drĭv′ē-əl) *adj.* **1.** Having four roads or ways leading out. **2.** Of or pertaining to the quadrivium.

quad·riv·i·um (kwŏ-drĭv′ē-əm) *n., pl.* **-ia** (-ē-ə). The higher division of the seven liberal arts in the Middle Ages, composed of geometry, astronomy, arithmetic, and music. Compare **trivium.** [Late Latin, from Latin, place where four ways meet : QUADRI- + *via,* road, way (see **wei-**[2] in Appendix*).]

quad·roon (kwŏ-drōōn′) *n.* A person having one quarter Negro ancestry. [From Spanish *cuarteron,* from *cuarto,* quarter, from Latin *quārtus.* See **kwetwer-** in Appendix.*]

quadru-. Indicates four; for example, **quadrumanous.** [Latin. See **kwetwer-** in Appendix.*]

quad·ru·ma·nous (kwŏ-drōō′mə-nəs) *adj.* Also **quad·ru·ma·nal** (-nəl). *Zoology.* Having four feet with opposable first digits, as primates other than man. [QUADRU- + Latin *manus,* hand (see **man-**[2] in Appendix*).]

quad·ru·ped (kwŏd′rŏŏ-pĕd′) *n.* A four-footed animal. —*adj.* Four-footed. [Latin *quadrupēs* : QUADRU- + -PED.] —**quad·ru′pe·dal** (kwŏ-drōō′pə-dəl, kwŏd′rŏŏ-pĕd′l) *adj.*

quad·ru·ple (kwŏ-drōō′pəl, -drŭp′əl, kwŏd′rŏŏ-pəl) *adj.* **1.** Having four parts. **2.** Multiplied by four; fourfold. **3.** *Music.* Having four beats to the measure. —*n.* A number or amount four times as many or as much as another. —*v.* **quadrupled, -pling, -ples.** —*tr.* To multiply or increase by four; to quadruplicate. —*intr.* To become quadrupled. [French, from Latin *quadruplus* : QUADRU- + *-plus,* "-fold" (see **pel-**[3] in Appendix*).] —**quad·ru′ply** *adv.*

quad·ru·plet (kwŏ-drŭp′lĭt, -drōō′plĭt, kwŏd′rŏŏ-plĭt) *n.* **1.** A group or combination of four associated by common properties or behavior. **2.** One of four offspring born in a single birth.

quad·ru·pli·cate (kwŏ-drōō′plĭ-kĭt) *adj.* **1.** Multiplied by four; quadruple. **2.** Fourth in a group or set. —*n.* One of a set or group of four. —*v.* (kwŏ-drōō′plĭ-kāt′) **quadruplicated, -cating, -cates.** —*tr.* To multiply four times. —*intr.* To become quadruplicated. [Latin *quadruplicātus,* past participle of *quadruplicāre,* to multiply by four, from *quadruplex,* fourfold : QUADRU- + *-plex,* "-fold" (see **plek-** in Appendix*).] —**quad·ru′pli·cate·ly** (-kĭt-lē) *adv.* —**quad·ru′pli·ca′tion** *n.*

quaes·tor (kwĕs′tər, kwē′stər) *n.* Any of various public officials in ancient Rome responsible for finance and administration in various areas of government and the military. [Middle English *questor,* from Latin *quaestor,* from *quaerere,* seek, to ask. See **quaerere** in Appendix.*] —**quaes·to′ri·al** (kwĕ-stôr′ē-əl, -stōr′ē-əl, kwē-) *adj.* —**quaes′tor·ship′** *n.*

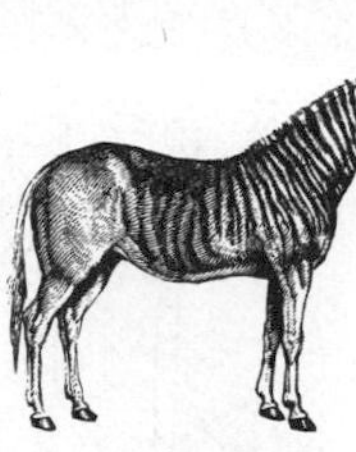
quagga

quaff (kwŏf, kwăf, kwôf) *v.* **quaffed, quaffing, quaffs.** —*tr.* To drink heartily. —*intr.* To drink something heartily. —*n.* A hearty draft. [Perhaps imitative.] —**quaff′er** *n.*

quag·ga (kwăg′ə, kwŏg′ə) *n.* A zebralike mammal, *Equus quagga,* of southern Africa, that has been extinct since the late 19th century. [Afrikaans, probably from Hottentot *quagga.*]

quag·gy (kwăg′ē, kwŏg′ē) *adj.* **-gier, -giest. 1.** Like a marsh; soggy. **2.** Soft; flabby. [From QUAGMIRE.]

quag·mire (kwăg′mīr′, kwŏg′-) *n.* **1.** A bog having a surface that yields when stepped on. Also called "quag." **2.** A difficult or precarious situation from which extrication is almost impossible. [Probably variant of *quabmire* : *quab-,* "wetness," "slime," probably akin to Middle Dutch *quac-,* unguent, liquor (see **gwēbh-**[2] in Appendix*) + MIRE.]

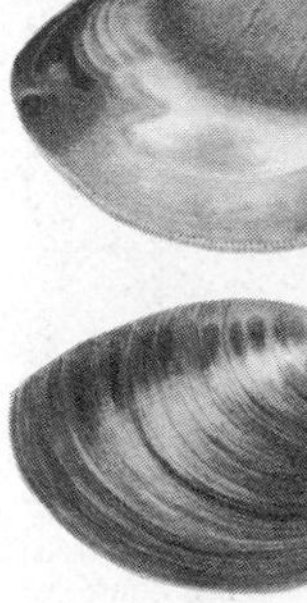
quahog

qua·hog (kwô′hôg′, -hŏg′, kwō′-, kō′-) *n.* Also **qua·haug.** An edible clam, *Venus mercenaria,* of the Atlantic coast of North America, having a hard, rounded shell. Also called "hard-shell clam," "round clam." See **cherrystone, littleneck.** [Narragansett *poquaûhock.*]

quaich (kwāKH) *n.* Also **quaigh.** A two-handled Scottish drinking cup of varying size. [Scottish Gaelic *cuach,* from Old Irish *cūach,* from Latin *caucus,* drinking cup, from Greek *kauka, kaukion.* See **keu-**[2] in Appendix.*]

Quai d'Or·say (kā dôr-sā′). The French Foreign Office.

quail[1] (kwāl) *n., pl.* **quail** or **quails. 1.** Any of various chickenlike Old World birds of the genus *Coturnix;* especially *C. coturnix,* a small bird having mottled brown plumage and a short tail. **2.** Any of various similar or related New World birds, such as the **bobwhite** and the **California quail** *(both of which see).* [Middle English *quaille,* from Old French, from Medieval Latin *quaccula,* from Gallo-Roman *coacula* (imitative of its cry).]

quail[2] (kwāl) *intr.v.* **quailed, quailing, quails.** To lose courage; cower: *"when his eyes beheld the Mountain and the desert, he quailed"* (J.R.R. Tolkien). See Synonyms at **recoil.** [Middle English *quailen,* to decline, fail, give way, perhaps from Old French *quailler,* from Latin *coāgulāre,* to curdle, COAGULATE.]

quaint (kwānt) *adj.* **quainter, quaintest. 1.** Agreeably curious, especially in an old-fashioned way: *"Smoke drifted lazily from a multitude of quaint chimneys."* (Stephen Crane). **2.** Unfamiliar or unusual in character; strange. **3.** Highly inappropriate or illogical. Used ironically: *They fought the war out of a quaint sense of honor.* —See Synonyms at **strange.** [Middle English *queinte, cointe,* clever, skillfully made, from Old French *cointe,* expert, elegant, from Latin *cognitus,* past participle of *cognōscere,* to be acquainted with : *com-,* with + *gnōscere,* to know (see **gnō-** in Appendix*).] —**quaint′ly** *adv.* —**quaint′ness** *n.*

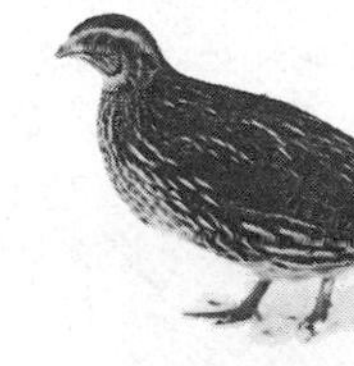
quail[1]
Coturnix coturnix

quake (kwāk) *intr.v.* **quaked, quaking, quakes. 1.** To shake or tremble with instability or shock. **2.** To shiver or tremble, as with cold or strong emotion. —See Synonyms at **shake.** —*n.* **1.** An instance of quaking; a shake. **2.** An earthquake. [Middle English *quaken,* Old English *cwacian,* from Germanic *kwei* (unattested), to shake.] —**quak′y** *adj.*

Quak·er (kwā′kər) *n.* A member of the Society of Friends. Not used officially by the Friends. [From QUAKE, probably in allusion to the admonition of George Fox, founder of the Society, to "tremble at the word of the Lord."] —**Quak′er·ism′** *n.* —**Quak′er·ly** *adv. & adj.*

Quaker gun. A dummy gun made of wood. [In allusion to the Quakers' opposition to war.]

Quak·er·la·dies (kwā′kər-lā′dēz) *pl.n.* A plant, **bluets** *(see).*

quaking aspen. See **aspen.**

qual·i·fi·ca·tion (kwŏl′ə-fĭ-kā′shən) *n.* **1. a.** The act of qualifying. **b.** The condition of being qualified. **2.** Any quality, accomplishment, or ability that suits a person to a specific position or task. **3.** A condition or circumstance that must be met or complied with. **4.** A restriction or modification.

qual·i·fied (kwŏl′ə-fīd′) *adj.* **1.** Competent, suited, or having met the requirements for a specific position or task. **2.** Limited, restricted, or modified: *a qualified plan for expansion.* —**qual′i·fied′ly** (-fīd′lē, -fī′ĭd-lē) *adv.*

qual·i·fi·er (kwŏl′ə-fī′ər) *n.* **1.** One that qualifies. **2.** *Grammar.* A word or phrase that qualifies, limits, or modifies the meaning of another word or phrase.

qual·i·fy (kwŏl′ə-fī′) *v.* **-fied, -fying, -fies.** —*tr.* **1.** To describe by enumerating the characteristics or qualities of; characterize. **2.** To make competent or suitable for an office, position, or task. **3.** To give legal power to; make legally capable. **4.** To modify, limit, or restrict, as by giving exceptions. **5.** To make less harsh or severe; moderate. **6.** *Grammar.* To modify the meaning of (a word or phrase). —*intr.* To be or to become qualified. [Old French *qualifier,* from Medieval Latin *quālificāre,* to attribute a quality to : Latin *quālis,* of what kind (see **quality**) + *facere,* to make (see **dhē-**[1] in Appendix*).]

qual·i·ta·tive (kwŏl′ə-tā′tĭv) *adj.* Of, pertaining to, or concerning quality or qualities. [Late Latin *quālitātivus,* from Latin *quālitās,* QUALITY.] —**qual′i·ta′tive·ly** *adv.*

qualitative analysis. Chemical determination of the constituents of a substance without regard to quantity.

qual·i·ty (kwŏl′ə-tē) *n., pl.* **-ties.** *Abbr.* **qlty. 1.** A characteristic or attribute of something; property; a feature. **2.** The natural or essential character of something. **3.** Excellence; superiority.

quarrel[2]

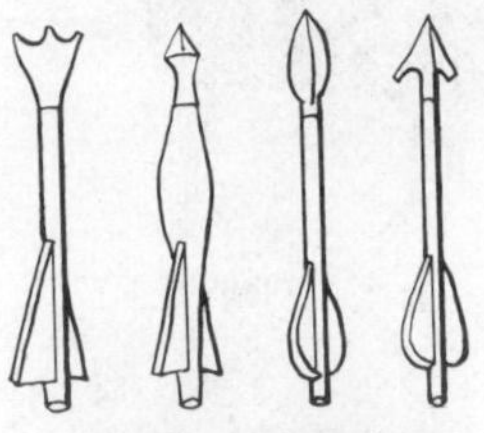

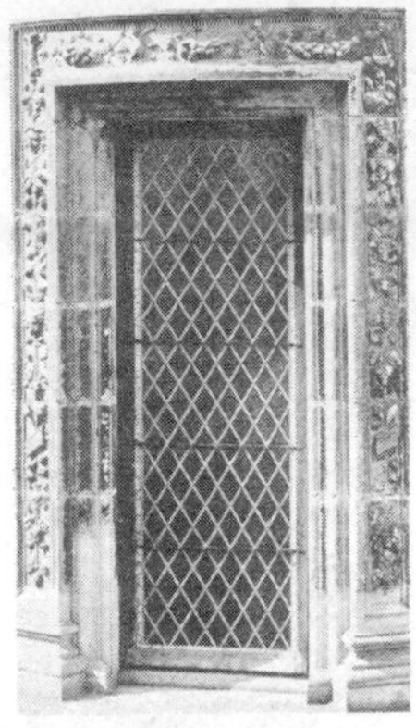

Above: Crossbow quarrels
Below: Window quarrels

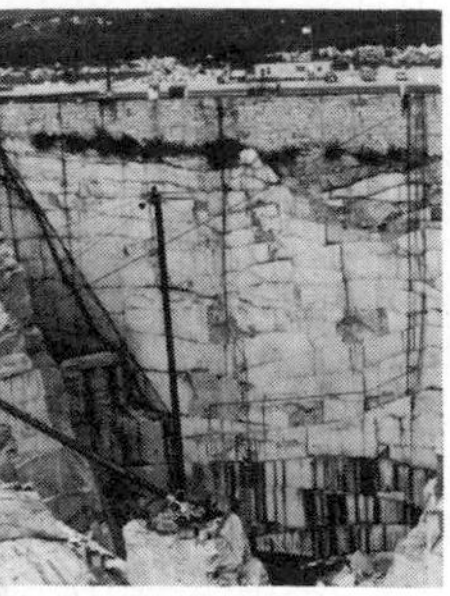

quarry[2]
Granite quarry at Barre, Vermont

4. Degree or grade of excellence: *yard goods of low quality.* **5. a.** High social position. **b.** People of high social position. Preceded by *the.* **6.** *Music.* Timbre, as determined by overtones. **7.** *Linguistics.* The character of a vowel sound determined by the size and shape of the oral cavity and the amount of resonance with which the sound is produced. **8.** *Logic.* The positive or negative character of a proposition. [Middle English *qualite,* from Old French, from Latin *quālitās,* from *quālis,* of what kind. See **kwo-** in Appendix.*]

Synonyms: *quality, property, attribute, character, trait.* The most inclusive of these terms, *quality,* is any feature that distinguishes or identifies someone or something. *Property* designates a specific quality that is basic to a thing and often makes it act in a certain way. An *attribute,* unlike a property, is a quality that is less precisely known and is only ascribed to someone or something: *properties of iron; attributes of God. Character* and *trait* stress distinctive features, but *character* usually applies to what distinguishes the whole of a thing, or a group, whereas *trait* refers to one particular feature, and is usually restricted to persons.

qualm (kwäm, kwôm) *n.* **1.** A sudden feeling of sickness, faintness, or nausea. **2.** A sensation of doubt or misgiving; uneasiness. **3.** A pang of conscience. [Origin obscure.]

Synonyms: *qualm, scruple, compunction, misgiving, reservation.* These nouns denote varying degrees of uncertainty felt by a person about his judgment in taking action. *Qualm* can be as slight as a feeling of uneasiness or as strong as a queasy sensation in its implication of self-doubt. *Scruple* adds the idea of conscience. *Compunction* increases the importance of conscience in deciding the rightness or wrongness of one's acts. *Misgiving* implies mistrust or apprehension as to one's ability, or fear that one has made a mistake. *Reservation* also connotes doubt about the fitness or correctness of an action, but refers to a rather well-defined limiting condition that one has arrived at.

qualm·ish (kwä′mĭsh, kwô′-) *adj.* **1.** Feeling qualms. **2.** Producing or tending to produce qualms. —**qualm′ish·ly** *adv.*

quam·ash. Variant of **camas.**

quan·da·ry (kwŏn′drē, -də-rē) *n., pl.* **-ries.** A state of uncertainty or perplexity; dilemma. See Synonyms at **predicament.** [Origin uncertain.]

quant. quantitative.

quan·ti·fy (kwŏn′tə-fī′) *tr.v.* **-fied, -fying, -fies. 1.** To determine or express the quantity of: *"human misery . . . is hard to quantify"* (Renata Adler). **2.** *Logic.* To limit the quantity of (a proposition) by prefixing an expression such as *all, some,* or *none.* [Medieval Latin *quantificāre* : *quantus,* how great (see **quantity**) + *facere,* to make (see **dhē-**[1] in Appendix*).] —**quan′ti·fi·ca′tion** *n.* —**quan′ti·fi′er** *n.*

quan·ti·ta·tive (kwŏn′tə-tā′tĭv) *adj. Abbr.* **quant. 1. a.** Expressed or capable of expression as a quantity. **b.** Of, pertaining to, or susceptible of measurement. **c.** Of or pertaining to number or quantity. **2.** *Prosody.* Pertaining to syllables in classical verse that are based upon duration of sound rather than stress. [Medieval Latin *quantitātivus,* from Latin *quantitās,* QUANTITY.] —**quan′ti·ta′tive·ly** *adv.*

quantitative analysis. Chemical determination of the amounts or proportions of constituents in a substance.

quantitative gene. *Genetics.* A **polygene** *(see).*

quan·ti·ty (kwŏn′tə-tē) *n., pl.* **-ties.** *Abbr.* **qt., qty. 1. a.** A number or amount of anything, either specified or indefinite. **b.** A sufficient or considerable amount or number: *sell wholesale drugs in quantity.* **c.** The exact amount of anything. **2.** The measurable, countable, or comparable property or aspect of a thing. **3.** *Mathematics.* Anything serving as the object of a mathematical operation. **4.** *Linguistics.* The length of a vowel or consonant sound expressed in terms of the time needed to produce it. **5.** *Logic.* The exact character of a proposition in reference to its universality, singularity, or particularity. [Middle English *quantite,* from Old French, from Latin *quantitās,* from *quantus,* how great. See **kwo-** in Appendix.*]

quan·tize (kwŏn′tīz′) *tr.v.* **-tized, -tizing, -tizes.** *Physics.* **1.** To limit the possible values of (a magnitude or quantity) to a discrete set of values by quantum mechanical rules. **2.** To replace the dynamic variables of a system by the corresponding quantum mechanical operators in order to calculate the behavior of the system. [QUANT(UM) + -IZE.] —**quan′ti·za′tion** *n.*

Quan·trill (kwŏn′trĭl), **William Clarke.** 1837–1865. American leader of Confederate raiders in Kansas and Missouri.

quan·tum (kwŏn′təm) *n., pl.* **-ta** (-tə). **1.** The quantity or amount of something. **2.** A specified portion of something. **3.** Something that may be counted or measured. **4.** *Physics.* **a.** An indivisible unit of energy, equal for radiation of frequency v to the product hv, where h is Planck's constant. **b.** The particle mediating a specific type of fundamental interaction: *The photon is the quantum of the electromagnetic field.* [Latin, neuter of *quantus,* how great. See **quantity.**]

quantum electrodynamics. *Physics.* The quantum mechanical theory of the properties and interactions of charged elementary particles, especially of the electron, with the electromagnetic field.

quantum jump. 1. *Physics.* The transition of an atomic or molecular system from one discrete energy level to another with concomitant absorption or emission of radiation having energy equal to the difference between the two levels. **2.** Any abrupt change or step, especially in knowledge or information.

quantum liquid. *Physics.* Any fluid exhibiting thermal, conductive, or kinetic behavior attributable to the quantum statistics obeyed by the particles of the fluid, especially a **superfluid** *(see).* Also called "quantum fluid."

quantum mechanics. *Physics.* **Quantum theory** *(see),* especially the quantum theory of the structure and behavior of atoms and molecules.

quantum number. *Physics.* Any of a set of real numbers that individually characterize the properties and collectively specify the state of a particle or of an atomic system.

quantum state. *Physics.* Any one of the possible states of a system described by quantum theory.

quantum theory. *Physics.* A mathematical theory of dynamic systems in which dynamic variables are represented by abstract mathematical operators having properties that specify the behavior of the system. The theory originated from, and includes as essential aspects, the hypothesis of energy quantization and the concept of wave-particle duality.

quar. 1. quarter. **2.** quarterly.

quar·an·tine (kwôr′ən-tēn′, kwŏr′-) *n.* **1. a.** A period of time, originally lasting 40 days, during which a vehicle, a person, or goods suspected of carrying a contagious disease are detained at their port of entry under enforced isolation to prevent disease from entering a country. **b.** A place for such detention. **2.** Enforced isolation or restriction of free movement imposed to prevent a contagious disease from spreading. **3.** Any enforced isolation. —*tr.v.* **quarantined, -tining, -tines. 1.** To isolate for the purpose of preventing the spread of contagious disease; place in quarantine. **2.** To isolate politically or economically. [Italian *quarantina (giorni),* forty (days), from *quaranta,* forty, from Latin *quadrāgintā.* See **kwetwer-** in Appendix.*]

quark (kwôrk) *n. Physics.* Any of three hypothetical subatomic particles having electric charges of magnitude one-third or two-thirds that of the electron, proposed as the fundamental units of matter. Also called "ace." [From a line in Joyce's *Finnegan's Wake,* "three quarks for Mr. Marks."]

quar·rel[1] (kwôr′əl, kwŏr′-) *n.* **1.** An angry dispute; disagreement; argument. **2.** A cause for a dispute or argument: *We have no quarrel with the findings.* —*intr.v.* **quarreled** or **-relled, -reling** or **-relling, -rels. 1.** To engage in a quarrel; argue angrily: *"He never quarrelled with his wife, but he never talked to her"* (Trollope). **2.** To disagree; differ. **3.** To find fault in something; complain. —See Synonyms at **argue.** [Middle English, (cause for) complaint, from Old French, from Latin *querēla,* from *querī,* to complain. See **kwes-** in Appendix.*] —**quar′rel·er, quar′rel·ler** *n.*

quar·rel[2] (kwôr′əl, kwŏr′-) *n.* **1.** A bolt for a crossbow. **2.** A tool having a squared head, as a stonemason's chisel. **3.** A small diamond-shaped or square pane of glass in a latticed window. [Middle English *quarel,* from Old French, from Vulgar Latin *quadrellus* (unattested), diminutive of Latin *quadrus,* square. See **kwetwer-** in Appendix.*]

quar·rel·some (kwôr′əl-səm, kwŏr′-) *adj.* Characterized by quarreling or tending to quarrel. See Synonyms at **belligerent.**

quar·ry[1] (kwôr′ē, kwŏr′ē) *n., pl.* **-ries. 1.** A bird or animal hunted; prey; game. **2.** Any object of pursuit. [Middle English *querre,* entrails of a beast given to the hounds, from Old French *cuiree,* variant of *co(u)ree,* from Late Latin *corāta,* viscera, from Latin *cor,* heart. See **kerd-**[1] in Appendix.*]

quar·ry[2] (kwôr′ē, kwŏr′ē) *n., pl.* **-ries.** An open excavation or pit from which stone is obtained by digging, cutting, or blasting. —*tr.v.* **quarried, -rying, -ries. 1.** To cut, dig, blast, or otherwise obtain (stone) from a quarry. **2.** To use (land) as a quarry. [Middle English *quarey, quarere,* from Old French *quarriere,* from *quarre* (unattested), "square stone," from Latin *quadrus,* square. See **kwetwer-** in Appendix.*] —**quar′ri·er** *n.*

quar·ry[3] (kwôr′ē, kwŏr′ē) *n., pl.* **-ries.** A square or diamond shape. [Variant of QUARREL, bolt.]

quart[1] (kwôrt) *n. Abbr.* **q., qt, qt. 1. a.** A unit of volume or capacity in the U.S. Customary System, used in liquid measure, equal to two pints or 57.75 cubic inches. **b.** A unit of volume or capacity in the U.S. Customary System, used in dry measure, equal to two pints or 67.2 cubic inches. **c.** A unit of volume or capacity in the British Imperial System, used in liquid and dry measure, equal to 1.201 U.S. liquid quarts, 1.032 U.S. dry quarts, or 69.354 cubic inches. See **measurement. 2.** A container having a capacity of one quart. [Middle English, from Old French *quarte,* "fourth part (of a gallon)," from Latin *quārtus,* fourth. See **kwetwer-** in Appendix.*]

quart[2] (kärt) *n.* A sequence of four playing cards in one suit. [French *quarte,* fourth, QUARTE.]

quar·tan (kwôrt′n) *adj.* Occurring every fourth day, counting inclusively, or every 72 hours. Said of a fever. —*n.* A recurrent malarial fever, occurring every 72 hours. Also called "quartan fever." [Middle English *quarteyne,* from Old French *quartaine,* from Latin *quārtāna (fēbris),* from *quārtānus,* of the fourth, from *quārtus,* fourth. See **kwetwer-** in Appendix.*]

quarte (kärt) *n.* The fourth regular position in fencing. [French, "fourth," "quart," from Old French. See **quart.**]

quar·ter (kwôr′tər) *n. Abbr.* **q., qr., quar. 1.** One of four equal parts of something. **2.** A coin equal to one-fourth of the dollar of the United States and Canada. **3. a.** One-fourth of an hour; 15 minutes. **b.** The moment marking either the beginning or the end of such a period of time. **4. a.** One-fourth of a year; three months. **b.** An academic term lasting for approximately three months. **5.** *Astronomy.* **a.** One-fourth of the period of the moon's revolution around the earth. **b.** Either of two of the visible phases of the moon: the *first quarter,* from new moon until it approaches fullness; and the *third quarter,* from after fullness until it has disappeared in the sunrise. **6.** *Sports.* One of four equal periods of playing time in which some games are divided. **7.** One-fourth of a yard; nine inches. **8.** One-fourth of a mile; two furlongs. **9.** One-fourth of a pound; four ounces.

ă pat/ā pay/âr care/ä father/b bib/ch church/d deed/ĕ pet/ē be/f fife/g gag/h hat/hw which/ĭ pit/ī pie/îr pier/j judge/k kick/l lid, needle/m mum/n no, sudden/ng thing/ŏ pot/ō toe/ô paw, for/oi noise/ou out/ŏŏ took/ōō boot/p pop/r roar/s sauce/sh ship, dish/

10. One-fourth of a ton; 500 pounds. Usually used as a measure of grain. **11.** *British.* A measure of grain equal to approximately eight bushels. **12. a.** One-fourth of a hundredweight; 25 pounds. **b.** One-fourth of a British hundredweight; 28 pounds. **13. a.** One of the four major divisions of the compass: north, south, east, or west. **b.** One-fourth of the distance between any two of the 32 divisions of the compass. Also called "quarter point." **c.** *Nautical.* The general direction on either side of a ship located 45 degrees off the stern. **d.** One of the four major divisions of the horizon as determined by the four points of the compass. **e.** Any region or area of the earth thought of as falling within a specific division of the compass. **14.** *Nautical.* **a.** The upper portion of the after side of a ship, usually between the aftermost mast and the stern. **b.** The part of a yard between the slings and the yardarm. **15.** *Heraldry.* Any of four equal divisions of a shield. **16.** One leg of a carcass of an animal, usually including the adjoining parts. **17.** Either side of a horse's hoof. **18.** The part of the side of a shoe between the heel and the vamp. **19.** *Plural.* A place of residence; specifically, the buildings or barracks housing military personnel. **20.** *Usually plural.* A proper or assigned station or place, as for officers and crew on a warship. **21.** A specific district or section, as of a city: *the Latin quarter.* **22.** *Usually plural.* An unspecified person or group of persons: *information from the highest quarters.* **23.** Mercy or clemency, especially when shown to an enemy. —*v.* **quartered, -tering, -ters.** —*tr.* **1. a.** To cut or otherwise divide into four equal or equivalent parts. **b.** To **quartersaw** *(see).* **2.** To divide or separate into a number of parts. **3.** To dismember (a human body) into four parts. **4.** *Heraldry.* **a.** To divide (a shield) into four equal areas with vertical and horizontal lines. **b.** To place (a charge) in a quarter or quarters. **5. a.** To mark or place (holes, for example) a fourth of a circle apart. **b.** To fix (one machine part) at right angles to its connecting part. **6.** To furnish with housing. **7.** To traverse (an area of ground) laterally back and forth while slowly advancing forward. Used especially of hunting dogs. —*intr.* **1.** To take up or be assigned lodgings. **2.** To cover an area of ground by ranging over it from side to side. —*adj.* **1.** Being one of four equal or equivalent parts. **2.** Being one-fourth of a standard or usual value. [Middle English, from Old French *quartier,* from Latin *quartārius,* from *quartus,* fourth. See **kwetwer-** in Appendix.*]

quar·ter·age (kwôr′tər-ĭj) *n.* A monetary allowance, wage, or payment made or received quarterly.

quar·ter·back (kwôr′tər-băk′) *n. Abbr.* **qb, q.b.** *Football.* The backfield player whose position is behind the line of scrimmage and who usually calls the signals for the plays.

quarter day. Any of the four days of the year regarded as the beginning of a new season or quarter, when most quarterly payments are due.

quar·ter·deck (kwôr′tər-dĕk′) *n.* The after part of the upper deck of a sailing ship, usually reserved for officers.

quar·ter·fi·nal (kwôr′tər-fī′nəl) *adj.* Designating one of four competitions in a tournament, whose winners go on to play in semifinal competitions.

quarter horse. One of a breed of strong saddle horses developed in the western United States. [Formerly trained for races up to a quarter of a mile.]

quar·ter·hour (kwôr′tər-our′) *n.* Also **quarter hour. 1.** Fifteen minutes. **2.** The point on a clock's face marking either 15 minutes after or 15 minutes before an hour.

quar·ter·ly (kwôr′tər-lē) *adj. Abbr.* **q., qr., quar. 1.** Made up of four parts. **2.** Being one of four parts. **3.** Occurring or appearing at regular intervals of three months: *a quarterly magazine.* —*n., pl.* **quarterlies.** *Abbr.* **q., qr., quar.** A publication issued regularly every three months. —*adv.* In or by quarters.

quar·ter·mas·ter (kwôr′tər-măs′tər, -mäs′tər) *n. Abbr.* **QM, Q.M. 1.** A military officer responsible for the food, clothing, and equipment of troops. **2.** A naval petty officer responsible for the navigation of a ship. [From QUARTER, in the sense of a residence.]

quartermaster corps. *Abbr.* **Q.C., QMC, Q.M.C.** A branch of the U.S. Army responsible for food, clothing, and equipment.

Quartermaster General. *Abbr.* **QMG, Q.M.G.** *U.S. Army.* A major general commanding a quartermaster corps.

quar·tern (kwôr′tərn) *n.* **1.** One-fourth of something. **2.** *British.* A loaf weighing about four pounds. [Middle English *quarteron,* from Old French, from *quartier,* QUARTER.]

quarter note. *Music.* A note having one-fourth the time value of a whole note. Also called "crotchet."

quar·ter·phase (kwôr′tər-fāz′) *adj. Electricity.* **Two-phase** *(see).*

quar·ter·saw (kwôr′tər-sô′) *tr.v.* **-sawed, -sawed** or **-sawn, -sawing, -saws.** To saw (a log) into quarters lengthwise along its axis.

quarter section. A quarter of a square mile of land.

quarter sessions. *Law.* Any of various courts, primarily in the United States and Great Britain, that sit every three months.

quar·ter·staff (kwôr′tər-stăf′, -stäf′) *n., pl.* **-staves** (-stāvz′). A long wooden staff, formerly used as a weapon.

quar·ter·tone (kwôr′tər-tōn′) *n. Music.* Half a **semitone** *(see).*

quar·tet (kwôr-tĕt′) *n.* Also **quar·tette. 1.** A musical composition for four instruments, especially stringed instruments. **2.** A group of four performing musicians. **3.** Any set of four persons or things. [Italian *quartetto,* diminutive of *quarto,* fourth, from Latin *quartus.* See **quarto.**]

quar·tic (kwôr′tĭk) *adj. Mathematics.* Of or designating the fourth degree. [From Latin *quartus,* fourth. See **quarto.**] —**quar′tic** *n.*

quar·tile (kwôr′tĭl, -tīl) *n. Statistics.* The value of the boundary

at the 25th, 50th, or 75th percentiles of a frequency distribution divided into four parts, each containing a quarter of the population. —*adj.* Of or pertaining to a quartile. [Medieval Latin *quārtilis,* of a quartile, from Latin *quārtus,* fourth. See **quarto.**]

quar·to (kwôr′tō) *n., pl.* **-tos.** *Abbr.* **q., Q., qto.,** *pl.* **Qq. 1.** The page size obtained by folding a whole sheet into four leaves. **2.** A book composed of pages of this size or folded in this way. Also written *4to,* 4°. [Latin *(in) quārtō,* in quarter, from *quārtus,* fourth. See **kwetwer-** in Appendix.*] —**quar′to** *adj.*

quartz (kwôrts) *n.* A hard, crystalline, vitreous mineral silicon dioxide, SiO_2, found worldwide as a component of sandstone and granite, or as pure crystals in such varieties as agate, chalcedony, chert, flint, opal, and rock crystal. [German *Quarz,* from Middle High German *quarz,* from West Slavic *kwardy.* See **twer-²** in Appendix.*]

quartz glass. A pure silica glass, highly transparent to ultraviolet radiations.

quartz·if·er·ous (kwôrt-sĭf′ər-əs) *adj.* Containing quartz.

quartz·ite (kwôrt′sīt′) *n.* A metamorphic rock resulting from the recrystallization of quartz sandstone.

qua·sar (kwā′zär′, -sär′, -zər, -sər) *n. Astronomy.* A **quasi-stellar object** *(see).* [QUAS(I) + (STELL)AR.]

quash¹ (kwŏsh) *tr.v.* **quashed, quashing, quashes.** *Law.* To set aside or annul. [Middle English *quassen,* from Old French *quasser, casser,* from Late Latin *cassāre,* from Latin *cassus,* empty, void. See **kes-²** in Appendix.*]

quash² (kwŏsh) *tr.v.* **quashed, quashing, quashes.** To put down or suppress forcibly and completely. [Middle English *quashen,* from Old French *quasser, casser,* from Latin *quassāre,* frequentative of *quatere* (past participle *quassus*), to shake, shatter. See **kwet-** in Appendix.*]

qua·si (kwā′zī′, -sī′, kwä′zē, -sē) *adv.* To some degree; almost or somewhat. Used in combination: *quasi-scientific literature.* —*adj.* Resembling but not being (the thing in question). Used in combination: *a quasi-victory.* [Latin *quasi,* contraction of *quānsei* (unattested), as if : *quam,* than, how, as (see **kwo-** in Appendix*) + *sī,* if (see **swo-** in Appendix*).]

qua·si-stel·lar object (kwā′zī-stĕl′ər, kwä′sī′-, kwä′zē-, kwä′-sē-). *Abbr.* **QSO** *Astronomy.* A member of any of several classes of starlike objects having exceptionally large red shifts that are often emitters of radio frequency as well as visible radiation and have apparently immense speeds, energies, and distances from earth. Also called "quasar."

quasi-stellar radio source. *Abbr.* **QSRS** *Astronomy.* A quasi-stellar object.

quas·sia (kwŏsh′ə) *n.* **1.** A tree, *Quassia amara,* of tropical America, having bright scarlet flowers. **2.** A bitter substance obtained from the wood and bark of this tree and related trees, used in medicine and as an insecticide. [New Latin, after Graman *Quassi,* name of an inhabitant of Surinam, who discovered its medicinal properties in the mid-18th century.]

quas·sin (kwŏs′ĭn) *n.* The bitter principle of quassia, used to denature alcohol. [QUASS(IA) + -IN.]

qua·ter·nar·y (kwŏt′ər-nĕr′ē, kwə-tûr′nə-rē) *adj.* **1.** Consisting of four; in fours. **2.** *Chemistry.* **a.** Designating a compound having four alkyl groups connected to a nitrogen or phosphorus atom. **b.** Designating a compound consisting of four different atoms or radicals. —*n., pl.* **quaternaries. 1.** The number four. **2.** That member of a group which is fourth in order. [Middle English, set of four, from Latin *quaternārius,* consisting of four each, from *quaternī,* four each, from *quater,* four times. See **kwetwer-** in Appendix.*]

Qua·ter·nar·y (kwŏt′ər-nĕr′ē, kwə-tûr′nə-rē) *adj. Geology.* Of, belonging to, or designating the geologic time, system of rocks, and sedimentary deposits of the second period of the Cenozoic era, from the end of the Tertiary through the present, characterized by the appearance and development of man, and including the Pleistocene and Holocene epochs. See **geology.** —*n. Geology.* The Quaternary period or system of deposits. Preceded by *the.* [From QUATERNARY (fourth).]

qua·ter·ni·on (kwə-tûr′nē-ən) *n.* **1.** A set of four persons or items. **2.** *Mathematics.* An element of a system of four dimensional vectors obeying laws similar to those of complex numbers. [Middle English, from Late Latin *quaterniō,* from Latin *quaternī,* four each. See **quaternary.**]

quat·rain (kwŏt′rān′, kwŏ-trān′) *n.* **1.** A stanza of four lines. **2.** Either of the two halves of the octave of a sonnet. **3.** A poem of four lines. [French, from Old French, from *quatre,* four, from Latin *quattuor.* See **kwetwer-** in Appendix.*]

quat·re·foil (kăt′ər-foil′, kăt′rə-) *n.* **1.** A figure of a flower with four petals or a leaf with four leaflets, especially in heraldry. **2.** *Architecture.* An ornament or tracery with four foils or lobes. [Middle English *quaterfoile,* set of four leaves : *quater-,* four, from Old French *quatre* (see **quatrain**) + FOIL (leaf).]

quat·tro·cen·to (kwŏt′rō-chĕn′tō) *n.* The 15th-century period of Italian art and literature. [Italian, short for *(mil)quattro cento,* "(one thousand) four hundred" : *quattro,* four, from Latin *quattuor* (see **kwetwer-** in Appendix*) + *cento,* hundred, from Latin *centum* (see **dekm** in Appendix).]

qua·ver (kwā′vər) *v.* **-vered, -vering, -vers.** —*intr.* **1.** To quiver, as from weakness; tremble. **2.** To speak in a quivering voice or utter a quivering sound. **3.** To produce a trill on a musical instrument or with the voice. —*tr.* To utter or sing in a trilling voice. —*n.* **1.** A quivering sound. **2.** A trill. **3.** *Music. Chiefly British.* An eighth note *(see).* [Middle English *quaveren,* frequentative of *quaven,* to tremble, from Germanic, akin to Low German *quabbeln,* to tremble. See **gwebh-²** in Appendix.*] —**qua′ver·y** *adj.*

quay (kē) *n.* A wharf or reinforced bank where ships are loaded

quartz
Rock crystal

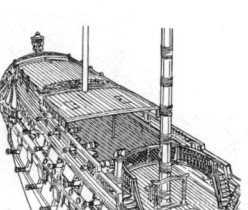

quarter-deck

quatrefoil
Window ornamented
with three quatrefoils

ă pat/ā pay/âr care/ä father/b bib/ch church/d deed/ĕ pet/ē be/f fife/g gag/h hat/hw which/ĭ pit/ī pie/îr pier/j judge/k kick/l lid, needle/m mum/n no, sudden/ng thing/ŏ pot/ō toe/ô paw, for/oi noise/ou out/ŏŏ took/ōō boot/p pop/r roar/s sauce/sh ship, dish/t tight/th thin, path/th this, bathe/ŭ cut/ûr urge/v valve/w with/y yes/z zebra, size/zh vision/ə about, item, edible, gallop, circus/à Fr. ami/œ Fr. feu, Ger. schön/ü Fr. tu, Ger. über/KH Ger. ich, Scot. loch/N Fr. bon. *Follows main vocabulary. †Of obscure origin.

or unloaded. [Earlier *key,* Middle English *key, kay,* from Old French *chai, cay,* from Gaulish *caio,* rampart, retaining wall. See **kagh-** in Appendix.*]

quay·age (kē′ĭj) *n.* **1.** A charge for the use of a quay. **2.** The space available on a system of quays. **3.** Quays collectively.

Que. Quebec.

quean (kwēn) *n.* **1.** *Archaic.* An impudent or disreputable woman. **2.** *Scottish.* A young woman. [Middle English *quen(e),* Old English *cwene,* woman, wife. See **gwen-** in Appendix.*]

quea·sy (kwē′zē) *adj.* **-sier, -siest.** Also **quea·zy. 1.** Nauseated. **2.** Easily nauseated. **3.** Causing nausea; sickening. **4. a.** Causing uneasiness. **b.** Uneasy; troubled. **5.** Easily troubled. [Middle English *coysy, qwesye,* perhaps originally "wounded," "tender," probably from Old Norse *kveisa,* whitlow. See **gweyə-** in Appendix.*] **—quea′si·ly** *adv.* **—quea′si·ness** *n.*

Que·bec (kwĭ-bĕk′). *French* **Qué·bec** (kā-bĕk′). **1.** *Abbr.* **Que., P.Q.** A province, 523,860 square miles in land area, of eastern Canada. Population, 5,657,000. See map at **Canada. 2.** The capital of this province, in the south on the St. Lawrence. Population, 331,000.

que·bra·cho (kā-brä′chō) *n., pl.* **-chos. 1.** Any of several South American trees having very hard wood; especially, *Aspidosperma quebracho-blanco,* the bark of which is used in medicine, and *Schinopsis lorentzii,* of which the wood yields tannin. **2.** The bark or wood of any of these trees. [American Spanish, variant of *quiebrahacha,* "ax-breaker" : *quiebra,* it breaks, from *quebrar,* to break, from Latin *crepāre,* to rattle, crack (see **ker-**[2] in Appendix*) + *hacha,* ax, from French *hache,* from Old French, from Germanic (see **skep-**[1] in Appendix*).]

Quech·ua (kĕch′wə, -wä′) *n.* Also **Kech·ua. 1.** A tribe or a member of a tribe of South American Indians originally constituting the ruling class of the Incan Empire. **2.** The language of these South American Indians, still spoken by other Indian peoples of Peru, Ecuador, Bolivia, Chile, and Argentina. [Spanish, from Quechua *kkechúwa,* "plunderer," "robber."] **—Quech′uan** *adj.*

queen (kwēn) *n. Abbr.* **qu. 1.** The wife or widow of a king. **2.** A female monarch or ruler. **3.** A woman, or a thing personified as a woman, who is eminent or supreme in a given domain. **4.** *Abbr.* **Q** The most powerful chessman, able to move in any direction in a straight line. **5.** A playing card bearing the figure of a queen, next above the jack and below the king in each suit. **6.** The fertile, developed female in a colony of social bees, ants, or termites. **7.** *Slang.* An effeminate male homosexual. —*v.* **queened, queening, queens.** —*tr.* **1.** To make (a woman) a queen. **2.** *Chess.* To raise (a pawn) to queen. —*intr.* To reign as queen. [Middle English *qu(e)ene,* Old English *cwēn,* woman, wife, queen. See **gwen-** in Appendix.*]

Queen Anne. The style of English architecture and furniture typical of the reign of Queen Anne (1702–14). Often used attributively.

Queen Anne's lace. A widely distributed plant, *Daucus carota,* native to Eurasia, having finely divided leaves and flat clusters of small white flowers. Also called "wild carrot."

Queen Anne's War. See **War of the Spanish Succession.**

Queen Char·lotte Islands (shär′lət). An island group of British Columbia, in the Pacific northwest of Vancouver Island.

queen consort. The wife of a reigning king.

queen-cup (kwēn′kŭp′) *n.* A plant, *Clintonia uniflora,* of northwestern North America, bearing a solitary white flower and a blue berry.

Queen E·liz·a·beth Islands (ĭ-lĭz′ə-bəth). A group of islands of the Northwest Territories, Canada, lying north of Viscount Melville and Lancaster sounds, and including the Parry and Sverdrup groups and Devon and Ellesmere islands.

queen·ly (kwēn′lē) *adj.* **-lier, -liest. 1.** Of or resembling a queen. **2.** Pertaining to or befitting a queen. **—queen′li·ness** *n.*

Queen Mar·y Coast (mâr′ē). A section of the coast of Antarctica fronting on the southern Indian Ocean.

Queen Maud Gulf (môd). A gulf between Victoria Island and the mainland, Northwest Territories, Canada.

Queen Maud Land (môd). A segment of Antarctica between Coats Land and Enderby Land, declared a dependency by Norway in 1949.

queen mother. A dowager queen who is the mother of the reigning monarch.

queen of the prairie. A plant, *Filipendula rubra,* of prairies and meadows of the central United States, having compound leaves and clusters of small pink flowers.

queen olive. A variety of olive having large fruit, used for eating rather than as a source of oil.

queen post. One of two upright supporting posts set vertically between the rafters and the tie beam at equal distances from the apex of a roof. Compare **king post.**

Queens (kwēnz). The largest (108 square miles) borough of New York City, on Long Island. Population, 1,810,000.

Queen's. The former name for **Laoighis.**

Queensberry Rules. The **Marquis of Queensberry Rules** *(see).*

Queen's Counsel. *Abbr.* **Q.C.** The **King's Counsel** *(see).* Used when the British sovereign is a queen.

queen's evidence. The **king's evidence** *(see).*

Queens·land (kwēnz′lănd′, -lənd). The second-largest state (670,500 square miles) of Australia, in the northeastern part of the country. Population, 1,589,000. Capital, Brisbane.

queen's metal. A form of britannia containing a small amount of zinc.

queen truss. A building truss having queen posts.

queer (kwîr) *adj.* **queerer, queerest. 1.** Deviating from the expected or normal; strange. **2.** Odd or unconventional in behavior; eccentric. **3.** Arousing suspicion. **4.** *Slang.* Homosexual. **5.** *Slang.* Fake; counterfeit. —See Synonyms at **strange.** —*n. Slang.* **1.** A homosexual. **2.** Counterfeit money. —*tr.v.* **queered, queering, queers.** *Slang.* **1.** To ruin or thwart. **2.** To put into a bad position. [Perhaps from German *quer,* perverse, cross, from Middle High German *twerch, querch,* from Old High German *twërh, dwerah.* See **terkw-** in Appendix.*] **—queer′ly** *adv.* **—queer′ness** *n.*

Queer Street. *Chiefly British.* Difficulties, especially financial ones.

quell (kwĕl) *tr.v.* **quelled, quelling, quells. 1.** To put down forcibly; suppress. **2.** To pacify; to quiet. [Middle English *quellen,* to kill, destroy, Old English *cwellan.* See **gwel-**[2] in Appendix.*]

Quel·part. The former name for **Cheju.**

Que·moy (kē-moi′). *Chinese* **Kin·men** (chĕn′mŭn′). An island off the coast of Fukien Province, China, about 15 miles east of Amoy, administered by Taiwan.

quench (kwĕnch) *tr.v.* **quenched, quenching, quenches. 1.** To put out; extinguish. **2.** To suppress; squelch. **3.** To put an end to; destroy. **4.** To slake; satisfy. **5.** To cool (hot metal) by thrusting in water or other liquid. [Middle English *quenchen,* Old English *ācwencan.* See **gweyə-** in Appendix.*] **—quench′a·ble** *adj.* **—quench′er** *n.*

que·nelle (kə-nĕl′) *n.* A ball or dumpling of forcemeat bound with eggs and poached in stock or water. [French, probably from Alsatian *Knödel,* dumpling, from Middle High German, diminutive of *knode,* knot, from Old High German *knodo.* See **gen-** in Appendix.*]

Quen·tin (kwĕnt′n, kwĭn′tĭn). A masculine given name. [Latin *Quintinus,* from *Quintus,* a Roman praenomen, from *quintus,* fifth. See **penkwe** in Appendix.*]

quer·ce·tin (kwûr′sə-tĭn) *n.* A yellow, powdered crystalline compound, $C_{15}H_{10}O_7$, synthesized or occurring as a glycoside in the rind and bark of numerous plants, and used medicinally to treat abnormal capillary fragility. [From Latin *quercētum,* oak forest, from *quercus,* oak. See **quercitron.**]

quer·ci·tron (kwûr′sə-trən, -trŏn′, kwər-sĭt′rən) *n.* **1.** A tree, the **black oak** *(see).* **2.** The bright-orange inner bark of this tree, from which a yellow dye is obtained. **3.** This dye. [Latin *quercus,* oak (see **perkwu-** in Appendix*) + CITRON (color).]

Que·ré·ta·ro (kā-rā′tä-rō). **1.** A central state of Mexico, occupying 4,432 square miles. Population, 379,000. **2.** The capital of this state. Population, 68,000.

que·rist (kwîr′ĭst) *n. Rare.* A questioner; an inquirer. [From Latin *quaerere,* to seek, ask. See **quaerere** in Appendix.*]

quern (kwûrn) *n.* **1.** A hand-turned grain mill consisting of two stone wheels, one resting upon the other. **2.** A small hand mill for grinding spices. [Middle English *querne,* Old English *cweorn.* See **gwer-**[2] in Appendix.*]

quer·u·lous (kwĕr′ə-ləs, kwĕr′yə-) *adj.* **1.** Given to complaining or fretting; peevish. **2.** Expressing a complaint or grievance; grumbling; fretful; plaintive. [Latin *querulus,* from *querī,* to complain. See **kwes-** in Appendix.*] **—quer′u·lous·ly** *adv.* **—quer′u·lous·ness** *n.*

que·ry (kwîr′ē) *n., pl.* **-ries. 1.** A question; an inquiry. **2.** A doubt in the mind. **3.** *Abbr.* **q., qu.** A notation, usually (?), calling attention to an item to question its validity or accuracy. —*tr.v.* **queried, -rying, -ries. 1.** To express doubt or uncertainty about; to question. **2.** To put a question to (a person). **3.** To mark (an item) with a question mark in order to question its validity or accuracy. —See Synonyms at **ask.** [Variant (influenced by INQUIRY) of earlier *quaere,* from Latin, imperative of *quaerere,* to seek, ask. See **quaerere** in Appendix.*]

ques. question.

quest (kwĕst) *n.* **1.** The act or instance of seeking or pursuing something; a search. **2.** In medieval romance, an expedition undertaken by a knight in order to perform some prescribed feat. **—in quest of.** In pursuit of; seeking. —*v.* **quested, questing, quests.** —*intr.* **1.** To make a search; go on a quest. **2.** To search for game. —*tr.* To seek; search for. [Middle English *queste,* from Old French, from Vulgar Latin *quaesta* (unattested), from Latin, feminine past participle of *quaerere,* to seek. See **quaerere** in Appendix.*] **—quest′er** *n.*

ques·tion (kwĕs′chən) *n. Abbr.* **q., qn., qu., ques.** *pl.* **qq. 1.** An expression of inquiry that invites or calls for a reply; an interrogative sentence, phrase, or gesture. **2.** A subject or point open to controversy; an unsettled issue. **3.** A difficult matter; problem: *a question of ethics.* **4.** A point or subject under discussion or being considered. **5. a.** A proposition brought up for consideration by an assembly. **b.** The act of bringing such a proposal to vote. **6.** Uncertainty; doubt: *no question about its validity.* **7.** Possibility: *out of the question.* **—call into question. 1.** To request debate on. **2.** To cast doubt upon. —*v.* **questioned, -tioning, -tions.** —*tr.* **1.** To put a question to. **2.** To interrogate, as a witness or suspect. **3.** To express doubt about; to dispute. —*intr.* To ask questions. —See Synonyms at **ask.** [Middle English, from Old French, from Latin *quaestiō,* from *quaerere* (past participle *quaestus*), to seek, ask. See **quaerere** in Appendix.*] **—ques′tion·er** *n.* **—ques′tion·ing·ly** *adv.*

ques·tion·a·ble (kwĕs′chən-ə-bəl) *adj.* **1.** Open to doubt; uncertain; problematic. **2.** Of dubious morality or respectability. —See Synonyms at **doubtful. —ques′tion·a·ble·ness, ques′tion·a·bil′i·ty** *n.* **—ques′tion·a·bly** *adv.*

question mark. A punctuation symbol (?) written at the end of a sentence or phrase to indicate a direct question. Also called "interrogation point."

ques·tion·naire (kwĕs′chə-nâr′) *n.* A printed form containing a

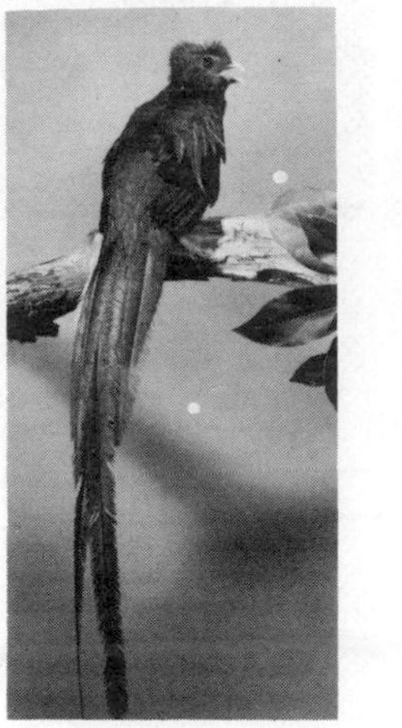

quetzal

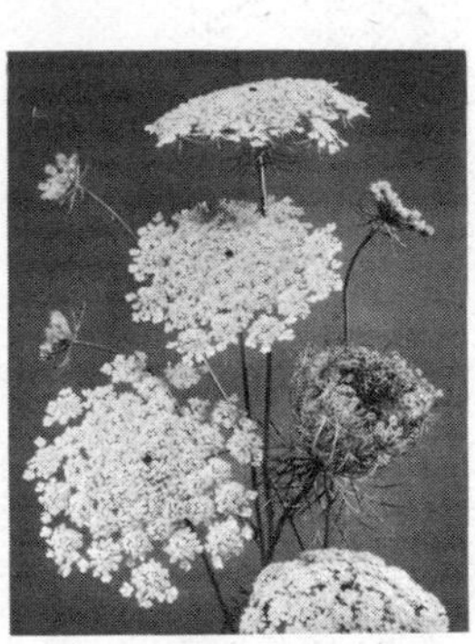

Queen Anne's lace

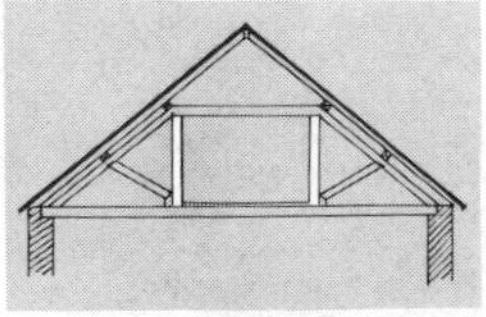

queen post

set of questions, especially one addressed to a statistically significant number of subjects by way of gathering information, as for a survey. [French, from *questionner,* to question, from *question,* QUESTION.]
Quet·ta (kwĕt′ə). A city of West Pakistan, 370 miles north of Karachi. Population, 107,000.
quet·zal (kĕt-säl′) *n., pl.* **-zals** or **-zales** (-sä′lās). Also **que·zal** (kā-zäl′). **1.** A Central American bird, *Pharomacrus mocino,* having brilliant bronze-green and red plumage and, in the male, long, flowing tail feathers. **2.** *Abbr.* **Q a.** The basic monetary unit of Guatemala, equal to 100 centavos. See table of exchange rates at **currency. b.** A coin worth one quetzal. [American Spanish, from Nahuatl *quetzall,* large brilliant tail feather.]
Quet·zal·co·a·tl (kĕt-säl′kō-ät′l). A god of the Toltecs and Aztecs, represented as a plumed serpent.
queue (kyōō) *n.* **1.** A line or file of people or vehicles awaiting turn, as at a ticket window. **2.** A long braid of real or artificial hair worn hanging down the back of the neck; pigtail. —*intr.v.* **queued, queuing, queues.** To get in line; wait in a queue. Often used with *up.* [French, tail, pigtail, line, from Old French *coe, cue,* tail, braid, from Latin *cauda,* tail. See **caudate.**]
Que·zon City (kā′sôn′). The capital of the Philippines (since 1948), on Luzon near Manila. Population, 398,000.
Que·zon (kā′sôn′), **Manuel Luis.** Also **Que·zon y Mo·li·na** (e mō-lē′nä). 1878–1944. Philippine statesman; first president of Commonwealth of the Philippines (1935–1944).
quib·ble (kwĭb′əl) *intr.v.* **-bled, -bling, -bles. 1.** To make exaggerated distinctions or raise objections to the unimportant details of a thing in order to avoid acknowledging its worth or importance. **2.** *Archaic.* To make a pun. —*n.* **1.** A petty distinction or irrelevant objection. **2.** *Archaic.* A pun. [Perhaps from obsolete *quib,* pun, perhaps from Latin *quibus,* plural of *qui,* who, which (used in legal documents and hence associated with quips and quibbles). See **kwo-** in Appendix.*]
quiche (kēsh) *n.* A custard dish baked in an unsweetened pastry shell, often with bacon or cheese. Also called "quiche Lorraine." [French, probably from German (dialectal) *Küche,* diminutive of *Kuchen,* cake, from Old High German *kuocho.* See **kak-**[2] in Appendix.*]
Qui·ché (kē-chā′) *n.* **1.** An Indian people of Guatemala. **2.** The Mayan language of this people.
quick (kwĭk) *adj.* **quicker, quickest. 1.** Moving or functioning rapidly and energetically; speedy. **2.** Occurring or achieved in a brief space of time. **3.** Understanding, thinking, or learning with speed and dexterity; bright. **4.** Perceiving with speed and sensitivity; alert; keen. **5.** Done or occurring immediately. **6.** Hasty or sharp in reacting. **7.** *Archaic.* Pregnant. **8.** *Archaic.* Alive. —See Synonyms at **fast, nimble.** —*n.* **1.** Sensitive or raw exposed flesh, as under the fingernails. **2.** The most personal and sensitive aspect of the emotions: *cut to the quick.* **3.** The living: *the quick and the dead.* **4.** The vital core of a thing; essence. Used especially in the phrase *the quick of the matter.* **5.** *British.* Quickset. —*adv.* Quickly; promptly. See Usage note below. [Middle English *qui(c)ke,* swift, lively, alive, Old English *cwic(u),* living, alive. See **gwei-** in Appendix.*] —**quick′ness** *n.*
Usage: *Quick* (adverb) is used frequently in speech and written dialogue: *Come quick!* In other written contexts, *quickly* is much more common: *By moving quickly, they hope to surprise him.* In this example the use of *quick* for *quickly* is termed unacceptable in writing by 90 per cent of the Usage Panel.
quick assets. Liquid assets, including cash on hand and assets readily convertible to cash.
quick bread. Any bread made with a leavening agent, such as baking powder, that expands during baking and does not require a leavening period beforehand.
quick·en (kwĭk′ən) *v.* **-ened, -ening, -ens.** —*tr.* **1.** To make more rapid; speed up; accelerate. **2.** To make alive; vitalize. **3.** To excite and stimulate; stir. —*intr.* **1.** To become more rapid. **2.** To show life; come or return to life. **3.** To reach the stage of pregnancy when the fetus can be felt to move. —See Synonyms at **speed.** —**quick′en·er** *n.*
quick-freeze (kwĭk′frēz′) *tr.v.* **-froze** (-frōz′), **-frozen** (-frō′zən), **-freezing, -freezes.** To freeze (food) by a process sufficiently rapid to retain natural flavor, nutritional value, or other properties.
quick grass. Couch grass *(see).* [Variant of QUITCHGRASS.]
quick·ie (kwĭk′ē) *n. Informal.* Something made, done, or consumed rapidly or hastily.
quick·lime (kwĭk′līm′) *n. Chemistry.* **Calcium oxide** *(see).* [Quicklime is the *first* product of heating limestone.]
quick·ly (kwĭk′lē) *adv.* **1.** Rapidly; fast. **2.** Soon; promptly. —See Usage note at **quick.**
quick·sand (kwĭk′sănd′) *n.* A bed of loose sand mixed with water forming a soft, shifting mass that yields easily to pressure and tends to suck down any object resting on its surface.
quick·set (kwĭk′sĕt′) *n. Chiefly British.* **1. a.** Cuttings or slips of a plant suitable for hedges. **b.** A single slip or cutting of such a plant. **2.** A hedge consisting of such plants.
quick·sil·ver (kwĭk′sĭl′vər) *n.* The element **mercury** *(see).* —*adj.* Unpredictable; mercurial. [Middle English *quicksilver,* Old English *cwicseolfor* (translation of Latin *argentum vivum*) : QUICK, "living" + SILVER.]
quick·step (kwĭk′stĕp′) *n. Music.* A march for accompanying military quick time.
quick-tem·pered (kwĭk′tĕm′pərd) *adj.* Easily aroused to anger.
quick time. A military marching pace of 120 steps per minute.
quick-wit·ted (kwĭk′wĭt′ĭd) *adj.* Mentally alert and sharp; keen. See Synonyms at **shrewd, intelligent.**
quid[1] (kwĭd) *n.* A cut of something to be chewed, such as tobacco. [Middle English *quide,* cud, Old English *cwidu, c(w)udu.* See **gwet-**[1] in Appendix.*]
quid[2] (kwĭd) *n., pl.* **quid** or **quids.** *British Slang.* A pound sterling. [Origin obscure.]
quid·di·ty (kwĭd′ə-tē) *n., pl.* **-ties. 1.** The real nature of a thing; essence. **2.** A hairsplitting distinction; a quibble. [Medieval Latin *quidditās,* from Latin *quid,* what, something, anything. See **kwo-** in Appendix.*]
quid·nunc (kwĭd′nŭngk′) *n.* A nosy person; busybody. [Latin *quid nunc?* "What now?" : *quid,* what (see **kwo-** in Appendix*) + *nunc,* now (see **nu-** in Appendix*).]
quid pro quo (kwĭd′ prō kwō′). An equal exchange or substitution. [Latin, "something for something."]
qui·es·cent (kwī-ĕs′ənt, kwē-) *adj.* Inactive or still; dormant. See Synonyms at **latent.** [Latin *quiēscens,* present participle of *quiēscere,* to be QUIET.] —**qui·es′cence** *n.* —**qui·es′cent·ly** *adv.*
qui·et (kwī′ĭt) *adj.* **-eter, -etest. 1.** Making no noise; silent. **2.** Free of noise; hushed. **3.** Calm and unmoving; still. **4.** Free of turmoil and agitation; untroubled. **5.** Restful; soothing. **6.** Characterized by tranquillity; serene; peaceful. **7.** Not showy or brash; restrained; unobtrusive. —See Synonyms at **calm, still.** —*n.* The quality or condition of being quiet; silence; tranquillity; repose. —*v.* **quieted, -eting, -ets.** —*tr.* To cause to become silent or at rest; to silence; allay. —*intr.* To become quiet. Often used with *down: The child had been crying but soon quieted down.* —See Synonyms at **pacify.** [Middle English, from Old French, from Latin *quiētus,* from the past participle of *quiēscere,* to be quiet, to be at rest, from *quiēs,* quiet. See **kweye-** in Appendix.*] —**qui′et·ly** *adv.* —**qui′et·ness** *n.*
qui·et·ism (kwī′ə-tĭz′əm) *n.* **1.** A form of Christian mysticism enjoining passive contemplation and the beatific annihilation of the will. **2.** A state of quietness and passivity. —**qui′et·ist** *adj.* & *n.* —**qui′et·is′tic** *adj.*
qui·e·tude (kwī′ə-tōōd′, -tyōōd′) *n.* A condition of tranquillity. [Medieval Latin *quiētūdō,* from Latin *quiētus,* QUIET.]
qui·e·tus (kwī-ē′təs) *n.* **1.** Something that serves to suppress, check, or eliminate. **2.** Release from life; death. **3.** Anything that kills or eliminates; deathblow. **4.** A final discharge, as of a duty or debt. [Medieval Latin *quiētus (est),* "(he is) discharged," from Latin *quiētus,* at rest, QUIET.]
quill (kwĭl) *n.* **1.** The hollow, stemlike main shaft of a feather. Also called "calamus." **2.** Any of the larger wing or tail feathers of a bird. **3.** A writing pen made from such a feather. **4.** A plectrum for a stringed musical instrument of the clavichord type. **5.** A toothpick made from the stem of a feather. **6.** One of the sharp hollow spines of a porcupine or hedgehog. **7.** A musical pipe having a hollow stem. **8.** A spindle or bobbin, originally a length of reed or cane, around which yarn is wound in weaving. **9.** A small roll of dried bark, especially cinnamon. **10.** *Machinery.* A hollow shaft that rotates on a solid shaft when gears are engaged. —*tr.v.* **quilled, quilling, quills. 1.** To wind (thread or yarn) onto a quill. **2.** To make or press small ridges in (fabric). [Middle English *quil(le),* akin to Middle Low German *quiele*†.]
quill·back (kwĭl′băk′) *n., pl.* **-backs** or **quillback.** A North American freshwater fish, *Carpiodes cyprinus,* having one ray of the dorsal fin extending conspicuously beyond the others.
Quil·ler-Couch (kwĭl′ĕr-kōōch′), Sir **Arthur Thomas.** Pen name, "Q." 1863–1944. English author and essayist.
quil·let (kwĭl′ĭt) *n.* A verbal nicety or subtlety; a quibble. [Perhaps short for obsolete *quillity,* variant of QUIDDITY.]
quill·wort (kwĭl′wûrt′, -wôrt′) *n.* Any of several aquatic or marsh plants of the genus *Isoetes,* having short, fleshy stems and grasslike leaves.
Quil·mes (kēl′mās′). A city of Argentina, near the Río de la Plata, southeast of Buenos Aires. Population, 115,000.
quilt (kwĭlt) *n.* **1.** A bed coverlet or blanket made of two layers of fabric with a layer of cotton, wool, feathers, or down in between, all stitched firmly together, usually in a crisscross design. **2.** Any thick cover of protective material. —*v.* **quilted, quilting, quilts.** —*tr.* **1.** To make into a quilt by stitching together (layers of fabric). **2.** To make like a quilt: *quilt a skirt.* **3.** To pad and stitch ornamentally, as in trapunto. —*intr.* **1.** To make a quilt. **2.** To do quilted work. [Middle English *quilte,* from Old French *cuilte,* from Latin *culcita,* sack filled with feathers, mattress. See **kwelek-** in Appendix.*]
quilt·ing (kwĭl′tĭng) *n.* **1.** The process of doing quilted work. **2. a.** Material used to make quilts. **b.** Quilted material.
quin–. Indicates cinchona or cinchona bark; for example, **quinidine.** [From Spanish *quina,* cinchona bark, short for *quinaquina,* perhaps from Quechua.]
quin·a·crine hydrochloride (kwĭn′ə-krēn′). A bright-yellow, bitter, crystalline compound, used primarily to treat malaria. [QUIN- + ACR(ID)INE.]
qui·nate (kwī′nāt′) *adj.* Arranged in groups of five: *quinate leaflets.* [From Latin *quīnī,* five each. See **penkwe** in Appendix.*]
quince (kwĭns) *n.* **1.** A tree, *Cydonia oblonga,* native to western Asia, having white flowers and applelike fruit. **2.** The aromatic, many-seeded fruit of this tree, edible only when cooked. [Middle English *quynce,* plural of *quyn,* quince, from Old French *c(o)oin,* from Latin *cotōneum, cydōneum (mālum),* "Cydonian (apple)," from Greek *kudōnion,* from *Kudōnia,* CYDONIA.]
quin·cun·cial (kwĭn-kŭn′shəl) *adj.* Of, pertaining to, or forming a quincunx. —**quin·cun′cial·ly** *adv.*
quin·cunx (kwĭn′kŭngks′) *n.* An arrangement of five objects, such as trees, with one at each corner of a rectangle and one at the center. [Latin *quincunx* (stem *quincunc-*), "five-twelfths of

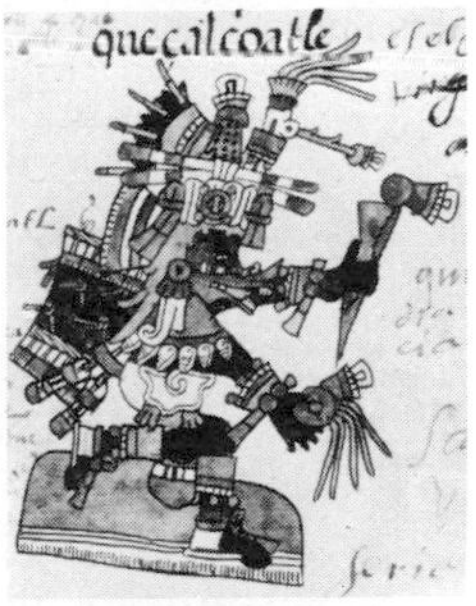
Quetzalcoatl
Aztec pictorial manuscript

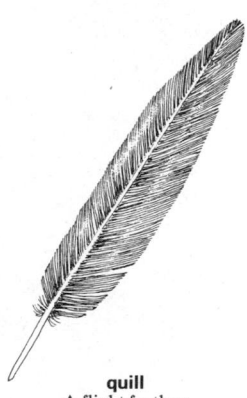

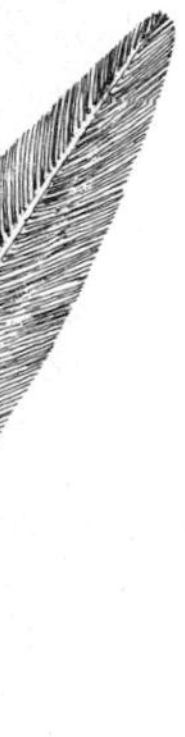
quill
A flight feather

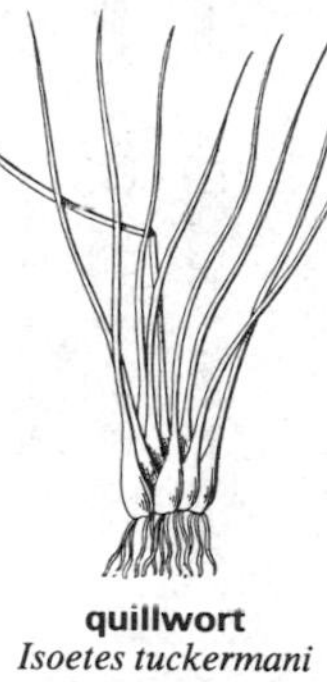
quillwort
Isoetes tuckermani

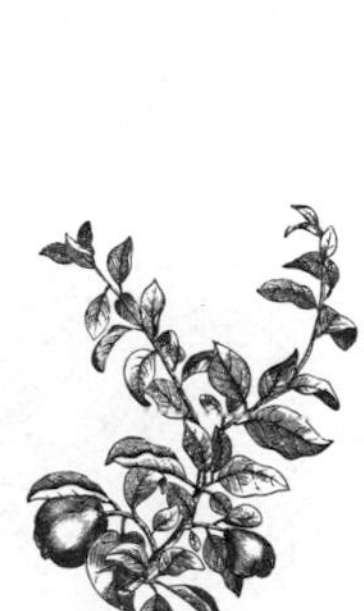
quince

the Roman coin (as denoted by five dots or dashes so arranged)" : *quinque,* five (see **penkwe** in Appendix*) + *uncia,* a twelfth part, from *ūnus,* one (see **oino-** in Appendix*).]

Quin·cy (kwĭn′sē; kwĭn′zē *for sense 2*). **1.** A city of Illinois, on the Mississippi. Population, 44,000. **2.** A city of eastern Massachusetts, the birthplace of John Adams and John Quincy Adams. Population, 87,000.

Quin·cy (kwĭn′zē), **Josiah.** 1772–1864. American political figure, author, and educator.

quin·de·cen·ni·al (kwĭn′dĭ-sĕn′ē-əl) *adj.* **1.** Occurring once every 15 years. **2.** Lasting 15 years. —*n.* A 15th anniversary. [From Latin *quindecim,* fifteen (see **penkwe** in Appendix*) + *annus,* year (see **at-** in Appendix*).]

quin·i·dine (kwĭn′ə-dēn′) *n.* A colorless crystalline alkaloid, $C_{20}H_{24}N_2O_2$, resembling quinine and used in treating certain heart disorders and malaria. [QUIN- + -ID(E) + -INE.]

qui·nine (kwī′nīn′; *British* kwĭ-nēn′) *n.* **1.** A bitter, colorless, amorphous powder or crystalline alkaloid, $C_{20}H_{24}N_2O_2 \cdot 3H_2O$, derived from certain cinchona barks and used in medicine to treat malaria. **2.** Any of various compounds or salts of this alkaloid. [QUIN- + -INE.]

quinine water. A carbonated beverage flavored with quinine.

quin·nat salmon (kwĭn′ăt′). The **chinook salmon** *(see).* [Salish *t'kwinnat.*]

quin·oid (kwĭn′oid′) *n. Chemistry.* A substance resembling quinone in structure or physical properties.

qui·noi·dine (kwĭ-noi′dēn′, -dĭn) *n.* A brownish-black mixture of alkaloids remaining after extraction of crystalline alkaloids from cinchona bark, used as a quinine substitute. [QUIN- + -OID + -INE.]

quin·o·line (kwĭn′ə-lēn′, -lĭn) *n.* An aromatic organic base, C_9H_7N, having a pungent tarlike odor, synthesized or obtained from coal tar, and used as a food preservative and in making antiseptics and dyes. [QUIN- + -OL + -INE.]

qui·none (kwĭ-nōn′, kwĭn′ōn′) *n. Chemistry.* Any of a class of aromatic compounds found widely in plants, especially the yellow crystalline form, $C_6H_4O_2$, used in making dyes, in tanning hides, and in photography. [QUIN- + -ONE.]

quin·o·noid (kwĭn′ə-noid′, kwĭ-nō′noid′) *adj.* Of, containing, or resembling quinone, in structure or properties.

quin·qua·ge·nar·i·an (kwĭng′kwə-jə-nâr′ē-ən) *n.* A person fifty years old, or in his fifties. —*adj.* Of or characteristic of a person in his fifties. [From Latin *quinquāgēnārius,* consisting of fifty, from *quinquāgēnī,* fifty each, from *quinquāginta,* fifty. See **penkwe** in Appendix.*]

Quin·qua·ges·i·ma (kwĭng′kwə-jĕs′ə-mə) *n.* Shrove Sunday, about 50 days before Easter. Also called "Quinquagesima Sunday." [Medieval Latin *quinquāgēsima,* from Latin, fiftieth, from *quinquāginta,* fifty. See **penkwe** in Appendix.*]

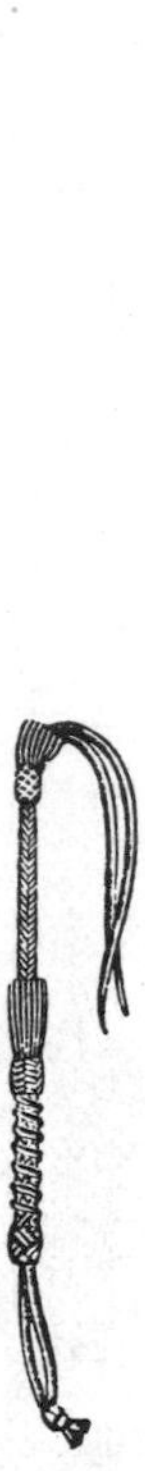

quirt

quinque–. Indicates five; for example, **quinquefoliate.** [From Latin *quinque,* five. See **penkwe** in Appendix.*]

quin·que·fo·li·ate (kwĭng′kwə-fō′lē-ĭt, -āt′) *adj. Botany.* Having five leaves, leaflets, or leaflike parts. [QUINQUE- + Late Latin *foliōlum,* diminutive of Latin *folium,* leaf, FOIL.]

quin·quen·ni·al (kwĭn-kwĕn′ē-əl, kwĭng-) *adj.* **1.** Happening once every five years. **2.** Lasting for five years. —*n.* **1.** A fifth anniversary. **2.** A period of five years. —**quin·quen′ni·al·ly** *adv.*

quin·quen·ni·um (kwĭn-kwĕn′ē-əm, kwĭng-) *n., pl.* **-ums** or **-quennia** (-kwĕn′ē-ə). A period of five years. [Latin : QUINQUE- + *annus,* year (see **at-** in Appendix*).]

quin·que·va·lent (kwĭng′kwə-vā′lənt) *adj.* Pentavalent. —**quin′que·va′lence** *n.*

quin·sy (kwĭn′zē) *n.* Acute inflammation of the tonsils and the surrounding tissue, often leading to the formation of an abscess. [Middle English *quinesye,* from Old French *quinencie,* from Medieval Latin *quinancia,* from Greek *kunanchē,* dog quinsy, sore throat : *kuōn,* hound (see **kwon-** in Appendix*) + *ankhein,* to strangle (see **angh-** in Appendix*).]

quint[1] (kwĭnt) *n.* In piquet, a sequence of five cards of the same suit in one hand. [French, from Latin *quinta,* feminine of *quintus,* fifth. See **penkwe** in Appendix.*]

quint[2] (kwĭnt) *n.* A shortened form of **quintuplet.**

quin·tain (kwĭnt′n) *n.* **1.** A post, or a target mounted on a post, to be tilted at by horsemen or footmen. **2.** The exercise of tilting. [Middle English *quintaine,* from Old French, from Latin *quintāna via,* the fifth street in a Roman camp, supposedly used for military exercises, from *quintānus,* fifth in rank, from *quintus,* fifth. See **penkwe** in Appendix.*]

quin·tal (kwĭnt′l) *n. Abbr.* **q., ql.** **1.** A unit of mass in the metric system equal to 100 kilograms. **2.** A **hundredweight** *(see).* [Middle English, from Old French, from Medieval Latin *quintāle,* from Arabic *qinṭār,* KANTAR.]

Quin·ta·na Ro·o (kēn-tä′nä rō′ō). A territory of Mexico, occupying 19,630 square miles on the eastern part of the Yucatán Peninsula. Population, 61,000. Capital, Chetumal.

quin·tar (kēn-tär′) *n.* A monetary unit, equal to 1/100 of the lek of Albania. See table of exchange rates at **currency.** [Albanian *qintar.*]

quin·tes·sence (kwĭn-tĕs′əns) *n.* **1.** The pure, highly concentrated essence of something. **2.** The purest or most typical instance: *"thou fiery-faced quintessence of all that is abominable!"* (Poe). **3.** *Ancient & Medieval Philosophy.* The fifth and highest essence (after the four elements of earth, air, fire, and water), thought to be the substance of the heavenly bodies and latent in all things. [Middle English, from Old French *quinte essence,* from Medieval Latin *quinta essentia* (translation of Greek *pemptē ousia,* fifth essence) : Latin *quinta,* feminine of *quintus,* fifth (see **penkwe** in Appendix*) + *essentia,* ESSENCE.]

quin·tes·sen·tial (kwĭn′tə-sĕn′shəl) *adj.* Having the nature of a quintessence; pure and concentrated in nature: *"The languor of youth! How unique and quintessential it is."* (Evelyn Waugh).

quin·tet (kwĭn-tĕt′) *n.* Also **quin·tette.** **1.** A group of five persons or things; especially, a group of five musicians. **2.** A musical composition for five voices or instruments. [Italian *quintetto,* from *quinto,* fifth, from Latin *quintus.* See **penkwe** in Appendix.*]

quin·tile (kwĭn′tīl′, kwĭnt′l) *n.* **1.** *Astrology.* The aspect of planets distant from each other by 72 degrees or one-fifth of the zodiac. **2.** *Statistics.* The portion of a frequency distribution containing one-fifth of the total sample. [From Latin *quintus,* fifth. See **penkwe** in Appendix.*]

Quin·til·ian (kwĭn-tĭl′yən). Full name, Marcus Fabius Quintilianus. Roman rhetorician of the first century A.D.

quin·til·lion (kwĭn-tĭl′yən) *n.* **1.** The cardinal number represented by 1 followed by 18 zeros; usually written 10^{18}. Called in British usage "trillion." **2.** In British usage, the cardinal number represented by 1 followed by 30 zeros; usually written 10^{30}. See **number.** [Latin *quintus,* fifth (see **penkwe** in Appendix*) + (M)ILLION.] —**quin·til′lion** *adj.*

quin·til·lionth (kwĭn-tĭl′yənth) *n.* The ordinal number quintillion in a series. See **number.** —**quin·til′lionth** *adj.*

quin·tu·ple (kwĭn-tōō′pəl, -tyōō′pəl, -tŭp′əl, kwĭn′tŏŏ-pəl) *adj.* **1.** Consisting of five parts or units. **2.** Multiplied by five; five times as much, as many, or as large. —*n.* A fivefold amount or number. —*v.* **quintupled, -pling, -ples.** —*tr.* To multiply by five. —*intr.* To be multiplied fivefold. [Old French, from Late Latin *quintuplex* : Latin *quintus,* fifth (see **penkwe** in Appendix*) + *-plex,* "-fold" (see **plek-** in Appendix*).]

quin·tu·plet (kwĭn-tŭp′lĭt, -tōō′plĭt, -tyōō′plĭt, kwĭn′tŏŏ-plĭt) *n.* **1.** A group or combination of five associated by common properties or behavior. **2.** One of five offspring born in a single birth. [From QUINTUPLE.]

quin·tu·pli·cate (kwĭn-tōō′plĭ-kĭt, kwĭn-tyōō′-) *adj.* **1.** Multiplied by five; fivefold. **2.** Being the fifth of a set of copies. —*n.* **1.** One of a set of five. **2.** A set of five copies. —*tr.v.* (kwĭn-tōō′plĭ-kāt′, kwĭn-tyōō′-) **quintuplicated, -cating, -cates.** To make five copies of. [Late Latin *quintuplicātus,* from *quintuplicāre,* to make fivefold, from *quintuplex,* QUINTUPLE.]

quip (kwĭp) *n.* **1.** A brief, witty remark delivered offhand. **2.** A cleverly sarcastic remark; a verbal thrust; a gibe. **3.** A quibble. **4.** Something curious or odd. —See Synonyms at **joke.** —*intr.v.* **quipped, quipping, quips.** To make quips. [Earlier *quippy,* perhaps from Latin *quippe,* indeed, certainly (often used ironically), from *quid,* what. See **kwo-** in Appendix.*]

quip·ster (kwĭp′stər) *n.* One known for making quips.

qui·pu (kē′pōō) *n.* Also **quip·pu.** A device consisting of variously colored and knotted cords attached to a base rope, used by the Incas of Peru for calculating and recording numbers. [Spanish *quipo,* from Quechua *quipu.*]

quire (kwīr) *n. Abbr.* **q., qr.** **1.** A set of 24 or sometimes 25 sheets of paper of the same size and stock; 1/20 ream. **2.** A set of all leaves required for a book. —*tr.v.* **quired, quiring, quires.** To fold or arrange in quires. [Middle English, from Old French *quaer,* set of four sheets, from Vulgar Latin *quaternum* (unattested), from Latin *quaternī,* set of four, from *quater,* four. See **kwetwer-** in Appendix.*]

Quir·i·nal[1] (kwĭr′ə-nəl). *Italian* **Qui·ri·na·le** (kē′rē-nä′lā). One of the seven hills of Rome, the site of the Quirinal Palace, the residence of the monarch or president of Italy since 1870.

Quir·i·nal[2] (kwĭr′ə-nəl) *n.* The Italian government.

quirk (kwûrk) *n.* **1. a.** A sudden sharp turn or twist. **b.** A flourish in handwriting, drawing, or music. **2.** A peculiarity of behavior that eludes prediction or suppression. **3.** An unpredictable or unaccountable act or event; vagary. **4.** An equivocation; quibble; subterfuge. **5.** *Architecture.* A lengthwise groove on a molding between the convex upper part and the soffit. —See Synonyms at **eccentricity.** [Origin obscure.] —**quirk′i·ly** *adv.* —**quirk′i·ness** *n.* —**quirk′y** *adj.*

quirt (kwûrt) *n.* A riding whip with a short handle and a lash of braided rawhide. [Perhaps from Spanish *cuerda,* whip, cord, from Latin *chorda,* CORD.]

quis·ling (kwĭz′lĭng) *n.* A traitor who serves as the puppet of the enemy occupying his country. [After Vidkun *Quisling* (1887–1945), head of the State Council of Norway during the German occupation (1940–45).]

quit (kwĭt) *v.* **quit** or **quitted, quitting, quits.** —*tr.* **1.** To end one's engagement in or occupation with; leave abruptly: *"You and I are on the point of quitting the theatre of our exploits"* (Lord Nelson). **2.** To give up; relinquish; put aside. **3.** To discontinue; cease; stop. **4.** To rid oneself of by paying: *quit a debt.* **5.** To release from a burden or responsibility. **6.** To conduct (oneself) in a specified way: *Quit yourselves like gentlemen.* —*intr.* **1.** To cease to perform. **2.** To give up as in defeat; stop. **3.** To leave a job. —*adj.* Absolved of a duty or obligation; free; released: *"Akaba became quit of all concern for its own present safety."* (T.E. Lawrence). —**call it quits.** To declare that one is ready to stop or give up. [Middle English *quiten,* to set free, release, deliver from, from Old French *quiter,* from Medieval Latin *quiētāre,* to set free, quit, discharge, from Latin *quiētus,* freed, QUIET.]

quitch grass (kwĭch). A plant, **couch grass** *(see).* [Middle English *quicche* (unattested), Old English *cwice.* See **gwei-** in Appendix.*]

quit·claim (kwĭt′klām′) *n. Law.* The transfer of a title, right, or claim to another. —*tr.v.* **quitclaimed, -claiming, -claims.** To renounce all claim to (a possession or right). [Middle English *quiteclaimen* (verb), from Old French *quiteclamer,* "to declare free" : *quite,* free (see **quite**) + *clamer,* to CLAIM.]

ă pat/ā pay/âr care/ä father/b bib/ch church/d deed/ĕ pet/ē be/f fife/g gag/h hat/hw which/ĭ pit/ī pie/îr pier/j judge/k kick/l lid, needle/m mum/n no, sudden/ng thing/ŏ pot/ō toe/ô paw, for/oi noise/ou out/ŏŏ took/ōō boot/p pop/r roar/s sauce/sh ship, dish/

quite (kwīt) *adv.* **1.** To the greatest extent; entirely; completely: *quite alone; not quite finished.* **2.** Actually; truly; really. **3.** Somewhat; rather; to a degree. See Usage note below. —**quite a** (or **an**). **1.** Considerable; notable. Used to qualify an indefinite noun: *quite a few; quite a gap.* See Usage note below. **2.** *Informal.* Exceptional; extraordinary; impressive: *quite an establishment.* [Middle English, from adjective, "free," rid of, from Old French, from Latin *quiētus,* freed, QUIET.]

   Usage: *Quite* is always proper in the senses *to the greatest extent* and *really, truly.* But it is more widely used, and accepted, in the less rigid sense of *somewhat* or *rather: quite warm for spring* (acceptable in writing to 81 per cent of the Usage Panel). In the expressions *quite all right* (accepted by 86 per cent of the Panel) and *quite similar* (accepted by 65 per cent), *quite* is construed in this nonrigid sense. (Some grammarians have contended that *quite all right* is redundant and that *quite* and *similar* are contradictory, according to rigid interpretations of the words.) *Quite a* (or *quite an*), indicating indefinite quantity, is acceptable in written usage to 61 per cent of the Panel in the example *Quite a few of the applicants failed to report. Quite a,* indicating extraordinary quality *(quite a fellow),* is informal.

Qui·to (kē′tō). The capital of Ecuador, situated on the Andean plateau at an altitude of over 9,000 feet. Population, 348,000.

quit·rent (kwĭt′rĕnt′) *n.* A rent paid by a freeman in lieu of services required of him by feudal custom. [Middle English *quiterent* : *quite,* free (see **quite**) + RENT.]

quits (kwĭts) *adj.* Even (with someone) by payment or requital. [Middle English, "discharged," "paid up," from Medieval Latin *quittus,* variant of *quiētus,* freed. See **quit.**]

quit·tance (kwĭt′ns) *n.* **1.** Release from a debt, obligation, or penalty. **2.** A document or receipt certifying such a release. **3.** Something given as requital or recompense; repayment. [Middle English *quitance,* from Old French, from *quiter,* to free, discharge a debt, QUIT.]

quit·ter (kwĭt′ər) *n.* One who gives up easily.

quit·tor (kwĭt′ər) *n.* An inflammation of the hoof cartilage of horses and other solid-hoofed animals, characterized by degeneration of hoof tissue, formation of a slough, and fistulous sores. [Middle English *quiture,* perhaps from Old French, decoction, from Latin *coctūra,* from *coquere* (past participle *coctus*), to cook. See **pekw-** in Appendix.*]

quiv·er[1] (kwĭv′ər) *v.* **-ered, -ering, -ers.** —*intr.* To shake with a rapid slight agitating motion; tremble; vibrate: *A drop of tea quivered at the tip of the spout.* —*tr.* To cause to quiver. —See Synonyms at **shake.** —*n.* The act or motion of quivering. [Middle English *quiveren,* perhaps from QUIVER (nimble).]

quiv·er[2] (kwĭv′ər) *n.* **1.** A portable case for arrows. **2.** A case full of arrows. [Middle English, from Norman French *quiveir,* variant of Old French *cuivre,* from Old Low Franconian *cocar,* probably from Medieval Latin *cucurum,* probably from Hunnish, akin to Mongolian *kökür,* quiver.]

quiv·er[3] (kwĭv′ər) *adj. Obsolete.* Nimble; brisk. [Middle English *quiver,* Old English *cwifer-.* See **gwei-** in Appendix.*]

qui vive (kē vēv′). *French.* A sentinel's challenge. —**on the qui vive.** On the alert; vigilant; watchful. [French, "(Long) live who?"]

quix·ot·ic (kwĭk-sŏt′ĭk) *adj.* Also **quix·ot·i·cal** (kwĭk-sŏt′ĭ-kəl). Caught up in the romance of noble deeds or unreachable ideals; romantic without regard to practicality. [After DON QUIXOTE.] —**quix·ot′i·cal·ly** *adv.* —**quix′o·tism** (kwĭk′sə-tĭz′əm) *n.*

quiz (kwĭz) *tr.v.* **quizzed, quizzing, quizzes. 1.** To question closely or repeatedly; interrogate. See Usage note below. **2.** To test the knowledge of by posing questions. **3.** *British.* To poke fun at; mock. —See Synonyms at **ask.** —*n., pl.* **quizzes. 1.** A questioning or inquiry. See Usage note below. **2.** A short oral or written test of knowledge. **3.** A practical joke. **4.** *Rare.* An eccentric person. [Origin obscure.] —**quiz′zer** *n.*

   Usage: The use, especially in journalism, of *quiz* to mean "interrogate," as in *police quizzed the suspect,* is acceptable in writing to 56 per cent of the Usage Panel. Its use as a noun equivalent to *investigation,* as in *the Senate quiz of automobile manufacturers,* is acceptable in writing to 43 per cent of the Panel.

quiz·zi·cal (kwĭz′ĭ-kəl) *adj.* **1.** Suggesting puzzlement; questioning. **2.** Teasing; mocking: *"his face wore a somewhat quizzical almost impertinent air"* (Lawrence Durrell). —**quiz′zi·cal′i·ty** *n.* —**quiz′zi·cal·ly** *adv.*

quizzing glass. A monocle.

Qum (ko͞om). A city and pilgrimage center of Iran, about 75 miles southwest of Teheran. Population, 96,000.

quod (kwŏd) *n. British Slang.* Prison. [Origin obscure.]

quod·li·bet (kwŏd′lĭ-bĕt′) *n.* A musical medley. [Middle English, scholastic debate, disputation, from Medieval Latin *quodlibetum,* from Latin *quodlibet,* what you please : *quod,* what (see **kwo-** in Appendix*) + *libet,* it pleases, from *libēre,* to please (see **leubh-** in Appendix*).]

quod vi·de (kwŏd vī′dē). *Abbr.* **q.v.** *Latin.* Which see. Usually abbreviated and inserted in parentheses after a cross-reference.

quoin (koin, kwoin) *n.* **1. a.** An exterior angle of a wall or other masonry. **b.** A stone serving to form such an angle; cornerstone. **2.** A keystone. **3.** *Printing.* A wedge-shaped block used

to lock type in a chase. **4.** A wedge used to raise the level of a gun. —*tr.v.* **quoined, quoining, quoins.** To provide, secure, or raise with a quoin or quoins. [Variant of COIN (corner).]

quoit (kwoit, koit) *n.* **1.** *Plural.* A game in which flat rings of iron or rope are pitched at a stake, with points awarded for encircling it. **2.** One of the rings used in this game. [Middle English *coite*†.]

quon·dam (kwŏn′dəm, -dăm′) *adj.* That once was; former: *"the quondam drunkard, now perfectly sober"* (Bret Harte). [Latin, formerly, from *quom,* when. See **kwo-** in Appendix.*]

Quon·set hut (kwŏn′sĭt). A trademark for a portable hut having a semicircular roof of corrugated metal that curves down to form walls. [First made in *Quonset,* Rhode Island.]

Quonset hut

quo·rum (kwôr′əm, kwōr′-) *n.* **1.** The minimum number of officers and members of a committee or organization, usually a majority, who must be present for the valid transaction of business. **2.** A select group; an elect body. [Middle English, a quorum of justices of the peace, from Latin texts of commissions reading *quorum vos . . . duos esse volumus,* "of whom we wish that you be . . . two," genitive plural of *quī,* who. See **kwo-** in Appendix.*]

quot. quotation.

quo·ta (kwō′tə) *n.* **1. a.** A share, as of goods, assigned to a group or to each member of a group; allotment. **b.** A production assignment. **2.** The maximum number or proportion of persons who may be admitted, as to a nation, group, or institution. [Medieval Latin, from Latin, feminine of *quotus,* of what number. See **quote.**]

quot·a·ble (kwō′tə-bəl) *adj.* Suitable for quoting. —**quot′a·bil′i·ty** *n.*

quo·ta·tion (kwō-tā′shən) *n. Abbr.* **quot. 1.** The act of quoting. **2.** A passage that is quoted. See Usage note at **quote. 3.** *Commerce.* **a.** The quoting of current prices and bids for securities and goods. **b.** The prices or bids cited. —**quo·ta′tion·al** *adj.* —**quo·ta′tion·al·ly** *adv.*

quotation mark. Either of a pair of punctuation marks used to mark the beginning and end of a passage attributed to another and repeated word for word. They usually appear in the form (" "). Single quotation marks (' ') are usually reserved to set off a quotation within a quotation. Also *informal* "quote."

   Usage: Quotation marks may also be used to enclose titles of works of art, literary and musical works, and names of ships and aircraft (except where such material is set off by italic type). They are also employed to distinguish a term or phrase from the rest of the text: *the word "liberal"; the saying "better late than never."* These marks may also be used to indicate irony or other double meaning: *this "leader" we elected.* When lengthy quoted material extends beyond one paragraph, each additional paragraph begins with quotation marks, but the marks that close the quotation appear only once. Usually a comma or period at the end of a quoted passage is placed inside quotation marks; usually a semicolon or colon is outside.

quote (kwōt) *v.* **quoted, quoting, quotes.** —*tr.* **1.** To repeat or copy the words of (another), usually with acknowledgment of the source. **2.** To cite or refer to for illustration or proof. See Usage note below. **3.** To state (a price) for securities, goods, or services. —*intr.* To give a quotation, as from a book. —*n. Informal.* **1.** A quotation. See Usage note below. **2.** A **quotation mark** (see). [Middle English *coten,* to mark (as chapters or references) with numbers, from Medieval Latin *quotāre,* from Latin *quotus,* of what number, from *quot,* how many. See **kwo-** in Appendix.*] —**quot′er** *n.*

   Usage: *Quote* (transitive verb) is used most accurately in the sense of exact citation. When less specific reference to something is intended, *cite* is more appropriate. *Quote* (noun), as a substitute for *quotation,* is considered unacceptable in writing to 85 per cent of the Usage Panel.

quoth (kwōth) *tr.v. Archaic.* Uttered; said. Used only in the first and third persons, with the subject following: *"Quoth the raven 'Nevermore!'"* (Poe). [Middle English *quoth,* Old English *cwæth,* he said, from *cwethan,* to say. See **gwet-**[2] in Appendix.*]

quo·tha (kwō′thə) *interj. Archaic.* Used to express surprise or sarcasm, after quoting the word or phrase of another. [Contraction of *quoth he.*]

quo·tid·i·an (kwō-tĭd′ē-ən) *adj.* **1.** Recurring daily. **2.** Everyday; commonplace. [Middle English *cotidien,* from Old French, from Latin *quotīdiānus,* from *quotīdiē,* each day : *quot,* how many, as many as (see **kwo-** in Appendix*) + *diēs,* day (see **deiw-** in Appendix*).]

quo·tient (kwō′shənt) *n.* The quantity resulting from division of one quantity by another. [Middle English *quocient,* from Latin *quotiēns,* how many times, from *quot,* how many. See **kwo-** in Appendix.*]

Qur·net es Sau·da (ko͞or′nĕt-ĕs-sä′o͞o-dä). The highest peak (10,131 feet) of the Lebanon Mountains, in northern Lebanon.

qu·rush (ko͞or′rəsh) *n., pl.* **-rush** or **-rushes.** A coin equal to 1/20 of the riyal of Saudi Arabia. See table of exchange rates at **currency.** [Arabic *qurūs,* plural of *qirš.*]

q.v. quod vide.

quiver[2]
Fifteenth-century German quiver with crossbow bolts

Rr

Ra

raccoon

999 99P PRR Rr RℛRℛrℛ

1 2 3	4 5 6	7 8 9	10 11	12 13 14 15
Phoenician	Greek	Roman	Medieval	Modern

Around 1000 B.C. the Phoenicians and other Semites of Syria and Palestine began to use a graphic sign in the forms (1,2,3). They gave it the name rēsh, *meaning "head," and used it for the consonant* r. *After 900 B.C. the Greeks borrowed the sign from the Phoenicians (4), straightened it out (5), and reversed its orientation (6). They also changed its name to* rhō. *The Greek forms passed via Etruscan to the Roman alphabet (7). The Romans added a tail running from the loop (8) so as to differentiate this sign from their sign* P. *The Roman Monumental Capital (9) is the prototype of our modern capital, printed (12) and written (13). The written form (8) developed into the late Roman and medieval Uncial (10) and then into the Cursive (11), which is the basis of our modern small letter, printed (14) and written (15).*

r, R (är) *n., pl.* **r's** or *rare* **rs, R's** or **Rs. 1.** The 18th letter of the modern English alphabet. See **alphabet. 2.** Any of the speech sounds represented by this letter.

r, R, r., R. *Note:* As an abbreviation or symbol, *r* may be a small or a capital letter, with or without a period. Established forms or those generally preferred precede the definition. When no form is given, all four forms are in general use in that sense. **1.** R *Chemistry.* gas constant. **2.** R. rabbi. **3.** R *Chemistry.* radical. **4.** r, R radius. **5.** r., R. railroad; railway. **6.** r. range. **7.** r. rare. **8.** R, R. Réaumur (scale). **9.** R. rector. **10.** R. regius. **11.** R Republican (party). **12.** r, R *Electricity.* resistance. **13.** R *Ecclesiastical.* response. **14.** r. retired. **15.** r., R. right. **16.** r., R. river. **17.** r., R. road. **18.** r. rod (unit of length). **19.** R roentgen (unit of radiation). **20.** R *Chess.* rook. **21.** r., R. rouble. **22.** R. royal. **23.** r. *Card Games.* rubber. **24.** r, R *Sports.* run. **25.** r., R. rupee. **26.** The 18th in a series; 17th when *J* is omitted.

Ra (rä). Also **Re** (rā). The sun god, the supreme deity of the ancient Egyptians, represented as a man with the head of a hawk crowned with a solar disk and uraeus. [Egyptian *ra'.*]

Ra The symbol for the element radium.

RA Regular Army.

R.A. 1. rear admiral. **2.** Regular Army. **3.** *Astronomy.* right ascension. **4.** Royal Academy; Royal Academician.

Raab. The German name for **Györ.**

R.A.A.F. Royal Australian Air Force.

Ra·bat (rä-bät'). The capital of Morocco, a seaport on the Atlantic coast. Population, 227,000.

ra·ba·to. Variant of **rebato.**

Rab·bah Am·mon, Rab·bath Am·mon. The Biblical names for **Amman.**

rab·bet (răb'ĭt) *n.* Also **re·bate** (rē'bāt, răb'ĭt). **1.** A cut or groove along or near the edge of a piece of wood that allows another piece to fit into it to form a joint. **2.** A joint made in this manner. —*v.* **rabbeted, -beting, -bets.** —*tr.* **1.** To cut a rabbet in. **2.** To join by a rabbet. —*intr.* To be joined by a rabbet. [Middle English *rabet,* from Old French *rabat,* a beating down, from *rabattre,* beat down, reduce : *re-,* back + *abattre,* beat down : *a-,* from Latin *ad-,* to + *battre,* beat, from Latin *battuere* (see **battuere** in Appendix*).]

rab·bi (răb'ī) *n., pl.* **-bis.** Also **rab·bin** (răb'ĭn). **1.** *Abbr.* **R.** The ordained spiritual leader of a Jewish congregation. **2.** Formerly, a person authorized to interpret Jewish law. [Hebrew *rabbi,* my master : *rabh,* great one + *-ī,* my.]

rab·bin·ate (răb'ĭn-āt') *n.* The office or function of a rabbi.

Rab·bin·ic (rə-bĭn'ĭk) *n.* The Hebrew language as used in the learned writings of the rabbis of the medieval period.

rab·bin·i·cal (rə-bĭn'ĭk-əl) *adj.* Also **rab·bin·ic** (-ĭk). Of, pertaining to, or characteristic of rabbis, or their views, learning, writings, or language. —**rab·bin'i·cal·ly** *adv.*

rab·bin·ism (răb'ĭn-ĭz'əm) *n.* Rabbinical teachings and traditions.

rab·bin·ist (răb'ĭn-ĭst) *n.* A strict observer of the Talmud and of rabbinical traditions. —**rab·bin·is'tic, rab·bin·is'ti·cal, rab·bin·it'ic** (-ĭt'ĭk) *adj.* —**rab·bin·is'ti·cal·ly** *adv.*

rab·bit (răb'ĭt) *n., pl.* **-bits** or **rabbit. 1.** Any of various long-eared, short-tailed, burrowing mammals of the family Leporidae, such as the commonly domesticated Old World species *Oryctolagus cuniculus,* or the **cottontail** *(see).* **2.** Loosely, a hare. **3.** The fur of a rabbit or hare. **4.** A cheese dish, **Welsh rabbit** *(see).* —*intr.v.* **rabbited, -biting, -bits.** To hunt rabbits. [Middle English *rabet,* probably from Walloon *robete,* diminutive of Flemish *robbe†.*] —**rab'bit·er** *n.*

rabbit brush. An aromatic shrub, *Chrysothamnus graveolens,* of western North America, having clusters of yellow flowers.

rabbit fever. A disease, **tularemia** *(see).*

rab·bit-foot clover (răb'ĭt-fŏŏt'). A clover, *Trifolium arvense,* native to the Old World, having pinkish-gray, furlike flowers resembling rabbits' paws.

rabbit punch. A chopping blow to the back of the neck.

rab·ble¹ (răb'əl) *n.* **1.** A tumultuous mob. **2.** A group of persons regarded with contempt: *a rabble of penniless aristocrats.* —**the rabble.** The nonpropertied classes. Used contemptuously. [Origin uncertain.]

rab·ble² (răb'əl) *n.* Also **rab·bler** (-lər). *Metallurgy.* **1.** An iron bar with one end bent like a rake, used to stir and skim molten iron in puddling. **2.** Any of various similar tools or mechanically operated devices used in roasting or refining furnaces. —*tr.v.* **rabbled, -bling, -bles.** *Metallurgy.* To stir or skim (molten iron) with a rabble. [French *râble,* fire shovel, from Old French *roable,* from Medieval Latin *rotabulum,* from Latin *rutābulum,* from *ruere†* (past participle *rutus*), to rake up.]

rab·ble-rous·er (răb'əl-rou'zər) *n.* A demagogue.

Rab·e·lais (răb'ə-lā; *French* rà-blā'), **François.** 1494?–1553. French humanist.

Rab·e·lai·si·an (răb'ə-lā'zē-ən, -zhən) *adj.* Pertaining to or characteristic of Rabelais; broadly and lustily humorous; satirical.

Ra·bi (rŭ'bē) *n.* Also **Ra·bi·a** (rə-bē'ə). Either the third or the fourth month of the Moslem calendar. See **calendar.** [Arabic *rabī,* spring.]

Ra·bi (rä'bē), **Isidor Isaac.** Born 1898. Austrian-born American atomic physicist.

rab·id (răb'ĭd) *adj.* **1.** Of or afflicted with rabies. **2.** Fanatical. **3.** Raging; uncontrollable: *rabid thirst.* [Latin *rabidus,* raving, from *rabere,* to rave. See **rabh-** in Appendix.*] —**ra·bid'i·ty** (rə-bĭd'ə-tē, rā-), **rab'id·ness** *n.* —**rab'id·ly** *adv.*

ra·bies (rā'bēz, -bĭ-ēz) *n.* An acute, infectious, often fatal, viral disease of most warm-blooded animals, especially wolves, cats, and dogs, that attacks the central nervous system and is transmitted by the bite of infected animals. Also called "hydrophobia." [New Latin, from Latin *rabiēs,* rage, from *rabere,* to rave. See **rabh-** in Appendix.*] —**ra·bi·et'ic** (-ĕt'ĭk) *adj.*

Ra·bin·o·witz, Solomon. See **Sholem Aleichem.**

rac·coon (ră-kōōn') *n., pl.* **-coons** or **raccoon.** Also **ra·coon. 1.** A carnivorous North American mammal, *Procyon lotor,* having grayish-brown fur, black, masklike facial markings, and a bushy, black-ringed tail. Also called "coon." **2.** The fur of this animal. **3.** Any of various similar or related animals. [Algonquian (Virginia) *aroughcoune, arathkone.*]

raccoon dog. A foxlike mammal, *Nyctereutes procyonoides,* of northeastern Asia, having raccoonlike facial markings.

race¹ (rās) *n.* **1.** A local geographic or global human population

ă pat/ā pay/âr care/ä father/b bib/ch church/d deed/ĕ pet/ē be/f fife/g gag/h hat/hw which/ĭ pit/ī pie/îr pier/j judge/k kick/l lid,
needle/m mum/n no, sudden/ng thing/ŏ pot/ō toe/ô paw, for/oi noise/ou out/ŏŏ took/ōō boot/p pop/r roar/s sauce/sh ship, dish/

distinguished as a more or less distinct group by genetically transmitted physical characteristics. **2.** Mankind as a whole. **3.** Any group of people united or classified together on the basis of common history, nationality, or geographical distribution. **4.** A genealogical line; lineage; family. **5.** Any group of people more or less distinct from all others: *the race of statesmen.* **6.** *Biology.* **a.** A plant or animal population that differs from others of the same species in the frequency of hereditary traits; subspecies. **b.** A breed or strain, as of domestic animals. **7.** A distinguishing or characteristic quality, such as the flavor of a wine. **8.** Sprightliness; style. —See Synonyms at **nation.** [French, group of people, generation, perhaps ultimately from Latin *ratiō,* a reckoning, account. See **ratio.**]

race[2] (rās) *n.* **1. a.** A competition of speed, such as in running or riding. **b.** *Plural.* A series of such competitions, usually horse races, held at a specified time on a regular course: *winning money at the races.* **2.** Any contest or pursuit of supremacy: *the Presidential race.* **3.** Steady or rapid onward movement. **4. a.** A strong or swift current of water. **b.** The channel of such a current. **c.** An artificial channel built to transport water and utilize its energy. **5.** A groovelike part of a machine in which a moving part slides or rolls. **6.** *Aviation.* A **slipstream** *(see).* —*v.* **raced, racing, races.** —*intr.* **1.** To compete in a contest of speed. **2.** To move rapidly or at top speed. **3.** *Machinery.* To run too rapidly because of decreased resistance or a lighter load. —*tr.* **1.** To compete against in a contest of speed. **2.** To cause to compete in such a contest. **3.** *Machinery.* To cause (an engine with the gears disengaged, for example) to run swiftly or too swiftly. [Middle English *ra(a)s,* from Old Norse *rās.* See **ers-**[1] in Appendix.*]

race[3] (rās) *n.* A root, especially of ginger. [Old French *rais, raiz,* root, from Latin *rādix.* See **werād-** in Appendix.*]

Race, Cape (rās). A cape at the southeastern extremity of Newfoundland, on Avalon Peninsula.

race·course (rās′kôrs′) *n.* A racetrack.

race·horse (rās′hôrs′) *n.* A horse bred and trained to race.

ra·ceme (rā-sēm′, rə-) *n. Botany.* An inflorescence in which stalked flowers are arranged singly along a common main axis, as in the lily of the valley. [Latin *racēmus*†, stalk of a cluster of grapes, bunch of berries.]

ra·ce·mic (rā-sē′mĭk, -sĕm′ĭk, rə-) *adj.* Of or pertaining to a chemical compound containing equal quantities of dextrorotatory and levorotatory isomers so that it does not rotate the plane of incident polarized light. [French *racémique,* from Latin *racēmus,* RACEME.]

racemic acid. An optically inactive form of tartaric acid, $C_4H_6O_6 \cdot H_2O$, that can be separated into dextrorotatory and levorotatory components and is sometimes found in grape juice during wine-making.

ra·ce·mi·form (rā-sē′mə-fôrm′) *adj. Botany.* Racemelike in form. [From RACEME + -FORM.]

rac·e·mism (răs′ə-mĭz′əm, rā-sē′-) *n. Chemistry.* The condition or state of being racemic.

rac·e·mi·za·tion (răs′ə-mĭ-zā′shən) *n. Chemistry.* The conversion of an optically active substance to a racemic form.

rac·e·mose (răs′ə-mōs′) *adj.* **1.** *Botany.* Resembling or growing in a raceme. **2.** *Anatomy.* Having a structure of clustered parts. Said of glands. [Latin *racēmōsus,* full of clusters, from *racēmus,* RACEME.] —**rac′e·mose′ly** *adv.*

rac·er (rā′sər) *n.* **1.** One that engages in races or is capable of great speed. **2.** Any of various fast-moving North American snakes of the genus *Coluber.*

race·run·ner (rās′rŭn′ər) *n.* Any of several fast-moving New World lizards of the genus *Cnemidophorus.*

race·track (rās′trăk′) *n.* A course laid out for racing.

race·way (rās′wā′) *n.* **1.** An artificial channel for transporting water. **2.** A usually rectangular tube for enclosing and protecting electric wires. **3.** A racetrack.

Ra·chel[1] (rā′chəl). A feminine given name. [Hebrew *rāḥēl,* "ewe."]

Ra·chel[2] (rā′chəl). The second wife of Jacob and mother of his sons Joseph and Benjamin. Genesis 29–35.

ra·chis (rā′kĭs) *n., pl.* **-chises** or **-chides** (-kə-dēz′). *Biology.* A main axis or shaft, such as the main stem of an inflorescence or the spinal column. [New Latin, from Greek *rhakhis,* spine, backbone. See **wrāgh-** in Appendix.*] —**ra′chi·al** *adj.*

ra·chi·tis (rə-kī′tĭs) *n.* A childhood and infant disease, **rickets** *(see).* [New Latin, from Greek *rhakhitis,* disease of the spine : RACHIS + -ITIS.] —**ra·chit′ic** (-kĭt′ĭk) *adj.*

Rach·ma·ni·noff (răKH-mä′nĭ-nôf), **Sergei Vassilievich.** 1873–1943. Russian composer and pianist.

ra·cial (rā′shəl) *adj.* **1.** Pertaining to or typical of an ethnic group or groups. **2.** Arising from or based upon differences between ethnic groups. —**ra′cial·ly** *adv.*

Ra·cine (rə-sēn′). An industrial city on Lake Michigan in southeastern Wisconsin. Population, 89,000.

Ra·cine (rà-sēn′), **Jean Baptiste.** 1639–1699. French playwright.

racing form. An information sheet about horse races.

ra·cism (rā′sĭz′əm) *n.* Also *chiefly British* **ra·cial·ism** (rā′shəl-ĭz′əm). The notion that one's own ethnic stock is superior. —**rac′ist, ra′cial·ist** *n. & adj.*

rack[1] (răk) *n.* **1.** A framework or stand in which to hold or display various articles, especially: **a.** A triangular frame for arranging billiard balls at the start of a game. **b.** A receptacle for livestock feed. **c.** A frame for holding bombs in an airplane. **d.** *Printing.* An upright framework for holding cases of type or galley proof. **2.** *Machinery.* A toothed bar that meshes with another toothed structure, such as a pinion or gearwheel. **3.** A framelike instrument of torture. Often used with *the.* **4.** A state or cause of intense anguish. **5.** The stress of storm. —**on the rack.** Under a great strain or in anguish. —*tr.v.* **racked, racking, racks. 1.** To place in or upon a rack. **2.** To torture by means of the rack. **3.** To torment. **4.** To strain with great effort: *rack one's brain.* —**rack up.** *Slang.* To accumulate or score: *rack up points.* [Middle English *rekke, rakke,* probably from Middle Dutch *rec,* framework. See **reg-**[1] in Appendix.*] —**rack′er** *n.*

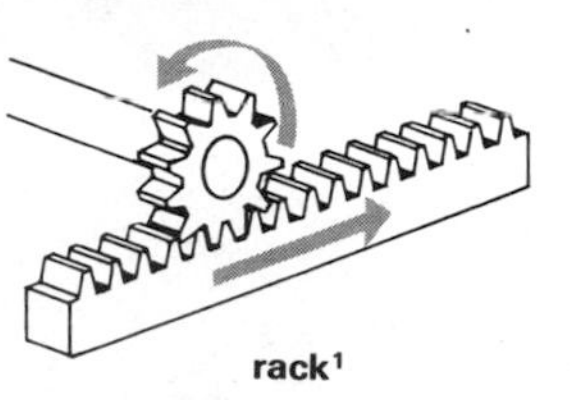

rack[1]

rack[2] (răk) *n.* Either of two gaits of horses, the **single-foot** or the **pace** *(both of which see).* —*intr.v.* **racked, racking, racks.** To go or move with either of these gaits. [Origin uncertain.]

rack[3] (răk) *n.* Also **wrack.** A thin mass of wind-driven clouds. —*intr.v.* **racked, racking, racks.** Also **wrack.** To be driven by the wind, as clouds. [Middle English *rak,* perhaps from Scandinavian, akin to Swedish *rak.* See **wreg-** in Appendix.*]

rack[4] (răk) *n.* Destruction. —**go to rack and ruin.** To fall apart. [Variant of WRACK (ruin).]

rack[5] (răk) *tr.v.* **racked, racking, racks.** To drain (wine or cider) from the dregs. [Middle English *rakken,* from Old Provençal *arracer,* from *raca*†, dregs, stems and husks of grapes.]

rack[6] (răk) *n.* **1.** A wholesale rib cut of lamb between the shoulder and the loin. **2.** A crown roast of lamb. [Perhaps from RACK (framework).]

rack and pinion. A device for the interconversion of rotary and linear motion, consisting of a pinion and a mated rack.

rack·et[1] (răk′ĭt) *n.* Also **rac·quet. 1.** A light bat with a nearly elliptical hoop strung with a network of catgut, nylon, or silk, used in various ball games. **2.** *Plural.* A game similar to tennis, played in a four-walled court. Used with a singular verb. [Old French *rachette, raquette,* from dialectal Arabic *râḥet,* palm of the hand.]

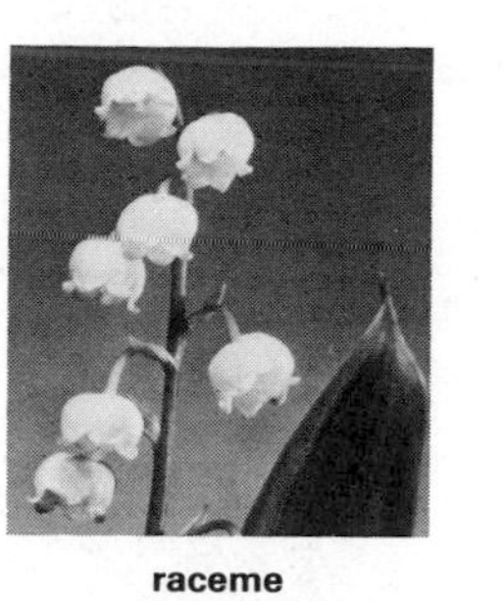

raceme
Raceme of
lily of the valley

rack·et[2] (răk′ĭt) *n.* **1.** A clamor; uproar. **2. a.** A business that obtains money through fraud or extortion. **b.** An illegal or dishonest practice. **3.** *Slang.* Any business or job. —See Synonyms at **noise.** —*intr.v.* **racketed, -eting, -ets.** To lead a gay life. [Origin obscure.]

rack·et·eer (răk′ə-tîr′) *n.* One engaged in an illegal business. —*intr.v.* **racketeered, -eering, -eers.** To engage in a racket.

rack·et·y (răk′ĭt-ē) *adj.* Noisy; raucous; rowdy.

rack railway. A **cog railway** *(see).*

rack-rent (răk′rĕnt′) *n.* Exorbitant rent. —*tr.v.* **rack-rented, -renting, -rents.** To exact exorbitant rent for or from. [From RACK (to torture).] —**rack′-rent′er** *n.*

rac·on·teur (răk′ŏn-tûr′; *French* rà-kôN-tœr′) *n.* One who recounts stories and anecdotes with skill and wit. [French, from Old French, from *raconter,* to tell : *re-,* again + *aconter,* tell, count : *a-,* from Latin *ad-,* to + *co(u)nter,* to COUNT.]

ra·coon. Variant of **raccoon.**

rac·y (rā′sē) *adj.* **-ier, -iest. 1.** Full-flavored, as wine or fruit. **2. a.** Piquant or pungent. **b.** Risqué; ribald. [From RACE (lineage, in the sense of a distinctive kind).] —**rac′i·ly** *adv.* —**rac′i·ness** *n.*

rad (răd) *n. Physics.* A unit of energy absorbed from ionizing radiation, equal to 100 ergs per gram of irradiated material. [Short for RADIATION.]

rad radian.

rad. 1. radical. **2.** radio. **3.** radius. **4.** radix.

ra·dar (rā′där) *n. Electronics.* **1.** A method of detecting distant objects and determining their position, velocity, or other characteristics by analysis of very high frequency radio waves reflected from their surfaces. **2.** The equipment used in such detection. [RA(DIO) D(ETECTING) A(ND) R(ANGING).]

radar beacon. A fixed device that sends or receives, amplifies, alters, and returns a radar signal, permitting a distant receiver to determine its bearing and sometimes its range.

ra·dar·scope (rā′där-skōp′) *n. Electronics.* The oscilloscope viewing screen of a radar receiver. [RADAR + (OSCILLO)SCOPE.]

Rad·cliffe (răd′klĭf), **Ann.** 1764–1823. English novelist.

rad·dle[1] (răd′l) *tr.v.* **-dled, -dling, -dles.** To twist together or interweave. [From Old French *rudelle, redelle,* rod twisted between upright stakes, perhaps from Middle High German *reidel.* See **reidh-** in Appendix.*]

rad·dle[2]. Variant of **ruddle.**

rad·dled (răd′əld) *adj.* Worn-out and broken-down, as by debauch or general deterioration. [Origin unknown.]

Ra·dha·krish·nan (rä′dŭ-krĭsh′nŭn), Sir **Sarvepali.** Born 1888. Indian statesman; president of India (1962–67).

ra·di·al (rā′dē-əl) *adj.* **1. a.** Of, pertaining to, or arranged like rays or radii. **b.** Radiating from or converging to a common center. **2.** Having or characterized by parts so arranged or so radiating. **3.** Moving or directed along a radius. **4.** *Anatomy.* Of, pertaining to, or near the radius or forearm. **5.** Developing symmetrically about a central point. —*n.* A radial part, such as a ray, spoke, or radius. [Medieval Latin *radiālis,* from Latin *radius,* rod, ray. See **radius.**] —**ra′di·al·ly** *adv.*

radial engine. An internal-combustion engine, as formerly used in propeller-driven aircraft, with radially arrayed cylinders.

radial symmetry. Symmetrical arrangement of constituents, especially of radiating parts, about a central point.

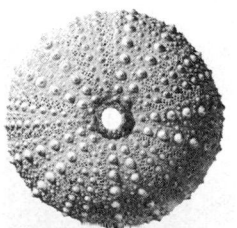

radial symmetry
Shell of sea urchin
showing radial symmetry

ra·di·an (rā′dē-ən) *n. Abbr.* **rad** *Mathematics.* A unit of angular measure equal to the angle subtended at the center of a circle by an arc of length equal to the radius of the circle. It is equal to $^{360}/_{2\pi}$ degrees, or approximately 57°17′44.6″. [RADI(US) + -AN.]

ra·di·ance (rā′dē-əns) *n.* Also **ra·di·an·cy** (-ən-sē). **1.** The quality or state of being radiant. **2.** *Physics.* The radiant energy emitted per unit time in a specified direction by a unit area of an emitting surface. In this sense, also called "radiant flux."

ra·di·ant (rā′dē-ənt) *adj.* **1.** Emitting heat or light. **2.** Consist-

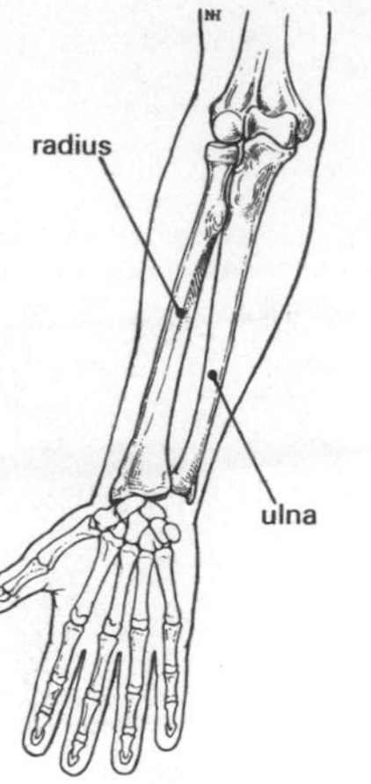

radius

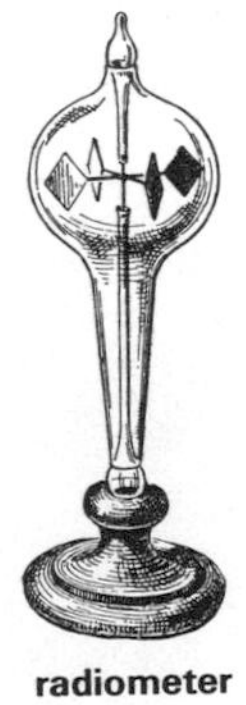

radiometer

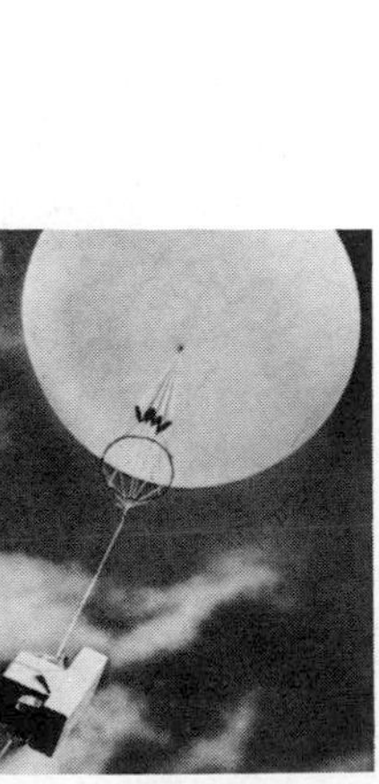

radiosonde

ing of or emitted as radiation: *radiant heat.* **3. a.** Filled with light; bright. **b.** Glowing; beaming. —See Synonyms at **bright.** —*n.* **1.** An object or point from which light or heat rays are emitted. **2.** *Astronomy.* The apparent celestial origin of a meteoric shower. [Latin *radiāns,* present participle of *radiāre,* to RADIATE.] —**ra'di·ant·ly** *adv.*

radiant energy. *Physics.* Energy transferred by radiation, especially by an electromagnetic wave, as of visible light, heat, or radio waves.

ra·di·ate (rā'dē-āt') *v.* **-ated, -ating, -ates.** —*intr.* **1.** To emit radiation. **2.** To issue or emerge in rays. **3.** To spread out or converge radially, as the spokes of a wheel. —*tr.* **1.** To emit (heat or light, for example). **2.** To diffuse or disseminate from or as if from a center. **3.** To irradiate or illuminate (an object). **4.** To manifest in a glowing manner: *He radiated confidence.* —*adj.* (rā'dē-ĭt). **1.** *Botany.* Having rays or raylike parts: *radiate flowers.* **2.** *Zoology.* Characterized by **radial symmetry** *(see).* **3.** Surrounded with rays, as a head represented on a coin. [Latin *radiāre,* to emit beams, furnish with spokes, from *radius,* ray. See **radius.**] —**ra'di·a'tive** *adj.*

ra·di·a·tion (rā'dē-ā'shən) *n.* **1.** The act or process of radiating. **2.** *Physics.* **a.** The emission and propagation of waves or particles. **b.** The propagating waves or particles, such as light, sound, radiant heat, or particles emitted by radioactivity. **3.** *Anatomy.* Radial arrangement of parts, as of a group of nerve fibers connecting different areas of the brain. **4.** *Biology.* A form of evolution, **adaptive radiation** *(see).*

radiation sickness. Illness induced by ionizing radiation, ranging in severity from nausea, vomiting, headache, and diarrhea to loss of hair and teeth, reduction in red and white blood cell count, extensive hemorrhaging, sterility, and death.

ra·di·a·tor (rā'dē-ā'tər) *n.* **1.** A heating device consisting of a series of connected pipes for the circulation of steam or hot water. **2.** A cooling device, as in automotive engines, through which water or other fluids circulate as a coolant. **3.** *Physics.* A body that emits radiation. **4.** A transmitting antenna.

rad·i·cal (răd'ĭ-kəl) *adj.* **1.** Arising from or going to a root or source; fundamental; basic. **2.** Carried to the farthest limit; extreme; sweeping: *radical social change.* **3.** Favoring or effecting revolutionary changes, as in political organization. **4.** Of or designating a word root. **5.** *Botany.* Of, pertaining to, or growing from the root. —*n.* **1.** One who advocates political and social revolution. **2.** *Mathematics. Abbr.* **rad.** The root of a quantity as indicated by the **radical sign** *(see).* **3.** *Chemistry. Abbr.* **R** An atom or group of atoms with at least one unpaired electron. **4.** *Abbr.* **rad.** A word element, **root** *(see).* [Middle English, of the root, fundamental, from Late Latin *rādīcālis,* having roots, from Latin *rādix* (stem *rādīc-*), root. See **werād-** in Appendix.*] —**rad'i·cal·ly** *adv.* —**rad'i·cal·ness** *n.*

radical expression. A mathematical expression or form in which radical signs appear.

rad·i·cal·ism (răd'ĭ-kəl-ĭz'əm) *n.* The doctrines or practices of political radicals.

radical sign. **1.** The sign √ placed before a quantity, indicating extraction of the root designated by a raised integral index. When extracting a square root, the index is customarily omitted. **2.** This sign together with a horizontal bar extending from its top to the end of the expression from which a root is to be extracted.

rad·i·cand (răd'ĭ-kănd') *n.* The quantity under a radical sign: *3 is the radicand of √3.* [Latin *rādīcandum,* neuter gerundive of *rādīcāre,* to take root, from **rādix,** root. See **radical.**]

rad·i·ces. Plural of **radix.**

rad·i·cle (răd'ĭ-kəl) *n.* **1.** *Botany.* The part of the plant embryo that develops into the primary root. **2.** *Anatomy.* A small structure resembling a root, such as a fibril of a nerve. [Latin *rādīcula,* diminutive of *rādix* (stem *rādīc-*), root. See **werād-** in Appendix.*]

ra·di·i. Plural of **radius.**

ra·di·o (rā'dē-ō) *n., pl.* **-os.** *Abbr.* **rad.** **1.** The use of electromagnetic waves in the approximate frequency range from 10 kilocycles/second to 300,000 megacycles/second to transmit or receive electric signals without wires connecting the points of transmission and reception. **2.** Communication of audible signals, such as music, encoded in electromagnetic waves so transmitted and received. **3.** Transmission of programs for the public by this means; radio broadcast. **4. a.** The equipment used to transmit radio signals; transmitter. **b.** The equipment used to receive radio signals; receiver. **c.** A complex of equipment capable of both transmitting and receiving radio signals. **5.** A message sent by radio. —*adj.* **1.** Of, pertaining to, designating, or sent by radio. **2.** Of, pertaining to, or designating oscillations of **radio frequency** *(see).* —*v.* **radioed, -oing, -os.** —*tr.* To transmit a message to, or communicate with, by radio. —*intr.* To transmit a message by radio. [Short for RADIOTELEGRAPHY.]

radio-. Indicates emission and propagation of radiation; for example, **radioactive.** [From RADIATION.]

ra·di·o·ac·tive (rā'dē-ō-ăk'tĭv) *adj. Physics.* Of, pertaining to, or exhibiting radioactivity: *radioactive tracer.* [RADIO- + ACTIVE.] —**ra'di·o·ac'tive·ly** *adv.*

radioactive decay. A progressive decrease in the number of radioactive atoms in a substance by spontaneous nuclear disintegration or transformation. Also called "decay."

radioactive series. A group of isotopes related by a sequence of radioactive decay processes in which the heavier members of the group are transformed into successively lighter ones, the lightest being stable.

ra·di·o·ac·tiv·i·ty (rā'dē-ō-ăk'tĭv'ə-tē) *n.* **1.** The spontaneous emission of radiation, either directly from unstable atomic nuclei or as a consequence of a nuclear reaction. **2.** Broadly, the radiation so emitted, including alpha particles, nucleons, electrons, and gamma rays.

radio astronomy. The study of celestial objects and phenomena by observation and analysis of emitted or reflected radio-frequency waves.

radio beacon. A fixed radio transmitter that broadcasts distinctive signals as a navigational aid.

radio beam. A focused beam of radio signals transmitted by a radio beacon to guide aircraft or ships. Also called "beam."

ra·di·o·bi·ol·o·gy (rā'dē-ō-bī-ŏl'ə-jē) *n.* **1.** The study of the effects of radiation on living organisms. **2.** The use of radioactive tracers to study biological processes. —**ra'di·o·bi'o·log'i·cal** (-ə-lŏj'ĭ-kəl) *adj.* —**ra'di·o·bi·ol'o·gist** *n.*

ra·di·o·broad·cast (rā'dē-ō-brôd'kăst', -käst') *v.* **-cast** or **-casted, -casting, -casts.** —*tr.* To broadcast (a program, for example) by radio; radiocast. —*intr.* To broadcast by radio. —**ra'di·o·broad'cast'er** *n.*

ra·di·o·car·bon (rā'dē-ō-kär'bən) *n.* Radioactive carbon, especially **carbon 14** *(see).*

ra·di·o·cast (rā'dē-ō-kăst', -käst') *tr.v.* **-cast** or **-casted, -casting, -casts.** To broadcast (a message, for example) by radio. [RADIO + (BROAD)CAST.] —**ra'di·o·cast'er** *n.*

ra·di·o·chem·is·try (rā'dē-ō-kĕm'ĭs-trē) *n.* The chemistry of radioactive materials. —**ra'di·o·chem'i·cal** *adj.*

radio compass. A navigational aid consisting of an automatic radio receiver that determines the transmission direction of incoming radio waves.

ra·di·o·el·e·ment (rā'dē-ō-ĕl'ə-mənt) *n.* Any naturally occurring or artificially produced radioactive element.

radio frequency. *Abbr.* **RF** **1.** The frequency of the waves transmitted by a specific radio station. **2.** Any frequency in the range within which radio waves may be transmitted, from about 10 kilocycles/second to about 300,000 megacycles/second. Radio frequency groups are: *very low frequency* (vlf), 10 to 30 kilocycles/second; *low frequency* (lf), 30 to 300 kilocycles/second; *medium frequency* (mf), 300 to 3,000 kilocycles/second; *high frequency* (hf), 3,000 to 30,000 kilocycles/second; *very high frequency* (vhf), 30 to 300 megacycles/second; *ultrahigh frequency* (uhf), 300 to 3,000 megacycles/second; *superhigh frequency* (shf), 3,000 to 30,000 megacycles/second; *extremely high frequency* (ehf), 30,000 to 300,000 megacycles/second.

ra·di·o·ge·nic (rā'dē-ō-jĕn'ĭk) *adj.* Caused by radioactivity. [RADIO- + -GENIC.]

ra·di·o·gram (rā'dē-ō-grăm') *n.* **1.** A message transmitted by wireless telegraphy. **2.** A **radiograph** *(see).*

ra·di·o·graph (rā'dē-ō-grăf', -gräf') *n.* An image produced on a radiosensitive surface, such as a photographic film, by radiation other than visible light, especially by x rays passed through an object, or by photographing a fluoroscopic image. Also called "radiogram." —*tr.v.* **radiographed, -graphing, -graphs.** To make a radiograph of. [RADIO- + -GRAPH.] —**ra'di·og'ra·pher** (-ŏg'rə-fər) *n.* —**ra'di·o·graph'ic** *adj.* —**ra'di·o·graph'i·cal·ly** *adv.* —**ra'di·og'ra·phy** (-ŏg'rə-fē) *n.*

ra·di·o·i·so·tope (rā'dē-ō-ī'sə-tōp') *n.* A naturally or artificially produced radioactive isotope of an element.

ra·di·o·lar·i·an (rā'dē-ō-lâr'ē-ən) *n.* Any of various marine protozoans of the order Radiolaria, having rigid siliceous skeletons and spicules. [New Latin *Radiolaria,* from Late Latin *radiolus,* small sunbeam, diminutive of Latin *radius,* ray. See **radius.**]

ra·di·o·lo·ca·tion (rā'dē-ō-lō-kā'shən) *n.* The detection of distant objects by radar. [RADIO- + LOCATION.]

ra·di·ol·o·gy (rā'dē-ŏl'ə-jē) *n.* **1.** The use of ionizing radiation for medical diagnosis, especially of x rays in medical radiography or fluoroscopy, and for radiotherapy. **2.** The use of radiation for the scientific examination of material structures, radioscopy. [RADIO- + -LOGY.] —**ra'di·o·log'i·cal** (-ə-lŏj'ĭ-kəl) *adj.* —**ra'di·ol'o·gist** *n.*

ra·di·o·man (rā'dē-ō-măn') *n., pl.* **-men** (-mĕn'). A radio technician or operator.

ra·di·om·e·ter (rā'dē-ŏm'ə-tər) *n.* A device that detects and measures radiation, consisting of a partially evacuated glass bulb containing lightweight vertical vanes, each blackened on one side, suspended radially about a central vertical axis to permit their revolution about the axis as a measure of incident radiation. [RADIO- + -METER.] —**ra'di·o·met'ric** (-ō-mĕt'rĭk) *adj.* —**ra'di·om'e·try** *n.*

ra·di·o·phone (rā'dē-ō-fōn') *n.* A **radiotelephone** *(see).* —**ra'di·o·phon'ic** (-fŏn'ĭk) *adj.*

ra·di·o·pho·to·graph (rā'dē-ō-fō'tə-grăf', -gräf') *n.* Also **ra·di·o·pho·to** (-fō'tō). A photograph transmitted by radio waves, each image point being reproduced by a received electric impulse. —**ra'di·o·pho·tog'ra·phy** (rā'dē-ō-fə-tŏg'rə-fē) *n.*

ra·di·o·scope (rā'dē-ō-skōp') *n.* A **fluoroscope** *(see).* [RADIO- + -SCOPE.]

ra·di·os·co·py (rā'dē-ŏs'kə-pē) *n.* The examination of the inner structure of optically opaque objects by x rays or other penetrating radiation; radiology. [RADIO- + -SCOPY.] —**ra'di·o·scop'ic** (-ō-skŏp'ĭk), **ra'di·o·scop'i·cal** *adj.*

ra·di·o·sen·si·tive (rā'dē-ō-sĕn'sə-tĭv) *adj.* Sensitive to radiation. Said especially of living structures.

ra·di·o·sonde (rā'dē-ō-sŏnd') *n.* An instrument carried aloft, chiefly by balloon, to gather and transmit meteorological data. [RADIO- + French *sonde,* sounding line, from Old French, from Old English *sund* (attested only in compounds), sea (see **swem-** in Appendix*).]

radio spectrum. The entire range of electromagnetic commu-

nications frequencies, including those used for radio, radar, and television; radio-frequency spectrum.
ra·di·o·tel·e·graph (rā′dē-ō-tĕl′ə-grăf′, -gräf′) *n.* The sending of messages by radiotelegraphy. **—ra′di·o·tel′e·graph′ic** *adj.*
ra·di·o·te·leg·ra·phy (rā′dē-ō-tə-lĕg′rə-fē) *n.* Wireless telegraphy, in which messages are sent by radio. [RADI(ATE) + TELEGRAPHY.]
ra·di·o·tel·e·phone (rā′dē-ō-tĕl′ə-fōn′) *n.* A telephone in which audible communication is established by radio. Also called "radiophone," "wireless telephone." **—ra′di·o·tel′e·phon′ic** (-ə-fŏn′ĭk) *adj.* **—ra′di·o·te·leph′o·ny** (-tə-lĕf′ə-nē) *n.*
radio telescope. A sensitive, directional radio-antenna system used to detect and analyze radio waves of extraterrestrial origin.
ra·di·o·ther·a·py (rā′dē-ō-thĕr′ə-pē) *n.* The treatment of disease with radiation, especially by selective irradiation with x rays or other ionizing radiation and by ingestion of radioisotopes.
radio wave. A radio-frequency electromagnetic wave. Formerly called "Hertzian wave."
rad·ish (răd′ĭsh) *n.* **1.** Any of various plants of the genus *Raphanus;* especially, *R. sativus,* having a thickened, edible root. **2.** The pungent root of this plant, eaten raw as an appetizer and in salads. [Middle English *radiche,* Old English *rædic,* from Latin *rādix* (stem *rādīc-*), root. See **werād-** in Appendix.*]
ra·di·um (rā′dē-əm) *n. Symbol* **Ra** A rare brilliant-white, luminescent, highly radioactive metallic element having 13 isotopes with mass numbers between 213 and 230, of which radium 226 with a half-life of 1,622 years is the most common. It is used in cancer radiotherapy, as a neutron source for some research purposes, and as a constituent of luminescent paints. Atomic number 88, melting point 700°C, boiling point 1,737°C, valence 2. See **element.** [New Latin, from Latin *radius,* ray (radium emits rays that penetrate opaque matter). See **radius.**]
radium therapy. The use of radium in radiotherapy, especially in treating cancer.
ra·di·us (rā′dē-əs) *n., pl.* **-dii** (-dē-ī′) or **-uses. 1.** *Abbr.* **R, r, rad. a.** A line segment that joins the center of a circle with any point on its circumference. **b.** A line segment that joins the center of a sphere with any point on its surface. **c.** A line segment that joins the center of a regular polygon to any of its vertices. **2.** The length of any such line segment. **3.** A measure of circular area or extent: *every family within a radius of 25 miles.* **4.** A measure of range of activity or influence. **5.** A radial part or structure, as a mechanically pivoted arm or the spoke of a wheel. **6.** *Anatomy.* **a.** A long, prismatic, slightly curved bone, the shorter and thicker of the two forearm bones, located on the lateral side of the ulna. **b.** A similar bone in many vertebrates. [Latin *radius*†, spoke of a wheel, ray.]
radius vector. 1. *Mathematics.* **a.** A line segment that joins any variable point to the origin of polar or spherical coordinates. **b.** The length of such a line segment. **2.** *Astronomy.* A line segment that joins the center of a satellite to the focus of its orbit.
ra·dix (rā′dĭks) *n., pl.* **radices** (răd′ə-sēz′, rā′də-) or **-dixes. 1.** *Biology.* A root or point of origin. **2.** *Abbr.* **rad.** *Mathematics.* The base of a system of numbers, as are 2 of the binary system and 10 of the decimal system. [Latin *rādix* (plural *rādīcēs*), root. See **werād-** in Appendix.*]
Rad·nor·shire (răd′nər-shîr, -shər). Also **Rad·nor** (răd′nər). A county in central Wales. Population, 18,000. County seat, Presteigne.
Ra·dom (rä′dôm). An industrial city in east-central Poland. Population, 141,000.
ra·dome (rā′dōm) *n.* A domelike protective housing for a radar antenna used especially in certain aircraft. [RA(DAR) + DOME.]
ra·don (rā′dŏn) *n. Symbol* **Rn** A colorless, radioactive, inert gaseous element formed by disintegration of radium. It is used as a radiation source in radiotherapy and to produce neutrons for research. Atomic number 86, atomic weight 222, melting point −71°C, boiling point −61.8°C, specific gravity (solid) 4, valence 0, half-life 3.823 days. See **element.** [New Latin : RADIUM + *-on,* suffix indicating inert gases.]
rad·u·la (răj′o͝o-lə) *n., pl.* **-lae** (-lē′). *Zoology.* In mollusks, a flexible, tonguelike organ with rows of horny teeth on the surface. [New Latin, from Latin *rādula,* scraper, from *rādere,* to scrape. See **rēd-** in Appendix.*] **—rad′u·lar** *adj.*
Rae·burn (rā′bərn), Sir **Henry.** 1756–1823. Scottish painter.
Rae·ti·a. See **Rhaetia.**
RAF, R.A.F. Royal Air Force.
Ra·fa·el, Raf·fa·el·lo. See **Raphael.**
raf·fi·a (răf′ē-ə) *n.* Also **raph·i·a. 1.** An African palm tree, *Raphia ruffia,* having large leaves that yield a useful fiber. Also called "raffia palm." **2.** The fiber of these leaves, used for mats, baskets, and other products. [Malagasy *rafia, rofia.*]
raf·fi·nose (răf′ə-nōs′) *n.* A white crystalline sugar, $C_{18}H_{32}O_{16}\cdot 5H_2O$, obtained from cottonseed meal and sugar beets. [French, from *raffiner,* to refine : *re-,* again + *affiner,* to refine : *a-,* to, from Latin *ad-* + *fin,* refined, from Old French, FINE.]
raff·ish (răf′ĭsh) *adj.* **1.** Vulgar; showy. **2.** Rakish. [Probably from dialectal *raff,* trash, from Middle English *raf.* See **raft.**] **—raff′ish·ly** *adv.* **—raff′ish·ness** *n.*
raf·fle¹ (răf′əl) *n.* A lottery in which a number of persons buy chances on a prize. *—v.* **raffled, -fling, -fles.** *—tr.* To dispose of in a raffle. Often used with *off.* *—intr.* To conduct or take part in a raffle. [Middle English *rafle,* from Old French *raffle,* act of snatching, probably from Middle Dutch *raffel,* a game of dice, from Germanic *hrap-* (unattested).] **—raf′fler** *n.*
raf·fle² (răf′əl) *n.* Rubbish; debris. [Probably from French *rafle,* a seizing, from Old French *raffle.* See **raffle** (lottery).]
raf·fle·si·a (rə-flē′zhē-ə, -zē-ə) *n.* Any of various parasitic leafless plants of the genus *Rafflesia,* of tropical Asia, having very large, often malodorous flowers. [New Latin, after Sir Stamford *Raffles* (1781–1826), British colonial administrator.]
raft¹ (răft, räft) *n.* **1.** A flat structure, typically made of planks, logs, or barrels, that floats on water and is used for transport or as a platform for swimmers. **2.** A **life raft** *(see).* *—v.* **rafted, rafting, rafts.** *—tr.* **1.** To convey on a raft. **2.** To make a raft from. *—intr.* To travel by raft. [Middle English *rafte,* from Old Norse *raptr,* beam, rafter. See **rēp-²** in Appendix.*]
raft² (răft, räft) *n. Informal.* A great number, amount, or collection; a lot. [Variant of Scottish *raff,* trash, from Middle English *raf,* perhaps from Scandinavian, akin to Old Norse *hreppa,* to catch, from Germanic *hrap-* (unattested). See **raffle.**]
raft·er (răf′tər, räf′-) *n.* One of the sloping beams that support a pitched roof. [Middle English *rafter,* Old English *ræfter.* See **rēp-²** in Appendix.*]
rag¹ (răg) *n.* **1.** A scrap of cloth. **2.** Cloth converted to pulp for papermaking: *the rag content of a sheet.* **3.** A scrap or fragment. **4.** *Slang.* A newspaper. **5.** *Plural.* Threadbare or tattered clothing. **6.** The stringy central portion and membranous walls of citrus fruits. **—the rag game.** *Slang.* The garment industry. [Middle English *ragge,* ultimately from Old Norse *rögg,* tuft. See **rugged.**]
rag² (răg) *tr.v.* **ragged, ragging, rags.** *Slang.* **1.** To tease; taunt. **2.** To scold. **3.** *British.* To play a practical joke upon. *—n. British.* A practical joke; prank. [Origin obscure.]
rag³ (răg) *n.* **1.** A roofing slate with one rough surface. **2.** *British.* Any coarsely textured rock. [Origin obscure.]
rag⁴ (răg) *tr.v.* **ragged, ragging, rags.** To compose or play (a piece of music) in ragtime. *—n.* A piece of music written in ragtime. [Short for RAGTIME.]
ra·ga (rä′gə) *n.* A traditional form in Hindu music, consisting of a theme that expresses some aspect of religious feeling and sets forth a tonal system on which variations are improvised within a prescribed framework of typical progressions, melodic formulas, and rhythmic patterns. [Sanskrit *rāga,* color, musical color. See **reg-³** in Appendix.*]
rag·a·muf·fin (răg′ə-mŭf′ĭn) *n.* A dirty or unkempt child. [After *Ragamoffyn,* demon in *Piers Plowman* (1393).]
rag·bag (răg′băg′) *n.* **1.** A bag for storing rags. **2.** A motley collection; mixture.
rage (rāj) *n.* **1. a.** Violent anger. **b.** A fit of anger. **2.** Furious intensity, as of a storm or disease. **3.** Burning desire or passion. **4.** A fad; craze. —See Synonyms at **anger.** *—intr.v.* **raged, raging, rages. 1.** To speak or act furiously. **2.** To move with great violence or intensity. **3.** To spread or prevail unchecked. [Middle English, from Old French, from Vulgar Latin *rabia* (unattested), from Latin *rabiēs,* madness, from *rabere,* to rave. See **rabh-** in Appendix.*]
rag·ged (răg′ĭd) *adj.* **1.** Tattered. **2.** Dressed in tattered or threadbare clothes. **3.** Unkempt or shaggy. **4.** Having a rough surface or edges. **5.** Imperfect; sloppy: *a ragged performance.* **6.** Harsh; rasping: *a ragged cry.* [Middle English, probably from *ragge,* RAG.] **—rag′ged·ly** *adv.* **—rag′ged·ness** *n.*
ragged robin. A plant, *Lychnis flos-cuculi,* native to Eurasia, having reddish or white flowers with deeply lobed petals. Also called "cuckooflower." [Perhaps from the narrow lobes which have a cut or ragged look.]
ra·gi (răg′ē) *n.* A grass, *Eleusine coracana,* of Africa and Asia, where it is cultivated for its edible grain. [Hindi *rāgī,* from Sanskrit, from Dravidian *rāki* (unattested).]
rag·lan (răg′lən) *n.* A loose coat, jacket, or sweater with slanted shoulder seams and with the sleeves extending in one piece to the neckline. *—adj.* Having the shoulder seams slanted and extending to the neckline: *a raglan sleeve.* [After Field Marshal Lord *Raglan* (1788–1855), British soldier.]
rag·man (răg′măn′) *n., pl.* **-men** (-mĕn′). A seller of rags. Also called "ragpicker."
ra·gout (ră-go͞o′) *n.* A meat and vegetable stew. [French *ragoût,* from *ragoûter,* to renew the taste : *re-,* again + *a-,* from Latin *ad,* to + *goût,* taste, from Latin *gustus* (see **geus-** in Appendix*).]
rag·tag (răg′tăg′) *n.* Rabble; riffraff. Also called "ragtag and bobtail." [RAG (scrap) + TAG.]
rag·time (răg′tīm′) *n.* A style of jazz characterized by elaborately syncopated rhythm in the melody and a steadily accented accompaniment. [Perhaps from *ragged time,* referring to the syncopation.]
Ra·gu·sa (rä-go͞o′zä). **1.** A city of Italy, situated in southeastern Sicily. Population, 55,000. **2.** The Italian name for **Dubrovnik.**
rag·weed (răg′wēd′) *n.* **1.** Any weed of the genus *Ambrosia;* especially, *A. artemisiifolia* or *A. trifida,* whose profuse pollen is one of the chief causes of hay fever. Sometimes called "bitterweed." **2.** *Chiefly British.* The ragwort. [From the raggedness of the leaves.]
rag·wort (răg′wûrt′, -wôrt′) *n.* Any of several plants of the genus *Senecio,* having yellow flowers; especially, *S. aureus,* the golden ragwort of eastern North America, and *S. jacobaea,* of Europe. [From the raggedness of the leaves.]
rah (rä) *interj.* Hurrah. Used chiefly in college and high-school cheers. [Short for HURRAH.]
raid (rād) *n.* **1.** A surprise attack, as one made by a commando force. **2.** A sudden and forcible invasion by police. **3.** A sudden predatory onset. **4.** An attempt by speculators to drive stock prices down by mutual selling. *—v.* **raided, raiding, raids.** *—tr.* To make a raid on. *—intr.* To conduct or participate in a raid. [Scottish dialect, raid on horseback, from Middle English *rade,* Old English *rād,* ride, road. See **reidh-** in Appendix.*] **—raid′er** *n.*

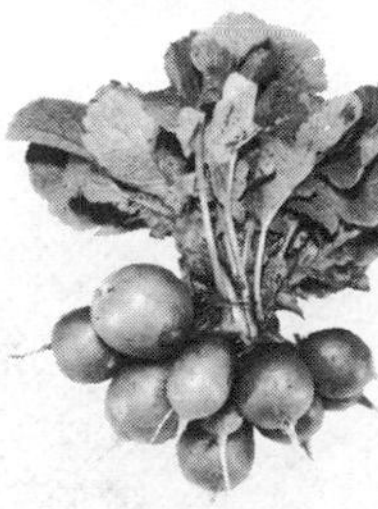
radish
Raphanus savitus

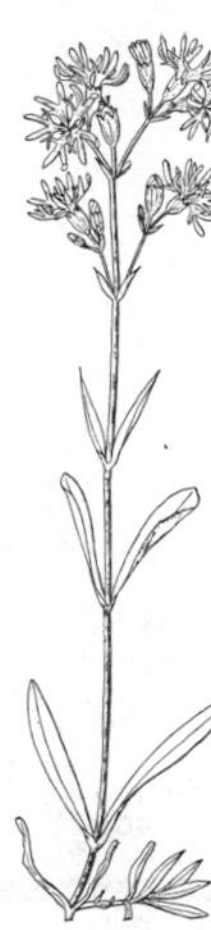
ragged robin

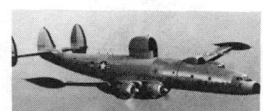

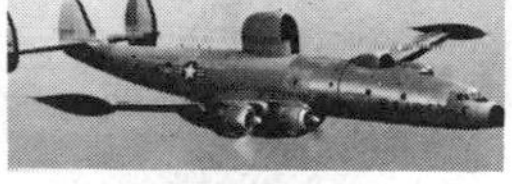
radome
Radome housing on a USAF Air Defense Command Super Constellation

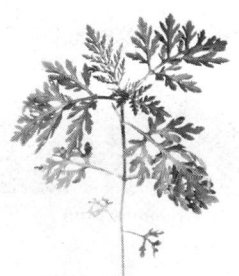

ragweed
Ambrosia artemisiifolia

rail[2]
Rallus limicola
Virginia rail

rail[1] (rāl) *n.* **1.** A horizontal bar supported by vertical posts, as in a fence. **2.** A railing or balustrade. **3.** A steel bar used, usually in pairs, as a track for railroad cars and similar vehicles. **4.** The railroad as a means of transportation: *goods transported by rail.* **5.** *Plural.* The stocks and bonds issued by railroads: *Rails are up two points today.* **6.** A horizontal piece of wood in a door or in paneling. —*tr.v.* **railed, railing, rails.** To supply or enclose with a rail or rails. [Middle English *raile,* from Old French *reille,* bar, from Latin *rēgula,* rod, straight piece of wood. See **reg-**[1] in Appendix.*]

rail[2] (rāl) *n.* Any of various marsh birds of the family Rallidae, characteristically having brownish plumage and short wings adapted for only short flights. [Middle English *ra(i)le,* from Old French *raale,* from Old Provençal *rascla,* from *rasclar,* to scrape, make a scraping noise, from Vulgar Latin *rasclāre, rasiculāre* (both unattested), from Latin *rādere* (past participle *rāsus*), to scrape, scratch. See **rēd-** in Appendix.*]

rail[3] (rāl) *intr.v.* **railed, railing, rails.** To use bitter, harsh, or abusive language. Used with *at* or *against.* See Synonyms at **scold.** [Middle English *railen,* from Old French *railler,* to mock, from Old Provençal *ralhar,* to scold, from Vulgar Latin *ragulāre* (unattested), to bray, from Late Latin *ragere*†, to neigh, roar.] —**rail′er** *n.*

rail fence. A fence of split logs secured to posts.

rail·head (rāl′hĕd′) *n.* **1.** The farthest point on a railroad to which rails have been laid. **2.** *Military.* The section of a railroad where supplies are unloaded.

rail·ing (rā′lĭng) *n.* **1. a.** A banister, balustrade, or fence made of rails. **b.** The upper, longitudinal part of a balustrade. **2.** Rails collectively. **3.** Material for making rails.

rail·ler·y (rā′lər-ē) *n., pl.* **-ies.** Good-natured teasing or ridicule; banter. [French *raillerie,* from Old French *railler,* RAIL (to use harsh language against).]

rail·road (rāl′rōd′) *n. Abbr.* **r., R., RR, R.R. 1.** A road composed of parallel steel rails supported by ties and providing a track for locomotive-drawn trains and other rolling stock. **2.** The entire system of such track, together with the land, stations, rolling stock, and other property used in rail transportation. —*v.* **railroaded, -roading, -roads.** —*tr.* **1.** To transport by railroad. **2.** To supply (an area) with railroads. **3.** *Informal.* **a.** To rush or push through quickly in order to prevent careful consideration: *railroad a law through Congress.* **b.** To cause (someone) to be imprisoned without a fair trial or on trumped-up charges. —*intr.* To work for a railroad company.

railroad flat. An apartment in which the rooms are connected in a line, with windows at the front and rear.

rake[1]
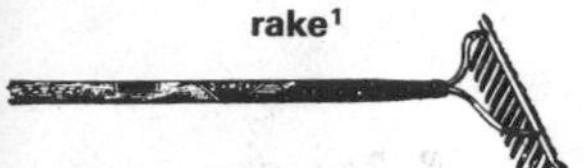
garden rake

rail-split·ter (rāl′splĭt′ər) *n.* One who splits logs for fences.

rail·way (rāl′wā′) *n. Abbr.* **r., R., Rwy., Ry. 1.** A railroad, especially one operated over a limited area, as a street railway. **2.** A track providing a runway for wheeled equipment.

rai·ment (rā′mənt) *n.* Clothing; garments. [Middle English *rayment,* short for *arrayment,* from Old French *araiement, araie,* an array, from *arayer,* to ARRAY.]

rain (rān) *n.* **1. a.** Water condensed from atmospheric vapor, falling to earth in drops. **b.** A fall of such water; a rainstorm or shower. **c.** The descent of such water. **d.** Rainy weather. **2.** The rapid falling of anything in this manner. **3.** *Plural.* The rainy season or seasonal rainfalls, as in certain tropical areas. —**rain or shine. 1.** Regardless of the weather. **2.** Under all circumstances. —*v.* **rained, raining, rains.** —*intr.* **1.** To fall in drops of water from the clouds. **2.** To fall like rain. **3.** To release rain. —*tr.* **1.** To send or pour down. **2.** To offer or give abundantly. —**rain cats and dogs.** To rain in great quantity; pour. —**rain out.** To force the postponement of (an outdoor event) because of rain. [Middle English *reyn, rain,* Old English *regn, rēn.* See **reg-**[2] in Appendix.*]

croupier with rake

rain·bow (rān′bō′) *n.* **1. a.** An arc of spectral colors appearing in the sky opposite the sun as a result of the refractive dispersion of sunlight in drops of rain or mist. **b.** Any similar arc, as in a waterfall mist or graded display of colors. **2.** An illusory hope: *the rainbow of making a quick fortune.* [Middle English *reinbowe,* Old English *rēnboga.* See **reg-**[2] in Appendix.*]

rainbow cactus. A tall, spiny, cylindrical cactus, *Echinocereus rigidissimus,* of the southwestern United States and Mexico, having showy pink flowers. [From its colorful flowers.]

rainbow trout. A North American food fish, *Salmo gairdneri,* having a reddish longitudinal band and black spots. See **steelhead.**

rain check. 1. A ticket stub for an outdoor sports event entitling the holder to admission at a future date if the original event is canceled because of rain. **2.** A postponement of the acceptance of an offer.

rainbow trout

rain·coat (rān′kōt′) *n.* A waterproof or water-resistant coat.

rain·drop (rān′drŏp′) *n.* A drop of rain.

rain·fall (rān′fôl′) *n.* **1.** A shower or fall of rain. **2.** *Meteorology.* The quantity of water, expressed in inches, precipitated as rain, snow, hail, or sleet in a specified area and time interval.

rain gauge. Also **rain gage.** A device for measuring rainfall. Also called "pluviometer."

Rai·nier III (rĕ-nyā′, rā-nyā′). Born 1923. Reigning prince of Monaco (since 1949).

Rai·nier, Mount (rā-nîr′, rā′nîr). Formerly **Mount Ta·co·ma** (tə-kō′mə). A volcanic peak, 14,408 feet high, of the Cascade Range, in west-central Washington.

rain·mak·er (rān′mā′kər) *n.* A person supposedly capable of producing rain, especially among American Indians.

rain·mak·ing (rān′mā′kĭng) *n.* **1.** The ceremony observed by a rainmaker. **2.** *Informal.* **Cloud seeding** *(see).*

rain·spout (rān′spout′) *n.* A spout draining a roof gutter.

rain·squall (rān′skwôl′) *n.* A squall accompanied by rain.

rain·storm (rān′stôrm′) *n.* A storm accompanied by rain.

rain-wash (rān′wŏsh′) *n. Geology.* **1.** Rock debris transported downhill by rain. **2.** Decomposed rock and similar matter washed down into the soil by rain. —*tr.v.* **rain-washed, -washing, -washes.** *Geology.* To wash (material) down a slope by rain.

rain·wat·er (rān′wô′tər, -wŏt′ər) *n.* Water precipitated as rain with little dissolved mineral matter.

rain·wear (rān′wâr′) *n.* Waterproof clothing.

rain·y (rā′nē) *adj.* **-ier, -iest.** Characterized by, full of, or bringing rain. —**rain′i·ly** *adv.* —**rain′i·ness** *n.*

rainy day. A time of need or trouble.

Rain·y Lake (rā′nē). A 50-mile-long lake partly in northern Minnesota and partly in southwestern Ontario.

Rais, Baron de. See Baron de **Retz.**

raise (rāz) *v.* **raised, raising, raises.** —*tr.* **1.** To move or cause to move upward or to a higher position; elevate; lift. **2.** To place or set upright; make erect. **3.** To erect or build. **4. a.** To cause to arise, appear, or exist. **b.** To awaken from or as if from death. **5.** To increase in size, quantity, or worth. **6.** To increase in intensity, degree, strength, or pitch. **7.** To improve in rank or dignity; promote. **8. a.** To grow or breed. **b.** To bring up; rear. See Usage note below. **9.** To put forward for consideration. **10.** *Law.* To begin or set (a lawsuit) in operation. **11.** To express or utter (a cry or shout, for example). **12.** To bring about; cause; provoke. **13.** To arouse or stir up: *raise a revolt.* **14.** To gather together; collect: *raise money.* **15.** To cause (dough) to puff up. **16.** To end (a siege) by withdrawing troops or forcing the enemy troops to withdraw. **17.** To remove or withdraw (an order). **18. a.** To increase (a poker bet). **b.** To bet more than (a preceding bettor in poker). **c.** To increase the bid of (one's bridge partner). **19.** *Nautical.* To bring (a shoreline or another ship, for example) into sight by approaching nearer. **20.** To alter and increase illegally the written value of (a check or the like). **21.** To cough up (phlegm). **22.** *Scottish.* To make angry; enrage. —*intr.* To increase the stakes in poker or gambling. —See Synonyms at **lift.** —*n.* **1.** An act of raising or increasing. **2.** An increase in salary. See Usage note below. [Middle English *reisen, raisen,* from Old Norse *reisa.* See **rīsan** in Appendix.*] —**rais′er** *n.*

Usage: *Raise* (verb), in the sense of rearing children, is acceptable in writing to 82 per cent of the Usage Panel. *Rear* is the more formal term. In formal usage, *raise* is almost exclusively transitive. Less strictly, it appears intransitively in examples such as *the windows raise easily,* which is acceptable to 48 per cent of the Panel. *Raise* (noun), for increase in salary, is approved in written usage by 91 per cent of the Panel; it is in much wider use in the United States than *rise.*

raised (rāzd) *adj.* **1.** Represented in relief, as a surface design; embossed. **2.** Made light and high by yeast or other leaven.

rai·sin (rā′zən) *n.* A sweet grape of several varieties, dried either in the sun or artificially. [Middle English *raisin,* from Old French, grape, from Latin *racēmus,* RACEME.]

rai·son d'ê·tre (rĕ-zôɴ′ dĕ′tr). *French.* Reason for being; reason or justification for existing.

raj (räj) *n.* In India, dominion; sovereignty. [Hindi *rāj,* from Sanskrit *rājā,* from *rājati,* he rules. See **reg-**[1] in Appendix.*]

Raj·ab (rŭj′əb) *n.* The seventh month of the Moslem calendar. See **calendar.** [Arabic.]

ra·jah, ra·ja (rä′jə) *n.* A prince, chief, or ruler in India or the East Indies. [Hindi *rājā,* from Sanskrit *rājan,* king. See **reg-**[1] in Appendix.*]

Ra·ja·sthan (rä′jə-stän). A state of the Republic of India, occupying 132,152 square miles in the northwestern part of the country. Population, 20,156,000. Capital, Jaipur.

Raj·put (räj′po͝ot) *n.* Also **Raj·poot.** One of a Hindu people claiming descent from the warlike and powerful rulers of northern India from the 8th to the 13th century.

rake[1] (rāk) *n.* **1.** A long-handled implement with a row of projecting teeth at its head, used to gather leaves or mowed grass, or to loosen or smooth earth. **2.** Any similarly shaped implement. —*v.* **raked, raking, rakes.** —*tr.* **1.** To gather or move with or as if with a rake. **2.** To smooth, scrape, or loosen with a rake or similar implement. **3.** To gain in abundance. Usually used with *in.* **4.** To revive or bring to light. Usually used with *up: rake up old gossip.* **5.** To search or examine thoroughly. **6.** To scrape; scratch; graze. **7.** To aim heavy gunfire along the length of. —*intr.* **1.** To use a rake. **2.** To conduct a search. **3.** To make one's way rapidly or roughly: *raked through the crowd.* [Middle English *rake,* Old English *raca, racu.* See **reg-**[1] in Appendix.*] —**rak′er** *n.*

rake[2] (rāk) *n.* A profligate man; roué. [Short for RAKEHELL.]

rake[3] (rāk) *v.* **raked, raking, rakes.** —*intr.* To slant or incline from the vertical, as a ship's mast. —*tr.* To cause to lean or slant. —*n.* **1.** Inclination from the vertical or from the horizontal. **2.** The angle between the cutting edge of a tool and a plane perpendicular to the working surface to which the tool is applied. [Origin unknown.]

rake·hell (rāk′hĕl′) *n.* A rake; roué. —*adj.* Dissolute; profligate. [Probably from the phrase, *to rake hell.*]

rake-off (rāk′ôf′) *n. Slang.* A percentage or share of the profits of an enterprise, especially one given or accepted as a bribe. [From the rake used by a croupier in a gambling house.]

rak·i (răk′ē, rä′kē, rä′kə) *n.* Also **rak·ee.** A brandy of Turkey and the Balkan Peninsula, distilled from grapes or plums and flavored with anise. [Turkish *rāqī.*]

rak·ish[1] (rā′kĭsh) *adj.* **1.** *Nautical.* Having a trim, streamlined appearance: *"We were schooner-rigged and rakish, with a long and lissome hull"* (Masefield). **2.** Gay and showy; jaunty;

smart. [From RAKE (to incline), from the raked masts on some fast pirate ships.] —**rak'ish·ly** *adv.* —**rak'ish·ness** *n.*
rak·ish[2] (rā'kĭsh) *adj.* Like a rake; debauched; libertine. —**rak'ish·ly** *adv.* —**rak'ish·ness** *n.*
rale (räl) *n.* Also **râle**. An abnormal or pathological respiratory sound. [French *râle*, from *râler*, to make a rattling sound in the throat, from Old French, probably from Vulgar Latin *rasclāre* (unattested), to scrape. See **rail** (bird).]
Ra·leigh (rô'lē). The capital of North Carolina, near the center of the state. Population, 94,000.
Ra·leigh (rô'lē), Sir **Walter**. Also **Ra·legh**. 1552?–1618. English courtier, navigator, colonizer, and writer.
ral·len·tan·do (răl'ən-tăn'dō; *Italian* räl'lĕn-tän'dō) *adj. Abbr.* **rall.** *Music.* Gradually slackening in tempo; ritardando. Used as a direction to the performer. —*n., pl.* **rallentandos.** *Music.* A passage or movement performed with a gradual reduction in tempo. [Italian, slowing down, from *rallentare*, to relax : *re-* (intensifier) + *allentare*, to slow down, from Late Latin *allentāre* : Latin *ad-*, to + *lentus*, slow (see **lento-** in Appendix*).] —**ral'len·tan'do** *adv.*
ral·li·form (răl'ə-fôrm') *adj. Ornithology.* Pertaining to or resembling the rails. [From Medieval Latin *rallus*, a rail, from Old French *raale*, RAIL + -FORM.]
ral·ly[1] (răl'ē) *v.* **-lied, -lying, -lies.** —*tr.* **1.** To call together for a common purpose; assemble. **2.** To reassemble and restore to order. **3.** To rouse or revive (one's strength, for example) from inactivity or decline. —*intr.* **1.** To meet for a common purpose. **2.** To join in an effort for a common cause: *"In the terror and confusion of change, society rallied round the kings."* (Garrett Mattingly). **3.** To recover abruptly from a setback or disadvantage. **4.** To show sudden improvement in health or spirits. **5.** *Tennis.* To exchange several strokes. —See Synonyms at **gather.** —*n., pl.* **rallies. 1.** An assembly, especially one intended to inspire enthusiasm for a cause. **2. a.** A reassembling, as of dispersed troops. **b.** The signal ordering this. **3.** A sharp improvement in health, vigor, or spirits. **4.** *Finance.* A notable rise in market prices and active trading after a decline. **5.** *Tennis.* An exchange of several strokes before one side scores a point. **6.** A race in which automobiles are driven over a fixed course with specified rules. [French *rallier*, from Old French *ralier* : *re-*, again + *alier*, to unite, ALLY.] —**ral'li·er** *n.*
ral·ly[2] (răl'ē) *v.* **-lied, -lying, -lies.** —*tr.* To tease good-humoredly; banter. —*intr.* To banter or jest. [French *railler*, from Old French, to RAIL (abuse).] —**ral'li·er** *n.*
Ralph (rălf; *British* rāf). A masculine given name. [Middle English *radulf*, from Old Norse *radhulfr* : *radh*, counsel (see **ar-** in Appendix*) + *ulfr*, wolf (see **wl̥kwo-** in Appendix*).]
ram (răm) *n.* **1.** A male sheep. **2.** *Capital* **R.** A constellation and sign of the zodiac, **Aries** *(see)*. **3.** Any of several devices used to drive, batter, or crush by forceful impact: **a.** A weapon, the **battering-ram** *(see)*. **b.** The weight that drops in a pile driver or steam hammer. **c.** The plunger or piston of a force pump or hydraulic press. **4. a.** A projection on the prow of a warship, used to batter or cut into an enemy vessel. **b.** A ship having such a projection. **5.** A pump, a **hydraulic ram** *(see)*. —*tr.v.* **rammed, ramming, rams. 1.** To strike or drive against with a heavy impact; to butt. **2.** To force or press into place. **3.** To cram; to stuff. [Middle English *ram*, Old English *ramm*, from Germanic *ramma-* (unattested).] —**ram'mer** *n.*
R.A.M. Royal Academy of Music.
Ra·ma (rä'mə) *n. Hinduism.* Any of three of the incarnations of Vishnu, regarded as heroes: **Balarama, Parashurama,** and especially **Ramachandra** *(all of which see)*. [From Sanskrit *Rāma*†, dark-colored, black.]
Ra·ma IX (rä'mə). Title of Phumiphol Aduldet (or Bhumibol Adulyade). Born 1927. King of Thailand (since 1946).
Ra·ma·chan·dra (rä'mə-chŭn'drə) *n. Hinduism.* The seventh of Vishnu's incarnations and hero of the Hindu epic poem *Ramayana*. Also called "Rama."
Ram·a·dan (răm'ə-dän') *n.* Also **Ram·a·dhan, Ram·a·zan** (-zän'). **1.** The ninth month of the Moslem year, spent in fasting from sunrise to sunset. See **calendar. 2.** The fasting itself. [Arabic *Ramaḍān*, the hot month, from *ramaḍ*, dryness.]
Ra·ma·krish·na (rä'mə-krĭsh'nə). 1834–1886. Hindu mystic; a leader of modern Hinduism.
Ra·man effect (rä'mən). *Physics.* The alteration in frequency and random alteration in phase of light scattered in a material medium. [Discovered by Sir Chandrasekhara Venkata *Raman* (born 1888), Indian physicist.]
ra·mate (rā'māt') *adj.* Having branches; branched. [From Latin *rāmus*, branch. See **werād-** in Appendix.*]
Ra·ma·ya·na (rä-mä'yə-nə) *n.* A Sanskrit epic poem of ancient India, regarded as a sacred text by Hindus. It relates the adventures of Ramachandra. Compare **Mahabharata.** [Sanskrit *Rāmāyana* : *Rāma*, RAMA + *-ayana*, suffix meaning "pertaining to."]
ram·ble (răm'bəl) *intr.v.* **-bled, -bling, -bles. 1.** To walk or wander aimlessly; stroll or roam. **2.** To follow an irregularly winding course of motion or growth. **3.** To speak or write at length and with many digressions. —See Synonyms at **wander.** —*n.* A leisurely stroll. [Variant of earlier *romble*, from Middle English *romblen*, frequentative of *romen*, to ROAM.]
ram·bler (răm'blər) *n.* **1.** One who rambles. **2.** A type of climbing rose having numerous red, pink, or white flowers. Also called "rambler rose."
ram·bling (răm'blĭng) *adj.* **1.** Roaming; roving; wandering. **2.** Extended over an irregular area; sprawling: *"a large, rambling Elizabethan house, in a misty-looking village of England"* (Poe). **3.** Lengthy and desultory: *"By my rambling digressions, I perceive myself to be grown old."* (Franklin). —**ram'bling·ly** *adv.*
Ram·bouil·let (răm'bo͞o-lā; *French* räN-bo͞o-yā') *n.* Any of a breed of merino sheep of French origin, raised for wool and meat. [After *Rambouillet*, town in northern France.]
ram·bunc·tious (răm-bŭngk'shəs) *adj.* Boisterous; disorderly. [Probably variant of earlier *rumbustious*, variant (influenced by *rumble*), of earlier *robustious*, boisterous, from Latin *robustus*, oaken, strong. See **reudh-** in Appendix.*]
Usage: Though usually humorous in application, *rambunctious* is not out of place in formal writing. It is acceptable to 84 per cent of the Usage Panel in this example: *Jackson's subordinates did not need whiskey to become rambunctious.*
ram·bu·tan (răm-bo͞o'tən) *n.* **1.** A tree, *Nephelium lappaceum*, of southeastern Asia, bearing edible, oval red fruit with soft spines. **2.** The fruit of this tree. [Malay *rambutan*, from *rambut*, hair, from the hairy covering of the fruit.]
ram·e·kin (răm'ə-kĭn) *n.* Also **ram·e·quin. 1.** A cheese preparation made with eggs, bread crumbs, or unsweetened puff pastry, baked and served in individual dishes. **2.** A small individual dish used for both baking and serving. [French *ramequin*, from Middle Dutch *rameken*, diminutive of *ram*, cream, from Middle Low German *rōm(e)*. See **reughmen-** in Appendix.*]
Ram·e·ses (răm'ə-sēz'). Also **Ram·ses** (răm'sēz). The name of 12 kings of Egypt, reigning from 1315? to 1090 B.C.

Rameses
One of the four giant statues of Rameses II at Abu Simbel, Egypt

ram·ie (răm'ē) *n.* **1.** A woody Asian plant, *Boehmeria nivea*, having broad leaves. **2.** The flaxlike fiber from the stem of this plant, used in making fabrics and cordage. [Malay *rami*.]
ram·i·fi·ca·tion (răm'ə-fə-kā'shən) *n.* **1.** The act or process of branching out or dividing into branches. **2.** A branch or other subordinate part extending from a main body. **3.** An arrangement of branches or branching parts. **4.** A development or consequence growing out of and often complicating a problem, plan, or statement: *"In the ramifications of Party doctrine she had not the faintest interest."* (George Orwell).
ram·i·form (răm'ə-fôrm') *adj.* Branchlike or branching. [From RAMUS + -FORM.]
ram·i·fy (răm'ə-fī') *v.* **-fied, -fying, -fies.** —*tr.* To divide into, or cause to extend in, branches or branchlike parts. —*intr.* To branch out. [Old French *ramifier*, from Medieval Latin *rāmificāre*, from Latin *rāmus*, branch. See **werād-** in Appendix.*]

ram

ram·jet (răm'jĕt') *n.* A jet engine that propels aircraft by igniting fuel with air taken and compressed by the engine in a fashion that produces greater exhaust than intake velocity.
Ra·mo·na (rə-mō'nə). A feminine given name. [Spanish *Ramona*, feminine of *Ramón*, from Old French *Raimund*, from Frankish *Raginmund*, RAYMOND.]
ra·mose (rā'mōs', rə-mōs') *adj.* Having many branches. [Latin *rāmōsus*, from *rāmus*, branch. See **werād-** in Appendix.*]
ra·mous (rā'məs) *adj.* **1.** Of or resembling branches. **2.** Branching; ramose. [Latin *rāmōsus*, RAMOSE.]
ramp[1] (rămp) *n.* **1.** An inclined passage or roadway connecting different levels, as of a building or road. **2.** *Architecture.* A concave bend of a handrail where a sharp change in level or direction occurs, such as at a stair landing. **3.** A mobile staircase for entering and leaving an airplane. [French *rampe*, from *ramper*, to slope, creep, from Old French, to RAMP.]
ramp[2] (rămp) *intr.v.* **ramped, ramping, ramps. 1.** To stand in the rampant position. **2.** To assume a threatening stance. **3.** To act threateningly or violently; to rage. —*n.* The act of ramping. [Middle English *rampen*, from Old French *ramper*, to climb, rear up, from Frankish *rampōn* (unattested). See **skerbh-** in Appendix.*]

Rama
Eleventh-century statuette of Ramachandra

ram·page (răm'pāj) *n.* A course of violent, frenzied action or behavior. —*intr.v.* (răm-pāj'). **rampaged, -paging, -pages.** To move about wildly or violently; to rage. [Scottish, perhaps from RAMP (to rear up).] —**ram·pag'er** (-pā'jər) *n.*
ram·pa·geous (răm-pā'jəs) *adj.* Raging; frenzied: *"The hot rampageous horses of my will"* (W.H. Auden). —**ram·pa'geous·ly** *adv.* —**ram·pa'geous·ness** *n.*
ram·pant (răm'pənt) *adj.* **1.** Extending unchecked; unrestrained; widespreading: *a rampant growth of vegetation.* **2.** Characterized by ungoverned vehemence and extravagance. **3.** Rearing or ramping on the hind legs. **4.** *Heraldry.* Rearing on the left hind leg with the forelegs elevated, the right above the left, and usually with the head in profile. **5.** *Architecture.* Springing from a support or abutment higher at one side than at the other. Said of an arch or vault. [Middle English *rampaunt*, from Old French *rampant*, present participle of *ramper*, to climb, to RAMP.] —**ram'pan·cy** *n.* —**ram'pant·ly** *adv.*
ram·part (răm'pärt) *n.* **1.** A fortification consisting of an elevation or embankment, often provided with a parapet. **2.** Anything that serves to protect or defend: *"the line of dark cliff, a long rampart against the Atlantic."* (H.C. Bailey). —See Synonyms at **bulwark.** —*tr.v.* **ramparted, -parting, -parts.** To defend with a rampart. [Old French *rampart*, from *ramparer*, to fortify : *re-* (intensifier) + *emparer*, to defend, fortify, from Old Provençal *antparar, amparar*, from Vulgar Latin *anteparāre* (unattested), to prepare for defense : Latin *ante-*, before + *parāre*, to prepare (see **per-**[4] in Appendix*).]

rampant
Lions rampant

ram·pike (răm'pīk') *n.* A standing dead tree or tree stump, especially one killed by fire. [Origin unknown.]
ram·pi·on (răm'pē-ən) *n.* **1.** A Eurasian plant, *Campanula rapunculus*, having clusters of bluish flowers and an edible root used in salads. **2.** Any of various similar plants of the genus *Phyteuma*. [Probably from Old French *raiponce*, from Old Italian *raponzo*, from *rapa*, turnip, from Latin *rāpa, rāpum*, turnip. See **rāp-** in Appendix.*]
Ram·pur (räm'po͝or). **1.** A former princely state of India, in Uttar Pradesh. **2.** Its capital. Population, 135,000.

ram·rod (răm′rŏd′) *n.* **1.** A metal rod used to force the charge into a muzzleloading firearm. **2.** A rod used to clean the barrel of a firearm. *—adj.* **1.** Like a rod in stiffness; inflexible. **2.** Severe; harsh.

Ram·say (răm′zē), Sir **William.** 1852–1916. British chemist; worked on inert gases.

Ram·ses. See **Rameses.**

ram·shack·le (răm′shăk′əl) *adj.* Likely to fall apart because of shoddy construction or upkeep; rickety. [Back-formation from *ramshackled, ransackled,* from *ransackle,* frequentative of Middle English *ransaken,* to RANSACK.]

ram's horn. *Judaism.* A **shofar** *(see).*

ram·son (răm′zən, -sən) *n.* A broad-leaved Eurasian garlic, *Allium ursinum,* having a bulbous root used in salads and relishes. Usually used in the plural. [Middle English *ramsyn,* Old English *hramsan* (plural). See **kerem-** in Appendix.*]

ram·til (răm′tĭl) *n.* An African plant, *Guizotia abyssinica,* grown for its oil-rich seeds. The seed is called "Niger seed." [Hindi *rāmtil* : Sanskrit *rāma,* dark (see **Rama**) + *tila*†, sesame.]

ram·u·lose (răm′yə-lōs′) *adj.* Having numerous small branches. [Latin *rāmulōsus,* from *rāmulus,* diminutive of *rāmus,* branch, RAMUS.]

ra·mus (rā′məs) *n., pl.* **-mi** (-mī′). *Biology.* A branchlike part of a structure. [New Latin, from Latin *rāmus,* branch. See **wrād-** in Appendix.*]

ran. Past tense of **run.** See Usage note at **run.**

Ran (rän). *Norse Mythology.* The goddess of the sea and of drowning persons.

ranch (rănch) *n.* **1.** An extensive farm, especially in the American West, on which large herds of cattle, sheep, or horses are raised. **2.** Any large farm on which a particular crop or kind of animal is raised. *—intr.v.* **ranched, ranching, ranches.** To work on or manage a ranch. [Mexican Spanish *rancho,* from Spanish, mess room, from Old Spanish *rancher, ranchar,* be billeted, from Old French *ranger,* to put in a line, from *renc,* line, row, from Frankish *hring* (unattested), circle, ring. See **sker-**[3] in Appendix.*]

ranch·er (răn′chər) *n.* One who owns or manages a ranch.

ran·che·ri·a (răn′chə-rē′ə) *n. Southwestern U.S.* **1.** A Mexican herdsman's hut. **2.** A village of such huts. **3.** An Indian village. [Mexican Spanish, from *ranchero,* RANCHERO.]

ran·che·ro (răn-châr′ō) *n., pl.* **-ros.** *Southwestern U.S.* A ranchman. [Mexican Spanish, from *rancho,* RANCH.]

ranch house. 1. The building on a ranch occupied by its operator. **2.** A rectangular, one-story house with a low-pitched roof, a style common on Western ranches and in suburbs.

ranch·man (rănch′mən) *n., pl.* **-men** (-mĭn). One who operates or works on a ranch.

ranch mink. A mink bred in captivity from Alaskan and Labrador strains for special pelt colors and qualities.

ran·cho (răn′chō) *n., pl.* **-chos.** *Southwestern U.S.* **1.** A hut or group of huts in which ranch workers live. **2.** A ranch. [Mexican Spanish, RANCH.]

ran·cid (răn′sĭd) *adj.* Having the disagreeable odor or taste of decomposed oils or fats; sour; stale; rank. [Latin *rancidus,* from *rancēre*†, to stink.] **—ran·cid′i·ty, ran′cid·ness** *n.*

ran·cor (răng′kər) *n.* Also *chiefly British* **ran·cour.** Bitter, long-lasting resentment; deep-seated ill will. See Synonyms at **enmity.** [Middle English *rancour,* from Old French, from Latin *rancor,* rancidity, from *rancēre,* to stink. See **rancid.**] **—ran′cor·ous** *adj.* **—ran′cor·ous·ly** *adv.* **—ran′cor·ous·ness** *n.*

randan

rand (rănd, ränd) *n.* **1.** The basic monetary unit of the Republic of South Africa, equal to 100 cents. See table of exchange rates at **currency. 2.** A coin worth one rand. [Afrikaans, from Dutch, strip, edge, from Germanic *randa* (unattested), rim, edge. See **Randolph.**]

Rand, The. See **Witwatersrand.**

ran·dan (răn′dăn) *n.* **1.** A type of boat designed to be rowed by three persons. **2.** The way of rowing this boat, in which the persons fore and aft use one oar each, and the person amidships uses two. [Origin uncertain.]

Ran·dolph (răn′dŏlf). A masculine given name. [Middle English *Randolph,* Old English *Randwulf* : *rand,* shield, border, from Germanic *randa* (unattested), edge, rim + *wulf,* WOLF.]

Ran·dolph (răn′dŏlf), **Edmund Jennings.** 1753–1813. American statesman; Attorney General and Secretary of State in cabinet of George Washington.

Ran·dolph (răn′dŏlf), **John.** Called "Randolph of Roanoke." 1773–1833. American political figure and orator.

ran·dom (răn′dəm) *adj.* **1.** Having no specific pattern or objective; lacking causal relationships; haphazard. **2.** *Statistics.* **a.** Of or designating a phenomenon that does not produce the same outcome or consequences every time it occurs under identical circumstances. **b.** Of or designating an event having a relative frequency of occurrence that approaches a stable limit as the number of observations of the event increases to infinity. **c.** Of or designating a sample drawn from a population so that each member of the population has an equal chance to be drawn. **d.** Of or pertaining to a member of such a sample: *a random number.* —See Synonyms at **chance. —at random.** Without definite method or purpose; unsystematically: *"accusations are not made at random, but form part of a coherent whole"* (Denis Baly). [Middle English *randoun,* from Old French *randon,* haphazard, from *randir,* to run, from Frankish *rant*† (unattested), a running.] **—ran′dom·ly** *adv.*

ran·dom·ize (răn′də-mīz′) *tr.v.* **-ized, -izing, -izes.** To make random, especially for scientific experimentation. **—ran′dom·i·za′tion** *n.*

random variable. *Statistics.* A variable having numerical values determined by the results of a chance experiment. Also called "stochastic variable."

ran·dy (răn′dē) *adj.* **1.** Lascivious; bawdy. **2.** *Scottish.* Ill-mannered. [Scottish, from *rand,* variant of RANT.]

ra·nee. Variant of **rani.**

rang. Past tense of **ring.** See Usage note at **ring.**

range (rānj) *n. Abbr.* **r. 1. a.** The extent of perception, knowledge, experience, or ability. **b.** The area or sphere in which any activity takes place; scope: *"The artistic range of Emerson is narrow, as every well-read critic must feel at once"* (James Russell Lowell). **c.** The full extent covered by something: *within the range of possibilities.* **2. a.** An amount or extent of variation: *a wide price range.* **b.** *Music.* The gamut of tones within the capacity of a voice or instrument. **3. a.** The maximum or effective distance that can be traversed, as by bullets or by radiation. **b.** The distance to a target. **4.** The maximum distance that a ship or other vehicle can travel before exhausting its fuel supply. **5.** A place for shooting at targets. **6.** *Aerospace.* A testing area in which rockets and missiles are fired and flown. **7.** An extensive area of open land on which livestock wander and graze. **8.** The geographical region in which a kind of plant or animal normally lives or grows. **9.** The act of wandering or roaming over a large area. **10.** *Mathematics.* The totality of points in a set established by a **mapping** *(see).* Compare **domain. 11.** *Statistics.* A measure of dispersion equal to the difference or interval between the smallest and largest of a set of quantities. **12.** A class, rank, or order. **13.** An extended group or series, especially of mountains. **14.** One of a series of double-faced bookcases in a library stack room. **15.** A single series or row of townships, each six miles square, extending parallel to, and numbered east and west from, a survey base meridian line. **16.** A type of large cooking stove on which several foods may be cooked at the same time. *—v.* **ranged, ranging, ranges.** *—tr.* **1.** To arrange or dispose in a particular order, especially in rows or lines. **2.** To assign to a particular category; classify. **3.** To align (a gun or telescope, for example) with a target; to train; to sight. **4. a.** To determine the distance of (a target). **b.** To be capable of reaching (a maximum distance). **5.** To move or travel over or through (a region), as in exploration. **6.** To turn (livestock) on a range to graze. **7.** *Nautical.* To uncoil (an anchor cable) on deck so the anchor may descend easily. *—intr.* **1.** To vary within specified limits: *"Joyce's humor ranges from subtle irony to boisterous horseplay."* (Richard Kain). **2.** To extend in a particular direction: *a river ranging to the east.* **3.** To extend in the same direction. **4.** To move over or through a given area as in exploration: *"his eye . . . ranged with delight over the treasures"* (Washington Irving). **5.** To roam or wander; rove. **6.** To live or grow within a particular region. —See Synonyms at **wander.** [Middle English, series, line, from Old French *range, renge,* range, rank, from *renc, reng,* line, row, from Frankish *hring* (unattested), circle, ring. See **sker-**[3] in Appendix.*]

range finder. Any of various optical, electronic, or acoustical instruments used to determine the distance of an object.

Range·ley Lakes (rānj′lē). A group of lakes in a recreation area in western Maine.

rang·er (rān′jər) *n.* **1.** A wanderer or rover. **2.** One of an armed troop employed in patrolling a specific region. **3.** *Capital* **R.** A member of a group of U.S. soldiers specially trained for making raids. Compare **commando. 4. a.** A warden employed to patrol and guard a forest. **b.** *British.* The keeper of a royal forest or park. **5.** One of a cattle herd that grazes on a range.

Ran·goon (răng-gōōn′). A coastal city and the capital of Burma, on the Rangoon River estuary. Population, 1,530,000.

rang·y (rān′jē) *adj.* **-ier, -iest. 1.** Inclined to rove. **2.** Having slender, long limbs. **3.** Providing ample range; roomy.

ra·ni (rä′nē) *n., pl.* **-nis.** Also **ra·nee. 1.** The wife of a rajah. **2.** A reigning Hindu princess or queen. [Hindi *rānī,* from Sanskrit *rājñī,* feminine of *rājan,* king. See **reg-**[1] in Appendix.*]

rank[1] (răngk) *n.* **1. a.** A relative position in society. **b.** An official position or grade: *the rank of sergeant.* **c.** A relative position or degree of value in any graded group: *"The critical power is of lower rank than the creative."* (Matthew Arnold). **d.** High or eminent station or position: *persons of rank.* **2.** A row, line, series, or range. **3.** *Military.* **a.** A line of soldiers, vehicles, or other military equipment standing side by side in close order. Compare **file. b.** *Plural.* The armed forces. **c.** *Plural.* Enlisted men. **4.** Any of the horizontal lines of squares on a chessboard. **—pull rank.** *Slang.* To use one's superior rank to gain an advantage. *—v.* **ranked, ranking, ranks.** *—tr.* **1.** To place in a row or rows. **2.** To give a particular order or position to; classify. **3.** To outrank or take precedence over. *—intr.* **1.** To hold a particular rank: *rank first.* **2.** To form or stand in a row or rows. [Old French *ranc, renc,* rank, RANGE.]

rank[2] (răngk) *adj.* **ranker, rankest. 1.** Growing profusely or with excessive vigor: *rank weeds.* **2.** Yielding a profuse, often excessive, crop; highly fertile: *rank earth.* **3.** Strong and offensive in odor or flavor. **4.** Indecent; disgusting. **5.** Absolute; complete: *a rank amateur.* —See Synonyms at **flagrant.** [Middle English *rank,* Old English *ranc,* haughty, full-grown, overbearing. See **reg-**[1] in Appendix.*] **—rank′ly** *adv.* **—rank′ness** *n.*

rank and file. 1. The common soldiers of an army. **2.** Those who form the major portion of any group or organization, excluding the leaders and officers.

rank·er (răngk′ər) *n. British.* **1.** An enlisted soldier. **2.** A commissioned officer.

Ran·kin (răng′kĭn), **Jeannette.** Born 1880. American feminist leader; first woman in U.S. House of Representatives.

Ran·kine scale (răng′kĭn). The scale of absolute temperature using Fahrenheit degrees, in which the freezing point of water is 491.69° and the boiling point of water is 671.69°. [After William J.M. *Rankine* (1820–1872), Scottish physicist.]

rank·ing (răngk'ĭng) *adj.* Of the highest rank; pre-eminent.

ran·kle (răng'kəl) *v.* **-kled, -kling, -kles.** —*intr.* **1.** To cause persistent irritation or resentment. **2.** To become sore or inflamed; fester. —*tr.* To embitter; irritate. [Middle English *ranclen,* from Old French *rancler, draoncler,* from *rancle, draoncle,* ulcer, festering sore, from Late Latin *dracunculus,* something twisted like a serpent, from Latin, diminutive of *dracō* (stem *dracon-*), serpent. See *derk-* in Appendix.*]

Rann of Cutch (rŭn; kŭch). Also **Rann of Kutch.** A salt marsh, 9,000 square miles in area, between the Republic of India and West Pakistan. Also called "Cutch," "Kutch."

ran·sack (răn'săk') *tr.v.* **-sacked, -sacking, -sacks. 1.** To search or examine thoroughly: *"the wearisomest . . . pharisee that ever ransacked a Bible"* (Emily Brontë). **2.** To search carefully for plunder; to pillage. —See Synonyms at **rob.** [Middle English *ransaken,* from Old Norse *rannsaka,* search a house : *rann,* house, from Common Germanic *razn-* (unattested) + *-saka,* search (see **sāg-** in Appendix*).] —**ran'sack·er** *n.*

ran·som (răn'səm) *n.* **1.** The release of a person or property in return for payment of a stipulated price. **2.** The price or payment demanded or paid. **3.** *Theology.* A redemption from sin and its consequences. —*tr.v.* **ransomed, -soming, -soms. 1.** To obtain the release of (a person or property) by paying a certain price. **2.** To release after receiving such a payment. **3.** *Theology.* To deliver from sin and its consequences. [Middle English *ransoun,* from Old French *rançon,* from Latin *redemptiō,* REDEMPTION.] —**ran'som·er** *n.*

rant (rănt) *v.* **ranted, ranting, rants.** —*intr.* To speak or declaim in a violent, loud, or vehement manner; rave. —*tr.* To exclaim with violence or extravagance. Often used with *out.* —*n.* **1.** Violent, loud, or extravagant speech. **2.** *British Regional.* Wild or uproarious merriment. —See Synonyms at **bombast.** [Probably from Dutch *ranten†.*] —**rant'er** *n.*

ra·nun·cu·lus (rə-nŭng'kyə-ləs) *n., pl.* **-luses** or **-li** (-lī'). Any plant of the genus *Ranunculus,* including the buttercups. [New Latin, from Latin *rānunculus,* diminutive of *rāna†,* frog.]

rap¹ (răp) *v.* **rapped, rapping, raps.** —*tr.* **1.** To hit sharply and swiftly; to strike. **2.** To utter sharply. Used with *out.* —*intr.* **1.** To strike a quick, light blow or blows; to knock. **2.** *Slang.* To talk discursively. —*n.* **1.** A quick, light blow or knock. **2.** A knocking or tapping sound. **3.** *Slang.* **a.** A reprimand or censure. **b.** A legal sentence to serve in prison. —**beat the rap.** *Slang.* To escape punishment or be acquitted of a charge. —**take the rap.** *Slang.* To accept punishment for a crime, especially when innocent. [Middle English *rappen,* akin to Norwegian *rappe,* Swedish *rappa,* (imitative).]

rap² (răp) *tr.v.* **rapt** or **rapped, rapping, raps. 1.** *Archaic.* To enchant or seize with rapture. Now used only in the past participle. **2.** *Obsolete.* To snatch. [Back-formation from RAPT.]

rap³ (răp) *n.* **1.** A counterfeit halfpenny passed in Ireland during the 18th century. **2.** *Informal.* The least bit: *I don't care a rap.* [Short for Irish-Gaelic *rapaire,* pike. See **rapparee.**]

ra·pa·cious (rə-pā'shəs) *adj.* **1.** Taking by force; plundering. **2.** Greedy; avaricious; ravenous. **3.** Subsisting on live prey. [From Latin *rapax* (stem *rapāc-*), from *rapere,* to seize. See **rep-** in Appendix.*] —**ra·pa'cious·ly** *adv.* —**ra·pa'cious·ness, ra·pac'i·ty** (rə-păs'ə-tē) *n.*

rape¹ (rāp) *n.* **1.** The crime of forcing a female to submit to sexual intercourse. See **statutory rape. 2.** The act of seizing and carrying off by force; abduction. **3.** Abusive or improper treatment; violation; profanation: *a rape of justice.* —*v.* **raped, raping, rapes.** —*tr.* **1.** To force (a female) to submit to sexual intercourse. **2.** To seize and carry off by force. **3.** To plunder or pillage. —*intr.* To commit rape. [Middle English, from *rapen,* to rape, from Old French *raper,* from Latin *rapere,* to seize. See **rep-** in Appendix.*] —**rap'ist** *n.*

rape² (rāp) *n.* A Eurasian plant, *Brassica napus,* cultivated for its seed, which yields a useful oil, and as fodder. Also called "colza." [Middle English, from Latin *rāpa, rāpum,* turnip. See **rāp-** in Appendix.*]

rape³ (rāp) *n.* The refuse of grapes left after the extraction of the juice in wine-making. [French *râpe,* grape stalk, from Old French *rasper,* to scrape off, RASP.]

rape oil. The edible oil extracted from rapeseed, also used as a lubricant and in the manufacture of various products. Also called "rapeseed oil."

rape·seed (rāp'sēd') *n.* The seed of the rape plant.

Raph·a·el¹ (răf'ē-əl, rä'fē-). Also **Raf·a·el** (rä'fä-ĕl), **Raf·fa·el·lo** (ra-fä-ĕl'lō). Original surname, Sanzio. 1483–1520. Italian Renaissance painter and architect.

Raph·a·el² (răf'ē-əl, rä'fē-). One of the archangels. [Hebrew *Rəphā'ēl,* "God has healed."]

Raph·a·el·esque (răf'ē-əl-ĕsk') *adj.* In the style of the painter Raphael. —**Raph·a·el·ism** *n.* —**Raph·a·el·ite** *n.*

ra·phe (rā'fē) *n., pl.* **-phae** (-fē). Also **rha·phe.** *Biology.* A seamlike line or ridge between two similar parts, as in the scrotum, the coat of certain seeds, or the valves of a diatom. [New Latin, from Greek *rhaphē,* seam, from *rhaptein,* to sew. See **wer-³** in Appendix.*]

raph·i·a. Variant of **raffia.**

ra·phide (rā'fīd) *n., pl.* **raphides** (răf'ə-dēz'). Also **ra·phis** (-fĭs). *Botany.* One of a bundle of needle-shaped crystals, composed chiefly of calcium oxalate, occurring in many plant cells. [Back-formation from *raphides,* plural, from New Latin, from Greek *rhaphis* (stem *rhaphid-*), needle, from *rhaptein,* to sew. See **wer-³** in Appendix.*]

rap·id (răp'ĭd) *adj.* Moving, acting, or occurring with great speed; swift. See Synonyms at **fast.** —*n. Usually plural.* An extremely fast-moving part of a river, caused by a steep descent in the riverbed. [Latin *rapidus,* hurrying, seizing, from *rapere,* to seize. See **rep-** in Appendix.*] —**rap'id·ly** *adv.* —**ra·pid·i·ty** (rə-pĭd'ə-tē), **rap'id·ness** *n.*

Rap·i·dan (răp'ə-dăn'). A river rising in northern Virginia and flowing 90 miles east to the Rappahannock.

Rap·id City (răp'ĭd sĭt'ē). A city in western South Dakota, near the Black Hills. Population, 42,000.

rap·id-fire (răp'ĭd-fīr') *adj.* **1.** Designed to fire shots in rapid succession. **2.** Marked by continuous, rapid occurrence: *rapid-fire questions.*

rapid transit. An urban passenger transportation system using elevated or underground trains or a combination of both.

ra·pi·er (rā'pē-ər, răp'yər) *n.* **1.** A long, slender, two-edged sword with a cuplike hilt, used in the 16th and 17th centuries. **2.** An 18th-century, lighter, sharp-pointed sword lacking a cutting edge and used only for thrusting. [French *rapière,* originally *(espée) rapière†,* rapier (sword).]

rap·ine (răp'ĭn) *n.* Forcible seizure of another's property; plunder. [Middle English *rapyne,* from Old French *rapine,* from Latin *rapīna,* from *rapere,* to RAPE (seize).]

Rap·pa·han·nock (răp'ə-hăn'ək). A river in Virginia, flowing 185 miles from the Blue Ridge Mountains to Chesapeake Bay.

rap·pa·ree (răp'ə-rē') *n.* **1.** A freebooting soldier of 17th-century Ireland. **2.** A bandit or robber. [Irish-Gaelic *rapaire,* either from English RAPIER or French *rapière,* RAPIER.]

rap·pee (ră-pē') *n.* A strong snuff made from a dark, coarse tobacco. [French *râpé,* "grated" (as tobacco), from *râper,* to grate, from Old French *rasper,* RASP.]

rap·pel (ră-pĕl') *n.* The act or method of descending from a mountainside or cliff by means of a double rope passed under one thigh and over the opposite shoulder. —*intr.v.* **rappeled, -pelling, -pels.** To descend from a steep height by rappel. [French, "recall," from Old French *rapel,* from *rapeler,* to summon, recall : *re-,* again + *apeler,* to summon, APPEAL.]

rap·pen (rä'pən) *n., pl.* **rappen.** A Swiss coin, the *centime (see).* [German *Rappen,* from *Rappe(n),* a raven (a jocular reference to the eagles on the earliest rappens), from Middle High German *rappe.* See **ker-²** in Appendix.*]

rap·per (răp'ər) *n.* One that raps; specifically, a doorknocker.

rap·port (ra-pôr', -pōr') *n.* Relationship; especially, one of mutual trust or emotional affinity. [French, from *rapporter,* to bring back, to yield, from Old French *raporter* : *re-,* back, again + *aporter,* to bring, from Latin *apportāre* : *ad-,* to + *portāre,* to carry (see **per-²** in Appendix*).]

rap·proche·ment (ra-prôsh-mäN') *n.* **1.** A reestablishing of cordial relations, as between two countries. **2.** The state of reconciliation or of cordial relations: *"During the New Deal the rapprochement between intellectuals and the public was restored."* (Richard Hofstadter). [French, from *rapprocher,* to bring together : *re-,* again + *approcher,* to approach, from Late Latin *appropriāre* : Latin *ad-,* to + *prope,* near (see **per¹** in Appendix*).]

rap·scal·lion (răp-skăl'yən) *n.* A rascal; scamp. [Variant of obsolete *rascallion,* from RASCAL.]

rapt (răpt). Past tense and past participle of **rap** (to enchant). —*adj.* **1.** Transported with strong, noble emotion; enraptured. **2.** Deeply absorbed; engrossed: *"I sat in my sunny doorway . . . rapt in a revery"* (Thoreau). **3.** Expressing or resulting from rapture: *"Alcaeus listened with rapt adoration"* (Allen Tate). [Middle English, from Latin *raptus,* "seized," from the past participle of *rapere,* to seize. See **rep-** in Appendix.*]

Rap·ti (räp'tē). A river rising in Nepal and flowing 400 miles to the Gogra River, Republic of India.

rap·tor (răp'tər) *n.* A bird of prey. [Latin, "one who seizes," from *raptus,* RAPT.]

rap·to·ri·al (răp-tôr'ē-əl, -tōr'ē-əl) *adj.* **1.** Subsisting by seizing prey; predatory. **2.** Adapted for the seizing of prey. **3.** Of, relating to, or characteristic of birds of prey.

rap·ture (răp'chər) *n.* **1.** The state of being transported by a lofty emotion; ecstasy. **2.** *Often plural.* An expression of ecstatic feeling. **3.** *Rare.* The transporting of a person from one place to another, especially to heaven. —See Synonyms at **ecstasy.** —*tr.v.* **raptured, -turing, -tures.** *Rare.* To enrapture. [Medieval Latin *raptūra,* "ecstasy," from Latin *raptus,* RAPT.]

rap·tur·ous (răp'chər-əs) *adj.* Filled with great joy or rapture; ecstatic. —**rap'tur·ous·ly** *adv.* —**rap'tur·ous·ness** *n.*

ra·ra a·vis (râr'ē ā'vĭs) *pl.* **rara avises** or **rarae aves** (râr'ē ā'vēz). A rare or unique person or thing. [Latin, "rare bird."]

rare¹ (râr) *adj.* **rarer, rarest. 1.** *Abbr.* **r.** Infrequently occurring; uncommon; unusual. **2.** Highly valued owing to uncommonness; special. **3.** Thin in density; rarefied. Said of gases. [Middle English, from Latin *rārus,* loose, thin, scarce, remarkable. See **erə-¹** in Appendix.*] —**rare'ness** *n.*

Usage: *Rare* and *scarce* both describe what is infrequent or in short supply. But *rare* usually implies unusual quality and value enhanced by permanent infrequency. *Scarce* emphasizes mere infrequency, with the implication that it is temporary.

rare² (râr) *adj.* **rarer, rarest.** Cooked a short time to retain juice and redness. Said of meat. [Originally used only of eggs and meaning "soft-boiled," later form of *rear,* Middle English *rere,* Old English *hrēr.* See **kerə-** in Appendix.*] —**rare'ness** *n.*

rare·bit (râr'bĭt) *n.* A cheese dish, **Welsh rabbit** *(see).* [Variant of (WELSH) RABBIT.]

rare earth. 1. Any of various oxides of the rare-earth elements. **2.** Any rare-earth element.

rare-earth element (râr'ûrth'). Any of the abundant metallic

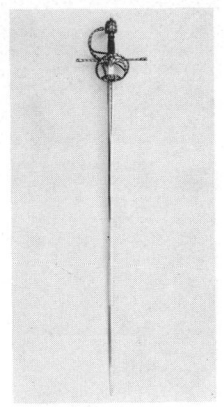

rapier
Late 16th-century
Spanish

Raphael¹
A self-portrait

elements of atomic number 57 through 71. See **element.** Also called "rare earth," "lanthanide." [Originally contrasted with the so-called "common-earth elements" (calcium, magnesium, and aluminum).]

Rasputin

rar·ee show (râr'ē). **1.** A **peepshow** *(see).* **2.** A street show. [From RARE (excellent).]

rar·e·fac·tion (râr'ə-făk'shən) *n.* Also **rar·e·fi·ca·tion** (-fĭ-kā'-shən). **1.** The act or process of rarefying. **2.** The state of being rarefied. —**rar'e·fac'tive** *adj.*

rar·e·fied (râr'ə-fīd) *adj.* **1.** Belonging to or reserved for a small and select group; esoteric. **2.** Elevated in character or style; exalted; lofty: *"Spiritual things, of a more rarefied nature than knowledge"* (Donne).

rar·e·fy (râr'ə-fī') *v.* **-fied, -fying, -fies.** —*tr.* **1.** To make thin, less compact, or less dense. **2.** To purify or refine. —*intr.* To become thin, less dense, or purer. [Middle English *rarefien,* from Old French *rarefier,* from Latin *rārēfacere* : *rārus,* RARE + *facere,* to make (see **dhē-**[1] in Appendix*).] —**rar'e·fi'a·ble** *adj.*

rare·ly (râr'lē) *adv.* **1.** Not often; seldom; infrequently: *"The truth is rarely pure and never simple."* (Oscar Wilde). **2.** In an unusual degree; exceptionally. **3.** With uncommon excellence.

Usage: The use of *ever* after *rarely* or *seldom* is redundant. Thus, the example *He rarely* (or *seldom*) *ever watches television* is unacceptable in writing to 87 per cent of the Usage Panel and in speech to 62 per cent. The following combinations are possible, however: *rarely if ever; rarely or never* (but not *rarely or ever*).

rare·ripe (râr'rīp') *adj.* Ripening early. —*n.* A fruit or vegetable that ripens early. [*Rare-,* variant (perhaps influenced by RARE, underdone) of RATHE.]

rat
Rattus norvegicus

rar·ing (râr'ĭng) *adj. Informal.* Full of eagerness; enthusiastic. Followed by an infinitive: *We're raring to get started.* [From dialectal *rare,* variant of REAR (to arouse, raise up).]

Rar·i·tan (răr'ə-tən). A river rising in northern New Jersey and flowing 75 miles generally eastward to Raritan Bay, the western arm of lower New York Bay.

rar·i·ty (râr'ə-tē) *n., pl.* **-ties. 1.** Something that is rare. **2.** The quality or state of being rare; infrequency of occurrence.

Ra·ro·ton·ga (rä'rô-tông'gə). A volcanic island in the South Pacific Ocean, site of Avarua, capital of the Cook Islands. Population, 10,000.

Ras As·sir. The Arabic name for Cape **Guardafui.**

ras·bo·ra (răz-bôr'ə, -bōr'ə) *n.* Any of various tropical fishes of the genus *Rasbora,* of which several brightly colored species are kept in home aquariums. [From a native East Indian name.]

ras·cal (răs'kəl) *n.* **1.** An unscrupulous or dishonest person; a scoundrel. **2.** One who is playfully mischievous; a scamp. **3.** *Archaic.* One belonging to the rabble. —*adj. Archaic.* Of or suited to the rabble; base. [Middle English *rascaille,* perhaps from Norman French, from *rasquer* (unattested), to scrape up, from Old French *rasque, rasche,* mud, filth. See **rash** (eruption).] —**ras'cal·ly** *adj.*

ratchet
Wheel and pawl

ras·cal·i·ty (răs-kăl'ə-tē) *n., pl.* **-ties. 1.** The behavior or character of a rascal. **2.** A base or mischievous act.

Ras Da·shan (räs dä-shän'). The highest elevation (15,157 feet) in Ethiopia, in the north, northeast of Lake Tana.

rase (rāz) *tr.v.* **rased, rasing, rases.** *Rare.* **1.** To erase. **2.** Variant of **raze.**

rash[1] (răsh) *adj.* **rasher, rashest. 1.** Acting without forethought or due caution; impetuous. **2.** Characterized by ill-considered haste or boldness. **3.** *Obsolete.* Quick in producing an effect. —See Synonyms at **reckless.** [Middle English *rasch,* nimble, quick, eager, perhaps from Middle Dutch, *rasch.* See **kret-**[1] in Appendix.*] —**rash'ly** *adv.* —**rash'ness** *n.*

rash[2] (răsh) *n.* **1.** Any skin eruption. **2.** An outbreak of many instances within a brief period: *"this current rash of criticism and disrespect"* (John F. Kennedy). [Possibly from obsolete French *rache,* from Old French *rasche,* scurf, from *raschier,* to scratch, from Vulgar Latin *rasciāre* (unattested), to scrape, from Latin *rādere* (past participle *rāsus*). See **rēd-** in Appendix.*]

rash·er (răsh'ər) *n.* **1.** A thin slice of bacon to be fried or broiled. **2.** A dish of such slices. [Origin unknown.]

Rasht. See **Resht.**

Rask (räsk), **Rasmus Christian.** 1787–1832. Danish philologist; a founder of the science of philology.

Ras·mus·sen (räs'mōōs-ən), **Knud Johan Victor.** 1879–1933. Danish ethnologist and explorer of the Arctic.

raspberry
Rubus idaeus

ra·so·ri·al (rə-zôr'ē-əl, rə-zōr'-, rə-sôr'-, rə-sōr'-) *adj.* Characteristically scratching the ground for food. Said of chickens and similar birds. [From Late Latin *rāsor,* "scraper," from Latin *rādere* (past participle *rāsus*), to scrape. See **rēd-** in Appendix.*]

rasp (răsp, räsp) *v.* **rasped, rasping, rasps.** —*tr.* **1.** To file or scrape with a rasp. **2.** To utter in a grating voice. **3.** To irritate; grate upon (nerves or feelings). —*intr.* **1.** To grate; scrape harshly. **2.** To make a harsh, grating sound. —*n.* **1.** A file having abrasive, pointed projections. **2.** The act of filing with a rasp. **3.** A harsh, grating sound. [Middle English *raspen,* from Old French *rasper,* from Old High German *raspōn,* from Germanic *hrap-* (unattested), to snatch. See **raffle.**] —**rasp'er** *n.* —**rasp'ing·ly** *adv.*

rasp·ber·ry (răz'bĕr'ē, -bə-rē, räz'-) *n., pl.* **-ries.** Also **razz·ber·ry** (for sense 4). **1.** Any of various shrubby, usually prickly plants of the genus *Rubus,* bearing edible berries, such as *R. strigosus,* of eastern North America, and *R. idaeus,* of Europe. **2.** The fruit of any of these plants, consisting of a mass of small, fleshy, usually red drupelets. **3.** Moderate to dark or deep purplish red. See **color. 4.** *Slang.* A derisive or contemptuous sound made by vibrating the extended tongue and the lips while exhaling. In this sense, also called "bird," "Bronx cheer," "razz." [From earlier *raspis*†.]

Ras·pu·tin (răs-pyōō'tĭn), **Grigori Efimovich.** 1871?–1916. Russian mystic monk; favorite of the imperial family; assassinated.

rasp·y (răs'pē, räs'-) *adj.* **-ier, -iest.** Grating; harsh; rough.

rat (răt) *n.* **1.** Any of various long-tailed rodents resembling, but larger than, mice; especially, one of the genus *Rattus.* **2.** Any of various similar animals. **3.** *Slang.* A despicable, sneaky person, especially one who betrays or informs upon his associates. **4.** *Informal.* A pad of hair or other material worn as part of a woman's coiffure to puff out the hair. —**smell a rat.** *Slang.* To suspect that something underhanded or treacherous is going on. —*intr.v.* **ratted, ratting, rats. 1.** To hunt for or catch rats, especially with the aid of dogs. **2.** *Slang.* To desert or betray one's comrades. Used with *on.* [Middle English *rat,* Old English *ræt,* from Germanic *ratt-* (unattested).]

rat·a·ble (ra'tə-bəl) *adj.* **1.** Capable of being rated, estimated, or appraised. **2.** Proportional. **3.** *British.* Liable to assessment; taxable. —**rat'a·bil'i·ty, rat'a·ble·ness** *n.* —**rat'a·bly** *adv.*

rat·a·fi·a (răt'ə-fē'ə) *n.* Also **rat·a·fee** (-ə-fē'). **1.** A sweet cordial flavored with fruit kernels or almonds. **2.** A biscuit flavored with this cordial. [French, from West Indian Creole.]

rat·a·plan (răt'ə-plăn') *n.* A tattoo, as of a drum, the hoofs of a galloping horse, or machine-gun fire. [French (imitative).]

rat-a-tat-tat (răt'ə-tăt'tăt') *n.* A series of short, sharp sounds, such as those made by knocking on a door. [Imitative.]

rat-bite fever (răt'bīt'). Either of two infectious diseases contractible from the bite of a rat: **a.** That arising from *Streptobacillus moniliformis* and characterized by skin inflammation, back and joint pains, headache, and vomiting. **b.** That from *Spirillum minus,* with ulceration at the site of the bite, a purplish rash, and recurrent fever. Also called "rat-bite disease."

ratch·et (răch'ĭt) *n.* **1.** A mechanism consisting of a pawl, or hinged catch, that engages the sloping teeth of a wheel or bar, permitting motion in one direction only. **2.** The pawl, wheel, or bar of such a mechanism. [French *rochet,* from Old French *rocquet,* head of a lance, from Frankish *rokko* (unattested), a distaff. See **ruk-**[1] in Appendix.*]

rate[1] (rāt) *n.* **1.** A measured quantity that occurs or is attained within the limits of a fixed quantity of something else: *a rate of speed of 60 miles an hour.* **2.** A quantitative measure of a part to a whole; proportion: *the birth rate; a tax rate.* **3.** The cost per unit of a commodity or service. **4.** A charge or payment calculated in relation to any particular sum or quantity. **5.** Level of quality. **6.** *British.* A property tax assessed locally. —**at any rate. 1.** Whatever the case may be. **2.** At least. —*v.* **rated, rating, rates.** —*tr.* **1.** To calculate the value of; appraise. **2.** To place in a particular rank or grade. **3.** To regard or account: *rated as a great success.* **4.** To value for purposes of taxation. **5.** To set a rate for (goods to be shipped). **6.** To specify the performance limits of (a machine or firearm, for example). **7.** *Informal.* To merit or deserve: *rate special treatment.* See Usage note below. —*intr.* **1.** To be ranked in a particular class. **2.** *Informal.* To have status, importance, or influence. See Usage note below. —See Synonyms at **estimate.** [Middle English, from Old French, from Medieval Latin *rata,* calculated, fixed, from the feminine past participle of Latin *rērī,* to calculate. See **ar-** in Appendix.*]

Usage: The informal senses of the verb are not appropriate to most writing. Typical examples involving *rate* in the sense of to merit or deserve and *rate* in the sense of to have status or influence were rejected by 74 per cent and 65 per cent of the Usage Panel, respectively.

rate[2] (rāt) *v.* **rated, rating, rates.** —*tr.* To berate. —*intr.* To express reproof. [Middle English *raten,* perhaps from Old Norse *hrata.* See **sker-**[2] in Appendix.*]

ra·tel (rät'l, rāt'l) *n.* An animal, the **honey badger** *(see).* [Afrikaans *ratel*†.]

rate of exchange. The ratio at which the unit of currency of one country may be, or is, exchanged for the unit of currency of another country. Also called "exchange rate."

rate·pay·er (rāt'pā'ər) *n. British.* One who pays rates.

rat·fink (răt'fĭngk') *n. Slang.* A contemptible, obnoxious, or otherwise undesirable person. [RAT (to betray) + FINK.]

rat·fish (răt'fĭsh') *n., pl.* **ratfish** or **-fishes.** A fish, *Hydrolagus colliei,* of Pacific waters, having a long, narrow tail.

rathe (rāth, răth) *adj. Archaic.* **1.** Appearing or ripening early in the year. **2.** Prompt; eager. [Middle English *rathe,* early, rapid, Old English *hræd, hræth.* See **kret-**[1] in Appendix.*]

rath·er (răth'ər, rä'*th*ər; rä'*th*ûr', rä'*th*ûr' *for sense 6*) *adv.* **1.** More readily; preferably. See Usage note below. **2.** With more reason, logic, wisdom, or other justification. **3.** With more accuracy: *He's my friend, or rather he was my friend.* **4.** To a certain extent; somewhat: *rather nice.* **5.** On the contrary. **6.** *Chiefly British.* Most certainly. Used as an emphatic affirmative reply. **7.** *Obsolete.* More quickly; earlier. [Middle English *rather,* Old English *hrathor,* comparative of *hrathe, hræth,* early, RATHE.]

Usage: *Rather* is usually preceded by *would* (or *should*) in constructions expressing preference: *He would rather not go.* But *had rather* is also possible: *He had rather be dead than be a slave.*

rat·i·fi·ca·tion (răt'ə-fĭ-kā'shən) *n.* The action of officially confirming something, such as a treaty or constitution.

rat·i·fy (răt'ə-fī') *tr.v.* **-fied, -fying, -fies.** To give formal sanction to; approve and so make valid. See Synonyms at **approve, confirm.** [Middle English *ratifien,* from Old French *ratifier,* from Medieval Latin *ratificāre* : Latin *ratus,* "fixed" (see **rate**) + *facere,* to make (see **dhē-**[1] in Appendix*).] —**rat'i·fi'er** *n.*

ă pat/ā pay/âr care/ä father/b bib/ch church/d deed/ĕ pet/ē be/f fife/g gag/h hat/hw which/ĭ pit/ī pie/îr pier/j judge/k kick/l lid, needle/m mum/n no, sudden/ng thing/ŏ pot/ō toe/ô paw, for/oi noise/ou out/ŏŏ took/ōō boot/p pop/r roar/s sauce/sh ship, dish/

rat·i·né (răt′ə-nā′) *n.* A loosely woven fabric with a nubby texture. [French, past participle of *ratiner*†, to adorn.]
rat·ing[1] (rā′tĭng) *n.* **1.** A place assigned on a scale; a standing. **2.** A classification according to specialty or proficiency, as of an armed serviceman. **3.** An evaluation of the financial status of a business or an individual. **4.** A specified performance limit, as of capacity, range, or operational capability: *power rating.* **5.** The popularity of a television or radio program as estimated by a poll of segments of the audience. **6.** *British.* An enlisted man in the navy.
rat·ing[2] (rā′tĭng) *n.* A scolding. [From RATE (scold).]
ra·tio (rā′shō, rā′shē-ō′) *n., pl.* **-tios.** **1.** Relation in degree or number between two similar things; rate. **2.** *Finance.* The relative value of silver and gold in a currency system that is bimetallic. **3.** *Mathematics.* The relative size of two quantities expressed as the quotient of one divided by the other: *The ratio of 7 to 4 is written 7:4 or 7/4.* [Latin *ratiō*, computation, from *rērī* (past participle *ratus*), to consider. See **ar-** in Appendix.*]
ra·ti·oc·i·nate (răsh′ē-ŏs′ə-nāt′) *intr.v.* **-nated, -nating, -nates.** To reason methodically and logically. [Latin *ratiōcinārī*, from *ratiō*, RATIO.] —**ra′ti·oc′i·na′tive** *adj.* —**ra′ti·oc′i·na′tion** *n.* —**ra′ti·oc′i·na′tor** (-nā′tər) *n.*
ra·tion (răsh′ən, rā′shən) *n.* **1.** A fixed portion; especially, an amount of food allotted to persons in military service or to civilians in times of scarcity. **2.** *Plural. Military.* Food. —*tr.v.* **rationed, -tioning, -tions.** **1.** To supply with rations. **2.** To distribute as rations. **3.** To restrict to limited allotments, as during wartime. —See Synonyms at **distribute.** [French, from Latin *ratiō* (stem *ratiōn-*), RATIO.]
ra·tion·al (răsh′ən-əl) *adj.* **1.** Having or exercising the ability to reason. **2.** Of sound mind; sane. **3.** Manifesting or based upon reason; logical. **4.** *Mathematics.* Designating an algebraic expression no variable of which appears in an irreducible radical or with a fractional exponent. [Latin *ratiōnālis*, from *ratiō*, reason, RATIO.] —**ra′tion·al·ly** *adv.* —**ra′tion·al·ness** *n.*
ra·tion·ale (răsh′ə-năl′) *n.* **1.** The fundamental reasons for something; a logical basis. **2.** An exposition of principles or reasons. [Latin *ratiōnāle*, neuter of *ratiōnālis*, RATIONAL.]
ra·tion·al·ism (răsh′ən-əl-ĭz′əm) *n.* The theory that the exercise of reason, rather than the acceptance of empiricism, authority, or spiritual revelation, provides the only valid basis for action or belief, and that reason is the prime source of knowledge and of spiritual truth. —**ra′tion·al·ist** *n.* —**ra′tion·al·is′tic** *adj.* —**ra′tion·al·is′ti·cal·ly** *adv.*
ra·tion·al·i·ty (răsh′ə-năl′ə-tē) *n., pl.* **-ties.** **1.** The quality or condition of being rational. **2.** A rational belief or practice.
ra·tion·al·i·za·tion (răsh′ən-əl-ə-zā′shən) *n.* **1.** The act, process, or practice of rationalizing. **2.** An instance of rationalizing.
ra·tion·al·ize (răsh′ən-əl-īz′) *v.* **-ized, -izing, -izes.** —*tr.* **1.** To make conformable to reason; make rational. **2.** To interpret from a rational standpoint. **3.** *Psychology.* To devise self-satisfying but incorrect reasons for (one's behavior). **4.** *Mathematics.* To remove radicals without changing the value of (an expression) or roots of (an equation). **5.** *Chiefly British.* To bring modern, efficient methods to (an industry, for example). —*intr.* **1.** To think in a rational or rationalistic way. **2.** *Psychology.* To devise self-satisfying but incorrect reasons for one's behavior. —**ra′tion·al·iz′er** *n.*
rational number. Any number capable of being expressed as an integer or quotient of integers. See **number.**
Rat·is·bon. See **Regensburg.**
rat·ite (răt′īt′) *adj.* Designating any of a group of flightless birds having a flat breastbone without the keellike prominence characteristic of most flying birds. —*n.* A ratite bird, such as the ostrich or emu. [New Latin *Ratitae* (group), from Latin *ratis*, raft (so named in allusion to the "keelless" sternum). See **ere-**[2] in Appendix.*]
rat·line (răt′lĭn) *n.* Also **rat·lin.** *Nautical.* **1.** Any of the small ropes fastened horizontally to the shrouds of a ship and forming a ladder for going aloft. **2.** The rope used for this purpose. [Origin uncertain.]
ra·toon (ră-to͞on′) *n.* Also **rat·toon.** A basal shoot sprouting from a plant such as the banana, pineapple, or sugar cane. —*v.* **ratooned, -tooning, -toons.** Also **rat·toon.** —*intr.* To produce or grow as a ratoon or ratoons. —*tr.* To propagate (a crop) from ratoons. [Spanish *retoño*, sprout, from *retoñar*, to sprout : *re-*, again + *otoñar*, to grow in the autumn, from *otoño*, autumn, from Latin *autumnus*, AUTUMN.]
rat race. *Slang.* A ceaseless round of rushed, competitive activity, such as the hectic routine of office workers.
rats·bane (răts′bān′) *n.* Rat poison, especially arsenic trioxide. [From RAT + BANE.]
rat snake. Any of several nonvenomous snakes of the genus *Elaphe.*
rat-tail (răt′tāl′) *adj.* Also **rat-tailed** (-tāld′). Shaped like a rat's tail: *a rat-tail file.* —*n.* A fish, the **grenadier** *(see).*
rat-tail cactus. A tropical American cactus, *Aporocactus flagelliformis*, having thin, creeping or hanging stems and brilliant crimson flowers.
rat·tan (ră-tăn′) *n.* **1.** Any of various climbing palms of the genera *Calamus, Daemonorops,* or *Plectomia,* of tropical Asia, having long, tough, slender stems. **2.** The stems of any of these palms, used to make wickerwork. **3.** A switch or cane made from such a stem. [Malay *rotan*, possibly from *raut*, trim.]
rat·teen (ră-tēn′) *n. Obsolete.* A thick, twilled woolen cloth. [French *ratine*†.]
rat·ter (răt′ər) *n.* **1.** A cat, dog, or person who catches or kills rats. **2.** *Slang.* A deserter, betrayer, or traitor.
rat·tle[1] (răt′l) *v.* **-tled, -tling, -tles.** —*intr.* **1.** To make or emit a quick succession of short, sharp sounds. **2.** To move with such sounds: *a train rattling along the track.* **3.** To talk rapidly and at length, usually without much thought. —*tr.* **1.** To cause to rattle. **2.** To utter or perform rapidly or effortlessly: *rattle off a list of names.* **3.** *Informal.* To fluster, unnerve. See Usage note below. —*n.* **1.** Short, percussive sounds produced in rapid succession. **2.** A device for producing these sounds, such as a baby's toy. **3.** A rattling sound in the throat caused by obstructed breathing. **4.** The series of horny structures at the end of a rattlesnake's tail. **5.** Loud or rapid talk; chatter. [Middle English *ratelen*, from Middle Low German *rattelen*, akin to Middle High German *razzeln*†.]
Usage: Though informal in tone, the verb *rattle* in the sense of to unnerve is not necessarily inappropriate to serious writing. The following example is approved by 86 per cent of the Usage Panel: *He was obviously rattled by her testimony.*
rat·tle[2] (răt′l) *tr.v.* **-tled, -tling, -tles.** *Nautical.* To secure ratlines to (shrouds). Used with *down.* [Back-formation from *rattling*, variant of RATLINE.]
rat·tle·box (răt′l-bŏks′) *n.* Any of various plants or shrubs of the genus *Crotalaria*, having inflated pods within which the seeds rattle.
rat·tle·brained (răt′l-brānd′) *adj.* Giddy and talkative; foolish.
rat·tler (răt′lər) *n.* **1.** One who or that which rattles. **2.** A rattlesnake. **3.** *Informal.* A freight train.
rat·tle·snake (răt′l-snāk′) *n.* Any of various venomous New World snakes of the genera *Crotalus* and *Sistrurus*, having at the end of the tail a series of loosely attached, horny segments that can be vibrated to produce a rattling or buzzing sound.
rattlesnake flag. Any of several flags bearing the motto "Don't Tread on Me" and a picture of a rattlesnake, used during the French and Indian War and the Revolutionary War.
rattlesnake master. Any of several plants supposedly effective against the venom of rattlesnakes, such as *Eryngium yuccifolium*, of the southeastern United States, having narrow leaves with spiny margins and pale-blue or white flowers. Also called "button snakeroot."
rattlesnake plantain. Any of various small orchids of the genus *Goodyera*, having mottled or striped leaves and spikes of whitish flowers. [From its leaves, which resemble a rattlesnake's skin.]
rattlesnake root. Any of various plants of the genus *Prenanthes*, having thick, bitter-tasting roots. [Because it was believed that the root cured rattlesnake bite.]
rattlesnake weed. A plant, *Hieracium venosum*, having red-veined or purple-veined leaves and yellow flowers. Also called "poor Robin's plantain."
rat·tle·trap (răt′l-trăp′) *n.* A rickety, worn-out vehicle.
rat·tling (răt′lĭng) *adj. Informal.* **1.** Animated; brisk: *rattling conversation.* **2.** Very good. —*adv. Informal.* Very; especially: *a rattling good party.*
rat·tly (răt′lē) *adj.* Rattling or apt to rattle; clattering.
rat·toon. Variant of **ratoon.**
rat·trap (răt′trăp′) *n.* **1.** A device for trapping rats. **2.** A dilapidated or unsanitary dwelling.
rat·ty (răt′ē) *adj.* **-tier, -tiest.** **1.** Of or characteristic of rats. **2.** Infested by rats. **3.** *Slang.* Disreputable; dilapidated; shabby. **4.** *Chiefly British.* Annoyed; irritable.
rau·cous (rô′kəs) *adj.* Rough-sounding and harsh: *raucous laughter.* [Latin *raucus*, hoarse, harsh. See **reu-** in Appendix.*] —**rau′cous·ly** *adv.* —**rau′cous·ness, rau′ci·ty** (rô′sə-tē) *n.*
raun·chy (rôn′chē, rän′-) *adj.* **-chier, -chiest.** *Slang.* **1.** Smutty; indecent. **2.** Lecherous. [Origin unknown.]
rau·wol·fi·a (rou-wo͝ol′fē-ə, rô-) *n.* Any of various tropical trees and shrubs of the genus *Rauwolfia*; especially, *R. serpentina*, of southeastern Asia. The root of this species is the source of tranquilizing alkaloid drugs such as reserpine. [New Latin, after Leonhard *Rauwolf* (died 1596), German botanist.]
rav·age (răv′ĭj) *v.* **-aged, -aging, -ages.** —*tr.* To destroy or despoil; devastate: *Invaders ravaged the countryside.* —*intr.* To wreak destruction. —*n.* **1.** The act or practice of ravaging. **2.** Grievous damage; havoc: *the ravages of disease.* [French, from Old French, from *ravir*, to RAVISH.] —**rav′ag·er** *n.*
rave (rāv) *v.* **raved, raving, raves.** —*intr.* **1.** To speak wildly, irrationally, or incoherently: *raving like a madman.* **2.** To roar; rage: *The storm raved in the forest.* **3.** To speak with wild enthusiasm: *He raved about her looks.* —*tr.* To utter frenziedly. —*n.* **1.** The state or act of raving. **2.** *Informal.* An extravagantly enthusiastic opinion or review: *The play got raves.* —*adj. Informal.* Wildly enthusiastic: *rave reviews.* [Middle English *raven*, to be delirious, to wander, from Old North French *raver*†.]
rav·el (răv′əl) *v.* **-eled, -eling, -els.** Also *chiefly British* **-elled, -elling.** —*tr.* **1.** To separate the fibers or threads of (cloth, for example); unravel. **2.** To clarify by separating the aspects of. Often used with *out: "Must I ravel out my weaved-up folly"* (Shakespeare). **3.** To tangle or complicate. —*intr.* **1.** To become separated into its component threads; unravel; fray. Used of cloth. **2.** To become tangled or confused. —*n.* **1.** A raveling. **2.** A broken or discarded thread. **3.** A tangle. [From Dutch *rafelen*, to unravel, from obsolete Dutch *ravelen*†, to entangle.] —**rav′el·er** *n.*
Ra·vel (rə-vĕl′, ră-), **Maurice Joseph.** 1875–1937. French composer of the impressionist school.
rave·lin (răv′lĭn) *n.* A triangular embanked salient outside the main ditch of a fortress. [Old French, from obsolete Italian *ravellino, rivellino*, diminutive of *riva*, bank, from Latin *rīpa*. See **rei-**[1] in Appendix.*]
rav·el·ing (răv′əl-ĭng) *n.* Also *chiefly British* **rav·el·ling.** **1.** A

rattle[1]
Eighteenth-century child's gold rattle with a coral handle

rattlesnake
Crotalus durissus
Detail of rattle shown above

rattlesnake flag

raven[1]
Painting by
John James Audubon

rawhide
Drawing by
Frederic Remington
of cowboy wielding rawhide

ray[2]

thread or fiber that has become separated from a woven material. **2.** The act of a person or thing that ravels.
rav·el·ment (răv′əl-mənt) *n.* Confusion or complexity; a tangle.
ra·ven[1] (rā′vən) *n.* A large bird, *Corvus corax,* having black plumage and a croaking cry. —*adj.* Black and shiny. [Middle English *raven,* Old English *hræfn.* See **ker-[2]** in Appendix.*]
rav·en[2] (răv′ən) *v.* **-ened, -ening, -ens.** —*tr.* **1.** To consume greedily; devour. **2.** To seek or seize as prey or plunder. —*intr.* **1.** To seek or seize prey or plunder. **2.** To eat ravenously; be voracious. —*n.* Variant of **ravin.** [Old French *raviner,* ravage, seize by force, from Vulgar Latin *rapīnāre* (unattested), from Latin *rapīna,* rapine, from *rapere,* to seize. See **rep-** in Appendix.*] —**rav′en·er** *n.*
rav·en·ing (răv′ən-ĭng) *adj.* **1.** Predatory; voracious. **2.** *Archaic.* Rabid. —**rav′en·ing·ly** *adv.*
Ra·ven·na (rä-vĕn′nä). A city of northern Italy, six miles inland from the Adriatic. Population, 124,000.
rav·en·ous (răv′ən-əs) *adj.* **1.** Extremely hungry; voracious. **2.** Predatory. **3.** Greedy for gratification: *ravenous for power.* [Middle English, rapacious, from Old French *ravineux,* from *raviner,* to RAVEN.] —**rav′en·ous·ly** *adv.* —**rav′en·ous·ness** *n.*
ra·vi·gote (rä-vē-gôt′) *n.* A vinegar sauce spiced with minced onion, capers, and herbs, used with boiled meats or fish. [French, from *ravigoter,* to add new vigor : *re-,* again + *a-,* to, from Latin *ad-* + *vigueur,* vigor, from Latin *vigor,* VIGOR.]
rav·in (răv′ən) *n.* Also **rav·en.** **1.** Voracity; rapaciousness. **2.** Something taken as prey. **3.** The act or practice of preying. [Middle English *ravine,* from Old French, rapine, from Latin *rapīna,* from *rapere,* to seize. See **rep-** in Appendix.*]
ra·vine (rə-vēn′) *n.* A deep, narrow cleft or gorge in the earth's surface, especially one worn by the flow of water. [French, mountain torrent, from Old French, rapine. See **ravin.**]
rav·ing (rā′vĭng) *adj.* **1.** Talking or behaving irrationally; wild: *a raving maniac.* **2.** *Informal.* Exciting admiration: *a raving beauty.* —*n.* Delirious, irrational speech. —**rav′ing·ly** *adv.*
ra·vi·o·li (ră′vē-ō′lē) *pl.n.* Small casings of pasta with various fillings, as chopped meat or cheese; often served with a sauce. [Italian, plural of dialectal *raviolo,* diminutive of *rava,* turnip, from Latin *rāpa,* turnip. See **rāp-** in Appendix.*]
Ra·vi River (rä′vē). A river rising in the Himalayas in northwestern Republic of India and flowing 450 miles southwest to the Chenab northeast of Multan, West Pakistan.
rav·ish (răv′ĭsh) *tr.v.* **-ished, -ishing, -ishes.** **1.** To seize and carry away by force. **2.** To rape; deflower; violate. **3.** To enrapture. [Middle English *ravisshen,* from Old French *ravir* (present stem *raviss-*), from Vulgar Latin *rapīre* (unattested), from Latin *rapere,* seize. See **rep-** in Appendix.*] —**rav′ish·er** *n.*
rav·ish·ing (răv′ĭsh-ĭng) *adj.* Entrancing. —**rav′ish·ing·ly** *adv.*
rav·ish·ment (răv′ĭsh-mənt) *n.* **1.** The act of seizing by force. **2.** Rape. **3.** Ecstasy; rapture; entrancement.
raw (rô) *adj.* **1.** Uncooked: *raw meat.* **2.** Being in a natural condition; not subjected to manufacturing, refining, or finishing processes: *raw wool.* **3.** Untrained and inexperienced: *a raw, unbroken colt.* **4.** Recently finished; fresh: *raw plaster.* **5.** Having subcutaneous tissue exposed: *a raw wound.* **6.** Penetratingly damp: *a raw wind.* **7.** Cruel and unfair: *a raw punishment.* **8.** Outspoken; crude: *a raw portrayal of truth.* —**in the raw.** **1.** In a crude or unrefined state: *nature in the raw.* **2.** *Informal.* Nude; naked. [Middle English *raw,* Old English *hrēaw.* See **kreu-[1]** in Appendix.*] —**raw′ly** *adv.* —**raw′ness** *n.*
Ra·wal·pin·di (rôl-pĭn′dĭ). An industrial and administrative city in the northern Punjab of West Pakistan; the interim capital of Pakistan (1960–66). Population, 340,000.
raw·boned (rô′bōnd′) *adj.* Having a lean, gaunt frame with prominent bones. See Synonyms at **lean.**
raw deal. *Slang.* An instance of unjust or cruel treatment.
raw·hide (rô′hīd′) *n.* **1.** The untanned hide of cattle or other animals. **2.** A whip or rope made of such hide. —*tr.v.* **rawhided, -hiding, -hides.** To beat with a rawhide whip.
raw material. **1.** Unprocessed natural products used in manufacture. **2.** Unprocessed data of any kind.
raw sienna. **1.** A brownish-yellow pigment. **2.** Brownish orange to light brown. Also called "sienna." See **color.**
raw silk. **1.** Untreated silk as reeled from the cocoon. **2.** Fabric woven from such silk.
ray[1] (rā) *n.* **1.** A thin line or narrow beam of radiation, especially of visible light. **2.** Any graphic or other representation of such a line. **3.** A foretaste, trace, hint, gleam, or glimpse: *a ray of hope.* **4.** *Geometry.* A straight line extending from a point. **5.** Any structure having this form. **6.** *Botany.* A **ray flower** *(see).* **7.** *Zoology.* One of the bony spines supporting the membrane of a fish's fin. —*tr.v.* **rayed, raying, rays.** **1.** To send out as rays; emit. **2.** To supply with rays or radiating lines. **3.** To cast rays upon; irradiate. [Middle English, from Old French *rai,* from Latin *radius.* See **radius.**]
ray[2] (rā) *n.* Any of various marine fishes of the order Rajiformes (or Batoidei), having cartilaginous skeletons, horizontally flattened bodies, and narrow tails. [Middle English *raye,* from Old French *raie,* from Latin *raia*†.]
Ray (rā). A masculine given name. [Short for RAYMOND.]
Ray, Cape (rā). A promontory in extreme southwestern Newfoundland, Canada.
Ray (rā), **John.** 1627?–1705. English naturalist; published thorough systematic descriptions of animal and vegetable life.
Ray (rā), **Satyajit.** Born 1921. Indian motion-picture director and writer; first to win audiences outside India.
Ray·burn (rā′bûrn), **Sam(uel Taliaferro).** 1882–1961. American political figure; served 48 years in U.S. House of Representatives.
ray flower. Any of the flat, strap-shaped marginal flowers around the head of certain flowers, such as the daisy. Also called "ray floret." Compare **disk flower.**
Ray·leigh (rā′lē), **Lord.** Title of John William Strutt. 1842–1919. British physicist; discoverer of argon.
Rayleigh scattering. The scattering of light waves by particles with dimensions much smaller than their wavelengths, resulting in angular separation of colors, and responsible for the reddish color of sunset and the blue of the sky. [Explained by Lord RAYLEIGH in 1871.]
ray·less (rā′lĭs) *adj.* **1.** Lacking rays: *a rayless flower.* **2.** Lacking light: *a rayless dungeon.*
Ray·mond (rā′mənd). A masculine given name. [Middle English *Reimond,* from Old French *Raimund,* from Frankish *Raginmund.* See **rēk-** in Appendix.*]
Ray·mond (rā′mənd), **Henry Jarvis.** 1814–1878. American journalist; co-founder of *The New York Times* (1851).
ray·on (rā′ŏn) *n.* **1.** Any of several similar synthetic textile fibers produced by forcing a cellulose solution through fine spinnerets and solidifying the resulting filaments. **2.** Any fabric woven or knit from such fibers. [From RAY (light).]
raze (rāz) *tr.v.* **razed, razing, razes.** Also **rase.** **1.** To tear down or demolish; level to the ground. **2.** To scrape or shave off. **3.** *Archaic.* To erase. —See Synonyms at **ruin.** [Middle English *rasen,* from Old French *raser,* from Vulgar Latin *rasāre* (unattested), from Latin *rādere* (past participle *rāsus*), to scrape. See **rēd-** in Appendix.*]
ra·zor (rā′zər) *n.* A sharp-edged cutting instrument, sometimes electrically driven, used especially for shaving the face. [Middle English *raso(u)r,* from Old French *rasor,* from *raser,* to scrape, RAZE.]
ra·zor·back (rā′zər-băk′) *n.* **1.** A semiwild hog of the southeastern United States, having a narrow body with a ridged back. **2.** A whale, the **rorqual** *(see).* **3.** A sharp, ridged hill.
ra·zor-billed auk (rā′zər-bĭld′). A sea bird, *Alca torda,* of the northern Atlantic, having black-and-white plumage and a flattened, white-ringed bill. Also called "razorbill."
razor clam. Any of various clams of the family Solenidae, characteristically having long, narrow shells.
razz (răz) *n. Slang.* A derisive sound, a **raspberry** *(see).* —*tr.v.* **razzed, razzing, razzes.** *Slang.* To deride, heckle, or tease. [Short for RAZZBERRY.]
razz·ber·ry. *Slang.* Variant of **raspberry.**
raz·zle-daz·zle (răz′əl-dăz′əl) *n. Slang.* An act, display, or condition of confusion, dazzling excitement, or bewilderment. [*Razzle,* perhaps blend of RATTLE and DAZZLE.]
Rb The symbol for the element rubidium.
RBE *Physics.* relative biological effectiveness.
r.b.i. *Baseball.* run batted in.
R.C. **1.** Red Cross. **2.** Roman Catholic.
RCAF, R.C.A.F. Royal Canadian Air Force.
R.C.Ch. Roman Catholic Church.
R.C.M.P. Royal Canadian Mounted Police.
rcpt. receipt.
rct. recruit.
rd rod (unit of length).
rd. **1.** road. **2.** round.
Rd. road.
R.D. rural delivery.
re[1] (rā) *n. Music.* A solmization syllable representing the second tone of the diatonic scale. [Middle English *re,* from Medieval Latin, short for *re(sonāre),* RESOUND. See **gamut.**]
re[2] (rē) *prep.* Concerning; in reference to; in the case of. [Latin *rē,* from *rēs,* thing. See **rei-[3]** in Appendix.*]
Usage: *Re* and the variant form *in re,* meaning in the case or matter of, are usually confined to commercial or legal usage.
Re The symbol for the element rhenium.
Re. Variant of **Ra.**
re-. Indicates: **1.** Restoration to a previous condition or position; for example, **repay, replace.** **2.** Repetition of a previous action; for example, **reactivate.** ***Note:*** Many compounds other than those entered here may be formed with *re-.* In forming compounds *re-* is normally joined with the following element without space or hyphen: *reopen.* If the second element begins with *e,* it is preferable to separate it with a hyphen: *re-entry.* However, such compounds may often be found written solid and are indicated here as fully acceptable variants. If a compound that resembles a familiar word is intended in a special sense, the hyphen is necessary to make the distinction: *re-creation,* meaning "creation anew." The hyphen may also be necessary to clarify an unusual nonce formation: *re-realignment,* or a compound that produces a series of three or more vowels: *reaerify.* [Middle English *re-,* from Old French, from Latin *re-, red-,* in the following senses: 1. Back, as in **rebuke.** 2. Back to an earlier state or condition, as in **repair.** 3. Back in place, as in **remain.** 4. Backward, away, as in **refract.** 5. Again, repeatedly, in return for, as in **respond.** 6. Behind, as in **relinquish.** 7. Contrary, in the sense of negating, as in **repeal.** 8. Against, as in **reluctant.** 9. In response to, as in **requiem.** 10. As an intensive, as in **revere.** See **re-** in Appendix.*]
Re. rupee.
R.E. real estate.
reach (rēch) *v.* **reached, reaching, reaches.** —*tr.* **1.** To stretch out or put forth (a bodily part); extend. **2.** To touch or take hold of by extending some bodily part, especially the hand or something held therein. **3.** To get to, go as far as, or arrive at: *reach maturity.* **4.** To succeed in communicating with: *They reached him by wire.* **5. a.** To extend as far as: *His property reached the shore.* **b.** To carry as far as: *His cry reached our*

ears. **6.** To aggregate or amount to: *Sales reached the thousands.* **7.** *Informal.* To give or hand over to someone: *Reach me the sugar.* **8.** To score a hit, as with a weapon. **9.** To make an impression on; affect. —*intr.* **1.** To extend or thrust out something. **2.** To try to grasp or touch something: *reach for a gun.* **3. a.** To have coextension in time or space: *Radio waves reach Mars.* **b.** To be extensive in influence or effect. **4.** To sail with the wind abeam. —*n.* **1.** The act or power of stretching or thrusting out. **2.** The extent or distance something can reach. **3.** The range or scope of influence or effect. **4.** An unbroken expanse: *a reach of prairie.* **5.** A pole connecting the rear axle of a vehicle with the front. **6.** *Nautical.* The tack of a sailing vessel with the wind abeam. **7.** The stretch of water visible between bends in a river or channel. [Middle English *rechen,* Old English *rǣcan.* See **reig-**[2] in Appendix.*] —**reach′er** *n.*

Synonyms: *reach, achieve, attain, gain, compass, accomplish.* These terms presuppose attainment of certain objectives. *Reach* connotes arriving at a goal through effort and progress. *Achieve* suggests the successful executing of an important enterprise through skill or initiative. *Attain* may imply great effort and pride in reaching a level or goal. *Gain* connotes arriving at a goal despite considerable effort in surmounting obstacles, often with the implication of deserved satisfaction. *Compass* implies mental rather than physical effort in attaining goals. *Accomplish* connotes successful completion.

re·act (rē-ăkt′) *intr.v.* **-acted, -acting, -acts. 1.** To act in response or in opposition to some former act or state. **2.** To be affected or influenced by circumstances or events. **3.** *Chemistry.* To undergo chemical change. [RE- + ACT, influenced by Late Latin *reagere* (past participle *reactus*), to react.]

re·ac·tance (rē-ăk′təns) *n.* Opposition to the flow of alternating electric current caused by the inductance and capacitance in a circuit. See **impedance.**

re·ac·tant (rē-ăk′tənt) *n.* A substance participating in a chemical reaction, especially a directly reacting substance present at the initiation of the reaction.

re·ac·tion (rē-ăk′shən) *n.* **1. a.** A response to a stimulus. **b.** The state resulting from such a response. **2.** A reverse or opposing action. **3. a.** A tendency to revert to a former state. **b.** Opposition to progress or liberalism. **4.** A chemical change or transformation in which a substance decomposes, combines with other substances, or interchanges constituents with other substances. **5.** *Physics.* A **nuclear reacton** *(see).*

re·ac·tion·ar·y (rē-ăk′shə-nĕr′ē) *adj.* Also **re·ac·tion·ist** (-nĭst). Characterized by reaction; especially, opposing progress or liberalism. —*n., pl.* **reactionaries.** Also **re·ac·tion·ist.** An opponent of progress or liberalism.

reaction engine. An engine that develops thrust by the focused expulsion of matter, especially ignited fuel gases. Also called "reaction motor."

reaction time. The time interval between the application of a stimulus and the detection of a response.

re·ac·ti·vate (rē-ăk′tə-vāt′) *tr.v.* **-vated, -vating, -vates. 1.** To make active again. **2.** To restore effectiveness or the ability to function of. —**re·ac′ti·va′tion** *n.*

re·ac·tive (rē-ăk′tĭv) *adj.* **1.** Tending to be responsive or to react to a stimulus. **2.** Characterized by reaction. **3.** *Chemistry & Physics.* Tending to participate in reactions.

re·ac·tor (rē-ăk′tər) *n.* **1.** A person or thing that reacts. **2.** *Electricity.* A circuit element, such as a coil, used to introduce reactance. **3.** *Physics.* A **nuclear reactor** *(see).*

read (rēd) *v.* **read** (rĕd), **reading, reads.** —*tr.* **1.** To comprehend or take in the meaning of (something written or printed). **2.** To utter or render aloud (something written or printed). **3.** To have the knowledge of (a language) necessary to understand printed or written material. **4.** To seek to interpret the true nature or meaning of (someone or something) through close scrutiny: *read the sky for signs of snow.* **5.** To ascertain the intent or mood of: *He read her mind.* **6.** To derive a special meaning from or ascribe a special significance to (something read, experienced, or observed): *"a tendency to read deep and nasty meanings into Robinson's words"* (Muriel Spark). **7.** To foretell or predict (the future). **8.** To perceive, receive, or comprehend (a signal, message, or the like): *I read you fine.* **9.** To study or make a study of: *read for a law exam.* **10.** To learn or get knowledge from (something written or printed): *He read that crime was rife.* **11.** To have or adopt as a reading in a particular passage: *For "colour" read "color."* **12.** To indicate, register, or show: *The dial reads 0°* —*intr.* **1.** To read printed or written characters, as of words or music. **2.** To utter or render aloud the words that one is reading. **3.** To learn by reading. Used with *about* or *of: He read about dogs.* **4.** To study. **5.** To have a particular wording: *The line reads thus.* **6.** To contain a specific meaning: *The law reads that he is guilty.* **7.** To have a specified character or quality for the reader: *His poems read well.* —**read between the lines.** To perceive or detect a meaning or implication that is obscure or unexpressed. —**read out.** To expel by proclamation from a social, political, or other group. —**read up on.** To acquire information by reading. —*adj.* (rĕd). Informed by reading; learned. [Read (infinitive), read (past tense and past participle); Middle English *reden, redde, red,* Old English *rǣdan,* advise, explain, read, *rǣdde, rǣden.* See **ar-** in Appendix.*]

Read (rēd), Sir **Herbert (Edward).** 1893–1968. British art curator, poet, editor, and critic.

read·a·ble (rē′də-bəl) *adj.* **1.** Capable of being read easily; legible. **2.** Pleasurable or interesting to read. —**read′a·bil′i·ty, read′a·ble·ness** *n.* —**read′a·bly** *adv.*

read·er (rē′dər) *n.* **1.** One who reads. **2.** A professional reciter of literary works. **3.** *Roman Catholic Church.* One of the minor orders, a cleric or layman who recites lessons or prayers in the church service. **4.** A person employed by a publisher to read and evaluate manuscripts. **5.** A corrector of printers' proofs. **6.** A teaching assistant who reads and grades examination papers. **7.** *Chiefly British.* A university lecturer. **8. a.** A textbook of reading exercises. **b.** A literary anthology.

read·er·ship (rē′dər-shĭp′) *n.* **1.** The readers of a publication or publications. **2.** *Chiefly British.* The office of a reader.

read·i·ly (rĕd′ə-lē) *adv.* **1.** Promptly. **2.** Willingly. **3.** Easily.

read·i·ness (rĕd′ē-nĭs) *n.* The quality or state of being ready.

read·ing (rē′dĭng) *n.* **1.** The act or practice of a reader. **2.** Written or printed material. **3.** The act of rendering aloud written or printed matter. **4.** An official or public recitation of literary or other written material: *the reading of a will.* **5.** A personal interpretation or appraisal. **6.** The specific form of a particular passage in a text. **7.** The information indicated by a gauge or graduated instrument. —*adj.* **1.** Designed or used for reading. **2.** Disposed or attracted to reading: *the reading man.*

Read·ing (rĕd′ĭng). **1.** The county seat of Berkshire, England, a university town 35 miles west of London. Population, 124,000. **2.** A city in Pennsylvania, 45 miles northwest of Philadelphia. Population, 98,000.

re·ad·just (rē′ə-jŭst′) *tr.v.* **-justed, -justing, -justs.** To adjust or arrange again. —**re′ad·just′er** *n.* —**re′ad·just′ment** *n.*

read-out (rēd′out′) *n.* Presentation of computer data, usually in digital form, from calculations or storage.

read·y (rĕd′ē) *adj.* **-ier, -iest. 1.** Prepared or available for service or action. **2.** Mentally disposed; willing: *He was ready to believe them.* **3.** Liable or about to do something. Used with an infinitive: *ready to leave.* **4.** Prompt in apprehending or reacting: *a ready intelligence; a ready response.* **5.** Available: *ready money.* —**at the ready.** Designating a rifle in position for aiming and firing. [Middle English *redy,* Old English *rǣde.* See **reidh-** in Appendix.*]

read·y-made (rĕd′ē-mād′) *adj.* **1.** Made to a set pattern, not custom-made. Compare **made-to-order. 2.** Preconceived.

read·y-wit·ted (rĕd′ē-wĭt′ĭd) *adj.* Quick-witted.

re·af·firm (rē′ə-fûrm′) *tr.v.* **-firmed, -firming, -firms.** To affirm or assert again. —**re′af·fir·ma′tion** (rē′ăf-ər-mā′shən) *n.*

re·a·gent (rē-ā′jənt) *n.* Any substance used in a chemical reaction to detect, measure, examine, or produce other substances. [RE- + AGENT, after REACT.]

re·al[1] (rē′əl, rēl) *adj.* **1.** Being or occurring in fact or actuality; having verifiable existence: *The child shows real intelligence.* **2.** True and actual; not illusory or fictitious: *real people.* **3.** Genuine and authentic; not artificial or spurious: *real mink; real humility.* **4.** *Philosophy.* Existing actually and objectively. **5.** *Optics.* Of, pertaining to, or designating an image formed by light rays that converge in space. **6.** *Mathematics.* Of, pertaining to, or designating the nonimaginary part of a complex quantity. **7.** *Law.* Of or pertaining to stationary or fixed property, as buildings or land. Compare **personal.** —*adv. Informal.* Very: *real sorry.* [Middle English, of real property or things, from Norman French, from Late Latin *reālis,* actual, real, from Latin *rēs,* thing. See **rei-**[3] in Appendix.*] —**real′ness** *n.*

Synonyms: *real, actual, true, authentic, concrete, existent, genuine, tangible, veritable. Real,* although frequently used interchangeably with the terms that follow, pertains basically to that which is not imaginary but is existent and identifiable as a thing, state, or quality. *Actual* connotes that which is demonstrable. *True* implies belief in that which conforms to fact. *Authentic* implies acceptance of historical or attributable reliability rather than visible proof. *Concrete* implies the reality of actual things. *Existent* applies to concepts or objects existing either in time or space: *existent tensions. Genuine* presupposes evidence or belief that a thing or object is what it is claimed to be. *Tangible* stresses the mind's acceptance of that which can be touched or seen. *Veritable,* which should be used sparingly, applies to persons and things having all the qualities claimed for them.

re·al[2] (rā-äl′) *n., pl.* **reals** or **-ales** (-ä′lās). A former Spanish silver monetary unit. [Spanish, from *real,* "royal," from Latin *rēgālis,* regal, from *rēx* (stem *rēg-*), king. See **reg-**[1] in Appendix.*]

re·al[3] (rā-äl′) *n., pl.* **reals** or **reis** (rās). Either of two former monetary units of Portugal and Brazil. [Portuguese, from *real,* "royal," from Latin *rēgālis,* regal. See **real** (Spanish coin).]

real estate. *Abbr.* **R.E.** Landed property, including all inherent natural resources and any man-made improvements established thereon. Also called "realty." —**re′al-es·tate′** *adj.*

re·al·gar (rē-ăl′gär′, -gər) *n.* A soft orange-red arsenic ore, As_2S_2, used in pyrotechnics, tanning, and as a pigment. [Middle English, from Medieval Latin, from Catalan, from Arabic *rajh al-ghār,* powder (of) the mine or cave: *rahj,* powder + *al,* the + *ghār,* cave.]

re·al·ism (rē′ə-lĭz′əm) *n.* **1.** Inclination toward literal truth and pragmatism. **2.** Artistic representation felt to be visually accurate. **3.** *Philosophy.* **a.** The doctrine that universal principles are more real than objects as sensed. **b.** The doctrine that names somehow denote the essences of things or categories of things. Compare **nominalism. c.** The doctrine that the objects of perception exist independently of the perceiver. Compare **idealism.** —**re′al·is′tic** *adj.* —**re′al·is′ti·cal·ly** *adv.*

re·al·ist (rē′ə-lĭst) *n.* **1.** One inclined to literal truth and pragmatism. **2.** A practitioner of artistic or philosophic realism.

re·al·i·ty (rē-ăl′ə-tē) *n., pl.* **-ties. 1.** The quality or state of being actual or true. **2.** A person, entity, or event that is actual. **3.** The totality of all things possessing actuality, existence, or

razor-billed auk
Painting by
John James Audubon

razor clam
Ensis siliqua

essence. **4.** That which exists objectively and in fact. **5.** *Philosophy.* The sum of all that is real, absolute, and unchangeable.
reality principle. *Psychoanalysis.* Awareness of and adjustment to environmental demands in a manner that assures ultimate satisfaction of instinctual needs.
re·al·i·za·tion (rē'ə-lə-zā'shən) *n.* **1.** The enactment or actualization of plans, ideals, or the like. **2.** The condition of being realized or the act of realizing. **3.** The result of realizing.
re·al·ize (rē'ə-līz') *v.* **-ized, -izing, -izes.** —*tr.* **1.** To comprehend completely or correctly. **2.** To make real or actualize (a plan or ambition, for example): *realize an ideal.* **3.** To make realistic. **4.** To obtain or achieve, as gain or profit: *realize a return on an investment.* **5.** To bring in (a sum) as profit by sale. —*intr.* To exchange holdings or goods for money. [French *réaliser,* from Old French *realiser,* from *real,* real, from Late Latin *reālis,* REAL.] —**re'al·iz'a·ble** *adj.* —**re'al·iz'er** *n.*
re·al·ly (rē'ə-lē', rē'lē) *adv.* **1.** In reality: *Man really needs his fellow man.* **2.** Truly: *a really enjoyable evening.* **3.** Indeed. Used as an intensive: *Really, you shouldn't have done it*
realm (rĕlm) *n.* **1.** A kingdom. **2.** Any field, sphere, or province: *the realm of science.* [Middle English *realme, reaume,* from Old French, from Latin *regimen,* system of government, from *regere,* rule. See **reg-**[1] in Appendix.*]
real number. Any rational or irrational **number** *(see).*

reamer

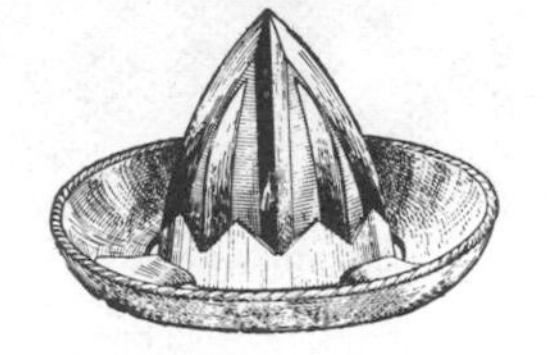

citrus-fruit reamer

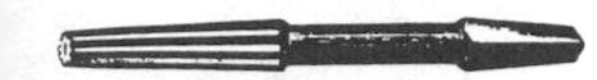

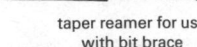

taper reamer for use with bit brace

re·al·po·li·tik (rā-äl'pō'lĭ-tēk') *n.* A usually expansionist national policy having as its sole principle the advancement of the national interest. [German, "realistic politics."]
real time. **1.** The actual time in which a physical process under computer study or control occurs. **2.** The time required for a computer to solve a problem, measured from the time data are fed in to the time a solution is received. —**real'-time'** *adj.*
Re·al·tor (rē'əl-tər, -tôr') *n.* Also **re·al·tor.** A real-estate agent affiliated with the National Association of Real Estate Boards. [From REALTY.]
re·al·ty (rē'əl-tē) *n., pl.* **-ties.** Landed property, **real estate** *(see).* [REAL + -TY.]
ream[1] (rēm) *n.* **1.** *Abbr.* **rm.** A quantity of paper, formerly 480 sheets, now 500 sheets or, in a printer's ream, 516 sheets. **2.** *Usually plural.* Very much: *reams of verse.* [Middle English *rem(e),* from Old French *remme,* from Arabic *rizmah,* bundle.]
ream[2] (rēm) *tr.v.* **reamed, reaming, reams.** **1.** To form, shape, taper, or enlarge (a hole) with or as if with a reamer. **2.** To remove (material) by reaming. **3.** To squeeze the juice out of (fruit) with a reamer. [Perhaps Middle English *remen,* to make room, Old English *rȳman,* to widen. See **rewə-** in Appendix.*]
ream·er (rē'mər) *n.* **1.** Any of various tools used to shape or enlarge holes. **2.** A utensil with a conical, ridged projection, used for extracting citrus-fruit juice. **3.** One that reams.
reap (rēp) *v.* **reaped, reaping, reaps.** —*tr.* **1.** To cut (grain or pulse) for harvest with a scythe, sickle, or reaper. **2.** To harvest (a crop so cut). **3.** To harvest a crop from: *reap a field.* **4.** To obtain as a result of effort. —*intr.* **1.** To cut or harvest grain or pulse. **2.** To obtain a return or reward. [Middle English *repen,* Old English *rīpan.* See **rei-**[1] in Appendix.*]
reap·er (rē'pər) *n.* **1.** One who reaps. **2.** A machine for harvesting grain or pulse crops.

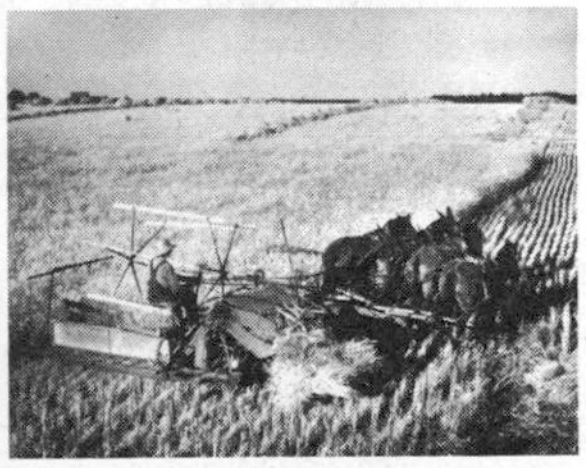

reaper
Horse-drawn reaper fitted with a binder, photographed in Kansas in 1937

re·ap·por·tion (rē'ə-pôr'shən) *tr.v.* **-tioned, -tioning, -tions.** To distribute anew. [RE- + APPORTION.]
re·ap·por·tion·ment (rē'ə-pôr'shən-mənt) *n.* **1.** The act of reapportioning or the state of being reapportioned. **2.** The redistribution of representation in a legislative body, especially the reallotment of U.S. Congressional seats as required by the Constitution.
re·ap·prais·al (rē'ə-prā'zəl) *n.* A new appraisal or evaluation.
rear[1] (rîr) *n.* **1.** The hind part of something. **2.** The point or area farthest from the front of something. **3.** The part of a military deployment usually farthest from the fighting front. **4.** *Informal.* The buttocks. —**bring up the rear.** To be last in a line. —*adj.* Of, at, or located in the rear. [Short for ARREAR.]
rear[2] (rîr) *v.* **reared, rearing, rears.** —*tr.* **1.** To care for (a child or children) during the early stages of life; bring up. See Usage note at **raise. 2.** To lift upright; raise. **3.** To build; erect. **4.** To tend (growing plants or animals). —*intr.* **1.** To rise on the hind legs, as a horse. **2.** To rise high in the air; to tower. —See Synonyms at **lift.** [Middle English *reren,* to lift up, raise, Old English *rǣran.* See **risan** in Appendix.*] —**rear'er** *n.*
rear admiral. *Abbr.* **Rear Adm., R.A.** A naval officer ranking below a vice admiral and above a captain.
rear guard. A detachment of troops that protects the rear of a military force. [Middle English *reregarde,* from Old French : *rere,* backward, behind, from Latin *retrō* (see **re-** in Appendix*) + *garde,* GUARD.] —**rear'guard'** (rîr'gärd') *adj.*
re·arm (rē-ärm') *v.* **-armed, -arming, -arms.** —*tr.* **1.** To arm again. **2.** To equip with better weapons. —*intr.* To arm oneself again. —**re·ar'ma·ment** (rē-är'mə-mənt) *n.*
rear·most (rîr'mōst') *adj.* Farthest in the rear; last.
re·ar·range (rē'ə-rānj') *tr.v.* **-ranged, -ranging, -ranges.** To arrange again; change the arrangement of. —**re'ar·range'ment** *n.*
rear·view mirror (rîr'vyōō'). **1.** A small rectangular adjustable mirror centrally attached above or below the windshield in a motor vehicle to allow the driver a rear view. **2.** A similar mirror attached to the handlebar of a motorcycle or bicycle.
rear·ward[1] (rîr'wərd) *adj.* Directed toward or situated at the rear. —*adv.* Also **rear·wards** (-wərdz). Toward, to, or at the rear. —*n.* A position or place at the rear.
rear·ward[2] (rîr'wôrd') *n. Rare.* The rear guard of an armed force. [Middle English *rerewarde,* from Norman French : *rere,* behind, from Latin *retrō* (see **re-** in Appendix*) + *warde,* guard, from Germanic (see **wer-**[4] in Appendix*).]
rea·son (rē'zən) *n.* **1.** The basis or motive for an action, decision, or conviction. **2.** A declaration made to explain or justify an action, decision, or conviction. See Usage note at **because. 3.** An underlying fact or cause that provides logical sense for a premise or occurrence. **4.** The capacity for rational thought, inference, or discrimination. **5.** Good judgment; sound sense; intelligence **6.** Normal mental state; sanity. **7.** *Logic.* A premise, usually the minor premise, of an argument. —See Synonyms at **cause, mind.** —**by reason of.** Because of. —**in reason.** With good sense or justification; reasonably. —**stand to reason.** To be logical or likely. Usually used impersonally: *It stands to reason that he will win.* —**within reason.** Within the bounds of good sense or practicality. —**with reason.** With good cause; justifiably. —*v.* **reasoned, -soning, -sons.** —*intr.* **1.** To use the faculty of reason; think logically. **2.** To talk or argue logically and persuasively. **3.** *Archaic.* To engage in conversation or discussion: *"Come . . . let us reason together"* (Isaiah 1:18). —*tr.* **1.** To determine or conclude by logical thinking. Often used with *out.* **2.** To persuade or dissuade (someone) with reasons. Used with *out* or *into* **3.** To discuss; to debate. [Middle English *reisun,* from Old French, from Vulgar Latin *ratiōne* (unattested), from Latin *ratiō,* calculation, judgment, reasoning, from *ratus,* past participle of *rērī,* to think, reason. See **ar-** in Appendix.*] —**rea'son·er** *n.*
Synonyms: *reason, intuition, understanding, discernment, judgment. Reason* in this comparison is the intellectual process of seeking truth or knowledge by inferring from either fact or logic. *Intuition* is instinctive knowing or perception without reference to the rational process. *Understanding* is the apprehension or comprehension of knowledge resulting from reason or thinking. *Discernment* is the faculty of discriminating, often through selection, what is apprehensible, relevant, or worthwhile. *Judgment* is the faculty of making sound conclusions.
rea·son·a·ble (rē'zən-ə-bəl) *adj.* **1.** Capable of reasoning; rational. **2.** Governed by or in accordance with reason or sound thinking. **3.** Within the bounds of common sense: *arrive home at a reasonable hour.* **4.** Not excessive or extreme; fair; moderate: *reasonable prices.* —**rea'son·a·bil'i·ty, rea'son·a·ble·ness** *n.* —**rea'son·a·bly** *adv.*
rea·son·ing (rē'zən-ĭng) *n.* **1.** The mental processes of one who reasons; especially, the drawing of conclusions or inferences from observation, facts, or hypotheses. **2.** The evidence or arguments used in this procedure.
re·as·sure (rē'ə-shōōr') *tr.v.* **-sured, -suring, -sures.** **1.** To restore confidence to. **2.** To assure again. **3.** To reinsure. —**re'as·sur'ance** *n.* —**re'as·sur'ing·ly** *adv.*
re·a·ta. Variant of **riata.**
Ré·au·mur (rā'ō-myōōr') *adj.* Also **Re·au·mur.** *Abbr.* **R, R., Réaum.** Denoting or indicated on a thermometer scale that registers the freezing point of water as 0° and the boiling point as 80°. [Introduced by René de RÉAUMUR.]
Ré·au·mur (rā-ō-mür'), **René Antoine Ferchault de.** 1683–1757. French physicist.
reave[1] (rēv) *v.* **reaved** or **reft** (rĕft), **reaving, reaves.** *Archaic.* —*tr.* **1.** To seize and carry off forcibly. **2.** To deprive of; bereave. —*intr.* To rob, plunder, or pillage. [Middle English *reven,* to plunder, Old English *rēafian.* See **reup-** in Appendix.*]
reave[2] (rēv) *tr.v.* **reaved** or **reft** (rĕft), **reaving, reaves.** *Archaic.* To break or tear apart. [Middle English *reven,* variant (influenced by *riven,* RIVE) of REAVE (seize).]
Reb[1] (rĕb) *n.* Also **reb.** *Informal.* A Confederate soldier in the Civil War. [Short for REBEL.]
Reb[2] (rĕb) *n.* A Jewish title of respect, approximately equivalent to "Mr." or "Sir," but used with the given name rather than the surname. [Yiddish, from Hebrew *rabbī,* my teacher, RABBI.]
re·bar·ba·tive (rē-bär'bə-tĭv) *adj.* Extremely unattractive; repellent; tending to irritate. [French *rébarbatif,* from Old French *rebarber,* "to face beard to beard," face an enemy, hence, to be repellent : *re-,* back, against + *barbe,* beard, from Latin *barba* (see **bhardhā** in Appendix*).]
re·bate[1] (rē'bāt') *n.* A deduction from an amount to be paid or a return of part of an amount given in payment. —*tr.v.* (rē'bāt', rĭ-bāt') **rebated, -bating, -bates.** **1.** To deduct or return (an amount) from a payment or bill. **2.** *Rare.* To dull or blunt (a weapon, for example). **3.** *Rare.* To lessen; diminish. [Middle English *rebaten,* deduct, subtract, from Old French *rabattre,* to beat down again, reduce : *re-,* again + *abattre,* to beat down : *a-,* to, from Latin *ad-* + *battre,* to beat, from Latin *battuere* (see **battuere** in Appendix*).] —**re'bat·er** (rē'bā'tər, rĭ-bā'tər) *n.*
re·bate[2]. Variant of **rabbet.**
re·ba·to (rĭ-bä'tō) *n., pl.* **-tos.** Also **ra·ba·to** (rə-bä'tō). A stiff, flaring collar of lace or other fabric, worn by both sexes early in the 17th century. [Old French *rabat,* turndown collar, from *rabattre,* to turn down again, REBATE.]
re·bec (rē'bĕk') *n.* Also **re·beck.** A pear-shaped, two- or three-stringed musical instrument of medieval times, played with a bow. [Old French *rebec,* variant (influenced by *bec,* beak, because of the shape of the instrument) of *rebebe,* from Old Provençal *rebab,* from Arabic (dialectal) *rebāb.*]
Re·bec·ca[1] (rĭ-bĕk'ə). A feminine given name. [Late Latin, from Greek *Rebekka,* from Hebrew *Ribqāh.*]
Re·bec·ca[2] (rĭ-bĕk'ə). Also **Re·bek·ah.** The wife of Isaac and the mother of Jacob and Esau. Genesis 24:1–67.
re·bel (rĭ-bĕl') *intr.v.* **-belled, -belling, -bels.** **1.** To refuse allegiance to and oppose by force an established government or ruling authority. **2.** To resist or defy any authority or generally accepted convention. **3.** To feel or express strong unwillingness or repugnance: *She rebelled at the unwelcome suggestion.* —*n.* **reb·el** (rĕb'əl). **1.** A person who rebels or is in rebellion.

ă pat/ā pay/âr care/ä father/b bib/ch church/d deed/ĕ pet/ē be/f fife/g gag/h hat/hw which/ĭ pit/ī pie/îr pier/j judge/k kick/l lid, needle/m mum/n no, sudden/ng thing/ŏ pot/ō toe/ô paw, for/oi noise/ou out/ŏŏ took/ōō boot/p pop/r roar/s sauce/sh ship, dish/

2. *Capital* **R.** A Confederate soldier in the Civil War. Used chiefly by Union sympathizers. —*adj.* **reb·el** (rĕb′əl). 1. Of, pertaining to, or consisting of rebels. 2. Rebellious; defiant. [Middle English *rebellen*, from Old French *rebeller*, from Latin *rebellāre*, to make war again : *re-*, again + *bellāre*, to make war, from *bellum*, war (see **duellum** in Appendix*).]

re·bel·lion (rĭ-bĕl′yən) *n.* **1.** An uprising or organized opposition intended to change or overthrow an existing government or ruling authority. **2.** An act or show of defiance toward any authority or established convention. [Middle English, from Old French, from Latin *rebelliō*, from *rebellāre*, to REBEL.]

Synonyms: *rebellion, revolution, revolt, riot, mutiny, insurrection, uprising, coup d'état, putsch.* These terms pertain in varying degree to opposition to an existing order or authority. *Rebellion* is defiance of authority in general or open but unorganized disobedience: *the teen-age rebellion;* also, it is open, armed, and organized insurrection against constituted political authority that usually fails of its purpose, as *Shays' Rebellion. Revolution* is a radical alteration in a system or in social conditions, such as the *Industrial Revolution;* also, it is the overthrowing by open, organized armed force of a government and replacing it with another, such as the *American Revolution. Revolt* is widespread opposition to prevailing standards: *a taxpayers' revolt;* also, it is an armed attempt to change authority. *Riot* is a sudden, violent, disorganized uprising, frequently unarmed and unplanned. *Mutiny* is forcible resistance to constituted authority, especially by subordinates in the armed forces. *Insurrection* and *uprising* are armed attempts to change authority. *Coup d'état* is a sudden, violent overthrow of a government. *Putsch* is an attempted *coup d'état.*

re·bel·lious (rĭ-bĕl′yəs) *adj.* **1.** Participating in or tending toward a rebellion. **2.** Of or characteristic of a rebel. **3.** Resisting management or control; unruly. —See Synonyms at **insubordinate.** —**re·bel′lious·ly** *adv.* —**re·bel′lious·ness** *n.*

re·bind (rē-bīnd′) *tr.v.* **-bound** (-bound′), **-binding, -binds.** To bind again; especially, to put a new binding on (a book). —*n.* (rē′bīnd′). A book that has been rebound.

re·birth (rē-bûrth′, rē′bûrth′) *n.* **1.** A second or new birth; reincarnation. **2.** A renaissance; resurgence; revival.

re·born (rē-bôrn′) *adj.* Born again; emotionally or spiritually revived or regenerated.

re·bound (rē′bound′, rĭ-) *v.* **-bounded, -bounding, -bounds.** —*intr.* **1.** To spring or bounce back after hitting or colliding with something. **2.** To recover, as from depression or disappointment. **3.** To re-echo; resound. —*tr.* To cause to rebound. —*n.* (rē′bound′, rĭ-bound′). **1.** A springing or bounding back; recoil. **2.** *Sports.* **a.** *Basketball.* The ball in the process of bouncing off the backboard after an unsuccessful attempt to score. **b.** *Hockey.* The rapid backward motion of the puck upon impact with the goalkeeper. **3.** A quick recovery from or reaction to disappointment or depression: *marriage on the rebound.* [Middle English *rebounden*, from Old French *rebondir* : *re-*, again, back + *bondir*, to resound, BOUND (leap).]

re·bo·zo (rĭ-bō′sō) *n., pl.* **-zos.** A long scarf worn over the head and shoulders chiefly by Mexican women. [Spanish *rebozo*†.]

re·broad·cast (rē-brôd′kăst′, -käst′) *tr.v.* **-cast** or **-casted, -casting, -casts.** **1.** To repeat the broadcast of (a program). **2.** To receive and send out (a broadcast) again. —*n.* A broadcast that is repeated or that is relayed from another station.

re·buff (rĭ-bŭf′) *n.* **1.** A blunt or abrupt repulse or refusal, as to an offer; a snub. **2.** Any check or abrupt setback to progress or action. —*tr.v.* **rebuffed, -buffing, -buffs.** **1.** To refuse bluntly or contemptuously; snub. **2.** To repel or drive back. —See Synonyms at **refuse.** [Old French *rebuffer*, from Italian *ribuffare*, scold, rebuff, from *ribuffo*, reprimand : *re-*, back, again, from Latin + *buffo*, puff, gust (imitative).]

re·build (rē-bĭld′) *tr.v.* **-built** (-bĭlt′), **-building, -builds.** **1.** To build again. **2.** To make extensive structural repairs on.

re·buke (rĭ-byo͞ok′) *tr.v.* **-buked, -buking, -bukes.** **1.** To criticize or reprove sharply; reprimand. **2.** *Obsolete.* To check; repress. —See Synonyms at **admonish.** —*n.* A sharp reproof. [Middle English *rebuken*, from Old North French *rebuker*†.]

re·bus (rē′bəs) *n., pl.* **-buses.** A riddle composed of words or syllables depicted by symbols or pictures that suggest the sound of the words or syllables they represent. [Latin *rēbus*, by things, from *rēs*, thing. See **rei-**[3] in Appendix.*]

re·but (rĭ-bŭt′) *v.* **-butted, -butting, -buts.** —*tr.* **1.** To refute, especially by offering opposing evidence or arguments, as in a legal case. **2.** *Obsolete.* To repel. —*intr.* To present opposing evidence or arguments. [Middle English *rebuten*, from Old French *rebuter* : *re-*, again, back + *buter*, to BUTT.]

re·but·tal (rĭ-bŭt′l) *n.* The act of rebutting.

re·but·ter (rĭ-bŭt′ər) *n.* **1.** One that refutes or rebuts. **2.** *Law.* The defendant's answer to the plaintiff's surrejoinder.

rec. **1.** receipt. **2.** recipe. **3.** record; recording. **4.** recreation.

re·cal·ci·trant (rĭ-kăl′sə-trənt) *adj.* Stubbornly resistant to authority, domination, or guidance; refractory. See Synonyms at **unruly.** —*n.* A recalcitrant person. [Latin *recalcitrāns*, present participle of *recalcitrāre*, to kick back : *re-*, back, again + *calcitrāre*, to kick, from *calx* (stem *calc-*), heel (see **calk**).] —**re·cal′ci·trance, re·cal′ci·tran·cy** *n.*

re·ca·les·cence (rē′kə-lĕs′əns) *n. Metallurgy.* A sudden increase of heat in a cooling metal caused by an exothermic structural change. [Latin *recalescens*, present participle of *recalescere*, to grow warm again : *re-*, back, again + *calescere*, become warm, from *calēre*, to be warm (see **kel-**[1] in Appendix*).] —**re′ca·les′cent** *adj.*

re·call (rĭ-kôl′) *tr.v.* **-called, -calling, -calls.** **1.** To call back; ask or order to return. **2.** To summon back to awareness of or concern with the subject or situation at hand. **3.** To remember or recollect. **4.** To cancel, take back, or revoke. **5.** To bring back; restore. —*n.* (rĭ-kôl′, rē′kôl′). **1.** The act of recalling or summoning back; especially, an official order to return. **2.** A signal, such as a bugle call, used to summon servicemen back to their posts. **3.** The ability to remember information or experiences. **4.** The act of revoking. **5. a.** The procedure by which a public official may be removed from office by popular vote. **b.** The right to employ this procedure. —**re·call′a·ble** *adj.*

re·cant (rĭ-kănt′) *v.* **-canted, -canting, -cants.** —*tr.* To make a formal retraction or disavowal of (a statement or belief to which one has previously committed oneself). —*intr.* To make a formal retraction or disavowal of a previously held belief. [Latin *recantāre* : *re-*, back + *cantāre*, sing, chant, frequentative of *canere*, sing (see **kan-** in Appendix*).] —**re′can·ta′tion** *n.* —**re·cant′er** *n.*

re·cap[1] (rē-kăp′) *tr.v.* **-capped, -capping, -caps.** **1.** To replace a cap or caplike covering on: *recap a bottle.* **2.** To restore (a used automobile tire) to usable condition by bonding new rubber onto the worn tread and lateral surface. Compare **retread.** —*n.* (rē′kăp′). A tire thus reconditioned.

re·cap[2] (rē′kăp′) *tr.v.* **-capped, -capping, -caps.** To summarize by recapitulating. —*n.* A summary or recapitualtion, as of a news report. [Short for RECAPITULATE.]

re·cap·i·tal·ize (rē-kăp′ə-təl-īz′) *tr.v.* **-ized, -izing, -izes.** To change the capital structure of (a corporation). —**re·cap′i·tal·i·za′tion** *n.*

re·ca·pit·u·late (rē′kə-pĭch′o͞o-lāt′) *v.* **-lated, -lating, -lates.** —*tr.* **1.** To repeat in concise form. **2.** *Biology.* To appear to repeat (the evolutionary stages of the species) during the embryonic development of the individual organism. —*intr.* To summarize. [Late Latin *recapitulāre* : *re-*, back, again + *capitulāre*, to put under headings, from Latin *capitulum*, heading, small head, diminutive of *caput*, head (see **kaput** in Appendix*).] —**re·ca·pit′u·la′tive, re·ca·pit′u·la·to′ry** (-lə-tôr′ē, -tōr′ē) *adj.*

re·ca·pit·u·la·tion (rē′kə-pĭch′o͞o-lā′shən) *n.* **1.** The act or process of recapitulating. **2.** A summary or concise review. **3.** *Biology.* The apparent repetition of some of the evolutionary stages of the species during embryonic development of the individual organism. **4.** *Music.* The restatement of the exposition that constitutes the third section of the typical sonata form.

re·cap·ture (rē-kăp′chər) *tr.v.* **-tured, -turing, -tures.** **1.** To capture again; retake or recover. **2.** To recall: *an attempt to recapture the past.* **3.** To acquire by the government procedure of recapture. —*n.* **1. a.** The act of recapturing. **b.** The condition of being recaptured. **2.** *International Law.* The retaking of booty or goods. **3.** Anything recaptured. **4.** The lawful taking by a government of a fixed amount of the profits of a public-service corporation in excess of a stipulated rate of return.

re·cast (rē-kăst′) *tr.v.* **-cast, -casting, -casts.** **1.** To mold again: *recast a bell.* **2.** To set down or present (ideas, for example) in a new or different arrangement. **3.** To change the cast of (a theatrical production). —*n.* (rē′kăst′). **1.** The act or process of recasting. **2.** Something produced by recasting.

recd. received.

re·cede (rē-sēd′) *tr.v.* **-ceded, -ceding, -cedes.** To cede back; yield or grant to one formerly in possession.

re·cede (rĭ-sēd′) *intr.v.* **-ceded, -ceding, -cedes.** **1.** To move back or away from a limit, point, or mark: *The tidal waters receded.* **2.** To slope backward. **3.** To become or seem to become more distant. **4.** To withdraw or retreat from an agreement, stated position, or the like. [Latin *recēdere*, to go back : *re-*, back, again + *cēdere*, to go (see **ked-**[1] in Appendix*).]

re·ceipt (rĭ-sēt′) *n. Abbr.* **rec., rcpt., rept., rec't, rect.** **1. a.** The act of receiving something. **b.** The fact of being received. **2.** *Usually plural.* The quantity or amount of something received: *cash receipts.* **3.** A written acknowledgment that a specified article, sum of money, or delivery of merchandise has been received. **4.** *Regional.* A recipe. —*v.* **receipted, -ceipting, -ceipts.** —*tr.* **1.** To mark (a bill) as having been paid. **2.** To give or write a receipt for (money paid or goods delivered). —*intr.* To give a receipt. [Middle English *receite*, from Old North French, from Medieval Latin *recepta*, from Latin *recipere* (past participle *receptus*), to take, RECEIVE.]

re·ceiv·a·ble (rĭ-sē′və-bəl) *adj.* **1.** Suitable for being received or accepted, especially as payment. **2.** Awaiting or requiring payment; due or collectable: *accounts receivable.* —*n. Plural.* Business assets representing the total amounts due from others.

re·ceive (rĭ-sēv′) *v.* **-ceived, -ceiving, -ceives.** —*tr.* **1.** To take or acquire (something given, offered, or transmitted); get. **2.** To acquire knowledge of or information about: *receive bad news.* **3.** To have bestowed on oneself as a title. **4.** To meet with; experience: *receive sympathetic treatment.* **5.** To have inflicted or imposed on oneself: *receive a penalty.* **6.** To bear the weight or force of; support. **7.** To take or intercept the impact of, as a blow. **8.** To take in, hold, or contain. **9.** To admit: *receive new members.* **10.** To greet or welcome. **11.** To perceive or acquire mentally: *receive a bad impression.* **12.** To regard with approval or disapproval: *theories well received.* **13.** To listen to and formally and authoritatively acknowledge: *receive an oath of allegiance.* —*intr.* **1.** To acquire or get something; be a recipient: *"It is more blessed to give than to receive"* (Acts 20:35). **2.** To admit or welcome guests or visitors. **3.** To partake of the Eucharist. **4.** *Electronics.* To convert incoming electromagnetic waves into visible or audible signals. [Middle English *receiven*, from Old North French *receivre*, from Latin *recipere*, to take back, regain : *re-*, back, again + *capere*, to take (see **kap-** in Appendix*).]

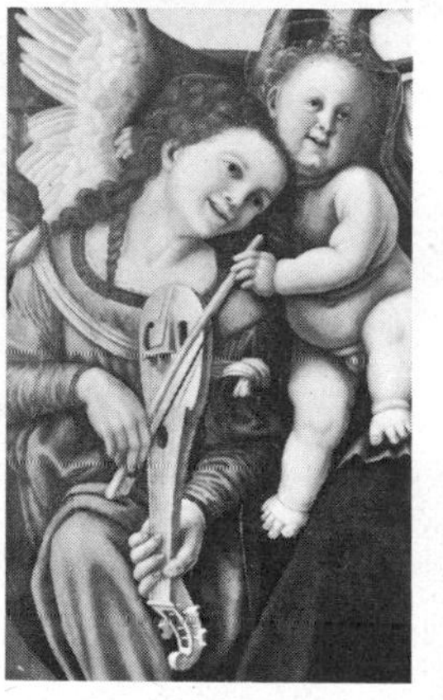

rebec
Detail from a painting by Piero di Cosimo

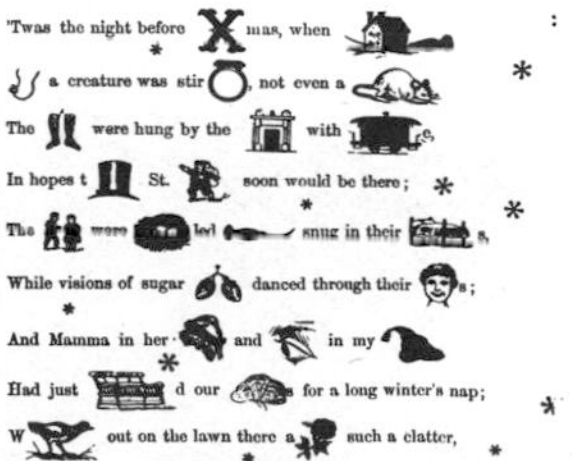

rebus
The first lines of the poem "A Visit from St. Nicholas" presented as a rebus

Received Standard English. The dialect spoken in British public schools and Oxford and Cambridge, usually accepted as the standard for educated Englishmen.

re·ceiv·er (rĭ-sē′vər) *n.* **1.** One who receives something; a recipient. **2.** An official appointed to receive and account for money due. **3.** *Law.* A person appointed by a court administrator to take into custody the property or funds of others, pending litigation. **4.** One who knowingly buys or receives stolen goods. **5.** A receptacle intended for a specific purpose. **6.** *Electronics.* A device, such as a part of a radio, television set, or telephone, that receives incoming electromagnetic signals and converts them to perceptible forms.

re·ceiv·er·ship (rĭ-sē′vər-shĭp′) *n. Law.* **1.** The office or functions of a receiver. **2.** The state of being held by a receiver.

re·cen·sion (rĭ-sĕn′shən) *n.* **1.** A critical revision of a text incorporating the most plausible elements found in varying sources. **2.** A text so revised. [Latin *recēnsiō*, a reviewing, an enumeration, from *recēnsēre*, survey again, review : *re-*, again, back + *cēnsēre*, estimate, assess (see **kens-** in Appendix*).]

re·cent (rē′sənt) *adj.* **1.** Of, belonging to, or occurring at a time immediately prior to the present. **2.** Modern; new. **3.** *Capital* **R.** *Geology.* Of, belonging to, or designating the Holocene epoch. [Latin *recēns* (stem *recent-*), fresh, new. See **ken-**[3] in Appendix.*] —**re′cen·cy, re′cent·ness** *n.* —**re′cent·ly** *adv.*

re·cept (rē′sĕpt′) *n.* A mental image formed from what is common to successive perceptions. [RE- + (CON)CEPT.]

re·cep·ta·cle (rĭ-sĕp′tə-kəl) *n.* **1.** Something that holds or contains; a container. **2.** *Botany.* The part of a flower stalk that bears and supports the floral organs. **3.** *Electricity.* A fitting connected to a power supply and equipped to receive a plug. [Latin *receptāculum*, from *receptāre*, to take again, frequentative of *recipere* (past participle *receptus*), to RECEIVE.]

re·cep·tion (rĭ-sĕp′shən) *n.* **1.** The act or process of receiving or of being received. **2.** A welcome, greeting, or acceptance: *a friendly reception.* **3.** A formal social function. **4.** Mental approval or acceptance: *the reception of a new theory.* **5.** *Electronics.* **a.** The action of receiving electromagnetic signals. **b.** The condition or quality of received signals. [Latin *receptiō*, from *recipere* (past participle *receptus*), to RECEIVE.]

re·cep·tion·ist (rĭ-sĕp′shə-nĭst) *n.* A person employed chiefly to receive callers and answer the telephone.

re·cep·tive (rĭ-sĕp′tĭv) *adj.* **1.** Capable of or qualified for receiving. **2.** Ready or willing to receive favorably: *receptive to their proposals.* —**re·cep′tive·ly** *adv.* —**re′cep·tiv′i·ty, re·cep′tive·ness** *n.*

re·cep·tor (rĭ-sĕp′tər) *n. Anatomy.* A nerve ending specialized to sense or to receive stimuli.

re·cess (rē′sĕs′, rĭ-sĕs′) *n.* **1.** A cessation of the customary activities of an engagement, occupation, or pursuit. **2.** The period of such cessation. **3.** *Usually plural.* A remote, secret, or secluded place. **4. a.** An indentation or small hollow. **b.** An alcove. —*v.* **recessed, -cessing, -cesses.** —*tr.* **1.** To place in a recess. **2.** To create or fashion a recess in. **3.** To suspend for a recess. —*intr.* To take a recess. [Latin *recessus*, from the past participle of *recēdere*, to RECEDE.]

re·ces·sion (rē-sĕsh′ən) *n.* The act of restoring possession to a former owner.

re·ces·sion (rĭ-sĕsh′ən) *n.* **1.** The act of withdrawing or going back. **2.** The filing out of clergy and choir members after a church service. **3.** A moderate and temporary decline in economic activity that occurs during a period of otherwise increasing prosperity, often in a recovery period following a depression. [Latin *recessiō*, from *recessus*, RECESS.]

re·ces·sion·al (rĭ-sĕsh′ən-əl) *adj.* Of or pertaining to recession. —*n.* **1.** A hymn that accompanies the exit of the clergy and choir after a service. **2.** A recession from a church.

re·ces·sive (rĭ-sĕs′ĭv) *adj.* **1.** Tending to go backward or recede. **2.** *Genetics.* Of, pertaining to, or designating an allele that does not produce a phenotypic effect when heterozygous with a dominant allele. Compare **dominant.** —*n. Genetics.* **1.** A recessive allele or trait. **2.** An organism having a recessive trait. —**re·ces′sive·ly** *adv.*

ré·chauf·fé (rā′shō-fā′) *n.* **1.** Warmed leftover food. **2.** Old material reworked or rehashed. [French, "warmed over," from *réchauffer*, to heat again, from Old French : *re-*, again, back + *chauffer*, to warm (see **chafe**).]

re·cher·ché (rə-shâr′shā′) *adj.* **1.** Intensely sought after; uncommon; rare. **2.** Exquisite or refined. **3.** Overrefined; forced. [French, past participle of *rechercher*, search for, from Old French *recercher*, to RESEARCH.]

re·cid·i·vism (rĭ-sĭd′ə-vĭz′əm) *n.* A tendency to relapse into a former pattern of behavior; especially, a tendency to return to criminal habits. [From *recidivist*, from French *récidiviste*, relapser, from *récidiver*, to relapse, from Medieval Latin *recidīvāre*, from Latin *recidīvus*, a falling back, from *recidere*, fall back : *re-*, back, again + *cadere*, fall (see **kad-** in Appendix*).] —**re·cid′i·vist** *n.* —**re·cid′i·vis′tic, re·cid′i·vous** *adj.*

Re·ci·fe (rə-sē′fē). A major city and seaport in northeastern Brazil, the capital of the state of Pernambuco. Population, 797,000.

recip. reciprocal; reciprocity.

rec·i·pe (rĕs′ə-pē′) *n.* **1.** *Abbr.* **rec.** A formula for preparing a mixture or compound, especially in cooking or pharmacology, with a list of measured ingredients and often a set of directions for their use or application. **2.** *Symbol* ℞ A medical prescription. **3.** A formula for or means to a desired end. [Latin, "take," imperative of *recipere*, to take, RECEIVE.]

re·cip·i·ence (rĭ-sĭp′ē-əns) *n.* Also **re·cip·i·en·cy** (-ən-sē). The capacity to receive; receptivity.

re·cip·i·ent (rĭ-sĭp′ē-ənt) *adj.* Functioning as a receiver; receptive. —*n.* One that receives or is receptive. [Latin *recipiēns*, present participle of *recipere*, to RECEIVE.]

re·cip·ro·cal (rĭ-sĭp′rə-kəl) *adj. Abbr.* **recip. 1.** Concerning each of two or more persons or things. **2.** Interchanged, given, or owed mutually: *reciprocal funds.* **3.** Performed, experienced, or felt by both sides: *reciprocal hatred.* **4.** Interchangeable; complementary. **5.** *Grammar.* Expressing mutual action or relationship. Said of some verbs and compound pronouns. **6.** *Mathematics.* Of or pertaining to a quantity divided into 1. —See Usage note at **mutual.** —*n.* **1.** Anything that is reciprocal to something else; a converse or complement. **2.** *Mathematics.* The quotient of a specific quantity divided into 1. For example, the reciprocal of 7 is $^1/_7$; the reciprocal of $^2/_3$ is $^3/_2$. [Latin *reciprocus*, alternating, returning. See **per**[1] in Appendix.*] —**re·cip′ro·cal′i·ty** (-kăl′ə-tē), **re·cip′ro·cal·ness** *n.* —**re·cip′ro·cal·ly** *adv.*

reciprocal pronoun. *Grammar.* A pronoun or pronominal phrase expressing mutual action or relationship, as *each other.*

re·cip·ro·cate (rĭ-sĭp′rə-kāt′) *v.* **-cated, -cating, -cates.** —*tr.* **1.** To give or take mutually; to interchange. **2.** To show or feel in response or return. —*intr.* **1.** To move back and forth alternately. **2.** To give and take something mutually. **3.** To make a return for something given or done. **4.** To be complementary or equivalent. [Latin *reciprocāre*, to move back and forth, from *reciprocus*, RECIPROCAL.] —**re·cip′ro·ca′tive** *adj.* —**re·cip′ro·ca′tor** (-kā′tər) *n.*

reciprocating engine. An engine having a crankshaft turned by linearly reciprocating pistons.

re·cip·ro·ca·tion (rĭ-sĭp′rə-kā′shən) *n.* **1.** An alternating back-and-forth movement. **2.** The act or fact of reciprocating; a mutual giving or receiving; an interchange.

rec·i·proc·i·ty (rĕs′ə-prŏs′ə-tē) *n. Abbr.* **recip. 1.** A reciprocal condition or relationship. **2.** A mutual or cooperative interchange of favors or privileges. **3.** A commercial policy or trade agreement between two or more parties.

re·ci·sion (rĭ-sĭzh′ən) *n.* The act of rescinding; an annulment or cancellation. [Latin *recīsiō*, a cutting off, from *recīsus*, past participle of *recīdere*, to cut down : *re-*, back, back down, again + *caedere*, to cut (see **skhai-** in Appendix*).]

re·cit·al (rĭ-sīt′l) *n.* **1.** A public reciting of rhetorical or elocutionary materials memorized or practiced previously. **2.** A retelling in detail; narration. **3.** Something thus told. **4.** A performance of music or dance, especially by one performer.

rec·i·ta·tion (rĕs′ə-tā′shən) *n.* **1.** The act of reciting memorized materials in a public performance. **2.** The material so recited. **3. a.** The oral delivery of prepared lessons by a pupil. **b.** The class period within which this recitation occurs.

rec·i·ta·tive[1] (rĕs′ə-tā′tĭv, rĭ-sī′tə-tĭv) *adj.* Pertaining to or having the character of a recital or recitation.

rec·i·ta·tive[2] (rĕs′ə-tə-tēv′) *n.* Also **re·ci·ta·ti·vo** (rĕs′ə-tə-tē′vō; *Italian* rā′chē-tä-tē′vō) *pl.* **-vi** (-vē) or **-vos** (-vōz). **1.** A musical style used in opera and oratorio, in which the text is declaimed in the rhythm of natural speech with slight melodic variation. **2.** A passage rendered in this form. [Italian *recitativo*, from *recitare*, to recite, from Latin *recitāre*, RECITE.]

re·cite (rĭ-sīt′) *v.* **-cited, -citing, -cites.** —*tr.* **1.** To repeat or utter aloud something rehearsed or memorized, especially publicly. **2.** To relate in detail. **3.** To list or enumerate. —*intr.* **1.** To deliver a recitation. **2.** To repeat lessons prepared or memorized. [Middle English *reciten*, from Old French *reciter*, from Latin *recitāre*, to read out, cite again : *re-*, back, again + *citāre*, to CITE.] —**re·cit′er** *n.*

reck (rĕk) *v.* **recked, recking, recks.** —*tr.* To take heed of; be concerned about: *He does not reck death.* —*intr.* To take heed; have caution. [Middle English *recken*, *recchen*, to be careful, to take care, Old English *reccan*, *recan*. See **reg-**[1] in Appendix.*]

reck·less (rĕk′lĭs) *adj.* **1. a.** Heedless or careless. **b.** Headstrong; rash: *a reckless lover.* **2.** Having no regard for consequences; uncontrolled; wild: *a reckless driver.* [Middle English *recheles*, *reckeles*, Old English *rēcelēas*. See **reg-**[1] in Appendix.*] —**reck′less·ly** *adv.* —**reck′less·ness** *n.*

Synonyms: *reckless, adventurous, rash, precipitate, foolhardy, audacious, daring, venturous, venturesome. Reckless* suggests heedlessness or thoughtlessness in action or decision. *Adventurous* implies willingness to incur risk and danger, but usually not mindlessly. *Rash* and *precipitate* connote haste and lack of deliberation in deed or decision. *Foolhardy* implies absence of sound judgment. *Audacious* and *daring* suggest fearlessness and confidence. *Venturous* and *venturesome* imply inclination to take risk that is recognized as such.

Reck·ling·hau·sen (rĕk′lĭng-hou′zən). A city in the Ruhr of North Rhine-Westphalia, West Germany. Population, 129,000.

reck·on (rĕk′ən) *v.* **-oned, -oning, -ons.** —*tr.* **1.** To count or compute. **2.** To consider as being; regard as. **3.** *Informal.* To think or assume. —*intr.* **1.** To make a calculation; to figure. **2.** To depend. Used with *on* or *upon: reckon on financial aid.* —See Synonyms at **calculate, consider, rely.** —**reckon for.** To be accountable for. —**reckon with.** To come to terms or settle accounts with. [Middle English *reknen*, Old English *gerecenian*, to enumerate. See **reg-**[1] in Appendix.*]

reck·on·er (rĕk′ən-ər) *n.* **1.** One that reckons. **2.** A handbook of mathematical tables to facilitate computation.

reck·on·ing (rĕk′ən-ĭng) *n.* **1.** The act of counting; a computation. **2.** An itemized bill or statement of a sum due. **3.** The settlement of a bill or account. **4. a.** The act or process of calculating the position of a ship, aircraft, or the like. **b.** The position so calculated.

re·claim (rē-klām′) *tr.v.* **-claimed, -claiming, -claims.** To

ă pat/ā pay/âr care/ä father/b bib/ch church/d deed/ĕ pet/ē be/f fife/g gag/h hat/hw which/ĭ pit/ī pie/îr pier/j judge/k kick/l lid, needle/m mum/n no, sudden/ng thing/ŏ pot/ō toe/ô paw, for/oi noise/ou out/ŏŏ took/ōō boot/p pop/r roar/s sauce/sh ship, dish/

demand the restoration or return of; claim again or back.

re·claim (rĭ-klām′) *tr.v.* **-claimed, -claiming, -claims. 1.** To make (marshland or desert, for example) suitable for cultivation or habitation, as by filling, irrigating, or fertilizing. **2.** To procure (usable substances) from refuse or waste products. **3.** To turn (a person) from error, evil, or barbarism; to reform. **4.** *Rare.* To tame (a falcon, for example). —See Synonyms at **recover, save.** [Middle English *reclamen,* to call back, from Old French *reclamer,* from Latin *reclāmāre,* to exclaim against : *re-,* back, against + *clāmāre,* call out (see **kel-**[3] in Appendix*).] —**re·claim′a·ble** *adj.* —**re·claim′ant, re·claim′er** *n.*

rec·la·ma·tion (rĕk′lə-mā′shən) *n.* **1.** The act or process of reclaiming. **2.** A restoration, as to productivity, usefulness, or morality. [Old French, a protest, from Latin *reclāmātiō,* cry of opposition, from *reclāmāre,* to RECLAIM.]

ré·clame (rā-kläm′) *n.* **1.** Public acclaim. **2.** A taste or flair for publicity. [French, publicity, from *réclamer,* to reclaim, from Old French *reclamer,* to RECLAIM.]

rec·li·nate (rĕk′lə-nāt′) *adj. Botany.* Bent or turned downward toward the base. [Latin *reclīnātus,* past participle of *reclīnāre,* to RECLINE.]

re·cline (rĭ-klīn′) *v.* **-clined, -clining, -clines.** —*tr.* To cause to assume a leaning or prone position. —*intr.* To lie back or down. [Middle English *reclinen,* from Old French *recliner,* from Latin *reclīnāre* : *re-,* back, again + *-clīnāre,* to bend (see **klei-** in Appendix*).] —**rec′li·na′tion** (rĕk′lə-nā′shən) *n.* —**re·clin′er** *n.*

re·cluse (rĕk′lo͞os′, rĭ-klo͞os′) *n.* One who withdraws from the world to live in solitude and seclusion, as a hermit. —*adj.* Withdrawn from the world; solitary. [Middle English *reclus(e),* from Old French, past participle of *reclure,* to shut up, from Latin *reclūdere,* to close off, unclose, open : *re-* (intensifier), again + *claudere,* to close (see **klēu-** in Appendix*).]

re·clu·sion (rĭ-klo͞o′zhən) *n.* **1.** The condition of being a recluse. **2.** The state of being in solitary confinement.

re·clu·sive (rĭ-klo͞o′sĭv, -zĭv) *adj.* **1.** Seeking or preferring seclusion or isolation. **2.** Providing seclusion: *a reclusive hut.*

rec·og·ni·tion (rĕk′əg-nĭsh′ən) *n.* **1.** The act of recognizing or state of being recognized. **2.** An awareness that something perceived has been perceived before. **3.** An acknowledgment, as of a claim. **4.** A giving of attention or favorable notice: *recognition of a speaker.* **5.** An acknowledgment or acceptance of the national status of a new government by another nation. [Latin *recognitiō,* from *recognōscere* (past participle *recognitus*), to RECOGNIZE.] —**re·cog′ni·to′ry** (rĭ-kŏg′nə-tôr′ē, -tōr′ē), **re·cog′ni·tive** *adj.*

re·cog·ni·zance (rĭ-kŏg′nə-zəns, -kŏn′ə-zəns) *n.* **1.** *Law.* **a.** An obligation of record entered into before a court or magistrate with the condition to perform a particular act, as to appear in court. **b.** A sum of money pledged to assure the performance of such an act. **2.** A recognition. [Middle English *recognizance, reconissaunce,* recognition, from Old French *reconoissance,* from *reconoistre,* to RECOGNIZE.] —**re·cog′ni·zant** *adj.*

rec·og·nize (rĕk′əg-nīz′) *tr.v.* **-nized, -nizing, -nizes. 1.** To know or be aware that something perceived has been perceived before: *recognize a face.* **2.** To know or identify from past experience or knowledge: *recognize a red-winged blackbird.* **3.** To perceive or acknowledge the validity or reality of: *recognize a demand.* **4.** To acknowledge as a speaker. **5.** To acknowledge or accept the national status of as a new government. **6.** To acknowledge, approve of, or appreciate: *recognize services rendered.* **7.** To admit the acquaintance of, as by salutation. **8.** *Law.* To enter into a recognizance. [Old French *reconoistre* (stem *reco(g)noiss-*), from Latin *recognōscere,* to know again : *re-,* again + *cognōscere,* to know : *co-,* with + *gnōscere,* become acquainted (see **gnō-** in Appendix*).] —**rec′og·niz′a·ble** *adj.* —**rec′og·niz′a·bly** *adv.* —**rec′og·niz′er** *n.*

re·coil (rĭ-koil′) *intr.v.* **-coiled, -coiling, -coils. 1.** To spring back, as a gun upon firing. **2.** To shrink back in fear or repugnance. **3.** To fall back; return. Used with *on* or *upon: Vice recoils upon the guilty men.* —*n.* (rē′koil′, rĭ-koil′). **1.** The amount of space used by a firearm as it recoils upon firing. **2.** The act or state of recoiling. [Middle English *recoilen, reculen,* from Old French *reculer* : *re-,* back, again + *cul,* backside, from Latin *cūlus* (see **skeu-** in Appendix*).] —**re·coil′er** *n.*

Synonyms: *recoil, blench, cower, quail, shrink, cringe, flinch. Recoil* implies instinctive, involuntary drawing back, as from something dangerous or repulsive. *Blench* applies to the act of shying back or turning away. *Cower, quail,* and *shrink* imply fear or despair, involving avoidance of that which is difficult by shying away, sinking downward, or huddling. *Cringe* suggests crouching or slinking resulting from cowardice or servility: *He cringed before the bully. Flinch* connotes instinctive drawing back from something painful: *He flinched from the blow.*

re-col·lect (rē′kə-lĕkt′) *tr.v.* **-lected, -lecting, -lects. 1.** To collect again. **2.** To calm or control (oneself). —**re′-col·lec′tion** *n.*

rec·ol·lect (rĕk′ə-lĕkt′) *v.* **-lected, -lecting, -lects.** —*tr.* To recall to mind; remember. —*intr.* To have a recollection; remember. [Medieval Latin *recolligere* (past participle *recollectus*), to recall, from Latin, to gather again : *re-,* again + *colligere,* to gather, COLLECT.] —**rec′ol·lec′tive** *adj.* —**rec′ol·lec′tive·ly** *adv.*

rec·ol·lec·tion (rĕk′ə-lĕk′shən) *n.* **1.** The act or power of recollecting. **2.** Something recollected. —See Synonyms at **memory.**

re·com·bi·na·tion (rē′kŏm-bə-nā′shən) *n.* The formation in offspring of genetic combinations not present in parents.

rec·om·mend (rĕk′ə-mĕnd′) *tr.v.* **-mended, -mending, -mends. 1.** To commend to the attention of another as reputable, worthy, or desirable. **2.** To make attractive or acceptable: *Honesty recommends any man.* **3.** To commit to the charge of another; entrust. **4.** To counsel or advise (that something be done). [Middle English *recommenden,* from Medieval Latin *recommendāre* : Latin *re-,* again + *commendāre,* to COMMEND.] —**rec′om·mend′a·ble** *adj.* —**rec′om·mend′er** *n.*

rec·om·men·da·tion (rĕk′ə-mĕn-dā′shən) *n.* **1.** The act of recommending. **2.** Something that recommends; specifically, a favorable statement concerning the character or qualifications of someone. —**rec′om·men′da·to′ry** (-də-tôr′ē, -tōr′ē) *adj.*

re·com·mit (rē′kə-mĭt′) *tr.v.* **-mitted, -mitting, -mits. 1.** To commit again. **2.** To refer to a committee again, as proposed legislation. —**re′com·mit′ment, re′com·mit′tal** *n.*

rec·om·pense (rĕk′əm-pĕns′) *tr.v.* **-pensed, -pensing, -penses. 1.** To award compensation to; to reward; pay. **2.** To award compensation for; make a return for. —*n.* **1.** Amends made for something, such as damage or loss. **2.** Payment in return for something given or done, as services. [Middle English *recompensen,* from Old French *recompenser,* from Late Latin *recompensāre* : Latin *re-,* back, again + *compensāre,* to COMPENSATE.]

re·com·pose (rē′kəm-pōz′) *tr.v.* **-posed, -posing, -poses. 1.** To compose again; reorganize or rearrange. **2.** To restore to composure; to calm. —**re′com·po·si′tion** (rē′kŏm-pə-zĭsh′ən) *n.*

rec·on·cil·a·ble (rĕk′ən-sī′lə-bəl, rĕk′ən-sī′lə-bəl) *adj.* Capable of or qualified for reconciliation. —**rec′on·cil′a·bil′i·ty, rec′on·cil′a·ble·ness** *n.* —**rec′on·cil′a·bly** *adv.*

rec·on·cile (rĕk′ən-sīl′) *tr.v.* **-ciled, -ciling, -ciles. 1.** To re-establish friendship between. **2.** To settle or resolve, as a dispute. **3.** To bring to acquiescence: *reconcile oneself to defeat.* **4.** To make compatible or consistent. Often used with *to* or *with: reconcile my way of thinking with yours.* [Middle English *reconcilen,* from Old French *reconcilier,* from Latin *reconciliāre* : *re-,* again + *conciliāre,* to CONCILIATE.] —**rec′on·cile′ment, rec′on·cil′i·a′tion** (-sĭl′ē-ā′shən) *n.* —**rec′on·cil′er** *n.* —**rec′on·cil′i·a·to′ry** (-sĭl′ē-ə-tôr′ē, -tōr′ē) *adj.*

rec·on·dite (rĕk′ən-dīt′, rĭ-kŏn′dīt′) *adj.* **1.** Not easily understood by the average person; abstruse: *the recondite origin of life.* **2.** Delving into abstruse concerns: *recondite scholarship.* **3.** Concealed; hidden. —See Synonyms at **ambiguous.** [Latin *reconditus,* past participle of *recondere,* to hide, put up again : *re-,* again + *condere,* bring together (see **dhē-**[1] in Appendix*).] —**rec′on·dite′ly** *adv.* —**rec′on·dite′ness** *n.*

re·con·di·tion (rē′kən-dĭsh′ən) *tr.v.* **-tioned, -tioning, -tions.** To restore by repairing, renovating, or rebuilding.

re·con·nais·sance (rĭ-kŏn′ə-səns, -zəns) *n.* Also **re·con·nois·sance. 1.** The process or activity of reconnoitering. **2.** An inspection of a land area prior to surveying. **3.** A survey made of a region to examine its terrain or to determine the disposition of military forces. [French, from Old French *reconoissance,* RECOGNIZANCE.]

re·con·noi·ter (rē′kə-noi′tər, rĕk′ə-) *v.* **-tered, -tering, -ters.** Also *chiefly British* **re·con·noi·tre.** —*tr.* To make a preliminary inspection of. —*intr.* To make a reconnaissance. [Obsolete French *reconnoître,* from Old French *reconoistre,* RECOGNIZE.] —**re′con·noi′ter·er** *n.*

re·con·sid·er (rē′kən-sĭd′ər) *v.* **-ered, -ering, -ers.** —*tr.* **1.** To consider again, especially with intent to alter or modify a previous decision. **2.** To take up for reconsideration, as a matter previously acted on by a legislature. —*intr.* To consider again. —**re′con·sid′er·a′tion** *n.*

re·con·struct (rē′kən-strŭkt′) *tr.v.* **-structed, -structing, -structs.** To construct again.

re·con·struc·tion (rē′kən-strŭk′shən) *n.* **1.** The act or result of reconstructing. **2.** *Capital* **R.** *U.S. History.* The period (1865–77) during which the states of the Southern Confederacy were controlled by the Federal government and forced to modify their political and social institutions as prerequisite to full readmission to the Union. —**re′con·struc′tive** *adj.*

re·con·vey (rē′kən-vā′) *tr.v.* **-veyed, -veying, -veys.** To convey back to a former owner or place. —**re′con·vey′ance** *n.*

rec·ord (rĕk′ərd) *n. Abbr.* **rec. 1.** An account made in an enduring form, especially in writing, that preserves the knowledge or memory of events or facts. **2.** Something on which such an account is made. **3.** Information or data on a particular subject collected and preserved: *the coldest day on record.* **4.** The known history of performance or achievement: *a horse with a fine record in trotting.* **5.** The best performance known, as in a sport. **6.** *Law.* **a.** An account officially written and preserved as evidence or testimony. **b.** An account of judicial or legislative proceedings written and preserved as evidence. **c.** The documents or volumes containing such evidence. **7.** A disk or cylinder structurally coded to reproduce sound; phonograph record. —**off the record.** Not for publication. —*v.* **re·cord** (rĭ-kôrd′) **-corded, -cording, -cords.** —*tr.* **1.** To set down for preservation in writing or other permanent form. **2.** To register or indicate: *A thermometer records temperatures.* **3.** To register (sound) in permanent form by mechanical or electrical means for reproduction. —*intr.* To record something. —*adj.* **rec·ord** (rĕk′ərd). *Abbr.* **rec.** Establishing a record: *a record crowd.* [Middle English *recorde,* from Old French *record,* from *recorder,* to record, from Latin *recordārī,* to remember, think over : *re-,* again + *cor* (stem *cord-*), mind, heart (see **kerd-**[1] in Appendix*).]

re·cord·er (rĭ-kôr′dər) *n.* **1.** One that records. **2.** A judge who has criminal jurisdiction in a city. **3.** A fipple flute with eight finger holes.

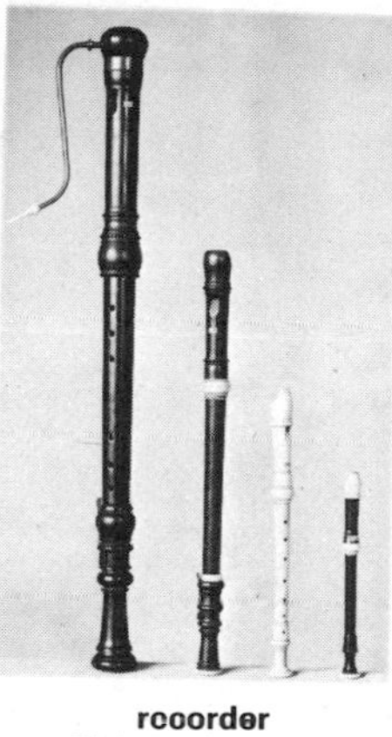

recorder
Eighteenth-century German recorders

re·cord·ing (rĭ-kôr′dĭng) *n. Abbr.* **rec. 1.** A phonograph record or magnetic tape or wire upon which sound has been recorded. **2.** The sound so recorded.

re-count (rē-kount′) *tr.v.* **-counted, -counting, -counts.** To count again. —*n.* (rē′kount′, rē-kount′). An additional count; especially, a second count of votes cast in an election.

re·count (rĭ-kount′) *tr.v.* **-counted, -counting, -counts. 1.** To narrate the facts or particulars of. **2.** To enumerate. [Middle English *recounten*, from Old French *reconter* : *re-*, again, back + *conter, compter*, relate, COUNT.] **—re·count′al** *n.*

re·coup (rĭ-ko͞op′) *v.* **-couped, -couping, -coups.** *—tr.* **1.** To receive an equivalent for; make up for: *recoup the loss.* **2.** To return as an equivalent for; reimburse. **3.** *Law.* To deduct or withhold (part of something due) for an equitable reason. *—intr.* To regain a former favorable position. —See Synonyms at **recover.** *—n.* The act of recouping. [Middle English *recoupen*, from Old French *recouper*, to cut back, retrench : *re-*, back + *couper*, to cut, strike, from *coup*, blow, COUP.] **—re·coup′a·ble** *adj.* **—re·coup′ment** *n.*

re·course (rē′kôrs′, -kōrs′, rĭ-kôrs′, -kōrs′) *n.* **1.** A turning or applying to a person or thing for aid or security: *have recourse to the courts.* **2.** One that is turned or applied to for aid or security: *His only recourse was the police department.* **3.** *Law.* The right to demand payment from the endorser of a commercial paper when the first party liable fails to pay. [Middle English *recours*, from Old French, from Latin *recursus*, a running back, from *recurrere*, to run back : *re-*, again, back + *currere*, to run (see **kers-**[2] in Appendix*).]

re·cov·er (rē-kŭv′ər) *tr.v.* **-ered, -ering, -ers.** To cover anew.

re·cov·er (rĭ-kŭv′ər) *v.* **-ered, -ering, -ers.** *—tr.* **1.** To get back; regain. **2.** To restore (oneself) to a normal state. **3.** To compensate for, as a loss. *—intr.* **1.** To regain a normal or usual condition or state, as of health. **2.** To receive a favorable judgment in a lawsuit. [Middle English *recoveren*, from Old French *recoverer*, from Latin *recuperāre*, to RECUPERATE.] **—re·cov′er·a·ble** *adj.* **—re·cov′er·er** *n.*

Synonyms: *recover, reclaim, regain, recoup, retrieve. Recover* refers to the getting back of something lost. *Reclaim* applies both to the act of demanding the return of something and to the restoration of a thing to good condition. *Regain* suggests effort in getting back something lost or taken from one, usually a quality or status rather than an object. *Recoup* means getting back the equivalent of something lost or damaged. *Retrieve* pertains either to the physical recovery of a thing or to the repair or remedy of the consequences of an act.

re·cov·er·y (rĭ-kŭv′ə-rē) *n., pl.* **-ies. 1.** An act, instance, process, or duration of recovering. **2.** A return to a normal condition. **3.** Something gained or restored in recovering. **4.** The obtaining of usable substances from unusable sources, such as waste material. **—final recovery.** *Law.* The final verdict or judgment in a case.

rec·re·ant (rĕk′rē-ənt) *adj.* **1.** Unfaithful or disloyal to belief, promise, or cause. **2.** Craven or cowardly. *—n.* **1.** A faithless or disloyal person; an apostate. **2.** A coward. [Middle English *recreant*, from Old French, present participle of *recroire*, to yield, surrender, from Medieval Latin *recrēdere* : Latin *re-*, back, contrarily + *crēdere*, entrust, believe (see **kerd-**[1] in Appendix*).] **—rec′re·ance, rec′re·an·cy** *n.* **—rec′re·ant·ly** *adv.*

re-cre·ate (rē′krē-āt′) *tr.v.* **-ated, -ating, -ates.** To create anew.

rec·re·ate (rĕk′rē-āt′) *v.* **-ated, -ating, -ates.** *—tr.* To impart fresh life to; refresh mentally or physically. *—intr.* To take recreation. [Latin *recreāre*, to create anew : *re-*, back, again + *creāre*, to CREATE.] **—rec′re·a′tive** *adj.*

rec·re·a·tion (rĕk′rē-ā′shən) *n. Abbr.* **rec.** Refreshment of one's mind or body after labor through diverting activity; play. **—rec′re·a′tion·al** *adj.*

rec·re·ment (rĕk′rə-mənt) *n.* Waste matter; refuse; dross. [Latin *recrēmentum* : *re-*, back, again + *cernere*, to separate, sift (see **skeri-** in Appendix*).] **—rec′re·men′tal** (-mĕn′təl) *adj.*

re·crim·i·nate (rĭ-krĭm′ə-nāt′) *v.* **-nated, -nating, -nates.** *—tr.* To accuse in return. *—intr.* To counter one accusation with another. [Medieval Latin *recrīmināre* : Latin *re-*, again, back + *crīmināre*, to accuse, from *crīmen*, accusation (see **ker-**[2] in Appendix*).] **—re·crim′i·na′tive, re·crim′i·na·to′ry** (-nə-tôr′ē, -tōr′ē) *adj.* **—re·crim′i·na′tor** (-nā′tər) *n.*

re·crim·i·na·tion (rĭ-krĭm′ə-nā′shən) *n.* **1.** The act of recriminating. **2.** A countercharge.

re·cru·desce (rē′kro͞o-dĕs′) *intr.v.* **-desced, -descing, -desces.** To break out anew after a dormant or inactive period. See Synonyms at **return.** [Latin *recrūdēscere* : *re-*, again + *crūdēscere*, to get worse, from *crūdus*, harsh, raw (see **kreu-**[1] in Appendix*).] **—re′cru·des′cence** *n.* **—re′cru·des′cent** *adj.*

re·cruit (rĭ-kro͞ot′) *v.* **-cruited, -cruiting, -cruits.** *—tr.* **1.** To engage (persons) for military service. **2.** To strengthen or raise (an armed force) by enlistment. **3.** To supply with new members or employees. **4.** To enroll (another) in support of oneself or one's ideas: *"That's the struggle of humanity, to recruit others to your vision of what's real."* (Saul Bellow). **5.** To replenish. **6.** To renew or restore (health or vitality). *—intr.* **1.** To raise a military force. **2.** To obtain replacements for or new supplies of anything lost, wasted, or needed. **3.** To regain lost health or strength; recover: *"I believe the brain stands as much in need of recruiting as the body."* (Sterne). *—n.* **1.** *Abbr.* **rct.** A newly engaged member of a military force; especially, one of the lowest rank or grade. **2.** A new member of any organization or body. [Old French *recruter*, from *recrute*, new growth, from *recrue*, past participle of *recroître*, to grow again, from Latin *recrēscere* : *re-*, again + *crēscere*, to grow (see **ker-**[3] in Appendix*).] **—re·cruit′er** *n.* **—re·cruit′ment** *n.*

rec't receipt.

rect. 1. receipt. **2.** rectangle; rectangular. **3.** rectified. **4.** rector; rectory.

rec·tal (rĕk′təl) *adj.* Pertaining to or near the rectum.

rec·tan·gle (rĕk′tăng′gəl) *n. Abbr.* **rect.** *Geometry.* A parallelogram with a right angle. [Medieval Latin *rēctangulum* : Latin *rēctus*, right (see **reg-**[1] in Appendix*) + *angulus*, ANGLE.]

rec·tan·gu·lar (rĕk-tăng′gyə-lər) *adj. Abbr.* **rect. 1.** Having the shape of a rectangle. **2.** Having right angles. **3.** Designating a geometric coordinate system with mutually perpendicular axes. **—rec·tan′gu·lar′i·ty** (-lăr′ə-tē) *n.* **—rec·tan′gu·lar·ly** *adv.*

rectangular coordinate. *Geometry.* A coordinate in a rectangular **Cartesian coordinate system** *(see).*

rec·ti·fi·er (rĕk′tə-fī′ər) *n.* **1.** A person or thing that rectifies. **2.** *Electricity.* A device, such as a diode, that converts alternating current to direct current. **3.** A worker who blends or dilutes whiskey or other alcoholic beverages.

rec·ti·fy (rĕk′tə-fī′) *tr.v.* **-fied, -fying, -fies. 1.** To set right; correct. **2.** To correct by calculation or adjustment. **3.** *Chemistry.* To refine or purify, especially by distillation. **4.** *Electricity.* To convert (alternating current) into direct current. **5.** To adjust (the proof of alcoholic beverages) by adding water or other liquids. —See Synonyms at **correct.** [Middle English *rectifien*, from Old French *rectifier*, from Medieval Latin *rēctificāre* : Latin *rēctus*, straight (see **reg-**[1] in Appendix*) + *facere*, to make (see **dhē-**[1] in Appendix*).] **—rec′ti·fi′a·ble** *adj.* **—rec′ti·fi·ca′tion** (-fə-kā′shən) *n.*

rec·ti·lin·e·ar (rĕk′tə-lĭn′ē-ər) *adj.* Moving in, consisting of, bounded by, or characterized by a straight line or lines. [From Late Latin *rēctilīneus* : *rēctus*, straight (see **reg-**[1] in Appendix*) + *līnea*, LINE.] **—rec′ti·lin′e·ar·ly** *adv.*

rec·ti·tude (rĕk′tə-to͞od′, -tyo͞od′) *n.* **1.** Moral uprightness. **2.** Rightness, as of intellectual judgment. **3.** Straightness. [Middle English, from Old French, from Late Latin *rēctitūdō*, from Latin *rēctus*, straight. See **reg-**[1] in Appendix.*]

rec·to (rĕk′tō) *n., pl.* **-tos.** The right-hand page of a book or front side of a leaf, as opposed to the **verso** *(see).* [Latin *rēctō (foliō)*, on the right side of (a page), ablative of *rēctus*, right, straight. See **reg-**[1] in Appendix.*]

rec·tor (rĕk′tər) *n. Abbr.* **R., rect. 1.** *Protestant Episcopal Church.* A clergyman in charge of a parish. **2.** *Anglican Church.* A clergyman who has charge of a parish and owns the tithes from it. **3.** *Roman Catholic Church.* A priest appointed to be managerial as well as spiritual head of a church or other institution such as a seminary or university. **4.** The principal of certain schools, colleges, and universities. [Latin *rēctor*, governor, from *rēctus*, past participle of *regere*, to rule. See **reg-**[1] in Appendix.*] **—rec′tor·ate** (-ĭt) *n.* **—rec·to′ri·al** (rĕk-tôr′ē-əl, -tōr′ē-əl) *adj.*

rec·to·ry (rĕk′tə-rē) *n., pl.* **-ries.** *Abbr.* **rect. 1.** The house in which a Roman Catholic parish priest or an Episcopal minister lives. **2.** *Anglican Church.* **a.** A rector's dwelling. **b.** A rector's office and benefice.

rec·trix (rĕk′trĭks) *n., pl.* **rectrices** (rĕk′trə-sēz′, rĕk-trī′sēz). One of the stiff main feathers of a bird's tail. [Latin, feminine of *rēctor*, governor (the feathers help regulate flight). See **rector.**]

rec·tum (rĕk′təm) *n., pl.* **-tums** or **-ta** (-tə). The portion of the large intestine extending from the sigmoid flexure to the anal canal. [New Latin *rectum (intestinum)*, straight (intestine), from Latin *rēctus*, straight. See **reg-**[1] in Appendix.*]

rec·tus (rĕk′təs) *n., pl.* **-ti** (-tī′). Any of various straight muscles, as of the abdomen, eye, neck, and thigh. [New Latin, from Latin *rēctus*, straight. See **reg-**[1] in Appendix.*]

re·cum·bent (rĭ-kŭm′bənt) *adj.* **1.** Lying down; reclining. **2.** Resting; idle. **3.** *Biology.* Resting upon the surface from which it arises: *a recumbent organ.* —See Synonyms at **prone.** [Latin *recumbēns*, present participle of *recumbere*, to lie down : *re-*, back, again + *-cumbere*, to lie (see **keu-**[2] in Appendix*).] **—re·cum′bence, re·cum′ben·cy** *n.* **—re·cum′bent·ly** *adv.*

re·cu·per·ate (rĭ-ko͞o′pə-rāt′, rĭ-kyo͞o′-) *v.* **-ated, -ating, -ates.** *—intr.* **1.** To return to health or strength; recover. **2.** To recover from financial loss. *—tr.* **1.** To restore to health or strength: *"The sparkling wine soon recuperated Ianthe"* (Wilkie Collins). **2.** To regain. [Latin *recuperāre*. See **kap-** in Appendix.*] **—re·cu′per·a′tion** *n.* **—re·cu′per·a′tive** (-pə-rā′tĭv, -pər-ə-tĭv, rĭ-kyo͞o′-), **re·cu′per·a·to′ry** (-pər-ə-tôr′ē, -tōr′ē) *adj.*

re·cur (rĭ-kûr′) *intr.v.* **-curred, -curring, -curs. 1.** To happen, come up, or show up again or repeatedly. **2.** To return to one's attention or memory. **3.** To return in thought or discourse. **4.** To have recourse: *recur to the use of force.* —See Synonyms at **return.** [Latin *recurrere*, run back : *re-*, back + *currere*, run (see **kers-**[2] in Appendix*).] **—re·cur′rence** *n.*

re·cur·rent (rĭ-kûr′ənt) *adj.* **1.** Occurring or appearing again or repeatedly; returning regularly. **2.** *Anatomy.* Running in a reverse direction. Said of arteries and nerves. **—re·cur′rent·ly** *adv.*

recurring decimal. *Mathematics.* A **repeating decimal** *(see).*

re·cur·sion (rĭ-kûr′zhən) *adj* Of, pertaining to, or designating: **a.** A mathematical expression, such as a polynomial, each term of which is determined by application of a formula to preceding terms. **b.** A formula that generates the successive terms of such an expression. [Late Latin *recursiō*, a return, from Latin *recurrere* (past participle *recursus*), to RECUR.] **—re·cur′sive** *adj.*

re·cur·vate (rĭ-kûr′vāt′, -vĭt) *adj.* Bent or curved backward. [Latin *recurvātus*, past participle of *recurvāre*, RECURVE.]

re·curve (rē-kûrv′) *v.* **-curved, -curving, -curves.** *—tr.* To bend or curve backward or downward. *—intr.* To become bent or curved backward or downward. [Latin *recurvāre* : *re-*, back, backward + *curvāre*, to curve, from *curvus*, CURVE.] **—re′cur·va′tion** (rē′kûr-vā′shən) *n.*

rec·u·sant (rĕk′yə-zənt, rĭ-kyo͞o′-) *n.* **1.** A Roman Catholic who refused to attend the services of the Church of England between the reigns of Henry VIII and George II. **2.** A dissenter; a nonconformist. [Latin *recusāns*, present participle of *recusāre*, to refuse : *re-*, contrary to, back + *causa*, CAUSE.] **—rec′u·san·cy**

ă pat/ā pay/âr care/ä father/b bib/ch church/d deed/ĕ pet/ē be/f fife/g gag/h hat/hw which/ĭ pit/ī pie/îr pier/j judge/k kick/l lid, needle/m mum/n no, sudden/ng thing/ŏ pot/ō toe/ô paw, for/oi noise/ou out/o͝o took/o͞o boot/p pop/r roar/s sauce/sh ship, dish/

(rĕk′yə-zən-sē, rĭ-kyo͞o′zən-se) *n.* —**rec′u·sant** *adj.*

red¹ (rĕd) *n.* **1.** Any of a group of colors that may vary in lightness and saturation, whose hue resembles that of blood; the hue of the long-wave end of the spectrum; one of the additive or light primaries; one of the psychological primary hues, evoked in the normal observer by the long-wave end of the spectrum. See **color, primary color. 2.** A pigment or dye having or giving this hue. **3.** Something that has this hue. **4.** *Often capital* **R.** A partisan of the red banner of revolution; a communist or revolutionary activist. —**in the red.** Operating at a loss; in debt. —**see red.** To be or become furious. —*adj.* **redder, reddest. 1.** Having a color resembling that of blood. **2.** Reddish in color, or having parts that are reddish in color. Used in animal and plant names: *red fox; red oak.* **3.** Having a coppery skin tone. **4.** Having a ruddy or flushed complexion. **5.** *Sometimes capital* **R.** Following or associated with the red banner of revolution: **a.** Revolutionary or governed in accordance with revolutionary principles: *the struggle to keep China red; Red Guard.* **b.** Of, pertaining to, or aroused by revolution or revolutionaries: *red scare.* **c.** Composed of or directed by Communists: *a red labor union in a defense project.* [Middle English *red, read,* Old English *rēad.* See **reudh-** in Appendix.*] —**red′ly** *adv.* —**red′ness** *n.*

red². Variant of **redd.**

red. reduced; reduction.

re·dact (rĭ-dăkt′) *tr.v.* **-dacted, -dacting, -dacts. 1.** To draw up or frame (a proclamation or edict, for example). **2.** To make ready for publication; edit or revise. [Latin *redigere* (past participle *redactus*), to collect, drive back : *re-,* back + *agere,* to drive, do (see **ag-** in Appendix*).] —**re·dac′tor** (rĭ-dăk′tər, -tôr′) *n.* —**re·dac′tion** (-dăk′shən) *n.*

red algae. Any of the algae of the division Rhodophyta, characteristically red or reddish in color.

red·bait (rĕd′bāt′) *tr.v.* **-baited, -baiting, -baits.** To denounce as Communist. —**red′bait′er** *n.*

red·bird (rĕd′bûrd′) *n.* Any of various birds with red plumage, such as the cardinal or scarlet tanager.

red blood cell. An **erythrocyte** *(see).*

red-blood·ed (rĕd′blŭd′ĭd) *adj.* Strong or virile.

red·breast (rĕd′brĕst′) *n.* **1.** A bird with a red breast, such as the robin. **2.** A freshwater sunfish, *Lepomis auritus,* of eastern North America.

Red·bridge (rĕd′brĭj′). A borough of London, England, comprising the former administrative divisions of Wanstead and Woodford, and of Ilford. Population, 249,000.

red·bud (rĕd′bŭd′) *n.* Any of several shrubs or small trees of the genus *Cercis,* having pinkish flowers that bloom before the leaves appear. Also called "Judas tree."

red·cap (rĕd′kăp′) *n.* A porter, usually in a railroad station.

red carpet. A carpet laid down for important visitors outside the door of a house or public establishment. —**roll out the red carpet.** To welcome with great hospitality or ceremony. —**red′-car′pet** *adj.*

red cedar. 1. An evergreen tree, *Juniperus virginiana,* of eastern North America. **2.** A tall evergreen tree, *Thuja plicata,* of western North America. **3.** The reddish, aromatic, durable wood of either of these trees, or of similar trees.

red cent. *Informal.* A copper penny. Used especially in the phrase *not worth a red cent.*

Red China. *Informal.* The People's Republic of China.

red clover. A Eurasian plant, *Trifolium pratense,* widely naturalized in North America, and frequently planted as a forage or cover crop. It has leaflets in groups of three and globular heads of fragrant, rose-purple flowers.

red·coat (rĕd′kōt′) *n.* A British soldier during the American Revolution and the War of 1812.

Red Cross. 1. *Abbr.* **R.C.** Officially, Red Cross Society. An international organization, formed according to the terms of the Geneva Convention of 1864, for the care of the wounded, sick, and homeless in wartime and now also during and following natural disasters. **2.** Any national branch of this organization. **3.** The emblem of the organization, a Geneva cross or red Greek cross on a white background.

redd¹ (rĕd) *tr.v.* **redded** or **redd, redding, redds.** Also **red, red, redding, reds.** *Regional.* To put in order; make tidy or clean. Often used with *up: Redd up the house before company comes.* [Middle English *redden,* probably variant of *ridden,* to RID.]

redd² (rĕd) *n.* A circular depression in sand or gravel, used as a spawning area or nest by certain fish, such as salmon and some trout. [Origin unknown.]

red deer. A common European deer, *Cervus elaphus,* having a reddish-brown coat and many-branched antlers.

Red Deer. A river rising in southwestern Alberta, Canada, and flowing 385 miles south to the South Saskatchewan River.

red·den (rĕd′n) *v.* **-dened, -dening, -dens.** —*tr.* To make red. —*intr.* To grow red; especially, to flush or blush.

red·dish (rĕd′ĭsh) *adj.* Mixed or tinged with red; somewhat red. —**red′dish·ness** *n.*

red·dle. Variant of **ruddle.**

red-dog (rĕd′dôg′, -dŏg′) *v.* **-dogged, -dogging, -dogs.** *Football.* —*intr.* To charge across the line of scrimmage in an attempt to overwhelm the opposing quarterback before he can throw a forward pass. Used of linebackers and sometimes of defensive backs. —*tr.* To charge (the passer).

red drum. A food fish, *Sciaenops ocellata,* of southern Atlantic coastal waters. Also called "channel bass."

rede (rēd) *tr.v.* **reded, reding, redes.** *Archaic.* **1.** To give advice to; to counsel. **2.** To interpret; explain or tell. —*n. Archaic.* **1.** Advice or counsel. **2.** An interpretation or narration. [Middle English *reden,* to guide, direct, Old English *rǣdan.* See **ar-** in Appendix.*]

re·dec·o·rate (rē-dĕk′ə-rāt′) *v.* **-rated, -rating, -rates.** —*tr.* To change the décor of, as by painting, rearranging furnishings, or the like. —*intr.* To change the décor of a room, building, or the like. —**re·dec′o·ra′tion** *n.*

re·deem (rĭ-dēm′) *tr.v.* **-deemed, -deeming, -deems. 1.** To recover ownership of by paying a specified sum. **2.** To pay off, as a promissory note. **3.** To turn in (coupons or trading stamps, for example) and receive something in exchange. **4.** To fulfill (an oath, pledge, or promise). **5.** To convert into cash, as stocks. **6.** To set free; to rescue or ransom. **7.** To save from a state of sinfulness and its consequences. **8.** To make up for. —See Synonyms at **save.** [Middle English *redemen,* from Latin *redimere,* to buy back : *red-, re-,* back, again + *emere,* to take, buy (see **em-** in Appendix*).] —**re·deem′a·ble** *adj.*

re·deem·er (rĭ-dē′mər) *n.* **1.** One who redeems; a savior. **2.** *Capital* **R.** Christ.

re·de·liv·er (rē′dĭ-lĭv′ər) *tr.v.* **-ered, -ering, -ers. 1.** To deliver again. **2.** To deliver in return; give back.

re·demp·tion (rĭ-dĕmp′shən) *n.* **1.** The act of redeeming or the condition of being redeemed. **2.** A recovery of something pawned or mortgaged; a repurchase. **3.** The payment of an obligation, such as a government's payment of the value of its bonds. **4.** Deliverance upon payment of ransom; a rescue. **5.** *Theology.* Salvation from sin through Christ's sacrifice. [Middle English *redempcioun,* from Old French *redemption,* from Latin *redemptiō,* from *redimere* (past participle *redemptus*), to REDEEM.] —**re·demp′tion·al, re·demp′tive, re·demp′to·ry** (-tə-rē) *adj.*

re·demp·tion·er (rĭ-dĕmp′shən-ər) *n.* In Colonial America, an emigrant from Europe who paid for his voyage by serving as a bondservant for a specified period.

Re·demp·tor·ist (rĭ-dĕmp′tər-ĭst) *n.* A member of a Roman Catholic order, the Congregation of the Most Holy Redeemer, founded by St. Alphonsus de Liguori in 1732.

re·de·ploy (rē′dĭ-ploi′) *tr.v.* **-ployed, -ploying, -ploys.** To move (military forces) from one combat zone to another. —**re′de·ploy′ment** *n.*

re·de·vel·op (rē′dĭ-vĕl′əp) *v.* **-oped, -oping, -opes.** —*tr.* **1.** To develop (something) again. **2.** *Photography.* To tone or intensify (a developed negative) by a second developing process. **3.** To restore (a slum area, for example) to a better condition; renew or reclaim. —*intr.* To develop again. —**re′de·vel′op·er** *n.* —**re′de·vel′op·ment** *n.*

red·eye (rĕd′ī′) *n.* **1.** *Informal.* A danger signal on a railroad. **2.** *Slang.* Whiskey of an inferior grade. **3.** Any of several red-eyed fishes, such as the **rock bass** *(see).*

red fir. 1. An evergreen tree, *Abies magnifica,* of California and Oregon, having reddish wood valued as timber. **2.** The wood of this tree, or of similar trees, such as the **Douglas fir** *(see).*

red fire. Any of various combustible compounds, especially salts of lithium or strontium, that burn bright red and are used in flares and fireworks.

red·fish (rĕd′fĭsh′) *n., pl.* **redfish** or **-fishes.** Any of several fishes that are reddish in color.

red fox. Any of several foxes of the genus *Vulpes,* characteristically having reddish fur; especially, *V. fulva,* of North America. See **silver fox.**

red gum¹. Any of several Australian trees of the genus *Eucalyptus,* especially, *E. rostrata,* which has been naturalized in California. [From its reddish wood.]

red gum². A disease, **strophulus** *(see).*

red-hand·ed (rĕd′hăn′dĭd) *adj.* In the act of committing, or having just committed, a crime; in flagrante delicto: *caught red-handed.* —**red′-hand′ed** *adv.* —**red′-hand′ed·ly** *adv.*

red·head (rĕd′hĕd′) *n.* **1.** A person with red hair. **2.** A North American duck, *Aythya americana,* of which the male has black and gray plumage and a reddish head.

red heat. 1. The temperature of a red-hot substance. **2.** The physical condition of a red-hot substance.

red herring. 1. A smoked herring having a reddish color. **2.** Something that draws attention from the matter or issue at hand. [From the use of red herring to distract hunting dogs from the scent.]

red-hot (rĕd′hŏt′) *adj.* **1.** Glowing hot; very hot. **2.** Heated, as with excitement, anger, or enthusiasm: *a red-hot speech.* **3.** New; very recent: *red-hot information.* —*n. Slang.* A hot dog.

Red Indian. A North American Indian.

red·in·gote (rĕd′ĭng-gōt′) *n.* **1.** A man's long double-breasted topcoat with full skirt. **2.** A woman's full-length unlined coat or dress open down the front to show a dress or underdress. [French, from English *riding coat.*]

re·dis·count (rē-dĭs′kount′) *tr.v.* **-counted, -counting, -counts.** To discount again. —*n.* **1. a.** The discounting of commercial paper that has previously been discounted. **b.** The discounting of bank-owned commercial paper at a Federal Reserve Bank in the United States. **2.** *Usually plural.* Commercial paper that is discounted a second time.

re·dis·trib·ute (rē′dĭs-trĭb′yo͞ot) *tr.v.* **-uted, -uting, -utes.** To distribute again in a different way; reallocate. —**re·dis′tri·bu′tion** *n.* —**re′dis·trib′u·tive** *adj.*

re·dis·trict (rē-dĭs′trĭkt) *tr.v.* **-tricted, -tricting, -tricts.** To give new boundaries to; divide again, as into administrative or election districts.

Red Jacket. Original name, Sagoyewatha. 1758?–1830. American Indian leader and orator; chief of the Seneca.

red lead. A bright-red powder, Pb_3O_4, used in paints, glass, pottery, and pipe-joint packing. Also called "minium."

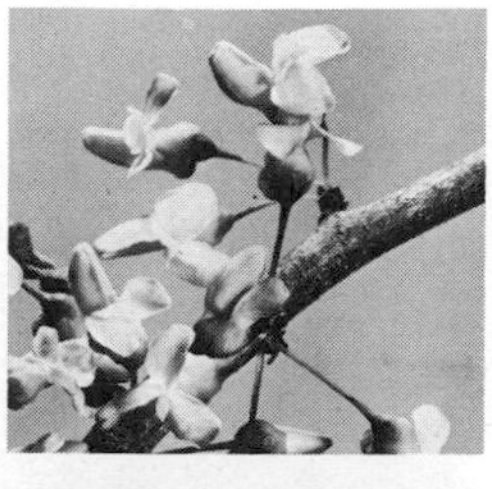

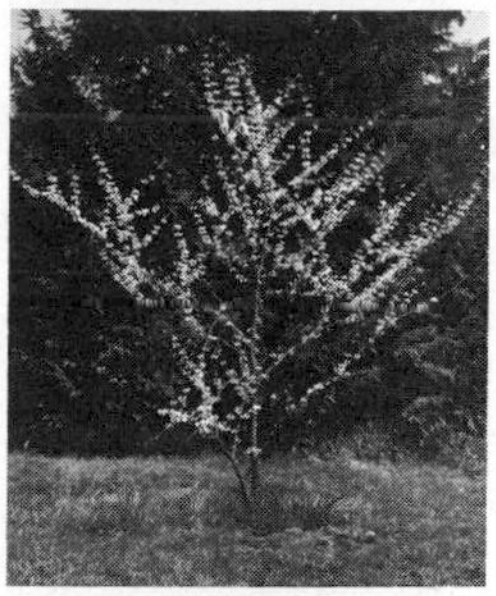

redbud
Cercis canadensis
Detail of flowers above

redingote

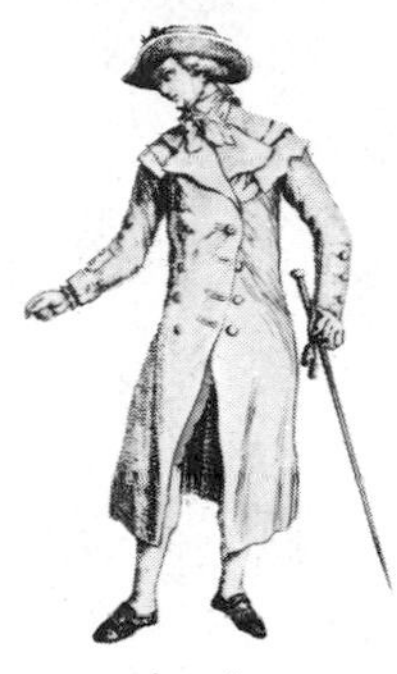

man's redingote, 19th century

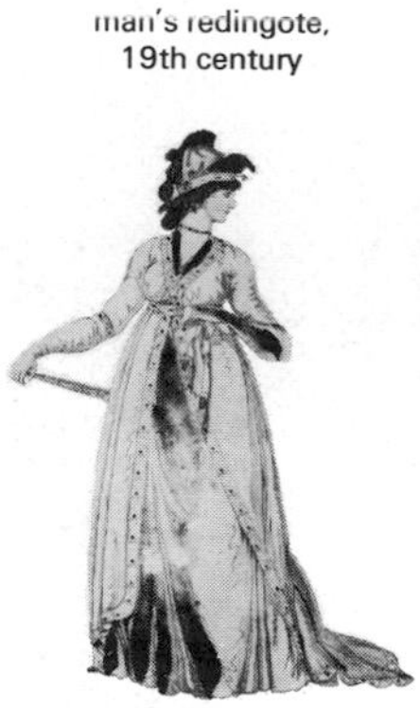

woman's redingote, 18th century

red-let·ter (rĕd′lĕt′ər) *adj.* Memorably happy: *a red-letter day.* [From the rubrication of feasts in church calendars.]
red light. A red traffic or danger signal indicating stop.
red-light district (rĕd′līt′). A neighborhood containing many brothels.
red mulberry. A tree, *Morus rubra,* of eastern and central North America, having irregularly lobed leaves and edible, blackberrylike fruit.
red mullet. *British.* Any fish of the family Mullidae; a goatfish.
red·neck (rĕd′nĕk′) *n. Slang.* One of the white rural laboring class in the southern United States. Used disparagingly.
re·do (rē′dōō′) *tr.v.* **-did** (-dĭd′), **-done** (-dŭn′), **-doing, -does** (-dŭz′). **1.** To do over again. **2.** To redecorate.
red ocher. 1. A natural red mixture of clay and iron oxide; an **ocher** *(see).* **2.** A refined form of this mixture used as pigment.
red·o·lent (rĕd′ə-lənt) *adj.* **1.** Having or emitting fragrance; pleasantly odorous. **2.** Smelling. Used with *of: boatyards redolent of tar.* [Middle English, from Old French, from Latin *redolēns,* present participle of *redolēre,* to emit an odor : *red-, re-,* in response, back + *olēre,* to smell (see **od-**¹ in Appendix*).] **—red′o·lence, red′o·len·cy** *n.* **—red′o·lent·ly** *adv.*
red osier. A North American shrub, *Cornus stolonifera,* often forming dense clumps, and having red branches, white flowers, and bluish-white, berrylike fruit.
re·dou·ble (rē-dŭb′əl) *v.* **-bled, -bling, -bles.** *—tr.* **1.** To double. **2.** To repeat. **3.** *Archaic.* To echo or re-echo. **4.** To double the doubling bid of (an opponent in bridge). *—intr.* **1.** To be doubled; become twice as much or as great. **2.** *Archaic.* To echo; reverberate. **3.** To double a double in bridge.
re·doubt (rĭ-dout′) *n.* **1.** A small, often temporary defensive fortification. **2.** A reinforcing earthwork or breastwork within a permanent rampart. **3.** Any protected place of refuge or defense. [Old French *redoute,* from Old Italian *ridotto,* from Medieval Latin *reductus,* concealed place, from Latin, withdrawn, from the past participle of *redūcere,* withdraw : *re-,* back + *dūcere,* to lead (see **deuk-** in Appendix*).]
re·doubt·a·ble (rĭ-dou′tə-bəl) *adj.* **1.** Awesome; formidable; fearsome. **2.** Worthy of respect or honor. [Middle English, from Old French *redoutable,* from *redouter,* to dread : *re-* (intensive) + *douter,* to fear, DOUBT.] **—re·doubt′a·bly** *adv.*
re·dound (rĭ-dound′) *intr.v.* **-dounded, -dounding, -dounds. 1.** To have an effect or consequence: *deeds that redound to one's discredit.* **2.** To return; recoil. Used with *upon: Glory redounds upon the brave.* **3.** To contribute; accrue. [Middle English *redounden,* to abound, from Old French *redonder,* from Latin *redundāre,* to overflow : *red-, re-* (intensifier) + *undāre,* to overflow, surge, from *unda,* wave (see **wed-**¹ in Appendix*).]
re·dox (rē′dŏks′) *n. Chemistry.* **Oxidation-reduction** *(see).*
red-pen·cil (rĕd′pĕn′səl) *tr.v.* **-ciled, -ciling, -cils.** To censor, revise, or correct with or as if with a red pencil.
red pepper. 1. The pungent, red, podlike fruit of any of several varieties of the pepper plant, *Capsicum frutescens.* **2. Cayenne pepper** *(see).*
red pine. An evergreen timber tree, *Pinus resinosa,* of northeastern North America. Also called "Norway pine."
red·poll (rĕd′pōl′) *n.* Any of several finches of the genus *Acanthis,* having brownish plumage and a red crown.

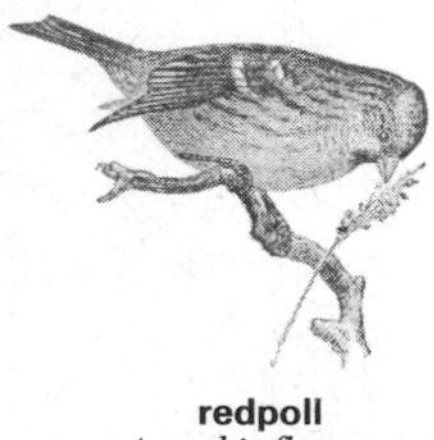

redpoll
Acanthis flammea

Red Poll. Any of a breed of reddish, hornless cattle developed in England and raised for dairy and meat products.
red puccoon. A plant, the **bloodroot** *(see).*
re·dress (rĭ-drĕs′) *tr.v.* **-dressed, -dressing, -dresses. 1.** To set right; remedy or rectify. **2.** To make amends to. **3.** To make amends for. **4.** To adjust (a balance, for example). —See Synonyms at **correct.** *—n.* (rĭ-drĕs′, rē′drĕs). **1.** Satisfaction or amends for wrong done. **2.** Correction or reformation. —See Synonyms at **reparation.** [Middle English *redressen,* from Old French *redresser* : *re-,* back + *dresser,* to make straight, DRESS.] **—re·dress′er, re·dres′sor** *n.*
Red River. 1. A river of the southwestern United States, rising in the Texas Panhandle and flowing 1,018 miles along the Texas-Oklahoma boundary, through Arkansas, and into Louisiana to join the Mississippi. **2.** A river of the United States and Canada, flowing northward 533 miles along the Minnesota-North Dakota boundary into Lake Winnipeg, Manitoba, Canada. Also called "Red River of the North." **3.** *Chinese* **Yu·an Kiang** (yōō-än′ jē-äng′); *Annamese* **Song Coi** (sông′koi′). A river of China and North Vietnam rising in Yunnan Province, China, and flowing in a southeasterly direction for about 730 miles past Hanoi to the Gulf of Tonkin.
red·root (rĕd′rōōt′) *n.* **1.** A bog plant, *Lachnanthes tinctoria,* of eastern North America, having red roots and woolly yellow flowers. **2.** Any of several plants having red roots, such as **pigweed** *(see).*
red salmon. The **sockeye salmon** *(see).*
Red Sea. An elongated body of water, about 170,000 square miles in area, separating the Arabian Peninsula from Africa and connected with the Mediterranean by the Suez Canal.

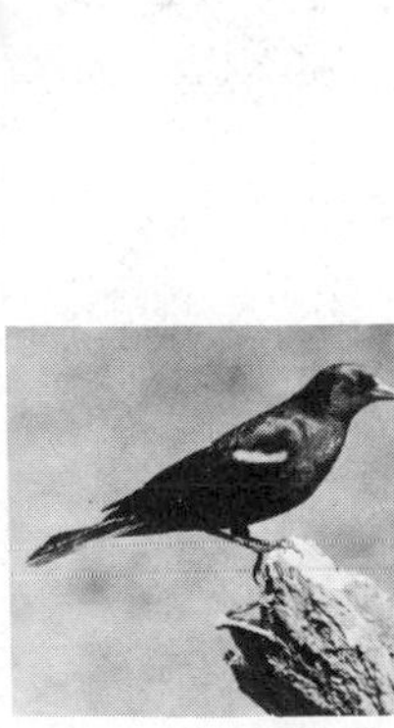

redwing
Agelaius phoeniceus

red·shank (rĕd′shăngk′) *n.* An Old World wading bird, *Tringa totanus,* having long red legs.
red shift. 1. An apparent increase in the wavelength of radiation emitted by a receding celestial body as a consequence of the **Doppler effect** *(see).* **2.** A similar increase in wavelength resulting from loss of energy by radiation moving against a gravitational field.
red·skin (rĕd′skĭn′) *n. Informal.* A North American Indian.
red snapper. Any of several marine food fishes of the genus *Lutjanus,* of tropical and semitropical waters, having red or reddish bodies.
red squill. 1. A plant, the **sea onion** *(see).* **2.** A powder prepared from the bulbs of this plant and used as a rat poison.
red squirrel. A North American squirrel, *Tamiasciurus hudsonicus,* having reddish or tawny fur. See **chickaree.**
red·start (rĕd′stärt′) *n.* **1.** A small North American bird, *Setophaga ruticilla,* the male of which has black plumage with orange patches on the wings and tail. **2.** A European bird, *Phoenicurus phoenicurus,* having grayish plumage and a rust-red breast and tail. [RED + obsolete *start,* tail, from Middle English *stert,* Old English *steort* (see **ster-**¹ in Appendix*).]
red tape. Impedimental use of official forms and procedures. [From the tape used to tie English governmental documents.]
red tide. Ocean waters colored by the proliferation of red, one-celled, plantlike animals in sufficient numbers to kill fish.
red·top (rĕd′tŏp′) *n.* A widely cultivated grass, *Agrostis alba,* native to Europe, having reddish flower clusters.
re·duce (rĭ-dōōs′, -dyōōs′) *v.* **-duced, -ducing, -duces.** *—tr.* **1.** To lessen in extent, amount, number, degree, price, or other quality; diminish. **2.** To gain control of; conquer. **3.** To put in order or arrange systematically. **4.** To separate into orderly components by analysis. **5.** To bring to a certain state or condition. **6.** To powder or pulverize. **7.** To thin (paint) with a solvent. **8.** *Chemistry.* **a.** To decrease the valence of (an atom) by adding electrons. **b.** To deoxidize. **c.** To add hydrogen to. **d.** To change to a metallic state by removing nonmetallic constituents; to smelt. **9.** *Mathematics.* To change the form of (an expression) without changing the value. **10.** *Photography.* To remove some of the silver from (an emulsion) forming a photographic image. **11.** *Surgery.* To restore (a fractured or displaced body part) to a normal condition. *—intr.* **1.** To become diminished. **2.** To lose weight, as by dieting. —See Synonyms at **decrease.** [Middle English *reducen,* bring back, from Latin *redūcere* : *re-,* back, again + *dūcere,* to lead (see **deuk-** in Appendix*).] **—re·duc′er** *n.* **—re·duc′i·bil′i·ty** *n.* **—re·duc′i·ble** *adj.* **—re·duc′i·bly** *adv.*
reducing agent. A substance that chemically reduces other substances. Also called "reductant."
re·duc·tase (rĭ-dŭk′tās′, -tāz′) *n.* Any enzyme that catalyzes biochemical reduction reactions. [REDUCT(ION) + -ASE.]
re·duc·ti·o ad ab·sur·dum (rĭ-dŭk′tē-ō ăd əb-sûr′dəm). Disproof of a proposition by showing the absurdity of its inevitable conclusion. [Latin, "reduction to absurdity."]
re·duc·tion (rĭ-dŭk′shən) *n. Abbr.* **red. 1.** The act or process of reducing. **2.** The result of reducing. **3.** The amount by which anything is lessened or diminished. **4.** *Biology.* The first meiotic division, in which the chromosome number is reduced. Also called "reduction division." **5.** *Chemistry.* A decrease in positive valence or an increase in negative valence by the gaining of electrons. Compare **oxidation. 6.** *Mathematics.* **a.** The canceling of common factors in the numerator and denominator of a fraction. **b.** The converting of a fraction to its decimal equivalent. [Middle English *reduccion,* from Old French *reduction,* from Late Latin *reductiō,* from Latin, from *redūcere,* to REDUCE.] **—re·duc′tion·al, re·duc′tive** *adj.*
reduction division. *Biology.* **1.** The first meiotic division, **reduction** *(see).* **2. Meiosis** *(see).*
re·dun·dan·cy (rĭ-dŭn′dən-sē) *n., pl.* **-cies.** Also **re·dun·dance** (-dəns). **1.** The state of being redundant. **2.** Superfluity or excess. **3.** Unnecessary repetition. **4.** *Technology.* **a.** Duplication or repetition of elements in electronic or mechanical equipment to provide alternative functional channels in case of failure. **b.** Repetition of parts or all of a message to circumvent transmission errors.
re·dun·dant (rĭ-dŭn′dənt) *adj.* **1.** Exceeding what is necessary or natural; superfluous. **2.** Needlessly repetitive; verbose. [Latin *redundāns,* present participle of *redundāre,* to overflow, run back : *red-, re-,* back + *undāre,* to overflow, from *unda,* wave (see **wed-**¹ in Appendix*).] **—re·dun′dant·ly** *adv.*
redupl. reduplicate; reduplication; reduplicative.
re·du·pli·cate (rĭ-dōō′plə-kāt′, rĭ-dyōō′-) *v.* **-cated, -cating, -cates.** *—tr.* **1.** To repeat over and over again; redouble. **2.** *Linguistics.* **a.** To double (the initial syllable or all of a root word) to produce an inflectional or derivational form. **b.** To form (a new word) by doubling all or part of a word. *—intr.* To be doubled. *—adj.* (rĭ-dōō′plə-kĭt, rĭ-dyōō′-). *Abbr.* **redupl.** Doubled. [Late Latin *reduplicāre* : Latin *re-,* again + *duplicāre,* to DUPLICATE.]
re·du·pli·ca·tion (rĭ-dōō′plə-kā′shən, rĭ-dyōō′-) *n. Abbr.* **redupl. 1.** A reduplicating or the state of being reduplicated. **2.** A product or result of reduplicating. **3.** A word formed by or containing a reduplicated element. **4.** The added element in a word form that is reduplicated. **—re·du′pli·ca′tive** *adj.* **—re·du′pli·ca′tive·ly** *adv.*
red·wing (rĕd′wĭng′) *n.* **1.** A North American blackbird, *Agelaius phoeniceus,* the male of which has scarlet patches on the wings. Also called "red-winged blackbird." **2.** A European thrush, *Turdus iliacus,* having reddish feathers under the wings.
red·wood (rĕd′wŏŏd′) *n.* **1.** A very tall evergreen tree, *Sequoia sempervirens,* of coastal and northern California. Compare **giant sequoia. 2.** The soft, reddish wood of this tree. **3.** Any of various woods of reddish color or yielding red dye.
re·ech·o (rĭ-ĕk′ō) *v.* **-oed, -oing, -oes.** *—intr.* To echo back; sound back or reverberate again. *—tr.* To echo back; send back; repeat.
reed (rēd) *n.* **1. a.** Any of various tall grasses having jointed, hollow stalks; especially, one of the genera *Phragmites* or *Arundo.* **b.** The stalk of one of these plants. **2.** A primitive wind instrument made of such a hollow stalk. **3.** *Music.* **a.** A flexible strip of cane or metal set into the mouthpiece of certain musical instruments to produce tone by vibrating in response to

a stream of air. **b.** An instrument, such as an oboe or clarinet, fitted with a reed. **4.** *Weaving.* A narrow, movable frame fitted with reed or metal strips that separate the warp threads. **5.** *Architecture.* A reeding. [Middle English *rede, reod,* Old English *hrēod.* See **kreut-** in Appendix.*]

Reed (rēd), **John.** 1887–1920. American journalist and poet.

Reed (rēd), **Walter.** 1851–1902. American physician; noted for research on yellow fever.

reed·bird (rēd′bûrd′) *n.* The **bobolink** *(see).*

reed·buck (rēd′bŭk′) *n.* Any of several African antelopes of the genus *Redunca.* [Translation of Afrikaans *rietbok.*]

reed·ing (rē′dĭng) *n. Architecture.* A convex decorative molding having parallel strips resembling thin reeds.

reed·ling (rēd′lĭng) *n.* A small Eurasian marsh bird, *Panurus biarmicus,* of which the male has mustachelike black markings.

reed mace. A plant, the **cattail** *(see).*

reed organ. A keyboard instrument in which free-beating reeds produce tones when acted upon by currents of air.

reed pipe. An organ pipe with a reed that vibrates and produces a tone when air is forced through it. Compare **flue pipe.**

reed stop. A stop on an organ made up of reed pipes having any of various tonal characteristics. Compare **flue stop.**

re·ed·u·cate (rē-ĕj′ŏŏ-kāt′) *tr.v.* **-cated, -cating, -cates. 1.** To instruct again. **2.** To retrain (a person) to function effectively; rehabilitate. —**re-ed′u·ca′tion** *n.*

reed·y (rē′dē) *adj.* **-ier, -iest. 1.** Full of reeds. **2.** Made of reeds. **3.** Resembling a reed. **4.** Having a tone like a reed instrument. —**reed′i·ness** *n.*

reef[1] (rēf) *n.* **1.** *Geology.* A strip or ridge of rocks, sand, or coral that rises to or near the surface of a body of water. **2.** *Mining.* A vein. —See Synonyms at **shoal.** [Earlier *riff,* from Middle Dutch *rif,* ridge, perhaps from Old Norse, rib, ridge. See **rebh-** in Appendix.*] —**reef′y** *adj.*

reef[2] (rēf) *n. Nautical.* A portion of a sail rolled and tied down to lessen the area exposed to the wind. —*tr.v.* **reefed, reefing, reefs. 1.** To reduce the size of (a sail) by tucking in a part and tying it to or rolling it around a yard. **2.** To shorten (a topmast or bowsprit) by taking part of it in. [Middle English *riff,* from Old Norse *rif,* ridge, rib. See **rebh-** in Appendix.*]

reef·er[1] (rē′fər) *n.* **1.** One who reefs, such as a midshipman. **2.** A short, heavy, close-fitting, double-breasted jacket.

reef·er[2] (rē′fər) *n. Slang.* A marijuana cigarette. [Perhaps from REEF (to roll up and shorten a sail).]

reef knot. A **square knot** *(see).*

reek (rēk) *v.* **reeked, reeking, reeks.** —*intr.* **1.** To smoke, steam, or fume. **2.** To be pervaded by something unpleasant. **3.** To give off or become permeated with a strong and unpleasant odor. —*tr.* **1.** To emit or exude (smoke, vapor, or odors, for example). **2.** To process or treat by exposing to the action of smoke. —*n.* **1.** A strong and offensive odor; stench. **2.** Vapor; steam. [Middle English *reken,* Old English *rēocan.* See **reug-** in Appendix.*] —**reek′er** *n.* —**reek′y** *adj.*

reel[1] (rēl) *n.* **1.** A cylinder, spool, or frame that turns on an axis and is used for winding rope, tape, or other flexible materials. **2.** Such a device attached to a fishing rod to let out or wind up the line. **3.** The quantity of wire, film, or other material wound on one reel. —*tr.v.* **reeled, reeling, reels. 1.** To wind upon a reel. **2.** To recover by winding on a reel. Used with *in: reel in the marlin.* **3.** To recite fluently. Used with *off: reel off the names and dates.* [Middle English *reel,* Old English *hrēol.* See **krek-**[1] in Appendix.*] —**reel′a·ble** *adj.*

reel[2] (rēl) *v.* **reeled, reeling, reels.** —*intr.* **1.** To be thrown off balance or fall back. **2.** To stagger, lurch, or sway, as from drunkenness. **3.** To go round and round in a whirling motion. **4.** To feel dizzy. —*tr.* To cause to reel. —*n.* A movement of staggering, swaying, or whirling. [Middle English *relen,* probably from REEL (spool).] —**reel′er** *n.*

reel[3] (rēl) *n.* **1.** A fast dance of Scottish origin. **2.** The Virginia reel. **3.** The music for a reel. [From REEL (whirl).]

re-en·force, re·en·force, re·ën·force. Variants of **reinforce.**

re-en·ter (rē-ĕn′tər) *v.* **-tered, -tering, -ters.** Also **re·en·ter, re·ën·ter.** —*intr.* To come in or enter again. —*tr.* To record again on a list or ledger. —**re-en′trance** *n.*

re-en·trant (rē-ĕn′trənt) *adj.* Also **re·en·trant, re·ën·trant.** Re-entering; pointing inward. —*n.* A re-entrant angle or part.

re-entrant angle. An interior angle of a polygon greater than 180 degrees.

re-en·try (rē-ĕn′trē) *n., pl.* **-tries.** Also **re·en·try, re·ën·try. 1.** The act of re-entering; a second or subsequent entry. **2.** *Law.* The recovery of possession under a right reserved in a previous property transaction. **3. a.** In bridge and whist, the act of regaining the lead by taking a trick. **b.** The card that will take a trick and thus regain the lead. **4.** *Aerospace.* The return of a missile or spacecraft into the earth's atmosphere.

reeve[1] (rēv) *n.* **1.** A high officer of local administration appointed by the Anglo-Saxon kings. **2.** In the later medieval period, a bailiff or steward of a manor. **3.** Any of various minor officers of parishes or other local authorities. **4.** The elected president of a town council in some parts of Canada. [Middle English *reve, reeve,* Old English *(ge)rēfa*†.]

reeve[2] (rēv) *tr.v.* **reeved** or **rove** (rōv), **reeving, reeves.** *Nautical.* **1.** To pass (a rope or rod) through a hole, ring, pulley, or block. **2.** To fasten by passing through or around. [Origin obscure.]

reeve[3] (rēv) *n.* A bird, the female **ruff** *(see).* [Possibly variant of RUFF.]

re-ex·am·ine (rē′ĭg-zăm′ĭn) *tr.v.* **-ined, -ining, -ines.** Also **re·ex·am·ine, re·ëx·am·ine. 1.** To examine again or anew; review. **2.** *Law.* To question (a witness) again after cross-examination. —**re′-ex·am′i·na′tion** *n.*

ref. **1.** referee. **2.** reference; referred. **3.** refining. **4.** reformation; reformed. **5.** refunding.

re·fect (rĭ-fĕkt′) *tr.v.* **-fected, -fecting, -fects.** *Obsolete.* To supply with food and drink. [Latin *reficere* (past participle *refectus*), to refresh : *re-,* again + *facere,* to make (see **dhē-**[1] in Appendix*).]

re·fec·tion (rĭ-fĕk′shən) *n.* **1.** Refreshment with food and drink. **2.** A light meal or repast. [Middle English *refeccioun,* from Old French *refection,* from Latin *refectiō,* a restoring, from *reficere,* to refresh. See **refect.**]

re·fec·to·ry (rĭ-fĕk′tə-rē) *n., pl.* **-ries.** A room where meals are served. [Late Latin *refectōrium,* from Latin *reficere,* to REFECT.]

re·fer (rĭ-fûr′) *v.* **-ferred, -ferring, -fers.** —*tr.* **1.** To direct to a source for help or information. **2.** To assign or attribute to; regard as originated by. **3.** To assign to or regard as belonging within a particular kind or class. **4.** To submit (a matter in dispute) to an authority for arbitration, decision, or examination. **5.** To direct the attention of. —*intr.* **1.** To pertain; concern; apply. **2.** To allude or make reference. **3.** To turn to, as for information or authority. —See Synonyms at **attribute.** [Middle English *refer(r)en,* from Old French *referer,* from Latin *referre,* refer to, carry back : *re-,* back, again + *ferre,* to carry (see **bher-**[1] in Appendix*).] —**ref′er·a·ble** (rĕf′ər-ə-bəl, rĭ-fûr′ə-bəl) *adj.* —**re·fer′ral** (rĭ-fûr′əl) *n.* —**re·fer′rer** *n.*

ref·e·ree (rĕf′ə-rē′) *n. Abbr.* **ref. 1.** One to whom something is referred, especially for settlement or decision; an arbitrator. **2.** *Sports.* An official supervising the play; umpire. **3.** *Law.* A person appointed by a court to examine and report on a case. —See Synonyms at **judge.** —*v.* **refereed, -reeing, -rees.** —*tr.* To judge as referee. —*intr.* To act as referee.

ref·er·ence (rĕf′ər-əns, rĕf′rəns) *n. Abbr.* **ref. 1.** An act of referring. **2. a.** One that is referred to. **b.** Significance in a specified context. **c.** Meaning (of a linguistic referent). **3.** The state of being related or referred. Used in the phrases *with reference to; in reference to.* **4.** A direction of attention; an allusion to an occurrence or situation. **5. a.** A note in a publication referring the reader to another passage or source. **b.** The passage or source so referred to. **c.** A mark or footnote used to direct a reader elsewhere for additional information. **6.** *Law.* **a.** The submission of a case to a referee. **b.** Legal actions conducted before or by a referee. **7. a.** One to whom another may refer for a recommendation when seeking employment or an introduction. **b.** A statement attesting to personal qualifications, character, and dependability. —**ref′er·enc·er** *n.* —**ref′er·en′tial** (-ə-rĕn′shəl) *adj.*

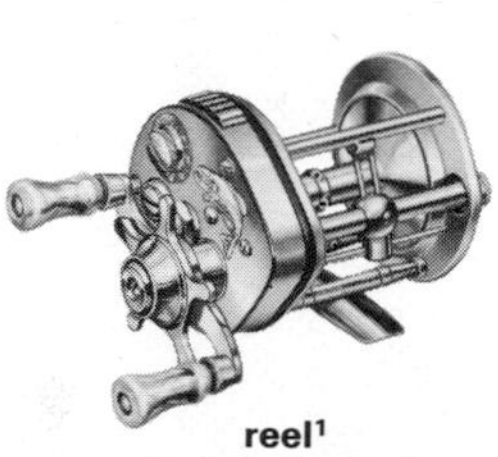

reel[1]
Bait-casting reel

ref·er·en·dum (rĕf′ə-rĕn′dəm) *n., pl.* **-dums** or **-da** (-də). **1.** The submission of a proposed public measure or actual statute to a direct popular vote. **2.** Such a vote. **3.** A note from a diplomat to his government requesting instructions. [Latin, neuter gerundive of *referre,* to REFER.]

ref·er·ent (rĕf′ər-ənt, rĭ-fûr′ənt) *n.* **1.** Something that refers, especially a linguistic item in its capacity of referring to a meaning. **2.** Something referred to. [Latin *referēns,* present participle of *referre,* REFER.]

re·fill (rē-fĭl′) *tr.v.* **-filled, -filling, -fills.** To fill again. —*n.* (rē′fĭl′). **1.** A product packaged to replace the used contents of a container. **2.** A second or subsequent filling.

re·fine (rĭ-fīn′) *v.* **-fined, -fining, -fines.** —*tr.* **1.** To reduce to a pure state; purify. **2.** To remove by purifying. Used with *out* or *away.* **3.** To free from coarse characteristics. —*intr.* **1.** To become free of impurities. **2.** To acquire polish or elegance. **3.** To use subtlety and precise distinctions in thought or speech. [RE- + FINE (verb).] —**re·fin′er** *n.*

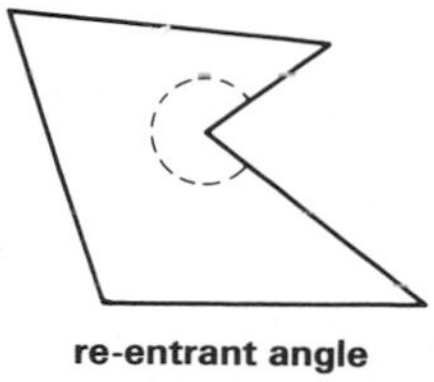

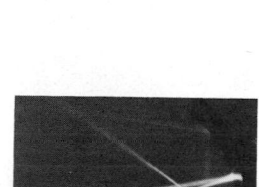

re-entrant angle

re·fined (rĭ-fīnd′) *adj.* **1.** Free from coarseness or vulgarity; polite; genteel. **2.** Free of impurities; purified. **3.** Precise to a fine degree; subtle; exact.

re·fine·ment (rĭ-fīn′mənt) *n.* **1. a.** An act of refining. **b.** The state of being refined. **2.** The result of refining; an improvement or elaboration. **3.** Fineness of thought or expression; polish; cultivation. **4.** A keen or precise phrasing; subtle distinction. —See Synonyms at **culture.**

re·fin·er·y (rĭ-fī′nə-rē) *n., pl.* **-ies.** An industrial plant for purifying a crude substance, such as petroleum, sugar, fat, or ore.

re·fin·ish (rē-fĭn′ĭsh) *tr.v.* **-ished, -ishing, -ishes.** To put a new finish on (furniture). —**re·fin′ish·er** *n.*

re·fit (rē-fĭt′) *v.* **-fitted, -fitting, -fits.** —*tr.* To prepare and equip for additional use. —*intr.* To be made fit again. —*n.* (rē′fĭt′, rē-fĭt′). **1.** The repair of damage or wear. **2.** A secondary or subsequent preparation of supplies and equipment.

refl. **1.** reflection; reflective. **2.** reflex; reflexive.

re·flect (rĭ-flĕkt′) *v.* **-flected, -flecting, -flects.** —*tr.* **1.** To throw or bend back (heat, light, or sound, for example) from a surface. **2.** To form an image of (an object); to mirror. **3.** To manifest as a result of one's actions: *His work reflects intelligence.* **4.** *Archaic.* To bend back. —*intr.* **1.** To be bent back. **2.** To give back a likeness; become mirrored. **3.** To think or consider seriously. **4.** To bring blame or reproach. [Middle English *reflecten,* from Old French *reflecter,* from Latin *reflectere,* to bend back : *re-,* back + *flectere,* to FLEX.]

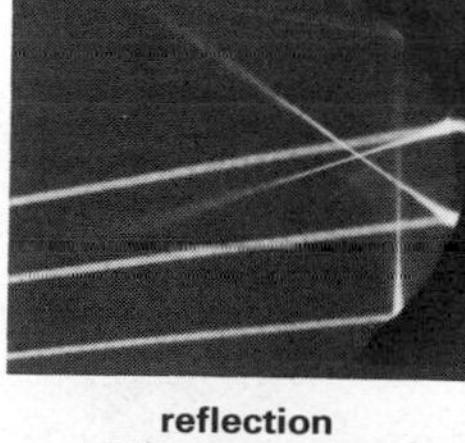

reflection
Differing angles of incidence cause different angles of reflection

re·flec·tance (rĭ-flĕk′təns) *n.* The ratio of the total radiant flux, as of light, reflected by a surface to the total incident on the surface. Compare **absorptance.**

reflecting telescope. An optical telescope in which the principal image-forming element is a parabolic or spherical mirror. Also called "reflector." Compare **refracting telescope.**

re·flec·tion (rĭ-flĕk′shən) *n.* Also *chiefly British* **re·flex·ion.** *Abbr.* **refl. 1.** The act or state of being reflected. **2.** Something reflected, as light, radiant heat, sound, or an image. **3. a.** Con-

centration of the mind; careful consideration. **b.** The results of such consideration, communicated or not. **4.** An imputation of censure or discredit. —**re·flec′tion·al** *adj.*

re·flec·tive (rĭ-flĕk′tĭv) *adj. Abbr.* **refl.** **1.** Of, pertaining to, produced by, or resulting from reflection. **2.** Meditative; pensive. —See Synonyms at **pensive.** —**re·flec′tive·ly** *adv.*

re·flec·tiv·i·ty (rē′flĕk-tĭv′ə-tē) *n., pl.* **-ties.** **1.** The quality of being reflective. **2.** The ability to reflect. **3.** *Physics.* The ratio of the intensity of the total radiation, as of light, reflected from a surface to the total incident on the surface.

re·flec·tor (rĭ-flĕk′tər) *n.* **1.** That which reflects. **2.** A surface that reflects radiation. **3.** A **reflecting telescope** *(see).*

re·flex (rē′flĕks′) *adj. Abbr.* **refl.** **1.** Turned, thrown, or bent backward. **2.** *Physiology.* Designating an involuntary action or response, such as a sneeze, blink, or hiccup. —*n.* (rē′flĕks′). *Abbr.* **refl.** **1.** Reflection or an image produced by reflection. **2.** *Physiology.* An involuntary response to a stimulus. **3.** *Psychology.* An unlearned or instinctive response to a stimulus. **4.** *Linguistics.* A form or feature that reflects or represents an earlier (often reconstructed) form or feature having undergone phonetic or other change. —*tr.v.* (rĭ-flĕks′) **reflexed, -flexing, -flexes.** **1.** To bend, turn back, or reflect. **2.** To cause to undergo a reflex process. [Latin *reflexus,* past participle of *reflectere,* to REFLECT.]

reflex angle. An angle greater than 180 degrees and less than 360 degrees.

reflex arc. *Physiology.* The neural path of a simple reflex.

reflex camera. A camera fitted with a mirror to reflect the exact focused image that can be recorded onto a coupled viewing screen.

re·flex·ive (rĭ-flĕk′sĭv) *adj.* **1.** *Abbr.* **refl.** *Grammar.* **a.** Designating a verb having an identical subject and direct object, as *dressed* in the sentence *She dressed herself.* **b.** Designating the pronoun used as direct object of a reflexive verb, as *herself* in the preceding example. **2.** Of or pertaining to a reflex. —*n.* A reflexive verb or pronoun. —**re·flex′ive·ly** *adv.* —**re·flex′ive·ness, re′flex·iv′i·ty** (rē′flĕk-sĭv′ə-tē) *n.*

ref·lu·ent (rĕf′lo͞o-ənt) *adj.* Flowing back; ebbing. [Latin *refluēns,* present participle of *refluere,* flow back : *re-,* back + *fluere,* flow (see **bhleu-** in Appendix*).] —**ref′lu·ence** *n.*

re·flux (rē′flŭks′) *n.* A flowing back; ebb. [Middle English, from Medieval Latin *refluxus* : Latin *re-,* back + *fluxus,* a flow, from *fluere,* to flow (see **bhleu-** in Appendix*).]

re·for·est (rē-fôr′ĭst, -fŏr′ĭst) *tr.v.* **-ested, -esting, -ests.** To replant (an area) with forest trees. —**re′for·es·ta′tion** *n.*

re-form (rē-fôrm′) *v.* **-formed, -forming, -forms.** —*tr.* To form again. —*intr.* To become formed again. [RE- + FORM.]

re·form (rĭ-fôrm′) *v.* **-formed, -forming, -forms.** —*tr.* **1.** To improve by alteration, correction of error, or removal of defects. **2.** To abolish abuse or malpractice in. **3.** To cause (a person) to abandon irresponsible or immoral practices. —*intr.* To behave better; give up irresponsible or immoral practices. —See Synonyms at **correct.** —*n.* **1.** A change for the better; a correction of evils or abuses. **2.** A movement that attempts to institute improved social and political conditions without revolutionary change. **3.** Moral improvement. [Middle English *reformen,* from Old French *reformer,* from Latin *refōrmāre* : *re-,* again, back + *fōrmāre,* to form, from *fōrma,* FORM.] —**re·for′ma·tive** *adj.* —**re·form′er** *n.*

ref·or·ma·tion (rĕf′ər-mā′shən) *n. Abbr.* **ref.** **1.** The act of reforming, or state of being reformed. **2.** *Capital* **R.** The effort in the 16th century to reconstitute the life and teaching of Western Christendom, resulting in the separation of the Protestant churches from the Roman Catholic Church. —**ref′or·ma′tion·al** *adj.*

re·for·ma·to·ry (rĭ-fôr′mə-tôr′ē, -tōr′ē) *n., pl.* **-ries.** A penal institution for the discipline, reformation, and training of juvenile and first offenders. Also called "reform school." —*adj.* Serving or intending to reform. [Latin *refōrmāre* (past participle *refōrmātus*), to REFORM + -ORY.]

re·formed (rĭ-fôrmd′) *adj. Abbr.* **ref.** **1.** Improved or amended by the removal of faults. **2.** Improved in conduct or character. **3.** *Capital* **R.** Of, pertaining to, or denoting the Protestant churches that follow the teachings of Calvin and Zwingli. **4.** *Capital* **R.** Of, pertaining to, or denoting Reform Judaism.

re·form·ism (rĭ-fôr′mĭz′əm) *n.* A doctrine or movement of reform. —**re·form′ist** *n.*

Reform Judaism. A branch of Judaism introduced in the 19th century that endeavors to reconcile historical Judaism with present-day life without requiring strict observance of traditional law. Compare **Conservative Judaism, Orthodox Judaism.**

re·fract (rĭ-frăkt′) *tr.v.* **-fracted, -fracting, -fracts.** To deflect (light, for example) by refraction. [Latin *refringere* (past participle *refractus*), to break off : *re-,* away, backward + *frangere,* to break (see **bhreg-** in Appendix*).]

refracting telescope. A telescope in which the final image is produced entirely by lenses. Also called "refractor." Compare **reflecting telescope.**

re·frac·tion (rĭ-frăk′shən) *n. Abbr.* **refr.** **1.** *Physics.* The deflection of a propagating wave, as of light or sound, at the boundary between two mediums with different refractive indices, or in passage through a medium of nonuniform density. **2.** *Astronomy.* The apparent positional elevation of celestial objects caused by deflection of light entering the earth's atmosphere. —**re·frac′tion·al, re·frac′tive** *adj.* —**re·frac′tive·ly** *adv.* —**re·frac′tive·ness, re′frac·tiv′i·ty** (rē′frăk-tĭv′ə-tē) *n.*

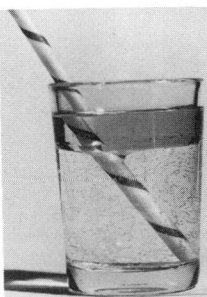

refraction
Differing indices of refraction for air, glass, oil, and water shown by displacement of a drinking straw

refractive index. *Physics.* **Index of refraction** *(see).*

re·frac·tom·e·ter (rē′frăk-tŏm′ə-tər) *n.* Any of several instruments that measure indices of refraction.

re·frac·tor (rĭ-frăk′tər) *n.* **1.** One that refracts. **2.** A **refracting telescope** *(see).*

re·frac·to·ry (rĭ-frăk′tə-rē) *adj.* **1.** Obstinate; unmanageable. **2.** Difficult to melt or work; resistant to heat. **3.** Not responsive to treatment: *a refractory disease.* —See Synonyms at **unruly.** —*n., pl.* **refractories.** **1.** Any of various materials such as alumina, silica, and magnesite that do not significantly deform or change chemically at high temperatures. **2.** *Plural.* Bricks of such materials and of various shapes used to line furnaces. [Earlier *refractary,* from Latin *refractārius,* from *refringere* (past participle *refractus*), to break off, REFRACT.] —**re·frac′to·ri·ly** *adv.* —**re·frac′to·ri·ness** *n.*

re·frain[1] (rĭ-frān′) *v.* **-frained, -fraining, -frains.** —*intr.* To hold oneself back; forbear. Used with *from: Kindly refrain from singing.* —*tr. Archaic.* To restrain or hold back; to curb. [Middle English *refreynen,* from Old French *refrener,* from Latin *refrēnāre,* hold back, bridle : *re-,* back + *frēnum,* bridle (see **ghren-** in Appendix*).] —**re·frain′er** *n.* —**re·frain′ment** *n.*

re·frain[2] (rĭ-frān′) *n.* **1. a.** A phrase or verse repeated at intervals throughout a song or poem, especially at the end of each stanza. **b.** Music for the refrain of a poem. **2.** A repetitious utterance or theme. [Middle English *refreyn,* from Old French *refrain,* from *refraindre,* echo, to break off (a refrain "breaks off" to recur at intervals), from Vulgar Latin *refrangere* (unattested), from Latin *refringere,* to break off, REFRACT.]

re·fran·gi·ble (rĭ-frăn′jə-bəl) *adj.* Capable of being refracted. [RE- + FRANGIBLE.] —**re·fran′gi·bil′i·ty, re·fran′gi·ble·ness** *n.*

re·fresh (rĭ-frĕsh′) *v.* **-freshed, -freshing, -freshes.** Also **re·freshen.** —*tr.* **1.** To revive (a person) with or as if with rest, food, or drink. **2.** To make cool, clean, or damp; freshen. **3.** To renew by stimulation: *refresh one's memory.* —*intr.* **1.** To take refreshment. **2.** To become revived; reinvigorate. [Middle English *refresshen,* from Old French *refreschir, refreschier* : *re-,* again + *freis, fresche,* FRESH.]

re·fresh·er (rĭ-frĕsh′ər) *n.* One who or that which refreshes. —*adj.* Serving to reacquaint one with material previously studied: *a refresher course.*

re·fresh·ing (rĭ-frĕsh′ĭng) *adj.* **1.** Serving to refresh. **2.** Pleasantly new and different; unusual. —**re·fresh′ing·ly** *adv.*

re·fresh·ment (rĭ-frĕsh′mənt) *n.* **1.** The act of refreshing or state of being refreshed; reinvigoration; revival. **2.** Something that refreshes, such as food or drink. **3.** *Plural.* A light meal or snack.

re·frig·er·ant (rĭ-frĭj′ər-ənt) *adj.* **1.** Cooling or freezing; refrigerating. **2.** *Medicine.* Reducing fever. —*n.* **1.** A substance such as air, ammonia, water, or carbon dioxide used to produce refrigeration, either as the working substance of a refrigerator or by direct absorption of heat. **2.** *Medicine.* Any agent used to reduce fever.

re·frig·er·ate (rĭ-frĭj′ə-rāt′) *tr.v.* **-ated, -ating, -ates.** **1.** To cool or chill (a substance). **2.** To preserve (food) by chilling. [Latin *refrigerāre* : *re-,* repeatedly, again + *frigerāre,* to make cool, from *frigus* (stem *frigor-*), cool (see **srig-** in Appendix*).] —**re·frig′er·a′tion** *n.* —**re·frig′er·a′tive** *adj.* & *n.* —**re·frig′er·a·to′ry** (-ər-ə-tôr′ē, -tōr′ē) *adj.*

re·frig·er·a·tor (rĭ-frĭj′ə-rā′tər) *n.* An apparatus for reducing and maintaining the temperature of a chamber below the temperature of the external environment.

re·frin·gent (rĭ-frĭn′jənt) *adj.* Of, pertaining to, or producing refraction; refractive. [Latin *refringens,* present participle of *refringere,* to REFRACT.]

reft. Alternate past tense and past participle of **reave.**

re·fu·el (rē-fyo͞o′əl) *v.* **-eled, -eling, -els.** —*tr.* To supply again with fuel. —*intr.* To take on a fresh supply of fuel.

ref·uge (rĕf′yo͞oj) *n.* **1.** Protection or shelter, as from danger or hardship. **2.** A place providing protection or shelter; haven or sanctuary. **3.** Anything to which one may turn for help, relief, or escape: *Silence was his only refuge.* —See Synonyms at **shelter.** —*v.* **refuged, -uging, -uges.** *Archaic.* —*tr.* To give refuge to. —*intr.* To take refuge. [Middle English, from Old French, from Latin *refugium,* from *refugere,* flee back : *re-,* away, back + *fugere,* to flee (see **bheug-**[1] in Appendix*).]

ref·u·gee (rĕf′yo͞o-jē′) *n.* A person who flees to find refuge; especially, one who escapes from invasion, oppression, or persecution. [French *réfugié,* from the past participle of *réfugier,* to put in a refuge, from *refuge,* REFUGE.]

re·ful·gent (rĭ-fŭl′jənt) *adj.* Shining radiantly; brilliant; resplendent. [Latin *refulgēns,* present participle of *refulgēre,* to flash back : *re-,* back + *fulgēre,* to flash (see **bhel-**[1] in Appendix*).] —**re·ful′gence, re·ful′gen·cy** *n.* —**re·ful′gent·ly** *adv.*

re·fund[1] (rĭ-fŭnd′, rē′fŭnd′) *v.* **-funded, -funding, -funds.** —*tr.* **1.** To return or repay; give back. **2.** To repay (a person); reimburse. —*intr.* To make repayment. —*n.* (rē′fŭnd′). **1.** A repayment of funds. **2.** The amount repaid. [Middle English *refunden,* to pour back, from Old French *refunder,* from Latin *refundere* : *re-,* back + *fundere,* to pour (see **gheu-** in Appendix*).] —**re·fund′er** *n.* —**re·rund′ment** *n.*

re·fund[2] (rē-fŭnd′) *tr.v.* **-funded, -funding, -funds.** **1.** To fund anew. **2.** *Finance.* To pay back (a debt) with new borrowing; especially, to replace (a bond issue) with a new bond issue.

re·fur·bish (rē-fûr′bĭsh) *tr.v.* **-bished, -bishing, -bishes.** To make clean, bright, or fresh again; renovate. —**re·fur′bish·ment** *n.*

re·fus·al (rĭ-fyo͞o′zəl) *n.* **1.** The act of refusing. **2.** The opportunity to accept or reject; option.

re·fuse[1] (rĭ-fyo͞oz′) *v.* **-fused, -fusing, -fuses.** —*tr.* **1.** To decline to do, accept, give, or allow. **2.** To decline to jump (an obstacle). Used of a horse. —*intr.* To decline to do, accept, allow, or give something. [Middle English *refusen,* from Old French *refuser,* from Vulgar Latin *refūsāre* (unattested), from Latin

refundere (past participle *refūsus*), to pour back. See **refund.**] **—re·fus′er** *n.*

Synonyms: *refuse, decline, reject, spurn, rebuff, ignore.* These verbs imply negation or denial in varying manner. *Refuse* is used of a positive, unyielding, sometimes brusque decision not to act, accept, or do something. *Decline* involves withholding consent but usually doing so courteously: *decline an invitation. Reject* applies to a blunt, even hostile, refusal to do something. *Spurn* is to reject scornfully, contemptuously. *Rebuff* pertains to the disdainful refusal to accept something offered. *Ignore* implies affront in not recognizing the presence or existence of a person or proposal.

ref·use[2] (rĕf′yo͞os) *n.* Anything discarded or rejected as useless or worthless; trash; rubbish. *—adj.* Discarded or rejected as useless or worthless. [Middle English, something rejected, from Old French *refus,* refusal, from *refuser,* to REFUSE.]

ref·u·ta·tion (rĕf′yo͞o-tā′shən) *n.* Also **re·fu·tal** (rĭ-fyo͞ot′l). **1.** The act of refuting. **2.** Something that refutes.

re·fute (rĭ-fyo͞ot′) *tr.v.* **-futed, -futing, -futes. 1.** To prove (a statement or argument) to be false or erroneous; disprove. **2.** To prove (a person) to be wrong. —See Synonyms at **deny.** [Latin *refūtāre,* rebut, drive back. See **bhau-** in Appendix.*] **—re·fut′a·bil′i·ty** (rĭ-fyo͞o′tə-bĭl′ə-tē, rĕf′yə-tə-) *n.* **—re·fut′a·ble** *adj.* **—re·fut′a·bly** *adv.* **—re·fut′er** *n.*

reg. 1. regent. **2.** regiment. **3.** region. **4.** register; registered. **5.** registrar. **6.** registry. **7.** regular; regularly. **8.** regulation. **9.** regulator.

re·gain (rē-gān′) *tr.v.* **-gained, -gaining, -gains. 1.** To recover possession of; get back again. **2.** To manage to reach again. —See Synonyms at **recover. —re·gain′er** *n.*

re·gal (rē′gəl) *adj.* **1.** Of or pertaining to a king; royal. **2.** Belonging to or befitting a king: *regal attire.* [Middle English, from Old French, from Latin *rēgālis,* royal, from *rēx* (stem *rēg-*), king. See **reg-**[1] in Appendix.*] **—re′gal·ly** *adv.*

re·gale (rĭ-gāl′) *v.* **-galed, -galing, -gales.** *—tr.* **1.** To delight or entertain; give pleasure to. **2.** To entertain sumptuously with food and drink; provide a feast for. *—intr.* To feast. —See Synonyms at **amuse.** *—n. Obsolete.* **1.** A great feast; a sumptuous repast. **2.** A choice food or drink; delicacy. **3.** Refreshment. [French *régaler,* from Old French *regaler,* from *regal,* REGAL.] **—re·gale′ment** *n.*

re·ga·lia (rĭ-gāl′yə, -gā′lē-ə) *n.* Plural in form, often used with a singular verb. **1.** The emblems and symbols of royalty, as the crown and scepter. **2.** The rights and privileges of royalty. **3.** The distinguishing symbols of any rank, office, order, or society. **4.** Magnificent or fancy attire; finery. [Medieval Latin *rēgālia,* plural of *rēgāle,* royal prerogative, from Latin, neuter of *rēgālis,* REGAL.]

re·gal·i·ty (rĭ-găl′ə-tē) *n., pl.* **-ties. 1.** Royalty or sovereignty; kingship. **2.** A country or area under the authority of a monarch; kingdom. **3.** The rights or privileges of a king.

re·gard (rĭ-gärd′) *v.* **-garded, -garding, -gards.** *—tr.* **1.** To look at attentively; observe closely. **2.** To look upon or consider in a particular way: *I regard him as a fool.* **3.** To have great affection or admiration for: *She regards her father highly.* **4.** To relate, concern, or refer to: *This item regards your question.* **5.** To consider or take into account: *regard the fact that man is mortal.* **6.** *Obsolete.* To take care of. *—intr.* **1.** To look; to gaze. **2.** To give heed; pay attention. —See Synonyms at **consider.** *—n.* **1.** A look or gaze. **2.** Careful thought or attention; concern; heed: *He gives little regard to his appearance.* **3.** Respect, affection, or esteem: *He has won the regard of all.* **4.** *Plural.* Sentiments of respect or affection; good wishes: *send one's regards.* **5.** Reference or relation: *in regard to this case.* **6.** A particular point or respect: *I agree in this regard.* **7.** *Obsolete.* Appearance or aspect. [Middle English *regarden,* from Old French *regarder, reguarder,* to look at, regard : *re-,* back, back at + *guarder, garder,* to GUARD.]

Synonyms: *regard, esteem, admiration, approbation.* These terms refer in varying degree to the appreciation of the worth of a person or thing. *Regard* is the least forceful, a general term implying affection and recognition of worth; in the plural it is often used as a courteous close to a letter or message: *with best regards. Esteem* connotes measured, considered, and pleasurable appraisal of worth: *esteem for a distinguished scholar. Admiration* is undisguised pleasure, delight, and wonder in contemplating something unusual, beautiful, or skillful. *Approbation* is the approval or commendation of something after careful consideration of its worth.

Usage: *Regard* (noun), in denoting reference, is found principally in the combinations *in* (or *with*) *regard to* (but not *in,* or *with, regards to*). The terms *regarding* and *respecting* (used as prepositions) and the expression *as regards* are acceptable in the same sense, though sometimes disparaged by stylists. Both *regard* and *respect* have the sense of *particular: In some respects the books are alike.* But *respect* is much more appropriate to such constructions; 84 per cent of the Usage Panel term *in some regards* unacceptable in the preceding example. *Regard,* as a verb equivalent to *consider,* is normally used with *as,* not with the infinitive *to be: I regard it as an insult* (rather than *I regard it an insult* or *regard it to be an insult*).

re·gar·dant (rĭ-gär′dənt) *adj. Heraldry.* With the face turned backward in profile. [Middle English, from Old French, from *regarder,* to REGARD.]

re·gard·ful (rĭ-gärd′fəl) *adj.* **1.** Showing regard; observant; heedful. Often used with *of.* **2.** Showing deference; respectful; considerate. **—re·gard′ful·ly** *adv.* **—re·gard′ful·ness** *n.*

re·gard·ing (rĭ-gär′dĭng) *prep.* In reference to; with respect to; concerning. See Usage note at **regard.**

re·gard·less (rĭ-gärd′lĭs) *adj.* Heedless; unmindful. Often used with *of.* *—adv.* In spite of everything; anyway.

re·gard·less·ly (rĭ-gärd′lĭs-lē) *adv.* In a regardless manner. **—re·gard′less·ness** *n.*

re·gat·ta (rĭ-gä′tə, -găt′ə) *n.* A boat race or an organized series of boat races. [Italian (Venetian dialect) *regatta, regata*†, gondola race.]

regd. registered.

re·ge·late (rē′jə-lāt′, rē′jə-lāt′) *intr.v.* **-lated, -lating, -lates.** To undergo regelation. [Back-formation from REGELATION.]

re·ge·la·tion (rē′jə-lā′shən) *n.* **1.** The fusion of two blocks of ice by pressure. **2.** Successive melting under pressure and freezing when pressure is relaxed at the interface of two blocks of ice. [RE- + GELATION.]

re·gen·cy (rē′jən-sē) *n., pl.* **-cies. 1.** The office, area of jurisdiction, or government of a regent or regents. **2.** A person or group selected to govern in place of a king or other ruler in case of minority, absence, incompetence, or sickness. **3.** The period during which a regent governs, as in England (1811–20) or France (1715–23). *—adj.* Also **Re·gen·cy.** Of, relating to, or characteristic of the style, especially in furniture, prevalent during the regency (1811–20) of George, Prince of Wales.

re·gen·er·a·cy (rĭ-jĕn′ər-ə-sē) *n.* The state of being regenerated.

re·gen·er·ate (rĭ-jĕn′ə-rāt′) *v.* **-ated, -ating, -ates.** *—tr.* **1.** To reform spiritually or morally. **2.** To form, construct, or create anew. **3.** *Biology.* To replace (a lost or damaged organ or part) by formation of new tissue. *—intr.* **1.** To become formed or constructed again. **2.** To undergo spiritual conversion or rebirth. **3.** To effect regeneration. *—adj.* (rĭ-jĕn′ər-ĭt). **1.** Spiritually or morally revitalized. **2.** Restored; refreshed; renewed. [Latin *regenerāre,* to reproduce : *re-,* again + *generāre,* to beget, GENERATE.] **—re·gen′er·a′tive** (-ə-rā′tĭv, -ər-ə-tĭv) *adj.* **—re·gen′er·a′tive·ly** *adv.*

re·gen·er·a·tion (rĭ-jĕn′ə-rā′shən) *n.* **1.** The act or process of regenerating or the state of being regenerated. **2.** Spiritual or moral revival or rebirth. **3.** *Biology.* The regrowth of lost or destroyed parts or organs.

re·gen·er·a·tor (rĭ-jĕn′ə-rā′tər) *n.* One that regenerates.

Re·gens·burg (rā′gəns-bo͝ork′). Also **Rat·is·bon** (răt′ĭs-bŏn′). A city on the Danube in eastern Bavaria, West Germany. Population, 125,000.

re·gent (rē′jənt) *n. Abbr.* **reg., Regt. 1.** One who rules during the absence or disability of a sovereign. **2.** One acting as a ruler or governor. **3.** A person serving on a board that governs a university or other educational institution or system in the United States. [Middle English, from Old French, ruling, from Medieval Latin *regēns,* from Latin, present participle of *regere,* to rule. See **reg-**[1] in Appendix.*] **—re′gent** *adj.*

Reg·gio di Ca·la·bri·a (răd′jō dē kä-lä′brē-ä). Also **Reg·gio, Reg·gio Ca·la·bri·a.** A city in southern Italy, on the Strait of Messina opposite Sicily. Population, 157,000.

Reg·gio nell′E·mi·lia (răd′jō nāl′lā-mē′lyä). Also **Reg·gio, Reg·gio E·mi·lia** (răd′jō ā-mē′lyä). A city and manufacturing center of north-central Emilia-Romagna, Italy. Population, 122,000.

reg·i·cide (rĕj′ə-sīd′) *n.* **1.** The killing of a king. **2.** One who kills or helps to kill a king. [Latin *rēx* (stem *rēg-*), king (see **reg-**[1] in Appendix*) + -CIDE.] **—reg′i·ci′dal** (-sīd′l) *adj.*

re·gime (rā-zhēm′, rĭ-) *n.* Also **ré·gime. 1.** A system of management of government; an administration. **2.** A social system or pattern. **3.** A regimen. [French *régime,* from Latin *regimen,* from *regere,* to rule. See **reg-**[1] in Appendix.*]

reg·i·men (rĕj′ə-mən, -mĕn′) *n.* **1.** Governmental rule or control. **2.** The systematic procedure of a natural phenomenon or process. **3.** A system of therapy: *a dietetic regimen.* [Middle English, from Latin, REGIME.]

reg·i·ment (rĕj′ə-mənt) *n. Abbr.* **reg., regt.** A military unit of ground troops, consisting of at least two battalions and sometimes other units. *—tr.v.* (rĕj′ə-mĕnt′) **reg·i·mented, -menting, -ments. 1.** To organize or form into a regiment or regiments. **2.** To appoint to a regiment. **3.** To put into order; systematize. **4.** To force uniformity and discipline upon. [Middle English, from Old French, from Late Latin *regimentum,* from Latin *regere,* to rule. See **reg-**[1] in Appendix.*] **—reg′i·men′tal** *adj.* **—reg′i·men·ta′tion** *n.*

reg·i·men·tals (rĕj′ə-mĕnt′əlz) *pl.n.* **1.** The uniform and insignia characteristic of a particular regiment. **2.** Military dress.

Re·gi·na (rĭ-jī′nə). The capital of Saskatchewan, Canada. Population, 112,000.

Reg·i·nald (rĕj′ə-nəld). A masculine given name. [Middle English *Reginaldus,* Old English *Regenweald* : *regen,* power (see **rēk-** in Appendix*) + *weald,* force (see **wal-** in Appendix*).]

Re·gi·o·mon·ta·nus (rē′jē-ō-mŏn-tā′nəs, -tä′nəs, -tăn′əs, rĕj′ē-). Original name, Johann Müller. 1436–1476. German mathematician and astronomer.

re·gion (rē′jən) *n. Abbr.* **reg. 1.** Any large, usually continuous segment of a surface or space; an area. **2.** A large and indefinite portion of the earth's surface. **3.** A specified district or territory. **4.** A field of interest or activity; sphere. **5.** A part of the earth characterized by distinctive animal or plant life. **6.** An area of the body having natural or arbitrarily assigned boundaries: *the abdominal region.* —See Synonyms at **area.** [Middle English *regioun,* kingdom, from Old French *region,* from Latin *regiō,* direction, boundary, from *regere,* to direct. See **reg-**[1] in Appendix.*]

re·gion·al (rē′jən-əl) *adj.* **1.** Of, pertaining to, or characteristic of a large geographic region. **2.** Of, pertaining to, or characteristic of a particular region or district; localized. **3.** Of, belonging to, or characteristic of a form of a language that is distributed in identifiable geographic areas and has identifiable phonetic, structural, and other differences from the standard form of the language; dialectal. —**re′gion·al·ly** *adv.*

ré·gis·seur (rā′zhē-sœr′) *n., pl.* **-seurs** (-sœr′). *French.* The director of a ballet.

reg·is·ter (rĕj′ĭ-stər) *n. Abbr.* **reg.** **1.** A formal or official recording of items, names, or actions. **2.** A book for such entries. **3.** An entry in a register. **4.** A device that automatically registers a quantity or number. **5.** An adjustable, grill-like device through which heated or cooled air is released into a room. **6.** *Music.* **a.** The range of an instrument or voice. **b.** A part of such a range that has similar quality. **c.** A group of matched organ pipes; a stop. —*v.* **registered, -tering, -ters.** —*tr.* **1.** To enter in a register; record officially; enroll. **2.** To indicate, as on an instrument or scale. **3.** To show (emotion). **4.** To cause (mail) to be officially recorded by payment of a fee. —*intr.* **1.** To place or cause placement of one's name in a register. **2.** To have one's name officially placed on a list of eligible voters. **3.** To create an impression. [Middle English *registre,* from Old French, from Medieval Latin *registrum, regest(r)um,* from Late Latin *regesta,* list, neuter plural past participle of Latin *regerere,* bring back : *re-,* back + *gerere,* bring, to carry (see **gerere** in Appendix*).] —**reg′is·ter·er** *n.* —**reg′is·tra·ble** (-ĭ-strə-bəl) *adj.*

reg·is·tered (rĕj′ĭ-stərd) *adj. Abbr.* **reg., regd. 1.** Having the owner's name listed in a register: *registered bonds.* **2.** Having the pedigree recorded in a breed association studbook: *a registered poodle.* **3.** Officially qualified or authenticated.

registered mail. Mail that is recorded by the post office when sent and is insured by payment of a fee against loss or damage.

registered nurse. *Abbr.* **R.N.** A graduate trained nurse who has passed a state registration examination.

reg·is·trant (rĕj′ĭ-strənt) *n.* One who registers or is registered.

reg·is·trar (rĕj′ĭ-strär′, rĕj′ĭ-strär′) *n. Abbr.* **reg., regr. 1.** An officer in a college or university who keeps records on the enrollment and academic standing of students. **2.** An officer of a corporation responsible for maintaining records of ownership of its securities.

reg·is·tra·tion (rĕj′ĭ-strā′shən) *n.* **1.** A registering, as of voters or students. **2.** The number of persons registered; enrollment. **3.** An entry in a register. **4. a.** A combination of organ stops selected to be used in playing a piece. **b.** The technique of selecting and adjusting organ stops.

reg·is·try (rĕj′ĭ-strē) *n., pl.* **-tries.** *Abbr.* **reg. 1.** Registration. **2.** A ship's registered nationality; flag. **3.** A place where registers are kept.

re·gius professor (rē′jəs, -jē-əs). One holding a professorship established by royal bounty at any of certain older British universities. [Latin *rēgius,* royal, from *rēx* (stem *rēg-*), king (see **reg-**[1] in Appendix*) + PROFESSOR.]

reg·let (rĕg′lĭt) *n.* **1.** *Architecture.* A narrow, flat molding. **2.** *Printing.* A flat piece of wood used to separate lines of type. [French *réglet,* from Old French *reglet,* from *regle,* rule, straightedge, from Latin *rēgula,* rule. See **reg-**[1] in Appendix.*]

reg·nal (rĕg′nəl) *adj.* Designating a specified year of a king's reign calculated from the date of his accession. [Medieval Latin *regnālis,* from Latin *rēgnum,* REIGN.]

reg·nant (rĕg′nənt) *adj.* **1.** Reigning; ruling. **2.** Predominant. **3.** Widespread; prevalent. [Latin *regnāns,* present participle of *regnāre,* to reign, from *rēgnum,* REIGN.]

reg·o·lith (rĕg′ə-lĭth′) *n.* The layer of loose rock material resting on bedrock that constitutes the surface of most land. [Greek *rhēgos,* blanket (see **reg-**[3] in Appendix*) + -LITH.]

re·gorge (rē-gôrj′) *tr.v.* **-gorged, -gorging, -gorges.** To disgorge. [French *regorger,* from Old French : *re-,* back + *gorger,* to gorge, from *gorge,* throat, GORGE.]

regr. registrar.

re·grate (rē-grāt′) *tr.v.* **-grated, -grating, -grates. 1.** To purchase (goods, especially foodstuffs) in order to resell at a profit at or near the same marketplace. **2.** To retail or sell again (goods so purchased). [Middle English *regraten,* from Old French *regrater,* from *regratier* : perhaps *re-,* against + *grater,* to scratch, from Germanic (see **grat-** in Appendix*).]

re·gress (rĭ-grĕs′) *intr.v.* **-gressed, -gressing, -gresses.** To go back; return to a previous condition or state. —*n.* (rē′grĕs′). **1.** Return or withdrawal. **2.** The act of reasoning from an effect to a cause. [Latin *regressus,* past participle of *regredī,* to go back : *re-,* back + *gradī,* to step, go (see **ghredh-** in Appendix*).]

re·gres·sion (rĭ-grĕsh′ən) *n.* **1.** Reversion; retrogression. **2.** Relapse to a less perfect or developed state. **3.** *Psychoanalysis.* Reversion to a more primitive or less mature behavior pattern. **4.** *Statistics.* The tendency for the expected value of one of two jointly correlated random variables to approach more closely the mean value of its set than the other. **5.** *Astronomy.* Retrogradation.

re·gres·sive (rĭ-grĕs′ĭv) *adj.* **1.** Tending to return or revert. **2.** Characterized by regression or a tendency to regress. **3.** Having the rate lessen as the amount taxed increases. —**re·gres′sive·ly** *adv.* —**re·gres′sive·ness** *n.*

re·gret (rĭ-grĕt′) *tr.v.* **-gretted, -gretting, -grets. 1.** To feel sorry, disappointed, or distressed about. **2.** To feel sorrow or grief over; mourn. —*n.* **1.** A sense of loss and longing for someone gone. **2.** Distress over a desire unfulfilled or an action performed or not performed. **3.** An expression of grief or disappointment. **4.** *Plural.* A courteous declining to accept an invitation. [Middle English *regretten,* from Old French *regreter,* to lament : perhaps *re-* (intensifier), again + Old Norse *grata,* to moan, sob (see **gher-**[3] in Appendix*).]

Synonyms: regret, sorrow, grief, anguish, woe, heartache. These nouns relate to mental distress. *Regret* has the broadest range of meanings, from mere disappointment in not being able to do something to painful sense of loss, bitterness, or longing for something lost or done or left undone. *Sorrow* connotes sadness caused by misfortune or the loss of a loved one and also implies contrition for something one regrets having done. *Grief* is deep, acute personal sorrow arising as from irreplaceable loss. *Anguish* implies an agonizing grief so painful as to be excruciating. *Woe* is intense, prolonged unhappiness or misery. *Heartache* is a state of unhappiness implying longing or pining for something out of reach.

re·gret·ful (rĭ-grĕt′fəl) *adj.* Full of regret or sorrow. —**re·gret′ful·ly** *adv.* —**re·gret′ful·ness** *n.*

re·gret·ta·ble (rĭ-grĕt′ə-bəl) *adj.* Eliciting or deserving regret. See Synonyms at **pathetic.** —**re·gret′ta·bly** *adv.*

regt. regiment.

Regt. regent.

reg·u·lar (rĕg′yə-lər) *adj. Abbr.* **reg. 1.** Customary, usual, or normal. **2.** Orderly or symmetrical. **3.** Conforming to set procedure, principle, or discipline. **4.** Methodical; well-ordered. **5.** Occurring at fixed intervals; periodic. **6.** Constant; not varying. **7.** Formally correct; proper. **8.** Having the required qualifications for an occupation. **9.** Perfect; complete; thorough: *a regular villain.* **10.** *Informal.* Good; nice: *a regular guy.* **11.** *Botany.* Having symmetrically arranged parts of similar size and shape: *regular flowers.* **12.** *Grammar.* Belonging to a standard mode of inflection or conjugation. **13.** Belonging to a religious order and bound by its rules: *the regular clergy.* Compare **secular. 14.** *Geometry.* **a.** Having equal sides and equal angles. Said of polygons. **b.** Having faces that are congruent regular polygons and congruent polyhedral angles. Said of polyhedra. **15.** Belonging to or constituting the permanent army of a nation. **16. a.** Of or pertaining to policies, candidates, or platforms authorized by a party leadership. **b.** Designating a person loyal to such leadership. —See Synonyms at **normal.** —*n. Abbr.* **reg. 1.** A clergyman or other member of a religious order. **2.** A soldier belonging to a regular army. **3.** A person loyal to the authorized candidates, policies, and the like, of a political party. **4.** *Informal.* A habitual customer. [Middle English *reguler,* under religious rule, from Old French, from Latin *rēgulāris,* containing rules, from *rēgula,* rule, ruler. See **reg-**[1] in Appendix.*] —**reg′u·lar′i·ty** (rĕg′yə-lăr′ə-tē) *n.* —**reg′u·lar·ly** *adv.*

Regular Army. *Abbr.* **RA, R.A.** The permanent part of the Army of the United States.

reg·u·lar·ize (rĕg′yə-lə-rīz′) *tr.v.* **-ized, -izing, -izes.** To make regular or cause to conform. —**reg′u·lar·i·za′tion** *n.*

regular year. In the Jewish calendar: **a.** An ordinary year of 354 days. **b.** A leap year of 384 days.

reg·u·late (rĕg′yə-lāt′) *tr.v.* **-lated, -lating, -lates. 1.** To control or direct according to a rule. **2.** To adjust in conformity to a specification or requirement. **3.** To adjust (a mechanism) for accurate and proper functioning. [Late Latin *rēgulāre,* from Latin *rēgula,* a rule. See **reg-**[1] in Appendix.*] —**reg′u·la′tive, reg′u·la·to′ry** (-lə-tôr′ē, -tōr′ē) *adj.*

reg·u·la·tion (rĕg′yə-lā′shən) *n. Abbr.* **reg. 1.** A principle, rule, or law designed to control or govern behavior. **2.** A governmental order having the force of law. —*adj. Abbr.* **reg.** Prescribed in accordance with a rule: *a regulation uniform.*

reg·u·la·tor (rĕg′yə-lā′tər) *n. Abbr.* **reg. 1.** One that regulates. **2. a.** The mechanism in a watch by which its speed is governed. **b.** An accurate clock used as a standard for timing other clocks. **3. a.** A device to maintain uniform speed in a machine; governor. **b.** A device to control the flow of gases, liquids, or electric current.

reg·u·lus (rĕg′yə-ləs) *n., pl.* **-li** (-lī′) or **-luses.** *Metallurgy.* **1.** The relatively pure metallic part of a charge that sinks to the bottom of a furnace or crucible. **2.** A relatively impure product of various ores in smelting, **matte** *(see).* [Medieval Latin *rēgulus,* from Latin, a petty king (this metallic antimony combines readily with gold, the king of metals), diminutive of *rēx,* king. See **reg-**[1] in Appendix.*] —**reg′u·line** (rĕg′yə-lĭn, -līn′) *adj.*

Reg·u·lus (rĕg′yə-ləs) *n.* A bright double star in the constellation Leo. Also designated "Alpha Leonis."

re·gur·gi·tate (rē-gûr′jə-tāt′) *v.* **-tated, -tating, -tates.** —*intr.* To rush or surge back; regorge. —*tr.* To cause to pour back; especially, to cast up (partially digested food); to vomit. [Medieval Latin *regurgitāre* : *re-,* back + Late Latin *gurgitāre,* to engulf, flood, from Latin *gurges,* a whirlpool (see **gwerə-**[2] in Appendix*).] —**re·gur′gi·ta′tion** *n.*

re·ha·bil·i·tate (rē′hə-bĭl′ə-tāt′) *tr.v.* **-tated, -tating, -tates. 1.** To restore (a handicapped or delinquent person) to useful life through education and therapy. **2.** To reinstate the good name of. **3.** To restore the former rank, privileges, or rights of. [Medieval Latin *rehabilitāre* : Late Latin *re-,* again + *habilitāre,* HABILITATE.] —**re′ha·bil′i·ta′tion** *n.* —**re′ha·bil′i·ta′tive** *adj.*

re·hash (rē-hăsh′) *tr.v.* **-hashed, -hashing, -hashes.** To repeat, rework, or rewrite (old material). —*n.* (rē′hăsh′). A repeated or redundant account. [RE- + HASH (to chop over).]

re·hear (rē-hîr′) *tr.v.* **-heard** (-hûrd′), **-hearing, -hears. 1.** To hear again. **2.** *Law.* To give a second consideration to.

re·hear·ing (rē-hîr′ĭng) *n. Law.* A second or new consideration of a case, plea, or suit in the same court.

re·hears·al (rĭ-hûr′səl) *n.* **1.** The act or process of practicing in preparation for a performance, especially for a public performance. **2.** A verbal repetition or recital.

re·hearse (rĭ-hûrs′) *v.* **-hearsed, -hearsing, -hearses.** —*tr.* **1.** To practice (all or part of a program) in preparation for a public performance. **2.** To perfect or cause to perfect (an action) by repetition. **3.** To retell or recite. —*intr.* To rehearse a song, play, dance, or the like. [Middle English *rehercen,* from Old French *rehercer,* to repeat, originally "to harrow again" : *re-,* again + *hercer,* to harrow, from *herce,* a harrow, from Latin *hirpex* (see **hearse**).] —**re·hears′er** *n.*

Re·ho·bo·am (rē′ō-bō′əm) *n.* A large wine bottle holding 156 ounces. [After *Rehoboam,* son of King Solomon (by analogy with JEROBOAM).]

re·house (rē-houz′) *tr.v.* **-housed, -housing, -houses.** To put or re-establish in a new, usually improved, dwelling or shelter.

Reich (rīk; *German* rīKH) *n.* The territory or government of a German empire or republic, as the First Reich, the Holy Roman Empire (from the ninth century to 1806); the Second Reich, the German Empire (1871–1919); the Weimar Republic (1919–33); and the Third Reich (1933–45). [German, from Old High German *rīhhi,* realm. See **reg-**[1] in Appendix.*]

reichs·mark (rīks′märk′; *German* rīKHs′märk′) *n., pl.* **reichs-mark** or **-marks.** *Abbr.* **RM.** A former monetary unit of Germany, until 1948, having a value of 100 reichspfennigs. See **Deutsche mark, ostmark.** [German : *Reichs,* genitive of REICH + MARK (money).]

reichs·pfen·nig (rīks′fĕn′ĭg; *German* rīKHs′pfĕn′ĭKH) *n.* A former bronze German coin of small denomination, worth 1/100 of a reichsmark. See **pfennig.** [German : *Reichs,* genitive of REICH + PFENNIG.]

re·i·fy (rē′ə-fī′, rā′-) *tr.v.* **-fied, -fying, -fies.** To regard or treat an abstraction or idea as if it had concrete or material existence. [Latin *rēs,* a thing (see **rei-**[3] in Appendix*) + -FY.] —**re′i·fi·ca′tion** *n.* —**re′i·fi′er** *n.*

reign (rān) *n.* **1.** The exercise of sovereign power, as by a monarch. **2.** The term during which sovereignty is held. **3.** Dominance or widespread influence: *the reign of reason.* —*intr.v.* **reigned, reigning, reigns. 1.** To exercise sovereign power. **2.** To hold the title of sovereign, but with limited authority. **3.** To be predominant or prevalent. [Middle English *rei(n)gne,* from Old French *reigne,* from Latin *rēgnum,* from *rēx* (stem *rēg-*), a king. See **reg-**[1] in Appendix.*]

Reign of Terror. 1. The period (1793–94) of the French Revolution during which thousands of persons were executed. **2.** *Small* **r,** *small* **t.** Any period of widespread violence.

Rei·kja·vik. See **Reykjavik.**

re·im·burse (rē′ĭm-bûrs′) *tr.v.* **-bursed, -bursing, -burses. 1.** To repay: *He reimbursed his creditors.* **2.** To pay back or compensate (a person) for money spent, or losses or damages incurred. [RE- + obsolete *imburse,* to pay, to pocket money, from Old French *embourser* : EN- + *borser,* to obtain money, from *borse,* a purse, from Late Latin *bursa,* "oxhide," from Greek, hide, skin (see **bursa** in Appendix*).] —**re′im·burs′a·ble** *adj.* —**re′im·burse′ment** *n.*

re·im·port (rē′ĭm-pôrt′, -pōrt′, rē-ĭm′pôrt′, -pōrt′) *tr.v.* **-ported, -porting, -ports.** To bring back into a country (goods made from raw materials originally exported from that country). —*n.* (rē-ĭm′pôrt′, -pōrt′). **1.** The act of reimporting. **2.** Goods reimported. —**re′im·por·ta′tion** *n.*

re·im·pres·sion (rē′ĭm-prĕsh′ən) *n.* **1.** A second or subsequent impression. **2.** A reprinting of a book from the original plates.

Reims (rēmz; *French* răNs). Also **Rheims.** A city of northeastern France. Population, 134,000.

rein (rān) *n.* **1.** *Usually plural.* A long, narrow leather strap attached to the bit of a bridle and used by a rider or driver to control a horse or other animal. See **harness. 2.** Any means of restraint, check, or guidance. —**draw in the reins. 1.** To exert pressure on the reins. **2.** To slow or stop. —**give (free) rein to.** To release from restraints. —**keep a (tight) rein on.** To exercise close control over. —*v.* **reined, reining, reins.** —*tr.* **1.** To check or hold back. **2.** To guide or control. **3.** To equip with reins. —*intr.* To control a horse or other animal with reins. Often used with *in* or *up.* [Middle English *re(i)ne,* from Old French *re(s)ne,* from Vulgar Latin *retina* (unattested), from Latin *retinēre,* to RETAIN.]

re·in·car·nate (rē′ĭn-kär′nāt′) *v.* **-nated, -nating, -nates.** To be reborn in another body; to incarnate again. —**re′in·car·na′tion** (rē′ĭn-kär-nā′shən) *n.*

rein·deer (rān′dîr′) *n., pl.* **reindeer** or **-deers.** A large deer, *Rangifer tarandus,* of arctic regions of the Old World and Greenland, having branched antlers in both sexes. It is identical to the caribou taxonomically, but is capable of being domesticated. [Middle English *reyndere,* from Old Norse *hreindýri* : *hreinn,* reindeer (see **ker-**[1] in Appendix*) + *dýr,* deer (see **dheu-**[1] in Appendix*).]

Reindeer Lake. A lake covering 2,436 square miles in northeastern Saskatchewan and northwestern Manitoba, Canada.

reindeer moss. An erect, grayish, branching lichen, *Cladonia rangiferina,* of arctic regions, forming the chief source of food for reindeer.

Rei·ner (rī′nər), **Fritz.** 1888–1963. Hungarian-born American conductor of opera and symphony orchestras.

re·in·force (rē′ĭn-fôrs′, -fōrs′) *tr.v.* **-forced, -forcing, -forces.** Also **re-en·force, re·en·force, re·ën·force. 1.** To give more force or effectiveness to; strengthen; support. **2.** *Military.* To strengthen with additional manpower or equipment. **3.** To strengthen as by adding extra support or padding. **4.** To increase in number. [RE- + *inforce,* variant of ENFORCE.]

reinforced concrete. Poured concrete containing steel bars or metal netting to increase its tensile strength. Also called "ferroconcrete."

re·in·force·ment (rē′ĭn-fôrs′mənt, -fōrs′mənt) *n.* **1.** The act or process of reinforcing, or the condition of being reinforced. **2.** Something that reinforces. **3.** *Often plural.* Additional troops, vessels, or equipment sent to support a military action. **4.** *Psychology.* **a.** The occurrence or experimental introduction of an unconditioned stimulus along with a conditioned stimulus. **b.** The strengthening of a conditioned response by such means. **c.** The strengthening of an instrumental or operant conditioned response leading to satisfaction; reward. **d.** Loosely, any event, circumstance, or condition that increases the likelihood that a response will recur in a situation like that in which the reinforcing condition originally occurred; any condition strengthening learning.

reins (rānz) *pl.n. Archaic.* **1.** The kidneys, loins, or lower back region. **2.** The seat of affections and passions, formerly regarded as having their source in the kidneys and loins. [Middle English, from Old French, from Latin *rēnēs.* See **renal.**]

re·in·state (rē′ĭn-stāt′) *tr.v.* **-stated, -stating, -states.** To restore to a previous condition or position. —**re′in·state′ment** *n.*

re·in·sure (rē-ĭn-shŏŏr′) *tr.v.* **-sured, -suring, -sures. 1.** To insure again. **2.** To insure by contracting to transfer in whole or in part a risk or contingent liability already covered under an existing contract. —**re′in·sur′ance** *n.* —**re′in·sur′er** *n.*

re·in·vest (rē′ĭn-vĕst′) *tr.v.* **-vested, -vesting, -vests.** To invest (capital or earnings) again. Used especially of receipts derived from a securities portfolio. —**re′in·vest′ment** *n.*

reis. Alternate plural of **real** (Portuguese monetary unit).

re·is·sue (rē-ĭsh′ōō) *tr.v.* **-sued, -suing, -sues.** To issue again. —*n.* **1.** A second or subsequent issue, as of a book altered in format or price. **2.** A reprinting of postage stamps from unchanged plates.

re·it·er·ate (rē-ĭt′ə-rāt′) *tr.v.* **-ated, -ating, -ates.** To say over again. [Latin *reiterāre* : *re-,* again + *iterāre,* ITERATE.] —**re·it′er·a′tion** *n.* —**re·it′er·a′tive** *adj.* —**re·it′er·a′tive·ly** *adv.*

re·ject (rĭ-jĕkt′) *tr.v.* **-jected, -jecting, -jects. 1.** To refuse to accept, recognize, or make use of; repudiate. **2.** To refuse to consider or grant; deny. **3.** To refuse affection or recognition to (a person). **4.** To discard as defective or useless; throw away. **5.** To spit out or vomit. —See Synonyms at **refuse.** —*n.* (rē′jĕkt). Something or someone that has been rejected. [Middle English *rejecten,* from Latin *rejicere* (past participle *rejectus*), to throw back : *re-,* back, away + *jacere,* to throw (see **yē-** in Appendix*).] —**re·ject′er, re·jec′tor** (-jĕk′tər) *n.*

re·jec·tion (rĭ-jĕk′shən) *n.* **1.** The act or process of rejecting. **2.** The condition of being rejected. **3.** Something rejected.

re·joice (rĭ-jois′) *v.* **-joiced, -joicing, -joices.** —*intr.* To feel or be joyful. —*tr.* To fill with joy; gladden. [Middle English *rejoicen,* from Old French *rejoir* (stem *rejoiss-*) : *re-* (intensifier), again + *joir,* to be joyful, from Latin *gaudēre* (see **gāu-** in Appendix*).] —**re·joic′er** *n.*

re·joic·ing (rĭ-joi′sĭng) *n.* The feeling or expressing of joy or an instance of this; joyful celebration.

re·join[1] (rē′join′) *v.* **-joined, -joining, -joins.** —*tr.* **1.** To come together again in company with. **2.** To join or put together again; reunite. —*intr.* To be or become joined again.

re·join[2] (rĭ-join′) *v.* **-joined, -joining, -joins.** —*tr.* To say as a reply. —*intr.* **1.** To respond; answer. **2.** *Law.* To answer a plaintiff's replication. [Middle English *rejoinen,* from Old French *rejoindre* : *re-,* back, again + *joindre,* to JOIN.]

re·join·der (rĭ-join′dər) *n.* **1.** An answer, especially in response to a reply. **2.** *Law.* A second pleading by a defendant, in answer to a plaintiff's replication. [Middle English *rejoyner,* from Old French *rejoindre* (substantive infinitive), to REJOIN (answer).]

re·ju·ve·nate (rĭ-jōō′və-nāt′) *tr.v.* **-nated, -nating, -nates. 1.** To restore the youthful vigor or appearance of. **2. a.** To stimulate (a stream) to renewed erosive activity, as by uplift. **b.** To develop youthful topographical features in (a previously leveled area). [From RE- + Latin *juvenis,* a youth (see **yeu-**[2] in Appendix*).] —**re·ju′ve·na′tion** *n.* —**re·ju′ve·na′tor** (-tər) *n.*

REK Airport code for Reykjavik, Iceland.

rel. 1. relating. **2.** relative. **3.** released. **4.** religion; religious.

re·lapse (rĭ-lăps′) *intr.v.* **-lapsed, -lapsing, -lapses. 1.** To fall back or revert to a former state. **2.** To regress after partial recovery from illness. **3.** To slip back into bad ways; backslide. —*n.* (rē′lăps, rĭ-lăps′). The act or result of relapsing. [Latin *relapsus,* past participle of *relābī,* to slide back : *re-,* back + *lābī,* to slide (see **leb-**[1] in Appendix*).] —**re·laps′er** *n.*

relapsing fever. Any of several infectious diseases characterized by chills and fever, and caused by spirochetes transmitted by lice and ticks. Also called "recurrent fever."

re·late (rĭ-lāt′) *v.* **-lated, -lating, -lates.** —*tr.* **1.** To narrate or tell. **2.** To bring into logical or natural association. —*intr.* **1.** To have connection, relation, or reference. Used with *to.* **2.** *Jargon.* To interact with others in a meaningful or coherent fashion. —See Synonyms at **join.** [Latin *relātus* (past participle of *referre,* to carry back, REFER) : *re-,* back + *-lātus,* "carried" (see **tel-**[1] in Appendix*).] —**re·lat′er** *n.*

re·lat·ed (rĭ-lā′tĭd) *adj.* **1.** Connected; associated. **2.** Connected by kinship, marriage, or common origin. **3.** Having a specified harmonic connection. —**re·lat′ed·ness** *n.*

re·la·tion (rĭ-lā′shən) *n.* **1.** A logical or natural association between two or more things; relevance of one to another; connection. **2.** The connection of people by blood or marriage; kinship. **3.** A person akin to another by blood or marriage; a relative. **4.** The mode in which a person or thing is connected with another: *relation of parent to child.* **5.** *Plural.* The connections or associations drawing together persons, groups, or nations in personal, business, or diplomatic affairs. **6.** Reference; regard. **7. a.** The act of telling or narrating. **b.** A narrative; an account. **8.** *Law.* **a.** A relator's statement of grounds for grievance or action to be taken. **b.** The assumption that an act or

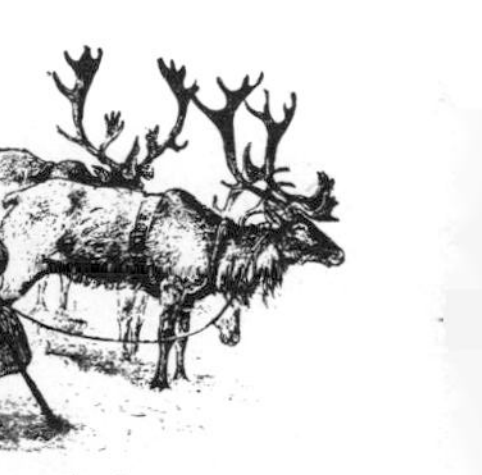

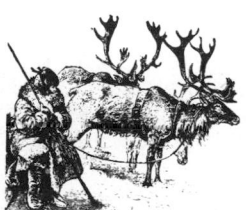

reindeer

proceeding has taken place prior to its completion or official enactment. **9.** *Plural.* Sexual intercourse.

re·la·tion·al (rĭ-lā′shən-əl) *adj.* **1.** Of or arising from kinship. **2.** Indicating or constituting relations. **3.** Expressing a syntactic relation.

re·la·tion·ship (rĭ-lā′shən-shĭp′) *n.* **1.** The condition or fact of being related. **2.** Connection by blood or marriage; kinship.

rel·a·tive (rĕl′ə-tĭv) *adj.* *Abbr.* **rel.** **1.** Having pertinence or relevance; connected; related. **2.** Considered in comparison to or relationship with something else. **3.** Dependent upon or interconnected with something else for intelligibility or significance; not absolute. **4.** Referring to or qualifying an antecedent. **5.** Having the same key signature. Said of major and minor scales and keys. —*n.* **1.** One related by kinship. **2.** One that is relative. **3.** A relative term. [Middle English *relatif,* from Old French, from Late Latin *relātīvus,* from Latin *relātus.* See **relate.**] —**rel′a·tive·ly** *adv.* —**rel′a·tive·ness** *n.*

relative biological effectiveness. *Abbr.* **RBE** *Physics.* A measure of the capacity of a specific ionizing radiation to produce a specific biological effect, usually expressed as the dose of radium gamma rays or 200-kilovolt x rays relative to the dose of the ionization in question required to produce the effect.

relative clause. A dependent clause introduced by a relative pronoun. In the sentence *He who hesitates is lost,* the relative clause is *who hesitates.*

relative humidity. *Abbr.* **r.h.** The ratio of the amount of water vapor in the air at a specific temperature to the maximum capacity of the air at that temperature.

relative pitch. **1.** The pitch of a tone as determined by its position in a scale. **2.** The ability to recognize or produce a tone by mentally establishing a relationship between its pitch and that of a recently heard tone. Compare **absolute pitch.**

relative pronoun. A pronoun that introduces a relative clause and has reference to an antecedent. In the sentence *He who hesitates is lost,* the relative pronoun is *who.*

rel·a·tiv·ism (rĕl′ə-tĭv-ĭz′əm) *n.* *Philosophy.* The theory that all truth is relative to the individual and to the time or place in which he acts.

rel·a·tiv·ist (rĕl′ə-tĭv-ĭst) *n.* **1.** A proponent of relativism. **2.** A physicist specializing in the theories of relativity.

rel·a·tiv·is·tic (rĕl′ə-tĭv-ĭs′tĭk) *adj.* **1.** Of or pertaining to relativism. **2.** *Physics.* **a.** Of, pertaining to, or resulting from speeds that are large with respect to the speed of light: *relativistic increase in mass.* **b.** Of or pertaining to phenomena explicable by special or general relativity: *relativistic mechanics.*

rel·a·tiv·i·ty (rĕl′ə-tĭv′ə-tē) *n.* **1.** The quality or state of being relative. **2.** *Philosophy.* Existence dependent solely upon relation to a thinking mind. **3.** A state of dependence in which the existence or significance of one entity is solely dependent upon that of another. **4.** *Physics.* **a.** **Special relativity** *(see).* **b.** **General relativity** *(see).*

re·la·tor (rĭ-lā′tər) *n.* One who relates or narrates.

re·lax (rĭ-lăks′) *v.* **-laxed, -laxing, -laxes.** —*tr.* **1.** To make lax or loose: *relax one's grip.* **2.** To make less severe or strict. **3.** To reduce in intensity; slacken. **4.** To relieve from effort or strain. —*intr.* **1.** To take one's ease; rest. **2.** To become lax or loose. **3.** To become less severe or strict. **4.** To become less formal, aloof, or tense. [Middle English *relaxen,* from Latin *relaxāre* : *re-,* back + *laxāre,* to loosen, from *laxus,* lax, loose (see **slēg-** in Appendix*).] —**re·lax′a·ble** *adj.* —**re·lax′er** *n.*

re·lax·ant (rĭ-lăk′sənt) *n.* A drug or therapeutic treatment that relaxes or relieves muscular or nervous tension. —*adj.* Tending to relax or to relieve tension.

re·lax·a·tion (rē′lăk′sā′shən) *n.* **1. a.** The act of relaxing. **b.** The state of being relaxed. **2.** Refreshment of body or mind; recreation: *play golf for relaxation.* **3.** A loosening or slackening. **4.** A reduction in strictness or severity. **5.** *Physiology.* The lengthening of inactive muscle or muscle fibers. **6.** *Physics.* The return or adjustment of a system to equilibrium following displacement or abrupt change. **7.** *Mathematics.* A numerical method in which the errors, or residuals, resulting from an initial approximation are reduced by succeeding approximations until all errors are within specified limits. —See Synonyms at **rest.** —**re·lax′a·tive** *adj.* & *n.*

relaxation time. *Physics.* The time required for an exponential variable to decrease to $1/e$ (0.368) of its initial value.

re·lax·in (rĭ-lăk′sən) *n.* A female hormone secreted by the corpus luteum that helps soften the cervix and relax the pelvic ligaments in childbirth. [RELAX + -IN.]

re·lay (rē′lā′) *tr.v.* **-laid** (-lād′), **-laying, -lays.** To lay again.

re·lay (rē′lā, rĭ-lā′) *n.* **1.** A fresh team, as of horses or dogs, to relieve weary animals in a hunt, task, or journey. **2.** A crew of laborers who relieve another crew at work; a shift. **3.** The act of passing something along from one person, group, or station to another. **4.** A relay race, or one of its lengths or laps. **5.** *Electricity.* An automatic electromagnetic or electromechanical device that responds to a small current or voltage change by activating switches or other devices in an electric circuit. —*tr.v.* **relaid** (rē′lād, rĭ-lād′), **-laying, -lays.** **1.** To pass or send along by or as if by relay: *relay a message.* **2.** To supply with fresh relays. **3.** *Electricity.* To control or retransmit by means of a relay. [Middle English *relai,* from Old French, from *relaier,* to relay, leave behind : *re-,* back + *laier,* to leave, variant of *laissier,* from Latin *laxāre,* to loosen, from *laxus,* lax, loose (see **slēg-** in Appendix*).]

relay race. A race between two or more teams, in which each team member runs only a set part of the race, and then is relieved by another member of his team.

re-lease (rē′lēs′) *tr.v.* **-leased, -leasing, -leases.** To lease again.

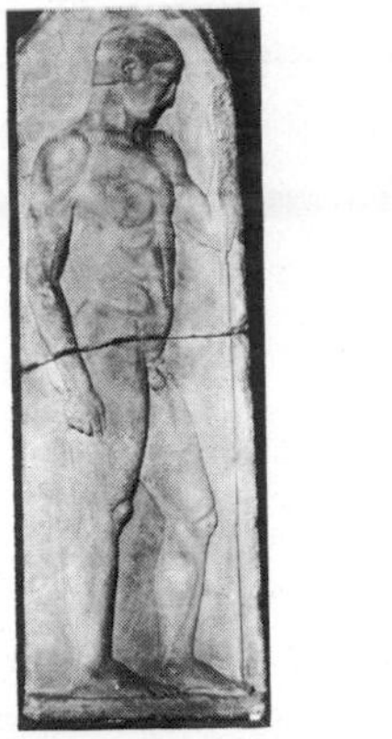

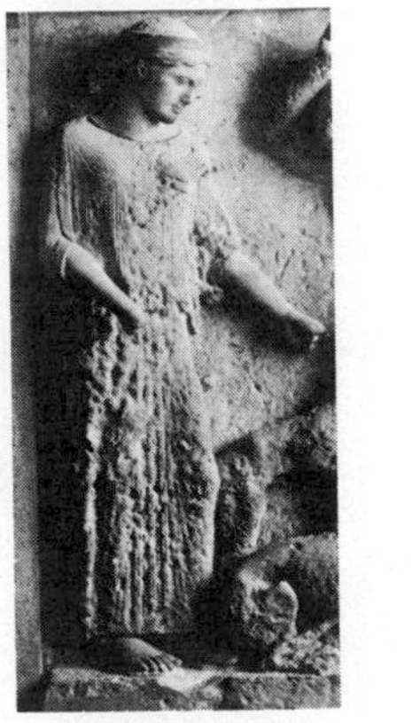

relief
Above: Low relief
Below: High relief

re·lease (rĭ-lēs′) *tr.v.* **-leased, -leasing, -leases.** **1.** To set free from confinement, restraint, or bondage; liberate. **2.** To free, unfasten, or let go of. **3.** To relieve from debt or obligation. **4.** To allow performance, sale, publication, or circulation of. **5.** To relinquish (a right or claim, for example). —*n.* **1** A deliverance; liberation. **2.** An authoritative discharge from an obligation or from prison. **3.** An unfastening or letting go of something caught or held fast. **4.** A device or catch for locking or releasing a mechanism. **5. a.** A freeing of something for general publication, use, or circulation. **b.** Something thus released: *a press release.* **6.** *Law.* **a.** The relinquishment of a right, title, or claim to another. **b.** The document thus relinquishing. [Middle English *relesen,* from Old French *relessier, relaissier,* from Latin *relaxāre,* to RELAX.] —**re·leas′er** *n.*

released time. In some U.S. public schools, a part of a regular school day during which children are excused from class attendance to receive outside religious instruction.

rel·e·gate (rĕl′ə-gāt′) *tr.v.* **-gated, -gating, -gates.** **1.** To send or consign, especially to an obscure place, position, or condition. **2.** To assign to a particular class or category; classify. **3.** To refer or assign (a matter or task, for example) for decision or performance. **4.** To cast out; banish; exile. —See Synonyms at **commit.** [Latin *relēgāre,* to send away : *re-,* back, away + *lēgare,* to send (see **leg-**[1] in Appendix*).] —**rel′e·ga′tion** *n.*

re·lent (rĭ-lĕnt′) *v.* **-lented, -lenting, -lents.** —*intr.* To become softened or gentler in attitude, temper, or determination. —*tr.* *Obsolete.* To cause to slacken or abate. —See Synonyms at **yield.** [Middle English *relenten,* from Medieval Latin *relentāre* (unattested) : *re-* (intensifier), again + *lentāre,* soften, from Latin, bend, from *lentus,* pliable (see **lento-** in Appendix*).]

re·lent·less (rĭ-lĕnt′lĭs) *adj.* **1.** Unyielding; pitiless: *relentless persecution.* **2.** Steady and persistent; unremitting: *the relentless advance of the tide.* —**re·lent′less·ly** *adv.* —**re·lent′less·ness** *n.*

rel·e·vant (rĕl′ə-vənt) *adj.* **1.** Related to the matter at hand; to the point; pertinent. **2.** *Linguistics.* Serving to distinguish one phoneme from others; distinctive. [Medieval Latin *relevāns,* from Latin, present participle of *relevāre,* to lift up, RELIEVE.] —**rel′e·vance, rel′e·van·cy** *n.* —**rel′e·vant·ly** *adv.*

Synonyms: *relevant, pertinent, germane, material, apt, apposite, apropos.* These terms are related by their varying degree of appropriateness to a subject. *Relevant* is that which has a bearing on the matter at hand. *Pertinent* implies a logical and precise bearing. *Germane* is that which is so closely akin to the subject as to reinforce it. *Material* has the sense of being needed to complete the subject: *material evidence. Apt* is that which is fitting, to the point. *Apposite* is strikingly appropriate or pertinent. *Apropos* is both relevant and opportune, frequently used with *of: apropos of the discussion.*

re·li·a·ble (rĭ-lī′ə-bəl) *adj.* That can be relied upon; dependable. —**re·li′a·bil′i·ty, re·li′a·ble·ness** *n.* —**re·li′a·bly** *adv.*

re·li·ance (rĭ-lī′əns) *n.* **1.** The act of relying. **2.** Confidence; dependence; trust. **3.** Something or someone depended on; a mainstay. —See Synonyms at **trust.**

re·li·ant (rĭ-lī′ənt) *adj.* Having or demonstrating reliance. —**re·li′ant·ly** *adv.*

rel·ic (rĕl′ĭk) *n.* Also *archaic* **rel·ique.** **1.** Something that has survived the passage of time; especially, an object or custom whose original cultural environment has disappeared: *"Corporal punishment was a relic of barbarism."* (Cyril Connolly). **2.** Something cherished for its age or associations with a person, place, or event; a keepsake. **3.** An object of religious veneration; especially, an article reputed to be associated with a saint or martyr. **4.** *Plural.* A corpse; remains. —See Synonyms at **remainder.** [Middle English *relik(e),* from Old French *relique,* from Late Latin *reliquiae,* remains (especially of a martyr), from Latin, from *relinquere,* to leave behind, RELINQUISH.]

rel·ict (rĕl′ĭkt, rĭ-lĭkt′) *n.* **1.** *Ecology.* An organism or species of an earlier time surviving in an environment that has undergone considerable change. **2.** *Rare.* A widow. —*adj.* *Geology.* Pertaining to something that has survived, such as structures or minerals after destructive processes. [Latin *relictus,* past participle of *relinquere,* to leave behind, RELINQUISH.]

re·lic·tion (rĭ-lĭk′shən) *n.* *Geology.* The gradual recession of water, leaving permanently dry land.

re·lief (rĭ-lēf′) *n.* **1.** Ease from or lessening of pain or discomfort: *"Steeped in misery . . . I shall be pardoned for seeking relief"* (Poe). **2.** Anything that lessens pain, discomfort, fear, anxiety, or the like. **3.** Assistance, in the form of money or food, given to the needy, aged, or to the inhabitants of any disaster-stricken region. **4. a.** A release from a job, post, or duty, as of a sentinel. **b.** The person or persons taking over the duties of another. **5.** *Art & Architecture.* **a.** The projection of figures or forms from a flat background, or such a projection that is apparent only, as in painting. **b.** Any art work fashioned in this manner. Also called "relievo." **6.** *Geography.* The variations in elevation of any area of the earth's surface. **7.** Distinction or prominence resulting from contrast: *"the light brought the white church . . . into relief from the flat ledges"* (Willa Cather). **8.** In feudal law, a payment made by the heir of a deceased tenant to a lord for the privilege of succeeding to the tenant's estate. —**on relief.** Receiving government funds because of need or poverty. [Middle English, from Old French, from *relever,* RELIEVE.]

relief map. A map that depicts land configuration, as with contour lines, shading, or colors.

re·lieve (rĭ-lēv′) *tr.v.* **-lieved, -lieving, -lieves.** **1.** To lessen or alleviate (anything that is painful, oppressive, or distressing); ease: *"hypnotic suggestion may relieve certain symptoms of hysteria"* (Norman L. Munn). **2.** To free from pain, anxiety, fear, or the like. **3.** To furnish assistance or aid to. **4.** To release (a person) from obligation or oppression, as by law or legislation. **5.** To free from a specified duty by providing or acting as a substitute. **6.** To make less unpleasant, monotonous, or tiresome: *"An explosive little laugh relieved the tension"* (F. Scott Fitzgerald). **7.** To make distinct or more effective through contrast; set off: *A black sash relieves a white gown* **8.** To ease (oneself) by eliminating bodily wastes. [Middle English *releven,* from Old French *relever,* relieve, raise again, from Latin *relevāre* : *re-,* again + *levāre,* to raise (see **legwh-** in Appendix*).] —**re·liev'a·ble** *adj.* —**re·liev'er** *n.*

Synonyms: *relieve, allay, alleviate, assuage, comfort, lighten, soothe, mitigate.* These terms have in common the sense of lessening a burden. *Relieve* implies making that which causes discomfort or distress more endurable by some positive action. *Allay* suggests giving comfort by laying at rest for the time being that which is causing distress: *allay one's fears. Alleviate* connotes temporary lessening of distress by some action without removing its cause. *Assuage, comfort, lighten,* and *soothe* imply the employment of moral or spiritual means to lessen distress, as through words or acts of cheer, consolation, or reassurance. *Mitigate* connotes moderating the severity of that which is distressing.

re·lie·vo (rĭ-lē'vō) *n., pl.* **-vos.** *Art & Architecture.* **Relief** *(see).* [Italian *rilievo,* from *rilievare,* to emphasize, raise, from Latin *relevāre,* RELIEVE.]

re·lig·ion (rĭ-lĭj'ən) *n. Abbr.* **rel., relig. 1.** The expression of man's belief in and reverence for a superhuman power recognized as the creator and governor of the universe. **2.** Any particular integrated system of this expression: *the Hindu religion.* **3.** The spiritual or emotional attitude of one who recognizes the existence of a superhuman power or powers. **4.** Any objective attended to or pursued with zeal or conscientious devotion: *A collector might make a religion of his hobby.* **5.** *Obsolete.* Sacred rites or practices. [Middle English *religioun,* from Old French *religion,* from Latin *religiō,* bond between man and the gods, perhaps from *religāre,* to bind back : *re-,* back + *ligāre,* to bind, fasten (see **leig-**[1] in Appendix*).]

re·lig·ion·ism (rĭ-lĭj'ən-ĭz'əm) *n.* Excessive or affected religious zeal. —**re·lig'ion·ist** *n.*

re·li·gi·ose (rĭ-lĭj'ē-ōs') *adj.* Overly religious, particularly in a conspicuous or sentimental manner. [From RELIGIOUS.]

re·lig·i·os·i·ty (rĭ-lĭj'ē-ŏs'ə-tē) *n., pl.* **-ties. 1.** The state of being religious. **2.** Excessive or affected piety.

re·lig·ious (rĭ-lĭj'əs) *adj. Abbr.* **rel. 1.** Of, pertaining to, or teaching religion: *a religious text.* **2.** Adhering to or manifesting religion; pious; godly. **3.** Extremely faithful; scrupulous; conscientious: *religious devotion to duty.* **4.** Pertaining to or belonging to a monastic order. —*n., pl.* **religious.** *Abbr.* **rel.** A person belonging to a monastic order, as a monk or nun. [Middle English, from Old French, from Latin *religiōsus,* from *religiō,* RELIGION.] —**re·li'gious·ly** *adv.* —**re·li'gious·ness** *n.*

Synonyms: *religious, devout, saintly, pious, sanctimonious, puritanical.* These terms have in common the sense of a mental, emotional, or reverential attitude about religion. *Religious* implies adherence to religion in both belief and practice. *Devout* connotes inward faith and outward sincere observance of rituals and requirements. *Saintly* implies an exceptional, exemplary quality of spiritual and religious integrity. *Pious* suggests basically a godly and reverential observance of religion, but when referring to ostentatious conduct, the term may imply derogation. *Sanctimonious,* in its modern usage, connotes sustained religious hypocrisy. *Puritanical* applies to a religious person who seeks to impose on others his own strict moral code.

re·line (rē-līn') *tr.v.* **-lined, -lining, -lines. 1.** To make new lines on. **2.** To put a new lining in.

re·lin·quish (rĭ-lĭng'kwĭsh) *tr.v.* **-quished, -quishing, -quishes. 1.** To retire from; leave; abandon. **2.** To put aside or desist from (something practiced, professed, or intended). **3.** To surrender; renounce: *"the papacy did not relinquish its claims for political power"* (George L. Mosse). **4.** To let go (a grasp, for example); release. [Middle English *relinquysshen,* from Old French *relinquir* (stem *relinquiss-*), from Latin *relinquere,* to leave behind : *re-,* behind + *linquere,* to leave (see **leikw-** in Appendix*).] —**re·lin'quish·er** *n.* —**re·lin'quish·ment** *n.*

Synonyms: *relinquish, yield, resign, abandon, surrender, cede, waive, forgo, renounce.* These terms have in common the sense of giving up something either voluntarily or involuntarily. *Relinquish* connotes giving up something desirable or prized unwillingly and regretfully. *Yield* implies giving way under contest or pressure with the hope that such action will be temporary. *Resign* suggests submission out of hopelessness. It may also refer to the giving up of office. *Abandon* and *surrender* agree in implying the giving up of something with no expectation of returning to it or recovering it, but differ in that the former action usually is voluntary and the latter the result of force. *Cede* connotes formal transfer of rights or territory. *Waive* implies a voluntary decision to dispense with a claim or a right. *Forgo* suggests abstaining or refraining from something mildly desirable or pleasurable: *forgo dessert. Renounce* means to turn down something or to dissociate oneself from it formally, usually as a matter of principle.

rel·i·quar·y (rĕl'ə-kwĕr'ē) *n., pl.* **-ies.** A receptacle, such as a coffer or shrine, for keeping or displaying relics. [French *reliquaire,* from Medieval Latin *reliquiārium,* from *reliquia,* singular of Late Latin *reliquiae,* remains. See **relic.**]

rel·ique. *Archaic.* Variant of **relic.**

re·liq·ui·ae (rĭ-lĭk'wĭ-ē') *pl.n. Latin.* Remains, especially of fossil organisms.

rel·ish (rĕl'ĭsh) *n.* **1.** An appetite for something; an appreciation or liking: *"a relish for luxury and splendor"* (Henry James). **2. a.** Pleasure; zest. **b.** Anything that lends pleasure or zest. **3.** A spicy or savory condiment served with other food. **4.** The flavor of a food, especially when appetizing. **5.** A trace or suggestion of some important quality. —*v.* **relished, -ishing, -ishes.** —*tr.* **1.** To enjoy; take pleasure in. **2.** To like the flavor of. **3.** To give flavor to; to spice. —*intr.* To have a pleasing or distinctive taste. —See Synonyms at **like.** [Middle English *reles,* a taste, from Old French *reles,* variant of *relais,* something remaining, from *relaissier,* to leave behind, release, from Latin *relaxāre,* to loosen, RELAX.] —**rel'ish·a·ble** *adj.*

re·live (rē-lĭv') *v.* **-lived, -living, -lives.** —*tr.* To undergo again (an experience, for example). —*intr.* To live again.

re·lo·cate (rē-lō'kāt') *v.* **-cated, -cating, -cates.** —*tr.* To establish in a new place. —*intr.* To become established in a new residence or place of business: *The company relocated in the suburbs.* —**re'lo·ca'tion** *n.*

re·lu·cent (rĭ-lo͞o'sənt) *adj.* Reflecting light; shining. [Latin *relūcēns,* present participle of *relūcēre,* to shine back : *re-,* back + *lūcēre,* to shine (see **leuk-** in Appendix*).]

re·luct (rĭ-lŭkt') *intr.v.* **-lucted, -lucting, -lucts.** *Rare.* To show reluctance or resistance. [Latin *reluctārī,* to struggle against : *re-,* against, back + *luctārī,* to struggle (see **leug-**[1] in Appendix*).]

re·luc·tance (rĭ-lŭk'təns) *n.* Also **re·luc·tan·cy** (-tən-sē). **1.** The state of being reluctant; unwillingness; disinclination. **2.** *Physics.* A magnetic quantity analogous to electric resistance and equal in a closed magnetic circuit to the ratio of circuit length to the product of cross-sectional area and permeability.

re·luc·tant (rĭ-lŭk'tənt) *adj.* **1.** Unwilling; averse: *reluctant to help.* **2.** Marked by unwillingness. **3.** *Obsolete.* Offering resistance; opposing. [Latin *reluctāns,* present participle of *reluctārī,* to struggle against, RELUCT.] —**re·luc'tant·ly** *adv.*

rel·uc·tiv·i·ty (rĕl'ək-tĭv'ə-tē) *n., pl.* **-ties.** *Physics.* A measure of the resistance of a material to the establishment of a magnetic field within it, equal to the reciprocal of **magnetic permeability** *(see).* [RELUCT(ANCE) + (CONDUCT)IVITY.]

re·lume (rĭ-lo͞om') *tr.v.* **-lumed, -luming, -lumes.** To make bright or clear again; illuminate again. [RE- + (IL)LUME.]

re·ly (rĭ-lī') *intr.v.* **-lied, -lying, -lies. 1.** To depend. Used with *on* or *upon.* **2.** To trust confidently. Used with *on* or *upon: rely on the children to behave.* [Middle English *relien,* to gather, rally, from Old French *relier,* from Latin *religāre,* to bind back : *re-,* back + *ligāre,* to fasten, to tie (see **leig-**[1] in Appendix*).]

Synonyms: *rely, trust, depend, bank, count, reckon. Rely* implies having complete confidence in the ability or veracity of another. *Trust* has the sense of belief based on inconclusive evidence. *Depend* implies confidence in the strength or support of another. *Bank* and *count,* informal terms, suggest assurance of the fulfillment of a promise. *Reckon* implies a sense of expectancy in the fulfillment of a promise or action.

rem (rĕm) *n. Physics.* The amount of ionizing radiation required to produce the same biological effect as one roentgen of high-penetration x rays. [R(OENTGEN) E(QUIVALENT IN) M(AN).]

rem. remittance.

re·main (rĭ-mān') *intr.v.* **-mained, -maining, -mains. 1.** To continue without change of condition, quality, or place: *"It were well if none remained boys all their lives"* (John Henry Newman). **2.** To stay or be left over after the removal, departure, loss, or destruction of others. **3.** To be left as still to be dealt with: *A cure remains to be found.* **4.** To endure or persist: *"Today fears of the capitalistic powers remain."* (John C. Bennett). —See Synonyms at **stay.** [Middle English *remaynen,* from Old French *remanoir, remaindre,* from Latin *remanēre,* to stay behind : *re-,* back in place + *manēre,* to stay (see **men-**[3] in Appendix*).]

re·main·der (rĭ-mān'dər) *n.* **1.** Something that is left over after other parts have been taken away; the rest. **2.** *Mathematics.* **a.** In division, the dividend minus the product of the divisor and quotient. **b.** In subtraction, the **difference** *(see).* **3.** *Law.* An estate effective and enjoyable only after the determination of another estate. **4.** The copy or copies of a book remaining with a publisher after sales have fallen off, sold at a reduction. —*adj.* Remaining; leftover. —*tr.v.* **remaindered, -dering, -ders.** To sell (books) as remainders. [Middle English *remaynder,* from Old French *remainder,* from *remaindre,* to REMAIN.]

Synonyms: *remainder, rest, residue, residuum, residuals, balance, remnant, leavings, tailings, remains, relic. Remainder,* the most general of these terms, is that which is left when something is taken away. *Rest* is used virtually interchangeably with *remainder* in its general meaning. *Residue* and *residuum* refer to what is left after something has undergone dissolution or diminution, as by combustion; also, both terms refer to what is left of an estate after probate costs and bequests have been satisfied. *Residuals* in modern usage refers to royalty payments made to artists on the remainder of the life of an artistic production after the original production or edition has run its course. *Balance* implies that which is left at a bank after withdrawals; also, the unpaid amount on a charge account. *Remnant* is any small piece or quantity remaining after the major part has been used. *Leavings* and *tailings* are the culls remaining after that which is valuable has been taken away: *the tailings of a gold mine. Remains* specifically refers to a corpse, although it also applies to monuments of the past. *Relic* is a treasured memento, cherished in memory of a person, event, or place.

re·main·der·man (rĭ-mān'dər-mən) *n., pl.* **-men** (-mĭn). *Law.* One who is in possession of a remainder.

re·mains (rĭ-mānz') *pl.n.* **1.** All that is left after other parts have

reliquary
Above: Fifteenth-century Italian
Below: Twelfth-century Spanish

been taken away, used up, or destroyed. **2.** A corpse. **3.** The unpublished writings of a deceased author. **4.** Ancient ruins or fossils. —See Synonyms at **body, remainder.**

re·make (rē-māk′) *tr.v.* **-made** (-mād′), **-making, -makes.** To make anew; reconstruct. —*n.* **1.** An instance of making anew. **2.** Something made again: *a remake of a motion picture.*

re·man (rē-măn′) *tr.v.* **-manned, -manning, -mans. 1.** To supply with a new contingent of men, as for work or defense. **2.** To renew the manliness or courage of.

re·mand (rĭ-mănd′) *tr.v.* **-manded, -manding, -mands. 1.** To send or order back. **2.** *Law.* **a.** To send back (one in custody) to prison, to another court, or to another agency for further proceedings. **b.** To send back (a case) to a lower court with instructions about further proceedings. —*n.* **1.** The state of being remanded. **2.** The act of remanding. **3.** A person remanded. [Middle English *remaunden,* from Old French *remander,* from Late Latin *remandāre,* to send back word : Latin *re-,* back + *mandāre,* to send word (see **man-**[2] in Appendix*).] —**re·mand′ment** *n.*

rem·a·nence (rĕm′ə-nəns) *n.* **1.** The state or quality of remaining or enduring. **2.** The remainder. **3.** *Physics.* The magnetic induction that remains in a material after removal of the magnetizing force. [From Middle English *remanent,* remaining, from Latin *remanens,* present participle of *remanēre,* to REMAIN.] —**rem′a·nent** *adj.*

re·mark (rĭ-märk′) *v.* **-marked, -marking, -marks.** —*tr.* **1.** To say or write briefly and casually as a comment. **2.** To take notice of; observe. **3.** *Obsolete.* To make identifiable; mark off. —*intr.* To make a comment or observation. Used with *on* or *upon.* —See Synonyms at **see.** —*n.* **1.** The act of noticing or observing; observation; mention: *a place worthy of remark.* **2.** A casual or brief expression of opinion; comment. **3.** *Engraving.* Variant of **remarque.** [French *remarquer,* from Old French : *re-* (intensifier), again + *marquer,* to note, mark, from *marque,* variant of *merche,* a mark, from Old Norse *merki* (see **merg-** in Appendix*).] —**re·mark′er** *n.*

re·mark·a·ble (rĭ-mär′kə-bəl) *adj.* **1.** Worthy of notice. **2.** Extraordinary; conspicuous; uncommon. —**re·mark′a·ble·ness** *n.* —**re·mark′a·bly** *adv.*

re·marque (rĭ-märk′) *n.* Also **re·mark.** *Engraving.* **1.** A mark made in the margin of a plate to indicate its stage of development prior to completion. **2.** A print or proof from a plate carrying such a mark. [French, "a remark," from *remarquer,* to REMARK.]

Re·marque (rə-märk′), **Erich Maria.** Original name, Erich Paul Kramer. Born 1898. German-born American novelist.

re·match (rē-măch′, rē′măch) *n.* A contest between opponents who had previously met each other in competition.

Rem·brandt (rĕm′brănt). In full, Rembrandt Harmensz or Harmenszoon van Rijn or van Ryn. 1606–1669. Dutch painter and graphic artist; produced over 3,000 works.

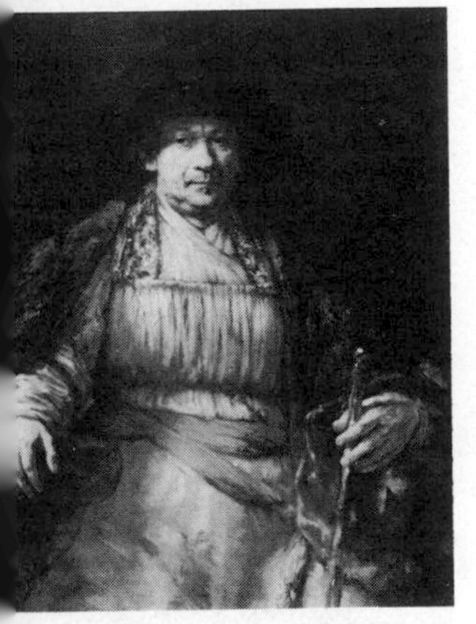

Rembrandt
Self-portrait, 1658
(detail)

re·me·di·a·ble (rĭ-mē′dē-ə-bəl) *adj.* Capable of being remedied. —**re·me′di·a·ble·ness** *n.* —**re·me′di·a·bly** *adv.*

re·me·di·al (rĭ-mē′dē-əl) *adj.* **1.** Supplying a remedy. **2.** Intended to correct something, especially study or reading habits. —**re·me′di·al·ly** *adv.*

rem·e·dy (rĕm′ə-dē) *n., pl.* **-dies. 1.** Something, such as medicine or therapy, that relieves pain, cures disease, or corrects a disorder. **2.** Something that corrects any evil, fault, or error. **3.** *Law.* A legal means of preventing or correcting a wrong or enforcing a right. **4.** A mint's allowance for deviation from the standard weight or quality of coins. —*tr.v.* **remedied, -dying, -dies. 1.** To relieve or cure (a disease or disorder). **2.** To counteract or rectify (an error or defect); set right. —See Synonyms at **correct.** [Middle English *remedie,* from Norman French, from Latin *remedium,* medicine : *re-,* again + *medērī,* to heal (see **med-** in Appendix*).]

re·mem·ber (rĭ-mĕm′bər) *v.* **-bered, -bering, -bers.** —*tr.* **1.** To recall to the mind through an act of memory; think of again. **2.** To recall to the mind with effort or determination. **3.** To retain in the mind; keep carefully in memory: *remember a poem.* **4.** To keep (someone) in mind as worthy of affection or recognition. **5.** To reward with a gift or tip. **6.** To mention (someone) to another as sending greetings. **7.** *Archaic.* To remind: *"One thing only . . . let me remember you of."* (Philip Sidney). —*intr.* To have or use the faculty of memory. [Middle English *remembren,* from Old French *remembrer,* from Late Latin *rememorārī,* to remember again : *re-,* again + *memorārī,* to remind, from Latin *memor,* mindful (see **smer-**[1] in Appendix*).] —**re·mem′ber·a·ble** *adj.* —**re·mem′ber·er** *n.*

re·mem·brance (rĭ-mĕm′brəns) *n.* **1.** The act of remembering. **2.** The state of being remembered. **3.** Something serving to celebrate or honor the memory of a person or event; a memorial. **4.** The length of time over which one's memory extends. **5.** Something remembered; a reminiscence. **6.** A memento or souvenir. **7.** *Plural.* Greetings: *Send remembrances to him.* —See Synonyms at **memory.** [Middle English, from Old French, from *remembrer,* REMEMBER.]

re·mem·branc·er (rĭ-mĕm′brən-sər) *n.* **1.** One that causes another to remember; a reminder. **2.** *Capital* **R. a.** One of several officers of the Court of Exchequer in England. **b.** An officer of the British judiciary responsible for collecting debts due to the Crown. In this sense, also called "King's (or Queen's) Remembrancer."

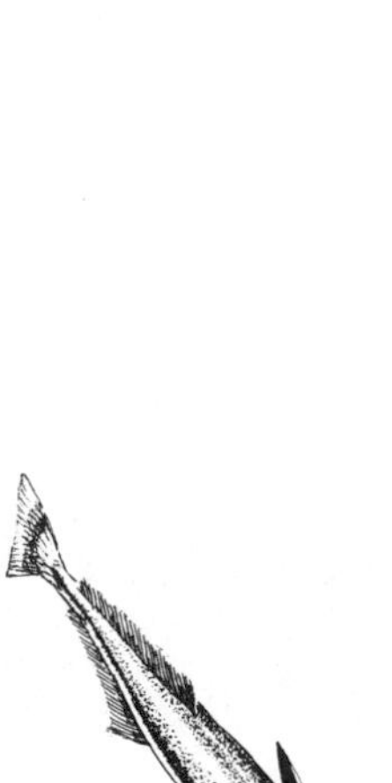

remora
Echeneis naucrates

re·mex (rē′mĕks′) *n., pl.* **remiges** (rĕm′ə-jēz′). *Ornithology.* A quill or flight feather of a bird's wing. [New Latin, from Latin *rēmex* (stem *rēmig-*), oarsman : *rēmus,* oar (see **erə-**[1] in Appendix*) + *agere,* to drive (see **ag-** in Appendix*).] —**re·mig′i·al** (rĭ-mĭj′ē-əl) *adj.*

re·mind (rĭ-mīnd′) *tr.v.* **-minded, -minding, -minds. 1.** To cause (someone) to remember. **2.** To bring into (someone's) mind: *"the lyric of a song might remind a man on the edge of insanity that soon he will be insane again"* (Norman Mailer). [RE- + MIND.] —**re·mind′er** *n.*

Rem·ing·ton (rĕm′ĭng-tən), **Eliphalet.** 1793–1861. American manufacturer of firearms.

Rem·ing·ton (rĕm′ĭng-tən), **Frederic.** 1861–1909. American painter, sculptor, and author; depicted American frontier life.

rem·i·nisce (rĕm′ə-nĭs′) *intr.v.* **-nisced, -niscing, -nisces.** To recollect and tell of past experiences or events. [Back-formation from REMINISCENT.]

rem·i·nis·cence (rĕm′ə-nĭs′əns) *n.* **1.** The act or process of recalling the past. **2.** A thing remembered; a memory. **3.** *Often plural.* A narration of past experiences. **4.** An event that brings to mind a similar, former event. —See Synonyms at **memory.**

rem·i·nis·cent (rĕm′ə-nĭs′ənt) *adj.* **1.** Having the quality of or containing reminiscence. **2.** Tending to recall or talk of the past. [Latin *reminiscens,* present participle of *reminiscī,* to recollect. See **men-**[1] in Appendix.*] —**rem′i·nis′cent·ly** *adv.*

re·mise (rĭ-mīz′) *tr.v.* **-mised, -mising, -mises.** *Law.* To relinquish a claim to; surrender by deed. [Middle English, from Old French, from the feminine past participle of *remettre,* to remit, from Latin *remittere,* REMIT.]

re·miss (rĭ-mĭs′) *adj.* **1.** Lax in attending to duty; negligent. **2.** Inclined to idleness; slack; sluggish. [Middle English, from Latin *remissus,* slack, past participle of *remittere,* REMIT.] —**re·miss′ness** *n.*

re·mis·si·ble (rĭ-mĭs′ə-bəl) *adj.* Capable of being remitted or forgiven. —**re·mis′si·bil′i·ty** *n.*

re·mis·sion (rĭ-mĭsh′ən) *n.* **1. a.** The act of remitting. **b.** The condition of being remitted. **2.** Release, as from a debt or obligation. **3.** A lessening of intensity or degree; abatement.

re·mit (rĭ-mĭt′) *v.* **-mitted, -mitting, -mits.** —*tr.* **1.** To send (money); transmit. **2. a.** To cancel (a penalty or punishment). **b.** To pardon; forgive. **3.** To restore to an original condition; put back. **4.** *Law.* To refer (a case) back to a lower court for further consideration. **5.** To relax; slacken. **6.** To defer; postpone. —*intr.* **1.** To transmit money. **2.** To diminish; abate. [Middle English *remitten,* from Latin *remittere,* to send back, release : *re-,* back + *mittere,* to send (see **smeit-** in Appendix*).] —**re·mit′ta·ble** *adj.* —**re·mit′tor** (rĭ-mĭt′ər) *n.*

re·mit·tal (rĭ-mĭt′l) *n.* Remission.

re·mit·tance (rĭ-mĭt′əns) *n. Abbr.* **rem. 1.** Money or credit sent to someone. **2.** The act of sending money or credit.

remittance man. 1. A person who lives abroad on funds sent from home. **2.** One paid to remain abroad.

re·mit·tent (rĭ-mĭt′ənt) *adj.* Characterized by temporary abatements in severity. Said especially of diseases. —*n.* A remittent fever. —**re·mit′tence, re·mit′ten·cy** *n.* —**re·mit′tent·ly** *adv.*

re·mit·ter (rĭ-mĭt′ər) *n. Law.* **1.** The principle or act by which an individual holds property by a valid title dated prior to a defective title under which he at first held ownership. **2.** The act of transferring a case for decision to another court, generally a lower one. **3.** One that remits.

rem·nant (rĕm′nənt) *n.* **1.** Something left over; a remainder. **2.** A surviving trace or vestige, as of a former time or condition. **3.** *Often plural.* A small, remaining group of people. —See Synonyms at **remainder.** —*adj.* Remaining; leftover: *"dropped the remnant flowers by the family monument"* (Ross Lockridge, Jr.). [Middle English *remenant,* from Old French, present participle of *remanoir, remaindre,* to REMAIN.]

re·mod·el (rē-mŏd′l) *tr.v.* **-eled, -eling, -els. 1.** To model again. **2.** To remake with a new structure; reconstruct; renovate. —**re·mod′el·er** *n.*

re·mo·lade. Variant of **rémoulade.**

re·mon·e·tize (rē-mŏn′ə-tīz′, rē-mŭn′-) *tr.v.* **-tized, -tizing, -tizes.** To restore (silver, for example) to use as legal tender. —**re·mon′e·ti·za′tion** *n.*

re·mon·strance (rĭ-mŏn′strəns) *n.* **1.** The act of remonstrating. **2.** A speech or gesture of protest, opposition, or reproof.

re·mon·strant (rĭ-mŏn′strənt) *adj.* Characterized by remonstrance; expostulatory. —*n.* **1.** Someone who remonstrates or signs a remonstrance. **2.** *Capital* **R. a.** One of the Dutch Arminians who, in 1610, formally stated the grounds of their dissent from strict Calvinism. **b.** A member of the Protestant denomination founded by these dissenters.

re·mon·strate (rĭ-mŏn′strāt′) *v.* **-strated, -strating, -strates.** —*tr.* To say or plead in protest, objection, or reproof. —*intr.* To make objections; argue against some action. —See Synonyms at **object.** [Medieval Latin *remōnstrāre,* to demonstrate : Latin *re-,* completely + *monstrāre,* to show, from *monstrum,* an omen, a portent, from *monēre,* to warn (see **men-**[1] in Appendix*).] —**re′mon·stra′tion** (rē′mŏn-strā′shən, rĕm′ən-) *n.* —**re·mon′stra·tive** (rĭ-mŏn′strə-tĭv) *adj.* —**re·mon′stra′tor** (rĭ-mŏn′strā′tər) *n.*

re·mon·tant (rĭ-mŏn′tənt) *adj. Horticulture.* Blooming more than once during a season, as certain roses. —*n.* A remontant rose. [French, "rising again," from the present participle of *remonter,* to rise again, REMOUNT.]

rem·o·ra (rĕm′ər-ə) *n.* Any of several marine fishes of the family Echeneidae, having on the head a sucking disk with which they attach themselves to sharks, whales, sea turtles, or the hulls of ships. Also called "suckerfish." [Latin, "delay" (they were believed to be able to delay ships by sticking to them) : *re-,* back + *mora,* a delay (see **merə-** in Appendix*).]

re·morse (rĭ-môrs′) *n.* **1.** Moral anguish arising from repentance for past misdeeds; bitter regret. **2.** *Obsolete.* Compassion. [Middle English, from Old French *remors,* from Medi-

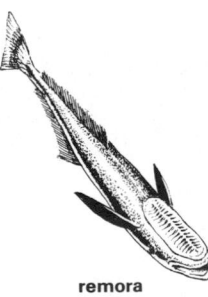

eval Latin *remorsus,* from Latin, a biting back, from the past participle of *remordēre,* to bite again : *re-,* again + *mordēre,* to bite (see **mer-**² in Appendix*).] —**re·morse′ful** *adj.* —**re·morse′ful·ly** *adv.* —**re·morse′ful·ness** *n.*

re·morse·less (rĭ-môrs′lĭs) *adj.* Having no pity or compassion; merciless. —**re·morse′less·ly** *adv.* —**re·morse′less·ness** *n.*

re·mote (rĭ-mōt′) *adj.* **-moter, -motest. 1.** Located far away; relatively distant in space: *"This room was . . . silent, because remote from the nursery and kitchens"* (Charlotte Brontë). **2.** Distant in time: *the remote past.* **3.** Barely discernible; slight: *"Europe has a set of primary interests which to us have none or a very remote relation."* (George Washington). **4.** Being distantly related by blood or marriage: *a remote descendant.* **5.** Distant in manner; aloof. —See Synonyms at **distant.** [Latin *remōtus,* past participle of *removēre,* to move back or away : *re-,* back, away + *movēre,* to move (see **mew-** in Appendix*).] —**re·mote′ly** *adv.* —**re·mote′ness** *n.*

remote control. The direction of a remote activity, process, or machine, as by radioed instructions or coded signals.

re·mo·tion (rĭ-mō′shən) *n.* **1.** The act of removing; a removal. **2.** *Obsolete.* Departure. [Middle English *remocion,* from Latin *remōtiō,* from *removēre* (past participle *remōtus*), REMOVE.]

ré·mou·lade (rā′mo͞o-läd′) *n.* Also **re·mo·lade** (rā′mə-läd′). A piquant cold sauce for cold poultry, meat, and shellfish, made of mayonnaise with chopped pickles, capers, anchovies, and herbs. [French *rémoulade,* variant of Picard dialect *ramolas,* horseradish, variant of Latin *armoracea,* of Italic origin.]

re·mount (rē-mount′) *tr.v.* **-mounted, -mounting, -mounts. 1.** To mount again. **2.** To supply with fresh horses. —*n.* (rē′-mount′, rē-mount′). A fresh horse. [Middle English *remounten,* from Old French *remonter* : *re-,* again + *monter, munter,* to MOUNT.]

re·mov·a·ble (rĭ-mo͞o′və-bəl) *adj.* Capable of being removed. —**re·mov′a·bil′i·ty, re·mov′a·ble·ness** *n.* —**re·mov′a·bly** *adv.*

re·mov·al (rĭ-mo͞o′vəl) *n.* **1. a.** The act of removing. **b.** The fact of being removed. **2.** Relocation, as of a residence or business. **3.** Dismissal, as from office.

re·move (rĭ-mo͞ov′) *v.* **-moved, -moving, -moves.** —*tr.* **1.** To move from a position occupied: *remove the dishes.* **2.** To convey from one place to another: *"Mr. Crane removed the family to Warren"* (Philip Horton). **3.** To take from one's person; doff: *remove one's hat.* **4.** To take away; to extract; separate: *remove stains.* **5.** To do away with; eliminate. **6.** To dismiss from office. —*intr.* **1.** To change one's place of residence or business; move: *"In 1751, I removed from the country to the town"* (Hume). **2.** *Poetic.* To depart; go away. —*n.* **1.** The act of removing; removal. **2.** The distance or degree of space, time, or status that separates persons or things: *"those who consider themselves to be at a safe remove from all the wretched"* (James Baldwin). [Middle English *removen,* from Old French *removoir,* from Latin *removēre,* to move back : *re-,* back + *movēre,* to move (see **mew-** in Appendix*).] —**re·mov′er** *n.*

re·moved (rĭ-mo͞ovd′) *adj.* **1.** Distant in space, time, or nature; remote. **2.** Separated in relationship by a given degree of descent: *My first cousin's child is my first cousin once removed.* —See Synonyms at **distant.** —**re·mov′ed·ly** (-mo͞o′vĭd-lē) *adj.* —**re·mov′ed·ness** (-mo͞o′vĭd-nĭs) *n.*

Rem·scheid (rĕm′shīt′). A city of West Germany, about 25 miles southeast of Düsseldorf. Population, 131,000.

re·mu·da (rĭ-mo͞o′də) *n. Southwestern U.S.* A herd of horses from which ranch hands select their mounts. [American Spanish, change of horses, from Spanish, an exchange, from *remudar,* to exchange : *re-,* again, "in return" + *mudar,* to change, from Latin *mūtāre* (see **mei-**¹ in Appendix*).]

re·mu·ner·ate (rĭ-myo͞o′nə-rāt′) *tr.v.* **-ated, -ating, -ates. 1.** To pay (a person) for goods provided, services rendered, or losses incurred. **2.** To compensate for; make up for: *remunerate his efforts.* [Latin *remūnerārē* : *re-,* intensive + *mūnerāre,* to give, from *mūnus,* a gift (see **mei-**¹ in Appendix*).] —**re·mu′ner·a·bil′i·ty** (-nər-ə-bĭl′ə-tē) *n.* —**re·mu′ner·a·ble** *adj.* —**re·mu′ner·a′tor** (-nə-rā′tər) *n.*

re·mu·ner·a·tion (rĭ-myo͞o′nə-rā′shən) *n.* **1.** An act of remunerating. **2.** That which remunerates; a recompense; payment.

re·mu·ner·a·tive (rĭ-myo͞o′nə-rā′tĭv, -nər-ə-tĭv) *adj.* **1.** Likely to be well remunerated; profitable. **2.** Serving to remunerate. —**re·mu′ner·a′tive·ly** *adv.* —**re·mu′ner·a′tive·ness** *n.*

Re·mus (rē′məs). *Roman Mythology.* The twin brother of **Romulus** *(see).*

ren·ais·sance (rĕn′ə-säns′, -zäns′; *British* rĭ-nā′səns) *n.* **1.** A rebirth; revival. **2.** *Capital* **R. a.** The humanistic revival of classical art, literature, and learning that originated in Italy in the 14th century and later spread through Europe. **b.** The period of this revival, roughly from the 14th through the 16th century. **3.** *Sometimes capital* **R.** Any similar period of revived intellectual or artistic achievement or enthusiasm: *the Celtic Renaissance.* —*adj. Capital* **R. 1.** Of, pertaining to, or characteristic of the Renaissance or its artistic and intellectual works and styles. **2.** Of or designating the style of architecture and decoration prevalent during the Renaissance. [French, a rebirth, from Old French, from *renaistre* (present stem *renais-*), to be born again, from Latin *renascī* : *re-,* again + *nascī,* to be born (see **gene-** in Appendix*).]

re·nal (rē′nəl) *adj.* Of, pertaining to, or in the region of the kidneys. [French *rénal,* from Late Latin *rēnālis,* from Latin *rēnēs*†, kidneys.]

Re·nan (rə-näN′), **Ernest.** 1823–1892. French philosopher.

re·nas·cence (rĭ-năs′əns, -nā′səns) *n.* **1.** A new birth or life; rebirth. **2.** A cultural revival; renaissance.

re·nas·cent (rĭ-năs′ənt, -nā′sənt) *adj.* Coming into being again; showing renewed growth or vigor. [Latin *renascēns,* present participle of *renascī,* to be born again. See **renaissance.**]

ren·coun·ter (rĕn-koun′tər) *n.* **1.** An unplanned meeting. **2.** *Obsolete.* A sudden encounter with an enemy. —*v.* **rencountered, -tering, -ters.** —*tr.* To meet unexpectedly. —*intr.* To have an unexpected meeting. [Old French *rencontre,* from *rencontrer,* to have a (hostile) meeting : *re-,* again, against + *encontrer,* to ENCOUNTER.]

rend (rĕnd) *v.* **rent** (rĕnt) or **rended, rending, rends.** —*tr.* **1.** To tear apart or into pieces violently; to split. **2.** To remove forcibly; wrest. **3.** To penetrate and disturb as if by tearing: *screams that rend the silence.* **4.** To distress (the heart, for example) painfully. —*intr.* To burst; come apart. —See Synonyms at **tear.** [Middle English *renden,* Old English *rendan.* See **rendh-** in Appendix.*] —**rend′er** *n.*

ren·der (rĕn′dər) *tr.v.* **-dered, -dering, -ders. 1.** To submit or present for consideration, payment, or the like: *render a bill.* **2.** To give or make available: *render assistance.* **3.** To give what is due or proper: *"He asked so much of his servants and rendered so little"* (Frederick Brechner). **4.** To give in return or retribution: *render an apology for his rudeness.* **5.** To surrender or relinquish; yield. **6.** To represent in a verbal or artistic form; depict: *"Joyce has attempted . . . to render . . . what our participation in life is like"* (Edmund Wilson). **7.** To perform an interpretation of (a musical piece, for example). **8.** To express in another language or form; translate. **9.** To pronounce formally; hand down (a verdict, for example). **10.** To cause to become; make: *"This study renders men acute, inquisitive"* (Burke). **11.** To reduce, convert, or melt down (fat) by heating. **12.** To coat (brick, for example) with plaster or cement. —See Synonyms at **perform.** —*n.* A payment in kind, services, or cash from a tenant to a feudal lord. [Middle English *rendren,* to give in return, relinquish, from Old French *rendre,* to give back, from Vulgar Latin *rendere* (unattested), variant of Latin *reddere* : *re-,* back + *dare,* to give (see **dō-** in Appendix*).] —**ren′der·a·ble** *adj.* —**ren′der·er** *n.*

ren·dez·vous (rän′dā-vo͞o′, rän′də-) *n., pl.* **-vous** (-vo͞oz′). **1.** A prearranged meeting place. **2.** The meeting itself. **3.** A popular gathering place. —*v.* **rendezvoused** (-vo͞od′), **-vousing** (-vo͞o′ĭng), **-vous** (-vo͞oz′). —*tr.* To bring together (persons or military units) at a specified time and place. —*intr.* To meet together at a specified time and place. [Old French, from *rendez vous,* "present yourselves" : *rendez,* imperative of *rendre,* to RENDER + *vous,* you, from Latin *vos* (see **wōs** in Appendix*).]

ren·di·tion (rĕn-dĭsh′ən) *n.* **1.** The act of rendering. **2.** An interpretation of a musical score or dramatic piece. **3.** A performance of a musical or dramatic work. See Usage note below. **4.** A translation, often interpretive. **5.** *Rare.* A surrender. [Obsolete French, from Old French *rendre,* to give back, RENDER.]

Usage: *Rendition,* applied to a musical or dramatic performance, is appropriate to the unusual, since it stresses both interpretation and distinctiveness. In its usual sense of *performance,* it is acceptable to 69 per cent of the Usage Panel.

Ren·don (rĕn′dən). A former administrative division of London, England, now part of **Barnet** *(see).*

ren·e·gade (rĕn′ə-gād′) *n.* **1.** One who rejects his religion, cause, allegiance, or group for another; a traitor; deserter. **2.** An outlaw. —*adj.* Of or like a renegade; traitorous. [Spanish *renegado,* from Medieval Latin *renegātus,* one who denies, renegade, from the past participle of *renegāre,* to deny : Latin *re-,* intensive + *negāre,* to deny (see **ne** in Appendix*).]

re·nege (rĭ-nĭg′, -nĕg′, -nēg′) *v.* **-neged, -neging, -neges.** —*intr.* **1.** To fail to carry out a promise or commitment. **2.** *Card Games.* To fail to follow suit when able and required by the rules to do so. —*tr. Obsolete.* To renounce; disown. —*n. Card Games.* The act of reneging. [Medieval Latin *renegāre,* to deny. See **renegade.**] —**re·neg′er** *n.*

Usage: *Renege* (to go back on one's word) is often followed by *on: renege on a commitment.* The preceding example is acceptable in writing to 74 per cent of the Usage Panel.

re·ne·go·ti·ate (rē′nĭ-gō′shē-āt′) *tr.v.* **-ated, -ating, -ates.** To negotiate anew; especially, to revise the terms of (a contract) so as to limit or get back excess profits gained by the contractor.

re·new (rĭ-no͞o′, -nyo͞o′) *v.* **-newed, -newing, -news.** —*tr.* **1.** To make new or as if new again; restore. **2.** To take up again; resume. **3.** To repeat so as to reaffirm. **4.** To regain (spiritual or physical vigor); revive. **5.** To arrange for the extension of: *renew a contract.* **6.** To replenish. **7.** To bring into being again; re-establish. —*intr.* **1.** To become new again. **2.** To start over. [RE- + NEW.] —**re·new′a·ble** *adj.*

re·new·al (rĭ-no͞o′əl, rĭ-nyo͞o′-) *n.* **1. a.** The act of renewing. **b.** The state of being renewed. **2.** Something renewed.

re·new·ed·ly (rĭ-no͞o′ĭd-lē, rĭ-nyo͞o′-) *adv.* Over again; anew.

Ren·frew (rĕn′fro͞o). Also **Ren·frew·shire** (-shĭr, -shər). A county of Scotland, occupying 242 square miles in the southwest. Population, 353,000. County seat, Paisley.

Re·ni (rā′nē), **Guido.** 1575–1642. Italian baroque painter.

ren·i·form (rĕn′ə-fôrm′, rē′nə-) *adj.* Shaped like a kidney. [Latin *rēnēs,* kidneys (see **renal**) + -FORM.]

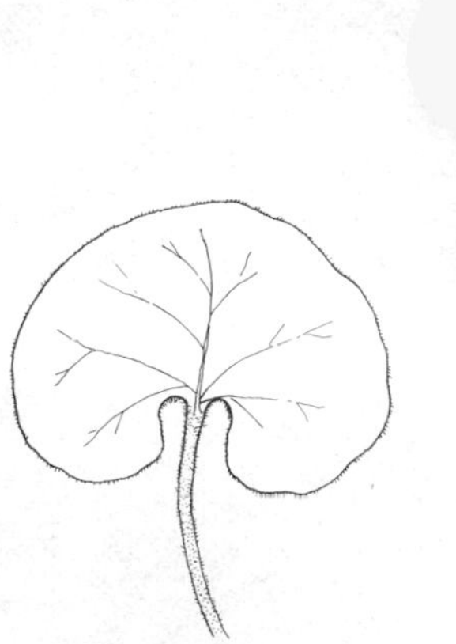

reniform
Reniform leaf of wild ginger

ren·in (rĕn′ĭn) *n.* A protein-digesting enzyme released by the kidney that acts to raise blood pressure. [Latin *rēnēs,* kidneys (see **renal**) + -IN.]

ren·i·tent (rĕn′ə-tənt, rĭ-nīt′ənt) *adj.* **1.** Resisting pressure; not pliant. **2.** Reluctant to yield or be swayed; recalcitrant. [Latin *renitens,* present participle of *renītī,* to struggle against, resist : *re-,* back, against + *nītī,* to press forward, push (see **kneigwh-** in Appendix*).] —**ren′i·tence, ren′i·ten·cy** *n.*

Rennes (rĕn). A city of Brittany, France. Population, 152,000.

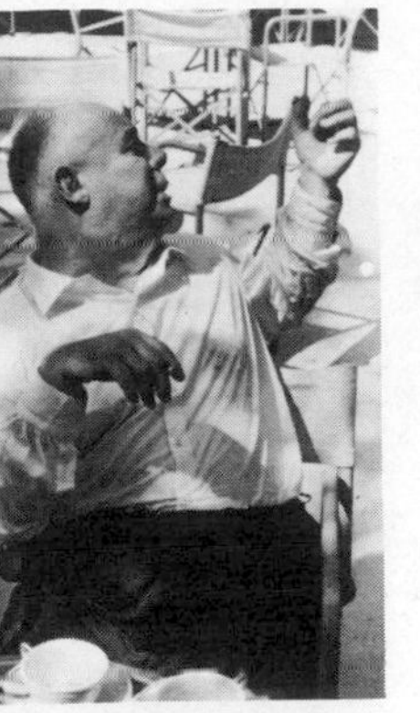
Jean Renoir

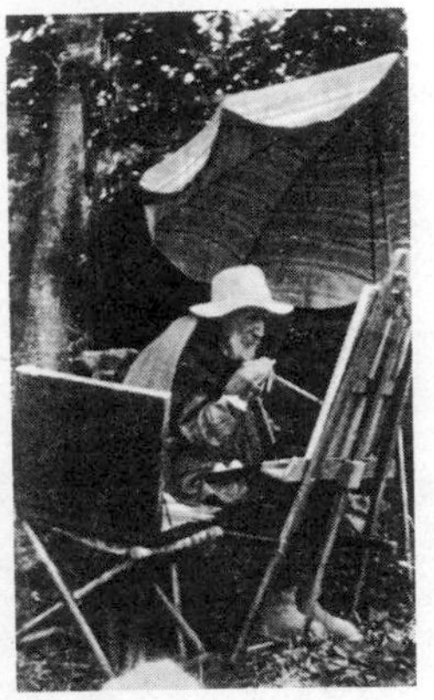
Pierre Auguste Renoir

ren·net (rĕn′ĭt) *n.* **1.** The inner lining of the fourth stomach of calves and other young ruminants. **2.** A dried extract of this lining, used to curdle milk. **3. Rennin** *(see).* [Middle English *rennet,* Old English *rynet* (unattested). See **er-**[1] in Appendix.*]

ren·nin (rĕn′ĭn) *n.* A milk-coagulating enzyme produced from rennet and used in making cheeses and junkets. Also called "chymosin," "rennase," "rennet." [RENN(ET) + -IN.]

Re·no (rē′nō). A tourist center of Nevada, 25 miles north of Carson City. Population, 51,000.

Re·noir (rĕn′wär′; *French* rə-nwàr′), **Jean.** Born 1894. French-born director of motion pictures; son of P.A. Renoir.

Re·noir (rĕn′wär′; *French* rə-nwàr′), **Pierre Auguste.** 1841–1919. French impressionist painter; father of J. Renoir.

re·nounce (rĭ-nouns′) *v.* **-nounced, -nouncing, -nounces.** —*tr.* **1.** To give up (a title or activity, for example), especially by formal announcement. **2.** To reject; disown. **3.** *Card Games.* To revoke. —*intr. Card Games.* To revoke. —See Synonyms at **relinquish.** —*n. Card Games.* A revoke. [Middle English *renouncen,* from Old French *renoncer,* from Latin *renūntiāre,* to bring back word, protest against, report : *re-,* back, against + *nūntiāre,* inform, from *nūntium,* message (see **neu-**[1] in Appendix*).] —**re·nounce′ment** *n.* —**re·nounc′er** *n.*

ren·o·vate (rĕn′ə-vāt′) *tr.v.* **-vated, -vating, -vates. 1.** To restore to an earlier condition; improve by repairing or remodeling. **2.** To impart new vigor to; revive. [Latin *renovāre* : *re-,* again + *novāre,* to make new, from *novus,* new (see **newo-** in Appendix*).] —**ren′o·va′tion** *n.* —**ren′o·va′tor** (-vā′tər) *n.*

re·nown (rĭ-noun′) *n.* **1.** The quality of being widely honored and acclaimed; celebrity. **2.** *Obsolete.* Report; rumor. —See Synonyms at **fame.** [Middle English *renoun(e),* from Old French *renon, renom,* from *renomer,* to name again, make famous : *re-,* again, from Latin + *nomer,* to name, from Latin *nōmināre,* from *nōmen,* a name (see **nomen** in Appendix*).]

re·nowned (rĭ-nound′) *adj.* Having renown; famous.

rent[1] (rĕnt) *n.* **1.** Payment, usually of an amount fixed by contract, made by one person or agency at specified intervals in return for the right to occupy or use the property of another. **2.** *Economics.* **a.** The return derived from cultivated or improved land after deduction of all production costs. **b.** The revenue yielded by a piece of land in excess of that yielded by the poorest or least favorably located land, under equal market conditions. In this sense, also called "economic rent." —*v.* **rented, renting, rents.** —*tr.* **1.** To obtain occupancy or use of (another's property) in return for regular payments. **2.** To grant temporary occupancy or use of (one's own property) in return for regular payments. —*intr.* To be for rent: *The cottage rents for $200 a month.* [Middle English *rente,* income from property, from Old French, from Vulgar Latin *rendita* (unattested), from the feminine past participle of *rendere* (unattested), to RENDER.] —**rent′a·ble** *adj.*

rent[2] (rĕnt). Past tense and past participle of **rend.** —*n.* **1.** An opening made by rending; a rip or gap. **2.** A breach of relations between persons.

rent·al (rĕnt′l) *n.* **1.** An amount paid out or taken in as rent. **2.** A list of tenants and schedule of rents. **3.** Property available for renting. —*adj.* Of, concerning, or available for rent.

rente (räNt) *n., pl.* **rentes** (räNt). *French.* **1.** Annual income; annuity. **2.** *Usually plural.* The bonds, stocks, and securities representing the national debt of France. **3.** The interest paid on this debt.

rent·er (rĕn′tər) *n.* **1.** One who receives payment in exchange for the use of his property by another. **2.** One who pays rent for the use of another's property; a tenant.

ren·tier (räN-tyā′) *n. French.* One who derives a fixed income from property rentals or returns on investments.

re·num·ber (rē-nŭm′bər) *tr.v.* **-bered, -bering, -bers.** To number again or in a different order.

re·nun·ci·a·tion (rĭ-nŭn′sē-ā′shən) *n.* **1.** The act or practice of renouncing: *"Reality imposes on human beings the necessity of renunciation of pleasures"* (Norman O. Brown). **2.** A declaration in which something is renounced. [Middle English, from Latin *renūntiātiō,* from *renūntiāre,* to RENOUNCE.] —**re·nun′ci·a′tive, re·nun′ci·a·to′ry** (-sē-ə-tôr′ē, -tōr′ē) *adj.*

re·o·pen (rē-ō′pən) *v.* **-pened, -pening, -pens.** —*tr.* To open or take up again. —*intr.* To start over; resume.

re·or·der (rē-ôr′dər) *v.* **-dered, -dering, -ders.** —*tr.* **1.** To order again. **2.** To straighten out or put in order again. **3.** To rearrange. —*intr.* To order the same goods again. —*n.* An order of goods like a previous one from the same supplier.

re·or·gan·i·za·tion (rē-ôr′gə-nə-zā′shən) *n.* **1.** The act or process of organizing again or differently. **2.** *Finance.* A thorough alteration of the structure of a business corporation, especially after a bankruptcy.

re·or·gan·ize (rē-ôr′gə-nīz′) *v.* **-ized, -izing, -izes.** —*tr.* To organize again or anew. —*intr.* To undergo or effect changes in organization. —**re·or′gan·iz′er** *n.*

rep[1] (rĕp) *n.* Also **repp.** A ribbed or corded fabric of various materials, such as cotton, wool, or silk. [French *reps*†.]

rep[2] (rĕp) *n. Informal.* A representative.

rep[3] (rĕp) *n. Physics.* A unit of absorbed radiation dose, equal to the absorbed dose in water that has been exposed to one roentgen. The rep has been largely replaced by the **rad** *(see).* [R(OENTGEN) + E(QUIVALENT) + P(HYSICAL).]

rep[4] (rĕp) *n. Informal.* A repertory theater; repertory.

rep. **1.** repair. **2.** report. **3.** reporter. **4.** representative. **5.** reprint. **6.** republic.

Rep. **1.** representative. **2.** republic. **3.** Republican (Party).

r.e.p. roentgen equivalent, physical.

re·pack·age (rē′păk′ĭj) *tr.v.* **-aged, -aging, -ages.** To package again or anew; especially, to put in a new kind of package.

re·pair[1] (rĭ-pâr′) *tr.v.* **-paired, -pairing, -pairs. 1.** To restore to sound condition after damage or injury; fix. **2.** To set right; remedy: *repair an error.* **3.** To renew or refresh. **4.** To make up for or compensate for (a loss or wrong, for example). —*n. Abbr.* **rep. 1.** The work, act, or process of repairing. **2.** General condition after use or repairing: *in good repair.* **3.** *Usually plural.* An instance of repairing. [Middle English *repairen,* from Old French *reparer,* from Latin *reparāre* : *re-,* back (to an earlier state) + *parāre,* to put in order, prepare (see **per-**[4] in Appendix*).] —**re·pair′a·ble** *adj.* —**re·pair′er** *n.*

re·pair[2] (rĭ-pâr′) *intr.v.* **-paired, -pairing, -pairs.** To betake oneself; go: *repair to the parlor.* —*n.* **1.** An act of going or sojourning. **2.** A place to which one goes frequently or habitually; a haunt. [Middle English *reparen,* to return, from Old French *repairer,* from Late Latin *repatriāre,* REPATRIATE.]

re·pair·man (rĭ-pâr′măn′, -mən) *n., pl.* **-men** (-mĕn′, -mĭn). A man whose occupation is making repairs.

re·pand (rĭ-pănd′) *adj. Botany.* Having a somewhat wavy margin: *a repand leaf.* [Latin *repandus,* bent backward : *re-,* back, backward + *pandus,* bent, turned, past participle of *pandere,* to spread (see **pet-**[2] in Appendix*).]

rep·a·ra·ble (rĕp′ər-ə-bəl) *adj.* Also **re·pair·a·ble** (rĭ-pâr′ə-bəl). Able to be repaired. —**rep′a·ra·bil′i·ty** *n.* —**rep′a·ra·bly** *adv.*

rep·a·ra·tion (rĕp′ə-rā′shən) *n.* **1.** The act or process of repairing, or the condition of being repaired. **2.** The act or process of making amends; expiation. **3.** Something done or paid to amend or make up for; compensation. **4.** *Plural.* Compensation or remuneration required from a defeated nation as indemnity for damage or injury during a war. [Middle English *reparacioun,* from Old French *reparation,* from Late Latin *reparātiō,* from Latin *reparāre,* REPAIR.]

Synonyms: *reparation, redress, amends, restitution, indemnity. Reparation* implies giving compensation to satisfy one who has suffered injury, loss, or wrong at the hands of another; in the plural form it applies to the compensation a defeated nation must make for damage to the enemy, especially civilians. *Redress* involves reparation without good will necessarily resulting, since it presupposes an act of retaliation to right a wrong: *He sought redress in the courts. Amends* does not have the force of *redress* or *reparation,* connoting the giving of satisfaction for a minor grievance or lesser injury, often apologetically. *Restitution* means returning to the rightful owner what has been taken illegally from him, or giving back something of equal worth: *The thief made restitution by returning the stolen goods. Indemnity* implies repayment or reimbursement for loss or damage.

re·par·a·tive (rĭ-păr′ə-tĭv) *adj.* Also **re·par·a·to·ry** (rĭ-păr′ə-tôr′ē, -tōr′ē). **1.** Tending to repair. **2.** Of, pertaining to, or of the nature of reparations.

rep·ar·tee (rĕp′ər-tē′, -ər-tā′, -är-tē′, -är-tā′) *n.* **1.** A swift, witty reply; a ready or spirited retort. **2.** Witty and spirited conversation characterized by such replies. **3.** Skill in making such replies or conversation. —See Synonyms at **wit.** [French *repartie,* from *repartir,* to reply readily, from Old French, to depart back again : *re-,* again + *partir,* to part, from Latin *partīre,* from *pars,* a part (see **pere-** in Appendix*).]

re·par·ti·tion (rē′pär-tĭsh′ən) *n.* **1.** Distribution; apportionment. **2.** A partitioning again or in a different way. —*tr.v.* **repartitioned, -tioning, -tions.** To partition again; redivide.

re·pass (rē-păs′, -päs′) *v.* **-passed, -passing, -passes.** —*tr.* **1.** To pass (something) again. **2.** To cause to pass again in the opposite direction. —*intr.* To pass again; go by again.

re·pas·sage (rē-păs′ĭj) *n.* **1.** The act or process of passing again. **2.** Passage back, or the right of passage back.

re·past (rĭ-păst′, -päst′) *n.* **1.** A meal, or the food eaten or provided at a meal. **2.** *Obsolete.* Food; nourishment. [Middle English, from Old French, from *repaistre,* to feed, from Late Latin *repascere,* to feed again : Latin *re-,* again + *pascere,* to feed (see **pā-** in Appendix*).]

re·pa·tri·ate (rē-pā′trē-āt′) *tr.v.* **-ated, -ating, -ates.** To return to the country of one's birth or citizenship: *repatriate war refugees.* —*n.* (rē-pā′trē-ət, -āt′). Someone who has been repatriated. [Late Latin *repatriāre* : Latin *re-,* back + *patria,* native country (see **patriot**).] —**re·pa′tri·a′tion** *n.*

re·pay (rĭ-pā′) *v.* **-paid** (-pād′), **-paying, -pays.** —*tr.* **1.** To pay back (money); refund. **2.** To pay (someone) back, either in return or in requital. **3.** To make compensation for; make a return for: *She repaid his anger with indignation.* **4.** To make or do in return: *repay a call.* —*intr.* To make repayment or requital. —**re·pay′a·ble** *adj.* —**re·pay′ment** *n.*

re·peal (rĭ-pēl′) *tr.v.* **-pealed, -pealing, -peals. 1.** To revoke or rescind; withdraw or annul officially or formally. **2.** *Obsolete.* To summon back or recall, especially from exile. —See Synonyms at **nullify.** —*n.* **1.** The act or process of repealing. **2.** *Capital* **R.** The repeal of the 18th amendment to the Constitution, which prohibited the manufacture and sale of alcoholic beverages. [Middle English *repelen,* from Norman French *repeler,* from Old French *rapeler* : *re-,* back, contrary + *apeler,* to APPEAL.] —**re·peal′a·ble** *adj.* —**re·peal′er** *n.*

re·peat (rĭ-pēt′) *v.* **-peated, -peating, -peats.** —*tr.* **1.** To utter or state again. **2.** To utter in duplication of another's utterance. **3.** To recite from memory. **4.** To tell to another. **5.** To do, experience, or produce again. **6.** To manifest or express in the same way or words. Used reflexively: *History repeats itself.* —*intr.* **1.** To do or say something again. **2.** To commit the fraudulent offense of voting more than once in a single election. —*n.* **1.** The act of repeating. **2.** Something repeated: *a repeat of a television program.* **3.** *Music.* **a.** A passage or section that is repeated. **b.** A sign usually consisting of two vertical dots, indicating a passage to be repeated. [Middle English *repeten,* from Old French *repeter,* from Latin *repetere,* to go back to, seek again : *re-,* again + *petere,* to go to, seek (see **pet-**[1] in Appendix*).]

re·peat·ed (rĭ-pē′tĭd) *adj.* Said, done, or occurring again and again. —**re·peat′ed·ly** *adv.*

re·peat·er (rĭ-pē′tər) *n.* **1.** Someone or something that repeats. **2.** A watch or clock with a pressure-activated mechanism that strikes the hour. **3.** A **repeating firearm** *(see).* **4.** A student who repeats a course, usually one that he has previously failed. **5.** Someone who fraudulently votes more than once in a single election. **6.** Someone who has been convicted of wrongdoing more than once, especially for the same offense.

repeating decimal. A decimal in which, after a certain digit, a pattern of one or more digits is repeated indefinitely. Also called "circulating decimal," "recurring decimal."

repeating firearm. A firearm capable of firing several times without reloading. Also called "repeater."

re·pel (rĭ-pĕl′) *v.* **-pelled, -pelling, -pels.** —*tr.* **1.** To drive back; ward off or keep away: *repel insects.* **2.** To offer resistance to; fight against: *repel an invasion.* **3.** To refuse to accept; reject: *repel an offer.* **4.** To turn away from; spurn. **5.** To cause aversion or distaste in: *His rudeness repels everyone.* See Usage note below. **6.** To be resistant to; be incapable of absorbing or mixing with. **7.** To present an opposing force to; push back or away by a force: *Electric charges of the same sign repel one another.* —*intr.* **1.** To offer a resistant force to something. **2.** To cause aversion or distaste. See Usage note below. [Middle English *repellen,* from Latin *repellere* : *re-,* back + *pellere,* to drive (see **pel-**[6] in Appendix*).] —**re·pel′ler** *n.*

Usage: *Repel* and *repulse* (verbs) both have the physical sense of driving back or off. *Repulse* also may apply to rebuffing or rejecting by discourtesy; but only *repel* is used in the sense of causing distaste or aversion.

re·pel·lent (rĭ-pĕl′ənt) *adj.* **1.** Serving or tending to repel; capable of repelling something. **2.** Inspiring aversion or distaste; repulsive. **3.** Resistant or impervious to some substance. Often used in combination: *a water-repellent fabric.* —See Synonyms at **hateful.** —*n.* Something that repels, especially: **a.** A substance used to repel insects. **b.** A substance or treatment for making a fabric or surface impervious or resistant to something. —**re·pel′lence, re·pel′len·cy** *n.*

re·pent[1] (rĭ-pĕnt′) *v.* **-pented, -penting, -pents.** —*intr.* **1.** To feel remorse or self-reproach for what one has done or failed to do; be contrite. **2.** To feel such remorse or regret for past conduct as to change one's mind regarding it. Used with *of: He repented of his severity.* **3.** To feel remorse or contrition for one's sins and to abjure sinful ways. —*tr.* **1.** To feel regret or self-reproach for. **2.** To change one's mind regarding (past conduct). [Middle English *repenten,* from Old French *repentir* : *re-,* in response to + *pentir,* to be sorry, from Vulgar Latin *penitīre* (unattested), to cause to repent, from Latin *paenitēre* (see **penitent**).] —**re·pent′er** *n.*

re·pent[2] (rē′pənt) *adj. Biology.* Creeping along the ground; prostrate. [Latin *rēpēns,* present participle of *rēpere,* to creep. See **rēp-**[1] in Appendix.*]

re·pen·tance (rĭ-pĕn′təns) *n.* **1.** Remorse or contrition for past conduct or sin. **2.** The act or process of repenting.

re·pen·tant (rĭ-pĕn′tənt) *adj.* Characterized by or demonstrating repentance; penitent. —**re·pen′tant·ly** *adv.*

re·per·cus·sion (rē′pər-kŭsh′ən) *n.* **1.** An indirect effect, influence, or result produced by an event or action. **2.** A recoil, rebounding, or reciprocal motion after impact. **3.** A reflection, especially of sound. [Latin *repercussiō,* from *repercussus,* past participle of *repercutere,* to cause to rebound : *re-,* back + *percutere,* to PERCUSS.] —**re′per·cus′sive** *adj.*

rep·er·toire (rĕp′ər-twär, -tôr) *n.* Also **rep·er·to·ry** (-ər-tôr′ē, -ər-tōr′ē). **1.** The stock of songs, plays, operas, readings, or other pieces that a player or company is prepared to perform. **2.** The range or number of skills, aptitudes, or special accomplishments of a particular person or group. [French *répertoire,* from Late Latin *repertōrium,* REPERTORY.]

rep·er·to·ry (rĕp′ər-tôr′ē, -tōr′ē) *n., pl.* **-ries. 1.** A repertoire. **2.** A theater or theatrical company that presents plays from a specified repertoire, usually in alternation. Also called "repertory theater." **3.** A storehouse or other place where a stock of things is kept. **4.** Something stored in or as if in such a place; a stock or collection. [Late Latin *repertōrium,* from Latin *repertus,* past participle of *reperīre,* to find out, find again : *re-,* again + *parīre,* to produce, invent (see **per-**[4] in Appendix*).] —**rep′er·to′rial** *adj.*

rep·e·tend (rĕp′ə-tĕnd, rĕp′ə-tĕnd′) *n.* **1.** A word, sound, or phrase that is repeated; refrain. **2.** *Mathematics.* The digit or group of digits that repeats infinitely in a repeating decimal. [Latin *repetendum,* neuter gerundive of *repetere,* to REPEAT.]

rep·e·ti·tion (rĕp′ə-tĭsh′ən) *n.* **1.** The act or process of repeating; the saying, doing, or producing of something again. **2.** A recitation or recital, especially of prepared or memorized material. **3.** Something repeated or produced by repeating; a copy or reproduction. [Latin *repetītiō,* from *repetere,* REPEAT.]

rep·e·ti·tious (rĕp′ə-tĭsh′əs) *adj.* Characterized by or filled with repetition, especially needless or tedious repetition. —**rep′e·ti′tious·ly** *adv.* —**rep′e·ti′tious·ness** *n.*

re·pet·i·tive (rĭ-pĕt′ə-tĭv) *adj.* Characterized by repetition; tending to repeat. —**re·pet′i·tive·ly** *adv.* —**re·pet′i·tive·ness** *n.*

re·phrase (rē-frāz′) *tr.v.* **-phrased, -phrasing, -phrases.** To phrase again; especially, to state in a new or different way.

re·pine (rĭ-pīn′) *intr.v.* **-pined, -pining, -pines.** To be discontented or low in spirits; complain or fret. [RE- + PINE (pain).]

repl. replacement.

re·place (rĭ-plās′) *tr.v.* **-placed, -placing, -places. 1.** To place again; put back in place. **2.** To take or fill the place of; supplant or supersede. **3.** To be or provide a substitute for. **4.** To pay back or return; to refund. —**re·place′a·ble** *adj.* —**re·plac′er** *n.*

Synonyms: *replace, supplant, displace, supersede. Replace* applies both to substituting something new or workable for that which is lost, depleted, or worn out and to placing another in the stead of one who leaves or is dismissed from a position. *Supplant,* in literal usage, suggests intrigue, but is now often used without such implication. It emphasizes the loss of prestige or power by what or who is replaced. *Displace* implies the involuntary yielding of a place to another or simply to mechanical movement: *Gas displaced the water. Supersede* pertains to the replacement of a person or thing by another held to be superior or more recent.

re·place·ment (rĭ-plās′mənt) *n. Abbr.* **repl. 1.** The act or process of replacing or of being replaced. **2.** One that replaces; especially, a person assigned to a vacant military position.

re·plant (rē-plănt′, -plänt′) *tr.v.* **-planted, -planting, -plants. 1.** To plant something again, or in a new place. **2.** To supply with new plants: *replant a window box.* —*n.* (rē′plănt′, -plänt′). Something that has been replanted.

re·play (rē-plā′) *tr.v.* **-played, -playing, -plays.** To play (something) over again. —*n.* (rē′plā′). **1.** The act or process of replaying something. **2.** Something replayed.

re·plead·er (rĭ-plē′dər) *n. Law.* **1.** A court order requiring parties to plead their case again because of some prior erroneous or miscarried pleading. **2.** The right of pleading again.

re·plen·ish (rĭ-plĕn′ĭsh) *tr.v.* **-ished, -ishing, -ishes.** To fill or make complete again; add a new stock or supply to: *replenish the larder.* [Middle English *replenisshen,* from Old French *replenir* (present stem *repleniss-*) : *re-,* again + *plenir,* to fill, from *plein,* full, from Latin *plēnus* (see **pel-**[8] in Appendix*).] —**re·plen′ish·er** *n.* —**re·plen′ish·ment** *n.*

re·plete (rĭ-plēt′) *adj.* **1.** Plentifully supplied; abounding. Used with *with.* See Usage note below. **2.** Filled to satiation; gorged. [Middle English *replet,* from Old French, from Latin *replētus,* past participle of *replēre,* to refill : *re-,* again + *plēre,* to fill (see **pel-**[8] in Appendix*).] —**re·plete′ness** *n.*

Usage: *Replete* stresses great abundance. It is not the equivalent of *complete* or *equipped (with),* for which *replete* is often used loosely.

re·ple·tion (rĭ-plē′shən) *n.* **1.** The condition of being fully supplied or completely filled. **2.** A state of excessive fullness.

re·plev·i·a·ble (rĭ-plĕv′ī-ə-bəl) *adj.* Also **re·plev·is·a·ble** (-ə-sə-bəl). *Law.* Capable of being recovered by replevin.

re·plev·in (rĭ-plĕv′ĭn) *n.* Also **re·plev·y** (-plĕv′ē). **1.** An action to recover personal property unlawfully taken. **2.** The recovery of property by this action. **3.** The writ or procedure by which the property is recovered. —*tr.v.* **replevined, -ining, -ins.** To replevy. [Middle English *replevyn,* from Norman French *replevine,* a pledge, from Old French *replevir,* to recover, "to pledge back" : *re-,* back + *plevir,* pledge, from (unattested) Frankish *plegan* (see **plegan** in Appendix*).]

re·plev·y (rĭ-plĕv′ē) *tr.v.* **-ied, -ying, -ies.** To regain possession of (goods) by a writ of replevin. —*n.* Replevin. [Norman French *replevir,* from Old French. See **replevin.**]

rep·li·ca (rĕp′lə-kə) *n.* **1.** A copy or reproduction of a work of art, especially one made by the original artist. **2.** Any copy or close reproduction. [Italian, from *replicare,* to repeat, from Latin *replicāre,* REPLICATE.]

Usage: *Replica* in its strictest sense is reserved for a copy by the original artist. But it is widely accepted for any close reproduction, and it is acceptable to 60 per cent of the Usage Panel in the still less literal sense of "close reproduction in miniature."

rep·li·cate (rĕp′lĭ-kāt′) *tr.v.* **-cated, -cating, -cates. 1.** To duplicate, copy, or repeat. **2.** To fold over or bend back upon itself. —*adj.* (rĕp′lĭ-kət). Also **rep·li·cat·ed** (-kā′tĭd). Folded over or bent back upon itself: *a replicate leaf.* [Late Latin *replicāre,* to repeat, from Latin, to fold back : *re-,* back + *plicāre,* to fold (see **plek-** in Appendix*).]

rep·li·ca·tion (rĕp′lə-kā′shən) *n.* **1.** A fold or a folding back. **2.** A reply; response, especially to an answer. **3.** *Law.* The plaintiff's response to the defendant's answer or plea. **4.** An echo or reverberation. **5.** A copy or reproduction. **6.** The act or process of duplicating or reproducing something.

re·ply (rĭ-plī′) *v.* **-plied, -plying, -plies.** —*intr.* **1.** To give an answer in speech or writing. **2.** To respond by some action or gesture: *He replied by shrugging his shoulders.* **3.** To echo. **4.** *Law.* To answer a defendant's plea. —*tr.* To say or give as an answer: *He replied that he was unable to help them.* —See Synonyms at **answer.** —*n., pl.* **replies. 1.** An answer in speech or writing. **2.** A response by action or gesture. **3.** *Law.* A plaintiff's speech or argument in answer to that of a defendant. [Middle English *replīen,* from Old French *replier,* to fold back, reply, from Latin *replicāre,* REPLICATE.] —**re·pli′er** *n.*

ré·pon·dez s'il vous plaît (rā-pôN-dā′ sēl vōō plĕ′). *Abbr.* **R.S.V.P., r.s.v.p.** *French.* Please reply. Used on formal invitations.

re·port (rĭ-pôrt′) *n. Abbr.* **rep., rept., rpt. 1.** An account or announcement that is prepared, presented, or delivered, usually in formal or organized form. **2.** A formal, detailed account of the proceedings or transactions of a group. **3.** *Usually plural. Law.* A published collection of authoritative accounts of court cases or of judicial decisions. **4.** Rumor or gossip; common talk: *According to report, they eloped.* **5.** Reputation; repute: *a man of bad report.* **6.** An explosive noise: *the rifle's report.* —*v.* **re-**

ported, -porting, -ports. —*tr.* 1. To make or present an account of (something), often officially, formally, or regularly. 2. To relate or tell about; to present: *report one's findings.* 3. To write or provide an account or summation of for publication or broadcast. 4. To submit or relate the results of considerations concerning: *The committee reported the bill.* 5. To carry back and repeat to another. 6. To complain about or denounce: *Report him to the police.* —*intr.* 1. To make a report. 2. To serve as a reporter for a newspaper or similar publication. 3. To present oneself: *report for duty.* [Middle English, from Old French, from *reporter,* to carry back, from Latin *reportāre,* "to carry back" : *re-,* back + *portāre,* to carry (see **per-**[2] in Appendix*).] —**re·port'a·ble** *adj.*

re·port·age (rĕp'ər-täzh', rĭ-pôr'tĭj) *n.* The reporting of news or information of general interest.

re·port·ed·ly (rĭ-pôr'tĭd-lē, rĭ-pōr'-) *adv.* By report; supposedly.

re·port·er (rĭ-pôr'tər, rĭ-pōr'-) *n. Abbr.* **rep.** 1. A person who reports. 2. A writer of news stories. 3. A person authorized to write and issue official accounts of judicial or legislative proceedings. —**rep'or·to'ri·al** (rĕp'ər-tôr'ē-əl, -tōr'ē-əl, rē'pôr-, rē'pōr-) *adj.*

re·pose[1] (rĭ-pōz') *n.* 1. a. The act of resting; a rest. b. The state of being at rest; relaxation. 2. Peace of mind; freedom from anxiety; composure. 3. Calmness; tranquillity. —See Synonyms at **rest.** —*v.* **reposed, -posing, -poses.** —*tr.* To lay (oneself) down. Used reflexively. —*intr.* 1. To lie at rest; relax. 2. To lie supported by something. [Middle English *reposen,* from Old French *reposer, repauser,* from Late Latin *repausāre* : *re-* (intensifier), again + *pausāre,* to rest, from Latin *pausa,* a stop, pause, from Greek *pausis,* from *pauein,* to stop (see **pauein** in Appendix*).] —**re·pos'al** (rĭ-pō'zəl) *n.* —**re·pos'er** *n.*

re·pose[2] (rĭ-pōz') *tr.v.* **-posed, -posing, -poses.** To place, as faith or trust in: *The nation had reposed its hopes in a single man.* [Middle English *reposen* : RE- + POSE (formed on analogy with Latin *repōnere,* to put back).]

re·pose·ful (rĭ-pōz'fəl) *adj.* Expressing repose; calm. —**re·pose'ful·ly** *adv.* —**re·pose'ful·ness** *n.*

re·pos·it (rĭ-pŏz'ĭt) *tr.v.* **-ited, -iting, -its.** To put away; store. [Latin *repōnere* (past participle *repositus*), to put back, replace : *re-,* back + *pōnere,* to place (see **apo-** in Appendix*).] —**re'po·si'tion** (rē'pə-zĭsh'ən, rĕp'ə-) *n.*

re·pos·i·to·ry (rĭ-pŏz'ə-tôr'ē, -tōr'ē) *n., pl.* **-ries.** 1. A place where things may be put for safekeeping. 2. A warehouse. 3. A museum. 4. A burial vault; tomb. 5. A person to whom a secret is told.

re·pos·sess (rē'pə-zĕs') *tr.v.* **-sessed, -sessing, -sesses.** 1. To take back possession of (property); regain possession of. 2. To give back possession to. —**re'pos·ses'sion** *n.*

re·pous·sé (rə-pōō-sā') *adj. Metalworking.* 1. Raised in relief. 2. Decorated with raised designs. —*n. Metalworking.* 1. A design hammered in relief. 2. The technique of hammering such a design. [French, past participle of *repousser,* to push back, from Old French : *re-,* back + *pousser,* to PUSH.]

repp. Variant of **rep** (fabric).

repr. representing.

rep·re·hend (rĕp'rĭ-hĕnd') *tr.v.* **-hended, -hending, -hends.** To reprove; censure. See Synonyms at **criticize.** [Middle English *reprehenden,* from Latin *reprehendere,* rebuke, hold back : *re-,* back + *prehendere,* to seize (see **ghend-** in Appendix*).]

rep·re·hen·si·ble (rĕp'rĭ-hĕn'sə-bəl) *adj.* Deserving of rebuke or censure; blameworthy. [Late Latin *reprehēnsibilis,* from Latin *reprehendere* (past participle *reprehēnsus*), to REPREHEND.] —**rep're·hen'si·bil'i·ty, rep're·hen'si·ble·ness** *n.* —**rep're·hen'si·bly** *adv.*

rep·re·hen·sion (rĕp'rĭ-hĕn'shən) *n.* Rebuke; reproof; censure.

rep·re·sent (rĕp'rĭ-zĕnt') *tr.v.* **-sented, -senting, -sents.** 1. To stand for; symbolize. 2. To depict; portray. 3. To present clearly to the mind. 4. To make representations (of something) to someone by way of remonstrance or expostulation. 5. To describe (a person or thing) as an embodiment of some specified quality. 6. To serve as the official and authorized delegate or agent for; act as a spokesman for. 7. To serve as an example of: *a mammal represented by seven species.* 8. To be the equivalent of. 9. a. To stage (a play, for example); to present; produce. b. To act the part or role of. —See Synonyms at **mean.** [Middle English *representen,* from Latin *repraesentāre,* show, bring back : *re-,* back, again + *praesentāre,* to PRESENT.] —**rep're·sent'a·ble** *adj.* —**rep're·sent'a·bil'i·ty** *n.*

rep·re·sen·ta·tion (rĕp'rĭ-zĕn-tā'shən, rĕp'rĭ-zən-) *n.* 1. The act of representing or the state of being represented. 2. That which represents. 3. a. An account or statement, as of facts, allegations, or arguments. b. An expostulation; protest. 4. A presentation or production, as of a play. 5. The state or condition of serving as an official delegate, agent, or spokesman. 6. *Government.* The right or privilege of being represented by delegates having a voice in a legislative body. 7. *Law.* A statement of fact made by one party in order to induce another party to enter into a contract.

rep·re·sen·ta·tion·al (rĕp'rĭ-zĕn-tā'shən-əl, rĕp'rĭ-zən-) *adj.* Of or pertaining to representation, especially to realistic graphic representation. —**rep're·sen·ta'tion·al·ism'** *n.*

rep·re·sen·ta·tive (rĕp'rĭ-zĕn'tə-tĭv) *n. Abbr.* **rep., Rep.** 1. A person or thing serving as an example or type for others of the same classification; a typical instance. 2. One qualified to serve as an authorized official delegate or agent. 3. a. A member of a governmental body, usually legislative, chosen by popular vote. b. In the United States, a member of the House of Representatives, the lower house of Congress, or of a state legislature. —*adj.* 1. Representing, depicting, portraying, or able to do so. 2. Authorized to act as an official delegate or agent. 3. Of, pertaining to, or characteristic of government by representation. 4. Exemplary of others in the same class; typical. —**rep're·sen'ta·tive·ly** *adv.* —**rep're·sen'ta·tive·ness** *n.*

re·press (rĭ-prĕs') *tr.v.* **-pressed, -pressing, -presses.** 1. To hold back; restrain: *repress a laugh.* 2. To suppress; quell: *repress a rebellion.* 3. To force (memories, ideas, or fears, for example) into the subconscious mind. [Middle English *repressen,* from Latin *reprimere* (past participle *repressus*) : *re-,* back + *premere,* to press (see **per-**[6] in Appendix*).] —**re·press'i·ble** *adj.*

re·pres·sion (rĭ-prĕsh'ən) *n.* 1. a. The action of repressing. b. The state of being repressed. 2. *Psychoanalysis.* The unconscious exclusion of painful impulses, desires, or fears from the conscious mind. —**re·pres'sive** (-prĕs'ĭv) *adj.* —**re·pres'sive·ly** *adv.* —**re·pres'sive·ness** *n.*

re·pres·sor (rĭ-prĕs'ər) *n.* Also **re·press·er.** 1. One that represses. 2. *Biology.* A chemical compound that prevents the synthesis of a protein by interfering with the action of DNA.

re·prieve (rĭ-prēv') *tr.v.* **-prieved, -prieving, -prieves.** To postpone the punishment of. —*n.* 1. a. The postponement of a punishment. b. A warrant for such a postponement. 2. Temporary relief, as from danger or pain. [Variant of earlier *reprive, repry,* from Middle English *repryen,* from Old French *reprendre* (past participle *repris*), to take back, from Latin *reprehendere,* to hold back, REPREHEND.] —**re·priev'a·ble** *adj.*

rep·ri·mand (rĕp'rə-mănd', -mänd') *tr.v.* **-manded, -manding, -mands.** To rebuke or censure severely. See Synonyms at **admonish.** —*n.* A severe or formal rebuke or censure. [Old French *reprimender,* from *reprimende,* a reprimand, from Latin *reprimenda,* neuter plural gerundive of *reprimere,* to REPRESS.]

re·print (rē'prĭnt') *n. Abbr.* **rep.** 1. Something that has been printed again, especially: a. A new or additional edition; a facsimile impression of an original. b. An offprint; a separately printed excerpt. 2. *Philately.* A facsimile of a stamp printed after the original issue of the stamp has ceased. —*tr.v.* (rē-prĭnt') **reprinted, -printing, -prints.** To print again; make a new copy or edition of. —**re·print'er** *n.*

re·pri·sal (rĭ-prī'zəl) *n.* 1. The forcible seizure of an enemy's goods or subjects in retaliation for inflicted injuries. 2. The practice of using political or military force without actually resorting to war. 3. Retaliation for an injury with the intent of inflicting at least as much injury in return. [Middle English *reprisail,* from Norman French *reprisaille,* from Medieval Latin *repraesālia,* contraction of *repraehensālia,* from Latin *reprehensus,* past participle of *reprehendere,* to REPREHEND.]

re·prise (rə-prēz') *n. Music.* A repetition of a phrase or verse; a return to an original theme. [Middle English, from Old French, "a taking back," from the feminine past participle of *reprendre,* to take back, from Latin *reprehendere,* to REPREHEND.]

re·pro (rē'prō) *n., pl.* **-pros.** A **reproduction proof** *(see).*

re·proach (rĭ-prōch') *tr.v.* **-proached, -proaching, -proaches.** 1. To blame for something; rebuke. 2. To bring shame upon; disgrace. —See Synonyms at **admonish.** —*n.* 1. Censure; rebuke; blame. 2. That which causes rebuke or blame. 3. Disgrace; shame. [Middle English *reprochen,* from Old French *reprochier,* from Vulgar Latin *repropiāre* (unattested), bring back near : Latin *re-,* back + *prope,* near (see **per**[1] in Appendix*).] —**re·proach'a·ble** *adj.* —**re·proach'a·ble·ness** *n.* —**re·proach'a·bly** *adv.* —**re·proach'er** *n.*

re·proach·ful (rĭ-prōch'fəl) *adj.* Expressing reproach or blame. —**re·proach'ful·ly** *adv.* —**re·proach'ful·ness** *n.*

rep·ro·bate (rĕp'rə-bāt') *n.* 1. A morally unprincipled person. 2. *Theology.* One who is predestined to damnation. —*adj.* 1. Morally unprincipled; profligate. 2. *Theology.* Rejected by God and without hope of salvation. —*tr.v.* **reprobated, -bating, -bates.** 1. To disapprove of; condemn. 2. *Theology.* To abandon to eternal damnation. [Late Latin *reprobātus,* past participle of *reprobāre,* to reprove : Latin *re-,* back, against + *probāre,* to test, PROVE.] —**rep'ro·ba'tion** *n.*

re·pro·duce (rē'prə-dōōs', -dyōōs') *v.* **-duced, -ducing, -duces.** —*tr.* 1. To produce a counterpart, image, or copy of. 2. *Biology.* To generate (offspring) by sexual or asexual means. 3. To produce again or anew; re-create. 4. To bring to mind again, as a memory. —*intr.* 1. To generate offspring. 2. To undergo copying. —**re'pro·duc'er** *n.* —**re'pro·duc'i·ble** *adj.*

re·pro·duc·tion (rē'prə-dŭk'shən) *n.* 1. The act of reproducing or of being reproduced. 2. That which is reproduced. 3. *Biology.* The sexual or asexual process by which organisms generate others of the same kind.

reproduction proof. *Printing.* A proof of metal type made for reproduction through a photographic process such as photo-offset lithography. Also called "repro."

re·pro·duc·tive (rē'prə-dŭk'tĭv) *adj.* 1. Of or pertaining to reproduction. 2. Tending to reproduce. —**re'pro·duc'tive·ly** *adv.* —**re'pro·duc'tive·ness** *n.*

re·proof (rĭ-prōōf') *n.* An act or expression of reproving.

re·prove (rĭ-prōōv') *tr.v.* **-proved, -proving, -proves.** 1. To rebuke for a fault or misdeed; scold. 2. To find fault with. —See Synonyms at **admonish.** [Middle English *reproven,* from Old French *reprover,* from Late Latin *reprobāre,* REPROBATE.] —**re·prov'a·ble** *adj.* —**re·prov'er** *n.* —**re·prov'ing·ly** *adv.*

rept. 1. receipt. 2. report.

rep·tant (rĕp'tənt) *adj. Biology.* Creeping or crawling; repent. [Latin *reptāns,* present participle of *reptāre,* to crawl, frequentative of *repere,* to crawl. See **rēp-**[1] in Appendix.*]

rep·tile (rĕp'tĭl, -tīl') *n.* 1. Any of various cold-blooded, usually egg-laying vertebrates of the class Reptilia, as a snake, lizard, crocodile, turtle, or dinosaur, having an external covering of scales or horny plates, and breathing by means of lungs. **2.** A sly or treacherous person. *—adj.* **1.** Of, pertaining to, or characteristic of reptiles. **2.** Creeping. **3.** Treacherous; sly. [Middle English *reptil,* from Old French *reptile,* from Late Latin *reptile,* neuter of *reptilis,* creeping, from Latin *repere,* to creep. See **rep-**[1] in Appendix.*]

rep·til·i·an (rĕp-tĭl′ē-ən, -tĭl′yən) *adj.* **1.** Of or pertaining to reptiles. **2.** Resembling or characteristic of a reptile. **3.** Sly; mean; vicious. *—n.* A reptile.

Repub. 1. republic. **2.** Republican (Party).

re·pub·lic (rĭ-pŭb′lĭk) *n. Abbr.* **rep., Rep., Repub. 1.** Any political order that is not a monarchy. **2.** A constitutional form of government, especially a democratic one. **3.** Any group of people working freely and equally for the same cause: *the republic of letters.* [Old French *republique,* from Latin *rēspublica* : *rēs,* a thing, matter, affair (see **rei-**[3] in Appendix*) + *pūblica,* feminine of *pūblicus,* PUBLIC.]

re·pub·li·can (rĭ-pŭb′lĭ-kən) *adj.* **1.** Of, pertaining to, or characteristic of a republic. **2.** In favor of a republican form of government. **3.** *Capital* **R.** *Abbr.* **R., Rep., Repub.** Of, pertaining to, characteristic of, or belonging to the Republican Party of the United States. *—n.* **1.** A person who favors a republican form of government. **2.** *Capital* **R.** A member of the Republican Party of the United States. **—re·pub′li·can·ism′** *n.*

Republican calendar. The **Revolutionary calendar** *(see).*

re·pub·li·can·ize (rĭ-pŭb′lĭ-kən-īz′) *tr.v.* **-ized, -izing, -izes.** To make republican. **—re·pub′li·can·i·za′tion** *n.*

Republican Party. 1. One of the two primary political parties of the United States, organized in 1854 to oppose slavery. **2.** The Democratic-Republican Party, a former political party of the United States, organized in 1792 by Thomas Jefferson. See **Democratic Party.**

Republican River. A river flowing 445 miles eastward from southwestern Nebraska to join the Smoky Hill River and form the Kansas River at Junction City, Kansas.

re·pub·li·ca·tion (rē′pŭb-lĭ-kā′shən) *n.* **1.** The act of republishing. **2.** That which is republished.

re·pub·lish (rē′pŭb′lĭsh) *tr.v.* **-lished, -lishing, -lishes. 1.** To publish anew or again. **2.** *Law.* To revive, as a canceled will. **—re′pub′lish·er** *n.*

re·pu·di·ate (rĭ-pyo͞o′dē-āt′) *tr.v.* **-ated, -ating, -ates. 1.** To reject the validity of. **2.** To refuse to recognize or pay. **3.** To disown, as a son. [Latin *repudiāre,* to reject, cast off, from *repudium,* a casting off. See **speud-** in Appendix.*] **—re·pu′di·a′tive** *adj.* **—re·pu′di·a′tor** (-ā′tər) *n.*

re·pu·di·a·tion (rĭ-pyo͞o′dē-ā′shən) *n.* **1.** The act of repudiating or the state of being repudiated. **2.** The act of refusing to acknowledge a contract or debt.

re·pugn (rĭ-pyo͞on′) *v.* **-pugned, -pugning, -pugns.** *Obsolete. —tr.* To oppose or resist. *—intr.* To be opposed; conflict. [Middle English *repugnen,* from Old French *repugner,* from Latin *repugnāre,* to fight against : *re-,* against + *pugnāre,* to fight (see **peuk-** in Appendix*).]

re·pug·nance (rĭ-pŭg′nəns) *n.* Also **re·pug·nan·cy** (-nən-sē). **1.** The state of feeling extreme dislike or aversion. **2.** *Logic.* The relationship of contradictory terms; inconsistency.

re·pug·nant (rĭ-pŭg′nənt) *adj.* **1.** Offensive; distasteful; repulsive. **2.** *Logic.* Contradictory; inconsistent. [Middle English, from Old French, from Latin *repugnāns,* present participle of *repugnāre,* REPUGN.] **—re·pug′nant·ly** *adv.*

re·pulse (rĭ-pŭls′) *tr.v.* **-pulsed, -pulsing, -pulses. 1.** To drive back; repel. **2.** To repel with rudeness, coldness, or denial. —See Usage note at **repel.** *—n* **1.** The act of repulsing or the state of being repulsed. **2.** Rejection; refusal. [Latin *repulsus,* past participle of *repellere,* to REPEL.] **—re·puls′er** *n.*

re·pul·sion (rĭ-pŭl′shən) *n.* **1.** The act of repulsing, or the condition of being repulsed. **2.** Extreme aversion or dislike.

re·pul·sive (rĭ-pŭl′sĭv) *adj.* **1.** Causing repugnance, extreme dislike, or aversion; disgusting. **2.** Tending to repel or drive off. **—re·pul′sive·ly** *adv.* **—re·pul′sive·ness** *n.*

rep·u·ta·ble (rĕp′yə-tə-bəl) *adj.* **1.** Having a good reputation; honorable; trustworthy. **2.** In correct usage. Said of words. **—rep′u·ta·bil′i·ty** *n.* **—rep′u·ta·bly** *adv.*

rep·u·ta·tion (rĕp′yə-tā′shən) *n.* **1.** The general estimation in which a person or thing is held by the public. **2.** The state or situation of being held in high repute. **3.** A specific character or trait ascribed to a person or thing: *a reputation for courtesy.* [Middle English *reputacion,* from Latin *reputātiō,* a reckoning, from *reputāre,* to consider, REPUTE.]

re·pute (rĭ-pyo͞ot′) *tr.v.* **-puted, -puting, -putes.** To assign a reputation to. Usually used in the passive. *—n.* **1.** Reputation. **2.** A good reputation. —See Synonyms at **fame.** [Middle English *reputen,* from Old French *reputer,* from Latin *reputāre,* to count over, consider : *re-,* over, again + *putāre,* to compute, consider (see **peue-**[2] in Appendix*).]

re·put·ed (rĭ-pyo͞o′tĭd) *adj.* Generally considered or supposed. **—re·put′ed·ly** *adv.*

req. 1. require; required. **2.** requisition.

re·quest (rĭ-kwĕst′) *tr.v.* **-quested, -questing, -quests. 1.** To ask for; express a desire for. **2.** To ask (a person) to do something. *—n.* **1.** An expressed desire; the act of asking. **2.** That which is asked for. **—by request.** In response to an expressed desire. **—in request.** In great demand. *—adj.* Having been desired or demanded: *a request performance.* [Old French *requester,* from *requeste,* a request, from Vulgar Latin *requaestia* (unattested), from Latin *requīrere,* to seek again, REQUIRE.]

Usage: *Request* (noun) is commonly followed by *for: a request for records.* But *request* (verb) is improperly followed by *for* in these constructions: *to request Jones for records; to request for Jones to supply records.* The sense is more properly expressed by any of these: *to request Jones to supply; to request that Jones supply; to request records from Jones.*

re·qui·em (rĕk′wē-əm, rē′kwē-) *n.* **1.** *Capital* **R.** *Roman Catholic Church.* **a.** A mass for a deceased person or persons. **b.** A musical composition for such a mass. **2.** Any hymn, composition, or service for the dead. [Middle English, from Latin (first word of the introit of the mass for the dead), accusative of *requiēs,* rest, "after-rest" : *re-,* after, in response to + *quiēs,* rest (see **kweyə-** in Appendix*).]

req·ui·es·cat (rĕk′wē-ĕs′kăt′, -kät′) *n.* A prayer for the repose of the souls of the dead. [Latin, "may he (or she) rest," from *requiescere,* to rest : *re-,* again + *quiescere,* to be quiet, rest, from *quiēs,* quiet, rest (see **kweyə-** in Appendix*).]

re·quire (rĭ-kwīr′) *tr.v.* **-quired, -quiring, -quires. 1.** To have use for as a necessity; need. **2.** To demand; insist upon. **3.** To command; to order. [Middle English *requiren,* from Old French *requere,* from Vulgar Latin *requaerere* (unattested), from Latin *requīrere,* to seek again, search for, inquire : *re-,* again + *quaerere,* to seek, to ask (see **quaerere** in Appendix*).] **—re·quir′a·ble** *adj.* **—re·quir′er** *n.*

re·quired (rĭ-kwīrd′) *adj. Abbr.* **req.** Needed; essential. See Synonyms at **necessary.**

re·quire·ment (rĭ-kwīr′mənt) *n.* **1.** That which is required; something needed. **2.** Something obligatory; a prerequisite.

req·ui·site (rĕk′wə-zĭt) *adj.* Required; absolutely needed; essential. See Synonyms at **necessary.** *—n.* A necessity; something absolutely essential. See Synonyms at **need.** [Middle English, from Latin *requīsītus,* past participle of *requīrere,* to REQUIRE.] **—req′ui·site·ly** *adv.* **—req′ui·site·ness** *n.*

req·ui·si·tion (rĕk′wə-zĭsh′ən) *n. Abbr.* **req. 1.** A formal written request for something that is needed. **2.** A necessity; requirement. **3.** The state or condition of being needed. **4.** A formal request of one government to another, demanding the return of a criminal. *—tr.v.* **requisitioned, -tioning, -tions. 1.** To demand, as for military needs. **2.** To make demands of.

re·qui·tal (rĭ-kwīt′l) *n.* **1.** The act of requiting. **2.** Return, as for an injury or for some friendly act.

re·quite (rĭ-kwīt′) *tr.v.* **-quited, -quiting, -quites. 1.** To make repayment or return for: *requite another's love.* **2.** To avenge. [RE- + obsolete *quite,* to repay, variant of QUIT.] **—re·quit′a·ble** *adj.* **—re·quit′er** *n.*

re·ra·di·a·tion (rē-rā′dē-ā′shən) *n.* Also **re·ra·di·a·tion.** *Physics.* Radiation emission resulting from radiation absorption.

rere·dos (rĭr′dŏs) *n.* **1.** A **retable** *(see).* **2.** The back of an open hearth of a fireplace. [Middle English, from Old French *areredos* : *arere,* back, behind, from Vulgar Latin *ad retrō* (unattested) : Latin *ad,* to + *retrō,* backward (see **re-** in Appendix*) + *dos,* back, from Latin *dorsum* (see **dorsum** in Appendix*).]

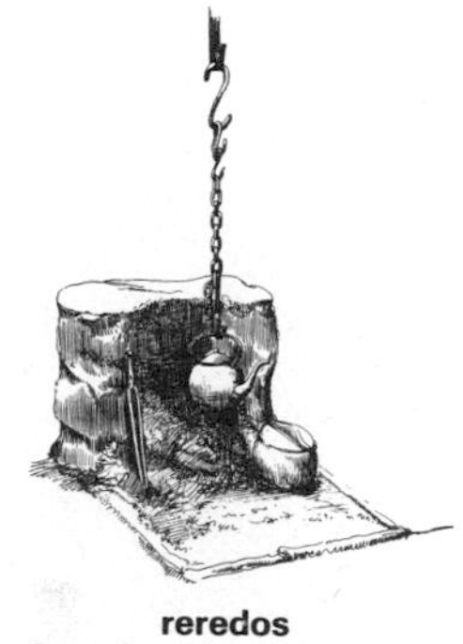

reredos
Open-hearth reredos from the Shetland Islands

re·run (rē′rŭn′) *n. Motion Pictures & Television.* A repetition of a recorded performance. *—tr.v.* (rē′rŭn′) **reran** (-răn′), **-running, -runs.** To present a second production of.

res. 1. research. **2.** reserve. **3.** residence; resident; resides. **4.** resolution.

RES reticuloendothelial system.

res ad·ju·di·ca·ta. Variant of **res judicata.**

re·sale (rē′săl, rē-săl′) *n.* The act of selling again.

re·scind (rĭ-sĭnd′) *tr.v.* **-scinded, -scinding, -scinds.** To void; repeal. See Synonyms at **nullify.** [Latin *rescindere,* to cut off, abolish : *re-* (intensifier), again + *scindere,* to cut (see **skei-** in Appendix*).] **—re·scind′a·ble** *adj.* **—re·scind′er** *n.*

re·scis·sion (rĭ-sĭzh′ən) *n.* The act of rescinding. [Late Latin *rescissiō,* from Latin *rēcissus,* past participle of *rescindere,* RESCIND.] **—re·scis′so·ry** (-sĭz′ə-rē, -sĭs′ə-rē) *adj.*

re·script (rē′skrĭpt) *n.* **1.** *Roman Catholic Church.* A response from the Pope or other ecclesiastical superior to a question regarding discipline or doctrine. **2.** Any formal decree or edict. **3.** A reply from the Roman emperor to a magistrate's query on a point of law. [Latin *rēscriptum,* from the neuter past participle of *rēscrībere,* to write back or in reply : *re-,* back + *scrībere,* to write (see **skeri-** in Appendix*).]

res·cue (rĕs′kyo͞o) *tr.v.* **-cued, -cuing, -cues. 1.** To save, as from danger or imprisonment. **2.** *Law.* To take from legal custody by force. —See Synonyms at **save.** *—n.* **1.** An act of freeing or saving; deliverance. **2.** *Law.* Removal from legal custody by force. [Middle English *rescuen,* from Old French *rescourre,* from Vulgar Latin *reexcutere* (unattested), to drive away, shake off : Latin *re-* (intensifier) + *excutere,* to shake out or off : *ex,* out + *quatere,* to shake (see **kwēt-** in Appendix*).] **—res′cu·a·ble** *adj.* **—res′cu·er** *n.*

rescue grass. A tall grass, *Bromus catharticus,* native to tropical America, cultivated in warm regions for hay. [Probably variant of FESCUE grass.]

re·search (rĭ-sûrch′, rē′sûrch) *n. Abbr.* **res.** Scholarly or scientific investigation or inquiry. *—v.* **researched, -searching, -searches.** *—intr.* To engage in or perform research. *—tr.* To study thoroughly. [Old French *recerche,* from *recercher,* to seek out, to search again : *re-,* again + *cerch(i)er,* to SEARCH.] **—re·search′er** *n.*

ré·seau, re·seau (rē-zō′, rĭ-zō′) *n., pl.* **-seaus** (-zōz′) or **-seaux** (-zō′). **1.** A net or mesh foundation for lace. **2.** *Astronomy.* A reference grid of fine lines forming uniform squares on a photographic plate or print, used to aid in measurement. **3.** *Photography.* A mosaic screen of fine lines of three colors, used in color photography. [French, from Old French *reseuil,* diminutive of *raiz, roiz,* a net, from Latin *rētis, rēte.* See **erə-**[2] in Appendix.*]

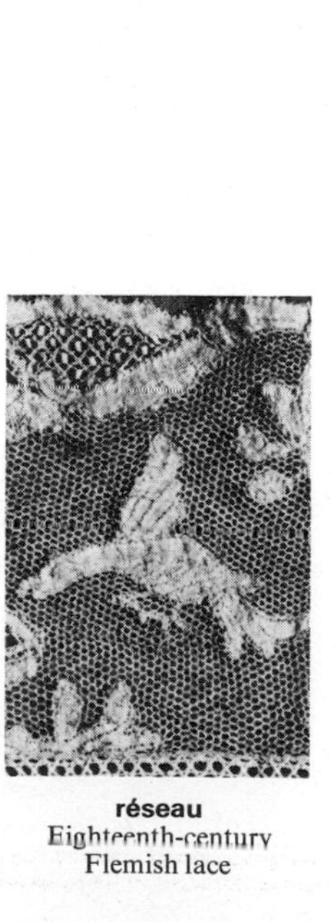

réseau
Eighteenth-century Flemish lace

re·sect (rĭ-sĕkt′) *tr.v.* **-sected, -secting, -sects.** To perform a resection; cut off or away. [Latin *resectus,* past participle of

resecāre, to cut off : *re-*, back, off + *secāre*, to cut (see **sek-** in Appendix*).]
re·sec·tion (rĭ-sĕk′shən) *n.* The surgical removal of part of an organ or structure.
re·se·da (rĭ-sē′də) *n.* **1.** Any plant of the genus *Reseda*, which includes the mignonette. **2.** Grayish or dark green to yellow green or light olive. See **color**. [New Latin, from Latin *resēda*†.] —**re·se′da** *adj.*
re·sem·blance (rĭ-zĕm′bləns) *n.* **1.** The condition or quality of resembling something; similarity in nature, form, or appearance; likeness. **2.** Something that resembles another; a likeness; semblance. —See Synonyms at **likeness**.
re·sem·ble (rĭ-zĕm′bəl) *tr.v.* **-bled, -bling, -bles.** To have a similarity to; be like. [Middle English *resemblen*, from Old French *resembler* : *re-* (intensifier) + *sembler*, to be like, from Latin *simulāre, similāre*, to imitate, from *similis*, like (see **sem-**¹ in Appendix*).] —**re·sem′bler** *n.*
re·sent (rĭ-zĕnt′) *tr.v.* **-sented, -senting, -sents.** To feel indignantly aggrieved at (an act, situation, or person). [Obsolete French *resentir*, to feel strongly : *re-* (intensive) + *sentir*, to feel, from Latin *sentīre* (see **sent-** in Appendix*).]
re·sent·ful (rĭ-zĕnt′fəl) *adj.* Full of, characterized by, or inclined to feel resentment. —**re·sent′ful·ly** *adv.* —**re·sent′ful·ness** *n.*
re·sent·ment (rĭ-zĕnt′mənt) *n.* Indignation or ill will felt as a result of a real or imagined offense. See Synonyms at **anger**.
re·ser·pine (rĭ-sûr′pĭn, -pēn′, rĕs′ər-pĭn, -pēn′) *n.* A white to yellowish powder, $C_{33}H_{40}N_2O_9$, isolated from the roots of certain species of rauwolfia, and used as a sedative and tranquilizer. [German *Reserpin*, from New Latin *Rauwolfia serpentina*, a species of snakeroot : RAUWOLFIA + Late Latin *serpentīna*, feminine of *serpentīnus*, SERPENTINE.]
res·er·va·tion (rĕz′ər-vā′shən) *n.* **1.** The act of reserving; a keeping back or withholding. **2.** Something that is kept back or withheld. **3.** A limiting qualification, condition, or exception. **4.** A tract of land set apart by the Federal government for a special purpose; especially, one for the use of an American Indian people or tribe. **5. a.** An arrangement by which accommodations are secured in advance, as in a hotel or on an airplane. **b.** The accommodations so secured. **c.** The record or promise of such an arrangement. —See Synonyms at **qualm**.
re·serve (rĭ-zûrv′) *tr.v.* **-served, -serving, -serves.** **1.** To keep back or save for future use or a special purpose. **2.** To set apart for a particular person or use. **3.** To keep or secure for oneself; retain: *I reserve the right to disagree.* —See Synonyms at **keep**. —*n. Abbr.* **res.** **1.** Something kept back or saved for future use or special purpose. **2.** The state of being kept back, set aside, or saved: *funds held in reserve.* **3.** The act of reserving; a reservation, condition, or exception. **4.** The keeping of one's feelings, thoughts, or affairs to oneself. **5.** Self-restraint in expression; reticence; discretion. **6.** Lack of enthusiasm; skeptical caution. **7.** An amount of capital held back from investment by a bank or company in order to meet probable or possible demands. **8.** A reservation of public land: *a forest reserve.* **9.** *Often plural.* **a.** A fighting force kept uncommitted until strategic need arises. **b.** The part of a country's armed forces not on active duty but subject to call in an emergency. —*adj.* Held in or forming a reserve: *a reserve supply of food.* [Middle English *reserven*, from Old French *reserver*, from Latin *reservāre*, to keep back : *re-*, back + *servāre*, to save, keep (see **ser-**¹ in Appendix*).] —**re·serv′a·ble** *adj.* —**re·serv′er** *n.*
reserve bank. Any of the 12 main banks of the U.S. Federal Reserve System.
re·served (rĭ-zûrvd′) *adj.* **1.** Held in reserve; kept back or set aside. **2.** Characterized by self-restraint or reticence; not outgoing in manner or speech; undemonstrative; reticent. —See Synonyms at **humble, silent**. —**re·serv′ed·ly** (rĭ-zûr′vĭd-lē) *adv.* —**re·serv′ed·ness** *n.*
Reserve Officers' Training Corps. *Abbr.* **ROTC, R.O.T.C.** A U.S. military corps that trains college students for commission as officers upon graduation.
re·serv·ist (rĭ-zûr′vĭst) *n.* A member of a military reserve.
res·er·voir (rĕz′ər-vwär′, -vwôr′, -vôr′) *n.* **1.** A body of water collected and stored in a natural or artificial lake. **2.** A receptacle or chamber for storing a fluid. **3.** *Anatomy.* A **cisterna** *(see).* **4.** A large supply of something; a reserve: *a reservoir of gratitude.* [French *réservoir*, from *réserver*, to RESERVE.]
re·set (rē-sĕt′) *tr.v.* **-set, -setting, -sets.** To set (as a broken bone, or matter in type) again. —*n.* (rē′sĕt′). **1.** The act of resetting. **2.** Something that is reset. —**re·set′ter** *n.*
res ges·tae (rās gĕs′tī). *Latin.* **1.** Things done; deeds. **2.** *Law.* The facts of a case that are admissible in evidence.
resh (rĕsh) *n.* The 20th letter of the Hebrew alphabet, corresponding to the letter *r* in English. See **alphabet**. [Hebrew *rēsh*, from *rōsh*, "head."]
Resht (rĕsht). Also **Rasht** (răsht). A major commercial city of Iran, in the north near the Caspian Sea. Population, 119,000.
re·side (rĭ-zīd′) *intr.v.* **-sided, -siding, -sides.** **1.** To live in a place for an extended or permanent period of time. **2.** To be inherently present; exist. Used with *in.* **3.** To be vested. Used with *in.* [Middle English *residen*, from Old French *resider*, from Latin *residēre*, "to sit back," "remain sitting" : *re-*, back, back in place + *sedēre*, to sit (see **sed-**¹ in Appendix*).] —**re·sid′er** *n.*
res·i·dence (rĕs′ə-dəns, -dĕns′) *n. Abbr.* **res.** **1.** The place in which one lives; a dwelling; an abode. **2.** The act or a period of residing somewhere. **3.** Medical residency.
res·i·den·cy (rĕz′ə-dən-sē, -dĕn′sē) *n., pl.* **-cies.** **1.** The period during which a physician receives specialized clinical training. **2. a.** The house of a colonial resident. **b.** The sphere of authority of a colonial resident. **3.** Residence.
res·i·dent (rĕz′ə-dənt, -dĕnt′) *n. Abbr.* **res.** **1.** One who makes his home in a particular place. **2.** A colonial official acting as adviser to the ruler of a protected state, often having quasi-gubernatorial powers. **3.** A nonmigratory bird or other animal. **4.** A physician serving his period of residency. —*adj.* **1.** Dwelling in a particular place; residing. **2.** Living somewhere in connection with duty or work. **3.** Inherently present. **4.** Nonmigratory. Said of birds and other animals.
res·i·den·tial (rĕz′ə-dĕn′shəl) *adj.* **1.** Of, relating to, or having residence. **2.** Of, characterized by, suitable for, or limited to residences.
res·i·den·ti·ar·y (rĕz′ə-dĕn′shē-ĕr′ē, -shə-rē) *adj.* **1.** Having a residence, especially an official one. **2.** Involving or requiring official residence. —*n., pl.* **residentiaries.** **1.** A resident. **2.** A clergyman required to have an official residence.
re·sid·u·al (rĭ-zĭj′o͞o-əl) *adj.* **1.** Pertaining to or characteristic of a residue. **2.** Remaining as a residue. —*n.* **1.** The quantity left over at the end of a process; remainder. **2.** *Usually plural.* Payment made to a performer on a recorded television show for repeat showings. —See Synonyms at **remainder**.
re·sid·u·ar·y (rĭ-zĭj′o͞o-ĕr′ē) *adj.* **1.** Of, pertaining to, or constituting a residue. **2.** *Law.* Entitled to the residue of an estate.
res·i·due (rĕz′ə-do͞o′, -dyo͞o′) *n.* **1.** The remainder of something after removal of a part. **2.** Matter remaining after completion of any abstractive chemical or physical process, such as evaporation, combustion, distillation, or filtration; a residuum. **3.** *Law.* The remainder of a testator's estate after all claims, debts, and bequests are satisfied. Also called "residuum." —See Synonyms at **remainder**. [Middle English, from Old French *residu*, from Latin *residuum*, from *residuus*, remaining, from *residēre*, RESIDE.]
re·sid·u·um (rĭ-zĭj′o͞o-əm) *n.* **1.** Something remaining after removal of a part; residue. **2.** *Law.* **Residue** *(see).* —See Synonyms at **remainder**. [Latin, RESIDUE.]
re·sign (rē-sīn′) *tr.v.* **-signed, -signing, -signs.** To sign anew.
re·sign (rĭ-zīn′) *v.* **-signed, -signing, -signs.** —*tr.* **1.** To give over or submit (oneself); force (oneself) to acquiesce. **2.** To give up (a position); quit. **3.** To relinquish (a privilege, right, or claim). —*intr.* To give up one's job or office; quit, especially by formal notice. Often used with *from: resign from the army.* —See Synonyms at **relinquish**. [Middle English *resignen*, from Old French *resigner*, from Latin *resignāre*, to unseal, resign : *re-*, back + *signāre*, to seal, sign, from *signum*, a mark, sign (see **sekw-**¹ in Appendix*).] —**re·sign′er** *n.*
res·ig·na·tion (rĕz′ĭg-nā′shən) *n.* **1.** The act of resigning. **2.** An oral or written statement that one is resigning a position or office. **3.** Unresisting acceptance; passive submission. —See Synonyms at **patience**.
re·signed (rĭ-zīnd′) *adj.* Feeling or marked by resignation; acquiescent. —**re·sign′ed·ly** (rĭ-zī′nĭd-lē) *adv.*
re·sile (rĭ-zīl′) *intr.v.* **-siled, -siling, -siles.** To spring back, especially to resume a prior position or form after being stretched or pressed. [Latin *resilīre*, to leap back, recoil : *re-*, back + *salīre*, to leap (see **sel-**⁴ in Appendix*).]
re·sil·ience (rĭ-zĭl′yəns) *n.* Also **re·sil·ien·cy** (-yən-sē). **1.** The ability to recover quickly from illness, change, or misfortune; buoyancy. **2.** The property of a material that enables it to resume its original shape or position after being bent, stretched, or compressed; elasticity. —**re·sil′ient** *adj.*
res·in (rĕz′ĭn) *n.* **1.** Any of numerous clear to translucent, yellow or brown, solid or semisolid, viscous substances of plant origin, such as copal, rosin, and amber, used principally in lacquers, varnishes, inks, adhesives, synthetic plastics, and pharmaceuticals. **2.** Any of numerous physically similar polymerized synthetics or chemically modified natural resins including thermoplastic materials, such as polyvinyl, polystyrene, and polyethylene, and thermosetting materials, such as polyesters, epoxies, and silicones, that are used with fillers, stabilizers, pigments, and other components to form plastics. —*tr.v.* **resined, -ining, -ins.** To treat or rub with a resin; apply resin to. [Middle English *resyn*, from Old French *resine*, from Latin *rēsīna*, from Greek *rhētinē*†.] —**res′in·ous** (rĕz′ə-nəs) *adj.*
res·in·ate (rĕz′ə-nāt′) *tr.v.* **-ated, -ating, -ates.** To impregnate, permeate, or flavor with a resin.
res·in·if·er·ous (rĕz′ə-nĭf′ər-əs) *adj.* Yielding resin.
res·in·oid (rĕz′ə-noid′) *adj.* Characteristic of, pertaining to, or containing resin. —*n.* A resinoid synthetic, especially a thermosetting resin.
re·sist (rĭ-zĭst′) *v.* **-sisted, -sisting, -sists.** —*tr.* **1.** To strive or work against; fight off; oppose actively. **2.** To remain firm against the action or effect of; withstand. **3.** To keep from giving in to or enjoying; abstain from. —See Synonyms at **oppose**. —*n.* A substance that can cover and protect a surface, as from corrosion. [Middle English *resisten*, from Latin *resistere*, to stand back, resist : *re-*, back, against + *sistere*, to set, place (see **stā-** in Appendix*).] —**re·sist′er** *n.*
re·sis·tance (rĭ-zĭs′təns) *n.* **1.** The act of resisting or the capacity to resist. **2.** Any force that tends to oppose or retard motion. **3.** *Abbr.* **r, R** *Electricity.* The opposition to electric current characteristic of a medium, substance, or circuit element. **4.** The underground organization engaged in the struggle for national liberation in a country under military occupation. **5.** *Psychoanalysis.* A process in which the ego opposes the conscious recall of unpleasant experiences. —**re·sis′tant** *adj.*
re·sist·i·ble (rĭ-zĭs′tə-bəl) *adj.* Capable of being resisted. —**re·sist′i·bil′i·ty** *n.* —**re·sist′i·bly** *adv.*
re·sis·tive (rĭ-zĭs′tĭv) *adj.* Capable of or tending toward resistance; resisting. —**re·sis′tive·ly** *adv.*
re·sis·tiv·i·ty (rē′zĭs-tĭv′ə-tē) *n.* **1.** The capacity for or tendency

toward resistance. **2.** *Electricity.* The resistance per unit length of a substance with uniform cross section. In this sense, also called "specific resistance."

re·sist·less (rĭ-zĭst′lĭs) *adj.* **1.** Incapable of being resisted; irresistible. **2.** Powerless to resist; unresisting. —**re·sist′less·ly** *adv.* —**re·sist′less·ness** *n.*

re·sis·tor (rĭ-zĭs′tər) *n.* An electric circuit element used to provide resistance.

res ju·di·ca·ta (rās jo͞o′dĭ-kä′tə, yo͞o′dĭ-kä′tə). Also **res ad·ju·di·ca·ta** (ăd-jo͞o′-, ăd-yo͞o′-). An adjudicated precedent in law. [Latin, "thing decided."]

re·sol·u·ble (rĭ-zŏl′yə-bəl) *adj.* Capable of being resolved; soluble. [Late Latin *resolūbilis,* from Latin *resolvere,* RESOLVE.] —**re·sol′u·bil′i·ty** (-bĭl′ə-tē), **re·sol′u·ble·ness** *n.*

res·o·lute (rĕz′ə-lo͞ot′) *adj.* Characterized by firmness or determination; pursuing a fixed purpose; unwavering. See Synonyms at **faithful.** [Latin *resolūtus,* past participle of *resolvere,* to RESOLVE.] —**res′o·lute′ly** *adv.* —**res′o·lute′ness** *n.*

res·o·lu·tion (rĕz′ə-lo͞o′shən) *n. Abbr.* **res.** **1.** The state or quality of being resolute; firm determination. **2.** The act of resolving to do something. **3.** A course of action determined or decided upon. **4.** A formal statement of a decision or expression of opinion put before or adopted by an assembly such as the U.S. Congress. **5.** The action or process of separating or reducing something into its constituent parts: *the prismatic resolution of sunlight into its spectral colors.* **6.** *Medicine.* The subsiding or termination of an abnormal condition, as of a fever or inflammation. **7.** A decision made by a court of law. **8.** An explanation, as of a problem or puzzle; a solution. **9.** *Music.* **a.** The progression of a dissonant tone or chord to a consonant tone or chord. **b.** The tone or chord to which such a progression is made. —See Synonyms at **courage.**

re·solv·a·ble (rĭ-zŏl′və-bəl) *adj.* Capable of being resolved; solvable. —**re·solv′a·bil′i·ty, re·solv′a·ble·ness** *n.*

re·solve (rĭ-zŏlv′) *v.* **-solved, -solving, -solves.** —*tr.* **1.** To make a firm decision about. **2.** To cause (a person) to reach a decision. **3.** To decide or express by formal vote. **4.** To separate (something) into constituent parts. **5.** To change or convert. Used with *into;* usually used reflexively: *His resentment resolved itself into resignation.* **6.** To find a solution to; to answer. **7.** To remove or dispel (doubts); explain away. **8.** To bring to a conclusion: *resolve a conflict.* **9.** *Medicine.* To cause reduction of (an inflammation). **10.** *Music.* To cause (a tone or chord) to progress from dissonance to consonance. **11.** *Chemistry.* To separate (a racemic compound or mixture) into its optically active constituents. **12.** *Optics.* To render visible and distinguish parts of (an image). **13.** *Mathematics.* To separate (a vector, for example) into coordinate components. **14.** *Obsolete.* To melt or dissolve (something). —*intr.* **1.** To reach a decision; make a determination. Used with *on* or *upon: resolve on a proposal.* **2.** To become separated or reduced to constituents. **3.** *Music.* To undergo resolution. —See Synonyms at **decide.** —*n.* **1.** Firmness of purpose; resolution; determination. **2.** A determination or decision; fixed purpose. **3.** A formal resolution made by a deliberative body. [Middle English *resolven,* to analyze, untie, solve, from Latin *resolvere,* to release, unbind, annul, resolve : *re-* (intensifier), again + *solvere,* untie, release (see **leu-**[1] in Appendix*).] —**re·solv′er** *n.*

re·solved (rĭ-zŏlvd′) *adj.* Fixed in purpose; firmly determined; resolute. —**re·solv′ed·ly** (rĭ-zŏl′vĭd-lē) *adv.*

re·sol·vent (rĭ-zŏl′vənt) *adj.* Causing or capable of causing separation into constituents; solvent. —*n.* A resolvent substance; especially, a medicine that reduces inflammation or swelling.

res·o·nance (rĕz′ə-nəns) *n.* **1.** The quality or condition of being resonant. **2.** *Physics.* **a.** The enhancement of the response of an electric or mechanical system to a periodic driving force when the driving frequency is equal to the natural undamped frequency of the system. **b.** The condition of a system of subatomic particles in which the probability of a particular reaction, as for nuclear capture of a neutron, is a maximum; the occurrence of a cross-section maximum. **c.** The event corresponding to such a maximum, especially the formation of a particle state having only a few possible modes of decay and characterized by a lifetime considerably longer than neighboring states. **3.** *Acoustics.* The intensification and prolongation of sound, especially of a musical tone, produced by sympathetic vibration. **4.** *Medicine.* The sound produced by diagnostic percussion of the normal chest. **5.** *Chemistry.* The phenomenon of interrelated alternative bond structures in certain molecules, produced by redistribution of valence electrons without change in the relative positions of bound atoms and resulting in highly stable compounds. **6.** *Phonetics.* The intensification of vocal tones during articulation.

res·o·nant (rĕz′ə-nənt) *adj.* **1.** Of, pertaining to, or exhibiting resonance. **2.** Producing resonance: *resonant frequency excitation.* **3.** Resulting from or as if from resonance: *resonant amplification; a resonant voice.* [Latin *resonāns,* present participle of *resonāre,* to RESOUND.] —**res′o·nant·ly** *adv.*

resonant circuit. An electric circuit with inductance and capacitance chosen to produce a specified value of the natural frequency of the circuit.

res·o·nate (rĕz′ə-nāt′) *intr.v.* **-nated, -nating, -nates.** **1.** To exhibit resonance or resonant effects. **2.** To resound. [Latin *resonāre,* to RESOUND.] —**res′o·na′tion** *n.*

res·o·na·tor (rĕz′ə-nā′tər) *n.* **1.** A resonating system. **2.** A hollow chamber or cavity with dimensions chosen to permit internal resonant oscillation of electromagnetic or acoustical waves of specific frequencies. **3.** *Electronics.* **a.** Any of various microwave generating tubes or devices containing such resonant chambers or cavities. **b.** A **resonant circuit** *(see).*

re·sorb (rē-sôrb′, -zôrb′) *v.* **-sorbed, -sorbing, -sorbs.** —*tr.* **1.** To absorb again. **2.** *Biology.* To dissolve and assimilate (bone tissue, for example). —*intr.* To undergo resorption. [Latin *resorbēre* : *re-,* back + *sorbēre,* to suck up (see **srebh-** in Appendix*).] —**re·sorp′tion** (-sôrp′shən, -zôrp′shən) *n.*

res·or·cin·ol (rə-zôr′sə-nôl′, -nōl′) *n.* Also **res·or·cin** (rə-zôr′sĭn). A white crystalline compound, $C_6H_4(OH)_2$, used to treat certain skin diseases and in dyes, resin adhesives, and pharmaceuticals. [RES(IN) + ORC(HIL) + -IN + -OL.]

re·sort (rĭ-zôrt′) *intr.v.* **-sorted, -sorting, -sorts.** **1.** To seek assistance or relief; have recourse. Used with *to: The government resorted to censorship of the press.* **2.** To go customarily or frequently; to repair. Used with *to.* —*n.* **1.** A place frequented by people for relaxation or recreation: *a winter resort.* **2.** A customary or frequent going or gathering; a repair: *a popular place of resort.* **3.** Recourse. **4.** A person or thing turned to for aid or relief: *a last resort.* [Middle English *resorten,* return, revert, from Old French *resortir,* to come out again, to resort : *re-,* again + *sortir,* to go out (see **sortie**).]

re·sound (rĭ-zound′) *v.* **-sounded, -sounding, -sounds.** —*intr.* **1.** To be filled with sound; reverberate. **2.** To make a loud, long, or reverberating sound. **3.** To sound loudly; to ring. **4.** To become famous, celebrated, or extolled. —*tr.* **1.** To send back (sound). **2.** To utter or emit loudly. **3.** To proclaim widely; extol; celebrate. [Middle English *resounen,* from Old French *resoner,* from Latin *resonāre,* to sound again, echo : *re-,* again + *sonāre,* to sound (see **swen-** in Appendix*).] —**re·sound′ing** *adj.* —**re·sound′ing·ly** *adv.*

re·source (rē′sôrs′, -sōrs′, -zôrs′, -zōrs′, rĭ-sôrs′, -sōrs′, -zôrs′, -zōrs′) *n.* **1.** Something that can be turned to for support or help. **2.** An available supply that can be drawn upon when needed. **3.** An ability to deal with a situation effectively. **4.** *Usually plural.* Means that can be used to advantage. **5.** Available capital; assets. —See Synonyms at **asset.** [French *ressource,* from Old French *ressourse,* relief, recovery, from *resourdre,* to rise again, from Latin *resurgere* : *re-,* again + *surgere,* to rise, SURGE.]

re·source·ful (rĭ-sôrs′fəl, rĭ-sōrs′-, rĭ-zôrs′-, rĭ-zōrs′-) *adj.* Readily able to act effectively. —**re·source′ful·ly** *adv.* —**re·source′ful·ness** *n.*

resp. **1.** respective; respectively. **2.** respiration.

re·spect (rĭ-spĕkt′) *tr.v.* **-spected, -specting, -spects.** **1.** To feel or show esteem for; to honor. **2.** To show consideration for; avoid violation of; treat with deference. **3.** To relate or refer to; to concern. —*n.* **1.** A feeling of deferential regard; honor; esteem. **2.** The state of being regarded with honor or esteem. **3.** Willingness to show consideration or appreciation. **4.** *Plural.* Polite expressions of consideration or deference: *pay one's respects.* **5.** A particular aspect, feature, or detail. **6.** Relation; reference. —See Usage note at **regard.** [Latin *respectus,* past participle of *respicere,* to regard, to look back : *re-,* back + *specere,* to look (see **spek-** in Appendix*).] —**re·spect′er** *n.* —**re·spect′ful** *adj.* —**re·spect′ful·ly** *adv.* —**re·spect′ful·ness** *n.*

re·spect·a·bil·i·ty (rĭ-spĕk′tə-bĭl′ə-tē) *n., pl.* **-ties.** **1.** The quality, state, or characteristic of being respectable. **2.** Respectable members of a community. **3.** *Plural.* Conventions and customs regarded as indicating respectability.

re·spect·a·ble (rĭ-spĕk′tə-bəl) *adj.* **1.** Meriting respect or esteem; worthy. **2.** Of or appropriate to good or proper behavior or conventional conduct. **3.** Of moderately good quality: *a respectable day's work.* **4.** Considerable in amount, number, or size: *a respectable sum of money.* **5.** Having an acceptable appearance; presentable: *a respectable hat.* —**re·spect′a·ble·ness** *n.* —**re·spect′a·bly** *adv.*

re·spect·ing (rĭ-spĕk′tĭng) *prep.* In relation to; concerning. See Usage note at **regard.**

re·spec·tive (rĭ-spĕk′tĭv) *adj. Abbr.* **resp.** Relating or pertaining to two or more persons or things regarded individually; several; particular: *"The two women stood by their respective telephones"* (Doris Lessing). —**re·spec′tive·ness** *n.*

re·spec·tive·ly (rĭ-spĕk′tĭv-lē) *adv. Abbr.* **resp.** Singly in the order designated or mentioned: *I'm referring to each of you respectively.*

re·spell (rē-spĕl′) *tr.v.* **-spelled** or **-spelt** (-spĕlt′), **-spelling, -spells.** To spell again or in a new way, especially by using a phonetic alphabet.

Re·spi·ghi (rĕ-spē′gē), **Ottorino.** 1879–1936. Italian composer.

res·pi·ra·ble (rĕs′pər-ə-bəl, rĭ-spīr′-) *adj.* **1.** Fit for breathing. **2.** Capable of breathing. —**res′pi·ra·bil′i·ty** *n.*

res·pi·ra·tion (rĕs′pə-rā′shən) *n. Abbr.* **resp.** **1.** The act or process of inhaling and exhaling; a breathing. **2.** The metabolic process by which an organism assimilates oxygen and releases carbon dioxide and other products of oxidation.

res·pi·ra·tor (rĕs′pə-rā′tər) *n.* **1.** An apparatus used in administering artificial respiration. **2.** A screenlike device worn over the mouth or nose, or both, to protect the respiratory tract.

res·pi·ra·to·ry (rĕs′pər-ə-tôr′ē, -tōr′ē, rĭ-spīr′ə-) *adj.* Of, pertaining to, affecting, or used in respiration.

re·spire (rĭ-spīr′) *v.* **-spired, -spiring, -spires.** —*intr.* **1.** To breathe in and out; inhale and exhale. **2.** To undergo the metabolic process of respiration. **3.** To breathe easily again, as after a period of exertion or trouble. —*tr.* To inhale and exhale (air); breathe. [Middle English *respyren,* to breathe again, from Latin *respīrāre* : *re-,* again + *spīrāre,* to breathe (see **spirāre** in Appendix*).]

res·pite (rĕs′pĭt) *n.* **1.** A temporary cessation or postponement, usually of something disagreeable; an interval of rest or relief.

2. *Law.* The temporary suspension of a death sentence; a reprieve. —*tr.v.* **respited, -piting, -pites. 1.** To provide with a period of temporary rest or relief; postpone. **2.** To grant a reprieve from (a punishment or sentence). [Middle English *respit,* from Old French, from Latin *respectus,* a looking back, a refuge, from the past participle of *respicere,* to look back : *re-,* back + *specere,* to look (see **spek-** in Appendix*).]

re·splend·ent (rĭ-splĕn′dənt) *adj.* Filled with splendor; brilliant. [Middle English, from Latin *resplendēns,* present participle of *resplendēre,* to shine brightly : *re-* (intensifier), again + *splendēre,* to shine (see **spel-²** in Appendix*).] —**re·splen′dence, re·splen′den·cy** *n.* —**re·splen′dent·ly** *adv.*

re·spond (rĭ-spŏnd′) *v.* **-sponded, -sponding, -sponds.** —*intr.* **1.** To make a reply; to answer. **2.** To act in return or in answer. **3.** To react positively or cooperatively: *"Every individual responds to confidence."* (Booker T. Washington). —*tr.* To say in reply; to answer. —See Synonyms at **answer.** —*n. Architecture.* A pilaster supporting an arch. [Latin *respondēre,* "to promise in return" : *re-,* back, in return + *spondēre,* to promise (see **spend-** in Appendix*).]

re·spon·dent (rĭ-spŏn′dənt) *adj.* **1.** Giving or given as an answer; responsive. **2.** *Law.* Being a defendant. —*n.* **1.** A person who responds. **2.** *Law.* A defendant, especially in divorce or equity cases. —**re·spon′dence, re·spon′den·cy** *n.*

re·spond·er (rĭ-spŏn′dər) *n.* One that responds.

re·sponse (rĭ-spŏns′) *n.* **1.** The act of responding; an answering. **2.** A reply or answer. **3.** A reaction, as that of an organism or mechanism, to a specific stimulus. **4.** *Abbr.* **R. a.** That which is spoken or sung by a congregation or choir in answer to the officiating minister or priest. **b.** An anthem sung after a reading; a responsory. [Middle English *respons,* from Old French, from Latin *responsum,* from past participle of *respondēre,* "to promise in return," RESPOND.]

re·spon·si·bil·i·ty (rĭ-spŏn′sə-bĭl′ə-tē) *n., pl.* **-ties. 1.** The state, quality, or fact of being responsible. **2.** A thing or person that one is answerable for; a duty, obligation, or burden. —See Synonyms at **obligation.**

re·spon·si·ble (rĭ-spŏn′sə-bəl) *adj.* **1.** Legally or ethically accountable for the care or welfare of another. **2.** Involving personal accountability or ability to act without guidance or superior authority. **3.** Being the source or cause of something. Used with *for.* See Usage note below. **4.** Capable of making moral or rational decisions on one's own, and therefore answerable for one's behavior. **5.** Able to be trusted or depended upon; reliable. **6.** Based upon or characterized by good judgment or sound thinking. **7.** Having the means to pay debts or fulfill obligations. **8.** Required to render account; answerable. Used with *to: The cabinet is responsible to the parliament.* [Obsolete French, correspondent to, from Latin *respondēre,* to RESPOND.] —**re·spon′si·bly** *adv.*

Synonyms: *responsible, answerable, liable, accountable, amenable.* These terms relate to obligations, usually to a superior authority. *Responsible* implies trustworthy performance of fixed duties and consequent awareness of the penalty for failure to do them. It may also refer to obligation for things or possessions. *Answerable* suggests a moral or contractual commitment subject to resolution by a higher authority. *Liable* may refer to legal responsibility, as in the payment of damages, or to obligation to perform service, such as military service. *Accountable* emphasizes liability for something of value either contractually or because of one's position of responsibility. *Amenable* refers to the condition of being subject to control or review.

Usage: *Responsible,* in the sense of *being the cause,* is applicable to both persons and things: *The workmen were responsible for the crash. Defective construction was responsible for the crash.* The second example, sometimes disputed, is acceptable to 70 per cent of the Usage Panel. Those who contend that *responsible,* like *answerable* and *accountable,* is properly limited to persons may prefer as an alternative: *Defective construction caused* (or *resulted in*) *the crash.*

re·spon·sive (rĭ-spŏn′sĭv) *adj.* **1.** Answering or replying; responding. **2.** Readily reacting to suggestions, influences, appeals, or efforts. **3.** Containing or using responses: *responsive reading.* —**re·spon′sive·ly** *adv.* —**re·spon′sive·ness** *n.*

re·spon·so·ry (rĭ-spŏn′sə-rē) *n., pl.* **-ries.** A responsive reading or anthem in a church service. [Middle English, from Late Latin *responsōria,* from Latin *respondēre* (past participle *responsus*), RESPOND.]

rest¹ (rĕst) *n.* **1.** The act or state of ceasing from work, activity, or motion; quiet. **2.** Peace, ease, or refreshment resulting from sleep or the cessation of an activity. **3.** Sleep. **4.** Death. **5.** Relief or freedom from disquiet or disturbance. **6.** Mental or emotional tranquility. **7.** Termination or absence of motion. **8.** *Music.* **a.** An interval of silence corresponding to one of the possible time values within the measure. **b.** The mark or symbol indicating such a pause and its length. **9.** *Prosody.* A short pause in the line; caesura. **10.** A device used as a support: *footrest.* **11.** *Billiards.* A **bridge** *(see).* **12.** *Military.* A command allowing troops to relax. —See Synonyms below. —**at rest. 1.** In a state or condition of repose, especially: **a.** Asleep. **b.** Dead. **2.** Motionless; inactive. **3.** Free from anxiety or distress. —**lay to rest. 1.** To bury (the dead). **2.** To quell or put down (a false assertion, belief, or the like): *lay a rumor to rest.* —*v.* **rested, resting, rests.** —*intr.* **1.** To refresh oneself by ceasing work or activity or by lying down, sleeping, or relaxing in some other manner. **2.** To cease temporarily from work or other activity. **3.** To sleep. **4.** To be at peace or ease; be tranquil. **5.** To be, become, or remain temporarily still, quiet, or inactive. **6.** To be supported or based; lie, lean, or sit. Used with *in, on, upon,* or *against.* **7.** To be imposed or placed as a responsibility or burden. Used with *on* or *upon.* **8.** To depend or rely. Used with *on* or *upon.* **9.** To be located or be in a specified place. **10.** To be fixed on something: *"His brown eyes rested on her for a moment"* (John LeCarré). **11.** To remain; linger. Used with *on* or *upon.* **12.** *Law.* To cease voluntarily the presentation of evidence in a case. —*tr.* **1.** To give rest or repose to; refresh by rest. **2.** To place, lay, or lean for ease, support, or repose. **3.** To base or ground. **4.** To fix or direct (the eyes or gaze, for example). **5.** To bring to rest; halt. **6.** *Law.* To cease voluntarily the introduction of evidence in (a case). [Middle English *reste,* Old English *reste, ræst,* rest, resting place, from Common Germanic *rast-* (unattested).] —**rest′er** *n.*

Synonyms: *rest, relaxation, repose, leisure, ease, comfort. Rest* refers to inactivity following work or other exertion and suggests mental and physical recuperation. *Relaxation* implies the seeking of release from tension, fatigue, or worry in something pleasurable. *Repose* connotes peace of mind, a complete absence of worry or effort. *Leisure* applies to a person's free time when he can do what pleases him. *Ease* implies effortless enjoyment of freedom from work or worry. *Comfort* suggests well-being and satisfaction with one's condition.

rest² (rĕst) *n.* **1.** That part which is left over after something has been removed; the remainder. **2.** Those people remaining. Used with a plural verb: *The rest are coming later.* —See Synonyms at **remainder.** —*intr.v.* **rested, resting, rests. 1.** To be or continue to be; remain: *rest easy.* **2.** *Obsolete.* To remain or be left over. [Middle English, from Old French *reste,* from *rester,* to remain, from Latin *restāre,* to keep back, stand firm : *re-,* back + *stāre,* to stand (see **stā-** in Appendix*).]

rest³ (rĕst) *n.* On medieval armor, a support for a lance on the side of the breastplate. [Middle English *(a)rest,* an arresting, from Old French, from *arester,* to ARREST.]

re·state (rē-stāt′) *tr.v.* **-stated, -stating, -states.** To state again or in a new form. —**re·state′ment** *n.*

res·tau·rant (rĕs′tər-ənt, -tə-ränt′) *n.* A place where meals are served to the public. [French, "restorative," from *restaurer,* to restore, from Old French *restorer,* to RESTORE.]

res·tau·ra·teur (rĕs′tər-ə-tûr′) *n.* The manager of a restaurant. [French, from *restaurer,* to restore. See **restaurant.**]

rest energy. The energy equivalent of the rest mass of a body, equal to the rest mass multiplied by the speed of light squared.

rest·ful (rĕst′fəl) *adj.* **1.** Affording tranquillity. **2.** At rest; quiet. —See Synonyms at **comfortable.** —**rest′ful·ly** *adv.* —**rest′ful·ness** *n.*

rest·har·row (rĕst′hăr′ō) *n.* Any of several Old World plants of the genus *Ononis,* having tough, woody stems and roots, and pink or purplish flowers. [Middle English *(a)resten,* ARREST + HARROW (because its roots obstruct or "arrest" the harrow).]

rest·ing (rĕs′tĭng) *adj.* **1. a.** In a state of inactivity or rest. **b.** Dead. **2.** *Botany.* Dormant. Said especially of spores that germinate after a prolonged period.

res·ti·tute (rĕs′tə-to͞ot′, -tyo͞ot′) *tr.v.* **-tuted, -tuting, -tutes.** To bring back to a former condition; restore. [Latin *restituere* (past participle *restitūtus*), to restore, set up again : *re-,* again + *statuere,* to set up, from *stāre* (past participle *stātus*), to stand (see **stā-** in Appendix*).]

res·ti·tu·tion (rĕs′tə-to͞o′shən, -tyo͞o′shən) *n.* **1.** The act of restoring to the rightful owner something that has been taken away, lost, or surrendered. **2.** The act of making good or compensating for loss, damage, or injury; indemnification; reparation. **3.** A return to or restoration of a previous state or position. —See Synonyms at **reparation.**

res·tive (rĕs′tĭv) *adj.* **1.** Impatient or nervous under restriction, delay, or pressure; uneasy; restless. **2.** Difficult to control; refractory; unruly. See Usage note below. **3.** Refusing to move, as a horse or other animal. [Middle English *restyffe,* unwilling to move, stationary, from Old French *restif,* from Vulgar Latin *restīvus* (unattested), remaining stationary, from Latin *restāre,* to keep back : *re-,* back + *stāre,* to stand (see **stā-** in Appendix*).] —**res′tive·ly** *adv.* —**res′tive·ness** *n.*

Usage: *Restive* and *restless* are now generally employed as equivalent terms. In more precise usage, however, *restive* emphasizes resistance to control, and is more nearly interchangeable with *refractory, obstinate,* and *balky.*

rest·less (rĕst′lĭs) *adj.* **1.** Without quiet, repose, or rest: *a restless night.* **2.** Incapable of or opposed to resting or relaxing: *a restless child.* **3.** Never still or motionless: *the restless sea.* —**rest′less·ly** *adv.* —**rest′less·ness** *n.*

rest mass. The physical mass of a body as observed in a reference system with respect to which the body is at rest.

re·stock (rē-stŏk′) *tr.v.* **-stocked, -stocking, -stocks.** To stock again; furnish new stock for.

res·to·ra·tion (rĕs′tə-rā′shən) *n.* **1.** The act of putting someone or something back into a prior position, place, or condition. **2.** The state of being reinstated, reconstructed, or otherwise restored. **3.** That which has been restored, such as a renovated building. —**the Restoration. 1.** The return of Charles II to the British throne in 1660. **2.** The period between the return of Charles II and the Revolution of 1688.

re·stor·a·tive (rĭ-stôr′ə-tĭv, rĭ-stōr′-) *adj.* **1.** Pertaining to a renewal or restoration. **2.** Tending to renew or restore something, such as health. —*n.* Something that restores.

re·store (rĭ-stôr′, -stōr′) *tr.v.* **-stored, -storing, -stores. 1.** To bring back into existence or use; re-establish: *restore law and order.* **2.** To bring back to a previous, normal condition: *restore a building.* **3.** To put (someone) back in a prior position: *restore the emperor to the throne.* **4.** To give or bring back; make restitution of: *restore the stolen funds.* [Middle English *restoren,* from Old French *restorer,* from Latin *restaurāre* : *re-,* back + *instaurāre,* to renew (see **stā-** in Appendix*).] —**re·stor'er** *n.*

re·strain (rĭ-strān') *tr.v.* **-strained, -straining, -strains. 1.** To control; check; repress. **2.** To deprive of freedom or liberty. **3.** To limit or restrict. [Middle English *restreynen,* from Old French *restraindre* (present stem *restrain-*), from Latin *restringere,* to bind back, RESTRICT.] —**re·strain'a·ble** *adj.* —**re·strain'ed·ly** (rĭ-strā'nĭd-lē) *adv.* —**re·strain'er** *n.*

Synonyms: *restrain, restrict, curb, check, snaffle, bridle, inhibit. Restrain* implies restriction of one's freedom of action by either moral or physical force, frequently for one's own good: *The groom restrained the frightened horse. Restrict* means to set bounds: *He restricted his son's allowance. Curb* and *check* imply a sudden or abrupt stoppage of an advance or forward motion. *Snaffle* applies to a gentler, less forcible stoppage. *Bridle* means holding in or governing one's emotions or passions. *Inhibit* usually connotes a self-imposed check on one's actions or emotions.

re·straint (rĭ-strānt') *n.* **1.** The act of holding back or restraining. **2.** Loss or abridgment of freedom. **3.** Any influence that inhibits or restrains; a limitation. **4.** An instrument or means of controlling or restraining. **5.** Control or repression of feelings; constraint. [Middle English *restreinte,* from Old French *restreinte,* from the past participle of *restraindre,* RESTRAIN.]

re·strict (rĭ-strĭkt') *tr.v.* **-stricted, -stricting, -stricts.** To hold down or keep within limits. See Synonyms at **limit, restrain.** [Latin *restringere* (past participle *restrictus*), to bind back tight : *re-,* back + *stringere,* to bind (see **streig-** in Appendix*).]

re·strict·ed (rĭ-strĭk'tĭd) *adj.* **1.** Confined; limited. **2.** Excluding or unavailable to members of ostracized minorities. Used euphemistically: *a restricted neighborhood.* —**re·strict'ed·ly** *adv.*

re·stric·tion (rĭ-strĭk'shən) *n.* **1.** The act of limiting or restricting. **2.** The state of being limited or restricted. **3.** That which restrains or restricts; a limitation.

re·stric·tive (rĭ-strĭk'tĭv) *adj.* **1.** Tending or serving to restrict. **2.** Denoting a subordinate clause, phrase, or term considered to limit the use of the word or word group that it modifies, thus being essential to the meaning of the sentence and generally not set off by commas. In the sentence *People who read a great deal have large vocabularies,* the restrictive clause is *who read a great deal.* Compare **nonrestrictive.** —**re·stric'tive·ly** *adv.*

rest room. A public lavatory.

re·sult (rĭ-zŭlt') *intr.v.* **-sulted, -sulting, -sults. 1.** To occur or exist as a consequence of a particular cause. **2.** To end in a particular way. Used with *in.* —See Synonyms at **follow.** —*n.* The consequence of a particular action, operation, or course; outcome. See Synonyms at **effect.** [Middle English *resulten,* from Medieval Latin *resultāre,* from Latin, to leap back, rebound : *re-,* back + *saltāre,* to leap, frequentative of *salīre,* to leap (see **sel-⁴** in Appendix*).]

re·sul·tant (rĭ-zŭl'tənt) *adj.* Issuing or following as a consequence or result. —*n.* **1.** That which results; an outcome. **2.** *Mathematics.* A vectorial sum.

re·sume (rĭ-zo͞om') *v.* **-sumed, -suming, -sumes.** —*tr.* **1.** To begin again; take up after interruption. **2.** To occupy or take again. **3.** To take on or take back again. —*intr.* To begin again or continue after interruption. [Middle English *resumen,* from Old French *resumer,* from Latin *resūmere,* to take up again : *re-,* again + *sūmere,* to take up (see **em-** in Appendix*).] —**re·sum'a·ble** *adj.* —**re·sum'er** *n.*

ré·su·mé (rĕz'o͝o-mā', rĕz'o͝o-mā') *n.* **1.** A summing up; a summary. **2.** A summary of experience submitted with a job application. [French, from the past participle of *résumer,* to resume, from Old French *resumer,* RESUME.]

re·sump·tion (rĭ-zŭmp'shən) *n.* The act of resuming, taking again, or taking back. [Middle English, from Old French, from Late Latin *resūmptiō,* from Latin *resūmere,* RESUME.]

re·su·pi·nate (rĭ-so͞o'pə-nāt', -nĭt) *adj. Biology.* Inverted or seemingly turned upside-down. [Latin *resupīnatus,* bent back, past participle of *resupīnāre,* to bend back : *re-,* back + *supīnus,* SUPINE.] —**re·su'pi·na'tion** *n.*

re·su·pine (rē'so͞o-pīn', rĕs'ə-) *adj.* Lying on the back; supine. [Latin *resupīnus,* from *resupīnāre.* See **resupinate.**]

re·surge (rĭ-sûrj') *intr.v.* **-surged, -surging, -surges. 1.** To rise again; be resurrected. **2.** To sweep or surge back again. [Latin *resurgere* : *re-,* again + *surgere,* SURGE.]

re·sur·gent (rĭ-sûr'jənt) *adj.* **1.** Rising or tending to rise again. **2.** Sweeping or surging back again. —**re·sur'gence** *n.*

res·ur·rect (rĕz'ə-rĕkt') *v.* **-rected, -recting, -rects.** —*tr.* **1.** To bring back to life; raise from the dead. **2.** To bring back into practice, notice, or use. —*intr.* To rise from the dead; return to life. [Back-formation from RESURRECTION.]

res·ur·rec·tion (rĕz'ə-rĕk'shən) *n.* **1.** A rising from the dead or returning to life. **2.** The state of those who have returned to life. **3.** A returning to practice, notice, or use; rebirth. **4.** *Capital* **R.** The rising again of Christ on the third day after the Crucifixion. **5.** *Capital* **R.** The rising again of the dead at the Last Judgment. [Middle English *resurreccion,* from Old French *resurrection,* from Late Latin *resurrēctiō,* from Latin *resurgere* (past participle *resurrēctus*), to RESURGE.] —**res'ur·rec'tion·al** *adj.*

resurrection fern. An American fern, *Polypodium polypoides,* of warm regions, having fronds that curl up and apparently die in prolonged dry weather and expand under moist conditions.

res·ur·rec·tion·ist (rĕz'ə-rĕk'shə-nĭst) *n.* One who steals bodies from the grave in order to sell them for dissection; a body snatcher.

resurrection plant. Any of several plants that appear dead during dry periods and expand and continue to grow under moist conditions; especially, the **rose of Jericho** *(see).*

re·sur·vey (rē'sər-vā', rē-sûr'vā') *tr.v.* **-veyed, -veying, -veys.** To study or survey anew. —*n.* (rē-sûr'vā'). A new survey or study.

re·sus·ci·tate (rĭ-sŭs'ə-tāt') *v.* **-tated, -tating, -tates.** —*tr.* To restore consciousness, vigor, or life to. —*intr.* To return to life or consciousness; revive. [Latin *resuscitāre,* to revive : *re-,* again + *suscitāre,* to raise, stir up : *sub-,* below, up from below + *citāre,* to set moving, from *citus,* quick, past participle of *ciēre, cīre,* to stir (see **kei-³** in Appendix*).] —**re·sus'ci·ta·ble** (-tə-bəl) *adj.* —**re·sus'ci·ta'tion** *n.* —**re·sus'ci·ta'tive** *adj.* —**re·sus'ci·ta'tor** (-tā'tər) *n.*

ret (rĕt) *tr.v.* **retted, retting, rets.** Also **rot** (rŏt). To moisten or soak (flax or hemp, for example) to soften and separate the fibers by partial rotting. [Middle English *reten,* perhaps from Old Norse *reyta* (unattested), from Germanic *rutjan* (unattested), to ROT.]

ret. 1. retain. **2.** retired. **3.** return.

re·ta·ble (rē'tā'bəl) *n.* A structure forming the back of an altar, especially: **a.** An overhanging shelf for lights and ornaments. **b.** A frame enclosing painted panels. Also called "reredos." [French, from Spanish *retablo,* from Medieval Latin *retabulum* (unattested), shortening of *retrōtabulum,* structure at the back of an altar : *retrō-,* back + *tabulum,* table, from Latin *tabula,* board, tablet (see **table**).]

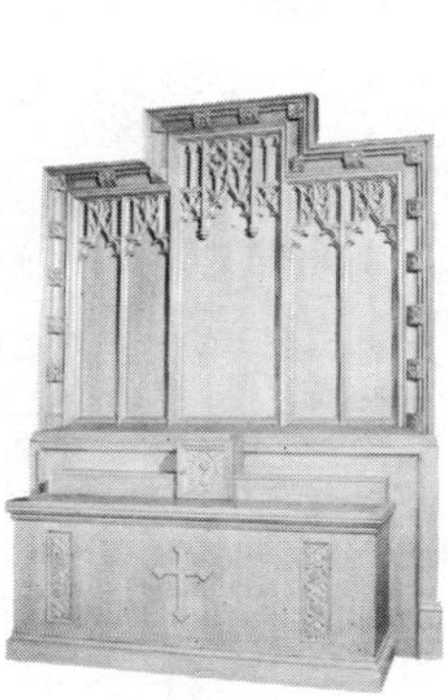
retable

re·tail (rē'tāl') *n.* The sale of commodities in small quantities to the consumer. —*adj.* Of or engaged in the sale of goods at retail. —*v.* (rē'tāl' *for sense 1;* rĭ-tāl' *for sense 2*) **retailed, -tailing, -tails.** —*tr.* **1.** To sell in small quantities. **2.** To tell and retell. —*intr.* To sell at retail. [Middle English *retaile,* "division," from Old French *retaille,* from *retailler,* to cut up : *re-* (intensive) + *tailler,* to cut (see **tailor**).] —**re'tail'er** *n.*

re·tain (rĭ-tān') *tr.v.* **-tained, -taining, -tains. 1.** To keep or hold in one's possession. **2.** To continue to practice, employ, or the like. **3.** To keep or hold in a particular place, condition, or position. **4.** To keep in mind; remember. **5.** To hire (a lawyer) by the payment of a fee. **6.** To keep in one's service or pay. —See Synonyms at **keep.** [Middle English *reteinen,* from Old French *retenir,* from Latin *retinēre* : *re-,* back + *tenēre,* to hold (see **ten-** in Appendix*).] —**re·tain'a·ble** *adj.* —**re·tain'ment** *n.*

retained object. An object in a passive construction that is identical to the object in the corresponding active construction, as *story* in *Susan was told the story by John.*

re·tain·er¹ (rĭ-tā'nər) *n.* **1.** A person or thing that keeps or retains. **2. a.** One who served in a noble household, as in the feudal period, but who ranked higher than a servant; an attendant. **b.** A domestic servant. **c.** An employee. **3.** Any device, frame, or groove that restrains or guides something.

re·tain·er² (rĭ-tā'nər) *n.* **1.** The act of retaining a lawyer or other adviser. **2.** The fee paid to engage the services of a lawyer, consultant, or other professional.

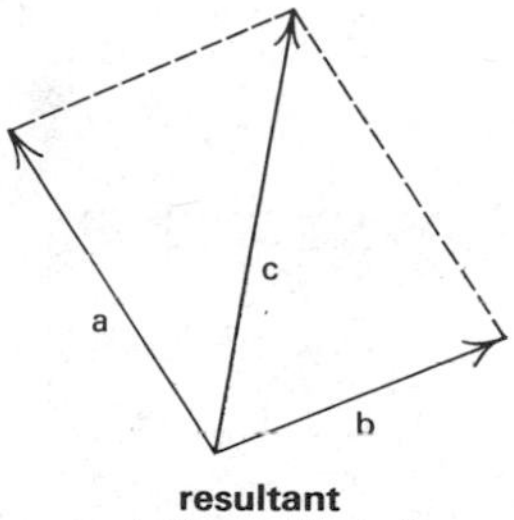

resultant
c is the resultant of vectors *a* and *b*

re·take (rē-tāk') *tr.v.* **-took** (-to͝ok'), **-taken** (-tāk'ən), **-taking, -takes. 1.** To take back or again. **2.** To photograph again. —*n.* (rē'tāk'). **1.** A taking again. **2.** A rephotographed scene. —**re·tak'er** *n.*

re·tal·i·ate (rĭ-tăl'ē-āt') *v.* **-ated, -ating, -ates.** —*intr.* To return like for like, especially to return evil for evil: *"my uncle Toby had scarce a heart to retaliate upon a fly"* (Sterne). —*tr.* To pay back (an injury) in kind. [Latin *retaliāre,* repay in kind : *re-,* back + *tāliō,* punishment in kind (see **tel-¹** in Appendix*).] —**re·tal'i·a'tion** *n.* —**re·tal'i·a·to'ry** (-ē-ə-tôr'ē, -tōr'ē) *adj.*

re·tard (rĭ-tärd') *v.* **-tarded, -tarding, -tards.** —*tr.* To impede or delay; cause to proceed slowly. —*intr.* To become delayed. —See Synonyms at **delay, hinder.** —*n.* **1.** Delay. **2.** *Music.* A slackening of tempo. [Middle English *retarden,* from Old French *retarder,* from Latin *retardāre* : *re-,* back, back in place + *tardāre,* to delay, from *tardus,* slow (see **tardy**).]

re·tar·date (rĭ-tär'dāt', -dĭt) *n.* A mentally retarded person.

re·tar·da·tion (rē'tär-dā'shən) *n.* **1.** The act of retarding. **2.** The condition of being retarded. **3. a.** That which retards; a delay or hindrance. **b.** The amount or time of delay or hindrance. **4.** *Music.* A diminishing of tempo; a retard. **5.** *Psychology.* **Mental deficiency** *(see).*

re·tard·ed (rĭ-tär'dĭd) *adj.* Relatively slow or backward in mental or emotional development or in academic achievement.

retch (rĕch) *v.* **retched, retching, retches.** —*intr.* To try to vomit; heave. —*tr.* To vomit. [Ultimately from Old English *hrǣcan,* to cough up phlegm. See **ker-²** in Appendix.*]

re·te (rē'tē) *n., pl.* **retia** (rē'tē-ə, rē'shə). An anatomical mesh or network, as of veins, arteries, or nerves. [New Latin, from Latin *rēte,* a net. See **ere-²** in Appendix.*]

re·tell (rē-tĕl') *tr.v.* **-told** (-tōld'), **-telling, -tells. 1.** To relate or tell again. **2.** To count again.

re·tene (rĕt'ēn) *n.* A crystalline compound, $C_{18}H_{18}$, derived from pine tar, fossil resins, and tar oils. [Greek *rhētinē,* RESIN.]

re·ten·tion (rĭ-tĕn'shən) *n.* **1.** The act of retaining. **2.** The condition of being retained. **3.** The capacity to remember; memory; remembrance. **4.** The ability to retain. **5.** *Pathology.* Involuntary withholding of normally eliminated wastes or secretions. [Middle English *retencion,* from Old French, from Latin *retentiō,* from *retinēre,* RETAIN.]

re·ten·tive (rĭ-tĕn'tĭv) *adj.* Having the ability or capacity to retain: *a retentive memory.* —**re·ten'tive·ness** *n.*

re·ten·tiv·i·ty (rē'tĕn-tĭv'ə-tē) *n.* The quality or state of being retentive.

re·ti·ar·y (rē'shē-ĕr'ē) *adj.* Of, resembling, or forming a net or web. [From Latin *rēte,* net. See **ere-²** in Appendix.*]

ret·i·cence (rĕt'ə-səns) *n.* **1.** Uncommunicativeness; reserve. **2.** An instance of silence or restraint.

ret·i·cent (rĕt′ə-sənt) *adj.* **1.** Characteristically silent in temperament. **2.** Restrained or reserved in style. —See Synonyms at **silent.** [Latin *reticēns,* present participle of *reticēre,* to keep silent : *re-* (intensifier), again + *tacēre,* to be silent (see **tak-¹** in Appendix*).] —**ret′i·cent·ly** *adv.*

ret·i·cle (rĕt′ĭ-kəl) *n.* A grid or pattern used to establish scale or position in the eyepiece of an optical instrument. Also called "reticule." [Latin *rēticulum,* diminutive of *rēte,* net. See **ere-²** in Appendix.*]

re·tic·u·lar (rĭ-tĭk′yə-lər) *adj.* **1.** Netlike. **2.** Intricate; entangled. [New Latin *reticulāris,* from Latin *rēticulum,* RETICLE.]

re·tic·u·late (rĭ-tĭk′yə-lĭt, -lāt′) *adj.* Resembling or forming a network: *reticulate veins of a leaf.* —*v.* (rĭ-tĭk′yə-lāt′) **reticulated, -lating, -lates.** —*tr.* **1.** To make a net or network of. **2.** To mark with lines resembling a network. —*intr.* To form a net or network. [Latin *rēticulātus,* from *rēticulum,* RETICLE.]

re·tic·u·la·tion (rĭ-tĭk′yə-lā′shən) *n.* A network.

ret·i·cule (rĕt′ĭ-kyo͞ol′) *n.* **1.** A woman's handbag or purse, originally made of a netted fabric. **2.** *Optics.* A **reticle** *(see).* [French *réticule,* from Latin *rēticulum,* RETICLE.]

re·tic·u·lo·en·do·the·li·al system (rĭ-tĭk′yə-lō-ĕn′də-thē′lē-əl). *Abbr.* **RES** The widely diffused bodily system comprising all phagocytic cells except the leukocytes. [From RETICUL(UM) + ENDOTHELIAL.]

re·tic·u·lum (rĭ-tĭk′yə-ləm) *n., pl.* **-la** (-lə). **1.** A netlike formation or structure; network. **2.** *Zoology.* The second compartment of the stomach of ruminant mammals, lined with a membrane having honeycombed ridges. [Latin *rēticulum,* RETICLE.]

Re·tic·u·lum (rĭ-tĭk′yə-ləm) *n.* A constellation in the Southern Hemisphere near Dorado and Horologium. [Latin *rēticulum,* RETICLE.]

re·ti·form (rē′tə-fôrm′, rĕt′ə-) *adj.* Arranged like a net; reticulate. [Latin *rēte,* net (see **ere-²** in Appendix*) + -FORM.]

ret·i·na (rĕt′n-ə) *n., pl.* **-nas** or **retinae** (rĕt′n-ē′). A delicate multilayer light-sensitive membrane lining the inner eyeball and connected by the optic nerve to the brain. [Middle English *rethina,* from Medieval Latin *retina,* possibly from Latin *rēte,* net. See **ere-²** in Appendix.*] —**ret′i·nal** *adj.*

ret·i·nene (rĕt′n-ēn′) *n.* A crystalline retinal pigment, $C_{19}H_{27}CHO$, a component of **rhodopsin** *(see).* [RETIN(O)- + -ENE.]

ret·i·ni·tis (rĕt′n-ī′tĭs) *n. Pathology.* Inflammation of the retina. [RETIN(O)- + -ITIS.]

retino–, retin–. Indicates the retina; for example, **retinitis.**

ret·i·no·scope (rĕt′n-ə-skōp′) *n.* An optical instrument, for examining refraction of light in the eye. Also called "skiascope." [RETINO- + -SCOPE.]

ret·i·nos·co·py (rĕt′n-ŏs′kə-pē) *n.* Medical examination and analysis of the refractive properties of the eye. Also called "skiascopy." [RETINO- + -SCOPY.] —**ret′i·no·scop′ic** (-ə-skŏp′ĭk) *adj.*

ret·i·nue (rĕt′n-o͞o′, rĕt′n-yo͞o′) *n.* The retainers accompanying a person of rank. [Middle English *retenue,* from Old French, from the feminine past participle of *retenir,* to RETAIN.]

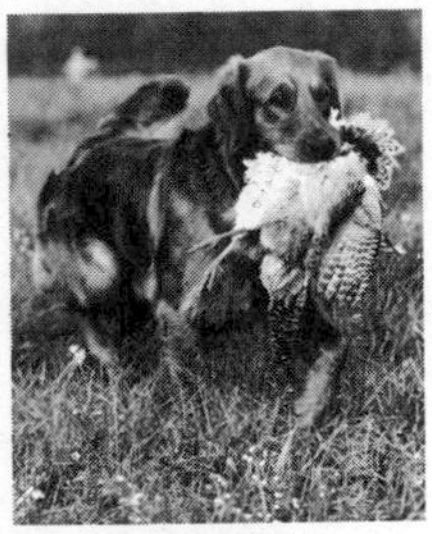

retriever
Golden retriever

re·tire (rĭ-tīr′) *v.* **-tired, -tiring, -tires.** —*intr.* **1.** To go away; depart, as for rest, seclusion, or shelter. **2.** To go to bed. **3.** To withdraw from business or public life so as to live at leisure on one's income, savings, or pension. **4.** To fall back; retreat. —*tr.* **1.** To remove from active service: *retire an old career officer.* **2.** To lead back or away (troops, for example) from action; withdraw. **3.** To take out of circulation: *retire bonds.* **4.** *Baseball.* To put out (a batter). [Old French *retirer* : *re-,* back + *tirer,* to draw (see **tier**).]

re·tired (rĭ-tīrd′) *adj. Abbr.* **r., ret.** **1.** Withdrawn; secluded. **2.** Withdrawn from business or public life. **3.** Received by one on retirement: *retired pay.*

re·tire·ment (rĭ-tīr′mənt) *n.* **1.** The act of retiring. **2.** The condition of being retired, as from one's former occupation or office. **3.** Seclusion or privacy. **4.** A retreat; a place of seclusion. —See Synonyms at **solitude.**

re·tir·ing (rĭ-tī′rĭng) *adj.* Shy and modest; soft-spoken; reticent. See Synonyms at **humble.** —**re·tir′ing·ly** *adv.*

re·tool (rē-to͞ol′) *tr.v.* **-tooled, -tooling, -tools.** **1.** To fit out anew with tools. **2.** To revise and reorganize.

re·tort¹ (rĭ-tôrt′) *v.* **-torted, -torting, -torts.** —*tr.* **1.** To return in kind; pay back. **2. a.** To reply; especially, to answer in a quick, direct manner. **b.** To present a counterargument to. —*intr.* **1.** To make a reply, especially one that is marked by sharpness or wit. **2.** To present a counterargument. —See Synonyms at **answer.** —*n.* **1.** A quick, incisive reply; especially, one that turns the first speaker's words to his own disadvantage. **2.** An act of retorting. [Latin *retorquēre* (past participle *retortus*), to bend back : *re-,* back + *torquēre,* to bend, twist (see **terkw-** in Appendix*).] —**re·tort′er** *n.*

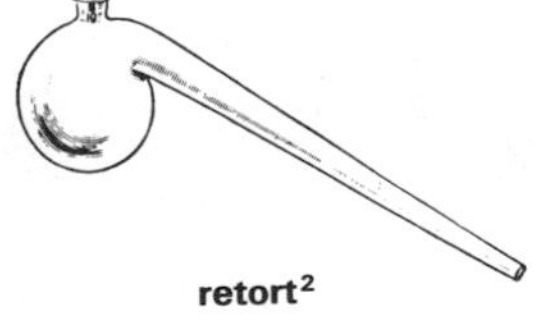

retort²

re·tort² (rĭ-tôrt′, rē′tôrt′) *n.* A closed laboratory vessel with an outlet tube, used for distillation, sublimation, or decomposition by heat. [Old French *retorte,* from Medieval Latin *retorta,* feminine of Latin *retortus,* "bent back" (the neck of the vessel is bent over), from *retorquēre,* to bend back, RETORT.]

re·touch (rē-tŭch′) *tr.v.* **-touched, -touching, -touches.** **1.** To add new details or touches to, for correction or improvement. **2.** *Photography.* To improve or change (a negative or print) by adding details or removing flaws. —*n.* (rē′tŭch′, rē-tŭch′). **1.** A detail changed or improved in a work of art. **2.** A work of art that has been retouched. **3.** The act of altering or retouching.

re·trace (rē-trās′) *tr.v.* **-traced, -tracing, -traces.** To trace again. —**re·trace′a·ble** *adj.*

re·tract (rĭ-trăkt′) *v.* **-tracted, -tracting, -tracts.** —*tr.* **1.** To take back or disavow (a statement, accusation, offer, or verbal contract); recant. **2.** To draw back or in: *The turtle retracted its head.* **3.** *Phonetics.* **a.** To utter (a sound) with the tongue drawn back. **b.** To draw back (the tongue). —*intr.* **1.** To take back or disavow a statement or the like. **2.** To shrink or draw back. [Middle English *retracten,* from Old French *retracter,* from Latin *retractāre,* to handle again, frequentative of *retrahere* (past participle *retractus*), to draw back : *re-,* back, again + *trahere,* to draw (see **tragh-** in Appendix*).] —**re·tract′a·ble, re·tract′i·ble** *adj.* —**re′trac·ta′tion** *n.*

re·trac·tile (rĭ-trăk′tĭl) *adj.* Capable of being drawn back or in: *Cats have retractile claws.* —**re′trac·til′i·ty** *n.*

re·trac·tion (rĭ-trăk′shən) *n.* **1.** The act of recanting. **2.** The power of drawing back or of being drawn back.

re·trac·tive (rĭ-trăk′tĭv) *adj.* Tending to retract.

re·trac·tor (rĭ-trăk′tər) *n.* **1.** One that retracts. **2.** *Anatomy.* A muscle, such as a flexor, that retracts an organ or part. **3.** *Surgery.* An instrument that holds back the edges of a wound.

re·tral (rē′trəl, rĕt′rəl) *adj.* **1.** At, close to, or toward the back. **2.** Backward; reverse. [From Latin *retrō,* backward, behind. See **re-** in Appendix.*] —**re′tral·ly** *adv.*

re·tread (rē-trĕd′) *tr.v.* **-trod** (-trŏd′), **-trodden** (-trŏd′n), **-treading, -treads.** To tread again.

re·tread (rē-trĕd′) *tr.v.* **-treaded, -treading, -treads.** To fit (a worn automobile tire) with a new tread. Compare **recap.** —*n.* (rē′trĕd′). A retreaded tire.

re·treat (rĭ-trēt′) *n.* **1.** The act of going backward or of withdrawing. **2.** A quiet, private, or secure place; a refuge. **3.** A period of seclusion, retirement, or solitude. **4. a.** The withdrawal of a military force from a dangerous position or from an enemy attack. **b.** The signal for such withdrawal, made on a drum or trumpet. **5.** *Military.* A trumpet call signaling the lowering of the flag at sunset. —See Synonyms at **shelter.** —**beat a retreat. 1.** *Military.* To give a signal for withdrawal of forces. **2.** To withdraw; flee. —*v.* **retreated, -treating, -treats.** —*intr.* **1.** To withdraw; retire; go back. **2.** To slope backward. —*tr. Chess.* To move (a piece) back. [Middle English *retret,* from Old French *retrait,* from the past participle of *retraire,* to draw back, from Latin *retrahere,* to RETRACT.]

re·trench (rĭ-trĕnch′) *v.* **-trenched, -trenching, -trenches.** —*tr.* **1.** To cut down; curtail; reduce. **2.** To remove, delete, or omit. —*intr.* To curtail expenses; economize. [Obsolete French *retrencher,* from Old French *retrenchier* : *re-* (intensifier), again + *trenchier,* to cut off (see **trench**).] —**re·trench′ment** *n.*

re·tri·al (rē-trī′əl) *n.* A second trial, as of a legal case.

ret·ri·bu·tion (rĕt′rə-byo͞o′shən) *n.* **1.** Something given or demanded in repayment; especially, punishment. **2.** *Theology.* Punishment or reward distributed in a future life based on performance in this one. [Middle English *retribucion,* from Old French *retribution,* from Late Latin *retribūtiō,* from Latin *retribuere,* to pay back : *re-,* back + *tribuere,* to grant, pay (see **tribute**).]

re·trib·u·tive (rĭ-trĭb′yə-tĭv) *adj.* Also **re·trib·u·to·ry** (-tôr′ē, -tōr′ē). Of, involving, or characterized by retribution.

re·triev·al (rĭ-trē′vəl) *n.* **1.** The act or process of regaining, restoring, remedying, or remembering. **2.** The possibility of repossession or restoration: *beyond retrieval.*

re·trieve (rĭ-trēv′) *v.* **-trieved, -trieving, -trieves.** —*tr.* **1.** To get back; regain. **2.** To revive; restore. **3.** To make good; put right; rectify. **4.** To recall to mind; remember. **5.** To find and carry back; fetch. —*intr.* To find and bring back game. —See Synonyms at **recover.** —*n.* The act of retrieving. [Middle English *retreven,* to find again, from Old French *retrover* : *re-,* again + *trover,* to find, perhaps from Vulgar Latin *tropāre* (unattested) to write, compose, from Latin *tropus,* trope, a manner of singing, a song, from Greek *tropos,* "a turning" (see **trep-²** in Appendix*).] —**re·triev′a·bil′i·ty** *n.* —**re·triev′a·ble** *adj.* —**re·triev′a·bly** *adv.*

re·triev·er (rĭ-trē′vər) *n.* **1.** One that retrieves. **2.** Any of several breeds of dog developed and trained to retrieve game.

retro–. Indicates: **1.** Backward or back; for example, **retrorocket. 2.** Situated behind; for example, **retrolental.** [From Latin *retrō,* backward, behind. See **re-** in Appendix.*]

ret·ro·ac·tion (rĕt′rō-ăk′shən) *n.* **1.** A retroactive action. **2.** An opposing or reciprocal action; a reaction.

ret·ro·ac·tive (rĕt′rō-ăk′tĭv) *adj.* Influencing or applying to a period prior to enactment: *a retroactive pay increase.* [French *rétroactif,* from Latin *retroactus,* past participle of *retroagere,* to drive back : RETRO- + *agere,* to drive (see **ag-** in Appendix*).] —**ret′ro·ac′tive·ly** *adv.* —**ret′ro·ac·tiv′i·ty** *n.*

ret·ro·cede (rĕt′rō-sēd′) *v.* **-ceded, -ceding, -cedes.** —*intr.* To go back; recede. —*tr.* To cede or give back; return. [Latin *retrōcēdere,* to go back : RETRO- + *cēdere,* to go (see **ked-¹** in Appendix*).] —**ret′ro·ces′sion** (-sĕsh′ən) *n.*

ret·ro·flex (rĕt′rə-flĕks′) *adj.* Also **ret·ro·flexed** (-flĕkst′). **1.** Bent, curved, or turned backward. **2.** *Phonetics.* Pronounced with the tip of the tongue turned back against the roof of the mouth. [New Latin *retroflexus,* from Late Latin *retrōflectere,* to bend back : RETRO- + Latin *flectere,* to bend, FLEX.] —**ret′ro·flex′ion, ret′ro·flec′tion** *n.*

ret·ro·grade (rĕt′rə-grād′) *adj.* **1.** Moving or tending backward; retiring; retreating. **2.** Inverted or reversed. **3.** Reverting to an earlier or inferior condition. **4.** *Astronomy.* Having a direction of motion opposite to that of the earth on its axis or of the planets around the sun. **5.** *Obsolete.* Opposed; contrary. —*intr.v.* **retrograded, -grading, -grades.** **1.** To move or seem to move backward. **2.** To decline; degenerate; deteriorate. [Middle English, from Latin *retrōgradus* : RETRO- + *gradus,* a step, grade (see **ghredh-** in Appendix*).] —**ret′ro·gra·da′tion** (-rō-grā-dā′shən) *n.*

ă pat/ā pay/âr care/ä father/b bib/ch church/d deed/ĕ pet/ē be/f fife/g gag/h hat/hw which/ĭ pit/ī pie/îr pier/j judge/k kick/l lid, needle/m mum/n no, sudden/ng thing/ŏ pot/ō toe/ô paw, for/oi noise/ou out/o͝o took/o͞o boot/p pop/r roar/s sauce/sh ship, dish/

ret·ro·gress (rĕt′rə-grĕs′, rĕt′rə-grĕs′) *intr.v.* **-gressed, -gressing, -gresses. 1.** To return to an earlier, inferior, or less complex condition. **2.** To go or move backward. [Latin *retrōgradī* (past participle *retrōgressus*), to go backward : RETRO- + *gradī*, to step (see **ghredh-** in Appendix*).]

ret·ro·gres·sion (rĕt′rə-grĕsh′ən) *n.* **1.** The act or process of deteriorating or declining. **2.** *Biology.* A return to a less complex or more primitive state or stage.

ret·ro·gres·sive (rĕt′rə-grĕs′ĭv) *adj.* Characterized by retrogression; tending to retrogress. **—ret′ro·gres′sive·ly** *adv.*

ret·ro·len·tal (rĕt′rō-lĕnt′l) *adj.* Behind a lens. [RETRO- + New Latin *lens* (stem *lent-*), LENS + -AL.]

ret·ro·rock·et (rĕt′rō-rŏk′ĭt) *n.* A rocket engine used to retard, arrest, or reverse the motion of an aircraft, missile, spacecraft, or other vehicle. Also called "braking rocket."

re·trorse (rĭ-trôrs′, rē′trôrs′) *adj.* Directed or turned backward or downward. [Latin *retrōrsus*, contraction of *retrōversus* : RETRO- + *versus*, "turned," past participle of *vertere*, to turn (see **wer-**[3] in Appendix*).] **—re·trorse′ly** *adv.*

ret·ro·spect (rĕt′rə-spĕkt′) *n.* A review, survey, or contemplation of things in the past. See Synonyms at **memory.** **—in retrospect.** Looking backward or reviewing the past. **—***v.* **retrospected, -specting, -spects.** **—***intr.* **1.** To contemplate the past. **2.** To refer back. Used with *to.* **—***tr.* To look back on or contemplate (things past). [Latin *retrōspectus*, past participle of *retrōspicere*, to look back at : RETRO- + *specere*, to look at (see **spek-** in Appendix*).] **—ret′ro·spec′tion** *n.*

ret·ro·spec·tive (rĕt′rə-spĕk′tĭv) *adj.* **1.** Looking back on, contemplating, or directed to the past. **2.** Looking or directed backward. **3.** Applying to or influencing the past; retroactive. **4.** Of or pertaining to an art show exhibiting the work of an artist or school over a period of years. **—***n.* A retrospective art exhibition. **—ret′ro·spec′tive·ly** *adv.*

re·trous·sé (rə-trōō-sā′, rĕt′rōō-sā′) *adj.* Turned up at the end. Said of the nose. [French, past participle of *retrousser*, to turn back, from Old French : *re-*, back + *trousser*, to TRUSS.]

ret·ro·ver·sion (rĕt′rō-vûr′zhən, -shən) *n.* **1.** A turning or tilting backward. **2.** The state of being turned or tilted back. [From Latin *retrōversus*, RETRORSE.]

re·try (rē-trī′) *tr.v.* **-tried, -trying, -tries.** To try again.

ret·si·na (rĕt′sĭ-nə) *n.* A resinated Greek wine. [Modern Greek, from Italian *resina*, resin, from Latin *rēsīna*, RESIN.]

re·turn (rĭ-tûrn′) *v.* **-turned, -turning, -turns.** **—***intr.* **1.** To go or come back, as to an earlier condition or place. **2.** To revert in speech, thought, or practice. **3.** To revert to a former owner. **4.** To answer; retort; respond. **—***tr.* **1.** To send, put, or carry back; replace; restore: *return bottles to the store.* **2.** To give or send back in reciprocation: *She returned his praise.* **3.** To produce or yield (profit or interest) as a payment for labor, investment, or expenditure. **4.** To reflect or send back (light or sound). **5.** To submit (a writ, report, or statement) to a judge or other person in authority. **6.** To render or deliver (a verdict). **7.** To elect or re-elect, as to a legislative body. **8.** *Card Games.* To respond to (a partner's lead) by leading the same suit. **9.** To turn away from or place at an angle to the previous line of direction. **—***n. Abbr.* **ret. 1.** The act or state of going, coming, bringing, or sending back. **2. a.** Something that is brought or sent back. **b.** Something that goes or comes back. **3.** A recurrence, as of a periodic occasion or event. **4.** Something exchanged for that received; repayment. **5.** A reply; response; answer. **6. a.** The profit made on an exchange of goods. **b.** *Often plural.* A profit or yield, as from labor or investments. **c.** Output or yield per unit rather than cost per unit, as in the manufacturing of a particular product. **7. a.** A report, list, or set of statistics; especially, one that is formal or official. **b.** *Usually plural.* A report on the vote in an election. **8.** *Card Games.* A lead that responds to the lead of one's partner. **9.** In tennis and certain other sports: **a.** The act of sending the ball back to one's opponent. **b.** The ball so returned. **10.** *Architecture.* **a.** The extension of a molding, projection, or other part at an angle (usually 90 degrees) to the main part. **b.** A part of a building set at an angle to the façade. **11.** *Informal.* A round-trip ticket. **12.** *Law.* **a.** The bringing or sending back of a writ, subpoena, or other document, generally with a short written report on it, by a sheriff or other officer, to the court from which it was issued. **b.** A certified report by an assessor, election officer, collector, or other official. **—***adj.* **1.** Of or for coming back: *the return voyage.* **2.** Given, sent, or done in reciprocation or exchange: *a return visit.* **3.** Performed, presented, or occurring again: *a return boxing match.* **4. a.** Reversing or changing direction. **b.** Formed by a reversal or change in direction, as a bend in a road. [Middle English *reto(u)rnen*, from Old French *retorner*, from Vulgar Latin *retornāre* (unattested), to turn back : Latin *re-*, back + *tornāre*, to turn in a lathe, from *tornus*, lathe, from Greek *tornos* (see **ter-**[2] in Appendix*).] **—re·turn′er** *n.*

Synonyms: *return, revert, recur, recrudesce. Return* denotes going back or coming back to a former place, position, or condition. *Revert* refers to returning to an earlier and less desirable condition. *Recur* applies to repeated occurrences of the same thing. *Recrudesce* is said of that which becomes active after a period of quiescence.

re·turn·a·ble (rĭ-tûr′nə-bəl) *adj.* **1.** Capable of being returned or brought back. **2.** Legally required to be returned.

re·tuse (rĭ-tōōs′, -tyōōs′) *adj.* Having a rounded or blunt apex with a shallow notch. Said chiefly of leaves. [Latin *retūsus*, past participle of *retundere*, to beat back : *re-*, back + *tundere*, to strike, beat (see **steu-** in Appendix*).]

Retz (rĕts), **Baron de.** Also **de Rais.** Title of Gilles de Laval. Often wrongly called "Bluebeard." 1404?–1440. Marshal of France; comrade in arms of Joan of Arc.

Retz (rĕts), **Cardinal de.** Title of Jean François Paul de Gondi. 1614–1679. French political leader and man of letters.

Reu·ben[1] (rōō′bĭn). A masculine given name. [Hebrew *Re'ūbēn*, "behold, a son" (from Genesis 29:32) : *rə'u*, imperative plural of *ra'ah*, to behold, see + *bēn*, son.]

Reu·ben[2] (rōō′bĭn). Jacob's eldest son, the ancestor of one of the tribes of Israel. Genesis 29:32.

Reu·ben[3] (rōō′bĭn) *n.* The tribe of Israel descended from Reuben.

re·un·ion (rē-yōōn′yən) *n.* **1.** The act of reuniting. **2.** The state of being reunited. **3.** A gathering of the members of a group who have been separated.

Ré·un·ion (rē-yōōn′yən; *French* rā-ü-nyôN′). An island and overseas department of France, 970 square miles in area, lying in the Indian Ocean 110 miles southwest of Mauritius. Population, 396,000. Capital, Saint-Denis.

re·u·nite (rē′yōō-nīt′) *v.* **-nited, -niting, -nites.** **—***tr.* To bring together again. **—***intr.* To come together again. [Medieval Latin *reūnīre* : *re-*, again + *ūnīre*, from Late Latin, to UNITE.]

Reu·ter (roi′tər), Baron **Paul Julius von.** Original name, Israel Beer Josaphat. 1816–1899. German-born founder of the British news agency, Reuters.

Reu·ther (rōō′thər), **Walter Philip.** Born 1907. American labor leader.

rev (rĕv) *n. Informal.* A revolution, as of a motor. **—***v.* **revved, revving, revs.** *Informal.* **—***tr.* To increase the speed of (a motor). Often used with *up.* **—***intr.* To operate at an increased speed. Often used with *up.*

rev. 1. revenue. **2.** reverse; reversed. **3.** review; reviewed. **4.** revise; revision. **5.** revolution. **6.** revolving.

Rev. 1. Revelation (New Testament). **2.** reverend (title). **3.** revolution.

re·vamp (rē-vămp′) *tr.v.* **-vamped, -vamping, -vamps. 1.** To patch up or restore; renovate. **2.** To revise or reconstruct (a manuscript, for example). **3.** To vamp (a shoe or boot) anew.

re·vanch·ism (rĭ-vănch′ĭz′əm) *n.* A foreign policy motivated by a desire to regain territory lost earlier to an enemy. [From French *revanche*, revenge, from *revancher*, to revenge, from Old French *revencher*, to REVENGE.]

re·veal (rĭ-vēl′) *tr.v.* **-vealed, -vealing, -veals. 1.** To divulge or disclose; make known. **2.** To bring to view; expose; show. [Middle English *revelen*, from Old French *reveler*, from Latin *revēlāre*, to unveil, reveal : *re-*, back, back to a prior condition + *vēlāre*, to veil, from *vēlum*, a veil (see **weg-**[1] in Appendix*).] **—re·veal′a·ble** *adj.* **—re·veal′er** *n.*

Synonyms: *reveal, expose, disclose, divulge, impart, betray. Reveal* is to make known what has heretofore been kept secret. *Expose* is a stronger term referring to making public something reprehensible, such as a crime or conspiracy. *Disclose* means to make known something that has been under consideration but for valid reasons has been kept from public knowledge. *Divulge* implies making known what has been a secret to a small circle. *Impart* refers to sharing knowledge or information with another. *Betray* implies making known and thereby breaking a trust or pledge.

rev·eil·le (rĕv′ə-lē) *n.* **1.** The sounding of a bugle early in the morning to awaken and summon persons in a camp or garrison. **2.** The first military formation of the day. [French *réveillez*, imperative of *réveiller*, to rouse, awaken, from Old French *reveiller* : *re-*, again + *veiller*, to rouse, from Latin *vigilāre*, to watch, from *vigil*, awake (see **weg-**[2] in Appendix*).]

rev·el (rĕv′əl) *intr.v.* **-eled** or **-elled, -eling** or **-elling, -els. 1.** To take great pleasure or delight. Used with *in: He reveled in his work.* **2.** To engage in uproarious festivities; make merry. **—***n. Often plural.* A noisy festivity. [Middle English *revelen*, from Old French *reveler*, to make noise, "to rebel," from Latin *rebellāre*, to REBEL.] **—rev′el·er** *n.*

rev·e·la·tion (rĕv′ə-lā′shən) *n.* **1.** Something revealed. **2.** An act of revealing, especially a dramatic disclosure of something not previously known or realized. **3.** *Theology.* A manifestation of divine will or truth. **4.** *Capital* **R.** *Abbr.* **Rev.** In full, The Revelation of Saint John the Divine. The last book in the New Testament, attributed to Saint John. In this sense, also called "Apocalypse." [Middle English, from Old French, from Late Latin *revēlātiō*, from Latin *revēlāre*, REVEAL.]

rev·el·ry (rĕv′əl-rē) *n., pl.* **-ries.** Boisterous merrymaking. **—rev′el·rous** (-rəs) *adj.*

rev·e·nant (rĕv′ə-nənt) *n.* **1.** One that returns after an absence. **2.** One who returns after death; a ghost. [French, from the present participle of *revenir*, to return, from Latin *revenīre* : *re-*, again, back + *venīre*, to come (see **gwā-** in Appendix*).]

re·venge (rĭ-vĕnj′) *tr.v.* **-venged, -venging, -venges. 1.** To inflict punishment in return for (injury or insult); avenge. **2.** To seek or take vengeance for (oneself or another person). —See Usage note at **avenge.** **—***n.* **1.** Vengeance; retaliation. **2.** The act of taking vengeance. **3.** A desire for revenge; vindictiveness. [Middle English *revengen*, from Old French *revenger, revencher*, from Late Latin *revindicāre*, to avenge : Latin *re-* (intensifier), again + *vindicāre*, to VINDICATE.]

re·venge·ful (rĭ-vĕnj′fəl) *adj.* Wishing revenge. See Synonyms at **vindictive.** **—re·venge′ful·ly** *adv.* **—re·venge′ful·ness** *n.*

rev·e·nue (rĕv′ə-nōō, -nyōō) *n. Abbr.* **rev. 1.** The income of a government from all sources appropriated for the payment of the public expenses. **2.** Yield from property or investment; income. **3.** A single source of income. **4.** A governmental department set up to collect public funds. [Middle English, return, return to place, from Old French, from the feminine past

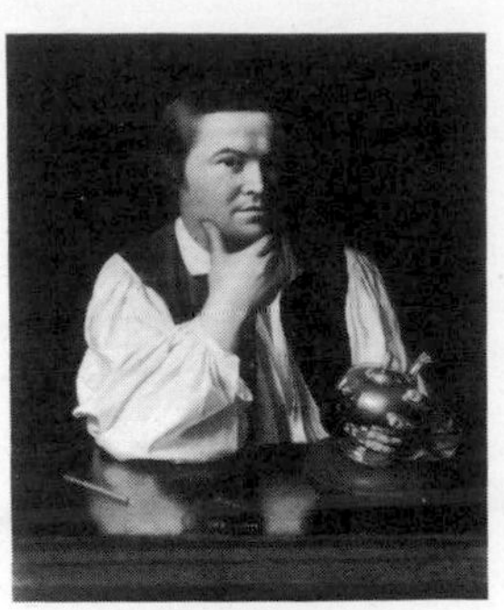

Paul Revere
Portrait by
John Singleton Copley

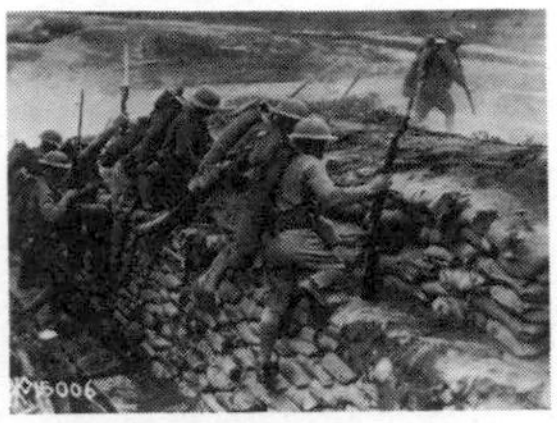

revetment
Sandbag revetment at U.S. Army training grounds, Fort Riley, Kansas

participle of *revenir,* to return, from Latin *revenīre* : *re-,* back, again + *venīre,* to come (see **gwā-** in Appendix*).]

re·ver·ber·ate (rĭ-vûr′bə-rāt′) *v.* **-ated, -ating, -ates.** —*intr.* **1.** To re-echo; resound. **2.** To be repeatedly reflected. **3.** To rebound or recoil; redound. —*tr.* **1.** To re-echo (a sound). **2.** To reflect (heat or light) repeatedly. [Latin *reverberāre,* to cause to rebound : *re-,* back + *verberāre,* to whip, lash, from *verbera,* whips, rods (see **wer-**^{3} in Appendix*).] —**re·ver′ber·a′tion** *n.* —**re·ver′ber·a·to′ry** (-bə-rə-tôr′ē, -tōr′ē), **re·ver′ber·ant, re·ver′ber·a′tive** *adj.*

re·vere^{1} (rĭ-vîr′) *tr.v.* **-vered, -vering, -veres.** To regard with awe, great respect, or devotion; venerate. [Latin *reverērī* : *re-* (intensifier), again + *verērī,* to respect, feel awe of (see **wer-**^{4} in Appendix*).] —**re·ver′er** *n.*

Synonyms: *revere, worship, venerate, adore, sanctify, idolize, idolatrize.* These terms imply the deepest respect and esteem for a person, an object, or a deity. *Revere* has a sense of treasuring with profound respect: *to revere the memory of Lincoln. Worship* implies intense, unquestioning esteem, love, and adoration, sometimes manifested in set forms. *Venerate* has the quality of love added to esteem. *Adore* is to love with rapturous and complete devotion. *Sanctify* connotes giving something a sacred character. *Idolize* or *idolatrize* implies worship of an object to which attributes of a deity are ascribed.

re·vere^{2}. Variant of **revers.**

Re·vere (rĭ-vîr′), **Paul.** 1735–1818. American silversmith, engraver, and Revolutionary patriot; rode (1775) from Charlestown to Lexington to warn colonists of British advance.

rev·er·ence (rĕv′ər-əns) *n.* **1.** A feeling of profound awe and respect and often of love; veneration. **2.** An act of showing respect; especially, an obeisance. **3.** The state of being revered. **4.** *Capital* **R.** A title of respect for a clergyman. Preceded by *His* or *Your.* —See Synonyms at **honor.** —*tr.v.* **reverenced, -encing, -ences.** To venerate: *"The Cherokees feared and reverenced snakes and took care not to kill them."* (Donald Davidson).

rev·er·end (rĕv′ər-ənd) *adj.* **1.** Deserving of reverence. **2.** Pertaining to or characteristic of the clergy; clerical. **3.** *Often capital* **R.** *Abbr.* **Rev.** Designating a member of the clergy. See Usage note below. —*n. Informal.* A cleric or minister. [Middle English, from Old French, from Latin *reverendus,* gerundive of *reverērī,* REVERE.]

Usage: *Reverend,* as a title, is an adjective, not a noun, and thus is properly preceded by *the* in formal usage. In writing, the preferred forms of address or first reference are expressed in the following examples: *the Reverend* (or *Rev.*) *Joseph Hames, the Rev. Dr. Joseph Hames.* The variant forms *Rev. Joseph Hames* and *Rev. Dr. Joseph Hames* are termed unacceptable by 59 per cent of the Usage Panel. For subsequent references, in written usage, the proper form is *the Rev. Mr.* (or *Dr.*) *Hames* (not *Rev. Hames* or merely *the Reverend*), according to 63 per cent of the Panel. As a form of address in speech, the term *Reverend,* unaccompanied by a name, is considered impolite.

rev·er·ent (rĕv′ər-ənt) *adj.* Feeling or showing reverence. [Middle English, from Latin *reverēns,* present participle of *reverērī,* REVERE.] —**rev′er·ent·ly** *adv.*

rev·er·en·tial (rĕv′ə-rĕn′shəl) *adj.* Expressing reverence; reverent. —**rev′er·en′tial·ly** *adv.*

rev·er·ie (rĕv′ər-ē) *n.* **1.** Abstracted musing; daydreaming. **2.** A daydream: *"I felt caught up in a reverie of years long past"* (William Styron). [Middle English, from Old French, from *rever*†, to dream.]

re·vers (rĭ-vîr′, -vâr′) *n., pl.* **revers.** Also **re·vere** *pl.* **-veres** (-vîrz′, -vârz′). A part of a garment turned back to show the reverse side, as a lapel. [French, from Old French, REVERSE.]

re·ver·sal (rĭ-vûr′səl) *n.* **1.** An act or instance of reversing. **2.** The state of being reversed. **3.** *Law.* A changing or setting aside, as of a lower court's decision by an appellate court.

re·verse (rĭ-vûrs′) *adj. Abbr.* **rev. 1.** Turned backward in position, direction, or order; opposite; contrary. **2.** Moving or acting in a manner contrary to the usual. **3.** Causing backward movement: *a reverse gear.* —*n. Abbr.* **rev. 1.** The opposite or contrary of something. **2.** The back or rear of something; specifically, the side of a coin not carrying the principal design. **3.** A change to an opposite position, condition, or direction. **4.** A change in fortune from better to worse; setback. **5. a.** A mechanism for reversing movement, as a gear in an automobile. **b.** The reverse position or operating condition of such a mechanism. —*v.* **reversed, -versing, -verses.** —*tr.* **1.** To turn to the opposite direction or tendency. **2.** To turn inside out or upside down. **3.** To exchange the positions of; transpose. **4.** *Law.* To revoke or annul (a decision or decree). —*intr.* **1.** To turn or move in the opposite direction. **2.** To reverse the action of an engine. [Middle English *revers,* from Old French, from Latin *reversus,* past participle of *revertere,* REVERT.] —**re·vers′er** *n.*

Synonyms: *reverse, invert, transpose. Reverse* implies a complete turning about to a contrary position with reference to action, direction, or policy. *Invert* basically means to turn something upside down or inside out but may imply placing something in a contrary order. *Transpose* applies to altering position in a sequence by reversing or changing the order.

re·verse·ly (rĭ-vûrs′lē) *adv.* **1.** In a reverse manner, position, or direction. **2.** On the contrary; on the other hand.

re·vers·i·ble (rĭ-vûr′sə-bəl) *adj.* **1.** Capable of being reversed. **2.** *Chemistry & Physics.* Capable of successively assuming or producing either of two states: *a reversible cell; a reversible reaction.* —*n.* A reversible item of clothing. —**re·vers′i·bil′i·ty, re·vers′i·ble·ness** *n.* —**re·vers′i·bly** *adv.*

re·ver·sion (rĭ-vûr′zhən) *n.* **1.** A return to a former condition, belief, or interest; a reverting. **2.** A turning away or in the opposite direction; reversal. **3.** *Genetics.* Loosely, **atavism** *(see).* **4.** *Law.* **a.** The return of an estate to the grantor or his estate after the grant has expired. **b.** The estate thus returned. **c.** The right to succeed to an estate.

re·ver·sion·ar·y (rĭ-vûr′zhə-nĕr′ē) *adj.* Also **re·ver·sion·al** (-zhən-əl). Of or connected with the reversion of an estate.

re·ver·sion·er (rĭ-vûr′zhən-ər) *n. Law.* A person entitled to receive an estate in reversion.

re·vert (rĭ-vûrt′) *intr.v.* **-verted, -verting, -verts. 1.** To return to a former condition, practice, subject, or belief. **2.** *Law.* To return to the former owner or his heirs. Used of money or property. —See Synonyms at **return.** [Middle English *reverten,* from Old French *revertir,* from Latin *revertere,* to turn back : *re-,* back + *vertere,* to turn (see **wer-**^{3} in Appendix*).] —**re·vert′er** *n.* —**re·vert′i·ble** *adj.* —**re·ver′tive** *adj.*

re·vest (rē-vĕst′) *tr.v.* **-vested, -vesting, -vests. 1.** To invest (someone) again with power or ownership; reinstate. **2.** To vest (power or possession, for example) once again in a person or agency. [Middle English *revesten,* to dress (in ecclesiastical garments), from Old French *revestir,* from Late Latin *revestīre,* to clothe again : Latin *re-,* again + *vestīre,* to clothe, from *vestis,* clothes (see **wes-**^{4} in Appendix*).]

re·vet (rĭ-vĕt′) *v.* **-vetted, -vetting, -vets.** —*tr.* To retain (a wall of earth) with a layer of stone or other suitable material. —*intr.* To construct a revetment. [French *revêtir,* from Old French *revestir,* to clothe again. See **revest.**]

re·vet·ment (rĭ-vĕt′mənt) *n.* **1.** A facing, as of masonry, used to support an embankment. **2.** A barricade against explosives.

re·view (rĭ-vyōō′) *v.* **-viewed, -viewing, -views.** —*tr.* **1.** To look over, study, or examine again. **2.** To consider retrospectively; look back on. **3.** To examine with an eye to criticism or correction. **4.** To write or give a critical report on (a new work or performance). **5.** *Law.* To examine (an action or determination), especially in a higher court, in order to correct possible errors. **6.** To subject to a formal inspection, especially a military inspection. —*intr.* **1.** To go over or restudy material. **2.** To act as a reviewer, especially for a newspaper or magazine. —*n. Abbr.* **rev. 1.** A re-examination or reconsideration. **2.** A retrospective view or survey. **3.** A restudying of subject matter. **4.** An inspection or examination for the purpose of evaluating something. **5.** A report or essay giving a critical estimate of a work or performance. **6.** A periodical publication devoted primarily to such reports. **7.** A formal military inspection. **8.** *Law.* An examination of an action or determination, especially by a higher court, in order to correct possible errors. **9.** An entertainment, a **revue** *(see).* [Old French *revoir* (past participle *reveu*), to see again, look over : *re-,* again, over + *voir,* to see, from Latin *vidēre* (see **weid-** in Appendix*).] —**re·view′a·ble** *adj.*

re·view·al (rĭ-vyōō′əl) *n.* The act or process of reviewing.

re·view·er (rĭ-vyōō′ər) *n.* One who reviews: especially, a newspaper or magazine critic.

re·vile (rĭ-vīl′) *v.* **-viled, -viling, -viles.** —*tr.* To denounce with abusive language; rail against. —*intr.* To use abusive language. —See Synonyms at **malign, scold.** [Middle English *revilen,* from Old French *reviler* : *re-* (intensifier), again + *vil,* VILE.] —**re·vile′ment** *n.* —**re·vil′er** *n.* —**re·vil′ing·ly** *adv.*

re·vis·al (rĭ-vī′zəl) *n.* The act of revising; revision.

re·vise (rĭ-vīz′) *tr.v.* **-vised, -vising, -vises. 1.** To prepare a newly edited version of (a text). **2.** To change or modify: *revise an earlier opinion.* —See Synonyms at **correct.** —*n. Abbr.* **rev** (rē′vīz′, rĭ-vīz′). *Printing.* A proof made from an earlier proof on which corrections have been made. [Latin *revīsere,* to look back : *re-,* again, back + *vīsere,* look at, from *vidēre* (past participle *vīsus*), to see (see **weid-** in Appendix*).] —**re·vis′a·ble** *adj.* —**re·vis′er, re·vi′sor** (rĭ-vī′zər) *n.*

Revised Standard Version. *Abbr.* **R.S.V.** A modern American version of the English Bible in the King James tradition.

Revised Version. *Abbr.* **R.V., Rev. Ver.** A British and American revision of the King James Version of the Bible.

re·vi·sion (rĭ-vĭzh′ən) *n. Abbr.* **rev. 1.** The act or procedure of revising. **2.** The result of revising; a corrected or new version. —**re·vi′sion·al, re·vi′sion·ar′y** *adj.*

re·vi·sion·ism (rĭ-vĭzh′ə-nĭz′əm) *n.* A recurrent tendency within the Communist movement to revise Marxist theory in such a way as to provide justification for a retreat from the revolutionary to the reformist position. —**re·vi′sion·ist** *n.* & *adj.*

re·vis·it (rē-vĭz′ĭt) *tr.v.* **-ited, -iting, -its.** To visit again. —*n.* A second or repeated visit. —**re′vis·i·ta′tion** *n.*

re·vi·so·ry (rĭ-vī′zə-rē) *adj.* Of, pertaining to, effecting, or having the power of revision.

re·vi·tal·ize (rē-vīt′l-īz′) *tr.v.* **-ized, -izing, -izes.** To impart new life or vigor to; restore the vitality of. —**re·vi′tal·i·za′tion** *n.*

re·viv·al (rĭ-vī′vəl) *n.* **1.** The act of reviving, or the condition of being revived. **2.** A restoration to use, acceptance, activity, or vigor after a period of obscurity or quiescence. **3.** A new presentation of an old play or motion picture. **4.** A reawakening of interest in religion. **5.** A meeting or series of meetings for the purpose of reawakening religious faith, often characterized by impassioned preaching and public professions of faith.

re·viv·al·ism (rĭ-vī′və-lĭz′əm) *n.* The spirit or activities characteristic of religious revivals.

re·viv·al·ist (rĭ-vī′və-lĭst) *n.* **1.** A person who promotes or leads religious revivals. **2.** A person who revives practices or ideas of an earlier time. —**re·viv′al·ist, re·viv′al·is′tic** *adj.*

re·vive (rĭ-vīv′) *v.* **-vived, -viving, -vives.** —*tr.* **1.** To bring back to life or consciousness; resuscitate. **2.** To impart new health, vigor, or spirit to. **3.** To restore to use, currency, activity, or notice. **4.** To restore the validity or effectiveness of. **5.** To

ă pat/ā pay/âr care/ä father/b bib/ch church/d deed/ĕ pet/ē be/f fife/g gag/h hat/hw which/ĭ pit/ī pie/îr pier/j judge/k kick/l lid, needle/m mum/n no, sudden/ng thing/ŏ pot/ō toe/ô paw, for/oi noise/ou out/ŏŏ took/ōō boot/p pop/r roar/s sauce/sh ship, dish/

renew in the mind; recall. **6.** To present (an old play or motion picture) again. —*intr.* **1.** To return to life or consciousness. **2.** To regain health, vigor, or good spirits. **3.** To return to use, currency, or notice; flourish again. **4.** To return to validity, effectiveness, or operative condition. [Middle English *reviven,* from Old French *revivre,* from Late Latin *revīvere* : Latin *re-,* again + *vīvere,* to live (see **gwei-** in Appendix*).] —**re·viv′er** *n.*

re·viv·i·fy (rē-vĭv′ə-fī′) *tr.v.* **-fied, -fying, -fies.** To impart new life to. [Old French *revivifier,* from Late Latin *revīvificāre* : *re-,* again + *vīvificāre,* to VIVIFY.] —**re·viv′i·fi·ca′tion** *n.*

rev·o·ca·ble (rĕv′ə-kə-bəl) *adj.* Also **re·vok·a·ble** (rĭ-vō′-). Capable of being revoked. —**rev′o·ca·bil′i·ty, rev′o·ca·ble·ness** *n.* —**rev′o·ca·bly** *adv.*

rev·o·ca·tion (rĕv′ə-kā′shən) *n.* The act of revoking, or the condition of being revoked; cancellation; repeal. —**rev′o·ca·to′ry** (rĕv′ə-kə-tôr′ē, -tōr′ē) *adj.*

re·voke (rĭ-vōk′) *v.* **-voked, -voking, -vokes.** —*tr.* To void or annul by recalling, withdrawing, or reversing; cancel; rescind: *revoke a license.* —*intr. Card Games.* To fail to follow suit when one is required and able to do so. —See Synonyms at **nullify.** —*n. Card Games.* An act of revoking; a failure to follow suit. [Middle English *revoken,* from Old French *revoquer,* from Latin *revocāre,* to call back : *re-,* back + *vocāre,* to call (see **wekw-** in Appendix*).] —**re·vok′er** *n.*

re·volt (rĭ-vōlt′) *v.* **-volted, -volting, -volts.** —*intr.* **1.** To institute or take part in a rebellion against state authority; to rebel or mutiny. **2.** To turn away in disgust or revulsion. Used with *against, at,* or *from.* —*tr.* To fill with disgust or abhorrence; repel. —*n.* **1.** An uprising against state authority; rebellion. **2.** Any act of protest or rejection. **3.** The state of a person or persons in rebellion: *be in revolt.* —See Synonyms at **rebellion.** [Old French *revolter,* from Italian *rivoltare,* from Vulgar Latin *revolvitāre* (unattested), from Latin *revolvere,* to roll back, REVOLVE.] —**re·volt′er** *n.*

re·volt·ing (rĭ-vōl′tĭng) *adj.* Causing disgust; repulsive; abhorrent. —**re·volt′ing·ly** *adv.*

rev·o·lute (rĕv′ə-lo͞ot′) *adj. Botany.* Rolled back on the undersurface from the tip or margins, as some leaves before they are expanded. [Latin *revolūtus,* past participle of *revolvere,* to roll back, REVOLVE.]

rev·o·lu·tion (rĕv′ə-lo͞o′shən) *n. Abbr.* **rev. 1. a.** Orbital motion about a point, especially as distinguished from axial rotation: *the planetary revolution about the sun.* **b.** A turning or rotational motion about an axis. **c.** A single complete cycle of such orbital or axial motion. **2.** An assertedly momentous change in any situation: *the revolution in physics.* **3.** A sudden political overthrow brought about from within a given system, especially: **a.** A forcible substitution of rulers or of ruling cliques: *a palace revolution.* **b.** Seizure of state power by the militant vanguard of a subject class or nation. **4.** *Capital* **R.** *Abbr.* **Rev. a.** See **American Revolution. b.** See **French Revolution.** —See Synonyms at **rebellion.** [Middle English *revolucioun,* from Old French *revolution,* from Late Latin *revolūtiō,* from Latin *revolvere* (past participle *revolūtus*), REVOLVE.]

rev·o·lu·tion·ar·y (rĕv′ə-lo͞o′shə-nĕr′ē) *adj.* **1.** Of, pertaining to, or bringing about a political or social revolution: *"Masscult is a dynamic, revolutionary force, breaking down the old barriers"* (Dwight Macdonald). **2.** Characterized by or resulting in radical change: *a revolutionary discovery.* —*n., pl.* **revolutionaries.** Also **rev·o·lu·tion·ist** (-nĭst). A militant in the struggle for revolution.

Revolutionary calendar. The calendar officially adopted in France during the French Revolution. Also called "Republican calendar." See **calendar.**

Revolutionary War. The **American Revolution** *(see).*

rev·o·lu·tion·ize (rĕv′ə-lo͞o′shə-nīz′) *tr.v.* **-ized, -izing, -izes. 1.** To bring about a radical change in; alter extensively or drastically. **2.** To cause (a country) to undergo a political or social revolution. **3.** To imbue with revolutionary principles.

re·volve (rĭ-vŏlv′) *v.* **-volved, -volving, -volves.** —*intr.* **1.** To orbit a central point. **2.** To turn on an axis; rotate. **3.** To recur in cycles or at periodic intervals. **4.** To be held in the mind and considered in turn. —*tr.* **1.** To cause to revolve. **2.** To think over; ponder or reflect on. —See Synonyms at **turn.** [Middle English *revolven,* from Latin *revolvere,* to roll back : *re-,* back + *volvere,* to roll (see **wel-**[3] in Appendix*).] —**re·volv′a·ble** *adj.*

re·volv·er (rĭ-vŏl′vər) *n.* **1.** A pistol having a revolving cylinder with several cartridge chambers. **2.** One that revolves.

re·vue (rĭ-vyo͞o′) *n.* A musical show consisting of skits, songs, and dances, often satirizing current events, trends, and personalities. Also called "review." See Synonyms at **musical comedy.** [French, from Old French, past participle of *revoir,* to REVIEW.]

re·vul·sion (rĭ-vŭl′shən) *n.* **1.** A sudden and strong change or reaction in feeling; especially, a feeling of violent disgust or loathing. **2.** A withdrawing or turning away from something. [Latin *revulsiō,* from *revellere* (past participle *revulsus*), to pull back or away : *re-,* back + *vellere,* to pull, tear (see **wel-**[4] in Appendix*).] —**re·vul′sive** *adj.*

Rev. Ver. Revised Version (of the Bible).

re·ward (rĭ-wôrd′) *n.* **1.** Something given or received in recompense for worthy behavior. **2.** Money offered for some special service, such as the return of a lost article or the capture of a criminal. **3.** A satisfying return or result; profit. —See Synonyms at **bonus.** —*tr.v.* **rewarded, -warding, -wards. 1.** To bestow a reward on. **2.** To give a reward because of or in return for. **3.** To satisfy or gratify. [Middle English *rewarden,* to heed, regard, reward, from Norman French *rewarder,* "to look at" : *re-* (intensifier) + *warder,* to watch over, from Germanic (see **wer-**[4] in Appendix*).] —**re·ward′er** *n.*

re·wind (rē-wīnd′) *tr.v.* **-wound** (-wound′), **-winding, -winds.** To wind again or anew. —*n.* (rē′wīnd′, rē-wīnd′). The act or process of rewinding something, such as film. —**re·wind′er** *n.*

re·wire (rē-wīr′) *tr.v.* **-wired, -wiring, -wires.** To provide with new wiring.

re·word (rē-wûrd′) *tr.v.* **-worded, -wording, -words. 1.** To state or express again in different words. **2.** To state or express again in the same words; repeat.

re·work (rē-wûrk′) *tr.v.* **-worked, -working, -works. 1.** To work over again; revise. **2.** To subject to a repeated or new process.

re·write (rē-rīt′) *tr.v.* **-wrote** (-rōt′), **-written** (-rĭt′n), **-writing, -writes. 1.** To write again, especially in a different form. **2.** *Journalism.* To write (an account given by a reporter) in a form suitable for publishing. —*n.* (rē′rīt′). An article so written. —**re·writ′er** *n.*

Rex (rĕks). A masculine given name. [Latin *rēx,* king. See **reg-**[1] in Appendix.*]

Rey·kja·vik (rā′kyə-vēk′). Also **Rei·kja·vik.** The capital of Iceland, in the south on Faxa Bay. Population, 17,000.

Rey·nard (rā′nərd, -närd′, rĕn′ərd). A name given to the fox in folklore and fable.

Reyn·olds (rĕn′əldz), Sir **Joshua.** 1723–1792. English portrait painter.

Rey·no·sa (rĕ-ə-nō′sä). A city of eastern Mexico, on the Rio Grande. Population, 109,000.

re·zone (rē-zōn′) *tr.v.* **-zoned, -zoning, -zones.** To divide (a municipality) into new or different zones.

RF radio frequency.

r.f. right field; right fielder.

RFD, R.F.D. rural free delivery.

Rh The symbol for the element rhodium.

r.h. **1.** relative humidity. **2.** right hand.

rhab·do·man·cy (răb′də-măn′sē) *n.* Divination by means of a wand or a rod, especially for discovering underground water or ores. [Late Greek *rhabdomanteia* : *rhabdos,* rod (see **wer-**[3] in Appendix*) + -MANCY.] —**rhab′do·man′cer** *n.*

rhab·do·my·o·ma (răb′dō-mī-ō′mə) *n., pl.* **-mas** or **-mata** (-mə-tə). *Pathology.* A tumor in striated muscular fibers. [Greek *rhabdos,* rod (see **wer-**[3] in Appendix*) + MYOMA.]

Rhad·a·man·thine (răd′ə-măn′thĭn, -thīn′) *adj.* Of or characteristic of Rhadamanthus; strictly and uncompromisingly just.

Rhad·a·man·thus (răd′ə-măn′thəs). Also **Rhad·a·man·thys.** *Greek Mythology.* The judge of the underworld.

Rhae·ti·a (rē′shē-ə, -shə). Also **Rae·ti·a.** An ancient Roman province that included portions of modern Switzerland and Austria. —**Rhae′tian** (rē′shən) *adj.* & *n.*

Rhae·tian Alps (rē′shən). A section of the central Alps along Switzerland's Italian and Austrian borders. Highest elevation, Piz Bernina (13,304 feet).

Rhae·to-Ro·man·ic (rē′tō-rō-măn′ĭk) *adj.* Also **Rhae·to-Ro·mance** (-rō-măns′). Of or pertaining to a group of closely related Romance dialects spoken in southern Switzerland, northern Italy, and the Tyrol. —*n.* Also **Rhae·to-Ro·mance.** These dialects considered as a distinct Romance language.

rha·phe. Variant of **raphe.**

rhap·sod·ic (răp-sŏd′ĭk) *adj.* Also **rhap·sod·i·cal** (-ĭ-kəl). **1.** Of, resembling, or characteristic of a rhapsody. **2.** Immoderately impassioned or enthusiastic; ecstatic. —**rhap·sod′i·cal·ly** *adv.*

rhap·so·dist (răp′sə-dĭst) *n.* Also **rhap·sode** (-sōd′). **1.** In ancient Greece, an epic singer. **2.** A person who uses extravagantly enthusiastic or impassioned language.

rhap·so·dize (răp′sə-dīz′) *v.* **-dized, -dizing, -dizes.** —*intr.* To express oneself in an immoderately enthusiastic manner. —*tr.* To recite (something) in the manner of a rhapsody.

rhap·so·dy (răp′sə-dē) *n., pl.* **-dies. 1.** Exalted or excessively enthusiastic expression of feeling in speech or writing. **2.** In ancient Greece, an epic poem, or a portion of one, suitable for uninterrupted recitation. **3.** A literary work written in an impassioned or exalted style. **4.** *Music.* A composition that is free or irregular in form, is often improvisatory in character, and typically has a melodic content based on folk tunes. [Latin *rhapsōdia,* from Greek *rhapsōidia,* from *rhapsōidos,* "weaver of songs," rhapsodist : *rhaptein,* to string or stitch together (see **wer-**[3] in Appendix*) + *ōidē,* ode, song (see **wed-**[2] in Appendix*).]

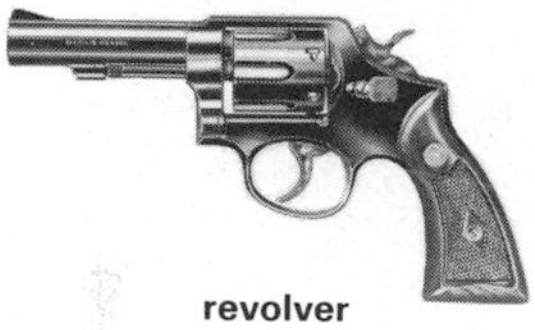

revolver

rhat·a·ny (răt′n-ē) *n., pl.* **-nies. 1.** Either of two South American shrubs, *Krameria triandra* or *K. argentea,* having thick, fleshy roots. **2.** The dried root of either of these plants, formerly used as an astringent. [Spanish *ratania,* from Quechua *ratánya.*]

rhbdr. rhombohedron.

rhe·a (rē′ə) *n.* Any of several flightless South American birds of the genus *Rhea,* resembling the ostrich but somewhat smaller and having three toes instead of two. [New Latin *Rhea,* arbitrarily named after RHEA.]

Rhe·a (rē′ə). *Greek Mythology.* The wife of Cronus.

Rhee (rē), **Syngman.** 1875–1965. Korean statesman; first president of Republic of Korea (1948–1960); deposed and exiled.

Rheims. See **Reims.**

Rhein. The German name for the **Rhine.**

Rhein·land-Pfalz. The German name for **Rhineland-Palatinate.**

rhe·mat·ic (rĭ-măt′ĭk) *adj.* **1.** Of or pertaining to word formation. **2.** Derived from or pertaining to a verb. [Greek *rhēmatikos,* from *rhēma,* word, verb. See **wer-**[6] in Appendix.*]

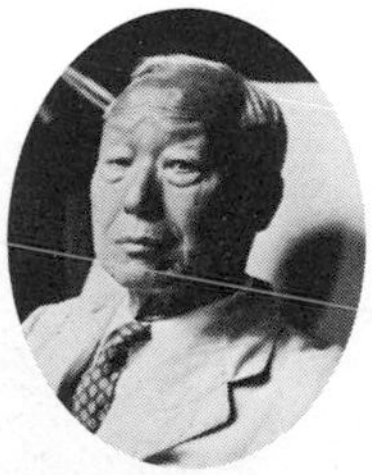

Syngman Rhee

Rhen·ish (rĕn′ĭsh) *adj.* Of or pertaining to the river Rhine or the lands bordering on it. —*n.* **Rhine wine** *(see).*

rhe·ni·um (rē′nē-əm) *n. Symbol* **Re** A rare dense silvery-white metallic element with a very high melting point. It is used for electrical contacts and with tungsten for high-temperature thermocouples. Atomic number 75, atomic weight 186.2, melt-

ing point 3,180°C, boiling point 5,627°C, specific gravity 21.02, valences 1, 2, 3, 4, 5, 6, 7. See **element**. [New Latin, from Latin *Rhēnus*, the RHINE.]

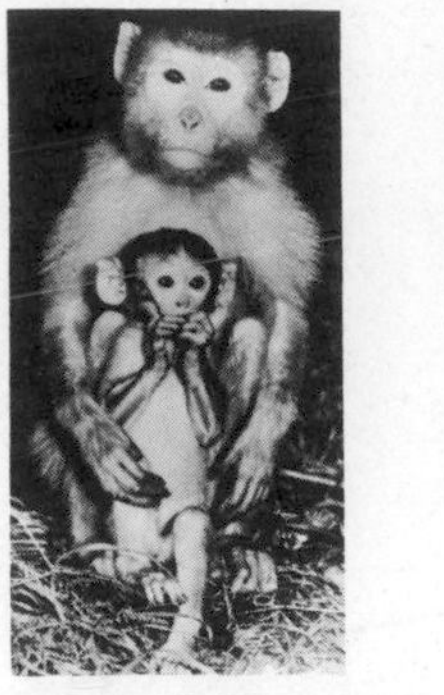

rhesus monkey
A female with young

rheo–. Indicates a flow or current; for example, **rheology**. [From Greek *rheos*, current, stream, from *rhein*, to flow. See **sreu-** in Appendix.*]

rheo. rheostat.

rhe·ol·o·gy (rē-ŏl′ə-jē) *n.* The study of the deformation and flow of matter. [RHEO- + -LOGY.] —**rhe′o·log′i·cal** (rē′ə-lŏj′ĭ-kəl) *adj.* —**rhe·ol′o·gist** *n.*

rhe·om·e·ter (rē-ŏm′ə-tər) *n.* An instrument for measuring the flow of viscous liquids, as of blood. [RHEO- + -METER.]

rhe·o·stat (rē′ə-stăt′) *n. Abbr.* **rheo.** A continuously variable electrical resistor used to regulate current. [RHEO- + -STAT.] —**rhe′o·stat′ic** *adj.*

rhe·o·tax·is (rē′ə-tăk′sĭs) *n.* The movement of an organism in response to the flow of a current. [RHEO- + -TAXIS.] —**rhe′o·tac′tic** (-tăk′tĭk) *adj.*

rhe·sus monkey (rē′səs). A brownish monkey, *Macaca mulatta*, of India, used extensively in biological experimentation. [New Latin *rhesus*, arbitrarily from Latin *Rhēsus*, name of a mythological king of Thrace.]

rhet. rhetoric.

rhe·tor (rē′tôr′, -tər) *n. Obsolete.* **1.** A teacher of rhetoric. **2.** An orator. [Middle English, from Medieval Latin *rēthor*, *rhētor*, from Greek *rhētōr*. See **wer-**[6] in Appendix.*]

rhet·o·ric (rĕt′ər-ĭk) *n. Abbr.* **rhet. 1.** The study of the elements used in literature and public speaking, such as content, structure, cadence, and style. **2.** The art of prose as distinct from that of poetry. **3. a.** Affectation or exaggeration in prose or verse. **b.** Unsupported or inflated discourse. **4.** The art of oratory, especially the persuasive use of language to influence the thoughts and actions of listeners. [Middle English *rethorik*, from Old French *rethorique*, from Latin *rhētorica*, from Greek *rhētorikē (tekhnē)*, "rhetorical (art)," from *rhētorikos*, rhetorical, from *rhētōr*, RHETOR.]

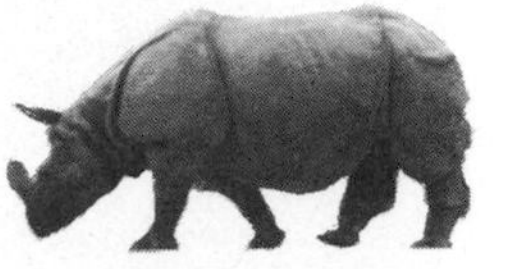

rhinoceros
Rhinoceros unicornis

rhe·tor·i·cal (rĭ-tôr′ĭ-kəl, rĭ-tŏr′-) *adj.* **1.** Concerned primarily with style or effect; showy or overelaborate. **2.** Resembling rhetoric; oratorical. —**rhe·tor′i·cal·ly** *adv.*

rhetorical question. A question to which no answer is expected, or to which only one answer may be made.

rhet·o·ri·cian (rĕt′ə-rĭsh′ən) *n.* **1.** An expert in or teacher of rhetoric. **2.** An eloquent speaker or writer. **3.** One given to verbal extravagance.

rheum (ro͞om) *n.* A watery or thin mucous discharge from the eyes or nose. [Middle English *reume*, from Old French, from Latin *rheuma*, from Greek, stream, humor of the body, rheum. See **sreu-** in Appendix.*] —**rheum′y** *adj.*

rheu·mat·ic (ro͞o-măt′ĭk) *adj.* Of, pertaining to, or afflicted with rheumatism. —*n.* **1.** A person afflicted with rheumatism. **2.** *Plural. Informal.* Pains due to rheumatism. [Middle English *rewmatyk*, from Latin *rheumaticus*, troubled with rheum, from Greek *rheumatikos*, subject to rheum, from *rheuma*, stream, body humor, RHEUM.]

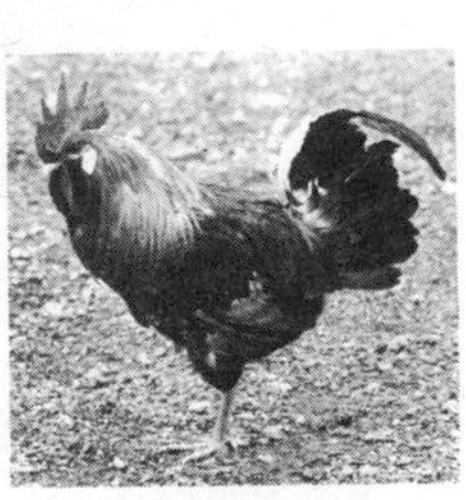

Rhode Island Red
Rooster

rheumatic fever. A severe infectious disease occurring chiefly in children, characterized by fever and painful inflammation of the joints, and frequently resulting in permanent damage to the valves of the heart.

rheu·ma·tism (ro͞o′mə-tĭz′əm) *n.* **1.** Any of several pathological conditions of the muscles, tendons, joints, bones, or nerves, characterized by discomfort and disability. **2.** Rheumatoid arthritis. [Latin *rheumatismus*, rheum, catarrh, from Greek *rheumatismos*, from *rheumatizesthai*, to suffer from a flux, from *rheuma*, stream, flux, RHEUM.]

rheu·ma·toid (ro͞o′mə-toid′). Also **rheu·ma·toi·dal** (ro͞o′mə-toid′l) *adj.* **1.** Of or resembling rheumatism. **2.** Afflicted with rheumatism. —**rheu′ma·toi′dal·ly** *adv.*

rheumatoid arthritis. A chronic disease marked by stiffness and inflammation of the joints, weakness, loss of mobility, and deformity.

Rh factor. Any of several substances on the surface of red blood cells that induce antigenic reactions with Rh negative blood cells. Also called "Rhesus factor." [First discovered in the blood of RHESUS MONKEYS.]

rhi·nal (rī′nəl) *adj.* Of or pertaining to the nose; nasal. [RHIN(O)- + -AL.]

Rhine (rīn). *German* **Rhein** (rīn); *French* **Rhin** (răN); *Dutch* **Rijn** (rīn). A river of Europe, rising in eastern Switzerland and flowing about 820 miles generally north through West Germany and the Netherlands to the North Sea via the Ijssel, Lek, and Waal rivers. [Latin *Rhēnus* and German *Rhein*, from Gaulish *Rēnos*. See **er-**[1] in Appendix.*]

Rhine·land (rīn′lănd′, -lənd). A general term for the regions along the Rhine in West Germany.

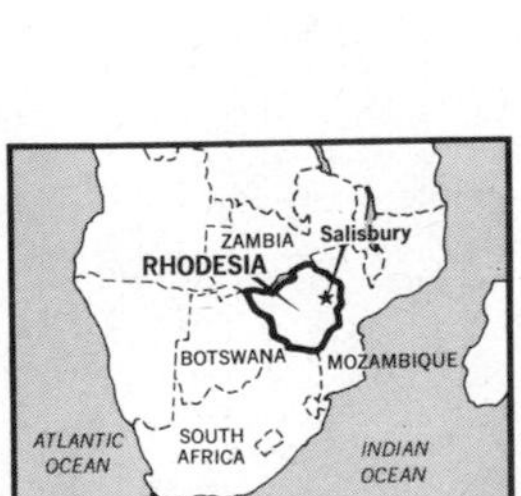

Rhodesia

Rhine·land-Pa·lat·i·nate (rīn′lănd′pə-lăt′n-āt′, -ĭt). *German* **Rhein·land-Pfalz** (rīn′länt′pfälts′). A state of West Germany, 7,666 square miles in area, formed in 1946 of the Lower Palatinate, Rhenish Hesse, and parts of Hesse-Nassau and the Prussian Rhine Province. Population, 3,545,000.

rhi·nen·ceph·a·lon (rī′nĕn-sĕf′ə-lŏn′, -lən) *n., pl.* **-la** (-lə). The olfactory region of the brain, in the cerebrum. [RHIN(O)- + ENCEPHALON.] —**rhi′nen·ce·phal′ic** (-sə-făl′ĭk) *adj.*

rhine·stone (rīn′stōn′) *n.* A colorless, artificial gem of paste or glass, often with facets that sparkle in imitation of diamond. [Translation of French *caillou du Rhin*; originally made at Strasbourg.]

Rhine wine. 1. Any of several wines produced in the Rhine valley. Also called "Rhenish." **2.** Any similar light, dry wine produced elsewhere.

rhi·ni·tis (rī-nī′tĭs) *n.* Inflammation of the nasal mucous membranes. [New Latin : RHIN(O)- + -ITIS.]

rhi·no[1] (rī′nō) *n., pl.* **-nos.** *Informal.* A rhinoceros.

rhi·no[2] (rī′nō) *n. British Slang.* Money; cash. [Probably short for *rhinocerical*, heavy as a rhinoceros, hence, (slang) rich, from RHINOCEROS.]

rhino–, rhin–. Indicates nose or nasal; for example, **rhinoscopy**, **rhinitis**. [From Greek *rhis*† (stem *rhin-*), nose.]

rhi·noc·er·os (rī-nŏs′ər-əs) *n., pl.* **rhinoceros** or **-oses.** Any of several large, thick-skinned, herbivorous mammals of the family Rhinocerotidae, of Africa and Asia, having one or two upright horns on the snout. [Middle English *rinoceros*, from Latin *rhīnocerōs*, from Greek *rhinokerōs*, "nose-horned" : RHINO- + *keras*, horn (see **ker-**[1] in Appendix*).]

rhi·nol·o·gy (rī-nŏl′ə-jē) *n.* The anatomy, physiology, and pathology of the nose. [RHINO- + -LOGY.] —**rhi·nol′o·gist** *n.*

rhi·nos·co·py (rī-nŏs′kə-pē) *n.* Examination of the nasal passages. [RHINO- + -SCOPY.]

rhizo-, rhiz–. Indicates a root; for example, **rhizomorphous**, **rhizoid**. [From Greek *rhiza*, root. See **werād-** in Appendix.*]

rhi·zo·bi·um (rī-zō′bē-əm) *n., pl.* **-bia** (-bē-ə). Any of various nitrogen-fixing bacteria of the genus *Rhizobium* that form nodules on the roots of leguminous plants such as clover and beans. [New Latin *Rhizobium* : RHIZO- + Greek *bios*, life (see **gwei-** in Appendix*).]

rhi·zo·ceph·a·lan (rī′zō-sĕf′ə-lən) *n.* Any of various small aquatic crustaceans of the order Rhizocephala that are parasitic on other crustaceans. [From New Latin *Rhizocephala*, "root-headed ones" (from the rootlike processes extending from the limbless body) : RHIZO- + *-cephala*, from *-cephalus*, -CEPHALOUS.] —**rhi′zo·ceph′a·lous** *adj.*

rhi·zo·gen·ic (rī′zō-jĕn′ĭk). Also **rhi·zo·ge·net·ic** (-jə-nĕt′ĭk), **rhi·zog·e·nous** (rī-zŏj′ə-nəs) *adj. Botany.* Giving rise to roots: *rhizogenic tissue.* [RHIZO- + -GENIC.]

rhi·zoid (rī′zoid′) *adj.* Rootlike. —*n.* **1.** A slender, rootlike filament by which mosses, liverworts, and ferns attach to the substratum and absorb nourishment. **2.** A rootlike extension of the thallus of a fungus. [RHIZ(O)- + -OID.] —**rhi·zoi′dal** *adj.*

rhi·zome (rī′zōm′) *n. Botany.* A rootlike, usually horizontal stem growing under or along the ground, and sending out roots from its lower surface, and leaves or shoots from its upper surface. Also called "rootstock," "rootstalk." [New Latin *rhizoma*, from Greek *rhizōma*, mass of roots of a tree, from *rhizousthai*, to take root, from *rhiza*, root. See **werād-** in Appendix.*] —**rhi·zom′a·tous** (-zŏm′ə-təs, -zō′mə-təs) *adj.*

rhi·zo·morph (rī′zō-môrf′) *n.* A rootlike part, such as a thread-like structure in fungi, consisting of strands of hyphae. [RHIZO- + -MORPH.]

rhi·zo·mor·phous (rī′zō-môr′fəs) *adj. Botany.* Having the form of a root. [RHIZO- + -MORPHOUS.]

rhi·zoph·a·gous (rī-zŏf′ə-gəs) *adj.* Feeding on roots. [RHIZO- + -PHAGOUS.]

rhi·zo·pod (rī′zō-pŏd′) *n.* Any protozoan of the class or subclass Rhizopoda, such as an amoeba or radiolarian, characteristically moving and taking in food by means of pseudopodia. [New Latin *Rhizopoda*, "root-footed" (from its rootlike pseudopodia) : RHIZO- + -POD.] —**rhi·zop′o·dan** (rī-zŏp′ə-dən) *adj.* & *n.* —**rhi·zop′o·dous** *adj.*

rhi·zo·pus (rī′zō-pəs) *n.* Any of various often destructive fungi of the genus *Rhizopus*, such as *R. nigricans*, the common bread mold. [New Latin, "one having rootlike feet" (from its rhizoids) : RHIZO- + Greek *pous*, foot (see **-pod**).]

rhi·zot·o·my (rī-zŏt′ə-mē) *n., pl.* **-mies.** Surgical severance of spinal nerve roots to relieve pain or hypertension. [RHIZO- + -TOMY.]

Rh negative. Lacking an **Rh factor** *(see).*

rho (rō) *n.* The 17th letter in the Greek alphabet written Ρ, ρ. Transliterated in English as *r*, or *rh* when aspirated. See **alphabet**. [Greek *rhō*, perhaps shortened from *rhōs*, head, of Semitic origin, akin to Hebrew *rēsh*, *rōsh*, "head," RESH.]

rho·da·mine (rō′də-mēn′) *n.* Any of several synthetic red to pink dyes. [RHOD(O)- + AMINE (the dyes are prepared from aminophenol).]

Rhode Island (rōd). **1.** *Abbr.* **R.I.** Officially, The State of Rhode Island and Providence Plantations. A southern New England state of the United States, 1,214 square miles in area, and one of the original 13 states. Population, 893,000. Capital, Providence. See map at **United States of America**. **2.** Formerly **A·quid·neck** (ə-kwĭd′nĕk). An island belonging to this state, in Narragansett Bay. —**Rhode Islander.**

Rhode Island Red. Any of an American breed of domestic fowls having dark reddish-brown feathers.

Rhodes (rōdz). **1.** The largest (542 square miles) of the Dodecanese Islands in the Aegean Sea, southwest of Turkey. It was ceded by Italy to Greece in 1947. **2.** The capital of this island. Population, 27,000. —**Rho′di·an** (rō′dē-ən) *adj.* & *n.*

Rhodes (rōdz), **Cecil (John).** 1853–1902. British financier and colonialist.

Rho·de·sia (rō-dē′zhə). **1.** A region of central-south Africa, formerly comprising the British protectorates of Northern Rhodesia and Southern Rhodesia. **2.** Formerly, **Southern Rhodesia**. A self-governing British protectorate, 150,333 square miles in area, in southern Africa. In 1965, it unilaterally declared its independence. Population, 3,849,000. Capital, Salisbury. —**Rho·de′sian** *adj.* & *n.*

Rhodesia and Nyasaland, Federation of. A former federation, dissolved in 1964, of the British protectorates of Northern Rhodesia, Southern Rhodesia, and Nyasaland, in southern Africa.

Rhodesian man. A fossil man, *Homo rhodesiensis* (or *Cyphanthropus rhodesiensis*), found in south-central Africa, having a large, low skull with massive brow ridges and skeletal bones similar to modern man.

Rhodesian ridgeback. A large dog of a breed developed in Africa, having short, yellowish-tan hair that forms a ridge along the back.

rho·di·um (rō′dē-əm) *n. Symbol* **Rh** A hard, durable, silvery-white metallic element that is used to form high-temperature alloys with platinum and is plated on other metals to produce a durable corrosion-resistant coating. Atomic number 45, atomic weight 102.905, melting point 1,966°C, boiling point 3,727°C, specific gravity 12.41, valences 2, 3, 4, 5. See **element.** [New Latin, "rose red" (from the color of its compounds), from Greek *rhodon,* rose. See **wrod-** in Appendix.*]

rhodo-, rhod-. Indicates rose or rose-red; for example, **rhodolite.** [From Greek *rhodon,* rose. See **wrod-** in Appendix.*]

rho·do·chro·site (rō′də-krō′sīt′) *n.* A naturally occurring impure manganese carbonate, MnCO$_3$, light-pink to rose-red in color with a pearly or vitreous luster, used as a manganese ore. Also called "manganese spar." [German *Rhodochrosit* : RHODO- + Greek *khrōsis,* coloring, from *khrōs, khroos,* color, skin (see **ghrēu-** in Appendix*) + -ITE.]

rho·do·den·dron (rō′də-děn′drən) *n.* Any of various evergreen shrubs of the genus *Rhododendron,* of the North Temperate Zone, having clusters of variously colored flowers. See **rosebay, azalea.** [New Latin, from Latin, from Greek, "rose tree" : RHODO- + Greek *dendron,* tree (see **deru-** in Appendix*).]

rho·do·lite (rō′də-līt′) *n.* A rose-red or pink variety of garnet, a silicate mineral used as a gem. [RHODO- + -LITE.]

rho·do·mon·tade. Variant of **rodomontade.**

rho·do·nite (rō′də-nīt′) *n.* A pink to rose-red mineral, essentially a glassy crystalline manganese silicate, MnSiO$_3$, used as an ornamental stone. Also called "manganese spar." [German *Rhodonit* : Greek *rhodon,* rose (see **rhod-**) + -ITE.]

Rhod·o·pe Mountains (rŏd′ə-pē). A mountain group in the Balkan Peninsula along the border of southern Bulgaria and northeastern Greece. Highest peak, Musala (9,596 feet).

rho·dop·sin (rō-dŏp′sĭn) *n.* The pigment sensitive to red light in the retinal rods of the eyes, consisting of opsin and retinene. Also called "visual purple." [RHODO- + Greek *opsis,* sight (see **okw-** in Appendix*) + -IN.]

rho·do·ra (rō-dôr′ə, -dōr′ə) *n.* A shrub, *Rhododendron canadense,* of eastern North America, having rose-purple flowers that bloom before the leaves appear. [New Latin, from Latin *rhodōra,* variant of *rodarum,* meadowsweet, from Gaulish.]

rhomb. rhombic.

rhom·ben·ceph·a·lon (rŏm′bĕn-sĕf′ə-lŏn′, -lən) *n.* The portion of the embryonic brain from which the metencephalon, myelencephalon, and subsequently the cerebellum, pons, and medulla oblongata develop. Also called "hindbrain." [New Latin : RHOMB(US) + ENCEPHALON.]

rhom·bic (rŏm′bĭk) *adj.* 1. *Abbr.* **rhomb.** Having the shape of a rhombus. 2. *Crystallography.* **Orthorhombic** (see).

rhom·bo·he·dron (rŏm′bō-hē′drən) *n., pl.* **-drons** or **-dra** (-drə). *Abbr.* **rhbdr.** A prism with six faces, each a rhombus. [New Latin : RHOMBUS + -HEDRON.] —**rhom′bo·he′dral** (-drəl) *adj.*

rhom·boid (rŏm′boid′) *n.* A parallelogram with unequal adjacent sides. —*adj.* Having a shape like a rhomboid. [Greek *rhomboeidēs* : RHOMBUS + -OID.] —**rhom·boi′dal** (-boid′l) *adj.*

rhom·bus (rŏm′bəs) *n., pl.* **-buses** or **-bi** (-bī′). An equilateral parallelogram. [Latin, from Greek *rhombos,* bullroarer, magic wheel, rhombus. See **wer-³** in Appendix.*]

rhon·chus (rŏng′kəs) *n., pl.* **-chi** (-kī′). A coarse rattling sound somewhat like snoring, usually caused by secretion in the bronchial tube; a rale. [Late Latin, snoring, from Greek *rhonkhos, rhonkos.* See **srenk-** in Appendix.*] —**rhon′chal, rhon′chi·al** (-kē-əl) *adj.*

Rhône (rōn). Also **Rhone.** A European river rising in central Switzerland and flowing 505 miles, first generally west and then south to the Mediterranean near Arles, France.

r.h.p. rated horsepower.

Rh positive. Containing an **Rh factor** (see).

rhu·barb (rōō′bärb′) *n.* 1. Any of several plants of the genus *Rheum,* characterized by large, long-stalked leaves; especially, *R. rhaponticum,* the common garden rhubarb, having long, green or reddish, acid leafstalks that are edible when sweetened and cooked. This species is sometimes called "pie plant." 2. The dried, bitter-tasting rhizome and roots of *R. palmatum* or *R. officinale,* of central Asia, used as a laxative. 3. *Slang.* A heated discussion, quarrel, or fight. [Middle English *rubarbe,* from Old French *r(e)ubarbe,* probably from Medieval Latin *reubarb(ar)um,* probably alteration of *rha barbarum,* barbarian rhubarb : Late Latin *rha, rhubarb,* from Greek *rha, rhēon,* probably from *Rha,* former name of the Volga, on whose banks rhubarb was grown, from Avestan *Ra(n)hā,* a mythical river (see **ers-²** in Appendix*) + Latin *barbarus,* BARBAROUS.]

rhumb (rŭm, rŭmb) *n.* 1. A rhumb line. 2. One of the points of the mariner's compass. [Earlier *rumb,* from Old Spanish *rumbo* and Old French *rumb,* modifications (influenced by Latin *rhombus,* RHOMBUS) of Middle Dutch *ruum, rume,* room, space. See **rewa-** in Appendix.*]

rhum·ba. Variant of **rumba.**

rhumb line. The path of a ship that maintains a fixed compass direction, shown on a map as a line crossing all meridians at the same angle. Also called "loxodromic curve."

rhyme (rīm) *n.* Also **rime.** 1. Correspondence of terminal sounds of words or of lines of verse. See **assonance, consonance.** 2. A poem or verse having a regular correspondence of sounds, especially at the ends of lines. 3. Poetry or verse of this kind. 4. A word that corresponds with another in terminal sound, such as *baboon* and *harpoon.* —*v.* **rhymed, rhyming, rhymes.** Also **rime.** —*intr.* 1. To form a rhyme; correspond in sound. 2. To compose rhymes or verse. 3. To make use of rhymes in composing verse. —*tr.* 1. To put into rhyme or compose with rhymes. 2. To use (a word or words) as a rhyme or rhymes. [Middle English *rime, ryme,* from *rime,* from Medieval Latin *rithmus,* variant of Latin *rhythmus,* rhythm, from Greek *rhuthmos.* See **sreu-** in Appendix.*]

rhym·er (rī′mər) *n.* Also **rim·er.** One who composes rhyming verses. See Synonyms at **poet.**

rhyme·ster (rīm′stər) *n.* Also **rime·ster.** One who makes up light verse that rhymes. See Synonyms at **poet.**

rhyn·cho·ce·pha·lian (rĭng′kō-sə-fāl′yən) *adj.* Of or belonging to the Rhynchocephalia, an order of mostly extinct lizardlike reptiles. —*n.* A rhynchocephalian reptile, such as the tuatara. [New Latin *Rhynchocephalia* : Greek *rhunkhos,* snout, bill, beak (see **srenk-** in Appendix*) + CEPHAL(O)- + -IA.]

rhy·o·lite (rī′ə-līt′) *n.* A glassy volcanic rock, similar to granite in composition and usually exhibiting flow lines. [German *Rhyolit* : irregularly from Greek *rhuax,* stream (of lava), from *rhein,* to flow (see **sreu-** in Appendix*) + -ITE.]

rhythm (rĭth′əm) *n.* 1. Any kind of movement characterized by the regular recurrence of strong and weak elements: *the rhythm of the tides.* 2. Nonrandom variation, especially uniform or regular variation, of any quantity or condition characterizing a process. 3. *Music.* **a.** A regulated pattern formed by long or short notes. **b.** A specific kind of such a pattern: *a waltz rhythm.* 4. *Poetry.* **a.** The metrical flow of sound with a regulated pattern of long and short, or accented and unaccented syllables. **b.** A specific kind of such a metrical flow. 5. In painting, sculpture, and other visual arts, a regular or harmonious pattern created by lines, forms, and colors: *"Aubrey Beardsley introduced a new sense of rhythm into black and white art"* (Holbrook Jackson). [Old French *rhythme,* from Latin *rhythmus,* from Greek *rhuthmos,* recurring motion, measure, rhythm. See **sreu-** in Appendix.*]

Synonyms: rhythm, meter, cadence, beat. Rhythm denotes the regular patterned flow, the ebb and rise, of sounds and movement in speech, music, writing, dance, and other physical activities, and in natural phenomena: *the rhythm of the heart. Meter* basically means measure, and applies to a system or pattern of measured recurrence of length, beat, or numbers in poetry and music. *Cadence* refers specifically to the pleasing rise and fall of the voice in speech or singing and to the harmonic sequence of chords in music indicating conclusion. *Beat* is the heavy stress in rhythm; it may also be used loosely for rhythm.

rhyth·mi·cal (rĭth′mĭ-kəl) *adj.* Also **rhyth·mic** (-mĭk). Pertaining to or having rhythm; recurring with measured regularity. —**rhyth′mi·cal·ly** *adv.*

rhyth·mics (rĭth′mĭks) *n.* Plural in form, used with a singular verb. The study of rhythm.

rhyth·mist (rĭth′mĭst) *n.* 1. One who is expert in, or has a keen sense of, rhythm. 2. One who studies or produces rhythm.

rhythm method. A birth-control method dependent on continence during the period of female ovulation.

RI Rhode Island (with Zip Code).

R.I. Rhode Island.

Ri·ad. See **Riyadh.**

ri·al (rē-ôl′, -äl′) *n.* 1. **a.** The basic monetary unit of Iran, equal to 100 dinars. See table of exchange rates at **currency. b.** A coin worth one rial. 2. Variant of **riyal.** [Persian, from Arabic *riyāl,* from Spanish *real,* REAL (coin).]

Ri·al·to (rē-ăl′tō; *Italian* rä-äl′tō). 1. An island in Venice, Italy, the oldest quarter in the city. 2. The legitimate theater district of New York City.

ri·a·ta (rē-ä′tə) *n.* Also **re·a·ta.** A lariat; lasso. [Spanish *(la) reata,* (the) lariat, LARIAT.]

rib (rĭb) *n.* 1. **a.** One of a series of long, curved bones, occurring in 12 pairs in man and extending from the spine to or toward the sternum. **b.** A similar bone in most vertebrates. 2. Some part or piece similar to a rib and serving to shape or support: *the rib of an umbrella.* 3. A cut of meat enclosing one or more ribs. 4. In a boat or ship, any one of many curved members attached to the keel and extending upward and outward to form the framework of the hull. 5. Any one of many formed transverse pieces along the length of an airplane wing used to establish shape. 6. *Architecture.* **a.** An arch or a projecting arched member of a vault. **b.** One of the curved pieces of an arch. 7. A raised ridge or wale in knitted material or in cloth. 8. *Botany.* One of the main veins of a leaf or other organ. 9. *Slang.* A joke. —*tr.v.* **ribbed, ribbing, ribs.** 1. To shape, support, or provide with a rib or ribs. 2. To make with ridges or raised markings. 3. *Slang.* To tease or make fun of. [Middle English *rib(be),* Old English *rib(b).* See **rebh-¹** in Appendix.*]

rib·ald (rĭb′ôld) *adj.* Pertaining to or indulging in vulgar, lewd humor. See Synonyms at **coarse.** —*n.* A ribald person. [Middle English *ribaud,* retainer of low rank, lewd person, rascal, blasphemer, from Old French *ribauld, ribaut,* from *riber,* to be wanton, from Old High German *riban,* to be in heat, copulate, "to rub." See **wer-³** in Appendix.*]

rib·ald·ry (rĭb′əl-drē) *n., pl.* **-ries.** Ribald language or joking.

rib·and (rĭb′ənd) *n. Archaic.* A ribbon, especially one used as a decoration. [Middle English *ribawnd, ryband,* variants (with parasitic -*d*) of *riban,* RIBBON.]

rib·band (rĭb′ănd, -ənd, -ən) *n.* A length of flexible wood or metal used to hold the ribs of a ship in place while the exterior planking or plating is being applied. [RIB + BAND (strip).]

Rhodesian ridgeback

rhododendron
Rhododendron carolinianum

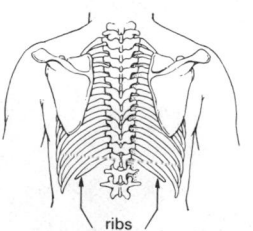

rib
The human ribs
viewed from behind

ă pat/ā pay/âr care/ä father/b bib/ch church/d deed/ĕ pet/ē be/f fife/g gag/h hat/hw which/ĭ pit/ī pie/îr pier/j judge/k kick/l lid, needle/m mum/n no, sudden/ng thing/ŏ pot/ō toe/ô paw, for/oi noise/ou out/ōō took/ōō boot/p pop/r roar/s sauce/sh ship, dish/

t tight/th thin, path/*th* this, bathe/ŭ cut/ûr urge/v valve/w with/y yes/z zebra, size/zh vision/ə about, item, edible, gallop, circus/ à *Fr.* ami/œ *Fr.* feu, *Ger.* schön/ü *Fr.* tu, *Ger.* über/KH *Ger.* ich, *Scot.* loch/N *Fr.* bon. *Follows main vocabulary. †Of obscure origin.

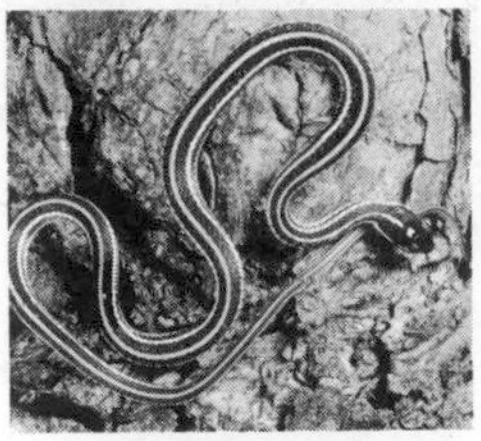

ribbon snake

ribgrass

Baron von Richthofen

Edward Rickenbacker
Photographed in 1918

Rib·ben·trop (rĭb′ən-trôp), **Joachim von.** 1893–1946. German Nazi diplomat; foreign minister (1938–45); executed.

rib·bing (rĭb′ĭng) *n.* **1.** Ribs collectively. **2.** An arrangement of ribs, as in a boat. **3.** *Slang.* An instance of joking or teasing.

rib·bon (rĭb′ən) *n.* **1.** A narrow strip or band of fine fabric, such as satin or velvet, finished at the edges and used for trimming or tying. **2.** Anything resembling a ribbon, as a measuring tape. **3.** *Plural.* Tattered or ragged strips: *a dress torn to ribbons.* **4.** An inked strip of cloth used for making the impression, as in a typewriter. **5. a.** A band of colored cloth signifying membership in an order or the award of a prize. **b.** In the armed forces, a strip of colored cloth worn on the left breast of a uniform to indicate the award of a medal or decoration. **6.** *Plural. Informal.* Reins for driving horses. —*tr.v.* **ribboned, -boning, -bons.** **1.** To decorate or tie with ribbons. **2.** To tear into ribbons or shreds. —*adj.* **1.** Resembling ribbon. **2.** Streaked with parallel bands, as certain minerals. [Middle English *riban,* from Old French *riban, ruban,* from Middle Dutch *ringhband,* necklace : *ringh-, rinc,* ring (see **sker-**[3] in Appendix*) + *band,* band (see **bhendh-** in Appendix*).]

rib·bon·fish (rĭb′ən-fĭsh′) *n., pl.* **ribbonfish** or **-fishes.** Any of several marine fishes, chiefly of the genus *Trachipterus,* having long, narrow, compressed bodies.

ribbon snake. A nonvenomous North American snake, *Thamnophis sauritus,* having yellow or reddish stripes along the body.

ribbon worm. A **nemertean** *(see).*

rib cage. The enclosing structure formed by the ribs and the bones to which they are attached.

Ri·bei·rão Pre·to (rē′bā-rouN prā′tōō). A city in southern Brazil, 175 miles north of São Paulo. Population, 116,000.

Ri·be·ra (rē-vĕ′rä), **José.** Called "Lo Spagnoletto." 1588–1656. Spanish painter.

rib·grass (rĭb′grăs′, -gräs′) *n.* A weedy plant, *Plantago lanceolata,* having lancelike, ribbed leaves and a dense spike of small whitish flowers. Also called "English plantain," "ribwort."

ri·bo·fla·vin (rī′bō-flā′vĭn) *n.* A crystalline orange-yellow pigment, $C_{17}H_{20}O_6N_4$, the principal growth-promoting factor in the vitamin B_2 complex, found in milk, leafy vegetables, fresh meat, and egg yolks, and produced synthetically. Also called "lactoflavin," "vitamin B_2," "vitamin G." [RIBO(SE) + FLAVIN.]

ri·bo·nu·cle·ase (rī′bō-nōō′klē-ās, rī′bō-nyōō′-, -āz) *n.* Any of various enzymes that decompose ribonucleic acids.

ri·bo·nu·cle·ic acid (rī′bō-nōō-klē′ĭk, rī′bō-nyōō-). *Abbr.* **RNA** A universal polymeric constituent of all living cells, consisting of a single-stranded chain of alternating phosphate and ribose units with the bases adenine, guanine, cytosine, and uracil bonded to the ribose, the structure and base sequence of which are determinants of protein synthesis. See **messenger RNA.** [RIBO(SE) + NUCLEIC ACID.]

ri·bose (rī′bōs′) *n.* A pentose sugar, $C_5H_{10}O_5$, occurring as a component of nucleic acids. [From German *Ribon(säure),* a tetrahydroxyl acid from which ribose is obtained : *Ribon-,* arbitrary alteration of English *arabinose,* ribose : (GUM) ARAB(IC) + -IN + -OSE + *Säure,* acid.]

ri·bo·some (rī′bə-sōm) *n.* A spherical cytoplasmic RNA-containing particle active in the synthesis of protein. Also called "microsome." [RIBO(SE) + -SOME (body).] —**ri·bo·so′mal** *adj.*

rib·wort (rĭb′wûrt′, -wôrt′). The **ribgrass** *(see).*

Ri·car·do (rĭ-kär′dō), **David.** 1772–1823. English economist.

Ric·cio·li (rēt-chō′lē), **Giovanni Battista.** 1598–1671. Italian astronomer; made telescopic lunar studies.

rice (rīs) *n.* **1.** A cereal grass, *Oryza sativa,* that is cultivated extensively in warm climates, and is a staple food throughout the world. **2.** The starchy edible seed of this grass. —*tr.v.* **riced, ricing, rices.** To sieve (food) to the consistency of rice. [Middle English *rys, ryce,* from Old French *ris,* from Italian *riso,* from Latin *orўza,* from Greek *oruzon, oruza,* from East Iranian *vriz-* (unattested), akin to Sanskrit *vrīhi*†.]

Rice (rīs), **Elmer.** Original surname, Reizenstein. 1892–1967. American playwright and novelist.

rice·bird (rīs′bûrd′) *n.* **1.** *Southern U.S.* The **bobolink** *(see).* **2.** Any of various other birds that frequent rice fields.

rice paper. A thin paper made chiefly from the pith of the rice-paper tree.

rice-pa·per tree (rīs′pā′pər). A shrub or small tree, *Tetrapanax papyriferum,* of eastern Asia, grown as a source of fiber for rice paper. Also called "rice-paper plant."

ric·er (rī′sər) *n.* A kitchen utensil used for ricing soft foods by extrusion through small holes.

rice weevil. A small, destructive insect, *Sitophilus oryzae,* that infests stored grain and cereal products.

rich (rĭch) *adj.* **richer, richest. 1.** Possessing great wealth; owning much money, goods, or land. **2.** Composed of rare or valuable materials; made with fine or elaborate craftsmanship; costly: *a rich brocade.* **3.** Of great worth; valuable. **4.** Elaborate or sumptuous: *a rich feast.* **5.** Plentiful; abundant; ample: *rich in ideas.* **6.** Abundantly or copiously supplied. Followed by *in* or *with: rich in tradition.* **7.** Abounding in natural resources: *a rich land.* **8.** Producing or yielding much; abundant: *a rich harvest.* **9.** Abounding in desirable qualities; specifically, of food containing a large or excessive proportion of tasty ingredients: *a rich sauce.* **10.** Pleasing and satisfying to the senses: *a rich tenor voice.* **11.** Containing a large proportion of fuel to air. Used of a fuel mixture. **12.** *Informal.* Full of amusement; satisfyingly funny: *a rich joke.* —*n.* Wealthy people considered collectively. Preceded by *the.* [Middle English *riche,* originally powerful, great, partly from Old French *riche,* from Frankish *rīki* (unattested), and partly from Old English *rīce.* See **reg-**[1] in Appendix.*] —**rich′ly** *adv.* —**rich′ness** *n.*

Rich·ard (rĭch′ərd). A masculine given name. [Middle English, from Old French, from Old High German *Ricohard* : *rīhhi,* powerful (see **reg-**[1] in Appendix*) + *-hard,* hardy, from Germanic (see **kar-**[1] in Appendix*).]

Rich·ard I (rĭch′ərd). Called "Coeur de Lion" or "the Lion-Hearted." 1157–1199. King of England (1189–99).

Rich·ard II (rĭch′ərd). 1367–1400. King of England (1377–99).

Rich·ard III (rĭch′ərd). 1452–1485. King of England (1483–85).

Rich·ard Roe. See **John Doe.**

Rich·ards (rĭch′ərdz), **Dickinson Woodruff.** Born 1895. American physician; pioneer in heart research.

Rich·ard·son (rĭch′ərd-sən), **Samuel.** 1689–1761. English author of novels in letter form.

Ri·che·lieu (rē-shə-lyœ′), **Duc de.** Title of Armand Jean du Plessis. 1585–1642. French cardinal and statesman; chief minister of Louis XIII and virtual dictator (1624–42).

Ri·che·lieu River (rē-shə-lyœ′, rĭsh-ə-lōō′). A river of southern Quebec, Canada, flowing north about 210 miles from Lake Champlain to the St. Lawrence.

rich·en (rĭch′ən) *tr.v.* **-ened, -ening, -ens.** To make rich.

rich·es (rĭch′ĭz) *pl.n.* **1.** Abundant wealth. **2.** Valuable or precious possessions. [Middle English *riches, richesse,* wealth, from Old French, from *riche,* powerful, RICH.]

Rich·mond (rĭch′mənd). **1.** The capital and largest city of Virginia, and a port on the James River; the capital of the American Confederacy (1861–65). Population, 220,000. **2.** A city and port of western California on San Francisco Bay. Population, 72,000. **3.** A borough of New York City, coextensive with Staten Island. Population, 222,000. **4.** A former administrative division of London, England, now part of Richmond-on-Thames.

Rich·mond-on-Thames (rĭch′mənd-ŏn-tĕmz′). A borough of London, England, comprising the former administrative divisions of Richmond, Barnes, and Twickenham. Population, 182,000.

Rich·ter (rĭKH′tər), **Jean Paul Friedrich.** Pen name, Jean Paul. 1763–1825. German humorist and novelist.

Richt·ho·fen (rĭKHt′hō-fən), Baron **Manfred von.** 1892–1918. German aviator; World War I air ace.

rich·weed (rĭch′wēd′) *n.* **1.** A plant, **clearweed** *(see).* **2.** A plant, **horse balm** *(see).* [Probably from its juicy stems or its rich fragrance.]

ri·cin (rī′sĭn, rĭ′-) *n.* A poisonous protein extracted from the castor bean and used as a biochemical reagent. [Latin *ricinus*†, castor-oil plant.]

ri·cin·o·le·ic acid (rĭs′ĭn-ō-lē′ĭk). An unsaturated fatty acid, $C_{18}H_{34}O_3$, prepared from castor oil and used in making soaps and in textile finishing. [Latin *ricinus,* castor-oil plant (see **ricin**) + OLEIC.]

rick (rĭk) *n.* A stack of hay, straw, or similar material, especially when covered or thatched for protection from the weather. —*tr.v.* **ricked, ricking, ricks.** To pile in ricks. [Middle English *reke,* Old English *hrēac,* akin to Old Norse *hraukr*†.]

Rick·en·back·er (rĭk′ən-băk′ər), **Edward Vernon.** Born 1890. American aviator; World War I ace.

rick·ets (rĭk′ĭts) *n.* A deficiency disease resulting from a lack of vitamin D and from insufficient exposure to sunlight, characterized by defective bone growth, and occurring chiefly in children. Also called "rachitis." [Variant of RACHITIS.]

rick·ett·si·a (rĭ-kĕt′sē-ə) *n., pl.* **-siae** (-sĭ-ē′). Any of various microorganisms of the genus *Rickettsia,* carried as parasites by many ticks, fleas, and lice. Transmitted to man, they cause diseases such as typhus, scrub typhus, and Rocky Mountain spotted fever. [New Latin; discovered by Howard T. *Ricketts* (1871–1910), American pathologist.] —**rick·ett′si·al** *adj.*

rick·et·y (rĭk′ĭt-ē) *adj.* **-ier, -iest. 1.** Likely to break or fall apart; shaky. **2.** Feeble with age; infirm: *a rickety old man.* **3.** Irregular. Said of movement. **4.** Of, having, or resembling rickets. [From RICKETS.] —**rick′et·i·ness** *n.*

rick·ey (rĭk′ē) *n., pl.* **-eys.** A drink of soda water, lime juice, and usually gin. [Probably after a Colonel *Rickey.*]

Rick·ey (rĭk′ē), **Branch Wesley.** 1881–1965. American baseball executive; founded the farm system.

Rick·o·ver (rĭk′ō-vər), **Hyman George.** Born 1900. Polish-born American naval officer; responsible for the development of the atomic submarine.

rick·rack (rĭk′răk′) *n.* A flat, narrow braid in zigzag form, used as a trimming. [Reduplication of RACK (to torture).]

rick·shaw, rick·sha (rĭk′shô) *n.* A **jinriksha** *(see).* [Short for JINRIKSHA.]

ric·o·chet (rĭk′ə-shā′, -shĕt′) *intr.v.* **-cheted** (-shād′) or **-chetted** (-shĕt′ĭd), **-cheting** (-shā′ĭng) or **-chetting** (-shĕt′ĭng), **-chets.** To rebound at least once from a surface or surfaces. —*n.* An instance of such deflection. [French *ricochet*†.]

ri·cot·ta (rē-kôt′tä) *n.* An Italian cottage cheese. [Italian, from Latin *recocta,* feminine past participle of *recoquere,* to cook again : *re-,* again + *coquere,* to cook (see **pekw-** in Appendix*).]

ric·tus (rĭk′təs) *n.* **1.** The expanse of an open mouth, a bird's beak, or similar structure. **2.** A cleft, split, or gap. [Latin *rictus,* from the past participle of *ringī*†, to gape.] —**ric′tal** *adj.*

rid (rĭd) *tr.v.* **rid** or **ridded, ridding, rids.** To free from something objectionable or undesirable. [Middle English *rud(d)en, rid(d)en,* from Old Norse *rythja* (past participle *ruddr*), from Germanic *rudjan* (unattested).] —**rid′der** *n.*

rid·a·ble (rī′də-bəl) *adj.* Capable of being ridden or ridden on.

rid·dance (rĭd′əns) *n.* A removal of or deliverance from something. —**good riddance.** A welcome removal of or deliverance from something. [RID + -ANCE.]

ă pat/ā pay/âr care/ä father/b bib/ch church/d deed/ĕ pet/ē be/f fife/g gag/h hat/hw which/ĭ pit/ī pie/îr pier/j judge/k kick/l lid, needle/m mum/n no, sudden/ng thing/ŏ pot/ō toe/ô paw, for/oi noise/ou out/ŏŏ took/ōō boot/p pop/r roar/s sauce/sh ship, dish/

rid·den (rĭd′n). Past participle of **ride**. —*adj.* Dominated. Usually used in combination: *disease-ridden; grief-ridden.*
rid·dle¹ (rĭd′l) *tr.v.* **-dled, -dling, -dles. 1.** To pierce with numerous holes; perforate: *riddle with bullets.* **2.** To put through a coarse sieve. **3.** To find or show weaknesses in; disprove or damage. —*n.* A coarse sieve for separating and grading materials such as gravel and the like: *a potato riddle.* [Middle English *rid(d)len,* to sift, from *riddil,* sieve, Old English *hriddel, hridder.* See **skeri-** in Appendix.*] —**rid′dler** *n.*
rid·dle² (rĭd′l) *n.* **1.** A question or statement requiring thought to answer or understand; conundrum. **2.** Something perplexing; an enigma. —*v.* **riddled, -dling, -dles.** —*tr.* To solve or explain. —*intr.* **1.** To solve or propound riddles. **2.** To speak in riddles. [Middle English *redel(es), ridil,* Old English *rǣdelse.* See **ar-** in Appendix.*] —**rid′dler** *n.*
ride (rīd) *v.* **rode** (rōd), **ridden** (rĭd′n), **riding, rides.** —*intr.* **1.** To sit on, control, and be conveyed by an animal or a machine. **2.** To be conveyed in a vehicle, such as an automobile, boat, aircraft, or the like. **3.** To travel over a surface: *This car rides well.* **4.** To float or move on or as if on water: *He rode into office on a tide of discontent.* **5.** To lie at anchor. **6.** To seem to be floating in space: *a star riding in the sky.* **7.** To carry a rider or support something in a particular manner. **8.** To lie over something; overlap. Used especially of bones. **9.** To work or move from the proper place. Used with *up.* **10.** To allow to continue undisturbed by any action: *We let the problem ride.* —*tr.* **1.** To sit on and drive. **2.** To be supported or carried upon: *a swimmer riding the waves.* **3.** To travel over, along, or through: *ride the highways.* **4.** To rest upon by overlapping; overlie. **5.** To take part in or do by riding: *He rode his last race.* **6.** To control or dominate. **7.** To cause to ride; especially, to cause to be carried: *ride him out of town on a rail.* **8.** To keep (a vessel) at anchor. **9.** *Informal.* To tease or ridicule. **10.** To copulate with. —**ride for a fall.** To court danger or disaster. —**ride herd on.** To keep watch or control over. —**ride out.** To withstand or survive successfully. —**ride roughshod over.** To take a course of action without regard for the feelings, opinions, or welfare of others. —**ride to hounds.** To follow foxhounds, harriers, or the like on horseback during a hunt. —*n.* **1.** An excursion or journey by any means of conveyance, as on horseback, in an automobile, or on a boat. **2.** A path made for riding on horseback, especially through woodlands. **3.** In amusement parks and similar places, any of various structures in which persons ride for pleasure or excitement. —**take for a ride.** *Slang.* **1.** To transport to a place and kill (someone). **2.** To deceive or swindle. [Ride, rode, ridden; Middle English *riden, rad* (or *rod*), *riden,* Old English *rīdan, rād, riden* (unattested). See **reidh-** in Appendix.*]
Ri·deau Canal (rĭ-dō′). A canal in Canada, linking the Ottawa River and Lake Ontario between Ottawa and Kingston.
rid·er (rī′dər) *n.* **1.** One who or that which rides. **2.** One who rides horses. **3.** A clause, usually having little relevance to the main issue, added to a legislative bill. **4.** An amendment or addition to a document or record. **5.** Anything that rests upon or is supported by something else, as the top rail of a fence.
ridge (rĭj) *n.* **1.** The long, narrow upper section or crest of something: *ridge of a wave.* **2.** A long, narrow land elevation; a long hill or chain of mountains. **3.** A long, narrow, or crested part of the body: *the ridge of the nose.* **4.** The horizontal line formed by the juncture of two sloping planes; especially, the line formed by the surfaces of a roof. **5.** Any narrow raised strip, as in cloth or on plowed ground. —*v.* **ridged, ridging, ridges.** —*tr.* To mark with, form into, or provide with ridges. —*intr.* To form ridges. [Middle English *rigge,* back, ridge, Old English *hrycg.* See **sker-³** in Appendix.*]
ridge·back (rĭj′băk′) *n.* An African breed of hunting dog, a **Rhodesian ridgeback** *(see).*
ridge·ling (rĭj′lĭng) *n.* Also **ridg·ling.** *Veterinary Medicine.* A male animal with one or two undescended testicles. [Obsolete *ridgel,* probably "(animal) with testes near the back," from RIDGE.]
ridge·pole (rĭj′pōl′) *n.* **1.** A horizontal beam at the ridge of a roof, to which the rafters are attached. **2.** The horizontal pole at the top of a tent. Also called "ridge beam," "ridge piece."
Ridg·way (rĭj′wā′), **Matthew Bunker.** Born 1895. American army officer.
ridg·y (rĭj′ē) *adj.* **-ier, -iest.** Having or forming ridges.
rid·i·cule (rĭd′ə-kyo͞ol′) *n.* Words or actions intended to evoke contemptuous laughter at or feelings toward a person or thing. —*tr.v.* **ridiculed, -culing, -cules.** To deride, mock, or make fun of. [French *ridicule,* from Latin *rīdiculum,* joke, jest, from *rīdiculus,* laughable, RIDICULOUS.] —**rid′i·cul′er** *n.*
Synonyms: *ridicule, mock, taunt, twit, deride, gibe.* These verbs concern the efforts of one to find amusement or delight at the expense of another; they vary from mere mischief to sheer malice. *Ridicule* refers to the attempt to arouse laughter or merriment at another's expense by making fun of or belittling him. *Mock* implies contempt through caricature. *Taunt* suggests reproach through sarcasm. *Twit* applies to an effort to ridicule by calling attention to something embarrassing. *Deride* implies scorn and contempt in demeaning another. *Gibe* refers to light taunting of someone over something trivial or humorous.
ri·dic·u·lous (rĭ-dĭk′yə-ləs) *adj.* Deserving or inspiring ridicule; absurd or preposterous; silly or laughable. See Synonyms at **foolish.** [Latin *rīdiculōsus, rīdiculus,* laughable, from *rīdēre*†, to laugh.] —**ri·dic′u·lous·ly** *adv.* —**ri·dic′u·lous·ness** *n.*
rid·ing¹ (rī′dĭng) *n.* **1.** The action of riding. **2.** Horseback riding. —*adj.* Suitable for, used in, or pertaining to riding.
rid·ing² (rī′dĭng) *n.* **1.** Any one of the three administrative divisions of Yorkshire, England: North Riding, East Riding, and West Riding. **2.** Any similar administrative division; specifically, in Canada, a constituency represented by a member of Parliament. [Middle English *riding, rithing* (in *Nortriding* for *Nort Trithing*), Old English *thrithing,* from Old Norse *thrithjungr,* third part, from *thrithi,* third. See **trei-** in Appendix.*]
riding habit. The costume worn by a horseback rider.
rid·ley (rĭd′lē) *n., pl.* **-leys.** A marine turtle, *Lepidochelys kempi,* of the Gulf of Mexico and Atlantic coastal waters. [Perhaps from the name *Ridley.*]
Rid·ley (rĭd′lē), **Nicholas.** 1500?–1555. English Protestant prelate and martyr.
Rie·ka. See **Rijeka.**
ri·el (rē-ĕl′) *n.* The basic monetary unit of Cambodia, equal to 100 sen. See table of exchange rates at **currency.** [Perhaps from Spanish *real,* REAL (coin).]
Ri·el (rē-ĕl′), **Louis.** 1844–1885. French Canadian rebel leader; executed for treason.
Rie·mann·ian geometry (rē-män′ē-ən). A non-Euclidean geometry based on the postulate that there are no parallel lines. Also called "elliptic geometry." [Introduced by Georg Friedrich Bernhard *Riemann* (1826–1866), German mathematician.]
Ri·en·zi (rē-ĕn′zē), **Cola di.** Also **Ri·en·zo** (rē-ĕn′zō). Original name, Niccolo Gabrini. 1313?–1354. Italian patriot; proclaimed tribune (1347); assassinated.
Ries·ling (rēs′lĭng) *n.* A dry white wine similar to Rhine wine. [German, earlier *Rüssling*†.]
Ries·man (rēs′mən, rēz-), **David.** Born 1909. American sociologist.
Rif (rĭf). Also **Riff, Er Rif** (ĕr rĭf), **Er Riff.** A coastal arc of hills in northern Morocco, Africa. —**Rif′fi·an** *adj.* & *n.*
rife (rīf) *adj.* **rifer, rifest. 1.** Frequently or commonly happening or appearing; widespread; prevalent. **2.** Abundant; numerous. **3.** Abounding; full. Used with *with: That department is rife with incompetents.* —See Synonyms at **prevailing.** [Middle English *rif, ryfe,* Old English *rȳfe.* See **rei-¹** in Appendix.*]
riff (rĭf) *n. Music.* A short rhythmic phrase repeated constantly. [Probably shortened variant of REFRAIN.]
Riff (rĭf) *n.* Also **Rif·fi·an** (rĭf′ē-ən) (for sense 1). **1.** A Berber tribesman of the Rif country in northern Morocco, Africa. **2.** See **Rif.**
rif·fle (rĭf′əl) *n.* **1.** A rocky shoal or sandbar lying just below the surface of a waterway. **2.** A stretch of choppy water caused by such a shoal or sandbar; a rapid. **3.** *Mining.* **a.** The sectional stone or wood bottom lining of a sluice, arranged to trap mineral particles, as of gold. **b.** A groove or block in such a lining. **4.** The act of shuffling cards. —*v.* **riffled, -fling, -fles.** —*tr.* **1.** To shuffle (playing cards) by holding part of a deck in each hand and raising up the edges before releasing them to fall alternately in one stack. **2.** To thumb through (the pages of a book, for example). —*intr.* **1.** To shuffle cards. **2.** To become choppy, as water. [Perhaps blend of RUFFLE (disturb) and RIPPLE.]
rif·fler (rĭf′lər) *n.* A file with curved ends suitable for scraping. [Old French *rifloir,* from *rifler*†, to scratch, file.]
riff·raff (rĭf′răf′) *n.* **1.** Worthless or disreputable persons. **2.** Rubbish; trash. [Middle English *riffe raffe, rif and raf,* one and all, from Old French *rif et raf* : *rifler,* to file (see **riffler**) + *raffe,* a sweeping, from Middle High German *raffen,* to snatch (see **raffle**).]
ri·fle¹ (rī′fəl) *n.* **1.** A firearm with a rifled bore designed to be fired from the shoulder. **2.** An artillery piece or naval gun with such spiral grooves. **3.** *Plural.* Troops armed with rifles. —*tr.v.* **rifled, -fling, -fles.** To cut spiral grooves within (a gun barrel, for example). [Originally "spiral groove," from *rifle,* to cut spiral grooves, from Old French *rifler,* to file. See **riffler.**]
ri·fle² (rī′fəl) *tr.v.* **-fled, -fling, -fles. 1.** To search with intent to steal. **2.** To ransack or plunder; pillage. **3.** To rob; strip bare: *rifle a safe.* [Middle English *riflen,* from Old French *rifler,* to scratch, file, plunder. See **riffler.**] —**ri′fler** *n.*
ri·fle·bird (rī′fəl-bûrd′) *n.* Any of several birds of paradise of the genera *Craspedophora* and *Ptiloris,* of Australia and New Guinea. [From its cry.]
ri·fle·ry (rī′fəl-rē) *n.* **1.** The art and practice of marksmanship. **2.** Rifle fire: *the sound of distant riflery.*
ri·fle·scope (rī′fəl-skōp′) *n.* A telescopic sight for a rifle.
ri·fling (rī′flĭng) *n.* **1.** The process or operation of cutting spiral grooves in a rifle barrel. **2.** Grooves so cut.
rift¹ (rĭft) *n.* **1. a.** *Geology.* A **fault** *(see).* **b.** A narrow fissure in rock. **2.** A break in friendly relations. —*v.* **rifted, rifting, rifts.** —*intr.* To split open; burst; break. —*tr.* To cause to split open or break. [Middle English *rift, ryft,* from Scandinavian, akin to Danish *rift,* breach. See **rei-¹** in Appendix.*]
rift² (rĭft) *n.* **1.** A shallow area in a waterway. **2.** The backwash of a wave that has broken upon a beach. [Probably variant of *riff,* dialectal variant of REEF.]
rift valley. A long, narrow depression in the earth's surface formed when the land sinks between two fairly parallel faults.
Rift Valley. See **Great Rift Valley.**
rig (rĭg) *tr.v.* **rigged, rigging, rigs. 1.** To fit out; provide with harness or equipment: *rigged out and ready for action.* **2. a.** To equip (a ship) with sails, shrouds, and yards. **b.** To fit (sails, shrouds, and the like) to masts and yards. **3.** *Informal.* To dress, clothe, or adorn: *rigged out in her best dress.* **4.** To make or construct in haste or in a makeshift manner. Often used with *up.* **5.** To manipulate dishonestly for personal gain: *rig a prize fight.* —*n.* **1.** The arrangement of masts, spars, and sails on a sailing vessel: *a square rig.* **2.** Any special equipment or gear for a particular purpose. **3.** A vehicle with one or more horses

rifle¹

Winchester 66

Springfield

M-1 (Garand)

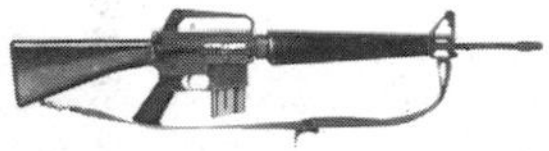

M-16

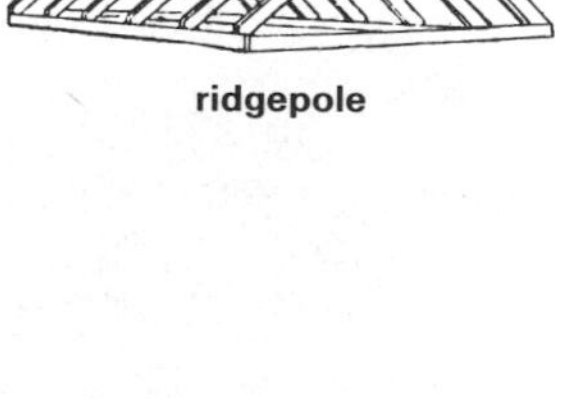

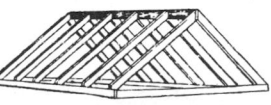

ridgepole

harnessed to it. **4.** The special apparatus used for drilling oil wells. **5.** *Western U.S.* A saddle. **6.** *Informal.* A costume or dress. **7.** Fishing tackle. [Middle English *riggen,* probably from Scandinavian, akin to Swedish *rigga.* See **reig-**[1] in Appendix.*]

Ri·ga (rē′gə). The capital of Latvia and a major seaport on the Baltic. Population, 658,000.

Ri·ga, Gulf of (rē′gə). An inlet of the Baltic Sea between Latvia and Estonia.

rig·a·doon (rĭg′ə-do͞on′) *n.* **1.** A lively jumping quickstep for one couple. **2.** Music for this dance, usually in rapid duple meter. [French *rigaudon, rigodon,* said to have been invented by a famous dancing master of Marseille named *Rigaud.*]

rig·a·ma·role. Variant of **rigmarole.**

rig·a·to·ni (rĭg′ə-tō′nē) *n.* Large, ribbed, macaroni tubes, slightly curved and cut into short lengths. [Italian, plural of *rigato,* past participle of *rigare,* to draw a line, corrugate, from *riga,* line, from Germanic. See **rei-**[1] in Appendix.*]

Ri·gel (rī′jəl) *n.* A bright double star in the constellation Orion. [Arabic *rijl,* (Orion's) foot.]

rig·ger (rĭg′ər) *n.* **1.** One who rigs, especially: **a.** One who fits rigging to sailing ships. **b.** One who assembles or aligns aircraft parts or parachutes. **c.** One who works with hoisting tackle, cranes, pulleys, and scaffolds. **2.** A protective scaffold set up against a building under construction.

rig·ging (rĭg′ĭng) *n.* **1.** The system of ropes, chains, and tackle used to support and control the masts, sails, and yards of a sailing vessel. **2.** Gear for a specific task.

Ri·ghi. See **Rigi.**

right (rīt) *adj.* **righter, rightest.** *Abbr.* **R., r., rt. 1.** In accordance with or conformable to justice, law, morality, or another standard: *right action.* **2.** In accordance with fact, reason, or truth; correct: *the right answer.* **3.** Fitting, proper, or appropriate: *It is not right to lie.* **4.** Most favorable, desirable, or convenient: *the right time to act.* **5.** In a satisfactory state or condition; in good order. **6.** Mentally sound or normal; sane: *in one's right mind.* **7.** Physically normal or healthy; well. **8.** Intended to be worn facing outward or toward an observer: *the right side of cloth.* **9.** *Archaic.* Genuine; not spurious. **10. a.** Of, pertaining to, or toward that side of the human body in which the liver is normally located. **b.** Of, pertaining to, or toward the corresponding side of something relative to the observer's point of view. **11.** *Often capital* **R.** Of or tending toward conservative or reactionary political policies or views. **12.** *Geometry.* **a.** Formed by or in reference to a line or plane that is perpendicular to another line or plane. **b.** Having the axis perpendicular to the base: *right cone.* **13.** Straight; uncurved; direct: *a right line.* —*n.* **1.** That which is just, morally good, legal, proper, or fitting. **2. a.** The right-hand side or direction. **b.** That which is on or toward the right-hand side. **3.** *Often capital* **R.** A faction, party, or other political group whose policies are conservative or reactionary. **4.** *Boxing.* The right hand or a blow given by the right hand. **5.** That which is due to anyone by law, tradition, or nature. **6.** A just or legal claim or title. **7.** *Finance.* **a.** A stockholder's privilege of buying additional stock in a corporation at a special price, usually at par or at a price below the current market value. **b.** The negotiable certificate on which this privilege is indicated. **c.** *Often plural.* A privilege of subscribing for a particular stock or bond. —**by right** (or **rights**). Justly; properly. —**to rights.** In a satisfactory or orderly condition: *set the place to rights.* —*adv.* **1.** In a straight line; directly; straight. Often used with *to, into,* or *through: He went right to the heart of the matter.* **2.** Properly; suitably; conveniently; well: *The suit doesn't fit right.* **3.** Exactly; just: *It happened right over there.* **4.** Immediately: *She will be right down.* **5.** Completely; thoroughly; quite: *The wind blew right through him.* **6.** According to law, morality, or justice. **7.** Accurately; correctly. **8.** On or toward the right side or direction. **9.** *Archaic.* Extremely: *He answered right well.* **10.** Very. Used in certain titles: *the Right Reverend.* —*v.* **righted, righting, rights.** —*tr.* **1.** To put in or restore to an upright or proper position: *They righted their boat.* **2.** To put in order or set right; to correct. **3.** To make reparation or amends for; redress: *right a wrong.* —*intr.* To regain an upright or proper position. [Middle English *riht, right,* Old English *riht.* See **reg-**[1] in Appendix.*] —**right′er** *n.*

Synonyms: *right, privilege, prerogative, perquisite, franchise, birthright, title.* These terms apply to powers and possession and one's established claim to them. *Right* refers to a just claim, legally, morally, or traditionally: *the right of free speech. Privilege* usually suggests an advantage not enjoyed by everyone: *his privilege to sit at the head table. Prerogative* connotes a prior right or privilege based on custom, law, office, sex, or recognition of precedence: *the President's prerogative to veto. Perquisite* applies to advantage accorded one by virtue of one's position or the needs of one's employment: *His perquisites included the use of an automobile. Franchise* denotes specific rights formally and legally granted. *Birthright* applies to heritable rights as a result of birth. *Title* refers to that which establishes the right to ownership of property.

right angle. An angle formed by the perpendicular intersection of two straight lines; an angle of 90 degrees.

right-an·gled (rīt′ăng′gəld) *adj.* Forming or containing one or more right angles: *a right-angled bend.*

right ascension. *Abbr.* **R.A.** The angular distance of a celestial body or point on the celestial sphere, measured eastward from the vernal equinox along the celestial equator to the hour circle of the body or point, and expressed in degrees or in hours.

right cone. A cone with the axis perpendicular to the base.

Jacob Riis

right·eous (rī′chəs) *adj.* Meeting the standards of what is right and just; morally right; guiltless: *a righteous action.* See Synonyms at **moral.** —*n.* Righteous individuals collectively. Preceded by *the: "The righteous shall inherit the land."* (Psalms 37:9). [Middle English *rightwise, ryghtuous,* Old English *rihtwīs* : *riht,* RIGHT + *wīs,* WISE (way).] —**right′eous·ly** *adv.* —**right′eous·ness** *n.*

right face. *Military.* A command to turn 90 degrees to the right.

right field. *Abbr.* **r.f.** *Baseball.* The part of the outfield that is to the right as viewed from home plate.

right fielder. *Abbr.* **r.f.** *Baseball.* An outfielder who defends right field.

right·ful (rīt′fəl) *adj.* **1.** Right or proper; just. **2.** Having a just or proper claim: *Return this dog to its rightful owner.* **3.** Held or owned by just or proper claim: *This dog is my rightful property.* —**right′ful·ly** *adv.* —**right′ful·ness** *n.*

right-hand (rīt′hănd′) *adj.* **1.** Located on the right side. **2.** Directed toward the right side: *a right-hand turn.* **3.** Of, for, or done by the right hand. **4.** Helpful; reliable: *my right-hand man.* **5.** Of rope, plain-laid. —**right′-hand′er** *n.*

right-hand·ed (rīt′hăn′dĭd) *adj.* **1.** Using the right hand more easily or skillfully than the left. **2.** Done with the right hand. **3.** Made to be used by the right hand. **4.** Turning or spiraling from left to right; clockwise. —**right′-hand′ed, right′-hand′ed·ly** *adv.* —**right′-hand′ed·ness** *n.*

right·ism (rī′tĭz′əm) *n.* Also **Right·ism.** Reactionary or conservative political activities or ideas. —**right′ist** *adj.* & *n.*

right·ly (rīt′lē) *adv.* **1.** With correctness. **2.** Uprightly; with honesty. **3.** Properly; suitably.

right-mind·ed (rīt′mīn′dĭd) *adj.* Having ideas and views based on what is right. —**right′-mind′ed·ness** *n.*

right·ness (rīt′nĭs) *n.* The state or quality of being right.

right of asylum. *International Law.* The right of receiving protection within a foreign embassy or other place recognized by custom, law, or treaty.

right of search. *International Law.* The right of a warring nation to stop any neutral vessel on the high seas and search it for contraband. Also called "right of visit and search."

right of way. Also **right-of-way** (rīt′əv-wā′). **1.** *Law.* **a.** The right to pass over property owned by another party. **b.** The path or thoroughfare on which such passage is made. **2.** The strip of land over which facilities such as highways, railroads, or power lines are built. **3.** The customary or legal right of a person, vessel, or vehicle to pass in front of another.

right triangle. A triangle containing an angle of 90 degrees.

right whale. Any of several whales of the family Balaenidae, characterized by a large head, absence of a dorsal fin, and whalebone plates in the mouth. [So called perhaps because it is rich in oil and is "right" for commercial purposes.]

right wing. A division holding relatively conservative views within a larger political group. —**right′-wing′** *adj.* —**right′-wing′er** *n.*

Ri·gi (rē′gē). Also **Ri·ghi.** A mountain and resort area in the Alps of north-central Switzerland, near the Lake of Lucerne.

rig·id (rĭj′ĭd) *adj.* **1.** Not bending; stiff; inflexible. **2.** Not moving; fixed. **3.** Rigorous; harsh; severe. **4.** Scrupulously strict; undeviating. —See Synonyms at **stiff.** [Old French *rigide,* from Latin *rigidus,* from *rigēre,* to be stiff. See **reig-**[1] in Appendix.*] —**rig′id·ly** *adv.* —**rig′id·ness** *n.*

ri·gid·i·ty (rĭ-jĭd′ə-tē) *n., pl.* **-ties. 1.** The state or quality of being rigid; stiffness; inflexibility. **2.** An instance of being rigid.

rig·ma·role (rĭg′mə-rōl) *n.* Also **rig·a·ma·role** (-ə-mə-rōl). **1.** Confused, rambling, or incoherent discourse; nonsense: *"'Eena, deena, dina, do,' or some such rigmarole."* (Richard Hughes). **2.** A complicated and petty set of procedures. [Alteration of obsolete *ragman roll,* list, catalog, from Middle English *Ragmane rolle,* scroll used in a medieval game and containing various items (such as verses describing various characters) : Old North French *Ragemon le bon,* Ragemon the good, name of one of the characters + Middle English *rolle,* a roll, from Old French, from Latin *rotulus,* wheel (see **roll**).]

rig·or (rĭg′ər) *n.* Also *British* **rig·our. 1.** Strictness or severity, as in temperament, action, or judgment. **2.** A harsh or trying circumstance; hardship. **3.** A severe or cruel act. **4.** *Medicine.* Shivering or trembling, as caused by a chill. **5.** *Physiology.* A state of rigidity in living tissues or organs that prevents response to stimuli. **6.** *Obsolete.* Stiffness or rigidity. [Middle English *rigour,* from Old French, from Latin *rigor,* stiffness, severity, from *rigēre,* to be stiff. See **reig-**[1] in Appendix.*]

rig·or·ism (rĭg′ə-rĭz′əm) *n.* Severity or strictness in conduct, judgment, or practice. —**rig′or·ist** *n.* —**rig′or·is′tic** *adj.*

rig·or mor·tis (rĭg′ər môr′tĭs) *n.* Muscular stiffening following death. [Latin, "the stiffness of death."]

rig·or·ous (rĭg′ər-əs) *adj.* **1.** Characterized by or acting with rigor; rigid and severe. **2.** Full of rigors; trying; harsh: *a rigorous climate.* **3.** Precisely accurate; strict. —See Synonyms at **burdensome.** —**rig′or·ous·ly** *adv.* —**rig′or·ous·ness** *n.*

Rig-Ve·da (rĭg-vā′də, -vē′də) *n.* The most ancient collection of Hindu sacred verses. [Sanskrit *ṛgveda* : *ṛc* (stem *ṛg-*), "praise," hymn (see **erkw-** in Appendix*) + *veda,* "knowledge," sacred writing, Veda (see **weid-** in Appendix*).]

Riis (rēs), **Jacob August.** 1849–1914. Danish-born American journalist, reformer, and author.

Ri·je·ka (rē-yĕ′kä). Also **Rie·ka** (ryĕ′kä). A seaport on the Adriatic, in northwestern Croatia, Yugoslavia. Population, 108,000.

Rijn. The Dutch name for the **Rhine.**

Riks·mål (rĕks′mōl) *n. Danish* **Rigs·mål.** One of the two officially recognized forms of Norwegian. Also called "Dano-

Norwegian." Compare **Landsmål.** [Norwegian *riksmål,* "language of the kingdom" : *rik,* kingdom, from Old Norse *rīki* (see **reg-**[1] in Appendix*) + *mål,* speech, from Old Norse *māl* (see **mōd-** in Appendix*).]

rile (rīl) *tr.v.* **riled, riling, riles. 1.** To vex; anger; irritate. **2.** To stir up (liquid); unsettle; roil. —See Synonyms at **annoy.** [Variant of ROIL.]

Usage: *Rile* in the sense of vex or anger, though sometimes disparaged as provincial, is not necessarily inappropriate to formal writing. It is acceptable to 69 per cent of the Usage Panel in the example *Her flippancy riled him.*

ril·ey (rī′lē) *adj.* **1.** Riled; upset. **2.** Roiled; turbid.

Ri·ley (rī′lē), **James Whitcomb.** 1849–1916. American dialectal poet, "The Hoosier Poet."

Ril·ke (rĭl′kə), **Rainer Maria.** 1875–1926. Austrian lyric poet and writer.

rill (rĭl) *n.* Also **rille. 1.** A small brook; rivulet. **2.** Any of various long, narrow, straight depressions on the moon's surface. [Dutch *ril* or Low German *rille.* See **er-**[1] in Appendix.*]

rill·et (rĭl′ĭt) *n.* A small rill.

rim (rĭm) *n.* **1.** The border, edge, or margin of an object. **2.** The circular outer part of a wheel, furthest from the axle. **3.** A circular metal structure around which a wheel tire is fitted. —See Synonyms at **border.** —*tr.v.* **rimmed, rimming, rims. 1.** To furnish with a rim; put a rim around; border. **2.** *Sports.* To roll around the rim of (a hole, basket, or cup) without falling in. [Middle English *rime, rym,* Old English *rima,* from Germanic *rimō* (unattested).]

Rim·baud (răN-bō′), **(Jean Nicolas) Arthur.** 1854–1891. French poet.

rime[1] (rīm) *n.* A frost or granular ice coating, as on grass and trees; hoarfrost. —*tr.v.* **rimed, riming, rimes.** To cover with or as if with rime. [Middle English *rim,* Old English *hrīm.* See **krei-**[1] in Appendix.*] —**rim′y** *adj.*

rime[2]. Variant of **rhyme.**

rim·er. Variant of **rhymer.**

rime riche (rēm rĕsh′) *pl.* **rimes riches** (rēm rĕsh′). Rhyme using words or parts of words that are pronounced identically but have different meanings, for example, *write-right* or *port-deport.* Also called "identical rhyme." [French, "rich rhyme."]

rime·ster. Variant of **rhymester.**

Rim·i·ni (rĭm′ĭ-nē; *Italian* rē′mē-nē). A resort and seaport on the Adriatic coast of north-central Italy. Population, 104,000.

Rim·i·ni, Francesca da. See **Francesca da Rimini.**

ri·mose (rī′mōs, rī-mōs′) *adj.* Full of chinks, cracks, or crevices. [Latin *rīmōsus,* from *rīma,* cleft, crevice, fissure. See **rei-**[1] in Appendix.*] —**ri′mose·ly** *adv.* —**ri·mos′i·ty** (rī-mŏs′ə-tē) *n.*

rim·ple (rĭm′pəl) *n.* A fold; wrinkle; crease. —*v.* **rimpled, -pling, -ples.** —*tr.* To wrinkle; rumple. —*intr.* To form wrinkles or creases. [Middle English *rymple,* Old English *hrympel.* See **skerbh-** in Appendix.*]

Rim·sky-Kor·sa·kov (rĭm′skē-kôr′sə-kôf; *Russian* rēm′skē-kôr′sä-kôf), **Nicholas Andreievich.** 1844–1908. Russian composer.

rind (rīnd) *n.* A tough outer covering, such as bark, the skin of some fruits, or the coating on cheese or bacon. [Middle English *rinde,* Old English *rind(e).* See **rendh-** in Appendix.*]

rin·der·pest (rĭn′dər-pĕst′) *n.* An acute, contagious virus disease, chiefly of cattle, characterized by ulceration of the intestinal tract. [German *Rinderpest* : *Rinder,* plural of *Rind,* ox, cow, from Old High German *(h)rind* (see **ker-**[1] in Appendix*) + *Pest,* pestilence, plague, from Latin *pestis,* PEST.]

rin·for·zan·do (rēn′fôr-tsän′dō) *adj. Music.* With a sudden increase of emphasis. Used as a direction. [Italian, present participle of *rinforzare,* to reinforce : *ri-,* from Latin *re-,* again + *inforzare,* from Old French *enforcier,* ENFORCE.]

ring[1] (rĭng) *n.* **1.** Any circular object, form, or arrangement with a vacant circular center. **2.** A small circular band, generally made of precious metal, often set with jewels, and worn on a finger. **3.** Any circular band used for carrying, holding, or containing something: *a napkin ring.* **4.** A circular movement or course, as in dancing. **5.** An enclosed, usually circular area in which exhibitions, sports, or contests take place: *a circus ring.* **6. a.** A rectangular arena set off by stakes and ropes, in which prize fights are held. **b.** The sport of prize fighting. **7. a.** An enclosed area in which bets are placed at a racetrack. **b.** Bookmakers collectively. **8.** An exclusive group of persons acting privately or illegally to advance their own interests, as in business or politics. **9.** A field of contenders; contest: *entered the ring of senate aspirants.* **10.** *Botany.* An **annual ring** *(see).* **11.** *Geometry.* The planar area between two concentric circles; an annulus. **12.** *Algebra.* An algebraic system consisting of a set with two binary operations in the set such that the set together with one operation, usually denoted *addition,* is a commutative group, together with the second, usually denoted *multiplication,* is a semigroup, and multiplication is distributive over addition. **13.** Any of the turns comprising a spiral or helix. **14.** *Chemistry.* A group of atoms chemically bound in a manner graphically representable as a circular form. Also called "closed chain." —*v.* **ringed, ringing, rings.** —*tr.* **1.** To surround with a ring; encircle. **2.** To form into a ring or rings. **3.** To ornament or supply with a ring or rings. **4.** To remove a circular strip of bark around the circumference of (a tree trunk or branch); girdle. **5.** To put a ring in the nose of (a pig, bull, or other animal). **6.** To hem in (cattle or other animals) by riding in a circle around them. **7.** *Games.* To toss a ring over (a peg). —*intr.* **1.** To form a ring or rings. **2.** To move, run, or fly in a spiral or circular course. [Middle English *ring,* Old English *hring.* See **sker-**[3] in Appendix.*]

ring[2] (rĭng) *v.* **rang** (răng) or *nonstandard* **rung** (rŭng), **rung, ringing, rings.** —*intr.* **1.** To give forth a clear, resonant sound when caused to vibrate. **2.** To cause a bell or bells to sound. **3.** To sound a bell in order to summon someone. **4.** To have a sound or character suggestive of a particular quality: *a perception that rings true.* **5.** To be filled with sound; resound. **6.** To hear a persistent humming or buzzing: *ears ringing from the blast.* —*tr.* **1.** To cause (a bell, chimes, or the like) to ring. **2.** To produce (a sound) by or as if by ringing: *"Sea-nymphs hourly ring his knell"* (Shakespeare). **3. a.** To announce, proclaim, or signal by or as if by ringing. **b.** To summon or usher in in this way. Used with *in* or *out: ring in the new year.* **4.** To call (someone) on the telephone. Often used with *up.* **5.** To test (a coin or the like) for quality by the sound it produces when struck against something. —**ring a bell.** *Informal.* To arouse a memory, often indistinct. —*n.* **1.** The sound created by a bell or other sonorous, vibrating object. **2.** Any loud sound, especially one that is repeated or continued. **3.** A telephone call. **4.** A suggestion of a particular quality: *His offer has a suspicious ring.* **5.** A set of bells. **6.** An act or instance of sounding a bell. [Middle English *ringen,* Old English *hringan.* See **ker-**[2] in Appendix.* Rang, rung; Middle English *rang, rungen,* analogous formations to verbs such as SING.]

Usage: *Rang* (not *rung*) is now the usual form in the past tense, especially in written usage: *The telephone rang repeatedly.* In the same example, in speech, *rung* is considered unacceptable by 85 per cent of the Usage Panel.

ring-billed gull (rĭng′bĭld′). A North American gull, *Larus delawarensis,* having a black ring around its bill.

ring·bolt (rĭng′bōlt′) *n.* A bolt having a ring fitted through an eye at its head.

ring·bone (rĭng′bōn′) *n.* A bony growth on the fetlock, pastern, or coffin bone of a horse's foot, usually causing lameness. [It tends to spread around a horse's foot like a ring.]

ring·dove (rĭng′dŭv′) *n.* **1.** An Old World pigeon, *Streptopelia risoria,* having black markings forming a half circle on the neck. **2.** The **wood pigeon** *(see).*

ringed (rĭngd) *adj.* **1.** Wearing or marked with a ring or rings. **2.** Encircled or surrounded by bands or rings.

rin·gent (rĭn′jənt) *adj. Biology.* Having gaping liplike parts, as the corolla of some flowers or the shells of certain bivalves. [Latin *ringens,* present participle of *ringī,* to open wide the mouth, gape. See **rictus.**]

ring·er[1] (rĭng′ər) *n.* **1.** Someone or something that rings. **2.** A horseshoe or quoit thrown so that it encircles the peg.

ring·er[2] (rĭng′ər) *n.* **1.** One that sounds a bell or chime. **2.** *Slang.* A contestant entered dishonestly into a competition. **3.** *Slang.* A person who bears a striking resemblance to another.

ring finger. The third finger of the left hand.

ring·hals (rĭng′hăls′) *n.* An African snake, *Haemachates haemachatus,* that spits forth its venom at its victims. [Afrikaans *ringhals, rinkals,* "ring-necked" : *ring,* ring, circle, from Middle Dutch *rinc* (see **sker-**[3] in Appendix*) + *hals,* neck, from Middle Dutch (see **kwel-**[1] in Appendix*).]

ring·lead·er (rĭng′lē′dər) *n.* A person who leads others, especially in unlawful or improper activities.

ring·let (rĭng′lĭt) *n.* **1.** A long, spirally curled lock of hair. **2.** A small circle or ring. —**ring′let·ed** *adj.*

ring·mas·ter (rĭng′măs′tər, -mäs′tər) *n.* A person in charge of the performances in a circus ring.

Ring Nebula. A planetary nebula in the constellation Lyra. [From its resemblance to a smoke ring.]

ring-necked pheasant (rĭng′nĕkt′). A widely distributed bird, *Phasianus colchicus,* native to the Old World, of which the male has a long, pointed tail, brightly colored plumage, and a white ring around the neck.

ring·side (rĭng′sīd′) *n.* **1.** The area or seats immediately outside an arena or ring, as at a prize fight. **2.** Any place providing a close view of a spectacle.

ring·tail (rĭng′tāl′) *n.* A ring-tailed animal, such as the **cacomistle** *(see).* Also called "ring-tailed cat."

ring-tailed (rĭng′tāld′) *adj.* **1.** Having a tail with ringlike markings. **2.** Having a tail that curls to form a ring.

ring·worm (rĭng′wûrm′) *n.* Any of a number of contagious skin diseases caused by several related fungi, and characterized by ring-shaped, scaly, itching patches on the skin.

rink (rĭngk) *n.* **1.** An area surfaced with smooth ice for skating, hockey, or curling. **2.** A smooth floor suited for roller-skating. **3.** A building that houses a surface prepared for skating. **4.** A section of a bowling green large enough for holding a match. **5.** A team of players in quoits, bowling, or curling. [Middle English (Scottish) *renk, rinc,* race course, from Old French *renc, ranc,* row, range, from Frankish *hring* (unattested), ring. See **sker-**[3] in Appendix.*]

rinse (rĭns) *tr.v.* **rinsed, rinsing, rinses. 1.** To wash lightly with water. **2.** To so remove (soap, dirt, or impurities). —*n.* **1.** The act of washing lightly. **2.** The water or other solution used in this process. **3.** A cosmetic solution used in conditioning or tinting the hair. [Middle English *ryncen,* from Old French *rincer, recincier,* probably from Vulgar Latin *recentiāre* (unattested), to refresh, from Latin *recēns,* fresh, RECENT.] —**rins·a·bil′i·ty, rins·i·bil′i·ty** *n.* —**rins′a·ble, rins′i·ble** *adj.* —**rins′er** *n.*

Ri·o Bran·co (rē′ō brăng′kō). **1.** A river rising in northern Roraima, Brazil, and flowing south 350 miles to the Rio Negro. **2.** The former name for **Roraima. 3.** The capital of Acre territory, western Brazil. Population, 17,000.

Rí·o Bra·vo. The Mexican name for the **Rio Grande.**

Ri·o de Ja·nei·ro (rē′ō dĭ jə-nâr′ō, zhə-nâr′ō; *Portuguese* rē′o͞o dĭ zhä-nā′ro͞o). **1.** A major city and seaport of Brazil, in the

ringmaster
Drawing of a ringmaster with clown, by A.B. Frost

ring-necked pheasant
A male of the species

southeast on Guanabara Bay. It is the capital of Guanabara State and the former capital of the country. Population, 3,223,000. Informally called "Rio." **2.** A state of Brazil occupying 16,372 square miles on the southeastern coast. Population, 4,103,000. Capital, Niterói.

Rí·o de la Pla·ta (rē′ō *thĕ* lä plä′tä). *English* **River Plate** (plāt). The estuary on the southeastern coast of South America, extending 225 miles between Argentina and Uruguay, formed by the merging of the Paraná and Uruguay rivers.

Rí·o de O·ro (rē′ō *thĕ* ō′rō). The southern zone of **Spanish Sahara.**

Rí·o Ga·lle·gos (rē′ō gäl-yĕ′gōs). The southernmost seaport of Argentina, on the Atlantic, north of the entrance to the Strait of Magellan.

Ri·o Grande (rē′ō grănd *for sense 1; Portuguese* rē′o͞o gräɴ′dĭ *for senses 2, 3*). **1.** *Mexican* **Rí·o Bra·vo** (rē′ō brä′vō). A river rising in southern Colorado and flowing 1,885 miles generally southeast to the Gulf of Mexico, forming much of the U.S.-Mexican border on its course. **2.** A river rising in the highlands of southeastern Brazil and flowing west 650 miles to the Paranaíba with which it forms the Paraná. **3.** A city and seaport of extreme southeastern Brazil, at the southern entrance of Lagoa dos Patos. Population, 83,000.

Ri·o Gran·de do Nor·te (rē′o͞o gräɴ′dĭ do͞o nôr′tĭ). A state of Brazil, occupying 20,482 square miles in the northeastern part of the country. Population, 1,157,000. Capital, Natal.

Ri·o Gran·de do Sul (rē′o͞o gräɴ′dĭ do͞o so͞ol′). A state of Brazil, occupying 103,482 square miles in the southernmost part of the country. Population, 5,449,000. Capital, Pôrto Alegre.

Rí·o Mu·ni (rē′ō mo͞o′nē). The mainland portion of Equatorial Guinea in western Africa. Population, 183,000.

Rí·o Ne·gro (rē′ō nā′grō). **1.** A river rising in eastern Colombia and flowing about 1,400 miles to the Amazon in northern Brazil. **2.** A river of Argentina formed by the confluence of the Limay and Neuquén rivers and flowing 400 miles southeast to the Atlantic Ocean. **3.** A river of Uruguay, rising northeast of Brazil and flowing about 500 miles to the Uruguay River.

Ri·o Roo·se·velt (rē′ō rō′zə-vĕlt, rōz′vĕlt, -vəlt). A river of western Brazil, rising in Rondônia Territory and flowing north for about 400 miles.

ri·ot (rī′ət) *n.* **1.** A wild or turbulent disturbance created by a large number of people. **2.** *Law.* A violent disturbance of the public peace by three or more persons assembled for a common private purpose. **3.** An unrestrained outbreak, as of laughter or passions. **4.** A profusion, as of colors. **5. a.** Unrestrained merrymaking; revelry. **b.** Debauchery. **6.** *Slang.* An irresistibly funny person or thing. —See Synonyms at **rebellion.** —**run riot. 1.** To move or act with wild abandon. **2.** To grow luxuriantly or abundantly. —*v.* **rioted, -oting, -ots.** —*intr.* **1.** To take part in a riot. **2.** To live wildly or engage in uncontrolled revelry. —*tr.* To waste (money or time) in wild or wanton living. [Middle English *riot(e),* debauchery, revel, riot, from Old French *ri(h)ot(e),* from *r(u)ihoter,* to quarrel, perhaps from *ruire,* to roar, from Latin *rūgīre.* See **reu-** in Appendix.*] —**ri′ot·er** *n.*

ripsaw

Riot Act. 1. An English law, enacted in 1715, providing that if 12 or more persons unlawfully assemble and disturb the public peace, they must disperse upon proclamation or be considered guilty of felony. **2.** *Small* **r,** *small* **a.** Any energetic or forceful warning or reproach.

ri·ot·ous (rī′ət-əs) *adj.* **1.** Of, pertaining to, or resembling a riot. **2.** Taking part in or inciting to riot or uproar. **3.** Uproarious; boisterous. **4.** Dissolute; profligate. **5.** Abundant or luxuriant: *a riotous growth.* —**ri′ot·ous·ly** *adv.* —**ri′ot·ous·ness** *n.*

rip[1] (rĭp) *v.* **ripped, ripping, rips.** —*tr.* **1.** To cut or tear apart roughly or energetically; slash. **2.** To remove by cutting or tearing roughly. **3.** To split or saw (wood) along the grain. **4.** *Informal.* To produce, display, or exclaim suddenly. Used with *out: ripped out a gun; ripped out a vicious oath.* —*intr.* **1.** To become torn or split apart. **2.** *Informal.* To move quickly or violently. **3.** *Informal.* To direct a vehement attack or censure. Used with *into: ripped into his opponent's record.* —See Synonyms at **tear.** —*n.* **1.** A torn or split place, especially along a seam; a tear. **2.** The act of ripping. **3.** A **ripsaw** *(see).* [Middle English *rippen,* probably from Flemish *rippen,* to rip, strip off roughly. See **reup-** in Appendix.*] —**rip′per** *n.*

rip[2] (rĭp) *n.* **1.** A stretch of broken water in a river, estuary, or tidal channel. **2.** A **rip current** *(see).* [Perhaps from RIP (the act of tearing).]

rip[3] (rĭp) *n.* **1.** A dissolute person. **2.** An old or worthless horse. [Perhaps shortened variant of REPROBATE.]

R.I.P. requiescat in pace.

ri·par·i·an (rĭ-pâr′ē-ən) *adj.* Of, on, or pertaining to the bank of a river, or of a pond or small lake. [From Latin *rīpārius,* from *rīpa,* bank, shore. See **rei-**[1] in Appendix.*]

riparian right. *Law.* A right, as to fishing or to the use of a river bed, of one who owns riparian land.

rip·cord (rĭp′kôrd′) *n.* **1.** A cord pulled to release the pack of a parachute. **2.** A cord pulled to release gas from a balloon.

rip current. A current of water disturbed by an opposing current, especially in tidal waters, or by passage over an irregular bottom. Also called "rip," "rip tide," "tide rip."

ripe (rīp) *adj.* **1.** Fully developed; mature. **2.** Resembling matured fruit, as in fullness: *a ripe figure.* **3.** Sufficiently advanced in preparation or aging to be used: *ripe cheese.* **4.** Thoroughly matured, as by study or experience; seasoned: *ripe judgment.* **5.** Advanced in years: *the ripe age of 85.* **6.** Fully prepared to do or undergo something; ready. **7.** Sufficiently advanced; opportune. Said of time. [Middle English *ripe,* Old English *rīpe.* See **rei-**[1] in Appendix.*] —**ripe′ly** *adv.* —**ripe′ness** *n.*

rip·en (rī′pən) *v.* **-ened, -ening, -ens.** —*tr.* To make ripe; cause to mature. —*intr.* To become ripe; to mature. —**rip′en·er** *n.*

Rip·ley (rĭp′lē), **George.** 1802–1880. American Unitarian minister and literary critic; founder of Brook Farm community.

Rip·on (rĭp′ən). A city of east-central Wisconsin, 20 miles west of Fond du Lac; site of a political meeting in 1854 that led to the formation of the Republican Party. Population, 6,000.

Rip·on Falls (rĭp′ən). A former waterfall of the Victoria Nile in southeastern Uganda, now submerged by Owen Falls Dam.

ri·poste (rĭ-pōst′) *n.* Also **ri·post. 1.** A quick thrust given after parrying an opponent's lunge. **2.** A retaliatory action, maneuver, or retort. —*intr.v.* **riposted, -posting, -postes. 1.** To make a return thrust. **2.** To retort quickly. [French, from Old French *risposte,* from Italian *risposta,* answer, feminine past participle of *rispondere,* to answer, from Latin *respondēre,* RESPOND.]

rip·ping (rĭp′ĭng) *adj. British Slang.* Fine; excellent; splendid. —**rip′ping·ly** *adv.*

rip·ple[1] (rĭp′əl) *v.* **-pled, -pling, -ples.** —*intr.* **1.** To form or display little undulations or waves on the surface, as does disturbed water. **2.** To flow with such undulations or waves on the surface. **3.** To rise and fall gently in tone or volume. —*tr.* To cause to form small waves or undulations. —*n.* **1.** A slight wave or undulation. **2.** An indistinct, vibrating sound. **3.** A small rapid. [Perhaps frequentative of RIP (to tear).] —**rip′pler** *n.* —**rip′pling·ly** *adv.*

rip·ple[2] (rĭp′əl) *n.* A comblike, toothed instrument for removing seeds from flax and other fibers. —*tr.v.* **rippled, -pling, -ples.** To remove seeds from (flax or other fibers) with a ripple. [Middle English *rip(e)len,* to remove seeds, from Germanic, akin to Middle Low German *repelen.* See **rei-**[1] in Appendix.*]

rip·plet (rĭp′lĭt) *n.* A little wave or ripple.

rip·ply (rĭp′lē) *adj.* **-lier, -liest.** Characterized by or sounding in ripples.

rip·rap (rĭp′răp′) *n.* **1.** A loose assemblage of broken stones erected in water or on soft ground as a foundation. **2.** The broken stones used for this. —*tr.v.* **riprapped, -rapping, -raps. 1.** To construct a riprap in or upon. **2.** To strengthen with a riprap. [Reduplication of RAP (to strike).]

rip-roar·ing (rĭp′rôr′ĭng, -rōr′ĭng) *adj.* Also **rip-roar·i·ous** (rĭp′-rôr′ē-əs, -rōr′ē-əs). Noisy, lively, and exciting. [From RIP + (UP)ROAR(IOUS).]

rip·saw (rĭp′sô′) *n.* A coarse-toothed saw for cutting wood along the grain. Also called "rip."

rip·snort·er (rĭp′snôr′tər) *n. Slang.* A person or thing remarkable for strength, intensity, or excellence. —**rip′snort′ing** *adj.*

Rip·u·ar·i·an (rĭp′yo͞o-âr′ē-ən) *adj.* Pertaining to a group of Franks who lived along the Rhine, near Cologne, in the fourth century. —*n.* A Ripuarian Frank. [Medieval Latin *Ripuārius*†.]

rise (rīz) *v.* **rose** (rōz), **risen** (rĭz′ən), **rising, rises.** —*intr.* **1.** To assume a standing position after lying, sitting, or kneeling. **2.** To get out of bed. **3.** To move from a lower to a higher position; ascend. **4.** To increase in value: *rise in prices.* **5.** To appear above the horizon. **6.** To extend upward; be prominent: *The tower rose above the hill.* **7.** To slant or slope upward. **8.** To originate; come into existence: *a storm rising in the north.* **9.** To be erected: *New buildings are rising in the city.* **10.** To appear at the surface of the water or the earth; emerge. **11.** To puff up or become larger; swell up: *Bread dough rises.* **12.** To become stiff and erect. **13.** To increase in quantity, value, or price. **14.** To increase in intensity, force, pitch, or prominence. **15.** To attain a higher status. **16.** To become apparent to the mind or senses: *Fears rose to haunt him.* **17.** To uplift oneself to meet a demand or challenge. **18.** To return to life. **19.** To rebel: *"the right to rise up, and shake off the existing government"* (Lincoln). **20.** To close a session of an official assembly; adjourn. —*tr.* **1.** To cause to rise. **2.** To cause (a distant object at sea) to become visible above the horizon by advancing closer. —*n.* **1.** The act of rising; an ascent. **2.** The degree of elevation or ascent; an upward slope. **3.** The appearance of the sun or other heavenly body above the horizon. **4.** An increase in height, as of the level of water. **5.** A gently sloped hill. **6.** An origin, beginning, or source: *the rise of a river.* **7.** Occasion or opportunity: *give rise to doubt.* **8.** The emergence of a fish seeking food or bait at the water's surface. **9.** An increase in price, worth, quantity, or degree. **10.** An increase in intensity, volume, or pitch. **11.** Elevation in social status, prosperity, or importance. **12.** The height of a flight of stairs or of a single riser. **13.** *British.* An increase in salary or wages; a raise. See Usage note at **raise.** —**get a rise out of.** *Slang.* To provoke or tease (someone) successfully. [Rise, rose, risen; Middle English *risen, ros, risen,* Old English *rīsan, rās, risen.* (*Rās* and *risen* are attested only in compounds.) See **rīsan** in Appendix.*]

Synonyms: *rise, ascend, climb, soar, tower, mount, surge, spring.* These verbs all denote a moving upward but differ widely in their connotations and metaphorical senses. *Rise* is applied to a great range of acts, chiefly involving steady or customary upward movement. *Ascend* connotes a rising step by step; *climb,* a steady progress against gravity or other resistance; *soar,* the effortless attainment of great height; and *tower,* admirable height or supremacy relative to the surroundings. With *mount,* the idea of a level or limit to be achieved is present. *Surge* implies ponderous, irresistible forward momentum, while to *spring* is to rise in a single, swift movement.

ris·er (rī′zər) *n.* **1.** A person who rises, especially from sleep: *a late riser.* **2.** The vertical part of a stair step.

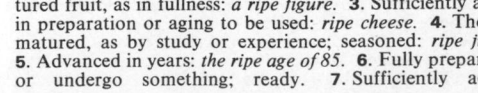

ă pat/ā pay/âr care/ä father/b bib/ch church/d deed/ĕ pet/ē be/f fife/g gag/h hat/hw which/ĭ pit/ī pie/îr pier/j judge/k kick/l lid, needle/m mum/n no, sudden/ng thing/ŏ pot/ō toe/ô paw, for/oi noise/ou out/o͝o took/o͞o boot/p pop/r roar/s sauce/sh ship, dish/

ris·i·bil·i·ty (rĭz′ə-bĭl′ə-tē) *n., pl.* **-ties. 1.** The ability or tendency to laugh. **2.** *Often plural.* A sense of the ludicrous or amusing. **3.** Laughter; hilarity.

ris·i·ble (rĭz′ə-bəl) *adj.* **1.** Capable of laughing or inclined to laugh. **2.** Pertaining to or used in laughter. **3.** Apt to excite laughter; ludicrous; laughable. [Late Latin *rīsibilis,* from Latin *rīdēre* (past participle *rīsus*), to laugh. See **ridiculous.**] **—ris′i·bly** *adv.*

ris·ing (rī′zĭng) *adj.* **1.** Ascending, sloping upward, or advancing: *a rising tide.* **2.** Coming to maturity; growing; emerging: *the rising generation.* **—***n.* **1.** The act of someone or something that rises. **2.** An uprising; insurrection; revolt. **3.** A prominence or projection. **4.** The leaven or yeast used to make dough rise in baking.

risk (rĭsk) *n.* **1.** The possibility of suffering harm or loss; danger. **2.** A factor, element, or course involving uncertain danger; hazard. **3.** *Insurance.* **a.** The danger or probability of loss to the insurer. **b.** The amount that the insurance company stands to lose. **c.** A person or thing considered with respect to the possibility of loss to an insurer: *a poor risk.* —See Synonyms at **danger.** **—***tr.v.* **risked, risking, risks. 1.** To expose to a chance of loss or damage; hazard: *"I had seen him risk his limbs blindly at a fox-hunt"* (Wilkie Collins). **2.** To incur the risk of: *His action risked a sharp reprisal.* [French *risque,* from Italian *risico,* from Vulgar Latin *resecum* (unattested), risk at sea, danger, rock, "that which cuts," from Latin *resecāre,* to cut off : *re-,* against + *secāre,* to cut (see **sek-** in Appendix*).] **—risk′er** *n.*

risk·y (rĭs′kē) *adj.* **-ier, -iest.** Accompanied by or involving risk or danger; hazardous. **—risk′i·ness** *n.*

Ri·sor·gi·men·to (rē-sôr′jē-mĕn′tō) *n.* The period of or the movement for the liberation and political unification of Italy, beginning about 1750 and lasting until 1870. [Italian, "resurrection," from *risorgere,* to resurrect, from Latin *resurgere,* to rise again : *re-,* again + *surgere,* to rise : *sub-,* up from under + *regere,* to lead straight (see **reg-**[1] in Appendix*).]

ri·sot·to (rē-sôt′tō) *n. Italian.* Rice cooked in broth with grated cheese and seasonings.

ris·qué (rĭs-kā′) *adj.* Suggestive of or bordering on indelicacy or impropriety: *a risqué joke.* [French, from the past participle of *risquer,* to risk, from *risque,* RISK.]

ris·sole (rĭ′sōl; *French* rē-sôl′) *n.* A small, pastry-enclosed croquette with a minced meat or fish filling, and usually fried in deep fat. [French, from Old French *roissole,* from (unattested) Vulgar Latin *russeola (pasta),* "reddish (pastry)," from the feminine of Late Latin *russeolus,* diminutive of Latin *russeus,* reddish, from *russus,* red. See **reudh-** in Appendix.*]

ris·so·lé (rē-sô-lā′) *adj.* Browned by frying. [French, past participle of *rissoler,* to brown by deep frying, from *rissole,* RISSOLE.]

rit. ritardando.

Ri·ta (rē′tə). A feminine given name. [Spanish, short for *Margarita,* from Latin *Margarīta,* MARGARET.]

ri·tar·dan·do (rē′tär-dän′dō) *adj. Abbr.* **rit., ritard.** *Music.* Gradually slowing in tempo; retarding. Used as a direction. [Italian, from Latin *retardandum,* gerund of *retardāre,* to RETARD.]

rite (rīt) *n.* **1.** The prescribed or customary form for conducting a religious or other solemn ceremony: *the rite of baptism.* **2.** A ceremonial act or series of acts: *fertility rites.* **3.** *Often capital* **R.** The liturgy of a Christian church, especially one of the historical forms of the Eucharistic service: *the Anglican Rite.* **4.** *Often capital* **R.** A branch or division of the Christian church as determined by specific liturgy and law: *Catholics of the Latin Rite.* **5.** Any formal practice, custom, or procedure. [Middle English *ryte,* from Latin *rītus.* See **ar-** in Appendix.*]

ri·tor·nel·lo (rē′tôr-nĕl′lō) *n., pl.* **-li** (-lē) or **-los.** *Music.* **1.** An instrumental interlude recurring after each stanza in a vocal work. **2.** A passage for full orchestra in a baroque concerto grosso. **3.** An instrumental interlude in early 17th-century opera. **4.** The refrain of a rondo. [Italian, a refrain, diminutive of *ritorno,* return, from *ritornare,* to return, from Vulgar Latin *retornāre* (unattested), to RETURN.]

Rit·ten·house (rĭt′ən-hous), **David.** 1732–1796. American astronomer and political figure; first director of U.S. Mint.

rit·ter (rĭt′ər) *n., pl.* **ritter.** A knight. [German *Ritter,* from Middle High German *riter,* from Middle Dutch *ridder(e),* rider, knight, probably from *rīden,* to ride. See **reidh-** in Appendix.*]

rit·u·al (rĭch′o͞o-əl) *n.* **1.** The prescribed form or order of conducting a religious or solemn ceremony. **2.** The body of ceremonies or rites used in a church, fraternal organization, or the like; a system of rites. **3.** A book of rites or ceremonial forms. **4.** *Often plural.* **a.** A ceremonial act or a series of such acts. **b.** The performance of such acts. **5.** Any detailed method of procedure faithfully or regularly followed: *Her household chores have become a ritual with her.* **—***adj.* **1.** Of or characterized by a rite or rites. **2.** Practiced as a rite: *a ritual fire dance.* [Latin *rituālis,* from *rītus,* RITE.] **—rit′u·al·ly** *adv.*

rit·u·al·ism (rĭch′o͞o-əl-ĭz′əm) *n.* **1.** The practice or observance of religious ritual. **2.** Insistence upon or adherence to ritual.

rit·u·al·ist (rĭch′o͞o-əl-ĭst) *n.* **1.** An authority on or student of ritual. **2.** A person who practices or advocates the observance of ritual. **—***adj.* Pertaining or devoted to ritual; ritualistic.

rit·u·al·is·tic (rĭch′o͞o-əl-ĭs′tĭk) *adj.* **1.** Pertaining to ritual or ritualism. **2.** Advocating or practicing ritual. **—rit′u·al·is′ti·cal·ly** *adv.*

ritz·y (rĭt′sē) *adj.* **-ier, -iest.** *Slang.* Elegant; fancy; fashionable. [From the *Ritz* hotels (especially, the *Ritz*-Carlton in New York City) founded by César *Ritz* (1850–1918), Swiss hotelier.]

riv. river.

riv·age (rĭv′ĭj) *n. Archaic.* A coast, shore, or bank. [Middle English, from Old French, from *rive,* bank, shore, from Latin *rīpa.* See **rei-**[1] in Appendix.*]

ri·val (rī′vəl) *n.* **1.** A person who attempts to equal or surpass another, or who pursues the same object as another; competitor. **2.** One that equals or almost equals another in some respect. **3.** *Obsolete.* Any companion or associate in a particular duty. —See Synonyms at **opponent.** **—***adj.* Acting as or being a rival; competing. **—***v.* **rivaled, -valing, -vals.** Also *chiefly British* **-valled, -valling. —***tr.* **1.** To attempt to equal or surpass: *"his ambition led him to rival the career of Edmund Burke."* (Henry Adams). **2.** To be the equal of; be a match for: *"rivalled the beauties of the best Grecian architecture"* (Fielding). **—***intr. Archaic.* To be a competitor or rival; compete. Used with *with.* [Old French, from Latin *rīvālis,* "one using the same brook as another," rival, from *rīvālis,* of a brook, from *rīvus,* brook. See **er-**[1] in Appendix.*]

Synonyms: *rival, compete, vie, emulate, match.* These verbs apply to the act of seeking to equal or surpass another. *Rival* is the most general, connoting an attempt to reach the same level of proficiency or recognition as another. *Compete* and the less forceful *vie* imply a common aim in attainment and usually a satisfaction in the effort involved: *They competed with each other for the honor. Emulate* connotes conscious imitation of excellence. *Match* is said of attainment of equality with a competitor in gradual steps.

ri·val·ry (rī′vəl-rē) *n., pl.* **-ries. 1.** The act of competing or emulating. **2.** The state or condition of being a rival.

rive (rīv) *v.* **rived, rived** or **riven** (rĭv′ən), **riving, rives. —***tr.* **1.** To rend or tear apart. **2.** To break into pieces, as by a blow; cleave or split asunder. **3.** To break or distress (the heart or spirit, for example). **—***intr.* To be or become split. [Middle English *riven,* from Old Norse *rīfa.* See **rei-**[1] in Appendix.*]

riv·er[1] (rĭv′ər) *n.* **1.** *Abbr.* **R., r., riv.** A large natural stream of water emptying into an ocean, lake, or other body of water, and usually fed along its course by converging tributaries. **2.** Any stream or abundant flow resembling this: *a river of tears.* **—sell down the river.** To betray or deceive. **—up the river.** *Slang.* In or to prison. [Middle English *rivere,* from Old French, riverbank, river, from Vulgar Latin *rīpāria* (unattested), feminine of Latin *rīpārius,* on a bank, from *rīpa,* bank. See **rei-**[1] in Appendix.*]

riv·er[2] (rī′vər) *n.* One who rives or splits.

Ri·ve·ra (rē-vĕ′rȧ), **Diego.** 1886–1957. Mexican artist.

river basin. The land area drained by a river and its tributaries.

riv·er·bed (rĭv′ər-bĕd′) *n.* The area covered or once covered by water, between the banks of a river.

riv·er·head (rĭv′ər-hĕd′) *n.* The source of a river.

river horse. The **hippopotamus** *(see).*

riv·er·ine (rĭv′ər-īn′, -ĭn) *adj.* **1.** Pertaining to or resembling a river. **2.** Located on or inhabiting the banks of a river; riparian.

River Plate. The English name for **Río de la Plata.**

riv·er·side (rĭv′ər-sīd′) *n.* The bank of a river. **—***adj.* On or close to a bank of a river.

Riv·er·side (rĭv′ər-sīd′). A city in southern California, 50 miles east of Los Angeles. Population, 84,000.

riv·er·weed (rĭv′ər-wēd′) *n.* A North American plant, *Podostemum ceratophyllum,* growing on rocks in rapidly flowing streams, and resembling seaweed.

riv·et (rĭv′ĭt) *n.* A metal bolt or pin, having a head on one end, used to fasten metal plates or other objects together by inserting the shank through a hole in each piece and hammering down the plain end so as to form a new head. **—***tr.v.* **riveted, -eting, -ets. 1.** To fasten or secure with, or as if with, a rivet. **2.** To hammer the headless end of (a bolt, pin, or similar device) so as to form a head and fasten something. **3.** To fasten or secure firmly; fix. **4.** To engross or hold (the attention, for example): *"His mind was ever riveted to his profession"* (Edward Brenton). [Middle English *ryvette,* from Old French *river*†, to fix.] **—riv′et·er** *n.*

Riv·i·er·a (rĭv′ē-âr′ə; *Italian* rē-vyā′rä). The narrow coastal strip and famous resort area extending along the Mediterranean coast from La Spezia, Italy, in the east, to Hyères, France, in the west, and including the towns of Nice, Monte Carlo, and Cannes. [Italian, "shore," from Vulgar Latin *rīpāria* (unattested). See **river.**]

ri·vière (rē-vyâr′) *n.* A necklace of diamonds or other precious stones, generally in one strand. [French, short for *rivière des diamants,* "stream of diamonds," from Old French *rivere,* RIVER.]

riv·u·let (rĭv′yə-lĭt) *n.* A small brook or stream; streamlet. [Earlier *rivelet,* probably from Italian *rivoletto,* diminutive of *rivolo,* small stream, from Latin *rīvulus,* diminutive of *rīvus,* brook, stream. See **er-**[1] in Appendix.*]

Ri·yadh (rē-yäd′). Also **Ri·yad, Ri·ad.** The capital of Saudi Arabia and of Nejd, located in the eastern part of the country, about 230 miles from the Persian Gulf. Population, 300,000.

ri·yal (rē-ôl′, -äl′) *n.* Also **ri·al** (for sense 1). **1.** The basic monetary unit of Saudi Arabia, equal to 20 qurush. See table of exchange rates at **currency. 2.** The basic monetary unit of Yemen, equal to 40 bugshas. See table of exchange rates at **currency.** [Arabic *riyāl,* from Spanish *real,* REAL (coin).]

Ri·zal (rē-säl′). Formerly **Pa·say** (pä′sī). A city of the Philippines, on Manila Bay south of Manila. Population, 132,000.

Ri·zal (rē-säl′), **José.** 1861–1896. Philippine national hero.

Riz·zio (rēt′tsyō), **David.** 1533?–1566. Italian musician; counselor of Mary, Queen of Scots.

RM reichsmark.

rm. 1. ream. **2.** room.

rms root mean square.

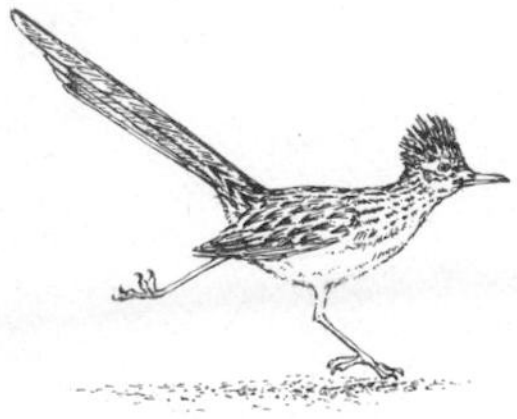

roadrunner

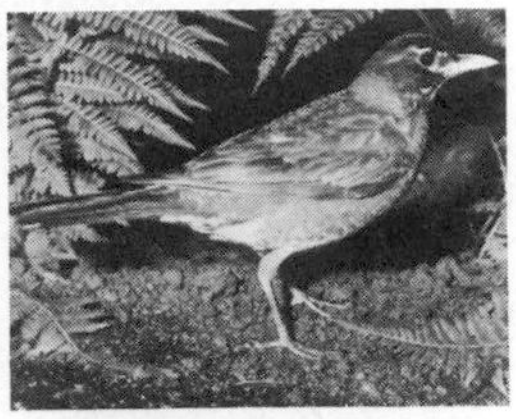

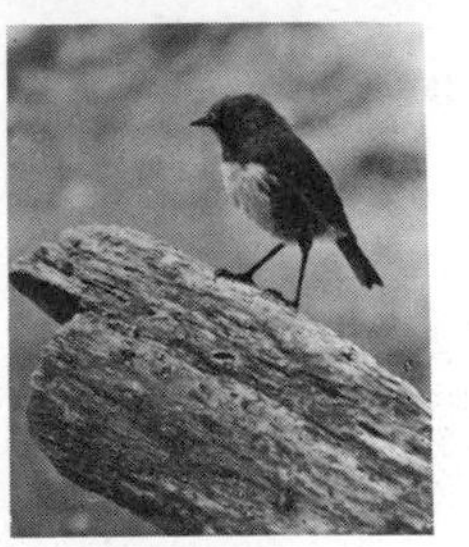

robin
Above: Turdus migratorius
Below: Erithacus rubecula

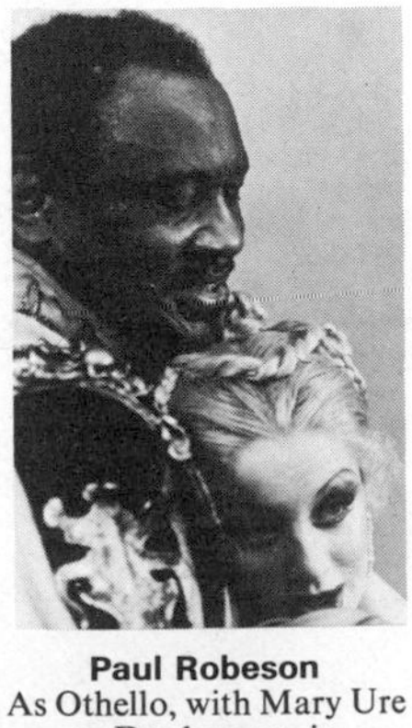

Paul Robeson
As Othello, with Mary Ure as Desdemona, in Shakespeare's *Othello*

R.M.S. 1. Railway Mail Service. 2. Royal Mail Service. 3. Royal Mail Steamship.
Rn The symbol for the element radon.
R.N. 1. registered nurse. 2. Royal Navy.
RNA *Biochemistry.* ribonucleic acid.
ro. rood (measure).
roach[1] (rōch) *n., pl.* **roach** or **roaches.** 1. A freshwater fish, *Rutilus rutilus,* of northern Europe. 2. Any of various similar or related fishes, such as some North American sunfishes. [Middle English *roche,* from Old French *roche*†.]
roach[2] (rōch) *n.* An insect, the **cockroach** *(see).*
roach[3] (rōch) *n.* 1. A roll of hair brushed up from the forehead or temple. 2. *Nautical.* A cut on the edge of a sail to prevent chafing. 3. *Slang.* The butt of a marijuana cigarette. —*tr.v.* **roached, roaching, roaches.** 1. To brush (hair) in a roach. 2. To shave (the mane of a horse) to a short bristle. [Origin unknown.]
road (rōd) *n. Abbr.* **Rd., rd., R., r.** 1. An open way, generally public, for the passage of vehicles, persons, and animals. 2. A course or path. 3. A railroad. 4. *Usually plural. Nautical.* A **roadstead** *(see).* —**on the road.** 1. On tour, as a theatrical company. 2. Traveling, especially as a salesman. 3. Wandering, as a vagabond. [Middle English *rood, rode,* riding, journey, Old English *rād.* See **reidh-** in Appendix.*]
road agent. A bandit who robbed stagecoaches.
road·bed (rōd′bĕd′) *n.* 1. a. The foundation upon which the ties, rails, and ballast of a railroad are laid. b. A layer of ballast directly under the ties. 2. The foundation and surface of a road.
road·block (rōd′blŏk′) *n.* 1. A barricade or obstruction across a road set up by the police to prevent the escape of a fugitive or by the military to prevent the passage of enemy troops. 2. Any obstruction in a road, as a fallen tree or rocks.
road hog. A driver who selfishly keeps his vehicle near the middle of the road.
road·house (rōd′hous′) *n.* An inn, restaurant, or night club located on a road outside a city.
road metal. Crushed or broken stone, cinders, or similar material used in the construction and repair of roads and roadbeds.
road·run·ner (rōd′rŭn′ər) *n.* A swift-running, crested bird, *Geococcyx californianus,* of southwestern North America, having streaked, brownish plumage and a long tail. Also called "chaparral cock."
road·side (rōd′sīd′) *n.* The area bordering on the side of a road.
road·stead (rōd′stĕd′) *n. Nautical.* A sheltered, offshore anchorage area for ships. Also called "roads."
road·ster (rōd′stər) *n.* 1. An open automobile having a single seat for two or three people, and a rumble seat or luggage compartment in the back. 2. A horse for riding on a road.
road·way (rōd′wā′) *n.* A road, especially the part over which vehicles travel.
road·work (rōd′wûrk′) *n.* Outdoor long-distance running as a form of physical exercise or conditioning.
roam (rōm) *v.* **roamed, roaming, roams.** —*intr.* To move or travel without purpose or plan; rove; wander. —*tr.* To wander over or through: *"mad dogs roam the streets; the plague year is here"* (William Demby). —See Synonyms at **wander.** —*n.* The act of roaming. [Middle English *romen*†.] —**roam′er** *n.*
roan (rōn) *adj.* 1. Having a chestnut, bay, or sorrel coat thickly sprinkled with white or gray. Said chiefly of horses. 2. Made or prepared from roan leather. —*n.* 1. The characteristic coloring of a roan horse. 2. A roan horse or other animal. 3. A soft, flexible sheepskin leather, often treated to resemble morocco, and used in bookbinding. In this sense, also called "roan leather." [Old French, from Old Spanish *roano*†.]
Ro·a·noke (rō′ə-nōk). A city of southwestern Virginia. Population, 97,000.
Ro·a·noke Island (rō′ə-nōk). An island off the coast of North Carolina, where Sir Walter Raleigh attempted to found a colony (1585–87).
Ro·a·noke River (rō′ə-nōk). A river rising in southwestern Virginia and flowing 410 miles generally southeast to Albemarle Sound off northeastern North Carolina.
roar (rôr) *v.* **roared, roaring, roars.** —*intr.* 1. To utter a loud, deep, prolonged sound, especially in distress, rage, or excitement. 2. To utter a loud, rumbling sound, as that characteristic of a lion. 3. To laugh loudly or excitedly. 4. To make or produce a loud noise or din. 5. To move or operate with a loud noise, as a vehicle or gun. 6. To breathe with a rasping sound. Used of a horse. —*tr.* 1. To utter or express with a deep, loud, and prolonged sound. 2. To put, bring, or force into a specified state by roaring: *The crowd roared itself hoarse.* —*n.* 1. A loud, deep sound or cry, as of a person in distress or rage. 2. The loud, deep cry characteristic of a lion. 3. A loud, prolonged noise, such as that produced by waves. 4. A loud burst of laughter. [Middle English *roren, raren,* Old English *rārian.* See **rei-**[3] in Appendix.*] —**roar′er** *n.*
roar·ing (rôr′ĭng) *adj.* Very lively or successful; thriving: *a roaring trade.* —*adv.* Extremely; very: *roaring drunk.*
roast (rōst) *v.* **roasted, roasting, roasts.** —*tr.* 1. a. To cook with dry heat, especially in an oven. b. To cook by direct exposure to dry heat, as over an open fire or in hot ashes. 2. To dry, brown, or parch by exposing to heat. 3. To expose to great or excessive heat. 4. *Metallurgy.* To heat (ores) in a furnace in order to dehydrate, purify, or oxidize. 5. *Informal.* To criticize or ridicule harshly. —*intr.* 1. To cook meat or other food in an oven. 2. To undergo roasting. —*n.* 1. Something roasted. 2. A cut of meat suitable or prepared for roasting. 3. The act or process of roasting, or the state of being roasted. —*adj.* Roasted. [Middle English *rosten,* from Old French *rostir,* probably from Old High German *rōsten,* from *rōst,* grate, gridiron, from Germanic *raust* (unattested).]
roast·er (rōs′tər) *n.* 1. One that roasts. 2. A special pan or apparatus for roasting. 3. Something fit for roasting.
rob (rŏb) *v.* **robbed, robbing, robs.** —*tr.* 1. To take property from (a person or persons) illegally, by using or threatening to use violence or force; commit robbery upon. 2. To take valuable or desired articles unlawfully from: *rob a bank.* 3. a. To deprive (a person) of something belonging, desired, or legally due by any unjust procedure: *rob a person of his reputation.* b. To deprive of something injuriously: *a parasite that robs a tree of its sap.* 4. To take as booty; steal. —*intr.* To commit or engage in robbery. [Middle English *robben,* from Old French *rober,* from Germanic. See **reup-** in Appendix.*] —**rob′ber** *n.*
Synonyms: *rob, burglarize, filch, pilfer, plunder, loot, ransack, steal, thieve.* All these verbs mean to take property from another or valuables from a place. *Rob* in its most common usage means to take property from another through fear, force, or violence; the term may also imply depriving another of property legally his, by fraud or stealth. *Burglarize* connotes entering a place to commit theft or other felony. *Filch* and *pilfer* both imply stealth in taking small sums of money or petty objects. *Plunder* refers to robbery on a large scale, in modern usage; it also applies to pillaging by victorious troops in conquered areas. *Loot* suggests in its primary sense the carrying away of property by undisciplined troops or mobs; the term also applies to the systematic pilfering of funds or property by trusted persons. *Ransack* pertains to a thorough search of a house or building by persons seeking to take valuable or desired articles. *Steal* and *thieve* both apply to the practice of taking property or belongings surreptitiously and without permission; *steal* also can mean to appropriate another's ideas as one's own or plagiarize.
rob·a·lo (rŏb′ə-lō, rō′bə-) *n., pl.* **-los** or **robalo.** Any of various chiefly tropical marine food fishes of the family Centropomidae, such as the **snook** *(see).* [Spanish *róbalo, robálo,* probably modification of *lobaro* (unattested), from *lobo,* wolf, "wolflike fish," from Latin *lupus.* See **wḷkwo-** in Appendix.*]
robber baron. 1. A feudal lord who robbed travelers passing through his domain. 2. One of the American industrial or financial magnates of the latter 19th century who became wealthy by unethical means, such as questionable stock-market operations, or exploitation of labor or political connections.
robber fly. Any of various predatory flies of the family Asilidae, characteristically having long, bristly legs.
rob·ber·y (rŏb′ər-ē) *n., pl.* **-ies.** 1. The act of unlawfully taking the property of another by the use of violence or intimidation. 2. An instance of this.
Rob·bia, della. See **della Robbia.**
Rob·bins (rŏb′ĭnz), **Frederick Chapman.** Born 1916. American microbiologist.
robe (rōb) *n.* 1. A long, loose, flowing outer garment, specifically: a. An official garment worn on formal occasions to show office or rank, as by a judge or high church official. b. An academic gown. c. A dressing gown or bathrobe. 2. *Plural.* Clothes in general; apparel; dress. 3. A blanket or covering made of fur, cloth, or other material: *a lap robe.* —*v.* **robed, robing, robes.** —*tr.* To clothe or dress in a robe or robes. —*intr.* To put on a robe or robes. [Middle English, from Old French, from Vulgar Latin *rauba* (unattested), "clothes taken away as booty," robe, from Germanic. See **reup-** in Appendix.*]
Rob·ert (rŏb′ərt). *Abbr.* **Robt.** A masculine given name. [Middle English, from Old North French (superseding Old English *Hreodbeorht*), from Old High German *Hrōdebert* : *Hrōd-,* fame (see **kar-**[2] in Appendix*) + *beraht,* bright (see **bherəg-** in Appendix*).]
Rob·ert I (rŏb′ərt). Called "the Bruce." 1274–1329. King of Scotland (1306–29); defeated English at Bannockburn (1314); won recognition of independent Scotland (1328).
Ro·ber·ta (rə-bûr′tə, rō-). A feminine given name. [Feminine of ROBERT.]
Robe·son (rōb′sən), **Paul.** Born 1898. American singer.
Robes·pierre (rōbz′pē-âr; *French* rô-bəs-pyâr′), **Maximilien François Marie Isidore de.** 1758–1794. French revolutionary leader; guillotined.
rob·in (rŏb′ĭn) *n.* 1. A North American songbird, *Turdus migratorius,* having a rust-red breast and gray and black upper plumage. 2. A small Old World bird, *Erithacus rubecula,* having an orange breast and a brown back. 3. Any of various birds resembling a robin. [Short for *Robin redbreast,* from ROBIN.]
Rob·in (rŏb′ĭn). A masculine or feminine given name. [Diminutive of ROBERT.]
Rob·in Good·fel·low. See **Puck.**
Rob·in Hood (rŏb′ĭn ho͝od). A legendary English outlaw of the 12th century, famous for his courage and chivalry, and for his practice of robbing the rich to aid the poor.
rob·in's-egg blue (rŏb′ĭnz-ĕg′). Pale to green to light bluish green to greenish or grayish blue. See **color.**
Rob·in·son (rŏb′ĭn-sən), **Edwin Arlington.** 1869–1935. American poet.
Rob·in·son (rŏb′ĭn-sən), **(Esmé Stuart) Lennox.** 1886–1958. Irish playwright, novelist, and theatrical manager.
Rob·in·son (rŏb′ĭn-sən), **Jack Washington ("Jackie").** Born 1919. American athlete; broke baseball's color line.
Rob·in·son (rŏb′ĭn-sən), Sir **Robert.** Born 1886. British chemist; worked on alkaloids.
Rob·in·son (rŏb′ĭn-sən), **Sugar Ray.** Original name, Walker Smith. Born 1921. American prize fighter.
Rob·in·son Cru·soe (rŏb′ĭn-sən kro͞o′sō). The hero of Daniel

ă pat/ā pay/âr care/ä father/b bib/ch church/d deed/ĕ pet/ē be/f fife/g gag/h hat/hw which/ĭ pit/ī pie/îr pier/j judge/k kick/l lid, needle/m mum/n no, sudden/ng thing/ŏ pot/ō toe/ô paw, for/oi noise/ou out/o͝o took/o͞o boot/p pop/r roar/s sauce/sh ship, dish/

Defoe's novel *Robinson Crusoe* (1719), a shipwrecked English sailor who lived for years on a small tropical island.

Robin's plantain. A plant, *Erigeron pulchellus,* of eastern North America, having many-rayed purplish flowers.

rob·le (rō'blā) *n.* **1.** An oak, *Quercus lobata,* of California, having leathery leaves and slender, pointed acorns. Also called "white oak." **2.** Any of various similar or related trees. [Spanish and Portuguese *roble,* oak, from Latin *rōbur,* oak, strength. See **reudh-** in Appendix.*]

rob·o·rant (rŏb'ər-ənt) *adj.* Restoring vigor or strength. —*n.* A roborant drug; tonic. [Latin *rōborāns,* present participle of *rōborāre,* to strengthen, from *rōbur,* strength. See **reudh-** in Appendix.*]

ro·bot (rō'bət, rŏb'ət) *n.* **1.** An externally manlike mechanical device capable of performing human tasks or behaving in a human manner. **2.** A person who works mechanically without original thought. **3.** Any machine or device that works automatically or by remote control. Also called "automaton." [Czech, from *robota,* compulsory labor, drudgery. See **orbh-** in Appendix.*] —**ro'bot·ism'** *n.* —**ro'bot·is'tic** *adj.*

robot bomb. **1.** A small, explosive-carrying, jet-propelled, gyroscopically guided winged missile. Also called "V-1," "buzz bomb," "flying bomb." **2.** A **guided missile** *(see).*

robot pilot. *Aviation.* An **automatic pilot** *(see).*

Rob Roy (rŏb roi). Original name, Robert Macgregor. 1671–1734. Scottish freebooter, leader of the clan Macgregor, and Jacobite hero of legends.

rob roy (rŏb roi). A cocktail made with Scotch whisky, sweet vermouth, and bitters. [After ROB ROY.]

Rob·son, Mount (rŏb'sən). A mountain in eastern British Columbia, Canada; the highest elevation in the Canadian Rockies (12,972 feet).

Robt. Robert.

ro·bust (rō-bŭst', rō'bŭst) *adj.* **1.** Full of health and strength; vigorous; hardy. **2.** Powerfully built; sturdy; husky. **3.** Requiring or suited to physical strength or endurance: *robust labor.* **4.** Boisterous; rough. **5.** Marked by richness and fullness; full-bodied: *a robust wine.* —See Synonyms at **healthy.** [Latin *rōbustus,* oaken, from *rōbur, rōbus,* oak, strength. See **reudh-** in Appendix.*] —**ro·bust'ly** *adv.* —**ro·bust'ness** *n.*

roc (rŏk) *n.* A legendary bird of prey of enormous size and strength. [Arabic *rukhkh,* from Persian *rukh*†.]

Ro·ca, Cape (rō'kə). *Portuguese* **Ca·bo da Ro·ca** (kä'bo͞o dä rô'kä). The westernmost point of continental Europe, 19 miles northwest of Lisbon, Portugal.

roc·am·bole (rŏk'əm-bōl') *n.* **1.** A European plant, *Allium scorodoprasum,* having a garliclike bulb. **2.** The bulb of this plant, used as a seasoning. [French, from German *Rockenbolle,* "distaff bulb" : *Rocken,* distaff, from Old High German *rocko* (see **ruk-**[1] in Appendix*) + *Bolle,* bulb, from Old High German *bolla,* ball (see **bhel-**[2] in Appendix*).]

Ro·cham·beau (rō-shäN-bō'), **Comte de.** Title of Jean Baptiste Donatien de Vimeur. 1725–1807. French army officer; led French forces in the American Revolution.

Roch·dale (rŏch'dāl). A textile manufacturing center in southeastern Lancashire, England, the home of the British cooperative movement, founded in 1844 by a group known as the Rochdale Pioneers. Population, 86,000.

Ro·chelle, La. See **La Rochelle.**

Ro·chelle powder (rô-shĕl'). A cathartic, **Seidlitz powder** *(see).*

Rochelle salt. A colorless efflorescent crystalline compound, $KNaC_4H_4O_6 \cdot 4H_2O$, used in making mirrors, in electronics, and as a laxative. [After LA ROCHELLE.]

roche mou·ton·née (rôsh mo͞o-tô-nā') *pl.* **roches moutonnées** (rôsh mo͞o-tô-nā'). A bedrock outcrop worn smooth by glacial abrasion. Also called "sheepback." [French, "fleecy rock."]

Roch·es·ter (rŏch'ĕs-tər). **1.** A city in western New York State, on the New York State Barge Canal near Lake Ontario. Population, 319,000. **2.** A city in Minnesota, 70 miles southeast of St. Paul; the site of the Mayo Clinic. Population, 41,000.

Roch·es·ter (rŏch'ĕs-tər), **Second Earl of.** Title of John Wilmot. 1647–1680. English satiric poet of the Restoration.

roch·et (rŏch'ĭt) *n.* A ceremonial vestment made of linen or lawn, worn by bishops and other church dignitaries. [Middle English, from Old French, from Frankish *rok* (unattested), coat. See **ruk-**[1] in Appendix.*]

rock[1] (rŏk) *n.* **1.** Any relatively hard naturally formed mass of mineral or petrified matter; stone. **2. a.** A relatively small piece or fragment of such material. **b.** A relatively large body of such material, as a cliff or peak. **3.** *Geology.* Any naturally formed mineral mass or aggregate that constitutes a significant part of the earth's crust. **4.** Anything similar to or suggesting a mass of stone in stability, such as a support, foundation, or source of strength. **5.** *Usually plural. Slang.* Money. **6.** *Slang.* A large gem, especially a diamond. **7.** *Chiefly British.* A kind of hard candy. **8.** A British youth, a **rocker** *(see).* —**on the rocks. 1.** In a state of destruction or ruin: *Their marriage is on the rocks.* **2.** Without money; bankrupt. **3.** Served over ice cubes without water or mix. —**The Rock. 1.** *Informal.* The Rock of **Gibraltar** *(see).* **2.** *Slang.* **Alcatraz** *(see).* [Middle English *rokke,* from Old North French *roque,* variant of Old French *roche,* from Vulgar Latin *rocca*† (unattested).]

rock[2] (rŏk) *v.* **rocked, rocking, rocks.** —*intr.* **1.** To move back and forth or from side to side, especially gently or rhythmically. **2.** To sway violently, as from a blow or shock; shake. **3.** *Mining.* To be washed and panned in a cradle or rocker. Used of ores. —*tr.* **1.** To sway back and forth or from side to side; especially, to soothe or lull to sleep. **2.** To cause to shake or sway violently. **3.** To disturb the emotions or mind of; upset: *The scandal rocked the town.* **4.** *Mining.* To wash or pan (ore) in a cradle or rocker. **5.** In mezzotint engraving, to roughen (a metal plate) with various rockers and roulettes. —See Synonyms at **swing.** —*n.* **1.** The act of rocking. **2.** A rocking motion. **3. Rock 'n' roll** *(see).* [Middle English *rokken,* Old English *roccian,* perhaps from Germanic *rukk-* (unattested).] —**rock'ing·ly** *adv.*

rock·a·by (rŏk'ə-bī') *interj.* Also **rock·a·bye, rock-a-bye.** Used to lull an infant to sleep. [ROCK + (LULL)ABY.]

rock-and-roll. Variant of **rock 'n' roll.**

rock and rye. A rye whiskey bottled commercially with rock candy and fruit.

rock·a·way (rŏk'ə-wā') *n.* A four-wheeled carriage with two seats and a standing top. [First made at *Rockaway,* town in New Jersey.]

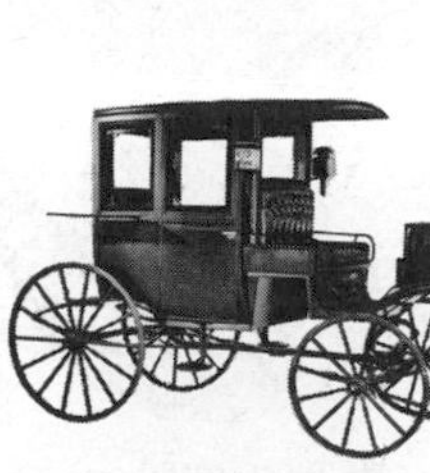

rockaway
Glass panel rockaway made about 1900

rock bass. **1.** A freshwater food fish, *Ambloplites rupestris,* of eastern and central North America. Also called "redeye." **2.** Any of various similar or related fishes.

rock bottom. The lowest level; the absolute bottom: *Prices have reached rock bottom.* —**rock'-bot'tom** *adj.*

rock-bound (rŏk'bound') *adj.* Hemmed in by or bordered with rocks: *a rock-bound lake.*

rock candy. Sugar in the form of large, hard, clear crystals.

Rock Cornish hen. A small fowl of a breed developed by crossing white Plymouth Rock and Cornish strains, and used especially as a roasting chicken.

Rock Creek Butte. A mountain in northeastern Oregon, the highest elevation in the Blue Mountains (9,097 feet).

rock crystal. Transparent quartz, especially when colorless.

rock dove. A bird, *Columba livia,* native to Europe but widely distributed elsewhere, having variously colored plumage with iridescent neck markings. It is the common pigeon seen in cities and frequently domesticated. [Such doves sometimes live on rocks by the seaside.]

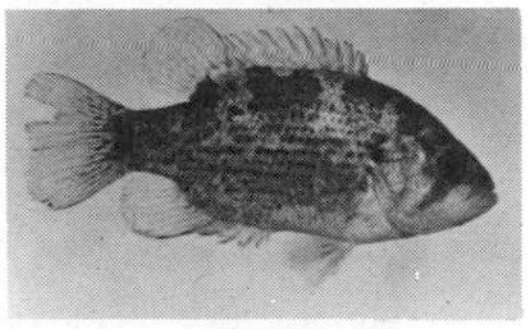

rock bass
Ambloplites rupestris

Rock·e·fel·ler (rŏk'ə-fĕl'ər), **John D(avison).** 1839–1937. American industrialist and philanthropist.

Rock·e·fel·ler (rŏk'ə-fĕl'ər), **Nelson Aldrich.** Born 1908. American diplomat and political figure; governor of New York (since 1959); grandson of John D. Rockefeller.

Rock·e·fel·ler (rŏk'ə-fĕl'ər), **Winthrop.** Born 1912. American investment manager and political figure; grandson of John D. Rockefeller.

rock·er (rŏk'ər) *n.* **1.** A person who rocks something, such as a cradle. **2.** A rocking chair. **3.** A rocking horse. **4.** One of the two curved pieces upon which a cradle, rocking chair, or similar device rocks. **5.** *Mining.* A cradle for washing or panning ores. **6.** A small steel plate with a curved, toothed edge, used to roughen a copper plate for a mezzotint. **7.** An ice skate with a curved blade. **8.** *Sometimes capital* **R.** A British youth who affects a rowdyish air and usually belongs to a gang of motorcycling enthusiasts. In this sense, also called "rock." —**off one's rocker.** *Slang.* Out of one's mind; crazy.

rocker arm. A pivoted lever, as in an automobile engine, used to transfer cam or pushrod motion to a valve stem.

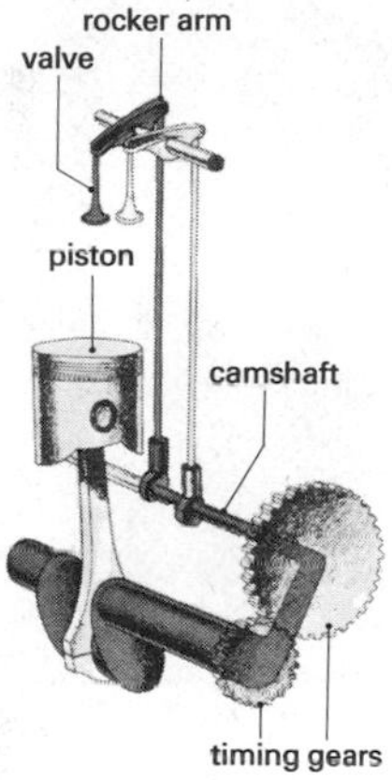
rocker arm
valve
piston
camshaft
timing gears

rocker arm

rocker cam. A cam on a rockshaft.

rock·er·y (rŏk'ər-ē) *n., pl.* **-ies.** A **rock garden** *(see).*

rock·et[1] (rŏk'ĭt) *n.* **1. a.** Any device propelled by ejection of matter, especially by the high-velocity ejection of the gaseous combustion products produced by internal ignition of solid or liquid fuels. **b.** An engine that propels in this manner; a rocket engine. **2. a.** A weapon carrying an explosive or other warhead, and using rocket power. **b.** An incendiary weapon with a rounded hollow warhead filled with explosives and formerly fired from a ship. **3.** A firework for aerial display. —*v.* **rocketed, -eting, -ets.** —*intr.* **1.** To move swiftly, as a rocket. **2.** To fly swiftly straight up, as a frightened game bird. **3.** To rise rapidly or unexpectedly, as in a career. —*tr.* **1.** To assault with rockets. **2.** To carry by means of a rocket. [Italian *rocchetta,* rocket, small distaff, diminutive of *rocca,* distaff, from Gothic *rukka* (unattested). See **ruk-**[1] in Appendix.*]

rock·et[2] (rŏk'ĭt) *n.* **1.** A plant, *Eruca sativa,* native to Eurasia, having yellowish-white flowers and leaves that are sometimes used in salads. **2.** Any of several related plants, especially one of the genus *Hesperis.* [Old French *roquette,* from Old Italian *ruchetta,* diminutive of *ruca,* from Latin *ērūca,* "caterpillar," perhaps from *er,* hedgehog. See **ghers-** in Appendix.*]

rock·et·eer (rŏk'ə-tîr') *n.* A person who designs, launches, studies, or pilots rockets.

rocket engine. An engine that propels, especially one that propels spacecraft or aircraft, by means of rockets.

rocket motor. A rocket engine, especially one using solid propellants.

rock·et·ry (rŏk'ĭt-rē) *n.* The science and technology of rocket design, construction, and flight.

rock·et·sonde (rŏk'ĭt-sŏnd') *n.* A rocket used for observation in the upper atmosphere. [ROCKET + French *sonde,* sounding line, from Old French, from Old English *sund(rāp),* "sounding rope," from *sund,* sea (see **swem-** in Appendix*).]

rock·fish (rŏk'fĭsh') *n., pl.* **rockfish** or **-fishes. 1.** Any of various fishes living among rocks. **2.** Any of various fishes, chiefly of the genus *Sebastodes,* of Pacific waters. **3.** The **striped bass** *(see).*

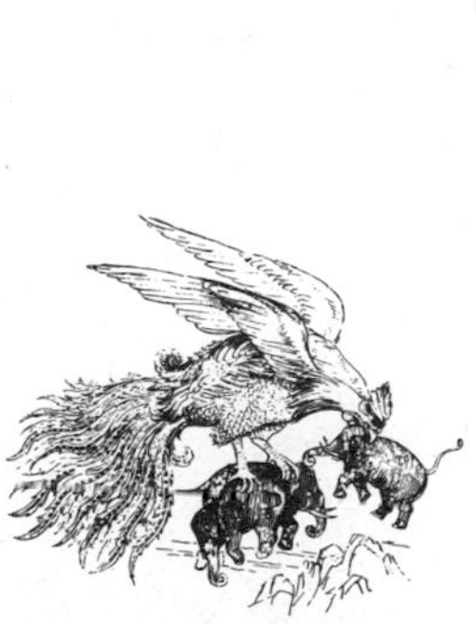

roc
Illustration by Edward W. Lane

rock flour. Pulverized rock produced by glacial abrasion.

Rock·ford (rŏk'fərd). A city and manufacturing center of northern Illinois. Population, 127,000.

rock garden. A rocky area in which plants especially adapted to such terrain are cultivated. Also called "rockery."

Rock·ies (rŏk'ēz). *Informal.* The Rocky Mountains.

rocking chair. A chair mounted on rockers or springs.

t tight/th thin, path/*th* this, bathe/ŭ cut/ûr urge/v valve/w with/y yes/z zebra, size/zh vision/ə about, item, edible, gallop, circus/ à *Fr.* ami/œ *Fr.* feu, *Ger.* schön/ü *Fr.* tu, *Ger.* über/KH *Ger.* ich, *Scot.* loch/N *Fr.* bon. *Follows main vocabulary. †Of obscure origin.

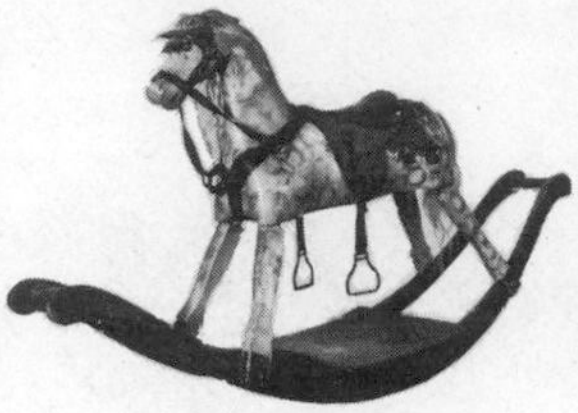
rocking horse

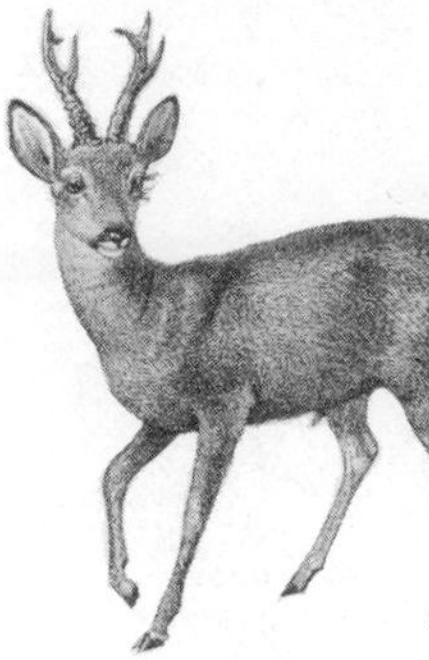
roe deer

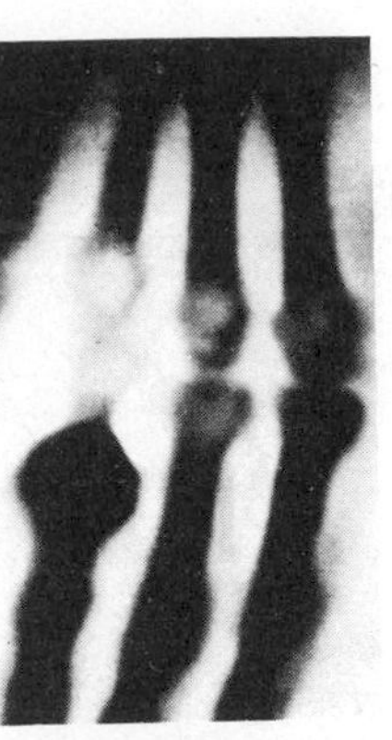
roentgenogram
X ray of his wife's hand taken by Roentgen in 1895

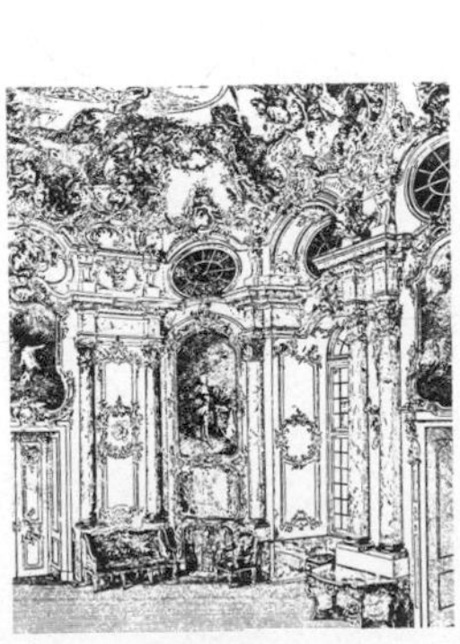
rococo

rocking horse. A toy horse large enough for a child to ride, mounted upon rockers or springs. Also called "hobbyhorse."
Rock Island (rŏk). A city on the Mississippi in northwestern Illinois. Population, 52,000.
rock·ling (rŏk′lĭng) *n., pl.* **-lings** or **rockling.** Any of various small marine fishes of the family Gadidae, of North Atlantic coastal waters. [ROCK (stone) + LING (fish).]
rock lobster. The **spiny lobster** *(see).*
rock maple. A tree, the **sugar maple** *(see),* or its tough, close-grained wood.
Rock·ne (rŏk′nē), **Knute Kenneth.** 1888–1931. Norwegian-born American athlete; football coach at University of Notre Dame.
rock 'n' roll (rŏk′ ən rōl′). Also **rock-and-roll** (rŏk′ən-rōl′). Popular music combining elements of rhythm and blues with country and western music, and having a heavily accented beat. Also called "rock." *—adj.* Of or pertaining to such music or dancing.
rock oil. *Chiefly British.* Petroleum.
rock-ribbed (rŏk′rĭbd′) *adj.* **1.** Having rocks or rock outcroppings. **2.** Stern and unyielding.
Rock River. A river rising in southeastern Wisconsin and flowing 300 miles generally south to the Mississippi in northwestern Illinois.
rock·rose (rŏk′rōz′) *n.* Any of various plants or shrubs of the genus *Helianthemum* and related genera, having roselike yellow, white, or reddish flowers. Also called "frostweed."
rock salt. Common salt, essentially sodium chloride, occurring in large solid masses. Also called "halite."
rock·shaft (rŏk′shăft′, -shäft′) *n.* A shaft that oscillates or rocks upon its bearings, but does not revolve.
rock·weed (rŏk′wēd′) *n.* Any of several coarse, brownish seaweeds of the genera *Fucus* and *Ascophyllum,* that grow on rocks in coastal areas.
rock·work (rŏk′wûrk′) *n.* **1.** A natural mass of rocks. **2.** Stonework imitating the irregular surface of natural rocks.
rock·y[1] (rŏk′ē) *adj.* **-ier, -iest. 1.** Consisting of, containing, or abounding in rock or rocks. **2.** Resembling or suggesting rock; firm or hard; tough; unyielding. **3.** Marked by obstructions or difficulties: *the rocky road to success.* **—rock′i·ness** *n.*
rock·y[2] (rŏk′ē) *adj.* **-ier, -iest. 1.** Inclined or prone to sway or totter; unsteady; unstable; shaky. **2.** Weak, dizzy, or nauseated. **—rock′i·ness** *n.*
Rocky Mountain goat. See **mountain goat.**
Rocky Mountain National Park. A resort region of Colorado, 405 square miles in area, established in 1915 in the Rocky Mountains, 50 miles northwest of Denver.
Rock·y Mountains (rŏk′ē). The major mountain system of North America, extending over 3,000 miles from northern Mexico to Alaska, and forming the Continental Divide. Highest elevation, Mt. McKinley (20,320 feet).
Rocky Mountain sheep. The **bighorn** *(see).*
Rocky Mountain spotted fever. An acute infectious disease caused by a microorganism, *Rickettsia rickettsii,* and transmitted by ticks. It is characterized by muscular pains, high fever, and skin eruptions, and is endemic throughout North America. Also called "spotted fever."
ro·co·co (rə-kō′kō, rō′kə-kō′) *n.* **1. a.** A style of art developed from the baroque that originated in France (about 1720) and soon spread throughout Europe; especially, this style used in architecture and decoration, characterized by elaborate, profuse designs intended to produce a delicate effect. **b.** A style of literature regarded as being similarly elaborate. **2.** *Music.* The style immediately following the baroque in Europe (about 1726 to 1775). *—adj.* **1.** Of or in rococo style. **2.** Profuse or elaborate; overdone; florid. [French, a fanciful alteration of *rocaille,* rockwork, from Old French *roche,* ROCK.]
rod (rŏd) *n.* **1.** A straight, thin piece or bar of metal, wood, or other material. **2.** A shoot or stem cut from, or growing as part of, a woody plant. **3. a.** A stick, or a bundle of sticks, used for chastisement. **b.** Punishment itself; correction. **4.** A **fishing rod** *(see).* **5.** A scepter or staff symbolizing power or authority; wand. **6.** Power or dominion, especially of a tyrannical nature: *"under the rod of a cruel slavery."* (John Henry Newman). **7.** A metal bar in a machine: *a piston rod.* **8.** A measuring stick. **9.** A **leveling rod** *(see).* **10.** A **lightning rod** *(see).* **11.** A **divining rod** *(see).* **12.** *Abbr.* **rd, r. a.** A linear measure equal to 5.5 yards, 16.5 feet, or 5.03 meters. Also called "pole," *British* "perch." **b.** A square perch or pole equal to 30.25 square yards. See **measurement. 13.** In Biblical usage, a line of family descent; a branch of a tribe. **14.** *Anatomy.* Any of various rod-shaped cells in the retina that respond to dim light. **15.** *Microbiology.* Any elongated microorganism. **16.** *Slang.* A pistol or revolver. **17.** A drawbar under a freight car. **—ride the rods.** *Slang.* To take an unauthorized free ride on the drawbars under a freight car. [Middle English *rodd,* Old English *rodd.* See **rēt-** in Appendix.*]
rode. Past tense of **ride.**
ro·dent (rōd′ənt) *n.* Any of various mammals of the order Rodentia, such as a mouse, rat, squirrel, or beaver, characterized by large incisors adapted for gnawing or nibbling. *—adj.* **1.** Gnawing. **2.** Of or pertaining to rodents. [New Latin *Rodentia,* from Latin *rōdens,* present participle of *rōdere,* to gnaw. See **rēd-** in Appendix.*]
ro·de·o (rō′dē-ō′, rō-dā′ō) *n., pl.* **-os. 1.** A cattle roundup. **2.** An enclosure for keeping cattle that have been rounded up. **3.** A public entertainment including riding broncos, lassoing, and the like. [Spanish, from *rodear,* to surround, from Latin *rotāre,* to ROTATE.]
Rod·er·ick (rŏd′ə-rĭk). A masculine given name. [Medieval Latin *Rodericus,* from Old High German *Hroderich* : *Hrōd-,* fame (see **kar-**[2] in Appendix*) + *-rich,* rule (see **reg-**[1] in Appendix*).]
Rodg·ers (rŏj′ərz), **Richard.** Born 1902. American composer.
Ro·din (rō-dăN′), **(François) Auguste (René).** 1840–1917. French sculptor.
rod·o·mon·tade (rŏd′ə-mŏn-tād′, -täd′) *n.* Also **rhod·o·mon·tade.** Pretentious boasting or bragging; bluster. See Synonyms at **bombast.** *—adj.* Pretentiously boastful or bragging. *—intr.v.* **rodomontaded, -tading, -tades.** To boast or brag; to bluster; to rant. [Old French, from Italian *rodomontada,* from *rodomonte,* braggart, after *Rodomonte,* a boastful Moorish king in the epics *Orlando Innamorato* (1487) and *Orlando Furioso* (1516).]
roe[1] (rō) *n.* **1.** The egg-laden ovary of a fish. **2.** The egg mass of certain crustaceans, such as the lobster. **3. Soft roe** *(see).* [Middle English *roof, roughe, row,* from Middle Low German or Middle Dutch *roge.* See **krek-**[2] in Appendix.*]
roe[2] (rō) *n.* The **roe deer** *(see).*
Roeb·ling (rōb′lĭng), **John Augustus.** 1806–1869. German-born American civil engineer.
roe·buck (rō′bŭk′) *n.* A male roe deer.
roe deer. A rather small, delicately formed Eurasian deer, *Capreolus capreolus,* having a brownish coat and short, branched antlers in the male. Also called "roe." [*Roe,* Middle English *ro, ra(a),* Old English *rā, rāha.* See **rei-**[2] in Appendix.*]
roent·gen (rĕnt′gən, rŭnt′-) *n.* Also **rönt·gen.** *Symbol* **R** *Physics.* An obsolete unit of radiation dosage, equal to the quantity of ionizing radiation that will produce one electrostatic unit of electricity in one cubic centimeter of dry air at 0°C and standard atmospheric pressure. [After Wilhelm Konrad ROENTGEN.] **—roent′gen** *adj.*
Roent·gen (rĕnt′gən, rŭnt′-; *German* rœnt′gən), **Wilhelm Konrad.** Also **Rönt·gen.** 1845–1923. German physicist; discovered and studied x rays.
roent·gen·ize (rĕnt′gən-īz′, rŭnt′-) *tr.v.* **-ized, -izing, -izes.** To subject to the action of x rays. **—roent′gen·i·za′tion** *n.*
roentgeno-. Indicates x rays; for example, **roentgenography.** [From ROENTGEN.]
roent·gen·o·gram (rĕnt′gən-ə-grăm′, rŭnt′-) *n.* Also **roent·gen·o·graph** (rĕnt′gən-ə-grăf′, rŭnt′-, -gräf′). A photograph made with x rays. [ROENTGENO- + -GRAM.]
roent·gen·og·ra·phy (rĕnt′gən-ŏg′rə-fē, rŭnt′-) *n.* Photography with the use of x rays. [ROENTGENO- + -GRAPHY.] **—roent′gen·o·graph′ic** (rĕnt′gən-ə-grăf′ĭk) *adj.* **—roent′gen·o·graph′ic·al·ly** *adv.*
roent·gen·ol·o·gy (rĕnt′gən-ŏl′ə-jē, rŭnt′-) *n.* Radiology with x rays. [ROENTGENO- + -LOGY.] **—roent′gen·o·log′ic** (-ə-lŏj′ĭk), **roent′gen·o·log′i·cal** *adj.* **—roent′gen·o·log′i·cal·ly** *adv.* **—roent′gen·ol′o·gist** *n.*
roent·gen·o·scope (rĕnt′gən-ō-skōp′, rŭnt′-) *n.* A **fluoroscope** *(see).* [ROENTGENO- + -SCOPE.]
roent·gen·o·ther·a·py (rĕnt′gən-ō-thĕr′ə-pē, rŭnt′-) *n.* The therapeutic use of x rays in treating disease.
Roentgen ray. **X ray** *(see).*
ro·ga·tion (rō-gā′shən) *n.* **1.** *Usually plural. Ecclesiastical.* Solemn prayer or supplication, especially as chanted during the rites of the Rogation Days. **2. a.** The proposal of a law by tribune or consul to the people of ancient Rome for acceptance or rejection. **b.** A law proposed in this manner. [Middle English *rogacioun,* from Latin *rogātiō,* from *rogāre,* to ask, supplicate. See **reg-**[1] in Appendix.*]
Rogation Days. *Ecclesiastical.* The three days preceding Ascension Day, designated as days of special prayer.
ro·ga·to·ry (rŏ′gə-tôr′ē, -tōr′ē) *adj.* Requesting information; questioning. [French *rogatoire,* from Medieval Latin *rogātōrius,* from Latin *rogāre,* to ask, supplicate. See **reg-**[1] in Appendix.*]
Rog·er[1] (rŏj′ər) *interj.* Also **rog·er.** Used in radio communications to indicate message received. [From the name ROGER, used as code word for the letter *R* meaning *received.*]
Rog·er[2] (rŏj′ər). A masculine given name. [Middle English, from Old North French (superseding Old English *Hrothgar*), from Old High German *Hrōdgar* : *Hrōd-,* fame (see **kar-**[2] in Appendix*) + *gairu,* spear (see **ghaiso-** in Appendix*).]
Roger of Coverley. **Coverley, Sir Roger de** *(see).*
Rog·ers (rŏj′ərz), **Robert.** 1731–1795. American frontiersman; commander of rangers in French and Indian War.
Rog·ers (rŏj′ərz), **Will(iam Penn Adair).** 1879–1935. American humorist, actor, and author.
Ro·get (rō-zhā′), **Peter Mark.** 1779–1869. English physician and scholar; author of *Thesaurus of English Words and Phrases.*
rogue (rōg) *n.* **1.** An unprincipled person; a scoundrel or rascal. **2.** A person who is playfully mischievous; scamp. **3.** *Archaic.* A wandering beggar; vagrant or vagabond. **4.** A vicious and solitary animal, especially an elephant that has separated itself from its herd. **5.** An organism, especially a plant, that shows an undesirable variation from a standard. *—v.* **rogued, roguing, rogues.** *—tr.* **1.** To defraud. **2.** To remove (diseased or abnormal specimens) from a group of plants of the same variety. *—intr.* To remove undesired plant specimens. [Originally "beggar," probably variant of obsolete *roger,* possibly from Latin *rogāre,* to ask, beg. See **reg-**[1] in Appendix.*]
Rogue River (rōg). A river rising in the Cascade Range in southwestern Oregon and flowing about 200 miles to the Pacific Ocean.
ro·guer·y (rō′gər-ē) *n., pl.* **-ies. 1.** Behavior characteristic of a rogue; trickery. **2.** A mischievous act.

rogues' gallery. A collection of photographs of criminals maintained in police files and used for making identifications.
ro·guish (rō′gĭsh) *adj.* **1.** Dishonest; unprincipled. **2.** Playfully mischievous. —**ro′guish·ly** *adv.* —**ro′guish·ness** *n.*
roil (roil) *v.* **roiled, roiling, roils.** —*tr.* **1.** To make (a liquid) muddy or cloudy by stirring up sediment. **2.** To displease or disturb; irritate; vex. —*intr.* To be in a state of turbulence or agitation: *"and moodily watched Lake Michigan roil beneath an April storm"* (New York Times). [Origin obscure.]
roil·y (roi′lē) *adj.* **-ier, -iest. 1.** Muddy; cloudy. **2.** Agitated.
roist·er (rois′tər) *intr.v.* **-ered, -ering, -ers. 1.** To engage in boisterous merrymaking; revel noisily. **2.** To behave in a blustering manner; to swagger. [Probably from Old French *rustre,* churl, boor, alteration of *ruste,* rude, rough, churlish, from Latin *rūsticus,* RUSTIC.] —**roist′er·er** *n.* —**roist′er·ous** *adj.*
Ro·land[1] (rō′lənd). A masculine given name. [Middle English *Rowland,* from Old North French *Roland,* from Old High German *Hrōdland* : *Hrōd-* "fame" (see **kar-**[2] in Appendix*) + *lant,* land (see **lendh-**[2] in Appendix*).]
Ro·land[2] (rō′lənd; *French* rô-läɴ′). A legendary paladin and nephew of Charlemagne killed in the battle against the Saracens at Roncesvalles (A.D. 778).
role (rōl) *n.* Also **rôle. 1.** A character or part played by an actor in a dramatic performance. **2.** The characteristic and expected social behavior of an individual. **3.** A function or position. [French *rôle,* from Old French *ro(lle),* roll (on which a part is written), from Medieval Latin *ro(tu)lus, ro(tu)la,* roll of parchment, from Latin *rotulus,* small wheel. See **roll.**]
Rolfe (rŏlf), **John.** 1585–1622. English colonist in America; husband of Pocahontas.
roll (rōl) *v.* **rolled, rolling, rolls.** —*intr.* **1.** To move forward along a surface by revolving on an axis or by repeatedly turning over. **2.** To travel or be moved on wheels or rollers. **3.** To travel around or wander: *roll from town to town.* **4. a.** To travel or be carried in a vehicle. **b.** To be carried on a stream: *The logs rolled down the cascading river.* **5.** To gain momentum: *The political campaign began to roll.* **6.** To go by; elapse. Used with *on, away,* or *by: The hours rolled on.* **7.** To recur periodically; move as in cycles: *Summer has rolled around again.* **8.** To move in a periodic revolution, as a planet in its orbit. **9.** To turn over and over: *The puppy rolled in the mud.* **10.** To rotate: *His eyes rolled with fright.* **11.** To turn around or revolve on or as on an axis. **12.** To advance with a rising and falling motion; undulate: *The waves rolled toward shore.* **13.** To extend or appear to extend in gentle rises and falls: *The hills roll to the sea.* **14.** To move or rock from side to side, as a ship. Compare **pitch. 15.** To walk with a swaying, unsteady motion. **16.** To form, when being wound, the shape of a ball or cylinder: *Yarn rolls easily.* **17.** To become flattened by or as if by pressure applied by a roller. **18.** To make a deep, prolonged, surging sound, as thunder. **19.** To make a sustained, trilling sound, as certain birds. **20.** To beat a drum in a continuous series of short blows. —*tr.* **1.** To cause to move forward along a surface by revolving on an axis, or by repeatedly turning over. **2.** To move or push along on wheels or rollers: *roll the plane out of the hangar.* **3.** To impel or send onward in a steady, swelling motion: *The sea rolls its waves onto the sand.* **4.** To impart a swaying, rocking motion to: *Heavy seas rolled the ship.* **5.** To turn around or partly turn around; rotate: *roll one's eyes.* **6.** To pronounce or utter with a trill: *You must roll your "r's" in Spanish.* **7.** To utter or emit in full, swelling tones. **8.** To beat (a drum) with a continuous series of short blows. **9.** To wrap (something) round and round upon itself or around something else: *roll up a scroll.* **10. a.** To envelop or enfold in a covering: *roll laundry in a sheet.* **b.** To make by shaping into a ball or cylinder: *roll a cigarette.* **11.** To spread, compress, or flatten by applying pressure with a roller: *roll dough.* **12.** *Printing.* To apply ink to (type) with a roller or rollers. **13.** To throw (dice) in craps or other games. **14.** *Slang.* To rob (a drunken, sleeping, or otherwise helpless person). —See Synonyms at **turn.** —**roll in. 1.** To arrive in large numbers; pour in: *Volunteers are rolling in.* **2.** *Informal.* To arrive home, as after a long night of carousing. **3.** *Informal.* To abound in; wallow: *rolling in money.* —**roll one's own.** *Slang.* To make one's own cigarettes. —**roll out. 1.** To unroll and spread out. **2.** To make flat by rolling. —**roll the bones.** To cast the dice, especially in craps. —**roll up. 1.** *Informal.* To arrive in a vehicle. **2.** To amass; collect; accumulate: *roll up a fortune.* —*n.* **1.** The act or an instance of rolling. **2.** Anything rolled up in the form of a cylinder: *a roll of tape.* **3.** A quantity of something, such as cloth or wallpaper, rolled into a cylinder, often considered as a unit of measure. **4.** A piece of parchment or paper that may be or is rolled up; scroll. **5.** A register or catalogue. **6.** A list of names of persons belonging to a given group. **7.** A mass of something in cylindrical or rounded form: *a roll of tobacco.* **8. a.** A small rounded portion of bread. **b.** A cake made by rolling up dough on which a filling has been spread: *jelly roll.* **c.** Any food that is prepared by rolling up: *an egg roll.* **9.** A rolling, swaying, or rocking motion. **10.** A gentle swell or undulation of a surface: *the roll of the plains.* **11.** A deep reverberation or rumble. **12.** A rapid succession of short sounds: *the roll of a drum.* **13.** A trill: *the roll of his "r's."* **14.** A resonant, rhythmical flow of words. **15.** A roller; especially, a cylinder on which to roll something up or with which to flatten something. **16.** *Aviation.* A maneuver in which an airplane makes a single, complete rotation about its longitudinal axis without changing direction or losing altitude. **17.** *Slang.* Money; especially, a wad of paper money. —**strike off the rolls.** To deprive of membership; expel. [Middle English *rol(l)en,* from Old French *rol(l)er,* from Vulgar Latin *rotulāre* (unattested), from Latin *rotulus, rotula,* small wheel, from *rota,* wheel. See **ret-** in Appendix.*]
Rol·land (rô-läɴ′), **Romain.** 1866–1944. French author of novels, plays, essays, and biographies.
roll·a·way (rōl′ə-wā′) *adj.* Set upon rollers for easy moving and storing: *a rollaway bed.*
roll back. 1. To reduce (prices or wages) to a previous lower level. **2.** To cause to retreat; turn back.
roll·back (rōl′băk′) *n.* A reduction of prices or wages to a previous lower level by governmental action or direction.
roll call. 1. The reading aloud of a list of names of people, as in a classroom or military post, to determine who is absent. **2.** The time fixed for such a reading.
roll·er (rō′lər) *n.* **1.** One that rolls. **2.** Any of various cylindrical devices, specifically: **a.** A small, spokeless wheel, such as that of a roller skate or caster. **b.** An elongated cylinder upon which something is wound, such as a window shade or towel. **c.** A heavy cylinder used to perform leveling or crushing operations. **d.** *Printing.* A cylinder, usually of hard rubber, used to ink the type before the paper is impressed. **e.** A cylinder of wire mesh, foam rubber, or other material around which a strand of hair is wound to produce a soft curl or wave. **3.** A long, rolled bandage. **4.** A heavy, swelling wave that breaks on the coast. **5.** Any of various African, Far-Eastern, and Australian birds of the family Coraciidae, having bright-blue wings, stocky bodies, and hooked bills, and noted for their aggressiveness.
roller bearing. A bearing using rollers to reduce friction between machine parts.
roller coaster. A steep, sharply banked, elevated railway with small open passenger cars, operated as an amusement park entertainment.
roller skate. A skate having four small wheels instead of a runner, for skating on sidewalks and hard floors.
roll·er-skate (rō′lər-skāt′) *intr.v.* **-skated, -skating, -skates.** To skate on roller skates. —**roller skater.**
roll film. Photographic film rolled on a spool.
rol·lick (rŏl′ĭk) *intr.v.* **-licked, -licking, -licks.** To behave or move in a carefree, frolicsome manner; to romp. —*n.* A carefree escapade; a lark. [Probably a blend of ROMP or ROLL and FROLIC.] —**rol′lick·some, rol′lick·y** *adj.*
rol·lick·ing (rŏl′ĭk-ĭng) *adj.* Carefree and high-spirited; boisterous. —**rol′lick·ing·ly** *adv.*
rolling mill. 1. A factory in which metal is rolled into sheets, bars, or other forms. **2.** A machine used for rolling metal.
rolling pin. A smooth cylinder, usually of wood, with a handle at each end, used for rolling out dough.
rolling stock. A railroad's wheeled vehicles.
roll·mops (rōl′mŏps′) *n., pl.* **rollmops.** A marinated fillet of herring wrapped around a gherkin or onion and served as an hors d'oeuvre. [German *Rollmops* : *rollen,* to roll, from Middle High German, from Old French *roller,* from Vulgar Latin *rotulāre* (unattested), to ROLL + *Mops,* pug dog, from Low German *mops,* fool, pug dog (see **mu-** in Appendix*).]
Rol·lo (rŏl′ō). Also **Hrolf** (hrŏlf, rŏlf). 860?–931? Norse chieftain; first duke of Normandy and ancestor of Charlemagne.
roll-top desk (rōl′tŏp′). A desk fitted with a flexible, sliding top made of parallel slats.
roll·way (rōl′wā′) *n.* Any surface along which cylinders or objects on rollers may be moved.
Röl·vaag (rōl′väg), **Ole Edvart.** 1876–1931. Norwegian-born American author of novels in Norwegian about Western pioneer life.
ro·ly-po·ly (rō′lē-pō′lē) *adj.* Short and plump; pudgy. —*n., pl.* **roly-polies. 1.** A roly-poly creature. **2.** *Chiefly British.* A pudding made by rolling up jam or fruit in pastry dough and cooking it. [Perhaps from ROLL + POLL (head).]
ROM Airport code for Rome, Italy.
rom. roman (type).
Rom. 1. Roman. **2.** Romance (language). **3.** Romans (New Testament).
Ro·ma. The Italian name for **Rome.**
Ro·ma·gna (rō-män′yä). A historical region of north-central Italy, now part of Emilia-Romagna. It was the center of the Byzantine authority in Italy (A.D. 540–751).
Ro·ma·ic (rō-mā′ĭk) *n.* Modern vernacular Greek. [Modern Greek *Rhōmaikos,* from Greek, Roman (especially, of the eastern Roman Empire at Byzantium), from *Rhōmē, Rhōma,* Rome, from Latin *Rōma,* ROME.] —**Ro·ma′ic** *adj.*
ro·maine (rō-mān′) *n.* A variety of lettuce, *Lactuca sativa longifolia,* having long crisp leaves forming a slender head. Also called "cos," "cos lettuce." [French, from the feminine of *Romain,* Roman, from Old French, ROMAN.]
Ro·mains (rô-măɴ′), **Jules.** Pen name of Louis Farigoule. Born 1885. French author of novels, poetry, and plays.
ro·man[1] (rô-mäɴ′) *n. French.* A metrical narrative of medieval France derived from the ancient epic poems.
ro·man[2] (rō′mən) *n.* Also **Ro·man,** *Abbr.* **rom.** The most common style of type, characterized by upright letters having serifs and vertical lines thicker than horizontal lines. This definition is printed in roman. Compare **italic.** —*adj.* Also **Ro·man.** *Abbr.* **rom.** Of, set, or printed in roman. [It represents the style used in ancient Roman inscriptions and manuscripts.]
Ro·man (rō′mən) *adj. Abbr.* **Rom. 1.** Of, pertaining to, derived from, or characteristic of Rome and its people, especially ancient Rome. **2.** Of, in, pertaining to, or characteristic of the Latin language. **3.** Of or pertaining to the Roman Catholic Church. **4.** Of or designating an architectural style developed by the ancient Romans, characterized by great, round arches and barrel vaults, concrete masonry construction, and classical

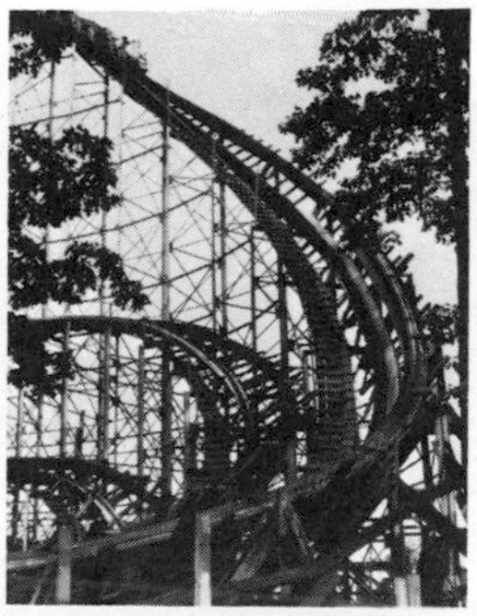
roller coaster

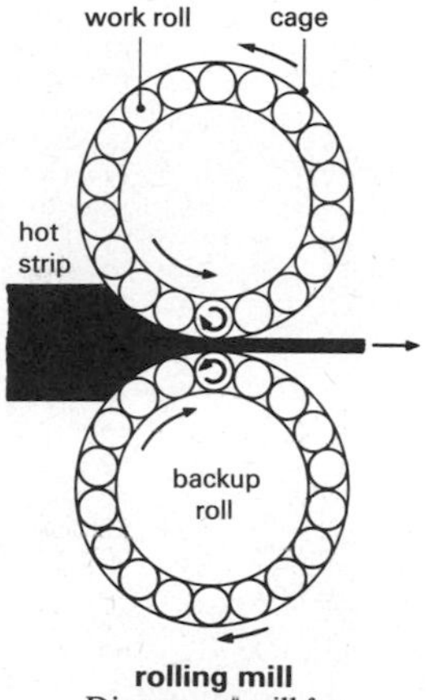
work roll
cage
hot strip
backup roll
rolling mill
Diagram of mill for rolling hot metal

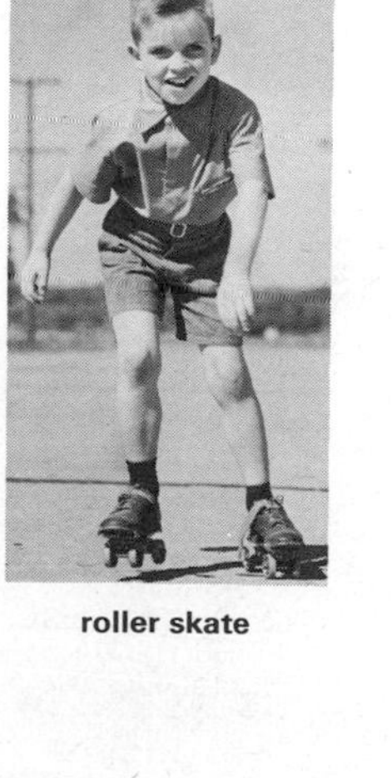
roller skate

orders as decorative features. —*n. Abbr.* **Rom.** **1.** A native, resident, or citizen of Rome, especially ancient Rome. **2.** The Italian language as spoken in Rome. **3.** The language of the ancient Romans; Latin. **4.** One belonging to the Roman Catholic Church. Sometimes used disparagingly. [Middle English *Roman* and *Romain*, respectively from Old English *Rōmān*, a Roman, and Old French *Romain*, Roman, a Roman, both from Latin *Rōmānus*, from *Rōma*, ROME.]
ro·man à clef (rô-mäɴ' à klĕ') *pl.* **romans à clef** (rô-mäɴ' à klĕ'). *French.* A novel in which actual persons or places are depicted in fictional guise. Literally, novel with a key.
Roman alphabet. The **Latin alphabet** *(see).*
Roman calendar. The lunar calendar used by the ancient Romans until the introduction of the Julian calendar in 46 B.C. See **calendar.**
Roman candle. A firework consisting of a tube from which balls of fire are ejected. [Originated in Italy.]
Roman Catholic. *Abbr.* **R.C.** **1.** Of, designating, or pertaining to the Roman Catholic Church. **2.** A member of the Roman Catholic Church.
Roman Catholic Church. *Abbr.* **R.C.Ch.** The Christian church that is characterized by a hierarchic structure of bishops and priests in which doctrinal and disciplinary authority are dependent upon apostolic succession, with the pope as head of the episcopal college. Also called "Catholic Church," "Church of Rome."
Roman Catholicism. The doctrines, practices, and organization of the Roman Catholic Church.
ro·mance (rō-măns', rō'măns) *n.* **1.** A long, medieval narrative in prose or verse, telling of the adventures of chivalric heroes. **2.** Any long, fictitious tale of heroes and extraordinary or mysterious events. **3.** The class of literature of such tales. **4.** A quality suggestive of the adventure and idealized exploits found in such tales: *"These fine old guns often have a romance clinging to them"* (Richard Jefferies). **5.** A novel, story, or film dealing with a love affair. **6.** The class or style of fictional works about idealized love. **7. a.** A love affair. **b.** Love; romantic involvement. **c.** A strong, usually short-lived attachment or enthusiasm. **8.** Inclination toward the romantic or adventurous; romantic spirit. **9.** A fictitiously embellished account or explanation. **10.** A short, lyrical song or instrumental piece. —*v.* (rō-măns') **romanced, -mancing, -mances.** —*intr.* **1.** To invent, write, or tell romances. **2.** To think or behave in a romantic manner. —*tr. Informal.* To make romantic love to; woo. [Middle English *roma(u)ns, roma(u)nce*, French, work written in French, from Old French *romanz, romant*, from Vulgar Latin *Rōmānicē* (unattested), in the Roman manner, from Latin *Rōmānicus*, Roman, made in Rome, from *Rōmānus*, ROMAN.] —**ro·manc'er** *n.*
Ro·mance (rō-măns', rō'măns) *adj. Abbr.* **Rom.** Of, designating, or belonging to any of the languages that developed from Vulgar Latin, the principal ones being French, Italian, Portuguese, Rumanian, and Spanish. Other Romance languages are Catalan, Provençal, Rhaeto-Romanic, and Sardinian. —*n.* The Romance languages. [From ROMANCE (French, "the Roman tongue").]
Ro·manche Deep (rō-mänsh'). An ocean depth of over 25,000 feet in the Atlantic, at the equator.
Roman Empire. The empire of the ancient Romans, established in 27 B.C. by Augustus and continuing until A.D. 395, when it became divided into the Western Roman Empire, with the capital at Rome, and the Eastern Roman Empire, with the capital at Constantinople.
Ro·man·esque (rō'mən-ĕsk') *adj.* **1.** Of, pertaining to, or designating a transitional style of European architecture prevalent from the 9th to the 12th century. **2.** Of, pertaining to, or designating corresponding styles in painting and sculpture. —*n.* This style of architecture, painting, or sculpture. [From ROMAN.]
ro·man-fleuve (rô-män'flœv') *n., pl.* **romans-fleuves** (rô-män'flœv'). A long novel, often in many volumes, chronicling the history of several generations of a family, community, or other group. Also called "saga novel." [French, "river-novel" (because the development of its plot is now rapid, now slow, like the flow of a river), coined by Romain Rolland.]
Roman holiday. A time of enjoyment derived from the suffering of others. [So called from the gladiatorial contests staged as entertainment for the ancient Romans.]
Ro·mâ·nia. The Rumanian name for **Rumania.**
Ro·man·i·an. Variant of **Rumanian.**
Ro·man·ic (rō-măn'ĭk) *adj.* **1.** Of or derived from the ancient Romans or their language. **2.** Of or pertaining to the Romance languages. [Latin *Rōmānicus*, from *Rōmānus*, ROMAN.]
Ro·man·ism (rō'mən-ĭz'əm) *n* Roman Catholicism. Usually used disparagingly.
Ro·man·ist (rō'mən-ĭst) *n.* **1.** One who professes Roman Catholicism. Usually used disparagingly. **2.** A student of or authority on Roman law, culture, and institutions.
Ro·man·ize (rō'mən-īz') *tr.v.* **-ized, -izing, -izes.** **1.** To convert (someone) to Roman Catholicism. **2.** To make Roman in character, allegiance, or style. **3.** To write or transliterate in the Latin alphabet. —**Ro'man·i·za'tion** *n.*
Roman law. The system of laws of ancient Rome, upon which the legal systems of many countries are based.
Roman nose. A nose with a high, prominent bridge.
Roman numeral. One of the letters employed in the ancient Roman system of numeration. The system is now used in certain formal contexts, as for dates on monuments; for distinctively separate numeration, as for the pagination of the front matter of a book; and as a subsidiary system in composite numeration, as *section 3.a.viii.*

Roman numeral

I	1
II	2
III	3
IV	4
V	5
VI	6
VII	7
VIII	8
IX	9
X	10
XI	11
XII	12
XIII	13
XIV	14
XV	15
XVI	16
XVII	17
XVIII	18
XIX	19
XX	20
XXI	21
XXIX	29
XXX	30
XL	40
XLVIII	48
IL	49
L	50
LX	60
XC	90
XCVIII	98
IC	99
C	100
CI	101
CC	200
D	500
DC	600
CM	900
M	1,000
MDCLXVI	1666
MCMLXX	1970

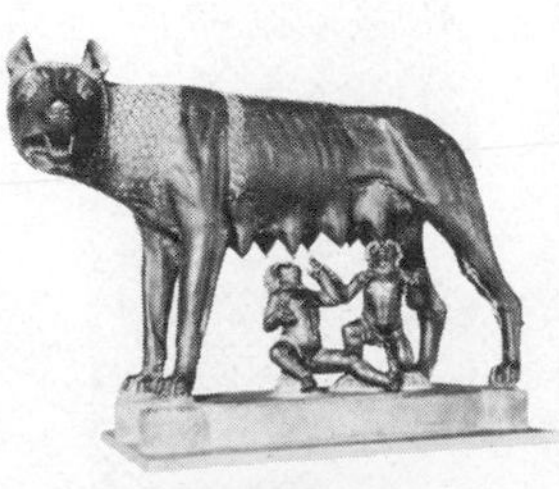

Romulus
She-wolf (Etruscan) with twins (added about 1500)

Ro·ma·no. See **Giulio Romano.**
Ro·ma·nov (rō-mä'nəf, rō'mə-nŏf). Also **Ro·ma·noff.** Family name of a Russian ruling dynasty (1613–1917).
Ro·mans (rō'mənz) *n.* Plural in form, used with a singular verb. *Abbr.* **Rom.** A book of the New Testament, an epistle of Saint Paul to the Christians of Rome.
Ro·mansch (rō-mänsh', rō-mänsh') *n.* Also **Ro·mansh.** The Rhaeto-Romanic dialects spoken in eastern Switzerland and in neighboring parts of Italy. [Romansch *Ruman(t)sch, Roman(t)sch*, "Roman," "Romance language," from Vulgar Latin *Rōmānicē* (unattested), in the Roman manner, in the Roman tongue. See **romance.**]
ro·man·tic (rō-măn'tĭk) *adj.* **1.** Of, pertaining to, or characteristic of romance. **2.** Given to thoughts or feelings of romance. **3.** Conducive to romance. **4.** Imaginative but impractical: *romantic notions.* **5.** Not based on fact; imaginary. **6.** Of or characteristic of romanticism in the arts. —*n.* **1.** A romantic person. **2.** A romanticist. [French *romantique*, from Old French *romant, romanz*, ROMANCE.] —**ro·man'ti·cal·ly** *adv.*
ro·man·ti·cism (rō-măn'tə-sĭz'əm) *n.* **1.** A literary and artistic movement originating in Europe toward the end of the 18th century that sought to assert the validity of subjective experience and to escape from the prevailing subordination of content and feeling to classical forms. **2.** The spirit and attitudes characteristic of romantic thought. —**ro·man'ti·cist** *n.*
ro·man·ti·cize (rō-măn'tə-sīz') *v.* **-cized, -cizing, -cizes.** —*tr.* To interpret romantically. —*intr.* To think in a romantic way.
Rom·a·ny (rŏm'ə-nē, rō'mə-) *n., pl.* **Romany** or **-nies.** Also **Rom·ma·ny.** **1.** A Gypsy **2.** The Indic language spoken by the Gypsies; Gypsy. —*adj.* Of or pertaining to the Gypsies, their culture, or their language. [Romany *romani*, plural of *romano*, gypsy, from *rom*, man, husband, gypsy man, from Sanskrit *ḍomba, ḍoma*, man of a low caste of musicians, from Dravidian, akin to Telegu *ṭamaṭama*, drum.]
ro·maunt (rō-mänt') *n. Archaic.* A verse romance. [Middle English, from Old French *romant, romanz*, ROMANCE.]
Rom·blon (rôm-blôn'). A province of the Republic of the Philippines comprising a group of the Visayan Islands. Capital, Romblon, on Romblon Island.
Rome[1] (rōm). **1.** *Italian* **Ro·ma** (rō'mä). The capital of Italy, on the Tiber in the west-central part of the country. It is the site of Vatican City, and was formerly the capital of the Roman Republic, the Roman Empire, and the Papal States. Population, 2,445,000. **2.** A city and cotton-marketing center in northwestern Georgia. Population, 32,000. **3.** An industrial city in central New York State. Population, 52,000. [Middle English *Rome*, Old English *Rome*, from Old French, from Latin *Rōma*, probably of Etruscan origin.]
Rome[2] (rōm) *n.* The Roman Catholic Church.
Ro·me·o (rō'mē-ō) *n., pl.* **-os.** A male lover. [After the tragic hero of Shakespeare's *Romeo and Juliet.*]
Rom·ford (rŭm'fərd, rŏm'-). A former administrative division of London, England, now part of **Havering** *(see).*
Rom·ish (rō'mĭsh) *adj.* Of or pertaining to the Roman Catholic Church. Often used disparagingly.
Rom·mel (rŏm'əl), **Erwin.** 1891–1944. German army officer.
Rom·ney (rŭm'nē). One of the **Cinque Ports** *(see).*
Rom·ney (rŏm'nē, rŭm'-), **George.** 1734–1802. English painter of portraits and historical scenes.
romp (rŏmp) *intr.v.* **romped, romping, romps.** **1.** To play or frolic boisterously. **2.** *Slang.* To win a race easily. —*n.* **1.** Lively, merry play; frolic. **2.** One who sports and frolics, especially a girl. **3.** *Slang.* An easy win. [Variant of RAMP (to rage).]
romp·er (rŏm'pər) *n.* **1.** One who romps; especially, a small child. **2.** *Plural.* A loose-fitting playsuit with short bloomers.
Ro·mu·lo (rŏm'yōō-lō), **Carlos Pena.** Born 1899. Philippine educator, journalist, army officer, author, and diplomat.
Rom·u·lus (rŏm'yə-ləs). *Roman Mythology.* The son of Mars and a vestal virgin, who, with his twin brother Remus, was abandoned as an infant to die but was raised by a she-wolf. He later killed Remus, founded Rome in 753 B.C., and became the first king of Rome.
Ron·ald (rŏn'əld). A masculine given name. [Scottish, from Old Norse *Rögnvaldr* : *rögn*, "decreeing powers," gods, plural of *regin*, decree (see **rēk-** in Appendix*) + *valdr*, ruler (see **wal-** in Appendix*).]
Ron·ces·valles (rŏn'sə-vălz; *Spanish* rôn-thĕz-vä'lyĕs). *French* **Ronce·vaux** (rôɴs-vō'). A village in Navarre, northern Spain, near the Pass of Roncesvalles through the Pyrenees, which has long served as an invasion and pilgrimage route.
ron·deau (rŏn'dō, rŏn-dō') *n., pl.* **-deaux** (-dōz, -dōz'). **1.** A lyrical poem of French origin having 13 or, sometimes, 10, lines with two rhymes throughout, and with the opening phrase repeated twice as a refrain. Also called "roundel." **2.** *Music.* A monophonic trouvère song. [Old French, variant of RONDEL.]
ron·del (rŏn'dəl, -dĕl) *n.* A rondeau that usually has 14 lines. Also called "roundel." [Middle English, from Old French, "small circle" (from the repetition of the first lines at the end of the poem), from *ronde, rounde*, ROUND.]
ron·de·let (rŏn'də-lĕt) *n.* A short rondeau having five or seven lines and one refrain in one stanza. [Old French, diminutive of RONDEL.]
ron·do (rŏn'dō, rŏn-dō') *n.* A musical composition having a refrain that occurs at least three times in its original key between contrasting couplets. [Italian *rondò*, from French *rondeau*, RONDEAU.]
Ron·dô·nia (rōn-dōn'yə). Formerly **Gua·po·ré** (gwä-pə-rā). A

federal territory occupying 96,986 square miles in western Brazil. Population, 2,602,000. Capital, Porto Velho.

ron·dure (rŏn′jər) *n.* Something circular or gracefully rounded. [Old French *rondeur,* from *rond, rounde,* ROUND.]

Ron·sard (rôN-sär′), **Pierre de.** 1524–1585. French poet.

rönt·gen. Variant of **roentgen.**

Rönt·gen, Wilhelm Konrad. See **Roentgen.**

rood (ro͞od) *n.* **1.** A crucifix symbolizing the cross on which Christ was crucified. **2.** Any cross or crucifix. **3.** A large crucifix or the representation of one over the altar screen of a medieval church. **4.** *Abbr.* **ro.** *British.* A measure of length that varies from 5½ to 8 yards. **5.** *Abbr.* **ro.** A measure of land equal to ¼ acre or 40 square rods. [Middle English *ro(o)d,* Old English *rōd,* rod, cross. See **rēt-** in Appendix.*]

Roo·de·poort-Ma·rais·burg (ro͞o′də-po͝ort′mə-rāz′bûrg). A city in southern Transvaal, Republic of South Africa, 12 miles west of Johannesburg. Population, 95,000.

rood screen. An ornamented altar screen, usually surmounted by a crucifix, separating the choir of a church from the nave.

roof (ro͞of, ro͝of) *n.* **1.** The exterior surface and its supporting structures on the top of a building. **2.** The top covering of anything: *the roof of a car.* **3.** A house or home. **—raise the roof.** *Slang.* **1.** To be extremely noisy and boisterous. **2.** To complain loudly and bitterly. *—tr.v.* **roofed, roofing, roofs.** To furnish or cover with a roof. [Middle English *ro(o)f,* Old English *hrōf.* See **krapo-** in Appendix.*]

roof·er (ro͞o′fər, ro͝of′ər) *n.* One who lays or repairs roofs.

roof garden. **1.** A garden on the roof of a building. **2.** A restaurant on the roof of a building

roof·ing (ro͞o′fĭng, ro͝of′ĭng) *n.* **1.** The act of constructing a roof. **2.** A roof. **3.** Materials used in building a roof.

roof·less (ro͞of′lĭs, ro͝of′lĭs) *adj.* **1.** Lacking a roof. **2.** Having no home or shelter; homeless; destitute.

roof·tree (ro͞of′trē′, ro͝of′-) *n.* **1.** A long horizontal beam extending along the ridge of a roof; ridgepole. **2.** A roof.

rook[1] (ro͝ok) *n.* A crowlike Old World bird, *Corvus frugilegus,* that nests in colonies near the tops of trees. *—tr.v.* **rooked, rooking, rooks.** *Slang.* To swindle. [Middle English *rok, ruke,* Old English *hrōc.* See **ker-**[2] in Appendix.*]

rook[2] (ro͝ok) *n. Abbr.* **R** A chess piece that may move in a straight line over any number of empty squares in a rank or file. Also called "castle." [Middle English *rok(e),* from Old French *roc(k),* from Arabic *rukh,* from Persian *rukh*†.]

rook·er·y (ro͝ok′ər-ē) *n., pl.* **-ies.** **1.** A place where rooks nest and breed. **2.** The breeding ground of certain other birds and animals, such as seals. **3.** *Informal.* A crowded tenement.

rook·ie (ro͝ok′ē) *n. Slang.* **1.** An untrained recruit. **2.** A novice player in baseball. **3.** Any inexperienced person. [Alteration of RECRUIT (influenced by the bird ROOK).]

room (ro͞om, ro͝om) *n. Abbr.* **rm.** **1.** A space that is or may be occupied by something; open space: *a desk that takes up too much room.* **2.** An area separated by walls or partitions from other similar parts of the structure or building in which it is located. **3.** The people present in such an area: *The whole room laughed.* **4.** *Plural.* Living quarters. **5.** Suitable opportunity: *room for error.* *—intr.v.* **roomed, rooming, rooms.** To occupy a room; to live or lodge. **—room in.** To live at the home where one is employed as a servant. [Middle English *roum,* Old English *rūm.* See **rewe-** in Appendix.*]

room·er (ro͞o′mər, ro͝om′ər) *n.* A lodger.

room·ette (ro͞o-mĕt′, ro͝om-ĕt′) *n.* A small private compartment in a railroad sleeping car.

room·ful (ro͞om′fo͝ol′, ro͝om′-) *n., pl.* **-fuls.** **1.** As much or as many as a room will hold. **2.** The number of people in a room.

rooming house. A house where lodgers may rent rooms.

room·mate (ro͞om′māt′, ro͝om′-) *n.* A person with whom one shares a room or apartment.

room·y (ro͞o′mē, ro͝om′ē) *adj.* **-ier, -iest.** Having plenty of room; spacious; large. **—room′i·ly** *adv.* **—room′i·ness** *n.*

roor·back (ro͝or′băk′) *n.* A false or slanderous story used for political advantage. [After Baron von *Roorback,* fictional author of an imaginary *Roorback's Tour Through the Western and Southern States,* from which a passage was quoted before the Presidential election of 1844 in an attempt to disparage candidate James K. Polk.]

Roo·se·velt (rō′zə-vĕlt, rōz′vĕlt, -vəlt), **(Anna) Eleanor.** 1884–1962. American diplomat, writer, humanitarian, and political figure; wife of Franklin Delano Roosevelt.

Roo·se·velt (rō′zə-vĕlt, rōz′vĕlt, -vəlt), **Franklin Delano.** 1882–1945. Thirty-second President of the United States (1933–45).

Roo·se·velt (rō′zə-vĕlt, rōz′vĕlt, -vəlt), **Theodore.** 1858–1919. Twenty-sixth President of the United States (1901–09).

Roo·se·velt Dam (rō′zə-vĕlt, rōz′vĕlt, -vəlt). A dam, 280 feet high and 1,080 feet long, on the Salt River in central Arizona, forming the Roosevelt Reservoir.

roost (ro͞ost) *n.* **1.** A perch on which domestic fowls or other birds rest or sleep. **2.** A place with perches for fowls or other birds. **3.** A place for temporary rest or sleep. **—rule the roost.** To be in charge; dominate. *—intr.v.* **roosted, roosting, roosts.** To rest or sleep on a perch or roost. [Middle English *rooste,* Old English *hrōst.* See **kred-** in Appendix.*]

roost·er (ro͞os′tər) *n.* **1.** The adult male of the common domestic fowl. **2.** The adult male of other birds; a cock. **3.** A pugnacious and cocky person.

root[1] (ro͞ot′, ro͝ot) *n.* **1. a.** The usually underground portion of a plant that serves as support, draws food and water from the surrounding soil, and stores food. **b.** Any similar underground plant part, such as a rhizome, corm, or tuber. **c.** One of many small, hairlike growths that serve to attach and support plants such as the ivy and other vines. **2.** The embedded part of an organ or structure such as a hair, tooth, or nerve. **3.** Any base or support. **4.** An essential part or element; a basic core. **5.** A primary source; origin. **6.** An antecedent or ancestor. **7.** The condition of being settled and of belonging to a particular place or society: *put down roots in a new town.* **8.** *Linguistics.* **a.** In etymology, a word or word element from which other words are formed. **b.** In morphology, a base to which prefixes and suffixes may be added. Also called "radical." **9.** *Mathematics.* **a.** A number that when multiplied by itself an indicated number of times forms a product equal to a specified number: *a fourth root of 4 is* $\sqrt{2}$. Also "numerical root," "*n*th root." **b.** A number that reduces a polynomial equation in one variable to an identity when it is substituted for the variable. **c.** A root *a* of the polynomial equation $f(x) = 0$ in which $(x\text{-}a)$ occurs at least twice as a factor of $f(x)$. Also called "multiple root." **10.** *Music.* **a.** The note from which a chord is built. **b.** The first or lowest note of a triad or chord. —See Synonyms at **origin.** **—take root.** **1.** To put forth roots and begin to grow. **2.** To become firmly fixed or established. *—v.* **rooted, rooting, roots.** *—intr.* **1.** To grow a root or roots. **2.** To become firmly established, settled, or entrenched. **3.** To come into existence; originate: *"Men's ideas root pretty far back."* (Clarence Darrow). *—tr.* **1.** To cause to put out roots and grow. **2.** To implant by or as if by the roots. **3.** To furnish a primary source or origin to. **4.** To pull or dig up by or as if by the roots. Used with *up* or *out.* [Middle English *rot(e),* Old English *rōt,* from Old Norse. See **wrād-** in Appendix.*] **—root′er** *n.*

root[2] (ro͞ot, ro͝ot) *v.* **rooted, rooting, roots.** *—tr.* To dig with or as with the snout or nose. *—intr.* **1.** To dig in the earth with or as with the snout or nose. **2.** To rummage for something. [Alteration (influenced by ROOT of a plant) of earlier *wroot,* Middle English *wroten,* Old English *wrōtan.* See **wrōd-** in Appendix.*] **—root′er** *n.*

root[3] (ro͞ot, ro͝ot) *intr.v.* **rooted, rooting, roots.** **1.** To give encouragement to a contestant or team; cheer. Used with *for.* **2.** To lend support to someone or something. Used with *for.* [Perhaps from ROOT (to dig with the snout).] **—root′er** *n.*

Root (ro͞ot), **Elihu.** 1845–1937. American lawyer and government official; Secretary of State (1905–09).

root·age (ro͞o′tĭj, ro͝ot-ĭj) *n.* **1.** A system or growth of roots. **2.** Establishment by or as if by roots.

root beer. A carbonated soft drink made from extracts of the roots of several plants.

root canal. A pulp-filled cavity in a root of a tooth.

root cap. *Botany.* A thimble-shaped mass of cells that covers and protects the tip of a growing root.

root cellar. A cellar, usually covered with earth, used for the storage of root crops and other vegetables.

root hair. *Botany.* A thin, hairlike outgrowth of a plant root, that absorbs water and minerals from the soil

root·less (ro͞ot′lĭs, ro͝ot′-) *adj.* **1.** Having no roots: *a rootless tooth.* **2.** Not belonging to a particular place or society: *the rootless refugees in a strange country.* **—root′less·ness** *n.*

root·let (ro͞ot′lĭt, ro͝ot′-) *n.* A small root or division of a root.

root mean square. *Abbr.* **rms** The square root of the arithmetic mean of the squares of a set of numbers.

root·stalk (ro͞ot′stôk′, ro͝ot′-) *n.* A plant part, a **rhizome** *(see).*

root·stock (ro͞ot′stŏk′, ro͝ot′-) *n.* **1.** A rootlike stem, a **rhizome** *(see).* **2.** A source or origin.

root·y (ro͞o′tē, ro͝ot′ē) *adj.* **-ier, -iest.** **1.** Full of roots. **2.** Consisting of a root or roots. **3.** Resembling roots. **—root′i·ness** *n.*

rope (rōp) *n.* **1.** A flexible, heavy cord of twisted hemp or other fiber. **2.** A cord with a noose at one end for hanging a person. **3.** Death by hanging. **4.** A lasso or lariat. **5.** *Plural.* Several cords strung between poles to enclose a boxing ring. **6.** Any string of items attached in one line by twisting or braiding: *a rope of onions.* **7.** A sticky glutinous formation of stringy matter in a liquid. **—know the ropes.** To be experienced with the details of an operation. **—on the ropes.** **1.** Knocked against the ropes that form the boxing ring. **2.** *Slang.* Nearing total collapse or ruin. *—v.* **roped, roping, ropes.** *—tr.* **1.** To tie or fasten with or as with rope. **2.** To enclose with a rope. Usually used with *off.* **3.** To catch with a rope or lasso. **4.** *Informal.* To trick or deceive. Usually used with *in.* *—intr.* To become ropy and sticky. [Middle English *rop(e),* Old English *rāp.* See **rei-**[1] in Appendix.*]

rope tow. A ski tow consisting of an endless rope.

rope·walk (rōp′wôk′) *n.* **1.** A long, usually covered path or alley where ropes are made. **2.** A long, narrow building containing such a path.

rop·y (rō′pē) *adj.* **-ier, -iest.** **1.** Resembling a rope or ropes. **2.** Forming sticky glutinous strings or threads, as some liquids. **—rop′i·ly** *adv.* **—rop′i·ness** *n.*

roque (rōk) *n.* A difficult form of croquet played on a hard court. [Alteration of CROQUET.]

Roque·fort (rōk′fərt; *French* rôk-fôr′). Full name, **Roque·fort-sur-Soul·zon** (rôk′fôr′sür-so͞ol′zôN′). A village in southern France, the center of manufacture of Roquefort cheese.

Roquefort cheese. A French cheese made from goat's and ewe's milk, and containing a blue mold, *Penicillium roqueforti.*

roqu·e·laure (rŏk′ə-lôr, rŏk′lôr, -lōr) *n.* A man's knee-length cloak popular during the 18th and early 19th century. [After Antoine Gaston Jean-Baptiste, Duc de *Roquelaure* (1656–1738), French marshal.]

Ro·rai·ma (rō-rī′mə). Formerly **Ri·o Bran·co** (rē′ō brăng′kō). A federal territory occupying 97,438 square miles in extreme northern Brazil. Population, 37,000. Capital, Boa Vista.

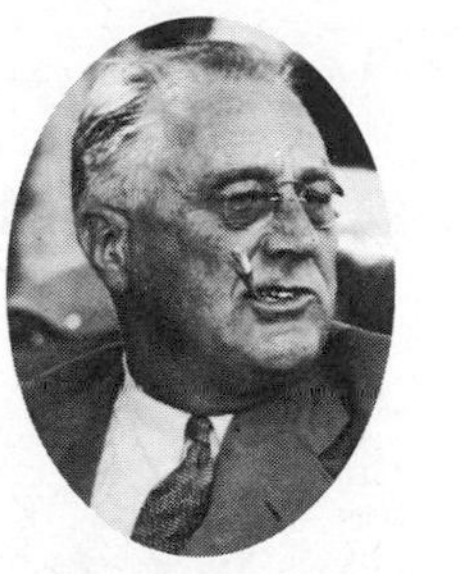

Franklin Delano Roosevelt

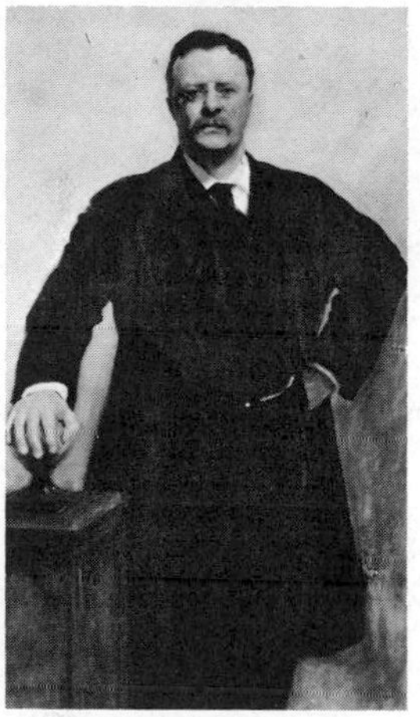

Theodore Roosevelt
Portrait by
John Singer Sargent

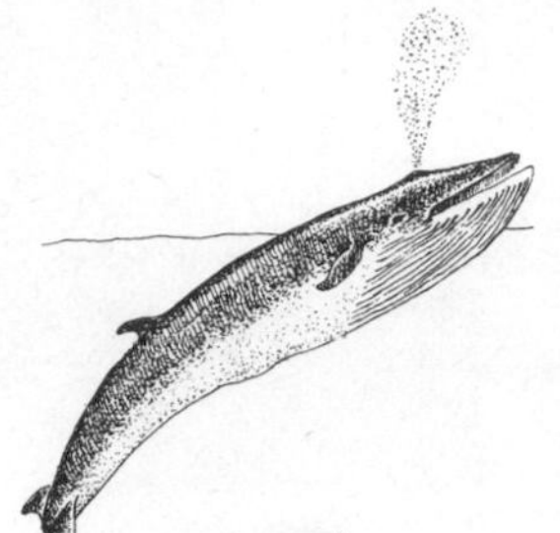

rorqual
Balaenoptera borealis

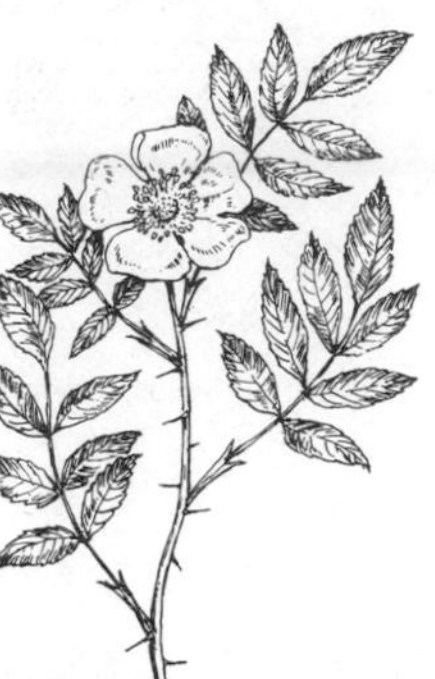

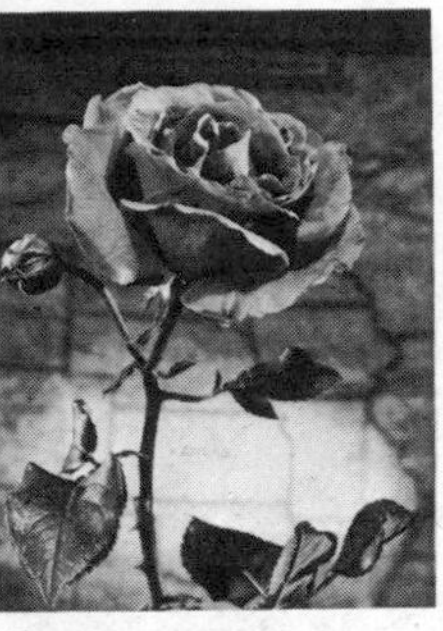

rose[1]
Above: Rosa carolina, a wild rose
Below: Cultivated hybrid tea rose "President Eisenhower"

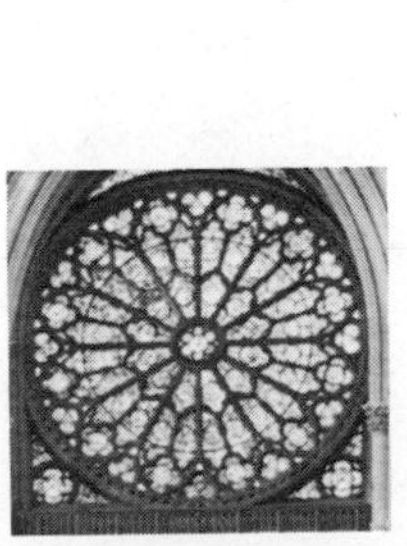

rose window
Reims Cathedral, France

ror·qual (rôr′kwəl) *n.* Any of several whalebone-bearing whales of the genus *Balaenoptera,* having longitudinal grooves on the throat, and a small, pointed dorsal fin. Also called "finback," "razorback." [French, from Norwegian *røhrval,* from Old Norse *reytharhvalr* : *reythr,* rorqual, "red whale" (from its red streaks), from *rauthr,* red (see **reudh-** in Appendix*) + *hvalr,* whale (see **skwalo-** in Appendix*).]

Ror·schach test (rôr′shäk, -shäkh, rōr′-). A psychological projective test of personality in which a subject's interpretations of ten standard abstract designs are analyzed as a measure of emotional and intellectual functioning and integration. [Devised by Hermann *Rorschach* (1884–1922), Swiss psychiatrist.]

Ro·sa, Mon·te (mŏn′tā rō′zə). The highest mountain (15,203 feet) in the Pennine Alps, on the border between Italy and Switzerland.

ro·sa·ceous (rō-zā′shəs) *adj.* **1.** *Botany.* Of or belonging to the Rosaceae, the plant family that includes the roses. **2.** Resembling the flower of a rose. [From New Latin *Rosaceae,* from Latin *rosāceus,* made of roses : ROSE + -ACEOUS.]

ros·an·i·line (rō-zăn′ə-lĭn) *n.* Also **ros·an·i·lin** (-lĭn). A brownish-red crystalline organic compound, $C_{20}H_{21}N_3O$, derived from aniline and used in the manufacture of dyes. [ROSE (flower) + ANILINE.]

Ro·sa·rio (rō-sä′ryō). A city and trade center of Argentina on the Paraná, about 170 miles northwest of Buenos Aires. Population, 604,000.

ro·sa·ry (rō′zə-rē) *n., pl.* **-ries. 1.** *Roman Catholic Church.* **a.** A form of devotion to the Virgin Mary, consisting of three sets of five decades each of the "Hail Mary," each decade preceded by an "Our Father" and ending with a "Glory Be to the Father." **b.** A string of beads on which these prayers are counted. **2.** Similar beads used by other religious groups. [Medieval Latin *rosārium,* the rosary beads (representing the crown of roses of the Virgin), from Latin, rose garden, from *rosa,* ROSE.]

rosary pea. A woody vine, *Abrus precatorius,* of tropical Asia, having scarlet, black-spotted, poisonous seeds that are used as beads. Also called "Indian licorice," "jequirity bean."

Ros·com·mon (rŏs-kŏm′ən). **1.** A county in west-central Ireland. Population, 59,000. **2.** The seat of this county. Population, 2,000.

rose[1] (rōz) *n.* **1.** Any of numerous shrubs or vines of the genus *Rosa,* usually having prickly stems, compound leaves, and variously colored, often fragrant flowers. **2.** The flower of any of these plants, occurring in a wide variety of colors, such as pink, red, yellow, and white. **3.** Any of various plants related to or resembling the rose. **4.** A dark pink to purplish pink, to moderate red or purplish red. It covers a variable range of medium lightness and moderate saturation. See **color. 5.** A rosy color of the cheeks. **6.** An ornament resembling a rose in form; a rosette. **7.** A perfume obtained from or having the odor of roses. **8.** A perforated nozzle for spraying water from a hose or sprinkling can. **9. a.** A form of gem cut, marked by a flat base and a faceted, hemispheric upper surface. **b.** A diamond so cut. **10.** A **rose window** *(see).* **11.** A **compass card** *(see).* —*adj.* Rose-colored. [Middle English *rose,* Old English *rose, rōse,* from Latin *rosa.* See **wrod-** in Appendix.*]

rose[2]. Past tense of **rise.**

ro·sé (rō-zā′) *n.* A pink, light wine made from red grapes from which the skins are removed during fermentation. [French "pink," from Old French *rose,* rosy, a rose, from Latin *rosa,* ROSE.]

Rose (rōz), **William Cumming.** Born 1887. American biochemist; experimented with amino acids.

rose acacia. A shrub, *Robinia hispida,* of the southern United States, having brittle, bristly branches and clusters of rose-colored flowers.

ro·se·ate (rō′zē-ĭt, -āt′) *adj.* **1.** Rose-colored. **2.** Cheerful; optimistic; rosy. [From Latin *roseus,* from *rosa,* ROSE.] —**ro′se·ate·ly** *adv.*

rose·bay (rōz′bā′) *n.* **1.** Any of several shrubs of the genus *Rhododendron;* especially, *R. maximum,* of northeastern North America, having large, glossy leaves and clusters of white or pink flowers. This species is also called "great laurel." **2.** A shrub, the **oleander** *(see).* **3.** *Chiefly British.* A plant, the **willow herb** *(see).*

rose-breast·ed grosbeak (rōz′brĕs′tĭd). A North American bird, *Pheucticus ludovicianus,* the male of which is black and white with a rose-red patch on the breast.

rose·bud (rōz′bŭd′) *n.* The bud of a rose.

rose·bush (rōz′bo͝osh′) *n.* A shrub that bears roses.

rose campion. A European plant, *Lychnis coronaria,* naturalized in northeastern North America. It is covered with white, woolly down and has rose-red flowers. Also called "mullein pink," "dusty miller."

rose chafer. A long-legged gray beetle, *Macrodactylus subspinosus,* that causes damage to garden plants, especially roses and grapes. Also called "rose beetle."

rose-col·ored (rōz′kŭl′ərd) *adj.* **1.** Having the color **rose** *(see).* **2.** Seeing or seen overoptimistically.

Rose·crans (rōz′krănz), **William Starke.** 1819–1898. Union general in the Civil War.

rose fever. A spring or early summer hay fever.

rose·fish (rōz′fĭsh′) *n., pl.* **rosefish** or **-fishes.** A bright-red marine food fish, *Sebastes marinus,* of North Atlantic waters.

rose geranium. A woody plant, *Pelargonium graveolens,* having rose-pink flowers and fragrant leaves used for flavoring and in perfumery.

ro·selle (rō-zĕl′) *n.* A tropical Old World plant, *Hibiscus sabdariffa,* with yellow flowers. Its immature floral bracts have a pleasantly acid flavor, and are used to make jelly and beverages. [Origin uncertain.]

rose mallow. A tall plant, *Hibiscus moscheutos,* growing in brackish marshes of eastern North America, and having leaves covered with whitish down and white or pink flowers.

rose·mar·y (rōz′mâr′ē) *n., pl.* **-ies.** An aromatic evergreen shrub, *Rosmarinus officinalis,* of southern Europe, having light-blue flowers and grayish-green leaves that are used in cooking and perfume manufacture. [Middle English, alteration (influenced by ROSE and MARY) of *rosmarine,* from Latin *rōs marīnus,* "sea dew" : *rōs,* dew (see **ers-**[2] in Appendix*) + *marīnus,* of the sea, from *mare,* sea (see **mori-** in Appendix*).]

rose moss. 1. Any moss of the genus *Rhodobryum;* especially, *R. roseum,* characterized by conspicuous terminal leaf rosettes. **2.** A garden plant, **portulaca** *(see).*

rose of Jericho. A fernlike desert plant, *Anastatica hierochuntica,* that forms a tight ball when dry, and unfolds and blooms under moist conditions. Also called "resurrection plant."

rose of Sharon. 1. A tall shrub, *Hibiscus syriacus,* having large reddish, purple, or white flowers. Also called "althea." **2.** A shrubby plant, *Hypericum calycinum,* native to Eurasia, having evergreen leaves and yellow flowers.

ro·se·o·la (rō-zē′ə-lə, -ō-lə) *n.* Any rose-colored skin rash. [New Latin, diminutive of Latin *roseus,* rosy, from *rosa,* ROSE.]

rose pink. A light purplish pink to moderate or strong pink. See **color.** —**rose′-pink′** *adj.*

rose quartz. A pinkish quartz used as a gemstone.

rose·root (rōz′ro͞ot′, -ro͝ot′) *n.* A plant, *Sedum roseum,* of the Northern Hemisphere, having fleshy leaves and greenish-yellow or purple flowers.

Roses, Wars of the. A sporadic dynastic war (1455–85) in England between the House of York (white rose) and the House of Lancaster (red rose).

Ro·set·ta stone (rō-zĕt′ə). A basalt tablet, inscribed with a decree of Ptolemy V of 196 B.C. in Greek, Egyptian hieroglyphic, and Demotic, that was discovered in 1799 near the town of Rosetta, Egypt, and provided the key to the decipherment of hieroglyphics.

ro·sette (rō-zĕt′) *n.* **1.** An ornament or badge made of ribbon or silk that is gathered and tufted to resemble a rose, and is used to decorate clothing, or worn in the buttonhole of civilian dress to indicate the possession of certain medals or honors. **2.** Any roselike marking or formation, such as one of the clusters of spots on a leopard's fur. **3.** *Architecture.* A painted, carved, or sculptured ornament having a circular arrangement of parts resembling the petals of a rose. **4.** *Botany* A circular cluster of leaves or other plant parts. [French, "small rose," from Old French, from *rose,* rose, from Latin *rosa,* ROSE.]

Rose·ville (rōz′vĭl). A city of Michigan, in the southeast about 13 miles from Detroit. Population, 50,000.

rose water. A fragrant preparation made by steeping or distilling rose petals in water, used in cosmetics and in cookery.

rose window. A circular window usually of stained glass with radiating tracery in the form of a rose.

rose·wood (rōz′wo͝od′) *n.* **1.** Any of various tropical or semi-tropical trees, chiefly of the genus *Dalbergia,* having hard reddish or dark wood with a strongly marked grain. **2.** The wood of any of these trees, used in cabinetwork.

Rosh Ha·sha·nah (rŏsh hə-shä′nə, rōsh). Also **Rosh Ha·sha·na, Rosh Ha·sho·na** (hə-shō′nə), **Rosh Ha·sho·nah.** The Jewish New Year, a solemn occasion celebrated by Orthodox and Conservative Jews on the first and second of Tishri (usually late September or early October), and by Reform Jews on the first of Tishri only. [Hebrew *rōsh hasshānāh,* beginning of the year : *rōsh,* head + *hash-shānāh,* the year.]

Ro·si·cru·cian (rō′zə-kro͞o′shən, rŏz′ə-) *n.* **1.** A member of an international fraternity of religious mysticism, the Rosicrucian Order, or Ancient Mystic Order Rosae Crucis (*Abbr.* AMORC), devoted to the application of esoteric religious doctrine to modern life. **2.** A member of any of several similar secret religious organizations active in the 17th and 18th centuries. —*adj.* Of or pertaining to Rosicrucians or their philosophy. [From Medieval Latin *(Frater) Rosae Crucis,* translation of the German name (Friar) Christian *Rosenkreutz,* supposed founder of the society in the 15th century.] —**Ro′si·cru′cian·ism′** *n.*

ros·in (rŏz′ĭn) *n.* A translucent yellowish to dark-brown resin derived from the sap of various pine trees, and used to increase sliding friction on the bows of certain stringed instruments and in a wide variety of manufactured products including varnishes, inks, linoleum, and soldering compounds. —*tr.v.* **rosined, -ining, -ins.** To coat or rub with rosin. [Middle English *rosyn, rosine,* variants of RESIN.] —**ros′in·y** *adj.*

rosin oil. A white to brown viscous liquid obtained by fractional distillation of rosin and used in lubricants, electrical insulation, and printing inks. Also called "rosinol."

ros·in·weed (rŏz′ĭn-wēd′) *n.* Any of several North American plants of the genus *Silphium* and related genera, having a resinous juice; especially, the **compass plant,** the **cup plant,** and the **gum plant** *(all of which see).*

Ros·kil·de (rō′skĭl-do͞o). A city in eastern Denmark, west of Copenhagen. It is the former capital of Denmark, and the burial place of many Danish kings. Population, 32,000.

Ross (rôs), **Betsy (Griscom).** 1752–1836. American patriot; legendary maker of the first American flag.

Ross (rôs), **Harold Wallace.** 1892–1951. American journalist and editor.

Ross (rôs), Sir **James Clark.** 1800–1862. British explorer of the Arctic and Antarctic; nephew of Sir John Ross.

ă pat/ā pay/âr care/ä father/b bib/ch church/d deed/ĕ pet/ē be/f fife/g gag/h hat/hw which/ĭ pit/ī pie/îr pier/j judge/k kick/l lid, needle/m mum/n no, sudden/ng thing/ŏ pot/ō toe/ô paw, for/oi noise/ou out/o͝o took/o͞o boot/p pop/r roar/s sauce/sh ship, dish/

Ross (rôs), Sir **John.** 1777–1856. British naval officer and explorer of the Arctic; uncle of Sir James Clark Ross.
Ross (rôs), **John.** Original name, Coowescoowe or Koowes-koowe. 1790–1866. American Indian leader; chief of the Cherokee; reluctant leader of their removal from Georgia to Oklahoma.
Ross (rôs), Sir **Ronald.** 1857–1932. British physician; discovered that mosquitoes transmit malaria.
Ross and Crom·ar·ty (rôs; krŏm′ər-tē; rŏs; krŭm′ər-tē). A county occupying 3,089 square miles in northwestern Scotland. Population, 57,000. County seat, Dingwall.
Ross Dependency (rôs). A part of Antarctica on the Ross Sea, claimed by Great Britain and administered by New Zealand.
Ros·set·ti (rō-zĕt′ē), **Christina Georgina.** 1830–1894. English lyric poet; sister of Dante Gabriel Rossetti.
Ros·set·ti (rō-zĕt′ē), **Dante Gabriel.** 1828–1882. English pre-Raphaelite poet and painter.
Ros·si·ni (rô-sē′nē), **Gioacchino Antonio.** 1792–1868. Italian composer of operas, opéra bouffe, and sacred music.
Ross Island (rôs). **1.** An island of Antarctica, about 1,200 square miles in area, in the Weddell Sea northeast of the Antarctic Peninsula. **2.** An island of Antarctica in the western part of the Ross Sea, and the site of Mount Erebus.
Ros·si·ya. The Russian name for **Russia.**
Ross Sea (rôs). A large inlet of the Pacific Ocean in Antarctica.
Ross Shelf Ice (rôs). Also **Ross Barrier.** An ice barrier about 400 miles long, forming the southern portion of the Ross Sea.
Ros·tand (rō-stäɴ′), **Edmond.** 1868–1918. French author.
ros·tel·late (rŏs′tə-lāt′, -lĭt) *adj.* Having a rostellum. [New Latin *rostellatus,* from ROSTELLUM.]
ros·tel·lum (rŏs-tĕl′əm) *n., pl.* **-tella** (-tĕl′ə). *Biology.* A small, beaklike part, as a projection on the stigma of an orchid, a tubular mouth part on some insects, or the hooked projection on the head of a tapeworm. [New Latin, from Latin, diminutive of *rostrum,* beak, ROSTRUM.] **—ros·tel′lar** *adj.*
ros·ter (rŏs′tər) *n.* **1.** A list of names. **2.** *Military.* A list of the names of officers and men enrolled for active duty. [Dutch *rooster,* gridiron, list (on a ruled sheet), from Middle Dutch, gridiron, from *roosten,* to roast, from *roost,* gridiron, from Germanic *raust* (unattested). See **roast.**]
Ros·tock (rŏs′tŏk; *German* rôs′tôk). A seaport of East Germany, on the Baltic Sea about 100 miles northeast of Hamburg. Population, 179,000.
Ros·tov (rŏs′tŏv). Also **Ros·tov-on-Don** (rŏs′tŏv-ŏn-dŏn′). A river port of the southeastern Soviet Union, on the Don about 25 miles east of the Sea of Azov. Population, 720,000.
ros·trate (rŏs′trāt′, -trət) *adj.* Having a rostrum or beaklike part. [Latin *rostrātus,* from *rostrum,* beak, ROSTRUM.]
ros·trum (rŏs′trəm) *n., pl.* **-trums** or **-tra** (-trə) (only form for sense 2). **1.** A dais, platform, or similar raised place for public speaking. **2.** In ancient Rome: **a.** The curved, beaklike prow of a ship. **b.** The speakers' platform in the Forum, which was decorated with the prows of captured enemy ships. **3.** *Biology.* A beaklike or snoutlike projection. [Latin, beak, ship's prow. See **rēd-** in Appendix.*] **—ros′tral** (-trəl) *adj.*
ros·y (rō′zē) *adj.* **-ier, -iest. 1.** Having the characteristic pink or red color of a rose. **2.** Consisting of, decorated with, or suggestive of roses. **3.** Flushed with a healthy glow. **4.** Bright; cheerful; optimistic. **—ros′i·ly** *adv.* **—ros′i·ness** *n.*
rot¹ (rŏt) *v.* **rotted, rotting, rots.** *—intr.* **1.** To undergo decomposition, especially organic decomposition; to decay. **2.** To disappear or fall by decaying. Used with *off* or *away.* **3.** To decay morally; become degenerate. *—tr.* To cause to decompose or decay. —See Synonyms at **decay.** *—n.* **1.** The process of rotting or the condition of being rotten. **2. a. Foot rot** *(see).* **b. Liver fluke** *(see).* **3.** Any of several plant diseases characterized by the breakdown of tissue, and caused by various bacteria, fungi, or microorganisms. **4.** *Medicine. Archaic.* Any disease causing the decay of flesh. **5.** Pointless talk. *—interj.* Used to express contempt or impatience. [Middle English *roten, rotyen,* Old English *rotian,* from Germanic *rutjan* (unattested).]
rot². Variant of **ret.**
rot. rotating; rotation.
ro·ta (rō′tə) *n., pl.* **-tas. 1.** *Chiefly British.* A roll call or roster of names. **2.** *Chiefly British.* A round or rotation of duties. **3.** *Capital* **R.** *Roman Catholic Church.* A tribunal of prelates, called in full the Sacred Roman Rota, that serves as an ecclesiastical court. [Latin, wheel. See **ret-** in Appendix.*]
Ro·tar·i·an (rō-târ′ē-ən) *n.* A member of a Rotary Club.
ro·ta·ry (rō′tə-rē) *adj.* Of, pertaining to, causing, or characterized by rotation, especially axial rotation. *—n., pl.* **rotaries. 1.** A part or device that rotates around an axis. **2.** A **traffic circle** *(see).* [Medieval Latin *rotārius,* from Latin *rota,* wheel. See **ret-** in Appendix.*]
Rotary Club. Any club belonging to Rotary International, a service organization.
rotary engine. An engine, such as a turbine, in which power is supplied directly to vanes or other rotary parts.
rotary harrow. A harrow, consisting of a series of freely turning wheels rimmed with spikes. Also called "rotary hoe."
rotary plow. A plow having a series of hoes arranged on a revolving power-driven shaft. Also called "rotary tiller."
rotary press. A printing press having a cylinder to which curved plates are attached so that, when revolving, they will print onto a continuous roll of paper.
ro·tate (rō′tāt′) *v.* **-tated, -tating, -tates.** *—intr.* **1.** To turn or spin on an axis. **2.** To proceed in sequence; to alternate. *—tr.* **1.** To cause rotation. **2.** To plant or grow (crops) in a fixed order of succession. —See Synonyms at **turn.** *—adj.* Having radiating parts; wheel-shaped. [Latin *rotāre,* to revolve, from *rota,* wheel. See **ret-** in Appendix.*] **—ro′tat′a·ble** *adj.*
ro·ta·tion (rō-tā′shən) *n. Abbr.* **rot. 1.** Motion in which the path of every point in the moving object is a circle or circular arc centered on a specified axis, especially on an internal axis: *the axial rotation of the earth.* **2.** A single complete cycle of such motion; revolution. **3.** *Geometry.* A coordinate transformation consisting of an angular displacement, or successive angular displacements, of coordinate axes with the origin remaining fixed. **4.** Uniform sequential variation; alternation. **—ro·ta′tion·al** *adj.*
ro·ta·tive (rō′tə-tĭv) *adj.* **1.** Of, pertaining to, causing, or characterized by rotation. **2.** Characterized by or occurring in alternation or succession. **—ro′ta·tive·ly** *adv.*
ro·ta·tor (rō′tā′tər) *n.* One who or that which rotates.
ro·ta·to·ry (rō′tə-tôr′ē, -tōr′ē) *adj.* **1.** Of, pertaining to, causing, or characterized by rotation. **2.** Occurring or proceeding in alternation or succession.
ROTC, R.O.T.C. Reserve Officers' Training Corps.
rote¹ (rōt) *n.* **1.** A memorizing process using routine or repetition without full comprehension: *learn by rote.* **2.** Mechanical routine; unthinking repetition. [Middle English, custom, rote, possibly from Latin *rota,* wheel. See **ret-** in Appendix.*]
rote² (rōt) *n. Rare.* The sound of surf breaking on the shore. [From Scandinavian, akin to Old Norse *rauta,* to roar. See **reu-** in Appendix.*]
rote³ (rōt) *n.* A medieval stringed instrument. [Middle English, from Old French, from Germanic. See **krut-** in Appendix.*]
ro·te·none (rō′tə-nōn′) *n.* A white crystalline compound, $C_{23}H_{22}O_6$, extracted from the roots of derris and cubé, and used as an insecticide. [Japanese *rōten,* derris plant + -ONE.]
rot·gut (rŏt′gŭt′) *n. Slang.* Raw, inferior liquor. [ROT + GUT.]
Rothe·say (rŏth′sē). The county seat of Bute, in southwestern Scotland. Population, 7,000.
Roth·ko (rŏth′kō), **Mark.** Born 1903. Russian-born American abstract expressionist painter.
Roth·schild (rŏth′chīld, rŏs-; *German* rōt′shĭlt), **Meyer Amschel.** 1743–1812. German banker; with his sons, **Nathan Meyer** (1777–1836) in London and **Salomon** (1774–1855) in Vienna, directed House of Rothschild.
ro·ti·fer (rō′tə-fər) *n.* Any of various minute, multicellular aquatic organisms of the phylum Rotifera, having at the anterior end a wheellike ring of cilia. Also called "wheel animalcule." [New Latin *Rotifera* : Latin *rota,* wheel (see **rotate**) + -FER.] **—ro·tif′er·al** (rō-tĭf′ər-əl), **ro·tif′er·ous** *adj.*
ro·ti·form (rō′tə-fôrm′) *adj.* Shaped like a wheel. [New Latin *rotiformis* : Latin *rota,* wheel (see **ret-** in Appendix*) + -FORM.]
ro·tis·se·rie (rō-tĭs′ə-rē) *n.* **1.** A cooking device equipped with a rotating spit on which meat or other food is roasted. **2.** A shop or restaurant where meats are roasted to order. [French *rôtisserie,* from Old French *rostisserie,* from *rostir* (present stem *rostiss-*), to ROAST.]
rot·l (rŏt′l) *n.* **1.** A unit of weight used in countries bordering on the Mediterranean and in nearby areas, varying in different regions from about one to five pounds. **2.** A varying unit of dry measure in these localities. [Arabic *raṭl, riṭl,* possibly altered by metathesis from Greek *litra.* See **liter.**]
ro·to·gra·vure (rō′tə-grə-vyŏŏr′, -grā′vyər) *n.* An intaglio printing process in which letters and pictures are transferred from an etched copper cylinder to a web of paper, plastic, or similar material in a rotary press. [Latin *rota,* wheel (see **ret-** in Appendix*) + GRAVURE.]
ro·tor (rō′tər) *n.* **1.** A rotating part of an electrical or mechanical device. Compare **stator. 2.** An assembly of rotating horizontal airfoils, such as that of a helicopter. [Short for ROTATOR.]
rotor ship. A ship propelled by one or more tall cylindrical rotors operated by wind power.
rot·ten (rŏt′n) *adj.* **-tener, -tenest. 1.** In a state of putrefaction or decay; decomposed. **2.** Having a foul odor resulting from or suggestive of decay; putrid; stinking. **3.** Made weak or unsound by rot. **4.** Morally corrupt or despicable. **5.** Very bad; wretched. [Middle English *roten, rotin,* from Old Norse *rotinn,* from Germanic *ruteno-* (unattested), akin to *rutjan* (unattested), to ROT.] **—rot′ten·ly** *adv.* **—rot′ten·ness** *n.*
rotten borough. In England prior to the Parliamentary reform of 1832, a borough having only a few voters but entitled to send a representative to Parliament.
rot·ten·stone (rŏt′n-stōn′) *n.* A friable variety of tripoli, the product of decomposed siliceous limestone, used for polishing.
Rot·ter·dam (rŏt′ər-dăm). A city and river port of the Netherlands, in the southwest on a distributary of the Rhine-Meuse delta. Population, 732,000.
rott·wei·ler (rŏt′wī-lər; *German* rôt′vī-lər) *n.* A dog of an ancient breed developed in Germany, having a stocky body, a short black coat, and tan face markings. [Originally bred in *Rottweil,* city in southwestern Germany.]
Ro·tu·ma (rō-tōō′mə). A volcanic island in the southwestern Pacific, part of the British colony of Fiji.
ro·tund (rō-tŭnd′) *adj.* **1.** Rounded; plump. **2.** Sonorous. —See Synonyms at **fat.** [Latin *rotundus,* round. See **ret-** in Appendix.*] **—ro·tund′ly** *adv.* **—ro·tund′ness** *n.*
ro·tun·da (rō-tŭn′də) *n.* **1.** A circular building or hall, especially one with a dome. **2.** A large room with a high ceiling, as a lobby of a hotel. [Italian *rotonda,* from Latin *rotunda,* feminine of *rotundus,* round. See **ret-** in Appendix.*]
ro·tun·di·ty (rō-tŭn′də-tē) *n., pl.* **-ties. 1.** The condition of being round or plump. **2.** A rotund protrusion or object.

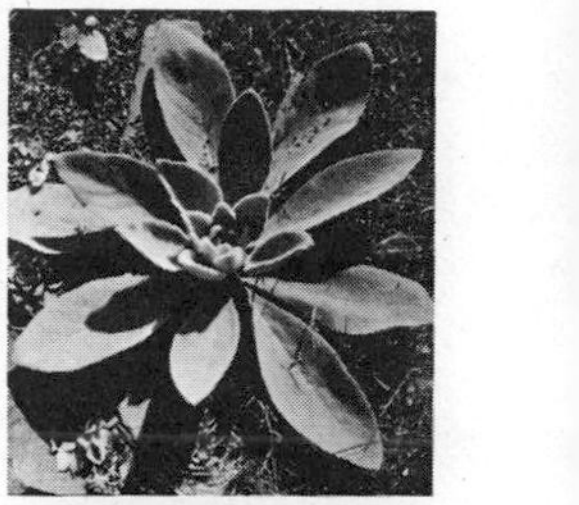
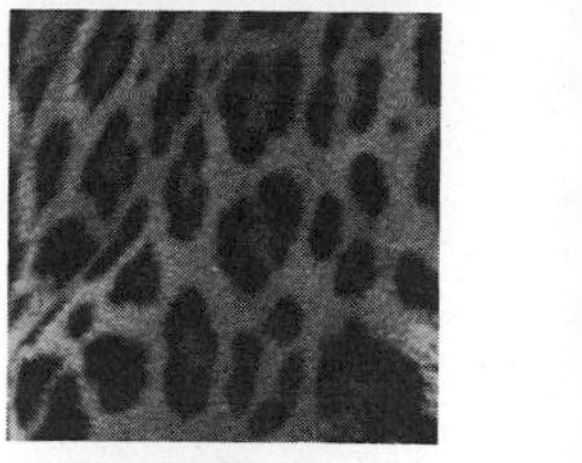

rosette
Above: Rosette of mullein leaves
Below: Markings on jaguar's fur

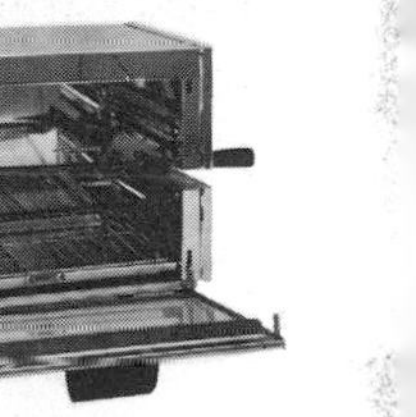

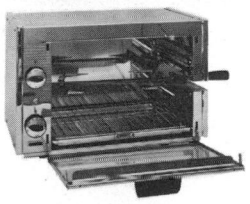

rotisserie

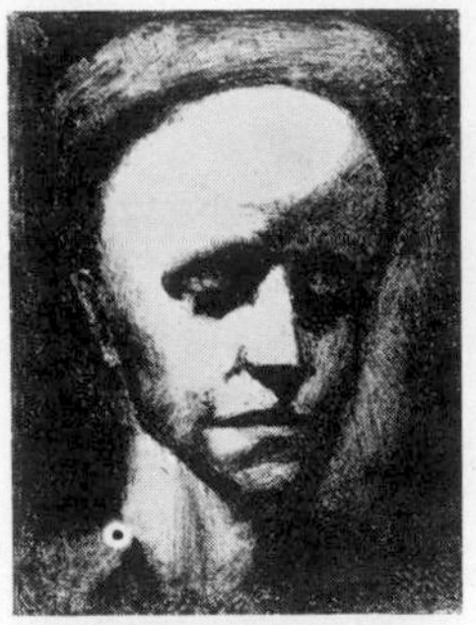

Georges Rouault
"Self Portrait with Cap,"
a 1926 lithograph

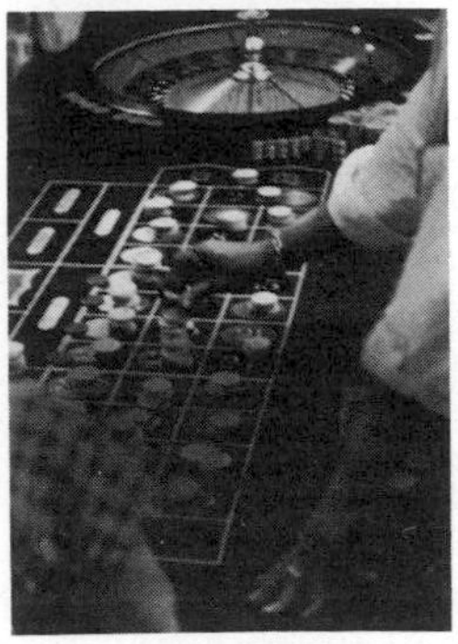

roulette

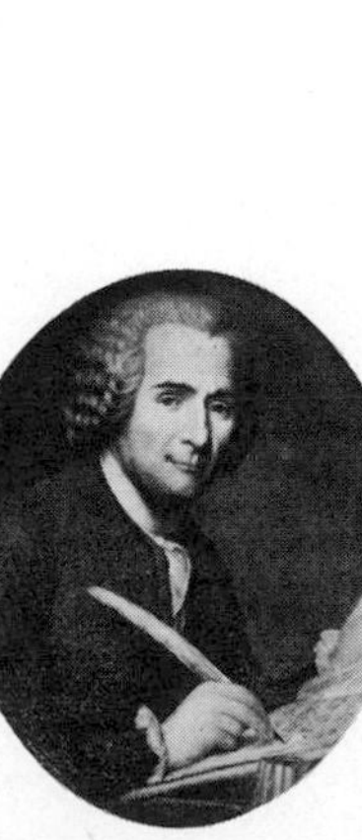

Jean Jacques Rousseau

ro·tu·rier (rō-tü-ryā′) *n.* A person of plebeian rank; commoner. [French, from Old French, from *roture,* newly broken land, obligation to a lord for land, hence, a commoner, from Vulgar Latin *ruptūra,* from Latin, a RUPTURE.]

Rou·ault (rōō-ō′), **Georges.** 1871–1958. French expressionist painter and graphic artist.

Rou·baix (rōō′bĕ′). A city and textile center in northern France, near Lille. Population, 113,000.

rou·ble, ru·ble (rōō′bəl) *n. Abbr.* **r., R. 1.** The basic monetary unit of the Union of Soviet Socialist Republics, equal to 100 kopecks. See table of exchange rates at **currency. 2.** A coin worth one rouble. [Russian *rubl′,* "silver bar," from Old Russian, "bar," "block," from *rubiti,* to cut up, build, from Balto-Slavic *romb-* (unattested).]

rouche. Variant of **ruche.**

rou·é (rōō-ā′) *n.* A lecherous and dissipated man; a profligate. [French, "broken on the wheel," completely tired, from the past participle of *rouer,* to break on the wheel, from Medieval Latin *rotāre,* to turn, from Latin, to ROTATE.]

Rou·en (rōō-äN′). A city in northern France, on the Seine, famous for its cathedral and as the place where Joan of Arc was executed. Population, 121,000.

rouge (rōōzh) *n.* **1.** A red or pink cosmetic for coloring the cheeks or lips. **2.** A reddish powder, chiefly ferric oxide, used to polish metals or glass. *—v.* **rouged, rouging, rouges.** *—tr.* To put rouge on; color with rouge. *—intr.* To use rouge as a cosmetic. [French, from Old French, red, from Latin *rubeus.* See **reudh-** in Appendix.*]

rouge et noir (rōōzh′ ā nwär′). A gambling card game played at a table marked with two red and two black diamond-shaped spots, on which bets are placed. Also called "trente et quarante." [French, "red and black."]

rough (rŭf) *adj.* **rougher, roughest. 1.** Having an uneven surface; full of bumps, ridges, or other irregularities; not smooth. **2.** Coarse, shaggy, or uneven in texture: *a rough bearskin.* **3.** Characterized by violent motion; turbulent; agitated: *rough waters.* **4.** Severely inclement; stormy: *a rough climate.* **5.** Boisterous, unruly, or rowdy in manner or behavior. **6.** Not gentle or careful; violent: *rough handling.* **7.** Savage; harsh; brutal: *a rough temper.* **8.** Rude; unmannerly; uncouth. **9.** *Informal.* Difficult or unpleasant: *a rough time.* **10.** Harsh to the ear. **11.** Harsh or sharp to the taste: *a rough wine.* **12.** Lacking polish or finesse. **13.** In a natural state: *rough diamonds.* **14.** Not perfected, elaborated, or completed: *a rough drawing.* **15.** Requiring physical strength rather than intelligence; unskilled: *rough work.* **16.** *Linguistics.* Pronounced with an aspirated sound like that of the letter *h.* *—n.* **1.** Uneven, overgrown ground. **2.** The part of a golf course left unmowed and uncultivated, as distinguished from the fairway and the greens. **3.** A rough, irregular, or difficult part or condition. **4.** Something in an unfinished or hastily worked-out state. **5.** A hoodlum or rowdy. **—in the rough.** In a crude or unfinished state. *—v.* **roughed, roughing, roughs.** *—tr.* **1.** To make rough; roughen. **2.** To treat roughly or with physical violence; especially, to subject (an opponent) unnecessarily and intentionally to such treatment. Used with *up.* **3.** To prepare or indicate in a rough or unfinished form: *rough in the illustrations for a book.* *—intr.* To behave roughly; especially, to treat an opponent with unnecessary roughness. **—rough it.** To get along without the usual comforts: *rough it on a camping trip.* *—adv.* In a rough manner; roughly. [Middle English *ruch, r(o)wgh,* Old English *rūh.* See **ruk-²** in Appendix.*] **—rough′er** *n.* **—rough′ly** *adv.* **—rough′ness** *n.*

Synonyms: *rough, harsh, jagged, rugged, scabrous, uneven. Rough* describes any surface that to the sight or touch has inequalities, irregularities, projections, ridges, or breaks: *a rough path. Harsh* in this context implies discordance to the senses, as grating to the ear. *Jagged* refers to an edge with irregular projections and depressions: *a jagged ridge. Rugged* refers to strength or endurance in persons, and to irregularity of terrain. *Scabrous* connotes that which is scaly or rough to the tactile sense and often repulsive or obscene in nature. *Uneven* refers to a fluctuation in line or, figuratively, in standards of production: *The quality was uneven.*

rough·age (rŭf′ĭj) *n.* **1.** Any rough or coarse material. **2.** The relatively coarse, indigestible parts of certain foods and fodder that contain cellulose and stimulate peristalsis.

rough-and-read·y (rŭf′ən-rĕd′ē) *adj.* Rough or crude but effective or usable.

rough-and-tum·ble (rŭf′ən-tŭm′bəl) *adj.* Characterized by roughness and disregard for order or rules: *a rough-and-tumble scuffle.*

rough breathing. 1. An aspirate sound in Greek like that of the letter *h* in English. **2.** The mark (ʻ) placed over initial sounds in Greek to indicate a preceding aspirate.

rough·cast (rŭf′kăst′, -käst′) *n.* **1.** A coarse plaster used for outside wall surfaces. **2.** A rough, preliminary model or form. *—tr.v.* **roughcast, -casting, -casts. 1.** To plaster (a wall, for example) with roughcast. **2.** To shape or work into a rough or preliminary form. **—rough′cast′er** *n.*

rough·dry (rŭf′drī′) *tr.v.* **-dried, -drying, -dries.** To dry (something laundered) without ironing or smoothing out. *—adj.* Laundered but not ironed.

rough·en (rŭf′ən) *v.* **-ened, -ening, -ens.** *—tr.* To make rough. *—intr.* To become rough.

rough·hew (rŭf′hyōō′) *tr.v.* **-hewed** or **-hewn** (-hyōōn′), **-hewing, -hews. 1.** To hew or shape (timber or stone, for example) roughly, without finishing. **2.** To make in rough form; to roughcast.

rough·house (rŭf′hous′) *n.* Rowdy, uproarious play or behavior. *—v.* **roughhoused, -housing, -houses.** *—intr.* To engage in boisterous or rowdy activity. *—tr.* To handle or treat roughly, usually in fun.

rough-leg·ged hawk (rŭf′lĕg′ĭd). A hawk, *Buteo lagopus,* having dark plumage and whitish feathers covering the legs.

rough·neck (rŭf′nĕk′) *n.* A pugnacious fellow; a rowdy.

rough·rid·er (rŭf′rī′dər) *n.* **1.** A skilled rider of little-trained horses; especially, one who breaks horses for riding. **2.** Any skilled Western horseman.

Rough Riders. The members of a volunteer cavalry regiment organized by Theodore Roosevelt and Leonard Wood for service in the Spanish-American War of 1898.

rough·shod (rŭf′shŏd′) *adj.* Shod with horseshoes having projecting nails or points to prevent slipping. **—ride roughshod over.** To treat inconsiderately or arrogantly.

roul. *Philately.* roulette.

rou·lade (rōō-läd′) *n.* **1. a.** A musical embellishment consisting of a rapid run of several notes sung to one syllable. **b.** A roll on a drum. **2.** A slice of meat rolled around a filling and cooked. [French, "a rolling," from *rouler,* to roll, from Old French *roller,* to ROLL.]

rou·leau (rōō-lō′) *n., pl.* **-leaux** (-lōz′) or **-leaus. 1.** A small roll, especially of coins wrapped in paper. **2.** A roll or fold or ribbon used for piping. [French, from Old French *rolel,* diminutive of *rol(l)e,* a roll, from Latin *rotulus,* small wheel. See **roll.**]

rou·lette (rōō-lĕt′) *n.* **1.** A gambling game played with a shallow bowl enclosing a rotating disk, that has numbered slots alternately colored red and black, the players betting on which slot, or which color, a small ball will come to rest in. **2.** A small, toothed disk of tempered steel attached to a handle and used to make rows of dots, slits, or perforations, as in engraving or on a sheet of postage stamps. **3.** *Abbr.* **roul.** *Philately.* Short consecutive incisions made between individual stamps in a sheet for easy separation. Compare **perforation.** *—tr.v.* **rouletted, -letting, -lettes.** To mark or divide with a roulette. [French, from Old French, from *rouelle,* from Late Latin *rotella,* diminutive of Latin *rota,* a wheel. See **ret-** in Appendix.*]

Rou·ma·ni·a. See **Rumania.**

Rou·ma·ni·an. Variant of **Rumanian.**

Rou·me·li·a. See **Rumelia.**

round¹ (round) *adj. Abbr.* **rd. 1.** Spherical; globular; ball-shaped. **2.** Circular or circular in cross section. **3.** Having a curved edge or surface; not flat or angular. **4.** Formed or articulated with the lips assuming an oval shape: *a round vowel.* **5.** Whole or complete; full; entire: *a round dozen.* **6. a.** Expressed or designated as a whole number or integer; not fractional; integral. **b.** Adjusted so as to express an exact number in an approximate, more convenient form: *"1900 is a good round date to choose"* (Arthur C. Clarke). **c.** Approximate; rough; not exact: *a round estimate.* **7.** Large; ample; considerable: *a round sum.* **8.** Brought to a satisfying perfection; finished: *a round, polished writing style.* **9.** Sonorous; full in tone. **10.** Brisk; rapid; smart: *a round pace.* **11.** Outspoken; candid; blunt. **12.** Made with full force; unrestrained: *a round thrashing.* *—n.* **1.** The state of being round. **2.** Something round, as a circle, disk, globe, or ring; a curved or rounded form or part. **3.** A rung or crossbar, as on a ladder or chair. **4.** The part of the thigh on a beef animal between the rump and shank, considered as meat. **5.** An assembly of people; group. **6.** Movement around a circle, or about an axis. **7.** A **round dance** *(see).* **8.** A complete course, succession, or series, often ending at the starting point: *a round of parties.* **9.** *Often plural.* A course of customary or prescribed actions, duties, or places. **10.** A complete range or extent. **11.** A single distribution, as of drinks. **12.** A single outburst of applause or cheering. **13. a.** A single shot or volley. **b.** Ammunition for a single shot; a **cartridge** *(see).* **14.** A rounded slice of bread. **15.** *Archery.* A specified number of arrows shot from a specified distance to a target. **16.** An interval of play in various games and sports that occupies a specified time, comprises a certain number of plays, or allows each player a turn. **17.** *Music.* A short, rhythmical canon in which each part enters in unison at equal time intervals. **—go** (or **make**) **the rounds.** To be in wide circulation. **—in the round. 1.** With the stage in the center of the audience: *theater in the round.* **2.** Not attached to a background; freestanding. Said of sculpture. *—v.* **rounded, rounding, rounds.** *—tr.* **1.** To make round. **2.** To pronounce with rounded lips; labialize. **3.** To lessen in angularity; fill out; make plump. **4.** To bring to completion or perfection; to finish. **5.** To make a complete circuit of; go or pass around. **6.** To make a turn about or to the other side of: *rounded a bend in the road.* **7.** To encompass; surround. **8.** To move or cause to proceed in a circular course. *—intr.* **1.** To become round. **2.** To take a circular course; complete or partially complete a circuit. **3.** To turn about, as on an axis; to reverse. **4.** To become curved, filled out, or plump. **5.** To come to completion or perfection. Often used with *into* or *out.* **—round off.** To express (a number) approximately, or only to a specified number of decimals. *—adv.* Around. See Synonyms at **about.** *—prep.* **1.** Around. **2.** From the beginning to the end of; throughout: *a plant that grows round the year.* —See Synonyms at **about.** [Middle English, from Old French *ronde,* from Latin *rotundus.* See **ret-** in Appendix.*] **—round′ness** *n.*

round² (round) *tr.v.* **rounded, rounding, rounds.** *Archaic.* To whisper. [Middle English *r(o)unen,* Old English *rūnian.* See **rūno-** in Appendix.*]

round·a·bout (round′ə-bout′) *adj.* Indirect; oblique; circuitous: *"this conclusion was reached in a roundabout but nevertheless perfectly reliable way"* (George Gamow). See Synonyms at **in-**

direct. —*n.* **1.** A short, close-fitting jacket. **2.** *Chiefly British.* A merry-go-round. **3.** *Chiefly British.* A traffic circle.

round clam. The **quahog** *(see).*

round dance. **1.** A folk dance performed with the dancers arranged in a circle. **2.** A ballroom dance performed with circular movements around the room.

round·ed (roun′dĭd) *adj.* **1.** Made round; shaped in a circle or sphere. **2.** Pronounced with the lips shaped ovally; labialized. **3.** Complete; balanced.

roun·del (roun′dəl) *n.* **1.** A curved form; especially, a semicircular panel, window, or recess. **2.** *Prosody.* **a.** A **rondel** *(see).* **b.** A **rondeau** *(see).* **c.** An English variation of the rondeau, consisting of three triplets with a refrain after the first and third. [Middle English, from Old French *rondel,* "small circle," RONDEL.]

roun·de·lay (roun′də-lā′) *n.* **1.** A poem or song with a regularly recurring refrain. **2.** A dance in a circle; round. [From Old French *rondelet,* diminutive of *rondel,* ROUNDEL.]

round·er (roun′dər) *n.* **1.** One that rounds, especially a tool for rounding corners and edges. **2.** One who makes rounds, as a watchman. **3.** *Capital* **R.** *British.* A Methodist preacher who travels a circuit among his congregations. **4.** *Informal.* A dissolute or dishonest person. **5.** *Plural.* An English ball game similar to baseball. Used with a singular verb.

round hand. A style of handwriting in which the letters are rounded and full, rather than angular.

Round·head (round′hĕd′) *n.* A member or supporter of the Parliamentary or Puritan party during the English Civil War (1642–49). Used as a term of derision by the Royalists in reference to the Puritans' close-cropped hair. Compare **Cavalier.**

round·house (round′hous′) *n.* **1.** A circular building for housing and switching locomotives. **2.** A cabin on the after part of the quarter-deck of a ship. **3.** A meld of four kings and four queens in the game of pinochle. **4.** *Slang.* A punch or swing delivered with a sweeping sidearm movement.

round·ish (roun′dĭsh) *adj.* Rather round. —**round′ish·ness** *n.*

round·let (round′lĭt) *n.* A little circle or a small circular object. [Middle English *roundelet,* from Old French *rondelet,* diminutive of *rondel,* small circle, RONDEL.]

round·ly (round′lē) *adv.* **1.** In the form of a circle or sphere. **2.** In a round manner; bluntly; candidly. **3.** Fully; thoroughly.

round robin. **1.** A tournament in which each contestant is matched against every other contestant. **2.** A petition or protest on which the signatures are arranged in the form of a circle in order to conceal the order of signing. **3.** A letter sent among members of a group, often with comments added by each person in turn. **4.** An extended sequence.

round-shoul·dered (round′shōl′dərd) *adj.* Having the shoulders and upper back rounded.

rounds·man (roundz′mən) *n., pl.* **-men** (-mĭn). **1.** A police officer in charge of several patrolmen. **2.** One who makes rounds, as a deliveryman.

round steak. A lean, oval cut of beef from between the rump and shank.

Round Table. **1.** The table of King Arthur, made circular in order to avoid disputes about precedence among his knights. **2.** King Arthur and his knights as a group. **3.** *Small* **r,** *small* **t.** A conference or discussion with several participants.

round-the-clock (round′*th*ə-klŏk′) *adj.* Also **a·round-the-clock** (ə-round′-). Throughout the entire day; continuous.

round trip. A trip from one place to another, and back; two-way trip. —**round′-trip′** *adj.*

round up. **1.** To seek out and bring together; gather. **2.** To herd (cattle) together for inspection, branding, or shipping.

round·up (round′ŭp′) *n.* **1. a.** The herding together of cattle for inspection, branding, or shipping. **b.** The cattle that are herded together. **c.** The cowboys and horses employed in such herding. **2.** Any similar gathering up, as of persons under suspicion by the police. **3.** A summing up; summation; résumé.

round·worm (round′wûrm′) *n.* A **nematode** *(see).*

roup (ro͞op) *n.* An infectious disease of poultry and pigeons characterized by inflammation and discharge from the mouth and eyes. [Origin unknown.]

rouse (rouz) *v.* **roused, rousing, rouses.** —*tr.* **1.** To cause to come out of a state of slumber, apathy, or depression. **2.** To excite, as to anger or action; to spur. **3.** To startle (game) from a covert or lair. —*intr.* **1.** To awaken, as from sleep, repose, or unconsciousness. **2.** To stir; to become active. **3.** To rise or start from cover, as game. —See Synonyms at **provoke.** —*n.* **1.** The act of rousing. **2.** A signal for rousing; reveille. [Originally "to startle (game) from cover," Middle English *rowsen*†, to shake feathers or body.] —**rous′er** *n.*

rous·ing (rou′zĭng) *adj.* **1.** Inducing enthusiasm or excitement; stirring: *a rousing sermon.* **2.** Active; lively; vigorous: *a rousing march tune.* **3.** *Informal.* Extraordinary; exceptional: *a rousing vacation; a rousing lie.* —**rous′ing·ly** *adv.*

Rous·seau (ro͞o-sō′), **Henri.** Called "Le Douanier." 1844–1910. French primitive painter.

Rous·seau (ro͞o-sō′), **Jean Jacques.** 1712–1778. French author of works on political philosophy, education, and morality.

Rous·sil·lon (ro͞o-sē-yôɴ′). A region and former province of France, bordering on Spain and the Mediterranean Sea.

roust (roust) *tr.v.* **rousted, rousting, rousts.** To rout, especially out of bed. [Alteration of ROUSE.]

roust·a·bout (rous′tə-bout′) *n.* **1.** A deck or wharf laborer, especially on the Mississippi River. **2.** A laborer in a circus. **3.** A laborer employed for transient or unskilled jobs, as in an oil field. [ROUST + ABOUT.]

rout[1] (rout) *n.* **1.** A disorderly retreat or flight following defeat. **2.** An overwhelming defeat. **3.** A disorderly crowd of persons; boisterous mob; rabble. **4.** A public disturbance; riot. **5.** *Archaic.* A company of people or animals, especially of knights or wolves. **6.** *Archaic.* A wild party. —See Synonyms at **flock.** —*tr.v.* **routed, routing, routs.** **1.** To put to disorderly flight or retreat: *"the flock of starlings which Jasper had routed with his gun"* (Virginia Woolf). **2.** To defeat overwhelmingly. —See Synonyms at **defeat.** [Middle English *route,* troop, disorderly crowd (influenced by French *deroute,* defeat), from Old French, dispersed group, troop, from Vulgar Latin *rupta* (unattested), from Latin *rumpere* (past participle *ruptus*), to break. See **reup-** in Appendix.*]

rout[2] (rout) *v.* **routed, routing, routs.** —*intr.* **1.** To dig for food with the snout; to root. **2.** To search; poke around; rummage. —*tr.* **1.** To dig up with the snout. **2.** To expose to view; uncover. **3.** To hollow, scoop, or gouge out. **4.** To drive or force out; eject. [Variant of ROOT (to dig up).]

rout[3] (rout, ro͞ot) *intr.v.* **routed, routing, routs.** *Chiefly Scottish.* To make a loud noise or clamor. [Middle English *r(o)uten,* from Old Norse *rauta,* to roar. See **reu-** in Appendix.*]

route (ro͞ot, rout) *n. Abbr.* **rte.** **1. a.** A road, course, or way for travel from one place to another. **b.** A highway. **2.** A customary line of travel. **3.** A fixed course or territory assigned to a salesman or deliveryman. —See Synonyms at **way.** —*tr.v.* **routed, routing, routes.** **1.** To send along; to forward. **2.** To schedule or dispatch on a sequence of procedures or stops: *The travel agency routed them to Paris by way of Luxembourg.* [Middle English, from Old French, from unattested Vulgar Latin *rupta (via),* "broken or beaten (way)." See **rout.**]

rout·er[1] (ro͞o′tər, rou′tər) *n.* One that routes.

rout·er[2] (rou′tər) *n.* One who or that which routs.

rou·tine (ro͞o-tēn′) *n.* **1.** A prescribed and detailed course of action to be followed regularly; a standard procedure. **2.** A set of customary and often mechanically performed procedures or activities. **3.** A set piece of entertainment, especially in a nightclub or theater. —See Synonyms at **method.** —*adj.* **1.** In accordance with established procedure. **2.** Habitual; regular. **3.** Lacking in interest or originality. [French, from Old French, from ROUTE (beaten path).] —**rou·tine′ly** *adv.* —**rou·tin′ism′** *n.* —**rou·tin′ist** *n.*

rou·tin·ize (ro͞o-tē′nīz′) *tr.v.* **-ized, -izing, -izes.** **1.** To establish a routine for. **2.** To reduce to a routine.

roux (ro͞o) *n.* A mixture of flour and butter or other fat, browned together and used as a thickening. [French *(beurre) roux,* browned (butter), from *roux,* reddish brown, from Old French *rous,* from Latin *russus,* red. See **reudh-** in Appendix.*]

rove[1] (rōv) *v.* **roved, roving, roves.** —*intr.* To wander about at random, especially over a wide area; roam. —*tr.* To roam or wander around, over, or through. —See Synonyms at **wander.** —*n.* A roaming; ramble. [Middle English *roven,* (in archery) to shoot at a random mark (sense influenced by ROVER, a pirate), probably from Scandinavian, akin to Icelandic *rāfa,* to wander, loiter. See **rei-**[1] in Appendix.*]

rove[2] (rōv) *tr.v.* **roved, roving, roves.** **1.** To card (wool). **2.** To put (fibers or thread) through an eye or opening. **3.** To stretch and twist (fibers), before spinning; ravel out. —*n.* A slightly twisted and extended fiber or sliver. [Origin obscure, possibly akin to REEVE (pass through a hole).]

rove[3]. Alternate past tense and past participle of **reeve.**

rove beetle. Any of numerous beetles of the family Staphylinidae, often found in decaying matter and having slender bodies and short wing covers. [Perhaps from ROVE (to wander about).]

rov·er (rō′vər) *n.* **1.** One who roves; wanderer; nomad. **2. a.** A pirate. **b.** A pirate vessel. **3.** *Archery.* A mark selected by chance. [As "pirate," Middle English *rover,* from Middle Dutch *rōver,* robber, from *rōven,* to rob. See **reup-** in Appendix.* As "random mark," Middle English *rover,* from *roven,* to shoot at a random mark. See **rove** (to wander about).]

row[1] (rō) *n.* **1.** A horizontal linear arrangement or array. **2.** A line of adjacent seats, as in a theater, auditorium, or classroom. **3.** A street flanked by a continuous line of buildings on both sides. —*tr.v.* **rowed, rowing, rows.** To place in a row or rows. Often used with *up.* [Middle English *raw, row,* Old English *rāw, rǣw.* See **rei-**[1] in Appendix.*]

row[2] (rō) *v.* **rowed, rowing, rows.** —*intr.* To propel a boat with or as if with oars. —*tr.* **1.** To propel (a boat) with or as if with oars. **2.** To carry in or on a boat propelled by oars. **3.** To propel or convey in a manner resembling rowing. **4.** To employ (a specified number of oars or oarsmen). **5.** To pull (an oar) as part of a racing crew. **6.** To race against by rowing. —*n.* **1.** An act of rowing; a shift at the oars of a boat. **2.** A trip or excursion in a rowboat. [Middle English *rowen,* Old English *rōwan.* See **erə-**[1] in Appendix.*] —**row′er** *n.*

row[3] (rou) *n.* **1.** A boisterous disturbance or quarrel; brawl. **2.** Noise; clamor; uproar. —*intr.v.* **rowed, rowing, rows.** To take part in a row. [Origin unknown.]

row·an (rou′ən) *n.* A small, deciduous tree, *Sorbus aucuparia,* native to Europe, having clusters of white flowers and orange-red berries. Also called "mountain ash." [Of Scandinavian origin, akin to Old Norse *reynir.* See **reudh-** in Appendix.*]

row·boat (rō′bōt′) *n.* A small boat propelled by oars.

row·dy (rou′dē) *n., pl.* **-dies.** A rough, disorderly person. —*adj.* **rowdier, -diest.** Disorderly; rough. [Probably from ROW (quarrel).] —**row′di·ness, row′dy·ism′** *n.*

Rowe (rō), **Nicholas.** 1674–1718. English poet and playwright.

row·el (rou′əl) *n.* A sharp-toothed wheel inserted into the end of the shank of a spur. —*tr.v.* **roweled** or **-elled, -eling** or

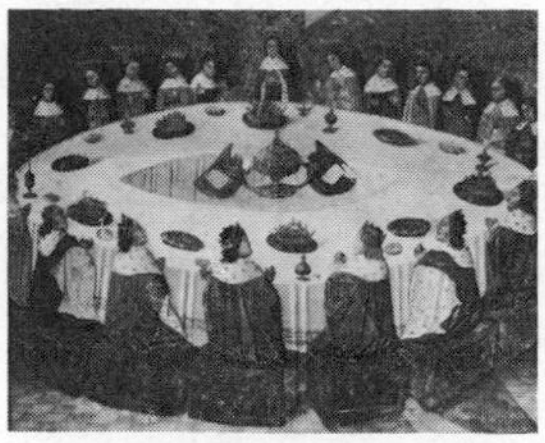

Round Table
Fifteenth-century manuscript illustration

rowan

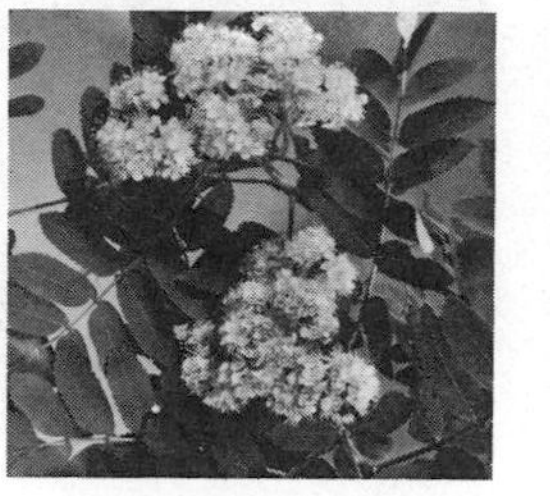

flowers

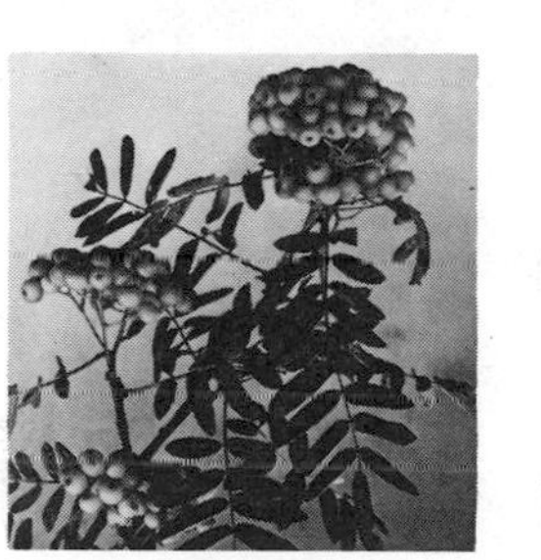

berries

-elling, -els. To spur; urge with a rowel. [Middle English *rowelle,* from Old French *roele,* from Late Latin *rotella,* diminutive of Latin *rota,* a wheel. See **ret-** in Appendix.*]

row·en (rou′ən) *n.* A second crop, as of hay, in a season. [Middle English *rewayn,* from Norman French, from Old French *regaīn* : *re-,* again + *gaīn,* rowen, from *gaaignier,* to till, "to obtain food," "gain" (see **wei-**[2] in Appendix*).]

Row·land·son (rō′lənd-sən), **Thomas.** 1756–1827. English caricaturist, illustrator, and portraitist.

row·lock (rō′lŏk′) *n. Chiefly British.* An **oarlock** *(see).*

Rox·burgh·shire (rŏks′bûr-ə-shîr, -shər). Also **Rox·burgh** (rŏks′bə-rə). A county of Scotland, occupying 665 square miles in the southeast on the border with England. Population, 43,000. County seat, Jedburgh.

roy·al (roi′əl) *adj. Abbr.* **R. 1.** Of or pertaining to a king, queen, or other monarch. **2.** Of the rank of a king or queen. **3.** Of, pertaining to, or in the service of a kingdom. **4.** Issued or performed by a king or sovereign. **5.** Founded, chartered, or authorized by a sovereign. **6.** Befitting a king; stately. **7.** Superior in size or quality. —*n.* **1.** A sail set on the royalmast. **2.** A paper size, 20 by 25 inches for printing, 19 by 24 inches for writing. [Middle English *roial,* from Old French, from Latin *rēgālis,* from *rēx* (stem *rēg-*), king. See **reg-**[1] in Appendix.*] —**roy′al·ly** *adv.*

royal blue. Deep to strong blue. See **color.** —**roy′al-blue′** *adj.*

royal fern. A deep-rooted fern, *Osmunda regalis,* of worldwide distribution, having tall, upright fronds.

royal flush. *Poker.* The highest hand attainable, consisting of the five highest cards of one suit.

Royal Gorge. A canyon with 1,000-foot walls formed by the Arkansas River in south-central Colorado, and extending for ten miles. Also called "Grand Canyon of the Arkansas."

roy·al·ism (roi′əl-ĭz′əm) *n.* Support of or adherence to the principles of rule by a monarch.

roy·al·ist (roi′əl-ĭst) *n.* A supporter of the cause or power of a king or monarchy. —*adj.* Also **roy·al·is·tic** (roi′əl-ĭs′tĭk). Of or pertaining to royalists.

Roy·al·ist (roi′əl-ĭst) *n.* **1.** An Englishman loyal to Charles I; a Cavalier. **2.** A supporter of the House of Bourbon's claims to the French throne since the French Revolution. **3.** A Colonial American loyal to British rule; a Tory.

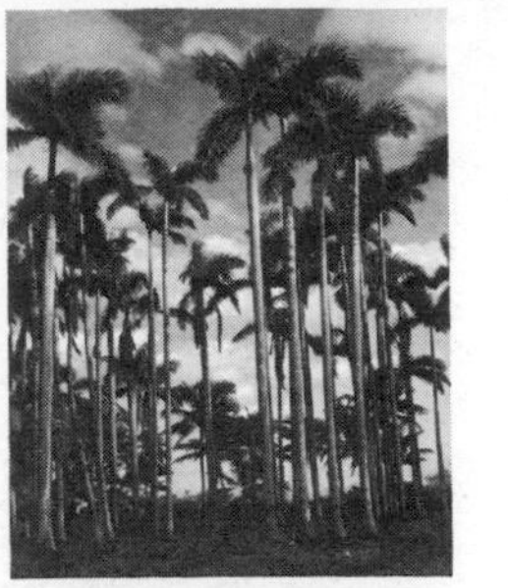

royal palm
Roystonea regia

royal jelly. A nutritious substance secreted in the pharyngeal glands of worker bees, serving as food for the young larvae, and as the only food for those that develop into queen bees.

roy·al·mast (roi′əl-măst′, -mäst′) *n.* Also **royal mast.** The small mast immediately above the topgallant mast.

Royal Oak. A city in southeastern Michigan, a suburb of Detroit. Population, 81,000.

royal palm. Any of several palm trees of the genus *Roystonea,* mostly from the West Indies, having a tall, naked trunk surmounted by a large tuft of pinnate leaves.

royal poinciana. A tropical and semitropical tree, *Delonix regia,* native to Madagascar, having clusters of large scarlet and yellow flowers and long pods. Also called "flamboyant."

royal purple. A moderate or strong violet to deep purple or dark reddish purple. See **color.** —**roy′al-pur′ple** *adj.*

roy·al·ty (roi′əl-tē) *n., pl.* **-ties. 1. a.** A king, queen, or other person of royal lineage. **b.** Monarchs and their families collectively. **2.** The lineage or rank of a king or queen. **3.** The power, status, or authority of monarchs. **4.** Royal quality or bearing; kingliness. **5.** A kingdom or possession ruled by a monarch. **6.** A right or prerogative of the crown, as that of receiving a percentage of the proceeds from mines in the royal domain. **7. a.** The granting of a right by a sovereign to a corporation or individual to exploit specified natural resources. **b.** The payment for such a right. **8. a.** A share paid to an author or composer out of the proceeds resulting from the sale or performance of his work. **b.** A share in the proceeds paid to an inventor or proprietor for the right to use his invention or services.

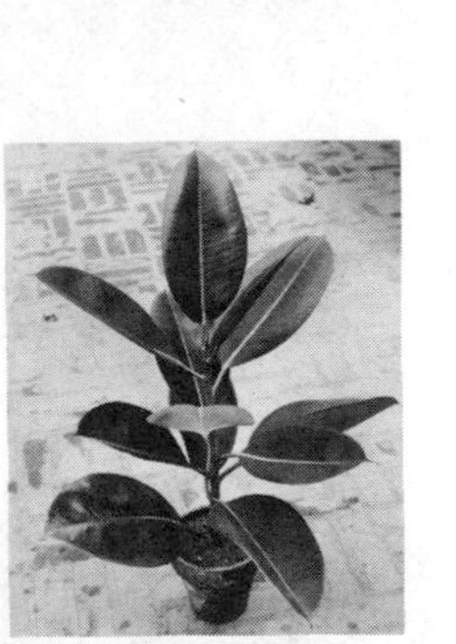

rubber plant
Ficus elastica

Royce (rois), **Josiah.** 1855–1916. American educator and philosopher.

r.p.m. revolutions per minute.

R.P.O. Railway Post Office.

r.p.s. revolutions per second.

rpt. report.

R.Q. respiratory quotient.

RR railroad.

R.R. 1. railroad. **2.** Right Reverend (title). **3.** rural route.

RRB Railroad Retirement Board.

-rrhagia. *Pathology.* Indicates an abnormal or excessive flow or discharge; for example, **menorrhagia.** [New Latin, from Greek, from *rhēgnunai,* to burst forth. See **wrēg-** in Appendix.*]

-rrhea, -rrhoea. *Pathology.* Indicates a flow or discharge; for example, **seborrhea, amenorrhoea.** [Middle English *-ria,* from Late Latin *-rrhoea,* from Greek *-rrhoia,* from *rhoia,* a flowing, flux, from *rhein,* to flow. See **sreu-** in Appendix.*]

R.S. 1. recording secretary. **2.** right side. **3.** Royal Society.

R.S.F.S.R. Russian Soviet Federated Socialist Republic.

R.S.V. Revised Standard Version (of the Bible).

r.s.v.p., R.S.V.P. répondez s'il vous plaît (English *please reply*).

rt. right.

rte. route.

Rt. Hon. Right Honorable (title).

Rt. Rev. Right Reverend (title).

Ru The symbol for the element ruthenium.

Ru·an·da-U·run·di (rōō-än′də-ōō-rōōn′dē). A former United Nations trust territory of east-central Africa, divided in 1962 into the independent countries of Burundi and Rwanda.

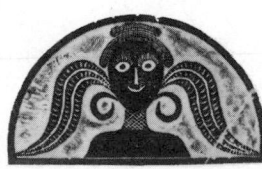

rubbing
Taken from a late
18th-century gravestone
in a Massachusetts cemetery

rub (rŭb) *v.* **rubbed, rubbing, rubs.** —*tr.* **1.** To apply pressure and friction to (a surface), manually or mechanically. **2.** To clean, polish, or manipulate by applying pressure and friction. **3.** To apply firmly and with friction upon a surface. **4.** To move (an object or objects) against another or each other repeatedly and with friction; scrape. **5.** To cause to become worn, chafed, or irritated. **6.** To remove or erase. Used with *out, off,* or *away.* —*intr.* **1.** To exert pressure and friction on something. **2.** To move along in contact with a surface; scrape. **3.** To become worn or chafed from friction. **4.** To be removed by pressure and friction. Used with *off* or *out.* —**rub it in.** To remind someone repeatedly of his mistake, shortcoming, or failure. —**rub out.** *Slang.* To murder. —*n.* **1.** The act of rubbing. **2.** An unevenness on a surface. **3.** An act or remark wounding to the feelings; a rebuke or sarcasm. **4.** Difficulty: *"Aye, there's the rub"* (Shakespeare). [Middle English *rubben,* perhaps from Middle Low German *rubben*†.]

Rub al Kha·li (rōōb′ äl KHä′lē). Also **Ar Ri·mal** (ûr rĭ-măl′). A vast desert occupying about 250,000 square miles in the southeastern interior of the Arabian Peninsula. Also called "Empty Quarter."

ru·basse (rōō-băs′, -bäs′) *n.* A quartz colored ruby red by its iron oxide content. [French *rubace,* from Old French *rubi, rubis,* RUBY.]

ru·ba·to (rōō-bä′tō) *n., pl.* **-tos.** *Music.* Rhythmic flexibility within a phrase or measure. —*adj. Music.* Containing or characterized by rubato. [Italian, *(tempo) rubato,* "stolen (time)," from the past participle of *rubare,* to rob, from Germanic. See **reup-** in Appendix.*]

rub·ber[1] (rŭb′ər) *n.* **1.** A light cream to dark amber, amorphous, elastic, solid polymer of isoprene, $(C_5H_8)_n$, generally prepared by coagulation and drying of the milky sap, or latex, of various tropical plants, especially the **rubber tree** *(see),* and subsequently vulcanized, pigmented, and otherwise modified for finishing as any of a wide variety of manufactured products including electric insulation, elastic bands and belts, tires, and containers. Also called "caoutchouc," "India rubber." **2.** Any of numerous synthetic elastic materials of varying chemical composition, with properties similar to those of natural rubber. **3.** *Usually plural.* A low overshoe made of rubber. **4.** *Slang.* A condom. **5.** *Baseball.* The oblong piece of hard rubber on which the pitcher must stand when he delivers the ball. **6. a.** One who rubs. **b.** One who gives a massage. **7.** Something used for rubbing; specifically, an eraser made of rubber. —*adj.* Made of rubber.

rub·ber[2] (rŭb′ər) *n. Abbr.* **r. 1.** In bridge, whist, and other games and sports, a series of games of which two out of three or three out of five must be won to terminate the play. **2.** The game that breaks a tie and ends such a series. [Origin unknown.]

rubber band. An elastic loop of natural or synthetic rubber, used to hold objects together.

rub·ber-base paint (rŭb′ər-bās′). **Latex paint** *(see).*

rubber check. A check returned by a bank because of insufficient funds in the account on which it is drawn.

rub·ber·ize (rŭb′ər-īz′) *tr.v.* **-ized, -izing, -izes.** To coat, treat, or impregnate with rubber.

rub·ber·neck (rŭb′ər-nĕk′) *n. Slang.* A gawking tourist or sightseer. —*intr.v.* **rubbernecked, -necking, -necks.** *Slang.* To stretch the neck in order to see better; to gawk.

rubber plant. 1. Any of several tropical plants yielding sap that can be coagulated to form crude rubber. **2.** A small tree, *Ficus elastica,* that has large, glossy, leathery leaves, and is popular as a house plant. It is not a source of commercial rubber.

rubber stamp. 1. A piece of rubber affixed to a handle and bearing raised characters, used to make ink impressions of names, dates, and the like. **2.** A person or body that gives perfunctory approval or endorsement of a policy without assessing its merit. **3.** A perfunctory approval or endorsement.

rub·ber-stamp (rŭb′ər-stămp′) *tr.v.* **-stamped, -stamping, -stamps. 1.** To mark with the imprint of a rubber stamp. **2.** To endorse, vote for, or approve without question or deliberation.

rubber tree. A tree, *Hevea brasiliensis,* native to tropical America but widely cultivated throughout the tropics, yielding a milky juice, or latex, that is a major source of commercial rubber.

rub·ber·y (rŭb′ər-ē) *adj.* Of or like rubber; elastic; resilient.

rub·bing (rŭb′ĭng) *n.* **1.** The act of polishing, cleaning, or drying. **2.** A representation of a raised or indented surface made by placing paper over the surface and rubbing the paper gently with a marking agent such as charcoal or chalk.

rub·bish (rŭb′ĭsh) *n.* **1.** Something discarded as refuse; garbage; litter. **2.** Worthless material. **3.** Foolish discourse; nonsense. [Middle English *robishe, robys, robous,* from Norman French *robbous,* plural of *robel* (unattested), RUBBLE.]

rub·bish·y (rŭb′ĭsh-ē) *adj.* **1.** Littered with rubbish. **2.** Of no value; worthless.

rub·ble (rŭb′əl) *n.* **1.** Fragments of rock or masonry crumbled by natural or man-made forces. **2. a.** Irregular fragments or pieces of rock used in masonry. **b.** The masonry made with such rocks. In this sense, also called "rubblework." [Middle English *robyl,* from Norman French *robel* (unattested), "rubbings," from Germanic. See **reup-** in Appendix.*] —**rub′bly** *adj.*

rub·down (rŭb′doun′) *n.* An energetic massage of the body.

rube (rōōb) *n. Slang.* An unsophisticated country fellow. [Probably from *Rube,* nickname of REUBEN.]

ru·be·fa·cient (rōō′bə-fā′shənt) *adj.* Producing redness, as of the skin. —*n.* A substance that irritates the skin, causing redness. [Latin *rubefaciēns,* present participle of *rubefacere,* to redden : *rubeus,* red, reddish (see **reudh-** in Appendix*) +

ă pat/ā pay/âr care/ä father/b bib/ch church/d deed/ĕ pet/ē be/f fife/g gag/h hat/hw which/ĭ pit/ī pie/îr pier/j judge/k kick/l lid, needle/m mum/n no, sudden/ng thing/ŏ pot/ō toe/ô paw, for/oi noise/ou out/ŏŏ took/ōō boot/p pop/r roar/s sauce/sh ship, dish/

facere, to make (see **dhē-**[1] in Appendix*).] **—ru′be·fac′tion** (-făk′shən) *n.*

Rube Gold·berg. See **Goldberg.**

ru·bel·la (ro͞o-bĕl′ə) *n.* A disease, **German measles** *(see).* [New Latin, from Latin, feminine of *rubellus,* reddish, from *rubeus,* red, reddish. See **reudh-** in Appendix.*]

ru·bel·lite (ro͞o′bə-līt′) *n.* A red tourmaline used as a gemstone. [Latin *rubellus,* reddish (see **rubella**) + -ITE.]

Ru·bens (ro͞o′bənz), **Peter Paul.** 1577–1640. Flemish painter.

ru·be·o·la (ro͞o-bē′ə-lə) *n.* **1. Measles** *(see).* **2. German measles** *(see).* [New Latin, neuter plural diminutive of Latin *rubeus,* red. See **reudh-** in Appendix.*] **—ru·be′o·lar** *adj.*

ru·bes·cent (ro͞o-bĕs′ənt) *adj.* Reddening. [Latin *rubescēns,* present participle of *rubescere,* to grow red, inchoative of *rubēre,* to be red. See **reudh-** in Appendix.*] **—ru·bes′cence** *n.*

Ru·bi·con (ro͞o′bĭ-kŏn). A small river of northern Italy rising just north of San Marino and flowing 15 miles northeast to the Adriatic Sea. Caesar's crossing it with his army in 49 B.C. constituted an illegal entry into Italy and thereby initiated civil war. **—cross** (or **pass**) **the Rubicon.** To embark on an undertaking from which one cannot turn back.

ru·bi·cund (ro͞o′bə-kənd) *adj.* Inclined to a healthy rosiness; ruddy. [Latin *rubicundus.* See **reudh-** in Appendix.*] **—ru′bi·cun′di·ty** (-kŭn′də-tē) *n.*

ru·bid·i·um (ro͞o-bĭd′ē-əm) *n. Symbol* **Rb** A soft silvery-white alkali element that ignites spontaneously in air and reacts violently with water. It is used in photocells and in the manufacture of vacuum tubes. Atomic number 37, atomic weight 85.47, melting point 38.89°C, boiling point 688°C, specific gravity (solid) 1.532, valences 1, 2, 3, 4. See **element.** [New Latin, from Latin *rubidus,* red (from the red lines in its spectrum). See **reudh-** in Appendix.*]

ru·big·i·nous (ro͞o-bĭj′ə-nəs) *adj.* Also **ru·big·i·nose** (-nōs′). Rust-colored; reddish-brown. [Latin *rūbīginōsus,* from *rūbīgo, rōbīgo,* rust. See **reudh-** in Appendix.*]

Ru·bin·stein (ro͞o′bən-stīn), **Anton Gregor.** 1829–1894. Russian concert pianist, composer, and educator.

Ru·bin·stein (ro͞o′bən-stīn), **Artur.** Born 1886. Polish-born American concert pianist.

ru·bi·ous (ro͞o′bē-əs) *adj.* Having the color of a ruby; red.

ru·ble. Variant of **rouble.**

ru·bric (ro͞o′brĭk) *n.* **1.** A part of a manuscript or book, such as a title, heading, or initial letter, that appears in decorative red lettering, or is otherwise distinguished from the rest of the text. **2.** A title or heading of a statute or chapter in a code of law, originally written or printed in red. **3.** A name for a class or category; title. **4.** *Ecclesiastical.* A direction in a missal, hymnal, or other liturgical book. **5.** Any brief, authoritative rule or direction. **6.** A short commentary or explanation covering a broad subject. **7.** *Rare.* Red ocher. *—adj.* **1.** Red or reddish. **2.** Written in red. [Middle English *rubrike,* from Old French *rubriche,* from Latin *rubrīca (terra),* "red earth," "red ocher," from *ruber,* red. See **reudh-** in Appendix.*] **—ru′bri·cal** *adj.*

ru·bri·cate (ro͞o′brə-kāt′) *tr.v.* **-cated, -cating, -cates. 1.** To arrange, write, or print as a rubric. **2.** To provide with rubrics. **3.** To establish rules for. [Late Latin *rubricāre,* from *rubrica,* RUBRIC.] **—ru′bri·ca′tion** *n.*

ru·bri·cian (ro͞o-brĭsh′ən) *n.* A person learned in the rubrics of ecclesiastical ritual.

ru·by (ro͞o′bē) *n., pl.* **-bies. 1.** A deep-red, translucent corundum, highly valued as a precious stone. Also called "Oriental ruby," "true ruby." **2.** Something made from a ruby, as a watch bearing. **3.** A dark or deep red to deep purplish red. See **color.** *—adj.* Of or having the color of rubies. [Middle English, from Old French *rubi,* from Medieval Latin *rubīnus (lapis),* "red stone," from Latin *rubeus,* red. See **reudh-** in Appendix.*]

ru·by-throat·ed hummingbird (ro͞o′bē-thrō′tĭd). A small bird, *Archilochus colubris,* of eastern North America, having metallic-green upper plumage and, in the male, a brilliant red throat.

ruche, rouche (ro͞osh) *n.* A ruffle or pleat of lace, muslin, or other fine fabric used for trimming women's garments. [French, beehive, frill (pleated like a straw beehive), from Old French *ruche,* bark of a tree, beehive made of barks, from Medieval Latin *rūsca,* from Gaulish *rūska* (unattested), akin to Old Irish *rūsc*†, bark.]

ruch·ing (ro͞o′shĭng) *n.* **1.** A ruche. **2.** Fabric for ruches.

ruck[1] (rŭk) *n.* **1.** A large number mixed together; a jumble. **2.** The multitude of ordinary people. [Middle English *ruke*†, heap, stack.]

ruck[2] (rŭk) *v.* **rucked, rucking, rucks.** *—tr.* **1.** To make a fold in; to crease. **2.** To disturb or ruffle; irritate. Often used with *up.* *—intr.* **1.** To become creased. **2.** To become irritated. *—n.* A crease or pucker, as in cloth. [Ultimately from Old Norse *hrukka,* wrinkle, crease. See **sker-**[3] in Appendix.*]

ruck·sack (rŭk′săk′, ro͝ok′-) *n.* A canvas sack for carrying supplies. [German *Rucksack* : *Rücken,* back, from Old High German *hrukki* (see **sker-**[3] in Appendix*) + *Sack,* sack, from Old High German *sac,* from Latin *saccus,* SACK.]

ruck·us (rŭk′əs) *n. Informal.* A noisy disturbance; commotion. [Probably RUC(TION) + (RUMP)US.]

ruc·tion (rŭk′shən) *n. Informal.* A riotous disturbance; noisy quarrel. [From *the Ruction,* Irish revolt in 1798, probably shortened from INSURRECTION.]

rudd (rŭd) *n.* A European freshwater fish, *Scardinius erythrophthalmus,* having a brownish body and red fins. [Probably from *rud,* a ruddy color. See **ruddle.**]

rud·der (rŭd′ər) *n.* **1.** A vertically hinged plate of metal or wood mounted at the stern of a vessel for directing its course. **2.** A similar structure at the tail of an aircraft, used for effecting horizontal changes in course. **3.** Anything that controls direction; a guide. [Middle English *rother, rodyr,* Old English *rōther,* steering oar. See **ere-**[1] in Appendix.*]

rud·der·stock (rŭd′ər-stŏk′) *n.* The vertical shaft of a rudder, allowing it to pivot when the tiller or steering gear is operated. Also called "rudderpost."

rud·dle (rŭd′l) *n.* Also **red·dle** (rĕd′l), **rad·dle** (răd′l). Red ocherous iron ore, used in dyeing and marking. *—tr.v.* **ruddled, -dling, -dles.** Also **red·dle, rad·dle.** To dye or mark with red ocher: *ruddle sheep.* [Diminutive of *rud,* a ruddy color, Middle English *rud(d)e,* Old English *rudu.* See **reudh-** in Appendix.*]

rud·dle·man (rŭd′l-mən) *n., pl.* **-men** (-mĭn). A man who sells ruddle, or red ocher.

rud·dock (rŭd′ək) *n. British Regional.* The Old World robin. [Middle English *ruddok,* Old English *rudduc.* See **reudh-** in Appendix.*]

rud·dy (rŭd′ē) *adj.* **-dier, -diest. 1.** Having a healthy, reddish color. **2.** Reddish; rosy. **3.** *Slang.* Confounded; darned. [Middle English *rudie,* Old English *rudig,* from *rudu,* red color. See **reudh-** in Appendix.*] **—rud′di·ly** *adv.* **—rud′di·ness** *n.*

ruddy duck. A North American duck, *Oxyura jamaicensis,* having stiff, pointed tail feathers and, in the male, brownish-red upper plumage and a black and white head.

rude (ro͞od) *adj.* **ruder, rudest. 1.** Primitive; uncivilized: *"the Lappians, a rude and savage nation, living in woods"* (Clemen Adams). **2.** Lowly; humble: *a rude thatched hut.* **3.** Lacking the graces of civilized life; unrefined; uncouth. **4.** Ill-mannered; uncivil; discourteous. **5.** Formed without skill or precision; makeshift; crude: *"A dead willow trunk thrown from bank to bank forms a rude bridge"* (Richard Jefferies). **6.** Approximate; rough: *"the height of the cliffs thus affording a rude measure of the age of the streams"* (Darwin). **7.** Vigorous; robust. **8.** Harsh; severe. **9.** Discordant: *"rude harsh-sounding rhymes"* (Shakespeare). [Middle English, from Old French, from Latin *rudis,* rough, raw, akin to *rūdus,* broken stone. See **ruderal.**] **—rude′ly** *adv.* **—rude′ness** *n.*

ru·der·al (ro͞o′də-rəl) *adj. Botany.* Growing in rubbish, poor land, or waste places. *—n. Botany.* A plant growing in such ground. [New Latin *rūderālis,* from Latin *rūdera,* ruins, rubbish, plural of *rūdus*†, broken stone.]

rudes·by (ro͞odz′bē) *n., pl.* **-bies.** *Archaic.* An ill-bred, insolent, or turbulent person: *"Commoved by the speech of this rudesby"* (Scott). [RUDE + *-by,* a suffix used to indicate personal appellations.]

ru·di·ment (ro͞o′də-mənt) *n.* **1.** *Often plural.* A fundamental element, principle, or skill, as of a field of learning. **2.** *Often plural.* Something in an incipient or undeveloped form; beginnings: *the rudiments of social behavior in children.* **3.** *Biology.* An imperfectly or incompletely developed organ or part. [Old French, from Latin *rudīmentum,* beginning (formed after *elementum,* ELEMENT), from *rudis,* RUDE.]

ru·di·men·ta·ry (ro͞o′də-mĕn′tər-ē) *adj.* Also **ru·di·men·tal** (-təl). **1.** Of or relating to basic facts or principles that must be learned first; elementary. **2.** In the earliest stages of development; incipient. **3.** *Biology.* Imperfectly or incompletely developed; vestigial: *a rudimentary organ.* **—ru′di·men·ta′ri·ly** *adv.* **—ru′di·men′ta·ri·ness** *n.*

Ru·dolf I (ro͞o′dŏlf). 1218–1291. Holy Roman Emperor (1273–91); founder of the Hapsburg Dynasty.

Ru·dolf, Lake (ro͞o′dŏlf). A salt lake of eastern Africa, occupying about 3,500 square miles in the Great Rift Valley in northwestern Kenya.

Ru·dolf of Haps·burg (ro͞o′dŏlf; hăps′bûrg). 1858–1889. Archduke and crown prince of Austria; son of Emperor Francis Joseph; murdered his mistress and committed suicide.

rue[1] (ro͞o) *v.* **rued, ruing, rues.** *—tr.* To feel remorse or sorrow for; to regret; repent. *—intr.* To feel remorse or sorrow; be penitent or regretful. *—n. Archaic.* Sorrow; regret. [Middle English *ruen,* Old English *hrēowan,* to make penitent, distress. See **kreu-**[2] in Appendix.*] **—ru′er** *n.*

rue[2] (ro͞o) *n.* An aromatic Eurasian plant of the genus *Ruta;* especially, *R. graveolens,* having evergreen leaves that yield an acrid, volatile oil formerly used in medicine. Formerly called "herb-of-grace." [Middle English, from Old French, from Latin *rūta,* from Greek *rhutē,* originally a Peloponnesian word.]

rue anemone. A small North American woodland plant, *Anemonella thalictroides,* having white or pinkish flowers.

rue·ful (ro͞o′fəl) *adj.* **1.** Inspiring pity or compassion. **2.** Causing, feeling, or expressing sorrow or regret. **3.** Expressive of a bitter, faintly sardonic compassion; wry. **—rue′ful·ly** *adv.* **—rue′ful·ness** *n.*

ru·fes·cent (ro͞o-fĕs′ənt) *adj.* Tinged with red. [Latin *rūfēscēns,* present participle of *rūfēscere,* to become reddish, from *rūfus,* reddish. See **reudh-** in Appendix.*] **—ru·fes′cence** *n.*

ruff[1] (rŭf) *n.* **1.** A stiffly starched, frilled or pleated circular collar of lace, muslin, or other fine fabric, worn by men and women in the 16th and 17th centuries. **2.** A distinctive collarlike projection around the neck, as of feathers on a bird or of fur on a mammal. **3.** The male of a Eurasian sandpiper, *Philomachus pugnax,* having collarlike, erectile feathers around the neck during the breeding season. The female is called a "reeve." [Short for RUFFLE (frill).] **—ruffed** *adj.*

ruff[2] (rŭf) *n. Card Games.* **1.** The playing of a trump card when one cannot follow suit. **2.** An old game resembling whist. *—v.* **ruffed, ruffing, ruffs.** *Card Games.* *—tr.* To trump. *—intr.* To play a trump. [Old French *roffle,* earlier *ronfle,* probably from Italian *ronfa,* perhaps alteration of *trionfa,* "triumph," trump card, from Latin *triumphus,* TRIUMPH.]

ruff[3] (rŭf) *n.* A European freshwater fish, *Acerina cernua,* re-

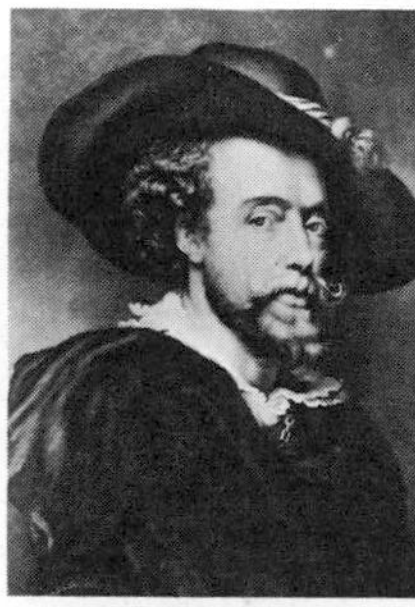

Peter Paul Rubens

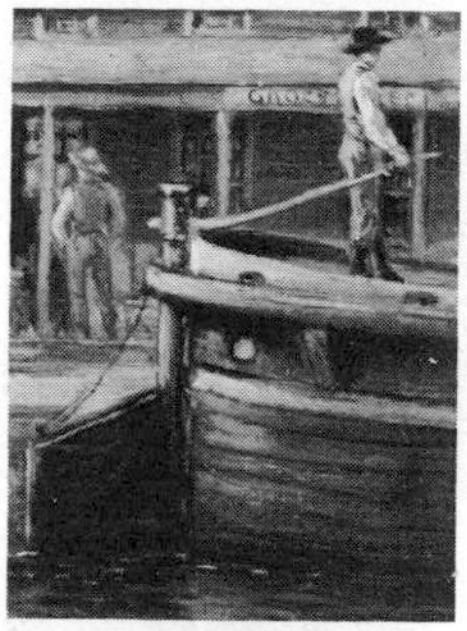

rudder
Detail from E.L. Henry painting, showing a man steering a barge on the Erie Canal

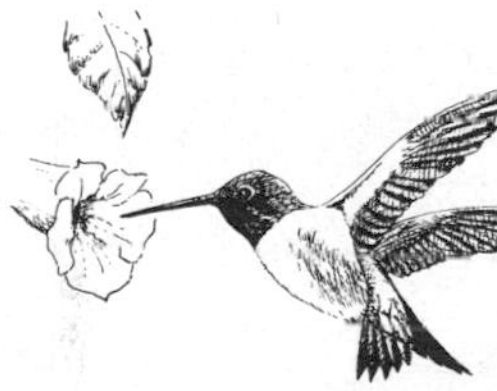

ruby-throated hummingbird

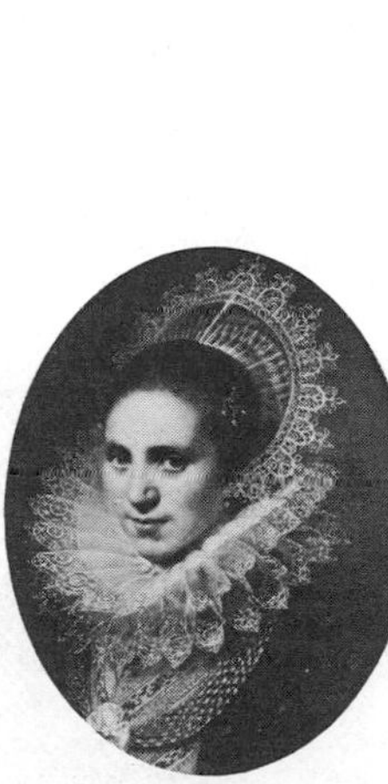

ruff[1]

lated to the perches. [Middle English *ruf, ruffe,* sea bream, perhaps from *ruch, r(o)wgh,* ROUGH (from its rough scales).]

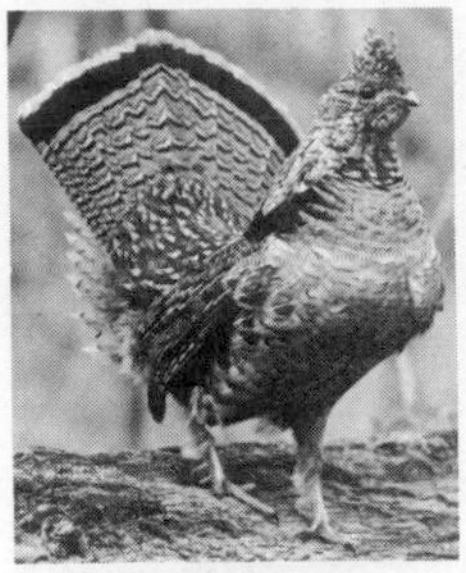

ruffed grouse

ruffed grouse. A chickenlike North American game bird, *Bonasa umbellus,* having mottled brownish plumage. Also called "partridge," sometimes "pheasant."

ruf·fi·an (rŭf′ē-ən, rŭf′yən) *n.* **1.** A tough or rowdy fellow. **2.** A thug or gangster. [Old French *rufien, ruf(f)ian,* from Italian *ruffiano,* pander, "filthy or scabby person," from *roffia, ruffia,* scab, filth, probably from Germanic. See **kreup-** in Appendix.*] —**ruf′fi·an·ism′** *n.* —**ruf′fi·an, ruf′fi·an·ly** *adj.*

ruf·fle¹ (rŭf′əl) *n.* **1.** A strip of frilled or closely pleated fabric used for trimming or decoration. **2.** Something resembling such trimming, as a bird's ruff. **3.** A slight discomposure; an agitation. **4.** An irregularity in smoothness; a slight disturbance. —*v.* **ruffled, -fling, -fles.** —*tr.* **1.** To disturb the smoothness or regularity of; to ripple. **2.** To pleat or gather (fabric) into a ruffle. **3.** To erect (the feathers). **4.** To discompose; fluster. **5.** To flip through (the pages of a book). **6.** To shuffle (cards). —*intr.* **1.** To become irregular or rough. **2.** To flutter. **3.** To become flustered. [Middle English *ruffelen,* to roughen, disarrange, from Germanic, akin to Middle Low German *ruffelen,* to crumple. See **kreup-** in Appendix.*]

ruf·fle² (rŭf′əl) *n.* A low continuous beating of a drum that is not as loud as a roll. —*tr.v.* **ruffled, -fling, -fles.** To beat a ruffle on (a drum). [Frequentative of earlier *ruff,* ruffle (imitative).]

ruf·fle³ (rŭf′əl) *intr.v.* **-fled, -fling, -fles.** To behave arrogantly or roughly; swagger. [Middle English *ruffelen,* perhaps extended use of RUFFLE (to roughen).] —**ruf′fler** *n.*

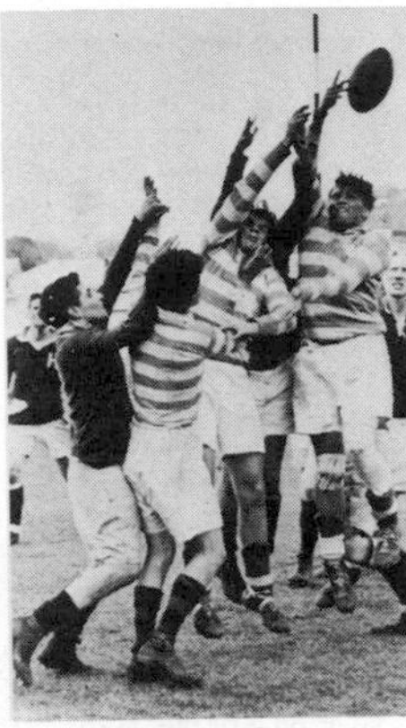

Rugby football

ru·fous (ro͞o′fəs) *adj.* Strong yellowish pink to moderate orange. See **color.** [Latin *rūfus,* red, reddish. See **reudh-** in Appendix.*]

Ru·fus (ro͞o′fəs). A masculine given name. [Latin *rūfus,* red, reddish. See **reudh-** in Appendix.*]

rug (rŭg) *n.* **1.** A piece of heavy fabric used to cover a portion of a floor. **2.** An animal skin used as a floor covering. **3.** *Chiefly British.* A piece of thick, warm fabric or fur used as a coverlet or lap robe. [Probably from Swedish *rugg,* ruffled hair, akin to Old Norse *rǫgg,* tuft. See **rugged.**]

ru·ga (ro͞o′gə) *n., pl.* **-gae** (-gē′, -gī′). *Usually plural. Biology.* A fold, crease, or wrinkle, as in the lining of the stomach. [Latin *rūga,* fold. See **ruk-²** in Appendix.*] —**ru′gate′** (-gāt′) *adj.*

Rug·by football (rŭg′bē). A British form of football in which players on two competing teams may kick, dribble, or run with the ball. Forward passing, substitution of players, and time-outs are not permitted. Also called "rugby," and, in Great Britain, "rugger." [Invented at *Rugby* School, Warwickshire.]

Rü·gen (rü′gən). An island (358 square miles) in the Baltic Sea connected with the mainland of East Germany by a dam.

rug·ged (rŭg′ĭd) *adj.* **1.** Having a rough, irregular surface. **2.** Having strong features marked with furrows or wrinkles. **3.** Tempestuous; stormy. **4.** Demanding great effort, ability, or endurance. **5.** Lacking culture or polish. **6.** Vigorously healthy; hardy. —See Synonyms at **rough.** [Middle English, shaggy, from Scandinavian, akin to Old Norse *rǫgg,* tuft, from Germanic *rawwō* (unattested).] —**rug′ged·ly** *adv.* —**rug′ged·ness** *n.*

rug·ger (rŭg′ər) *n. British.* **Rugby football** *(see).*

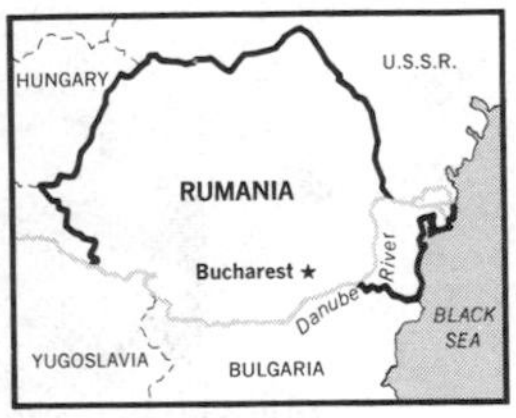

Rumania

ru·gose (ro͞o′gōs) *adj.* Also **ru·gous** (ro͞o′gəs). **1.** Having many wrinkles or creases. **2.** *Botany.* Having a rough and ridged surface, as certain prominently veined leaves do. [Latin *rūgōsus,* creased, from *rūga,* fold. See **ruk-²** in Appendix.*] —**ru′gose·ly** *adv.* —**ru·gos′i·ty** (-gŏs′ə-tē) *n.*

Ruhr (ro͝or). **1.** A river of West Germany flowing west for 145 miles through North Rhine-Westphalia to join the Rhine at Duisburg. **2.** The major coal-mining and industrial region of West Germany, bounded on the south by the Ruhr River.

ru·in (ro͞o′ĭn) *n.* **1.** Total destruction or disintegration, rendering something formless, useless, or valueless. **2.** The cause of such destruction: *A single flaw is the ruin of a diamond.* **3.** A condition of total destruction or collapse. **4.** *Often plural.* The remains of something destroyed, disintegrated, or decayed. **5.** A person whose physical or mental capacities have been destroyed. **6.** The loss or severe impairment of one's health, position, or honor. **7.** The cause of such loss. —*v.* **ruined, -ining, -ins.** —*tr.* **1.** To destroy or demolish; reduce to ruin or disintegrate. **2.** To harm irreparably. **3.** To reduce to poverty or bankruptcy. **4.** To deprive of chastity. —*intr.* To fall into ruin. [Middle English *ruine,* from Old French, from Latin *ruīna,* "fall," from *ruere,* to fall, crumble. See **rabble.**] —**ru′in·a·ble** *adj.* —**ru′in·er** *n.*

Synonyms: *ruin, raze, demolish, destroy, devastate, damage, wreck.* These verbs mean to cause serious injury to a thing or, less often, to a person. *Ruin* implies depriving of usefulness, soundness, or integrity without altogether doing away with the object injured. *Raze* means to level to the ground, and *demolish,* to pull down or break or tear to pieces. *Destroy* is less specific but stresses an end to usefulness if not utter elimination of something. *Devastate* means to lay waste, and implies severe and widespread injury and desolation. *Damage* is nonspecific with respect to extent of injury, but in general is the weakest of these terms. *Wreck* suggests severe, usually irreparable, injury, often incurred violently or willfully.

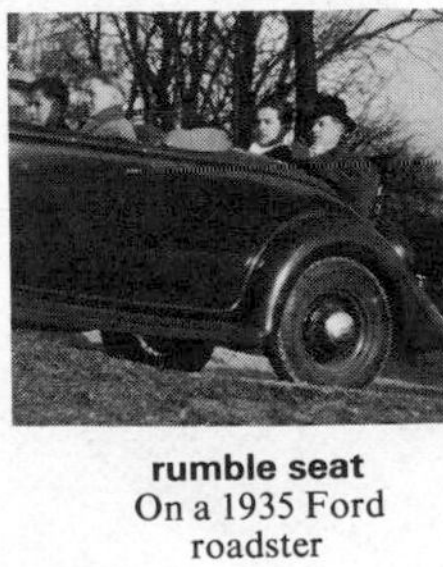

rumble seat
On a 1935 Ford roadster

ru·in·ate (ro͞o′ĭ-nāt′) *adj.* Ruined. [Medieval Latin *ruīnātus,* from *ruīnāre,* to ruin, from Latin *ruīna,* RUIN.]

ru·in·a·tion (ro͞o′ĭ-nā′shən) *n.* **1. a.** The act of ruining. **b.** The condition of being ruined. **2.** The cause of ruin.

ru·in·ous (ro͞o′ĭ-nəs) *adj.* **1.** Causing or apt to cause ruin; destructive. **2.** Falling to ruin; dilapidated or decayed. —**ru′in·ous·ly** *adv.* —**ru′in·ous·ness** *n.*

Ruis·dael. See **Ruysdael.**

Ruis·lip and North·wood (rī′slĭp; nôrth′wo͝od). A former administrative division of London, England, now part of **Hillingdon** *(see).*

rule (ro͞ol) *n.* **1.** Governing power, or its possession or use; authority; control: *under the rule of Henry VIII.* **2.** An authoritative direction for conduct or procedure, specifically: **a.** One of the regulations governing procedure in a legislative body. **b.** A principle of conduct observed by the members of a group. **c.** A regulation observed by the players in a game, sport, or contest. **3.** A code of principles for the conduct of religious services or activities. **4.** An established standard or habit of behavior. **5.** Something that generally prevails or obtains. **6.** A standard method or procedure for solving a class of mathematical problems. **7.** *Law.* **a.** A court order limited in application to a specific case. **b.** A subordinate regulation governing a particular matter. **8.** A straightedge; ruler. **9.** *Printing.* A thin metal strip of various widths and designs, used to print borders or lines, as between columns. —*v.* **ruled, ruling, rules.** —*tr.* **1.** To exercise control over; govern. **2.** To dominate by powerful influence; hold sway over. **3.** To keep within proper limits; restrain. **4.** To decide or declare judicially; decree. **5. a.** To mark with straight parallel lines: *ruled note paper.* **b.** To mark (a straight line), as with a ruler. —*intr.* **1.** To exercise authority; be in control or command. **2.** To formulate and issue a decree or decision. **3.** To maintain a specified rate or level: *Prices ruled low.* —See Synonyms at **decide.** [Middle English *riule, reule,* from Old French, from Latin *rēgula,* straight stick, ruler, rule, pattern. See **reg-¹** in Appendix.*] —**rul′a·ble** *adj.*

ruled surface. A surface, such as a cone or a cylinder, generated by the motion of a straight line.

rule of thumb. A useful principle with wide application, not intended to be strictly accurate. [From the use of the thumb in measuring.]

rul·er (ro͞o′lər) *n.* **1.** A person or thing that rules or governs, as a sovereign. **2.** A straight-edged strip, as of wood or metal, for drawing straight lines and measuring lengths.

rul·ing (ro͞o′lĭng) *adj.* Exercising control or dominion; predominant. —*n.* **1.** The act of governing or controlling. **2.** An authoritative or official decision. **3. a.** The drawing, grinding, or other marking of straight, parallel lines. **b.** The lines so ruled.

rum¹ (rŭm) *n.* **1.** An alcoholic liquor distilled from fermented molasses or sugar cane. **2.** Intoxicating beverages. [Perhaps shortened from earlier *rumbullion*†.]

rum² (rŭm) *adj.* Also **rum·my** (rŭm′ē). *British Slang.* Odd; queer. [Perhaps from Romany *rom,* gypsy man. See **Romany.**]

Rum. The Arabic name for the **Byzantine Empire.**

Ru·ma·ni·a (ro͞o-mā′nē-ə, -nyə). Also **Ro·ma·ni·a** (rō-), **Rou·ma·ni·a** (ro͞o-). *Rumanian* **Ro·mâ·ni·a** (rô-mû′nyä). Officially, the Rumanian People's Republic. *Abbr.* **Rum.** A country of southeastern Europe, 91,700 square miles in area, with a short eastern border on the Black Sea. Population, 18,927,000. Capital, Bucharest. [Rumanian *Romania,* from *Roman, Ruman,* a Rumanian, "Roman," from Latin *Rōmānus,* ROMAN.]

Ru·ma·ni·an (ro͞o-mā′nē-ən, ro͞o-mān′yən) *adj.* Also **Ro·ma·ni·an** (rō-mā′nē-ən, -nyən), **Rou·ma·ni·an** (ro͞o-mā′nē-ən, -nyən). *Abbr.* **Rum.** Of or pertaining to Rumania, its people, or their language. —*n.* Also **Ro·ma·ni·an, Rou·ma·ni·an.** **1.** An inhabitant or native of Rumania. **2.** The Romance language of the Rumanian people.

rum·ba (rŭm′bə; *Spanish* ro͞om′bä) *n.* Also **rhum·ba.** **1.** A complex rhythmical dance that originated among Cuban Negroes. **2.** A modern ballroom adaptation of this dance. [American Spanish, from *rumbo,* carousel, from Spanish, pomp, perhaps extended use of *rumbo,* bearing, rhumb line, from Middle Dutch *rume.* See **rewe-** in Appendix.*]

rum·ble (rŭm′bəl) *v.* **-bled, -bling, -bles.** —*intr.* **1.** To make a continuous, deep, heavy, reverberating sound, as thunder does. **2.** To move or proceed with such a sound. **3.** *Slang.* To engage in a gang fight. —*tr.* **1.** To utter with a rumbling sound. **2.** To polish or mix (metal parts) in a tumbling box. —*n.* **1.** A continuous, deep, heavy, rolling sound. **2.** A **tumbling box** *(see).* **3.** A luggage compartment or servant's seat in the rear of a carriage. **4.** *Slang.* A gang fight. [Middle English *romblen,* probably from Middle Dutch *rommelen* (imitative).] —**rum′bler** *n.* —**rum′bling·ly** *adv.* —**rum′bly** *adj.*

rumble seat. An uncovered passenger seat that opens out from the rear of an automobile.

Ru·me·li·a (ro͞o-mē′lē-ə). Also **Rou·me·li·a.** The possessions of the former Ottoman Empire in the Balkan Peninsula, including Macedonia, Albania, and Thrace.

ru·men (ro͞o′mĕn) *n., pl.* **-mina** (-mə-nə) or **-mens.** The first division of the stomach of a ruminant animal, in which food is partly digested before being regurgitated for further chewing. Also called "paunch." [Latin *rūmen*†, throat, gullet.]

ru·mi·nant (ro͞o′mə-nənt) *n.* Any of various hoofed, even-toed, usually horned mammals of the suborder Ruminantia, such as cattle, sheep, goats, deer, and giraffes, characteristically having a stomach divided into four compartments, and chewing a cud consisting of regurgitated, partially digested food. —*adj.* **1.** Characterized by the chewing of cud. **2.** Of or belonging to the Ruminantia. **3.** Meditative; contemplative. [Latin *rūminans,* present participle of *rūmināre,* to chew cud, RUMINATE.]

ru·mi·nate (ro͞o′mə-nāt′) *v.* **-nated, -nating, -nates.** —*intr.* **1.** To chew cud. **2.** To meditate at length; muse. —*tr.* To meditate or reflect on. —See Synonyms at **ponder.** [Latin *rūmināre,* from *rūmen,* RUMEN.] —**ru′mi·nat′ing·ly, ru′mi·na·tive·ly** *adv.* —**ru′mi·na′tive** *adj.* —**ru′mi·na′tor** (-nā′tər) *n.*

ru·mi·na·tion (ro͞o′mə-nā′shən) *n.* **1.** The act or process of chewing cud. **2.** The act of pondering; meditation.

rum·mage (rŭm′ĭj) *v.* **-maged, -maging, -mages.** —*tr.* **1.** To search thoroughly by handling, turning over, or disarranging the contents of. **2.** To discover by searching thoroughly. Used with *up* or *out.* —*intr.* To make an energetic, usually hasty search. —*n.* **1.** An act of rummaging; a thorough search among a number of things. **2.** A confusion of miscellaneous articles. [Originally "arrangement of cargo in a ship's hold," odds and ends, from Norman French *rumage* (unattested), variant of Old French *arrumage,* from *arrumer, arimer,* to put in a ship's hold : *a-,* from Latin *ad-,* to, at + *-rimer,* ship's hold, "space," from Germanic (see **rewe-** in Appendix*).] —**rum′mag·er** *n.*

rummage sale. **1.** A sale of secondhand miscellaneous objects, contributed by donors to raise money for a charity. **2.** A sale of unclaimed or excess goods, as at a warehouse or wharf.

rum·mer (rŭm′ər) *n.* A large drinking cup or glass. [German *Römer,* from Dutch *roemer,* "glass for drinking toasts," from *roemen,* to praise, extol. See **kar-**[2] in Appendix.*]

rum·my[1] (rŭm′ē) *n.* A card game, played in many variations, in which the object is to obtain sets of three or more cards of the same denomination or suit. [Origin uncertain.]

rum·my[2] (rŭm′ē) *n., pl.* **-mies.** *Slang.* A drunkard.

rum·my[3]. *British Slang.* Variant of **rum** (odd).

ru·mor (ro͞o′mər) *n.* Also *chiefly British* **ru·mour.** Unverified information of uncertain origin usually spread by word of mouth; gossip; hearsay. —*tr.v.* **rumored, -moring, -mors.** Also *chiefly British* **ru·mour.** To spread or tell by rumor. [Middle English *rumo(u)r,* from Old French, from Latin *rūmor.* See **reu-** in Appendix.*]

ru·mor·mon·ger (ro͞o′mər-mŭng′gər, -mŏng′gər) *n.* One who spreads rumors.

rump (rŭmp) *n.* **1.** The fleshy hindquarters of an animal. **2.** A cut of beef or veal from this part. **3.** The human buttocks. **4.** The part of a bird's back nearest the tail. **5.** The last or inferior part of something. **6.** A legislature having only a small part of its original membership and so unrepresentative or lacking authority. [Middle English *rumpe,* from Scandinavian, akin to Danish *rumpe*†, buttocks.]

rum·ple (rŭm′pəl) *v.* **-pled, -pling, -ples.** —*tr.* To wrinkle or form into folds or creases. —*intr.* To become wrinkled or creased. —*n.* An uneven fold; an irregular or untidy crease. [Dutch *rompelen,* from Middle Dutch *rompelen, rumpelen.* See **skerbh-** in Appendix.*] —**rum′ply** *adj.*

Rump Parliament. The part of the Long Parliament that remained after Pride's Purge (1648) until dismissed by Cromwell (1653). It was recalled (1659), but again disbanded at the restoration of Charles II (1660).

rum·pus (rŭm′pəs) *n.* A noisy clamor. [Origin unknown.]

rumpus room. A room for play and parties.

rum·run·ner (rŭm′rŭn′ər) *n.* **1.** One who illegally transports liquor across a border. **2.** A boat used for this purpose.

Rum·sey (rŭm′zē), **James.** 1743–1792. American engineer; inventor of practical steamboat (1787) and steam boiler.

run (rŭn) *v.* **ran** (răn), **running, runs.** —*intr.* **I.** To move rapidly. **1. a.** To move on foot at a pace faster than the walk and in such a manner that both feet leave the ground during each stride. **b.** To move at a gait faster than the canter; to gallop. Used of a horse. **2.** To retreat rapidly; flee: *turn and run.* **3.** To move without hindrance or restraint: *The cattle ran on good pasture all summer.* **4.** To make a short, quick trip or visit: *run down to the shore.* **5. a.** To swim rapidly: *A trout took the fly and ran upstream.* **b.** To shoal or migrate inshore or upstream, especially prior to spawning: *The shad are running.* **6. a.** To move, act, or occur quickly or fleetingly; to hurry; hasten: *She ran through her mail.* **b.** To have frequent recourse to someone or something: *He is always running to his lawyer.* **II.** To compete. **7.** To take part in a race: *His horse ran in the Derby.* **8.** To compete for elected office: *He ran for mayor.* **9.** To finish a race in a specified position: *He ran second.* **III.** To move in a specified way. **10.** To move freely, as by rolling or sliding: *The car ran downhill.* **11.** To be in operation: *The car's engine is running.* **12.** To go regularly; to ply: *The ferry runs every hour.* **13.** *Nautical.* To sail or steer before the wind or on an indicated course: *run before the storm; run into port.* **IV.** To flow. **14.** To flow in a steady stream, as fluids or loose particles. **15.** To melt and flow: *Tin must be hot for the solder to run.* **16.** To flow and spread, as dyes in a fabric: *The colors ran.* **17.** To be wet with; stream with: *The street ran with blood.* **18.** To overflow. **19.** To discharge; carry off; drain: *The sink isn't running.* **20.** To surge, as waves or the tides: *A heavy surf was running.* **V.** To extend in space. **21.** To extend, stretch, or reach: *"the houses run down one side and the Park runs down the other"* (Pamela Travers). **22.** To spread or climb, as vines: *Poison ivy ran all over the yard.* **23.** To spread rapidly: *Rumors ran through the town.* **24.** *Law.* To be valid in a given area: *The writ runs only to the county line.* **25.** To unravel along a line: *Her stocking ran.* **VI.** To extend in time. **26.** To continue: *The lease has two years to run.* **27.** To pass. *Days ran into weeks.* **28.** To persist or recur: *Gout runs in the family.* **29.** *Law.* **a.** To be effective. **b.** To be concurrent with: *Fishing rights run with ownership of the land.* **30. a.** To accumulate or accrue. **b.** To become payable: *Your note runs, with interest, to June 1st.* **31.** To be expressed in a given way: *His reasoning ran thus.* **32.** To tend or incline: *His tastes run to the macabre.* **33.** To be channeled: *"His mind seemed to run monotonously on women, or rather, sex."* (Katherine Anne Porter). **34.** To vary or range in quality, price, size, proportion, or the like: *Hog prices were running high.* **35.** To come into or out of a specified condition: *We ran into debt.* —*tr.* **I. 1. a.** To traverse on foot at a pace faster than the walk: *run the entire distance.* **b.** To cause (a horse) to move at a gait faster than the canter: *run a horse.* **2.** To allow to move without restraint: *He runs his sheep on hill pasture.* **3.** To do or accomplish by or as if by running: *run errands.* **4.** To hunt or pursue (game or the like): *Wolves ran the sheep in the night.* **5.** To bring to a given condition by or as if by running: *She ran him ragged.* **6.** To cause to move quickly: *He ran his fingers over the keyboard.* **7.** To compel to leave: *They ran him out of town.* **II. 8.** To cause to compete in or as if in a race: *He ran two horses in the Derby.* **9.** To present or nominate for elective office: *They ran him for mayor.* **10.** To compete in a given manner against: *He ran them a close second.* **III. 11.** To cause to move or progress freely: *run up the jib.* **12.** To cause to function; operate: *He ran his engine.* **13.** To convey or transport: *Run me into town.* **14.** To cause to ply: *They don't run the ferries here in winter.* **15.** *Nautical.* To cause to move on a course: *We ran our boat into a cove.* **16. a.** To smuggle: *run rifles.* **b.** To evade and pass through (a blockade, for example). **17.** To move swiftly down or through: *run the rapids.* **IV. 18.** To cause to flow: *run water into a tub.* **19.** To emit or flow with: *The fountains ran wine.* **20. a.** To melt, fuse, or smelt (metal). **b.** To mold or cast (molten metal): *run gold into ingots.* **V. 21.** To cause to extend in a specified way: *run a road into the hills.* **22.** To mark or trace on a surface: *run a pencil line between two points.* **23.** To sew with a continuous line of stitches: *run a seam.* **24.** To cause to unravel along a line: *She ran her stocking on a splinter.* **25.** To cause to penetrate: *She ran a pin into her thumb.* **VI. 26.** To cause to continue: *They ran the film for a month.* **27.** To publish in a periodical: *run an advertisement.* **28.** To cause to accumulate. Often used with *up: He ran his winnings up to $500.* **29.** To subject or be subjected to (risk, for example). **30.** To have (a fever) as a symptom. **31. a.** To score (balls or points) consecutively in billiard games: *run 15 balls.* **b.** To clear (the table) in pool by consecutive scores. **32.** To conduct or perform (a test or experiment, for example). **33.** To control, manage, or direct **34.** To unite or combine: *We ran two companies into one* —**run across.** To meet or find by chance. —**run after. 1.** To pursue; to chase. **2.** *Informal.* To seek the company or attentions of. —**run away with. 1.** To make off with. **2.** To win (an election or competition) by a large margin. —**run for it.** To attempt to escape. —**run into. 1.** To meet by chance. **2.** To collide with. —**run out (of).** To become used up; exhaust the supply of. —**run over. 1.** To drive or ride over, as with an automobile. **2.** To overflow. **3.** To examine or rehearse. **4.** To extend beyond. —*n.* **I. 1. a.** A pace faster than the walk. **b.** A gait faster than the canter. **2.** An act of running. **3. a.** A distance covered by or as if by running. **b.** The time taken to cover it: *a two minutes' run from the subway.* **4.** A quick trip or visit: *a run into town.* **5.** *Abbr.* **r, r.** *Baseball.* **a.** The process of scoring a point by running from home plate around the bases and back to home plate. **b.** The point so scored. **6.** *Football.* A player's attempt to carry the ball past or through the opposing team: *an end run.* **7.** *Cricket.* **a.** A successful act of running from one popping crease to the other by both batsmen. **b.** The point so scored. **8.** A shoaling or migrating of fish inshore or upstream, especially prior to spawning: *the shad run.* **9.** Unrestricted freedom or use of: *I had the run of their library.* **II. 10.** A stretch or period of riding, as in a race or to hounds. **III. 11.** A track or slope along or down which something can travel: *a ski run.* **12.** *Golf.* The distance a ball rolls after hitting the ground. **13. a.** A journey between points on a scheduled or regular route. **b.** The distance so covered. **c.** The time taken to cover this distance. **14. a.** A continuous period of operation by a machine, factory, or the like. **b.** The production achieved during such a period. **15.** The terminal approach of a military aircraft to its target: *a bombing run.* **16.** A transit of smuggled goods. **IV. 17. a.** A movement or flow, as of fluid or sand. **b.** The duration of such a flow. **c.** The amount of such a flow. **18.** A pipe or channel through which something flows: *a mill run.* **19.** A small, fast-flowing stream or brook **20.** *Mining.* A fall or slide, as of sand or mud. **V. 21.** A continuous length or extent of something: *a ten-foot run of tubing.* **22.** *Mining.* A vein or seam, as of ore or rock. **23.** The direction, configuration, or lie of something: *the run of the grain in leather.* **24.** A trail or burrow made or frequented by animals: *a rabbit run.* **25.** An outdoor enclosure for domestic animals or poultry. **26.** A length of torn or unraveled stitches in a knitted fabric. **VI. 27.** An unbroken series or sequence: *a run of dry summers.* **28.** An unbroken sequence of theatrical performances. **29.** *Music.* A rapid sequence of notes; roulade. **30.** A series of unexpected and urgent demands by depositors, customers, or the like: *a run on a bank.* **31. a.** In certain games, a continuous set or sequence, as of playing cards in one suit. **b.** A successful sequence of shots or points. **32.** A sustained state or condition: *a run of good luck.* **33.** A trend or tendency: *the run of events.* **34.** The average type, group, or category; majority: *The broad run of voters want him to win.* —**a run for one's money.** Strong competition. —**in the long run.** In the final analysis or outcome. —**on the run. 1. a.** In rapid retreat. **b.** In hiding, as a fugitive. **2.** Hurrying busily from place to place. —**the runs.** *Slang.* Diarrhea. —*adj.* **1.** In a liquid state; melted. **2.** Poured into a mold while liquid: *run metal.* **3.** Drained; extracted: *run honey.* **4.** Smuggled: *run liquor.* [Run, ran, run; Middle English *runnen, ran, runnen,* Old English *rinnan* (but influenced by the past participle), *ran(n), gerunnen,* reinforced by Old Norse cognate verb *rinna.* See **er-**[1] in Appendix.*]

run·a·bout (rŭn′ə-bout′) *n.* **1. a.** A small, open automobile or carriage. **b.** A small motorboat. **c.** A light aircraft. **2.** A vagabond or gadabout.

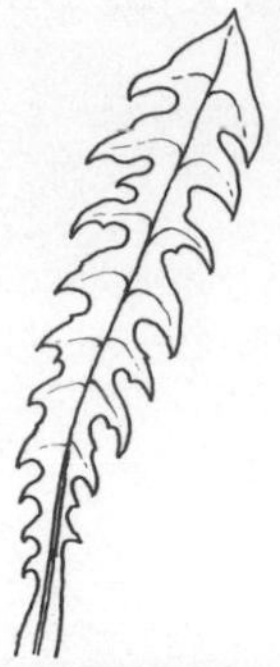

runcinate
Runcinate leaf of dandelion

rune

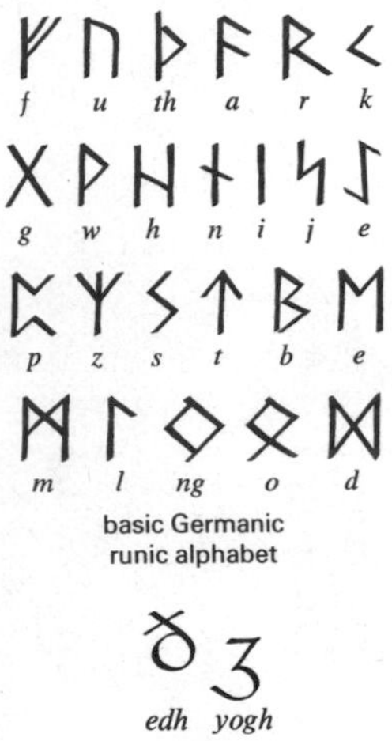
f u th a r k
g w h n i j e
p z s t b e
m l ng o d
edh yogh

basic Germanic runic alphabet

two later runes used in English

run·a·gate (rŭn′ə-gāt′) *n. Archaic.* **1.** A renegade or deserter. **2.** A vagabond. [Variant of RENEGADE (influenced by RUN).]
run·a·round (rŭn′ə-round′) *n.* Also **run·round** (rŭn′round′). **1.** Deception, usually in the form of evasive excuses. **2.** *Printing.* Type set in a column narrower than the body of the text, as on either side of a picture.
run·a·way (rŭn′ə-wā′) *n.* **1.** One that runs away. **2.** An act of running away. **3.** *Informal.* An easy victory. *—adj.* **1.** Escaping or having escaped from captivity or control. **2.** Of or done by running away. **3.** Easily won, as a race. **4.** Of or pertaining to a rapid price rise.
run·back (rŭn′băk′) *n.* **1.** The act of returning a kickoff, punt, or intercepted forward pass. **2.** The distance so covered.
run·ci·ble spoon (rŭn′sə-bəl). A three-pronged fork, as a pickle fork, curved like a spoon and having a cutting edge. [*Runcible,* a nonsense word coined by Edward Lear.]
run·ci·nate (rŭn′sə-nāt′, -nĭt) *adj. Botany.* Having saw-toothed divisions directed backward: *runcinate leaves.* [Latin *runcinātus,* past participle of *runcināre,* to plane, from *runcina,* carpenter's plane (formerly taken also to mean a saw), from Greek *rhukanē*†.]
run down. **1. a.** To slow down and stop, as a machine. **b.** To exhaust or wear out. **c.** To lessen in value. **2.** To pursue and capture. **3.** To hit with a moving vehicle. **4.** To disparage; decry. **5.** To give a brief or summary account of. **6.** *Baseball.* To put out a runner after trapping him between two bases.
run-down (rŭn′doun′) *n.* **1.** A summary or résumé. **2.** *Baseball.* A play in which a runner is put out when he is trapped between bases. *—adj.* **1.** In poor physical condition; weak or exhausted. **2.** Unwound and not running.
rune (ro͞on) *n.* **1.** One of the letters of an alphabet used by ancient Germanic peoples, especially by the Scandinavians and Anglo-Saxons. **2.** Any poem, riddle, or the like written in runic characters. **3.** Any occult characters. **4.** A Finnish poem or canto. [In sense 4, from Finnish *runo.* In other senses, Middle English *roun, rune,* secret writing, rune, from Old Norse *rūn* (unattested). See **rūno-** in Appendix.*] *—run′ic adj.*
rung[1] (rŭng) *n.* **1.** A rod or bar forming a step of a ladder. **2.** A crosspiece supporting the legs or back of a chair. **3.** The spoke in a wheel. **4.** *Nautical.* One of the spokes or handles on a ship's steering wheel. [Middle English *rung, rong,* Old English *hrung,* akin to Old High German *runga,* Gothic *hrugga*†.]
rung[2]. Past tense and past participle of **ring.** See Usage note at **ring.**
run in. **1.** To insert or include as something extra. **2.** *Printing.* To make a solid body of text without a paragraph or other break. **3.** *Slang.* To take into legal custody.
run-in (rŭn′ĭn′) *n.* **1.** A quarrel; an argument; a fight. **2.** *Printing.* Matter added to a text. *—adj.* Added or inserted in text.
run·let (rŭn′lĭt) *n.* A rivulet. [Diminutive of RUN (stream).]
run·nel (rŭn′əl) *n.* **1.** A rivulet; a brook. **2.** A narrow channel or course, as for water. [Middle English *rynel,* Old English *rynel,* from *rinnan,* to run, flow. See **er-**[1] in Appendix.*]
run·ner (rŭn′ər) *n.* **1.** One who or that which runs, as: **a.** One that competes in a race. **b.** A fugitive. **c.** A messenger or errand boy. **2.** An agent or collector, as for a bank or brokerage house. **3.** One who solicits business, as for a hotel or store. **4.** A smuggler. **5.** A vessel engaged in smuggling. **6.** One who operates or manages something. **7.** A device in or on which a mechanism slides or moves, as: **a.** The blade of a skate. **b.** The supports on which a drawer slides. **8.** A long narrow carpet. **9.** A long narrow tablecloth. **10.** A roller towel. **11.** *Metallurgy.* A channel along which molten metal is poured into a mold; gate. **12.** *Botany.* **a.** A slender, creeping stem that puts forth roots from nodes spaced at intervals along its length. **b.** A plant, such as the strawberry, having such a stem. **c.** A twining vine, such as the **scarlet runner** *(see).* **13.** Any of several marine fishes of the family Carangidae, such as the blue runner, *Caranx crysos,* of temperate waters of the American Atlantic coast.
run·ner-up (rŭn′ər-ŭp′) *n.* One that takes second place.
run·ning (rŭn′ĭng) *n.* **1.** The act of one that runs. **2.** The power or ability to run. **3.** Competition: *in the running.* **4.** An operating or controlling: *the running of a machine.* **5. a.** That which runs or flows. **b.** The amount that runs.
running board. A narrow footboard extending under and beside the doors of some automobiles and other conveyances.
running gear. **1.** The working parts, including the engine, of an automobile, locomotive, or other vehicle, as distinguished from the body. **2.** **Running rigging** *(see).*
running hand. Writing done rapidly without lifting the pen from the paper.
running head. *Printing.* A title printed at the top of every page or every other page. Also called "running title."
running knot. A **slipknot** *(see).*
running light. **1.** One of several lights on a boat or ship kept lighted between dusk and dawn. **2.** One of several similar lights on an aircraft; a navigation light.
running mate. **1.** A horse used to set the pace in a race for another horse. **2.** The candidate or nominee for the lesser of two closely associated political offices.
running rigging. The part of a ship's rigging that comprises the ropes with which sails are raised, lowered, or trimmed, booms and gaffs are operated, etc. Also called "running gear."
running stitch. One of a series of small, even stitches.
run·ny (rŭn′ē) *adj.* **-nier, -niest.** Inclined to run or flow.
Run·ny·mede (rŭn′ĭ-mēd). A meadow on the Thames, 19 miles west of London, where King John is thought to have signed the Magna Carta in 1215. [Middle English *Runimede,* "meadow on the council island" : Old English *Rūnīeg,* council island : *rūn,* secret, secret council (see **rūno-** in Appendix*) + *īeg, īg,* island (see **akwā-** in Appendix*) + *mede,* MEAD (meadow).]
run off. **1.** To print, duplicate, or copy. **2.** To run away; elope. **3.** To spill over; to overflow. **4.** To decide a contest or competition by a run-off.
run-off (rŭn′ôf′, -ŏf′) *n.* **1. a.** The overflow of a fluid from a container. **b.** Rainfall that is not absorbed by the soil. **2.** Eliminated waste products from manufacturing processes. **3.** An extra competition held to break a tie.
run-of-the-mill (rŭn′əv-*th*ə-mĭl′) *adj.* Ordinary; not special; average. See Synonyms at **average.** [From *run of (the) mill,* products of a mill that are not graded for quality.]
run on. **1.** To continue on and on. **2.** *Printing.* To continue a text without a formal break.
run-on (rŭn′ŏn′, -ôn′) *n. Printing.* Matter that is appended or added without a formal break. *—adj.* Being run on.
run·round. Variant of **run-around.**
runt (rŭnt) *n.* **1.** An undersized animal; especially, the smallest animal of a litter. **2.** A person of small stature. Often used disparagingly. [Possibly from Dutch *rund,* small ox. See **ker-**[1] in Appendix.*] *—runt′i·ness n. —runt·y adj.*
run through. **1.** To pierce. **2.** To use up (money, for example) quickly. **3.** To examine or rehearse quickly.
run-through (rŭn′thro͞o′) *n.* A complete but rapid review or rehearsal of something, such as a theatrical work.
run·way (rŭn′wā′) *n.* **1.** A path, channel, or track over which something runs. **2.** The bed of a water course. **3.** A chute down which logs are skidded. **4.** *Bowling.* A narrow track on which balls are returned after they are bowled. **5.** A smooth ramp for wheeled vehicles. **6.** A narrow walkway extending from a stage into an auditorium. **7.** A strip of level ground, usually paved, on which aircraft take off and land.
Run·yon (rŭn′yən), **(Alfred) Damon.** 1884–1946. American journalist and author of short stories.
ru·pee (ro͞o-pē′, ro͞o′pē) *n. Abbr.* **Re., r., R.** **1. a.** The basic monetary unit of Ceylon and Mauritius, equal to 100 cents. **b.** The basic monetary unit of India, equal to 100 paise. **c.** The basic monetary unit of Nepal, equal to 100 pice. **d.** The basic monetary unit of Pakistan, equal to 100 paisas. See table of exchange rates at **currency.** **2.** A coin worth one rupee. [Hindi *rupaīyā,* from Sanskrit *rūpya,* wrought silver, from *rūpa*†, shape, image.]
Ru·pert (ro͞o′pərt). A river of Quebec, Canada, flowing 380 miles westward from Mistassini Lake to James Bay.
Ru·pert (ro͞o′pərt), **Prince.** 1619–1682. German-born English military, naval, and political leader; supporter of Charles I; inventor.
Ru·pert's Land (ro͞o′pərts). The Canadian territory granted the Hudson's Bay Company in 1670, most of which was incorporated in The Northwest Territories after its purchase by Canada in 1870.
ru·pi·ah (ro͞o-pē′ä) *n., pl.* **rupiah** or **-ahs.** **1.** The basic monetary unit of Indonesia, equal to 100 sen. See table of exchange rates at **currency.** **2.** A note worth one rupiah. [Hindi *rupaīyā,* RUPEE.]
rup·ture (rŭp′chər) *n.* **1. a.** The act of breaking open or bursting. **b.** The state of being broken open or burst. **2.** A break in friendly relations between individuals or nations. **3.** *Pathology.* **a.** A **hernia** *(see),* especially of the groin or intestines. **b.** A tear in bodily tissue. *—v.* **ruptured, -turing, -tures.** *—tr.* To break open; burst. *—intr.* To undergo or suffer a rupture. —See Synonyms at **break.** [Middle English *ruptur,* from Old French *rupture,* from Latin *ruptūra,* from *rumpere* (past participle *ruptus*), to break. See **reup-** in Appendix.*] *—rup′tur·a·ble adj.*
ru·ral (ro͝or′əl) *adj.* **1.** Of or pertaining to the country as opposed to the city; rustic. **2.** Of or pertaining to people who live in the country. **3.** Of or relating to farming; agricultural. Compare **urban.** [Middle English, from Old French, from Latin *rūrālis,* from *rūs* (stem *rūr-*), country. See **rewe-** in Appendix.*] *—ru′ral·ism′ n. —ru′ral·ist n. —ru′ral·ly adv.*
Synonyms: *rural, arcadian, bucolic, rustic, pastoral, sylvan.* These adjectives are all descriptive of existence or environment which is close to nature; those with a literary flavor are often used facetiously. *Rural* applies to sparsely settled or agricultural country, as distinct from settled communities. *Arcadian* implies ideal or simple country living. *Bucolic* is often used derisively of country people or manners. *Rustic,* sometimes uncomplimentary, applies to country people who seem unsophisticated, but may also apply favorably to living conditions or to natural environments which are pleasingly primitive. *Pastoral* implies the supposed peace of rural living and the shepherd's life, with a suggestion of artificiality. *Sylvan* refers to wooded as opposed to cultivated country, and carries the sense of unspoiled beauty.
rural free delivery. *Abbr.* **R.F.D., RFD** Free government delivery of mail in rural areas.
ru·ral·i·ty (ro͞o-răl′ə-tē) *n., pl.* **-ties.** **1.** The state or quality of being rural. **2.** A rural trait or characteristic.
ru·ral·ize (ro͝or′əl-īz′) *v.* **-ized, -izing, -izes.** *—tr.* To make rural. *—intr.* To live or visit in the country. *—ru′ral·i·za′tion n.*
rural route. *Abbr.* **R.R.** A rural mail route.
Ru·rik (ro͞o′rĭk). The Russian royal family (1462–1598), reputedly descended from a viking chieftain of the same name.
Rus. Russia; Russian.
Ru·se (ro͞o′sä). *Turkish* **Rus·chuk** (ro͞os′cho͝ok). A Danubian port in northeastern Bulgaria. Population, 118,000.
ruse (ro͞oz) *n.* An action or device meant to confuse or mislead. See Synonyms at **artifice.** [Middle English, detour of a hunted animal, from Old French, from *ruser,* to repulse, detour. See **rush** (to dash off).]

ă pat/ā pay/âr care/ä father/b bib/ch church/d deed/ĕ pet/ē be/f fife/g gag/h hat/hw which/ĭ pit/ī pie/îr pier/j judge/k kick/l lid, needle/m mum/n no, sudden/ng thing/ŏ pot/ō toe/ô paw, for/oi noise/ou out/o͝o took/o͞o boot/p pop/r roar/s sauce/sh ship, dish/

rush[1] (rŭsh) *v.* **rushed, rushing, rushes.** —*intr.* **1.** To move or act swiftly. **2.** To make a sudden or swift attack or charge. Used with *on* or *upon.* **3.** *Football.* To move the ball by running rather than passing. —*tr.* **1.** To cause to move or act with unusual haste or violence. **2.** To perform with great haste. **3.** To attack swiftly and suddenly. **4.** To attempt to impress or seek the favor of. **5.** To entertain; to court. —*n.* **1.** The act of rushing; a sudden forward motion or turbulent movement. **2.** An anxious and eager movement to get to or from a place. **3.** General haste or busyness. **4.** A sudden attack; an onslaught. **5.** *Football.* An attempt to move the ball by running with it. **6.** *Often plural.* The first, unedited print of a motion-picture scene. **7.** A great flurry of activity or press of business. —*adj.* Requiring or marked by haste or urgency: *a rush job.* [Middle English *russhen,* from Norman French *russher,* variant of Old French *ruser,* to repulse, from Latin *recusāre,* to object to (in Vulgar Latin, "to repel") : *re-,* back + *causārī,* to plead, give as a reason, from *causa,* CAUSE.] —**rush'er** *n.*

rush[2] (rŭsh) *n.* **1.** Any of various grasslike marsh plants of the family Juncaceae, having pliant, hollow, or pithy stems. **2.** Any of various similar, usually aquatic plants. **3.** The stem of a rush, used in making baskets, mats, and chair seats. [Middle English *rush, rish,* Old English *rysc* See **rezg-** in Appendix.*]

Rush (rŭsh), **Benjamin.** 1745–1813. American physician, educator, political leader, and author.

rush hour. A period of heavy traffic. —**rush'-hour'** *adj.*

rush·light (rŭsh'līt') *n.* A candle consisting of a rush wick in tallow. Also called "rush candle."

Rush·more, Mount (rŭsh'mōr). A mountain in the Black Hills of western South Dakota; a national memorial with 60-foot-high carved likenesses of Washington, Jefferson, Lincoln, and Theodore Roosevelt.

rush·y (rŭsh'ē) *adj.* **-ier, -iest. 1.** Resembling or characteristic of rushes; rushlike. **2.** Abounding in rushes: *a rushy marsh.*

rusk (rŭsk) *n.* **1.** A light, soft-textured sweetened biscuit. **2.** Sweet raised bread dried and browned in an oven. [Spanish and Portuguese *rosca*†, a coil, twisted roll.]

Rusk (rŭsk), **(David) Dean.** Born 1909. American diplomat; Secretary of State (1961–1969).

Rus·kin (rŭs'kĭn), **John.** 1819–1900. English writer, art critic, sociologist, and philanthropist.

Russ. Russia; Russian.

Rus·sell (rŭs'əl), Lord **Bertrand (Arthur William).** Born 1872. English pacifist, philosopher, author, and mathematician.

Rus·sell (rŭs'əl), Lord **John.** 1792–1878. British statesman; prime minister (1846–52); advocate of parliamentary reform.

Rus·sell (rŭs'əl), **Lillian.** Original name, Helen Louise Leonard. 1861–1922. American soprano.

Rus·sell Cave National Monument (rŭs'əl). An area in northeastern Alabama, the site of the discovery of artifacts dating from 6200 B.C. to A.D. 1650.

rus·set (rŭs'ĭt) *n.* **1.** Moderate to strong brown. See **color. 2.** A coarse reddish-brown to brown homespun cloth. **3.** A winter apple with a rough reddish-brown skin. —*adj.* **1.** Moderate-brown to strong-brown. **2.** Made from russet cloth. [Middle English, from Old French *rousset,* from *rous,* red, from Latin *russus.* See **reudh-** in Appendix.*]

Rus·sia (rŭsh'ə). *Russian* **Ros·si·ya** (rŭ-syē'yə). *Abbr.* **Rus., Russ. 1.** The name commonly applied to the **Union of Soviet Socialist Republics** *(see).* **2.** The **Russian Soviet Federated Socialist Republic** *(see).* **3.** Historically, the Russian Empire until its termination in 1917 by the Russian Revolution. Capital, St. Petersburg (Petrograd). [Medieval Latin *Russi,* Russians, from Old Russian *Rus',* "Norsemen," Norse founders of the Russian principalities, from Old Norse *Rōthsmenn,* "sea-farers," from *rōthr,* to row. See **erə-**[1] in Appendix.*]

Rus·sian (rŭsh'ən) *n. Abbr.* **Rus., Russ. 1.** A native or inhabitant of Russia. **2.** One who is of Russian descent. **3.** The Slavic language of the Russian people that is the official language of the Soviet Union. —*adj.* Of or relating to Russia, its people, or their language.

Russian dressing. Mayonnaise with chili sauce, chopped pickles, and pimientos.

Russian olive. A tree, the **oleaster** *(see).*

Russian Orthodox Church. 1. An independent branch of the Eastern Orthodox Church in Russia headed by the Patriarch of Moscow. **2.** A branch of this church outside Russia.

Russian Revolution. 1. The seizure of the central organs of state power in Petrograd by the Bolsheviks under the leadership of Lenin on November 7, 1917 (October 25, Old Style). Also called "October Revolution." **2.** The sequence of events in Russia following the overthrow of czarism by the uprising of March 1917 (the February Revolution), evolving with the transformation of the democratic revolution as embodied by the provisional government into a socialist revolution led by the Bolsheviks, and culminating with the defeat of counterrevolution in the civil war (1918–22).

Russian roulette. A stunt in which a person spins the cylinder of a revolver loaded with one bullet, aims the muzzle at his head, and pulls the trigger.

Russian Soviet Federated Socialist Republic. *Abbr.* **Russian S.F.S.R., R.S.F.S.R.** The largest (6,322,350 square miles) constituent republic of the Soviet Union, in Europe and Asia. Also called "Russia." Population, 125,800,000. Capital, Moscow.

Russian thistle. A red-stemmed, prickly plant, *Salsola kali tenuifolia,* native to Asia, and a troublesome weed in western North America.

Russian Turkestan. See **Turkestan.**

Russian wolfhound. A dog, the **borzoi** *(see).*

Russo–. Indicates Russia or that which pertains to Russia; for example, **Russophilia.** [From RUSSIA.]

Rus·so-Jap·a·nese War (rŭs'ō-jăp'ə-nēz', -nēs'). A war (1904–05) between Russia and Japan.

Rus·so·phil·i·a (rŭs'ə-fĭl'ĭ-ə) *n.* Interest in or enthusiasm about Russia, its culture, people, government, or language. [RUSSO- + -PHILIA.] —**Rus'so·phile** (fĭl, -fīl) *n.*

Rus·so·pho·bi·a (rŭs'ə-fō'bē-ə) *n.* Dislike or fear of Russia or its policies. [RUSSO- + -PHOBIA.] —**Rus'so·phobe'** *n.*

rust (rŭst) *n.* **1.** Any of various powdery or scaly reddish-brown or reddish-yellow hydrated ferric oxides formed on iron and iron-containing materials by low-temperature oxidation in the presence of water. **2.** Any of various metallic coatings, especially oxides, formed by corrosion. **3.** A stain or coating resembling iron rust. **4.** Any deterioration of ability or character resulting from inactivity or neglect. **5. a.** Any of various parasitic fungi of the order Uredinales, that are injurious to a wide variety of plants. **b.** A plant disease caused by such fungi, characterized by reddish or brownish spots on leaves, stems, and other parts. **6.** Strong brown. See **color.** —*v.* **rusted, rusting, rusts.** —*intr.* **1.** To become corroded. **2.** To deteriorate or degenerate through inactivity or neglect. **3.** To become the color of rust. **4.** To develop a disease caused by a rust fungus. —*tr.* **1.** To corrode or subject (a metal) to rust formation. **2.** To impair or spoil by misuse, inactivity, and the like. **3.** To color something strong brown. —*adj.* Strong-brown. [Middle English *rust,* Old English *rūst.* See **reudh-** in Appendix.*] —**rust'a·ble** *adj.*

rus·tic (rŭs'tĭk) *adj.* **1.** Typical of country life. **2.** Simple; unsophisticated; bucolic. **3.** Made of rough tree branches: *rustic furniture.* **4.** *Masonry.* Having a rough surface with deep or chamfered joints. —See Synonyms at **rural.** —*n.* **1.** A rural person. **2.** An awkward or mannerless simpleton. [Middle English *rustyk,* from Old French *rustique,* from Latin *rūsticus,* from *rūs,* country. See **rewə-** in Appendix.*] —**rus'ti·cal·ly** *adv.*

rus·ti·cate (rŭs'tĭ-kāt') *v.* **-cated, -cating, -cates.** —*intr.* To go to or live in the country. —*tr.* **1.** To send to the country. **2.** *British.* To suspend (a student) from a university. **3.** To construct (masonry) in the rustic style. [Latin *rūsticārī,* from *rūsticus,* RUSTIC.] —**rus'ti·ca'tion** *n.* —**rus'ti·ca'tor** (-kā'tər) *n.*

rus·tic·i·ty (rŭs-tĭs'ə-tē) *n., pl.* **-ties. 1.** The state or condition of being rustic. **2.** An especially rustic trait or mannerism.

rus·tle[1] (rŭs'əl) *v.* **-tled, -tling, -tles.** —*intr.* To move with soft whispering sounds. —*tr.* To cause to make such sounds. —*n.* A soft whispering sound: *The gentle rustle of a silken gown.* [Middle English *rustlen, rustelen,* akin to Frisian *russelje,* Dutch *ridselen* (imitative).] —**rus'tler** *n.* —**rus'tling·ly** *adv.*

rus·tle[2] (rŭs'əl) *v.* **-tled, -tling, -tles.** —*tr.* To steal (cattle). —*intr.* **1.** To steal cattle. **2.** *Informal.* To forage. [Probably from RUSTLE (to move with soft sounds).] —**rus'tler** *n.*

rust·less (rŭst'lĭs) *adj.* Free from rust.

rust·proof (rŭst'prōōf') *adj.* Incapable of rusting.

rust·y (rŭs'tē) *adj.* **-ier, -iest. 1.** Covered with rust; corroded. **2.** Consisting of or produced by rust. **3.** Having a yellowish-red or brownish-red color. **4.** Working or operating stiffly or incorrectly because of or as if because of rust. **5.** Weakened or impaired by neglect, disuse, or lack of practice. —**rust'i·ly** *adv.* —**rust'i·ness** *n.*

rut[1] (rŭt) *n.* **1.** A sunken track or groove made by the passage of vehicles. **2.** A fixed routine of thought or action. —*tr.v.* **rutted, rutting, ruts.** To furrow. [Old French *rote, route,* way, ROUTE.]

rut[2] (rŭt) *n.* **1.** A cyclically recurring condition of sexual excitement and reproductive activity in male mammals, such as deer. **2.** Any comparable condition of mammalian sexual activity; estrus. —*intr.v.* **rutted, rutting, ruts.** To be in rut. [Middle English *rutte,* from Old French *rut, ruit,* "roar," "bellowing (of stags in rut)," from Late Latin *rūgitus,* from Latin *rūgīre,* to roar. See **reu-** in Appendix.*]

Rut. Rutland.

ru·ta·ba·ga (rōō'tə-bā'gə) *n.* **1.** A plant, *Brassica napobrassica,* native to Eurasia, having a thick, bulbous root used as food and livestock feed. **2.** The edible root of this plant. Also called "Swedish turnip," "swede." [Swedish (dialectal) *rotabagge,* "baggy root" : *rot,* root, from Old Norse *rōt* (see **werād-** in Appendix*) + *bagge,* from Old Norse *baggi,* BAG.]

Rutd. Rutland.

ruth (rōōth) *n. Archaic.* **1.** Compassion or pity. **2.** Sorrow; misery; grief. [Middle English *ruthe, rewthe,* from *rewen,* to rue, from Old English *hrēowan.* See **kreu-**[2] in Appendix.*]

Ruth[1] (rōōth). A feminine given name. [Hebrew *Rūth,* perhaps contracted from *rə'ūth,* companion.]

Ruth[2] (rōōth). In the Old Testament, a Moabite widow who left home with her mother-in-law and went to Bethlehem where she later married Boaz.

Ruth[3] (rōōth) *n.* A book of the Old Testament in which the story of Ruth is told.

Ruth (rōōth), **George Herman ("Babe").** Called "the Bambino." 1895–1948. American baseball player.

Ru·the·ni·a (rōō thē'nē-ə). A historic region of eastern Europe, in western Ukraine, south of the Carpathian Mountains, part of which constituted a province of Czechoslovakia (1918–39) and was also called Carpatho-Ukraine, and all of which was annexed by the Soviet Union in 1945. [Medieval Latin, Russia, from *Rut(h)enī,* Russians, from Russian *Rusin,* from Old Russian *Rus',* "Norsemen." See **Russia.**]

Ru·the·ni·an (rōō-thē'nē-ən) *n.* **1.** A member of a group of Ukrainians living in Ruthenia. **2.** A Ukrainian dialect spoken by these people. —**Ru·the'ni·an** *adj.*

ru·the·ni·um (rōō-thē'nē-əm) *n. Symbol* **Ru** A hard white acid-

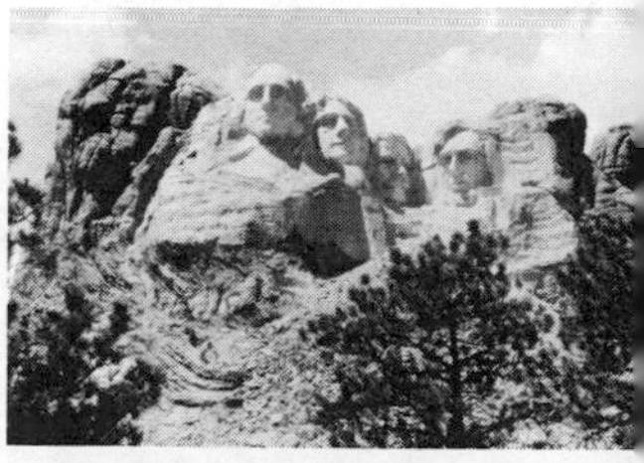

Mount Rushmore
From left: Washington, Jefferson, Roosevelt, Lincoln

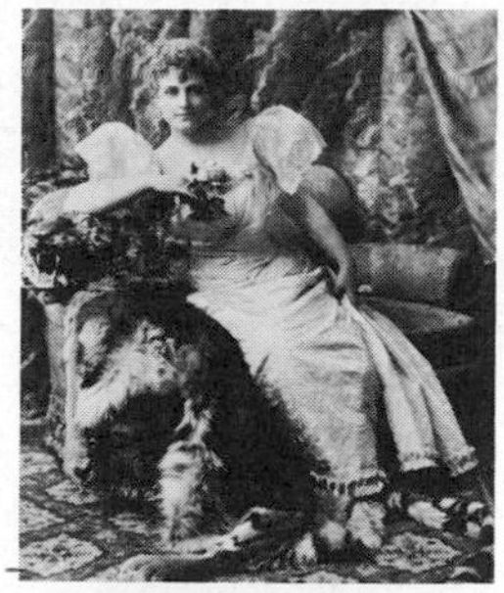

Lillian Russell

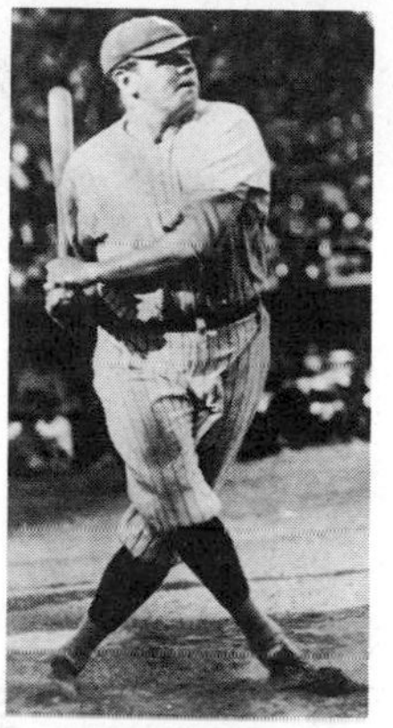

Babe Ruth
Playing for the American League in 1922

t tight/th thin, path/*th* this, bathe/ŭ cut/ûr urge/v valve/w with/y yes/z zebra, size/zh vision/ə about, item, edible, gallop, circus/ à *Fr.* ami/œ *Fr.* feu, *Ger.* schön/ü *Fr.* tu, *Ger.* über/KH *Ger.* ich, *Scot.* loch/N *Fr.* bon. ***Follows main vocabulary. †Of obscure origin.**

resistant metallic element found in platinum ores. It is used to harden platinum and palladium for jewelry and in alloys for nonmagnetic wear-resistant instrument pivots and electrical contacts. Atomic number 44, atomic weight 101.07, melting point 2,250°C, boiling point 3,900°C, specific gravity 12.41, valences 0, 1, 2, 3, 4, 5, 6, 7, 8. See **element**. [New Latin; first discovered in the Ural Mountains in Russia, from Medieval Latin *Ruthenia,* Russia. See **Ruthenia**.]

ruth·er·ford (rŭ*th*′ər-fərd) *n.* A unit of radioactivity equal to the quantity of radioactive material that undergoes one million disintegrations per second. [After Ernest RUTHERFORD.]

Ruth·er·ford (rŭ*th*′ər-fərd), **Daniel.** 1749–1819. Scottish chemist; credited with the discovery of nitrogen.

Ruth·er·ford (rŭ*th*′ər-fərd), **Ernest.** First Baron Rutherford of Nelson. 1871–1937. British physicist; theorized existence of the atomic nucleus.

ruth·ful (rōōth′fəl) *adj. Archaic.* **1.** Full of sorrow; rueful. **2.** Causing sorrow or pity. —**ruth′ful·ly** *adv.* —**ruth′ful·ness** *n.*

ruth·less (rōōth′lĭs) *adj.* Having no compassion or pity; merciless. See Synonyms at **cruel**. —**ruth′less·ly** *adv.* —**ruth′less·ness** *n.*

ru·ti·lant (rōō′tə-lənt) *adj. Rare.* Bright-red in color. [Middle English *rutilaunt,* from Latin *rutilāns,* from *rutilāre,* to make reddish, from *rutilus,* reddish. See **reudh-** in Appendix.*]

ru·tile (rōō′tĭl, -tēl, -tīl) *n.* The lustrous red, reddish-brown, or black natural mineral form of titanium dioxide, TiO₂, used as a gemstone, as a source of titanium, and in paints and fillers. [German *Rutil,* from Latin *rutilus,* reddish. See **rutilant**.]

Rut·land (rŭt′lənd). **1.** Also **Rut·land·shire** (-shîr, -shər). *Abbr.* **Rut., Rutd., Rutl.** The smallest county in England, located in the eastern Midlands. Population, 24,000. County seat, Oakham. **2.** A city in western Vermont, the site of two American Revolutionary forts. Population, 18,000.

rut·tish (rŭt′ĭsh) *adj.* Lustful; libidinous.

rut·ty (rŭt′ē) *adj.* **-tier, -tiest.** Full of ruts. —**rut′ti·ness** *n.*

Ru·vu·ma (rōō-vōō′mə). A river of Africa flowing 450 miles generally east to the Indian Ocean from its source in the northern highlands of Mozambique, and forming most of the boundary between that country and Tanzania.

Ru·wen·zo·ri (rōō′wən-zôr′ē, -zōr′ē). A mountain group of east-central Africa, on the border between the Democratic Republic of the Congo and Uganda. It was known by the ancients as the "Mountains of the Moon," and was the supposed source of the Nile. Highest elevation, Mount Stanley (16,795 feet).

Ruys·dael (rois′däl; *Dutch* rœis′däl), **Jacob van.** Also **Ruis·dael.** 1628?–1682. Dutch landscape painter.

Ru·žič·ka (rōō-zhĭch′kə), **Leopold.** Born 1887. Austrian-born Swiss chemist; shared the Nobel Prize in chemistry (1939) with Adolf **Butenandt** *(see)* for work on sex hormones.

R.V. Revised Version (of the Bible).

R.W. 1. Right Worshipful (title). **2.** Right Worthy (title).

Rwan·da (rwän′dä, rōō-än′-). A republic, independent since 1962, of east-central Africa, with an area of 10,166 square miles. Population, 3,000,000. Capital, Kigali.

Rwy., Ry. railway.

Rya·zan (rē-ä-zän′; *Russian* ryä-zän′y′). A city of the Soviet Union, in the Russian S.F.S.R., 115 miles southeast of Moscow. Population, 287,000.

Ry·binsk (rē′byĭnsk). Formerly **Shcher·ba·kov** (shâr′bə-kôf′). A city and transportation center of the Soviet Union, in the Russian S.F.S.R., on the Volga River south of the Rybinsk Reservoir. Population, 208,000.

Ry·binsk Reservoir (rē′byĭnsk). A large (1,800 square miles) artificial lake in north-central Russian S.F.S.R. on the Volga.

Ry·der (rī′dər), **Albert Pinkham.** 1847–1917. American painter; noted for landscape and marine paintings.

rye¹ (rī) *n.* **1.** A widely cultivated cereal grass, *Secale cereale,* the seeds of which are valued as grain. **2.** The grain of this plant, used in making flour and whiskey and for livestock feed. **3.** Whiskey made from rye. [Middle English *rye, ruge,* Old English *ryge.* See **wrughyo-** in Appendix.*]

rye² (rī) *n.* A gentleman among the Gypsies. [Romany *rai,* from Sanskrit *rājan,* king. See **reg-¹** in Appendix.*]

rye bread. Bread made partially or entirely from rye flour.

rye grass. Any of several pasture or meadow grasses of the genus *Lolium,* native to Eurasia.

rynd (rĭnd, rīnd) *n.* An iron bar supporting an upper millstone. [Middle English, from Middle Low German *rin* and Middle Dutch *rijn†.*]

ry·ot (rī′ət) *n.* A peasant or tenant farmer in India. [Hindi *ra′iyat,* from Arabic *ra′iyah,* herd, peasants, from *ra′ā,* pasture.]

Ryu·kyu Islands (ryōō′kyōō′). *Japanese* **Nan·sei Sho·to** (nän′sä shō′tō). A 650-mile-long archipelago occupying about 1,800 square miles in the Pacific between Kyushu, Japan, and Taiwan. Population, 908,000. —**Ryu′kyu′an** *adj. & n.*

ă pat/ā pay/âr care/ä father/b bib/ch church/d deed/ĕ pet/ē be/f fife/g gag/h hat/hw which/ĭ pit/ī pie/îr pier/j judge/k kick/l lid, needle/m mum/n no, sudden/ng thing/ŏ pot/ō toe/ô paw, for/oi noise/ou out/ŏŏ took/ōō boot/p pop/r roar/s sauce/sh ship, dish/

Rwanda

Ss

| 1 | 2 | 3 | 4 | 5 | 6 | 7 | 8 | 9 | 10 | 11 | 12 | 13 | 14 | 15 | 16 |
Phoenician   Greek   Roman   Medieval   Modern

Around 1000 B.C. the Phoenicians and other Semites of Syria and Palestine began to use a graphic sign in the form (1). They gave it the name shin or śin, meaning "tooth," and used it for their consonant sh or ś. After 900 B.C. the Greeks borrowed the sign from the Phoenicians, writing it with three, four, or five strokes in various forms (2,3,4,5), and ending with the symmetrical classical form (6). They used the sign for their consonant s. They also renamed it sigma, confusing it with the name of another Semitic character sāmekh (see X). The Greek form (4) passed via Etruscan to the Roman alphabet (7). The Romans changed the angular into a rounded form (8). Their Monumental Capital (9) is the prototype of our modern capital, printed (13) and written (14). The written Roman form (8) developed into the late Roman and medieval Uncial (10,11) and Cursive (12), which are the bases of our modern small letter, printed (15) and written (16).

s, S (ĕs) *n., pl.* **s's, S's** or **Ss. 1.** The 19th letter of the modern English alphabet. See **alphabet. 2.** Any of the speech sounds represented by this letter. **3.** Anything shaped like the letter **S,** as a curve in a road.

s, S, s., S. Note: As an abbreviation or symbol, *s* may be a small or a capital letter, with or without a period. Established forms or those generally preferred precede the definition. When no form is given, all four forms are in general use in that sense. **1. S.** Sabbath. **2. S.** saint. **3. S.** Saturday. **4. S.** Saxon. **5. s., S.** school. **6. s., S.** sea. **7. S** seaman. **8. s** second (unit of time). **9. s** second of arc. **10. s.** see. **11. s.** semi-. **12. S** September. **13. s.** shilling. **14. S.** *Medicine.* signature. **15. S.** signor; signorc. **16. s.** singular. **17. s.** sire. **18. s.** sister. **19. s.** small. **20. s., S.** society. **21. s** solo. **22. s.** son. **23. s., S** soprano. **24. s.** sou. **25. s.** south; southern. **26. s** stere. **27. s.** stock. **28. S** *Physics.* strangeness. **29. s.** substantive. **30. S** The symbol for the element sulfur. **31. S.** Sunday. **32. s.** surplus. **33.** The 19th in a series; 18th when *J* is omitted.

–s¹. Indicates the plural form, for which it is used in most nouns not ending in a sibilant, an affricate, or a postconsonantal *y;* for example, **charms, toys.** Compare **-es** (in nouns). [Middle English *-es, -s,* Old English *-as,* nominative and accusative plural ending of some nouns.]

–s². Indicates the third person singular form of the present indicative, for which it is used in most verbs not ending in a sibilant, an affricate, or a postconsonantal *y;* for example, she **sleeps,** one **stays.** Compare **-es** (in verbs). [Middle English *-es,* Old English *-es, -as.*]

–s³. Used in the formation of certain adverbs from nouns and adjectives; for example, **nights** (in *He works nights*), **unawares.** [In Middle and Old English the genitive singular ending *-es* was used to form adverbs from some nouns and adjectives.]

–'s¹. Indicates the possessive case, for which it is used in singular nouns and in irregularly formed plural nouns; for example, **nation's, men's.** See Usage note at **possessive.** [Middle English *-es,* genitive singular ending, Old English *-es.*]

–'s². 1. Contraction of **is:** *She's here.* **2.** Contraction of **has:** *He's been eating.* **3.** Contraction of **us:** *Let's go.*

s.a. *Library Service.* without date (Latin *sine anno*).

S.A. 1. Salvation Army. **2.** South Africa. **3.** South America. **4.** Sturmabteilung.

Saa·nen (sä′nən) *n.* A dairy goat of a breed developed in Switzerland, having a white, short-haired coat and no horns. [From *Saanen,* a town in southwest Switzerland.]

Saar (sär). *French* **Sarre** (sär). **1.** A river rising in northeastern France and flowing about 150 miles north to the Moselle in western West Germany. **2.** See **Saarland.**

Saar·brück·en (sär′brŏŏk-ən; *German* zär′brük-ən). The capital of Saarland, West Germany, an industrial city on the Saar River in the southeastern part of the state. Population, 133,000.

Saar·e·maa (sä′rə-mä′). Also **Saa·re** (sä′rə). *Swedish* **Ö·sel** (œ′sĕl). An island of Estonia, 1,046 square miles in area, at the mouth of the Gulf of Riga.

Saa·ri·nen (sär′ĭ-nĕn′), **Eero.** 1910–1961. Finnish-born American architect.

Saar·land (sär′länd′). *French* **Sarre** (sär). Formerly **Saar Territory.** A former region of Europe between France and Germany and, since 1957, a state of West Germany, occupying 988 square miles in the Saar Valley in the west. Also called "Saar." Population, 2,200,000. Capital, Saarbrücken.

Sab. Sabbath.

Sa·ba (sä′bä). **1.** An island of the northern Netherlands Antilles, five square miles in area, between St. Martin and St. Eustatius. Population, 1,000. **2.** The Arabic name for **Sheba.**

sab·a·dil·la (săb′ə-dĭl′ə) *n.* **1.** A tropical American plant, *Schoenocaulon officinale,* having poisonous seeds used in insecticides. **2.** The dry, ripe seeds of this plant. [Spanish *cebadilla,* diminutive of *cebada,* barley, from *cebo,* feed, from Latin *cibust,* food, probably of non-Indo-European origin.]

Sa·bah (sä′bä). Formerly **British North Bor·ne·o** (bôr′nē-ō, bôr′-), **North Borneo.** A state of Malaysia, occupying 29,388 square miles in northern Borneo. Population, 454,000. Capital, Kota Kinabalu.

Sab·a·oth (săb-ā′ōth) *pl.n.* Hosts; armies: *the Lord of Sabaoth.* Romans 9:29; James 5:4. [Latin *Sabaôth,* from Greek, from Hebrew *ṣəbhā′ôth,* host, army.]

Sa·ba·tier (sà-bà-tyā′), **Paul.** 1854–1941. French chemist.

Sa·ba·ti·ni (săb′ə-tē′nē), **Rafael.** 1875–1950. Italian-born English author of romantic historical novels and plays.

sab·bat (săb′ət) *n.* The **witches' Sabbath** *(see).* [French, "Sabbath," from Latin *sabbatum,* SABBATH.]

Sab·ba·tar·i·an (săb′ə-tĕr′ē-ən) *n.* **1.** A person who observes Saturday as the Sabbath, as in Judaism and some sects of Christianity. **2.** A person who believes in strict observance of the Sabbath. —*adj.* Pertaining to the Sabbath or to Sabbatarians. [From Late Latin *sabbatārius,* from Latin *sabbatum,* SABBATH.] —**Sab′ba·tar′i·an·ism′** *n.*

Sab·bath (săb′əth) *n. Abbr.* **S., Sab. 1.** The seventh day of the week, Saturday, named in the Ten Commandments as the day of rest and worship and observed as such by the Jews and some Christian sects. **2.** The first day of the week, Sunday, observed as the day of rest by most Christian churches. [Middle English *sabat(h),* from Old French *sab(b)at* and Old English *sabat,* both from Latin *sabbatum,* from Greek *sabbaton,* from Hebrew *shabbāth,* from *shābhath,* to rest.]

sab·bat·i·cal (sə-băt′ĭ-kəl) *adj.* Also **sab·bat·ic** (-ĭk). **1.** *Capital* **S.** Pertaining or appropriate to the Sabbath as the day of rest. **2.** Pertaining to a sabbatical year. —*n.* A sabbatical year. [From Late Latin *sabbaticus,* from Greek *sabbatikos,* from *sabbaton,* SABBATH.]

sabbatical year. 1. *Often capital* **S.** A year during which land remained fallow, observed every seven years by the ancient Jews. **2.** A leave of absence with pay, usually granted every seventh year, as to a college professor, for travel, research, or rest. In this sense, also called "sabbatical leave."

Sa·be·an, Sa·bae·an (sə-bē′ən) *adj.* Pertaining to ancient Sheba, its inhabitants, or their language. —*n.* **1.** An inhabitant of Sheba in the first millennium B.C. **2.** The Semitic language of ancient Sheba. [From Latin *Sabaeus,* from Greek *Sabaios,* from *Saba,* SHEBA.]

---

t tight/th thin, path/*th* this, bathe/ŭ cut/ûr urge/v valve/w with/y yes/z zebra, size/zh vision/ə about, item, edible, gallop, circus/ à *Fr.* ami/œ *Fr.* feu, *Ger.* schön/ü *Fr.* tu, *Ger.* über/KH *Ger.* ich, *Scot.* loch/N *Fr.* bon. ***Follows main vocabulary. †Of obscure origin.**

Sa·bel·li·an (sə-bĕl′ē-ən) *n.* **1.** An extinct division of the subfamily of Italic Indo-European languages, including ancient Aequian, Sabine, and Volscian. **2.** A speaker of one of these ancient Italic languages. [From Latin *Sabellus*†, Sabine.] —**Sa·bel′li·an** *adj.*

sa·ber (sā′bər) *n.* Also *chiefly British* **sa·bre.** **1.** A heavy cavalry sword with a one-edged, slightly curved blade. **2.** *Fencing.* A two-edged sword used in both thrusting and slashing. —*tr.v.* **sabered, -bering, -bers.** Also *chiefly British* **sa·bre, -bred, -bring, -bres.** To hit, injure, or kill with a saber. [French *sabre,* variant of German *Säbel,* from Middle High German *sabel, sebel,* possibly from Hungarian *szablya.*]

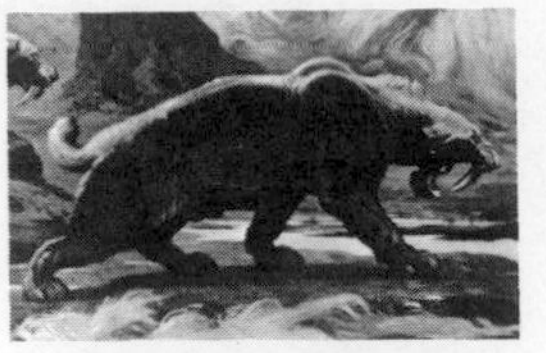
saber-toothed tiger

saber rattling. An ostentatious display of military power or the threatening of war.

sa·ber-toothed tiger (sā′bər-to͞otht′). Any of various extinct cats of the Oligocene to the Pleistocene epoch, characterized by long upper canine teeth; especially, one of the larger members of the genus *Smilodon.* Also called "saber-toothed cat."

sa·bin (sā′bĭn) *n.* A unit of acoustic absorption, equivalent to the absorption by one square foot of a surface that absorbs all incident sound. [After W.C.W. SABINE.]

Sa·bin (sā′bĭn), **Albert Bruce.** Born 1906. Polish-born American physician and microbiologist; developed oral vaccine against polio.

Sa·bine¹ (sā′bīn′) *n.* **1.** A member of an ancient tribe of central Italy, conquered and assimilated by the Romans in 290 B.C. **2.** The language of this people, one of the Sabellian Italic tongues. —*adj.* Of or pertaining to the Sabine people or language. [Middle English *Sabyn,* from Latin *Sabīnus*†.]

Sa·bine² (sə-bēn′). A river rising in northeastern Texas and flowing 578 miles southeast and then south along the Texas-Louisiana border, forming Sabine Lake (about 17 miles long) just north of its mouth on the Gulf of Mexico.

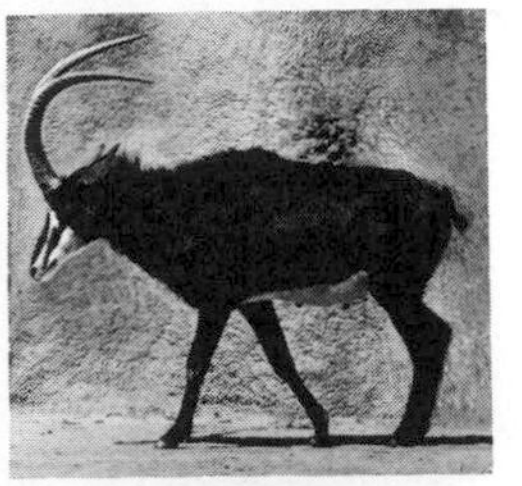
sable antelope

Sa·bine (sā′bĭn), **Wallace Clement Ware.** 1868–1919. American physicist; considered the founder of the science of architectural acoustics.

Sa·bin vaccine (sā′bĭn). A live attenuated virus taken orally to immunize against poliomyelitis. [Developed by A.B. SABIN.]

sa·ble (sā′bəl) *n.* **1. a.** A carnivorous mammal, *Martes zibellina,* of northern Europe and Asia, having soft, dark fur. **b.** The highly valued pelt or fur of this animal. **c.** The similar fur of other species of martens. **2. a.** The color black, especially in heraldry. **b.** *Usually plural.* Black garments worn in mourning. **3.** Grayish yellowish brown. See **color. 4.** A **sablefish** *(see).* —*adj.* **1.** Made of or trimmed with sable fur. **2.** Having the color of sable fur. **3. a.** Of the color black, as in heraldry or mourning. **b.** Dark; somber: *"The sable simplicity that generally characterized the Puritanic modes of dress"* (Hawthorne). [Middle English, from Old French, from Medieval Latin *sabelum,* from Slavic, akin to Russian *sobol*†.]

Sable, Cape (sā′bəl). **1.** A cape in extreme southern Florida, the southernmost point of continental United States. **2.** A promontory in extreme southern Nova Scotia, Canada.

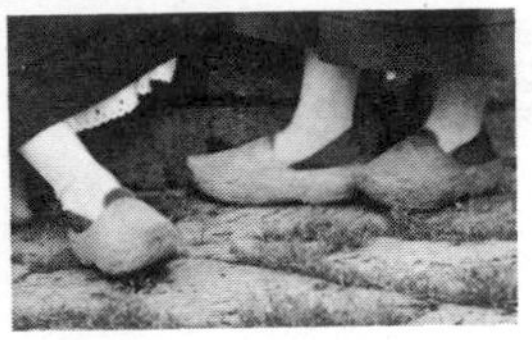
sabot

sable antelope. A large African antelope, *Hippotragus niger,* having a usually dark coat and backward-curving horns.

sa·ble·fish (sā′bəl-fĭsh′) *n., pl.* **sablefish** or **-fishes.** A dark-colored marine food fish, *Anoplopoma fimbria,* of North American Pacific waters. Also called "sable."

sa·bot (săb′ət; *French* sà-bō′) *n.* **1.** A shoe carved from a single piece of wood, worn in several European countries. **2.** A sandal or shoe having a band of leather or other material across the instep. [French, from Old French, perhaps blend of *savate,* old shoe, akin to Italian *ciabatta,* old shoe, Spanish *zapáto,* shoe, perhaps of Oriental origin, and *bot, bote,* BOOT.]

sab·o·tage (săb′ə-täzh′) *n.* **1.** The damaging of property or procedure so as to obstruct productivity or normal functioning, such as that committed by enemy agents against a nation in war. **2.** Any underhanded effort to defeat or do harm to an endeavor; deliberate subversion. —*v.* **sabotaged, -taging, -tages.** —*tr.* To commit sabotage against; do harm to underhandedly or maliciously. —*intr.* To carry on sabotage. [French, from *saboter,* "to clatter shoes," work clumsily, from SABOT.]

sab·o·teur (săb′ə-tûr′; *French* sà-bô-tœr′) *n.* A person who commits sabotage. [French, from *saboter,* to work clumsily, SABOTAGE.]

sa·bra (sä′brə, -brä) *n.* A native-born Israeli. [Hebrew *Ṣabēr,* "prickly pear," a plant widespread in the Negev.]

sa·bre. *Chiefly British.* Variant of **saber.**

sab·u·lous (săb′yə-ləs) *adj.* Also **sab·u·lose** (-lōs′). Gritty; sandy. [Latin *sabulōsus,* from *sabulum,* coarse sand. See **bhes-¹** in Appendix.*] —**sab′u·los′i·ty** (-lŏs′ə-tē) *n.*

sac (săk) *n.* A pouch or pouchlike structure in a plant or animal, sometimes filled with fluid. [French, a bag, from Latin *saccus,* a SACK.]

SAC 1. Airport code for Sacramento, California. **2.** Strategic Air Command.

Sac. Variant of **Sauk.**

Sac·a·ga·we·a (săk′ə-jə-wē′ə). 1788?–1812. American Indian woman of the Shoshone tribe; served as guide and interpreter for the Lewis and Clark expedition.

sac·a·ton (săk′ə-tōn′) *n.* A grass, *Sporobolus wrightii,* of the southwestern United States, used for pasture and hay in saline areas. [American Spanish *zacatón,* from *zacate,* coarse grass, from Nahuatl *zacatl,* straw.]

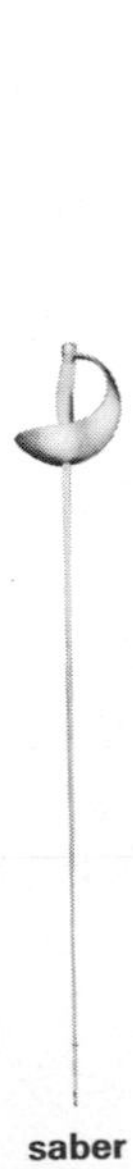
saber
A fencing saber

sac·cate (săk′āt′) *adj.* Shaped like or having a pouch or sac. [New Latin *saccatus,* from Latin *saccus,* a bag, SACK.]

sac·cha·rase (săk′ə-rās′) *n.* An enzyme, **invertase** *(see).* [SACCHAR(O)- + -ASE.]

sac·cha·rate (săk′ə-rāt′) *n.* A salt or ester of saccharic acid. [SACCHAR(IC ACID) + -ATE.]

sac·char·ic acid (sə-kăr′ĭk). A white crystalline acid, $CO\text{-}OH(CHOH)_4COOH$, formed by the oxidation of glucose, sucrose, or starch. [From SACCHAR(O)- + -IC.]

sac·cha·ride (săk′ə-rīd′, -rĭd) *n.* Any of a series of compounds of carbon, hydrogen, and oxygen in which the atoms of the latter two elements are in the ratio of 2:1, especially those containing the group $C_6H_{10}O_5$. [SACCHAR(O)- + -IDE.]

sac·char·i·fy (sə-kăr′ə-fī′, săk′ər-ə-) *tr.v.* **-fied, -fying, -fies.** Also **sac·cha·rize** (săk′ə-rīz′), **-rized, -rizing, -rizes.** To convert (starch, for example) into sugar. [SACCHAR(O)- + -FY.] —**sac·char′i·fi·ca′tion** (sə-kăr′ə-fə-kā′shən) *n.*

sac·cha·rim·e·ter (săk′ə-rĭm′ə-tər) *n.* **1.** A polarimeter that indicates the concentration of sugar in a solution. **2.** An instrument that determines the sugar content of a fermenting sample from carbon dioxide measurements. [From SACCHAR(O)- + -METER.]

sac·cha·rin (săk′ə-rĭn) *n.* A white crystalline powder, $C_7H_5NO_3S$, having a taste about 500 times sweeter than cane sugar, used as a calorie-free sweetener. [SACCHAR(O)- + -IN.]

sac·cha·rine (săk′ə-rĭn, -rīn′) *adj.* **1.** Of, relating to, or of the nature of sugar or saccharin; sweet. **2.** Having a cloyingly sweet attitude, tone, or character: *a saccharine smile.* [SACCHAR(O)- + -INE.] —**sac′cha·rine·ly** *adv.* —**sac′cha·rin′i·ty** *n.*

saccharo-, sacchar-. Indicates sugar; for example, **saccharometer, saccharide, saccharin.** [From Latin *saccharum,* sugar, from Greek *sakkharon,* from Pali *sakkharā,* from Sanskrit *śarkarā,* gravel, SUGAR.]

sac·cha·roid (săk′ə-roid′) *adj.* Also **sac·cha·roi·dal** (săk′ə-roid′l). Designating rocks and minerals having a granular structure similar to that of loaf sugar. [SACCHAR(O)- + -OID.]

sac·cha·rom·e·ter (săk′ə-rŏm′ə-tər) *n.* A hydrometer that determines the amount of sugar in a solution from density measurements. [SACCHARO- + -METER.]

sac·cha·ro·my·cete (săk′ə-rō-mī′sēt′) *n.* Any of various yeast fungi, especially of the genus *Saccharomyces,* many of which ferment sugar. [SACCHARO- + -MYCETE.] —**sac′cha·ro·my·ce′tic** (-mī-sē′tĭk), **sac′cha·ro·my·ce′tous** (-mī-sē′təs) *adj.*

sac·cha·rose (săk′ə-rōs′) *n.* A sugar, **sucrose** *(see).* [SACCHAR(O)- + -OSE.]

Sac·co (săk′ō; *Italian* säk′kō), **Nicola.** 1891–1927. Italian-born American political activist; with his friend, Bartolomeo **Vanzetti** *(see),* executed after a controversial murder trial.

sac·cu·late (săk′yə-lāt′) *adj.* Also **sac·cu·lat·ed** (-lā′tĭd), **sac·cu·lar** (-lər). Formed of or divided into a series of saclike dilations or pouches. [New Latin *sacculus,* SACCULE + -ATE.]

sac·cule (săk′yo͞ol) *n.* Also **sac·cu·lus** (săk′yə-ləs) *pl.* **-li** (-lī′). **1.** A small sac. **2.** The smaller of two membranous sacs in the vestibule of the labyrinth of the ear. [New Latin *sacculus,* from Latin, diminutive of *saccus,* a bag, SACK.]

sac·er·do·tal (săs′ər-dōt′l, săk′-) *adj.* **1.** Of or pertaining to priests or the priesthood; priestly. **2.** Of or pertaining to sacerdotalism. [Middle English, from Old French, from Latin *sacerdōtālis,* from *sacerdōs* (stem *sacerdōt-*), a priest. See **sak-** in Appendix.*] —**sac′er·do′tal·ly** *adv.*

sac·er·do·tal·ism (săs′ər-dōt′l-ĭz′əm, săk′-) *n.* **1.** The belief that priests act as mediators between God and man. **2.** The doctrine based on such a belief.

SACEUR Supreme Allied Commander, Europe.

sa·chem (sā′chəm) *n.* **1.** The chief of a tribe or confederation among some North American Indians, such as the Algonquins or Wampanoags. **2.** Any of the high officials of the Tammany Society. [Narraganset *sâchim,* "chief," from Proto-Algonquian *saakimaawa* (unattested). See also **sagamore.**]

Sa·cher-Ma·soch (zä′KHər-mä′zôKH), **Leopold von.** 1836–1895. Austrian author of popular novels characterized by the theme of sexual pleasure induced by submission to inflicted pain.

sa·cher tor·te (sä′kər tôr′tə; *German* zä′KHər tôr′tə). A rich chocolate cake filled with cream or jam and chocolate and topped with chocolate icing. [German *Sachertorte* : *Sacher,* 19th- and 20th-century family of hotel owners + TORTE.]

sa·chet (să-shā′) *n.* A small bag or packet containing perfumed powder and used to scent clothes, as in trunks or closets. [French, from Old French, a small bag, diminutive of *sac,* a bag, from Latin *saccus,* SACK.]

Sachs (zäks), **Hans.** 1494–1576. German poet, dramatist, and Meistersinger; author of over 6,000 works.

Sach·sen. The German name for **Saxony.**

sack¹ (săk) *n.* Also **sacque** (for sense 3). **1.** *Abbr.* **sk. a.** A large bag of strong, coarse material for holding foodstuffs or other objects in bulk. **b.** The contents of such a bag. **c.** A variable measure, equivalent to the amount a sack will hold. **2.** A similar but smaller container, often of paper or plastic. **3. a.** A short, loose-fitting coat for women and children. **b.** A woman's loose-fitting dress. **4.** *Slang.* A dismissal from employment: *His boss finally gave him the sack.* **5.** *Slang.* A bed, mattress, or sleeping bag. **6.** *Baseball.* A base. —**hit the sack.** *Slang.* To go to bed. —*v.* **sacked, sacking, sacks.** —*tr.* **1.** To place in a sack. **2.** *Slang.* To discharge from employment. —*intr. Slang.* To sleep. Often used with *out.* [Middle English *sack, sak,* Old English *sæcc, sacc,* from Latin *saccus,* from Greek *sakkos,* from Semitic, akin to Hebrew *śaq,* sack, sackcloth.]

sack² (săk) *tr.v.* **sacked, sacking, sacks.** To loot or pillage (a captured city, for example). —*n.* **1.** The looting or pillaging of a captured town. **2.** Plunder; loot. [Old French *(mettre a) sac,* (to put in) a sack, to plunder, from Italian *sacco,* bag, from Latin *saccus,* SACK.]

sack[3] (săk) *n.* Any of various light, dry, strong wines from Spain and the Canary Islands, imported to England in the 16th and 17th centuries. [Earlier *seck,* from Old French *(vin) sec,* dry (wine), from Latin *siccus,* dry. See **seikw-** in Appendix.*]

sack·but (săk′bŭt′) *n.* **1.** A medieval musical instrument resembling the trombone. **2.** A triangular stringed instrument. Daniel 3:5. [Old French *saqueboute,* "hooked lance" : *saquer, sachier*†, to pull, draw + *bouter,* to push, thrust against, from Common Romance *bottāre* (unattested), from Germanic (see **bhau-** in Appendix*).]

sack·cloth (săk′klôth′) *n.* **1.** Sacking. **2. a.** A rough cloth of camel's hair, goat hair, hemp, cotton, or flax. **b.** Garments made of this cloth, worn as a symbol of mourning or penitence.

sack·ing (săk′ĭng) *n.* A coarse, stout woven cloth, such as burlap or gunny, used for making sacks.

Sack·ville (săk′vĭl), **Thomas.** First Earl of Dorset and Baron Buckhurst. 1536–1608. English poet, dramatist, and diplomat.

sa·cral[1] (sā′krəl) *adj.* Of, near, or pertaining to the sacrum. [New Latin *sacralis,* from SACRUM.]

sa·cral[2] (sā′krəl) *adj.* Pertaining to sacred rites or observances. [From Latin *sacer* (stem *sacr-*), SACRED.]

sac·ra·ment (săk′rə-mənt) *n.* **1.** Any of seven rites of the historical Christian Church considered to have been instituted or observed by Jesus as a testament to inner grace or as a channel that mediates grace. In the liturgical churches these rites include baptism, confirmation, the Eucharist, matrimony, orders, penance, and extreme unction. **2.** *Often capital* **S. a.** The Eucharist. **b.** The consecrated elements of the Eucharist; especially, the bread or host. **3.** Something considered to have sacred significance; a spiritual symbol or bond. [Middle English, from Old French *sacrement,* from Latin *sacrāmentum,* from Latin, oath, solemn obligation, from *sacrāre,* to consecrate, from *sacer* (stem *sacr-*), SACRED.]

sac·ra·men·tal (săk′rə-mĕn′təl) *adj.* **1.** Pertaining to, of the nature of, or used in a sacrament. **2.** Consecrated or bound by or as if by a sacrament: *a sacramental duty.* **3.** Having the force or efficacy of a sacrament. —*n.* Any rite, action, or sacred object instituted by some Christian churches for use in worship. —**sac′ra·men′tal·ly** *adv.*

sac·ra·men·tal·ism (săk′rə-mĕn′tə-lĭz′əm) *n.* **1.** The doctrine that observance of the sacraments is necessary for salvation and that such participation can confer grace. **2.** The emphasis upon the efficacy of a sacramental. —**sac′ra·men′tal·ist** *n.*

sac·ra·men·tar·i·an (săk′rə-mĕn-târ′ē-ən) *n.* Also **Sac·ra·men·tar·i·an.** A person who regards the sacraments as merely visible symbols, not inherently efficacious nor corporeally manifesting Christ. —*adj.* **1.** *Often capital* **S.** Of or pertaining to sacramentarians. **2.** Of or pertaining to sacramentalism or sacramentalists. [Translation of German *Sakramenter, Sakramentierer.*] —**sac′ra·men′tar′i·an·ism′** *n.*

Sac·ra·men·to (săk′rə-mĕn′tō). **1.** The capital of California, on the Sacramento River in the north-central part of the state. Population, 192,000. **2.** The longest river in California, rising near the state's northern border and flowing 382 miles generally south to the Pacific northeast of San Francisco.

sa·crar·i·um (sə-krâr′ē-əm) *n., pl.* **-ia** (-ē-ə). **1.** The sanctuary or sacristy of a church. **2.** A **piscina** *(see).* [Medieval Latin *sacrārium,* from Latin, a place for keeping holy things, from *sacer,* SACRED.]

sa·cred (sā′krĭd) *adj.* **1.** Dedicated to or set apart for the worship of a deity. **2.** Made or declared holy: *sacred bread and wine.* **3.** Dedicated or devoted exclusively to a single use, purpose, or person. **4.** Worthy of reverence or respect; venerable: *the sacred teachings of Buddha.* **5.** Of or pertaining to religious objects, rites, or practices; not secular or profane. [Middle English, from the past participle of *sacren,* to consecrate, from Old French *sacrer,* from Latin *sacrāre,* from *sacer* (stem *sacr-*), dedicated, holy, sacred. See **sak-** in Appendix.*] —**sa′cred·ly** *adv.* —**sa′cred·ness** *n.*

Sacred College. The **College of Cardinals** *(see).*

sacred cow. A person, idea, or object sarcastically regarded as immune from reasonable criticism.

sac·ri·fice (săk′rə-fīs′) *n.* **1. a.** The act of offering something to a deity in propitiation or homage; especially, the ritual slaughter of an animal or person for this purpose. **b.** That which is so offered. **2. a.** The forfeiture of something highly valued, as an idea, object, or friendship, for the sake of someone or something considered to have a greater value or claim. **b.** Something so forfeited. **3. a.** A relinquishing of something at less than its presumed value. **b.** Something so relinquished. **c.** A loss so sustained. **4.** *Baseball.* A **sacrifice hit** *(see).* —*v.* **sacrificed, -ficing, -fices.** —*tr.* **1.** To offer as a sacrifice to a deity. **2.** To forfeit (something of value) for something considered to have a greater value or claim. **3.** To sell or give away at a loss: *"She would have sacrificed her soul for a good dinner"* (Katherine Mansfield). —*intr.* **1.** To make or offer a sacrifice. **2.** *Baseball.* To make a sacrifice hit. [Middle English, from Old French, from Latin *sacrificium* : *sacer,* holy, SACRED + *facere,* to do, to make (see **dhē-**[1] in Appendix*).] —**sac′ri·fic′er** *n.*

sacrifice fly. *Baseball.* A fly ball enabling a runner to score after it is caught by a fielder.

sacrifice hit. *Baseball.* A bunt batted to allow a runner to gain a base while the batter is retired.

sac·ri·fi·cial (săk′rə-fĭsh′əl) *adj.* Pertaining to or concerned with a sacrifice: *a sacrificial lamb.* —**sac′ri·fi′cial·ly** *adv.*

sac·ri·lege (săk′rə-lĭj) *n.* The misuse, theft, desecration, or profanation of anything consecrated to a deity or regarded as sacred. [Middle English, from Old French, from Latin *sacrilegium,* from *sacrilegus,* one who steals sacred things : *sacer,* SACRED + *legere,* to gather, pluck, steal (see **leg-** in Appendix*).] —**sac′ri·le′gist** (săk′rə-lē′jĭst) *n.*

sac·ri·le·gious (săk′rə-lē′jəs) *adj.* **1.** Disrespectful or irreverent toward anything regarded as sacred; impious; profane. **2.** Having committed sacrilege. —See Synonyms at **profane.** —**sac′ri·le′gious·ly** *adv.* —**sac′ri·le′gious·ness** *n.*

Usage: *Sacrilegious* is frequently misspelled through confusion with *religious.*

sa·cring bell (sā′krĭng). A bell rung at the elevation of the Host in Mass. [Middle English *sacringe belle* : *sacringe,* gerund of *sacren,* to consecrate (see **sacred**) + BELL.]

sac·ris·tan (săk′rĭs-tən) *n.* Also **sa·crist** (sā′krĭst). **1.** A person in charge of a sacristy. **2.** A sexton. [Middle English, from Medieval Latin *sacristānus,* from *sacrista,* "one in charge of sacred vessels," from Latin *sacer* (stem *sacr-*), SACRED.]

sac·ris·ty (săk′rĭs-tē) *n., pl.* **-ties.** A room in a church housing the sacred vessels and vestments; vestry. [French *sacristie,* from Medieval Latin *sacristia,* from *sacrista,* SACRISTAN.]

sac·ro·il·i·ac (săk′rō-ĭl′ē-ăk′, sā′krō-) *adj.* Of, pertaining to, or affecting the sacrum and ilium, their articulation, or associated ligaments. —*n.* The sacroiliac region or cartilage. [SACR(UM) + ILI(UM) + -AC.]

sac·ro·sanct (săk′rō-săngkt′) *adj.* Regarded as sacred and inviolable. See Usage note below. [Latin *sacrōsanctus,* consecrated with religious ceremonies : *sacrō,* by a sacred rite, ablative of *sacrum,* a holy thing, religious rite, from *sacer,* SACRED + *sanctus,* past participle of *sancīre,* to consecrate (see **sak-** in Appendix*).] —**sac′ro·sanc′ti·ty** (săk′rō-săngk′tə-tē) *n.*

Usage: *Sacrosanct,* when not applied specifically to religious objects, is sometimes used ironically, and thus may imply undeserved immunity to questioning or attack.

sa·crum (sā′krəm) *n., pl.* **-cra** (-krə). A triangular bone made up of five fused vertebrae and forming the posterior section of the pelvis. [New Latin, from Late Latin *(os) sacrum* (translation of Greek *hieron osteon,* "sacred bone," because it was used in sacrifice), from Latin, a sacred thing, from *sacer,* SACRED.]

sad (săd) *adj.* **sadder, saddest. 1.** Low in spirit; dejected; sorrowful; unhappy. **2.** Expressive of sorrow or unhappiness. **3.** Causing sorrow or gloom; depressing. **4.** Deplorable; sorry: *"Gertrude Stein was in a sad state of indecision and worry."* (Alice B. Toklas). **5.** Dark-hued; somber. [Middle English *sad,* grave, sad, full (of something), Old English *sæd,* sated, weary. See **sā-** in Appendix.*] —**sad′ly** *adv.* —**sad′ness** *n.*

Synonyms: *sad, melancholy, depressed, blue, dejected, downcast, sorrowful, doleful, woebegone, desolate, miserable, wretched.* These adjectives all mean to be in low spirits. *Sad* is the most general. *Melancholy* can refer to a lingering state resulting from temperament, or a condition marked merely by somber thoughts. The first of these senses is often described by *depressed. Blue* less formally applies to lowness of spirits. *Dejected* and *downcast* suggest dark moods of rather short duration, often triggered abruptly by something external and marked by disheartenment. *Sorrowful* applies broadly to manifestation of extreme sadness. *Doleful* describes what is mournful, gloomy, or dismal; especially with reference to appearance or nature, it sometimes suggests unintentionally comic effects. *Woebegone* suggests the appearance of one overcome by woe. *Desolate* implies extreme sorrow due to an irreparable loss. *Miserable* and *wretched* pertain to any state of profound unhappiness.

sad·den (săd′n) *v.* **-dened, -dening, -dens.** —*tr.* To make sad. —*intr.* To grow sad; darken: *"the sky saddens with the gathered storm"* (James Thomson).

sad·dhu. Variant of **sadhu.**

sad·dle (săd′l) *n.* **1. a.** A leather seat for a rider, secured on an animal's back by a girth. **b.** Similar tack used for attaching a pack to an animal. **2.** The padded part of a driving harness fitting over a horse's back. **3.** The part of an animal's back upon which a saddle is placed. **4.** Something resembling or suggestive of a saddle in position, function, or shape. **a.** The seat of a bicycle, motorcycle, or similar vehicle. **b.** A cut of meat, consisting of part of the backbone and both loins. **c.** The lower part of a male fowl's back. **d.** A saddle-shaped depression in the ridge of a hill; a col. **e.** A ridge between two peaks. —**in the saddle.** In a position of control or dominant influence. —*v.* **saddled, -dling, -dles.** —*tr.* **1.** To put a saddle on (a horse, for example). **2.** To load or burden; encumber: *saddled with ten children.* **3.** To impose (a burdensome responsibility) upon another: *She saddled her debts on him.* —*intr.* To saddle a horse or get into a saddle. Often used with *up.* [Middle English *sadel,* Old English *sadol.* See **sed-**[1] in Appendix.*]

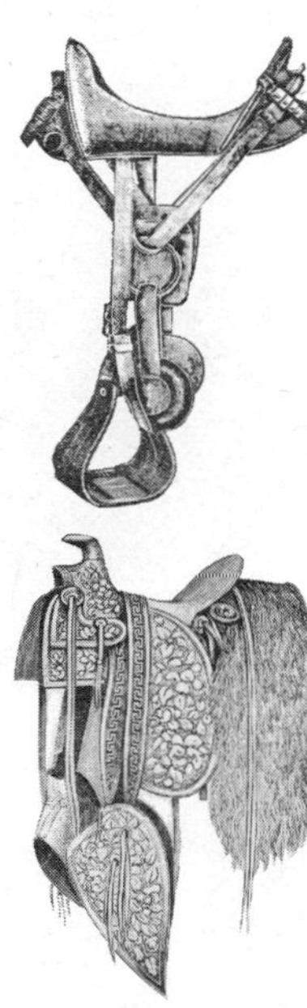

saddle
Above: Civil War cavalryman's saddle
Below: Western saddle

sad·dle·bag (săd′l-băg′) *n.* A pouch of leather or other material, usually one of a pair hung across a saddle.

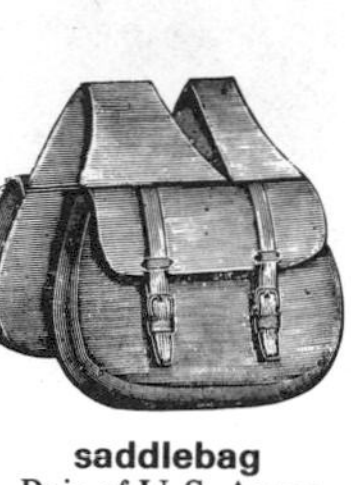

saddlebag
Pair of U.S. Army leather saddlebags

saddle blanket. A blanket placed between a saddle and a horse's back to prevent galling.

sad·dle·bow (săd′l-bō′) *n.* The arched upper front part of a saddle; pommel. [Middle English *sadelbowe,* Old English *sadulboga* : *sadul, sadol,* SADDLE + *boga,* BOW (arch).]

sad·dle·cloth (săd′l-klôth′, -klŏth′) *n.* A cloth placed under the saddle of a racehorse and bearing its number.

saddle horse. A horse bred or schooled for riding.

sad·dler (săd′lər) *n.* One who makes, repairs, or sells saddles.

saddle roof. A roof having a ridge and two gables.

sad·dler·y (săd′lə-rē) *n., pl.* **-ies. 1.** Saddles, harnesses, and other furnishings for horses; tack. **2.** A shop selling such equipment. **3.** The craft or business of a saddler.

saddle shoe. A flat casual shoe, usually white, having a band of leather in a contrasting color across the instep.

saddle soap. A preparation containing mild soap and neat's-foot oil, used for cleaning and softening leather.

t tight/th thin, path/*th* this, bathe/ŭ cut/ûr urge/v valve/w with/y yes/z zebra, size/zh vision/ə about, item, edible, gallop, circus/ à *Fr.* ami/œ *Fr.* feu, *Ger.* schön/ü *Fr.* tu, *Ger.* über/KH *Ger.* ich, *Scot.* loch/N *Fr.* bon. ***Follows main vocabulary. †Of obscure origin.**

safety pin

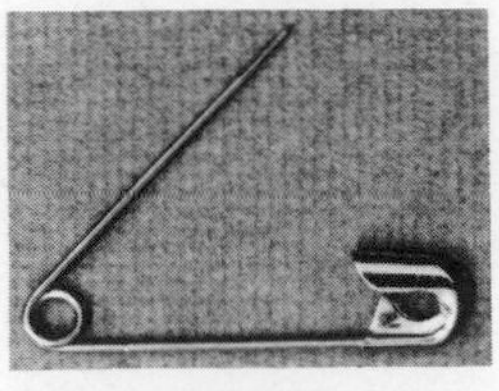

open pin

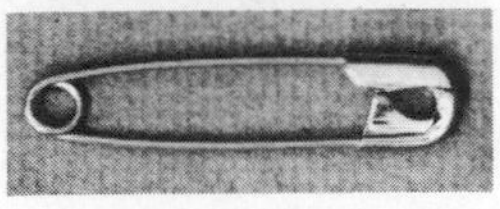

closed pin

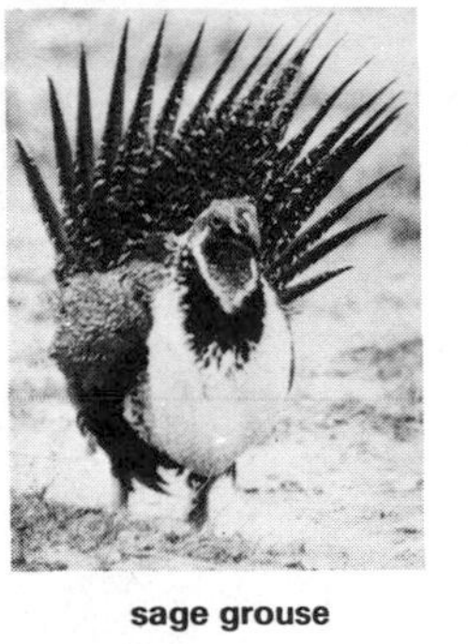

sage grouse

saddle sore. 1. A sore on a horse's back caused by an improperly fitted saddle. 2. A sore on the rider caused by saddle chafing.

saddle stitch. 1. A simple overcasting stitch used primarily as ornament on clothing, and usually of a thread contrasting in color with the fabric of the garment. 2. *Bookbinding.* A stitch used in sewing together the leaves of a book at the fold lines, either with thread or wire.

sad·dle·tree (săd'l-trē') *n.* The frame of a saddle.

Sad·du·cee (săj'ŏŏ-sē, săd'yŏŏ-) *n.* A Jewish sect flourishing from the second century B.C. through the first century A.D., that retained the older interpretation of the written Mosaic law against the oral tradition and denied the resurrection of the dead. Compare **Pharisee.** [Middle English *Saducee,* Old English *Sadducēas* (plural), from Late Latin *Saddūcaeus,* from Late Greek *Saddoukaios,* from Hebrew *Ṣaddūqī,* probably from *Ṣādōq,* Zadok, "righteous," high priest of Israel in King David's time, and supposedly the founder of the sect.] —**Sad'du·ce'an** (-sē'ən) *adj.* —**Sad'du·cee'ism'** (-ĭz'əm) *n.*

sa·de, sa·dhe (sä'də, -dē) *n.* Also **tsa·de** (tsä'də, -dē). The 18th letter of the Hebrew alphabet. See **alphabet.** [Hebrew *ṣadhe.*]

Sade (sȧd), Comte **Donatien Alphonse François de.** Known as Marquis de Sade. 1740–1814. French man of letters, novelist, and libertine.

sad·hu (sä'dōō) *n.* Also **sad·dhu.** A Hindu ascetic holy man. [Sanskrit *sādhu,* from adjective, "straight," right, holy, from Indo-Iranian *sādh* (unattested).]

sad·i·ron (săd'ī'ərn) *n.* A heavy flatiron, having points at both ends and a removable handle. [SAD (in the dialectal sense of "heavy") + IRON.]

sa·dism (sā'dĭz'əm, săd'ĭz'əm) *n.* 1. *Psychology.* The association of sexual satisfaction with the infliction of pain on others. Compare **masochism.** 2. Broadly, delight in cruelty. [After Comte Donatien de SADE, who expounded principles of anarchic sexual violence.] —**sa'dist** *n.* & *adj.*

sa·dis·tic (sə-dĭs'tĭk) *adj.* Characterized by sadism; deliberately cruel. See Synonyms at **cruel.** —**sa·dis'ti·cal·ly** *adv.*

sa·do·mas·och·ism (sā'dō-măs'ə-kĭz'əm, săd'ō-) *n. Psychology.* A tendency to simultaneous sadism and masochism. [SAD(ISM) + MASOCHISM.] —**sa'do·mas'och·ist** *n.* —**sa'do·mas'och·is'tic** (sā'dō-măs'ə-kĭs'tĭk, săd'ō-) *adj.*

Sa·do·va (sä-dō'vä). *German* **Sa·do·wa** (zä-dō'vä). A village in northern Bohemia, Czechoslovakia, the site of a battle in which the Prussians defeated the Austrians (1866).

SAF Airport code for Santa Fe, New Mexico.

Sa·far (sə-fär') *n.* Also **Sa·phar.** The second month of the Moslem calendar. See **calendar.** [Arabic.]

sa·fa·ri (sə-fä'rē) *n., pl.* **-ris.** An overland expedition, especially for hunting or exploring in East Africa. [Arabic *safarīy,* a journey, from *safara,* to travel, set out.]

safe (sāf) *adj.* **safer, safest.** 1. Not apt or able to cause or incur danger, harm, or evil; secure: *"Time was when the unguarded door was safe"* (Cowper). 2. Free from danger or injury; unhurt: *safe and sound.* 3. Free from hazard; sure: *a safe bet.* 4. Affording protection: *a safe place.* 5. *Baseball.* Having reached a base without being put out, as a batter or base runner. —*n.* 1. A metal container usually having a lock, used for storing valuables; strongbox. 2. Any repository for protecting stored items; especially, a cooled compartment for perishable foods. 3. *Slang.* A condom. [Middle English *sauf,* from Old French, from Latin *salvus,* healthy, uninjured, safe. See **sol-** in Appendix.*] —**safe'ly** *adv.* —**safe'ness** *n.*

safe-con·duct (sāf'kŏn'dŭkt) *n.* 1. An official document or an escort assuring unmolested passage, as through enemy territory. 2. The protection thus afforded. —*tr.v.* (sāf'kən-dŭkt') **safe-conducted, -ducting, -ducts.** 1. To grant a safe-conduct to. 2. To escort with a safe-conduct.

safe-de·pos·it (sāf'dĭ-pŏz'ĭt) *adj.* Pertaining to or constituting a fireproof metal box or vault for the safe storage of papers, jewelry, or other valuables.

safe·guard (sāf'gärd') *n.* 1. a. One that serves as a guard or protection. b. Any mechanical device or technical improvement designed to prevent accidents. c. Any precaution. 2. A safe-conduct. 3. A protective stipulation, as in a contract. —*tr.v.* **safeguarded, -guarding, -guards.** To insure the safety of; to guard; protect. See Synonyms at **defend.**

safe·keep·ing (sāf'kē'pĭng) *n.* The act of keeping in safety or the state of being kept safe; protection; care.

safe·light (sāf'līt') *n.* A lamp having one or more color filters capable of permitting moderate darkroom illumination without exposure of photosensitive film or paper.

safe·ty (sāf'tē) *n., pl.* **-ties.** 1. Freedom from danger, risk, or injury. 2. Any of various devices designed to prevent accident; specifically, a lock on a firearm preventing accidental firing. 3. *Football.* a. A play in which a member of the offensive team downs the ball, willingly or unwillingly, behind his own goal line, resulting in two points for the defensive team. Compare **touchback.** b. One of two defensive backs, usually positioned closest to the goal line they defend. 4. *Slang.* A condom. —*adj.* Contributing to or insuring safety; protective.

safety belt. A **seat belt** *(see).*

safety glass. A composite of two sheets of glass with an intermediate layer of transparent plastic used to prevent shattering. Also called "shatterproof glass."

safety lamp. 1. A miner's lamp with a protective wire gauze surrounding the flame to prevent ignition of flammable gases. 2. Any specially protected lamp.

safety match. A match that can be lighted only by being struck against a chemically prepared friction surface.

safety pin. 1. A pin in the form of a clasp, having a sheath to cover and hold the point. 2. A pin that prevents the premature or accidental detonation of a bomb, grenade, or other explosive.

safety razor. A razor in which the blade is fitted into a holder with guards to prevent cutting of the skin.

safety valve. 1. A valve in a pressure container, as in a steam boiler, that automatically opens when pressure reaches a dangerous level. 2. Any outlet for the release of an excess, as of emotion.

safety zone. An area from which automotive traffic is prohibited for the safety of pedestrians.

saf·flow·er (săf'lou'ər) *n.* 1. A plant, *Carthamus tinctorius,* native to Asia, having orange flowers that yield a dyestuff and seeds that are the source of an oil used in cooking, cosmetics, paints, and medicine. 2. The dried flowers of this plant. [Earlier *safflore,* from Dutch *saffloer,* from Old French *saffleur,* variant (influenced by *safran,* saffron, and *fleur,* flower) of *safour,* from Old Italian *saffiore,* saffron, variant of *asfiore,* from Arabic *aṣfar,* yellow, a yellow plant.]

saf·fron (săf'rən) *n.* 1. A plant, *Crocus sativus,* native to the Old World, having purple or white flowers with orange stigmas. 2. The dried stigmas of this plant, used to color foods and as a cooking spice and a dyestuff. 3. Moderate or strong orange-yellow to moderate orange. In this sense, also called "saffron yellow." See **color.** [Middle English *saffran,* from Old French *safran,* from Medieval Latin *safranum,* from Arabic *za'farān.*] —**saf'fron** *adj.*

Sa·fi (sä'fī). A city and seaport of Morocco, in the west, 85 miles northwest of Marrakesh. Population, 100,000.

saf·ra·nine (săf'rə-nēn', -nĭn) *n.* Also **saf·ra·nin** (-nən). Any of a family of dyes based on phenazine, used in the textile industry and as a biological stain. [French *safran,* SAFFRON + -INE.]

saf·role (săf'rōl') *n.* A colorless or pale-yellow oily liquid, $C_{10}H_{10}O_2$, derived from oil of sassafras and other essential oils and used in making perfume and soap. [French *safran,* SAFFRON + -OLE.]

sag (săg) *v.* **sagged, sagging, sags.** —*intr.* 1. To sink, curve downward, or settle from pressure, weight, or slackness. 2. To hang loosely or unevenly; to droop. 3. To diminish in firmness or strength; weaken. 4. To decline in value or price. 5. *Nautical.* To drift to leeward. —*tr.* To cause to sag. —*n.* 1. The act, degree, or extent of sagging. 2. A sagging or sunken place or area; a depression. 3. *Nautical.* A drift to leeward. [Middle English *saggen,* perhaps of Scandinavian origin, akin to Swedish *sacka.* See **sengw-** in Appendix.*]

sa·ga (sä'gə) *n.* 1. An Icelandic prose narrative of the 12th and 13th centuries recounting historical and legendary events and exploits. 2. Any long narrative. [Old Norse, a story, legend. See **sekw-**[3] in Appendix.*]

sa·ga·cious (sə-gā'shəs) *adj.* Possessing or showing sound judgment and keen perception; wise. See Synonyms at **shrewd.** [From Latin *sagāx* (stem *sagāc-*). See **sāg-** in Appendix.*] —**sa·ga'cious·ly** *adv.* —**sa·ga'cious·ness** *n.*

sa·gac·i·ty (sə-găs'ə-tē) *n.* Keen intelligence; shrewdness.

sag·a·more (săg'ə-môr', -mōr') *n.* A subordinate chief among the Algonquian Indians of North America. [Eastern Abnaki *sàkama,* from Proto-Algonquian *saakimaawa* (unattested). See also **sachem.**]

Sa·gan (sā'gən), **Carl.** Born 1934. American astronomer.

Sa·gan (sȧ-gän'), **Françoise.** Original name, Françoise Quoirez. Born 1935. French writer.

saga novel. The **roman-fleuve** *(see).*

sage[1] (sāj) *n.* A person, usually an elderly man, who is venerated for his experience, judgment, and wisdom. —*adj.* **sager, sagest.** 1. Having, proceeding from, or showing wisdom and calm judgment; judicious; wise. 2. *Obsolete.* Serious; solemn. [Middle English, from Old French, from Vulgar Latin *sapius* (unattested), from Latin *sapere,* to be sensible, be wise. See **sap-** in Appendix.*] —**sage'ly** *adv.* —**sage'ness** *n.*

sage[2] (sāj) *n.* 1. Any of various plants and shrubs of the genus *Salvia;* especially, *S. officinalis,* having aromatic grayish-green leaves and used as a cooking herb. 2. The leaves of this plant, used as seasoning. [Middle English *sauge,* from Old French *sauge,* from Latin *salvia,* "the healing plant," from *salvus,* healthy, safe. See **sol-** in Appendix.*]

sage·brush (sāj'brŭsh') *n.* Any of several aromatic plants of the genus *Artemisia;* especially, *A. tridentata,* a shrub of arid regions of western North America, having silver-green leaves and large clusters of small white flowers.

sage green. Grayish or moderate yellow green to grayish or moderate olive green. See **color.** —**sage'-green'** *adj.*

sage grouse. A chickenlike bird, *Centrocercus urophasianus,* of western North America, having long, pointed tail feathers that can be spread fanwise. Also called "sage hen."

sag·ger (săg'ər) *n.* Also **sag·gar.** 1. A protective casing of fire clay in which delicate ceramic articles are fired. 2. Clay used to make such casings. —*tr.v.* **saggered, -gering, -gers.** To place or bake in a sagger. [Perhaps a contraction of SAFEGUARD.]

Sa·ghal·ien. The former name for **Sakhalin.**

Sag·i·naw (săg'ə-nô). A city of Michigan, on the Saginaw River about 20 miles south of Saginaw Bay of Lake Huron. Population, 98,000.

Sa·git·ta (sə-jĭt'ə) *n.* A constellation in the Northern Hemisphere near Aquila and Vulpecula. [Latin *sagitta*†, Sagitta, arrow.]

sag·it·tal (săj'ə-təl) *adj.* 1. Of, pertaining to, or like an arrow or arrowhead. 2. *Anatomy.* Relating to the suture uniting the two parietal bones of the skull. 3. *Zoology.* Pertaining to or des-

ă pat/ā pay/âr care/ä father/b bib/ch church/d deed/ĕ pet/ē be/f fife/g gag/h hat/hw which/ĭ pit/ī pie/îr pier/j judge/k kick/l lid, needle/m mum/n no, sudden/ng thing/ŏ pot/ō toe/ô paw, for/oi noise/ou out/ŏŏ took/ōō boot/p pop/r roar/s sauce/sh ship, dish/

ignating the longitudinal vertical plane that divides the body of a bilaterally symmetrical animal into right and left halves. [From Latin *sagitta*, arrow. See **Sagitta**.] —**sag′it·tal·ly** *adv.*

Sag·it·ta·ri·us (săj′ə-târ′ē-əs) *n.* **1.** A constellation in the Southern Hemisphere near Scorpius and Capricornus. **2.** The ninth sign of the **zodiac** *(see)*. Also called the "Archer." [Middle English, from Latin *sagittārius*, an archer, Sagittarius, from *sagitta*, an arrow. See **Sagitta**.]

sag·it·tate (săj′ə-tāt′) *adj.* Also **sa·git·ti·form** (sə-jĭt′ə-fôrm′). *Botany.* Having the shape of an arrowhead: *sagittate leaves.* [From Latin *sagitta*, arrow. See **Sagitta**.]

sa·go (sā′gō) *n.* A powdery starch obtained from the trunks of the sago palm and used in Asia as a food thickener and textile stiffener. [Malay *sagu*.]

sago palm. **1.** Any of various palm trees of the genera *Metroxylon, Arenga*, and *Caryota*, of tropical Asia. **2.** A palmlike cycad, *Cycas revoluta*, of southeastern Asia.

sa·gua·ro (sə-gwär′ō, sə-wär′ō) *n., pl.* **-ros.** Also **sa·hua·ro** (sə-wär′ō). **1.** A very large cactus, *Carnegiea gigantea*, of the southwestern United States and northern Mexico, having upward-curving branches, white flowers, and edible red fruit. **2.** The fruit of this cactus. [Mexican Spanish, probably of Piman origin.]

Saguaro National Monument. An area occupying about 84 square miles in southeastern Arizona, reserved to protect the numerous saguaros growing there.

Sag·ue·nay (săg′ə-nā′). A river of south-central Quebec, Canada, flowing 110 miles southeast from Lake Saint John to the St. Lawrence.

Sa·gui·a el Ham·ra (sə-gwē′ə ăl hăm′rə). The northern zone of **Spanish Sahara** *(see)*.

Sa·gun·to (sä-go͞on′tō). Ancient name **Sa·gun·tum** (-təm). Formerly **Mur·vie·dro** (mo͞or-vyā′*th*rō). A city of Spain, captured by Hannibal in 219 B.C. Population, 30,000.

Sa·hap·tin (sä-hăp′tən) *n., pl.* **Sahaptin** or **-tins.** Also **Sha·hap·tin** (shä-), **Sha·hap·ti·an** (shä-hăp′tē-ən). **1.** A member of a North American Indian people of Idaho, Washington, and Oregon. **2.** The language of this people.

Sa·har·a (sə-hâr′ə, -här′ə). *Arabic* **Sah·ra** (sŏ′hrä). A vast arid area of northern Africa, occupying over 3,000,000 square miles and extending from the Atlantic coast to the Nile Valley and from the Atlas Mountains south to the Sudan. [Arabic *aṣḥar*, color of desert sand, from *ṣaḥrá*, desert.]

Usage: *Sahara*, or *the Sahara*, is the preferred form, especially in formal and scholarly usage. *Sahara Desert*, though widely used, involves redundancy, since *desert* is implicit in *Sahara*.

Sa·ha·ran·pur (sə-hä′rən-po͝or). A city of India, in northern Uttar Pradesh. Population, 197,000.

sa·hib (sä′ĭb) *n.* A title of respect equivalent to *master* or *sir*. Used for Europeans in colonial India. [Hindi *ṣāḥib*, master, lord, from Arabic, friend, companion, master.]

said (sĕd). Past tense and past participle of **say**. —*adj. Law.* Named or mentioned before; aforementioned. See Usage note.

Usage: *Said* (adjective) is seldom appropriate to any but legal or business writing: *the said tenant* (named in a lease); *said property*. In general usage, in similar contexts, *said* is usually unnecessary, and *the tenant* or *the property* will suffice. Where clarity demands an equivalent of *said*, preferable alternatives are *aforementioned* and *specified*.

Sa·i·da (sä-ē′dä). A seaport of Lebanon, on the Mediterranean 25 miles southwest of Beirut on the site of ancient **Sidon** *(see)*. Population, 32,000.

sai·ga (sī′gə) *n.* Either of two small antelopes, *Saiga tatarica* or *S. mongolia*, of the plains of northern Eurasia, having a stubby, proboscislike nose. [Russian *saĭga*, from Chagatai *saigak*.]

Sai·gon (sī-gŏn′). The capital and a port of South Vietnam, in the south on the Saigon River about 50 miles upstream from the South China Sea. Population, 1,400,000.

sail (sāl) *n.* **1.** A length of shaped canvas or other strong material attached to a ship, iceboat, or the like, to catch the wind and propel or aid in maneuvering the vessel. **2.** A sailing vessel. **3. a.** Sails collectively. **b.** Sailing vessels collectively. **4.** A trip or voyage in a sailing craft. **5.** Something resembling a sail in form or function, such as the blade of a windmill. —**in sail.** Having the sails set. —**make sail. 1.** To unfurl a ship's sail or sails. **2.** To begin a voyage. —**set sail. 1.** To hoist the sails preparatory to a voyage. **2.** To begin a trip or voyage. —**take in sail.** To reduce the area of sail exposed to the wind; to reef. —**under sail** (or **sails**). With sails set and catching the wind; sailing. —*v.* **sailed, sailing, sails.** —*intr.* **1.** To move across the surface of water, especially by means of a sail. **2.** To travel by water in a vessel. **3.** To start out on a voyage or journey; set sail. **4.** To operate a sailing craft, especially for sport. **5.** To glide through the air; soar. **6.** To move in a swift, dignified manner, like a ship in full sail: *sail through a room.* **7.** *Informal.* To plunge into vigorous action. Used with *in: The efficiency expert sailed in and made sweeping changes.* —*tr.* **1.** To navigate or manage (a vessel). **2.** To voyage upon or across (a body of water): *sail the Pacific.* —**sail into. 1.** To begin with vigor or force; enter into with energy. **2.** To attack violently with words or physical force. [Middle English *sail(le)*, Old English *segl*, from Germanic *seglam* (unattested).]

sail·boat (sāl′bōt′) *n.* A small boat propelled partly or wholly by sail.

sail·cloth (sāl′klôth′, -klŏth′) *n.* Cotton canvas or other strong fabric suitable for making sails, tents, or the like.

sail·fish (sāl′fĭsh′) *n., pl.* **sailfish** or **-fishes.** Any of various large marine fishes of the genus *Istiophorus*, having the upper jaw prolonged into a spearlike bone and a large, saillike dorsal fin.

sail·ing (sā′lĭng) *n.* **1.** The act of one that sails. **2.** The skill required to operate and navigate a sailing vessel; navigation. **3.** The departure or time of departure of a vessel or person on board: *The sailing is at 2:00* P.M.

sail·or (sā′lər) *n.* **1.** One who serves in a navy or who earns his living by working on a ship; especially, an ordinary seaman. **2.** One traveling by water, especially with reference to his susceptibility to seasickness: *a poor sailor.* **3.** A low-crowned straw hat with a flat top and flat brim. In this sense, also called "sailor hat." [Variant of earlier *sailer*, from Middle English, from *sailen*, to sail, Old English *seglan*, from Germanic *segljan* (unattested), from *seglam* (unattested), SAIL (noun).] —**sail′or·ly** *adj.*

sail·or's-choice (sā′lərz-chois′) *n., pl.* **sailor's-choice.** Any of various fishes of the North American Atlantic coast, such as the **pinfish** *(see)* or *Haemulon parrai* of more southerly waters.

sain·foin (sān′foin′, săn′-) *n.* A plant, *Onobrychis viciaefolia*, native to Eurasia, that has compound leaves and pink or white flowers and is often used as fodder. [French, from Old French, from Medieval Latin *sānum faenum*, "wholesome hay" (formerly used as a medicinal herb) : Latin *sānum, sānus*, healthy, whole (see **sānos** in Appendix*) + *faenum, fēnum*, hay (see **dhēi-** in Appendix*).]

saint (sānt) *n.* **1.** *Abbr.* **S., St.** *Theology.* **a.** A person officially recognized by the Roman Catholic Church and certain other Christian churches as being entitled to public veneration and as being capable of interceding for men on earth; one who has been canonized. **b.** Any person who has died and gone to heaven. **c.** Any baptized believer in Christ, according to the New Testament. **d.** *Capital* **S.** A member of any of various religious groups; especially, a **Latter-Day Saint** *(see)*. **2.** A very holy person. **3.** A charitable, unselfish, or patient person. —*tr.v.* **sainted, sainting, saints.** To name, recognize, or venerate as a saint; canonize. [Middle English, from Old French, from Latin *sanctus*, sacred, from the past participle of *sancire*, to sanctify, consecrate. See **sak-** in Appendix.*]

Saint. Entries not found under **Saint** may appear at **St.** Biographies of Saints appear at the name of the individual Saint; for **Saint Paul**, see **Paul**.

Saint Agnes' Eve. The night of January 20th, when, according to legend, a woman will dream of her future husband. [After Saint *Agnes* (died A.D. 304), Roman Catholic child martyr, who was beheaded for refusing to marry.]

Saint Anthony's cross. A **tau cross** *(see)*.

Saint Bernard. A large, strong dog of a breed developed in Switzerland, having a thick brown and white coat, and originally used by monks of the hospice of Saint Bernard in the Swiss Alps to help patrol the snow-covered region.

Saint-De·nis (săɴ-də-nē′). **1.** An industrial city north of Paris, France, of which it is a suburb; the site of a Gothic basilica containing the tombs of many French monarchs. Population, 93,000. **2.** The capital of Réunion. Population, 75,000.

saint·dom (sānt′dəm) *n.* The condition or quality of being a saint.

Sainte-Beuve (săɴt-bœv′), **Charles Augustin.** 1804–1869. French literary critic, poet, and historian.

saint·ed (sān′tĭd) *adj.* **1.** Enrolled among the saints; canonized. **2.** Of saintly character; holy.

Saint-É·tienne (săɴ-tā-tyĕn′). An industrial city in a coal-mining area of southeastern France, about 31 miles southwest of Lyon. Population, 204,000.

Saint-Ex·u·pé·ry (săɴ-tĕg-zü-pā-rē′), **Antoine de.** 1900–1944. French author and aviator.

Saint-Gau·dens (sānt-gô′dənz), **Augustus.** 1848–1907. Irish-born American sculptor.

saint·hood (sānt′ho͝od′) *n.* **1.** The status, character, or condition of being a saint. **2.** Saints collectively.

Saint John (sānt′ jŏn′). The largest city and a major port of New Brunswick, Canada, in the south on the Bay of Fundy. Population, 55,000.

Saint John, Lake (sānt′ jŏn′). *French* **Lac Saint-Jean** (lăk săɴ-zhäɴ′). A lake occupying 375 square miles in south-central Quebec, Canada.

Saint Johns (sānt′ jŏnz′). The capital of Antigua, on the northern coast of the island. Population, 21,000.

Saint-Just (săɴ-zhüst′), **Louis Antoine Léon de.** 1767–1794. French revolutionary; guillotined.

Saint-Laur·ent (săɴ-lō-räɴ′). A city of Canada in southern Quebec near Montreal. Population, 50,000.

Saint-Lo (săɴ-lō′). A town in Normandy, northwestern France; the site of an Allied breakthrough in World War II (1944). Population, 12,000.

Saint-Lou·is (săɴ-lo͞o-ē′). A port of Senegal, on the Senegal River near the border with Mauritania. Population, 58,000.

saint·ly (sānt′lē) *adj.* **-lier, -liest.** Resembling, pertaining to, or befitting a saint. See Synonyms at **religious**. —**saint′li·ness** *n.*

Saint Mar·ys. The former name for **St. Marys City**.

Saint-Maur-des-Fos·sés (săɴ-môr-dā-fô-sā′). A city and industrial center of France, southeast of Paris, of which it is a suburb. Population, 70,000.

Saint-Mi·hiel (săɴ-mē-yĕl′). A town on the Meuse in northeastern France; the site of a successful American offensive against German forces in World War I (1918).

Saint-Na·zaire (săɴ-nà-zâr′). A city and major shipbuilding center of France, in the west at the mouth of the Loire. It was the leading German submarine base on the Atlantic during World War II, until demolished by Allied bombs (1943). Population, 49,000.

Saint Nicholas, Saint Nick. **Santa Claus** *(see)*.

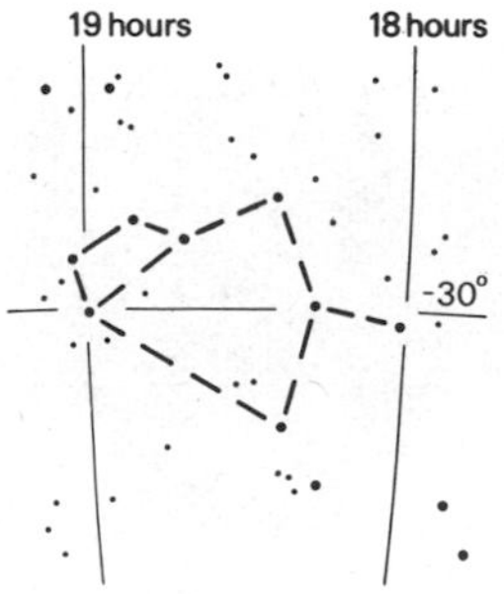

Sagittarius

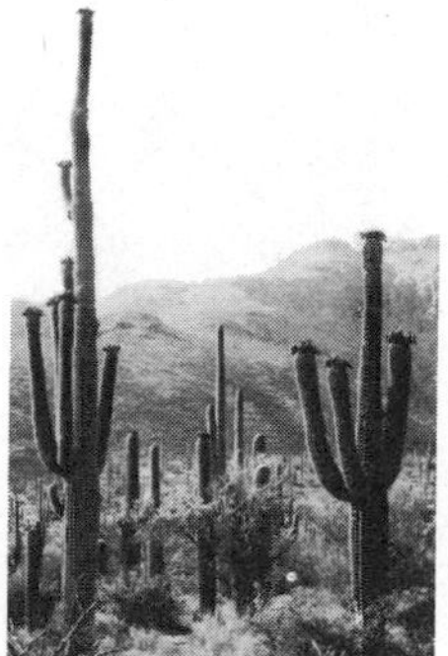
saguaro

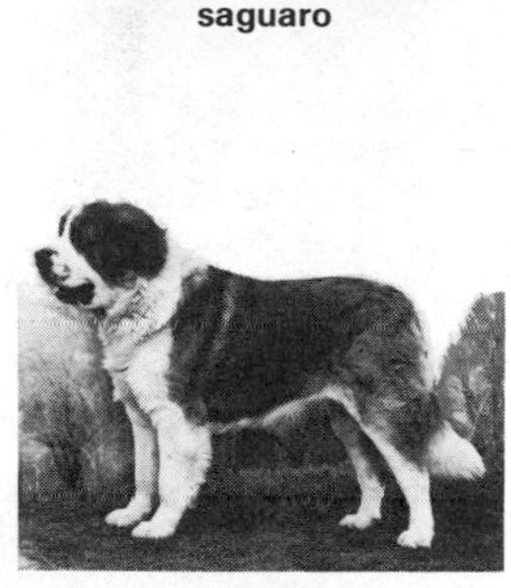
Saint Bernard

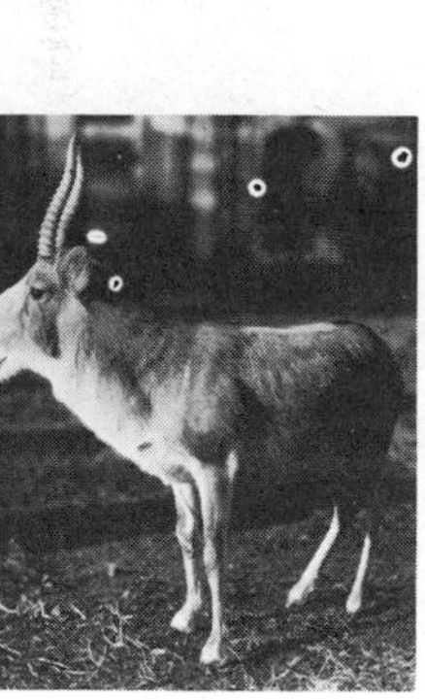
saiga
Saiga tatarica

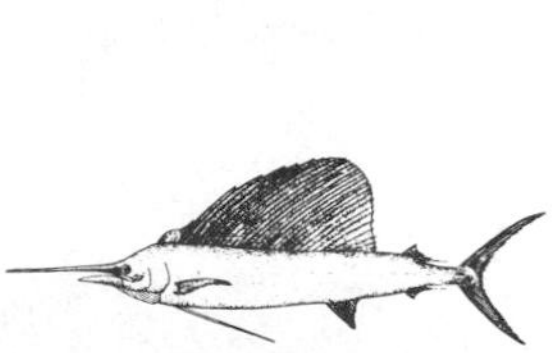
sailfish

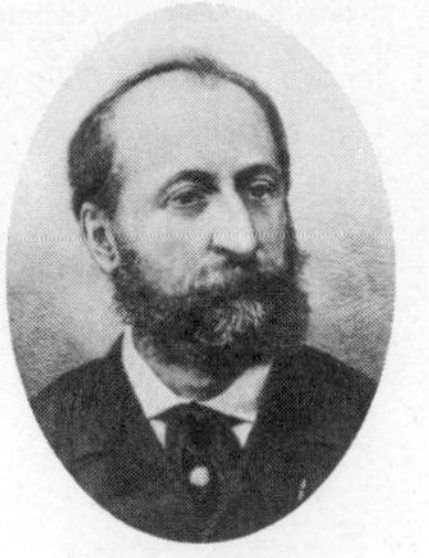

Saint-Saëns
Contemporary portrait etched by Albert Rosenthal, Philadelphia, 1889

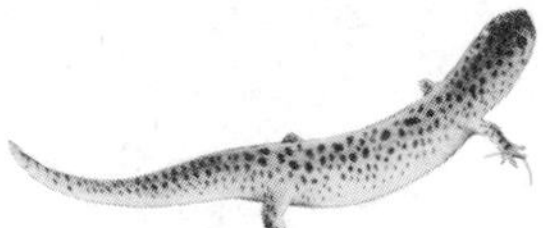

salamander
Pseudotriton ruber

Saint Patrick's Day. March 17, observed in honor of Saint Patrick, the patron saint of Ireland.
Saint Paul (sānt' pôl'). The capital of Minnesota, in the east on the Mississippi opposite Minneapolis. Population, 313,000.
Saint-Pierre. The French name for **St. Pierre.**
Saint-Saëns (săN-săNs'), **(Charles) Camille.** 1835–1921. French composer, pianist, and organist.
Saint-Si·mon (săN-sē-môN'), **Comte de.** Title of Claude Henri de Rouvroy. 1760–1825. French social philosopher; regarded as the founder of French socialism.
Saint-Si·mon (săN-sē-môN'), **Duc de.** Title of Louis de Rouvroy. 1675–1755. French army officer and public official; author of *Mémoires* of life under Louis XIV and Louis XV.
Saint-Tro·pez (săN-trô-pā'). A resort town of France, in the southeast on the Mediterranean.
Saint Valentine's Day. February 14, on which valentines are traditionally exchanged.
Sai·pan (sī-păn', -păn', sī'păn). The largest (47 square miles) of the Mariana Islands in the western Pacific; the site of a U.S. air base in World War II after its capture from the Japanese (1944).
Sa·is (sā'ĭs). An ancient Egyptian city on the Nile delta; a capital of Lower Egypt (663–525 B.C.). **—Sa'ite'** (-īt') *n.* **—Sa·it'ic** (sā-ĭt'ĭk) *adj.*
Sai·shu. The Japanese name for **Cheju.**
saith. *Archaic.* Third person singular present indicative of **say.**
Sai·va (sī'və, shī'-) *n.* A member of the cult of Shiva.
Sa·ja·ma (sä-hä'mä). A mountain rising to 21,390 feet in western Bolivia, near the border with Chile.
Sa·kai (sä'kī'). A city and seaport of Japan, on southern Honshu. Population, 439,000.
Sa·kar·ya (sə-kär'yə). A river rising in west-central Turkey and flowing 490 miles, first in two wide loops and then generally north, to the Black Sea.
sake¹ (sāk) *n.* **1.** Purpose; motive; end: *a quarrel only for the sake of argument.* **2.** Advantage; good: *for the sake of his health.* **3.** Personal benefit or interest; welfare: *for his own sake.* [Middle English *sake,* contention, lawsuit, guilt (the phrase "for the sake of" probably originated in legal usage), Old English *sacu,* lawsuit. See **sāg-** in Appendix.*]
sa·ke² (sä'kē) *n.* Also **sa·ki.** A Japanese liquor made from fermented rice. [Japanese, "liquor."]
Sa·kel (zä'kəl), **Manfred Joshua.** 1906–1957. Austrian-born American psychiatrist; first used shock therapy for schizophrenia.
sa·ker (sā'kər) *n.* A Eurasian falcon, *Falco cherrug,* having brown plumage and often trained for falconry. [Middle English *sagre,* from Old French *sacre,* from Arabic *ṣaqr.*]
Sa·kha·lin (săk'ə-lēn; *Russian* sə-KHä-lyēn'). Formerly **Sa·ghal·ien** (säg'əl-yĕn'). An island of the Soviet Union, 29,700 square miles in area, in the Sea of Okhotsk north of Hokkaido, Japan. Divided between Russia and Japan in 1905, the southern half became known as Karafuto until restored to the Soviet Union in 1945. Population, 630,000. Administrative center, Yuzhno-Sakhalinsk.
Sa·ki (sä'kē). Pen name of H.H. **Munro** *(see).*
Sa·ki·shi·ma Islands (sä'kē-shē'mä). The southern group of the Ryukyu Islands, between the East China Sea and the Pacific Ocean east of northern Taiwan.
Sak·ta. Variant of **Shakta.**
Sak·ti. Variant of **Shakti.**
sal (săl) *n.* Salt. [Latin *sāl.* See **sal-¹** in Appendix.*]
SAL Airport code for San Salvador, El Salvador.
sa·laam (sə-läm') *n.* **1.** A Moslem salutation or ceremonial greeting performed by bowing low while placing the right palm on the forehead. **2.** A respectful or ceremonial greeting. *—v.* **salaamed, -laaming, -laams.** *—tr.* To greet (someone) with a salaam. *—intr.* To greet with or perform a salaam. [Arabic *salām,* "peace" (part of *assalām 'alaikum,* "peace to you"). See **slm** in Appendix.*]
sal·a·ble (sā'lə-bəl) *adj.* Also **sale·a·ble.** Offered or suitable for sale; marketable. **—sal'a·bil'i·ty** (sā'lə-bĭl'ə-tē), **sal'a·ble·ness** *n.* **—sal'a·bly** *adv.*
sa·la·cious (sə-lā'shəs) *adj.* **1.** Stimulating to the sexual imagination; especially, morbidly appealing to lust. **2.** Lustful; lecherous; bawdy: *"He was restless and active, endowed with an easy, salacious humour."* (T.E. Lawrence). [From Latin *salāx* (stem *salāc-*), fond of leaping (said of male animals), lustful, from *salīre,* to leap. See **sel-⁴** in Appendix.*] **—sa·la'cious·ly** *adv.* **—sa·la'cious·ness, sa·lac'i·ty** (sə-lăs'ə-tē) *n.*
sal·ad (săl'əd) *n.* **1.** A dish consisting of green, leafy raw vegetables, often with radish, cucumber, or tomato, tossed with a dressing. **2.** The course consisting of this dish. **3.** A cold dish of chopped fruit, meat, fish, eggs, or other food, usually prepared with mayonnaise or other dressing. **4.** Any green vegetable or herb used in salad; especially, lettuce. [Middle English *salade,* from Old French, from Old Provençal *salada,* from Vulgar Latin *salāta* (unattested), from the feminine past participle of *salāre* (unattested), to salt, from Latin *sāl,* salt. See **sal-¹** in Appendix.*]
salad days. The time of youth, innocence, and inexperience. [From *"my* salad days *when I was green in judgment, cold in blood"* (Shakespeare).]
salad dressing. A sauce, as of mayonnaise or oil and vinegar, served on salad.
Sal·a·din (săl'ə-dĭn). Arabic name, Salah-al-Din Yusuf ibn-Ayyub. 1138?–1193. Sultan of Egypt and Syria; captured Jerusalem (1187); defeated by the Third Crusade under Richard I of England and Philip II of France.
Sa·la·do (sä-lä'*thō*). **1.** In full **Sa·la·do del Nor·te** (dĕl nôr'tā). A river of Argentina, rising in the Andes in the northwest and flowing 1,250 miles generally southeast to the Paraná. **2.** A river of Argentina, rising as the Desaguadero near the Chilean border and flowing 750 miles south and southeast to the Colorado.
Sal·a·man·ca (sä-lä-mäng'kä). A city of Spain 110 miles west of Madrid; the Nationalist capital during the Spanish Civil War (1937–38). Population, 101,000.
sal·a·man·der (săl'ə-măn'dər) *n.* **1.** Any of various small, lizardlike amphibians of the order Caudata, having porous, scaleless skin and four legs that are often weak or rudimentary. **2.** A mythical creature, generally resembling a lizard, once thought capable of living in or withstanding fire. **3.** An object used in fire or capable of withstanding heat, as a poker. **4.** *Metallurgy.* A mass of solidified material, largely metallic, left in a blast-furnace hearth. **5.** A portable stove used to heat or dry buildings under construction. [Middle English *salamandre,* from Old French, from Latin *salamandra,* from Greek *salamandra*†.]
sa·la·mi (sə-lä'mē) *n.* A highly spiced and salted sausage, either hard or soft in consistency, that originated in Italy. [Italian, plural of *salame,* "salted pork," from *salare,* to salt, from Vulgar Latin *salāre* (unattested). See **salad.**]
Sal·a·mis (săl'ə-mĭs). **1.** An ancient city on the eastern coast of Cyprus near Famagusta. **2.** An island of Greece, 39 square miles in area, in the Saronic Gulf east of Athens, off which the Greeks defeated the Persians (480 B.C.).
sal ammoniac. *Chemistry.* **Ammonium chloride** *(see).* [Middle English *sal armoniak,* from Medieval Latin *sāl armōniacum,* from Latin *sāl ammōniacum* : SAL + AMMONIAC.]
sal·a·ried (săl'ə-rēd) *adj.* Earning or yielding a regular salary.
sal·a·ry (săl'ə-rē, săl'rē) *n., pl.* **-ries.** A fixed compensation for services, paid to a person on a regular basis. Compare **wage.** *—tr.v.* **salaried, -rying, -ries.** To assign or pay a fixed salary to. [Middle English *salarie,* from Norman French, from Latin *salārium,* originally "money given to Roman soldiers to buy salt," from *salārius,* of salt, from *sāl,* salt. See **sal-¹** in Appendix.*]
Sa·la·zar (sä'lə-zär'), **Antonio de Oliveira.** Born 1889. Portuguese statesman; prime minister and virtual dictator (1932–68).
Sal·can·tay (säl'kän-tī'). The highest mountain (20,500 feet) in the Cordillera Oriental in southeastern Peru.
sale (sāl) *n.* **1.** The exchange of property or services for a determined amount of money or its equivalent; the act of selling. **2.** An opportunity for selling; a market; a demand. **3.** Availability for purchase. Often used with *for* or *on.* **4.** A selling of property to the highest bidder; auction. **5.** A special disposal of goods at lowered prices. Often used with *on.* [Middle English *sale,* Old English *sala,* from Old Norse. See **sel-³** in Appendix.*]
Sa·lé (sà-lā'). Also **Sla** (slä). A seaport of Morocco, on the Atlantic just north of Rabat. Population, 76,000
sale·a·ble. Variant of **salable.**
Sa·lem (sā'ləm). **1.** A seaport of Massachusetts on Cape Ann; the site, in the 17th century, of witch trials and executions. Population, 39,000. **2.** The capital of Oregon, in the northwest on the Willamette River. Population, 63,000. **3.** A city of the Republic of India, in north-central Madras State. Population, 249,000. **4.** An ancient name for Jerusalem.
sal·ep (săl'əp, sə-lĕp') *n.* A starchy meal ground from the dried roots of various Old World orchids of the genera *Orchis* and *Eulophia,* used for food and formerly as medicine. [French or Spanish, from Turkish *sālep,* from Arabic *saḥleb,* variant of *khasyu ath-tha'lab,* "the fox's testicles," a kind of orchid.]
sal·e·ra·tus (săl'ə-rā'təs) *n.* Sodium or potassium bicarbonate used as a leavening agent; baking soda. [New Latin *sal aeratus,* "aerated salt" : Latin *sāl,* SAL + AERATED.]
Sa·ler·no (sä-lâr'nō). Ancient name **Sa·ler·num** (sə-lûr'nəm; *Latin* sä-lâr'nōōm). A city and seaport of Italy, in the southwest on the Gulf of Salerno, an inlet of the Tyrrhenian Sea. Population, 131,000.
sales check. A piece of paper given by a store to serve as a record or receipt of a purchase or sale.
sales·clerk (sālz'klûrk') *n.* A salesman or saleswoman.
Sa·le·sian (sə-lē'zhən, sā-lē'-) *n.* A member of the Society of St. Francis de Sales, a Roman Catholic congregation founded in Turin in 1845 and dedicated chiefly to education and missionary work. *—adj.* Of or pertaining to the Salesians.
sales·man (sālz'mən) *n., pl.* **-men** (-mĭn). A man employed to sell merchandise in a store or in a designated territory.
sales·man·ship (sālz'mən-shĭp') *n.* **1.** The work or occupation of a salesman. **2.** Skill or ability in selling.
sales·per·son (sālz'pûr'sən) *n.* A salesman or saleswoman.
sales talk. Argument or other persuasion intended to induce a person to purchase a product or service or accept an idea or suggestion. Also called "sales pitch."
sales tax. A tax levied on the retail price and collected by the retailer.
sales·wom·an (sālz'wōōm'ən) *n., pl.* **-women** (-wĭm'ĭn). A woman or girl employed to sell merchandise, especially in a store. Also called "salesgirl," "saleslady."
Sal·ford (sôl'fərd). A city of England, in southeastern Lancashire. Population, 148,000.
sali-. Indicates salt; for example, **salimeter.** [From Latin *sāl* (stem *sali-*), salt. See **sal-¹** in Appendix.*]
Sa·li·an (sā'lē-ən) *adj.* Of or pertaining to the tribe of Franks, the Salii, who settled in the Rhine region of the Netherlands in the fourth century A.D. *—n.* A Salian Frank. [From Late Latin *Saliī,* the Salian Franks. See **Salic.**]

ă pat/ā pay/âr care/ä father/b bib/ch church/d deed/ĕ pet/ē be/f fife/g gag/h hat/hw which/ĭ pit/ī pie/îr pier/j judge/k kick/l lid, needle/m mum/n no, sudden/ng thing/ŏ pot/ō toe/ô paw, for/oi noise/ou out/ŏŏ took/ōō boot/p pop/r roar/s sauce/sh ship, dish/

sal·ic (săl′ĭk) *adj.* Pertaining to igneous rocks, such as quartz and the feldspars, containing large amounts of silica and alumina. [S(ILICA) + AL(UMINA) + -IC.]

Sal·ic (săl′ĭk, sā′lĭk) *adj.* Also **Sal·ique** (sə-lēk′, sâl′ĭk, sā′lĭk). **1.** Designating or pertaining to the Salian Franks. **2.** Of or pertaining to the Salic law or to the legal code of the Salian Franks. [Old French *salique,* from Medieval Latin *Salicus,* from Late Latin *Saliī*†, the Salian Franks.]

sal·i·cin (săl′ə-sən) *n.* A bitter glucoside, $C_{13}H_{18}O_7$, obtained mainly from the bark of poplar and willow trees and formerly used as an analgesic. [French *salicine* : Latin *salix* (stem *salic-*), willow (see **salik-** in Appendix*) + -IN.]

Salic law. Also **Salique law.** A law, thought to derive from the code of laws of the ancient Salic Franks, prohibiting a woman from succession to the throne and later used to exclude women from the thrones of France and Spain.

sal·i·cyl·ate (sə-lĭs′ə-lāt′, -lĭt, săl′ə-sĭl′ĭt) *n.* A salt or ester of salicylic acid. [SALICYL(IC ACID) + -ATE.]

sal·i·cyl·ic acid (săl′ə-sĭl′ĭk). A white crystalline acid, $C_7H_6O_3$, used in making aspirin, as a preservative and flavoring agent, and in the external treatment of certain skin conditions such as eczema. [From French *salicyle,* the radical of salicylic acid : SALIC(IN) + -YL.]

sa·li·ence (sā′lē-əns) *n.* Also **sa·li·en·cy** (-ən-sē). **1.** The quality or condition of being salient. **2.** A pronounced feature or part; a highlight.

sa·li·ent (sā′lē-ənt) *adj.* **1.** Projecting or jutting beyond a line or surface; protruding up or out. **2.** Striking; conspicuous. **3.** Springing; jumping: *salient tree toads.* —*n.* **1.** The area of a battle line, trench, fortification, or other military defense that projects closest to the enemy. **2.** A projecting angle or part. [Latin *saliēns,* present participle of *salīre,* to leap, jump. See **sel-⁴** in Appendix.*] —**sa′li·ent·ly** *adv.* —**sa′li·ent·ness** *n.*

sa·li·en·ti·an (sā′lē-ĕn′shē-ən) *n.* An amphibian of the order Salientia (formerly Anura or Batrachia), which includes the frogs and toads. —*adj.* Of or belonging to the Salientia. [New Latin *Salientia,* from Latin, neuter plural of *saliēns,* SALIENT.]

sa·lif·er·ous (sə-lĭf′ər-əs) *adj.* Containing or yielding salt. [SALI- + -FEROUS.]

sal·i·fy (săl′ə-fī′) *tr.v.* **-fied, -fying, -fies. 1.** To form or convert into a salt, as by chemical combination. **2.** To mix or impregnate with a salt. [French *salifier* : SALI- + -FY.] —**sal′i·fi′a·ble** *adj.* —**sal′i·fi·ca′tion** (săl′ə-fə-kā′shən) *n.*

sa·lim·e·ter (sə-lĭm′ə-tər) *n. Chemistry.* A specially graduated hydrometer that indicates directly the percentage of a salt in a salt solution. [SALI- + -METER.] —**sal′i·met′ric** (săl′ə-mĕt′rĭk) *adj.* —**sal′im′e·try** *n.*

sa·li·na (sə-lī′nə) *n.* **1.** A salt marsh, spring, pond, or lake. **2.** A land area encrusted with salt. [Spanish, from Latin *salīnae,* salt pits, feminine plural of *salīnus,* SALINE.]

sa·line (sā′lēn′, -līn′) *adj.* **1.** Of, relating to, or containing salt; salty. **2.** Pertaining to mineral salts having the characteristics of common salt. —*n.* **1.** Any salt of magnesium or of the alkalis, used in medicine as a cathartic. **2.** A saline solution, especially one that is isotonic with blood and is used in medicine and surgery. [Middle English *salyne,* from Latin *salīnus,* from *sāl,* salt. See **sal-¹** in Appendix.*] —**sa·lin′i·ty** (sə-lĭn′ə-tē) *n.*

Sal·in·ger (săl′ən-jər), **J(erome) D(avid).** Born 1919. American author of short stories and novels.

sal·i·nom·e·ter (săl′ə-nŏm′ə-tər) *n.* An instrument, especially a salimeter, used to measure the amount of salt in a solution. [SALIN(E) + -METER.] —**sal′i·no·met′ric** (săl′ə-nə-mĕt′rĭk) *adj.* —**sal·i·nom′e·try** *n.*

Salis·bur·y (sôlz′bĕr-ē, -brē). The capital of Rhodesia, in the northeastern part of the country. Population, 314,000.

Salis·bur·y Plain (sôlz′bĕr′ē, -brē). A plateau occupying about 300 square miles in southern Wiltshire, England; the site of Stonehenge.

Salis·bur·y steak (sôlz′bĕr′ē, -brē). A patty of ground beef mixed with various seasonings and broiled or fried. [After J.H. *Salisbury,* 19th-century English nutritionist.]

Sa·lish (sā′lĭsh) *n.* Also **Sa·lish·an** (sā′lĭsh-ən, săl′ĭsh-). **1.** A family of languages spoken by North American Indian tribes, including the Flathead, in the northwestern United States and British Columbia. **2.** The Indians speaking languages of this family. —**Sa′lish·an** *adj.*

sa·li·va (sə-lī′və) *n.* The watery, tasteless liquid mixture of salivary and oral mucous gland secretions that lubricates chewed food, moistens the oral walls, and contains the enzyme ptyalin, which functions in the predigestion of starches. [Latin *salīva*†.] —**sal′i·var′y** (săl′ə-vĕr′ē) *adj.*

salivary gland. A gland that secretes saliva; especially, any of three pairs of large glands, the parotid, submandibular, and sublingual, the secretions of which enter the mouth and mingle in saliva.

sal·i·vate (săl′ə-vāt′) *v.* **-vated, -vating, -vates.** —*intr.* To secrete or produce saliva. —*tr.* To produce an excessive salivation in. [Latin *salīvāre,* to spit out, from *salīva,* SALIVA.]

sal·i·va·tion (săl′ə-vā′shən) *n.* **1.** The act or process of secreting saliva. **2.** An abnormally abundant flow of saliva.

Salk (sôlk), **Jonas Edward.** Born 1914. American microbiologist; introduced first successful poliomyelitis vaccine.

Salk vaccine. A killed-virus vaccine used to immunize actively against poliomyelitis. [Introduced by Jonas SALK.]

sal·let (săl′ĭt) *n.* A light medieval helmet, with a brim flaring in the back, sometimes fitted with a visor. [Middle English *sal(l)et,* from Old French *salade,* from Old Italian *celata,* perhaps from Vulgar Latin *caelāta* (unattested), from Latin, feminine past participle of *caelāre,* to engrave (as on the metal of a helmet), from *caelum,* chisel. See **skhai-** in Appendix.*]

sal·low¹ (săl′ō) *adj.* **lower, -lowest.** Of a sickly yellowish hue or complexion. —*tr.v.* **sallowed, -lowing, -lows.** To make sallow. [Middle English *salowe,* Old English *salo.* See **sal-²** in Appendix.*] —**sal′low·ly** *adv.* —**sal′low·ness** *n.*

sal·low² (săl′ō) *n.* Any of several European willows, especially *Salix caprea,* the wood of which is a source of charcoal. [Middle English *salwe,* Old English *sealh.* See **salik-** in Appendix.*]

Sal·lust (săl′əst). Full name, Gaius Sallustius Crispus. 86–34 B.C. Roman historian and politician.

sal·ly (săl′ē) *intr.v.* **-lied, -lying, -lies. 1.** To rush or leap forth suddenly. **2.** To issue suddenly from a defensive or besieged position to make an attack upon an enemy. **3.** To emerge spiritedly, as from a resting place. **4.** To set out on a trip or excursion. Often used with *forth.* —*n., pl.* **sallies. 1.** A sudden rush forward; a leap. **2.** An assault from a defensive position; a sortie. **3.** A sudden emergence into action or expression; an outburst. **4.** A quick witticism or bantering remark; a quip. **5.** A venturing forth; an excursion; jaunt. —See Synonyms at **joke.** [From Old French *saillie,* a sally, from the feminine past participle of *salir, saillir,* to leap or rush forward, from Latin *salīre,* to leap. See **sel-⁴** in Appendix.*]

Sal·ly (săl′ē). A feminine given name. [Pet form of SARAH.]

sal·ly lunn (săl′ē lŭn′). A muffinlike tea cake. [Supposedly invented by *Sally Lunn,* 18th-century English baker.]

sally port. A gate in a fortification designed for sorties.

sal·ma·gun·di (săl′mə-gŭn′dē) *n.* Also **sal·ma·gun·dy. 1.** A salad of chopped meat, anchovies, eggs, and onions, often arranged in rows on lettuce, and served with vinegar and oil. **2.** Any mixture or assortment; a potpourri. [French *salmigondis, salmigondin*†.]

sal·mi (săl′mē) *n.* Also **sal·mis** (-mē; *French* sȧl-mē′). **1.** A highly spiced dish consisting of roasted game birds, minced and stewed in wine. **2.** A sauce of butter, vinegar, brown sugar, and various spices, served with wild fowl. [French *salmis,* short for *salmigondis,* SALMAGUNDI.]

salm·on (săm′ən) *n., pl.* **salmon** or **-ons. 1.** Any of various large food and game fishes of the genera *Salmo* and *Oncorhynchus,* of northern waters, characteristically swimming from salt to fresh water to spawn, and having a delicate pinkish flesh. **2.** Moderate, light, or strong yellowish pink to moderate reddish orange or light orange. In this sense, also called "salmon pink." See **color.** [Middle English *samoun, salmon,* from Old French *saumon,* from Latin *salmō.* See **sel-⁴** in Appendix.*] —**salm′on** *adj.*

salm·on·ber·ry (săm′ən-bĕr′ē) *n., pl.* **-ries. 1.** A prickly shrub, *Rubus spectabilis,* of western North America, having compound leaves and fragrant reddish flowers. **2.** The edible salmon-colored, raspberrylike fruit of this shrub. [From the yellowish-pink color of the fruit.]

sal·mo·nel·la (săl′mə-nĕl′ə) *n., pl.* **salmonella** or **-las** or **-lae** (-lē). Any of various rod-shaped bacteria of the genus *Salmonella,* many of which are pathogenic. [New Latin, after Daniel E. *Salmon* (1850–1914), American veterinarian.]

sal·mo·noid (săm′ə-noid′) *adj.* **1.** Resembling or characteristic of a salmon. **2.** Of or belonging to the family Salmonidae, which includes the salmon, trout, and whitefishes. —*n.* A salmonoid fish.

Salmon River. A river rising in central Idaho and flowing 425 miles north, then west, and again north to the Snake River on the Oregon-Idaho border.

salmon trout. Broadly, any of various salmonlike fish, such as the brown trout, the lake trout, or the steelhead.

sal·ol (săl′ōl) *n.* A white crystalline powder, $C_{13}H_{10}O_3$, derived from salicylic acid, and used in the manufacture of plastics and sun-tan oils and medicinally as an analgesic and antipyretic. [Originally a trademark : SAL(ICYLIC ACID) + -OL.]

Sa·lo·me (sə-lō′mē, săl′ə-mā′). Daughter of Herodias and niece of Herod Antipas, who granted her the head of John the Baptist in return for her dancing. Matthew 14:6-11. [Late Latin *Salōmē,* from Greek. See **salama** in Appendix.*]

sa·lon (sə-lŏn′; *French* sȧ-lôN′) *n.* **1.** A drawing room or other large room or hall for receiving and entertaining guests. **2.** An assemblage of persons, usually of social or intellectual distinction, who frequent such a room. **3.** A hall or gallery for the exhibition of works of art. **4.** *Often capital* **S.** Any of various exhibitions of art works held annually in France. **5.** A commercial establishment offering some product or service related to fashion: *a beauty salon.* [French, from Italian *salone,* augmentative of *sala,* a hall, room, from Germanic. See **sel-¹** in Appendix.*]

Sa·lo·ni·ka (sə-lŏn′ĭ-kə, săl′ō-nē′kə). Ancient name **Thes·sa·lo·ni·ca** (thĕs′ə-lō′nĭ-kə). A city and seaport of Greece, in the northeast on the Gulf of Salonika, an inlet of the Aegean. Population, 251,000.

sa·loon (sə-lo͞on′) *n.* **1.** A place where alcoholic drinks are sold and drunk; a bar; tavern. **2.** A large room or hall for receptions, public entertainment, or exhibitions. **3. a.** The officers' dining and social room on a cargo ship. **b.** A large social lounge on a passenger ship. **4.** *British.* A sedan automobile. [French *salon,* SALON.]

sa·loon·keep·er (sə-lo͞on′kē′pər) *n.* One who owns or operates a saloon for drinking.

sa·loop (sə-lo͞op′) *n.* A hot drink, formerly used medicinally, made from salep, sassafras, or similar aromatic herbs. [Variant of SALEP.]

Sa·lop. See **Shropshire.**

Sa·lo·te (sä-lō′tā). 1900–1965. Queen of Tonga (1918–65).

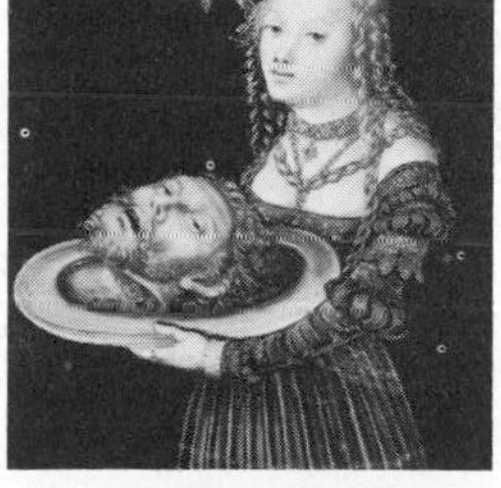

Salome
Carrying the head of John the Baptist in a painting by Lucas Cranach

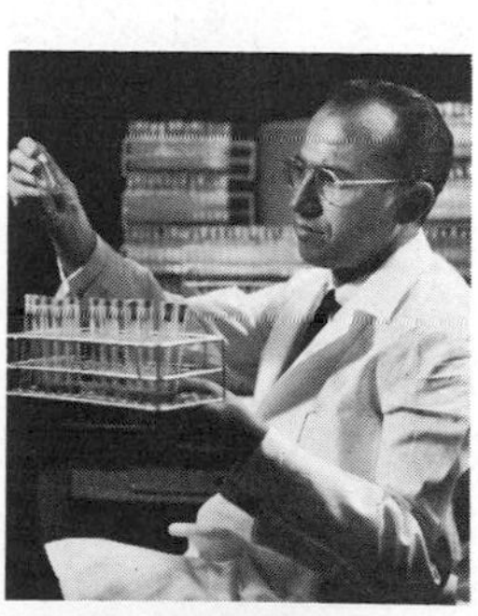

Jonas Salk
In a laboratory at the University of Pittsburgh in 1954

t tight/th thin, path/*th* this, bathe/ŭ cut/ûr urge/v valve/w with/y yes/z zebra, size/zh vision/ə about, item, edible, gallop, circus/ ȧ *Fr.* ami/œ *Fr.* feu, *Ger.* schön/ü *Fr.* tu, *Ger.* über/KH *Ger.* ich, *Scot.* loch/N *Fr.* bon. ***Follows main vocabulary.** †**Of obscure origin.**

salp (sălp) *n.* Also **sal·pa** (săl′pə). Any of various free-swimming chordates of the genus *Salpa,* of warm seas, having a translucent, somewhat flattened, keglike body. [New Latin *salpa,* from Latin, a kind of stockfish, from Greek *salpē*†.] —**sal′pi·form′** (-pə-fôrm′) *adj.*

saltire

sal·pin·gec·to·my (săl′pĭn-jĕk′tə-mē) *n., pl.* **-mies.** The surgical removal of the Fallopian tube. [New Latin *salpinx* (stem *salping-*), SALPINX + -ECTOMY.]

sal·pin·gi·tis (săl′pĭn-jī′tĭs) *n. Pathology.* Inflammation of the Fallopian or Eustachian tube. [New Latin : *salpinx* (stem *salping-*), SALPINX + -ITIS.]

sal·pinx (săl′pĭngks) *n., pl.* **salpinges** (săl′pĭn′jēz). **1.** The Fallopian tube. **2.** The Eustachian tube. [New Latin, from Greek *salpinx*†, trumpet.] —**sal·pin′gi·an** (-pĭn′je-ən) *adj.*

sal·si·fy (săl′sə-fī′) *n.* **1.** A plant, *Tragopogon porrifolius,* native to Europe, having grasslike leaves, purple flowers, and an edible taproot. **2.** The root of this plant, eaten as a vegetable. Also called "vegetable oyster," "oyster plant." [French *salsifis,* from (obsolete) Italian *salsifica*†.]

sal soda. A hydrated **sodium carbonate** *(see)* used as a general cleanser.

salt (sôlt) *n.* **1.** A colorless or white crystalline solid, chiefly **sodium chloride** *(see),* extensively used as a food seasoning and preservative. **2.** A chemical compound formed by replacing all or part of the hydrogen ions of an acid with one or more cations of a base. **3.** *Plural.* Any of various mineral salts used as a laxative or cathartic. **4.** *Plural.* **Smelling salts** *(see).* **5.** *Plural.* **Epsom salts** *(see).* **6.** An element that gives flavor or zest. **7.** Sharp, lively wit; pungency of expression. **8.** *Informal.* A sailor, especially when old or experienced. **9.** A saltshaker or saltcellar. —**with a grain of salt.** With reservations concerning truthfulness or accuracy; skeptically. —**worth one's salt.** Worthy of continued support; deserving of sustenance. —*adj.* **1.** Tasting of, containing, or filled with salt; salty. **2.** Preserved in salt or a salt solution: *salt mackerel.* **3. a.** Flooded with sea water. **b.** Found in or near such a flooded area: *salt grasses.* —*tr.v.* **salted, salting, salts. 1.** To add salt to; season or sprinkle with salt. **2.** To cure or preserve by treating with salt or a salt solution. **3.** *Informal.* To stock up or store away (money, for example); to hoard. Often used with *away* or *down.* **4.** To provide salt for (deer or cattle, for example). **5.** To add zest or liveliness to; to season: *salt a lecture with anecdotes.* **6.** To give an appearance of value to by fraudulent means; especially, to place valuable minerals in (a mine, for example) for the purpose of deceiving. —**salt out.** To separate (a dissolved substance) by adding salt to the solution. [Middle English *salt,* Old English *sealt.* See **sal-**[1] in Appendix.*] —**salt′ness** *n.*

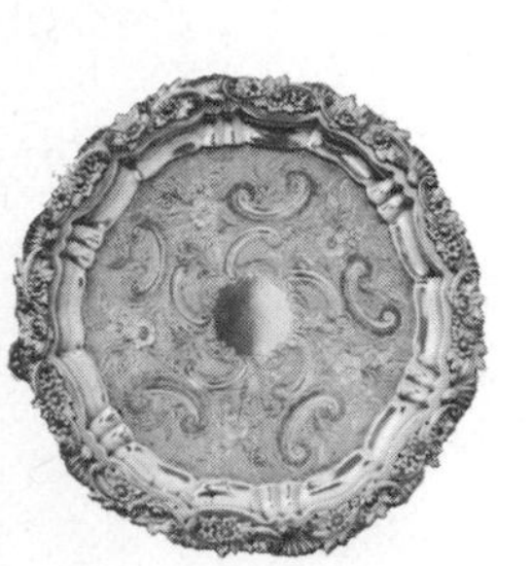

salver[1]
Early 19th-century Sheffield

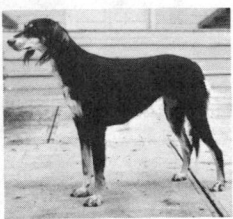

Sal·ta (säl′tä). A city and commercial center of northwestern Argentina. Population, 121,000.

salt-and-pep·per. See **pepper-and-salt.**

sal·tant (săl′tənt, sôl′-) *adj.* Jumping or dancing. [Latin *saltāns,* present participle of *saltāre,* to leap, dance, frequentative of *salīre* (past participle *saltus*), to jump. See **sel-**[4] in Appendix.*]

sal·ta·rel·lo (săl′tə-rĕl′ō; *Italian* säl′tä-rĕl′lō) *n., pl.* **-relli** (-rĕl′ē; *Italian* -rĕl′lē). **1.** A lively Italian dance with a skipping step at the beginning of each measure. **2.** Music for this dance, generally in triple or sextuple time. [Italian, from *saltare,* to leap, from Latin *saltāre.* See **saltant.**]

sal·ta·tion (săl-tā′shən, sôl′-) *n.* **1.** The act of leaping, jumping, or dancing. **2.** Discontinuous movement, transition, or development; advancement by leaps. **3.** *Biology.* A mutation or discontinuous variation. [Latin *saltātiō,* from *saltātus,* past participle of *saltāre,* to leap. See **saltant.**]

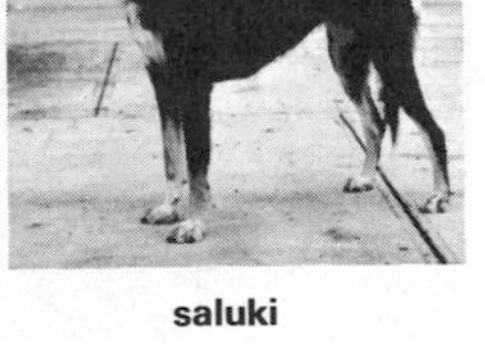

saluki

sal·ta·to·ri·al (săl′tə-tôr′ē-əl, -tōr′ē-əl, sôl′-) *adj.* **1.** Of or relating to leaping or dancing. **2.** *Zoology.* Adapted for or characterized by leaping.

sal·ta·to·ry (săl′tə-tôr′ē, -tōr′ē, sôl′-) *adj.* **1.** Of, pertaining to, or adapted for leaping or dancing. **2.** Proceeding by leaps, hops, or abrupt movements. [Latin *saltātōrius,* from *saltātus,* past participle of *saltāre,* to leap. See **saltant.**]

salt·box (sôlt′bŏks′) *n.* A frame house of square plan having two stories in front and one in back, topped by a roof with a long rear slope.

salt·bush (sôlt′bo͝osh′) *n.* Any of several salt-tolerant plants of the genus *Atriplex;* especially, *A. hortensis.* [So called because it grows in saline or alkaline soils.]

salt cake. Impure sodium sulfate, used in making paper pulp, soaps and detergents, glass, ceramic glazes, and dyes.

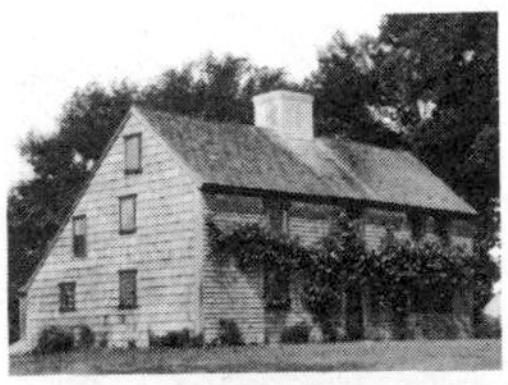

saltbox
The Major John Bradford House, built in 1675 at Kingston, Massachusetts

salt·cel·lar (sôlt′sĕl′ər) *n.* A small dish or shaker for holding and dispensing salt. [Variant (influenced by CELLAR) of Middle English *salt saler* : SALT + *saler,* saltcellar, from Old French *saliere,* from Latin *salārius,* of salt, from *sāl,* salt (see **sal-**[1] in Appendix*).]

salt·er (sôl′tər) *n.* **1.** A person who manufactures or sells salt. **2.** A person who treats meat, fish, or other foods with salt.

salt·ern (sôl′tərn) *n.* A building or place of salt manufacture; saltworks. [Ultimately from Old English *sealtærn, sealtern* : *sealt,* SALT + *ærn, ern,* house, from (unattested) Common Germanic *razn-* (see **ransack**).]

salt grass. Any of various grasses, such as those of the genus *Distichlis,* that grow in salt marshes and alkaline regions.

salt hay. 1. The wiry, tough stems of several species of salt-marsh rushes, especially *Juncus gerardi,* used as a garden mulch and packing material. **2.** Hay prepared from salt grass.

sal·ti·grade (săl′tə-grād′, sôl′-) *adj.* Adapted for or proceeding by leaping. Said of certain insects and spiders. [New Latin *Saltigradae,* former designation for saltigrade spiders : Latin *saltus,* a leap, from the past participle of *salīre,* to leap (see **sel-**[4] in Appendix*) + *gradī,* to step (see **ghredh-** in Appendix*).]

Sal·ti·llo (säl-tē′yō). The capital of Coahuila, Mexico, in the southeastern part of the state. Population, 118,000.

sal·tine (sôl-tēn′) *n.* A thin, crisp cracker sprinkled with coarse salt. [SALT + -INE.]

sal·tire (săl′tîr, sôl′-) *n.* Also **sal·tier.** *Heraldry.* An ordinary in the shape of a St. Andrew's cross, formed by the crossing of a bend and a bend sinister. [Middle English *sawturoure, sawtire,* from Old French *sau(l)toir,* originally a cross-shaped stile to keep cattle from straying, but which people could jump over, from *sau(l)ter,* to jump, from Latin *saltāre.* See **saltant.**]

salt·ish (sôl′tĭsh) *adj.* Somewhat salty.

Salt Lake. See **Great Salt Lake.**

Salt Lake City. The capital and largest city of Utah, in the north-central part of the state near the southeastern shore of Great Salt Lake. Population, 349,000.

salt lick. 1. A natural deposit of exposed salt that animals lick. **2.** A block of salt or an artificial medicated saline preparation set out for cattle, sheep, or deer to lick.

salt marsh. Low coastal grassland frequently overflowed by the tide. Also called "salt meadow."

salt of the earth. The most admirable element of mankind; the exemplary people. Matthew 5:13.

Sal·ton Sea (sôl′tən). A shallow salt lake about 300 square miles in area, in southeastern California, formed by the flooding of the Colorado (1905–06) into Salton Sink, a depression reaching as low as 280 feet below sea level.

salt·pe·ter (sôlt′pē′tər) *n.* Also *chiefly British* **salt·pe·tre. 1. Potassium nitrate** *(see).* **2. Sodium nitrate** *(see).* **3. Niter** *(see).* [Variant of earlier *salpetre,* from Middle English, from Old French, from Medieval Latin *salpetra,* probably "salt rock" (so called because it appears as a saltlike crust on rocks) : Latin *sāl,* salt (see **sal-**[1] in Appendix*) + *petra,* rock, from Greek (see **petra** in Appendix*).]

salt rheum. Eczema *(see).*

salt-ris·ing bread (sôlt′rī′zĭng). A bread made of coarse flour, water or milk, and salt, in which leavening is produced by allowing a salted batter to rise before mixing with additional flour and liquid.

Salt River. 1. A river rising in eastern Arizona and flowing 200 miles generally west to the Gila River. **2.** A river rising in northeastern Missouri and flowing about 200 miles generally southeast to the Mississippi.

salt·shak·er (sôlt′shā′kər) *n.* A container with a perforated top for sprinkling table salt.

salt·water (sôlt′wô′tər, -wŏt′ər) *adj.* Pertaining to, consisting of, or inhabiting salt water.

salt·works (sôlt′wûrks′) *n.* Plural in form, used with a singular or plural verb. A place or building where salt is manufactured commercially.

salt·wort (sôlt′wûrt′, -wôrt′) *n.* Any of several plants of the genus *Salsola;* especially, *S. kali,* native to the Old World, having stiff, prickly leaves, and growing on sandy seashores.

salt·y (sôl′tē) *adj.* **-ier, -iest. 1.** Pertaining to, containing, or tasting of salt. **2.** Suggestive of the sea or sailing life. **3.** Piquant; witty; pungent: *salty humor.* —**salt′i·ly** *adv.* —**salt′i·ness** *n.*

sa·lu·bri·ous (sə-lo͞o′brē-əs) *adj.* Conducive or favorable to health or well-being; wholesome; healthful. [From Latin *salūbris,* from *salūs,* health. See **sol-** in Appendix.*] —**sa·lu′bri·ous·ly** *adv.* —**sa·lu′bri·ous·ness, sa·lu′bri·ty** (-brə-tē) *n.*

Sa·lu·da (sə-lo͞o′də). A river of South Carolina, rising in the Blue Ridge Mountains and flowing southeast 200 miles.

sa·lu·ki (sə-lo͞o′kē) *n., pl.* **-kis.** A tall, slender dog of an ancient breed developed in Arabia and Egypt, having a smooth, sand-colored coat. [Arabic *salūqīy,* (dog) of *Salūq,* ancient southern Arabian city.]

sal·u·tar·y (săl′yə-tĕr′ē) *adj.* **1.** Effecting or designed to effect an improvement; beneficially corrective; remedial: *salutary advice.* **2.** Favorable or conducive to health; wholesome: *a salutary climate.* [Old French *salutaire,* from Latin *salūtāris,* of health, from *salūs* (stem *salūt-*), health. See **sol-** in Appendix.*] —**sal′u·tar′i·ly** *adv.* —**sal′u·tar′i·ness** *n.*

sal·u·ta·tion (săl′yə-tā′shən) *n.* **1.** A polite expression of greeting or good will. **2.** A gesture of greeting, as a bow or kiss. **3.** The word or phrase of greeting, as *Dear Sir* in a letter or *Ladies and Gentlemen* in a speech. [Middle English *salutacioun,* from Latin *salūtātiō,* from *salūtātus,* past participle of *salūtāre,* to SALUTE.]

sa·lu·ta·to·ri·an (sə-lo͞o′tə-tôr′ē-ən, -tōr′ē-ən) *n.* The student who delivers the salutatory at graduation exercises, usually the one ranking second highest in the class.

sa·lu·ta·to·ry (sə-lo͞o′tə-tôr′ē, -tōr′ē) *n., pl.* **-ries.** An opening or welcoming address, such as that delivered by a graduating student at commencement exercises in some schools and colleges. —*adj.* Pertaining to, of the nature of, or expressing a salutation. [From Medieval Latin *salūtātōrius,* of a salutation, from Latin *salūtātus,* past participle of *salūtāre,* to SALUTE.]

sa·lute (sə-lo͞ot′) *v.* **-luted, -luting, -lutes.** —*tr.* **1.** To greet or address with an expression of welcome, good will, or respect. **2.** To recognize (a military superior) with a gesture prescribed by regulations, as by raising the hand to the cap. **3.** To honor formally and ceremoniously. **4.** To come forth as if to greet: *"and all the joyful world salutes the rising day"* (Cowley). —*intr.* To make a gesture of greeting. —*n.* **1.** An act or gesture of welcome, honor, or courteous recognition. **2.** A formal military display of honor or greeting, as firing cannon or presenting arms. [Middle English *saluten,* from Latin *salūtāre,* to preserve, salute, wish health to, from *salūs* (stem *salūt-*), health, safety. See **sol-** in Appendix.*] —**sa·lut′er** *n.*

sal·va·ble (săl′və-bəl) *adj.* **1.** Capable of being saved. **2.** Able to be salvaged. [From Late Latin *salvāre,* to save, SALVAGE.]

Sal·va·dor (săl′və-dôr; *Portuguese* säl′vä′dōr′). **1.** Formerly **Ba·hi·a** (bə-ē′ä), **São Sal·va·dor** (souɴ). The capital of the state of Bahia, Brazil, a commercial center and Atlantic seaport. Population, 631,000. **2.** See **El Salvador.**

Sal·va·do·ri·an (săl′və-dôr′ē-ən, -dōr′-ē-ən) *adj.* Also **Sal·va·do·ran** (-dôr′ən, -dōr′ən). Pertaining to El Salvador, its people, or their culture. —*n.* Also **Sal·va·do·ran.** A native or inhabitant of El Salvador.

sal·vage (săl′vĭj) *tr.v.* **-vaged, -vaging, -vages. 1.** To save (a ship or its cargo, for example) from loss or destruction. **2.** To save (discarded or damaged material) for further use. —*n.* **1. a.** The rescue of a ship or its crew or cargo from fire or shipwreck. **b.** The ship, crew, or cargo so rescued. **2.** Compensation given to those who voluntarily aid in such a rescue. **3. a.** The act of saving any imperiled property from loss. **b.** The property so saved. [From French, the act of saving, from Old French, from *salver,* to save, from Late Latin *salvāre,* from Latin *salvus,* unharmed, safe. See **sol-** in Appendix.*] —**sal′vage·a·ble** *adj.* —**sal′vag·er** *n.*

Sal·var·san (săl′vər-săn′) *n.* A trademark for an organic compound, **arsphenamine** *(see).* [German trademark : Latin *salvus,* safe (see **sol-** in Appendix*) + German *Arsen,* from Latin *arsenicum,* ARSENIC.]

sal·va·tion (săl-vā′shən) *n.* **1.** Preservation or deliverance from evil or difficulty. **2.** A source, means, or cause of such deliverance or preservation. **3. a.** *Theology.* The deliverance of man or his soul from the power or penalty of sin; redemption. **b.** *Christian Science.* The realization and demonstration of Life, Truth, and Love as supreme over all, carrying with it the destruction of the illusions of sin, sickness, and death. [Middle English, from Old French, from Late Latin *salvātiō,* from *salvāre,* to save, to SALVAGE.] —**sal·va′tion·al** *adj.*

Salvation Army. *Abbr.* **S.A.** An international evangelical and charitable organization founded (1865) by William Booth.

sal·va·tion·ist (săl-vā′shən-ĭst) *n.* **1.** *Usually capital* **S.** A member of the Salvation Army. **2.** An evangelist.

salve[1] (săv, säv) *n.* **1.** An analgesic or medicinal ointment. **2.** Anything that soothes or heals; balm. **3.** Flattery or commendation. —*tr.v.* **salved, salving, salves. 1.** To soothe as if with salve; quiet; appease. **2.** To dress (a wound or sore) with salve. [Middle English *salf, salve,* Old English *salf, sealf.* See **selp-** in Appendix.*]

salve[2] (sălv) *tr.v.* **salved, salving, salves.** *Archaic.* To save (a ship, for example) from danger, loss, or destruction; safeguard. [Back-formation from SALVAGE.]

sal·ver[1] (săl′vər) *n.* A tray or serving platter. [From French *salve,* a tray for presenting food (to the king), from Spanish *salva,* originally "foretasting of food to detect poison," from *salvar,* to foretaste food or drink, "to save," from Late Latin *salvāre,* to save, to SALVAGE.]

sal·ver[2]. Variant of **salvor.**

sal·vi·a (săl′vē-ə) *n.* Any of various plants and shrubs of the genus *Salvia;* especially, *S. splendens,* native to South America and widely cultivated for its showy scarlet flowers. This species is also called "scarlet sage." [New Latin, from Latin, "the healing plant," SAGE.]

sal·vo (săl′vō) *n., pl.* **-vos** or **-voes. 1.** A simultaneous discharge of firearms. **2. a.** The simultaneous release of a rack of bombs from an aircraft. **b.** The bombs thus released. **3.** A sudden outburst of cheers or the like. [Earlier *salve, salva,* from Italian *salva,* salute, volley, from Latin *salvē,* hail, imperative of *salvēre,* to be in good health, from *salvus,* safe, well. See **sol-** in Appendix.*]

sal·vor (săl′vər) *n.* Also **sal·ver.** A person or ship that salvages a ship or cargo at sea. [From SALVE (to salvage).]

Sal·ween (săl′wēn′). Also **Sal·win.** A river of southeastern Asia, rising in eastern Tibet and flowing 1,750 miles southeastward to the Gulf of Martaban at Moulmein in Burma.

Salz·burg (sôlz′bûrg′; *German* zälts′bo͝orкн′). A city and resort in west-central Austria. Population, 108,000.

Salz·git·ter (zälts′gĭt′ər). A city and industrial center of northeastern West Germany. Population, 110,000.

Sam. Samuel (Old Testament).

Sa·mar (sä′mär). The third-largest (5,050 square miles) of the Philippines, in the eastern Visayan Island group.

sam·a·ra (săm′ə-rə, sə-mâr′ə) *n. Botany.* A winged, usually one-seeded fruit that does not split open, as of the ash or maple. Also called "key fruit." [New Latin, from Latin *samara*†, seed of the elm.]

Sa·ma·ra. The former name for **Kuibyshev.**

Sa·ma·rang. See **Semarang.**

Sa·mar·i·a (sə-mâr′ē-ə). **1.** A division of ancient Palestine, now in western Jordan. **2.** The ancient northern kingdom of Israel. **3.** The capital of this kingdom in the ninth century B.C.

Sa·mar·i·tan (sə-măr′ĭ-tən) *n.* **1.** A native or inhabitant of Samaria. **2.** A **Good Samaritan** *(see).* —*adj.* Of or relating to Samaria or to Samaritans. [Middle English, from Late Latin *Samaritānus,* from Greek *Samaritēs,* from *Samareia,* Samaria, perhaps from Hebrew *Shomərown.*]

sa·mar·i·um (sə-mâr′ē-əm) *n. Symbol* **Sm** A silvery or pale-gray metallic rare-earth element found in monazite and bastnaesite and used as a dopant for laser materials, in infrared absorbing glass, and as a neutron absorber in certain nuclear reactors. Atomic number 62, atomic weight 150.35, melting point 1,072°C, boiling point 1,900°C, specific gravity (approximately) 7.50, valences 2, 3. See **element.** [New Latin : SAMAR(SKITE) + -IUM.]

Sam·ar·kand (săm′ər-kănd′; *Russian* sä′mär-känt′). A city and former capital of the Uzbek S.S.R.; served as capital of Tamerlane's empire in the late 14th and early 15th centuries. Population, 233,000.

sa·mar·skite (sə-mär′skīt′) *n.* A velvet-black mineral oxide with red-brown streaks that is a source of several rare-earth metals. [French, after Colonel von *Samarski,* 19th-century Russian mine official.]

sam·ba (săm′bə, säm′bä) *n.* **1.** An African dance, modified in Brazil as a ballroom dance. **2.** Music in 4/4 time for dancing the samba. —*intr.v.* **sambaed, -baing, -bas.** To dance the samba. [Portuguese, of African origin.]

sam·bar (săm′bər, säm′-) *n.* Also **sam·bur.** A large deer, *Cervus unicolor,* of southeastern Asia, having a reddish-brown coat. [Hindi *sābar, sāmbar,* from Sanskrit *śambara*†.]

Sam Browne belt. A belt worn as part of a military or police uniform, having a shoulder strap that runs diagonally across the chest. [Modeled after the sword belt invented by Sir *Samuel* James *Browne* (1824–1901), British general who having lost his left arm could not support his sword with his left hand.]

same (sām) *adj.* Usually preceded by *the.* **1.** Being the very one; not different; identical. **2.** Similar in kind, quality, quantity, or degree; equivalent; corresponding. **3.** Conforming absolutely; unaltered; unchanged. Often used with *as: playing according to the same rules as before.* **4.** Identical with someone or something previously mentioned or indicated; aforesaid. —*pron.* Usually preceded by *the.* See Usage note below. **1.** A person, thing, or event identical with or similar to another. **2.** A person or thing previously mentioned or described. —**all the same. 1.** Nevertheless. **2.** Of no importance; of little significance. —**just the same. 1.** Nevertheless. **2.** Identical or corresponding; unchanged. —*adv.* Preceded by *the.* In like manner; in the identical way: *He walks the same as his father.* [Middle English, from Old Norse *samr.* See **sem-**[1] in Appendix.*]

Synonyms: *same, selfsame, identical, equal, equivalent.* These adjectives refer to the absence of difference or disparity. *Same, selfsame,* and *identical* are all applicable, when only one object is under consideration, in the sense of one and the same: *the same man I saw this morning* (or *selfsame* or *identical*). *Same* and *identical* are also used when two or more objects are considered. In this sense, *same* implies absence of difference with respect to kind, quality, quantity, or the like; *identical* specifies strict agreement in every respect and detail. *Equal* refers more generally to absence of difference between two or more with respect to extent, amount, value, force, or the like. *Equivalent,* referring to two or more, means not identical but having the same worth, effect, force, or meaning.

Usage: *Same* (pronoun) is usually preceded by *the: Each received the same.* A less acceptable construction employs *same* or *the same* in place of another pronoun, with the sense of *aforesaid thing or person: Thank you for the pen; I shall return same shortly. Land is plentiful, but is there great demand for the same?* Although grammatically possible, this usage is usually considered inappropriate outside legal or commercial contexts. In general usage, in such examples, *it* or another appropriate pronoun is preferable to *same.*

sa·mekh (sä′mĕk) *n.* Also **sa·mech, sa·mek.** The 15th letter of the Hebrew alphabet. See **alphabet.** [Hebrew *sāmekh.*]

same·ness (sām′nĭs) *n.* **1.** The condition of being the same; uniformity; identity. **2.** A lack of variety or change; monotony.

Sam Hill (săm′ hĭl′). *Regional.* Euphemism for **hell.**

sam·iel (săm′yĕl′) *n.* **1.** The **simoom** *(see).* **2.** A name for the Devil. [Turkish *samyeli* : *sam,* poisonous + *yel,* wind.]

sam·i·sen (săm′ĭ-sĕn′) *n.* A Japanese musical instrument resembling a banjo, having a very long neck and three strings played with a plectrum. [Japanese, "three-stringed" : *sam,* three + *-mi,* taste, touch + *sen,* string, chord, from Ancient Chinese *sam, mjwei, siän.*]

sa·mite (sā′mīt′, săm′īt′) *n.* A heavy silk fabric, often interwoven with gold or silver, worn in the Middle Ages. [Middle English *samit,* from Old French, from Medieval Latin *examitum,* from Medieval Greek *hexamiton,* from Greek *hexamitos,* of six threads : HEXA- (six) + *mitos,* thread of the warp (see **mei-**[4] in Appendix*).]

sam·let (săm′lĭt) *n.* A young salmon. [Irregular diminutive of SALMON.]

Sam·nite (săm′nīt′) *n.* **1.** A member of an Italic people, related to the Sabines, who inhabited Samnium. **2.** The Oscan language spoken by this people. [Latin *Samnītēs,* the Samnites, from SAMNIUM.] —**Sam′nite** *adj.*

Sam·ni·um (săm′nē-əm). An ancient region of east-central Italy. [Latin *Samnium*†.]

Sa·mo·a (sə-mō′ə). An island group in the South Pacific Ocean, divided into two political units, **American Samoa** and **Western Samoa** *(both of which see).*

Sa·mo·an (sə-mō′ən) *adj.* Of or pertaining to Samoa, its Polynesian inhabitants, or their language. —*n.* **1.** A native or inhabitant of Samoa. **2.** The Polynesian language of the Samoans.

Sa·mos (sā′mŏs; *Greek* sä′môs). An island of Greece, 194 square miles in area, in the Aegean off the western coast of Turkey. Population, 53,000. —**Sa′mi·an** (sā′mē-ən) *adj.* & *n.*

Sam·o·set (săm′ə-sĕt′, sə-mŏs′ĭt). American Indian chief of the early 17th century; aided Pilgrim colonists at Plymouth.

Sam·o·thrace (săm′ō-thrās). *Greek* **Sam·o·thra·ke** (sä′mô-thrä′-kyē). An island of Greece, 71 square miles in area, in the northeastern Aegean.

sam·o·var (săm′ə-vär′, săm′ə-vär′) *n.* A metal urn with a

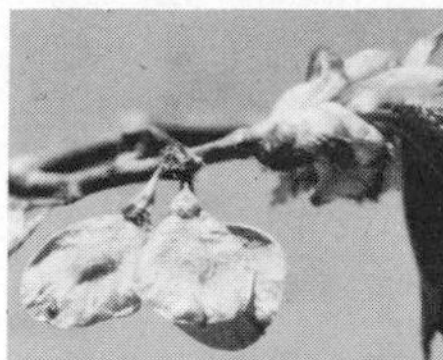

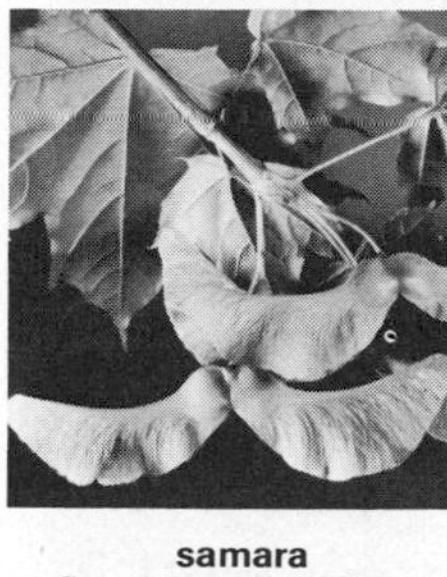

samara
Samaras of elm *(above)* and maple *(below)*

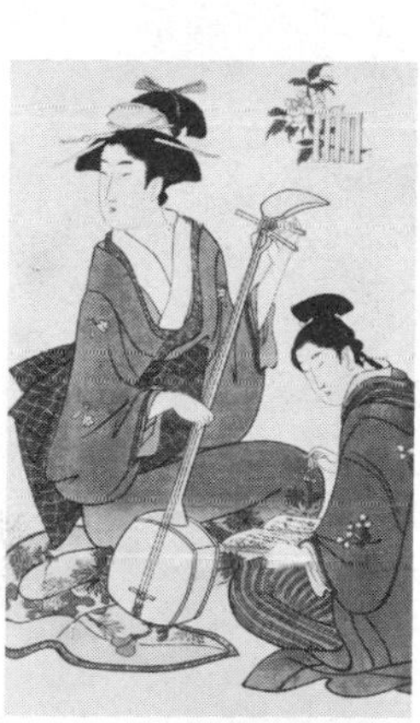

samisen

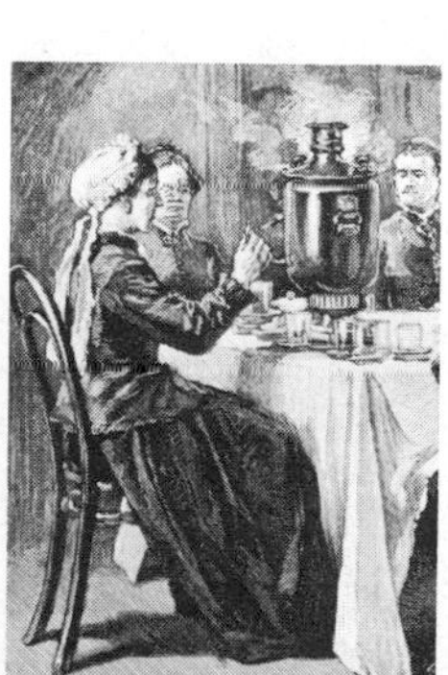

samovar

spigot, used to boil water for tea. [Russian, "self-boiler" : *samo-*, self (see **sem-¹** in Appendix*) + *varit'*, to boil, cook, probably from Old Church Slavonic *variti* (see **wer-⁹** in Appendix*).]

Sam·o·yed (săm'ə-yĕd') *n.* Also **Sam·o·yede.** **1.** A member of a Ural-Altaic people inhabiting the tundra lands of the northeastern European Soviet Union and northwestern Siberia. **2.** A branch of the Uralic family of languages represented by four living languages spoken by the Samoyed tribes inhabiting this region. **3.** A dog of a breed originally developed in northern Eurasia, having a thick, long white coat. [Russian *samoed*, from Lapp *Sāme-Āednàma*, "of Lapland."]

Sam·o·yed·ic (săm'ə-yĕd'ĭk) *adj.* Of or pertaining to the Samoyeds or their Uralic language.

samp (sămp) *n.* **1.** A coarse hominy. **2.** A porridge made from it. [Narraganset *nasàump*, "corn mush," akin to Western Abnaki *nsôbôn*.]

sam·pan (săm'păn') *n.* Any of various flat-bottomed skiffs used on the waterways of the Orient. [Chinese *san¹ pan³* (obsolete; now *shan¹ pan³*) : *san¹*, small boat + *pan³*, board.]

sam·phire (săm'fīr') *n.* **1.** A plant, the **glasswort** *(see)*. **2.** Any of several Old World plants of coastal areas; especially, *Crithmium maritimum*, having fleshy divided leaves and small white flowers. [Variant (perhaps influenced by earlier *camphire*, camphor) of earlier *sampere*, from Old French *(herbe de) Saint Pierre*, "Saint Peter's herb."]

sam·ple (săm'pəl) *n.* **1. a.** A portion, piece, or segment regarded as representative of a whole. **b.** An entity representative of a class; a specimen. **2.** *Statistics.* A set of elements drawn from and analyzed to estimate the characteristics of a population. Also called "sampling." —See Synonyms at **example.** —*tr.v.* **sampled, -pling, -ples.** To take a sample of; especially, to test or examine by a sample. [Middle English, short for Old French *essample*, EXAMPLE.]

sam·pler (săm'plər) *n.* **1.** One employed to take and appraise samples, as of a food product. **2.** A mechanical device for obtaining and analyzing samples. **3.** A piece of cloth embroidered with various designs or mottoes.

sam·pling (săm'plĭng) *n.* **1.** *Statistics.* A sample *(see).* **2.** The process of selecting a sample.

sam·sa·ra (sŭm-sä'rə) *n. Hinduism & Buddhism.* The eternal cycle of birth, suffering, death, and rebirth. [Sanskrit *saṁsāra*, "a passing through" : *sam*, together, completely (see **sem-¹** in Appendix*) + *sarati*, it runs, it flows (see **ser-²** in Appendix*).]

Sam·son¹ (săm'sən). An Israelite judge of extraordinary strength, betrayed to the Philistines by Delilah. Judges 14–16. [Late Latin *Sampsōn*, from Greek, from Hebrew *Shimshōn*, "like the sun," from *shemesh*, sun.]

Sam·son² (săm'sən) *n.* A man of great physical strength. [After SAMSON.]

Sam·u·el¹ (săm'yoō-əl). A masculine given name. [Late Latin, from Greek *Samouēl*, from Hebrew *shəmū'el*, "name of God" : *shēm*, name + *'el*, God.]

Sam·u·el² (săm'yoō-əl). Hebrew judge and prophet of the 11th century B.C.

Sam·u·el³ (săm'yoō-əl) *n. Abbr.* **Sam.** Either of two books, I and II Samuel, of the Old Testament.

sam·u·rai (săm'oō-rī') *n., pl.* **samurai** or **-rais.** **1.** The military aristocracy of feudal Japan. **2.** A warrior belonging to this social category. [Japanese, "a warrior."]

San (sän). A river of Poland, rising in the Carpathian Mountains and flowing about 280 miles to the Vistula.

San·a (sä-nä'). Also **Sa·naa, San·a.** One of the two capitals of Yemen, on a central plateau at an altitude of 7,750 feet. Population, 75,000

San An·dre·as Fault (săn ăn-drā'əs). A series of cracks in the earth's crust extending about 600 miles from the Gulf of California northward along the California coast, the movement of part of which caused the San Francisco earthquake in 1906.

San An·ge·lo (săn ăn'jə-lō). A city and resort in Texas, 77 miles southwest of Abilene. Population, 59,000.

San An·to·ni·o (săn' ăn-tō'nē-ō). **1.** A major industrial and commercial center of south-central Texas. Population, 588,000. **2.** A river of Texas flowing about 200 miles southeast from San Antonio to the Gulf of Mexico.

san·a·to·ri·um (săn'ə-tôr'ē-əm, -tōr'ē-əm) *n., pl.* **-ums** or **-toria** (-tôr'ē-ə, -tōr'ē-ə). Also **san·a·ta·ri·um** (-târ'ē-əm). **1.** An institution for the treatment of chronic diseases, such as tuberculosis, or for medically supervised recuperation. **2.** A sanitarium. [New Latin, from Late Latin *sānātōrium*, neuter of *sānātōrius*, from Latin *sānātus*, past participle of *sānāre*, to heal, from *sānus*, healthy, SANE.]

san·be·ni·to (săn-bə-nē'tō) *n., pl.* **-tos.** A garment of sackcloth worn at an auto-da-fé of the Spanish Inquisition by condemned heretics, being yellow with red crosses for the penitent and black with painted flames and devils for the impenitent. [Spanish *sambenito*, after *San Benito*, Saint BENEDICT (from its resemblance to the Benedictine scapular).]

San Ber·nar·di·no (săn bûr'nər-dē'nō, -nə-dē'nō). A city of southeastern California. Population, 92,000.

San Ber·nar·di·no Mountains (săn bûr'nər-dē'nō, -nə-dē'nō). A range in southern California, extending about 55 miles south of the Mojave Desert. Highest elevation, San Gorgonio (11,485 feet).

San Ber·nar·di·no Pass (săn bûr'nər-dē'nō, -nə-dē'nō). A pass in the Lepontine Alps of southeastern Switzerland. Highest elevation, 6,770 feet.

San Blas, Gulf of (săn blăs'; *Spanish* sän bläs'). An inlet of the Caribbean Sea in north-central Panama.

San·cho Pan·za (săn'chō păn'zə; *Spanish* sän'chō pän'thä). The ignorant yet realistic squire of Don Quixote in Cervantes' *Don Quixote*.

San Cris·tó·bal (săn' krĭs-tō'bəl; *Spanish* säng' krēs-tō'väl). **1.** An island of Ecuador, 195 square miles in area, in the Galápagos Islands. Also called "Chatham Island." **2.** A city of Venezuela in the extreme west. Population, 116,000.

sanc·ti·fied (săngk'tə-fīd') *adj.* **1.** Made holy; dedicated to sacred use; consecrated. **2.** Sanctimonious.

sanc·ti·fy (săngk'tə-fī') *tr.v.* **-fied, -fying, -fies.** **1.** To reserve for sacred use; consecrate. **2.** To make holy; purify. **3.** To give religious sanction to, as with an oath: *sanctify a marriage.* **4.** To cause (a practice, for example) to be piously observed or revered. **5.** To make productive of holiness or blessing. —See Synonyms at **revere.** [Middle English *sanctifien*, from Old French *sanctifier*, from Late Latin *sanctificāre* : Latin *sanctus*, holy, sacred, from the past participle of *sancīre*, to consecrate (see **sak-** in Appendix*) + *facere*, to make (see **dhē-¹** in Appendix*).] —**sanc'ti·fi·ca'tion** *n.* —**sanc'ti·fi·er** *n.*

sanc·ti·mo·ni·ous (săngk'tə-mō'nē-əs) *adj.* Making a pretense of piety or righteousness. See Synonyms at **religious.** —**sanc'ti·mo'ni·ous·ly** *adv.* —**sanc'ti·mo'ni·ous·ness** *n.*

sanc·ti·mo·ny (săngk'tə-mō'nē) *n.* Affected piety or righteousness; pompous high-mindedness. [Old French *sanctimonie*, from Latin *sanctimōnia*, sacredness, sanctity, from *sanctus*, sacred. See **sanctify.**]

sanc·tion (săngk'shən) *n.* **1.** Authoritative permission or approval that makes a course of action valid. **2.** Support or encouragement, as from public opinion or established custom. **3.** A consideration, influence, or principle that dictates an ethical choice. **4.** A law or decree. **5.** The penalty for noncompliance specified in a law or decree. **6.** Any penalty, specified or in the form of moral pressure, that acts to insure compliance or conformity. **7.** A coercive measure adopted usually by several nations acting together against a nation violating international law. —*tr.v.* **sanctioned, -tioning, -tions.** **1.** To authorize; legitimize. **2.** To maintain or encourage by an indication of approval. —See Synonyms at **approve.** [Old French, from Latin *sanctiō*, an ordaining, a sanction, from *sanctus*, sacred. See **sanctify.**]

sanc·ti·ty (săngk'tə-tē) *n., pl.* **-ties.** **1.** Saintliness or godliness. **2.** Sacredness: *the sanctity of a church.* **3.** The quality or condition of being considered sacred; inviolability. **4.** Anything considered sacred. [Middle English *saunctite*, from Old French *sainctite*, from Latin *sanctitās*, from *sanctus*, sacred. See **sanctify.**]

sanc·tu·ar·y (săngk'choō-ĕr'ē) *n., pl.* **-ies.** **1.** A sacred place, such as a church, temple, or mosque. **2.** The most holy part of a sacred place. **3.** A church or other sacred place in which fugitives formerly were immune to arrest or punishment. **4.** Immunity from arrest or punishment, as by taking refuge in a sacred place. **5.** Any place of refuge or asylum. **6.** A reserved area in which animals or birds are protected from hunting or other molestation. —See Synonyms at **shelter.** [Middle English *sanctuarie*, from Old French *sainctuarie*, from Late Latin *sanctuārium*, from Latin *sanctus*, sacred. See **sanctify.**]

sanc·tum (săngk'təm) *n., pl.* **-tums** or **-ta** (-tə). **1.** A sacred or holy place. **2.** A private room or study where one is not to be disturbed. [Latin, neuter of *sanctus*, sacred. See **sanctify.**]

sanctum sanc·to·rum (săngk'tôr'əm, -tōr'əm). **1.** The place in the Jewish tabernacle and temple where the Ark of the Covenant was located; the holy of holies. **2.** An inviolably private place. Often used facetiously. [Late Latin, "the holy of holies" (translation of Greek *to hagion tōn hagiōn*, translation of Hebrew *qōdesh ha-qqodashīm*).]

Sanc·tus (săngk'təs) *n.* The hymn of praise that culminates the Preface in many eucharistic liturgies. [Middle English, from Medieval Latin, first word of the last part of the Preface, from Late Latin, "holy" (first word of the hymn sung by the angels in Isaiah 6:3), from Latin. See **sanctify.**]

sand (sănd) *n.* **1.** Loose, granular, gritty particles of worn or disintegrated rock, finer than gravel and coarser than dust. **2.** *Usually plural.* A tract or stretch of land covered with this material, as a beach or desert. **3.** This material in an hourglass. **4.** *Plural.* Moments of allotted time or duration: *"The sands are number'd that make up my life"* (Shakespeare). **5.** *Slang.* Grit; courage. **6.** Light grayish brown to yellowish gray, including grayish and dark grayish yellow. See **color.** —*tr.v.* **sanded, sanding, sands.** **1.** To sprinkle or cover with sand or similar particles. **2.** To polish or scrape with sand or sandpaper. **3.** To mix with sand. **4.** To fill up (a harbor) with sand. [Middle English *sand*, Old English *sand*. See **bhes-¹** in Appendix*.]

Sand (sănd; *French* sänd), **George.** Pen name of Amandine Aurore Lucie Dupin, Baroness Dudevant. 1804–1876. French novelist.

san·dal¹ (săn'dəl) *n.* **1.** A shoe consisting of a sole fastened to the foot by thongs or straps. **2.** A light slipper or low-cut shoe. **3.** A rubber overshoe, cut very low and covering little more than the sole of the shoe. **4.** A strap or band for fastening a low shoe or slipper on the foot. [Middle English *sandalie*, from Latin *sandalium*, from Greek *sandalion*, diminutive of *sandalon*, sandal, perhaps from Lydian *sāndāl*, the shoe of Sandal (name of a Lydian god).]

san·dal² (săn'dəl) *n.* Sandalwood. [Middle English, from Old French, from Medieval Latin *sandalum, santalum*, from Greek *santalon, sandanon*, probably from Sanskrit *candanaḥ*. See **kand-** in Appendix.]

san·dal·wood (săn'dəl-woŏd') *n.* **1.** Any of several Asian trees of the genus *Santalum;* especially, *S. album*, having aromatic yellowish heartwood that is used in cabinetmaking and wood carving, and that yields an oil used in perfumery. **2.** The wood of this tree or of similar trees. **3.** Light to moderate or grayish brown. See **color**.

Sandalwood Island. The former name for **Sumba**.

san·da·rac (săn′də-răk′) *n.* Also **san·da·rach.** **1.** A tree, *Tetraclinis articulata* (or *Callitris quadrivalvis*), of northern Africa, having wood yielding a brittle, translucent resin used in varnishes. **2.** The resin of this tree. [Latin *sandaraca*, red pigment, beebread, from Greek *sandarak(h)ē*, (red pigment derived from) realgar, perhaps from Sanskrit *candra-rāga* (unattested), possibly "bright red" : *candráḥ*, shining (see **kand-** in Appendix*) + *raga*, red (see **reg-**[3] in Appendix*).]

sand·bag (sănd′băg′) *n.* **1.** A bag filled with sand, used in piles to form protective walls. **2.** A small, narrow bag partially filled with sand, used as a weapon. —*tr.v.* **sandbagged, -bagging, -bags. 1.** To put sandbags in or around. **2. a.** To hit with, or as if with, a sandbag. **b.** To force by crude means.

sand·bar (sănd′bär′) *n.* An offshore shoal of sand built up by the action of waves or currents; a bar.

sand·blast (sănd′blăst′, -bläst′) *n.* **1.** A blast of air or steam carrying sand at high velocity to etch glass or to clean stone or metal surfaces. **2.** A machine used to apply such a blast. **3.** A strong wind carrying sand along. —*tr.v.* **sandblasted, -blasting, -blasts.** To apply a sandblast to for the purpose of cleaning or engraving. —**sand′blast′er** *n.*

sand·blind (sănd′blīnd′) *adj.* Partially blind. [Middle English *sand-blind*, Old English *sāmblind* (unattested) : *sām-*, half (see **sēmi-** in Appendix*) + BLIND.] —**sand blindness.**

sand·box (sănd′bŏks′) *n.* A low box filled with sand for children to play in.

sandbox tree. A tropical American tree, *Hura crepitans*, having a spiny trunk and woody seed capsules that split explosively when ripe. [So called because the capsules were formerly used to hold sand for drying ink.]

sand·bur (sănd′bûr′) *n.* **1.** Any of several grasses of the genus *Cenchrus*; especially, *C. tribuloides*, of the eastern United States and tropical America, having burlike, spiny fruiting clusters. **2.** A plant, *Solanum rostratum*, of the western United States and Mexico, having prickly fruit.

Sand·burg (sănd′bûrg′, săn′-), **Carl.** 1878–1967. American poet and biographer.

sand-cast (sănd′kăst′, -käst′) *tr.v.* **-cast, -casting, -casts.** To make (a casting) by pouring molten metal into a sand mold.

sand crack. A fissure in the side of a horse's hoof, often causing lameness.

sand dab. Any of several small food fishes of the genus *Citharichthys*, of Pacific waters, related to and resembling the flounders.

sand dollar. Any of various thin, circular echinoderms of the order Exocycloida (or Clypeasteroidea); especially, *Echinarachnius parma*, of sandy ocean bottoms of the northern Atlantic and Pacific.

sand eel. A fish, the **sand lance** *(see)*.

sand·er (săn′dər) *n.* **1. a.** One that spreads sand. **b.** One that sands surfaces, as of wood. **2.** A **sanding machine** *(see)*.

san·der·ling (săn′dər-lĭng) *n.* A small shore bird, *Crocethia alba*, having predominantly gray and white plumage. [Perhaps from SAND + -LING.]

sand flea. 1. Broadly, any of various small crustaceans living on sandy beaches. **2.** The **chigoe** *(see)*.

sand fly. Any of various small biting flies of the genus *Phlebotomus*, of tropical areas, some of which transmit diseases.

sand grouse. Any of various pigeonlike birds of the genus *Pterocles* and related genera, of arid and semiarid regions of the Old World.

san·dhi (săn′dē, sän′-) *n. Linguistics.* The modification of the sound of a morpheme in certain phonetic contexts. The difference between the pronunciation of *the* in *the house* and in *the other house* is an instance of sandhi. [Sanskrit *saṁdhi*, "a placing together" : *sam*, together (see **sem-**[1] in Appendix*) + *dadhāti*, he places (see **dhē-**[1] in Appendix*).]

sand·hog (sănd′hôg′, -hŏg′) *n.* A laborer who works under compressed air, as in the construction of underwater tunnels.

sand hopper. A small crustacean, the **beach flea** *(see)*.

Sand·hurst (sănd′hûrst). A town in southeast Berkshire, England; site of the Royal Military College, founded in 1802.

San Di·e·go (săn′ dē-ā′gō). A city and seaport in southern California on San Diego Bay, an inlet of the Pacific, 15 miles north of the Mexican border. Population, 573,000.

sanding machine. A machine having a powered abrasive-covered disk or belt, used for smoothing, polishing, or refinishing. Also called "sander."

sand lance. Any of several small marine fishes of the genus *Ammodytes*, having a slender body with a forked tail fin, and often burrowing in the sand of tidelands. Also called "launce," "sand launce," "sand eel."

sand lily. A low-growing plant, *Leucocrinum montanum*, of the western United States, having grasslike leaves and fragrant white, star-shaped flowers.

sand-lot (sănd′lŏt′) *adj.* Designating a game played by amateurs, especially children, usually in a vacant lot: *sand-lot baseball.*

sand·man (sănd′măn′) *n.* A character in fairy tales and folklore who puts children to sleep by sprinkling sand in their eyes.

sand painting. 1. A ceremonial design of the Navaho Indians made by trickling fine colored sand onto a base of neutral sand. **2.** The art of making such designs.

sand·pa·per (sănd′pā′pər) *n.* Heavy paper coated on one side with sand or other abrasive material, used for smoothing. —*tr.v.* **sandpapered, -pering, -pers.** To rub with sandpaper for the purpose of smoothing, polishing, or finishing.

sand·pi·per (sănd′pī′pər) *n.* Any of various small wading birds of the family Scolopacidae, usually having a long, straight bill, and often frequenting the seashore in flocks.

San·dra (săn′drə, sän′-). A feminine given name. [Pet form of ALEXANDRA.]

San·dring·ham (săn′drĭng-əm). A village in northeastern Norfolk, England, the site of a royal estate and residence.

sand·stone (sănd′stōn′) *n.* Variously colored sedimentary rock composed predominantly of sandlike quartz grains cemented by lime, silica, or other materials.

sand·storm (sănd′stôrm′) *n.* A strong wind carrying clouds of sand through the air near the ground.

sand table. 1. A table with raised edges, used for holding sand with which children play. **2.** A table on which a relief model of terrain is built out of sand for the study of military maneuvers. **3.** An inclined table in which sand-bearing ore is shaken to separate out the ore.

sand trap. A hazard on a golf course consisting of a depression filled with sand.

sand verbena. Any of several plants of the genus *Abronia*, of western North America, having fragrant, usually pink flowers.

sand viper. Any of various snakes of sandy areas, such as *Vipera ammodytes*, a venomous species of southern Europe and Asia Minor, or the **horned viper** *(see)*.

sand·wich (sănd′wĭch, săn′-) *n.* **1.** Two or more slices of bread with meat, cheese, or other filling placed between them. **2.** An arrangement resembling an edible sandwich; for example, two slabs of one material holding a slab of different material between them, as in certain electronic devices. —*tr.v.* **sandwiched, -wiching, -wiches. 1.** To insert tightly between two things. **2.** To place in tight, alternating layers. **3.** To fit between two other things that allow little time: *sandwich a meeting between two others.* [After the Fourth Earl of *Sandwich* (1718–92), for whom sandwiches were made so that he could stay at the gambling table without interruptions for meals.]

Sand·wich (sănd′wĭch, săn′-). **1.** A town in eastern Kent, England, near the Strait of Dover; the most ancient of the Cinque Ports. **2.** One of the oldest settlements (incorporated 1639) on Cape Cod, Massachusetts.

sandwich board. Two large boards bearing advertising placards, hinged at the top by straps for hanging on a carrier's shoulders.

Sand·wich Islands (sănd′wĭch, săn′-). The name given by Captain Cook to the Hawaiian Islands.

sandwich man. A man hired to carry a sandwich board.

sand·worm (sănd′wûrm′) *n.* Any of various segmented worms, especially of the genera *Nereis* and *Arenicola*, generally inhabiting coastal mud or sand, and often used as fishing bait.

sand·wort (sănd′wûrt′, -wôrt′) *n.* Any of numerous low-growing plants of the genus *Arenaria*, having small, usually white flowers.

sand·y (săn′dē) *adj.* **-ier, -iest. 1.** Covered with, full of, or consisting of sand. **2.** Like sand, as in being unstable. **3.** Having the color of sand; yellowish red. —**sand′i·ness** *n.*

Sandy Hook. A narrow low and sandy peninsula of eastern New Jersey, at the entrance to Lower New York Bay.

sane (sān) *adj.* **saner, sanest. 1.** Mentally healthy; of sound mind. **2.** Having or showing sound judgment; reasonable; rational. [Latin *sānus*, sound, whole, healthy. See **sānos** in Appendix.*] —**sane′ly** *adv.* —**sane′ness** *n.*

San Fer·nan·do Valley (săn′ fər-năn′dō). A fertile valley in southwestern California, part of which is within the Los Angeles city limits.

San·ford, Mount (săn′fərd). A mountain rising to 16,208 feet in the western Wrangell Mountains of southern Alaska.

San·for·ized (săn′fə-rīzd′) *adj.* Designating a trademark for fabric preshrunk by a patented mechanical process before being made into clothing so as to minimize later shrinkage. [Invented by *Sanford* L. Cluett (born 1874), U.S. manufacturer.]

San Fran·cis·co (săn′ frən-sĭs′kō). A city and seaport of California, in the west on the Pacific, the Golden Gate, and San Francisco Bay. Population, 743,000. —**San Franciscan.**

San Fran·cis·co Bay (săn′ frən-sĭs′kō). An inlet of the Pacific in California, connected with the ocean by the Golden Gate.

San Fran·cis·co Peaks (săn′ frən-sĭs′kō). Three peaks of an extinct volcano in northern Arizona, the highest being Humphreys Peak (12,655 feet), the highest point in the state.

sang. Past tense of **sing.**

San Ga·bri·el Mountains (săn′ gā′brē-əl). A range between the Mojave Desert and the Los Angeles area in southern California. Highest elevation, San Antonio Peak (10,080 feet).

San·ga·mon (săng′gə-mən). A river rising in east-central Illinois and flowing about 250 miles generally west to the Illinois River.

san·ga·ree (săng′gə-rē′) *n.* A beverage made of wine, often Madeira, or other alcoholic liquor and grated nutmeg. [Spanish *sangría*, "a bleeding," from *sangre*, blood, from Latin *sanguis*. See **sanguine.**]

San·gay (säng-gī′). An active volcano, 17,454 feet high, in the Andes of east-central Ecuador.

Sang·er (săng′ər), **Frederick.** Born 1918. British biochemist; studied the insulin molecule.

Sang·er (săng′ər), **Margaret (Higgins).** 1883–1966. American social reformer; a pioneer in the birth-control movement.

sang-froid (säN-frwä′) *n.* Composure; imperturbability. See Synonyms at **equanimity.** [French, "cold blood" : Old French

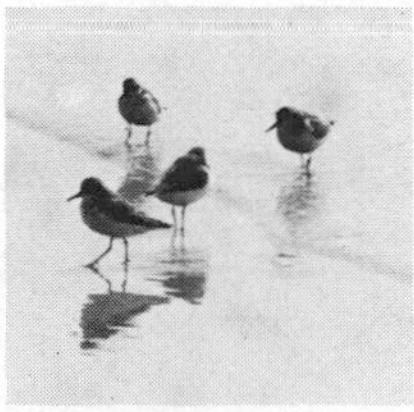

sandpiper
Ereunetes pusillus
Semipalmated sandpiper

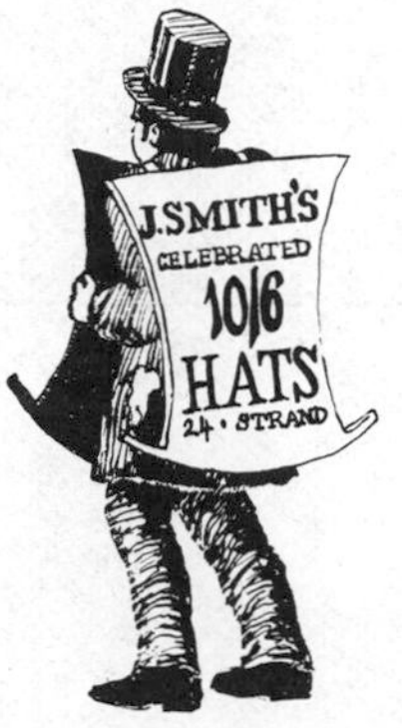

sandwich man

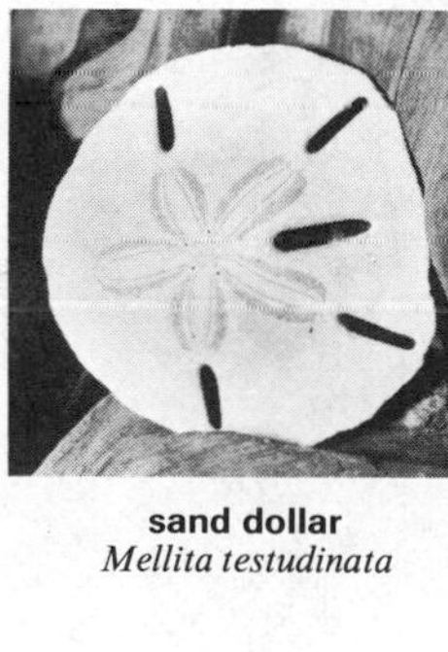

sand dollar
Mellita testudinata

t tight/th thin, path/*th* this, bathe/ŭ cut/ûr urge/v valve/w with/y yes/z zebra, size/zh vision/ə about, item, edible, gallop, circus/ à *Fr.* ami/œ *Fr.* feu, *Ger.* schön/ü *Fr.* tu, *Ger.* über/KH *Ger.* ich, *Scot.* loch/N *Fr.* bon. ***Follows main vocabulary. †Of obscure origin.**

sang, blood, from Latin *sanguis* (see **sanguine**) + *froid,* cold, from Latin *frīgidus,* FRIGID.]

sangh (săng) *n.* An association in India that promotes the consolidation of the different groups in Hinduism. [Hindi *sāg,* from Sanskrit *saṅga,* association, from *sajati,* he adheres. See **gwhen-**^{1} in Appendix.*]

San·gi·he (săng-gē′ə). Also **Sang·i** (săng′ē). **1.** A group of Indonesian islands, with a combined area of 314 square miles, northeast of Sulawesi. Population, 127,000. **2.** The largest (217 square miles) of these islands.

San·gre de Cris·to Mountains (săng′grē də krĭs′tō). The southernmost range of the Rocky Mountains, extending 220 miles south from central Colorado to northern New Mexico. Highest elevation, Blanca Peak in Colorado (14,363 feet).

san·gri·a (săng-grē′ə) *n.* A cold drink made of red or white wine mixed with brandy and sugar, and garnished with orange and lemon slices. [Spanish *sangría,* "bleeding," from *sangre,* blood, from Latin *sanguis.* See **sanguine.**]

san·gui·nar·y (săng′gwə-nĕr′ē) *adj.* **1.** Accompanied by carnage. **2.** Bloodthirsty. **3.** Consisting of or stained with blood. [Latin *sanguinārius,* of blood, from *sanguis* (stem *sanguin-*), blood. See **sanguine.**] —**san′gui·nar′i·ly** *adv.*

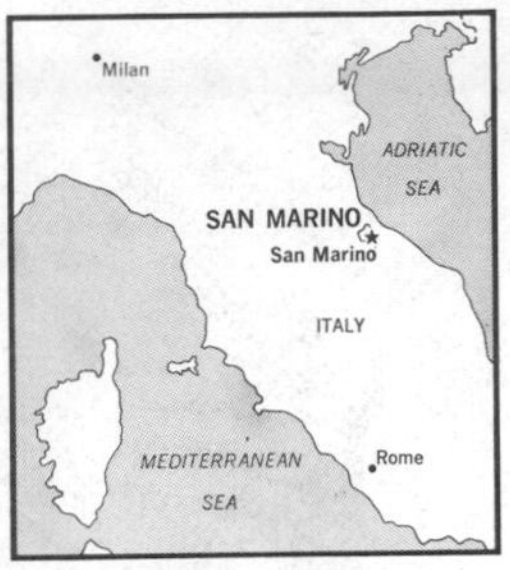

San Marino

san·guine (săng′gwĭn) *adj.* **1. a.** Of the color of blood; red. **b.** Ruddy. Said of the complexion. **2.** *Archaic.* Dominated by the humor of blood in terms of medieval physiology. See **humor. 3.** Having the temperament and ruddy complexion formerly thought to be characteristic of a man dominated by this humor; passionate. **4.** Eagerly optimistic; cheerful. [Middle English *sanguin,* from Old French, from Latin *sanguineus,* of blood, bloody, from *sanguis*† (stem *sanguin-*), blood.] —**san′guine·ly** *adv.* —**san′guine·ness, san·guin′i·ty** *n.*

san·guin·e·ous (săng-gwĭn′ē-əs) *adj.* **1.** Pertaining to or involving blood or bloodshed. **2.** Blood-red. [Latin *sanguineus,* SANGUINE.]

san·guin·o·lent (săng-gwĭn′ə-lənt) *adj.* Mixed or tinged with blood. [Latin *sanguinolentus,* full of blood, from *sanguis* (stem *sanguin-*), blood. See **sanguine.**]

San·he·drin (săn′hĭ-drĭn, săn′ĭ-, săn-hē′drĭn, -hĕd′rĭn) *n.* Also **San·he·drim** (-drĭm). **1.** The highest judicial and ecclesiastical council of the ancient Jewish nation, composed of from 70 to 72 members. Also called "Great Sanhedrin." **2.** Any assembly or council. [Hebrew *sanhedhrīn,* from Greek *sunedrion,* a council, from *sunedros,* sitting within council : SYN- (together) + *hedra,* a seat, a sitting (see **sed-**^{1} in Appendix*).]

san·i·cle (săn′ĭ-kəl) *n.* Any of various plants of the genus *Sanicula,* having clusters of small, greenish flowers and reputedly having medicinal value as an astringent. [Middle English, from Old French, from Medieval Latin *sanicula,* probably from Latin *sānus,* healthy, SANE (because the plant was once thought to have healing powers).]

sa·ni·es (sā′nĭ-ēz) *n.* A thin, fetid, greenish fluid consisting of serum and pus discharged from a wound, ulcer, or fistula. [Latin *saniēs*†.] —**sa′ni·ous** (-əs) *adj.*

San Il·de·fon·so (sän ēl′*th*ā-fōn′sō). A town in central Spain, 38 miles northwest of Madrid, the scene of the signing of two treaties between Spain and France (1796 and 1800).

San I·si·dro (sän ē-sē′*th*rō). A city of eastern Argentina, near Buenos Aires, of which it is a suburb. Population, 196,000.

san·i·tar·i·an (săn-ə-târ′ē-ən) *n.* A public health or sanitation expert. [From SANITARY.]

san·i·tar·i·um (săn′ə-târ′ē-əm) *n., pl.* **-ums** or **-ia** (-ē-ə). **1.** A health resort. **2.** A sanatorium. [New Latin, from Latin *sānitās,* health, SANITY.]

san·i·tar·y (săn′ə-tĕr′ē) *adj.* **1.** Pertaining to or used for the preservation of health. **2.** Clean; hygienic. [French *sanitaire,* from Latin *sānitās,* health, SANITY.] —**san′i·tar′i·ly** *adv.*

sanitary belt. A band, usually of elastic, for holding a sanitary napkin in place.

sanitary engineer. An engineer specializing in the maintenance of urban environmental conditions conducive to the preservation of public health, such as the disposal of sewage and provision of pure water. —**sanitary engineering.**

sanitary napkin. A disposable pad of absorbent material worn to absorb menstrual flow.

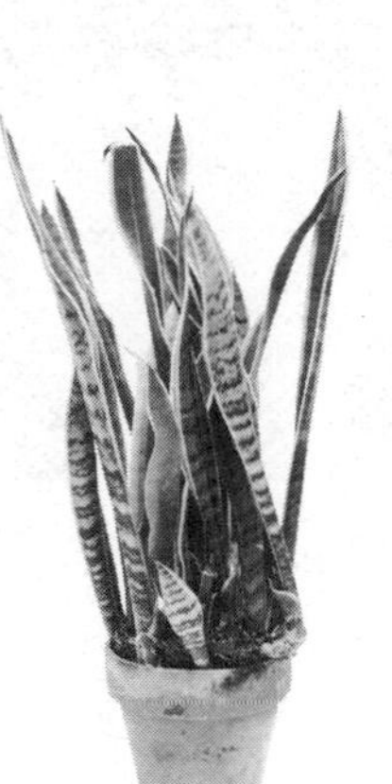
sansevieria
Sansevieria trifasciata

san·i·ta·tion (săn′ə-tā′shən) *n.* **1.** The formulation and application of measures designed to protect public health. **2.** The disposal of sewage. [From SANITARY.]

san·i·tize (săn′ə-tīz′) *tr.v.* **-tized, -tizing, -tizes.** To make sanitary.

san·i·ty (săn′ə-tē) *n.* **1.** The condition of having sound mental health; saneness. **2.** Soundness of judgment or reason. [Middle English *sanite,* from Old French, from Latin *sānitās,* health, sanity, from *sānus,* healthy, SANE.]

San Ja·cin·to (săn′ jə-sĭn′tō). A battle site in southern Texas, 16 miles east of Houston, where the Texans under Sam Houston defeated the Mexicans led by Santa Anna (1836).

San Joa·quin (săn′ wô-kēn′, wä-kēn′). A river of California, rising in the Sierra Nevada and flowing about 350 miles generally northwest to join the Sacramento near its mouth.

San Jo·se (săn′ hō-zā′). A city of California, near the southern end of San Francisco Bay. Population, 204,000.

San Jo·sé (săn′ hō-zā′). The capital of Costa Rica, situated on the country's central plateau. Population, 114,000.

San Jose scale. A destructive scale insect, *Aspidiotus perniciosus,* that does considerable damage to fruit trees and fruit-bearing plants. [First seen in the United States in SAN JOSE, California.]

San Juan (săn′ hwän′). **1.** The capital of Puerto Rico, a major city and seaport on the northern coast of the Commonwealth. Population, 452,000. **2.** A city and commercial center of Argentina, in the west, 600 miles northwest of Buenos Aires. Population, 107,000.

San Juan Hill (săn′ hwän′). A battle site east of Santiago de Cuba where U.S. forces won a victory over the Spanish in the Spanish-American War (1898).

San Juan Islands (săn′ hwän′). A group of about 170 islands at the northern end of Puget Sound in northwestern Washington. Also called "San Juans."

San Juan Mountains (săn′ hwän′). A range of the Rocky Mountains in southwestern Colorado and northern New Mexico. Highest elevation, Uncompahgre Peak (14,306 feet).

San Juan River (săn′ hwän′). A river rising in the San Juan Mountains, in Colorado, and flowing 400 miles generally westward through New Mexico and Utah to the Colorado.

sank. Past tense of **sink.**

San·key (săng′kē), **Ira David.** 1840–1908. American evangelist and hymn writer; associate of Dwight L. **Moody** *(see).*

San·khya (säng′kyə) *n.* A system of Hindu philosophy based on a dualism involving the ultimate principles of soul and potential matter. [Sanskrit *sāṁkhya-,* "based on calculation," from *saṁkhyā-,* calculation, from *saṁkhyāti*†, he counts up.]

San·ku·ru (säng-ko͞o′ro͞o). A river rising as the Lubilash in the south-central part of the Congo (Kinshasa) and flowing about 750 miles generally north and then west to the Kasai.

San Le·an·dro (săn′ lē-ăn′drō). A city of California, in a dairy-farming region southeast of Oakland. Population, 66,000.

San Lu·cas, Cape (sän lo͞o′käs). A cape on the Pacific at the southernmost tip of Baja California Sur, Mexico.

San Lu·is Po·to·sí (sän lwēs′ pō′tō-sē′). **1.** A state of Mexico, occupying 24,415 square miles in the north-central part of the country. Population, 1,048,000. **2.** The capital of this state, situated in the southwest. Population, 177,000.

San Ma·ri·no (săn′ mə-rē′nō; *Italian* sän′ mä-rē′nō). **1.** An independent republic occupying 23 square miles in the Apennines near the Adriatic coast of Italy. Population, 17,000. **2.** The capital of this republic.

San Ma·te·o (săn′ mə-tā′ō). A residential city of California, in the west on San Francisco Bay. Population, 70,000.

san·nup (săn′əp) *n.* A married male American Indian. [From a Massachusetts word akin to Eastern Abnaki *sénape,* "man."]

San Pab·lo Bay (săn′ păb′lō). The northern section of San Francisco Bay, western California.

San Pe·dro (săn′ pē′drō). A seaport section of southern Los Angeles, California. Population, 60,000.

San Re·mo (săn′ rē′mō, rā′mō; *Italian* sän′ rā′mō). A seaport and resort on the Gulf of Genoa in northwestern Italy. Population, 40,000.

sans (sănz; *French* säN) *prep.* Without. [Middle English *saunz, san(s),* from Old French *san(s), sen(s),* from Vulgar Latin *sene* (unattested), from Latin *sine* (influenced by Latin *absentiā,* in the absence of). See **sen-**^{2} in Appendix.*]

San Sal·va·dor (săn′ săl′və-dôr; *Spanish* sän′ säl′vä-*th*ôr′). **1.** The capital of El Salvador, centrally located 20 miles inland from the Pacific. Population, 281,000. **2.** A volcano, 6,400 feet high, near this city.

San Sal·va·dor Island (săn′ săl′və-dôr). An island, 60 square miles in area, in the central Bahamas, the site of Columbus' first landing in the New World (1492).

sans-cu·lotte (sănz′kyo͞o-lŏt′; *French* säN-kü-lôt′) *n.* **1.** An extreme republican during the French Revolution. **2.** A revolutionary extremist. [French *sans-culotte,* "without breeches" (the revolutionaries wore pantaloons instead of the knee-breeches worn by members of the upper classes) : SANS + CULOTTES.] —**sans′-cu·lot′tic** *adj.* —**sans′-cu·lot′tism′** *n.*

San Se·bas·tián (săn′ sə-băs′chĭn; *Spanish* sän′ sā′väs-tyän′). A city of Spain, on the Bay of Biscay ten miles from the French border. Population, 149,000.

San·sei (sän′sā′) *n., pl.* **Sansei** or **-seis.** Also **san·sei.** The U.S.-born grandchild of Japanese immigrants to America; a third-generation Japanese-American. Compare **Nisei.** [Japanese *sansei* : *san,* three, third, from Ancient Chinese *sam* (Mandarin Chinese *san*^{1}) + *sei,* generation, age, from Ancient Chinese *śiäi* (Mandarin Chinese *shih*^{4}).]

san·se·vie·ri·a (săn′sə-vĭr′ē-ə) *n.* Any of various tropical Old World plants of the genus *Sansevieria,* having thick, lance-shaped leaves and often cultivated as a house plant. [New Latin, after Raimondo di Sangro (1710–1771), Prince of *San Severo,* Italy.]

San·skrit (săn′skrĭt′) *n.* Also **San·scrit.** *Abbr.* **Skt., Skr. 1.** An ancient language of India, belonging to the Indic branch of the Indo-Iranian subfamily of Indo-European languages. It is the language of the Vedas and of Hinduism. **2.** The literary language of India, classical Sanskrit, the grammar of which was fixed by Indian grammarians before the fourth century B.C., now used only for sacred or scholarly writings. [Sanskrit *saṁskṛta,* put together, well-formed, refined : *sam,* together (see **sem-**^{1} in Appendix*) + *kṛ,* to make, do (see **kwer-**^{1} in Appendix*).] —**San′skrit·ist** *n.*

San·skrit·ic (săn-skrĭt′ĭk) *adj.* **1.** Designating a large group of Indian languages and dialects, both ancient and modern, such as Hindi, Pali, Bengali, and Punjabi. **2.** Of, relating to, or written in Sanskrit.

sans serif. A typeface without serifs. Also called "Gothic."

San Ste·fa·no (săn′ stā-fä′nō). *Turkish* **Ye·şil·köy** (yĕ′shēl-kû′ē). A village of Turkey near Istanbul, the site of the signing of a treaty between Russia and Turkey (1878).

San·ta An·a (săn′tə ăn′ə; *Spanish* sän′tä ä′nä). **1.** The second largest city in El Salvador, situated about 30 miles west of San

Salvador. Population, 73,000. **2.** A city of California in the southwest, east of Long Beach. Population, 100,000.

San·ta An·na (săn′tə ä′nə), **Antonio Lopez.** Also **San·ta A·na.** 1795?–1876. Mexican statesman; four times president and three times exiled; victor at the Alamo but defeated at San Jacinto.

San·ta Bar·ba·ra (săn′tə bär′bə-rə, bär′brə). A city and seaside resort of California, about 80 miles northwest of Los Angeles. Population, 59,000.

San·ta Bar·ba·ra Channel (săn′tə bär′bə-rə, bär′brə). A channel between mainland California and the northern Santa Barbara Islands.

San·ta Bar·ba·ra Islands (săn′tə bär′bə-rə, bär′brə). A chain of islands extending about 150 miles along the coast of California.

San·ta Cat·a·li·na (săn′tə kăt-ə-lē′nə). One of the Santa Barbara Islands, a resort center 75 square miles in area, lying about 24 miles southwest of Los Angeles, California. Also called "Catalina," "Catalina Island."

San·ta Ca·ta·ri·na (săn′tə kăt′ə-rē′nə; *Portuguese* săn′tä kä′tä-rē′nä). A state of Brazil, occupying 36,435 square miles in the southern part of the country. Population, 2,502,000. Capital, Florianópolis.

San·ta Cla·ra (săn′tə klăr′ə; *Spanish* săn′tä klä′rä *for sense 2*). **1.** A city of California, in the west, south of the southern end of San Francisco Bay. Population, 59,000. **2.** A city of Cuba, in the central part of the country. Population, 142,000.

San·ta Claus (săn′tə klôz′). The personification of the spirit of Christmas, usually represented as a jolly, fat old man with a white beard and a red suit. Also called "Saint Nicholas," "Saint Nick." [Variant of Dutch (dialectal) *Sinterklaas,* from Middle Dutch *Sinterclaes,* unexplained shortening of *Sint Nicolaes,* Saint Nicholas, the patron saint of children, who, according to legend, threw purses of gold into the house of three poor maidens to serve as their dowries.]

San·ta Cruz (săn′tə krōoz′; *Spanish* săn′tä krōos′ *for senses 1, 4, 5*). **1.** A city of Bolivia, east of the Andes in the center of the country. Population, 83,000. **2.** A city and seaside resort in west-central California, south of San Francisco. Population, 26,000. **3.** An island of California in the northwestern part of the Santa Barbara Islands. **4.** A river in southern Argentina, flowing about 250 miles from Lake Argentino to the Atlantic. **5.** The Spanish name for **St. Croix.**

San·ta Cruz de Ten·er·ife (săn′tə krōoz′ də těn′ə-rǐf′; *Spanish* săn′tä krōoth′ *th*ä tā-nä-rē′fä). A city, seaport, and resort in the Canary Islands, on the northeastern coast of Tenerife. Population, 133,000.

San·ta Cruz Islands (săn′tə krōoz′). A group of volcanic islands with an area of 380 square miles, in the southwestern Pacific, administered as part of the Solomon Islands.

San·ta Fe (săn′tə fā′). The capital of New Mexico, in the north-central part of the state. Population, 35,000.

San·ta Fé (săn′tä fā′). A port in east-central Argentina, on the Salado River. Population, 199,000.

San·ta Fe Trail (săn′tə fā′). A wagon and trade route much used in the 19th century (1821–80) between Independence, Missouri, and Santa Fe, New Mexico.

San·ta Is·a·bel (săn′tə ĭz′ə-běl′; *Spanish* săn′tä ē′sä-věl′). The capital and chief port of Equatorial Guinea, on the island of Fernando Po in the Gulf of Guinea. Population, 20,000.

San·ta Ma·ri·a[1] (săn′tə mə-rē′ə; *Spanish* săn′tä mä-rē′ä). The flagship of the flotilla with which Columbus made his maiden voyage to America.

San·ta Ma·ri·a[2] (săn′tä mä-rē′ä). An active volcano, 12,362 feet high, in southwestern Guatemala.

San·ta Mon·i·ca (săn′tə mŏn′ĭ-kə). A suburban city of California, west of Los Angeles. Population, 83,000.

San·tan·der (săn′tän-děr′). A seaport of Spain, in the north on the Bay of Biscay. Population, 118,000.

San·ta·ya·na (săn′tə-yä′nä), **George.** 1863–1952. Spanish-born American philosopher and poet.

San·ti·a·go (săn·tyä′gō). **1.** Officially, Santiago de Chile. The capital of Chile, at the foot of the Andes in the central part of the country. Population, 1,907,000; metropolitan area, 2,314,000. **2.** In full **San·ti·a·go de los Ca·ba·lle·ros** (săn-tyä′gō *th*ě lōs kä-bä-lyě′ōs, -lyěr′ōs, dě). A city of the Dominican Republic, in the northern part of the country. Population, 114,000.

San·ti·a·go de Com·pos·te·la (săn-tyä′gō dě kōm-pō-stě′lä). Also **San·ti·a·go.** A city of northwestern Spain, a pilgrimage center and the site of the tomb of Saint James, the country's patron saint. Population, 31,000.

San·ti·a·go de Cu·ba (săn-tyä′gō dě kōo′bä). A city and seaport of Cuba and the capital of Oriente Province, in the southeast on the Caribbean. Population, 213,400.

San·ti·a·go del Es·te·ro (săn-tyä′gō děl ěs-těr′ō). A city of north-central Argentina. Population, 103,000.

San·to Do·min·go (săn′tō dō-mēng′gō). **1.** Formerly **Ciu·dad Tru·ji·llo** (sě′ōo-*th*ä′ trōo-hē′ōo, sě′ōo-däd′). The capital of the Dominican Republic, a seaport in the southeastern part of the country. Population, 478,000. **2.** A former Spanish colony on the island of Hispaniola, now the Dominican Republic.

san·ton·i·ca (săn-tŏn′ĭ-kə) *n.* **1.** A wormwood, *Artemisia maritima,* of the Old World, having flowers that yield santonin. **2.** The dried unopened flowers of this plant. [New Latin, from Latin (*herba*) *santonica,* from the feminine of *santonicus,* of the *Santoni,* a people of Aquitania.]

san·to·nin (săn′tə-nĭn) *n.* A colorless crystalline compound, $C_{15}H_{18}O_3$, obtained from species of wormwood, especially *santonica,* and used as an anthelmintic. [SANTON(ICA) + -IN.]

San·tos (săn′tōos). A city and major coffee port of Brazil, on an island of São Paulo in the southeastern part of the state. Population, 266,000.

San·tur·ce (săn-tōor′sě). The principal suburb of San Juan, Puerto Rico.

SAO Airport code for São Paulo, Brazil.

São Fran·cis·co (soun frän-sēs′kōo). A major river of Brazil, rising in southwestern Minas Gerais and flowing about 1,800 miles, first northeast and then generally east, to the Atlantic.

São Lu·is (soun lōo-ēs′). A city and seaport of Brazil and the capital of Maranhão, on an island in the north-central part of the state. Population, 125,000.

São Ma·nuel. The former name for the **Teles Pires.**

São Mi·guel (soun mē-gěl′). The largest island (288 square miles) of the Azores, in the eastern part of the group.

Saône (sōn). A river of east-central France, rising in the Vosges Mountains and flowing 268 miles southwest to the Rhône.

São Pau·lo (soun pou′lōo). **1.** A state of Brazil, occupying 95,453 square miles in the southeastern part of the country. Population, 15,326,000. **2.** The capital of this state and Brazil's largest city. Population, 3,825,000.

São Pau·lo de Lo·an·da. A former name for **Luanda.**

São Sal·va·dor. A former name for **Salvador.**

São Ti·a·go (soun tyä′gōo). The largest (383 square miles) of the Cape Verde Islands. Principal town, Praia, the capital of the archipelago.

São To·mé (soun tōo-mě′). **1.** An island, 319 square miles in area, in the Gulf of Guinea. **2.** The principal town on this island, the capital of São Tomé e Principe. Population, 8,000.

São To·mé e Prin·ci·pe (soun tōo-mě′ ě prěn′sē-pĭ). A Portuguese Overseas Province consisting of the islands of São Tomé and Principe, in the Gulf of Guinea about 175 miles west of Gabon. Population, 63,000. Capital, São Tomé, on São Tomé island.

sap[1] (săp) *n.* **1. a.** The watery fluid that circulates through a plant, carrying food and other substances to the tissues. **b.** Any plant juice or fluid. **2.** Any essential bodily fluid. **3.** Health and energy; vitality. **4.** *Slang.* An easy victim; a dupe; fool. [Middle English *sap,* Old English *sæp.* See **sab-** in Appendix.*]

sap[2] (săp) *n.* **1.** A covered trench or tunnel dug to a point within an enemy position. **2.** A narrow trench dug for protection while approaching a point under enemy fire. —*v.* **sapped, sapping, saps.** —*tr.* **1.** To undermine the foundations of (a fortification). **2.** To deplete or weaken gradually; devitalize. —*intr.* To dig a sap. [Earlier *sappe,* trench, from Old French *sappe,* "an undermining" or Old Italian *zappa†.*]

s. ap. apothecaries' scruple.

sap·a·jou (săp′ə-jōo) *n.* A monkey, the **capuchin** (*see*). [French, from Tupi.]

sa·pan·wood. Variant of **sappanwood.**

Sa·phar. Variant of **Safar.**

sap·head (săp′hěd′) *n. Slang.* A fool. [SAP (dupe) + HEAD.]

sa·phe·na (sə-fē′nə) *n., pl.* **-nae** (-nē′). Either of two large superficial veins of the leg. [Middle English, from Medieval Latin, from Arabic *ṣāfin.*] —**sa·phe′nous** *adj.*

sap·id (săp′ĭd) *adj.* **1.** Pleasantly flavorful; savory. **2.** Pleasing to the mind; engaging. [Latin *sapidus,* tasty, from *sapere,* to taste, savor. See **sap-** in Appendix.*] —**sa·pid′i·ty** *n.*

sa·pi·ent (sā′pē-ənt) *adj.* Having wisdom; wise; discerning. Usually used ironically. [Middle English, from Old French, from Latin *sapiēns,* present participle of *sapere,* to taste, to have good taste, to be sensible or wise. See **sap-** in Appendix.*] —**sa′pi·ence** *n.* —**sa′pi·ent·ly** *adv.*

Sa·pir (sə-pîr′), **Edward.** 1884–1939. American anthropologist, ethnologist, and linguist; studied American Indians.

sap·less (săp′lĭs) *adj.* **1.** Devoid of sap; dry. **2.** Lacking spirit or energy.

sap·ling (săp′lĭng) *n.* **1.** A young tree. **2.** A youth. **3.** A greyhound less than one year old. [SAP (juice) + -LING.]

sap·o·dil·la (săp′ə-dĭl′ə) *n.* **1.** An evergreen tree, *Achras zapota,* of tropical America, having latex that yields chicle. **2.** The edible russet fruit of this tree. Also called "naseberry," "sapota." [Spanish *zapotillo,* diminutive of *zapote,* sapodilla fruit, from Nahuatl *tzapotl.*]

sap·o·na·ceous (săp′ə-nā′shəs) *adj.* Having the qualities of soap. [New Latin *saponaceus* : Latin *sāpō* (stem *sāpōn-*), soap (see **sib-** in Appendix*) + -ACEOUS.]

sa·po·na·ted (săp′ə-nā′tĭd) *adj.* Combined or treated with a soap. [From Latin *sāpō* (stem *sāpōn-*), soap. See **sib-** in Appendix.*]

sa·pon·i·fi·ca·tion (sə-pŏn′ə-fə-kā′shən) *n. Chemistry.* The hydrolysis of an ester by an alkali, producing a free alcohol and an acid salt; especially, alkaline hydrolysis of fats to make soap.

sa·pon·i·fy (sə-pŏn′ə-fī′) *v.* **-fied, -fying, -fies.** *Chemistry.* —*tr.* **1.** To convert (an ester) by saponification. **2.** To convert (fats) into soap. —*intr.* To undergo saponification. [French *saponifier* : Latin *sāpō* (stem *sāpōn-*), soap (see **sib-** in Appendix*) + -FY.] —**sa·pon′i·fi′a·ble** *adj.* —**sa·pon′i·fi′er** *n.*

sap·o·nin (săp′ə-nĭn) *n.* Any of various plant glucosides that form soapy colloidal solutions when mixed and agitated with water, used in detergents, synthetic sex hormones, foaming agents, and emulsifiers. [French *saponine* : Latin *sāpō* (stem *sāpōn-*), soap (see **sib-** in Appendix*) + -IN.]

sap·o·nite (săp′ə-nīt′) *n.* An amorphous, hydrous silicate of magnesium, occurring as a soaplike mass in the cavities of certain rocks, such as diabase. [Swedish *saponit* : Latin *sāpō* (stem *sāpōn-*), soap (see **sib-** in Appendix*) + -ITE.]

sa·por (sā′pər, -pôr) *n.* Also *British* **sa·pour.** A quality perceptible to the sense of taste; flavor. [Middle English, from Latin

Santa Claus
Drawing by Thomas Nast

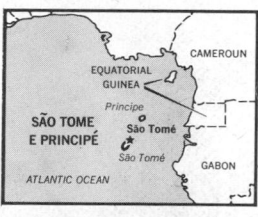

São Tomé e Principe

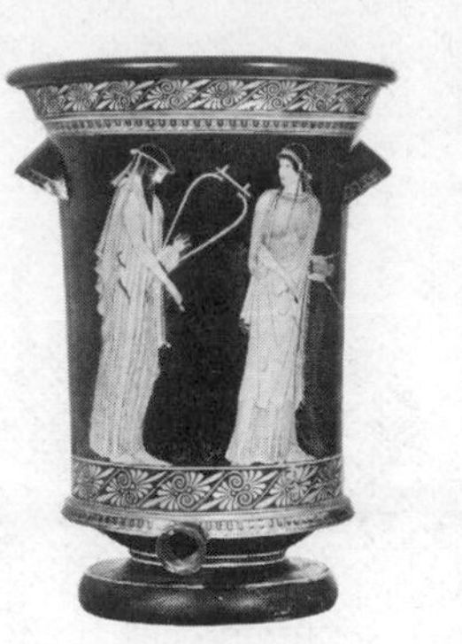

Sappho
Sappho *(right)* with Alcaeus

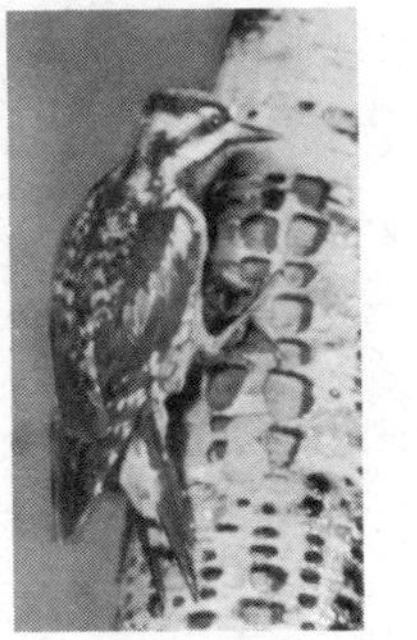

sapsucker
Sphyrapicus varius
Yellow-bellied sapsucker

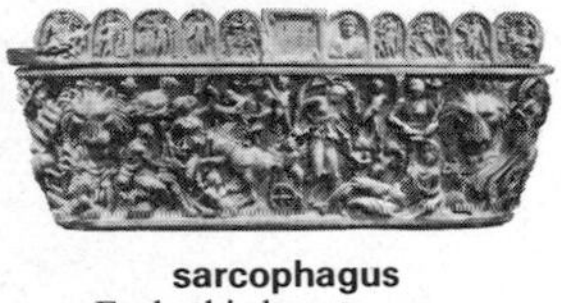

sarcophagus
Early third-century A.D. Roman sarcophagus of marble

sapor, taste, from *sapere,* to taste. See **sap-** in Appendix.*] —**sap′o·rif′ic, sap′o·rous** *adj.*

sap·pan·wood (sə-păn′wo͝od′, săp′ăn-) *n.* Also **sa·pan·wood.** **1.** A tree, *Caesalpina sappan,* of tropical Asia, having wood that yields a red dye. **2.** The wood of this tree. [Malay *sapang,* sappanwood + WOOD.]

sap·per (săp′ər) *n.* A military engineer, especially in the British armed forces. [Originally one who digs saps (fortifications).]

Sap·phic (săf′ĭk) *adj.* **1.** Of or pertaining to the Greek poet Sappho. **2. a.** Designating a verse of dactyls combined with trochees or anapests with iambs, especially one of 11 syllables. **b.** Designating a stanza of three such verses followed by an Adonic. **c.** Designating an ode made up of such stanzas. **3.** *Usually small* **s.** Of or pertaining to homosexuality among women; lesbian. —*n.* **1.** A Sapphic meter, verse, stanza, or ode. **2.** *Usually small* **s.** A lesbian.

sap·phire (săf′īr) *n.* **1.** Any of several relatively pure forms of corundum, especially a blue form used as a gemstone. **2.** A corundum gem. **3.** The blue color of a gem sapphire. —*adj.* Having the color of a blue sapphire. [Middle English *saphir, safir,* from Old French *safir,* from Latin *sapphīrus,* from Greek *sappheiros,* perhaps from Hebrew *sappīr,* perhaps from Sanskrit *śanipriya,* "precious to the planet Saturn" : *Śani*†, the planet Saturn + *priya-,* precious (see **prī-** in Appendix*).]

sap·phi·rine (săf′ər-ĭn, -ə-rēn′) *adj.* Of or resembling sapphire. —*n.* A rare light-blue or green aluminum-magnesium silicate mineral.

Sap·pho (săf′ō). Greek lyric poet of the seventh century B.C.

Sap·po·ro (säp-pō′rō). The capital and largest city of Hokkaido, Japan, in the southwestern part of the island southeast of Ishikari Bay. Population, 704,000.

sap·py (săp′ē) *adj.* **-pier, -piest. 1.** Full of sap; juicy. **2.** Vital; vigorous. **3.** *Slang.* Insipid or mawkish. **4.** *Slang.* Silly or foolish. —**sap′pi·ly** *adv.* —**sap′pi·ness** *n.*

sa·pre·mi·a (sə-prē′mē-ə) *n.* Also **sa·prae·mi·a. Septicemia** *(see).* [New Latin : SAPR(O)- + -EMIA.] —**sa·pre′mic** *adj.*

sapro–, sapr–. Indicates dead or decaying material; for example, **saprophyte, sapremia.** [Greek, from *sapros,* rotten, putrid, akin to *sēpein,* to rot. See **septic.**]

sap·robe (săp′rōb′) *n.* An organism that derives its nourishment from nonliving or decaying organic matter. [SAPRO- + Greek *bios,* life (see **gwei-** in Appendix*).] —**sa·pro′bic** (sə-prō′bĭk) *adj.* —**sa·pro′bi·cal·ly** *adv.*

sap·ro·gen·ic (săp′rō-jĕn′ĭk) *adj.* Also **sa·prog·e·nous** (sə-prŏj′ə-nəs). **1.** Producing decay or putrefaction. **2.** Resulting from decay or putrefaction. [SAPRO- + -GENIC.] —**sap′ro·ge·nic′i·ty** (săp′rə-jə-nĭs′ə-tē) *n.*

sap·ro·lite (săp′rə-līt′) *n.* Clay, silt, or other rock remnants, unmoved from the site of disintegration. [SAPRO- + -LITE.]

sap·ro·pel (săp′rə-pĕl) *n.* **1.** An aquatic sludge rich in organic matter. **2.** A fluid slime found in swamps as a product of putrefaction. [SAPRO- + Greek *pēlos,* clay, mud (see **pel-²** in Appendix*).] —**sa′pro·pel′ic** (săp′rə-pĕl′ĭk) *adj.*

sa·proph·a·gous (sə-prŏf′ə-gəs) *adj.* Feeding on decaying matter. [SAPRO- + -PHAGOUS.]

sap·ro·phyte (săp′rə-fīt′) *n.* A plant that lives on and derives its nourishment from dead or decaying organic matter. [SAPRO- + -PHYTE.] —**sap′ro·phyt′ic** (-fĭt′ĭk) *adj.*

sap·ro·zo·ic (săp′rə-zō′ĭk) *adj.* **1.** Pertaining to or designating nutrition by absorption of dissolved organic and inorganic materials, as in protozoans and some fungi. **2.** Feeding on dead or decaying animal matter. [SAPRO- + -ZOIC.]

sap·sa·go (săp-sā′gō, săp′sə-gō′) *n.* A hard cheese made from skim-milk curd, colored and flavored with sweet clover. [Corruption of German *Schabzieger* : *schaben,* to scrape, from Old High German *skaban* (see **skep-** in Appendix*) + German (dialect) *Zi(e)ger,* whey, whey cheese, from Middle High German *ziger,* probably from Celtic (see **gwher-** in Appendix*).]

sap·suck·er (săp′sŭk′ər) *n.* Either of two small North American woodpeckers, *Sphyrapicus varius* or *S. thyrsoides,* that drill holes in and drink the sap of certain trees.

sap·wood (săp′wo͝od′) *n.* Newly formed outer wood that lies just inside the cambium of a tree or woody plant and is usually lighter in color and more active in nutrition than the heartwood. Sometimes called "alburnum."

SAR, S.A.R. Sons of the American Revolution.

sar·a·band (săr′ə-bănd′) *n.* **1.** A stately court dance of the 17th and 18th centuries, in slow triple time. **2.** The music for this dance. [French *sarabande,* from Spanish *zarabanda*†.]

Sa·ra·bat. See **Gediz.**

Sar·a·cen (săr′ə-sən) *n.* **1.** A member of a pre-Islamic nomadic people of the Syrian-Arabian deserts. **2.** An Arab. **3.** Any Moslem, especially of the time of the Crusades. [Middle English, from Old French *Saracin,* from Late Latin *Saracēnus,* from Late Greek *Sarakēnos,* probably from Arabic *sharqīyīn,* "Easterners," from *sharq,* sunrise, east, from *shāraqa,* to rise.] —**Sar′a·cen′ic** (-sĕn′ĭk) *adj.*

Sa·ra·gat (sä′rä-gät′), **Giuseppe.** Born 1898. Italian statesman; president (since 1964).

Sar·a·gos·sa (săr′ə-gŏs′ə). *Spanish* **Za·ra·go·za** (thä′rä-gō′thä). The major city of the Aragon region in northeastern Spain. Population, 377,000.

Sar·ah¹ (sâr′ə). Also **Sar·a.** A feminine given name. [Hebrew *Sārāh,* "princess."]

Sar·ah² (sâr′ə). The wife of Abraham and mother of Isaac. Genesis 7:15.

Sa·ra·je·vo (sä′rä-yĕ-vō). Also **Se·ra·je·vo** (sĕ′-). A city in central Yugoslavia and the capital of Bosnia and Herzegovina. Population, 213,000.

sa·ran (sə-răn′) *n.* Any of various thermoplastic resins derived from vinyl compounds and used to make packaging films, corrosion-resistant pipes, fittings, and bristles, and as a fiber in screens, carpets, drapery materials, and other heavy fabrics. [From the trademark *Saran,* coined by Dow Chemical Co., by which it was first developed.]

Sar·a·nac Lakes (săr′ə-năk). Three lakes in a resort region of northeastern New York State, known as Upper Saranac, Middle Saranac, and Lower Saranac, and linked by the Saranac River, which flows from the Lower Saranac northeast to Lake Champlain.

Sar·ansk (sŭ-ränsk′). The capital of the Mordvinian A.S.S.R., in the central part of the republic. Population, 124,000.

sa·ra·pe. Variant of **serape.**

Sar·a·so·ta (săr′ə-sō′tə). A city and resort of Florida, in the west on the Gulf of Mexico. Population, 77,000.

Sar·a·to·ga. The former name for **Schuylerville.**

Sar·a·to·ga Springs (săr′ə-tō′gə). A resort center in eastern New York State, 30 miles north of Albany; the site of a racetrack opened in 1864. Population, 17,000.

Saratoga trunk. A large traveling trunk, formerly used by women. [First popularized in SARATOGA SPRINGS.]

Sa·ra·tov (sŭ-rä′təf). A city and industrial center of the Soviet Union, on the Volga about 220 miles north of Volgograd. Population, 683,000.

Sa·ra·wak (sə-rä′wäk). The largest (48,250 square miles) of the states of Malaysia, formerly a British colony, on northwestern Borneo. Population, 818,000. Capital, Kuching.

sar·casm (sär′kăz′əm) *n.* **1.** A sharply mocking or contemptuous remark, typically utilizing statements or implications pointedly opposite or irrelevant to the underlying purport. **2.** The quality of such remarks. **3.** The use of such remarks. —See Synonyms at **wit.** [French *sarcasme,* from Greek *sarkasmos,* from *sarkazein,* "to tear flesh," bite the lips in rage, speak bitterly, from *sarx* (stem *sark-*), flesh. See **twerk-** in Appendix.*]

sar·cas·tic (sär-kăs′tĭk) *adj.* Also **sar·cas·ti·cal** (-tĭ-kəl). **1.** Expressing sarcasm. **2.** Given to using sarcasm. [French *sarcastique,* from *sarcasme,* SARCASM.] —**sar·cas′ti·cal·ly** *adv.*

Synonyms: *sarcastic, ironic, caustic, satirical, sardonic.* These adjectives apply to personal expression that is bitter, cutting, or derisive. *Sarcastic* and *ironic* both pertain to a form of expression in which meanings are conveyed obliquely. *Sarcastic* suggests open taunting and ridicule; *ironic* suggests a milder and subtler form of mockery. *Caustic* can apply to any expression that is biting or corrosive. *Satirical* refers to expression that seeks to expose wrong or folly to ridicule, often by means of sarcasm or irony. *Sardonic* can describe both the content and manner of expression and is associated with scorn, derision, mockery, and cynicism.

sarce·net (särs′nĭt) *n.* A fine, soft silk cloth. [Middle English *sarsenet,* from Norman French *sarzinett,* perhaps diminutive of *(drap) Sarzin,* Saracen (cloth), from Late Latin *Saracēnus,* SARACEN.]

sar·co·carp (sär′kō-kärp′) *n. Botany.* The fleshy pulp surrounding the seed of a drupaceous fruit such as a peach or plum. [French *sarcocarpe* : Greek *sarx* (stem *sark-*), flesh (see **twerk-** in Appendix*) + -CARP.]

sar·coid (sär′koid′) *adj.* Pertaining to or resembling flesh. [Greek *sarkoeidēs* : *sarx* (stem *sark-*), flesh (see **twerk-** in Appendix*) + -OID.]

sar·co·ma (sär-kō′mə) *n., pl.* **-mata** (-mə-tə) or **-mas.** A malignant tumor arising from nonepithelial connective tissues. [New Latin, from Greek *sarkōma,* fleshy excrescence : *sarkoun,* to make fleshy, from *sarx* (stem *sark-*), flesh (see **twerk-** in Appendix*) + -OMA.] —**sar·co′ma·toid, sar·co′ma·tous** *adj.*

sar·co·ma·to·sis (sär-kō′mə-tō′sĭs) *n. Pathology.* The formation of numerous sarcomatous growths in the body. [New Latin : *sarcoma* (stem *sarcomat-*), SARCOMA + -OSIS.]

sar·coph·a·gus (sär-kŏf′ə-gəs) *n., pl.* **-gi** (-jī′). A stone coffin. [Latin *sarcophagus (lapis),* "flesh-eating (stone)," from Greek *(lithos) sarkophagos* : *sarx* (stem *sark-*), flesh (see **twerk-** in Appendix*) + -PHAGOUS.]

sar·cop·tic mange (sär-kŏp′tĭk). *Veterinary Medicine.* A mange caused by the mite *Sarcoptes scabiei.* [From New Latin *Sarcoptes,* "flesh-cutter" : Greek *sarx* (stem *sark-*), flesh (see **twerk-** in Appendix*) + *koptein,* to cut (see **skep-** in Appendix*).]

sar·cous (sär′kəs) *adj.* Of, pertaining to, or consisting of flesh or muscle. [From Greek *sarx* (stem *sark-*), flesh. See **twerk-** in Appendix.*]

sard (särd) *n.* A clear or translucent deep orange-red to brownish red **chalcedony** *(see).* Also called "sardius." [French *sarde,* from Latin *sarda,* perhaps variant of Greek *sardion,* "the Sardian stone," from *Sardeis,* SARDIS.]

sar·dine (sär-dēn′) *n.* **1.** Any of various small or half-grown edible herrings or related fishes of the family Clupeidae, frequently canned in oil. **2.** Any of numerous unrelated small, silvery freshwater or marine fishes that are similarly processed. [Middle English *sardeyn,* from Old French *sardine,* from Latin *sardīna,* from Greek *sardinos,* possibly from *Sardō,* SARDINIA.]

Sar·din·i·a (sär-dĭn′ē-ə). *Italian* **Sar·de·gna** (sär-dān′yä). The second-largest (9,196 square miles) island in the Mediterranean, an autonomous region of Italy, from which it is separated by the Tyrrhenian Sea. Population, 1,420,000. Capital, Cagliari.

Sar·din·i·an (sär-dĭn′ē-ən) *adj.* Of or pertaining to Sardinia or its people. —*n.* **1.** A native or inhabitant of Sardinia. **2.** The dialect spoken in Sardinia.

Sar·dis (sär′dĭs). Also **Sar·des** (sär′dēz). An ancient city in western Asia Minor, the capital of the Lydian Empire.

ă pat/ā pay/âr care/ä father/b bib/ch church/d deed/ĕ pet/ē be/f fife/g gag/h hat/hw which/ĭ pit/ī pie/îr pier/j judge/k kick/l lid, needle/m mum/n no, sudden/ng thing/ŏ pot/ō toe/ô paw, for/oi noise/ou out/o͝o took/o͞o boot/p pop/r roar/s sauce/sh ship, dish/

sar·di·us (sär′dē-əs) *n.* A variety of chalcedony, **sard** *(see).* [Middle English, from Late Latin, from Greek *sardios,* the Sardian stone, from *Sardeis,* SARDIS.]

sar·don·ic (sär-dŏn′ĭk) *adj.* Scornful; mocking; cynical. See Synonyms at **sarcastic.** [French *sardonique,* from Latin *Sardonius (risus),* bitter (laugh), from Late Greek *Sardonios,* alteration (influenced by Latin *herba Sardonia,* "Sardinian herb," a poisonous plant supposed to distort the face of the eater) of *Sardanios,* bitter, scornful. See **sward-** in Appendix.*] —**sar·don′i·cal·ly** *adv.* —**sar·don′i·cism′** (-ə-sĭz′əm) *n.*

sar·do·nyx (sär-dŏn′ĭks, sär′də-nĭks) *n.* An onyx with alternating brown and white bands of sard and other minerals. [Middle English *sardonix,* from Latin *sardonyx,* from Greek *sardonux* : probably *sardion,* SARD + *onux,* ONYX.]

sar·gas·so (sär-găs′ō) *n.* A seaweed, **gulfweed** *(see).* [Portuguese *sargaço,* perhaps from Latin *salix* (stem *salic-*), willow, sallow (supposedly from a resemblance to the leaves of the sallow). See **salik-** in Appendix.*]

Sargasso Sea. A section of the North Atlantic between the West Indies and the Azores, an area with an abundance of seaweed floating on its comparatively calm waters.

sarge (särj) *n. Informal.* Sergeant.

Sar·gent (sär′jənt), **John Singer.** 1856–1925. American painter.

sa·ri (sär′ē) *n., pl.* **-ris.** An outer garment worn chiefly by women of India and Pakistan, consisting of a length of lightweight cloth with one end wrapped about the waist to form a skirt and the other draped over the shoulder or covering the head. [Hindi *sāṛī,* from Sanskrit *śāṭī*†, "cloth," sari.]

Sark (särk). A small (1,274 acres) island in the Channel Islands, seven miles east of Guernsey; a feudal manor governed by the Dame of Sark. Population, 556.

Sar·ma·ti·a (sär-mā′shē-ə, -shə). An ancient region in eastern Europe between the Vistula and the Volga in present-day Poland and the Soviet Union.

sar·men·tose (sär-mĕn′tōs′) *adj. Botany.* Having slender, prostrate stems that root at intervals, as in the strawberry. [Latin *sarmentōsus,* full of twigs, from *sarmentum,* twigs, from *sarpere,* to cut off, prune. See **serp-¹** in Appendix.*]

Sar·ni·a (sär′nē-ə). A city and industrial center of Ontario, Canada, in the southeast at the southern end of Lake Huron. Population, 51,000.

Sar·noff (sär′nôf), **David.** Born 1891. Russian-born American broadcasting executive.

sa·rong (sə-rông′, -rŏng′) *n.* A length of brightly colored cloth wrapped about the waist and hanging as a skirt, worn by both men and women of the Malay Archipelago and the Pacific islands. [Malay, sarong, sheath, covering.]

Sa·ron·ic Gulf (sə-rŏn′ĭk). An inlet of the Aegean in Greece, extending 50 miles between Attica and the Peloponnesus.

Sa·ros, Gulf of (sä′rôs). An inlet of the Aegean, extending 37 miles into Turkey, north of the Gallipoli Peninsula.

Sa·roy·an (sə-roi′ən), **William.** Born 1908. American novelist and playwright.

Sarre. 1. The French name for the **Saar. 2.** The French name for **Saarland.**

sar·sa·pa·ril·la (săs′pə-rĭl′ə, sär′sə-pə-rĭl′ə) *n.* **1.** The dried roots of any of several tropical American plants of the genus *Smilax,* especially *S. aristolochiaefolia,* of Mexico, used as a flavoring. **2.** A sweet soft drink flavored with sarsaparilla. **3.** Either of two North American plants, *Aralia hispida* or *A. nudicaulis,* having clusters of small white flowers. [Spanish *zarzaparrilla* : *zarza,* bramble, from Arabic *sharaṣ,* thorny plant + *parrilla,* diminutive of *parra*†, vine.]

Sar·to, Andrea del. See **Andrea del Sarto.**

sar·to·ri·al (sär-tôr′ē-əl, -tōr′ē-əl) *adj.* **1.** Of or relating to a tailor or tailoring. **2.** Of or pertaining to clothing or dress, especially men's. **3.** *Anatomy.* Of or pertaining to the sartorius. [From Latin *sartor,* a tailor. See **sartorius.**] —**sar·to′ri·al·ly** *adv.*

sar·to·ri·us (sär-tôr′ē-əs, -tōr′ē-əs) *n.* A flat, narrow thigh muscle, the longest of the human anatomy, crossing the front of the thigh obliquely from the hip to the inner side of the tibia. [New Latin *sartorius (musculus),* "tailor's (muscle)" (because it enables one to sit in a cross-legged position like a tailor at work), from Latin *sartor,* a tailor, from *sartus,* past participle of *sarcīre,* to mend. See **serk-** in Appendix.*]

Sar·tre (sȧr′tr′), **Jean Paul.** Born 1905. French philosopher and man of letters.

Sa·se·bo (sä′sĕ-bō′). A city and seaport of Japan, on the western coast of Kyushu. Population, 284,000.

sash¹ (săsh) *n.* A band or ribbon worn about the waist, as for ornament, or over the shoulder as a symbol of rank. [Earlier *shash,* from Arabic *shāsh,* muslin.]

sash² (săsh) *n.* A frame in which the panes of a window or door are set. —*tr.v.* **sashed, sashing, sashes.** To furnish with a sash. [Variant of earlier *shashes* (plural), from French *châssis,* a frame, CHASSIS.]

sa·shay (să-shā′) *intr.v.* **-shayed, -shaying, -shays.** *Informal.* **1.** To strut or flounce. **2.** To perform the chassé in dancing. —*n. Informal.* An excursion; a sally. [Variant of CHASSÉ.]

Sas·katch·e·wan (săs-kăch′ə-wän′, -wən). *Abbr.* **Sask.** A province of Canada, occupying 237,975 square miles in the south-central part of the country. Population, 953,000. Capital, Regina. See map at **Canada.**

Sas·katch·e·wan River (săs-kăch′ə-wän′, -wən). A river of Canada, formed by the confluence of the North and South Saskatchewan rivers near Prince Albert in north-central Saskatchewan and flowing 340 miles generally east to Lake Winnipeg in Manitoba.

sas·ka·toon (săs′kə-to͞on′) *n.* A shrub, *Amelanchier alnifolia,* of northwestern North America, having white flowers and edible dark-purple fruit. [Cree *misāskwatomin,* saskatoon berry : *misāskwat,* saskatoon willow + *-min,* berry.]

Sas·ka·toon (săs′kə-to͞on′). A city of Canada in south-central Saskatchewan. Population, 116,000.

sass (săs) *n. Informal.* Impertinence; back talk. —*tr.v.* **sassed, sassing, sasses.** *Informal.* To argue impudently with; talk back to. [Back-formation from SASSY (impudent).]

sas·sa·by (săs′ə-bē) *n., pl.* **-bies.** An African antelope, *Damaliscus lunatus,* having curved, ridged horns. [Bantu (Tswana) *tshêsêbê.*]

sas·sa·fras (săs′ə-frăs′) *n.* **1.** A North American tree, *Sassafras albidum,* having irregularly lobed leaves and aromatic bark. **2.** The dried root bark of this tree, used as flavoring and as a source of a volatile oil. [New Latin, from Spanish *sasafrás*†.]

Sas·sa·nid (săs′ə-nĭd) *n., pl.* **-nids** or **Sassanidae** (să-săn′ə-dē). Also **Sas·sa·ni·an** (sə-sā′nē-ən), **Sas·sa·nide** (săs′ə-nīd′). A member of the dynasty of Persian kings ruling from the third through the middle of the seventh century A.D. [Medieval Latin *Sassanidae* (plural), from *Sassan,* grandfather of Ardashir I, founder of the dynasty.] —**Sas′sa·nid** *adj.*

Sas·se·nach (săs′ə-năKH) *n. Irish & Scottish.* An Englishman. [Irish *Sasanach,* from *Sasan-,* Saxon, from Late Latin *Saxonēs,* SAXON(s).] —**Sas′se·nach** *adj.*

Sas·soon (să-so͞on′), **Siegfried.** 1886–1967. English poet and novelist.

sas·sy¹ (săs′ē) *adj.* **-sier, -siest.** *Informal.* **1.** Impudent. **2.** Jaunty. [Variant of SAUCY.] —**sas′si·ly** *adv.* —**sas′si·ness** *n.*

sas·sy² (săs′ē) *n.* A tree, *Erythrophloeum guineense,* of western Africa, having bark that yields a poison. Also called "sasswood," "sassy bark." [Probably of African origin.]

sas·tru·ga (sə-stro͞o′gə) *n., pl.* **-gi** (-jē). Also **zas·tru·ga** (zə-). A long, wavelike ridge of snow formed by the wind and found on the polar plains. [Russian *zastruga,* groove : *za,* by, to (see **ghō** in Appendix*) + *struga,* deep place (see **ster-²** in Appendix*).]

sat. Past tense and past participle of **sit.**

SAT 1. Airport code for San Antonio, Texas. **2.** Scholastic Aptitude Test.

Sat. Saturday.

S.A.T. Scholastic Aptitude Test.

Sa·tan (sāt′n) *n.* Also **Sa·than, Sath·a·nas** (săth′ə-nəs). The Devil. [Middle English *Satan,* Old English *Satan,* from Late Latin *Satān,* from Greek *Satan,* from Hebrew *śāṭān,* devil, adversary, from *śāṭan,* to accuse.]

sa·tang (sä-tăng′) *n., pl.* **satang.** A coin equal to 1/100 of the baht of Thailand. See table of exchange rates at **currency.** [Thai *satāṅ.*]

sa·tan·ic (sə-tăn′ĭk) *adj.* Also **sa·tan·i·cal** (-ĭ-kəl). **1.** Pertaining to or suggestive of Satan or evil. **2.** Profoundly cruel or evil; fiendish. **3.** Designating a group of 19th-century writers, including Byron and Shelley, whose impiety was deplored by their contemporaries. —**sa·tan′i·cal·ly** *adv.*

Sa·tan·ism (sāt′n-ĭz′əm) *n.* Worship of Satan. —**Sa′tan·ist** *n.*

satch·el (săch′əl) *n.* A small valise or bag, often having a shoulder strap, and used for carrying books, clothing, or the like. [Middle English *sachel,* from Old French, from Latin *saccelus,* diminutive of *saccus,* a bag, SACK.]

sate¹ (sāt) *tr.v.* **sated, sating, sates. 1.** To indulge (an appetite) fully. **2.** To indulge to excess; glut. —See Synonyms at **satiate.** [Probably variant (influenced by SATIATE) of obsolete *sade,* Middle English *sad(d)en,* Old English *sadian.* See **sā-** in Appendix.*]

sate². *Archaic.* Past tense of **sit.**

sa·teen (să-tēn′) *n.* A cotton fabric with a satin finish. [Variant of SATIN (influenced by VELVETEEN).]

sat·el·lite (săt′l-īt′) *n.* **1.** *Astronomy.* A relatively small body orbiting a planet; a moon. **2.** *Aerospace.* A man-made object orbiting, or intended to orbit, a celestial body. **3.** One who attends a powerful dignitary. **4.** A subservient follower. **5.** A nation that is dominated politically by another. [Old French, from Latin *satelles* (stem *satellit-*), an attendant, escort, probably from Etruscan *śatnal.*]

sa·tem (sä′təm, sā′-) *adj.* Designating those Indo-European languages, including the Indo-Iranian, Armenian, Albanian, and Balto-Slavic subfamilies, in which original velar stops became fricatives (as $k > s$ or *ś*) and labiovelar stops became velars (as $kw > k$). Compare **centum.** [From Avestan *satəm,* hundred (an arbitrarily chosen word in which initial *s* represents initial Indo-European *k*). See **dekm̥** in Appendix.*]

sa·ti·a·ble (sā′shē-ə-bəl) *adj.* Capable of being satiated. [Late Latin *satiābilis,* from Latin *satiāre,* SATIATE.] —**sa′ti·a·bil′i·ty, sa′ti·a·ble·ness** *n.* —**sa′ti·a·bly** *adv.*

sa·ti·ate (sā′shē-āt′) *tr.v.* **-ated, -ating, -ates. 1.** To satisfy (an appetite or desire) fully. **2.** To gratify to excess; sate. —*adj.* Filled to satisfaction; satiated. [Latin *satiāre,* from *satis,* sufficient, enough. See **sā-** in Appendix.*] —**sa′ti·a′tion** *n.*

Synonyms: *satiate, sate, cloy, glut, gorge, surfeit.* These verbs mean to fill or supply to the utmost or, more often, to excess. *Satiate* and *sate* are generally interchangeable. Although they can mean merely to satisfy fully, both usually imply satisfaction beyond natural desire, or overindulgence. *Cloy* invariably stresses the discomfort or ennui produced by gratification beyond desire. *Glut* emphasizes the sheer volume of oversupply more than its effects, especially with respect to overeating or flooding a market with goods. *Gorge* refers principally to greedy overstuffing with food. *Surfeit* implies oversupply and consequent dissatisfaction, though less strongly than *cloy.*

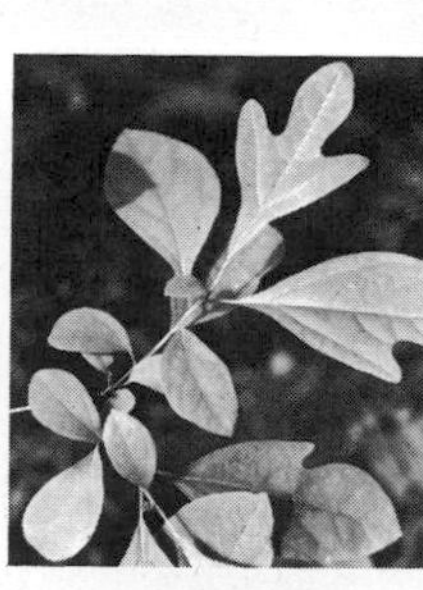

sassafras

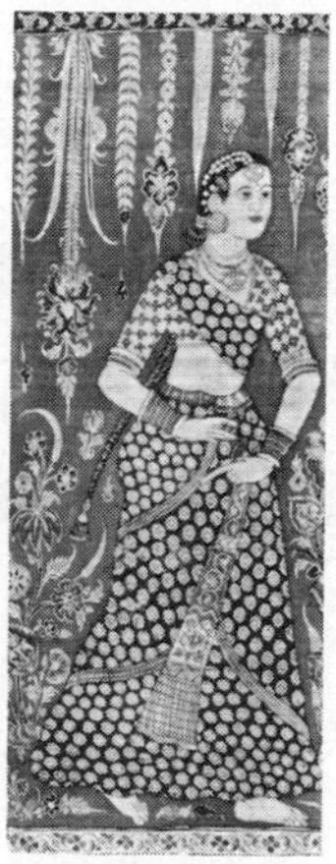

sari
Detail of a 17th-century Indian textile hanging

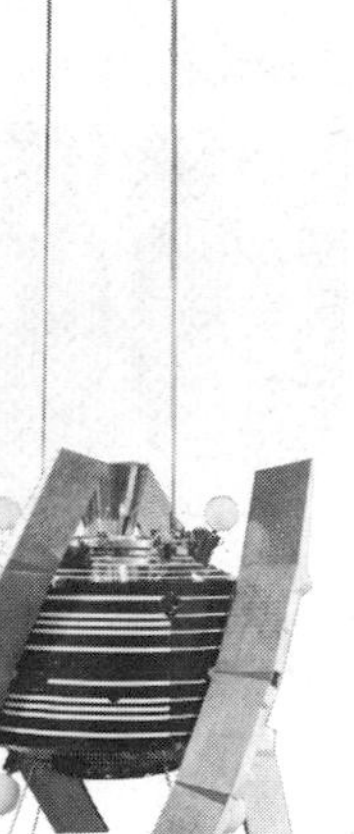

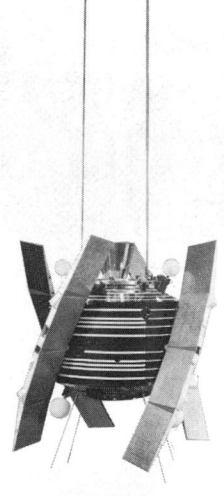

satellite
Prototype NASA satellite designed to monitor radio-frequency signals from space

t tight/th thin, path/*th* this, bathe/ŭ cut/ûr urge/v valve/w with/y yes/z zebra, size/zh vision/ə about, item, edible, gallop, circus/ à *Fr.* ami/œ *Fr.* feu, *Ger.* schön/ü *Fr.* tu, *Ger.* über/KH *Ger.* ich, *Scot.* loch/N *Fr.* bon. ***Follows main vocabulary. †Of obscure origin.**

Sa·tie (sà-tē′), **Erik.** Full name, Alfred Erikit Leslie Satie. 1866–1925. French composer.

sa·ti·e·ty (sə-tī′ə-tē) *n.* **1.** The condition of being full to satisfaction, as with food. **2.** The condition of being gratified beyond the point of satisfaction; surfeit. [Old French *satiete*, from Latin *satietās*, sufficiency, from *satis*, sufficient, enough. See **sā-** in Appendix.*]

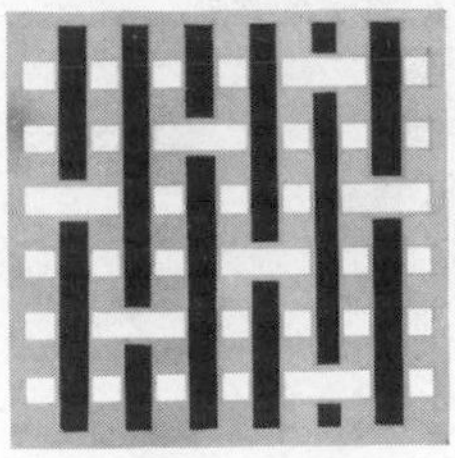

satin weave

sat·in (săt′n) *n.* A smooth silk, cotton, rayon, or nylon fabric woven with a glossy face and a dull back. —*adj.* Made of or resembling satin. [Middle English, from Old French, probably from Spanish *acetuni*, probably from Arabic *zaytūnī*, of Zaytun, from *Zaytūn*, Arabic form of Chinese *Tseutung*, former name of *Tsinkiang*, city in southern China, where it was probably first exported.]

sat·i·net (săt′n-ĕt′) *n.* Also **sat·i·nette**. A thin satin or an imitation satin, such as a blend of cotton and silk or cotton and wool. [French, from Old French, diminutive of SATIN.]

sat·in·flow·er (săt′n-flou′ər) *n.* A plant, *Godetia grandiflora*, of California, having showy red-blotched flowers.

sat·in·pod (săt′n-pŏd′) *n.* A plant, **honesty** *(see)*.

satin stitch. An embroidery stitch worked in close parallel lines to give a solid satin finish.

satin weave. A basic weave construction with the interlacing of the threads so arranged that the face of the cloth is covered with warp yarn or filling yarn and no twill line is distinguishable.

sat·in·wood (săt′n-wo͝od′) *n.* **1. a.** A tree, *Chloroxylon swietenia*, of southern Asia, having hard, yellowish, close-grained wood. **b.** The wood of this tree, used in cabinetwork. **2. a.** Any of several other trees having similar wood. **b.** The wood of any of these trees.

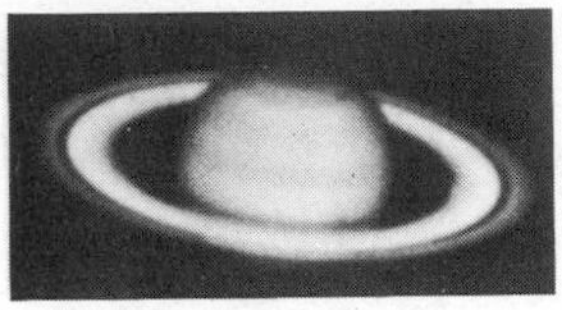

Saturn[2]

sat·in·y (săt′n-ē) *adj.* Lustrous and smooth like satin.

sat·ire (săt′īr) *n.* **1.** A literary work in which irony, derision, or wit in any form is used to expose folly or wickedness. **2.** The branch of literature comprising such works. **3.** The use of derisive wit in any context to attack folly or wickedness. —See Synonyms at **caricature**. [Old French, from Latin *satira*, *satura*, satire, medley, mixture, mixed fruits, from the feminine of *satur*, full of food, sated. See **sā-** in Appendix.*]

sa·tir·i·cal (sə-tîr′ĭ-kəl) *adj.* Also **sa·tir·ic** (-tîr′ĭk). Based on, characteristic of, or inclined to the use of satire. See Synonyms at **sarcastic**. —**sa·tir′i·cal·ly** *adv.* —**sa·tir′i·cal·ness** *n.*

sat·i·rist (săt′ə-rĭst) *n.* A writer of satirical works.

sat·i·rize (săt′ə-rīz′) *tr.v.* **-rized, -rizing, -rizes.** To ridicule or attack by means of satire.

sat·is·fac·tion (săt′ĭs-făk′shən) *n.* **1.** The fulfillment or gratification of a desire, need, or appetite. **2.** Pleasure derived from the gratification of a desire or appetite. **3.** Reparation in the form of penance for sin; atonement. **4.** Compensation for injury or loss; amends. **5.** A source of gratification.

sat·is·fac·to·ry (săt′ĭs-făk′tə-rē) *adj.* **1.** Giving satisfaction; sufficient to meet a demand or requirement; adequate. **2.** Warranting some pleasure; gratifying. —**sat′is·fac′to·ri·ly** *adv.* —**sat′is·fac′to·ri·ness** *n.*

sat·is·fy (săt′ĭs-fī′) *v.* **-fied, -fying, -fies.** —*tr.* **1.** To gratify the need, desire, or expectation of. **2.** To fulfill (a need or desire). **3.** To relieve of doubt or question; assure. **4.** To suffice to dispel (a doubt or question). **5.** To fulfill or discharge (an obligation, contract, or debt). **6.** To discharge an obligation to (a creditor). **7.** To conform to the requirements of (a standard or rule, for example). **8.** To make reparation for; redress (a wrong). —*intr.* To give satisfaction. [Middle English *satisfien*, from Old French *satisfier*, from Latin *satisfacere* : *satis*, sufficient, enough (see **sā-** in Appendix*) + *facere*, to do, make (see **dhē-**[1] in Appendix*).] —**sat′is·fi′er** *n.* —**sat′is·fy′ing·ly** *adv.*

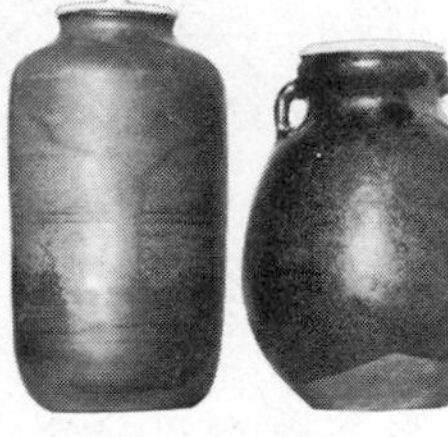

Satsuma ware

Sa·to (sä′tō), **Eisaku.** Born 1901. Japanese statesman; premier (since 1964).

sa·to·ri (sä-tôr′ē) *n.* A state of spiritual enlightenment sought in Zen Buddhism. [Japanese, "insight."]

Sat·pu·ra Range (săt′po͞o-rə). A series of hills in central India, extending about 600 miles along the northern edge of the Deccan Plateau. Highest elevation, 4,429 feet.

sa·trap (sā′trăp, săt′răp) *n.* **1.** A governor of a province in ancient Persia. **2.** Any subordinate ruler. [Middle English *satrape*, from Old French, from Latin *satrapēs*, from Greek, from Old Persian *khshathrapāvan*, "protector of the country" : *khshathra-*, province, country (see **ksei-**[2] in Appendix*) + *-pāvan*, protector (see **pōi-**[2] in Appendix*).]

sa·trap·y (sā′trə-pē, săt′rə-) *n.*, *pl.* **-ies.** The territory or sphere under the rule of a satrap. [French *satrapie*, from Latin *satrapia*, from Greek *satrapeia*, from *satrapēs*, SATRAP.]

Sa·tsu·ma (sä-tso͞o′mä). A former feudal province of southern Kyushu, Japan.

Sa·tsu·ma ware (săt-so͞o′mə). A yellow porcelain ware originally made at Satsuma, Japan.

Sat·ta·hip (sä′tə-hēp′). A former fishing village, site of a seaport development in southeastern Thailand, on the Gulf of Siam. Population, 23,000.

Sa·tu-Ma·re (sä′to͞o-mä′rĕ). *Hungarian* **Szat·már-Né·me·ti** (sôt′-mär-nā′mĕ-tē). A city of Rumania in the northwest near the Hungarian border; part of Hungary (1940–45). Population, 64,000.

sat·u·rant (săch′ər-ənt) *adj.* Serving to saturate; impregnating. —*n.* A substance used to saturate. [Latin *saturāns*, present participle of *saturāre*, SATURATE.]

sat·u·rate (săch′ə-rāt′) *tr.v.* **-rated, -rating, -rates.** **1.** To cloy with an excess; to surfeit; sate. **2.** To soak, imbue, or impregnate thoroughly: *"The recollection was saturated with sunshine"* (Vladimir Nabokov). **3.** To fill to capacity or beyond. **4.** *Chemistry.* **a.** To cause (a solution) to be saturated. **b.** To cause (a compound) to be saturated. [Latin *saturāre*, to fill, satiate, from *satur*, full of food, sated. See **sā-** in Appendix.*] —**sat′u·ra·ble** (săch′ər-ə-bəl) *adj.* —**sat′u·ra′tor** (-rā′tər) *n.*

sat·u·rat·ed (săch′ə-rā′tĭd) *adj.* **1.** Unable to hold or contain more of a substance; full. **2.** Soaked with moisture; drenched. **3.** *Chemistry.* **a.** Containing all the solute that can normally be dissolved at a given temperature. Said of solutions. **b.** Having all available valence bonds filled. Said especially of organic compounds. **4.** *Geology.* Of or pertaining to minerals that can crystallize from magmas even in the presence of excess silica. **5.** In a state of saturation. Said of colors.

sat·u·ra·tion (săch′ə-rā′shən) *n.* **1. a.** The act or process of saturating. **b.** The condition of being saturated. **2.** *Physics.* A state of a ferromagnetic substance in which an increase in applied magnetic field strength does not produce an increase in magnetic intensity. **3.** *Chemistry.* The state of a compound or solution that is fully saturated. **4.** *Meteorology.* A condition in which air at a specific temperature contains all the moisture vapor possible without precipitating; 100 per cent relative humidity. **5.** *Color Technology.* Vividness of hue; degree of difference from a gray of the same lightness or brightness. See **color**. **6.** *Military.* The striking of a target with so many missiles that it is totally destroyed. **7.** The flooding of a market with all of a commodity that its consumers can possibly purchase.

Sat·ur·day (săt′ər-dē, -dā′) *n.* *Abbr.* **Sat.** The seventh day of the week. [Middle English *Saterday*, Old English *Sæterdæg*, short for *sæternesdæg*, "Saturn's day" : *Sætern*, *Saturnus*, SATURN + *dæg*, DAY.]

Sat·urn[1] (săt′ərn). An Italic and Roman deity identified with the Greek god Cronus. —**reign of Saturn.** The golden age. [Middle English *Saturnus*, *Satourn*, Old English *Saturnus*, from Latin *Sāturnus*, Saturn (the god), Saturn (the planet), probably of Etruscan origin.]

Sat·urn[2] (săt′ərn) *n.* The sixth planet from the sun and the second-largest in the solar system, having a diameter of 74,000 miles, a mass 95 times that of Earth, and an orbital period of 29.5 years at a mean distance of about 886,000,000 miles. It has nine satellites and is encircled by a system of rings composed of many small solid bodies. See **solar system**.

sat·ur·na·li·a (săt′ər-nā′lē-ə) *pl.n.* Usually used with a singular verb. Any occasion or period of unrestrained or orgiastic revelry and licentiousness. [Latin *sāturnālia*, from the neuter plural of *Sāturnālis*, of Saturn, from *Sāturnus*, SATURN (from the festival of Saturn in ancient Rome, which was celebrated with feasting and revelry).]

Sa·tur·ni·an (sə-tûr′nē-ən) *adj.* **1.** Of or pertaining to the planet Saturn or to its supposed astrological influence. **2.** Of or pertaining to the god Saturn or his reign.

sa·tur·ni·id (sə-tûr′nē-ĭd) *n.* Any of various often large and colorful moths of the family Saturniidae. —*adj.* Of or belonging to the Saturniidae. [New Latin *Saturniidae*, from *Saturnia* (type genus), from Latin *Sāturnia*, daughter of Saturn, from the feminine of *Sāturnius*, of Saturn, from *Sāturnus*, SATURN.]

sat·ur·nine (săt′ər-nīn′) *adj.* **1.** Having the temperament of one born under the supposed astrological influence of Saturn; gloomy; taciturn. **2.** Pertaining to or resembling lead or produced by the absorption of lead. —See Synonyms at **glum**.

sat·urn·ism (săt′ər-nĭz′əm) *n.* *Pathology.* **Lead poisoning** *(see)*. [From Middle English *saturne*, from Medieval Latin *sāturnus*, lead, from Latin *Sāturnus*, SATURN (the planet, astrologically associated with lead).]

Sat·ya·gra·ha (sŭt′yə-grŭ′hə) *n.* The policy of nonviolent resistance initiated in India by Mahatma Gandhi as a means of pressing for political reform. [Sanskrit *satyāgraha*, "insistence on truth" : *satya*, truth, reality, from *sat*, *sant*, existing, true (see **es-** in Appendix*) + *āgraha*, the act of holding firmly to, insistence : *ā*, to + *gṛbhṇāti*, he seizes (see **ghrebh-**[1] in Appendix*).]

sat·yr (săt′ər, sā′tər) *n.* **1.** *Greek Mythology.* One of a category of anthropomorphic woodland gods or demons often having the pointed ears, legs, and short horns of a goat. **2.** A lecher. **3.** A man afflicted with satyriasis. **4.** Any of various butterflies of the family Satyridae, having brown wings marked with eyelike spots. [Middle English, from Latin *satyrus*, from Greek *saturos*†.] —**sa·tyr′ic** (sə-tîr′ĭk), **sa·tyr′i·cal** *adj.*

sat·y·ri·a·sis (săt′ə-rī′ə-sĭs) *n.* An excessive and often uncontrollable sexual desire in men. [Late Latin, from Greek *saturiasis* : *saturos*, SATYR + -IASIS.]

sauce (sôs) *n.* **1.** Any flavorful soft or liquid dressing or relish served as an accompaniment to food. **2.** Stewed or puréed sweetened fruit, often served with other foods. **3.** *Regional.* Vegetables; greens. **4.** Anything that adds zest, flavor, or piquancy to something. **5.** *Informal.* Impudence; sauciness. **6.** *Slang.* Alcoholic liquor. —*tr.v.* **sauced, saucing, sauces.** **1.** To season or flavor with sauce. **2.** To add piquancy or zest to. **3.** *Informal.* To be impertinent or impudent to. [Middle English, from Old French, from Latin *salsa*, feminine of *salsus*, salted, from the past participle of *sallere*, to salt, from *sāl*, salt. See **sal-**[1] in Appendix.*]

sauce bé·ar·naise (bā-är-nāz′). A sauce similar to hollandaise but flavored with tarragon, shallots, and chervil. Also called "béarnaise sauce." [From French *béarnaise*, feminine of *béarnais*, of Béarn, region in southwestern France.]

sauce bor·de·laise (bôr-də-lĕz′). A brown sauce highly flavored with Bordeaux wine. Also called "bordelaise sauce." [From French *Bordelaise*, feminine of *Bordelais*, of Bordeaux, from BORDEAUX.]

sauce·box (sôs′bŏks′) *n.* *Informal.* An impertinent child.

sauce·pan (sôs′păn′) *n.* A long-handled cooking pan.

sau·cer (sô′sər) *n.* **1.** A small, shallow dish having a slight circular depression in the center for holding a cup. **2.** Any dish or other object having a similar shape. [Middle English, sauce dish, from Old French *saussier,* from *sausse, sauce,* SAUCE.]

sau·cy (sô′sē) *adj.* **-cier, -ciest. 1.** Impertinent or disrespectful; impudent. **2.** Piquant; pert. —**sau′ci·ly** *adv.* —**sau′ci·ness** *n.*

Sa·ud (sä-ōōd′), **Abdul Aziz ibn**[1]. 1880–1953. King of Saudi Arabia (1932–53); succeeded by his son Abdul Aziz.

Sa·ud (sä-ōōd′), **Abdul Aziz ibn**[2]. 1901?–1969. King of Saudi Arabia (1953–64); deposed by his half brother, Faisal.

Sa·u·di A·ra·bi·a (sä-ōō′dē ə-rā′bē-ə). A kingdom occupying some 800,000 square miles on the Arabian peninsula. Population, 6,000,000. Capitals, Riyadh and Mecca.

sauer·bra·ten (sour′brät′n; *German* zou′ər-brät′n) *n.* A pot roast of beef marinated in vinegar, water, wine, and spices before being cooked. [German *Sauerbraten* : *sauer,* sour, from Old High German *sūr* (see **sūro-** in Appendix*) + *Braten,* roast meat, from Middle High German, variant (influenced by *braten,* to roast), of *brāte,* soft edible meat, from Old High German *brāto* (see **bhreu-**[2] in Appendix*).]

sauer·kraut (sour′krout′) *n.* Also **sour·crout.** Chopped or shredded cabbage that is salted and fermented in its own juice. [German *Sauerkraut* : *sauer,* sour, from Old High German *sūr* (see **sūro-** in Appendix*) + *Kraut,* cabbage, from Old High German *krūt,* from Germanic *krūda-* (unattested).]

sau·ger (sô′gər) *n.* A small North American freshwater fish, *Stizostidion canadense,* having a spotted, spiny dorsal fin. [Origin obscure.]

Sauk (sôk) *n., pl.* **Sauk** or **Sauks.** Also **Sac** (sôk, säk). **1.** A tribe of Algonquian-speaking North American Indians living originally in Michigan, Wisconsin, and Illinois and now settled in Iowa and Oklahoma. **2.** A member of this tribe. **3.** The language of this tribe. [French, from earlier *Saki,* short for Ojibwa-Algonquian *osākī,* "person of the river mouth," from *sākī,* "river mouth," from Proto-Algonquian *sāk-* (unattested), to come out.]

Saul (sôl). First king of Israel during the 11th century B.C.; proclaimed by Samuel; succeeded by David.

Saul of Tarsus. See Saint **Paul.**

Sault Sainte Ma·rie Canals (sōō′ sānt′ mə-rē′). One Canadian and two U.S. canals by-passing the rapids of the St. Marys River and providing ship passage between Lake Huron and Lake Superior. Also called "Soo Canals."

sau·na (sou′nə) *n.* **1.** A steam-bath treatment originating in Finland, in which the bather is subjected to steam produced usually by running water over heated rocks. **2.** A room for taking this treatment. [Finnish.]

saun·ter (sôn′tər) *intr.v.* **-tered, -tering, -ters.** To walk at a leisurely pace; to stroll. —*n.* A leisurely pace; stroll. [Probably Middle English *santeren*†, to muse.]

–saur, –saurus. Indicates lizard; for example, **brontosaur, plesiosaurus.** [From New Latin *saurus,* lizard. See **saurel.**]

sau·rel (sôr′əl) *n.* **1.** A marine fish, *Trachurus trachurus,* of eastern Atlantic waters. **2.** A related fish, the **jack mackerel** *(see).* [French, from New Latin *saurus,* horse mackerel, lizard, from Greek *sauros*†.]

sau·ri·an (sôr′ē-ən) *n.* Any of various reptiles of the suborder Sauria, which includes the true lizards. —*adj.* Of, belonging to, or characteristic of the Sauria; lizardlike. [From New Latin *Sauria,* from *saurus,* lizard. See **saurel.**]

sau·ro·pod (sôr′ə-pŏd′) *n.* Any of various large semiaquatic dinosaurs of the suborder Sauropoda, of the Jurassic and Cretaceous periods. —*adj.* Of or belonging to the Sauropoda. [New Latin *Sauropoda* : *saurus,* a lizard (see **saurel**) + -POD.] —**sau·rop′o·dous** (sô-rŏp′ə-dəs) *adj.*

–saurus. Variant of **-saur.**

sau·ry (sôr′ē) *n., pl.* **-ries.** Any of several offshore marine fishes of the family Scomberesocidae, related to the needlefishes. [From New Latin *saurus,* saury, lizard. See **saurel.**]

sau·sage (sô′sĭj) *n.* **1.** Finely chopped and seasoned meat, especially pork, usually stuffed into a prepared animal intestine or other casing and cooked or cured. **2.** An observation balloon. [Middle English *sausige,* from Old North French *saussiche,* from Late Latin *salsīcia,* from *salsīcius,* prepared by salting, from Latin *salsus,* salted. See **sauce.**]

Saus·sure (sō-sür′), **Ferdinand de.** 1857–1913. Swiss linguist.

sau·té (sō-tā′, sô-) *tr.v.* **-téed, -téing, -tés.** To fry lightly in fat in a shallow, open pan. —*n.* Sautéed food. [French, "tossed (in a pan)," from the past participle of *sauter,* to leap, from Old French, from Latin *saltāre,* frequentative of *salīre* (past participle *saltus*), to leap. See **sel-**[4] in Appendix.*]

sau·terne, sau·ternes (sō-tûrn′, sô-; *French* sō-tĕrn′) *n.* A delicate, sweet white dessert wine. [French, made in *Sauternes,* commune in southwestern France.]

Sa·va (sä′vä). A river of Yugoslavia, rising near the Italian border in the northwest and flowing about 580 miles east to the Danube near Belgrade.

sav·age (săv′ĭj) *adj.* **1.** Untouched by man and civilization; not domesticated or cultivated; wild. **2.** Not civilized; primitive; barbaric. **3.** Ferocious; fierce. **4.** Vicious or merciless; brutal. **5.** Lacking polish or manners; rude. —*n.* **1.** A primitive or uncivilized person. **2.** A brutal, fierce, or vicious person. **3.** A rude person; a boor. —*tr.v.* **savaged, -aging, -ages. 1.** To attack violently. **2.** To make angry or fierce. **3.** To bite or trample ferociously. [Middle English *sauvage,* from Old French, from Common Romance *salvāticus* (unattested), from Latin *silvāticus,* of the woods, wild, from *silva,* woods, forest. See **sylvan.**] —**sav′age·ly** *adv.* —**sav′age·ness** *n.*

Savage Island. See **Niue.**

sav·age·ry (săv′ĭj-rē) *n., pl.* **-ries. 1.** The condition of being savage; barbarism. **2.** Savage action, behavior, or nature; barbarity.

Sav·age's Station (săv′ĭ-jəz). The site of one of the Seven Days' Battles (June 29, 1862), near Richmond, Virginia.

Sa·vai·i (sä-vī′ē). The largest (703 square miles) island of Samoa, part of Western Samoa.

sa·van·na (sə-văn′ə) *n.* Also **sa·van·nah.** A flat, treeless grassland of tropical or subtropical regions. [Earlier *zavana,* from Spanish, from Taino *zabana.*]

Sa·van·nah (sə-văn′ə). A seaport and the oldest city of Georgia, at the mouth of the Savannah River. Population, 149,000.

Sa·van·nah River (sə-văn′ə). A river flowing 314 miles southeast from northwestern South Carolina to the Atlantic, forming most of the Georgia-South Carolina border.

sa·vant (sə-vänt′, săv′ənt; *French* sȧ-väɴ′) *n.* A learned scholar; a wise man. [French, from the present participle of *savoir,* to know, from Vulgar Latin *sapēre* (unattested), from Latin *sapere,* to be sensible, be wise. See **sap-** in Appendix.*]

save[1] (sāv) *v.* **saved, saving, saves.** —*tr.* **1.** To rescue from harm, danger, or loss; bring to a safe condition. **2.** To keep in a safe, intact condition; safeguard. **3.** To prevent or reduce the waste, loss, or expenditure of. **4.** To keep for future use or enjoyment; store. Often used with *up.* **5.** To treat with care in order to avoid fatigue, wear, or damage; to spare. **6.** To make unnecessary; obviate: *This will save you an extra trip.* **7.** *Theology.* To deliver from sin or the wages of sin; redeem. —*intr.* **1.** To avoid wasting, losing, or spending something, especially habitually; be economical. **2.** To accumulate money or goods. **3.** To preserve a person or thing from harm or loss. **4.** To admit of preservation; keep, as certain foods. [Middle English *saven, salven,* from Old French *sauver, salver,* from Late Latin *salvāre,* from Latin *salvus,* safe. See **sol-** in Appendix.*] —**sav′a·ble, save′a·ble** *adj.* —**sav′a·ble·ness** *n.* —**sav′er** *n.*

Synonyms: *save, rescue, reclaim, redeem, deliver.* These verbs are compared in the sense of freeing a person or thing from danger, evil, confinement, or servitude. *Save,* the most general, applies to any act of preserving from the consequences of danger or evil, including sin. *Rescue* usually implies saving from immediate harm or danger by direct action. *Reclaim,* applied to persons, usually means to restore to an earlier state of moral and physical soundness or to reform after a lapse; it can also mean to return or convert a thing to usefulness or productivity. *Redeem* refers to freeing from captivity, pawn, or the consequences of sin, error, or misuse, in every case by the expenditure of money or effort. *Deliver* applies chiefly to freeing persons from confinement, restraint, or evil.

save[2] (sāv) *prep.* With the exception of; except; but: *"No man enjoys self-reproach save a masochist."* (Philip Wylie). —*conj.* **1.** Were it not; except; but. Usually used with *that.* **2.** *Archaic.* Unless. [Middle English *save, sa(u)f,* from Old French *sa(u)f, salf,* from Latin *salvō,* without injury or prejudice to, except, ablative singular of *salvus,* safe, sound, healthy. See **sol-** in Appendix.*]

save-all (sāv′ôl′) *n.* **1.** Any device or contrivance that prevents the waste, damage, or loss of something, or that catches the waste products of a process for further use in manufacture. **2.** *Regional.* Overalls or a pinafore.

sav·e·loy (săv′ə-loi′) *n.* A highly seasoned smoked pork sausage. [Variant of obsolete French *cervelat,* from Italian *cervellato,* from *cervello,* brain (the sausage is sometimes made from the brain of pigs), from Latin *cerebellum,* diminutive of *cerebrum,* brain. See **ker-**[1] in Appendix.*]

sav·in, sav·ine (săv′ĭn) *n.* **1.** An evergreen Eurasian shrub, *Juniperus sabina,* the young shoots of which yield an oil formerly used medicinally. **2.** Any of several related shrubs or trees. [Middle English *savin,* from Old English *safīne* and Old French *savine,* both from Latin *(herba) Sabīna,* "Sabine (plant)," from *Sabīnus,* SABINE.]

sav·ing (sā′vĭng) *adj.* **1.** Serving to save; preserving or rescuing. **2.** Redeeming; compensating: *saving graces.* **3.** Careful about expenditures; economical; thrifty. **4.** Making or containing a reservation; excepting; qualifying: *a saving clause.* —*n.* **1.** Preservation or rescue from harm, danger, or loss. **2.** Avoidance of excess expenditure; economy. **3.** A reduction in expenditure or cost: *a saving of six per cent.* **4.** *Plural. Abbr.* **svgs.** Sums of money saved. See Usage note below. **5.** Anything that is saved. **6.** *Law.* An exception or reservation. —*prep.* With the exception of. —*conj.* Except; save.

Usage: *Savings* (plural noun) is not preceded by the singular *a,* except loosely: *The price represents a savings* (properly *saving*) *of ten dollars.* In the foregoing, considered as an example in writing, *savings* is unacceptable to 89 per cent of the Usage Panel.

savings account. An account that draws interest at a bank.

savings bank. 1. A bank that receives and invests the savings of private depositors and pays interest on the deposits. **2.** A receptacle for saving coins; a coin bank.

savings bond. A nontransferable registered bond issued by the U.S. Government in denominations of $25 to $1,000.

sav·ior (sāv′yər) *n.* Also *chiefly British* **sav·iour** (common U.S. for sense 2). **1.** A person who rescues someone or something from dire circumstances. **2.** *Capital* **S.** Christ. Usually preceded by *the.* [Middle English *saviour, sauveur,* from Old French *sauveour,* from Late Latin *salvātor,* from *salvāre,* to SAVE.]

sa·voir-faire (sȧ-vwär-fâr′) *n. French.* The ability to say and do the right thing in any situation; courteous adroitness; tact. See Synonyms at **tact.**

Sav·o·na·ro·la (săv′ə-nə-rō′lə; *Italian* sä′vō-nä-rō′lä), **Girolamo.** 1452–1498. Italian Dominican monk; religious, politi-

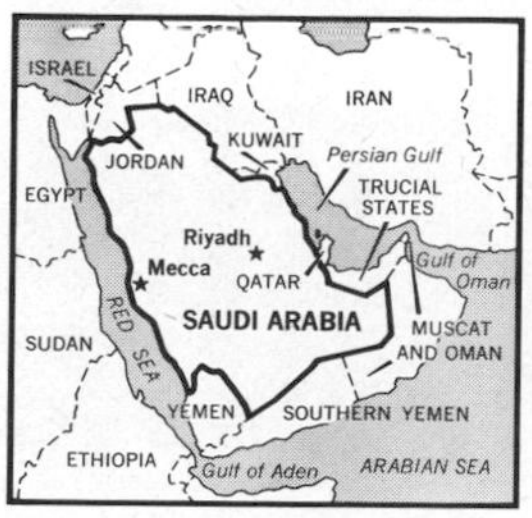

Saudi Arabia

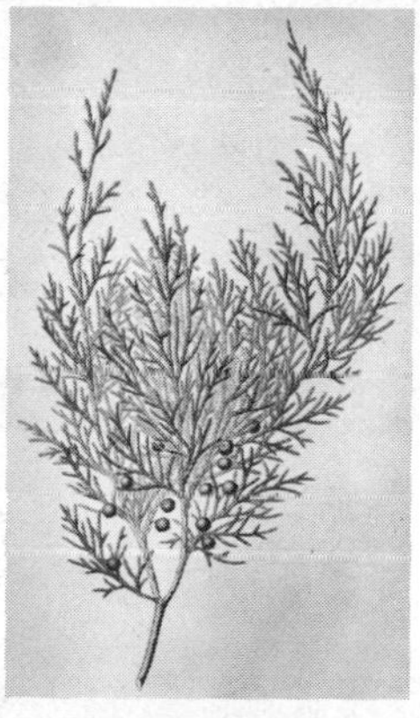
savin
Juniperus sabina

cal, and social reformer; excommunicated and burned as a heretic.

sa·vor (sā'vər) *n.* Also *chiefly British* **sa·vour.** **1.** The quality of a thing which affects the sense of taste or smell; taste or aroma. **2.** A specific taste or smell. **3.** A distinctive or typical quality. **4.** Power or quality of exciting interest; zestfulness. —See Synonyms at **smell.** —*v.* **savored, -voring, -vors.** Also *chiefly British* **sa·vour.** —*intr.* **1.** To have a particular savor. Used with *of: The kitchen savored of fresh bread.* **2.** To exhibit a specified quality or characteristic. Used with *of: "it savours much more of vanity or insolence to publish a book for any other end"* (Locke). —*tr.* **1.** To impart a flavor or scent to. **2.** To taste or enjoy with zest; to relish. **3.** To have or show the savor of. [Middle English *savour,* from Old French, from Latin *sapor,* taste, savor, from *sapere,* to taste, to savor. See **sap-** in Appendix.*] —**sa'vor·er** *n.* —**sa'vor·ous** *adj.*

sa·vor·y¹ (sā'vər-ē) *adj.* Also *chiefly British* **sa·vour·y.** **1.** Appetizing to the taste or smell. **2.** Piquant, pungent, or salty to the taste; not sweet. **3.** Morally respectable; inoffensive. —*n., pl.* **savories.** Also *chiefly British* **sa·vour·y.** A savory dish such as anchovies on toast sometimes served in Britain as an hors d'oeuvre or instead of a dessert. [Middle English *savory, savure,* from Old French *savoure,* from the past participle of *savourer,* to savor, from Late Latin *sapōrāre,* from Latin *sapor,* SAVOR.] —**sa'vor·i·ly** *adv.* —**sa'vor·i·ness** *n.*

sa·vor·y² (sā'vər-ē) *n., pl.* **-ies.** **1.** Either of two aromatic herbs, *Satureja hortensis* or *S. montana,* native to the Old World. The former species is also called "summer savory" and the latter "winter savory." **2.** The leaves of either of these plants, used as seasoning. [Middle English *saverey,* variant (perhaps influenced by SAVORY, pungent) of Old English *sætherie,* from Latin *saturēia†.*]

Sa·voy (sə-voi'). A region of France, in the southeast, bordering on Switzerland and Italy; a duchy in the Middle Ages and later part of the Kingdom of Sardinia (1720–1860).

Sa·voy Alps (sə-voi'). A section of the Alps in southeastern France. Highest elevation, Mont Blanc (15,781 feet).

Sa·voy·ard (sə-voi'ərd; *French* sà-vwà-yàr') *n.* **1.** A native or inhabitant of Savoy. **2.** A southeastern dialect of French. **3.** Any performer in or enthusiastic admirer of Gilbert and Sullivan operas, most of which were first staged at London's Savoy Theatre. —*adj.* Of or pertaining to Savoy, its inhabitants, or their dialect.

sav·vy (săv'ē) *intr.v.* **-vied, -vying, -vies.** *Slang.* To understand or know; comprehend. —*n. Slang.* Practical understanding or knowledge; common sense. [Corruption of Spanish *sabe (usted),* (you) know, from *saber,* to know, from Latin *sapere,* to be sensible, be wise. See **sap-** in Appendix.*]

saw¹ (sô) *n.* **1.** A portable tool, either hand-operated or power-operated, having a thin metal blade or disk with a sharp-toothed edge, used for cutting wood, metal, or other hard materials. **2.** A powered disk tool lacking teeth, used for cutting metal. **3.** A fixed machine for the operation of a saw or series of saws. —*v.* **sawed, sawed** or **sawn** (sôn), **sawing, saws.** —*tr.* **1.** To cut or divide with or as if with a saw. **2.** To produce or shape with or as if with a saw. **3.** To handle with a sawlike motion; use as one would a saw. —*intr.* **1.** To use a saw. **2.** To cut. Used of a saw itself. **3.** To be cut with a saw: *This board saws evenly.* [Middle English *sawe,* Old English *sagu, sage.* See **sek-** in Appendix.*] —**saw'er** *n.*

saw² (sô) *n.* A familiar saying, especially one worn out through repetition. See Synonyms at **saying.** [Middle English *sawe,* Old English *sagu,* speech, talk. See **sekw-³** in Appendix.*]

saw³. Past tense of **see.**

Sa·watch Range (sə-wŏch'). A section of the Rocky Mountains in central Colorado. Highest elevation, Mount Elbert (14,431 feet).

saw·bones (sô'bōnz') *n. Slang.* A surgeon.

saw·buck (sô'bŭk') *n.* **1.** A sawhorse, especially one having X-shaped legs projecting above the crossbar. **2.** *Slang.* A ten-dollar bill. [Sense 1, translation of Dutch *zaagbok;* sense 2, referring to the Roman numeral X.]

saw·dust (sô'dŭst') *n.* The small particles of wood or other material that fall from an object as a result of sawing.

sawed-off (sôd'ôf', -ŏf') *adj.* **1.** Having one end sawed off: *a sawed-off shotgun.* **2.** *Slang.* Short; runty.

saw·fish (sô'fĭsh') *n., pl.* **sawfish** or **-fishes.** Any of various marine fishes of the genus *Pristis,* related to the rays and skates, and having a bladelike snout with teeth along both sides.

saw·fly (sô'flī') *n., pl.* **-flies.** Any of various destructive insects, chiefly of the family Tenthredinidae, the females of which have sawlike ovipositors used for cutting into plant tissue to deposit their eggs.

saw grass. Any of several grasses or sedges, especially *Cladium jamaicense,* having leaves with minutely toothed margins.

saw·horse (sô'hôrs') *n.* A rack or trestle used to support a piece of wood being sawed; sawbuck.

saw log. A log of a size large enough for sawing into boards.

saw·mill (sô'mĭl') *n.* **1.** A plant where lumber is machine-cut into boards. **2.** A large machine for sawing lumber.

sawn. Alternate past participle of **saw.**

saw palmetto. Any of several low-growing, prickly palms of the genus *Sabal,* of the southeastern United States.

saw set. An instrument used to give set to the teeth of a saw by bending each alternate tooth slightly outward.

saw-toothed (sô'tōōtht') *adj.* Having teeth resembling the teeth of a saw; serrate.

saw-whet owl (sô'hwĕt'). A small brown and white owl, *Aegolius acadicus,* of western North America, having no ear

saxophone

sawfish
Pristis pectinatus

sawhorse

tufts. [The owl's call resembles the sound of filing a saw.]

saw·yer (sô'yər) *n.* **1.** One employed at sawing wood, as in a lumber camp or sawmill. **2.** Any of several longicorn beetles having larvae that bore large holes in living or dead wood. [Middle English *sawier,* from *sawen,* to saw, from *sawe,* a SAW.]

sax (săks) *n. Informal.* A saxophone.

Sax. Saxon; Saxony.

sax·a·tile (săk'sə-tĭl', -tĭl) *adj. Ecology. Rare.* Saxicolous. [Latin *saxātilis,* from *saxum,* rock. See **sek-** in Appendix.*]

Saxe. The French name for **Saxony.**

Saxe-Al·ten·burg (săks'äl'tən-bûrg, -bŏŏrk). A former duchy of central Germany, now in East Germany.

Saxe-Co·burg (săks'kō'bûrg). A former duchy of central Germany, combined with Saxe-Gotha to form Saxe-Coburg-Gotha and divided in 1918 between Bavaria and Thuringia.

Saxe-Mei·ning·en (săks'mī'nĭng-ən). A former duchy of central Germany, now in East Germany.

Saxe-Wei·mar-Ei·se·nach (săks'vī'mär'ī'zə-näκH). A former grand duchy of central Germany, now part of East Germany.

sax·horn (săks'hôrn') *n.* Any of a family of valved brass wind instruments, resembling the bugle and having a full, even tone and wide compass. [Invented (1845) by Adolphe *Sax* (1814-1894), Belgian musical instrument maker.]

sax·ic·o·lous (săk-sĭk'ə-ləs) *adj.* Also **sax·ic·o·line** (-lĭn'). *Ecology.* Growing on or living among rocks. [Latin *saxum,* rock (see **sek-** in Appendix*) + -COLOUS.]

sax·i·frage (săk'sə-frĭj, -frāj') *n.* Any of numerous plants of the genus *Saxifraga,* of temperate regions, having small flowers and leaves often forming a basal rosette. [Middle English, from Old French, from Late Latin *saxifraga (herba),* "rock-breaking (herb)" (because it grows in rock crevices), from Latin *saxifragus,* rock-breaking : *saxum,* rock (see **sek-** in Appendix*) + *frangere* (stem *frag-*), to break (see **bhreg-** in Appendix*).]

Sax·o Gram·mat·i·cus (săk'sō grə-măt'ĭ-kəs). Danish historian of the 13th century; transmitter of the Hamlet legend.

Sax·on (săk'sən) *n. Abbr.* **S., Sax.** **1.** A member of a West Germanic tribal group that inhabited northern Germany and invaded England in the fifth century with the Angles and Jutes. See **Anglo-Saxon.** **2.** An Englishman as distinguished from an Irishman, Welshman, or Scot. **3.** A native or inhabitant of Saxony. **4.** The West Germanic language or dialect spoken by any Saxon people. **5.** The Germanic elements present in Modern English as distinguished from French or Latin elements. —*adj.* **1.** Of or pertaining to the Anglo-Saxons or their language. **2.** Of Anglo-Saxon origin. **3.** Of or pertaining to Saxony, the German Saxons, or their language. [Middle English, from Old French, from Late Latin *Saxō* (akin to Old English *Seaxan,* Saxons), from Germanic. See **sek-** in Appendix.*]

Sax·on·ism (săk'sə-nĭz'əm) *n.* An English word, phrase, or idiom of Anglo-Saxon origin.

sax·o·ny (săk'sə-nē) *n.* Also **Sax·o·ny.** **1.** A high-grade wool fabric, originally made from the wool of sheep raised in Saxony. **2.** A fine soft woolen fabric similar in weave to tweed.

Sax·o·ny (săk'sə-nē). *German* **Sach·sen** (zäk'sən); *French* **Saxe** (säks). *Abbr.* **Sax.** **1.** A former region with undefined boundaries in northwestern Germany. **2.** A former duchy, kingdom, and electorate in central Germany. **3.** A former province of Prussia in central Germany. Capital, Magdeburg. **4.** A former state of the Weimar Republic in east-central Germany. **5.** A former state of East Germany.

sax·o·phone (săk'sə-fōn') *n.* A wind instrument having a single-reed mouthpiece, a usually curved conical metal bore, and finger keys, and made in a variety of sizes. [Invented (1846) by Adolphe *Sax.* See **saxhorn.**] —**sax'o·phon'ist** (-fō'nĭst) *n.*

sax·tu·ba (săks'tōō'bə, -tyōō'bə) *n.* A large bass saxhorn. [SAX(HORN) + TUBA.]

say (sā) *v.* **said** (sĕd), **saying, says** (sĕz). —*tr.* **1.** To utter aloud; pronounce; speak. **2.** To express in words; state; declare. **3.** To state (an opinion, for example) with positive assurance or conviction. **4.** To repeat or recite: *say grace.* **5.** To report or maintain; allege: *"They say that falling in love is wonderful"* (Irving Berlin). **6.** To estimate or suppose; assume: *Let's say that you're right.* —*intr.* To make a statement or express an opinion. —**go without saying.** To be so self-evident as to need no justification or explanation. —**that is to say.** In other words; meaning. —*n.* **1.** A positive assertion or assurance: *We're risking this on your say.* **2.** One's turn or chance to speak. **3.** The right or power to influence a decision; voice; authority: *have one's own say in the matter.* —*adv.* **1.** Approximately: *There were, say, 500 people present.* See Usage note below. **2.** For instance: *a woodwind, say an oboe.* —*interj.* Used to gain the attention of someone. [Say, said (past tense and past participle); Middle English *seggen* (later *sayen*), *saide,* Old English *secgan, sægde,* (ge)*sægd* (past participle). See **sekw-³** in Appendix.*] —**say'er** *n.*

Usage: Say is used adverbially in the following examples to express an estimate or approximation: *a very large shipment, say five carloads* or an assumption, supposition, or hypothetical illustration: *Say he becomes restless.*

SAY Airport code for Salisbury, Rhodesia.

Say (sā), **Thomas.** 1787-1834. American entomologist.

Sa·yan Mountains (sä-yän'). A mountain range of the Soviet Union, partly on the border between Mongolia and Siberia. Highest elevation, Munku Sardyk (11,453 feet).

Say·ers (sā'ərz), **Dorothy L(eigh).** 1893-1957. English writer of detective stories and annotator of Dante.

say·ing (sā'ĭng) *n.* **1. a.** An adage; maxim. **b.** A word of wit or wisdom; mot. **2.** The act or manner of saying something.
Synonyms: saying, maxim, adage, saw, motto, epigram, prov-

erb, aphorism. These nouns denote concise, familiar expressions believed to contain truth or wisdom. *Saying,* the most general, is any such expression that is often repeated. *Maxim* refers particularly to a rule of conduct grounded in practical experience. *Adage* is applicable to a saying the wisdom of which has gained credit through long use. *Saw* usually refers to a saying that is discredited through long repetition. *Motto* is usually a moral maxim that expresses the aims or principles of a person, group, or institution. *Epigram* is a terse, witty expression, often paradoxical or satirical and neatly or brilliantly phrased. *Proverb* refers to an old and unpretentious statement that illustrates something such as a basic truth. *Aphorism,* an expression of a truth or principle, implies depth of content and stylistic distinction. *Aphorisms* and *epigrams* are frequently of known authorship; the other terms of this group more often imply anonymous sources.

say-so (sā′sō) *n., pl.* **-sos.** *Informal.* **1.** An unsupported statement or assurance. **2.** An authoritative assertion; dictum. **3.** A right of final decision; authority.

say·yid (sä′yĭd, sā′ĭd) *n.* Also **say·id.** Lord; sir. Used as a title of respect for an Islamic dignitary. [Arabic, "lord."]

Sb The symbol for the element antimony (Latin *stibium*).

sb. substantive.

S.B. Bachelor of Science.

SBA Small Business Administration.

SbE south by east.

'sblood (zblŭd) *interj. Archaic.* Used as an oath. [Contraction of *God's blood.*]

SbW south by west.

Sc The symbol for the element scandium.

SC 1. Security Council (United Nations). **2.** South Carolina (with Zip Code).

sc. 1. scene. **2.** scilicet. **3.** scruple (weight). **4.** sculpsit.

Sc. Scotch; Scottish.

s.c. *Printing.* small capitals.

S.C. 1. South Carolina. **2.** Supreme Court.

scab (skăb) *n.* **1.** The crustlike exudate that covers a healing wound. **2.** Scabies or mange in domestic animals or livestock. **3. a.** Any of various plant diseases caused by fungi or bacteria and resulting in crustlike spots on fruit, leaves, or roots. **b.** The spots caused by such a disease. **4.** *Informal.* **a.** A worker who refuses membership in a labor union. **b.** An employee who works while others are on strike; a strikebreaker. **c.** A low or contemptible person. *—intr.v.* **scabbed, scabbing, scabs. 1. a.** To form a scab. **b.** To become covered with a scab. **2.** *Informal.* To take a job held by a worker on strike; act as a scab. [Middle English *scabbe,* from Old Norse *skabb.* See **skep-** in Appendix.*]

scab·bard (skăb′ərd) *n.* A sheath or container for a dagger, sword, or other similar arm. *—tr.v.* **scabbarded, -barding, -bards.** To put into or furnish with a sheath. [Middle English *scauberc,* from Norman French *escaubers* (plural) : probably Old High German *scār,* scissors, sword (see **sker-**[1] in Appendix*) + *-berc,* protection, from *bergan,* to protect (see **bhergh-**[1] in Appendix*).]

scabbard fish. Any of several narrow-bodied marine fishes of the family Trichiuridae; especially, *Lepidopus xantusi,* of Pacific waters. [From its narrow, sheathlike body.]

scab·ble (skăb′əl) *tr.v.* **-bled, -bling, -bles.** To work or dress (stone) to any stage prior to that of fine tooling. [Earlier *scapple,* Middle English *scaplen,* from Old French *eschapler,* "to cut off," dress timber : *es-,* from Latin *ex-,* off + *chapler,* to cut, from Late Latin *capulāre* (see **skep-** in Appendix*).]

scab·by (skăb′ē) *adj.* **-bier, -biest. 1.** Having, consisting of, or covered with scabs or something resembling scabs. **2.** Afflicted with scabies. **3.** *Informal.* Low; mean; vile: *a scabby trick.* **—scab′bi·ly** *adv.* **—scab′bi·ness** *n.*

sca·bies (skā′bēz′) *n.* Plural in form, used with a singular verb. **1.** A contagious skin disease caused by a mite, *Sarcoptes scabiei,* and characterized by intense itching. **2.** A similar disease in animals, especially sheep. Also called "seven-year itch." [Latin *scabiēs,* roughness, scurf, itch, from *scabere,* to scratch. See **skep-** in Appendix.*] **—sca′bi·et′ic** (skā′bē-ĕt′ĭk) *adj.*

sca·bi·ous[1] (skā′bē-əs, skăb′ē-əs) *adj.* **1.** Of or pertaining to scabies. **2.** Having scabs. [Latin *scabiōsus,* scabby, from *scabiēs,* SCABIES.]

sca·bi·ous[2] (skā′bē-əs) *n.* Any of various plants of the genus *Scabiosa;* especially, *S. pratensis* or *S. atropurpureus,* having opposite leaves and variously colored flower heads. [Middle English *scabiose,* from Medieval Latin *scabiōsa (herba),* "(herb) for scabies," from Latin, feminine of *scabiōsus,* SCABIOUS.]

scab·rous (skăb′rəs, skā′brəs) *adj.* **1.** Roughened with small projections; rough to the touch; scaly. **2.** Difficult to handle tactfully; knotty. **3.** Indelicate or salacious; off-color: *a scabrous novel.* —See Synonyms at **rough.** [Latin *scabrōsus,* rough, from *scaber,* rough, scurfy. See **skep-** in Appendix.*] **—scab′rous·ly** *adv.* **—scab′rous·ness** *n.*

scad (skăd) *n., pl.* **scad** or **scads.** Any of several marine fishes of the family Carangidae, related to the jacks and pompanos. [Origin unknown.]

scads (skădz) *pl.n. Informal.* A large number or amount: *scads of people.* [Origin obscure.]

Sca·fell Pike (skô′fĕl′). The highest (3,210 feet) of the Cumbrian Mountains and the highest point in England.

scaf·fold (skăf′əld, -ōld′) *n.* **1.** A temporary platform used by workers in the construction, repair, or cleaning of a building. **2.** Any raised wooden framework or platform. **3.** A platform for the execution of condemned prisoners. *—tr.v.* **scaffolded, -folding, -folds. 1.** To provide or support with a scaffold. **2.** To place on a scaffold. [Middle English, from Old North French *escafaut,* variant of Old French *eschafaud* (influenced by *eschace,* tilt), from *chafaud,* scaffold, from Vulgar Latin *catafalicum* (unattested), CATAFALQUE.]

scaf·fold·ing (skăf′əl-dĭng, skăf′ōl′-) *n.* **1.** A scaffold or system of scaffolds. **2.** The materials for scaffolds.

scagl·io·la (skăl-yō′lə) *n.* Plasterwork in imitation of ornamental marble, consisting of ground gypsum and glue colored with marble or granite dust. [Italian, diminutive of *scaglia,* scale, chip, small piece of marble, from Germanic. See **skel-**[1] in Appendix.*]

sca·lade (skə-lād′, -läd′) *n.* Also **sca·la·do** (skə-lā′dō, -lä′dō) *pl.* **-dos.** An **escalade** *(see).* [Italian *scalada,* obsolete spelling of *scalata,* ESCALADE.]

scal·age (skā′lĭj) *n.* **1.** The percentage by which a deduction from listed weights or prices of goods is figured to compensate for loss, as by shrinkage. **2.** The estimated amount of lumber in a log or logs being scaled.

sca·lar (skā′lər) *n.* A quantity, such as mass, length, time, or temperature, completely specified by a number on an appropriate scale. Compare **vector.** [Latin *scālāris,* of a staircase, from *scālae,* stairs, SCALE.] **—sca′lar** *adj.*

sca·la·re (skə-lâr′ē, -lär′ē) *n.* The **angelfish** *(see).* [New Latin, "ladderlike" (from its parallel stripes), from Latin, neuter of *scālāris,* of a staircase, from *scālae,* stairs, SCALE.]

sca·lar·i·form (skə-lăr′ə-fôrm′) *adj.* Ladderlike; having rungs. Said of certain vessels and tissues. [New Latin *scalariformis* : Latin *scālāris,* of a ladder (see **scalar**) + FORM.]

scalar product. The numerical product of the lengths of two vectors and the cosine of the angle between them. Also called "dot product," "inner product." Compare **vector product.**

scal·a·wag (skăl′ə-wăg′) *n.* Also **scal·la·wag, scal·ly·wag** (skăl′ē-wăg′). **1.** *Informal.* A reprobate; rascal. **2.** A white Republican Southerner during Reconstruction. Used disparagingly. Compare **carpetbagger.** [Originally "an undersized, worthless animal," perhaps from *Scalloway,* Shetland, in allusion to its undersized ponies.]

scald[1] (skôld) *v.* **scalded, scalding, scalds.** *—tr.* **1.** To burn with or as if with hot liquid or steam. **2.** To subject to or treat with boiling water; specifically, to sterilize (instruments, for example). **3.** To heat (a liquid) almost to the boiling point. *—intr.* To be or become scalded. *—n.* **1.** The lesion or injury caused by scalding. **2. a.** A superficial discoloration on fruit, vegetables, leaves, or tree trunks caused by sudden exposure to intense sunlight or the action of gases. **b.** A disease of some cereal grasses, caused by a fungus of the genus *Rhynchosporium.* [Middle English *scalden,* from Old North French *escalder,* from Late Latin *excaldāre,* to wash in hot water : Latin *ex-,* to bring into a certain condition + *cal(i)da,* hot water, from the feminine of *calidus,* warm (see **kel-**[1] in Appendix*).]

scald[2]. **1.** Variant of **skald. 2.** Variant of **scall.**

scale[1] (skāl) *n.* **1. a.** A small, platelike dermal or epidermal structure characteristically forming the external covering of fishes, reptiles, and certain mammals. **b.** A similar part, such as one of the minute structures overlapping to form the covering on the wings of butterflies and moths. **2.** *Pathology.* A dry, thin flake of epidermis shed from the skin. **3.** A small, thin piece of anything. **4.** *Botany.* Any of various thin, often overlapping parts, such as one of the protective rudimentary leaves covering the buds of certain trees, or a membranous bract. **5. a.** A scale insect. **b.** A plant disease or infestation caused by scale insects. **6. a.** A flaky oxide film formed on a metal, as on iron, heated to high temperatures. **b.** A flake of rust. **7.** A coating or incrustation formed inside boilers, kettles, and other similar containers after extensive use. *—v.* **scaled, scaling, scales.** *—tr.* **1.** To clear or strip of scale or scales. **2.** To remove in layers or scales. **3.** To cover with scales; cause incrustation to form on. **4.** To throw (a thin, flat object) so that it soars through the air or skips along the surface of a body of water. *—intr.* **1.** To come off in layers or scales; to flake. **2.** To become covered with incrustation. [Middle English, from Old French *escale,* "shell," "husk," from Germanic. See **skel-**[1] in Appendix.*]

scale[2] (skāl) *n.* **1.** A system of ordered marks at fixed intervals used as a reference standard in measurement. **2.** An instrument or device bearing such marks. **3. a.** The proportion used in determining the relationship of a representation to that which it represents. **b.** A calibrated line, as on a map or architectural plan, to indicate such a proportion. **4.** A progressive classification, as of size, amount, importance, or rank. **5.** A relative level or degree: *entertain on a lavish scale.* **6. Wage scale** *(see).* **7.** *Mathematics.* A system of notation in which the value of numbers is determined by their place relative to the fixed constant of the system: *decimal scale.* **8.** *Music.* An ascending or descending series of tones proceeding by a specified scheme of intervals and varying in pitch arrangement and interval size. In this sense, see **chromatic, diatonic.** *—v.* **scaled, scaling, scales.** *—tr.* **1.** To climb up to the top of or over, with or as if with a ladder, rope, or other device. **2.** To draw or reproduce in accordance with a particular proportion or scale. **3.** To adjust according to a proportion; regulate. **4.** To estimate or measure the quantity of lumber in (logs or uncut trees). *—intr.* **1.** To go up; climb; ascend. **2.** To ascend in steps or stages. [Middle English, ladder, graduation, from Late Latin *scāla,* ladder, from Latin *scālae,* stairs. See **skand-** in Appendix.*]

scale[3] (skāl) *n.* **1.** Any instrument or machine for weighing: *a bathroom scale; a truck scale.* **2.** Either of the pans, trays, or dishes of a balance. **—turn** (or **tip**) **the scales.** To determine; decide. *—v.* **scaled, scaling, scales.** *—tr.* **1.** To weigh with scales. **2.** To have a weight of. *—intr.* To have as a weight, as

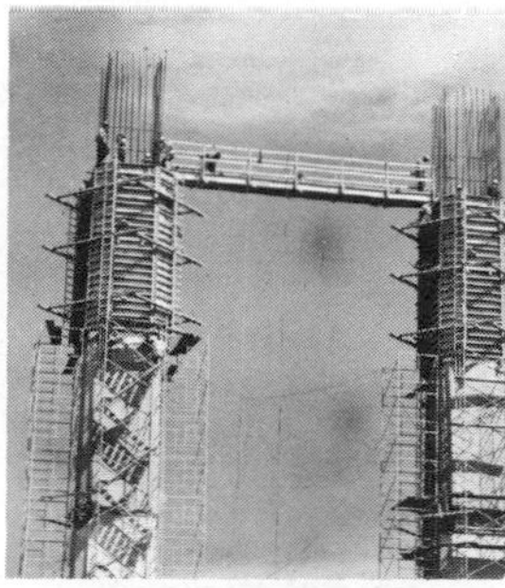

scaffolding
In use in raised highway construction

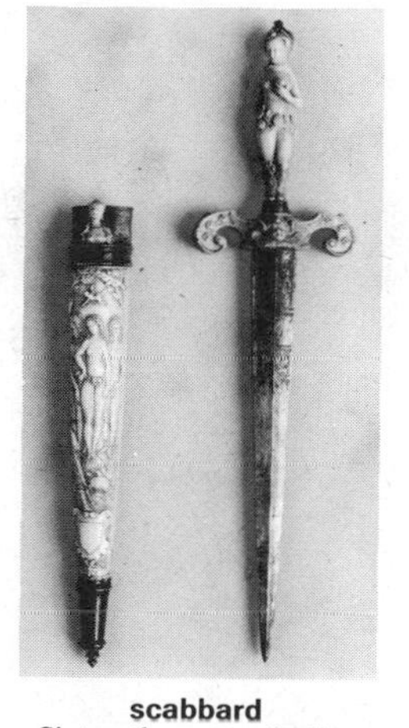

scabbard
Sixteenth-century Italian scabbard and dagger

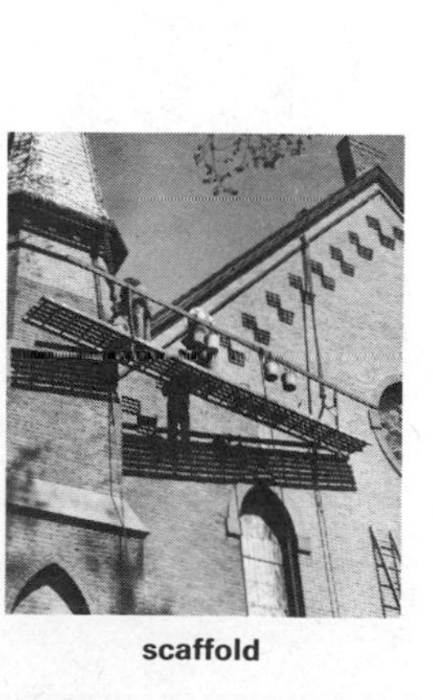

scaffold

t tight/th thin, path/*th* this, bathe/ŭ cut/ûr urge/v valve/w with/y yes/z zebra, size/zh vision/ə about, item, edible, gallop, circus/ à *Fr.* ami/œ *Fr.* feu, *Ger.* schön/ü *Fr.* tu, *Ger.* über/KH *Ger.* ich, *Scot.* loch/N *Fr.* bon. ***Follows main vocabulary. †Of obscure origin.**

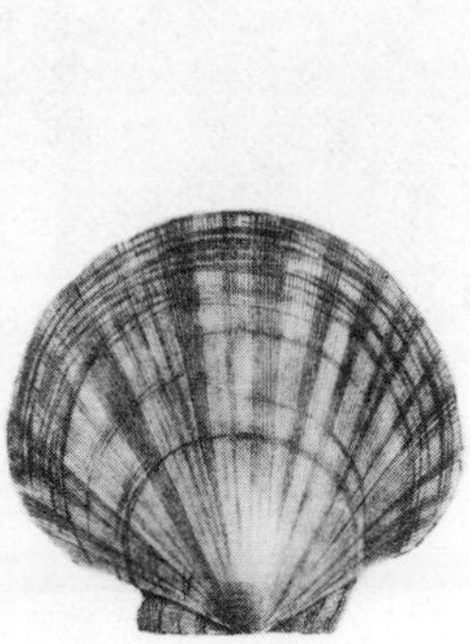

scallop
Pecten grandis

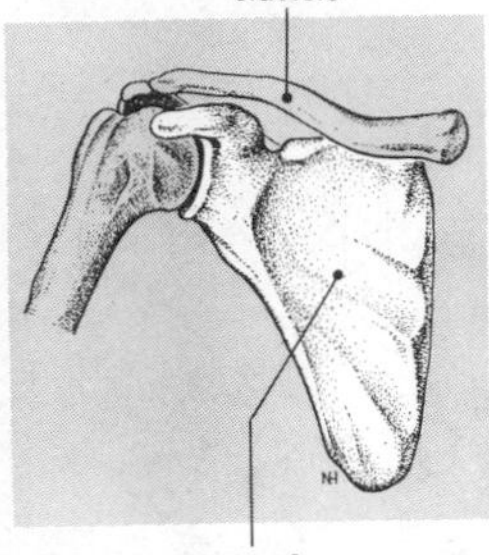

scapula

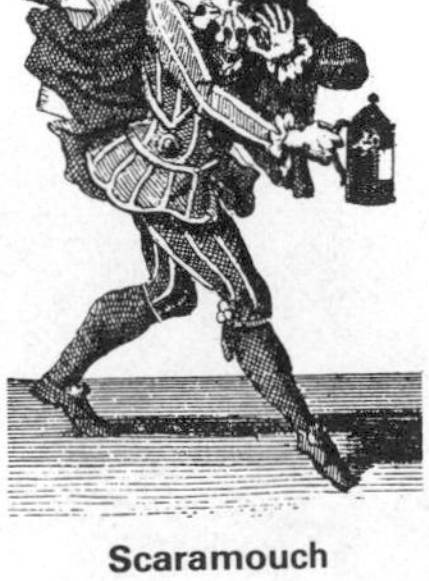

Scaramouch

determined by a scale. [Middle English, from Old Norse *skāl,* bowl, scale of a balance. See **skel-¹** in Appendix.*]

scale insect. Any of various destructive sucking insects of the family Coccidae, the females of which secrete and remain under waxy scales on plant tissue.

scale moss. Any of various leafy liverworts of the order Jungermanniales.

sca·lene (skā′lēn′, skā-lēn′) *adj.* Having three unequal sides. Said of triangles. [Late Latin *scalēnus,* from Greek *skalēnos,* uneven. See **skel-³** in Appendix.*]

scal·er (skā′lər) *n.* An electronic circuit that records the aggregate of a specific number of signals that occur too rapidly to be recorded individually. [From SCALE (to measure).]

Scales (skālz) *pl.n.* The constellation and sign of the zodiac, **Libra** *(see).*

scall (skôl) *n.* Also **scald** (skôld). A scaly eruption of the skin or scalp. [Middle English *scalle,* from Old Norse *skalli,* bald-head. See **skel-¹** in Appendix.*]

scal·la·wag. Variant of **scalawag.**

scal·lion (skăl′yən) *n.* **1.** A young onion before the enlargement of the bulb. **2.** Any of several similar onionlike plants, such as a leek or shallot. [Middle English *scalo(u)n,* from Norman French, from Vulgar Latin *escalōnia* (unattested), from Latin *Ascalōnia (caepa),* "Ascalonian (onion)," from *Ascalō,* Ascalon, port in southern Palestine.]

scal·lop (skŏl′əp, skăl′-) *n.* Also **es·cal·lop** (ĕ-skŏl′əp, ĕ-skăl′-) (for sense 5), **scol·lop** (skŏl′əp). **1.** Any of various free-swimming marine mollusks of the family Pectinidae, having fan-shaped bivalve shells with a radiating fluted pattern. **2.** The edible adductor muscle of a scallop. **3.** A scallop shell, or a similarly shaped dish, used for baking and serving seafood. **4.** Any of a series of variously curved projections forming an ornamental border, as on fabrics or lace. **5.** A thin, boneless slice of meat. —*tr.v.* **scalloped, -loping, -lops.** Also **es·cal·lop** (for sense 2), **scol·lop.** **1.** To design or border (cloth) with scallops. **2.** To bake in a casserole with milk or a sauce and often with bread crumbs. [Middle English *scalop,* from Old French *escalope,* shell, probably from Germanic.] —**scal′lop·er** *n.*

scal·ly·wag. Variant of **scalawag.**

sca·lop·pi·ne (skăl′ə-pē′nē, skä′lə-) *pl.n.* Also **sca·lop·pi·ni.** Small, thinly sliced pieces of veal or other meat, especially when cooked in a sauce of wine or tomatoes and seasonings. [Italian, plural of *scaloppina,* diminutive of *scaloppa,* fillet of meat, from Old French *escalope,* shell (because such fillets are served curled like shells). See **scallop.**]

scalp (skălp) *n.* **1.** *Anatomy.* The skin covering the top of the human head. **2.** This integument with attached hair formerly cut or torn from an enemy as a battle trophy by certain North American Indians. **3.** A piece of hide from the skull of certain animals, such as the fox, shown as proof of killing in order to collect a bounty. **4.** Any trophy of victory. **5.** *Informal.* The profit made by a ticket scalper. —*v.* **scalped, scalping, scalps.** —*tr.* **1.** To cut or tear the scalp from. **2.** To deprive of top growth or of a top layer. **3.** *Informal.* To be victorious over (an opponent), especially in a spectacular manner. **4.** *Informal.* To sell (tickets) at a price higher than the established value. **5.** *Informal.* To buy and sell quickly (stocks or bonds, for example) in order to make many small profits. —*intr. Informal.* To scalp bonds or tickets. [Middle English, probably from Scandinavian, akin to Old Norse *skalpr,* sheath, "shell." See **skel-¹** in Appendix.*] —**scalp′er** *n.*

scal·pel (skăl′pəl, skăl-pĕl′) *n.* A small straight knife with a very thin, sharp, usually removable blade, used in surgery and dissection. [Latin *scalpellum,* diminutive of *scalper,* knife, from *scalpere,* to cut, scratch. See **skel-¹** in Appendix.*]

scalp lock. A long lock of hair left on the shaven head by certain North American Indians as a challenge to an enemy.

scal·y (skā′lē) *adj.* **-ier, -iest. 1.** Covered or partially covered with scales. **2.** Shedding scales or flakes; flaking. **3.** *Slang.* Mean; despicable. —**scal′i·ness** *n.*

scaly anteater. A mammal, the **pangolin** *(see).*

Sca·man·der. The ancient name for the **Menderes.**

scam·mo·ny (skăm′ə-nē) *n., pl.* **-nies. 1.** A plant, *Convolvulus scammonia,* of the eastern Mediterranean region, having large roots formerly used as a cathartic. **2.** A preparation made from the roots of this plant. [Middle English *scamonie,* from Latin *scammōnea,* from Greek *skammōnia*†.]

scamp¹ (skămp) *n.* **1.** A rogue; rascal. **2.** A mischievous or prankish youngster. [Originally "highwayman," "robber," from obsolete *scamp,* to slip away, bolt, probably from Middle Dutch *schampen,* from Old French *escamper,* to SCAMPER.]

scamp² (skămp) *tr.v.* **scamped, scamping, scamps.** To perform in a careless or superficial way. [Probably a blend of SCANT and SKIMP.] —**scamp′er** *n.*

scam·per (skăm′pər) *intr.v.* **-pered, -pering, -pers.** To run or go hurriedly. —*n.* A hasty run or departure. [Flemish *scamperen,* to decamp, from Old French *escamper,* from Vulgar Latin *excampāre* (unattested) : Latin *ex-,* out of, away + *campus,* field (see **camp**).] —**scam′per·er** *n.*

scam·pi (skăm′pē) *pl.n.* Large shrimps, especially as used in Italian cooking. [Italian *scampi*†.]

scan (skăn) *v.* **scanned, scanning, scans.** —*tr.* **1.** To examine (a small area) closely; scrutinize. See Usage note below. **2.** To look (a wide area) over quickly but thoroughly, as from one end to another. See Usage note below. **3.** To analyze (verse) into metrical feet and rhythm patterns. **4.** *Electronics.* **a.** To move a finely focused beam of light or electrons in a systematic pattern over (a surface) in order to reproduce, or sense and subsequently transmit, an image. **b.** To move a radar beam over (a sector of sky) in search of a target. **c.** To search (a series of punched cards or a magnetic tape) automatically for specific data. **5.** To look over or leaf through hastily. See Usage note below. —*intr.* **1.** To analyze verse into metrical feet. **2.** To conform to a metrical pattern. Used of verse. **3.** *Electronics.* To undergo electronic scanning. —See Synonyms at **see.** —*n.* **1.** An act or instance of scanning; a searching look. **2.** A scope or field of vision. [Middle English *scannen,* from Late Latin *scandere,* "to analyze the rising and falling rhythm in verses," from Latin, to climb. See **skand-** in Appendix.*] —**scan′na·ble** *adj.* —**scan′ner** *n.*

Usage: *Scan* (transitive verb) is applicable both to close examination of something and to quick inspection. The context in which it appears must make clear which of these opposing senses is intended if ambiguity is to be prevented. The sense "to look over quickly" is the less formal of the two, but is now well established in American usage; it is acceptable to 85 per cent of the Usage Panel in *to scan the newspapers,* as an example in writing.

Scand. Scandinavia; Scandinavian.

scan·dal (skăn′dəl) *n.* **1.** Any act or set of circumstances that brings about disgrace or offends the morality of the social community; a public disgrace. **2.** The reaction caused by such an act or set of circumstances; outrage; shame. **3.** Any talk damaging to the character; malicious gossip. **4.** Damage to reputation or character caused by offensive or grossly improper behavior; a disgrace. **5.** One whose conduct brings about disgrace or defamation. —See Synonyms at **disgrace.** —*tr.v.* **scandaled** or **-dalled, -daling** or **-dalling, -dals. 1.** *Archaic.* To spread scandal about; defame. **2.** *Obsolete.* To scandalize. **3.** *Obsolete.* To disgrace or dishonor. [French *scandale,* from Late Latin *scandalum,* from Greek *skandalon,* trap, snare, stumbling block. See **skand-** in Appendix.*]

scan·dal·ize (skăn′də-līz′) *tr.v.* **-ized, -izing, -izes. 1.** To shock the propriety or moral sense of. **2.** *Archaic.* To dishonor; disgrace. —**scan′dal·i·za′tion** *n.* —**scan′dal·iz′er** *n.*

scan·dal·ous (skăn′də-ləs) *adj.* **1.** Causing scandal; shocking; offensive. **2.** Containing defamatory or libelous information. —**scan′dal·ous·ly** *adv.* —**scan′dal·ous·ness** *n.*

scandal sheet. A newspaper or other periodical that habitually prints stories of a defamatory, scandalous nature.

scan·dent (skăn′dənt) *adj. Botany.* Climbing: *a scandent vine.* [Latin *scandēns,* present participle of *scandere,* to climb. See **skand-** in Appendix.*]

scan·di·a (skăn′dē-ə) *n. Chemistry.* **Scandium oxide** *(see).* [New Latin, from SCANDIUM.]

Scan·di·an (skăn′dē-ən) *adj.* Scandinavian. [From Latin *Scandia,* variant of *Scandinavia,* SCANDINAVIA.]

Scan·di·na·vi·a (skăn′də-nā′vē-ə, -nāv′yə). *Abbr.* **Scand. 1.** See **Scandinavian Peninsula. 2.** The northwestern European countries of Norway, Sweden, and Denmark. **3.** These countries and Iceland considered as a linguistic and cultural unit. **4.** Broadly, Norway, Sweden, Denmark, Iceland, Finland, and the Faeroe Islands. [Latin, from German *Skandinaujā* (unattested), name of the southernmost part of Sweden. See **akwā-** in Appendix.*]

Scan·di·na·vi·an (skăn′də-nā′vē-ən, -nāv′yən) *adj. Abbr.* **Scand.** Pertaining or relating to Scandinavia, its inhabitants, culture, or languages. —*n. Abbr.* **Scand. 1.** A native or inhabitant of Scandinavia. **2.** The North Germanic languages.

Scandinavian Peninsula. The peninsula in northwestern Europe occupied by Norway and Sweden. Also called "Scandinavia."

scan·di·um (skăn′dē-əm) *n. Symbol* **Sc** A silvery-white, very lightweight metallic element found in various rare minerals and separated as a by-product in the processing of certain uranium ores. An artificially radioactive isotope is used as a tracer in oil-well and pipeline studies. Atomic number 21, atomic weight 44.956, melting point 1,539°C, boiling point 2,727°C, specific gravity 2.992, valence 3. See **element.** [New Latin, from Latin *Scandia,* ancient name for Scandinavia, where it was discovered. See **Scandian.**] —**scan′dic** *adj.*

scandium oxide. A white amorphous powder, Sc_2O_3, used as a source of scandium and in the manufacture of ceramics. Also called "scandia."

scan·ning (skăn′ĭng) *n.* Any of various electronic or optical techniques by which images or recorded information are sensed for subsequent modification, integration, or transmission.

scan·sion (skăn′shən) *n.* The analysis of verse into metrical feet and rhythm patterns. [Late Latin *scansiō,* from Latin, a climbing, from *scandere* (past participle *scansus*), to climb. See **skand-** in Appendix.*]

scan·so·ri·al (skăn-sôr′ē-əl, -sōr′ē-əl) *adj. Zoology.* Adapted to or specialized for climbing. [Latin *scansōrius,* from *scandere* (past participle *scansus*), to climb. See **skand-** in Appendix.*]

scant (skănt) *adj.* **scanter, scantest. 1.** Deficient in quantity or amount; meager; inadequate. **2.** Being just short of a specific measure: *a scant three miles.* **3.** Inadequately supplied. Used with *of: scant of breath.* —See Synonyms at **meager.** —*tr.v.* **scanted, scanting, scants. 1.** To provide with an inadequate portion or allowance; skimp. **2.** To limit, as in amount or share; stint. **3.** To reduce the size or amount of; cut down. **4.** To deal with or treat inadequately or neglectfully. [Middle English, from Old Norse *skamt,* neuter of *skammr,* short. See **kem-¹** in Appendix.*] —**scant′ly** *adv.* —**scant′ness** *n.*

scant·ling (skănt′lĭng, -lĭn) *n.* **1.** A small piece of timber, usually one having a cross section no more than five inches square. **2.** This kind of timber collectively. **3.** The dimensions of building materials such as stone or timber, especially in breadth and thickness. **4.** A small upright piece of timber in the frame of a house; a stud. **5.** *Usually plural. Nautical.* The dimensions of the structural parts of a vessel, as frames, plates, and girders. **6.** A very small amount. [Earlier *scantlon,* Middle English *scantilon,* carpenter's gauge, dimension, from Old French *escantillon, eschandillon,* probably from Vulgar Latin *scandilia* (unattested), measure, scale, from Latin *scandere,* to climb. See **skand-** in Appendix.*]

scant·y (skăn′tē) *adj.* **-ier, -iest. 1.** Barely sufficient or adequate. **2.** Deficient in extent or degree; small; insufficient. —See Synonyms at **meager.** —**scant′i·ly** *adv.* —**scant′i·ness** *n.*

SCAP Supreme Commander for the Allied Powers.

Scap·a Flow (skăp′ə flō′). An anchorage of some 50 square miles in the Orkney Islands, Scotland; a British naval base.

scape¹ (skāp) *n.* **1.** *Botany.* A leafless flower stalk growing directly from the ground. **2.** A similar stalklike part, such as a feather shaft or a segment of an insect's antenna. **3.** *Architecture.* The shaft of a column. [Latin *scāpus*†, stalk.]

scape². *Archaic.* Variant of **escape.**

-scape. Indicates scene or view; for example, **seascape.** [Back-formation from LANDSCAPE.]

scape·goat (skāp′gōt′) *n.* **1.** A live goat over whose head Aaron confessed all the sins of the children of Israel and which was sent into the wilderness symbolically bearing their sin on the Day of Atonement. Leviticus 16. **2.** A person or group bearing blame for others. [(E)SCAPE + GOAT (improper translation of Hebrew *azāzēl,* probably "goat for Azazel, demon of the desert," but misconstrued as *ēz-ōzēl,* "goat that escapes").]

scape·grace (skāp′grās′) *n.* An unprincipled or incorrigible person; reprobate. [(E)SCAPE + GRACE.]

scaph·oid (skăf′oid′) *adj.* Boat-shaped. —*n. Anatomy.* The **navicular** *(see).* [New Latin *scaphoides,* from Greek *skaphoeidēs : skaphē,* tub, boat (see **skep-** in Appendix*) + -OID.]

scap·o·lite (skăp′ə-līt′) *n.* Any of a series of variously colored, often fluorescent mineral silicates of aluminum, calcium, and sodium. Also called "wernerite." [French : Latin *scāpus,* stalk, SCAPE (from its prismatic crystals) + -ITE.]

sca·pose (skā′pōs′) *adj.* Resembling or consisting of a scape.

scap·u·la (skăp′yə-lə) *n., pl.* **-las** or **-lae** (-lē′). *Anatomy.* Either of two large, flat, triangular bones forming the back part of the shoulder. Also called "shoulder blade." [Latin, shoulder blade, shoulder. See **skep-** in Appendix.*]

scap·u·lar (skăp′yə-lər) *n.* Also **scap·u·lar·y** (-lĕr′ē) *pl.* **-ies. 1.** A monk's sleeveless outer garment hanging from the shoulders and sometimes having a cowl. **2.** A badge worn by members of certain religious orders, consisting of two pieces of cloth joined by strings and worn under the clothing about the shoulders. **3.** One of the feathers covering the shoulder of a bird. —*adj. Anatomy.* Of or pertaining to the shoulder or scapula. [Middle English *scapulare,* from Medieval Latin *scapulāre, scapulārium,* "shoulder cloak," from Latin *scapula,* shoulder, SCAPULA.]

scar¹ (skär) *n.* **1.** A mark left on the skin following the healing of a surface injury or wound. **2.** Any sign of damage remaining as evidence of injury or an injurious mental or physical condition. **3.** *Botany.* A mark indicating a former attachment, as of a leaf to a stem. **4.** A mark, dent, or other blemish made by use, motion, or contact. —*v.* **scarred, scarring, scars.** —*tr.* To mark with a scar. —*intr.* To become marked with a scar. [Middle English *(e)scare,* from Old French *esc(h)are,* scab, from Late Latin *eschara,* from Greek *eskhara*†, hearth, scab caused by burning.]

scar² (skär) *n. Scottish* **scaur** (skär, skôr). *Geology.* **1.** A protruding, isolated rock. **2.** A bare, rocky place on a mountain side or some other steep slope. [Middle English *skerre,* from Old Norse *sker,* low reef. See **sker-¹** in Appendix.*]

scar·ab (skăr′əb) *n.* Also **scar·a·bae·us** (skăr′ə-bē′əs) *pl.* **-uses** or **-baei** (-bē′ī′). **1.** Any scarabaeid beetle; especially, *Scarabaeus sacer,* regarded as sacred by the ancient Egyptians. **2.** A representation of a scarab beetle, as a ceramic or stone sculpture, used in ancient Egypt as a talisman and a symbol of the soul. [Old French *scarabee,* from Latin *scarabaeus*†.]

scar·a·bae·id (skăr′ə-bē′ĭd) *n.* Any of the numerous beetles of the family Scarabaeidae, which includes the June bugs and dung beetles. —*adj.* Of or belonging to the Scarabaeidae. [New Latin *Scarabaeidae,* from Latin *scarabaeus,* SCARAB.] —**scar′a·bae′oid′** (-bē′oid′) *adj.*

scar·a·boid (skăr′ə-boid′) *adj.* Resembling or characteristic of a scarabaeid beetle; scarablike.

Scar·a·mouch (skăr′ə-mōōsh′, -mōōch′, -mouch′). A stock character in old Italian comedy and pantomime, depicted as a boastful, cowardly braggart or buffoon. [French *Scaramouche,* from Italian *Scaramuccia,* jocular use of *scaramuccia,* SKIRMISH.]

scarce (skârs) *adj.* **scarcer, scarcest. 1.** Uncommonly or infrequently seen or found. **2.** Insufficient to meet a demand or requirement; not plentiful or abundant. See Usage note at **rare.** —**make oneself scarce.** *Informal.* To get out or away; stay away. [Middle English *scars,* from Norman French *escars,* from Vulgar Latin *excarpsus* (unattested), "picked," "choice," hence "rare," variant of Latin *excerptus,* past participle of *excerpere,* to pick out, select : *ex-,* out + *carpere,* to pick, pluck (see **kerp-** in Appendix*).] —**scarce′ness** *n.*

scarce·ly (skârs′lē) *adv.* **1.** By a small margin; just; barely. **2.** Almost not; hardly. **3.** Assuredly not. —See Synonyms at **hardly.**

Usage: *Scarcely* has a negative sense, and is therefore not preceded by another negative in standard usage: *He could scarcely hear* (not *couldn't scarcely*). *She assented with scarcely a word* (not *without scarcely*). *Scarcely* is preferably followed by *when* or (less often) *before,* rather than by *than,* in constructions such as: *Scarcely had he entered, when the telephone rang.* Especially in written usage, *scarcely* is preferably placed just before the word, or group of words, that it modifies: *He saw scarcely anyone.*

scar·ci·ty (skâr′sə-tē) *n., pl.* **-ties. 1.** Insufficient amount or supply; shortage. **2.** Infrequency of appearance or occurrence; uncommonness.

scare (skâr) *v.* **scared, scaring, scares.** —*tr.* **1.** To startle with fear; frighten; alarm; terrify. **2.** To force, drive, or evoke by frightening. Used with *away, off, out.* **3.** *Informal.* To cause to be in a specified state by frightening. —*intr.* To become frightened. —See Synonyms at **frighten.** —**scare up.** *Informal.* To gather or prepare hurriedly or with little effort. —*n.* **1.** A condition or sensation of sudden fear. **2.** A general state of alarm, especially when exaggerated or unreasonable; panic. [Middle English *skerren,* from Old Norse *skirra,* from *skjarr,* shy, timid, from North Germanic *skerza-* (unattested).] —**scar′er** *n.* —**scar′ing·ly** *adv.*

scare·crow (skâr′krō′) *n.* **1.** A crude figure of a man set up in a field to scare birds away from growing crops. **2.** Something frightening but not inherently dangerous. **3.** A person resembling a scarecrow; especially, a very thin, haggard person.

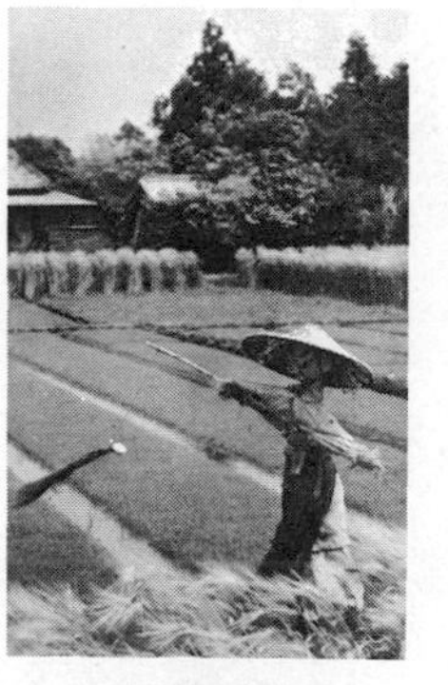
scarecrow
In a Japanese rice paddy

scare·mon·ger (skâr′mŭng′gər, -mŏng′gər) *n.* A person who spreads frightening rumors; an alarmist.

scarf¹ (skärf) *n., pl.* **scarfs** or **scarves** (skärvz). **1.** A rectangular or triangular piece of cloth, worn about the neck or head for protection, warmth, or adornment. **2.** Any piece of neckwear, such as a cravat or muffler. **3.** A runner, as for a bureau or table. **4.** *Military.* A sash denoting rank. —*tr.v.* **scarfed, scarfing, scarfs. 1.** To dress, cover, or decorate with or as with a scarf. **2.** To wrap around loosely; put on like a scarf. [Old North French *escarpe,* variant of Old French *escherpe,* originally "pilgrim's wallet suspended from the neck," from Frankish *skirpja* (unattested), from Latin *scirpea,* basket made of rushes, from *scirpeus,* of rushes, from *scirpus*†, rush, bulrush. See also **scrip** (wallet).]

scarf² (skärf) *n., pl.* **scarfs. 1.** A joint made by cutting and notching the ends of two timbers and strapping or bolting them together to make a continuous piece. Also called "scarf joint." **2.** The end of a timber notched in this fashion. —*tr.v.* **scarfed, scarfing, scarfs. 1.** To join by means of a scarf joint. **2.** To cut a scarf in. [Middle English *skarf*†.]

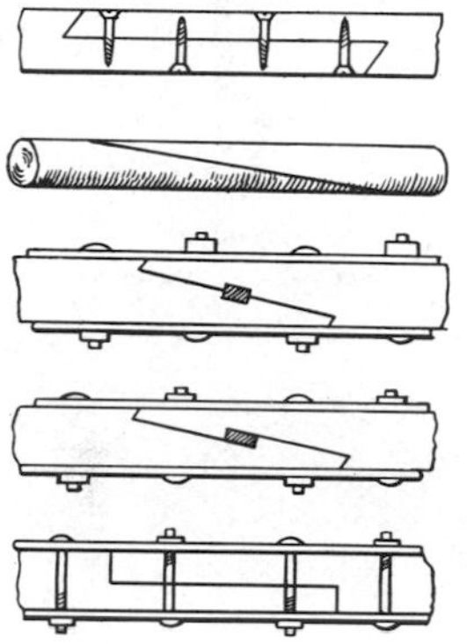
scarf²

scarf·skin (skärf′skĭn′) *n.* The epidermis or outermost layer of skin, especially the cuticle.

scar·i·fi·ca·tor (skăr′ə-fĭ-kā′tər) *n.* A surgical instrument with several spring-operated lancets, used for skin scarification.

scar·i·fy (skăr′ə-fī′) *tr.v.* **-fied, -fying, -fies. 1.** To make superficial incisions in (the skin), as when vaccinating. **2.** To break up the surface of (topsoil, for example). **3.** To criticize severely. **4.** *Botany.* To slit or soften the outer coat of (seeds) to speed germination. [Middle English *scarifien,* to make incisions on the bark of a tree, from Old French *scarifier,* from Late Latin *scarīficāre,* variant of Latin *scarīfāre,* from Greek *skariphasthai,* to scratch an outline, sketch, from *skariphos,* pencil. See **skeri-** in Appendix.*] —**scar′i·fi′er** *n.* —**scar′i·fi·ca′tion** *n.*

scar·i·ous (skâr′ē-əs) *adj.* Also **scar·i·ose** (-ōs′). Thin, membranous, and dry: *scarious bracts.* [New Latin *scariosus*†.]

scar·la·ti·noid (skär′lə-tē′noid′) *adj.* Resembling scarlet fever or its rash. [New Latin *(febris) scarlatina,* scarlet fever, from Medieval Latin *scarlata,* SCARLET + -OID.]

Scar·lat·ti (skär-lät′ē), **Alessandro.** 1659–1725. Italian composer; father of Domenico Scarlatti.

Scar·lat·ti (skär-lät′ē), **(Giuseppe) Domenico.** 1683–1757. Italian harpsichordist and composer; son of Alessandro Scarlatti.

scar·let (skär′lĭt) *n.* **1.** Strong to vivid red or reddish orange. See **color. 2.** Clothing or cloth having this color. —*adj.* **1.** Having a scarlet color. **2.** Sinful or unchaste; whorish. [Middle English, from Old French *escarlate,* from Medieval Latin *scarlata, scarletum,* scarlet cloth, from Persian *sāqirlāṭ,* silk material dyed red with cochineal, from Arabic *siqillāṭ,* from Latin *sigillātus,* adorned with little images, from *sigilla,* little images, from *signum,* sign. See **sekw-¹** in Appendix.*]

scarlet fever. An acute contagious disease caused by a hemolytic streptococcus, occurring predominantly among children and characterized by a scarlet skin eruption and high fever. Also called "scarlatina."

scarlet pimpernel. See **pimpernel.**

scarlet runner. A climbing bean plant, *Phaseolus coccineus,* native to tropical America, having scarlet flowers and long pods containing edible seeds.

scarlet sage. A species of **salvia** *(see).*

scarlet tanager. A New World bird, *Piranga olivacea,* of which the male has bright scarlet plumage with a black tail and wings.

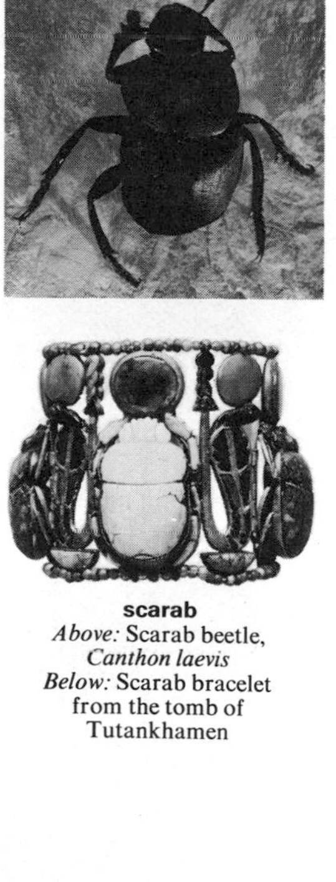
scarab
Above: Scarab beetle, *Canthon laevis*
Below: Scarab bracelet from the tomb of Tutankhamen

scarp (skärp) *n.* **1.** A steep slope; cliff; abrupt declivity. **2.** A steep slope at the outer portion of a fortification. —*tr.v.* **scarped, scarping, scarps.** To cut or make into a steep slope. [Italian *scarpa,* probably from Gothic *skarpō* (unattested), pointed object. See **sker-¹** in Appendix.*]

Scar·ron (skȧ-rôɴ′), **Paul.** 1610–1660. French poet, novelist, and playwright.

scar tissue. A dense, often hard layer of connective tissue formed over a healing wound or cut.

scar·y (skâr′ē) *adj.* **-ier, -iest.** *Informal.* **1.** Frightening; alarming. **2.** Easily scared; very timid.

scat¹ (skăt) *intr.v.* **scatted, scatting, scats.** *Informal.* To go away hastily; leave at once. Usually used in the imperative. [Possibly short for SCATTER.]

t tight/th thin, path/*th* this, bathe/ŭ cut/ûr urge/v valve/w with/y yes/z zebra, size/zh vision/ə about, item, edible, gallop, circus/ ȧ *Fr.* ami/œ *Fr.* feu, *Ger.* schön/ü *Fr.* tu, *Ger.* über/KH *Ger.* ich, *Scot.* loch/N *Fr.* bon. ***Follows main vocabulary. †Of obscure origin.**

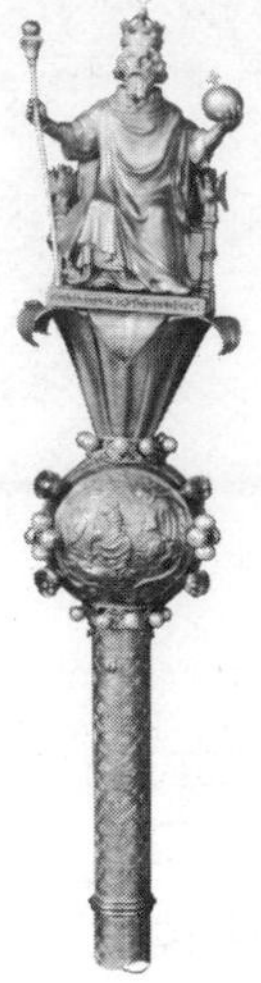

scepter
Scepter of Charles V
of France

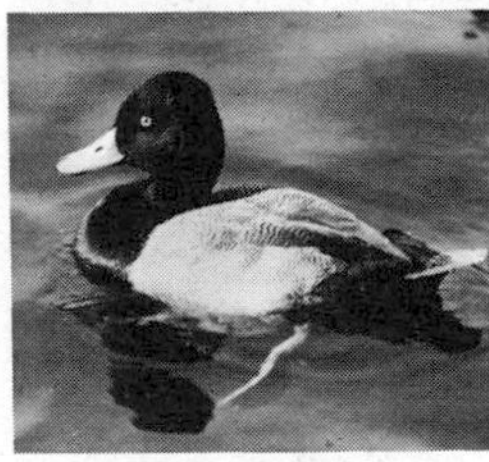

scaup
Aythya affinis
Lesser scaup

scat[2] (skăt) *n.* A type of jazz singing consisting of the improvisation and repetition of meaningless syllables sung to a melody. —*intr.v.* **scatted, scatting, scats.** To sing in this manner. [Perhaps imitative.]

scat[3] (skăt) *n.* Any of several freshwater fishes of the genus *Scatophagus,* of tropical Asia and adjacent areas, having a flat, rounded, spotted or striped body, and popular as an aquarium fish. [Shortened from New Latin *Scatophagus,* from Greek *skatophagos,* SCATOPHAGOUS.]

scat[4] (skăt) *n.* The excrement of an animal, especially a game animal. [Probably from SCATO-.]

scathe (skāth) *tr.v.* **scathed, scathing, scathes. 1.** To harm or injure severely, especially by fire or heat; wither; sear. **2.** To criticize severely. —*n.* Harm; injury. [Middle English *skathen,* from Old Norse *skadha.* See **skēth-** in Appendix.*] —**scathe′ful** *adj.*

scath·ing (skā′thĭng) *adj.* **1.** Extremely severe or harsh; bitterly denunciatory: *"a scathing tract on the uselessness of war"* (Pierre Brodin). **2.** Harmful or painful; injurious.

scato–. Indicates feces or excrement; for example, **scatology.** [Greek *skato-,* from *skōr* (genitive *skatos*), dung, ordure. See **sker-**[4] in Appendix.*]

sca·tol·o·gy (skə-tŏl′ə-jē, skă-) *n.* **1.** The study of fecal excrement, as in medicine or paleontology. **2. a.** An obsession with excrement or excretory functions. **b.** The psychiatric study of such an obsession. **3.** Preoccupation with obscenity, as in literature. [SCATO- + -LOGY.] —**scat′o·log′i·cal** (skăt′ə-lŏj′ĭ-kəl), **scat′o·log′ic** *adj.* —**sca·tol′o·gist** *n.*

sca·toph·a·gous (skə-tŏf′ə-gəs, skă-) *adj.* Feeding on dung, as a beetle or fly. [Greek *skatophagos* : SCATO- + -PHAGOUS.]

scat·ter (skăt′ər) *v.* **-tered, -tering, -ters.** —*tr.* **1.** To cause to separate and go in various directions; disperse. **2.** To distribute loosely by or as if by sprinkling or strewing. **3.** *Physics.* To deflect (radiation or particles). —*intr.* **1.** To separate and go in several directions; disperse. **2.** To appear, occur, or fall at widely spaced intervals. —*n.* **1.** The act of scattering. **2.** The condition or extent of being scattered. **3.** That which is scattered. [Middle English *scateren,* possibly variant of *schateren,* SHATTER.] —**scat′ter·er** *n.*

Synonyms: *scatter, disperse, dissipate, dispel.* These verbs are compared as they mean to cause something, considered as a mass or aggregate, to break up. *Scatter* usually refers to widespread and often haphazard distribution of components, as persons fleeing a storm or physical objects blown by wind. *Disperse* makes a stronger implication of complete breaking up of the mass, as a crowd of persons routed by police or a mass of clouds acted on by sunlight. *Dissipate* usually implies reduction to nothing, as by squandering (a fortune, time, or energy) or causing something (such as fog or mist) to evaporate. *Dispel* suggests making disappear as if by scattering; often it takes as its object something nonphysical, as a rumor, fear, joy, or doubt.

scat·ter·brain (skăt′ər-brān′) *n.* A person lacking the power of concentration or attention; a flighty, disorganized, or thoughtless person. —**scat′ter·brained′** *adj.*

scat·ter·good (skăt′ər-gŏŏd′) *n.* One who wastes money; spendthrift; wastrel.

scat·ter·ing (skăt′ər-ĭng) *n.* **1. a.** The act or process of dispersing or scattering. **b.** The state of being dispersed or scattered. **2.** A sparse distribution or irregular occurrence of something: *a scattering of applause.* **3.** *Physics.* The dispersal of a beam of particles or of radiation into a range of directions resulting from physical interactions. —*adj.* Placed at intervals or occurring irregularly. —**scat′ter·ing·ly** *adv.*

scatter pin. A small brooch often worn in groups of two or three as a decorative accessory for a woman.

scatter rug. A small rug for carpeting a part of a floor. Also called "throw rug."

scaup (skôp) *n.* Either of two diving ducks, *Aythya marila* or *A. affinis,* having predominantly black and white plumage. Sometimes called "bluebill." [Perhaps from *scaup,* variant of SCALP (rare sense "bed of mussels"), because these ducks feed on shellfish.]

scaur. *Scottish.* Variant of **scar** (rock).

scav·enge (skăv′ĭnj) *v.* **-enged, -enging, -enges.** —*tr.* **1.** To collect and remove refuse from; clean up. **2.** To search through for salvageable material. **3.** To collect (salvageable material) by searching. **4.** To expel (exhaust gases) from a cylinder of an internal-combustion engine. **5.** *Metallurgy.* To clean (molten metal) by chemically removing impurities. —*intr.* To search through discarded material for edible or useful things. [Back-formation from SCAVENGER.]

scav·en·ger (skăv′ĭn-jər) *n.* **1.** An animal that feeds on dead animal flesh or other decaying organic matter. **2.** One who scavenges. **3.** *Chemistry.* A substance added to a mixture to remove impurities or to counteract the undesirable effects of other constituents. [Earlier *scavager,* street-cleaner, Middle English *skawager,* collector of tolls, from Norman French *scawager,* from *scawage,* a toll levied on foreign merchants, variant of Old North French *escauwage,* inspection, from *escauwer,* to inspect, from Flemish *scawuen,* to look at. See **keu-**[1] in Appendix.*]

sce·nar·i·o (sĭ-nâr′ē-ō′, sĭ-när′-) *n., pl.* **-os. 1.** An outline of the plot of a dramatic or literary work. **2.** A **screenplay** *(see).* **3.** An outline of a hypothesized chain of events. [Italian, "scenery," from Late Latin *scaenārius,* of the stage, from Latin *scaena,* stage, SCENE.]

sce·nar·ist (sĭ-nâr′ĭst, sĭ-när′-) *n.* A writer of screenplays.

scend (sĕnd) *intr.v.* **scended, scending, scends.** Also **send.** To heave upward on a wave or swell. —*n.* Also **send.** The rising movement of a ship on a wave or swell. [Perhaps from earlier *'scend,* short for DESCEND or ASCEND.]

scene (sēn) *n.* **1.** A locality as seen by a viewer; view. **2.** The surroundings and place where an action or event occurs. **3.** *Abbr.* **sc.** The place in which the action of a narrative occurs; setting; locale. **4.** *Abbr.* **sc.** A subdivision of an act in a dramatic presentation in which the setting is fixed and the time continuous. **5.** *Abbr.* **sc.** A shot or series of shots in a film constituting a unit of continuous related action. **6.** The scenery and properties for a dramatic presentation. **7.** *Archaic.* A theater stage. **8.** A real or fictitious episode, especially when described. **9.** A public display of passion or temper. **10.** *Slang.* A place or realm of the currently fashionable or exciting. —**behind the scenes. 1.** Backstage. **2.** In private. —**make the scene.** *Slang.* To participate in an activity or event. [French *scène,* from Old French *scene,* stage, stage performance, from Latin *scaena,* stage, scene, theater, from Greek *skēnē*†, "tent."]

scen·er·y (sē′nə-rē) *n.* **1.** The landscape. **2.** The painted backdrops on a theatrical stage. [Italian *scenario,* SCENARIO.] —**sce′nic** *adj.* —**sce′ni·cal·ly** *adv.*

scent (sĕnt) *n.* **1.** A distinctive odor. **2.** A perfume. **3.** An odor left by the passing of an animal. **4.** The trail of a hunted animal or fugitive. **5.** The sense of smell. **6.** A hint of something imminent; suggestion. —See Synonyms at **smell.** —*v.* **scented, scenting, scents.** —*tr.* **1.** To perceive or identify by the sense of smell. **2.** To suspect or detect as if by smelling: *scent danger.* **3.** To perfume. —*intr.* To hunt by means of the sense of smell. Used of hounds. [Middle English *sent,* from *senten,* to smell, scent, from Old French *sentir,* from Latin *sentire,* to feel. See **sent-** in Appendix.*]

scep·ter (sĕp′tər) *n.* Also *chiefly British* **scep·tre. 1.** A staff held by a sovereign on ceremonial occasions as an emblem of authority. **2.** Sovereign office or power. —*tr.v.* **sceptered, -tering, -ters.** Also *chiefly British* **scep·tre, -tred, -tring, -tres.** To invest with royal authority. [Middle English *(s)ceptre,* from Old French, from Latin *scēptrum,* from Greek *skēptron*†, "staff," "stick."]

scep·tic. Variant of **skeptic.**

sch. school.

Schau·dinn (shou′dĭn), **Fritz.** 1871–1906. German zoologist; discovered organism that causes syphilis.

Schaum·burg-Lip·pe (shoum′bŏŏrk′lĭp′ə). A former state of northwestern Germany, now part of Lower Saxony, West Germany.

schav (shäv) *n.* A chilled soup made with sorrel, onions, lemon juice, eggs, and sugar, and served with sour cream. [Polish *szczaw,* sorrel, akin to Russian *ščavel*†.]

sched·ule (skĕj′ōōl, -ōō-əl, skĕj′əl; *British* shĕd′yōōl) *n.* **1.** A formal written list of items, usually in tabular form; especially, a listing of rates or prices. **2. a.** A program of forthcoming events or appointments. **b.** A student's program of classes. **3.** A timetable of departures and arrivals. **4.** A production plan allotting work to be done and specifying deadlines. **5.** A supplemental statement of details appended to a document. —*tr.v.* **scheduled, -uling, -ules. 1.** To enter on a schedule. **2.** To make up a schedule for. **3.** To plan or appoint for a certain time or date. [Middle English *cedule, sedule,* slip of parchment or paper, short note, from Old French *cedule,* from Late Latin *schedula,* diminutive of Latin *scheda, scida,* papyrus leaf, from Greek *skhidē* (unattested), splinter of wood, from *skhizein,* to split. See **skei-** in Appendix.*]

Schee·le (shā′lə), **Karl Wilhelm.** 1742–1786. Swedish chemist; discovered many acids, gases, and elements.

schee·lite (shā′līt′) *n.* A variously colored natural form of calcium tungstate, $CaWO_4$, found in igneous rocks and used as a source of tungsten. [Discovered by Karl SCHEELE.]

Sche·her·a·za·de (shə-hĕr′ə-zä′də, -zäd′). The fictional narrator of *The Arabian Nights' Entertainments.*

Scheldt (skĕlt). *Flemish & Dutch* **Schel·de** (skĕl′də); *French* **Es·caut** (ĕs-kō′). A river rising in northern France and flowing 270 miles generally north through Belgium and the southern Netherlands to the North Sea.

Schel·ling (shĕl′ĭng), **Friedrich Wilhelm Joseph von.** 1775–1854. German philosopher.

sche·ma (skē′mə) *n., pl.* **-mata** (-mə-tə). A summarized or diagrammatic representation of something; an outline. [German *Schema,* from Greek *skhēma,* form. See **scheme.**]

sche·mat·ic (skē-măt′ĭk) *adj.* Pertaining to or in the form of a scheme or schema; diagrammatic. —*n.* A structural or procedural diagram, especially of an electrical or mechanical system.

sche·ma·tism (skē′mə-tĭz′əm) *n.* The patterned disposition of constituents within a given system.

sche·ma·tize (skē′mə-tīz′) *tr.v.* **-tized, -tizing, -tizes.** To form into a scheme. [Greek *skhēmatizein,* to give a form to, from *skhēma,* form, manner. See **scheme.**] —**sche′ma·ti·za′tion** *n.*

scheme (skēm) *n.* **1.** A systematic plan of action. **2.** An orderly combination of related or successive parts or things; system. **3.** An underhand or secret plan; plot; intrigue. **4.** A visionary plan. **5.** A chart, diagram, or outline of a system or object. —*v.* **schemed, scheming, schemes.** —*tr.* **1.** To contrive a plan or scheme for. **2.** To plot. —*intr.* To make devious plans. [Latin *schēma,* form, figure, manner, from Greek *skhēma.* See **segh-** in Appendix.*] —**schem′er** *n.*

Sche·nec·ta·dy (skə-nĕk′tə-dē). A city and industrial center of New York State, in the east on the Mohawk River. Population, 82,000.

scher·zan·do (skĕr-tsän′dō) *adj. Music.* Playful; sportive. Used as a direction to the performer. —*n., pl.* **scherzandos.** *Music.* A scherzando passage. [Italian, gerund of *scherzare,* to joke, from *scherzo,* joke, SCHERZO.] —**scher·zan′do** *adv.*

scher·zo (skĕr′tsō) *n., pl.* **-zos** or **-zi** (-tsē). *Music.* A lively movement commonly in ¾ time. [Italian, joke, from Middle High German *scherz,* from *scherzen,* to joke, leap with joy. See **sker-**[2] in Appendix.*]

Schick test (shĭk). An intracutaneous skin test of susceptibility to diphtheria. [Invented by Bela *Schick* (1877–1967), American pediatrician.]

schil·ler (shĭl′ər) *n.* A lustrous, almost metallic reflection from certain planes in a mineral grain, caused by internal reflections from microscopic inclusions. [German *Schiller,* iridescence, from Middle High German *schilher,* iridescent taffeta, from *schilhen,* to wink, blink, from Old High German *scilihen.* See **skel-**[3] in Appendix.*] —**schil′ler·i·za′tion** *n.*

Schil·ler (shĭl′ər), **Johann Christoph Friedrich von.** 1759–1805. German poet and dramatist.

schil·ling (shĭl′ĭng) *n.* **1.** The basic monetary unit of Austria, equal to 100 groschen. See table of exchange rates at **currency. 2.** A coin worth one schilling. [German *Schilling,* from Middle High German *schillinc,* from Old High German *skilling,* from Germanic *skillingaz* (unattested), SHILLING.]

schip·per·ke (skĭp′ər-kē, -kə) *n.* A small dog, having a dense, long black coat, of a breed developed in Belgium. [Flemish, "little skipper" (so called because it is often trained as a watchdog on a boat), from *schipper,* skipper, from Middle Dutch, from *schip,* ship. See **skipam-** in Appendix.*]

schism (sĭz′əm, skĭz′-) *n.* **1.** A separation or division into factions, especially a formal breach of union within a Christian church. **2.** The offense of attempting to produce such a split within a church or religious group. **3.** A schismatic body or sect. [Middle English *(s)cisme,* from Old French, from Late Latin *schisma,* from Greek *skhisma,* a split, division, from *skhizein,* to split. See **skei-** in Appendix.*] —**schis·mat′ic** (sĭz-măt′ĭk, skĭz-) *adj.* —**schis·mat′i·cal·ly** *adv.*

schist (shĭst) *n.* Also **shist.** Any of various medium- to coarse-grained metamorphic rocks composed of laminated, often flaky, parallel layers of chiefly micaceous minerals. [French *schiste,* from Latin *(lapis) schistos,* "fissile (stone)," from Greek *skhistos (lithos),* talc, from *skhizein,* to split. See **skei-** in Appendix.*] —**schis′tose′** (shĭs′tōs′), **schis′tous** (shĭs′təs) *adj.*

schis·to·some (shĭs′tə-sōm′) *n.* Any of several chiefly tropical trematode worms of the genus *Schistosoma,* many of which are parasitic in the blood of man and other mammals. Also called "blood fluke." [New Latin *Schistosoma,* "having a cleft body" : Greek *skhistos,* cleft, from *skhizein,* to split (see **schism**) + -SOME (body).]

schis·to·so·mi·a·sis (shĭs′tō-sō-mī′ə-sĭs) *n.* Any of various generally tropical diseases caused by infestation with schistosomes. Also called "bilharziasis." [New Latin : *Schistosoma,* SCHISTOSOME + -IASIS.]

schizo-, schiz-. Indicates division, split, or cleavage; for example, **schizophrenia, schizont.** [New Latin, from Greek *skhizo-,* from *skhizein,* to split. See **skei-** in Appendix.*]

schiz·o·carp (skĭz′ə-kärp′) *n.* A dry seed that splits at maturity into two or more closed carpels, each usually containing one seed, as in the fruit of the carrot or mallow. [SCHIZO- + -CARP.] —**schiz′o·car′pous** (-kär′pəs), **schiz′o·car′pic** *adj.*

schiz·o·gen·e·sis (skĭz′ō-jĕn′ə-sĭs) *n. Biology.* Reproduction by fission. [New Latin : SCHIZO- + -GENESIS.]

schi·zog·o·ny (skĭ-zŏg′ə-nē) *n. Biology.* Reproduction by multiple asexual fission, characteristic of many sporozoans. [New Latin *schizogonia* : SCHIZO- + -GONY.]

schiz·oid (skĭt′soid′) *adj.* Characteristic of or resembling schizophrenia. —*n.* A schizophrenic. [SCHIZ(O)- + -OID.]

schiz·o·my·cete (skĭz′ō-mī′sēt′) *n.* Any of numerous one-celled microorganisms of the class Schizomycetes, which includes the bacteria. [New Latin *Schizomycetes,* "fission fungi" (from their multiplying by fission) : SCHIZO- + -MYCETE.] —**schiz′o·my·ce′tous** (-mī-sē′təs) *adj.*

schiz·o·my·co·sis (skĭz′ō-mī-kō′sĭs) *n.* Any disease caused by bacteria. [New Latin : SCHIZO(MYCETE) + MYCOSIS.]

schiz·ont (skĭz′ŏnt′) *n.* A protozoan cell produced by schizogony in the life cycle of a sporozoan. [SCHIZO- + *-ont,* being, from Greek *ōn* (stem *ont-*), present participle of *einai,* to be (see **es-** in Appendix*).]

schiz·o·phre·ni·a (skĭt′sə-frē′nē-ə, -frĕn′ē-ə) *n.* Any of a group of psychotic reactions characterized by withdrawal from reality with highly variable accompanying affective, behavioral, and intellectual disturbances. Formerly called "dementia praecox." [New Latin, "split mind" : SCHIZO- + -PHRENIA.] —**schiz′o·phren′ic** (-frĕn′ĭk) *adj. & n.*

schiz·o·phyte (skĭz′ə-fīt′) *n.* Any of various one-celled or simple colonial organisms of the division Schizophyta, including bacteria and the blue-green algae, reproducing asexually, usually by fission. [New Latin *Schizophyta* : SCHIZO- + -PHYTE.] —**schiz′o·phyt′ic** (-fĭt′ĭk) *adj.*

schiz·o·pod (skĭz′ə-pŏd′) *n.* Any of various shrimplike crustaceans of the orders Euphausiacea and Mysidacea (formerly included in the single order Schizopoda). [New Latin *Schizopoda,* "split-footed ones" (from the splitting of the thoracic limbs) : SCHIZO- + -POD.] —**schiz·op′o·dous** (skĭ-zŏp′ə-dəs) *adj.*

schiz·o·thy·mi·a (skĭt′sə-thī′mē-ə) *n.* Schizoid behavior that resembles schizophrenia in the tendency to autistic thinking but remains within the limits of normality. [New Latin, "split spirit" : SCHIZO- + -THYMIA.] —**schiz′o·thy′mic** (-thī′mĭk) *adj.*

Schle·gel (shlā′gəl), **August Wilhelm von.** 1767–1845. German critic, poet, and translator; brother of **Karl Wilhelm Friedrich von Schlegel** (1772–1829), German philosopher, poet, and critic.

schle·miel (shlə-mēl′) *n. Slang.* An unlucky and habitual bungler; dolt. [Yiddish, perhaps from Hebrew *Shelūmīel,* character in the Bible.]

schlep (shlĕp) *v.* **schlepped, schlepping, schleps.** *Slang.* —*tr.* To carry clumsily or with difficulty; to lug. —*intr.* To carry something clumsily. —*n. Slang.* **1.** An arduous journey. **2.** A clumsy or stupid person. [Yiddish *shleppen,* to drag, trail, from Middle Low German *slēpen.* See **lei-** in Appendix.*]

Schle·si·en. The German name for **Silesia.**

Schles·in·ger (shlĕs′ĭn-jər), **Arthur Meier.** 1888–1965. American historian and educator; father of **Arthur Meier, Jr.** (born 1917), also American historian and educator.

Schles·wig (shlĕs′wĭg; *German* shlās′vĭKH). *Danish* **Sles·vig** (slĭs′vē). **1.** A city of West Germany, in northern Schleswig-Holstein. Population, 34,000. **2.** The southern part of the Jutland Peninsula, formerly a duchy belonging to Denmark and now divided between Denmark and West Germany.

Schles·wig-Hol·stein (shlĕs′wĭg-hōl′stīn′; *German* shlās′vĭKH-hôl′shtīn′). A state of West Germany, occupying 6,045 square miles in the north. Population, 2,406,000. Capital, Kiel.

Schlie·mann (shlē′män′), **Heinrich.** 1822–1890. German archaeologist; excavated the sites of Troy and Mycenae.

schlie·ren (shlîr′ən) *pl.n.* **1.** *Geology.* Irregular tabular bodies occurring as essential components of plutonic rock but differing in texture or composition from the principal mass. **2.** Regions of a transparent medium, as of a flowing gas, that exhibit densities different from that of the bulk of the medium. [German *Schlieren,* plural of *Schliere,* streak, from dialectal German *Schlier,* "slimy mass," from Middle High German *slier,* mud, slime. See **sleu-** in Appendix.*]

schli·ma·zel (shlĭ-mä′zəl) *n. Slang.* An extremely unlucky or inept person; a habitual failure: *A schlemiel is a waiter who spills hot soup, and the schlimazel is the one who gets it in his lap.* [Yiddish *shlimazel,* bad luck, probably from Hebrew *š-l-msl,* "that which is not luck."]

schlock (shlŏk) *n. Slang.* Merchandise of meretricious or obviously inferior quality. [Yiddish, "broken merchandise," perhaps from German *Schlag,* a blow, from Middle High German *slac,* from Old High German *slag.* See **slak-** in Appendix.*] —**schlock** *adj.*

schmaltz (shmälts) *n.* Also **schmalz. 1.** Animal fat used as food, especially chicken fat. **2.** *Slang.* **a.** Excessive sentimentality in art or music. **b.** Maudlin sentimentality. **3.** *Slang.* Excessively profuse flattery or praise. [German, "melted fat," from Middle High German *smalz,* from Old High German. See **mel-**[1] in Appendix.*] —**schmaltz′y** *adj.*

schmeer (shmîr) *n. Slang.* **1.** An aggregate of persons or things. **2.** A bribe. —*tr.v.* **schmeered, schmeering, schmeers.** *Slang.* To bribe. [From German *Schmer, Schmiere,* grease, bribe, gang, from Middle High German *smer,* from Old High German *smero.* See **smer-**[3] in Appendix.*]

Schmidt (shmĭt), **Bernhard.** 1879–1935. Swedish-born German astronomer and optician; invented telescope corrector plate.

Schmidt system. A system consisting of a concave spherical mirror and a transparent plate of glass at its center of curvature, used in reflecting telescopes to offset spherical aberration, coma, and astigmatism. [Invented by Bernhard SCHMIDT.]

schmo (shmō) *n., pl.* **schmoes.** Also **schmoe, shmo.** *Slang.* A dull or stupid person. [Yiddish *shmok,* from Slovenian *šmok.*]

schmoose (shmōōz) *intr.v.* **schmoosed, schmoosing, schmooses.** Also **schmooze.** *Slang.* To chat idly or gossip. —*n.* Also **schmooze.** *Slang.* A chat. [Yiddish *shmuesn,* to chat, from *shmues,* a chat, from Hebrew *shemu′ōth,* plural of *shemu′āh,* rumor, from *shāmō′a,* to hear.]

schmuck (shmŭk) *n. Slang.* A clumsy, self-assertive, or stupid person; oaf. [Yiddish *schmuck,* "penis," from German *Schmuck,* ornament, from Middle Low German *smuck.* See **meug-**[2] in Appendix.*]

schnap·per (shnăp′ər, snăp′-) *n.* A large, reddish marine food fish, *Chrysophrys auratus,* of Australian waters. [Pseudo-German spelling of SNAPPER (fish).]

schnapps (shnäps, shnăps) *n.* Any of various strong liquors. [German *Schnaps,* from Low German *snaps,* mouthful, dram, from *snappen,* to snap, from Middle Low German, SNAP.]

schnau·zer (shnou′zər) *n.* A dog of a breed developed in Germany, having a wiry gray coat and a blunt muzzle and ranging in size from fairly small to quite large. [German *Schnauzer,* from *Schnauze,* snout. See **snē-**[2] in Appendix.*]

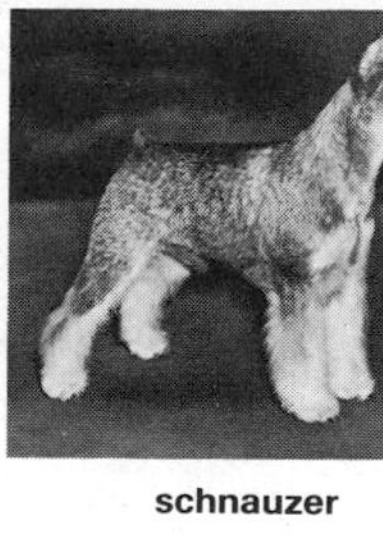

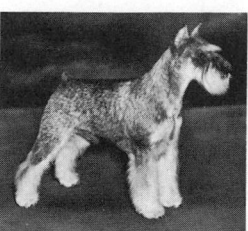

schnauzer

schneck·en (shnĕk′ən) *pl.n.* Sweet cinnamon rolls cut in a coiled shape like that of a snail shell. [German, plural of *Schnecke,* "snail," from Middle High German *snecke,* from Old High German *snecko.* See **sneg-** in Appendix.*]

schnit·zel (shnĭt′səl) *n.* A thin cutlet of veal fried lightly in butter. [German *Schnitzel,* diminutive of *Schnitz,* slice, from Middle High German *sniz.* See **sneit-** in Appendix.*]

Schnitz·ler (shnĭts′lər), **Arthur.** 1862–1931. Austrian playwright and novelist.

schnook (shnōōk) *n.* A stupid or easily victimized person; a dupe. [Yiddish *shnok,* variant of *shmok,* SCHMO.]

schnor·rer (shnôr′ər) *n. Slang.* One who takes advantage of the generosity of friends; parasite or beggar. [Yiddish, from *schnorren,* to beg (while playing a pipe or harp), from Middle High German *snurren,* to hum, whir. See **sner-**[1] in Appendix.*]

schnoz·zle (shnŏz′əl) *n. Slang.* The nose. [Probably alteration (influenced by NOZZLE) of Yiddish *shnoitsl,* diminutive of *shnoits,* snout, from German *Schnauze.* See **snē-**[2] in Appendix.*]

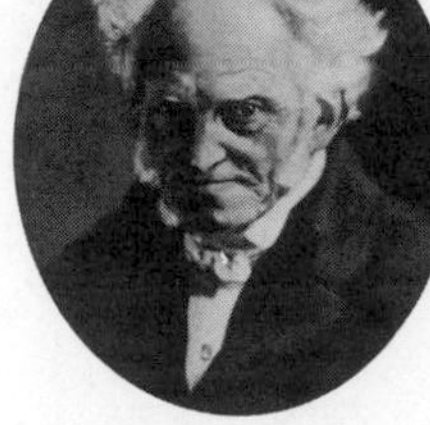
Schopenhauer

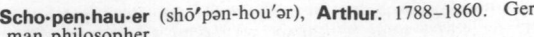

Schoen·heim·er (shōn′hī′mər), **Rudolf.** 1898–1941. German-born American biochemist.

schol·ar (skŏl′ər) *n.* **1. a.** A learned or erudite person. **b.** A specialist in some given branch of the humanities. **2.** One considered in the light of his aptness at learning. **3.** A pupil in elementary or Sunday school. **4.** A student who holds or has held a particular scholarship. [Middle English *scoler,* from Old French *escoler,* from Late Latin *scholāris,* of a school, from Latin *schola,* SCHOOL.]

schol·ar·ly (skŏl′ər-lē) *adj.* Pertaining to, characteristic of, or befitting scholars or scholarship. —**schol′ar·li·ness** *n.*

schol·ar·ship (skŏl′ər-shĭp′) *n.* **1.** The methods, discipline, and attainments of a scholar; learning; erudition. **2.** Existing knowledge resulting from scholarly research in a particular field. **3.** A grant-in-aid awarded to a student, as by a college. —See Synonyms at **knowledge.**

scho·las·tic (skə-lăs′tĭk) *adj.* **1.** Of or pertaining to schools; academic. **2.** *Usually capital* **S.** Pertaining to or characteristic of the Schoolmen. **3.** Pedantic; dogmatic. —*n.* **1.** *Usually capital* **S.** A Schoolman. **2.** A dogmatist; pedant. **3.** A formalist in art. [Latin *scholasticus,* from Greek *skholastikos,* academic, from *skholazein,* to study, attend lectures, from *skholē,* school. See **segh-** in Appendix.*] —**scho·las′ti·cal·ly** *adv.*

scho·las·ti·cism (skə-lăs′tə-sĭz′əm) *n.* Also **Scho·las·ti·cism.** The dominant theological and philosophical school of the High Middle Ages, based on the authority of the Latin Fathers and of Aristotle and his commentators.

scho·li·ast (skō′lē-ăst′) *n.* One of the ancient commentators who annotated the classical authors. [Late Greek *skholiastēs,* from *skholiazein,* to comment on, from *skholion,* SCHOLIUM.]

scho·li·um (skō′lē-əm) *n., pl.* **-ums** or **-lia** (-lē-ə). **1.** An explanatory note or commentary, as on a Greek or Latin text. **2.** A note amplifying a proof or process, as in mathematics. [New Latin, from Greek *skholion,* diminutive of *skholē,* lecture, SCHOOL.]

Schön·berg (shœn′bûrg), **Arnold.** 1874–1951. Austrian composer and musical theorist.

school[1] (sko͞ol) *n. Abbr.* **s., S., sch. 1.** An institution for the instruction of children. **2.** An institution for instruction in a skill or business. **3.** A college or university. **4.** An institution within a college or university for instruction in a specialized field. **5.** The student body of an educational institution. **6.** A place of instruction; the building or group of buildings in which instruction is given or in which students work and live. **7.** The process of being educated; especially, formal education comprising a planned series of courses over a number of years. **8.** A session of instruction. **9.** A group of persons, especially intellectuals or artists, whose thought, work, or style demonstrates some common influence or unifying belief. **10.** A class of people distinguished by a convention of manner, custom, or opinion. **11.** The education provided by a set of circumstances or experiences. **12.** A division comprising several grades or classes in a private school. **13.** The prescribed regulations and drill instructions applying to individuals or to a unit of an army or navy. —*tr.v.* **schooled, schooling, schools. 1.** To instruct; educate. **2.** To train; discipline. —See Synonyms at **teach.** [Middle English *scole,* Old English *scōl,* from Medieval Latin *scōla,* from Latin *schola,* leisure, school, from Greek *skholē,* leisure (devoted to learning), lecture, school. See **segh-** in Appendix.*]

school[2] (sko͞ol) *n.* A large group of aquatic animals, especially fish, swimming together; a shoal. See Synonyms at **flock.** —*intr.v.* **schooled, schooling, schools.** To swim in, or form into, a school. [Middle English *scole,* from Middle Dutch *schōle,* troop, group. See **skel-**[1] in Appendix.*]

school·boy (sko͞ol′boi′) *n.* A boy attending school.

school·child (sko͞ol′chīld′) *n., pl.* **-children** (-chĭl′drən). A child attending school.

school·girl (sko͞ol′gûrl′) *n.* A girl attending school.

school·house (sko͞ol′hous′) *n.* A building used as a school.

school·ing (sko͞o′lĭng) *n.* **1.** Instruction or training given at school; especially, a program of formal education. **2.** Training or instruction obtained through experience or exposure. **3.** The training of a horse or of a horse and rider in specific techniques.

school·man (sko͞ol′mən) *n., pl.* **-men** (-mĭn). **1.** *Often capital* **S.** A philosopher or theologian of a medieval university. **2.** A professional educator or scholar.

school·marm (sko͞ol′märm′) *n.* Also **school·ma′am** (-mäm, -măm). *Informal.* A woman schoolteacher, especially one who is pedantic, old-fashioned, or a priggish disciplinarian. [Dialectal *marm,* variant of *ma'am,* MADAM.]

school·mas·ter (sko͞ol′măs′tər, -mäs′tər) *n.* **1.** A male teacher. **2.** A headmaster of a school. **3.** A reddish-brown food fish, the snapper *Lutjanus apodus,* of the tropical Atlantic and the Gulf of Mexico.

school·mate (sko͞ol′māt′) *n.* A school companion or associate.

school·mis·tress (sko͞ol′mĭs′trĭs) *n.* **1.** A woman teacher. **2.** A headmistress of a school.

school·room (sko͞ol′ro͞om′, -ro͝om′) *n.* A classroom.

school·teach·er (sko͞ol′tē′chər) *n.* One who teaches in a school below the college level.

school year. The period of the year that constitutes a complete annual session of school.

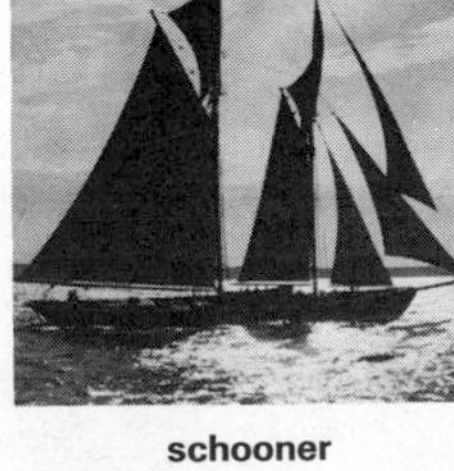
schooner

schoo·ner (sko͞o′nər) *n.* **1.** A ship with two or more masts, all of which are fore-and-aft-rigged, the mainmast being abaft of and taller than the foremast. **2.** A large beer glass, generally holding a pint or more. [Earlier *scooner,* probably from New England dialectal *scoon,* to glide, slide, from Scottish *scon*†, to make a flat stone skip along the surface of water.]

Scho·pen·hau·er (shō′pən-hou′ər), **Arthur.** 1788–1860. German philosopher.

schorl (shôrl) *n.* Also **shorl.** Tourmaline, especially black tourmaline. [German *Schörl*†.] —**schor·la′ceous** (-lā′shəs) *adj.*

schot·tische (shŏt′ĭsh) *n.* **1.** A round dance in 2/4 time. **2.** Music for this dance. [German *Schottische,* short for *(der) schottische (Tanz),* (the) Scottish (dance), from Middle High German *schottesch,* Scottish, from *Schotte,* Scot, from Old High German *Scotto,* from Late Latin *Scottus.* See **Scot.**]

Schou·ten Islands (skhou′tən). A group of islands with a combined area of 1,231 square miles, in the Pacific off the northern coast of West Irian.

Schrö·ding·er (shrœ′dĭng-ər), **Erwin.** 1887–1961. Austrian physicist and philosopher.

Schu·bert (sho͞o′bərt), **Franz.** 1797–1828. Austrian composer.

Schulz (sho͝olts), **Charles M(onroe).** Born 1922. American cartoonist; creator of *Peanuts.*

Schu·man (shü-män′), **Robert.** 1886–1963. French statesman; premier (1947–48).

Schu·man (sho͞o′mən), **William (Howard).** Born 1910. American composer, educator, and administrator.

Schu·mann (sho͞o′män), **Clara Josephine (Wieck).** 1819–1896. German pianist; wife of Robert Schumann.

Schu·mann (sho͞o′män), **Robert.** 1810–1856. German composer.

Schurz (sho͝orts), **Carl.** 1829–1906. German-born American political leader, reformer, and journalist.

schuss (sho͝os) *intr.v.* **schussed, schussing, schusses.** To make a fast straight run in skiing. —*n.* **1.** A straight, steep course for skiing. **2.** The act of skiing such a course. [German *Schuss,* shot, from Middle High German *schuz,* from Old High German *scuz.* See **skeud-** in Appendix.*]

Schutz·staf·fel (sho͝ots′shtä′fəl) *n., pl.* **-feln** (-fəln). *German. Abbr.* **SS** The elite military and police unit of the Nazi Party.

Schuy·ler (skī′lər), **Philip John.** 1733–1804. American statesman; a commander in the Revolutionary War.

Schuy·ler·ville (skī′lər-vĭl). Formerly **Sar·a·to·ga** (săr′ə-tō′gə). A village in eastern New York State, on the Hudson; the site of General Burgoyne's surrender to General Gates (1777) in the Revolutionary War.

schwa (shwä, shvä) *n.* **1.** A symbol (ə) for certain English vowel sounds, as: **a.** An indeterminate sound in many unstressed syllables (as indicated in the pronunciation key below). **b.** In some phonological systems, a phoneme representing the mid-central vowel whether stressed or unstressed, as the vowel in the word *cut.* ***Note:*** This stressed vowel is represented in this Dictionary by the symbol (ŭ). **2.** An indistinct vowel sound in Hebrew, transliterated as *ĕ.* **3.** A symbol used to render an Indo-European laryngeal. [German *Schwa,* from Hebrew *shəwā',* probably from Syriac *shəwayyā,* "equal."]

Schwa·ben. The German name for **Swabia.**

Schwann (shvän), **Theodor.** 1810–1882. German physiologist; regarded as founder of the cell theory.

Schwarz·wald. The German name for the **Black Forest.**

Schwei·tzer (shwīt′sər, shvīt′sər), **Albert.** 1875–1965. French philosopher and musicologist; awarded the Nobel Peace Prize (1952).

Schweiz. The German name for **Switzerland.**

Schwe·rin (shvā-rēn′). A city of East Germany, 60 miles east of Hamburg. Population, 94,000.

Schwin·ger (shwĭng′ər), **Julian Seymour.** Born 1918. American theoretical physicist; worked on quantum electrodynamics; awarded the Nobel Prize in physics (1965).

Schwyz (shvēts). **1.** A canton occupying 351 square miles in central Switzerland north of Lake Lucerne. Population, 80,000. **2.** The capital of this canton. Population, 11,000.

sci. science; scientific.

sci·at·ic (sī-ăt′ĭk) *adj.* **1.** Of or pertaining to the **ischium** *(see).* **2.** Of or pertaining to sciatica. [Old French *sciatique,* from Late Latin *(i)sc(h)iaticus,* variant of Latin *ischiadicus,* from Greek *iskhiadikos,* from *iskhion,* hip joint, ISCHIUM.]

sci·at·i·ca (sī-ăt′ĭ-kə) *n.* **1.** Neuralgia of the sciatic nerve. **2.** Chronic neuralgic pain in the area of the hip or thigh. [Middle English, from Medieval Latin *sciatica (passiō),* "(suffering) in the hip," from Late Latin *sciaticus,* SCIATIC.]

sciatic nerve. *Anatomy.* A sensory and motor nerve originating in the sacral plexus and running through the pelvis and upper leg.

sci·ence (sī′əns) *n. Abbr.* **sci. 1.** The observation, identification, description, experimental investigation, and theoretical explanation of natural phenomena. **2.** Such activity restricted to a class of natural phenomena. **3.** Such activity applied to any class of phenomena. **4.** Any methodological activity, discipline, or study. **5.** Any activity that appears to require study and method. **6.** Knowledge; especially, knowledge gained through experience. [Middle English, knowledge, learning, from Old French, from Latin *scientia,* from *sciēns,* present participle of *scire,* to know. See **skei-** in Appendix.*]

science fiction. *Abbr.* **SF** Fiction in which scientific discoveries and developments form an element of plot or background; especially, a work of fiction based on prediction of future scientific possibilities. —**sci′ence-fic′tion** *adj.*

sci·en·tial (sī-ĕn′shəl) *adj.* **1.** Of or producing knowledge or science. **2.** Capable; skillful.

sci·en·tif·ic (sī′ən-tĭf′ĭk) *adj. Abbr.* **sci. 1.** Of, relating to, or used in science. **2.** Broadly, having or appearing to have an exact, objective, factual, systematic, or methodological basis. [Medieval Latin *scientificus,* "producing knowledge" : Latin *scientia,* knowledge, SCIENCE + -FIC.] —**sci′en·tif′i·cal·ly** *adv.*

scientific empiricism. The philosophical view that there are no ultimate differences among the various sciences. Also called "Unity of Science Movement."

scientific method. The totality of principles and processes regarded as characteristic of or necessary for scientific investigation, generally taken to include rules for concept formation, conduct of observations and experiments, and validation of hypotheses by observations or experiments.

sci·en·tism (sī′ən-tĭz′əm) *n.* The theory that investigational methods used in the natural sciences should be applied in all fields of inquiry. —**sci′en·tis′tic** (sī′ən-tĭs′tĭk) *adj.*

sci·en·tist (sī′ən-tĭst) *n.* **1.** A person having expert knowledge of one or more sciences. **2.** *Capital* **S.** A Christian Scientist.

scil·i·cet (sĭl′ĭ-sĕt′, skē′lĭ-kĕt′) *adv. Abbr.* **sc., scil., ss** That is to say; namely. [Latin, short for *scīre licet,* "it is permitted to know," it is evident, of course, namely : *scīre,* to know (see **skei-** in Appendix*) + *licet,* third person singular present of *licēre,* to be allowed (see **leisure**).]

Scil·ly Islands (sĭl′ē). A group of islets at the entrance to the English Channel off Cornwall.

scim·i·tar (sĭm′ə-tər, -tär′) *n.* Also **scim·i·ter** (-tər). A curved Oriental sword with an edge on the convex side. [French *cimeterre,* from Italian *scimitarra,* from Persian *shimshīr*†.]

scin·til·la (sĭn-tĭl′ə) *n.* A minute amount; trace; iota. [Latin, spark. See **skī-** in Appendix.*]

scin·til·late (sĭn′tə-lāt′) *v.* **-lated, -lating, -lates.** —*intr.* **1.** To throw off sparks; flash. **2.** To sparkle or shine. **3.** To be animated and brilliant. —*tr.* To give off (sparks or flashes). —See Synonyms at **flash.** [Latin *scintillāre,* from *scintilla,* spark. See **skī-** in Appendix.*] —**scin′til·lat′ing·ly** *adv.*

scin·til·la·tion (sĭn′tə-lā′shən) *n.* **1.** The action of scintillating. **2.** A spark; flash. **3.** *Astronomy.* Rapid variation in the light of a celestial body caused by turbulence in the earth's atmosphere; a twinkling. **4.** *Physics.* A flash of light produced in certain media by absorption of an ionizing particle or photon.

scintillation counter. A device for detecting and counting scintillations produced by ionizing radiation.

sci·o·lism (sī′ə-lĭz′əm) *n.* A pretentious attitude of scholarship; superficial knowledgeability. [From Late Latin *sciolus,* smatterer, diminutive of *scius,* knowing, from *scīre,* to know. See **skei-** in Appendix.*] —**sci′o·list** *n.* —**sci′o·lis′tic** (-lĭs′tĭk) *adj.*

sci·on (sī′ən) *n.* Also **ci·on** (for sense 2). **1.** A descendant or heir. **2.** A detached shoot or twig containing buds from a woody plant and used in grafting. [Middle English, from Old French *ciun, cion,* from Germanic. See **gēi-**[1] in Appendix.*]

Sci·o·to (sī-ō′tə, -tō). A river rising in central Ohio and flowing 237 miles south to the Ohio River.

Scip·i·o Ae·mil·i·a·nus Af·ri·ca·nus Nu·man·ti·nus (skĭp′ē-ō′ ē-mĭl′ē-ā′nŭs ăf′rĭ-kā′nəs nōō′mən-tī′nəs, sĭp′ē-ō′), **Publius Cornelius.** Known as Scipio the Younger. 185–129 B.C. Roman consul and general; victor in the third Punic War; adopted grandson of Scipio the Elder.

Scip·i·o Af·ri·ca·nus (skĭp′ē-ō′ ăf′rĭ-kā′nəs, sĭp′ē-ō′), **Publius Cornelius.** Known as Scipio the Elder. 237–183 B.C. Roman general; victor in the second Punic War.

sci·re fa·ci·as (sī′rē fā′shē-əs, fā′shəs). *Law.* **1.** A writ requiring the party against whom it is issued to appear and show cause why a judicial record should not be enforced, repealed, or annulled. **2.** A judicial proceeding under such a writ. [Latin *scīre facias,* "you are to cause (him) to know" (phrase commonly used in the writ) : *scīre,* to know (see **skei-** in Appendix*) + *facias,* second person singular present subjunctive of *facere,* to make, do (see **dhē-**[1] in Appendix*).]

sci·roc·co. Variant of **sirocco.**

scir·rhus (skĭr′əs, sĭr′-) *n., pl.* **scirrhi** (skĭr′ī′, sĭr′ī′) or **-rhuses.** A hard cancerous growth usually associated with connective tissue. [New Latin, from Greek *skirros, skiros*†, hard.] —**scir′rhous, scir′rhoid′** (skĭr′oid′, sĭr′-) *adj.*

scis·sile (sĭs′əl, -īl′) *adj.* Capable of being cut or split easily. [French, from Latin *scissilis,* from *scindere* (past participle *scissus*), to cut. See **scission.**]

scis·sion (sĭzh′ən, sĭsh′-) *n.* The act of cutting or severing; division; fission. [French, from Late Latin *scissiō,* from Latin *scindere* (past participle *scissus*), to cut. See **skei-** in Appendix.*]

scis·sor (sĭz′ər) *tr.v.* **-sored, -soring, -sors.** To cut or clip with scissors or shears. —*n.* Scissors.

scis·sors (sĭz′ərz) *n.* Plural in form, used with a singular or plural verb. **1.** A cutting implement consisting of two blades, each with a loop handle and joined by a swivel pin that allows the cutting edges to be opened and closed. Also called "pair of scissors." **2.** A wrestling hold in which the legs are locked about the head or body of the opponent. **3.** Any of various gymnastic exercises or jumps in which the movement of the legs suggests the opening and closing of scissors. [Middle English *sisoures,* from Old French *cisoires,* from Medieval Latin *cisōria,* plural of Late Latin *cīsōrium,* cutting instrument, from Latin *caedere* (past participle *caesus,* in compounds *-cīsus*), to cut. See **skhai-** in Appendix.*]

scissors kick. A swimming kick used chiefly with the side stroke in which one leg is swung forward, the other bent back at the knee, and then both are straightened and snapped together.

scis·sor·tail (sĭz′ər-tāl′) *n.* A bird, *Muscivora forficata,* of the southwestern United States, Mexico, and Central and South America, having a long, forked tail. Also called "scissor-tailed flycatcher."

sci·u·roid (sī′yə-roid′, sī-yŏŏr′oid′) *adj.* **1.** Resembling or characteristic of a squirrel. **2.** *Botany.* Similar in shape to a squirrel's tail; bushy and curved. [Latin *sciūrus,* SQUIRREL + -OID.]

SCL Airport code for Santiago, Chile.

sclaff (sklăf) *v.* **sclaffed, sclaffing, sclaffs.** *Golf.* —*intr.* To scrape or strike the ground with the club behind the ball before hitting it. —*tr.* **1.** To hit (the club) against the ground before striking the ball. **2.** To strike (the ground) with the club before hitting the ball. —*n.* A stroke made in this manner. [Scottish, to strike with a flat surface (imitative).] —**sclaff′er** *n.*

Sclav. *Obsolete.* Variant of **Slav.**

S.C.L.C. Southern Christian Leadership Conference.

scle·ra (sklîr′ə) *n.* Also **scle·rot·i·ca** (sklə-rŏt′ĭ-kə). The tough, white, fibrous outer envelope of tissue covering all of the eyeball except the cornea. [New Latin, from Greek *sklēros,* hard. See **skel-**[4] in Appendix.*]

scle·ren·chy·ma (sklə-rĕng′kə-mə) *n.* Supportive or protective plant tissue consisting of thick-walled, usually lignified cells. [New Latin : SCLER(O)- + -ENCHYMA.] —**scle′ren-chym′a·tous** (sklîr′ən-kĭm′ə-təs) *adj.*

scle·rite (sklîr′īt) *n.* One of the hard outer plates forming part of the exoskeleton of an arthropod, especially an insect. [SCLER(O)- + -ITE.]

scle·ri·tis (sklə-rī′tĭs) *n.* Inflammation of the sclera. [New Latin : SCLER(O)- + -ITIS.] —**scle·rit′ic** (sklə-rĭt′ĭk) *adj.*

sclero–, scler–. Indicates: **1.** Hardness; for example, **scleroderma, sclerite. 2.** Of or affecting the sclera; for example, **sclerotomy, scleritis.** [New Latin, from Greek *sklēros,* hard. See **skel-**[4] in Appendix.*]

scle·ro·der·ma (sklîr′ō-dûr′mə) *n.* Pathological thickening and hardening of the skin. [New Latin : SCLERO- + -DERMA.]

scle·ro·der·ma·tous (sklîr′ō-dûr′mə-təs) *adj.* **1.** Characterizing or afflicted with scleroderma. **2.** *Zoology.* Having an outer covering of hard plates or bony scales.

scle·roid (sklîr′oid′) *adj. Biology.* Hard or hardened; indurated. [SCLER(O)- + -OID.]

scle·ro·ma (sklə-rō′mə) *n., pl.* **-mata** (-mə-tə). An abnormally hard patch of bodily tissue. [New Latin, from Greek *sklērōma,* hardening, from *sklēroun,* to harden, from *sklēros,* hard. See **skel-**[4] in Appendix.*]

scle·rom·e·ter (sklə-rŏm′ə-tər) *n.* An instrument used to determine relative hardness by measurement of the pressure required on a standard diamond stylus to achieve penetration. [SCLERO- + -METER.]

scle·ro·pro·tein (sklîr′ō-prō′tēn′, -tē-ĭn) *n.* Any of a large class of proteins, such as keratin, elastin, and collagen, found in skeletal and connective tissue.

scle·rosed (sklə-rōst′) *adj.* **1.** Affected with sclerosis; hardened. **2.** Lignified. [From SCLEROSIS.]

scle·ro·sis (sklə-rō′sĭs) *n., pl.* **-ses** (-sēz′). **1. a.** *Pathology.* A thickening or hardening of a body part, as of an artery or the spinal cord, especially from tissue overgrowth or disease. **b.** A disease characterized by sclerosis. **2.** *Botany.* The hardening of an outer cell wall by formation or deposit of lignin. [Middle English *sclirosis,* from Medieval Latin *sclīrōsis,* from Greek *sklērōsis,* hardening, from *sklēroun,* to harden, from *sklēros,* hard. See **skel-**[4] in Appendix.*] —**scle·ro′sal** *adj.*

scle·rot·ic (sklə-rŏt′ĭk) *adj.* **1.** Affected or characterized by sclerosis. **2.** *Anatomy.* Of or pertaining to the sclera. [New Latin *scleroticus,* from SCLEROSIS and SCLERA.]

scle·rot·i·ca. Variant of **sclera.**

scle·ro·ti·um (sklə-rō′shē-əm) *n., pl.* **-tia** (-shē-ə). A dense mass of branching filaments, or hyphae, in certain fungi, containing stored food and capable of remaining dormant for long periods. [New Latin, from Greek *sklērotēs,* hardness, from *sklēros,* hard, SCLEROUS.] —**scle·ro′tial** (-shəl) *adj.*

scle·rot·o·my (sklə-rŏt′ə-mē) *n., pl.* **-mies.** Surgical incision of the sclera. [SCLERO- + -TOMY.]

scle·rous (sklîr′əs) *adj.* Hardened; toughened; bony. [Greek *sklēros,* hard. See **skel-**[4] in Appendix.*]

scoff (skôf, skŏf) *v.* **scoffed, scoffing, scoffs.** —*tr.* To mock at or treat with derision. —*intr.* To laugh or mock at. —*n.* An expression of derision or scorn; a jeer. [Middle English *scoffen,* from *scof,* mockery, probably from Scandinavian, akin to Danish *skof,* jest. See **skeubh-** in Appendix.*] —**scoff′er** *n.* —**scoff′ing·ly** *adv.*

scoff·law (skôf′lô′, skŏf′-) *n.* One who habitually violates the law or fails to answer court summonses.

scold (skōld) *v.* **scolded, scolding, scolds.** —*tr.* To reprimand harshly. —*intr.* To find fault habitually and openly. —*n.* One who persistently rails against others. [Middle English *scalden, scolden,* from *scald, scold,* ribald or abusive person, perhaps from Old Norse *skāld,* poet. See **sekw-**[3] in Appendix.] —**scold′er** *n.* —**scold′ing·ly** *adv.*

Synonyms: *scold, upbraid, berate, revile, nag, rail.* These verbs mean to express criticism or disfavor. *Scold* implies anger or irritation and the tone and manner of one correcting a child at fault. *Upbraid* is stronger and generally implies rather formal criticism, such as that made by an official or a superior. *Berate* suggests scolding or rebuking angrily and abusively at length. *Revile* especially stresses the idea of abusive language; usually it implies deliberate and prolonged verbal assault. *Nag* refers to complaining and faultfinding, usually prolonged and persistent. *Rail* also suggests persistent criticism but is much stronger through its implication of scorn and abuse.

scold·ing (skōl′dĭng) *n.* A sharp or rude reprimand.

sco·lex (skō′lĕks′) *n., pl.* **-leces** (-lə-sēz′) or **-lices** (-lə-sēz′). The knoblike anterior end of a tapeworm, having suckers or hooklike parts that in the adult stage serve as organs of attachment to the host on which the tapeworm is parasitic. [New Latin, from Greek *skōlēx,* worm, grub. See **skel-**[3] in Appendix.*]

sco·li·o·sis (skō′lē-ō′sĭs, skŏl′ē-) *n.* Also **sco·li·o·ma** (skō′lē-ō′mə, skŏl′ē-ō′mə). Abnormal lateral curvature of the spine.

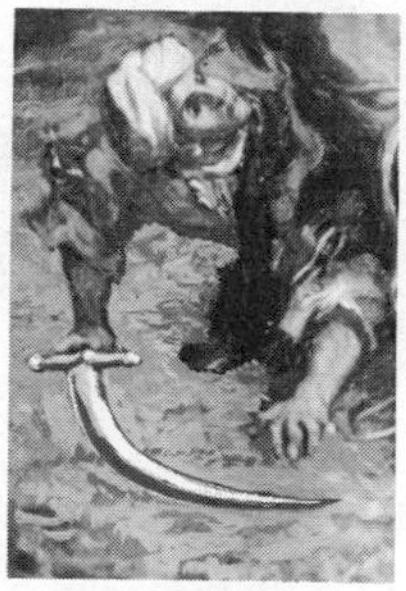

scimitar
Detail from "The Lion Hunt," by Delacroix

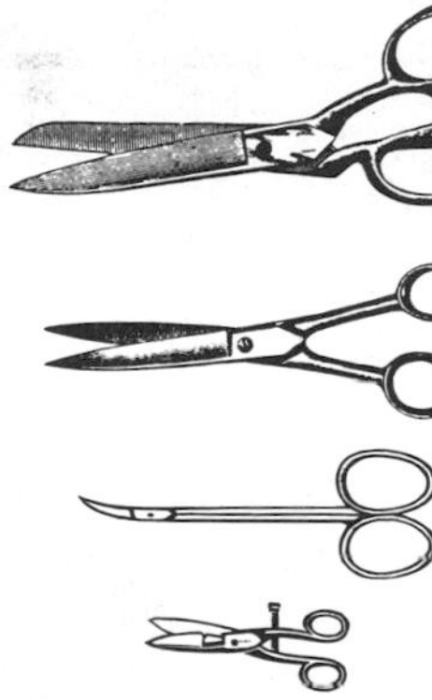

scissors
From top: Trimming scissors; barber scissors; manicure scissors; buttonhole scissors

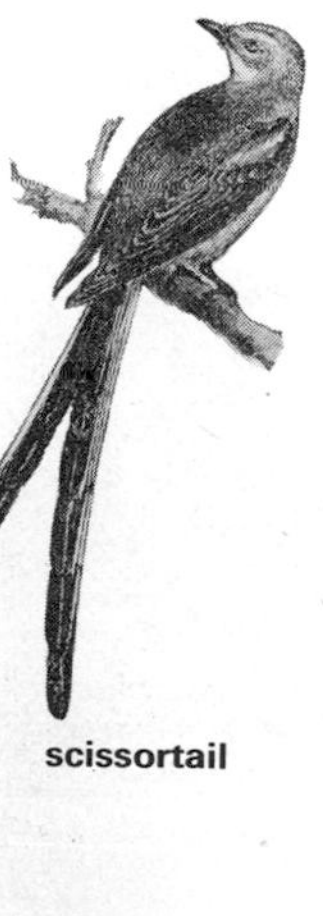

scissortail

[New Latin, from Greek *skiliōsis*, crookedness, from *skolios*, crooked. See **skel-³** in Appendix.] **—sco'li·ot'ic** (-ŏt'ĭk) *adj.*

scol·lop. Variant of **scallop.**

scol·o·pen·drid (skŏl'ə-pĕn'drĭd) *n.* Any of numerous arthropods of the family Scolopendridae, which includes the centipedes. [New Latin *Scolopendridae*, from Latin *scolopendra*, millipede, from Greek *skolopendra*†.] **—scol'o·pen'drid, scol'o·pen'drine'** (-drīn', -drĭn) *adj.*

scom·broid (skŏm'broid') *adj.* Of or belonging to the suborder Scombroidei, which includes marine fishes such as the mackerel. *—n.* A scombroid fish. [New Latin *Scombroidei*, from Latin *scomber*, mackerel, from Greek *skombros*†.]

sconce¹ (skŏns) *n.* A small defense earthwork or fort. [Dutch *schans*, from German *Schanze*, fortification originally made of latticework, from Italian *scanso*, defense, from *scansare*, to turn off, ward off, from Vulgar Latin *excampsāre* (unattested) : Latin *ex-*, out + *campsāre*, to turn around a place, sail by, from Greek *kamptein* (aorist stem *kamps-*), to bend, curve, turn (see **kamp-** in Appendix*).]

sconce² (skŏns) *n.* A decorative wall bracket for candles or lights. [Middle English, from Old French *esconse*, lantern, hiding place, from Medieval Latin *(a)sconsa*, from Latin *absconsus*, past participle of *abscondere*, to hide away : *ab(s)-*, away + *condere*, to hide (see **dhē-¹** in Appendix*).]

sconce³ (skŏns) *n. Informal.* The head or skull. [Jocular use of SCONCE (wall bracket).]

scone (skōn, skŏn) *n.* **1.** A round, soft, doughy pastry. **2.** Originally, in Scotland, a thin cake of oatmeal baked on a griddle. [Short for Dutch *schoonbrood*, fine white bread, from Middle Dutch *schoonbroot*, from *schoon*, beautiful, bright, white (see **keu-¹** in Appendix*) + *broot*, bread.]

Scone (sko͞on). A village in eastern Perthshire, Scotland, site of a royal residence and place of coronation (1150–1488).

Scone, Stone of. The stone on which Scottish kings were seated for coronation. It was removed to London by Edward I in 1297 and has been kept under the seat of the coronation chair in Westminster Abbey ever since, except for a brief period (1950–51) when it was stolen by Scottish Nationalists.

scoop

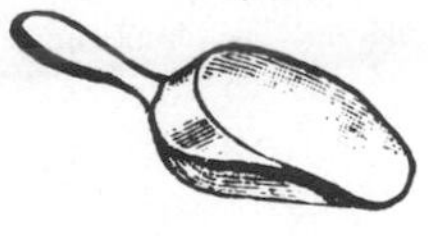

covered metal scoop

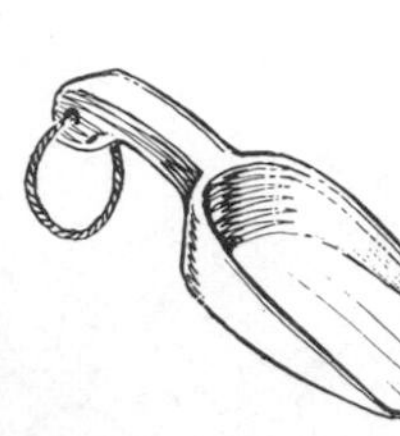

basswood scoop

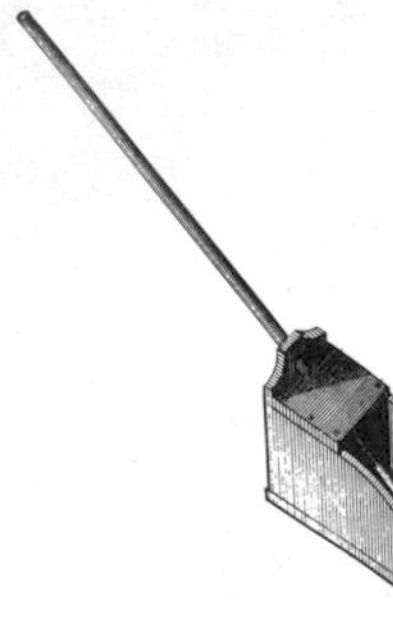

early 18th-century dredging scoop

scoop (sko͞op) *n.* **1.** A small, shovellike utensil, usually having a deep, curved dish and short handle, used for drawing on various stores. **2.** A long-handled utensil with a round bowl, especially one for liquids; a ladle; dipper. **3.** An implement for bailing water from a boat. **4.** A narrow, spoon-shaped instrument for surgical extraction in cavities or cysts. **5. a.** A thick-handled kitchen utensil for dispensing balls of ice cream, mashed potatoes, or the like, usually having a sweeping band in the dish which is levered by the thumb to free the contents. **b.** A portion gathered in this manner. **6.** The bucket or shovel of a steam shovel or dredge. **7.** A scooping movement or action; a sweep. **8.** A wide hole or bowl-shaped cavity. **9.** *Informal.* A large profit gained through speculation. **10.** *Slang.* **a.** An exclusive news story acquired by luck or initiative. **b.** Any sensational piece of news. **11.** *Slang.* The substance or details of a given occurrence or situation. *—tr.v.* **scooped, scooping, scoops.** **1.** To take up or dip into with or as with a scoop; to spoon. **2.** To hollow out or excavate; form by digging. Used with *out.* **3.** To gather or collect swiftly and unceremoniously; to grab. Used with *up* or *in.* **4.** To empty or deplete; to bail; clean out. Used with *out.* **5.** *Slang.* To top or outmaneuver (a competitor) in acquiring and publishing an important news story. [Middle English, from Middle Low German and Middle Dutch *schōpe*. See **skep-** in Appendix.*] **—scoop'er** *n.*

scoot (sko͞ot) *intr.v.* **scooted, scooting, scoots.** To go speedily; to dart or scurry off; to hurry. *—n.* A darting or scurrying off; a hurried departure. [Probably from Scandinavian, akin to Old Norse *skjōta*, to shoot, throw, push. See **skeud-** in Appendix.*]

scoot·er (sko͞o'tər) *n.* **1.** A child's vehicle consisting of a long footboard between two small end wheels, the forward wheel controlled by an upright steering handle. **2.** A **motor scooter** *(see).* **3.** A sailboat, flat-bottomed, with runners that can skim over water or ice. [From SCOOT.]

scop (skŏp) *n.* A bard or minstrel of Anglo-Saxon England. [Middle English *scop(e)*, Old English *scop*. See **skeubh-** in Appendix.*]

scope (skōp) *n.* **1.** The range of one's perceptions, thoughts, or actions. **2.** Breadth or opportunity to function. **3.** The area covered by a given activity or subject. **4.** The length or sweep of a mooring cable. **5.** *Informal.* A shortened form for microscope, periscope, telescope, or the like. [Originally "something aimed at," "purpose," from Italian *scopo*, from Greek *skopos*, watcher, goal, aim. See **spek-** in Appendix.*]

-scope. Indicates an instrument for observing or detecting; for example, **oscilloscope, telescope, microscope.** [Latin *-scopium*, from Greek *-skopion*, from *skopein*, to see. See **spek-** in Appendix.*]

Scopes (skōps), **John Thomas.** Born 1901. American teacher; convicted (1925) for teaching evolution in a Tennessee school.

sco·pol·a·mine (skō-pŏl'ə-mēn', -mĭn) *n.* A thick, syrupy, colorless alkaloid, $C_{17}H_{21}NO_4$, extracted from such plants as henbane and used as a mydriatic, sedative, and truth serum. Also called "hyoscine." [German *Scopolamin* : New Latin *Scopolia*, genus of plants from which the alkaloid is extracted, named after Giovanni *Scopoli* (1723–88), Italian naturalist + -AMINE.]

sco·po·line (skō'pə-lēn', -lĭn) *n.* A crystalline alkaloid, $C_8H_{13}O_2N$, derived from scopolamine and used as a narcotic. [SCOPOL(AMINE) + -INE.]

sco·po·phil·i·a (skō'pə-fĭl'ē-ə) *n.* Also **scop·to·phil·i·a** (skŏp'tə-fĭl'ē-ə). The derivation of sexual pleasure from viewing sexual organs or erotic scenes; voyeurism. [New Latin : Greek *skopein*, to see (see **spek-** in Appendix*) + -PHILIA.]

scop·u·la (skŏp'yə-lə) *n., pl.* **-lae** (-lē'). A dense, brushlike tuft of hairs, as in certain insects. [Late Latin *scōpula*, diminutive of Latin *scopa*†, twigs, broom.] **—scop'u·late'** (-lāt') *adj.*

Sco·pus, Mount (skō'pəs). A mountain of Israel, 2,736 feet high, in western Jordan northeast of Jerusalem.

-scopy. Indicates viewing, seeing, or observing; for example, **microscopy, telescopy.** [Greek *-skopia*, from *skopein*, to look into, behold. See **spek-** in Appendix.*]

scor·bu·tic (skôr-byo͞o'tĭk) *adj.* Also **scor·bu·ti·cal** (-tĭ-kəl). Related to, resembling, or afflicted with scurvy. [New Latin *scorbuticus*, from Late Latin *scorbūtus*, scurvy, from Russian *skrobota*, "scratch," from *skrest'*, to scratch, scrape. See **sker-¹** in Appendix.*] **—scor·bu'ti·cal·ly** *adv.*

scorch (skôrch) *v.* **scorched, scorching, scorches.** *—tr.* **1.** To burn slightly so as to alter the color or taste. **2.** To wither or parch with intense heat; char. **3.** To subject to severe censure or anger; excoriate. *—intr.* To become scorched or singed. —See Synonyms at **burn.** *—n.* **1.** A slight or surface burn. **2.** A discoloration caused by heat. **3.** Brown spotting on plant leaves caused by fungi, heat, or lack of water. [Middle English *scorchen, scorcnen*, perhaps from Old Norse *skorpna*, to shrivel. See **skerbh-** in Appendix.*] **—scorch'ing·ly** *adv.*

scorched-earth policy (skôrcht'ûrth'). A military policy of devastating all land and buildings in the course of an advance or retreat, so as to leave nothing salvageable to the enemy.

scorch·er (skôr'chər) *n.* **1.** One that scorches. **2.** *Informal.* An extremely hot day.

score (skôr, skōr) *n.* **1.** A notch or incision, especially one made to keep a tally. **2.** An evaluative record, usually numerical, of any competitive event: *keeping score.* **3. a.** The total number of points made by each competitor or side in a contest, either final or at a given stage. **b.** The number of points attributed to any one competitor or team. **4.** A result, usually expressed numerically, of a test or examination. **5. a.** An amount due; a debt. **b.** A harbored grievance; a grudge demanding satisfaction. **6.** A ground; reason; account. **7.** A group of 20 items. **8.** *Plural.* Large numbers. **9.** The written form of a musical composition for orchestral or vocal parts, either complete or for a particular instrument or voice. **10.** The music composed for a stage show or film. **—know the score.** *Informal.* To be aware of the realities of a situation. *—v.* **scored, scoring, scores.** *—tr.* **1.** To mark with lines or notches, especially for the purpose of keeping a record. **2.** To cancel or eliminate by or as if by superimposing lines. Used with *out* or *off.* **3.** *Cooking.* To mark the surface of (meat, for example) with usually parallel cuts. **4. a.** To gain (a point) in a game or contest. **b.** To count or be worth as points. **5.** To achieve; win. **6.** To evaluate and assign a grade to. **7.** *Music.* **a.** To orchestrate. **b.** To arrange for a specific instrument. **8.** To criticize cuttingly; berate. *—intr.* **1.** To make a point in a game or contest. **2.** To keep the score of a game or contest. **3. a.** To achieve a purpose or advantage; succeed. **b.** *Informal.* To make a surprising gain or coup. [Middle English *scor*, Old English *scoru* (attested only in plural *scora*), twenty, from Old Norse *skor*, notch, twenty. See **sker-¹** in Appendix.*] **—scor'er** *n.*

score·card (skôr'kärd', skōr'-) *n.* **1.** A printed program or card enabling a spectator to identify players and record the progress of a game. **2.** A small card used by an individual player or by partners, as in golf, to record one's own performance.

score·less (skôr'lĭs, skōr'-) *adj.* With no points scored by a competing team or teams: *a scoreless game.*

Scores·by Sound (skôrz'bē, skōrz'-). A fjord system extending about 200 miles into eastern Greenland.

sco·ri·a (skôr'ē-ə, skōr'-) *n., pl.* **scoriae** (skôr'ē-ē', skōr'-). **1.** *Geology.* Rough fragments of burnt, crustlike lava. Also called "cinder," "slag." **2.** *Metallurgy.* The refuse of a smelted metal or ore; slag. [Middle English, slag, dross, from Latin *scōria*, from Greek *skōria*, from *skōr*, excrement. See **sker-⁴** in Appendix.*] **—sco'ri·a'ceous** (skôr'ē-ā'shəs, skōr'-) *adj.*

sco·ri·fy (skôr'ə-fī', skōr'-) *tr.v.* **-fied, -fying, -fies.** To separate (an ore) into scoria and a precious metal. [SCORI(A) + -FY.] **—sco'ri·fi·ca'tion** *n.*

scorn (skôrn) *n.* **1.** Contempt or disdain, as felt toward a person or object considered despicable or inferior. **2.** The expression of such an attitude in behavior or speech; derision. **3.** A person or thing treated or spoken of with contempt. *—v.* **scorned, scorning, scorns.** *—tr.* **1.** To consider or treat as contemptible or unworthy. **2.** To reject or refuse with derision. *—intr.* To express contempt; to scoff. [Middle English *scornen, schornen*, to despise, from Old French *escharnir*, from Vulgar Latin *escarnīre* (unattested), from Germanic *skarnjan* (unattested).] **—scorn'er** *n.* **—scorn'ful** *adj.* **—scorn'ful·ly** *adv.* **—scorn'ful·ness** *n.*

scor·pae·noid (skôr-pē'noid') *adj.* Of or belonging to the suborder Scorpaenoidei, which includes the scorpion fishes and rockfishes. *—n.* A scorpaenoid fish. [New Latin *Scorpaenoidei* : *Scorpaena* (genus), from Latin, a fish, from Greek *skorpaina*, feminine of *skorpios*, a sea fish, SCORPION + *-oidei*, plural of Latin *-oidēs*, -OID (likeness).]

scor·pi·oid (skôr'pē-oid') *adj.* **1.** Pertaining to or resembling a scorpion. **2.** *Botany.* Curved or curled like the tail of a scorpion: *a scorpioid inflorescence.* [Greek *skorpioeidēs*, scorpionlike : *skorpios*, SCORPION + -OID.]

scor·pi·on (skôr'pē-ən) *n.* **1.** Any of various arachnids of the order Scorpionida, of warm, dry regions, having a segmented body and an erectile tail tipped with a venomous sting. **2.** *Capital* **S.** The constellation and sign of the zodiac **Scorpius** *(see).*

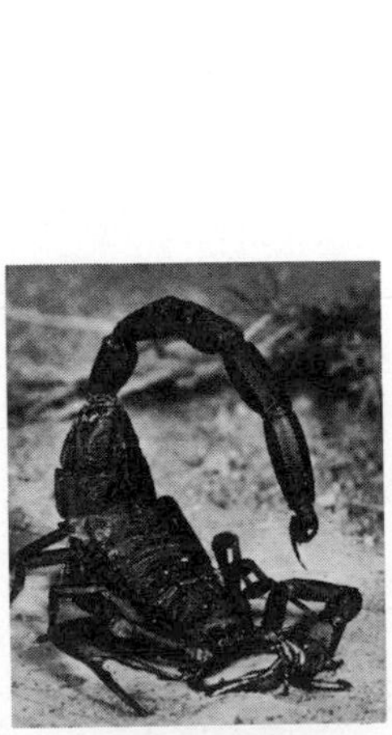

scorpion
Centruroides gracilis
Scorpion and prey

[Middle English *scorpioun,* from Old French *scorpion,* from Latin *scorpiō,* from Greek *skorpios*†.]

scorpion fish. Any of numerous small, often brilliantly colored marine fishes of the family Scorpaenidae, having poisonous spines in the dorsal fin in most species.

scorpion fly. Any insect of the order Mecoptera, having in the male of most species a curved genital structure that resembles the sting of a scorpion.

Scor·pi·us (skôr′pē-əs) *n.* Also **Scor·pi·o** (skôr′pē-ō′). **1.** A constellation in the Southern Hemisphere near Libra and Sagittarius. It contains the star Antares. **2.** The eighth sign of the **zodiac** *(see).* Also called the "Scorpion." [New Latin, from Latin *scorpius, scorpiō,* SCORPION.]

Scot (skŏt) *n.* **1.** A native or inhabitant of Scotland. See Usage note at **Scotsman. 2.** A member of the ancient Gaelic tribe that migrated to the northern part of Great Britain from Ireland in about the sixth century A.D. [Middle English *Scottes,* Scots, Old English *Scottas,* from Late Latin *Scōti, Scotti* (singular *Scottus*), from Old Irish *Scuit*†, Scots, Irishmen.]

Scot. Scotch; Scotland; Scottish.

scot and lot (skŏt). A municipal tax formerly levied in Great Britain on the members of a community proportionate to their ability to pay. **—pay scot and lot.** To pay in full; settle all obligations. [Middle English *scot,* tax, contribution, partly from Old Norse *skot* and partly from Old French *escot,* from Frankish *skot* (unattested). See **skeud-** in Appendix.*]

scotch[1] (skŏch) *tr.v.* **scotched, scotching, scotches. 1.** To cut or score; to scratch. **2.** To injure so as to render harmless; cripple. **3.** To put an abrupt end to; to crush; stifle. *—n.* **1.** A surface cut or abrasion; a gash or scratch. **2.** A line drawn on the ground, as one used in playing hopscotch. [Middle English *scocchen,* from Norman French *escocher,* to cut a notch : *es-,* from Latin *ex-* (intensifier) + Old French *coche,* notch, from Vulgar Latin *cocca*† (unattested).]

scotch[2] (skŏch) *tr.v.* **scotched, scotching, scotches.** To block (a wheel, barrel, or log, for example) with a prop to prevent rolling or slipping. *—n.* A block or wedge used as a prop behind or under a wheel or other object likely to roll. [Perhaps variant of *scatch,* stilt, from Old French *escache,* "wooden leg," from Frankish *skakkja* (unattested), from *skakan* (unattested), to run fast, from Germanic *skakan* (unattested), to SHAKE.]

Scotch (skŏch) *n. Abbr.* **Sc., Scot. 1.** The people of Scotland. Used with *the.* See Usage note at **Scotsman. 2.** Any of the English dialects spoken in Scotland. **3.** Scotch whisky. *—adj.* **1.** Of or pertaining to the people, language, or culture of Scotland; Scottish; Scots. **2.** Tight with one's money; frugal. [Contraction of SCOTTISH.]

Scotch·man (skŏch′mən) *n., pl.* **-men** (-mĭn). A Scot. See Usage note at **Scotsman.**

Scotch tape. A trademark for a transparent cellulose adhesive tape.

Scotch terrier. A **Scottish terrier** *(see).*

Scotch verdict. 1. *Scottish Law.* A verdict permissible in certain criminal cases indicating only that guilt is not proven. **2.** Any inconclusive judgment or pronouncement.

Scotch whisky. A smoky-flavored whiskey distilled in Scotland from malted barley, the malt having been dried over a peat fire. See Usage note at **whiskey.**

Scotch woodcock. A savory dish consisting of scrambled eggs on toast with anchovies or anchovy paste. [By humorous analogy with WELSH RABBIT.]

sco·ter (skō′tər) *n.* Any of several dark-colored diving ducks of the genera *Oidemia* and *Melanitta,* of northern coastal areas. Sometimes called "coot." [Perhaps related to Old Norse *skoti,* shooter, and *skjōta,* to shoot (from its swiftness). See **skeud-** in Appendix.*]

scot-free (skŏt′frē′) *adj.* **1.** Without having to pay; free from obligation. **2.** Without incurring any penalty; unpunished. [From Middle English *scot,* tax. See **scot and lot.**]

Sco·tia (skō′shə) *n. Poetic.* Scotland. [Medieval Latin, from Late Latin *Scottus,* Scotsman, Irishman. See **Scot.**]

Sco·tism (skō′tĭz′əm) *n.* The scholastic philosophy of John Duns Scotus. **—Sco′tist** *n.*

Scot·land (skŏt′lənd). *Abbr.* **Scot.** A constituent country of the United Kingdom of Great Britain and Northern Ireland, occupying 30,405 square miles in northern Great Britain and including in its territory the Hebrides, Shetland, and Orkney island groups. It was an independent kingdom from 1122 until the Act of Union with England in 1707. Population, 5,178,000. Capital, Edinburgh.

Scotland Yard. 1. The headquarters of the London Metropolitan Police, housed at New Scotland Yard on the Thames embankment. **2.** The London Metropolitan Police, especially the Criminal Investigation Department (C.I.D.).

sco·to·ma (skə-tō′mə) *n., pl.* **-mas.** An area of pathologically diminished vision within the visual field. [New Latin, from Medieval Latin, dim sight, from Greek *skotōma,* dizziness, vertigo, from *skotoun,* to darken, from *skotos,* darkness. See **skot-** in Appendix.*]

sco·to·pi·a (skə-tō′pē-ə) *n.* Ability to see in dim light; night-adaptive vision. [New Latin : Greek *skotos,* darkness (see **scotoma**) + -OPIA.]

Scots (skŏts) *adj.* Scottish. See Usage note at **Scotsman.** *—n.* The English dialect spoken in Scotland. [Middle English *scottis,* variant of *Scottisc,* SCOTTISH.]

Scots·man (skŏts′mən) *n., pl.* **-men** (-mĭn). A Scot.

Usage: *Scotsman, Scot,* and *Scotchman* are all employed to designate one of the people of Scotland. *Scotsman* is the term generally preferred in Scotland; *Scotchman* is sometimes considered mildly offensive. *Scots* and *(the) Scotch* are the usual collective plural forms. Of the corresponding adjectives, *Scottish* and *Scots* are generally preferred to *Scotch* in Scotland, in general usage. But each has become an established form in certain well-known combinations *(Scotch broth, Scotch whisky, Scottish rite, Scots Guards). Scot* is not an adjective.

Scott (skŏt), **Dred.** 1795?–1858. American Negro slave; subject of a proslavery decision by Supreme Court (1857).

Scott (skŏt), **Robert Falcon.** 1868–1912. British explorer of the Antarctic; reached South Pole.

Scott (skŏt), Sir **Walter.** 1771–1832. Scottish poet and historical novelist.

Scott (skŏt), **Winfield.** 1786–1866. American military officer; commander in chief in the Mexican War.

Scot·ti·cism (skŏt′ə-sĭz′əm) *n.* An idiom or other expression characteristic of Scottish English.

Scot·tie (skŏt′ē) *n.* **1.** A Scotsman. **2.** A Scottish terrier.

Scot·tish (skŏt′ĭsh) *adj. Abbr.* **Sc., Scot.** Of, pertaining to, or characteristic of Scotland, its people, or its language. See Usage note at **Scotsman.** *—n.* **1.** A dialect of English spoken by the Lowlanders of Scotland; Scots. **2.** The people of Scotland. Preceded by *the.* See Usage note at **Scotsman.** [Middle English *Scottisc,* from *Scottes,* Scots. See **Scot.**]

Scottish Gaelic. The Gaelic language of the Scottish Highlanders. Sometimes called "Erse."

Scottish terrier. A terrier of a breed originating in Scotland, having a heavy-set body, short legs, blunt muzzle, and a dark, wiry coat. Sometimes called "Scotch terrier."

Sco·tus, Duns. See John **Duns Scotus.**

scoun·drel (skoun′drəl) *n.* A villain. *—adj.* Of or befitting a scoundrel. [Origin unknown.] **—scoun′drel·ly** *adj.*

scour[1] (skour) *v.* **scoured, scouring, scours.** *—tr.* **1. a.** To clean, polish, or wash by scrubbing vigorously, usually with an abrasive. **b.** To remove by scrubbing. **2.** To remove dirt or grease from (cloth or fibers) by means of a detergent. **3.** To clean (wheat) before the milling process. **4.** To clear (an area) by freeing of weeds or the like. **5.** To clear (a channel or pipe) by flushing. *—intr.* **1.** To scrub something in order to clean or polish it. **2.** To have diarrhea. Used of livestock. *—n.* **1.** A scouring action or effect. **2.** A place that has been scoured, as by flushing with water. **3.** A cleansing agent for wool. **4.** *Usually plural.* Diarrhea in livestock. Used with a singular or plural verb. [Middle English *scouren,* from Middle Dutch *schūren,* from Old French *escurer,* from Late Latin *excūrāre,* to clean out : Latin *ex-,* out + Late Latin *cūrāre,* to clean, from Latin, to take care of, from *cūra,* care, cure (see **cūra** in Appendix*).]

scour[2] (skour) *v.* **scoured, scouring, scours.** *—tr.* **1.** To range over (an area) quickly and energetically. **2.** To search through or over thoroughly. *—intr.* **1.** To range over or about an area, especially in a search. **2.** To move swiftly; to scurry; run. [Middle English *scouren,* probably from Old Norse *skȳra,* to rush in. See **kewero-** in Appendix.*]

scour·er[1] (skour′ər) *n.* A workman or device that scours.

scour·er[2] (skour′ər) *n.* **1.** A person who ranges about, especially a scout. **2.** A rowdy prankster of a kind that prowled the nighttime streets of 18th-century England.

scourge (skûrj) *n.* **1.** A whip used to inflict punishment. **2.** Any means of inflicting severe suffering, vengeance, or punishment. **3.** A cause of widespread and dreaded affliction, as pestilence or war. *—tr.v.* **scourged, scourging, scourges. 1.** To flog. **2.** To chastise severely; excoriate. **3.** To ravage; devastate. [Middle English, from Old French *escorge,* from *escorgier,* to whip, from Vulgar Latin *excorrigiāre* (unattested) : Latin *ex-* (intensive) + *corrigia,* thong, shoelace, "whip," from Celtic (see **reig-**[1] in Appendix*).] **—scourg′er** *n.*

scouring rush. Any of several species of horsetail; especially, *Equisetum hyemale,* having rough-ridged stems formerly used for scouring utensils.

scour·ings (skour′ĭngz) *pl.n.* **1.** The refuse that remains after scouring grain. **2.** Dregs; scum.

scouse (skous) *n.* A sailor's stew, **lobscouse** *(see).* [Short for LOBSCOUSE.]

scout[1] (skout) *n.* **1. a.** A person, aircraft, or ship dispatched from a main body to gather information, as about the terrain or enemy ahead. **b.** The action so performed; a reconnoitering. **2.** A watchman or sentinel. **3.** A person employed to discover and recruit persons with talent, as in sports or entertainment. **4. a.** A member of the Boy Scouts. **b.** A member of the Girl Scouts. **5.** *British.* A student's servant at Oxford University. *—tr.v.* **scouted, scouting, scouts. 1.** To spy upon or explore carefully in order to obtain information; reconnoiter. **2.** To observe and evaluate (a young actor, for example) for possible hiring. **3.** To search. Often used with *around.* [Middle English *scoute,* from Old French *escoute,* "listener," spy, from *escouter,* to listen, from Vulgar Latin *ascultāre* (unattested), variant of Latin *auscultāre.* See **ous-** in Appendix.*] **—scout′er** *n.*

scout[2] (skout) *v.* **scouted, scouting, scouts.** *—tr.* To reject contemptuously; dismiss with disdain or derision. *—intr.* To scoff. Used with *at.* [From Scandinavian, akin to Old Norse *skūta, skūti,* mockery, taunt. See **skeud-** in Appendix.*]

scout·ing (skou′tĭng) *n.* Participation in the activities of the Boy Scouts or Girl Scouts.

scout·mas·ter (skout′măs′tər, -mäs′tər) *n.* The adult leader in charge of a troop of Boy Scouts.

scow (skou) *n.* A large flat-bottomed boat with square ends, used chiefly for transporting freight. [Dutch *schouw,* from Middle Dutch *scoude, scouwe,* akin to Old Saxon *skaldan*†, to push a boat from the shore.]

scowl (skoul) *n.* A look of anger, sullenness, or strong dis-

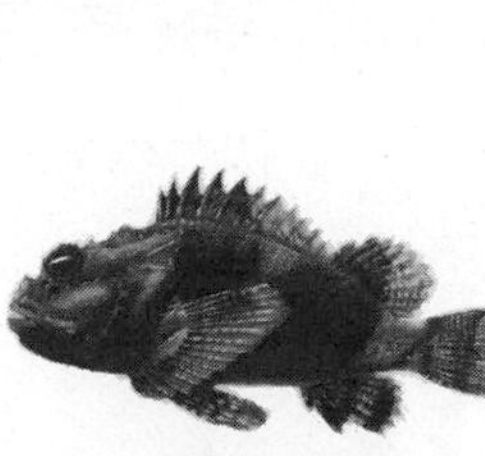

scorpion fish
Scorpaena plumieri

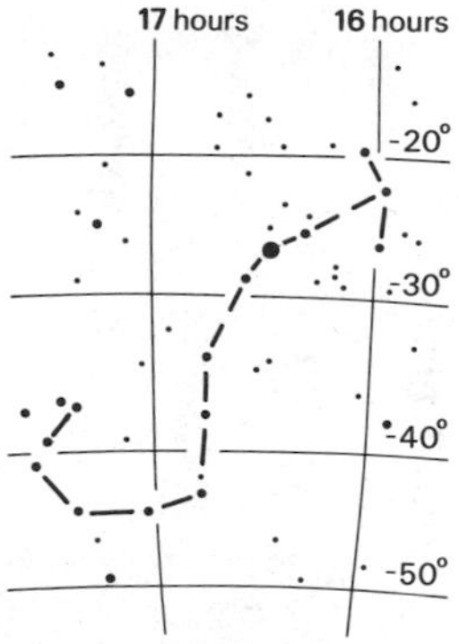

Scorpius

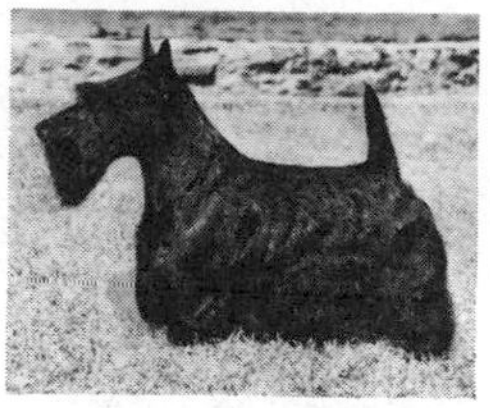

Scottish terrier

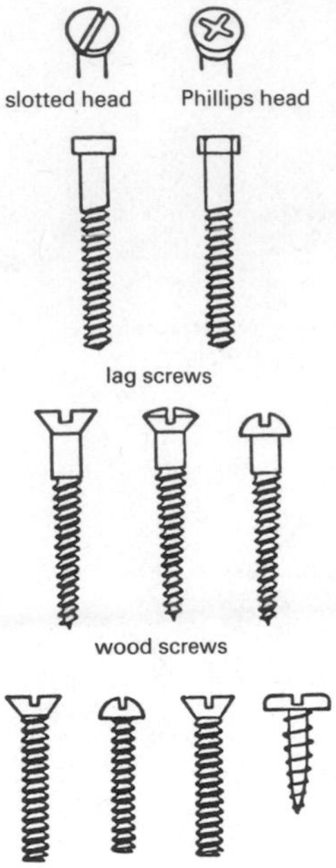
slotted head
Phillips head
lag screws
wood screws
metal screws
screw

approval; an angry frown. —*v.* **scowled, scowling, scowls.** —*intr.* To lower or contract the brow in an expression of anger, disapproval, or bitterness; frown angrily. —*tr.* To express or utter with a scowl. [Middle English *scoulen,* probably from Scandinavian, akin to Danish *skule*†, to scowl.] —**scowl'er** *n.* —**scowl'ing·ly** *adv.*

scr. scruple (unit of weight).

scrab·ble (skrăb'əl) *v.* **-bled, -bling, -bles.** —*intr.* **1.** To scrape or grope about frenetically with the hands. **2.** To struggle. **3.** To make hasty, disordered markings; to scribble. —*tr.* **1.** To make or obtain by scraping together. Often used with *up.* **2.** To scribble on; scrawl over. —*n.* **1.** The act or an instance of scrabbling. **2.** A scribble; a doodle. [Middle Dutch *schrabbelen,* frequentative of *schrabben,* to scrape. See **sker-**[1] in Appendix.*]

Scrab·ble (skrăb'əl) *n.* A trademark for a board game in which players build words with small lettered blocks of varying count values.

scrag (skrăg) *n.* **1.** A bony or scrawny person or animal. **2.** A piece of lean or bony meat, especially a neck of mutton. **3.** *Slang.* The human neck. —*tr.v.* **scragged, scragging, scrags.** *Informal.* To wring the neck of; kill by strangling. [Variant of obsolete *crag(ge),* neck, throat, Middle English *crag, crage,* from Middle Dutch *crāghe.* See **gwere-**[2] in Appendix.*]

scrag·gly (skrăg'lē) *adj.* **-glier, -gliest.** Ragged; irregular; untended or unkempt. [From SCRAG.]

scrag·gy (skrăg'ē) *adj.* **-gier, -giest. 1.** Jagged; ragged; rough. **2.** Bony and lean. —**scrag'gi·ly** *adv.* —**scrag'gi·ness** *n.*

scram (skrăm) *intr.v.* **scrammed, scramming, scrams.** *Slang.* To leave a scene at once; go abruptly. Usually used in the imperative. [Short for SCRAMBLE.]

scram·ble (skrăm'bəl) *v.* **-bled, -bling, -bles.** —*intr.* **1.** To move or climb hurriedly, especially on the hands and knees. **2.** To vie in free-for-all competition; to struggle urgently. **3.** *Military.* To take off with all possible haste in order to intercept enemy aircraft. —*tr.* **1.** To mix or throw together confusedly. **2.** To gather together in a hurried or disorderly fashion. Often used with *up.* **3.** *Electronics.* To distort or garble (a signal) so as to render it unintelligible without a special receiver. —*n.* **1.** The act or an instance of scrambling. **2.** An arduous hike or climb over rough terrain. **3.** An unceremonious scuffle or struggle for something. [Blend of obsolete *scamble*†, to struggle for, and *cramble*†, to crawl.]

scrambled eggs. 1. Eggs fried with the yolks and whites mixed together. **2.** *Slang.* The gold braid worn on the bill of the cap of high-ranking officers in the armed services.

scram·bler (skrăm'blər) *n.* **1.** One that scrambles. **2.** An electronic device that scrambles telecommunication signals to make them unintelligible to an eavesdropper.

Scran·ton (skrăn'tən). A city and manufacturing center in an anthracite-producing region of northeastern Pennsylvania. Population, 111,000.

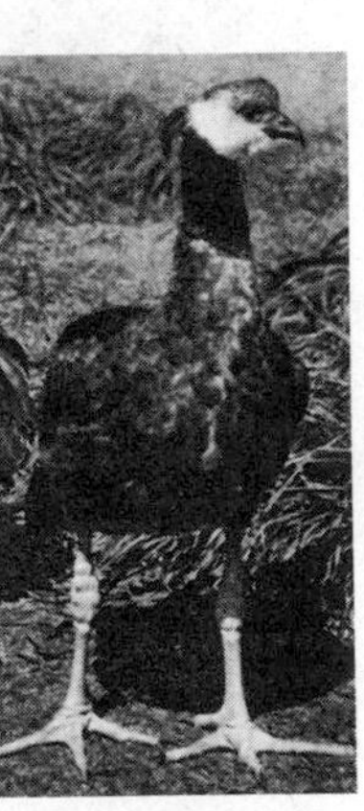
screamer
Chauna chavaria

scrap[1] (skrăp) *n.* **1. a.** A small detached piece or bit; a fragment. **b.** A shred; particle. **2.** An unincorporated fragment of writing. **3.** *Plural.* Leftover and unwanted bits of food. **4.** Construction material left over or discarded as refuse; especially, discarded metal suitable for reprocessing. **5.** *Plural.* Crisp pieces of rendered animal fat; cracklings. —*tr.v.* **scrapped, scrapping, scraps. 1.** To break down into parts for disposal or salvage. **2.** To discard as useless or worthless; to junk. —*adj.* **1.** Consisting of a scrap or scraps. **2.** For the collection or disposal of scrap: *scrap basket.* [Middle English, from Old Norse *skrap,* trifles, remains. See **sker-**[1] in Appendix.*]

scrap[2] (skrăp) *intr.v.* **scrapped, scrapping, scraps.** *Slang.* To fight, often with the fists; to quarrel. —*n.* *Slang.* A fight; a scuffle. [Perhaps variant of SCRAPE.] —**scrap'per** *n.*

scrap·book (skrăp'bo͝ok') *n.* A book with blank pages for the mounting and preserving of pictures or other mementos.

scrape (skrāp) *v.* **scraped, scraping, scrapes.** —*tr.* **1.** To rub (a surface) with considerable pressure. **2.** To draw (a hard or abrasive object) forcefully over a surface. **3.** To remove (an outer layer or adherent matter) by this procedure. **4.** To abrade or smooth by rubbing with a sharp or rough instrument. **5.** To injure the skin of by rubbing against something rough or sharp. **6.** To amass or produce with difficulty. Used with *together* or *up.* —*intr.* **1.** To come into sliding, abrasive contact. **2.** To rub or move with a harsh grating noise. **3.** To give forth a harsh grating noise. **4.** To draw the foot backward along the floor when bowing: *bow and scrape.* **5.** To scrimp; be parsimonious. **6.** To proceed or manage precariously. Usually used with *through* or *along.* —*n.* **1.** The act of scraping. **2.** The sound of scraping. **3.** An abrasion on the skin. **4.** *Slang.* **a.** An embarrassing predicament. **b.** A fight; scuffle. [Middle English *scrapen,* from Old Norse *skrapa.* See **sker-**[1] in Appendix.*]

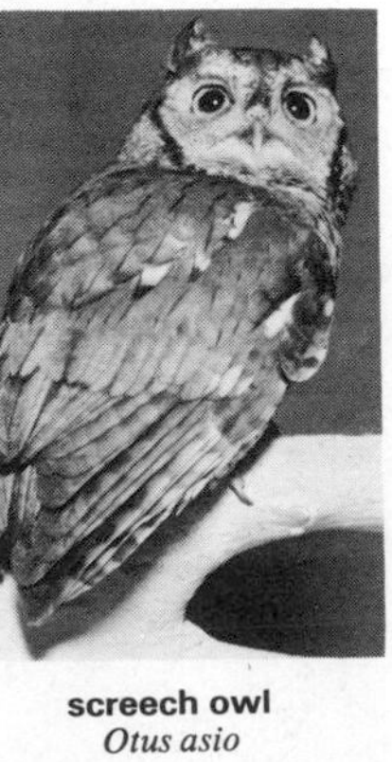
screech owl
Otus asio

scrap·er (skrā'pər) *n.* **1.** One that scrapes. **2.** A tool for scraping off paint or other adherent matter.

scrap·ing (skrā'pĭng) *n.* **1.** The action of one that scrapes. **2.** Something that is scraped, or left to be scraped. Often used in the plural. **3.** The sound made by something being scraped.

scrap·ple (skrăp'əl) *n.* A mush of pork scraps and cornmeal that is allowed to set and then sliced and fried. [Diminutive of SCRAP (bit).]

scrap·py[1] (skrăp'ē) *adj.* **-pier, -piest.** Composed of scraps; fragmentary. —**scrap'pi·ly** *adv.* —**scrap'pi·ness** *n.*

scrap·py[2] (skrăp'ē) *adj.* **-pier, -piest. 1.** Quarrelsome; contentious. **2.** Full of fighting spirit. —**scrap'pi·ly** *adv.* —**scrap'pi·ness** *n.*

scratch (skrăch) *v.* **scratched, scratching, scratches.** —*tr.* **1.** To make a thin, shallow cut or mark on (a surface) with a sharp instrument. **2.** To rub (the skin) to relieve itching. **3.** To scrape or strike on an abrasive surface. **4.** To write or draw hurriedly or haphazardly. **5.** To strike out or cancel (a word, name, or passage) by or as if by drawing lines through. **6.** To withdraw (an entry) from a contest. —*intr.* **1.** To use the nails or claws to dig, scrape, or wound. **2.** To rub the skin to relieve itching. **3.** To make a harsh, scraping sound. **4.** To claw and scrape the ground searching for food, as chickens do. **5.** To withdraw from a contest. **6.** *Billiards.* To make a scratch. —*n.* **1. a.** A linelike mark produced by scratching. **b.** A slight wound of this sort. **2.** A mark or scribble hastily made. **3.** A sound made by scratching, as on a phonograph record. **4.** *Sports.* **a.** A starting line for a race. **b.** A line formerly drawn across a prize ring at which the boxers began each round. **5.** A contestant who has been withdrawn from the running. **6.** *Billiards.* **a.** A shot that results in a penalty, as when the cue ball falls into a pocket or jumps the cushion. **b.** A fluke or chance shot. **7.** Poultry feed. **8.** *Slang.* Money. —**from scratch.** From the beginning. —**up to scratch.** *Informal.* **1.** Meeting the requirements or standards. **2.** In fit condition. —*adj.* **1.** Done haphazardly or by chance. **2.** Assembled at random; heterogeneous. **3.** *Sports.* Without handicap. **4.** Used for hasty jottings or sketches: *scratch paper.* [Blend of obsolete *scrat,* to scratch, from Middle English *scratten*†, and obsolete *cratch,* to scratch, from Middle English *cracchen,* from Middle Dutch *cratsen,* scrape (see **grat-** in Appendix*).] —**scratch'er** *n.*

scratch hit. *Baseball.* A batted ball that is not squarely struck or cleanly fielded but is counted as a hit.

scratch line. 1. A starting line for a race. **2.** A line beyond which a contestant must not step.

scratch sheet. A **dope sheet** *(see).*

scratch test. A test for allergy performed by scratching the skin and applying an allergen to the wound.

scratch·y (skrăch'ē) *adj.* **-ier, -iest. 1.** Characterized by or consisting of scratches. **2.** Making a harsh, scratching noise: *a scratchy record.* **3.** Irregular; rough. **4.** Harsh and irritating: *a scratchy fabric.* —**scratch'i·ly** *adv.* —**scratch'i·ness** *n.*

scrawl (skrôl) *v.* **scrawled, scrawling, scrawls.** —*tr.* To write hastily or illegibly. —*intr.* To write in a sprawling, irregular manner. —*n.* Irregular, often illegible handwriting. . [Blend of SPRAWL and CRAWL.] —**scrawl'er** *n.* —**scrawl'y** *adj.*

scraw·ny (skrô'nē) *adj.* **-nier, -niest.** Gaunt and bony; skinny. See Synonyms at **lean.** [Origin unknown.] —**scraw'ni·ness** *n.*

screak (skrēk) *intr.v.* **screaked, screaking, screaks.** To screech; shriek. —*n.* A screech. [Middle English *skricken,* from Old Norse *skrækja.* See **ker-**[2] in Appendix.*] —**screak'y** *adj.*

scream (skrēm) *v.* **screamed, screaming, screams.** —*intr.* **1.** To utter a long, loud, piercing cry, as of pain. **2.** To make a loud, piercing sound. **3.** To speak or write in a heated, hysterical manner. **4.** To have or produce a blatantly arresting effect. —*tr.* To utter or say in or as if in a screaming voice. —*n.* **1.** A long, loud, piercing cry or sound. **2.** *Slang.* Someone or something hilariously or ridiculously funny. [Middle English *scremen,* from Old Norse *skræma.* See **ker-**[2] in Appendix.*]

Synonyms: *scream, shriek, screech, yell.* These verbs mean to make a loud, piercing sound, usually vocal. *Scream* generally implies sudden, piercing, prolonged sound indicative of intense pain, anger, or surprise. *Shriek* differs principally in its stronger implication of shrillness, inarticulateness, and lack of control. *Screech* stresses shrill, raucous, rasping sound. Both *screech* and *shriek* chiefly express pain, terror, or anger, or they can apply to violent laughter. *Yell* suggests a vigorous outcry expressive of any of the emotional conditions mentioned in the foregoing but also, more specifically, of joy.

scream·er (skrē'mər) *n.* **1.** One that screams. **2.** *Slang.* A sensational headline. **3.** *Slang.* Something that evokes screams or laughter. **4.** Any of several large aquatic birds of the family Anhimidae, of South America, having a harsh, resonant call.

scree (skrē) *n.* **1.** Loose rock debris. **2.** A slope of this at the base of a steep incline or cliff. [Back-formation from *screes* (plural), contraction of *screethes* (unattested), from Old Norse *skrīdha,* landslide, from Germanic *skrīth-* (unattested).]

screech (skrēch) *n.* **1.** A high-pitched, harsh, piercing cry; a shriek. **2.** A sound resembling this. —*v.* **screeched, screeching, screeches.** —*tr.* To say or utter in or as if in a screeching voice. —*intr.* **1.** To scream in a high-pitched, strident voice. **2.** To make a prolonged shrill, grating noise. —See Synonyms at **scream.** [Earlier *scritch,* Middle English *scrichen,* from Old Norse *skraekja.* See **ker-**[2] in Appendix.*] —**screech'er** *n.* —**screech'y** *adj.*

screech owl. Any of various small owls of the genus *Otus;* especially, *O. asio,* of North America, having ear tufts and a quavering, whistlelike call.

screed (skrēd) *n.* **1.** A long, monotonous harangue or piece of writing. **2.** A strip of wood, plaster, or metal placed on a wall or pavement as a guide for the even application of plaster or concrete. **3.** *Scottish.* A rent; a tear. [Middle English *screde,* fragment, strip, Old English *scrēade.* See **skeru-** in Appendix.*]

screen (skrēn) *n.* **1.** A movable device, especially a framed construction, designed to divide, conceal, or protect, as a hinged or sliding room divider. **2.** Something that serves to divide, conceal, or protect, as a body of troops or ships. **3. a.** A coarse sieve used for sifting out fine particles, as of sand, gravel, or coal. **b.** A system for appraising and selecting personnel. **4.** A window insertion of framed wire or plastic mesh used to keep out insects. **5.** The large flat-white or silver surface upon which a picture is projected for viewing. **6.** The motion-picture industry. **7.** *Electronics.* The phosphorescent surface upon which the image is formed in a cathode-ray tube. **8.** *Printing.* A glass

ă pat/ā pay/âr care/ä father/b bib/ch church/d deed/ĕ pet/ē be/f fife/g gag/h hat/hw which/ĭ pit/ī pie/îr pier/j judge/k kick/l lid, needle/m mum/n no, sudden/ng thing/ŏ pot/ō toe/ô paw, for/oi noise/ou out/o͝o took/o͞o boot/p pop/r roar/s sauce/sh ship, dish/

plate marked off with crossing lines, placed before the lens of a camera when photographing for halftone reproduction. —*tr.v.* **screened, screening, screens.** **1.** To provide with a screen: *screen a porch.* **2. a.** To conceal from view. **b.** To protect, guard, or shield. **3. a.** To separate or sift out by means of a sieve or screen. **b.** To examine systematically in order to determine suitability. **4.** To show on a screen, as a motion picture. —See Synonyms at **hide.** [Middle English *screne,* from Old French *escren, escran,* from Middle Dutch *scherm,* "shield," "protection." See **sker-**[1] in Appendix.*] —**screen′er** *n.*

screen·ing (skrē′nĭng) *n.* **1.** *Plural.* Refuse, such as waste coal, separated out by a screen; siftings. Used with a singular or plural verb. **2.** The mesh material used to make door or window screens. **3.** A presentation of a motion picture.

screen·land (skrēn′lănd′) *n.* The motion-picture industry.

screen·play (skrēn′plā′) *n.* The script for a motion picture. Also called "scenario."

screen test. A brief motion-picture sequence filmed to test the ability of an aspiring actor.

screen-test (skrēn′tĕst′) *tr.v.* **-tested, -testing, -tests.** To subject to a screen test.

screen·writer (skrēn′rī′tər) *n.* A writer of screenplays.

screw (skrōō) *n.* **1. a.** A cylindrical rod incised with one or more helical or advancing spiral threads, as a lead screw or worm screw. **b.** The tapped collar or socket that receives this. **2.** A metal pin with incised thread or threads, having a broad slotted head so that it can be driven as a fastener by turning it with a screwdriver, especially: **a.** A tapered and pointed wood screw. **b.** A cylindrical and flat-tipped machine screw. **3.** A device having helical form, as a corkscrew. **4.** A **propeller** *(see).* **5.** A twist or turn of or as if of a screw. **6.** *Vulgar Slang.* **a.** An act of sexual intercourse. **b.** A partner in sexual intercourse. **7.** *British Slang.* Salary; wages. **8.** *British.* A small paper packet, as of tobacco. **9.** *British.* An old broken-down horse. **10.** *Chiefly British.* A stingy or crafty bargainer. **11.** *Slang.* The warder or turnkey of a jail. —**have a screw loose.** *Slang.* To behave in an eccentric or whimsical manner. —**put** (or **apply**) **the screws on** (or **to**). To apply coercion to; put pressure on (someone). —*v.* **screwed, screwing, screws.** —*tr.* **1.** To drive or tighten (a screw). **2. a.** To fasten, tighten, or attach by or as if by means of a screw. **b.** To attach (a tapped or threaded fitting or cap) by twisting into place. Used with *on* or *in.* **c.** To rotate (a part) on a threaded axis. **3.** To contort (one's face). Used with *up.* **4.** *Slang.* To make a mess of (an undertaking). Used with *up.* **5.** *Vulgar Slang.* To have sexual intercourse with. **6.** *Slang.* To take advantage of; to cheat. —*intr.* **1.** To turn or twist. Used with *around.* **2. a.** To become attached by means of screw threads. Used with *into, on,* or *to.* **b.** To be capable of such attachment. **3.** *Vulgar Slang.* To engage in sexual intercourse. —**screw out of.** *Slang.* **1.** To use force or guile on (one) to obtain something. **2.** To extort (something) using pressure. [Middle English *skrewe,* from Old French *escroue,* originally "female screw," from West Germanic *scrūva* (unattested), from Latin *scrōfa,* sow (probably because screw threads coil like a sow's tail, and perhaps influenced in sense by Latin *scrobis,* ditch, pudenda, hence, in Vulgar Latin, female screw). See **sker-**[1] in Appendix.*] —**screw′er** *n.*

screw·ball (skrōō′bôl′) *n.* **1.** *Baseball.* A pitched ball with an erratic flight. **2.** *Slang.* An eccentric, impulsively whimsical, or irrational person. —*adj. Slang.* Odd; eccentric; zany.

screw bean. 1. A mesquite, *Prosopis pubescens,* of the southwestern United States, having compound leaves, tiny yellowish-white flowers, and twisted pods used as fodder. **2.** The pod of this tree.

screw·driv·er (skrōō′drī′vər) *n.* **1.** A tool used for turning screws. **2.** A cocktail of vodka and orange juice.

screw eye. A wood screw with an eyelet in place of a head.

screw jack. A jackscrew.

screw log. *Nautical.* An instrument with rotary fins that is dragged from the stern of a vessel to measure the speed or distance traveled. Also called "patent log," "taffrail log."

screw pine. A plant, the **pandanus** *(see).*

screw propeller. A **propeller** *(see).*

screw thread. 1. The continuous helical groove on a screw or on the inner surface of a nut. **2.** One complete turn of a screw thread.

screw·worm (skrōō′wûrm′) *n.* The larva of the screwworm fly.

screwworm fly. A blue-green fly, *Cochliomyia hominivorax,* of the New World, that breeds in the living tissue of mammals, having penetrated chiefly through open wounds. The parasitic larvae cause serious injury or death to livestock.

screw·y (skrōō′ē) *adj.* **-ier, -iest.** *Slang.* **1.** Eccentric; crackbrained; crazy. **2.** Ludicrously odd, unlikely, inappropriate, or absurd.

Scria·bin (skryä′bĭn), **Alexander.** 1872–1915. Russian composer.

scrib·ble (skrĭb′əl) *v.* **-bled, -bling, -bles.** —*tr.* **1.** To write hurriedly without heed to legibility or grammatical form. **2.** To cover with such writing or with meaningless marks. —*intr.* To write or draw in a hurried, careless way. —*n.* **1.** Careless, hurried writing. **2.** Meaningless marks and lines. [Middle English *scriblen,* from Medieval Latin *scrībillāre,* frequentative of Latin *scrībere,* to write. See **skeri-** in Appendix.*]

scrib·bler (skrĭb′lər) *n.* **1.** One who scribbles. **2.** A very minor or disreputable author.

scribe (skrīb) *n.* **1.** A public clerk or secretary. **2.** A professional copyist of manuscripts and documents. **3.** A writer or journalist. **4.** A scriber. —*v.* **scribed, scribing, scribes.** —*tr.* **1.** To mark with a scriber. **2.** To write or inscribe. —*intr.* To work as a scribe. [Middle English, from Latin *scrība,* official writer, clerk, scribe, from *scrībere,* to write. See **skeri-** in Appendix.*] —**scrib′al** *adj.*

Scribe (skrēb), **Augustin Eugène.** 1791–1861. French author.

scrib·er (skrī′bər) *n.* A sharply pointed tool used for marking lines on wood, metal, ceramic, or the like.

scrim (skrĭm) *n.* **1.** A durable, loosely woven cotton or linen fabric used for curtains, upholstery lining, or in industry. **2.** *Theater.* A similar fabric used as a transparent drop. [Origin unknown.]

scrim·mage (skrĭm′ĭj) *n.* **1. a.** A rough-and-tumble struggle; a tussle. **b.** A skirmish. **2.** *Football.* **a.** The contest between two teams from the time the ball is snapped back until it becomes out of play. **b.** A team's practice session. **3.** *Rugby.* A scrummage. —**line of scrimmage.** *Football.* An imaginary line across the field on which the ball rests and at which the teams line up for a new play. —*intr.v.* **scrimmaged, -maging, -mages.** *Football.* To engage in a scrimmage. [Alteration of *scrimish,* obsolete variant of SKIRMISH.]

scrimp (skrĭmp) *v.* **scrimped, scrimping, scrimps.** —*intr.* To economize severely. —*tr.* **1.** To be excessively sparing with or of. **2.** To cut or make too small or scanty. [Perhaps from Scandinavian, akin to Swedish *skrympa,* to shrink. See **skerbh-** in Appendix.*] —**scrimp′y** *adj.* —**scrimp′i·ness** *n.*

scrim·shaw (skrĭm′shô′) *v.* **-shawed, -shawing, -shaws.** —*tr.* To decorate (whale ivory, bone, or shells) with intricate carvings or designs. —*intr.* To turn out such meticulously executed work. —*n.* A bone or ivory article fashioned in this way. [Earlier *scrimshander*†.]

scrip[1] (skrĭp) *n.* **1.** A small scrap of paper, especially one with writing, as a list or a schedule. **2.** Paper money issued for temporary, emergency use. See **shinplaster.** [Variant of SCRIPT (influenced by SCRAP).]

scrip[2] (skrĭp) *n.* **1.** A provisional certificate entitling the holder to a fractional share of stock or of other jointly owned property. **2.** Such certificates collectively. [Short for *subscription (receipt),* receipt for portion of a loan.]

scrip[3] (skrĭp) *n. Archaic.* A wallet, small satchel, or bag. [Middle English *scrippe,* from Old French *escreppe,* variant of Old North French *escarpe,* "pilgrim's knapsack." See **scarf.**]

Scripps (skrĭps). Family of American newspaper editors and publishers, pioneers in syndication, including **James Edmund** (English-born; 1835–1906), his half brother, **E(dward) W(yllis)** (1854–1926), and E.W.'s son, **Robert Paine** (1895–1938).

scrip·sit (skrĭp′sĭt). *Latin.* He (or she) wrote (it). Placed after the author's name on a manuscript.

script (skrĭpt) *n.* **1. a.** Handwriting as distinguished from print. **b.** A style of writing with cursive characters. **c.** Alphabet. **2. a.** A type that imitates handwriting. **b.** Matter printed with this type. **3.** *Law.* An original document. **4.** The text of a play, broadcast, or motion picture; especially, the copy of a text used by a director or performer. —*tr.v.* **scripted, scripting, scripts.** To prepare (a text) for filming: *Perelman scripted several Marx Brothers movies.* [Middle English *skript,* from Old French *escript,* from Latin *scrīptum,* from *scrīptus,* past participle of *scrībere,* to write. See **skeri-** in Appendix.*]

Script. Scriptural; Scriptures.

scrip·to·ri·um (skrĭp-tôr′ē-əm, -tōr′ē-əm) *n., pl.* **-ums** or **-toria** (-tôr′ē-ə, -tōr′ē-ə). A room in a monastery set aside for the copying, writing, or illuminating of manuscripts and records. [Medieval Latin, from Latin *scrībere* (past participle *scrīptus*), to write. See **skeri-** in Appendix.*]

scrip·tur·al (skrĭp′chər-əl) *adj.* **1.** Of or pertaining to writing; written. **2.** *Capital* **S.** *Abbr.* **Script.** Of, relating to, based upon, or contained in the Scriptures. —**scrip′tur·al·ly** *adv.*

Scrip·ture (skrĭp′chər) *n.* **1.** *Often plural. Abbr.* **Script. a.** A sacred writing or book; especially, the **Holy Scripture** *(see).* **b.** A passage from such a writing or book. **2.** *Small* **s.** A statement regarded as authoritative and definitive, as a code of regulations. [Middle English, from Late Latin *scrīptūra,* from Latin, act of writing, from *scrībere* (past participle *scrīptus*), to write. See **skeri-** in Appendix.*]

script·writ·er (skrĭpt′rī′tər) *n.* A person who writes copy to be used by an announcer, performer, or director.

scriv·en·er (skrĭv′nər) *n. Archaic.* **1.** A professional copyist; scribe. **2.** A notary. [Middle English *scriveiner,* from *scrivein,* scribe, from Old French *escrevein,* from Vulgar Latin *scrībānem* (unattested), accusative of Latin *scrība,* SCRIBE.]

scro·bic·u·late (skrō-bĭk′yə-lĭt, -lāt′) *adj. Biology.* Marked with many shallow depressions, grooves, or pits. [From Latin *scrobiculus,* diminutive of *scrobis,* trench. See **sker-**[1] in Appendix.*]

scrod (skrŏd) *n.* A young cod or haddock, especially one split and boned for cooking. [Obsolete Dutch *schrood,* slice, shred, from Middle Dutch *schrode.* See **skeru-** in Appendix.*]

scrof·u·la (skrŏf′yə-lə) *n. Rare.* A constitutional condition affecting the tissues in the young, characterized by predisposition to tuberculosis, lymphatism, glandular swellings, and respiratory catarrhs. Also called "struma." [Middle English *scrophulas* (plural), from Medieval Latin *scrōfulae,* swelling of the glands, "small sows," from Latin *scrōfa,* sow (probably after Greek *khoirades,* scrofula, from *khoiras,* like a hog's back). See **sker-**[1] in Appendix.*]

scrof·u·lous (skrŏf′yə-ləs) *adj.* **1.** Pertaining to, affected with, or resembling scrofula. **2.** Morally degenerate; corrupt. —**scrof′u·lous·ly** *adv.* —**scrof′u·lous·ness** *n.*

scroll (skrōl) *n.* **1.** A roll of parchment, papyrus, or the like used especially for writing a document. **2. a.** *Archaic.* A piece of writing, as a letter. **b.** A list or schedule of names. **3.** Ornamentation resembling a partially rolled scroll of paper, espe-

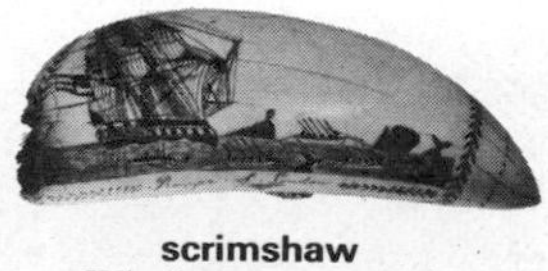

scrimshaw
Whaling scene carved on a whale's tooth

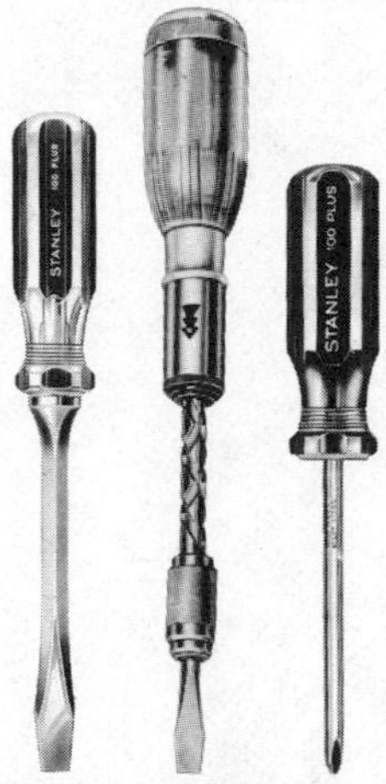

screwdriver
From left: Square-bar standard; spiral ratchet; Phillips

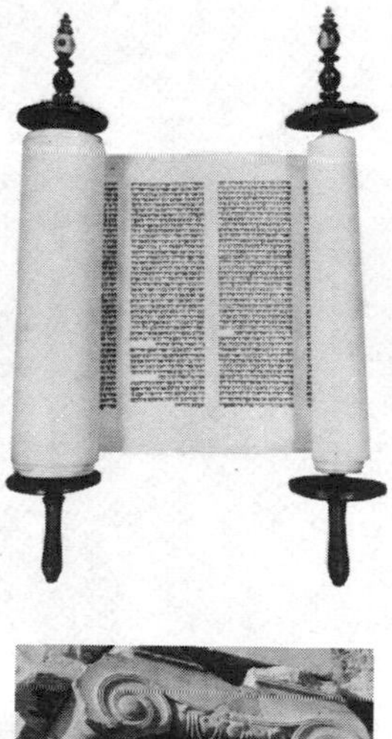

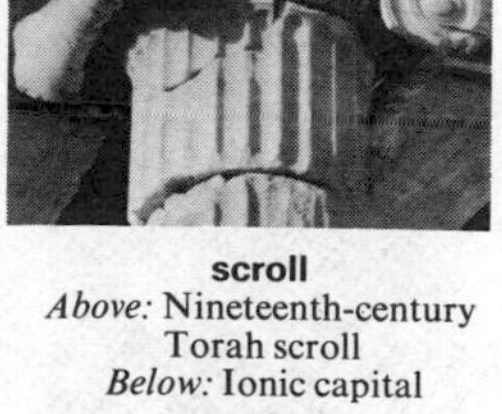

scroll
Above: Nineteenth-century Torah scroll
Below: Ionic capital

cially: **a.** The volute in Ionic and Corinthian capitals. **b.** The curved head on an instrument of the violin family. **c.** *Heraldry.* A ribbon inscribed with a motto. [Middle English *scrowle,* variant (influenced by *rowle,* a roll) of *scrow,* from Old French *escro(u)e,* strip of parchment, from Frankish *skrōda* (unattested), piece, shred. See **skeru-** in Appendix.*]

scroll saw. A hand or power saw with a narrow ribbonlike blade for cutting curved or irregular shapes. See **fretsaw, jigsaw.**

scroll·work (skrōl′wûrk′) *n.* Embellishment with a scroll motif; especially, ornamentation executed in wood with a scroll saw.

Scrooge (skrōōj) *n.* A mean-spirited, miserly person; skinflint. [From the miserly character Ebenezer *Scrooge* in Charles Dickens' *Christmas Carol.*]

scro·tum (skrō′təm) *n., pl.* **-ta** (-tə) or **-tums.** The external sac of skin enclosing the testes in most mammals. [Latin *scrōtum.* See **skeru-** in Appendix.*] —**scro′tal** (skrōt′l) *adj.*

scrounge (skrounj) *v.* **scrounged, scrounging, scrounges.** *Slang.* —*tr.* **1.** To obtain by salvaging or foraging; round up. **2.** To wheedle; cadge. —*intr.* **1.** To forage about in an effort to acquire something at no cost. **2.** To wheedle. [Variant of dialectal *scrunge*†, to steal.] —**scroung′er** *n.*

scroung·y (skroun′jē) *adj.* **-ier, -iest.** *Slang.* **1.** Given to pilfering or sponging. **2.** Dirty or unkempt; grubby.

scrub[1] (skrŭb) *v.* **scrubbed, scrubbing, scrubs.** —*tr.* **1.** To rub hard, as with a brush, soap, and water, in order to clean. **2.** To remove (dirt or stains) by such rubbing. **3.** To cleanse (a gas). **4.** *Slang.* To cancel; drop. —*intr.* To clean or wash something by hard rubbing. —*n.* An act of scrubbing. [Middle English *scrobben,* from Middle Low German or Middle Dutch *schrobben, schrubben.* See **sker-**[1] in Appendix.*]

scrub[2] (skrŭb) *n.* **1.** A straggly, stunted tree or shrub. **2.** A growth or tract of stunted vegetation. **3.** A domestic animal of inferior breeding or poor appearance. **4.** An undersized or insignificant person. **5.** *Sports.* A player not on the varsity or first team. —*adj.* **1.** Undersized, stunted, or inferior. **2.** Made up of or participated in by scrubs: *a scrub team.* [Middle English, variant of *schrubbe,* SHRUB.]

scrub·ber (skrŭb′ər) *n.* **1.** One that scrubs. **2.** An apparatus for removing impurities from a gas.

scrub·by (skrŭb′ē) *adj.* **-bier, -biest.** **1.** Covered with or consisting of scrub or underbrush. **2.** Small; straggly; stunted. **3.** Shabby or paltry; wretched. —**scrub′bi·ness** *n.*

scrub oak. Any of several shrubby or small oaks; especially, *Quercus ilicifolia,* of eastern North America, having sharply lobed leaves.

scrub pine. Any of several small, straggling pine trees; especially, *Pinus virginiana,* of the eastern United States, having prickly cones.

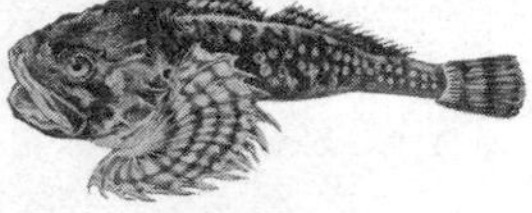

sculpin
Cottus scorpius

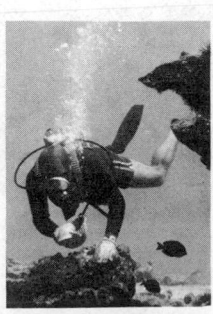

scrub typhus. An acute infectious disease common in Asia, transmitted by a mite and characterized by sudden fever, painful swelling of the lymphatic glands, skin lesions, and skin rash. Also called "tsutsugamushi disease," "Japanese river fever."

scrub·wom·an (skrŭb′wŏŏm′ən) *n., pl.* **-women** (-wĭm′ĭn). A woman hired to clean; charwoman.

scruff (skrŭf) *n.* The back of the neck; nape. [Variant of obsolete *scuff,* perhaps from Old Norse *skopt,* hair on the head. See **skeup-** in Appendix.*]

scruf·fy (skrŭf′ē) *adj.* **-fier, -fiest.** **1.** Shabby. **2.** *Chiefly British.* Scaly; scabby. [From *scruff,* scurf, Middle English *scrofe,* Old English *scruf,* variant of *scurf,* SCURF.]

scrum·mage (skrŭm′ĭj) *n.* Also *informal* **scrum** (skrŭm). A Rugby formation in which the two sets of forwards mass together around the ball and, with their heads down, try to shoulder their opponents off the ball and kick it to their own team. —*intr.v.* **scrummaged, -maging, -mages.** To tussle in such a play; engage in a scrummage. [Variant of SCRIMMAGE.] —**scrum′mag·er** *n.*

scrump·tious (skrŭmp′shəs) *adj. Slang.* Splendid; delectable. [Perhaps alteration of SUMPTUOUS.]

scrunch (skrŭnch, skrŏŏnch) *v.* **scrunched, scrunching, scrunches.** —*tr.* **1.** To crush or crunch. **2.** To hunch, as the shoulders. Often used with *up.* —*intr.* **1.** To hunch. **2.** To move with or make a crunching sound. —*n.* A crunching sound. [Variant of CRUNCH.]

scru·ple (skrōō′pəl) *n.* **1.** Ethical objection to certain actions; principle; dictate of conscience. **2.** *Abbr.* **sc., scr.** A unit of apothecary weight equal to 20 grains. See **measurement.** **3.** A minute part or amount. —See Synonyms at **qualm.** —*intr.v.* **scrupled, -pling, -ples.** To hesitate through the demands of conscience or principle. [Old French *scrupule,* from Latin *scrūpulus,* small, sharp stone, small weight, scruple, from *scrūpus*†, rough stone.]

scru·pu·lous (skrōō′pyə-ləs) *adj.* **1.** Having scruples; principled. **2.** Very conscientious and exacting; punctilious. —See Synonyms at **meticulous.** [Middle English, from Latin *scrūpulōsus,* from *scrūpulus,* SCRUPLE.] —**scru′pu·los′i·ty** (-lŏs′ə-tē), **scru′pu·lous·ness** *n.* —**scru′pu·lous·ly** *adv.*

scuba

scru·ta·ble (skrōō′tə-bəl) *adj.* Comprehensible through scrutiny. [Medieval Latin *scrūtābilis,* searchable, from Latin *scrūtārī,* to search. See **scrutiny.**]

scru·ti·nize (skrōōt′n-īz′) *tr.v.* **-nized, -nizing, -nizes.** To examine or observe with great care; inspect minutely or critically. —**scru′ti·niz′er** *n.* —**scru′ti·niz′ing·ly** *adv.*

scru·ti·ny (skrōōt′n-ē) *n., pl.* **-nies.** **1.** A close, careful examination or study; a critical, sustained look. **2.** Close observation; surveillance. [Latin *scrūtinium,* from *scrūtārī,* to search, examine (originally said of ragpickers), "to rummage in a heap of trash," from *scrūta,* trash. See **skeru-** in Appendix.*]

scu·ba (skōō′bə) *n.* An apparatus containing compressed air and used for free-swimming underwater breathing. [S(ELF) C(ONTAINED) U(NDERWATER) B(REATHING) A(PPARATUS).]

scud (skŭd) *intr.v.* **scudded, scudding, scuds.** **1.** To run or skim along swiftly and easily. **2.** *Nautical.* To run before a gale with little or no sail set. —*n.* **1.** The act of scudding. **2. a.** Wind-driven clouds, mist, or rain. **b.** A sudden light shower. [Perhaps variant of SCUT (rabbit's tail, hence "run like a rabbit").]

scu·do (skōō′dō) *n., pl.* **-di** (-dē). A former monetary unit and coin of Italy and Sicily. [Italian, "shield," from Latin *scūtum.* See **skei-** in Appendix.*]

scuff (skŭf) *v.* **scuffed, scuffing, scuffs.** —*intr.* To scrape the feet while walking; to shuffle. —*tr.* **1.** To scrape with the feet. **2.** To shuffle (the feet). **3.** To scrape and roughen the surface of (shoes, for example). —*n.* **1.** The sound or act of scuffing. **2.** A worn or rough spot resulting from scuffing. **3.** A flat, backless house slipper. [Probably from Scandinavian, akin to Old Norse *skūfa,* to push. See **skeubh-** in Appendix.*]

scuf·fle[1] (skŭf′əl) *intr.v.* **-fled, -fling, -fles.** **1.** To fight or struggle confusedly at close quarters. **2. a.** To shuffle. **b.** To scoot with shuffling steps. —*n.* A rough, disorderly struggle at close quarters. See Synonyms at **conflict.** [Probably from Scandinavian, akin to Old Norse *skūfa,* to push. See **skeubh-** in Appendix.*] —**scuf′fler** *n.*

scuf·fle[2] (skŭf′əl) *n.* A type of hoe manipulated by pushing rather than pulling. Also called "scuffle hoe." [Dutch *schoffel,* from Middle Dutch *schoffel, schuffel,* shovel. See **skeubh-** in Appendix.*]

scull (skŭl) *n.* **1.** A long oar twisted from side to side over the stern of a boat to propel it. **2.** One of a pair of short-handled oars used by a single rower. **3.** A small, light boat for sculling, especially a racing boat. —*v.* **sculled, sculling, sculls.** —*tr.* To propel (a boat) with a scull or sculls. —*intr.* To use a scull or sculls to propel a boat. [Middle English *sculle*†.] —**scull′er** *n.*

scul·ler·y (skŭl′ə-rē) *n., pl.* **-ies.** A room adjoining the kitchen in large houses, where dishwashing and other kitchen chores are done. [Middle English, from Norman French *squillerie,* from Old French *escuelerie,* from *escuelier,* keeper of dishes, from *escuele,* dish, from (unattested) Vulgar Latin *scūtella,* variant (influenced by Latin *scūtum,* SCUTUM) of Latin *scutella,* salver, diminutive of *scutra*†, platter.]

scul·lion (skŭl′yən) *n. Archaic.* A servant employed to do menial tasks in a kitchen. [Middle English *sculyon,* probably from Old French *escovillon,* dishcloth, diminutive of *escouve,* broom, from Latin *scopa.* See **scopula.**]

sculp. sculpsit; sculptor; sculptress; sculpture.

scul·pin (skŭl′pĭn) *n., pl.* **-pins** or **sculpin.** **1.** Any of various marine and freshwater fishes of the family Cottidae, having a large, flattened head and prominent spines. Sometimes called "bullhead." **2.** A scorpion fish, *Scorpaena guttata,* of California coastal waters. [Perhaps variant of obsolete *scorpene,* from Latin *scorpaena,* sea scorpion. See **scorpaenoid.**]

sculp·sit (skŭlp′sĭt). *Latin. Abbr.* **sc., sculp., sculpt.** He (or she) sculptured (it). Placed after the artist's name.

sculpt (skŭlpt) *tr.v.* **sculpted, sculpting, sculpts.** To sculpture. [French *sculpter, sculper,* from Latin *sculpere,* to carve. See **sculpture.**]

sculpt. sculpsit.

sculp·tor (skŭlp′tər) *n. Abbr.* **sculp.** **1.** One who sculptures; especially, an artist who works in stone or metal. **2.** *Capital* **S.** A constellation in the Southern Hemisphere near Cetus and Phoenix. Also called "Sculptor's Workshop." [Latin, from *sculpere* (past participle *sculptus*), to carve. See **sculpture.**]

sculp·tress (skŭlp′trĭs) *n. Abbr.* **sculp.** A woman who sculptures.

sculp·ture (skŭlp′chər) *n. Abbr.* **sculp.** **1.** The art or practice of shaping figures or designs in the round or in relief, as by carving wood, chiseling marble, modeling clay, or casting in metal. **2. a.** A work of art created in this manner. **b.** Such works collectively. **3.** Ridges, indentations, or other markings, as on a shell, formed by natural processes. —*tr.v.* **sculptured, -turing, -tures.** **1.** To fashion into a three-dimensional figure. **2.** To represent in sculpture. **3.** To ornament with sculpture. **4.** To give sculptural shape or contour to, as by erosion. [Middle English, from Latin *sculptūra,* from *sculpere* (past participle *sculptus*), to carve. See **skel-**[1] in Appendix.*] —**sculp′tur·al** *adj.* —**sculp′tur·al·ly** *adv.*

sculp·tur·esque (skŭlp′chə-rĕsk′) *adj.* Suggestive of sculpture; having the qualities of sculpture. —**sculp′tur·esque′ly** *adv.* —**sculp′tur·esque′ness** *n.*

scum (skŭm) *n.* **1.** A filmy layer of extraneous or impure matter that forms on or rises to the surface of a liquid or body of water. **2.** The refuse or dross of molten metals. **3.** Any refuse or worthless matter. **4.** An element of society regarded as being vile or worthless. —*v.* **scummed, scumming, scums.** —*tr.* To remove the scum from; to skim. —*intr.* To become covered with scum. [Middle English *scume, scome,* from Middle Dutch *schūm.* See **skeu-** in Appendix.*] —**scum′mer** *n.*

scum·ble (skŭm′bəl) *tr.v.* **-bled, -bling, -bles.** *Painting & Drawing.* To soften the colors or outlines of by covering with a film of opaque or semiopaque color or by rubbing. —*n.* **1.** The effect produced by scumbling. **2.** Material used for scumbling. [Probably frequentative formation from *scum,* to cover with scum, from SCUM.]

scun·ner (skŭn′ər) *n.* A strong dislike; aversion: *I took an immediate scunner to him.* [Middle English *skunner*†.]

scup (skŭp) *n., pl.* **scup** or **scups.** A food fish, *Stenotomus chrysops,* of western Atlantic waters, related to and resembling the porgies. [Short for Narraganset *mishcùp.*]

scup·per (skŭp′ər) *n. Nautical.* An opening in the side of a ship

at deck level to allow water to run off. [Middle English *skopper,* perhaps from Old French *escopir,* to spit (imitative).]
scup·per·nong (skŭp′ər-nông′, -nŏng′) *n.* **1.** A grape, the **muscadine** *(see);* especially, a cultivated variety having sweet, yellowish fruit. **2.** A wine made from these grapes. [Short for *Scuppernong grape,* grown in the *Scuppernong* River basin, North Carolina.]
scurf (skûrf) *n.* **1.** Scaly or shredded dry skin, such as dandruff. **2.** Any loose, scaly crust coating a surface, especially of a plant. [Middle English *scurf, scorf,* Old English *scurf,* variant (probably influenced by Old Norse *skurfōttr,* scurfy) of *sceorf.* See **sker-**[1] in Appendix.*] —**scurf′y** *adj.* —**scurf′i·ness** *n.*
scur·rile (skûr′əl) *adj.* Also **scur·ril.** *Archaic.* Scurrilous. [French, from Latin *scurrīlis,* SCURRILOUS.]
scur·ril·i·ty (skə-rĭl′ə-tē) *n., pl.* **-ties. 1.** The quality of being scurrilous. **2.** A scurrilous remark or passage.
scur·ri·lous (skûr′ə-ləs) *adj.* **1.** Given to the use of vulgar or low abusive language; foul-mouthed. **2.** Expressed in coarse and abusive language. [From Latin *scurrīlis,* buffoonlike, jeering, from *scurra,* buffoon, possibly from Etruscan.] —**scur′ri·lous·ly** *adv.* —**scur′ri·lous·ness** *n.*
scur·ry (skûr′ē) *intr.v.* **-ried, -rying, -ries. 1.** To go with light running steps; hurry; scamper. **2.** To flurry or swirl about: *"the snow underfoot scurries before the wind"* (Henry Miller). —*n., pl.* **scurries. 1.** The act or noise of scurrying. **2.** A short run or race on horseback. [Probably short for HURRY-SCURRY.]
scur·vy (skûr′vē) *n.* A disease caused by deficiency of vitamin C, characterized by spongy and bleeding gums, bleeding under the skin, and extreme weakness. —*adj.* **scurvier, -viest. 1.** Mean; worthless; contemptible. **2.** *Obsolete.* Scurfy. [From SCURF (but used later to render like-sounding French *scorbut,* the skin disease, from Medieval Latin *scorbūtus.* See **scorbutic**).] —**scur′vi·ly** *adv.* —**scur′vi·ness** *n.*
scurvy grass. A plant, *Cochlearia officinalis,* of northern regions, having bitter foliage, formerly used to cure scurvy.
scut (skŭt) *n.* A stubby erect tail, such as that of a hare, rabbit, or deer. [Middle English *scut*†, hare.]
scu·tage (skyōō′tĭj) *n.* In feudal times, a tax paid in lieu of military service. [Middle English, from Medieval Latin *scūtāgium,* "shield money," from Latin *scūtum,* shield, SCUTUM.]
scu·tate (skyōō′tāt′) *adj.* **1.** *Zoology.* Covered with bony plates or scales. **2.** *Botany.* Shaped like a buckler or shield. [New Latin *scutatus,* from Latin *scūtātus,* equipped with a shield, from *scūtum,* shield, SCUTUM.]
scutch (skŭch) *tr.v.* **scutched, scutching, scutches.** To separate the valuable fibers of (flax or other textile material) from the woody parts by beating. —*n.* An implement for scutching. [Obsolete French *escoucher,* from Old French *escousser,* from Vulgar Latin *excussāre* (unattested), frequentative of Latin *excutere* (past participle *excussus*), to shake out : *ex-,* out + *quatere,* to shake (see **kwēt-** in Appendix*).] —**scutch′er** *n.*
scutch·eon (skŭch′ən) *n.* **1.** Variant of **escutcheon. 2.** A shield-shaped object, such as a scute.
scutch grass. Bermuda grass *(see).*
scute (skyōōt) *n. Zoology.* A horny, chitinous, or bony external plate or scale, such as one of those on the shell of a turtle. [New Latin *scutum,* from Latin *scūtum,* shield, SCUTUM.]
scu·tel·late (skyōō-tĕl′ĭt, skyōōt′l-āt′) *adj.* Also **scu·tel·lat·ed** (skyōōt′l-ā′tĭd) (for sense 1). **1.** *Zoology.* **a.** Covered with bony plates or scales. **b.** Having a scutellum. **2.** *Botany.* Shaped like a shield or platter. [From SCUTELLUM.]
scu·tel·la·tion (skyōōt′l-ā′shən) *n.* An arrangement or covering of scales, as on a bird's leg.
scu·tel·lum (skyōō-tĕl′əm) *n., pl.* **-tella** (-tĕl′ə). **1.** *Zoology.* A shieldlike bony plate or scale, as on the thorax of some insects. **2.** *Botany.* Any of several shield-shaped structures, such as the cotyledon of a grass. [New Latin, diminutive of Latin *scūtum,* shield, SCUTUM.]
scu·ti·form (skyōō′tə-fôrm′) *adj.* Having the shape of a shield. [New Latin *scutiformis* : Latin *scūtum,* SCUTUM + -FORM.]
scut·ter (skŭt′ər) *intr.v.* **-tered, -tering, -ters.** *British Informal.* To bustle about; scuttle. [Variant (influenced by SCATTER) of SCUTTLE (to run).]
scut·tle[1] (skŭt′l) *n.* **1.** A small opening or hatch with a movable lid in the deck, side, wall, or roof of a ship or in the roof or floor of a house. **2.** The lid or hatch for this. —*tr.v.* **scuttled, -tling, -tles. 1.** To cut or open a hole or holes in (a ship's hull). **2.** To sink (a ship) by this means. **3.** *Informal.* To scrap; discard. [Middle English *skottell,* from Old French *escoutille,* from Spanish *escotilla,* diminutive of *escote,* opening in a garment, "seam," probably from Gothic *skaut,* seam, hem. See **skeud-** in Appendix.*]
scut·tle[2] (skŭt′l) *n.* **1.** A metal pail for carrying coal. **2.** A shallow open basket for carrying vegetables, flowers, grain, or the like. [Middle English *scutel,* Old English *scutel,* from Latin *scutella,* salver. See **scullery.**]
scut·tle[3] (skŭt′l) *intr.v.* **-tled, -tling, -tles.** To run hastily; scurry. —*n.* A hurried run; a scurrying pace. [Variant of dialectal *scuddle,* frequentative of SCUD.]
scut·tle·butt (skŭt′l-bŭt′) *n.* **1.** A drinking fountain on a ship. **2.** Formerly, a cask on a ship used to hold the day's supply of drinking water. **3.** *Slang.* Gossip; rumor. [SCUTTLE (hatch) + BUTT (cask).]
scu·tum (skyōō′təm) *n., pl.* **-ta** (-tə). **1.** *Zoology.* A bony, calcareous, chitinous, or horny scale or plate, as on certain barnacles. **2.** *Capital* **S.** *Astronomy.* A constellation in the equatorial region of the southern sky near Sagittarius and Serpens Cauda. [Latin *scūtum,* shield. See **skei-** in Appendix.*]
Scyl·la (sĭl′ə) *n.* A rock on the Italian side of the Strait of Messina, opposite the whirlpool Charybdis, personified by Homer as a female sea monster who devoured sailors. —**between Scylla and Charybdis.** In a spot where avoidance of one danger exposes one to destruction by the other.
scy·pho·zo·an (sī′fə-zō′ən) *n.* Any of various marine coelenterates of the class Scyphozoa, including the jellyfishes, and usually having a well-developed medusoid stage. [New Latin *Scyphozoa,* "cuplike creatures" : Greek *skuphos,* cup (see **skep-** in Appendix*) + -ZOA.]
scythe (sīth) *n.* An implement consisting of a long, curved single-edged blade with a long, bent handle, used for mowing or reaping. —*tr.v.* **scythed, scything, scythes.** To cut with a scythe. [Middle English *sithe, sythe,* Old English *sīthe.* See **sek-** in Appendix.*]
Scyth·i·a (sĭth′ē-ə). An ancient region of Asia and southeastern Europe, on the lower courses of the Don and Dnieper.
Scyth·i·an (sĭth′ē-ən) *n.* **1.** A member of the ancient nomadic people inhabiting Scythia. **2.** The extinct Iranian language of these people. —*adj.* Of or pertaining to the Scythians, their land, or their language.
Scyth·o-Drav·id·i·an (sĭth′ō-drə-vĭd′ē-ən) *adj.* Of or pertaining to an ethnic group of northwestern India having mixed Iranian and Dravidian characteristics.
SD South Dakota (with Zip Code).
s.d. sine die.
S.D. 1. special delivery. **2.** South Dakota (unofficial).
S.Dak. South Dakota.
Se The symbol for the element selenium.
SE southeast; southeastern.
sea (sē) *n.* **1.** *Abbr.* **s., S. a.** The continuous body of salt water covering most of the earth's surface, especially this body regarded as a geophysical entity distinct from earth and sky. Usually preceded by *the.* **b.** A tract of water within an ocean, such as the Sargasso Sea. **c.** A relatively large body of salt water completely or partly landlocked, such as the Caspian Sea or the Red Sea. **d.** A body of fresh water, such as the Sea of Galilee. **2.** The condition of the ocean's surface with regard to its course, flow, swell, or turbulence: *a high sea.* **3.** Something that suggests the sea in its overwhelming sweep or vastness. **4.** Seafaring as a way of life. **5.** A lunar **mare** *(see).* —**at sea. 1.** On the open waters of the ocean. **2.** At a loss; perplexed. —**follow the sea.** To pursue a career as a sailor. —**go to sea. 1.** To become a sailor. **2.** To set out on an ocean voyage. —**put to sea.** To leave port. [Middle English *se(e),* Old English *sǣ,* from Common Germanic *saiwa-* (unattested).]
SEA Airport code for Seattle/Tacoma, Washington.
sea anchor. *Nautical.* A drag, usually a canvas-covered conical frame, floating behind a vessel to prevent drifting or to maintain a heading into the wind. Also called "drag anchor," "drift anchor," "drogue."
sea anemone. Any of numerous flowerlike marine coelenterates of the class Anthozoa (or Actinozoa), having a flexible, cylindrical body and tentacles surrounding a central mouth.
sea bass. Any of various marine food fishes of the genus *Centropristes* and related genera; especially, *C. striatus,* of coastal Atlantic waters of the United States.
Sea·bee (sē′bē′) *n.* A member of one of the U.S. Navy's construction battalions, established in 1941 to build naval aviation bases and facilities. [Variant of *cee bee,* from the initials of *C*onstruction *B*attalion.]
sea bird. A bird, such as a petrel or albatross, that frequents the ocean, especially far from shore.
sea biscuit. Hardtack.
sea·board (sē′bôrd′, -bōrd′) *n.* **1.** The seacoast. **2.** The land near the sea. —*adj. Rare.* Adjoining the sea. [SEA + BOARD (obsolete sense "border").]
Sea·borg (sē′bôrg′), **Glenn Theodore.** Born 1912. American physicist; studied transuranic elements.
sea·borne (sē′bôrn′, -bōrn′) *adj.* **1.** Conveyed by sea; transported by ship. **2.** Carried on or over the sea.
sea bread. Sea biscuit; hardtack.
sea bream. Any of various marine food fishes of the family Sparidae; especially, *Pagellus centrodontus,* of European waters, and *Archosargus rhomboidalis,* of western Atlantic coastal waters.
sea breeze. A cool breeze blowing inland from the sea.
Sea·bur·y (sē′bĕr′ē, -bə-rē), **Samuel.** 1729–1796. American religious leader; first bishop of Protestant Episcopal Church in America (consecrated 1784).
sea butterfly. A marine organism, a **pteropod** *(see).*
sea card. 1. A map of the sea. **2.** The card of a mariner's compass.
sea·coast (sē′kōst′) *n.* Land bordering the sea.
sea coconut. The **double coconut** *(see).*
sea cow. 1. Any of several marine mammals of the order Sirenia, such as a manatee or dugong. **2.** Broadly, any of several other aquatic animals, such as a walrus or hippopotamus.
sea cradle. A mollusk, the **chiton** *(see).*
sea cucumber. Any of various cucumber-shaped echinoderms of the class Holothuroidea, having a flexible body with tentacles surrounding the mouth. See **trepang.**
sea dog. 1. Broadly, any of various seals or similar marine mammals. **2.** A sailor with long experience of the sea.
sea·dog (sē′dôg′, -dŏg′) *n.* A **fogbow** *(see).*
sea duck. Any of various diving ducks, such as the eider or scoter, of coastal areas.
sea eagle. Any of various fish-eating eagles or similar birds, such as the bald eagle or the osprey.
sea elephant. The **elephant seal** *(see).*

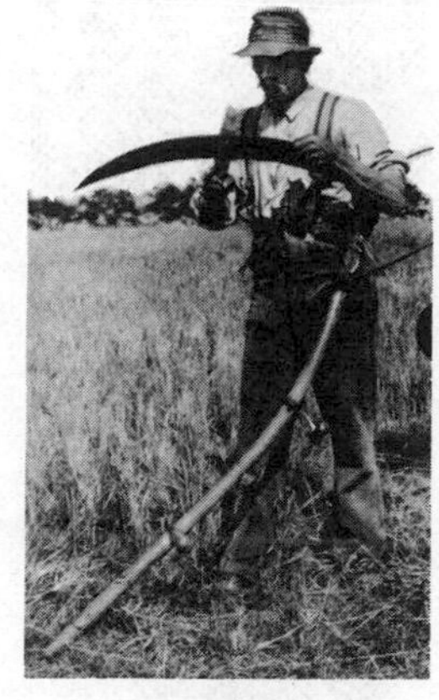
scythe

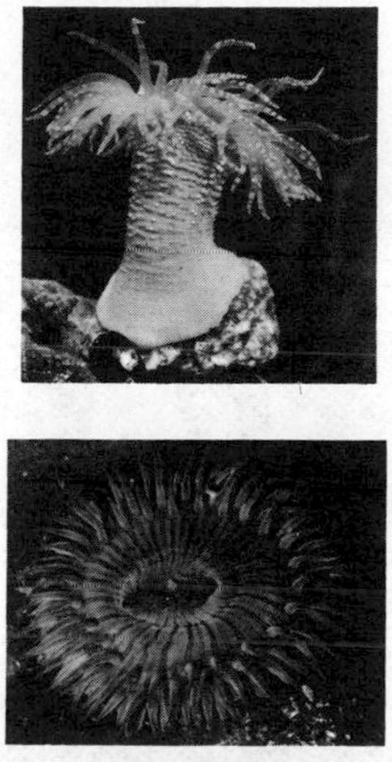
sea anemone
Above: Side view of *Bunodactis verrucosa*
Below: Top view of *Anthopleura elegantissima*

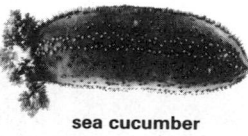

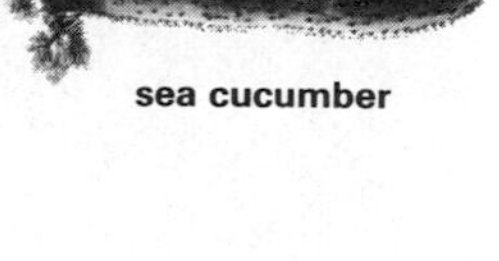
sea cucumber

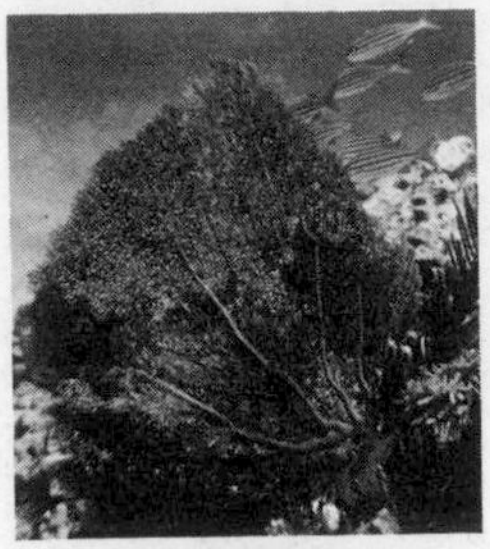
sea fan
Gorgonia flabellum

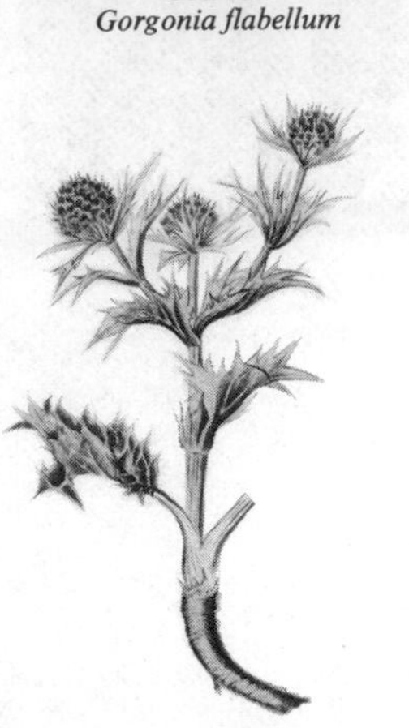
sea holly

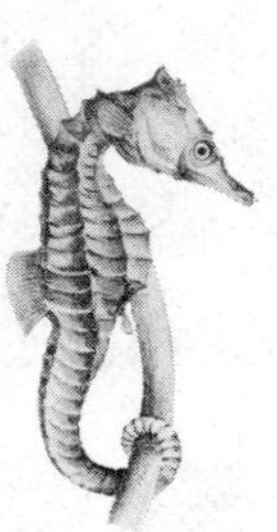
sea horse
Hippocampus hudsonius

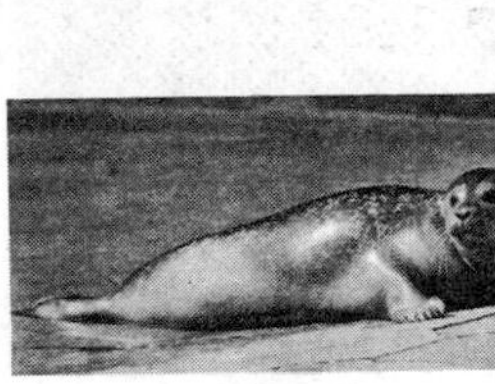
seal[2]
Phoca vitulina
Harbor seal

sea fan. Any of various yellowish to reddish fan-shaped corals of the genus *Gorgonia;* especially, *G. flabellum,* of coastal waters of Florida and the West Indies.
sea·far·er (sē′fâr′ər) *n.* A sailor or mariner.
sea·far·ing (sē′fâr′ĭng) *n.* **1.** Travel by sea. **2.** The calling of a sailor. *—adj.* Following a life at sea.
sea feather. Any of several anthozoans of the family Pennatulidae, having a featherlike shape.
sea·food (sē′fōōd′) *n.* Also **sea food.** Edible fish or shellfish from the sea.
sea·fowl (sē′foul′) *n.* **1.** A sea bird. **2.** Sea birds collectively.
sea front. A strip of land at the very edge of the sea, especially land desirable for a resort.
sea·girt (sē′gûrt′) *adj.* Surrounded by the sea.
sea·go·ing (sē′gō′ĭng) *adj.* **1.** Made or used for ocean voyages. **2.** Seafaring.
sea gooseberry. A marine organism of the genus *Pleurobrachia,* having two tentacles and a round, iridescent body. [From its round, berrylike shape.]
sea grant college. Any of several state colleges and universities that receive grants from the National Science Foundation to aid in developing programs for increasing the use of marine resources in accordance with the National Sea Grant College and Program Act of 1966.
sea grape. A tropical American shrub or small tree, *Coccolobis uvifera,* of sandy beaches, having broad, rounded leaves and hard, purplish fruit in grapelike clusters.
sea gull. A gull, especially one appearing near coastal areas.
sea holly. An Old World plant, *Eryngium maritimum,* growing on seashores and having prickly leaves and clusters of blue or purplish flowers.
sea horse. 1. Any small marine fish of the genus *Hippocampus,* characteristically swimming in an upright position, and having a prehensile tail, a horselike head, and a body covered with bony plates. **2.** Broadly, a walrus. **3.** A mythical animal, half fish and half horse, ridden by Neptune and other sea gods. **4.** A large white-capped wave.
Sea Island cotton. A species of cotton, *Gossypium barbadense,* native to tropical America and widely cultivated for its fine, long-staple fibers. [From the SEA ISLANDS.]
Sea Islands. A chain of islands in the Atlantic off the coasts of South Carolina, Georgia, and northern Florida.
sea kale. A European plant, *Crambe maritima,* having edible, cabbagelike leaves.
sea king. A viking pirate chief of the early Middle Ages.
seal[1] (sēl) *n.* **1. a.** A die or signet having a raised or incised emblem, used to stamp an impression upon a receptive substance such as wax or lead. **b.** The impression made. **c.** The design or emblem itself, belonging exclusively to the user: *the king's seal.* **d.** A small disk or wafer of wax, lead, or paper bearing such an imprint and affixed to a document to prove authenticity or to seal it shut. **2.** Something (as a commercial hallmark) that serves similarly to authenticate, confirm, or attest. **3.** An adhesive agent such as wax, paraffin, or putty used to close or secure something or to prevent seepage of moisture or air. **4.** A device or fluid in a drainpipe preventing the upward passage of gas. **5.** An airtight closure. **6.** A small decorative paper sticker: *a Christmas seal.* **—under seal.** Secured with an official seal. *—tr.v.* **sealed, sealing, seals. 1.** To affix a seal to so as to prove authenticity or attest to accuracy, legal weight, quality, or other standard. **2. a.** To close or seal as if with a seal: *seal an envelope; seal one's lips.* **b.** To close hermetically. **c.** To make fast or fill up as with plaster or cement. **3.** To grant, certify, or designate under seal or authority. **4.** To establish or determine irrevocably. **5.** *Mormon Church.* To make binding for life; to solemnize forever, as a marriage. [Middle English *seel,* from Old French, from Latin *sigillum,* seal, diminutive of *signum,* sign. See **sekw-**[1] in Appendix.*] **—seal′a·ble** *adj.*
seal[2] (sēl) *n.* **1.** Any of various aquatic, carnivorous mammals of the families Phocidae and Otariidae, having a sleek, torpedo-shaped body and limbs that are modified into paddlelike flippers. **2.** The pelt or fur of a seal, especially a fur seal. **3.** Leather made from the hide of a seal. *—intr.v.* **sealed, sealing, seals.** To hunt seals. [Middle English *selch, seel,* Old English *seolh.* See **selk-** in Appendix.*]
seal·ant (sē′lənt) *n.* A sealing agent.
sea lavender. Any of several salt-marsh plants of the genus *Limonium,* having clusters of small lavender or pinkish flowers.
sea legs. *Informal.* The ability to walk on board ship with steadiness, especially in rough seas.
seal·er[1] (sē′lər) *n.* **1.** One that seals. **2.** An undercoat of paint or varnish used to size a surface. **3.** An officer who inspects, tests, and certifies weights and measures.
seal·er[2] (sē′lər) *n.* A person or ship engaged in seal hunting.
seal·er·y (sē′lə-rē) *n., pl.* **-ies. 1.** The occupation of hunting seals. **2.** A place where seals are hunted.
sea lettuce. Any of several green seaweeds of the genus *Ulva,* having thin, leaflike, irregularly shaped fronds sometimes used as food.
sea level. The level of the ocean's surface; especially, the mean level halfway between high and low tide, used as a standard in reckoning land elevation or sea depths.
sea lily. Any of various marine crinoids, usually anchored to the ocean floor in deep water, and having a flowerlike body supported by a long stalk.
sealing wax. A resinous preparation of shellac and turpentine that is soft and fluid when heated but solidifies upon cooling, used to seal letters, batteries, jars, and the like.
sea lion. Any of several seals of the family Otariidae, having small but distinct external ears; especially, *Zalophus californianus,* of the Northern Pacific.
seal ring. A **signet ring** *(see).*
seal·skin (sēl′skĭn′) *n.* **1.** The pelt or fur of a fur seal, especially the underfur. **2.** A coat or other garment made of this skin. **—seal′skin′** *adj.*
Sea·ly·ham terrier (sē′lē-hăm′, -lē-əm). A terrier of a breed developed in Wales, having a wiry white coat, a long head, and short legs. [Originally bred at *Sealyham,* Pembrokeshire, Wales.]
seam (sēm) *n.* **1. a.** A line of junction formed by sewing together two pieces of material along their margins. **b.** A similar line, ridge, or groove made by fitting, joining, or lapping together two sections along their edges. **c.** A suture. **d.** A scar. **2.** Any line across a surface, as a crack, fissure, or wrinkle. **3.** A thin layer or stratum, as of coal or rock. *—v.* **seamed, seaming, seams.** *—tr.* **1.** To put together with or as with a seam. **2.** To mark with a groove, wrinkle, scar, or other seamlike line. **3.** *Knitting.* To form ridges in by purling. *—intr.* **1.** To crack open; become fissured or furrowed. **2.** *Knitting.* To purl. [Middle English *se(e)m,* Old English *sēam.* See **syū-** in Appendix.*] **—seam′er** *n.*
sea·maid·en (sē′mād′n) *n.* Also **sea-maid** (sē′mād′). A mermaid or a sea nymph.
sea·man (sē′mən) *n., pl.* **-men** (-mĭn). **1.** A mariner or sailor. **2.** *Abbr.* **S** *U.S. Navy.* An enlisted man ranking above seaman apprentice and below petty officer.
Sea·man (sē′mən), **Elizabeth (Cochrane).** Pen name, Nellie Bly. 1867–1922. American journalist.
seaman apprentice. *U.S. Navy.* An enlisted man ranking above a seaman recruit and below a seaman.
seaman recruit. *U.S. Navy.* An enlisted man of the lowest rank.
sea·man·ship (sē′mən-shĭp′) *n.* Skill in managing or navigating a boat or ship.
sea·mark (sē′märk′) *n.* **1.** A landmark visible from the sea, used as a guide in navigation. **2.** The mark along a coastline indicating the upper tidal limits.
sea mew. Any of various gulls frequenting coastal areas; especially, *Larus canus,* of Europe.
sea milkwort. A fleshy plant, *Glaux maritima,* of shores and brackish marshes, having pink or white flowers.
seam·less (sēm′lĭs) *adj.* **1.** Without seams; woven without a seam. **2.** Perfectly consistent. **—seam′less·ness** *n.*
sea·mount (sē′mount′) *n.* A submarine mountain rising to more than 3,000 feet above the ocean floor but having a summit at least 1,000 feet below sea level.
sea mouse. Any of various segmented marine worms of the genus *Aphrodite;* especially, *A. aculeata,* having a flattened elliptical body with overlapping scales covered by long hairs.
seam·ster (sēm′stər) *n.* A tailor. [Middle English *semester,* Old English *sēamestre* : *sēam,* SEAM + -STER.]
seam·stress (sēm′strĭs) *n.* A woman who makes her living by sewing.
seam·y (sē′mē) *adj.* **-ier, -iest. 1.** Having, marked with, or showing a seam or seams. **2.** Unattractive, like the wrong side of a garment; rough and raw; sordid: *the seamy side of life.* **—seam′i·ness** *n.*
Sean·ad Eir·eann (săn′əd âr′ĭn). The Senate, or upper house, of the Irish parliament. [Irish *seanad,* senate, from Latin *senātus,* SENATE + *Éireann,* of Ireland (see **Dail Eireann**).]
sé·ance (sā′äns′) *n.* **1.** A meeting of persons to receive spiritualistic messages. **2.** A meeting, session, or sitting. [French, "a sitting," from Old French, from *seoir,* to sit, from Latin *sedēre,* sit. See **sed-**[1] in Appendix.*]
sea onion. 1. A plant, *Urginea maritima,* of the Mediterranean area, cultivated for its bulb that yields a powder used medicinally and as a rat poison. Also called "squill," "red squill." **2.** A small European bulbous plant, *Scilla verna,* having fragrant blue flowers.
sea otter. A large, nearly extinct marine otter, *Enhydra lutris,* of northern Pacific coasts, having a soft dark-brown coat valued as fur.
sea pen. Any of various marine anthozoans of the families Stylatulidae and Funiculinidae, resembling and related to the sea feathers. [From its resemblance to a quill pen.]
sea·plane (sē′plān′) *n.* An aircraft equipped with floats for landing on or taking off from a body of water.
sea·port (sē′pôrt′, -pōrt′) *n.* *Abbr.* **spt.** A harbor or town having facilities for seagoing ships.
sea power. 1. A nation having naval strength. **2.** Naval strength.
sea purse. The purse-shaped egg case of skates or of certain sharks.
sea·quake (sē′kwāk′) *n.* An earthquake under the sea floor.
sear[1] (sîr) *v.* **seared, searing, sears.** *—tr.* **1.** To make withered; dry up or shrivel. **2.** To char, scorch, or burn the surface of with or as with a hot instrument. *—intr.* To become withered or dried up, as vegetation; shrivel. —See Synonyms at **burn.** *—adj.* Variant of **sere.** *—n.* Also **sere.** Any condition, as a scar, produced by searing. [Middle English *seren,* Old English *sēarian,* from *sēar,* withered. See **saus-** in Appendix.*]
sear[2] (sîr) *n.* The catch in a gunlock that keeps the hammer halfcocked or fully cocked. [Probably from Old French *serre,* grasp, lock, from *serrer,* to grasp, from Vulgar Latin *serrāre* (unattested), from Late Latin *serāre,* to bolt, bar, from Latin *sera,* bar, door, bolt. See **ser-**[3] in Appendix.*]
sea raven. A large sculpin, *Hemitripterus americanus,* of the western Atlantic.

ă pat/ā pay/âr care/ä father/b bib/ch church/d deed/ĕ pet/ē be/f fife/g gag/h hat/hw which/ĭ pit/ī pie/îr pier/j judge/k kick/l lid, needle/m mum/n no, sudden/ng thing/ŏ pot/ō toe/ô paw, for/oi noise/ou out/ŏŏ took/ōō boot/p pop/r roar/s sauce/sh ship, dish/

search (sûrch) *v.* **searched, searching, searches.** —*tr.* **1.** To make a thorough examination of or look over carefully in order to find something; explore. **2.** To make a careful examination or investigation of; probe: *search one's conscience.* **3.** To make a thorough check of (a legal document or records, for example); scrutinize: *search a title.* **4. a.** To examine (a house, ship, area, or the like) in order to find something lost or concealed. **b.** To examine the person or personal effects of in order to find something lost or concealed. **5.** To come to know; learn. Used with *out.* —*intr.* To conduct a thorough investigation; seek. Often used with *for.* —*n.* **1.** An act of searching; investigation; examination; probe. **2.** The exercise of **right of search** *(see).* [Middle English *serchen,* from Norman French *sercher,* variant of Old French *cerchier,* "to go around," from Late Latin *circāre,* from Latin *circus,* circle. See **sker-**[3] in Appendix.*] —**search'a·ble** *adj.* —**search'er** *n.*

search·light (sûrch'līt') *n.* **1.** An apparatus containing a light source and a reflector for projecting a bright beam of approximately parallel rays of light. **2.** The beam of light so projected. **3.** A flashlight.

search warrant. A warrant giving legal authorization for a search.

sea robin. Any of various marine fishes of the family Triglidae, having a bony head and extremely long pectoral fins with fingerlike rays.

sea room. Space at sea adequate for maneuvering a ship.

sea·scape (sē'skāp') *n.* A view or picture of the sea. [SEA + -SCAPE.]

Sea Scout. A member of a program designed to train Boy Scouts in seamanship.

sea serpent. A large snakelike marine animal often reported by mariners since antiquity but never positively identified.

sea·shell (sē'shĕl') *n.* The calcareous shell of a marine mollusk or similar marine organism.

sea·shore (sē'shôr', -shōr') *n.* **1.** Land by the sea. **2.** *Law.* Ground lying between high-water and low-water marks; foreshore.

sea·sick·ness (sē'sĭk'nĭs) *n.* Nausea and other malaise provoked by the motion of a vessel at sea. —**sea'sick'** *adj.*

sea·side (sē'sīd') *n.* The seashore. —*adj.* Of, pertaining to, or situated at the seashore.

sea slug. Any of various shell-less marine gastropods of the suborder Nudibranchia, having a colorful body with fringelike projections. Also called "nudibranch."

sea snake. Any of various venomous tropical marine snakes of the family Hydrophidae, chiefly of the Pacific and Indian oceans.

sea·son (sē'zən) *n.* **1. a.** One of the four equal natural divisions of the year, spring, summer, autumn, and winter, indicated by the passage of the sun through an equinox or solstice and derived from the apparent north-south movement of the sun caused by the fixed direction of the earth's axis in solar orbit. **b.** The two divisions of the year, rainy and dry, in tropical climates. **2.** A recurrent period that is characterized by certain occupations, festivities, or crops. **3.** A suitable, natural, or convenient time. **4.** Any period of time. —**in season. 1.** Available or ready for eating or other use. **2.** Legally available to the hunter, fisherman, or trapper. **3.** At the right moment; opportunely. **4.** In heat. Said of animals. —**out of season. 1.** Not available or ready for eating or hunting. **2.** Not at the right or proper moment; inopportunely. —*v.* **seasoned, -soning, -sons.** —*tr.* **1.** To improve or enhance the flavor of (food) by adding salt, spices, herbs, or other flavorings. **2.** To add zest, piquancy, or interest to. **3.** To dry (lumber) until it is usable; cure. **4.** To render competent through trial and experience. **5.** To accustom; inure. **6.** To moderate; temper. —*intr.* To become usable, competent, tempered, or the like. [Middle English *sesoun,* from Old French *seson,* from Latin *satiō,* act of sowing (in Vulgar Latin, "sowing time"), from *serere* (past participle *satus*), to sow, plant. See **sē-**[1] in Appendix.*]

sea·son·a·ble (sē'zə-nə-bəl) *adj.* **1.** In keeping with the time or the season. **2.** Occurring or performed at the proper time; timely. —**sea'son·a·bly** *adv.*

Usage: *Seasonable* and *seasonal,* though closely related, are differentiated in usage. *Seasonable* stresses appropriateness to a season *(heavy snow, seasonable in Michigan in January)* or timeliness *(seasonable rains assure a good crop). Seasonal* largely applies to what depends on, and is controlled by, seasons or a particular season *(seasonal variations in employment).*

sea·son·al (sē'zə-nəl) *adj.* Of or dependent upon a particular season. See Usage note at **seasonable.** —**sea'son·al·ly** *adv.*

sea·son·ing (sē'zə-nĭng) *n.* **1.** Anything used to flavor food. **2.** The act or process by which something is seasoned.

season ticket. A ticket valid for a specified period of time.

sea spider. Any of various marine arachnids of the class Pycnogonida, having long legs and a relatively small body.

sea squirt. Any of various sedentary marine animals of the class Ascidiacea, having a transparent, sac-shaped body with two siphons. [It squirts water when disturbed.]

seat (sēt) *n.* **1.** Something that may be sat upon, as a chair, bench, or the like. **2.** A place in which one may sit. **3.** The part of something on which one rests in sitting. **4. a.** The buttocks. **b.** That part of a garment covering the buttocks. **5. a.** A part serving as the base of something. **b.** The surface or part upon which another part sits or rests. **6. a.** The place where anything is located or based. **b.** A center of authority; capital. **7.** A place of abode or residence; especially, a large house that is part of an estate. **8.** Membership in a legislative body, stock exchange, or other organization, obtained by purchase, appointment, or election. **9.** The manner of sitting on a horse. —*tr.v.* **seated, seating, seats. 1. a.** To place in or on a seat. **b.** To cause or assist to sit down. **2.** To provide with a particular seat. **3.** To have or provide seats for: *We can seat 300.* **4.** To repair or replace the seat of. **5.** To install in a position of authority or eminence. **6.** To fix firmly in place. [Middle English *sete,* from Old Norse *sæti.* See **sed-**[1] in Appendix.*]

sea tangle. Any of various brown seaweeds, especially of the genus *Laminaria.*

seat belt. A safety strap attached to the seat of a passenger vehicle. Also called "safety belt."

seat·ing (sē'tĭng) *n.* **1.** The act of providing or furnishing with a seat or seats. **2.** The arrangement of seats in a room, auditorium, banquet hall, or the like. **3.** The member or part upon or within which another part is seated. **4.** Material for upholstering seats.

SEATO (sē'tō) Southeast Asia Treaty Organization.

sea trout. 1. Any of several marine fishes of the genus *Cynoscion;* especially, the **weakfish** *(see).* **2.** Broadly, any of several trouts or similar fishes that live in the sea but migrate to fresh water to spawn.

Se·at·tle[1] (sē-ăt'l). 1786?–1866. American Indian chief of the Suquamish and other tribes.

Se·at·tle[2] (sē-ăt'l). A major city and seaport in west-central Washington, on the eastern shore of Puget Sound. Population, 567,000.

sea urchin. Any of various echinoderms of the class Echinoidea, having a soft body enclosed in a round, symmetrical, limy shell covered with long spines.

sea wall. An embankment to prevent erosion of a shoreline.

sea walnut. Any of several ctenophores of the genus *Mnemiopsis* and related genera, having a translucent, ovoid body with lengthwise ridges and rows of hairlike cilia.

sea·ward (sē'wərd) *adv.* Also **sea·wards** (-wərdz). Toward the sea. —**sea'ward** *adj.*

sea·ware (sē'wâr') *n.* Sea wrack used as fertilizer. [SEA + *ware,* seaweed, Middle English *ware,* Old English *wār* (see **wei-**[1] in Appendix*).]

sea·way (sē'wā') *n.* **1.** A sea route. **2.** An inland waterway for ocean shipping. **3.** The headway of a ship. **4.** A rough sea.

sea·weed (sē'wēd') *n.* **1.** Any of numerous marine algae, such as a kelp, rockweed, or gulfweed. **2.** Any of various other marine plants.

sea·wor·thy (sē'wûr'thē) *adj.* Designating a vessel that is fit to sail. —**sea'wor'thi·ness** *n.*

sea wrack. Any material cast ashore, especially seaweed.

se·ba·ceous (sĭ-bā'shəs) *adj. Physiology.* **1.** Of, pertaining to, or resembling fat or sebum; fatty. **2.** Secreting fat or sebum. [Latin *sēbāceus* : *sēbum,* tallow (see **sebum**) + -ACEOUS.]

sebaceous gland. Any of various glands in the corium of the skin that open into a hair follicle and produce and secrete sebum.

se·bac·ic acid (sĭ-bā'sĭk). A white crystalline acid, $C_{10}H_{18}O_4$, used in the manufacture of certain synthetic resins and fibers, various plasticizers, and polyester rubbers. [*Sebacic,* from SEBACEOUS (because originally obtained from melted suet).]

Se·bas·tian (sĭ-băs'chən), **Saint.** Roman martyr of the late third century A.D.

Se·bas·to·pol. See **Sevastopol.**

SEbE southeast by east.

sebi-, sebo-. Indicates fat or fatty material; for example, **sebiferous, seborrhea.** [New Latin, from Latin *sēbum,* tallow. See **sebum.**]

se·bif·er·ous (sĭ-bĭf'ər-əs) *adj.* Also **se·bip·a·rous** (sĭ-bĭp'-). Producing or secreting fatty, oily, or waxy matter; sebaceous. [SEBI- + -FEROUS.]

seb·or·rhe·a (sĕb'ə-rē'ə) *n.* Also **seb·or·rhoe·a.** A disease of the sebaceous glands characterized by excessive secretion of sebum or an alteration in its quality, resulting in an oily coating, crusts, or scales on the skin. [*Sebo-,* variant of SEBI- + -RRHEA.]

SEbS southeast by south.

se·bum (sē'bəm) *n.* The semifluid secretion of the sebaceous glands. [Latin *sēbum*†, tallow.]

sec (sĕk) *adj. French.* Dry. Said of wines, especially champagne. Compare **brut.**

sec 1. secant. **2.** second (unit of time). **3.** second (unit of angular measure).

SEC Securities and Exchange Commission.

sec. 1. secretary. **2.** sector. **3.** secundum.

se·cant (sē'kənt, -kănt') *n. Abbr.* **sec 1.** *Geometry.* **a.** A straight line intersecting a curve at two or more points. **b.** The straight line drawn from the center through one end of a circular arc and intersecting the tangent to the other end of the arc. **2.** *Trigonometry.* **a.** The reciprocal of the cosine of an angle. **b.** For an acute angle, the ratio of the hypotenuse to the side of a right triangle adjacent to the acute angle. [French *(ligne) secante,* "cutting line," from Latin *secāns,* present participle of *secāre,* to cut. See **sek-** in Appendix.*]

Sec·chi (săk'kē), **Pietro Angelo.** 1818–1878. Italian astronomer; made first spectroscopic classification of the stars.

sec·co (sĕk'ō) *n., pl.* **-cos.** The art or an example of painting on dry plaster. Compare **fresco.** [Italian, "dry," from Latin *siccus.* See **seikw-** in Appendix.*]

se·cede (sĭ-sēd', sē'-) *intr.v.* **-ceded, -ceding, -cedes.** To withdraw formally from membership in an organization, association, or alliance. [Latin *sēcēdere,* to go away : *sē,* apart (see **seu-**[2] in Appendix*) + *cēdere,* to go (see **ked-**[1] in Appendix*).]

se·cern (sĭ-sûrn') *tr.v.* **-cerned, -cerning, -cerns. 1.** *Rare.* To dis-

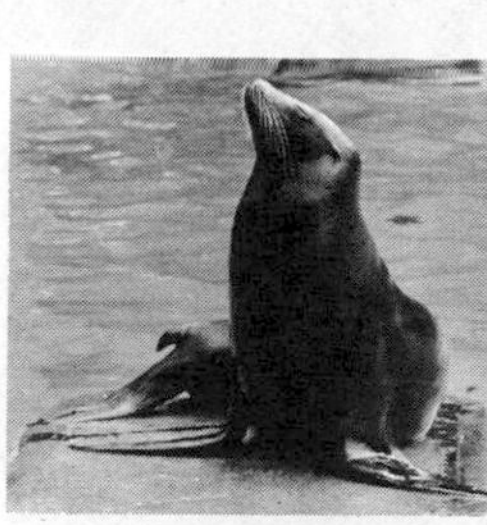

sea lion
Zalophus californianus

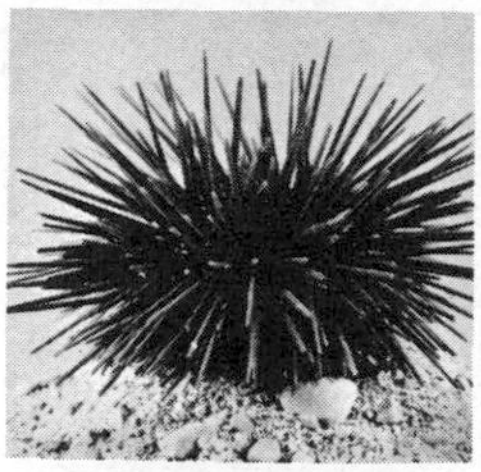

sea urchin
Centrostephanus rogersi

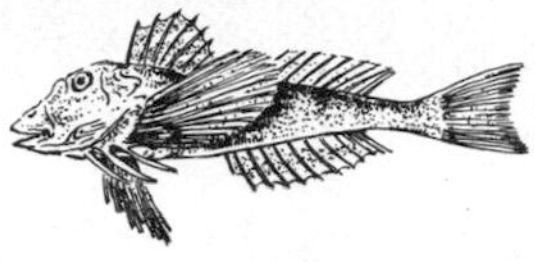

sea robin
Prionotus carolinus

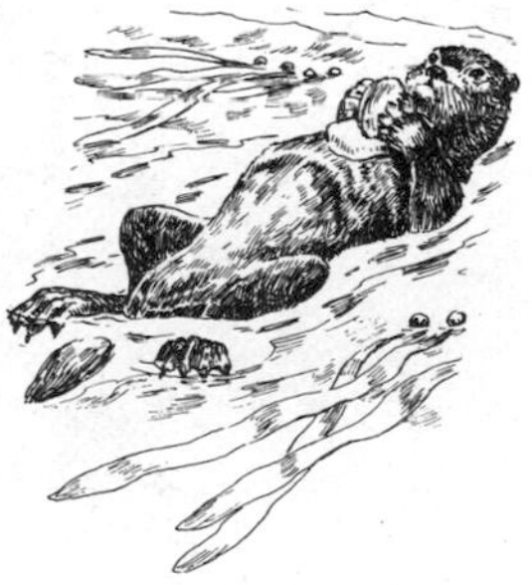

sea otter

cern as separate; to discriminate. **2.** *Physiology.* To secrete. Used of a gland or follicle. [Latin *sēcernere*, to separate : *sē*, apart (see **seu-²** in Appendix*) + *cernere*, to separate, discern (see **skeri-** in Appendix*).] —**se·cern′ment** *n.*

se·ces·sion (sĭ-sĕsh′ən) *n.* **1.** The act of seceding. **2.** *Usually capital* S. The withdrawal of 11 Southern states from the Federal Union in 1860–61, precipitating the Civil War. [Latin *sēcessiō*, from *sēcēdere* (past participle *secessus*), SECEDE.] —**se·ces′sion·al** *adj.*

se·ces·sion·ism (sĭ-sĕsh′ə-nĭz′əm) *n.* The policy of those maintaining the right of secession. —**se·ces′sion·ist** *adj. & n.*

Seck·el pear (sĕk′əl, sĭk′əl). A variety of pear having small, sweet, reddish-brown fruit. [Originally grown by a Pennsylvania farmer named *Seckel.*]

se·clude (sĭ-klōōd′) *tr.v.* **-cluded, -cluding, -cludes. 1.** To remove or set apart from others; to place in solitude. **2.** To screen from view; make private. [Middle English *secluden*, to shut off, keep away, from Latin *sēclūdere* : *sē*, apart (see seu-² in Appendix*) + *claudere*, to shut (see **kleu-** in Appendix*).]

se·clud·ed (sĭ-klōō′dĭd) *adj.* **1.** Removed or remote from others; solitary. **2.** Screened from view; sequestered; hidden. —**se·clud′ed·ly** *adv.* —**se·clud′ed·ness** *n.*

se·clu·sion (sĭ-klōō′zhən) *n.* **1. a.** The act of secluding. **b.** The state of being secluded; solitude; privacy. **2.** A secluded place or abode. —See Synonyms at **solitude.** [Medieval Latin *sēclūsiō*, from Latin *sēclūdere* (past participle *sēclūsus*), SECLUDE.]

se·clu·sive (sĭ-klōō′sĭv, -zĭv) *adj.* Fond of, seeking, or tending to seclusion.

sec·ond¹ (sĕk′ənd) *n.* **1.** *Abbr.* **s, sec** *Symbol* ″ A unit of time equal to ¹⁄₆₀ of a minute. **2.** *Informal.* A brief lapse of time; a moment. **3.** *Abbr.* **s, sec** *Symbol* ″ *Geometry.* A unit of angular measure equal to ¹⁄₆₀ of a minute of arc. See **measurement.** —See Synonyms at **moment.** [Middle English *seconde*, unit in geometry, from Old French, from Medieval Latin *(pars minūta) secunda*, "second (small part)" (after the second sexagesimal division), from Latin, feminine of *secundus*, SECOND.]

sec·ond² (sĕk′ənd) *adj.* **1.** Coming next after the first in order, place, rank, time, or quality. Also written 2nd. See **number. 2.** Repeating an initial instance; another. **3.** Inferior to another; subordinate: *second to none.* **4.** *Music.* **a.** Having a lower pitch. **b.** Singing or playing a part having a lower range. **5.** Having the second-highest ratio. Said of gears in a sequence. —*n.* **1.** The ordinal number two in a series. Also written 2nd. See **number. 2.** One that is next in order, place, time, or quality after the first. **3.** *Often plural.* An article of merchandise of inferior quality. **4.** The official attendant of a contestant in a duel or boxing match. **5.** *Music.* **a.** The interval between consecutive tones on the diatonic scale. **b.** A tone separated by this interval from another tone. **c.** A combination of two such tones in notation or in harmony. **d.** The second part, instrument, or voice in a harmonized composition. **6.** *Parliamentary Procedure.* An utterance of endorsement. **7.** The forward gears in an automobile transmission having the second-highest ratio. —*tr.v.* **seconded, -onding, -onds. 1.** To attend (a duelist, for example) as an aide or assistant. **2.** To promote or encourage; reinforce. **3.** *Parliamentary Procedure.* To endorse (a motion or nomination) as a required preliminary to discussion or vote. —*adv.* **1.** In the second order, place, or rank. **2.** But for one other; save one: *the second-highest peak.* [Middle English, from Old French, from Latin *secundus*, following, coming next. See **sekw-¹** in Appendix.*]

Second Advent. The **Second Coming** (see).

sec·on·dar·y (sĕk′ən-dĕr′ē) *adj.* **1. a.** One step removed from the first; of the second rank; not primary: **b.** Inferior; minor; lesser. **2.** Derived from what is primary or original: *a secondary source.* **3.** *Ornithology.* Of, pertaining to, or designating the shorter flight feathers projecting along the inner part of the edge of a bird's wing. **4.** *Electricity.* Having an induced current that is generated by an inductively coupled primary. Said of a circuit or coil. **5.** *Chemistry.* Formed by replacement of two atoms or radicals within a molecule. Said of a compound. **6.** *Geology.* Resulting from changes in the pre-existing minerals. **7.** Of or relating to education between the elementary school and the college: *secondary school.* —*n., pl.* **secondaries. 1.** One that acts in an auxiliary, subordinate, or inferior capacity. **2.** *Ornithology.* One of the shorter flight feathers projecting along the inner part of the edge of a bird's wing. **3.** *Electricity.* A coil or circuit having an induced current. **4.** *Astronomy.* A body that orbits a primary; a satellite. **5.** *Football.* The defensive backfield. —**sec′on·dar′i·ly** *adv.* —**sec′on·dar′i·ness** *n.*

secondary battery. *Electricity.* A **storage battery** (see).

secondary cell. A rechargeable electric cell that converts chemical energy into electrical energy by a reversible chemical reaction. Also called "storage cell." Compare **primary cell.**

secondary color. A color produced by mixing two primary colors in approximately equal proportions.

secondary electron. An electron produced in secondary emission.

secondary emission. *Physics.* Emission of electrons from the surface of a substance bombarded by electrons or ions.

secondary sex characteristic. Any of various genetically transmitted anatomical, physiological, or behavioral characteristics, as voice quality, abundance of facial hair, or breast development, that first appear in humans at puberty and differentiate between the sexes without having a direct reproductive function. Also called "secondary sex character."

second base. *Baseball.* **1.** The base across the diamond from home plate, to be touched second by a runner. **2.** The position played by a second baseman.

second baseman. The infielder who positions himself near and usually to the first-base side of second base.

second childhood. Senility; dotage.

sec·ond-class (sĕk′ənd-klăs′, -kläs′) *adj.* **1.** In the rank or class that is next below the first or best; of secondary status; inferior. Also called "second-rate." **2.** Of or pertaining to travel accommodations ranking next below the highest or first class. **3.** Of or pertaining to a class of U.S. and Canadian mail consisting of newspapers and periodicals. —*adv.* By means of second-class mail or travel accommodations.

Second Coming. The return of Christ as judge upon the last day; millennium. Also called "Second Advent."

sec·ond-de·gree burn (sĕk′ənd-də-grē′). A burn that blisters the skin. See **burn.**

Second Empire. A heavily ornate style of furniture, architecture, and decoration that was developed in mid-19th-century France.

second fiddle. 1. A secondary role. **2.** One who plays such a role.

second growth. Trees that cover an area after the removal of the original stand, as by cutting or fire.

sec·ond-guess (sĕk′ənd-gĕs′) *v.* **-guessed, -guessing, -guesses.** —*tr.* **1.** To criticize (a decision or decision-maker) after the outcome is known; reconsider from hindsight. **2.** To anticipate the moves of; outguess. —*intr.* To criticize a decision after its outcome is known. —**sec′ond-guess′er** *n.*

second hand¹. The hand of a timepiece that marks the seconds.

second hand². An intermediary person or source. Usually preceded by *at: heard at second hand.*

sec·ond-hand (sĕk′ənd-hănd′) *adj.* Also **sec·ond-hand, second hand. 1.** Previously used by another; not new. **2.** Dealing in previously used merchandise. **3.** Obtained or derived from another; not original; borrowed. —*adv.* In an indirect manner; indirectly.

second lieutenant. An officer in the U.S. Army and Marine Corps of the lowest commissioned grade, ranking below a first lieutenant.

sec·ond·ly (sĕk′ənd-lē) *adv.* In the second place; second.

second mortgage. A mortgage on property that is already mortgaged.

second nature. An acquired personal disposition, tendency, or habit so long practiced as to seem innate.

se·con·do (sā-kôn′dō) *n., pl.* **-di** (-dē). *Music.* **1.** The second part in a concerted piece; especially, the lower part in a piano duet. **2.** One who performs such a part. [Italian, "second," from Latin *secundus*, SECOND (next).]

second person. *Grammar.* The form of a pronoun or verb used in referring to the person addressed; for example, *you* and *shall* in *you shall not enter.*

second sight. Clairvoyance.

sec·ond-sto·ry man (sĕk′ənd-stôr′ē, -stōr′ē). A burglar adept at entering through upstairs windows.

Second World War. World War II (see).

se·cre·cy (sē′krə-sē) *n.* **1.** The quality or condition of being secret or hidden; concealment. **2.** The ability or habit of keeping secrets; closeness. [Earlier *secretie*, Middle English *secretee*, from *secre(t)*, SECRET.]

se·cret (sē′krĭt) *adj.* **1.** Concealed from general knowledge or view; kept hidden. **2.** Dependably close-mouthed; discreet. **3.** Operating in a hidden or confidential manner: *secret agent.* **4.** Not visibly expressed; private; inward. **5.** Not frequented; secluded. **6.** Known or shared only by the initiated: *secret rites.* **7.** Beyond ordinary understanding; mysterious. **8.** *Military.* Designating the security classification below top-secret and above confidential. —*n.* **1.** Something kept hidden from others or known only to oneself or to a few. **2.** Something that remains beyond understanding or explanation; mystery. **3.** A method or formula on which success is based. **4.** *Capital* S. A variable prayer said after the Offertory and before the Preface in the liturgy of the Mass. —**in secret.** Secretly; in secrecy. [Middle English *secre(t)*, from Old French, from Latin *sēcrētus*, separate, out of the way, secret, from the past participle of *sēcernere*, to put apart, separate : *sē*, apart (see **seu-²** in Appendix*) + *cernere*, to separate (see **skeri-** in Appendix*).] —**se′cret·ly** *adv.*

Synonyms: secret, stealthy, covert, clandestine, furtive, surreptitious, underhand. These adjectives apply to what is purposely concealed from view or knowledge. *Secret* is the most general and therefore least strong in suggesting anything beyond this basic sense. *Stealthy* is most often applied to action designed to achieve an end without attracting notice. *Covert* describes any act not taken openly. *Clandestine* implies secrecy for the purpose of concealing illegal or improper actions. *Furtive* applies to action and suggests the slyness and evasiveness of a thief. *Surreptitious* usually describes quick, secret, often nefarious action. *Underhand* describes action or means involving unfairness, deceit, or fraud as well as concealment.

sec·re·tar·i·at (sĕk′rə-târ′ē-ĭt) *n.* Also **sec·re·tar·i·ate** (-ĭt). **1.** The department administered by a governmental secretary, especially for an international organization: *secretariat of the United Nations.* **2.** The office occupied by such a department. **3.** The office or position of a governmental secretary. [French *secrétariat*, from Medieval Latin *sēcrētāriātus*, from *sēcrētārius*, SECRETARY.]

sec·re·tar·y (sĕk′rə-tĕr′ē) *n., pl.* **-ies.** *Abbr.* **sec., secy. 1.** A person employed to handle correspondence, keep files, and do clerical work for an individual or company. **2.** An officer who keeps records of the meetings, stock transfers, and legal transactions of a company or other organization. **3.** An official presiding over an administrative department of state. **4.** A desk with a small bookcase on top. [Middle English *secretarie*, from Medieval Latin *sēcrētārius*, confidential officer, secretary, from Latin *sēcrētus*, SECRET.] —**sec′re·tar′i·al** (-târ′ē-əl) *adj.*

secretary bird. A large African bird of prey, *Sagittarius serpentarius*, with long legs and a crest of quills at the back of the head.

sec·re·tar·y-gen·er·al (sĕk′rə-tĕr′ē-jĕn′ər-əl) *n., pl.* **secretaries-general.** A principal executive officer, as in certain political parties or governmental bodies such as the United Nations.

se·crete[1] (sĭ-krēt′) *tr.v.* **-creted, -creting, -cretes.** To generate and separate out (a substance) from cells or bodily fluids. [Back-formation from SECRETION.] —**se·cre′tor** (-krē′tər) *n.*

se·crete[2] (sĭ-krēt′) *tr.v.* **-creted, -creting, -cretes.** To conceal in a hiding place; cache. See Synonyms at **hide.** [Earlier *secret*, to conceal, keep secret, from SECRET.]

se·cre·tin (sĭ-krē′tĭn) *n.* A hormone secreted in the duodenum to stimulate the flow of pancreatic juice. [SECRET(ION) + -IN.]

se·cre·tion (sĭ-krē′shən) *n.* **1.** The process of secreting a substance, especially one that is not a waste, from blood or cells. **2.** The substance so secreted. [Latin *sēcrētiō*, separation, from *sēcernere*, to separate. See **secret.**]

se·cre·tive (sē′krə-tĭv, sĭ-krē′tĭv *for sense 1; only* sĭ-krē′tĭv *for sense 2*) *adj.* **1.** Close-mouthed. **2.** Secretory. —See Synonyms at **silent.** —**se′cre·tive·ly** *adv.* —**se′cre·tive·ness** *n.*

se·cre·to·ry (sĭ-krē′tə-rē) *adj.* Pertaining to or performing the function of secretion.

secret service. Intelligence work conducted secretly by a governmental agency.

Secret Service. A branch of the U.S. Treasury Department concerned with the suppression of counterfeiters and the protection of the President and his immediate family.

sect (sĕkt) *n.* **1.** A group of people forming a distinct unit within a larger group by virtue of certain refinements or distinctions of belief or practice. **2.** A schismatic religious body. **3.** Any small faction united by common interests or beliefs. [Middle English *secte*, from Old French, from Latin *secta*, "following," from *sectus*, archaic past participle of *sequi*, to follow. See **sekw-**[1] in Appendix.*]

-sect. Indicates cut or divide; for example, **trisect, bisect.** [From Latin *sectus*, past participle of *secāre*, to cut. See **sek-** in Appendix.*]

sec·tar·i·an (sĕk-târ′ē-ən) *adj.* **1.** Pertaining to or characteristic of a sect or sects. **2.** Adhering or confined to the dogmatic limits of a sect; partisan. **3.** Narrow-minded; parochial. —*n.* **1.** A member of a sect. **2.** One characterized by bigoted adherence to a factional viewpoint. —**sec·tar′i·an·ism′** *n.*

sec·ta·ry (sĕk′tə-rē) *n., pl.* **-ries. 1.** A sectarian. **2.** A dissenter from an established church; specifically, a Protestant nonconformist. [Medieval Latin *sectārius*, from Latin *secta*, sect.]

sec·tile (sĕk′tĭl, -tīl′) *adj.* Capable of being cut or severed smoothly by a knife. [Latin *sectilis*, from *secāre*, to cut. See **sek-** in Appendix.*] —**sec·til′i·ty** (-tĭl′ə-tē) *n.*

sec·tion (sĕk′shən) *n.* **1.** One of several component parts of something; piece; portion. **2.** A subdivision of a written work. **3.** A division of a statute or legal code. **4.** A distinct portion of a newspaper. **5.** A distinct area of a town, county, or country. **6.** *Surveying.* A land unit of 640 acres or one square mile, equal to ¹⁄₃₆ of a township. **7.** The act or process of separating or cutting; especially, the surgical separation of tissue. **8.** A thin slice, as of tissue, suitable for microscopic examination. **9.** A segment of a fruit, especially a citrus fruit. **10.** The representation of a solid object as it would appear if cut by an intersecting plane, so that the internal structure is displayed. **11.** *Geometry.* The planar configuration formed by the intersection of a solid by a plane. Also called "plane section." **12. a.** A portion of a railroad track maintained by a single crew. **b.** An area in a sleeping car containing an upper and lower berth. **13.** *Military.* An army tactical unit smaller than a platoon and larger than a squad. **14.** A unit of vessels or aircraft within a military division. **15. a.** The character (§) used in printing to mark the beginning of a section. **b.** This character used as the fourth in a series of reference marks for footnotes. —*tr.v.* **sectioned, -tioning, -tions. 1.** To separate or divide into parts. **2.** To separate (tissue) surgically. **3.** To shade or crosshatch (part of a drawing) to indicate sections. [French, from Latin *sectiō*, a cutting, from *secāre*, to cut. See **sek-** in Appendix.*]

-section. Indicates the act or process of dividing or cutting; for example, **vivisection.** [From SECTION.]

sec·tion·al (sĕk′shən-əl) *adj.* **1.** Pertaining to or characteristic of a particular district. **2.** Composed of or divided into component sections. —*n.* A piece of furniture made up of sections that can be used separately or together. —**sec′tion·al·ly** *adv.*

sec·tion·al·ism (sĕk′shən-ə-lĭz′əm) *n.* Excessive devotion to local interests and customs. —**sec′tion·al·ist** *n.*

sec·tion·al·ize (sĕk′shən-ə-līz′) *tr.v.* **-ized, -izing, -izes. 1.** To compose of sections. **2.** To divide into sections, particularly into geographical sections. —**sec′tion·al·i·za′tion** *n.*

section gang. A work crew assigned to a section of railroad track.

sec·tor (sĕk′tər, -tôr′) *n. Abbr.* **sec. 1.** *Geometry.* The portion of a circle bounded by two radii and one of the intercepted arcs. **2.** *Military.* **a.** A division of a defensive position for which one unit is responsible. **b.** A division of an offensive position; a zone of action. **3.** A part or division of something, such as a city, resembling a military sector. —*tr.v.* **sectored, -toring, -tors.** To divide into sectors. [Late Latin, from Latin, cutter, from *secāre*, to cut. See **sek-** in Appendix.*] —**sec·tor′i·al** (-tôr′ē-əl, -tŏr′ē-əl) *adj.*

sec·u·lar (sĕk′yə-lər) *adj.* **1.** Of or pertaining to the temporal rather than to the spiritual. **2.** Not specifically pertaining to religion or to a religious body: *secular schools.* **3.** Pertaining to or advocating secularism. **4.** Not living in a monastery or religious community. Said of the clergy. Compare **regular. 5.** Occurring or observed once in an age or century. **6.** Lasting from century to century. —*n.* **1.** A secular clergyman. **2.** A layman. [Middle English *seculer*, from Old French, from Latin *saeculāris*, from *saeculum*†, generation, age.]

sec·u·lar·ism (sĕk′yə-lə-rĭz′əm) *n.* The view that consideration of the present well-being of mankind should predominate over religious considerations in civil affairs or public education. —**sec′u·lar·ist** *n.* —**sec′u·lar·is′tic** *adj.*

sec·u·lar·i·ty (sĕk′yə-lăr′ə-tē) *n., pl.* **-ties. 1.** The condition or quality of being secular. **2.** Something secular.

sec·u·lar·ize (sĕk′yə-lə-rīz′) *tr.v.* **-ized, -izing, -izes. 1.** To convert from ecclesiastical or religious to civil or lay use or ownership. **2.** To cause to draw away from religious orientation; make worldly. **3.** To lift the monastic restrictions from (a member of the clergy); make secular. —**sec′u·lar·i·za′tion** *n.*

se·cund (sē′kŭnd′, sĭ-kŭnd′) *adj.* Arranged on or turned to one side of an axis. [Latin *secundus*, going the same way, following, second. See **sekw-**[1] in Appendix.*]

sec·un·dines (sĕk′ən-dīnz′, sĭ-kŭn′dĭnz) *pl.n. Physiology.* The afterbirth *(see).* [Late Latin *secundīnae*, from Latin *secundus*, second, following. See **secund.**]

se·cure (sĭ-kyŏŏr′) *adj.* **-curer, -curest. 1.** Free from danger or risk of loss; safe. **2.** Free from fear or doubt; not anxious or unsure. **3. a.** Not likely to fail or give way; stable; strong. **b.** Well-fastened. **4.** Assured; certain; guaranteed. **5.** *Archaic.* Careless or overconfident. —*tr.v.* **secured, -curing, -cures. 1.** To guard from danger or risk of loss. **2.** To make firm or tight; to fasten. **3.** To make certain; guarantee; ensure. **4.** To make a pledge on, as a loan. **5.** To get possession of; acquire; procure. **6.** To bring about; effect. [Latin *sēcūrus*, "without care" : *sē*, without (see **seu-**[2] in Appendix*) + *cūra*, care (see **cūra** in Appendix*).] —**se·cur′a·ble** *adj.* —**se·cure′ly** *adv.* —**se·cure′ment** *n.* —**se·cur′er** *n.*

Securities and Exchange Commission. *Abbr.* **SEC** A U.S. governmental agency that supervises the exchange of securities so as to protect investors against malpractice.

se·cu·ri·ty (sĭ-kyŏŏr′ə-tē) *n., pl.* **-ties. 1.** Freedom from risk or danger; safety. **2.** Freedom from doubt, anxiety, or fear; confidence. **3.** Anything that gives or assures safety. **4.** Something deposited or given as assurance of the fulfillment of an obligation; a pledge. **5.** One who undertakes to fulfill the obligation of another; surety. **6.** *Plural.* Written evidence of ownership or creditorship; especially, a stock certificate. **7.** Measures adopted to guarantee freedom of secrecy of action, communication, or the like, as in wartime. [Middle English *securite*, from Latin *sēcūritās*, from *sēcūrus*, SECURE.]

Security Council. *Abbr.* **SC** The permanent peace-keeping organ of the United Nations, composed of five permanent members and ten elected members.

secy. secretary.

sed. sediment.

se·dan (sĭ-dăn′) *n.* **1.** A closed automobile having two or four doors and a front and rear seat. **2.** A portable enclosed chair for one person, having poles front and rear and carried by two men. [Perhaps obscurely from Vulgar Latin *sedda* (unattested), variant of Latin *sella*, seat, chair. See **sed-**[1] in Appendix.*]

Se·dan (sĭ-dăn′; *French* sə-dän′). A town on the Meuse in northern France, 50 miles northeast of Reims; the scene of the defeat of the French in the Franco-Prussian War and of the capture of Napoleon III (1870).

se·date[1] (sĭ-dāt′) *adj.* Serenely deliberate in character or manner; composed; collected. See Synonyms at **serious.** [Latin *sēdātus*, past participle of *sēdāre*, to settle, calm, compose. See **sed-**[1] in Appendix.*] —**se·date′ly** *adv.* —**se·date′ness** *n.*

se·date[2] (sĭ-dāt′) *tr.v.* **-dated, -dating, -dates.** To administer a sedative to (a patient). [Back-formation from SEDATIVE.]

se·da·tion (sĭ-dā′shən) *n.* **1.** The reduction of stress or excitement by administration of a sedative. **2.** The state or condition induced by a sedative.

sed·a·tive (sĕd′ə-tĭv) *adj.* Having a soothing, calming, or tranquilizing effect. —*n.* A sedative agent or drug.

sed·en·tar·y (sĕd′n-tĕr′ē) *adj.* **1.** Characterized by or requiring much sitting: *a sedentary job.* **2.** Accustomed to sitting or to taking little exercise. **3.** Remaining in one area; not migratory. **4.** *Zoology.* Attached to a surface and not free-moving, as a barnacle. [French *sédentaire*, from Latin *sedentārius*, from *sedēns*, present participle of *sedēre*, to sit. See **sed-**[1] in Appendix.*] —**sed′en·tar′i·ly** *adv.* —**sed′en·tar′i·ness** *n.*

Se·der (sā′dər) *n., pl.* **Seders** or **Sedarim** (sĭ-där′ĭm). *Judaism.* The feast commemorating the exodus of the Israelites from Egypt, celebrated on the eve of the first day of Passover, and by Orthodox and Conservative Jews again on the eve of the second day. [Hebrew *sēdher*, "order," "arrangement."]

sedge (sĕj) *n.* Any of numerous plants of the family Cyperaceae, resembling grasses but having solid rather than hollow stems. [Middle English *segge*, Old English *secg*. See **sek-** in Appendix.*]

Sedge·moor (sĕj′mŏŏr). A marsh area in central Somerset, England; the scene of a battle in which James II defeated the Duke of Monmouth (1685).

se·di·li·a (sə-dĕl′ē-ə) *pl.n.* A set of seats, generally three, built into the wall on the south side of the choir near the altar in Gothic-style churches for the use of the celebrant and his min-

secretary bird

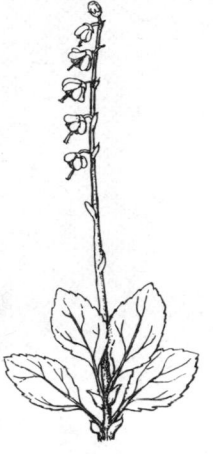

secund
Secund raceme of
Pyrola secunda

sedan

sedilia

ă pat/ā pay/â care/ä father/b bib/ch church/d deed/ĕ pet/ē be/f fife/g gag/h hat/hw which/ĭ pit/ī pie/îr pier/j judge/k kick/l lid, needle/m mum/n no, sudden/ng thing/ŏ pot/ō toe/ô paw, for/oi noise/ou out/ŏŏ took/ōō boot/p pop/r roar/s sauce/sh ship, dish/
t tight/th thin, path/th this, bathe/ŭ cut/ûr urge/v valve/w with/y yes/z zebra, size/zh vision/ə about, item, edible, gallop, circus/
à *Fr.* ami/œ *Fr.* feu, *Ger.* schön/ü *Fr.* tu, *Ger.* über/KH *Ger.* ich, *Scot.* loch/N *Fr.* bon. *Follows main vocabulary. †Of obscure origin.

isters. [Latin *sedīlia,* plural of *sedīle,* seat, from *sedēre,* to sit. See **sed-**[1] in Appendix.*]

sed·i·ment (sĕd′ə-mənt) *n. Abbr.* **sed. 1.** Material that settles to the bottom of a liquid; dregs; lees. **2. a.** Material suspended in water or in the air. **b.** The deposition of such material onto the surface underlying this water or air. **c.** The material so deposited. [Old French, from Latin *sedimentum,* a settling, from *sedēre,* to sit, settle. See **sed-**[1] in Appendix.*]

sed·i·men·ta·ry (sĕd′ə-mĕn′tə-rē, -mĕn′trē) *adj.* Also **sed·i·men·tal** (-mĕnt′l). **1.** Of, containing, resembling, or derived from sediment. **2.** *Geology.* Of or pertaining to rocks formed from sediment or from transported fragments deposited in water.

sed·i·men·ta·tion (sĕd′ə-mən-tā′shən, sĕd′ə-mĕn-) *n.* The act or process of depositing sediment.

se·di·tion (sĭ-dĭsh′ən) *n.* **1.** Conduct or language inciting to rebellion against the authority of the state. **2.** *Rare.* Insurrection; rebellion. [Middle English *sedicioun,* from Old French *sedition,* from Latin *sēditiō,* "a going apart," separation : *sē, sēd,* apart (see **seu-**[2] in Appendix*) + *itiō,* act of going, from *ire* (past participle *itus*), to go (see **ei-**[1] in Appendix*).]

se·di·tious (sĭ-dĭsh′əs) *adj.* **1.** Of, or having the nature of, sedition. **2.** Engaged in sedition. —See Synonyms at **insubordinate.** —**se·di′tious·ly** *adv.* —**se·di′tious·ness** *n.*

se·duce (sĭ-do͞os′, -dyo͞os′) *tr.v.* **-duced, -ducing, -duces. 1.** To lead (a person) away from duty or proper conduct; entice into wrongful behavior; corrupt. **2. a.** To induce to have sexual intercourse. **b.** To persuade (a virgin) to submit to being deflowered. **3. a.** To entice or beguile into a desired state or position. **b.** To win over; attract. —See Synonyms at **lure.** [Middle English *seduisen,* from Old French *seduire* (present stem *seduis-*), from Latin *sēdūcere,* to lead away : *sē,* apart (see **seu-**[2] in Appendix*) + *dūcere,* to lead (see **deuk-** in Appendix*).] —**se·duc′er** *n.* —**se·duc′i·ble, se·duce′a·ble** *adj.*

se·duc·tion (sĭ-dŭk′shən) *n.* Also **se·duce·ment** (sĭ-do͞os′mənt, sĭ-dyo͞os′-). **1.** The act of seducing or the condition of being seduced. **2.** Something that seduces or has the qualities to seduce; a means of seducing; temptation; enticement.

se·duc·tive (sĭ-dŭk′tĭv) *adj.* Tending to seduce; alluring; beguiling. —**se·duc′tive·ly** *adv.* —**se·duc′tive·ness** *n.*

se·duc·tress (sĭ-dŭk′trĭs) *n.* A woman who seduces.

sed·u·lous (sĕj′o͝o-ləs) *adj.* Diligent; painstaking; industrious. See Synonyms at **busy.** [Latin *sēdulus,* diligent, zealous, from *sē dolō,* "without guile," hence with zeal : *sē,* without (see **seu-**[2] in Appendix*) + *dolus,* guile (see **del-**[2] in Appendix*).] —**se·du′li·ty** (sĭ-do͞o′lə-tē, sĭ-dyo͞o′-), **sed′u·lous·ness** *n.* —**sed′u·lous·ly** *adv.*

se·dum (sē′dəm) *n.* Any of numerous plants of the genus *Sedum,* having thick, fleshy leaves. [Latin *sedum*†, houseleek.]

see[1] (sē) *v.* **saw** (sô), **seen** (sēn) (see Usage note below), **seeing, sees.** —*tr.* **1.** To perceive with the eye. **2.** To apprehend as if by the sense of sight: *see with one's fingers.* **3.** To have a mental image of; visualize. **4.** To understand; comprehend. **5.** To regard; view. **6.** To imagine; believe possible: *I don't see him as a teacher.* **7.** To foresee. **8.** To know through first-hand experience; undergo: *"He saw some service on the king's side"* (Tucker Brooke). **9.** To be characterized by or bring forth: *"Her long reign saw the heyday of verbal humor."* (Richard Kain). **10.** To find out; ascertain. **11.** *Abbr.* **s.** To refer to; read: *See page xi of the Introduction.* **12.** To take note of. **13.** To meet or be in the company of. **14.** To be together socially often or regularly. **15.** To visit socially or for consultation: *see a doctor.* **16.** To receive socially or for consultation. **17.** To attend; view. **18.** To escort; attend: *see someone off.* **19.** To make sure; take care: *See that it gets done right away.* **20.** *Card Games.* **a.** To meet (a bet). **b.** To meet the bet of (another player). —*intr.* **1.** To have the power of sight. **2.** To understand; comprehend. **3.** To consider; think it over: *Let's see, which should we take?* **4.** To wait and ascertain how things go: *We probably can do it, but we'll have to see.* **5.** To have foresight: *"No man can see to the end of time."* (John F. Kennedy). **6.** To take note. —**see about. 1.** To attend to. **2.** To investigate. —**see through.** To understand the true character or nature of. —**see to.** To attend to. [See, saw, seen; Middle English *se(e)n, sauh, seyen,* Old English *sēon, seah* (plural *sāwon*), *gesewen.* See **sekw-**[2] in Appendix.*]

Synonyms: *see, behold, note, notice, espy, descry, observe, contemplate, survey, view, perceive, discern, remark, scan, skim.* These verbs refer to being visually or mentally aware of something. *See,* the most general, can mean merely to look at, but more often implies recognition, understanding, or appreciation. *Behold,* usually in literary or other formal contexts, is stronger in implying real awareness of what is seen. *Note* and *notice* go further by suggesting close attention and rather detailed visual or mental impression. *Note,* in particular, implies careful and systematic recording in the mind of what is seen. *Espy* and *descry* both stress acuteness of sight that permits detection of something distant or obscure. *Observe* emphasizes attention that is both careful and closely directed. *Contemplate* implies looking attentively and meditatively. *Survey* stresses detailed examination of something on a wide or full scale. *View* usually also implies close attention but suggests examination in a special way or with a particular purpose in mind. *Perceive* and *discern* both imply not only visual recognition but mental observation and understanding. *Perceive* is especially associated with insight, and *discern* with the mental capacity for distinguishing, discriminating, and making judgments. *Remark* suggests directing the attention closely, usually to some specific detail. *Scan* usually refers to quick visual inspection of something but can also mean to examine closely. *Skim* is limited to the sense of looking quickly to get the gist of something.

Usage: The phrase *see where* is nonstandard for *see that* in constructions such as *I see that* (not *where*) *your principal has decided to retire.* The past participle *seen* is nonstandard as a past tense (for *saw*): *I saw* (not *seen*) *the movie last night;* but *I have seen many films that were better.*

see[2] (sē) *n.* **1.** The official seat, center of authority, jurisdiction, or office of a bishop. **2.** *Obsolete.* A cathedra. [Middle English, from Norman French *se, sed,* from Vulgar Latin *sedem* (unattested), from Latin *sēdem,* accusative of *sēdes,* "seat," "residence." See **sed-**[1] in Appendix.*]

see·catch (sē′kăch′) *n., pl.* **-catchie** (-kăch′ē). An adult male Alaskan fur seal. [Russian *sekach*†.]

seed (sēd) *n., pl.* **seeds** or **seed. 1.** A fertilized and ripened plant ovule containing an embryo capable of germinating to produce a new plant. **2.** Broadly, any propagative part of a plant, as a tuber or spore. **3.** Seeds collectively. **4.** The seed-bearing stage of a plant. **5.** A source or beginning; germ. **6.** Offspring; progeny. **7.** Ancestry; family stock. **8.** Sperm; semen. **9.** A young oyster or oysters used for propagating a new oyster bed. —**go** (or **run**) **to seed. 1.** To pass into the seed-bearing stage. **2.** To become weak or devitalized; deteriorate. —*v.* **seeded, seeding, seeds.** —*tr.* **1.** To plant seeds in (land); sow. **2.** To plant in soil. **3.** To remove the seeds from (fruit). **4.** To sprinkle (a cloud) with particles, as of silver iodide, in order to disperse it or produce rain. **5.** *Sports.* **a.** To arrange (the drawing for positions in a tournament) so that the more skilled contestants meet in the later rounds. **b.** To rank (a contestant) in this way. —*intr.* **1.** To sow seed. **2.** To go to seed. [Middle English *seed, seid,* Old English *sǣd.* See **sē-**[1] in Appendix.*]

seed cake. A sweet cake or cooky containing aromatic seeds, such as sesame or caraway.

seed coat. The outer protective covering of a seed.

seed·er (sē′dər) *n.* **1.** A machine or implement used for planting seeds. **2.** A machine or implement used to remove the seeds from fruit.

seed leaf. *Botany.* A **cotyledon** *(see).*

seed·ling (sēd′lĭng) *n.* A young plant that develops soon after germination of a seed.

seed oyster. A young oyster, especially one suitable for transplanting to another bed.

seed pearl. A very small, often imperfect, pearl.

seed plant. A seed-bearing plant; a spermatophyte.

seed vessel. *Botany.* A **pericarp** *(see).*

seed·y (sē′dē) *adj.* **-ier, -iest. 1.** Having many seeds. **2.** Seedlike. **3.** Worn and shabby in appearance; unkempt: *"He was soiled and seedy and fragrant with gin."* (Mark Twain). **4.** Tired or sick; out of sorts; low. **5.** Somewhat disreputable; squalid: *a seedy hotel.* —**seed′i·ly** *adv.* —**seed′i·ness** *n.*

See·ger (sē′gər), **Alan.** 1888–1916. American poet.

see·ing (sē′ĭng) *conj.* Inasmuch as. Often used with *that.*

Seeing Eye. A trademark for a dog trained to lead a blind person. [After The *Seeing Eye,* Inc., an institution with headquarters in Morristown, New Jersey, that trains such dogs.]

seek (sēk) *v.* **sought** (sôt), **seeking, seeks.** —*tr.* **1.** To try to locate or discover; search for. **2.** To endeavor to obtain or reach. **3.** To move to; go to or toward: *Water seeks its own level.* **4.** To inquire for; request. **5.** To try; endeavor. **6.** *Obsolete.* To explore. —*intr.* To make a search or investigation. [Seek, sought, sought; Middle English *seken, so(u)hte, soht,* Old English *sēcan, sōhte, sōht.* See **sāg-** in Appendix.*] —**seek′er** *n.*

seel (sēl) *tr.v.* **seeled, seeling, seels.** To stitch closed the eyes of (a falcon). [Middle English *silen,* from Old French *ciller,* from Medieval Latin *ciliāre,* from Latin *cilium,* eyelid. See **kel-**[4] in Appendix.*]

seem (sēm) *intr.v.* **seemed, seeming, seems. 1.** To give the impression of being; appear. **2.** To appear to one's own mind: *I can't seem to get the story straight.* **3.** To appear to be so; be evident: *It seems you object to the plan.* **4.** To appear to exist: *There seems no reason to postpone it.* [Middle English *semen,* to beseem, seem, from Old Norse *sœma,* to conform to, honor, from *sœmr,* fitting. See **sem-**[1] in Appendix.*]

Usage: *Seem,* a linking verb, is followed by an adjective (not by an adverb) in constructions such as *This one seems different; These seem good.* In the present tense, *seem* is often followed by the present infinitive *(He seems to enjoy his job)* or perfect infinitive *(seems to have changed his mind);* in the past tense, it is usually followed by the present infinitive *(seemed to find the experience stimulating).* The construction *cannot* (or *can't*) *seem* plus infinitive is common in speech and informal writing: *I can't seem to locate it.* Its use, especially in writing on a higher level, is sometimes objected to on the ground of illogicality, however. The following, as an example in writing, is acceptable to 51 per cent of the Usage Panel: *He could never seem to consolidate his early gains.* Alternative constructions, retaining *seem,* are *do not seem able, seem to be unable,* and *seem unable.*

seem·ing (sē′mĭng) *adj.* Apparent; ostensible. —*n.* Outward appearance; semblance. —**seem′ing·ly** *adv.* —**seem′ing·ness** *n.*

seem·ly (sēm′lē) *adj.* **-lier, -liest. 1.** Conforming to standards of conduct and good taste; proper; suitable. **2.** Of pleasing appearance; handsome. —*adv.* In a seemly manner; suitably. [Middle English *semely, semeliche,* from Old Norse *sœmiligr,* from *sœmr,* fitting. See **sem-**[1] in Appendix.*] —**seem′li·ness** *n.*

seen. Past participle of **see.**

seep (sēp) *intr.v.* **seeped, seeping, seeps. 1.** To pass slowly through small openings or pores; to ooze. **2.** To enter, depart, or become diffused gradually. —*n.* A spot where water or petroleum trickles out of the ground to form a pool. [Perhaps

ă pat/ā pay/âr care/ä father/b bib/ch church/d deed/ĕ pet/ē be/f fife/g gag/h hat/hw which/ĭ pit/ī pie/îr pier/j judge/k kick/l lid, needle/m mum/n no, sudden/ng thing/ŏ pot/ō toe/ô paw, for/oi noise/ou out/o͝o took/o͞o boot/p pop/r roar/s sauce/sh ship, dish/

variant of dialectal *sipe*, from Middle English *sipen*, Old English *sipian*. See **sib-** in Appendix.*]

seep·age (sē′pĭj) *n.* **1.** The act or process of seeping or oozing; a trickle; leakage. **2.** A quantity of something that has seeped.

seer (sē′ər *for sense 1;* sîr *for sense 2*) *n.* **1.** A prophet. **2.** A clairvoyant. [Middle English, from *seen*, to SEE.]

seer·ess (sîr′ĭs) *n.* A woman seer or clairvoyant.

seer·suck·er (sîr′sŭk′ər) *n.* A light, thin fabric, generally cotton or rayon, with a crinkled surface and striped pattern. [Hindi *sirsakar*, from Persian *shīr-o-shakar*, "milk and sugar" : *shīr*, milk, from Avestan *khshīra*, perhaps from Dravidian + *shakar*, sugar, akin to Sanskrit *śarkāra*, SUGAR.]

see·saw (sē′sô′) *n.* **1.** A long plank balanced on a central fulcrum so that with a person riding on either end, one end goes up as the other goes down. Also called "teeter," "teeter board," "teeter-totter." **2.** The act or game of riding a seesaw. **3.** A back-and-forth or up-and-down movement. —*intr.v.* **seesawed, -sawing, -saws.** **1.** To play on a seesaw. **2.** To move back and forth or up and down. [Reduplication of SAW (to cut), from the up-and-down movement of sawing.]

seethe (sēth) *v.* **seethed** or *obsolete* **sod** (sŏd), **seethed** or *obsolete* **sodden** (sŏd′n), **seething, seethes.** —*intr.* **1.** To churn and foam as if boiling. **2.** To move in confusion; ferment; moil: *"The seething of propaganda began."* (Carl Sandburg). **3.** To be violently excited or agitated. **4.** *Archaic.* To come to a boil. —*tr.* **1.** To soak in liquid. **2.** *Archaic.* To boil. —See Synonyms at **boil.** —*n.* The act of seething. [Seethe, sod, sodden; Middle English *sethen, sothe, sodden*, Old English *sēothan, sēath, soden*. See **seu-¹** in Appendix.*]

Se·fe·ri·a·des (sĕf′ə-rī′ə-dēz′), **Giorgos Stylianou.** Pen name, George Seferis. Born 1900. Greek poet and diplomat.

seg·ment (sĕg′mənt) *n.* **1.** Any of the parts into which something can be divided. **2.** *Geometry.* A portion of a figure cut off by a line or plane, especially: **a.** The area bounded by a chord and the arc of a curve subtended by the chord. **b.** The portion of a curve between any two points on the curve. **c.** The portion of a sphere bounded by two parallel planes intersecting or tangent to the sphere. **3.** *Biology.* A clearly differentiated subdivision of an organism or part, such as a metamere. —*v.* (sĕg-mĕnt′) **segmented, -menting, -ments.** —*tr.* To divide into segments. —*intr.* To become divided into segments. [Latin *segmentum*, from *secāre*, to cut. See **sek-** in Appendix.*] —**seg′men·tar′y** *adj.*

seg·men·tal (sĕg-mĕnt′l) *adj.* **1.** Of or relating to segments. **2.** Divided or organized into segments. —**seg·men′tal·ly** *adv.*

seg·men·ta·tion (sĕg′mən-tā′shən) *n.* **1.** Division into segments. **2.** *Biology.* **Cleavage** *(see).*

segmentation cavity. *Biology.* A **blastocoel** *(see).*

se·gno (sā′nyō) *n., pl.* **-gni** (-nyē). *Music.* A notational sign; especially, the sign marking the beginning or end of a repeat. [Italian, sign, from Latin *signum*. See **sekw-¹** in Appendix.*]

se·go (sē′gō′) *n., pl.* **-gos.** The succulent, edible bulb of the sego lily. [Of Ute origin.]

sego lily. A plant, *Calochortus nuttallii*, of western North America, having showy, variously colored flowers.

Se·go·vi·a (sĕ-gō′vē-ä). **1.** A city of Spain, northwest of Madrid. Population, 34,000. **2.** A former name for the **Coco.**

Se·go·vi·a (sĕ-gō′vē-ä), **Andrés.** Born 1893. Spanish classical guitarist.

Se·grè (sĕ-grā′), **Emilio.** Born 1905. Italian-born American physicist; detected antiproton with Owen **Chamberlain** *(see).*

seg·re·gate (sĕg′rə-gāt′) *v.* **-gated, -gating, -gates.** —*tr.* **1.** To separate or isolate from others or from a main body or group. **2.** To impose the separation of (a race or class) from the rest of society. —*intr.* **1.** To become separated from a main body or mass. **2.** To practice a policy of racial segregation. —See Synonyms at **separate.** —*adj.* Separated; isolated. [Latin *sēgregāre*, "to separate from the flock" : *sē*, apart (see **seu-²** in Appendix*) + *grex* (stem *greg-*), flock (see **ger-¹** in Appendix*).] —**seg′re·ga′tive** *adj.* —**seg′re·ga′tor** (-gā′tər) *n.*

seg·re·ga·tion (sĕg′rə-gā′shən) *n.* **1.** The act or process of segregating or the condition of being segregated. **2.** The policy and practice of imposing the social separation of races, as in schools, housing, and industry; especially, discriminatory practices against nonwhites in a predominantly white society. **3.** *Genetics.* The separation of paired alleles in meiosis.

seg·re·ga·tion·ist (sĕg′rə-gā′shən-ĭst) *n.* One who advocates or practices a policy of racial segregation.

se·gui·di·lla (sĕg′ə-dē′yä) *n.* **1.** A Spanish stanza form of four to seven short verses. **2.** A lively Spanish dance. **3.** The music for this dance, in ¾ time. [Spanish, from *seguida*, "sequence," from the feminine past participle of *seguir*, to follow, from Vulgar Latin *sequere* (unattested), from Latin *sequī*. See **sekw-¹** in Appendix.*]

sei·cen·to (sā-chĕn′tō) *n.* The 17th century, with reference to the Italian literature and art of that period. [Italian *(mil) seicento*, (one thousand) six hundred : *sei*, six, from Latin *sex* (see **sweks** in Appendix*) + *cento*, hundred, from Latin *centum* (see **dekm** in Appendix*).]

seiche (sāsh) *n.* A wave that oscillates in lakes, bays, or gulfs from a few minutes to a few hours as a result of seismic or atmospheric disturbances. [Swiss French *seiche*†.]

sei·del (sīd′l, zīd′l) *n.* A beer mug. [German *Seidel*, from Middle High German *sīdel*, from Latin *situla*†, bucket.]

Seid·litz powder (sĕd′lĭts). Also **Seid·litz powders.** A cathartic consisting of Rochelle salts, sodium bicarbonate, and tartaric acid. Also called "Rochelle powder." [So called because it has laxative properties similar to those of the spring water of *Seidlitz*, village in Bohemia.]

seign·ior (sān′yôr) *n.* A man of rank; specifically, a feudal lord. [Middle English *seignour*, from Old French *seigneur*, from Medieval Latin *senior*, from Latin, older, comparative of *senex*, old. See **sen-¹** in Appendix.*] —**sei·gnio′ri·al** *adj.*

seign·ior·age (sān′yər-ĭj) *n.* A profit or revenue taken from the minting of coins, usually the difference between the value of the bullion used and the face value of the coin. [Middle English *seigneurage*, duty imposed by a lord as his prerogative, from Old French, from *seigneur*, SEIGNIOR.]

seign·ior·y (sān′yə-rē) *n., pl.* **-ies.** **1.** The feudal estate of a lord; a manor. **2.** The authority and power of a feudal lord.

seine (sān) *n.* A large fishing net made to hang vertically in the water by weights at the lower edge and floats at the top. —*v.* **seined, seining, seines.** —*intr.* To fish with a seine. —*tr.* To fish for or catch with a seine. [Middle English *seine*, Old English *segne*, from West Germanic *sagina* (unattested), from Latin *sagēna*, from Greek *sagēnē*†.]

Seine (sĕn). A river of northern France, rising in the east and flowing 482 miles generally northwest to its estuary on the English Channel near Le Havre.

Sei·shin. The Japanese name for **Chongjin.**

seism (sī′zəm) *n.* An **earthquake** *(see).* [Greek *seismos*, from *seiein*, to shake. See **twei-** in Appendix.*]

seis·mic (sīz′mĭk) *adj.* Of, subject to, or caused by an earthquake or earth vibration. [SEISM(O)- + -IC.] —**seis′mi·cal·ly** *adv.* —**seis·mic′i·ty** (sīz-mĭs′ə-tē) *n.*

seis·mism (sīz′mĭz′əm) *n.* The collective phenomena involved in earthquakes. [SEISM(O)- + -ISM.]

seismo–, seism–. Indicates earthquake; for example, **seismograph, seismism.** [From Greek *seismos*, SEISM.]

seis·mo·gram (sīz′mə-grăm′) *n.* The record of an earth tremor made by a seismograph. [SEISMO- + -GRAM.]

seis·mo·graph (sīz′mə-grăf′, -gräf′) *n.* An instrument for automatically detecting and recording the intensity, direction, and duration of any movement of the ground, especially of an earthquake. [SEISMO- + -GRAPH.] —**seis′mo·graph′ic** *adj.* —**seis·mog′ra·pher** (sīz-mŏg′rə-fər) *n.* —**seis·mog′ra·phy** *n.*

seis·mol·o·gy (sīz-mŏl′ə-jē) *n.* The geophysical science of earthquakes and of the mechanical properties of the earth. [SEISMO- + -LOGY.] —**seis′mo·log′ic** (-mə-lŏj′ĭk), **seis′mo·log′i·cal** *adj.* —**seis′mo·log′i·cal·ly** *adv.* —**seis·mol′o·gist** *n.*

seis·mom·e·ter (sīz-mŏm′ə-tər) *n.* A detecting device that receives seismic impulses. [SEISMO- + -METER.] —**seis′mo·met′ric** (sīz′mə-mĕt′rĭk), **seis′mo·met′ri·cal** *adj.*

seis·mo·scope (sīz′mə-skōp′) *n.* An instrument that indicates the occurrence or time of occurrence of an earthquake. [SEISMO- + -SCOPE.] —**seis′mo·scop′ic** (-skŏp′ĭk) *adj.*

seize (sēz) *v.* **seized, seizing, seizes.** Also **seise** (for sense 5b). —*tr.* **1.** To grasp suddenly and forcibly; lay hold of; take or grab. **2.** To grasp with the mind; comprehend. **3.** To have a sudden effect upon; possess or overwhelm. **4.** To take into custody; make a prisoner of; capture. **5. a.** To take quick and forcible possession of: *seize arms.* **b.** *Law.* To take into legal custody; confiscate; put in seizin. **c.** *Obsolete.* To put in possession of a feudal property. **6.** To put to immediate advantage, as an opportunity; act swiftly upon. **7.** *Nautical.* To bind with turns of small line. —*intr.* **1.** To lay sudden or forcible hold. Used with *on* or *upon.* **2.** To cohere or fuse with another part as a result of high pressure or temperature, restricting or preventing further motion. [Middle English *saisen, seisen*, from Old French *seisir, saisir*, from Gallo-Latin *sacīre* (unattested), to claim, from Germanic. See **sāg-** in Appendix.*] —**seiz′a·ble** *adj.*

seiz·er (sē′zər) *n.* Also **seiz·or, seis·or** (for sense 2). **1.** One that seizes. **2.** *Law.* One who takes seizin.

sei·zin (sē′zĭn) *n.* Also **sei·sin.** *Law.* **1. a.** Legal possession of land, as a freehold estate. **b.** The act of taking such possession. **2.** Property thus legally possessed. [Middle English *sesin, seisine*, from Old French *seisine, saisine*, from *seisir*, to SEIZE.]

seiz·ing (sē′zĭng) *n. Nautical.* A binding of larger lines made with multiple turns of smaller line.

sei·zure (sē′zhər) *n.* **1.** The act of seizing or being seized. **2.** A sudden paroxysm, as an epileptic convulsion or heart attack. **3.** Any sudden onset, cognition, or sensation of a subjective nature: *"His mother had sudden strange seizures of uneasiness about him"* (D.H. Lawrence).

Sejm (sām) *n.* The unicameral legislature of the Polish People's Republic. [Polish, assembly. See **em-** in Appendix.*]

sel. select; selected.

se·la·chi·an (sĭ-lā′kē-ən) *adj.* Of or belonging to the order Selachii (or Squaliformes), which includes the sharks and rays. —*n.* A member of the Selachii. [From New Latin *Selachii*, from Greek *selakhē*, plural of *selakhos*†, cartilaginous fish.]

sel·a·gi·nel·la (sĕl′ə-jə-nĕl′ə) *n.* Any of numerous fernlike, usually prostrate plants of the genus *Selaginella*, having small scalelike leaves and bearing spores. [New Latin, from Latin *selāgō*† (stem *selāgin-*), plant resembling the savin.]

se·lah (sē′lə) *n.* A Hebrew word of unknown meaning often marking the end of a verse in the Psalms and thought to be a term indicating a pause or rest. [Hebrew *selāh*.]

Se·lan·gor (sə-lăng′ər). A state of Malaysia, occupying 3,166 square miles on the western Malay Peninsula. Population, 1,276,000. Capital, Kuala Lumpur.

Sel·den (sĕl′dən), **George Baldwin.** 1846–1922. American inventor; first to patent gasoline-driven automobile (1895).

Sel·den (sĕl′dən), **John.** 1584–1654. English jurist and antiquary.

sel·dom (sĕl′dəm) *adv.* Not often; infrequently; rarely. See Usage note at **rarely.** —*adj. Archaic.* Infrequent; rare. [Mid-

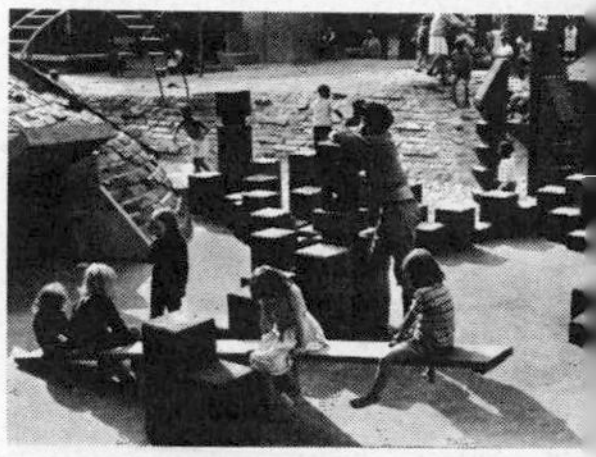

seesaw
Children on a seesaw at Riis Plaza, New York City

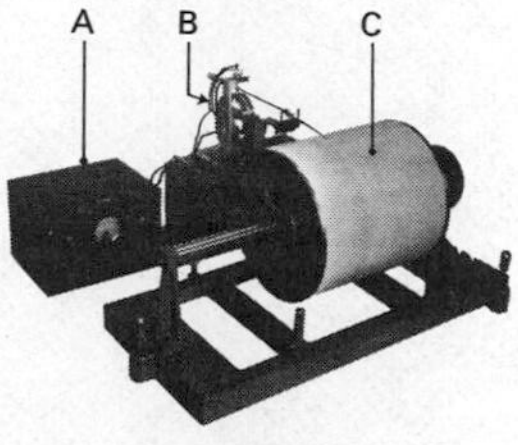

seismograph
A. Coordinating electronic circuitry
B. Pen assembly
C. Recording drum

dle English *selden, seldom,* Old English *seldan,* from Common Germanic *seldo-* (unattested).] —**sel′dom·ness** *n.*

se·lect (sĭ-lĕkt′) *v.* **-lected, -lecting, -lects.** —*tr.* To choose from among several; take in preference; pick out. —*intr.* To make a choice or selection; choose. —See Synonyms at **choose.** —*adj.* Also **se·lect·ed** (sĭ-lĕk′tĭd). *Abbr.* **sel. 1.** Singled out in preference; chosen; picked out. **2.** Of special value or quality; preferred. [Latin *sēligere* (past participle *sēlectus*), to choose out : *sē,* apart (see **seu-**[2] in Appendix*) + *legere,* to choose (see **leg-** in Appendix*).] —**se·lect′ness** *n.*

se·lec·tee (sĭ-lĕk′tē′) *n.* One who is selected, especially for military service; inductee.

se·lec·tion (sĭ-lĕk′shən) *n.* **1. a.** The act of selecting or the fact of being selected; choosing; choice. **b.** That which is selected. **2.** A carefully chosen or representative collection of persons or things. **3.** A literary or musical text chosen for reading or performance. **4.** *Biology.* A process that favors or induces the survival and perpetuation of one kind of organism in competition with others. —See Synonyms at **choice.**

se·lec·tive (sĭ-lĕk′tĭv) *adj.* **1.** Of or characterized by selection; discriminating. **2.** Empowered or tending to select; fastidious; particular. **3.** *Electronics.* Capable of rejecting frequencies other than that selected or tuned. —**se·lec′tive·ly** *adv.* —**se·lec′tive·ness** *n.*

selective service. Compulsory military service according to stipulated requirements for induction.

se·lec·tiv·i·ty (sĭ-lĕk′tĭv′ə-tē) *n.* **1.** The state or quality of being selective. **2.** *Electronics.* The degree to which an electronic receiver is selective.

se·lect·man (sĭ-lĕkt′mən) *n., pl.* **-men** (-mĭn). One of a board of town officers chosen annually in New England communities to manage local affairs.

se·lec·tor (sĭ-lĕk′tər) *n.* One that selects.

sel·e·nate (sĕl′ə-nāt′) *n.* A salt or ester of selenic acid. [From SELENIUM.]

Se·len·ga (sĕ′lĕng-gä′). A river rising in the Mongolian People's Republic and flowing 897 miles generally northeast to Lake Baikal in the Soviet Union.

se·len·ic acid (sĭ-lĕn′ĭk, -lē′nĭk). A highly corrosive, hygroscopic, white solid acid with composition H_2SeO_4. [From SELENIUM.]

sel·e·nite (sĕl′ə-nīt′) *n.* Gypsum in the form of colorless clear crystals. [Latin *selēnītēs,* from Greek *selēnītēs (lithos),* "moon (stone)" (because it supposedly waxed and waned with the moon), from *selēnē,* moon. See **selenium.**]

se·le·ni·um (sĭ-lē′nē-əm) *n. Symbol* **Se** A nonmetallic element, red in powder form, black in vitreous form, and metallic gray in crystalline form, resembling sulfur and obtained primarily as a by-product of electrolytic copper refining. It is widely used in rectifiers, as a semiconductor, and in xerography, and certain forms exhibit photovoltaic and photoconductive action, making it useful in photocells, photographic exposure meters, and solar cells. Atomic number 34, atomic weight 78.96, melting point (of gray selenium) 217°C, boiling point (gray) 684.9°C, specific gravity (gray) 4.79, (vitreous) 4.28, valence 2, 4, or 6. See **element.** [New Latin, from Greek *selēnē,* moon (named by analogy to a related element, tellurium, which is from Latin *tellus,* earth), akin to Greek *selas*†, brightness.]

selenium cell. A photoconductive cell consisting of an insulated selenium strip between two suitable electrodes.

sel·e·nog·ra·phy (sĕl′ə-nŏg′rə-fē) *n.* The study of the physical features of the moon. [New Latin *selenographia* : Greek *selēnē,* moon (see **selenium**) + -GRAPHY.] —**sel′e·nog′ra·pher, sel′e·nog′ra·phist** *n.* —**sel′e·no·graph′ic** (-nə-grăf′ĭk), **sel′e·no·graph′i·cal** *adj.* —**sel′e·no·graph′i·cal·ly** *adv.*

sel·e·nol·o·gy (sĕl′ə-nŏl′ə-jē) *n.* The astronomical study of the moon. [Greek *selēnē,* moon (see **selenium**) + -LOGY.] —**se′le·no·log′i·cal** (sĕ′lē-nə-lŏj′ĭ-kəl) *adj.* —**sel′e·nol′o·gist** *n.*

se·le·nous acid (sĭ-lē′nəs, sĕl′ə-). Also **se·le·ni·ous acid** (sĭ-lē′nē-əs). A transparent, colorless crystalline acid, H_2SeO_3, used as a chemical reagent. [From SELENIUM.]

Se·leu·ci·a (sĭ-lo͞o′shē-ə). An ancient city of Mesopotamia, on the Tigris, 20 miles southeast of Baghdad.

Se·leu·cids (sĭ-lo͞o′sĭdz) *pl.n.* Also **Se·leu·ci·dae** (-sĭ-dē′). The six dynastic leaders in Asia Minor from 312 B.C. to 64 B.C. —**Se·leu′cid, Se·leu′ci·dan** *adj.*

self (sĕlf) *n., pl.* **selves** (sĕlvz). **1.** The total, essential, or particular being of one person; the individual. **2.** The qualities of one person distinguishing him from another; personality or character; individuality. **3.** An individual's consciousness of his own being or identity; subjectivity; ego. **4.** One's own interests, welfare, or advantage; private or personal concerns; selfishness: *thinking of self alone.* —*pron.* Myself, yourself, himself, or herself: *a living wage for self and family.* —*adj.* **1.** *Obsolete.* Same or identical. **2.** Like, attached to, or made from that with which it is used; homogeneous. Said mostly of clothes: *a self scarf.* [Middle English *se(o)lf, silf,* noun, pronoun, and adjective, Old English *self, silf.* See **seu-**[2] in Appendix.*]

self-heal
Prunella vulgaris

self-. Forms hyphenated compounds indicating: **1.** Oneself or itself; for example, **self-evident, self-government. 2.** Of, to, toward, in, on, with, by, for, or from the self, oneself, or itself; for example, **self-educated, self-denial, self-imposed. 3.** Autonomous, automatic, or automatically; for example, **self-driven, self-winding.** ***Note:*** Many compounds other than those entered here may be formed with *self-.* When *self-* is joined with a word that can stand alone, it is joined by a hyphen: *self-deception.* In the rare cases when *self-* is joined with a form that cannot stand alone as a word, it is joined without space or hyphen: *selfhood.* [Middle English *self-,* Old English *self-,* from SELF.]

self-ab·ne·ga·tion (sĕlf′ăb′nĭ-gā′shən) *n.* The setting aside of self-interest for the sake of others or for a belief or principle. —**self′-ab′ne·gat′ing** *adj.*

self-a·buse (sĕlf′ə-byo͞os′) *n.* **1.** Abuse of oneself or one's abilities. **2.** Masturbation.

self-ad·dressed (sĕlf′ə-drĕst′) *adj.* Addressed to oneself.

self-ag·gran·dize·ment (sĕlf′ə-grăn′dĭz-mənt) *n.* The act or practice of enhancing one's own importance, power, or reputation. —**self′-ag·gran′diz·ing** *adj.*

self-ap·point·ed (sĕlf′ə-poin′tĭd) *adj.* Designated or chosen by oneself rather than by due authority; unsanctioned and usually ill-qualified: *a self-appointed arbiter.*

self-as·ser·tion (sĕlf′ə-sûr′shən) *n.* Determined advancement of one's own personality, wishes, or views. —**self′-as·ser′tive** *adj.* —**self′-as·ser′tive·ly** *adv.*

self-as·sured (sĕlf′ə-sho͝ord′) *adj.* Having or showing confidence and sureness. —**self′-as·sur′ance** *n.*

self-cen·tered (sĕlf′sĕn′tərd) *adj.* Engrossed in oneself and one's affairs. —**self′-cen′tered·ly** *adv.* —**self′-cen′tered·ness** *n.*

self-col·ored (sĕlf′kŭl′ərd) *adj.* **1.** In the natural or original color. **2.** Of only one color.

self-com·mand (sĕlf′kə-mănd′, -mänd′) *n.* Full presence of mind; self-control.

self-con·fessed (sĕlf′kən-fĕst′) *adj.* According to one's own admission.

self-con·fi·dence (sĕlf′kŏn′fə-dəns) *n.* Confidence in oneself or one's abilities. See Synonyms at **confidence.** —**self′-con′fi·dent** *adj.* —**self′-con′fi·dent·ly** *adv.*

self-con·scious (sĕlf′kŏn′shəs) *adj.* **1.** Excessively conscious of one's appearance or manner; socially ill at ease. **2.** Showing the effects of such consciousness; stilted: *"the dialect became a self-conscious prose poetry in her plays"* (Richard Kain). **3.** Aware of oneself or one's own being, actions, or thoughts. —See Synonyms at **humble.** —**self′-con′scious·ly** *adv.* —**self′-con′scious·ness** *n.*

self-con·tained (sĕlf′kən-tānd′) *adj.* **1.** Possessing within oneself or itself all that is necessary; self-sufficient. **2.** Keeping to oneself; reserved.

self-con·tent (sĕlf′kən-tĕnt′) *adj.* Also **self-con·tent·ed** (-tĕn′tĭd). Satisfied with oneself and one's condition; complacent. —*n.* Also **self-con·tent·ment** (-tĕnt′mənt). Self-satisfaction; complacency. —**self′-con·tent′ed·ly** *adv.*

self-con·tra·dic·tion (sĕlf′kŏn′trə-dĭk′shən) *n.* **1.** The act, state, or fact of contradicting oneself or itself. **2.** An idea or statement containing contradictory elements. —**self′-con′tra·dic′to·ry** (-tə-rē) *adj.*

self-con·trol (sĕlf′kən-trōl′) *n.* Control of one's emotions, desires, or actions by one's own will. —**self′-con·trolled′** *adj.*

self-crit·i·cal (sĕlf′krĭt′ĭ-kəl) *adj.* Critical of oneself; watchful for one's own faults and weaknesses. —**self′-crit′i·cal·ly** *adv.* —**self′-crit′i·cism′** *n.*

self-de·ceived (sĕlf′dĭ-sēvd′) *adj.* Deceived by one's own illusion or error.

self-de·ceiv·ing (sĕlf′dĭ-sē′vĭng) *adj.* Given to or promoting mistaken notions about oneself.

self-de·cep·tion (sĕlf′dĭ-sĕp′shən) *n.* Also **self-de·ceit** (sĕlf′dĭ-sēt′). The act of deceiving oneself or the state of being deceived by oneself. —**self′-de·cep′tive** *adj.*

self-de·feat·ing (sĕlf′dĭ-fē′tĭng) *adj.* Injurious to one's or its own purposes or welfare.

self-de·fense (sĕlf′dĭ-fĕns′) *n.* **1.** Defense of oneself when physically attacked. **2.** Defense of what belongs to oneself, as one's works or reputation. **3.** *Law.* The right to protect oneself against violence or threatened violence with whatever force or means are reasonably necessary. —**self′-de·fen′sive** *adj.*

self-de·ni·al (sĕlf′dĭ-nī′əl) *n.* Sacrifice of one's own comfort or gratification; restraint of one's natural desires. See Synonyms at **abstinence.** —**self′-de·ny′ing** *adj.* —**self′-de·ny′ing·ly** *adv.*

self-de·ter·mi·na·tion (sĕlf′dĭ-tûr′mə-nā′shən) *n.* **1.** Determination of one's own fate or course of action without compulsion; free will. **2.** Freedom of a people or area to determine its own political status; independence.

self-dis·ci·pline (sĕlf′dĭs′ə-plĭn) *n.* Training and control of oneself and one's conduct, usually for personal improvement.

self-driv·en (sĕlf′drĭv′ən) *adj.* Driven by itself; automotive.

self-ed·u·cat·ed (sĕlf′ĕj′o͞o-kā′tĭd) *adj.* Educated by one's own efforts, without formal instruction. —**self′-ed′u·ca′tion** *n.*

self-ef·fac·ing (sĕlf′ĭ-fā′sĭng) *adj.* Not drawing attention to oneself; modest; humble. —**self′-ef·face′ment** *n.*

self-em·ployed (sĕlf′ĕm-ploid′) *adj.* Earning and directing one's own livelihood; working for oneself, rather than an employer.

self-es·teem (sĕlf′ə-stēm′) *n.* Pride in oneself.

self-ev·i·dent (sĕlf′ĕv′ə-dənt) *adj.* Requiring no proof or explanation. —**self′-ev′i·dence** *n.* —**self′-ev′i·dent·ly** *adv.*

self-ex·plan·a·to·ry (sĕlf′ĭk-splăn′ə-tôr′ē, -tōr′ē) *adj.* Needing no explanation; obvious in meaning.

self-ex·pres·sion (sĕlf′ĭk-sprĕsh′ən) *n.* Expression of one's own personality, as through speech or art.

self-fer·til·i·za·tion (sĕlf′fûr′tə-lə-zā′shən) *n.* Fertilization by sperm from the same animal, as in some hermaphrodites, or by pollen from the same flower.

self-gov·ern·ment (sĕlf′gŭv′ərn-mənt) *n.* **1.** Political independence; autonomy. **2.** Popular or representative government; democracy. **3.** *Archaic.* Self-control. —**self′-gov′erned** *adj.* —**self′-gov′ern·ing** *adj.*

self-hard·en·ing (sĕlf′här′d′n-ĭng) *adj.* Of or pertaining to materials, as certain steels, that harden without special treatment.

self-heal (sĕlf′hēl′) *n.* Any of several plants reputed to have

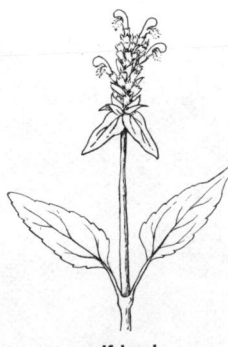

healing powers; especially, *Prunella vulgaris*, a low-growing plant native to Europe, having tightly clustered violet-blue flowers. Also called "heal-all," "all-heal."

self·hood (sĕlf′hŏŏd′) *n.* **1.** The state of having a distinct identity; individuality. **2.** The fully developed self; achieved personality. **3.** Self-centeredness. [Translation of German *Selbheit.*]

self-im·por·tance (sĕlf′ĭm-pôr′təns) *n.* Excessively high opinion of one's own importance or station; pomposity; conceit. —**self′-im·por′tant** *adj.* —**self′-im·por′tant·ly** *adv.*

self-im·posed (sĕlf′ĭm-pōzd′) *adj.* Imposed by oneself; voluntarily assumed or endured.

self-im·prove·ment (sĕlf′ĭm-prōōv′mənt) *n.* Improvement of one's condition through one's own efforts.

self-in·duced (sĕlf′ĭn-dōōst′, -dyōōst′) *adj.* **1.** Induced by oneself or itself; willfully acquired or brought on: *a self-induced wound.* **2.** *Electricity.* Produced by self-induction.

self-in·duc·tion (sĕlf′ĭn-dŭk′shən) *n.* The generation by a changing current of an electromotive force in the same circuit tending to counteract such change. —**self′-in·duc′tive** *adj.*

self-in·dul·gence (sĕlf′ĭn-dŭl′jəns) *n.* Excessive indulgence of one's own appetites and desires. —**self′-in·dul′gent** *adj.* —**self′-in·dul′gent·ly** *adv.*

self-in·flict·ed (sĕlf′ĭn-flĭk′tĭd) *adj.* Inflicted or imposed upon oneself: *a self-inflicted punishment.* —**self′-in·flic′tion** *n.*

self-in·ter·est (sĕlf′ĭn′trĭst, -ĭn′tər-ĭst) *n.* **1.** Personal advantage or interest; selfish motive or gain. **2.** Pursuit of or excessive regard for such advantage or interest. —**self′-in′ter·est·ed** *adj.*

self·ish (sĕl′fĭsh) *adj.* **1.** Concerned chiefly or only with oneself, without regard for the well-being of others; egotistic. **2.** Arising from, characterized by, or showing such concern: *a selfish whim.* —**self′ish·ly** *adv.* —**self′ish·ness** *n.*

self-knowl·edge (sĕlf′nŏl′ĭj) *n.* Knowledge of one's own nature, abilities, and limitations; insight into oneself.

self·less (sĕlf′lĭs) *adj.* Without concern for oneself; unselfish. —**self′less·ly** *adv.* —**self′less·ness** *n.*

self-liq·ui·dat·ing (sĕlf′lĭk′wə-dā′tĭng) *adj.* **1.** Involving goods convertible into cash in a short time. Said of business transactions. **2.** Producing a return equal to the sum invested to create or maintain it: *a self-liquidating toll-bridge project.*

self-load·ing (sĕlf′lō′dĭng) *adj.* Automatically ejecting the shell and chambering the next round from the magazine; automatic or semiautomatic. Said of firearms.

self-love (sĕlf′lŭv′) *n.* The instinct or desire to promote one's own well-being; regard for or love of self. —**self′-lov′ing** *adj.*

self-made (sĕlf′mād′) *adj.* **1.** Having achieved success unaided: *a self-made man.* **2.** Made by oneself or itself.

self-mas·ter·y (sĕlf′măs′tər-ē, -mäs′tər-ē) *n.* Self-command.

self-or·dained (sĕlf′ôr-dānd′) *adj.* Ordained by oneself rather than by others; practicing by one's own authority.

self-pit·y (sĕlf′pĭt′ē) *n.* Pity for oneself. —**self′-pit′y·ing** *adj.* —**self′-pit′y·ing·ly** *adv.*

self-pol·li·na·tion (sĕlf′pŏl′ə-nā′shən) *n.* The transfer of pollen from an anther to a stigma of the same flower. —**self′-pol′li·nat′ed** (-nā′tĭd) *adj.*

self-por·trait (sĕlf′pôr′trĭt, sĕlf′pōr′-, -trāt′) *n.* A portrait, pictorial or verbal, of oneself created by oneself.

self-pos·ses·sion (sĕlf′pə-zĕsh′ən) *n.* Full command of one's faculties, feelings, and behavior; presence of mind; poise. See Synonyms at **confidence.** —**self′-pos·sessed′** *adj.*

self-pres·er·va·tion (sĕlf′prĕz′ər-vā′shən) *n.* **1.** Protection of oneself from harm or destruction. **2.** The instinct for such individual preservation; innate desire to stay alive.

self-pro·pelled (sĕlf′prə-pĕld′) *adj.* Containing its own means of propulsion, as an automobile.

self-re·al·i·za·tion (sĕlf′rē′ə-lə-zā′shən) *n.* The complete development or fulfillment of the self's potential.

self-re·cord·ing (sĕlf′rĭ-kôr′dĭng) *adj.* Automatically recording its own functions or operations. Said of a machine or instrument.

self-re·li·ance (sĕlf′rĭ-lī′əns) *n.* Reliance upon one's own capabilities, judgment, or resources; moral independence. See Synonyms at **confidence.** —**self′-re·li′ant** *adj.* —**self′-re·li′ant·ly** *adv.*

self-re·proach (sĕlf′rĭ-prōch′) *n.* The act or an instance of charging oneself with a fault or mistake. —**self′-re·proach′ful** *adj.* —**self′-re·proach′ful·ly** *adv.*

self-re·spect (sĕlf′rĭ-spĕkt′) *n.* Due respect for oneself, one's character, and one's conduct. —**self′-re·spect′ing** *adj.*

self-re·straint (sĕlf′rĭ-strānt′) *n.* Restraint of one's emotions, desires, or inclinations; self-control.

self-right·eous (sĕlf′rī′chəs) *adj.* Piously sure of one's righteousness. —**self′-right′eous·ly** *adv.* —**self′-right′eous·ness** *n.*

self-rule (sĕlf′rōōl′) *n.* Self-government.

self-sac·ri·fice (sĕlf′săk′rə-fīs′) *n.* Sacrifice of one's personal interests or well-being for the sake of others or for a cause. —**self′-sac′ri·fic′ing** *adj.*

self·same (sĕlf′sām′) *adj.* Exactly identical; the very same: *"Just as my fingers on these keys/Make music, so the selfsame sounds/On my spirit make a music, too"* (Wallace Stevens). See Synonyms at **same.** [Middle English *selve same* : *self,* SELF (obsolete sense "same") + SAME.] —**self′same′ness** *n.*

self-sat·is·fac·tion (sĕlf′săt′ĭs-făk′shən) *n.* Satisfaction with oneself or with one's own accomplishment.

self-seek·ing (sĕlf′sē′kĭng) *adj.* Pursuing or seeking only for oneself. —*n.* The characteristics or activities of a self-seeking person. —**self′-seek′er** *n.*

self-serv·ice (sĕlf′sûr′vĭs) *adj.* Being a retail commercial enterprise in which the customers serve themselves and pay a cashier: *a self-service cafeteria.*

self-start·er (sĕlf′stär′tər) *n.* *Machinery.* A **starter** (*see*).

self-styled (sĕlf′stīld′) *adj.* As characterized by oneself: *"Poets, real or self-styled"* (Constantine Fitzgibbon).

self-suf·fi·cient (sĕlf′sə-fĭsh′ənt) *adj.* Also **self-suf·fic·ing** (-fī′sĭng). **1.** Able to provide for oneself without the help of others; not dependent. **2.** Having undue confidence; smug or overbearing. —**self′-suf·fi′cien·cy** *n.*

self-sup·port (sĕlf′sə-pôrt′, -pōrt′) *n.* The act of or capacity for supporting oneself financially without the help of others. —**self′-sup·port′ed** *adj.* —**self′-sup·port′ing** *adj.*

self-sus·tain·ing (sĕlf′sə-stā′nĭng) *adj.* Capable of sustaining oneself or itself independently.

self-taught (sĕlf′tôt′) *adj.* Having taught oneself without formal instruction or the help of others.

self-will (sĕlf′wĭl′) *n.* Willfulness, especially in satisfying one's own desires; obstinacy. —**self′-willed′** *adj.*

self-wind·ing (sĕlf′wīn′dĭng) *adj.* Not requiring any conscious manual effort to wind up the mainspring. Said of clocks and watches.

Sel·juk (sĕl′jōōk′, sĕl-jōōk′) *n.* A member of one of several Turkish dynasties ruling over central and western Asia from the 11th to the 13th century. [Turkish, after *Seljūk,* the reputed eponymous ancestor.]

Sel·kirk (sĕl′kûrk). **1.** Also **Sel·kirk·shire** (-shîr, -shər). A county occupying 266 square miles in southern Scotland. Population, 20,000. **2.** Its county seat. Population, 6,000.

Sel·kirk (sĕl′kûrk), **Alexander.** 1676–1721. Scottish sailor; marooned on one of Juan Fernandez islets (1704–09); regarded as model of Defoe's *Robinson Crusoe.*

Sel·kirk (sĕl′kûrk), **Fifth Earl of.** Title of Thomas Douglas. 1771–1820. Scottish philanthropist; colonizer in Prince Edward Island and the valley of the Red River of the North.

Sel·kirk Mountains (sĕl′kûrk). A range of the Rocky Mountains extending some 200 miles through southeastern British Columbia, Canada. Highest elevation, Mount Sir Sandford (11,590 feet).

sell (sĕl) *v.* **sold** (sōld), **selling, sells.** —*tr.* **1.** To exchange or deliver for money or its equivalent, as goods, services, or property; dispose of for a price. **2.** To offer for sale, as for one's business or livelihood: *He sells textiles.* **3.** To give up or surrender in exchange for a price or reward: *"The witches had sold themselves to Satan"* (Karl A. Menninger). **4.** To be responsible for the sale of; promote; render successfully: *Publicity sold that product.* **5.** To convince of. Used with *on: They sold him on the idea.* **6.** *Slang.* To cheat or dupe. —*intr.* **1.** To exchange ownership for money or its equivalent; engage in selling. **2.** To be sold or be on sale. **3.** To attract prospective buyers; be popular on the market: *an item that sells well.* **4.** To be approved of; gain acceptance. —**sell off.** To get rid of by selling, often at reduced prices; deplete. —*n.* **1.** The activity of selling. **2.** *Slang.* A hoax or swindle. [Sell, sold, sold; Middle English *sellen, sold, sold,* Old English *sellan, sealde, seald,* to give, betray, sell. See **sel-**[3] in Appendix.*]

sell·er (sĕl′ər) *n.* **1.** A person who sells; salesman; vender. **2.** An item that sells in a particular manner: *a best seller.*

sell out. 1. To sell all one's goods or possessions. **2.** *Slang.* To betray one's cause or colleagues: *"It meant that the intellectual had sold out"* (Robert Warshow).

sell·out (sĕl′out′) *n.* **1.** The act of selling out. **2.** An event the tickets for which are all sold. **3.** One who has betrayed his principles or an espoused cause.

sell short. 1. *Finance.* To contract for the sale of securities or commodities one expects to own at a later date and at more advantageous terms. **2.** To underestimate the true value or worth of.

sel·syn (sĕl′sĭn′) *n.* A device for the instantaneous transmission and reception, from a generator to a motor, of the angular movement of rotating parts. Also called "synchro." [Short for *self-synchronous.*]

selt·zer (sĕlt′sər) *n.* **1.** A natural effervescent spring water of high mineral content. **2.** Such water artificially prepared and containing carbon dioxide. Also called "seltzer water." [German *Selterser (Wasser),* "(water) of Nieder Selters," a district near Wiesbaden, West Germany, locality of the springs.]

sel·vage (sĕl′vĭj) *n.* Also **sel·vedge. 1.** The edge of a fabric woven so that it will not ravel, especially an ornamental fringe at either end of an oriental carpet. **2.** Any edge similar to this, usually a tapelike one. **3.** The edge plate of a lock with a slot for a bolt. [Middle English : *selve, self,* SELF + *egge,* EDGE (after obsolete Dutch *selfegghe*).]

selves. Plural of **self.**

sem. seminary.

se·man·teme (sə-măn′tēm) *n.* An irreducible linguistic unit of meaning. [SEMANT(IC) + -EME.]

se·man·tic (sə-măn′tĭk) *adj.* **1.** Pertaining to meaning, especially meaning in language. **2.** Of, relating to, or according to the science of semantics. [Greek *sēmantikos,* significant, from *sēmainein,* to signify, show by a sign, from *sēma,* sign. See **dheye-** in Appendix.*]

se·man·ti·cist (sə-măn′tə-sĭst) *n.* A specialist in semantics.

se·man·tics (sə-măn′tĭks) *n.* Plural in form, used with a singular verb. **1.** *Linguistics.* The study or science of meaning in language forms, particularly with regard to its historical change. **2.** *Logic.* The study of relationships between signs and symbols and what they represent. Also called "semasiology," "semiotics."

sem·a·phore (sĕm′ə-fôr′, -fōr′) *n.* **1.** Any visual signaling apparatus with flags, lights, or mechanically moving arms, as on a railroad. **2.** A system for flag signaling using various designated positions of the (person's) arms. —*v.* **semaphored,**

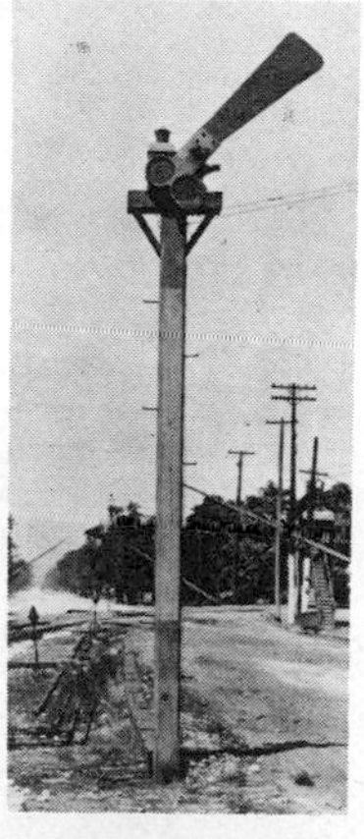

semaphore
Three-position railway semaphore shown in "caution" position

semidome
In a reconstruction of a section of the baths of Caracalla

-phoring, -phores. —*tr.* To send (a message) by semaphore. —*intr.* To signal with a semaphore. [Greek *sēma*, sign (see dheye- in Appendix*) + -PHORE.]

Se·ma·rang (sə-mä′räng). Also **Sa·ma·rang.** A city and port of Indonesia, in northern Java. Population, 374,000.

se·ma·si·ol·o·gy (sĭ-mā′sē-ŏl′ə-jē) *n. Logic.* **Semantics** (*see*). [Greek *sēmasia*, meaning, from *sēmainein*, to signify, mean (see **semantic**) + -LOGY.] —**se·ma′si·o·log′i·cal** (-ə-lŏj′ĭ-kəl) *adj.* —**se·ma′si·ol′o·gist** *n.*

se·mat·ic (sĭ-măt′ĭk) *adj.* Serving as a warning or signal of danger. Said especially of the coloring of certain animals. [From Greek *sēma* (stem *sēmat-*), sign. See dheye- in Appendix.*]

sem·bla·ble (sĕm′blə-bəl) *adj.* **1.** Resembling; like. **2.** Appearing real; seeming; apparent. —*n.* That which closely resembles something else. [Middle English, from Old French, from *sembler*, to resemble, seem, from Latin *similāre, simulāre,* to SIMULATE.] —**sem′bla·bly** *adv.*

sem·blance (sĕm′bləns) *n.* **1.** An outward or token appearance; superficial aspect; a show: "*Foolish men mistake transitory semblance for eternal fact*" (Carlyle). **2.** A representation; resemblance; copy. **3.** The barest trace; a modicum. [Middle English, from Old French, from *semblant,* present participle of *sembler,* to resemble, seem. See **semblable.**]

se·mé (sĕ-mā′) *adj. Heraldry.* Having a design embellished with small, delicate figures, as a lacing of stars or flowers. [French, past participle of *semer,* to sow, scatter, from Latin *sēmināre,* from *sēmen,* seed. See sē-¹ in Appendix.*]

se·mei·ol·o·gy (sē′mē-ŏl′ə-jē). Variant of **semiology.**
se·mei·ot·ic (sē′mē-ŏt′ĭk). Variant of **semiotic.**

se·meme (sē′mēm′) *n.* The meaning expressed by a morpheme. [Greek *sēmainein,* to signify, mean (see **semantic**) + -EME.]

se·men (sē′mən) *n.* A viscous whitish secretion of the male reproductive organs, the transporting medium for spermatozoa. Also called "sperm." [Middle English, from Latin *sēmen,* "seed." See sē-¹ in Appendix.*]

Se·me·nov (sĭ-myŭn′əf), **Nikolai Nikolayvich.** Born 1896. Soviet physical chemist.

se·mes·ter (sə-mĕs′tər) *n.* One of two divisions of 15 to 18 weeks each of an academic year. Compare **trimester.** [German *Semester,* from Latin (*cursus*) *sēmēstris,* "(period) of six months" : *sex,* six (see **sweks** in Appendix*) + *mēnsis,* month (see mē-² in Appendix*).]

semi-. *Abbr.* **s.** Indicates: **1.** Partly or partially; for example, **semiaquatic. 2.** Half of; for example, **semicircle. 3.** Occurring twice within a particular period of time; for example, **semimonthly.** *Note:* Many compounds other than those entered here may be formed with *semi-.* In forming compounds, *semi-* is normally joined with the following element without space or hyphen: *semiannual.* However, if the second element begins with a capital letter or with *i,* it is separated with a hyphen: *semi-Americanized, semi-idle.* [Latin *sēmi-.* See sēmi- in Appendix.*]

sem·i·an·nu·al (sĕm′ē-ăn′yōō-əl, sĕm′ī-) *adj.* Happening or issued twice a year.

sem·i·a·quat·ic (sĕm′ē-ə-kwăt′ĭk, sĕm′ī-) *adj.* Adapted for living or growing in or near water; not entirely aquatic.

sem·i·au·to·mat·ic (sĕm′ē-ô′tə-măt′ĭk, sĕm′ī-) *adj.* **1.** Partially automatic. **2.** Having an automatic reloading mechanism but requiring a pull of the trigger for each shot. Said of firearms. Also "autoloading." Compare **automatic.** —*n.* A semiautomatic firearm.

sem·i·breve (sĕm′ē-brĕv′, sĕm′ī-) *n. Chiefly British. Music.* A whole note.

sem·i·cen·ten·ni·al (sĕm′ē-sĕn-tĕn′ē-əl, sĕm′ī-) *adj.* Marking the 50th anniversary of some event. —*n.* **1.** A 50th anniversary. **2.** A celebration honoring this.

sem·i·cir·cle (sĕm′ĭ-sûr′kəl) *n.* **1.** A half of a circle as divided by a diameter. **2.** An object or arrangement of objects in the shape of a half-circle. —**sem′i·cir′cu·lar** (-sûr′kyə-lər) *adj.*

semicircular canal. Any of the three tubular and looped structures in the labyrinth of the inner ear, together functioning in the maintenance of a sense of balance and orientation.

sem·i·civ·i·lized (sĕm′ē-sĭv′ə-līzd′, sĕm′ī-) *adj.* Partly civilized.

sem·i·co·lon (sĕm′ĭ-kō′lən) *n.* A mark of punctuation (;) indicating a degree of separation intermediate in value between the comma and the period.
Usage: Semicolons are frequently used to separate parallel expressions in a series that concludes a sentence, especially if the sentence is long and structurally involved or if the expressions in the series contain commas: *The shipment comprises 40 watches, including some discontinued models; 23 gold rings, cased as specified; and 110 pieces of costume jewelry.* A semicolon is also employed to separate independent elements, especially when they are closely related and not joined by a conjunction: *War seldom produces lasting solutions; conciliation usually does.* A semicolon is sometimes used between two such independent elements when the second begins or ends with *however, nevertheless,* or *moreover: He was frequently ill during that period; nevertheless, he completed two symphonies and much chamber music.*

sem·i·con·duc·tor (sĕm′ē-kən-dŭk′tər, sĕm′ī-) *n.* Any of various solid crystalline substances, such as germanium or silicon, having electrical conductivity greater than insulators but less than good conductors.

sem·i·con·scious (sĕm′ē-kŏn′shəs, sĕm′ī-) *adj.* Half-conscious. —**sem′i·con′scious·ly** *adv.* —**sem′i·con′scious·ness** *n.*

sem·i·de·tached (sĕm′ē-dĭ-tăcht′, sĕm′ī-) *adj.* Attached to something on one side only. Said of either of a pair of houses joined by a common wall.

sem·i·di·am·e·ter (sĕm′ē-dī-ăm′ə-tər, sĕm′ī-) *n.* The apparent radius of a celestial body when viewed as a disk from Earth.

sem·i·di·ur·nal (sĕm′ē-dī-ûr′nəl, sĕm′ī-) *adj.* **1.** Of, pertaining to, occurring, or performed during a half-day. **2.** Occurring or coming approximately once every 12 hours, as the tides. **3.** Designating the arc described by a celestial body between its meridian passage and its point of rising or setting.

sem·i·di·vine (sĕm′ē-dī-vīn′, sĕm′ī-) *adj.* Not fully divine, but more than mortal, as a demigod in Greek mythology.

sem·i·dome (sĕm′ē-dōm′, sĕm′ī-) *n.* A roof covering a semicircular space; half a dome.

sem·i·el·lip·ti·cal (sĕm′ē-ĭ-lĭp′tĭ-kəl, sĕm′ī-) *adj.* Having the form or shape of half of an ellipse, especially when divided along the major axis.

sem·i·fi·nal (sĕm′ē-fī′nəl, sĕm′ī-) *adj.* Immediately preceding the final, as in a series of competitions or examinations. —*n.* **1.** A match, competition, or other event that precedes the final event. **2.** One of the two competitions of the next to the last round in an elimination tournament. —**sem′i·fi′nal·ist** *n.*

sem·i·flu·id (sĕm′ē-flōō′ĭd, sĕm′ī-) *adj.* Also **sem·i·flu·id·ic** (-flōō-ĭd′ĭk). Intermediate in flow properties between solids and liquids; highly viscous. —*n.* A semifluid substance.

sem·i·for·mal (sĕm′ē-fôr′məl, sĕm′ī-) *adj.* **1.** Partly formal. Said of an occasion. **2.** Suitable for such an occasion.

sem·i·group (sĕm′ē-grōōp′) *n. Algebra.* A nonempty set with an associative binary multiplication.

sem·i·in·fi·nite (sĕm′ē-ĭn′fĭn-ĭt, sĕm′ī-) *adj.* Unbounded in one direction or dimension.

sem·i·liq·uid (sĕm′ē-lĭk′wĭd, sĕm′ī-) *adj.* Intermediate in properties, especially flow properties, between liquids and solids. —*n.* A semiliquid substance.

sem·i·log·a·rith·mic (sĕm′ē-lôg′ə-rĭth′mĭk, sĕm′ī-) *adj.* **1.** Having one logarithmic and one arithmetic scale: *semilogarithmic graph paper.* **2.** Characteristic of a relationship expressed using such scales.

sem·i·lu·nar (sĕm′ē-lōō′nər, sĕm′ī-) *adj.* Also **sem·i·lu·nate** (-lōō′nāt′). Shaped like a half-moon; crescent.

semilunar bone. *Anatomy.* The **lunate bone** (*see*).

semilunar valve. Either of two crescent-shaped valves, each having three cusps, located in the aorta and in the pulmonary artery and preventing blood from flowing back into the heart. See **heart.**

sem·i·month·ly (sĕm′ē-mŭnth′lē, sĕm′ī-) *adj.* Occurring or issued twice a month. See Usage note at **bimonthly.** —*n., pl.* **semimonthlies.** A semimonthly publication. —*adv.* Twice monthly; at half-monthly intervals. See Usage note at **bimonthly.**

sem·i·nal (sĕm′ə-nəl) *adj.* Also *rare* **sem·i·nar·y** (-nĕr′ē). **1.** Of, relating to, or containing semen or seed. **2.** Of, pertaining to, or having the power of origination; germinative. [Middle English, from Old French, from Latin *sēminālis,* from *sēmen* (stem *sēmin-*), seed, SEMEN.]

sem·i·nar (sĕm′ə-när′) *n.* **1. a.** A small group of advanced students in a college or graduate school engaged in original research under the guidance of a professor who meets regularly with them for reports and discussions. **b.** A course of study so pursued. **c.** A scheduled meeting of such a group. **2.** A meeting for an exchange of ideas in some area; conference. [German *Seminar,* from Latin *sēminārium,* seed plot, nursery. See **seminary.**]

sem·i·nar·i·an (sĕm′ə-nâr′ē-ən) *n.* A seminary student.

sem·i·nar·y (sĕm′ə-nĕr′ē) *n., pl.* **-ies.** *Abbr.* **sem. 1. a.** A school; especially, a theological school for the training of priests, ministers, or rabbis. **b.** A school of higher education; especially, a private school for girls. **2.** A place or environment in which something is developed or nurtured. —*adj.* **1.** Of or relating to a seminary. **2.** *Rare.* Variant of **seminal.** [Middle English, seed plot, place for cultivation, nursery garden, from Latin *sēminārium,* garden, seed plot, nursery, from *sēminārius,* of seeds, from *sēmen* (stem *sēmin-*), seed. See sē-¹ in Appendix.*]

sem·i·na·tion (sĕm′ə-nā′shən) *n. Rare.* The dispersal or production of seed. [Latin *sēminātiō,* propagation, from *sēminātus,* past participle of *sēmināre,* to sow, from *sēmen* (stem *sēmin-*), seed. See sē-¹ in Appendix.*]

sem·i·nif·er·ous (sĕm′ə-nĭf′ər-əs) *adj. Biology.* **1.** Conveying or producing semen. **2.** Bearing seed. [Latin *sēmen* (stem *sēmin-*), SEMEN + -FEROUS.]

Sem·i·nole (sĕm′ə-nōl′) *n., pl.* **Seminole** or **-noles. 1.** A tribe of Muskhogean-speaking North American Indians, a late Creek offshoot, originally living in Alabama, later in Florida, but now chiefly in Oklahoma. **2.** A member of this tribe. **3.** The language of this tribe. [Creek *simanóli, simalóni,* from American Spanish *cimarrón,* wild, runaway. See **maroon** (to abandon).] —**Sem′i·nole′** *adj.*

sem·i·no·mad (sĕm′ē-nō′măd, sĕm′ī-) *n.* One of a people whose living habits are largely nomadic but who plant some crops at a base point. —**sem′i·no·mad′ic** (-nō-măd′ĭk) *adj.*

sem·i·of·fi·cial (sĕm′ē-ə-fĭsh′əl, sĕm′ī-) *adj.* Having some official authority or sanction. —**sem′i·of·fi′cial·ly** *adv.*

se·mi·ol·o·gy (sē′mē-ŏl′ə-jē, sĕ′mī-, sĕm′ē-, sĕm′ī-) *n.* Also **mei·ol·o·gy.** **1. a.** The science dealing with signs or sign language. **b.** The use of signs in signaling, as with a semaphore. **2. Symptomatology** (*see*). [New Latin *semaeologia* : Greek *sēmeion,* mark, sign, from *sēma,* sign, signal (see dheye- in Appendix*) + -LOGY.]

sem·i·o·paque (sĕm′ē-ō-pāk′, sĕm′ī-) *adj.* Almost opaque.

se·mi·ot·ic (sē′mē-ŏt′ĭk, sē′mī-, sĕm′ē-, sĕm′ī-) *adj.* Also **se·mi-**

ot·i·cal (-ĭ-kəl), **se·mei·ot·ic** (sē′mī-ŏt′ĭk, sĕm′ī-), **se·mei·ot·i·cal.** **1.** *Logic.* Of or relating to semantics. **2.** *Medicine.* Relating to symptomatology. [Greek *sēmeiōtikos,* observant of signs, from *sēmeioun,* to mark, give signals, to note, from *sēmeion,* sign. See **semiology.**]

se·mi·ot·ics (sē′mē-ŏt′ĭks, sē′mī-, sĕm′ē-, sĕm′ī-) *n.* Also **se·mei·ot·ics** (sē′mī-ŏt′ĭks, sĕm′ī-). Plural in form, used with a singular verb. **1.** *Logic.* **Semantics** *(see).* **2.** *Medicine.* Symptomatology. **—se′mi·o·ti′cian** (-ə-tĭsh′ən) *n.*

Sem·i·pa·la·tinsk (sĕm′ĭ-pə-lä′tĭnsk). A city of the Soviet Union, on the Irtish River in northeastern Kazakhstan. Population, 192,000.

sem·i·pal·mate (sĕm′ē-păl′māt′, sĕm′ī-) *adj.* Also **sem·i·pal·mat·ed** (-mā′tĭd). Having partial or reduced webbing between the toes, as do some wading birds.

sem·i·par·a·site (sĕm′ē-păr′ə-sīt′, sĕm′ī-) *n. Biology.* A **hemiparasite** *(see).* **—sem′i·par′a·sit′ic** (-sĭt′ĭk) *adj.*

sem·i·per·me·a·ble (sĕm′ē-pûr′mē-ə-bəl, sĕm′ī-) *adj.* **1.** Partially permeable. **2.** Of or relating to a natural or artificial membrane that is permeable to some molecules in a mixture or solution but not to all. See **osmosis.**

sem·i·por·ce·lain (sĕm′ē-pôr′sə-lĭn, -pōr′sə-lĭn, -pôrs′lĭn, -pōrs′lĭn, sĕm′ī-) *n.* Any of several glazed ceramic wares resembling porcelain but having little or no translucency.

sem·i·post·al (sĕm′ē-pōs′təl, sĕm′ī-) *adj.* Designating a postage stamp sold for more than its postal value to raise money for some charitable purpose. *—n.* Such a stamp.

sem·i·pre·cious (sĕm′ē-prĕsh′əs, sĕm′ī-) *adj.* Designating stones of less value than precious stones, as a topaz.

sem·i·pri·vate (sĕm′ē-prī′vĭt, sĕm′ī-) *adj.* Shared with usually one to three other hospital patients: *a semiprivate room.*

sem·i·pro (sĕm′ē-prō′, sĕm′ī-) *adj. Informal.* Semiprofessional. **—sem′i·pro′** *n.*

sem·i·pro·fes·sion·al (sĕm′ē-prə-fĕsh′ən-əl, sĕm′ī-) *adj.* **1.** Taking part in a sport for pay but not on a full-time basis. **2.** Composed of or engaged in by semiprofessional players. **3.** Designating an apartment which may be used by a resident professionally but for only part of his income. *—n.* **1.** A semiprofessional player. **2.** One whose occupation or work has some of the characteristics of a profession or of a professional.

sem·i·qua·ver (sĕm′ē-kwā′vər) *n. Music. Chiefly British.* A **sixteenth note** *(see).*

Se·mir·a·mis (sĭ-mîr′ə-mĭs). The legendary founder of Babylon and wife of Ninus.

sem·i·rig·id (sĕm′ē-rĭj′ĭd, sĕm′ī-) *adj.* **1.** Moderately rigid. **2.** Having some rigid components.

sem·i·round (sĕm′ē-round′, sĕm′ī-) *adj.* Having a round side and a flat side. *—n.* Something having this shape.

sem·i·skilled (sĕm′ē-skĭld′, sĕm′ī-) *adj.* Possessing some skills but not enough to do specialized work.

sem·i·sol·id (sĕm′ē-sŏl′ĭd, sĕm′ī-) *adj.* Intermediate in properties, especially in rigidity, between solids and liquids. *—n.* A semisolid substance, such as a stiff dough or firm gelatin.

Sem·ite (sĕm′īt′) *n.* Also **Shem·ite** (shĕm′īt′). **1.** One of a people of Caucasian stock comprising chiefly Jews and Arabs but in ancient times also including Babylonians, Assyrians, Phoenicians, and others of the eastern Mediterranean area. **2.** One of the people descended from Shem. [New Latin *semita,* from Late Latin *Sēm,* Shem (traditional ancestor of the Semites), from Greek, from Hebrew *Shem.*]

Se·mit·ic (sə-mĭt′ĭk) *adj.* **1.** Of or pertaining to the Semites; especially, Jewish or Arabic. **2.** Of, pertaining to, or designating a subfamily of the Afro-Asiatic family of languages including Arabic, Hebrew, Ethiopic, Amharic, and Aramaic. *—n.* **1.** The Semitic subfamily of languages. **2.** Any one of these languages.

Se·mit·ics (sə-mĭt′ĭks) *n.* Plural in form, used with a singular verb. The study of the history, languages, and cultures of the Semitic peoples.

Sem·i·tism (sĕm′ə-tĭz′əm) *n.* **1.** A Semitic word or idiom. **2.** Semitic traits, attributes, or customs. **3.** A disposition in favor of the Jews, as a political policy.

Sem·i·to-Ha·mit·ic (sĕm′ə-tō′hă-mĭt′ĭk) *n.* **Afro-Asiatic** *(see).* **—Sem′i·to′-Ha·mit′ic** *adj.*

sem·i·tone (sĕm′ē-tōn′, sĕm′ī-) *n. Music.* An interval equal to half a tone in the standard diatonic scale. Also called "half step," "half tone." **—sem′i·ton′ic** (-tŏn′ĭk) *adj.*

sem·i·trail·er (sĕm′ē-trā′lər, sĕm′ī-) *n.* A trailer with a set or sets of wheels at the rear only, the forward portion supported by the truck tractor or towing vehicle.

sem·i·trans·par·ent (sĕm′ē-trăns-păr′ənt, -pâr′ənt, sĕm′ī-) *adj.* Not completely transparent.

sem·i·trop·i·cal (sĕm′ē-trŏp′ĭ-kəl, sĕm′ī-) *adj.* Partly tropical; subtropical.

sem·i·vow·el (sĕm′ĭ-vou′əl) *n. Phonetics.* A letter or vocal sound having the sound of a vowel but used as a consonant, as *w, y,* and *r.* Also called "glide."

sem·i·week·ly (sĕm′ē-wēk′lē, sĕm′ī-) *adj.* Issued or happening twice a week. See Usage note at **bimonthly.** *—n., pl.* **semiweeklies.** A semiweekly publication. *—adv.* Twice weekly. See Usage note at **bimonthly.**

sem·i·year·ly (sĕm′ē-yîr′lē, sĕm′ī-) *adj.* Happening or issued twice a year or once every half year. See Usage note at **bimonthly.** *—n., pl.* **semiyearlies.** A semiyearly event or publication. *—adv.* Every half year. See Usage note at **bimonthly.**

Sem·mel·weis (zĕm′əl-vīs′), **Ignaz Philipp.** 1818–1865. Hungarian obstetrician; pioneered in obstetrical antisepsis.

Semmes (sĕmz), **Raphael.** 1809–1877. American naval officer; a commander of Confederate Navy in the Civil War.

sem·o·li·na (sĕm′ə-lē′nə) *n.* The gritty, coarse particles of wheat left after the finer flour has passed through the bolting machine, used for pasta. [Variant of Italian *semolino,* diminutive of *semola,* bran, from Latin *simila,* fine flour. See **simnel.**]

sem·per fi·de·lis (sĕm′pər fĭ-dā′lĭs). *Latin.* Always faithful. The motto of the U.S. Marine Corps.

sem·per pa·ra·tus (sĕm′pər pə-rä′təs). *Latin.* Always prepared. The motto of the U.S. Coast Guard.

sem·pi·ter·nal (sĕm′pĭ-tûr′nəl) *adj.* Eternal; perpetual. [Middle English, from Old French *sempiternel,* from Late Latin *sempiternālis,* from Latin *sempiternus* : *semper,* always (see **sem-**[1] in Appendix*) + *aeternus,* eternal (see **aiw-** in Appendix*).] **—sem′pi·ter′ni·ty** (-pĭ-tûr′nə-tē) *n.*

sem·pli·ce (sĕm′plĭ-chā′) *adv. Music.* Simply; plainly. Used as a direction. [Italian, from Latin *simplex* (stem *simplic-*), simple. See **sem-**[1] in Appendix.*] **—sem′pli·ce′** *adj.*

sem·pre (sĕm′prā) *adv. Music.* In the same manner throughout. Used as a direction. [Italian, "always," from Latin *semper.* See **sem-**[1] in Appendix.*]

semp·stress (sĕmp′strĭs, sĕm′-) *n. Rare.* A seamstress. [Variant of SEAMSTRESS.]

sen (sĕn) *n., pl.* **sen. 1.** A coin equal to 1/100 of the yen of Japan. **2.** A coin equal to 1/100 of the rupiah of Indonesia. **3.** A monetary unit equal to 1/100 of the riel of Cambodia. —See table of exchange rates at **currency.** [Japanese, from Chinese (Mandarin) *ch′ ien*[2], money, coin.]

sen., Sen. 1. senate; senator. **2.** senior.

se·nar·i·us (sə-nâr′ē-əs) *n., pl.* **-narii** (-nâr′ē-ī′). A Greek or Latin verse consisting of six feet. [Latin *sēnārius,* from adjective, SENARY.]

sen·a·ry (sĕn′ə-rē) *adj.* Of or relating to the number six; having six things or parts. [Latin *sēnārius,* from *sēnī,* six each, from *sex,* six. See **sweks** in Appendix.*]

sen·ate (sĕn′ĭt) *n. Abbr.* **sen., Sen. 1.** An assembly or council of citizens having the highest deliberative and legislative functions in a government, specifically: **a.** *Capital* **S.** The upper house of Congress in the United States, to which two members are elected from each state by popular vote for a six-year term. **b.** *Capital* **S.** The upper house in the bicameral legislature of many U.S. states. **c.** *Capital* **S.** The upper legislative house in Canada, France, and other countries. **d.** The supreme council of state of the ancient Roman republic and later of the empire. **2.** The building or hall in which a senate meets. **3.** A governing, advisory, or disciplinary body of some colleges and universities composed of faculty members and sometimes student representatives. [Middle English *senat,* from Old French, from Latin *senātus,* from *senex* (stem *sen-*), old, an old man, an elder. See **sen-**[1] in Appendix.*]

sen·a·tor (sĕn′ə-tər) *n.* Also **Sen·a·tor.** *Abbr.* **Sen., sen.** A member of a senate. **—sen′a·tor·ship′** *n.*

sen·a·to·ri·al (sĕn′ə-tôr′ē-əl, -tōr′ē-əl) *adj.* **1.** Of, concerning, or befitting a senator or a senate. **2.** Composed of senators. **—sen′a·to′ri·al·ly** *adv.*

senatorial courtesy. The custom in the U.S. Senate of refusing to confirm a Presidential appointment to office opposed by both senators from the state of the appointee or by the senior senator of the President's party.

se·na·tus con·sul·tum (sə-nā′to͞os kōn-so͞ol′to͞om, sə-nā′təs kən-sŭl′təm) *pl.* **senatus consulta** (kōn-so͞ol′tə, kən-sŭl′tə). *Latin.* A decree of the ancient Roman senate.

send[1] (sĕnd) *v.* **sent** (sĕnt), **sending, sends.** *—tr.* **1. a.** To cause to be conveyed by an intermediary to a destination: *send goods by plane.* **b.** To express for conveyance: *She sends her love.* **2.** To dispatch, as by mail or telegraph. **3. a.** To direct to go on a mission. **b.** To require or enable to go: *send a son to college.* **c.** To command or request to go: *Send the guard away.* **d.** To cause or force to depart: *The news sent them hurrying home.* **e.** To direct (a person) to a source of information; refer. **4.** To give off; emit (heat or smoke, for example). Often used with *forth* or *out.* **5.** To direct or propel with force; drive: *The batter sent the ball to left field.* **6.** To cause to take place or befall; bestow; inflict. **7. a.** To put or drive into some state or condition. **b.** *Slang.* To transport with delight; carry away. *—intr.* To dispatch a messenger or message. **—send (one) about his business.** To send away curtly; dismiss with displeasure. **—send away for.** To order by mail. **—send down.** *British.* To suspend or dismiss from a university. **—send flying. 1.** To scatter or knock in all directions with great force or violence. **2.** To cause to flee. **—send for. 1.** To order. **2.** To summon by means of a message or messenger. **—send out for.** To dispatch (an order or delivery, for example). **—send packing.** To dismiss summarily or abruptly. **—send up.** *Informal.* To send to jail. [Send, sent, sent; Middle English *senden, sente, sent,* Old English *sendan, sende, sended.* See **sent-** in Appendix.*] **—send′er** *n.*

send[2]. Variant of **scend.**

Sen·dai (sĕn′dī′). A city and cultural center of Japan, on Honshu, 180 miles north of Tokyo. Population, 464,000.

sen·dal (sĕnd′l) *n.* A light, thin silk used in the Middle Ages for fine garments, church vestments, and banners. [Middle English *cendal,* from Old French, obscurely akin to Greek *sindōn*†, a fine linen cloth.]

send·off (sĕnd′ôf′, -ŏf′) *n.* **1.** An event or demonstration of affection and good wishes for one about to leave on a journey or to begin a new undertaking. **2.** A start given to someone or something.

Sen·e·ca (sĕn′ĭ-kə) *n., pl.* **Seneca** or **-cas. 1.** A tribe of Iroquoian-speaking North American Indians formerly inhabiting western New York; one of the **Five Nations** *(see).* **2.** A member of this tribe. **3.** The language of this tribe. [Colonial Dutch

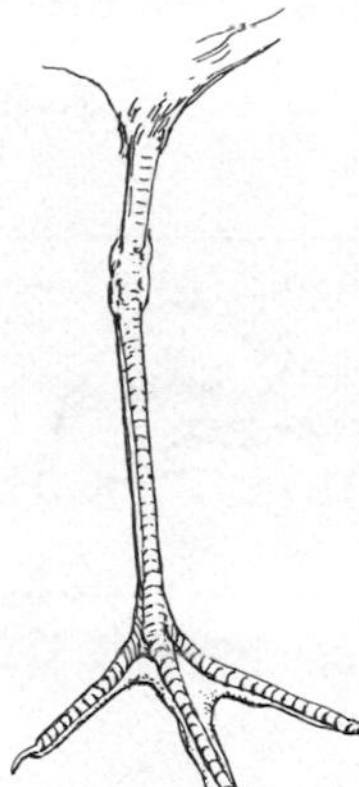

semipalmate
Semipalmate foot of a plover

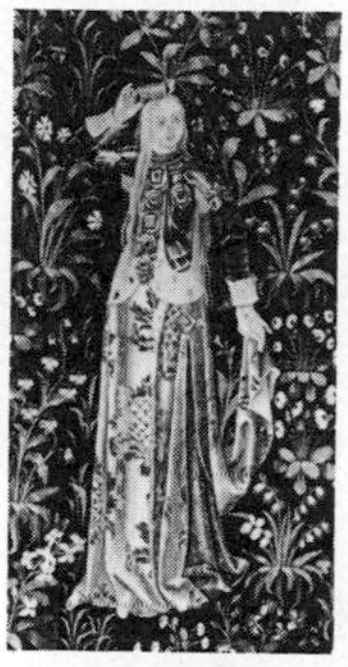

Semiramis
Detail of a 15th-century Flemish tapestry

t tight/th thin, path/*th* this, bathe/ŭ cut/ûr urge/v valve/w with/y yes/z zebra, size/zh vision/ə about, item, edible, gallop, circus/ à *Fr.* ami/œ *Fr.* feu, *Ger.* schön/ü *Fr.* tu, *Ger.* über/KH *Ger.* ich, *Scot.* loch/N *Fr.* bon. ***Follows main vocabulary.** †**Of obscure origin.**

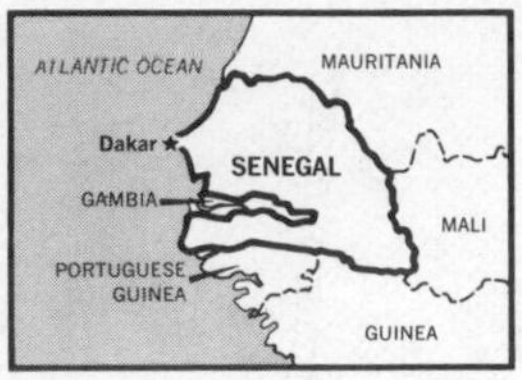

Senegal

Sinnekens, Sennecaas, perhaps of Algonquian origin.]
Sen·e·ca (sĕn′ə-kə), **Lucius Annaeus.** 4?B.C.–A.D. 65. Roman philosopher, political leader, and author of tragedies.
Sen·e·ca Lake (sĕn′ə-kə). The largest, 67 square miles in area, of the Finger Lakes, in west-central New York State.
Seneca snakeroot. A North American plant, *Polygala senega,* having a terminal cluster of small white flowers. [So called because the Senecas used it as a snakebite remedy.]
se·nec·ti·tude (sĭ-nĕk′tə-to͞od′, -tyo͞od′) *n.* Old age. [Medieval Latin *senectitūdō,* from Latin *senectūs,* from *senex,* old. See **sen-**[1] in Appendix.*]
sen·e·ga (sĕn′ə-gə) *n.* The dried roots of the Seneca snakeroot, used medicinally as an expectorant. [Variant of SENECA.]
Sen·e·gal, Republic of (sĕn′ə-gôl′). A republic, 76,124 square miles in area, in western Africa. Formerly part of French West Africa, it became independent in 1960. Population, 3,100,000. Capital, Dakar.
Sen·e·gal River (sĕn′ə-gôl′). A river of Africa, flowing over 1,000 miles from western Mali to the Atlantic in Senegal.
Sen·e·gam·bi·a (sĕn′ə-găm′bē-ə). A region of western Africa around the Senegal and Gambia rivers, now mainly in Senegal and Mali.
se·nes·cent (sĭ-nĕs′ənt) *adj.* Aging; growing old; elderly. [Latin *senēscēns,* present participle of *senēscere,* to grow old, inceptive of *senēre,* to be old, from *senex,* old. See **sen-**[1] in Appendix.*] —**se·nes′cence** *n.*
sen·e·schal (sĕn′ə-shəl) *n.* An official in a medieval noble household in charge of domestic arrangements and the administration of servants; a steward. [Middle English, from Old French, from Medieval Latin *siniscalcus,* from Germanic. See **sen-**[1] in Appendix.*]
Sen·ghor (säN-gôr′), **Léopold Sédar.** Born 1906. Senegalese poet and statesman; president of Senegal (since 1960).
se·nile (sē′nīl′, sĕn′īl′) *adj.* **1.** Pertaining to, characteristic of, or proceeding from old age. **2.** Exhibiting senility. **3.** *Geology.* Worn away nearly to the base level, as at the end of an erosion cycle. [Old French, from Latin *senīlis,* from *senex* (stem *sen-*), old. See **sen-**[1] in Appendix.*] —**se′nile′ly** *adv.*
senile dementia. Progressive, abnormally accelerated deterioration of mental faculties and emotional stability in old age.
se·nil·i·ty (sĭ-nĭl′ə-tē) *n.* **1.** The state of being senile. **2.** Mental and physical deterioration with old age.
sen·ior (sēn′yər) *adj. Abbr.* **Sr., sr., Sen., sen. 1.** Of or designating the older of two; especially, denoting the older of two persons having the same name, as father and son. **2. a.** Above others in rank or length of service. **b.** Having precedence in making certain decisions. **3.** Of or pertaining to the fourth and last year of high school or college. —*n.* **1.** A senior person. **2.** A student in his fourth year of high school or college. [Latin, comparative of *senex,* old. See **sen-**[1] in Appendix.*]
Usage: When *senior* is used with a personal name to denote the older of two it is usually written *James Smith, Sr.*
senior citizen. A person of or over the age of retirement.
Usage: *Senior citizen* is objected to by some as a euphemism associated with the worlds of politics and advertising. It is acceptable in general usage to 47 per cent of the Usage Panel.
senior high school. A high school comprising, usually, grades 10, 11, and 12. Also called "senior high."
sen·ior·i·ty (sēn-yôr′ə-tē, -yŏr′ə-tē) *n., pl.* **-ties. 1.** The state of being older or higher in rank. **2.** Precedence of position; especially, precedence over others of the same rank by reason of a longer span of service.
Sen·lac (sĕn′lăk). A hill in Sussex, England, near Hastings; the site of the Battle of Hastings (1066).
sen·na (sĕn′ə) *n.* **1.** Any of various plants of the genus *Cassia,* having compound leaves and usually yellow flowers. **2.** The dried leaves of *C. angustifolia* or *C. acutifolia,* used medicinally as a cathartic. [New Latin, from Arabic *sanā′.*]
Sen·nach·er·ib (sĭ-năk′ər-ĭb′). King of Assyria (705–681 B.C.); invaded Judea; subjugated Babylon; rebuilt Nineveh.
sen·net[1] (sĕn′ĭt) *n.* A call on a trumpet or cornet signaling the ceremonial exits and entrances of actors in Elizabethan drama. [Perhaps variant of SIGNET.]
sen·net[2] (sĕn′ĭt) *n.* Any of several barracudas, especially *Sphyraena borealis,* of the western Atlantic. [Origin obscure.]
Sen·nett (sĕn′ĭt), **Mack.** 1884–1960. Canadian-born American producer and director of motion pictures.
sen·night (sĕn′īt′) *n.* Also **se′n·night.** *Archaic.* A week. [Middle English *seoveniht, sennet,* Old English *seofon nihta* : *seofon,* SEVEN + *nihta,* plural of *niht,* NIGHT.]
sen·nit (sĕn′ĭt) *n.* **1.** *Nautical.* Braided cordage formed by plaiting several strands of rope fiber or similar material. **2.** Plaited straw, grass, or palm leaves for making hats. [Origin unknown.]
sen·o·pi·a (sĕn-ō′pē-ə) *n.* Improvement of near vision sometimes occurring in the aged because of swelling of the crystalline lens in incipient cataract. [Latin *senex,* old (see **sen-**[1] in Appendix*) + -OPIA.]
se·ñor (sān-yôr′) *n., pl.* **señores** (sān-yôr′ās). *Abbr.* **Sr. 1.** The Spanish title of courtesy for a man, equivalent to the English *Mr.* or *sir.* It may be used alone or prefixed to a name. **2.** A Spanish or Spanish-speaking man.
se·ño·ra (sān-yôr′ä) *n., pl.* **señoras** (sān-yôr′äs). *Abbr.* **Sra. 1.** The Spanish title of courtesy for a married woman, equivalent to the English *Mrs.* or *madam.* It may be used alone or prefixed to a name. **2.** A Spanish or Spanish-speaking woman.
se·ño·ri·ta (sän′yō-rē′tä) *n., pl.* **-tas** (-täs). *Abbr.* **Srta. 1.** The Spanish title of courtesy for an unmarried young woman or a girl, equivalent to the English *Miss.* It may be used alone or prefixed to a name. **2.** A Spanish or Spanish-speaking unmarried woman or girl.
sen·sate (sĕn′sāt′) *adj.* Also **sen·sat·ed** (-sā′tĭd). Perceived by the senses. [Late Latin *sēnsātus,* gifted with sense, from Latin *sēnsus,* SENSE.] —**sen′sate′ly** *adv.*
sen·sa·tion (sĕn′sā′shən, sən-) *n.* **1. a.** A perception associated with stimulation of a sense organ or with a specific bodily condition: *the sensation of heat.* **b.** The faculty to feel or perceive; physical sensibility: *He had little sensation left in his leg.* **2.** A state of heightened interest or emotion: *"The anticipation produced in me a sensation somewhat between bliss and fear."* (James Weldon Johnson). **3. a.** A condition of intense public interest and excitement: *"The purser made a sensation as sailors like to do, by predicting a storm."* (Evelyn Waugh). **b.** An event or object causing such public excitement. [Medieval Latin *sēnsātiō,* from Late Latin *sēnsātus,* SENSATE.]
sen·sa·tion·al (sĕn′sā′shən-əl, sən-) *adj.* **1.** Of or pertaining to sensation. **2.** Arousing or intended to arouse strong curiosity, interest, or reaction, especially by exaggerated or lurid details. **3.** Outstanding; spectacular. —**sen′sa′tion·al·ly** *adv.*
sen·sa·tion·al·ism (sĕn′sā′shən-əl-ĭz′əm, sən-) *n.* **1. a.** The use of sensational matter or methods in writing, art, politics, or the like. **b.** Sensational subject matter. **c.** Interest in or the effect of such subject matter. **2.** *Philosophy.* The theory that sensation is the only source of knowledge. Also called "sensualism." **3.** The ethical doctrine that feeling is the only criterion of good. —**sen′sa′tion·al·ist** *n.* —**sen·sa′tion·al·is′tic** *adj.*
sense (sĕns) *n.* **1.** Any of the animal functions of hearing, sight, smell, touch, and taste. **2.** The faculty of external or self-perception exemplified by these functions. **3.** *Plural.* The faculties of sensation as means of providing physical gratification and pleasure. **4. a.** Intuitive or acquired perception or ability to estimate: *a sense of timing.* **b.** A capacity to appreciate or understand: *a sense of humor.* **c.** A vague feeling, as of coming danger. **d.** Recognition or perception either through the senses or through the intellect; consciousness: *a sense of guilt.* **5. a.** *Usually plural.* Normal ability to think or reason soundly; correct judgment: *Come to your senses.* **b.** That which is sound or reasonable: *There's no sense in waiting.* **6. a.** Import; point; signification. **b.** Lexical meaning: *"Let us take 'useful,' as Locke takes it, in its proper and popular sense"* (John Henry Newman). **c.** The meaning of a word in a particular context. **7.** Judgment; view; consensus. —See Synonyms at **meaning, mind.** —*tr.v.* **sensed, sensing, senses. 1.** To become aware of; perceive. **2.** *Informal.* To grasp; understand. **3.** To detect something automatically: *sense radioactivity.* [Latin *sēnsus,* the faculty of perceiving, from the past participle of *sentīre,* to perceive by senses, to feel. See **sent-** in Appendix.*]
sense datum. A basic unanalyzable experience resulting from the stimulation of a sense organ.
sense·less (sĕns′lĭs) *adj.* **1.** Without sense or meaning; meaningless. **2.** Foolish; lacking sense: *a senseless boy.* **3.** Insensate; unconscious. —**sense′less·ly** *adv.* —**sense′less·ness** *n.*
sense organ. A specialized organ or structure, such as the eye or ear, the stimulation of which initiates a process of sensory perception.
sense perception. Perception by the bodily senses.
sen·si·bil·i·ty (sĕn′sə-bĭl′ə-tē) *n., pl.* **-ties. 1.** The ability to feel or perceive. **2. a.** Keen intellectual perception: *the sensibility of a painter to color.* **b.** Mental or emotional responsiveness toward something, as the feelings of another. **3.** *Often plural.* Receptiveness to impression, whether pleasant or unpleasant; acuteness of feeling: *"The sufferings of the Cuban people shocked our sensibilities"* (George F. Kennan). **4.** Delicate, sensitive responsiveness to the pathetic or to artistic or aesthetic values. **5.** The aptness of plant organisms and instruments to be affected by environment.
sen·si·ble (sĕn′sə-bəl) *adj.* **1.** Perceptible by the senses or by the mind. **2.** Readily perceived; appreciable. **3.** Having the faculty of sensation; able to feel or perceive. **4.** Having a perception of something; cognizant; aware: *"But I am sensible that a good deal more is still to be done."* (Burke). **5.** Acting with or showing good sense: *a sensible choice.* —See Synonyms at **aware.** [Middle English, from Old French, from Latin *sēnsibilis,* from *sēnsus,* SENSE.] —**sen′si·ble·ness** *n.* —**sen′si·bly** *adv.*
sen·si·tive (sĕn′sə-tĭv) *adj.* **1.** Capable of perceiving with a sense or senses. **2.** Responsive to external conditions or stimulation. **3.** Susceptible to the attitudes, feelings, or circumstances of others. **4.** Quick to take offense; touchy. **5.** Easily irritated: *sensitive skin.* **6.** Readily altered by the action of some agent: *sensitive to light.* **7.** Registering very slight differences or changes of condition. Said of an instrument. **8.** Fluctuating or tending to fluctuate, as stock prices. **9.** Dealing with classified governmental information, usually involving national security: *a sensitive post in the State Department.* —See Usage note at **sensitivity.** [Middle English, from Old French *sensitif,* from Medieval Latin *sēnsitīvus,* from Latin *sēnsus,* SENSE.] —**sen′si·tive·ly** *adv.* —**sen′si·tive·ness** *n.*
sensitive plant. 1. A woody tropical American plant, *Mimosa pudica,* having leaflets and stems that fold and droop when touched. **2.** Any of various similar plants, such as *Cassia nictitans,* of eastern North America.
sen·si·tiv·i·ty (sĕn′sə-tĭv′ə-tē) *n., pl.* **-ties. 1.** The quality or condition of being sensitive. See Usage note below. **2.** Organic or organismic responsiveness to stimulation. **3.** *Electronics.* The minimum input signal required to produce a specified output signal. **4.** *Photography.* The degree of response of a plate or film to light, especially to light of a specified wavelength.
Usage: *Sensitivity* can be used as the noun equivalent of any

of the senses at *sensitive.* However, *sensitiveness,* rather than *sensitivity,* is usually employed for the personal tendency to be offended easily or to react readily to criticism.

sen·si·tize (sĕn′sə-tīz′) *v.* **-tized, -tizing, -tizes.** —*tr.* **1.** To make sensitive. **2.** *Photography.* To make (a film or plate) sensitive to light, especially to light of a specific wavelength. —*intr.* To become sensitive. —**sen′si·ti·za′tion** *n.* —**sen′si·tiz′er** *n.*

sen·si·tom·e·ter (sĕn′sə-tŏm′ə-tər) *n.* **1.** A device used for measuring the sensitivity of photographic film to light. **2.** A similar device for measuring the sensitivity of eyes to light. [SENSIT(IVE) + -METER.]

sen·sor (sĕn′sər, -sôr′) *n.* A device, such as a photoelectric cell, that receives and responds to a signal or stimulus. [From Latin *sēnsus,* SENSE.]

sen·so·ri·mo·tor (sĕn′sə-rē-mō′tər) *adj.* Also **sen·so·mo·tor** (sen′sō-mō′tər), **sen·si·mo·tor** (sĕn′sĭ-mō′tər). Of, pertaining to, or combining the functions of the sensing and motor activities. Said of nerves. [SENSOR(Y) + MOTOR.]

sen·so·ri·um (sĕn-sôr′ē-əm, sĕn-sōr′-) *n., pl.* **-ums** or **-soria** (-sôr′ē-ə, -sōr′ē-ə). **1.** The part of the brain that receives and correlates the impressions conveyed to various sensory areas. **2.** The entire sensory system. [Late Latin *sēnsōrium,* organ of sensation, from Latin *sēnsus,* SENSE.]

sen·so·ry (sĕn′sər-ē) *adj.* Also **sen·sor·i·al** (sĕn-sôr′ē-əl, sĕn-sōr′-). **1.** Of or pertaining to the senses or sensation. **2.** Transmitting impulses from sense organs to nerve centers; afferent.

sen·su·al (sĕn′shŏŏ-əl) *adj.* **1.** Pertaining to or affecting any of the senses or a sense organ. **2. a.** Pertaining to or given to the gratification of the physical appetites, especially sexual appetites. **b.** Suggesting sexuality; voluptuous. **c.** Carnal rather than spiritual or intellectual; worldly. **3.** Sensory. —See Synonyms at **sensuous.** —**sen′su·al·ly** *adv.* —**sen′su·al·ness** *n.*

sen·su·al·ism (sĕn′shŏŏ-əl-ĭz′əm) *n.* **1.** Sensuality. **2.** The ethical doctrine that the pleasures of the senses are the highest good. **3.** *Philosophy.* **Sensationalism** *(see).* —**sen′su·al·ist** *n.* —**sen′su·al·is′tic** *adj.*

sen·su·al·i·ty (sĕn′shŏŏ-ăl′ə-tē) *n., pl.* **-ties. 1.** The quality or state of being sensual. **2. a.** Excessive devotion to sensual pleasures. **b.** Lasciviousness.

sen·su·al·ize (sĕn′shŏŏ-ə-līz′) *tr.v.* **-ized, -izing, -izes.** To make sensual. —**sen′su·al·i·za′tion** *n.*

sen·su·ous (sĕn′shŏŏ-əs) *adj.* **1.** Pertaining to or derived from the senses. **2.** Having qualities that appeal to the senses: *the sensuous beauty of a spring day.* **3.** Readily susceptible through the senses; highly appreciative of the pleasures of sensation. —**sen′su·ous·ly** *adv.* —**sen′su·ous·ness** *n.*

Synonyms: *sensuous, sensual, luxurious, voluptuous, sybaritic, epicurean.* These adjectives refer to satisfaction of the senses. *Sensuous* can refer to any of the senses but more often applies to those involved in aesthetic enjoyment of art, music, nature, and the like. *Sensual* specifically applies to gratification of the physical senses, particularly those associated with sexual pleasure. *Luxurious* in this comparison is applicable to gratification of physical comfort, aesthetic fulfillment, or sense of extreme well-being. *Voluptuous* refers principally to satisfaction of physical senses and stresses indulgence in pleasure. The term also describes extremely shapely women. *Sybaritic* suggests devotion to pleasure and luxury even more strongly. *Epicurean* stresses gratification of a taste for good food and drink.

sent. Past tense and past participle of **send.**

sen·tence (sĕn′təns) *n.* **1.** *Abbr.* **sent.** *Grammar.* A grammatical unit comprising a word or a group of words that is separate from any other grammatical construction, and usually consists of at least one subject with its predicate and contains a finite verb or verb phrase; for example, *The door is open* and *Go!* are sentences. **2. a.** A court judgment; especially, a judicial decision of what punishment is to be inflicted on a convicted person. **b.** The penalty meted out. **3.** An opinion; especially, one given formally after deliberation. **4.** *Archaic.* An aphorism. —*tr.v.* **sentenced, -tencing, -tences.** To pass sentence upon (a convicted person). [Middle English, opinion, judgment, thought, from Old French, from Latin *sententia,* a way of thinking, opinion, from *sentīre,* to feel. See **sent-** in Appendix.*] —**sen·ten·tial** (sĕn-tĕn′shəl) *adj.* —**sen·ten′tial·ly** *adv.*

sen·tenc·er (sĕn′tən-sər) *n.* One who pronounces sentence.

sentence stress. The variation in emphasis or vocal stress on the syllables of words within a sentence. Also called "sentence accent."

sen·ten·tious (sĕn-tĕn′shəs) *adj.* **1.** Terse and energetic in expression; pithy. **2.** Abounding in aphorisms. **3. a.** Fond of aphoristic utterances. **b.** Given to pompous moralizing. [Latin *sententiōsus,* full of meaning, from *sententia,* opinion, SENTENCE.] —**sen·ten′tious·ly** *adv.* —**sen·ten′tious·ness** *n.*

sen·ti·ence (sĕn′chĭ-əns) *n.* Also **sen·ti·en·cy** (-ən-sē). **1.** The quality or state of being sentient; consciousness. **2.** Feeling as distinguished from perception or thought.

sen·ti·ent (sĕn′chĭ-ənt) *adj.* **1.** Having sense perception; conscious: *"the living knew themselves just sentient puppets on God's stage"* (T.E. Lawrence). **2.** Experiencing feeling or sensation. —*n.* **1.** A sentient person or thing. **2.** The mind. [Latin *sentiēns,* present participle of *sentīre,* to feel. See **sent-** in Appendix.*] —**sen′ti·ent·ly** *adv.*

sen·ti·ment (sĕn′tə-mənt) *n.* **1. a.** A cast of mind regarding something; general mental disposition: *"But how about counter-revolutionary sentiment inside Cuba? Does it exist?"* (C. Wright Mills). **b.** An opinion about a specific matter; a view. **2.** A thought, view, or attitude based on feeling or emotion instead of reason. **3.** The emotional import of a passage as distinguished from the words used. **4. a.** Susceptibility to tender, romantic, or nostalgic feeling. **b.** An expression of this. **5.** Emotion that borders on mawkishness. **6.** The expression of delicate and sensitive feeling in art and literature. **7.** *Rare.* A vague feeling or awareness; sensation: *"overpowered by an intense sentiment of horror"* (Poe). —See Synonyms at **opinion.** [Middle English *sentement,* from Old French, from Medieval Latin *sentīmentum,* from Latin *sentīre,* to feel. See **sent-** in Appendix.*]

sen·ti·men·tal (sĕn′tə-mĕnt′l) *adj.* **1. a.** Characterized by or swayed by sentiment. **b.** Affectedly or extravagantly emotional; mawkish. **2.** Resulting from or colored by emotion rather than reason or realism. **3.** Appealing to the sentiments, especially to romantic feelings: *sentimental music.* —**sen′ti·men′tal·ly** *adv.*

sen·ti·men·tal·ism (sĕn′tə-mĕnt′l-ĭz′əm) *n.* **1.** A predilection for the sentimental. **2.** An idea or expression marked by excessive sentiment. —**sen′ti·men′tal·ist** *n.*

sen·ti·men·tal·i·ty (sĕn′tə-mĕn-tăl′ə-tē) *n., pl.* **-ties. 1.** The condition or quality of being excessively or affectedly sentimental. **2.** Any expression of this.

sen·ti·men·tal·ize (sĕn-tə-mĕnt′l-īz) *v.* **-ized, -izing, -izes.** —*tr.* To regard with sentiment; be sentimental about. —*intr.* To behave in a sentimental manner. —**sen′ti·men′tal·i·za′tion** *n.*

sen·ti·nel (sĕnt′n-əl) *n.* One that keeps guard; a sentry. —*tr.v.* **sentineled, -neling, -nels.** Also *chiefly British* **-nelled, -nelling. 1.** To watch over as a sentinel. **2.** To provide with a sentinel. **3.** To post as a sentinel. [French *sentinelle,* from Italian *sentinella,* perhaps from *sentire,* to perceive, watch, from Latin *sentīre,* to perceive, feel. See **sent-** in Appendix.*]

sen·try (sĕn′trē) *n., pl.* **-tries. 1.** A guard, especially a soldier posted at some spot to prevent the passage of unauthorized persons. **2.** The duty of a sentry; a watch. [Perhaps short for obsolete *centrinell,* variant of SENTINEL.]

sentry box. A small shelter for a sentry on his post.

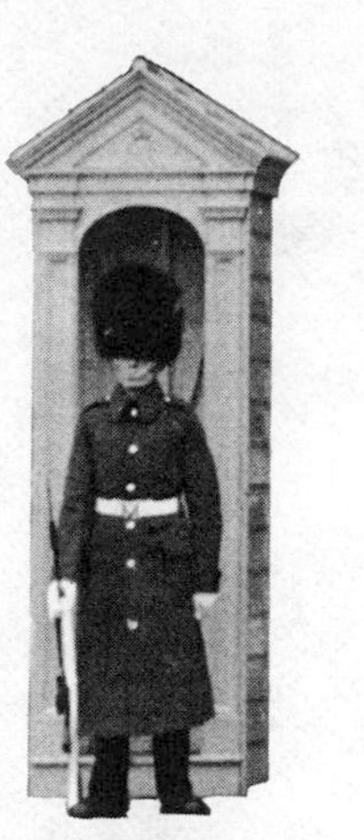

sentry box
At an entrance to
Buckingham Palace, London

Seoul (sōl). *Japanese* **Kei·jo** (kā′jō). The capital of South Korea and former capital of Korea, in the northwest on the Han River. Population, 3,376,000. Also called "Kyongsong."

Sep. September (unofficial).

se·pal (sē′pəl) *n.* One of the usually green segments forming the calyx of a flower. Compare **petal.** [New Latin *sepalum* : *sepa,* sepal, variant of Greek *skepē*†, covering + (PET)AL, misnamed by N.J. de Necker (died 1790), who combined the terms petal and sepal, not distinguishing between the corolla and calyx.] —**se′paled, sep′a·lous** (sĕp′ə-ləs) *adj.*

se·pal·oid (sē′pə-loid′, sĕp′ə-) *adj.* Also **se·pal·ine** (sē′pə-līn′, -lĭn, sĕp′ə-). Resembling or characteristic of a sepal.

-sepalous. Indicates sepals (of a certain type or number); for example, **monosepalous.**

sep·a·ra·ble (sĕp′ər-ə-bəl, sĕp′rə-) *adj.* Capable of being separated. —**sep′a·ra·bil′i·ty** *n.* —**sep′a·ra·bly** *adv.*

sep·a·rate (sĕp′ə-rāt′) *v.* **-rated, -rating, -rates.** —*tr.* **1. a.** To set or keep apart; divide; disunite. **b.** To space apart. **c.** To sort. **2.** To differentiate or discriminate between; distinguish. **3.** To remove from a mixture or combination; isolate. **4.** To part (a married couple) by decree: *He was separated from his wife last March.* **5.** To terminate a contractual relationship, as military service or employment; discharge. —*intr.* **1.** To become disconnected or severed; come apart; part. **2.** To withdraw: *The state threatened to separate from the Union.* **3.** To part company; disperse. **4.** To cease a conjugal relationship. **5.** To become divided into components or parts: *Oil and water tend to separate.* —*adj.* (sĕp′ər-ĭt, sĕp′rĭt). **1.** Set apart from the rest; not connected; disjoined; detached. **2.** *Archaic.* Withdrawn from others; solitary; isolated. **3.** Existing as an entity; independent. **4.** Dissimilar; distinct. **5.** Not shared; individual. —See Synonyms at **single.** —*n.* (sĕp′ər-ĭt, sĕp′rĭt). A garment, such as a skirt, jacket, or pair of slacks, that may be purchased separately and worn in various combinations with other garments. Usually used in the plural. [Middle English *separaten,* from Latin *sēparāre* (past participle *sēparātus*) : *sē,* apart (see **seu-**[2] in Appendix*) + *parāre,* to make ready, prepare (see **per-**[4] in Appendix*).] —**sep′a·rate·ly** *adv.* —**sep′a·rate·ness** *n.*

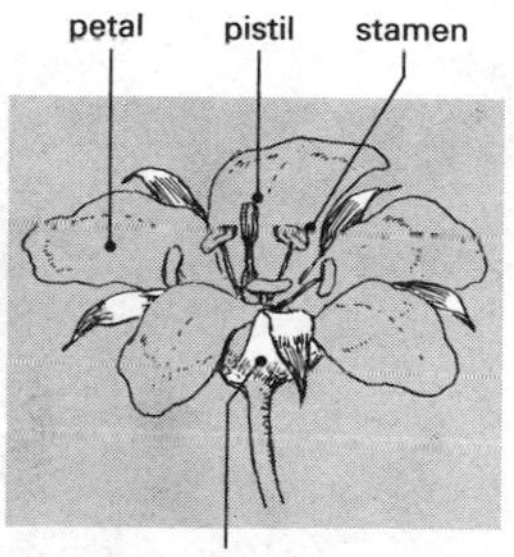

Synonyms: *separate, divide, part, sever, sunder, divorce, diverge, segregate.* These verbs refer to disjoining or disuniting. *Separate* applies both to putting apart by removing one or more components from a mass or by the act of dissociating, and to keeping apart by occupying a position between things: *The Pyrenees separate France and Spain. Divide* also has both these senses. With respect to putting apart, *divide* usually implies separation into predetermined portions or groups. The term can also refer to voluntary splitting or branching off. With respect to keeping apart, *divide* often implies separation into opposing or hostile groups. *Part* refers most often to separation of persons or of segments: *The curtains parted. Sever* usually applies to cutting a part from the whole or cutting a whole into sections; or it can refer figuratively to ending a relationship. In every case, abruptness and force are implied. *Sunder* stresses violent separation by tearing or wrenching apart. *Divorce* most often refers to the dissolution of a marriage or other close union. *Diverge* involves disjoining by going off in different directions from a common starting point or norm. *Segregate* principally refers to setting a group of persons apart from the mass or community at large; usually it implies discriminatory action against a racial group or social class thus isolated.

sep·a·ra·tion (sĕp′ə-rā′shən) *n.* **1. a.** The act or process of separating. **b.** The state of being separated. **2.** The place where a division or parting occurs. **3.** An interval or space that separates; a gap. **4. a.** *Law.* An agreement or court decree terminating the conjugal relationship of a husband and wife. **b.** Discharge, as from employment or military service.

separation center. An armed forces center handling the discharge of servicemen.

sep·a·ra·tist (sĕp′ər-ə-tĭst, sĕp′rə-, sĕp′ə-rā′tĭst) *n.* Also **sep·a·ra·tion·ist** (sĕp′ə-rā′shən-ĭst). One who secedes or advocates separation, especially from an established church; sectarian; schismatic. —**sep′a·ra·tism′** *n.* —**sep′a·ra·tis′tic** *adj.*

sep·a·ra·tive (sĕp′ə-rā′tĭv, sĕp′ər-ə-tĭv, sĕp′rə-) *adj.* Tending to separate or causing separation.

sep·a·ra·tor (sĕp′ə-rā′tər) *n.* **1.** One that separates. **2.** A device for separating cream from milk.

Se·phar·di (sə-fär′dē) *n., pl.* **-dim** (-dĭm). Also **Se·phar·a·di** (sə-fär′ə-dē). A member of one of the two main divisions of Jews; a Spanish or Portuguese Jew or one of his descendants. Compare **Ashkenazi.** [Modern Hebrew *Səphāradhī*, Spaniard, from *Səphāradh*, Spain.] —**Se·phar′dic** *adj.*

se·pi·a (sē′pē-ə) *n.* **1.** A dark-brown ink or pigment originally prepared from the secretion of the cuttlefish. **2. a.** A drawing or picture done in this pigment. **b.** A photograph in a brown tint. **3.** Dark grayish yellowish brown to dark or moderate olive brown. See **color.** —*adj.* **1.** Of the color sepia. **2.** Done in sepia. [Italian *seppia*, from Latin *sēpia*, cuttlefish, dark-brown pigment prepared from its secretion, from Greek, akin to *sēpein*, to rot. See **septic.**]

Se·pik (sā′pĭk). A river of New Guinea, rising at the western boundary of the Territory of New Guinea and flowing 700 miles generally east to the Pacific Ocean.

se·pi·o·lite (sē′pē-ə-līt′) *n. Mineralogy.* **Meerschaum** *(see).* [German *Sepiolith* : Greek *sēpion*, cuttlebone, from *sēpia*, cuttlefish (see **sepia**) + -LITE.]

se·poy (sē′poi′) *n.* In some Middle Eastern countries, a native regular soldier; especially, a native Indian soldier formerly serving under British command. [Perhaps from Portuguese *sipae*, from Urdu *sipāhī*, from Persian, from *sipāh*, army, from Old Persian *spāda*†.]

sep·pu·ku (sĕp′pōō-kōō) *n. Japanese.* **Hara-kiri.**

sep·sis (sĕp′sĭs) *n.* The presence of pathogenic organisms, or their toxins, in the blood or tissues. [New Latin, from Greek *sēpsis*, putrefaction, from *sēpein*, to make rotten. See **septic.**]

sept (sĕpt) *n.* A division of a tribe, especially in ancient and medieval Ireland; clan. [Perhaps variant of SECT.]

Sept. September.

sep·ta. Plural of **septum.**

sep·tal (sĕp′təl) *adj.* Of or pertaining to a septum.

sep·tar·i·um (sĕp-târ′ē-əm) *n., pl.* **-ia** (-ē-ə). An irregular polygonal system of calcite-filled cracks occurring in certain rock concretions. [New Latin : SEPT(I)- (septum) + -ARIUM.] —**sep·tar′i·an** *adj.*

sep·tate (sĕp′tāt′) *adj.* Having a septum or septa. [New Latin *septatus*, from SEPTUM.]

Sep·tem·ber (sĕp-tĕm′bər) *n. Abbr.* **Sept.** The ninth month of the year, according to the Gregorian calendar. September has 30 days. See **calendar.** [Middle English *Septembre*, from Old French, from Latin *September*, the seventh month (of the Roman calendar), from *septem*, seven. See **septm̥** in Appendix.*]

Sep·tem·brist (sĕp-tĕm′brĭst) *n.* **1.** One of the mob that massacred the imprisoned royalists in Paris, September 1792. **2.** A bloodthirsty revolutionist.

sep·te·nar·i·us (sĕp′tə-nâr′ē-əs) *n., pl.* **-narii** (-nâr′ē-ī′). *Prosody.* A Greek or Latin verse containing seven feet. [Latin *septēnārius*, SEPTENARY.]

sep·te·nar·y (sĕp′tə-nĕr′ē) *adj.* **1.** Of or pertaining to the number seven. **2.** Forming a group of seven or based on the number seven. —*n., pl.* **septenaries. 1.** A set or group of seven. **2.** A period of seven years or, rarely, weeks or days. [Latin *septēnārius*, from *septēnī*, seven each, from *septem*, seven. See **septm̥** in Appendix.*]

sep·ten·ni·al (sĕp-tĕn′ē-əl) *adj.* **1.** Occurring every seven years. **2.** Of or for seven years. —*n.* An event that occurs every seven years. [From Latin *septennium*, period of seven years, from *septennis*, of seven years : *septem*, seven (see **septm̥** in Appendix*) + *annus*, year (see **at-** in Appendix*).] —**sep·ten′ni·al·ly** *adv.*

sep·ten·tri·on (sĕp-tĕn′trē-ŏn′, -ən) *n. Archaic.* The north; northern regions. [Middle English *septemtrioun*, from Old French *septentrion*, from Latin *septentriōnēs*, "seven plowoxen," northern constellation : *septem*, seven (see **septm̥** in Appendix*) + *triōnēs*, plow oxen, plural of *triō*, plow ox (see **ter-**[2] in Appendix*).] —**sep·ten′tri·o·nal** (-trē-ə-nəl) *adj.*

sep·tet (sĕp-tĕt′) *n.* Also **sep·tette. 1.** A group of seven. **2.** *Music.* **a.** A composition for seven voices or instruments. **b.** The musicians performing such a composition. [German *Septet*, from Latin *septem*, seven. See **septm̥** in Appendix.*]

septi-[1]. Indicates seven; for example, **septilateral.** [Latin, from *septem*, seven. See **septm̥** in Appendix.*]

septi-[2], **sept-.** Indicates partition or septum; for example, **septarium, septifragal.** [From SEPTUM.]

sep·tic (sĕp′tĭk) *adj.* **1.** Of, pertaining to, or of the nature of sepsis. **2.** Causing sepsis; putrefactive. —*n.* A putrefactive substance. [Latin *sēpticus*, putrefying, septic, from Greek *sēptikos*, from *sēptos*, rotten, from *sēpein*†, to make rotten.] —**sep·tic′i·ty** (sĕp-tĭs′ə-tē) *n.*

sep·ti·ce·mi·a (sĕp′tĭ-sē′mē-ə) *n.* A systemic disease caused by pathogenic organisms or their toxins in the bloodstream. Also called "sapremia," "blood poisoning." [New Latin : Latin *sēpticus*, SEPTIC + -EMIA.] —**sep′ti·ce′mic** (-sē′mĭk) *adj.*

sep·ti·ci·dal (sĕp′tĭ-sīd′l) *adj. Botany.* Splitting along or through the septa. Said of a seed capsule. [SEPTI- (partition) + *-cidal*, from -CIDE.] —**sep′ti·ci′dal·ly** *adv.*

septic sore throat. An infection of the throat, often epidemic, caused by hemolytic streptococci and characterized by fever and inflammation of the tonsils. Also called "strep throat."

septic tank. A sewage disposal tank in which a continuous flow of waste material is decomposed by anaerobic bacteria.

sep·tif·ra·gal (sĕp-tĭf′rə-gəl) *adj. Botany.* Characterized by the breaking away of certain parts of the plant from its dividing walls. [From SEPTI- (partition) + Latin *frangere*, to break (see **bhreg-** in Appendix*).]

sep·ti·lat·er·al (sĕp′tə-lăt′ər-əl) *adj.* Seven-sided. [SEPTI- (seven) + LATERAL.]

sep·til·lion (sĕp-tĭl′yən) *n.* **1.** The cardinal number represented by 1 followed by 24 zeros, usually written 10^{24}. Called in British usage "quadrillion." See **number. 2.** In British usage, the cardinal number represented by 1 followed by 42 zeros, usually written 10^{42}. See **number.** [French : SEPTI- (seven) + (MI)LLION.] —**sep·til′lion** *adj.*

sep·til·lionth (sĕp-tĭl′yənth) *n.* **1.** The ordinal number one septillion in a series. **2.** One of a septillion equal parts. See **number.** —**sep·til′lionth** *adj.*

sep·tu·a·ge·nar·i·an (sĕp′chōō-ə-jə-nâr′ē-ən, sĕp′tōō-) *n.* A person seventy years old or between the ages of seventy and eighty. —*adj.* **1.** Seventy years old or between seventy and eighty. **2.** Pertaining or relating to a septuagenarian. [From Latin *septuāgēnārius*, noun and adjective, from *septuāgēnī*, seventy each, from *septuāgintā*, seventy. See **Septuagint.**]

Sep·tu·a·ges·i·ma (sĕp′chōō-ə-jĕs′ə-mə, sĕp′tōō-) *n.* The third Sunday before Lent. Also called "Septuagesima Sunday." [Middle English *Septuagesime*, Septuagesima, the seventy days following it, from Old French, from Late Latin *septuāgēsima*, from Latin, feminine of *septuāgēsimus*, seventieth, from *septuāgintā*, seventy. See **Septuagint.**]

Sep·tu·a·gint (sĕp′chōō-ə-jĭnt′, sĕp′tōō-) *n. Abbr.* **LXX.** A Greek translation of the Old Testament made in the third century B.C. [Latin *septuāgintā*, seventy, "the Seventy," designation of the 70 or 72 Jewish scholars who, according to an unhistorical tradition, completed the translation in 72 days on the island of Pharos : *septem*, seven (see **septm̥** in Appendix*) + *-gintā*, decimal suffix, ten times (see **dekm̥** in Appendix*).]

sep·tum (sĕp′təm) *n., pl.* **-ta** (-tə). A thin partition or membrane between two cavities or soft masses of tissue in a plant or animal. [Latin *sēptum, saeptum*, partition, from *sēpīre, saepīre*, to surround with a hedge, from *sēpes, saepes*†, hedge.]

sep·tu·ple (sĕp′tōō-pəl, -tyōō-pəl, sĕp-tōō′pəl, -tyōō′pəl) *adj.* **1.** Consisting of or containing seven. **2.** Multiplied by seven. —*tr.v.* **septupled, -pling, -ples.** To multiply by seven. [Late Latin *septuplus*, sevenfold : Latin *septem*, seven (see **septm̥** in Appendix*) + *-plus*, "-fold" (see **pel-**[3] in Appendix*).]

sep·ul·cher (sĕp′əl-kər) *n.* Also *chiefly British* **sep·ul·chre. 1.** A burial vault. **2.** A receptacle for sacred relics, especially in an altar. —*tr.v.* **sepulchered, -chering, -chers.** Also *chiefly British* **sep·ul·chre, -chred, -chring, -chres.** To place in a sepulcher; inter. [Middle English *sepulcre*, from Old French, from Latin *sepulcrum*, from *sepultus*, past participle of *sepelīre*, to bury. See **sep-** in Appendix.*]

se·pul·chral (sə-pŭl′krəl) *adj.* **1.** Of or pertaining to a sepulcher. **2.** Suggestive of the grave; funereal. —**se·pul′chral·ly** *adv.*

sep·ul·ture (sĕp′əl-chər) *n. Archaic.* **1.** The act of interment; burial. **2.** A sepulcher. [Middle English, from Old French, from Latin *sepultūra*, from *sepultus*, "buried." See **sepulcher.**]

seq. 1. sequel. **2.** the following (Latin *sequēns*).

seqq. the following (things) (Latin *sequentia*).

se·qua·cious (sĭ-kwā′shəs) *adj.* **1.** *Archaic.* Disposed to follow any leader; dependent. **2.** Following in logical sequence and regularity. [From Latin *sequāx* (stem *sequāc-*), pursuing, sequacious, from *sequī*, to follow. See **sekw-**[1] in Appendix.*] —**se·qua′cious·ly** *adv.* —**se·quac′i·ty** (sĭ-kwăs′ə-tē) *n.*

se·quel (sē′kwĕl) *n. Abbr.* **seq. 1.** Anything that follows; a continuation. **2.** A literary work complete in itself but continuing the narrative of an earlier work. **3.** A result or consequence. —See Synonyms at **effect.** [Middle English *sequele*, from Old French *sequelle*, from Latin *sequēla*, from *sequī*, to follow. See **sekw-**[1] in Appendix.*]

se·que·la (sĭ-kwĕl′ə) *n., pl.* **-lae** (-lē). Something that follows; especially, a pathological condition resulting from a disease. [Latin *sequēla*, SEQUEL.]

se·quence (sē′kwəns) *n.* **1.** A following of one thing after another; succession. **2.** An order of succession; arrangement. **3.** A related or continuous series. **4.** Three or more playing cards in consecutive order; a run. **5.** *Motion Pictures.* A series of single shots so edited as to constitute an aesthetic or dramatic unit; an episode. **6.** *Music.* A melodic or harmonic pattern successively repeated at different pitches, with or without a key change. **7.** *Roman Catholic Church.* A hymn read between the gradual and the gospel. **8.** *Mathematics.* An ordered set of quantities, as x, $2x^2$, $3x^3$, $4x^4$. —See Synonyms at **series.** [Late Latin *sequentia*, from Latin *sequēns*, present participle of *sequī*, to follow. See **sekw-**[1] in Appendix.*]

se·quent (sē′kwənt) *adj.* **1.** Following in order or time; subsequent. **2.** Following as a result; consequent. —*n.* A result; consequence. [Latin *sequēns*. See **sequence.**]

se·quen·tial (sĭ-kwĕn′shəl) *adj.* **1.** Forming or characterized by a sequence, as of notes or units. **2.** Sequent. —**se·quen′ti·al′i·ty** *n.* —**se·quen′tial·ly** *adv.*

se·ques·ter (sĭ-kwĕs′tər) *v.* **-tered, -tering, -ters.** —*tr.* **1.** To remove or set apart; segregate. **2.** *Law.* To take temporary possession of (property) as security against legal claims. **3.** *International Law.* To requisition and confiscate (enemy property). **4.** To withdraw into seclusion: *"there was a time . . . when*

ă pat/ā pay/âr care/ä father/b bib/ch church/d deed/ĕ pet/ē be/f fife/g gag/h hat/hw which/ĭ pit/ī pie/îr pier/j judge/k kick/l lid, needle/m mum/n no, sudden/ng thing/ŏ pot/ō toe/ô paw, for/oi noise/ou out/ŏŏ took/ōō boot/p pop/r roar/s sauce/sh ship, dish/

a man might properly sequester himself, to review his life and purify his heart" (Samuel Johnson). —*intr. Chemistry.* To undergo sequestration. [Late Latin *sequestrāre*, to separate, give up for safekeeping, from Latin *sequester*, depository. See **sekw-**[1] in Appendix.*]

se·ques·trant (sĭ-kwĕs'trənt) *n.* A chemical that promotes sequestration. [From SEQUESTER.]

se·ques·trate (sĭ-kwĕs'trāt') *tr.v.* **-trated, -trating, -trates.** 1. *Law.* To seize; confiscate. 2. *Archaic.* To sequester. [Late Latin *sequestrāre*, SEQUESTER.] —**se'ques·tra'tor** (sē'kwĕs-trā'tər, sĭ-kwĕs'trā-tər) *n.*

se·ques·tra·tion (sē'kwĕs-trā'shən) *n.* 1. The act of sequestering; segregation. 2. *Law.* **a.** Seizure of property. **b.** A writ authorizing seizure of property. 3. *Chemistry.* The inhibition or prevention of normal ion behavior by combination with added materials, especially the prevention of metallic ion precipitation from solution by formation of a coordination complex with a phosphate.

se·ques·trum (sĭ-kwĕs'trəm) *n., pl.* **-tra** (-trə). A dead bone fragment separated from healthy bone. [New Latin, from Latin, deposit, "something separated," from *sequester*, depository. See **sekw-**[1] in Appendix.*]

se·quin (sē'kwĭn) *n.* 1. A small shiny decorative disk, often sewn on cloth; a spangle. 2. A gold coin of the Venetian Republic. In this sense, also called "zecchino." [French, from Italian *zecchino*, from *zecca*, the mint, from Arabic *sikkah*, coin die.]

se·quoi·a (sĭ-kwoi'ə) *n.* Any very large evergreen tree of the genus *Sequoia*, which includes the **redwood** and the **giant sequoia** (*both of which see*). [After SEQUOYA.]

Sequoia National Park. An area occupying 604 square miles in the Sierra Nevada of central California, noted for its stands of sequoias and its mountain scenery.

Se·quoy·a (sĭ-kwoi'ə). Also **Se·quoy·ah.** Known as George Guess. 1770?–1843. American Indian leader and scholar; recorded the Cherokee language of his tribe.

ser. 1. serial. 2. series. 3. sermon.

se·ra. Alternate plural of **serum.**

sé·rac (sə-răk'; *French* sā-räk') *n.* A large mass of ice broken off the main body of a glacier and remaining behind in a crevasse after glacial movement or melting. [Swiss French, piece of white cheese (which the ice resembles), perhaps from Latin *serum*, whey. See **ser-**[2] in Appendix.*]

se·ra·glio (sĭ-răl'yō, -räl'yō) *n., pl.* **-glios.** 1. A large harem. 2. A sultan's palace. [Italian *serraglio*, probably from Turkish *serai†*, a palace, lodging, from Persian.]

Se·ra·je·vo. See **Sarajevo.**

se·ra·pe (sə-rä'pē) *n.* Also **sa·ra·pe.** A woolen cloak or poncho worn by Latin-American men. [Mexican Spanish *sarape†*.]

ser·aph (sĕr'əf) *n., pl.* **-aphs** or **-aphim** (-ə-fĭm) or **-aphin** (-ə-fĭn). 1. A celestial being having three pairs of wings. Isaiah 6:2. 2. One of the nine orders of angels. See **angel.** [Back-formation from plural seraphim, from Middle English *seraphin*, Old English *seraphin*, from Late Latin *seraphim, seraphin*, from Hebrew *Səraphīm*, plural of *sārāph*.] —**se·raph'ic** (sĭ-răf'ĭk), **se·raph'i·cal** *adj.* —**se·raph'i·cal·ly** *adv.*

Se·ra·pis (sĭ-rā'pĭs). An ancient Egyptian god of the lower world, also worshiped in ancient Greece and Rome.

Serb (sûrb) *n.* A Serbian. [Serbo-Croatian *Srb†*.]

Serb. Serbia; Serbian.

Ser·bi·a (sûr'bē-ə). *Abbr.* **Serb.** Formerly **Ser·vi·a** (sûr'vē-ə). *Serbo-Croatian* **Srbi·ja** (sûr'bē-yä'). A constituent republic of Yugoslavia, formerly an independent state, occupying 34,194 square miles in the eastern part of the country. Population, 7,642,000. Capital, Belgrade. [Russian *Serbija*, from Serbo-Croatian *Srb*, SERB.]

Ser·bi·an (sûr'bē-ən) *n. Abbr.* **Serb.** 1. A member of a southern Slavic people that is the dominant ethnic group of Serbia and adjacent republics of Yugoslavia. 2. A Serbo-Croatian. —*adj.* 1. Of Serbia or the Serbians. 2. Serbo-Croatian.

Ser·bo-Cro·a·tian (sûr'bō-krō-ā'shən) *n.* The Slavic language of the Serbs and Croats of Yugoslavia, generally written in Cyrillic letters in Serbia and in Roman letters in Croatia. Also called "Croatian." —*adj.* Of or pertaining to this language or those who speak it.

Serbs, Cro·ats, and Slo·venes, Kingdom of the. The former name for **Yugoslavia.**

sere¹ (sîr) *adj.* Also **sear.** Withered; dry. —*n.* Variant of **sear.** [Middle English *sere*, Old English *sēar*. See **saus-** in Appendix.*]

sere² (sîr) *n.* The entire sequence of ecological communities successively occupying an area. [From SERIES.]

ser·e·nade (sĕr'ə-nād', sĕr'ə-nād') *n.* 1. An honorific musical performance; especially, one given by a lover for his sweetheart. 2. An instrumental form comprising characteristics of the suite and the sonata. —*v.* (sĕr'ə-nād') **serenaded, -nading, -nades.** —*tr.* To perform a serenade for. —*intr.* To perform a serenade. [French *sérénade*, from Italian *serenata*, evening serenade, from *sereno*, serene (influenced in meaning by *sera*, evening), from Latin *serēnus*, SERENE.] —**ser'e·nad'er** *n.*

ser·en·dip·i·ty (sĕr'ən-dĭp'ə-tē) *n.* The faculty of making fortunate and unexpected discoveries by accident. [Coined by Horace Walpole after the characters in the fairy tale *The Three Princes of Serendip*, who made such discoveries.] —**ser'en·dip'i·tous** *adj.*

se·rene (sĭ-rēn') *adj.* 1. Unruffled; tranquil; dignified. 2. Unclouded; fair; bright. 3. *Often capital* **S.** August. Used as part of a title of respect for certain royal personages: *His Serene Highness.* —See Synonyms at **calm.** [Latin *serēnus*, serene,

bright, clear. See **ksero-** in Appendix.*] —**se·rene'ly** *adv.* —**se·rene'ness** *n.*

se·ren·i·ty (sĭ-rĕn'ə-tē) *n., pl.* **-ties.** 1. The state or quality of being serene; dignity; tranquillity; quiet: *"this best and meekest woman bore/With such serenity her husband's woes"* (Byron). 2. Clearness; brightness. —See Synonyms at **equanimity.**

Se·reth. See **Siret.**

serf (sûrf) *n.* 1. A slave, especially a member of the lowest feudal class in medieval Europe, bound to the land and owned by a lord. 2. Any person in servitude. [Old French, from Latin *servus*, slave. See **servus** in Appendix.*] —**serf'dom** *n.*

serge (sûrj) *n.* A twilled cloth of worsted or worsted and wool, often used for suits. [Middle English *sarge, serge*, from Old French, from Vulgar Latin *sārica* (unattested), from Latin *sērica*, feminine of *sēricus*, of Seres (a people), from Greek *sērikos*, from *Sēres*, Seres. See **silk.**]

ser·geant (sär'jənt) *n.* Also *chiefly British* **ser·jeant** (for senses 2, 3). *Abbr.* **Sgt.** 1. **a.** Any of several ranks of noncommissioned officers in the U.S. Army, Air Force, or Marine Corps. **b.** One holding any of these ranks. 2. **a.** The rank of police officer next below a captain, lieutenant, or inspector. **b.** One holding this rank. 3. A **sergeant at arms** (*see*). [Middle English *sergeaunte, sergant*, from Old French *sergent*, from Latin *serviēns*, present participle of *servire*, to serve, from *servus*, slave. See **servus** in Appendix.*] —**ser'gean·cy, ser'geant·ship'** *n.*

sergeant at arms. An officer appointed to keep order within an organization, such as a legislative, judicial, or social body. Also called "sergeant."

sergeant first class. *Abbr.* **Sfc.** A noncommissioned officer next below master sergeant in the U.S. Army.

sergeant fish. The **cobia** (*see*).

sergeant major. *Abbr.* **Sgt. Maj.** 1. A noncommissioned officer serving as chief administrative assistant of a headquarters unit of the U.S. Army, Air Force, or Marine Corps. 2. *British.* A noncommissioned officer of the highest rank. 3. A fish, *Abudefduf saxatilis*, of warm seas, having a flattened body with dark vertical stripes.

Ser·gi·pe (sər-zhē'pə). The smallest state (8,130 square miles) of Brazil, in the northeastern part of the country. Population, 821,000. Capital, Aracajú.

se·ri·al (sîr'ē-əl) *adj.* 1. Of, forming, or arranged in a series: *serial numbers.* 2. Published or produced in installments, as a novel or television drama. 3. Pertaining to such publication or production. 4. *Music.* Pertaining to or based on a 12-tone row. —*n. Abbr.* **ser.** A literary or dramatic work published or produced in installments. [From SERIES.] —**se'ri·al·ly** *adv.*

se·ri·al·ize (sîr'ē-əl-īz') *tr.v.* **-ized, -izing, -izes.** To write or publish in serial form. —**se'ri·al·i·za'tion** (sîr'ē-əl-ĭ-zā'shən) *n.*

se·ri·ate (sîr'ē-āt', -ĭt) *adj.* Arranged or occurring in a series or in rows. [From SERIES.]

se·ri·a·tim (sîr'ē-ā'tĭm, -ă'təm, sĕr'-) *adv.* One after another; in a series. [Medieval Latin, from Latin *seriēs*, SERIES.]

se·ri·ceous (sĭ-rĭsh'əs) *adj.* 1. Silky. 2. *Botany.* Covered with soft, silky hairs. [Late Latin *sēriceus*, from Latin *sēricus*, of Seres. See **serge.**]

ser·i·cin (sĕr'ə-sĭn) *n.* A viscous, gelatinous protein that forms on the surface of raw-silk fibers. [Latin *sēricus*, silken, of Seres (see **serge**) + -IN.]

ser·i·cul·ture (sĕr'ə-kŭl'chər) *n.* The production of raw silk and the raising of silkworms for this purpose. [French *sériculture*: Latin *sēricus*, silken, of Seres (see **serge**) + CULTURE.] —**ser'i·cul'tur·al** *adj.* —**ser'i·cul'tur·ist** *n.*

ser·i·e·ma (sĕr'ĭ-ē'mə) *n.* Either of two cranelike South American birds, *Cariama cristata* or *Chunga burmeisteri*, having a tuftlike crest at the base of the bill. [Tupi *seriema, çariama*, "crested."]

se·ries (sîr'ēz) *n., pl.* **series.** See Usage note below. *Abbr.* **ser.** 1. **a.** A group of events, or objects corresponding to such events, related by order of occurrence, especially by succession: *a series of accidents; a series of wrecks.* **b.** A group of thematically connected works or performances. 2. A group of objects related by a linearly varying morphological or configurational characteristic: *a radioactive decay series; the paraffin series; stratigraphic series.* 3. *Mathematics.* The indicated sum of a finite or of a sequentially ordered infinite set of terms. 4. *Grammar.* A succession of coordinate elements in a sentence. [Latin *seriēs*, from *serere*, to join. See **ser-**[3] in Appendix.*]

Synonyms: *series, succession, progression, sequence, chain, train, string, set.* These nouns denote groups of things considered from the standpoint of order or arrangement. *Series* refers to like or related things or events arranged or occurring in order. *Succession* applies to like or related things or events that follow each other, generally in order of time and without interruption. A *progression* is a series that reveals a definite pattern of advance. In a *sequence*, things follow one another in chronological or numerical order or in order that indicates causal or logical relationship or a recurrent pattern. *Chain* suggests a series of things closely linked or a sequence of closely related ideas or events. *Train* can apply to a procession of persons or vehicles or to a sequence of ideas or events. *String* refers to a continuous series or succession of like things or events, sometimes with the suggestion of impressive length. *Set* applies to a number of matching or similar things that have a common function or purpose or that form a whole. It can also denote a group of persons closely associated.

Usage: *Series* is both a singular and a plural form. When it has the singular sense of "one set," it takes a singular verb, even when *series* is followed by *of* and a plural noun: *A series of lectures is scheduled.*

sergeant major

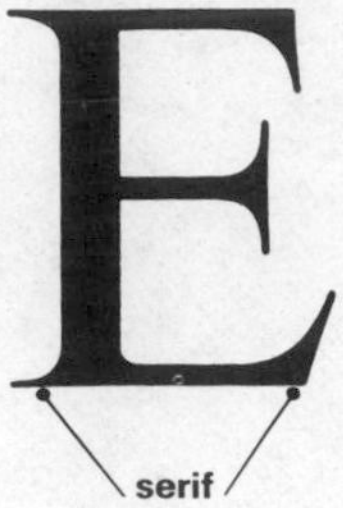

series circuit. An electric circuit connected so that current passes through each circuit element in turn without branching.
se·ries-wound (sîr′ēz-wound′) *adj.* Designating an electric motor or dynamo in which the armature circuit and the field circuit are connected in series with the external circuit. Compare **shunt-wound.**
ser·if (sĕr′ĭf) *n.* Also *chiefly British* **cer·iph.** *Printing.* A fine line finishing off the main strokes, as at the top and bottom of *M* or ending the cross stroke of *T.* [Perhaps from Dutch *schreef,* line, from Middle Dutch *screve,* from *scriven,* to write, from Latin *scribere.* See **skeri-** in Appendix.*]
ser·i·graph (sĕr′ə-grăf, -gräf) *n.* A print made by the silk-screen process. [Latin *sēri(cum),* SILK + -GRAPH.] —**se·rig′ra·phy** (sə-rĭg′rə-fē) *n.*
ser·in (sĕr′ən) *n.* Any of several Old World finches of the genus *Serinus,* having yellowish plumage. See **canary.** [French, from Old French, perhaps from Old Provençal *serena,* bee-eater, from Latin *sīrēn,* a kind of bird, from *Sīrēn,* SIREN (the Sirens were thought to be birds with the faces of virgins).]
ser·ine (sĕr′ēn′) *n.* An amino acid, $C_3H_7NO_3$, that is a common constituent of many proteins. [SER(ICIN) + -INE.]
Se·rin·ga·pa·tam (sə-rĭng′gə-pə-tăm′). A town in the southern part of Mysore State, Republic of India, the former seat of the sultans of Mysore. Population, 11,000.
se·ri·o·com·ic (sîr′ē-ō-kŏm′ĭk) *adj.* Also **se·ri·o·com·i·cal** (-ĭ-kəl). Both serious and comic. [SERIO(US) + COMIC.]
se·ri·ous (sîr′ē-əs) *adj.* **1.** Grave in character, quality, or mien; sober. **2.** Said or done in earnest; sincere. **3.** Concerned with important rather than trivial matters; weighty. **4.** Requiring extensive effort or consideration; difficult. **5.** Causing anxiety; critical; dangerous. —See Synonyms at **critical.** [Middle English *seryous,* from Old French *serieux,* from Late Latin *sēriōsus,* from Latin *sērius.* See **wer-²** in Appendix.*] —**se′ri·ous·ly** *adv.* —**se′ri·ous·ness** *n.*

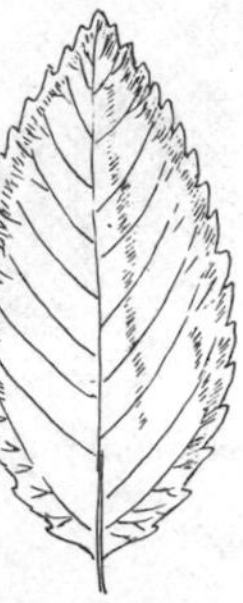
serrate
Serrate leaf

Synonyms: *serious, sober, grave, solemn, earnest, sedate, staid.* These adjectives are compared as they refer to the appearance, air, manner, or disposition of persons. *Serious* applies broadly to one whose main concern is with responsibility and work as opposed to play. *Sober* strengthens the implications of dedication to purpose, circumspect behavior, and self-control. *Grave* suggests dignity and somberness associated with weighty affairs, especially those that give cause for deep concern. *Solemn* adds to the foregoing the suggestion of formality and impressiveness. *Earnest* implies manifest sincerity and intensity of purpose. *Sedate* implies a calm, dignified manner. *Staid* emphasizes unvarying dignity and observance of propriety.
ser·jeant. *Chiefly British.* Variant of **sergeant.**
ser·mon (sûr′mən) *n. Abbr.* **ser. 1.** A religious discourse delivered as part of a church service. **2.** Any discourse or speech; especially, a lengthy and tedious reproof or exhortation. [Middle English *sermun,* from Norman French, from Latin *sermō* (stem *sermōn-*), a speaking, a discourse. See **ser-³** in Appendix.*] —**ser·mon′ic** (-mŏn′ĭk), **ser·mon′i·cal** *adj.*
ser·mon·ize (sûr′mən-īz′) *v.* **-ized, -izing, -izes.** —*tr.* To deliver a sermon to (someone). —*intr.* To deliver, or speak as though delivering, a sermon. —**ser′mon·iz′er** *n.*
Sermon on the Mount. A discourse of Jesus, delivered on the Mount of Olives. Matthew 5–7.

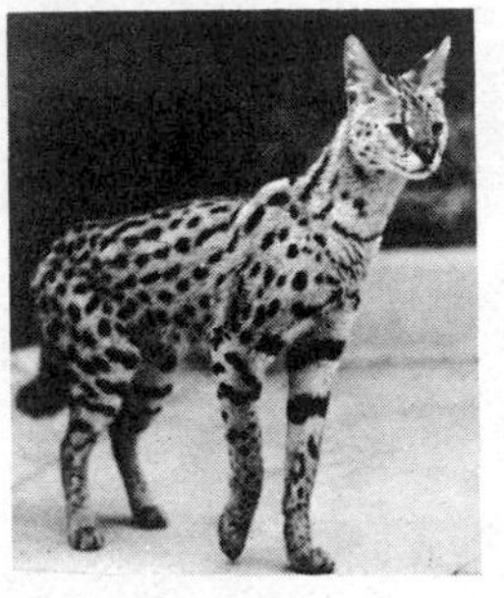
serval

sero–. Indicates serum; for example, **serology.** [From SERUM.]
se·rol·o·gy (sĭ-rŏl′ə-jē) *n.* The medical study of serum. [SERO- + -LOGY.] —**ser′o·log′ic** (sîr′ə-lŏj′ĭk), **ser′o·log′i·cal** *adj.* —**se·rol′o·gist** *n.*
se·ro·sa (sĭ-rō′sə, -zə) *n., pl.* **-sas** or **sae** (-sē′). A **serous membrane** *(see).* [New Latin, feminine of *serosus,* SEROUS.]
se·ro·ther·a·py (sîr′ō-thĕr′ə-pē) *n.* Treatment of disease by administration of a serum or antitoxin. [SERO- + THERAPY.]
se·rot·i·nous (sĭ-rŏt′ə-nəs) *adj.* Also **se·rot·i·nal** (-nəl). *Biology.* Late in developing or blooming. [Latin *sērōtinus,* late, from *sērō,* late, from *sērus,* late. See **sē-²** in Appendix.]
ser·o·to·nin (sĕr′ə-tō′nĭn) *n.* An organic compound, $C_{10}H_{12}N_2O$, found in animal and human tissue, especially the brain, blood serum, and gastric mucosa, and capable of raising the blood pressure. [SERO- + TON(IC) + -IN.]
se·rous (sîr′əs) *adj.* Containing, secreting, or resembling serum. [New Latin *serosus,* from SERUM.]
serous membrane. A thin membrane lining a closed bodily cavity. Also called "serosa."
se·row (sə-rō′) *n.* Any of several goatlike antelopes of the genus *Capricornis,* of mountainous regions of eastern Asia, having short horns and a dark coat. [Lepcha *să-ro,* Tibetan goat.]
Ser·pens (sûr′pənz, -pĕnz′) *n.* A constellation in the equatorial region of the northern sky, made up of two parts: *Serpens Cauda,* the "tail," and *Serpens Caput,* the "head," both near Hercules and Ophiuchus. Also called the "Serpent." [Latin *serpēns,* SERPENT.]

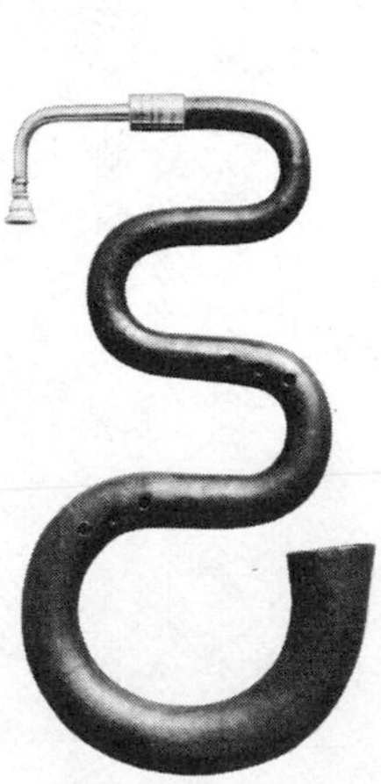
serpent
Belgian brass serpent of the early 18th century

ser·pent (sûr′pənt) *n.* **1.** A snake. **2.** *Often capital* **S. a.** The creature that tempted Eve. Genesis 3. **b.** Satan. **3.** A subtle, sly, or treacherous person. **4.** A kind of firework that writhes while burning. **5.** *Music.* A deep-voiced wind instrument of serpentine shape, used principally in the 18th century, approximately eight feet in length and made of brass or wood. [Middle English, from Old French, from Latin *serpēns* (stem *serpent-*), "crawling thing," from the present participle of *serpere,* to crawl, creep. See **serp-²** in Appendix.*]
ser·pen·tine (sûr′pən-tēn′, -tīn′) *adj.* **1.** Of or resembling a serpent, as in form or movement; sinuous; winding. **2.** Having the qualities of a serpent; subtle, sly, and slinky. —*n.* A greenish, brownish, or spotted mineral, $3MgO \cdot 2SiO_2 \cdot 2H_2O$, used as a source of magnesium and in architecture as a decorative stone. [Middle English, from Old French *serpentin,* from Late Latin *serpentīnus,* from Latin *serpēns,* SERPENT.]
serpent star. A marine animal, the **brittle star** *(see).*
ser·pi·go (sər-pī′gō) *n.* A spreading skin eruption or lesion, such as ringworm. [Middle English, from Medieval Latin *serpīgo,* from Latin *serpere,* to creep. See **serp-²** in Appendix.*] —**ser·pig′i·nous** (sər-pĭj′ə-nəs) *adj.*
Ser·ra (sĕr′ə), **Junipero.** Original name, Miguel José Serra. 1713–1784. Spanish Franciscan missionary; established nine missions in California.
ser·ra·nid (sə-rā′nĭd, -răn′ĭd) *adj.* Of or belonging to the family Serranidae, which includes the sea basses and groupers. —*n.* A fish of this family. [New Latin *Serranidae,* from *Serranus* (genus), from Latin *serra,* saw (perhaps from its serrated dorsal fin). See **serrate.**]
ser·rate (sĕr′āt′, -ĭt) *adj.* Also **ser·rat·ed** (-rā′tĭd). **1.** Having notched, toothlike projections. **2.** Having the edge or margin notched with toothlike projections: *serrate leaves.* [Latin *serrātus,* saw-shaped, from Latin *serra*†, saw.]
ser·ra·tion (sĕ-rā′shən) *n.* **1.** The state of being serrate. **2.** A series or set of teeth or notches. **3.** A single such tooth or notch in a serrate edge.
ser·ried (sĕr′ēd) *adj.* Pressed together in rows; in close order: *"Troops in serried ranks assembled"* (W.S. Gilbert). [Perhaps from the past participle of obsolete *serry,* to press together, from Old French *serré,* past participle of *serrer,* to crowd, from Vulgar Latin *serrāre* (unattested), from Latin *sērāre,* to fasten with a bolt, from *sera,* lock. See **ser-³** in Appendix.*]
ser·ru·late (sĕr′yə-lĭt, -lāt′, sĕr′ə-) *adj.* Also **ser·ru·lat·ed** (-lā′tĭd). Having small, toothlike notches along the edge; minutely serrate. [New Latin *serrulatus,* from Latin *serrula,* diminutive of *serra,* saw. See **serrate.**]
ser·tu·lar·i·an (sûr′cho͝o-lâr′ē-ən, sûr′tə-lâr′-) *n.* Any of various colonial hydroids of the genus *Sertularia,* having stalkless polyps arranged in pairs along a long, branching stem. [From New Latin *Sertularia,* from Latin *sertula,* diminutive of *serta,* melilot, garland, from the feminine past participle of *serere,* to join, entwine. See **ser-³** in Appendix.*]
se·rum (sîr′əm) *n., pl.* **-rums** or **sera** (sîr′ə). **1.** The clear yellowish fluid obtained upon separating whole blood into its solid and liquid components. **2.** The fluid from the tissues of immunized animals, used especially as an antitoxin. **3.** Any watery fluid from animal tissue, as is found in edema. **4. Whey** *(see).* [Latin, whey, serum. See **ser-²** in Appendix.*]
serum albumin. A protein fraction of blood serum involved in maintaining osmotic pressure, used in the treatment of shock.
serum globulin. A protein fraction of blood serum chiefly containing antibodies.
serv. 1. servant. **2.** service.
ser·val (sûr′vəl, sər-văl′) *n.* A long-legged wild cat, *Felis serval,* of Africa, having a yellowish coat with black spots. [French, from Portuguese *(lobo) cerval,* deerlike (wolf), from *cervo,* deer, from Latin *cervus.* See **ker-¹** in Appendix.*]
ser·vant (sûr′vənt) *n. Abbr.* **serv. 1.** Someone privately employed to perform domestic services. **2.** Someone publicly employed to perform services, as for a government. **3.** Someone expressing submission, recognizance, or debt to another: *your obedient servant.* [Middle English, from Old French, from the present participle of *servir,* to SERVE.]
serve (sûrv) *v.* **served, serving, serves.** —*tr.* **1.** To work for; be a servant to. **2. a.** To prepare and offer, as food: *serve tea.* **b.** To place food before (someone); wait on: *serve the vicar tea.* **3. a.** To provide goods and services for (customers): *serve the public at the same location for 30 years.* **b.** To supply (goods or services) to customers. **c.** To assist (the celebrant) during Mass. **4.** To be of assistance to; promote the interests of; aid: *"Both major parties today seek to serve the national interest"* (John F. Kennedy). **5.** To spend or complete (time), as in prison or in elective office: *serve four terms in Congress.* **6.** To fight or undergo military service for: *serve one's country as an airman.* **7.** To give homage and obedience to: *"Go thy ways, wench. Serve God."* (Shakespeare). **8.** To requite: *Punish her; it will serve her right.* **9.** To copulate with. Used of male animals: *The buck served the doe.* **10.** To meet a need or requirement for; suffice: *serve the purpose.* **11.** To be used by: *One phone serves the whole office.* **12.** To function for: *His cunning served him well.* **13.** *Law.* **a.** To deliver or present (a legal writ or summons). **b.** To present such a writ to. **14.** To put (the ball) in play, as in tennis, badminton, and jai alai. **15.** To bind or whip (a rope) with fine cord or wire. —*intr.* **1.** To be employed as a servant. **2.** To do a term of duty: *serve in the U.S. Air Force.* **3.** To act in a particular capacity: *serve as a clerk.* **4.** To be of service or use; to function: *serve as a reminder.* **5.** To meet requirements or needs; satisfy; suffice: *"'Tis not so deep as a well . . . but 'twill serve"* (Shakespeare). **6.** To wait on table: *serve at luncheon.* **7.** To put a ball or the like into play, as in games played on a court. **8.** To assist the celebrant during Mass. —*n.* The right, manner, or act of serving in many games played on a court. [Middle English *serven,* from Old French *servir,* from Latin *servīre,* from *servus,* slave. See **servus** in Appendix.*]
serv·er (sûr′vər) *n.* **1.** One that serves. **2.** Something used in serving, as a tray. **3.** An attendant to the celebrant at a Mass. **4.** The player who serves, as in tennis or badminton.
Ser·ve·tus (sər-vē′təs), **Michael.** Spanish name, Miguel Serveto. 1511–1553. Spanish theologian and physician; described circulation of the blood; executed for heresy.
Ser·vi·a. The former name for **Serbia.**
serv·ice (sûr′vĭs) *n. Abbr.* **serv. 1.** The occupation or duties of a servant. **2.** Employment in duties or work for another; espe-

ă pat/ā pay/âr care/ä father/b bib/ch church/d deed/ĕ pet/ē be/f fife/g gag/h hat/hw which/ĭ pit/ī pie/îr pier/j judge/k kick/l lid, needle/m mum/n no, sudden/ng thing/ŏ pot/ō toe/ô paw, for/oi noise/ou out/o͝o took/o͞o boot/p pop/r roar/s sauce/sh ship, dish/

cially, such employment for a government. **3.** A government branch or department and its employees: *civil service.* **4.** The armed forces of a nation, or any branch thereof. **5.** Work or duties performed for a superior. **6.** Work done for others as an occupation or business: *a shoe-repair service.* **7.** Installation, maintenance, or repairs provided or guaranteed by a dealer or manufacturer. **8.** A facility providing the public with the use of something, such as water or transportation. **9.** Acts of devotion to God; witness. **10.** A religious rite. **11.** An act of assistance or benefit to another or others; favor. **12.** The serving of food or the manner in which it is served. **13.** A set of dishes or utensils: *a silver tea service.* **14.** The act, manner, or right of serving in many games, as tennis, volleyball, and jai alai, that are played on a court; a serve. **15.** Copulation with a female. Used of male animals. **16.** *Law.* The serving of a writ or summons. **17.** Any material, as cord, used in binding or wrapping rope. *—adj.* **1.** Of or for service; useful. **2.** Not for use by the general public; reserved for employees, deliveries, or the like: *a service elevator.* **3.** Of or pertaining to the armed forces. *—tr.v.* **serviced, -vicing, -vices. 1.** To make fit for use; adjust; repair; maintain: *service a car.* **2.** To provide services to, as a commodity used by the public. **3.** To copulate with. Used of male animals. [Middle English *servis(e),* from Old French *service,* from Latin *servitium,* servitude, slavery, from *servus,* slave. See **servus** in Appendix.*]

Usage: *Service* (verb) is well established in the sense dealing with work, such as installation or maintenance, necessary for the continuing operation of something, but is not invariably interchangeable with the more general *serve. Serve* is preferable to *service* when the benefit involved is more general: *A radio network serves three states* or *Two newspapers serve this area.*

Ser·vice (sûr′vĭs), **Robert W(illiam).** 1874–1958. English-born Canadian writer of novels and ballads.

serv·ice·a·ble (sûr′vĭs-ə-bəl) *adj.* **1.** Ready for service; usable. **2.** Able to give good service; long-wearing; durable. **—serv′ice·a·bil′i·ty. serv′ice·a·ble·ness** *n.* **—serv′ice·a·bly** *adv.*

serv·ice·ber·ry (sûr′vĭs-bĕr′ē, sär′vĭs-) *n., pl.* **-ries.** The **shadbush** *(see),* or one of its fruit. [SERVICE (TREE) + BERRY.]

service cap. A visored flat-topped military cap.

serv·ice·man (sûr′vĭs-măn′, -mən) *n., pl.* **-men** (-mĕn′, -mĭn). Also **service man** (for sense 2). **1.** A member of the armed forces. **2.** A man whose work is the maintenance and repair of equipment.

service mark. A device that identifies a service offered to the public, as by an airline or insurance company.

service station. 1. A **filling station** *(see).* **2.** A place where services can be obtained, as repair, maintenance, or replacement of electrical or mechanical devices.

serv·ice tree (sûr′vĭs, sär′-). Either of two Old World trees, *Sorbus domestica* or *S. torminalis,* having clusters of white flowers and brownish, edible fruit. [From Middle English *serves,* plural of *serve,* Old English *syrfe,* from Vulgar Latin *sorbea* (unattested), from Latin *sorbus*†.]

ser·vi·ette (sûr′vē-ĕt′) *n.* A table napkin. [French, from Old French, towel, napkin, from *servir,* to SERVE.]

ser·vile (sûr′vəl, -vīl′) *adj.* **1.** Slavish in character or attitude; obsequious; submissive. **2.** Of or suitable to a slave or servant: *"freed from servile bands / of hope to rise or fear to fall"* (Bunyan). —See Synonyms at **obedient.** [Middle English, from Latin *servīlis,* from *servus,* slave. See **servus** in Appendix.*] **—ser′vile·ly** *adv.* **—ser′vile·ness, ser·vil′i·ty** (sər-vĭl′ə-tē) *n.*

serv·ing (sûr′vĭng) *n.* **1.** The act of one that serves. **2.** An individual portion or helping of food or drink: *This recipe makes four servings.* *—adj.* Pertaining to, related to, or used for serving: *a serving dish.*

ser·vi·tor (sûr′və-tər, -tôr′) *n.* One who performs the duties of a servant to another; an attendant. [Middle English, from Old French, from Latin *servitor,* from Latin *servīre,* to SERVE.] **—ser′vi·tor·ship′** *n.*

ser·vi·tude (sûr′və-to͞od′, -tyo͞od′) *n.* **1.** Submission to a master; slavery. **2.** Forced labor imposed as a punishment for crime: *penal servitude.* **3.** *Law.* A right that grants use of another's property. [Old French, from Latin *servitūdō,* from *servus,* slave. See **servus** in Appendix.*]

Synonyms: *servitude, bondage, slavery.* These nouns state a condition of being involuntarily under the power of another. *Servitude* sometimes refers broadly to the absence of liberty but generally implies involuntary service. *Bondage* emphasizes being bound to the service of another with virtually no hope of freedom. To be held in *slavery* is to be owned bodily by the person one serves and treated as his property. Less literally, *slavery* and *bondage* can refer to subjection to any person, economic system, or vice.

ser·vo·mech·a·nism (sûr′vō-mĕk′ə-nĭz′əm) *n.* A feedback system that consists of a sensing element, an amplifier, and a servomotor, and is used in the automatic control of a mechanical device. Also called "servo." [SERVO(MOTOR) + MECHANISM.]

ser·vo·motor (sûr′vō-mō′tər) *n.* An electric motor or hydraulic piston that supplies power to a servomechanism. Also called "servo." [French *servo-moteur* : Latin *servus,* slave (see **servus** in Appendix*) + MOTOR.]

ses·a·me (sĕs′ə-mē) *n.* **1.** A plant, *Sesamum indicum,* of tropical Asia, bearing small, flat seeds used as food and as a source of oil. **2.** The seeds of this plant. Also called "benne." [Latin *sēsamum, sīsamum,* from Greek *sēsamon, sēsamē,* of Semitic origin, akin to Arabic *simsim,* Akkadian *shamashshamu.*]

ses·a·moid (sĕs′ə-moid′) *adj.* Of or designating a small bone, such as the kneecap, that develops in a tendon or in the capsule of a joint. [Greek *sēsamoeidēs,* shaped like a sesame seed : SESAME + -OID.] **—ses′a·moid** *n.*

sesqui-. Indicates one and a half; for example, **sesquicentennial.** [Latin, from *semisque* (unattested), one-half more : *sēmis,* half (see **sēmi-** in Appendix*) + *-que* (enclitic), and (see **kwe** in Appendix*).]

ses·qui·cen·ten·ni·al (sĕs′kwə-sĕn-tĕn′ē-əl) *adj.* Of or pertaining to a period of 150 years. *—n.* A 150th anniversary or its celebration. [SESQUI- + CENTENNIAL.]

ses·qui·pe·da·li·an (sĕs′kwə-pə-dā′lē-ən) *adj.* Also **ses·quip·e·dal** (sĕs′kwĭp′ĭ-dəl). **1.** Long and ponderous; polysyllabic. **2.** Given to using long words. *—n.* A long word. [From Latin *sesquipedalis,* of a foot and a half in length : SESQUI- + *pes* (stem *ped-*), foot (see **ped-**[1] in Appendix*).]

sess. session.

ses·sile (sĕs′ĭl′, -əl) *adj.* **1.** *Botany.* Stalkless and attached directly at the base: *sessile leaves.* **2.** *Zoology.* Permanently attached or fixed; not free-moving. [Latin *sessilis,* of sitting, low (said of plants), from *sessus,* past participle of *sedēre,* to sit. See **sed-**[1] in Appendix.*]

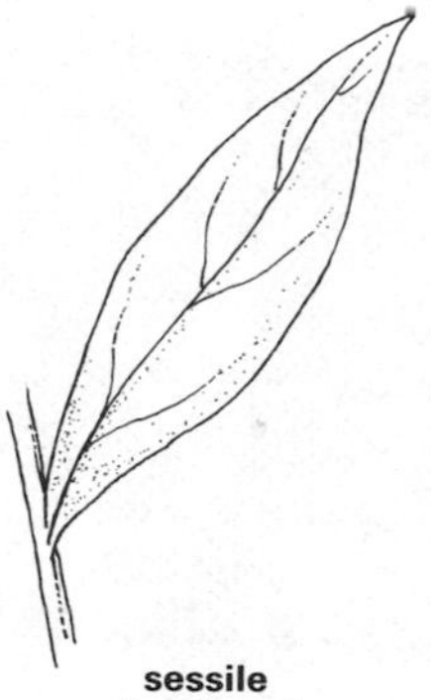

sessile
Sessile leaf

ses·sion (sĕsh′ən) *n. Abbr.* **sess. 1.** A meeting of a legislative or judicial body for the purpose of transacting business. **2.** A series of such meetings. **3.** The term or duration of time that is taken by such a series of meetings. **4.** The part of a year or of a day during which a school holds classes. **5.** A group of persons assembled for a common purpose or with a common interest: *a gossip session.* **6.** A court of criminal jurisdiction in the United States: *the court of sessions.* **7.** Any period of time devoted to a specific activity. [Middle English *sessioun,* a session, a sitting, from Old French *session,* from Latin *sessiō,* from *sessus,* past participle of *sedēre,* to sit. See **sed-**[1] in Appendix.*] **—ses′sion·al** *adj.* **—ses′sion·al·ly** *adv.*

ses·terce (sĕs′tərs) *n.* A silver or bronze coin of ancient Rome, equivalent to 1/4 denarius. [Latin *sestertius,* (coin) worth two and a half (asses) (i.e., two plus a half of a third ass) : *sēmis,* a half (see **sēmi-** in Appendix*) + *tertius,* a third (see **trei-** in Appendix*).]

ses·ter·ti·um (sĕs-tûr′shē-əm) *n., pl.* **-tia** (-shē-ə). A monetary unit of ancient Rome, equivalent to 1,000 sesterces. [Latin *(mille) sestertium,* (a thousand) sesterces, from the genitive plural of *sestertius,* SESTERCE.]

ses·tet (sĕs-tĕt′) *n.* A stanza constituting the last six lines of a sonnet. Compare **octet.** [Italian *sestetto,* from *sesto,* sixth, from Latin *sextus.* See **sweks** in Appendix.*]

ses·ti·na (sĕs-tē′nə) *n.* An originally Provençal verse form consisting of six six-line stanzas and a three-line envoi, repeating the end words of the first stanza throughout according to a scheme of cruciate retrogradation. [Italian, from *sesto,* sixth, from Latin *sextus.* See **sweks** in Appendix.*]

Ses·tos (sĕs′təs). An ancient town on the Hellespont, at the narrowest part of the strait.

set[1] (sĕt) *v.* **set, setting, sets.** *—tr.* **1.** To put in a specified position; to place. **2.** To put into a specified state. **3.** To put into a stable position; fix. **4.** To put into a position that will restore a proper and normal state. **5. a.** To adjust for proper functioning. **b.** To adjust (a saw) by deflecting the teeth. **6.** To adjust according to a standard. **7.** To adjust (an instrument) to a specific point or calibration. **8.** To arrange tableware upon (a table) preparatory to eating. **9.** To apply equipment, as curlers and clips, to (one's hair) in order to style. **10.** *Printing.* **a.** To arrange (type) into words and sentences preparatory to printing; compose. **b.** To transpose into type. **11. a.** To compose (music) to fit a given text. **b.** To write (words) to fit a given melodic line. **12.** To arrange scenery upon (a theater stage). **13.** To prescribe or establish. **14.** To prescribe the unfolding of (a scene) in a specific place. **15.** To prescribe as a time for. **16.** To prescribe or assign. **17.** To detail or assign to a particular duty, service, or station. **18.** To direct. **19.** To put forth as a model to be emulated. **20. a.** To put in a mounting; mount. **b.** To apply jewels to; to stud. **21.** To cause to sit. **22. a.** To put (a hen) on eggs for the purpose of hatching them. **b.** To put (eggs) beneath a hen or in an incubator. **23. a.** To affix (a price or value). Used with *on* or *upon.* **b.** To hold or have (anticipation or hope). Used with *on* or *upon.* **24.** To point to the location of (game) by holding a fixed attitude. Used of a hunting dog. **25.** *Horticulture.* To produce, as after pollination: *set seed.* *—intr.* **1.** To disappear below the horizon. Used of the sun. **2.** To diminish or decline; wane. **3.** To sit on eggs. Used of fowl. See Usage note below. **4.** To become fixed; harden or congeal. **5.** To embark upon a journey. Used with *out, forth,* or *off.* **6.** To become restored to a normal state; knit. **7.** *Horticulture.* To mature or develop, as after pollination. **8.** *Regional.* To sit. See Usage note below. **—set about.** To start or begin doing. **—set against. 1.** To compare; weigh. **2.** To make unfriendly or hostile to. **—set aside. 1.** To separate and reserve for a special purpose. **2.** To dismiss or discard. **3.** To declare invalid or void; annul. **—set down. 1.** To put upon a surface; to seat. **2.** To put into written or printed form; to record. **3.** To regard or consider. **4.** To attribute. **—set forth.** To utter or express, as a declaration. **—set in. 1.** To begin to happen. **2.** To move toward the shore. Used of wind or water. **—set on.** To instigate or urge. **—set out. 1.** To display for exhibition or sale. **2.** To define the boundaries of. **3.** To lay out (a room, town, or garden, for example); to plan. **4.** To plant (slips or seedlings, for example). **5.** To begin any procedure or progress, especially a journey; to start. *—adj.* **1.** Fixed or established by agreement. **2.** Established by convention; stereotyped. **3.** Established deliberately; formal; purposeful. **4.** Fixed and rigid; unflinching. **5.** Fixed and rigid in disposition; unyielding; firm.

6. Assembled or formed. 7. Ready: *get set.* —*n.* 1. a. The act or process of setting. b. The condition resulting from setting. 2. A permanent firming or hardening of a substance, as by cooling. 3. The deflection of the teeth of a saw. 4. The manner in which something is positioned. 5. The carriage or bearing of a part of the body. 6. A descent below the horizon. 7. The direction or course of wind or water. 8. A seedling, slip, or cutting that is ready for planting. [Set (infinitive, past tense, past participle); Middle English *setten, sette, sette,* to cause to sit, to place, Old English *settan, sette, sett.* See **sed-**[1] in Appendix.*]

Usage: *Set* is largely, though by no means exclusively, transitive. *Sit* is principally intransitive. In the following typical examples of intransitive usage, *sit* is proper; *set* would not be standard in them (though it sometimes appears, especially in speech): *Come and sit awhile* (addressed to a person). *The castle sits atop a hill. The meal did not sit well. His remarks did not sit well with me.* But either *set* or *sit* is possible in these: *The hen sets* (or *sits*) *on eggs. The jacket sets* (or *sits*) *perfectly* (referring to fit or hang).

set[2] (sĕt) *n.* 1. A group of persons or things connected by or collected for their similar appearance, interest, importance, or the like: *a chess set.* 2. A group of persons sharing social status and a common interest; clique: *the jet set.* 3. A group of objects related in function and generally used together. 4. A group of circumstances, situations, events, or the like joined to be treated as a whole. 5. A group of books published as a unit by virtue of their common authorship, relevance, subject, or the like. 6. a. A number of couples required for participation in a square dance. b. The movements constituting a square dance. 7. a. The scenery constructed for a theatrical performance. b. The entire enclosure in which a motion picture is being filmed; a sound stage; studio. 8. The collective receiving apparatus assembled to operate a radio or television. 9. *Mathematics.* Any collection of distinct elements: *a set of positive integers.* 10. In tennis and other games, a group of games constituting one division or unit of a match. —See Synonyms at **circle, series.** [Middle English *sette,* sect, set, from Old French, from Latin *secta,* SECT (later confused with set, to place, taken as "a group or number set together").]

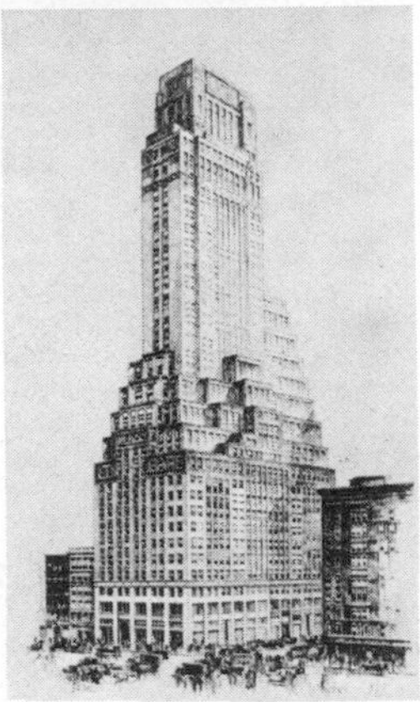

setback
The Fred F. French Building, New York City

se·ta (sē′tə) *n., pl.* **setae** (sē′tē′). *Biology.* A stiff hair, bristle, or bristlelike process. [New Latin, from Latin *sēta, saeta*†, bristle.] —**se′tal** *adj.*

se·ta·ceous (sĭ-tā′shəs) *adj.* 1. Having or consisting of bristles; bristly. 2. Resembling a bristle or bristles; bristlelike. [New Latin *setaceus* : SET(A) + -ACEOUS.]

set back. To impede the progress or advance of.

set·back (sĕt′băk′) *n.* 1. An unanticipated or sudden check in progress; a reverse. 2. a. A steplike recession in a wall. b. Any of a series of such recessions in the rise of a tall building.

set chisel. A chisel with a broad cutting edge on a tapered shaft.

Seth (sĕth). A masculine given name. [Hebrew, "appointed."]

se·ti·form (sē′tə-fôrm′) *adj.* Having the shape of a seta or bristle. [SET(A) + -FORM.]

set·line (sĕt′lĭn′) *n.* A long fishing line towed by a boat and supporting many smaller lines bearing baited hooks. Also called "trawl," "trawl line," "trotline."

set off. 1. To show to best advantage; enhance by contrast. 2. To separate from others. 3. To cause to explode.

set·off (sĕt′ôf′) *n.* 1. Anything, such as an object, situation, or the like, that sets off something else by contrast. 2. Anything that offsets or compensates for something else. 3. a. A counterclaim. b. The settlement of a debt by a debtor's establishing such a claim against his creditor. 4. *Architecture.* A flat projection from a wall or the like; ledge; offset.

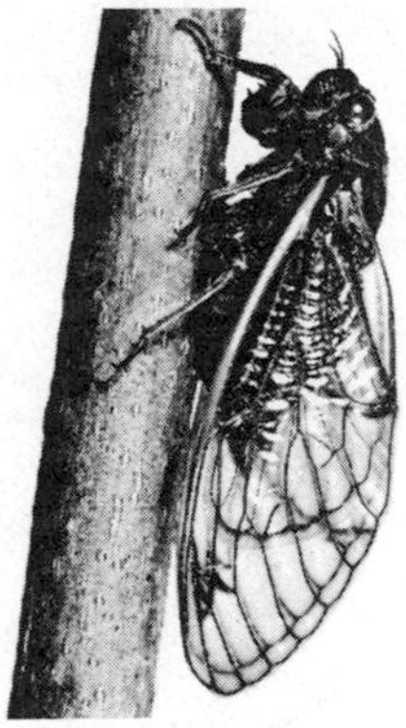

seventeen-year locust

Se·to Nai·kai. The Japanese name for the **Inland Sea.**

se·tose (sē′tōs′) *adj.* Bristly or bristlelike; setaceous. [Latin *sētōsus,* from *sēta,* bristle, SETA.]

set·screw (sĕt′skrōō′) *n.* 1. A screw, often without a head, used to hold two parts in a position relative to each other without motion. 2. A screw used to regulate the tension of a spring.

set·tee (sĕ-tē′) *n.* 1. A long wooden bench with a high back. 2. A small sofa. [Perhaps variant of SETTLE (bench).]

set·ter (sĕt′ər) *n.* 1. One that sets. 2. Any of several breeds of long-haired dogs, originally trained to indicate the presence of game by crouching in a set position.

set theory. The study of the mathematical properties of sets.

set·ting (sĕt′ĭng) *n.* 1. The act of a person or thing that sets. 2. The context in which a situation is set. 3. A mounting, as for a jewel. 4. The scenery constructed for a theatrical performance. 5. Music composed or arranged to fit a text. 6. A set of eggs in a hen's nest. 7. The descent of the sun or other celestial body below the horizon.

set·tle (sĕt′l) *v.* **-tled, -tling, -tles.** —*tr.* 1. To put into order; arrange or fix definitely as desired. 2. To put firmly in a desired position or place; establish; situate. 3. To establish as a resident or residents. 4. To establish residence in. 5. To establish in a residence, business, profession, or the like. 6. To remove the disturbance of; restore calmness or comfort to. 7. a. To cause to come to rest, sink, or become compact. b. To cause (a liquid) to become clear by forming a sediment. 8. *Informal.* To subdue or make orderly. 9. To establish on a permanent basis; stabilize; assure. 10. a. To make compensation for (a claim). b. To pay (a debt). 11. To conclude (a dispute, for example) by a final decision. 12. To decide (a law suit) by mutual agreement of the involved parties without court action. 13. *Law.* To secure or assign (property or title, for example) by legal action. Used with *on* or *upon.* —*intr.* 1. To discontinue moving and come to rest in one place. 2. To descend or subside gradually. 3. To sink and become more compact: *The dust settled.* 4. a. To become clear. Used of liquids. b. To be separated from a solution or mixture as a sediment. 5. To establish one's residence. 6. To reach a decision; determine. Used with *on, upon,* or *with.* 7. To compensate for a claim or pay a debt. —See Synonyms at **decide.** —**settle down.** 1. To begin living a more orderly life, as by marrying or taking a permanent job. 2. To become less nervous or restless. 3. To apply one's attention purposefully and diligently. —**settle for.** To accept in spite of incomplete satisfaction. —*n.* A long wooden bench with a high back, often including storage space beneath the seat. [Middle English *setlen,* to place in order, to seat, Old English *setlan,* from *setl,* seat. See **sed-**[1] in Appendix.*]

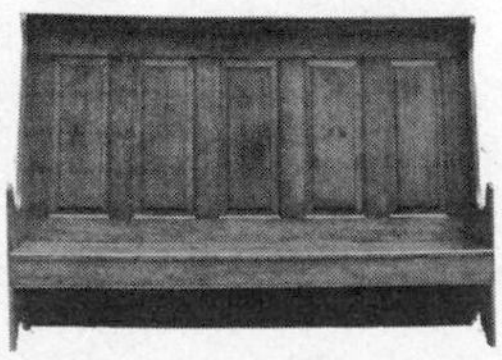

settle
Eighteenth-century American

set·tle·ment (sĕt′l-mənt) *n.* 1. The act or process of settling. 2. a. Establishment, as of a person in a business or of people in a new region. b. A newly colonized region. 3. A small community. 4. An adjustment or other understanding reached in financial matters, business proceedings, or the like. 5. a. The transfer of property to provide for the future needs of a person. b. Property thus transferred. 6. A welfare center providing community services in an underprivileged area. In this sense, also called "settlement house."

set·tler (sĕt′l-ər, sĕt′lər) *n.* 1. A person or thing that settles, decides, or determines something. 2. A person who settles in a new region; colonist.

set·tlings (sĕt′l-ĭngz, sĕt′lĭngz) *pl.n.* Matter that has settled at the bottom of a liquid; sediment; dregs.

set to. 1. To begin working; start in. 2. To begin fighting.

set-to (sĕt′tōō′) *n., pl.* **-tos.** A brief but usually heated contest.

set up. 1. To place in an upright position. 2. To elevate or raise. 3. To raise to authority or power; invest with power. 4. To assemble and erect. 5. To establish; found. 6. To establish (a person) in business by providing capital, equipment, and the like. 7. To put forth or propose. 8. *Informal.* a. To provide a person with drinks; treat to drinks. b. To provide drinks for a person. 9. *Informal.* To stimulate or exhilarate.

set·up (sĕt′ŭp′) *n.* 1. *Informal.* The way in which anything is constituted, arranged, or planned. 2. The way in which a person or animal carries itself; bearing; carriage. 3. Physical make-up; physique. 4. *Usually plural. Informal.* The collective ingredients and mixers necessary for serving a variety of alcoholic drinks, as ice and soda water. 5. *Slang.* a. A contest prearranged to result in an easy or faked victory. b. Any endeavor that is, or is prearranged to be, easy to accomplish.

Seu·rat (sœ-rä′), **Georges Pierre.** 1859–1891. French painter.

Se·van, Lake (sĕ-vän′). *Turkish* **Gök·cha** (gœk′chä). A lake in the Armenian S.S.R., occupying 546 square miles in the eastern part of the republic.

Se·vas·to·pol (sĕ-väs′tō-pōl). Also **Se·bas·to·pol** (sĕ-bäs′tō-pōl). A city and port of the Soviet Union, in the southern Crimea on the Black Sea. Population, 192,000.

sev·en (sĕv′ən) *n.* The cardinal number written 7 or in Roman numerals VII. See **number.** [Middle English *seven,* Old English *seofon.* See **septm̥** in Appendix.*] —**sev′en** *adj. & pron.*

seven deadly sins. The sins of pride, lust, envy, anger, covetousness, gluttony, and sloth. Also called "cardinal sins."

sev·en·fold (sĕv′ən-fōld′) *adj.* 1. Consisting of seven parts or members. 2. Having seven times as many or as much. —**sev′en·fold′** *adv.*

Seven Pines. See **Fair Oaks.**

seven seas. Also **Seven Seas.** All the oceans of the world.

sev·en·teen (sĕv′ən-tēn′, sĕv′ən-tēn′) *n.* The cardinal number written 17 or in Roman numerals XVII. See **number.** [Middle English *seventene,* Old English *seofontīne* : SEVEN + -TEEN.] —**sev′en·teen′** *adj.* & *pron.*

sev·en·teenth (sĕv′ən-tēnth′, sĕv′ən-tēnth′) *n.* 1. The ordinal number 17 in a series. Also written 17th. 2. One of 17 equal parts. See **number.** —**sev′en·teenth′** *adj.* & *adv.*

sev·en·teen-year locust (sĕv′ən-tēn-yîr′). A cicada, *Magicicada septendecim,* of the eastern United States, having a nymphal stage in which it remains underground for 17 or sometimes 13 years.

sev·enth (sĕv′ənth) *n.* 1. The ordinal number seven in a series. Also written 7th. 2. One of seven equal parts. See **number.** 3. A musical interval encompassing seven diatonic degrees. —**sev′enth** *adj.* & *adv.*

Sev·enth-Day Adventist (sĕv′ənth-dā′). A member of a sect of Adventism distinguished chiefly for its observance of the Sabbath on Saturday. See **Adventist.**

seventh heaven. 1. The furthest of the concentric spheres containing the stars and comprising the dwelling place of God and the angels in the Moslem and cabalist systems. 2. A state of great joy and satisfaction.

sev·en·ty (sĕv′ən-tē) *n.* The cardinal number written 70 or in Roman numerals LXX. See **number.** —**sev′en·ty** *adj.* & *pron.*

sev·en-up (sĕv′ən-ŭp′) *n.* A card game for two, three, or four players, originally requiring seven points to win. Also called "all fours," "pitch."

sev·en-year itch (sĕv′ən-yîr′). A disease, **scabies** *(see).*

sev·er (sĕv′ər) *v.* **-ered, -ering, -ers.** —*tr.* 1. To divide or separate into parts; keep apart or make distinct. 2. To cut or break forcibly into two or more parts. 3. To break off (a relationship, for example); dissolve. —*intr.* 1. To become cut or broken apart. 2. To divide; separate or go apart. —See Synonyms at **separate, tear.** [Middle English *severen,* from Norman French *severer,* from Vulgar Latin *sēperāre* (unattested), from Latin *sēparāre,* to SEPARATE.] —**sev′er·a·ble** (sĕv′ər-ə-bəl) *adj.*

sev·er·al (sĕv′ər-əl) *adj.* 1. Being of a number more than two or three, but not many; of an indefinitely small number. 2. Single;

ă pat/ā pay/âr care/ä father/b bib/ch church/d deed/ĕ pet/ē be/f fife/g gag/h hat/hw which/ĭ pit/ī pie/îr pier/j judge/k kick/l lid, needle/m mum/n no, sudden/ng thing/ŏ pot/ō toe/ô paw, for/oi noise/ou out/ŏŏ took/ōō boot/p pop/r roar/s sauce/sh ship, dish/

distinct: *"Pshaw! said I, with an air of carelessness, three several times"* (Sterne). **3.** Respectively different; diverse; various. **4.** *Law.* Pertaining separately to each party of a bond or note. —*n.* Several persons or things; a few. [Middle English *severall,* separate, distinct, from Norman French *several,* from Medieval Latin *sēparālis,* from Latin *sēpār,* separate, from *sēparāre,* to SEPARATE.] —**sev′er·al·ly** *adv.*

sev·er·ance (sĕv′ər-əns) *n.* **1. a.** The act or process of severing. **b.** The condition of being severed. **2.** Separation; partition.

se·vere (sə-vîr′) *adj.* **-verer, -verest. 1.** Unsparing and harsh in treating others; stern; strict. **2.** Corresponding strictly to established rule; maintained rigidly; accurate. **3.** Austere or dour in appearance, manner, or temperament; grave; forbidding. **4.** Extremely plain in substance, dress, or style; conservatively presented; uniform. **5.** Causing intense pain or distress; sharp; violent. **6.** Extremely difficult to perform or accomplish; trying; rigorous. [Old French, from Latin *sevērus.* See **wēros** in Appendix.*] —**se·vere′ly** *adv.* —**se·vere′ness** *n.*

Synonyms: *severe, stern, austere, ascetic, strict, exacting.* These adjectives mean to be unsparing, especially with respect to discipline or control. *Severe* is broadly applicable to persons or things that adhere rigidly to established standards, often rigorous standards, or high principles, or that impose harsh or taxing conditions. *Stern* is often interchangeable with *severe* but especially suggests unyielding disposition, unshakable resolution, and forbidding appearance or nature. *Austere* implies, in persons, self-restraint or self-denial, extreme reserve, and often rigid moral standards. In things it implies severe simplicity. *Ascetic* applies principally to the character and life of a person who practices extreme self-denial and who usually renounces worldly interests for spiritual or intellectual pursuits. *Strict* stresses the idea of rigid observance of rules or standards. *Exacting* applies to persons or things that make rigorous demands on one's time, labor, or attention.

se·ver·i·ty (sə-vĕr′ə-tē) *n., pl.* **-ties. 1.** Harshness; rigor. **2.** Extreme strictness; rigid conformity. **3.** Austerity; gravity. **4.** Intensity; violence.

Sev·ern (sĕv′ərn). **1.** A river rising in central Wales and flowing 210 miles northeast, southeast, south, and finally southwest through western England to the Bristol Channel. **2.** A river rising in western Ontario, Canada, and flowing 420 miles generally northeast to Hudson Bay. **3.** An inlet of Chesapeake Bay in central Maryland, on the right bank of which Annapolis is situated.

Se·ver·na·ya Dvi·na. The Russian name for the Northern **Dvina.**

Se·ver·na·ya Zem·lya (sĕv′ər-nə-yä′ zĕm′lē-ä′). An archipelago of the Soviet Union, 14,300 square miles in area, in the Arctic Ocean north of the Taimyr Peninsula.

Se·vier (sə-vîr′). A river flowing about 325 miles from southern Utah north and then southwest to Lake Sevier, in the west-central part of the state.

Sé·vi·gné (sā-vē-nyā′), **Marquise de.** Born Marie de Rabutin-Chantal. 1626–1696. French woman of letters.

Se·ville (sə-vĭl′). *Spanish* **Se·vil·la** (sā-vēl′yä). A city and inland port of Spain, in the southwest on the Guadalquivir. Population, 532,000.

Sè·vres (sĕv′rə) *n.* A fine porcelain made in Sèvres, France. Also called "Sèvres ware."

sew (sō) *v.* **sewed, sewn** (sōn) or **sewed, sewing, sews.** —*tr.* **1.** To make, repair, or fasten with a needle and thread. **2.** To furnish with stitches for the purpose of closing, fastening, attaching, or the like. Often used with *up: sew up a wound.* —*intr.* To work with a needle and thread or with a sewing machine. —**sew up.** *Informal.* **1.** To bring a business deal or the like to a successful close. **2.** To control. [Middle English *sewen,* Old English *seowian.* See **syū-** in Appendix.*]

sew·age (so͞o′ĭj) *n.* Liquid and solid waste carried off with ground water in sewers or drains. [SEW(ER) + -AGE.]

Sew·all (so͞o′əl), **Samuel.** 1652–1730. American jurist in colonial Massachusetts; presided at Salem witchcraft trials.

Sew·ard (so͞o′ərd), **William Henry.** 1801–1872. American statesman; Secretary of State (1861–69).

Sew·ard Peninsula (so͞o′ərd). A projection of Alaska extending 210 miles westward to Cape Prince of Wales, the westernmost point on the North American mainland.

sew·er[1] (so͞o′ər) *n.* An artificial, usually underground conduit for carrying off sewage or rainwater. [Middle English *sewer,* from Norman French *sever(e),* from Vulgar Latin *exaquāria* (unattested) : Latin *ex-,* out of + *aqua,* water (see **akwā-** in Appendix*).]

sew·er[2] (so͞o′ər) *n.* A medieval servant who supervised the serving of meals. [Middle English *sewer,* from Norman French *asseour,* from Old French *asseoir,* cause to sit (seating of guests was a sewer's responsibility), from Latin *assidēre,* to sit down : *ad-,* to + *sedēre,* sit (see **sed-**[1] in Appendix*).]

sew·er[3] (sō′ər) *n.* One that sews.

sew·er·age (so͞o′ər-ĭj) *n.* **1.** A system of sewers. **2.** The removal of waste materials by means of a sewer system. **3.** Sewage.

sew·ing (sō′ĭng) *n.* **1.** The act, occupation, or hobby of a person who sews. **2.** The article upon which one is working with needle and thread; needlework.

sewing circle. A group of women who meet regularly for the purpose of sewing, often for charitable causes.

sewing machine. A machine for sewing, often having additional attachments for special stitching.

sewn. Past participle of **sew.**

sex (sĕks) *n.* **1. a.** The property or quality by which organisms are classified according to their reproductive functions. **b.** Either of two divisions, designated *male* and *female,* of this classification. **2.** Males or females collectively. **3.** The condition or character of being male or female; the physiological, functional, and psychological differences that distinguish the male and the female. **4.** The sexual urge or instinct as it manifests itself in behavior. **5.** Sexual intercourse. —*tr.v.* **sexed, sexing, sexes.** To determine the sex of (young chickens). [Middle English, from Old French *sexe,* from Latin *sexus*†.]

sex-. Indicates six; for example, **sexpartite.** [Latin *sex,* six. See **sweks** in Appendix.*]

sex·a·ge·nar·i·an (sĕk′sə-jə-nâr′ē-ən) *n.* A person sixty or between sixty and seventy years old. —*adj.* **1.** Sixty years old or between sixty and seventy. **2.** Of or relating to a sexagenarian. [From Latin *sexāgēnārius,* SEXAGENARY.]

sex·ag·e·nar·y (sĕk-săj′ə-nĕr′ē) *adj.* **1.** Pertaining to or proceeding by sixties. **2.** Sexagenarian. —*n., pl.* **sexagenaries.** A sexagenarian. [Latin *sexāgēnārius,* adjective and noun, from *sexāgēnī,* sixty each, from *sexāgintā,* sixty : SEX- + *-gintā,* ten times (see **dekm̥** in Appendix*).]

Sex·a·ges·i·ma (sĕk′sə-jĕs′ə-mə) *n.* The second Sunday before Lent. Also called "Sexagesima Sunday." [Late Latin *sexāgēsima,* sixtieth (day before Easter), from Latin, feminine of *sexāgēsimus,* sixtieth, from *sexāgintā,* sixty. See **sexagenary.**]

sex·a·ges·i·mal (sĕk′sə-jĕs′ə-məl) *adj.* Relating to or based upon the number 60. —*n.* A fraction whose denominator is 60 or a power of 60. [From Latin *sexāgēsimus,* sixtieth, from *sexāgintā,* sixty. See **sexagenary.**]

sex appeal. Physical attractiveness that arouses sexual interest in a member of the opposite sex.

sex·cen·te·nar·y (sĕk′sĕn′tə-nĕr′ē) *adj.* Pertaining to 600 or to a 600-year period. —*n., pl.* **sexcentenaries.** A 600th anniversary or its commemoration. [From Latin *sexcentēnī,* six hundred each : SEX- + *centēnī,* a hundred each, from *centum,* hundred (see **dekm̥** in Appendix*).]

sex chromosome. Either of a pair of chromosomes, usually designated X or Y, in the germ cells of man, most animals, and some plants, that combine to determine the sex of an individual, XX resulting in a female and XY in a male.

sex·en·ni·al (sĕk-sĕn′ē-əl) *adj.* **1.** Occurring every six years. **2.** Of or for six years. —*n.* An event that occurs every six years. [From Latin *sexennium,* (period of) six years : SEX- + *annus,* year (see **at-** in Appendix*).] —**sex·en′ni·al·ly** *adv.*

sex gland. A gonad; a testis or ovary.

sex hormone. Any of various animal hormones, such as estrogen and androgen, affecting the growth or function of the reproductive organs and the development of secondary sex characteristics.

sex·less (sĕks′lĭs) *adj.* **1.** Lacking sexual characteristics; asexual; neuter. **2.** Arousing or exhibiting no sexual interest or desire. —**sex′less·ly** *adv.* —**sex′less·ness** *n.*

sex linkage. The condition in which a gene responsible for a specific phenotypic trait is located on the X chromosome, resulting in sexually dependent inheritance of the trait.

sex-linked (sĕks′lĭngkt′) *adj.* **1.** Carried by a sex chromosome, especially an X chromosome. Said of genes. **2.** Broadly, sexually determined. Said especially of inherited traits.

sex·ol·o·gy (sĕk-sŏl′ə-jē) *n.* The study of human sexual behavior. [SEX + -LOGY.] —**sex′o·log′ic** (-sə-lŏj′ĭk), **sex′o·log′i·cal** (-ĭ-kəl) *adj.* —**sex·ol′o·gist** *n.*

sex·par·tite (sĕks-pär′tīt′) *adj.* Composed of or divided into six parts, such as a groined vault. [SEX- + PARTITE.]

sex reversal. The natural, artificial, or pathological functional transformation from one sex to another.

sext (sĕkst) *n.* Also **Sext.** *Ecclesiastical.* **1.** The fourth of the seven **canonical hours** *(see).* **2.** The time of day set aside for this prayer, usually the sixth hour, or noon. [Middle English *sexte,* from Latin *sexta (hora),* sixth (hour), from the feminine of *sextus,* sixth. See **sweks** in Appendix.*]

sex·tan (sĕks′tən) *adj.* Occurring or recurring every six days. —*n.* A malarial fever with paroxysms recurring every six days. [New Latin *sextana (febris),* sextan (fever), from Latin *sextus,* sixth. See **sweks** in Appendix.*]

Sex·tans (sĕks′təns) *n.* A constellation in the equatorial region of the sky near Leo and Hydra. Also called the "Sextant." [New Latin, SEXTANT.]

sex·tant (sĕks′tənt) *n.* **1.** A navigational instrument used for measuring the altitudes of celestial bodies. **2.** *Capital* **S.** The constellation **Sextans** *(see).* [New Latin *sextans* (stem *sextant-*), from Latin *sextāns,* a sixth part (the instrument has an arc graduated in sixths of a circle), from *sextus,* sixth. See **sweks** in Appendix.*]

sex·tet (sĕks-tĕt′) *n.* **1. a.** A group composed of six vocalists or musicians. **b.** A musical composition written for six performers. **2.** Any gathering or collection of six persons or things. [Learned respelling of SESTET, after Latin *sex,* six.]

sex·tile (sĕks′tĭl′) *adj.* Designating the position of two celestial bodies when they are 60 degrees apart. [Latin *sextīlis,* one sixth (of a circle), from *sextus,* sixth. See **sweks** in Appendix.*]

sex·til·lion (sĕks-tĭl′yən) *n.* **1.** The cardinal number represented by 1 followed by 21 zeros, usually written 10^{21}. **2.** In British usage, the cardinal number represented by 1 followed by 36 zeros, usually written 10^{36}. See **number.** [French : SEX- + (M)ILLION.] —**sex·til′lion** *adj.*

sex·til·lionth (sĕks-tĭl′yənth) *n.* **1.** The ordinal number sextillion in a series. **2.** One of sextillion equal parts. See **number.** —**sex·til′lionth** *adj.* & *adv.*

sex·to·dec·i·mo (sĕks′tō-dĕs′ə-mō′) *n., pl.* **-mos. 1.** The page size (4½ by 6⅞ inches) of a book composed of printer's sheets folded into 16 leaves or 32 pages. **2.** A book composed of pages

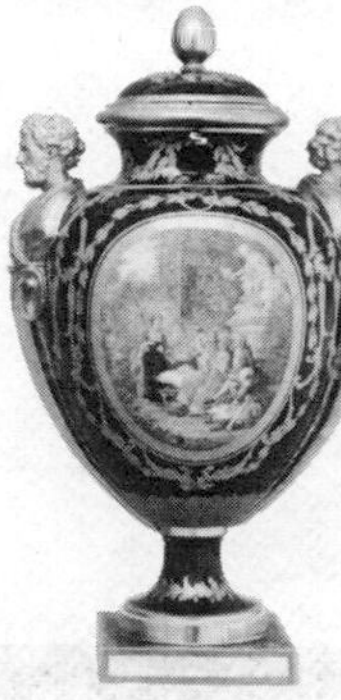

Sèvres
Eighteenth-century urn-shaped vase

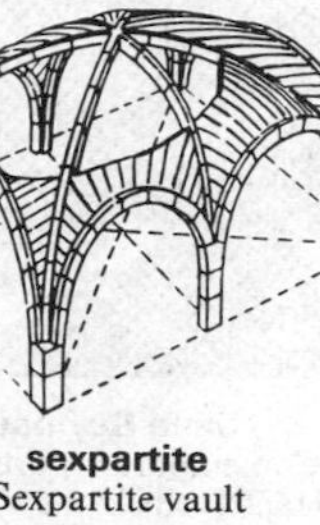

sexpartite
Sexpartite vault

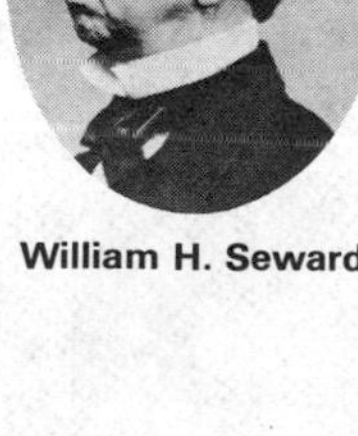

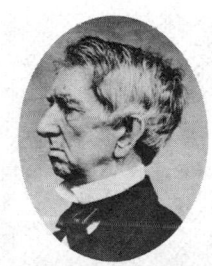

William H. Seward

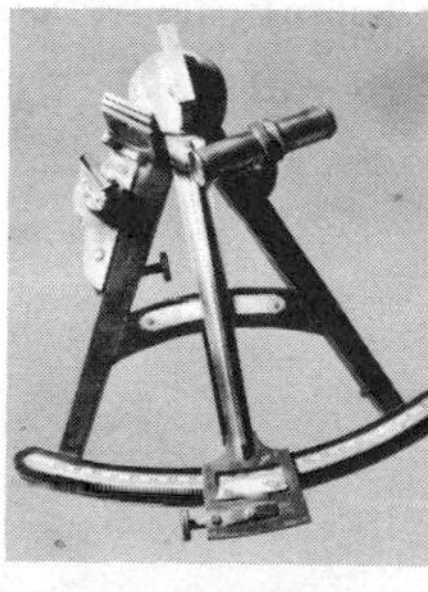

sextant
Instrument used by Nelson

t tight/th thin, path/*th* this, bathe/ŭ cut/ûr urge/v valve/w with/y yes/z zebra, size/zh vision/ə about, item, edible, gallop, circus/ à *Fr.* ami/œ *Fr.* feu, *Ger.* schön/ü *Fr.* tu, *Ger.* über/KH *Ger.* ich, *Scot.* loch/N *Fr.* bon. ***Follows main vocabulary.** †**Of obscure origin.**

of this size. Also called "sixteenmo." Also written *16 mo, 16°*. [Latin *sextōdecimō*, ablative of *sextusdecimus*, a sixteenth : *sextus*, sixth (see **sweks** in Appendix*) + *decimus*, tenth, from *decem*, ten (see **dekm̥** in Appendix*).] —**sex'to·dec'i·mo'** *adj.*

sex·ton (sĕks'tən) *n.* **1.** A maintenance man in a church, responsible for the care and upkeep of the church property and sometimes for bell-ringing or supervising burials in the churchyard. **2.** Formerly, a gravedigger. [Middle English *segerstone, sexton*, from Norman French *segerstaine*, from Medieval Latin *sacristānus*, SACRISTAN.]

sexton beetle. The **burying beetle** *(see)*.

sex·tu·ple (sĕks-to͞o'pəl, -tyo͞o'pəl, -tŭp'əl, sĕks'to͞o-pəl) *v.* **-pled, -pling, -ples.** —*tr.* To multiply by six. —*intr.* To become multiplied by six. —*adj.* **1.** Containing or consisting of six parts; sixfold. **2.** Larger or greater by sixfold; multiplied by six. **3.** *Music.* Having six beats to the measure. —*n.* A number six times larger than another. [Probably SEX- + (QUIN)TUPLE.] —**sex'tu·ply** *adv.*

sex·tu·plet (sĕks-tŭp'lĭt, -to͞o'plĭt, -tyo͞o'plĭt, sĕks'to͞o-plĭt) *n.* **1.** One of six offspring delivered at one birth. **2.** *Plural.* The six offspring of one birth. **3.** A collection or set of six similar persons or things; sextet. [SEXTU(PLE + TRI)PLET.]

sex·tu·pli·cate (sĕks-to͞o'plĭ-kĭt, sĕks-tyo͞o'-) *adj.* **1.** Six times as many or as much; sixfold. **2.** Raised to the sixth power. —*tr.v.* (sĕks-to͞o'plĭ-kāt', sĕks-tyo͞o'-) **sextuplicated, -cating, -cates.** To sextuple. —*n.* (sĕks-to͞o'plĭ-kĭt, sĕks-tyo͞o'-). One of six similar things. [SEXTU(PLE + DU)PLICATE.] —**sex·tu'pli·cate·ly** *adv.* —**sex·tu'pli·ca'tion** *n.*

sex·u·al (sĕk'sho͞o-əl) *adj.* **1.** Pertaining to, affecting, or characteristic of sex, the sexes, or the sex organs and their functions. **2.** Having a sex or sexual organs. **3.** Implying or symbolizing erotic desires or activity. **4.** Pertaining to or designating reproduction involving the union of male and female gametes. [Late Latin *sexuālis*, from Latin *sexus*, SEX.] —**sex'u·al·ly** *adv.*

sexual intercourse. Coitus, especially between humans.

sex·u·al·i·ty (sĕk'sho͞o-ăl'ə-tē) *n.* **1.** The condition of being characterized and distinguished by sex. **2.** Concern or preoccupation with sex. **3.** The quality of possessing a sexual character or potency.

sexual selection. A Darwinian adjunct of natural selection hypothesizing the preferred hereditary selection of characteristics involved in male courtship displays and combat.

sex·y (sĕk'sē) *adj.* **-ier, -iest.** *Slang.* Arousing or intending to arouse sexual desire or interest.

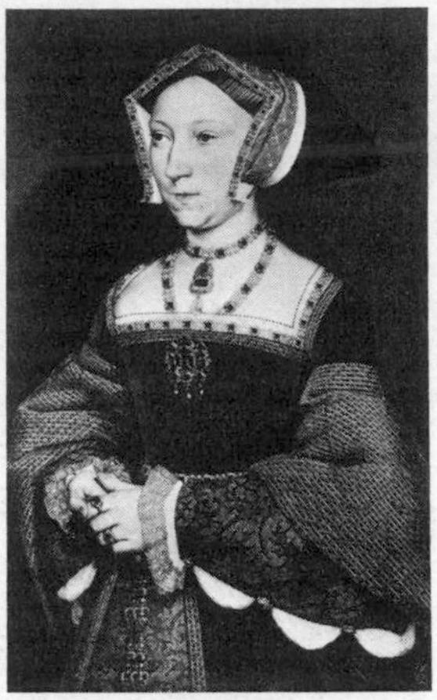

Jane Seymour
Contemporary portrait by Hans Holbein the Younger

Sey·chelles (sā-shĕl', -shĕlz'). A group of islands with a combined area of 156 square miles, constituting a British colony in the Indian Ocean about 1,000 miles east of Zanzibar. Population, 46,000. Capital, Victoria on Mahé.

Sey·han (sā-hän'). A river rising in south-central Turkey and flowing 320 miles to the Mediterranean south of Adana.

Sey·mour (sē'môr', -mōr'), **Jane.** 1510?–1537. Queen of England as third wife of Henry VIII; mother of Edward VI.

SF science fiction.

sf. *Music.* sforzando.

Sfax (sfäks). A city and seaport of Tunisia, in the east on the Gulf of Gabès. Population, 66,000.

Sfc. sergeant first class.

sfer·ics (sfîr'ĭks, sfĕr'-) *n.* Also **spher·ics.** Plural in form, used with a singular verb. **1.** The study of atmospherics, especially using electronic detectors. **2.** **Atmospherics** *(see)*. [Short for ATMOSPHERICS.]

SFO Airport code for San Francisco, California.

Sfor·za (sfôr'tsä). Italian family; rulers of Milan (1450–1535).

sfor·zan·do (sfôr-tsän'dō) *adj.* Also **for·zan·do** (fôr-). *Abbr.* **sf., sfz.** Suddenly and strongly accented. Used as a musical direction. —*n.* Also **for·zan·do.** A sforzando tone or chord. [Italian, gerund of *sforzare*, to use force : *s-*, from Latin *ex-*, out of + *forzare*, to force, from Vulgar Latin *fortiāre* (unattested), from *fortia* (unattested), FORCE.] —**sfor·zan'do** *adv.*

S.G. solicitor general.

sgd. signed.

SGN Airport code for Saigon, South Vietnam.

sgraf·fi·to (zgrä-fē'tō) *n., pl.* **-fiti** (-fē'tē). **1.** Decoration produced on pottery or ceramic by scratching through a surface of plaster or glazing to reveal a different color beneath. **2.** Ware having this decoration. [Italian, from the past participle of *sgraffire*, to scratch, from *sgraffio*, a scratch, from *sgraffiare*, to produce sgraffito : *s-*, from Latin *ex-*, out of + *graffiare*, to scratch (see **graffito**).]

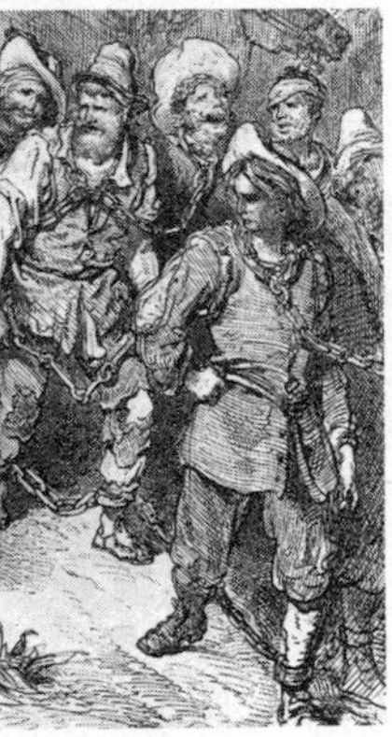

shackle
Illustration by Gustave Doré for *Don Quixote*, showing prisoners in shackles

's Gra·ven·ha·ge. The Dutch name for The **Hague.**

Sgt. sergeant.

Sgt. Maj. sergeant major.

sh (sh) *interj.* Used to urge silence.

sh. 1. share (capital stock). **2.** sheet. **3.** shilling.

Sha·ban (shə-bän') *n.* Also **Shaa·ban.** The eighth month of the year on the Moslem calendar. See **calendar.** [Arabic *sha'bān.*]

Shab·bat (shä-bät', shä'bəs) *n., pl.* **-batim** (-bä'tĭm, -bô'sĭm). The Jewish Sabbath. [Hebrew *shabbāth*, SABBATH.]

shab·by (shăb'ē) *adj.* **-bier, -biest. 1.** Threadbare; worn-out. **2.** Wearing worn garments; seedy. **3.** Dilapidated; deteriorated. **4.** Despicable; paltry; mean. **5.** Unfair. [From obsolete *shab*, a scab, from Middle English *schab(be)*, Old English *sceabb*. See **skep-** in Appendix.*] —**shab'bi·ly** *adv.* —**shab'bi·ness** *n.*

Sha·bu·oth. Variant of **Shavuot.**

shack (shăk) *n.* A small, crudely built cabin; shanty. [Short for Mexican Spanish *jacal*, from Aztec *xacalli*, thatched cabin.]

shack·le (shăk'əl) *n.* **1.** A metal fastening, usually one of a pair, for encircling and confining the ankle or wrist of a prisoner or captive; fetter; manacle. **2.** A hobble for an animal. **3.** Any of several devices, as a clevis, used to fasten or couple. **4.** Anything that confines or restrains. —*tr.v.* **shackled, -ling, -les. 1.** To put shackles on; to hobble; to fetter. **2.** To fasten or connect with a shackle. **3.** To restrict; to confine; to hamper. [Middle English *schackle*, Old English *sceacel*, fetter, from Germanic *skakulo-* (unattested).] —**shack'ler** *n.*

Shack·le·ton (shăk'əl-tən), Sir **Ernest Henry.** 1874–1922. British explorer of the Antarctic.

shack·o. Variant of **shako.**

shack up. *Slang.* **1.** To live, room, or stay at a place. **2.** To live in sexual intimacy with another person, especially for a short duration. Used with *with*.

shad (shăd) *n., pl.* **shad** or **shads. 1.** Any of several food fishes of the genus *Alosa*, related to the herrings but atypical in swimming up streams from marine waters to spawn. **2.** Broadly, any of various unrelated silvery fishes. [Middle English *shad*, Old English *sceadd*†.]

shad·ber·ry (shăd'bĕr'ē) *n., pl.* **-ries.** The fruit of the shadbush.

shad·bush (shăd'bo͝osh') *n.* Any of various North American shrubs or trees of the genus *Amelanchier*, having white flowers and edible blue-black or purplish fruit. Also called "shadblow," "serviceberry," "Juneberry." [So called because the flowers bloom at about the same time shad appear in U.S. rivers.]

shad·dock (shăd'ək) *n.* **1.** A tropical tree, *Citrus maxima* (or *C. grandis*), closely related to the grapefruit. **2.** The edible yellow, pear-shaped fruit of this tree. Also called "pompelmous." [After Captain *Shaddock*, commander of an East India Company ship, who took the seed to Jamaica in 1696.]

shade (shād) *n.* **1.** Light diminished in intensity as a result of the interception of the rays; comparative darkness or obscurity. **2.** An area or space of such partial darkness or obscurity. **3.** Cover or shelter provided by an object's interception of sun or its rays. **4.** Any of various devices used to reduce or screen light or heat. **5.** *Plural. Slang.* Sunglasses. **6.** Relative obscurity. **7.** *Plural.* Dark shadows gathering at dusk: *"The shades of night are falling fast"* (Longfellow). **8.** The part of a picture or photograph depicting darkness or shadow. **9.** The degree to which a color is mixed with black or is decreasingly illuminated; gradation of darkness. **10.** A slight difference or variation; nuance. **11.** A small amount; trace; jot. **12.** A disembodied spirit; ghost. —*tr.v.* **shaded, shading, shades. 1.** To screen from light or heat. **2.** To obscure or darken. **3.** To cause shade in or on. **4. a.** To represent degrees of darkness in (a picture). **b.** To produce (gradations of light or color) in (a picture). **5.** To change or vary by slight degrees: *shade the meaning.* **6.** *Informal.* To make a slight reduction in: *shade prices.* [Middle English *schade*, Old English *sceadu, scead*. See **skot-** in Appendix.*]

shad·fly (shăd'flī') *n., pl.* **-flies.** An insect, the **mayfly** *(see)*.

shad·ing (shā'dĭng) *n.* **1.** Screening against light or heat. **2.** The lines or other marks used to fill in outlines of a sketch, engraving, or painting to represent gradations of colors or darkness. **3.** Any small variation, gradation, or difference.

shad·ow (shăd'ō) *n.* **1.** An area that is not, or is only partially, irradiated or illuminated because of the interception of radiation by an opaque object between the area and the source of radiation. **2.** The rough image of the intervening object, especially the umbral image, that delimits the shaded area. **3.** An imperfect imitation or copy of something else. **4.** *Plural.* The darkness following sunset. **5.** Gloom or unhappiness or an influence that causes such feeling. **6.** A shaded area in a picture or photograph. **7.** A mirrored image or reflection. **8.** A phantom; ghost. **9.** A detective; spy. **10.** A faint indication; premonition. **11.** A vestige; remnant. **12.** An insignificant portion or amount; slight trace. **13.** Shelter; protection. —*tr.v.* **shadowed, -owing, -ows. 1.** To cast a shadow upon; shade. **2.** To make gloomy or dark; to cloud. **3.** To represent vaguely, mysteriously, or prophetically. **4.** To darken in a painting or drawing; shade in. **5.** To follow after, especially in secret; to trail. [Middle English *schadow*, Old English *sceaduwe*, oblique case of *sceadu*, SHADE.] —**shad'ow·er** *n.*

shad·ow·box (shăd'ō-bŏks') *intr.v.* **-boxed, -boxing, -boxes.** To spar with an imaginary opponent, as for exercise.

shad·ow·graph (shăd'ō-grăf', -gräf') *n.* An image produced by casting a shadow on a screen.

shad·ow·y (shăd'ō-ē) *adj.* **-ier, -iest. 1.** Pertaining to or resembling a shadow. **2.** Full of shadows; dark; shady. **3.** Vague; indistinct; dim. —See Synonyms at **dark.** —**shad'ow·i·ness** *n.*

Sha·drach (shăd'răk). A Hebrew captive who, with Meshach and Abednego, miraculously escaped death in Nebuchadnezzar's fiery furnace. Daniel 3.

Shad·well (shăd'wəl), **Thomas.** 1640?–1692. English poet and dramatist; poet laureate (1688–92).

shad·y (shā'dē) *adj.* **-ier, -iest. 1.** Full of shade; shaded. **2.** Casting shade. **3.** Quiet, dark, or concealed; hidden. **4.** Of dubious character or honesty; questionable. —See Synonyms at **dishonest, dark.** —**shad'i·ly** *adv.* —**shad'i·ness** *n.*

shaft[1] (shăft, shäft) *n.* **1.** The long, narrow stem or body of a spear or arrow. **2.** A spear or arrow. **3.** Something suggestive of a missile in appearance or effect; a bolt. **4.** A ray or beam of light. **5.** The handle of any of various tools or implements. **6.** The rib of a feather. **7.** *Anatomy.* **a.** The midsection of a long bone; diaphysis. **b.** The section of a hair projecting from the surface of the body. **8.** A column or obelisk or the section of a column between the capital and base. **9.** One of two parallel poles between which an animal is harnessed. **10.** *Machinery.* A long, generally cylindrical bar, especially one that rotates and transmits power: *a drive shaft.* [Middle English *shaft*, Old English *sceaft*. See **skep-** in Appendix.*]

shaft[2] (shăft, shäft) *n.* **1.** A long, narrow passage sunk into the earth; tunnel. **2.** A vertical passage housing an elevator. **3.** A duct or conduit for the passage of air, as for ventilation or heating. [Probably from Middle Low German *schacht.* See **skep-** in Appendix.*]

shaft·ing (shăf′tĭng, shäf′-) *n.* **1.** A system of shafts, as in a mechanical device, for transmitting motion or power. **2.** Material from which shafts are made.

shag[1] (shăg) *n.* **1.** A tangle or mass, especially of rough, matted hair. **2. a.** A coarse long nap, as on some woolen cloth. **b.** Cloth having such a nap. **3.** Coarse shredded tobacco. —*tr.v.* **shagged, shagging, shags. 1.** To make shaggy; roughen. **2.** *Baseball.* To chase and catch (fly balls) in batting practice. [Middle English *shagge* (unattested), Old English *sceacga,* from Germanic *skag-* (unattested).] —**shag** *adj.*

shag[2] (shăg) *n.* A dance step of the 1930's consisting of a hop on each foot in alternation. —*intr.v.* **shagged, shagging, shags.** To dance the shag. [Origin obscure.]

shag[3] (shăg) *n.* A bird, the **cormorant** *(see).* [Perhaps from its shaggy crest.]

shag·bark (shăg′bärk′) *n.* A North American hickory tree, *Carya ovata,* having shaggy bark, compound leaves, and edible nuts with a hard shell. Also called "shellbark."

shag·gy (shăg′ē) *adj.* **-gier, -giest. 1.** Having, covered with, or resembling long, rough hair or wool. **2.** Bushy and matted: *shaggy hair.* **3.** Poorly groomed; unkempt. —**shag′gi·ly** *adv.* —**shag′gi·ness** *n.*

shag·gy-dog story (shăg′ē-dôg′, -dŏg′). A long, drawn-out anecdote depending for humor upon an absurd or anticlimactic punch line.

shaggy mane. An edible mushroom, *Coprinus comatus,* having shaggy scales covering the cap. Also called "shaggy cap."

sha·green (shə-grēn′) *n.* **1.** The rough hide of a shark or ray, covered with numerous bony denticles, and used as an abrasive and as leather. **2.** Leather with a granular surface, prepared from the skins of various animals. [French *chagrin,* from Turkish *sağri,* leather.] —**sha·green′** *adj.*

shah (shä) *n.* The monarch of certain lands of the Middle East, especially Iran. [Persian *shāh,* from Old Persian *khshāyathiya.* See **ksei-** in Appendix.*]

Sha·hap·tin, Sha·hap·ti·an. Variants of **Sahaptin.**

Shah Ja·han (shä yə-hän′). Also **Je·han.** 1592?–1666. Mogul emperor of Hindustan (1628–58).

Shah·ja·han·pur (shä′jə-hän′po͝or). A city of the Republic of India, in central Uttar Pradesh. Population, 110,000.

Shahn (shän), **Ben.** 1898–1969. Russian-born American artist.

shai·tan, shei·tan (shī-tän′) *n.* **1.** *Often capital* **S.** *Islam.* Satan, the Devil. **2.** An evil spirit; a fiend. [Arabic *shaiṭān,* from Hebrew *sāṭān,* SATAN.]

Shak. Shakespeare.

shake (shāk) *v.* **shook** (sho͝ok), **shaken** (shā′kən), **shaking, shakes.** —*tr.* **1.** To cause to move to and fro with short jerky movements. **2.** To cause to quiver or tremble; vibrate or rock: *A severe tremor shook the ground.* **3.** To cause to stagger or waver; unsettle. **4.** To remove or dislodge by jerky movements: *shake the dust out.* **5.** To bring to a specified condition by or as if by jerky movements: *"It is not easy to shake one's heart free of the impression"* (John Middleton Murry). **6.** To disturb or agitate; unnerve. Often used with *up.* **7.** To brandish or wave: *shake one's fist.* **8.** To clasp (hands or another's hand) in greeting or leave-taking or as a sign of agreement. **9.** To free oneself from; get rid of. Usually used with *off.* **10.** *Music.* To trill (a note). **11.** *Dice.* To rattle and mix (the dice) before casting. —*intr.* **1.** To move to and fro in short jerky movements. **2.** To tremble, as from cold or in anger. **3.** To totter or waver; become unsteady. **4.** *Music.* To trill. **5.** To shake hands. —*n.* **1.** An act of shaking. **2.** A trembling or quivering movement. **3.** *Informal.* An earthquake. **4.** A fissure in rock. **5.** A crack in timber caused by wind or frost. **6.** *Slang.* A moment or instant; trice: *I'll do it in a shake.* **7.** *Music.* A trill. **8.** A beverage in which the ingredients are mixed by shaking: *a milk shake.* **9.** A rough shingle used to cover barns and other rustic buildings. —**give (someone** or **something) the shake.** *Slang.* To escape from or get rid of. —**get a fair** (or **good**) **shake.** *Slang.* To be treated with fairness. —**no great shakes.** *Slang.* Unexceptional; ordinary; mediocre. —**the shakes.** *Informal.* **1.** The chill accompanying intermittent fever. **2.** Uncontrollable trembling, especially as a symptom of alcoholism. [Shake, shook, shaken; Middle English *schaken, schook, schaken,* Old English *sceacan, sceōc, sceacen,* from Germanic *skakan* (unattested).] —**shak′a·ble, shake′a·ble** *adj.*

Synonyms: *shake, tremble, quake, quiver, shiver, shudder, wobble.* These verbs mean to give evidence of agitation in the form of involuntary vibratory movement. *Shake,* the most general, applies to any such pronounced movement in a thing or a person, especially one moved by strong emotion. *Tremble* implies quick and rather slight movement like that of a person affected by fear, anger, or awe. *Quake* refers to violent convulsive movement caused by physical or emotional upheaval. *Quiver* suggests a slight and tremulous movement. *Shiver* involves rapid and rather slight movement, as of a person experiencing chill or fear. Whereas *trembling* implies localized movement in persons, *shivering* affects a wide area of the body. *Shudder* chiefly applies to sudden strong, convulsive shaking in a person, caused by fear, horror, or a revolting sight or thought. *Wobble* refers to pronounced and very unsteady movement.

shake down. *Informal.* **1.** To extort money from. See Usage note at **shakedown. 2.** To make a thorough search of. **3.** To subject to a shakedown cruise.

shake·down (shāk′doun′) *n. Informal.* **1.** An extortion of money by blackmail or other means. **2.** A thorough search of a place or person. **3.** A period of appraisal followed by adjustments to improve efficiency or functioning. —*adj.* Designed to test the performance of a ship or airplane and familiarize the crew with the operation: *a shakedown cruise.*

Usage: *Shakedown* (noun) in the sense of extortion and the related verb form *shake down* are not appropriate to deliberately formal usage, but have won increasing acceptance on all other levels. As examples in writing, the following are acceptable to majorities of the Usage Panel: *The committee found no evidence of a shakedown* (accepted by 80 per cent). *He was convicted of shaking down three film executives* (accepted by 67 per cent).

shak·er (shā′kər) *n.* **1.** One that shakes. **2.** A container used for shaking something out: *a salt shaker.* **3.** A container used to mix or blend by shaking: *a cocktail shaker.*

Shak·er (shā′kər) *n.* A member of a religious sect originating in England in 1747, practicing communal living and observing celibacy. The official name of the sect is "The United Society of Believers in Christ's Second Coming." [From the former custom of dancing with shaking movements during ceremonies.]

Shak·er Heights (shā′kər). A city of northern Ohio, a residential suburb of Cleveland. Population, 36,000.

Shake·speare (shāk′spîr), **William.** Also **Shak·spere.** 1564–1616. English dramatist and poet.

Shake·spear·e·an, Shake·spear·i·an (shāk-spîr′ē-ən) *adj.* Of, pertaining to, or like Shakespeare, his works, or his style. —*n.* A scholar of Shakespeare or his works.

Shakespearean sonnet. The sonnet form perfected by Shakespeare, composed of three quatrains and a terminal couplet with the rhyme pattern *abab cdcd efef gg,* and retaining the break or pause in theme that falls between the octave and sestet in earlier sonnet forms. Also called "Elizabethan sonnet," "English sonnet."

shake up. *Informal.* To reorganize or rearrange drastically.

shake-up (shāk′ŭp′) *n.* A thorough or drastic reorganization, as in the personnel of a business or government.

Shakh·ty (shäKH′tē). Formerly **A·lek·san·drovsk-Gru·shev·ski** (ăl′ĭk-săn′drəfsk-gro͞o-shĕf′skē). A city of the southwestern Soviet Union, northeast of Rostov. Population, 207,000.

shak·o (shăk′ō, shā′kō) *n., pl.* **-os** or **-oes.** Also **shack·o.** A stiff, cylindrical military dress hat with a metal plate in front, a short visor, and a plume. [French *schako,* from Hungarian *csákó,* from *csákó (süveg),* pointed (cap), from *csák,* peak, from German *Zacken,* point, from Middle High German *zacke.* See **dek-**[2] in Appendix.*]

Shak·ta (shäk′tə) *n.* Also **Sak·ta** (säk′tə). A member of a Hindu sect that worships Shakti. [Sanskrit *śākta,* from *śakti,* SHAKTI.] —**Shak′tism′** *n.* —**Shak′tist** *n.*

Shak·ti (shŭk′tē, shäk′-). Also **Sak·ti** (sŭk′tē, säk′-). *Hinduism.* A name for the wife of the god Shiva, the personification of nature and generative power. [Sanskrit *śakti,* from *śaknōti,* he is strong. See **kak-**[1] in Appendix.*]

shak·y (shā′kē) *adj.* **-ier, -iest. 1.** Trembling or quivering; tremulous; shaking. **2.** Unsteady or unsound; weak: *a shaky table.* **3.** Not to be depended upon; wavering; insecure: *a shaky alliance.* —**shak′i·ly** *adv.* —**shak′i·ness** *n.*

shale (shāl) *n.* A fissile rock composed of laminated layers of claylike, fine-grained sediments. [Probably Middle English *shale,* a dish, shell, Old English *sc(e)alu.* See **skel-**[1] in Appendix.*]

shall (shăl) *v.* past **should** (sho͝od) or *archaic* **shouldst** (sho͝odst) or **shouldest** (sho͝od′ĭst) for second person singular, present **shall** or *archaic* **shalt** (shălt) for second person singular. Used as an auxiliary followed by a simple infinitive or, in reply to a question or suggestion, with the infinitive understood. It can indicate: **1.** In the first person singular or plural, simple futurity: *I shall be twenty-eight tomorrow.* See Usage note below. **2.** In the second and third persons: **a.** Determination or promise: *Your service shall be rewarded.* **b.** Inevitability: *That day shall come.* **c.** Command: *Thou shalt not kill.* **d.** Compulsion, with the force of *must,* in statutes, deeds, and other legal documents: *The penalty shall not exceed two years in prison.* See Usage note below. **3.** In all persons, indefinite futurity, in conditional clauses and in clauses expressing doubt, anxiety, or desire: *If you shall ever change your opinion, come to me again.* [Shall, shalt, should; Middle English *schal, schalt, scholde,* Old English *sceal, scealt, sceolde.* See **skel-**[2] in Appendix.*]

Usage: In expressly formal usage, *shall* is employed as indicated above. In the first person it expresses simple futurity (unstressed intention or normal expectation); in the second and third persons it expresses any of the following: determination, promise, obligation, command, compulsion, permission, or inevitability. *Will,* as an auxiliary verb, is used in the opposite way: to express simple futurity in the second and third persons and to indicate one of the other conditions in the first person. However, these distinctions are not closely observed in general usage, including much serious writing. On this somewhat lower level, to indicate mere futurity, *will* is widely employed in all three persons (and *shall* is largely neglected): *We will be in London next week* (acceptable to 62 per cent of the Usage Panel as an example in writing on all levels). *Will,* in all three persons, is also employed more often than *shall* in expressing any of the forms of emphatic futurity. In speech, the degree of stress on the auxiliary verb is usually more indicative of intended meaning than the choice of *shall* or *will.* In writing, a condition other than mere futurity is often expressed more clearly by an al-

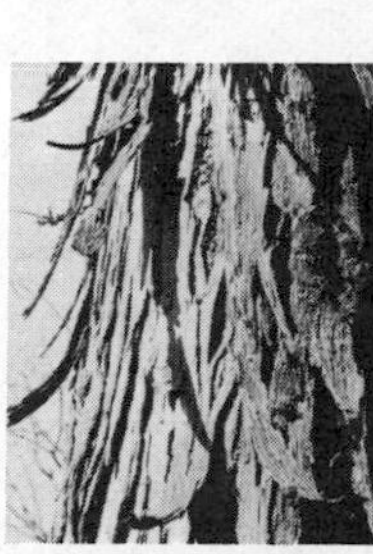

shagbark
Detail of bark

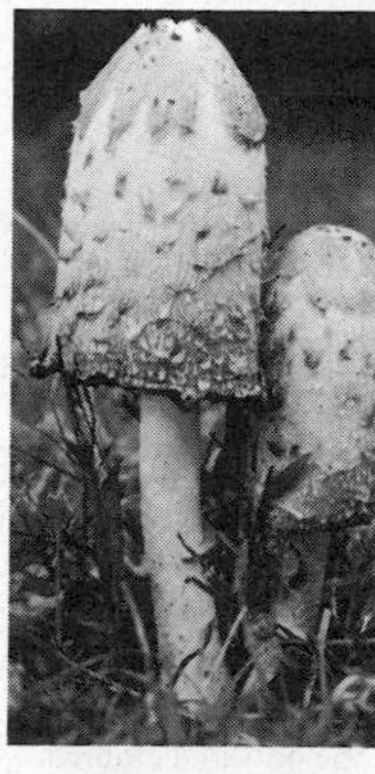

shaggy mane

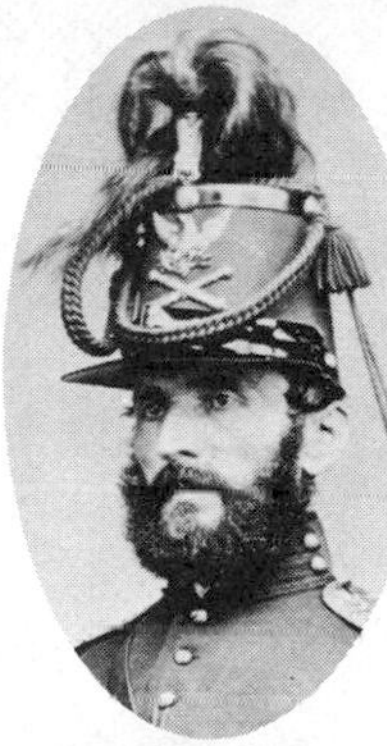

shako

ternative to *shall* or *will,* such as *must* or *have to* (indicating determination, compulsion, or obligation) or by use of an intensifying word, such as *certainly* or *surely,* with *shall* or *will.* Informally, contractions such as *I'll, we'll,* and *you'll* are generally employed without distinction between the functions of *shall* and *will* as defined formally.

shal·loon (shă-lo͞on′) *n.* A lightweight wool or worsted twill fabric, used chiefly for coat linings. [French *chalon,* from *Châlons*-sur-Marne, France.]

shal·lop (shăl′əp) *n.* An open boat fitted with oars, sails, or both. [French *chaloupe,* from Dutch *sloep,* SLOOP.]

shal·lot (shə-lŏt′) *n.* **1.** A plant, *Allium ascalonicum,* closely related to the onion, cultivated for its edible bulb that divides into smaller sections. **2.** The mildly flavored bulb of this plant, used in cookery. [Obsolete *eschalot,* from obsolete French *eschalotte,* from Old French *eschaloigne,* from Vulgar Latin *iscalōnia* (unattested), from Latin *Ascalōnia (caepa),* (onion) of Ascalon. See **scallion.**]

shal·low (shăl′ō) *adj.* **-lower, -lowest. 1.** Measuring little from bottom to top or surface; not deep. **2.** Lacking depth, as in intellect or significance: *"His intellect was of the shallowest order . . . his mind was in its original state of white paper."* (Lamb). —See Synonyms at **superficial.** —*n.* A shallow part of a body of water; a shoal. —*v.* **shallowed, -lowing, -lows.** —*tr.* To make shallow. —*intr.* To become shallow. [Middle English *schalowe,* ultimately akin to Old English *sceald,* shallows. See **shoal.**] —**shal′low·ly** *adv.* —**shal′low·ness** *n.*

sha·lom (shä-lōm′) *interj. Hebrew.* Peace. Used as a greeting or farewell. [Hebrew *shālōm,* peace, "completeness." See **slm** in Appendix.*]

sha·lom a·lei·chem (shô′ləm ä-lā′KHəm, shä-lōm′). *Hebrew.* Peace be with you. Used as a greeting or farewell.

shalt (shălt). *Archaic.* Second person singular present tense of **shall.** Used with *thou.*

sham (shăm) *n.* **1.** Something false or empty purporting to be genuine; a spurious imitation. **2.** The quality of deceitfulness; empty pretense. **3.** A person who assumes a false character; a pretender or impostor: *"He a man! Hell! He was a hollow sham!"* (Conrad). **4.** A decorative cover made to simulate an article of household linen and used over or in place of it: *a pillow sham.* —*adj.* Not genuine; fake, pretended, or counterfeit. —*v.* **shammed, shamming, shams.** —*tr.* **1.** To put on the false appearance of; feign. **2.** *Obsolete.* To deceive. —*intr.* To assume a false appearance or character; dissemble. [Possibly variant of SHAME.] —**sham′mer** *n.*

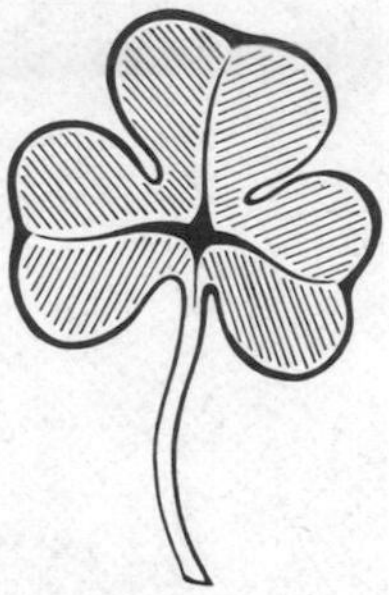

shamrock
Stylized representation of the national emblem of Ireland

sha·man (shä′mən, shā′-, shăm′ən) *n.* **1.** A priest of shamanism. **2.** A medicine man among certain North American Indians. [German *Schamane,* from Russian *shaman,* from Tungus *šaman,* from Tocharian *ṣamāne,* from Prakrit *samaṇa,* from Sanskrit *śramaṇás*†, "ascetic."]

sha·man·ism (shä′mə-nĭz′əm, shā′-, shăm′ə-) *n.* **1.** The religious practices of certain native peoples of northern Asia who believe that good and evil spirits pervade the northern world and can be summoned or heard through inspired priests acting as mediums. **2.** Any similar form of primitive spiritualism, such as that practiced among certain North American Indian tribes. —**sha′man·ist** *n.* —**sha′man·is′tic** *adj.*

Sha·mash (shä′mäsh). The sun god of Assyro-Babylonian religion, worshiped as the author of justice and compassion. [Akkadian, "sun," akin to Hebrew *shémesh.*]

sham·ble (shăm′bəl) *intr.v.* **-bled, -bling, -bles.** To walk in an awkward, lazy, or unsteady manner, shuffling the feet. —*n.* A shambling walk; shuffling gait. [From earlier *shamble,* ungainly, perhaps from *shamble legs,* probably referring to legs which were ungainly like those of a meat table. See **shambles.**]

sham·bles (shăm′bəlz) *n.* Plural in form, used with a singular verb. **1.** A scene or condition of complete disorder or ruin: *The brawlers left the bar in a shambles.* See Usage note below. **2.** A place or scene of bloodshed or carnage. **3.** A slaughterhouse. **4.** *British.* A meat market or butcher shop. [From plural of earlier *shamble,* table for display or sale of meat, from Middle English *shamel,* Old English *sc(e)amel,* table, from West Germanic *skamel* (unattested), from Latin *scamellum,* diminutive of *scamnum,* bench. See **skabh-** in Appendix.*]

Usage: *Shambles* is well established in the sense of scene or condition of complete disorder or ruin, without reference to actual bloodshed or carnage (which are inherent in earlier and still current senses of the term). Although this extended and weaker sense is sometimes objected to, it is acceptable to 85 per cent of the Usage Panel in the following, as a typical example in writing: *The painter is here, and the apartment is a shambles.*

shame (shām) *n.* **1.** A painful emotion caused by a strong sense of guilt, embarrassment, unworthiness, or disgrace. **2.** Capacity for such a feeling: *Have you no shame?* **3.** A person or thing that brings dishonor, disgrace, or condemnation. **4.** A condition of disgrace or dishonor; ignominy. **5.** A great disappointment. —See Synonyms at **disgrace.** —**put to shame. 1.** To fill with shame; to disgrace. **2.** To outdo thoroughly; surpass. —*tr.v.* **shamed, shaming, shames. 1.** To cause to feel shame; put to shame. **2.** To bring dishonor or disgrace upon. **3.** To force by making ashamed. Used with *into* or *out of: He was shamed into an apology.* [Middle English *s(c)hame,* Old English *sc(e)amu,* from Germanic *skamō* (unattested).]

shame·faced (shām′fāst′) *adj.* **1.** Indicative of shame; ashamed: *a shamefaced explanation.* **2.** Extremely modest or shy; bashful. [Variant (influenced by FACE) of earlier *shamefast,* from Middle English *sham(e)fast,* Old English *sceamfæst,* : *sceamu,* SHAME + *fæst,* FAST (firm), as if held firm by shame.] —**shame′fac′ed·ly** (-fā′sĭd-lē) *adv.* —**shame′fac′ed·ness** *n.*

shame·ful (shām′fəl) *adj.* **1.** Bringing or deserving shame; disgraceful; indecent. **2.** *Archaic.* Full of shame; shamefaced; ashamed. —**shame′ful·ly** *adv.* —**shame′ful·ness** *n.*

shame·less (shām′lĭs) *adj.* **1.** Not subject to the restraint of shame; impudent or immodest; brazen. **2.** Done without shame; indicating a lack of pride or decency: *a shameless lie.* —**shame′less·ly** *adv.* —**shame′less·ness** *n.*

Synonyms: *shameless, brazen, barefaced, brash, bold, impudent, unblushing, forward.* These adjectives describe personal behavior that is in defiance of social and moral proprieties. *Shameless* implies lack of both modesty and sense of decency, together with contempt for the rights of others. *Brazen* is somewhat stronger in its suggestion of open display of conscienceless behavior. *Barefaced* specifies absence of any attempt to conceal misconduct. *Brash* stresses impetuousness, lack of tact and forethought, and reckless indifference to consequences of action. *Bold,* as compared here, implies undue presumption. *Impudent* suggests pertness that verges on insolence. *Unblushing* implies lack of embarrassment where grounds for it clearly exist. *Forward* applies less forcefully to one who is unduly self-assertive.

sham·mes (shä′məs) *n., pl.* **shammosim** (shä-mô′sĭm). *Judaism.* **1.** A sexton in a synagogue. Also called "beadle." **2.** The candle used to light the other eight candles of the Chanukah Menorah. [Yiddish *shames,* from Hebrew *shammāsh,* from Aramaic *shəmmāsh,* to serve.]

sham·my. Variant of **chamois.**

sham·poo (shăm-po͞o′) *n., pl.* **-poos. 1.** Any of various liquid or cream preparations of soap or detergent used to wash the hair and scalp. **2.** Any of various cleaning agents for rugs or upholstery. **3.** The act or process of washing or cleaning with shampoo. —*v.* **shampooed, -pooing, -poos.** —*tr.* To wash or clean with shampoo. —*intr.* To wash the hair with shampoo. [Hindi *chāmpo,* from *chāmpnā,* massage, press, mark, from *chāp-nā,* stamp, from *chap-nā,* to be stamped, from Indo-Aryan *chapp-* (unattested), to press, cover.]

sham·rock (shăm′rŏk′) *n.* Any of several plants, such as a clover or wood sorrel, having compound leaves with three small leaflets, considered the national emblem of Ireland. [Irish *seamrog,* diminutive of *seamar,* clover, from Old Irish *semar*†.]

sha·mus (shä′məs, shā′-) *n. Slang.* A policeman or private detective. [Perhaps variant of SHAMMES.]

Shan (shän, shăn) *n.* **1.** One of a group of Mongoloid tribes living in Burma, Thailand, and southern China. **2.** A member of one of these tribes. **3.** The northern Thai language spoken by these tribes. —*adj.* Of or pertaining to this people or to their Thai language.

shan·dy·gaff (shăn′dē-găf′) *n.* A drink made of beer or ale mixed with ginger beer, ginger ale, or lemonade. Also called "shandy." [Origin unknown.]

Shang (shäng) *n.* A Chinese dynasty (1766–1122 B.C.). Its capital was **An-yang** *(see).*

shang·hai (shăng-hī′) *tr.v.* **-haied, -haiing, -hais. 1.** To kidnap (a man) for compulsory service aboard a ship, especially after rendering him insensible. **2.** To induce or compel (someone) to do something, especially by fraud or force. [After SHANGHAI (city), from the former custom of kidnaping sailors to man ships going to that city.]

Shang·hai[1] (shăng-hī′). The leading seaport of China, in the east on the Yangtze estuary. Population, 7,000,000.

Shang·hai[2] (shăng-hī′) *n.* A red and black domestic fowl of a breed said to have been imported from Asia. [From SHANGHAI (city).]

Shang·kiu (shäng′kyo͞o′). A city of eastern China, in northeastern Honan Province; the imperial residence of the Northern Sung dynasty (A.D. 960–1127). Population, 165,000.

Shan·gri-la (shăng′grĭ-lä′) *n.* An imaginary, remote paradise on earth; utopia. [After *Shangri-La,* the imaginary land in *Lost Horizon* (1933) by James Hilton (1900–1954).]

shank (shăngk) *n.* **1.** *Anatomy.* The part of the human leg between the knee and ankle or the corresponding part in other vertebrates. **2.** The whole leg of a man. **3.** A cut of meat from the leg of a steer, calf, sheep, or lamb. **4.** The long, narrow part of a nail or pin. **5.** A stem, stalk, or similar part. **6.** The stem of an anchor. **7.** The long shaft of a fishhook. **8.** That part of a tobacco pipe between the bowl and stem. **9.** The shaft of a key. **10.** The narrower section of a spoon's handle. **11. a.** The narrow part of a shoe's sole under the instep. **b.** A piece of metal or other material used to reinforce or shape this part. **12.** The ring or other projection on the back of some buttons by which they are sewn to the cloth. **13. a.** The part of a drill or other tool that connects the functioning head to the handle. **b.** A **tang** *(see).* **14. a.** The latter or remaining part of anything, especially of a period of time. **b.** The early or best part of a period of time: *the shank of the evening.* [Middle English *shanke,* Old English *sc(e)anca.* See **skeng-** in Appendix.*]

Shan·kar (shän′kär′), **Ravi.** Born 1920. Indian sitarist and composer; leader of renaissance in Indian music.

Shan·ka·ra (shŭng′kə-rä′). Also **Shan·ka·ra·char·ya** (shŭng′kə-rä-chär′yə). Indian philosopher of the early ninth century A.D.

shank·piece (shăngk′pēs′) *n.* An arch support inserted into the shank of a shoe.

shanks' mare (shăngks). *Informal.* One's own legs as a means of transportation: *go on shanks' mare.*

Shan·non (shăn′ən). A river of the Republic of Ireland, rising in the central part of the country and flowing 220 miles southwest to the Atlantic.

Shan·non (shăn′ən), **Claude Elwood.** Born 1916. American mathematician; pioneer in information theory.

Shan·si (shän′sē′). A province of China occupying 50,000

ă pat/ā pay/âr care/ä father/b bib/ch church/d deed/ĕ pet/ē be/f fife/g gag/h hat/hw which/ĭ pit/ī pie/îr pier/j judge/k kick/l lid, needle/m mum/n no, sudden/ng thing/ŏ pot/ō toe/ô paw, for/oi noise/ou out/o͝o took/o͞o boot/p pop/r roar/s sauce/sh ship, dish/

square miles in the northeast. Population, 15,960,000. Capital, Taiyüan.

Shan State (shän, shăn). Also **Shan States.** A state of Burma occupying 60,090 square miles in eastern Upper Burma and divided politically into Northern Shan State and Southern Shan State. Population, 1,506,000. Capital, Taunggyi.

shan't, sha'nt (shănt, shänt). Contractions of *shall not.*

shan·tey. Variant of **chantey.**

shan·tung (shăn′tŭng′) *n.* **1.** A heavy silk fabric with a rough, nubby surface, made of spun wild silk. **2.** An imitation of this fabric, made of rayon or cotton. [Manufactured in SHANTUNG.]

Shan·tung (shăn′tŭng′; *Chinese* shän′dōong′). A province of China occupying 59,200 square miles in the east, including the Shantung Peninsula, a projection of land between the Yellow Sea on the south and the Gulf of Po Hai on the north. Population, 54,030,000. Capital, Tsinan.

shan·ty[1] (shăn′tē) *n., pl.* **-ties.** A roughly built or ramshackle cabin; shack. [Perhaps from Irish *sean tig,* "old house" : *sean,* old (see **sen-[1]** in Appendix*) + *tig,* house, from Old Irish *tech* (see **steg-[1]** in Appendix*).]

shan·ty[2]. Variant of **chantey.**

shan·ty·man (shăn′tē-mən, -măn′) *n., pl.* **-men** (-mĭn, -mĕn′). A man who lives in a shanty; especially, a lumberjack.

shan·ty·town (shăn′tē-toun′) *n.* A town or section of a town consisting of ramshackle huts or shanties.

Shao·hing (shou′shĭng′). Also **Shao·hsing.** A city of China, in north-central Chekiang Province. Population, 160,000.

shape (shāp) *n.* **1.** The outline or characteristic surface configuration of a thing; a contour; form. **2.** The contour of a person's body; figure. **3.** Developed, definite, or proper form. **4.** Any form or condition in which something may exist or appear; embodiment. **5.** Assumed or false appearance; guise. **6.** An imaginary or ghostly form; phantom. **7.** Something used to give or determine form, as a mold or pattern. **8.** *Informal.* Condition as regards efficiency or state of repair; form. —See Synonyms at **form.** —*v.* **shaped, shaped** or *archaic* **shapen** (shā′pən), **shaping, shapes.** —*tr.* **1.** To give a particular form to. **2.** To cause to conform to a particular form or pattern; modify; adapt to fit. **3.** To plan and supervise. —*intr.* **1.** *Informal.* To take a definite form; develop. Often used with *into* or *up.* **2.** *Informal.* To proceed or develop in a satisfactory or desirable manner. Used with *up.* [Middle English *schap, shape,* Old English *(ge)sceap.* See **skep-** in Appendix.*]

SHAPE (shāp) Supreme Headquarters Allied Powers, Europe.

shape·less (shāp′lĭs) *adj.* **1.** Having no distinct shape. **2.** Lacking symmetrical or attractive form; not shapely. —**shape′less·ly** *adv.* —**shape′less·ness** *n.*

shape·ly (shāp′lē) *adj.* **-lier, -liest.** Having a pleasing shape; well-proportioned: *a shapely figure.* —**shape′li·ness** *n.*

shape·up (shāp′ŭp′) *n.* An assembled group of longshoremen from which the day's work crew will be chosen by a representative of the union.

Shap·ley (shăp′lē), **Harlow.** Born 1885. American astronomer; worked in photometry, spectroscopy, and cosmology.

shard (shärd) *n.* Also **sherd** (shûrd). **1.** A piece of broken pottery; a **potsherd** *(see).* **2.** A fragment of a brittle substance, as of glass or metal. **3.** *Zoology.* A tough sheath; especially, the outer wing covering of a beetle. [Middle English *sherd,* Old English *sceard.* See **sker-[1]** in Appendix.*]

share[1] (shâr) *n.* **1.** A part or portion belonging to, distributed to, contributed by, or owed by a person or group. **2.** An equitable, reasonable, or full portion. **3.** *Abbr.* **sh., shr.** Any of the equal parts into which the capital stock of a corporation or company is divided. —**go shares.** To be concerned or partake equally or jointly, as in a business venture. —**on shares.** With each individual concerned taking a share, usually equal, of any profit or loss. Said of an enterprise. —*v.* **shared, sharing, shares.** —*tr.* **1.** To divide and parcel out in shares; apportion. **2.** To participate in, use, or experience in common. —*intr.* To have or take a part; participate; join. Usually used with *in: share in an effort.* [Middle English *share,* division, share, Old English *sceāru,* division or fork of the body, tonsure. See **sker-[1]** in Appendix.*] —**shar′er** *n.*

Synonyms: *share, participate, partake.* These verbs refer to forms of joint activity, such as having, using, or experiencing something with others. *Share* applies both to possession, use, and enjoyment of physical things and to division of what is nonphysical, such as responsibility or work. *Participate* implies taking an active part in activities or experiences with others. *Partake,* a less common term, usually refers to having a portion of something, especially food or drink, but can be applied to involvement in intangible things, such as emotional experiences.

share[2] (shâr) *n.* A plowshare. [Middle English *shaar,* Old English *scēar.* See **sker-[1]** in Appendix.*]

share·crop·per (shâr′krŏp′ər) *n.* A tenant farmer who gives a share of his crop to the landlord in lieu of rent.

share·hold·er (shâr′hōl′dər) *n.* A person who owns or holds a share or shares of stock; a stockholder.

Sha·rett (shə-rĕt′), **Moshe.** 1894–1965. Russian-born Israeli statesman; prime minister (1953–55).

Sha·ri (shä′rē). *French* **Cha·ri** (shȧ-rē′). A river of western Africa flowing from the Central African Republic about 1,400 miles northwest through Chad to Lake Chad.

sha·rif. Variant of **sherif.**

shark[1] (shärk) *n.* Any of numerous chiefly marine fishes of the order Squaliformes (or Selachii), having a cartilaginous skeleton and tough skin covered with small, toothlike scales, and sometimes large and voracious. [Origin obscure.]

shark[2] (shärk) *n.* **1.** A ruthless, greedy, or dishonest person; a vicious usurer. **2.** *Slang.* A person with unusually great skill in some field of activity. —*intr.v.* **sharked, sharking, sharks.** To live by fraud and trickery. [Probably from SHARK (fish).]

shark·skin (shärk′skĭn′) *n.* **1.** A shark's skin. **2.** Leather made from a shark's skin. **3.** A rayon and acetate fabric having a smooth, somewhat shiny surface.

Sharm el Sheik (shärm′ ĕl shāk′). An Egyptian military station at the southeastern tip of the Sinai Peninsula, seized by Israeli forces in 1967.

Shar·on (shăr′ən). A feminine given name. [Hebrew *Shārōn,* short for *yəshārōn,* "the plain."]

Shar·on, Plain of (shăr′ən). A section of the coastal plain of western Israel, extending southward about 50 miles from Mount Carmel.

sharp (shärp) *adj.* **sharper, sharpest.** **1.** Having a thin, keen edge or a fine, acute point; suitable for or capable of cutting or piercing: *a sharp knife.* **2.** Having an acute edge or point; not rounded or blunt; peaked: *a sharp nose.* **3.** Abrupt or acute; not gradual; sudden. **4.** Clear or marked; distinct. **5.** Shrewd; astute. **6.** Artful; underhand. **7.** Vigilant; alert. **8.** Brisk; ardent; vigorous. **9.** Harsh; biting; acrimonious. **10.** Fierce or impetuous; violent. **11.** Intense; severe. **12.** Sudden and shrill. **13.** Composed of hard, angular particles: *sharp sand.* **14.** *Music.* **a.** Raised in pitch by a semitone. **b.** Above the proper pitch. **c.** Having the key signature in sharps. Compare **flat.** **15.** *Phonetics.* Voiceless. Said of a consonant. **16.** *Slang.* Pleasing in appearance or personality; attractive or stylish: *a sharp jacket.* —*adv.* **1.** In a sharp manner. **2.** Punctually; exactly. **3.** *Music.* Above the true or proper pitch. —*n.* **1. a.** A musical note or tone raised one semitone above its normal pitch. **b.** A sign (♯) indicating this. Compare **flat.** **2.** A slender sewing needle with a very fine point. **3.** *Informal.* A shrewd cheater; a sharper. —*v.* **sharped, sharping, sharps.** *Music.* —*tr.* To raise in pitch by a half step. —*intr.* To sound above the proper pitch. [Middle English *s(c)harp,* Old English *scearp.* See **sker-[1]** in Appendix.*] —**sharp′ly** *adv.* —**sharp′ness** *n.*

Synonyms: *sharp, keen, acute.* These adjectives describe edges or points that are not dull; they may also indicate degrees of mental awareness. *Sharp* applies to a point or an edge that can easily pierce or cut. *Keen* usually specifies a long, sharp cutting edge. *Acute* applies both to what has a pointed tip or end and to an angle of less than 90 degrees. Figuratively, *sharp* suggests quickness of perception or cleverness. *Keen* implies both mental vigor and discernment. *Acute* implies even more strongly a penetrating analytical ability.

sharp·en (shär′pən) *v.* **-ened, -ening, -ens.** —*tr.* To make sharp or sharper. —*intr.* To grow sharp or sharper. —**sharp′en·er** *n.*

sharp·er (shär′pər) *n.* One who deals dishonestly with others; especially, a gambler who cheats.

sharp-eyed (shärp′īd′) *adj.* **1.** Having keen eyesight. **2.** Keenly perceptive or observant; alert.

sharp·ie (shär′pē) *n.* **1.** A long, narrow, flat-bottomed fishing boat used in New England, having a centerboard and one or two masts, each rigged with a triangular sail. **2.** *Informal.* An alert or quick-witted person. [From SHARP.]

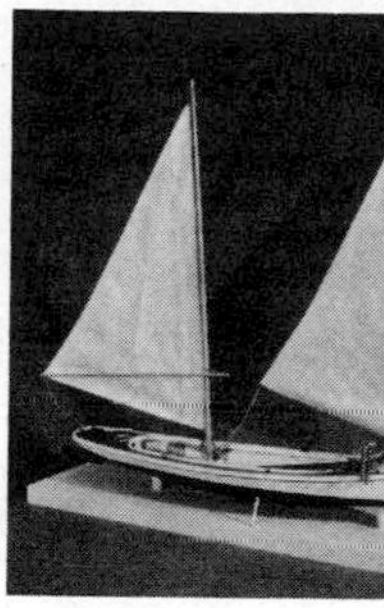

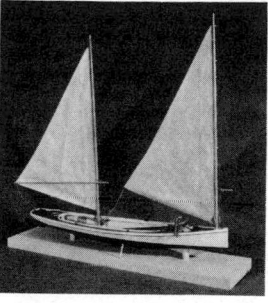

sharpie

Sharps·burg (shärps′bûrg). A town in western Maryland; site of the Civil War battle of Antietam (1862).

sharp-shinned hawk (shärp′shĭnd′). A small North American hawk, *Accipiter striatus,* having short, rounded wings and a long tail.

sharp·shoot·er (shärp′shōō′tər) *n.* **1.** An expert marksman. **2.** *Military.* **a.** The second grade of proficiency in the use of rifles and other small arms. Compare **expert, marksman. b.** A person having this grade of proficiency.

sharp-tongued (shärp′tŭngd′) *adj.* Harsh, critical, or sarcastic.

shash·lik, shash·lick (shäsh-lĭk′, shäsh′lĭk) *n.* A dish consisting of marinated cubes of mutton or veal, grilled or roasted on a spit, often with slices of eggplant, onion, and tomato; shish kebab. [Russian *shashlyk,* of Turkic origin.]

Shas·ta, Mount (shăs′tə). An extinct volcano, 14,162 feet high, in the Cascade Range of northern California.

Shas·ta daisy (shăs′tə). A cultivated variety of *Chrysanthemum maximum,* of the Pyrenees, having large, white, daisylike flowers. [From Mt. SHASTA, named by Luther Burbank, who lived in California.]

Shas·tri (shäs′trē), **Lal Bahadur.** 1904–1966. Indian statesman; prime minister (1964–66).

shat. *Vulgar.* Alternate past tense and past participle of **shit.**

Shatt-al-Ar·ab (shăt′ăl-ăr′əb). A river formed by the confluence of the Tigris and the Euphrates in southeastern Iraq and flowing southeast about 120 miles to the Persian Gulf, forming part of the Iran-Iraq border.

shat·ter (shăt′ər) *v.* **-tered, -tering, -ters.** —*tr.* **1.** To cause to break or burst suddenly into pieces, as with a violent blow. **2.** To damage seriously; disable; ruin. —*intr.* To break into pieces; smash or burst. —See Synonyms at **break.** —*n.* **1.** The act of shattering. **2.** *Usually plural.* A splintered or fragmented condition. [Middle English *schateren,* Old English *sc(e)aterian.* See **skhed-** in Appendix.*]

shat·ter·proof glass (shăt′ər-prōōf′). **Safety glass** *(see).*

shave (shāv) *v.* **shaved, shaved** or **shaven** (shā′vən), **shaving, shaves.** —*tr.* **1.** To remove the beard or other body hair from, as with a razor. **2.** To cut (the beard, for example) at the surface of the skin with a razor. Often used with *off* or *away.* **3.** To crop, trim, or mow closely: *shave a meadow.* **4.** To remove thin slices from. **5.** To cut or scrape into thin slices; shred. **6.** To come close to or graze in passing. **7.** *Informal.* To purchase (a note) at a reduction greater than the legal or customary rate.

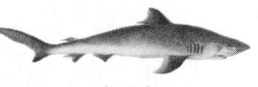

shark[1]
Prionace glauca

t tight/th thin, path/*th* this, bathe/ŭ cut/ûr urge/v valve/w with/y yes/z zebra, size/zh vision/ə about, item, edible, gallop, circus/ ȧ *Fr.* ami/œ *Fr.* feu, *Ger.* schön/ü *Fr.* tu, *Ger.* über/KH *Ger.* ich, *Scot.* loch/N *Fr.* bon. ***Follows main vocabulary.** †**Of obscure origin.**

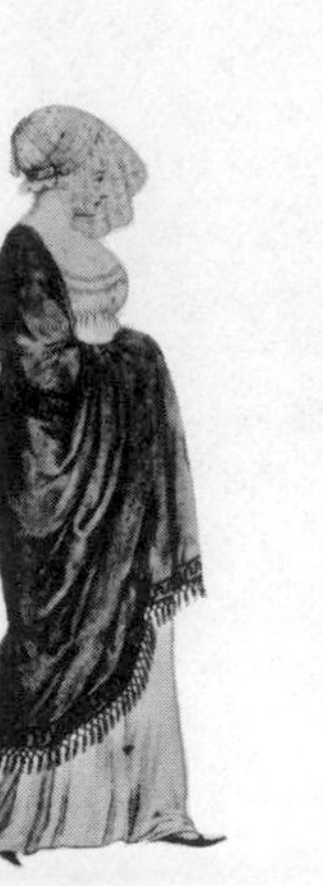
shawl
Late 18th-century French

8. *Informal.* To cut (a price) by a slight margin. —*intr.* To remove a beard or hair with a razor. —*n.* **1.** The act, process, or result of shaving. **2.** A thin slice or scraping; a shaving. **3.** Any of various tools used for shaving. —**close shave.** *Informal.* A narrow escape. [Middle English *shaven,* to scrape, shave, Old English *sceafan.* See **skep-** in Appendix.*]

shav·er (shā′vər) *n.* **1. a.** A person who shaves. **b.** An electric or mechanical device used to shave. **2.** *Informal.* A small child, especially a boy.

Sha·vi·an (shā′vē-ən) *adj.* Of or characteristic of George Bernard Shaw or his works: *Shavian wit.* —*n.* An admirer or disciple of George Bernard Shaw. [From *Shavius,* pseudo-Latin form of the name *Shaw.*]

shav·ing (shā′vĭng) *n.* **1.** A thin slice; sliver. **2.** The action of one that shaves.

Sha·vu·ot (shə-vo͞o′ōt, -ōth′, -əs) *n.* Also **Sha·bu·oth.** A Jewish holiday commemorating the revelation of the Law on Mount Sinai and the celebration of the wheat festival in ancient times, observed on the sixth and seventh of Sivan. Also called "Feast of Weeks." [Hebrew *shābhū′ōth,* from *shābhūa′,* week.]

Shaw (shô), **George Bernard.** 1856–1950. Irish-born English dramatist, critic, and essayist.

Shaw (shô), **Henry Wheeler.** See **Josh Billings.**

shawl (shôl) *n.* A square or oblong piece of cloth worn by women as a covering for the head, neck, and shoulders. [Earlier *shal, shaul,* from Urdu, from Persian *shāl*†.]

shawm (shôm) *n.* Any of various early double-reed wind instruments, forerunners of the modern oboe. [Middle English *schallemele, schalme,* from Old French *chalemel,* from Vulgar Latin *calamellus* (unattested), diminutive of Latin *calamus,* reed, from Greek *kalamos.* See **kolem-** in Appendix.*]

Shaw·nee (shô-nē′) *n., pl.* **Shawnee** or **-nees.** **1.** A tribe of Algonquian-speaking North American Indians, formerly living in the Tennessee Valley and adjacent areas, now surviving in Oklahoma. **2.** A member of this tribe. **3.** The language of this tribe. [Obsolete *Shawanese, Shawnoes,* from Delaware *šāonu,* from Shawnee *šăwanwa,* a Shawnee, from Proto-Algonquian *šāwanw-* (unattested), "south."]

Shaw·wal (shə-wäl′) *n.* The tenth month of the year in the Moslem calendar. See **calendar.** [Arabic *Shawwāl.*]

shay (shā) *n. Regional.* A chaise. [Back-formation from CHAISE, which was mistaken for a plural.]

Shays (shāz), **Daniel.** 1747?–1825. American military officer in the Revolutionary War; led rebellion in the Commonwealth of Massachusetts (1786–87).

Sha·zar (shə-zär′), **Schneor Zalman.** Original surname, Rubashev. Born 1889. Russian-born Israeli journalist and statesman; president of Israel (since 1963).

Shcher·ba·kov. The former name for **Rybinsk.**

she (shē) *pron.* The third person singular pronoun in the nominative case, feminine gender. **1.** Used to represent the female person, animal, or other being last mentioned or implied. **2.** Used traditionally of certain objects and institutions such as ships and nations. **3.** Applied in a certain informal style to things not usually personified: *That problem, she was a mean one!* —*n.* **1.** A female animal or person: *Is the cat a she?* **2.** Often used in combination: *a she-cat.* [Middle English *s(c)ho, s(c)he,* Old English *sēo,* she (Old English *hēo,* she, remained in some Middle English dialects but only appears in Modern English HER). See **so-** in Appendix.*]

shea butter (shē, shā). A whitish or yellowish fat obtained from the nut of the **shea tree** *(see),* used as food and for making soap and candles.

sheaf (shēf) *n., pl.* **sheaves** (shēvz). **1.** A bundle of cut stalks of grain or similar plants bound with straw or twine. **2.** Any gathering or collection of articles held or bound together. **3.** An archer's quiver of arrows. —*tr.v.* **sheafed, sheafing, sheafs.** To bind into a sheaf. [Middle English *sheef, shefe,* Old English *scēaf.* See **skeup-** in Appendix.*]

shear (shîr) *v.* **sheared** or *archaic* **shore** (shôr, shōr), **sheared** or **shorn** (shôrn, shōrn), **shearing, shears.** —*tr.* **1.** To remove (fleece, hair, or the like) by cutting or clipping with a sharp instrument. **2.** To remove the hair or fleece from. **3.** To cut with or as if with shears. **4.** To strip, divest, or deprive of. —*intr.* **1.** To use shears or a similar cutting tool. **2.** To move or proceed by or as if by cutting. Used with *through.* **3.** *Physics.* To become deformed by forces tending to produce a **shearing strain** *(see).* —*n.* **1.** The act, process, or result of shearing. **2.** Something cut off by shearing. **3.** A shearing. Used to indicate a sheep's age: *a two-shear ram.* **4.** *Physics.* **a.** An applied force or system of forces that tends to produce a **shearing strain** *(see).* In this sense, also called "shear stress," "shearing stress." **b.** Shearing strain. [Shear, shore, shorn; Middle English *sc(h)eren, share, shorn,* Old English *sceran, scǣron* (third person plural), *scoren.* See **sker-**[1] in Appendix.*] —**shear′er** *n.*

shearing strain. A condition in or deformation of an elastic body caused by forces that tend to produce an opposite but parallel sliding motion of the body's planes.

shear legs. Also **sheer-legs** (shîr′lĕgz′). An apparatus used to lift heavy weights, consisting of two or more spars joined at the top and spread at the base, the tackle being suspended from the top. Also called "shears."

shear·ling (shîr′lĭng) *n.* **1.** A year-old sheep that has been once shorn. **2.** The skin of such a sheep, or of any newly shorn sheep, tanned and with the wool on. [Middle English *scherling* : *scheren,* to SHEAR + -LING.]

shears (shîrz) *pl.n.* Also **sheers** (for sense 3). **1.** Large-sized scissors. Also called a "pair of shears." **2.** Any of various other implements or machines that cut with scissorlike action. **3.** A lifting crane, a **shear legs** *(see).* [From Middle English *s(c)here* (singular), scissors, Old English *scēara* (plural). See **sker-**[1] in Appendix.*]

shear·wa·ter (shîr′wô′tər, -wŏt′ər) *n.* Any of various oceanic birds of the family Procellariidae, especially of the genus *Puffinus,* having long wings and a hooked bill. [From its habit of skimming close to the water.]

sheat·fish (shēt′fĭsh′) *n., pl.* **sheatfish** or **-fishes.** A large freshwater catfish, *Silurus glanis,* of Eurasia. [Variant of obsolete *sheath-fish* : SHEATH (probably from its shell-like covering or its sheathlike shape) + FISH.]

sheath (shēth) *n., pl.* **sheaths** (shē*th*z, shēths). **1.** A case for the blade of a knife, sword, or similar instrument. **2.** Any of various coverings applied like or resembling a sheath. **3.** *Biology.* An enveloping structure or part, such as the tubular base of a leaf surrounding a stem. **4.** A close-fitting dress, usually having a straight skirt and no belt. —*tr.v.* **sheathed, sheathing, sheaths.** To sheathe. [Middle English *s(c)hethe,* Old English *scēath, scǣth.* See **skei-** in Appendix.*]

sheath·bill (shēth′bĭl′) *n.* Either of two shore birds, *Chionia alba* or *C. minor,* of Antarctic regions, having white plumage and a horny covering on the base of the bill.

sheathe (shē*th*) *tr.v.* **sheathed, sheathing, sheathes.** **1.** To insert into or provide with a sheath. **2.** To retract (a claw) into a sheath or sheaths. **3.** To encase in sheathing. —**sheath′er** *n.*

sheath·ing (shē′*th*ĭng) *n.* **1.** A layer of boards or of other wood or fiber materials applied to the outer studs, joists, and rafters of a building to strengthen the structure and serve as a base for an exterior weatherproof cladding. **2.** An exterior covering, usually metal, on the underwater part of a ship's hull, to protect against marine growths. **3.** The action of providing sheathing for something.

sheath knife. A knife having a fixed blade and fitting into a sheath.

shea tree (shā, shē). An African tree, *Butyrospermum parkii,* having fruit containing oily seeds that yield an edible fat called shea butter. [From Bambara *si.*]

sheave[1] (shēv) *tr.v.* **sheaved, sheaving, sheaves.** To bind into a sheaf or sheaves; gather; collect.

sheave[2] (shĭv) *n.* A wheel or disk with a grooved rim, especially one used as a pulley. [Middle English *shive, sheve,* Old English *scife* (unattested). See **skei-** in Appendix.*]

sheaves (shēvz *for sense 1,* shĭvz *for sense 2*). **1.** Plural of **sheaf.** **2.** Plural of **sheave.**

She·ba (shē′bə). *Arabic* **Sa·ba** (sä′bä). The Biblical name for a region of the Arabian peninsula now occupied by Yemen.

She·ba (shē′bə), **Queen of.** A queen who came from southern Arabia to test the wisdom of King Solomon. I Kings 10:1.

she·bang (shĭ-băng′) *n. Informal.* A situation, organization, contrivance, or set of facts or things. Chiefly used in the phrase *the whole shebang.* [Origin uncertain.]

She·bat. Variant of **Shevat.**

shed[1] (shĕd) *v.* **shed, shedding, sheds.** —*tr.* **1.** To pour forth or cause to pour forth: *"If you have tears, prepare to shed them now"* (Shakespeare). **2.** To send forth; diffuse or radiate: *shed light; shed confidence.* **3.** To repel without allowing penetration: *A duck's feathers shed water.* **4.** To lose by natural process: *"He was a middle-aged child that had never shed its baby fat."* (Truman Capote). —*intr.* **1.** To lose a natural growth or covering by natural process. **2.** To pour forth, fall off, or drop out: *All the leaves have shed.* —**shed blood.** To take life; to kill. —*n.* **1.** Something that sheds; especially, an elevation in the earth's surface from which water flows in two directions; a watershed. **2.** Something that has been shed. [Shed, shed (past tense and past participle); Middle English *sheden, schede, scheden,* shed, divide, Old English *scēadan, scēad, sceāden,* to divide. See **skei-** in Appendix.*]

shed[2] (shĕd) *n.* **1.** A small structure, either freestanding or attached to a larger structure, serving for storage or shelter. **2.** A large structure, often open on all sides, for storage or shelter. [Earlier *shadde,* perhaps specialized use of SHADE.]

she'd (shēd). **1.** Contraction of *she had.* **2.** Contraction of *she would.*

shed·der (shĕd′ər) *n.* One that sheds, as a long-haired animal or a molting snake.

shed dormer. A dormer having a roof that slopes in the same direction as the one in which the dormer is located.

she-dev·il (shē′dĕv′əl) *n.* A malicious or cruel woman.

sheen (shēn) *n.* **1.** Glistening brightness; shininess: *"And the sheen of their spears was like stars on the sea"* (Byron). **2.** *Poetic.* Splendid attire. [From Middle English *shene,* beautiful, bright, Old English *sciene, scēne.* See **keu-**[1] in Appendix.*]

sheen·y (shē′nē) *n., pl.* **-ies.** A Jew. An offensive term, used derogatorily. [Origin unknown.]

sheep (shēp) *n., pl.* **sheep.** **1.** Any of various usually horned, ruminant mammals of the genus *Ovis;* especially, the domesticated species *O. aries,* raised in many breeds for its wool, edible flesh, or skin. **2.** The skin of a sheep or leather made from it. **3.** One who is meek and submissive. [Middle English *she(e)p,* Old English *scē(a)p,* from West Germanic *skǣpa* (unattested).]

sheep·back (shēp′băk′) *n. Geology.* **Roche moutonnée** *(see).*

sheep·ber·ry (shēp′bĕr′ē) *n., pl.* **-ries.** A North American shrub or tree, *Viburnum lentago,* having clusters of white flowers and blue-black edible berries. Also called "nannyberry." [From the supposed resemblance of its berries to sheep droppings.]

sheep·cote (shēp′kōt′, -kŏt′) *n.* A sheepfold. [Middle English *shepcote* : *shep,* SHEEP + *cote,* shed, COTE.]

sheep dip. Any of various liquid disinfectants used to destroy parasites in the wool of sheep prior to shearing.

sheep dog. Also **sheep·dog** (shēp′dôg′, -dŏg′). A dog trained to guard and herd sheep. See **Old English sheepdog.**
sheep·fold (shēp′fōld′) *n.* A pen for sheep.
sheep·herd·er (shēp′hûr′dər) *n.* One who herds a large flock of sheep in open range; a shepherd. **—sheep′herd′ing** *n.*
sheep·ish (shē′pĭsh) *adj.* **1.** Embarrassed, as by consciousness of a fault: *a sheepish grin.* **2.** Resembling a sheep in meekness or stupidity. **—sheep′ish·ly** *adv.* **—sheep′ish·ness** *n.*
sheep laurel. An evergreen shrub, *Kalmia angustifolia,* of eastern North America, having rose-pink flowers and poisonous foliage. Also called "lambkill."
sheep's eyes. Shyly amorous glances.
sheep·shank (shēp′shăngk′) *n.* A knot used to shorten a line.
sheeps·head (shēps′hĕd′) *n.* **1.** A food fish, *Archosargus probatocephalus,* of American Atlantic waters, having dark, vertical markings. **2.** *Archaic.* A silly or stupid person. [Sense 1, from the resemblance of its teeth to those of a sheep.]
sheep·shear·ing (shēp′shîr′ĭng) *n.* **1.** The act of shearing sheep. **2. a.** The time or season when sheep are sheared. **b.** The festivities held at this time. **—sheep′shear′er** *n.*
sheep·skin (shēp′skĭn′) *n.* **1.** The skin of a sheep either tanned with the fleece left on or in the form of leather or parchment. **2.** A diploma.
sheep·weed (shēp′wēd′) *n.* A plant, the **butterwort** *(see).*
sheer[1] (shîr) *v.* **sheered, sheering, sheers.** *—intr.* To swerve or deviate from a course. *—tr.* To cause to swerve or deviate. *—n.* **1.** A swerving or deviating course. **2.** *Nautical.* **a.** The upward curve, or the amount of upward curve, of the longitudinal lines of a ship's hull as viewed from the side. **b.** The position in which a ship is placed to enable it to keep clear of a single bow anchor. [Perhaps a variant of SHEAR.]
sheer[2] (shîr) *adj.* **sheerer, sheerest. 1.** Thin, fine, and transparent; diaphanous. Said of a fabric. **2.** Not mixed or blended with anything; undiluted; pure: *"the mole waggled his toes from sheer happiness"* (Kenneth Grahame). **3.** Perpendicular or nearly perpendicular; steep: *"Sheer greystone walls . . . against the pale yellow sky"* (Dodie Smith). *—adv.* Perpendicularly or nearly perpendicularly: *"A stone . . . would have fallen sheer downward one thousand feet"* (Ambrose Bierce). [Perhaps Middle English *schir,* bright, shining, Old English *scīr.* See **skī-** in Appendix.*] **—sheer′ly** *adv.* **—sheer′ness** *n.*
sheer·legs. Variant of **shear legs.**
sheers. Variant of **shears.**
sheet[1] (shēt) *n. Abbr.* **sh. 1.** A rectangular piece of linen or similar material serving as a basic article of bedding, commonly used in pairs, one above and one below the body of the sleeper. **2.** A broad, thin, usually rectangular mass or piece of any material, as paper, metal, glass, or plywood. **3.** A broad, flat, continuous surface or expanse: *a sheet of rain.* **4.** A newspaper; especially, a tabloid. **5.** *Geology.* A broad, relatively thin deposit or layer of igneous or sedimentary rock. **6.** *Philately.* The large block of stamps printed by a single impression of a plate before the individual stamps have been separated. *—tr.v.* **sheeted, sheeting, sheets.** To cover with, wrap in, or provide with a sheet or sheets. [Middle English *s(c)hete,* cloth, sheet, towel, Old English *scēte.* See **skeud-** in Appendix.*]
sheet[2] (shēt) *n. Nautical.* A rope or chain attached to one or both of the lower corners of a sail, serving to move or extend it. **—three sheets to the wind.** *Informal.* Drunk. *—intr.v.* **sheeted, sheeting, sheets.** *Nautical.* To extend in a certain direction. Used of the sheets of a sail. [Middle English *s(c)hete,* Old English *scēata,* corner of a sail. See **skeud-** in Appendix.*]
sheet anchor. 1. A large extra anchor intended for use in emergency. **2.** A person or thing that can be turned to in time of emergency. [Perhaps SHEET (rope) + ANCHOR.]
sheet bend. A knot in which one rope or piece of yarn is made fast to the bight of another.
sheet glass. Molten glass drawn into a wide sheet which, after annealing and hardening, is cut into required lengths.
sheet·ing (shē′tĭng) *n.* **1.** Any material, as metal or cloth, used to make a sheet. **2.** The act or process of sheeting.
sheet lightning. Lightning that appears as a broad, sheetlike illumination of parts of a thundercloud, caused by the reflection of a lightning flash.
sheet music. Music printed on unbound sheets of paper.
sheets (shēts) *pl.n. Nautical.* The spaces at the bow and stern of an open rowboat that are not occupied by oarsmen.
Shef·field (shĕf′ēld). A city and cutlery-manufacturing center of the West Riding, Yorkshire, England. Population, 489,000.
she·getz (shā′gĭts) *n., pl.* **shkotzim** (shkôt′sĭm). **1.** A non-Jewish boy or young man. Usually used disparagingly. **2.** A Jewish boy or young man who fails to live up to traditional Jewish teachings or practices. Usually used disparagingly. [Yiddish *sheygets,* from Hebrew *sheqeṣ,* blemish.]
sheik (shēk, shāk) *n.* Also **sheikh. 1. a.** A Moslem religious official. **b.** The leader of an Arab family, village, or tribe. **2.** *Slang.* A romantically alluring man. [Arabic *shaikh,* old man, from *shākha,* to be old.]
sheik·dom (shēk′dəm, shāk′-) *n.* The area ruled by a sheik.
Shei·la (shē′lə). Also **Shei·lah.** A feminine given name. [Irish, variant of CELIA.]
shei·tan. Variant of **shaitan.**
shek·el (shĕk′əl) *n.* **1.** Any of several ancient units of weight; especially, a Hebrew unit equal to about half an ounce. **2.** A gold or silver coin equal in weight to one of these units; especially, the chief silver coin of the Hebrews. **3.** *Slang.* A coin; cash; money. [Hebrew *sheqel,* from *shāqal,* to weigh, akin to Akkadian *shiqlu,* a weight.]
She·ki·nah (shĭ-kē′nə) *n.* A visible manifestation of the divine presence as described in Jewish theology. [Hebrew *shəkhīnāh,* from *shākhan,* to dwell.]
shel·drake (shĕl′drāk′) *n.* **1.** Any of various large Old World ducks of the genus *Tadorna;* especially, *T. tadorna,* having predominantly black and white plumage. Also called "shelduck." **2.** Any of several other ducks; especially, the **merganser** *(see).* [Middle English *sheldedrake* : *sheld-,* variegated, perhaps of Low German origin, akin to Middle Dutch *schillede* (see **skel-**[1] in Appendix*) + DRAKE (duck).]
shelf (shĕlf) *n., pl.* **shelves** (shĕlvz). **1.** A flat, usually rectangular structure of a rigid material, as of wood, glass, or metal, fixed at right angles to a wall or other vertical surface and used to hold or store objects. **2.** The contents or capacity of such a structure. **3.** Anything resembling such an object, as a balcony or a ledge of rock. **4.** A reef, sandbar, or shoal. **5.** *Mining.* Bedrock. **—on the shelf. 1.** In a state of disuse; put aside. **2.** Unemployed; out of circulation; retired. [Middle English *shelf(e),* perhaps from Middle Low German *schelf.* See **skel-**[1] in Appendix.*]
shelf ice. An extension of glacial ice into coastal waters, in contact with the bottom near the shore but not toward the outer edge of the shelf.
Shel·i·kof Strait (shĕl′ĭ-kôf′). A strait 30 miles wide between the Alaska Peninsula and the Kodiak and Afognak islands.
shell (shĕl) *n.* **1. a.** The usually hard outer covering that encases certain organisms. **b.** A similar outer covering on an egg, fruit, or nut. **2.** The material composing such a covering. **3.** Anything resembling or having the form of such a covering, especially: **a.** A framework or exterior, as of a building. **b.** A thin layer of pastry. **c.** The hull of a ship. **d.** The external part of the ear. **e.** A long, narrow racing boat propelled by oarsmen. **4. a.** A projectile or piece of ammunition; especially, the hollow tube containing explosives used to propel such a projectile. **b.** A metal or cardboard case, containing the charge, primer, and shot, fired from a shotgun. **5.** An attitude or manner adopted to mask one's true feelings. **6.** *Physics.* **a.** Any of the set of hypothetical spherical surfaces centered on the nucleus of an atom that contain the orbits of electrons having the same principal quantum number; hence, all the electrons in an atom that have the same principal quantum number. **b.** Any of a set of groupings of nucleon energy states in a nucleus, or of nucleons occupying such states, in which the binding energies of states differ from one another by much less than from the binding energies of states in another grouping. *—v.* **shelled, shelling, shells.** *—tr.* **1. a.** To remove the shell of; to shuck. **b.** To remove from a shell, pod, or the like. **2.** To separate the kernels of (corn) from the cob. **3.** To fire shells at; bombard. **4.** *Informal.* To pay. Used with *out.* *—intr.* To shed or become free of a shell. [Middle English *shell,* Old English *scell, scill.* See **skel-**[1] in Appendix.*] **—shell′er** *n.* **—shell′y** *adj.*
she'll (shēl). **1.** Contraction of *she will.* **2.** Contraction of *she shall.*
shel·lac (shə-lăk′) *n.* Also **shel·lack, shell-lac. 1.** A purified lac formed into thin yellow or orange flakes, often bleached white, and widely used in varnishes, paints, stains, inks, and sealing wax, as a binder, and in phonograph records. **2.** A thin varnish made by dissolving flake shellac in denatured alcohol, used as a wood coating and sealer and for finishing floors. *—v.* **shellacked, -lacking, -lacs.** *—tr.* **1.** To apply shellac to. **2.** *Slang.* To defeat decisively. Usually used of a sporting contest. **3.** *Slang.* To administer blows to; batter mercilessly. *—intr.* To apply shellac. [SHEL(L) + LAC (lacquer).]
shell·back (shĕl′băk′) *n.* A veteran sailor; especially, one who has crossed the equator. [Originally an old sailor hardened by experience.]
shell·bark (shĕl′bärk′) *n.* A tree, the **shagbark** *(see).*
shell bean. Any of various beans cultivated for their edible seeds rather than for their pods.
Shel·ley (shĕl′ē), **Mary Wollstonecraft (Godwin).** 1797–1851. English novelist; author of *Frankenstein;* wife of P.B. Shelley.
Shel·ley (shĕl′ē), **Percy Bysshe.** 1792–1822. English poet.
shell·fire (shĕl′fīr′) *n.* The firing of artillery projectiles at, or their reception in, a target area.
shell·fish (shĕl′fĭsh′) *n., pl.* **shellfish** or **-fishes.** Any aquatic animal having a shell or shell-like exoskeleton, as a mollusk or crustacean.
shell·flow·er (shĕl′flou′ər) *n.* **1.** A tall plant, *Molucella laevis,* native to Asia, having tiny flowers and conspicuous green calyxes. Also called "bells of Ireland." **2.** A tall plant, *Alpina speciosa,* native to tropical Asia, having showy, variously colored flowers. [From the shell-like appearance of the flowers.]
shell game. 1. A swindling game, **thimblerig** *(see).* **2.** Any scheme in which the customer cannot win; a swindle. [The game is sometimes played by placing a pea under one of three shells and requiring the bettor to guess its location.]
shell jacket. A man's short, fitted jacket worn for semiformal occasions.
shell pink. Pinkish white to strong yellowish pink, including grayish and light yellowish pinks. See **color. —shell′-pink′** *adj.*
shell·proof (shĕl′prōōf′) *adj.* Able to withstand shellfire.
shell shock. 1. Any of various usually acute, often hysterical neuroses originating in trauma suffered under fire in modern warfare. **2. Combat fatigue** *(see).* **—shell′-shocked′** *adj.*
shel·ter (shĕl′tər) *n.* **1. a.** Something that provides cover or protection, as from the weather. **b.** A refuge; haven. **2.** The state of being covered or protected. *—v.* **sheltered, -tering, -ters.** *—tr.* To provide cover or protection for. *—intr.* To take cover; to find refuge. [Origin uncertain.] **—shel′ter·er** *n.*
Synonyms: *shelter, cover, retreat, refuge, asylum, sanctuary,*

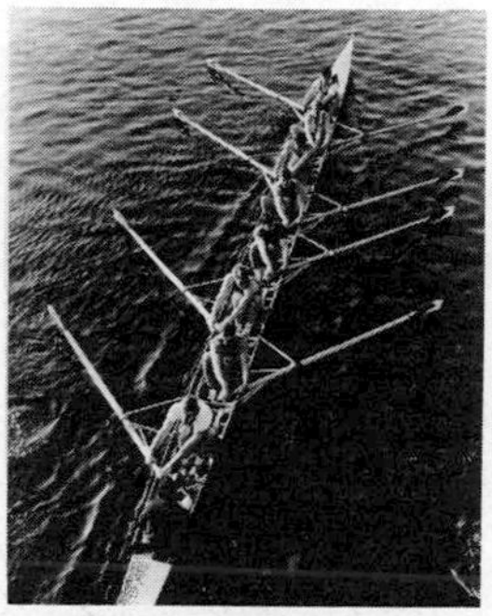

shell
A Harvard University racing crew

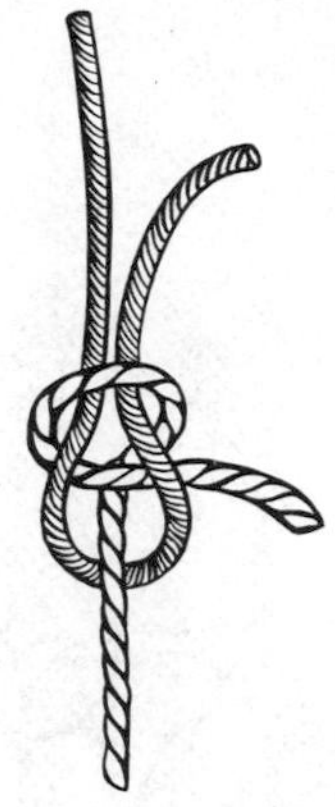

sheet bend

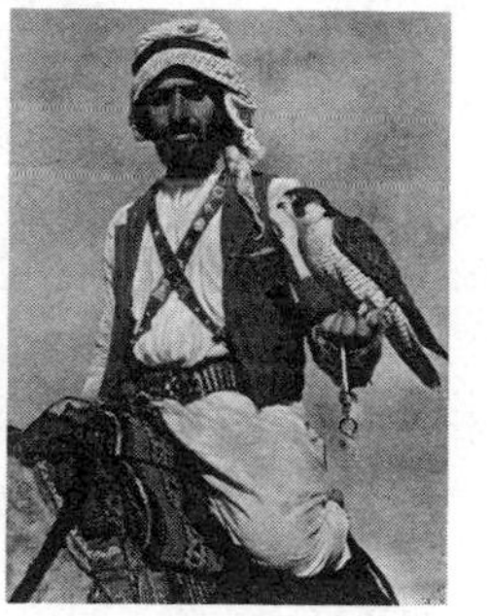

sheik
From the Persian Gulf

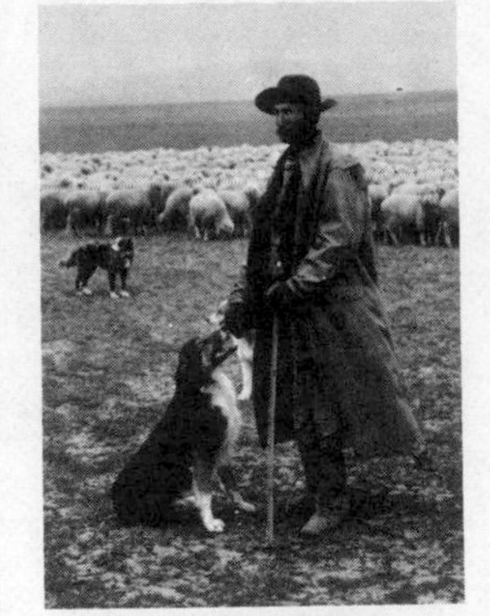

shepherd
In the American West

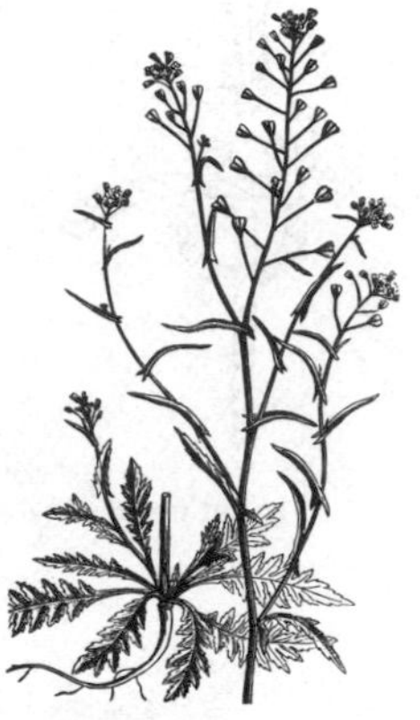

shepherd's-purse

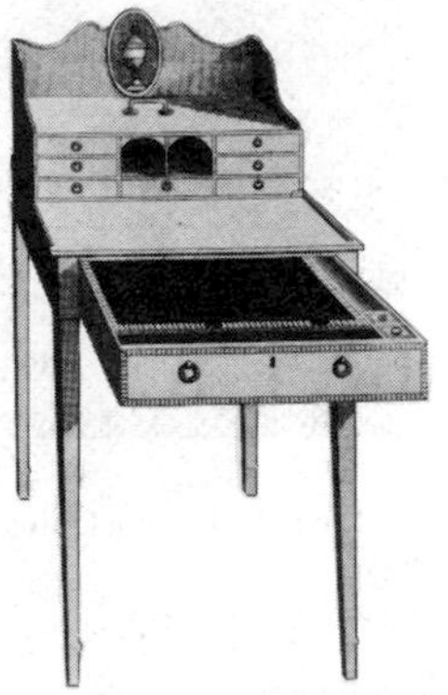

Sheraton
Sheraton writing table

haven. These nouns refer to places that afford protection or to the condition of being protected. *Shelter* usually implies an enclosed area that protects temporarily against a specific threat, such as a storm or air raid. *Cover* suggests a concealed place resorted to hastily for temporary protection. *Retreat* applies chiefly to a place of seclusion to which one retires for meditation or to escape the demands of worldly affairs. *Refuge* suggests a place of escape, real or figurative, from actual pursuit or from harassment. *Asylum* adds to *refuge* the idea of legal protection against a pursuer or of immunity to prosecution. *Sanctuary* denotes a sacred or inviolable place of refuge. *Haven* can apply to an anchorage or broadly to any sheltered place.

shelter tent. A small tent usually formed of two or more pieces of waterproof material. Also called "pup tent."

shel·tie (shĕl′tē) *n.* Also **shel·ty** *pl.* **-ties. 1.** A **Shetland pony** *(see).* **2.** A **Shetland sheepdog** *(see).* [Norn *sjalti,* shetland pony, Shetlander, from Old Norse *Hjalti,* Shetlander, from *Hjaltland,* Shetland, probably from *hjalt,* hilt, from Germanic *heltaz* (unattested), HILT.]

shelve (shĕlv) *v.* **shelved, shelving, shelves.** *—tr.* **1.** To place or arrange on a shelf or shelves. **2.** To put away as though on a shelf; put aside; postpone: *"as usual, Dixon shelved this question"* (Kingsley Amis). **3.** To retire from service; dismiss. **4.** To furnish or outfit with shelves. *—intr.* To slope gradually; to incline. [From SHELVES.]

shelves. Plural of **shelf.**

shelv·ing (shĕl′vĭng) *n.* **1.** Shelves collectively. **2.** Material for shelves. **3.** The act of arranging or putting away on a shelf or shelves. **4.** An incline or slope.

Shem (shĕm). The eldest son of Noah. Genesis 5:32.

Shem·ite. Variant of **Semite.**

Shen·an·do·ah (shĕn′ən-dō′ə). A river flowing 55 miles northeast from northern Virginia to the Potomac at Harpers Ferry, West Virginia.

Shen·an·do·ah National Park (shĕn′ən-dō′ə). A scenic area occupying 302 square miles in northern Virginia, including part of the Blue Ridge Mountains.

she·nan·i·gan (shə-năn′ĭ-gən) *n. Informal.* **1.** *Usually plural.* Prankishness; mischief. **2.** Treachery; deceit. [Origin unknown.]

Sheng·king. A former name for **Liaoning.**

Shen·si (shĕn′shē′). A province of China occupying 75,000 square miles in the north-central part of the country. Population, 15,960,000. Capital, Sian.

Shen·yang (shŭn′yäng′). Formerly **Feng·tien** (fŭng′tyĕn′), **Muk·den** (mŏŏk′dən, -dĕn′). A city of northeastern China, the capital of Liaoning Province and, formerly, of Manchuria. Population, 2,411,000.

she-oak (shē′ōk′) *n.* A tree, the **beefwood** *(see).* [SHE (used in the obsolete sense of a lesser plant) + OAK.]

she·ol (shē′ōl′) *n.* **1.** Hell. **2.** *Capital* **S.** A place described in the Old Testament as the abode of the dead. [Hebrew *sheʾōl.*]

Shep·ard (shĕp′ərd), **Alan Bartlett, Jr.** Born 1923. American naval officer and astronaut; first American in space (1961).

shep·herd (shĕp′ərd) *n.* **1.** One who herds, guards, and cares for sheep. **2.** One who cares for a group of people, as a minister or teacher. *—tr.v.* **shepherded, -herding, -herds.** To herd, guard, or care for as or in the manner of a shepherd. [Middle English *sheepherde,* Old English *scēaphirde* : *scēap,* SHEEP + *hirde,* HERD (herdsman).]

shepherd dog. Any of various dogs trained to tend sheep.

shep·herd·ess (shĕp′ər-dĭs) *n.* A woman shepherd.

shepherd's pie. A casserole consisting of cooked cubes of beef or lamb with gravy, topped by a layer or surrounding border of mashed potatoes.

shep·herd's-purse (shĕp′ərdz-pûrs′) *n.* A common weed, *Capsella bursa-pastoris,* having small white flowers and flat, heart-shaped fruit. [From its pouchlike pods.]

Sher·a·ton (shĕr′ə-tən) *adj.* Of or designating a style of English furniture originated by Thomas Sheraton (1751–1806) and characterized by straight lines and graceful proportions.

sher·bet (shûr′bĭt) *n.* **1.** A sweet-flavored water ice to which milk, egg white, or gelatin has been added. **2.** *British.* A beverage made of sweetened diluted fruit juice. **3.** A stemmed glass in which desserts are served. [Turkish *sherbet* and Persian *sharbat,* from Arabic *sharbah,* drink, from *shariba,* to drink. See also **syrup, shrub.**]

Sher·brooke (shûr′brŏŏk). A city and commercial center of Quebec, Canada, on the St. Francis River, in the southern part of the province. Population, 67,000.

sherd. Variant of **shard.**

Sher·i·dan (shĕr′ə-dən), **Philip Henry.** 1831–1888. American commander of Union cavalry in the Civil War.

Sher·i·dan (shĕr′ə-dən), **Richard Brinsley.** 1751–1816. English dramatist.

she·rif (shə-rēf′) *n.* Also **sha·rif. 1. a.** A descendant of the prophet Mohammed through his daughter Fatima. **b.** The title of certain Arab princes claiming such descent. **2.** The chief magistrate of Mecca. Also called "grand sherif." **3.** A Moroccan prince or ruler. [Arabic *sharīf,* "noble," from *sharafa,* to be highborn.]

sher·iff (shĕr′ĭf) *n.* **1.** The chief executive of the courts of superior jurisdiction in a U.S. county. **2.** An officer of a shire or county in England, Scotland, and Northern Ireland. [Middle English *shir(r)eve, shirrif,* Old English *scīrgerēfa* : *scīr,* SHIRE + *gerēfa,* officer, REEVE.]

Sher·lock Holmes (shûr′lŏk′ hōmz′). English detective, central character in stories and novels by Sir Arthur Conan Doyle.

Sher·man (shûr′mən), **James Schoolcraft.** 1855–1912. Vice President of the United States under William Howard Taft (1909–12).

Sher·man (shûr′mən), **John.** 1823–1900. American statesman; as senator from Ohio, author of the Sherman Antitrust Act (1890).

Sher·man (shûr′mən), **Roger.** 1721–1793. American jurist, statesman, and patriot.

Sher·man (shûr′mən), **William Tecumseh.** 1820–1891. American commander of Union troops in the Civil War.

she·root. Variant of **cheroot.**

Sher·pa (shûr′pə) *n., pl.* **Sherpa** or **-pas.** A member of a Tibetan people living in northern Nepal.

sher·ry (shĕr′ē) *n., pl.* **-ries.** Also *archaic* **sher·ris** (-ĭs). **1.** A fortified Spanish wine ranging from very dry to sweet, and amber in color. **2.** A similar wine made outside of Spain. [Earlier *sherris,* "wine of Jerez," from *Xeres,* older form of JEREZ.]

's Her·to·gen·bosch (sĕr′tō-gən-bôs′). *French* **Bois-le-Duc** (bwä-lə-dük′). The capital of North Brabant Province, the Netherlands. Population, 76,000.

Sher·wood (shûr′wŏŏd′), **Robert Emmet.** 1896–1955. American playwright.

Sher·wood Forest (shûr′wŏŏd′). Formerly an extensive royal forest in Nottinghamshire, Derbyshire, and Yorkshire, England, traditionally the retreat of Robin Hood.

Shet·land (shĕt′lənd) *adj.* Of or from the Shetland Islands. *—n.* **1.** A fine, loosely twisted yarn made from the wool of Shetland sheep and used for knitting and weaving. **2.** A garment, especially a sweater, made of Shetland wool.

Shet·land Islands (shĕt′lənd). A group of islands with a combined area of 550 square miles, in the North Atlantic 105 miles northeast of Scotland, forming the Scottish county of Shetland or Zetland. Population, 18,000. Capital, Lerwick, on Mainland Island.

Shetland pony. A small, compactly built pony of a breed originating in the Shetland Islands. Also called "sheltie."

Shetland sheepdog. A dog of a breed developed in the Shetland Islands, having a rough coat and resembling a small collie. Also called "sheltie."

She·vat (shə-vät′) *n.* Also **She·bat** (-bät′, -vät′). The fifth month of the Hebrew calendar. See **calendar.** [Hebrew *shəbhāṭ.*]

shew·bread. *Archaic.* Variant of **showbread.**

Shey·enne (shī-ăn′, -ĕn′). A river rising in central North Dakota and flowing 325 miles to the Red River near Fargo.

shf, SHF superhigh frequency.

Shi·ah (shē′ə) *n.* Also **Shi·a. 1.** The principal minority sect of Islam, composed of the followers of Ali, the cousin and son-in-law of Mohammed, who regard the heirs of Ali as the legitimate successors to the Prophet and reject the other caliphs and the Sunnite legal and political institutions. Compare **Sunni. 2.** A **Shiite** *(see).* [Arabic *shīʿah,* "following," "sect," from *shāʿa,* to follow, accompany.]

shi·bah. Variant of **shiva.**

shib·bo·leth (shĭb′ə-lĭth, -lĕth′) *n.* **1.** A password, phrase, custom, or usage that reliably distinguishes the members of one group or class from another. **2.** A slogan, catchword, or saying, especially one distinctive of a particular group. [Hebrew *shibbōleth,* an ear of corn, stream (password used by the Gileadites in the Bible).]

shield (shēld) *n.* **1.** An article of protective armor made of leather, metal, or wood, carried on the forearm to ward off blows or missiles. **2.** A means of defense; protection. **3.** Something resembling a shield in shape. **4.** *Military.* A steel sheet attached to a gun to protect the gunners from small-arms fire. **5.** *Zoology.* A protective plate or similar hard outer covering. **6.** A piece of rubberized or absorbent cloth worn at the armpits of a garment as protection from perspiration. **7.** *Physics.* A mass of material, such as lead or cement, that encloses a nuclear reactor in order to reduce the amount of radiation that escapes into the surrounding area. *—v.* **shielded, shielding, shields.** *—tr.* **1.** To protect or defend with or as if with a shield; to guard. **2.** To cover up; conceal. *—intr.* To act or serve as a shield or safeguard. —See Synonyms at **defend.** [Middle English *shild, sheld,* Old English *scild, sceld.* See **skel-**[1] in Appendix.*] **—shield′er** *n.*

Shield of David. A six-pointed star, the **Magen David** *(see).*

shiel·ing (shē′lĭng) *n. Scottish.* A shepherd's hut. [From Scottish *shiel,* shed, hut, Middle English *schele, shale,* probably from Scandinavian, akin to Old Norse *skjol,* shelter, hut. See **skeu-**[1] in Appendix.*]

shift (shĭft) *v.* **shifted, shifting, shifts.** *—tr.* **1.** To move or transfer (something material or immaterial) from one place or position to another. **2.** To exchange for or replace with something similar in quality or kind; to switch. **3.** To change (gears) in an automobile. **4.** *Linguistics.* To alter phonetically or as part of a systematic change. *—intr.* **1.** To change position, direction, place, form, or the like. **2. a.** To provide for one's needs; get along; manage. **b.** To get along by tricky or evasive means. **3.** To change gears, as when driving an automobile. *—n.* **1.** A change, transference, or displacement from one individual, position, or configuration to another. **2.** A change of direction or form. **3. a.** A change or relay of workers. **b.** The working period or time of such a group: *the night shift.* **4.** *Music.* A change of the position of the hand in playing the violin or a similar instrument. **5.** *Linguistics.* **a.** A systematic change of the phonetic or phonemic structure of a language. **b. Functional shift** *(see).* **6.** *Football.* A lateral movement of the offensive backfield from one formation to another just prior to putting the ball in play. **7.** A dodge, evasion, artifice, or trick. **8. a.** A dress, a **chemise** *(see).* **b.** A woman's undergarment; slip; chemise. **9.** An ingenious, evasive, or fraudulent expedient; a trick. [Middle English *shiften,* to arrange, apportion, change, Old English *sciftan,* to arrange, from German *skip-* (unattested).] **—shift'er** *n.*

shift·less (shĭft'lĭs) *adj.* **1.** Showing a lack of ambition or purpose; lazy. **2.** Showing a lack of resourcefulness or efficiency; not capable. [From SHIFT (archaic sense "resourcefulness").] **—shift'less·ly** *adv.* **—shift'less·ness** *n.*

shift·y (shĭf'tē) *adj.* **-ier, -iest. 1.** Tricky; crafty. **2.** Suggesting craft or guile; furtive. **3.** Full of expedients; resourceful. **—shift'i·ly** *adv.* **—shift'i·ness** *n.*

Shih Huang Ti (shîr' hwäng' tē'). 259–210 B.C. Emperor of China (246–210 B.C.); builder of the Great Wall. [Chinese *shih^{3}huang^{2}ti^4,* "the first emperor" : *shih^3,* beginning + *huang^{2}ti^4,* emperor.]

Shih·kia·chwang (shîr'jē-ä'jwäng'). A city of east-central China, in Hopei Province. Population, 623,000.

Shi·ism (shē'ĭz'əm) *n.* Also **Shi'·ism.** The religion or doctrines of the **Shiah** *(see).*

Shi·ite (shē'īt') *n.* Also **Shi'·ite.** A member of the Shiah branch of Islam. Also called "Shiah." **—Shi·it'ic** (-ĭt'ĭk) *adj.*

shi·ka·ree (shĭ-kär'ē) *n.* Also **shi·kar·ree, shi·ka·ri.** *Anglo-Indian.* A big-game hunting guide. [Hindi, from Persian *shikārī,* from *shikār,* hunting, from Middle Persian *shkār*†.]

Shi·ko·ku (shĭ-kō'ko͞o). The smallest (7,280 square miles) of the major islands of Japan, between southwestern Honshu and eastern Kyushu. Population, 4,192,000.

shik·sa (shĭk'sə) *n.* Also **shik·se, shick·sa. 1.** A non-Jewish girl or young woman. Usually used disparagingly. **2.** A Jewish girl or young woman who fails to live up to traditional Jewish teachings or practices. Usually used disparagingly. [Yiddish *shikse,* feminine of *sheygets,* SHEGETZ.]

Shil·ka (shĭl'kə). A river of the Soviet Union in Asia, rising north of the border with Mongolia and flowing 345 miles northeast to the Argun, with which it forms the Amur.

shill (shĭl) *n. Slang.* One who works as a decoy, as in a confidence game, by posing as a customer or an innocent bystander. [Probably short for *shillaber*†, decoy, impostor.]

shil·le·lagh (shə-lā'lē, -lə) *n.* Also **shil·la·lah.** A club or cudgel, especially one of oak or blackthorn. [Such clubs were originally made from the oaks or blackthorns of *Shillelagh,* town in County Wicklow, Ireland.]

shil·ling (shĭl'ĭng) *n. Abbr.* **s., sh. 1.** The basic monetary unit of Kenya, the Somali Republic, Tanzania, and Uganda, equal to 100 cents. See table of exchange rates at **currency. 2.** A coin equal to $1/20$ of the pound of the United Kingdom, Gambia, Republic of Ireland, Jamaica, Malawi, Malta, Nigeria, Rhodesia, and of various dependent territories of the United Kingdom, such as Bermuda. See table of exchange rates at **currency. 3.** *Printing.* A **virgule** *(see).* [Middle English *shilling,* Old English *scilling,* from Germanic *skillingaz* (unattested).]

Shil·long (shĭ-lông'). The capital of Assam, India, in the south-central part of the state. Population, 117,000.

shil·ly-shal·ly (shĭl'ē-shăl'ē) *intr.v.* **-lied, -lying, -lies. 1.** To put off acting; hesitate or waver. **2.** To idle or poke; dawdle. *—adj.* Hesitant; vacillating. *—n., pl.* **shilly-shallies.** Procrastination; hesitation. *—adv.* In a hesitant manner; irresolutely. [Short for *to stand* (or *go*), *shall I? shall I?* reduplication of *shall I?*] **—shil'ly-shal'li·er** *n.*

Shi·loh (shī'lō). **1.** An ancient village of central Palestine, on the eastern slope of Mount Ephraim, northwest of the Black Sea. **2.** Officially, Shiloh National Military Park. An area occupying 3,729 acres in southwestern Tennessee; the site of the Civil War battle at Pittsburg Landing, in which Union forces defeated the Confederates (1862).

shim (shĭm) *n.* A thin, often tapered piece of metal, wood, stone, or other material, used as leveler or filler between materials such as stone or metal or between pieces of furniture and the floor. *—tr.v.* **shimmed, shimming, shims.** To level or fill in by inserting a shim or shims. [Origin unknown.]

Shi·mi·zu (shē-mē'zo͞o). A city of Japan, a seaport in south-central Honshu. Population, 210,000.

shim·mer (shĭm'ər) *intr.v.* **-mered, -mering, -mers.** To shine with a flickering light. See Synonyms at **flash.** *—n.* A flickering or tremulous light; a glimmer. [Middle English *schimeren,* Old English *scimerian, scimrian.* See **skī-** in Appendix.*] **—shim'mer·y** *adj.*

shim·my (shĭm'ē) *n., pl.* **-mies. 1.** A dance popular in the 1920's, characterized by rapid shaking of the body. Also called "shimmy shake." **2.** Abnormal vibration or wobbling, as in the chassis of an automobile. **3.** *Regional.* A chemise. *—intr.v.* **shimmied, -mying, -mies. 1.** To vibrate or wobble. **2.** To shake the body in or as if in dancing the shimmy. [Short for *shimmy-shake,* "to shake one's chemise," from *shimmy,* incorrect form of CHEMISE.]

Shim·o·no·se·ki (shē-mō'nō-sĕk'ē). A city and seaport of southwestern Honshu, Japan. Population, 263,000.

shin[1] (shĭn) *n.* **1.** *Anatomy.* **a.** The front part of the leg below the knee and above the ankle. **b.** The **tibia** *(see).* **2.** The lower part of the foreleg in beef cattle, as opposed to the upper foreleg or shank. Said of cuts of meat. *—v.* **shinned, shinning, shins.** *—tr.* **1.** To climb (a rope or pole, for example) by gripping and pulling alternately with the hands and legs. **2.** To kick or hit in the shins. *—intr.* To climb something by shinning. [Middle English *shine,* Old English *scinu.* See **skei-** in Appendix.*]

shin[2] (shēn) *n.* The 22nd letter in the Hebrew alphabet. See **alphabet.** [Hebrew *shīn,* variant of *shēn,* tooth (from the shape of the letter).]

Shi·nar (shī'när'). The Biblical name for an ancient country on the lower courses of the Tigris and Euphrates, probably comprising the Babylonian plain. Genesis 10:10.

shin·bone (shĭn'bōn') *n. Anatomy.* The **tibia** *(see).*

shin·dig (shĭn'dĭg') *n. Slang.* A festive party or celebration. Also called "shindy." [Probably an alteration of SHINDY.]

shin·dy (shĭn'dē) *n., pl.* **-dies.** *Slang.* **1.** A commotion; row; uproar. **2.** A **shindig** *(see).* [Alteration of SHINNY (game).]

shine (shīn) *v.* **shone** (shōn) or **shined, shining, shines.** *—intr.* **1.** To emit light; be radiant; beam. **2.** To reflect light; glint or glisten. **3.** To distinguish oneself in some sphere; be eminent; excel. **4.** To become clearly apparent. *—tr.* **1.** To aim or cast the beam or glow of. **2.** To make glossy or bright by polishing. **—shine up to.** *Slang.* To be attentive to; attempt to please. *—n.* **1.** Brightness; radiance; luster. **2.** A shoeshine. **3.** Fair weather. Used in the phrase *rain or shine.* **4.** *Plural. Informal.* Foolish pranks or tricks. **5.** *Slang.* Whiskey; moonshine. **—take a shine to.** To like spontaneously. [Shine, shone (past tense); Middle English *shinen, schon,* Old English *scīnan, scān* (past singular). The past participle *shone* is formed in Modern English from the past tense *shone.* See **skī-** in Appendix.*]

shin·er (shī'nər) *n.* **1.** One that shines. **2.** *Slang.* A black eye. **3. a.** Any of numerous small, often silvery North American freshwater fishes of the family Cyprinidae, especially one of the genus *Notropis.* **b.** Any of various other small silvery fishes.

shin·gle[1] (shĭng'gəl) *n.* **1.** A thin oblong piece of wood, asbestos, or other material, laid in overlapping rows to cover the roofs and sides of houses. **2.** *Informal.* A small signboard, as one indicating a doctor's office. Used especially in the phrase *hang out a shingle.* **3.** A woman's close-cropped haircut. *—tr.v.* **shingled, -gling, -gles. 1.** To cover (a roof or building) with shingles. **2.** To cut (hair) short and close to the head. [Middle English *scincle, scingle,* from Latin *scindula,* variant of *scandula.* See **skhed-** in Appendix.*] **—shin'gler** *n.*

shin·gle[2] (shĭng'gəl) *n.* **1.** Beach gravel consisting of large smooth pebbles unmixed with finer material. **2.** Any gravel that is coarser than ordinary gravel. **3.** A stretch of shore or beach covered with coarse, smooth gravel. [Probably from Middle Low German *singele, tsingele,* outermost wall, hence sandbank, from Medieval Latin *cingulum,* curtain-wall, from Latin, belt, zone, from *cingere,* to encompass. See **kenk-**[1] in Appendix.*] **—shin'gly** *adj.*

shin·gles (shĭng'gəlz) *n.* Plural in form, used with a singular or plural verb. *Pathology.* A skin eruption, **herpes zoster** *(see).* [Middle English *schingles, cingules,* from Medieval Latin *cingulus,* "belt" (translation of Greek *zōnē,* shingles, belt, ZONE), from Latin, girdle, belt, from *cingere,* to gird. See **kenk-**[1] in Appendix.*]

shin·leaf (shĭn'lēf') *n.* A North American woodland plant, *Pyrola elliptica,* having rounded basal leaves and white flowers. [From the use of its leaves in plasters for sore legs.]

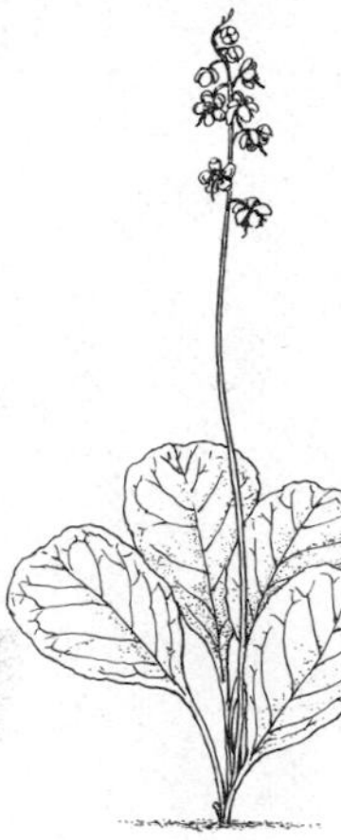
shinleaf

shin·ny[1] (shĭn'ē) *n., pl.* **-nies. 1.** A simple form of hockey played by schoolboys. **2.** The curved stick used in this game. [Probably from *shin ye, shin t'ye,* "shin to you," a cry used in the game.]

shin·ny[2] (shĭn'ē) *intr.v.* **-nied, -nying, -nies.** To climb by shinning.

shin·plas·ter (shĭn'plăs'tər, -pläs'tər) *n.* Paper currency issued privately; especially, such currency devalued by lack of backing or by inflation. [From the comparison of such bank notes to small squares of brown paper soaked with vinegar or tobacco juice and used by poor people to treat sore legs.]

Shin·to (shĭn'tō) *n.* Also **Shin·to·ism** (-ĭz'əm). The aboriginal religion of Japan, marked by the veneration of nature spirits and of ancestors. [Japanese *shintō,* "the way of the gods" : *shin,* god(s), from Chinese (Mandarin) *shên^2* + *tō,* for *dō,* way, from Chinese (Mandarin) *tao^4.*] **—Shin'to·ist** *n.*

shin·y (shī'nē) *adj.* **-ier, -iest. 1.** Bright; glistening. **2.** Clear; shining. **—shin'i·ness** *n.*

ship (shĭp) *n.* **1.** Any vessel of considerable size adapted for deep-water navigation. **2.** A three-masted sailing vessel with square mainsails on all masts. **3.** *Maritime Law.* A vessel intended for marine transportation, without regard to form, rig, or means of propulsion. **4.** A ship's company. **5.** An airplane; airship. *—v.* **shipped, shipping, ships.** *—tr.* **1.** To place or take on board a ship. **2. a.** To send or cause to be transported. **b.** *Informal.* To dispatch to a specified destination. **3.** To hire for work on a ship. **4.** To take in (water) over the side. **5.** To set in place for use, as the mast or rudder. *—intr.* **1.** To go aboard or travel by means of a ship. **2.** To hire oneself out or enlist for service on a ship. [Middle English *s(c)hip,* Old English *scip.* See **skipam** in Appendix.*]

-ship. Indicates: **1.** The quality or condition of; for example, **friendship, scholarship. 2.** The status, rank, or office of; for example, **professorship, authorship. 3.** The art or functioning of; for example, **penmanship, leadership.** [Middle English *-s(c)hip(e),* Old English *-scipe.* See **skep-** in Appendix.*]

ship biscuit. A type of bread, **hardtack** *(see).*

ship·board (shĭp'bôrd', -bōrd') *n. Obsolete.* The side of a ship. **—on shipboard.** On board a ship. *—adj.* Occurring on board a ship: *a shipboard romance.*

ship·build·ing (shĭp'bĭl'dĭng) *n.* The business of constructing ships. **—ship'build'er** *n.*

ship canal. A canal deep enough to serve ships. Also called "shipway."

ship chandler. A person who deals in equipment for ships.

ship·load (shĭp'lōd') *n.* A capacity cargo for a ship.

ship·man (shĭp'mən) *n., pl.* **-men** (-mĭn). *Archaic.* **1.** A sailor. **2.** A **shipmaster** *(see).*

ship·mas·ter (shĭp′măs′tər, -mäs′tər) *n.* The commander or captain of a merchant ship. Also called "shipman."

ship·mate (shĭp′māt′) *n.* A sailor serving on the same ship as another; fellow sailor.

ship·ment (shĭp′mənt) *n. Abbr.* **shpt.** **1.** The act of sending or transporting goods. **2.** The goods or cargo transported.

ship money. A former tax on English maritime towns and shires to provide revenue for the construction of warships.

ship of the line. Formerly, a warship large enough to take a position in the line of battle.

ship·per (shĭp′ər) *n.* A person who consigns or receives goods for transportation; shipping agent.

ship·ping (shĭp′ĭng) *n.* **1.** The act or business of transporting goods. **2.** The body of ships belonging to one port, industry, or country, often referred to in aggregate tonnage. **3.** *Obsolete.* A voyage.

shipping clerk. A person employed to manage the shipment or receipt of goods.

ship-rigged (shĭp′rĭgd′) *adj. Nautical.* Rigged as a ship, with three or more masts and square sails.

ship·shape (shĭp′shāp′) *adj.* Neatly arranged; orderly; tidy. [Originally, "arranged in a manner befitting a ship" (said of rigging).] **—ship′shape′** *adv.*

ship's papers. The documents that international law requires a ship to carry and be able to provide on demand for inspection.

ship·way (shĭp′wā′) *n.* **1.** The structure supporting a ship during construction or in dry dock. **2.** A **ship canal** *(see).*

ship·worm (shĭp′wûrm′) *n.* Any of various wormlike marine mollusks of the genera *Teredo* and *Bankia,* having rudimentary bivalve shells with which they bore into wood, often doing extensive damage.

ship·wreck (shĭp′rĕk′) *n.* **1.** The remains of a wrecked ship. **2.** The destruction of a ship, as by storm or collision. **3.** Complete failure or ruin. **—*tr.v.*** **shipwrecked, -wrecking, -wrecks.** **1.** To cause (a ship or its passengers) to suffer shipwreck. **2.** To ruin utterly. [Earlier *shipwrack,* Middle English *shipwrak,* Old English *scipwræc,* cargo thrown overboard to lighten a ship in danger : SHIP + *wræc,* thing driven by the sea, WRACK.]

ship·wright (shĭp′rīt′) *n.* A carpenter employed in the construction or maintenance of ships.

ship·yard (shĭp′yärd′) *n.* A yard or area where ships are built or repaired.

Shi·raz (shĭ-räz′). A city of southwestern Iran, famous for carpets. Population, 230,000.

shire (shīr) *n.* One of the counties of Great Britain. [Middle English *shir(e),* Old English *scīr,* official charge, province, shire, akin to Old High German *scīra*†, care.]

Shi·re (shē′rā). Also **Shi·ré.** *Portuguese* **Chi·re** (shē′rĭ). A river of Africa, flowing about 250 miles from the southern end of Lake Nyasa in Malawi to the Zambezi in Mozambique.

shire horse. A large, powerful draft horse of a breed originating in the shires or midland region of England.

shirk (shûrk) *v.* **shirked, shirking, shirks.** **—*tr.*** To put off or avoid discharging: *"A number of high civil servants shirked their duty to preserve their jobs."* (Nevil Shute). **—*intr.*** To put off or avoid work or duty. **—*n.*** A person who avoids work or duty. Also called "shirker." [From obsolete *shirk,* parasite, rogue, probably from German *Schurke,* scoundrel, perhaps from Old High German *(fiur)-scurgo,* "fire stirrer," stoker, hence devil (as an infernal stoker), from *scurigen,* to poke. See **skeu-** in Appendix.*]

Shir·ley (shûr′lē), **William.** 1694–1771. British colonial administrator; governor of Massachusetts (1741–49 and 1753–56).

Shirley poppy. A variety of the corn poppy having scarlet, pink, or salmon flowers.

shirr (shûr) *tr.v.* **shirred, shirring, shirrs.** **1.** To gather (cloth) into three or more decorative parallel rows. **2.** To cook (eggs) by baking unshelled in molds. **—*n.*** A decorative gathering of cloth into three or more parallel rows. Also called "shirring." [Origin unknown.]

shirt (shûrt) *n.* **1.** A garment for the upper part of the body, typically having a collar, sleeves, and a front opening. **2.** An undershirt. **3.** A night shirt. **4.** A protective cloth casing, as for use in shipping perishable goods. **—keep one's shirt on.** *Slang.* To remain calm or patient. **—lose one's shirt.** *Slang.* To lose everything one has or owns. [Middle English *sherte, scurte,* Old English *scyrte.* See **sker-**[1] in Appendix.*]

shirt·ing (shûr′tĭng) *n.* Fabric, such as broadcloth, suitable for making shirts.

shirt·waist (shûrt′wāst′) *n.* **1.** A woman's tailored shirt, with details copied from men's shirts. **2.** A woman's dress with the bodice styled like a tailored shirt.

shish ke·bab (shĭsh′ kə-bŏb′). Also **shish ke·bob, shish ka·bob.** A dish consisting of pieces of seasoned meat roasted and served with condiments on skewers. [Turkish *şiş kebabı* : *şiş,* skewer + *kebap,* roast meat.]

shist. Variant of **schist.**

shit (shĭt) *v.* **shit** or **shat** (shăt) or **shitted, shitting, shits.** **—*intr.*** *Vulgar.* To defecate. **—*tr.*** *Vulgar Slang.* To deceive or mislead. **—*n.*** **1.** *Vulgar.* Excrement. **2.** *Vulgar.* An act of defecating. **3.** *Vulgar Slang.* Worthless matter; junk. **4.** *Vulgar Slang.* Foolish or misleading talk; nonsense. **5.** *Vulgar Slang.* A highly objectionable person. **6.** *Vulgar Slang.* A narcotic drug; especially, heroin. **—*interj.*** *Vulgar Slang.* Used to express anger or disappointment. [Middle English *shiten,* to void excrement, Old English *scītan* (attested only in compound *bescītan,* to befoul). See **skei-** in Appendix.*]

shit·tim·wood (shĭt′əm-wo͝od′) *n.* **1.** A tree, probably a species of acacia, that was a source of a wood mentioned frequently in the Bible. Also called "shittah tree." **2.** The wood of this tree, used to make the ark of the Tabernacle. Exodus 25:10. [From Hebrew *shiṭṭīm,* plural of *shiṭṭāh,* related to Egyptian *sont,* acacia.]

shiv (shĭv) *n.* Also **chiv.** *Slang.* A knife or razor, especially as a weapon. [Romany *chiv*†, "blade."]

shi·va (shĭv′ə) *n.* Also **shi·vah, shi·bah.** *Judaism.* A seven-day period of formal mourning observed after the funeral of a close relative. [Yiddish, from Hebrew *shiv'āh,* seven.]

Shi·va (shē′və). Also **Si·va** (shē′və, sē′-). *Hinduism.* The god of destruction and reproduction, a member of the Hindu triad along with Brahma and Vishnu. [Sanskrit *Śiva,* "the auspicious (one)," from *śiva,* auspicious, dear. See **kei-**[1] in Appendix.*] **—Shi′va·ism′** *n.* **—Shi′va·ist** *n.*

shiv·a·ree. Variant of **charivari.**

shive[1] (shīv) *n.* **1.** A thin, flat cork used to stop wide-mouthed bottles. **2.** *Archaic.* A slice. [Middle English, slice, probably from Middle Dutch or Middle Low German *schīve.* See **skei-** in Appendix.*]

shive[2] (shīv) *n.* A sliver of woody matter, as of flax, separated in breaking. [Middle English *schyff,* probably of Low German origin, akin to Middle Low German *schīve,* slice. See **shive** (cork).]

shiv·er[1] (shĭv′ər) *v.* **-ered, -ering, -ers.** **—*intr.*** **1.** To shudder or shake from cold or a cold sensation; tremble. **2.** To quiver or vibrate, as by the force of wind. **—*tr.*** *Nautical.* To cause (a sail) to flutter in the wind. —See Synonyms at **shake.** **—*n.*** An act of shivering; a tremble. [Middle English *shiveren,* earlier *chiveren,* perhaps alteration of *chevelen,* to shiver, originally "to chatter" (said of teeth), from Old English *ceafl,* the jaw. See **geph-** in Appendix.*]

shiv·er[2] (shĭv′ər) *v.* **-ered, -ering, -ers.** **—*intr.*** To break suddenly into fragments or splinters; shatter: *"Suddenly a few feet away the entire plate-glass window shivered into confetti."* (Ian Fleming). **—*tr.*** To cause to break into fragments. —See Synonyms at **break.** [Middle English, from *scivre,* fragment, perhaps of Low German origin, akin to Middle Low German *schever.* See **skei-** in Appendix.*]

shiv·er·y[1] (shĭv′ər-ē) *adj.* **1.** Trembling, as from cold or fear. **2.** Making one shiver with cold or fear; chilling.

shiv·er·y[2] (shĭv′ər-ē) *adj.* Easily broken; brittle.

Shi·zu·o·ka (shē-zo͞o-ō′kä). An industrial city in central Honshu, Japan. Population, 359,000.

shkotz·im. Plural of **shegetz.**

shmo. Variant of **schmo.**

shoal[1] (shōl) *n.* **1.** A place in any body of water where the water is especially shallow. **2.** A sandy elevation of the bottom of a body of water, constituting a hazard to navigation; a sandbank or sandbar. **—*v.*** **shoaled, shoaling, shoals.** **—*intr.*** To become shallow: *"The water, already brackish, shoaled and became turbid."* (Samuel E. Morison). **—*tr.*** **1.** To make shallow. **2.** To come or sail into a shallower part of: *The ship shoaled water.* **—*adj.*** Having little depth; shallow. [Middle English *schald, sholde,* originally "shallow," Old English *sc(e)ald,* from Germanic *skaldez* (unattested).]

Synonyms: *shoal, reef, bar, bank.* These nouns have reference to elevations of ground under water. A *shoal* is an elevation of land coming close to but not above the surface of the water. The term also is applied to the shallow area thus formed. A *reef* is a ridge, usually of rock or coral, extending near or slightly above the water's surface. A *bar* is a ridge, usually of sand, near the surface and often exposed at low water. A *bank* in this comparison is a large, totally submerged plateau that rises from the floor of the sea or other large body of water, but is well below the water level.

shoal[2] (shōl) *n.* **1.** A large group; a crowd. **2.** A school of fish or other marine animals. —See Synonyms at **flock.** **—*intr.v.*** **shoaled, shoaling, shoals.** To come together in large numbers; to school. [Probably from Middle Dutch or Middle Low German *schōle.* See **school** (of fish).]

shoat (shōt) *n.* Also **shote.** A young pig just after weaning. [Middle English *shote,* probably of Low German origin, akin to West Flemish *schote.* See **skeud-** in Appendix.*]

shock[1] (shŏk) *n.* **1.** A violent collision or impact; heavy blow. **2.** Something that jars the mind or emotions as if with a violent, unexpected blow. **3.** The disturbance of function, equilibrium, or mental faculties caused by such a blow; violent agitation. **4.** A severe offense to one's sense of propriety or decency; an outrage. **5.** *Pathology.* A generally temporary state of massive physiological reaction to bodily trauma, usually characterized by marked loss of blood pressure and the depression of vital processes. **6.** The sensation and muscular spasm caused by an electric current passing through the body or through a bodily part. **7.** **Shock therapy** *(see).* **—*v.*** **shocked, shocking, shocks.** **—*tr.*** **1.** To strike with great surprise and agitation. **2.** To strike with disgust; offend; scandalize: *"His actions shocked the bartender, who hurriedly asked them to go."* (Nathanael West). **3.** To induce a state of shock in (a person). **4.** To subject (an animal or person) to an electric shock. **—*intr.*** *Archaic.* To come into contact violently, as in battle; collide. [Old French *choc,* from *choquer*†, to strike (with fear).]

shock[2] (shŏk) *n.* A number of sheaves of grain stacked upright in a field for drying: *"A few shocks of corn in a corner of a fallow mead stood up as if alive."* (D.H. Lawrence). **—*tr.v.*** **shocked, shocking, shocks.** To gather (grain) into shocks. [Middle English *shokke,* probably from Middle Dutch or Middle Low German *schok,* shock, group of sixty, akin to Old Saxon *scok*†.] **—shock′er** *n.*

shock[3] (shŏk) *n.* A thick, heavy mass: *"The wind moving gently*

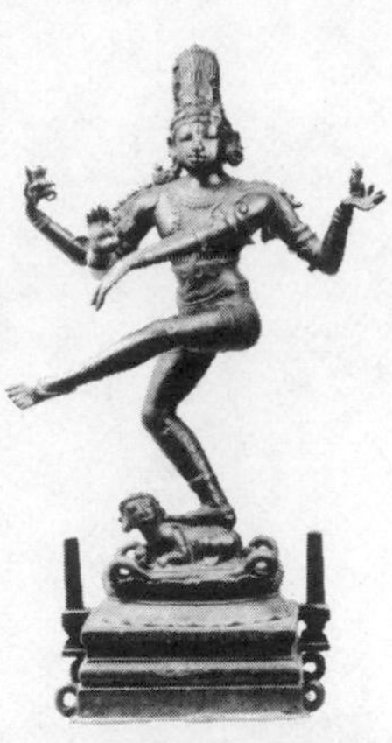

Shiva

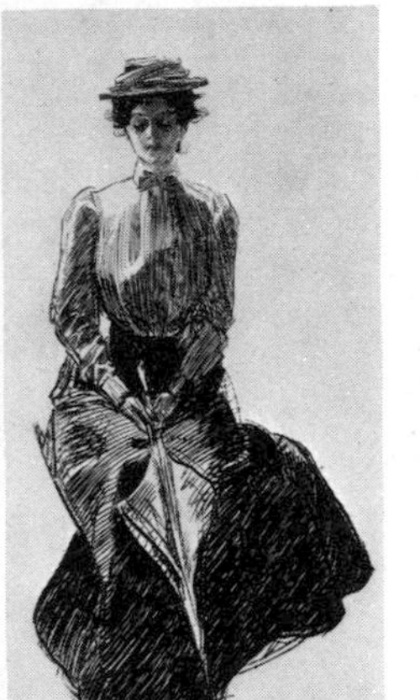

shirtwaist
Drawing by Charles Dana Gibson

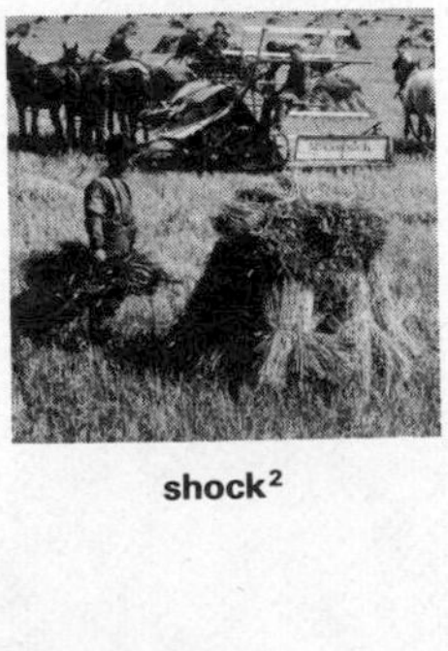

shock[2]

his great shock of voluminous white hair'' (Melville D. Post). —*adj.* Thick and shaggy. [Perhaps from SHOCK (stack).]

shock absorber. Any of various devices used to absorb mechanical shocks, especially a hydraulically damped coupling used to absorb impulsive forces generated by the contact of automotive wheels with irregular road surfaces.

shock·er (shŏk′ər) *n.* One that startles, shocks, or horrifies; especially, a sensational story or novel.

shock·ing (shŏk′ĭng) *adj.* **1.** Highly disturbing emotionally. **2.** Highly offensive; indecent or distasteful. **3.** Very vivid or intense in tone: *shocking pink.* —**shock′ing·ly** *adv.*

Shock·ley (shŏk′lē), **William Bradford.** Born 1910. British-born American physicist; discovered the transistor effect with J. Bardeen and W.H. Brattain *(see).*

shock therapy. The inducing of shock by electric current or drugs, sometimes with convulsions, as a therapy for mental illness. Also called "shock treatment."

shock troops. *Military.* Highly experienced and capable men specially trained to lead attacks.

shock wave. A large-amplitude compression wave, such as that produced by an explosion, caused by supersonic motion of a body in a medium.

shod·dy (shŏd′ē) *n., pl.* **-dies. 1.** Wool fibers obtained by shredding unfelted woolen or worsted rags or worn garments. **2.** Yarn, fabric, or garments made from or containing such reclaimed wool fibers. **3.** Inferior or imitation goods; cheap, derivative material. —*adj.* **shoddier, -iest. 1.** Made of or containing shoddy or other inferior material. **2.** Transparently imitative or inferior; ersatz. **3.** Unsound; inept: *shoddy construction.* **4.** Shabby; run-down. [Origin unknown.] —**shod′di·ly** *adv.* —**shod′di·ness** *n.*

shoe (shōō) *n., pl.* **shoes** or *archaic* **shoon** (shōōn). **1.** A durable covering for the human foot; especially, one of a matched pair made of leather or similar material reaching about to the ankle and having a rigid sole and heel. **2.** A horseshoe. **3.** A part or device placed at an end, foot, or bottom, especially: **a.** A strip of metal fitted onto the bottom of a sled runner. **b.** A skid placed under the wheel of a vehicle to retard its motion. **c.** The outer covering, casing, or tread of a pneumatic rubber tire. **4.** The part of a brake that presses against the wheel or drum to retard its motion. **5.** The sliding contact plate on an electric train or streetcar that conducts electricity from the third rail. —*tr.v.* **shod** (shŏd), **shod** or **shodden** (shŏd′n), **shoeing, shoes. 1.** To furnish or fit with shoes. **2.** To cover with a wooden or metal guard to protect against wear. [Middle English *sho(o)*, Old English *scōh*, from Germanic *skōhaz* (unattested).]

shoe·bill (shōō′bĭl′) *n.* A tall wading bird, *Balaeniceps rex*, native to swampy regions of eastern tropical Africa, and having slaty plumage, long black legs, a stubby neck, and a large shoe-like bill with a hook on the upper mandible.

shoe·horn (shōō′hôrn′) *n.* A curved implement, often of horn or smooth metal, used at the heel to help slip on a shoe.

shoe·lace (shōō′lās′) *n.* A string or cord used for lacing and fastening shoes.

shoe·mak·er (shōō′mā′kər) *n.* A person who makes or repairs shoes and boots as an occupation. —**shoe′mak′ing** *n.*

sho·er (shōō′ər) *n.* A person who shoes horses; blacksmith.

shoe·string (shōō′strĭng′) *n.* **1.** A shoelace. **2.** A small sum of money; barely adequate capital: *The company started on a shoestring.* —*adj.* Cut to or in the shape of a shoestring; long and slender: *shoestring potatoes.*

shoe·tree (shōō′trē′) *n.* A foot-shaped form inserted into a shoe to preserve its shape. Also called "boot tree."

sho·far (shō′fär, -fər) *n., pl.* **-fars** or **shofroth** (shō-frōt′, -frōth′). Also **sho·phar.** *Judaism.* A trumpet made of a ram's horn, blown for warning, summoning, and ritual purposes by the ancient Hebrews, and now sounded in the synagogue at Rosh Hashanah and Yom Kippur. [Hebrew *shōphār*, "ram's horn."]

sho·gun (shō′gŭn′, -gōōn′) *n.* Any of a line of military leaders of Japan who, until 1868, exercised absolute rule under the nominal leadership of the emperor. [Japanese *shōgun*, "general," from Ancient Chinese *tsiang kiuən* (Mandarin Chinese *chiang¹ chün¹*) : *tsiang*, to lead, command + *kiuən*, army.]

sho·gun·ate (shō′gən-ĭt, -āt′) *n.* The office or government of a shogun.

sho·ji (shō′jē) *n., pl.* **shoji** or **-jis.** A translucent paper screen forming a sliding door or partition in a Japanese house. [Japanese *shōji*, from (Mandarin) Chinese *chang⁴ tzŭ⁰.*]

Sho·la·pur (shō′lə-pōōr′). A city and cotton-milling center of India, in central Maharashtra State. Population, 338,000.

Sho·lem A·lei·chem (shō′ləm ə-lā′ᴋʜəm, shō′-). Pen name of Solomon Rabinowitz. 1859–1916. Russian-born American author of humorous tales and sketches in Yiddish.

Sholes (shōlz), **Christopher Latham.** 1819–1890. American inventor; awarded patent for typewriter (1868).

Sho·lo·khov (shô′lə-ᴋʜôf′), **Mikhail Aleksandrovich.** Born 1905. Soviet novelist.

shone. Past tense and past participle of **shine.**

shoo (shōō) *interj.* Used to scare away animals or birds. —*v.* **shooed, shooing, shoos.** —*tr.* To drive or scare away, as by crying "shoo." —*intr.* To cry "shoo." [Middle English *schowe* (imitative).]

shoo·fly (shōō′flī′) *n., pl.* **-flies. 1.** A child's rocker having the seat made between two sides cut in the shape of an animal. **2.** *Slang.* An undercover policeman who checks on the honesty and performance of other policemen. [SHOO + FLY (insect). Originally name of a popular song, later used loosely for something remarkable or nice, such as a child's hobbyhorse.]

shoofly pie. A pie having a filling consisting of layers of molasses and brown sugar mixed with flour, topped with a crumbly crust of the sugar mixture. [So called because it attracts flies that have to be shooed away.]

shoo·in (shōō′ĭn′) *n. Informal.* A contestant or candidate who seems certain of winning.

shook¹ (shŏŏk) *n.* **1.** A set of parts for assembling a barrel or packing box. **2.** A shock of grain. [Origin unknown.]

shook². Past tense of **shake.**

shook-up (shŏŏk′ŭp′) *adj. Slang.* Emotionally upset; shaken.

shoon. *Archaic.* Plural of **shoe.**

shoot¹ (shōōt) *v.* **shot** (shŏt), **shooting, shoots.** —*tr.* **1.** To hit, wound, or kill with a missile fired from a weapon. **2.** To fire or let fly (a missile) from a weapon. **3.** To discharge (a weapon). **4.** To put forcefully or swiftly: *He shot his hands into his pockets.* **5.** To send forth swiftly or dartingly: *She shot a retort to the insult.* **6.** To pass over or through swiftly: *shoot the rapids.* **7.** To cover (country) in hunting for game. **8.** To record on film (a scene, motion picture, or the like). **9.** To cause to project or protrude; extend. **10.** To put forth; begin to grow or produce; generate. **11.** To pour, empty out, or discharge down or as if down a chute. **12.** To variegate with streaks or threads of a different color: *a black coat shot with gray.* **13. a.** To move or propel (a marble or ball) toward its objective. **b.** To score (a point or goal). **c.** To play (golf, craps, or pool). **14.** To slide into or out of a fastening: *shoot a door bolt.* **15.** To measure the altitude of with a sextant or other instrument: *shoot a star.* —*intr.* **1.** To discharge a missile from a weapon. **2.** To discharge fire; go off. **3.** To move swiftly; to dart. **4.** To protrude; extend; project. **5.** To hunt with a weapon: *shoot in the marshes.* **6.** To put forth new growth; germinate; sprout. **7.** To take pictures; to film. **8.** To propel a ball or other object toward the goal. **9.** To take one's turn at play. —**shoot down. 1.** To bring down (an aircraft, for example) by hitting and damaging with a missile. **2.** *Slang.* To ruin the aspirations of; disappoint. —**shoot for** (or **at**). To strive or aim for; have as a goal: *"Such girls are usually championship material, shooting for the Nationals."* (Terry Southern). —**shoot up. 1.** *Informal.* To grow or get taller rapidly. **2.** *Informal.* To hit many times with shot or other projectiles. **3.** *Informal.* To terrorize by lawless, wild shooting. **4.** *Slang.* To inject (a narcotic drug) directly into a vein. —**shot through with.** Filled with; riddled with. —*n.* **1.** The motion or movement of something that is shot; a forward or upward advance. **2. a.** The young growth arising from a germinating seed; sprout. **b.** A bud or young leaf on a plant. **3.** Any new growing part. **4.** A narrow and swift or turbulent section of a stream; a rapid. **5.** An inclined channel through which something, such as timber, can be shot; chute. **6.** A skeet tournament, hunt, or other organized shooting activity. **7.** *Informal.* The launching of a rocket or similar missile. **8.** The distance a shot travels; a range. **9.** *Rowing.* The interval between strokes. —*interj.* Used to express readiness to listen. [Middle English *shoten*, past *shote*, past participle *shote(n)*, Old English *scēotan*, *scēat* (past singular), *scoten*. See **skeud-** in Appendix.*] —**shoot′er** *n.*

shoot². (shōōt). Euphemism for **shit.**

shooting gallery. An enclosed target range for firearms practice or competition.

shooting iron. *Informal.* A six-shooter *(see).*

shooting star. 1. A briefly visible **meteor** *(see).* **2.** Any of several North American plants of the genus *Dodecatheon*, having nodding flowers with reflexed petals. In this sense, also called "American cowslip."

shooting stick. A stick pointed at one end and opening into a seat at the other, typically used by spectators at races.

shop (shŏp) *n.* Also *archaic* **shoppe** (for sense 1). **1.** A small retail store or a specialty department in a large store. **2.** An atelier; studio. **3.** A place for the manufacture or repair of machinery or the like: *a machine shop.* **4. a.** Any commercial or industrial establishment. **b.** A business or other similar activity: *set up shop.* **5.** A home workshop. **6. a.** A schoolroom fitted with machinery and tools for instruction in the manual arts. **b.** The manual arts as a technical science or course of study. —**talk shop.** To talk about one's business. —*v.* **shopped, shopping, shops.** —*intr.* **1.** To visit stores for the purpose of inspecting and buying merchandise. **2.** To look for anything with the intention of acquiring it. —*tr.* To visit or buy from (a particular store). [Middle English *shoppe*, Old English *sceoppa*, booth, stall, from Germanic *skupp-* (unattested).]

sho·phar. Variant of **shofar.**

shop·keep·er (shŏp′kē′pər) *n.* An owner or manager of a shop.

shop·lift·er (shŏp′lĭf′tər) *n.* One who steals goods on display in a store. —**shop′lift′ing** *n.*

shop·per (shŏp′ər) *n.* **1.** A customer or purchaser. **2.** A commercial agent sent to compare the merchandise and prices of competing merchants. **3.** A commercial employee who fills mail or telephone orders.

shopping center. A group of stores and shops forming a central retail market within a given rural or suburban area.

shop steward. A union member chosen by his fellow workers to represent them in their dealings with the management. Also called "shop chairman."

shop·talk (shŏp′tôk′) *n.* Talk or conversation concerning one's business or occupation.

shop·worn (shŏp′wôrn′, -wōrn′) *adj.* **1.** Tarnished, frayed, faded, or otherwise defective from being on display in a store. **2.** Worn-out; exhausted. —See Synonyms at **trite.**

sho·ran (shôr′ăn′, shōr′-) *n.* A relatively short-range navigation system by which a ship or aircraft can determine its position

shoebill

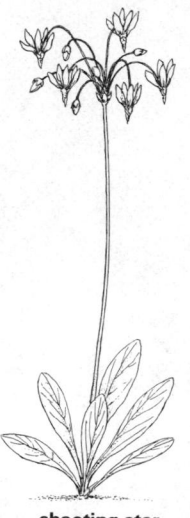
shooting star
Dodecatheon meadia

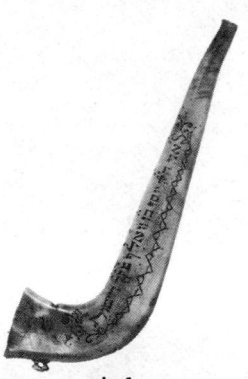
shofar
Late 18th-century
German

ă pat/ā pay/âr care/ä father/b bib/ch church/d deed/ĕ pet/ē be/f fife/g gag/h hat/hw which/ĭ pit/ī pie/îr pier/j judge/k kick/l lid, needle/m mum/n no, sudden/ng thing/ŏ pot/ō toe/ô paw, for/oi noise/ou out/
t tight/th thin, path/th this, bathe/ŭ cut/ûr urge/v valve/w with/y yes/z zebra, size/zh vision/ə about, item, edible, gallop, circus/
à *Fr.* ami/œ *Fr.* feu, *Ger.* schön/ü *Fr.* tu, *Ger.* über/ᴋʜ *Ger.* ich, *Scot.* loch/ɴ *Fr.* bon. *Follows main vocabulary. †Of obscure origin.

with high precision by measuring the times required for a radio signal to reach each of two ground stations of known position and to return. [SHO(RT) RA(NGE) N(AVIGATION).]

shore[1] (shôr, shōr) *n.* **1.** The land along the edge of an ocean, sea, lake, or river; a coast. **2.** Land: *native shore.* —*tr.v.* **shored, shoring, shores.** To put or set on shore. [Middle English, from Middle Dutch and Middle Low German *schore*†.]

shore[2] (shôr, shōr) *tr.v.* **shored, shoring, shores.** To prop up, as with an inclined timber. Usually used with *up.* —*n.* A beam or timber propped against a ship, wall, or other structure as a temporary support. [Middle English, *shoren,* from Middle Dutch *schōren*†.]

shore[3]. *Archaic.* Past tense of **shear.**

shore bird. Any of various birds, such as a sandpiper, plover, or snipe, that frequent the shores of coastal or inland waters.

Shore·ditch (shôr′dĭch′, shōr′-). A former administrative division of London, England, now part of **Hackney** *(see).*

shore·line (shôr′līn′, shōr′-) *n.* The line marking the edge of a body of water.

shore patrol. *Abbr.* **SP** A detail of the U.S. Navy, Marine Corps, or Coast Guard serving as military police ashore.

shor·ing (shôr′ĭng, shōr′-) *n.* **1.** The act or operation of propping with shores. **2.** A system of supporting shores.

shorl. Variant of **schorl.**

shorn. Alternate past participle of **shear.**

short (shôrt) *adj.* **shorter, shortest. 1.** Having little length; not long. **2.** Having little height; not tall; low. **3.** Having a small extent in time; brief. **4.** Not attaining that which is required; inadequate; insufficient. **5.** Lacking in length or amount: *a board short two inches.* **6.** Lacking in breadth or scope. **7.** Not lengthy; concise; succinct: *short and to the point.* **8.** *Finance.* **a.** Not owning the stocks or commodities one is selling. **b.** Pertaining to or designating a sale of stocks or goods not yet owned by the seller, but which he must produce to meet the terms of a contract. **9.** Lacking in retentiveness: *a short memory.* **10.** Rudely brief; abrupt; curt. **11.** Containing shortening; crisp; friable, as pastry. **12. a.** In Greek and Latin verse, indicating a syllable of relatively brief duration. **b.** In English prosody, unstressed. **13.** Designating a particular pronunciation of the letters for the vowel sounds, such as the sound of (ă) in *pan,* of (ĕ) in *pen,* of (ĭ) in *pin,* of (ŏ) in *pond,* and of (ŭ) in *puck,* as distinguished from the sound of (ā) in *pane,* of (ē) in *penal,* of (ī) in *pine,* of (ō) in *post,* and of (ū) in *pure.* **14.** *Phonetics.* Describing a speech sound of relatively brief duration, as opposed to the same or similar sound of relatively long duration. —See Usage note at **brief.** —**short of. 1.** Not equivalent to; less than: *something short of a mile.* **2.** Lacking a sufficient amount of: *short of breath.* **3.** Without reaching an extreme of: *"a simpler manner of life and thought could hardly exist, short of cave-dwelling"* (Henry Adams). **4.** Without reaching as an end or goal. —*adv.* **1.** Abruptly; quickly: *stop short.* **2.** Rudely; crossly. **3.** Concisely. **4.** So as not to meet the requirements of. **5.** Without getting to; before reaching. **6.** Without owning what one is selling: *sell short.* —**caught short.** Unexpectedly lacking what is necessary. —**fall** (or **come**) **short.** To fail to meet expectations or requirements. —*n.* **1.** Anything that is short, especially: **a.** A briefly articulated or unaccented syllable. **b.** A short vowel. **c.** A short sale, or a person who sells short. **d.** *Plural.* Short trousers extending to the knee or above. **e.** *Plural.* Men's undershorts. **f.** A short motion picture, **short subject** *(see).* **2.** *Plural.* A by-product of wheat processing, consisting of bran mixed with coarse meal or flour. **3.** *Plural.* Clippings or trimmings that remain as by-products in various manufacturing processes, often used to make an inferior variety of the product. **4.** *Electricity.* **a.** A **short circuit** *(see).* **b.** A malfunction caused by a short circuit. **5.** *Baseball.* A shortstop. —*v.* **shorted, shorting, shorts.** —*tr.* **1.** To cause a short circuit in. **2.** *Informal.* To give (a person) less than he is entitled to; shortchange. —*intr.* To short-circuit. [Middle English *short,* Old English *scort.* See **sker-**[1] in Appendix.*] —**short′ness** *n.*

short account. 1. The account of a person who sells short. **2.** The total open short sales, as of a particular commodity or security, or on the market as a whole.

short·age (shôr′tĭj) *n. Abbr.* **shtg.** A deficiency in amount; deficit; insufficiency.

short·bread (shôrt′brĕd′) *n.* A kneaded dough of flour, sugar, and butter, rolled thickly, cut into cookies, and baked.

short·cake (shôrt′kāk′) *n.* A dessert consisting of a cake made with rich biscuit dough, split and filled with strawberries or other fruit, and topped with cream.

short·change (shôrt′chānj′) *tr.v.* **-changed, -changing, -changes.** *Informal.* **1.** To give (someone) less change than is due. **2.** To swindle, cheat, or trick. —**short′chang′er** *n.*

short circuit. An accidentally established low-resistance connection between two points in an electric circuit. Also called "short."

short-cir·cuit (shôrt′sûr′kĭt) *v.* **-cuited, -cuiting, -cuits.** —*tr.* To cause to have a short circuit. —*intr.* To become affected with a short circuit.

short·com·ing (shôrt′kŭm′ĭng) *n.* A deficiency or flaw.

short covering. The buying of securities, stocks, or commodities in order to close out a short sale.

short cut. 1. A more direct route than the customary one. **2.** Any means of saving time or effort: *"The American liking for short cuts in speech"* (H.L. Mencken).

short division. A division of one number by another, usually no more than two digits, without writing out the remainders.

short·en (shôrt′n) *v.* **-ened, -ening, -ens.** —*tr.* **1.** To make short or shorter. **2.** To take in (a sail) so that less canvas is exposed to the wind. **3.** To reduce in force, efficacy, or intensity. **4.** To add shortening to (dough) so as to make crumbly. —*intr.* To become short or shorter.

shortened form. An abbreviated form of a polysyllabic word; for example, *auto* for *automobile.* Also called "clipped form."

short·en·ing (shôrt′n-ĭng, shôrt′nĭng) *n.* **1.** A fat, such as butter, lard, or vegetable oil, used to make cake or pastry light or flaky. **2.** A shortened form of something, as an abbreviation. **3.** The act of one that shortens.

short·hand (shôrt′hănd′) *n.* **1.** A system of rapid handwriting employing symbols to represent words, phrases, and letters; stenography. **2.** Any system, form, or instance of abbreviated or formulaic reference: *"The classical error is to regard a scientific law as only a shorthand for its instances."* (J. Bronowski). —**short′hand′** *adj.*

short·hand·ed (shôrt′hăn′dĭd) *adj.* Lacking the usual or necessary number of workmen, employees, or assistants.

short·horn (shôrt′hôrn′) *n.* One of a breed of beef or dairy cattle originating in northern England and having short, curved horns. Also called "Durham."

short hundredweight. A **hundredweight** *(see).*

shor·ti·a (shôr′tē-ə) *n.* A plant of the genus *Shortia;* especially, *S. galacifolia,* of the southeastern United States, having evergreen leaves and a solitary white flower. [Identified by Charles Wilkins *Short* (1794–1863), American botanist.]

short-lived (shôrt′līvd′, -lĭvd′) *adj.* Living or lasting only a short time; ephemeral.

short·ly (shôrt′lē) *adv.* **1.** In a short time; soon; presently. **2.** In a few words; concisely. **3.** Abruptly or curtly.

short order. Food quickly prepared and served, as in a diner. —**in short order.** Quickly; immediately. —**short′-or′der** *adj.*

short rib. A cut of meat consisting of the area between the rib roast and the plate.

short sale. A sale of securities or commodities not in the immediate possession of the seller but whose delivery is anticipated before the close of the contract.

short shrift. 1. a. A short respite, as from death. **b.** *Archaic.* The short space of time granted a condemned prisoner for his confession before execution. **2.** Summary and unsympathetic treatment or dismissal. —**make** (or **give**) **short shrift of** (or **to**). **1.** To dispose of summarily or without consideration. **2.** To make quick work of; dispatch.

short·sight·ed (shôrt′sī′tĭd) *adj.* **1.** Near-sighted; myopic. **2.** Lacking foresight. **3.** Resulting from a lack of foresight. —**short′sight′ed·ly** *adv.* —**short′sight′ed·ness** *n.*

short-spo·ken (shôrt′spō′kən) *adj.* Given to shortness or abruptness in manner or speech; laconic; curt.

short·stop (shôrt′stŏp′) *n. Baseball.* **1.** The field position between second and third bases. **2.** The player who occupies this position.

short story. A short prose fiction aiming at unity of characterization, theme, and effect.

short subject. A brief motion picture intended to be shown between showings of longer motion pictures.

short-tem·pered (shôrt′tĕm′pərd) *adj.* Easily or quickly moved to anger; irascible.

short-term (shôrt′tûrm′) *adj.* Payable or reaching maturity within a relatively short time, such as a year: *a short-term loan.*

short ton. *Abbr.* **s.t.** A unit of weight, a **ton** *(see).*

short wave. *Abbr.* **sw** An electromagnetic wave with wavelength in the short-wave region.

short-wave (shôrt′wāv′) *adj. Abbr.* **sw 1.** Having a wavelength of less than approximately 80 meters. **2.** Capable of receiving or transmitting at such wavelengths.

short-wind·ed (shôrt′wĭn′dĭd) *adj.* **1.** Having shortness of breath; easily winded. **2.** Choppy; disconnected: *lines adapted to a strident, short-winded delivery.*

Sho·sho·ne (shō-shō′nē) *n., pl.* **Shoshone** or **-nes.** Also **Sho·sho·ni. 1.** A tribe of Uto-Aztecan-speaking North American Indians, formerly occupying parts of Nevada, Oregon, Idaho, Utah, Wyoming, and Texas. **2.** A member of this tribe. **3.** The language of this tribe.

Sho·sho·ne·an (shō-shō′nē-ən) *n.* An Indian linguistic group in western North America, comprising most of the Uto-Aztecan languages found in the United States. —**Sho·sho′ne·an** *adj.*

Sho·sho·ne Falls (shō-shō′nē). A cascade (over 200 feet high) on the Snake River in southern Idaho.

Sho·sho·ne River (shō-shō′nē). A river of northwest Wyoming flowing about 120 miles northeast to the Bighorn.

Shos·ta·ko·vich (shŏs′tə-kō′vĭch), **Dmitri.** Born 1906. Soviet composer.

shot[1] (shŏt) *n., pl.* **shots** or **shot** (for sense 2). **1.** The firing or discharge of a weapon, as of a gun or a bow. **2.** A pellet, bullet, or similar material trajected from various firearms; a round as distinguished from a cartridge or casing. **3.** *Informal.* Something that resembles the directed discharge of a weapon in force and carry, as a throw, hit, or drive in any of several games. **4.** One who shoots, considered with regard to the accuracy of his aim: *a good shot.* **5.** The distance over which something is shot; range. **6.** An attempt to hit or land on something with a missile or rocket: *a moon shot.* **7.** An attempt, guess, or opportunity. **8.** The heavy metal ball that is put for distance in the shot-put. **9.** *Mining.* A charge of explosives used in blasting. **10. a.** A photograph or one in a series of photographs. **b.** A single cinematic view or take. **11.** A hypodermic injection. **12.** A drink of liquor, especially a jigger. **13.** *Nautical.* A unit designating chain length, in the United States 15 fathoms, in Great Britain 12½ fathoms. —*tr.v.* **shotted, shotting, shots. 1.** To load or weight with shot. **2.** To clean (bottles) by shaking when full of shot. [Middle English *shot*, Old English *scot*. See **skeud-** in Appendix.*]

shot² (shŏt) *adj.* **1.** Of changeable, variegated, or iridescent color, as fabric having different-colored warp and weft. **2.** *Informal.* Worn-out; ruined.

shot³. Past tense and past participle of **shoot.**

shote. Variant of **shoat.**

shot·gun (shŏt'gŭn') *n.* A shoulder-held firearm that fires multiple pellets through a smooth bore.

shot-put (shŏt'pŏŏt') *n.* **1.** An athletic event in which the contestants attempt to throw or put a shot or heavy ball as far as possible. **2.** One such throw; a heave. **3.** The standard ball used in this competition; the shot. —**shot'-put'ter** *n.*

shott. Variant of **chott.**

shot·ten (shŏt'n) *adj.* **1.** Having recently spawned and thus less desirable as food. Said of fish, especially herring. **2.** *Archaic.* Of no value; worthless. [Originally a variant past participle of SHOOT (specialized sense "to spawn").]

should (shŏŏd). Past tense of **shall**, but more often used as an auxiliary verb expressing degrees of the present and future and for various shades of attendant meaning indicating: **1.** Obligation; duty; necessity. **2.** Anticipation of a probable occurrence; expectation: *They should arrive at noon.* **3.** Condition; contingency of one condition upon another: *If he should fall, then so would I.* **4.** Uncertainty in a future event: *Would he like to go? I should think he would.* **5.** Moderation of the directness or bluntness of a statement with some implication of the unusual or surprising: *After sailing, what should we encounter first but a storm.* **6.** *Informal.* An ironic negative, asserting the negative in a positive way: *With his ability, he should worry* (meaning *should not worry*) *about winning.*

Usage: *Should,* in indicating obligation or necessity, is somewhat weaker than *ought* and appreciably weaker than *must* and *have to.* In sentences expressing simple conditions (contingency of one clause on another clause or phrase), both *would* and *should* are employed, but *would* is much more frequent in American usage: *If I had known that, I would* (or *should*) *have made a different reply. We would* (or *should*) *not have succeeded without your assistance.* Either *would* or *should* (indicating condition, not obligation) is acceptable on all levels of usage in the preceding examples, according to 80 per cent of the Usage Panel. *Would* is employed in such constructions in all three grammatical persons, whereas *should* is limited to the first person. (In this respect, current American usage departs from earlier rules of grammar and, to some extent, from formal British practice. Grammarians often specify that the choice between *should* and *would* is based on the distinctions they make between *shall* and *will* as auxiliary verbs. Thus, they use *should* in the first person and *would* in the second and third, in sentences, like the preceding ones, that merely make statements based on conditions. When something more than a conditional future is intended, such as determination, volition, or compulsion, they employ *would* in the first person and *should* in the second and third.) In the same way, either *would* or *should* is possible in the first person, as an auxiliary, with *like, be inclined, be glad, prefer,* and related verbs: *I would* (or *should*) *like to call your attention to an oversight.* Here *would* is acceptable on all levels to 77 per cent of the Usage Panel, and is more common in American usage than *should.* In such constructions, both the present and perfect infinitives often occur: *I would* (or *should*) *have liked to go. I would* (or *should*) *like to have gone.* But not *I would* (or *should*) *have liked to have gone.*

shoul·der (shōl'dər) *n.* **1.** *Anatomy.* **a.** The part of the human body between the neck and upper arm. **b.** The joint connecting the arm with the trunk. **2.** The corresponding part of an animal. **3.** *Plural.* The two shoulders and the area of the back between them. **4.** The forequarter of some animals. **5.** The portion of a garment that covers the shoulder. **6.** The angle between the face and the flank of a bastion in fortifications. **7.** *Printing.* The extended flat surface on the body of type beyond the letter or character. **8.** A kind of leather from that portion of the hide anterior to the butt. **9. a.** The edge or ridge running on either side of a roadway. **b.** Any shoulderlike projection or slope. —*v.* **shouldered, -dering, -ders.** —*tr.* **1.** To carry (a burden, for example) on or as on the shoulders; bear or support; assume. **2.** To push through or apply force to with or as with the shoulder: *shoulder one's way through.* **3.** To make or form a shoulder or abutment on. —*intr.* To push with the shoulder or shoulders. [Middle English *shulder*, Old English *sculdor*, from Germanic *skuldra-* (unattested).]

shoulder blade. The **scapula** *(see).*

shoulder girdle. The **pectoral girdle** *(see).*

shoulder patch. A military identification patch worn on the upper portion of the sleeve to designate one's unit or branch.

should·n't (shŏŏd'ənt). Contraction of **should not.**

shouldst (shŏŏdst). Also **should·est** (shŏŏd'ĭst). *Archaic.* Second person singular past tense of **shall.** Used with *thou.*

shout (shout) *n.* A loud cry, often expressing strong emotion or a command. —*v.* **shouted, shouting, shouts.** —*tr.* To say with a shout. —*intr.* To utter a loud cry; to yell; speak loudly. —**shout down.** To overwhelm or silence another by shouting loudly. [Middle English *shouten*†.] —**shout'er** *n.*

shove (shŭv) *v.* **shoved, shoving, shoves.** —*tr.* To prod or give thrust to, as forward or along a surface; push roughly or rudely. —*intr.* To push someone or something with sudden force. —**shove off. 1.** To set a beached boat afloat. **2.** *Informal.* To leave. —*n.* The act of shoving; especially, a rude push. [Middle English *sho(u)ven*, Old English *scūfan.* See **skeubh-** in Appendix.*] —**shov'er** *n.*

shov·el (shŭv'əl) *n.* **1.** A tool with a handle and a somewhat flattened scoop for picking up dirt, snow, or the like. **2.** A large mechanical device or vehicle for heavy digging or excavation, usually a jawed scoop suspended from a boom or crane. **3.** *Informal.* A **shovel hat** *(see).* —*v.* **shoveled** or **-elled, -eling** or **-elling, -els.** —*tr.* **1.** To dig into or move with a shovel. **2.** To clear away or make with a shovel. **3.** To set down or into in a hasty or careless way; unload: *"Bond shovelled the great wad of notes out on to the table"* (Ian Fleming). **4.** To convey in a rough way, as with a shovel. —*intr.* To dig or work with a shovel. [Middle English *shovel*, Old English *scofl.* See **skeubh-** in Appendix.*]

shov·el·board. Variant of **shuffleboard.**

shov·el·er (shŭv'ə-lər) *n.* Also **shov·el·ler. 1.** One who works with a shovel. **2.** A widely distributed duck, *Spatula clypeata* (or *Anas clypeata*), having a long, broad bill.

shov·el·ful (shŭv'əl-fŏŏl') *n.* The amount a shovel will hold.

shovel hat. A stiff, broad-brimmed, low-crowned hat, turned up at the sides and projecting in front, worn by some English clergymen. Also informally called "shovel."

shov·el·head (shŭv'əl-hĕd') *n.* A shark, *Sphyrna tiburo,* of Atlantic and Pacific waters.

shov·el·nose (shŭv'əl-nōz') *n.* A sturgeon, *Scaphirhynchus platorynchus,* of the Mississippi River, having a broad, flat snout. Also called "shovelnose sturgeon."

shov·el·nosed (shŭv'əl-nōzd') *adj.* Having a broad, flattened snout, bill, or head.

show (shō) *v.* **showed, shown** (shōn) or **showed, showing, shows.** —*tr.* **1. a.** To cause or allow to be seen or viewed; to display; make visible. **b.** To present in public exhibition or competition. **2.** To conduct; guide. **3.** To point out; demonstrate. **4. a.** To manifest; reveal. **b.** To indicate; to register. **5.** To grant; confer; bestow. **6.** *Law.* To plead; allege: *show cause.* —*intr.* **1.** To be or become visible or evident. **2.** *Informal.* To come to a rendezvous; make an appearance. **3.** *Informal.* To manifest or display; respond with: *His face showed red.* **4.** To be exhibited; to run: *The film will show three days.* **5.** *Sports.* To finish third or better for betting purposes. Compare **win, place.** —**show (someone) out.** To usher out. —**show up. 1.** To expose or reveal faults or the like. **2.** To be clearly or ultimately visible. **3.** To put in an appearance; arrive. **4.** *Informal.* To prove that one is superior to (another); outdo. —*n.* **1.** The act of showing or revealing. **2.** A display; manifestation; demonstration. **3.** An appearance; semblance: *a show of kindness.* **4.** A striking appearance or display; spectacle. **5.** A pompous or ostentatious display. **6. a.** Any public exhibition or entertainment. **b.** A troupe or company. **7.** A trace; indication. **8.** *Informal.* Any affair or undertaking; a result: *a poor show.* **9.** *Sports.* Third place or better for betting purposes: *win, place, and show.* —**show of hands.** A raising of hands among the members of a group to indicate a vote. —*adj.* Of, pertaining to, in, or used for a show or shows: *show business.* [Middle English *shewen, showen,* to look at, cause to look at, show, Old English *scēawian,* to look at, see. See **keu-¹** in Appendix.*]

Synonyms: *show, display, expose, parade, exhibit, flaunt.* These verbs mean to present something to view. *Show* is the most general, since it makes no clear implication as to manner or method of presentation. *Display* usually suggests an attempt to present something to best advantage, but it can imply ostentation or even the making obvious of something better concealed, such as ignorance. *Expose* usually involves uncovering or bringing from concealment or unmasking. *Parade* generally suggests a blatant or boastful presentation. *Exhibit* implies open, rather formal presentation that invites inspection. *Flaunt* implies a prideful, arrogant attempt to gain attention.

show bill. An advertising poster.

show biz. *Slang.* Show business.

show·boat (shō'bōt') *n.* A river steamboat having a troupe of actors and a theater aboard for performances on the river.

show·bread (shō'brĕd') *n.* Also *archaic* **shew·bread.** The 12 loaves of blessed unleavened bread placed every Sabbath in the sanctuary of the Tabernacle by the ancient Hebrew priests. Exodus 25:30. [Translation of German *Schaubrot,* translation of Hebrew *lehem pānim,* "bread of the Divine Presence" : *lehem,* bread + *pānim,* presence.]

show business. The entertainment industry or arts.

show·case (shō'kās') *n.* **1.** A display case or cabinet, as in a store or museum. **2.** A setting in which something may be displayed to advantage.

show·down (shō'doun') *n.* **1.** *Poker.* The laying down of the players' hands of cards for the purpose of determining the winner of the pot. **2.** Any event or circumstance that forces an issue to a conclusion.

show·er¹ (shou'ər) *n.* **1. a.** A brief fall of rain, hail, or sleet. **b.** A downfall of a group of objects, especially of a large group, from the sky: *a meteor shower.* **2.** Any brief or sudden downpour. **3.** An abundant flow; outpouring: *a shower of abuse.* **4.** A party held to honor and present gifts to someone: *a bridal shower.* **5.** A shower bath. —*v.* **showered, -ering, -ers.** —*tr.* **1.** To sprinkle; spray. **2.** To bestow abundantly. —*intr.* **1.** To fall or pour down in a shower. **2.** To take a shower bath. [Middle English *shour,* Old English *scūr.* See **kēwero-** in Appendix.*] —**show'er·y** *adj.*

show·er² (shō'ər) *n.* One that shows.

shower bath. 1. A bath in which water is sprayed on the bather from an overhead nozzle. **2.** A room or booth equipped for such baths.

show·girl (shō'gûrl') *n.* A chorus girl or similar entertainer.

Show·hsien. The former name for **Hwainan.**

shoveler

ă pat/ā pay/âr care/ä father/b bib/ch church/d deed/ĕ pet/ē be/f fife/g gag/h hat/hw which/ĭ pit/ī pie/îr pier/j judge/k kick/l lid, needle/m mum/n no, sudden/ng thing/ŏ pot/ō toe/ô paw, for/oi noise/ou out/ŏŏ took/ōō boot/p pop/r roar/s sauce/sh ship, dish/t tight/th thin, path/th this, bathe/ŭ cut/ûr urge/v valve/w with/y yes/z zebra, size/zh vision/ə about, item, edible, gallop, circus/ à *Fr.* ami/œ *Fr.* feu, *Ger.* schön/ü *Fr.* tu, *Ger.* über/KH *Ger.* ich, *Scot.* loch/N *Fr.* bon. *Follows main vocabulary. †Of obscure origin.

show·ing (shō′ĭng) *n.* **1. a.** The action of presenting or displaying. **b.** An instance of this. **2.** Performance, as in a competition or test of skill: *a poor showing.* **3.** A presentation of evidence, facts, or figures.
show·man (shō′mən) *n., pl.* **-men** (-mĭn). **1.** A theatrical producer. **2.** A person having a flair for dramatic or visual effectiveness. **—show′man·ship′** *n.*
Show Me State. The nickname for Missouri.
shown. Past participle of **show.**
show off. 1. To display in a showy fashion. **2.** To behave in an impudent and exhibitionistic manner.
show-off (shō′ôf′, -ŏf′) *n.* **1.** Ostentatious display or exhibitionistic behavior. **2.** An exhibitionist.
show·piece (shō′pēs′) *n.* An exhibition piece.
show place. A place that is viewed and frequented for its beauty, historical interest, or the like.
show room. A room in which merchandise is on display.
show·y (shō′ē) *adj.* **-ier, -iest. 1.** Making a conspicuous display; striking: *showy flowers.* **2.** Displaying brilliance and virtuosity of ability or performance. **3.** Ostentatious; gaudy; flashy. —See Synonyms at **ornate. —show′i·ly** *adv.* **—show′i·ness** *n.*
shp shaft horsepower.
shpt. shipment.
Shqi·pe·ri. The Albanian name for **Albania.**
shr. share (capital stock).
shrank. Past tense of **shrink.**
shrap·nel (shrăp′nəl) *n., pl.* **shrapnel.** *Military.* **1. a.** An antipersonnel projectile containing metal balls, fused to explode in the air above enemy troops. **b.** The metal balls in such a weapon. **2.** Shell fragments from any high-explosive shell. [Invented by General Henry *Shrapnel* (1761–1842), British artillery officer.]
shred (shrĕd) *n.* **1.** A long, irregular strip cut or torn off. **2.** A small amount; particle. *—tr.v.* **shredded** or **shred, shredding, shreds.** To cut or tear into shreds. [Middle English *shrede,* Old English *scrēade.* See **skeru-** in Appendix.*] **—shred′der** *n.*
Shreve·port (shrēv′pôrt′, -pōrt′). A city of northwestern Louisiana, on the Red River. Population, 178,000.

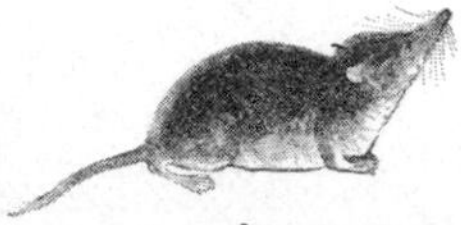

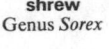

shrew
Genus *Sorex*

shrew (shrōō) *n.* **1.** Any of various small, chiefly insectivorous mammals of the family Soricidae, having a long, pointed nose and small, often poorly developed eyes. Sometimes called "shrewmouse." **2.** A woman with a violent, scolding, or nagging temperament; a scold. [Middle English *shrewe* (unattested), Old English *scrēawa.* See **skeru-** in Appendix.*]
shrewd (shrōōd) *adj.* **shrewder, shrewdest. 1.** Having keen insight; discerning; astute. **2.** Artful; cunning; tricky. **3.** Sharp; penetrating; searching. —See Synonyms at **clever.** [Middle English *shrewed(e),* wicked, dangerous, serious, from SHREW (evil person).] **—shrewd′ly** *adv.*
Synonyms: *shrewd, sagacious, astute, quick-witted.* These adjectives refer to the possession of a keen, searching intelligence combined usually with sound judgment. *Shrewd* stresses perceptiveness, hardheadedness, cunning, and an intuitive knack in practical matters. *Sagacious* emphasizes more profound wisdom based on wide experience and a gift for discernment and farsightedness. *Astute* suggests qualities associated with practical wisdom, such as acute understanding, insight, discernment, and immunity to being deceived. *Quick-witted,* the narrowest term, refers to alertness and mental adroitness.
shrewd·ness (shrōōd′nĭs) *n.* **1.** The quality of being shrewd. **2.** An aggregation of apes. See Synonyms at **flock.**
shrew·ish (shrōō′ĭsh) *adj.* Like a shrew in temperament; ill-tempered; nagging. **—shrew′ish·ly** *adv.* **—shrew′ish·ness** *n.*
shrew mole. Any of several shrewlike moles of the family Talpidae; especially, *Neurotrichus gibbsi,* of western North America, or *Uropsilus soricipes,* of eastern Asia.

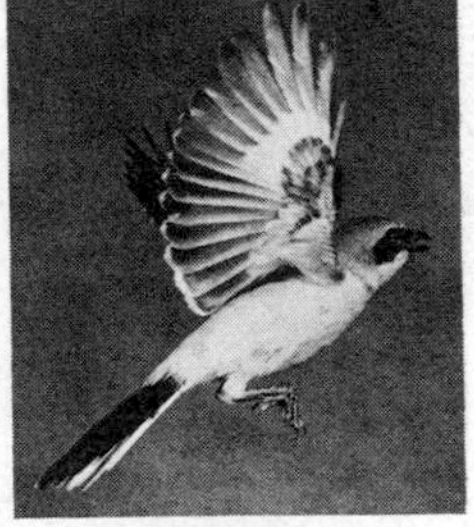

shrike
Lanius ludoviscianus
Loggerhead shrike

shriek (shrēk) *n.* **1.** A shrill outcry; screech. **2.** Any sound suggestive of a shriek: *"the shearing surflike shriek of the saw"* (James Agee). *—v.* **shrieked, shrieking, shrieks.** *—intr.* **1.** To utter such a cry. **2.** To make a sound similar to such a cry: *"the winds shriek through the clouds"* (Ezra Pound). *—tr.* To utter with a shriek. —See Synonyms at **scream.** [Middle English *shriken,* probably from Old Norse *skrækja.* See **ker-**[2] in Appendix.*] **—shriek′er** *n.*
shriev·al (shrē′vəl) *adj.* Of or pertaining to a sheriff or his jurisdiction. **—shriev′al·ty** *n.*
shrift (shrĭft) *n. Archaic.* **1.** The act of shriving. **2.** Confession to a priest. **3.** Absolution given by a priest. [Middle English *shrift(e),* Old English *scrift,* from *scrīfan,* SHRIVE.]
shrike (shrīk) *n.* Any of various carnivorous birds of the family Laniidae, having a hooked bill, and often impaling its prey on sharp-pointed thorns or barbs of wire fencing. Some species are also called "butcherbird." [Probably from Middle English *shrik* (unattested), from Old English *scrīc,* thrush. See **ker-**[2] in Appendix.*]
shrill (shrĭl) *adj.* **1.** High-pitched and piercing in quality. **2.** Producing a sharp, high-pitched tone or sound. **3.** Sharp or keen to any of the senses. *—v.* **shrilled, shrilling, shrills.** *—tr.* To utter in a shrill manner; to scream; shriek. *—intr.* To produce a shrill cry or sound. [Middle English *shrille,* from *shrillen,* to shriek, probably from Scandinavian, akin to Norwegian *skrylla.* See **ker-**[2] in Appendix.*] **—shrill′ness** *n.* **—shril′ly** *adv.*
shrimp (shrĭmp) *n., pl.* **shrimp** or **shrimps. 1. a.** Any of various small, slender-bodied, chiefly marine decapod crustaceans of the suborder Natantia, many species of which are edible. **b.** Any of various similar crustaceans. **2.** *Slang.* A diminutive or unimportant person. [Middle English *shrimpe,* pigmy, shrimp, perhaps of Low German origin, akin to Middle Low German *schrempen,* to shrink, wrinkle. See **skerbh-** in Appendix.*]
shrimp·fish (shrĭmp′fĭsh′) *n., pl.* **shrimpfish** or **-fishes.** Any of various small, slender, tropical marine fishes of the family Centriscidae, related to the sea horses and pipefish.
shrimp plant. A shrubby plant, *Beloperone guttata,* having inconspicuous flowers borne between a series of reddish bracts.
shrine (shrīn) *n.* **1.** A container or receptacle for sacred relics; reliquary. **2.** The tomb of a saint or other venerated person. **3.** A site hallowed by a venerated object or its associations. *—tr.v.* **shrined, shrining, shrines.** To enshrine. [Middle English *shrin(e),* box, chest, reliquary, Old English *scrīn,* from Latin *scrīnium*†, box, bookcase.]
Shrine (shrīn) *n.* A U.S. secret fraternal order established in 1872. Also called "Ancient Arabic Order of Nobles of the Mystic Shrine." **—Shrin′er** *n.*
shrink (shrĭngk) *v.* **shrank** (shrăngk) or **shrunk** (shrŭngk), **shrunk** or **shrunken** (shrŭng′kən), **shrinking, shrinks.** *—intr.* **1.** To draw together or constrict from heat, moisture, or cold; to contract. **2.** To become reduced in amount or value; dwindle. **3.** To draw back; recoil. **4.** To be reluctant to do or say something. *—tr.* To cause to shrink. —See Synonyms at **contract, decrease, recoil.** *—n.* **1.** A shrinking or shrinkage. **2.** *Slang.* A psychiatrist or psychologist. [Shrink, shrank, shrunk; Middle English *shrinken, shrank* (also *shrunk*), *shrunken,* Old English *scrincan, scranc* (plural *scruncon*), *(ge)scruncen.* See **sker-**[3] in Appendix.*] **—shrink′a·ble** *adj.* **—shrink′er** *n.*
shrink·age (shrĭng′kĭj) *n.* **1.** The process of shrinking; constriction, as of clothing in laundering. **2.** A reduction in value; depreciation. **3. a.** The total weight loss sustained by livestock in shipment to a market. **b.** The amount of any loss by shrinkage.
shrinking violet. *Informal.* A shy or retiring person.
shrink package. A transparent form-fitting plastic wrapping, especially of polyethylene or polyvinyl chloride, used to protect a commodity from dust, moisture, and abrasion. Also called "shrink wrap."
shrink-pack·age (shrĭngk′păk′ĭj) *tr.v.* **-aged, -aging, -ages.** To enclose (a commodity) in a protective film of extruded plastic sealed and shrunk to a form-fitting envelope by the application of heat; shrink-wrap.
shrink-wrap (shrĭngk′răp′) *tr.v.* **-wrapped, -wrapping, -wraps.** To shrink-package.
shrive (shrīv) *v.* **shrove** (shrōv) or **shrived, shriven** (shrĭv′ən) or **shrived, shriving, shrives.** *—tr.* **1.** To confess and give absolution to (a penitent). **2.** To obtain absolution for (oneself) by confessing and doing penance. *—intr.* **1.** To make or go to confession. **2.** To hear confessions. [Shrive, shrove, shriven; Middle English *shriven, shrove, shriven,* Old English *scrīfan, scrāf* (past singular), *scrifen(e),* from West Germanic *skrīban* (unattested), to write, "prescribe (penance)," from Latin *scrībere,* to write. See **skeri-** in Appendix.*] **—shriv′er** *n.*
shriv·el (shrĭv′əl) *v.* **-eled** or **-elled, -eling** or **-elling, -els.** *—intr.* **1.** To shrink and wrinkle, often in drying. Often used with *up.* **2.** To lose vitality or intensity: *"Their spirits shrivelled in the numbing breath of a military government"* (T.E. Lawrence). *—tr.* To cause to become shriveled. [Possibly from Old Norse *skrīfla* (unattested), to wrinkle. See **skeri-** in Appendix.*]
Shrop·shire[1] (shrŏp′shĭr, -shər). A county occupying 1,337 square miles in western England. Population, 297,000. County seat, Shrewsbury. Also called "Salop."
Shrop·shire[2] (shrŏp′shĭr, -shər) *n.* A large, hornless, black-faced sheep of a breed developed in Shropshire, England, now found chiefly in North America. It is raised for meat and wool.
shroud (shroud) *n.* **1.** A cloth used to wrap a body for burial; winding sheet. **2.** Something that conceals, protects, or screens in the manner of a garment. **3.** *Usually plural.* One of a set of ropes or wire cables stretched from the masthead to a vessel's sides to support the mast. **4.** A similar support for a smokestack or comparable structure. **5.** One of the ropes connecting the harness and canopy of a parachute. *—v.* **shrouded, shrouding, shrouds.** *—tr.* **1.** To wrap (a corpse) in burial clothing. **2.** To envelop; screen; hide. **3.** *Archaic.* To shelter; protect. *—intr. Archaic.* To take cover; find shelter. [Middle English *sc(h)rud,* garment, clothing, Old English *scrūd.* See **skeru-** in Appendix.*]
Shrove·tide (shrōv′tīd′) *n.* The three days, Shrove Sunday, Shrove Monday, and Shrove Tuesday, preceding Ash Wednesday. [Middle English *schroftyde* : *schrof-,* "shriving," irregularly from *schrov-,* past stem of *shriven,* SHRIVE + *tyde, tid(e),* TIDE (time).]
shrub[1] (shrŭb) *n.* A woody plant of relatively low height, distinguished from a tree by having several stems rather than a single trunk; a bush. [Middle English *schrubbe,* Old English *scrybb.* See **sker-**[1] in Appendix.*]
shrub[2] (shrŭb) *n.* A beverage made from fruit juice, sugar, and a liquor such as rum or brandy. [Arabic *shurb,* a drink, from *shariba,* to drink. See also **sherbet, syrup.**]
shrub·ber·y (shrŭb′ə-rē) *n., pl.* **-ies. 1.** Shrubs collectively. **2.** A group or planting of shrubs.
shrub·by (shrŭb′ē) *adj.* **-bier, -biest. 1.** Consisting of, planted, or covered with shrubs. **2.** Of or resembling a shrub; shrublike. **—shrub′bi·ness** *n.*
shrug (shrŭg) *v.* **shrugged, shrugging, shrugs.** *—tr.* To raise (the shoulders) as a gesture of doubt, disdain, or indifference. *—intr.* To make this gesture. **—shrug off. 1.** To minimize the importance of. **2.** To get rid of. **3.** To wriggle out of clothing. *—n.* **1.** The expressive gesture constituted by this movement. **2.** A short jacket or sweater, open down the front. [Middle English *shruggen,* to shiver, shrug, perhaps from Scandinavian,

ă pat/ā pay/âr care/ä father/b bib/ch church/d deed/ĕ pet/ē be/f fife/g gag/h hat/hw which/ĭ pit/ī pie/îr pier/j judge/k kick/l lid, needle/m mum/n no, sudden/ng thing/ŏ pot/ō toe/ô paw, for/oi noise/ou out/ŏŏ took/ōō boot/p pop/r roar/s sauce/sh ship, dish/

akin to Danish *skrugge*, to duck the head. See **sker-**[3] in Appendix.*]

shrunk. Past participle and alternate past tense of **shrink.**

shrunken. Alternate past participle of **shrink.**

shtg. shortage.

shtick (shtĭk) *n. Slang.* **1.** A characteristic attribute, talent, or trait. **2.** A striking portion or detail. **3.** The method of doing something. [Yiddish, probably from Middle High German *stich*, a thrust, puncture, from Old High German *stih*. See **steig-** in Appendix.*]

shuck (shŭk) *n.* The outer covering of something, such as a pea pod, corn husk, or oyster shell. —**not worth shucks.** Of little or no value; worthless. —*tr.v.* **shucked, shucking, shucks. 1.** To remove the husk or shell from. **2.** *Informal.* To cast off (clothing, for example). [Origin unknown.] —**shuck′er** *n.*

shucks (shŭks) *interj.* Used to express disappointment, disgust, or annoyance. [From SHUCK (thing of no value).]

shud·der (shŭd′ər) *intr.v.* **-dered, -dering, -ders. 1.** To tremble or shiver convulsively, as from fear or aversion: *"They shuddered at the thought of hard work"* (Conrad). **2.** To vibrate; quiver. —See Synonyms at **shake.** —*n.* A convulsive shiver, as from fear or cold; a tremor. [Middle English *shoddren, shudren*, from Middle Low German *schōderen*. See **skut-** in Appendix.*] —**shud′der·ing·ly** *adv.*

shuf·fle (shŭf′əl) *v.* **-fled, -fling, -fles.** —*tr.* **1.** To drag (the feet) along the floor or ground while walking or dancing; to scuffle. **2.** To move (something) from one place to another. **3.** To mix together or otherwise handle in a disordered, haphazard fashion. **4.** To put aside or conceal hastily; cover up. **5.** To mix together (playing cards, tiles, or dominoes) to change their order of arrangement. —*intr.* **1.** To move with a shambling, idle gait; to scuffle. **2.** To dance the shuffle. **3.** To shift about from place to place. **4.** To act in a shifty or deceitful manner; equivocate. —*n.* **1.** A shuffling gait or movement. **2.** A dance in which the feet scrape along the floor at each step. **3.** An evasive or deceitful irresponsible action; a dodge; an equivocation. **4. a.** The act of mixing cards, dominoes, or tiles. **b.** A player's right or turn to do this. [Probably from Low German *schüffeln*, to walk clumsily, shuffle cards. See **skeubh-** in Appendix.*] —**shuf′fler** *n.*

shuf·fle·board (shŭf′əl-bôrd′, -bōrd′) *n.* Also **shov·el·board** (shŭv′əl-). **1.** A game in which disks are pushed or slid along a smooth, level surface toward numbered squares with a pronged cue. **2.** The surface on which this game is played. [Alteration (influenced by SHUFFLE) of earlier *shove-board* : SHOVE + BOARD.]

shul (shŏŏl, shōōl) *n. Yiddish.* A synagogue.

shun (shŭn) *tr.v.* **shunned, shunning, shuns.** To avoid (a person, group, or thing) deliberately and consistently; keep away from: *"Avoid the reeking herd, / Shun the polluted flock"* (Elinor Wylie). See Synonyms at **escape.** [Middle English *shun(n)en*, Old English *scunian*†, to avoid, be afraid, abhor.] —**shun′ner** *n.*

shun·pike (shŭn′pīk′) *n.* A side road taken to avoid the tollgates on a major artery.

shunt (shŭnt) *n.* **1.** The act of shunting. **2.** A railroad switch. **3.** *Electricity.* A low-resistance connection between two points in an electric circuit that forms an alternative path for a portion of the current. In this sense, also called "by-pass." —*v.* **shunted, shunting, shunts.** —*tr.* **1.** To turn or move (something) aside or onto another course. **2.** To shift or switch (a train or car) from one track to another. **3.** *Electricity.* To provide or divert (current) by means of a shunt. **4.** To evade or avoid (a task, for example) by refusing or putting aside. —*intr.* **1.** To move or turn aside. **2.** *Electricity.* To become diverted by means of a shunt. Used of a circuit. **3.** To shift one's views or direction. [Middle English *shunten*, to flinch, shy, run away, perhaps from *shun(n)en*, SHUN.]

shunt-wound (shŭnt′wound′) *adj.* Of or pertaining to a direct-current motor or generator in which the field coil is connected in parallel with the armature so that the same voltage appears across each. Compare **series-wound.**

shush (shŭsh) *interj.* Used to express a demand for silence. —*tr.v.* **shushed, shushing, shushes.** To demand silence from by saying "shush": *"Simon shushed him quickly as though he had spoken too loudly in church."* (William Golding).

Shu·shan. The Biblical name for **Susa.**

shut (shŭt) *v.* **shut, shutting, shuts.** —*tr.* **1.** To move (a door, lid, valve, or the like) into closed position over or within a conjoined aperture. **2.** To block passage or access to; close. **3.** To fasten or secure with a lock, catch, or latch. **4.** To prevent or forbid access to; to bar. **5.** To prevent or forbid egress from; confine. **6.** To close (a business establishment). —*intr.* To move or become moved to a closed position; close. —**shut up. 1.** To demand silence from a person. Usually used in the imperative. **2.** To silence (a person). **3.** To be or become silenced. **4.** To close (a business or enterprise). —*n.* **1.** The act or time of closing or shutting. **2.** The line of connection between welded pieces of metal. [Middle English *shutten*, originally a West Midland form of *shitten, shetten*, Old English *scyttan*. See **skeud-** in Appendix.*]

shut·down (shŭt′doun′) *n.* **1.** A temporary closing of an industrial plant. **2.** The failure or intentional cessation of operation of any apparatus or equipment.

shut-eye (shŭt′ī′) *n. Slang.* Sleep.

shut-in (shŭt′ĭn′) *n.* An invalid. —*adj.* **1.** Confined to a house or hospital, as by illness. **2.** *Psychiatry.* Disposed to avoid other people; excessively introverted.

shut·off (shŭt′ôf′, -ŏf′) *n.* **1.** A device that shuts something off. **2.** A stoppage; cessation; interruption.

shut·out (shŭt′out′) *n.* **1.** A **lockout** *(see).* **2.** *Sports.* A game in which one side does not score.

shut·ter (shŭt′ər) *n.* **1.** One that shuts. **2.** A hinged cover or screen for a window, usually fitted with louvers. **3.** *Plural.* The movable louvers on a pipe organ, controlled by pedals, that open and close the swell box. **4.** A mechanical device that opens and shuts the lens aperture of a camera to expose a plate or film. —*tr.v.* **shuttered, -tering, -ters.** To furnish or close with a shutter or shutters.

shut·ter·bug (shŭt′ər-bŭg′) *n. Informal.* An amateur photographer.

shut·tle (shŭt′l) *n.* **1.** A device used in weaving to carry the woof thread back and forth between the warp threads. **2.** A device for holding the thread in tatting, in netting, and in a sewing machine. **3.** A train, bus, or plane making short, frequent trips between two points. **4.** The act of shuttling. —*v.* **shuttled, -tling, -tles.** —*intr.* To go, move, or travel back and forth by or as if by a shuttle. —*tr.* To move by or as if by a shuttle. [Middle English *schutylle*, Old English *scytel*, dart, missile. See **skeud-** in Appendix.*]

shut·tle·cock (shŭt′l-kŏk′) *n.* **1.** A small rounded piece of cork or similar material with a crown of feathers, used in the games of badminton and battledore. Also called "bird," "birdie." **2.** The game of battledore. —*tr.v.* **shuttlecocked, -cocking, -cocks.** To bandy back and forth like a shuttlecock. [SHUTTLE + COCK (bird).]

shy[1] (shī) *adj.* **shier** or **shyer, shiest** or **shyest. 1.** Easily startled; timid. **2.** Bashful; reserved. **3.** Distrustful; wary; cautious. **4.** *Informal.* Not having paid an amount due, as one's ante in poker. **5.** *Informal.* Short; lacking. —*intr.v.* **shied, shying, shies. 1.** To move suddenly, as if startled. **2.** To draw back, as from fear or caution. —*n., pl.* **shies.** A sudden movement, as from fright; a start. [Middle English *schey*, easily frightened, timid, Old English *scēoh*, from Germanic *skiuhwaz* (unattested).] —**shi′er, shy′er** *n.* —**shy′ly, shi′ly** *adv.* —**shy′ness** *n.*

Synonyms: *shy, bashful, diffident, modest, coy, demure.* These adjectives describe persons who are markedly unobtrusive. *Shy* implies either a retiring or withdrawn nature or timidity resulting from lack of social experience. *Bashful* suggests obvious embarrassment or awkwardness in the presence of others. *Diffident* implies lack of self-confidence. *Modest* is associated with a retiring nature, absence of vanity, and a dislike of personal ostentation. *Coy* usually implies false modesty or feigned shyness that may be calculated to stimulate attention or attract the interest of others. *Demure* implies a sedate, modest manner or decorous appearance.

shy[2] (shī) *v.* **shied, shying, shies.** —*tr.* To throw (something) with a swift sidewise motion. —*intr.* To throw in this manner. —*n., pl.* **shies. 1.** A quick throw; fling. **2.** *Informal.* A gibe; sneer. **3.** *Informal.* An experiment; a try. [Earliest senses, "to take a sudden fright," "shrink," "flinch," probably from SHY (easily frightened).]

shy·lock (shī′lŏk′) *n.* Also **Shy·lock.** A heartless, exacting creditor. [After *Shylock*, the ruthless usurer in Shakespeare's *Merchant of Venice* (1595).]

shy·ster (shī′stər) *n. Slang.* An unethical or unscrupulous practitioner, especially of law or politics. [Possibly after *Scheuster*, an unscrupulous 19th-century New York lawyer.]

si (sē) *n. Music.* The former name for **ti** *(see).*

Si The symbol for the element silicon.

SI International System of measurement (French *Système International*). See **measurement.**

si·al (sī′ăl′) *n.* A layer of rock rich in silica and alumina underlying all continental land masses. [SI(LICON) + AL(UMINUM).] —**si·al′ic** *adj.*

Si·al·kot (sĭ-äl′kōt). A city in northeastern West Pakistan; site of a shrine to Nanak, founder of Sikhism. Population, 168,000.

Si·am. The former name for **Thailand.**

Si·am, Gulf of (sī-ăm′). An arm of the South China Sea, extending 450 miles between the Malay Peninsula and Indochina.

si·a·mang (sē′ə-măng′) *n.* A large black gibbon, *Symphalangus syndactylus* (or *Hylobates syndactylus*), of Sumatra and the Malay Peninsula, having an inflatable throat sac. [Malay.]

si·a·mese (sī′ə-mēz′, -mēs′) *n.* An external automatic water pipe with a twin hose connection. —*adj.* Connecting two hoses or pipes to a larger hose or pipe.

Si·a·mese (sī′ə-mēz′, -mēs′) *adj.* **1. Thai** *(see).* **2.** Closely connected or very similar; twin. —*n., pl.* **Siamese. Thai** *(see).*

Siamese cat. A short-haired cat of a breed developed in the Orient, having blue eyes and a pale fawn or gray coat with darker ears, face, tail, and feet.

Siamese fighting fish. A small, often brightly colored freshwater fish, *Betta splendens*, native to tropical Asia and popular in home aquariums.

Siamese twins. Twins born with their bodies joined together in any manner. [After Chang and Eng (1811–1874), joined Chinese twins born in Siam.]

Si·an (shē′än′). Ancient name **Hsien·yang** (shē-ĕn′yäng′). Formerly **Chang·an** (chäng′än′). The capital of Shensi Province, central China; one of China's oldest cities and, as Changan, an ancient national capital of the Han Dynasty (206 B.C.–A.D. 220). Population, 1,310,000.

Siang (shē-äng′). Also **Hsiang. 1.** A river of southeastern China, flowing 715 miles northeast through Hunan Province to Lake Tungting. **2.** The former name for the **Yü Kiang.**

Siang·tan (shē-äng′tän′). A city of southeastern China, on the Siang in Hunan Province. Population, 247,000.

sib (sĭb) *n.* **1. a.** A blood relation; kinsman. **b.** Relatives collectively; kinfolk. **2.** A brother or sister; sibling. —*adj.* Re-

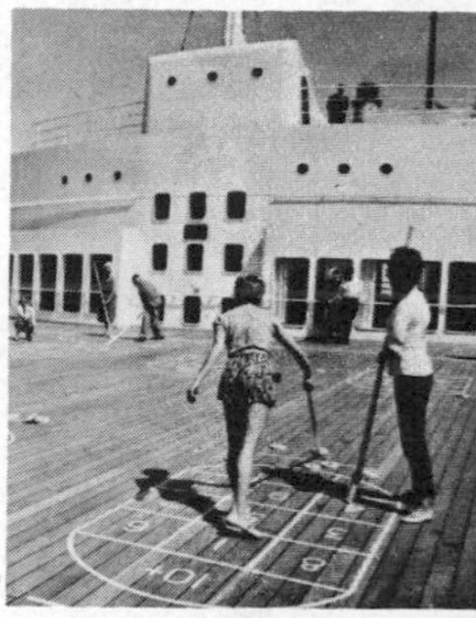

shuffleboard
Playing shuffleboard on a ship's deck

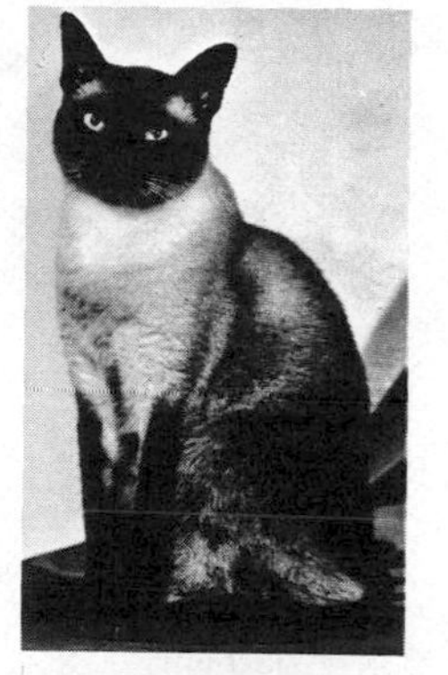

Siamese cat

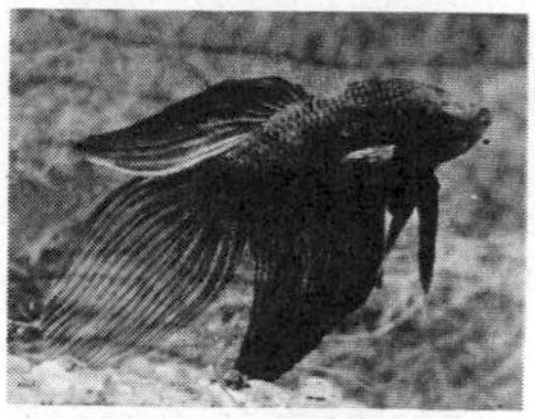

Siamese fighting fish

lated by blood; akin. Used with *to.* [Middle English *sib(be),* Old English *sibb.* See **seu-**² in Appendix.*]

Sib. Siberia; Siberian.

Si·be·li·us (sĭ-bā′lē-əs, -bāl′yəs), **Jean.** 1865–1957. Finnish composer.

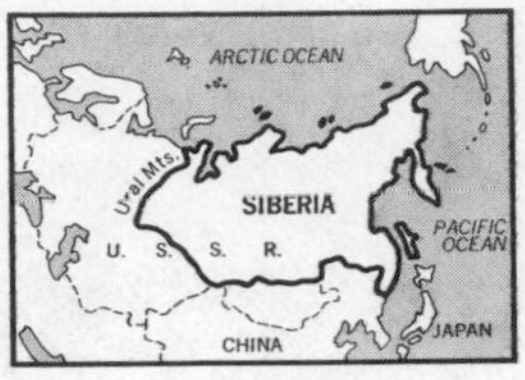

Siberia

Si·be·ri·a (sī-bîr′ē-ə). *Russian* **Si·bir** (sĭ-bēr′). *Abbr.* **Sib.** A large region (over 5,000,000 square miles) of the Soviet Union in Asia, extending from the Ural Mountains to the Pacific Ocean. —**Si·be′ri·an** *adj.* & *n.*

sib·i·lant (sĭb′ə-lənt) *adj.* Producing a hissing sound; characterized by the sound of (s) or (sh). —*n. Phonetics.* **1.** A speech sound that suggests hissing, as (s), (sh), (z), or (zh). **2.** A sibilant consonant. [Latin *sibilāns,* present participle of *sibilāre,* to hiss, whistle, SIBILATE.] —**sib′i·lance, sib′i·lan·cy** *n.* —**sib′i·lant·ly** *adv.*

sib·i·late (sĭb′ə-lāt′) *v.* **-lated, -lating, -lates.** —*intr.* To hiss; utter a hissing sound. —*tr.* To pronounce with a hissing sound. [Latin *sibilāre,* to hiss, whistle. See **swei-**¹ in Appendix.*] —**sib′i·la′tion** *n.*

Si·biu (sē-byōō′). *German* **Her·mann·stadt** (hĕr′män-shtät′). A city in Transylvania, central Rumania, founded as a Saxon colony in the 12th century. Population, 103,000.

sib·ling (sĭb′lĭng) *n.* One of two or more persons having one or especially both parents in common; a brother or sister. [Middle English *siblyng,* Old English *sibling* : SIB + -LING.]

Si·bu·yan Sea (sē′bōō-yän′). A body of water in the Philippines bordered by southern Luzon, Mindoro, and the Visayans.

sib·yl (sĭb′əl) *n.* **1.** One of a number of women regarded as oracles or prophetesses by the ancient Greeks and Romans. **2.** A prophetess. [Middle English *Sibile, Sybylle,* from Old French *Sibile, Sebile,* from Latin *Sibylla,* from Greek *Sibulla*†.]

sib·yl·line (sĭb′ə-līn′, -lēn′) *adj.* Also **si·byl·ic** (sĭ-bĭl′ĭk), **si·byl·lic. 1.** Pertaining to, coming from, or characteristic of a sibyl. **2.** Prophetic; oracular; mysterious.

sic¹ (sĭk, sēk) *adv. Latin.* Thus; so. Used in written texts to indicate that a surprising or paradoxical word, phrase, or fact is not a mistake and is to be read as it stands. [Latin *sīc.* See **so-** in Appendix.*]

sic² (sĭk) *tr.v.* **sicced, siccing, sics.** Also **sick, sicked, sicking, sicks. 1.** To urge to attack or chase. **2.** To set upon or chase. Used only in the imperative, as a command to a dog. [Dialectal variant of SEEK.]

Sic. Sicilian; Sicily.

Si·ca·ni·an (sĭ-kā′nē-ən) *adj.* Sicilian.

sic·ca·tive (sĭk′ə-tĭv) *n.* A substance added to paints and some medicines to promote drying; a drier. —*adj.* Drying. [Latin *siccātīvus,* drying, from *siccāre,* to dry, from *siccus,* dry. See **seikw-** in Appendix.*]

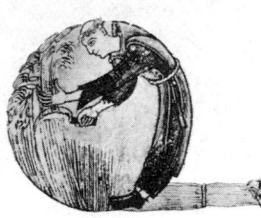

sideburns
Ambrose Burnside

Si·cil·ian (sĭ-sĭl′yən, -sĭl′ē-ən) *adj. Abbr.* **Sic.** Of or pertaining to Sicily or its inhabitants. —*n. Abbr.* **Sic. 1.** A native of Sicily. **2.** The dialect of Italian spoken in Sicily.

Sic·i·lies, The Two (sĭs′ə-lēz). A former kingdom consisting of the kingdoms of Sicily and Naples.

Sic·i·ly (sĭs′ə-lē). *Italian* **Si·ci·lia** (sē-chē′lyä). Ancient name **Tri·nac·ri·a** (trĭ-năk′rē-ə, trī-). *Abbr.* **Sic.** The largest island (9,831 square miles) in the Mediterranean, an autonomous region of Italy, from which it is separated by the Strait of Messina. Population, 4,712,000. Capital, Palermo.

sick¹ (sĭk) *adj.* **sicker, sickest. 1. a.** Ailing; ill; unwell. **b.** Violently nauseated. **2.** Of or for sick persons: *sick leave.* **3. a.** Mentally ill or disturbed. **b.** Morbid or unwholesome: *a sick joke.* See Usage note below. **c.** Culturally ailing or unsound: *"he is one man who knows he is sick in a civilization that doesn't know it is sick"* (Colin Wilson). **4. a.** Deeply distressed; chagrined; upset. **b.** Disgusted; revolted. **c.** Weary; tired. Usually used with *of: sick of it all.* **d.** Pining; longing. Used with *for.* **5.** In need of repairs. Said of a ship. **6.** Unable to produce a profitable yield of crops. [Middle English *sēk, sīk,* Old English *sēoc,* from Germanic *siukaz* (unattested).]

Synonyms: *sick, ill, indisposed, unwell.* These adjectives describe persons not in good health. *Sick* applies to such a condition of any nature or severity. It sometimes specifies nausea and may also suggest an alien attitude toward society. *Ill* can be used as a polite equivalent of *sick* or as a term intended to emphasize the severity of a condition. *Indisposed* refers to minor sickness. *Unwell,* sometimes considered euphemistic, has the wide range of *sick.*

Usage: *Sick at one's stomach* and *sick to one's stomach* are both widely employed. The Usage Panel expresses a slight preference for the first form. *Sick* (adjective) is standard usage in the newer sense of *perverted, morbid (sick humor),* according to 81 per cent of the Panel.

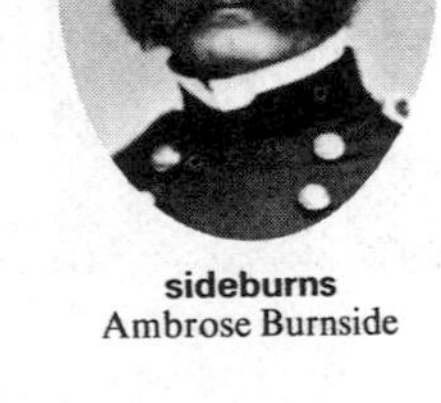

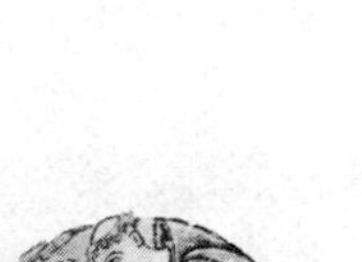

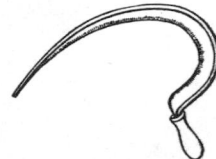

sickle
Above: Eleventh-century manuscript initial letter *Q* showing monk using sickle
Below: Hand sickle

sick². Variant of **sic** (to urge to attack).

sick·bay (sĭk′bā′) *n.* The hospital and dispensary of a ship.

sick·bed (sĭk′bĕd′) *n.* A sick person's bed.

sick call. *Military.* **1.** The daily line-up of personnel requiring medical attention. **2.** The signal announcing this.

sick·en (sĭk′ən) *v.* **-ened, -ening, -ens.** —*tr.* To make sick. —*intr.* To become sick. —**sick′en·er** *n.*

sick·en·ing (sĭk′ə-nĭng) *adj.* **1.** Causing sickness or nausea. **2.** Revolting or disgusting; loathsome. —**sick′en·ing·ly** *adv.*

sick headache. A headache accompanied by nausea.

sick·ish (sĭk′ĭsh) *adj.* **1.** Somewhat sick or nauseated. **2.** Somewhat revolting or nauseating. —**sick′ish·ly** *adv.*

sick·le (sĭk′əl) *n.* **1.** An implement having a semicircular blade attached to a short handle, for cutting grain or tall grass. **2.** The cutting mechanism of a reaper or mower. —*tr.v.* **sickled, -ling, -les.** To cut with a sickle. [Middle English *sikel,* Old English *sicol, sicel,* from West Germanic, from Vulgar Latin *sicila* (unattested), variant of Latin *sēcula.* See **sek-** in Appendix.*]

sick leave. Time off from work with pay allowed an employee because of sickness.

sick·le·bill (sĭk′əl-bĭl′) *n.* Any of several birds having sharply curved bills; especially, *Falculea palliata,* of Madagascar.

sickle cell. An abnormal crescent-shaped red blood cell.

sickle cell anemia. A hereditary anemia characterized by the presence of oxygen-deficient sickle cells, episodic pain, and leg ulcers. Also called "sicklemia."

sickle feather. Any of the long, curving feathers in the tail of a cock.

Sick·les (sĭk′əlz), **Daniel Edgar.** 1825–1914. American military and political leader; commanded Union troops in the Civil War.

sick list. A list of sick personnel, as in the army.

sick·ly (sĭk′lē) *adj.* **-lier, -liest. 1.** Prone to sickness; ailing. **2.** Of, caused by, or associated with sickness: *a sickly pallor.* **3.** Conducive to sickness; unhealthful. **4.** Nauseating; sickening. **5.** Enervated; feeble; weak. —*adv.* Also **sick·li·ly** (sĭk′lə-lē). In a sick manner. —*tr.v.* **sicklied, -lying, -lies.** *Rare.* To render sickly: *"timidity . . . sicklies the whole cast of thought in action"* (Henry Adams). —**sick′li·ness** *n.*

sick·ness (sĭk′nĭs) *n.* **1.** The condition of being sick; illness. **2.** A disease; malady. **3.** Nausea.

sick·room (sĭk′rōōm′, -rŏŏm′) *n.* A room occupied by an invalid.

sic pas·sim (sĭk păs′ĭm, sēk pä′sĭm). *Latin.* Thus everywhere. Used in textual annotation to indicate that a term or idea is to be found throughout the work cited.

sid·dur (sĭd′ŏŏr′, sĭd′ər) *n.* A Jewish prayer book containing prayers for the various days of the year. Compare **mahzor.** [Hebrew *siddūr,* "order," "arrangement (of prayers)," from *siddēr,* to arrange.]

side (sīd) *n.* **1.** *Geometry.* **a.** A line bounding a plane figure. **b.** A surface bounding a solid figure. **2.** A surface of an object; especially, a surface joining a top and bottom. **3.** A surface of an object that extends more or less perpendicularly from an observer standing in front: *the side of the ship.* **4.** Either of the two surfaces of a flat object, such as a piece of paper. **5. a.** The part within an object or area to the left or right of the observer, or of its vertical axis. **b.** The left or right half of the trunk of a human or animal body. **6.** The space immediately next to someone or something: *stood at her side.* **7.** One of two or more contrasted parts or places within an area, identified by its location with respect to a center: *the north side of the park.* **8.** An area separated from another area by some intervening line, barrier, or other feature: *on this side of the Atlantic.* **9. a.** One of two or more opposing groups, teams, or sets of opinions. **b.** One of the positions maintained in a dispute or debate. **10.** A distinct aspect of something: *the cruel side of her nature.* **11.** Line of descent: *my aunt on my mother's side.* **12.** *British Slang.* Nerve; swagger. —See Synonyms at **phase.** —**on the side.** In addition to the main portion, occupation, or arrangement. —**side by side.** Next to each other; close together. —**take sides.** To associate oneself with a faction, contested opinion, or cause. —**this side (of).** Up to but not beyond; short of: *this side of madness.* —*adj.* **1.** Located on a side: *a side door.* **2.** From or to one side; oblique: *a side view.* **3.** Minor; incidental: *a side interest.* **4.** In addition to the main part; supplementary: *a side benefit.* —*tr.v.* **sided, siding, sides.** To provide sides or siding for: *side a barn.* —**side with** (or **against**). To align oneself with (or against). [Middle English *side,* Old English *sīde.* See **sē-**² in Appendix.*]

side arm. A small weapon carried at the side or waist, as a sword, bayonet, or pistol.

side·arm (sīd′ärm′) *adj. Baseball.* Thrown with or marked by a sweep of the arm between shoulder and hip height: *a sidearm curve ball.*

side·band (sīd′bănd′) *n.* Also **side band.** A frequency band immediately adjacent to a specified frequency, especially to a carrier frequency.

side·board (sīd′bôrd′, -bōrd′) *n.* A piece of dining-room furniture for holding dishes of food and usually having drawers and shelves for linens and tableware.

side·burns (sīd′bûrnz′) *pl.n.* Growths of hair down the sides of the face in front of the ears, especially when worn with the rest of the beard shaved off. [Alteration of BURNSIDES.]

side·car (sīd′kär′) *n.* **1.** A one-wheeled car for a single passenger, attached to the side of a motorcycle. **2.** A cocktail combining brandy, an orange-flavored liqueur, and lemon juice.

sid·ed (sī′dĭd) *adj.* Having sides usually of a specified number or kind. Used in combination: *many-sided; marble-sided.*

side effect. A peripheral or secondary effect; especially, an undesirable secondary effect of a drug or therapy.

side·kick (sīd′kĭk′) *n. Slang.* A close friend and follower with whom one shares adventures.

side·light (sīd′līt′) *n.* **1.** A light coming from the side. **2.** *Nautical.* Either of two lights, red to port, green to starboard, shown by ships at night. **3.** Incidental information.

side·line (sīd′līn′) *n.* Also **side line. 1. a.** A line along either of the two sides of a playing court or field, marking its limits. **b.** *Plural.* The space outside such limits, occupied by spectators and inactive players. **c.** *Plural.* The position or point of view of those who observe rather than participate in some activity. **2.** A subsidiary line of merchandise. **3.** An activity pursued in addition to one's regular occupation. —*tr.v.* **sidelined, -lining, -lines.** To remove or keep from active participation, as in athletic contests.

ă pat/ā pay/âr care/ä father/b bib/ch church/d deed/ĕ pet/ē be/f fife/g gag/h hat/hw which/ĭ pit/ī pie/îr pier/j judge/k kick/l lid, needle/m mum/n no, sudden/ng thing/ŏ pot/ō toe/ô paw, for/oi noise/ou out/ŏŏ took/ōō boot/p pop/r roar/s sauce/sh ship, dish/

side·ling (sīd′lĭng) *adj.* **1.** Directed to one side; oblique. **2.** Sloping; inclined. —*adv.* Obliquely; sideways. [Middle English *sideling* : SIDE + -LING (adverbial suffix).]
side·long (sīd′lông′, -lŏng′) *adj.* **1.** Directed to one side; sideways: *a sidelong glance.* **2.** Slanting; sloping. —*adv.* On or toward the side; obliquely; sideways. [Alteration of SIDELING.]
side·man (sīd′măn′) *n., pl.* **-men** (-mĕn′). An instrumentalist in a jazz band.
si·de·re·al (sī-dîr′ē-əl) *adj.* **1.** Of, pertaining to, or concerned with the stars or constellations; stellar. **2.** Measured or determined by means of the stars: *sidereal time.* **3.** Relative to the stars. [From Latin *sīdereus,* from *sīdus* (stem *sīder-*), constellation. See **sweid-**[1] in Appendix.*]
sidereal day. The time required for a complete rotation of the earth, measured as the interval between two successive meridian transits of the vernal equinox, or 23 hours, 56 minutes, 4.09 seconds in units of mean solar time.
sidereal hour. A 24th part of a sidereal day.
sidereal month. See **month.**
sidereal time. Time based upon the axial and orbital rotation of the earth with reference to the background of stars.
sidereal year. The time required for one complete revolution of the earth about the sun, relative to the fixed stars, or 365 days, 6 hours, 9 minutes, 9.54 seconds in units of mean solar time.
sid·er·ite (sĭd′ə-rīt′) *n.* **1.** An impure yellowish-brown iron carbonate mineral. **2.** An iron meteorite. [SIDER(O)- + -ITE.] —**sid′er·it′ic** (-ə-rĭt′ĭk) *adj.*
sidero–, sider–. Indicates iron; for example, **siderolite, siderosis.** [From Greek *sidēros*†, iron.]
sid·er·o·lite (sĭd′ər-ə-līt′) *n.* A meteorite that contains iron, nickel, silicon, magnesium, and small amounts of other elements. [SIDERO- + -LITE.]
sid·er·o·sis (sĭd′ə-rō′sĭs) *n.* Chronic inflammation of the lungs caused by excessive inhalation of dust containing iron salts or particles. [SIDER(O)- + -OSIS.]
sid·er·o·stat (sĭd′ər-ə-stăt′) *n.* An optical system consisting of a rotating clock-driven mirror that reflects light from a celestial body in a relatively fixed direction to a fixed telescope or other bulky astronomical instrument. [Latin *sīdus* (stem *sīder-*), constellation (see **sidereal**) + -STAT.]
side·sad·dle (sīd′săd′l) *n.* A saddle designed so that a woman may sit with both legs on one side of the horse. —*adv.* On a sidesaddle.
side show. **1.** A small show offered in addition to the main attraction, as at a circus. **2.** A diverting incident or spectacle.
side·slip (sīd′slĭp′) *intr.v.* **-slipped, -slipping, -slips.** To slip or skid to one side. —*n.* **1.** A sideways skid, as of an automobile. **2.** *Aviation.* A flying sideways and downward along the lateral axis to reduce altitude without gaining speed or as the result of banking too deeply.
side·spin (sīd′spĭn′) *n.* A rotary motion that spins a ball horizontally.
side·split·ting (sīd′splĭt′ĭng) *adj.* Causing one's sides to ache, as with laughter. —**side′split′ting·ly** *adv.*
side step. **1.** A step to one side. **2.** A step on the side of something.
side·step (sīd′stĕp′) *v.* **-stepped, -stepping, -steps.** —*intr.* **1.** To step aside. **2.** To dodge an issue or responsibility. —*tr.* **1.** To step out of the way of. **2.** To evade; skirt. —**side′step′per** *n.*
side stroke. A swimming stroke in which a person swims on one side and thrusts his arms forward alternately while performing a scissors kick.
side·swipe (sīd′swīp′) *tr.v.* **-swiped, -swiping, -swipes.** To strike along the side in passing. —*n.* A glancing blow on or along the side.
side·track (sīd′trăk′) *v.* **-tracked, -tracking, -tracks.** —*tr.* **1.** To switch from a main track to a siding. **2.** To divert from a main issue or course. **3.** To divert (a person) to a lesser position. —*intr.* **1.** To run into a siding. **2.** To deviate from the main subject or course. —*n.* A railroad siding.
side·walk (sīd′wôk′) *n.* A walk or raised path along the side of a road for pedestrians.
sidewalk superintendent. *Informal.* A pedestrian who stops to watch construction or demolition work.
side wall. A side surface of an automobile tire.
side·ward (sīd′wərd) *adj.* Moving or directed toward one side. —*adv.* Also **side·wards** (-wərdz). Toward or from one side.
side·ways (sīd′wāz′) *adv.* Also **side·way** (-wā′), **side·wise** (-wīz′). **1.** From one side. **2.** Toward one side; in a sideward direction. **3.** Presenting the side instead of the front or back. —*adj.* Also **side·way, side·wise.** Toward or from one side.
side wheel. One of a pair of paddle wheels on the side of a steamboat. —**side′-wheel′** *adj.* —**side′-wheel′er** *n.*
side·wind·er (sīd′wīn′dər) *n.* **1.** A small rattlesnake, *Crotalus cerastes,* of the southwestern United States and Mexico, that moves by a distinctive lateral looping motion of its body. **2.** A powerful blow by the fist delivered from the side. **3.** *Military.* A short-range supersonic air-to-air missile.
Si·di-bel-Ab·bès (sē′dĭ-bĕl-ə-bĕs′). A city of northwestern Algeria. Population, 105,000.
Si·di If·ni (sē′dĭ ĭf′nĭ). The capital of the Spanish enclave of Ifni, southwestern Morocco. Population, 13,000.
sid·ing (sī′dĭng) *n.* **1.** A short section of railroad track connected by switches with a main track. **2.** Material, such as boards or shingles, used for surfacing a frame building.
si·dle (sīd′l) *intr.v.* **-dled, -dling, -dles.** **1.** To move sideways; edge along furtively or indirectly. **2.** To make advances in a fawning manner. —*n.* A sidelong step or movement. [Back-formation from SIDELING and SIDELONG.] —**si′dling·ly** *adv.*
Sid·ney (sĭd′nē), Sir **Philip.** 1554–1586. English courtier, soldier, poet, and essayist.
Si·don (sīd′n). An ancient city and seaport of Phoenicia, on the Mediterranean on the site of modern Saida, Lebanon.
Sid·ra, Gulf of (sĭd′rə). Ancient name **Syr·tis Ma·jor** (sûr′tĭs mā′jər). An inlet of the Mediterranean in the coast of Libya west of Bengasi.
Sie·ben·ge·bir·ge (zē′bən-gə-bîr′gə). A range of hills in West Germany, along the Rhine, south of Bonn.
Sieg·bahn (sēg′bän), **Karl Manne Georg.** Born 1886. Swedish physicist; worked in x-ray spectroscopy.
siege (sēj) *n.* **1.** The surrounding and blockading of a town or fortress by an army bent on capturing it. **2.** A prolonged period, as of illness or adversity. **3.** *Obsolete.* **a.** A seat. **b.** A seat of rule. —*tr.v.* **sieged, sieging, sieges.** To lay siege to; besiege. [Middle English *sege,* from Old French, "seat," from Vulgar Latin *sedicum* (unattested), from *sedicāre* (unattested), "to seat oneself," from Latin *sedēre,* to be seated. See **sed-**[1] in Appendix.*]
Siege Perilous. A seat at King Arthur's Round Table for the knight destined to find the Holy Grail and fatal for any other occupant.
Sieg·fried (sēg′frēd′). A principal character of the **Nibelungenlied** *(see)* and other medieval epics. [German, from Old High German *Sigifrith* : *sigu, sigo,* victory (see **segh-** in Appendix*) + *fridu,* peace (see **prī-** in Appendix*).]
Sie·mens (zē′mənz), **Ernst Werner von.** 1816–1892. German manufacturer, inventor, and pioneer in telegraphy; brother of Sir William Siemens.
Sie·mens (zē′mənz), Sir **William.** 1823–1883. German-born British engineer; invented open-hearth steelmaking process.
Si·en·a (sē-ĕn′ə). A city and cultural center in Tuscany, central Italy, about 40 miles south of Florence. Population, 49,000. —**Si′en·ese′** (sē′ə-nēz′, -nēs′) *adj.* & *n.*
Sien·kie·wicz (shĕn-kyĕ′vĭch), **Henryk.** 1846–1916. Polish novelist.
si·en·na (sē-ĕn′ə) *n.* **1.** A special clay containing iron and manganese oxides, used as a pigment for oil and water-color painting. **2.** **Raw sienna** *(see).* **3.** **Burnt sienna** *(see).* [From *terra-sienna,* from Italian *terra di Sienna,* "earth of SIENA."]
si·er·ra (sē-ĕr′ə) *n.* **1.** A rugged range of mountains having an irregular or serrated profile. **2.** Any of several mackerellike fishes of the genus *Scomberomorus,* of tropical seas. [Spanish, "a saw," from Latin *serra.* See **serrate.**] —**si·er′ran** *adj.*
Usage: After a reference to a mountain chain or range, such as the Sierra Madre or Sierra Nevada, the form often used for further reference is *the Sierras* (preferable to *Sierra mountains,* a redundance, since *mountains* is inherent in *sierra*).
Sier·ra de Cór·do·ba (syĕr′rä *thä* kôr′dō-vä). A mountain range extending about 300 miles in central Argentina. Highest elevation, 9,450 feet.
Sier·ra de Gua·da·lu·pe. The Spanish name for **Guadalupe Mountains.**
Sier·ra de Gua·dar·ra·ma (syĕr′rä *thä* gwä-*thär*-rä′mä′). A mountain range in Spain, extending about 120 miles on the central plateau, northwest of Madrid. Highest elevation, Peñalara (7,972 feet).
Si·er·ra Le·one (sē-ĕr′ə lē-ōn′). A country occupying 27,925 square miles on the Atlantic coast of northwestern Africa. Formerly a British colony, it became independent in 1961. Population, 2,183,000. Capital, Freetown.
Si·er·ra Ma·dre (sē-ĕr′ə mä′drā; *Spanish* syĕr′rä mä′*th*rā). The major mountain system of Mexico, comprising three ranges: **1.** The *Sierra Madre del Sur,* in the south along the Pacific from northern Guerrero State to the Isthmus of Tehuantepec. **2.** The *Sierra Madre Oriental,* extending from Coahuila State south to the Isthmus of Tehuantepec. Highest elevation, Pico de Orizaba (18,700 feet). **3.** The *Sierra Madre Occidental,* extending along the Pacific coast into Michoacán State.
Si·er·ra Ne·vad·a (sē-ĕr′ə nə-vä′də, -văd′ə; *also Spanish* syĕr′rä nā-vä′*thä for sense 2*). **1.** A mountain range extending about 400 miles in eastern California. Highest elevation, Mount Whitney (14,495 feet). **2.** A mountain range in southern Spain. Highest elevation, Mulhacén (11,411 feet).
Sier·ra Ne·va·da de Mé·ri·da. See **Cordillera de Mérida.**
si·es·ta (sē-ĕs′tə) *n.* A rest, usually taken after the midday meal. [Spanish, from Latin *sexta (hora),* sixth (hour after sunrise), noon, from *sextus,* sixth. See **sweks** in Appendix.*]
sieve (sĭv) *n.* Any meshwork, especially a utensil of wire mesh or closely perforated metal, used for straining, sifting, ricing, or puréeing. —*v.* **sieved, sieving, sieves.** —*tr.* To pass (something) through a sieve; sift. —*intr.* To sift. [Middle English *sive,* Old English *sife.* See **sib-** in Appendix.*]
sieve tube. A series of cells joined end to end, forming a tube through which food is conducted in vascular plants.
sift (sĭft) *v.* **sifted, sifting, sifts.** —*tr.* **1.** To put through a sieve or other straining device in order to separate the fine from the coarse particles. **2.** To distinguish as if separating with a sieve; to screen. **3.** To apply by scattering with or as if with a sieve. **4.** To examine closely and carefully: *sift the evidence.* —*intr.* **1.** To sift something. **2.** To pass through or as if through a sieve: *"The troops, sifting through the forest"* (Stephen Crane). **3.** To make a careful and critical examination. Used with *through.* [Middle English *siften,* Old English *siftan.* See **sib-** in Appendix.*] —**sift′er** *n.*
sift·ings (sĭf′tĭngz) *pl.n.* Material removed or separated with or as if with a sieve.
sig. **1.** signal. **2.** signature. **3.** signor; signore.
Sig. **1.** signor; signore. **2.** *Medicine.* signature.

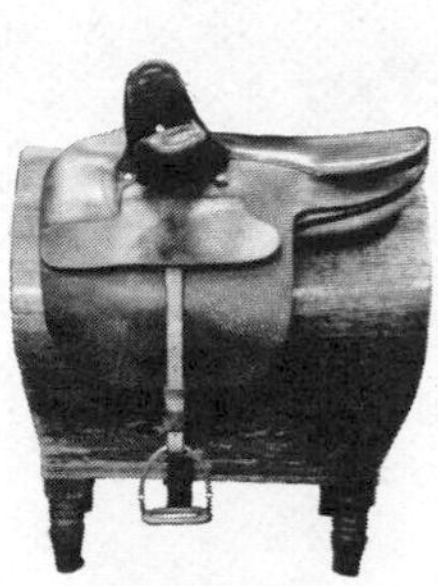
sidesaddle

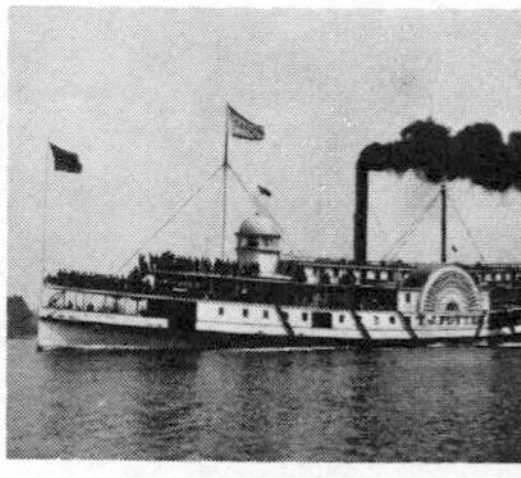
side wheel

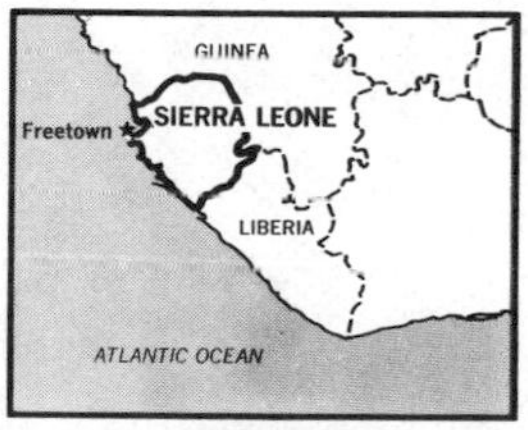

Sierra Leone

sigh (sī) *v.* **sighed, sighing, sighs.** —*intr.* **1.** To exhale audibly in a long, deep breath, as in sorrow, weariness, or relief. **2.** To emit a similar sound: *willows sighing in the wind.* **3.** To feel yearning, longing, or grief; mourn. —*tr.* **1.** To express with or as if with an audible exhalation. **2.** *Archaic.* To lament. —*n.* The act or sound of sighing. [Middle English *sighen*, probably altered from *siken* (weak past tense *sighte*), Old English *sīcan*, from West Germanic *sīk-* (unattested).]

sight (sīt) *n.* **1.** The ability to see; the faculty of vision. **2.** The act or fact of seeing. **3.** The field of one's vision. **4.** The field of one's mental vision; point of view; estimation. **5.** Something that is seen; a view. **6.** Something worth seeing; a spectacle: *the sights of London.* **7.** *Informal.* Something unsightly: *Her hair was a sight.* **8.** A device used to assist aim by guiding the eye, as on a firearm or surveying instrument. **9.** An aim or observation taken with such a device. **10.** An opportunity to observe or inspect. —**at** (or **on**) **sight. 1.** When first seen; as soon as seen. **2.** On presentation or demand for payment: *a bill payable at sight.* —**out of sight.** *Slang.* Extreme; remarkable; incredible. —**sight unseen.** Without seeing the object in question: *buy a car sight unseen.* —*tr.v.* **sighted, sighting, sights. 1.** To see or observe within one's field of vision: *sight land.* **2.** To observe or take a sight of with an instrument: *sight a target.* **3.** To adjust the sights of, as a rifle. **4.** To take aim with (a firearm). [Middle English *si(g)ht*, Old English *sihth, gesiht*, eyesight, vision, thing seen. See **sekw-**[2] in Appendix.*]

sight draft. A draft or bill payable upon demand or presentation.

sight·ed (sī′tĭd) *adj.* **1.** Having sight; not blind. **2.** Having eyesight of a specified kind. Used in combination: *keen-sighted.*

sight·less (sīt′lĭs) *adj.* **1.** Blind. **2.** Invisible. —**sight′less·ly** *adv.* —**sight′less·ness** *n.*

sight·ly (sīt′lē) *adj.* **-lier, -liest. 1.** Pleasing to see; handsome. **2.** Affording a fine view. —**sight′li·ness** *n.*

sight-read (sīt′rēd′) *v.* **-read** (-rĕd′), **-reading, -reads.** —*tr.* To read or perform (music, for example) without preparation or prior acquaintance. —*intr.* To read or perform something at sight. —**sight′-read′er** *n.*

sight·see·ing (sīt′sē′ĭng) *n.* The act or pastime of touring places of interest. —*adj.* Used or engaged in seeing sights. —**sight′-se′er** *n.*

sig·il (sĭj′əl, sĭg′ĭl) *n.* **1.** A seal; signet. **2.** A supposedly magical sign or image. [Latin *sigillum*, diminutive of *signum*, SIGN.]

sigill. seal (Latin *sigillum*).

sig·ma (sĭg′mə) *n.* **1.** The 18th letter in the Greek alphabet, written Σ,σ. Transliterated in English as *S, s.* See **alphabet. 2.** *Symbol* Σ *Physics.* Any of three subatomic particles in the baryon family. See **particle.** [Greek, from Semitic, akin to Hebrew *sāmekh*, SAMEK.] —**sig′mate′** (-māt′) *adj.*

sig·moid (sĭg′moid′) *adj.* Also **sig·moi·dal** (sĭg-moid′l). **1.** Having the shape of the letter S. **2.** Of or pertaining to the sigmoid flexure of the colon. [Greek *sigmoeidēs* : SIGMA + -OID.]

sigmoid flexure. *Anatomy.* An S-shaped bend in the colon between the descending section and the rectum.

sign (sīn) *n., pl.* **signs** or **sign** (for sense 5 only). **1.** Something that suggests the presence or existence of a fact, condition, or quality not immediately evident; an indication: *"Her silence . . . is a sign that she has a weapon"* (J.P. Donleavy). **2.** An action or gesture used to convey an idea, desire, information, or a command. **3.** A board, poster, or placard displayed in a public place to advertise or to convey information or a direction: *a stop sign.* **4.** A conventional figure or device that stands for a word, phrase, or operation; a symbol, as in mathematics or musical notation. **5.** An indicator, such as a spoor or scent, of the presence or trail of an animal: *deer sign.* **6.** A trace or vestige: *no sign of life.* **7.** A portentous incident or event; a presage. **8.** *Medicine.* Any bodily manifestation that serves to indicate the presence of a malfunction or disease. **9.** *Astrology.* One of the 12 divisions of the zodiac, each named for a constellation and represented by a symbol. —*v.* **signed, signing, signs.** —*tr.* **1.** To affix one's signature to. **2.** To write (one's signature). **3.** To approve or ratify (a document) by affixing a signature, seal, or other mark: *a bill signed into law.* **4. a.** To hire by means of obtaining a signature on a contract: *sign a new player.* **b.** To hire (oneself). Often used with *on: I signed myself on as a field hand.* **5.** To relinquish or transfer title to by signature. Used with *away, off,* or *over.* **6.** To express or signify with a sign. **7.** To consecrate with the sign of the cross. —*intr.* **1.** To make a sign or signs; to signal. **2.** To write one's signature. —**sign off.** *Broadcasting.* To stop transmission after identifying the broadcasting station. —**sign up.** To volunteer one's services; enlist. [Middle English *signe*, from Old French, from Latin *signum*, distinctive mark or figure, seal, signal. See **sekw-**[1] in Appendix.*] —**sign′er** *n.*

Synonyms: *sign, badge, mark, token, indication, symptom, note.* These nouns are compared as they denote outward evidence of something. *Sign*, the most general, can mean virtually any such manifestation. *Badge* usually refers to something worn that denotes membership in a group, or rank, achievement, or condition: *Her mink coat was a badge of success. Mark* can refer to a personal characteristic or indication of character: *Intolerance is the mark of a bigot.* It can also denote evidence of an experience: *Poverty had left its mark on him. Token* usually refers to a symbol, pledge, or proof of something intangible: *a token of affection. Indication* refers to evidence of a condition. *Symptom* suggests visible evidence of an adverse condition, such as a disease. *Note* applies to a distinguishing characteristic or feature: *the note of mysticism in his novels.*

Si·gnac (sē-nyăk′), **Paul.** 1863–1935. French painter.

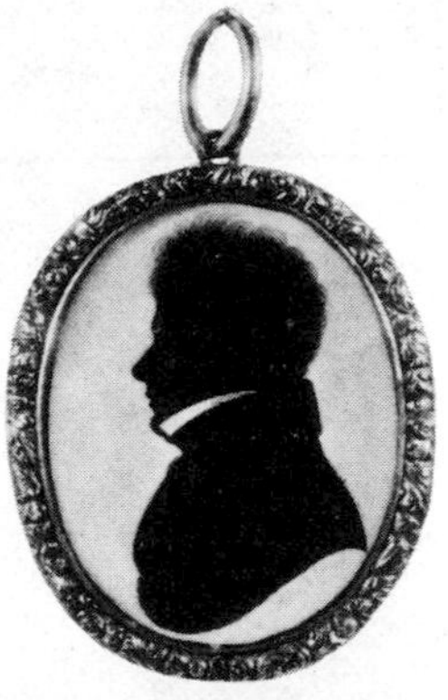

silhouette

sig·nal (sĭg′nəl) *n. Abbr.* **sig. 1. a.** A sign, gesture, mechanical device, or other indicator serving as a means of communication. **b.** A message communicated by such means. **2.** That which incites action: *The execution was the signal for mass protests.* **3.** *Electronics.* An impulse or fluctuating electric quantity, such as voltage, current, or electric field strength, the variations of which represent coded information. **4.** The sound, image, or message transmitted or received in telegraphy, telephony, radio, television, or radar. —*adj.* **1.** Out of the ordinary; remarkable; conspicuous: *a signal feat.* **2.** Used or acting as a signal: *a signal flare.* —*v.* **signaled** or **-nalled, -naling** or **-nalling, -nals.** —*tr.* **1.** To make a signal or signals to (a person or thing); to communicate with by signals. **2.** To relate or make known by signals; to communicate (information). —*intr.* To make a signal or signals. [French, from Old French *s(e)ignal*, from Medieval Latin *signāle*, from Latin *signālis*, of a sign, from *signum*, SIGN.] —**sig′nal·er, sig′nal·ler** *n.*

Signal Corps. The branch of the U.S. Army that handles communications.

sig·nal·ize (sĭg′nə-līz′) *tr.v.* **-ized, -izing, -izes. 1.** To make remarkable or conspicuous. **2.** To point out particularly.

sig·nal·ly (sĭg′nə-lē) *adv.* Conspicuously.

sig·nal·ment (sĭg′nəl-mənt) *n.* A detailed description of the appearance of a person, as for police files. [French *signalement*, from *signaler*, to mark out, describe, from *signal*, SIGNAL.]

sig·na·to·ry (sĭg′nə-tôr′ē, -tōr′ē) *adj.* Bound by signed agreement. —*n., pl.* **signatories.** A person or nation that has signed a treaty or other document. [Latin *signātōrius*, from *signāre*, to mark, affix one's seal to, from *signum*, SIGN.]

sig·na·ture (sĭg′nə-cho͝or′) *n. Abbr.* **sig. 1.** The name of a person as written by himself. **2.** A distinctive mark, characteristic, or sound effect indicating identity. **3.** The act of signing one's name. **4.** *Abbr.* **S., Sig.** The part of a physician's prescription containing directions to the patient. **5.** *Music.* **a.** A sign used to indicate key. **b.** A sign used to indicate tempo. **6.** *Printing.* **a.** A letter, number, or symbol placed at the bottom of the first page of each form of printed pages of a book as a guide to the proper sequence of the sheets in binding. **b.** A large sheet printed with four or a multiple of four pages. When folded it becomes a section of the book. [Old French, from *signer*, to sign, from Latin *signāre*, to mark with a sign, from *signum*, SIGN.]

sign·board (sīn′bôrd′, -bōrd′) *n.* A board bearing a sign.

sig·net (sĭg′nĭt) *n.* **1.** A seal; especially, a seal used on a document. **2.** The impression made with such a seal. —*tr.v.* **signeted, -neting, -nets.** To mark or endorse with a signet. [Middle English, from Old French, diminutive of *signe*, SIGN.]

signet ring. A finger ring bearing a signet. Also called "seal ring."

sig·nif·i·cance (sĭg-nĭf′ĭ-kəns) *n.* Also **sig·nif·i·can·cy** (-kən-sē). **1.** The state or quality of being significant; importance; consequence. **2.** Meaning; import. **3.** Implied meaning; suggestiveness. —See Synonyms at **importance, meaning.**

sig·nif·i·cant (sĭg-nĭf′ĭ-kənt) *adj.* **1.** Having or expressing a meaning; meaningful. **2.** Having or expressing a covert meaning; suggestive: *a significant glance.* **3.** Important; notable; valuable. [Latin *significāns*, present participle of *significāre*, SIGNIFY.] —**sig·nif′i·cant·ly** *adv.*

significant digits. *Mathematics.* The digits of the decimal form of a number beginning with the leftmost nonzero digit and extending to the right to include all digits warranted by the accuracy of measuring devices used to obtain the numbers.

sig·ni·fi·ca·tion (sĭg′nə-fĭ-kā′shən) *n.* **1.** The intended meaning; sense. **2.** The act of signifying; indication; communication. —See Synonyms at **meaning.**

sig·nif·i·ca·tive (sĭg-nĭf′ĭ-kā′tĭv) *adj.* **1.** Indicative; significant. **2.** Suggestive; symbolic.

sig·ni·fy (sĭg′nə-fī′) *v.* **-fied, -fying, -fies.** —*tr.* **1.** To serve as a sign of; to betoken; denote. **2.** To make known; to intimate. —*intr.* To have meaning or importance. —See Synonyms at **mean** (convey sense). [Middle English *signifien*, from Old French *signifier*, from Latin *significāre* : *signum*, SIGN + *facere*, to make (see **dhē-**[1] in Appendix*).] —**sig′ni·fi′er** *n.*

sign language. A system of communication by means of hand gestures.

sign manual *pl.* **signs manual.** A signature; especially, that of a monarch at the top of a royal decree.

sign of the cross. A gesture describing the form of a cross, made in token of faith in Christ or as an invocation of blessing; especially, in the Roman Catholic Church, such a gesture of the right hand from the forehead to the breast and from the left to the right shoulder.

si·gnor (sēn-yôr′, -yōr′) *n., pl.* **signori** (sēn-yôr′ē, -yōr′ē) or **-gnors.** Also **si·gnior.** *Abbr.* **S., sig., Sig.** The English form of the Italian title *signore.*

si·gno·ra (sēn-yôr′ə, -yōr′ə) *n., pl.* **signore** (sēn-yôr′ā, -yōr′ā) or **-ras.** The Italian title of courtesy for a married woman, equivalent to the English *Mrs.* or *madam.* [Italian, feminine of SIGNORE.]

si·gno·re (sēn-yôr′ā, -yōr′ā) *n., pl.* **signori** (sēn-yôr′ē, -yōr′ē). *Abbr.* **S., sig., Sig.** The Italian title of courtesy for a man, equivalent to the English *Mr.* or *sir.* [Italian, from Latin *senior*, older, SENIOR.]

Si·gno·rel·li (sē′nyō-rĕl′lē), **Luca.** 1441–1523. Italian painter.

si·gno·ri·na (sēn′yō-rē′nə) *n., pl.* **-ne** (-nā) or **-nas.** The Italian title of courtesy for an unmarried woman, equivalent to the English *Miss.* [Italian, diminutive of SIGNORA.]

sign·post (sīn′pōst′) *n.* **1.** A post supporting a sign. **2.** Anything that serves as an indication, sign, or guide.

ă pat/ā pay/âr care/ä father/b bib/ch church/d deed/ĕ pet/ē be/f fife/g gag/h hat/hw which/ĭ pit/ī pie/îr pier/j judge/k kick/l lid, needle/m mum/n no, sudden/ng thing/ŏ pot/ō toe/ô paw, for/oi noise/ou out/o͝o took/o͞o boot/p pop/r roar/s sauce/sh ship, dish/

Sig·urd (sĭg′o͝ord′, -ərd). *Norse Mythology.* The hero who slays Fafnir. He corresponds to Siegfried, hero of the *Nibelungenlied.*
Si·ha·nouk (sē′ə-no͝ok′), Prince **Norodom.** Born 1922. Cambodian statesman; king (1941–55); prime minister (1955–60); chief of state (since 1960).
Sikh (sēk) *n.* An adherent of Sikhism. —*adj.* Of or pertaining to the Sikhs. [Hindi, from Sanskrit *śiṣya,* "disciple," from *śikṣati,* he helps, pays homage, learns, serves, desiderative of *śaknōti,* he can, is able to do. See **kak-**[1] in Appendix.*]
Sikh·ism (sē′kĭz′əm) *n.* The doctrines and practices of a monotheistic Hindu religious sect founded in the 16th century.
Si·kho·te-A·lin Range (sē′kə-tā′ə-lēn′). A mountain range of the Soviet Union, extending 650 miles parallel to the Sea of Japan between Vladivostok and the lower course of the Amur river.
Si Kiang (shē′ jyäng′). A river of southeastern China formed by the confluence of the Hungshui and the Siang and flowing 300 miles generally east to the South China Sea near Macao. Also called "West River."
Sik·kim (sĭk′ĭm). A kingdom, a protectorate of the Republic of India, occupying 2,744 square miles between India and Tibet, China. Population, 162,000. Capital, Gangtok.
Si·kor·sky (sĭ-kôr′skē), **Igor Ivanovich.** Born 1889. Russian-born American aeronautical engineer and manufacturer.
si·lage (sī′lĭj) *n.* Fodder prepared by storing and fermenting green forage plants in a silo.
si·lence (sī′ləns) *n.* **1.** The condition or quality of being or keeping silent; avoidance of speech or noise. **2.** The absence of sound; stillness. **3.** A period of time without speech or noise. **4.** Refusal or failure to speak out; secrecy. —*tr.v.* **silenced, -lencing, -lences. 1.** To make silent or bring to silence. **2.** To curtail the expression of; suppress: *silencing all criticism.*
si·lenc·er (sī′lən-sər) *n.* **1.** One that silences. **2.** A device attached to the muzzle of a firearm to muffle the report.
si·lent (sī′lənt) *adj.* **1.** Making no sound or noise; quiet. **2.** Not disposed to speak; taciturn. **3.** Unable to speak; mute. **4.** Refusing or failing to give information or an opinion; secretive. **5.** Not voiced or expressed; tacit: *silent declarations of love.* **6.** Inactive or undisturbed; quiescent: *a silent volcano.* **7.** Having no phonetic value; unpronounced, as the *b* in *subtle.* **8.** Having no sound track. Said of some motion pictures. —See Synonyms at **still.** [Latin *silēns,* present participle of *silēre,* to be silent. See **silo-** in Appendix.*] —**si′lent·ly** *adv.* —**si′lent·ness** *n.*
Synonyms: *silent, reticent, reserved, taciturn, secretive, uncommunicative, noncommittal, tightlipped.* These adjectives describe persons who are sparing with speech. *Silent* can refer to literal speechlessness but more often merely implies habitual reluctance to speak. *Reticent* does not necessarily imply silence as a trait but rather suggests reluctance to speak out at a given time, particularly about one's personal affairs. *Reserved* suggests aloofness and habitual restraint in communicating. *Taciturn* also implies unsociableness and a characteristic tendency to be grudging of speech. *Secretive* implies an unwillingness to speak about matters that could be openly discussed and suggests deliberate concealment. *Uncommunicative* suggests the deliberate withholding of information. *Noncommittal* describes one who abstains from taking a stand or committing himself in a discussion. *Tightlipped* implies rigid self-restraint in speech.
silent butler. A small receptacle with a handle and a hinged cover, used for collecting ashes and crumbs.
silent partner. One who makes financial investments in a business enterprise but does not participate in its management.
si·le·nus (sī-lē′nəs) *n., pl.* **-ni** (-nī′). *Greek Mythology.* Any of various minor woodland deities or spirits and companions of Dionysus.
Si·le·nus (sī-lē′nəs). *Greek Mythology.* A satyr, the foster father of Bacchus.
si·le·sia (sī-lē′zhə, -shə) *n.* **1.** A smooth linen fabric first produced in Silesia. **2.** A twilled cotton fabric used for linings.
Si·le·sia (sī-lē′zhə, -shə, sĭ-). *German* **Schle·si·en** (shlā′zē-ən); *Polish* **Śląsk** (shlônsk). A region of central Europe, now chiefly within southwestern Poland.
si·lex (sī′lĕks′) *n.* **1.** *Obsolete.* **Silica** *(see).* **2.** Finely ground tripoli, used as an inert paint filler. [Latin *silex*†, hard stone, flint.]
Si·lex (sī′lĕks′) *n.* A trademark for a vacuum coffee maker.
sil·hou·ette (sĭl′o͞o-ĕt′) *n.* A representation of the outline of something, usually filled in with black or another solid color. —*tr.v.* **silhouetted, -etting, -ettes.** To cause to be seen as a silhouette; to outline. [French, short for *portrait à la silhouette,* from *silhouette,* object intentionally marred or made incomplete, something of ephemeral value, after Étienne de *Silhouette* (1709–67), with reference to his evanescent career (March–November 1759) as French controller-general.]
sil·i·ca (sĭl′ĭ-kə) *n.* A white or colorless crystalline compound, SiO_2, occurring abundantly as quartz, sand, flint, agate, and many other minerals, and used to manufacture a wide variety of materials, notably glass and concrete. Also called "silicon dioxide" and, formerly, "silex." [New Latin, from Latin *silex* (stem *silic-*), flint, SILEX.]
silica gel. Amorphous silica that resembles white sand and is used as a drying and dehumidifying agent, a catalyst and catalyst carrier, an anticaking agent in cosmetics, and in chromatography.
sil·i·cate (sĭl′ĭ-kāt′, -kĭt) *n.* Any of numerous compounds containing silicon, oxygen, and a metallic or organic radical, occurring in most rocks except limestone and dolomite, and forming the basis of common glass and bricks. [SILIC(A) + -ATE.]
si·li·ceous (sĭ-lĭsh′əs) *adj.* Containing, resembling, pertaining to, or consisting of silica. [Latin *siliceus,* of flint or limestone, from *silex,* flint, SILEX.]
silici-, silic-. Indicates silica or silicon; for example, **siliciferous, silicide.** [From SILICA.]
si·lic·ic (sĭ-lĭs′ĭk) *adj.* Pertaining to, resembling, or derived from silica or silicon.
silicic acid. A jellylike substance, $SiO_2.nH_2O$, produced when sodium silicate solution is acidified and used as is silica gel.
sil·i·cide (sĭl′ə-sīd′) *n.* A compound of silicon with another element or radical. [SILIC(I)- + -IDE.]
sil·i·cif·er·ous (sĭl′ə-sĭf′ər-əs) *adj.* Bearing, producing, or in partial combination with silica. [SILICI- + -FEROUS.]
si·lic·i·fy (sĭ-lĭs′ə-fī′) *v.* **-fied, -fying, -fies.** —*tr.* To convert into silica. —*intr.* To be or become converted into silica. [SILICI- + -FY.] —**si·lic′i·fi·ca′tion** *n.*
sil·i·cle (sĭl′ĭ-kəl) *n. Botany.* A short, flat silique. [Latin *silicula,* diminutive of *siliqua,* seed pod, SILIQUE.]
sil·i·con (sĭl′ĭ-kən, -kŏn′) *n. Symbol* **Si** A nonmetallic element occurring extensively in the earth's crust in silica and silicates, having both an amorphous and a crystalline allotrope, and used doped or in combination with other materials in glass, semiconducting devices, concrete, brick, refractories, pottery, and silicones. Atomic number 14, atomic weight 28.086, melting point 1,410°C, boiling point 2,355°C, specific gravity 2.33, valence 4. See **element.** [From SILICA.]
silicon carbide. A bluish-black crystalline compound, SiC, one of the hardest known substances, used as an abrasive and heat-refractory material, and in single crystals as semiconductors, especially in high-temperature applications.
silicon dioxide. *Chemistry.* **Silica** *(see).*
sil·i·cone (sĭl′ĭ-kōn′) *n.* Any of a group of semi-inorganic polymers based on the structural unit R_2SiO, where R is an organic group, characterized by wide-range thermal stability, high lubricity, extreme water repellence, and physiochemical inertness, used in adhesives, lubricants, protective coatings, paints, electrical insulation, synthetic rubber, and prosthetic replacements for bodily parts. Compare **siloxane.** [SILIC(I)- + -ONE.]
sil·i·co·sis (sĭl′ĭ-kō′sĭs) *n.* Fibrosis of the lungs caused by long-term inhalation of silica dust and resulting in a chronic shortness of breath. [New Latin : SILIC(I)- + -OSIS.]
si·lique (sĭ-lēk′) *n.* A long pod that is divided by a membranous partition and splits at both seams, characteristic of fruit of the mustards and related plants. [French, from Latin *siliqua*†, pod.] —**sil′i·quous** (sĭl′ə-kwəs), **sil′i·quose′** (-kwōs′) *adj.*
silk (sĭlk) *n.* **1.** The fine, lustrous fiber produced by certain insect larvae and spiders; especially, that produced by a silkworm to form its cocoon. **2.** Thread or fabric made from this fiber. **3. a.** A garment made from this fabric. **b.** *Plural.* The brightly colored identifying garments of a jockey or harness driver. **4.** Any silky, filamentous material, such as the styles forming a tuft on an ear of corn. —*adj.* Of, resembling, or pertaining to silk. —*intr.v.* **silked, silking, silks.** To develop silk. Used of corn. [Middle English *silk, selk,* Old English *sioloc, seoluc,* probably from Old Slavic *šelkŭ,* akin to Greek *Sēres,* the Chinese (probably originally meaning "the silk people"), Mongolian *sirkek,* silk, Korean *sir,* all ultimately from Chinese *ssŭ*[1], silk. See also **sericeous, serge.**]
silk cotton. A silky fiber, such as kapok, attached to the seeds of certain trees.
silk-cot·ton tree (sĭlk′kŏt′n). Any of several trees of the family Bombacaceae; especially, *Ceiba pentandra,* native to tropical America, cultivated for its leathery fruit containing the silklike fiber kapok.
silk·en (sĭl′kən) *adj.* **1.** Made of silk. **2.** Resembling silk in texture or appearance; smooth and lustrous. **3.** Delicately pleasing or caressing in effect. **4.** Luxurious.
silk hat. A man's silk-covered top hat.
silk oak. A tree, *Grevillea robusta,* native to Australia, having divided leaves and showy clusters of orange flowers.
silk-screen process (sĭlk′skrēn′). A method of producing a stencil in which a design is imposed upon a screen of silk or other fine fabric, with blank areas coated with an impermeable substance, and ink is forced through the cloth onto the printing surface.
silk-stock·ing (sĭlk′stŏk′ĭng) *n.* **1.** An aristocratic or wealthy person. **2.** *Informal.* A member or supporter of the Whig party formed during the early 19th century in the United States.
silk tree. A tree, *Albizzia julibrissin,* native to the eastern Mediterranean area, having feathery compound leaves and clusters of pinkish flowers. Sometimes called "mimosa."
silk·weed (sĭlk′wēd′) *n.* The **milkweed** *(see).*
silk·worm (sĭlk′wûrm′) *n.* Any of various caterpillars that produce silk cocoons; especially, the larva of a moth, *Bombyx mori,* native to Asia, that spins a cocoon of fine, lustrous fiber that is the source of commercial silk.
silk·y (sĭl′kē) *adj.* **-ier, -iest. 1.** Resembling silk; soft; smooth; lustrous. **2.** Made of silk; silken. **3.** Having long, silklike hairs or a silky covering. **4.** Ingratiating; seductive. —**silk′i·ly** *adv.* —**silk′i·ness** *n.*
sill (sĭl) *n.* **1.** *Architecture.* The horizontal member that bears the upright portion of a frame; especially, the base of a window. **2.** *Geology.* A relatively thin sheet of igneous rock intruded between beds of other rock. [Middle English *sille, selle,* Old English *syll(e),* threshold, sill. See **swel-**[3] in Appendix.*]
sil·la·bub. Variant of **syllabub.**
Sil·li·man (sĭl′ə-mən), **Benjamin.** 1779–1864. American chemist and geologist; pioneer in scientific education.

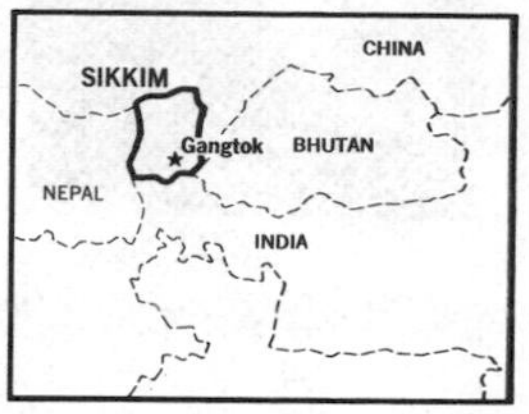

Sikkim

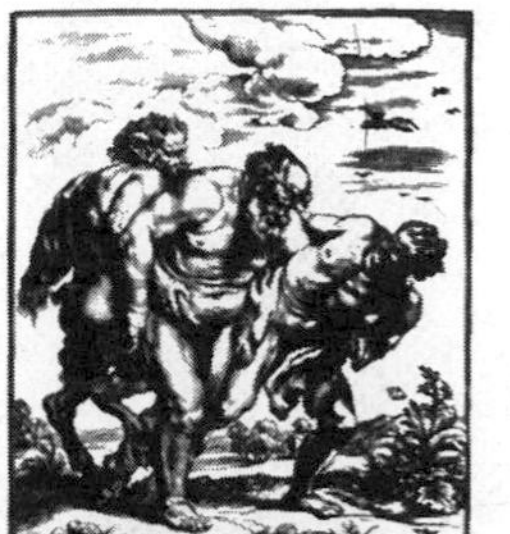
Silenus
Woodcut after a painting by Rubens

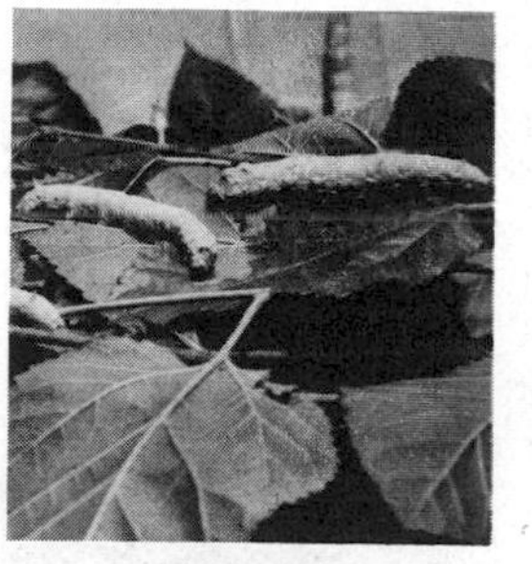
silkworm
Larvae of *Bombyx mori* feeding on mulberry leaves

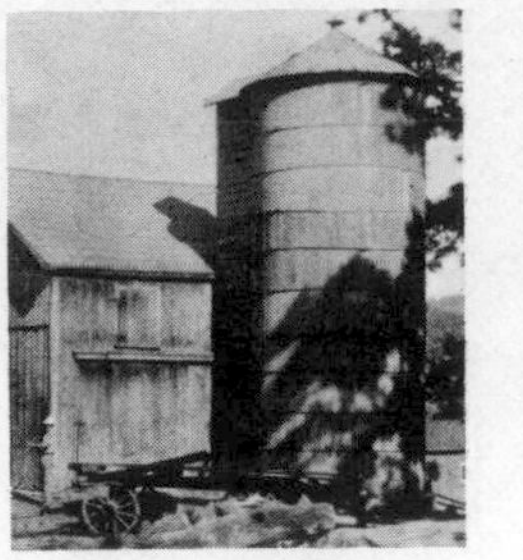

silo

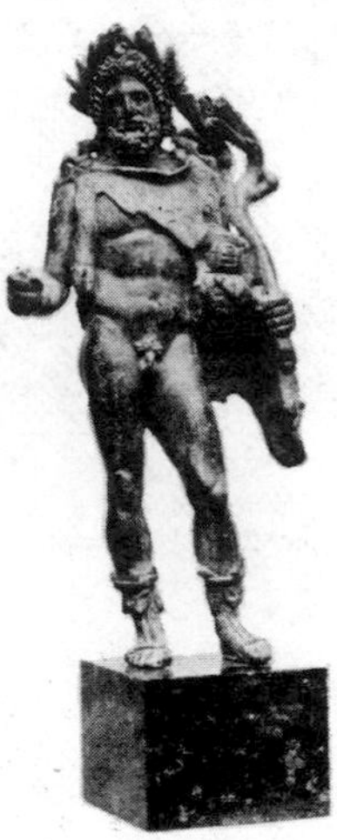

Silvanus

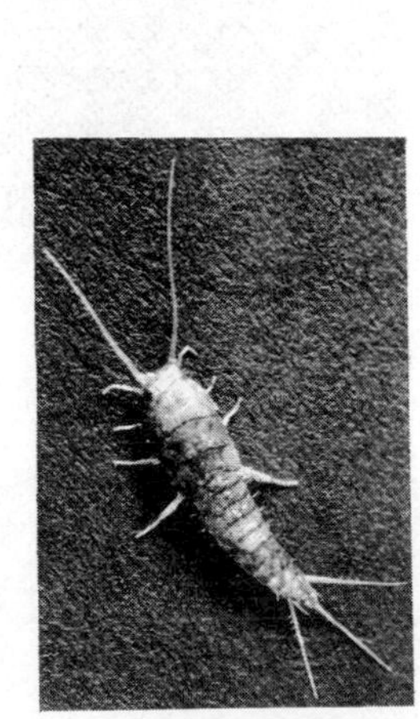

silverfish
Lepisma saccharina

sil·ly (sĭl′ē) *adj.* **-lier, -liest. 1.** Showing a lack of good sense; unreasoning; stupid. **2.** Frivolous. **3.** Semiconscious; dazed. —See Synonyms at **foolish.** [Middle English, "pitiable," originally variant of *seely,* happy, blessed, Old English *gesǣlig.* See **sel-**[2] in Appendix.*] —**sil′li·ly** (sĭl′ə-lē) *adv.* —**sil′li·ness** *n.*

si·lo (sī′lō) *n., pl.* **-los. 1. a.** A tall, cylindrical structure in which fodder is stored. **b.** A pit dug for the same purpose. **2.** *Military.* A sunken missile shelter with facilities either for lifting the missile to a launch position or for launch from underground. —*tr.v.* **siloed, -loing, -los.** To store in a silo. [Spanish, from Latin *sirus,* from Greek *sirost*, pit for keeping grain in.]

Si·lo·am (sĭ-lō′əm, sī-). A pool outside Jerusalem. John 9:7.

Si·lo·ne (sē-lō′nā), **Ignazio.** Born 1900. Italian novelist; resident in Switzerland.

si·lox·ane (sĭ-lŏk′sān′) *n.* Any of a class of organic or inorganic chemical compounds of silicon, oxygen, and usually carbon and hydrogen, based on the structural unit R_2SiO, where R is CH_3, H, C_2H_5, or a more complex group. Compare **silicone.** [SIL(ICON) + OX(YGEN) + (METH)ANE.]

silt (sĭlt) *n.* A sedimentary material consisting of fine mineral particles intermediate in size between sand and clay. —*v.* **silted, silting, silts.** —*intr.* To become filled with silt. Usually used with *up.* —*tr.* To fill with silt. Usually used with *up.* [Middle English *cylte,* probably from Scandinavian, akin to Danish and Norwegian *sylt,* salt marsh. See **sal-**[1] in Appendix.*]

Sil·u·res (sĭl′yə-rēz′) *pl.n.* A people described by Tacitus as occupying southwestern Britain at the time of the Roman invasion.

Si·lu·ri·an (sĭ-lo͝or′ē-ən, sī-) *adj.* **1.** Of, belonging to, or designating the geologic time, system of rocks, or sedimentary deposits of the third period of the Paleozoic era, characterized by the appearance of land plants. See **geology. 2.** Of or relating to the Silures or their culture. —*n. Geology.* The Silurian period or system of deposits. Preceded by *the.* [After the SILURES, the rocks having been first identified in the part of Wales supposed to have been inhabited by them.]

si·lu·rid (sĭ-lo͝or′ĭd, sī-) *adj.* Of or belonging to the family Siluridae, which includes various freshwater catfishes of Europe and Asia. —*n.* A silurid fish. [New Latin *Siluridae,* from Latin *silurus,* a large freshwater fish, probably the sheatfish, from Greek *silouros.* See **ors-** in Appendix.*]

sil·va. Variant of **sylva.**

sil·van. Variant of **sylvan.**

Sil·va·nus (sĭl-vā′nəs) *n.* Also **Syl·va·nus.** *Roman Mythology.* A god of forests, fields, and herding. [Latin, from *silva,* forest. See **sylvan.**]

sil·ver (sĭl′vər) *n.* **1.** *Symbol* **Ag** A lustrous white, ductile, malleable metallic element, occurring both uncombined and in ores such as argentite, having the highest thermal and electrical conductivity of the metals. It is highly valued for jewelry, tableware, and other ornamental use, and is widely used in coinage, photography, dental and soldering alloys, electrical contacts, and printed circuits. Atomic number 47, atomic weight 107.870, melting point 960.8°C, boiling point 2,212°C, specific gravity 10.50, valences 1, 2. See **element. 2.** This metal as a commodity or medium of exchange. **3.** Coins made of this metal. **4. a.** Tableware and other domestic articles made of this metal. See **sterling silver. b.** Any tableware. **5.** The color medium gray. See **color. 6.** *Photography.* A silver salt, especially silver nitrate, used to sensitize paper. —*adj.* **1.** Made of, containing, or coated with silver. **2.** Of, pertaining to, or based on silver: *the silver standard.* **3.** Having a lustrous medium-gray color: *silver hair.* **4.** Having a bell-like sound. **5.** Eloquent; persuasive: *a silver tongue.* **6.** Favoring the adoption of silver as a standard of currency. **7.** Of or designating a 25th anniversary. —*v.* **silvered, -vering, -vers.** —*tr.* **1.** To cover, plate, or adorn with silver or a similar lustrous substance. **2.** To cause to resemble silver. **3.** To coat (photographic paper) with a film of silver nitrate or other silver salt. —*intr.* To become silvery. [Middle English *silver,* Old English *siolfor, seolfor,* Common Germanic *silubhra-* (unattested), ultimately from Akkadian *sarpu,* refined silver, from *ṣarāpu,* to smelt, refine.]

sil·ver-bell tree (sĭl′vər-bĕl′). Any of several trees or shrubs of the genus *Halesia;* especially, *H. carolina,* of the southeastern United States, having drooping, bell-shaped white flowers. Also called "snowdrop tree."

sil·ver·ber·ry (sĭl′vər-bĕr′ē) *n., pl.* **-ries.** A North American shrub, *Elaeagnus commutata,* with silvery flowers, leaves, and berries.

silver bromide. A pale-yellow crystalline compound, AgBr, turning black on exposure to light, and used as the light-sensitive component on ordinary photographic films and plates.

silver certificate. A paper money bill, formerly issued as legal tender by the U.S. Government in representation of deposited silver bullion.

silver chloride. A white granular powder, AgCl, that turns dark on exposure to light and is used in photography, photometry, and optics.

sil·ver·fish (sĭl′vər-fĭsh′) *n., pl.* **silverfish** or **-fishes. 1.** Any of various fishes having silvery scales, such as a tarpon. **2.** A silvery, wingless insect, *Lepisma saccharina,* that often causes extensive damage to bookbindings, starched clothing, and similar material.

silver fox. 1. A color phase of the North American red fox, *Vulpes fulva,* having black fur tipped with white. **2.** The fur of this animal.

silver iodide. A pale-yellow, odorless powder, AgI, that darkens on exposure to light and is used in artificial rainmaking, in photography, and as an antiseptic.

sil·ver·ly (sĭl′vər-lē) *adv.* With a silvery appearance or tone.

sil·vern (sĭl′vərn) *adj. Poetic.* Like silver; silvery.

silver nitrate. A poisonous, colorless crystalline compound, $AgNO_3$, that becomes grayish black when exposed to light in the presence of organic matter and is used in photography, mirror manufacturing, hair dyeing, silver plating, and as an external medicine.

silver perch. A fish, the **mademoiselle** *(see).*

silver plate. Tableware or other household articles made of silver or of base metal plated with silver.

sil·ver·rod (sĭl′vər-rŏd′) *n.* A North American plant, *Solidago bicolor,* related to the goldenrods but having white rather than yellow flowers.

sil·ver·side (sĭl′vər-sīd′) *n.* Also **sil·ver·sides** (-sīdz′). Any of various marine and freshwater fishes of the family Atherinidae, characteristically having a silvery band along each side.

sil·ver·smith (sĭl′vər-smĭth′) *n.* A person who makes, repairs, or replates articles of silver.

Silver Spring. A city of Maryland north of Washington, D.C., of which it is a suburb. Population, 66,000.

silver standard. A monetary standard under which a specified quantity of silver constitutes the basic unit of currency.

Silver Star. A U.S. military decoration awarded for gallantry in action.

sil·ver-tongued (sĭl′vər-tŭngd′) *adj.* Having the power of fluent and persuasive speech; eloquent.

sil·ver·ware (sĭl′vər-wâr′) *n.* Articles made of or plated with silver; especially, tableware.

sil·ver·weed (sĭl′vər-wēd′) *n.* A plant, *Potentilla anserina,* having yellow flowers and leaves that are silvery beneath.

sil·ver·y (sĭl′və-rē) *adj.* **1.** Containing or coated with silver. **2.** Like silver in luster; shining; glittering: *"a fountain threw high its silvery water"* (Harriet Beecher Stowe). **3.** Having a clear, ringing sound. —**sil′ver·i·ness** *n.*

sil·vi·cul·ture (sĭl′vĭ-kŭl′chər) *n.* The care and cultivation of forest trees; forestry. [French : Latin *silva, sylva,* forest, SYLVA + CULTURE.] —**sil′vi·cul′tur·al** *adj.* —**sil′vi·cul′tur·al·ly** *adv.* —**sil′vi·cul′tur·ist** *n.*

si·ma (sī′mə) *n.* The lower layer of the earth's outer crust, rich in silica, iron, and magnesium, that underlies the **sial** *(see).* [German *Sima* : New Latin SI(LICA) + MA(GNESIUM).]

Sim·birsk. The former name for **Ulyanovsk.**

Sim·chath To·rah (sĭm′KHäs tôr′ə, tōr′ə). A Jewish holiday celebrated on the 23rd day of Tishri, marking the end of the Feast of Tabernacles. [Hebrew *shimḥath tōrāh,* "rejoicing over the Law" : *śimḥath,* inflectional form of *śimḥāh,* joy, merriment, from *śāmaḥ,* he rejoiced + TORAH.]

Si·me·non (sēm′nôN′), **Georges.** Born 1903. Belgian-born French novelist.

Sim·e·on (sĭm′ē-ən). **1.** In the Old Testament, the second son of Jacob and Leah and the name of the tribe of Israel descended from him. Genesis 29:33. **2.** The man who, upon seeing the infant Jesus, spoke the **Nunc Dimittis** *(see).* Luke 2:25–32.

Sim·e·on Sty·li·tes (sĭm′ē-ən stī-lī′tēz), **Saint.** A.D. 390?–459. Syrian Christian ascetic; constructed, dwelt upon, and preached from a 60-foot pillar (A.D. 429–459).

Sim·fe·ro·pol (sĭm′fə-rô′pəl). A city of the Soviet Union, in the Crimea. Population, 203,000.

sim·i·an (sĭm′ē-ən) *adj.* Pertaining to, characteristic of, or resembling an ape or monkey. —*n.* An ape or monkey. [From Latin *simia,* ape, perhaps from *sīmus,* snub-nosed, from Greek *simost*, bent upward, snub-nosed.]

sim·i·lar (sĭm′ə-lər) *adj.* **1.** Showing some resemblance; related in appearance or nature; alike though not identical. See Usage note below. **2.** *Geometry.* Designating figures having corresponding angles equal and corresponding line segments proportional. [French *similaire,* from Latin *similis,* like. See **sem-**[1] in Appendix.*] —**sim′i·lar·ly** *adv.*

Usage: *Similar* is often misused in nontechnical contexts where *same* or *identical* would convey the sense actually intended. *Similar* and *corresponding* are sometimes interchangeable, but the latter is a narrower, more precise term. *Similar* is an adjective only, and is not employed adverbially in standard usage: *The heating mechanism is similar to that of a drier* or *works like that* (or *similarly to that*) *of a drier,* but not *works similar to that of a drier.*

sim·i·lar·i·ty (sĭm′ə-lăr′ə-tē) *n., pl.* **-ties. 1.** The condition or quality of being similar; resemblance. **2.** An instance in which objects are similar. —See Synonyms at **likeness.**

sim·i·le (sĭm′ə-lē) *n.* A figure of speech in which two essentially unlike things are compared, the comparison being made explicit typically by the use of the introductory *like* or *as: "Like ancient trees, we die from the top"* (Gore Vidal). Compare **metaphor.** [Latin, neuter of *similis,* SIMILAR.]

si·mil·i·tude (sĭ-mĭl′ə-to͞od′, -tyo͞od′) *n.* **1.** Similarity. **2.** Something closely resembling another; a counterpart; double. **3.** *Archaic.* A simile, allegory, or parable. —See Synonyms at **likeness.** [Middle English, from Old French, from Latin *similitūdo,* from *similis,* SIMILAR.]

sim·lin. Variant of **cymling.**

sim·mer (sĭm′ər) *v.* **-mered, -mering, -mers.** —*intr.* **1.** To cook gently below or just at the boiling point. **2.** To be filled with barely controlled anger or resentment; seethe. —*tr.* To cook below or just at the boiling point. —See Synonyms at **boil.** —**simmer down. 1.** To reduce the liquid volume of by boiling slowly. **2.** To become calm after excitement or anger. —*n.* The state or process of simmering. [Earlier *simper,* Middle English *simperen* (imitative).]

sim·nel (sĭm′nəl) *n. British.* **1.** A crisp bread made of fine wheat flour. **2.** A fruitcake eaten on festive occasions. [Middle English *simenel,* from Old French, from Latin *simila,* fine flour, probably from Semitic, akin to Akkadian *samīdu.* See also **semolina.**]

si·mo·le·on (sĭ-mō′lē-ən) *n. Slang.* A dollar. [Perhaps from earlier synonymous *Simon*†.]

Si·mon (sī′mən). A masculine given name. [Latin, from Greek *Simōn,* from Hebrew *Shimə'ōn,* "harkening," from *shāma',* "he heard."]

si·mo·ni·ac (sĭ-mō′nē-ăk′) *n.* A person who practices simony. —**si·mo′ni·ac, sim′o·ni′a·cal** (sĭm′ə-nī′ə-kəl) *adj.* —**sim′o·ni′a·cal·ly** *adv.*

si·mon·ize (sī′mə-nīz′) *tr.v.* **-ized, -izing, -izes.** To clean and wax the surface of (an automobile, for example). [From *Simoniz,* trademark for an automobile wax.]

Si·mon Le·gree (sī′mən lə-grē′). A slave driver or a brutal master. [Name of a cruel slave dealer in the novel *Uncle Tom's Cabin* (1852) by Harriet Beecher Stowe.]

Si·mon Ma·gus (sī′mən mā′gəs). Samaritan sorcerer of the first century A.D.; converted to Christianity.

Si·mo·nov (sē′mə-nôf), **Konstantin Mikhailovich.** Born 1915. Soviet author of novels, plays, and poetry.

Si·mon Pe·ter. See Saint **Peter.**

si·mon-pure (sī′mən-pyŏŏr′) *adj.* Genuine; thoroughgoing; real. [From the *real Simon Pure,* after *Simon Pure,* a character who is impersonated by a rival in Susanna Centlivre's play *A Bold Stroke for a Wife* (1718).]

sim·o·ny (sĭm′ə-nē, sī′mə-) *n.* The buying or selling of ecclesiastical pardons, offices, or emoluments. [Middle English *simonie,* from Old French, from Late Latin *sīmōnia,* after *Simon Magus,* a Samaritan who offered money to the Apostles Peter and John for the power of conferring the Holy Ghost on whomever he wished. Acts 8:18–19.] —**sim′o·nist** *n.*

Si·mon Ze·lo·tes (sī′mən zē-lō′tēz). Known as Simon the Canaanite. Christian leader of the first century A.D.; one of the Twelve Apostles.

si·moom (sĭ-mōōm′) *n.* Also **si·moon** (-mōōn′). A strong hot, sand-laden wind of the Sahara and Arabian deserts. Also called "samiel." [Arabic *samūm,* "poisonous," from *samma,* "he poisoned," from *sam,* poison, from Aramaic *sammā,* drug, poison.]

simp (sĭmp) *n. Slang.* A simpleton; a fool.

sim·pa·ti·co (sĭm-pä′tĭ-kō′, -păt′ĭ-kō′) *adj.* **1.** Of like mind or temperament; compatible. **2.** Having attractive qualities; pleasing. [Italian, from *simpatia,* sympathy, from Latin *sympathīa,* SYMPATHY.]

sim·per (sĭm′pər) *v.* **-pered, -pering, -pers.** —*intr.* To smile in a silly or self-conscious manner. —*tr.* To utter or express with a simper. —*n.* A silly or self-conscious smile. See Synonyms at **smile.** [From Scandinavian, akin to Danish dialectal *simper*†, affected.] —**sim′per·er** *n.* —**sim′per·ing·ly** *adv.*

sim·ple (sĭm′pəl) *adj.* **-pler, -plest. 1.** Having or composed of one thing or part only; not combined or compound. **2.** Not involved or complicated; easy: *"All that was intricate and false; the truth was simple."* (W.H. Auden). **3.** Without additions or modifications; bare; mere. **4.** Without embellishment; not ornate or adorned. **5.** Not elaborate, elegant, or luxurious. **6.** Not affected; unassuming or unpretentious. **7.** Not guileful or deceitful; sincere. **8.** Humble or lowly in condition or rank: *a simple peasant.* **9.** Ordinary or common: *a simple head cold.* **10.** Not important or significant; trivial. **11.** Having or manifesting little sense or intellect; silly. **12.** *Biology.* Having no divisions or subdivisions; not compound: *a simple leaf.* **13.** *Music.* Without overtones: *a simple tone.* —See Synonyms at **easy, naive.** —*n.* **1.** Something uncomplex or unmixed. **2.** A fool; simpleton. **3.** *Archaic.* A person of humble birth or condition. **4.** *Archaic.* A medicinal plant or the medicine obtained from it. [Middle English, from Old French, from Latin *simplus.* See **sem-[1]** in Appendix.*]

simple fraction. A fraction in which both the numerator and the denominator are integers.

simple fruit. A fruit, such as a pea pod, grape, or almond, that develops from a single pistil.

simple harmonic motion. *Physics.* A periodic motion that may be described as a sinusoidal function of time; specifically, the motion of a particle that obeys the equation $x = A\cos(kt + \phi)$, where x is the displacement of the particle from the origin at any time t, A is the maximum displacement, ϕ is the initial phase or angular displacement at $t = 0$, and k is a constant equal to 2π times the frequency of the oscillation.

simple honors. *Bridge.* Three honors in trump, or three aces at no-trump, held by the same side.

simple interest. Interest paid only on the original principal, not on the interest accrued. Compare **compound interest.**

simple machine. A **machine** *(see).*

simple microscope. A microscope having one lens or lens system, as a magnifying glass or hand lens.

sim·ple-mind·ed (sĭm′pəl-mīn′dĭd) *adj.* **1.** Not sophisticated; artless. **2.** Stupid or silly. **3.** Mentally defective. —**sim′ple-mind′ed·ly** *adv.* —**sim′ple-mind′ed·ness** *n.*

simple pendulum. A **pendulum** *(see).*

simple sentence. A sentence having no coordinate or subordinate clauses; for example: *The cat purred.*

Simple Simon. A foolish fellow; simpleton. [After *Simple Simon,* title character of a nursery rhyme.]

sim·ple·ton (sĭm′pəl-tən) *n.* A silly or stupid person; a fool. [SIMPLE + *-ton,* "town" (appearing in surnames derived from place names).]

sim·plex (sĭm′plĕks′) *adj.* Denoting a system of telegraphy in which only one message may be sent in either direction at one time. [From Latin *simplex,* simple, single. See **sem-[1]** in Appendix.*]

sim·plic·i·ty (sĭm-plĭs′ə-tē) *n., pl.* **-ties. 1.** The state or quality of being simple; absence of complexity, intricacy, or artificiality. **2.** Lack of good sense or intelligence; foolishness. [Middle English *symplicite,* from Old French, from Latin *simplicitās,* from *simplex,* simple. See **sem-[1]** in Appendix.*]

sim·pli·fy (sĭm′plə-fī′) *tr.v.* **-fied, -fying, -fies.** To make simple or simpler; render less complex or intricate. [French *simplifier,* from Medieval Latin *simplificāre* : Latin *simplus,* SIMPLE + *facere,* to make (see **dhē-[1]** in Appendix*).] —**sim′pli·fi·ca′tion** *n.* —**sim′pli·fi′er** *n.*

sim·plism (sĭm′plĭz′əm) *n.* The tendency to oversimplify an issue or problem by ignoring complexities or complications. [French *simplisme,* from Old French *simple,* SIMPLE.] —**sim·plis′tic** (sĭm-plĭs′tĭk) *adj.* —**sim·plis′ti·cal·ly** *adv.*

Sim·plon Pass (sĭm′plŏn′; *French* săN-plôN′). A pass between the Lepontine and Pennine Alps, connecting Switzerland and Italy and reaching a maximum elevation of 6,598 feet. Nearby is the Simplon Tunnel (12.25 miles long) through Mount Leone.

sim·ply (sĭm′plē) *adv.* **1.** In a simple manner; plainly. **2.** Foolishly. **3.** Merely; only. **4.** Absolutely; altogether. **5.** Frankly; candidly: *You are, quite simply, inadequate for this job.*

Simp·son (sĭmp′sən), Sir **James Young.** 1811–1870. British physician; first used anesthesia in childbirth.

sim·u·la·crum (sĭm′yə-lā′krəm) *n., pl.* **-cra** (-krə). Also *archaic* **sim·u·la·cre** (-kər) *pl.* **-cres. 1.** An image or representation of something. **2.** An unreal or vague semblance of something. [Latin, from *simulāre,* SIMULATE.]

sim·u·lar (sĭm′yə-lər, -lär′) *n. Archaic.* A simulator. —*adj. Archaic.* Simulated; sham.

sim·u·late (sĭm′yə-lāt′) *tr.v.* **-lated, -lating, -lates. 1.** To have or take on the appearance, form, or sound of; imitate. **2.** To make a pretense of; feign: *simulate an interest.* —See Synonyms at **imitate, pretend.** —*adj.* (sĭm′yə-lĭt, -lāt′). Simulated; assumed; pretended. [Latin *simulāre,* from *similis,* SIMILAR.] —**sim′u·la′tive** *adj.* —**sim′u·lant** (-lənt) *adj.* & *n.*

sim·u·la·tion (sĭm′yə-lā′shən) *n.* **1.** The act or process of simulating. **2.** An imitation. **3.** The assumption of a false appearance; a feigning or pretending.

sim·u·la·tor (sĭm′yə-lā′tər) *n.* One that simulates; especially, an apparatus that generates test conditions approximating actual or operational conditions.

si·mul·cast (sī′məl-kăst′, -käst′, sĭm′əl-) *tr.v.* **-casted, -casting, -casts.** To broadcast simultaneously by FM and AM radio or by radio and television. —*n.* A broadcast so transmitted. [SIMUL(TANEOUS) + (BROAD)CAST.]

si·mul·ta·ne·ous (sī′məl-tā′nē-əs, sĭm′əl-) *adj.* **1.** Happening, existing, or done at the same time. **2.** *Mathematics.* Collectively restricting the values of a set of variables: *simultaneous equations.* —See Synonyms at **contemporary.** [Formed by analogy with INSTANTANEOUS from Latin *simul,* at the same time. See **sem-[1]** in Appendix.*] —**si′mul·ta′ne·ous·ly** *adv.* —**si′mul·ta′ne·ous·ness, si′mul·ta·ne′i·ty** (sī′məl-tə-nē′ə-tē, sĭm′əl-) *n.*

Usage: *Simultaneous* is an adjective only: *Simultaneous with the election was a referendum on daylight-saving time.* Its use as an adverb, for *simultaneously,* though common, is not standard. The following paraphrase of the original example is termed unacceptable by all members of the Usage Panel: *The referendum was conducted simultaneous with the general election.*

sin[1] (sĭn) *n.* **1.** A transgression of a religious or moral law, especially when deliberate. **2.** *Theology.* A condition of estrangement from God as a result of breaking His law. **3.** Any offense, violation, fault, or error. —See Synonyms at **offense.** —*intr.v.* **sinned, sinning, sins. 1.** To commit a sinful act; violate a religious or moral law. **2.** To commit an offense or violation; do wrong. [Middle English *sinne, sunne,* Old English *syn(n).* See **es-** in Appendix.*]

sin[2] (sēn) *n.* The 21st letter of the Hebrew alphabet. See **alphabet.** [Hebrew *sin,* variant of *shīn,* "tooth," SHIN (letter).]

sin *Trigonometry.* sine.

SIN Airport code for Singapore.

Si·nai (sī′nī′). A peninsula comprising the Asian part of Egypt, extending about 140 miles between the Gulf of Suez and the Gulf of Aqaba. It was the scene of an Israeli victory in 1967.

Si·nai, Mount (sī′nī′). The mountain where Moses received the law from God (Exodus 19), believed to be one of the mountains on the southern Sinai Peninsula.

Si·na·lo·a (sē′nə-lō′ə; *Spanish* sē′nä-lō′ä). A state of Mexico occupying 22,582 square miles in the west on the Gulf of California. Population, 913,000. Capital, Culiacán.

sin·an·thro·pus (sī-năn′thrə-pəs, sĭ-, sī′năn-thrō′pəs, sĭn′ăn-) *n.* An extinct manlike primate of the genus *Sinanthropus,* which includes Peking man. [New Latin *Sinanthropus,* "Chinese man" : SIN(O)- + -ANTHROPUS.]

sin·a·pism (sĭn′ə-pĭz′əm) *n.* A mustard plaster. [French *sinapisme,* from Late Latin *sināpismus,* from Greek *sinapismos,* use of a mustard plaster, from *sinapizein,* to apply a mustard plaster, from *sinapi,* mustard, related to earlier *napu,* probably from Egyptian.]

since (sĭns) *adv.* **1.** From a time in the past up to the present; from then until now. Often preceded by *ever: He arrived last week and has been here ever since.* **2.** At a time between a past time or event and the present; between then and now. **3.** At some past time; before now; ago: *long since forgotten.* —*prep.* **1.** During the time following a past time or event: *He has not been home since Easter.* **2.** Continuously throughout the time following: *since midnight.* —*conj.* **1.** During the time after

Simple Simon
Woodcut illustrations

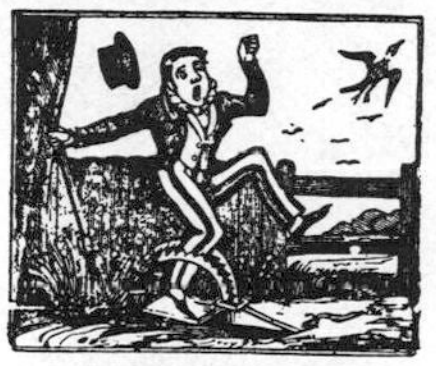

"Simple Simon went a poaching/For to shoot some game/A mantrap caught him by the leg/Which gave poor Simon pain."

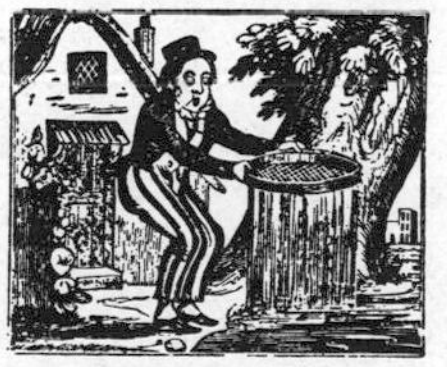

"He went for water with a sieve/But soon it all ran through . . ."

which: *He hasn't been home since he graduated.* **2.** Continuously from the time when: *He hasn't spoken since he sat down.* **3.** As a result of the fact that; inasmuch as. See Usage note at **because.** [Middle English *sin(ne)s,* contraction of *sithen(es),* Old English *siththan,* "after that." See **sē-**[2] in Appendix.*]

sin·cere (sĭn-sîr′) *adj.* **-cerer, -cerest. 1.** Not feigned or affected; true: *sincere indignation.* **2.** Presenting no false appearance; not hypocritical; honest: *a sincere believer.* **3.** *Archaic.* Pure; unadulterated. [Latin *sincērus,* clean, pure, genuine, honest. See **ker-**[3] in Appendix.*] **—sin·cere′ly** *adv.*

Synonyms: *sincere, natural, unaffected, unfeigned, wholehearted, hearty, heartfelt.* These adjectives describe what is genuine and free from dissimulation or artifice. *Sincere* emphasizes honesty of expression or behavior. It implies freedom from hypocrisy and usually a disposition to be constructive. *Natural* and *unaffected* stress absence of artificiality. *Natural* usually applies to appearance or behavior thought to express one's true nature, whereas *unaffected* may imply genuineness where the opposite could be expected. *Unfeigned* especially suggests freedom from falseness or deceit. *Wholehearted* and *hearty* imply not only genuineness of feeling but also its expression in convincing terms. *Wholehearted* suggests total commitment and unstinting devotion to a cause or the like. *Hearty* especially stresses convincing expression of feeling openly displayed. *Heartfelt,* in contrast, emphasizes depth of feeling rather than its display.

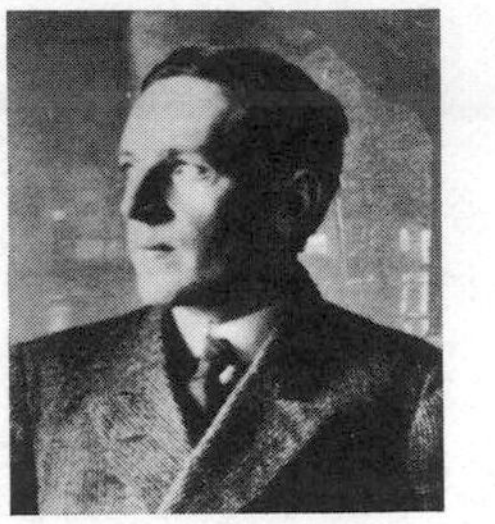

Upton Sinclair

sin·cer·i·ty (sĭn-sĕr′ə-tē, -sîr′ə-tē) *n., pl.* **-ties.** Also **sin·cere·ness** (sĭn-sîr′nĭs) (for sense 1). **1.** The quality or condition of being sincere. **2.** A sincere feeling or expression.

sin·ci·put (sĭn′sə-pət) *n., pl.* **-puts** or **sincipita** (sĭn-sĭp′ə-tə). **1.** The upper half of the cranium, especially the anterior portion above and including the forehead. **2.** The forehead. [Latin, from earlier *sēmicaput* (unattested) : SEMI + *caput,* head (see **kaput** in Appendix*).] **—sin·cip′i·tal** (-sĭp′ə-təl) *adj.*

Sin·clair (sĭn-klâr′), **Upton (Beall).** 1878–1968. American novelist, political leader, and social reformer.

Sind (sĭnd). A former province of Pakistan, now constituting two administrative divisions of West Pakistan.

Sin·dhi (sĭn′dē) *n., pl.* **Sindhi** or **-dhis. 1. a.** The predominantly Moslem people of Sind. **b.** A member of this people. **2.** The Indic language of Sind. **—Sin′dhi** *adj.*

sine (sīn) *n. Abbr.* **sin 1.** The ordinate of the endpoint of an arc of a unit circle centered at the origin of a Cartesian coordinate system, the arc being of length *x* and measured counterclockwise from the point (1, 0) if *x* is positive, or clockwise if *x* is negative. **2.** In a right triangle, the function of an acute angle that is the ratio of the opposite side to the hypotenuse. [Medieval Latin *sinus,* "fold of a garment" (mistranslation of Arabic *jayb,* chord of an arc, sine, through confusion with Arabic *jayb,* fold of a garment), from Latin, curve, fold, hollow. See **sinus.**]

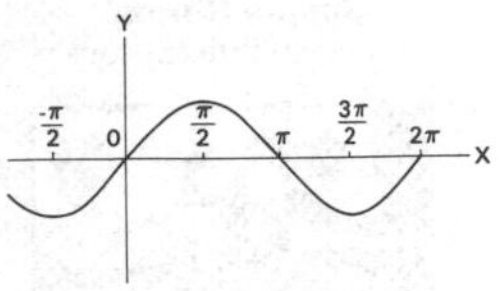

sine curve

si·ne·cure (sī′nə-kyŏŏr′, sĭn′ə-) *n.* **1.** An ecclesiastical benefice not attached to the spiritual duties of a parish. **2.** An office, commission, or charge that requires no work yet provides compensation. [Medieval Latin *(beneficium) sine cūrā,* (benefice) without cure (of souls) : *sine,* without (see **sen-**[2] in Appendix*) + *cūrā,* ablative of *cūra,* cure, care (see **cūra** in Appendix*).] **—si′ne·cur·ism′** *n.* **—si′ne·cur·ist** *n.*

sine curve (sīn). The graph of the equation $y = \sin x$. Also called "sinusoid."

si·ne di·e (sī′nē dī′ē, sĕn′ā dē′ā). *Abbr.* **s.d.** Indefinitely: *Parliament was dismissed sine die.* [Latin, "without a day."]

si·ne qua non (sĭn′ā kwä nōn′, sī′nē kwā nŏn′). An essential element or condition. [Latin, "without which not."]

sin·ew (sĭn′yōō) *n.* **1.** A tendon. **2.** Vigorous strength; muscular power. **3.** *Often plural.* The source or mainstay of vitality and strength: *"good company and good discourse are the very sinews of virtue"* (Walton). [Middle English *sin(e)we, sen(e)ue,* Old English *sinu, seonu.* See **snēu-** in Appendix.*]

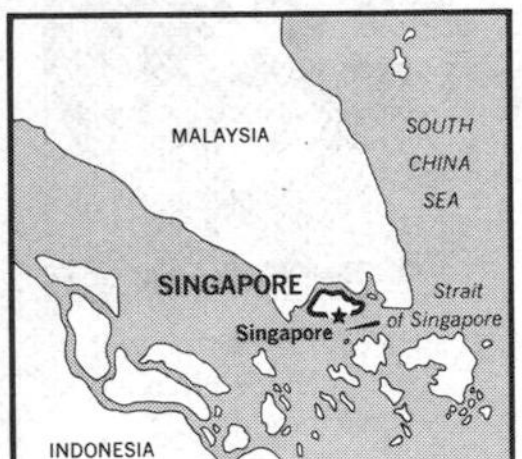

Singapore

sine wave (sīn). *Physics.* A waveform with deviation that can be expressed as the sine or cosine of a linear function of time or space or both.

sin·ew·y (sĭn′yōō-ē) *adj.* **1.** Like or consisting of sinew. **2.** Lean and muscular. **3.** Strong; vigorous.

sin·ful (sĭn′fəl) *adj.* Marked by or full of sin; wicked. **—sin′ful·ly** *adv.* **—sin′ful·ness** *n.*

sing (sĭng) *v.* **sang** (săng) or **sung** (sŭng), **sung, singing, sings.** *—intr.* **1.** To utter a series of words or sounds in musical tones. **2.** To vocalize songs or musical selections. **3.** To give or have the effect of melody; lilt. **4.** To produce musical sounds when played. **5.** To make a high whine or hum. **6.** To be filled with a buzzing sound. **7.** To proclaim or extol something in verse. **8.** *Slang.* To give information or evidence against someone. *—tr.* **1.** To render in tones with musical inflections of the voice. **2.** To produce the musical sound of. **3.** To intone; chant. **4.** To proclaim or extol, especially in verse. **5.** To bring to a specified state by singing. *—n.* A gathering of people for group singing. [Sing, sang, sung; Middle English *singen, sang, sungen,* Old English *singan, sang* (past singular), *sungen.* See **sengwh-** in Appendix.*] **—sing′a·ble** *adj.*

sing. singular.

Sin·ga·pore (sĭng′gə-pôr′, -pōr′, sĭng′ə-). **1.** An island, 224 square miles in area, off the southern tip of the Malay Peninsula. **2.** An independent state comprising this island and smaller neighboring islands, formerly a British colony and, from 1963 to 1965, a state of Malaysia. Population, 1,844,000. **3.** The capital of this state, a seaport on the Strait of Singapore. Population, 1,775,000. [Literally "lion city" : Sanskrit *simha,* lion (see **Singhalese**) + *pūr,* city (see **pele-**[2] in Appendix*).]

Sin·ga·ra·dja (sĭng′gä-rä′jä). The capital of Bali, Indonesia, on the northern coast of the island. Population, 15,000.

singe (sĭnj) *tr.v.* **singed, singeing, singes. 1.** To burn superficially; scorch. **2.** To burn the ends of. **3.** To burn off the feathers or bristles of by subjecting briefly to flame. —See Synonyms at **burn.** *—n.* A scorch. [Middle English *sengen,* Old English *sengan.* See **senk-** in Appendix.*] **—sing′er** (sĭn′jər) *n.*

sing·er (sĭng′ər) *n.* **1.** A person who sings, especially a trained or professional vocalist. **2.** A poet. **3.** A songbird.

Sing·er (sĭng′ər), **Isaac Merrit.** 1811–1875. American manufacturer and inventor of a sewing machine.

Sin·gha·lese (sĭng′gə-lēz′, -lēs′) *n., pl.* **Singhalese.** Also **Sin·ha·lese** (sĭn′hə-). **1.** A people constituting the major portion of the population of Ceylon. **2.** The Indic language of these people. *—adj.* Of or pertaining to the Singhalese or their language. [Sanskrit *Simhala,* "of lions," Ceylon, from *simha,* lion, perhaps of African origin, akin to Swahili *simba,* lion.]

sin·gle (sĭng′gəl) *adj.* **1.** Not accompanied by another or others; solitary. **2.** Consisting of one form or part; not double or multiple: *a single thickness.* **3.** One throughout; not divided. **4.** Undiversified; uniform. **5.** Separate from others; distinct; individual: *"The great single subject of the sonnets is Time."* (Mark Van Doren). **6.** Intended or designed to accommodate one person: *a single bed.* **7.** Unmarried. **8.** Of or pertaining to celibacy. **9.** *Botany.* Having only one rank or row of petals: *a single flower.* **10.** One-against-one; man-to-man: *single combat.* *—n.* **1.** A separate unit; individual. **2.** An accommodation for one person. **3.** A one-dollar bill. **4.** *Baseball.* A **one-base hit** *(see).* **5.** *Cricket.* A hit for one run. **6.** A golf match between two players. **7.** *Plural.* A tennis match between two players. *—v.* **singled, -gling, -gles.** *—tr.* To separate or distinguish from among others. Used with *out.* *—intr. Baseball.* To make a one-base hit. [Middle English *sengle,* from Old French, from Latin *singulus.* See **sem-**[1] in Appendix.*] **—sin′gle·ness** *n.*

Synonyms: *single, sole, unique, solitary, individual, separate.* These adjectives refer in various ways to the condition of being one in number. *Single* means one only, that is, not in accompaniment or association or combination with another or others. *Sole* stresses the idea of one and only, either in the sense of being the only one in existence or the only one involved in what is under consideration. *Unique* applies to what is the only one of its kind in existence. *Solitary* applies to what stands alone or to the condition of isolation. *Individual* makes specific reference to one person or thing distinguished from the mass to which it belongs or from all others. *Separate,* as compared here, implies the condition of being one and distinct by reason of being disunited from all others under consideration.

sin·gle-breast·ed (sĭng′gəl-brĕs′tĭd) *adj.* Closing with a narrow overlap and a single row of fasteners. Said of a coat or jacket.

single entry. A system of bookkeeping in which a business keeps only a single account showing amounts due and amounts owed. **—sin′gle-en′try** *adj.*

single file. A line of people, animals, or things standing or moving one behind the other. Also called "Indian file."

sin·gle-foot (sĭng′gəl-fŏŏt′) *n.* A rapid gait of a horse in which each foot strikes the ground separately. Also called "rack." *—intr.v.* **single-footed, -footing, -foots.** To go at this gait.

sin·gle-hand·ed (sĭng′gəl-hăn′dĭd) *adj.* **1.** Working or done without help; unassisted. **2.** Designed for use with one hand. **3.** Having or using only one hand. **—sin′gle-hand′ed·ly** *adv.*

single knot. An **overhand knot** *(see).*

sin·gle-mind·ed (sĭng′gəl-mīn′dĭd) *adj.* **1.** Having one overriding purpose or opinion. **2.** Steadfast. **—sin′gle-mind′ed·ly** *adv.* **—sin′gle-mind′ed·ness** *n.*

sin·gle-phase (sĭng′gəl-fāz′) *adj.* Producing, carrying, or powered by a single alternating voltage.

sin·gle-space (sĭng′gəl-spās′) *v.* **-spaced, -spacing, -spaces.** *—tr.* To type (copy) without leaving a blank line between lines. *—intr.* To type copy without line spaces.

sin·gle·stick (sĭng′gəl-stĭk′) *n.* **1.** A one-handed fencing stick fitted with a hand guard. Also called "backsword." **2.** The art, sport, or exercise of fencing with such a stick.

sin·gle·stick·er (sĭng′gəl-stĭk′ər) *n. Informal.* A sailboat with one mast; a sloop.

sin·glet (sĭng′glĭt) *n.* **1.** *Chiefly British.* A man's jersey undershirt. **2.** *Physics.* A multiplet with a single member. [From SINGLE (referring to an unlined garment), after DOUBLET.]

single tax. *Economics.* A system by which all revenue is derived from a tax on one object, especially on land.

sin·gle·ton (sĭng′gəl-tən) *n.* **1.** A playing card that is the only one of its suit in a player's hand. **2.** An individual separated or distinguished from two or more of its group. [From *single* (after SIMPLETON).]

sin·gle·tree (sĭng′gəl-trē) *n.* A **whiffletree** *(see).*

sin·gly (sĭng′glē) *adv.* **1.** Without company or help; alone. **2.** One by one; individually.

Sing Sing (sĭng′ sĭng′). A state prison in Ossining, New York.

sing·song (sĭng′sông′, -sŏng′) *n.* **1.** Verse characterized by mechanical regularity of rhythm and rhyme. **2.** Enunciation marked by the monotonously repetitive qualities of incantation or patter. *—adj.* Characterized by monotonous cadence.

sin·gu·lar (sĭng′gyə-lər) *adj.* **1. a.** Being only one; separate; individual. **b.** Deviating strongly from a norm; rare; extraordinary. **2.** *Abbr.* **s., sing.** *Grammar.* Of or being a word form denoting a single person or thing or several considered as a single unit. Compare **plural. 3.** *Logic.* Of or relating to the specific as distinguished from the general; individual. **4.** Peculiar. —See Synonyms at **strange.** *—n. Abbr.* **s., sing.** *Grammar.* The singular number, a form denoting it, or a word

having a singular number. [Middle English *singuler,* solitary, single, separate, from Old French, from Latin *singulāris,* from *singulus,* SINGLE.] —**sin′gu·lar·ly** *adv.* —**sin′gu·lar·ness** *n.*
sin·gu·lar·i·ty (sĭng′gyə-lăr′ə-tē) *n., pl.* **-ties.** **1.** The condition or quality of being singular. **2.** A trait marking one as distinct from others; peculiarity. **3.** Something uncommon or unusual.
sin·gu·lar·ize (sĭng′gyə-lə-rīz′) *tr.v.* **-ized, -izing, -izes.** To make conspicuous; distinguish.
sinh hyperbolic sine.
Sin·hai·lien (shĭng′hī′lē-ĕn′). Formerly **Tung·hai** (tŏŏng′hī′). A city of eastern China, in Kiangsu Province near the Yellow Sea coast. Population, 210,000.
Sin·ha·lese. Variant of **Singhalese.**
Sin·i·cism (sī′nə-sĭz′əm, sĭn′ə-) *n.* A custom or trait peculiar to the Chinese. [From Medieval Latin *Sinicus,* Chinese, from Late Latin *Sinae,* the Chinese. See **Sino-.**]
Si·ning (shē′nĭng′). A city of China, the capital of Tsinghai, in the northeastern part of the province. Population, 150,000.
sin·is·ter (sĭn′ĭ-stər) *adj.* **1.** Suggesting an evil force or motive: *a sinister smile.* **2.** Presaging trouble; ominous. **3.** *Rare.* On the left side; left. **4.** *Heraldry.* On the left of the bearer and hence on the right of the observer. Compare **dexter.** [Middle English *sinistre,* from Old French, from Latin *sinister*†, left, on the left, hence evil, unlucky (in augury the left side being regarded as inauspicious).] —**sin′is·ter·ly** *adv.* —**sin′is·ter·ness** *n.*
Synonyms: *sinister, baleful, malign, dire.* These adjectives apply to what is indicative of, or threatens, disaster or evil. *Sinister* usually implies impending or lurking danger that makes its presence felt indirectly by signs or portents. *Baleful* intensifies the sense of menace by suggesting a direct threat. The term can also refer to evil already present. *Malign* is generally applied to what is present and either is causing harm or exercising a great potential for evil. *Dire* describes what is in itself disastrous or the cause of great suffering or what represents a grave and direct threat of calamity.
sin·is·tral (sĭn′ĭ-strəl) *adj.* **1.** Of or facing the left side. **2.** Left-handed. Compare **dextral.** **3.** *Zoology.* Designating or pertaining to a gastropod shell that has its aperture to the left when facing the observer with the apex upward. —**sin′is·tral·ly** *adv.*
sin·is·trorse (sĭn′ĭ-strôrs′, sĭn′ĭ-strôrs′) *adj.* Growing upward in a spiral that turns from right to left: *a sinistrorse vine.* Compare **dextrorse.** [New Latin *sinistrorsus,* from Latin, turned toward the left : SINISTER (left) + *versus,* past participle of *vertere,* to turn (see **wer-**[3] in Appendix*).] —**sin′is·trorse′ly** *adv.*
sin·is·trous (sĭn′ĭ-strəs) *adj.* Sinister; ill-omened: *"The arrival of a beggar on an island is accounted a sinistrous event."* (Samuel Johnson). —**sin′is·trous·ly** *adv.*
Si·nit·ic (sī-nĭt′ĭk, sĭ-) *n.* One of the two branches of the Sino-Tibetan linguistic group, comprising all the various Chinese languages and dialects, including Mandarin, Cantonese, and Fukien. —**Si·nit′ic** *adj.*
sink (sĭngk) *v.* **sank** (săngk) or **sunk** (sŭngk), **sunk** or **sunken** (sŭng′kən), **sinking, sinks.** See Usage note below. —*intr.* **1.** To descend beneath the surface or to the bottom of a liquid or soft substance. **2.** To move to a lower level; go down slowly or in stages. **3.** To appear to move downward. **4.** To slope downward; to incline. **5.** To pass into a worsened physical condition; approach death. **6.** To become weaker, quieter, or less forceful. **7.** To diminish, as in value. **8.** To decline, as in morale. **9.** To seep; penetrate. Used with *in* or *into.* **10.** To make an impression; become understood. Used with *in* or *into.* **11.** To be hollowed or sunken, as the cheeks. —*tr.* **1.** To cause to descend beneath the surface. **2.** To cause or allow to fall; to drop or lower. **3.** To force into the ground: *sink a piling.* **4.** To dig or drill (a mine or well) in the earth. **5.** To make weaker, quieter, or less forceful. **6.** To degrade; debase the nature of. **7.** To suppress; hide; conceal. **8.** *Informal.* To defeat, as in sports. **9.** To invest. **10.** To lose part or all of an investment. **11.** To pay off (a debt). **12.** *Sports.* To get the ball into the hole or basket, as in golf, pool, or basketball. —*n.* **1.** A water basin fixed to a wall or floor and having a drainpipe and generally a piped supply of water. **2.** A cesspool. **3.** A sink hole. **4.** Any place regarded as an abode of wickedness and corruption. [Sink, sank, sunk (or sunken); Middle English *sinken, sank, sunken,* Old English *sincan, sanc* (past singular), *suncen.* See **sengw-** in Appendix.*] —**sink′a·ble** *adj.*
Usage: As the past tense, *sank* is now preferable to the alternative form *sunk,* especially in formal usage: *The bow sank beneath the water. Sunk* (not *sank*) is the past participle: *They have sunk both destroyers; The skiff may have sunk.*
Sin·kao Shan. The Chinese name for Mount **Morrison.**
sink·er (sĭng′kər) *n.* **1.** One that sinks. **2.** A weight used for sinking fishing lines, nets, or the like. **3.** *Slang.* A doughnut.
sink·hole (sĭngk′hōl′) *n.* A natural depression in a land surface communicating with a subterranean passage, generally occurring in limestone regions and formed by solution or by collapse of a cavern roof.
Sin·kiang-Ui·gur Autonomous Region (shĭn′jē-äng′wē′gər). Formerly **Sin·kiang.** A division of China occupying 636,000 square miles in the northwest. Population, 5,640,000. Capital, Urumchi.
sinking fund. A fund accumulated to pay off a public or corporate debt.
sin·less (sĭn′lĭs) *adj.* Free from or without sin. —**sin′less·ly** *adv.* —**sin′less·ness** *n.*
sin·ner (sĭn′ər) *n.* One who sins.
Sinn Fein (shĭn′ fān′). An Irish political and cultural society founded in about 1905 to promote political and economic independence and the renewal of culture in Ireland. [Irish *sinn féin,* "we ourselves" : *sinn,* we, reshaped from Old Irish *snī* (see **nes-**[2] in Appendix*) + *féin,* self, from Old Irish (see **seu-**[2] in Appendix*).] —**Sinn Feiner.** —**Sinn Feinism.**
Sino-. Indicates Chinese; for example, **Sinophile.** [French, from Late Latin *Sinae,* the Chinese, from Greek *Sinai,* from Arabic *Sīn,* China, from Chinese (Mandarin) *Ch'in*[2], dynastic name of the country. See also **China.**]
Sin·o·logue (sī′nə-lôg′, -lŏg′, sĭn′ə-) *n.* Also **Sin·o·log.** A student of Sinology. [French *sinologue* : SINO- + -LOGUE.]
Si·nol·o·gy (sī-nŏl′ə-jē, sĭ-nŏl′-) *n.* The study of Chinese language, literature, or civilization. [French *sinologie* : SINO- + -LOGY.] —**Sin′o·log′i·cal** (sĭn′ə-lŏj′ĭ-kəl, sī′-) *adj.* —**Si·nol′o·gist** *n.*
Sin·o·phile (sī′nō-fīl′, sĭn′ə-) *n.* One friendly to the Chinese and their interests. [SINO- + -PHILE.]
Sin·o-Ti·bet·an (sī′nō-tĭ-bĕt′n, sĭn′ō-) *n.* A linguistic group that includes the Sinitic and Tibeto-Burman language families. —**Sin′o-Ti·bet′an** *adj.*
sin·ter (sĭn′tər) *n.* **1.** *Geology.* A chemical sediment or crust, as of porous silica, deposited by a mineral spring. **2.** A mass formed by sintering. —*v.* **sintered, -tering, -ters.** —*tr.* To weld together (metallic powder, for example) partially and without melting. —*intr.* To form a homogeneous mass by heating without melting. [German *Sinter,* iron dross, from Old High German *sintar.* See **sendhro-** in Appendix.*]
sin·u·ate (sĭn′yōō-ĭt, -āt′) *adj.* Also **sin·u·at·ed** (-ā′tĭd). Having a wavy indented margin, as a leaf. [Latin *sinuātus,* past participle of *sinuāre,* to bend, wind, from *sinus,* a bend, curve, fold. See **sinus.**] —**sin′u·ate·ly** *adv.* —**sin′u·a′tion** *n.*
Sin·ui·ju (shĭn′ē-jōō′). A city in northwestern North Korea, on the Yalu opposite Antung, China. Population, 118,000.
sin·u·os·i·ty (sĭn′yōō-ŏs′ə-tē) *n., pl.* **-ties.** **1.** The quality of being sinuous. **2.** A bending or curving shape or movement.
sin·u·ous (sĭn′yōō-əs) *adj.* **1.** Characterized by many curves or turns; winding. **2.** Supple and lithe in movement. **3.** Sinuate. [Latin *sinuōsus,* from *sinus,* a bend, curve, fold. See **sinus.**] —**sin′u·ous·ly** *adv.* —**sin′u·ous·ness** *n.*
si·nus (sī′nəs) *n.* **1.** A depression or cavity formed by a bending or curving. **2.** *Anatomy.* **a.** A dilated channel for the passage of chiefly venous blood. **b.** Any of various air-filled cavities in the cranial bones, especially one communicating with the nostrils. **3.** *Pathology.* A fistula or channel to a suppurating cavity. **4.** *Botany.* A notch or indentation between lobes of a leaf or corolla. [Latin *sinus*†, a bend, curve, fold, hollow.]
si·nus·i·tis (sī′nə-sī′tĭs) *n.* Inflammation of a sinus membrane, especially in the nasal region.
si·nus·oid (sī′nyōō-soid′, -nə-soid′) *n. Mathematics.* A **sine curve** *(see).* [Medieval Latin *sinus,* sine, from Latin, a curve (see **sinus**) + -OID.] —**si′nus·oi′dal** (-soid′l) *adj.*
sinusoidal projection. A map projection in which areas are equal to corresponding areas on a globe. The parallels and the prime meridian are straight lines; the other meridians are increasingly curved outward from the prime meridian.
Si·on. Variant of **Zion.**
Siou·an (sōō′ən) *n.* A large North American Indian language family spoken from Lake Michigan to the Rocky Mountains and southward to Arkansas by many tribes including the Omaha, Iowa, Winnebago, Sioux, and Crow groups. —*adj.* Of or pertaining to this language group.
Sioux (sōō) *n., pl.* **Sioux.** **1.** Any of the various groups of Siouan-speaking North American Indian peoples formerly occupying parts of the Great Plains in the Dakotas, Minnesota, and Nebraska. **2.** An individual member of one of the Sioux groups. **3.** The language of one of the Sioux groups. See **Dakota.** [French, short for *Nadowessioux,* from Ojibwa *nātowēssiwak,* Dakotas, from Proto-Algonquian *nātowē(hsi)wa* (unattested), name applied to different Siouan and Iroquoian tribes.] —**Sioux** *adj.*
Sioux City (sōō). A city and meat-packing center on the Missouri in western Iowa. Population, 89,000.
Sioux Falls (sōō). The largest city of South Dakota, in the southeastern part of the state. Population, 65,000.
sip (sĭp) *v.* **sipped, sipping, sips.** —*tr.* **1.** To drink delicately and in small quantities: *She sipped the hot tea.* **2.** To drink from in sips. —*intr.* To drink in sips. —*n.* **1.** The act of sipping. **2.** A small quantity of liquid sipped. [Middle English *sippen,* probably of Low German origin, akin to Low German *sippen,* to sip. See **sib-** in Appendix.*]
si·phon (sī′fən) *n.* Also **sy·phon.** **1.** A pipe or tube fashioned or deployed in an inverted U shape and filled until atmospheric pressure is sufficient to force a liquid from a reservoir in one end of the tube over a barrier higher than the reservoir and out the other end. **2.** *Zoology.* A tubular organ, especially of aquatic invertebrates such as squids or clams, by which water is taken in or expelled. —*v.* **siphoned, -phoning, -phons.** Also **sy·phon.** —*tr.* To draw off or convey through or as if through a siphon. —*intr.* To pass through a siphon. [French, from Latin *sīphō, sīphōn,* from Greek *siphōn*†, pipe, tube.] —**si′phon·al, si·phon′ic** (sī-fŏn′ĭk) *adj.*

siphon

si·pho·no·phore (sī-fŏn′ə-fôr′, sī′fə-nə-, -fōr′) *n.* Any of various colonial marine coelenterates of the order Siphonophora, which includes the Portuguese man-of-war. [New Latin *Siphonophora,* "tube-bearers" (from their feeding tube) : Latin *sīphō, sīphōn,* tube, SIPHON + New Latin *-phora,* neuter plural of *-phorus,* -PHOROUS.]
si·pho·no·stele (sī-fŏn′ə-stēl′, sī′fə-nə-stē′lē) *n.* A vascular tube surrounding the pith in the stems of certain plants. [SIPHON + STELE (vascular tissue).] —**si′pho·no·ste′lic** *adj.*
si·phun·cle (sī′fŭng′kəl) *n. Zoology.* **1.** A tubelike structure in

t tight/th thin, path/*th* this, bathe/ŭ cut/ûr urge/v valve/w with/y yes/z zebra, size/zh vision/ə about, item, edible, gallop, circus/ à *Fr.* ami/œ *Fr.* feu, *Ger.* schön/ü *Fr.* tu, *Ger.* über/KH *Ger.* ich, *Scot.* loch/N *Fr.* bon. *Follows main vocabulary. †Of obscure origin.

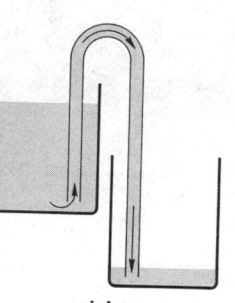

the body of a shelled cephalopod, such as a chambered nautilus, extending through each chamber of the shell. **2.** A dorsal tube in an aphid, secreting a waxy fluid. In this sense, formerly called "nectary." [Latin *sīphunculus*, diminutive of *sīphō, siphōn*, tube, SIPHON.]

sip·pet (sĭp′ĭt) *n.* A small piece of toast or bread soaked in gravy or other juice. [*Sip*, alteration of SOP + -ET.]

Si·quei·ros (sē-kyâr′ōs), **David Alfaro.** Born 1898. Mexican muralist.

sir (sûr) *n.* **1.** *Sometimes capital* **S.** A respectful form of address used instead of a man's name. **2.** *Capital* **S.** A title of honor used before the given name or the full name of baronets and knights. **3.** *Obsolete.* A form of address used with a noun indicating a man's profession, rank, or the like. Sometimes used humorously or disparagingly: *"Sir boy, now let me see your archery"* (Shakespeare). **4.** *Archaic.* A gentleman of rank. [Middle English, unstressed variant of SIRE.]

sir·dar (sûr′där′) *n.* A person of rank in India, Pakistan, or Afghanistan. [Hindi *sardār*, from Persian : *sar*, head (see **ker-**[1] in Appendix*) + *dār*, possession, from Old Persian, from *dar-*, to hold, possess (see **dher-**[2] in Appendix*).]

sire (sīr) *n.* **1.** A father or forefather. **2.** *Abbr.* **s.** The male parent of an animal, especially a domesticated mammal, such as a horse. **3.** *Archaic.* A gentleman of rank. **4.** *Archaic.* A title and form of address to a superior, used especially in addressing a king. —*tr.v.* **sired, siring, sires.** To beget. Used especially of domestic animals. [Middle English, from Old French, from Vulgar Latin *seior* (unattested), variant of Latin *senior*, older, from *senex*, old. See **sen-**[1] in Appendix.*]

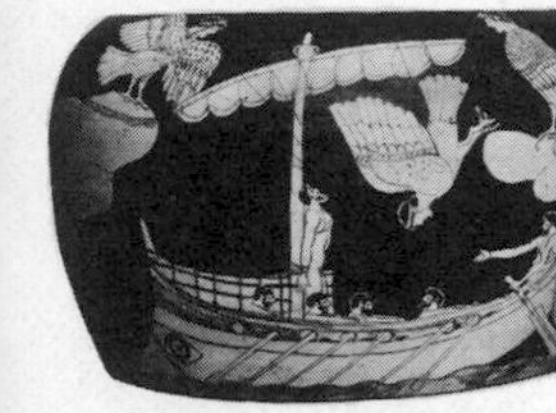

siren
Detail of a Greek vase painting of Odysseus tied to his ship's mast while listening to the sirens sing

si·ren (sī′rən) *n.* **1.** *Often capital* **S.** *Greek Mythology.* One of a group of sea nymphs who by their sweet singing lured mariners to destruction on the rocks surrounding their island. **2.** A beautiful, seductive woman; temptress. **3.** A device in which compressed air or steam is driven against a rotating perforated disk to create a loud, penetrating whistle, wailing, or other sound as a signal or warning. **4.** Any instrument producing a similar sound as a signal or warning. **5.** Any of several North American amphibians of the family Sirenidae, having an eellike body and no hind limbs. —*adj.* Suggesting the effect of the mythological sirens; bewitching. [Middle English *ser(e)yne, siren*, from Old French *sereine*, from Late Latin *sirēna*, from Latin *Sīrēn*, from Greek *Seirēn*. See **twer-**[2] in Appendix.*]

si·re·ni·an (sə-rē′nē-ən) *n.* Any herbivorous aquatic mammal of the order Sirenia, which includes the manatee and the dugong. —*adj.* Of or belonging to the Sirenia. [From New Latin *Sīrēnia* (order), from Latin *Sīrēn*, SIREN.]

Si·ret (sē-rĕt′). *German* **Se·reth** (zā′rĕt). A river rising in the eastern Carpathians of the Ukraine and flowing 280 miles through eastern Rumania to the Danube.

Sir·i·us (sĭr′ē-əs) *n.* A star in the constellation Canis Major, the brightest star in the sky, approximately 8.7 light years distant from Earth. Also called "Canicula," "Dog Star." [Latin, from Greek *Seirios*, from *seirios*†, burning, glowing.]

sir·loin (sûr′loin′) *n.* A cut of meat, especially of beef, from the upper part of the loin between the rump and the porterhouse. [Earlier *surloyn(e)*, from Old French *surlonge* : *sur*, above, from Latin *super* (see **uper** in Appendix*) + *longe, loigne*, loin, from Latin *lumbus* (see **lendh-**[1] in Appendix*).]

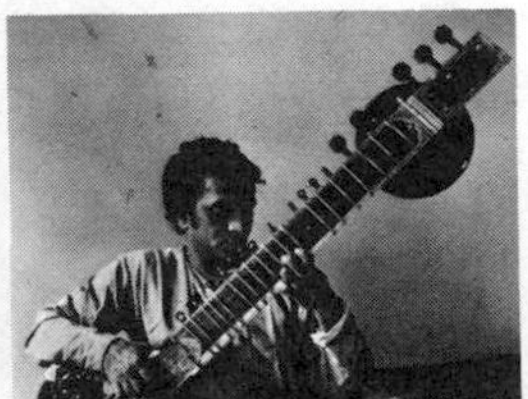

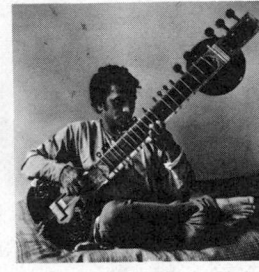

sitar
Ravi Shankar playing a sitar

si·roc·co (sə-rŏk′ō) *n., pl.* **-cos.** Also **sci·roc·co** (shə-). **1.** A hot, humid south or southeast wind of southern Italy, Sicily, and the Mediterranean islands, originating in the Sahara as a dry, dusty wind but becoming moist as it passes over the Mediterranean. **2.** A hot or warm southerly wind, especially one moving toward a low barometric pressure center. [Italian *sirocco*, from Arabic *sharq, sharuq*, "east (wind)," from *sharaqa*, (the sun) rose.]

Si·ros. See **Syros.**

sir·rah (sĭr′ə) *n. Obsolete.* Fellow. Used as a contemptuous form of address. [Earlier *syrra*, probably alteration of Middle English SIRE (sir).]

sir·ree (sə-rē′) *n.* Also **sir·ee.** *Informal.* Sir. Used with *yes* or *no* for emphasis.

Sir Sand·ford, Mount (săn′fərd). The highest mountain (11,590 feet) in the Selkirk Mountains, British Columbia, Canada.

sir·up. Variant of **syrup.**

sir·vente (sĭr-vänt′, -vĕnt′) *n., pl.* **-ventes** (-vänt′, -vĕnts). Also **sir·ventes.** A form of lyric verse of the Provençal troubadours satirizing political, social, or moral themes. [French, from Provençal *sirventes*, "a servant's song," from *sirvent, servent*, servant, from Latin *serviēns*, present participle of *servīre*, to serve, from *servus*, servant. See **servus** in Appendix.*]

sis (sĭs) *n. Informal.* Sister.

si·sal (sī′zəl, -səl) *n.* **1.** A fleshy plant, *Agave sisalana*, native to Mexico, widely cultivated for its large leaves that yield a stiff fiber used for cordage and rope. **2. a.** The fiber of this plant. **b.** The fiber of certain similar or related plants. [Mexican Spanish, after *Sisal*, town in Yucatán, Mexico.]

sis·kin (sĭs′kĭn) *n.* Any of several small birds of the family Fringillidae; especially, *Carduelis spinus*, of Eurasia, or the **pine siskin** *(see)*. [Middle Dutch *siseken*, formed as diminutive of Middle Low German *sisek*, from Slavic, akin to Czech *čiž*, Russian *chizh* (imitative).]

Sis·ki·you Mountains (sĭs′kĭ-yōō). A range of the Klamath Mountains in northern California and southwestern Oregon. Highest elevation, 7,530 feet.

Sis·ley (sēs-lē′), **Alfred.** 1840–1899. French impressionist painter of English descent.

sis·si·fied (sĭs′ĭ-fīd′) *adj.* Womanish; effeminate.

sis·sy (sĭs′ē) *n., pl.* **-sies.** **1.** An effeminate boy or man; a milksop. **2.** A timid or cowardly person. **3.** *Informal.* Sister. [From *sis*, short for SISTER.] —**sis′sy** *adj.*

sis·ter (sĭs′tər) *n.* **1.** *Abbr.* **s.** A female having the same mother and father as another, *full sister*, or having one parent in common with another, *half sister*. **2.** A female who shares a common ancestry, allegiance, character, or purpose with another or others, specifically: **a.** A kinswoman. **b.** A female fellow member, as of a sorority. **c.** A fellow woman, friend, or companion. **3.** *Informal.* A girl or woman. Often used humorously or disparagingly as a form of direct address. **4.** *Capital* **S.** *Ecclesiastical.* **a.** *Abbr.* **Sr.** A member of a religious order of women; a nun. **b.** A form of address for such a person. **5.** *British.* The head nurse in a ward. **6.** One identified as female and closely related to another: *"the sisters Death and Night"* (Walt Whitman). —*adj.* Standing in the relationship of a sister; related by or as if by sisterhood: *"Our sister civilization, Orthodox Christendom"* (Arnold Toynbee). [Middle English *suster, sister*, Old English *sweostor, swuster*. See **swesor-** in Appendix.*]

sis·ter·hood (sĭs′tər-hŏŏd′) *n.* **1.** The state or relationship of being a sister or sisters. **2.** The quality of being sisterly. **3.** A society of women; especially, a religious society of women.

sis·ter-in-law (sĭs′tər-ĭn-lô′) *n., pl.* **sisters-in-law.** **1.** The sister of one's husband or wife. **2.** The wife of one's brother. **3.** The wife of the brother of one's spouse.

sis·ter·ly (sĭs′tər-lē) *adj.* Characteristic of or befitting a sister or sisters. —*adv.* As a sister. —**sis′ter·li·ness** *n.*

Sis·tine (sĭs′tēn′) *adj.* Also **Six·tine** (sĭk′stēn′). **1.** Of or concerning one of the popes named Sixtus. **2.** Of or relating to the Sistine Chapel in the Vatican. [Italian *sistino*, from New Latin *sixtinus*, from the name *Sixtus*.]

Sis·y·phus (sĭs′ĭ-fəs) *n. Greek Mythology.* A cruel king of Corinth condemned forever to roll a huge stone up a hill in Hades only to have it roll down again on nearing the top. —**Sis′y·phe′an** (-fē′ən) *adj.*

sit (sĭt) *v.* **sat** (săt) or *archaic* **sate** (săt, sāt), **sat, sitting, sits.** —*intr.* **1.** To rest with the body supported upon the buttocks and the torso vertical. **2.** To rest with the hindquarters lowered onto a supporting surface. Used of animals. **3.** To perch. Used of birds. **4.** To cover eggs for hatching; to brood. **5.** To be situated; lie. **6.** To take and maintain a position for an artist or photographer; to pose. **7. a.** To occupy a seat as a member of a deliberative body. **b.** To be in session. **8.** To remain inactive or unused. **9.** To lie or rest in a specified manner. Used with *on* or *upon.* **10.** To affect one with or as if with a burden; weigh. Used with *on* or *upon: Official duties sat heavily on him.* **11.** To fit, fall, or drape in a specified manner. Used of clothing. **12.** To be agreeable to one; to please. Usually used with *with: The idea didn't sit well with him.* **13.** *Chiefly British.* To take an examination, as for a degree. **14.** To blow from a particular direction. Used of the wind. **15.** To baby-sit or watch with an invalid. —*tr.* **1.** To cause to sit; to seat. Often used reflexively: *Sit yourself over there.* **2.** To keep one's seat upon (a horse or other animal). —See Usage note at **set.** —**sit in on.** To attend or participate in. —**sit on** (or **upon**). **1.** *Informal.* To suppress or repress. **2.** *Informal.* To rebuke sharply; to reprimand. —**sit out.** **1.** To stay until the end of: *sit out a speech.* **2.** To remain seated throughout; take no part in a dance, game, or the like. —**sit tight.** *Informal.* To be patient and await the next move. —**sit up.** **1.** To sit straight or erect. **2.** To stay up later than the customary bedtime. **3.** To become suddenly alert; to be startled. [Sit, sat (past); Middle English *sitten, sat(e)*, Old English *sittan, sæt* (plural *sǣton*). Sat (past participle); Middle English *sat*, adopted from the past tense *sat(e)* and replacing the regular past participle *seten*, Old English *(ge)seten*. See **sed-**[1] in Appendix.*]

si·tar (sĭ-tär′) *n.* A Hindu stringed instrument made of seasoned gourds and teak and having a track of 20 metal frets with 6 or 7 main playing strings above and 13 sympathetic resonating strings below. [Hindi *sitār*, "three-stringed" : Persian *si*, three (see **trei-** in Appendix*) + *tār*, string, from Avestan (unattested) *tąthra-* (see **ten-** in Appendix*).] —**si·tar′ist** *n.*

sit-down strike (sĭt′doun′). A work stoppage in which the workers refuse to leave their place of employment pending agreement. Also called "sit-down."

site (sīt) *n.* **1.** The place or plot of land where something was, is, or is to be located: *"the archaeologist's fundamental unit of study is the site."* (James Deetz). **2.** The place or setting of an event. [Middle English, from Old French, from Latin *situs*, place, locality, from *situs*, past participle of *sinere*†, to allow (to remain in a place), hence lay, put.]

sith (sĭth) *conj. Archaic.* Since. [Middle English *sith(th)e*, Old English *siththa, siththan*, SINCE.] —**sith** *adv. & prep.*

sit-in (sĭt′ĭn′) *n.* A protest demonstration in which participants seat themselves in an appropriate place and refuse to move until their objectives are considered; especially, a civil-rights demonstration of this kind.

Sit·ka (sĭt′kə). A town of Alaska, in the southeast on the west coast of Baranof Island; site of a major U.S. naval base. Population, 3,000.

Sitka cypress. The **Nootka cypress** *(see)*.

Sit·ka National Monument (sĭt′kə). An area occupying 57 acres south of Sitka, Alaska, reserved to protect its Indian and Russian relics.

si·tol·o·gy (sī-tŏl′ə-jē) *n.* The science of foods, nutrition, and diet. [Greek *sitos*†, food, grain + -LOGY.]

Si·tsang. The Chinese name for **Tibet.**

Sit·tang (sĭt′täng′). A major river of Burma, rising in the north and flowing 350 miles south to the Gulf of Martaban.

sit·ter (sĭt′ər) *n.* **1.** One that sits; especially, a **baby-sitter** *(see).* **2.** A brooding hen.

Sit·ter (sĭt′ər), **Willem de.** 1872–1934. Dutch astronomer.

sit·ting (sĭt′ĭng) *n.* **1.** The act or position of one that sits. **2.** A period during which one is seated and occupied with a single activity, as posing for a portrait or reading a book. **3.** A term or session, as of a legislature or court. **4. a.** An incubation period. **b.** The number of eggs under a brooding bird.

Sit·ting Bull (sĭt′ĭng bŏŏl). 1834?–1890. American Indian leader; chief of the Dakota; leader in Sioux war (1876–77), at the battle of Little Bighorn, and in ghost-dance uprising (1890).

sitting duck. *Informal.* An easy target or victim.

sitting room. A small living room.

sit·u·ate (sĭch′ōō-āt′) *tr.v.* **-ated, -ating, -ates. 1.** To determine a site for; place in a certain spot or position; locate. **2.** To place under particular circumstances or in a given condition. *—adj.* (sĭch′ōō-ĭt, -āt′). *Archaic.* Situated. [Medieval Latin *situāre,* to put, place, from *situs,* place, SITE.]

sit·u·a·tion (sĭch′ōō-ā′shən) *n.* **1.** The place or position in which something is situated; location. **2.** A position or status with regard to conditions and attendant circumstances. **3.** A combination of circumstances at a given moment; state of affairs. **4.** A critical or problematic combination of circumstances. **5.** A position of employment; post. —See Synonyms at **state.** **—sit′u·a′tion·al** *adj.*

si·tus (sī′təs) *n., pl.* **situs.** Position or location; especially, the proper or normal position, as of a bodily organ or part. [Latin *situs,* place, SITE.]

Sit·well (sĭt′wəl). Family of English poets and critics; Dame **Edith** (1887–1964) and her brothers, Sir **Osbert** (1892–1969) and **Sacheverell** (born 1897).

sitz bath (sĭts). **1.** A tub in which one bathes in a sitting position. **2.** A bath taken in such a tub. [Partial translation of German *Sitzbad* : *Sitz,* a sitting, from Old High German *siz,* from *sizzen,* to sit (see **sed-¹** in Appendix*) + *Bad,* bath.]

Si·va. Variant of **Shiva.**

Si·van (sĭv′ən) *n.* Also **Si·wan.** The ninth month of the Hebrew year. See **calendar.** [Hebrew *Sīwān,* from Assyro-Babylonian *Simānu,* possibly related to Persian *Sefend,* an Iranian deity.]

Si·wa (sē′wə). Ancient name **Am·mo·ni·um** (ə-mō′nē-əm). An oasis north of the Libyan Desert of western Egypt, the seat of the classical oracle of Jupiter Ammon.

Si·wa·lik Range (sĭ-wä′lĭk). The southernmost foothills of the Himalayas in south-central Asia, extending 1,050 miles from southwestern Kashmir in the west to southern Nepal in the east.

six (sĭks) *n.* The cardinal number written 6 or in Roman numerals VI. See **number.** **—at sixes and sevens.** In a state of confusion or disorder. [Middle English *six, sex,* Old English *s(i)ex, six.* See **sweks** in Appendix.*] **—six** *adj. & pron.*

six-gun (sĭks′gŭn′) *n.* A revolver, the **six-shooter** *(see).*

Six Nations. The **Five Nations** *(see)* of the Iroquois confederacy plus the Tuscarora tribe, which joined them in the 18th century. Also called "Six Allied Nations."

six-pack (sĭks′păk′) *n.* Six units of a commodity; especially, six cans or bottles of a beverage sold in a pack.

six·pence (sĭk′spəns) *n. British.* **1.** A coin worth six pennies. **2.** The sum of six pennies.

six·pen·ny (sĭk′spə-nē; sĭks′pĕn′ē *for sense 3*) *adj.* **1.** Valued at, selling for, or worth sixpence. **2.** Of little worth; cheap; paltry. **3.** Denoting a size of nails, generally two inches.

six-shoot·er (sĭks′shōō′tər) *n. Informal.* A six-chambered revolver. Also called "six-gun," "shooting iron."

six·teen (sĭk′stēn′) *n.* The cardinal number written 16 or in Roman numerals XVI. See **number.** [Middle English *sixtene,* Old English *sixtȳne* : SIX + -TEEN.] **—six′teen′** *adj. & pron.*

six·teen·mo (sĭk-stēn′mō) *n., pl.* **-mos. Sextodecimo** *(see).*

six·teenth (sĭk′stēnth′) *n.* **1.** The ordinal number 16 in a series. Also written 16th. **2.** One of 16 equal parts. See **number.** **—six′teenth′** *adj. & adv.*

sixteenth note. *Music.* A note having $1/16$ the time value of a whole note. Also *chiefly British* "semiquaver."

sixth (sĭksth) *n.* **1.** The ordinal number six in a series. Also written 6th. **2.** One of six equal parts. See **number.** **3.** *Music.* **a.** An interval of six degrees in a diatonic scale. **b.** A tone separated by this interval from a given tone. **c.** The harmonic combination of two tones separated by this interval. **d.** The sixth tone of a scale; submediant. **—sixth** *adj. & adv.*

sixth sense. A power of perception seemingly independent of the five senses; intuition.

six·ti·eth (sĭk′stē-ĭth) *n.* **1.** The ordinal number 60 in a series. Also written 60th. **2.** One of 60 equal parts. See **number.** **—six′ti·eth** *adj. & adv.*

Six·tine. Variant of **Sistine.**

six·ty (sĭk′stē) *n.* The cardinal number written 60 or in Roman numerals LX. See **number.** **—six′ty** *adj. & pron.*

six·ty-fourth note (sĭk′stē-fôrth′, -fōrth′). *Music.* A note having $1/64$ the time value of a whole note. Also *chiefly British* "hemidemisemiquaver."

six·ty-nine (sĭk′stē-nīn′) *n.* **1.** The cardinal number written 69. **2.** *Vulgar Slang.* Simultaneous and mutual oral stimulation of genitalia by two members of the same or opposite sex. In this sense, also called "soixante-neuf."

siz·a·ble (sī′zə-bəl) *adj.* Also **size·a·ble.** Of considerable size; fairly large. **—siz′a·ble·ness** *n.* **—siz′a·bly** *adv.*

size¹ (sīz) *n.* **1.** The physical dimensions, proportions, magnitude, or extent of something. **2.** Any of a series of graduated categories of dimension whereby manufactured articles are classified. **3.** Considerable extent, amount, or dimensions. **4.** Moral or mental qualities, rank, or status with reference to relative importance or the capacity to meet certain requirements. **5.** Actual state of affairs; true situation: *That's about the size of the situation.* *—tr.v.* **sized, sizing, sizes. 1.** To arrange, classify, or distribute according to size. **2.** To make, cut, or shape to a required size. **—size up. 1.** To make an estimate, opinion, or judgment of. **2.** To meet certain specifications or requirements. [Middle English *syse,* fixed amount, assize, from Old French *sise,* short for *assise,* ASSIZE.]

size² (sīz) *n.* Any of several gelatinous or glutinous substances usually made from glue, wax, or clay and used as a glaze or filler for porous materials such as paper, cloth, or wall surfaces. Also called "sizing." *—tr.v.* **sized, sizing, sizes.** To treat or coat with size or a similar substance. [Middle English *cyse, syse,* probably a specialized use of SIZE (dimension).] **—siz′y** *adj.*

sized (sīzd) *adj.* Having a particular or specified size. Often used in combination: *medium-sized.*

siz·ing (sī′zĭng) *n.* **1.** A glaze or filler, **size** *(see).* **2.** The treatment of a fabric or other surface with size.

siz·zle (sĭz′əl) *intr.v.* **-zled, -zling, -zles. 1.** To make the hissing sound characteristic of frying fat. **2.** To seethe with anger or indignation. *—n.* A hissing sound. [Imitative.]

siz·zler (sĭz′lər) *n. Informal.* A very hot day.

S.J. Society of Jesus.

Sjael·land (shĕl′län). *English* **Zea·land** (zē′lənd). The largest (2,709 square miles) of the islands of Denmark and site of Copenhagen, the country's capital and chief city.

S.J.D. Doctor of Juridical Science (Latin *Scientiae Juridicae Doctor*).

SJO Airport code for San José, Costa Rica.

SJU Airport code for San Juan, Puerto Rico.

sk. sack.

Ska·gen, Cape (skä′gən). The northern tip of Jutland, Denmark, at the junction of the Skagerrak and Kattegat.

Skag·er·rak (skăg′ə-răk′). An arm of the North Sea, about 80 miles wide, extending 150 miles between Norway and Jutland.

Skag·way (skăg′wā′). A town in southeastern Alaska, 80 miles north of Juneau, a point of departure for the Yukon gold fields in the late-19th-century Klondike gold rush.

skald (skôld, skäld) *n.* Also **scald.** An ancient Scandinavian poet; bard. [Old Norse *skāld.* See **sekw-³** in Appendix.*] **—skald′ic** *adj.*

skat (skăt) *n.* **1.** A card game for three persons played with 32 cards, sevens through aces. **2.** One of the combinations of cards occurring in this game. [German *Skat,* from Italian *scarto,* a discard (said of cards), from *scartare,* to reject, discard : *s-,* negative prefix, from Latin *ex-,* out of + *carta,* card, from Latin *charta,* leaf of papyrus (see **card**).]

skate¹ (skāt) *n.* **1.** A shoe having a bladelike metal runner fixed to its sole, enabling the wearer to glide easily over ice. **2.** Such a runner having clamps and straps for attaching it to a shoe or boot. **3.** A **roller skate** *(see).* *—intr.v.* **skated, skating, skates.** To glide or move along on or as on skates. [Mistaken as singular of earlier *scates,* from Dutch *schaats,* a skate, from Old North French *escace,* stilt, from Frankish *skakkja* (unattested), from *skakan* (unattested), to run fast. See **scotch** (block).]

skate² (skāt) *n.* Any of various marine fishes of the family Rajidae, having a cartilaginous skeleton and a flattened body with the pectoral fins forming winglike lateral extensions. [Middle English *scate,* from Old Norse *skata*†.]

skate³ (skāt) *n.* A chap; fellow. [Perhaps variant of dialectal *skite,* contemptible person, probably from *skite,* to void excrement, Middle English *skyten,* from Old Norse *skīta.* See **skei-** in Appendix.*]

skat·or (skā′tər) *n.* **1.** One who skates. **2.** An insect, the **water strider** *(see).*

skat·ole (skăt′ōl′) *n.* Also **skat·ol.** A white crystalline organic compound, C_9H_9N, having a strong fecal odor, found naturally in feces, beets, and coal tar, and used as a fixative in the manufacture of perfume. [Greek *skōr* (stem *skat-*), dung (see **sker-⁴** in Appendix*) + -OLE.]

skean (shkēn) *n.* A type of double-edged dagger formerly used in Ireland and Scotland. [Irish Gaelic *scian, sgian,* from Old Irish *scīan.* See **skei-** in Appendix.*]

Skeat (skēt), **Walter William.** 1835–1912. English philologist.

Skee·na River (skē′nə). A river of British Columbia, rising in the northwest and flowing 360 miles to Hecate Strait.

skeet (skēt) *n.* A variety of trapshooting in which clay targets are thrown from traps to simulate birds in flight and are fired at from eight different stations by the shooter. [Ultimately from Old Norse *skjōta,* to shoot. See **skeud-** in Appendix.*]

skeg (skĕg) *n.* **1.** A timber that connects the keel and the sternpost of a ship. **2.** An arm extending to the rear of the keel to support the rudder and protect the propeller. **3.** A series of timbers attached to the stern of a small boat, serving as a keel to keep the boat on course. [Dutch *scheg(ge),* from Old Norse *skegg,* beard, projection. See **skek-** in Appendix.*]

skein (skān) *n.* **1.** A length of thread or yarn wound in a loose, elongated coil. **2.** Something like or suggestive of this: *a skein of hair.* **3.** A flock of geese or similar birds in flight. [Middle English *skeyne,* from Old French *escaigne*†.]

skel·e·tal (skĕl′ə-təl) *adj.* Pertaining to, forming, or of the nature of a skeleton. **—skel′e·tal·ly** *adv.*

skel·e·ton (skĕl′ə-tən) *n.* **1. a.** The internal vertebrate structure composed of bone and cartilage that protects and supports the soft organs, tissues, and parts. **b.** The hard external supporting and protecting structure in many invertebrates and certain vertebrates, such as turtles; exoskeleton. **2.** Any supporting structure or framework. **3.** An outline or sketch. **4.** A very thin or emaciated person or animal. *—adj.* **1.** Of or resembling a

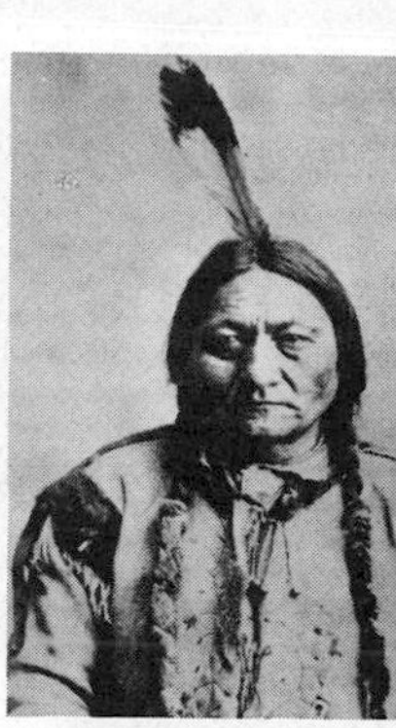

Sitting Bull

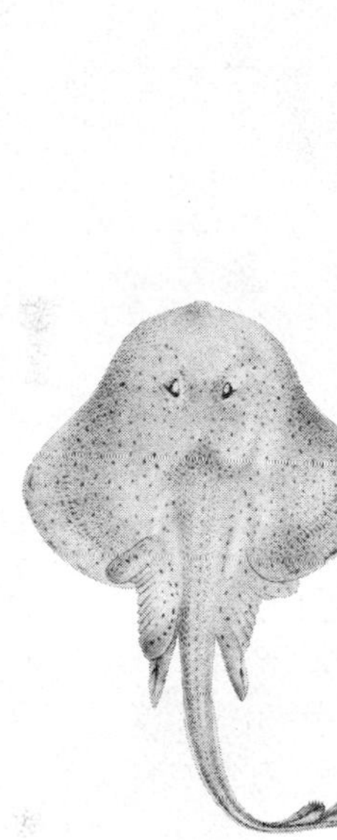

skate²
Raja ocellata

skeleton. **2.** Meager; emaciated. **3.** Having or consisting only of an outline, essential parts, or the smallest number of members: *a skeleton staff.* [New Latin, from Greek, neuter of *skeletos,* dried up, withered. See **skel-**[4] in Appendix.*]

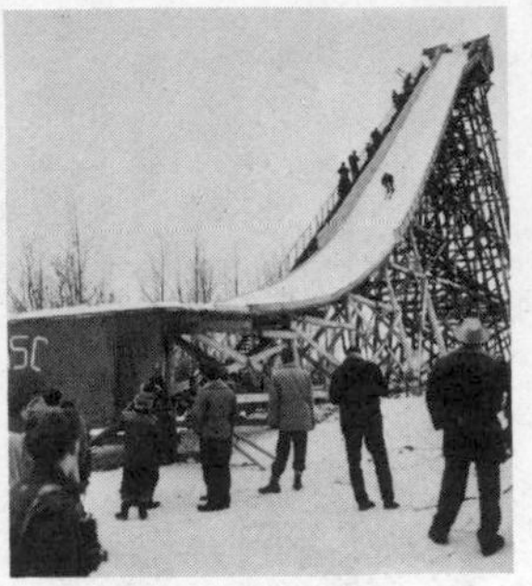

ski jump
Man-made course at Midland, Ontario

skeleton key. A key with a large portion of the bit filed away so that it can open different locks. Also called "passkey."

Skel·ton (skĕl′tən), **John.** 1460?–1529. English poet.

skep (skĕp) *n.* A beehive, particularly one of straw. [Middle English *skep(pe),* Old English *sceppe,* the quantity held by a skep, from Old Norse *skeppa*†, basket.]

skep·tic (skĕp′tĭk) *n.* Also **scep·tic. 1.** One who instinctively or habitually doubts, questions, or disagrees with assertions or generally accepted conclusions. **2.** One inclined to skepticism in religious matters. **3. a.** *Often capital* **S.** An adherent of any philosophical school of skepticism. **b.** *Capital* **S.** A member of an ancient Greek school of philosophical skepticism, especially that of Pyrrho of Elis. [Latin *Scepticus,* singular of *Sceptici,* followers of Pyrrho, from Greek *Skeptikoi,* from *skeptesthai,* to examine, consider. See **spek-** in Appendix.*]

skep·ti·cal (skĕp′tĭ-kəl) *adj.* **1.** Doubting; questioning; disbelieving. **2.** Pertaining to or characteristic of skeptics or skepticism. **—skep′ti·cal·ly** *adv.*

skep·ti·cism (skĕp′tə-sĭz′əm) *n.* **1.** A doubting or questioning attitude or state of mind; dubiety. **2.** The philosophical doctrine that absolute knowledge is impossible and that inquiry must be a process of doubting in order to acquire approximate or relative certainty. **3.** Doubt or disbelief of the tenets of Christianity. —See Synonyms at **uncertainty.**

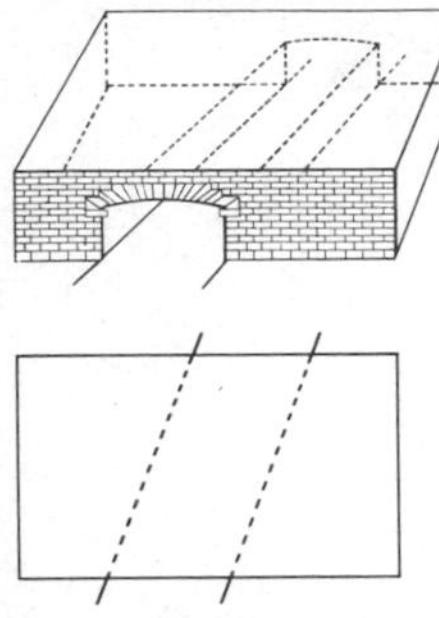

skew arch

sketch (skĕch) *n.* **1.** A hasty or undetailed drawing or painting made as a preliminary study. **2.** A brief, incomplete delineation or presentation, as of a book to be completed; an outline. **3. a.** A brief, light, or informal short story, essay, or other literary composition. **b.** *Music.* A brief composition, especially for the piano. **c.** A short scene or play, often satirical in tone, in a revue or variety show; a skit. **4.** *Informal.* An amusing person. **—*v.* sketched, sketching, sketches.** **—*tr.*** To make a sketch of; to outline. **—*intr.*** To make a sketch or sketches. [Dutch *schets* or German *Skizze,* from Italian *schizzo,* from *schizzare,* to sketch, from Vulgar Latin *schediāre* (unattested), from Latin *schedius,* hastily put together, from Greek *skhedios,* impromptu. See **segh-** in Appendix.*] **—sketch′er** *n.*

sketch·book (skĕch′bo͝ok′) *n.* Also **sketch book. 1.** A pad of paper used for sketching. **2.** A book of literary sketches.

sketch·y (skĕch′ē) *adj.* **-ier, -iest. 1.** Resembling a sketch; giving only major points or parts. **2.** Incomplete; slight; superficial. **—sketch′i·ly** *adv.* **—sketch′i·ness** *n.*

skew (skyo͞o) *v.* **skewed, skewing, skews.** **—*intr.* 1.** To take an oblique course or direction. **2.** To look obliquely or sideways. **—*tr.* 1.** To turn or place at an angle. **2.** To give a bias to; distort. **—*adj.* 1.** Placed or turned to one side; asymmetric. **2.** Distorted or biased in meaning or effect. **3.** Having a part that diverges from a straight line, a right angle, or the like, as gearing. **4. a.** *Geometry.* Neither parallel nor intersecting. Said of straight lines in space. Compare **parallel. b.** *Statistics.* Not symmetric about the mean. Said of distributions. **—*n.*** An oblique or slanting movement, position, or direction. [Middle English *skewen,* to skew, escape, from Old North French *eskuer,* from Germanic *skiuhwan* (unattested). See **eschew.**] **—skew′ness** *n.*

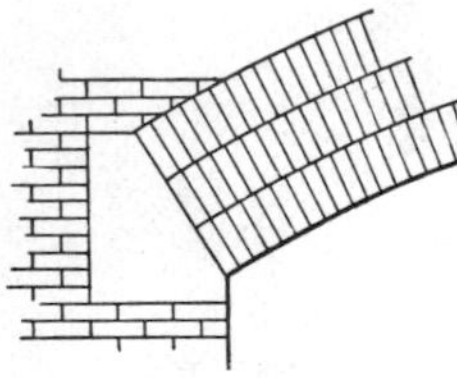

skewback

skew arch. *Architecture.* An arch having sides not at right angles with the face of its abutments.

skew·back (skyo͞o′băk′) *n.* *Architecture.* Either of two inset abutments sloped to support a segmental arch.

skew·bald (skyo͞o′bôld′) *adj.* Having spots or patches of white on a coat other than black: *a skewbald horse.* [From earlier *skued*† + BALD.]

skew·er (skyo͞o′ər) *n.* **1.** A long metal or wooden pin used to secure or suspend meat during cooking; a spit. **2.** Any of various picks or rods having a similar function or shape. **—*tr.v.* skewered, -ering, -ers.** To hold together or pierce with or as if with a skewer. [Variant of dialectal *skiver*†.]

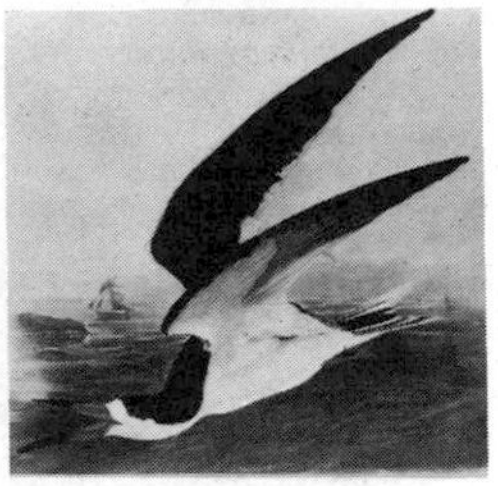

skimmer
Rynchops nigra
Black skimmer
Painting by
John James Audubon

ski (skē, shē) *n., pl.* **skis** or **ski.** One of a pair of long, flat runners of wood, metal, or other material that curve upward in front and may be attached to a boot for gliding or traveling over snow. **—*v.* skied, skiing, skis.** **—*intr.*** To travel on skis, especially as a sport. **—*tr.*** To travel over on skis. [Norwegian *ski(d),* from Old Norse *skīth,* ski, snowshoe. See **skei-** in Appendix.*] **—ski′er** *n.*

ski·a·gram (skī′ə-grăm′) *n.* Also **ski·a·graph** (-grăf′, -gräf′). A picture or photograph made up of shadows or outlines. [Greek *skia,* shadow (see **skī-** in Appendix*) + -GRAM.]

ski·ag·ra·phy (skī-ăg′rə-fē) *n.* The art or technique of making skiagrams. [SKIA(GRAM) + -GRAPHY.]

ski·a·scope (skī′ə-skōp′) *n.* *Optometry.* A **retinoscope** *(see).* [Greek *skia,* shadow (see **skī-** in Appendix*) + -SCOPE.]

ski·as·co·py (skī-ăs′kə-pē) *n.* *Optometry.* **Retinoscopy** *(see).*

skid (skĭd) *n.* **1.** The act of sliding or slipping over a surface, often sideways. **2. a.** A plank, log, or timber, usually one of a pair, used as a support or as a track for sliding or rolling heavy objects. **b.** A small platform for stacking merchandise to be moved or temporarily stored. **c.** *Lumbering.* One of several logs or timbers forming a skid road. **3.** *Plural. Nautical.* A wooden framework attached to the side of a ship to prevent damage, as when unloading. **4.** A shoe or drag applying pressure to a wheel to brake a vehicle. **5.** A runner in the landing gear of certain aircraft. **—on the skids.** *Slang.* On a downward path to ruin, failure, or depravity. **—*v.* skidded, skidding, skids.** **—*intr.* 1.** To slip or slide sideways while moving because of loss of traction, as a vehicle. **2.** To slide without revolving. Said of a wheel that does not turn while the vehicle is in motion. **3.** *Aviation.* To move sideways in a turn because of insufficient banking. —See Synonyms at **slide.** **—*tr.* 1.** To brake (a wheel) with a skid. **2.** To haul on a skid or skids. [Origin uncertain.]

skid fin. An upright auxiliary airfoil formerly placed above the upper wing in biplanes to increase lateral stability.

skid road. 1. A track made of logs laid transversely, spaced about five feet apart, and used to haul logs to a loading platform or a mill. **2.** *Slang.* Skid row.

skid row. *Slang.* A squalid district inhabited by derelicts and vagrants. [Variant (influenced by ROW) of SKID ROAD.]

skiff (skĭf) *n.* *Nautical.* A flat-bottomed open boat of shallow draft, having a pointed bow and a square stern and propelled by oars, sail, or motor. [French *esquif,* from Italian *schifo,* from Lombardic *skif* (unattested). See **skipam** in Appendix.*]

ski·jor·ing (skē′jôr′ĭng, -jōr′ĭng) *n.* A sport in which a skier is drawn over ice or snow by a horse or vehicle. [Norwegian *skikjøring* : SKI + *kjøring,* driving, from *kjøre,* to drive, from Old Norse *keyra* (see **geu-** in Appendix*).]

ski jump. 1. A jump or leap made by a skier. **2.** A course or chute prepared for such a jump.

ski lift. Any of various power-driven conveyors, usually with attached towing bars, suspended chairs, or gondolas, used to carry skiers to the top of a trail or slope. Also called "ski tow."

skill (skĭl) *n.* **1.** Proficiency, ability, or dexterity; expertness. **2.** An art, trade, or technique, particularly one requiring use of the hands or body. **3.** *Obsolete.* Understanding. —See Synonyms at **ability.** [Middle English *skil(e),* reason, skill, from Old Norse *skil.* See **skel-**[1] in Appendix.*]

skilled (skĭld) *adj.* **1.** Having or showing skill; expert. **2.** Having or requiring specialized ability or training, as in an industrial occupation. —See Synonyms at **proficient.**

skil·let (skĭl′ĭt) *n.* **1.** A frying pan. **2.** *Chiefly British.* A long-handled stewing pan or saucepan sometimes having legs. [Middle English *skelet,* probably from *skele,* pail, from Scandinavian, akin to Old Norse *skjōla.* See **skeu-** in Appendix.*]

skill·ful (skĭl′fəl) *adj.* Also **skil·ful. 1.** Possessing or exercising skill; able; expert. **2.** Characterized by, showing, or requiring skill. —See Synonyms at **proficient.** **—skill′ful·ly** *adv.* **—skill′ful·ness** *n.*

skim (skĭm) *v.* **skimmed, skimming, skims.** **—*tr.* 1.** To remove floating matter from (a liquid). **2.** To remove (floating matter) from a liquid. **3.** To coat or cover with or as with a thin layer, as of scum. **4. a.** To hurl across and close to the surface of, so as to bounce on water or slide on ice: *skimming stones.* **b.** To glide or pass quickly and lightly over. **5.** To read or glance through quickly or superficially; peruse hastily. **—*intr.* 1.** To move or pass swiftly and lightly over or near a surface; to glide; to graze. **2.** To give a quick and superficial reading, scrutiny, or consideration; to glance. Used with *over* or *through.* **3.** To become coated with a thin layer. Used with *over.* —See Synonyms at **see.** **—*n.* 1.** The act of skimming. **2.** Something that has been skimmed, as skim milk. **3.** A thin layer or film. **—*adj.*** Skimmed, as milk. [Middle English *skymen,* from Old French *escumer,* from *escume,* foam, from Old High German *scūm.* See **skeu-** in Appendix.*]

skim·mer (skĭm′ər) *n.* **1.** One that skims. **2.** A flat utensil, usually perforated and resembling a ladle, used in skimming liquids. **3.** A wide-brimmed hat with a flat shallow crown. **4.** Any of several chiefly coastal birds of the genus *Rynchops,* having long narrow wings and a long bill with a longer lower mandible for skimming the water's surface for food.

skim milk. Milk from which the cream has been removed.

skim·ming (skĭm′ĭng) *n.* **1.** *Usually plural.* That which is skimmed off a liquid. **2.** The action of skimming.

skimp (skĭmp) *v.* **skimped, skimping, skimps.** **—*tr.* 1.** To do hastily, carelessly, or with poor material; scamp. **2.** To be extremely sparing with; scrimp. **—*intr.*** To be very or unduly thrifty. Usually used with *on: skimp on the budget.* **—*adj.*** Scanty; skimpy. [Possibly a variant of SCRIMP.]

skimp·y (skĭm′pē) *adj.* **-ier, -iest. 1.** Inadequate in size, fullness, or amount; scanty. **2.** Unduly thrifty; stingy; niggardly. —See Synonyms at **meager.** **—skimp′i·ly** *adv.* **—skimp′i·ness** *n.*

skin (skĭn) *n.* **1.** The membranous tissue forming the external covering of the animal body; integument. **2.** An animal pelt, especially the comparatively pliable pelt of a small or young animal. **3.** Anything resembling skin in function or appearance; any outer layer, accretion, or protection, such as the rind of fruit, the surface film on boiled milk, or the plating on a ship or rocket. **4.** A liquid container made of animal skin. **—by the skin of one's teeth.** By the smallest margin; very closely; scarcely or barely. **—get under one's skin. 1.** To anger or irritate. **2.** To be or become an obsession. **—have a thick skin.** To be unperturbed by criticism or insults; be insensitive. **—have a thin skin.** To be easily hurt by criticism, unkindness, or rebuke. **—save one's skin.** To escape harm or avoid death. **—*v.* skinned, skinning, skins.** **—*tr.* 1.** To remove skin from; flay or peel. **2.** To cover with or as if with skin. **3.** To remove or peel off (skin or any outer covering). **4.** *Slang.* To fleece; swindle. **5.** To bruise, cut, or injure the skin or surface of. **—*intr.* 1.** To become covered with or as if with skin. **2.** To pass narrowly; squeeze through. Used with *by* or *through.* **3.** To go hurriedly; slip off. Often used with *out.* [Middle English, from Old Norse *skinn.* See **sek-** in Appendix.*]

skin-deep (skĭn′dēp′) *adj.* Superficial or shallow. **—*adv.*** In a shallow manner; superficially.

skin-dive (skĭn′dīv′) *intr.v.* **-dived** or *informal* **-dove** (-dōv′), **-dived, -diving, -dives.** To participate in skin diving.

skin diving. Underwater swimming, exploration, or fishing in which the diver is equipped with goggles, flippers, and a snorkel or other breathing device. **—skin diver.**

skin effect. The tendency of electric current density in a conductor carrying alternating current to be greater at the surface than at the center.

skin·flint (skĭn′flĭnt′) *n.* A miser. [From the notion that one would go so far as to try to skin a flint for money.]

skin friction. Friction caused by air crossing the surface of aircraft or rockets at high speeds. Also called "skin drag."

skin game. **1.** A crooked or fraudulent gambling game. **2.** Any trick or swindle.

skin graft. A surgical graft of skin from one part of the body to another or from one individual to another.

skink (skĭngk) *n.* Any of numerous smooth, shiny lizards of the family Scincidae, having a cylindrical body and short or rudimentary legs. [Latin *scincus,* from Greek *skinkos*†.]

skin·ner (skĭn′ər) *n.* **1.** A person who flays, dresses, or sells animal skins. **2.** *Western U.S.* A mule driver.

Skin·ner (skĭn′ər), **B(urrhus) F(rederic).** Born 1904. American behavioral psychologist.

skin·ny (skĭn′ē) *adj.* **-nier, -niest.** Very thin. See Synonyms at **lean.** **—skin′ni·ness** *n.*

skin test. A test for an allergy or infectious disease, performed by means of a **patch test, scratch test** *(both of which see),* or an intracutaneous injection of an allergen or extract of the disease-causing organism.

skin·tight (skĭn′tīt′) *adj.* Fitting or clinging closely to the skin.

skip (skĭp) *v.* **skipped, skipping, skips.** *—intr.* **1.** To bound or trip lightly, especially by taking two steps at a time with each foot; hop and step; caper. **2.** To bounce over or be deflected from a surface; skim or ricochet. **3. a.** To pass from point to point omitting or disregarding what intervenes. **b.** To be promoted in school beyond the next regular class or grade. **4.** *Informal.* To leave hastily; abscond. *—tr.* **1.** To leap or jump lightly over. **2.** To pass over, omit, or disregard. **3.** To cause to ricochet or skim. **4.** To be promoted beyond (the next grade or level). *—n.* **1.** A leaping or jumping movement; especially, a gait in which hops and steps alternate. **2.** A passing over or omission. [Middle English *skippen*†.]

skip distance. The smallest separation between a transmitter and a receiver that permits radio signals of a specific frequency to travel from one to the other by reflection from the ionosphere.

skip·jack (skĭp′jăk′) *n., pl.* **skipjack** or **-jacks.** **1.** Any of several marine food fishes of the genus *Euthynnus,* related to and resembling the tuna. **2.** Any of various other fishes, as certain herrings. [Originally "a fop" : SKIP + JACK (fellow).]

skip·per[1] (skĭp′ər) *n.* The master of a ship, especially of a small one. [Middle English *skypper,* from Middle Dutch *schipper,* from *schip,* ship. See **skipam** in Appendix.*]

skip·per[2] (skĭp′ər) *n.* **1.** One that skips. **2.** Any of numerous butterflies of the families Hesperiidae and Megathymidae, having a hairy, mothlike body and a darting flight pattern. **3.** Any of several related marine fishes, especially a saury, *Cololabis saira,* of Pacific waters.

skirl (skûrl) *v.* **skirled, skirling, skirls.** *—intr.* To produce a shrill, piercing tone. Used of a bagpipe. *—tr.* To play on the bagpipe. *—n.* **1.** The shrill sound made by a bagpipe. **2.** Any shrill, piercing sound: *"the skirl of a police whistle split the stillness."* (Sax Rohmer). [Middle English *skirlen, skrillen,* probably of Scandinavian origin, akin to Norwegian dialectal *skrylla.* See **ker-**[2] in Appendix.*]

skir·mish (skûr′mĭsh) *n.* **1.** A minor encounter in war between small bodies of troops, often as part of larger movements. **2.** Any minor or preliminary conflict or dispute. *—intr.v.* **skirmished, -mishing, -mishes.** To engage in a skirmish. [Middle English *skirmisshe, skarmuch,* from Old French *eskermir* (present stem *eskirmiss-*), to fight with the sword, from Germanic. See **sker-**[1] in Appendix.*] **—skir′mish·er** *n.*

skir·ret (skûr′ĭt) *n.* An Old World plant, *Sium sisarum,* having a sweetish, edible root. [Middle English *skirwhite,* variant (influenced by *skir,* bright, and *whit,* white) of Old French *eschervi,* probably a variant of *carvi,* caraway, from Arabic *alkarawyā,* CARAWAY.]

skirt (skûrt) *n.* **1.** That part of a garment, such as a dress or gown, that hangs from the waist down. **2.** A separate garment hanging from the waist and worn by women and girls. **3. a.** One of the leather flaps hanging from the side of a saddle. **b.** The lower outer section of a rocket vehicle. **4.** A border, margin, or outer edge. **5.** *Plural.* The edge or outskirts, as of a town. **6.** *Slang.* A woman or girl. *—v.* **skirted, skirting, skirts.** *—tr.* **1.** To lie along, form the border of, or surround; bound. **2.** To move or pass around rather than across or through. **3.** To evade or elude (a topic of conversation, for example) by circumlocution. *—intr.* To be near or move along the edge or border of something. [Middle English, from Old Norse *skyrta,* shirt. See **sker-**[1] in Appendix.*]

skit (skĭt) *n.* **1.** A short, usually comic theatrical sketch. **2.** A short humorous or satirical piece of writing. [Origin obscure.]

ski tow. **1.** A type of ski lift in which skiers cling to a continuous rope as they are hauled up a slope. **2.** A **ski lift** *(see).*

skit·ter (skĭt′ər) *v.* **-tered, -tering, -ters.** *—intr.* **1.** To skip, glide, or move lightly or rapidly along a surface; to dart; flit. **2.** To fish by drawing a lure or baited hook over the surface of the water with a skipping movement. *—tr.* To cause to skitter. [Probably a frequentative of dialectal *skite,* to run rapidly, to shoot about, perhaps from Old Norse *skjōta,* to shoot. See **skeud-** in Appendix.*]

skit·tish (skĭt′ĭsh) *adj.* **1.** Excitable or nervous. **2.** Shy, coy, or timid. **3. a.** Extremely lively or frivolous in action or character. **b.** Undependable or fickle. [Middle English, perhaps ultimately from Old Norse *skjōta,* to shoot, shoot about. See **skeud-** in Appendix.*] **—skit′tish·ly** *adv.* **—skit′tish·ness** *n.*

skit·tle (skĭt′l) *n. Chiefly British.* **1.** *Plural.* The game of ninepins, in which a wooden disk or ball is thrown to knock down the pins. Used with a singular verb. **2.** One of the pins used in this game. **—all beer and skittles.** Pure pleasure or carefree enjoyment; all drink and play. [Origin uncertain.]

skive (skīv) *tr.v.* **skived, skiving, skives.** To shave or cut off the surface of (leather or rubber); pare. [Ultimately from Old Norse *skīfa,* to slice. See **skei-** in Appendix.*]

skiv·er (skī′vər) *n.* **1.** A soft, thin leather split off the outside of sheepskin and used for bookbinding. **2.** A person who skives. **3.** A knife or other cutting device used in skiving.

skiv·vy (skĭv′ē) *n., pl.* **-vies.** *Slang.* **1.** A man's cotton knit undershirt. Also called "skivvy shirt." **2.** *Plural.* A man's underwear consisting of shirt and shorts. [Origin unknown.]

skoal (skōl) *interj.* Used as a drinking toast. [Norwegian and Danish *skaal* and Swedish *skål,* from Old Norse *skāl,* drinking cup. See **skel-**[1] in Appendix.*]

Skop·lje (skôp′lyĕ, skōp′-). *Macedonian* **Skop·je** (skŏp′yä, skōp′-), *Turkish* **Üs·küb** (üs-küb′). A city of Yugoslavia, the capital of Macedonia, in the south on the Vardar River. Almost completely destroyed by an earthquake in 1963, it has since been largely rebuilt. Population, 270,000.

Skr., Skt. Sanskrit.

sku·a (skyōō′ə) *n.* **1.** A predatory gull-like sea bird, *Catharacta skua,* of northern regions, having brownish plumage. **2.** *British.* A related bird, the jaeger. [New Latin, from Faroese *skūvur,* from Old Norse *skūfr*†, skua, tassel.]

skulk (skŭlk) *intr.v.* **skulked, skulking, skulks.** **1.** To lurk; lie in hiding. **2.** To move about stealthily. **3.** To evade work or obligation; malinger. *—n.* **1.** One who skulks. **2.** *Obsolete.* A company of stealthily moving creatures, especially of foxes. —See Synonyms at **flock.** [Middle English *skulken,* from Scandinavian, akin to Danish *skulke*†.] **—skulk′er** *n.*

skull (skŭl) *n.* **1.** The framework of the head of vertebrates, made up of the bones of the brain case and face. **2.** The head, especially regarded as the seat of thought or intelligence. Usually used disparagingly. **3.** A death's-head. [Middle English *schulle, skulle*†.]

skull and crossbones. A representation of a human skull above two long crossed bones, a symbol of death once used by pirates and now used as a warning label on poisons.

skull·cap (skŭl′kăp′) *n.* **1.** A light, close-fitting, brimless cap sometimes worn indoors. **2.** Any of various plants of the genus *Scutellaria,* having clusters of two-lipped, usually blue or purplish flowers.

skull·dug·ger·y (skŭl-dŭg′ə-rē) *n.* Also **skul·dug·ger·y.** Crafty deception or trickery. [Origin unknown.]

skunk (skŭngk) *n.* **1.** Any of several small, carnivorous New World mammals of the genus *Mephitis* and related genera, having a bushy tail and black fur with white markings and ejecting a malodorous secretion from glands near the anus. Sometimes called "polecat." **2.** *Slang.* A mean or despicable person. *—tr.v.* **skunked, skunking, skunks.** *Slang.* **1.** To defeat overwhelmingly, especially by keeping from scoring. **2.** To cheat, as by failing to pay. [Massachuset *squnck,* from Proto-Algonquian *shekākwa* (unattested) : *shek-* (unattested), to urinate + *-ākw-* (unattested), small mammal.]

skunk cabbage. **1.** An ill-smelling swamp plant, *Symplocarpus foetidus,* of eastern North America, having minute flowers enclosed in a mottled greenish or purplish spathe. **2.** A similar plant, *Lysichitum americanum,* of western North America. Also called "skunkweed."

Skunk River. A river rising in north-central Iowa and flowing 260 miles southeast to the Mississippi.

sky (skī) *n., pl.* **skies.** **1.** The upper atmosphere, appearing as a hemisphere above the earth. **2.** The highest level or degree of something; the ultimate: *reaching for the sky.* **3.** The celestial or heavenly regions. **4. a.** The appearance of the upper air: *blue skies.* **b.** Climate; weather. *—tr.v.* **skied, skying, skies.** **1.** To hit or throw (a ball, for example) high in the air. **2.** To hang (a painting, for example) high up on the wall, above the line of vision, especially in an exhibition. [Middle English, cloud, sky, from Old Norse *sk*ȳ, cloud, from Common Germanic *skewja-* (unattested).]

sky blue. Light to pale blue, from light greenish to light purplish blue. See **color.** **—sky′-blue′** *adj.*

sky·borne (skī′bôrn′, -bōrn′) *adj.* Airborne.

sky·coach (skī′kōch′) *n.* A commercial airliner that offers minimal cabin service and low fares.

sky·dive (skī′dīv′) *intr.v.* **-dived** or *informal* **-dove** (-dōv′), **-dived, -diving, -dives.** *Sports.* To jump from an airplane, performing various maneuvers before pulling the ripcord of a parachute. **—sky′div′er** *n.*

Skye, Isle of (skī). An island of Scotland, the largest (670 square miles) of the Inner Hebrides.

Skye terrier. A small terrier of a breed native to the Isle of Skye, having a long, low body, short legs, and shaggy hair.

sky·ey (skī′ē) *adj.* **1.** Of or from the skies: *skyey influences.* **2.** Resembling the sky. **3.** Lofty.

sky-high (skī′hī′) *adv.* **1.** Exceptionally high. **2.** In a lavish or enthusiastic manner. **3.** In pieces or to pieces; apart. *—adj.* **1.** High up in the air. **2.** Exorbitantly high.

sky·lark (skī′lärk′) *n.* An Old World bird, *Alauda arvensis,* having brownish plumage and noted for its singing while in flight. *—intr.v.* **skylarked, -larking, -larks.** To indulge in frolic.

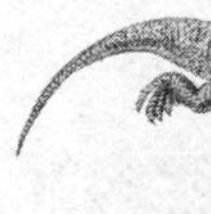

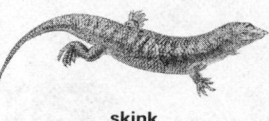

skink

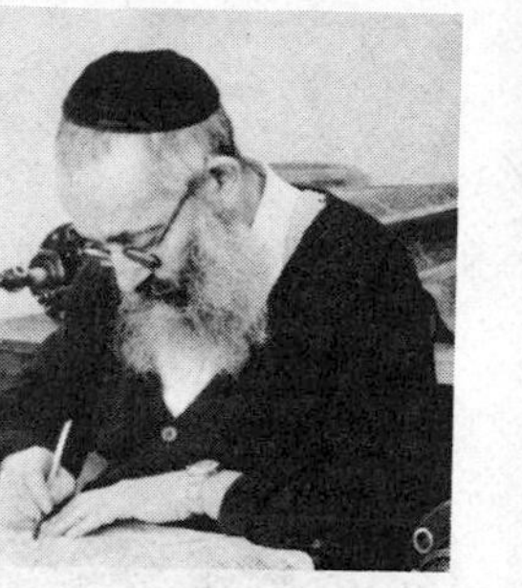

skullcap

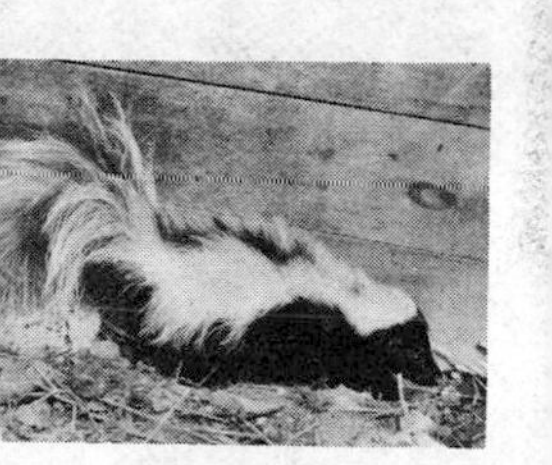

skunk
Mephitis mephitis

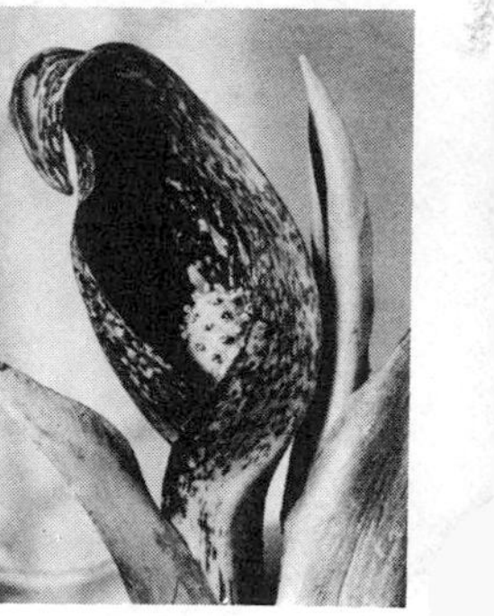

skunk cabbage
Symplocarpus foetidus

sky·light (skī′līt′) *n.* An overhead window admitting daylight.
sky·line (skī′līn′) *n.* **1.** The line along which the surface of the earth and sky appear to meet; the horizon. **2.** The outline of a group of buildings or a mountain range seen against the sky.
sky pilot. *Slang.* A clergyman; a chaplain.
sky·rock·et (skī′rŏk′ĭt) *n.* A firework that ascends high into the air, where it explodes in a brilliant cascade of flares and starlike sparks. —*v.* **skyrocketed, -eting, -ets.** —*intr.* To rise rapidly or suddenly, as in amount, position, reputation, or the like. —*tr.* To cause to rise rapidly.
Sky·ros (skī′rəs, skē′rôs). An island of Greece in the Aegean, the largest (81 square miles) of the Sporades group.
sky·sail (skī′səl, -sāl′) *n.* A small square sail above the royal in a square-rigged vessel.
sky·scrap·er (skī′skrā′pər) *n.* A very tall building.
sky·ward (skī′wərd) *adv.* Also **sky·wards** (-wərdz). Toward the sky. —**sky′ward** *adj.*
sky·way (skī′wā′) *n.* **1.** An airline route; air lane. **2.** An elevated highway.
sky·writ·ing (skī′rī′tĭng) *n.* **1.** The process of writing in the sky by releasing a visible vapor from a flying airplane. **2.** The letters or words thus formed. —**sky′writ′er** *n.*

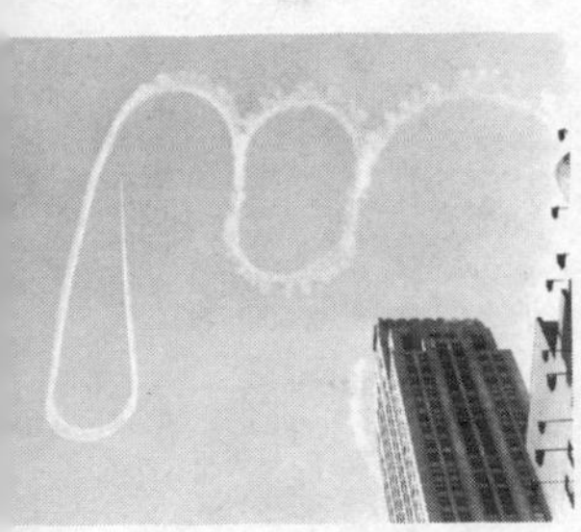
skywriting

sl. slightly.
Sla. See **Salé.**
slab[1] (slăb) *n.* **1.** A broad, flat, somewhat thick piece, as of cake, stone, or cheese. **2.** An outside piece cut from a log when squaring it for lumber. **3.** *Baseball.* The pitcher's plate. —*tr.v.* **slabbed, slabbing, slabs. 1.** To make or shape into a slab or slabs. **2.** To cover or pave with slabs. **3.** To dress (a log) by cutting slabs. [Middle English *s(c)labbe*†.]
slab[2] (slăb) *adj. Archaic.* Viscid. Used in the phrase *thick and slab.* [Probably of Scandinavian origin, akin to Danish *slab,* mud. See **leb-[1]** in Appendix.*]
slab-sid·ed (slăb′sī′dĭd) *adj. Informal.* **1.** Having flat sides. **2.** Tall and slim; lanky; lean.
slack[1] (slăk) *adj.* **1.** Not lively or moving; slow; dull; sluggish. **2.** Not busy; lacking in work: *a slack business season.* **3.** Not tense or taut; loose: *a slack rope.* **4.** Lacking firmness; weak; relaxed: *a slack grip.* **5.** Lacking in diligence; careless; negligent: *a slack secretary.* **6.** Flowing or blowing with little speed. Said of the wind or tide. —*v.* **slacked, slacking, slacks.** —*tr.* **1.** To slacken. **2.** To be remiss about; fail to give proper attention to. **3.** To slake (lime). —*intr.* To be or become slack. —**slack off.** To decrease in activity or intensity; fall off; abate. —*n.* **1.** A loose or slack part or portion of something, such as a rope or sail. **2.** A lack of tension; looseness. **3.** A period of little activity; a lull. **4. a.** A cessation of movement in a current of air or water. **b.** An area of still water. **5.** *Plural.* Separate trousers not part of a suit, for casual wear. —*adv.* In a slack manner: *"His mouth hung slack between laughter and surprise."* (Ivan Gold). [Middle English *slak,* Old English *slæc.* See **slēg-** in Appendix.*] —**slack′ly** *adv.* —**slack′ness** *n.*
slack[2] (slăk) *n.* A mixture of coal fragments, coal dust, and dirt that remains after screening coal. [Middle English *sleck,* probably from Middle Dutch *slacke.* See **slak-** in Appendix.*]
slack[3] (slăk) *n. Scottish & British Informal.* **1.** A small dell or hollow. **2.** A bog; morass. [Middle English *slak,* from Old Norse *slakki*†.]

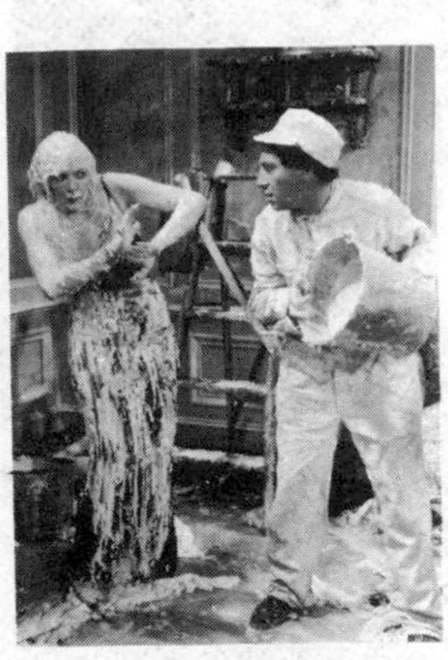
slapstick
"Chico" Marx dousing a girl with paste in a Marx Brothers film

slack-baked (slăk′bākt′) *adj.* **1.** Not perfectly baked; underdone; half-baked. Said chiefly of bread. **2.** Imperfectly made.
slack·en (slăk′ən) *v.* **-ened, -ening, -ens.** —*tr.* **1.** To make slower; slow down: *"As they approached the haystack he very slightly slackened his pace."* (Michael Gilbert). **2.** To make less vigorous, intense, firm, severe, or the like. **3.** To reduce the tension or tautness of; loosen. —*intr.* **1.** To slow down. **2.** To become less energetic, active, firm, strict, or the like. **3.** To become less tense or taut; loosen.
slack·er (slăk′ər) *n.* A person who shirks work or responsibility; especially, one who tries to evade military service in wartime.
slack water. 1. The period at high or low tide when there is no visible flow of water. **2.** An area in a sea or river unaffected by currents; still water.
slag (slăg) *n.* **1.** The vitreous mass left as a residue by the smelting of metallic ore. Also called "cinder." **2.** Volcanic refuse, **scoria** *(see).* —*v.* **slagged, slagging, slags.** —*tr.* To change into slag. —*intr.* To form slag; become slaglike. [Middle Low German *slagge.* See **slak-** in Appendix.*] —**slag′gy** *adj.*
slain. Past participle of **slay.**
slake (slāk) *v.* **slaked, slaking, slakes.** —*tr.* **1.** To quench; allay; satisfy. **2.** To lessen the force or activity of; moderate. **3.** To cool or refresh by wetting or moistening. **4.** To combine (lime) chemically with water or moist air. —*intr.* To undergo a slaking process; crumble or disintegrate, as lime. [Middle English *slaken,* to lessen, diminish, Old English *slacian,* from *slæc,* SLACK (loose).]
slaked lime. *Chemistry.* **Calcium hydroxide** *(see).*
sla·lom (slä′ləm) *n.* **1.** Skiing in a zigzag course. **2.** A race along such a course, laid out with flag-marked poles. [Norwegian, "sloping path" : *sla(d)*†, sloping + *lom, låm,* path, from Northwest Germanic *lanu-* (unattested).]
slam[1] (slăm) *v.* **slammed, slamming, slams.** —*tr.* **1.** To shut with force and loud noise. **2.** To put, throw, or otherwise forcefully move so as to produce a loud noise. **3.** To hit or strike with great force. **4.** *Slang.* To criticize harshly; attack verbally. —*intr.* **1.** To close or swing into place with force so as to produce a loud noise. **2.** To hit something with force; crash. —*n.* **1. a.** A forceful closing or other movement that produces a loud noise. **b.** The noise so produced. **2.** A harsh or devastating criticism. [Perhaps from Scandinavian, akin to Old Norse *slam(b)ra,* to strike at. See **leb-[1]** in Appendix.*]
slam[2] (slăm) *n.* In bridge and other whist-derived card games, the winning of all the tricks *(grand slam)* or all but one *(little slam)* during the play of one hand. [Origin unknown.]
slam-bang (slăm′băng′) *adv.* **1.** Swiftly and noisily. **2.** Recklessly.
s.l.a.n. *Library Service.* without place, year, or name (Latin *sine loco, anno, vel nomine*).
slan·der (slăn′dər) *n.* **1.** *Law.* The utterance of defamatory statements injurious to the reputation or well-being of a person. Compare **libel. 2.** A malicious statement or report. —*v.* **slandered, -dering, -ders.** —*tr.* To utter damaging reports about. —*intr.* To utter or spread slander. —See Synonyms at **malign.** [Middle English *s(c)laundre,* from Old French *esclandre,* variant of *escandle,* from Latin *scandalum,* SCANDAL.] —**slan′der·er** *n.* —**slan′der·ous** *adj.* —**slan′der·ous·ly** *adv.*
slang (slăng) *n.* **1.** The nonstandard vocabulary of a given culture or subculture, consisting typically of arbitrary and often ephemeral coinages and figures of speech characterized by spontaneity and raciness. **2.** Language peculiar to a group; argot or jargon. [Origin obscure.] —**slang′i·ly** *adv.* —**slang′i·ness** *n.* —**slang′y** *adj.*
slant (slănt, slänt) *v.* **slanted, slanting, slants.** —*tr.* **1.** To give an oblique direction to. **2.** To present so as to conform with a particular bias. —*intr.* To incline obliquely. —*n.* **1. a.** A sloping direction, plane, or course; an incline. **b.** Slope; obliquity. **2.** A bias or point of view. [Variant of earlier *slent,* from Middle English *slenten*†.] —**slant′ing·ly** *adv.*
slant·wise (slănt′wīz′, slänt′-) *adv.* Also **slant·ways** (-wāz′). At a slant or slope; obliquely. —*adj.* Slanting; oblique.
slap (slăp) *n.* **1. a.** A smacking blow made with the open hand or with any flat thing. **b.** The sound so made. **2.** An injury, as to one's pride. —*v.* **slapped, slapping, slaps.** —*tr.* **1.** To strike with a flat object, as the palm of the hand. **2.** To criticize or insult sharply. **3.** To put or place with a slapping sound: *"He took a clipping from his wallet and slapped it on the bar."* (Nathanael West). —*intr.* To strike or beat with the force and sound of a slap. —**slap down. 1.** To prohibit from acting in a specific way by means of a sharp blow or emphatic censure. **2.** To put a sudden end to; squelch; suppress. —*adv. Informal.* Directly and with force. [Low German *slapp.* See **leb-[1]** in Appendix.*] —**slap′per** *n.*
slap·dash (slăp′dăsh′) *adj.* Characterized by haste or carelessness. —*adv.* In a reckless, haphazard manner.
slap·hap·py (slăp′hăp′ē) *adj.* **-pier, -piest.** *Slang.* Dazed, silly, or incoherent from or as if from blows to the head.
slap·jack (slăp′jăk′) *n.* **1.** A pancake; flapjack. **2.** A simple card game. [SLAP + (FLAP)JACK.]
slap·stick (slăp′stĭk′) *n.* **1.** Comedy characterized by loud and boisterous farce. **2.** A paddle designed to produce a loud whacking sound, formerly used by actors in farces.
slash (slăsh) *v.* **slashed, slashing, slashes.** —*tr.* **1.** To cut or form by cutting with violent sweeping strokes. **2.** To lash violently with sweeping strokes. **3.** To make a gash or gashes in. **4.** To cut a slit or slits in. **5.** To criticize sharply. **6.** To reduce or curtail drastically. —*intr.* To make violent and sweeping strokes with or as with a sharp instrument. —See Synonyms at **tear.** —*n.* **1.** A sweeping stroke made with a sharp instrument. **2.** A cut or other injury made by such a stroke; a gash; a slit. **3.** An ornamental slit in a fabric or article of clothing. **4.** Branches and other residue left on a forest floor after the cutting of timber. **5.** *Often plural.* Wet or swampy ground overgrown with bushes and trees. **6.** *Printing.* A **virgule** *(see).* [Middle English *slaschen,* perhaps from Old French *esclaschier, esclachier,* to break (imitative).] —**slash′er** *n.*
slash pine. Any of several pine trees of the southeastern United States and adjacent regions, growing in swampy coastal areas.
Śląsk. The Polish name for **Silesia.**
slat (slăt) *n.* **1.** A narrow strip of metal or wood, as in a Venetian blind. **2.** A movable auxiliary airfoil running along the leading edge of the wing of an airplane. **3.** *Plural. Slang.* The ribs. —*tr.v.* **slatted, slatting, slats.** To provide or make with slats. [Middle English *s(c)lat,* from Old French *esclat,* splinter, fragment, from *esclater*†, to splinter.]
slatch (slăch) *n. New England.* **1.** A momentary lull between breaking waves, to be taken advantage of in launching a boat. **2.** A lull in a high windstorm. [Variant of SLACK (not tight).]
slate (slāt) *n.* **1.** A fine-grained metamorphic rock that splits into thin, smooth-surfaced layers. **2. a.** A piece of this material cut for use as roofing material or a writing surface. **b.** A writing tablet made of any material similar to slate. **3.** A record of past performance or activity: *a clean slate.* **4.** A list of the candidates of a particular political party running for various offices. **5.** Dark gray to bluish gray, to dark bluish or dark purplish gray. See **color.** —*tr.v.* **slated, slating, slates. 1.** To cover (a roof, for example) with slate. **2.** To put on a list of candidates. **3.** To designate or destine: *"I was slated to amass wealth beyond the dreams of avarice"* (S.J. Perelman). [Middle English *s(c)late,* from Old French *esclate,* feminine of *esclat,* fragment, splinter. See **slat.**]
slate blue. Grayish blue to dark bluish gray. See **color.** —**slate′-blue′** *adj.*
slat·er (slā′tər) *n.* **1.** One employed to lay slate roofs. **2.** Any of several small isopod crustaceans, such as a sow bug.
slath·er (slăth′ər) *tr.v.* **-ered, -ering, -ers.** *Informal.* **1.** To use great amounts of; to lavish. **2. a.** To spread thickly with. **b.** To spread thickly on. —*n. Slang.* A great amount; a lot. Used in the plural: *slathers of money.* [Origin uncertain.]

slat·ing (slā′tĭng) *n.* **1.** The act, process, or occupation of laying slates. **2.** Slates collectively, used as a building material.

slat·tern (slăt′ərn) *n.* A woman untidy or slovenly in person or habits; slut. [Perhaps variant of dialectal *slattering,* present participle of *slatter,* to spill awkwardly.]

slat·tern·ly (slăt′ərn-lē) *adj.* **1.** Slovenly; untidy: *"electricity took the place of candles and slatternly hearth-fires"* (Sinclair Lewis). **2.** Characteristic of or befitting a slattern. —See Synonyms at **dirty, sloppy.** —**slat′tern·li·ness** *n.*

slaugh·ter (slô′tər) *n.* **1.** The killing of animals for food. **2.** The killing of a large number of persons; carnage; massacre. —*tr.v.* **slaughtered, -tering, -ters. 1.** To kill (animals) for food; to butcher. **2. a.** To kill (persons) in large numbers; massacre. **b.** To kill in a violent or brutal manner. [Middle English *slau(g)hter,* probably from Old Norse *slātr.* See **slak-** in Appendix.*] —**slaugh′ter·er** *n.* —**slaugh′ter·ous** *adj.*

slaugh·ter·house (slô′tər-hous′) *n.* **1.** A place where animals are butchered. **2.** A scene of massacre or carnage.

Slav (släv) *n.* Also *obsolete* **Sclav** (sklăv). Any of the peoples who speak Slavic languages. [Middle English *Sclave,* from Medieval Latin *S(c)lavus,* from Late Greek *Sklabos†.*]

Slav. Slavic.

slave (slāv) *n.* **1.** One bound in servitude to a person or household as an instrument of labor. **2.** One who is submissive or subject to a specified person or influence. **3.** One whose condition is likened to that of slavery. **4.** A machine or component that is controlled by another machine or component. —*intr.v.* **slaved, slaving, slaves.** To work like a slave; to drudge. [Middle English *sclave,* from Old French *esclave,* slave, from Medieval Latin *sclavus,* from *Sclavus,* SLAV (the Slavs were reduced to slavery by conquest).]

slave driver. 1. A severely exacting employer or supervisor. **2.** An overseer of slaves at work.

slav·er[1] (slăv′ər) *intr.v.* **-ered, -ering, -ers. 1.** To slobber. **2.** To fawn; drivel. —*n.* **1.** Saliva drooling from the mouth. **2.** Slobbering flattery or drivel. [Middle English *slaveren,* probably from Old Norse *slafra.* See **leb-**[1] in Appendix.*]

slav·er[2] (slā′vər) *n.* **1.** A ship engaged in slave traffic. **2.** A trafficker of slaves.

Slave River. A river of Canada, flowing 258 miles north from northeastern Alberta to Great Slave Lake in the Northwest Territories.

slav·er·y (slā′və-rē, slāv′rē) *n., pl.* **-ies. 1.** Bondage to a master or household. **2.** A mode of production in which slaves constitute the principal work force. **3.** The condition of being subject or addicted to a specified influence. **4.** A condition of subjection likened to that of a slave: *wage slavery.* —See Synonyms at **servitude.**

Slave State. Any of the 15 states of the Union in which slavery was legal before the Civil War, including Alabama, Arkansas, Delaware, Florida, Georgia, Kentucky, Louisiana, Maryland, Mississippi, Missouri, North Carolina, South Carolina, Tennessee, Texas, and Virginia.

slave trade. Traffic in slaves; specifically, the transportation of black Africans to America for sale as slaves.

Slav·ic (slăv′ĭk) *adj.* Of or pertaining to the Slavs or their languages. —*n. Abbr.* **Slav.** A branch of the Indo-European language family, divided into East Slavic, South Slavic, and West Slavic.

slav·ish (slā′vĭsh) *adj.* **1.** Pertaining to or characteristic of a slave; servile. **2.** Pertaining to or characteristic of the institution of slavery; oppressive. **3.** Blindly dependent on or imitative: *a slavish copy of the original.* **4.** Extremely laborious or difficult. —**slav′ish·ly** *adv.* —**slav′ish·ness** *n.*

Slav·ism (slä′vĭz′əm) *n.* Anything peculiar to or characteristic of the Slavs or the Slavic languages.

Slav·kov. The Czech name for **Austerlitz.**

slav·oc·ra·cy (slă-vŏk′rə-sē) *n., pl.* **-cies.** The power structure formed by the advocates of slavery in the United States before the Civil War. [SLAVE + -CRACY.] —**slav′o·crat′** (-və-krăt′) *n.* —**slav′o·crat′ic** *adj.*

Sla·vo·ni·a (slə-vō′nē-ə). A region of Croatia, Yugoslavia, lying between the Drava and the Sava rivers. —**Sla·vo′ni·an** *adj.* & *n.*

Sla·von·ic (slə-vŏn′ĭk) *adj.* Slavic. —*n.* A Slavic language.

Slav·o·phile (slăv′ə-fīl′) *n.* Also **Slav·o·phil** (-fĭl). **1.** A person who admires the Slavs. **2.** A person who advocates the supremacy of the Slavic, and especially Russian, culture. [SLAV + -PHILE.] —**Sla·voph′i·lism′** (-vŏf′ə-lĭz′əm) *n.*

slaw (slô) *n.* Coleslaw *(see).*

slay (slā) *tr.v.* **slew** (slōō), **slain** (slān), **slaying, slays. 1.** To kill violently, as in battle. **2.** *Slang.* To overwhelm, as with laughter or love: *He slays all the girls.* [Slay, slew, slain; Middle English *slen(en),* slew, slayn, Old English *slēan, slōh, slægen.* See **slak-** in Appendix.*] —**slay′er** *n.*

SLC Airport code for Salt Lake City, Utah.

sld. 1. sailed. **2.** sealed.

sleave (slēv) *tr.v.* **sleaved, sleaving, sleaves.** To separate or disentangle, as a twisted mass of threads. —*n.* **1.** Any tangled or knotted thread or ravel. **2.** A thin thread. [Middle English *sleven* (unattested), Old English *slæfan,* to cut, cut up, akin to *-slīfan,* to splice. See **sliver.**]

sleave silk. Raw untwisted silk; floss, as for embroidery.

slea·zy (slē′zē) *adj.* **-zier, -ziest. 1.** Lacking in firmness; flimsy or thin. Said of fabric. **2.** Made of low-quality materials; cheap; shoddy. **3.** Not substantial or valid: *a sleazy excuse.* [Origin unknown.] —**slea′zi·ly** *adv.* —**slea′zi·ness** *n.*

sled (slĕd) *n.* **1.** A vehicle mounted on runners, used for carrying people or loads over ice and snow; sledge. **2.** A light wooden frame on runners, used by children for coasting over snow or ice. —*v.* **sledded, sledding, sleds.** —*tr.* To carry on or convey by a sled. —*intr.* To ride or use a sled. [Middle English *sledde,* from Middle Low German. See **sleidh-** in Appendix.*] —**sled′der** *n.*

sled·ding (slĕd′ĭng) *n.* **1.** The act of using a sled for hauling, transportation, or sport. **2.** The weather or snow conditions under which one may use a sled. **3.** *Informal.* The going: *The sledding gets tougher every year in this business.*

sledge (slĕdj) *n.* A vehicle on low runners drawn by horses, dogs, or other work animals and used for transporting loads across ice and snow. —*v.* **sledged, sledging, sledges.** —*tr.* To convey on a sledge. —*intr.* To travel on a sledge. [Dutch (dialectal) *sleeds,* from Middle Dutch *sleedse.* See **sleidh-** in Appendix.*]

sledge
Early 18th-century Russian

sledge·ham·mer (slĕdj′hăm′ər) *n.* A long, heavy hammer, often wielded with both hands, used for driving wedges and posts and for other heavy work. —*tr.v.* **sledgehammered, -mering, -mers.** To strike with such a hammer. —*adj.* Ruthlessly severe; crushing. [From Middle English *sleg(g)e,* Old English *slecg.* See **slak-** in Appendix.*]

sleek (slēk) *adj.* **sleeker, sleekest. 1.** Smooth and lustrous as if polished; glossy: *"your small head how sleek and cold with water"* (Edna St. Vincent Millay). **2.** Well-groomed and neatly tailored in appearance. **3.** Healthy or well-fed; thriving. **4.** Polished or smooth in behavior, especially in an unctuous way; slick. —*tr.v.* **sleeked, sleeking, sleeks. 1.** To make lustrous or smooth; to polish. **2.** To gloss over; conceal. [Variant of SLICK.] —**sleek′ly** *adv.* —**sleek′ness** *n.*

sleep (slēp) *n.* **1.** A natural, periodically recurring physiological state of rest, characterized by relative physical and nervous inactivity, unconsciousness, and lessened responsiveness to external stimuli. **2.** A period of this form of rest. **3.** Any similar condition of inactivity, such as unconsciousness, dormancy, or hibernation. **4.** *Botany.* The folding together of leaves or petals at night or in the absence of light. —*v.* **slept** (slĕpt, slēp), **sleeping, sleeps.** —*intr.* **1.** To be in the state of sleep or to fall asleep. **2.** To be in a condition resembling sleep, such as hibernation, dormancy, or death. —*tr.* **1.** To pass or get rid of by sleeping: *went home to sleep it off.* **2.** To provide with accommodations for sleeping. —**sleep around.** *Informal.* To be sexually promiscuous. —**sleep in.** To sleep at one's place of employment. Used of a household servant. —**sleep out.** To sleep at one's own home, not at one's place of employment. Used of a household servant. —**sleep with.** To have sexual intercourse with. [Middle English *slep(e),* sleep, Old English *slæp.* See **leb-**[1] in Appendix.*]

sleep·er (slē′pər) *n.* **1.** A person or animal that sleeps. **2.** A sleeping car on a railroad train. **3.** Any of various usually small marine and freshwater fishes of the family Eleotridae. **4.** *Football.* An offensive player who is stationed in an obscure field position with the hope that he will not be noticed by the other team until after he has performed his function in the play. **5.** *British.* A heavy beam used as a support for rails in a railroad track; crosstie. **6.** *Informal.* Someone or something that achieves unexpected recognition or success, as a race horse, book, or marketed product. **7.** An earmarked unbranded calf.

sleeping bag. A large, warmly lined, usually zippered bag in which a person may sleep outdoors.

sleeping car. A railroad car having accommodations to sleep passengers.

sleeping pill. A sedative, especially a barbiturate, in the form of a pill or capsule used to relieve insomnia.

sleeping sickness. 1. An often fatal, endemic infectious disease of man and animals in tropical Africa, caused by either of two protozoans of the genus *Trypanosoma,* transmitted by the tsetse fly, and characterized by fever and lethargy. **2.** *Pathology.* **Encephalitis lethargica** *(see).*

sleep·less (slēp′lĭs) *adj.* **1.** Without sleep; wakeful; restless; unquiet. **2.** Never sleeping or resting; always alert or active. —**sleep′less·ly** *adv.* —**sleep′less·ness** *n.*

sleep·walk·ing (slēp′wô′kĭng) *n. Pathology.* **Somnambulism** *(see).* —**sleep′walk′er** *n.*

sleep·y (slē′pē) *adj.* **-ier, -iest. 1.** Ready for or needing sleep; drowsy. **2.** Inactive; dull. **3.** Inducing sleep. **4.** Quiet: *a sleepy little town.* —**sleep′i·ness** *n.* —**sleep′i·ly** *adv.*

sleep·y·head (slē′pē-hĕd′) *n. Informal.* A sleepy person.

sleet (slēt) *n.* **1.** Precipitation consisting of generally transparent frozen or partially frozen raindrops. **2.** A mixture of rain and snow or hail. **3.** A thin icy coating that forms when rain or sleet freezes, as on trees or streets. —*intr.v.* **sleeted, sleeting, sleets.** To shower sleet. [Middle English *slete,* Old English *slēte* (unattested). See **sleu-** in Appendix.*] —**sleet′y** *adj.*

sleeve (slēv) *n.* **1.** The part of a garment that covers all or a part of the arm. **2.** Any encasement or shell into which a piece of equipment fits. —**up one's sleeve.** Hidden but accessible. —*tr.v.* **sleeved, sleeving, sleeves.** To furnish or fit with a sleeve or sleeves. [Middle English *slefe,* sleve, Old English *slīf, slēf.* See **sleubh-** in Appendix.*] —**sleeve′less** *adj.*

sleeve coupling. A thin steel cylinder uniting two lengths of shafting or pipe.

sleigh (slā) *n.* A light vehicle mounted on runners for use on snow or ice, having one or more seats and usually drawn by a horse. —*intr.v.* **sleighed, sleighing, sleighs.** To ride in or drive a sleigh. [Dutch (colonial) *slee,* short for *slede,* from Middle Dutch *slēde.* See **sleidh-** in Appendix.*] —**sleigh′er** *n.*

sleight (slīt) *n.* **1.** Deftness; dexterity; skill. **2.** A clever or skillful trick or deception; an artifice; stratagem. [Middle English *sle(i)ght,* from Old Norse *slœgdh,* from *slœgr,* sly. See **slak-** in Appendix.*]

sled
Woodcut of children coasting on sleds

sleigh
Sleighing in Central Park, New York City, in the mid-19th century

ă pat/ā pay/âr care/ä father/b bib/ch church/d deed/ĕ pet/ē be/f fife/g gag/h hat/hw which/ĭ pit/ī pie/îr pier/j judge/k kick/l lid, needle/m mum/n no, sudden/ng thing/ŏ pot/ō toe/ô paw, for/oi noise/ou out/ōō took/ōō boot/p pop/r roar/s sauce/sh ship, dish/
t tight/th thin, path/th this, bathe/ŭ cut/ûr urge/v valve/w with/y yes/z zebra, size/zh vision/ə about, item, edible, gallop, circus/
à *Fr.* ami/œ *Fr.* feu, Ger. schön/ü *Fr.* tu, Ger. über/κH Ger. ich, Scot. loch/N *Fr.* bon. *Follows main vocabulary. †Of obscure origin.

sleight of hand. **1.** Tricks or feats performed by jugglers or magicians so quickly that their manner of execution cannot be observed; legerdemain. **2.** Skill in performing such feats. **3.** The performance of such feats. —**sleight′-of-hand′** *adj.*

slen·der (slĕn′dər) *adj.* **1.** Having little width in proportion to the height or length; gracefully slim: *"She was slender as a willow shoot is slender—and equally graceful, equally erect."* (Frank Norris). **2.** Spare or small in amount or extent; meager; inadequate: *slender wages.* **3.** Having little force or justification; feeble; frail: *only a slender chance for success.* [Middle English *s(c)lendre*†.] —**slen′der·ly** *adv.* —**slen′der·ness** *n.*

slen·der·ize (slĕn′də-rīz′) *v.* **-ized, -izing, -izes.** —*intr.* To become slender or more slender. —*tr.* **1.** To make slender or slim. **2.** To make appear slender.

slept. Past tense and past participle of **sleep.**

Sles·vig. The Danish name for **Schleswig.**

sleuth (slo͞oth) *n.* **1.** *Informal.* A detective. **2.** A **sleuthhound** *(see).* —*v.* **sleuthed, sleuthing, sleuths.** —*tr.* To track or follow. —*intr.* To act as a detective. [Short for SLEUTHHOUND.]

sleuth·hound (slo͞oth′hound′) *n.* **1.** Formerly, a dog used for tracking or pursuing, as a bloodhound. Also called "sleuth." **2.** A detective. [Middle English : *sleuth,* track of an animal, from Old Norse *slōdh*† + HOUND.]

slew[1] (slo͞o) *n.* Also **slue.** *Informal.* A large amount or number; a lot: *a whole slew of her friends.* [Irish Gaelic *sluagh,* from Old Irish *slúag, slóg.* See **sloug-** in Appendix.*]

slew[2]**.** Past tense of **slay.**

slew[3]**.** Variant of **slough** (depression).

slew[4]**.** Variant of **slue** (twist).

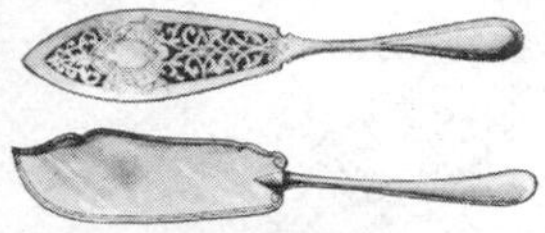

slice
Slices for serving fish

slice (slīs) *n.* **1.** A thin, broad piece cut from a larger object. **2.** A portion or share. **3. a.** A knife with a broad, thin, flexible blade, used for cutting and serving food. **b.** A similar implement for spreading printing ink. **4.** *Sports.* **a.** A stroke that causes a ball to curve off course to the right or, if the player is left-handed, to the left. **b.** The course followed by such a ball. —*v.* **sliced, slicing, slices.** —*tr.* **1.** To cut or divide into slices. **2.** To cut or remove from a larger piece. Often used with *off* or *away.* **3.** To cut through or across with or as if with a knife. **4.** To divide into portions or shares; parcel out. **5.** To spread, work at, or clear away with a bladed tool such as a slice bar. **6.** *Sports.* To hit (a ball) with a slice. —*intr. Sports.* To hit a ball with a slice. [Middle English *s(c)lice,* slice, splinter, from Old French *esclice,* from *esclicer,* to reduce to splinters, from West Germanic *slītjan* (unattested), from Germanic *slītan* (unattested), to SLIT.] —**slice′a·ble** *adj.* —**slic′er** *n.*

slice bar. An iron tool with a flat, broad end, used to loosen and clear out clinkers from furnace grates.

slick (slĭk) *adj.* **1.** Smooth, glossy, and slippery, as if covered with oil or ice. **2.** Deftly executed; adroit; facile. **3.** Shrewd; wily. **4.** Superficially attractive or skillful but without depth or sound quality; meretricious. —*n.* **1.** A smooth or slippery surface or area. **2.** Any of various implements used to make a surface slick; specifically, a chisel used for smoothing and polishing. Also called "slick chisel." **3.** *Informal.* A magazine printed on glossy, high-quality paper, featuring articles and fiction of popular appeal but small literary merit. Compare **pulp. 4.** A racing automobile tire with a smooth tread. —*tr.v.* **slicked, slicking, slicks. 1.** To make smooth, glossy, or oily. **2.** *Informal.* To make neat, trim, or tidy; spruce. Usually used with *up.* [Middle English *slike,* perhaps Old English *slice* (unattested). See **lei-** in Appendix.*]

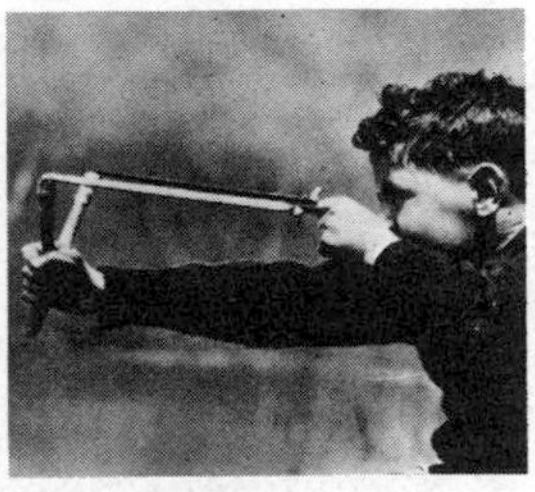

slingshot

slick·en·side (slĭk′ən-sīd′) *n.* A polished and striated rock surface caused by one rock mass sliding over another in a fault plane. [Dialectal *slicken,* glossy, variant of SLICK + SIDE.]

slick·er (slĭk′ər) *n.* **1.** A glossy raincoat, especially one made of oilskin. **2.** A tool for dressing hides. **3.** *Informal.* A cheat; swindler; crook. **4.** *Informal.* A stylish city dweller; a dude.

slide (slīd) *v.* **slid** (slĭd), **slid** or **slidden** (slĭd′n), **sliding, slides.** —*intr.* **1.** To move in smooth, continuous contact with a surface. **2.** To coast on a slippery surface, such as ice or snow. **3.** To pass smoothly and quietly; glide. **4.** To go unattended or unacted upon: *Let it slide.* **5.** To lose one's balance or intended direction on a slippery surface. **6.** *Baseball.* To drop down and skid, usually feet first, into a base to avoid being tagged out. —*tr.* To cause to slide or slip. —*n.* **1.** A sliding movement or action. **2.** A smooth surface or track for sliding, usually inclined: *a toboggan slide.* **3.** A playground apparatus for children to slide upon, typically consisting of a smooth metal chute mounted by means of a ladder. **4.** A part that operates by sliding, as the U-shaped section of tube on a trombone that is moved to produce various tones. **5.** An image on a transparent celluloid plate for projection on a screen. **6.** A small glass plate for mounting specimens to be examined under a microscope. **7.** An avalanche. **8.** *Music.* **a.** A portamento. **b.** An ornamentation consisting of two grace notes approaching the main note. [Slide, slid, slid or slidden; Middle English *sliden, slydde, slide* or *sliden,* Old English *slīdan, -slād, -sliden.* See **sleidh-** in Appendix.*] —**slid′er** *n.*

Synonyms: *slide, slip, glide, coast, skid.* These verbs mean to move smoothly over a surface. *Slide* usually implies rapid and easy movement without loss of contact with the surface. *Slip* more often is applied to accidental movement causing a fall, or threat of a fall, to the surface. *Glide* refers to smooth, free-flowing, and seemingly effortless movement. *Coast* applies specifically to effortless movement due to gravity or inertia. *Skid* generally implies involuntary and uncontrolled movement with much friction.

Slide Mountain. The highest (4,204 feet) of the Catskill Mountains in southeastern New York State.

slide rule. A device consisting essentially of two logarithmically scaled rules mounted to slide along each other so that multiplication, division, and sometimes more complex computations may be reduced to the mechanical equivalent of addition or subtraction.

slide valve. A valve that slides back and forth over ports in the cylinder wall of a steam engine, permitting the intake and outflow of steam to move the piston.

sliding scale. A scale in which indicated prices, taxes, or wages vary in accordance with some other factor, as wages with the cost-of-living index or medical charges with a patient's income.

slight (slīt) *adj.* **slighter, slightest. 1.** Small in size, degree, or amount; meager. **2.** Of small importance or consideration; trifling. **3.** Slender or frail; delicate: *"Slight are her arms, yet they have bound me straitly"* (Ezra Pound). —*tr.v.* **slighted, slighting, slights. 1.** To treat with discourteous reserve or inattention. **2.** To do negligently or thoughtlessly; shirk. **3.** To give insufficient weight or consideration to. —*n.* An act of pointed disrespect or discourtesy; an affront to one's self-esteem. [Middle English *sl(e)ight,* smooth, slight, from Old Norse *slēttr,* smooth, sleek. See **lei-** in Appendix.*] —**slight′ness** *n.*

slight·ing (slī′tĭng) *adj.* Constituting or conveying a slight; disrespectful; discourteous. —**slight′ing·ly** *adv.*

slight·ly (slīt′lē) *adv.* **1.** Carelessly. **2.** *Abbr.* **sl.** To a small degree or extent; somewhat.

Sli·go (slī′gō). **1.** A county of the Republic of Ireland, occupying 694 square miles in the northwest. Population, 54,000. **2.** The county seat of this county, a seaport on the Atlantic coast. Population, 13,000.

slim (slĭm) *adj.* **slimmer, slimmest. 1.** Small in girth or thickness in proportion to height or length; slender. **2.** Small in quality or amount; scant; meager. —*v.* **slimmed, slimming, slims.** —*tr.* To make slim or thin. —*intr.* To become slim. [Dutch, small, inferior, from Middle Dutch *slim,* slanting, bad. See **leb-**[1] in Appendix.*] —**slim′ly** *adv.* —**slim′ness** *n.*

slime (slīm) *n.* **1.** Viscous mud or a similar substance. **2.** A mucous substance secreted by certain animals, as fish or slugs. —*tr.v.* **slimed, sliming, slimes. 1.** To smear with slime. **2.** To remove slime from, as from fish to be canned. [Middle English *slim(e),* Old English *slīm.* See **lei-** in Appendix.*]

slime mold. Any of various fungi of the class Myxomycetes, having a vegetative body consisting of a slimy, motile, multinucleate mass of protoplasm. Also called "slime fungus," "myxomycete," and sometimes "mycetozoan."

slim·sy (slĭm′zē) *adj.* **-sier, -siest.** Also **slimp·sy** (slĭmp′-). *Informal.* Frail; flimsy. [Blend of SLIM and FLIMSY.]

slim·y (slī′mē) *adj.* **-ier, -iest. 1.** Consisting of or resembling slime; viscous. **2.** Covered with or exuding slime. **3.** Vile; filthy; foul. —**slim′i·ly** *adv.* —**slim′i·ness** *n.*

sling[1] (slĭng) *n.* **1. a.** A weapon consisting of a looped strap in which a stone is whirled and then let fly. **b.** A slingshot. **2.** A looped rope, strap, or chain for supporting, cradling, or hoisting something, specifically: **a.** A strap over the heel to hold a shoe in place. **b.** A strap used to carry a rifle over the shoulder. **c.** *Nautical.* A rope or chain for supporting a yard. **d.** A band suspended from the neck to support an injured arm or hand. **3.** The act of slinging. —*tr.v.* **slung** (slŭng), **slinging, slings. 1.** To hurl from or as if from a sling; fling. **2.** To place or carry in a sling. **3.** To move by means of a sling; raise or lower in a sling. **4.** To hang loosely or freely; let swing. —See Synonyms at **throw.** [Middle English, perhaps from Middle Low German *slinge.* See **slenk-** in Appendix.*] —**sling′er** *n.*

sling[2] (slĭng) *n.* A drink of brandy, whiskey, or gin, sweetened and usually lemon-flavored. [Origin unknown.]

sling·shot (slĭng′shŏt′) *n.* A Y-shaped stick with an elastic strap attached to the prongs, used for flinging small stones.

slink (slĭngk) *v.* **slunk** (slŭngk), **slinking, slinks.** —*intr.* To move in a quiet, furtive manner; to sneak: *"Back to the thicket slunk/ The guilty Serpent"* (Milton). —*tr.* To give birth to prematurely. Used especially of cows. —*n.* An animal, especially a calf, born prematurely. —*adj.* Born prematurely. [Middle English *slynken,* Old English *slincan.* See **slenk-** in Appendix.*] —**slink′ing·ly** *adv.*

slink·y (slĭng′kē) *adj.* **-ier, -iest. 1.** Stealthy; furtive; sneaking. **2.** *Informal.* Of feline sleekness and grace.

slip[1] (slĭp) *v.* **slipped, slipping, slips.** —*intr.* **1.** To move quietly and smoothly; glide. **2.** To pass swiftly and imperceptibly. **3. a.** To slide unexpectedly and by accident; lose one's balance. **b.** To slide out of place; shift position. **c.** To escape, as from a fastening or grip. **4.** To get away completely; be lost: *letting chances slip by.* **5.** To go gradually into or out of an opinion, practice, or condition. **6.** *Informal.* To decline in physical or mental ability, strength, or keenness. **7.** *Informal.* To decline; fall off. **8.** To fall behind a scheduled production rate. **9.** To fall into fault or error. —*tr.* **1.** To cause to move in a smooth, easy, or sliding motion. **2.** To place or insert smoothly and quietly. **3.** To put on or remove (clothing) easily or quickly. **4.** To free oneself or itself from; get loose from. **5.** To pass out of; escape unnoticed. **6.** To bring forth (young) prematurely. Used of animals. **7.** To unleash or free (a dog or hawk) to pursue game. **8.** To release; loose; unfasten: *slip the knot.* **9.** To dislocate (a bone). **10.** *Knitting.* To pass (a stitch) from one needle to another without knitting it. —See Synonyms at **slide.** —**let slip.** To say inadvertently. —**slip one over on.** *Informal.* To hoodwink; trick. —**slip over.** To omit; neglect. —**slip up.** *Informal.* **1.** To make a mistake; err. **2.** To go awry; miscarry. —*n.* **1.** The act of slipping or sliding. **2.** An accident; mishap; especially, a falling down. **3. a.** An error in conduct or thinking; a deviation. **b.** A slight error or oversight in speech or writing. **4. a.** A docking place for a ship; pier. **b.** A space for a ship between two docks or wharves. **c.** A **slipway** (*see*). **5.** The difference between a vessel's actual speed through water and the speed at which the vessel would move if the screw were propelling against a solid. **6.** A woman's undergarment of any of various lengths, serving as a lining for a dress. **7.** A pillowcase. **8.** *Geology.* **a.** A smooth crack at which rock strata have moved on each other. **b.** A small fault. **9.** The difference between optimal and actual output in a mechanical device. **10.** Movement between two parts where none should exist, as between a pulley and belt. **11.** *Aviation.* The sliding movement of an airplane in certain attitudes of the plane. See **sideslip.** —**give (someone) the slip.** *Slang.* To escape the company of. [Middle English *slippen,* to slip, slip away, probably from Middle Low German. See **lei-** in Appendix.*]

slip² (slĭp) *n.* **1.** A part of a plant cut or broken off for grafting or planting; a scion or cutting. **2.** Any long, narrow piece; a strip. **3.** A youthful, slender person: *a slip of a girl.* **4.** A small piece of paper; especially, a small form or list: *a sales slip.* **5.** A narrow pew in a church. —*tr.v.* **slipped, slipping, slips.** To make a slip from (a plant or plant part). [Middle English *slippe,* a strip.]

slip³ (slĭp) *n.* Thinned potter's clay used for decorating or coating ceramics. [Middle English *slyppe,* a soft mass, curds, mud, Old English *slypa,* slime. See **sleubh-** in Appendix.*]

slip·case (slĭp′kās′) *n.* An open-ended protective box for a book.

slip·cov·er (slĭp′kŭv′ər) *n.* A fitted, removable cover of cloth or other material for a piece of upholstered furniture. —*tr.v.* **slipcovered, -ering, -ers.** To provide with a slipcover.

slip·knot (slĭp′nŏt′) *n.* **1.** A knot made with a loop so that it slips easily along the rope or cord around which it is tied. Also called "running knot." **2.** A knot made so that it can readily be untied by pulling one free end.

slip-on (slĭp′ŏn′, -ôn′) *adj.* Designed to be easily donned or removed. —*n.* A slip-on garment, such as a blouse.

slip·o·ver (slĭp′ō′vər) *adj.* Designed to be put on or taken off over the head. —*n.* A slipover garment, such as a sweater.

slip·page (slĭp′ĭj) *n.* **1.** A slipping. **2.** The amount or extent of slipping. **3.** Loss of motion or power due to slipping.

slip·per (slĭp′ər) *n.* A light, low shoe, worn mainly indoors, that may be slipped on and off easily.

slip·per·wort (slĭp′ər-wûrt′, -wôrt′) *n.* A plant, the **calceolaria** (*see*).

slip·per·y (slĭp′ə-rē) *adj.* **-ier, -iest. 1.** Causing or tending to cause sliding or slipping, as a waxed, greasy, or wet surface. **2.** Tending to slip or slide, as from one's grasp. **3.** Elusive; evasive; untrustworthy: *"how extraordinarily slippery a liar the camera is"* (James Agee). [Variant of obsolete *slipper,* from Middle English *sli(p)per,* Old English *slipor.* See **lei-** in Appendix.*] —**slip′per·i·ly** *adv.* —**slip′per·i·ness** *n.*

slippery elm. A tree, *Ulmus rubra,* of eastern North America, having twigs and leaves with a mucilaginous, aromatic juice formerly used medicinally.

slip ring. A metal ring mounted on a rotating part of a machine to provide a continuous electrical connection through brushes on stationary contacts.

slip-sheet (slĭp′shēt′) *n. Printing.* A blank sheet of paper slipped between newly printed sheets to prevent offsetting. —*tr.v.* **slip-sheeted, -sheeting, -sheets.** *Printing.* To insert blank sheets between (printed sheets).

slip·shod (slĭp′shŏd′) *adj.* **1.** Poorly made or done; careless. **2.** Slovenly in appearance; shabby; seedy. [Originally "wearing slippers or loose shoes" : SLIP + SHOD.]

slip·slop (slĭp′slŏp′) *n.* **1.** *Archaic.* Unappetizing liquid or watery food; slops. **2.** Trivial conversation or writing; twaddle. [Reduplication of SLOP.]

slip-stitch (slĭp′stĭch′) *n.* A stitch used wherever stitching must be invisible on the right side of a garment, as on hems and facings, made by picking up one or two threads of fabric and then loosely catching the needle in the hem edge.

slip-stream (slĭp′strēm′) *n.* The turbulent flow of air driven backward by the propeller or propellers of an aircraft. Also called "race."

slip-up (slĭp′ŭp′) *n. Informal.* An error; oversight; mistake.

slip·way (slĭp′wā′) *n.* A sloping incline leading down to the water, on which ships are built or repaired. Also called "slip."

slit (slĭt) *n.* **1.** A long, narrow cut or tear. **2.** A long, narrow opening. —*tr.v.* **slit, slitting, slits. 1.** To make a long, narrow incision in. **2.** To cut lengthwise into strips; split. —See Synonyms at **tear.** [Middle English *slitte,* perhaps Old English *geslit,* a tearing, akin to *slītan,* to slit, from German *slīzan* (unattested).]

slith·er (slĭth′ər) *v.* **-ered, -ering, -ers.** —*intr.* **1.** To slip and slide, as on a loose or uneven surface: *"I tried mechanically to get my body on its feet but they slithered under me"* (William Golding). **2.** To move along by gliding, as a snake. —*tr.* To cause to slither or glide. —*n.* A slithering movement or gait. [Middle English *slideren,* Old English *slid(o)rian,* frequentative of *slidan,* to SLIDE.] —**slith′er·y** *adj.*

slit trench. A narrow, shallow trench dug during combat for the protection of a single soldier or a small group.

sliv·er (slĭv′ər) *n.* **1.** A slender piece cut, split, or broken off; a splinter. **2.** A continuous strand of loose wool, flax, or cotton, ready for drawing and twisting. —*v.* **slivered, -ering, -ers.** —*tr.* To split, cut, or form into splinters. —*intr.* To become split into slivers. [Middle English *slivere,* from *slyven,* to cleave, split, Old English *-slīfan* (unattested). See also **sleave.**]

sli·vo·vitz (slĭv′ə-vĭts) *n.* A dry, colorless plum brandy. [Ser-

bo-Croatian *šljivovica,* from *šljiva,* plum. See **slī-** in Appendix.*]

Sloan (slōn), **Alfred Pritchard.** 1875–1966. American industrialist and philanthropist; chairman of the board of General Motors Corporation (1937–56).

Sloan (slōn), **John.** 1871–1951. American painter.

slob (slŏb) *n. Informal.* An obnoxious, crude, or slovenly person. [Irish *slab,* mud, probably from Scandinavian. See **leb-¹** in Appendix.*]

slob·ber (slŏb′ər) *v.* **-bered, -bering, -bers.** —*intr.* **1.** To let saliva dribble from the mouth; to slaver. **2.** To spill (liquid or food, for example) from the mouth while eating or drinking. **3.** To indulge in mawkish sentimentality in speech or writing. —*tr.* To wet or smear with or as if with saliva or food dribbled from the mouth. —*n.* **1.** Saliva or liquid running from the mouth; drivel; slaver. **2.** Oversentimental speech or writing. [Middle English *sloberen,* perhaps of Low German origin, akin to Low German *slubberen.* See **leb-¹** in Appendix.*] —**slob′ber·er** *n.* —**slob′ber·y** *adj.*

sloe (slō) *n.* **1.** A shrub, the **blackthorn** (*see*). **2.** The tart, blue-black, plumlike fruit of this shrub. [Middle English *slo(o),* Old English *slā(h).* See **slī-** in Appendix.*]

sloe-eyed (slō′īd′) *adj.* Having soft, slanted, dark eyes.

sloe gin. A liqueur having a gin base, flavored with fresh sloes.

slog (slŏg) *v.* **slogged, slogging, slogs.** —*tr.* To strike with heavy blows, as in boxing. —*intr.* **1.** To walk with a slow, plodding gait. **2.** To work diligently for long hours. —*n.* **1.** Long, hard work. **2.** A long, exhausting march or hike. [Origin unknown.] —**slog′ger** *n.*

slo·gan (slō′gən) *n.* **1.** Originally, a battle cry of the Scottish clans. **2.** The catchword or motto of a political party, fraternity, school, or other group. **3.** A catch phrase used in advertising or promotion. [Earlier (Scottish) *slog(g)orne,* from Gaelic *sluagh-ghairm* : *sluagh,* host (see **sloug-** in Appendix*) + *gairm,* shout, cry, call, from Old Irish (see **gar-** in Appendix*).]

sloop (sloōp) *n. Nautical.* A single-masted, fore-and-aft-rigged sailing boat with a short standing bowsprit or none at all and a single headsail set from the forestay. Compare **cutter.** [Dutch *sloep.* See **sleubh-** in Appendix.*]

sloop of war. A small, armed vessel larger than a gunboat, carrying guns on one deck only.

slop¹ (slŏp) *n.* **1.** Liquid spilled or splashed. **2.** Soft mud or slush. **3.** Unappetizing, watery food or soup. **4.** *Usually plural.* Waste food used to feed pigs or other animals; swill. **5.** *Often plural.* Mash remaining after the process of alcohol distillation. **6.** *Often plural.* Human excrement. **7.** Repulsively effusive writing or speaking. —*v.* **slopped, slopping, slops.** —*intr.* **1.** To spill or splash, as a liquid. **2.** To spill over; overflow. **3.** To gush with excessive sentimentality. Often used with *over.* **4.** To plod or tramp awkwardly as if walking through mud: *"he slopped along in broken slippers, hands in pockets, whistling"* (Alan Sillitoe). —*tr.* **1.** To spill (liquid). **2.** To spill liquid upon. **3.** To dish out or serve unappetizingly or clumsily. **4.** To feed slops to (animals). [Middle English *sloppe,* a muddy place, probably Old English *sloppe* (unattested). See **sleubh-** in Appendix.*]

slop² (slŏp) *n.* **1.** *Plural.* Articles of clothing and bedding issued to sailors from a ship's stores. **2.** *Plural.* Short, full trousers or breeches worn in the 16th century. **3.** A loose outer garment, as a smock or overalls. **4.** *Plural. Chiefly British.* Cheap, ready-made garments. [Middle English *sloppe,* a kind of garment, perhaps Old English *(ofer)slop,* surplice. See **sleubh-** in Appendix.*]

slope (slōp) *v.* **sloped, sloping, slopes.** —*intr.* **1.** To incline upward or downward; lie on a slant. **2.** To move on a slant; ascend or descend. —*tr.* To cause to slope. —*n.* **1.** Any inclined line, surface, plane, position, or direction. **2.** A stretch of ground forming a natural or artificial incline: *ski slopes.* **3.** Any deviation from the horizontal. **4.** The amount or degree of such deviation. **5.** *Mathematics.* The rate at which an ordinate of a point of a line on a coordinate plane changes with respect to a change in its abscissa. [From Middle English *slope,* sloping, short for *aslope,* perhaps Old English *āslopen* (unattested), past participle of *āslūpan,* to slip away : *ā-,* away + *slūpan,* to slip (see **sleubh-** in Appendix*).] —**slop′er** *n.* —**slop′ing·ly** *adv.*

slop·py (slŏp′ē) *adj.* **-pier, -piest. 1.** Of, like, or covered with slop; splashy; muddy. **2.** Watery and unappetizing: *a sloppy stew.* **3.** Spotted or splashed with liquid or slop. **4.** *Informal.* Untidy; messy. **5.** *Informal.* Careless; slipshod. **6.** *Informal.* Oversentimental; maudlin. —**slop′pi·ly** *adv.* —**slop′pi·ness** *n.*

Synonyms: *sloppy, slovenly, slatternly, blowzy, frowzy, dowdy, unkempt, untidy.* These adjectives refer principally to appearance and indicate lack of care and of qualities that constitute neatness. *Sloppy* informally describes persons or things deficient in cleanliness or orderliness or both. Applied to things, it can also describe inferior quality caused by careless or slipshod work. *Slovenly* is often interchangeable with *sloppy* but applies more often to personal appearance and habits. *Slatternly* refers to lack of cleanliness and neatness in women. *Blowzy* suggests the appearance of a stout, coarse, ruddy-faced woman with disheveled attire. *Frowzy* implies disordered personal appearance and, often, uncleanliness that is offensive. *Dowdy* suggests drabness and tasteless dress in women. *Unkempt* applies to appearance of both persons and things and implies marked lack of care or maintenance. *Untidy,* the least forceful of these terms, refers to persons and things in the broad sense of being deficient in orderliness and care.

slop·work (slŏp′wûrk′) *n.* **1.** The manufacture of cheap ready-made clothes. **2.** Such clothes themselves. **3.** Any work of inferior quality.

John Sloan

sloop
The *Intrepid,* winner of the America's Cup in 1967

ă pat/ā pay/âr care/ä father/b bib/ch church/d deed/ĕ pet/ē be/f fife/g gag/h hat/hw which/ĭ pit/ī pie/îr pier/j judge/k kick/l lid, needle/m mum/n no, sudden/ng thing/ŏ pot/ō toe/ô paw, for/oi noise/ou out/ŏŏ took/

t tight/th thin, path/*th* this, bathe/ŭ cut/ûr urge/v valve/w with/y yes/z zebra, size/zh vision/ə about, item, edible, gallop, circus/ à Fr. ami/œ Fr. feu, Ger. schön/ü Fr. tu, Ger. über/KH Ger. ich, *Scot.* loch/N Fr. bon. *Follows main vocabulary. †Of obscure origin.

slosh (slŏsh) *v.* **sloshed, sloshing, sloshes.** —*tr.* **1.** To stir or splash (a liquid). **2.** To agitate in a liquid: *slosh clothes in a bleach solution.* —*intr.* To splash or flounder in water or another liquid. —*n.* **1.** Slush. **2.** The sound of splashing liquid. [Variant of SLUSH.] —**slosh'y** *adj.*

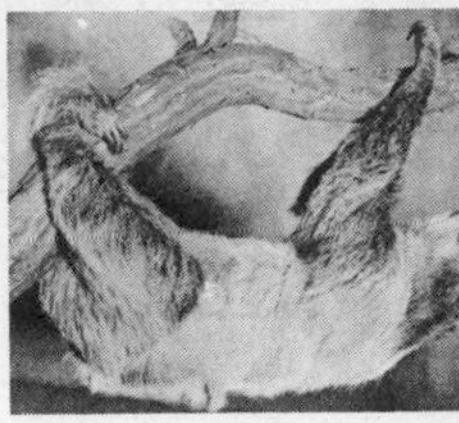

sloth
Choloepus didactylus
Two-toed sloth

slot[1] (slŏt) *n.* **1.** A long, narrow groove, opening, or notch, as for receiving coins in a vending machine. **2.** A gap between a main and an auxiliary airfoil to provide space for airflow and facilitate the smooth passage of air over the wing. —*tr.v.* **slotted, slotting, slots.** To cut or make a slot or slots in. [Middle English, hollow between the breasts, from Old French *esclot*†.]
slot[2] (slŏt) *n.* The track or trail of an animal, especially a deer. [Old French *esclot*, horse's hoofprint, probably from Old Norse *slōdh*, animal's track. See **sleuthhound.**]
sloth (slōth, slôth, slŏth) *n.* **1.** Aversion to work or exertion; laziness; indolence; sluggishness. **2.** Any of various slow-moving, arboreal mammals of the family Bradypodidae, of tropical America, including: **a.** Any member of the genus *Bradypus*, having three long-clawed toes on each foot. Also called "ai." **b.** Any member of the genus *Choloepus*, having two toes on the forefeet and three on the hind feet. Also called "unai." **3.** A company of bears. —See Synonyms at **flock.** [Middle English *slowthe*, from *slow*, SLOW.]
sloth bear. A bear, *Melursus ursinus*, of south-central Asia, having a long snout and dark, shaggy hair.

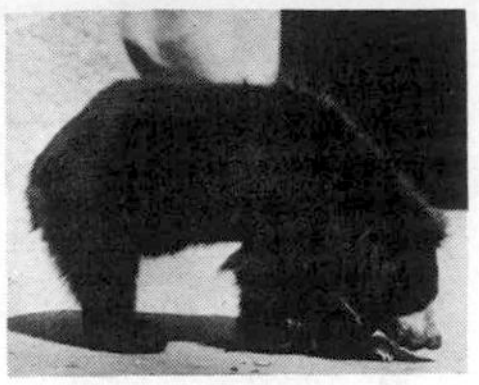

sloth bear

sloth·ful (slōth'fəl, slôth'-, slŏth'-) *adj.* Lazy; indolent; sluggish. —**sloth'ful·ly** *adv.* —**sloth'ful·ness** *n.*
slot machine. A vending or gambling machine having a slot or slots through which coins are inserted in order to operate it.
slouch (slouch) *v.* **slouched, slouching, slouches.** —*intr.* **1.** To sit, stand, or walk with an awkward, drooping posture; assume an excessively relaxed position. **2.** To droop or hang carelessly, as a hat. —*tr.* To cause to droop. —*n.* **1.** A drooping posture or position. **2.** An awkward, lazy, or inept person. [Origin uncertain.] —**slouch'i·ly** *adv.* —**slouch'i·ness** *n.* —**slouch'y** *adj.*
slouch hat. A soft hat with a broad, flexible brim.
slough[1] (slo͞o, slou *for senses 1, 2;* slou, slo͞o *for sense 3; British* slou) *n.* Also **slew** (slo͞o), **slue** (for sense 2). **1.** A depression or hollow, usually filled with deep mud or mire. **2.** A stagnant swamp, marsh, bog, or pond, especially as part of a bayou, inlet, or backwater. **3.** A state of deep despair or moral degradation. [Middle English *slo(g)h*, Old English *slōh*. See **slek-** in Appendix.*]
slough[2] (slŭf) *n.* **1.** The dead outer skin shed by a snake or amphibian. **2.** *Medicine.* Dead tissue separated from a living structure. **3.** Any outer layer or covering that is shed. —*v.* **sloughed, sloughing, sloughs.** —*intr.* **1.** To be cast off or shed; come off. **2.** To shed a slough. **3.** *Medicine.* To separate from surrounding tissue. Used of dead tissue. —*tr.* To get rid of; discard as undesirable or unfavorable. Often used with *off.* [Middle English *slugh(e), slouh*, possibly of Low German origin, akin to Low German *slu(we)*, husk, shell, from Common Germanic *slūhwō* (unattested).] —**slough'y** *adj.*

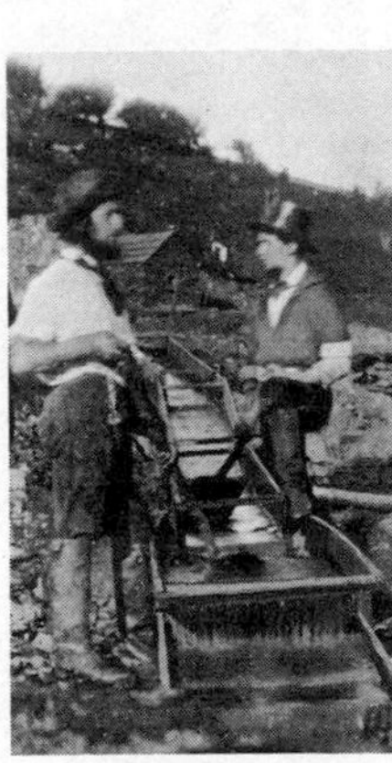

sluice
Daguerreotype of gold miners at a sluice for separating the ore

Slough (slou). A city in southeastern Buckinghamshire, England, 18 miles west of London. Population, 86,000.
Slo·vak (slō'väk', -văk') *n.* Also **Slo·vak·i·an** (slō-vä'kē-ən, -văk'ē-ən). **1.** Any of a Slavic people living in Slovakia. **2.** The West Slavic language of these people, closely related to Czech. —*adj.* Also **Slo·vak·i·an.** Of or pertaining to Slovakia, the Slovaks, or their language. [Slovak *Slovák.*]
Slo·vak·i·a (slō-vä'kē-ə). *Czech* **Slo·ven·sko** (slô-vĕn'skô). The eastern region and a former province of Czechoslovakia.
slov·en (slŭv'ən) *n.* One who is careless in his personal appearance or work. [Middle English *sloveyn*, perhaps from Middle Dutch *sloft*†, negligent.]
Slo·vene (slō'vēn') *n.* **1.** A native or inhabitant of Slovenia. **2.** The South Slavic language spoken in Slovenia. —*adj.* Of or pertaining to the language or inhabitants of Slovenia.
Slo·ve·ni·a (slō-vē'nē-ə). A republic of Yugoslavia, occupying 7,796 square miles in the northwest. Population, 1,592,000. Capital, Ljubljana. —**Slo·ve'ni·an** *adj. & n.*
slov·en·ly (slŭv'ən-lē) *adj.* **-lier, -liest. 1.** Having the habits or appearance of a sloven. **2. a.** Untidy; messy. **b.** Careless; marked by negligence; slipshod. —See Synonyms at **dirty, sloppy.** —**slov'en·li·ness** *n.* —**slov'en·ly** *adv.*

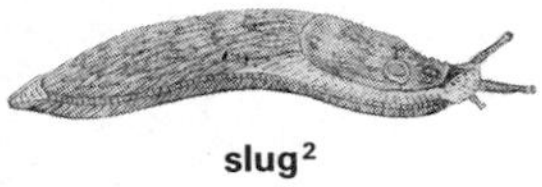

slug[2]

slow (slō) *adj.* **slower, slowest. 1. a.** Not moving or able to move quickly; proceeding at a low speed: *a slow boat.* **b.** Marked by a low speed or tempo: *a slow waltz.* **2. a.** Taking or requiring a long time: *the slow job of making bread.* **b.** Taking more time than is usual: *a slow worker.* **c.** Gradual: *slow progress.* **3. a.** Registering a time or rate behind or below the correct one: *a slow clock.* **b.** Not on time; tardy: *The train is slow today.* **4.** Lacking in promptness or willingness; not precipitate: *slow to accept.* **5.** Sluggish; inactive: *Business was slow.* **6.** *Informal.* Lacking in life or interest; boring: *a slow party.* **7.** Mentally dull; obtuse: *a slow student.* **8.** Only moderately warm; low: *a slow oven.* —See Synonyms at **stupid.** —*adv.* **1.** So as to fall behind: *The watch runs slow.* **2.** Slowly. —See Usage note below. —*v.* **slowed, slowing, slows.** —*tr.* **1.** To make slow or slower. **2.** To delay; retard. Often used with *up* or *down.* —*intr.* To become slow or slower; go slowly or more slowly. Often used with *up* or *down.* —See Synonyms at **delay.** [Middle English *slow, slaw*, Old English *slāw*, from Germanic *slǣwaz* (unattested).] —**slow'ly** *adv.* —**slow'ness** *n.*
Synonyms: *slow, dilatory, leisurely, laggard, deliberate.* These adjectives describe persons or their actions that in general take more time than is necessary. *Slow* is the least specific and not necessarily unfavorable in its implication. *Dilatory* implies fault, such as waste of time, procrastination, or indifference. *Leisurely* suggests lack of pressure or of awareness of a deadline. *Laggard* implies loitering or falling behind through indifference or lack of effort. *Deliberate* applies to one whose lack of speed in acting traces to self-restraint, careful consideration of each move, desire to avoid error, or the like.
Usage: *Slow* and *slowly* are both adverbs. *Slow* is more often encountered in speech and dialogue, in commands and exhortations *(Drive slow)*, and where forcefulness is otherwise sought. In general, *slowly* is preferred in written usage, especially formal, when it accommodates the sense desired as well as *slow.* Sense and established idiom are the main factors in determining a choice. Often *slow* and *slowly* are interchangeable. But *slow* is the established idiomatic form with certain senses of common verbs: *This watch runs slow* (loses time); *Trains are running slow* (behind schedule); *Go slow* or *Take it slow* (figuratively, proceed on a course of action).
slow·down (slō'doun') *n.* A slackening of pace; especially, an intentional slowing down of production by labor or management.
slow match. A fuse that burns slowly, used to set off explosives.
slow-mo·tion (slō'mō'shən) *adj.* **1.** Denoting motion pictures in which the action as projected appears to be slower than the original action. **2.** Moving or operating at below normal speed.
slow neutron. A neutron in thermal equilibrium with the surrounding medium, especially one produced by fission, slowed by a moderator, and having an average speed of approximately 2,200 meters per second. Also called "thermal neutron."
slow·poke (slō'pōk') *n. Informal.* One who moves, works, or acts slowly.
slow-wit·ted (slō'wĭt'ĭd) *adj.* Slow to comprehend; dull; stupid. —**slow'wit'ted·ly** *adv.* —**slow'wit'ted·ness** *n.*
slow·worm (slō'wûrm') *n.* A limbless European lizard, *Anguis fragilis*, having a smooth, snakelike body. Also called "blindworm." [Middle English *slowurm*, Old English *slāwyrm* : *slā*, perhaps "slime" (see **lei-** in Appendix*) + *wyrm*, WORM.]
sloyd (sloid) *n.* A system of manual training developed in Sweden, based upon woodcarving and joinery as exercises in the use of tools. [Swedish *slöjd*, skill, skilled labor, from Old Norse *slœgdh*, SLEIGHT.]
slub (slŭb) *tr.v.* **slubbed, slubbing, slubs.** To draw out and twist (a sliver of silk or other textile fiber) in preparation for spinning. —*n.* **1.** A soft, thick nub in yarn that is either an imperfection or purposely set for a desired effect. **2.** A slightly twisted roll of fiber, as of silk or cotton. [Origin unknown.]
sludge (slŭj) *n.* **1.** Mud, mire, or ooze covering the ground or forming a deposit, as on a river bed. **2.** Slushy matter or sediment such as that precipitated by the treatment of sewage or collected in a boiler. **3.** Finely broken or half-formed ice on a body of water. [Probably an expressive formation.] —**sludg'y** *adj.*
slue[1] (slo͞o) *v.* **slued, sluing, slues.** Also **slew.** —*tr.* **1.** To turn or twist (something) sideways. **2.** To twist (a mast or boom) around on its axis. —*intr.* To turn, twist, move, or skid to the side. —*n.* Also **slew. 1.** The act of sluing. **2.** The position to which something has slued. [Origin unknown.]
slue[2]. Variant of **slew** (a large number).
slue[3]. Variant of **slough** (backwater).
slug[1] (slŭg) *n.* **1.** A round bullet larger than buckshot. **2.** *Informal.* A shot of liquor. **3.** A small metal disk for use in a slot machine; especially, one used illegally. **4.** A lump of metal or glass ready to be processed. **5.** *Printing.* **a.** A strip of type metal, less than type-high and thicker than a lead, used for spacing. **b.** A line of cast type in a single strip of metal. **c.** A compositor's type line of identifying marks or instructions, inserted temporarily in copy. **6.** *Physics.* The unit of mass that is accelerated at the rate of one foot per second per second when acted upon by a force of one pound weight. Also called "geepound." —*tr.v.* **slugged, slugging, slugs.** *Printing.* To add slugs to. [Probably from the animal SLUG (from its shape).]
slug[2] (slŭg) *n.* **1.** Any of various terrestrial gastropod mollusks of the genus *Limex* and related genera, having an elongated body with no external shell. **2.** The smooth, soft larva of certain insects, such as the sawfly. **3.** *Informal.* A lazy person; a sluggard. [Middle English *slugge*, slow-moving person or animal, probably from Scandinavian, akin to Norwegian (dialectal) *slugg.* See **sleu-** in Appendix.*]
slug[3] (slŭg) *tr.v.* **slugged, slugging, slugs.** To strike heavily, especially with the fist. —*n.* A hard, heavy blow, as with the fist or a baseball bat. [Perhaps from SLUG (bullet).]
slug·a·bed (slŭg'ə-bĕd') *n.* One inclined to stay in bed out of laziness. [SLUG (sluggard) + ABED.]
slug·fest (slŭg'fĕst') *n. Slang.* **1.** A fight marked by a vicious exchange of blows. **2.** A baseball game in which many hits and runs are scored.
slug·gard (slŭg'ərd) *n.* A slothful person; an idler. —*adj.* Lazy. [Middle English *sluggart*, probably from *sluggen*, to be lazy, from Scandinavian, akin to Swedish (dialectal) *slugga.* See **sleu-** in Appendix.*] —**slug'gard·ly** *adv.* —**slug'gard·ness** *n.*
slug·ger (slŭg'ər) *n.* **1.** One that slugs, as a fighter who swings out with his fists. **2.** *Baseball.* A hard hitter.
slug·gish (slŭg'ĭsh) *adj.* **1.** Displaying little movement or activity; slow; inactive. **2.** Lacking in alertness, vigor, or energy; dull; lazy. **3.** Slow to perform or respond to stimulation. [Middle English, perhaps from *sluggen*, to be lazy. See **sluggard.**] —**slug'gish·ly** *adv.* —**slug'gish·ness** *n.*
sluice (slo͞os) *n.* **1.** A man-made channel for conducting water with a valve or gate to regulate the flow. **2.** The body of water

ă pat/ā pay/âr care/ä father/b bib/ch church/d deed/ĕ pet/ē be/f fife/g gag/h hat/hw which/ĭ pit/ī pie/îr pier/j judge/k kick/l lid, needle/m mum/n no, sudden/ng thing/ŏ pot/ō toe/ô paw, for/oi noise/ou out/o͝o took/o͞o boot/p pop/r roar/s sauce/sh ship, dish/

so regulated or held back. **3.** The valve or gate used in a sluice. Also called "sluice gate." **4.** Any artificial channel, especially one for carrying off excess water. Also called "sluiceway." **5.** A long inclined trough, as for carrying logs or separating gold ore. —*v.* **sluiced, sluicing, sluices.** —*tr.* **1. a.** To flood or drench by means of a sluice. **b.** To wash with a sudden flow of water; to flush. **2.** To draw off or let out by a sluice. **3.** To send (logs) down a sluice. —*intr.* To flow out from or as if from a sluice. [Middle English *scluse,* from Old French *excluse,* from Gallo-Roman *exclūsa* (unattested), from the feminine past participle of Latin *exclūdere,* to shut out, EXCLUDE.]

slum (slŭm) *n.* A heavily populated urban area characterized by poor housing and squalor. —*intr.v.* **slummed, slumming, slums.** To visit a slum, especially from curiosity or for amusement. Usually used in the phrase *go slumming.* [Origin obscure.]

slum·ber (slŭm′bər) *v.* **-bered, -bering, -bers.** —*intr.* **1.** To sleep or doze. **2.** To be dormant or quiescent. —*tr.* To pass (time) in sleep. —*n.* **1.** Sleep. **2.** A state of inactivity or dormancy. [Middle English *slum(b)eren,* perhaps frequentative of *slumen,* to doze, probably from *slume,* sleep, Old English *slūma.* See **sleu-** in Appendix.*] —**slum′ber·er** *n.* —**slum′ber·ing·ly** *adv.*

slum·ber·ous (slŭm′bər-əs) *adj.* Also **slum·ber·y** (-bə-rē), **slum·brous** (-brəs). **1.** Sleepy; drowsy. **2. a.** Suggestive of or like sleep. **b.** Quiet; tranquil. **3.** Causing or inducing sleep; soporific. —**slum′ber·ous·ly** *adv.* —**slum′ber·ous·ness** *n.*

slum·gul·lion (slŭm′gŭl′yən) *n.* **1.** *Slang.* A watery meat stew. **2.** *British Slang.* A weak beverage. [Earlier *slum,* slime, perhaps from German *Schlamm,* mud, from Middle High German *slam* (see **leb-**[1] in Appendix*) + *gullion*†.]

slum·lord (slŭm′lôrd′) *n. Informal.* A landlord of slum property, usually an absentee owner.

slump (slŭmp) *intr.v.* **slumped, slumping, slumps. 1.** To fall or sink suddenly, as into a bog or through a crust of snow or ice. **2.** To decline suddenly; collapse. **3.** To slide down suddenly. **4.** To droop, as in sitting or standing; to slouch. —*n.* A sudden falling off or decline, as in interest, activity, prices, or business. [Probably from Scandinavian, akin to Norwegian *slumpa.* See **leb-**[1] in Appendix.*]

slung. Past tense and past participle of **sling.**

slung·shot (slŭng′shŏt′) *n.* A small, heavy weight attached to a thong, used as a weapon.

slunk. Past tense and past participle of **slink.**

slur (slûr) *tr.v.* **slurred, slurring, slurs. 1.** To pass over lightly or carelessly; treat without due consideration. Often used with *over.* **2.** To pronounce indistinctly. **3.** To speak slightingly of; disparage; calumniate. **4.** *Music.* **a.** To glide over (a series of notes) smoothly without a break. **b.** To mark with a slur. **5.** *Printing.* To blur or smear. —*n.* **1.** A disparaging remark; an aspersion; stigma. **2.** A slurred utterance or sound. **3.** *Music.* **a.** A curved line connecting notes on a score to indicate that they are to be played or sung legato. **b.** A passage played or sung in this manner. **4.** *Printing.* A smeared or blurred impression. [From Middle English *sloor, slore,* mud, possibly from Middle Dutch. See **sleu-** in Appendix.*]

slurp (slûrp) *v.* **slurped, slurping, slurps.** —*tr.* To eat or drink in a noisy manner. —*intr.* To eat or drink something noisily. [Dutch *slurpen,* to slurp, lap, from Middle Dutch *slorpen.* See **srebh-** in Appendix.*]

slur·ry (slûr′ē) *n., pl.* **-ries.** A thin mixture of a liquid, especially water, and any of several finely divided substances, such as cement, plaster of Paris, or clay particles. [Middle English *slory,* probably akin to *sloor,* mud. See **slur.**]

slush (slŭsh) *n.* **1.** Partially melted snow or ice. **2.** Soft mud; slop; mire. **3.** Refuse grease or fat from a ship's galley. **4.** A greasy compound used as a lubricant for machinery. **5.** Maudlin speech or writing; sentimental drivel. —*v.* **slushed, slushing, slushes.** —*tr.* **1.** To daub (machinery) with slush. **2.** To fill (joints in masonry) with mortar. Usually used with *up.* **3.** To wash down (a deck) by dashing water upon. **4.** To splash or soak with slush or mud. —*intr.* **1.** To walk or proceed through slush. **2.** To make a splashing or slushy sound. [Middle English *sloche,* perhaps from Scandinavian, akin to Norwegian *slusk,* sloppy weather. See **sleu-** in Appendix.*] —**slush′i·ness** *n.* —**slush′y** *adv.*

slush fund. 1. A fund raised for undesignated purposes; especially: **a.** A fund used by a group, such as office employees, for entertainment or the like. **b.** A fund raised by a political group for bribery or other corrupt practices. **2.** Formerly, money raised by the sale of garbage from a warship to buy little items of luxury for the crew. [From SLUSH (refuse grease on a ship).]

slut (slŭt) *n.* **1.** A slovenly, dirty woman; slattern. **2. a.** A woman of loose morals. **b.** A prostitute. **3.** A bold, brazen girl. Used humorously. **4.** *Rare.* A female dog. [Middle English *slutte*†.] —**slut′tish** *adj.* —**slut′tish·ly** *adv.* —**slut′tish·ness** *n.*

sly (slī) *adj.* **slier** or **slyer, sliest** or **slyest. 1.** Stealthily clever; crafty; cunning. **2.** Secretive rather than open; underhand; deceitful. **3.** Playfully mischievous; roguish; arch. [Middle English *sli, sleih,* from Old Norse *slœgr,* cunning, clever. See **slak-** in Appendix.*] —**sly′ly** *adv.* —**sly′ness** *n.*

Synonyms: *sly, cunning, tricky, crafty, wily, foxy, artful, guileful.* These adjectives describe persons disposed to be indirect or devious in dealing with others. *Sly* usually implies stealth and absence of candor but in general suggests roguishness more strongly than outright deceit. *Cunning* stresses mental acuteness and practical skill in gaining an end, often at the expense of moral principles. *Tricky* emphasizes shiftiness, deception, and general absence of scruples. *Crafty* suggests one who is a master of devious methods in general. *Wily* suggests subterfuge or stratagem intended to trap another. *Foxy* implies shrewdness and usually long experience in the use of trickery, but is often less derogatory than most of these terms. *Artful* emphasizes adroitness and ingenuity, but not necessarily deceit, in maneuvering to gain an advantage. *Guileful,* in contrast, implies a designing, deceitful, and often treacherous nature.

sly·boots (slī′bōōts′) *n. Informal.* A sly person.

slype (slīp) *n. Architecture.* A covered passage, especially one between the transept and chapter house of a cathedral. [Origin uncertain.]

Sm The symbol for the element samarium.

sm. small.

S.M. Soldier's Medal.

smack[1] (smăk) *v.* **smacked, smacking, smacks.** —*tr.* **1.** To make a sound by pressing together the lips and pulling them apart quickly. **2.** To kiss noisily. **3.** To strike heartily and noisily. —*intr.* To make or give a smack. —*n.* **1.** The loud, sharp sound of smacking. **2.** A noisy kiss. **3.** A sharp blow or slap. —*adv.* **1.** With a smack: *fell smack on her head.* **2.** Directly: *went smack against the rules.* [From Middle Low German or Middle Dutch *smacken.* See **smeg-** in Appendix.*]

smack[2] (smăk) *n.* **1. a.** A distinctive flavor or taste. **b.** A suggestion or trace. **2.** A small amount; smattering. —*intr.v.* **smacked, smacking, smacks. 1.** To have a distinctive flavor or taste. Used with *of.* **2.** To give an indication; suggest. Used with *of: This smacks of foul play.* [Middle English *smack,* Old English *smæc.* See **smeg-** in Appendix.*]

smack[3] (smăk) *n.* A small sailing vessel; especially, a fishing vessel fitted with a well for live fish. [Dutch *smak,* from Middle Dutch *smacke*†.]

smack-dab (smăk′dăb′) *adv. Slang.* Squarely; directly.

smack·er (smăk′ər) *n.* **1.** A loud kiss. **2.** A resounding blow. **3.** *Slang.* A dollar.

smack·ing (smăk′ĭng) *adj.* Brisk; vigorous; spanking: *a smacking good breeze.*

small (smôl) *adj.* **smaller, smallest.** *Abbr.* **s., sm. 1.** Measurably less in size, number, quantity, magnitude, or extent; little. **2.** Limited in importance or significance; trivial. **3.** Limited in degree, scope, or intensity. **4.** Lacking position, influence, or status; minor: *"A crowd of small writers had vainly attempted to rival Addison."* (Macaulay). **5.** Engaged in business or other activity on a limited scale. **6.** Unpretentious; modest. **7.** Not fully grown; very young. **8.** Characterized by littleness of mind or character; petty. **9.** Belittled; humiliated. **10.** Diluted; weak. Said of alcoholic beverages. **11.** Soft; low: *a small voice.* —*adv.* **1.** In small pieces: *Cut it up small.* **2.** Softly. **3.** In a small manner. —*n.* **1.** Something smaller than the rest: *the small of the back.* **2.** *Plural.* **a.** Small things collectively. **b.** *British.* **Smallclothes** *(see).* [Middle English *smal(l),* Old English *smæl.* See **mēlo-** in Appendix.*] —**small′ness** *n.*

Synonyms: *small, little, diminutive, minute, miniature, minuscule, tiny, wee, petite.* These adjectives describe persons or things whose physical size is markedly below that of the average. *Small* and *little* can often be used interchangeably. In general, *small* has the wider application; with reference to physical size, *little* is usually more emphatic in implying sharp reduction from the average. *Little* is sometimes used also to add a sense of charm, endearment, or pathos to the term modified. *Diminutive* means very, often abnormally, small. *Minute* describes what is small to the point of being difficult to see. *Miniature* applies to a representation of something on a greatly reduced scale. *Minuscule* refers to what is very small, and is occasionally used in the sense of miniature. *Tiny* and *wee* both mean exceptionally small and are often interchangeable, though *wee* generally implies endearment or humor. *Petite* is applied principally to the feminine figure in the sense of small and trim.

small arms. Firearms carried in the hand.

small calorie. A **calorie** *(see).*

small capital. *Abbr.* **s.c.** A smaller letter having the form of a capital letter, for example: SMALL CAPITALS.

small change. 1. Coins of low denomination. **2.** Something of little value or significance.

small·clothes (smôl′klōthz′, -klōz′) *pl.n.* **1.** *Archaic.* Men's close-fitting knee breeches worn in the 18th century. **2.** *British.* Small items of clothing, such as underclothes, handkerchiefs, or the like. Also called "smalls."

small fry. 1. Young or small fish. **2.** Small children. **3.** Unimportant or insignificant persons or things.

small hours. The early postmidnight hours.

small intestine. The part of the intestine in which digestion is completed, extending from the pylorus to the cecum and consisting of the duodenum, the jejunum, and the ileum.

small-mind·ed (smôl′mīn′dĭd) *adj.* **1.** Having a narrow or selfish attitude; prejudiced. **2.** Characterized by pettiness or selfishness. —**small′-mind′ed·ly** *adv.* —**small′-mind′ed·ness** *n.*

small·mouth bass (smôl′mouth′). A North American freshwater food and game fish, *Micropterus dolomieui.*

small potatoes. *Informal.* Unimportant persons or things.

small·pox (smôl′pŏks′) *n.* An acute, highly infectious disease caused by a virus and initially characterized by chills, high fever, headache, and backache, with subsequent widespread eruption of pimples which eventually blister, produce pus, and form pockmarks.

small talk. Casual or trivial conversation.

small-time (smôl′tīm′) *adj. Informal.* Insignificant or unimportant; minor: *a smalltime comedian.* —**small′tim′er** *n.*

smalt (smôlt) *n.* A deep-blue paint and ceramic pigment produced by pulverizing a glass made of silica, potash, and cobalt oxide. [French, from Italian *smalto,* from Germanic. See **mel-**[1] in Appendix.*]

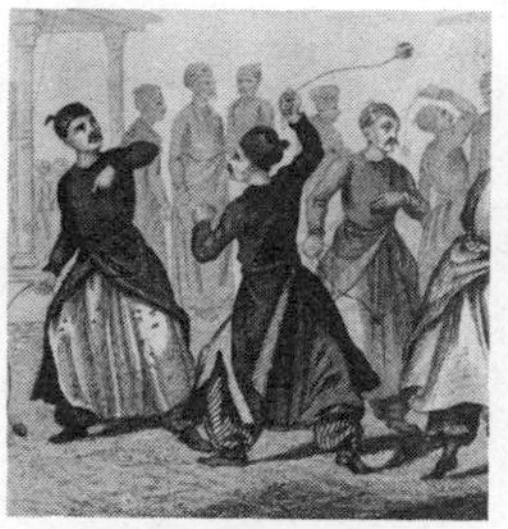

slungshot
Ottoman soldiers engaged in war games with slungshots

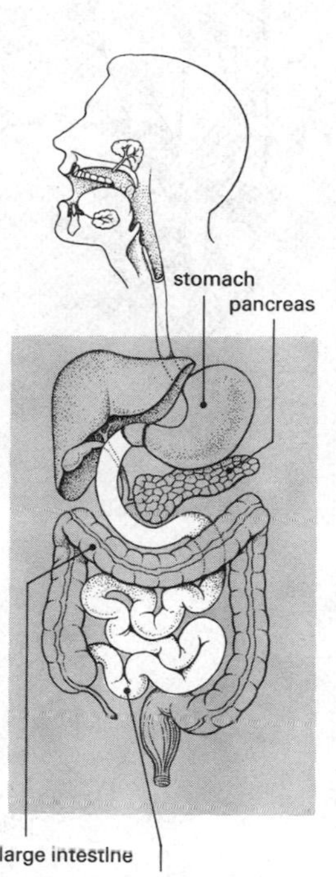
stomach
pancreas
large intestine

small intestine

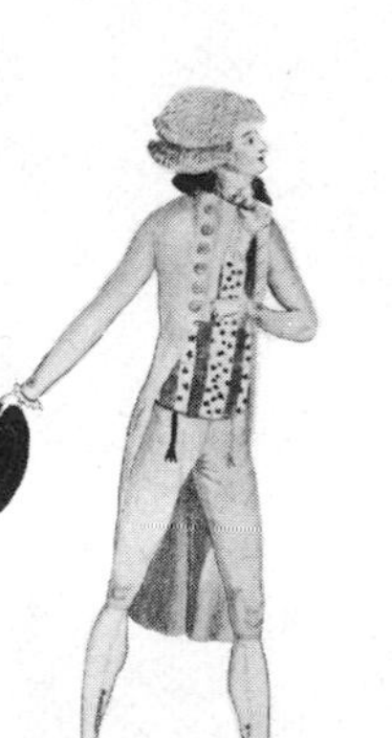

smallclothes
French dandy of the late 18th century

smalt·ite (smôl′tīt′) *n.* Also **smalt·ine** (smôl′tĭn, -tēn′). A white to silver-gray ore of nickel and cobalt, essentially $(Co,Ni)As_2$. [Originally smaltine, from French : SMALT + -INE.]

sma·rag·dite (smə-răg′dīt′) *n.* A thin, foliated, light-green amphibole mineral. [French, from Latin *smaragdus*, a kind of precious stone. See **emerald**.]

smart (smärt) *intr.v.* **smarted, smarting, smarts. 1.** To cause a sharp, usually superficial, stinging pain, as an acrid liquid or a slap. **2.** To be the source of such a pain, as a wound. **3.** To feel such a pain. **4.** To suffer acutely, as from mental distress, wounded feelings, remorse, or the like: *"No creature smarts so little as a fool."* (Pope). **5.** To suffer or pay a heavy penalty. Usually used with *for.* —*n.* Sharp mental or physical pain. —*adj.* **smarter, smartest. 1. a.** Characterized by sharp, quick thought; bright. **b.** Amusingly or impertinently clever; witty: *a smart answer.* **2.** Characterized by sharp, quick movement; energetic: *a smart pace.* **3.** Characterized by sharpness in dealings; shrewd: *a smart businessman.* **4.** Characterized by sharpness in dress; trim; elegant. **5.** Associated with, characteristic of, or patronized by persons of fashion; fashionable: *a smart restaurant.* —See Synonyms at **intelligent**. [Middle English *smarten, smerten,* Old English *smeortan.* See **smerd-** in Appendix.*] —**smart′ly** *adv.* —**smart′ness** *n.*

smart al·eck (ăl′ĭk). *Informal.* One who is obnoxiously self-assertive and arrogant. [SMART + *Aleck,* pet form of ALEXANDER.] —**smart′-al′eck·y** *adj.*

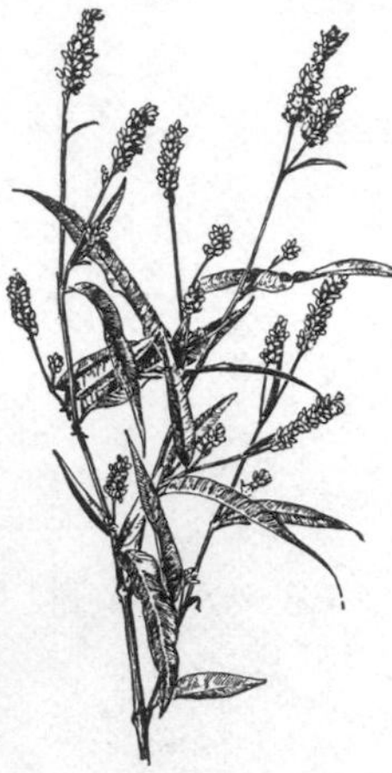
smartweed

smart·en (smärt′n) *v.* **-ened, -ening, -ens.** —*tr.* **1.** To improve in appearance or stylishness; spruce up. Usually used with *up.* **2.** To make brighter or quicker: *smarten the pace.* —*intr.* To make oneself smart or smarter. Usually used with *up.*

smart money. 1. Compensation beyond the value of actual harm, awarded by jury in cases of gross negligence or willful misconduct. **2.** A bet or bets placed by experienced gamblers or those having privileged information.

smart·weed (smärt′wēd′) *n.* Any of various marsh plants of the genus *Polygonum* (or *Persicaria*), having small, densely clustered pink, white, or green flowers. [So called because some species have a sharp, stinging taste.]

smash (smăsh) *v.* **smashed, smashing, smashes.** —*tr.* **1.** To break into pieces suddenly, noisily, and violently; shatter. **2. a.** To throw or dash (something) violently so as to shatter or crush. **b.** To strike with a heavy blow; batter. **3.** To hit (a ball or shuttlecock) in a violent overhand stroke. **4.** To crush or destroy completely; ruin. —*intr.* **1.** To move or be moved suddenly, noisily, and violently. **2.** To break into pieces, as from a violent blow or collision. **3.** To hit, as a ball or shuttlecock, in a violent overhand stroke. **4.** To be crushed or destroyed. **5.** To go bankrupt. Usually used with *up.* —See Synonyms at **break**. —*n.* **1. a.** The act or sound of smashing. **b.** The condition of having been smashed. **2. a.** Total defeat or destruction; ruin. **b.** Financial failure; bankruptcy. **3.** A collision or crash. **4. a.** A drink made of mint, sugar, soda water, and alcoholic liquor, usually brandy. **b.** A soft drink made of crushed fruit. **5.** A violent overhand stroke in tennis, badminton, or the like. **6.** *Informal.* A resounding success. —*adj. Informal.* Of, relating to, or being a resounding success. —*adv.* With a sudden, violent crash. [Perhaps blend of SMACK and CRASH.] —**smash′er** *n.*

smash·ing (smăsh′ĭng) *adj. Informal.* Extraordinarily or unusually impressive or fine; wonderful; admirable.

smash·up (smăsh′ŭp′) *n.* **1.** A total collapse or defeat. **2.** A serious collision between vehicles; a wreck.

smat·ter (smăt′ər) *v.* **-tered, -tering, -ters.** —*tr.* **1.** To speak (a language) without fluency. **2.** To study or approach superficially; dabble in. —*intr.* To prattle. —*n.* A smattering. [Middle English *smat(e)ren* (probably imitative).] —**smat′ter·er** *n.*

smat·ter·ing (smăt′ər-ĭng) *n.* Fragmented or superficial knowledge. [From SMATTER.]

smaze (smāz) *n.* A relatively dry atmospheric mixture of smoke and haze. [Blend of SMOKE and HAZE.]

smear (smîr) *v.* **smeared, smearing, smears.** —*tr.* **1.** To spread or daub with a sticky, greasy, or dirty substance. **2.** To stain by or as if by spreading or daubing with a sticky, greasy, or dirty substance. **3.** To stain or attempt to destroy the reputation of; vilify. **4.** *Slang.* To defeat utterly; smash. —*intr.* To be or become stained or dirtied. —*n.* **1.** A mark made by smearing; a spot; blot. **2.** A substance to be spread on a surface. **3.** A substance or preparation placed on a slide for microscopic examination. **4.** An attempt to destroy a reputation; vilification; slander. [Middle English *smeren,* to anoint, cover, daub, Old English *smierwan, smerian.* See **smer-**[3] in Appendix.*]

smear·case (smîr′kās′) *n.* Cottage cheese. [German *Schmierkäse* : *schmieren,* to smear, spread, from Old High German *smirwen* (see **smer-**[3] in Appendix*) + *Käse,* cheese, from Old High German *kāsi,* from Germanic *kasjūs* (unattested), from Latin *cāseus,* CHEESE.]

smear·y (smîr′ē) *adj.* **-ier, -iest. 1.** Smeared. **2.** Tending to smear or soil. —**smear′i·ness** *n.*

smell (smĕl) *v.* **smelled** or **smelt** (smĕlt), **smelling, smells.** —*tr.* **1.** To perceive the scent of (something) by means of the olfactory nerves. **2.** To sense the presence of by or as if by the olfactory nerves; detect; discover: *"It has been said of him that he could smell an isosceles triangle"* (Nathanael West). —*intr.* **1.** To use the sense of smell; perceive the scent of something. **2.** To have or emit an odor. **3.** To be suggestive; have a touch of something. Used with *of.* **4.** To have or emit an unpleasant odor; stink. **5.** To appear to be dishonest; to suggest evil or corruption. —See Usage note below. —*n.* **1.** The sense by which odors are perceived; the olfactory sense. **2.** That quality of something that may be perceived by the olfactory sense; odor; scent. **3.** The act or an instance of smelling. **4.** A distinctive quality enveloping or characterizing something; an aura; a trace. [Middle English *smellen, smullen*†.]

Synonyms: *smell, odor, scent, aroma, fragrance, perfume, bouquet, savor, stink, stench.* These nouns denote properties of things by means of which the things are perceived by the olfactory organs. *Smell* and *odor,* the most general and most nearly neutral, are frequently interchangeable except in technical and scientific contexts, where *odor* is more common. *Scent* refers to a distinctive or identifying odor, usually delicate and thought of especially as a physical emanation from the thing in question. *Aroma* suggests a pleasant odor, pungent, pervasive, and often spicy. *Fragrance, perfume,* and *bouquet* are applicable to pleasing, sweet odors or scents. *Fragrance* and *perfume* suggest the scent of flowers, and *fragrance* usually implies a lighter, less penetrating scent. *Bouquet* can refer to any aroma but occurs most often with reference to wine. *Savor* is the property of a thing that makes it strongly appealing to both smell and taste. *Stink* and *stench* both apply to highly unpleasant odors, especially those resulting from putrefaction. *Stench* is generally the stronger term.

Usage: *Smell* (intransitive verb, "to emit an odor") is modified by an adjective: *The flowers smell good* (not *well*), or *bad* (not *badly*), or *sweet* (not *sweetly*). The adjective in such constructions may in turn be modified by an adverb: *smells unbelievably bad.* An adverb may also occur in *smells of* constructions: *smells strongly of garlic. Smell* (intransitive verb, "to emit an unpleasant odor; stink") is modified by an adverb: *The fish smells disgustingly* (indicating degree of foul smell, in contrast with *smells disgusting,* which merely specifies an odor).

smelling salts. Any of several preparations based on spirits of ammonia, sniffed as a restorative.

smell·y (smĕl′ē) *adj.* **-ier, -iest.** *Informal.* Having an unpleasant or offensive odor.

smelt[1] (smĕlt) *v.* **smelted, smelting, smelts.** —*tr.* To melt or fuse (ores), separating the metallic constituents. —*intr.* To melt or fuse. Used of ores. [Dutch or Low German *smelten,* from Middle Dutch or Middle Low German. See **mel-**[1] in Appendix.*]

smelt[2] (smĕlt) *n., pl.* **smelts** or **smelt.** Any of various small silvery marine and freshwater food fishes of the family Osmeridae; especially, *Osmerus mordax,* of North America and *O. eperlanus,* of Europe. [Middle English *smelt,* Old English *smelt, smylt.* See **mel-**[1] in Appendix.*]

smelt[3]. Alternate past tense and past participle of **smell**.

smelt·er (smĕl′tər) *n.* Also **smelt·er·y** (smĕl′tə-rē) (for sense 1b). **1. a.** Any apparatus for smelting. **b.** An establishment for smelting. **2.** A person engaged in the smelting industry.

Sme·ta·na (smĕt′ə-nə), **Bedřich.** 1824–1884. Czech composer.

smew (smyōō) *n.* A small, crested Old World duck, *Mergus albellus,* having a narrow bill and white and black plumage in the male. [Origin uncertain.]

Smi·bert (smī′bərt), **John.** 1688–1751. Scottish-born American portraitist.

smid·gen (smĭj′ən) *n.* Also **smid·geon, smid·gin.** *Informal.* A very small quantity or portion; a bit; a mite. [Probably variant of British dialectal *smitch,* probably variant of SMUTCH.]

smi·lax (smī′lăks′) *n.* **1.** Any plant of the genus *Smilax,* which includes climbing vines such as the catbrier. **2.** A vine, *Asparagus asparagoides,* that has glossy foliage and is popular as a floral decoration. [New Latin, from Latin *smilax,* a kind of oak, smilax, bindweed, from Greek *smilax*†.]

smile (smīl) *n.* **1.** A facial expression characterized by an upward curving of the corners of the mouth and motivated by emotions or attitudes ranging from pleasure to derision. **2.** A pleasant or favorable disposition or aspect. —*v.* **smiled, smiling, smiles.** —*intr.* **1.** To have or form a smile. **2.** To express or appear to express approval or beneficence. Often used with *at, upon,* or *on.* —*tr.* **1.** To express with a smile. **2.** To effect or accomplish with or as if with a smile. [Middle English *smilen,* perhaps from Scandinavian, akin to Swedish *smila.* See **smei-** in Appendix.*] —**smil′er** *n.* —**smil′ing·ly** *adv.* —**smil′ing·ness** *n.*

Synonyms: *smile, grin, simper, smirk.* These nouns denote facial expressions in which the mouth is widened and curved upward slightly at the corners. *Smile* is the most general, since it can cover a wide range of feeling, from affection to malice, and can even refer to a mask for one's true feelings. A *grin* is a broad smile that exposes the teeth. Usually it is a spontaneous expression of good humor, approval, or triumph. A *simper* is a tight-lipped, affected, silly smile expressing self-indulgence. A *smirk* is an affected but bolder smile that expresses derision or suggests smugness or conceit.

smirch (smûrch) *tr.v.* **smirched, smirching, smirches. 1.** To soil, stain, or dirty with a smearing agent: *"their tough, hostile faces, smirched by the grime and rust"* (Henry Roth). **2.** To dishonor or defame. —*n.* Something that smirches; a blot, smear, or stain. [Middle English *smorchen*†.]

smirk (smûrk) *intr.v.* **smirked, smirking, smirks.** To smile in a self-conscious, knowing, or simpering manner. —*n.* A knowing, simpering smile. See Synonyms at **smile**. [Middle English *smirken,* Old English *smearcian,* to smile. See **smei-** in Appendix.*] —**smirk′er** *n.* —**smirk′ing·ly** *adv.*

smite (smīt) *v.* **smote** (smōt) or *archaic* **smit** (smĭt), **smitten** (smĭt′n) or **smit** or **smote, smiting, smites.** —*tr.* **1. a.** To inflict a heavy blow on with or as if with the hand, a tool, a weapon, or the like. **b.** To drive or strike (a tool, weapon, or the like) forcefully onto or into something else. **2.** To attack, damage, or destroy by or as if by blows. **3. a.** To afflict: *smitten with* *mumps.* **b.** To afflict retributively; chasten or chastise. **4.** To affect sharply with deep feeling: *"thou canst never know the anguish that smote my heart"* (Edgar Lee Masters). *—intr.* To strike or beat. [Smite, smote or smit, smitten; Middle English *smiten, smot* or *smite, smitten,* Old English *smītan, smiton* (plural) or *smāt* (singular), *smiten.* See **smē-** in Appendix.*] **—smit′er** *n.*

smith (smĭth) *n.* **1.** A metalworker; especially, one who works metal when it is hot and malleable. Often used in combination: *silversmith, goldsmith.* **2.** A **blacksmith** *(see).* [Middle English *smith,* Old English *smith.* See **smi-** in Appendix.*]

Smith (smĭth), **Adam.** 1723–1790. Scottish political economist and philosopher.

Smith (smĭth), **Alfred Emanuel.** 1873–1944. American political leader; governor of New York (1919–20 and 1923–28); Democratic Presidential candidate (1928).

Smith (smĭth), **Bessie.** 1898?–1937. American blues singer.

Smith, Edmund Kirby. See **Kirby-Smith.**

Smith (smĭth), **Jedediah Strong.** 1798–1831. American fur trader and explorer of the West.

Smith (smĭth), **John.** 1580–1631. English adventurer, colonist in Virginia, explorer of North Atlantic coast, and author.

Smith (smĭth), **Joseph.** 1805–1844. American religious leader; founder of the Church of Jesus Christ of the Latter-day Saints.

Smith (smĭth), **Margaret Chase.** Born 1898. American political leader; U.S. Senator from Maine (since 1949).

Smith (smĭth), **Sydney.** 1771–1845. English writer, clergyman, and wit.

smith·er·eens (smĭth′ə-rēnz′) *pl.n. Informal.* Fragments or splintered pieces; bits: *the dish broke into smithereens.* [Irish *smidirin,* diminutive of *smiodar*†, small fragment.]

smith·er·y (smĭth′ə-rē) *n., pl.* **-ies. 1.** The occupation or craft of a smith. **2.** A smithy.

Smith·son (smĭth′sən), **James.** Original name, James Lewis Macie. 1765–1829. British chemist and mineralogist; left bequest resulting in founding (1846) of the Smithsonian Institution in Washington, D.C.

smith·son·ite (smĭth′sə-nīt′) *n.* A white or yellow-to-brown mineral, chiefly $ZnCO_3$, used as a source of zinc. Also called "dry-bone ore." [After James SMITHSON.]

smith·y (smĭth′ē, smĭth′ē) *n., pl.* **-ies.** A blacksmith's shop; a forge. [Middle English *smythy,* from Old Norse *smidhja.* See **smi-** in Appendix.*]

smock (smŏk) *n.* A loose coatlike outer garment, often worn to protect the clothes while working. *—tr.v.* **smocked, smocking, smocks. 1.** To clothe in a smock. **2.** To decorate (fabric) with smocking. [Middle English *smok,* women's undergarment, smock, Old English *smoc.* See **meug-²** in Appendix.*]

smock·ing (smŏk′ĭng) *n.* Needlework decoration accomplished by stitching small regularly spaced gathers into a honeycomb pattern. [From SMOCK (verb).]

smog (smŏg, smôg) *n.* Fog that has become mixed and polluted with smoke. [Blend of SMOKE and FOG.] **—smog′gy** *adj.*

smoke (smōk) *n.* **1.** The vaporous system made up of small particles of carbonaceous matter in the air, resulting mainly from the incomplete combustion of organic material, such as wood or coal. **2.** A suspension of particles in a gaseous medium. **3.** Any cloud of fine particles. **4.** Anything insubstantial, unreal, or transitory. **5. a.** The act of smoking any form of tobacco. **b.** The duration of this act. **6.** *Informal.* Tobacco in any form that can be smoked; especially, a cigarette. **7.** A substance used in warfare to produce a smoke screen. **8.** Pale to grayish blue to bluish gray or dark gray. See **color.** *—v.* **smoked, smoking, smokes.** *—intr.* **1.** To emit smoke or a smokelike substance. **2.** To emit smoke excessively. **3.** To draw in and exhale smoke from a cigarette, cigar, pipe, or the like. *—tr.* **1.** To draw in and exhale the smoke of (tobacco or the like). **2.** To preserve (meat or fish) by exposure to the aromatic smoke of burning hardwood, usually after pickling in salt or brine. **3.** To fumigate (a house or the like). **4.** To expose (glass) to smoke in order to darken or change its color. **—smoke out. 1.** To force out of a place of hiding or concealment by or as if by the use of smoke. **2.** To detect and bring to public view; expose; reveal. [Middle English *smoke,* Old English *smoca.* See **smeug-** in Appendix.*]

smoke·house (smōk′hous′) *n.* A structure in which meat or fish is cured with smoke.

smoke·jack (smōk′jăk′) *n.* A device for turning a roasting spit in a chimney, activated by the current of rising gases.

smoke·jump·er (smōk′jŭm′pər) *n.* A firefighter who drops by parachute into a forest fire.

smoke·less (smōk′lĭs) *adj.* Emitting little or no smoke.

smokeless powder. A propellant charge composed mainly of nitrocellulose, which produces little or no smoke, used in projectiles and small artillery rockets.

smok·er (smō′kər) *n.* **1.** One that smokes. **2.** A railroad car in which smoking is permitted. Also called "smoking car." **3.** An informal social gathering for men.

smoke screen. 1. A mass of dense artificial smoke used to conceal military areas or operations from an enemy. **2.** Any action or statement used to conceal plans or intentions.

smoke·stack (smōk′stăk′) *n.* A large chimney or vertical pipe through which combustion vapors, gases, and smoke are discharged.

smoke tree. Either of two trees, *Cotinus obovatus,* of the southern United States, or *C. coggygria,* of Eurasia, having plumelike clusters of small yellowish flowers. The former species is also called "chittamwood." [So called because the flower clusters resemble puffs of smoke.]

smoking jacket. A man's evening jacket, often made of a fine fabric, elaborately trimmed, and usually worn at home.

smok·y (smō′kē) *adj.* **-ier, -iest. 1.** Emitting smoke in profuse volume. **2.** Mixed or filled with smoke. **3.** Resembling or similar to smoke. **4.** Discolored or soiled with smoke. **5.** Tasting of smoke. **—smok′i·ly** *adv.* **—smok′i·ness** *n.*

Smoky Hill River. A river rising in eastern Colorado and flowing 560 miles generally east through Kansas to join the Republican River and form the Kansas River.

Smoky Mountains. See **Great Smoky Mountains.**

smoky quartz. *Mineralogy.* **Cairngorm** *(see).*

smol·der (smōl′dər) *intr.v.* **-dered, -dering, -ders.** Also **smoul·der. 1.** To burn with little smoke and no flame. **2.** To exist in a suppressed state. **3.** To manifest repressed anger or hatred. *—n.* Also **smoul·der.** Thick smoke resulting from a slow fire. [Middle English *smolderen,* from *smolder*†, a smolder.]

Smo·lensk (smō-lĕnsk′). A city of the Soviet Union, on the Dnieper about 220 miles southwest of Moscow. Population, 183,000.

Smol·lett (smŏl′ĭt), **Tobias George.** 1721–1771. British novelist.

smolt (smōlt) *n.* A young salmon at the stage at which it migrates from fresh water to the sea. [Middle English, obscurely related to Old English *smelt,* SMELT (fish).]

smooch (smo͞och) *n. Slang.* A kiss. *—intr.v.* **smooched, smooching, smooches.** *Slang.* To kiss. [Perhaps imitative of a kiss.]

smooth (smo͞o*th*) *adj.* **smoother, smoothest. 1.** Having a surface free from irregularities, roughness, or projections; even. **2.** Having a surface whose roughness or projections have been worn level by use. **3.** Having a fine consistency or texture. **4.** Having an even or gentle motion or movement. **5.** Having no obstructions or difficulties. **6.** Serene. **7.** Mellifluous. **8.** Pleasing to the taste. **9.** Flatteringly bland; insinuating: *"With her smooth talk she compels him"* (Proverbs 7:21). **10.** Having no grossness or coarseness in dress or manner. **11.** Not aspirated. —See Synonyms at **easy, level, suave.** *—v.* **smoothed, smoothing, smoothes.** *—tr.* **1.** To make (something) even, level, unwrinkled, or the like. **2.** To rid of obstructions, hindrances, difficulties, or the like. **3.** To soothe or tranquilize; make calm. **4.** To make less harsh or crude; refine. *—intr.* To become smooth. *—n.* **1.** A smooth part of something; a smooth surface. **2.** The act of smoothing. [Middle English *smoth(e),* Old English *smōth,* akin to Old Saxon *smōthi*†.] **—smooth′er** *n.* **—smooth′ly** *adv.* **—smooth′ness** *n.*

smooth·bore (smo͞o*th*′bôr′, -bōr′) *adj.* Having no rifling within the barrel. Said of a firearm. *—n.* Also **smooth bore.** A firearm having no rifling.

smooth breathing. 1. The symbol (') written over some initial vowels in classical Greek to indicate that they are not aspirated. **2.** Such a vowel.

smooth·en (smo͞o′*th*ən) *v.* **-ened, -ening, -ens.** *—tr.* To smooth. *—intr.* To become smooth.

smooth muscle. The unstriated involuntary muscle of the internal organs, as of the intestine, bladder, and blood vessels, excluding the heart.

smor·gas·bord (smôr′gəs-bôrd′, -bōrd′) *n.* Also *Swedish* **smör·gås·bord** (smœr′gōs-bo͞ord′). A meal featuring a varied number of dishes served buffet-style. [Swedish *smörgåsbord* : *smörgås,* (open-faced) sandwich, bread and butter : *smör,* butter, from Old Norse *smör, smjör,* fat (see **smer-³** in Appendix*) + *gås,* goose, from Old Norse *gās* (see **ghans-** in Appendix*) + *bord,* table, from Old Norse *bordh* (see **bherdh-** in Appendix*).]

smote. Past tense and alternate past participle of **smite.**

smoth·er (smŭ*th*′ər) *v.* **-ered, -ering, -ers.** *—tr.* **1. a.** To suffocate (another). **b.** To deprive (a fire) of the oxygen necessary for combustion. **2.** To conceal, suppress, or hide. **3.** To cover (a foodstuff) thickly with another foodstuff. **4.** To lavish a surfeit of a given emotion upon (someone). *—intr.* **1. a.** To suffocate. **b.** To be extinguished. **2.** To be concealed or suppressed. **3.** To be surfeited with a given emotion. *—n.* Anything that smothers, as a dense cloud of smoke or dust or a welter of spume. [Middle English *smotheren, smortheren,* from *smorther,* a smother, from Old English *smorian*†, to suffocate, smother.] **—smoth′er·y** *adj.*

smoul·der. Variant of **smolder.**

smudge (smŭj) *v.* **smudged, smudging, smudges.** *—tr.* **1.** To make dirty, especially in one small area. **2.** To smear or blur. **3.** To fill (an orchard or other planted area) with dense smoke from a smudge pot in order to prevent damage from insects or frost. *—intr.* **1.** To smear, as with dirt, soot, or ink. **2.** To be smudged. *—n.* **1.** A blotch or smear. **2.** A smoky fire used as a protection against insects or frost. [Middle English *smogen*†.] **—smudg′i·ly** *adv.* **—smudg′i·ness** *n.* **—smudg′y** *adj.*

smudge pot. A receptacle in which oil or other smoky fuel is burned, as to protect an orchard from insects or frost or to indicate wind direction.

smug (smŭg) *adj.* **smugger, smuggest.** Complacent or self-righteous. [Probably from Low German *smuck,* neat, smooth, sleek, from Middle Low German, from *smucken,* to adorn. See **meug-²** in Appendix.*] **—smug′ly** *adv.* **—smug′ness** *n.*

smug·gle (smŭg′əl) *v.* **-gled, -gling, -gles.** *—tr.* **1.** To import or export without paying lawful customs charges or duties. **2.** To bring in or take out illicitly or by stealth. *—intr.* To engage in smuggling. [Earlier *smuckle,* from Low German *smukkelen, smuggeln* and Dutch *smokkelen.* See **meug-²** in Appendix.*] **—smug′gler** *n.*

smut (smŭt) *n.* **1. a.** A particle of dirt. **b.** A smudge made by soot, smoke, or dirt. **2.** Obscenity in speech or writing. **3. a.** Any of various plant diseases caused by fungi of the order

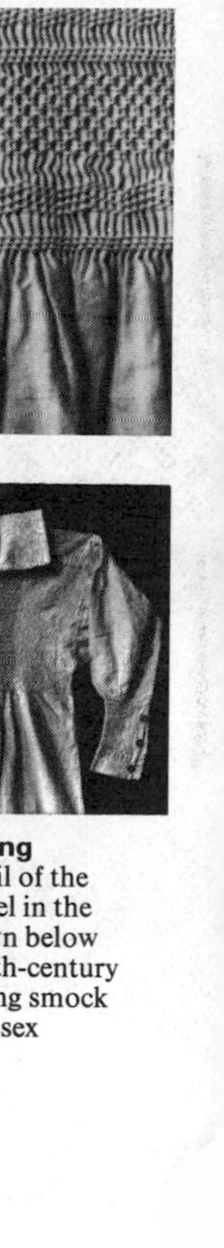

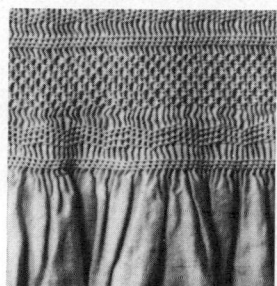

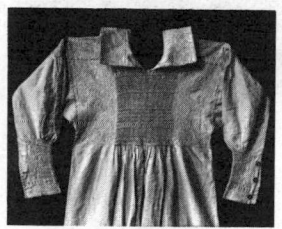

smocking
Above: Detail of the smocked panel in the garment shown below
Below: Mid-19th-century English wedding smock from Sussex

Ustilaginales and resulting in the formation of black, powdery masses of spores on the affected parts. **b.** A fungus causing such a disease. —*v.* **smutted, smutting, smuts.** —*tr.* **1.** To blacken or smudge, as with smoke or grime. **2.** To affect (a plant) with smut. **3.** To free (grain, for example) from smut. **4.** To make obscene. —*intr.* **1.** To emit smut. **2.** To be or become blackened or smudged. **3.** To become affected with smut, as a plant. [Perhaps from Low German *smutt†*.] —**smut'ti·ly** *adv.* —**smut'ti·ness** *n.* —**smut'ty** *adj.*

smutch (smŭch) *tr.v.* **smutched, smutching, smutches.** To soil or stain. —*n.* A stain or spot of dirt. [Perhaps related to SMUDGE.] —**smutch'y** *adj.*

Smuts (smŭts), **Jan Christiaan.** 1870–1950. A founder and prime minister of the Union of South Africa (1919–24 and 1939–48).

Smyr·na. The former name for **Izmir.**

Sn The symbol for the element tin (Latin *stannum*).

s.n. *Library Service.* without name (Latin *sine nomine*).

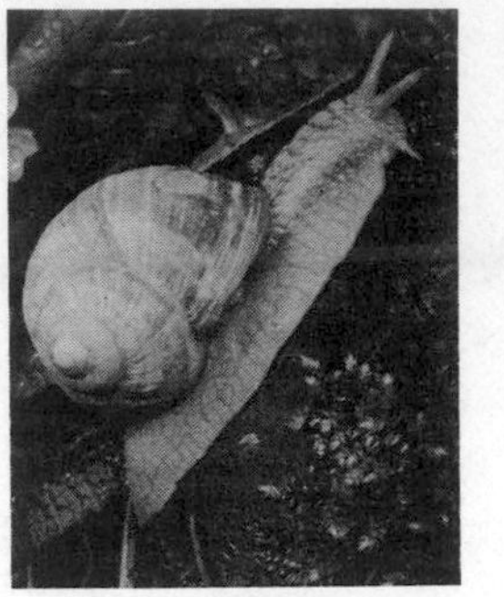

snail

snack (snăk) *n.* **1.** A hurried or light meal. **2.** Food eaten between meals. —*intr.v.* **snacked, snacking, snacks.** To eat a hurried or light meal. [Middle English *snake,* a snatch with the teeth, bite (especially of a dog), from Middle Dutch *snac(k).* See **snē-²** in Appendix.*]

snack bar. A lunch counter where light meals are served.

snaf·fle (snăf'əl) *n.* A bit for a horse, consisting of two bars jointed at the center. Also called "snafflebit." —*tr.v.* **snaffled, -fling, -fles.** To put on or control with a snaffle. See Synonyms at **restrain.** [Origin obscure.]

sna·fu (snă-fo͞o') *adj. Slang.* In a state of complete confusion. —*tr.v.* **snafued, -fuing, -fus.** *Slang.* To make chaotic or confused. —*n., pl.* **snafus.** *Slang.* Any chaotic or confused situation. [S(ITUATION) N(ORMAL) A(LL) F(UCKED) U(P).]

snag (snăg) *n.* **1.** Any rough, sharp, or jagged protuberance. **2.** A tree or a part of a tree that protrudes above the surface in a body of water. **3.** A snaggletooth. **4.** A break, pull, or tear in a fabric. **5.** An unforeseen or hidden obstacle. —See Synonyms at **obstacle.** —*v.* **snagged, snagging, snags.** —*tr.* **1.** To hinder, break, tear, or destroy by or as if by a snag. **2.** To free of snags. **3.** *Informal.* To catch unexpectedly and quickly. —*intr.* To be damaged by a snag. [Probably from Scandinavian, akin to Old Norse *snagi†,* peg.] —**snag'gy** *adj.*

snag·gle·tooth (snăg'əl-to͞oth') *n., pl.* **-teeth** (-tēth'). A tooth that is broken or not in alignment with the others. [British (dialectal) *snaggled,* snaggletoothed, from SNAG.]

snail (snāl) *n.* **1.** Any of numerous aquatic or terrestrial mollusks of the class Gastropoda, characteristically having a spirally coiled shell, a broad retractile foot, and a distinct head. **2.** A slow-moving, lazy, or sluggish person. [Middle English *snail,* Old English *snæg(e)l, sneg(e)l.* See **sneg-** in Appendix.*]

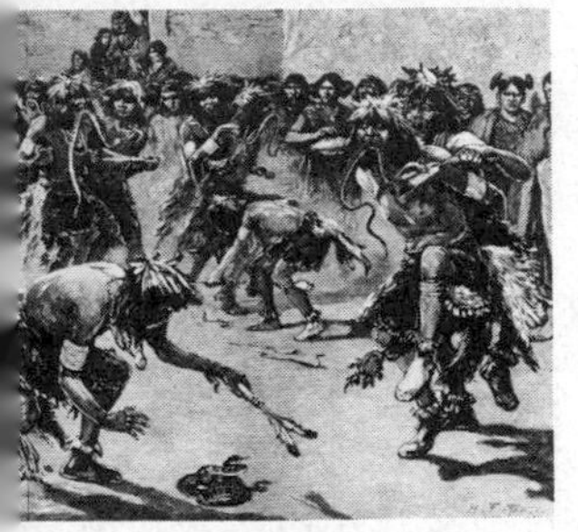

snake dance

snake (snāk) *n.* **1.** Any of various scaly, legless, sometimes venomous reptiles of the suborder Serpentes, having a long, tapering, cylindrical body. **2.** *Capital* **S.** The constellation **Hydra** *(see).* **3.** A treacherous person. **4.** A long, highly flexible metal wire used for cleaning drains. —*v.* **snaked, snaking, snakes.** —*tr.* **1.** To drag or pull lengthwise; especially, to drag with a rope or chain. **2.** To pull with quick jerks. **3.** To move in the manner of a snake. —*intr.* To move with a snakelike motion; crawl. [Middle English *snake,* Old English *snaca.* See **sneg-** in Appendix.*]

snake·bird (snāk'bûrd') *n.* Any of several long-necked, long-billed birds of the genus *Anhinga,* such as the **water turkey** *(see).* [From its snakelike, elongated neck.]

snake·bite (snāk'bīt') *n.* **1.** The bite of a snake. **2.** Poisoning resulting from the bite of a venomous snake.

snake charmer. One who utilizes rhythmic music and bodily movements to control snakes.

snake dance. 1. A dance performed as part of a biennial religious ceremony of the Hopi Indians, in which the dancers carry live rattlesnakes in their mouths. **2.** A procession of persons who join hands and move forward in a zigzag line.

snake fence. A **worm fence** *(see).*

snake·head (snāk'hĕd') *n.* A plant, the **turtlehead** *(see).*

snake·mouth (snāk'mouth') *n., pl.* **-mouths** (-mouthz'). An orchid, *Pogonia ophioglossoides,* of eastern North America, having a solitary rose-purple flower with a fringed lip.

snake oil. Any liquid falsely represented as having medicinal properties and usually hawked at a carnival or fair.

snake pit. *Slang.* A mental institution.

snake plant. Any of several tropical Old World plants of the genus *Sansevieria,* having narrow, rigid, often mottled leaves and widely cultivated as a house plant.

Snake River. A river of the northwestern United States, flowing 1,038 miles generally west from northwestern Wyoming through southern Idaho, then north along the Oregon-Idaho border, and finally west to the Columbia in southeastern Washington.

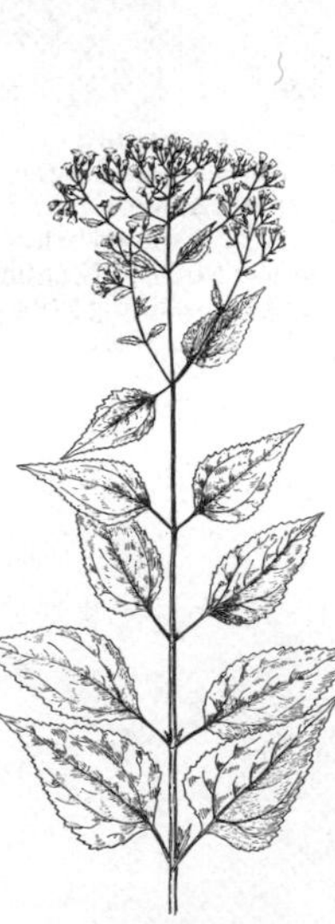

snakeroot
Eupatorium rugosum
White snakeroot

snake·root (snāk'ro͞ot', -ro͝ot') *n.* Any of various plants having roots reputed to cure snakebite; especially, a plant of the genus *Eupatorium* or the genus *Rauwolfia.*

snake·skin (snāk'skĭn') *n.* The skin of a snake, especially when prepared as leather.

snake·stone (snāk'stōn') *n.* **1.** A small stone or piece of porous substance reputed to cure snakebite. **2.** A whetstone.

snake·weed (snāk'wēd') *n.* Any of various plants having reputed power to cure snakebite.

snak·y (snā'kē) *adj.* **-ier, -iest. 1.** Pertaining to or characteristic of snakes. **2.** Having the form or movement of a snake; serpentine. **3.** Overrun with snakes. **4.** Treacherous; sly. —**snak'i·ly** *adv.* —**snak'i·ness** *n.*

snap (snăp) *v.* **snapped, snapping, snaps.** —*intr.* **1.** To make a brisk sharp cracking sound. **2.** To break suddenly with a brisk, sharp sound. **3.** To give way abruptly under pressure or tension. **4.** To bring the jaws briskly together, often with a clicking sound; to bite. Often used with *up* or *at.* **5.** To snatch or grasp suddenly and with eagerness. Often used with *up* or *at.* **6.** To speak abruptly or sharply. Often used with *at.* **7.** To move swiftly and smartly: *snap to attention.* **8.** To flash light or to appear to flash; to sparkle, as the eyes. **9.** To open or close with a click: *The lock snapped shut.* —*tr.* **1.** To snatch at with or as if with the teeth; to bite. **2.** To come apart or break with a snapping sound. **3.** To utter abruptly or sharply. **4. a.** To cause to emit a snapping sound: *snap a whip.* **b.** To close or latch with a snapping sound. **5.** To cause to move abruptly and smartly: *"His head was snapped back by a sudden scream from the bed"* (James Michener). **6.** To take (a photograph). **7.** *Football.* To center (the ball). —**snap out of it.** *Informal.* To recover quickly from a state of depression or an illness. —*n.* **1.** A brisk sudden, sharp cracking sound or the action producing such a sound. **2.** A sudden breaking of something. **3.** A clasp, catch, or other fastening device that operates with a snapping sound. **4.** A sudden attempt to bite, snatch, or grasp. **5. a.** The sound produced by rapid movement of the second finger from the thumb tip to the base of the thumb. **b.** The act of producing this sound. **6.** The sudden release of anything held under pressure or tension. **7.** A thin, crisp, usually circular cooky: *a ginger snap.* **8.** *Informal.* Briskness, liveliness, or energy. **9.** A brief spell of brisk, cold weather. **10.** *Informal.* An effortless task. **11. a.** A snapshot. **b.** The taking of a snapshot. **12.** A snap bean. **13.** *Football.* The passing of the ball from the center to a back that initiates each play. —*adj.* **1.** Made or done on the spur of the moment: *a snap decision.* **2.** Fastening with a snap. **3.** *Informal.* Simple; easy. —*adv.* With a snap. [Probably from Middle Low German or Middle Dutch *snappen,* to seize, speak hastily. See **snē-²** in Appendix.*]

snap bean. A bean, such as the **string bean** *(see),* cultivated for its crisp, edible pods.

snap-brim (snăp'brĭm') *n.* A hat having a flexible brim, usually turned down in front and up at the back.

snap·drag·on (snăp'drăg'ən) *n.* Any of several plants of the genus *Antirrhinum;* especially, a widely cultivated species, *A. majus,* of the Mediterranean region, having showy clusters of two-lipped, variously colored flowers. [From a fanciful likening of the flower to a dragon's mouth.]

snap·per (snăp'ər) *n., pl.* **snappers** or **snapper** (for sense 2). **1.** One that snaps. **2.** Any of numerous widely distributed marine fishes of the family Lutjanidae, many of which are prized as food and game fishes. **3.** A snapping turtle.

snapping beetle. The **click beetle** *(see).*

snapping turtle. Any of several New World freshwater turtles of the family Chelydridae; especially, *Chelydra serpentina* or *Macrochelys temmincki,* of North America, having a rough shell and powerful hooked jaws.

snap·pish (snăp'ĭsh) *adj.* **1.** Liable to snap or bite, as a dog. **2.** Liable to speak sharply or curtly; irritable; curt. —**snap'pish·ly** *adv.* —**snap'pish·ness** *n.*

snap·py (snăp'ē) *adj.* **-pier, -piest. 1.** *Informal.* Lively or energetic; brisk. **2.** *Informal.* Smart or chic in appearance. **3.** Snappish. —**snap'pi·ly** *adv.* —**snap'pi·ness** *n.*

snap roll. An aerial maneuver in which an aircraft is put through a sharp roll of 360 degrees about its longitudinal axis.

snap·shot (snăp'shŏt') *n.* An informal photograph taken with a small hand-held camera.

snare¹ (snâr) *n.* **1.** A trapping device, often consisting of a noose, used for capturing birds and small animals. **2.** Anything that serves to entangle the unwary. **3.** A surgical instrument with a wire loop controlled by a mechanism in the handle, used to remove growths, such as tumors and polyps. —*tr.v.* **snared, snaring, snares. 1.** To trap with a snare. **2.** To entrap (someone). [Middle English *snare,* Old English *sneare,* from Old Norse *snara.* See **sner-²** in Appendix.*] —**snar'er** *n.*

snare² (snâr) *n.* **1.** Any of the wires or cords stretched across the lower skin of a snare drum to increase reverberation. **2.** A snare drum. [Probably Dutch *snaar,* string, from Middle Dutch *snare.* See **sner-²** in Appendix.*]

snare drum. A small double-headed drum having a snare or snares stretched across the bottom head to increase reverberation.

snarl¹ (snärl) *v.* **snarled, snarling, snarls.** —*intr.* **1.** To growl viciously while baring the teeth. **2.** To speak angrily or threateningly. —*tr.* To utter with anger or hostility. —*n.* **1.** A vicious growl. **2.** Any vicious or hostile utterance. [From obsolete *snar,* to snarl, from Middle Low German *snarren.* See **sner-¹** in Appendix.*] —**snarl'er** *n.* —**snarl'ing·ly** *adv.* —**snarl'y** *adj.*

snarl² (snärl) *n.* **1.** A tangled mass, as of hair or yarn. **2.** Any confused, complicated, or tangled situation; a predicament. —*v.* **snarled, snarling, snarls.** —*intr.* To become tangled or confused. —*tr.* **1.** To tangle or knot (hair or yarn, for example). **2.** To confuse; complicate. [Middle English *snarle,* probably from SNARE (trap).] —**snarl'er** *n.* —**snarl'y** *adj.*

snatch (snăch) *v.* **snatched, snatching, snatches.** —*tr.* **1.** To grasp or seize hastily, eagerly, or suddenly. **2.** To grasp or seize illicitly. —*intr.* To make grasping or seizing motions. Used with *at.* —*n.* **1.** The act of snatching; a quick grasp or grab. **2.** A brief period of time: *"At the end we preferred to travel all night, sleeping in snatches"* (T.S. Eliot). **3.** A small amount; bit or fragment: *a snatch of dialogue.* **4.** *Slang.* A kidnaping. [Middle English *snacchen, snecchen,* make a sudden gesture, snap at, perhaps of Low German origin, akin to Middle Dutch *snakken.* See **snē-²** in Appendix.*] **—snatch′er** *n.*

snatch block. *Nautical.* A block that can be opened on one side to receive the looped part of a rope.

snatch·y (snăch′ē) *adj.* **-ier, -iest.** Occurring in snatches; intermittent; spasmodic.

snaz·zy (snăz′ē) *adj. Slang.* **-zier, -ziest.** Determinedly fashionable or flashy. [Perhaps a blend of SNAPPY and JAZZY.]

SNCC (*often* snĭk). Student Nonviolent Coordinating Committee.

sneak (snēk) *v.* **sneaked** or *nonstandard* **snuck** (snŭk), **sneaking, sneaks.** *—intr.* **1.** To go or move in a quiet, stealthy way; slink. **2.** To behave in a cowardly or servile manner. *—tr.* To move, give, take, or put in a quiet, stealthy manner: *sneak candy into one's mouth.* *—n.* **1.** One who sneaks; a stealthy, cowardly, or underhand person. **2.** An instance of sneaking; a quiet, stealthy movement. **3.** *Plural. Informal.* Sneakers. *—adj.* Secretly planned; stealthy. [Of dialectal origin, perhaps ultimately akin to Old English *snīcan,* to crawl, Old Norse *snīkja*†.]

sneak·er (snē′kər) *n.* **1.** One who sneaks. **2.** *Plural.* Canvas shoes with soft rubber soles. Also called "tennis shoes."

sneak·ing (snē′kĭng) *adj.* **1.** Acting in a stealthy, furtive way. **2.** Unavowed; secret. **3.** Gradually growing or persistent. **—sneak′ing·ly** *adv.*

sneak preview. A single public showing of a motion picture prior to its general release, usually as an addition to an announced program.

sneak thief. A burglar who enters without breaking in.

sneak·y (snē′kē) *adj.* **-ier, -iest.** Furtive; surreptitious. **—sneak′i·ly** *adv.* **—sneak′i·ness** *n.*

sneer (snîr) *n.* **1.** A scornful facial expression characterized by a slight raising of one corner of the upper lip. **2.** Any contemptuous facial expression, sound, or statement. *—v.* **sneered, sneering, sneers.** *—tr.* To utter with a sneer or in a sneering manner. *—intr.* **1.** To assume a scornful, contemptuous, or derisive facial expression. **2.** To speak in a scornful, contemptuous, or derisive manner. [Perhaps from North Frisian *sneere.* See **sner-¹** in Appendix.*] **—sneer′er** *n.* **—sneer′ful** *adj.* **—sneer′ing·ly** *adv.*

sneeze (snēz) *intr.v.* **sneezed, sneezing, sneezes.** To expel air forcibly from the mouth and nose in an explosive, spasmodic, involuntary action resulting from irritation of the nasal mucosa. *—n.* An instance of sneezing. [Middle English *snesen,* misreading of *fnesen,* Old English *fnēosan.* See **pneu-** in Appendix.*] **—sneez′er** *n.* **—sneez′y** *adj.*

sneeze·weed (snēz′wēd′) *n.* **1.** Any of several North American plants of the genus *Helenium,* having yellow, rayed flowers. **2.** The **sneezewort** *(see).* [The odor supposedly causes sneezing.]

sneeze·wort (snēz′wûrt′, -wôrt′) *n.* A plant, *Achillea ptarmica,* native to Europe, having clusters of white flowers.

snell (snĕl) *n.* A length of fine, threadlike material, such as monofilament or gut, that connects a fishhook to a heavier line; a leader. [Origin unknown.]

snib (snĭb) *tr.v.* **snibbed, snibbing, snibs.** *Chiefly Scottish & Canadian.* To latch (a door). [Origin obscure.]

snick·er (snĭk′ər) *n.* Also **snig·ger** (snĭg′ər). A snide, slightly stifled laugh. *—intr.v.* **snickered, -ering, -ers.** Also **snig·ger, -gered, -gering, -gers.** To utter a partly stifled laugh. [Imitative.] **—snick′er·ing·ly** *adv.*

snick·er·snee (snĭk′ər-snē′) *n.* Also **snick-a-snee, snick-or-snee.** **1.** A knife resembling a sword. **2.** *Archaic.* Fighting with knives. [Earlier *stick or snee* : Dutch *steken,* to stick, stab, from Middle Dutch (see **steig-** in Appendix*) + *snijden,* to cut, from Middle Dutch *sniden* (see **sneit-** in Appendix*).]

snide (snīd) *adj.* Derogatory in a malicious, superior way; sarcastic. [Origin unknown.]

sniff (snĭf) *v.* **sniffed, sniffing, sniffs.** *—intr.* **1.** To inhale a short, audible breath through the nose, as in smelling something. **2.** To indicate ridicule, contempt, or doubt by or as if by sniffing. Often used with *at.* **3.** To savor an odor by sniffing. *—tr.* **1.** To inhale forcibly through the nose. **2.** To smell or try to smell by sniffing. **3.** To perceive or detect by or as if by sniffing. *—n.* **1.** An instance or the sound of sniffing. **2.** Anything that is sniffed or perceived by sniffing; an odor; a whiff. [Middle English *sniffen.* See **snē-²** in Appendix.*]

snif·fle (snĭf′əl) *intr.v.* **-fled, -fling, -fles.** **1.** To breathe audibly through a congested nose, as when suffering from a head cold. **2.** To weep or whimper lightly with spasmodic sniffing. *—n.* An act or sound of sniffling. **—the sniffles.** *Informal.* A condition, such as a head cold, accompanied by sniffles. Also called "the snuffles." [Frequentative of SNIFF.]

snif·fy (snĭf′ē) *adj.* **-fier, -fiest.** *Informal.* Disposed to showing arrogance or contempt; haughty; disdainful.

snif·ter (snĭf′tər) *n.* **1.** A pear-shaped glass with a narrow top, used in serving brandy or other aromatic liquors. **2.** *Slang.* A small portion of liquor. [From dialectal *snifter,* to sniff, possibly from Middle Swedish *snypta* or Middle Danish *snyfte.* See **snē-²** in Appendix.*]

snip (snĭp) *v.* **snipped, snipping, snips.** *—tr.* To cut, clip, or separate in a short, quick stroke or strokes with scissors or shears. *—intr.* To cut or clip with short, quick strokes. *—n.* **1.** An instance of snipping or the sound produced by snipping. **2. a.** A small cut made with scissors or shears. **b.** A small piece cut or clipped off. **3.** *Informal.* **a.** A small or slight person or thing. **b.** A small person who is mischievous or annoying. **4.** *Plural.* Small hand shears used in cutting sheet metal. **5.** *Slang.* Something easily accomplished. [Low German or Dutch *snippen,* to snap. See **snē-²** in Appendix.*]

snipe (snīp) *n., pl.* **snipe** or **snipes.** **1.** Any of various long-billed wading birds of the genus *Capella;* especially, the common, widely distributed species *C. gallinago.* **2.** Any of various similar or related birds. **3.** A shot, especially a gunshot, from a concealed place. *—intr.v.* **sniped, sniping, snipes.** **1.** To shoot at individuals from a concealed place. **2.** To shoot snipe. [Middle English, perhaps from Old Norse *(mýri)snīpa*†, (moor) snipe.]

snip·er (snī′pər) *n.* **1.** *Military.* A skilled rifleman detailed to spot and pick off enemy soldiers from a concealed place. **2.** One who shoots at other people from a concealed place.

snip·pet (snĭp′ĭt) *n.* **1.** A tidbit or morsel. **2.** *Informal.* A small or mischievous person; a snip. [From SNIP (noun).]

snip·py (snĭp′ē) *adj.* **-pier, -piest.** Also **snip·pet·y** (snĭp′ĭ-tē), **-ier, -iest.** *Informal.* **1.** Impertinent. **2.** Composed of snips or scraps; fragmentary. **—snip′pi·ness** *n.*

snit (snĭt) *n. Slang.* A state of agitation or irritation. Usually used in the phrase *to be in a snit.*

snitch (snĭch) *v.* **snitched, snitching, snitches.** *Slang.* *—tr.* To steal (something of little or no value). *—intr.* To turn informer. Usually used with *on.* [Origin unknown.] **—snitch′er** *n.*

sniv·el (snĭv′əl) *intr.v.* **-eled** or **-elled, -eling** or **-elling, -els.** **1.** To cry or weep with sniffling. **2.** To complain or whine tearfully. **3.** To run at the nose. **4.** To snuffle or sniffle. *—n.* **1.** The act of sniffling or sniveling. **2.** Nasal mucus. [Middle English *snevelen,* Old English *snyflan* (unattested), akin to *snyflung,* nasal mucus. See **snē-²** in Appendix.*] **—sniv′el·er, sniv′el·ler** *n.*

snob (snŏb) *n.* **1.** An arrogant or affected person who strives to flatter, imitate, or associate with people of higher station or prestige. **2.** One who despises his inferiors and whose condescension arises from class or intellectual pretension. [Originally a shoemaker (origin unknown).] **—snob′ber·y** *n.*

snob·bish (snŏb′ĭsh) *adj.* Characteristic of or resembling a snob; pretentious. **—snob′bish·ly** *adv.* **—snob′bish·ness** *n.*

snood (snōōd) *n.* **1.** A small netlike cap worn by women to keep the hair in place. **2.** A headband or fillet. *—tr.v.* **snooded, snooding, snoods.** To hold (the hair) in place with a snood. [Middle English *snood* (unattested), Old English *snōd*†.]

snook (snŏŏk, snōōk) *n., pl.* **snook** or **snooks.** Any of several chiefly marine fishes of the family Centropomidae; especially, *Centropomus undecimalis,* of warm Atlantic waters. Also called "robalo." [Dutch *snoek,* pike, from Middle Dutch *snoec*†.]

snook·er (snŏŏk′ər) *n.* A pocket billiards game in which 15 red and 6 nonred balls are used. [Origin unknown.]

snoop (snōōp) *intr.v.* **snooped, snooping, snoops.** *Informal.* To pry into the private affairs of others, especially by prowling about. *—n. Informal.* One who snoops. [Dutch *snoepen,* to eat on the sly. See **snē-²** in Appendix.*] **—snoop′er** *n.*

snoop·y (snōō′pē) *adj.* **-ier, -iest.** *Informal.* Inclined, likely, or known to snoop. See Synonyms at **curious.**

snoot·y (snōō′tē) *adj.* **-ier, -iest.** *Informal.* **1.** Snobbish or aloof; haughty. **2.** High-class; exclusive. [From Middle English *snute,* SNOUT.]

snooze (snōōz) *intr.v.* **snoozed, snoozing, snoozes.** *Informal.* To take a light nap; to doze. *—n. Informal.* A brief light sleep. [Origin unknown.]

Sno·qual·mie Falls (snō-kwŏl′mē). A waterfall about 270 feet high on the Snoqualmie, a river flowing about 45 miles through west-central Washington.

snore (snôr, snōr) *intr.v.* **snored, snoring, snores.** To breathe through the nose and mouth while sleeping, making snorting noises caused by the vibration of the soft palate. *—n.* An instance of snoring or the noise produced by snoring. [Middle English *snoren,* to snort. See **sner-¹** in Appendix.*] **—snor′er** *n.*

snor·kel (snôr′kəl) *n.* **1.** A retractable vertical tube in a submarine, containing air-intake and exhaust pipes for the engines and for ventilation and which permits extended periods of submergence at periscope depth. **2.** A breathing apparatus used by skin divers, consisting of a long tube held in the mouth. *—intr.v.* **snorkeled, -keling, -kels.** To dive using a skin-diving snorkel. [German *Schnorchel,* from (dialectal) German, snout, from *schnarchen,* to snore, from Middle High German *snarche(l)n.* See **sner-¹** in Appendix.*]

snort (snôrt) *v.* **snorted, snorting, snorts.** *—intr.* **1. a.** To exhale forcibly and noisily through the nostrils, as a horse. **b.** To inhale forcibly through the nose or mouth and so produce from the soft palate a vibratory snoring noise. **2.** To express scorn, ridicule, or contempt with or as if with a snort. **3.** *Informal.* To emit a loud outburst of laughter. *—tr.* **1.** To express with a snort. **2.** To eject from the nostrils with or as with a snort. *—n.* **1.** The act or sound of snorting. **2.** *Slang.* A small drink of liquor, especially when swallowed in one gulp. [Middle English *snorten.* See **sner-¹** in Appendix.*] **—snort′er** *n.*

snot (snŏt) *n.* **1.** *Vulgar.* Nasal mucus; phlegm. **2.** *Vulgar Slang.* An untrustworthy, devious, or malicious person; one who is treacherous in a haughty or indifferent way. [Middle English *snot(te),* Old English *gesnot.* See **snē-²** in Appendix.*]

snot·ty (snŏt′ē) *adj.* **-tier, -tiest.** **1.** *Vulgar.* Dirtied with nasal mucus. **2.** *Vulgar Slang.* Nasty.

snout (snout) *n.* **1.** The projecting nose, jaws, or anterior facial part of an animal's muzzle. **2.** A similar prolongation of the anterior portion of the head in certain insects, such as weevils. **3.** A spout or nozzle likened to a snout. **4.** *Slang.* The human nose. [Middle English *sn(o)ute,* probably from Middle Dutch *snūt(e).* See **snē-²** in Appendix.*]

snout beetle. Any of numerous weevils of the family Curculionidae, having the front of the head elongated to form a snout.

snow (snō) *n.* **1.** Solid precipitation in the form of white or translucent ice crystals of various shapes originating in the

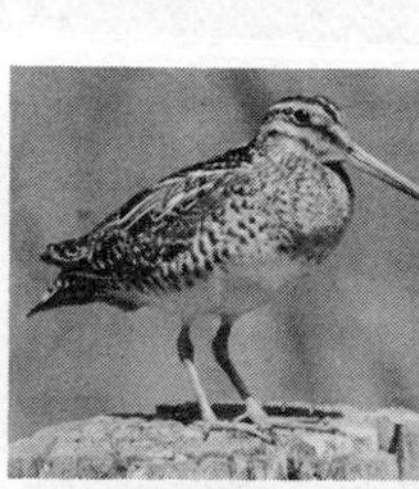

snipe
Capella gallinago

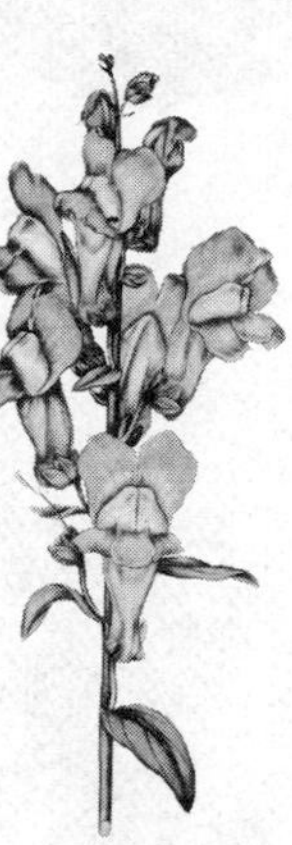

snapdragon
Antirrhinum majus

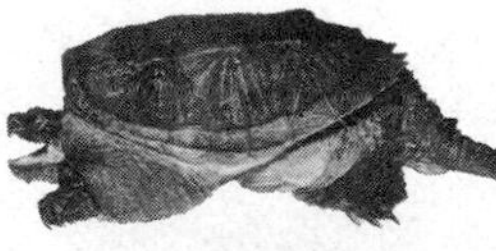

snapping turtle
Chelydra serpentina

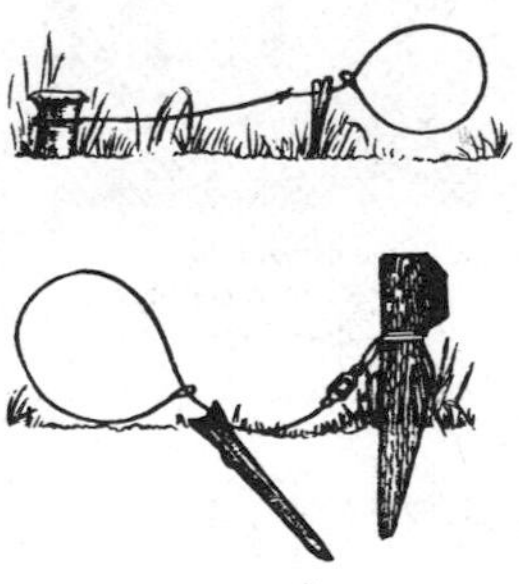

snare¹
Rabbit snares

upper atmosphere as frozen particles of water vapor. **2. a.** Anything resembling snow. **b.** The white specks on a television screen resulting from weak reception. **3.** A falling of snow; snowstorm. —*v.* **snowed, snowing, snows.** —*intr.* To fall as snow. —*tr.* **1.** To cover, shut off, or close off with snow. Used with *in, over, under,* or *up.* **2.** *Slang.* To overwhelm with insincere talk, especially with flattery. [Middle English *snawe, snow,* Old English *snāw.* See **sneigwh-** in Appendix.*]

snow apple. A variety of apple, the **Fameuse** *(see).*

snow·ball (snō′bôl′) *n.* **1.** A mass of soft, wet snow packed into a ball that can be thrown, as in play. **2.** Any of several plants or shrubs having rounded clusters of white flowers; especially, a cultivated variety of *Viburnum opulus.* —*v.* **snowballed, -balling, -balls.** —*intr.* **1.** To throw snowballs. **2.** To grow rapidly in significance, importance, or size, as a snowball rolling over snow. —*tr.* To throw snowballs at.

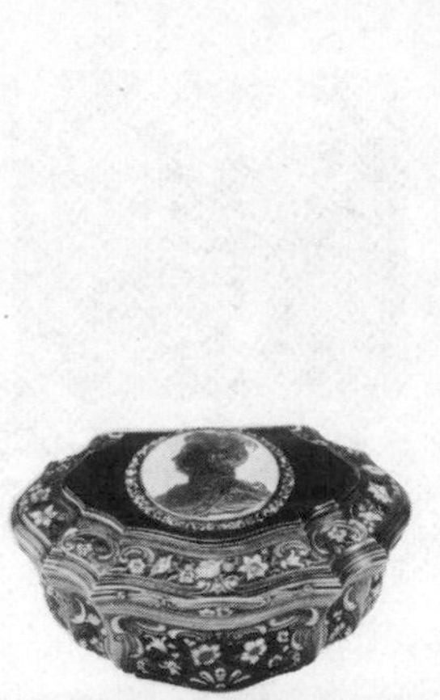

snuffbox
Eighteenth-century French

snow·bell (snō′bĕl′) *n.* Either of two shrubs, *Styrax grandifolia* or *S. americana,* of the southeastern United States, having bell-shaped white flowers.

snow·ber·ry (snō′bĕr′ē) *n., pl.* **-ries.** Any of various shrubs of the genus *Symphoricarpos;* especially, *S. albus,* having small pinkish flowers and white berries.

snow·bird (snō′bûrd′) *n.* Broadly, any of several birds, such as the junco, seen under snowy winter conditions.

snow blindness. Conjunctivitis and deteriorated vision caused by sunlight reflected from snow or ice. —**snow′-blind′** *adj.*

snow·blink (snō′blĭngk′) *n.* A white sky glow reflected from snowfields.

snow·bound (snō′bound′) *adj.* Confined in one place by heavy snow; snowed-in.

snow·broth (snō′brôth′, -brŏth′) *n.* Melted snow; slush.

snow bunting. A bird, *Plectrophenax nivalis,* of northern regions, having predominantly white winter plumage.

snow·bush (snō′bo͝osh′) *n.* Also **snow·brush** (-brŭsh′). A shrub, *Ceanothus velutinus,* of western North America, having large clusters of small white flowers.

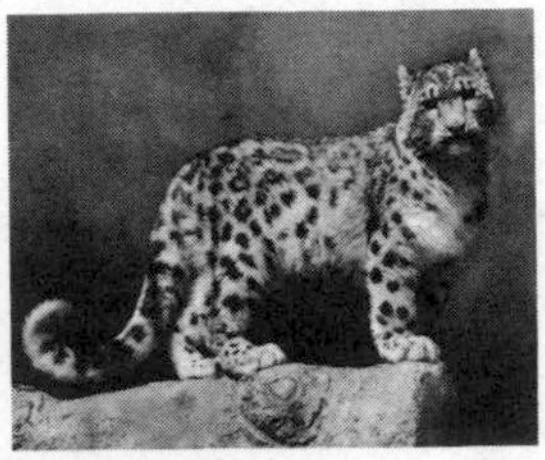

snow leopard

snow·cap (snō′kăp′) *n.* A cap of snow, as on a mountaintop. —**snow′capped′** *adj.*

Snow·don (snōd′n). A massif in Caernarvonshire, Wales, rising to 3,560 feet, the highest elevation in England and Wales.

snow·drift (snō′drĭft′) *n.* Snow banked up by the wind.

snow·drop (snō′drŏp′) *n.* Any of several bulbous plants of the genus *Galanthus,* native to Eurasia, having solitary, nodding white flowers that bloom early in spring.

snowdrop tree. The **silver-bell tree** *(see).*

snow·fall (snō′fôl′) *n.* **1.** The amount of snow that falls during a given period or in a specified area. **2.** A fall of snow.

snow fence. Temporary fencing composed of thin upright slats, used to prevent snow drifting onto walks or roads.

snow·flake (snō′flāk′) *n.* **1.** A single flake or crystal of snow. **2.** Any of several bulbous plants of the genus *Leucojum,* native to Europe, having white or whitish flowers.

snow goose. A goose, *Chen hyperborea,* that breeds in northern regions, having white plumage with black wing tips.

snow job. *Slang.* An effort to overwhelm with insincere talk, especially flattery.

snow leopard. A large feline mammal, *Uncia uncia,* of the highlands of central Asia, having long, thick, whitish fur with dark markings. Also called "ounce."

snow lily. The **fawn lily** *(see).*

snow line. **1.** The lower altitudinal boundary of a snow-covered area, especially of one which is perennially covered, as the snowcap of a mountain. **2.** The fluctuating latitudinal boundaries around the polar regions marking the extent of snow cover.

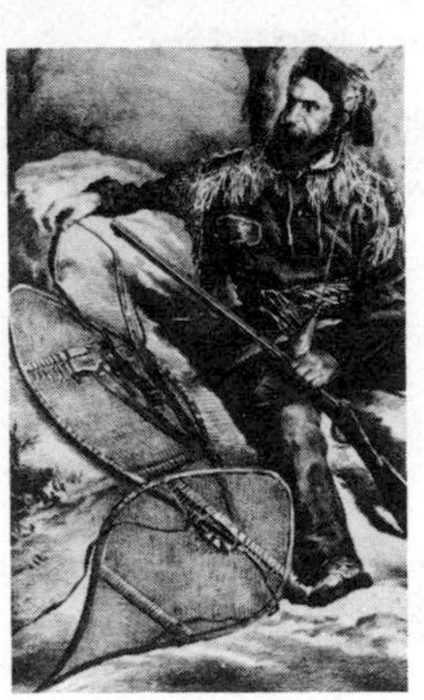

snowshoe
Nineteenth-century
Canadian fur trapper

Snow Mountains. The collective name for the mountain ranges extending over 400 miles through central New Guinea, including the Nassau and Orange ranges. Highest elevation, Mount Carstensz (16,400 feet).

snow-on-the-moun·tain (snō′ŏn-*thə*-moun′tən, snō′ôn-) *n.* A widely cultivated plant, *Euphorbia marginata,* of central North America, having white-margined leaves and showy white bracts.

snow pellets. **Graupel** *(see).*

snow plant. A saprophytic plant, *Sarcodes sanguinea,* of the mountains of western North America, having a fleshy, scaly, reddish stalk and scarlet flowers.

snow·plow (snō′plou′) *n.* Any plowlike device or vehicle used to remove snow, especially from roads and railroad tracks.

snow pudding. A light, fluffy pudding made of beaten egg whites, flavored gelatin, and sugar.

snow·shed (snō′shĕd′) *n.* A roofing built over portions of a railroad track to protect them from snowslides.

snow·shoe (snō′sho͞o′) *n.* A racket-shaped frame containing interlaced leather strips that can be attached to the foot to facilitate walking on deep snow. —*intr.v.* **snowshoed, -shoeing, -shoes.** To go or walk on snowshoes. —**snow′sho′er** *n.*

snowshoe rabbit. A hare, *Lepus americanus,* of northern North America, having large, heavily furred feet and fur that is white in winter and brown in summer. Also called "snowshoe hare," "varying hare."

snow·slide (snō′slīd′) *n.* An avalanche of ice or snow.

snow·storm (snō′stôrm′) *n.* A storm marked by heavy snowfall and high winds; blizzard.

snow·suit (snō′so͞ot′) *n.* A child's zippered winter coverall.

snow-white (snō′hwīt′) *adj.* White as snow.

snow·y (snō′ē) *adj.* **-ier, -iest.** **1.** Abounding in snow; covered with or subject to snow. **2.** Resembling or suggestive of snow; white; pure. —**snow′i·ly** *adv.* —**snow′i·ness** *n.*

snub (snŭb) *tr.v.* **snubbed, snubbing, snubs.** **1.** To treat with scorn or contempt; slight by ignoring or behaving coldly toward. **2.** To dismiss or rebuke in a decisive way; turn down or frustrate the expectations of. **3. a.** To check suddenly the movement of (a rope or cable running out) by turning it about a post. **b.** To secure (a vessel or animal, for example) in this manner. **4.** *Obsolete.* To clip or stunt: *snub cattle horns.* —*n.* **1.** A deliberate slight or affront: *"He was in distinct need of a snub"* (Henry James). **2.** A sudden checking, as of a rope or cable running out. [Middle English *snubben,* to rebuke, from Old Norse *snubba.* See **snē-²** in Appendix.*] —**snub′ber** *n.*

snub-nosed (snŭb′nōzd′) *adj.* Having a short, turned-up nose.

snuck (snŭk). *Nonstandard.* Past tense and past participle of **sneak.**

snuff¹ (snŭf) *v.* **snuffed, snuffing, snuffs.** —*tr.* **1.** To inhale through the nose; sniff. **2.** To sense or examine by smelling; to smell; sniff at. —*intr.* To snort or sniff. —*n.* An act of snuffing or the sound produced in snuffing; a sniff. [Probably from Middle Dutch *snuffen.* See **snē-²** in Appendix.*]

snuff² (snŭf) *n.* The charred portion of a candlewick. —*tr.v.* **snuffed, snuffing, snuffs.** **1.** To cut off the charred portion of (a candlewick). **2.** To extinguish (a candle or lamp, for example); put out. Used with *out.* **3.** To put a sudden end to; destroy. Used with *out.* [Middle English *snoffe*†.]

snuff³ (snŭf) *n.* **1.** A preparation of finely pulverized tobacco that can be drawn up into the nostrils by inhaling. **2.** The quantity of this inhaled at a single time; a pinch of snuff. **3.** Any powdery substance, such as a medicine, taken by inhaling. —**up to snuff.** *Informal.* **1.** Normal in health or usual in quality. **2.** *Chiefly British.* Not easily deceived. —*intr.v.* **snuffed, snuffing, snuffs.** To use or inhale snuff. [Dutch *snuf,* short for *snuf(tabak),* (tobacco) for snuffing, from Middle Dutch *snuffen,* to SNUFF.]

snuff·box (snŭf′bŏks′) *n.* A small, often highly decorative box with a hinged lid that is used for carrying snuff in the pocket.

snuff·er¹ (snŭf′ər) *n.* One who uses snuff.

snuff·er² (snŭf′ər) *n.* **1.** One that snuffs out candles. **2.** *Plural.* An instrument resembling a pair of shears that is used for cutting the snuff from or for extinguishing candles.

snuf·fle (snŭf′əl) *v.* **-fled, -fling, -fles.** —*intr.* **1.** To breathe noisily, as through a blocked nose or as a dog following a trail; to sniff; to sniffle. **2.** To talk or sing nasally; to whine. —*tr.* To utter (something) in a snuffling tone. —*n.* **1.** An act of snuffling. **2.** The sound produced in snuffling. —**the snuffles.** *Informal.* The **sniffles** *(see).* [Probably from Low German or Dutch *snuffelen.* See **snē-²** in Appendix.*] —**snuf′fler** *n.*

snug (snŭg) *adj.* **snugger, snuggest.** **1.** Comfortably sheltered from the cold and the weather; cozy: *"They looked so snug, sitting there together in the firelight"* (Frank O'Connor). **2.** Small but well-arranged: *a snug apartment.* **3. a.** Closely secured and well-built; compact. **b.** Seaworthy. **c.** Close-fitting, as a garment. —See Synonyms at **comfortable.** —*v.* **snugged, snugging, snugs.** —*tr.* To make snug or secure. —*intr.* To nestle or snuggle. —**snug down.** To prepare (a vessel) to weather a storm, as by taking in sail or securing movable gear. [Originally a nautical term meaning neat, tight, perhaps from Scandinavian, akin to Old Norse *snöggr,* "close-cropped." See **kes-¹** in Appendix.*] —**snug, snug′ly** *adv.* —**snug′ness** *n.*

snug·ger·y (snŭg′ə-rē) *n., pl.* **-ies.** A snug position or place.

snug·gle (snŭg′əl) *v.* **-gled, -gling, -gles.** —*intr.* To lie or press close together; nestle or cuddle. Often used with *together, with,* or *up.* —*tr.* To draw close or hold closely, as for comfort or in affection; to hug. [Frequentative of SNUG (verb).]

so¹ (sō) *adv.* **1.** In the manner described, shown, expressed, implied, or indicated; thus: *"She became his loyal friend and remained so to the end"* (Constantine Fitzgibbon). **2.** To the amount or degree expressed or understood; in such quantity or to such an extent: *He was so weary that he fell.* **3.** To a great extent; to such an evident degree: *But the idea is so obvious.* **4.** Because of the reason given; consequently; as a result: *He was weary and so he fell.* **5.** Approximately that quantity, amount, or number; thereabouts: *ten dollars or so.* **6.** Too; also; likewise: *You were on time and so was I.* **7.** Then; apparently. Used in expressing astonishment, disapproval, or sarcasm: *So you think you've got troubles?* **8.** In truth. Used to reply to doubt: *You aren't. I am so.* —*adj.* True; factual: *It is so.* —*conj.* **1.** With the purpose or reason that; in order that. Usually used with *that: I stopped so that you could catch up.* **2.** With the result or consequence that: *He agreed, so they went ahead with plans.* —*interj.* Used to express surprise or comprehension. [Middle English *so, s(w)a,* Old English *swā.* See **swo-** in Appendix.*]

Usage: *So* (conjunction) is preferably followed by *that* when it introduces a clause stating the purpose of, or reason for, an action expressed earlier: *He stayed a day longer so that he could avoid the holiday traffic.* This is especially true of formal written usage; informally, *so* often functions alone to express purpose. The preceding example, employing *so* in place of *so that,* is acceptable in written usage to only 44 per cent of the Usage Panel. *So* is better able to stand alone in introducing a clause that states a result or consequence of something that precedes: *The traffic was unusually heavy, so he stayed a day longer* (acceptable to 83 per cent of the Panel as an example in writing). In such an example in usage that is expressly formal, some grammarians consider an alternative construction, such as *and therefore* or *and consequently,* preferable to *so.* See Usage note at **as.**

so². *Music.* Variant of **sol.**

So. south; southern.

s.o. **1.** seller's option. **2.** strikeout.

soak (sōk) *v.* **soaked, soaking, soaks.** —*tr.* **1.** To make thoroughly wet or saturated by or as by placing in liquid; to im-

ă pat/ā pay/âr care/ä father/b bib/ch church/d deed/ĕ pet/ē be/f fife/g gag/h hat/hw which/ĭ pit/ī pie/îr pier/j judge/k kick/l lid, needle/m mum/n no, sudden/ng thing/ŏ pot/ō toe/ô paw, for/oi noise/ou out/o͝o took/o͞o boot/p pop/r roar/s sauce/sh ship, dish/

merse, often for a period of time. **2.** To absorb (liquid) through pores or interstices. Usually used with *up.* **3.** *Informal.* To take in or accept mentally, especially eagerly and easily; assimilate; absorb; devour. Used with *up.* **4.** *Informal.* **a.** To drink (alcoholic liquor), especially to excess. **b.** To make (a person) drunk. **5.** *Slang.* To overcharge (a person) for something; force to pay too much. —*intr.* **1.** To be immersed until thoroughly saturated. **2.** To penetrate or permeate; seep. Used with *in* or *into.* **3.** *Slang.* To drink to excess. —*n.* **1.** The act or process of soaking or the condition of being soaked. **2.** Liquid in which something may be soaked; a rinse. **3.** *Slang.* A drunkard. [Middle English *soken,* Old English *socian.* See **seu-**[4] in Appendix.*] —**soak′er** *n.*

soak·age (sō′kĭj) *n.* **1.** The process of soaking or the condition of being soaked. **2.** The amount of liquid that soaks into or through an object or seeps out of it; capacity; drainage.

so-and-so (sō′ən-sō′) *n., pl.* **-sos.** **1.** A figurative person or thing to be considered as unspecified or as a general example for discussion purposes. **2.** *Informal.* A euphemism used for various unsavory epithets: *a real so-and-so.*

soap (sōp) *n.* **1.** A cleansing agent, manufactured in bars, granules, flakes, or liquid form, made from a mixture of the sodium salts of various fatty acids of natural oils and fats. **2.** Any metallic salt of a fatty acid, as of aluminum or iron. **3.** *Slang.* Money, especially money used for bribery. —**no soap.** *Slang.* **1.** Not possible or permissible; categorically rejected. **2.** Unsuccessful; futile. —*tr.v.* **soaped, soaping, soaps.** To treat or cover with soap. [Middle English *sope, saip,* Old English *sāpe.* See **sib-** in Appendix.*]

soap·bark (sōp′bärk′) *n.* **1.** A tree, *Quillaja saponaria,* of western South America, having bark used as soap and as a source of saponin. **2.** The bark of this tree. **3.** Any of several other trees or shrubs having similar bark.

soap·ber·ry (sōp′bĕr′ē) *n., pl.* **-ries.** **1.** Any of various chiefly tropical New World trees of the genus *Sapindus,* having pulpy fruit that lathers like soap. **2.** The fruit of any of these trees.

soap·box (sōp′bŏks′) *n.* Also **soap box.** **1.** A carton or wooden crate in which soap is packed. **2.** Any box or crate used as a temporary platform for making an impromptu or nonofficial public speech. —*adj.* Designating oratory or an orator characterized by ranting, fanaticism, or eccentricity; demagogic. —**soap′box′er** *n.*

soap bubble. **1.** A bubble, especially a large one, formed from soapy water. **2.** Anything beautiful but transient, insubstantial, or illusory.

soap opera. A daytime radio or television serial drama, characterized by sentimentality. [So called because many of them were originally sponsored by soap companies.]

soap plant. **1.** A plant, *Chlorogalum pomeridianum,* of California, having small white flowers and a bulbous root formerly used as soap. Also called "amole." **2.** Any of several other plants having parts used as soap.

soap·stone (sōp′stōn′) *n.* A type of rock, **steatite** *(see).* [From its soapy texture.]

soap·suds (sōp′sŭdz′) *pl.n.* Suds from soapy water.

soap·wort (sōp′wûrt′, -wôrt′) *n.* A plant, the **bouncing Bet** *(see).* [So called because the leaves yield a soapy substance when bruised.]

soap·y (sō′pē) *adj.* **-ier, -iest.** **1.** Containing or consisting of soap; covered or filled with soap. **2.** Pertaining to or resembling soap. **3.** *Slang.* Unctuous; oily. —**soap′i·ly** *adv.* —**soap′i·ness** *n.*

soar (sôr, sōr) *intr.v.* **soared, soaring, soars.** **1.** To fly upward or rise high into the air; climb swiftly or powerfully. **2.** To fly or glide high in the air without visibly moving the wings. **3.** *Aviation.* To glide while maintaining altitude. **4.** To ascend suddenly above the normal or usual level; increase abnormally. **5.** To be inspired. —See Synonyms at **rise.** —*n.* **1.** The act of soaring. **2.** The altitude or scope attained in soaring. [Middle English *soren,* from Old French *esorer,* from Vulgar Latin *exaurāre* (unattested) : Latin *ex-,* out of + *aura,* the air, a gentle breeze, from Greek, a breeze (see **wē-** in Appendix*).] —**soar′er** *n.* —**soar′ing·ly** *adv.*

so·a·ve (sō-ä′vā) *n.* A dry white Italian table wine. [Italian, "sweet," from Latin *suāvis.* See **swād-** in Appendix.*]

sob (sŏb) *v.* **sobbed, sobbing, sobs.** —*intr.* **1.** To weep aloud with convulsive gasping and sniffling; cry uncontrollably. **2.** To make a sound resembling that of sobbing. —*tr.* **1.** To utter with sobs. **2.** To put or bring (oneself) into a specified condition by sobbing: *sob oneself to sleep.* —See Synonyms at **cry.** —*n.* The act of sobbing or the sound produced in sobbing; a short, audible gasp of the breath. [Middle English *sobben,* to catch breath, probably of Low German origin, akin to Dutch dialectal *sobben*†, to suck.] —**sob′bing·ly** *adv.*

S.O.B. *Slang.* son of a bitch.

So·bat (sō′băt). A river flowing 205 miles from southwestern Ethiopia to the White Nile in southeastern Sudan.

so·be·it (sō-bē′ĭt) *conj. Archaic.* Provided that; if it be so that.

so·ber (sō′bər) *adj.* **-berer, -berest.** **1.** Habitually abstemious in the use of alcoholic liquors; temperate. **2.** Not intoxicated. **3.** Straightforward in character; serious or grave; sedate: *"My sober mind was no longer intoxicated by the fumes of politics"* (Gibbon). **4.** Plain or subdued; not garish or gay. Said of colors. **5.** Without frivolity, excess, exaggeration, or speculative imagination: *"sober history provides no certain link between Arthur and Cornwall."* (Hugh Hencken). **6.** Characterized by self-control or sanity; reasonable; rational. —See Synonyms at **serious.** —*v.* **sobered, bering, -bers.** —*tr.* To make (someone) sober. Often used with *up.* —*intr.* To become sober. Often used with *up.* [Middle English *sobre,* from Old French, from Latin *sōbrius.* See **seu-**[2] in Appendix.*] —**so′ber·ly** *adv.* —**so′ber·ness** *n.*

So·bran·je (sə-brän′yə) *n.* Also **So·bran·ye, So·bran·i·ye** (sə-brän′ĭ-yə). The Bulgarian national assembly. [Bulgarian, "assembly."]

so·bri·e·ty (sō-brī′ə-tē) *n.* **1.** Seriousness or gravity in bearing, manner, or treatment; solemnity. **2.** Absence of alcoholic intoxication. —See Synonyms at **abstinence.**

so·bri·quet (sō′brĭ-kā′, -kĕt′, sō′brĭ-kā′, -kĕt′) *n.* Also **sou·bri·quet.** **1.** An affectionate or humorous nickname. **2.** An assumed name. —See Synonyms at **name.** [French *sobriquet,* earlier *soubriquet*†.]

sob sister. **1.** A journalist, especially a woman, employed as a writer or editor of sob stories. **2.** A sentimental and ineffective person who seeks to do good.

sob story. **1.** A tale of personal hardship or misfortune intended to arouse pity. **2.** A maudlin plea given as an explanation or rationalization.

soc. **1.** socialist. **2.** society.

Soc. society.

soc·age (sŏk′ĭj) *n.* In medieval feudalism, land tenure by a tenant not a knight, in return for agricultural or other nonmilitary services or for payment. [Middle English *sokage,* from *soke,* SOKE.] —**soc′ag·er** *n.*

so-called (sō′kôld′) *adj.* Designated thus or known by this term. Often implies a purported or dubious designation: *a so-called teetotaler.*

Usage: So-called is written thus when it precedes a noun and the noun is not enclosed in quotation marks, even when sarcasm is intended: *these so-called friends.* An alternative construction is *these "friends." So called* (without a hyphen) may be used in still another alternative: *these friends, so called.*

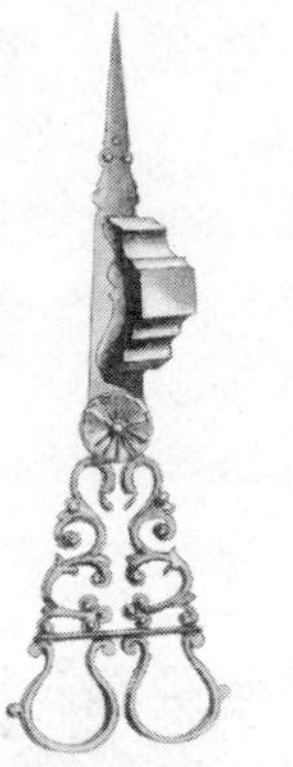
snuffer[2]
English silver snuffers

soc·cer (sŏk′ər) *n.* The most common international type of football, in which two teams of 11 men each on a rectangular field with net goals at either end maneuver a round ball mainly by kicking, butting, or by using any part of the body except the arms and hands in attempts to score points. Also *chiefly British* "association football," "football." [Shortened variant of ASSOCIATION (football).]

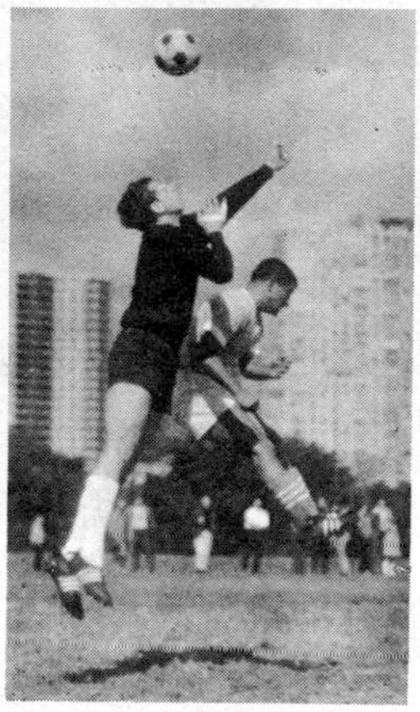
soccer
Heading the ball in a game at Columbia University, New York City

So·che. The Chinese name for **Yarkand.**

So·chi (sō′chē). A port and health resort of the Soviet Union, in the southwest on the Black Sea. Population, 179,000.

so·cia·bil·i·ty (sō′shə-bĭl′ə-tē) *n., pl.* **-ties.** **1.** The disposition or quality of being sociable. **2.** An instance of being sociable.

so·cia·ble (sō′shə-bəl) *adj.* **1.** Pleasant, friendly, or affable. **2.** Providing occasion for conversation and conviviality. —*n.* A **social** *(see).* [Old French, from Latin *sociābilis,* from *sociāre,* to join, to share, from *socius,* partner, sharer. See **sekw-**[1] in Appendix.*] —**so′cia·ble·ness** *n.* —**so′cia·bly** *adv.*

so·cial (sō′shəl) *adj.* **1. a.** Living together in communities. **b.** Characterizing such communal living. **c.** Of or pertaining to society. **2.** Living in an organized group or similar close aggregate: *social insects.* **3.** Involving allies or members of a confederacy. **4.** Of or pertaining to the upper classes. **5.** Sociable; fond of the company of others. **6.** Intended for convivial activities. **7.** Pertaining to or occupied with welfare work: *a social worker.* —*n.* An informal social gathering, as of the members of a church congregation. Also called "sociable." [Latin *sociālis,* of companionship, from *socius,* companion, partner. See **sekw-**[1] in Appendix.*]

social climber. One striving for acceptance in fashionable society.

social contract. The republican idealist theory, formulated by Rousseau (1762), that government should rest on the consent of the governed.

social disease. **1.** Venereal disease. Used as a euphemism. **2.** A disease having its highest incidence among social classes predisposed to it by a given set of adverse living or working conditions.

so·cial·ism (sō′shə-lĭz′əm) *n.* **1.** A social system in which the producers possess both political power and the means of producing and distributing goods. **2.** The theory or practice of those who support such a social system. **3.** In Marxist-Leninist theory, the building, under the dictatorship of the proletariat, of the material base for communism.

so·cial·ist (sō′shə-lĭst) *n.* **1.** An advocate of socialism. **2.** *Abbr.* **soc.** A member of a socialist party. —*adj.* **1.** Of, promoting, or practicing socialism. **2.** *Capital* **S.** Of, belonging to, or constituting a socialist party.

so·cial·is·tic (sō′shə-lĭs′tĭk) *adj.* Of, advocating, or tending toward socialism. —**so′cial·is′ti·cal·ly** *adv.*

Socialist Party. Any of certain political parties advocating socialism to be achieved by democratic process; specifically, an American party growing out of an earlier Socialist Labor Party and achieving its greatest electoral support in the Presidential election of 1912.

so·cial·ite (sō′shə-līt′) *n.* One prominent in fashionable society.

so·ci·al·i·ty (sō′shē-ăl′ə-tē) *n., pl.* **-ties.** **1. a.** The state or quality of being sociable; sociability. **b.** An instance of sociableness. **2.** The tendency to form communities and societies.

so·cial·ize (sō′shə-līz′) *v.* **-ized, -izing, -izes.** —*tr.* **1.** To place under government or group ownership or control; establish on a socialist basis. **2.** To fit for companionship with others; make sociable in attitude or manners. **3.** To convert or adapt to the needs of society. —*intr.* To take part in social activities. —**so′cial·i·za′tion** *n.* —**so′cial·iz′er** *n.*

socialized medicine. The provision of medical and hospital care for the people at nominal cost by means of government

t tight/th thin, path/*th* this, bathe/ŭ cut/ûr urge/v valve/w with/y yes/z zebra, size/zh vision/ə about, item, edible, gallop, circus/ à *Fr.* ami/œ *Fr.* feu, *Ger.* schön/ü *Fr.* tu, *Ger.* über/KH *Ger.* ich, *Scot.* loch/N *Fr.* bon. *Follows main vocabulary. †Of obscure origin.

regulation of health services and subsidies derived from taxation.

so·cial·ly (sō′shə-lē) *adv.* **1.** In a social manner. **2.** With regard to society: *socially important.* **3.** By society.

social register. A directory listing persons of social prominence in a community.

social science. The study of society and of individual relationships in and to society, generally regarded as including sociology, psychology, anthropology, economics, political science, and history.

social security. Measures by which the U.S. Government provides economic assistance to persons faced with unemployment, disability, or old age, financed by assessment of employers and employees.

social service. Organized efforts to advance human welfare; social work. —**so′cial-ser′vice** *adj.*

social studies. A course of study including geography, history, government, and sociology, taught in secondary and elementary schools.

social work. Welfare work usually involving casework.

so·ci·e·tal (sə-sī′ə-təl) *adj.* Of or pertaining to the structure, organization, or functioning of society. —**so·ci′e·tal·ly** *adv.*

so·ci·e·ty (sə-sī′ə-tē) *n., pl.* **-ties.** *Abbr.* **S., s., Soc., soc. 1. a.** The totality of social relationships among human beings. **b.** A group of human beings broadly distinguished from other groups by mutual interests, participation in characteristic relationships, shared institutions, and a common culture. **c.** The institutions and culture of a distinct self-perpetuating group. **2. a.** The rich, privileged, and fashionable social class. **b.** The socially dominant members of a community. **3.** Companionship; company. **4.** *Biology.* A colony or community of organisms, usually of the same species. —See Synonyms at **circle.** [Old French *societe*, from Latin *societās*, fellowship, union, society, from *socius*, a sharing. See **sekw-¹** in Appendix.*]

Society Islands. A group of islands with a combined area of 650 square miles, in the South Pacific Ocean, comprising part of French Polynesia. Population, 68,000. Capital, Papeete on Tahiti.

Society of Friends. A Christian sect founded in about 1650 in England by George Fox. It rejects ritual, formal sacraments, a formal creed, a priesthood, and violence. Also known informally as "Quakers."

Society of Jesus. *Abbr.* **S.J.** The Jesuits *(see).*

So·cin·i·an (sō-sĭn′ē-ən) *n.* An adherent of a sect holding unitarian views, including denial of the divinity of Jesus, founded by Laelius and Faustus Socinus, Italian theologians of the 16th century. —*adj.* Of or pertaining to the Socinians or their doctrines. —**So·cin′i·an·ism′** *n.*

socio-. Indicates: **1.** Society; for example, **sociometry. 2.** Social; for example, **socioeconomic.** [French, from Latin *socius,* a sharing. See **sekw-¹** in Appendix.*]

so·ci·o·ec·o·nom·ic (sō′sē-ō-ĕk′ə-nŏm′ĭk, -ē′kə-nŏm′ĭk, sō′-shē-) *adj.* Both social and economic.

so·ci·ol·o·gy (sō′sē-ŏl′ə-jē, sō′shē-) *n. Abbr.* **sociol. 1.** The study of human social behavior; especially, the study of the origins, organization, institutions, and development of human society. **2.** The analysis of a social institution or societal segment as a self-contained entity or in relation to society as a whole. [French *sociologie* : SOCIO- + -LOGY.] —**so′ci·o·log′ic** (-ə-lŏj′ĭk), **so′ci·o·log′i·cal** *adj.* —**so′ci·o·log′i·cal·ly** *adv.* —**so′ci·ol′o·gist** *n.*

so·ci·om·e·try (sō′sē-ŏm′ə-trē, sō′shē-) *n.* The quantitative study of interpersonal relationships in populations, especially the study and measurement of preferences. [SOCIO- + -METRY.]

so·ci·o·po·li·ti·cal (sō′sē-ō′pə-lĭt′ĭ-kəl, sō′shē-) *adj.* Both social and political.

sock¹ (sŏk) *n., pl.* **socks** (for all senses) or **sox** (for sense 1). **1.** A short stocking reaching a point between the ankle and the knee. **2. a.** A light shoe worn by comic actors in ancient Greek and Roman plays. Compare **buskin. b.** Comic drama; comedy. **3.** A windsock *(see).* —*tr.v.* **socked, socking, socks. 1.** To provide with socks. **2.** *Informal.* To stash (money); save. Usually used with *away.* —**socked in.** Closed in by bad weather. Used of an airport. [Middle English *socke,* Old English *socc,* a kind of light shoe, from Latin *soccus,* probably from Greek *sukkhos†.*]

sock² (sŏk) *v.* **socked, socking, socks.** *Slang.* —*tr.* To hit or strike forcefully; punch. —*intr.* To deliver a blow. —*n. Slang.* A hard blow or punch. [Origin obscure.]

sock·dol·a·ger (sŏk′dŏl′ə-jər) *n.* Also **sock·dol·o·ger.** *Archaic Slang.* **1.** A conclusive blow or remark. **2.** Something outstanding. [Perhaps a fanciful blend of SOCK (blow) and DOXOLOGY.]

sock·et (sŏk′ĭt) *n.* **1.** An opening or cavity that acts as the receptacle for an inserted part: *a light-bulb socket.* **2.** *Anatomy.* **a.** The hollow part of a joint that receives the end of a bone. **b.** A hollow or concavity into which a part, such as the eye, fits. —*tr.v.* **socketed, -eting, -ets.** To furnish with or insert into a socket. [Middle English *soket,* spearhead shaped like a plowshare, socket, from Norman French *soket,* diminutive of Old French *soc,* plowshare, probably from Celtic origin. See **su-¹** in Appendix.*]

sock·eye salmon (sŏk′ī′). A salmon, *Oncorhynchus nerka,* of northern Pacific coastal waters, that is a commercially valuable food fish. Also called "blueback salmon," "red salmon." [By folk etymology from Salish (dialectal) *suk-kegh.*]

so·cle (sō′kəl) *n. Architecture.* **1.** A plain square block higher than a plinth, serving as a pedestal for sculpture, a vase, or a

soda fountain

column. **2.** A plain plinth supporting a wall. [French *socle,* from Italian *zoccolo,* "wooden shoe," from Latin *socculus,* diminutive of *soccus,* a kind of light shoe. See **sock** (stocking).]

soc·man (sŏk′mən) *n., pl.* **-men** (-mĭn). Also **soke·man** (sōk′-). Formerly, in England, a tenant holding land in socage. [Medieval Latin *sokemannus* : Old English *sōcn,* SOKE + *mann,* MAN.]

So·co·tra (sō-kō′trə). Also **So·ko·tra, So·qo·tra.** An island, part of Southern Yemen, occupying 1,400 square miles in the Indian Ocean, off the horn of Africa. Population, 14,000. Administrative center, Tamrida.

Soc·ra·tes (sŏk′rə-tēz′). 470?–399 B.C. Greek philosopher and teacher; condemned to death for impiety and corrupting youth.

So·crat·ic (sō-krăt′ĭk). Also **So·crat·i·cal** (-ĭ-kəl). Of or pertaining to Socrates or his philosophical method of repeated questioning to elicit truths assumed to be implicit in all rational beings: *Socratic method.* —*n.* A disciple of Socrates. —**So·crat′i·cal·ly** *adv.* —**Soc′ra·tism′** (sŏk′rə-tĭz′əm), **So·crat′i·cism′** (sō-krăt′ə-sĭz′əm) *n.* —**Soc′ra·tist** *n.*

sod¹ (sŏd) *n.* **1.** A section of grass-covered surface soil held together by matted roots; turf. **2.** The ground, especially when covered with grass. —*tr.v.* **sodded, sodding, sods.** To cover with sod. [Middle English *sod(de),* from Middle Low German or Middle Dutch *sode,* akin to Old Frisian *sāda†.*]

sod². *Obsolete.* Past tense of **seethe.**

sod³ (sŏd) *n. British Slang.* An obnoxious or contemptible person. [Shortened from SODOMITE.]

so·da (sō′də) *n.* **1. a.** Any of various forms of sodium carbonate. **b.** Loosely, chemically combined sodium. **2.** Carbonated water or a soft drink containing it. **3.** A refreshment made from carbonated water, ice cream, and sometimes flavoring. **4.** In faro, the card turned face up at the beginning of the game. [Medieval Latin *soda†,* barilla (from which soda is made).]

soda ash. Crude anhydrous **sodium carbonate** *(see),* used especially as an industrial chemical.

soda biscuit. 1. A breadlike biscuit leavened with baking soda. **2.** A soda cracker.

soda cracker. A thin, usually square cracker leavened slightly with baking soda.

soda fountain. 1. An apparatus with faucets for dispensing soda water. **2.** A counter equipped for preparing and serving soft drinks, ice-cream dishes, sandwiches, and the like.

soda jerk. *Slang.* One who works at a soda fountain. [Short for *soda jerker.*]

soda lime. *Chemistry.* A mixture of calcium hydroxide and sodium or potassium hydroxide, used as a drying agent and carbon dioxide absorbent.

so·da·list (sō′də-lĭst) *n.* A member of a sodality.

so·da·lite (sō′də-līt′) *n.* A blue-white vitreous mineral, essentially $Na_4Al_3Si_3O_{12}Cl$, found in igneous rocks. [SODA + -LITE.]

so·dal·i·ty (sō-dăl′ə-tē) *n., pl.* **-ties. 1.** A society or association; especially, in the Roman Catholic Church, a devotional or charitable society. **2.** Brotherhood; fellowship. [Latin *sodālitās,* fellowship, brotherhood, from *sodālis,* fellow, intimate. See **seu-²** in Appendix.*]

so·da·mide (sō′də-mīd′) *n. Chemistry.* Sodium amide.

soda niter. *Chemistry.* Sodium nitrate *(see).*

soda pop. *Informal.* A soft drink; soda.

soda water. 1. Effervescent water charged under pressure with purified carbon dioxide gas, used as a beverage or mixer. Also called "carbonated water." **2.** A solution of water, sodium bicarbonate, and acid.

sod·den (sŏd′n). *Obsolete.* Past participle of **seethe.** —*adj.* **1.** Thoroughly soaked; saturated. **2.** Soggy and heavy from improper cooking; doughy. **3.** Bloated and dull, especially from drink. **4.** *Archaic.* Boiled. —*v.* **soddened, -dening, -dens.** —*tr.* To make sodden. —*intr.* To become sodden. [Middle English *soden,* from the past participle of *sethen,* to SEETHE.] —**sod′den·ly** *adv.* —**sod′den·ness** *n.*

sod·dy (sŏd′ē) *n., pl.* **-dies.** A house built of sod.

Sod·dy (sŏd′ē), **Frederick.** 1877–1956. British chemist; worked on radioactivity and isotopes.

so·di·um (sō′dē-əm) *n. Symbol* **Na** A soft, light, extremely malleable silver-white metallic element that reacts explosively with water. It is naturally abundant in combined forms, especially in common salt, and is used in the production of a wide variety of industrially important compounds. Atomic number 11, atomic weight 22.99, melting point 97.8°C, boiling point 892°C, specific gravity 0.971, valence 1. See **element.** [New Latin : SOD(A) + -IUM.]

sodium ammonium phosphate. A colorless, odorless crystalline compound, $NaNH_4HPO_4 \cdot 4H_2O$, used as an analytical reagent.

sodium benzoate. The sodium salt of benzoic acid, $C_6H_5CO\text{-}ONa$, used as a food preservative, antiseptic, and intermediate in dye manufacture, and in the production of pharmaceuticals. Also called "benzoate of soda."

sodium bicarbonate. A white crystalline compound, $NaHCO_3$, with a slightly alkaline taste, used in making effervescent salts and beverages, artificial mineral water, baking soda, pharmaceuticals, and in fire extinguishers. Also called "baking soda," "bicarbonate of soda."

sodium borate. A crystalline compound, $Na_2B_4O_7 \cdot 10H_2O$, used in the manufacture of glass, detergents, and pharmaceuticals. Also called "borax."

sodium carbonate. 1. A white powdery compound, Na_2CO_3, used in the manufacture of sodium bicarbonate, sodium nitrate, glass, ceramics, detergents, and soap. The dehydrated form is also called "soda ash." **2.** Any of various hydrated carbonates of sodium, such as sal soda.

ă pat/ā pay/âr care/ä father/b bib/ch church/d deed/ĕ pet/ē be/f fife/g gag/h hat/hw which/ĭ pit/ī pie/îr pier/j judge/k kick/l lid/ needle/m mum/n no, sudden/ng thing/ŏ pot/ō toe/ô paw, for/oi noise/ou out/ŏŏ took/ōō boot/p pop/r roar/s sauce/sh ship, dish/

sodium chlorate. A colorless crystalline compound, NaClO₃, used as a bleaching and oxidizing agent and in explosives.

sodium chloride. A colorless crystalline compound, NaCl, used in the manufacture of chemicals and as a food preservative and seasoning. Also called "common salt," "table salt."

sodium cyanide. A poisonous white crystalline compound, NaCN, used in extracting gold and silver from ores and in dye manufacture.

sodium cyclamate. A soluble white crystalline powder, C₆H₁₁NHSO₃Na, 30 times as sweet as sugar and a major constituent of low-calorie sweetening agents.

sodium dichromate. A red-orange crystalline compound, Na₂Cr₂O₇·2H₂O, used as an oxidizing agent.

sodium glutamate. A white crystalline compound, COOH-(CH₂)₂CH(NH₂)COONa, having a meatlike taste, used in cooking. Also called "monosodium glutamate."

sodium hydrosulfite. A yellowish powder, Na₂S₂O₄, used as a bleaching and reducing agent. Also called "hydrosulfite," "sodium hyposulfite."

sodium hydroxide. A strongly alkaline compound, NaOH, used in the manufacture of chemicals and soaps and in petroleum refining. Also called "caustic soda," "lye."

sodium hypochlorite. An unstable salt, NaOCl, usually stored in solution and used as a fungicide and an oxidizing bleach.

sodium hyposulfite. **1.** Sodium hydrosulfite *(see).* **2.** Sodium thiosulfate *(see).*

sodium nitrate. A white crystalline compound, NaNO₃, used in solid rocket propellants and in the manufacture of explosives and tobacco. Also called "saltpeter," "soda niter," "Chile saltpeter," "caliche."

sodium pentothal. *Chemistry.* Thiopental sodium *(see).*

sodium perborate. A white odorless crystalline compound, NaBO₂·H₂O₂·3H₂O, used as a mild alkaline oxidizing agent in dentifrices, as a topical antiseptic and deodorant, and as an industrial reagent.

sodium peroxide. A yellowish-white powder, Na₂O₂, employed industrially as an oxidizing and bleaching agent and medically as a germicide, antiseptic, and disinfectant.

sodium phosphate. Any of the three sodium salts of phosphoric acid, NaH₂PO₄, Na₂HPO₄, and Na₃PO₄, widely used in industry, pharmaceutical manufacturing, medicine, and chemistry.

sodium propionate. A clear crystalline compound, C₂H₅CO-ONa, capable of retarding the growth of molds and bacteria and used to prevent food spoilage.

sodium silicate. Any of various water-soluble silicate glass compounds used as a preservative for eggs, in plaster and cement, and in various purification and refining processes. Also called "soluble glass," "water glass."

sodium sulfate. A white crystalline compound, Na₂SO₄, used to manufacture paper, glass, dyes, and pharmaceuticals.

sodium sulfide. A hygroscopic yellow compound, Na₂S, used as a metal ore reagent and in photography, engraving, and printing.

sodium sulfite. A white crystalline or powdered compound, Na₂SO₃, used in preserving foods, silvering mirrors, developing photographs, and making dyes.

sodium thiosulfate. A white, translucent crystalline compound, Na₂S₂O₃·5H₂O, used as a photographic fixing agent and as a bleach. Also called "hypo," "hyposulfite," "sodium hyposulfite."

so·di·um-va·por lamp (sō′dē-əm-vā′pər). An electric lamp containing a small amount of sodium and neon gas, used in generating yellow light for lighting streets and highways.

Sod·om (sŏd′əm). A city of ancient Palestine that with Gomorrah was destroyed by fire because of the depravity of its inhabitants. Genesis 19:24.

sod·om·ite (sŏd′ə-mīt′) *n.* One who practices sodomy.

Sod·om·ite (sŏd′ə-mīt′) *n.* An inhabitant of Sodom.

sod·om·y (sŏd′ə-mē) *n.* **1.** Anal copulation of one male with another. **2.** In some legal usage, anal or oral copulation with a member of the opposite sex or any copulation with an animal. [Middle English, from Old French *sodomie,* from Late Latin *Sodoma,* SODOM.]

Soem·ba. The Dutch name for **Sumba.**

Soem·ba·wa. The Dutch name for **Sumbawa.**

Soe·ra·ba·ja. The Dutch name for **Surabaya.**

Soe·ra·kar·ta. The Dutch name for **Surakarta.**

so·ev·er (sō-ĕv′ər) *adv.* At all; in any way. Used to generalize or emphasize a word or phrase, usually in combination with *how, what, when, where,* or the like: *"Space to breathe, how short soever"* (Jonson). [SO + EVER.]

so·fa (sō′fə) *n.* A long upholstered seat with a back and arms. [Originally a raised dais furnished with carpets and cushions, ultimately from Arabic *suffah,* possibly akin to Hebrew *sapāh,* carpet, divan.]

sofa bed. A sofa, the seat of which unfolds to form a bed.

so·far (sō′fär′) *n.* A system for detecting and locating underwater explosions propagated over long distances through deep ocean layers, used to find survivors lost at sea. [SO(UND) F(IXING) A(ND) R(ANGING).]

sof·fit (sŏf′ĭt) *n.* The underside of a structural component, such as a beam, arch, staircase, or cornice. [French *soffite,* from Italian *soffito, soffitta,* from Vulgar Latin *suffictus* (unattested), from Latin *suffixus,* "something fastened beneath." See suffix.]

So·fi·a (sō′fē-ə, sō-fē′ə). Bulgarian **So·fi·ya** (sō′fī-yä). The capital of Bulgaria, situated in the west. Population, 747,000.

S. of Sol. Song of Solomon (Old Testament).

soft (sôft, sŏft) *adj.* **softer, softest. 1. a.** Offering little resistance;

easily molded, cut, or worked; malleable; plastic; not hard. **b.** Yielding readily to pressure or weight; not firm. **2.** Out of condition; flabby. **3. a.** Smooth or fine to the touch; not harsh or coarse. **b.** Not irritating; bland. **4.** Not loud or strident; low-toned. **5.** Not brilliant or glaring; subdued. **6.** Not sharply drawn or delineated. **7.** Gentle and caressing; mild; balmy. **8. a.** Of a gentle disposition; yielding. **b.** Easily touched; compassionate. **c.** Sentimental; affectionate: *a soft glance.* **d.** Not stern; lenient. **e.** Weak; unmanly. **f.** *Informal.* Simple; feeble: *soft in the head.* **9.** *Informal.* Easy: *a soft job.* **10.** Of or pertaining to a paper currency as distinct from a hard currency backed by gold. **11.** Having low dissolved mineral content. **12. a.** Sibilant rather than guttural, as *c* in *certain* and *g* in *gem.* **b.** Voiced and weakly articulated: *a soft consonant.* **c.** Palatalized, as certain consonants in Slavic languages. —*n.* A soft object or part. —*adv.* Softly; gently. [Middle English *soft(e),* agreeable, pleasant, Old English *sōfte, sēfte,* from Germanic *samfti-* (unattested).] —**soft′ly** *adv.* —**soft′ness** *n.*

soft·ball (sôft′bôl′, sŏft′-) *n.* **1.** A variation of baseball played on a smaller diamond with a larger, softer ball that is pitched underhand. **2.** The ball used.

soft·boiled (sôft′boild′, sŏft′-) *adj.* **1.** Boiled to a soft consistency. Said of an egg. **2.** *Informal.* Softhearted; not tough; lenient.

soft clam. The soft-shell clam *(see).*

soft coal. Bituminous coal *(see).*

soft drink. A nonalcoholic, usually carbonated beverage.

sof·ten (sôf′ən, sŏf′-) *v.* **-tened, -tening, -tens.** —*tr.* To make less severe or softer. —*intr.* To become soft or softer. —**sof′ten·er** *n.*

soft-finned (sôft′find′, sŏft′-) *adj. Zoology.* Having fins supported by flexible cartilaginous rays. Also "soft-rayed." Compare spiny-finned.

soft focus. A slightly blurred photographic effect obtained by setting a lens slightly out of focus.

soft goods. Dry goods *(see).*

soft hail. Graupel *(see).*

soft·head (sôft′hĕd′, sŏft′-) *n.* A foolish or feeble-minded person; a simpleton.

soft·head·ed (sôft′hĕd′ĭd, sŏft′-) *adj.* Lacking judgment, realism, or firmness: *a softheaded concession.* —**soft′head′ed·ly** *adv.* —**soft′head′ed·ness** *n.*

soft·heart·ed (sôft′här′tĭd, sŏft′-) *adj.* Easily moved; tender; merciful. —**soft′heart′ed·ly** *adv.* —**soft′heart′ed·ness** *n.*

soft landing. The landing of a space vehicle on a celestial body in such a way as to prevent damage or destruction.

soft palate. The movable fold, consisting of muscular fibers enclosed in mucous membrane, that is suspended from the rear of the hard palate and closes off the nasal cavity from the oral cavity during swallowing or sucking.

soft paste. Also **soft-paste** (sôft′pāst′, sŏft′-). Any of various ceramics containing first and refined clay.

soft pedal. A pedal used to mute tone, as on a piano.

soft-ped·al (sôft′pĕd′l, sŏft′-) *tr.v.* **-aled** or **-alled, -aling** or **-alling, -als. 1.** To soften or mute the tone of by depressing the soft pedal. **2.** *Informal.* To make less emphatic or obvious; to moderate; play down.

soft roe. The spermatozoa or testes of a fish; milt.

soft sell. *Informal.* A subtly persuasive and low pressure method of selling or advertising.

soft-shell (sôft′shĕl′, sŏft′-) *adj.* Also **soft-shelled** (-shĕld′). Having a soft, brittle, or unhardened shell.

soft-shell clam. A common edible clam, *Mya arenaria,* having a thin, elongated shell. Also called "soft clam."

soft-shell crab. A marine crab before its shell has hardened after molting; especially, the edible species, *Callinectes sapidus,* of eastern North America, in this stage.

soft-shelled turtle. Any of various freshwater turtles of the family Trionychidae, having a flat carapace covered with leathery skin.

soft-shoe (sôft′shōō′, sŏft′-) *adj.* Of or pertaining to a type of tap dancing performed without metal taps on the shoes.

soft shoulder. A border of soft earth running along the edge of a road.

soft soap. **1.** A fluid or semifluid soap. **2.** *Informal.* Cajolery.

soft-soap (sôft′sōp′, sŏft′-) *tr.v.* **-soaped, -soaping, -soaps.** *Informal.* To cajole or flatter. —**soft′soap′er** *n.*

soft-spo·ken (sôft′spō′kən, sŏft′-) *adj.* **1.** Speaking with a soft or gentle voice. **2.** Smooth; suave; ingratiating.

soft spot. **1.** A place in one's heart or affections; tender or sentimental feeling. **2.** In the skull of an infant, either of the points of juncture of the sagittal and lambdoid or the sagittal and coronal sutures.

soft·ware (sôft′wâr′, sŏft′-) *n.* **1.** Written or printed data, such as programs, routines, and symbolic languages, essential to the operation of computers. **2.** Documents containing information on the operation and maintenance of computers, such as manuals, circuit diagrams, and flow charts. [Coined after HARDWARE ("the machines").]

soft water. Water containing little or no dissolved salts of calcium or magnesium, especially water containing less than 85.5 parts per million of calcium carbonate. Compare **hard water.**

soft·wood (sôft′wŏŏd′, sŏft′-) *n.* **1.** The wood of a coniferous tree. **2.** A coniferous tree. Compare **hardwood.**

soft·y (sôf′tē, sŏft′-) *n., pl.* **-ies.** *Informal.* A weak, effeminate, or sentimental person.

Sog·di·an (sŏg′dē-ən) *n.* **1.** One of an ancient Iranian people who inhabited Sogdiana. **2.** Their extinct Iranian language.

soft-shell clam

sofa
Eighteenth-century American

Sog·di·a·na (sŏg'dē-ā'nə). Modern name **Trans·ox·i·a·na** (trăns'ŏk-sĭ-ā'nə). An ancient region of central Asia and a province of the Persian Empire. Capital, Maracanda (modern Samarkand).

sog·gy (sŏg'ē) *adj.* **-gier, -giest.** 1. Saturated or sodden with moisture; soaked. 2. Lacking spirit; dull. 3. Humid; sultry. [Either from dialectal *sog*†, a marsh, or from dialectal *sog*†, to soak.] —**sog'gi·ly** *adv.* —**sog'gi·ness** *n.*

Sog·ne Fjord (sông'nə). The longest (112 miles) and deepest (to 4,081 feet) of the Norwegian fjords, on the west coast, north of Bergen.

So·ho (sō'hō, sō-hō'). A district of London, England, noted for its night life and foreign restaurants.

soi-di·sant (swä-dē-zäɴ') *adj. French.* Self-styled; so-called.

soi·gné (swà-nyā') *adj.* Feminine **soi·gnée.** *French.* 1. Showing sophisticated care in performance, detail, or design. 2. Well-groomed; polished; elegant.

soil[1] (soil) *n.* 1. The top layer of the earth's surface, suitable for the growth of plant life. 2. A particular kind of earth or ground: *sandy soil.* 3. Country; territory; region: *native soil.* 4. Land, usually with nostalgic rural connotations: *a man of the soil.* 5. A place or condition favorable to growth; breeding ground. [Middle English, from Norman French, from Latin *solium,* seat (influenced in meaning by *solum,* base, ground). See **sed-**[1] in Appendix.*]

soil[2] (soil) *v.* **soiled, soiling, soils.** —*tr.* 1. To make dirty, particularly on the surface; begrime; smudge. 2. To disgrace; tarnish: *"I will not soil thy purple with my dust"* (Elizabeth Barrett Browning). 3. To pollute with sin; defile. —*intr.* To become dirty, stained, or tarnished. —*n.* 1. a. The state of being soiled. b. A stain or discoloration caused by dirt and grime. 2. Moral stain. 3. Filth, sewage, or refuse matter. 4. Manure, especially human excrement, used as fertilizer. [Middle English *soilen,* from Old French *souiller, suill(i)er,* from Vulgar Latin *suculāre* (unattested), from Latin *suculus, sucula,* diminutives of *sūs,* pig. See **su-**[1] in Appendix.*]

soil[3] (soil) *tr.v.* **soiled, soiling, soils.** 1. To feed (livestock) with soilage. 2. To purge (livestock) by feeding with green food. [Perhaps from obsolete *soil,* to manure, from SOIL (manure).]

soil·age (soi'lĭj) *n.* Green crops cut for feeding penned livestock.

soil pipe. A drain pipe that carries off wastes from a plumbing fixture, especially from a toilet.

soil·ure (soil'yər) *n.* 1. Soiling or the condition of being soiled. 2. A blot, stain, or smudge.

soi·ree (swä-rā') *n.* Also **soi·rée.** An evening party or reception. [French *soirée,* from *soir,* evening, from Latin *sērum,* late hour, neuter of *sērus,* late. See **sē-**[2] in Appendix.*]

Sois·sons (swà-sôɴ'). A city of France, in the north on the Aisne River. It was almost destroyed by German bombardment in World War I. Population, 23,000.

soix·ante-neuf (swä-säɴt'nœf') *n.* **Sixty-nine** *(see).*

so·journ (sō'jûrn, sō-jûrn') *intr.v.* **-journed, -journing, -journs.** To stay for a time; reside temporarily: *"such as cross the seas and sojourn in a land of strangers"* (Sterne). See Synonyms at **stay.** —*n.* (sō'jûrn, sō-jûrn', sŏ'jûrn). A temporary stay; brief residence. [Middle English *sojournen,* from Old French *sojorner,* from Vulgar Latin *subdiurnāre* (unattested) : Latin *sub-,* during, under + Late Latin *diurnum,* day, from Latin *diurnus,* daily, from *diēs,* day (see **deiw-** in Appendix*).] —**so'journ·er** *n.*

soke (sōk) *n.* 1. In early English law, the right of local jurisdiction, generally one of the feudal rights of lordship. 2. The district over which such jurisdiction was exercised. [Middle English, from Medieval Latin *sōca,* from Old English *sōcn,* inquiry, right of local jurisdiction. See **sāg-** in Appendix.*]

soke·man. Variant of **socman.**

Soke of Pe·ter·bor·ough (sōk; pē'tər-bə-rə, -brə). A former administrative county of Northamptonshire, England, now part of Huntingdon and Peterborough.

So·ko·to (sō-kō'tō). 1. A sultanate occupying some 36,477 square miles in northern Nigeria, formerly the center of a 19th-century Fula empire. 2. A city of northwestern Nigeria, the capital of that former empire. Population, 48,000.

So·ko·tra. See **Socotra.**

sol[1] (sōl) *n.* Also **so** (sō). *Music.* 1. The syllable used to represent the fifth tone of a diatonic scale. 2. The tone G. [Middle English, from Medieval Latin, from *solve,* "purge" (imperative), occurring in a hymn to St. John the Baptist (see **gamut**), from Latin, from *solvere,* to loosen, SOLVE.]

sol[2] (sŏl) *n.* 1. A former monetary unit of France, equal to 12 deniers. 2. An old French coin of this value. [Middle English, from Old French, from Latin *solidus,* SOLIDUS.]

sol[3] (sōl) *n., pl.* **soles** (sō'lās). 1. The basic monetary unit of Peru, equal to 100 centavos. See table of exchange rates at **currency.** 2. A coin or note worth one sol. [Spanish, "sun" (from the drawing on the coin), from Latin *sōl.* See **sāwel-** in Appendix.*]

sol[4] (sŏl) *n. Chemistry.* A liquid colloidal dispersion. [Short for HYDROSOL.]

sol[5] (sōl) *n. Alchemy.* Gold. [Middle English, from Medieval Latin *sōl,* from Latin, sun. See **sāwel-** in Appendix.*]

Sol (sŏl) *n.* The sun. [Middle English, from Latin *sōl.* See **sāwel-** in Appendix.*]

sol. solicitor.

so·la. 1. Feminine of **solus.** 2. A plural of **solum.**

sol·ace (sŏl'ĭs) *n.* Also **sol·ace·ment** (-mənt). 1. Comfort in sorrow, misfortune, or distress; consolation. 2. That which furnishes comfort or consolation: *"Solace of kisses and cookies and cabbage"* (Theodore Roethke). —*tr.v.* **solaced, -acing, -aces.**

1. To comfort, cheer, or console, as in trouble or sorrow. 2. To allay or assuage: *"They solaced their wretchedness, however, by duets after supper"* (Jane Austen). [Middle English *solas,* from Old French, from Latin *sōlācium, sōlātium,* from *sōlārī,* to comfort, console. See **sel-**[2] in Appendix.*] —**sol'ac·er** *n.*

so·lan (sō'lən) *n. Archaic.* A gannet, *Morus bassanus,* of northern Atlantic coastal regions. Also called "solan goose." [Middle English *soland* : probably Old Norse *sūla*†, gannet, pillar + *ŏnd,* duck (see **anet-** in Appendix*).]

so·lan·der (sə-lăn'dər) *n.* A book-shaped box used to protect books, library materials such as maps, or botanical specimens. It may be hinged or may have two parts, one sliding into the other. Also called "solander case." [After Daniel C. *Solander* (1736–1782), Swedish botanist.]

so·la·nine (sō'lə-nēn', -nĭn) *n.* A bitter poisonous alkaloid, $C_{45}H_{73}NO_{15}$, derived from potato sprouts, tomatoes, and nightshade, formerly used to treat epilepsy. [French : Latin *sōlānum,* nightshade, from *sōl,* sun (see **sāwel-** in Appendix*) + -INE.]

so·lar (sō'lər) *adj.* 1. Of, pertaining to, or proceeding from the sun: *solar rays.* 2. Utilizing or operated by energy derived from the sun. 3. Determined or measured with respect to the sun. [Middle English, from Latin *sōlāris,* from *sōl,* sun. See **sāwel-** in Appendix.*]

solar battery. A system consisting of a large number of connected solar cells.

solar cell. A semiconductor device that converts the energy of sunlight into electric energy, and is used mainly as a power supply in space vehicles.

solar constant. The amount of solar radiation perpendicularly impinging on a surface of unit area at a distance of one astronomical unit from the sun in a unit interval of time, having an average value of 1.94 calories per minute per square centimeter.

solar day. The interval between two successive meridian passages of the sun.

solar flare. A temporary outburst of solar gases from a small area of the sun's surface, a source of intense radiation.

solar furnace. A parabolic reflector that focuses solar radiation at a point to obtain temperatures as high as 4,000°C.

solar house. A house having large quantities of heat-absorbing material behind large glass areas, designed to supplement or replace conventional heating methods.

so·lar·im·e·ter (sō'lə-rĭm'ə-tər) *n.* An instrument used to measure the flux of solar radiation through a surface. [SOLAR + -METER.]

so·lar·i·um (sō-lâr'ē-əm) *n., pl.* **-laria** (-lâr'ē-ə) or **-iums.** A room, gallery, or glassed-in porch exposed to the sun, as in a sanitarium. [Latin *sōlārium,* sundial, terrace, balcony, from *sōl,* sun. See **sāwel-** in Appendix.*]

so·lar·ize (sō'lə-rīz') *v.* **-ized, -izing, -izes.** —*tr.* To affect by exposing to the sun's rays. —*intr. Photography.* To be over-exposed. —**so'lar·i·za'tion** *n.*

solar month. One-twelfth of a tropical year.

solar plexus. 1. The large network of sympathetic nerves and ganglia located in the peritoneal cavity behind the stomach and having branching tracts that supply nerves to the abdominal viscera. 2. *Informal.* The pit of the stomach. [From the radially branching ganglia.]

solar system. The sun together with the nine planets and all other celestial bodies that orbit the sun.

solar year. A tropical year *(see).*

so·la·ti·um (sō-lā'shē-əm) *n., pl.* **-tia** (-shē-ə). *Law.* Compensation for damage to the feelings as distinct from financial loss or physical suffering. [Late Latin *sōlātium,* SOLACE.]

sold. Past tense and past participle of **sell.**

sol·dan (sōl'dən, sŏl'-) *n.* Also **sou·dan** (sōō'dən). *Archaic.* A sultan. [Middle English *soldan, soudan,* from Old French, from Arabic *sulṭān,* SULTAN.]

sol·der (sŏd'ər, sôd'-) *n.* 1. Any of various fusible alloys, usually tin and lead, used to join metallic parts when applied in the melted state to the solid metal. 2. Anything that joins or cements. —*v.* **soldered, -dering, -ders.** —*tr.* To serve as a bond between; join closely together. —*intr.* 1. To unite or repair things with solder. 2. To be joined by or as by solder. [Middle English *souldour, soudur,* from Old French *soudure, soldure,* from *souder, solder,* to solder, from Latin *solidāre,* to make solid, from *solidus,* SOLID.] —**sol'der·er** *n.*

sol·dier (sōl'jər) *n.* 1. One who serves in an army. 2. An enlisted man or a noncommissioned officer as distinguished from a commissioned officer. 3. An active and loyal follower or worker. 4. A sexually undeveloped form of certain ants and termites, having the jaws specialized to serve as fighting weapons. —*intr.v.* **soldiered, -diering, -diers.** 1. To be or serve as a soldier. 2. To make a show of working in order to escape punishment. [Middle English *souldeour,* mercenary, from Old French *soud(i)er, soldier,* from *soulde,* pay, from Latin *solidus,* SOLIDUS.]

sol·dier·ly (sōl'jər-lē) *adj.* Befitting a good soldier.

soldier of fortune. One who serves in a military capacity wherever there may be profit or adventure.

Soldier's Medal. *Abbr.* **S.M.** A U.S. military decoration awarded for heroic deeds not involving conflict with the enemy.

sol·dier·y (sōl'jə-rē) *n., pl.* **-ies.** 1. Soldiers collectively. 2. A body of soldiers. 3. The military profession.

sole[1] (sōl) *n.* 1. The undersurface of the foot. 2. The undersurface of a shoe or boot. 3. The part on which something rests while standing, especially: a. The bottom surface of a plow. b. The bottom surface of the head of a golf club. —*tr.v.* **soled, soling, soles.** 1. To furnish (a shoe or boot) with a sole.

2. *Golf.* To put the sole of (a club) on the ground, as in preparing to make a stroke. [Middle English, from Old French *sole,* from Vulgar Latin *sola* (unattested), from Latin *solea,* sandal, from *solum,* bottom, ground, sole of the foot. See **sel-**[1] in Appendix.*]

sole[2] (sōl) *adj.* **1.** Being the only one; existing or functioning without another or others; only. **2.** Of or pertaining to only one individual or group; exclusive: *The court has the sole right to decide.* **3.** *Law.* Single or unmarried. **4.** *Archaic.* Solitary. —See Synonyms at **single.** [Middle English *soul(e), sole,* unmarried, alone, from Old French, from Latin *sōlus,* alone, single. See **seu-**[2] in Appendix.*]

sole[3] (sōl) *n., pl.* **sole** or **soles. 1.** Any of various chiefly marine flatfishes of the family Soleidae, related to and resembling the flounders; especially, any of several European species, such as *Solea solea,* valued as food fishes. **2.** Any of various other flatfishes. [Middle English, from Old French, sole (fish), SOLE (of the foot), from the shape of the fish.]

sol·e·cism (sŏl′ə-sĭz′əm, sō′lə-) *n.* **1.** A nonstandard usage or grammatical construction. **2.** A violation of etiquette. **3.** Any impropriety, mistake, or incongruity. [Latin *soloecismus,* from Greek *soloikismos,* from *soloikos,* speaking incorrectly, referring to the corrupt Attic dialect spoken by Athenian colonists at *Soloi,* in Cilicia.] —**sol′e·cist** *n.* —**sol′e·cis′tic** *adj.*

sole·ly (sōl′lē, sō′lē) *adv.* **1.** Alone; singly. **2.** Entirely; exclusively.

sol·emn (sŏl′əm) *adj.* **1.** Deeply earnest; serious; grave: *a solemn voice.* **2.** Of impressive and serious nature: *a solemn occasion.* **3.** Performed with full ceremony: *a Solemn High Mass.* **4.** Invoking the force of religion; sacred: *a solemn vow.* **5.** Gloomy; somber. —See Synonyms at **serious.** [Middle English *solem(p)ne,* from Old French, from Latin *sollemnis,* stated, established, appointed. See **sol-** in Appendix.*] —**sol′emn·ness** *n.* —**sol′emn·ly** *adv.*

so·lem·ni·ty (sə-lĕm′nə-tē) *n., pl.* **-ties. 1.** The condition or quality of being solemn; gravity; seriousness. **2.** A solemn observance or proceeding.

sol·em·nize (sŏl′əm-nīz′) *tr.v.* **-nized, -nizing, -nizes. 1.** To celebrate or observe with formal ceremonies or rites, as a religious occasion. **2.** To perform with formal ceremony: *solemnize a marriage.* **3.** To make serious or grave. —See Synonyms at **observe.** —**sol′em·ni·za′tion** *n.*

so·le·noid (sō′lə-noid′) *n.* **1.** A cylindrical coil of insulated wire in which an axial magnetic field is established by a flow of electric current. **2.** An assembly often used as a switch, consisting essentially of such a coil and a metal core free to slide along the coil axis under the influence of the magnetic field. [French *solénoïde,* from Greek *sōlēnoeidēs,* pipe-shaped, grooved, tubular : *sōlēn*†, channel, pipe + -OID.] —**so′le·noi′dal** *adj.* —**so′le·noi′dal·ly** *adv.*

So·lent, The (sō′lənt). A channel about 15 miles long between the Isle of Wight and Hampshire, England.

sole·plate (sol′plāt′) *n.* The undersurface of a clothes iron.

sol-fa (sōl′fä′) *n. Music.* **1.** The set of syllables *do, re, mi, fa, sol, la, ti,* used to represent the tones of the scale. **2.** The use of the sol-fa syllables. —*v.* **sol-faed, -faing, -fas.** —*intr.* To use the sol-fa syllables. —*tr.* To sing using the sol-fa syllables. [SOL (note) + FA.]

sol·fa·ta·ra (sōl′fə-tär′ə) *n.* A volcanic fissure that emits sulfurous vapors, steam, and, at times, hot mud. [Italian *Solfatara,* name of a sulfurous volcano near Naples, from *solfo,* sulfur, from Latin *sulfur, sulphur,* SULFUR.] —**sol′fa·ta′ric** *adj.*

sol·feg·gio (sōl-fĕj′ē-ō′, -fĕj′ō) *n., pl.* **-feggi** (-fĕj′ē) or **-gios.** Also **sol·fège** (sōl-fĕzh′, -fāzh′). *Music.* **1.** The use of the sol-fa syllables to note the tones of the scale; solmization. **2.** A singing exercise in which the sol-fa syllables are used. [Italian, from *solfeggiare,* to sol-fa, from *solfa,* sol-fa : SOL (note) + Medieval Latin *fa,* FA.]

sol·fe·ri·no (sŏl′fə-rē′nō) *n.* Moderate purplish red. See **color.** [From a dye discovered in the year of the Battle of *Solferino* (1859). Compare **magenta.**] —**sol′fe·ri′no** *adj.*

so·lic·it (sə-lĭs′ĭt) *v.* **-ited, -iting, -its.** —*tr.* **1.** To seek to obtain by persuasion, entreaty, or formal application: *solicit votes.* **2.** To petition (a person) persistently; entreat; importune. **3.** To entice or incite (a person) to action, particularly to an immoral or illegal action. **4.** To approach or accost (a person) with an offer of sexual services. —*intr.* To make solicitation or petition for something desired. [Middle English *soliciten,* to disturb, fill with concern, from Old French *solliciter,* from Latin *sollicitāre,* to disturb, agitate, from *sollicitus,* SOLICITOUS.] —**so·lic′i·ta′tion** *n.*

so·lic·i·tor (sə-lĭs′ə-tər) *n. Abbr.* **sol. 1.** One who solicits; especially, one who seeks trade, contributions, magazine subscriptions, or the like. **2.** The chief law officer of a city, town, or government department. **3.** *British.* A lawyer who is not a member of the bar and who may be heard only in the lower courts. Compare **barrister.** —See Synonyms at **lawyer.**

solicitor general *pl.* **solicitors general.** *Abbr.* **S.G. 1.** A law officer assisting an attorney general. **2.** The chief law officer in a state not having an attorney general.

so·lic·i·tous (sə-lĭs′ə-təs) *adj.* **1.** Anxious and concerned; attentive. **2.** Full of desire; eager. —See Synonyms at **thoughtful.** [Latin *sollicitus,* thoroughly moved, agitated : *sollus,* whole, entire (see **sol-** in Appendix*) + *citus,* past participle of *ciēre,* to put in motion, move (see **kei-**[3] in Appendix*).] —**so·lic′i·tous·ly** *adv.* —**so·lic′i·tous·ness** *n.*

so·lic·i·tude (sə-lĭs′ə-to͞od′, -tyo͞od′) *n.* **1.** The state of being solicitous; care; concern. **2.** *Usually plural.* That which causes anxiety or concern. —See Synonyms at **anxiety.**

sol·id (sŏl′ĭd) *adj.* **1.** Of definite shape and volume; not liquid or gaseous. **2.** Not hollowed out: *a solid block of wood.* **3.** Being the same substance throughout: *solid gold.* **4.** Of or pertaining to three-dimensional geometric figures or bodies. **5.** Without gaps or breaks; continuous: *a solid line of people.* **6.** Of good quality and substance; well-made: *solid foundations.* **7.** Forceful; hearty: *a solid slap.* **8.** Substantial; complete: *a solid meal.* **9.** Sound; reliable; concrete: *solid facts.* **10.** Financially sound. **11.** Upstanding and dependable: *a solid citizen.* **12.** Written without a hyphen or space. Said of words. **13.** *Printing.* Without leads between the lines. **14.** Uniform in tone. Said of a color. **15.** Acting together; unanimous: *a solid voting bloc.* —*n.* **1.** A substance that is neither liquid nor gaseous; a solid substance. **2.** A geometric figure having three dimensions. [Middle English *solide,* whole, solid, from Old French, from Latin *solidus.* See **sol-** in Appendix.*] —**sol′id·ly** *adv.* —**sol′id·ness** *n.*

solid angle. An angle subtended at a point by a surface, measured in steradians with respect to the area delimited on the unit sphere centered on that point by the locus of points of intersection of the sphere with the lines joining the point to the perimeter of the surface. Compare **polyhedral angle.**

sol·i·dar·i·ty (sŏl′ə-dăr′ə-tē) *n., pl.* **-ties.** A union of interests, purposes, or sympathies among members of a group; fellowship of responsibilities and interests: *"The savage depends upon the group . . . for practical cooperation and mental solidarity"* (Bronislaw Malinowski). See Synonyms at **unity.**

sol·i·dar·y (sŏl′ə-dĕr′ē) *adj.* Characterized by solidarity; united. [French *solidaire,* from *solide,* SOLID.]

solid geometry. The geometry of three-dimensional figures and surfaces.

so·lid·i·fy (sə-lĭd′ə-fī′) *v.* **-fied, -fying, -fies.** —*tr.* **1.** To make solid, compact or hard. **2.** To make strong or united. —*intr.* To become solid or united. —**so·lid′i·fi·ca′tion** *n.*

so·lid·i·ty (sə-lĭd′ə-tē) *n., pl.* **-ties. 1.** The condition or property of being solid. **2.** Soundness of mind, moral character, or finances; stability.

solid of revolution. A volume generated by the rotation of a plane figure about an axis in its plane.

solid propellant. A rocket propellant in solid form, combining both fuel and oxidizer in the form of a compact, cohesive grain.

solid solution. *Chemistry.* A homogeneous crystalline structure in which one or more types of atoms or molecules may be partly substituted for the original atoms and molecules without changing the structure.

sol·id-state (sŏl′ĭd-stāt′) *adj.* **1.** Characteristic of or pertaining to the physical properties of solid materials, especially to the electromagnetic, thermodynamic, and structural properties of crystalline solids. **2.** Based on or consisting chiefly or exclusively of semiconducting materials, components, and related devices.

sol·i·dus (sŏl′ə-dəs) *n., pl.* **-di** (-dī′). **1.** An ancient Roman coin used until the fall of the Byzantine Empire. **2.** A virgule; a slash. [Middle English, from Latin, from adjective, SOLID.]

sol·i·fid·i·an (sŏl′ə-fĭd′ē-ən) *n.* A person who believes that faith alone is sufficient to ensure salvation. [From New Latin *solifidius* : Latin *sōlus,* alone (see **seu-**[2] in Appendix*) + *fidēs,* faith (see **bheidh-** in Appendix*).] —**sol′i·fid′i·an·ism′** *n.*

so·lil·o·quize (sə-lĭl′ə-kwīz′) *v.* **-quized, -quizing, -quizes.** —*intr.* To utter or deliver a soliloquy. —*tr.* To put into the form of a soliloquy. —**so·lil′o·quist, so·lil′o·quiz′er** *n.*

so·lil·o·quy (sə-lĭl′ə-kwē) *n., pl.* **-quies. 1.** A literary or dramatic form of discourse in which a character talks to himself or reveals his thoughts in the form of a monologue without addressing a listener. **2.** The act of speaking to oneself in or as in solitude. [Late Latin *sōliloquium* : Latin *sōlus,* alone (see **seu-**[2] in Appendix*) + *loquī,* to speak (see **tolkw-** in Appendix*).]

So·li·mões (so͞o-lē-moinsh′). The upper Amazon from the Rio Negro to the Peruvian boundary.

So·ling·en (zō′lĭng-ən). A city of West Germany, in western North Rhine-Westphalia. Population, 173,000.

sol·ip·sism (sŏl′əp-sĭz′əm, sō′ləp-) *n. Philosophy.* **1.** The theory that the self is the only thing that can be known and verified. **2.** The theory or view that the self is the only reality. Compare **objectivism.** [Latin *sōlus,* alone (see **seu-**[2] in Appendix*) + *ipse*†, self + -ISM.] —**sol′ip·sist** *n.* —**sol′ip·sis′tic** *adj.*

sol·i·taire (sŏl′ə-târ′) *n.* **1.** A diamond or other gemstone set alone, as in a ring. **2.** Any of a number of card games played by one person. [French, from Old French, solitary, from Latin *sōlitārius,* SOLITARY.]

sol·i·tar·y (sŏl′ə-tĕr′ē) *adj.* **1.** Existing, living, or going without others; alone. **2.** Happening, done, or made alone. **3.** Remote from civilization; secluded; lonely: *a solitary retreat.* **4.** Having no companions; lonesome; lonely. **5.** Single; sole. —See Synonyms at **alone, single.** —*n., pl.* **solitaries. 1.** A person who lives alone; a recluse. **2.** *Informal.* Solitary confinement. [Middle English, from Latin *sōlitārius,* from *sōlus,* alone. See **seu-**[2] in Appendix.*] —**sol′i·tar′i·ly** *adv.* —**sol′i·tar′i·ness** *n.*

solitary confinement. The confinement of a prisoner in a cell in which he is isolated from all others.

sol·i·tude (sŏl′ə-to͞od′, -tyo͞od′) *n.* **1.** The state of being alone or remote from others; isolation. **2.** A lonely or secluded place. [Middle English, from Old French, from Latin *sōlitūdo,* from *sōlus,* alone. See **seu-**[2] in Appendix.*]

Synonyms: *solitude, isolation, seclusion, retirement.* These nouns denote the state of being alone or of being withdrawn or remote from society. *Solitude* implies the absence of all other persons but is otherwise not very specific. *Isolation* can refer to the condition of one person, a group, or even a unit such as a country. In every case it emphasizes total detachment from

others. *Seclusion* can apply to one person or a group and suggests being removed or apart from others though not necessarily completely inaccessible. Sometimes it implies surroundings that conceal. *Retirement* usually refers to the condition of one person who withdraws from regular activity or from society. The term does not necessarily imply physical detachment.

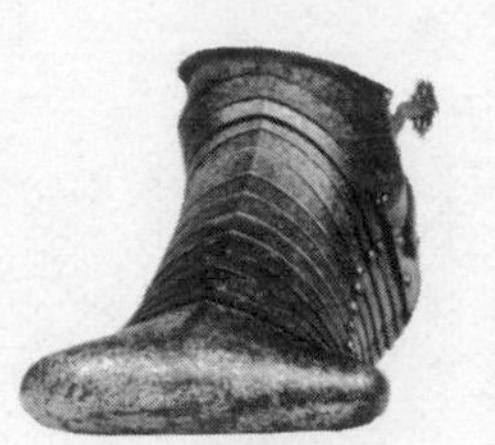

solleret
Sixteenth-century French

sol·ler·et (sŏl′ə-rĕt′) *n.* A steel shoe made of overlapping plates, forming a part of a medieval suit of armor. [Old French, diminutive of *soller,* shoe, from Medieval Latin *subtēlāris,* from Late Latin *subtēl,* hollow of the foot : Latin *sub-,* under + *tālus,* ankle (see **talus**).]

sol·mi·za·tion (sŏl′mə-zā′shən) *n. Music.* The act or a system of using syllables, such as *do, re, mi,* to note the tones of the scale. [French *solmisation,* from *solmiser,* to sol-fa : SOL (note) + MI.]

soln solution.

so·lo (sō′lō) *n., pl.* **-los.** **1.** *Abbr.* **s.** A musical composition or passage for an individual voice or instrument, with or without accompaniment. **2.** Any performance accomplished by a single individual. **3.** Any of various card games in which one player singly opposes others. *—adj.* **1.** Composed, arranged for, or performed by a single voice or instrument. **2.** Made or done by a single individual. *—adv.* Unaccompanied; alone. *—intr.v.* **soloed, -loing, -los.** To perform alone; especially, to fly an airplane without a companion or instructor. [Italian, from Latin *sōlus,* alone. See **seu-²** in Appendix.*]

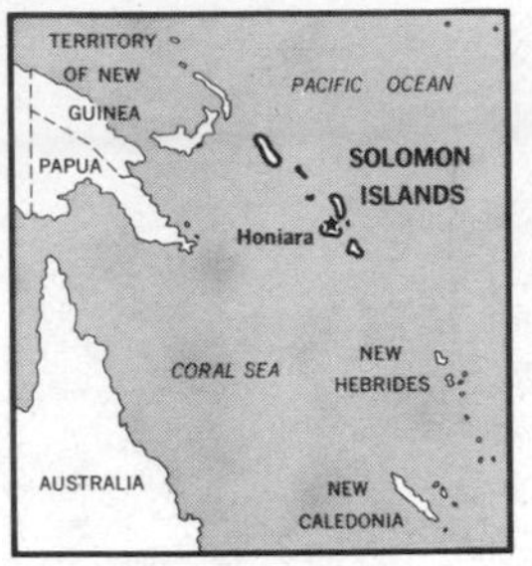

Solomon Islands

So·lo (sō′lō). **1.** The largest river (335 miles) of Java, Indonesia, rising in the south and flowing north and then northeast to the Java Sea. **2.** See **Surakarta.**

so·lo·ist (sō′lō-ĭst) *n.* One who performs a solo or solos.

Sol·o·mon¹ (sŏl′ə-mən). A masculine given name. [Hebrew *Shəlōmōh,* from *shālōm,* peace. See **slm** in Appendix.*]

Sol·o·mon² (sŏl′ə-mən). King of Israel in the tenth century B.C.; son of King David; noted for his wealth and wisdom; reputed author of three books of the Bible.

Sol·o·mon Islands (sŏl′ə-mən). A group of volcanic islands with a combined area of about 16,000 square miles in the southwestern Pacific, comprising, in the southeast, the British Solomon Islands with their capital at Honiara on Guadalcanal; and, in the northwest, part of the Trust Territory of New Guinea.

Solomon's seal. **1.** A six-pointed star or hexagram supposed to possess mystical powers and sometimes used as a charm or amulet. **2.** Any of several plants of the genus *Polygonatum,* having paired, drooping, greenish or yellowish flowers. [The plant is probably so called from the seallike markings on the root stocks.]

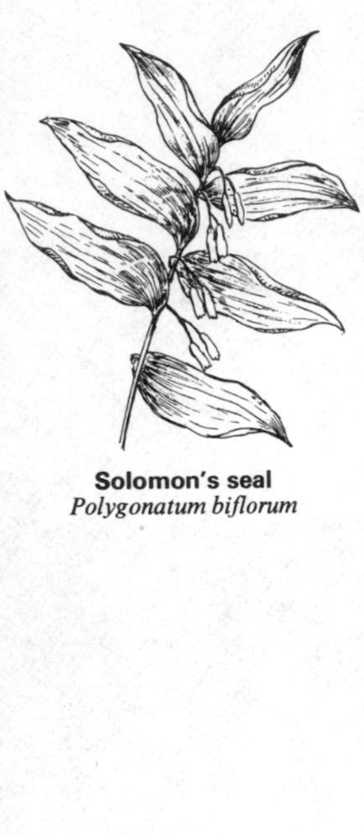

Solomon's seal
Polygonatum biflorum

So·lon (sō′lən). Athenian statesman and poet of the late seventh and early sixth centuries B.C.; instituted legal reforms.

so long. *Informal.* Good-by.

sol·stice (sŏl′stəs, sōl′-) *n.* **1.** *Astronomy.* Either of two times of the year when the sun has no apparent northward or southward motion, at the most northern or most southern point of the ecliptic. The summer solstice, when the sun is in the zenith at the tropic of Cancer, occurs about June 22, and the winter solstice, when it is over the tropic of Capricorn, occurs about December 22. **2.** A highest point or culmination; a limit. [Middle English, from Old French, from Latin *sōlstitium.* See **sāwel-** in Appendix.*] **—sol·sti′tial** (-stĭsh′əl) *adj.*

sol·u·bil·i·ty (sŏl′yə-bĭl′ə-tē) *n., pl.* **-ties.** **1.** The quality or condition of being soluble. **2.** The amount of a substance that can be dissolved in a given amount of solvent.

sol·u·bil·ize (sŏl′yə-bə-līz′) *tr.v.* **-ized, -izing, -izes.** To make soluble in water (such substances as fats and lipids, which are not appreciably soluble under standard conditions) by the action of a detergent or similar agent.

sol·u·ble (sŏl′yə-bəl) *adj.* **1.** Capable of being dissolved; especially, easily dissolved. **2.** Capable of being solved or explained. [Middle English, from Old French, from Late Latin *solūbilis,* from *solvere,* to loosen. See **leu-¹** in Appendix.*] **—sol′u·ble·ness** *n.* **—sol′u·bly** *adv.*

Usage: *Soluble* is applicable both to things that can be dissolved in liquids and to things, such as problems, that are capable of being solved or explained. *Solvable,* in modern usage, is largely restricted to the second category (problems).

soluble glass. *Chemistry.* **Sodium silicate** *(see).*

so·lum (sō′ləm) *n., pl.* **-la** (-lə) or **-lums.** The surface layers of a soil profile in which topsoil formation occurs. [New Latin, from Latin, base, foundation. See **sole** (of a shoe).]

so·lus (sō′ləs) *adj. Feminine* **so·la** (-lə). *Latin.* Alone; by oneself. Used especially as a stage direction.

sol·ute (sŏl′yo͞ot′, sŏl′o͞ot′) *n. Chemistry.* A substance dissolved in another substance, usually the component of a solution present in the lesser amount. Compare **solvent.** *—adj.* Dissolved; in solution. [Latin *solūtus,* past participle of *solvere,* to loosen. See **leu-¹** in Appendix.*]

so·lu·tion (sə-lo͞o′shən) *n.* **1.** *Abbr.* **soln** A spontaneously forming homogeneous mixture of two or more substances, retaining its constitution in subdivision to molecular volumes, displaying no settling, and having various possible proportions of the constituents, which may be solids, liquids, gases, or intercombinations. **2.** The process of forming such a mixture. **3.** The state of being dissolved. **4.** The method or process of solving a problem. **5.** The answer to or disposition of a problem. **6.** *Law.* The payment or satisfaction of a claim or debt. **7.** The action of separating or breaking up; a dissolution. [Middle English, from Old French, from Latin *solūtiō,* from *solūtus.* See **solute.**]

So·lu·tre·an (sə-lo͞o′trē-ən) *adj.* Also **So·lu·tri·an.** *Anthropology.* Of or relating to the Old World Upper Paleolithic culture that succeeded the Aurignacian and was characterized by improved flint implements and stylized symbolic forms of art. [Classified from finds made at *Solutré,* France.]

solv·a·ble (sŏl′və-bəl) *adj.* Capable of being solved. See Usage note at **soluble.** **—solv′a·bil′i·ty, solv′a·ble·ness** *n.*

sol·va·tion (sŏl-vā′shən) *n.* Any of a class of chemical reactions, such as the formation of hydrated copper sulfate in aqueous solution, in which solute and solvent molecules combine with relatively weak covalent bonds. Compare **solvolysis.** [SOLV(ENT) + -ATION.]

Sol·vay (sŏl′vā), **Ernest.** 1838–1922. Belgian chemist and philanthropist.

Solvay process. A process used to produce large quantities of sodium bicarbonate from salt, ammonia, carbon dioxide, and limestone. [Invented by Ernest SOLVAY.]

solve (sŏlv) *tr.v.* **solved, solving, solves.** **1.** To find a solution to; answer; explain. **2.** To work out a correct solution to (a problem). [Middle English *solven,* to loosen, unbind, from Latin *solvere.* See **leu-¹** in Appendix.*] **—solv′er** *n.*

sol·vent (sŏl′vənt) *adj.* **1.** Able to meet financial obligations. **2.** Capable of dissolving another substance. *—n.* **1.** *Chemistry.* **a.** The component of a solution that is present in excess or that undergoes no change of state. **b.** A liquid capable of dissolving another substance. Compare **solute.** **2.** Something that solves. [Latin *solvēns,* present participle of *solvere,* loosen. See **solve.**] **—sol′ven·cy** *n.*

sol·vol·y·sis (sŏl-vŏl′ə-sĭs) *n.* Any of a class of ionic chemical reactions, such as hydrolysis, in which solute and solvent react and alter the acidity or relative ionic concentrations of the solution. Compare **solvation.** [SOLV(ENT) + -LYSIS.]

Sol·way Firth (sŏl′wā′). An arm of the Irish Sea extending inland about 40 miles between England and Scotland.

Sol·y·man. See **Suleiman** I.

so·ma (sō′mə) *n., pl.* **-mata** (-mə-tə) or **-mas.** *Biology.* The physical entity of an organism, exclusive of the germ cells. [New Latin, from Greek *sōma,* body. See **teuə-** in Appendix.*]

So·ma·li (sō-mä′lē) *n., pl.* **Somali** or **-lis.** Also **So·mal** (sō′mäl′). **1.** A member of one of a group of Hamitic tribes of Somaliland. **2.** Their Hamitic language.

So·ma·li·a (sō-mä′lē-ə). Officially, Somali Republic. A country occupying 250,000 square miles in eastern Africa, on the Indian Ocean, formed in 1960 by the union of British Somaliland and Italian Somaliland. Population, about 2,000,000. Capital, Mogadishu.

So·ma·li·land (sō-mä′lē-lănd′). A region of eastern Africa, including Somalia, French Somaliland, and parts of Ethiopia.

so·mat·ic (sə-măt′ĭk) *adj.* **1.** Of or pertaining to the body, especially as distinguished from a bodily part, the mind, or the environment; physical. **2.** Of or pertaining to the wall of the body cavity, especially as distinguished from the head, limbs, or viscera. **3.** Of or pertaining to somatoplasm. [Greek *sōmatikos,* from *sōma,* body, SOMA.]

somatic cell. Any bodily cell other than a germ cell.

somato-. Indicates body; for example, **somatology.** [From Greek *sōma* (stem *sōmat-*), body. See **teuə-** in Appendix.*]

so·ma·to·gen·ic (sō′mə-tə-jĕn′ĭk, sō-măt′ə-) *adj.* Also **so·ma·to·ge·net·ic** (-jə-nĕt′ĭk). Arising within the body in response to environment. [SOMATO- + -GENIC.]

so·ma·tol·o·gy (sō′mə-tŏl′ə-jē) *n.* **1.** The physiological and anatomical study of the body. **2. Physical anthropology** *(see).* [SOMATO- + -LOGY.] **—so′ma·to·log′i·cal** (-tə-lŏj′ĭ-kəl) *adj.*

so·ma·to·plasm (sō′mə-tə-plăz′əm, sō-măt′ə-) *n.* **1.** The entirety of specialized protoplasm, other than germ plasm, constituting the body. **2.** The protoplasm of a somatic cell. [SOMATO- + -PLASM.]

so·ma·to·pleure (sō′mə-tə-plo͝or′, sō-măt′ə-) *n.* A complex sheet of embryonic cells in certain vertebrates, formed by association of part of the mesoderm with the ectoderm and developing as the internal body wall. [New Latin *somatopleura* : SOMATO- + PLEURA.]

so·ma·to·type (sō′mə-tə-tīp′, sō-măt′ə-) *n.* The morphological type of a human body; physique. **—so′ma·to·typ′ic** (-tĭp′ĭk) *adj.*

som·ber (sŏm′bər) *adj.* Also **som·bre,** *archaic* **som·brous** (-brəs). **1.** Dark; gloomy: *"A city takes on that sombre garb of grey"* (Dreiser). **2.** Melancholy; dismal. [French *sombre,* from Old French, shade, from Vulgar Latin *subombrāre* (unattested), to shade : Latin *sub-,* under + *umbra,* shade (see **andho-** in Appendix*).]

som·bre·ro (sŏm-brâr′ō) *n., pl.* **-ros.** A broad-brimmed Spanish or Mexican hat of felt or straw. [Spanish, hat, from *sombra,* shade, from Vulgar Latin *subombrāre* (unattested), to shade. See **somber.**]

some (sŭm) *adj.* **1.** Being an unspecified number or part: *Some laws are bad.* **2.** Being unknown or unspecified by name: *Some fool laughed.* **3.** *Logic.* Being part and perhaps all of a class. **4.** *Informal.* Remarkable: *He is some skier.* *—pron.* **1.** An indefinite or unspecified number or portion. **2.** An indefinite additional quantity: *three and some.* *—adv.* **1.** Approximately; about: *some 40 people.* **2.** *Informal.* Somewhat. See Usage note. [Middle English *som(e),* Old English *sum,* one, a certain one. See **sem-¹** in Appendix.*]

Usage: *Some,* employed adverbially in the sense of *somewhat,* is not appropriate to formal usage, though it is common informally. Thus, formally, *He is somewhat* (not *some*) *better. The situation has improved somewhat* (not *some*). As an example in writing, *The situation has improved some* is unacceptable to 87 per cent of the Usage Panel. Where idiom prevents the substitution of *somewhat* for *some,* alternative phrasing is necessary to convey formally the sense of indefinite degree or extent: *He watches television sometimes* (informally, *some*).

ă pat/ā pay/âr care/ä father/b bib/ch church/d deed/ĕ pet/ē be/f fife/g gag/h hat/hw which/ĭ pit/ī pie/îr pier/j judge/k kick/l lid, needle/m mum/n no, sudden/ng thing/ŏ pot/ō toe/ô paw, for/oi noise/ou out/o͝o took/o͞o boot/p pop/r roar/s sauce/sh ship, dish/

–some[1]. Indicates being or tending to be; for example, **burdensome.** [Middle English *-som*, Old English *-sum.* See sem-[1] in Appendix.*]

–some[2]. Indicates body; for example, **chromosome.** [New Latin *-soma*, from Greek *sōma*, body. See teue- in Appendix.*]

–some[3]. Indicates a group of. Used with numerals; for example, **threesome.** [Middle English *-sum*, from *sum, som,* SOME.]

some·bod·y (sŭm′bŏd′ē, -bŭd′ē, -bə-dē) *pron.* An unspecified or unknown person; someone. —*n., pl.* **somebodies.** *Informal.* A person of importance.
  Usage: Somebody (pronoun) and *someone* are usually construed as singular, in formal usage, and thus take singular verbs and related personal pronouns or pronominal adjectives: *Somebody has his coat draped across the chair.* Informally, especially in speech, such examples sometimes employ plural pronouns or adjectives: *Someone has their porch light turned on.* See Usage note at **someone.**

some·day (sŭm′dā′) *adv.* At a time in the future.
  Usage: Someday (adverb) and *sometime* express future time indefinitely. This sense can also be conveyed by *some day* and *some time.* The two-word forms are always used when *some* is an adjective modifying and specifying a more particular *day* or *time* (used as nouns). For example: *We'll succeed someday. Come sometime. Let's meet sometime* (or *some time*) *when your schedule permits. Come some day* (not *someday*) *soon. Choose some day* (not *someday*) *that is not so busy.*

some·how (sŭm′hou′) *adv.* In a way not specified, understood, or known.

some·one (sŭm′wŭn′, -wən) *pron.* Some person; somebody. —*n. Informal.* A somebody.
  Usage: Someone (pronoun) and *somebody* refer indefinitely to some person: *Someone* (or *somebody*) *will pick it up tomorrow.* The form *some one* refers specifically to a person or thing singled out of a group: *Some one of us will have to accept responsibility.* With *someone* and *somebody,* the stress is on *some;* with *some one,* the stress is on *one.* See Usage note at **somebody.**

some·place (sŭm′plās′) *adv. Informal.* Somewhere.
  Usage: Someplace (or *some place*), used adverbially for *somewhere,* is appropriate principally to informal speech and writing and to dialogue. Otherwise *somewhere* is clearly preferable. As an example in writing, the following is unacceptable to 83 per cent of the Usage Panel: *an unspecified target someplace between Inchon and Seoul.* But *some place,* as adjective plus noun, is acceptable on any level, as in *Choose some place cozy.*

som·er·sault (sŭm′ər-sôlt′) *n.* Also **sum·mer·sault, som·er·set** (-sĕt), **sum·mer·set.** 1. An acrobatic stunt in which the body rolls in a complete circle, heels over head. 2. Any complete reversal, as of sympathies or opinions. —*intr.v.* **somersaulted, -saulting, -saults.** Also **sum·mer·sault, som·er·set, sum·mer·set. -setted, -setting, -sets.** To execute a somersault. [Old French *sombresau(l)t,* variant of *sobresault,* from Old Provençal *sobresaut* (unattested) : *sobre-,* over, above, from Latin *suprā* (see **uper** in Appendix*) + *saut,* leap, from Latin *saltus,* from *salīre,* to leap (see **sel-**[4] in Appendix*).]

Som·er·set (sŭm′ər-sĕt′). Also **Som·er·set·shire** (-shîr, -shər). A county occupying 1,613 square miles in southwestern England. Population, 599,000. County seat, Taunton.

Som·er·set Island (sŭm′ər-sĕt′). An island of Canada, 9,594 square miles in area, in the Northwest Territories just north of the Boothia Peninsula.

Som·ers Islands. The former name for **Bermuda.**

So·mer·ville (sŭm′ər-vĭl). An industrial city of Massachusetts, in the northeast near Boston. Population, 95,000.

some·thing (sŭm′thĭng) *pron.* An undetermined or unspecified thing. —*n.* An important person or thing.

some·time (sŭm′tīm′) *adv.* 1. At an indefinite or unstated time. 2. At an indefinite time in the future. 3. *Rare.* Sometimes. 4. *Archaic.* Formerly. —*adj.* 1. Having been at some prior time; former: *a sometime secretary.* 2. *Nonstandard.* Occasional. See Usage note.
  Usage: Sometime (adjective) is also employed in the sense of being occasional or being such now and then: *the team's sometime star and sometime problem child.* It is acceptable in that sense to only 30 per cent of the Usage Panel. See Usage note at **someday.**

some·times (sŭm′tīmz′) *adv.* 1. Upon occasion; at times; now and then. 2. *Obsolete.* At some prior time; once; formerly.

some·way (sŭm′wā′) *adv.* Also **some·ways** (-wāz′). *Informal.* In some way or another; somehow.
  Usage: Someway and *someways* are largely appropriate to informal usage. As an example in writing that is not deliberately informal, the following is unacceptable to 83 per cent of the Usage Panel: *Someway we must find time to do it.* Here *somehow* would be preferable.

some·what (sŭm′hwät′, sŭm-hwät′) *adv.* To some extent or degree; rather. See Usage note at **some.** —*n.* Some amount, part, or degree; something: *He is somewhat of a fool.*

some·where (sŭm′hwĕr′) *adv.* 1. At, in, or to a place not specified or known; some place. See Usage note at **someplace.** 2. At or to some unspecified point in time, amount, or degree. Used with *in* or *about.* —*n.* An unknown or unspecified place.

so·mite (sō′mīt′) *n.* 1. *Zoology.* A body segment, a **metamere** (*see*). 2. *Embryology.* One of the segmental masses of mesoderm in the vertebrate embryo, occurring in pairs along the notochord. [SOM(A) + -ITE.]

Somme (sôm). A river of northern France, in the valley of which were fought major battles in World War I (1916 and 1918) and World War II (1940 and 1944).

som·me·lier (sôm′ə-lyā′) *n.* A wine steward in a restaurant. [French, from Old French, officer in charge of provisions, pack-animal driver, from *somme,* "pack," from Late Latin *sagma,* from Greek, "packsaddle." See sumpter.]

Som·mer·feld (sŭm′ər-fĕld′), **Arnold Johannes Wilhelm.** 1868–1951. German physicist; studied electromagnetic phenomena and atomic spectra.

som·nam·bu·late (sŏm-năm′byə-lāt′) *intr.v.* **-lated, -lating, -lates.** To walk while asleep. [SOMN(I)- + AMBULATE.]

som·nam·bu·lism (sŏm-năm′byə-lĭz′əm) *n.* Walking while asleep or in a sleeplike condition. Also called "noctambulism," "sleepwalking." —**som·nam′bu·list** *n.* —**som·nam′bu·lis′tic, som·nam′bu·lar** *adj.*

somni–, somn–. Indicates sleep; for example, **somnifacient, somnambulate.** [From Latin *somnus,* sleep. See swep-[1] in Appendix.*]

som·ni·fa·cient (sŏm′nə-fā′shənt) *adj.* Tending to produce sleep; hypnotic. [SOMNI- + -FACIENT.]

som·nif·er·ous (sŏm-nĭf′ər-əs) *adj.* Also **som·nif·ic** (-nĭf′ĭk). Inducing sleep; soporific. [From Latin *somnifer:* SOMNI- + -FEROUS.]

som·no·lence (sŏm′nə-ləns) *n.* Drowsiness; sleepiness.

som·no·lent (sŏm′nə-lənt) *adj.* 1. Drowsy; sleepy. 2. Inducing or tending to induce sleep; soporific. [Middle English *sompnolent,* from Old French, from Latin *somnolentus,* from *somnus,* sleep. See swep-[1] in Appendix.*] —**som′no·lent·ly** *adv.*

So·mo·za (sō-mō′sä). A family of Nicaraguan statesmen, including **Anastasio Somoza Garcia** (1896–1956), president (1937–47 and 1950–56); and his sons, **Luis Anastasio Somoza Debayle** (1922–1967), president (1956–63); and **Anastasio Somoza Debayle** (born 1925), president (since 1967).

son (sŭn) *n. Abbr.* **s.** 1. A male offspring. 2. Any male descendant. 3. a. An adopted male child. b. A son-in-law. 4. A male person strongly influenced by or associated with a place, cause, race, or school. 5. A young man. Used as a familiar term of address. —**the Son.** The second person of the Trinity, Christ. [Middle English *son(e),* Old English *sunu.* See seu-[3] in Appendix.*]

so·nance (sō′nəns) *n.* Sound.

so·nant (sō′nənt) *adj. Phonetics.* Voiced. —*n. Phonetics.* 1. A voiced speech sound. 2. A syllabic consonant; sonorant. [Latin *sonāns,* present participle of Latin *sonāre,* to sound. See swen- in Appendix.*]

so·nar (sō′när′) *n.* 1. A system using transmitted and reflected acoustic waves to detect and locate submerged objects. 2. An apparatus using such a system, as in a submarine. [SO(UND) NA(VIGATION) R(ANGING).]

so·na·ta (sō-nä′tä) *n.* A musical composition consisting of three or four independent movements varying in key, mood, and tempo. [Italian, from the feminine past participle of *sonare,* to sound, from Latin *sonāre.* See swen- in Appendix.*]

sonata form. A musical form consisting of three sections, the exposition, development, and recapitulation, often followed by a coda.

so·na·ti·na (sō′nä-tē′nä) *n., pl.* **-nas** or **-ne** (-nā). A sonata having shorter movements than the typical sonata. [Italian, diminutive of SONATA.]

sone (sōn) *n.* A subjective unit of loudness, equal to the loudness of a pure tone having a frequency of 1,000 cycles per second at 40 decibels above the listener's threshold of audibility. [From Latin *sonus,* a sound. See swen- in Appendix.*]

song (sông, sŏng) *n.* 1. A brief musical composition written or adapted for singing. 2. The act or art of singing. 3. A melodious utterance, such as a bird call. 4. a. Poetry; verse. b. A lyric poem or ballad. [Middle English *song, sang,* Old English *sang.* See sengwh- in Appendix.*]

song and dance. *Slang.* An overelaborate effort to explain or justify.

song·bird (sông′bûrd′, sŏng′-) *n.* A bird, especially one of the suborder Passeres, having a melodious song or call.

Song Bo. The Annamese name for the **Black River.**

Song Coi. The Annamese name for the **Red River.**

song·fest (sông′fĕst′, sŏng′-) *n.* A casual gathering for group singing.

song·ful (sông′fəl, sŏng′-) *adj.* Melodious; tuneful.

Song of Solomon. *Abbr.* **S. of Sol.** A book of the Old Testament consisting of a dramatic love poem traditionally attributed to Solomon. Also called "Canticle of Canticles," "Song of Songs."

song sparrow. A North American songbird, *Melospiza melodia,* having streaked brownish plumage.

song·ster (sông′stər, sŏng′-) *n.* 1. One that sings. 2. A songwriter.

song thrush. An Old World songbird, *Turdus philomelos,* having brown upper plumage and a spotted breast. Also called "mavis."

song·writ·er (sông′rī′tər, sŏng′-) *n.* One who writes lyrics or composes tunes for songs.

Son·ia (sō′nyə, sŭn′yə). Also **Son·ya.** A feminine given name. [Russian, diminutive of SOPHIA.]

son·ic (sŏn′ĭk) *adj.* 1. Of or relating to audible sound: *a sonic wave.* 2. Having a speed approaching or being that of sound in air, approximately 738 miles per hour at sea level. [Latin *son(us),* sound (see swen- in Appendix*) + -IC.]

sonic barrier. The sudden sharp increase in aerodynamic drag experienced by aircraft approaching the speed of sound. Also called "sound barrier."

sonic boom. A loud transient explosive sound caused by the shock wave preceding an aircraft traveling at supersonic speeds.

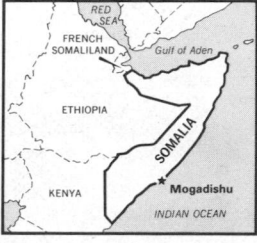
Somalia

sombrero

---

t tight/th thin, path/*th* this, bathe/ŭ cut/ûr urge/v valve/w with/y yes/z zebra, size/zh vision/ə about, item, edible, gallop, circus/ à *Fr.* ami/œ *Fr.* feu, *Ger.* schön/ü *Fr.* tu, *Ger.* über/KH *Ger.* ich, *Scot.* loch/N *Fr.* bon. *Follows main vocabulary. †Of obscure origin.

Sophocles

son-in-law (sŭn'ĭn-lô') n., pl. **sons-in-law** (sŭnz'-). The husband of one's daughter.

son·net (sŏn'ĭt) n. A 14-line poetic form usually made up of an octave and a sestet embodying the statement and the resolution of a single theme. [French, from Italian *sonetto*, from Old Provençal *sonet*, diminutive of *son*, song, from Latin *sonus*, sound. See swen- in Appendix.*]

son·net·eer (sŏn'ə-tîr') n. 1. A composer of sonnets. 2. An inferior poet.

son·ny (sŭn'e) n., pl. **-nies.** Little boy; young man. Used as a familiar form of address. [Diminutive of SON.]

son of a bitch pl. **sons of bitches.** Abbr. **S.O.B.** Slang. 1. A person regarded with strong disapproval. 2. Used to express astonishment.

So·no·ra (sō-nō'rä). A state of Mexico occupying 70,484 square miles in the northwest on the Gulf of California. Population, 893,000. Capital, Hermosillo.

so·no·rant (sə-nôr'ənt, sə-nōr'-, sŏn'ər-) n. Phonetics. A voiced consonant regarded as a syllabic sound, as the last sound in the word *sudden* (sŭd'n). [SONOR(OUS) + -ANT.]

so·nor·i·ty (sə-nôr'ə-tē, sə-nōr'-) n., pl. **-ties.** 1. The quality or state of being sonorous; resonance. 2. A sound.

so·no·rous (sə-nôr'əs, sə-nōr'-, sŏn'ər-) adj. 1. Having or producing sound. 2. Having or producing a full, deep, or rich sound. 3. Impressive; grandiloquent. [Latin *sonōrus*, from *sonor*, sound, from *sonāre*, to sound. See swen- in Appendix.*] —**so·no'rous·ly** adv.

son·ship (sŭn'shĭp') n. The fact or relationship of being a son.

Soo Canals. See **Sault Sainte Marie Canals.**

soo·chong. Variant of **souchong.**

Soo·chow (sōo'jō'). A city of China, in southern Kiangsu Province about 50 miles west of Shanghai. Population, 651,000.

soon (sōon) adv. **sooner, soonest.** 1. In the near future; shortly. 2. Without hesitation; promptly. 3. Before the usual or appointed time; early. 4. With willingness; readily. 5. Obsolete. Immediately. [Middle English *sone, soon(e)*, Old English *sōna*, from West Germanic *sǣnō* (unattested).]
  Usage: No sooner is preferably followed by *than*, rather than by *when*, as in the following typical examples: *No sooner had she come than the maid knocked. I had no sooner left than she called.*

soon·er[1] (sōo'nər) n. Slang. 1. A person who settled homestead land in the early West before it was officially made available, in order to have first choice of location. 2. Capital **S.** An Oklahoman. [From SOON.]

soon·er[2]. Comparative of **soon.**

Soon·er State (sōo'nər). The nickname for Oklahoma.

Soong (sōong). A Chinese family, including **Charles Jones Soong** (died 1927), missionary and merchant; and his daughters, **Mayling** (born 1898; married **Chiang Kai-Shek**); **Ai-Ling** (born 1888; married **H.H. Kung**); and **Soong Ching-Ling** (born 1890; married **Sun Yat-Sen**), deputy chairman of the People's Republic of China since 1959.

soot (sŏot, sŭt, sōot) n. A fine dispersion of black particles, chiefly carbon, produced by the incomplete combustion of coal, oil, wood, or other fuels. —tr.v. **sooted, sooting, soots.** To cover or smudge with soot. [Middle English *so(o)t*, Old English *sōt*. See sed-¹ in Appendix.*]

sooth (sōoth) adj. Archaic. 1. Real; true. 2. Soft; soothing; sweet. —n. Archaic. Truth; reality. [Middle English *so(o)th*, Old English *sōth*. See es- in Appendix.*] —**sooth'ly** adv.

soothe (sōoth) v. **soothed, soothing, soothes.** —tr. 1. To calm; mollify; placate. 2. To ease or relieve the pain of. —intr. To bring comfort, composure, or relief. —See Synonyms at re·lieve. [Middle English *sothen*, to show to be true, Old English *sōthian*, from *sōth*, truth, SOOTH.] —**sooth'er** n.

sooth·fast (sōoth'făst') adj. Archaic. 1. Truthful; honest. 2. True; real. [Middle English *sothfast*, Old English *sōthfæst* : *sōth*, SOOTH + *fæst*, FAST (firm).]

sooth·say (sōoth'sā') intr.v. **-said** (-sĕd'), **-saying, -says** (-sĕz'). To foretell future events; predict; prophesy. [Back-formation from SOOTHSAYER.]

sooth·say·er (sōoth'sā'ər) n. One who claims to foretell events; prophet; seer. [Middle English *sothsayer* : *soth*, SOOTH + *sayer*, one who says, from *sayen*, to SAY.]

soot·y (sōo'tē, sŏo'-, sŭt'ē) adj. **-ier, -iest.** 1. Covered with soot. 2. Of or producing soot. 3. Black or dark like soot.

sooty grouse. A bird, the **blue grouse** (see).

sooty mold. A black fungus of the genus *Capnodium*, growing on plants in the droppings of sucking insects such as aphids.

sop (sŏp) v. **sopped, sopping, sops.** —tr. 1. To dip, soak, or drench in a liquid; saturate. 2. To take up by absorption. Usually used with *up*. —intr. To be or become thoroughly soaked or saturated. —n. 1. A bit of bread or other food soaked in a liquid. 2. Anything thoroughly soaked; something soggy. 3. Something of little value yielded to placate an importunate person. [From Middle English *soppe*, dipped bread, Old English *sopp*. See seu-⁴ in Appendix.*]

SOP standard operating procedure.

sop. soprano.

soph. sophomore.

So·phi·a (sō-fī'ə, -fē'ə). Also **So·phie** (sō'fē). A feminine given name. [Middle English, from Greek, wisdom, from *sophos*, wise. See sophist.]

soph·ism (sŏf'ĭz'əm) n. 1. A plausible but fallacious argument. 2. Any deceptive or fallacious argumentation. [Middle English *sophime*, from Old French *sophi(s)me*, from Latin *sophisma*, from Greek, acquired skill, clever device, from *sophizesthai*, to play subtle tricks. See sophist.]

soph·ist (sŏf'ĭst) n. 1. Capital **S. a.** A member of a pre-Socratic

school of philosophy in ancient Greece. **b.** Any of a class of later Greek teachers of rhetoric and philosophy who came to be disparaged for their oversubtle, self-serving reasoning. 2. A scholar or thinker, especially one skillful in devious argumentation. [Latin *sophistēs*, from Greek, expert, deviser, from *sophizesthai*, to play subtle tricks, from *sophos*†, skilled, clever.]

so·phis·tic (sə-fĭs'tĭk) adj. Also **so·phis·ti·cal** (-tĭ-kəl). 1. Of, pertaining to, or characteristic of sophists. 2. Specious; fallacious. —**so·phis'ti·cal·ly** adv.

so·phis·ti·cate (sə-fĭs'tĭ-kāt') v. **-cated, -cating, -cates.** —tr. 1. To cause to become less natural or simple; especially, to make less naive; make worldly-wise. 2. To corrupt or pervert; adulterate. 3. To make more complex or inclusive; refine. —intr. To use sophistry. —n. (sə-fĭs'tĭ-kĭt). A sophisticated person. [Medieval Latin *sophisticāre*, from Latin *sophisticus*, sophistic, from Greek *sophistikos*, from *sophistēs*, SOPHIST.] —**so·phis'ti·ca'tor** (-kā'tər) n. —**so·phis'ti·ca'tion** n.

so·phis·ti·cat·ed (sə-fĭs'tĭ-kā'tĭd) adj. 1. Having acquired worldly knowledge or refinement; lacking natural simplicity or naiveté: *"We considered ourselves very sophisticated and talked of sex and morality in a superior way"* (Jawaharlal Nehru). 2. Complex or complicated; refined: *a sophisticated machine.* 3. Suitable for or appealing to the tastes of sophisticates. —**so·phis'ti·cat·ed·ly** adv.

soph·is·try (sŏf'ĭs-trē) n., pl. **-tries.** 1. A plausible but misleading or fallacious argument. 2. Plausible but fallacious argumentation; faulty reasoning.

Soph·o·cle·an (sŏf'ə-klē'ən) adj. Pertaining to or characteristic of Sophocles or his works.

Soph·o·cles (sŏf'ə-klēz'). 496?-406 B.C. Greek dramatist; author of seven extant tragedies.

soph·o·more (sŏf'ə-môr') n. Abbr. **soph.** 1. A second-year student in a four-year American college or high school. 2. A person in his second year of any endeavor. [Probably from earlier *sophumer*, arguments, from *sophum*, variant of SOPHISM.]

soph·o·mor·ic (sŏf'ə-môr'ĭk) adj. Also **soph·o·mor·i·cal** (-ĭ-kəl). Characteristic of a sophomore; especially, immature and overconfident. —**soph'o·mor'i·cal·ly** adv.

So·phy (sō'fē) n., pl. **-phies.** Also **So·phi.** A title formerly given to kings of Persia. [Persian *Safī*, surname of ruling Persian dynasty (1500-1736), from Arabic *Safī-ud-din*, "purity of religion."]

-sophy. Indicates knowledge or a system of thought; for example, **anthroposophy.** [From Greek *sophia*, wisdom, and *sophos*, wise. See sophist.]

so·por (sō'pôr', -pər) n. An abnormally deep sleep; stupor. [Latin *sopor*, sleep. See swep-¹ in Appendix.*]

so·po·rif·er·ous (sŏp'ə-rĭf'ər-əs) adj. Inducing sleep; soporific. [From Latin *soporifer* : SOPOR + -FEROUS.] —**so'po·rif'er·ous·ly** adv. —**so'po·rif'er·ous·ness** n.

so·po·rif·ic (sŏp'ə-rĭf'ĭk) adj. 1. Inducing or tending to induce sleep. 2. Drowsy. —n. A sleep-inducing drug. [SOPOR + -FIC.]

sop·ping (sŏp'ĭng) adj. Soaked thoroughly; drenched.

sop·py (sŏp'ē) adj. **-pier, -piest.** 1. Soaked; sopping. 2. Rainy. 3. Slang. Mawkish.

so·pran·o (sə-prăn'ō, -prä'nō) n., pl. **-os** or **-prani** (-prä'nē). Abbr. **sop., S., s.** Music. 1. The highest melodic line in a harmony. 2. A singer having such a voice. 3. A part for such a voice in four-part harmony. 4. The tonal range characteristic of a soprano. —adj. Of, pertaining to, for, or in the range of a soprano. [Italian, from *sopra*, above, from Latin *suprā*. See uper in Appendix.*]

So·qo·tra. See Socotra.

so·ra (sôr'ə) n. A North American marsh bird, *Porzana carolina*, having grayish-brown plumage. [Probably of American Indian origin.]

So·ra·ta. See Illampu.

sorb[1] (sôrb) tr.v. **sorbed, sorbing, sorbs.** To take up and hold, as by absorption or adsorption. [Back-formation from ADSORB and ABSORB.]

sorb[2] (sôrb) n. 1. Any of several Old World trees of the genus *Sorbus* or related genera, such as the service tree or the rowan. 2. The fruit of such a tree. In this sense, also called "sorb apple." [French *sorbe*, from Latin *sorbus*, SERVICE (tree).]

Sorb (sôrb) n. A Wend (see). [German *Sorbe*, perhaps variant of *Serbe*, Serb, from Serbian *Srb*, SERB.]

sor·bet (sôr'bĭt) n. 1. Sherbet. 2. A frozen dessert similar to a frappé and having a mushy consistency. [French, from Italian *sorbetto*, from Turkish *sherbet*, SHERBET.]

Sor·bi·an (sôr'bē-ən) n. 1. A Wend (see). 2. Wendish (see). [From SORB.] —**Sor·bi·an** adj.

sor·bic acid (sôr'bĭk). A white crystalline solid, $C_6H_8O_2$, found in the berries of the mountain ash and also synthesized, and used as a food preservative and fungicide. [From SORB (tree).]

sor·bose (sôr'bōs') n. A white sweetish sugar, $C_6H_{12}O_6$, used in the manufacture of ascorbic acid. [SORB (tree) + -OSE.]

sor·cer·er (sôr'sər-ər) n. One who practices sorcery; a wizard; enchanter. [Middle English *sorser*, from Old French *sorcier*, from Vulgar Latin *sortiārius* (unattested), caster of lots, from *sors* (stem *sort-*), lot. See ser-³ in Appendix.*]

sor·cer·ess (sôr'sər-ĭs) n. A female sorcerer.

sor·cer·y (sôr'sər-ē) n., pl. **-ies.** The use of supernatural power over others through the assistance of evil spirits; witchcraft; black magic. See Synonyms at magic. [Middle English *sorcerie*, from Old French, from *sorcier*, SORCERER.] —**sor'cer·ous** adj. —**sor'cer·ous·ly** adv.

sord (sôrd) n. A flight of mallards. See Synonyms at flock.

ă pat/ā pay/âr care/ä father/b bib/ch church/d deed/ĕ pet/ē be/f fife/g gag/h hat/hw which/ĭ pit/ī pie/îr pier/j judge/k kick/l lid/ needle/m mum/n no, sudden/ng thing/ŏ pot/ō toe/ô paw, for/oi noise/ou out/ŏŏ took/ōō boot/p pop/r roar/s sauce/sh ship, dish/

[Middle English *sorde,* from *sorden,* to rise up in flight, from Old French *sordre,* from Latin *surgere,* to rise, SURGE.]

sor·did (sôr′dĭd) *adj.* **1.** Filthy or dirty; foul: *"the great part of what happens is just muck and filth, sordid as any garbage can"* (Henry Miller). **2.** Depressingly squalid; wretched: *sordid shantytowns.* **3.** Morally degraded; vile; base: *"the sordid details of his orgies stank under his very nostrils"* (Joyce). **4.** Exceedingly mercenary; grasping; selfish. [French *sordide,* from Latin *sordidus,* from *sordēre,* to be dirty. See **swordo-** in Appendix.*] —**sor′did·ly** *adv.* —**sor′did·ness** *n.*

sor·di·no (sôr-dē′nō, sôr-) *n., pl.* **-ni** (-nē). Also **sor·dine** (sôr′dēn, sôr-dēn′). A mute for a musical instrument. [Italian, from *sordo,* deaf, mute, from Latin *surdus.* See **swer-**[2] in Appendix.*]

sore (sôr, sōr) *adj.* **sorer, sorest. 1.** Painful to the touch; tender. **2.** Feeling physical pain; hurting: *"sore in my feet with going till I was hardly able to stand"* (Pepys). **3.** Causing misery, sorrow, or distress; grievous: *sore need.* **4.** Causing embarrassment, irritation, or the like: *a sore subject.* **5.** Full of distress; grieved; sorrowful. **6.** *Informal.* Angered; offended. —*adv. Archaic.* Sorely. —*n.* **1.** An open skin lesion, wound, or ulcer. **2.** Any source of pain, distress, or irritation. [Middle English *sar, sor,* Old English *sār.* See **sai-** in Appendix.*] —**sore′ness** *n.*

sore·head (sôr′hĕd′, sōr′-) *n. Slang.* A person who is easily offended, annoyed, or angered.

sor·el. Variant of **sorrel** (color).

Sor·el (sô-rĕl′), **Georges.** 1847–1922. French syndicalist philosopher; influenced Nazism and Fascism.

sore·ly (sôr′lē, sōr′-) *adv.* **1.** Severely; painfully; grievously. **2.** Extremely; greatly: *His skill was sorely needed.*

Sör·en·sen (sû′rən-sən), **Sören Peter Lauritz.** 1868–1939. Danish biochemist; studied hydrogen ion and devised pH scale.

Sor·en·son (sôr′ən-sən), **Theodore Chaikin.** Born 1928. American lawyer and author.

sore throat. Any of various inflammations of the tonsils, pharynx, or larynx characterized by pain in swallowing.

sor·ghum (sôr′gəm, sōr′-) *n.* **1.** An Old World grass, *Sorghum vulgare,* several varieties of which are widely cultivated as grain and forage or as a source of syrup. **2.** Syrup made from the juice of this plant. [New Latin, from Italian *sorgo,* from Vulgar Latin *syricum (grānum)* (unattested), Syrian (grain), from Latin *Syricum,* SYRIAN.]

sor·go (sôr′gō, sōr′-) *n., pl.* **-gos.** Also **sor·gho.** Any of various sorghums cultivated as a source of syrup; especially, *Sorghum vulgare saccharatum.* [Italian *sorgo,* SORGHUM.]

so·ri. Plural of **sorus.**

sor·i·cine (sôr′ə-sēn′) *adj.* Of or belonging to the family Soricidae, which includes the shrews. [Latin *sōricinus,* from *sōrex* (stem *sōric-*), shrew, akin to Greek *hurax,* HYRAX.]

so·ri·tes (sō-rī′tēz′) *n., pl.* **sorites.** *Logic.* A form of argument in which a series of incomplete syllogisms is so arranged that the predicate of each premise forms the subject of the next, until the subject of the first is joined with the predicate of the last in the conclusion. [Latin *sōrītēs,* from Greek *sōreitēs,* from *sōros,* heap, pile. See **teuə-** in Appendix.*]

So·ro·ca·ba (sôr′ō-cä′bä). A city and commercial center of Brazil in southeastern São Paulo. Population, 109,000.

so·ro·ral (sə-rôr′əl, -rōr′əl) *adj.* Pertaining to or like a sister; sisterly. [From Latin *soror,* sister. See **swesor-** in Appendix.*]

so·ror·ate (sə-rôr′ĭt, -rōr′ĭt) *n.* The custom of marriage of a man to his wife's sister or sisters, usually after the wife has died or proved sterile. [From Latin *soror,* sister. See **sororal.**]

so·ror·i·cide (sə-rôr′ə-sīd′, sə-rōr′-) *n.* **1.** The killing of one's sister. **2.** One who kills his own sister. [Medieval Latin *sororicidium* : Latin *soror,* sister (see **sororal**) + -CIDE.] —**so·ror′i·cid′al** *adj.*

so·ror·i·ty (sə-rôr′ə-tē, sə-rōr′-) *n., pl.* **-ties.** A social club for female students, as at a college. Compare **fraternity.** [Medieval Latin *sororitās,* from Latin *soror,* sister. See **swesor-** in Appendix.*]

so·ro·sis (sə-rō′sĭs) *n., pl.* **-ses** (-sēz′). A women's club or organization. [From such an organization incorporated in 1869, from Greek *sōros,* heap. See **teuə-** in Appendix.*]

sorp·tion (sôrp′shən) *n. Chemistry.* **1.** The process of sorbing. **2.** The state of being sorbed. [Back-formation from ABSORPTION and ADSORPTION.]

sor·rel[1] (sôr′əl) *n.* **1.** Any of several plants of the genus *Rumex,* having acid-flavored leaves sometimes used as salad greens; especially, *R. acetosella,* a widely naturalized species native to Eurasia. **2.** Any of various plants of the genus *Oxalis.* [Middle English *sorel,* from Old French *surele,* from *sur,* sour, from Germanic. See **sūro-** in Appendix.*]

sor·rel[2] (sôr′əl) *n.* Also **sor·el. 1.** Brownish orange to light brown. See **color. 2.** A horse of this color. [From Middle English *sorelle,* sorrel-colored, from Old French *sorel,* from *sor,* red-brown, from Germanic. See **saus-** in Appendix.*]

sorrel tree. The **sourwood** *(see).*

Sor·ren·to (sô-rĕn′tō). A resort town of Italy, in the south on the Bay of Naples.

sor·row (sŏr′ō, sôr′ō) *n.* **1.** Mental anguish or suffering because of injury or loss; sadness. **2.** Something that causes such suffering; misfortune. **3.** The expression of such suffering; grieving. —See Synonyms at **regret.** —*intr.v.* **sorrowed, -rowing, -rows.** To feel or display sorrow; grieve. [Middle English *sorge, sorow,* Old English *sorh, sorg,* anxiety, sorrow. See **swergh-** in Appendix.*] —**sor′row·er** *n.*

sor·row·ful (sŏr′ō-fəl, sôr′-) *adj.* Causing, feeling, or expressing sorrow; mournful. See Synonyms at **sad.** —**sor′row·ful·ly** *adv.* —**sor′row·ful·ness** *n.*

sor·ry (sŏr′ē, sôr′ē) *adj.* **-rier, -riest. 1.** Feeling or expressing sympathy, pity, or regret; sorrowful. Often used to express apology: *I am sorry to be late.* **2.** Worthless or inferior; poor; paltry: *a sorry attempt at apology.* **3.** Causing sorrow, grief, or misfortune; grievous; sad: *"He brought the sorry news of another terrible slide in Georgia phosphates."* (Louis Auchincloss). [Middle English *sary, sory,* Old English *sārig,* painful, sad. See **sai-** in Appendix.*] —**sor′ri·ly** *adv.* —**sor′ri·ness** *n.*

sort (sôrt) *n.* **1.** A group or collection of similar persons or things; class; kind; set. **2.** The character or nature of something; type; quality. **3.** A method of acting or behaving; manner; style. **4.** *Usually plural. Printing.* One of the characters in a font of type. —See Synonyms at **type.** —**after a sort.** In a haphazard or imperfect way. —**of sorts. 1.** Of a mediocre or inferior kind. **2.** Of one kind or another. —**out of sorts.** *Informal.* **1.** Somewhat ill; slightly sick. **2.** In a bad mood; irritable; cross. —**sort of.** *Informal.* Somewhat; rather. —*tr.v.* **sorted, sorting, sorts. 1.** To arrange according to class, kind, or size; classify. **2.** To separate (one kind, for example) from the others. Often used with *out: sort out the wheat from the chaff.* [Middle English, from Old French *sorte,* probably from Common Romance *sorta* (unattested), "kind," from Latin *sors* (stem *sort-*), lot, fortune. See **ser-**[3] in Appendix.*] —**sort′a·ble** *adj.* —**sort′er** *n.*

Usage: *Sort* (noun), in written usage that is not deliberately informal, now usually is used with a singular modifier and verb: *This sort of problem is not new.* In the plural: *These sorts of problems are not new.* An alternative form, *these sort of problems are,* is more common to speech but also has literary precedent, and is defended by some grammarians. *All sort of problems* (for *all sorts*) has less standing.

sor·tie (sôr′tē) *n. Military.* **1.** A sally by besieged forces upon the besiegers. **2.** A single flight of an airplane on a combat mission. [French, "a going out," from Old French, from *sortir*†, go out.]

sor·ti·lege (sôr′tə-lĭj) *n.* **1.** The act or practice of foretelling the future by drawing lots. **2.** Sorcery; witchcraft. [Middle English, from Old French, from Medieval Latin *sortilegium,* from *sortilegus,* diviner : Latin *sors,* lot (see **ser-**[3] in Appendix*) + *legere,* to read (see **leg-** in Appendix*).]

so·rus (sôr′əs) *n., pl.* **sori** (sôr′ī′). *Botany.* **1.** A cluster of spore cases borne by ferns on the undersides of the fronds. **2.** A similar structure in certain fungi and lichens. [New Latin, from Greek *sōros,* heap. See **teuə-** in Appendix.*]

S O S 1. The letters represented by the radiotelegraphic signal ···———···, used internationally as a distress signal, particularly by ships and aircraft. **2.** Any call or signal for help.

So·sno·wiec (sō-snō′vyĕts). A city and metallurgical and coal-mining center in southern Poland. Population, 138,000.

so-so (sō′sō′) *adj.* Neither very good nor very bad; mediocre; passable. See Synonyms at **average.** —*adv.* Indifferently; tolerably; passably.

sos·te·nu·to (sō′stĕ-nōō′tō) *adv. Abbr.* **sost.** *Music.* In a sustained or prolonged manner. Used as a direction. —*n., pl.* **sostenutos** or **-ti** (-tē). *Abbr.* **sost.** *Music.* A passage played or sung in this manner. [Italian, past participle of *sostenere,* to sustain, from Latin *sustinēre,* SUSTAIN.] —**sos′te·nu′to** *adj.*

sot (sŏt) *n.* A chronic drunkard. [Middle English *sot,* a fool, Old English *sott,* from Medieval Latin *sottus*†.]

so·te·ri·ol·o·gy (sō-tîr′ē-ŏl′ə-jē) *n.* The theological doctrine of salvation as effected by Christ. [Greek *sōtērion,* deliverance, from *sōtēr,* savior, from *sōzein,* to save, from *saos,* safe (see **teuə-** in Appendix*) + -LOGY.] —**so·te′ri·o·log′ic** (-ə-lŏj′ĭk), **so·te′ri·o·log′i·cal** *adj.*

So·thic (sō′thĭk, sŏth′ĭk) *adj.* **1.** Of, pertaining to, or deriving from the name of Sothis. **2.** Designating the ancient Egyptian year, consisting of 365¼ days. **3.** Designating a cycle consisting of 1,460 years of 365 days in the ancient Egyptian calendar. [From Greek *Sōthis,* the star Sirius, which appeared on the eastern horizon at sunrise when the year commenced.]

So·this (sō′thĭs) *n.* Sirius, the Dog Star. [Greek *Sōthis,* the star Sirius. See **Sothic.**]

So·tho (sō′thō) *n.* A group of Bantu languages spoken in Lesotho, Botswana, and South Africa.

so·tol (sō-tōl′) *n.* Any of several tall, woody plants of the genus *Dasylirion,* of the southwestern United States and adjacent Mexico, having prickly-margined leaves and a large cluster of whitish flowers. [Mexican Spanish, from *sotole,* maguey leaf, from Nahuatl *tzotolli.*]

sot·tish (sŏt′ĭsh) *adj.* **1.** Stupefied from or as if from drink. **2.** Tending to drink excessively; drunken. —**sot′tish·ly** *adv.*

sot·to vo·ce (sŏt′ō vō′chē). Very softly; especially, so as not to be overheard; in an undertone. [Italian, "under the voice."]

sou (sōō) *n. Abbr.* **s.** A former French coin. [French, back-formation from Old French *sous,* plural of *sout,* from Latin *solidus,* SOLIDUS.]

Sou. southern.

sou·a·ri nut (sōō-är′ē). **1.** A South American tree, *Caryocar nuciferum,* bearing nuts used as food and a source of cooking oil. **2.** The nut of this tree. Sometimes called "butternut." [French *saouari,* from Galibi *sawarra.*]

sou·brette (sōō-brĕt′) *n.* **1. a.** A saucy, coquettish, and intriguing lady's maid in comedies or comic opera. **b.** An actress or singer taking such a part. **2.** Any flirtatious or frivolous young woman. [French, from Provençal *soubreto,* feminine of *soubret,* conceited, from *soubra,* to leave aside, from Old Provençal *sobras,* to be excessive, from Latin *superāre,* from *super,* above. See **uper** in Appendix.*]

sou·bri·quet. Variant of **sobriquet.**

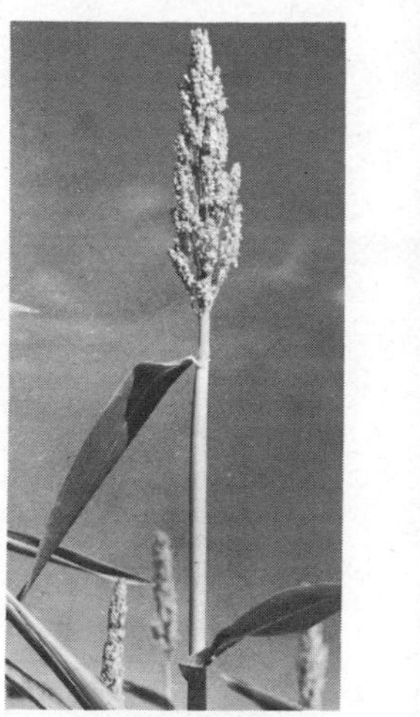

sorghum

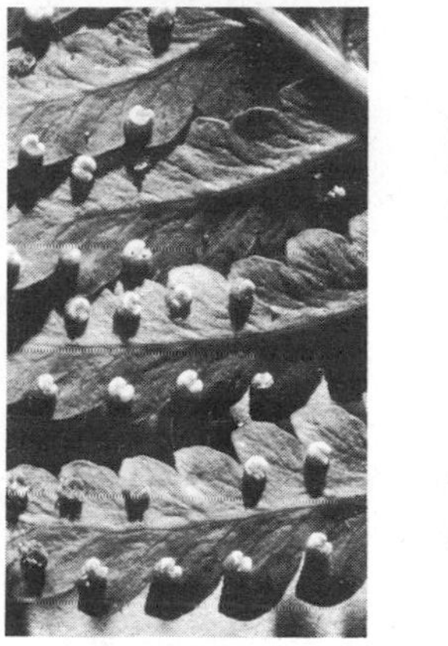

sorus
Fern sori

t tight/th thin, path/*th* this, bathe/ŭ cut/ûr urge/v valve/w with/y yes/z zebra, size/zh vision/ə about, item, edible, gallop, circus/ à *Fr.* ami/œ *Fr.* feu, *Ger.* schön/ü *Fr.* tu, *Ger.* über/KH *Ger.* ich, *Scot.* loch/N *Fr.* bon. *Follows main vocabulary. †Of obscure origin.

sou·chong (so͞o′chông′) *n.* Also **soo·chong.** One of several varieties of black tea native to China and adjacent regions. [Chinese (Mandarin) *hsiao[3]chung[3]*, small kind : *hsiao[3]*, small + *chung[3]*, kind.]

sou·dan. Variant of **soldan.**

Sou·dan. The French name for **Sudan.**

souf·flé (so͞o-flā′) *n.* A light, fluffy baked dish made with egg yolks and beaten egg whites combined with various other ingredients and served as a main dish or sweetened as a dessert. —*adj.* Also **souf·fléed** (-flād′). Made light and puffy by beating and baking or cooking. [French, from the past participle of *souffler*, to puff up, from Latin *sufflāre* : *sub-*, up, up from under + *flāre*, to blow (see **bhlē-[2]** in Appendix*).]

sough (sŭf, sou) *intr.v.* **soughed, soughing, soughs.** To make a soft murmuring or rustling sound: *"when the wind soughed through the thick foliage"* (Henry Miller). —*n.* A deep, soft murmuring sound, as of the wind or a gentle surf. [Middle English *swoghen*, Old English *swōgan*. See **swagh-** in Appendix.*]

sought. Past tense and past participle of **seek.**

soul (sōl) *n.* **1.** The animating and vital principle in man credited with the faculties of thought, action, and emotion and conceived as forming an immaterial entity distinguished from but temporally coexistent with his body. **2.** *Theology.* The spiritual nature of man considered in relation to God, regarded as immortal, separable from the body at death, and susceptible to happiness or misery in a future state. **3.** The disembodied spirit of a dead human being; a ghost; shade. **4.** *Capital* **S.** *Christian Science.* God. **5.** A human being: *"A soul as full of warmth as void of pride"* (Pope). **6.** A central or integral part of something; vital core. **7.** A person considered as the perfect embodiment of an intangible quality; personification. **8.** A person considered as an inspiring force; leader. **9.** The emotional nature in man as distinguished from his mind or intellect. **10.** *Slang.* An aggregate of elemental qualities that enables one to be in harmony with oneself and to convey to others the honest and unadorned expression of the hard side of life: *"Soul is bein' true to yourself . . . is . . . that uninhibited self-expression that goes into practically every Negro endeavor."* (Claude Brown). —*adj.* *Slang.* Of, pertaining to, characteristic of, or derived from the Negro or his culture: *soul food; soul music.* [Middle English *soul*, Old English *sāwol*, from Common Germanic *saiwalō* (unattested).]

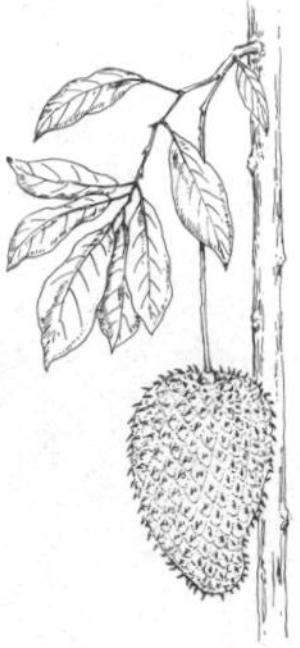

soursop

soul brother. *Slang.* A fellow Negro of the male sex.

soul·ful (sōl′fəl) *adj.* Full of or expressing a deep feeling; profoundly emotional. —**soul′ful·ly** *adv.* —**soul′ful·ness** *n.*

soul·less (sōl′lĭs) *adj.* Devoid of sensitivity or the capacity for deep feeling. —**soul′less·ly** *adv.* —**soul′less·ness** *n.*

soul mate. One of two persons compatible with each other in disposition, point of view, or sensitivity.

soul-search·ing (sōl′sûr′chĭng) *n.* The penetrating examination of oneself, one's motives, convictions, and emotional attitudes.

soul sister. *Slang.* A fellow Negro of the female sex.

sound[1] (sound) *n.* **1. a.** A vibratory disturbance in the pressure and density of a fluid, or in the elastic strain in a solid, with frequency in the approximate range between 20 and 20,000 cycles per second, and capable of being detected by the organs of hearing. **b.** Loosely, such a disturbance of any frequency. **2. a.** The sensation stimulated in the organs of hearing by such a disturbance. **b.** Such sensations collectively. **3.** A distinctive noise: *the sound of the whistle.* **4.** The distance over which something can be heard; earshot: *within sound of cannon fire.* **5. a.** An articulation made by the vocal apparatus. **b.** The distinctive character of such an articulation. For example, *bear* and *bare* have the same sound. **6.** A mental impression conveyed; import; implication. **7.** Auditory material that is recorded, as for a motion picture. **8.** Meaningless noise. **9.** *Archaic.* Rumor; report. —*v.* **sounded, sounding, sounds.** —*intr.* **1.** To make or give forth a sound. **2.** To present a particular impression; seem to be: *That argument sounds reasonable.* See Usage note below. —*tr.* **1.** To cause to give forth or produce a sound. **2.** To summon, announce, or signal by a sound: *sound a warning.* **3.** To articulate; pronounce. **4.** To make known; celebrate. **5.** To examine (a bodily organ or part) by causing to emit sound; auscultate. —**sound off. 1.** *Military Slang.* To speak in a loud, vigorous tone; shout. **2.** *Slang.* To speak loudly in a complaining or abusive way. [Middle English *sun*, *soun*, from Old French *son*, from Latin *sonus*. See **swen-** in Appendix.*]

Usage: *Sound* (intransitive verb: "convey an impression; seem to be") is followed by an adjective, not an adverb: *The news sounds good. His account sounds strange. The report sounds false.*

sound[2] (sound) *adj.* **sounder, soundest. 1.** Free from defect, decay, or damage; in good condition. **2.** Free from disease or injury; healthy: *sound in body and mind.* **3.** Having a firm basis; solid; unshakable: *a sound foundation.* **4.** Financially secure or safe; reliable: *a sound economy.* **5.** Founded on valid reasoning; free from misapprehension; sensible and correct: *a sound observation.* **6.** Thorough; complete: *a sound flogging.* **7.** Deep and unbroken; undisturbed: *a sound sleep.* **8.** Free from moral defect; upright; honorable: *"You know it is not sound and that you would never act in this way yourself"* (Jane Austen). **9.** Worthy of confidence; trustworthy. **10.** Marked by or showing common sense and good judgment; level-headed. **11.** Compatible with an accepted point of view; conservative. **12.** *Law.* Valid; legal. —See Synonyms at **healthy, valid.** [Middle English *sund*, Old English *gesund*. See **swento-** in Appendix.*] —**sound′ly** *adv.* —**sound′ness** *n.*

sound[3] (sound) *n.* **1.** A long, relatively wide body of water larger than a strait or a channel, connecting larger bodies of water. **2.** A long, wide ocean inlet. **3.** The air bladder of a fish. [Middle English *sound*, sound, swimming, Old English *sund*, swimming. See **swem-** in Appendix.*]

sound[4] (sound) *v.* **sounded, sounding, sounds.** —*tr.* **1.** To measure the depth of (water), especially by means of a weighted line; to fathom. **2.** To try to learn the attitudes or opinions of a person. Usually used with *out.* See Usage note below. **3.** *Surgery.* To probe (a bodily cavity) with a sound. —*intr.* **1.** To measure depth. **2.** To dive swiftly downward. Used of a whale or fish. **3.** To investigate; look into. —*n.* *Surgery.* An instrument used to examine body cavities. [Middle English *sounden*, from Old French *sonder*, from *sonde*, a sounding line, probably from Old English *sund-*, from *sund*, sea. See **swem-** in Appendix.*] —**sound′a·ble** *adj.*

Usage: *Sound out* is well established in the transitive sense of investigating or searching for attitudes or opinions, though the construction is sometimes held to be redundant. (Earlier, *sound* alone was used in this sense.) As an example in writing, *sound out the chairman of each delegation* is acceptable to 87 per cent of the Usage Panel.

sound barrier. The **sonic barrier** *(see).*

sound box. A hollow chamber in the body of a musical instrument, such as a violin or cello, that intensifies the resonance of the tone.

sound camera. A motion-picture camera equipped to record sound and image synchronously.

sound effects. Imitative sounds, as of thunder or an explosion, produced artificially for theatrical purposes.

sound·er[1] (soun′dər) *n.* One that sounds; especially, a device for making soundings of the sea.

sound·er[2] (soun′dər) *n.* A herd of wild boar. See Synonyms at **flock.** [Middle English, from Old French *sun(d)re*, from Germanic. See **seu-[2]** in Appendix.*]

sound·ing[1] (soun′dĭng) *n.* **1.** The act of one that sounds. **2.** An environmental probe for scientific observation. **3. a.** A measured depth of water. **b.** *Usually plural.* Water shallow enough for depth measurements to be taken by a hand line.

sound·ing[2] (soun′dĭng) *adj.* **1.** Emitting a full sound; resonant. **2.** Noisy but with little significance; high-sounding.

sounding board. 1. A thin board forming the upper portion of the resonant chamber in a musical instrument, such as a violin or piano, and serving to increase resonance. Also called "sound board." **2.** A dome or other structure suspended behind or over a podium, pulpit, or platform to reflect the speaker's voice to the audience. **3.** Any person or group whose reactions to an idea, opinion, or point of view will serve as a measure of its effectiveness or acceptability. **4.** Any device or agency serving to spread or popularize an idea or point of view.

sounding lead. The metal weight at the end of a sounding line.

sounding line. A line marked at intervals of fathoms and weighted at one end, used to determine the depth of water.

sounding rocket. A rocket used to make observations anywhere within the earth's atmosphere.

sound·less (sound′lĭs) *adj.* Having or making no sound; quiet; silent. —**sound′less·ly** *adv.* —**sound′less·ness** *n.*

sound·proof (sound′pro͞of′) *adj.* Not penetrable by audible sound. —*tr.v.* **soundproofed, -proofing, -proofs.** To make soundproof.

sound ranging. The electronic location of a sound source, as of enemy weapons, by checking time intervals indicated by microphones of known position.

sound stage. A room or studio, usually soundproof, used for the production of motion pictures.

sound·track (sound′trăk′) *n.* The narrow strip at one side of a motion-picture film that carries the sound recording.

sound truck. A truck or other vehicle having one or more loud-speakers, usually on top, for area broadcasting.

sound wave. A wave of **sound** *(see).*

soup (so͞op) *n.* **1.** A liquid food prepared from meat, fish, or vegetable stock sometimes combined with milk or a cream sauce, with various other ingredients added, as pieces of solid food, and served either hot or cold. **2.** *Slang.* Anything suggestive of the consistency of soup, especially: **a.** Dense fog. **b.** Nitroglycerine. —**in the soup.** *Slang.* In trouble; having difficulties. —**soup up.** *Slang.* To add horsepower or greater speed potential to (an engine). [French *soupe*, from Old French, broth, sop, from Germanic. See **seu-[4]** in Appendix.*]

soup·çon (so͞op-sôɴ′) *n. French.* A very small amount; a trace; a touch.

soup kitchen. A place where food is offered freely or at very low cost to the needy.

soup·spoon (so͞op′spo͞on′) *n.* A spoon somewhat larger than a teaspoon, used for eating soup.

soup·y (so͞o′pē) *adj.* **-ier, -iest. 1.** Having the consistency or appearance of soup. **2.** Foggy. **3.** *Informal.* Sentimental.

sour (sour) *adj. Rare* **sourer, sourest. 1.** Having a taste characteristic of that produced by acids; sharp, tart, or tangy, as lemons or vinegar. **2.** Made acid or rancid by fermentation; spoiled; rank. **3.** Having the characteristics of fermentation or rancidity; tasting or smelling of decay. **4.** Bad-tempered and morose; cross; peevish: *a sour temper.* **5.** Not up to the expected or usual ability or quality; bad: *His pitching went sour.* **6.** Designating soil that is excessively acid and damaging to crops. **7.** Containing an excess of sulfur compounds. Said of gasoline. —*n.* **1.** The sensation of sour taste, one of the four primary tastes. **2.** Anything that is sour. **3.** An alcoholic cocktail of whiskey, lime or lemon juice, and sugar. —*v.* **soured, souring, sours.** —*tr.* To make sour: *"Continued adversity had soured*

Johnson's temper" (Macaulay). —*intr.* To become sour. [Middle English *so(u)r,* Old English *sūr.* See **sūro-** in Appendix.*] —**sour'ly** *adv.* —**sour'ness** *n.*

source (sôrs, sōrs) *n.* **1.** A place or thing from which something comes or derives; point of origin. **2.** A spring, lake, or other body of water at which a stream or river originates. **3.** One that causes, creates, or initiates something; an author; a maker. **4.** A person or place that supplies information. **5.** A book, document, or other record supplying primary or firsthand information. —See Synonyms at **origin.** [Middle English *sours, source,* from Old French *sourse,* from the feminine past participle of *sourdre,* to rise, from Latin *surgere,* to SURGE.]

sour cherry. **1.** A tree, *Prunus cerasus,* native to Eurasia, having white flowers and tart red fruit. **2.** The edible fruit of this tree.

sour cream. **1.** Cream that has soured naturally by the action of lactic acid bacteria, and used in baking certain breads and cakes. **2.** A smooth, thick, artificially soured cream, widely used as an ingredient in soups, salads, and various meat dishes.

sour·crout. Variant of **sauerkraut.**

sour·dine (so͝or-dēn') *n.* **1.** An obsolete double-reed instrument with a soft tone. **2.** A mute, especially one for a violin. **3.** A stop on an organ producing a low, soft, muted tone. [French, from Italian *sordina,* from *sordo,* deaf, from Latin *surdus.* See **swer-**[2] in Appendix.*]

sour·dough (sour'dō') *n.* **1.** *Regional.* Sour fermented dough used as leaven in making bread. **2.** *Slang.* An old-time settler or prospector, especially in Alaska and northwestern Canada.

sour gum. A tree, *Nyssa sylvatica,* of eastern North America, having glossy, somewhat leathery leaves and soft wood. Also called "black gum," "pepperidge," and sometimes "beetlebung."

Sou·ris (so͝or'ĭs). A river rising in southeastern Saskatchewan, Canada, and flowing 435 miles first south into North Dakota and then north into Manitoba, where it joins the Assiniboine. Also called "Mouse River" in North Dakota.

sour mash. **1.** A mixture of new mash and mash from a preceding run used to distill certain malt whiskeys. **2.** The whiskey distilled from this mash.

sour·puss (sour'po͝os') *n. Slang.* A person with a habitually gloomy or sullen expression or attitude. [SOUR + PUSS (face).]

sour salt. Crystals of citric acid used in cooking.

sour·sop (sour'sŏp') *n.* **1.** A tropical American tree, *Annona muricata,* bearing spiny fruit with tart, edible pulp. **2.** The fruit of this tree.

sour·wood (sour'wo͝od') *n.* A tree, *Oxydendrum arboreum,* of the southeastern United States, having clusters of small white flowers. Also called "sorrel tree." [So called from its sour-tasting leaves.]

Sou·sa (so͞o'zə, -sə), **John Philip.** 1854–1932. American bandmaster and composer.

sou·sa·phone (so͞o'zə-fōn', so͞o'sə-) *n.* A large brass wind instrument similar to the tuba, having a flaring bell. [After John Philip SOUSA.]

souse[1] (sous) *v.* **soused, sousing, souses.** —*tr.* **1.** To plunge in a liquid. **2.** To make soaking wet; drench. **3.** To steep in a mixture, as in pickling. **4.** *Slang.* To make intoxicated. —*intr.* To become immersed or soaking wet. —*n.* **1.** The act or process of sousing. **2. a.** Food steeped in pickle; especially, the feet, ears, and head of a pig. **b.** The liquid used in pickling; brine. **3.** *Slang.* A drunkard. [Middle English *sousen,* to souse, to pickle, from *souse,* pickled meat, from Old French *sous, souz,* from Old High German *sulza,* brine. See **sal-**[1] in Appendix.*]

souse[2] (sous) *v.* **soused, sousing, souses.** *Archaic.* —*tr.* To pounce upon; attack. —*intr.* To swoop down, as an attacking hawk. Used with *on* or *upon.* —*n. Obsolete.* A swooping motion of attack, as of a hawk. [Middle English *souce,* swooping motion, perhaps variant of *sours,* SOURCE.]

Sousse (so͞os). Ancient name **Had·ru·me·tum** (hăd'ro͞o-mē'təm). A port city of northeastern Tunisia founded by the Phoenicians in the ninth century B.C. and later an important Roman colony. Population, 48,000.

sou·tache (so͞o-tăsh') *n.* A narrow flat braid in a herringbone effect, used for trimming and embroidery. [French, from Hungarian *sujtás.*]

sou·tane (so͞o-tän') *n.* A cassock worn by Roman Catholic priests. [French, from Italian *sottana,* garment worn under (religious vestments), from *sotto,* under, from Latin *subtus,* beneath, from *sub,* under. See **upo** in Appendix.*]

south (south) *n. Abbr.* **s, S, s., S., So.** **1. a.** The direction along a meridian to the right of an observer facing in the direction of the earth's rotation; the direction to the right of sunrise. **b.** The cardinal point on the mariner's compass, 180 degrees clockwise from north. See **compass card.** **2.** Any area or region lying in this direction. **3.** *Often capital* **S. a.** The southern part of the earth. **b.** The southern part of any country or region. —**the South.** In the United States, the states lying south of Pennsylvania and the Ohio River and east of the Mississippi, including those that fought for the Confederacy against the Union (or the North) in the Civil War. —*adj.* **1.** To, toward, of, facing, or in the south. **2.** Coming from or originating in the south. Said of wind. **3.** *Capital* **S.** Officially designating the southern part of a country, continent, or other geographical area: *South America.* —*adv.* In, from, or toward the south. [Middle English *south,* Old English *sūth.* See **sāwel-** in Appendix.*]

South Af·ri·ca, Republic of (ăf'rĭ-kə). Formerly **Union of South Af·ri·ca.** *Abbr.* **S.A.** A country occupying 471,445 square miles in southernmost Africa. Population, 17,474,000. Capital, Pretoria; seat of legislature, Cape Town.

South Af·ri·can (ăf'rĭ-kən). **1.** A native of the Republic of South Africa, especially one of European descent; an Afrikaner. **2.** Of or pertaining to South Africa or its inhabitants.

South African Dutch. **1.** See **Boer.** **2. Afrikaans** *(see).*

South African Republic. A former state of South Africa, coextensive with the modern province of **Transvaal.**

South African War. The **Boer War** *(see).*

South·all (south'ôl). A former administrative division of London, England, now part of **Ealing** *(see).*

South A·mer·i·ca (ə-mĕr'ĭ-kə). *Abbr.* **S.A.** The southern of the two continents of the Western Hemisphere, about 6,850,000 square miles in area, lying mostly south of the equator. —**South American.**

South·amp·ton (south-hămp'tən, sou-thămp'-). **1.** A city and major seaport in southern Hampshire, England. Population, 210,000. **2.** The official name for Hampshire.

South·amp·ton (south-hămp'tən, sou-thămp'-), **Third Earl of.** Title of Henry Wriothesley. 1573–1624. English courtier and military leader; treasurer of the Virginia Company (1620–24); literary patron, especially of Shakespeare.

South A·ra·bi·a. The former name for **Southern Yemen.**

South Aus·tra·lia (ô-strāl'yə). A state of the Commonwealth of Australia, occupying 380,000 square miles in the south-central part of the country. Population, 969,000. Capital, Adelaide.

South Bend. A city and educational and industrial center in northern Indiana. Population, 132,000.

south·bound (south'bound') *adj.* Going toward the south.

south by east. *Abbr.* **SbE** The direction, or point on the mariner's compass, halfway between due south and south-southeast. It is 168 degrees 45 minutes east of due north. See **compass card.**

south by west. *Abbr.* **SbW** The direction, or point on the mariner's compass, halfway between due south and south-southwest. It is 168 degrees 45 minutes west of due north. See **compass card.**

South Car·o·li·na (kăr'ə-lī'nə). *Abbr.* **S.C.** A Southeastern state of the United States, occupying 31,055 square miles on the Atlantic seaboard; one of the original 13 states. Population, 2,523,000. Capital, Columbia. See map at **United States of America.** —**South Car'o·lin'i·an** (-lĭn'ē-ən).

South China Sea. A section of the Pacific bordered by China, Vietnam, Cambodia, Thailand, Malaysia, Indonesia, and the Republic of the Philippines.

South Da·ko·ta (də-kō'tə). *Abbr.* **S.Dak.** A Middle Western state of the United States, occupying 77,047 square miles in the north-central part of the country. It joined the Union in 1889. Population, 715,000. Capital, Pierre. See map at **United States of America.** —**South Dakotan.**

South·down (south'doun') *n.* Any of a breed of small, hornless sheep of English origin, having dense, short, fine-textured wool. [From SOUTH DOWNS.]

South Downs. A range of hills extending west to east in southeastern England.

south·east (south-ēst'; *Nautical* sou-ēst') *n. Abbr.* **SE** **1.** The direction, or point on the mariner's compass, halfway between south and east. It is 135 degrees east of due north. See **compass card.** **2.** Any area or region lying in this direction. —*adj.* **1.** Situated, toward, facing, or in the southeast. **2.** Coming from or originating in the southeast, as a wind. —*adv.* In, from, or toward the southeast. —**south·east'ern** *adj.*

Southeast A·sia (ā'zhə, ā'shə). A region generally considered to include Indochina, Malaysia, Singapore, Indonesia, the Republic of the Philippines, Brunei, and Portuguese Timor.

Southeast Asia Treaty Organization. *Abbr.* **SEATO** The signatories to the Southeast Asian Collective Defense Treaty of 1954. They are Australia, France, Great Britain, New Zealand, Pakistan, the Philippines, Thailand, and the United States.

southeast by east. *Abbr.* **SEbE** The direction, or point on the mariner's compass, halfway between southeast and east-southeast. It is 123 degrees 45 minutes east of due north. See **compass card.**

southeast by south. *Abbr.* **SEbS** The direction, or point on the mariner's compass, halfway between southeast and south-southeast. It is 146 degrees 15 minutes east of due north. See **compass card.**

south·east·er (south-ē'stər; *Nautical* sou-ē'-) *n.* A storm or gale blowing from the southeast.

south·east·er·ly (south-ē'stər-lē; *Nautical* sou-ē'-) *adj.* **1.** Toward or in the southeast. **2.** From the southeast. —**south·east'er·ly** *adv.*

south·east·ward (south-ēst'wərd; *Nautical* sou-ēst'-) *adv.* Also **south·east·wards.** Toward the southeast. —*adj.* Situated toward or facing the southeast. —*n.* **1.** A direction or point toward the southeast. **2.** A region or part situated in or toward the southeast. —**south·east'ward·ly** *adj.* & *adv.*

South·end-on-Sea (south'ĕnd'ŏn-sē', -ôn-sē'). A residential and resort city on the Thames, in southeastern Essex, England. Population, 166,000.

south·er (sou'*th*ər) *n.* A strong wind coming from the south.

south·er·ly (sŭ*th*'ər-lē) *adj.* **1.** Situated toward the south. **2.** From the south. Said of wind. —*n., pl.* **southerlies.** A storm or wind from the south. —**south'er·ly** *adv.*

south·ern (sŭ*th*'ərn) *adj. Abbr.* **s, S, s., S., So., Sou.** **1.** Situated toward, in, or facing the south. **2.** Coming from the south. Said of wind. **3.** Native to or growing in the south. **4.** *Often capital* **S.** Of, pertaining to, or characteristic of southern regions or the South. **5.** South of the equator. [Middle English *southerne,* Old English *sūtherne.* See **sāwel-** in Appendix.*]

Southern Alps (ălps). A mountain range in west-central South

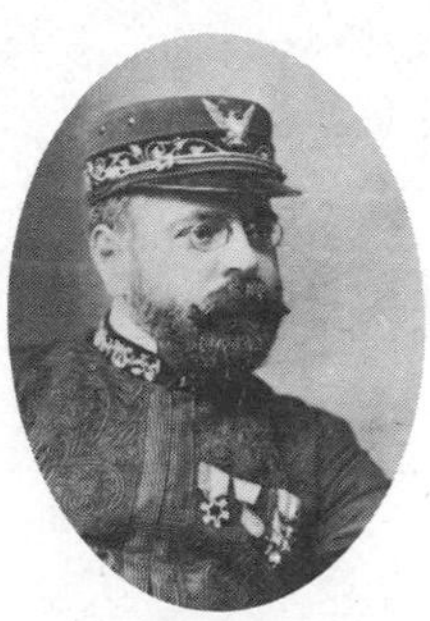

John Philip Sousa

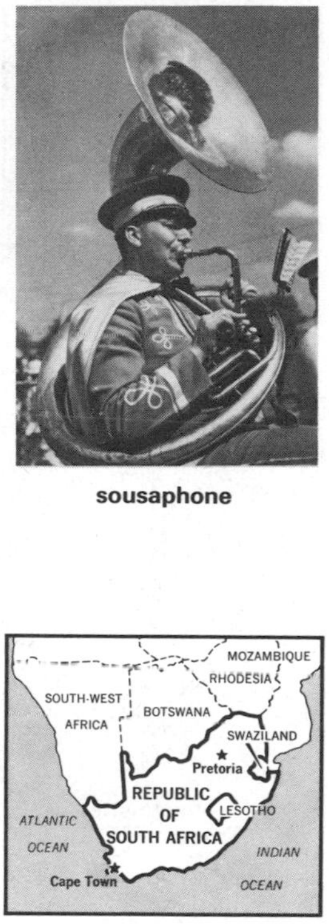

sousaphone

South Africa

Island, New Zealand. Highest elevation, Mount Cook, or Aorangi (12,349 feet).

Southern Bug. See **Bug.**

Southern Confederacy. The **Confederate States of America** (see).

Southern Cross. A constellation, **Crux** (see).

Southern Crown. A constellation, **Corona Australis** (see).

south·ern·er (sŭth′ər-nər) n. **1.** A native or inhabitant of the south. **2.** Often capital **S.** A native or inhabitant of the southern United States.

Southern Hemisphere. The half of the earth south of the equator.

Southern Kar·roo. See **Karroo.**

southern lights. The **aurora australis** (see).

Southern Protectorate of Mo·roc·co (mə-rŏk′ō). A former Spanish protectorate in southern Morocco, a part of Morocco since 1958.

Southern Rho·de·sia. The former name for **Rhodesia.**

south·ern·wood (sŭth′ərn-wŏŏd′) n. An aromatic woody plant, *Artemisia abrotanum,* native to Europe, having finely divided grayish foliage. Also called "old man."

Southern Ye·men (yĕm′ən, yā′mən). Officially, People's Republic of Southern Yemen. Formerly **South A·ra·bi·a** (ə-rā′bē-ə). A nation, independent since 1967, covering about 130,000 square miles in southern Arabia and consisting of 16 sheikdoms, the former British colony of Aden, and the island of Socotra. Population, 1,000,000. Capital, Madinat ash Sha'b.

South·ey (sŭth′ē), **Robert.** 1774–1843. English poet; poet laureate (1813–43).

South Gate. A city in southwestern California, near Los Angeles, of which it is a suburb. Population, 54,000.

South·gate (south′gət, -gāt). A former administrative division of London, England, now part of **Enfield** (see).

South Geor·gia (jôr′jə). A barren island, 1,450 square miles in area, in the South Atlantic, part of the British Antarctic Territory.

South Hol·land (hŏl′ənd). A province, 1,085 square miles in area, of the Netherlands, in the west on the North Sea. Population, 2,847,000. Capital, The Hague.

south·ing (sou′thĭng) n. Navigation. **1.** The difference in latitude between two positions as a result of a movement to the south. **2.** Progress toward the south.

South Island. The larger (58,093 square miles) of the two main islands of New Zealand. Population, 786,000.

South Ko·re·a. The unofficial name for the Republic of **Korea.**

South Mountain. A section of the Blue Ridge Mountains in southern Pennsylvania and western Maryland; the site of a Civil War battle in which the Confederates were defeated in their first attempt to invade the North (1862).

South Na·han·ni (nə-hän′ē). A river in the Northwest Territories, Canada, rising in the Mackenzie Mountains and flowing 250 miles southeast to the Liard.

South Ork·ney Islands (ôrk′nē). An island group in the South Atlantic, about 400 square miles in area, part of the British Antarctic Territory.

south·paw (south′pô′) n. Slang. A left-handed player, especially a left-handed baseball pitcher. —adj. Slang. Left-handed.

South Platte (plăt). A river flowing 450 miles from central Colorado northeast to central Nebraska, where it joins the North Platte to form the Platte.

South Pole. 1. The southern end of the earth's axis of rotation. **2.** The celestial zenith of the heavens as viewed from the south terrestrial pole. **3.** Small s, small p. The south-seeking **magnetic pole** (see) of a magnet.

South·port (south′pôrt, -pōrt). A seaport of England, on the Irish Sea coast of western Lancashire. Population, 80,000.

south·ron (sŭth′rən, south′-) n. **1.** Often capital **S.** Chiefly Scottish. A person who lives in the south, especially an Englishman as called by a Scotsman. **2.** A native or inhabitant of the American South. Used by the Confederate side in the Civil War. —adj. Chiefly Scottish. Southern. [Middle English (Scottish), variant of *southren, southerne,* SOUTHERN.]

South Sand·wich Islands (sănd′wĭch, săn′-, -wĭj). A group of islets in the South Atlantic, part of the British Antarctic Territory.

South Sas·katch·e·wan (săs-kăch′ə-wŏn). A river of Canada, flowing from south-central Alberta 550 miles generally northeast through Saskatchewan Province to join the North Saskatchewan and form the Saskatchewan River.

South Sea Islands. The islands of the South Pacific.

South Seas. 1. All seas south of the equator. **2.** The South Pacific.

South Shet·land Islands (shĕt′lənd). An archipelago in the South Atlantic between South America and the Antarctic Peninsula; claimed both by the United Kingdom and the republics of Argentina and Chile.

South Shields (shēldz). A port in northeastern Durham, England, on the Tyne estuary. Population, 109,000.

South Slavic. The southern division of the Slavic languages, consisting of Old Church Slavonic, Bulgarian, Macedonian, Serbo-Croatian, and Slovene.

south-south·east (south′south-ēst′; Nautical sou′sou-ēst′) n. Abbr. **SSE** The direction, or point on the mariner's compass, halfway between due south and southeast. It is 157 degrees 30 minutes east of due north. See **compass card.** —adj. Situated toward, facing, or in this direction. —adv. In, from, or toward this direction.

south-south·west (south′south-wĕst′; Nautical sou′sou-wĕst′) n. Abbr. **SSW** The direction, or point on the mariner's com-

pass, halfway between due south and southwest. It is 157 degrees 30 minutes west of due north. See **compass card.** —adj. Situated toward, facing, or in this direction. —adv. In, from, or toward this direction.

South Vi·et·nam. The unofficial name for the Republic of **Vietnam.**

south·ward (south′wərd; Nautical sŭth′ərd) adv. Also **southwards** (south′wərdz; Nautical sŭth′ərdz). Toward the south. —adj. Situated toward, facing, or in the south. —n. **1.** A direction toward the south. **2.** A region situated in or toward the south. —**south′ward·ly** adj. & adv.

South·wark (sŭth′ərk). A borough of London, England, comprising the former administrative divisions of Southwark, Bermondsey, and Camberwell. Population, 313,000.

south·west (south-wĕst′; Nautical sou-wĕst′) n. Abbr. **SW 1.** The direction, or point on the mariner's compass, halfway between south and west. It is 135 degrees west of due north. See **compass card. 2.** Any area or region lying in this direction. —**the Southwest.** A region of the southwestern United States generally considered to include New Mexico, Arizona, Texas, California, Nevada, Utah, and Colorado. —adj. **1.** To, toward, of, facing, or in the southwest. **2.** Coming from or originating in the southwest. Said of wind. —adv. In, from, or toward the southwest. —**south·west′ern** adj.

South-West Af·ri·ca (ăf′rĭ-kə). Abbr. **S.W.A.** Formerly **German Southwest Af·ri·ca.** A territory of 317,725 square miles in southwestern Africa, administered by South Africa under a League of Nations mandate. Population, 526,000. Capital, Windhoek.

southwest by south. Abbr. **SWbS** The direction, or point on the mariner's compass, halfway between southwest and south-southwest. It is 146 degrees 15 minutes west of due north. See **compass card.**

southwest by west. Abbr. **SWbW** The direction, or point on the mariner's compass, halfway between southwest and west-southwest. It is 123 degrees 45 minutes west of due north. See **compass card.**

south·west·er (south-wĕs′tər) n. Also **sou·west·er** (sou-wĕs′tər). **1.** A storm or strong wind from the southwest. **2.** A sailor's waterproof hat of material such as oilskin or canvas with a broad brim behind to protect the neck.

south·west·er·ly (south-wĕs′tər-lē; Nautical sou-wĕs′-) adj. **1.** Toward or in the southwest. **2.** From the southwest. —**south·west′er·ly** adv.

south·west·ward (south-wĕst′wərd; Nautical sou-wĕst′-) adv. Also **south·west·wards.** Toward the southwest. —adj. Situated toward, facing, or in the southwest. —n. **1.** A direction or point toward the southwest. **2.** A region or part situated in or toward the southwest. —**south·west′ward·ly** adj. & adv.

Sou·tine (sōō-tēn′), **Chaim.** 1894–1943. Lithuanian expressionist painter; resident in Paris (from 1913).

Sou·van·na Phou·ma (sōō-vä′nä pōō′mä), **Prince.** Born 1901. Laotian statesman and party leader; premier (1956–58, 1960, and since 1962).

sou·ve·nir (sōō′və-nîr′) n. Something serving as a token of remembrance, as of a place, occasion, or experience; a memento. [French, "memory," from *souvenir,* come to mind, recall, from Latin *subvenīre,* come to aid, come to mind : *sub-,* up to + *venīre,* to come (see **gwā-** in Appendix*).]

sov. sovereign.

sov·er·eign (sŏv′ər-ən) n. Also poetic **sov·ran** (sŏv′rən) (for sense 1). **1.** The chief of state in a monarchy; a king or queen; monarch. **2.** Abbr. **sov.** A British gold coin worth one pound. —adj. Also poetic **sov·ran. 1.** Paramount; supreme: *"beneath the sovereign brightness of the sky"* (Ronald Firbank). **2.** Having supreme rank or power. **3.** Self-governing; independent: *a sovereign state.* **4. a.** Of superlative strength or efficacy: *a sovereign remedy.* **b.** Unmitigated: *sovereign contempt.* [Middle English *souverein,* from Old French, from Vulgar Latin *superānus* (unattested), from Latin *super,* above. See **uper** in Appendix.*] —**sov′er·eign·ly** adv.

sov·er·eign·ty (sŏv′ər-ən-tē) n., pl. **-ties. 1.** Supremacy of authority or rule, as exercised by a sovereign or a sovereign state. **2.** Royal rank, authority, or power. **3.** Complete independence and self-government. **4.** A territory existing as an independent state.

so·vi·et (sō′vē-ĕt′, -vyĕt′, sŏv′ē-ĕt′) n. In the Soviet Union, one of the popularly elected legislative assemblies existing at local, regional, and national levels, organized on the basis of the workers', soldiers', and peasants' councils of the revolutionary period. See **Supreme Soviet.** [Russian *sovet,* "council," from Old Russian *suvětu.* See **sem-¹** in Appendix.*]

So·vi·et (sō′vē-ĕt′, sō-vyĕt′, sŏv′ē-ĕt′) adj. **1.** Of or pertaining to the Union of Soviet Socialist Republics. **2.** Small **s.** Of or pertaining to a soviet.

Soviet Central Asia. The region of the Soviet Union occupied by the republics of Kirghiz, Tadzhik, Turkmen, Uzbek, and Kazakh.

Soviet Union. See **Union of Soviet Socialist Republics.** Also called "Soviet Russia."

sow¹ (sō) v. **sowed, sown** (sōn) or **sowed, sowing, sows.** —tr. **1.** To scatter (seed) over the ground for growing. **2.** To impregnate (a growing medium) with seed. **3.** To propagate; disseminate; disperse. **4.** To strew or cover with anything; spread thickly. —intr. To scatter seed for growing. [Middle English *sowen, sawan,* Old English *sāwan.* See **sē-¹** in Appendix.*] —**sow′er** n.

sow² (sou) n. **1.** An adult female hog. **2. a.** A channel that conducts molten iron to the molds in a pig bed. **b.** The mass of

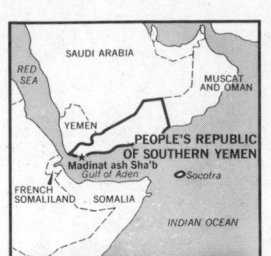

Southern Yemen

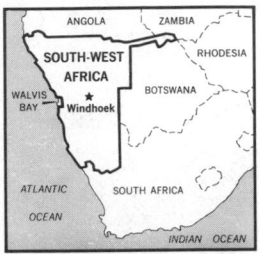

South-West Africa

sow thistle
Sonchus oleraceus

metal solidified in such a channel or mold. [Middle English *sow(e)*, Old English *sugu*. See **su-**¹ in Appendix.*]
sow·bel·ly (sou'bĕl'ē) *n. Informal.* Salt pork.
sow·bread (sou'brĕd') *n.* A plant, the **cyclamen** *(see).* [From the belief that pigs eat its roots.]
sow bug. Any of various small terrestrial crustaceans, chiefly of the genera *Oniscus* and *Porcellio*, commonly found under logs or stones and having an oval, segmented body. Also called "wood louse." [From its piglike shape.]
sow thistle. Any of various plants of the genus *Sonchus*; especially, *S. oleraceus*, native to Europe, having prickly leaves and yellow flowers.
sox. Alternate plural of **sock.**
soy (soi) *n.* **1.** The soybean. **2.** A salty brown liquid condiment made by fermenting soybeans in brine. In this sense, also called "soy sauce." [Japanese *shō-yu*, from Chinese (Mandarin) *chiang*⁴ *yu*² : *chiang*⁴, paste, sauce + *yu*², sauce.]
soy·bean (soi'bēn') *n.* **1.** A leguminous Asiatic plant, *Glycine max*, widely cultivated for forage, soil improvement, and for its nutritious, edible seeds. **2.** The seed of this plant. Also called "soya," "soya bean."
SP shore patrol; shore police.
sp. **1.** special. **2.** specialist. **3.** species. **4.** specific. **5.** spelling.
Sp. Spain; Spanish.
s.p. *Genealogy.* without issue (Latin *sine prole*).
spa (spä) *n.* **1.** A mineral spring. **2.** A resort area where such springs exist; a watering place. [After SPA (Belgium).]
Spa (spä). A resort town in eastern Belgium, site of the German headquarters in 1918 and scene of a conference of the Allied Supreme Council in 1920.
Spaak (späk), **Paul Henri.** Born 1899. Belgian statesman; premier (1938–39, 1946, and 1947–50).
space (spās) *n.* **1. a.** A set of elements or points satisfying specified geometric postulates: *non-Euclidean space.* **b.** The intuitive three-dimensional field of everyday experience. **c.** The infinite extension of the three-dimensional field. **2.** The expanse in which the solar system, stars, and galaxies exist; the universe. **3.** Broadly, the distance between two points or the area or volume between specified boundaries. **4.** An area provided for a particular purpose; room: *parking space.* **5.** Reserved or available accommodation on a public transportation vehicle. **6. a.** A period or interval of time. **b.** A little while. Used in the phrase *for a space.* **7.** *Music.* One of the intervals between the lines of a staff. **8.** *Printing.* One of the blank pieces of type or other means used for separating words or characters. **9.** One of the intervals during the telegraphic transmission of a message when the key is open or not in contact. —*tr.v.* **spaced, spacing, spaces.** **1.** To organize or arrange with spaces between. **2.** To separate or keep apart. [Middle English, time interval, from Old French *espace*, from Latin *spatium*†, space, distance.] —**spac'er** *n.*
space biology. **Exobiology** *(see).*
space capsule. *Aerospace.* A **capsule** *(see).*
space charge. An electric charge in a vacuum or region of low gas pressure, as in a vacuum tube, carried by a stream of electrons or ions.
space·craft (spās'krăft, -kräft) *n., pl.* **spacecraft.** A vehicle designed to be launched into space. Also called "space vehicle," "spaceship."
space flight. A flight of a vehicle into space.
space heater. A usually self-contained heating unit that warms the space in which it is located or to which it is connected.
space lattice. Any of the 14 possible geometric arrangements of points at which the atoms of a crystal may occur.
space·man (spās'măn') *n., pl.* **-men** (-mĕn'). **1.** Someone who travels in outer space; an astronaut. **2.** Someone who comes to Earth from outer space. A term used in science fiction.
space medicine. The medical science of the biological, physiological, and psychological effects of space flight upon human beings.
space·port (spās'pôrt', -pōrt') *n.* An installation for testing and launching spacecraft.
space probe. A spacecraft carrying instruments designed to explore the physical properties of outer space or of celestial bodies other than Earth.
space science. **1.** Any of several scientific disciplines, such as exobiology, that study phenomena occurring in the upper atmosphere, in space, or on celestial bodies other than Earth. **2.** Disciplines related to or dealing with the problems of space flight.
space sickness. Any of various ailments resulting from manned space flight, such as nausea resulting from prolonged weightlessness.
space station. A large manned satellite designed for permanent orbit around Earth and used for scientific research, military reconnaissance, or as an assembly point for long-range spacecraft.
space suit. A protective pressure suit having an independent air supply and other devices designed to permit the wearer relatively free movement in space.
space-time (spās'tīm') *n.* The four-dimensional continuum of one temporal and three spatial coordinates, in which any event or physical object is located. Also called the "space-time continuum." —**space'-time'** *adj.*
spa·cial. Variant of **spatial.**
spac·ing (spā'sĭng) *n.* **1. a.** The action or result of arranging by spaces. **b.** A procedure in time; system of or allowance for intervals. **2.** A space or spaces, as in print.
spa·cious (spā'shəs) *adj.* **1.** Providing or having much space or room; extensive. **2.** Vast in range or scope; all-inclusive. —**spa'cious·ly** *adv.* —**spa'cious·ness** *n.*
Spack·le (spăk'əl) *n.* A trademark for a powder to be mixed with water, or a ready-to-use plastic paste, designed to fill cracks and holes in plaster before painting or papering. —*tr.v.* **Spackled, -ling, -les.** To fill or repair with Spackle.
spade¹ (spād) *n.* **1.** A sturdy digging tool having a thick handle and a heavy, flat iron blade that can be pressed into the ground with the foot. **2.** Any of various digging or cutting tools resembling the spade. **3.** *Military.* A sharp metal piece at the back of a gun-carriage trail that embeds into the ground to retard the backward motion of the carriage during recoil. —**call a spade a spade.** To call a thing by its proper name; speak frankly and truly. —*tr.v.* **spaded, spading, spades.** To dig or cut with a spade. [Middle English *spade*, Old English *spadu*. See **sphē-** in Appendix.*] —**spad'er** *n.*
spade² (spād) *n.* **1.** The black symbol appearing on one of the four suits of playing cards, in the shape of an inverted heart with a short stalk at the fissure of the two lobes. **2.** *Plural.* The suit of cards identified by this mark. **3.** A card bearing this mark. [Italian *spada*, "broad sword" (from its flat, broad shape), from Latin *spatha*, spatula, from Greek *spathē*, broad blade. See **sphē-** in Appendix.*]
spade·fish (spād'fĭsh') *n., pl.* **spadefish** or **-fishes.** Any of several marine food fishes of the family Ephippidae; especially, *Chaetodipterus faber*, of the Atlantic, or *C. zonatus*, of the Pacific. [So called because of their flat, spade-shaped bodies.]
spade·work (spād'wûrk') *n.* **1.** Work requiring a spade. **2.** Any preparatory work necessary to a project or activity.
spa·dix (spā'dĭks) *n., pl.* **spadices** (spā'dĭ-sēz'). *Botany.* A club-like spike bearing minute flowers, usually enclosed within a sheathlike spathe, as in the calla and the jack-in-the-pulpit. [Latin *spādīx*, broken-off palm branch, from Greek *spadix*, akin to Greek *spasmos*, SPASM.]
spa·ghet·ti (spə-gĕt'ē) *n.* **1.** An Italian pasta consisting of long, solid strings of flour paste, cooked by boiling. **2.** *Electricity.* A slender tube of insulating material into which bare wire is inserted, especially in radio circuits. [Italian, plural diminutive of *spago*†, string.]
spa·ghet·ti·ni (spä-gĕ-tē'nē) *n.* A form of Italian pasta, thinner than spaghetti but not as thin as vermicelli. [Italian, diminutive of SPAGHETTI.]
spa·gyr·ic (spə-gîr'ĭk) *adj.* Also **spa·gyr·i·cal** (-ĭ-kəl). Pertaining to or resembling alchemy; alchemical. [New Latin *spagiricus*†, coined by Paracelsus.]
Spain (spān). *Spanish* **Es·pa·ña** (ās-pän'yä). *Abbr.* **Sp.** A country of western Europe occupying 194,400 square miles on the Iberian Peninsula and including politically the Balearic and Canary islands. Population, 30,903,000. Capital, Madrid.
spait. Variant of **spate.**
spake. *Archaic.* Past tense of **speak.**
Spa·la·to. The Italian name for **Split.**
spall (spôl) *n.* A chip, fragment, or flake from a piece of stone or ore. —*v.* **spalled, spalling, spalls.** —*tr.* To break up into chips or fragments. —*intr.* To chip or crumble. [Middle English *spalle*†.]
Spal·lan·za·ni (spä-län-zä'nē), **Lazzaro.** 1729–1799. Italian physiologist and anatomist; produced experimental evidence contradicting the theory of spontaneous generation.
spal·la·tion (spô-lā'shən) *n.* A nuclear reaction in which many particles are ejected from an atomic nucleus by an incident particle of sufficiently high energy. [SPALL + -ATION.]
Spam (spăm) *n.* A trademark for spiced pork products. [SP(ICED) (H)AM.]
span¹ (spăn) *n.* **1.** The extent or measure of space between two points or extremities, as of a bridge or roof; breadth. **2.** The distance between the tips of an airplane's wings. **3.** The section between two intermediate supports of a bridge. **4.** Something that spans, as a railroad trestle or bridge. **5.** *Archaic.* A unit of measure equal to the length of the fully extended hand from the tip of the thumb to the tip of the little finger, generally considered as nine inches. **6.** A period of time: *a life span.* —*tr.v.* **spanned, spanning, spans.** **1.** To measure by, or as if by, the fully extended hand. **2.** To encircle with the hand or hands, in or as if in measuring. **3.** To reach or extend over or from one side to the other of: *"a fallen tree that spans the moat of the palace"* (Tucker Brooke). **4.** To provide with something that extends over; bridge. [Middle English *span(ne)*, short interval, distance, Old English *spann*. See **spen-** in Appendix.*]
span² (spăn) *tr.v.* **spanned, spanning, spans.** To bind or fetter. —*n.* **1.** *Nautical.* A stretch of rope made fast at either end. **2.** A pair of animals, such as oxen, matched in size, strength, or color. [Middle Dutch *spannen*. See **spen-** in Appendix.*]
span³. *Archaic.* Past tense and past participle of **spin.**
Span. Spanish.
span·drel (spăn'drəl) *n.* Also **span·dril.** *Architecture.* **1.** The triangular space between the left or right exterior curve of an arch and the rectangular framework surrounding it. **2.** The space between two arches and a horizontal molding or cornice above them. [Middle English *spaundrell*, diminutive of Norman French *spaund(e)re*, from Old French *espandre*, to spread out, expand, from Latin *expandere*, EXPAND.]
spang (spăng) *adv.* Precisely; squarely; firmly: *spang in the middle of the table.* [Origin unknown.]
span·gle (spăng'gəl) *n.* **1.** A small, often circular piece of sparkling metal or plastic that may be sewn on stage costumes or other garments for decoration; a sequin. **2.** Any small sparkling object, drop, or spot: *spangles of sunlight.* —*v.* **spangled, -gling, -gles.** —*tr.* To adorn or cause to sparkle by covering with or as

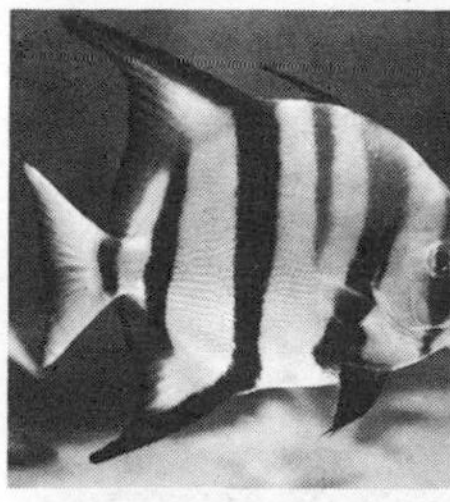
spadefish
Chaetodipterus faber

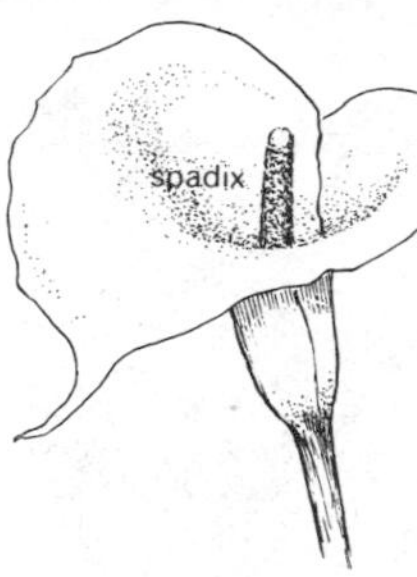

spadix
Calla lily

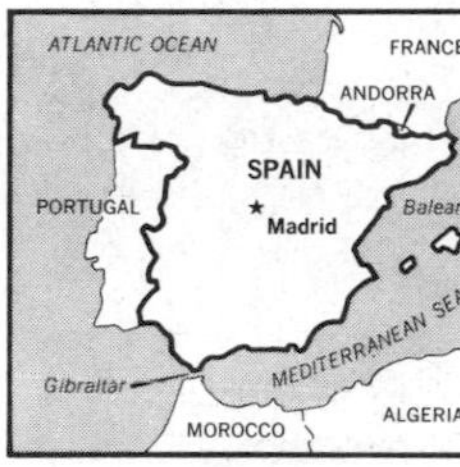

Spain

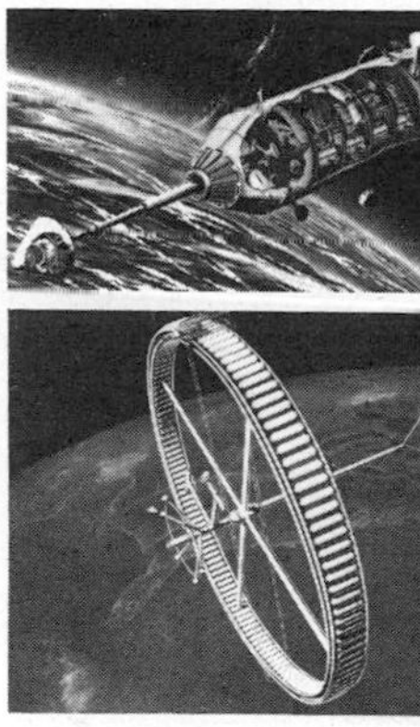
space station
Designs for space stations

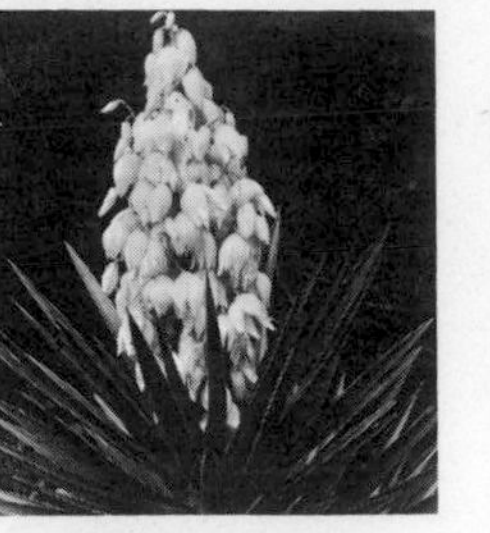

Spanish bayonet
Yucca aloifolia

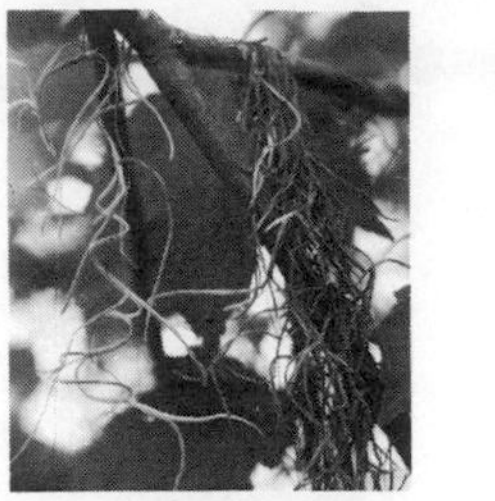

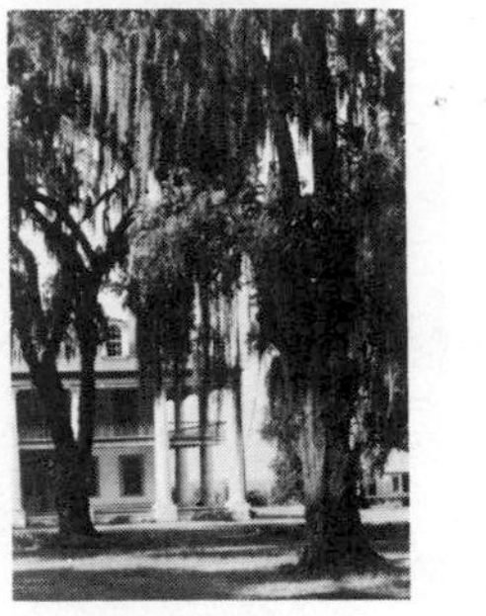

Spanish moss
Above: Close-up view
Below: Trees with Spanish moss

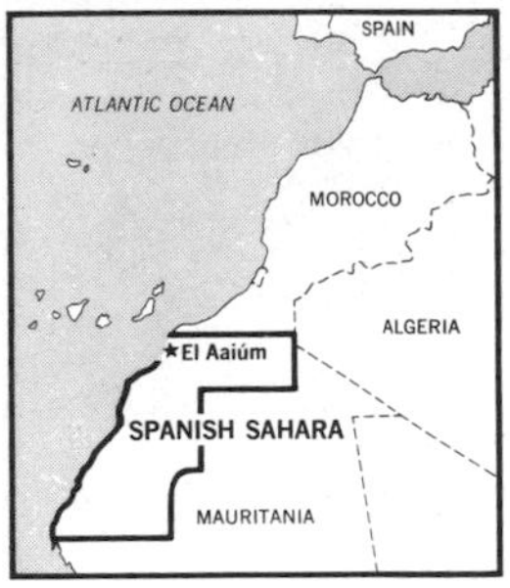

Spanish Sahara

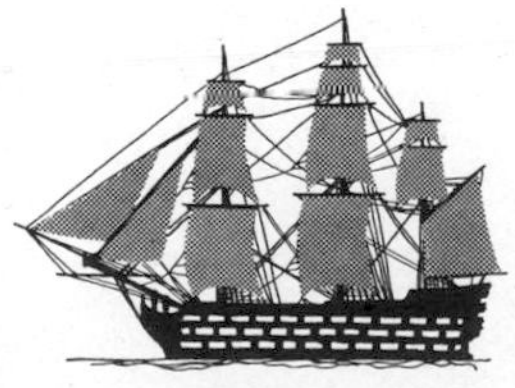

spanker
Spanker at the stern of a U.S. frigate

with spangles: *"the network of lights spangled the long, straight streets"* (Alec Waugh). —*intr.* To sparkle in the manner of spangles. [Middle English *spangele,* diminutive of *spange,* from Middle Dutch, ornament, clasp, buckle. See **spen-** in Appendix.*] —**span′gly** *adv.*

Span·iard (spăn′yərd) *n.* A native or inhabitant of Spain.

span·iel (spăn′yəl) *n.* **1.** Any of several breeds of small to medium-sized dogs, usually having drooping ears, short legs, and a silky, wavy coat. **2.** A docile or servile person. [Middle English *spaynel,* from Old French *espaignol,* "Spanish," from Vulgar Latin *spāniōlūs* (unattested), from Latin *Hispāniōlus,* from *Hispānia,* SPAIN.]

Span·ish (spăn′ĭsh) *adj. Abbr.* **Sp., Span.** Of or pertaining to Spain, its inhabitants, or their language or culture. —*n.* **1.** The Romance language of Spain and Spanish America. **2.** The inhabitants of Spain. Preceded by *the.*

Spanish America. The parts of the Western Hemisphere inhabited mostly by Spanish-speaking people and including: **a.** South America, excepting Brazil, Guyana, Surinam, and French Guiana. **b.** Central America, excepting British Honduras. **c.** Mexico, Cuba, Puerto Rico, and the Dominican Republic.

Span·ish-A·mer·i·can (spăn′ĭsh-ə-mĕr′ĭ-kən) *adj.* **1.** Of or pertaining to the countries or people of Spanish America. **2.** Of or pertaining to people of Spanish descent residing in the United States. —*n.* **1.** A native or inhabitant of a Spanish-American country. **2.** A person of Spanish descent who lives in the United States.

Spanish-American War. The war between Spain and the United States in 1898, as a result of which Spain ceded Puerto Rico, the Philippine Islands, and Guam to the United States and abandoned all claim to Cuba, which became independent in 1902. See Treaty of **Paris.**

Spanish Armada. A fleet sent against England by Philip II of Spain in 1588, considered invincible but defeated and subsequently destroyed by storms. Also called "the Armada."

Spanish bayonet. **1.** Any of several New World plants of the genus *Yucca;* especially, *Y. aloifolia,* having a tall, woody stem, stiff, pointed leaves, and a large cluster of white flowers. **2.** A similar plant, *Y. filamentosa.* In this sense, also called "Adam's needle."

Spanish cedar. **1.** Any of several tropical American trees of the genus *Cedrela;* especially, *C. odorata,* having reddish, aromatic wood used for cabinetwork and cigar boxes. **2.** The wood of this tree.

Spanish chestnut. **1.** A tree, *Castanea sativa,* of the Mediterranean area, bearing edible nuts. **2.** The nut of this tree. Sometimes called "marron."

Spanish fly. **1.** A European blister beetle, *Lytta vesicatoria.* **2.** A preparation, **cantharides** *(see),* produced from these beetles.

Spanish Guin·ea. The former name for **Equatorial Guinea.**

Spanish Inquisition. The state tribunal of the Roman Catholic Church, instituted in Spain in 1480 to suppress heresy and infamous for its ruthless methods. It was abolished by Joseph Bonaparte in 1808. See **Inquisition.**

Spanish mackerel. Any of various marine food fishes of the genus *Scomberomorus;* especially, a commercially important species, *S. maculatus,* of American Atlantic coastal waters.

Spanish Main. **1.** The coast of northern South America between Panama and the Orinoco, the area from which freebooters attacked Spanish ships. **2.** Those parts of the Caribbean traversed by Spanish ships in colonial times.

Spanish Mo·roc·co (mə-rŏk′ō). A former Spanish colony on the northern coast of Morocco, part of Morocco since 1956.

Spanish moss. An epiphytic plant, *Tillandsia usneoides,* growing on trees of the southeastern United States and tropical America, having gray, threadlike stems drooping in long, densely matted clusters. Sometimes called "old-man's-beard."

Spanish needles. Plural in form, used with a singular or plural verb. A North American plant, *Bidens bipinnata,* having yellowish flowers and slender, barbed fruit.

Spanish onion. A mild-flavored, yellow-skinned onion, probably derived from *Allium fistulosum.*

Spanish paprika. A mild seasoning made from pimientos.

Spanish rice. A dish consisting of rice, tomatoes, spices, chopped onions, and green peppers.

Spanish Sa·ha·ra (sə-hăr′ə). A Spanish Overseas Province, occupying 103,000 square miles on the northwestern coast of Africa, comprising two zones, Río de Oro and Saguia el Hamra. Population, 156,000. Capital, El Aaiúm.

Spanish West Af·ri·ca (ăf′rĭ-kə). The region on the northwestern coast of Africa occupied by Spanish Sahara and Ifni.

spank (spăngk) *v.* **spanked, spanking, spanks.** —*tr.* To slap on the buttocks with a flat object or with the open hand as punishment. —*intr.* To move briskly or spiritedly. —*n.* A smart slap on the buttocks. [Perhaps imitative.]

spank·er (spăng′kər) *n.* **1.** One that spanks. **2.** *Nautical.* A quadrilateral gaff sail set abaft the after mast of a square-rigged sailing ship. In this sense, also called "driver."

spank·ing (spăng′kĭng) *adj.* **1.** *Informal.* Exceptional of its kind in size, strength, quality, or, especially, smartness. **2.** Moving quickly and smartly; lively. Said of a horse. **3.** Brisk and fresh. Said of a breeze. [Origin unknown.]

span·ner (spăn′ər) *n.* **1.** One that spans. **2.** *Chiefly British.* A wrench, adjustable wrench, or the like. **3.** A measuring worm. [Obsolete *spanner,* winding tool, from German *Spanner,* from *spannen,* to stretch, tighten, from Old High German *spannan.* See **spen-** in Appendix.*]

span-new (spăn′no͞o′, -nyo͞o′) *adj. Regional.* Entirely new. [Middle English *spannewe,* from Old Norse *spānnýr* : *spānn,* chip (see **sphē-** in Appendix*) + *nýr,* new (see **newo-** in Appendix*).]

span·worm (spăn′wûrm′) *n.* A **measuring worm** *(see).* [From SPAN (bind).]

spar[1] (spär) *n.* **1.** *Nautical.* A wooden or metal pole, used as a mast, boom, yard, or bowsprit, or in any other way to support rigging. **2.** A similar pole, used as part of a crane or derrick. **3.** *Aviation.* A principal structural member in an airplane wing that runs from tip to tip or from root to tip. —*tr.v.* **sparred, sparring, spars.** **1.** To supply with spars. **2.** *Archaic.* To fasten with a bolt. [Middle English *sparre,* rafter, pole, from Old Norse *sperra,* beam. See **sper-[1]** in Appendix.*]

spar[2] (spär) *intr.v.* **sparred, sparring, spars.** **1.** To box; go through the motions of boxing. **2.** To bandy words about in argument; to dispute. **3.** To fight by striking with the feet and spurs. Used of cocks. —*n.* **1.** The act of sparring. **2.** A boxing match. [Middle English *sparren,* to thrust or strike rapidly, Old English *sperran†,* to strike.]

spar[3] (spär) *n.* Any of various nonmetallic, readily cleavable minerals with a vitreous luster, as feldspar. [Low German, from Middle Low German, akin to Old English *spær†,* gypsum.]

Spar (spär) *n.* Also **SPAR.** A member of the women's reserve of the U.S. Coast Guard. [S(EMPER) PAR(ATUS).]

spare (spâr) *v.* **spared, sparing, spares.** —*tr.* **1. a.** To treat mercifully; deal with leniently. **b.** To refrain from harming or destroying: *"Gather the Flow'rs, but spare the Buds"* (Marvell). **2.** To save or relieve (one) from pain, shame, trouble, or the like. **3.** To refrain from using or applying; use with restraint. **4.** To give or grant out of one's resources; afford; do without: *Can you spare ten minutes?* —*intr.* **1.** To be frugal. **2. a.** To be merciful or lenient. **b.** To refrain or forbear. —*adj.* **sparer, sparest.** **1. a.** Not in immediate or regular use but ready when needed. **b.** In excess of what is needed; extra: *spare cash.* **c.** Unoccupied; leisure. Said of time. **2. a.** Economical; meager. **b.** Thin or lean: *"give me the spare men, and spare me the great ones"* (Shakespeare). —See Synonyms at **lean, meager.** —*n.* **1.** A replacement, such as a spare tire, reserved for future use. **2.** *Bowling.* **a.** The act of knocking down all ten pins with two successive rolls of the ball by a single player. **b.** The score so made. [Middle English *sparen,* to leave unharmed, to show mercy, Old English *sparian,* from Germanic *sparōjan* (unattested).] —**spare′ly** *adv.* —**spare′ness** *n.* —**spar′er** *n.*

spare·ribs (spâr′rĭbz′) *pl.n.* A cut of pork consisting of the ribs with most of the meat trimmed off. [Inverted variant of Low German *ribbespēr,* from Middle Low German : *ribbe,* rib (see **rebh-** in Appendix*) + *spēr,* spit (see **sper-[1]** in Appendix*).]

sparge (spärj) *tr.v.* **sparged, sparging, sparges.** **1.** To spray or sprinkle. **2.** To introduce air or gas into (a liquid). —*n.* A sprinkling. [Old French *espargier,* from Latin *spargere.* See **sphereg-** in Appendix.*]

spar·id (spĕr′ĭd, spăr′-) *adj.* Of or belonging to the family Sparidae, which includes the porgies and similar fishes. —*n.* A member of the Sparidae. [New Latin *sparidae* : *Sparus* (genus), from Latin, gilthead, from Greek *sparos†* + -ID.]

spar·ing (spâr′ĭng) *adj.* **1.** Thrifty; frugal. **2.** Forbearing; lenient. —**spar′ing·ly** *adv.* —**spar′ing·ness** *n.*

Synonyms: *sparing, frugal, thrifty, economical.* These adjectives mean exercising or reflecting care in the management of money, time, or other resources. They are frequently interchangeable. *Sparing* stresses restraint in expenditure in general. *Frugal* implies self-denial and consequent abstention from luxury. *Thrifty* applies to a person who is industrious, saving, and otherwise diligent in conserving his means. *Economical* emphasizes prudence, skillful management, and in particular the avoidance of waste.

spark[1] (spärk) *n.* **1.** An incandescent particle, especially: **a.** One thrown off from a burning substance. **b.** One resulting from friction. **c.** One remaining in an otherwise extinguished fire; an ember. **2.** A glistening particle of something, as metal. **3. a.** A flash of light; especially, a flash produced by electric discharge. **b.** A short pulse or flow of electric current. **4.** A trace or suggestion, as: **a.** A quality or feeling with latent potential; seed: *the spark of genius.* **b.** A vital, animating factor or activating factor: *the spark of revolt.* **5.** *Plural. Usually capital* **S.** *Informal.* A ship's radio operator. Used with a singular verb. **6.** *Electricity.* **a.** The luminous phenomenon resulting from a disruptive discharge through an insulating material. **b.** The discharge itself. —*v.* **sparked, sparking, sparks.** —*intr.* **1.** To give off sparks. **2.** To operate correctly. Used of the ignition system of an internal-combustion engine. —*tr.* **1.** To set in motion; activate; ignite. **2.** To rouse to action. —See Synonyms at **flash.** [Middle English *sparke,* Old English *spearca, spærca,* akin to Middle Dutch *sparke†.*] —**spark′er** *n.*

Usage: *Spark* (verb) is widely employed on all levels in the newer transitive sense of to cause to come about. As an example in writing, the following is acceptable to 71 per cent of the Usage Panel: *The imposition of new taxes sparked the revolt.*

spark[2] (spärk) *n.* **1.** A young dandy or gallant. **2.** A lover; suitor. —*v.* **sparked, sparking, sparks.** —*tr.* To court or woo. —*intr.* To play the suitor. [Perhaps ultimately from Old Norse *sparkr,* lively, perhaps akin to Old English *spearca,* SPARK.]

spark arrester. **1.** A device to keep sparks from escaping, as at a chimney opening. **2.** A device to control electric sparking at a point where a circuit is made or broken.

spark chamber. A device consisting of electrically charged parallel metal plates in a chamber filled with inert gas, used to

ă pat/ā pay/âr care/ä father/b bib/ch church/d deed/ĕ pet/ē be/f fife/g gag/h hat/hw which/ĭ pit/ī pie/îr pier/j judge/k kick/l lid, needle/m mum/n no, sudden/ng thing/ŏ pot/ō toe/ô paw, for/oi noise/ou out/o͝o took/o͞o boot/p pop/r roar/s sauce/sh ship, dish/

detect and measure charged subatomic particles as they pass from one plate to another, leaving a trail of sparks.

spark coil. An induction coil used to produce a spark, as in an internal-combustion engine.

spark gap. A gap in an otherwise complete electric circuit across which a discharge occurs at some prescribed voltage.

spar·kle (spär′kəl) *intr.v.* **-kled, -kling, -kles. 1.** To give off sparks. **2.** To give off or reflect flashes of light; to glitter. **3.** To shine with animation. **4.** To flash with wit. **5.** To effervesce. —See Synonyms at **flash.** —*n.* **1.** A small spark or gleaming particle. **2.** A glittering quality. **3.** Shining animation; vivacity. **4.** Effervescence. [Middle English *sparklen,* frequentative of *sparken,* to spark, from *sparke,* SPARK.]

spar·kler (spär′klər) *n.* **1.** One that sparkles. **2.** A firework that burns slowly and gives off a shower of sparks. **3.** *Informal.* A diamond.

sparkling wine. Any of various effervescent wines, such as champagne, produced by a process that involves fermentation in the bottle.

spark plug. Also *British* **sparking plug. 1.** A device inserted in the head of an internal-combustion-engine cylinder that ignites the fuel mixture by means of an electric spark. **2.** *Informal.* A person who gives life or energy to an undertaking.

spark·plug (spärk′plŭg′) *tr.v.* **-plugged, -plugging, -plugs.** *Informal.* To inspire or energize (an undertaking, for example).

Sparks (spärks), **Jared.** 1789–1866. American historian.

spark transmitter. 1. A source of alternating current that derives its output from the discharge of a condenser across a spark gap. Also called "spark generator." **2.** *Electronics.* A now obsolete radio transmitter using a discharge across a spark gap to create a signal.

spar·ling (spär′lĭng) *n.* **1.** A fish, the European smelt. **2.** A young herring. [Middle English *sperlinge,* from Old French *esperlinge,* from Germanic. See **spei-** in Appendix.*]

spar·row (spăr′ō) *n.* **1.** Any of various small New World birds of the genera *Spizella, Zonotrichia, Melospiza,* and other closely related genera within the family Fringillidae, having grayish or brownish plumage. **2.** Any of several similar or related birds, such as the common **house sparrow** *(see).* [Middle English *sparowe,* Old English *spearwa.* See **sper-**[3] in Appendix.*]

spar·row·grass (spăr′ō-grăs′, -gräs′) *n.* Also **spar·ry·grass** (spăr′ē-). *Regional.* Asparagus. [By folk etymology from ASPARAGUS.]

sparrow hawk. 1. A small North American falcon, *Falco sparverius,* that preys on small birds and animals. **2.** A similar European hawk, *Accipiter nisus.*

sparse (spärs) *adj.* **sparser, sparsest.** Growing or settled at widely spaced intervals; not dense or crowded: *a sparse crop.* See Synonyms at **meager.** [Latin *sparsus,* past participle of *spargere,* to strew, scatter. See **sphereg-** in Appendix.*] —**sparse′ly** *adv.* —**sparse′ness, spar′si·ty** (spär′sə-tē) *n.*

Spar·ta (spär′tə). Also **Lac·e·dae·mon** (lăs′ə-dē′mən). A Dorian city-state of ancient Greece, in the southeastern Peloponnesus, renowned for military prowess, political rigidity, and cultural austerity.

Spar·ta·cus (spär′tə-kəs). Died 71 B.C. Thracian gladiator, leader of a large slave revolt against Rome (73–71 B.C.).

Spar·tan (spärt′n) *adj.* **1.** Of or pertaining to Sparta or its people. **2.** Resembling the Spartans in fortitude or self-discipline; rigorous; austere. —*n.* **1.** A citizen of Sparta. **2.** Someone of Spartan character. —**Spar′tan·ism′** *n.*

spar varnish. A waterproof varnish.

spasm (spăz′əm) *n.* **1.** A sudden, involuntary contraction of a muscle or group of muscles. **2.** Any sudden burst of energy, activity, or emotion. [Middle English *spasme,* from Old French, from Latin *spasmus,* from Greek *spasmos,* from *span*†, to draw, pull.]

spas·mod·ic (spăz-mŏd′ĭk) *adj.* **1.** Pertaining to, affected by, or having the character of a spasm; convulsive. **2.** Happening intermittently; fitful: *spasmodic rifle fire.* **3.** Given to sudden outbursts of energy or feeling; excitable. [New Latin *spasmodicus,* from Greek *spasmodikos,* from *spasmos,* SPASM.] —**spas·mod′i·cal·ly** *adv.*

spas·tic (spăs′tĭk) *adj.* Pertaining to or characterized by spasms; continuously convulsing or contracting. —*n.* **1.** A person suffering from muscular spasms. **2.** A person afflicted with spastic paralysis. [Latin *spasticus,* from Greek *spastikos,* from *span,* pull, draw. See **spasm.**] —**spas′ti·cal·ly** *adv.*

spastic paralysis. A chronic pathological condition involving exaggerated tendon reflexes and muscular spasms accompanying sclerosis of the spinal cord.

spat[1]. Past tense and past participle of **spit** (eject saliva).

spat[2] (spăt) *n., pl.* **spat** or **spats.** An oyster or similar bivalve mollusk in the larval stage, especially when it settles to the bottom and begins to develop a shell. —*intr.v.* **spatted, spatting, spats.** To spawn. Used of oysters and similar mollusks. [Origin obscure.]

spat[3] (spăt) *n.* A cloth or leather gaiter covering the shoe upper and the ankle and fastening under the shoe with a strap. Usually used in the plural. [Short for earlier *spatterdash* : SPATTER + DASH.]

spat[4] (spăt) *n.* **1.** A brief, petty quarrel. **2.** *Informal.* A slap or smack. **3.** A spattering sound, as of raindrops. —*v.* **spatted, spatting, spats.** —*intr.* **1.** To engage in a brief, petty quarrel. **2.** To strike with a light spattering sound; slap. —*tr. Informal.* To slap. [Origin obscure.]

spate, spait (spāt) *n.* **1.** A sudden flood, rush, or outpouring: *"this excess of essays, this spate of essays, this monstrous regiment of essays"* (Hilaire Belloc). **2.** *British.* **a.** A flash flood or a freshet resulting from a downpour of rain or melting of snow. **b.** A sudden heavy fall of rain. [Middle English *spate*†.]

spa·tha·ceous (spă-thā′shəs) *adj.* Also **spa·those** (spā′thōs′). *Botany.* Bearing or resembling a spathe. [SPATH(E) + -ACEOUS.]

spathe (spāth) *n. Botany.* A leaflike organ that encloses or spreads from the base of the spadix of certain plants, such as the jack-in-the-pulpit or the calla. [Latin *spatha,* broad flat instrument, from Greek *spathē,* broad blade. See **sphē-** in Appendix.*]

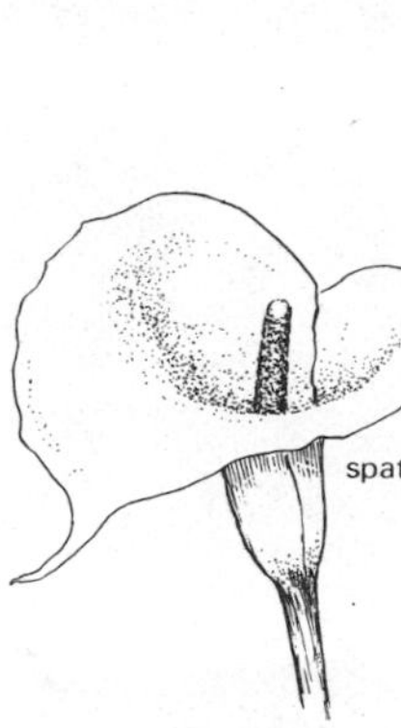
spathe

spathe
Calla lily

spath·ic (spăth′ĭk) *adj.* Having good cleavage. Said of minerals. [From obsolete *spath,* spar, from German *Spat(h),* from Middle High German *spat.* See **sphē-** in Appendix.*]

spa·tial (spā′shəl) *adj.* Also **spa·cial.** Of, pertaining to, involving, or having the nature of space. [From Latin *spatium,* SPACE.] —**spa′ti·al′i·ty** (-shə-ăl′ə-tē) *n.* —**spa′tial·ly** *adv.*

spa·ti·o·tem·po·ral (spā′shē-ō-tĕm′pə-rəl) *adj.* **1.** Of, pertaining to, or existing in both space and time. **2.** Of or relating to space-time. [Latin *spatium,* SPACE + TEMPORAL.]

spat·ter (spăt′ər) *v.* **-tered, -tering, -ters.** —*tr.* **1.** To scatter (a liquid substance) in drops or small splashes. **2.** To spot, splash, or soil. **3.** To sully the reputation of; defame. —*intr.* **1.** To spit off drops or small splashes; splatter. **2.** To fall with a splash or a splashing sound. —*n.* **1.** The act of spattering. **2.** A spattering sound. **3.** A drop or splash of something spattered; a spot or stain. [Perhaps a frequentative of Dutch *spatten,* from Middle Dutch (perhaps imitative).]

spat·ter·dock (spăt′ər-dŏk) *n.* An aquatic plant, *Nuphar advena,* of eastern North America, having broad leaves and globe-shaped yellow flowers. [SPATTER + DOCK (plant).]

spat·u·la (spăch′ə-lə) *n.* **1.** A small implement having a broad, flat, flexible blade that is used to spread or mix frosting, plaster, paint, or the like. **2.** *Medicine.* An implement, such as a small wooden paddle, used to press down the tongue. [Latin *spat(h)ula,* diminutive of *spatha,* blade, broad sword, from Greek *spathē.* See **sphē-** in Appendix.*] —**spat′u·lar** *adj.*

spat·u·late (spăch′ə-lĭt) *adj.* Shaped like a spatula.

spav·in (spăv′ən) *n.* Either of two diseases affecting the hock joint of horses: *bog spavin,* an infusion of lymph that enlarges the joint, and *bone spavin,* a bony deposit that stiffens the joint. [Middle English *spaveyne,* from Old French *espavin*†.] —**spav′ined** *adj.*

spawn (spôn) *n.* **1.** The eggs of aquatic animals such as bivalve mollusks, fishes, and amphibians. **2.** Offspring occurring in numbers; brood. **3.** A person regarded as the issue of some parent or family. Usually used disparagingly. **4.** The product or outcome of something. **5.** Fragments of mycelia used to start a mushroom culture. —*v.* **spawned, spawning, spawns.** —*intr.* **1.** To deposit eggs; produce spawn. **2.** To produce offspring in numbers like spawn. —*tr.* **1.** To produce (spawn). **2.** To give birth to. Usually used disparagingly of human beings. **3.** To give rise to; engender. **4.** To bring forth; produce. **5.** To plant with mycelia. [Middle English *spawne,* from *spawnen,* to spawn, from Norman French *espaundre,* to shed roe, from Old French *espandre,* to shed, spread, from Latin *expandere,* to spread out, EXPAND.]

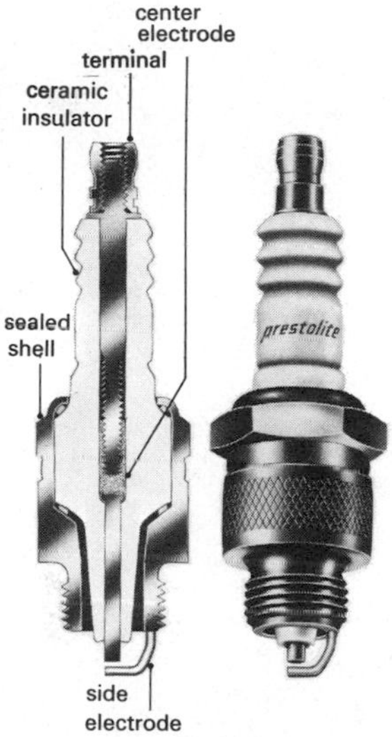
center
electrode
terminal
ceramic
insulator
sealed
shell
prestolite
side
electrode

spark plug
Left: Cross section
Right: Exterior

spay (spā) *tr.v.* **spayed, spaying, spays.** To excise the ovaries of (a female animal). [Middle English *spayen,* from Old French *espeer,* to cut with a sword, from *espee,* sword, from Latin *spatha,* broad sword, from Greek *spathē.* See **sphē-** in Appendix.*]

S.P.C.A. Society for the Prevention of Cruelty to Animals.

S.P.C.C. Society for the Prevention of Cruelty to Children.

speak (spēk) *v.* **spoke** (spōk) or *archaic* **spake** (spāk), **spoken** (spō′kən) or *archaic* **spoke, speaking, speaks.** —*intr.* **1.** To utter words with ordinary speech modulation; talk. **2. a.** To express oneself; engage in discussion; converse; talk. **b.** To recognize another; be on good terms: *They are no longer speaking.* **3.** To deliver an address or lecture; make a speech. **4.** To convey a message: *Actions speak louder than words.* **5.** To be expressive. **6.** To emit a report on firing: *"Our cannons speak and the enemy's now open in full chorus"* (Ambrose Bierce). **7. a.** To make communicative sounds. **b.** To give an impression of speaking: *teach a dog to speak for a bone.* —*tr.* **1.** To articulate in a speaking voice. **2.** To converse in or be able to converse in (a language). **3. a.** To express aloud; declare; tell. **b.** To express in writing. **4.** To reveal; show to be. **5.** *Nautical.* To hail and communicate with (another vessel) at sea. —**so to speak.** That is to say. —**speak for. 1.** To speak in behalf of; represent. **2.** To claim: *This ticket is spoken for.* —**speak one's mind.** To express one's opinion. —**speak out** (or **up**). **1.** To speak more clearly or louder. **2.** To speak without hesitation or fear. —**speak well for.** To express or indicate something favorable about. —**to speak of.** Worthy of mention or discussion. [Speak, spake, spoken; Middle English *speken, spake, spoken,* Old English *specan, spæc, gespecen.* See **spreg-** in Appendix.* Past tense spoke was formed on analogy with BREAK, BROKE, BROKEN.] —**speak′a·ble** *adj.*

Synonyms: *speak, talk, converse, discourse, chatter, gossip.* These verbs mean to express oneself or to communicate orally. *Speak* and *talk,* the most general, are often interchangeable. *Speak,* however, can refer to rather formal or authoritative utterance; *talk,* more often than *speak,* implies an ordinary or even idle exchange involving two or more persons. *Converse* stresses interchange of thoughts and ideas. *Discourse* usually refers to formal, extended, well-organized speech. *Chatter* refers to incessant and idle talk. *Gossip* is sometimes interchangeable with *chatter* but especially applies to unflattering or malicious talk about someone not present.

t tight/th thin, path/*th* this, bathe/ŭ cut/ûr urge/v valve/w with/y yes/z zebra, size/zh vision/ə about, item, edible, gallop, circus/ à *Fr.* ami/œ *Fr.* feu, *Ger.* schön/ü *Fr.* tu, *Ger.* über/KH *Ger.* ich, *Scot.* loch/N *Fr.* bon. ***Follows main vocabulary.** †**Of obscure origin.**

speak·eas·y (spēk′ē′zē) *n., pl.* **-ies.** *Slang.* A place for the illegal sale of alcoholic drinks, as during U.S. Prohibition.
speak·er (spē′kər) *n.* **1. a.** One who speaks. **b.** A spokesman. **2.** One who delivers a public speech. **3.** The presiding officer of a legislative assembly. **4.** A **loud-speaker** *(see).*
Speaker of the House. Presiding officer of the U.S. House of Representatives.
speak·ing (spē′kĭng) *adj.* **1.** Expressive or telling; eloquent. **2.** Striking; true to life: *a speaking likeness.* **—on speaking terms.** Sufficiently acquainted or friendly to permit speaking. *—n.* **1.** Speech. **2.** Oratory.
speaking tube. A tube or pipe used for speaking from one room or building to another.
spear (spîr) *n.* **1.** A weapon consisting of a long shaft with a sharply pointed head. **2.** A shaft with a sharp point and barbs for spearing fish. **3.** A spearman. **4.** A slender stalk, as of asparagus. *—v.* **speared, spearing, spears.** *—tr.* **1.** To pierce with or as if with a spear. **2.** To catch (a football, for example) with a thrust of the arm. *—intr.* **1.** To stab with or as with a spear. **2.** To sprout like a spear. [Middle English *spere,* Old English *spere.* See **sper-**[1] in Appendix.*] **—spear′er** *n.*

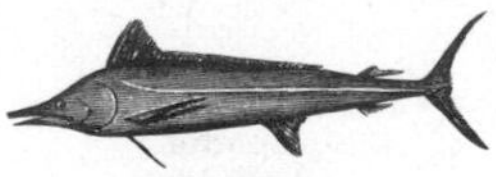
spearfish
Tetrapturus belone

spear·fish (spîr′fĭsh′) *n., pl.* **spearfish** or **-fishes.** Either of two large marine game fishes, *Tetrapturus angustirostris* or *T. belone,* having the upper jaw elongated into a spearlike projection.
spear·head (spîr′hĕd′) *n.* **1.** The sharpened head of a spear. **2. a.** The vanguard in a military thrust. **b.** A person or group seen as the driving force in a given action or endeavor. *—tr.v.* **spearheaded, -heading, -heads.** To be the leader of (a drive or an attack).
spear·man (spîr′mən) *n., pl.* **-men** (-mĭn). A soldier armed with a spear.
spear·mint (spîr′mĭnt′) *n.* An aromatic plant, *Mentha spicata,* native to Europe, having clusters of small purplish flowers and yielding an oil widely used as flavoring. [Perhaps so called from the sharpness of the leaf.]
spear side. The male side of a family. Compare **distaff side.**
spear·wort (spîr′wûrt′, -wôrt′) *n.* Any of several plants related to the buttercups; especially, *Ranunculus flammula,* native to Eurasia, having lance-shaped leaves and yellow flowers.
spec. 1. special. **2.** specification. **3.** speculation.
spe·cial (spĕsh′əl) *adj. Abbr.* **sp., spec. 1.** Surpassing what is common or usual; exceptional. **2. a.** Distinct among others of a kind; singular. **b.** Primary: *one's special interest.* **3.** Peculiar to a specific person or thing; particular. See Usage note below. **4. a.** Having a limited or specific function, application, or scope. **b.** Arranged for a particular occasion or purpose: *a special audience.* **5.** Esteemed; close: *special friends.* **6.** Additional; extra: *a special holiday flight.* *—n. Abbr.* **sp., spec. 1.** Something arranged, issued, or appropriated to a particular service or occasion. **2.** A featured attraction, such as a reduced price: *a special on lamb chops.* **3.** A single television production of unusual length and importance. [Middle English, from Old French *especial,* from Latin *speciālis,* special, of a particular kind, from *speciēs,* kind, SPECIES.] **—spe′cial·ly** *adv.*
Usage: *Special* and *specially* have wider application than *especial* and *especially. Special* and *specially* are always the choice when the desired sense is merely in opposition to what is general or ordinary (that is, particular or specific), without further emphasis: *a special occasion. Foremen are specially trained. Especial* and *especially* are often preferred, but not the only possibilities, when the sense is that of pre-eminence or exceptional degree: *an especial friend; especially talented. Especial* and *especially* are even more preferable when the sense stresses individuality or a particular circumstance: *for his especial benefit. Jones especially is implicated. Prudence is the best policy, especially now.*
special act. A legislative act that applies only to a particular person or area.
special court-mar·tial (kôrt′mär′shəl, kōrt′-) *pl.* **special courts-martial.** A court-martial consisting of at least three officers for trying intermediate offenses.
special delivery. *Abbr.* **S.D.** The delivery of a piece of mail, for an additional charge, by a special messenger rather than by scheduled delivery. **—spe′cial-de·liv′er·y** *adj.*
spe·cial·ism (spĕsh′ə-lĭz′əm) *n.* **1.** Confinement or limitation to some field of study or occupation. **2.** A field of specialization.
spe·cial·ist (spĕsh′ə-lĭst) *n. Abbr.* **sp. 1. a.** One who has devoted himself to a particular branch of study or research. **b.** A physician certified to limit his practice to a specified field. **2.** *U.S. Army.* An enlisted man whose pay corresponds to that of a noncommissioned officer but who ranks below a corporal and above a private first class. **—spe′cial·is′tic** *adj.*
spe·ci·al·i·ty (spĕsh′ē-ăl′ə-tē) *n., pl.* **-ties. 1.** A distinguishing mark or feature; special characteristic; peculiarity. **2.** *Plural.* Special points of consideration; details; particulars. **3.** *Chiefly British.* A specialty.
spe·cial·i·za·tion (spĕsh′ə-lə-zā′shən) *n.* The action of specializing or the process of becoming specialized.
spe·cial·ize (spĕsh′ə-līz′) *v.* **-ized, -izing, -izes.** *—intr.* **1.** To train or employ oneself in a special study or activity. **2.** *Biology.* To develop so as to become adapted to a specific environment or function. *—tr.* **1.** To make specific mention of; particularize; specify. **2.** To give a particular character or function to. **3.** *Biology.* To adapt by specialization. **4.** To specify the payee in endorsing (a check).
special jury. A jury drawn from a list of presumably better qualified candidates for a case involving unusually abstruse issues of fact, and chosen by the court upon request.
special pleading. 1. *Law.* The assertion of new or special matter to offset the opposing party's allegations, as an alternative to direct denial. **2.** A presentation of an argument that emphasizes only a favorable or a single aspect of the question at issue.
special relativity. The physical theory of space and time developed by Albert Einstein, based on the postulates that all the laws of physics are equally valid in all nonaccelerated frames of reference and that light is propagated rectilinearly in all directions at a constant speed, and having as consequences the relativistic mass increase of rapidly moving objects, the Lorentz contraction, time dilatation, and the principle of mass-energy equivalence. Also called "special theory of relativity." Compare **general relativity.**
special session. An extraordinary session of a court or of a legislative body.
spe·cial·ty (spĕsh′əl-tē) *n., pl.* **-ties. 1.** A special pursuit, occupation, service, product, or the like. **2.** An aspect of medicine to which physicians confine their practice after certification of special knowledge by examination. **3.** A special feature or characteristic; peculiarity. **4.** The state or quality of being special. **5.** *Law.* A special contract or agreement, especially a deed, kept under seal.
spe·ci·a·tion (spē′sē-ā′shən, spē′shē-) *n. Biology.* The evolutionary process by which new species are formed. [SPECI(ES) + -ATION.]
spe·cie (spē′shē, -sē) *n.* Coined money; coin. **—in specie. 1.** In coin. **2.** *Law.* In kind; in the same kind or shape. [Latin *(in) specie,* (in) kind, from the ablative of *speciēs,* kind, SPECIES.]
spe·cies (spē′shēz, -sēz) *n., pl.* **species.** *Abbr.* **sp. 1.** *Biology.* **a.** A fundamental category of taxonomic classification, ranking after a genus, and consisting of organisms capable of interbreeding. **b.** An organism belonging to such a category, represented in taxonomic nomenclature by a Latin adjective or epithet following a genus name. **2.** *Logic.* A class of individuals or objects grouped by virtue of their common attributes and assigned a common name; a division subordinate to a genus. **3.** A kind, variety, or type. **4.** *Obsolete.* An outward form or appearance. **5.** *Roman Catholic Church.* **a.** The outward appearance or form of the Eucharistic elements that is retained after their consecration. **b.** Either of the consecrated elements of the Eucharist. **6.** *Obsolete.* Specie. [Latin *speciēs,* a seeing, appearance, likeness, a particular sort, kind, species, from *specere,* to look at. See **spek-** in Appendix.*]
specif. specifically.
spec·i·fi·a·ble (spĕs′ə-fī′ə-bəl) *adj.* Capable of being specified.
spe·cif·ic (spə-sĭf′ĭk) *adj. Abbr.* **sp. 1.** Explicitly set forth; particular; definite. **2.** Pertaining to, characterizing, or distinguishing a species. **3.** Special, distinctive, or unique, as a quality or attribute. **4.** Intended for, applying to, or acting upon a particular thing. **5.** Denoting a disease produced by a particular microorganism or condition. **6. a.** Denoting a customs charge levied upon merchandise by unit or weight rather than according to value. **b.** Denoting a commodity rate applicable to the transportation of a single commodity between named points. *—n.* **1.** Something specific, such as a quality, statement, attribute, or the like. **2.** A remedy intended for some particular ailment or disorder. [Medieval Latin *specificus,* from Latin *speciēs,* kind, SPECIES.] **—spe·cif′i·cal·ly** *adv.* **—spec′i·fic′i·ty** (spĕs′ə-fĭs′ə-tē) *n.*
spec·i·fi·ca·tion (spĕs′ə-fĭ-kā′shən) *n. Abbr.* **spec. 1.** An act of specifying. **2. a.** *Usually plural.* A detailed and exact statement of particulars; especially, a statement prescribing materials, dimensions, and workmanship for something to be built, installed, or manufactured. **b.** A single item or article that has been specified. **3.** An exact written description of an invention by an applicant for a patent.
specific gravity. *Abbr.* **sp gr** The ratio of the mass of a solid or liquid to the mass of an equal volume of distilled water at 4°C, or of a gas to an equal volume of air or hydrogen under prescribed conditions of temperature and pressure.
specific heat. *Abbr.* **sp ht 1.** The ratio of the amount of heat required to raise the temperature of a unit mass of a substance by one unit of temperature to the amount of heat required to raise the temperature of a similar mass of a reference material, usually water, by the same amount. **2.** The amount of heat, measured in calories, required to raise the temperature of one gram of a substance by one centigrade degree.
specific impulse. A performance measure for rocket propellants, equal to units of thrust per unit weight of propellant consumed per unit time. Also called "specific thrust."
specific performance. The performance of a legal contract as specified in its terms.
specific resistance. *Electricity.* **Resistivity** *(see).*
spec·i·fy (spĕs′ə-fī′) *tr.v.* **-fied, -fying, -fies. 1.** To state explicitly. **2.** To include in a specification. [Middle English *specifien,* from Old French *specifier,* from Medieval Latin *specificāre,* from *specificus,* SPECIFIC.]
spec·i·men (spĕs′ə-mən) *n.* **1.** An individual, item, or part representative of a class, genus, or whole; instance; example; a sample. **2.** A sample, as of tissue, blood, or urine, used for analysis and diagnosis. —See Synonyms at **example.** [Latin *specimen,* mark, token, example, from *specere,* to look at. See **spek-** in Appendix.*]
spe·cious (spē′shəs) *adj.* **1.** Seemingly fair, attractive, sound, or true, but actually not so; deceptive: *"Daydreaming bears a specious resemblance to the workings of the creative imagination."* (Cyril Connolly). **2.** Having the ring of truth or plausibility but actually fallacious. —See Synonyms at **artificial.** [Middle English, attractive, fair, from Latin *speciōsus,* good-looking,

from *speciēs*, outward appearance, from *specere*, to look at. See **spek-** in Appendix.*] —**spe′cious·ly** *adv.* —**spe′cious·ness** *n.*

speck (spĕk) *n.* 1. A small spot, mark, or discoloration. 2. A very small bit of something; particle. —*tr.v.* **specked, specking, specks.** To mark with specks; to spot; to speckle. [Middle English *specke,* Old English *specca.*]

speck·le (spĕk′əl) *n.* A speck or small spot, especially a natural dot of color on skin, plumage, or foliage. —*tr.v.* **speckled, -ling, -les.** To mark or cover with or as if with speckles. [Middle Dutch *spekkel,* akin to Old English *specca,* SPECK.]

speck·led (spĕk′əld) *adj.* 1. Dotted or covered with speckles; especially, flecked with small spots of contrasting color. 2. Of a mixed character; motley.

speckled trout. The **brook trout** (*see*).

specs (spĕks) *pl.n.* Also **specks** (for sense 1). *Informal.* 1. Eyeglasses; spectacles. 2. Specifications, as for construction work.

spec·ta·cle (spĕk′tə-kəl) *n.* 1. A public performance or display. 2. **a.** An object of interest; a marvel or curiosity. **b.** An object or scene regrettably exposed to the public gaze: *made a spectacle of himself.* 3. **a.** Something seen or able to be seen. **b.** The sight of something: *"We pleased ourselves with the spectacle of Dublin's commerce"* (Joyce). 4. *Plural.* A pair of eyeglasses. 5. *Usually plural.* Something resembling eyeglasses in shape or suggesting them in function. [Middle English, from Old French, from Latin *spectāculum,* from *spectāre,* to look at, frequentative of *specere.* See **spek-** in Appendix.*]

spec·ta·cled (spĕk′tə-kəld) *adj.* 1. Wearing spectacles. 2. Having markings suggesting spectacles. Said of animals.

spec·tac·u·lar (spĕk-tăk′yə-lər) *adj.* Of the nature of a spectacle; sensational. —*n.* A single television production of unusual length and importance. —**spec·tac′u·lar·ly** *adv.* —**spec·tac′u·lar·i·ty** (-lăr′ə-tē) *n.*

spec·ta·tor (spĕk′tā-tər) *n.* 1. One who attends and views a show, sports event, or the like. 2. An observer of an event; eyewitness; onlooker. [Latin *spectātor,* from *spectāre,* look at. See **spectacle.**]

spec·ter (spĕk′tər) *n.* Also *chiefly British* **spec·tre.** 1. A ghost; phantom; apparition. 2. A mental image; phantasm: *"floating spectres of long forgotten spelling books"* (Lewis Carroll). 3. A foreboding. [French *spectre,* from Latin *spectrum,* appearance, image. See **spectrum.**]

spec·tral (spĕk′trəl) *adj.* 1. Of or resembling a specter; ghostly. 2. Of, pertaining to, or produced by a spectrum. —**spec·tral′i·ty** (-trăl′ə-tē), **spec′tral·ness** *n.* —**spec′tral·ly** *adv.*

spectral line. *Physics.* An isolated peak of intensity in a spectrum; especially, one of the visible dispersed images of the slit through which light enters the collimator of a spectroscope, produced by light of a single wavelength.

spectro-. Indicates spectrum; for example, **spectrograph, spectroscope.** [From SPECTRUM.]

spec·tro·gram (spĕk′trə-grăm′) *n. Physics.* A graph or photograph of a spectrum. [SPECTRO- + -GRAM.]

spec·tro·graph (spĕk′trə-grăf′, -gräf′) *n. Physics.* 1. A spectroscope equipped to photograph spectra. 2. A spectrogram. [SPECTRO- + -GRAPH.] —**spec′tro·graph′ic** *adj.* —**spec′tro·graph′i·cal·ly** *adv.* —**spec·trog′ra·phy** (-trŏg′rə-fē) *n.*

spec·tro·he·li·o·gram (spĕk′trə-hē′lē-ō-grăm′) *n. Physics.* A photograph of the sun taken in a narrow wavelength band centered on a selected wavelength.

spec·tro·he·li·o·graph (spĕk′trə-hē′lē-ō-grăf′, -gräf′) *n. Physics.* An instrument used to make spectroheliograms. —**spec′tro·he·li·o·graph′ic** *adj.* —**spec′tro·he·li·o·graph′i·cal·ly** *adv.*

spec·tro·he·li·o·scope (spĕk′trə-hē′lē-ō-skōp′) *n. Physics.* An instrument used to observe solar radiation. —**spec′tro·he·li·o·scop′ic** *adj.*

spec·trom·e·ter (spĕk-trŏm′ə-tər) *n. Physics.* A spectroscope equipped with scales for measuring the positions of spectral lines. [SPECTRO(SCOPE) + -METER.] —**spec′tro·met′ric** (-trō-mĕt′rĭk) *adj.* —**spec·trom′e·try** *n.*

spec·tro·pho·tom·e·ter (spĕk′trə-fō-tŏm′ə-tər) *n. Physics.* An instrument used to determine the distribution of energy in a spectrum of luminous radiation. —**spec′tro·pho′to·met′ric** (-tō-mĕt′rĭk) *adj.* —**spec′tro·pho·tom′e·try** *n.*

spec·tro·scope (spĕk′trə-skōp′) *n. Physics.* Any of various instruments for resolving and observing or recording spectra. [SPECTRO- + -SCOPE.] —**spec′tro·scop′ic** (-skŏp′ĭk), **spec′tro·scop′i·cal** *adj.* —**spec′tro·scop′i·cal·ly** *adv.*

spectroscopic analysis. *Physics.* The analysis of a spectrum to determine characteristics of its source, such as the analysis of the optical spectrum of an incandescent body to determine its composition or motion.

spec·tros·co·py (spĕk-trŏs′kə-pē) *n. Physics.* The study of spectra, especially the experimental observation of optical spectra. [SPECTRO- + -SCOPY.] —**spec·tros′co·pist** *n.*

spec·trum (spĕk′trəm) *n., pl.* **-tra** (-trə) or **-trums.** 1. *Physics.* The distribution of a characteristic of a physical system or phenomenon, especially: **a.** The distribution of energy emitted by a radiant source, as by an incandescent body, arranged in order of wavelengths. **b.** The distribution of atomic or subatomic particles in a system, as in a magnetically resolved molecular beam, arranged in order of masses. **c.** A graphic or photographic representation of any such distribution. See **continuous spectrum, line spectrum.** 2. **a.** A range of values of a quantity or set of related quantities. **b.** A broad sequence or range of related qualities, ideas, or activities: *the whole spectrum of 20th-century thought.* [Latin, appearance, image, form, from *specere,* to look at. See **spek-** in Appendix.*]

spec·u·lar (spĕk′yə-lər) *adj.* Of, resembling, or produced by a mirror or speculum.

spec·u·late (spĕk′yə-lāt′) *intr.v.* **-lated, -lating, -lates.** 1. To meditate on a given subject; reflect. 2. To engage in the buying or selling of a commodity with an element of risk on the chance of great profit. —See Synonyms at **conjecture.** [Latin *speculārī,* to spy out, watch, observe, from *specula,* watchtower, from *specere,* to look at. See **spek-** in Appendix.*]

spec·u·la·tion (spĕk′yə-lā′shən) *n. Abbr.* **spec.** 1. **a.** The act of speculating; consideration of some subject or idea. **b.** Contemplation of a profound nature. **c.** A conclusion, opinion, or theory reached by speculating. 2. **a.** Engagement in risky business transactions on the chance of quick or considerable profit. **b.** An instance of speculating.

spec·u·la·tive (spĕk′yə-lə-tĭv, -lā′tĭv) *adj.* 1. Of, characterized by, or based upon contemplative speculation; conjectural in nature rather than pragmatic or positive. 2. **a.** Given to speculation or conjecture. **b.** Spent in speculation. 3. **a.** Engaging in, given to, or involving financial speculation. **b.** Characteristic of speculation in the involvement of chance; risky. —**spec′u·la·tive·ly** *adv.* —**spec′u·la·tive·ness** *n.*

spec·u·lum (spĕk′yə-ləm) *n., pl.* **-la** (-lə) or **-lums.** 1. A mirror or polished metal plate, used as a reflector in optical instruments. 2. An instrument for dilating the opening of a body cavity for medical examination. 3. *Biology.* **a.** A bright, often iridescent patch of color on the wings of certain birds, especially ducks. **b.** A transparent spot in the wings of some butterflies or moths. [Latin, mirror, from *specere,* to look at. See **spek-** in Appendix.*]

sped. Past tense and past participle of **speed.**

speech (spēch) *n.* 1. **a.** The faculty or act of speaking; utterance of articulate sounds. **b.** The faculty or act of expressing or describing thoughts, feelings, or perceptions by the articulation of words. 2. That which is spoken; an utterance. 3. Conversation; vocal communication. 4. **a.** A talk or public address. **b.** A printed copy of an address. 5. A person's habitual manner or style of speaking. 6. The language or dialect of a nation or region. 7. The sounding of a musical instrument. 8. The study of oral communication, speech sounds, and vocal physiology. 9. *Archaic.* Rumor. [Middle English *speche,* Old English *spēc, spræc.* See **spreg-** in Appendix.*]

speech community. All speakers of a particular language or dialect, whether located in one area or scattered.

speech·i·fy (spēch′ə-fī′) *intr.v.* **-fied, -fying, -fies.** To orate; harangue. —**speech′i·fi′er** *n.*

speech·less (spēch′lĭs) *adj.* 1. Lacking the faculty of speech; dumb. 2. Temporarily unable to speak, as through astonishment. 3. Refraining from speech; silent. 4. Unexpressed or inexpressible in words: *speechless admiration.* —See Synonyms at **dumb.** —**speech′less·ly** *adv.* —**speech′less·ness** *n.*

speech·mak·er (spēch′mā′kər) *n.* One who makes a speech or speeches; an orator. Often used derisively, as of one who talks or promises much. —**speech′mak′ing** *n.*

speed (spēd) *n.* 1. *Mathematics & Physics.* The rate or a measure of the rate of motion, especially: **a.** Distance traveled divided by the time of travel. Also called "average speed." **b.** The limit of this quotient as the time of travel becomes vanishingly small; the first derivative of distance with respect to time. Also called "instantaneous speed." **c.** The magnitude of a **velocity** (*see*). 2. A rate of performance; swiftness of action. 3. The act or state of moving rapidly; rapidity; swiftness. 4. A transmission gear or set of gears in a motor vehicle. 5. *Photography.* **a.** A numerical expression of the sensitivity of a film, plate, or paper to light. **b.** The capacity of a lens to accumulate light at an appropriate aperture. See **f-stop.** **c.** The length of time required or permitted for a camera shutter to open and admit light. 6. *Slang.* Any amphetamine taken to produce euphoria. 7. *Archaic.* Prosperity; success; luck. —*v.* **sped** (spĕd) or **speeded, speeding, speeds.** —*tr.* 1. **a.** To hasten. **b.** To send or dispatch with speed or haste. 2. **a.** To increase the speed or rate of; accelerate. Often used with *up.* **b.** To set the speed of (a machine). 3. To drive (a motor vehicle) at a high or illegal rate of speed. 4. **a.** To wish Godspeed to. **b.** *Archaic.* To help to succeed or prosper; to aid. **c.** To further, promote, or expedite (a matter or legal action). —*intr.* 1. **a.** To go or move rapidly. **b.** To drive fast; exceed a traffic speed limit. 2. To pass quickly. 3. To move, perform, or happen at a faster rate; accelerate. Usually used with *up.* 4. *Obsolete.* **a.** To prove successful; prosper. **b.** To go well or poorly with a person; fare. [Middle English *sped(e),* success, prosperity, speed, Old English *spēd, spēd.* See **spēi-** in Appendix.*]

Synonyms: *speed, hurry, hasten, quicken, accelerate, precipitate, expedite.* These verbs mean to move or cause to move rapidly or to increase the pace of a person or thing. *Speed* refers directly to very rapid movement. *Hurry* implies movement or action at a rate markedly faster than usual, sometimes accompanied by commotion or confusion. *Hasten* refers to stepped-up activity that increases progress or brings a desired result much closer to fulfillment. Even more than *hurry,* it stresses urgency. *Quicken* and especially *accelerate* refer to increase in rate of activity, growth, or progress. *Precipitate* implies sudden or impetuous action that causes or impels rapid movement or that causes something to happen suddenly or prematurely. *Expedite* refers to action that furthers the quick and efficient accomplishment of something or accelerates its fulfillment.

speed·ball (spēd′bôl′) *n. Slang.* An intravenous dose of cocaine and heroin.

speed·boat (spēd′bōt′) *n.* A fast motorboat.

speed·er (spē′dər) *n.* One that speeds; especially, a driver who exceeds a legal or safe speed.

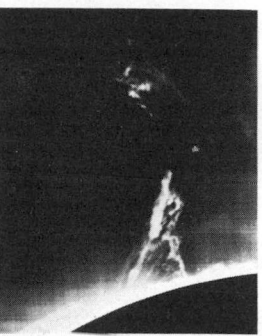

spectroheliogram
Eruptive prominence of the sun photographed in 1931

speed·ing (spē′dĭng) *adj.* Moving with speed. —*n.* The act of driving faster than is allowed by law.
speed limit. The maximum vehicular speed legally permitted on a given stretch of road.
speed·om·e·ter (spē-dŏm′ə-tər, spĭ-) *n.* **1.** An instrument for indicating speed. **2.** An instrument for indicating the distance traveled; odometer. [SPEED + -METER.]
speed·ster (spēd′stər) *n.* **1.** A speeder. **2.** A fast automobile, usually a sports car.
speed trap. A stretch of road where traffic speed is secretly checked by police using electronic or other devices.
speed·up (spēd′ŭp′) *n.* Acceleration of production without increase in pay.
speed·way (spēd′wā′) *n.* **1.** A course for automobile racing. **2.** A road designed for fast-moving traffic; an expressway.
speed·well (spēd′wĕl′) *n.* Any of various plants of the genus *Veronica,* having clusters of small, usually blue flowers.
speed·y (spē′dē) *adj.* **-ier, -iest. 1.** Characterized by rapid motion; swift. **2.** Accomplished or arrived at without delay; prompt; quick. —See Synonyms at **fast.** —**speed′i·ly** *adv.* —**speed′i·ness** *n.*

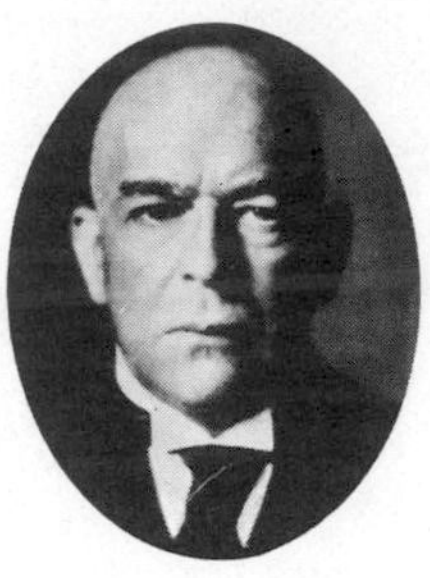

Oswald Spengler

speiss (spīs) *n.* Also *German* **Spei·se** (shpī′zə). A basic arsenic or antimony compound of iron, often with nickel, copper, or other metals, having a metallic luster and a strong tendency to crystallize, produced during the smelting of various ores. [German *Speise,* "food," from Old High German *spīsa,* from Medieval Latin *spēsa, spensa,* "provisions," from Latin *expēnsa,* spent, from the past participle of *expendere,* to EXPEND.]
spe·le·ol·o·gy (spē′lē-ŏl′ə-jē) *n.* **1.** The study of the physical, geologic, and biological aspects of caves. **2.** The exploration of caves. [Latin *spēleum,* cave, from Greek *spēlaion*† + -LOGY.] —**spe′le·o·log′i·cal** (-lē-ə-lŏj′ĭ-kəl) *adj.* —**spe′le·ol′o·gist** *n.*
spell[1] (spĕl) *v.* **spelled** or **spelt** (spĕlt), **spelling, spells.** —*tr.* **1.** To name or write in order the letters constituting (a word or part of a word). **2.** To be the letters of; form (a word). **3.** To mean; signify. —*intr.* To form a word or words correctly by means of letters. —**spell out. 1.** To make perfectly clear and understandable. See Usage note below. **2.** To read slowly, letter by letter. **3.** To puzzle out; comprehend by study. [Middle English *spellen,* read out, from Old French *espelir, espeller,* from Germanic. See **spel-**[3] in Appendix.*]
Usage: *Spell out* has long been used in the senses of reading closely or with difficulty and of deciphering (a difficult passage). It is used even more widely now, on all levels, in the newer sense of stating explicitly or in detail: *spell out provisions of the new code.* This is acceptable, as an example in writing, to 79 per cent of the Usage Panel. But *spell out details* is redundant.
spell[2] (spĕl) *n.* **1.** An incantational word or formula. **2.** Compelling attraction; fascination. **3.** A bewitched state; trance. —*tr.v.* **spelled, spelling, spells.** To put under a spell. [Middle English *spell,* discourse, Old English *spel(l),* story, fable. See **spel-**[3] in Appendix.*]
spell[3] (spĕl) *n.* **1.** A short, indefinite period of time. **2.** *Informal.* A period of weather of a particular kind: *a dry spell.* **3.** A short turn of work; turn; shift: *a spell at the helm.* **4.** *Informal.* A period, bout, or fit of illness, indisposition, or irritability. **5.** *Informal.* A short distance. —*v.* **spelled, spelling, spells.** —*tr.* **1.** To relieve (someone) from work temporarily by taking a turn. **2.** To allow to rest a while. —*intr.* To rest for a time from some activity. Usually used with *off: spell off for a while.* [Perhaps from Middle English *spelen,* relieve at work, Old English *spelian*†, to substitute.]

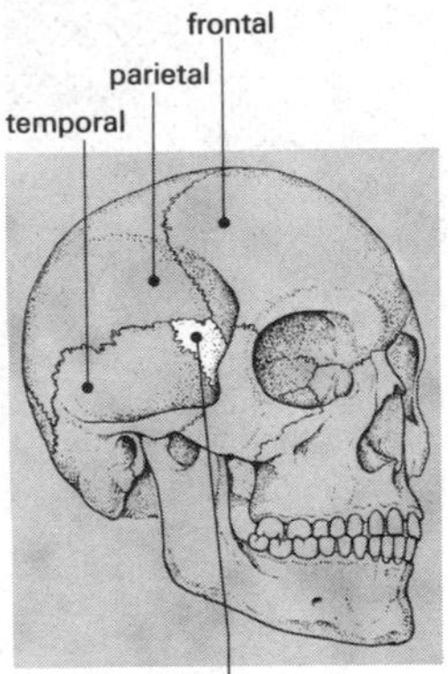
frontal
parietal
temporal
sphenoid bone

spell·bind (spĕl′bīnd′) *tr.v.* **-bound** (-bound′), **-binding, -binds.** To hold under or as if under a spell; enthrall; enchant.
spell·bind·er (spĕl′bīn′dər) *n.* One who holds others spellbound.
spell·bound (spĕl′bound′) *adj.* Entranced; fascinated.
spell down. To defeat in a spelldown.
spell·down (spĕl′doun′) *n.* A contest in which competitors are eliminated as they fail to spell a given word correctly.
spell·er (spĕl′ər) *n.* **1.** One who spells words. **2.** An elementary textbook to teach spelling.
spell·ing (spĕl′ĭng) *n. Abbr.* **sp. 1. a.** The forming of words with letters in an accepted order; orthography. **b.** The art or study of orthography. **2.** The way in which a word is spelled.
spelt[1] (spĕlt) *n.* A hardy wheat, *Triticum spelta,* grown mostly in Europe. [Probably from Middle Dutch *spelte.* See **spel-**[1] in Appendix.*]
spelt[2]. Alternate past tense and past participle of **spell** (to form words).
spel·ter (spĕl′tər) *n.* Zinc, especially in the form of ingots, slabs, or plates. [Obscurely akin to Middle Dutch *speauter*†, akin to Old French *peautre,* PEWTER.]
spe·lun·ker (spĭ-lŭng′kər, spē′lŭng-kər) *n.* One who explores and studies caves; a speleologist. [From obsolete *spelunk,* cave, from Middle English, from Latin *spelunca,* from Greek *spēlunx,* akin to Greek *spēlaion.* See **speleology.**]
spe·lunk·ing (spĭ-lŭng′kĭng, spē′lŭng-kĭng) *n.* The activity or hobby of exploring caves.
spen·cer[1] (spĕn′sər) *n. Nautical.* A **trysail** *(see).* [Perhaps from the surname *Spencer.*]
spen·cer[2] (spĕn′sər) *n.* **1.** A short double-breasted overcoat worn by men in the early 19th century. **2.** A close-fitting waist-length jacket worn by women. [After George *Spencer,* Earl Spencer (1758–1834).]
Spen·cer (spĕn′sər), **Herbert.** 1820–1903. British philosopher.
Spen·cer (spĕn′sər), **Platt Rogers.** 1800–1864. American calligrapher; originator of an ornate style of penmanship.
Spen·cer Gulf (spĕn′sər). A large inlet of the Indian Ocean in Australia, extending about 200 miles into South Australia.
Spen·ce·ri·an[1] (spĕn-sîr′e-ən) *adj.* Of or pertaining to Herbert Spencer or to his philosophy. —*n.* A follower of Herbert Spencer.
Spen·ce·ri·an[2] (spĕn-sîr′e-ən) *adj.* Of or relating to an ornate style of penmanship employing rounded letters slanted to the right, taught by Platt Rogers Spencer.
Spen·cer·ism (spĕn′sər-ĭz′əm) *n.* Also **Spen·ce·ri·an·ism** (spĕn-sîr′ē-ən-ĭz′əm). The system of logical positivism developed by Herbert Spencer, setting forth the idea that evolution is the passage from the simple, indefinite, and incoherent to the complex, definite, and coherent. Also called "synthetic philosophy."
spend (spĕnd) *v.* **spent** (spĕnt), **spending, spends.** —*tr.* **1.** To incur the expenditure of; use up or put out; devote; expend. **2.** To pay out (money); disburse. **3.** To deprive of force or strength; exhaust; wear out. **4.** To pass (time) in a specified manner or place. **5. a.** To throw away; waste; squander. **b.** To sacrifice. —*intr.* **1.** To pay out or expend money. **2.** *Obsolete.* To be exhausted or consumed. [Spend, spent, spent; Middle English *spenden, spente, spent,* partly from Old English *spendan,* from Latin *expendĕre,* to EXPEND, and partly from Old French *despendre,* to DISPEND.] —**spend′a·ble** *adj.* —**spend′er** *n.*
Spen·der (spĕn′dər), **Stephen.** Born 1909. English poet and critic.
spending money. Cash for small personal needs.
spend·thrift (spĕnd′thrĭft′) *n.* One who squanders money; a prodigal spender. —*adj.* Wasteful or extravagant. [SPEND + THRIFT (accumulated wealth).]
Speng·ler (spĕng′glər; *German* shpĕng′glĕr), **Oswald.** 1880–1936. German philosopher; author of *The Decline of the West.*
Spen·ser (spĕn′sər), **Edmund.** 1552?–1599. English poet.
Spen·se·ri·an sonnet (spĕn-sîr′ē-ən). A sonnet form comprising three interlocking quatrains and a couplet with the rhyme pattern *abab bcbc cdcd ee.* [After Edmund SPENSER.]
Spenserian stanza. A stanza consisting of eight lines of iambic pentameter and a final Alexandrine, rhymed *ababbcbcc,* used by Edmund Spenser in *The Faerie Queene.*
spent (spĕnt). Past tense and past participle of **spend.** —*adj.* **1.** Consumed; used up; expended. **2.** Passed; come to an end; over with: *"Like the episodes of a spent dream"* (George Santayana). **3.** Depleted of energy, force, or strength; exhausted. **4.** *Nautical.* The state of a vessel at the end of a voyage, with fuel, stores, and water consumed and cargo discharged.
sperm[1] (spûrm) *n.* **1.** The male gamete or reproductive cell, **spermatozoon** *(see).* **2.** The male fluid of fertilization, **semen** *(see).* [Middle English *sperme,* from Old French *esperme,* from Late Latin *sperma,* seed, sperm, from Greek *sperma.* See **sper-**[4] in Appendix.*] —**sperm′ous** *adj.*
sperm[2] (spûrm) *n.* The sperm whale or a substance associated with it, such as spermaceti. [Short for SPERMACETI.]
-sperm. *Botany.* Indicates a seed; for example, **gymnosperm.** [From SPERM (semen).]
sper·ma·ce·ti (spûr′mə-cĕt′ē) *n.* A white, waxy substance consisting of various esters of fatty acids, obtained from the head of the sperm whale and used for making candles, ointments, and cosmetics. [Middle English, from Medieval Latin *spermacētī,* "sperm of the whale" : Late Latin *sperma,* SPERM + Latin *cētī,* genitive of *cētus,* whale (see **cetacean**).]
sper·ma·ry (spûr′mə-rē) *n., pl.* **-ries.** An organ in which male gametes are formed, especially in invertebrate animals. [New Latin *spermarium,* from Late Latin *sperma,* SPERM.]
sper·ma·the·ca (spûr′mə-thē′kə) *n.* A receptacle for storing spermatozoa in certain female invertebrates, especially insects. [New Latin : Late Latin *sperma,* SPERM + THECA.] —**sper′ma·the′cal** *adj.*
sper·mat·ic (spûr-măt′ĭk) *adj.* **1.** Of, pertaining to, or resembling sperm; spermous. **2.** Of or pertaining to a spermary. [Old French *spermatique,* from Late Latin *spermaticus,* from Greek *spermatikos,* from *sperma* (stem *spermat-*), SPERM.]
spermatic cord. A cordlike structure consisting of the vas deferens and its accompanying arteries, veins, nerves, and lymphatic vessels that passes from the abdominal cavity through the inguinal canal, down into the scrotum to the back of the testicle.
spermatic fluid. *Physiology.* Semen.
sper·ma·tid (spûr′mə-tĭd′) *n.* One of four haploid cells formed during mitosis in the male that develop into spermatozoa without further division. [SPERMAT(O)- + -ID.]
sper·ma·ti·um (spûr-mā′shē-əm) *n., pl.* **-tia** (-shē-ə). A nonmotile, sporelike structure in red algae and certain fungi, generally acting as a male gamete. [New Latin, from Greek *spermation,* diminutive of *sperma* (stem *spermat-*), SPERM.] —**sper·ma′tial** *adj.*
spermato-, spermat-, spermo-. Indicates: **1.** Sperm; for example, **spermatogonium, spermatid. 2.** Seed; for example, **spermatophyte, spermophile.** [Late Latin *sperma* (stem *spermat-*), SPERM.]
sper·ma·to·cyte (spûr-măt′ə-sīt′, spûr′mə-tə-) *n.* A diploid cell that is converted by meiotic division into four spermatids. [SPERMATO- + -CYTE.]
sper·ma·to·gen·e·sis (spûr-măt′ə-jĕn′ə-sĭs, spûr′mə-tə-) *n.* The generation of sperm by male meiosis and spermiogenesis. [New Latin : SPERMATO- + -GENESIS.] —**sper′ma·to·ge·net′ic** (spûr′măt-ə-jə-nĕt′ĭk, -mə-tə-jə-nĕt′ĭk) *adj.*
sper·ma·to·go·ni·um (spûr-măt′ə-gō′nē-əm, spûr′mə-tə-) *n., pl.* **-nia** (-nē-ə). Any of the cells of the gonads in male animals that are the progenitors of primary spermatocytes. [New Latin : SPERMATO- + -GONIUM.] —**sper′ma·to·go′ni·al** *adj.*

ă pat/ā pay/âr care/ä father/b bib/ch church/d deed/ĕ pet/ē be/f fife/g gag/h hat/hw which/ĭ pit/ī pie/îr pier/j judge/k kick/l lid, needle/m mum/n no, sudden/ng thing/ŏ pot/ō toe/ô paw, for/oi noise/ou out/ŏŏ took/ōō boot/p pop/r roar/s sauce/sh ship, dish/

sper·ma·toid (spûr′mə-toid′) *adj.* Resembling sperm. [SPERMAT(O)- + -OID.]

sper·ma·to·phore (spûr-măt′ə-fôr′, -fōr′, spûr′mə-tə-) *n.* An extruded mass or capsule of spermatozoa in certain invertebrates and primitive vertebrates. [SPERMATO- + -PHORE.] —**sper′ma·toph′or·al** (spûr′mə-tŏf′ər-əl) *adj.*

sper·ma·to·phyte (spûr-măt′ə-fīt′, spûr′mə-tə-) *n.* Any plant of the division Spermatophyta, which includes all seed-bearing plants. [New Latin *Spermatophyta* : SPERMATO- + -PHYTE.] —**sper′mat′o·phyt′ic** (spûr′mə-fĭt′ĭk, spûr′mə-tə-) *adj.*

sper·ma·tor·rhe·a (spûr-măt′ə-rē′ə, spûr′mə-tə-rē′ə) *n.* Also **sper·ma·tor·rhoe·a.** Involuntary seminal discharge without orgasm. [New Latin : SPERMATO- + -RRHEA.]

sper·ma·to·zo·id (spûr-măt′ə-zoid′, spûr′mə-tə-) *n. Botany.* A ciliated male gamete produced in an antheridium. —*adj.* Resembling a spermatozoon. [SPERMATOZO(ON) + -ID.]

sper·ma·to·zo·on (spûr-măt′ə-zō′ŏn, spûr′mə-tə-zō′ən) *n., pl.* **-zoa** (-zō′ə). The fertilizing gamete of a male animal, usually a long nucleated cell with a thin, motile tail. Also called "sperm," "sperm cell," "zoosperm." [New Latin : SPERMATO- + -ZOON.] —**sper′ma·to·zo′al, sper′ma·to·zo′an, sper′ma·to·zo′ic** *adj.*

sper·mine (spûr′mēn′) *n.* A crystalline compound, $C_{10}H_{26}N_4$, found as a phosphate in semen, yeast, and ox pancreas. [SPERM + -INE.]

sper·mi·o·gen·e·sis (spûr′mē-ə-jĕn′ə-sĭs) *n.* The transformation of a spermatid into a spermatozoon. [New Latin : *spermium,* spermatozoon, probably from SPERM + -GENESIS.]

spermo–. Variant of **spermato-.**

sper·mo·go·ni·um (spûr′mə-gō′nē-əm) *n., pl.* **-nia** (-nē-ə). *Botany.* A hollow structure in which spermatia are formed. [SPERMO- + -GONIUM.]

sperm oil. A yellow, waxy oil, obtained chiefly from the head of the sperm whale and used as an industrial lubricant.

sperm·o·phile (spûr′mə-fīl′) *n.* Any of various North American ground squirrels of the genus *Citellus* (or *Spermophilus*). [New Latin *spermophilus,* "fond of seed" : SPERMO- + -PHILE.]

–spermous. Indicates having (a specified number of) seeds; for example, **monospermous.** [From -SPERM.]

sperm whale. A whale, *Physeter catodon,* having a very large head, with cavities containing sperm oil and spermaceti, and a long, narrow, toothed lower jaw. Also called "cachalot."

Sper·ry (spĕr′ē), **Elmer Ambrose.** 1860–1930. American inventor of a gyroscopic compass, gyroscopic stabilizers, and a high-intensity searchlight.

sper·ry·lite (spĕr′ĭ-līt′) *n.* A white crystalline platinum mineral, essentially PtAs₂. [After F.L. *Sperry,* 19th-century Canadian mineralogist.]

spes·sar·tite (spĕs′ər-tīt′) *n.* Also **spes·sar·tine** (-tēn′). A mineral silicate of manganese and aluminum, usually containing some iron. [French, from *Spessart,* mountain range in Germany.]

spew (spyōō) *v.* **spewed, spewing, spews.** Also **spue, spued, spuing, spues.** —*tr.* **1. a.** To vomit or cast out through the mouth. **b.** To force out in a stream; eject: *"I was spewed forth with the mob into the bright courtyard"* (James Baldwin). **2.** To eject or spit out with loathing or contempt; *"That the land spue not you out also, when ye defile it"* (Leviticus 18:28). —*intr.* To vomit. —*n.* Also **spue.** That which is spewed; vomit. [Middle English *spewen,* Old English *spīwan* and *spīowan.* See spyeu- in Appendix.*]

Spey·er (shpī′ər). Also **Spires** (spīrz). A city of West Germany, in southeastern Rhineland-Palatinate, site of three German Diets during the Protestant Reformation (1526, 1529, and 1544). Population, 37,000.

Spe·zia. See La Spezia.

Spe·zia, Gulf of (spāt′sē-ä). An inlet of the Gulf of Genoa in northwestern Italy.

sp gr specific gravity.

sphag·num (sfăg′nəm) *n.* Any of various pale or ashy mosses of the genus *Sphagnum,* the decomposed remains of which form peat. [New Latin, from Latin *sphagnos,* a kind of moss, from Greek *sphagnos†.*] —**sphag′nous** *adj.*

sphal·er·ite (sfăl′ər-īt′) *n.* A yellow, brown, black, or red zinc ore, essentially ZnS with some cadmium, iron, and manganese. Also called "blende," "zinc blende." [German *Sphalerit* : Greek *sphaleros,* slippery, from *sphallein†,* to trip + -ITE.]

sphene (sfēn) *n.* A titanium ore, chiefly CaTiSiO₅, sometimes used as a gemstone. Also called "titanite." [French *sphène,* from Greek *sphēn,* wedge. See sphē- in Appendix.*]

sphe·nic (sfĕn′ĭk) *adj.* Shaped like a wedge. [SPHEN(O)- + -IC.]

spheno–, sphen–. Indicates wedge-shaped; for example, **sphenogram, sphenodon.** [From Greek *sphēn,* wedge. See sphē- in Appendix.*]

sphe·no·don (sfĕn′ə-dŏn′) *n.* A reptile, the **tuatara** *(see).* [SPHEN(O)- + -ODON.]

sphe·no·gram (sfĕn′ə-grăm′) *n.* A cuneiform character. [SPHENO- + -GRAM.]

sphe·noid (sfē′noid′) *n.* The sphenoid bone *(see).* —*adj.* Also **sphe·noid·al** (sfē-noid′l). **1.** Wedge-shaped. **2.** Of or pertaining to the sphenoid bone. [New Latin *sphenoides,* from Greek *sphēnoeides* : SPHEN(O)- + -OID.]

sphenoid bone. A compound bone with winglike processes, situated at the base of the skull. Also called "sphenoid."

spher·al (sfîr′əl) *adj.* **1.** Of, pertaining to, or having the shape of a sphere; spherical. **2.** Symmetrical.

sphere (sfîr) *n.* **1.** *Geometry.* A three-dimensional surface, all points of which are equidistant from a fixed point. **2.** A spherical object or figure. **3.** A planet, star, or other heavenly body.

4. The sky, appearing as a hemisphere to an observer: *the sphere of the heavens.* **5.** In ancient astronomy, any of a series of concentric, transparent, revolving globes which together were thought to contain the moon, sun, planets, and stars. **6.** The environment in which one exists, acts, or has influence; range; domain. **7.** One's social stratum, rank, or position. —*tr.v.* **sphered, sphering, spheres. 1.** To form into a sphere. **2.** To put in or within a sphere. **3.** To surround or encompass. [Middle English *spere, sphere,* from Old French *espere,* from Latin *sphaera, sphēra,* ball, globe, from Greek *sphaira†.*] —**sphe·ric′i·ty** (sfîr-ĭs′ə-tē) *n.*

–sphere. Indicates the shape of a sphere; for example, **bathysphere.** [From SPHERE.]

spher·i·cal (sfîr′ĭ-kəl, sfĕr′-) *adj.* Also **spher·ic** (sfîr′ĭk, sfĕr′-). **1. a.** Having the shape of a sphere; globular. **b.** Having a shape approximating that of a sphere. **2.** Of or pertaining to a sphere or spheres. **3.** Of or pertaining to heavenly bodies; celestial. —**spher′i·cal·ly** *adv.* —**spher′i·cal·ness** *n.*

spherical aberration. An optical defect of refracting and reflecting spherical surfaces in which light rays from one axial point, incident on the surface at different distances from the optical axis, do not come to a common focus.

spherical angle. The angle formed at the intersection of the arcs of two great circles.

spherical astronomy. The branch of astronomy dealing with positions on the celestial sphere.

spher·i·cal-co·or·di·nate system (sfîr′ĭ-kəl-kō-ôr′də-nĭt, sfĕr′-, -nāt′). A three-dimensional system for locating points in space by means of a radius vector and two angles measured from the center of a sphere with respect to two arbitrary, fixed, perpendicular directions.

spherical excess. The difference between the sum of the angles of a spherical triangle and the sum of the angles of a plane triangle.

spherical geometry. The geometry of circles, angles, and figures on the surface of a sphere.

spherical polygon. Any part of a spherical surface that is bounded by arcs of three or more great circles.

spherical triangle. A triangle the three sides of which are arcs of great circles.

spherical trigonometry. The modified form of trigonometry applied to spherical triangles.

spher·ics (sfîr′ĭks, sfĕr′-) *n.* Plural in form, used with a singular verb. **1.** Spherical geometry or trigonometry. **2.** Variant of **sferics.**

sphe·roid (sfîr′oid′, sfĕr′-) *n.* An ellipsoid that is generated by revolving an ellipse around one of its axes. [Late Latin *sphaeroīdēs,* from Greek *sphaeroeidēs* : SPHERE + -OID.] —**sphe·roi′dal, sphe·roi′dic, sphe·roi′di·cal** *adj.* —**sphe·roi′dal·ly** *adv.* —**sphe′roi·dic′i·ty** (sfîr′oi-dĭs′ə-tē, sfĕr′-) *n.*

sphe·rom·e·ter (sfîr-ŏm′ə-tər, sfər-) *n.* An instrument for measuring the curvature of a surface, as of a sphere or cylinder. [SPHER(E) + -METER.]

spher·ule (sfîr′ool, -yool, sfĕr′-) *n.* A miniature sphere; globule. [Late Latin *sphaerula,* diminutive of Latin *sphaera,* SPHERE.] —**spher′u·lar** *adj.*

spher·u·lite (sfîr′ə-līt′, -yə-līt′, sfĕr′-) *n.* A small, usually spheroid, crystalline body having a radiating structure and found in obsidian and some silicic lava flows. [SPHERUL(E) + -ITE.] —**spher′u·lit′ic** (-lĭt′ĭk) *adj.*

spher·y (sfîr′ē) *adj.* **-ier, -iest. 1.** Of or pertaining to the celestial spheres. **2.** Resembling a heavenly body; starlike.

sphinc·ter (sfĭngk′tər) *n.* A ringlike muscle that normally maintains constriction of a bodily passage or orifice and that relaxes as required by normal physiological functioning. [Late Latin, from Greek *sphinktēr,* that which binds tight, from *sphingein†,* to bind tight.] —**sphinc′ter·al** *adj.*

sphinx (sfĭnks) *n., pl.* **sphinxes** or **sphinges** (sfĭn′jēz′). **1. a.** *Egyptian Mythology.* A figure having the body of a lion and the head of a man, ram, or hawk. **b.** *Capital* **S.** The monumental sphinx having the head of a man at Giza. **2.** *Greek Mythology.* A winged monster having the head of a woman and the body of a lion that destroyed all who could not answer its riddle. **3.** Any enigmatic person. [Middle English *spynx,* from Latin *Sphinx,* from Greek, with dialectal variants *Phix* and *Bix,* perhaps originally a deity from Mount *Phikion* in Boeotia.]

sphinx moth. The hawk moth *(see).*

sphra·gis·tics (sfră-jĭs′tĭks) *n.* Plural in form, used with a singular verb. The study of seals and signets. [French *sphragistique,* from Late Greek *sphragistikos,* from Greek *sphragist†,* seal, signet.]

sp ht specific heat.

sphyg·mic (sfĭg′mĭk) *adj. Physiology.* Pertaining to the pulse. [Greek *sphugmikos,* from *sphugmos,* pulsation, from *sphuzein†,* to throb.]

sphygmo–, sphygm–. Indicates the pulse; for example, **sphygmograph, sphygmoid.** [From Greek *sphugmos,* pulsation. See **sphygmic.**]

sphyg·mo·gram (sfĭg′mə-grăm′) *n.* The record or tracing produced by a sphygmograph. [SPHYGMO- + -GRAM.]

sphyg·mo·graph (sfĭg′mə-grăf′, -gräf′) *n.* An instrument for recording the character and variations of the arterial pulse. [SPHYGMO- + -GRAPH.]

sphyg·moid (sfĭg′moid′) *adj. Physiology.* Resembling a pulse; pulselike. [SPHYGM(O)- + -OID.]

sphyg·mo·ma·nom·e·ter (sfĭg′mō-mə-nŏm′ə-tər) *n.* Also **sphyg·mom·e·ter** (-mŏm′ə-tər). An instrument for measuring blood pressure in the arteries. [SPHYGMO- + MANOMETER.]

spic (spĭk) *n.* Also **spick.** *Slang.* A Spanish-speaking person. An

sperm whale

sphinx
The sphinx of
Queen Hatshepsut

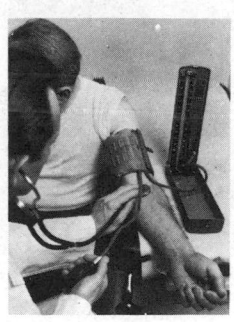

sphygmomanometer

offensive term used derogatorily. [Variant of obsolete *spig*†, Mexican.]

spi·ca (spī′kə) *n.* A bandage applied in overlapping opposite spirals to immobilize a digit or limb. [Latin *spīca*, "point," ear of grain (from the resemblance of the V-shaped bandage to the V-shaped spikelets on an ear of grain). See **spei-** in Appendix.*]

Spi·ca (spī′kə) *n.* The brightest star in the constellation Virgo, 212 light-years distant from Earth. [Latin *spīca*, "point," ear of grain. See **spica**.]

spi·cate (spī′kāt′) *adj. Botany.* Borne in or forming a spike. [Latin *spīcātus*, from the past participle of *spīcāre*, provide with spikes, from *spīca*, ear of grain, SPIKE.]

spic·ca·to (spĭ-kä′tō) *n., pl.* **-tos.** *Music.* A technique of bowing in which the bow is made to bounce slightly from the string. —*adj. Music.* Of or employing such a technique. [Italian, from the past participle of *spiccare*†, to separate.]

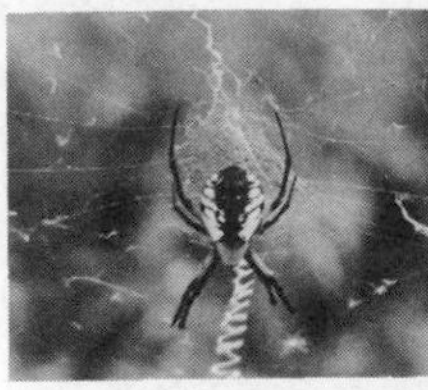

spider
Argiope riparia

spice (spīs) *n.* **1.** Any of various aromatic and pungent vegetable substances, such as cinnamon or nutmeg, used to flavor foods or beverages. **2.** These substances collectively. **3.** Something that adds zest or flavor. **4.** A pungent aroma; perfume. —*tr.v.* **spiced, spicing, spices. 1.** To season with spices. **2.** To add zest or flavor to. [Middle English, from Old French *espice*, from Late Latin *speciēs*, goods, spices, from Latin, appearance, kind, SPECIES.]

spice·ber·ry (spīs′bĕr′ē) *n., pl.* **-ries.** Any of various plants or shrubs having spicy berries, such as the wintergreen.

spice·bush (spīs′bo͝osh′) *n.* **1.** An aromatic shrub, *Lindera benzoin*, of eastern North America, having clusters of small, early-blooming yellow flowers. Also called "benjamin bush." **2.** An aromatic shrub, *Calycanthus occidentalis*, of California, having fragrant, brownish flowers.

Spice Islands. The former name for the **Molucca Islands.**

spic·er·y (spī′sə-rē) *n., pl.* **-ies. 1.** Spices collectively. **2.** The aromatic or pungent quality of spices. **3.** *Obsolete.* A place where spices are stored.

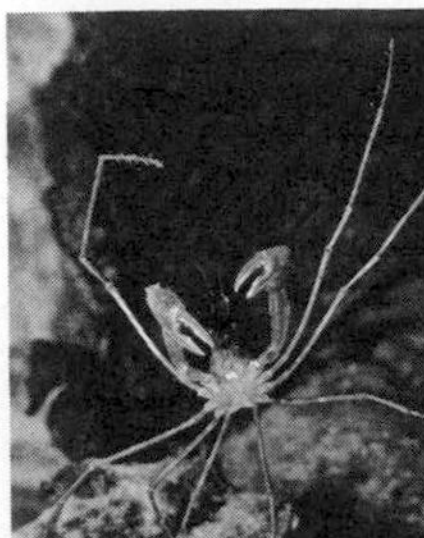

spider crab
Inachus scorpio

spick-and-span (spĭk′ən-spăn′) *adj.* Also **spic-and-span. 1.** Neat and clean; spotless. **2.** Brand-new; fresh. [Short for obsolete *spick and spannew* : *spick*, variant of SPIKE (nail) (influenced by Dutch *spiksplinter niew* "spike-splinter-new") + SPAN-NEW.]

spic·ule (spĭk′yo͞ol) *n.* Also **spic·u·la** (-yə-lə) *pl.* **-lae** (-lē′). A small needlelike structure or part, such as one of the silicate or calcium carbonate processes supporting the soft tissue of certain invertebrates, especially sponges. [Latin *spīculum*, SPICULUM.] —**spic′u·lar, spic′u·late** (spĭk′yə-lĭt, -lāt′) *adj.*

spic·u·lum (spĭk′yə-ləm) *n., pl.* **-la** (-lə). A spicule or similar needlelike structure. [Latin *spīculum*, diminutive of *spīca*, point. See **spei-** in Appendix.*]

spic·y (spī′sē) *adj.* **-ier, -iest. 1.** Having the characteristics of spice, such as flavor and aroma. **2.** Piquant; zesty. **3.** Slightly scandalous; risqué. —**spic′i·ly** *adv.* —**spic′i·ness** *n.*

spi·der (spī′dər) *n.* **1.** Any of numerous arachnids of the order Araneae, having eight legs, a body divided into a cephalothorax and an abdomen, and several spinnerets that produce silk used to make nests, cocoons, or webs for trapping insects. **2.** One that is similar to a spider, as in appearance, character, or movement. **3.** A frying pan equipped with a long handle and short legs. **4.** A trivet. [Middle English *spither*, *spithre*, Old English *spīthra*. See **spen-** in Appendix.*]

spider crab. Any of various crabs, such as those of the genera *Libinia* and *Macrocheira*, having long legs and a relatively small body.

spi·der·flow·er (spī′dər-flou′ər) *n.* The **cleome** *(see)*.

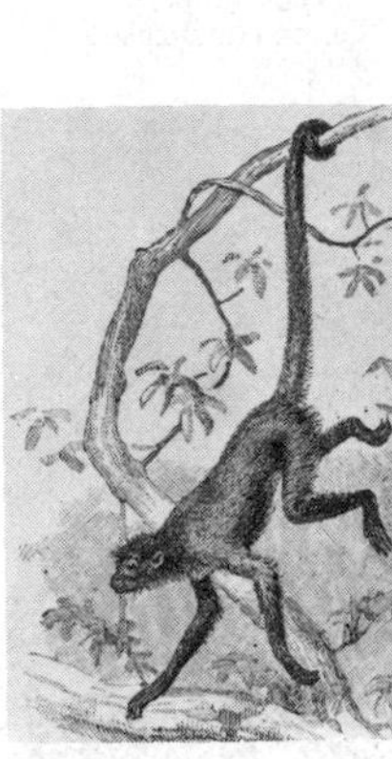

spider monkey
Ateles paniscus

spider lily. Any of various chiefly tropical American plants of the genus *Hymenocallis*, having narrow leaves and clusters of white flowers.

spider monkey. Any of several tropical American monkeys of the genus *Ateles*, having long legs and a long, prehensile tail.

spi·der·wort (spī′dər-wûrt′, -wôrt′) *n.* Any of various New World plants of the genus *Tradescantia*; especially, *T. virginiana*, having three-petaled blue or purple flowers.

spi·der·y (spī′də-rē) *adj.* **1.** Like or suggesting a spider. **2. a.** Resembling a spider's legs; long and slender. **b.** Resembling a spider's web; very fine. **3.** Infested with spiders.

spie·gel·ei·sen (spē′gə-lī′sən) *n.* An alloy of iron with approximately 15 per cent manganese and small quantities of carbon and silicon, used in the Bessemer process. Also called "spiegel." [German *Spiegeleisen*, "mirror-iron" : *Spiegel*, mirror, from Old High German *spiagal*, from Medieval Latin *spēglum*, from Latin *speculum*, SPECULUM + *Eisen*, iron, from Old High German *īsan*, *īsarn* (see **eis-**[1] in Appendix*).]

spiel (spēl) *n. Slang.* A voluble dissertation usually intended to persuade. —*v.* **spieled, spieling, spiels.** *Slang.* —*intr.* To talk at length or extravagantly. —*tr.* To say at length. [German *Spiel*, "play," from Old High German *spil*, from Germanic *spillōn* (unattested), to play.] —**spiel′er** *n.*

spif·fy (spĭf′ē) *adj.* **-fier, -fiest.** *Slang.* Smart in appearance or dress; stylish. [Origin unknown.] —**spiff′fi·ness** *n.*

spig·ot (spĭg′ət) *n.* **1.** A faucet. **2.** The vent plug of a cask. **3.** A wooden faucet placed in the bunghole of a cask. [Middle English, perhaps from Latin *spīca*, SPIKE (ear of grain).]

spike[1] (spīk) *n.* **1. a.** A long, thick, sharp-pointed piece of wood or metal. **b.** A heavy nail. **2. a.** A sharp-pointed member projecting outward, as from the top of a wall. **b.** A sharp metal projection set in the sole of a shoe for grip. **3. a.** A very high thin heel, used on a woman's shoe. Also called "spike heel." **b.** *Plural.* A pair of shoes having such heels. **4.** An unbranched antler of a young deer. **5.** A small young mackerel. —*tr.v.* **spiked, spiking, spikes. 1.** To secure or provide with a spike. **2.** To impale, pierce, or injure with a spike. **3.** To render (a muzzleloading gun) useless by driving a spike into the vent. **4.** To put an end to; thwart; block: *spike a plot.* **5.** *Slang.* To add alcoholic liquor to. [Middle English *spyk*, either from Old Norse *spīk*, nail, or Old English *spīcing*. See **spei-** in Appendix.*]

spike[2] (spīk) *n.* **1.** An ear of grain. **2.** *Botany.* A usually elongated inflorescence with stalkless or nearly stalkless flowers arranged along an axis. [Middle English *spik*, from Latin *spīca*, point, ear of grain. See **spei-** in Appendix.*]

spike lavender. An aromatic plant, *Lavandula latifolia*, of southern Europe, yielding an oil similar to that of true lavender. [From SPIKE (inflorescence).]

spike·let (spīk′lət) *n. Botany.* A small or secondary spike, especially one of those forming the inflorescence of grasses or similar plants.

spike·nard (spīk′närd′) *n.* **1.** An aromatic plant, *Nardostachys jatamansi*, of India, having rose-purple flowers. Also called "nard." **2.** A costly ointment of antiquity, probably prepared from this plant. Also called "nard." **3.** A North American plant, *Aralia racemosa*, having small, greenish flowers and an aromatic root. [Middle English, from Medieval Latin *spīca nardi*, spike of a nard (translation of Greek *nardostakhus*) : Latin *spīca*, SPIKE + *nardus*, NARD.]

spik·y (spī′kē) *adj.* **-ier, -iest.** Having a projecting sharp point or points. —**spik′i·ness** *n.*

spile (spīl) *n.* **1.** A post used as a foundation; a pile. **2.** A wooden plug; a bung. **3.** A spigot used in sapping a tree. —*tr.v.* **spiled, spiling, spiles.** To support, plug, or tap with a spile. [Perhaps from Middle Dutch or Middle Low German *spile*, bar. See **spei-** in Appendix.*]

spil·i·kin (spĭl′ĭ-kən) *n.* Also **spil·li·kin. 1.** A **jackstraw** *(see)*. **2.** *Plural.* **Jackstraws** *(see)*. [Perhaps SPILL (wood) + -KIN.]

spill[1] (spĭl) *v.* **spilled** or **spilt** (spĭlt), **spilling, spills.** —*tr.* **1.** To cause or allow (a substance) to run or fall out of a container. **2.** To shed (blood). **3.** To let the wind out of (a sail). **4.** To cause to fall: *The horse spilled his rider.* **5.** *Informal.* To divulge. —*intr.* To run or fall out of a container. —*n.* **1.** An act of spilling. **2.** The amount spilled. **3.** A fall, as from a horse. [Middle English *spillen*, destroy, kill, shed (blood), spill, Old English *spillan*. See **spel-**[1] in Appendix.*] —**spill′er** *n.*

spill[2] (spĭl) *n.* **1.** A piece of wood or rolled paper used to light a fire. **2.** A small peg used as a plug; a spile. [Probably from Middle Low German or Middle Dutch *spile*. See **spei-** in Appendix.*]

spill·age (spĭl′ĭj) *n.* **1.** An act of spilling. **2.** The amount spilled.

spill·way (spĭl′wā′) *n.* A channel for reservoir overflow.

spilth (spĭlth) *n.* Spillage. [From SPILL.]

spin (spĭn) *v.* **spun** (spŭn) or *archaic* **span** (spăn), **spinning, spins.** —*tr.* **1.** To draw out and twist (fibers) into thread. **2.** To form (thread or yarn) in this manner. **3.** To form (a thread, web, cocoon, or the like) by extruding viscous filaments. **4.** To make or produce by or as by drawing out and twisting. **5.** To prolong or extend. Used with *out.* **6.** To relate, especially imaginatively: *"fellows who spin interminable yarns"* (Melville). **7.** To cause to rotate swiftly; twirl. —*intr.* **1.** To make thread or yarn by the drawing out and twisting of fibers. **2.** To extrude viscous filaments, forming thread. Used of an insect. **3.** To rotate rapidly; whirl. **4.** To seem to be whirling, as from dizziness; to reel. **5.** To ride or drive rapidly. **6.** To fish with spinning tackle. —See Synonyms at **turn.** —*n.* **1.** The act of spinning. **2.** A swift whirling motion. **3.** A state of mental confusion. **4.** *Informal.* A short excursion in a vehicle. **5.** The flight condition of an aircraft in a nose-down, spiraling, stalled descent. **6.** *Physics.* **a.** The intrinsic angular momentum of a subatomic particle. **b.** The total angular momentum of an atomic nucleus. **c.** A nonnegative integral or half-integral quantum number that specifies the value of such momenta in units of Planck's constant divided by 2π. [Spin, spun, spun; Middle English *spinnen*, *spon* (plural), *spunne*, Old English *spinnan*, *spunnon* (plural), *gespunnen*. See **spen-** in Appendix.*]

spin·ach (spĭn′ĭch) *n.* **1.** A widely cultivated plant, *Spinacia oleracea*, native to Asia, having succulent, edible leaves. **2.** The leaves of this plant, eaten as a vegetable. [Old French *espinache*, from Old Spanish *espinaca*, from Arabic *isfānākh*.]

spi·nal (spī′nəl) *adj.* **1.** Of, pertaining to, or situated near the spine or spinal cord; vertebral. **2.** Resembling a spine or spinous part. —*n.* A spinal anesthetic. —**spi′nal·ly** *adv.*

spinal anesthesia. Partial or complete anesthesia produced by injecting an anesthetic substance into the spinal canal.

spinal canal. The canal formed by the successive openings in the vertebrae through which the spinal cord and its membranes pass. Also called "vertebral canal."

spinal column. The columnar assemblage of articulated vertebrae extending from the cranium to the coccyx or the end of the tail, encasing the spinal cord and forming the supporting axis of the body; the backbone. Also called "vertebral column."

spinal cord. The part of the central nervous system contained within the spinal canal and continuous at its cranial end with the medulla oblongata. Also called "spinal marrow."

spinal meningitis. *Pathology.* **Cerebrospinal meningitis** *(see)*.

spin·dle (spĭnd′l) *n.* **1. a.** A notched stick for spinning fibers into thread by hand. **b.** A pin or rod holding a bobbin or spool upon which thread is wound on a spinning wheel or spinning machine. **2.** Any of various slender mechanical parts that revolve or serve as axes for larger revolving parts, as in a lock or an axle. **3.** *Biology.* The axis between cytoplasm centers, along which the chromosomes are distributed in mitosis. —*v.* **spindled, -dling, -dles.** —*tr.* To impale or perforate on the spike of

ă pat/ā pay/âr care/ä father/b bib/ch church/d deed/ĕ pet/ē be/f fife/g gag/h hat/hw which/ĭ pit/ī pie/îr pier/j judge/k kick/l lid, needle/m mum/n no, sudden/ng thing/ŏ pot/ō toe/ô paw, for/oi noise/ou out/o͝o took/o͞o boot/p pop/r roar/s sauce/sh ship, dish/

a spindle: *Do not fold, spindle, or mutilate this card.* —*intr.* To grow into a thin, elongated, or weakly form. [Middle English *spindel,* rod of a spinning wheel, Old English *spinel.* See **spen-** in Appendix.*]

spin·dle·legs (spĭnd′l-lĕgz′) *pl.n.* Long, thin legs. Also called "spindleshanks."

spindle tree. Any of various shrubs or trees of the genus *Euonymus,* many species of which have brightly colored fruit. [So called because the wood is often used to make spindles.]

spin·dling (spĭnd′lĭng) *adj.* Spindly.

spin·dly (spĭnd′lē) *adj.* **-dlier, -dliest. 1.** Slender and elongated. **2.** Of weak growth.

spin·drift (spĭn′drĭft′) *n.* Wind-blown sea spray. Also called "spoondrift." [Variant of SPOONDRIFT.]

spine (spīn) *n.* **1.** The spinal column of a vertebrate. **2.** *Zoology.* Any of various pointed projections, processes, or appendages of animals. **3.** *Botany.* A sharp-pointed, usually woody process arising from the stem of a plant; a thorn. **4.** The hinged back of a book. **5.** Anything that resembles a spine. [Middle English, from Old French *espine,* from Latin *spīna,* thorn, prickle, spine. See **spei-** in Appendix.*]

spi·nel (spə-nĕl′) *n.* Any of several hard white, orange, red, green, blue, or black minerals with composition $MgAl_2O_4$, the red variety being valued as a gem. [Italian *spinella,* diminutive of *spina,* thorn (from its sharply pointed crystals), from Latin *spīna.* See **spei-** in Appendix.*]

spine·less (spīn′lĭs) *adj.* **1.** Lacking a vertebral column. **2.** Having no spiny processes. **3.** Lacking in courage or will power. —**spine′less·ness** *n.*

spi·nes·cent (spī-nĕs′ənt) *adj. Biology.* **1.** Having a spine or spines. **2.** Having or tending toward the form of a spine. [Late Latin *spīnescens,* present participle of *spīnescere,* to grow thorny, from Latin *spīna,* thorn, SPINE.] —**spi·nes′cence** *n.*

spin·et (spĭn′ĭt) *n.* **1.** A small, compact upright piano. **2.** A small harpsichord with a single keyboard. [Obsolete French *espinette,* from Italian *spinetta,* perhaps after its inventor, Giovanni *Spinetti,* Venetian spinet maker, about 1503.]

spi·nif·er·ous (spī-nĭf′ər-əs) *adj.* Also **spi·nig·er·ous** (-nĭj′ər-əs). Spine-bearing; spiny. [From Latin *spīnifer* : Latin *spīna,* thorn, SPINE + -FEROUS.]

spin·i·fex (spī′nə-fĕks′) *n.* Any of various Australian grasses, chiefly of the genus *Spinifex,* growing in arid regions and having spiny leaves or seeds. [New Latin : SPIN(E) + Latin *-fex,* "maker" (see **dhē-¹** in Appendix*).]

spin·na·ker (spĭn′ə-kər) *n.* A large triangular sail set on a spar that swings out opposite the mainsail, used on racing yachts when running before the wind. [Probably from *Sphinx,* name of the first yacht to carry a spinnaker sail, in about 1866.]

spin·ner (spĭn′ər) *n.* **1.** One that spins. **2.** An angler's lure that spins rapidly. **3.** A fairing fitted over the hub of the propeller in some aircraft. **4.** A device consisting of a dial and an arrow that is spun to indicate the next move in a board game.

spin·ner·et (spĭn′ə-rĕt′) *n.* **1.** *Zoology.* A posterior structure in spiders and certain insect larvae, containing passages through which silky filaments are secreted. **2.** A device for making rayon, nylon, and other synthetic fibers, consisting of a plate pierced with holes through which plastic material is extruded in filaments. [SPINNER + -ET.]

spin·ner·y (spĭn′ə-rē) *n., pl.* **-ies.** A spinning mill.

spin·ney (spĭn′ē) *n., pl.* **-neys.** *Chiefly British.* A small grove; copse. [Old French *espinei,* thicket, from Vulgar Latin *spīnēta* (unattested), from Latin *spīnētum,* thorn hedge, from *spīna,* thorn. See **spei-** in Appendix.*]

spin·ning (spĭn′ĭng) *n.* The process of making fibrous material into yarn or thread. —*adj.* Of, for, or used in spinning.

spinning frame. A machine that draws and twists fibers into yarn and winds it on spindles.

spinning jenny. An early form of spinning machine having several spindles.

spinning wheel. An apparatus for making yarn or thread, consisting of a foot- or hand-driven wheel and a single spindle.

spin-off (spĭn′ôf′, -ŏf′) *n.* An object, product, or enterprise derived from a larger, more or less unrelated entity or enterprise.

spi·nose (spī′nōs′) *adj.* Bearing spines; spiny. [Latin *spīnōsus,* from *spīna,* thorn, SPINE.] —**spi′nose′ly** *adv.* —**spi·nos′i·ty** (-nŏs′ə-tē) *n.*

spi·nous (spī′nəs) *adj.* **1.** Resembling a spine or thorn. **2.** Having spines or similar projections; spiny.

spinous process. The rearward projection from the arch of a vertebra, which with those of the other vertebrae forms the spine.

Spi·no·za (spĭ-nō′zə), **Baruch.** Known as Benedict de Spinoza. 1632–1677. Dutch philosopher and theologian.

Spi·no·zism (spĭ-nō′zĭz′əm) *n.* The philosophy of Spinoza; monistic idealism.

spin·ster (spĭn′stər) *n.* **1.** A woman who has remained single beyond the conventional age for marrying. **2.** *British Law.* Any single woman. **3.** A woman whose occupation is spinning. [Middle English *spinnester* : *spinnen,* SPIN + -STER.] —**spin′ster·hood′** *n.*

spin·thar·i·scope (spĭn-thăr′ə-skōp′) *n.* A device for observing individual scintillations produced by ionizing radiation, consisting of a tube with a magnifying lens at one end and a phosphorescent screen and a speck of radioactive salt at the other. [Greek *spintharis*†, spark + -SCOPE.] —**spin·thar′i·scop′ic** (spĭn-thăr′ə-skŏp′ĭk) *adj.*

spi·nule (spīn′yo͞ol) *n.* A small spine or thorn. [Latin *spīnula,* diminutive of *spīna,* thorn, SPINE.]

spin-the-bottle (spĭn′*th*ə-bŏt′l) *n.* A game in which a spinning bottle is used to determine one's partner, as for kissing.

spin·u·lose (spĭn′yə-lōs′) *adj.* Also **spin·u·lous** (spĭn′yə-ləs). **1.** Having spinules; minutely spiny. **2.** Shaped like a spinule.

spin·y (spī′nē) *adj.* **-ier, -iest. 1.** Bearing or covered with spines, thorns, or similar stiff projections. **2.** Shaped like a spine. **3.** Difficult; troublesome. —**spin′i·ness** *n.*

spiny anteater. A mammal, the **echidna** *(see).*

spin·y-finned (spī′nē-fĭnd′) *adj.* Having fins supported by sharp, spiny, inflexible rays. Also "spiny-rayed." Compare **soft-finned.**

spiny lobster. Any of various edible marine decapod crustaceans of the family Palinuridae, having a spiny carapace and lacking the large pincers characteristic of true lobsters. Also called "langouste," "rock lobster," and sometimes "crayfish."

spir·a·cle (spī′rə-kəl, spĭr′ə-) *n.* **1.** *Zoology.* A respiratory aperture, such as: **a.** Any of several tracheal openings in the exoskeleton of an insect or spider. **b.** A small respiratory opening behind the eye of fishes, such as sharks, rays, and skates. **c.** The blowhole of a cetacean. **2.** *Geology.* A small volcanic vent formed by gases on a lava flow. **3.** Any aperture or opening through which air is admitted and expelled. [Latin *spīrāculum,* a breathing hole, from *spīrāre,* to breathe. See **spīrāre** in Appendix.*] —**spi·rac′u·lar** (spī-răk′yə-lər, spĭ-) *adj.*

spi·ral (spī′rəl) *n.* **1.** The locus in a plane of a point moving around a fixed center at a monotonically increasing or decreasing distance from the center. **2.** The three-dimensional locus of a point moving parallel to and about a central axis at a constant or continuously varying distance; a helix. **3.** Something having the form of such a curve: *spirals of smoke.* **4.** The course or flight path of an object rotating on its longitudinal axis, as of an airplane or football. **5.** A continuously accelerating increase or decrease: *the wage-price spiral.* —*adj.* **1.** Of or resembling a spiral. **2.** Coiling in a constantly changing plane; helical. **3.** Circling around to form a series of constantly changing planes, as a spring. —*v.* **spiraled** or **-ralled, -raling** or **-ralling, -rals.** —*intr.* **1.** To take a spiral form or course. **2.** To rise or fall with steady acceleration. See Usage note below. —*tr.* To cause to take a spiral form or course. [Medieval Latin *spīrālis,* from Latin *spīra,* coil, SPIRE (spiral).] —**spi·ral′i·ty** *n.* —**spi′ral·ly** *adv.*

Usage: *Spiral* (verb) is widely used intransitively in the sense of steady upward movement of prices, costs, wages, and the like, without accompanying terms to specify direction: *Prices are spiraling* (acceptable to 78 per cent of the Usage Panel).

spiral binding. A binding for notebooks and booklets in which a cylindrical spiral of wire or plastic is passed through a row of punched holes at the edge of each sheet.

spiral galaxy. A galaxy having a spiral structure with spiral arms consisting mainly of gas, dust, and stars. Formerly called "spiral nebula."

spi·rant (spī′rənt) *n. Phonetics.* A **fricative** *(see).* —*adj. Phonetics.* Fricative. [Latin *spīrāns,* present participle of Latin *spīrāre,* to breathe. See **spiracle.**]

spire¹ (spīr) *n.* **1.** The top part or point of something that tapers upward; a pinnacle. **2.** A formation or structure that tapers to a point at the top, as a steeple. **3.** A slender, tapering part, such as a newly sprouting blade of grass. —*v.* **spired, spiring, spires.** —*tr.* To furnish with a spire or spires. —*intr.* To rise taperingly, like a spire. [Middle English *spir(e),* slender stalk, Old English *spīr.* See **spei-** in Appendix.*]

spire² (spīr) *n.* **1.** A spiral, especially a single turn of a spiral; a whorl. **2.** *Zoology.* The area farthest from the aperture and nearest the apex on a coiled gastropod shell. [French, from Latin *spīra,* a coil, twist, spire, from Greek *speira.* See **sper-²** in Appendix.*]

spi·re·a (spī-rē′ə) *n.* Also **spi·rae·a.** Any of various plants or shrubs of the genus *Spiraea,* having clusters of small white or pink flowers, and including the bridal wreath, hardhack, and meadowsweet. [Latin *spīraea,* meadowsweet, from Greek *speiraia,* from *speira,* coil, SPIRE.]

spi·reme (spī′rēm′) *n.* Also **spi·rem** (spī′rĕm). *Biology.* **1.** The tangle of filaments that appears at the beginning of the prophase portion of meiosis or mitosis. **2.** One of these filaments. [German *Spirem,* from Greek *speirēma,* coil, from *speira,* coil, SPIRE.]

Spires. See **Speyer.**

spi·rif·er·ous (spī-rĭf′ər-əs) *adj.* Having a spire, spiral structure, or spiral parts. [SPIR(E) + -FEROUS.]

spi·ril·lum (spī-rĭl′əm) *n., pl.* **-rilla** (-rĭl′ə). Any of various flagellated aerobic bacteria of the genus *Spirillum,* having an elongated spiral form. [New Latin, diminutive of Latin *spīra,* SPIRE (spiral).]

spir·it (spĭr′ĭt) *n.* **1.** That which is traditionally believed to be the vital principle or animating force within living beings. **2.** *Capital* **S.** The Holy Ghost. Preceded by *the.* **3.** *Capital* **S.** *Christian Science.* God. **4.** Any supernatural being, such as a ghost. **5. a.** That which constitutes one's unseen, intangible being. **b.** The essential and activating principle of a person; the will. **6.** A person as characterized by some stated quality: *He is a proud spirit.* **7.** An inclination or tendency of a specified kind. **8.** *Plural.* One's mood or emotional state. **9.** A particular mood or emotional state characterized by vigor and animation. **10.** Strong loyalty or dedication. **11.** The predominant mood of an occasion or period: *"The spirit of 1776 is not dead."* (Jefferson). **12.** The real sense or significance of something: *the spirit of the law.* **13.** *Often plural.* An alcohol solution of an essential or volatile substance. **14.** *Plural.* An alcoholic beverage. —*tr.v.* **spirited, -iting, -its. 1.** To carry off mysteriously or

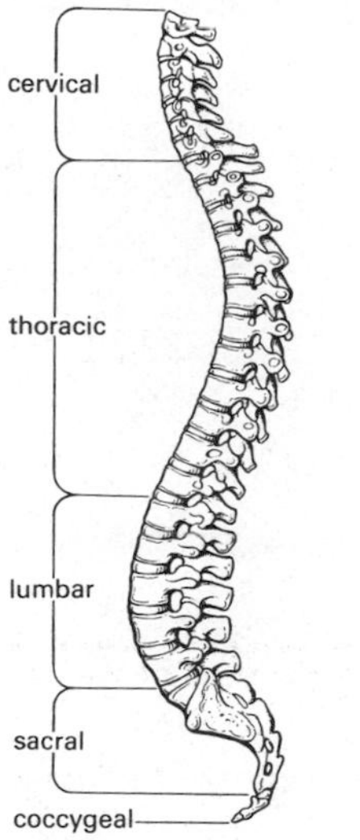
cervical
thoracic
lumbar
sacral
coccygeal

spine
Side view of the human spine

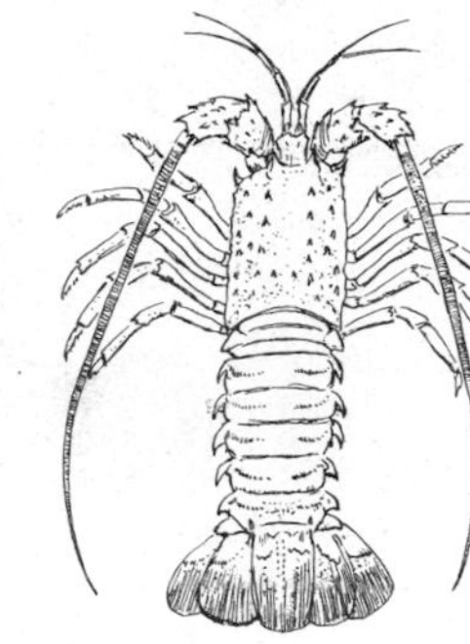

spiny lobster
Genus *Panulirus*

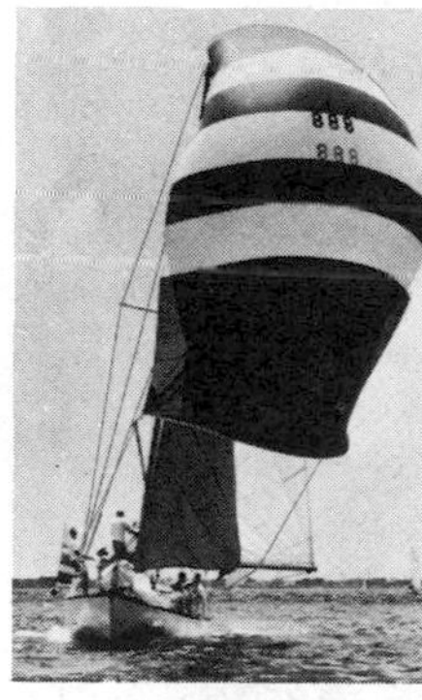

spinnaker

t tight/th thin, path/*th* this, bathe/ŭ cut/ûr urge/v valve/w with/y yes/z zebra, size/zh vision/ə about, item, edible, gallop, circus/ à *Fr.* ami/œ *Fr.* feu, *Ger.* schön/ü *Fr.* tu, *Ger.* über/KH *Ger.* ich, *Scot.* loch/N *Fr.* bon. ***Follows main vocabulary.** †**Of obscure origin.**

secretly. Used with *away* or *off.* **2.** To impart courage, animation, or determination to; stimulate; encourage. [Middle English, from Norman French, from Latin *spīritus,* breath, breath of a god, inspiration, from *spīrāre,* to breathe. See **spīrāre** in Appendix.*]

spir·it·ed (spĭr′ĭ-tĭd) *adj.* **1.** Full of or characterized by animation, vigor, or courage: *"Many of the men engaged in a spirited debate"* (Stephen Crane). **2.** Having a specified mood or nature. Used in combination: *high-spirited.* —**spir′it·ed·ly** *adv.* —**spir′it·ed·ness** *n.*

spir·it·ism (spĭr′ĭ-tĭz′əm) *n.* Spiritualism. —**spir′it·ist** *n.* —**spir′it·is′tic** *adj.*

spirit lamp. A lamp using alcohol or other liquid fuel.

spir·it·less (spĭr′ĭt-lĭs) *adj.* Lacking energy or enthusiasm; listless. —**spir′it·less·ly** *adv.* —**spir′it·less·ness** *n.*

spirit level. A leveling device, a **level** *(see).*

spir·it·ous (spĭr′ĭ-təs) *adj.* **1.** Spirituous. **2.** *Archaic.* Highly refined; pure.

spirits of ammonia. Also **spirit of ammonia.** A colorless aromatic solution made from ammonium carbonate, ammonia water, alcohol, and water, with small amounts of various aromatic agents, used as a remedy for faintness.

spirits of turpentine. Also **spirit of turpentine.** Refined turpentine.

spirits of wine. Also **spirit of wine.** Rectified ethyl alcohol.

spir·i·tu·al (spĭr′ĭ-cho͞o-əl) *adj.* **1.** Of, relating to, consisting of, or having the nature of spirit; not tangible or material. **2.** Of, concerned with, or affecting the soul. **3.** Of, from, or pertaining to God; deific. **4.** Of or belonging to a church or religion; ecclesiastical; sacred. **5.** Pertaining to or having the nature of spirits; supernatural. —*n.* **1. a.** A religious folk song of American Negro origin. **b.** Any work composed in imitation of a Negro spiritual. **2.** *Usually plural.* Religious, spiritual, or ecclesiastical matters. —**spir′i·tu·al·ly** *adv.* —**spir′i·tu·al·ness** *n.*

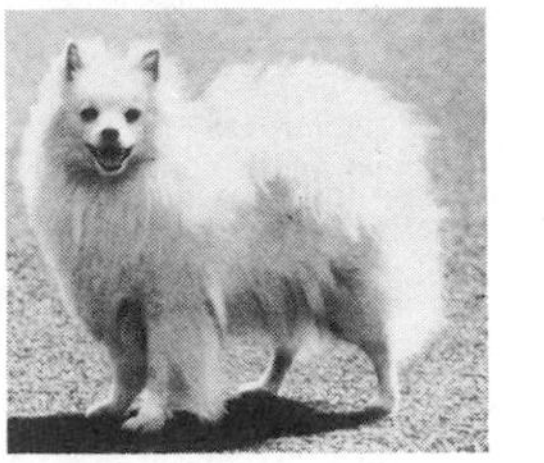

spitz

spir·i·tu·al·ism (spĭr′ĭ-cho͞o-ə-lĭz′əm, -chə-lĭz′əm) *n.* **1. a.** The belief that the dead communicate with the living, usually through a medium. **b.** The practices or doctrines of those holding such a belief. **2.** Any philosophy, doctrine, or religion emphasizing the spiritual rather than the material. —**spir′i·tu·al·ist** *n.* —**spir′i·tu·al·is′tic** *adj.*

spir·i·tu·al·i·ty (spĭr′ĭ-cho͞o-ăl′ə-tē) *n., pl.* **-ties.** **1.** The state, quality, or fact of being spiritual. **2.** Ecclesiastics collectively; the clergy; spiritualty. **3.** *Often plural.* Something belonging to the church or to an ecclesiastic, as property or revenue.

spir·i·tu·al·ize (spĭr′ĭ-cho͞o-ə-līz′, -chə-līz′) *tr.v.* **-ized, -izing, -izes.** **1.** To impart a spiritual nature to; refine; purify. **2.** To invest with or treat as having a spiritual sense or meaning. —**spir′i·tu·al·i·za′tion** *n.* —**spir′i·tu·al·iz′er** *n.*

spir·i·tu·al·ty (spĭr′ĭ-cho͞o-əl-tē, -chəl-tē) *n., pl.* **-ties.** Spiritualty.

spir·i·tu·el (spĭr′ĭ-cho͞o-ĕl′; *French* spē-rē-tü-ĕl′) *adj. Feminine* **spir·i·tu·elle.** Having or evidencing a refined mind and wit. [French, "spiritual."]

spir·i·tu·ous (spĭr′ĭ-cho͞o-əs) *adj.* Having the nature of or containing alcohol; alcoholic. —**spir′i·tu·os′i·ty** (-ŏs′ə-tē), **spir′i·tu·ous·ness** *n.*

spiro–. Indicates spiral or coiled form; for example, **spirochete.** [Latin *spīra,* coil, SPIRE.]

spi·ro·chete (spī′rə-kēt′) *n.* Also **spi·ro·chaete.** Any of various slender, nonflagellated, twisted microorganisms of the order Spirochaetales, many of which are pathogenic, causing syphilis, relapsing fever, yaws, and other diseases. [New Latin *Spirochaeta* (genus) : SPIRO- + CHAETA.] —**spi′ro·che′tal** *adj.*

spi·ro·che·to·sis (spī′rə-kē-tō′sĭs) *n.* Any of various diseases, such as syphilis, caused by a spirochete. [New Latin : SPIROCHET(E) + -OSIS.]

splay

spi·ro·graph (spī′rə-grăf′, -gräf′) *n.* An instrument for registering the depth and rapidity of respiratory movements. [Latin *spīr(āre),* to breathe (see **spirit**) + -GRAPH.]

spi·ro·gy·ra (spī′rə-jī′rə) *n.* Any of various green, filamentous freshwater algae of the genus *Spirogyra,* having chloroplasts in spirally twisted bands. [New Latin : SPIRO- + Greek *guros,* ring (see **ku-** in Appendix*).]

spi·roid (spī′roid) *adj.* Having resemblance to a spiral. [New Latin *spiroides,* from Greek *speiroeidēs* : *speira,* SPIRE + -OID.]

spi·rom·e·ter (spī-rŏm′ə-tər) *n.* An instrument for measuring the volume of air entering and leaving the lungs. [Latin *spīr(āre),* to breathe (see **spirit**) + -METER.]

spirt. *Chiefly British.* Variant of **spurt.**

spir·u·la (spĭr′ə-lə, -yə-lə) *n., pl.* **-lae** (-lē′). Any small cephalopod mollusk of the genus *Spirula,* having a spirally coiled, partitioned internal shell. [Late Latin *spīrula,* small twisted cake or cracknel, diminutive of Latin *spīra,* coil, SPIRE.]

spit[1] (spĭt) *n.* **1.** Saliva, especially when expectorated; spittle. **2.** The act of spitting. **3.** Something resembling saliva, such as the frothy secretion of certain insects. **4.** A brief, scattered fall of rain or snow. —*v.* **spat** (spăt) or **spit, spitting, spits.** —*tr.* **1.** To eject from the mouth. Often used with *out.* **2. a.** To eject as if by spitting. **b.** To utter in a violent manner. Often used with *out: spit out an insult.* —*intr.* **1.** To expectorate. **2.** To express contempt or animosity by or as if by spitting. **3.** To make a hissing or sputtering noise. **4.** To rain or snow in light, scattered drops or flakes. [Middle English *spitten,* Old English *spittan.* See **spyeu-** in Appendix.*]

spit[2] (spĭt) *n.* **1.** A slender, pointed rod on which meat is impaled for broiling. **2.** A narrow point of land extending into a body of water. —*tr.v.* **spitted, spitting, spits.** To impale on or as if on a spit. [Middle English *spit(e),* Old English *spitu.* See **spei-** in Appendix.*]

spit·al (spĭt′l) *n. Obsolete.* A hospital; especially, one for contagious diseases. [Variant of obsolete *spittle,* shortened variant of HOSPITAL.]

spit·ball (spĭt′bôl′) *n.* **1.** A piece of paper chewed and shaped into a lump for use as a projectile. **2.** *Baseball.* An illegal pitch in which the ball is moistened on one side with spit. In this sense, also called "spitter."

spite (spīt) *n.* **1.** Malicious ill will prompting an urge to hurt or humiliate another. **2.** An instance of such feeling. —**in spite of.** Regardless of; despite. See Synonyms at **notwithstanding.** —*tr.v.* **spited, spiting, spites.** **1.** To show spite toward or vent spite upon. **2.** To fill with spite; annoy. [Middle English, insult, ill will, short for Old French *despit.* See **despite.**]

spite·ful (spīt′fəl) *adj.* Filled with, prompted by, or showing spite; malicious. See Synonyms at **vindictive.** —**spite′ful·ly** *adv.* —**spite′ful·ness** *n.*

spit·fire (spĭt′fīr′) *n.* A quick-tempered or highly excitable person, especially a girl or woman.

Spits·ber·gen (spĭts′bûr′gən). Also **Spitz·ber·gen.** A Norwegian archipelago in the Arctic Ocean, 23,658 square miles in area, located between Greenland and Franz Josef Land.

spit·ter (spĭt′ər) *n.* **1.** One that spits. **2.** *Baseball.* A **spitball** *(see).* **3.** A young deer with unbranched horns; pricket.

spitting image. Also **spit and image.** A perfect likeness or counterpart. [Perhaps from the phrase *the very spit of,* an exact likeness, as if the image has been "spit out."]

spit·tle (spĭt′l) *n.* **1.** Spit; saliva. **2.** The frothy liquid secreted by spittlebugs. [Middle English *spetil,* Old English *spātl.* See **spyeu-** in Appendix.*]

spit·tle·bug (spĭt′l-bŭg′) *n.* Any of various insects of the family Cercopidae, the nymphs of which form frothy masses of liquid on plant stems. Also called "spittle insect," "froghopper."

spit·toon (spĭ-to͞on′) *n.* A bowl-shaped, usually metal vessel for spitting into. Also called "cuspidor." [SPIT + *-oon,* in such words as BALLOON and DOUBLOON.]

spitz (spĭts) *n.* A dog of a breed originating in Germany, having a long, thick, usually white coat and a tail curled over the back. [German *Spitz,* from *spitz,* "pointed" (from its pointed muzzle), from Old High German *spizzi.* See **spei-** in Appendix.*]

Spitz·en·burg (spĭts′ən-bûrg′) *n.* Also **spitz·en·burg, Spitz·en·berg, spitz·en·berg.** A variety of apple having red and yellow fruit. [Probably from American Dutch : *spits,* pointed (from the apple's shape), from Middle Dutch *spitz* (see **spei-** in Appendix*) + *berg,* hill (from its discovery on a hill near Esopus, New York), from Middle Dutch *berch* (see **bhergh-**[2] in Appendix*).]

spiv (spĭv) *n. British Slang.* A flashy swindler or black marketeer. [From dialectal *spiff*†, dandy.]

splanch·nic (splăngk′nĭk) *adj.* Of or relating to the viscera; visceral: *a splanchnic nerve.* [Greek *splankhnikos,* of the bowels, from *splankhna,* inward parts. See **spelgh-** in Appendix.*]

splash (splăsh) *v.* **splashed, splashing, splashes.** —*tr.* **1.** To dash or scatter (a liquid) about in flying masses. **2.** To dash liquid upon; wet or soil with flying masses of liquid. **3.** To cause to dash a liquid about. —*intr.* **1.** To cause a liquid to fly in scattered masses. **2.** To fall into or move through liquid with this effect. **3.** To move, spill, or fly about in scattered masses. —*n.* **1.** The act or sound of splashing. **2.** A flying mass of liquid. **3.** A marking produced by or as if by scattered liquid: *a splash of light.* **4.** A great though often short-lived impression; a stir. [Variant of PLASH (splash).] —**splash′er** *n.*

splash·board (splăsh′bôrd′, -bōrd′) *n.* **1.** A structure that protects a vehicle from splashes of mud. **2.** A screen on a boat to keep water from splashing on the deck. **3.** A board for closing a spillway or sluice.

splash·down (splăsh′doun′) *n.* The landing of a missile or spacecraft on water or its moment of impact.

splash·y (splăsh′ē) *adj.* **-ier, -iest.** **1.** Making or liable to make splashes. **2.** Covered with splashes of color. **3.** Showy; ostentatious. —**splash′i·ly** *adv.* —**splash′i·ness** *n.*

splat[1] (splăt) *n.* A slat of wood, such as one in the middle of a chair back. [Origin uncertain.]

splat[2] (splăt) *n.* A slapping noise. —*adv.* With a splat. [Origin uncertain.]

splat·ter (splăt′ər) *v.* **-tered, -tering, -ters.** —*tr.* To spatter (something); especially, to soil with splashes of liquid. —*intr.* To spatter; especially, to move or fall so as to cause heavy splashes. —*n.* A splash of liquid. [Perhaps a blend of SPLASH and SPATTER.]

splay (splā) *adj.* **1.** Spread or turned out. **2.** Clumsy or clumsily formed; awkward. —*n.* **1.** Expansion; spread. **2.** *Architecture.* An oblique slope given to the sides of an opening in a wall so that the opening is wider at one face than at the other. —*v.* **splayed, splaying, splays.** —*tr.* **1.** To spread (the limbs, for example) out or apart, especially clumsily. **2.** To make slanting or sloping; to bevel. **3.** To dislocate (a bone). Used of an animal. —*intr.* **1.** To be spread out or apart. **2.** To slant or slope. [From Middle English *spluyen,* to spread out, short for *displayen,* to DISPLAY.]

splay·foot (splā′fo͝ot′) *n., pl.* **-feet** (-fēt′). **1.** A physical deformity characterized by abnormally flat and turned-out feet. **2.** A foot of this kind. —**splay′foot′ed** *adj.*

spleen (splēn) *n.* **1.** One of the largest lymphoid structures, a visceral organ composed of a white pulp of lymphatic nodules and tissue and a red pulp of venous sinusoids in a framework of fibrous partitions lying on the left side below the diaphragm, functioning as a blood filter and to store blood. **2.** A homologous organ or tissue in other vertebrates. Also called "milt." **3.** *Obsolete.* **a.** This organ considered as the seat of mirth.

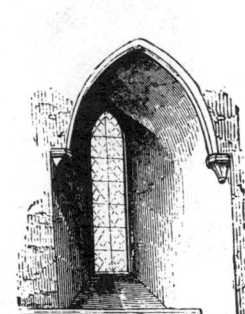

b. Merriment. c. Caprice. 4. *Archaic.* a. This organ considered as the seat of melancholy. b. Melancholy. 5. Ill temper. [Middle English *splen(e)*, from Old French *esplen*, from Latin *splēn*, from Greek. See **spelgh-** in Appendix.*] —**spleen'y** *adj.*

spleen·ful (splēn'fəl) *adj.* Ill-humored; peevish; irritable. [The spleen was once thought of as the seat of negative emotions.] —**spleen'ful·ly** *adv.*

spleen·wort (splēn'wûrt', -wôrt') *n.* Any of various ferns of the genus *Asplenium*, having featherlike, often evergreen fronds. [So called because it was thought to cure spleen disorders.]

splen·dent (splĕn'dənt) *adj.* 1. Shining or lustrous; brilliant. 2. Celebrated; illustrious. [Middle English, from Latin *splendēns*, present participle of *splendēre*, to shine. See **splendid.**]

splen·did (splĕn'dĭd) *adj.* 1. Brilliant with light or color; radiant. 2. Imposing by reason of showiness or grandeur; magnificent. 3. Glorious; illustrious. 4. Admirable for boldness or purity; transcendent. 5. Very good or satisfying; praiseworthy. [French *splendide*, from Latin *splendidus*, from *splendēre*, to shine. See **spel-**[2] in Appendix.*] —**splen'did·ly** *adv.* —**splen'did·ness** *n.*

splen·dif·er·ous (splĕn-dĭf'ər-əs) *adj.* Splendid. Often used ironically. [Middle English, from Medieval Latin *splendiferus* : SPLENDID + -FEROUS.]

splen·dor (splĕn'dər) *n.* Also *British* **splen·dour.** 1. Great light or luster; brilliance. 2. a. Magnificent appearance or display; grandeur. b. Something grand or magnificent. 3. Illustriousness; glory. [Middle English *splendure*, from Old French *splendeur*, from Latin *splendor*, from *splendēre*, to shine. See **splendid.**] —**splen'dor·ous, splen'drous** (splĕn'drəs) *adj.*

sple·net·ic (splĭ-nĕt'ĭk) *adj.* Also **sple·net·i·cal** (-nĕt'ĭ-kəl), *rare* **splen·i·tive** (splĕn'ə-tĭv). 1. Of or pertaining to the spleen. 2. Ill-humored; peevish; irritable. —*n.* An ill-humored person. [Late Latin *splēnēticus*, from Latin *splēn*, SPLEEN.] —**sple·net'i·cal·ly** *adv.*

splen·ic (splĕn'ĭk) *adj.* Of, in, near, or pertaining to the spleen. [Latin *splēnicus*, from Greek *splēnikos*, from *splēn*, SPLEEN.]

sple·ni·tis (splĭ-nī'tĭs) *n.* Inflammation of the spleen. [Greek *splēnitis* : *splēn*, SPLEEN + -ITIS.]

sple·ni·us (splē'nē-əs) *n., pl.* **-nii** (-nē-ī'). Either of two muscles of the back of the neck, extending from the vertebral column to the skull, that rotate and extend the head and neck. [New Latin, from Latin *splēnium*, patch, plaster, spleenwort, from Greek *splēnion*, from *splēn*, SPLEEN.] —**sple'ni·al** *adj.*

sple·no·meg·a·ly (splē'nō-mĕg'ə-lē) *n.* Enlargement of the spleen. [Latin *splēn*, SPLEEN + MEGAL(O)- + -Y.]

splice (splīs) *tr.v.* **spliced, splicing, splices.** 1. a. To join (film or wire, for example) at the ends. b. To join ropes by interweaving strands. 2. To join (pieces of wood) by overlapping and binding at the ends. 3. *Informal.* To unite in marriage. —*n.* 1. A joint made by splicing. 2. The place where parts have been spliced. [Probably from Middle Dutch *splissen.* See **splei-** in Appendix.*] —**splic'er** *n.*

spline (splīn) *n.* 1. a. Any of a series of projections on a shaft that fit into slots on a corresponding shaft, enabling both to rotate together. b. The groove or slot for such a projection. 2. A flexible piece of wood, hard rubber, or metal used in drawing curves. 3. A wooden or metal strip; a slat. [Origin obscure.]

splint (splĭnt) *n.* 1. A thin piece split off from a larger piece; a splinter. 2. Any rigid device used to prevent motion of a joint or the ends of a fractured bone. 3. A thin, flexible wooden strip, such as one used in the making of baskets and chair bottoms. 4. A plate or strip of metal. 5. A bony enlargement of the cannon bone or splint bone of a horse. —*tr.v.* **splinted, splinting, splints.** To support or restrict with or as if with a splint. [Middle English *splent, splint*, small strip of metal, splint, from Middle Low German or Middle Dutch *splinte.* See **splei-** in Appendix.*]

splint bone. Either of two small metacarpal or metatarsal bones in horses or related animals.

splin·ter (splĭn'tər) *n.* 1. A sharp, slender piece, as of wood, bone, glass, or metal, split or broken off from a main body. 2. A group that has broken away from a parent group, as a church or political party. In this sense, also called "splinter group." —*v.* **splintered, -tering, -ters.** —*intr.* To split or break into sharp, slender pieces; form splinters. —*tr.* To cause to splinter. —See Synonyms at **break.** [Middle English, from Middle Dutch. See **splei-** in Appendix.*] —**splin'ter·y** *adj.*

split (splĭt) *v.* **split, splitting, splits.** —*tr.* 1. To divide sharply or cleanly, especially into lengthwise sections or into two parts of approximately equal size. 2. To break, burst, or rip apart with force; rend. 3. To separate (persons or groups); disunite. 4. To divide and share: *split a meal.* 5. To separate (leather, for example) into layers. 6. To mark (a vote or ballot) in favor of candidates from different parties. 7. *Sports.* To win half the games of (a series or double-header). —*intr.* 1. To become separated into parts; especially, to divide lengthwise. 2. To become broken or ripped apart, especially from internal pressure. 3. To become divided or part company as a result of discord or disagreement. Often used with *up.* 4. To divide or share something with others. —See Synonyms at **break, tear.** —**split hairs.** To see or make trivial distinctions; to quibble. —*n.* 1. The act or result of splitting. 2. A breach or rupture in a group; schism. 3. A splinter. 4. Something divided and portioned out; a share. 5. A split strip of flexible wood used in basketmaking. 6. *Informal.* a. A bottle of an alcoholic or carbonated beverage half the usual size, usually about six ounces. b. A drink of half the usual quantity. c. A half pint. 7. A dessert of sliced fruit, ice cream, and toppings: *banana split.* 8. *Often plural.* An acrobatic feat in which the legs are stretched out in opposite directions at right angles to the trunk. 9. A single thickness of a split hide. 10. *Bowling.* An arrangement of pins left standing after the first bowl with one or more intermediate pins knocked down. —*adj.* 1. Divided or separated. 2. Fissured longitudinally; cleft. 3. *Stock Market.* Quoted in 16ths rather than in 8ths. [Dutch *splitten*, from Middle Dutch. See **splei-** in Appendix.*] —**split'ter** *n.*

Split (splĭt). *Italian* **Spa·la·to** (spä'lä-tō'). A city and seaport of Yugoslavia, in southern Croatia. Population, 133,000.

split infinitive. *Grammar.* An infinitive verb form with an element, usually an adverb, interposed between *to* and the verb form.

Usage: The split infinitive (as in *to readily accept*) is not a grammatical error, and it has ample precedent in literature. But it is still avoided, where possible, by many writers and editors, especially in its more extreme forms. It is least desirable, according to a majority of the Usage Panel, when *to* and its verb are separated by a succession of modifying words that slow the reader's comprehension needlessly and produce a clumsy effect: *We are seeking a plan to gradually, systematically, and economically relieve the burden.* In this example, termed unacceptable by 77 per cent of the Usage Panel, simple transposition of the adverbs (*to relieve the burden gradually, systematically . . .*) would improve both clarity and style without changing the desired sense. Most splits are not so extreme, and in such cases usage is divided: *If you want to really help a patient, you must respect his feelings* (accepted by 41 per cent of the Panel). *To better understand the miners' plight, he went to live in their district* (acceptable to 50 per cent). The split infinitive has greatest acceptance when it expresses concisely and clearly a sense that would be achieved less concisely by alternate phrasing: *We expect our output to more than double in a year* (acceptable to 66 per cent). In many examples of less extreme splitting (where only one adverb comes between *to* and its verb), a simple transposition of the adverb is possible. In all such cases, however, the writer should be sure that the revised construction does not distort the intended meaning or create ambiguity by having the adverb modify what it is not intended to modify or by making the function of the adverb unclear. He should also seek to avoid creating awkward passages through shifting the adverb's position. *To be really sure* and *to have just seen* are not split infinitives, though they are often mistaken for such (split variants would be *to really be* and *to just have*).

split-lev·el (splĭt'lĕv'əl) *adj.* Designating a style of house in which the floor levels of adjoining rooms are separated by about a half story.

split personality. A form of hysteria in which an individual manifests two or more relatively distinct identities.

split rail. A fence rail split lengthwise from a log.

split second. An instant; a flash.

split ticket. 1. A ballot cast for candidates of two or more political parties. 2. A ballot that includes the names of candidates of more than one party. Compare **straight ticket.**

split·ting (splĭt'ĭng) *adj.* 1. Acute; piercing. 2. Extremely painful; very severe, as a headache.

splotch (splŏch) *n.* An irregularly shaped stain, spot, or discolored area. —*tr.v.* **splotched, splotching, splotches.** To mark with a splotch or splotches. [Perhaps a blend of SPOT and BLOTCH.] —**splotch'y** *adj.*

splurge (splûrj) *v.* **splurged, splurging, splurges.** —*intr.* 1. To indulge in an extravagant expense or luxury. 2. To be showy or ostentatious. —*tr.* To spend extravagantly or wastefully. —*n.* 1. An extravagant display. 2. An expensive indulgence; a spree. [Origin uncertain.] —**splurg'y** *adj.*

splut·ter (splŭt'ər) *v.* **-tered, -tering, -ters.** —*intr.* 1. To make a spitting sound. 2. To speak incoherently, as when confused or angry. —*tr.* To utter or express hastily and incoherently. —*n.* A spluttering noise. [Perhaps alteration (influenced by SPLASH) of SPUTTER.] —**splut'ter·er** *n.*

Spock (spŏk), **Benjamin McLane.** Born 1903. American pediatrician and educator.

spode (spōd) *n.* Also **Spode.** A porcelain or chinaware of fine quality. [Originally produced in Staffordshire, England, by Josiah *Spode* (1754–1827), British potter.]

spod·u·mene (spŏd'yə-mēn') *n.* A greenish to pinkish or lilac mineral, essentially $LiAlSi_2O_6$, used as a source of lithium and in transparent varieties as a gemstone. [French *spodumène*, from Greek *spodoumenos*, present participle of *spodousthai*, to be burned to ashes (because the mineral becomes ash-gray when exposed to flame), from *spodos*†, wood ashes.]

spoil (spoil) *v.* **spoiled** or **spoilt** (spoilt), **spoiling, spoils.** —*tr.* 1. To impair the value or quality of; to damage. 2. To impair the completeness, perfection, or unity of; to flaw grievously. 3. To disrupt; disturb. 4. To overindulge or overpraise so as to do harm to the character. 5. *Obsolete.* a. To plunder; despoil. b. To take by force. —*intr.* 1. To become tainted, rotten, or otherwise unfit for use; to decay. Used especially of food. 2. *Obsolete.* To pillage. —See Synonyms at **decay, injure, pamper.** —**spoil for.** To be eager for; crave. —*n.* 1. *Plural.* Goods or property seized from a victim after a conflict, especially after a military victory. 2. *Plural.* Incidental benefits reaped by a winner; specifically, political patronage enjoyed by a successful party or candidate. 3. *Archaic.* The act of plundering; spoliation. 4. An object of plunder; prey. 5. Refuse material removed from an excavation. [Middle English *spoilen*, to despoil, plunder, from Old French *espoillier*, from Latin *spoliāre*, from *spolium*, hide torn from an animal, booty. See **spel-**[1] in Appendix.*]

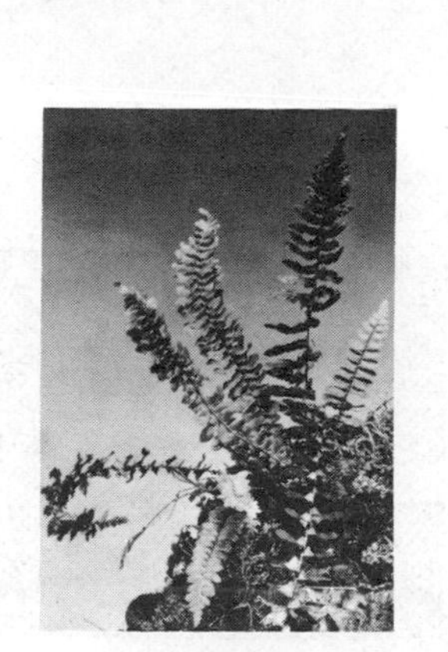
spleenwort
Asplenium platyneuron

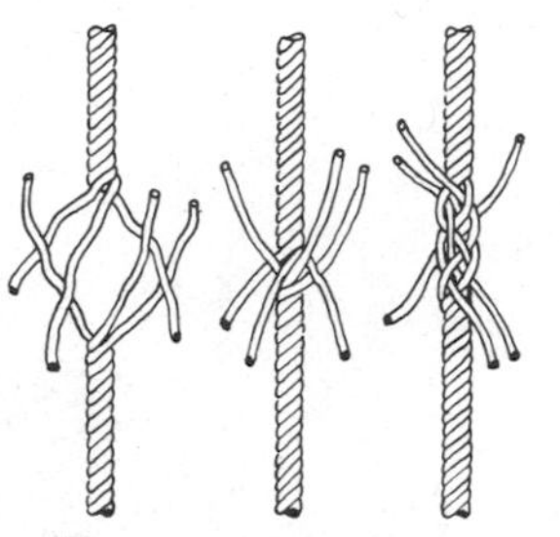
splice
Left to right: Three steps in making a short splice

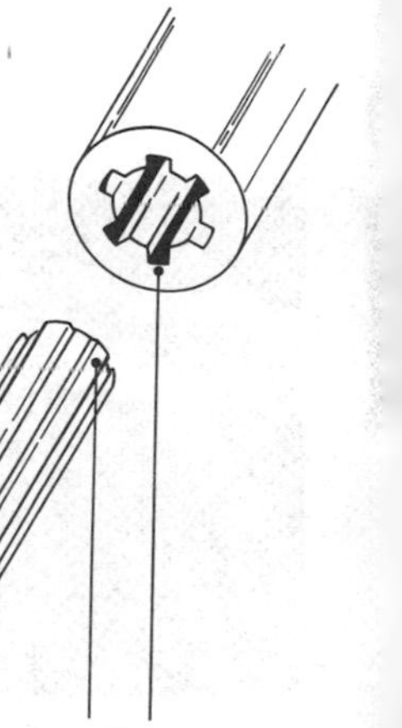
spline

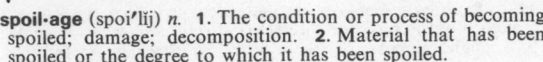

spoil·age (spoiʹlĭj) *n.* **1.** The condition or process of becoming spoiled; damage; decomposition. **2.** Material that has been spoiled or the degree to which it has been spoiled.
spoil·er (spoiʹlər) *n.* **1.** One who seizes spoils or booty. **2.** Something that causes spoilage; a corrupting agent. **3.** A long, narrow hinged plate on the upper surface of an airplane wing, the position of which affects the lift.
spoil·sport (spoilʹspôrt′) *n.* One whose prudence or sobriety mars the pleasure of others.
spoils system. The practice after an election of rewarding loyal supporters of the winning candidates and party with appointive public offices. Compare **merit system.**
Spo·kane (spō-kănʹ). A city of eastern Washington, near the Idaho border. Population, 182,000.
spoke[1] (spōk) *n.* **1.** One of the rods or braces that connect the hub and the rim of a wheel. **2.** One of the handles that project from the rim of a ship's steering wheel. **3.** A rod or stick that may be inserted into a wheel to prevent it from turning. **4.** A rung of a ladder. —*tr.v.* **spoked, spoking, spokes. 1.** To equip with spokes. **2.** To impede (a wheel) by inserting a rod. [Middle English *spake, spoke,* Old English *spāca.* See **spei-** in Appendix.*]

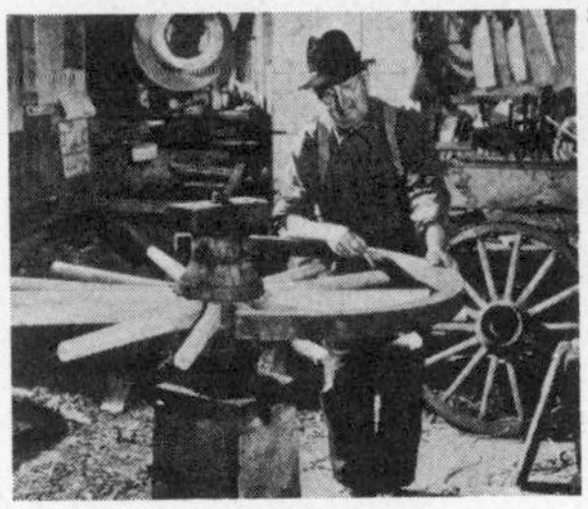

spoke[1]
Pennsylvania Dutch wheelwright attaching rim of a wheel to spokes

spoke[2]. Past tense and *archaic* past participle of **speak.**
spo·ken (spōʹkən). Past participle of **speak.** —*adj.* **1.** Uttered; expressed orally. **2.** Speaking or using speech in a specified manner or voice. Used in combination: *soft-spoken.*
spoke·shave (spōkʹshāv′) *n.* A **drawknife** *(see).*
spokes·man (spōksʹmən) *n., pl.* **-men** (-mĭn). A person who speaks on behalf of another or others. [*Spokes,* possessive case of *spoke,* "speaking," from *spoke,* obsolete past participle of SPEAK + MAN.]
spo·li·a·tion (spō′lē-āʹshən) *n.* **1.** The act of despoiling or plundering; especially, the seizure of neutral vessels at sea by a belligerent power in time of war. **2.** *Law.* The intentional alteration or destruction of a document. [Middle English *spoliacioun,* from Latin *spoliātiō,* from *spoliāre,* to despoil. See **spoil.**] —**spoʹli·a′tor** (-ā′tər) *n.*
spon·da·ic (spŏn-dāʹĭk) *adj.* Also **spon·da·i·cal** (-ĭ-kəl). Of, pertaining to, or consisting of spondees. [French *spondaïque,* from Late Latin *spondaicus, spondiăcus,* from Greek *spondeiakos,* from *spondeios,* SPONDEE.]
spon·dee (spŏnʹdē′) *n Prosody.* A metrical foot consisting of two long or stressed syllables. [Middle English *sponde,* from Old French *spondee,* from Latin *spondeum,* from Greek *spondeios (pous),* "(meter) used at a libation," from *spondē,* libation. See **spend-** in Appendix.*]
spon·dy·li·tis (spŏn′də-līʹtĭs) *n.* Inflammation of one or more of the vertebrae. [New Latin : Greek *spondulos, sphondulos*†, vertebra + -ITIS.]
sponge (spŭnj) *n.* **1.** Any of numerous primitive, chiefly marine animals of the phylum Porifera, characteristically having a porous skeleton composed of fibrous material or siliceous or calcareous spicules, and often forming irregularly shaped colonies attached to an underwater surface. **2.** The light, fibrous, absorbent connective structure of certain of these organisms, used for bathing, cleaning, and other purposes. **3.** Any of various substances having spongelike qualities, such as certain forms of plastics, rubber, or cellulose. **4.** A gauze pad used to absorb blood and other fluids, as in surgery and wound dressing. **5.** Dough that is leavened or in the process of being leavened. **6.** Any of various light cakes, such as sponge cake. **7.** A sponge bath. **8.** *Informal.* A glutton or drunkard. **9.** One who habitually depends on others for his maintenance. —**throw** (or **toss) in the sponge.** *Informal.* To give up; abandon an effort. —*v.* **sponged, sponging, sponges.** —*tr.* **1.** To moisten, wipe, or clean with a sponge. **2.** To wipe out; erase. **3.** *Informal.* To obtain free: *sponge a meal.* —*intr.* **1.** To fish for sponges. **2.** *Informal.* To live by relying on the generosity of others. [Middle English *spo(u)ng(e),* Old English *sponge,* from Latin *spongia,* from Greek *sphongos,* sponge, from the same Mediterranean origin as Latin *fungus,* FUNGUS.]

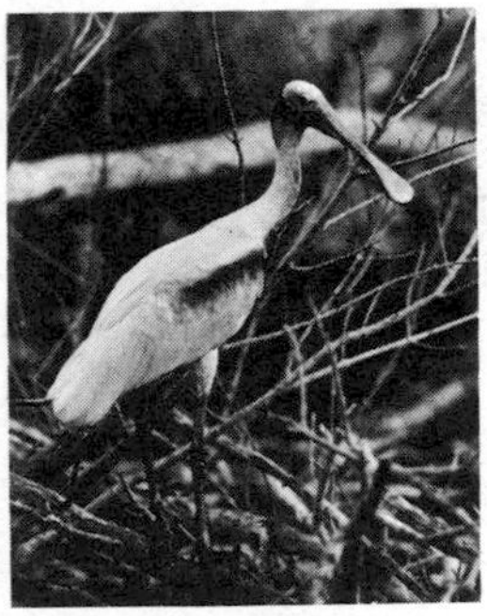

spoonbill
Ajaia ajaja
Roseate spoonbill

sponge bath. A washing of the body with a sponge or cloth, without immersion.
sponge cake. A very light, porous cake made of flour, sugar, beaten eggs, and flavoring, but containing no shortening.
sponge mushroom. The **morel** *(see).*
spong·er (spŭnʹjər) *n.* **1.** A person or boat engaged in gathering sponges. **2.** *Informal.* A person who lives by relying on the generosity of others; a parasite.
sponge rubber. A soft, porous rubber used in toys, in cushions and upholstery, as a vibration dampener, in gaskets, and in weather stripping.
spon·gin (spŭnʹjĭn) *n.* The fibrous material that forms the skeletal structure of sponges. [German *Spongin* : Latin *spongia,* SPONGE + -IN.]
spon·gi·o·blast (spŭnʹjĭ-ō-blăst′) *n.* Embryonic epithelial cells that give rise to the neuroglia cells. [Latin *spongia,* SPONGE + -BLAST.]
spon·gy (spŭnʹjē) *adj.* **gier, -giest.** Like a sponge in elasticity, absorbency, or porousness. —**sponʹgi·ness** *n.*
spon·son (spŏnʹsən) *n.* **1.** Any of several structures that project from the side of a boat or ship, especially a gun platform or flotation chamber. **2.** A short, curved, air-filled projection on the hull of a seaplane, imparting stability in the water. [Origin uncertain.]
spon·sor (spŏnʹsər) *n.* **1.** One who assumes responsibility for a person or group during a period of instruction, apprenticeship, or probation. **2.** One who vouches for the suitability of a candidate for admission. **3.** A legislator who proposes and urges the adoption of a bill. **4.** One who presents a candidate for baptism or confirmation; a godparent. **5.** A business enterprise that pays for a radio or television program, usually in return for advertising time. —*tr.v.* **sponsored, -soring, -sors.** To act as a sponsor for. [Latin, from *spondēre,* to make a solemn pledge. See **spend-** in Appendix.*] —**spon·soʹri·al** (-sôrʹē-əl, -sōrʹē-əl) *adj.* —**sponʹsor·ship** *n.*
spon·ta·ne·i·ty (spŏn′tə-nēʹə-tē) *n., pl.* **-ties. 1.** The condition or quality of being spontaneous. **2.** Spontaneous behavior, impulse, or movement.
spon·ta·ne·ous (spŏn-tāʹnē-əs) *adj.* **1.** Happening or arising without apparent external cause; self-generated. **2.** Voluntary and impulsive; unpremeditated: *spontaneous applause.* **3.** Unconstrained and unstudied in manner or behavior. **4.** Growing without cultivation or human labor; indigenous. —See Synonyms at **voluntary.** [Late Latin *spontāneus,* from Latin *sponte,* of one's own accord, out of free will. See **spen-** in Appendix.*] —**spon·taʹne·ous·ly** *adv.* —**spon·taʹne·ous·ness** *n.*
Synonyms: *spontaneous, impulsive, instinctive, involuntary, automatic.* These adjectives describe response, in actions or words, either uninfluenced by forethought or seemingly so. *Spontaneous* applies to what comes naturally to a person by reason of temperament or native tendency, and not from constraint or external stimulus. *Impulsive* refers to action prompted by a sudden urge not governed by reason and sometimes contrary to reason. *Instinctive* implies behavior guided not by one's reason but by natural consequence of being a member of a given species. Usually the term suggests behavior that promotes one's welfare or that traces to reflex action. *Involuntary* refers to what is not subject to the control of the will, as does *automatic.* The latter also suggests unvarying, mechanical response.
spontaneous abortion. Miscarriage *(see).*
spontaneous combustion. Ignition in a thermally isolated substance, as in oily rags or hay, caused by a localized heat-increasing reaction between the oxidant and the fuel.
spontaneous generation. *Biology.* **Abiogenesis** *(see).*
spon·toon (spŏn-to͞onʹ) *n.* A short pike carried by infantry officers in the 18th century. [French *sponton,* from Italian *spuntone,* from *spuntare,* to blunt, remove the point : *s-,* from Latin *ex-* (removal) + *punto,* point, from Latin *punctum,* from *pungere,* to pierce (see **peuk-** in Appendix*).]
spoof (spo͞of) *n.* **1.** Nonsense; tomfoolery. **2.** A hoax. **3.** A gentle satirical imitation; light parody. See Usage note below. —See Synonyms at **caricature.** —*tr.v.* **spoofed, spoofing, spoofs. 1.** To deceive. **2.** To do a spoof of; satirize gently. See Usage note. [From *spoof,* a card game characterized by nonsense and hoaxing, invented by Arthur Roberts (1852–1933), British comedian.]
Usage: *Spoof,* in the specific sense of parody, is not confined to expressly informal usage, despite its jocular tone. As a noun it is acceptable in writing to 82 per cent of the Usage Panel in the example *a spoof of a spy drama.* As a verb, as in *a sketch that spoofs Wagnerian opera,* it is acceptable to 66 per cent.
spook (spo͞ok) *n. Informal.* A ghost; specter. —*tr.v.* **spooked, spooking, spooks.** *Informal.* **1.** To haunt. **2.** To frighten; startle; especially, to startle and cause nervous activity among (cattle). [Dutch, from Middle Dutch *spoocke,* akin to Middle Low German *spōk*†.] —**spookʹish** *adj.*
spook·y (spo͞oʹkē) *adj.* **-ier, -iest.** *Informal.* **1.** Ghostly; eerie; unnatural. **2.** Easily startled; skittish; nervous. —**spookʹi·ly** *adv.* —**spookʹi·ness** *n.*
spool (spo͞ol) *n.* **1.** A small wood or cardboard cylinder upon which wire, thread, or string is wound. **2.** The amount of thread or other material on a particular spool. **3.** Anything similar to a spool in shape or function. —*tr.v.* **spooled, spooling, spools.** To wind on a spool. [Middle English *spole, spule,* from Old French *espole,* from Middle Dutch *spoele,* akin to Old High German *spuolo*†.]
spoon (spo͞on) *n.* **1.** A utensil consisting of a small, shallow bowl on a handle, used in preparing, serving, or eating food. **2.** Something similar to a spoon or its bowl, specifically: **a.** A shiny, curved metallic fishing lure. Also called "spoon bait," "trolling spoon." **b.** A paddle or oar with a curved blade. **3.** A wooden golf club with more loft than a brassie. Now commonly called "three wood." —*v.* **spooned, spooning, spoons.** —*tr.* **1.** To lift, scoop up, or carry with or as if with a spoon. **2.** To shove or scoop (a ball) into the air, as in certain games. —*intr.* **1.** To fish with a spoon lure. **2.** To give the ball an upward scoop in certain games. **3.** *Informal.* To make love, as by kissing or caressing. [Middle English *spo(o)n,* Old English *spōn,* chip of wood. See **sphē-** in Appendix.*].
spoon·bill (spo͞onʹbĭl′) *n.* **1.** Any of several long-legged wading birds of the subfamily Plataleinae, having a long, flat bill with a broadly spatulate tip. **2.** Any of various broad-billed ducks, such as the shoveler. **3.** The **paddlefish** *(see).*
spoon bread. A soft, custardlike bread made with corn meal, eggs, and buttermilk, and often served in place of mashed potatoes.
spoon·drift (spo͞onʹdrĭft′) *n.* **Spindrift** *(see).* [Obsolete *spoon*†, to drive back and forth (said of a boat) + DRIFT.]
spoon·er·ism (spo͞oʹnə-rĭzʹəm) *n.* An unintentional transposition of sounds in spoken language, as *Let me sew you to your sheet* for *Let me show you to your seat.* [After William A. *Spooner* (1844–1930), English clergyman, noted for such slips.]
spoon-fed (spo͞onʹfĕd′) *adj.* **1.** Fed with a spoon. **2.** Overindulged; coddled. **3.** Given no chance to think or act independently.
spoon·ful (spo͞onʹfo͝ol′) *n., pl.* **-fuls.** The amount a spoon will hold.

ă pat/ā pay/âr care/ä father/b bib/ch church/d deed/ĕ pet/ē be/f fife/g gag/h hat/hw which/ĭ pit/ī pie/îr pier/j judge/k kick/l lid, needle/m mum/n no, sudden/ng thing/ŏ pot/ō toe/ô paw, for/oi noise/ou out/o͝o took/o͞o boot/p pop/r roar/s sauce/sh ship, dish/

spoon·y (spōō′nē) *adj.* **-ier, -iest.** Also **spoon·ey, -eyier, -eyiest.** **1.** Enamored in a silly or sentimental way. **2.** Feebly sentimental; gushy. [From SPOON (to caress).]

spoor (spo͝or) *n.* The track or trail of an animal, especially a wild animal. See Synonyms at **trace.** —*v.* **spoored, spooring, spoors.** —*tr.* To track by following a spoor. —*intr.* To track an animal by its spoor. [Afrikaans, from Middle Dutch *spo(o)r.* See **spher-** in Appendix.*]

Spor·a·des (spôr′ə-dēz′; *Greek* spô-rä′*th*ěs). All the Greek islands in the Aegean, excepting the Cyclades.

spo·rad·ic (spô-răd′ĭk, spō-) *adj.* Also **spo·rad′i·cal** (-ĭ-kəl). **1.** Occurring at irregular intervals; having no pattern or order. **2.** Appearing singly or at widely scattered localities, as a plant. **3.** Not widespread; isolated: *a sporadic disease.* —See Synonyms at **periodic.** [Medieval Latin *sporadicus,* from Greek *sporadikos,* isolated, scattered, from *sporas,* scattered, dispersed. See **sper-**[4] in Appendix.*] —**spo·rad′i·cal·ly** *adv.* —**spo·rad′i·cal·ness** *n.*

spo·ran·gi·um (spô-răn′jē-əm, spō-) *n., pl.* **-gia** (-jē-ə). A spore-bearing structure in certain plants, such as fungi, mosses, and ferns. [New Latin : SPOR(O)- + Greek *angeion,* vessel, container (see **angiology**).] —**spo·ran′gi·al** *adj.*

spore (spôr, spōr) *n.* **1.** An asexual, usually single-celled reproductive organ characteristic of nonflowering plants such as fungi, mosses, or ferns. **2.** A microorganism, as a bacterium, in a dormant or resting state. —*intr.v.* **spored, sporing, spores.** To produce spores. [New Latin *spora,* from Greek, a sowing, seed. See **sper-**[4] in Appendix.*] —**spo·ra′ceous** *adj.*

spore case. A structure containing spores; a sporangium.

sporo-, spor-. Indicates spore; for example, **sporocarp, sporangium.** [New Latin *spora,* spore, from Greek, a sowing, seed. See **sper-**[4] in Appendix.*]

spo·ro·carp (spôr′ə-kärp′, spōr′-) *n. Botany.* A multicellular structure in which spores are formed. [SPORO- + -CARP.]

spo·ro·cyst (spôr′ə-sĭst, spōr′-) *n. Biology.* **1.** A resting cell that produces asexual plant spores. **2.** A protective case containing spores of certain protozoans. **3.** A saclike larval stage in many trematode worms.

spo·ro·cyte (spôr′ə-sīt′, spōr′-) *n. Biology.* A cell that produces haploid spores during meiosis. [SPORO- + -CYTE.]

spo·ro·gen·e·sis (spôr′ə-jĕn′ə-sĭs, spōr′-) *n.* The production or formation of spores. [SPORO- + -GENESIS.]

spo·ro·go·ni·um (spôr′ə-gō′nē-əm, spōr′-) *n., pl.* **-nia** (-nē-ə). A structure in mosses that produces asexual spores. [New Latin : SPORO- + -GONIUM.]

spo·rog·o·ny (spô-rŏg′ə-nē, spō-) *n.* The production of spores resulting from sexual fusion of gametes prior to multiple fission, characteristic of certain protozoans. [SPORO- + -GONY.]

spo·ro·phore (spôr′ə-fôr′, spōr′-) *n.* A spore-bearing structure, especially in fungi. [SPORO- + -PHORE.]

spo·ro·phyll (spôr′ə-fĭl′, spōr′-) *n.* A leaf or leaflike organ that bears spores. [SPORO- + -PHYLL.]

spo·ro·phyte (spôr′ə-fīt′, spōr′-) *n.* The spore-producing phase in plants that reproduce by metagenesis. [SPORO- + -PHYTE.] —**spo′ro·phyt′ic** (-fĭt′ĭk) *adj.*

-sporous. Indicates having spores, especially a specified number or kind; for example, **homosporous.** [From SPORE.]

spo·ro·zo·an (spôr′ə-zō′ən, spōr′-) *n.* Any of numerous parasitic protozoans of the class Sporozoa, many of which have complex reproductive processes. [New Latin *Sporozoa* : SPORO- + -ZOA.] —**spo′ro·zo′an** *adj.*

spo·ro·zo·ite (spôr′ə-zō′īt′, spōr′-) *n.* A sporozoan that has been released from a spore and is ready to penetrate a new host cell. [SPOROZO(A) + -ITE.]

spor·ran (spŏr′ən) *n.* A leather or fur pouch worn at the front of the kilt by Scottish Highlanders. [Scottish Gaelic *sporan,* from Late Latin *bursa,* bag, from Greek, leather, hide. See **bursa** in Appendix.*]

sport (spôrt, spōrt) *n.* **1.** An active pastime; diversion; recreation. **2.** A specific diversion, usually involving physical exercise and having a set form and body of rules; a game. **3.** Light mockery; raillery; jest. **4.** A person known for the manner of his acceptance of the rules of a game or of a difficult situation: *a poor sport.* **5.** *Informal.* A person who lives a gay, extravagant life. **6.** *Genetics.* An organism that shows a marked change from the parent stock; a mutation. **7.** *Archaic.* Amorous dalliance; lovemaking. —**in sport.** In jest; jokingly. —**make sport of.** To treat lightly and mockingly. —*v.* **sported, sporting, sports.** —*intr.* **1.** To play; to frolic. **2.** To joke or trifle. **3.** To mutate. —*tr.* To display or show off: *"His shoes sported elevated heels"* (Truman Capote). —*adj.* Of, relating to, or appropriate for sports: *a sport shirt.* [Middle English *sporten,* to amuse, divert, short for *disporten,* DISPORT.] —**sport′ful** *adj.* —**sport′ful·ly** *adv.* —**sport′ful·ness** *n.*

sport·ing (spôr′tĭng, spōr′-) *adj.* **1.** Used in or appropriate for sports. **2.** Characterized by sportsmanship. **3.** Of or associated with gambling. —**sport′ing·ly** *adv.*

sporting chance. *Informal.* A fair chance for success.

spor·tive (spôr′tĭv, spōr′-) *adj.* **1.** Playful; frolicsome. **2.** Pertaining to or interested in sports. **3.** *Obsolete.* Amorous; wanton. —**spor′tive·ly** *adv.* —**spor′tive·ness** *n.*

sports car. An automobile equipped for racing, especially an aerodynamically shaped one- or two-passenger vehicle having a low center of gravity and steering and suspension designed for precise control at high speeds on curving roads.

sports·man (spôrts′mən, spōrts′-) *n., pl.* **-men** (-mĭn). **1.** A man who is enthusiastic about and participates in sports. **2.** One who abides by the rules of a contest and accepts victory or defeat graciously. —**sports′man·ly** *adj.*

sports·man·ship (spôrts′mən-shĭp′, spōrts′-) *n.* The qualities and conduct befitting a sportsman.

sports·wear (spôrts′wâr′, spōrts′-) *n.* Clothes designed for comfort and casual wear.

sports·wom·an (spôrts′wo͝om′ən, spōrts′-) *n., pl.* **-women** (-wĭm′ĭn). A woman who is active in sports.

sport·y (spôr′tē, spōr′-) *adj.* **-ier, -iest.** *Informal.* **1.** Appropriate to sport or participation in sports. **2.** Casual in style. Said of clothes. **3.** Gay; carefree; loose.

spor·u·late (spôr′yə-lāt′, spōr′-) *intr.v.* **-lated, -lating, -lates.** To produce or release spores. [From New Latin *sporula,* small spore, from *spora,* SPORE.] —**spor′u·la′tion** *n.*

spot (spŏt) *n., pl.* **spots** or **spot** (for sense 6 only). **1.** A particular place of relatively small and definite limits. **2.** A mark on a surface differing sharply in color from the surroundings; especially, a stain or blot. **3.** A position; location. **4.** *Informal.* A set of circumstances; a situation, especially a troublesome one. **5.** A personal defect or injury, as in one's reputation. **6.** An edible marine fish, *Leiostomus xanthurus,* of North American Atlantic waters, having a dark spot above each pectoral fin. **7.** *Chiefly British Informal.* A small amount; a bit: *a spot of tea.* **8.** *Informal.* A spotlight. —**hit the spot.** *Informal.* To be just what is needed; be quite satisfying. —**in spots.** Now and then; here and there; occasionally. —**on the spot.** **1.** Without delay or movement; at once. **2.** At the scene of action. **3.** Under pressure or attention; in a pressed position. —*v.* **spotted, spotting, spots.** —*tr.* **1.** To cause a spot or spots to appear upon, especially: **a.** To soil with spots. **b.** To decorate with spots; to dot. **2.** To place in a particular location; situate precisely. **3.** To detect; locate; discern. **4.** *Sports.* To yield as a handicap: *spotted their opponents 11 points.* —*intr.* **1.** To become marked with spots. **2.** To cause a discoloration; make a stain. **3.** *Military.* To locate targets from the air. —*adj.* **1.** Made, paid, or delivered immediately: *spot cash.* **2.** Presented between major programs, especially by a local station on a network broadcast: *a spot announcement.* [Middle English *spot(te),* perhaps of Low German origin, akin to Middle Dutch *spotte,* from Common Germanic *sput-* (unattested).] —**spot′ta·ble** *adj.*

spot check. A random and hasty inspection or investigation.

spot-check (spŏt′chĕk′) *tr.v.* **-checked, -checking, -checks.** To subject to a spot check; inspect at random.

spot·less (spŏt′lĭs) *adj.* **1.** Perfectly clean. **2.** Free from blemish; impeccable. —**spot′less·ly** *adv.* —**spot′less·ness** *n.*

spot·light (spŏt′līt′) *n.* **1.** A strong beam of light that illuminates only a small area around a selected object, used especially to illuminate or center attention upon a stage actor. **2.** A lamp that produces such a light. **3.** Public notoriety or prominence. **4.** Any artificial source of light with a strongly focused beam, as on an automobile.

Spots·wood (spŏts′wo͝od), **Alexander.** 1676–1740. British colonial administrator; acting governor of Virginia (1710–22).

Spot·syl·va·ni·a (spŏt′səl-vā′nē-ə). A village in northeastern Virginia, scene of an indecisive Civil War battle (1864).

spot·ted (spŏt′ĭd) *adj.* **1.** Having or marked with spots. **2.** Discolored; stained.

spotted cranesbill. A plant, the **wild geranium** *(see).*

spotted fever. **1.** Any of various, often fatal infectious diseases, such as typhus and Rocky Mountain spotted fever, caused by *Rickettsiae,* that are transmitted by ticks and mites and are characterized by skin eruptions. **2.** An epidemic form of **cerebrospinal meningitis** *(see).*

spotted sandpiper. A small brownish-gray North American shore bird, *Actitis macularia.* Also called "peetweet."

spot·ter (spŏt′ər) *n.* **1.** One that applies spots. **2.** One that looks for, locates, and reports something, especially: **a.** A military or civil-defense lookout. **b.** *Informal.* A person hired to detect dishonest acts by employees, as in a bank. **3.** *Sports.* One who identifies players on the field, as for a radio and television announcer. **4.** One employed by a dry cleaner to remove spots.

spot·ty (spŏt′ē) *adj.* **-tier, -tiest.** **1.** Having or marked with spots; spotted. **2.** Lacking consistency; uneven. —**spot′ti·ly** *adv.* —**spot′ti·ness** *n.*

spous·al (spou′zəl, -səl) *adj.* Of or pertaining to marriage; nuptial. —*n.* Marriage; nuptials. Usually used in the plural.

spouse (spous, spouz) *n.* One's marriage partner; a husband or wife. —*tr.v.* (spouz, spous) **spoused, spousing, spouses.** *Archaic.* To marry; wed. [Middle English *sp(o)use,* from Old French *(e)spous,* from Latin *spōnsus,* betrothed (person), betrothal, from *spondēre,* to make a solemn pledge, betroth. See **spend-** in Appendix.*]

spout (spout) *v.* **spouted, spouting, spouts.** —*intr.* **1.** To gush forth in a rapid stream or in spurts. **2.** To discharge a liquid or other substance continuously or in spurts. **3.** *Informal.* To speak volubly and tediously. —*tr.* **1.** To cause to flow or spurt out. **2.** To utter pompously and volubly. **3.** *British Slang.* To pawn. —*n.* **1.** A tube, mouth, or pipe through which liquid is released or discharged. **2.** A continuous stream of liquid. **3.** *British Slang.* A pawnbroker's shop. [Middle English *spouten,* perhaps from Middle Dutch *spouten, spoiten.* See **spyeu-** in Appendix.*] —**spout′er** *n.*

spp. species (plural).

S.P.Q.R. The Senate and the People of Rome (Latin *Senatus Populusque Romanus*).

S.P.R. Society for Physical Research.

sprach·ge·fühl (shpräKH′gə-fül′) *n.* A feeling for language; an ear for the idiomatically correct or appropriate. [German *Sprachgefühl,* "language feeling."]

sprag (sprăg) *n.* **1. a.** A piece of wood or metal wedged beneath

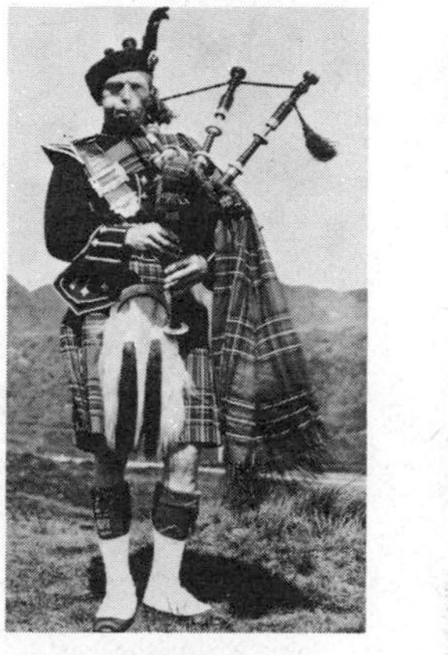

sporran

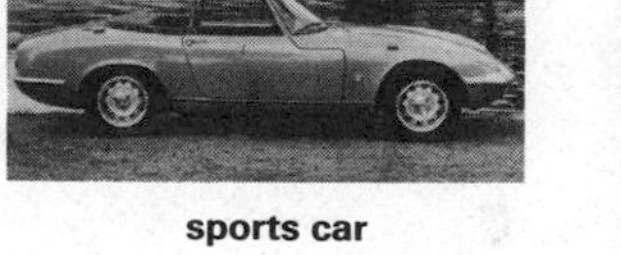

sports car

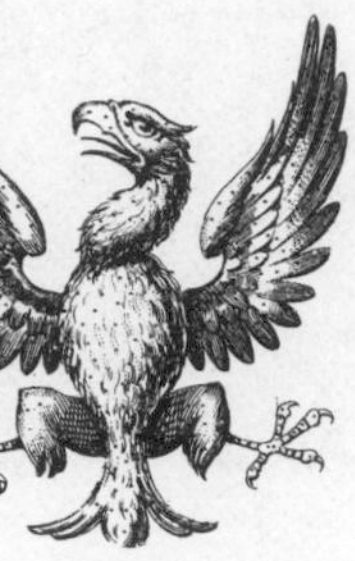

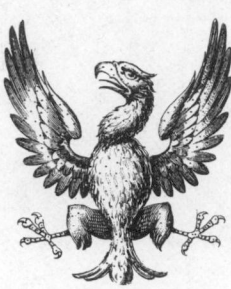

spread eagle

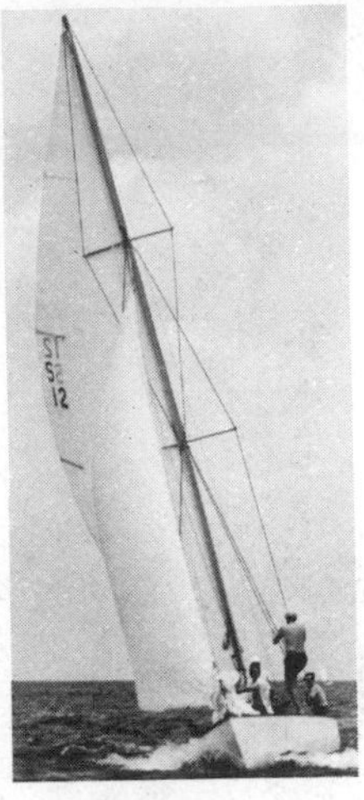

spreader
Spreaders on the mast of a racing sloop

spring

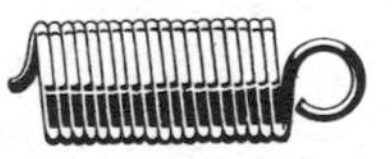

extension coil

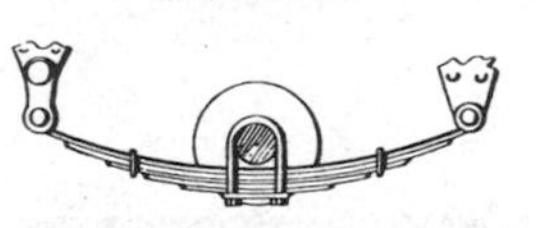

leaf

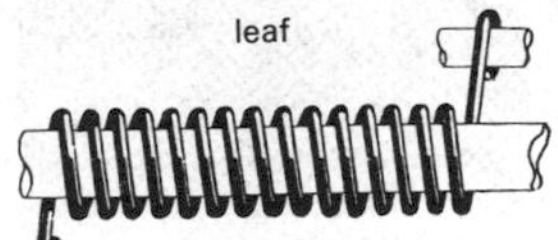

torsional

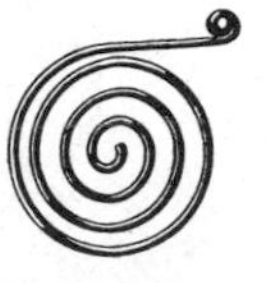

flat spiral

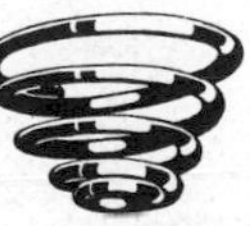

spiral coil

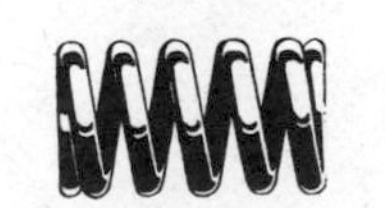

compression coil

a wheel or between spokes to keep a vehicle from rolling. **b.** A pointed stake lowered at an angle into the ground from a vehicle to prevent movement. **2.** A prop to support a mine roof. [Perhaps from Scandinavian, akin to Swedish dialectal *spragg*, twig. See **sphereg-** in Appendix.*]

Sprague (sprăg), **Frank Julian.** 1857–1934. American electrical engineer and inventor.

sprain (sprān) *n.* **1.** A painful wrenching or laceration of the ligaments of a joint. **2.** The condition resulting from such an injury. *—tr.v.* **sprained, spraining, sprains.** To cause a sprain in (a muscle or joint). [Perhaps from Old French *espraindre*, to squeeze out, strain, from Vulgar Latin *expremere* (unattested), variant of Latin *exprimere*, to press out : *ex-*, out + *premere*, to press (see **per-**[6] in Appendix*).]

sprang. Past tense of **spring.**

sprat (sprăt) *n.* **1.** A small marine food fish, *Clupea sprattus*, of northeastern Atlantic waters. Also called "brisling." **2.** Broadly, any of various similar fish, such as a young herring. [Earlier *sprot*, Middle English *sprotte*, Old English *sprott*, akin to Middle Low German or Middle Dutch *sprott*†.]

sprawl (sprôl) *v.* **sprawled, sprawling, sprawls.** *—intr.* **1.** To sit or lie with the body and limbs spread out awkwardly. **2.** To spread out in a straggling or disordered fashion, as handwriting or a mass of people. *—tr.* To cause to spread out in a straggling or disordered fashion. *—n.* A sprawling position or posture. [Middle English *sprewlen, spraulen*, Old English *sprēawlian*. See **sper-**[4] in Appendix.*] **—sprawl′er** *n.*

spray[1] (sprā) *n.* **1.** Water or other liquid moving in a mass of dispersed droplets, as from a wave. **2.** A fine jet of liquid discharged from a pressurized container. **3.** Such a pressurized container; an atomizer. **4.** Any of numerous commercial products, including paints, cosmetics, and insecticides, that are dispensed from containers in this manner. *—v.* **sprayed, spraying, sprays.** *—tr.* **1.** To disperse (a liquid) in a mass or jet of droplets. **2.** To apply a spray to (a surface). *—intr.* **1.** To discharge sprays of liquid. **2.** To move in the form of a spray. [Originally "to sprinkle," from Middle Dutch *spraeyen*†.] **—spray′er** *n.*

spray[2] (sprā) *n.* **1.** A small branch bearing buds, flowers, or berries. **2.** Any design similar to this. [Middle English *spray*, Old English *sprǣg*† (unattested).]

spray gun. A gunlike device for applying sprays.

spread (sprĕd) *v.* **spread, spreading, spreads.** *—tr.* **1.** To open to a fuller extent or width; stretch. **2.** To make wider the gap between; move farther apart. **3. a.** To distribute over a surface in a layer; apply. **b.** To cover with a thin layer. **4.** To extend over a considerable area or period of time; distribute widely. **5.** To cause to become widely known; disseminate. **6. a.** To prepare (a table) for eating; to set. **b.** To arrange (food or a meal) on a table. *—intr.* **1.** To be extended or enlarged. **2.** To become distributed or widely dispersed. **3.** To increase in range of occurrence; become known or prevalent over a wider area. **4.** To become distributed in a thin layer. **5.** To become separated; be forced farther apart. *—n.* **1. a.** The act of spreading; extension; dispersion. **b.** Diffusion; dissemination, as of news. **2. a.** An open area of land; expanse. **b.** The ranch or farmland under one owner. **3.** The extent or limit to which something is or can be spread; a range. **4.** A cloth covering for a bed, table, or other piece of furniture. **5.** *Informal.* An abundant meal laid out on a table. **6.** A food to be spread on bread or crackers. **7. a.** Facing pages of a magazine or newspaper with related matter extending across the fold. **b.** A story or advertisement running across two or more columns. **8.** The difference, as between two figures or totals. [Middle English *spred(d)en*, Old English *sprǣdan* (only in compounds, such as *tō-sprǣdan*). See **sper-**[4] in Appendix.*]

spread eagle. 1. The figure of an eagle with wings and legs spread, the emblem on the Great Seal of the United States. **2.** A posture or design resembling this.

spread-ea·gle (sprĕd′ē′gəl) *adj.* **1.** With the arms and legs stretched out. **2.** *Informal.* Full of patriotic or jingoistic rhetoric. *—v.* **spread-eagled, -gling, -gles.** *—tr.* To place in a spread-eagle position, especially as a means of punishment. *—intr.* To make a grandiloquent, patriotic speech.

spread·er (sprĕd′ər) *n.* One that spreads, especially: **a.** A butter knife. **b.** A farm implement for scattering fertilizer or seed. **c.** A device, such as a bar of wood or metal, for keeping wires or stays apart.

spree (sprē) *n.* **1.** A gay, lively outing. **2.** A drinking bout; carousal. **3.** An overindulgence in some activity; a rash outburst: *a buying spree.* [Earlier *spray*, perhaps alteration of Scottish *spreath*, cattle taken as booty, raid, plunder, from Irish Gaelic *sprēidh*, from Latin *praeda*, spoil, booty. See **ghend-** in Appendix.*]

Spree (shprā). A river of East Germany, rising in Saxony near the Czech border and flowing 250 miles north to join the Havel in Berlin.

sprig (sprĭg) *n.* **1. a.** A small shoot or twig of a plant. **b.** An ornament in this shape. **2.** A small brad without a head. **3.** A young, immature person. *—tr.v.* **sprigged, sprigging, sprigs. 1.** To decorate with a design of sprigs. **2.** To remove a sprig or sprigs from (a bush or tree). **3.** To fasten with a small headless brad. [Middle English *sprigg(e)*†.] **—sprig′ger** *n.*

spright. Variant of **sprite.**

spright·ly (sprīt′lē) *adj.* **-lier, -liest.** Buoyant or animated; full of life. See Synonyms at **nimble.** *—adv.* With briskness; gaily. **—spright′li·ness** *n.*

spring (sprĭng) *v.* **sprang** (sprăng) or **sprung** (sprŭng), **sprung, springing, springs.** *—intr.* **1.** To move upward or forward in a single quick motion; leap. **2.** To appear or emerge suddenly. **3.** To shift position suddenly: *The door sprang shut.* **4.** To arise from a source; develop; to issue. **5.** To become warped, bent, or cracked. Used of wood. **6.** To move out of place; come loose, as a part of a machine. *—tr.* **1.** To cause to leap, dart, or come forth suddenly. **2.** To jump over; to vault. **3.** To release from a checked or inoperative position; actuate: *Motion will spring the trap.* **4.** To cause to warp, bend, or crack, as by force. **5.** To bring to bear abruptly; present unexpectedly: *spring a surprise.* **6.** *Slang.* To cause to be released from prison. —See Synonyms at **rise.** *—n.* **1.** An elastic device, such as a coil of wire, that regains its original shape after being compressed or extended. **2.** An actuating force or factor; a motive. **3.** The quality of elasticity; resilience. **4. a.** The act of springing; especially, a jump or leap. **b.** The distance covered by a leap. **5.** A flock of teal. **6.** The return to normal shape after removal of stress; recoil. **7.** A natural fountain or flow of water. **8.** A source, origin, or beginning. **9.** The season of the year, occurring between winter and summer, during which the weather becomes warmer and plants revive, extending in the Northern Hemisphere from the vernal equinox to the summer solstice and popularly considered to comprise March, April, and May. **10.** A warping, bending, or cracking, such as that caused by excessive force. —See Synonyms at **flock.** *—adj.* **1.** Of or acting like a spring. **2.** Having or supported by springs. **3.** Coming from a spring: *spring water.* **4.** Of, occurring in, or characteristic of the season of spring. [Spring, sprang, sprung; Middle English *springen, sprang, sprungen*, Old English *springan, sprang* (past singular), *sprungen.* See **spergh-** in Appendix.*]

spring beauty. Any of several plants of the genus *Claytonia*; especially, *C. virginica*, of eastern North America, having narrow leaves and white or pinkish flowers.

spring·board (sprĭng′bôrd′, -bōrd′) *n.* **1.** A flexible board mounted on a fulcrum with one end secured, used by gymnasts to gain momentum, as in tumbling. **2.** A **diving board** *(see).*

spring·bok (sprĭng′bŏk′) *n.* Also **spring·buck** (-bŭk′). A small brown and white gazelle, *Antidorcas marsupialis*, of southern Africa, that is capable of leaping high into the air. [Afrikaans : *spring*, to leap up, from Middle Dutch *springen* (see **spergh-** in Appendix*) + *bok*, male deer, buck, from Middle Dutch *boc* (see **bhugo-** in Appendix*).]

spring chicken. 1. A young chicken, especially one from two to ten months old, having tender meat. **2.** *Slang.* A young or naive person: *At her age, she's no spring chicken.*

springe (sprĭnj) *n.* A device for snaring small game, made by attaching a noose to a branch under tension. *—v.* **springed, springeing** or **springing, springes.** *—tr.* To trap with a springe; ensnare. *—intr.* To prepare a springe. [Middle English *sprenge, springe*, Old English *sprencg* (unattested). See **spergh-** in Appendix.*]

spring·er (sprĭng′ər) *n.* **1.** One who or that which springs. **2.** A springer spaniel. **3.** *Western U.S.* A cow about to give birth. **4.** *Architecture.* **a.** The impost of an arch. **b.** The bottom stone of an arch resting on the impost.

springer spaniel. A dog of a breed originating in England or Wales, having drooping ears and a silky brown and white or black and white coat.

spring fever. The feelings of languor, rejuvenation, or yearning that may affect people at the advent of spring.

Spring·field (sprĭng′fēld). **1.** The capital of Illinois, in the center of the state; the home and burial place of Abraham Lincoln. Population, 83,000. **2.** A city in southwestern Massachusetts, the scene of Shays' Rebellion (1786–87). Population, 174,000. **3.** A city and trade center in southwestern Missouri. Population, 96,000. **4.** An industrial city and transportation center in west-central Ohio. Population, 84,000.

Springfield rifle. A magazine-fed breech-loading, bolt-action .30-caliber U.S. Army rifle. Also called "Springfield." [First made at the former U.S. Armory at SPRINGFIELD, Massachusetts.]

spring·halt (sprĭng′hôlt′) *n.* A **stringhalt** *(see).* [Alteration of STRINGHALT.]

spring·head (sprĭng′hĕd′) *n.* A fountainhead or source.

spring·house (sprĭng′hous′) *n.* A small house constructed over a spring and used to keep food cool.

spring·let (sprĭng′lĭt) *n.* A small spring of water; rill.

spring lock. A lock in which the bolt shoots automatically by means of a spring.

spring peeper. A small, brownish tree frog, *Hyla crucifer*, of eastern North America, having a characteristic shrill, high-pitched call.

Springs (sprĭngz). A city of South Africa, in a gold-mining region of southern Transvaal. Population, 135,000.

spring·tail (sprĭng′tāl′) *n.* Any of various small wingless insects of the order Collembola, having abdominal appendages that act as springs to catapult them through the air.

spring tide. 1. The tide generally having the greatest rise and fall, occurring at or shortly after the new moon or the full moon when the sun, moon, and earth are approximately aligned. Compare **neap tide. 2.** Any great flood or rush, as of emotion.

spring·time (sprĭng′tīm′) *n.* The season of spring. Also called "springtide."

spring·wood (sprĭng′wo͝od′) *n.* Young, usually soft wood that lies directly beneath the bark and develops in early spring.

spring·y (sprĭng′ē) *adj.* **-ier, -iest. 1.** Resilient; elastic. **2.** Having many springs of water. **—spring′i·ly** *adv.* **—spring′i·ness** *n.*

sprin·kle (sprĭng′kəl) *v.* **-kled, -kling, -kles.** *—tr.* **1.** To scatter or release in drops or small particles, as water or sand. **2.** To

scatter drops or particles upon. —*intr.* **1.** To scatter small drops or particles of something. **2.** To fall or rain in small or infrequent drops. —*n.* **1.** The act of sprinkling. **2.** A light, sparse rainfall. **3.** A small amount; a sprinkling. [Middle English *sprenklen,* probably from Middle Dutch *sprenkelen.* See **sphereg-** in Appendix.*]
sprin·kler (sprĭng′klər) *n.* One that sprinkles, especially: **a.** An outlet on a sprinkler system. **b.** A device, attached to the end of a water hose, for sprinkling water on lawns.
sprinkler system. A fire-extinguishing system consisting of a network of water pipes, usually equipped to release water automatically at temperatures above a predetermined limit.
sprin·kling (sprĭng′klĭng) *n.* **1.** Something that is sprinkled. **2.** A small amount or quantity, especially when tossed or sparsely distributed. **3.** The act of one who sprinkles.
sprint (sprĭnt) *n.* A short race run at top speed. —*intr.v.* **sprinted, sprinting, sprints.** To run at top speed. [Of Scandinavian origin, akin to Swedish dialectal *sprinta,* to jump, akin to Old Norse *spretta,* from Germanic *sprintan* (unattested).] —**sprint′er** *n.*
sprit (sprĭt) *n.* **1.** A pole extending diagonally across a fore-and-aft sail from the lower part of the mast to the peak of the sail. **2.** A **bowsprit** *(see).* [Middle English *spret(te), spryt(t),* Old English *sprēot,* pole. See **sper-**[4] in Appendix.*]
sprite (sprīt) *n.* Also **spright. 1.** A small or elusive supernatural being; an elf or pixie. **2.** *Archaic.* A specter or ghost. [Middle English *spr(e)it,* from Old French *esp(i)rit,* from Latin *spīritus,* SPIRIT.]
sprit·sail (sprĭt′səl, -sāl′) *n.* A sail extended by a sprit.
sprock·et (sprŏk′ĭt) *n.* Any of various toothlike projections arranged on a wheel rim to engage the links of a chain. [Origin unknown.]
sprocket wheel. A wheel rimmed with sprockets, to engage the links of a chain in a pulley or drive system.
sprout (sprout) *v.* **sprouted, sprouting, sprouts.** —*intr.* **1.** To begin to grow; give off shoots or buds. **2.** To grow or develop quickly; burgeon. —*tr.* To cause to grow or sprout. —*n.* **1.** A young plant growth, such as a bud or shoot. **2.** Something resembling or suggestive of a sprout. **3.** *Plural.* A vegetable, **Brussels sprouts** *(see).* [Middle English *spruten,* Old English *sprūtan.* See **sper-**[4] in Appendix.*]
spruce[1] (sprōōs) *n.* **1.** Any of various coniferous evergreen trees of the genus *Picea,* having needlelike foliage, drooping cones, and soft wood often used for paper pulp. **2.** Any of various similar or related trees. **3.** The wood of any of these trees. **4.** Grayish or dark grayish to greenish black. See **color.** [Short for *Spruce fir,* "Prussian fir," from *Spruce,* Prussia, Middle English *Sprewse,* alteration of *Pruce,* from Old French, from Medieval Latin *Prussia,* PRUSSIA.]
spruce[2] (sprōōs) *adj.* **sprucer, sprucest.** Having a neat, trim, or dapper appearance. —*v.* **spruced, sprucing, spruces.** —*tr.* To make spruce; dress neatly. —*intr.* To become spruce. Used with *up.* [Perhaps from *Spruce,* Prussia, Prussian leather (from the fineness of the leather).] —**spruce′ly** *adv.* —**spruce′ness** *n.*
spruce beer. A slightly fermented beverage made with an extract of spruce needles and twigs with molasses or sugar.
spruce pine. A tree, the **black spruce** *(see).*
sprue (sprōō) *n.* A chronic, chiefly tropical disease characterized by diarrhea, emaciation, and anemia. [Dutch *spruw,* from Middle Dutch *sprouwe,* akin to Middle Low German *sprūwe*†.]
sprung. Past participle and alternate past tense of **spring.**
sprung rhythm. A forcefully accentual verse rhythm in which a stressed syllable is followed by an irregular number of unstressed or slack syllables to form a foot having a metrical value equal to that of the other feet in the line. [Coined by Gerard Manley Hopkins.]
spry (sprī) *adj.* **sprier** or **spryer, spriest** or **spryest.** Active; nimble; lively; brisk. See Synonyms at **nimble.** [Perhaps from Scandinavian, akin to Swedish dialectal *sprygg,* brisk, active. See **sphereg-** in Appendix.*] —**spry′ly** *adv.* —**spry′ness** *n.*
spt. seaport.
spud (spŭd) *n.* **1.** A sharp tool resembling a spade for rooting or digging out weeds. **2.** *Slang.* A potato. —*tr.v.* **spudded, spudding, spuds.** To remove with a spud, as weeds. [Middle English *spudde*†, short knife.]
spue. Variant of **spew.**
spume (spyōōm) *n.* Foam or froth on a liquid. —*intr.v.* **spumed, spuming, spumes.** To froth or foam. [Middle English, from Old French *(e)spume,* from Latin *spūma.* See **spoimo-** in Appendix.*] —**spu′mous, spum′y** *adj.*
spu·mo·ne (spə-mō′nē; *Italian* spōō-mō′nā) *n., pl.* **-ni** (-nē). Also **spu·mo·ni.** An Italian frozen dessert of ice cream containing fruit, nuts, or candies. [Italian, from *spuma,* foam, from Latin *spūma,* SPUME.]
spun. Past tense and past participle of **spin.**
spun glass. 1. Fiber glass *(see).* **2.** Fine blown glass having delicate, often spiral threading or filigree.
spunk (spŭngk) *n.* **1.** Punk, touchwood, or other tinder. **2.** *Informal.* Spirit; pluck; mettle. [Scottish Gaelic *spong,* tinder, sponge, from Latin *spongia,* SPONGE.]
spunk·y (spŭng′kē) *adj.* **-ier, -iest.** Having spunk; spirited; plucky. —**spunk′i·ly** *adv.* —**spunk′i·ness** *n.*
spun silk. A yarn made from short-fibered silk.
spun sugar. Sugar threaded into a confectionary fluff. Also called "cotton candy."
spun yarn. A lightweight line made of several rope yarns loosely wound together, used for seizings on board ship.
spur (spûr) *n.* **1.** One of a pair of spikes or spiked wheels attached to a rider's heels and used to urge the horse forward. **2.** An incentive; a stimulus; goad. **3.** A spurlike attachment or projection, as: **a.** A spinelike process on the leg of some birds. **b.** A climbing iron; crampon. **c.** The gaff attached to the leg of a gamecock. **d.** A short or stunted branch of a tree. **e.** An ergot growing on rye. **4.** A lateral ridge projecting from a mountain or mountain range. **5.** An oblique reinforcing prop or stay of timber or masonry. **6.** *Botany.* A tubular extension of the corolla or calyx of a flower, as in a columbine or larkspur. **7.** A **spur track** *(see).* —**on the spur of the moment.** On a sudden impulse. —*v.* **spurred, spurring, spurs.** —*tr.* **1.** To urge (a horse) on by the use of spurs. **2.** To incite; prompt; stimulate. —*intr.* To ride quickly on horseback by making use of the spurs. [Middle English *spore, spure,* Old English *spora, spura.* See **spher-** in Appendix.*]
spurge (spûrj) *n.* Any of various chiefly tropical plants of the genus *Euphorbia,* characteristically having milky juice and small flowers that in some species are surrounded by showy bracts. [Middle English, from Old French *(e)spurge,* "purge" (certain species were formerly used as purgatives), from *espurgier,* to purge, from Latin *expurgāre* : *ex-,* away + *purgāre,* to purge, purify (see **peue-**[1] in Appendix*).]
spur gear. A gear with teeth radially arrayed on the rim parallel to its axis.
spurge laurel. A low-growing shrub, *Daphne laureola,* of southern Europe, having glossy evergreen leaves and small yellowish-green flowers.
spu·ri·ous (spyŏŏr′ē-əs) *adj.* **1.** Lacking authenticity or validity; counterfeit; false. **2.** Constituting a forgery or interpolation. **3.** Illegitimate; bastard. **4.** *Botany.* Similar in appearance but unlike in structure or function. —See Synonyms at **artificial.** [Late Latin *spurius,* false, from Latin, illegitimate, perhaps from Etruscan, akin to *spurcus,* dirty, impure.] —**spu′ri·ous·ly** *adv.* —**spu′ri·ous·ness** *n.*
spurn (spûrn) *v.* **spurned, spurning, spurns.** —*tr.* **1.** To reject or refuse disdainfully; scorn. **2.** *Archaic.* **a.** To kick disdainfully. **b.** To tread on; trample. —*intr.* To refuse something contemptuously. —See Synonyms at **refuse.** —*n.* **1.** A contemptuous rejection. **2.** *Archaic.* A kick. [Middle English *spurnen, spornen,* Old English *spurnan, spornan.* See **spher-** in Appendix.*] —**spurn′er** *n.*
spurred (spûrd) *adj.* **1.** Wearing spurs. **2.** Having a spur or spurs: *spurred flowers.*
spur·ri·er (spûr′ē-ər) *n.* A maker of spurs. [Middle English *sporior,* from *spore,* SPUR.]
spur·ry (spûr′ē) *n., pl.* **-ries.** Also **spur·rey** *pl.* **-reys.** Any of several weedy, low-growing plants of the genera *Spergula* or *Spergularia;* especially, *Spergula arvensis,* native to Europe, having whorled leaves and small white flowers. [Dutch *spurrie,* from Middle Dutch *sporie, speurie,* probably from Medieval Latin *spergula,* perhaps from Latin *spergere, spargere,* to scatter. See **sphereg-** in Appendix.*]
spurt (spûrt) *n.* Also *chiefly British* **spirt. 1.** A sudden and forcible gush, as of water. **2.** Any sudden outbreak or short burst of energy or activity. —*v.* **spurted, spurting, spurts.** —*intr.* To make a burst. —*tr.* To force out in a burst; to squirt. [Earlier *spirt, sprit,* to sprout, Middle English *sprutten,* Old English *spryttan.* See **sper-**[4] in Appendix.*]
spur track. A short side track that connects with the main track of a railroad system. Also called "spur."
sput·nik (spŭt′nĭk, spŏŏt′-) *n.* Any of the artificial Earth satellites launched by the U.S.S.R., especially the first, launched October 4, 1957. [Russian *sputnik (zemlyi),* "fellow traveler (of Earth)" : *s-,* for *so,* with (see **ksun** in Appendix*) + *put′,* path, way (see **pent-** in Appendix*) + *-nik,* agent noun suffix.]
sput·ter (spŭt′ər) *v.* **-tered, -tering, -ters.** —*intr.* **1.** To spit out small particles in short bursts, often with corresponding sounds or noises. **2.** To make the sporadic coughing noise characteristic of such activity. **3.** To speak in a hasty or confusing fashion; stammer. —*tr.* **1.** To spit out (saliva, for example) in short bursts. **2.** To utter in a hasty or confused fashion. —*n.* **1.** The act of sputtering. **2.** The sound of sputtering. **3.** The particles that are emitted during sputtering. **4.** Hasty or confused utterances. [From Dutch *sputteren.* See **spyeu-** in Appendix.*] —**sput′ter·er** *n.*
spu·tum (spyōō′təm) *n., pl.* **-ta** (-tə). **1.** Expectorated saliva; spit; spittle. **2.** Expectorated matter, including saliva, substances from the respiratory tract, and foreign material. [Latin *spūtum,* from *spūtus,* past participle of *spuere,* to spit. See **spyeu-** in Appendix.*]
spy (spī) *n., pl.* **spies. 1.** A clandestine agent employed by a state to obtain intelligence relating to its eventual or actual enemies at home or abroad. **2.** One who secretly watches another or others. **3.** The act of watching covertly or secretly. —*v.* **spied, spying, spies.** —*tr.* **1.** To keep under surveillance with hostile intent. Often used with *out.* **2.** To catch sight of; see; descry. —*intr.* **1. a.** To observe secretly and closely. Often used with *on, into,* or *upon.* **b.** To engage in espionage. **2.** To investigate; pry. Used with *into: spying into their activities.* [Middle English *spie,* from Old French *espie,* from *espier,* to spy, watch, from Frankish *spehōn* (unattested). See **spek-** in Appendix.*]
spy·glass (spī′glăs′, -gläs′) *n.* **1.** A small telescope. **2.** *Plural.* Binoculars.
sq. 1. squadron. **2.** square.
squab (skwŏb) *n.* **1.** A young, unfledged pigeon. **2.** A short, fat person. **3.** A soft cushion. **4.** A couch; sofa. —*adj.* **1.** Short and broad; squat. **2.** Newly hatched or unfledged. [Probably from Scandinavian, akin to Swedish dialectal *sqvabb*†, fat flesh, soft mass.]
squab·ble (skwŏb′əl) *intr.v.* **-bled, -bling, -bles.** To engage in a

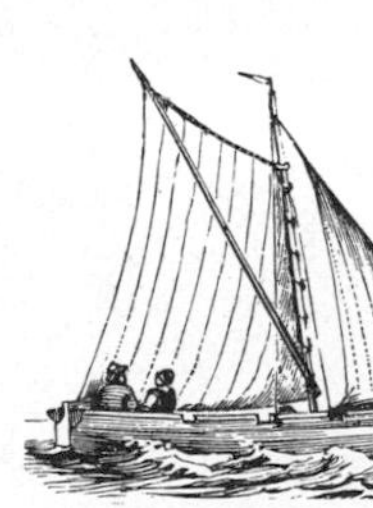

sprit

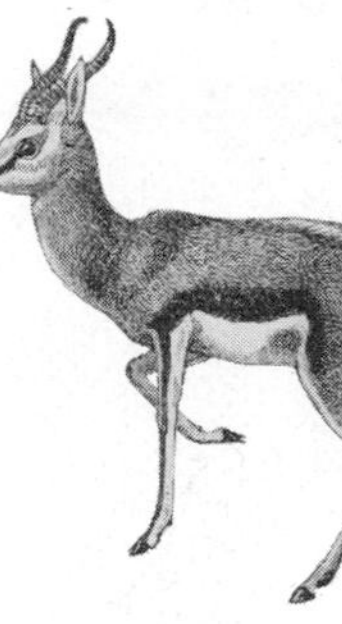

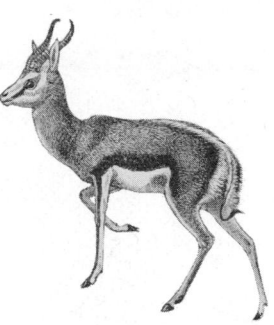

springbok

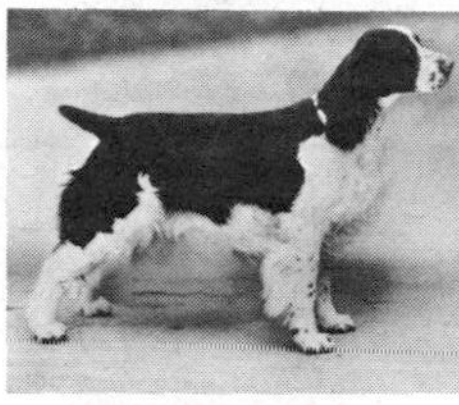

springer spaniel

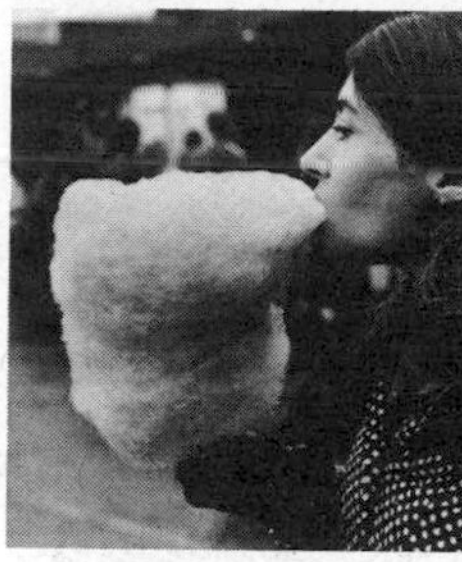

spun sugar

minor quarrel; bicker. See Synonyms at **argue.** —*n.* A trivial quarrel. [Probably from Scandinavian, akin to Swedish dialectal *sqvabbel,* to quarrel (imitative).] —**squab'bler** *n.*

squab·by (skwŏb'ē) *adj.* **-bier, -biest.** Short and fat; squat.

squad (skwŏd) *n.* **1.** A small group of persons organized for a specific purpose. **2.** *Military.* The smallest unit of personnel, frequently designated as a line or rank in formation. **3.** An athletic team. —*tr.v.* **squadded, squadding, squads. 1.** To form into a squad or squads. **2.** To assign to a squad. [Old French *esquad(r)e,* from Old Spanish *escuadra,* "square," "square formation (of troops)," from *escuadrar,* to square, form a squad, from Vulgar Latin *exquadrāre* (unattested) : *ex-* (intensive) + Latin *quadrāre,* to make square, from *quadrus,* a square (see **kwetwer-** in Appendix*).]

squad car. A police patrol car connected by radiotelephone with headquarters. Also called "cruiser," "prowl car."

squad·ron (skwŏd'rən) *n. Abbr.* **sq. 1.** A group of naval vessels constituting two or more divisions of a fleet. **2.** An armored cavalry unit consisting of two to four troops, a headquarters, and certain auxiliary units. **3.** *U.S. Air Force.* The basic tactical unit, subordinate to a group and consisting of two or more flights. **4.** Any organized multitude; a legion: *"squadrons of flies like particles of dust danced up and down"* (T.E. Lawrence). —*tr.v.* **squadroned, -roning, -rons.** To form into a squadron or squadrons. [Italian *squadrone,* "square formation (of troops)," from *squadra,* squad, "square," from Old Italian, from *squadrare,* to square, from Vulgar Latin *exquadrāre* (unattested). See **squad.**]

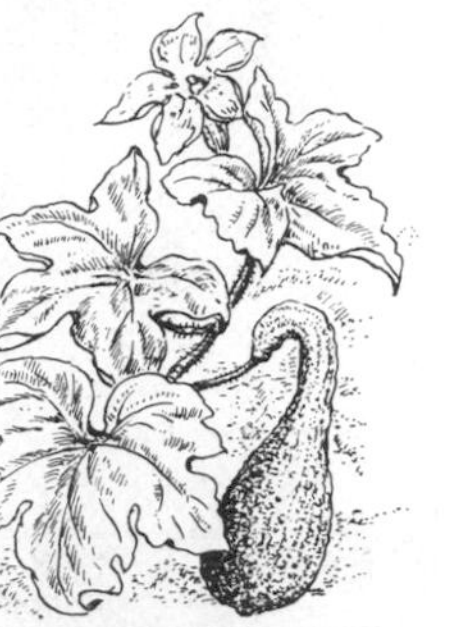

squash[1]
Cucurbita pepo
Crookneck squash

squa·lene (skwā'lēn') *n.* A natural unsaturated aliphatic hydrocarbon, $C_{30}H_{50}$, found in human sebum and other fatty deposits, that is an intermediate in the biosynthesis of cholesterol and is used in biochemical research. [New Latin *Squalus,* genus of sharks (because squalene is found in the liver oil of sharks), from Latin *squalus,* a sea fish (see **skwalo-** in Appendix*) + -ENE.]

squal·id (skwŏl'ĭd) *adj.* **1.** Having a dirty or wretched appearance. **2.** Morally repulsive; sordid. —See Synonyms at **dirty.** [Latin *squālidus,* from *squālēre,* to be filthy, from *squālus*†, scabby, filthy.] —**squal'id·ly** *adv.* —**squa·lid'i·ty** (skwŏ-lĭd'ə-tē), **squal'id·ness** *n.*

squall[1] (skwôl) *n.* A loud, harsh outcry. —*intr.v.* **squalled, squalling, squalls.** To scream or cry harshly and loudly. [Probably from Scandinavian, akin to Old Norse *skvala,* to SQUEAL.] —**squall'er** *n.*

squall[2] (skwôl) *n.* **1.** A brief, sudden, and violent windstorm, often accompanied by rain or snow. **2.** *Informal.* A disturbance or commotion. —*intr.v.* **squalled, squalling, squalls.** To blow strongly for a brief period; blow a squall. [Probably from Scandinavian, akin to Swedish and Norwegian *skval,* splash, akin to Old Norse *skvala,* SQUEAL.]

squall line. A zone of squalls and other violent changes in weather that marks the replacement of a warm air current by cold air.

squall·y (skwôl'ē) *adj.* **-ier, -iest. 1.** Characterized by squalls; stormy; gusty. **2.** *Informal.* Marked by disturbance or trouble.

squal·or (skwŏl'ər) *n.* The state or quality of being squalid; filth and misery. [Latin, from *squālēre,* to be filthy. See **squalid.**]

squa·ma (skwā'mə) *n., pl.* **-mae** (-mē'). **1.** A scale or scalelike structure. **2.** A thin plate of bone. [Latin *squāma*†, scale.] —**squa'mate'** (-māt') *adj.*

squa·ma·tion (skwə-mā'shən) *n.* **1.** The condition of being scaly. **2.** An arrangement of scales, as on a fish.

Squa·mish. Variant of **Suquamish.**

squa·mo·sal (skwə-mō'səl) *adj.* Of or pertaining to the squamous area of the temporal bone. —*n.* A squamosal bone. [From Latin *squāmōsus,* SQUAMOUS.]

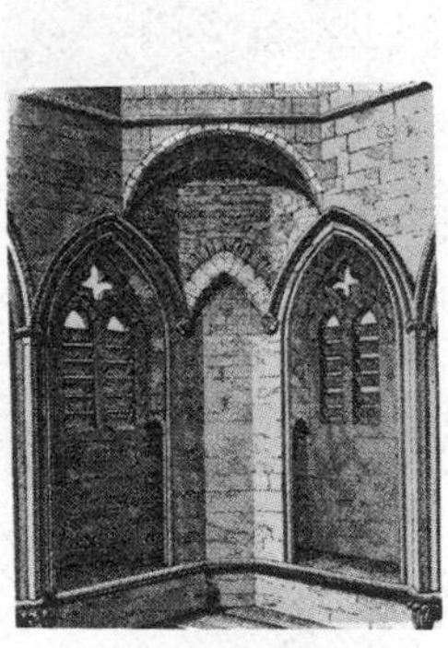

squinch
In the cathedral at
Oxford, England

squa·mous (skwā'məs) *adj.* Also **squa·mose** (-mōs'). **1.** Covered with or formed of scales; scaly. **2.** Resembling a scale or scales; scalelike. [Latin *squāmōsus,* from *squāma,* scale, SQUAMA.] —**squa'mous·ly** *adv.* —**squa'mous·ness** *n.*

squam·u·lose (skwăm'yə-lōs') *adj.* Having or consisting of minute scales; minutely scaly. [From New Latin *squāmula,* diminutive of Latin *squāma,* scale, SQUAMA.]

squan·der (skwŏn'dər) *tr.v.* **-dered, -dering, -ders. 1.** To spend wastefully or extravagantly; dissipate. **2.** *Obsolete.* To scatter. —*n.* Extravagant expenditure; prodigality. [Origin unknown.] —**squan'der·er** *n.* —**squan'der·ing·ly** *adv.*

square (skwâr) *n. Abbr.* **sq. 1.** A rectangle having four equal sides. **2.** Anything characterized by this form. **3.** A T-shaped or L-shaped instrument for drawing or testing right angles. **4.** The product of a number or quantity multiplied by itself. **5.** Any of the quadrilateral spaces dividing a checkerboard. **6. a.** An open, often quadrilateral area at the intersection of two or more streets. **b.** A rectangular space enclosed by streets and occupied by buildings; a block. **7.** *Slang.* One characterized by rigid conventionality or lack of sophistication. —**on the square. 1.** At right angles. **2.** Honestly and openly. —**out of square.** Not at a precise right angle. —*adj.* **squarer, squarest.** *Abbr.* **sq. 1.** Having four equal sides and four right angles. **2.** Forming a right angle. **3. a.** Expressed in units measuring area: *square feet.* **b.** Having a specified length in each of two equal dimensions. **4.** Set at right angles to the mast and keel, as the yards of a square-rigged ship. **5. a.** Of more or less quadrate dimensions: *a square house.* **b.** Characterized by blocklike solidity or sturdiness. **6.** Honest; direct: *a square answer.* **7.** Just; equitable: *a square deal.* **8.** Paid-up; settled. **9.** *Golf.* Even; tied. **10.** *Slang.* Rigidly conventional; unsophisticated. —**square peg in a round hole.** A misfit. —*v.* **squared, squaring, squares.** —*tr.* **1.** To cut to a square or rectangular shape. **2.** To test for conformity to a desired plane, straight line, or right angle. **3.** To test by comparison. **4.** To bring into conformity or agreement. **5.** To set straight or at right angles: *square one's cap.* **6.** To bring into balance; settle: *square a debt.* **7.** *Golf.* To even the score of; tie. **8.** To raise (a number or quantity) to the second power. **9.** To find a square equal in area to (the area of a given figure). —*intr.* **1.** To be at right angles. **2.** To agree or conform; balance. —**square away. 1.** To square the yards of a sailing vessel. **2.** To put away or in order. —**square off.** To assume a fighting stance. —**square up.** To settle or adjust, as a debt. —*adv.* **1.** At right angles. **2.** In a square shape. **3.** Solidly. **4.** Directly; straight. **5.** In an honest manner; straightforwardly. [Middle English, from Old French *esquare,* from Vulgar Latin *exquadra* (unattested), from *exquadrāre* (unattested), to square : Latin *ex-* (intensive) + *quadrāre,* to square, from *quadrus,* a square (see **kwetwer-** in Appendix*).] —**square'ly** *adv.* —**square'ness** *n.* —**squar'er** *n.*

square bracket. A written symbol, **bracket** *(see).*

square dance. 1. A dance in which sets of four couples form squares. **2.** Any of various similar group dances of English rural origin.

square-dance (skwâr'dăns') *intr.v.* **-danced, -dancing, -dances.** To perform a square dance.

square knot. A common double knot with the loose ends parallel to the standing parts. Also called "reef knot."

square measure. A system of units used in measuring area.

square rig. A sailing-ship rig with sails of rectangular cut set approximately at right angles to the keel line from horizontal yards. —**square'-rigged'** *adj.*

square-rig·ger (skwâr'rĭg'ər) *n.* A square-rigged vessel.

square root. A divisor of a quantity that when squared gives the quantity.

square sail. A four-sided sail bent to a yard set athwart the mast.

squar·rose (skwăr'ōs', skwŏ-rōs') *adj.* **1.** *Biology.* Having rough or spreading scalelike processes. **2.** *Botany.* Spreading or recurved at the tip: *squarrose bracts.* [Latin *squarrōsus,* alteration (influenced by Latin *squāma,* scale) of *escharōsus* (unattested), scabby, from Greek *eskhara,* hearth, scab, SCAR.]

squash[1] (skwŏsh, skwôsh) *n.* **1.** Any of various plants of the genus *Cucurbita,* having fleshy edible fruit with a hard rind. **2.** The fruit of such a plant, used as a vegetable. [Short for *isquoutersquash,* from Massachuset *askōōtasquash* : *askōt-* (unidentified root) + Proto-Algonquian *aškw-,* plant + *-ash,* inanimate plural ending.]

squash[2] (skwŏsh, skwôsh) *v.* **squashed, squashing, squashes.** —*tr.* **1.** To beat, squeeze, or flatten to a pulp; crush. **2.** To put down or suppress; quash. **3.** To silence (a person), as with crushing words. —*intr.* **1.** To be crushed or flattened. **2.** To move with a squelching sound. —*n.* **1.** The impact or sound of a soft body dropping against a surface. **2.** The sound of water being squeezed out, as from spongy ground or wet shoes. **3.** A crush; press. Said of persons. **4.** *Chiefly British.* A citrus-base soft drink. **5. a.** A game played in a walled court with a racket and a hard rubber ball. Also called "squash rackets." **b.** A similar game played with an inflated rubber ball. In this sense, also called "squash tennis." —*adv.* With a squashing sound. [Old French *esquasser,* from Vulgar Latin *exquassāre* (unattested), "to break to pieces" : Latin *ex-* (intensive) + *quassāre,* frequentative of *quatere,* to shake, beat, shatter (see **kwēt-** in Appendix*).] —**squash'er** *n.*

squash bug. A blackish North American insect, *Anasa tristis,* that is destructive to squash, pumpkins, and other crops.

squash·y (skwŏsh'ē, skwôsh'ē) *adj.* **-ier, -iest. 1.** Easily squashed. **2.** Overripe and soft; pulpy. **3.** Boggy; squishy. —**squash'i·ly** *adv.* —**squash'i·ness** *n.*

squat (skwŏt) *v.* **squatted** or **squat, squatting, squats.** —*intr.* **1.** To sit on one's heels. **2.** To settle on unoccupied land without legal claim. **3.** To occupy a given piece of public land in order to acquire title to it. —*tr.* **1.** To put (oneself) in a crouching posture. **2.** To occupy as a squatter. —*adj.* **squatter, squattest. 1.** Seated in a squatting position. **2.** Short and thick; low and broad. —*n.* **1.** A squatting or crouching posture. **2. a.** The act of squatting or crouching. **b.** The lair of a hare; form. **3.** The land occupied by a squatter. [Middle English *squatten,* to crush, flatten, hence to squat, from Old French *esquatir* : *es-,* from Latin *ex-* (intensive) + *quatir, catir,* to press flat, from Vulgar Latin *coactīre* (unattested), to press together, from Latin *cogere* (past participle *coāctus*), to drive together : *com-,* together + *agere,* to drive (see **ag-** in Appendix*).]

squat·ter (skwŏt'ər) *n.* **1.** One who settles on unoccupied land without legal claim. **2.** One who occupies a piece of public land so as to acquire title.

squaw (skwô) *n.* **1.** A North American Indian woman. **2.** A woman; wife. Used humorously or disparagingly. [Massachuset *squa, eshqua,* from Proto-Algonquian *ethkwēwa* (unattested), "woman."]

squaw·fish (skwô'fĭsh') *n., pl.* **squawfish** or **-fishes.** Any of several large freshwater fishes of the genus *Ptychocheilus,* of western North America.

squawk (skwôk) *v.* **squawked, squawking, squawks.** —*intr.* **1.** To utter a harsh scream; screech. **2.** To make a loud or angry protest. —*tr.* To utter with or as if with a squawk. —*n.* **1.** A loud screech; squall. **2.** A loud or insistent protest. [Perhaps blend of SQUALL and SQUEAK.] —**squawk'er** *n.*

squaw man. A frontiersman having an Indian wife.

squaw·root (skwô'rōōt', -rŏŏt') *n.* A plant, *Conopholis americana,* of eastern North America, that has yellowish flowers, a stem covered with brownish scales, and is parasitic on the roots of oaks and other trees. [Formerly used by Indians to cure female disorders.]

squeak (skwēk) *v.* **squeaked, squeaking, squeaks.** —*intr.* **1.** To utter or make a brief thin, shrill cry or sound. **2.** To pass or win by a slight margin. Used with *through* or *by.* **3.** *Slang.* To turn informer. —*tr.* To utter in a squeaky voice. —*n.* **1.** A brief thin, shrill cry or sound. **2.** An escape: *a close squeak.* [Middle English *squeken,* probably from Scandinavian, akin to Old Norse *skvakka,* to croak (imitative).] —**squeak'er** *n.*

squeak·y (skwē'kē) *adj.* **-ier, -iest.** Characterized by squeaking tones; tending to squeak. —**squeak'i·ly** *adv.* —**squeak'i·ness** *n.*

squeal (skwēl) *v.* **squealed, squealing, squeals.** —*intr.* **1.** To utter or produce a loud, shrill cry or sound. **2.** *Slang.* To betray a friend or a secret; turn informer. —*tr.* To utter or produce with a squeal. —*n.* A loud, shrill cry or noise. [Middle English *squelen,* probably from Scandinavian, akin to Old Norse *skvala,* to shriek (probably imitative).] —**squeal'er** *n.*

squeam·ish (skwē'mĭsh) *adj.* **1. a.** Easily nauseated or sickened. **b.** Nauseated. **2.** Easily offended or disgusted; prudish. **3.** Excessively fastidious; oversensitive. [Middle English *squaymisch,* variant of *squaymous, sweymous,* from Old English *swīma,* dizziness. See **swei-**[2] in Appendix.*] —**squeam'ish·ly** *adv.* —**squeam'ish·ness** *n.*

squee·gee (skwē'jē') *n.* **1.** A T-shaped implement having a crosspiece edged with rubber or leather, used to remove water from a surface, as a window. **2.** A similar implement or a rubber roller used in printing and photography. —*tr.v.* **squeegeed, -geeing, -gees.** To wipe or smooth with a squeegee. [Probably from *squeege,* perhaps intensive variant of SQUEEZE.]

squeeze (skwēz) *v.* **squeezed, squeezing, squeezes.** —*tr.* **1.** To press hard upon or together; to compress. **2.** To exert pressure on, as by way of extracting liquid: *squeeze an orange.* **3.** To extract from by applying pressure. Often used with *from: squeeze juice from a lemon.* **4.** To extract by dishonest means; extort. **5.** To obtain room or passage for by pressure; cram. **6.** To oppress with burdensome exactions. **7.** *Bridge.* To force (an opponent) to use a potentially winning card in a trick he cannot take. —*intr.* **1.** To give way under pressure. **2.** To exert pressure. **3.** To force one's way, as through a crowd. —*n.* **1.** An act or instance of compressing; compression. **2.** A handclasp or brief embrace. **3.** A group crowded together; a crush; press. **4. a.** An amount squeezed out of something. **b.** A minor ingredient; pinch. **5.** Pressure exerted to obtain some concession or goal. Also called "squeeze play." **6.** A forced discard of a potentially winning card in bridge. [Earlier *squease,* intensive form of *quease,* to press, Middle English *queysen,* Old English *cwȳsan.* See **gweyə-** in Appendix.*] —**squeez'er** *n.*

squeeze play. **1.** *Baseball.* A play in which the batter attempts to bunt so that a runner on third base may score. **2.** Extortive pressure, a **squeeze** *(see).*

squelch (skwĕlch) *v.* **squelched, squelching, squelches.** —*tr.* **1.** To crush by or as if by trampling; suppress; squash. **2.** To put down or silence, as with a crushing remark. **3.** To cause to make a squishing sound. —*intr.* To make or move with a splashing, squashing, or sucking sound. —*n.* **1.** A squishing sound. **2.** A crushing reply. **3.** An electric circuit that cuts off a radio receiver when the signal is too weak for reception of anything but noise. [Imitative.] —**squelch'er** *n.*

sque·teague (skwĭ-tēg') *n., pl.* **squeteague. 1.** The **weakfish** *(see).* **2.** Any of several related fishes. [Probably from an unidentified Algonquian word in southeastern New England.]

squib (skwĭb) *n.* **1. a.** A firecracker. **b.** A broken firecracker that burns but does not explode. **2.** A brief, sometimes witty literary effort, such as a lampoon. [Probably imitative.]

squid (skwĭd) *n., pl.* **squids** or **squid.** Any of various marine cephalopod mollusks of the genera *Loligo, Rossia,* and related genera, having a usually elongated body, ten arms surrounding the mouth, a vestigial internal shell, and a pair of triangular or rounded fins. Compare **octopus.** [Origin unknown.]

squig·gle (skwĭg'əl) *n.* A small wiggly mark or scrawl. —*intr.v.* **squiggled, -gling, -gles.** To squirm and wriggle. [Blend of SQUIRM and WRIGGLE.] —**squig'gly** *adj.*

squill (skwĭl) *n.* **1.** Any of several bulbous plants of the genus *Scilla,* native to Eurasia, having narrow leaves and bell-shaped blue, white, or pink flowers. **2.** A related plant, the **sea onion** *(see).* **3.** The dried inner scales of the bulbs of this plant, used as rat poison and formerly as a cardiac stimulant, expectorant, and diuretic. [Middle English, from Latin *squilla, scilla,* from Greek *skilla*†.]

squil·la (skwĭl'ə) *n., pl.* **-las** or **squillae** (skwĭl'ē'). Any of various burrowing marine crustaceans of the order Stomatopoda, having a pair of jointed grasping appendages. Also called "mantis shrimp," "mantis crab." [New Latin *Squilla,* type genus, from Latin *squilla*†, shrimp, prawn.]

squinch (skwĭnch) *n.* A quarter-spherical segment of masonry vaulting or corbeling thrown across the upper inside corners of a square tower as the transition to a circular or octagonal superstructure. [Variant of *scunch,* short for SCUNCHEON.]

squint (skwĭnt) *v.* **squinted, squinting, squints.** —*intr.* **1.** To look with the eyes partly open: *"Crabbe squinted at the Arabic letters, deciphering slowly"* (Anthony Burgess). **2.** To look or glance to the side. **3.** To suffer from strabismus. **4.** To have an indirect or implicit tendency. Usually used with *toward* or *at.* —*tr.* **1.** To cause to squint. **2.** To close (the eyes) partly. —*n.* **1.** The act of squinting. **2.** An inclination; tendency. **3.** Strabismus. —*adj.* **1.** Looking obliquely or askance. **2.** Affected with strabismus. [Short for ASQUINT.] —**squint'er** *n.*

squint-eyed (skwĭnt'īd') *adj.* **1.** Having strabismus. **2.** With narrowed or squinting eyes. **3.** Looking askance; biased.

squire (skwīr) *n.* **1.** A young nobleman attendant upon a knight and ranked next below a knight in the feudal hierarchy. **2.** An English country gentleman. Often used as a term of address. **3.** A judge or other local dignitary. Often used as a term of address. **4.** A man who attends or escorts a woman; a gallant. —*tr.v.* **squired, squiring, squires.** To attend as a squire or escort. [Middle English *squier, esquier,* from Old French *esquier, escuier,* "shield-bearer," from Late Latin *scūtārius,* from Latin *scūtum,* a shield. See **skei-** in Appendix.*]

squire·ar·chy, squir·ar·chy (skwīr'är-kē) *n., pl.* **-chies. 1.** Squires collectively; especially, English landed proprietors. **2.** Government by landed proprietors.

squirm (skwûrm) *intr.v.* **squirmed, squirming, squirms. 1.** To twist about in a wriggling, snakelike motion; writhe. **2.** To feel or exhibit signs of humiliation or embarrassment. —*n.* The act of squirming or a squirming movement; a wriggle. [Perhaps expressive.] —**squirm'er** *n.* —**squirm'y** *adj.*

squir·rel (skwûr'əl, skwĭr'əl) *n.* **1.** Any of various arboreal rodents of the genus *Sciurus* and related genera, usually with gray or reddish-brown fur and a long, flexible, bushy tail. **2.** Any of various related animals of the family Sciuridae, such as the **ground squirrel** or the **flying squirrel** *(both of which see).* **3.** The fur of a squirrel. [Middle English *squyrel,* from Norman French *esquirel,* from Vulgar Latin *scūriōlus* (unattested), diminutive of *scūrius* (unattested), variant of Latin *sciūrus,* squirrel, from Greek *skiouros,* "shadow-tail" : *skia,* shadow (see **skī-** in Appendix*) + *oura,* tail (see **ors-** in Appendix*).]

squirrel corn. A low-growing North American plant, *Dicentra canadensis,* having finely divided leaves, cream-colored flowers, and tubers resembling grains of corn.

squir·rel·fish (skwûr'əl-fĭsh', skwĭr'-) *n., pl.* **squirrelfish** or **-fishes.** Any of various fishes of the genus *Holocentrus* and related genera, of warm marine waters, having large eyes and a usually reddish body.

squir·rel·ly (skwûr'əl-ē, skwĭr'-) *adj. Slang.* Crazy; eccentric.

squirrel monkey. Either of two tropical American monkeys, *Saimiri sciureus* or *S. örstedii,* having short, thick fur and a long, nonprehensile tail.

squirt (skwûrt) *v.* **squirted, squirting, squirts.** —*intr.* **1.** To be ejected in a thin swift stream. **2.** To eject a thin swift stream. —*tr.* **1.** To eject (liquid) in a thin swift stream. **2.** To wet with liquid so ejected. —*n.* **1.** The act of squirting. **2.** A device used to squirt. **3.** The stream squirted. **4.** *Informal.* An insignificant but arrogant person. [Middle English *squirten, swirten,* of Low German origin, akin to Low German *swirtjen* (imitative).] —**squirt'er** *n.*

squirting cucumber. A hairy vine, *Ecballium elaterium,* of the Mediterranean region, having fruit that discharges its seeds and juice explosively when ripe.

squish (skwĭsh) *v.* **squished, squishing, squishes.** *Informal.* —*tr.* To squash noisily. —*intr.* To emit a sound like that of soft mud being compressed. —*n.* Such a sound. [Variant of SQUASH.] —**squish'y** *adj.*

sr steradian.

Sr The symbol for the element strontium.

sr. senior.

Sr. **1.** senior (after a surname). **2.** señor. **3.** sister (religious).

Sra. señora.

Sr·bi·ja. The Serbo-Croatian name for **Serbia.**

Sri·nag·ar (srē'nŭg'ər). The winter capital of Jammu and Kashmir, northwestern India, on the Jhelum River. Population, 285,257.

S.R.O. standing room only.

Srta. señorita.

ss scilicet.

SS **1.** Schutzstaffel. **2.** steamship.

S.S. **1.** steamship. **2.** Sunday school.

SSA Social Security Administration.

SSE south-southeast.

S.S.R. Soviet Socialist Republic.

SSS Selective Service System.

SSW south-southwest.

st. **1.** stanza. **2.** state. **3.** statute. **4.** stet. **5.** stitch. **6.** stone. **7.** street. **8.** strophe.

-st. Variant of **-est** (verb inflection).

St. **1.** saint. **2.** statute. **3.** strait. **4.** street.

s.t. short ton.

sta. **1.** station. **2.** stationary.

stab (stăb) *v.* **stabbed, stabbing, stabs.** —*tr.* **1.** To pierce or wound with or as if with a pointed weapon. **2.** To plunge (a weapon) into a body. —*intr.* **1.** To lunge with or as if with a pointed weapon. **2.** To inflict a wound in this way. —**stab in the back.** To betray. —*n.* **1.** A thrust made with a pointed instrument or weapon. **2.** A wound inflicted by stabbing. **3.** An attempt; an effort. [From Middle English *stabbe,* wound by stabbing, obscurely related to dialectal *stob,* to stab, perhaps from Middle English *stob,* stake, stick, variant of STUB.] —**stab'ber** *n.*

Sta·bat Ma·ter (stä'bät' mä'tər, stā'băt' mā'tər). **1.** A medieval Latin hymn on the sorrows of the Virgin Mary at the Crucifixion. **2.** A musical setting for this hymn. [Latin, "the mother was standing" (opening words of the hymn).]

sta·bile (stā'bĭl, stā'bīl') *adj.* Immobile; stable; unchangeable. —*n.* (stā'bēl'). An abstract sculpture, usually of sheet metal, with no moving parts. [Latin *stabilis,* STABLE.]

sta·bil·i·ty (stə-bĭl'ə-tē) *n., pl.* **-ties. 1.** Resistance to sudden change, dislodgment, or overthrow. **2. a.** Constancy of character or purpose; tenacity; steadfastness. **b.** Reliability; depend-

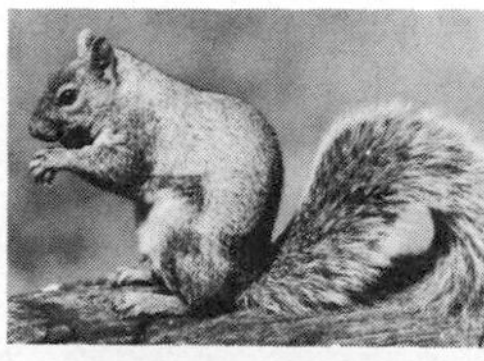

squirrel
Sciurus carolinensis
Eastern gray squirrel

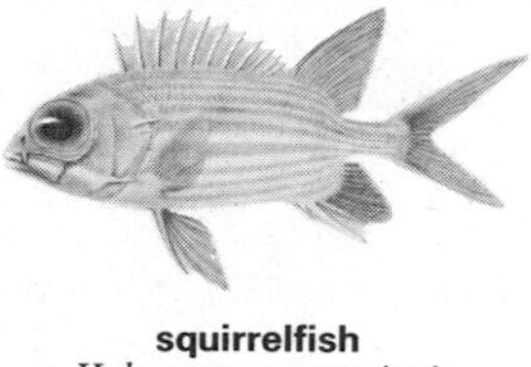

squirrelfish
Holocentrus ascensionis

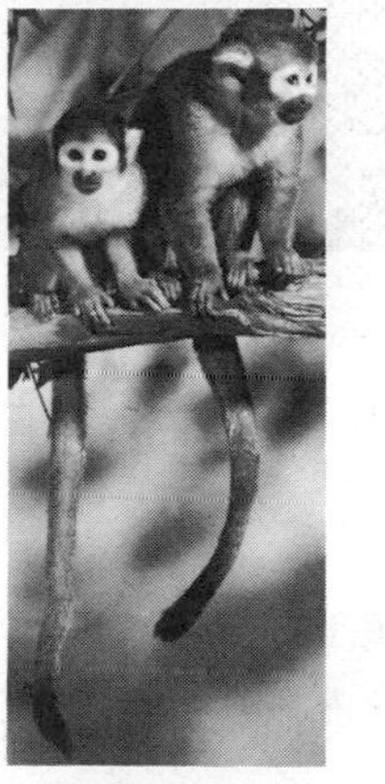

squirrel monkey
Saimiri sciureus

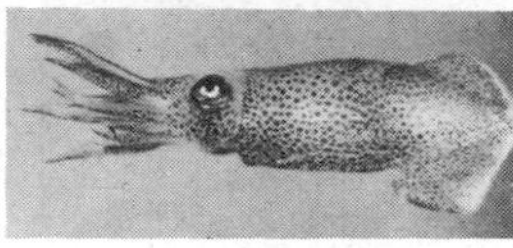

squid
Loligo pealei

ability. **3.** A vow committing a monk to one monastery for life.

sta·bi·lize (stā′bə-līz′) *v.* **-lized, -lizing, -lizes.** —*tr.* **1.** To make stable. **2.** To maintain the stability of. —*intr.* To become stable. —**sta′bi·li·za′tion** *n.*

sta·bi·liz·er (stā′bə-lī′zər) *n.* **1.** One that stabilizes. **2.** *Nautical.* A device in a ship or boat, such as a gyroscopically controlled fin, used to prevent excessive rolling. **3.** *Aviation.* Any airfoil used to stabilize an aircraft in flight. **4.** *Chemistry.* A substance that renders or maintains a solution, mixture, suspension, or state resistant to chemical change.

sta·ble[1] (stā′bəl) *adj.* **-bler, -blest. 1. a.** Resistant to sudden change of position or condition. **b.** Maintaining equilibrium; self-restoring. **2.** *Physics.* Having no known mode of decay; indefinitely long-lived. Said of atomic particles. **3.** Immutable and permanent; enduring. **4.** *Chemistry.* Not easily decomposed or otherwise modified chemically. **5.** Consistently dependable. [Middle English, from Old French *estable,* from Latin *stabilis,* standing firm. See **stā-** in Appendix.*] —**sta′ble·ness** *n.* —**sta′bly** *adv.*

sta·ble[2] (stā′bəl) *n.* **1.** A building for the shelter and feeding of domestic animals, especially horses and cattle. **2.** The animals lodged in such a building, collectively. **3.** All of the racehorses belonging to a single owner or racing establishment. **4.** The personnel employed to keep and train such a collection of racehorses. **5.** Any group that serves under a single authority, as prize fighters or prostitutes. —See Synonyms at **flock.** —*v.* **stabled, stabling, stables.** —*tr.* To put or keep (an animal) in a stable. —*intr.* To live or be kept in a stable. [Middle English, from Old French *estable,* from Latin *stabulum,* "standing place," enclosure, stable. See **stā-** in Appendix.*]

sta·bling (stā′blĭng) *n.* **1.** Stables collectively. **2.** Accommodations in a stable for animals.

stab·lish. *Archaic.* Variant of **establish.**

stac·ca·to (stə-kä′tō) *adj.* **1.** *Abbr.* **stac.** *Music.* Performed with a crisp, sharp attack to simulate rests between successive tones. Used as a direction to the performer. **2.** Composed of abrupt, distinct, emphatic parts or sounds: *"The man was walking with the staccato steps of someone carrying a load too heavy for him."* (Harper Lee). —*n., pl.* **staccatos** or **-ti** (-tĭ). An abrupt, emphatic manner or sound. [Italian, past participle of *(di)staccare,* to detach, from Old French *destach(i)er.* See **detach.**] —**stac·ca′to** *adv.*

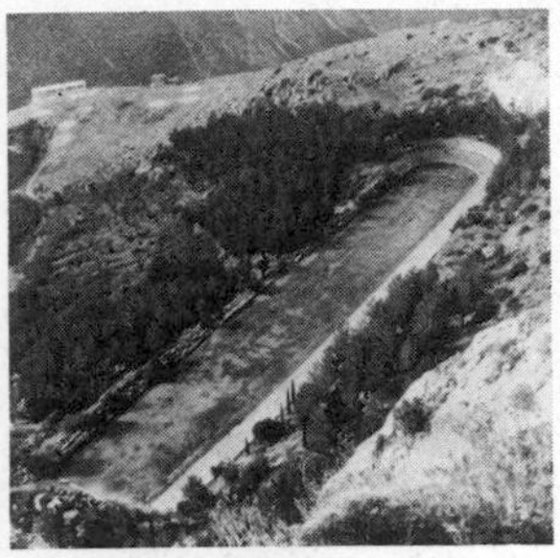

stadium
Ancient stadium at Delphi, Greece, built for the quadrennial Pythian games

stack (stăk) *n.* **1.** A large, usually conical pile of straw or fodder arranged for outdoor storage. **2.** Any orderly pile, especially one arranged in layers. **3.** A group of three or more unslung rifles, supporting each other butt downward and forming a cone. **4. a.** A chimney or flue. **b.** A group of chimneys. **5.** A vertical exhaust pipe, as on a ship or locomotive. **6.** Several rows of enclosed bookshelves; a bookcase. **7.** *Plural.* The area of a library in which most of the books are shelved. **8.** An English measure of coal or cut wood, equal to 108 cubic feet. **9.** *Informal.* A large quantity. —*tr.v.* **stacked, stacking, stacks. 1.** To arrange in a stack; to pile. **2.** To load with stacks of some material. **3.** To prearrange the order of (playing cards); to cheat. —**stack up. 1.** To add up or total. **2.** To measure up or equal. [Middle English *stak, sta(ke),* from Old Norse *stakkr.* See **steg-**[2] in Appendix.*] —**stack′er** *n.*

stac·te (stăk′tē) *n.* A spice used by the ancient Jews in making incense. Exodus 30:34. [Latin *stactē,* from Greek *staktē,* from the feminine of *staktos,* oozing, distilling, from *stazein,* to ooze. See **stag-** in Appendix.*]

stad·dle (stăd′l) *n.* A foundation; especially, a platform upon which hay or straw is stacked. [Middle English *stathel,* Old English *stathol.* See **stā-** in Appendix.*]

stad·hold·er (stăd′hōl′dər) *n.* Also **stadt·hold·er** (stăt′-). **1.** Formerly, a governor or viceroy in a province of the Netherlands. **2.** The chief magistrate of the Netherlands. [Partial translation of Dutch *stadhouder,* translation of Latin *locum tenens,* "(one) holding the place (of another)," lieutenant : *stad,* place, from Middle Dutch *stad, stat* (see **stā-** in Appendix*) + *houder,* holder.]

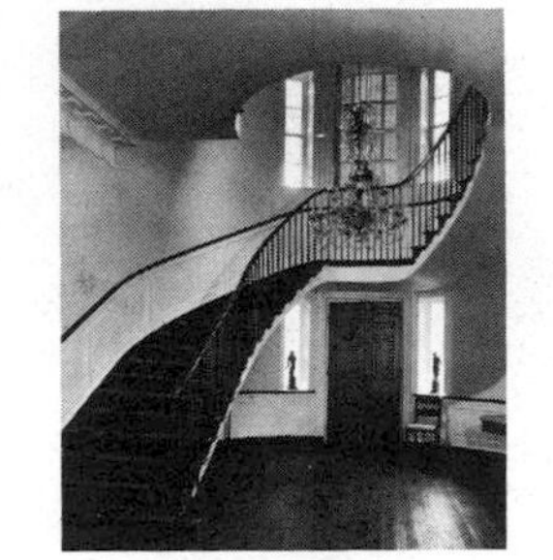

staircase
Circular staircase in the Joseph Manigault House, built in 1803, Charleston, South Carolina

sta·di·a (stā′dē-ə) *n.* **1.** A method of surveying distances with a telescopic instrument having two parallel lines used to intercept intervals on a calibrated rod, the intervals being proportional to the intervening distance. **2.** The graduated rod used. Also called "stadia rod." **3.** The parallel lines in the telescope. In this sense, also called "stadia hairs." [Italian, probably from Latin, plural of STADIUM (measure of length).]

sta·di·um (stā′dē-əm) *n., pl.* **-dia** (-dē-ə) or **-diums** (for sense 3). **1.** In ancient Greece, a course on which foot races were held, usually semicircular and having tiers of seats for spectators. **2.** An ancient Greek measure of distance, based on the length of such a course and equal to about 607 feet. **3.** A large, often unroofed structure in which athletic events are held. **4.** A stage in the progress of a disease. [Middle English, measure of distance, from Latin, from Greek *stadion,* alteration (probably influenced by the neuter of *stadios,* firm) of *spadion,* racetrack (particularly the racetrack of this length at Olympia), from *span,* to draw, pull. See **spasm.**]

Staël (stäl), **Madame de.** In full, Baronne Anne Louise Germaine Necker de Staël-Holstein. 1766–1817. French critic, novelist, and literary patron.

staff[1] (stăf) *n., pl.* **staffs** (except sense 4) or **staves** (stāvz) (except sense 3). **1.** A pole, rod, or stick carried for various purposes, specifically: **a.** A stick or cane carried as an aid in walking or climbing. **b.** A stick used as a weapon; a cudgel. **c.** A pole upon which a flag is displayed. **d.** A rod, baton, or the like carried as a symbol of authority. **2.** A rule or similar graduated stick used for testing or measuring, as in surveying. **3. a.** A group of assistants who aid an executive or other person of authority. **b.** A group of military or naval officers who serve a commanding officer but do not participate in combat and have no authority to command. **c.** The personnel who carry out a specific enterprise: *the nursing staff of a hospital.* **4.** *Music.* The set of horizontal lines and their intermediate spaces upon which notes are written or printed. In this sense, also called "stave." —*tr.v.* **staffed, staffing, staffs.** To provide (an office, for example) with a staff of employees. [Middle English *staf,* Old English *stæf,* stick, rod. See **stebh-** in Appendix.*]

staff[2] (stăf) *n.* A building material that resembles stucco, composed of plaster and fiber and used as a wall covering over the skeleton of temporary buildings, as at expositions. [Probably from German *staffieren,* to dress, trim, adorn, from Middle Low German *stafferen, stofferen,* from Middle Dutch *stofferen,* from Old French *estoffer,* to STUFF.]

Staf·fa (stăf′ə). An uninhabited island of the Inner Hebrides, Scotland; the site of Fingal's Cave.

staff of life. A staple or necessary food, especially bread.

Staf·ford (stăf′ərd). **1.** Also **Staf·ford·shire** (-shîr, -shər). A county occupying 1,153 square miles in west-central England. Population, 1,734,000. Also called "Staffs." **2.** The county seat of this county. Population, 49,000.

Staf·ford·shire terrier (stăf′ərd-shîr). A dog of a breed developed in England, having a short, variously colored coat and widely set forelegs.

staff sergeant. 1. *U.S. Army.* A noncommissioned officer of the rank above a sergeant and below a sergeant first class. **2.** *U.S. Air Force.* A noncommissioned officer of the rank above an airman first class and below a technical sergeant. **3.** *U.S. Marine Corps.* A noncommissioned officer of the rank above a sergeant and below a gunnery sergeant.

stag (stăg) *n.* **1.** The adult male of various deer, especially the red deer. **2.** An animal, especially a pig, castrated after reaching sexual maturity. **3.** A man who attends a social affair without escorting a woman. **4.** A social affair for men only. —*adj.* For or attended by men only: *a stag party.* —*adv.* As a single male; alone: *go stag.* —*intr.v.* **stagged, stagging, stags.** To attend a social affair without escorting a woman. [Middle English *stag(ge),* Old English *stagga.* See **stegh-** in Appendix.*]

stag beetle. Any of numerous large beetles of the family Lucanidae, having long, powerful, antlerlike mandibles.

stage (stāj) *n.* **1.** Any raised and level floor or platform. **2.** A platform on a microscope on which slides to be viewed are mounted. **3.** A workmen's scaffold. **4. a.** The raised platform upon which theatrical performances are presented. **b.** Any area in which actors perform. **c.** The acting profession. **d.** Dramatic literature or performance; the theater. **5.** The scene or setting of an event or series of events. **6.** A resting place on a journey, especially one providing overnight accommodations. **7.** The distance between stopping places on a journey; a leg of a journey. **8.** A stagecoach. **9.** A level or story of a building. **10.** The level of the surface of a river or other fluctuating body of water in relation to some datum: *at flood stage.* **11.** A level, degree, or period of time in the course of a process; a step in development. **12.** *Aerospace.* One of two or more successive propulsion units of a rocket vehicle that fires after the preceding one has been jettisoned. See **multistage rocket. 13.** *Geology.* A subdivision in the classification of stratified rocks, ranking just below a series and representing rock formed during a chronological age. **14.** *Electronics.* An element or group of elements in a complex arrangement of parts, especially a single tube or transistor and its accessory components in an amplifier. —See Synonyms at **phase.** —*v.* **staged, staging, stages.** —*tr.* **1.** To exhibit, present, or perform on or as if on a stage: *stage a boxing match.* **2.** To produce or direct (a theatrical performance). **3.** To arrange and carry out: *stage an invasion.* —*intr.* To be adaptable to or suitable for theatrical presentation. [Middle English, from Old French *estage,* from Vulgar Latin *staticum* (unattested), "standing place," position, from Latin *stāre,* to stand. See **stā-** in Appendix.*]

stage·coach (stāj′kōch′) *n.* A four-wheeled horse-drawn vehicle formerly used to transport mail, parcels, and passengers.

stage·craft (stāj′krăft′, -kräft′) *n.* The practice of or skill in theatrical techniques.

stage·hand (stāj′hănd′) *n.* A person who works backstage in a theater.

stage-man·age (stāj′măn′ĭj) *tr.v.* **-aged, -aging, -ages. 1.** To serve as overall supervisor of the stage and actors for (a theatrical production). **2.** To supervise (a political campaign, for example) from behind the scenes. —**stage manager.**

stag·er (stā′jər) *n.* One who possesses the wisdom of long experience. [Probably from Old French *estagier,* a monk long residing in an infirmary, from *estage,* infirmary, STAGE.]

stage-struck (stāj′strŭk′) *adj.* Enthralled with the stage or with hopes of becoming an actor.

stage whisper. 1. The conventional whisper of an actor, intended to be heard by the audience. **2.** Any whisper intended to be overheard.

stage·y. Variant of **stagy.**

Stagg (stăg), **Amos Alonzo.** 1862–1965. American athletic coach; developed modern football tactics.

stag·gard (stăg′ərd) *n.* A full-grown male red deer. [Middle English : STAG + -ARD.]

stag·ger (stăg′ər) *v.* **-gered, -gering, -gers.** —*intr.* **1.** To move or stand unsteadily, as if under a great weight; totter. **2.** To lose strength or confidence; begin to yield. —*tr.* **1.** To cause to totter, sway, or reel. **2.** To overwhelm with emotion or surprise. **3.** To place regularly on alternating sides of a midline; set

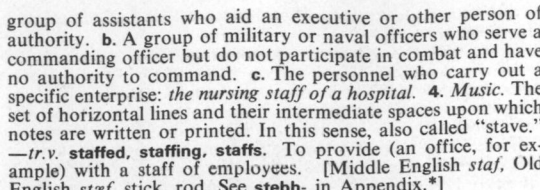

ă pat/ā pay/âr care/ä father/b bib/ch church/d deed/ĕ pet/ē be/f fife/g gag/h hat/hw which/ĭ pit/ī pie/îr pier/j judge/k kick/l lid, needle/m mum/n no, sudden/ng thing/ŏ pot/ō toe/ô paw, for/oi noise/ou out/ŏŏ took/ōō boot/p pop/r roar/s sauce/sh ship, dish/

in a zigzag row or rows: *theater seats staggered for clear viewing.* **4.** To arrange in alternating or overlapping time periods. —*n.* **1.** The act of staggering; a tottering, swaying, or reeling motion. **2.** A staggered pattern, arrangement, or order. [Earlier *stacker,* Middle English *stakeren,* from Old Norse *stakra,* frequentative of *staka,* to push, cause to stumble. See **steg-**[2] in Appendix.*] —**stag'ger·er** *n.* —**stag'ger·ing·ly** *adv.*

stag·ger·bush (stăg'ər-bo͝osh') *n.* A shrub, *Lyonia mariana,* of the eastern United States, having poisonous foliage.

stag·gers (stăg'ərz) *n.* Plural in form, usually used with a singular verb. **1.** Any of various diseases marked by vertigo, confusion, and weakness. **2.** Any of various diseases of the nervous system in animals, especially a cerebrospinal disease in horses, in which the animal loses coordination, staggers, and often falls. In this sense, also called "blind staggers."

stag·horn fern (stăg'hôrn'). Any of several tropical epiphytic ferns of the genus *Platycerium,* having large divided fronds that resemble antlers.

stag·hound (stăg'hound') *n.* Any of several dogs, such as a deerhound, formerly used in hunting deer.

stag·ing (stā'jĭng) *n.* **1.** A temporary platform; scaffold. **2. a.** The operation of stagecoaches as an enterprise. **b.** Travel by stagecoach. **3.** The process of producing and directing a stage play. **4.** The act of jettisoning a stage of a multistage rocket.

Sta·gi·ra (stə-jī'rə). Also **Sta·gi·rus** (-jī'rəs). An ancient city of Macedonia, on the eastern Chalcidice peninsula, in northeastern Greece; the birthplace of Aristotle. —**Stag'i·rite'** (stăj'ə-rīt') *adj.* & *n.*

stag·nant (stăg'nənt) *adj.* **1.** Not moving or flowing; without a current; motionless. **2.** Foul from standing still; polluted; stale: *"As long as the water is troubled it cannot become stagnant"* (James Baldwin). **3.** Lacking liveliness or briskness; inactive; sluggish. [Latin *stagnāns,* present participle of *stagnāre,* to be stagnant, from *stagnum,* pond, swamp. See **stag-** in Appendix.*] —**stag'nan·cy** *n.* —**stag'nant·ly** *adv.*

stag·nate (stăg'nāt') *intr.v.* **-nated, -nating, -nates. 1.** To be or become stagnant. **2.** To lie inactive; fail to progress or develop. [Latin *stagnāre.* See **stagnant.**] —**stag·na'tion** *n.*

St. Ag·nes' Eve (sānt ăg'nəs). Also **St. Ag·nes's Eve** (ăg'nə-səz). The night of January 20, when, according to legend, a maiden will dream of her future husband.

stag·y (stā'jē) *adj.* **-ier, -iest.** Also **stage·y.** Having a theatrical character or quality; especially, artificial and affected. —**stag'i·ly** *adv.* —**stag'i·ness** *n.*

Stahl (stäl), **Georg Ernst.** 1660–1734. German chemist and physician; publicized the phlogiston theory of combustion.

staid (stād) *adj.* **1.** Prudently reserved and colorless in style, manner, or behavior; grave; sober. **2.** Fixed; permanent: *"There is nothing settled, nothing staid in this universe"* (Virginia Woolf). —See Synonyms at **serious.** [From *staid,* obsolete past participle of STAY.] —**staid'ly** *adv.* —**staid'ness** *n.*

stain (stān) *v.* **stained, staining, stains.** —*tr.* **1.** To discolor, soil, or spot. **2.** To taint; tarnish; corrupt. **3.** To color with a coat of penetrating liquid dye or tint. **4.** To treat (specimens for the microscope) with a reagent or dye that makes visible certain parts without affecting others. —*intr.* To produce or receive discolorations. —*n.* **1.** A spot or smudge of foreign matter. **2.** A blemish upon one's moral character, personality, or reputation; stigma. **3.** A liquid substance applied especially to wood that penetrates the surface and imparts a rich color. **4.** A colored solution used for staining microscopic specimens. [Middle English *steynen,* short for *disteynen,* to deprive of color, stain, from Old French *desteindre,* from Vulgar Latin *distingere* (unattested) : Latin *dis-* (reversal) + *tingere,* to dye (see **teng-** in Appendix*).] —**stain'a·ble** *adj.* —**stain'er** *n.*

stained glass. Glass colored by mixing pigments inherently in the glass, by fusing colored metallic oxides onto the glass, or by painting and baking transparent colors on the glass surface. It is widely used in church windows. —**stained'-glass'** *adj.*

stain·less (stān'lĭs) *adj.* **1.** Without stain or blemish. **2.** Resistant to stain or corrosion. —**stain'less·ly** *adv.*

stainless steel. Any of various steels alloyed with sufficient chromium to resist corrosion, oxidation, or rusting associated with exposure of ordinary steel to water and moist air.

stair (stâr) *n.* **1.** *Usually plural.* A series or flight of steps; a staircase. **2.** One of a flight of steps. [Middle English *steir(e), stair(e),* Old English *stǣger.* See **steigh-** in Appendix.*]

stair·case (stâr'kās') *n.* A flight or series of flights of steps connecting separate levels, and its supporting structure.

stair·way (stâr'wā') *n.* A flight of stairs; a staircase.

stair·well (stâr'wĕl') *n.* A vertical shaft around which a staircase has been built.

stake[1] (stāk) *n.* **1.** A piece of wood or metal sharpened at one end for driving into the ground, as a marker, a fence pole, or a tent peg. **2. a.** A vertical post to which an offender is bound for execution by burning. **b.** Execution by burning. **3.** A vertical post secured at the edge of a platform, as on a truck. **4.** *Mormon Church.* A territorial division consisting of a group of wards under the jurisdiction of a bishop. —**pull up stakes.** To conclude one's affairs and move on. —*tr.v.* **staked, staking, stakes. 1.** To indicate the location or limits of with or as if with stakes. Often used with *out: stake out a claim.* **2.** To attach or support with a stake or stakes. **3.** To tether or tie to a stake. [Middle English *stake,* Old English *staca.* See **steg-**[2] in Appendix.*]

stake[2] (stāk) *n.* **1.** *Often plural.* **a.** Money or property risked in a wager or gambling game. **b.** The reward or prize awarded the winner of a contest or race; purse. **2.** A race offering a reward or prize to the winner. **3.** A share or interest in any enterprise; especially, a financial share. **4.** A grubstake. —**at stake.** In jeopardy. —*tr.v.* **staked, staking, stakes. 1.** To gamble or risk; to hazard; to bet. **2.** To provide working capital for; to finance. [Perhaps originally "something placed on a post as a wager in a game," from STAKE (post).]

Staked Plain. See **Llano Estacado.**

Sta·kha·nov·ite (stə-kä'nə-vīt') *n.* A worker whose diligence and zeal earn him high governmental esteem. [After Alexei *Stakhanov,* Russian miner who devised a worker-incentive system in 1935.]

sta·lac·tite (stə-lăk'tīt', stăl'ək-) *n.* A cylindrical or conical deposit, usually of calcite or aragonite, projecting downward from the roof of a cavern as a result of the dripping of mineral-rich water. [New Latin *stalactites,* from Greek *stalaktos,* dripping, from *stalassein*†, to drip.] —**sta·lac'ti·form'** (-tə-fôrm') *adj.* —**stal'ac·tit'ic** (stăl'ăk-tĭt'ĭk), **stal'ac·tit'i·cal** *adj.*

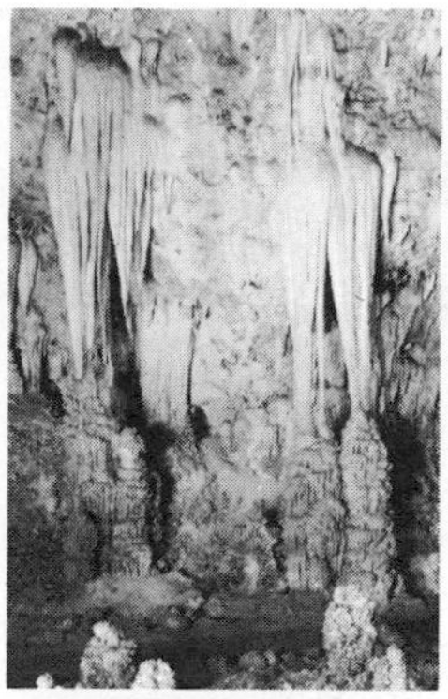

stalactite
Carlsbad Caverns
of southeastern New Mexico

sta·lag (stăl'ăg; *German* shtä'läk) *n.* A German prisoner-of-war camp for noncommissioned and enlisted personnel. [German *Stalag,* short for *Stammlager,* "base camp" : *Stamm,* a base, stem, from Old High German *stam* (see **stebh-** in Appendix*) + *Lager,* a camp, sleeping place, from Old High German *legar,* a bed (see **legh-** in Appendix*).]

sta·lag·mite (stə-lăg'mīt', stăl'əg-) *n.* A cylindrical or conical deposit, usually of calcite or aragonite, projecting upward from the floor of a cavern as a result of the dripping of mineral-rich water. [New Latin *stalagmites,* from Greek *stalagma,* a drop, from *stalagmos,* dripping, from *stalassein,* to drip. See **stalactite.**] —**stal'ag·mit'ic** (stăl'əg-mĭt'ĭk), **stal'ag·mit'i·cal** *adj.*

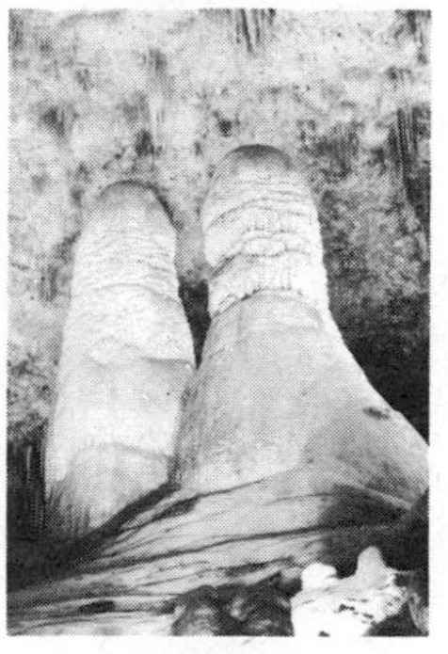

stalagmite
Carlsbad Caverns

St. Al·bans (sānt' ôl'bənz). A town in Hertfordshire, England, about 21 miles northwest of London. Population, 50,000.

stale[1] (stāl) *adj.* **staler, stalest. 1.** Having lost freshness, effervescence, or palatability; flat or dry. **2.** Lacking in originality or spontaneity: *a stale joke.* **3.** Impaired in efficacy or strength. **4.** Having lost legal efficacy or force through lack of exercise or action. —See Synonyms at **trite.** —*v.* **staled, staling, stales.** —*tr.* To make stale. —*intr.* To become stale. [Middle English, old enough to clear, well-aged (said of liquor), probably from Norman French, from Old French *estale,* not moving, slack, from *estaler,* to halt, stop, from *estal,* a stand, fixed place, from Frankish *stal* (unattested), position. See **stel-**[1] in Appendix.*] —**stale'ly** *adv.* —**stale'ness** *n.*

stale[2] (stāl) *intr.v.* **staled, staling, stales.** To urinate. Used of horses and camels. —*n.* Urine of horses or camels. [Middle English *stalen,* from Germanic, akin to Middle Low German *stallen.*]

stale·mate (stāl'māt') *n.* **1.** *Chess.* A drawing position in which only the king can move and although not in check can move only into check. **2.** A situation in which further action by either of two opponents is impossible; a deadlock. —*tr.v.* **stalemated, -mating, -mates.** To bring into a stalemate. [Obsolete *stale,* stalemate, from Middle English, from Norman French *estale,* fixed position, from Old French *estal* (see **stale**) + MATE (checkmate).]

Sta·lin. **1.** The former name for **Varna. 2.** The former name for **Brașov.**

Sta·lin (stä'lĭn; *Russian* stä'lyĭn'), **Joseph.** Original name, Iosif Vissarionovich Dzhugashvili. 1879–1953. General secretary of the Communist Party of the Soviet Union (1922–53); premier (1941–53).

Sta·li·na·bad. The former name for **Dushanbe.**

Sta·lin·grad. A former name for **Volgograd.**

Sta·lin·ism (stä'lə-nĭz'əm) *n.* The bureaucratic and authoritarian exercise of state power and mechanistic application of Marxist-Leninist principles associated with the period of Stalin's leadership, especially in the Soviet Union and the socialist states of central Europe. —**Sta'lin·ist** *n.* & *adj.*

Sta·li·no. A former name for **Donetsk.**

Sta·lin Peak. The former name for Mount **Communism.**

Sta·linsk. The former name for **Novo Kuznetsk.**

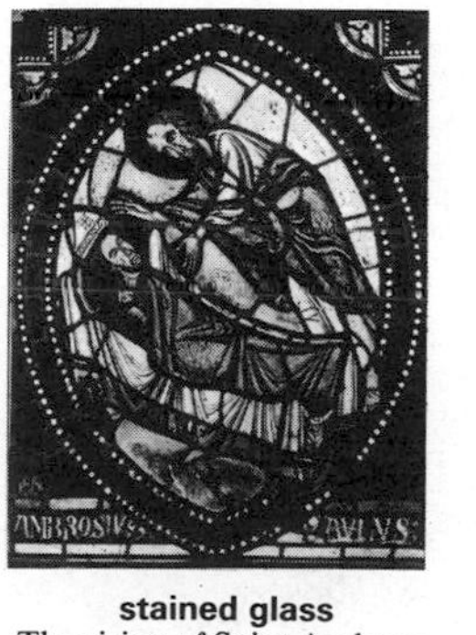

stained glass
The vision of Saint Ambrose
depicted in stained glass,
Cathedral of Le Mans,
France

stalk[1] (stôk) *n.* **1. a.** A stem or main axis of a herbaceous plant. **b.** A stem or similar structure that supports a plant part such as a flower, flower cluster, or leaf. **2.** Any slender or elongated support or structure. [Middle English *stalk(e),* probably from Scandinavian, akin to Norwegian dialectal *stalk.* See **stel-**[1] in Appendix.*] —**stalk'y** *adj.*

stalk[2] (stôk) *v.* **stalked, stalking, stalks.** —*intr.* **1.** To walk with a stiff, haughty, or angry gait. **2.** To move threateningly or menacingly; to steal. **3.** To track game. —*tr.* **1.** To pursue by tracking. **2.** To go through (a tract of country) in pursuit of game or other quarry. [Middle English *stalken,* Old English *(be)stealcian,* to walk cautiously. See **ster-**[4] in Appendix.*] —**stalk'er** *n.*

stalk·ing-horse (stô'kĭng-hôrs') *n.* **1.** A horse trained to conceal the hunter while stalking. **2.** A canvas screen made in the figure of a horse, used for similar concealment. **3.** Anything used to cover one's true purpose; a decoy. **4.** Any sham candidate put forward to conceal the candidacy of another or to divide the opposition.

stall (stôl) *n.* **1.** A compartment for one domestic animal in a barn or shed. **2.** Any small compartment, booth, or cubicle. **3. a.** An enclosed seat in the chancel of a church. **b.** A pew in a church. **4.** *Chiefly British.* A seat in the front part of the orchestra in a theater. **5.** A parking space for an automobile. **6.** A protective sheath of rubber or similar material for a finger or thumb; a cot. **7.** The condition in which the increase in incidence of an airplane wing gives little or no increase in lift and may cause loss of control and decrease in altitude. **8.** *Informal.* A ruse or delaying tactic employed to mislead interrogators or postpone action. —*v.* **stalled, stalling, stalls.** —*tr.* **1.** To put or lodge (an animal) in a stall. **2.** To maintain (an animal) in a stall for fattening. **3.** To check the motion or progress of; bring to a standstill. **4.** To employ delaying tactics against. Often used with *off: stall off creditors.* See Usage note below. **5.** Accidentally to cause (an engine) to stop running. **6.** To cause (an airplane) to go into a stall. —*intr.* **1.** To live or be lodged in a stall. **2.** To stick fast in mud or snow. **3.** To come to a standstill. **4.** To employ delaying tactics. See Usage note below. **5.** To stop running from mechanical failure. Said of an engine. **6.** *Aviation.* To lose forward speed causing a stall. [Middle English *stal(l),* Old English *steall,* standing place, stable. See **stel-**[1] in Appendix.*]

Usage: *Stall,* in sense 4 of both the transitive and intransitive verb, is common in informal contexts but not necessarily limited to them. The following, as examples in writing, are acceptable to a majority of the Usage Panel: *Realizing that help was on the way, he tried to stall* (accepted by 75 per cent). *She sought to stall off her creditors* (accepted by 62 per cent).

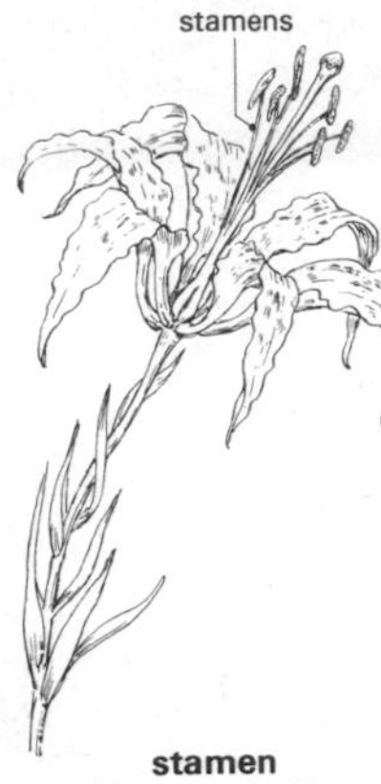

stamen
Stamens of a lily

stall-feed (stôl′fēd′) *tr.v.* **-fed** (-fĕd′), **-feeding, -feeds.** To lodge and feed (an animal) in a stall for the purpose of fattening.

stal·lion (stăl′yən) *n.* An adult male horse that has not been castrated. [Middle English *stalo(u)n,* from Old French *estalon,* from Frankish *stallo* (unattested), from *stal* (unattested), standing-place, stable. See **stel-**[1] in Appendix.*]

stal·wart (stôl′wərt) *adj.* **1.** Having physical strength; sturdy; robust. **2.** Resolute; uncompromising. —See Synonyms at **strong.** —*n.* **1.** One who is physically and morally strong. **2.** One who actively supports an organization or cause. [Middle English (Scottish dialect) variant of *stalworth, stalwurth,* Old English *stælwierthe,* serviceable, probably contraction of *statholwierthe,* "worthy in the foundation," firm : *stathol,* foundation (see **stā-** in Appendix*) + *wierthe, weorth,* worth (see **wer-**[3] in Appendix*).] —**stal′wart·ly** *adv.* —**stal′wart·ness** *n.*

Stam·bul (stäm-bo͞ol′). Also **Stam·boul.** **1.** The old section of Istanbul, south of the Golden Horn. **2.** See **Istanbul.**

sta·men (stā′mən) *n., pl.* **-mens** or *rare* **stamina** (stăm′ə-nə). The pollen-producing reproductive organ of a flower, usually consisting of a filament and an anther. [Latin *stāmen,* thread of the warp, stamen. See **stā-** in Appendix.*]

Stam·ford (stăm′fərd). A city of Connecticut, in the southwest on Long Island Sound. Population, 93,000.

stam·i·na (stăm′ə-nə) *n.* **1.** The physical or moral strength required to resist or withstand disease, fatigue, or hardship; endurance. **2.** *Rare.* Plural of **stamen.** [Latin, plural *stāmen,* thread of the warp, thread of human life. See **stamen.**]

stam·i·nal (stăm′ə-nəl) *adj.* **1.** Pertaining to, showing, or producing stamina. **2.** Pertaining to a stamen or stamens.

stam·i·nate (stăm′ə-nĭt, -nāt′) *adj. Botany.* **1.** Having a stamen or stamens. **2.** Bearing stamens but lacking pistils: *staminate flowers.*

stam·i·node (stăm′ə-nōd′) *n.* Also **stam·i·no·di·um** (stăm′ə-nō′dē-əm) *pl.* **-dia** (-dē-ə). *Botany.* A sterile functionless stamen. [New Latin *staminodium,* from Latin *stāmen,* STAMEN.]

stam·mel (stăm′əl) *n. Obsolete.* **1.** A coarse, red woolen cloth formerly used for undergarments. **2.** The red color of this cloth. —*adj. Obsolete.* Dull-red. [Probably variant of *stamin,* Middle English *stamyn,* from Latin *stāminea,* feminine of *stāmineus,* made of threads, from *stāmen,* thread of the warp. See **stā-** in Appendix.*]

stamp
Revenue stamp used under the Stamp Act

stam·mer (stăm′ər) *v.* **-mered, -mering, -mers.** —*intr.* To intrude involuntary pauses and sometimes syllabic repetitions into one's speaking; falter; stumble. —*tr.* To utter or say with a stammer. —*n.* An instance or habit of stammering. [Middle English *stameren,* Old English *stamerian.* See **stam-** in Appendix.*] —**stam′mer·er** *n.* —**stam′mer·ing·ly** *adv.*

Synonyms: *stammer, stutter.* These verbs apply to hesitant, stumbling, or repetitive speech. *Stammer* generally refers to involuntary pauses or breaks in speech. *Stutter* usually refers to spasmodic repetition or exaggeration of sounds or syllables, especially initial consonants.

stamp (stămp) *v.* **stamped, stamping, stamps.** —*tr.* **1.** To bring down (the foot) forcibly. **2.** To bring the foot down upon (an object or surface) forcibly. **3.** To bring into a specified condition by or as if by thrusting downward forcibly with the foot. **4.** To form or cut out by application of a mold, form, or die. **5.** To imprint or impress with a mark, design, or seal. **6.** To impress forcibly or permanently. **7.** To affix an adhesive stamp to. **8.** To identify, characterize, or reveal. —*intr.* **1.** To thrust the foot forcibly downward. **2.** To walk with forcible, heavy steps. —See Usage note at **stomp.** —*n.* **1.** The act of stamping. **2. a.** An implement or device used to impress, cut out, or shape something to which it is applied. **b.** The impression or shape thus formed. **3.** A mark, design, or seal, the impression of which indicates ownership, approval, completion, or the like. **4. a.** A small piece of gummed paper sold by a government for attachment to an article that is to be mailed; postage stamp. **b.** Any similar piece of gummed paper issued for a specific purpose: *trading stamp.* **5.** Any identifying or characterizing mark or impression. **6.** Characteristic nature or quality; class; kind. [Middle English *stampen,* Old English *stampian* (unattested), to pound, stamp. See **stebh-** in Appendix.*]

Stamp Act. An act passed (1765) by the British Parliament requiring that revenue stamps be affixed to all official documents and printed matter in the American colonies.

stam·pede (stăm′pēd′) *n.* **1.** A sudden headlong rush of startled animals, especially cattle or horses. **2.** A sudden headlong rush of a crowd of people. **3.** Any precipitous mass movement. —*v.* **stampeded, -peding, -pedes.** —*intr.* To participate in a stampede. —*tr.* To cause to stampede. [Mexican Spanish *estampida,* from Spanish, uproar, crash, "a stamping or pounding," from *estampar,* to pound, stamp, from Germanic. See **stebh-** in Appendix.*] —**stam′ped′er** *n.*

stamping ground. One's customary environment or favorite gathering place.

stamp mill. **1.** A machine that crushes ore. **2.** A building in which ore is crushed.

stance (stăns) *n.* **1.** The attitude or position of a standing person or animal; especially, the position assumed by an athlete or sportsman in action. **2.** One's emotional or intellectual attitude or position. [Old French *estance,* position, place, from Italian *stanza,* from Vulgar Latin *stantia* (unattested), a standing, from Latin *stāre.* See **stā-** in Appendix.*]

stanch (stänch, stănch) *tr.v.* **stanched, stanching, stanches.** Also **staunch.** **1.** To stop or check the flow of (a bodily fluid, especially blood). **2.** To check the flow of blood from (a wound). —*adj.* Variant of **staunch.** See Usage note at **staunch.** [Middle English *staunchen,* to stop from flowing, from Old French *estanch(i)er,* from Vulgar Latin *stanticāre* (unattested), from Latin *stāns,* present participle of *stāre,* to stand. See **stā-** in Appendix.*] —**stanch′er** *n.*

stan·chion (stăn′chən, -shən) *n.* **1.** An upright pole, post, or support. **2.** One of the vertical posts used to secure cattle in a stall. —*tr.v.* **stanchioned, -chioning, -chions.** **1.** To build stanchions for; equip with stanchions. **2.** To confine (cattle) in stanchions. [Middle English *stanchon,* from Norman French, from Old French *estanchon,* from *estanc(h)e,* a stay, prop, from *ester,* to stand, prop, from Latin *stāre.* See **stā-** in Appendix.*]

stand (stănd) *v.* **stood** (sto͝od), **standing, stands.** —*intr.* **1. a.** To take or maintain an upright position on the feet. **b.** To be placed in or maintain an erect position upon a base, support, or bottom. **c.** To grow in a vertical direction. **2.** To assume a standing position in a manner specified: *stand straight.* **3.** *Hunting.* To point or range. **4.** To measure or equal a specified height when in a standing position: *stand five feet tall.* **5. a.** To remain stable, valid, intact, or unchanged. **b.** To be or remain sure of or committed to. Used with *on: to stand on an argument.* **6.** To have a specified position, expectation, or opportunity: *stand to gain.* **7.** To be situated or placed. **8.** To be in a specified class or degree; to rank. **9.** To remain in a stationary position. **10. a.** To remain without flowing or being disturbed. **b.** To stagnate. **11.** To assume or maintain an attitude, conviction, or course. **12.** *Chiefly British.* To be a candidate for public office. **13.** To take or hold a particular course or direction; to steer: *a ship standing to windward.* —*tr.* **1.** To cause to stand; place upright. **2.** To encounter; meet; engage in: *stand battle.* **3. a.** To resist; withstand: *stand siege.* **b.** To tolerate; endure; bear. **4.** To be subjected to; undergo: *stand trial.* **5.** *Informal.* To pick up the check for; treat: *stand someone to a drink.* —See Synonyms at **bear.** —**stand a chance.** To have any hopes or likelihood of gaining or accomplishing. —**stand down.** *Law.* To leave the witness stand, as after giving testimony. —**stand for.** To represent; symbolize. —**stand in for.** To take someone's place; substitute for. —**stand on.** **1.** To depend upon; rest on. **2.** To insist upon or demand, as observance of formalities or one's due rights. **3.** To maintain the same tack or course in navigation. —**stand one's ground.** To hold out against attack. —**stand on one's own (two) feet** (or **legs**). To be independent and responsible for one's own affairs. —**stand over.** **1.** To keep close surveillance on; watch closely. **2.** To hold over or be held over; postpone. —**stand pat.** **1.** In poker, to keep one's original hand without drawing new cards. **2.** To remain unchanged. **3.** To oppose all change. —**stand to reason.** To be consistent with reason. —**stand up for.** To side with; defend. —**stand up to.** To face up to. —**stand up with.** To act as best man or bridesmaid for. —*n.* **1.** The act of standing. **2.** A halt. **3.** A ceasing of work or activity; standstill. **4.** A stop on a performance tour: *one-night stands in summer stock.* **5.** The place where a person stands. **6.** A booth, stall, or counter for the display of goods for sale. **7.** A parking space reserved for taxis. **8.** A desperate or decisive halt for defense or resistance, as in a battle. **9.** A position or opinion one is prepared to defend: *take a stand.* **10.** *Usually plural.* The bleachers at a playing field or stadium. **11.** A **witness stand** *(see).* **12.** A small rack, prop, or table for holding various articles: *music stand.* **13.** A group or growth of tall plants or trees: *a stand of pine.* [Stand, stood (past tense); Middle English *standen, sto(o)d,* Old English *standan, stōd* (past singular). See **stā-** in Appendix.*] —**stand′er** *n.*

stan·dard (stăn′dərd) *n. Abbr.* **std.** **1.** A flag, banner, or ensign, specifically: **a.** The ensign of a chief of state, nation, or city. **b.** A long, tapering flag bearing heraldic devices distinctive of a person or corporation. **c.** The colors of a mounted or motorized military unit. **2. a.** An acknowledged measure of comparison for quantitative or qualitative value; criterion; norm. **b.** An object that under specified conditions defines, represents, or records the magnitude of a **unit** *(see).* See **measurement.** **3.** The set proportion by weight of gold or silver to alloy metal prescribed for use in coinage. **4.** The commodity or commodities used to back a monetary system. See **gold standard, silver standard, bimetallism.** **5. a.** A degree or level of requirement, excellence, or attainment. **b.** A requirement of moral conduct. Often used in the plural to indicate moral character: *maintain standards in the face of temptation.* **6.** *British.* A grade level in elementary schools. **7.** A pedestal, stand, or base. **8.** *Botany.* **a.** The large upper petal of the flower of a pea or related plant. Also called "banner." **b.** One of the narrow, upright petals of an iris. **9.** *Horticulture.* A shrub or small tree that through grafting or training has a single stem of limited height with a crown of leaves and flowers at its apex. —See Synonyms at **ideal.** —*adj.* **1. a.** Serving as a standard of measurement or value. **b.** Commonly used and accepted as an authority: *a standard atlas.* **c.** Of average but acceptable quality. **d.** Of normal or prescribed size or quantity. **e.** Designating the U.S. Government grade of meat higher than *commercial* and lower than *good.* **2.** *Linguistics.* Conforming to established educated usage in speech or writing. —See Synonyms at **normal.** [Middle English, from Old French *estandard,* flag marking a place for rallying, probably from Frankish *standhard* (unattested), "standing firmly" : *standan* (unattested), to stand (see **stā-** in Appendix*) + *hard* (unattested), hard, firm (see **kar-**[1] in Appendix*).]

stan·dard-bear·er (stăn′dərd-bâr′ər) *n.* **1.** One who bears the colors of a military unit. **2.** One who is in the vanguard of a political or religious movement.

stan·dard·bred (stăn′dərd-brĕd′) *n.* One of an American breed of horses developed for harness racing.

standard candle. *Optics.* A **candela** *(see).*

standard deviation. *Symbol* σ, **s** *Statistics.* **1.** The square root of the **variance** *(see).* **2.** A statistic used as a measure of dispersion in a distribution, the square root of the arithmetic average of the squares of the deviations from the mean. In this sense, also called "root mean square deviation."

standard gauge. **1.** A railroad track having a width of 56½ inches. **2.** A railroad or railroad car built to the above specification. —**stan′dard-gauge′** *adj.*

stan·dard·ize (stăn′dər-dīz′) *tr.v.* **-ized, -izing, -izes.** To make, cause, or adapt to fit a standard. —**stan′dard·i·za′tion** *n.*

standard time. The time in any of 24 time zones, usually the mean solar time at the central meridian of each zone. In the continental United States, there are four standard time zones: Eastern (E.S.T., E.T.), using the 75th meridian; Central (C.S.T., C.T.), using the 90th meridian; Mountain (M.S.T., M.T.), using the 105th meridian; and Pacific (P.S.T., P.T.), using the 120th meridian.

stand by. **1.** To be available and ready for action if needed. **2.** To aid; support. **3.** To keep or maintain (one's word, policy, or promise). **4.** To wait for the resumption of transmission.

stand·by (stănd′bī′) *n., pl.* **-bys.** **1.** One that can always be depended upon. **2.** A favorite or frequent choice. **3.** One kept in readiness to serve as a substitute.

stand·ee (stăn-dē′) *n.* One using standing room.

stand in. To act as a stand-in.

stand-in (stănd′ĭn′) *n.* **1.** One who substitutes for an actor during lights and camera adjustments. **2.** A substitute.

stand·ing (stăn′dĭng) *n.* **1.** The act or position of one that stands. **2.** Standing room. **3. a.** Status with respect to credit, rank, or reputation. **b.** High reputation; esteem. **4.** Length of time; duration. —*adj.* **1.** Remaining upright; erect. **2.** Made or performed from an upright position: *standing jumps.* **3.** Permanent and unchanging. **4.** Not movable; stationary. **5.** Not flowing or circulating; stagnant.

standing army. A permanent army of paid soldiers.

standing room. Space in which to stand, as in a public place where all seats are filled.

standing wave. A wave in which the amplitude of the resultant of a transmitted and a reflected wave is stationary in time and in which some of the energy of the transmitted wave is absorbed by the reflecting boundary.

stand off. **1.** To maintain a distance from; avoid: *"standing the canoe off the rocks and speeding it into the channel"* (James Michener). **2.** To fail in or deny compliance or agreement. **3.** To put off; evade. **4.** To take or maintain a course away from the shore.

stand-off (stănd′ôf′, -ŏf′) *n.* **1.** A tie, as in a contest; a draw. **2.** An effect that neutralizes or counterbalances.

stand-off·ish (stănd-ôf′ĭsh, -ŏf′ĭsh) *adj.* Unsociable; aloof.

stand oil. A drying oil, such as linseed, tung, or soya, heated with minimum oxidation until thickened and used in oil enamel paints.

stand out. **1.** To protrude; stick out. **2.** To be conspicuous. **3.** To refuse compliance; maintain opposition: *stand out against a verdict.* **4.** To take or maintain a course away from shore.

stand·out (stănd′out′) *n.* One that is outstanding or excellent.

stand·pipe (stănd′pīp′) *n.* A large vertical pipe into which water is pumped in order to produce a desired pressure.

stand·point (stănd′point′) *n.* A position from which things are considered or judged; point of view. [Translation of German *Standpunkt.*]

St. An·drews (sānt′ ăn′dro͞oz). A town in eastern Fife, Scotland, the site of the Royal and Ancient Golf Club and of St. Andrews University. Population, 10,000.

St. An·drew's cross (sānt′ ăn′dro͞oz). **1.** A cross shaped like the letter X. **2.** A shrubby New World plant, *Ascyrum hypericoides,* having four-petaled yellow flowers.

stand·still (stănd′stĭl′) *n.* A halt: *came to a standstill.*

stand up. **1.** To assume a standing position; rise. **2.** To prove valid, satisfactory, or durable. **3.** *Informal.* To fail to keep an appointment with (someone).

stand·up, stand-up (stănd′ŭp′) *adj.* **1.** Erect; upright. **2.** Taken standing: *a stand-up supper.* **3.** Designating a fist fight confined largely to heavy blows with little maneuvering. **4.** Designating a theatrical performance, especially of a comedian performed without costume, stage properties, or assisting performers.

Stan·ford-Bi·net scale (stăn′fərd-bĭ-nā′). A revision of the **Binet-Simon scale** *(see)* used in one form or another since 1916. Also called "Stanford-Binet test," "Stanford Revision of the Binet scale." [Prepared at *Stanford* University, California.]

stang. *Obsolete.* Past tense of **sting.**

stan·hope (stăn′hōp′) *n.* A light open carriage with one seat and two or four wheels. [First built for the Reverend Fitzroy *Stanhope* (1787–1864), English clergyman.]

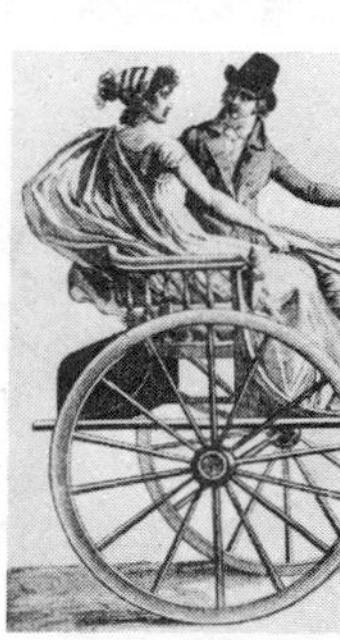

stanhope

Stan·is·lav·sky (stăn′ə-släv′skē, -släf′skē; *Russian* stə-nĭ-släf′skĭ), **Konstantin.** Original name, Konstantin Sergeivitch Alexeyev. 1863–1938. Russian actor and director.

stank. Past tense of **stink.**

Stan·ley (stăn′lē). The administrative center of the British Antarctic Territory, situated in the Falkland Islands.

Stan·ley (stăn′lē), Sir **Henry Morton.** Original name, John Rowlands. 1841–1904. Welsh-born journalist and explorer; founded Congo Free State (1879) for Belgium.

Stan·ley, Mount (stăn′lē). The highest elevation (16,795 feet) in the Ruwenzori, central Africa.

Stan·ley (stăn′lē), **Wendell Meredith.** Born 1904. American biochemist; worked on enzymes.

Stan·ley Falls (stăn′lē). A series of cataracts on the Lualaba River, in south-central Africa, below which the river becomes the Congo.

Stan·ley Pool (stăn′lē). A broadening of the Congo River forming a 320-square-mile lake between the two Congo Republics.

Stan·ley·ville. The former name for **Kisangani.**

stan·na·ry (stăn′ə-rē) *n., pl.* **-ries.** Also **Stan·na·ry.** One of the tin-producing districts of England. Usually used in the plural. [Medieval Latin *stannāria,* neuter plural of Late Latin *stannum,* tin. See **stannic.**]

stan·nic (stăn′ĭk) *adj.* Of, pertaining to, or containing tin, especially with valence 4. [Probably from French *stannique,* from Late Latin *stannum,* tin, from Latin *stannum*†, an alloy of silver and lead.]

stannic chloride. A colorless caustic liquid, $Na_2SnCl_6 \cdot H_2O$, made from tin treated with chlorine and used in the manufacture of textiles, sensitized papers, and perfumes.

stan·nite (stăn′īt′) *n.* A gray to black mineral, chiefly Cu_2-FeSnS, having a metallic luster. Also called "tin pyrites." [German *Stannit* : Late Latin *stannum,* tin (see **stannic**) + -ITE.]

stan·nous (stăn′əs) *adj.* Of or pertaining to tin, especially with valence 2. [From Late Latin *stannum,* tin. See **stannic.**]

Stan·o·voi Range (stăn′ə-voi′). A mountain range of the Soviet Union, extending about 450 miles in southeastern Siberia. Highest elevation, 8,143 feet.

St. An·tho·ny's fire. *Pathology.* **Erysipelas** *(see).*

Stan·ton (stăn′tən), **Edwin McMasters.** 1814–1869. American public official and jurist; Secretary of War (1862–68).

Stan·ton (stăn′tən), **Elizabeth Cady.** 1815–1902. American feminist and social reformer.

stan·za (stăn′zə) *n. Abbr.* **st.** One of the divisions of a poem, composed of two or more lines usually characterized by a common pattern of meter, rhyme, and number of lines. [Italian, "a stopping or standing," from Vulgar Latin *stantia* (unattested), from Latin *stāns,* present participle of *stāre,* to stand. See **stā-** in Appendix.*] —**stan·za′ic** (-zā′ĭk) *adj.*

sta·pes (stā′pēz′) *n., pl.* **stapes** or **stapedes** (stə-pē′dēz′). A small bone of the inner ear, shaped somewhat like a stirrup. Also called "stirrup bone." [New Latin, from Medieval Latin *stapēs,* perhaps variant of *staffa, stapha, stapeda,* stirrup : Latin *stāre,* to stand (see **stā-** in Appendix*) + *pēs* (stem *ped-*), foot (see **ped-**[1] in Appendix*).] —**sta·pe′di·al** (stə-pē′dē-əl) *adj.*

staphylo-. Indicates: **1.** *Anatomy.* The uvula; for example, **staphylorrhaphy.** **2.** *Microbiology.* Resembling a bunch of grapes; clustered; for example, **staphylococcus.** [New Latin, from Greek *staphulē,* bunch of grapes, grapevine, uvula. See **stebh-** in Appendix.*]

staph·y·lo·coc·cus (stăf′ə-lō-kŏk′əs) *n., pl.* **-cocci** (-kŏk′sī′). Any of various Gram-positive, spherical parasitic bacteria of the genus *Staphylococcus,* occurring in grapelike clusters and causing boils, septicemia, and other infections. Also called "staph." [New Latin : STAPHYLO- + -COCCUS.] —**staph′y·lo·coc′cal** (-kŏk′əl), **staph′y·lo·coc′cic** (-kŏk′sĭk) *adj.*

staph·y·lo·plas·ty (stăf′ə-lō-plăs′tē) *n.* Corrective surgery of the uvula and the soft palate. [STAPHYLO- + -PLASTY.] —**staph′y·lo·plas′tic** *adj.*

staph·y·lor·rha·phy (stăf′ə-lôr′ə-fē, -lŏr′ə-fē) *n.* Also **staph·y·lor·a·phy.** The correction of a cleft palate or divided uvula by plastic surgery. [STAPHYLO- + Greek *-rrhaphia,* sewing, suture, from *rhaptein,* to sew (see **wer-**[3] in Appendix*).]

sta·ple[1] (stā′pəl) *n.* **1.** A major commodity grown or produced in a region. **2.** A major item of trade in steady demand, as salt, flour, or coffee. **3.** A major part, element, or feature. **4.** Raw material. **5.** The fiber of cotton, wool, or flax, graded as to length and fineness. —*adj.* **1.** Being in constant supply and demand. **2.** Important as an article of trade, production, or consumption in a specified region. **3.** Principal; leading: *staple exports.* —*tr.v.* **stapled, -pling, -ples.** To grade (fibers) according to length and fineness. [Middle English *staple, estapel,* market town, trade center, from Old French *estaple,* from Middle Dutch *stapel,* pillar, foundation, pile, emporium. See **stebh-** in Appendix.*]

sta·ple[2] (stā′pəl) *n.* **1.** A U-shaped metal loop with pointed ends, driven into a surface to hold a bolt, hook, or hasp, or to hold wiring in place. **2.** A thin piece of wire having the shape of a square bracket, used as a fastening for papers, cloth, and similar materials. —*tr.v.* **stapled, -pling, -ples.** To fasten by means of a staple or staples. [Middle English *stapel, stapul,* Old English *stapol,* post, pillar. See **stebh-** in Appendix.*]

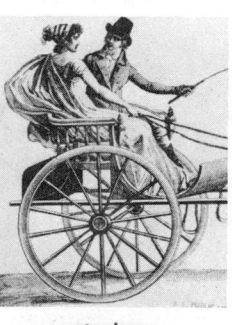

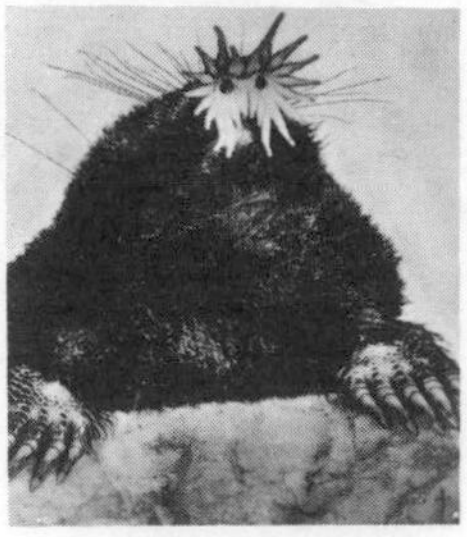

star-nosed mole

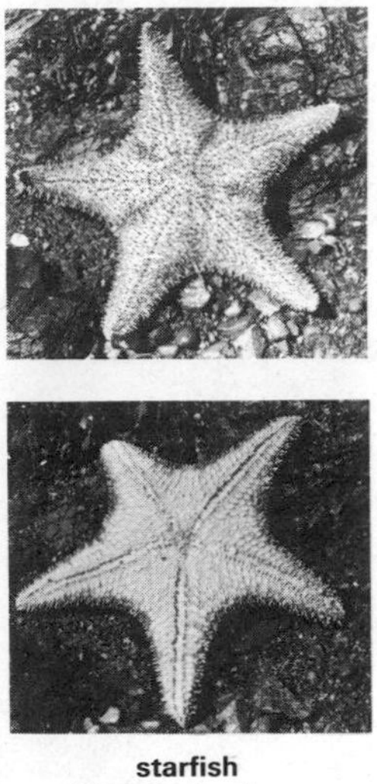

starfish
Hippasteria spinosa
Above: Dorsal view
Below: Ventral view

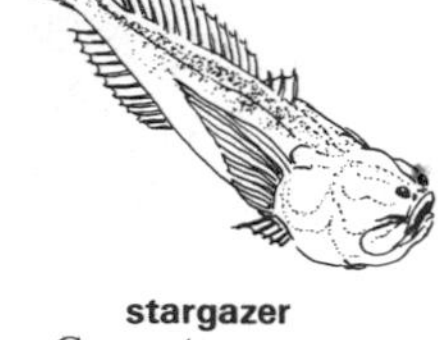

stargazer
Genus *Astroscopus*

sta·pler[1] (stā′plər) *n.* A person who deals in staple goods or staple fibers.

sta·pler[2] (stā′plər) *n.* A machine or hand-operated device used to bind material together by means of staples.

star (stär) *n.* **1.** *Astronomy.* A self-luminous, self-containing mass of gas in which the energy generated by nuclear reactions in the interior is balanced by the outflow of energy to the surface and the inward-directed gravitational forces are balanced by the outward-directed gas and radiation pressures. **2.** Any of the celestial bodies visible at night from Earth as relatively stationary, usually twinkling points of light. **3.** Anything regarded as resembling such a body. **4.** A graphic design having five or more radiating points, often used as a symbol. **5.** An artistic performer or athlete whose leading role or superior performance is acknowledged. **6.** An asterisk (*). **7.** A white spot on the forehead of a horse. **8.** *Plural. Astrology.* **a.** The constellations of the zodiac believed to influence personal destiny. **b.** Loosely, the planets in relation to them. **9.** The future; destiny. **—see stars.** To experience bright, flashing sensations, as from a blow on the head. **—thank one's (lucky) stars.** To be thankful for one's good fortune. —*v.* **starred, starring, stars.** —*tr.* **1. a.** To ornament with stars. **b.** To award or mark with a star for excellence. **2.** To mark with an asterisk. **3.** To present or feature (a performer) in a leading role. —*intr.* **1.** To play the leading role in a theatrical production. **2.** To do an outstanding job; perform excellently. —*adj.* **1.** Of or pertaining to a star. **2.** Pre-eminent. [Middle English *ste(o)rre,* Old English *steorra.* See **ster-**[3] in Appendix.*]

star anise. 1. An aromatic tree, *Illicium verum,* of eastern Asia, having purple-red flowers and starlike clusters of anise-scented fruit. **2.** The fruit of this tree, used in Oriental cooking. Also called "Chinese anise."

Sta·ra Pla·ni·na. The Bulgarian name for the **Balkan Mountains.**

star apple. 1. A tropical American tree, *Chrysophyllum cainito,* bearing smooth-skinned greenish-purple fruit. **2.** The edible fruit of this tree.

star·board (stär′bərd) *n. Abbr.* **stbd.** The right-hand side of a ship or aircraft as one faces forward. Compare **port.** —*adj. Abbr.* **stbd.** On the right-hand side. —*adv. Abbr.* **stbd.** To or toward the right-hand side. [Middle English *sterbord,* Old English *stēorbord,* "rudder side" (early Teutonic ships had rudders on the right sides) : *stēor,* rudder (see **stā-** in Appendix*) + *bord,* ship's side, board (see **bherdh-** in Appendix*).]

starch (stärch) *n.* **1.** A naturally abundant nutrient carbohydrate, $(C_6H_{10}O_5)_n$, found chiefly in the seeds, fruits, tubers, roots, and stem pith of plants, notably in corn, potatoes, wheat, and rice, varying widely in appearance according to source but commonly prepared as a white, amorphous, tasteless powder. **2.** Any of various substances, including natural starch, used to stiffen fabrics. Often specified as "laundry starch." **3.** Foods having a high content of starch. **4.** Stiff behavior. **5.** Vigor; mettle. —*tr.v.* **starched, starching, starches.** To stiffen with starch. [Middle English *sterche, starche,* from *sterchen,* to stiffen (with starch), Old English *stercan* (attested only by past participle *sterced-*). See **ster-**[1] in Appendix.*]

Star Chamber. A former English court (abolished in 1641) consisting of judges who were appointed by the Crown and sat in closed session on cases involving the security of the state. [Middle English *Sterred Chambre,* translation of Norman French *chambre d'estoiles* and Anglo-Latin *camera stellata,* so called because the ceiling of the original courthouse was decorated with gilded stars.]

star-cham·ber (stär′chām′bər) *adj.* Characterized by secret, harsh, or arbitrary procedures. [From STAR CHAMBER.]

starch·y (stär′chē) *adj.* **-ier, -iest. 1.** Of, of the nature of, or like starch. **2.** Containing starch. **3.** Stiffened with starch. **4.** *Informal.* Stiff; formal. **—starch′i·ly** *adv.* **—starch′i·ness** *n.*

star·dom (stär′dəm) *n.* **1.** The status of an actor or entertainer acknowledged as a star. **2.** Stars collectively, as of the stage, motion pictures, or television.

stare (stâr) *v.* **stared, staring, stares.** —*intr.* **1.** To fix with a steady, often wide-eyed gaze. **2.** *Chiefly British.* To stand out; be conspicuous or glaring. **3.** To stand on end; bristle, as hair or feathers. —*tr.* **1.** To look at insistently: *to stare someone up and down.* **2.** To affect by staring at: *He stared the boy into submission.* —See Synonyms at **gaze.** —*n.* The act of staring; an intent or fixed gaze. [Middle English *staren,* Old English *starian.* See **ster-**[1] in Appendix.*] **—star′er** *n.*

sta·rets (stär′yəts) *n., pl.* **startsy** (stärt′sē). *Eastern Orthodox Church.* A respected spiritual adviser, often a monk or religious hermit. [Russian, "old man," from *staryĭ,* old. See **stā-** in Appendix.*]

star facet. One of the eight small triangular facets in the crown of a brilliant-cut gem.

star·fish (stär′fĭsh′) *n., pl.* **starfish** or **-fishes.** Any of various marine echinoderms of the class Asteroidea, characteristically having a radially symmetrical form with five arms extending from a central disk.

star·flow·er (stär′flou′ər) *n.* **1.** Any of several small North American plants of the genus *Trientalis,* having white, starlike flowers. **2.** Any of several other plants having starlike flowers.

star·gaze (stär′gāz′) *intr.v.* **-gazed, -gazing, -gazes. 1.** To gaze at the stars. **2.** To daydream.

star·gaz·er (stär′gā′zər) *n.* **1.** An astronomer or astrologer. Used humorously. **2.** Any of various marine bottom-dwelling fishes of the families Uranoscopidae and Dactyloscopidae, having eyes on the top of the head.

star grass. 1. Any of various plants of the genus *Hypoxis,* having grasslike leaves and star-shaped flowers. **2.** Any of various similar plants, such as the **colicroot** *(see).*

stark (stärk) *adj.* **starker, starkest. 1.** Bare; blunt: *stark truth.* **2.** Complete or utter; extreme: *stark poverty.* **3.** Harsh in appearance; barren; grim: *stark cliffs.* —*adv.* Utterly; entirely; absolutely: *stark raving mad.* [Middle English *stark(e), sterk(e),* Old English *stearc,* hard, stern, severe, cruel. See **ster-**[1] in Appendix.*] **—stark′ly** *adv.* **—stark′ness** *n.*

stark naked. Completely naked. [Earlier *start naked,* Middle English *start naked, stert naked,* "naked to the tail" : *start, stert,* tail, Old English *steort* (see **ster-**[1] in Appendix*) + NAKED.]

star·let (stär′lĭt) *n.* **1.** A small star. **2.** A young motion-picture actress publicized as a future star.

star·light (stär′līt′) *n.* The light given by the stars. —*adj.* **1.** Of or like starlight. **2.** Illuminated by starlight; starlit.

star·ling[1] (stär′lĭng) *n.* Any of various Old World birds of the family Sturnidae, characteristically having dark, often iridescent plumage; especially, *Sturnus vulgaris,* widely naturalized in North America. [Middle English *sterling, starling,* Old English *stærlinc* : *stær,* starling (see **storos** in Appendix*) + -LING.]

star·ling[2] (stär′lĭng) *n.* A protective structure of pilings surrounding a pier of a bridge. [Probably alteration of Middle English *stadelinge,* from Middle English *stadel, stathel,* foundation, Old English *stathol.* See **stā-** in Appendix.*]

star·lit (stär′lĭt) *adj.* Illuminated by starlight.

star-nosed mole (stär′nōzd′). A mole, *Condylura cristata,* of eastern North America, having 22 small fleshy tentacles encircling the end of its nose.

star-of-Beth·le·hem (stär′əv-bĕth′lə-hĕm′) *n.* **1.** A plant, *Ornithogalum umbellatum,* native to Europe, having narrow leaves and a cluster of star-shaped white flowers. **2.** Any of several similar or related plants. [Probably from a fancied resemblance to the star that guided the Magi to the infant Jesus in Bethlehem (Matthew 2:2).]

Star of David. The **Magen David** *(see).*

Starr (stär), **Belle.** Original name, Myra Belle Shirley. 1848–1889. Legendary American frontierswoman and outlaw.

star·ry (stär′ē) *adj.* **-rier, -riest. 1.** Marked or set with stars or starlike objects. **2.** Shining or glittering like stars. **3.** Shaped like a star; starlike. **4.** Lighted by stars; starlit. **5.** Of, pertaining to, or from the stars; stellar. **—star′ri·ness** *n.*

star·ry-eyed (stär′ē-īd′) *adj.* Naively enthusiastic or visionary.

Stars and Stripes, The. The flag of the United States.

star sapphire. A sapphire with a polished convex surface exhibiting asterism.

star shell. An artillery shell that explodes in midair with a shower of lights, used for illumination and signaling.

Star-Span·gled Banner, The (stär′spăng′gəld). **1.** The flag of the United States. **2.** The national anthem of the United States, written by Francis Scott Key during the bombardment of Fort McHenry (1814) in the War of 1812; officially adopted in 1931.

start (stärt) *v.* **started, starting, starts.** —*intr.* **1.** To begin an activity or movement; set out. **2.** To have a beginning; commence. **3.** To move suddenly or involuntarily. **4.** To come quickly into view, life, or activity; spring forth. **5.** To be in the line-up for a race. **6.** To protrude or bulge. **7.** To become loosened or disengaged. —*tr.* **1.** To commence; begin. **2.** To set into motion, operation, or activity. **3.** To introduce; originate. **4.** To enter into a race; cause to be a starter. **5.** To help in beginning an activity or venture. **6.** To found; establish: *start a business.* **7.** To tend in an early stage of development: *start seedlings.* **8.** To rouse (game) from its hiding place or lair; flush. **9.** To cause to start from a fastening; displace; warp. —See Synonyms at **begin.** **—start in.** To begin work or an activity. **—start off.** To set out on a journey. **—start out.** To set out on a journey, a course of action, or a career. **—start up. 1.** To stand up, appear, or come into existence suddenly; spring up. **2.** To start a procedure or operation. **3.** To start an engine or motor. —*n.* **1.** A beginning; commencement. **2.** A startled reaction or movement. **3.** *Plural.* Quick, brief spurts of effort or activity. Used chiefly in the phrase *by fits and starts.* **4.** A part that has become dislocated or loosened. **5.** A place or time of beginning; starting line or starting point. **6.** A signal to begin a race. **7.** A position of advantage over others, as in a race or endeavor; an edge; lead. **8.** An opportunity granted to pursue a career or course of action. [Middle English *sterten,* Old English *styrtan* (attested only in the present participle *sturtende*), to leap up. See **ster-**[1] in Appendix.*]

start·er (stär′tər) *n.* **1.** One that starts. **2.** A worker who supervises departures of public transportation vehicles. **3.** An attachment for starting an internal-combustion engine without hand cranking. Also called "self-starter." **4.** One who signals the start of a race. **5.** A person or animal that starts in a race.

star thistle. Any of several plants of the genus *Centaurea;* especially, *C. calcitrapa,* native to Eurasia, having spiny purplish flower heads.

star·tle (stär′təl) *v.* **-tled, -tling, -tles.** —*tr.* **1.** To cause to make a quick involuntary movement or start; rouse suddenly. **2.** To alarm, frighten, or surprise. —*intr.* To become startled. —See Synonyms at **frighten.** —*n.* A sudden mild shock; a start. [Middle English *stertlen,* Old English *steartlian,* to kick, struggle. See **ster-**[1] in Appendix.*]

star tracker. A telescopic instrument, used chiefly on rockets, that provides a guidance reference by remaining fixed on a celestial body.

star·tsy. Plural of **starets.**

star·va·tion (stär-vā′shən) *n.* **1.** The act or process of starving. **2.** The condition of being starved.

starve (stärv) *v.* **starved, starving, starves.** —*intr.* **1.** To suffer or die from extreme or prolonged lack of food. **2.** To suffer from deprivation; be in need. **3.** *Informal.* To be hungry. **4.** *Archaic.* To suffer or die from cold. —*tr.* **1.** To cause to starve. **2.** To compel or force to a specified state by starving. [Middle English *ste(o)rven,* Old English *steorfan,* to die. See **ster-**[1] in Appendix.*]

starve·ling (stärv′lĭng) *n.* One that is starving or being starved. —*adj.* **1.** Starving. **2.** Poor in quality; inadequate.

star·wort (stär′wûrt′, -wôrt′) *n.* Any of various plants having star-shaped flowers.

stash (stăsh) *tr.v.* **stashed, stashing, stashes.** To hide or store away in a secret place. —*n.* A store or cache of money or valuables. [Origin unknown.]

sta·sis (stā′sĭs) *n., pl.* **-ses** (-sēz′). **1.** *Pathology.* Stagnation of a bodily fluid, especially of blood. **2.** A condition of balance among various forces; motionlessness. [New Latin, from Greek, a standing, standstill. See **stā-** in Appendix.*]

-stasis. Indicates: **1.** Slowing or stoppage; for example, **hemostasis. 2.** A stable state or a balance; for example, **homeostasis.** [New Latin, from Greek *stasis,* a standing, standstill. See **stasis.**]

-stat. Indicates stationary or making stationary; for example, **rheostat, thermostat.** [New Latin *-stata,* from Greek *-statēs,* one that causes to stand. See **stā-** in Appendix.*]

stat. **1.** immediately (Latin *statim*). **2.** stationary. **3.** statistics. **4.** statuary. **5.** statute.

state (stāt) *n. Abbr.* **st.** **1.** A condition or mode of being with regard to a set of circumstances; position. **2.** A condition of being in a stage or form, as of structure, growth, or development: *the fetal state.* **3.** A mental or emotional condition or disposition. **4.** *Informal.* A condition of excitement or distress. **5.** *Physics.* The condition of a physical system as specified by a set of appropriate macroscopic or quantum variables: *the proton state of the nucleon.* **6.** A social position or rank; estate. **7.** Ceremony; pomp; formality: *robes of state.* **8. a.** The supreme public power within a sovereign political entity. **b.** The sphere of supreme civil power within a given polity: *matters of state.* **9.** A specific mode of government: *a welfare state.* **10.** A body politic; specifically, one constituting a nation: *the states of eastern Europe.* **11.** One of the more or less internally autonomous territorial and political units composing a federation under a sovereign government: *the United States of America.* —See Synonyms at **nation.** —**lie in state.** To be placed in public view for honors prior to burial. —*tr.v.* **stated, stating, states.** To set forth in words; declare. [Middle English *stat(e),* from Old French *estat,* from Latin *status,* manner of standing, condition, position, attitude. See **stā-** in Appendix.*]

Synonyms: *state, condition, situation, status.* These nouns denote the mode of being or form of existence of a person or thing. *State* and *condition* are the most general and are largely interchangeable. *Situation* more narrowly refers to a state or condition, at a particular time, determined by a combination of circumstances that have special bearing on the person or thing in question. *Status* usually applies to a person or thing considered in relation to others of the same class. With reference to persons, it implies relative standing in a group. With respect to things, it implies a state or condition, as of a specified time.

State attorney. A prosecuting attorney for the state. Also called "State's attorney."

state·hood (stāt′ho͝od′) *n.* The status of being a state (rather than a territory or dependency) of the United States.

State House. A building in which a state legislature holds sessions; state capitol.

state·ly (stāt′lē) *adj.* **-lier, -liest.** **1.** Dignified; formal. **2.** Majestic; lofty. —See Synonyms at **grand.** —*adv.* In a ceremonious or imposing manner. [Middle English *statly,* suitable to a person of rank, from *stat,* person of rank, STATE.] —**state′li·ness** *n.*

state·ment (stāt′mənt) *n.* **1.** The act of stating or declaring. **2.** Something stated; a declaration; an account. **3.** *Law.* A formal pleading. **4.** An abstract of a commercial or financial account showing an amount due; a bill. **5.** A monthly report sent to a debtor or bank depositor.

Stat·en Island (stăt′n). An island, 57 square miles in area, in New York Bay, coextensive with the County and New York City Borough of Richmond. Population, 270,000.

State prison. A prison maintained by a state for the confinement of persons convicted of felonies. Also called "State penitentiary."

state·room (stāt′ro͞om′) *n.* A private cabin or compartment with sleeping accommodations on a ship or train.

state's evidence. Also **State's evidence.** **1.** Evidence for the prosecution in U.S. state or Federal trials. **2.** A person who gives evidence for the state in criminal proceedings.

States-Gen·er·al (stāts′jĕn′ər-əl) *n.* **1.** A legislative assembly of representatives from the estates of the nation, as opposed to a provincial assembly. **2.** The legislative assembly in France before the Revolution. Also called "Estates-General." **3.** The two-chamber parliament of the Netherlands.

state·side (stāt′sīd′) *adj.* Also **State·side.** Of or in the continental United States. —*adv.* Also **State·side.** *Informal.* To, toward, or in the continental United States.

states·man (stāts′mən) *n., pl.* **-men** (-mĭn). **1.** One who is a leader in national or international affairs. **2.** A political leader regarded as a disinterested promoter of the public good. —Compare **politician.** —**states′man·like′, states′man·ly** *adj.* —**states′man·ship′** *n.*

States of the Church. The **Papal States** *(see).*

States' rights. Also **State rights.** **1.** All rights not delegated to the Federal Government by the Constitution nor denied by it to the states. **2.** The political position advocating strict interpretation of the Constitution with regard to the limitation of Federal powers and the extension of the autonomy of the individual state to the greatest possible degree. —**States' righter.**

States' Rights Party. A former political party founded in 1948 by Southern Democrats to consolidate opposition to civil rights policies of the regular Democratic Party.

states·wom·an (stāts′wo͝om′ən) *n., pl.* **-women** (-wĭm′ĭn). A woman who is a leader in the affairs of a nation.

State university. A university that is maintained as part of the public education system of a state.

stat·ic (stăt′ĭk) *adj.* Also **stat·i·cal** (-ĭ-kəl). **1.** Having no motion; at rest; quiescent. **2.** *Electricity.* Of, pertaining to, or producing stationary charges; electrostatic. **3.** Of, pertaining to, or produced by random radio noise. —*n.* **1.** Random noise produced in a receiver, such as hissing or crackling in a radio or specks on a television screen. **2.** *Slang.* **a.** Back talk. **b.** Interference; obstruction. [New Latin *staticus,* from Greek *statikos,* causing to stand, from *statos,* placed, standing. See **stā-** in Appendix.*] —**stat′i·cal·ly** *adv.*

static electricity. **1.** An accumulation of electric charge on an insulated body. **2.** Electric discharge resulting from such accumulation.

stat·ics (stăt′ĭks) *n.* Plural in form, used with a singular verb. The equilibrium mechanics of stationary bodies. [New Latin *statica,* from Greek *statikē (tekhnē),* (science) of weighing, from *statikos,* causing to stand, skilled in weighing. See **static.**]

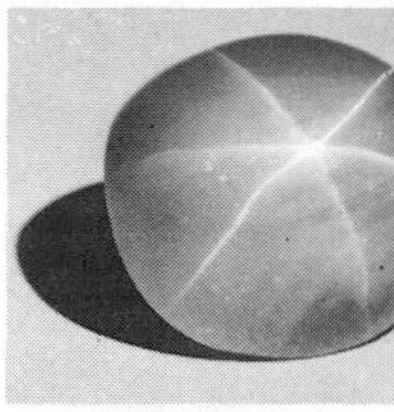

star sapphire
The 563.35-carat "Star of India"

sta·tion (stā′shən) *n. Abbr.* **sta.** **1.** The place or position where a person or thing stands or is assigned to stand; a post: *a sentry station.* **2.** The place, building, or establishment from which a service is provided or operations are directed: *a police station.* **3.** A stopping place along a route; especially, a stop for refueling or for taking on passengers; depot. **4.** Social position; status; rank. **5.** An establishment equipped for observation and study: *a radar station.* **6.** An establishment equipped for radio or television transmission. —*tr.v.* **stationed, -tioning, -tions.** To assign to a position; to post. [Middle English *stacioun,* a standstill, standing place, post, from Old French *(e)station,* from Latin *statiō.* See **stā-** in Appendix.*]

sta·tion·ar·y (stā′shə-nĕr′ē) *adj. Abbr.* **sta., stat.** **1.** Fixed in a position; not moving. **2.** Remaining in a fixed condition or state. —*n., pl.* **stationaries.** One that is stationary. [Middle English *stationarye,* from Latin *statiōnārius,* from *statiō,* a standstill, STATION.]

stationary front. A transition zone between two nearly stationary air masses of different density.

stationary orbit. *Aerospace.* **Synchronous orbit** *(see).*

stationary satellite. An artificial satellite in a synchronous orbit.

station break. An intermission in a radio or television program for identification of the network or station.

sta·tion·er (stā′shən-ər) *n.* **1.** One who sells stationery. **2.** *Obsolete.* **a.** A publisher. **b.** A bookseller. [Middle English *staciouner,* from Medieval Latin *statiōnārius,* shopkeeper, from *statiō,* shop, from Latin, STATION.]

sta·tion·er·y (stā′shə-nĕr′ē) *n.* **1.** Writing paper and envelopes. **2.** Writing materials and office supplies. **3.** A retail establishment that sells stationery and related items.

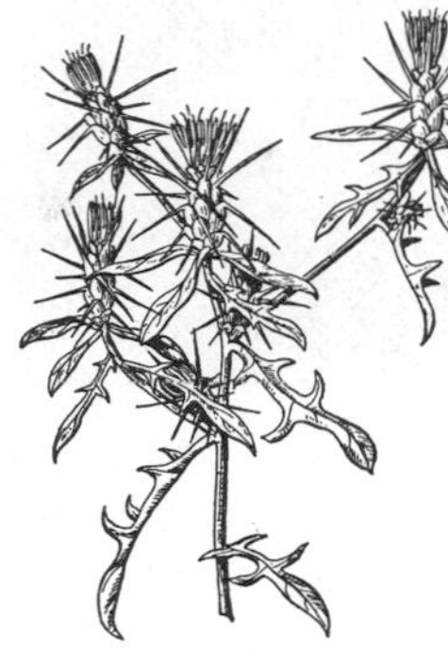

star thistle
Centaurea calcitrapa

station house. A police station.

sta·tion·mas·ter (stā′shən-măs′tər, -mäs′tər) *n.* An official in charge of a railroad or bus station.

Stations of the Cross. *Ecclesiastical.* **1.** A devotion consisting of meditating before each of 14 crosses set up in a church or along a path commemorating 14 events in the Passion of Jesus. **2.** The 14 crosses, often accompanied by images, before which the devotion is performed.

station wagon. An automobile having an extended interior with a third seat or luggage platform and a tailgate.

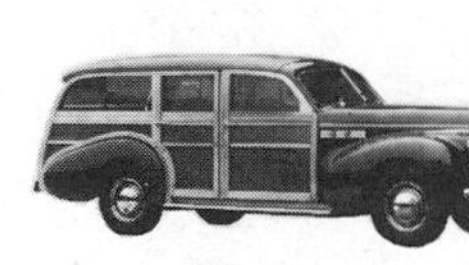

station wagon
Classic wooden-sided station wagon

sta·tis·tic (stə-tĭs′tĭk) *n.* **1.** Any numerical datum. **2.** An estimate of a parameter, as of the population mean or variance, obtained from a sample. [Back-formation from STATISTICS.] —**sta·tis′ti·cal** (-tĭ-kəl) *adj.* —**sta·tis′ti·cal·ly** *adv.*

stat·is·ti·cian (stăt′ə-stĭsh′ən) *n.* **1.** A mathematician specializing in statistics. **2.** A compiler of statistical data.

sta·tis·tics (stə-tĭs′tĭks) *n. Abbr.* **stat.** **1.** The mathematics of the collection, organization, and interpretation of numerical data; especially, the analysis of population characteristics by inference from sampling. Used with a singular verb. **2.** A collection of numerical data. Used with a plural verb. [German *Statistik,* originally "political science dealing with state affairs," from New Latin *statisticus,* of state affairs, from Latin *status,* manner of standing, position, state. See **stā-** in Appendix.*]

sta·tive (stā′tĭv) *adj.* Belonging to or designating a class of verbs which express a state or condition. —*n.* A verb of this class.

stato-. Indicates: **1.** Position; for example, **statocyst.** **2.** Resting, remaining, or surviving; for example, **statoblast.** [From Greek *statos,* placed, standing. See **stā-** in Appendix.*]

stat·o·blast (stăt′ə-blăst′) *n.* An asexually produced encapsulated bud of a freshwater bryozoan, from which new individuals develop after the parent colony has disintegrated. [STATO- + -BLAST.]

stat·o·cyst (stăt′ə-sĭst′) *n.* A small organ of balance in many invertebrates, consisting of a fluid-filled sac containing statoliths that help indicate position when the animal moves. Also called "otocyst." [STATO- + CYST.]

stat·o·lith (stăt′l-ĭth′) *n.* A small, movable concretion of calcium carbonate, found in statocysts. [STATO- + -LITH.]

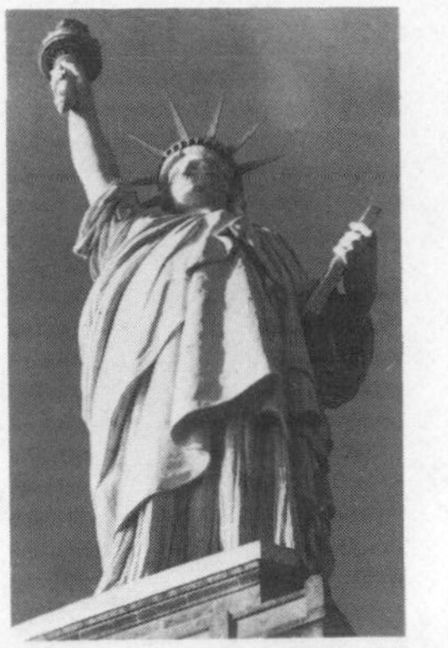

Statue of Liberty

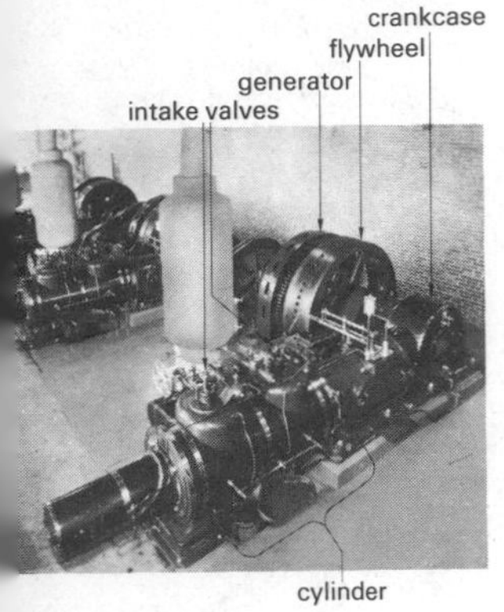
crankcase
flywheel
generator
intake valves
cylinder

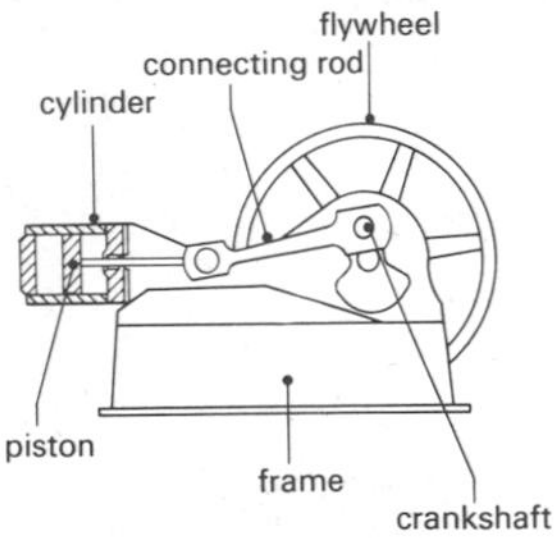
flywheel
connecting rod
cylinder
piston
frame
crankshaft

steam engine
Principal parts of a horizontal steam engine

sta·tor (stā′tər) *n.* The stationary part of a motor, dynamo, turbine, or other working machine about which a rotor turns. [New Latin, from Latin, one that stands, from *stāre* (past participle *status*), to stand. See **stā-** in Appendix.*]

stat·u·ar·y (stăch′o͞o-ĕr′ē) *n., pl.* **-ies.** *Abbr.* **stat. 1.** Statues collectively. **2.** A sculptor. **3.** The art of making statues. *—adj.* Of, pertaining to, or suitable for a statue or statues. [Latin *statuāria*, the art of making statues, and *statuārius*, sculptor, from *statuārius*, of a statue, from *statua*, STATUE.]

stat·ue (stăch′o͞o) *n.* A form or likeness sculpted, modeled, carved, or cast in material such as stone, clay, wood, or bronze. [Middle English, from Old French, from Latin *statua*, from *statuere*, to set up, erect. See **stā-** in Appendix.*]

Statue of Liberty. A statue representing liberty as a woman with a torch upraised in one hand and a book in the other arm. It is located in the Statue of Liberty National Monument, which includes Liberty Island, its site, and Ellis Island in New York harbor.

stat·u·esque (stăch′o͞o-ĕsk′) *adj.* Suggestive of a statue, as in proportion, grace, or dignity; stately. **—stat′u·esque′ly** *adv.* **—stat′u·esque′ness** *n.*

stat·u·ette (stăch′o͞o-ĕt′) *n.* A small statue.

stat·ure (stăch′ər) *n.* **1.** The natural height of a human or animal body in an upright position. **2.** A level achieved; status; caliber. —See Synonyms at **height.** [Middle English *statur(e)*, from Old French *(e)stature*, from Latin *statūra*. See **stā-** in Appendix.*]

stat·us (stā′təs, stăt′əs) *n.* **1.** The legal character or condition of a person or thing: *the status of a minor.* **2.** A relative position; standing; especially, social standing: *"She despised the status of her parents and looked to marry out of it."* (Israel Zangwill). **3.** High standing; prestige. **4.** A state of affairs; situation. —See Synonyms at **state.** [Latin *status*, manner of standing, posture, condition. See **stā-** in Appendix.*]

sta·tus quo (stā′təs kwō′, stăt′əs). The existing condition or state of affairs. [Latin, "state in which."]

stat·u·ta·ble (stăch′o͞o-tə-bəl) *adj.* Statutory.

stat·ute (stăch′o͞ot) *n. Abbr.* **st., St., stat. 1.** A law enacted by the legislative body of a representative government. Often distinguished from **common law** *(see)*, constitutional requirement, or judicial precedent. **2.** A decree or edict, as of a ruler. **3.** An established law or rule, as of a corporation. [Middle English *statut(e)*, from Old French *(e)statut*, from Late Latin *statūtum*, from the neuter of *statūtus*, past participle of *statuere*, to set up, decree. See **stā-** in Appendix.*]

statute law. A law established by legislative enactment. Compare **common law.**

statute mile. The standard mile, 5,280 feet.

statute of limitations. *Law.* A statute setting a time limit on enforcement of a right in certain cases.

stat·u·to·ry (stăch′ə-tôr′ē, -tōr′ē) *adj.* **1.** Of or pertaining to a statute. **2.** Enacted, regulated, or authorized by statute.

statutory rape. Sexual relations with a female who has not yet reached the statutory age of consent.

Stau·ding·er (shtou′dĭng-ər), **Herman.** 1881–1965. German chemist; worked on macromolecules.

St. Au·gus·tine (sānt′ ô′gəs-tēn′). A seaport and resort in northeastern Florida; the oldest permanent European settlement in the United States (founded 1565). Population, 15,000.

staunch (stônch, stänch) *adj.* **stauncher, staunchest.** Also **stanch** (stänch, stănch). **1.** Firm and steadfast; true. **2.** Having a strong or substantial construction or constitution. —See Synonyms at **faithful.** *—tr.v.* Variant of **stanch.** [Middle English *staunche, stanch*, watertight, firm, strong, from Old French *estanche*, feminine of *estanc*, from *estanch(i)er*, STANCH.] **—staunch′ly** *adv.* **—staunch′ness** *n.*

Usage: *Staunch* is more common than *stanch* as the spelling of the adjective. The reverse is true of the verb *stanch*, meaning to stop the flow.

Staun·ton (stănt′n). A city of north-central Virginia, in the Shenandoah Valley; the capital of the Northwest Territory (1738–70). Population, 22,200.

stau·ro·lite (stôr′ə-līt′) *n.* A brownish-black mineral, chiefly $FeAl_4Si_2O_{10}(OH)_2$, often having crossed intergrown crystals and sometimes used as a gem. [French : Greek *stauros*, cross (see **stā-** in Appendix*) + -LITE.] **—staur′o·lit′ic** (-lĭt′ĭk) *adj.*

stave (stāv) *n.* **1.** A narrow strip of wood forming part of the sides of a barrel, tub, or the like. **2.** A rung of a ladder or chair. **3.** A staff or cudgel. **4.** A musical **staff** *(see)*. **5.** A set of verses; stanza. *—v.* **staved** or **stove** (stōv), **staving, staves.** *—tr.* **1.** To break in or puncture the staves of. **2.** To break or smash a hole in. **3.** To crush or smash inward. **4.** To furnish with staves. **5.** To ward or keep off, as if with a staff. Usually used with *off.* *—intr.* To be or become crushed in. [Back-formation from *staves*, plural of STAFF.]

staves. Alternate plural of **staff.**

staves·a·cre (stāvz′ā′kər) *n.* **1.** A larkspur, *Delphinium staphisagria*, of southern Europe, having greenish-white flowers. **2.** The poisonous seeds of this plant, formerly used externally as a parasiticide. [Middle English *staphisagre, stafisagre*, from Latin *staphis agria*, from Greek, "a wild raisin" : *staphis, astaphis†*, raisin + *agria*, feminine of *agrios*, wild, "of the field," from *agros*, field (see **agro-** in Appendix*).]

Stav·ro·pol (stäv-rô′pəl, stäv′rə-). Formerly **Vo·ro·shi·lovsk** (vôr′ō-shē′lôfsk, vŏr′-). A city of the Soviet Union in the northern Caucasus. Population, 165,000.

stay[1] (stā) *v.* **stayed, staying, stays.** *—intr.* **1.** To remain or continue in a given place or condition. **2.** To remain or sojourn as a guest or lodger. **3.** To stop moving; cease; halt. **4.** To wait; pause. **5.** To hold on; endure. **6.** To keep up in a race or contest. **7.** *Poker.* To meet a bet without raising it. *—tr.* **1.** To stop or halt; check. **2.** To postpone; delay. **3.** To delay or stop the effect of (an order, for example) by legal action or mandate. **4.** To satisfy or appease temporarily. **5.** To wait for; await. *—n.* **1.** The action of halting; a check. **2.** The action of coming to a halt. **3.** A sojourn or visit. **4.** A suspension or postponement of a legal action or execution. [Middle English *steyen*, to stop moving, halt, from Old French *ester* (present stem *estei-*), to stand, stop, from Latin *stāre*. See **stā-** in Appendix.*]

Synonyms: *stay, remain, wait, abide, tarry, linger, sojourn.* These verbs mean to continue in a given place. *Stay* often suggests nothing beyond that, though it can imply that the person involved is a guest or visitor, as *remain* usually does not. *Remain* sometimes implies continuing residence after others have gone, but often it, like *stay*, is employed in the general sense of continuing. *Wait* suggests continuing for a purpose, often as a prelude to activity or in expectation of something. *Abide* implies continuing for a lengthy period, as *wait* generally does not. *Tarry* and *linger* both imply delaying departure beyond an indicated time, but *linger* is somewhat stronger in suggesting reluctance to leave. *Sojourn* implies temporary residence in a place, as that of a person in a foreign country.

stay[2] (stā) *tr.v.* **stayed, staying, stays. 1.** To brace, support, or prop up. **2.** To strengthen or sustain mentally or spiritually; to comfort. **3.** To rest or fix on for support. *—n.* **1.** A support or brace. **2.** A strip of bone, plastic, or metal, used to stiffen a garment or part, as a corset or shirt collar. **3.** *Plural.* A corset. [Old French *estayer*, to support, from *estaie*, support, from Middle Dutch *stæye*, rope used to support a mast. See **stak-** in Appendix.*]

stay[3] (stā) *n.* **1.** A heavy rope or cable, usually of wire, used as a brace or support for a mast or spar. **2.** Any rope used for a similar purpose; a guy line. **—in stays.** In the process of coming about. Said of a ship. *—v.* **stayed, staying, stays.** *—tr.* **1.** To brace or support with a stay or stays. **2.** To put (a ship) on the opposite tack. *—intr.* To come about. [Middle English *stey, stay*, Old English *stæg*. See **stak-** in Appendix.*]

staying power. The ability to endure or last.

stay·sail (stā′səl, -sāl′) *n.* A triangular sail hoisted on a stay.

stbd. starboard.

St. Ber·nard Pass (sānt′ bər-närd′). Either of two Alpine passes: the Great Saint Bernard Pass (highest elevation, 8,110 feet) east of Mont Blanc between Italy and Switzerland, and the Little Saint Bernard Pass (highest elevation, 7,180 feet) south of Mont Blanc between Italy and France.

St. Cath·a·rines (sānt′ kăth′ər-ĭnz). A city of Ontario, Canada, in the south on the Welland Ship Canal. Population, 84,000.

St. Chris·to·pher. See **St. Kitts.**

St. Clair, Lake (sānt′ klâr′). A lake, about 460 square miles in area, lying between southwestern Ontario, Canada, and southeastern Michigan.

St. Clair Shores (sānt′ klâr′). A city of Michigan, in the southeast on Lake St. Clair. Population, 77,000.

St. Croix (sānt′ kroi′). *Spanish* **San·ta Cruz** (sän′tä kro͞os′). The largest island (81 square miles) of the Virgin Islands of the United States.

St. Croix River (sānt′ kroi′). **1.** A river rising in northwestern Wisconsin and flowing 164 miles generally south, forming part of the Minnesota-Wisconsin border before joining the Mississippi. **2.** A river rising in east-central Maine and flowing 75 miles generally south to Passamaquoddy Bay, forming part of the border between Maine and New Brunswick, Canada.

std. standard.

St. Den·is (sānt′ dĕn′ĭs), **Ruth.** Original surname, Dennis. 1880–1968. American dancer and choreographer.

stead (stĕd) *n.* **1.** The place, position, or function properly or customarily occupied by another. **2.** Advantage; avail. Used chiefly in the phrase *stand one in good stead.* *—tr.v.* **steaded, steading, steads.** To be of advantage or service to; to benefit; to help: *"No face which we can give to a matter will stead us so well at last as the truth."* (Thoreau). [Middle English *stede*, Old English *stede*. See **stā-** in Appendix.*]

stead·fast (stĕd′făst′; *chiefly British* stĕd′fəst) *adj.* Also **sted·fast. 1.** Fixed or unchanging; steady. **2.** Firmly loyal or constant; unswerving. —See Synonyms at **faithful.** [Middle English *stedefast*, Old English *stedefæst*, fixed in one place : *stede*, place, STEAD + *fæst*, fixed, FAST.] **—stead′fast′ly** *adv.* **—stead′fast′ness** *n.*

stead·ing (stĕd′ĭng) *n. Regional.* **1.** A farmhouse. **2.** A small farm. [Middle English *steding*, from *stede*, STEAD.]

stead·y (stĕd′ē) *adj.* **-ier, -iest. 1.** Firm in position or place; stable; fixed. **2.** Direct and unfaltering; sure. **3.** Having a continuous movement, quality, or pace. **4.** Not easily excited or upset; controlled. **5.** Reliable; dependable. **6.** Temperate; sober. *—v.* **steadied, -ying, -ies.** *—tr.* To make steady; stabilize. *—intr.* To become steady. *—interj.* **1.** Used to urge self-control. **2.** *Nautical.* Used to direct the helmsman to keep the ship's head in the same direction. *—n., pl.* **steadies.** *Slang.* The boy or girl whom one dates regularly and exclusively. **—go steady.** To date regularly and exclusively. [From STEAD, place (after Middle Low German *stēdig*, stable).] **—stead′i·er** *n.* **—stead′i·ly** *adv.* **—stead′i·ness** *n.*

Synonyms: *steady, even, equable, uniform, constant.* These adjectives refer to things or persons that show stability or lack of change. *Steady* can imply continuity of activity, regularity of movement or behavior, or the manifestation of firmness or self-control. *Even* suggests the maintenance of a level of activity or behavior and the consequent absence of irregularity or fluctuation. *Equable* implies an inherent tendency to be regular in movement or activity, to avoid extremes, or (in persons) to be tranquil. *Uniform* emphasizes sameness in form, character, degree, regularity of occurrence, or the like. This sameness can apply to one thing that shows no variation within itself, or it can refer to a group that reveals no diversity. *Constant* describes a thing incapable of, or not given to, change or a person who is firm and steadfast in purpose. It also can imply continuity or regularity of activity or occurrence.

stead·y-state theory (stĕd′ē-stāt′). A cosmological theory that assumes that the large-scale view of the universe is independent of the position of the observer in space and time and that the expansion of the universe, required on other grounds, is compensated for by the continuous creation of matter.

steak (stāk) *n.* **1.** A slice of meat, beef unless otherwise indicated, typically cut thick and across the muscle grain and usually broiled or fried. **2.** A thick slice of a large fish cut across the body. **3.** A dish suggesting beefsteak, especially a cake of ground meat broiled or fried. [Middle English *ste(y)ke, styke,* from Old Norse *steik,* piece of meat roasted on a spit, from *steikja,* to roast on a spit. See **steig-** in Appendix.*]

steak tar·tare (tär′tär′, tär′tər). Raw ground beef mixed with onion, seasoning, and raw egg, eaten as an appetizer. Also called "tartare steak."

steal (stēl) *v.* **stole** (stōl), **stolen** (stō′lən), **stealing, steals.** —*tr.* **1.** To take without right or permission, generally in a surreptitious way. **2.** To get or effect secretly or artfully. **3.** To move, carry, or place surreptitiously. **4.** *Baseball.* To gain (a base) without the aid of a hit, error, or wild pitch. Used of a base runner. —*intr.* **1.** To commit theft. **2.** To move, happen, or elapse stealthily or unobtrusively. **3.** *Baseball.* To steal a base. —See Synonyms at **rob.** —*n.* **1.** The act of stealing; theft. **2.** *Baseball.* The act of stealing a base. **3.** *Slang.* A bargain. [Steal, stolen; Middle English *stelen, stole(n),* Old English *stelan, stolen.* Stole, Middle English *stole,* adopted from the past participle *stole(n)* and superseding the more regular form *stal,* Old English *stæl* (plural *stælon*). See **ster-**[4] in Appendix.*] —**steal′er** *n.*

stealth (stĕlth) *n.* **1.** The act of moving, proceeding, or acting in a covert way. **2.** Furtiveness; covertness. **3.** *Archaic.* The act of stealing. [Middle English *stalth, stelth,* probably from Old English *stǣlth* (unattested). See **ster-**[4] in Appendix.*]

stealth·y (stĕl′thē) *adj.* **-ier, -iest.** Characterized by clandestine or secret movement; avoiding notice. See Synonyms at **secret.** —**stealth′i·ly** *adv.* —**stealth′i·ness** *n.*

steam (stēm) *n.* **1. a.** The vapor phase of water. **b.** The mist of cooling water vapor. **2. Steam heating** *(see).* **3.** Power; energy. —**let** (or **blow**) **off steam.** To release pent-up emotions or energy. —*v.* **steamed, steaming, steams.** —*intr.* **1.** To produce or emit steam. **2.** To become or rise up as steam. **3.** To become misted or covered with steam. Used with *up.* **4.** To move by means of steam power. **5.** *Informal.* To move energetically and rapidly. —*tr.* To expose to steam, as in cooking. [Middle English *steme,* vapor, exhalation, Old English *stēam,* from West Germanic *stauma* (unattested).]

steam·boat (stēm′bōt′) *n.* A **steamship** *(see).*

steam boiler. A closed tank in which water is converted into steam under pressure.

steam chest. A compartment in a steam engine through which steam is delivered from the boiler to a cylinder. Also called "steam box."

steam engine. An engine that converts the heat energy of pressurized steam into mechanical energy, especially one in which steam drives a piston in a closed cylinder.

steam·er (stē′mər) *n. Abbr.* **str. 1.** A **steamship** *(see).* **2.** A container in which something is steamed. **3.** A soft-shell clam cooked by steaming.

steamer trunk. A small trunk originally designed to fit under the bunk of a steamship cabin.

steam·fit·ter (stēm′fĭt′ər) *n.* One whose occupation is the installation and repair of heating, ventilating, refrigerating, and air-conditioning systems.

steam heating. A heating system by which steam is generated in a boiler and piped to radiators. Compare **hot-water heat.**

steam iron. A pressing iron that holds and heats water to be emitted as steam on the cloth being pressed.

steam radio. *British slang.* Radio broadcasting considered as being old-fashioned by comparison with television.

steam·rol·ler (stēm′rō′lər) *n.* Also **steam roller. 1.** A steam-driven machine used chiefly for rolling road surfaces flat. **2.** A ruthless or irresistible force or power. —*v.* **steamrollered, -lering, -lers.** —*tr.* **1.** To work or roll (a road) with a steamroller. **2.** To overwhelm or suppress ruthlessly; crush. —*intr.* To move or proceed with overwhelming or crushing force.

steam·ship (stēm′shĭp′) *n. Abbr.* **SS, S.S.** A large vessel propelled by one or more steam-driven screws or propellers. Also called "steamboat," "steamer."

steam shovel. A steam-driven machine for digging.

steam table. A table equipped to hold containers of cooked food kept warm by hot water or steam circulating below.

steam turbine. A turbine operated by highly pressurized steam directed against or through vanes on a rotor.

steam·y (stē′mē) *adj.* **-ier, -iest. 1.** Filled with or emitting steam. **2.** *Informal.* Erotic. —**steam′i·ly** *adv.* —**steam′i·ness** *n.*

Ste. Anne de Beau·pré (sānt ăn′ də bō-prā′). A village and shrine on the St. Lawrence in southern Quebec, Canada.

ste·ap·sin (stē-ăp′sən) *n.* An enzyme of pancreatic juice that catalyzes the hydrolysis of fats to fatty acids and glycerol. [Greek *stear,* solid fat, suet, tallow (see **stearic**) + (PE)PSIN.]

ste·a·rate (stē′ə-rāt′) *n.* A salt or ester of stearic acid. [STEAR(IC) + -ATE.]

ste·ar·ic (stē-ăr′ĭk) *adj.* Of, pertaining to, or similar to stearin or fat. [French *stéarique,* from Greek *stear*†, solid fat, suet, tallow.]

stearic acid. A colorless, odorless, waxlike fatty acid, $CH_3(CH_2)_{16}COOH$, occurring in natural animal and vegetable fats.

ste·a·rin (stē′ə-rən) *n.* **1.** A colorless, odorless, tasteless ester of glycerol and stearic acid, $C_3H_5(C_{18}H_{35}O_2)_3$, used in the manufacture of soap and candles and for textile sizing. Also called "tristearin." **2.** Stearic acid, especially as used commercially. **3.** The solid form of fat. [French *stéarine* : Greek *stear,* solid fat, suet, tallow (see **stearic**) + -INE.]

ste·a·rop·tene (stē′ə-rŏp′tēn′) *n.* The portion of a natural essential oil that separates out as a white, crystalline solid on cooling or standing. [STEAR(IC) + Greek *ptēnos,* flying, winged, "volatile" (see **pet-**[1] in Appendix*).]

ste·a·tite (stē′ə-tīt′) *n.* A massive, white-to-green talc used in paints, ceramics, and insulation. Also called "soapstone." [Latin *steatītis, steatītēs,* from Greek *steatītis, steatītēs,* "tallow stone" : STEAT(O)- + -ITE.] —**ste′a·tit′ic** (-tĭt′ĭk) *adj.*

steato–. Indicates fat; for example, **steatopygia.** [Greek, from *stear* (stem *steat-*), solid fat, tallow. See **stearic.**]

ste·a·tol·y·sis (stē′ə-tŏl′ə-sĭs) *n.* The digestive emulsification of fats prior to assimilation. [New Latin : STEATO- + -LYSIS.]

ste·a·to·py·gi·a (stē′ə-tō-pĭj′ē-ə) *n.* An excessive accumulation of fat on the buttocks. [New Latin : STEATO- + Greek *pugē,* rump (see **pygidium**).] —**ste′a·to·pyg′ic, ste′a·to·py′gous** (-pī′gəs) *adj.*

ste·a·tor·rhe·a (stē′ə-tə-rē′ə) *n.* Also **ste·a·tor·rhoe·a. 1.** Overaction of the sebaceous glands. **2.** Excessive discharge of fat in the feces. [New Latin : STEATO- + -RRHEA.]

Stę·bark (stĕNm′bärk′). *German* **Tan·nen·berg** (tän′ən-bĕrk′). A town in northeastern Poland, formerly in East Prussia; site of a defeat of the Russians by the Germans (1914).

sted·fast. Variant of **steadfast.**

steed (stēd) *n.* A horse, especially one that is spirited. [Middle English *stede,* Old English *stēda,* stallion. See **stā-** in Appendix.*]

steel (stēl) *n.* **1.** Any of various generally hard, strong, durable, malleable alloys of iron and carbon, usually containing between 0.2 and 1.5 per cent carbon, often with other constituents such as manganese, chromium, nickel, molybdenum, copper, tungsten, cobalt, or silicon, depending on the desired alloy properties, and widely used as a structural material. **2.** A quality suggestive of steel; especially, a hard, unflinching character. **3.** Something made of steel, as a sword. **4.** A knife sharpener consisting of a handled steel rod. **5.** A slender strip or band of steel used for stiffening. **6.** Dark gray to purplish gray. See **color.** —*adj.* **1.** Made of or with steel. **2. a.** Resembling the properties of steel. **b.** Of the color steel. **3.** Of or pertaining to the production of steel. —*tr.v.* **steeled, steeling, steels. 1.** To cover, plate, edge, or point with steel. **2.** To make hard, strong, or obdurate; strengthen: *"Its direct business is not to steel the soul against temptation"* (John Henry Newman). [Middle English *stel(le), stiel,* Old English *stēli, stȳle.* See **stāk-** in Appendix.*]

steel band. A musical band of Trinidadian origin, composed chiefly of percussion instruments fashioned from oil drums.

Steele (stēl), Sir **Richard.** 1672–1729. English essayist.

steel engraving. 1. The art or process of engraving on a steel plate. **2.** An impression produced with an engraved steel plate.

steel·head (stēl′hĕd′) *n.* The rainbow trout when occurring in marine waters or large inland lakes.

steel wool. Fine fibers of steel woven or matted together to form an abrasive for cleaning, smoothing, or polishing.

steel·work (stēl′wûrk′) *n.* **1.** Something made of steel. **2.** *Plural.* A plant where steel is made.

steel·work·er (stēl′wûr′kər) *n.* One who works in a place where steel is manufactured.

steel·y (stē′lē) *adj.* **-ier, -iest. 1.** Made of steel. **2.** Like steel, as in coldness or hardness: *steely eyes.* —**steel′i·ness** *n.*

steel·yard (stēl′yärd′) *n.* A balance consisting of a scaled arm suspended off center, a hook at the shorter end on which to hang the object being weighed, and a counterbalance at the longer end that can be moved to find the weight. [STEEL + YARD (rod).]

Steen (stēn), **Jan.** 1626?–1679. Dutch genre painter.

steen·bok (stēn′bŏk′, stān′-) *n.* Also **stein·bok** (stīn′-). An African antelope, *Raphicerus campestris,* having a brownish coat and short, pointed horns in the male. [Afrikaans *steenbok,* from Middle Dutch *steenboc,* "stone buck," ibex : *steen,* stone (see **stei-** in Appendix*) + *boc,* buck (see **bhugo-** in Appendix*).]

steep[1] (stēp) *adj.* **steeper, steepest. 1.** Having a sharp inclination; nearly perpendicular; precipitous. **2.** Rising or falling rapidly or precipitously. **3. a.** Excessive; stiff; exorbitant: *a steep price.* **b.** Ambitious; difficult. Said of a goal or undertaking. —*n.* A precipitous slope; steep place. [Middle English *stepe,* Old English *stēap,* lofty, deep, projecting. See **steu-** in Appendix.*] —**steep′ly** *adv.* —**steep′ness** *n.*

steep[2] (stēp) *v.* **steeped, steeping, steeps.** —*tr.* **1.** To soak in liquid in order to cleanse, soften, or extract some property from. **2.** To infuse or subject thoroughly to. **3.** To make thoroughly wet; saturate. —*intr.* To undergo a soaking in liquid. —*n.* **1. a.** The process of steeping. **b.** The state of being steeped. **2.** A liquid, bath, or solution in which something is steeped. [Middle English *stepen,* perhaps from Old Norse *steypa,* to pour out. See **staup-** in Appendix.*] —**steep′er** *n.*

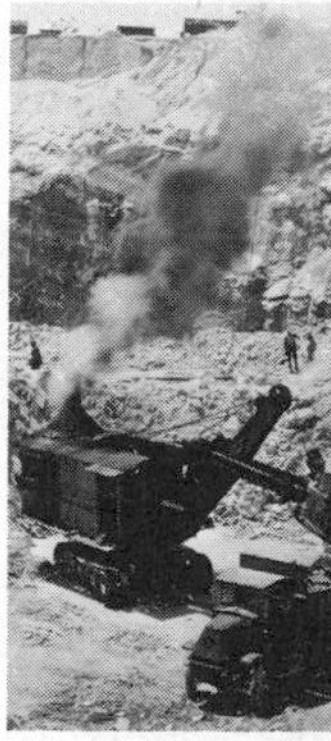

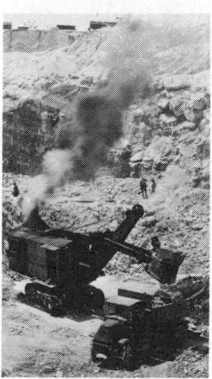

steam shovel

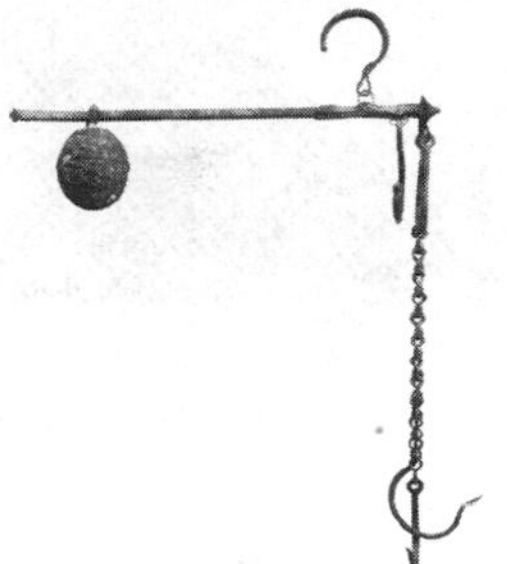

steelyard
Roman steelyard of bronze

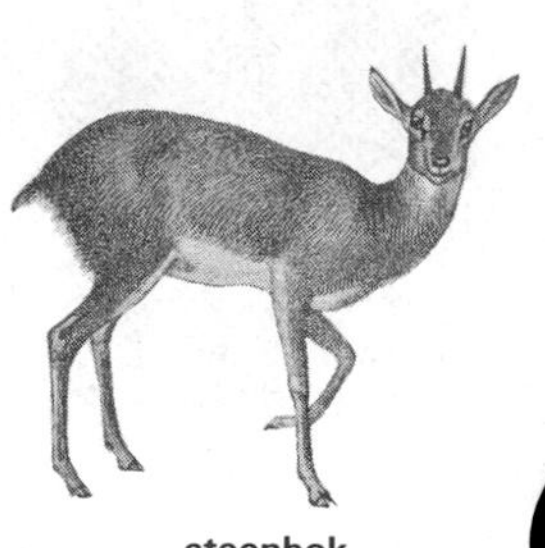

steenbok

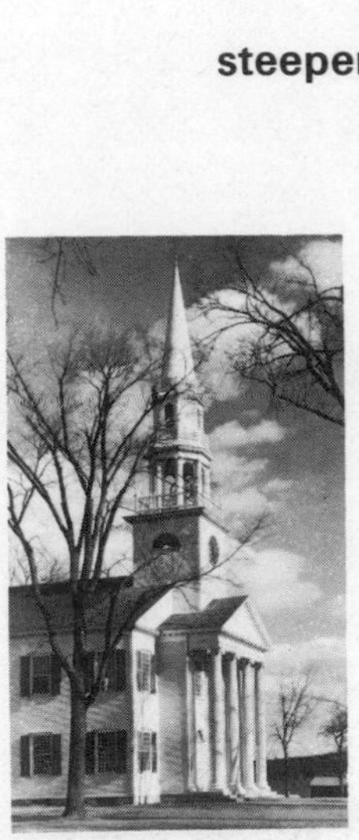

steeple
Congregational Church in Litchfield, Connecticut

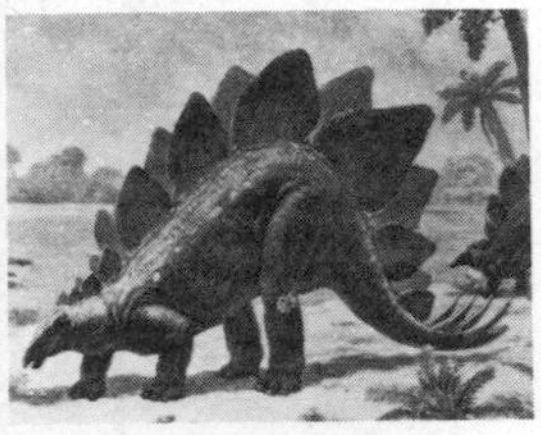

stegosaur

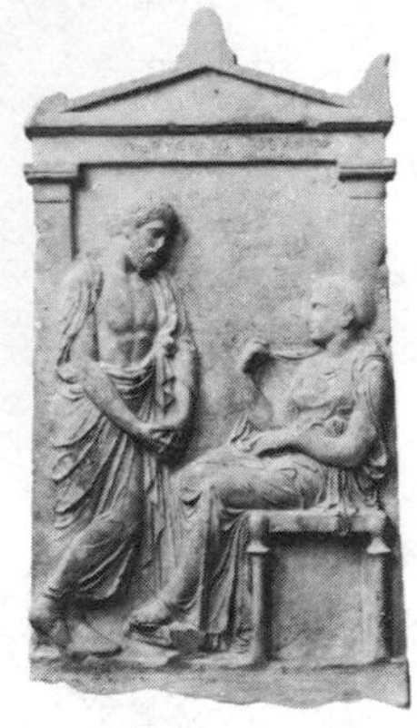

stele
Ancient Greek marble tombstone

steep·en (stē′pən) *v.* **-ened, -ening, -ens.** —*tr.* To make steeper. —*intr.* To become steeper.

stee·ple (stē′pəl) *n.* **1.** A tall tower forming the superstructure of a building, such as a church or temple, and usually surmounted by a spire. **2.** A spire. [Middle English *stepel, stepyl,* Old English *stīpel, stȳpel.* See **steu-** in Appendix.*]

stee·ple·bush (stē′pəl-bo͝osh′) *n.* A plant, the **hardhack** *(see).*

stee·ple·chase (stē′pəl-chās′) *n.* A horse race across open country or over a course provided artificially with obstacles. [Church steeples were originally used as goals in such races.] —**stee′ple·chas′er** *n.*

stee·ple·jack (stē′pəl-jăk′) *n.* A worker on steeples or other very high structures. [STEEPLE + JACK (laborer).]

steer¹ (stîr) *v.* **steered, steering, steers.** —*tr.* **1.** To guide (a vessel or vehicle) by means of a device such as a rudder, paddle, or wheel. **2. a.** To direct the course of. **b.** To maneuver (a person) into a place or course of action. —*intr.* **1.** To guide a vessel or vehicle. **2.** To follow or move in a set course. **3.** To allow of being steered or guided: *a craft that steers easily.* —**steer clear of.** To avoid. —*n.* A piece of advice. [Middle English *steren,* Old English *stīeran.* See **stā-** in Appendix.*] —**steer′a·ble** *adj.* —**steer′er** *n.*

steer² (stîr) *n.* A young ox, especially one castrated before sexual maturity and raised for beef. [Middle English *stere, steer,* Old English *stēor.* See **tauro-** in Appendix.*]

steer·age (stîr′ĭj) *n.* **1.** The action or practice of steering. **2.** The effect of the helm on a ship. **3.** The steering apparatus of a ship. **4.** The section of a passenger ship, originally near the rudder, providing the cheapest accommodations for passengers.

steer·age·way (stîr′ĭj-wā′) *n.* The minimum rate of motion required for the helm of a ship or boat to have effect.

steering committee. A committee whose function it is to suggest issues to be considered and to arrange the order of business, as for a legislative body or other assemblage.

steering gear. The mechanism by which dispositions of the steering controls of a vehicle are transferred to the part that interacts with the external medium.

steering wheel. A wheel that is turned to control the steering gear of an automotive vehicle, ship, or aircraft.

steers·man (stîrz′mən) *n., pl.* **-men** (-mĭn). A helmsman.

steeve¹ (stēv) *n.* A spar or derrick with a block at one end, used for stowing cargo. —*tr.v.* **steeved, steeving, steeves.** To stow or pack (cargo) in the hold of a ship. [Middle English *steven,* to stow, pack, from Old French *estiver,* from Spanish *estibar,* to cram, pack tightly, from Latin *stīpāre,* to compress, stuff fully. See **steip-** in Appendix.*]

steeve² (stēv) *n. Nautical.* The angle formed by the bowsprit and the horizon or the keel. —*v.* **steeved, steeving, steeves.** *Nautical.* —*tr.* To incline (a bowsprit) upward at an angle with the horizon or the keel. —*intr.* To have an upward inclination. Used of a bowsprit. [Origin unknown.]

Stef·ans·son (stĕf′ən-sən), **Vilhjalmur.** 1879–1962. Canadian Arctic explorer and ethnologist.

Stef·fens (stĕf′ənz), **(Joseph) Lincoln.** 1866–1936. American journalist.

steg·o·don (stĕg′ə-dŏn′) *n.* Also **steg·o·dont** (-dŏnt′). Any of various extinct elephantlike mammals of the genus *Stegodon* and related genera, of the Pliocene to Pleistocene epoch. [New Latin *Stegodon,* "ridge-toothed" (from the distinctive broad enamel ridges on its molars) : Greek *stegos,* roof, "ridge," from *stegein,* to cover (see **steg-¹** in Appendix*) + -ODONT.]

steg·o·saur (stĕg′ə-sôr′) *n.* Also **steg·o·sau·rus** (stĕg′ə-sôr′əs). Any of several herbivorous dinosaurs of the genus *Stegosaurus* and related genera, of the Triassic to the Cretaceous period, having a double row of upright bony plates along the back. [New Latin *Stegosaurus* : Greek *stegos,* roof, "ridge of plates" (see **stegodon**) + -SAUR.]

Stei·chen (stī′kən), **Edward.** Born 1879. American photographer and painter.

Stei·er·mark. The German name for **Styria.**

stein (stīn) *n.* An earthenware mug, especially one for beer, usually holding about a pint. [German *Stein,* probably short for *Steingut,* stoneware, earthenware : *Stein,* stone, from Old High German (see **stei-** in Appendix*) + *Gut,* goods, ware.]

Stein (stīn), **Gertrude.** 1874–1946. American author of experimental novels, essays, and plays; resident in France.

Stein·am·ang·er. The German name for **Szombathely.**

Stein·beck (stīn′bĕk), **John Ernst.** 1902–1969. American novelist.

Stein·berg (stīn′bûrg), **Saul.** Born 1914. Rumanian-born American graphic artist and cartoonist.

stein·bok. Variant of **steenbok.**

Stein·er (stī′nər), **Rudolf.** 1861–1925. Austrian social philosopher; founder of anthroposophy.

Stein·man (stīn′mən), **David Barnard.** 1886–1960. American civil engineer; designed and built bridges.

Stein·metz (stīn′mĕts), **Charles Proteus.** Original given names, Karl August Rudolf. 1865–1923. German-born American electrical engineer, mathematician, and inventor.

ste·le (stē′lē) *n., pl.* **-les** or **-lae** (-lē). Also **ste·la** (stē′lə) (for sense 1) *pl.* **-lae. 1.** An upright stone or slab with an inscribed or sculptured surface, used as a monument or as a commemorative tablet in the face of a building. **2.** *Botany.* The central core of vascular tissue in a plant stem. [Latin *stēla,* from Greek *stēlē,* pillar. See **stel-¹** in Appendix.*] —**ste′lar** (-lər) *adj.*

St. E·li·as, Mount (sānt′ ĭ-lī′əs). A peak rising to 18,008 feet in the St. Elias Mountains, on the border between Yukon Territory, Canada, and Alaska.

St. E·li·as Mountains (sānt′ ĭ-lī′əs). A range extending about 200 miles in southwestern Yukon Territory, Canada, and southeastern Alaska. Highest elevation, Mount Logan (19,850 feet).

Stel·la (stĕl′ə). A feminine given name. [Latin, from *stella,* star. See **ster-³** in Appendix.*]

stel·lar (stĕl′ər) *adj.* **1.** Of, relating to, or consisting of stars. **2. a.** Of or relating to a star performer. **b.** Outstanding; principal; leading. [Late Latin *stellāris,* from *stella,* star. See **ster-³** in Appendix.*]

stel·late (stĕl′āt′) *adj.* Also **stel·lat·ed** (-ā′tĭd). Arranged or shaped like a star; radiating from a center. [Latin *stellātus,* from *stella,* star. See **ster-³** in Appendix.*] —**stel′late·ly** *adv.*

stel·li·form (stĕl′ə-fôrm′) *adj.* Star-shaped. [New Latin *stelliformis* : Latin *stella,* star (see **stellate**) + -FORM.]

stel·li·fy (stĕl′ə-fī′) *tr.v.* **-fied, -fying, -fies.** To transform into a star. [Middle English *stellifien,* from Old French *stellifier,* from Medieval Latin *stellificāre* : Latin *stella,* star (see **stellate**) + *facere,* to do, make (see **dhē-¹** in Appendix*).]

stel·lu·lar (stĕl′yə-lər) *adj.* **1.** Having the form of a small star or stars. **2.** Bespangled with small stars. [From Late Latin *stellula,* diminutive of Latin *stella,* star. See **stellate.**]

St. El·mo's fire (sānt′ ĕl′mōz). A bluish electrical glow caused by corona discharge on masts and other high parts of a ship at sea before and during electrical storms. Also called "corposant." [After *St. Elmo,* patron saint of sailors.]

stem¹ (stĕm) *n.* **1. a.** The main ascending axis of a plant; a stalk or trunk. **b.** A slender stalk supporting or connecting another plant part, such as a leaf or flower. **2.** A banana stalk bearing several bunches of bananas. **3.** Something analogous to a plant stem, especially: **a.** The tube of a tobacco pipe. **b.** The slender upright support of a wine glass or goblet. **c.** The small projecting shaft with an expanded crown by which a watch is wound. **d.** The rounded rod in the center of certain locks about which the key fits and is turned. **e.** The shaft of a feather or hair. **f.** The main line of descent of a family as distinguished from a branch. **g.** The upright stroke of a typeface or letter. **h.** The vertical line extending from the head of a musical note. **i.** The main part of a word to which affixes are added. **j.** The curved upright beam at the fore of a vessel into which the hull timbers are scarfed to form the prow. **k.** In an incandescent bulb or vacuum tube, the tubular glass structure mounting the filament or electrodes. —**from stem to stern.** From one end to the other. —*v.* **stemmed, stemming, stems.** —*tr.* **1.** To remove the stem or stems of. **2.** To provide with a stem or stems. **3.** To make headway against (a tide, current, or comparable force); to breast: *"The gale increases as we stem the main"* (Philip Freneau). —*intr.* To derive from or originate in; develop from. Used with *from.* [Middle English *stem,* Old English *stemn, stefn,* stem, tree trunk, (timber used to build the) prow or stern of a ship. See **stā-** in Appendix.*] —**stem′less** *adj.*

stem² (stĕm) *v.* **stemmed, stemming, stems.** —*tr.* **1.** To stop or hold back (a flow, onrush, or movement) by or as if by damming; check the course of; stanch. **2.** To plug or tamp (a blast hole, for example). **3.** To point (skis) inward. —*intr.* To point skis inward by shifting one's weight in order to check one's speed, stop, or make a turn. [Middle English *stemmen,* from Old Norse *stemma.* See **stam-** in Appendix.*]

stem·ma (stĕm′ə) *n., pl.* **stemmata** (stĕm′ə-tə) or **-mas. 1.** In ancient Rome, a scroll recording the genealogy of a family; family tree. **2.** The genealogy of the manuscripts of a literary work. [Latin, garland, wreath, from Greek, from *stephein,* to encircle, crown, wreathe. See **stebh-** in Appendix.*]

stemmed (stĕmd) *adj.* **1.** Having the stems removed. **2.** Provided with a stem.

stem·mer (stĕm′ər) *n.* One that removes stems, as from fruit or tobacco.

stem·son (stĕm′sən) *n. Nautical.* A piece of supporting timber bolted to the stem and keelson at their junction near the bow of a wooden vessel. [STEM (prow) + (KEEL)SON.]

stem turn. In skiing, a turn made by stemming the downhill ski and placing one's weight upon it while bringing the other ski into a parallel position.

stem·ware (stĕm′wâr′) *n.* Glassware mounted on a stem.

stem-wind·er (stĕm′wīn′dər) *n.* A stem-winding watch.

stem-wind·ing (stĕm′wīn′dĭng) *adj.* Wound by turning an expanded crown on the stem.

sten. stenographer; stenography.

stench (stĕnch) *n.* A strong and foul odor; stink. See Synonyms at **smell.** [Middle English *stench,* Old English *stenc,* from Germanic *stenkw-* (unattested), akin to *stinkwan* (unattested), to STINK.]

sten·cil (stĕn′səl) *n.* **1.** A sheet of celluloid, cardboard, or other material in which a desired lettering or design has been cut so that when ink or paint is passed over the sheet the pattern will be reproduced on the surface placed below. **2.** The lettering or design so produced. —*tr.v.* **stenciled** or **-cilled, -ciling** or **-cilling, -cils. 1.** To mark with a stencil. **2.** To produce by stencil. [Middle English *stencel,* to adorn with brilliant colors, from Old French *estenceler,* "to cause to sparkle," from *estencele,* spark, from Vulgar Latin *stincilla* (unattested), variant of Latin *scintilla,* spark. See **skī-** in Appendix.*] —**sten′cil·er, sten′cil·ler** *n.*

Sten·dhal (stăN-dȧl′). Pen name of Marie Henri Beyle. 1783–1842. French novelist and biographer.

sten·o (stĕn′ō) *n., pl.* **-os. 1.** A stenographer. **2.** Stenography.

steno-. Indicates narrowness; for example, **stenophagous.** [From Greek *stenos,* narrow. See **sten-** in Appendix.*]

steno, stenog. stenographer; stenography.

sten·o·graph (stĕn′ə-grăf′, -gräf′) *n.* **1.** A keyboard machine for reproducing letters in a shorthand system. **2.** A particular character in shorthand. —*tr.v.* **stenographed, -graphing, -graphs.** To write in shorthand. [Back-formation from STENOGRAPHY.]

ste·nog·ra·pher (stə-nŏg′rə-fər) *n. Abbr.* **sten., steno., stenog.** A person skilled in shorthand; especially, one employed to take and transcribe dictation in an office or court.

ste·nog·ra·phy (stə-nŏg′rə-fē) *n. Abbr.* **sten., steno., stenog.** **1.** The art or process of writing in shorthand. **2.** Material written down in shorthand. [STENO- + -GRAPHY.] —**sten′o·graph′ic** (stĕn′ə-grăf′ĭk), **sten′o·graph′i·cal** *adj.* —**sten′o·graph′i·cal·ly** *adv.*

ste·noph·a·gous (stə-nŏf′ə-gəs) *adj.* Feeding on a single kind or limited range of food. [STENO- + -PHAGOUS.]

sten·o·ther·mal (stĕn′ō-thûr′məl) *adj. Biology.* Of or pertaining to organisms adapted to living only within a limited range of temperature. [From German *stenotherm* : STENO- + *thermē*, heat, THERM.]

sten·o·top·ic (stĕn′ō-tŏp′ĭk) *adj. Biology.* Having narrow limits of adaptation to environmental conditions. [Probably from German *stenotop* : STENO- + Greek *topos*, place (see **topic**).]

sten·o·type (stĕn′ō-tīp′) *n.* **1.** A symbol or combination of symbols representing a sound, word, or phrase, especially in shorthand. **2.** A Stenotype.

Sten·o·type (stĕn′ō-tīp′) *n.* A trademark for a keyboard machine used to record dictation by a phonetic system. [STENO- (GRAPHY) + TYPE.]

sten·tor (stĕn′tôr′) *n.* Any of several trumpet-shaped aquatic microorganisms of the genus *Stentor*, having cilia around the oral cavity. [New Latin *Stentor*, from Greek *Stentōr*. See **stentorian**.]

sten·to·ri·an (stĕn-tôr′ē-ən, stĕn-tōr′-) *adj.* Extremely loud. Said of the voice. [Greek *Stentōr*, name of a loud-voiced herald in the *Iliad*, from *stenein*, to groan, moan. See **steno-** in Appendix.*]

step (stĕp) *n.* **1. a.** The single complete movement of raising one foot and putting it down in another spot in the act of walking, running, or dancing. **b.** A manner of walking; gait. **c.** The rhythm or pace of another or others, as in a march or dance: *keep step.* **d.** The sound of a tread. **e.** A footprint. **2. a.** The distance traversed by moving one foot ahead of the other. **b.** A very short distance: *just a step away.* Course; path: *followed in his father's steps.* **3. a.** A rest for the foot in ascending or descending. **b.** *Plural.* Stairs. **4. a.** One of a series of actions or measures taken toward some end. **b.** A stage in a process. **5.** A degree in progress or a grade or rank in a scale: *a step ahead of the others.* **6.** *Music.* A degree in a scale or on a staff. **7.** *Nautical.* The block in which the heel of a mast is fixed. —**in step.** **1.** Moving in rhythm. **2.** *Informal.* In conformity with one's environment. —**out of step.** Not in step. —**step by step.** By degrees. —*v.* **stepped, stepping, steps.** —*intr.* **1.** To put or press the foot: *step on the gas.* **2.** To shift or move slightly by taking a step or two: *step back.* **3.** To walk a short distance to a specified place or in a specified direction: *step over to the corner.* **4.** To move with the feet in a particular manner: *step lively.* **5.** To move into a new situation by or as if by taking a single step: *stepping into a life of ease.* **6.** To treat with arrogant indifference. Used with *on*: *He either steps on people or patronizes them.* —*tr.* **1.** To put or set (the foot) down: *step foot on land.* **2.** To measure by pacing. Usually used with *off*: *step off ten yards.* **3.** To furnish with steps; make steps in. **4.** *Nautical.* To place (a mast) in its step. —**step on it.** *Informal.* To hurry up; speed up. —**step out.** **1.** To go outside briefly. **2.** *Informal.* To go out for an evening of entertainment or sociability. **3.** To walk with brisk strides. **4.** To withdraw; quit. [Middle English *step(pe)*, *stap(p)e*, Old English *stæpe*, *stepe*. See **stebh-** in Appendix.*]

step–. Indicates relationship through the previous marriage of a spouse or through the remarriage of a parent, rather than by blood; for example, **stepbrother.** [Middle English *step-*, *stip-*, Old English *stēop-*. See **steu-** in Appendix.*]

step·broth·er (stĕp′brŭth′ər) *n.* The son of one's stepparent by a previous marriage.

step·child (stĕp′chīld′) *n., pl.* **-children** (-chĭl′drən). The child of one's spouse by a former marriage.

step·daugh·ter (stĕp′dô′tər) *n.* The daughter of one's spouse by a former marriage.

step down. **1.** To take a lesser position. **2.** To abdicate; resign. **3.** To reduce (power, for example) by stages.

step-down (stĕp′doun′) *adj.* Decreasing in stages: *a step-down gear.* —*n.* A reduction in amount or size.

step-down transformer. A transformer that has a greater number of turns in the primary winding than in the secondary, used to transform high voltage to low voltage. Compare **step-up transformer.**

step·fa·ther (stĕp′fä′thər) *n.* The husband of one's mother by a later marriage.

Ste·phen, Ste·ven (stē′vən). A masculine given name. [Latin *Stephanus*, from Greek *Stephanos*, from *stephanos*, crown, from *stephein*, to encircle, crown. See **stebh-** in Appendix.*]

Ste·phen (stē′vən), **Saint.** First Christian martyr.

Stephen I (stē′vən). Also known as Saint Stephen. A.D. 975?-1038. First king of Hungary (997-1038); canonized (1087).

Stephen of Blois (stē′vən; blwä). 1097?-1154. King of England (1135-54); grandson of William the Conqueror; last Norman king.

Ste·phens (stē′vənz), **Alexander Hamilton.** 1812-1883. American political leader; vice president of the Confederacy (1861-65).

Ste·phens (stē′vənz), **James.** 1882-1950. Irish poet and novelist.

Ste·phen·son (stē′vən-sən), **George.** 1781-1848. British inventor; builder of first practical steam locomotive and first railroad; father of Robert Stephenson.

Ste·phen·son (stē′vən-sən), **Robert.** 1803-1859. British engineer; constructed railways, locomotives, and bridges.

step in. **1.** To enter into an activity. **2.** To intervene.

step-in (stĕp′ĭn′) *adj.* Put on by stepping into: *a step-in robe.* —*n.* **1.** *Plural.* Panties with wide legs. **2.** A step-in garment.

step·lad·der (stĕp′lăd′ər) *n.* A portable ladder with a hinged supporting frame and usually topped with a small platform.

step·moth·er (stĕp′mŭth′ər) *n.* The wife of one's father by a later marriage.

Step·ney (stĕp′nē). A former administrative division of London, England, now part of **Tower Hamlets** (*see*).

Step·noi. The former name for **Elista.**

step·par·ent (stĕp′pâr′ənt) *n.* A stepfather or a stepmother.

steppe (stĕp) *n.* A vast semiarid grass-covered plain, usually lightly wooded, as found in southeastern Europe and Siberia. [Russian *step*†, from Old Russian, lowland.]

step·per (stĕp′ər) *n.* **1.** One that steps, especially in a spirited manner. **2.** *Slang.* A dancer.

Steppes, The. See **Kirghiz Steppe.**

step·ping·stone (stĕp′ĭng-stōn′) *n.* **1.** A stone that provides a place to step, as in crossing a stream. **2.** An advantageous position for advancement toward some goal; something that assists an ambition.

step rocket. *Aerospace.* A **multistage rocket** (*see*).

step·sis·ter (stĕp′sĭs′tər) *n.* The daughter of one's stepparent by a previous marriage.

step·son (stĕp′sŭn′) *n.* The son of one's spouse by a former marriage.

step turn. A skiing turn made by lifting a ski, putting it down again pointed in the direction of the turn, and placing one's weight on it while bringing the other ski into parallel position.

step up. **1.** To increase by stages: *step up production by increasing weekly quotas. Production is stepping up.* **2.** To make oneself known; put oneself forward: *step up and be counted.*

step-up (stĕp′ŭp′) *adj.* Increasing in steps or by stages. —*n.* An increase in size, amount, or activity.

step-up transformer. A transformer that has fewer turns in the primary winding than in the secondary, used to transform low voltage to high voltage. Compare **step-down transformer.**

step·wise (stĕp′wīz′) *adj.* **1.** Marked by a gradual progression as if step by step. **2.** Moving from one musical tone to an adjacent one. —**step′wise′** *adv.*

–ster. Indicates: **1.** One who does, operates, or is engaged in; for example, **teamster.** **2.** One who takes part in or is associated with; for example, **gangster.** **3.** One who is given to making; for example, **prankster.** **4.** One who is; for example, **youngster.** [Middle English *-ster(e)*, *-estere*, Old English *-estre*, *-ister*, from West Germanic *-strjōn* (unattested), agent-noun suffix (primarily feminine).]

ster. sterling.

ste·ra·di·an (sti-rā′dē-ən) *n. Abbr.* **sr** A unit of measure equal to the solid angle subtended at the center of a sphere by an area equal to the radius squared on the surface of the sphere: *The total solid angle of a sphere is 4π steradians.* [STE(REO)- + RADIAN.]

ster·co·ra·ceous (stûr′kə-rā′shəs) *adj.* Also **ster·co·rous** (stûr′kər-əs). Consisting of or relating to excrement. [Latin *stercus* (stem *stercor-*), dung (see **sker-⁴** in Appendix*) + -ACEOUS.]

stere (stîr) *n. Abbr.* **s** A unit of volume equal to one cubic meter. See **measurement.** [French *stère*, from Greek *stereos*, solid, hard. See **ster-¹** in Appendix.*]

ste·re·o (stĕr′ē-ō′, stîr′-) *n., pl.* **-os.** **1. a.** A stereophonic sound-reproduction system. **b.** Stereophonic sound. **2.** A stereotype. **3.** A stereoscopic system or photograph. —**ste′re·o′** *adj.*

stereo-, stere-. Indicates solid, firm, or three-dimensional; for example, **stereophonic, stereoscope.** [From Greek *stereos*, solid, hard. See **ster-¹** in Appendix.*]

ster·e·o·bate (stĕr′ē-ō-bāt′, stîr′-) *n. Classical Architecture.* **1.** A stylobate. **2.** The foundation of a stone building, its top course sometimes being a stylobate. [Latin *stereobata*, from Greek *stereobatēs*, "solid base" : *stereos*, solid, STEREO- + *-batēs*, "one that is based" (see **gwā-** in Appendix*).]

ster·e·o·chem·is·try (stĕr′ē-ō-kĕm′ĭs-trē, stîr′-) *n.* The chemical study of spatial arrangements of atoms in molecules and of the effects of these arrangements on the molecule's properties.

ster·e·o·chro·my (stĕr′ē-ō-krō′mē, stîr′-) *n.* The art or process of mural painting with pigments mixed with water glass. [STEREO- + -CHROME + -Y.] —**ster′e·o·chrome′** *n.* —**ster′e·o·chro′mic** *adj.* —**ster′e·o·chro′mi·cal·ly** *adv.*

ster·e·o·gram (stĕr′ē-ō-grăm′, stîr′-) *n.* **1.** A picture or diagram designed to give the impression of solidity. **2.** A stereograph. [STEREO- + -GRAM.]

ster·e·o·graph (stĕr′ē-ō-grăf′, -gräf′, stîr′-) *n.* Two stereoscopic pictures, or one picture with two superposed stereoscopic images, designed to give a three-dimensional effect when viewed through a stereoscope or special glasses. —*tr.v.* **stereographed, -graphing, -graphs.** To make (a stereographic picture). [STEREO- + -GRAPH.]

ster·e·og·ra·phy (stĕr′ē-ŏg′rə-fē, stîr′-) *n.* **1.** The art or technique of depicting solid bodies on a plane surface. **2.** Photography involving stereoscopic equipment. [STEREO- + -GRAPHY.] —**ster′e·o·graph′ic** (-ə-grăf′ĭk), **ster′e·o·graph′i·cal** *adj.* —**ster′e·o·graph′i·cal·ly** *adv.*

ster·e·o·i·so·mer (stĕr′ē-ō-ī′sə-mər, stîr′-) *n. Chemistry.* An **isomer** (*see*).

ster·e·o·i·som·er·ism (stĕr′ē-ō-ī-sŏm′ə-rĭz′əm, stîr′-) *n.* Isom-

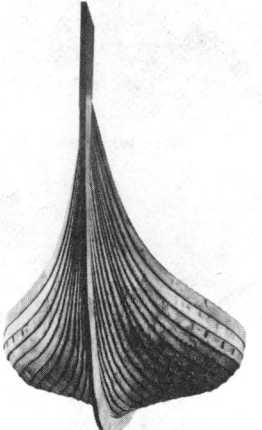

stentor
Stentor coeruleus

stem¹
The stem of a Viking ship

erism created by differences in the spatial arrangement of atoms in a molecule. —**ster′e·o·i′so·mer′ic** (-sə-mĕr′ĭk) *adj.*

ster·e·o·mi·cro·scope (stĕr′ē-ō-mī′krə-skōp′, stîr′-) *n.* A microscope optically equipped for stereoscopic viewing.

ster·e·o·phon·ic (stĕr′ē-ō-fŏn′ĭk, -fō′nĭk, stîr′-) *adj.* Having or rendering the illusion of having a natural distribution of sources of sound. Compare **binaural.** [STEREO- + -PHONIC.] —**ster′e·o·phon′i·cal·ly** *adv.* —**ster′e·oph′on·y** (-ē-ŏf′ə-nē) *n.*

ster·e·op·sis (stĕr′ē-ŏp′sĭs, stîr′-) *n.* Stereoscopic vision. [New Latin : STEREO- + -OPSIS.]

ster·e·op·ti·con (stĕr′ē-ŏp′tĭ-kŏn′, stîr′-) *n.* A **magic lantern** *(see),* especially one made double so as to produce dissolving views. [New Latin : STEREO- + Greek *optikon,* neuter of *optikos,* OPTIC.]

ster·e·o·scope (stĕr′ē-ə-skōp′, stîr′-) *n.* An optical instrument used to impart a three-dimensional effect to two photographs of the same scene taken at slightly different angles and viewed through two eyepieces. [STEREO- + -SCOPE.]

ster·e·o·scop·ic (stĕr′ē-ə-skŏp′ĭk, stîr′-) *adj.* Also **ster·e·o·scop·i·cal** (-ĭ-kəl). **1.** Of or pertaining to stereoscopy; especially, three-dimensional. **2.** Of or pertaining to a stereoscope. —**ster′e·o·scop′i·cal·ly** *adv.*

ster·e·os·co·py (stĕr′ē-ŏs′kə-pē, stîr′-) *n.* **1.** The viewing of objects as three-dimensional. **2.** The technique of making or using stereoscopes and stereoscopic slides. [STEREO- + -SCOPY.] —**ster′e·os′co·pist** *n.*

ster·e·o·tax·is (stĕr′ē-ə-tăk′sĭs, stîr′-) *n.* Also **ster·e·o·tax·y** (stĕr′ē-ə-tăk′sē, stîr′-). *Biology.* **Thigmotaxis** *(see).* —**ster′e·o·tac′tic** (-tăk′tĭk), **ster′e·o·tac′ti·cal** *adj.* —**ster′e·o·tac′ti·cal·ly** *adv.*

ster·e·ot·ro·pism (stĕr′ē-ŏt′rə-pĭz′əm, stîr′-) *n. Biology.* **Thigmotropism** *(see).* —**ster′e·o·trop′ic** (-ē-ə-trŏp′ĭk) *adj.*

ster·e·o·type (stĕr′ē-ə-tīp′, stîr′-) *n.* **1.** A metal printing plate cast from a matrix that is molded from a raised printing surface, such as type. **2.** A conventional, formulaic, and usually oversimplified conception, opinion, or belief. **3.** A person, group, event, or issue considered to typify or conform to an unvarying pattern or manner, lacking any individuality: *the very stereotype of a college sophomore.* —*tr.v.* **stereotyped, -typing, -types. 1.** To make a stereotype of. **2.** To print from a stereotype. **3.** To develop a fixed, unvarying idea about. [French *stéréotype* : STEREO- + TYPE.] —**ster′e·o·typ′er** *n.* —**ster′e·o·typ′ic** (-tĭp′ĭk), **ster′e·o·typ′i·cal** *adj.*

ster·e·o·typed (stĕr′ē-ə-tīpt′, stîr′-) *adj.* **1.** Printed or reproduced from stereotype plates. **2.** Not individualized; unoriginal; conventional. —See Synonyms at **trite.**

ster·e·o·typ·y (stĕr′ē-ə-tī′pē, stîr′-) *n.* **1.** The process or art of making stereotype plates. **2.** *Psychology.* Excessive repetition or lack of variation in movements, ideas, or patterns of speech.

ster·e·o·vi·sion (stĕr′ē-ō-vĭzh′ən, stîr′-) *n.* Visual perception of or exhibition in three dimensions.

ster·ic (stĕr′ĭk, stîr′-) *n.* Also **ster·i·cal** (-ĭ-kəl). Of or pertaining to the spatial arrangement of atoms in a molecule. [STER(EO)- + -IC.] —**ster′i·cal·ly** *adv.*

ster·ile (stĕr′əl; *chiefly British* stĕr′īl′) *adj.* **1.** Incapable of reproducing sexually; barren; infertile. **2.** Capable of producing little or no vegetation; unfruitful. **3.** Free from bacteria or other microorganisms. **4.** Lacking in imagination or vitality; not stimulating; dry. **5.** Lacking any power to function; not productive or effective. [Old French, from Latin *sterilis,* unfruitful. See **ster-**[5] in Appendix.*] —**ster′ile·ly** *adv.* —**ste·ril′i·ty** (stə-rĭl′ə-tē), **ster′ile·ness** *n.*

Synonyms: *sterile, infertile, barren, unfruitful, impotent.* These adjectives, in literal usage, mean lacking or seemingly lacking in power to produce offspring. Figuratively they suggest absence of a productive result. *Sterile* means being unable to procreate because of some defect in the reproductive organs; by extension it describes any lack of creativity. *Infertile* means *sterile* in the literal sense of the latter term. *Barren* describes, in particular, a woman who has tried and failed to have children. It can also apply to what is devoid of profit, enjoyment, or any other desirable thing. *Unfruitful* literally means not bearing fruit and figuratively means not having a useful result. *Impotent* specifies inability of a male to engage in sexual intercourse; in a general sense, it means powerless to act effectively.

ster·il·i·za·tion (stĕr′ə-lə-zā′shən, -lī-zā′shən) *n.* **1.** The procedure or act of sterilizing. **2.** The condition of being sterile or sterilized.

ster·il·ize (stĕr′ə-līz′) *tr.v.* **-ized, -izing, -izes. 1.** To render sterile. **2.** *Economics.* To place (gold) in safekeeping so as not to affect the supply of money or credit. —**ster′il·iz′er** *n.*

ster·let (stûr′lĭt) *n.* A sturgeon, *Acipenser ruthenus,* of the Black Sea and adjacent waters, used as food and as a source of caviar. [Russian *sterlyad′,* possibly akin to Germanic *sturjōn* (unattested), STURGEON.]

ster·ling (stûr′lĭng) *n. Abbr.* **ster., stg. 1.** British money; especially, the pound as the basic monetary unit of the United Kingdom. **2.** British coinage of silver or gold, having as a standard of fineness 0.500 for silver and 0.91666 for gold. **3. a.** Sterling silver. **b.** Articles made of sterling silver, such as tableware. —*adj. Abbr.* **ster., stg. 1.** Consisting of or relating to sterling or British money. **2.** Made of sterling silver. **3.** Of the highest quality. [Middle English *sterling, starling,* "small star" (from the small star stamped on the silver pennies), probably from Old English *steorling* (unattested) : *steorra,* STAR + -LING.]

sterling silver. 1. An alloy of 92.5 per cent silver with copper or another metal. **2.** Collectively, objects made of this alloy.

stern[1] (stûrn) *adj.* **sterner, sternest. 1.** Firm or unyielding; inflexible. **2.** Grave or severe in manner or appearance; austere: *"She was silent, cold, and stern, and yet in an odd way very close to her pupils"* (Sherwood Anderson). **3.** Grim, gloomy, or forbidding in appearance or outlook. **4.** Inexorable; relentless: *stern demands on his time.* —See Synonyms at **severe.** [Middle English *sterne, stierne,* Old English *styrne, stierne.* See **ster-**[1] in Appendix.*]

stern[2] (stûrn) *n.* **1.** The rear part of a ship or boat. **2.** The rear part of anything. [Middle English *sterne,* probably from Old Norse *stjōrn,* steering, rudder. See **stā-** in Appendix.*]

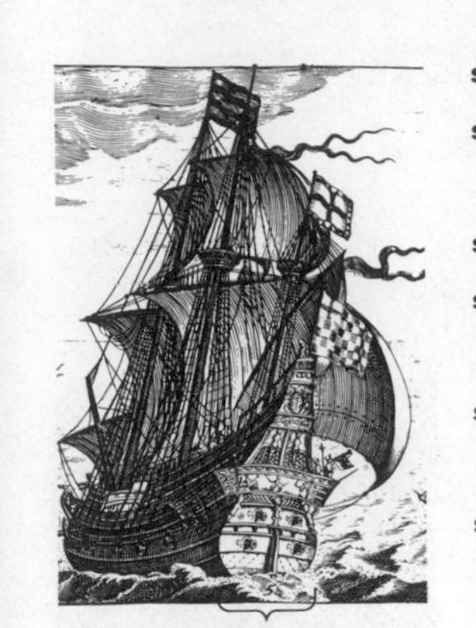

stern[2]
Seventeenth-century Dutch engraving

Stern (stûrn), **Otto.** Born 1888. German-born American physicist; discovered magnetic moment of the proton.

ster·nal (stûr′nəl) *adj. Anatomy.* Of, near, or pertaining to the sternum. [New Latin *sternalis,* from STERNUM.]

Stern·berg (stûrn′bûrg′), **George Miller.** 1838–1915. American physician; established Army Medical School, Dental Corps, and Nurse Corps; organized Yellow Fever Commission.

stern chaser. A gun or cannon mounted on the stern of a ship for firing at a pursuing vessel.

Sterne (stûrn), **Laurence.** 1713–1768. English satiric novelist.

stern·fore·most (stûrn′fôr′mōst′, -məst, stûrn′fōr′-) *adv.* With the stern foremost; backward.

stern·most (stûrn′mōst′, -məst) *adj.* Farthest astern.

stern·post (stûrn′pōst′) *n.* The principal upright post at the stern of a vessel, usually serving to support the rudder.

stern sheets. The stern area of an open boat.

stern·son (stûrn′sən) *n.* A bar of metal or wood set between the keelson and the sternpost to fortify the joint. Also called "stern knee," "sterson knee." [STERN + (KEEL)SON.]

ster·num (stûr′nəm) *n., pl.* **-na** (-nə) or **-nums.** A long flat bone articulating with the cartilages of and forming the midventral support of most of the ribs in tetrapod vertebrates, and also of the collarbone in man and certain other vertebrates. Also called "breastbone." [New Latin, from Greek *sternon,* breast, breastbone. See **ster-**[2] in Appendix.*]

ster·nu·ta·tion (stûr′nyə-tā′shən) *n.* **1.** The act of sneezing. **2.** A sneeze. [Latin *sternūtātiō,* from *sternūtāre,* frequentative of *sternuere,* to sneeze. See **pster-** in Appendix.*]

ster·nu·ta·tor (stûr′nyə-tā′tər) *n.* A substance that irritates the nasal and respiratory passages and causes coughing, sneezing, lachrimation, and sometimes vomiting.

ster·nu·ta·to·ry (stûr-nyo͞o′tə-tôr′ē, -tōr′ē) *adj.* Also **ster·nu·ta·tive** (-tĭv). Causing or tending to cause sneezing. —*n., pl.* **sternutatories.** A sternutatory substance, such as pepper.

stern·ward (stûrn′wərd) *adv.* Also **stern·wards** (-wərdz). Toward the stern; astern. —*adj.* In or at the stern.

stern·way (stûrn′wā′) *n.* The backward movement of a vessel.

stern-wheel·er (stûrn′hwē′lər) *n.* A steamboat propelled by a paddle wheel at the stern.

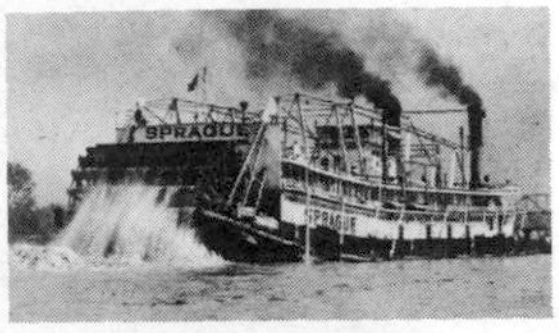

stern-wheeler

ster·oid (stĕr′oid′) *n.* Any of numerous naturally occurring, fat-soluble organic compounds having a 17-carbon-atom ring as a basis, and including the sterols and bile acids, many hormones, certain natural drugs such as digitalis compounds, and the precursors of certain vitamins. [STER(OL) + -OID.]

ster·ol (stĕr′ōl′) *n.* Any of a group of predominantly unsaturated solid alcohols of the steroid group, as cholesterol and ergosterol, occurring in the fatty tissues of plants and animals. [Short for CHOLESTEROL.]

Ster·o·pe[1] (stĕr′ə-pē′). Also **As·ter·o·pe** (ă-stĕr′ə-pē′). *Greek Mythology.* One of the seven **Pleiades** *(see).* [Greek *(A)steropē,* from *(a)steropē, astrapē,* lightning, "twinkling." See **ster-**[3] in Appendix.*]

Ster·o·pe[2] (stĕr′ə-pē′) *n.* One of the stars in the constellation **Pleiades** *(see).*

sterson knee. A **sternson** *(see).*

ster·tor (stûr′tər) *n.* A heavy snoring sound in respiration. [New Latin, from Latin *stertere,* to snore. See **pster-** in Appendix.*] —**ster′tor·ous** *adj.* —**ster′tor·ous·ly** *adv.*

stet (stĕt) *n. Abbr.* **st.** A printer's term directing that a letter, word, or other matter marked for omission or correction is to be retained. See table of Proofreaders' Marks at **proofread.** —*tr.v.* **stetted, stetting, stets.** To nullify a correction or omission previously made in (printed matter) by marking with the word *stet* and with a row of dots. Compare **dele.** [Latin, let it stand, from *stāre,* to stand. See **stā-** in Appendix.*]

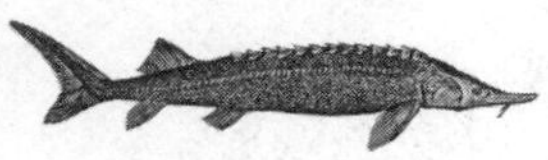

sterlet

steth·o·scope (stĕth′ə-skōp′) *n.* An instrument used for listening to sounds produced within the body. [French *stéthoscope* : Greek *stēthos*†, chest, breast + -SCOPE.] —**steth′o·scop′ic** (-skŏp′ĭk), **steth′o·scop′i·cal** *adj.* —**steth′o·scop′i·cal·ly** *adv.* —**ste·tho′sco·py** (stĕ-thŏs′kə-pē) *n.*

Stet·son (stĕt′sən) *n.* A trademark for a hat having a high crown and wide brim, popular in the western United States. [Designed by John *Stetson* (1830–1906), American hatmaker.]

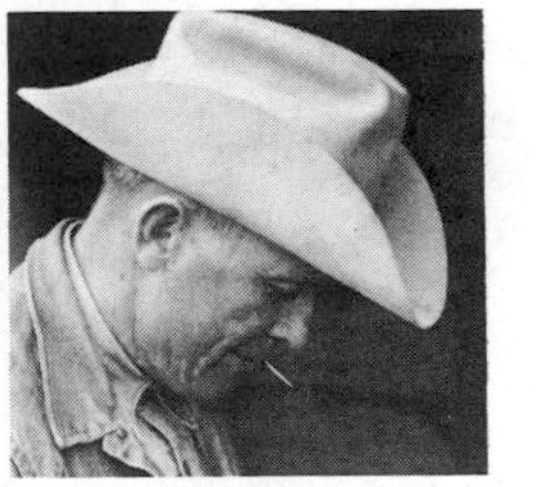

Stetson

Stet·tin. The former name for **Szczecin.**

Steu·art. Variant of **Stuart.**

Steu·ben (sto͞o′bən, styo͞o′-; *German* shtoi′bən), Baron **Friedrich Wilhelm Ludolf Gerhard Augustin von.** 1730–1794. Prussian-born military leader; trained and organized Continental Army under Washington; naturalized American citizen (1783).

Steu·ben·ville (sto͞o′bən-vĭl, styo͞o′-). A city and industrial center of Ohio, in the east on the Ohio River. Population, 32,000.

ste·ve·dore (stē′və-dôr′, -dōr′) *n.* A person employed in the loading or unloading of ships. —*v.* **stevedored, -doring, -dores.** —*tr.* To load or unload the cargo of (a ship). —*intr.* To load or unload a ship. [Spanish *estibador,* from *estivar,* to stow, pack, from Latin *stīpāre,* to compress, stuff, pack. See **steip-** in Appendix.*]

ă pat/ā pay/âr care/ä father/b bib/ch church/d deed/ĕ pet/ē be/f fife/g gag/h hat/hw which/ĭ pit/ī pie/îr pier/j judge/k kick/l lid, needle/m mum/n no, sudden/ng thing/ŏ pot/ō toe/ô paw, for/oi noise/ou out/o͝o took/o͞o boot/p pop/r roar/s sauce/sh ship, dish/

stevedore's knot. Also **stevedore knot.** A knot used to prevent a line from coming out of a pulley.
Ste·ven. Variant of **Stephen.**
Ste·vens (stē'vənz), **John.** 1749–1838. American inventor.
Ste·vens (stē'vənz), **Thaddeus.** 1792–1868. American political leader; U.S. congressman (1849–53 and 1859–68); led the impeachment of President Andrew Johnson.
Ste·vens (stē'vənz), **Wallace.** 1879–1955. American poet.
Ste·ven·son (stē'vən-sən), **Adlai Ewing[1].** 1835–1914. Vice President of the United States under Grover Cleveland (1893–97); grandfather of A.E. Stevenson.
Ste·ven·son (stē'vən-sən), **Adlai Ewing[2].** 1900–1965. American statesman; twice Democratic candidate for President (1952 and 1956); U.S. ambassador to United Nations (1961–65).
Ste·ven·son (stē'vən-sən), **Robert Louis (Balfour).** 1850–1894. Scottish poet and novelist; resident of Samoa (1889–94).
Ste·vin (stə-vīn'), **Simon.** Known as Stevinus. 1548–1620. Flemish mathematician; studied decimal fractions, hydrostatics, perpetual motion, and gravity.
stew (sto͞o, styo͞o) *v.* **stewed, stewing, stews.** *—tr.* To cook (food) by simmering or boiling slowly. *—intr.* **1.** To undergo cooking by boiling slowly or simmering. **2.** *Informal.* To suffer with oppressive heat or stuffy confinement; swelter. **3.** *Informal.* To worry; fret. —See Synonyms at **boil.** **—stew in one's own juice.** To suffer from problems of one's own making. *—n.* **1.** A dish cooked by stewing; especially, a mixture of meat or fish and vegetables with stock. **2.** *Informal.* Mental agitation: *in a stew over her lost keys.* **3.** *Usually plural. Archaic.* A brothel. [Middle English *stewen,* originally to bathe in hot water or steam, from Old French *estuver,* from Vulgar Latin *extūfāre* (unattested) : probably *ex-,* out of + *tufus* (unattested), hot vapor, from Greek *tuphos,* smoke, vapor, from *tuphein,* to smoke (see **dheu-**[1] in Appendix*).]
stew·ard (sto͞o'ərd, styo͞o'-) *n.* **1.** One who manages another's property, finances, or other affairs; an administrator; supervisor. **2.** One in charge of the household affairs of a large estate, club, hotel, or resort. **3.** An officer on a ship in charge of provisions and dining arrangements. **4.** Any male member of the staff of a ship, airplane, or bus who waits on the passengers. **5.** A **shop steward** *(see).* *—v.* **stewarded, -arding, -ards.** *—tr.* To serve as steward of; manage; administer. *—intr.* To serve as a steward. [Middle English *stuarde, stywarde,* Old English *stigweard,* "keeper of the hall" : *stig,* hall (see **sty**) + *weard,* keeper, ward (see **wer-**[4] in Appendix*).]
stew·ard·ess (sto͞o'ərd-ĭs, styo͞o'-) *n.* A female steward; especially, a young woman who assists airline passengers in flight.
Stew·art[1] (sto͞o'ərt, styo͞o'-). A river of Canada, rising in the Mackenzie Mountains in the Yukon and flowing 320 miles generally west to the Yukon River.
Stew·art[2]. Variant of **Stuart.**
Stew·art Island (sto͞o'ərt, styo͞o'-). A volcanic island of New Zealand, 670 square miles in area, lying south of South Island.
stewed (sto͞od, styo͞od) *adj.* **1.** Cooked by stewing: *stewed prunes.* **2.** *Slang.* Drunk; intoxicated.
St. Ex. stock exchange.
St. Fran·cis, Lake (sānt frăn'sĭs, frän'-, sənt). A lake formed by the widening of the St. Lawrence in southern Quebec and southeastern Ontario, Canada.
St. Fran·cis River (sānt frăn'sĭs, frän'-, sənt). A river rising in southeastern Missouri and flowing 470 miles generally south through eastern Arkansas to the Mississippi, forming part of the Missouri-Arkansas border on its course.
stg. sterling.
St. Gal·len (sānt găl'ən; *German* zängkt gä'lən). Also **St. Gall** (sānt gôl; *French* săɴ gàl'). A city and religious and educational center in northeastern Switzerland, the site of a seventh-century Benedictine abbey. Population, 76,000.
stge. storage.
St. George's (sānt jôr'jĭz, sənt). The capital and principal seaport of Grenada in the West Indies. Population, 7,000.
St. George's Channel (sānt jôr'jĭz, sənt). A strait between southeastern Ireland and Wales, connecting the Atlantic Ocean and the Irish Sea.
St. George's cross. The Greek cross, red on a white ground, as used in the flag of Great Britain.
St. Gott·hard (sānt gŏt'ərd; *German* zängkt gôt'härt'). Also **St. Got·hard.** A group of mountains in southeast-central Switzerland, crossed by the St. Gotthard Pass. Highest elevation, Pizzo Rotondo, 10,483 feet.
St. He·le·na (sānt' hə-lē'nə, sənt). A volcanic island, 47 square miles in area, in the South Atlantic, the administrative center of a British Colony including the dependencies of Ascension and other islands. It was the site of Napoleon Bonaparte's exile (1815–21). Population, 5,000. Capital, Jamestown.
St. Hel·ens (sānt hĕl'ənz, sənt). An urban area of southwestern Lancashire, England. Population, 110,000.
St. Hel·ens, Mount (sānt hĕl'ənz, sənt). A volcanic peak, 9,671 feet high, in the Cascade range in southwestern Washington.
St. Hel·ier (sānt hĕl'yər, sənt). The capital of the Channel Islands, on Jersey. Population, 26,000.
Sthe·no (sthē'nō). One of the three Gorgons.
stib·ine (stĭb'ēn) *n.* A colorless, flammable poisonous gas, SbH_3, often used as a fumigant. [Latin *stibium,* variant of *stibi, stimmi,* antimony, from Greek, from Egyptian *stm* + -INE.]
stib·nite (stĭb'nīt') *n.* A lead-gray mineral, Sb_2S_3, sometimes containing silver and gold, that is the chief source of antimony. Also called "antimony glance." [French *stibine,* stibnite, from Latin *stibium,* antimony (see **stibine**) + -ITE.]
stich (stĭk) *n.* A line of verse. [Greek *stikhos,* row, line, verse. See **steigh-** in Appendix.*]
stich·ic (stĭk'ĭk) *adj.* Pertaining to verse composed in homogeneous and recurrent lines, as in recitative poetry.
sti·chom·e·try (stĭ-kŏm'ə-trē) *n.* The division of a prose piece into lines whose lengths correspond to the natural divisions of sense or to the natural cadences, as in manuscripts written before the adoption of punctuation. [Greek *stikhos,* STICH + -METRY.] **—stich'o·met'ric** (stĭk'ə-mĕt'rĭk) *adj.*
stich·o·myth·i·a (stĭk'ə-mĭth'ē-ə) *n.* Also **sti·chom·y·thy** (stĭ-kŏm'ə-thē). An ancient Greek arrangement of dialogue in drama, poetry, and disputation in which single lines of verse are spoken by alternate speakers. [Greek *stikhomuthia,* from *stikhomuthein,* to speak in alternating lines : *stikhos,* STICH + *muthos,* speech, tale, MYTH.] **—stich'o·myth'ic** *adj.*
-stichous. Indicates rows; for example, **polystichous.** [Greek *-stikhos,* from *stikhos,* row, line, verse. See **steigh-** in Appendix.*]
stick (stĭk) *n.* **1.** A long, slender piece of wood, especially: **a.** A branch or stem cut from a tree or shrub. **b.** A tree branch or other piece of wood used for fuel, cut for lumber, or shaped for a specific purpose. **c.** A wand, staff, or rod. **d.** Any of various sticklike implements used in games or sports: *a hockey stick.* **2.** A cane or walking stick. **3.** Something cut into or having the shape of a stick: *a stick of dynamite.* **4.** *Slang.* A marijuana cigarette. **5.** *Aviation.* An airplane control that operates the elevators and ailerons. **6.** *Nautical.* A mast or a part of a mast. **7.** *Printing.* **a.** A composing stick. **b.** The type contents of a composing stick. Also called "stickful." **8.** *Military.* A group of bombs released to fall across a target in a straight row. **9.** A timber tree. **10.** A poke, thrust, or stab with a stick or similar object: *a stick in the ribs.* **11.** The state, condition, or power of adhering: *a glue with plenty of stick.* **12.** *Plural. Informal.* An area far from a city or town; backwoods: *They live way out in the sticks.* **13.** *Informal.* A stiff, spiritless, or boring person. **14.** *Archaic.* A difficulty or obstacle; delay; stoppage. *—v.* **stuck** (stŭk) or **sticked** (for senses 11, 12), **sticking, sticks.** *—tr.* **1.** To pierce, puncture, or penetrate with a pointed instrument, such as a knife or pin. **2.** To kill by piercing. **3.** To thrust or push (a knife, pin, or other pointed instrument) into or through another object. **4.** To fasten into place by forcing an end or point into something: *stick a hook on the wall.* **5.** To fasten or attach with or as with pins, nails, or similar instruments. **6.** To fasten or attach with an adhesive material, glue, or tape: *stick a picture on the wall.* **7.** To cover or decorate with objects piercing the surface. **8.** To fix, impale, or transfix on a pointed object: *stick an olive on a toothpick.* **9.** To put, thrust, or poke into a specified place or position: *"So I grabbed up the skeleton thick sunflower and stuck it at my side like a scepter"* (Allen Ginsberg). **10.** To detain or delay. **11.** To prop (a vine or other plant) with sticks or brush on which to grow. **12.** *Printing.* To set (type) in a composing stick. **13.** *Informal.* To confuse, baffle, or puzzle: *Even simple questions stick him.* **14.** To cover or smear with something sticky. **15.** To put blame or responsibility on; burden: *stuck with paying the bill.* **16.** *Slang.* To defraud or cheat. *—intr.* **1.** To be or become fixed or embedded in place by having the point thrust in. **2.** To become or remain attached or in close association by or as if by adhesion; cling: *"I'm all for us English sticking together when we're abroad"* (Maugham). **3.** To remain firm, determined, or resolute: *"I stuck to that resolution for seven long years."* (H.G. Wells). **4.** To persist, endure, or persevere. Used with *at, to,* or *with.* **5.** *Informal.* To remain in the vicinity; linger. Usually used with *around: Stick around here until I get back.* **6.** To scruple or hesitate. Used with *at* or *to: She sticks at nothing.* **7.** To be at or come to a standstill; become fixed, blocked, checked, or obstructed. **8.** To extend, project, or protrude. Used with *out, up, down,* or *through.* **—be stuck on.** *Informal.* **1.** To reach an impasse concerning: *I'm stuck on my income tax calculations.* **2.** To be in love with. **—stick by.** To remain loyal or faithful to. **—stick it out.** *Informal.* To persist or persevere to the end. **—stick to the ribs.** *Informal.* To be substantial or filling. Used of food. **—stick up for.** To defend or support. [Noun, Middle English *styk(ke),* Old English *sticca.* Verb, Middle English *stykken,* to pierce with a stick, cause to adhere, Old English *stician,* to pierce, stab. See **steig-** in Appendix.*]
stick·ball (stĭk'bôl') *n.* A form of baseball played with a rubber ball and a stick or the handle of a broom for a bat.
stick·er (stĭk'ər) *n.* **1.** A person or thing that sticks. **2.** A gummed or adhesive label or patch. **3.** A tenacious, diligent, or persistent person. **4.** A thorn, prickle, or barb.
sticking plaster. Adhesive tape.
stick insect. Any of several insects of the family Phasmidae, resembling sticks or twigs, such as the **walking stick** *(see).*
stick-in-the-mud (stĭk'ĭn-*thə*-mŭd') *n. Informal.* A person who lacks initiative, imagination, or enthusiasm; an old fogy.
stick·le (stĭk'əl) *intr.v.* **-led, -ling, -les.** **1.** To argue or contend stubbornly, particularly about trifles. **2.** To have or raise objections; scruple. [Earlier *stightle,* to arbitrate, intervene, umpire, Middle English *stightlen,* frequentative of *stighten,* to arrange, Old English *stihtan, stihtian.* See **steigh-** in Appendix.*]
stick·le·back (stĭk'əl-băk') *n.* Any of various small freshwater and marine fishes of the family Gasterosteidae, having erectile spines along the back. [Middle English *stykylbak,* "prickly back" : *stykyl-,* from Old English *sticel,* prick, sting (see **steig-** in Appendix*) + *bak,* BACK.]
stick·ler (stĭk'lər) *n.* **1.** A person who insists on or contends for something unyieldingly: *a stickler for neatness.* **2.** Anything puzzling or difficult.

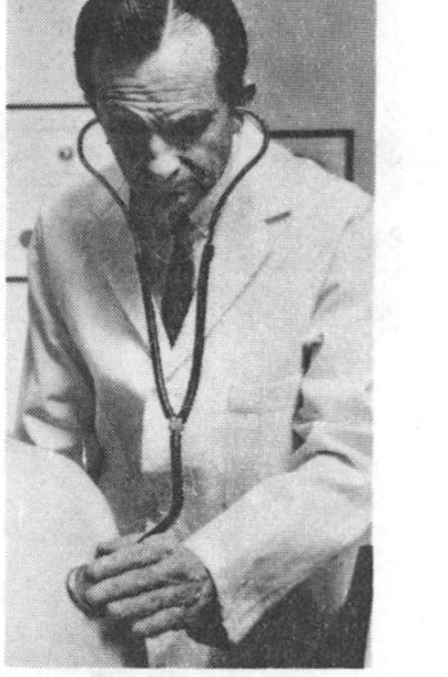
stethoscope

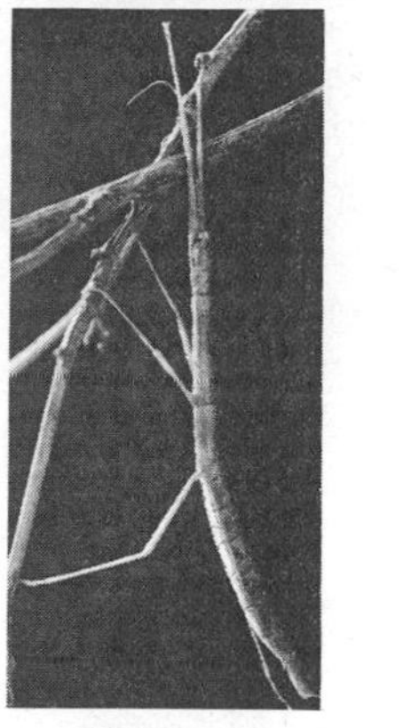
stick insect

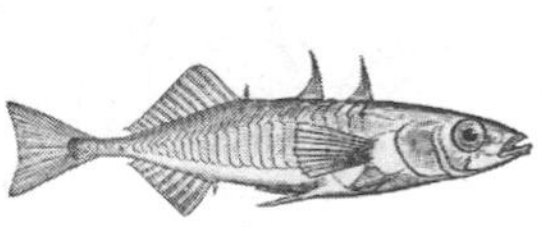
stickleback
Gasterosteus aculeatus

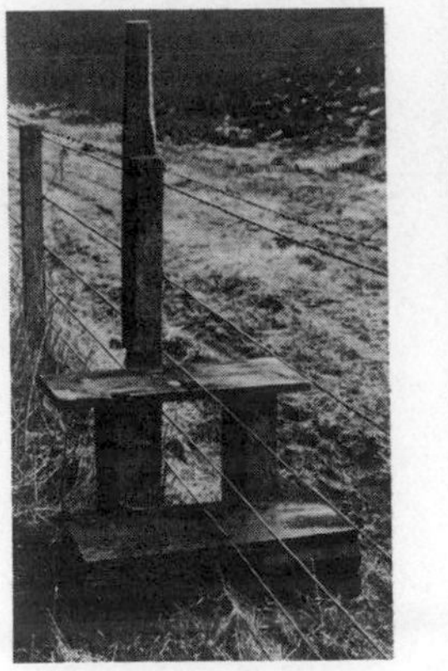

stile[1]

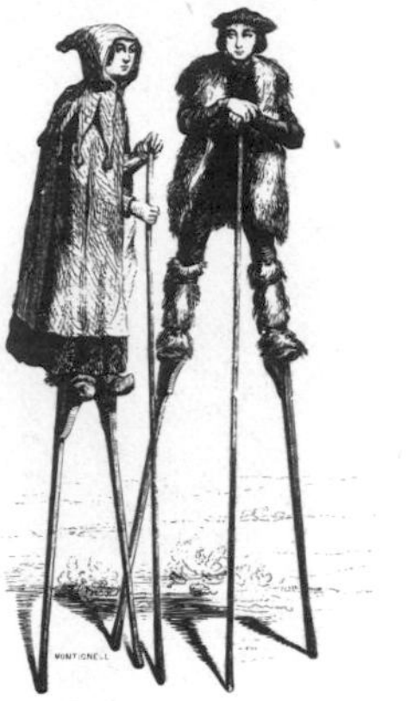

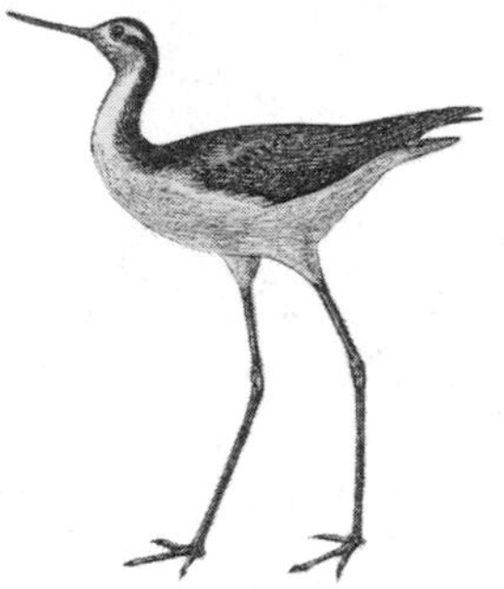

stilt
Above: Nineteenth-century French peasants on stilts
Below: Himantopus mexicanus

stick·pin (stĭk′pĭn′) *n.* A decorative pin worn on a necktie.
stick·seed (stĭk′sēd′) *n.* Any of various plants of the genus *Lappula,* having small prickly fruits that cling to clothing or fur. Also called "beggar's-lice," and sometimes "burseed."
stick·tight (stĭk′tĭt′) *n.* Any of various plants having barbed, clinging seeds or fruit, such as the **bur marigold** *(see).*
stick-to-it-ive·ness (stĭk-tō͞o′ə-tĭv-nĭs) *n. Informal.* Unwavering pertinacity; perseverance. —**stick-to′-it-ive·ly** *adv.*
stick up. *Informal.* To rob, especially at gunpoint.
stick·up (stĭk′ŭp′) *n. Slang.* A robbery, especially at gunpoint.
stick·weed (stĭk′wēd′) *n.* Broadly, any of various plants having clinging seeds or fruit.
stick·y (stĭk′ē) *adj.* **-ier, -iest. 1.** Having the property of adhering or sticking to a surface; adhesive. **2.** Covered with an adhesive agent: *a sticky floor.* **3.** Warm and humid; muggy. **4.** *Informal.* Painful or difficult. —**stick′i·ly** *adv.* —**stick′i·ness** *n.*
Stieg·litz (stēg′lĭts), **Alfred.** 1864–1946. American photographer, editor, and publisher.
stiff (stĭf) *adj.* **stiffer, stiffest. 1.** Difficult to bend or stretch; not flexible, pliant, or limp; rigid: *"his yellow moustache was as stiff as a toothbrush"* (Ford Madox Ford). **2.** Not moving or operating easily; not limber: *a stiff joint.* **3.** Drawn tightly; taut. **4.** Rigidly or excessively formal, awkward, or constrained; without ease or grace. **5.** Not liquid, loose, or fluid; firm; thick. **6.** Firm in purpose or resistance; stubborn; unyielding. **7.** Having a strong, swift, steady force or movement: *a stiff current.* **8.** Potent or strong, as a medicine or alcoholic beverage. **9.** Difficult, laborious, or arduous: *a stiff hike.* **10.** Difficult to carry through, comprehend, or accept; harsh or severe: *a stiff penalty.* **11.** Excessively high, as a price. **12.** *Nautical.* Not heeling over much in spite of great wind or the press of the sail. —*adv.* **1.** In a stiff manner. **2.** Completely; totally: *bored stiff.* —*n. Slang.* **1.** A corpse. **2.** An overformal, constrained, or priggish person. **3.** A drunk. **4.** A fellow; a man: *He's a lucky stiff.* **5.** A hobo; tramp. **6.** A person who tips poorly. [Middle English *stif(fe),* Old English *stīf.* See **steip-** in Appendix.*] —**stiff′ly** *adv.* —**stiff′ness** *n.*
Synonyms: *stiff, rigid, inflexible, inelastic, tense, taut.* These adjectives are compared as they relate to physical stress and to human behavior and attitudes. Anything *stiff* cannot easily be bent. In reference to persons, *stiff* suggests firmness of position and either lack of ease in manner or cold formality. *Rigid* and *inflexible* apply to what cannot be bent physically, at least without damage or deformation; figuratively they describe unyielding positions or attitudes. *Inelastic* refers largely to what cannot be stretched, bent, or expanded without marked physical change. *Tense* describes the condition of being stretched tight; it is applied literally to muscles and other bodily structures and figuratively to persons under nervous strain. *Taut* is used both in the physical sense of being tightly drawn or stretched and in the related sense of nervous tension.
stiff·en (stĭf′ən) *v.* **-ened, -ening, -ens.** —*tr.* To make stiff or stiffer. —*intr.* To become stiff or stiffer. —**stiff′en·er** *n.*
stiff-necked (stĭf′nĕkt′) *adj.* Stubborn; unyielding. See Synonyms at **obstinate.**
sti·fle[1] (stī′fəl) *v.* **-fled, -fling, -fles.** —*tr.* **1.** To kill by preventing respiration; smother or suffocate. **2.** To interrupt or cut off (the voice or breath). **3.** To keep or hold back; suppress; repress: *stifle one's views.* —*intr.* **1.** To die of suffocation. **2.** To feel smothered or suffocated by or as if by close confinement in a stuffy room. —See Synonyms at **suppress.** [Middle English *stufflen,* probably formed as a frequentative from Old French *estouffer,* to choke, smother, from Vulgar Latin *extuffāre* (unattested), perhaps alteration (influenced by unattested *extūfāre,* to bathe in hot vapor, STEW) of *stuppāre* (unattested), to stop up with tow, from Latin *stuppa,* tow, from Greek *stuppē.* See **stewe-** in Appendix.*] —**sti′fler** *n.* —**sti′fling·ly** *adv.*
sti·fle[2] (stī′fəl) *n.* The joint of the hind leg analogous to the human knee in certain quadrupeds, such as the horse. Also called "stifle joint." [Middle English *stifle*†.]
stig·ma (stĭg′mə) *n., pl.* **stigmata** (stĭg-mä′tə, stĭg′mə-tə) or **-mas** (especially for sense 6). **1.** *Archaic.* A mark burned into the skin of a criminal or slave; a brand. **2.** A mark or token of infamy, disgrace, or reproach. **3.** Any small mark; a scar or birthmark. **4.** *Medicine.* **a.** A mark or spot on the skin that bleeds as a symptom of hysteria. **b.** A mark indicative of a history of a disease or abnormality. **5.** *Biology.* A small mark, spot, or pore, such as the respiratory spiracle of an insect or an eyespot in certain algae. **6.** *Botany.* The apex of the pistil of a flower, upon which pollen is deposited at pollination. **7.** *Plural.* Marks or sores corresponding to and resembling the crucifixion wounds of Jesus, sometimes impressed on the bodies of certain persons in a state of religious ecstasy or hysteria. [Latin *stigma* (plural *stigmata*), from Greek, tattoo mark, from *stizein,* to prick, tattoo. See **steig-** in Appendix.*]
stig·mas·ter·ol (stĭg-măs′tə-rôl′, -rōl′, -rŏl′) *n.* A sterol, $C_{29}H_{48}O$, obtained from soybeans or Calabar beans. [New Latin *(Physo)stigma,* genus of the Calabar bean (see **physostigmine**) + STEROL.]
stig·mat·ic (stĭg-măt′ĭk) *adj.* Also **stig·mat·i·cal** (-ĭ-kəl). **1.** Pertaining to, resembling, or having a stigma or stigmata. **2.** **Anastigmatic** *(see).* —*n.* Also **stig·ma·tist** (-mə-tĭst). A person marked with religious stigmata.
stig·ma·tism (stĭg′mə-tĭz′əm) *n.* **1.** The state or condition of being affected by stigmata. **2.** *Optics.* The state of a refracting or reflecting system that focuses at a point light rays from an off-axis point.
stig·ma·tize (stĭg′mə-tīz′) *tr.v.* **-tized, -tizing, -tizes. 1.** To characterize or brand as disgraceful or ignominious. **2.** To brand or mark with a stigma or stigmata. **3.** To cause stigmata to appear on. [Medieval Latin *stigmatizāre,* to brand, from Greek *stigmatizein,* to mark, tattoo, from *stigma,* tattoo mark, STIGMA.] —**stig′ma·ti·za′tion** *n.* —**stig′ma·tiz′er** *n.*
Sti·kine (stĭ-kēn′). A river rising in northwestern British Columbia, Canada, and flowing 335 miles west and southwest through southern Alaska to the Pacific.
stil·bene (stĭl′bēn′) *n.* A colorless or yellowish crystalline compound, $C_{14}H_{12}$, used in the manufacture of dyes and optical bleaches and as a phosphor. [Greek *stilbos,* shining, shimmering, from *stilbein*†, to shimmer + -ENE.]
stil·bes·trol (stĭl-bĕs′trôl′) *n. Chemistry.* **Diethylstilbestrol** *(see).* [STILB(ENE) + ESTR(US) + -OL.]
stil·bite (stĭl′bīt′) *n.* A white or yellow lustrous zeolite mineral, essentially $(Ca,Na)_2Al_2Si_7O_{18}\cdot 7H_2O$. [French : Greek *stilbos,* shining, shimmering (see **stilbene**) + -ITE.]
stile[1] (stīl) *n.* **1.** A set or series of steps for getting over a fence or wall. **2.** A turnstile. [Middle English *stile,* Old English *stigel.* See **steigh-** in Appendix.*]
stile[2] (stīl) *n.* A vertical member of a panel or frame, as in a door or window sash. [Probably from Dutch *stijl,* doorpost, from Middle Dutch, probably from Latin *stilus,* pole, post. See **style.**]
sti·let·to (stĭ-lĕt′ō) *n., pl.* **-tos** or **-toes. 1.** A small dagger with a slender, tapering blade. **2.** A small, sharp-pointed instrument used for making eyelet holes in needlework. [Italian, diminutive of *stilo,* dagger, from Latin *stilus,* sharp-pointed post, pole, stake. See **style.**]
still[1] (stĭl) *adj.* **stiller, stillest. 1.** Free from sound; silent; quiet. **2.** Low in sound; hushed; subdued. **3.** Without movement; at rest: *A still flag hung from the mast.* **4.** Free from disturbance, commotion, or agitation; tranquil; serene. **5.** Free from a noticeable current, as a body of water. **6.** Not carbonated; lacking effervescence: *a still wine.* **7.** *Photography.* Of or pertaining to a single or static photograph as opposed to a motion picture. —See Synonyms at **calm.** —*n.* **1.** Silence; quiet; calm: *the still of the night.* **2.** A still photograph, especially one from a scene of a motion picture used for advertising purposes. **3.** A still-life picture. **4.** A still alarm. —*adv.* **1.** Without movement; motionlessly: *stand still.* **2.** Up to or at the time indicated; now as before; yet: *"The river was still belly-swollen from last week's rain"* (Alan Sillitoe). **3.** In increasing amount or degree: *still further complaints.* **4.** Nevertheless; all the same. **5.** *Archaic & Regional.* Always; constantly. —*conj.* Nevertheless; but yet: *It was difficult; still, he tried.* —See Synonyms at **but.** —*v.* **stilled, stilling, stills.** —*tr.* **1.** To make still or tranquil. **2.** To make quiet; to silence. **3.** To make motionless. **4.** To allay; calm. —*intr.* To become still. [Middle English *still(e),* Old English *stille.* See **stel-**[1] in Appendix.*] —**still′ness** *n.*
Synonyms: *still, quiet, silent, noiseless, hushed, tranquil.* These adjectives refer to the relative absence of sound or movement. *Still* can apply to what is without sound or activity or both, as can *quiet. Still* is usually the more emphatic in all senses; *quiet* often implies merely the absence of noise, bustle, or customary activity. *Silent* refers only to what is without sound or noise. Like *noiseless* and *hushed,* it makes no clear indication with respect to movement or the absence thereof. *Noiseless* can mean without sound but usually implies freedom from excessive or disturbing sound. *Hushed* suggests a sudden condition of silence, especially one following noise or excitement. *Tranquil* primarily implies calm and lack of agitated movement.
still[2] (stĭl) *n.* **1.** An apparatus for distilling liquids, particularly alcohols, consisting of a vessel in which the substance is vaporized by heat and a cooling device in which the vapor is condensed. **2.** A distillery. [From *still,* to distill, Middle English *stillen,* short for *distillen,* DISTILL.]
Still (stĭl), **Andrew Taylor.** 1828–1917. American physician; founder of osteopathy.
still alarm. A fire alarm transmitted by means other than sounding the regular signal apparatus, as by telephone.
still·birth (stĭl′bûrth′) *n.* **1.** The birth of a dead child or fetus. **2.** A child or fetus dead at birth. —**still′born′** *adj.*
still hunt. 1. The hunting of game by stalking or ambushing. **2.** *Informal.* A stealthy, quiet, or cautious pursuit of anything.
still-hunt (stĭl′hŭnt′) *v.* **-hunted, -hunting, -hunts.** —*tr.* To pursue (game) stealthily. —*intr.* To engage in a still hunt.
stil·li·form (stĭl′ə-fôrm′) *adj.* Drop-shaped. [Latin *stillis,* a drop (see **distill**) + -FORM.]
still life *pl.* **still lifes. 1.** The representation of inanimate objects, such as flowers or fruit, in painting or photography. **2.** A painting or picture of inanimate objects. —**still′-life′** *adj.*
still·man (stĭl′măn′) *n., pl.* **-men** (-mĕn′). **1.** A person who owns or manages a still or distillery. **2.** A person who operates a distillation apparatus, as in an oil refinery.
Still·son wrench (stĭl′sən). A trademark for a monkey wrench with serrated jaws, one of which has slight angular movement to facilitate gripping pipes and other round objects.
still·y (stĭl′ē) *adj. Poetic.* Quiet; calm. —**stil′ly** *adv.*
stilt (stĭlt) *n., pl.* **stilts** or **stilt** (for sense 3). **1.** Either of a pair of long, slender poles, each equipped with a raised footrest to permit walking elevated above the ground. **2.** Any of various tall posts or pillars used as support, as for a dock or building. **3. a.** A long-legged wading bird, *Himantopus mexicanus* (or *H. himantopus*), having black and white plumage and a long slender bill. **b.** A related bird, *Cladorhyncus leucocephala,* of Australia. —*tr.v.* **stilted, stilting, stilts.** To place or raise on stilts. [Middle English *stilte,* stilt, crutch, perhaps of Low German origin, akin to Low German and Flemish *stilte.* See **stel-**[3] in Appendix.*]

stilt·ed (stĭl′tĭd) *adj.* **1.** Stiffly or artificially dignified or formal; pompous: *"Standard English must always strike an American as a bit stilted"* (H.L. Mencken). **2.** *Architecture.* Having some vertical length between the impost and the beginning of the curve. Said of an arch. —**stilt′ed·ly** *adv.* —**stilt′ed·ness** *n.*

Stil·ton cheese (stĭlt′n). A rich, waxy cheese having a blue-green mold and a wrinkled rind. [Originally made at *Stilton,* a parish in Huntingdonshire, England.]

Stil·well (stĭl′wĕl′), **Joseph Warren.** 1883–1946. American military leader; commander of China-Burma-India forces in World War II.

Stim·son (stĭm′sən), **Henry Lewis.** 1867–1950. American public official; Secretary of War (1911–13 and 1940–45); Secretary of State (1929–33).

stim·u·lant (stĭm′yə-lənt) *n.* **1.** Anything that temporarily arouses or accelerates physiological or organic activity. **2.** A stimulus or incentive: *"An age of political excitement is usually a stimulant to literature"* (Will Durant). **3.** An alcoholic beverage. —*adj.* Serving as a stimulant. [Latin *stimulāns,* present participle of *stimulāre,* STIMULATE.]

stim·u·late (stĭm′yə-lāt′) *v.* **-lated, -lating, -lates.** —*tr.* To rouse to activity or heightened action, as by spurring or goading; excite. —*intr.* To act or serve as a stimulant or stimulus. —See Synonyms at **provoke.** [Latin *stimulāre,* to goad on, from *stimulus,* a STIMULUS.] —**stim′u·lat′er, stim′u·la′tor** (-lā′tər) *n.* —**stim′u·la′tion** *n.*

stim·u·la·tive (stĭm′yə-lā′tĭv) *adj.* Serving or tending to stimulate. —*n.* Anything that stimulates; a stimulus.

stim·u·lus (stĭm′yə-ləs) *n., pl.* **-li** (-lī′, -lē′). **1.** Anything causing or regarded as causing a response. **2.** An agent, action, or condition that elicits or accelerates a physiological or psychological activity. **3.** Something that incites or rouses to action; an incentive: *"works which were in themselves poor have often proved a stimulus to the imagination"* (W.H. Auden). [Latin *stimulus*†, a goad.]

sting (stĭng) *v.* **stung** (stŭng) or *obsolete* **stang** (stăng), **stung, stinging, stings.** —*tr.* **1.** To pierce or wound painfully with or as if with a sharp-pointed structure or organ, such as that of certain insects. **2.** To cause to feel a sharp, smarting pain by or as by pricking with a sharp point. **3.** To cause to suffer keenly in the mind or feelings: *Her words stung him bitterly.* **4.** To spur on by or as if by sharp irritation. **5.** *Slang.* To cheat or overcharge. —*intr.* **1.** To have, use, or wound with a sting. **2.** To cause or feel a sharp, smarting pain. —*n.* **1.** The act of stinging. **2.** The wound or pain caused by or as if by stinging. **3.** A sharp, piercing organ or part, often ejecting a venomous secretion, such as the modified ovipositor of a bee or wasp or the spine of certain fishes. **4.** Something that causes a sharp pain, either physical or mental; stinging power, quality, or capacity: *"The sting of fear is anxiety"* (Paul Tillich). **5.** A keen stimulus or incitement; a goad or spur. [Sting, stang or stung, stung; Middle English *stingen, stang* (past plural *stungen*), *stungen,* Old English *stingan, stang* (past plural *stungon*), *stungen.* See **stegh-** in Appendix.*] —**sting′ing·ly** *adv.*

sting·a·ree (stĭng′ə-rē) *n.* A fish, the **stingray** *(see).* [Variant of STINGRAY.]

sting·er (stĭng′ər) *n.* **1.** One that stings. **2.** A stinging organ or part. **3.** *Informal.* Anything that stings or wounds mentally, as an insult. **4.** A cocktail of crème de menthe and brandy.

sting·ray (stĭng′rā′) *n.* Any of various rays of the family Dasyatidae, having a whiplike tail armed with a venomous spine capable of inflicting severe injury. Also called "stingaree."

stin·gy[1] (stĭn′jē) *adj.* **-gier, -giest.** **1.** Giving or spending reluctantly or unwillingly; penurious. **2.** Scanty or meager: *"A rain though stingy had begun to fall"* (Robert Frost). [Perhaps originally "sharp," "bad-tempered," from dialectal *stinge,* act of stinging, Middle English *sting,* Old English *sting, styng,* from *stingan,* to STING.] —**stin′gi·ly** *adv.* —**stin′gi·ness** *n.*

Synonyms: *stingy, close, close-fisted, niggardly, miserly, parsimonious, penny-pinching.* These adjectives, which are often interchangeable, suggest reluctance to spend one's money or part with one's possessions. *Stingy,* the most general, often implies, besides absence of generosity, an inclination toward meanness in dealings. *Close* and *close-fisted* describe one who is exceedingly and usually annoyingly cautious in money matters. *Niggardly* implies a tendency to be grudging, petty, and covetous. *Miserly* suggests greediness and hoarding of wealth for its own sake. *Parsimonious* emphasizes frugality carried to an extreme. *Penny-pinching* adds to *niggardly* the implication of foolish economy.

sting·y[2] (stĭng′ē) *adj. Informal.* Stinging or able to sting; piercing. —**sting′i·ly** *adv.*

stink (stĭngk) *v.* **stank** (stăngk) or **stunk** (stŭngk), **stunk, stinking, stinks.** —*intr.* **1.** To emit a strong foul odor. **2. a.** To be highly offensive or abhorrent. **b.** To be in extremely bad repute. **3.** *Slang.* To have something to an extreme or offensive degree. Usually used with *of* or *with.* **4.** *Slang.* To be of an extremely low or bad quality: *This movie stinks.* —*tr.* To cause to stink. Usually used with *up.* —**stink out.** To drive or force out by a strong foul or suffocating smell. —*n.* A strong offensive odor; a stench. —See Synonyms at **smell.** —**make** (or **raise**) **a stink.** *Slang.* To create trouble by complaining or criticizing; make a great fuss. [Stink, stank (or stunk), stunk; Middle English *stinken, stank* (past plural *stunken*), *stunken,* Old English *stincan, stanc* (past plural *stuncon*), *stuncen,* from Germanic *stinkwan* (unattested).] —**stink′ing·ly** *adv.*

stink·bug (stĭngk′bŭg′) *n.* Any of numerous insects of the family Pentatomidae, having a broad, flattened body and emitting a foul odor.

stink·er (stĭng′kər) *n.* **1.** One that stinks. **2.** *Slang.* A contemptible, disgusting, or irritating person. **3.** *Slang.* Something very difficult: *The exam was a real stinker.*

stink·horn (stĭngk′hôrn′) *n.* Any of several foul-smelling fungi of the order Phallales, such as *Phallus impudicus* or *P. ravenelii,* having a thick, cylindrical stalk and a narrow cap.

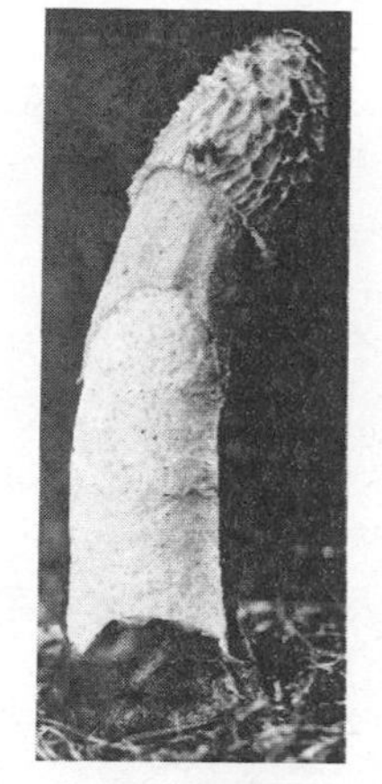

stinkhorn
Phallus impudicus

stink·ing (stĭng′kĭng) *adj.* **1.** Having a foul smell; fetid; rank. **2.** *Slang.* Very drunk. —*adv. Slang.* To an offensive or extreme degree: *"proceeded to get stinking drunk"* (James Jones). —**stink′ing·ly** *adv.* —**stink′ing·ness** *n.*

stinking chamomile. A plant, the **mayweed** *(see).*

stink·pot (stĭngk′pŏt′) *n.* **1.** An earthenware jar containing combustibles emitting a suffocating smoke, formerly used in warfare. **2.** *Slang.* A despised or mean person. **3.** A musk turtle, *Sternotherus odoratus,* of eastern North America.

stink stone. A variety of limestone that emits a disagreeable odor when struck or rubbed.

stink·weed (stĭngk′wēd′) *n.* Any of various plants having flowers or foliage with an unpleasant odor.

stink·wood (stĭngk′wo͝od′) *n.* **1. a.** A tree, *Ocotea bullata,* of southern Africa, having wood with an unpleasant odor. **b.** The hard, heavy wood of this tree, used in cabinetwork. **2.** Broadly, any of several other trees having wood with an unpleasant odor.

stint[1] (stĭnt) *v.* **stinted, stinting, stints.** —*tr.* **1.** To restrict or limit, as in amount or number; be sparing with: *"He was not the kind of youth to stint his praise of work he admired"* (Stanislaus Joyce). **2.** *Archaic.* To stop; desist. —*intr.* **1.** To subsist on a meager allowance; be frugal. **2.** *Archaic.* To stop or desist. —*n.* **1.** A fixed amount or share of work or duty to be performed within a given period of time. **2.** A limitation or restriction: *"when God opens the floodgates and pours Himself without stint into the soul"* (Walter J. Ong). —See Synonyms at **task.** [Middle English *stinten,* to stop, cut short, Old English *styntan,* to blunt, dull. See **steu-** in Appendix.*] —**stint′er** *n.*

stint[2] (stĭnt) *n.* Any of several small sandpipers of the genera *Erolia* or *Calidris,* of northern regions. [Middle English *stynt*†.]

stip. **1.** stipend. **2.** stipulation.

stipe (stīp) *n. Botany.* A stalk or stalklike structure, such as the stemlike support of the cap of a mushroom or the main stem of a fern frond. [French, from Latin *stīpes,* post, tree trunk. See **steip-** in Appendix.*]

sti·pel (stī′pəl) *n. Botany.* A minute or secondary stipule at the base of a leaflet. [New Latin *stipella,* diminutive of *stipula,* STIPULE.] —**sti·pel′late** (stī-pĕl′ĭt, stī′pə-lĭt, -lāt′) *adj.*

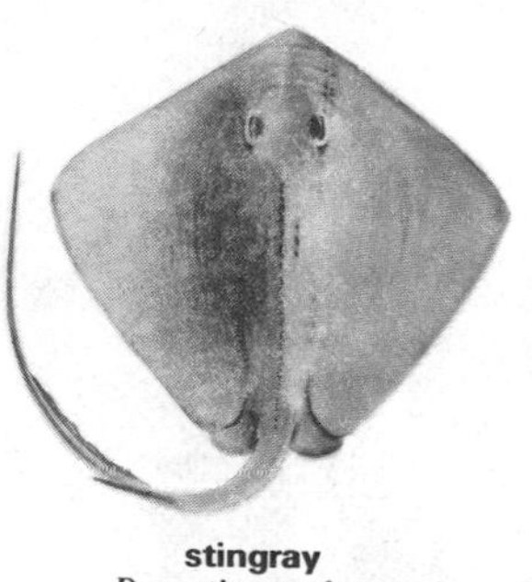

stingray
Dasyatis americana

sti·pend (stī′pĕnd′, -pənd) *n. Abbr.* **stip.** A fixed or regular payment, such as a salary for services rendered or an allowance. [Middle English *stipendie,* from Old French, from Latin *stīpendium,* tax, tribute, akin to *stipulārī,* to STIPULATE.]

sti·pen·di·ar·y (stī-pĕn′dē-ĕr′ē) *adj.* **1.** Receiving a stipend. **2.** Compensated for by stipend: *stipendiary services.* —*n., pl.* **stipendiaries.** A person who receives a stipend, as a clergyman. [Latin *stīpendiārius,* from *stīpendium,* tribute, STIPEND.]

sti·pes (stī′pēz′) *n., pl.* **stipites** (stĭp′ə-tēz′). *Zoology.* **1.** The basal segment of the maxilla of an insect. **2.** Any stalklike support or structure. [New Latin, from Latin *stīpes,* post, tree trunk. See **steip-** in Appendix.*] —**sti′pi·form′** (-pə-fôrm′), **stip′i·ti·form′** (stĭp′ə-tə-fôrm′) *adj.*

stip·i·tate (stĭp′ə-tāt′) *adj.* Having or supported on a stipe. [From Latin *stīpes* (stem *stīpit-*), post, tree trunk. See **stipes.**]

stip·ple (stĭp′əl) *tr.v.* **-pled, -pling, -ples.** **1.** To draw, engrave, or paint in dots or short touches. **2.** To apply (paint, for example) in dots or short strokes. **3.** To dot, fleck, or speckle: *"They crossed a field stippled with purple weeds"* (Flannery O'Connor). —*n.* **1.** The method of painting, drawing, or engraving by stippling. **2.** The effect produced by stippling or a work performed in this manner. [Dutch *stippelen,* frequentative of *stippen,* to speckle, dot, from *stip,* dot, point, from Middle Dutch. See **steip-** in Appendix.*] —**stip′pler** *n.*

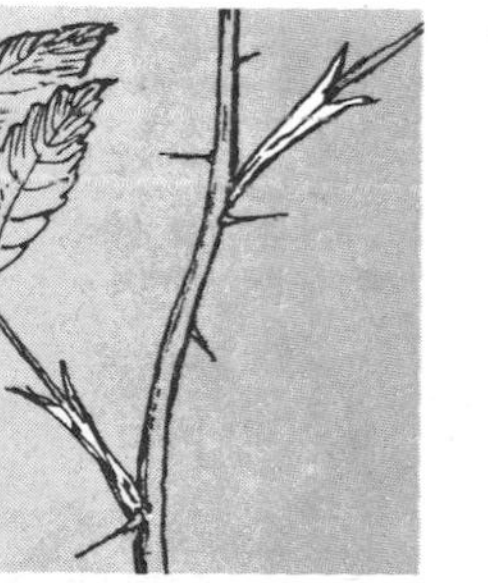

stipule

stip·u·lar (stĭp′yə-lər) *adj. Botany.* Of, pertaining to, or resembling a stipule or stipules.

stip·u·late[1] (stĭp′yə-lāt′) *v.* **-lated, -lating, -lates.** —*tr.* **1.** To specify as a condition of an agreement; require by contract. **2.** To guarantee in an agreement. —*intr.* **1.** To make an express demand or provision in an agreement. Used with *for.* **2.** To form an agreement. [Latin *stipulārī*†, to bargain, demand.] —**stip′u·la′tor** (-lā′tər) *n.*

stip·u·late[2] (stĭp′yə-lĭt) *adj. Botany.* Having stipules.

stip·u·la·tion (stĭp′yə-lā′shən) *n. Abbr.* **stip.** **1.** The act of stipulating. **2.** Something stipulated; a term or condition in an agreement. —**stip′u·la·to′ry** (-lə-tôr′ē, -tôr′ē) *adj.*

stip·ule (stĭp′yo͞ol′) *n. Botany.* One of the usually small, paired leaflike appendages at the base of a leaf or leafstalk in certain plants. [New Latin *stipula,* from Latin, stalk, stem, akin to *stipulārī,* to STIPULATE.]

stir[1] (stûr) *v.* **stirred, stirring, stirs.** —*tr.* **1.** To pass an implement through (a liquid) in circular motions, so as to mix or cool the contents. **2.** To alter the placement of slightly; disarrange. **3.** To move briskly or vigorously; bestir. **4.** To rouse (someone), as from sleep or indifference. **5.** To incite, provoke, or instigate. Often used with *up: stir up trouble.* **6.** To excite the emotions of; move or affect strongly: *"These mild sonnets stirred Coleridge"* (J.D. Campbell). —*intr.* **1.** To change position slightly: *"The woman stirred in her sleep, and called his name"* (Alan Paton). **2.** To move about actively; to venture. **3.** To take place; happen. **4.** To admit of being stirred. —See Synonyms at **provoke.** —*n.* **1.** An act of stirring; a mixing or poking movement. **2.** A disturbance or commotion. **3.** An excited reaction; a ferment. [Middle English *stiren,* Old English *styrian,* to move, agitate, excite. See **twer-**[1] in Appendix.*] **—stir′rer** *n.*

stir[2] (stûr) *n. Slang.* Prison. [Origin unknown.]

stir crazy. *Slang.* Distraught or restless from long confinement in or as if in prison.

stirk (stûrk) *n.* A yearling heifer or, sometimes, a bullock. [Middle English *stirk,* Old English *stirc.* See **ster-**[5] in Appendix.*]

Stir·ling (stûr′lĭng). **1.** Also **Stir·ling·shire** (-shîr, -shər). A county occupying 252 square miles in south-central Scotland. Population, 198,000. **2.** Its county seat. Population, 28,000.

stirps (stûrps) *n., pl.* **stirpes** (stûr′pēz). **1.** A line of descendants of common ancestry; stock. **2.** *Law.* One from whom a family is descended. [Latin *stirps*†, stem, root, lineage.]

stir·ring (stûr′ĭng) *adj.* **1.** Rousing; exciting; thrilling. **2.** Active; lively. —See Synonyms at **moving.** **—stir′ring·ly** *adv.*

stir·rup (stûr′əp, stĭr′-) *n.* **1.** A flat-based loop or ring hung from either side of a horse's saddle to support the rider's foot in mounting and riding. **2.** Any of various parts or devices shaped like an inverted U, in which something is supported. **3.** *Nautical.* A rope on a ship hanging from a yard and having an eye at the end through which a footrope is passed for support. [Middle English *stirope,* Old English *stigrāp.* See **steigh-** in Appendix.*]

stirrup bone. *Anatomy.* The **stapes** *(see).*

stir·rup-cup (stûr′əp-kŭp′, stĭr′-) *n.* **1.** A farewell drink for a rider already mounted to depart. **2.** Any farewell drink.

stirrup leather. The strap used to fasten a stirrup to a saddle. Also called "stirrup strap."

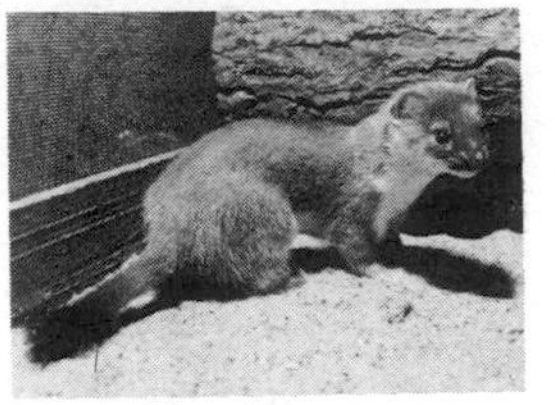
stoat

stitch (stĭch) *n. Abbr.* **st. 1.** A single complete movement of a threaded needle in sewing or surgical suturing. **2.** A single loop of yarn around a knitting needle or similar implement. **3.** The link, loop, or knot made in this way. **4.** A mode of arranging the threads in sewing, knitting, or crocheting: *a purl stitch.* **5.** A sudden sharp pain in the side. **6.** *Informal.* An article of clothing: *not a stitch on.* **7.** *Informal.* The least part; a bit: *He didn't do a stitch of work.* **8.** A ridge or rising between two furrows. **—in stitches.** *Informal.* Laughing uncontrollably. **—***v.* **stitched, stitching, stitches.** **—***tr.* **1:** To fasten or join with stitches. **2.** To ornament with stitches. **3.** To fasten with staples. **—***intr.* To make stitches; sew. [Middle English *stiche,* Old English *stice,* a sting, prick. See **steig-** in Appendix.*] **—stitch′er** *n.*

stitch·wort (stĭch′wûrt′, -wôrt′) *n.* Any of several low-growing plants of the genus *Stellaria,* having small, white, star-shaped flowers. [Middle English *stichewort,* Old English *sticwyrt,* agrimony : STITCH + WORT (from its alleged ability to cure sharp pains in the side).]

stith·y (stĭth′ē) *n., pl.* **-ies. 1.** An anvil. **2.** A forge or smithy. [Middle English *stethy,* from Old Norse *stedhi.* See **stā-** in Appendix.*]

sti·ver (stī′vər) *n.* **1.** An obsolete Dutch coin worth 1/20 of a guilder. **2.** Anything of small value. [Dutch *stuiver,* from Middle Dutch *stuyver.* See **steu-** in Appendix.*]

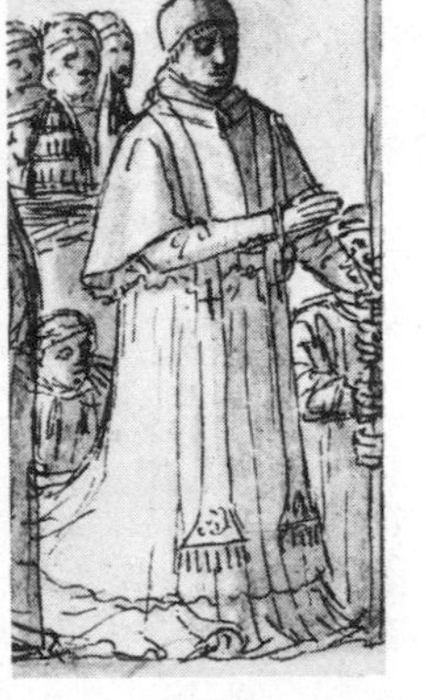
stole[1]
Detail from a drawing by Vittore Carpaccio showing Pope Alexander III in ceremonial robes and stole

St. John (sānt jŏn′). An island, 20 square miles in area, of the Virgin Islands of the United States, lying east of St. Thomas.

St. John River (sānt jŏn′). A river rising in northwestern Maine and flowing 450 miles, first northeast, then southeast through New Brunswick, Canada, to the Bay of Fundy, forming part of the U.S.-Canadian border on its course.

St. Johns (sānt jŏnz′). A river of eastern Florida, flowing 285 miles north to the Atlantic east of Jacksonville.

St. John's (sānt jŏnz′). The capital and chief seaport of Newfoundland, Canada, in the southeast. Population, 64,000.

St. John's bread. The long blackish, sugary, edible pod of the **carob** *(see).* [After St. JOHN the Baptist, who lived on honey and locusts while preaching (through confusion of the locusts with the carob, known also as locust bean). Matthew 3:4.]

St. Johns·wort (sānt′ jŏnz′wûrt′, -wôrt′). Any of various plants or shrubs of the genus *Hypericum,* having yellow flowers. [So called because it was gathered on *St. John's* Eve to ward off evil spirits.]

St. Joseph (sānt jō′zəf, -səf). A city of Missouri, in the northwest on the Missouri River. Population, 80,000.

stk. stock.

St. Kitts (sānt kĭts′). An island, 68 square miles in area, in the Leeward Islands of the West Indies. Population, 38,000. Also called "St. Christopher."

St. Kitts-Ne·vis (sānt kĭts′ nē′vĭs, nĕv′ĭs). Formerly **St. Kitts-Ne·vis-An·guil·la** (-ăng-gwĭl′ə). An island group in the Caribbean about 150 miles east of Puerto Rico; former British colony that included Anguilla, it became one of the West Indies Associated States in 1967. Anguilla declared itself an independent republic in 1969. Population, 51,000. Capital, Basseterre, on St. Kitts.

STL Airport code for St. Louis, Missouri.

St. Law·rence, Gulf of (sānt lôr′əns). A gulf of the North Atlantic between the St. Lawrence River estuary on the west and Newfoundland on the east.

St. Law·rence Island (sānt lôr′əns). An Alaskan island, 90 miles long and up to 22 miles wide, just south of Bering Strait.

St. Law·rence River (sānt lôr′əns). A river of Canada flowing 744 miles northeast from Lake Ontario to the Gulf of St. Lawrence and forming for 114 miles the border between New York State and Ontario, Canada.

St. Law·rence Seaway (sānt lôr′əns). **1.** A canal and river route extending 182 miles along the St. Lawrence River between Montreal, Canada, and Lake Ontario, established and administered jointly by the United States and Canada. **2.** Broadly, the entire inland waterway of rivers, canals, and lakes extending from the Atlantic through the Great Lakes.

St. Lou·is (sānt lo͞o′ĭs). An industrial city of Missouri, in the east on the Mississippi. Population, 750,000.

St. Lou·is River (sānt lo͞o′ĭs). A river rising in northeastern Minnesota and flowing 220 miles in a wide southward bend to Lake Superior at Duluth.

St. Lu·ci·a (sānt lo͞o′shə, lo͞o-sē′ə). An island, 233 square miles in area, in the West Indies, a former British colony, with internal self-government as one of the West Indies Associated States since 1967. Population, 100,000. Capital, Castries.

St. Mar·tin (sānt märt′n). A Leeward Island of the West Indies, about 33 square miles in area, constituting part of the Netherlands Antilles in the south and of the French Overseas Department of Guadeloupe in the north. Population, 4,000.

St. Mar·y·le·bone (sānt mĕr′ə-lə-bən). A former administrative division of the city of London, England, now part of **Westminster** *(see).*

St. Mar·ys City (sānt mâr′ēz). Formerly **Saint Mar·ys.** A village in southern Maryland, the site of the first settlement in Maryland (1634) and of the state's first capital.

St. Mar·ys River (sānt mâr′ēz). **1.** A river rising in Okefenokee Swamp, southeastern Georgia, and flowing 175 miles east to the Atlantic, forming part of the Georgia-Florida border. **2.** A river flowing 63 miles from Lake Superior to Lake Huron, forming the boundary between northeastern Michigan and Ontario, Canada.

St. Mau·rice (sānt mə-rēs′; *French* săN mô-rēs′). A river rising in central Quebec and flowing 325 miles southward to the St. Lawrence at Trois Rivières.

St. Mo·ritz (sānt mə-rĭts′; *French* săN mô-rēts′). *German* **Sankt Mo·ritz** (zängt′ mō-rĭts′). A resort in southeastern Switzerland, on the Inn River. Population, 3,000.

STO Airport code for Stockholm, Sweden.

sto·a (stō′ə) *n., pl.* **stoae** (stō′ē′) or **-as.** An ancient Greek covered walk or colonnade, usually having columns on one side and a wall on the other. [Greek, porch. See **stā-** in Appendix.*]

stoat (stōt) *n. Chiefly British.* The ermine, especially when in its brown color phase. [Middle English *stote*†.]

sto·chas·tic (stō-kăs′tĭk) *adj.* **1.** Of, denoting, or characterized by conjecture; conjectural. **2.** *Statistics.* **a.** Random. **b.** Statistical. [Greek *stokhastikos,* capable of aiming, conjectural, from *stokhazesthai,* to aim at, guess at, from *stokhos,* target, aim. See **stegh-** in Appendix.*]

stochastic variable. *Statistics.* A **random variable** *(see).*

stock (stŏk) *n. Abbr.* **s., stk. 1.** A supply accumulated for future use; a store or stores. **2.** The total merchandise kept on hand by a merchant or commercial establishment. **3.** All the animals kept or raised on a farm; livestock. **4.** *Economics.* **a.** The capital or fund that a corporation raises through the sale of shares entitling the holder to dividends and to other rights of ownership. **b.** The number of shares that each stockholder possesses. **c.** A certificate that shows ownership of a stated number of shares. **d.** Formerly, the part of a tally or record of account given to a creditor. **e.** A debt symbolized by a tally or tallies. **5.** The trunk or main stem of a tree or other plant as distinguished from the branches and roots. **6. a.** A plant or stem onto which a graft is made. **b.** A plant or tree from which cuttings and slips are taken. **7. a.** The original progenitor of a family line. **b.** Ancestry or lineage; antecedents. **c.** The type from which a group of animals or plants has descended. **d.** A race, family, or other related group of animals or plants. **e.** An ethnic group or other major division of mankind. **f.** A group of related languages. **g.** A group of related families of languages. **8.** The raw material out of which something is made. **9.** The broth from boiled meat or fish, used as a base in preparing soup, gravy, or sauces. **10. a.** The chief upright part of something, particularly a supporting structure or block. **b.** *Plural.* The timber frame that supports a ship during construction. **c.** A frame in which a horse or other animal is held for shoeing or for veterinary treatment. **11.** *Plural.* A former instrument of punishment, consisting of a heavy timber frame with holes for confining the ankles and, sometimes, the wrists. **12.** *Nautical.* A crosspiece at the end of an anchor's shank. **13.** The wooden block from which a bell is suspended. **14. a.** The rear wooden or metal handle or part of a rifle, pistol, or automatic weapon, to which the barrel and mechanism are attached. Also called "gunstock." **b.** The long mooring beam of field-gun carriages that trails along the ground. **15.** Any handle, as of a whip, fishing rod, or various carpenter's tools. **16.** The frame of a plow, to which the share, handles, colter, and other parts are fastened. **17. a.** *Theater.* A stock company. **b.** The repertoire of such a company. **c.** Any theater or theatrical activity, especially outside of a main theatrical center such as New York City: *a small role in summer stock.* **18.** Any of several plants of the genus *Mathiola,* native to the Old World; especially, *M. incana,* widely cultivated for its clusters of showy, variously colored flowers. **19.** That portion of a pack of cards or group of dominoes that is not dealt out but is drawn from during a game. **20.** *Geology.* A body of intrusive igneous rock of which less than 40 square miles is exposed. **21.** Personal reputation or status: *His stock with the students is falling.* **—in stock.** Available for sale or use; on hand. **—out of stock.** Not available for sale or use, generally temporarily. **—stock in trade. 1.** The merchandise kept on hand for sale. **2.** A person's resources for any purpose. **—take stock. 1.** To take an inventory. **2.** To make an estimate or reappraisal, as of resources, prospects, or the like. **—take stock in. 1.** To purchase a share or shares of stock in. **2.** *Informal.* To trust, believe in, or attach importance to. —*v.* **stocked, stocking, stocks.** —*tr.* **1.** To provide (a store or farm, for example) with merchandise or livestock. **2.** To keep for future sale or use. **3.** To provide (a rifle or plow, for example) with a stock. **4.** *Obsolete.* To put (someone) in the stocks as a punishment. —*intr.* **1. a.** To gather and store a supply of something. Used with *up* or *up on.* **b.** To hoard. Used with *up* or *up on.* **2.** To put forth or sprout new shoots. Used of plants. —*adj.* **1.** Kept regularly in stock. **2.** Commonplace; ordinary: *a stock answer.* **3.** Employed in dealing with or caring for stock or merchandise: *a stock clerk.* **4. a.** Of or pertaining to the raising of livestock: *stock farming.* **b.** Used for breeding: *a stock mare.* **5.** Of or pertaining to investment shares or stock: *a stock list.* **6.** *Theater.* Of or pertaining to a stock company or its repertoire. —*adv.* Utterly; completely. Used in combination: *stock-still.* [Middle English *stok(ke),* Old English *stocc,* tree trunk. See **steu-** in Appendix.*]

stock·ade (stŏk'ād') *n.* **1.** A defensive barrier made of strong posts or timbers driven upright side by side in the ground. **2.** Any similarly fenced or enclosed area, especially one used for protection or imprisonment. —*tr.v.* **stockaded, -ading, -ades.** To fortify, protect, or surround with a stockade. [Obsolete French *estocade,* from Spanish *estacada,* from *estaca,* stake, from Germanic. See **steg-²** in Appendix.*]

stock·breed·ing (stŏk'brē'dĭng) *n.* The raising of livestock. —**stock'breed'er** *n.*

stock·bro·ker (stŏk'brō'kər) *n.* A person who acts as an agent in the buying and selling of stocks or other securities. —**stock'-bro'ker·age, stock'bro'king** *n.*

stock car. 1. An automobile of a standard make, modified for racing. **2.** A railroad car carrying livestock.

stock certificate. A certificate establishing ownership of a stated number of shares in a corporation's stock.

stock company. 1. A company or corporation whose capital is divided into shares. **2.** *Theater.* A permanent company of actors and technicians attached to a single theater and performing in repertory.

stock dove. A common Old World bird, *Columba oenas,* having grayish plumage. [So called probably because it lives in hollow tree trunks.]

stock exchange. *Abbr.* **St. Ex. 1.** A place where stocks, bonds, or other securities are bought and sold. **2.** An association of stockbrokers who meet to buy and sell stocks and bonds according to fixed regulations.

stock·fish (stŏk'fĭsh') *n.* A fish, such as cod or haddock, cured by being split and air-dried without salt.

stock·hold·er (stŏk'hōl'dər) *n.* One who owns a share or shares of stock in a company. —**stock'hold'ing** *adj.* & *n.*

Stock·holm (stŏk'hōlm). The capital of Sweden, in the east on the Baltic Sea. Population, 794,000.

stock·i·net (stŏk'ə-nĕt') *n.* Also **stock·i·nette.** An elastic knitted fabric used in making undergarments, bandages, or the like. [Perhaps variant of earlier *stocking-net* : STOCKING + NET.]

stock·ing (stŏk'ĭng) *n.* **1.** A close-fitting, usually knitted covering for the foot and leg. **2.** Something resembling such a covering. —**in one's stocking feet.** Wearing socks or stockings but no shoes. [From dialectal *stock,* stocking, Middle English *stokke(s),* stocking(s), probably humorous use of *stokkes,* the stocks (instrument of punishment), from *stokke,* STOCK (tree trunk).]

stock·job·ber (stŏk'jŏb'ər) *n.* **1.** *British.* A stock-exchange operator who deals only with brokers and not with the public. **2.** A stockbroker. Often used disparagingly. —**stock'job'ber·y, stock'job'bing** *n.*

stock·man (stŏk'mən) *n., pl.* **-men** (-mĭn). **1.** One who owns or raises livestock. **2.** A man having charge of livestock or working on a stock farm. **3.** One employed in a stockroom or warehouse; a stock clerk.

stock market. 1. A stock exchange. **2.** The business transacted at a stock exchange. **3.** The prices offered for stocks and bonds: *The stock market fell today.*

stock·pile (stŏk'pīl') *n.* Also **stock pile.** A supply of material stored for future use, usually carefully accrued and maintained. —*v.* **stockpiled, -piling, -piles.** —*tr.* To accumulate a stockpile of. —*intr.* To accumulate a stockpile of a given material.

Stock·port (stŏk'pōrt). A city in northeastern Cheshire, England, southeast of Manchester. Population, 142,000.

stock·room (stŏk'rōōm') *n.* Also **stock room.** A room in which a store of goods or materials is kept.

Stock·ton (stŏk'tən). **1.** A city and commercial center of California, in the center of the state on the San Joaquin River. Population, 86,000. **2.** Also **Stockton-on-Tees** (stŏk'tən-ŏn-tēz', -ŏn-tēz'). A city and shipbuilding center of England, in the north in Durham county. Population, 83,000.

stock·y (stŏk'ē) *adj.* **-ier, -iest.** Solidly built; sturdy; thickset. —**stock'i·ly** *adv.* —**stock'i·ness** *n.*

stock·yard (stŏk'yärd') *n.* A large enclosed yard, usually with pens or stables, in which cattle, horses, sheep, or pigs are temporarily kept until they are slaughtered or shipped elsewhere.

stodg·y (stŏj'ē) *adj.* **-ier, -iest. 1. a.** Dull, narrow, and commonplace. **b.** Prim or pompous; stuffy: *"Why is the middle-class so stodgy—so utterly without a sense of humour!"* (Katherine Mansfield). **2.** Crammed full; packed or distended. **3.** Heavy; indigestible and starchy. Said of food. **4.** Solidly built; thickset; stocky. [From *stodge,* thick food or mud, anything dull, from *stodge*†, to cram, gorge.] —**stodg'i·ly** *adv.* —**stodg'i·ness** *n.*

sto·gy (stō'gē) *n., pl.* **-gies.** Also **sto·gie, sto·gey** *pl.* **-geys. 1.** A long, thin, inexpensive cigar. **2.** A roughly made heavy shoe or boot. [After *Conestoga,* town in Pennsylvania.]

sto·ic (stō'ĭk) *n.* **1.** A person seemingly indifferent to or unaffected by joy, grief, pleasure, or pain. **2.** *Capital* **S.** A member of a Greek school of philosophy founded by Zeno about 308 B.C., holding that men should be free from passion and calmly accept all occurrences as the unavoidable result of divine will. —*adj.* Also **sto·i·cal** (-ĭ-kəl) (for sense 1). **1.** Indifferent to or unaffected by pleasure or pain; impassive; enduring; brave: *"stoic resignation in the face of hunger"* (John F. Kennedy). **2.** *Capital* **S.** Of or pertaining to the Stoics or their beliefs. [Latin *Stōicus,* a Stoic, from Greek *Stōikos,* from *stoa,* portico, the porch where Zeno taught. See **stā-** in Appendix.*] —**sto'i·cal·ly** *adv.* —**sto'i·cal·ness** *n.*

stoi·chi·om·e·try (stoi'kē-ŏm'ə-trē) *n.* The methodology and technology by which the quantities of reactants and products in chemical reactions are determined. [Greek *stoikheion,* element (see **steigh-** in Appendix*) + -METRY.] —**stoi'chi·o·met'ric** (-ō-mĕt'rĭk) *adj.* —**stoi'chi·o·met'ri·cal·ly** *adv.*

sto·i·cism (stō'ĭ-sĭz'əm) *n.* **1.** Indifference to pleasure or pain; impassivity; an attitude of endurance or bravery: *"as soon as they knew the full hideousness of their doom, their stoicism forsook them"* (H. Rider Haggard). **2.** *Capital* **S.** The philosophy or doctrines of the Stoics.

stoke (stōk) *v.* **stoked, stoking, stokes.** —*tr.* **1.** To stir up and feed (a fire or furnace). **2.** To tend the fire of (a furnace). —*intr.* **1.** To feed a furnace with fuel. **2.** To tend a fire or furnace. [Back-formation from STOKER.]

stoke·hold (stōk'hōld') *n.* *Nautical.* The area or compartment into which the ship's furnaces or boilers open.

stoke·hole (stōk'hōl') *n.* **1.** The space about the opening in a furnace or boiler or the opening itself. **2.** A stokehold. [Translation of Dutch *stookgat.*]

Stoke New·ing·ton (stōk' nōō'ĭng-tən). A former administrative division of London, England, now part of **Hackney** *(see).*

Stoke-on-Trent (stōk'ŏn-trĕnt'). Also **Stoke-up·on-Trent** (-ə-pôn-trĕnt'). A city of west-central England, in Staffordshire; the center of the ceramics industry. Population, 277,000.

stok·er (stō'kər) *n.* **1.** One who feeds fuel to and tends a furnace, as a fireman on a locomotive. **2.** A mechanical device for feeding coal to a furnace. [Dutch, from *stoken,* to poke, thrust, from Middle Dutch. See **steu-** in Appendix.*]

Sto·ker (stō'kər), **Bram.** Original given name, Abraham. 1847–1912. British writer; creator of *Dracula.*

Stokes (stōks), Sir **George Gabriel.** 1819–1903. British mathematician and physicist; studied hydrodynamics.

Sto·kow·ski (stə-kou'skē), **Leopold Antoni Stanislaw.** Born 1882. British-born American conductor.

STOL (stōl) short takeoff and landing. Said of aircraft.

stole¹ (stōl) *n.* **1.** *Ecclesiastical.* A long scarf, usually of embroidered silk or linen, worn over the left shoulder by deacons and over both shoulders by priests and bishops while officiating. **2.** A women's long scarf of cloth or fur, worn about the shoulders. **3.** A long robe or outer garment worn by matrons in ancient Rome. [Middle English *stole,* long robe, Old English *stol,* from Latin *stola,* from Greek *stolē,* garment, array, equipment. See **stel-¹** in Appendix.*]

stole². Past tense of **steal.**

sto·len. Past participle of **steal.**

stol·id (stŏl'ĭd) *adj.* Having or showing little emotion; impassive: *"they suffered the eternal pleasantries with stolid patience"* (Thornton Wilder). [Latin *stolidus.* See **stel-¹** in Appendix.*] —**sto·lid'i·ty** (stə-lĭd'ə-tē), **stol'id·ness** *n.* —**stol'id·ly** *adv.*

stol·len (stō'lən) *n.* A rich yeast bread, often containing raisins, citron, and chopped nut meats. [German *Stollen,* loaf-shaped Christmas cake (symbolizing the Christ child in swaddling clothes), from Middle High German *stolle,* from Old High German *stollo,* post, support. See **stel-¹** in Appendix.*]

sto·lon (stō'lŏn', -lən) *n.* **1.** *Botany.* A stem growing along or under the ground and taking root at the nodes or apex to form new plants. **2.** *Zoology.* A stemlike structure of certain colonial organisms, from which new individuals develop by budding. [Latin *stolō* (stem *stolon-*), branch, shoot. See **stel-¹** in Appendix.*]

sto·lon·i·fer·ous (stō'lə-nĭf'ər-əs) *adj.* Bearing or forming stolons. —**sto'lon·if'er·ous·ly** *adv.*

sto·ma (stō'mə) *n., pl.* **-mata** (-mə-tə) or **-mas. 1.** *Botany.* One of the minute pores in the epidermis of a leaf or stem, through which gases and water vapor pass. **2.** *Anatomy.* **a.** A small aperture in the surface of a membrane. **b.** A minute opening in the surface of the peritoneum, thought to be for the passage of fluid into the lymphatic vessels. **3.** *Zoology.* A mouthlike opening, such as the oral cavity of a nematode. [New Latin, from Greek, mouth. See **stomen-** in Appendix.*]

stom·ach (stŭm'ək) *n.* **1. a.** The enlarged, saclike portion of the alimentary canal, one of the principal organs of digestion, located in vertebrates between the esophagus and the small intestine. **b.** A similar digestive structure of many invertebrates. **2.** *Informal.* The abdomen or belly. **3.** An appetite for food. **4.** Any desire or inclination; predilection. **5.** *Obsolete.* Courage or spirit. **6.** *Obsolete.* Pride or haughtiness. —*tr.v.* **stomached, -aching, -achs. 1.** To bear; tolerate; endure. **2.** To take into or hold in the stomach; digest. **3.** *Obsolete.* To resent. [Middle English *stomak,* from Old French *stomaque,* from Latin *stomachus,* from Greek *stomakhos,* throat, mouth, gullet, from *stoma,* mouth. See **stomen-** in Appendix.*]

stom·ach·ache (stŭm'ək-āk') *n.* Pain in the abdomen.

stom·ach·er (stŭm'ə-kər) *n.* A decorative, heavily embroidered or jeweled garment formerly worn over the chest and stomach, especially by women.

sto·mach·ic (stə-măk'ĭk) *adj.* Also **stom·ach·al** (stŭm'ə-kəl),

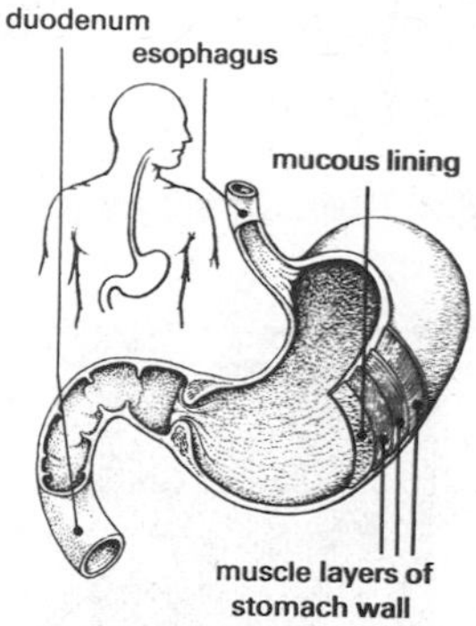
duodenum
esophagus
mucous lining
muscle layers of
stomach wall
stomach

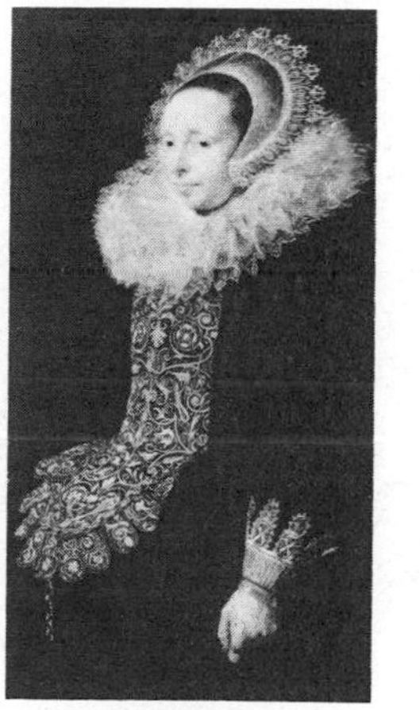
stomacher
Detail of painting by
Frans Hals

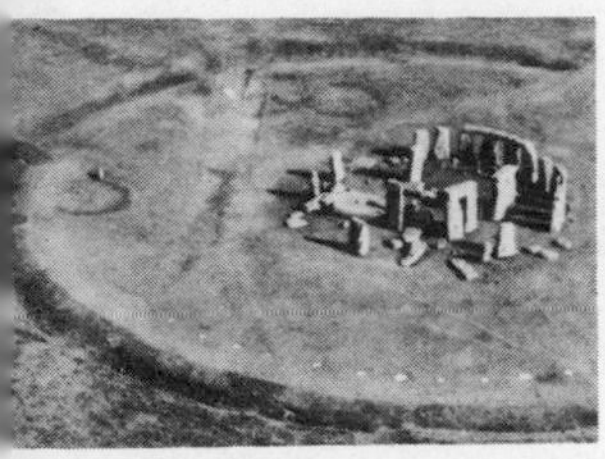
Stonehenge

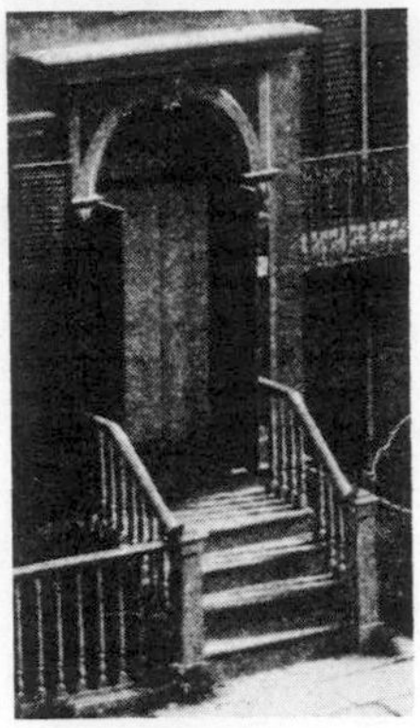
stoop²

sto·mach·i·cal (stə-măk′ĭ-kəl). **1.** Of or pertaining to the stomach; gastric. **2.** Beneficial to or stimulating digestion in the stomach. —*n.* Any medicine or agent that strengthens or stimulates the stomach.

stomach pump. A suction pump with a flexible tube inserted into the stomach through the mouth and esophagus to empty the stomach in an emergency, as in a case of poisoning.

stomach worm. Any of various parasitic nematode worms that infest the stomachs of animals; especially, *Haemonchus contortus,* a parasite of sheep and other ruminants.

sto·ma·ta. Plural of **stoma.**

sto·ma·tal (stō′mə-təl) *adj.* Of or having a stoma or stomata.

sto·mat·ic (stō-măt′ĭk) *adj.* **1.** Of or relating to the mouth. **2.** Stomatal.

sto·ma·ti·tis (stō′mə-tī′tĭs) *n.* Inflammation of the mucous tissue of the mouth. [New Latin : STOMAT(O)- + -ITIS.]

stomato–, stomat–. Indicates the mouth; for example, **stomatopod, stomatitis.** [From Greek *stoma* (stem *stomat-*), mouth. See **stomen-** in Appendix.*]

sto·ma·tol·o·gy (stō′mə-tŏl′ə-jē) *n.* The medical study of the physiology and pathology of the mouth. [STOMATO- + -LOGY.]

sto·ma·to·pod (stō-măt′ə-pŏd′) *n.* Any of various marine crustaceans of the order Stomatopoda, which includes the squilla. [New Latin *stomatopoda* : STOMATO- + -POD.]

sto·ma·tous (stō′mə-təs) *adj.* Having a stoma or stomata.

–stome. Indicates the mouth or a mouthlike opening; for example, **cyclostome.** [From Greek *stoma,* opening, mouth. See **stomen-** in Appendix.*]

sto·mo·de·um (stō′mə-dē′əm) *n., pl.* **-dea** (-dē′ə). Also **sto·mo·dae·um.** *Embryology.* The primitive oral cavity of an embryo. [New Latin : Greek *stoma,* mouth (see **stoma**) + *hodaios,* on the way, from *hodos,* way (see **sed-²** in Appendix*).]

stomp (stômp, stŏmp) *v.* **stomped, stomping, stomps.** —*tr.* To tread or trample heavily or violently on or upon. See Usage note below. —*intr.* To tread or trample heavily or violently. —*n.* **1.** A dance involving a rhythmical and heavy step. **2.** The jazz music for this dance. [Variant of STAMP (to pound).]

Usage: *Stomp* (verb) is established in the sense of trampling or violent treading: *stomped to death by waterfront hoodlums; stomping wild horses. Stamp* would also be possible in these examples, and it is the form used in the related sense of eliminating: *stamp out a fire; stamp out poverty.* In the sense of striking the ground with the human foot, as in a fit of temper, *stamp* is the standard form: *She stamped her foot and began to cry.* Here *stomped* would be unacceptable, in writing, to 76 per cent of the Usage Panel, though it sometimes occurs in speech.

–stomy. Indicates a surgical operation in which an artificial opening is made into (a specified organ or part); for example, **colostomy.** [From -STOME.]

stone (stōn) *n., pl.* **stones** or **stone** (for sense 10). *Abbr.* **st. 1.** Concreted earthy or mineral matter; rock. **2.** Such material used for construction. **3.** A small piece of rock. **4.** Rock or a piece of rock shaped or finished for a particular purpose, especially: **a.** A gravestone or tombstone. **b.** A grindstone, millstone, or whetstone. **c.** A milestone or boundary. **5.** A gem or precious stone. **6.** Something like a stone in shape or hardness, as a hailstone. **7.** *Botany.* The hard covering enclosing the kernel in certain fruits, such as the cherry or plum. **8.** *Usually plural. Archaic.* A testicle. **9.** *Pathology.* A mineral concretion in a hollow organ, as in the kidney. See **calculus. 10.** A unit of weight in Britain, 14 pounds avoirdupois. **11.** *Printing.* A table with a smooth surface on which page forms are composed, originally made of stone. —*adj.* **1.** Pertaining to or made of stone: *a stone wall.* **2.** Made of stoneware or earthenware. —*adv.* Utterly; completely. Used in combination: *stone-blind.* —*tr.v.* **stoned, stoning, stones. 1.** To hurl or throw stones at; pelt or kill with stones. **2.** To remove the stones or pits from. **3.** To geld or castrate (a hog, for example). **4.** To furnish, fit, pave, or line with stones. **5.** To rub on or with a stone in order to polish or sharpen. **6.** *Obsolete.* To make hard like stone; make pitiless or indifferent. [Middle English *stane, stone,* Old English *stān.* See **stei-** in Appendix.*] —**ston′er** *n.*

Stone (stōn), **Edward Durell.** Born 1902. American architect.

Stone (stōn), **Harlan Fiske.** 1872–1946. American jurist and educator; Chief Justice of the United States (1941–46).

Stone (stōn), **Lucy.** 1818–1893. American feminist leader.

Stone Age. *Archaeology.* The earliest known period of human culture, characterized by the use of stone tools.

stone·chat (stōn′chăt′) *n.* A small Old World bird, *Saxicola torquata,* having dark plumage, and a black head and reddish breast in the male. [From the bird's cry resembling the sound of falling pebbles.]

stone·crop (stōn′krŏp′) *n.* **1.** Any of various plants of the genus *Sedum,* having fleshy leaves and variously colored flowers. **2.** Any of various similar or related plants. [Middle English *stoncrop,* Old English *stāncropp* : *stān,* STONE + *cropp,* cluster, CROP.]

stone·cut·ter (stōn′kŭt′ər) *n.* One that cuts or carves stone; especially, a machine that dresses stone. —**stone′cut′ting** *n.*

stoned (stōnd) *adj. Slang.* Intoxicated; drunk.

stone·fish (stōn′fĭsh′) *n., pl.* **stonefish** or **-fishes.** Any of several tropical marine fishes of the family Scorpaenidae, having spines that eject a deadly venom. [From their resemblance to encrusted stones.]

stone·fly (stōn′flī′) *n., pl.* **-flies.** Any of numerous winged insects of the order Plecoptera, occurring on banks of streams and used as fishing bait both in the larval and adult stage. [From their aquatic larvae, found under stones.]

Stone·henge (stōn′hĕnj′) *n.* A prehistoric ceremonial ruin on the Salisbury Plain in Wiltshire, England, constructed at its first stage in the megalithic period, 1900–1700 B.C., of circular formations of huge upright stone slabs and lintels.

stone lily. A fossil crinoid.

stone marten. 1. A Eurasian mammal, *Martes foina,* having brown fur with lighter underfur. **2.** The fur of this animal.

stone·ma·son (stōn′mā′sən) *n.* One who prepares and lays stones in building. —**stone′ma′son·ry** *n.*

stone mint. A North American plant, *Cunila origanoides,* having clusters of small purplish or white flowers. Also called "dittany." [It grows in rocky places.]

Stone Mountain. A dome-shaped mountain of granite, 1,686 feet high, in northwest-central Georgia. A Confederate monument has been carved on one side of the mountain.

stone parsley. A Eurasian plant, *Sison amomum,* having clusters of small whitish flowers and aromatic seeds.

stone roller. A North American freshwater minnow, *Campostoma anomalum.*

Stones River (stōnz). A tributary of the Cumberland, flowing 39 miles in central Tennessee; the scene of a Union victory in the Civil War (1862–63).

stone's throw. A short distance.

stone·ware (stōn′wâr′) *n.* A heavy, nonporous pottery.

stone·work (stōn′wûrk′) *n.* **1.** The technique or process of working in stone. **2.** Work made of stone; stone masonry. **3.** *Plural.* A place where stone is cut and prepared for masonry. —**stone′work′er** *n.*

stone·wort (stōn′wûrt′, -wôrt′) *n.* Any of various green algae of the genus *Chara,* that grow submerged in fresh or brackish water and are frequently encrusted with calcium carbonate deposits.

ston·y (stō′nē) *adj.* **-ier, -iest.** Also **ston·ey. 1.** Covered with or full of stones. **2.** Hard as a stone. **3.** Hard-hearted; unemotional. **4.** Rigid; impassive: *a stony face.* **5.** Emotionally numbing or paralyzing: *a stony fear.* —**ston′i·ly** *adv.* —**ston′i·ness** *n.*

Stony Point. A village on the Hudson in southeastern New York State; the scene of a victory by American forces in the Revolutionary War (1779).

stood. Past tense and past participle of **stand.**

stooge (stōōj) *n.* **1.** The straight man to a comedian. **2.** Anyone who allows himself to be used for another's profit; an underling or puppet. **3.** A planted spy. —*intr.v.* **stooged, stooging, stooges.** To be or behave as a stooge. [Origin unknown.]

stool (stōōl) *n.* **1.** A backless and armless single seat supported on legs or a pedestal. **2.** A low bench or support for the feet or knees in sitting or kneeling, as a footrest or hassock. **3.** A toilet seat; privy. **4. a.** A bowel movement. **b.** Fecal matter. **5.** *Horticulture.* **a.** A stump or rootstock that produces shoots or suckers. **b.** A shoot or growth from such a stump or rootstock. —*intr.v.* **stooled, stooling, stools. 1.** To send up shoots or suckers. **2.** To evacuate the bowels; defecate. **3.** *Slang.* To act as a stool pigeon. [Middle English *stol,* Old English *stōl.* See **stā-** in Appendix.*]

stool pigeon. 1. A pigeon used as a decoy. **2.** *Slang.* A person acting as a decoy. **3.** *Slang.* An informer; especially, a spy for the police. In this sense, also called "stoolie." [Decoy pigeons were originally tied to a stool.]

stoop¹ (stōōp) *v.* **stooped, stooping, stoops.** —*intr.* **1.** To bend forward and down from the waist or middle of the back. **2.** To walk or stand with the head and upper back bent forward. **3.** To bend or sag downward. **4.** To lower or debase oneself; condescend. **5.** *Rare.* To yield; submit. **6.** To swoop down, as a bird in pursuing its prey. —*tr.* **1.** To bend (one's head or body) forward and down. **2.** *Archaic.* To debase or subdue; to humble. —*n.* **1.** The act of stooping. **2.** A forward bending of the head and upper back, especially when habitual. **3.** A self-abasement or condescension. **4.** A swooping down, as of a bird of prey. [Middle English *stupen,* Old English *stūpian.* See **steu-** in Appendix.*]

stoop² (stōōp) *n.* A small porch, platform, or staircase leading to the entrance of a house or building. [Dutch *stoep,* front verandah, from Middle Dutch. See **stebh-** in Appendix.*]

stoop³. Variant of **stoup.**

stop (stŏp) *v.* **stopped, stopping, stops.** —*tr.* **1.** To close (an opening) by covering, filling in, or plugging up. **2.** To close (a hole on a wind instrument) with the finger in sounding a desired tone. **3.** To constrict (an opening or orifice). **4.** To obstruct or block passage on (a road, for example). **5.** To prevent the flow or passage of. **6.** To cause to halt, cease, or desist. **7.** To desist from; cease doing. Often used with a gerund: *stop running.* **8.** To cause (a motor, for example) to cease operation or function; to halt. **9.** To press down (a string on a stringed instrument) on the fingerboard to produce a desired tone. —*intr.* **1.** To cease moving, progressing, acting, or operating; come to a halt or pause. **2.** To put an end to what one is doing; cease. **3.** To interrupt one's course or journey for a brief visit or stay. Often used with *off* or *over: stop off at the store.* —*n.* **1.** The act of stopping or the condition of being stopped; a cessation; a halt. **2.** A finish; an end. **3.** A stay or visit, as during a trip. **4.** Any place stopped at. **5.** A device or means that obstructs, blocks, or plugs up. **6.** An order given to a bank to withhold payment on a check. **7. a.** A part in a machine that stops or regulates movement. **b.** A perforated screen or diaphragm that limits the effective aperture of a lens, producing an image of improved definition but lowered intensity. **8.** A mark of punctuation, especially a period. **9.** *Music.* **a.** The act of stopping a string or hole on a musical instrument. **b.** A hole on a wind instrument or a fret on a stringed instrument. **c.** A device such as a key for closing the hole on a wind instrument. **10.** *Music.*

ă pat/ā pay/âr care/ä father/b bib/ch church/d deed/ĕ pet/ē be/f fife/g gag/h hat/hw which/ĭ pit/ī pie/îr pier/j judge/k kick/l lid, needle/m mum/n no, sudden/ng thing/ŏ pot/ō toe/ô paw, for/oi noise/ou out/ŏŏ took/ōō boot/p pop/r roar/s sauce/sh ship, dish/

a. A tuned set of pipes, as in an organ. **b.** A knob, key, or pull that regulates such a set of pipes. **11.** *Nautical.* A line used for securing something temporarily: *a sail stop.* **12.** *Phonetics.* A consonant articulated with a complete obstruction of the passage of breath; specifically, English *p, b, t, d, k,* or *g.* Compare **continuant. 13.** The depression between the muzzle and top of the skull of a dog. [Middle English *stoppen,* Old English *-stoppian,* from West Germanic *stoppōn* (unattested), to plug up, from Late Latin *stuppāre,* to stop up with a tow, from Latin *stuppa,* tow, from Greek *stuppē.* See **stewe-** in Appendix.*]

stop·cock (stŏp′kŏk′) *n.* A valve that regulates the flow of fluid through a pipe; a faucet.

stope (stōp) *n.* An excavation in the form of steps, made by the mining of ore from steeply inclined or vertical veins. —*v.* **stoped, stoping, stopes.** —*tr.* To remove (ore) from a stope. —*intr.* To mine by means of a stope. [Perhaps from Low German *stope,* a step, from Middle Low German *stōpe.* See **stebh-** in Appendix.*]

Stopes (stōps), **Marie Carmichael.** 1880–1958. British paleobotanist, social reformer, and advocate of birth control.

stop·gap (stŏp′găp′) *n.* An improvised substitute for something lacking; a temporary expedient.

stop·light (stŏp′līt′) *n.* **1.** A traffic signal. **2.** A light on the rear of a vehicle, lighted when the brakes are applied.

stop order. An order to a broker to buy or sell a stock when it reaches a specified level of decline or gain.

stop·o·ver (stŏp′ō′vər) *n.* **1.** An interruption in the course of a journey for stopping or visiting at a certain place. **2.** A place visited briefly in the course of a journey.

stop·page (stŏp′ĭj) *n.* The act of stopping or the condition of being stopped; a halt.

stop payment. An order to one's bank not to honor a check.

stop·per (stŏp′ər) *n.* **1.** Any device, as a cork or plug, inserted to close an opening. **2.** One that causes something to stop. —*tr.v.* **stoppered, -pering, -pers.** To close with a stopper.

stop·ple (stŏp′əl) *n.* A stopper; a plug. —*tr.v.* **stoppled, -pling, -ples.** To close with a stopple. [Middle English *stoppell,* from *stoppen,* to STOP.]

stop sign. A traffic sign that orders traffic to come to a stop.

stop·watch (stŏp′wŏch′) *n.* A timepiece with a sweep hand operated by an external trigger to measure duration of time.

stor·age (stôr′ĭj, stōr′-) *n. Abbr.* **stge., stor. 1. a.** The act of storing goods, as in a warehouse for safekeeping. **b.** The state of being stored. **2.** A space for storing goods. **3.** The price charged for keeping goods stored. **4.** The charging or regenerating of a storage battery. **5.** *Computers.* The part of a computer that stores information for subsequent use or retrieval.

storage battery. A group of reversible or rechargeable **secondary cells** *(see)* acting as a unit. Also called "secondary battery."

storage cell. A **secondary cell** *(see).*

sto·rax (stôr′ăks′, stōr′-) *n.* **1.** Any of various trees of the genus *Styrax,* some of which yield an aromatic resin. **2.** An aromatic resin obtained from any of these trees. **3.** A brownish, aromatic resin used in perfume and medicine and obtained from any of several trees of the genus *Liquidambar;* especially, *L. orientalis,* of Asia Minor. In this sense, also called "styrax." [Middle English, from Latin, from Greek, variant of *sturax,* probably from Semitic, akin to Hebrew *tzŏrī.*]

store (stôr, stōr) *n.* **1.** A place where merchandise is offered for sale; a shop. **2.** A stock or supply reserved for future use. **3.** *Plural.* Supplies, especially of food, clothing, or arms. **4.** A place where commodities are kept; a warehouse or storehouse. **5.** A great quantity or number; an abundance. —**in store.** Set aside or reserved for the future; forthcoming. —**set store by.** To regard with esteem; value. —*tr.v.* **stored, storing, stores. 1.** To reserve or put away for future use. **2.** To fill, supply, or stock with something. **3.** To deposit or receive in a storehouse or warehouse for safekeeping. [Middle English *stor,* from Old French *estor,* from *estorer,* to build, restore, from Latin *instaurāre.* See **stā-** in Appendix.*]

store-bought (stôr′bôt′, stōr′-) *adj.* Also **store-bought·en** (-bôt′n). *Nonstandard.* Manufactured and purchased at retail.

store·front (stôr′frŭnt′, stōr′-) *n.* **1.** The side of a store facing a street. **2.** A room or suite of rooms in a store building at street level: *a political office in a storefront.* —**store′front′** *adj.*

store·house (stôr′hous′, stōr′-) *n.* **1.** A place or building in which goods are stored; a warehouse. **2.** An abundant source or supply: *a storehouse of knowledge.*

store·keep·er (stôr′kē′pər, stōr′-) *n.* **1.** One who keeps a retail store or shop; a shopkeeper. **2.** A person in charge of receiving or distributing stores or supplies, as military or naval supplies.

store·room (stôr′ro͞om′, -ro͝om′, stōr′-) *n.* A room in which things are stored.

sto·rey. *Chiefly British.* Variant of **story** (level).

sto·ried[1] (stôr′ēd, stōr′-) *adj.* **1.** Celebrated or famous in history or story. **2.** Ornamented with designs representing scenes from history, legend, or story: *storied tapestry.*

sto·ried[2] (stôr′ēd, stōr′-) *adj.* Having or consisting of a specified number of stories. Usually used in combination: *a three-storied house.*

stork (stôrk) *n.* Any of various large wading birds of the family Ciconiidae, chiefly of warm regions, having long legs and a long straight bill. [Middle English *stork,* Old English *storc.* See **ster-**[1] in Appendix.*]

stork's-bill (stôrks′bĭl′) *n.* Any of various plants of the genus *Erodium,* having fruit with a narrow, beaklike point.

storm (stôrm) *n.* **1.** An atmospheric disturbance manifested in strong winds accompanied by rain, snow, or other precipitation, and often by thunder and lightning. **2.** *Meteorology.* A wind ranging from 64 to 72 miles per hour. **3.** A heavy shower of objects, such as bullets or missiles. **4.** A strong or violent outburst, as of emotion or excitement. **5.** A violent disturbance or upheaval, as in political, social, or domestic affairs. **6.** *Military.* A violent, sudden attack on a fortified place. —*v.* **stormed, storming, storms.** —*intr.* **1.** To blow forcefully; to rain, snow, hail, or otherwise precipitate violently. Used with *it: It stormed last night.* **2.** To be extremely angry; to rant and rage. **3.** To move or rush tumultuously, violently, or angrily: *She stormed into the room.* —*tr. Military.* To capture or try to capture by a violent, sudden attack. —See Synonyms at **attack.** [Middle English *storm,* Old English *storm.* See **twer-** in Appendix.*]

storm·bound (stôrm′bound′) *adj.* Delayed, confined, or cut off from communication by a storm.

storm cellar. A **cyclone cellar** *(see).*

storm center. 1. *Meteorology.* The central area covered by a storm; especially, the point of lowest barometric pressure within a storm. **2.** The center of trouble, disturbance, or argument.

storm door. An outer or additional door added for protection against inclement weather.

storm petrel. Any of various small sea birds of the family Hydrobatidae; especially, *Hydrobates pelagicus,* of the North Atlantic and the Mediterranean. Also called "stormy petrel," "Mother Carey's chicken."

storm troopers. A Nazi militia, the **Sturmabteilung** *(see).*

storm window. A secondary window attached over the usual window to protect against the wind and cold.

storm·y (stôr′mē) *adj.* **-ier, -iest. 1.** Subject to, characterized by, or affected by storms; tempestuous. **2.** Characterized by violent emotions, passions, speech, or actions: *a stormy argument.* —**storm′i·ly** *adv.* —**storm′i·ness** *n.*

stormy petrel. 1. A bird, the **storm petrel** *(see).* **2.** A person who brings discord or appears at the onset of trouble; a rebel.

sto·ry[1] (stôr′ē, stōr′ē) *n., pl.* **-ries. 1.** The narrating or relating of an event or series of events, either true or fictitious. **2.** A prose or verse narrative, usually fictional, intended to interest or amuse the hearer or reader; a tale. **3.** A type of fictional literary composition, a **short story** *(see).* **4.** Such compositions collectively, as a form of literature. **5.** The plot of a novel, play, or the like. **6.** A report, statement, or allegation of facts. **7. a.** A news article. **b.** The event, situation, or other material for such an article. **8.** An anecdote. **9.** A lie. **10.** Romantic legend or tradition. —*tr.v.* **storied, -rying, -ries. 1.** To decorate with scenes representing historical or legendary events. **2.** *Archaic.* To tell as a story. [Middle English *storie,* from Norman French *estorie,* from Latin *historia,* from Greek, from *histōr,* wisdom. See **weid-** in Appendix.*]

sto·ry[2] (stôr′ē, stōr′ē) *n., pl.* **-ries.** Also *chiefly British* **sto·rey** *pl.* **-reys. 1.** A complete horizontal division of a building, comprising the area between two adjacent levels. **2.** The set of rooms on the same level of a building. [Middle English *storye,* from Medieval Latin *historia,* originally a row of windows with pictures on them, from Latin *historia,* STORY (tale).]

sto·ry·book (stôr′ē-bo͝ok′, stōr′-) *n.* A book containing a collection of stories, usually for children. —*adj.* Occurring in or resembling the style of a storybook; romantic.

story line. The plot of a story or a dramatic work.

sto·ry·tell·er (stôr′ē-tĕl′ər, stōr′-) *n.* **1.** A person who tells or writes stories. **2.** *Informal.* A person who tells lies; fibber. —**sto′ry·tell′ing** *n.*

stoss (stŏs, shtōs) *adj.* Facing the direction from which a glacier moves. Said of a rock or slope in its path. [From German *stossen,* to push, thrust, from Old High German *stōzan.* See **steu-** in Appendix.*]

sto·tin·ka (stō-tĭng′kä) *n., pl.* **-ki** (-kē). A monetary unit equal to 1/100 of the lev of Bulgaria. See table of exchange rates at **currency.** [Bulgarian : *sto-,* from *suto,* hundred (see **dekm̥** in Appendix*) + suffixes *-tin, -ka.*]

Stough·ton (stōt′n), **William.** 1631–1701. American colonial jurist; presiding judge at Salem witchcraft trials.

stound (stound) *n. Obsolete.* A short time; a while. [Middle English *sto(u)nd,* Old English *stund.* See **stā-** in Appendix.*]

stoup (sto͞op) *n.* Also **stoop, stowp** (stōp). **1.** *Ecclesiastical.* A basin or font for holy water at the entrance of a church. **2.** *Scottish.* A bucket or pail. **3.** A cup, tankard, or other drinking vessel. [Middle English *stowp,* vessel, pail, from Old Norse *staup.* See **staup-** in Appendix.*]

stout (stout) *adj.* **stouter, stoutest. 1.** Determined, bold, or brave: *"It was enough to place horror upon the stoutest heart in the world."* (Defoe). **2.** Strong in body; sturdy. **3.** Strong in structure or substance; substantial; solid. **4.** Bulky in figure; thickset; corpulent. **5.** Powerful; forceful. **6.** Stubborn; staunch; firm. —See Synonyms at **strong, fat.** —*n.* **1.** A stout person. **2.** A garment size for a thickset person. **3.** A strong, very dark beer or ale. [Middle English, from Old French *estout,* from Germanic. See **stel-**[1] in Appendix.*] —**stout′ly** *adv.* —**stout′ness** *n.*

stout·heart·ed (stout′här′tĭd) *adj.* Brave; courageous; dauntless. —**stout′heart′ed·ly** *adv.* —**stout′heart′ed·ness** *n.*

stove[1] (stōv) *n.* **1.** An apparatus in which electricity or a fuel is used to furnish heat, as for cooking or comfort. **2.** A heated room or box used for a particular purpose, as a kiln or hothouse. [Middle English, heated chamber, from Middle Low German or Middle Dutch. See **staup-** in Appendix.*]

stove[2]**.** Alternate past tense and past participle of **stave.**

stove·pipe (stōv′pīp′) *n.* **1.** A pipe, usually of thin sheet iron, used to conduct smoke or fumes from a stove into a chimney flue. **2.** A tall silk man's hat. Also called "stovepipe hat."

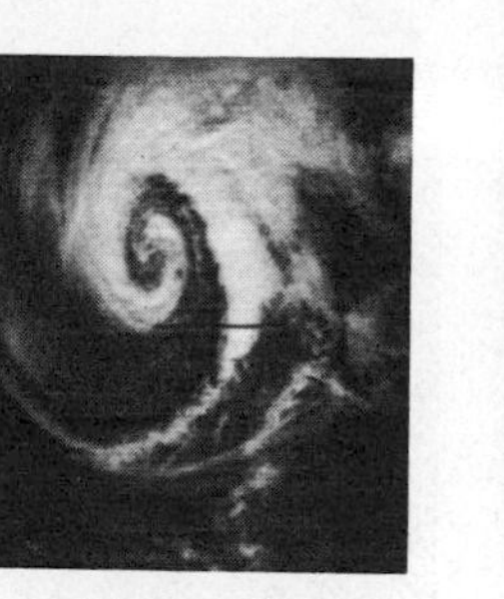

storm center
Satellite photograph

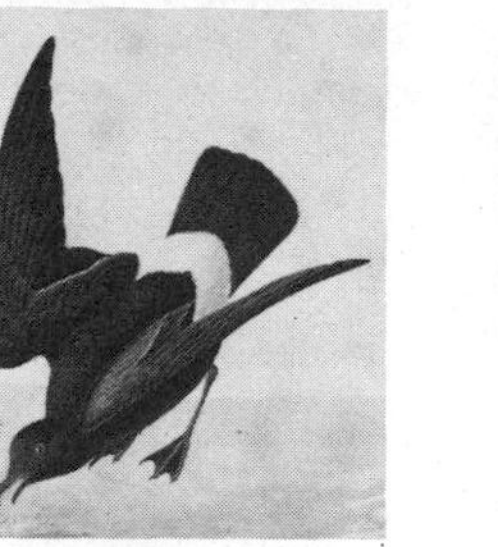

storm petrel
Hydrobates pelagicus
Painting by
John James Audubon

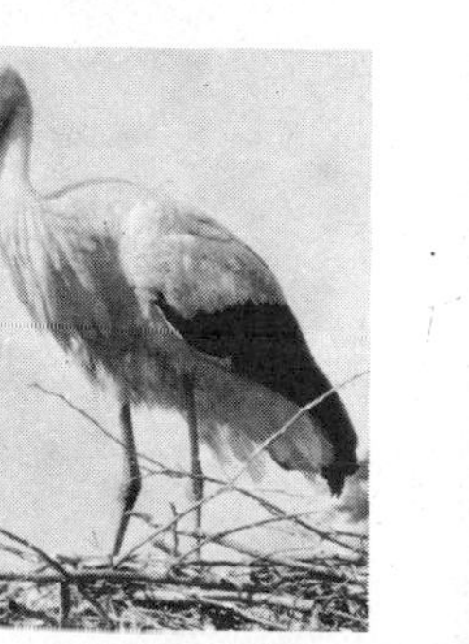

stork
Ciconia ciconia

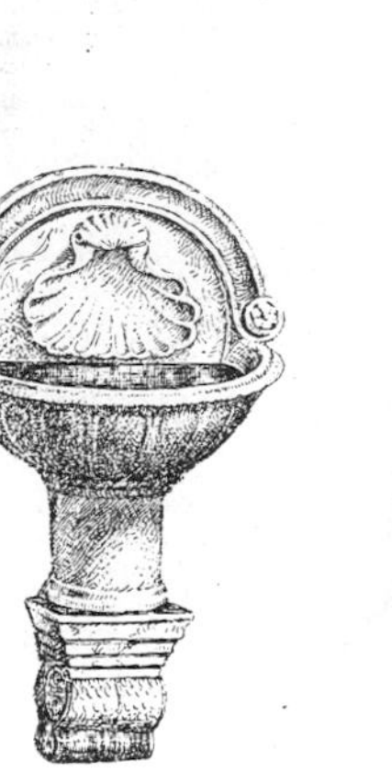

stoup

t tight/th thin, path/*th* this, bathe/ŭ cut/ûr urge/v valve/w with/y yes/z zebra, size/zh vision/ə about, item, edible, gallop, circus/
à *Fr.* ami/œ *Fr.* feu, *Ger.* schön/ü *Fr.* tu, *Ger.* über/KH *Ger.* ich, *Scot.* loch/N *Fr.* bon. ***Follows main vocabulary. †Of obscure origin.**

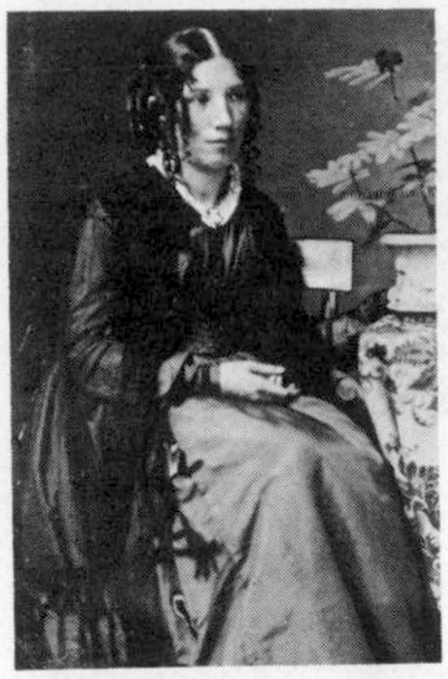

Harriet Beecher Stowe

sto·ver (stō′vər) *n.* The dried stalks and leaves of a cereal crop, used as fodder after the grain has been harvested. [Middle English, food, provisions, short for Norman French *estovers,* supplies, from Old French *estovier,* to be necessary, from Latin *est opus,* it is necessary : *est* (it) is, from *esse,* to be (see **es-** in Appendix*) + *opus,* need, necessity (see **op-**[1] in Appendix*).]

stow (stō) *tr.v.* **stowed, stowing, stows. 1.** To place, arrange, or store away, especially in a neat, compact way: *stow various articles into his knapsack.* **2.** To fill by packing tightly. **3.** To have room or space for; to hold. Used of a receptacle. **4.** *Slang.* To cease; stop. **5.** *Obsolete.* To provide lodging for; to quarter. **6.** *Slang.* To consume (food) greedily. Often used with *away.* [Middle English *stowen,* to place, put, from *stowe,* a place, Old English *stōw.* See **stā-** in Appendix.*]

stow·age (stō′ĭj) *n.* **1. a.** The act, manner, or process of stowing. **b.** The state of being stowed. **2.** Space or room for storage. **3.** Goods in storage. **4.** A charge for storing goods.

stow away. 1. To put or hide away, as in a safe place. **2.** To be a stowaway.

stow·a·way (stō′ə-wā′) *n.* One who hides aboard a ship or other conveyance in order to obtain free passage.

Stowe (stō), **Harriet (Elizabeth) Beecher.** 1811–1896. American novelist; author of *Uncle Tom's Cabin.*

stowp. Variant of **stoup.**

STP standard temperature and pressure.

St. Pan·cras (sānt păng′krəs). A former administrative division of London, England, now part of **Camden** *(see).*

St. Paul (sānt pôl′). The capital and an industrial and transportation center of Minnesota, in the east on the Mississippi opposite Minneapolis. Population, 313,000.

St. Pe·ter, Lake (sānt pē′tər). An expansion of the St. Lawrence, 130 square miles in area, in southern Quebec, Canada.

St. Peter Port (sānt pē′tər). The capital of Guernsey in the Channel Islands; the residence of Victor Hugo (1855–70).

St. Pe·ters·burg (sānt pē′tərz-bûrg′). **1.** A former name for **Leningrad. 2.** A city and resort of Florida, in the west on Tampa Bay. Population, 181,000.

St. Pierre (sānt pîr′). *French* **Saint-Pierre** (săN-pyâr′). **1.** A town in northwestern Martinique, destroyed by the eruption of Mount Pelée. **2.** An island of the St. Pierre and Miquelon group off Newfoundland, Canada. **3.** A fishing port on Réunion Island in the Indian Ocean. Population, 39,000.

St. Pierre and Mi·que·lon (sānt pîr′; mĭk′ə-lŏn). A group of 8 small islands with a combined area of 93 square miles, lying off the southern coast of Newfoundland, Canada, and constituting an Overseas Territory of France. Population, 5,000. Capital, St. Pierre.

STR Airport code for Stuttgart, Germany.

str. 1. steamer. **2.** strait. **3.** stringed (instruments).

stra·bis·mus (strə-bĭz′məs) *n.* A visual defect in which one eye cannot focus with the other on an objective because of imbalance of the eye muscles. See **walleye.** [New Latin, from Greek *strabismos,* from *strabizein,* to squint, from *strabos,* squinting. See **strebh-** in Appendix.*] —**stra·bis′mal, stra·bis′mic** *adj.*

Stra·bo (strā′bō). Greek geographer of the late first century B.C. and the early first century A.D.

stra·bot·o·my (strə-bŏt′ə-mē) *n., pl.* **-mies.** *Surgery.* The cutting of an ocular muscle or tendon to correct strabismus. [Greek *strabos,* squinting (see **strebh-** in Appendix*) + -TOMY.]

Stra·chey (strā′chē), **(Giles) Lytton.** 1880–1932. English biographer, historian, and critic.

strad·dle (străd′l) *v.* **-dled, -dling, -dles.** —*tr.* **1.** To sit astride of; bestride. **2.** To appear to favor both sides of (an issue). **3.** To fire shots behind and in front of (a target) in order to determine the range. —*intr.* **1.** To sit astride. **2.** To be wide apart; sprawl. **3.** To appear to favor both sides of an issue. —*n.* **1.** The act or posture of sitting astride. **2.** An equivocal or noncommittal position. **3.** *Stock Market.* The privileged option of either delivering or buying at a specified price within a stated period of time. Compare **call, put.** [Frequentative of *strad-,* obsolete past stem of STRIDE.] —**strad′dler** *n.*

Usage: *Straddle* (verb), in the figurative sense of appearing to favor both sides of an issue, is not confined to expressly informal contexts despite its casual tone. Employed transitively, it is acceptable to 87 per cent of the Usage Panel in the following, as an example in writing: *politicians who straddle every controversial question.* An intransitive variant of the same example (without an expressed object) is accepted by 57 per cent of the Panel.

strainer

Strad·i·var·i·us (străd′ə-vâr′ē-əs) *n.* One of the famed violins made in the workshop of Antonio Stradivari (1644–1737).

strafe (strāf, sträf) *tr.v.* **strafed, strafing, strafes.** To attack (ground troops, for example) with machine-gun fire from low-flying aircraft. —*n.* A rake of machine-gun fire from low-flying aircraft. [From German *(Gott) strafe (England),* "(God) punish (England)," from *strafen,* to punish, from Middle High German *strāfen*†, to rebuke.]

Straf·ford (străf′ərd), **First Earl of.** 1593–1641. Title of Thomas Wentworth. English statesman; principal minister to Charles I; executed for treason.

strag·gle (străg′əl) *intr.v.* **-gled, -gling, -gles. 1.** To stray or fall behind. **2.** To proceed or spread out in a scattered or irregular group. [Middle English *straglen,* perhaps frequentative of *straken,* to go, move, perhaps related to Old English *streccan,* to STRETCH.] —**strag′gler** *n.*

strag·gly (străg′lē) *adj.* **-glier, -gliest.** Spread out or proceeding irregularly.

straight (strāt) *adj.* **straighter, straightest. 1.** Extending continuously in the same direction without curving; having no curvature. **2.** Having no irregularities. **3.** Erect; upright. **4.** Direct and candid. **5.** Uninterrupted; unbroken. **6.** In poker, made up of five cards constituting a sequence: *a straight flush.* **7.** Politically undeviating: *a straight party line.* **8.** Correctly ordered; accurate; true. **9.** Upright; honorable. **10.** *Slang.* Not homosexual. **11.** *Slang.* **a.** Having the necessary amount of anything. **b.** Intoxicated by a narcotic. **12.** Unmodified, unaltered, or unqualified: *a straight answer.* **13.** Undiluted or unmixed: *straight whiskey.* **14.** Neatly arranged; orderly. **15.** Sold without discount regardless of the amount purchased. —*adv.* **1.** In a straight line; directly. **2.** In an erect posture; upright. **3.** Without detour or delay. **4.** Without circumlocution; candidly. Often used with *out.* **5.** Honestly or virtuously. **6.** Continuously. —**go straight.** *Informal.* To reform after having been a criminal. —**straight off.** Immediately; without hesitation. —*n.* **1.** The straight part of a racecourse between the winning post and the last turn. **2.** A straight line. **3.** A straight part, piece, or position. **4.** In poker: **a.** A numerical sequence of five cards of various suits. **b.** A hand containing this. [Middle English *streit, streight,* from the past participle of *strecchen,* to STRETCH.] —**straight′ly** *adv.* —**straight′ness** *n.*

straight angle. An angle having sides lying in the same straight line but extending in opposite directions from the vertex; an angle of 180 degrees.

straight-arm (strāt′ärm′) *tr.v.* **-armed, -arming, -arms.** *Football.* To ward off (a tackler) by holding the arm out straight.

straight-a·way (strāt′ə-wā′) *adj.* **1.** Extending in a straight line or course without a curve or turn. **2.** Unhesitating; immediate. —*n.* (strāt′ə-wā′). A straight course, stretch, or track. —*adv.* (strāt′ə-wā′). At once; immediately.

straight chain. An open linear organic molecular structure with no side chains.

straight·edge (strāt′ĕj′) *n.* A rigid flat rectangular bar, as of wood or metal, with a straight edge for testing or drawing straight lines. —**straight′edged′** *adj.*

straight·en (strāt′n) *v.* **-ened, -ening, -ens.** —*tr.* To make straight. —*intr.* To become straight. —**straighten out. 1.** To put to rights or restore order to; rectify. **2.** To reform or improve. —**straight′en·er** *n.*

straight face. A face that betrays no sign of emotion. —**straight′-faced′** (strāt′fāst′) *adj.*

straight·for·ward (strāt-fôr′wərd) *adj.* **1.** Proceeding in a straight course; direct. **2.** Honest; frank; candid. —See Synonyms at **frank, fair.** —*adv.* Also **straight·for·wards** (-wərdz). In a straightforward course or manner. —**straight·for′ward·ly** *adv.* —**straight·for′ward·ness** *n.*

straight jacket. Variant of **strait jacket.**

straight-line (strāt′līn′) *adj.* **1.** Lying in a straight line. **2.** Pertaining to a device whose linkage produces or copies motion in straight lines. **3.** Designating a mode of amortization by equal payments at stated intervals over a given period of time.

straight man. An actor who serves as a foil for a comedian.

straight razor. A razor consisting of a blade hinged to a handle into which it slips when not in use.

straight ticket. A ballot cast for all the candidates of one party. Compare **split ticket.**

straight·way (strāt′wā′, -wā′) *adv.* Without delay; at once.

strain[1] (strān) *v.* **strained, straining, strains.** —*tr.* **1.** To pull, draw, or stretch tight. **2.** To exert or tax to the utmost. **3.** To injure or impair by overuse or overexertion; to wrench: *strain a muscle.* **4.** To stretch or force beyond the proper or legitimate point or limit: *strain a point.* **5.** To alter the relations between the parts of a structure or shape by applying an external force; deform. **6.** To pass (a substance) through a strainer or other filtering agent. **7.** To draw off or remove by filtration. **8.** To embrace or clasp tightly; to hug. —*intr.* **1.** To make violent or steady efforts; strive hard. **2.** To be or become wrenched or twisted. **3.** To be subjected to great stress. **4.** To pull forcibly or violently. **5.** To stretch or exert one's muscles or nerves to the utmost. **6.** To filter, trickle, or ooze. —**strain at. 1.** To push or pull with great effort. **2.** To strive or contend for. **3.** To be extremely hesitant at accepting; balk at. —*n.* **1. a.** The act of straining. **b.** The state of being strained. **2.** A great or extreme effort, exertion, or tension. **3.** A wrench or other injury resulting from excessive effort or use. **4.** *Physics.* A deformation produced by stress. **5.** Any pressure, stress, or force. **6.** A great or excessive pressure or demand on one's emotions, resources, or the like. —See Synonyms at **effort.** [Middle English *streynen,* from Old French *estreindere,* from Latin *stringere,* to draw tight, tie. See **streig-** in Appendix.*]

strain[2] (strān) *n.* **1.** The collective descendants of a common ancestor; a race, stock, line, or breed. **2.** Any of the various lines of ancestry united in an individual or family; ancestry; lineage. **3.** *Biology.* A group of organisms of the same species, having distinctive characteristics but not usually considered a separate breed or variety. **4.** A kind; sort. **5. a.** An inborn or inherited tendency or character. **b.** A streak; trace. **6.** The tone or tenor of a verbal utterance. **7.** *Often plural.* A passage of musical expression; an air; a tune. **8.** A passage of poetic expression. **9.** An outburst or flow of eloquent or impassioned language. [Middle English *stren(e),* Old English *strēon,* acquisition, generation, offspring. See **ster-**[2] in Appendix.*]

strain·er (strā′nər) *n.* **1.** A filter, sieve, colander, or the like having meshes or porous parts and used to separate liquids from solids. **2.** One that strains. **3.** An apparatus for tightening, stretching, or strengthening.

strain gauge. A device in which mechanical motion, as of a thin wire or piezoelectric crystal, is converted into an electric variation that is used as a sensitive measure of strain.

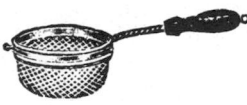

straining beam. *Architecture.* A horizontal tie beam connecting two queen posts in a roof truss. Also called "straining piece."

strait (strāt) *n. Abbr.* **St., str. 1.** *Often plural.* A narrow passage of water joining two larger bodies of water. **2.** *Often plural.* A position of difficulty, perplexity, distress, or need: *He was in desperate straits for money.* —*adj. Archaic.* **1.** Narrow or constricted. **2.** Affording little space or room; restricted, confined, or close. **3.** Strict, rigid, or righteous. [Middle English *streit,* from Old French *estreit,* tight, narrow, from Latin *strictus,* from the past participle of *stringere,* to draw tight. See **streig-** in Appendix.*]

strait·en (strāt′n) *tr.v.* **-ened, -ening, -ens. 1.** To make narrow; to limit, contract, or restrict. **2.** To put or bring into difficulties or distress, particularly financial hardship. Usually used in the past participle, especially in the phrase *in straitened circumstances.*

strait jacket. Also **straight jacket.** A long-sleeved jacketlike garment used to bind the arms tightly against the body as a means of restraining a violent patient or prisoner.

strait-laced (strāt′lāst′) *adj.* **1.** Excessively strict in behavior, morality, or opinions; puritanical; prudish. **2.** *Archaic.* Having or wearing a tightly laced garment.

Straits, The. 1. The waterway connecting the Black Sea and the Mediterranean, formed by the Bosporus and the Dardanelles. **2.** The former name for the **Strait of Gibraltar. 3.** See **Straits Settlements.**

Straits Settlements. Also **The Straits.** A former British crown colony, a division of British Malaya, including Singapore, Penang, Malacca, Labuan, and a number of smaller islands.

strake (strāk) *n. Nautical.* A single continuous line of planking or metal plating extending on a vessel's hull from stem to stern. [Middle English *strake,* perhaps "thing stretched," related to Old English *streccan,* to STRETCH.]

Stral·sund (shträl′zo͞ont, shträl-zo͞ont′). A city and port of East Germany, in the north on the Baltic. Population, 67,000.

stra·mo·ni·um (strə-mō′nē-əm) *n.* **1.** A plant, the **jimsonweed** *(see).* **2.** The dried poisonous leaves of the jimsonweed, used in the treatment of asthma. [New Latin, possibly an alteration of Tatar *turman,* horse medicine.]

strand[1] (strănd) *n.* **1.** Land bordering a body of water; a beach; especially, the area between tide marks: *"The strand and the waves exist no more, the summer is dead"* (Samuel Beckett). **2.** *Chiefly Poetic.* A foreign country. —*v.* **stranded, stranding, strands.** —*tr.* **1.** To drive or run aground, as a ship; to beach. **2.** To bring into or leave in a difficult or helpless position. Usually used in the passive: *The troupe was stranded in Peoria.* —*intr.* **1.** To be driven or run ashore or aground. **2.** To be left in or brought into a helpless position. [Middle English *strand,* Old English *strand,* shore, akin to Old Norse *strǫnd*†.]

strand[2] (strănd) *n.* **1.** Each of the fibers or filaments that are twisted together to form a rope, cable, or the like. **2.** Any single fiber, thread, or other filament: *"She wore her light hair in a bun from which strands slipped"* (Bernard Malamud). **3. a.** A string of beads, pearls, or the like. **b.** The material on which they are strung. **4.** Anything that is plaited or twisted, as a rope, cable, or braid of hair. —*tr.v.* **stranded, stranding, strands. 1.** To make or form (a rope or cable, for example) by twisting strands together. **2.** To break a strand or strands of (a rope, cable, or the like). [Middle English *strond*†.]

strand line. A shore line; especially, one marking an earlier and higher water level.

strange (strānj) *adj.* **stranger, strangest. 1.** Previously unknown; unfamiliar. **2.** Unusual; extraordinary; striking. **3.** Peculiar; queer. **4.** Not of one's own or a particular locality, environment, or kind; exotic. **5.** *Archaic.* Alien or foreign. **6.** Lacking experience; unskilled. —*adv.* In a strange manner. [Middle English *straunge,* from Old French *estrange,* from Latin *extrāneus,* foreign, strange, from *extrā,* outside, beyond. See **eghs** in Appendix.*] —**strange′ly** *adv.*

Synonyms: *strange, peculiar, odd, queer, quaint, outlandish, singular, eccentric.* These adjectives describe persons or things that are notably unusual. *Strange* refers especially to what is unfamiliar, unknown, or inexplicable. *Peculiar,* though often applied to anything unusual, is most applicable to what distinguishes a given person or thing from others. *Odd* suggests the quality of not fitting in, or lack of accord with associates, surroundings, or circumstances. *Queer* implies difference from the norm. *Quaint* often refers to peculiarity that seems old-fashioned but endearing. *Outlandish* suggests alien appearance or manner and often implies uncouthness. *Singular* describes what is unique, unparalleled, or unusual and thus arouses curiosity or wonder. *Eccentric* refers particularly to striking peculiarity of behavior.

strange·ness (strānj′nĭs) *n.* **1.** The quality of being strange. **2.** *Symbol* **S** *Physics.* A quantum number equal to hypercharge minus baryon number. [Sense 2, from the original lack of understanding of the nature of the particles which it describes.]

stran·ger (strān′jər) *n.* **1.** One who is neither friend nor acquaintance. **2.** A foreigner, newcomer, or outsider. **3.** One who is unaccustomed to or unacquainted with something specified; a novice. Used with *to: a stranger to our language.* **4.** A visitor or guest. **5.** *Law.* One who is neither privy nor party to an act, proceeding, or the like. [Middle English *straunger,* from Old French *estrangier,* from Vulgar Latin *extrāneārius* (unattested), from Latin *extrāneus,* STRANGE.]

stran·gle (străng′gəl) *v.* **-gled, -gling, -gles.** —*tr.* **1. a.** To kill by choking or suffocating; to throttle. **b.** To cut off the oxygen supply of; smother. **2.** To suppress, repress, or stifle. **3.** To inhibit the growth or action of; restrict: *"That artist is strangled who is forced to deal with human beings solely in social terms"* (James Baldwin). —*intr.* To die or suffer from suffocation or strangulation; to choke. [Middle English *stranglen,* from Old French *estrangler,* from Latin *strangulāre,* STRANGULATE.] —**stran′gler** *n.*

strangle hold. 1. *Wrestling.* An illegal hold used to choke an opponent. **2.** Any force, influence, or action that chokes, restricts, or suppresses freedom or progress.

stran·gles (străng′gəlz) *n.* Plural in form, used with a singular verb. An infectious disease of horses and related animals, caused by the bacterium *Streptococcus equi* and characterized by nasal inflammation and abscesses in the mouth. [From Middle English *strangle* (singular), strangulation, from *stranglen,* STRANGLE.]

stran·gu·late (străng′gyə-lāt′) *v.* **-lated, -lating, -lates.** —*tr.* **1.** To strangle. **2.** *Pathology.* To compress, constrict, or obstruct (a tube, duct, intestine, or other part) so as to cut off the flow of blood or other fluid. —*intr.* To be or become strangled or constricted. [Latin *strangulāre,* from Greek *strangalan,* from *strangalē,* halter. See **strenk-** in Appendix.*]

stran·gu·la·tion (străng′gyə-lā′shən) *n.* **1.** The act of strangling. **2.** The state of being strangled.

stran·gu·ry (străng′gyə-rē) *n.* Slow, painful urination with spasms of the urethra and bladder. [Middle English, from Latin *strangūria,* from Greek *strangouria* : *stranx* (stem *strang-*), drop (see **strenk-** in Appendix*) + -URIA.]

strap (străp) *n.* **1. a.** A long, narrow strip of leather or other similar material. **b.** Such a strip equipped with a buckle or similar fastener for binding or securing objects. **2.** A flat, thin metal band used for fastening or clamping objects together or into position. **3.** A narrow band formed into a loop for grasping with the hand. **4.** A razor strop. **5.** A strip of leather used in flogging. —*tr.v.* **strapped, strapping, straps. 1.** To fasten or secure with a strap. **2.** To beat with a strap. **3.** To strop or sharpen (a razor, for example). [Variant of STROP.]

strap·hang·er (străp′hăng′ər) *n.* A passenger, as on a bus or subway, who grips a hanging strap for support.

strap·less (străp′lĭs) *adj.* **1.** Without a strap. **2.** Of or pertaining to a dress or undergarment designed to leave the shoulders bare. —*n.* A strapless garment.

strap·pa·do (stră-pä′dō, stră-pā′-) *n., pl.* **-does. 1.** A torture in which the victim's hands are tied behind his back and attached to a pulley by means of which he is pulled up off the ground and then dropped halfway down with a jerk. **2.** The apparatus so employed. [French *(e)strapade,* from Italian *strappata,* from *strappare,* to drag, from Old French *estraper,* variant of *estreper,* from Latin *extirpāre,* to pluck up by the stem : *ex-,* out + *stirps,* stem (see **stirps**).]

strapped (străpt) *adj. Informal.* Lacking financial resources; penniless. [From STRAP (rare sense "to make penniless").]

strap·per (străp′ər) *n.* **1.** One who grooms or straps horses. **2.** A tall, sturdy person.

strap·ping (străp′ĭng) *adj.* Tall and sturdy.

Stras·berg (străs′bərg), **Lee.** Born 1901. Austrian-born American theatrical producer, director, and teacher.

Stras·bourg (străs′bûrg, sträz′-). *German* **Strass·burg** (shträs′-bo͝ork). A city of France, in the northeast on the Rhine, two miles west of the German border. Population, 226,000.

strass (străs) *n.* A type of lead glass, **paste** *(see).* [German, invented by Joseph *Strasser,* 18th-century German jeweler.]

stra·ta. Plural of **stratum.** See Usage note at **stratum.**

strat·a·gem (străt′ə-jəm) *n.* **1.** A military maneuver designed to deceive or surprise an enemy. **2.** A deception. —See Synonyms at **artifice.** [French *stratagème,* from Latin *stratēgēma,* from Greek, "act of a general," from *stratēgein,* to be a general, from *stratēgos,* general : *stratos,* army (see **ster-**[2] in Appendix*) + *agein,* to lead (see **ag-** in Appendix*).]

stra·te·gic (strə-tē′jĭk) *adj.* Also **stra·te·gi·cal** (-jĭ-kəl). **1.** Of or pertaining to strategy. **2. a.** Important or essential in relation to strategy: *a strategic withdrawal.* **b.** Essential to the effective conduct of war. **c.** Designed to destroy the military potential of an enemy: *strategic bombing.* —**stra·te′gi·cal·ly** *adv.*

stra·te·gics (strə-tē′jĭks) *n.* Plural in form, used with a singular verb. The art of strategy.

strat·e·gist (străt′ə-jĭst) *n.* One who is skilled in strategy.

strat·e·gy (străt′ə-jē) *n., pl.* **-gies. 1.** The science or art of military command as applied to the overall planning and conduct of large-scale combat operations. Compare **tactics. 2.** A plan of action resulting from the practice of this science. **3.** The art or skill of using stratagems in politics, business, courtship, or the like. [French *stratégie,* from Greek *stratēgia,* office of a general, from *stratēgos,* general. See **stratagem.**]

Strat·ford (străt′fərd). **1.** See **Stratford-on-Avon. 2.** A city of Connecticut, in the southeast on Long Island Sound; site of the American Shakespeare Festival. Population, 45,000. **3.** A city in southeastern Ontario, Canada; site of the Stratford Festival. Population, 20,000.

Strat·ford-on-A·von (străt′fərd-ŏn-ā′vŏn, -ā′vən). Also **Stratford.** A town on the Avon in southern Warwickshire, England; the birthplace and burial place of Shakespeare.

strath (străth) *n. Scottish.* A wide, flat river valley. [Scottish Gaelic *srath.* See **ster-**[2] in Appendix.*]

strati-. Indicates stratum or strata; for example, **stratigraphy.** [From STRATUM.]

stra·tic·u·late (stră-tĭk′yə-lĭt) *adj.* Having thin strata. [From New Latin *straticulus* (unattested), diminutive of STRATUM.] —**stra·tic′u·la′tion** (-lā′shən) *n.*

strat·i·fi·ca·tion (străt′ə-fĭ-kā′shən) *n.* **1.** The act or process of stratifying. **2.** A stratified configuration.

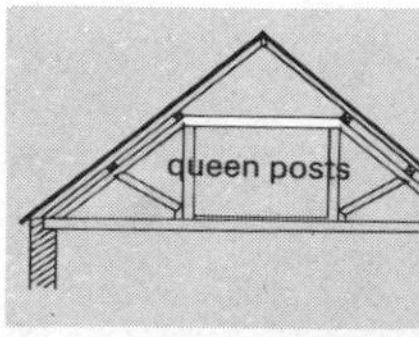

straining beam

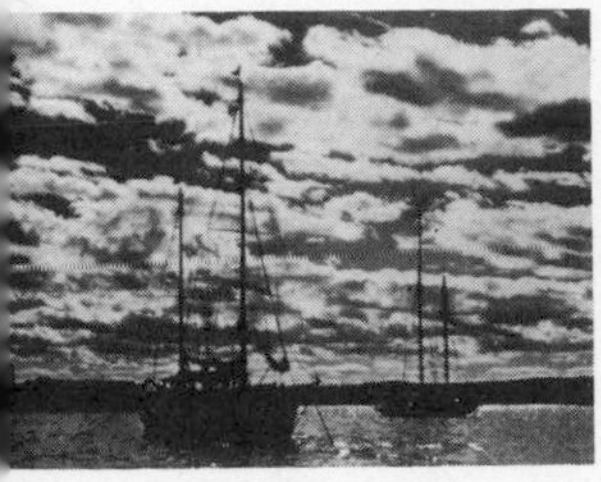

stratocumulus

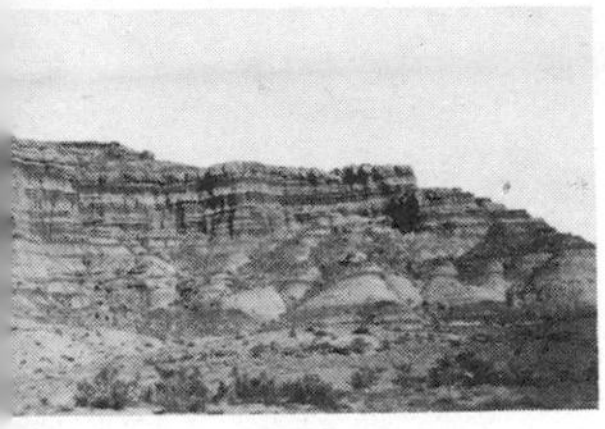

stratum
Cliff showing strata bared by erosion

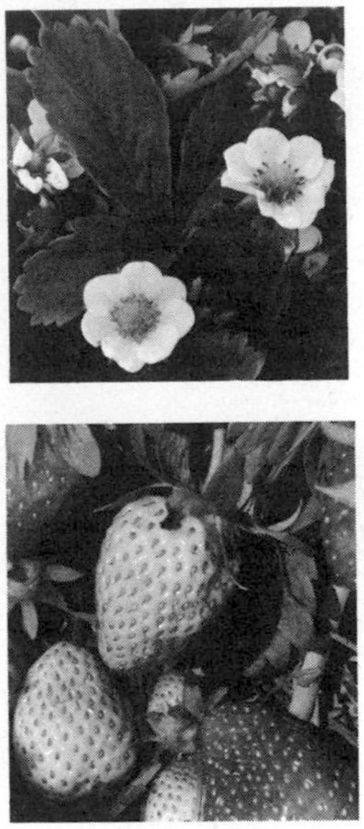

strawberry
Above: Flowers
Below: Fruit

strat·i·form (străt′ə-fôrm′) *adj.* Having the form of strata. [STRATI- + -FORM.]

strat·i·fy (străt′ə-fī′) *v.* **-fied, -fying, -fies.** —*tr.* **1.** To form, arrange, or deposit in strata. **2.** *Horticulture.* To preserve (seeds) by placing them between layers of moist sand or similar material. —*intr.* **1.** To become layered; form strata. **2.** *Sociology.* To develop different levels of caste, class, privilege, or status. [French *stratifier,* from New Latin *stratificare* : STRATUM + Latin *facere,* to make, do (see **dhē-**[1] in Appendix*).]

stra·tig·ra·phy (strə-tĭg′rə-fē) *n.* The study of rock strata, especially of their distribution, deposition, and age. [STRATI- + -GRAPHY.] —**strat′i·graph′ic** (străt′ĭ-grăf′ĭk), **strat′·i·graph′i·cal** *adj.* —**strat′i·graph′i·cal·ly** *adv.*

stra·toc·ra·cy (strə-tŏk′rə-sē) *n., pl.* **-cies.** Government by the army. [Greek *stratos,* army (see **ster-**[2] in Appendix*) + -CRACY.] —**strat′o·crat′ic** (străt′ə-krăt′ĭk) *adj.*

stra·to·cu·mu·lus (străt′ō-kyōōm′yə-ləs) *n., pl.* **-li** (-lī′). A low-lying cloud occurring in extensive horizontal layers with massive, rounded summits. [From STRAT(US) + CUMULUS.]

strat·o·sphere (străt′ə-sfîr′) *n.* The relatively isothermal part of the atmosphere above the troposphere and below the mesosphere. [French *stratosphère* : STRAT(UM) + (ATM)OSPHERE.] —**strat′o·spher′ic** (-sfîr′ĭk, -sfĕr′ĭk) *adj.*

Strat·ton (străt′n), **Charles Sherwood.** Known as General Tom Thumb. 1838–1883. American circus performer.

stra·tum (strā′təm, strä′-, străt′əm) *n., pl.* **-ta** (-tə) or *rare* **-tums.** **1.** A horizontal layer of any material; especially, one of several parallel layers arranged one on top of another. **2.** *Geology.* **a.** A bed or layer of rock having the same composition throughout. **b.** A formation containing a number of beds or layers of rock of the same kind of material. **3.** A category regarded as occupying a level in a hierarchy: *"He will dote on sophistication and relegate low comedy to a stratum beneath contempt"* (Charles Marowitz). [New Latin, from Latin *strātum,* neuter of *strātus,* stretched out. See **stratus.**] —**stra′tal** *adj.*

Usage: *Strata* is standard as a plural form but not as a singular: *All strata of society are represented. Each stratum is accounted for. Stratas* (plural) is not a standard form.

stra·tus (strā′təs, străt′əs) *n., pl.* **-ti** (-tī′). A low-altitude cloud typically resembling a horizontal layer of fog. [Latin *strātus,* past participle of *sternere,* to stretch out, extend. See **ster-**[2] in Appendix.*]

Straus (strous), **Oscar.** 1870–1954. Austrian-born composer of operettas and comic operas; naturalized French citizen (1939); resident of America (1940–48).

Strauss (strous), **Johann**[1]. Known as the Elder. 1804–1849. Austrian conductor, violinist, and composer; father of Johann Strauss the Younger.

Strauss (strous), **Johann**[2]. Known as the Younger. 1825–1899. Austrian violinist and conductor; composer of operettas and more than 300 waltzes; son of Johann Strauss the Elder.

Strauss (strous), **Richard.** 1864–1949. German composer.

Stra·vin·sky (strə-vĭn′skē), **Igor Fedorovich.** Born 1882. Russian-born composer; resident in France (1920–39); naturalized American citizen (1945).

straw (strô) *n.* **1. a.** Stalks of threshed grain. **b.** Such stalks used in the plaiting of hats, baskets, and the like. **c.** One such stalk. **2.** A slender tube used for sucking up a liquid. **3.** Something of minimal value or importance. —**catch** (or **clutch** or **grasp**) **at a straw** (or **straws**). To make a final desperate effort. —**straw in the wind.** A slight hint of something to come. —**the last straw.** The final blow to be withstood. —*tr.v.* **strawed, strawing, straws.** **1.** To cover (a surface, for example) with straw; strew. **2.** To provide with straw. —*adj.* **1.** Pertaining to, used for, or like straw. **2.** Made of straw. **3.** Of the color of straw; yellowish. **4.** Having little or no value or substance; unimportant. [Middle English *strawe,* Old English *strēaw.* See **ster-**[2] in Appendix.*]

straw·ber·ry (strô′bĕr′ē, -bə-rē) *n., pl.* **-ries.** **1.** Any of various low-growing plants of the genus *Fragaria,* having white flowers and red, fleshy, edible fruit. **2.** The fruit of any of these plants. [Middle English *strawberry,* Old English *strēawberige* : STRAW (possibly from the strawlike slender runners trailing on the ground) + BERRY.]

strawberry bass. A fish, the **black crappie** *(see).*

strawberry blite. A weedy plant, *Chenopodium capitatum,* of northern regions, having minute, petalless flowers and red, berrylike fruit.

straw·ber·ry-blond (strô′bĕr′ē-blŏnd′, strô′bə-rē-) *adj.* Reddish-blond. Said of hair.

strawberry bush. A North American shrub, *Euonymus americanus,* having inconspicuous flowers and showy pinkish fruit.

strawberry mark. A small reddish birthmark.

strawberry roan. A horse having reddish hair mixed with white.

strawberry shrub. Any of several North American shrubs of the genus *Calycanthus,* having aromatic reddish-brown flowers.

strawberry tomato. **1.** A North American plant, *Physalis pruinosa,* having yellow flowers and edible yellowish fruit enclosed in a husk. **2.** The fruit of this plant.

strawberry tree. A tree, *Arbutus unedo,* native to southern Europe, having evergreen leaves and strawberrylike fruit.

straw·board (strô′bôrd′, -bōrd′) *n.* A coarse yellow cardboard made of straw pulp.

straw boss. *Informal.* A worker who acts as a boss or assistant foreman in addition to his regular duties.

straw·flow·er (strô′flou′ər) *n.* A plant, *Helichrysum bracteatum,* native to Australia, having flowers with showy, variously colored bracts that retain their color when dried.

straw-hat (strô′hăt′) *adj.* Of or pertaining to a summer theater that operates in suburban or resort areas: *The show was a hit on the straw-hat circuit.* [So called because straw hats are worn in the summer.]

straw man. **1.** A bundle of straw made into the likeness of a man and often used as a scarecrow. **2.** One who is set up as cover or front man for a questionable enterprise. **3.** One set up as an opponent to be easily defeated or refuted.

straw vote. An unofficial vote or poll indicating the trend of opinion on a candidate or issue.

straw wine. A dessert wine made from grapes that have been dried on straw.

straw·worm (strô′wûrm′) *n.* The destructive larva of a fly, *Harmolita grandis,* of western North America, that infests stalks of grain.

stray (strā) *intr.v.* **strayed, straying, strays.** **1. a.** To wander from a given place or group or beyond established limits; roam. **b.** To become lost. **2.** To rove, wander about, or meander. **3.** To deviate from a course that is regarded as right or moral; go astray; err. **4.** To deviate from the subject matter at hand; digress. —See Synonyms at **wander.** —*n.* One that has strayed; especially, a domestic animal at large or lost. —*adj.* **1. a.** Straying or having strayed; out of place. **b.** Lost. **2.** Scattered or separate: *"A few stray white bread crumbs lay on the cleanly washed floor"* (Sherwood Anderson). [Middle English *straien,* from Old French *estraier,* from Vulgar Latin *estragāre* (unattested) : Latin *extrā-,* outside of + *vagārī,* to wander, roam, from *vagus,* wandering, VAGUE.] —**stray′er** *n.*

streak (strēk) *n.* **1.** A line, mark, smear, or band differentiated by color or texture from its surroundings. **2.** A slight trace or tendency; trait: *"We've got quite a little streak of self-reliance in our family"* (Arthur Miller). **3.** *Informal.* A brief stretch of time; a run: *a streak of good luck.* **4.** *Mineralogy.* The color of the powder of a mineral, used as a distinguishing characteristic. —*v.* **streaked, streaking, streaks.** —*tr.* To mark with a streak or streaks; stripe; striate. —*intr.* **1.** To form a streak or streaks: *"The engine smoke streaked out on dawn like a cold breath"* (Thomas Wolfe). **2.** To be or become streaked. **3.** To move at high speed; rush. [Middle English *strick(e),* Old English *strica.* See **streig-** in Appendix.*]

streak·y (strē′kē) *adj.* **-ier, -iest.** **1.** Marked with, characterized by, or occurring in streaks; streaked. **2.** Variable or uneven in character or quality. —**streak′i·ly** *adv.* —**streak′i·ness** *n.*

stream (strēm) *n.* **1.** A body of running water; especially, such a body moving over the earth's surface in a channel or bed, as a brook, rivulet, or river. **2.** A steady current in such a body of water. **3.** A steady current of any fluid. **4.** A steady flow or succession of anything: *a stream of invective.* **5.** A trend, course, or drift, as of opinion, thought, or history. —*v.* **streamed, streaming, streams.** —*intr.* **1.** To flow in or as in a stream: *"From the paddocks . . . there streamed the milky scent of ripe grass"* (Katherine Mansfield). **2.** To pour forth or give off a stream; flow. Used with *with: eyes streaming with tears.* **3.** To move or proceed in large numbers: *"Hundreds of people were streaming by our house in wild panic"* (James Thurber). **4.** To extend, wave, or float outward: *The banner streamed in the breeze.* **5. a.** To leave a continuous trail of light. **b.** To give forth a continuous stream of light rays or beams; shine. —*tr.* To emit, discharge, or exude. [Middle English *streme,* Old English *strēam.* See **sreu-** in Appendix.*] —**stream′y** *adj.*

stream·er (strē′mər) *n.* **1.** A long, narrow flag, banner, or pennant. **2.** Any long, narrow pendant strip of material. **3.** A shaft or ray of light extending upward from the horizon. **4.** A newspaper headline that runs across a full page.

stream·line (strēm′līn′) *n.* **1.** A fluid line having the property that the tangent at every point on the line is aligned with the fluid's local velocity. **2.** The path of one particle in a flowing fluid. **3.** Any contour of a body constructed so as to offer minimum resistance to a fluid flow. —*adj.* **1.** Indicating a flow characterized by lack of turbulence or interruption. **2.** Variant of **streamlined.** —*tr.v.* **streamlined, -lining, -lines.** **1.** To construct or design in a streamlined form. **2.** To improve the appearance or efficiency of; modernize.

stream·lined (strēm′līnd′) *adj.* Also **stream·line** (-līn′). **1.** Designed or arranged to offer the least resistance to fluid flow. **2.** Improved in appearance or efficiency; modernized.

stream of consciousness. **1.** *Psychology.* The conscious experience of an individual regarded as a continuous rather than a discrete series of events. **2.** A technique of composition in the novel, recording by means of first-person narration the formulated thoughts reflecting a given character's psychic process at some point significant to the development of the plot.

street (strēt) *n. Abbr.* **st., St.** **1.** A public way or thoroughfare in a city or town, usually including the sidewalks and buildings lining one or both sides. **2.** Such a roadway for vehicles apart from the buildings and sidewalks: *Don't play in the street.* **3.** The people living, working, or habitually gathering in or along such a roadway: *The whole street protested the new regulations.* —**the Street.** The financial section of New York City, centering on Wall Street. [Middle English *strete,* Old English *strǣt,* from West Germanic *strāta* (unattested), from Late Latin *strāta,* from Latin *strātus,* past participle of *sternere,* to extend, stretch out. See **ster-**[2] in Appendix.*]

street Arab. A homeless child; street urchin.

street·car (strēt′kär′) *n.* A public passenger car operated on rails along a regular route, usually through the streets of a city. Also called "trolley," "trolley car," *British* "tramcar," "tram."

street·walk·er (strēt′wô′kər) *n.* A prostitute who solicits in the streets. —**street′walk′ing** *n.*

ă pat/ā pay/âr care/ä father/b bib/ch church/d deed/ĕ pet/ē be/f fife/g gag/h hat/hw which/ĭ pit/ī pie/îr pier/j judge/k kick/l lid, needle/m mum/n no, sudden/ng thing/ŏ pot/ō toe/ô paw, for/oi noise/ou out/ŏŏ took/ōō boot/p pop/r roar/s sauce/sh ship, dish/

stre·ga (strā′gə) *n.* A sweet, orange-flavored Italian liqueur having a rich golden color. [From *Strega,* a trademark.]

strength (strĕngkth, strĕngth) *n.* **1.** The state, quality, or property of being strong; physical power; muscularity. **2.** The power of resisting force, attack, strain, or stress; durability; solidity; impregnability. **3.** Power in general, such as that deriving from the intellect, the law, or the possession of resources. **4. a.** A source of power or force; that which makes strong. **b.** One that is regarded as the embodiment of protective or supportive power; a stay. **5.** Firmness of will, character, mind, or purpose; moral courage or power. **6.** Effective or binding force; efficacy: *the strength of an argument.* **7.** The power or capability of generating a reaction or effect; operative potency: *the strength of a vise.* **8.** Degree of concentration, distillation, or saturation; potency. **9.** Intensity or vehemence, as in emotion, language, or action. **10. a.** A concentration of available numerical force or supportive personnel: *"their strength was in the provinces, particularly Ontario"* (W.L. Morton). **b.** Military force in terms of numbers in personnel or material: *a platoon at half strength.* **11.** Firmness of or a continuous rising tendency in prices. **12.** *Card Games.* Power derived from the value of cards held. **—on the strength of.** Relying or depending on; based on. [Middle English *strengthe,* Old English *strengthu.* See **strenk-** in Appendix.*]

Synonyms: *strength, power, might, force, energy, puissance, potency.* These nouns are compared as they relate to the ability to act effectively. *Strength* is the capacity for thus acting, considered especially as the means of physical accomplishment. *Power* is also the source of effective action but has even wider application than *strength,* as in contexts where it implies authority or the ability to control work by superhuman or supernatural means. *Might* implies abundant or overmastering power. *Force* is the application of power or physical strength. *Energy* is power considered either as something expended or as a latent source of action. *Puissance* is approximately equivalent to *might. Potency* is power considered as a means of achieving a desired result, and is often used to imply authority, influence, or chemical or medicinal value.

strength·en (strĕngk′thən, strĕng′-) *v.* **-ened, -ening, -ens.** *—tr.* To make strong or stronger. *—intr.* To become strong or stronger. **—strength′en·er** *n.*

stren·u·ous (strĕn′yo͞o-əs) *adj.* **1.** Requiring or characterized by great effort, energy, or exertion: *a strenuous task.* **2.** Vigorously active; energetic or zealous: *a strenuous child.* [Latin *strēnuus*†, brisk, nimble, quick.] **—stren′u·os′i·ty** (-yo͞o-ŏs′ə-tē), **stren′u·ous·ness** *n.* **—stren′u·ous·ly** *adv.*

strep throat (strĕp). *Pathology.* **Septic sore throat** *(see).* [Strep, short for STREPTOCOCCAL.]

strepto-. Indicates: **1.** A twisted chain; for example, **streptococcus. 2.** Streptococcus; for example, **streptokinase.** [From Greek *streptos,* twisted, from *strephein,* to turn. See **strebh-** in Appendix.*]

strep·to·coc·cal (strĕp′tə-kŏk′əl) *adj.* Also **strep·to·coc·cic** (-kŏk′sĭk). Of, pertaining to, or caused by a streptococcus.

strep·to·coc·cus (strĕp′tə-kŏk′əs) *n., pl.* **-cocci** (-kŏk′sī′). Any of various round to ovoid, often pathogenic bacteria of the genus *Streptococcus,* occurring in pairs or chains. [New Latin : STREPTO- + -COCCUS.]

strep·to·ki·nase (strĕp′tə-kĭn′ās′, -āz′, -kī′nās′, -kī′nāz′) *n.* A proteolytic enzyme derived from hemolytic streptococci, capable of dissolving fibrin and used to dissolve blood clots. [STREPTO- + KINASE.]

strep·to·ly·sin (strĕp′tə-lī′sən) *n.* An antigenic hemolysin derived from some strains of streptococci.

strep·to·my·cin (strĕp′tə-mī′sən) *n.* An antibiotic, $C_{21}H_{39}N_7O_{12}$, produced from mold cultures of bacteria of the genus *Streptomyces* and used medicinally to combat various Gram-positive and Gram-negative bacteria and tuberculosis. [New Latin *Streptomyces* : STREPTO- + Greek *mukēs,* fungus (see **meug-**[2] in Appendix*) + -IN.]

strep·to·thri·cin (strĕp′tə-thrī′sən, -thrĭs′ən) *n.* An antibiotic isolated from a soil fungus, *Streptomyces lavendulae,* and active against both Gram-positive and Gram-negative bacteria and some fungi. [New Latin *Streptothrix,* a genus of bacteria : STREPTO- + Greek *thrix,* hair (see **thrix** in Appendix*) + -IN.]

stress (strĕs) *n.* **1.** Importance, significance, or emphasis placed upon something: *"This misplaced stress upon realism might seem to find its proper corrective"* (Cleanth Brooks). **2.** *Phonetics.* **a.** The relative force with which a sound or syllable is spoken. **b.** The emphasis placed upon the sound or syllable spoken loudest in a given word or phrase. **3. a.** The relative emphasis given a syllable or word in accordance with a metrical pattern. **b.** A syllable receiving a strong relative emphasis. **4.** *Music.* An accent. **5.** *Physics.* An applied force or system of forces that tends to strain or deform a body. **6.** A mentally or emotionally disruptive or disquieting influence; distress. *—tr.v.* **stressed, stressing, stresses. 1.** To place emphasis on; to accent. **2.** To subject to pressure or strain; to distress. **3.** To subject to mechanical pressure or force. **4.** To construct so as to withstand a (specified) stress. [Middle English *stresse,* hardship, distress, from Old French *estresse,* narrowness, from Vulgar Latin *strictia* (unattested), from Latin *strictus,* STRICT.]

-stress. Indicates a feminine agent; for example, **seamstress.** [-ST(ER) + -ESS.]

stretch (strĕch) *v.* **stretched, stretching, stretches.** *—tr.* **1.** To lengthen, widen, or distend by pulling: *stretch a woolen sweater.* **2.** To cause to extend from one place to another or across a given space. **3.** To make taut; tighten. **4.** To reach or put forth; extend. Often used with *out: He stretched out his hand.* **5.** To extend (oneself) at full length, usually in a prone position. Often used with *out: "when I am stretched beneath the pines"* (Emerson). **6.** To flex the muscles of. Often used reflexively: *stretch one's arms.* **7.** To exert (oneself) to the utmost; strain: *stretch every nerve to win.* **8.** To wrench or strain (a muscle or ligament, for example); sprain: *stretch a tendon.* **9.** *Informal.* To fell by a blow: *He was stretched in the first round.* **10.** *Slang.* **a.** To cause to be hanged. **b.** To put to torture on the rack. **11. a.** To cause to suffice; make do with: *stretch the budget by careful spending.* **b.** To increase the quantity of by admixture or dilution: *stretch a meal by thinning the soup.* **12.** To extend the limits of credulity, law, conscience, or the like: *stretch the rules a little.* **13.** To prolong: *stretch out an argument.* *—intr.* **1.** To become lengthened, widened, or distended. **2.** To extend or reach over a given distance or area or in a given direction: *"On both sides of us stretched the wet plain"* (Hemingway). **3.** To lie down at full length. Usually used with *out.* **4.** To flex or extend one's muscles or limbs. **5.** To extend over a given period of time: *"This story stretches over a whole generation"* (William Golding). **6.** *Slang.* To be hanged. **—stretch one's legs.** To stroll about after a sedentary period. *—n.* **1.** The act of stretching or the state of being stretched. **2.** The extent or scope to which something can be stretched; elasticity. **3.** A continuous or unbroken length, area, or expanse: *"The stretch from Bent's Fort to the summit of Raton Pass was the most difficult of the entire trail"* (Bernard De Voto). **4.** A straight section of a racecourse or track, especially that section leading to the finish line. **5. a.** A continuous period of time. **b.** *Slang.* A term of imprisonment: *a two-year stretch.* **c.** *Informal.* The last stage of any event, period, or process. *—adj.* Capable of being stretched; elastic: *a stretch sock.* [Middle English *strecchen,* Old English *streccan,* to spread out, extend, from Germanic *strakkjan* (unattested).] **—stretch′a·ble** *adj.* **—stretch′y** *adj.*

stretch·er (strĕch′ər) *n.* **1.** One that stretches. **2.** A litter, usually of canvas stretched over a frame, used to transport the sick, wounded, or dead. **3.** Any of various devices used for stretching and shaping, such as the wooden framework upon which canvas is stretched for an oil painting. **4. a.** A usually horizontal tie beam or brace serving to support or extend a framework. **b.** A brick or stone laid parallel to the face of a wall.

stretch·er-bear·er (strĕch′ər-bâr′ər) *n.* One who helps carry a stretcher or litter.

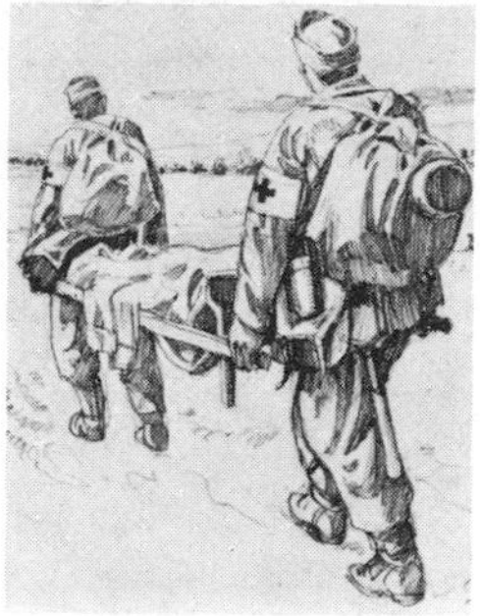

stretcher-bearer
Stretcher-bearers in World War I

stretch-out (strĕch′out′) *n.* An increase in the work required of industrial workers without a commensurate pay increase.

stret·to (strĕt′tō) *n., pl.* **-ti** (-tē) or **-tos.** *Music.* **1.** A close succession or overlapping of voices in a fugue, especially in the final section. **2.** A final section, as of an oratorio, performed with an acceleration in tempo to produce a climax. Also called "stretta." [Italian, "tight," from Latin *strictus,* STRICT.]

streu·sel (stroi′zəl, stro͞o′-; *German* shtroi′səl) *n.* A crumblike topping for coffee cakes and rich breads, consisting of flour, sugar, butter, cinnamon, and sometimes chopped nutmeats. [German *Streusel,* "something strewn together," from Middle High German *ströusel,* from *ströuwen,* to sprinkle, strew, from Old High German *strouwen.* See **ster-**[2] in Appendix.*]

strew (stro͞o) *tr.v.* **strewn** (stro͞on) or **strewed, strewing, strews. 1.** To spread here and there; scatter; sprinkle. **2.** To cover (a surface) with things scattered or sprinkled: *"Italy . . . was strewn thick with the remains of Roman buildings"* (Bernard Berenson). **3.** To be or become dispersed over (a surface). [Middle English *strewen,* Old English *strēowian.* See **ster-**[2] in Appendix.* The past participle strewn is an analogous formation in Modern English, from strew.]

stri·a (strī′ə) *n., pl.* **striae** (strī′ē′). **1.** A thin, narrow groove or channel. **2.** A thin line or band, especially one of several that are parallel or close together. [Latin, furrow, channel. See **streig-** in Appendix.*]

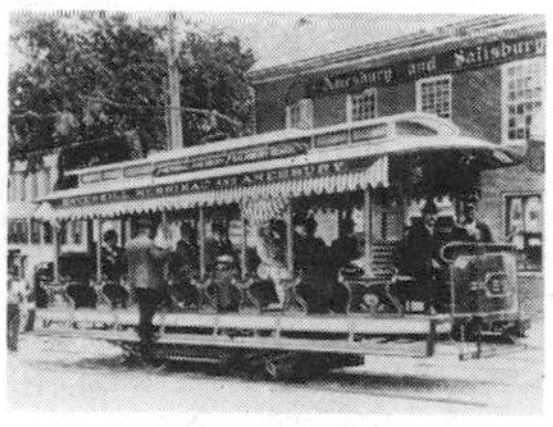

streetcar
Single-track open-sided streetcar built about 1900

stri·ate (strī′āt′) *adj.* Also **stri·at·ed** (-ā′tĭd). **1.** Marked with striae; striped, grooved, or ridged. **2.** Consisting of a stria or striae. *—tr.v.* **striated, -ating, -ates.** To mark with striae. [Latin *striātus,* past participle of *striāre,* to make furrows, from *stria,* furrow, STRIA.]

striated muscle. Skeletal, voluntary, and cardiac muscle, distinguished from smooth muscle by transverse striations of the fibers.

stri·a·tion (strī-ā′shən) *n.* **1.** The state of being striated or having striae. **2.** The form taken by striae. **3.** A stria.

strick·en (strĭk′ən) *adj.* **1.** Struck or wounded, as by a projectile. **2.** Afflicted with something overwhelming, such as strong emotion, disease, or trouble. **3.** Having the contents made even with the top of a measuring device or container; level. [Past participle of STRIKE.]

Strick·land (strĭk′lənd), **William.** 1787?–1854. American architect, engineer, and graphic artist; leader of Greek Revival.

strick·le (strĭk′əl) *n.* **1.** An instrument used to level off grain or other material in a measure; a strike. **2.** A foundry tool used to shape a mold in sand or loam. **3.** A tool for sharpening scythes. *—tr.v.* **strickled, -ling, -les.** To apply a strickle to. [Middle English *strikelle,* Old English *stricel.* See **streig-** in Appendix.*]

strict (strĭkt) *adj.* **stricter, strictest. 1.** Precise; accurate; exact. **2.** Complete; absolute: *strict loyalty.* **3.** Kept within narrow and specific limits: *a strict application of a law.* **4.** Imposing an exacting discipline; not permissive. **5.** Enforced or maintained rigorously; stringent: *strict standards.* **6.** Rigidly conforming; devout. **7.** *Botany.* Stiff, narrow, and upright. —See Synonyms at **severe.** [Latin *strictus,* tight, narrow, from the past participle of *stringere,* to draw tight, to tighten. See **streig-** in Appendix.*] **—strict′ly** *adv.* **—strict′ness** *n.*

stric·ture (strĭk′chər) *n.* **1.** Something that restrains, limits, or restricts. **2.** An adverse remark or criticism; censure. **3.** *Pathology.* An abnormal narrowing of a duct or passage. [Middle English, from Latin *strictūra,* contraction, compression, from *strictus,* STRICT.]

stride (strīd) *v.* **strode** (strōd) or *obsolete* **strid** (strĭd), **stridden** (strĭd'n) or *obsolete* **strid, striding, strides.** —*intr.* **1.** To walk with long steps, especially in a hasty or vigorous manner. **2.** To take a single long step, as in passing over an obstruction. —*tr.* **1.** To stride on, along, or through. **2.** To straddle; be astride of. —*n.* **1.** The act of striding. **2. a.** A single long step. **b.** The distance traveled in such a step. **3. a.** A single coordinated movement of the four legs of a horse or other animal, completed when the legs are returned to their initial relative position. **b.** The distance traveled in such a cycle of movements. **4.** A step forward; an advance. [Stride, strode (or strid), stridden; Middle English *striden, strode* (or *stride*), *stridden,* Old English *strīdan, strād* (singular, only in *bestrād*), *stridon* (plural, unattested), *striden* (unattested), from Germanic *strīdan* (unattested).] —**strid'er** *n.*

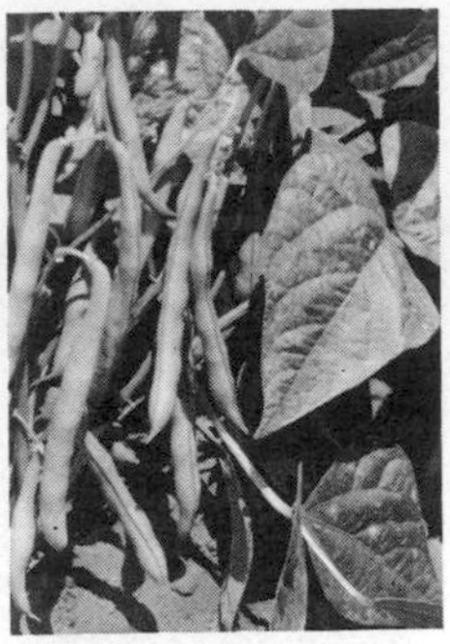

string bean
Phaseolus vulgaris

stri·dent (strīd'ənt) *adj.* Loud, harsh, and grating; shrill: *"His bluff strident words struck the note sailors understand"* (J.M. Barrie). See Synonyms at **vociferous.** [Latin *strīdēns,* present participle of *strīdēre,* to make a harsh sound. See **strei-** in Appendix.*] —**stri'dence, stri'den·cy** *n.* —**stri'dent·ly** *adv.*

stri·dor (strī'dər) *n.* **1.** A strident sound. **2.** *Pathology.* A harsh, high-pitched sound in inhalation or exhalation. [Latin *strīdor,* from *strīdēre,* to make a harsh sound. See **strident.**]

strid·u·late (strĭj'ōō-lāt') *intr.v.* **-lated, -lating, -lates.** To produce a shrill grating or creaking sound; chirp. Used especially of insects such as crickets or katydids. [From Latin *strīdulus,* creaking, STRIDULOUS.] —**strid'u·la'tion** *n.* —**strid'u·la·to'ry** (-lə-tôr'ē, -tōr'ē) *adj.*

strid·u·lous (strĭj'ōō-ləs) *adj.* Making or characterized by a strident sound or chirp. [Latin *strīdulus,* creaking, from *strīdēre,* to make a harsh sound. See **strident.**]

strife (strīf) *n.* **1.** Heated, often violent dissension; bitter conflict. **2.** A contention; struggle between rivals. **3.** *Rare.* Earnest endeavor or striving. —See Synonyms at **discord.** [Middle English *strif,* from Old French *estrif*†.]

strig·il (strĭj'əl) *n.* An instrument used in ancient Greece and Rome for scraping the skin after a bath. [Latin *strigilis,* from *stringere,* to draw tight. See **streig-** in Appendix.*]

stri·gose (strī'gōs', strĭ'gōs') *adj.* **1.** Marked with fine, close-set grooves or streaks. **2.** *Botany.* Having stiff, closely pressed hairs or bristles. [New Latin *strigosus,* from Latin *striga,* swath, furrow. See **streig-** in Appendix.*]

strike (strīk) *v.* **struck** (strŭk), **struck** or **stricken** (strĭk'ən), **striking, strikes.** —*tr.* **1. a.** To hit sharply, as with the hand, fist, or a weapon. **b.** To inflict (a blow). **2. a.** To collide with or crash into: *struck the desk with her knee.* **b.** To move into violent contact; to dash: *struck her knee against the desk.* **3. a.** To attack; assault. **b.** *Obsolete.* To do (battle). **4.** To afflict suddenly with a disease or impairment. **5.** To wound by biting. Used of a snake. **6.** To hook (a fish) that has taken the bait. **7.** To impress by stamping, printing, or punching: *strike a medallion.* **8.** To produce by hitting some agent, such as a key on a musical instrument or a typewriter: *strike a B flat.* **9.** To indicate by a percussive sound: *The clock struck nine.* **10. a.** To produce (a flame, light, or spark) by friction. **b.** To produce flame, light, or a spark from by friction. **11.** To eliminate or expunge. Often used with *out* or *off.* **12.** To come upon; discover: *struck gold.* **13.** To reach; fall upon: *A bright light struck her face.* **14.** To impress abruptly or freshly, causing an immediate response: *strikes me as a good idea.* **15.** To cause (an emotion) to penetrate deeply: *struck terror into their hearts.* **16. a.** To make or conclude (a bargain). **b.** To achieve (a balance, for example) by careful weighing or reckoning. **17.** To fall into or assume (a pose, for example). **18.** *Nautical.* **a.** To haul down (a mast or sail). **b.** To lower (a flag or sail) in salute or surrender. **c.** To lower (cargo) into a hold. **19.** To remove (theatrical properties, scenery, or the like) from the playing area. **20.** To pack up; break (camp). **21.** To undertake a strike against (an employer). **22.** To level or smooth (a measure, as of grain); strickle. **23.** To send out or send down (roots, for example). —*intr.* **1.** To deal a blow or blows with or as if with the fist or a weapon; hit. **2.** To aim a stroke or blow. **3.** To make contact suddenly or violently; collide: *"Just at this moment her head struck against the roof of the hall"* (Lewis Carroll). **4.** To begin an attack. **5.** To pierce; penetrate. **6.** To take the bait. **7. a.** To make a percussive sound. **b.** To be indicated by sounds: *The hour has struck.* **8.** To become ignited. **9.** To come suddenly or unexpectedly. Used with *on* or *upon.* **10.** To fall; impinge. Used with *on* or *upon.* **11.** To proceed, especially in a new direction; set out; to head. Sometimes used with *out: The hikers struck out at dawn.* **12.** To engage in a strike against an employer: *"The waiters in Paris cafés had the courage to strike for the right to grow beards"* (Roger Shattuck). —See Synonyms at **affect.** —**strike dumb.** To astound; astonish. —**strike it rich.** To gain sudden wealth. —**strike up. 1.** To start to play or sound vigorously: *Strike up the band.* **2.** To initiate (a friendship, for example). —*n.* **1.** An act or gesture of striking; a hit or thrust. **2.** An attack; especially, a military air attack upon a single group of targets. **3. a.** A cessation of work by employees in support of demands made upon their employer, as for higher pay or improved conditions. **b.** Any cessation of normal activity undertaken as a protest against the conduct of those in power. **4.** A sudden achievement or valuable discovery, as of a precious mineral. **5. a.** A taking of bait by a fish. **b.** A pull on the line indicating this. **6.** A quantity of coins or medals struck at the same time. **7.** *Baseball.* A pitched ball that is counted against the batter, typically one swung at and missed or one taken and judged to have been in the **strike zone** *(see).* **8.** *Bowling.* The knocking down of all the pins with the first bowl of a frame. **9.** *Geology.* The direction of a horizontal line in the plane of an inclined structural feature such as a rock bed or vein. **10.** A strickle. [Strike, struck (earlier stroke), stricken (or struck); Middle English *striken, strok* (or *strak*), *striken* (rare Scottish variant *strukkin*), Old English *strīcan,* to stroke, rub, *strāc, stricen.* See **streig-** in Appendix.*]

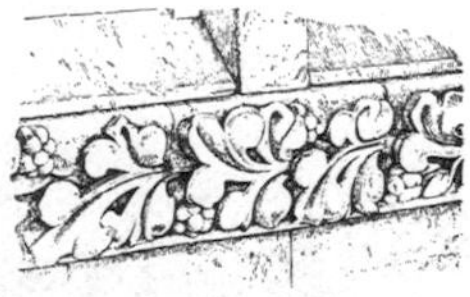

stringcourse

strike·bound (strīk'bound') *adj.* Closed, immobilized, or slowed down by a strike.

strike·break·er (strīk'brā'kər) *n.* One who works or provides an employer with workers during a strike. —**strike'break'ing** *n.*

strike figure. *Geology.* A **percussion figure** *(see).*

strike out. *Baseball.* To retire (a batter) or be retired by the recording of three strikes.

strike·out (strīk'out') *n. Abbr.* **s.o.** *Baseball.* The act or an instance of striking out.

strik·er (strī'kər) *n.* **1.** One that strikes. **2.** An employee who is on strike against his employer. **3.** Any device for striking, as the clapper in a bell or the firing pin in a gun. **4. a.** A harpooner. **b.** The harpoon. **5.** *U.S. Navy.* An enlisted man in training for a specified technical rating.

strike zone. *Baseball.* The area over the plate through which a pitch must pass to be called a strike, now defined as being between the batter's armpits and his knees.

strik·ing (strī'kĭng) *adj.* Impressing the mind or senses with immediacy; prominent in its effect: *"The most striking thing about this work is its Spartan honesty"* (Robert Brustein). —**strik'ing·ly** *adv.* —**strik'ing·ness** *n.*

Stri·mon. A Greek name for the **Struma.**

Strind·berg (strĭnd'bûrg'; *Swedish* strēn'bĕr-y'), **(Johan) August.** 1849–1912. Swedish playwright and novelist.

string (strĭng) *n.* **1.** A cord usually made of fiber, thicker than thread, used for fastening, tying, or lacing. **2.** Anything shaped into a long, thin line: *strings of spaghetti.* **3.** A set of objects threaded together: *a string of beads.* **4.** A series of related acts, events, or items arranged or falling in a line: *"Everything has a string of precedents"* (Glen Hughes). **5.** *Informal.* A set of animals, especially racehorses, belonging to a single owner; a stable. **6.** *Sports.* A group of players constituting a ranked team within a team: *He made the second string.* **7.** *Music.* **a.** A cord stretched across the sounding board of an instrument, that is struck, plucked, or bowed to produce tones. **b.** *Plural.* Instruments having such strings; especially, the instruments of the violin family. **8.** *Architecture.* **a.** A stringboard. **b.** A stringcourse. **9.** *Billiards.* The balk line. **10.** *Informal.* A limiting or hidden condition: *a gift with no strings attached.* —See Synonyms at **series.** —**pull strings.** To use one's influence, often in secret, to gain an advantage. —*v.* **strung** (strŭng), **stringing, strings.** —*tr.* **1.** To fit or furnish with a string or strings. **2.** To thread on a string. **3.** To arrange in a string or series. **4.** To fasten, tie, or hang with a string or strings. **5.** To extend; stretch out: *string a wire across a room.* **6.** To strip (vegetables) of strings. **7.** *Informal.* To fool or deceive. Usually used with *along.* **8.** *Informal.* To hang (someone). Usually used with *up.* —*intr.* **1.** To form strings or become stringlike. **2.** To extend or progress in a string, line, or succession. —**string along. 1.** To follow another's lead. **2.** To keep (someone) waiting or dangling. **3.** To cheat; deceive. [Middle English *stringe,* Old English *streng.* See **strenk-** in Appendix.*]

string bass. A **double bass** *(see).*

string bean. 1. A bushy or climbing plant, *Phaseolus vulgaris,* widely cultivated for its narrow, green, edible pods. **2.** The green pod of any bean prepared for cooking by breaking into sections that retain the beans. Also called "green bean," "snap bean." **3.** *Slang.* A tall, thin person. [From the stringy fibers on the pod.]

string·board (strĭng'bôrd', -bōrd') *n.* A board that runs along the side of a staircase to support or cover the ends of the steps.

string·course (strĭng'kôrs', -kōrs') *n. Architecture.* A horizontal band or molding set in the face of a building as a design element. Also called "cordon."

stringed instrument. A musical instrument played by plucking, striking, or bowing taut strings.

strin·gen·do (strĭn-jĕn'dō) *adj. Music.* Played with an accelerating tempo. Used as a direction to the performer. [Italian, "tightening," from *stringere,* to press together, to tighten, from Latin. See **streig-** in Appendix.*] —**strin·gen'do** *adv.*

strin·gent (strĭn'jənt) *adj.* **1.** Imposing rigorous standards of performance; severe. **2.** Constricted; tight: *"For the time grows stringent, frightfully pressing."* (Carlyle). **3.** Characterized by scarcity of money, credit restrictions, or the like: *stringent economic policies.* [Latin *stringēns,* present participle of *stringere,* to tighten. See **streig-** in Appendix.*] —**strin'gen·cy** *n.* —**strin'gent·ly** *adv.*

string·er (strĭng'ər) *n.* **1.** A person or thing that strings. **2.** *Architecture.* **a.** A long, heavy horizontal timber used for any of several connective or supportive purposes. **b.** A stringboard. **3.** A lengthwise timber used to support rails. **4.** A member of a specified string or squad on a team. Used in combination: *a second-stringer.* **5.** A part-time representative for a news publication who is stationed out of town or abroad.

string·halt (strĭng'hôlt') *n.* Lameness accompanied by spasmodic movements in the hind legs of a horse. Also called "springhalt." [Perhaps STRING + HALT.]

string quartet. 1. A quartet of musicians playing stringed instruments, traditionally including a first and second violinist, a violist, and a cellist. **2.** A composition for such a quartet of performers.

string tie. A narrow necktie, usually tied in a bow.

string·y (strĭng′ē) *adj.* **-ier, -iest. 1.** Resembling, forming, or consisting of a string or strings. **2.** Slender and sinewy; wiry. **—string′i·ly** *adv.* **—string′i·ness** *n.*

strip[1] (strĭp) *v.* **stripped** or *rare* **stript** (strĭpt), **stripping, strips.** *—tr.* **1. a.** To remove the clothing or other covering from. **b.** To remove (clothing or other covering). **2.** To deprive of honors, rank, or the like; divest. **3.** To reduce to essentials; remove all excess detail from. **4.** To remove the leaves from the stalks of. Used especially of tobacco. **5.** To dismantle (something) piece by piece. **6.** To damage or break the threads or teeth of (a nut, bolt, screw, or gear). **7.** To milk (a cow or other milk-giving creature); to dry. **8.** To rob; to plunder; despoil. *—intr.* **1. a.** To undress completely. **b.** To perform a striptease. **2.** To fall away or be removed; peel. *—n.* A striptease. [Middle English *stripen,* Old English *(be)strīepan,* to plunder, from Germanic *straupjan* (unattested).]

Synonyms: *strip, divest, denude, bare.* These verbs refer to the act of removing coverings or possessions. *Strip* often suggests force or abrupt action and applies to removal of such diverse things as clothing, natural covering such as bark or foliage, components of machinery, and attributes such as honor, rank, or position. *Divest* more often specifies deprivation of authority or rank or of the physical things that symbolize them. *Denude* generally refers to making land barren by depriving it of natural covering, such as vegetation or topsoil. *Bare* usually implies uncovering, literally or figuratively, and exposing to view.

strip[2] (strĭp) *n.* **1.** A long, narrow piece, usually of uniform width: *a strip of paper.* **2.** A **comic strip** *(see).* **3.** An **airstrip** *(see).* *—tr.v.* **stripped, stripping, strips.** To cut or tear into strips. [Perhaps variant of STRIPE (line).]

strip-crop·ping (strĭp′krŏp′ĭng) *n.* The growing of a cultivated crop, such as cotton, and a sod-forming crop, such as alfalfa, in alternating strips following the contour of the land, in order to minimize erosion.

stripe[1] (strīp) *n.* **1.** A long, narrow band distinguished, as by color or texture, from the surrounding material or surface. **2. a.** A fabric having such a band or bands. **b.** *Plural.* A garment of such fabric; especially, a prisoner's uniform. **3.** A strip of cloth or braid worn on a uniform to indicate rank, awards given, or length of service; a chevron. **4.** Sort; kind: *"All Fascists are not of one mind, one stripe"* (Lillian Hellman). *—tr.v.* **striped, striping, stripes.** To mark with a stripe or stripes. [Middle English *strype* (unattested), from Middle Dutch *strīpe,* akin to Middle High German *strīfe*†.]

stripe[2] (strīp) *n.* A stroke or blow, as with a whip. [Middle English *strype,* perhaps from Middle Low German *strippe,* a lash, strap, from Germanic *strip-* (unattested).]

striped (strīpt, strī′pĭd) *adj.* Having a stripe or stripes.

striped bass. A food and game fish, *Roccus saxatilis,* of North American coastal waters, having dark longitudinal stripes along its sides. Also called "rockfish."

striped maple. A tree, the **moosewood** *(see).*

strip·er (strī′pər) *n.* **1.** *Slang.* A member of the armed forces who wears stripes designating rank or length of service. Usually used in combination: *a four-striper.* **2.** *Informal.* A striped bass.

strip·ling (strĭp′lĭng) *n.* An adolescent youth. [Middle English, probably "slender as a strip," *strype,* STRIPE.]

strip mine. An open mine, especially a coal mine, the seams or outcrops of which run close to ground level and are exposed by the removal of topsoil and overburden.

strip·per (strĭp′ər) *n.* **1.** One that strips. **2.** *Slang.* One who performs a striptease.

strip·tease (strĭp′tēz′) *n.* Also **strip tease.** A theatrical performance featuring one who slowly removes clothing to a musical accompaniment. **—strip′teas′er** *n.*

strip·y (strī′pē) *adj.* **-ier, -iest.** Suggestive of or marked with stripes; striped.

strive (strīv) *intr.v.* **strove** (strōv) or *rare* **strived, striven** (strĭv′ən) or **strived, striving, strives. 1.** To exert much effort or energy: *"She strove to make him moral, religious"* (D.H. Lawrence). **2.** To struggle; contend: *"Good nature now and passion strive/Which of the two should be above"* (Suckling). [Middle English *striven,* from Old French *estriver,* perhaps from *estrif,* STRIFE. Strove, striven; Middle English *stroof, streven,* analogous formations, from *striven.*] **—striv′er** *n.*

strobe (strōb) *n.* **1.** Stroboscope. **2.** Strobe light.

strobe light. A flash lamp that produces high-intensity short-duration light pulses by electric discharge in a gas. Also called "electronic flash."

stro·bi·la (strō-bī′lə) *n., pl.* **-lae** (-lē′). A part or structure that buds to form a series of segments, such as the main body part of a tapeworm or the polyp stage in certain jellyfish. [New Latin, from Greek *strobilē,* plug of lint resembling a pine cone, from *strobilos,* pine cone, STROBILE.]

strob·i·la·ceous (strŏ′bə-lā′shəs) *adj. Botany.* Of or resembling a strobile; conelike.

strob·i·la·tion (strō′bə-lā′shən) *n.* Asexual reproduction by division into body segments, as in tapeworms and jellyfish.

strob·ile (strŏ′bəl, -bīl′) *n.* Also **strob·i·lus** (-bĭl′əs) *pl.* **-bili** (-bĭl′ī). *Botany.* A fruiting structure characterized by rows of overlapping scales, such as a pine cone or the fruit of the hop. [New Latin *strobilus,* from Late Latin, a pine cone, from Greek *strobilos,* "round ball," from *strobos,* a whirling around, whirlwind. See **strebh-** in Appendix.*]

strob·o·scope (strŏ′bə-skōp′) *n.* Any of various instruments used to view, calibrate, balance, or otherwise adjust moving, rotating, or vibrating objects by making them appear stationary, especially with pulsed illumination or mechanical devices that intermittently interrupt observation. [Greek *strobos,* a whirling round (see **strebh-** in Appendix*) + -SCOPE.] **—strob′o·scop′ic** (-skŏp′ĭk) *adj.* **—strob′o·scop′i·cal·ly** *adv.*

strode. Past tense of **stride.**

stro·gan·off (strô′gə-nôf′, strô-gä′nôf) *adj.* Sliced thin and cooked with onions, mushrooms, and seasonings, with a thick sour-cream sauce. [After Count *Stroganoff,* 19th-century Russian diplomat.]

Stro·heim (strō′hīm′), **Erich von.** 1885–1957. Austrian-born American motion-picture director and actor.

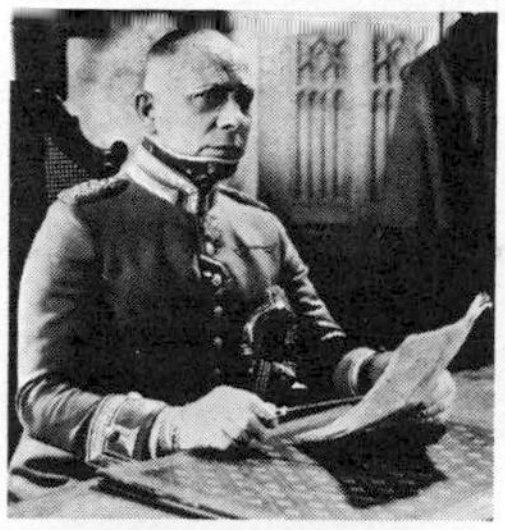

Erich von Stroheim

stroke (strōk) *n.* **1.** An impact; blow; strike. **2.** An act of striking. **3. a.** The striking of a bell, gong, or the like. **b.** The sound so produced. **c.** The time so indicated: *the stroke of midnight.* **4.** An event having a powerful immediate effect for good or ill: *a stroke of luck.* **5. a.** The sudden severe onset of a malady, as apoplexy or sunstroke. **b.** Apoplexy. Not in technical use. **6.** An inspired or effective idea or act: *a stroke of genius.* **7. a.** A single completed movement of the limbs and body, as in swimming or rowing. **b.** The rate or manner of executing such a movement. **8. a.** The member of a rowing crew who sits nearest the coxswain or the stern and sets the tempo of the oarsmen. **b.** The position he occupies. **9. a.** A movement of the upper torso and arms for the purpose of striking a ball, as in golf or tennis. **b.** The manner of executing such a movement. **10.** Any completed act or movement: *"All his life he had never done a stroke of work"* (E.M. Forster). **11.** *Machinery.* Any of a series of movements of a piston from one end of the limit of its motion to the other. **12. a.** A single mark made by a pen or other marking implement. **b.** The action of making such a mark: *"The stroke of his brush was like a caress"* (Sherwood Anderson). **13.** A single deft touch, as in literary composition. **14.** A light caressing movement, as of the hand. *—tr.v.* **stroked, stroking, strokes. 1.** To rub lightly, as with the hand or something held in the hand; caress. **2.** To set the pace for (a rowing crew). [Middle English *stroke,* Old English *strāc* (unattested). See **streig-** in Appendix.*]

stroll (strōl) *v.* **strolled, strolling, strolls.** *—intr.* To go for a leisurely walk: *stroll in the park.* *—tr.* To walk through at a leisurely pace: *stroll the streets.* *—n.* A leisurely walk. [Perhaps from German dialectal *strollen*†.]

stroll·er (strō′lər) *n.* **1.** One who strolls. **2.** A strolling player. **3.** A vagabond. **4.** A light four-wheeled chair for transporting small children.

stro·ma (strō′mə) *n., pl.* **-mata** (-mə-tə). The tissue framework, as distinguished from the specific substance, of an organ, gland, or other structure. [New Latin, from Latin *strōma,* coverlet, from Greek, mattress, bed. See **ster-**[2] in Appendix.*] **—stro·mat′ic** (-măt′ĭk) *adj.*

Strom·bo·li (strŏm-bō′lē). **1.** An island of Italy, about five square miles in area, lying off the northeastern coast of Sicily. **2.** An active volcano, 3,038 feet high, on this island.

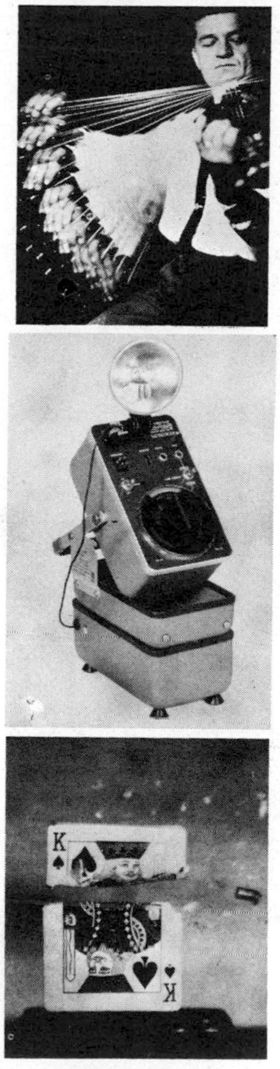

stroboscope
Above: Multiple-flash stroboscopic photograph
Center: The instrument
Below: Single-flash stroboscopic photograph

strong (strông) *adj.* **stronger, strongest. 1.** Having great physical strength; muscular; brawny. **2. a.** In sound health; robust. **b.** Economically or financially sound or thriving. **3.** Having force of character, will, morality, or intelligence. **4.** Manifesting ability or achievement in a specified field: *He is strong in chemistry.* **5.** Capable of enduring; solid: *a strong building.* **6.** Capable of being defended: *a strong flank.* **7.** Having a specified number of units or members: *"Marched them along, fifty-score strong"* (Robert Browning). **8.** Having force of motion or action: *a strong current.* **9. a.** Persuasive, effective, and cogent: *a strong argument.* **b.** Forceful and pointed; emphatic: *a strong statement.* **10.** Extreme; drastic: *strong measures.* **11.** Capable of exerting authority effectively: *strong leadership.* **12.** Having force of conviction or feeling: *a strong faith.* **13.** Intense in degree or quality: *a strong emotion.* **14. a.** Having an intense effect on the senses: *a strong smell.* **b.** Containing a considerable percentage of alcohol: *strong punch.* **15.** Characterized by a high degree of saturation. See **color. 16.** *Linguistics.* Designating those verbs in Germanic languages that form a past tense other than by means of a dental suffix. For example, *fly, flew; sing, sang.* In this sense, compare **weak.** *—adv.* In a strong, powerful, or vigorous manner; forcibly; forcefully. [Middle English *strong,* Old English *strang.* See **strenk-** in Appendix.*] **—strong′ly** *adv.*

Synonyms: *strong, stout, sturdy, tough, stalwart, hale, tenacious.* These adjectives are compared as they relate to vigor, durability, or power of body or spirit. *Strong* is the most general. *Stout* stresses ability to endure by muscular strength, solid construction, or resoluteness. *Sturdy* is closely related to *stout* in its implications of rugged health, solidity, or firmness of spirit or purpose. *Tough* suggests strength of physique or moral fiber that resists opposition or hardship. *Stalwart* implies imposing strength, courage, or unwavering determination, dependability, or loyalty. *Hale* suggests robust health. *Tenacious* stresses ability to hold fast to positions, goals, or opinions.

strong-arm (strông′ärm′) *adj. Informal.* Using physical force or coercion: *strong-arm tactics.* *—tr.v.* **strong-armed, -arming, -arms.** To use physical force or coercion against.

strong·box (strông′bŏks′) *n.* A stoutly made box or safe in which valuables are deposited.

strong·hold (strông′hōld′) *n.* **1.** A fortress. **2.** An area of predominance: *"The prairie region . . . has been the stronghold of the farmers' movement"* (Walter Prescott Webb).

strong-mind·ed (strông′mīn′dĭd) *adj.* **1.** Having a determined will. **2.** Having a vigorous mentality. **—strong′-mind′ed·ly** *adv.* **—strong′-mind′ed·ness** *n.*

t tight/th thin, path/*th* this, bathe/ŭ cut/ûr urge/v valve/w with/y yes/z zebra, size/zh vision/ə about, item, edible, gallop, circus/ à *Fr.* ami/œ *Fr.* feu, *Ger.* schön/ü *Fr.* tu, *Ger.* über/KH *Ger.* ich, *Scot.* loch/N *Fr.* bon. ***Follows main vocabulary. †Of obscure origin.**

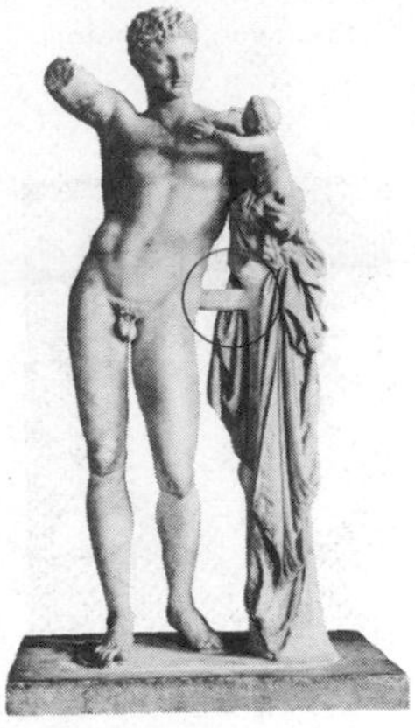

strut
The Hermes of Praxiteles

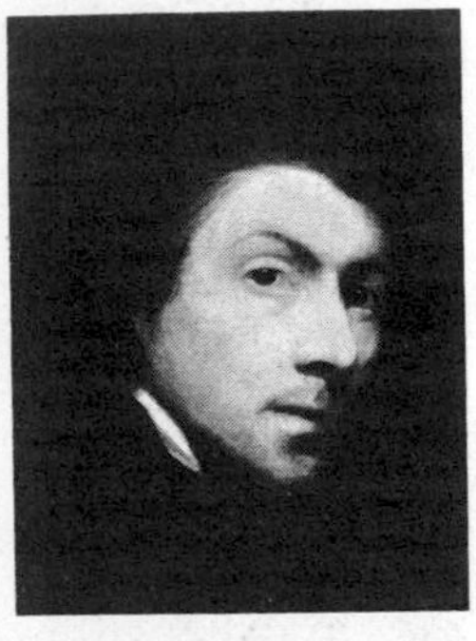

Gilbert Stuart
A self-portrait

stron·gyle (strŏn′jīl′) *n.* Also **stron·gyl** (-jəl). Any of various nematode worms of the family Strongylidae, often parasitic in the gastrointestinal tract of mammals, especially horses. [New Latin *Strongylus* (genus), from Greek *strongulos*†, round, compactly formed.]

stron·ti·an·ite (strŏn′chē-ə-nīt′, -tē-ə-nīt′) *n.* A gray to yellowish-green strontium ore, essentially $SrCO_3$. [*Strontian*, variant of STRONTIUM + -ITE.]

stron·ti·um (strŏn′chē-əm, -tē-əm) *n. Symbol* **Sr** A soft, silvery, easily oxidized metallic element that ignites spontaneously in air when finely divided. Strontium is used in pyrotechnic compounds and various alloys. Atomic number 38, atomic weight 87.62, melting point 769°C, boiling point 1,384°C, specific gravity 2.54, valence 2. See **element**. [Discovered in *Strontian*, mining village in Argyllshire, Scotland.] —**stron′tic** (-tĭk) *adj.*

strontium 90. The strontium isotope with mass 90, having a half-life of 28 years, used for its high-energy beta emission in certain nuclear electric power sources and constituting a radiation hazard in fallout.

strop (strŏp) *n.* A flexible strip of leather or canvas used for sharpening a razor. —*tr.v.* **stropped, stropping, strops.** To sharpen (a razor) on a strop. [Middle English *stroppe*, band of leather, from Middle Low German or Middle Dutch *strop*, from West Germanic *strupa* (unattested), from Latin *stroppus*, from Greek *strophos*, twisted cord, from *strephein*, to turn. See **strebh-** in Appendix.*]

stro·phan·thin (strō-făn′thən) *n.* A toxic glycoside or mixture of glycosides used medicinally as a cardiac tonic. [New Latin *Strophanthus* (genus) : Greek *strophos*, twisted cord (see **strop**) + *anthos*, flower (see **andh-** in Appendix*) + -IN.]

stro·phe (strō′fē, strō′fē′) *n. Abbr.* **st. 1. a.** A stanza, especially the first of a pair of stanzas of alternating form on which the structure of a given poem is based. **b.** A rhythmic system constituting a section of a poem, typically consisting of a series of asymmetric lines. **2.** The first division of the triad (strophe, antistrophe, and epode) constituting a section of a Pindaric ode. **3. a.** The movement of the chorus in classical Greek drama while turning from one side of the orchestra to the other. **b.** The part of a choral ode sung while this movement is executed. [Greek *strophē*, a turning, from *strephein*, to turn. See **strebh-** in Appendix.*] —**stroph′ic** *adj.*

stroph·u·lus (strŏf′yə-ləs) *n.* A disease, especially common among children, sometimes associated with intestinal disturbances and characterized by a papular eruption of the skin. Also called "red gum." [New Latin, from Greek *strophos*, twisted cord, from *strephein*, to turn. See **strebh-** in Appendix.*]

stroud (stroud) *n.* A coarse woolen cloth or blanket. [After *Stroud*, textile manufacturing center in Gloucestershire, England.]

strove. Past tense of **strive.**

struck (strŭk). Past tense and past participle of **strike.** —*adj.* Affected or shut down by a labor strike.

struck jury. *Law.* A jury, particularly a special jury, selected from an original panel of 48 members from which each party strikes off names until the list is reduced to 12.

struck measure. A dry measure having the contents leveled off and not heaped.

struc·tur·al (strŭk′chər-əl) *adj.* **1.** Of, relating to, having, or characterized by structure. **2.** Used in or necessary to construction. **3.** *Geology.* Pertaining to the structure of rocks and other aspects of the earth's crust. **4.** *Biology.* Of or relating to organic structure; morphological. —**struc′tur·al·ly** *adv.*

structural formula. A chemical formula that represents the configuration of atoms and bonds in a molecule.

struc·tur·al·ize (strŭk′chər-ə-līz′) *tr.v.* **-ized, -izing, -izes.** To incorporate into a structure. —**struc′tur·al·i·za′tion** *n.*

structural steel. Steel shaped for use in construction.

struc·ture (strŭk′chər) *n.* **1.** A complex entity. **2. a.** The configuration of elements, parts, or constituents in such an entity; organization; arrangement. **b.** Constitution; make-up. **3.** The interrelation of parts or the principle of organization in a complex entity. **4.** Relatively intricate or extensive organization: *an elaborate electric structure.* **5.** Something constructed, especially a building or part. —See Synonyms at **building.** —*tr.v.* **structured, -turing, -tures.** To construct; give form or arrangement to. [Middle English, from Old French, from Latin *structūra*, from *struere* (past participle *structus*), to construct. See **ster-²** in Appendix.*]

struc·tured (strŭk′chərd) *adj.* **1.** Highly organized: *a structured environment.* **2.** *Psychology.* Having a limited number of correct or nearly correct answers. Said of a test. Compare **unstructured.**

stru·del (strōōd′l) *n.* A kind of pie made with fruit or cheese rolled up in a thin sheet of dough and baked. [German *Strudel*, from Middle High German *strudel*, whirlpool. See **ser-²** in Appendix.*]

strug·gle (strŭg′əl) *v.* **-gled, -gling, -gles.** —*intr.* **1.** To exert muscular energy, as against a material force or mass; grapple; wrestle. **2.** To be strenuously engaged with a problem, task, undertaking, or the like. **3.** To make any strenuous effort; strive: *struggling to be polite.* **4. a.** To contend against: *"the human being struggles with his environment"* (Karl A. Menninger). **b.** To compete with. **5.** To progress or penetrate with difficulty. —*tr.* To move or place (something) with an effort: *struggle a trunk into a car.* —*n.* **1.** An act of struggling. **2.** Strenuous effort. **3.** Combat; strife. [Middle English *struglen*†.] —**strug′gler** *n.* —**strug′gling·ly** *adv.*

strum (strŭm) *v.* **strummed, strumming, strums.** —*tr.* To play idly on or as if on (a stringed musical instrument) by plucking the strings with the fingers. —*intr.* To play an instrument in this manner. —*n.* The act or sound of strumming. [Perhaps blend of STRING and THRUM.] —**strum′mer** *n.*

stru·ma (strōō′mə) *n., pl.* **-mae** (-mē′) or **-mas. 1.** *Pathology.* **a.** **Scrofula** *(see).* **b.** **Goiter** *(see).* **2.** *Botany.* A cushionlike swelling at the base of a moss capsule. [Latin *strūma*†, tumor.] —**stru·mat′ic** (-măt′ĭk), **stru′mose′** (-mōs′), **stru′mous** (-məs) *adj.*

Stru·ma (strōō′mə). *Greek* **Stry·mon** (strī′mən), **Stri·mon.** A river rising in southwestern Bulgaria near Sofia and flowing 215 miles generally southeast through Greece to the Aegean.

strum·pet (strŭm′pĭt) *n.* A whore. [Middle English *strompet*†.]

strung. Past tense and past participle of **string.**

strut (strŭt) *v.* **strutted, strutting, struts.** —*intr.* To walk with pompous bearing; to swagger. —*tr.* To brace with a strut or struts. —*n.* **1.** A stiff, self-important gait. **2.** A bar or rod used to strengthen a framework by resisting longitudinal thrust. [Middle English *strouten*, to swell, stand out, protrude, Old English *strūtian*, to stand out stiffly. See **ster-¹** in Appendix.*] —**strut′ter** *n.* —**strut′ting·ly** *adv.*

stru·thi·ous (strōō′thē-əs, -thē-əs) *adj.* Of, pertaining to, or resembling the ostrich or a related bird. [From Latin *strūthiō*, ostrich, from Greek *strouthion*, from *strouthos*†, sparrow, ostrich. See **trozdos-** in Appendix.*]

Strutt, John William. See Lord **Rayleigh.**

Stru·ve (shtrōō′və), **Friedrich Georg Wilhelm von.** 1793–1864. German-born Russian astronomer; first measured the parallax of Vega; great-grandfather of Otto Struve.

Stru·ve (strōō′vē), **Otto.** 1897–1963. Russian-born American astronomer; discovered interstellar matter.

strych·nine (strĭk′nīn′, -nən, -nēn′) *n.* An extremely poisonous white crystalline alkaloid, $C_{21}H_{22}N_2O_2$, derived from nux vomica and related plants, and used as a poison for rodents and other pests and medicinally as a stimulant for the central nervous system. [French, from New Latin *Strychnos*, genus of plants including nux vomica, from Latin *strychnos*, nightshade, from Greek *strukhnos*†.]

St. Thomas (sānt′ tŏm′əs). **1.** The second-largest (28 square miles) of the Virgin Islands of the United States. Population, 16,000. **2.** The former name for **Charlotte Amalie.**

Stu·art (stōō′ərt, styōō′-). Also **Steu·art, Stew·art.** Family name of rulers of Scotland (1371–1707), England (1603–1707), and Great Britain (1707–14).

Stu·art (stōō′ərt, styōō′-), **Charles Edward.** Called "Bonnie Prince Charlie" and "the Young Pretender." 1720–1788. Pretender to the British throne; son of James Francis Edward Stuart.

Stu·art (stōō′ərt), **Gilbert Charles.** 1755–1828. American portraitist; noted for his portraits of George Washington.

Stu·art (stōō′ərt), **James Ewell Brown ("Jeb").** 1833–1864. American Confederate general in the Civil War.

Stu·art (stōō′ərt, styōō′-), **James Francis Edward.** Called "the Old Pretender." 1688–1766. Pretender to the British throne; son of James II; father of Charles Edward Stuart.

stub (stŭb) *n.* **1. a.** The short blunt end remaining after something has been cut, broken off, or worn down, as the stump of a tree, tooth, or pencil. **b.** A cigar or cigarette butt. **c.** Any article that has been shortened, blunted, or worn down. **2. a.** The counterfoil of a check or receipt. **b.** The part of a ticket returned as a voucher of payment. —*tr.v.* **stubbed, stubbing, stubs. 1.** To pull up (weeds) by the roots. **2.** To clear (a field) of stubs. **3.** To strike (one's toe or foot) against something. **4.** To snuff out (a cigarette butt) by crushing. [Middle English *stubbe*, Old English *stybb, stubb*. See **steu-** in Appendix.*]

stub·ble (stŭb′əl) *n.* **1.** The short, stiff stalks of a grain or hay crop remaining on a field after the crop has been harvested. **2.** Anything resembling stubble. [Middle English *stuble*, from Old French, from Latin *stup(u)la*, variant of *stipula*, straw. See **stipule.**] —**stub′bly** *adj.*

stub·born (stŭb′ərn) *adj.* **1. a.** Unduly determined to exert one's will; refractory. **b.** Not easily persuaded; obstinate. **2.** Characterized by perseverance; persistent. **3.** Difficult to handle or work; resistant: *stubborn soil.* —See Synonyms at **contrary, obstinate.** [Middle English *stoborne*†.]

stub·by (stŭb′ē) *adj.* **-bier, -biest. 1.** Having the nature of a stub; short and stocky. **2.** Covered with or consisting of stubs. **3.** Short and bristly. —**stub′bi·ly** *adv.* —**stub′bi·ness** *n.*

stub nail. A short, thick nail.

stuc·co (stŭk′ō) *n., pl.* **-coes** or **-cos. 1.** A durable finish for exterior walls, applied wet and usually composed of cement, sand, and lime. **2.** A fine plaster for interior wall ornamentation, such as moldings. **3.** Any plaster or cement finish for interior walls. —*tr.v.* **stuccoed, -coing, -coes** or **-cos.** To finish or decorate with stucco. [Italian, from Old High German *stukki*, fragment, crust, covering. See **steu-** in Appendix.*] —**stuc′co·er** *n.*

stuck. Past tense and past participle of **stick.**

stuck-up (stŭk′ŭp′) *adj. Informal.* Snobbish; conceited.

stud¹ (stŭd) *n.* **1.** An upright post in the framework of a wall for supporting sheets of lath, wallboard, or the like. **2.** A small knob, nail head, rivet, or the like fixed in and slightly projecting from a surface. **3. a.** A small ornamental button mounted on a short post for insertion through an eyelet, as on a dress shirt. **b.** A buttonlike earring. **4.** Any of various protruding pins or pegs in machinery. **5.** A metal crosspiece used as a brace in a link, as in a chain cable. —*tr.v.* **studded, studding, studs. 1.** To provide with or construct with a stud or studs. **2.** To set with a stud or studs; fix a stud in: *stud a bracelet with rubies.* **3.** To be dotted about on, especially ornamentally; strew: *Daisies studded* *the meadow.* [Middle English *stode,* post, prop, Old English *studu, stuthu.* See **stā-** in Appendix.*]

stud[2] (stŭd) *n.* **1. a.** A group of animals, especially horses, kept for breeding. **b.** A stable or farm where they are kept. **2.** A stallion or other male animal kept for breeding. **3.** Stud poker. **—at** (or **in**) **stud.** Available or offered for breeding. *—adj.* **1.** Of or pertaining to a stud or studs. **2.** Kept for breeding. [Middle English *stod,* Old English *stōd,* stable for breeding. See **stā-** in Appendix.*]

stud. student.

stud·book (stŭd′bo͝ok′) *n.* A book registering the pedigrees of thoroughbred animals, especially of horses.

stud·ding (stŭd′ĭng) *n.* **1. a.** The wood framework of a wall or partition. **b.** Lumber cut for studs. **2.** That with which a surface is studded.

stud·ding·sail (stŭn′səl) *n. Nautical.* A narrow rectangular sail set from extensions of the yards of square-rigged ships. [Perhaps from Middle Low German and Middle Dutch *stōtinge,* a thrusting, from *stōten,* to force. See **steu-** in Appendix.*]

stu·dent (sto͞od′ənt, styo͞o′-) *n. Abbr.* **stud. 1.** One who attends a school, college, or university. **2.** One who makes a study of something. [Middle English, from Latin *studēns,* present participle of *studēre,* to study, be diligent. See **steu-** in Appendix.*]

student teacher. A college student who practices teaching under supervision.

stud·fish (stŭd′fĭsh′) *n., pl.* **studfish** or **-fishes.** Either of two small, brightly colored freshwater fishes, *Fundulus catenatus* or *F. stellifer,* of the southeastern United States. [Perhaps from STUD (post).]

stud·horse (stŭd′hôrs′) *n.* Also **stud horse.** A stallion.

stud·ied (stŭd′ēd) *adj.* **1. a.** Carefully contrived; deliberate; calculated: *a studied effect.* **b.** Lacking spontaneity: *a studied smile.* **2.** *Rare.* Learned. **—stud′ied·ly** *adv.* **—stud′ied·ness** *n.*

stu·di·o (sto͞o′dē-ō, styo͞o′-) *n., pl.* **-os. 1.** An artist's workroom. **2.** A photographer's establishment. **3.** An establishment where an art is taught or studied: *a dance studio.* **4.** A room or building for motion-picture, television, or radio productions. [Italian, from Latin *studium,* STUDY.]

studio couch. A couch that can serve as a bed.

stu·di·ous (sto͞o′dē-əs, styo͞o′-) *adj.* **1.** Devoted to study. **2.** Earnest; diligent. **3.** Giving or evincing careful attention; heedful: *"the major . . . was very studious of his appearance"* (H.E. Bates). **4.** *Rare.* Deliberate. **5.** Conducive to study. [Middle English, from Latin *studiōsus,* from *studium,* STUDY.] **—stu′di·ous·ly** *adv.* **—stu′di·ous·ness** *n.*

stud poker. Poker in which the first round of cards (and often the last) is dealt face down and the others face up. [From STUD (breeding).]

stud·work (stŭd′wûrk′) *n.* **1.** Work ornamented or covered with studs. **2.** The supportive framework of a wall or partition.

stud·y (stŭd′ē) *n., pl.* **-ies. 1.** The act or process of studying; the pursuit of knowledge, as by reading, observation, or research. **2.** Attentive scrutiny. **3.** A branch of knowledge. **4.** *Plural.* A branch or department of learning; something to be studied: *graduate studies.* **5. a.** A work resulting from studious endeavor, as a monograph or thesis. **b.** A literary work on a particular subject. **c.** A preliminary sketch, as for a work of art. **6.** A musical composition designed as a technical exercise; an étude. **7.** A state of mental absorption: *He's in a deep study.* **8.** A room intended or equipped for studying. **9. a.** One who memorizes something; especially, an actor with reference to his ability to memorize a part. **b.** The memorizing of a part in a play. *—v.* **studied, -ying, -ies.** *—tr.* **1.** To apply one's mind purposefully to the acquisition of knowledge or understanding of (any subject): *study a language.* **2.** To read carefully: *study a book.* **3.** To memorize. **4.** To take (a course) at a school. **5.** To inquire into; investigate: *study the mood of the country.* **6.** To examine closely; scrutinize: *study a diagram.* **7.** To give careful thought to; contemplate: *study the next move.* *—intr.* **1.** To apply oneself to learning, especially by reading. **2.** To pursue a course of study. **3.** To ponder; reflect; meditate. [Middle English *studie,* from Old French *estudie,* from Latin *studium,* from *studēre,* to be eager, study. See **steu-** in Appendix.*]

study hall. 1. A schoolroom reserved for study. **2.** A period set aside for study.

stuff (stŭf) *n.* **1.** The material out of which something is made or formed; substance. **2.** The basic substance or essential elements of anything; essence: *the stuff heroes are made of.* **3.** Material not specifically identified. **4.** *Informal.* Household or personal articles collectively; belongings. **5.** Worthless objects; refuse or junk. **6.** Foolish or empty words or ideas. Used to express impatience or derision in the interjection *stuff and nonsense.* **7.** *British.* Woven material; especially, woolens. **8.** *Slang.* Money; cash. *—v.* **stuffed, stuffing, stuffs.** *—tr.* **1. a.** To pack tightly; fill up; cram: *stuff a Christmas stocking.* **b.** To block (a passage); obstruct. **2. a.** To fill with an appropriate stuffing: *stuff a pillow; stuff a cabbage.* **b.** To fill (an animal skin) to restore its natural form. **3.** To cram with food. **4.** To fill (the mind). Often used derogatorily: *His head is stuffed with silly notions.* **5.** To put fraudulent votes into (a ballot box). **6.** To apply a preservative and softening agent to (leather). *—intr.* To overeat; gorge. [Middle English *stuff(e),* from Old French *estoffe,* provisions, from *estoffer,* to cram, pad, from Germanic *stopfōn* (unattested), from Late Latin *stuppāre,* to plug up, from Latin *stuppa,* plug, cork, from Greek *stuppē.* See **stewə-** in Appendix.*] **—stuff′er** *n.*

stuffed derma. Derma *(see).*

stuffed shirt. *Informal.* A stiff, pompous person.

stuff·ing (stŭf′ĭng) *n.* Material used to stuff or fill, especially. **a.** Padding put in cushions and upholstered furniture. **b.** Food put in the cavity of meat or vegetables.

stuffing box. An enclosure containing packing to prevent leakage around a moving machine part.

stuff·y (stŭf′ē) *adj.* **-ier, -iest. 1.** Lacking sufficient ventilation; airless; close. **2.** Having the respiratory passages blocked. **3.** *Informal.* **a.** Dull: *a stuffy dinner party.* **b.** Formal; strait-laced. **—stuff′i·ly** *adv.* **—stuff′i·ness** *n.*

stull (stŭl) *n.* **1.** A timber or other prop supporting the roof of a mine opening. **2.** A platform braced against the sides of a working area in a mine. [Perhaps from German *Stollen,* a prop, from Old High German *stollo.* See **stel-**[3] in Appendix.*]

stul·ti·fy (stŭl′tə-fī′) *tr.v.* **-fied, -fying, -fies. 1.** To render useless or ineffectual; cripple. **2.** To cause to appear stupid, inconsistent, or ridiculous. **3.** *Law.* To allege or prove insane and so not legally responsible. [Late Latin *stultificāre* : Latin *stultus,* foolish (see **stel-**[1] in Appendix*) + *facere,* to make (see **dhē-**[1] in Appendix*).] **—stul′ti·fi·ca′tion** *n.* **—stul′ti·fi′er** *n.*

stum (stŭm) *n.* **1.** Unfermented or partly fermented grape juice; must. **2.** Vapid wine renewed by an admixture of stum. *—tr.v.* **stummed, stumming, stums.** To ferment (vapid wine) by adding stum. [Dutch, from *stom,* unfermented, dumb, mute, translation of French *(vin) muet,* "mute (wine)," from Middle Dutch. See **stam-** in Appendix.*]

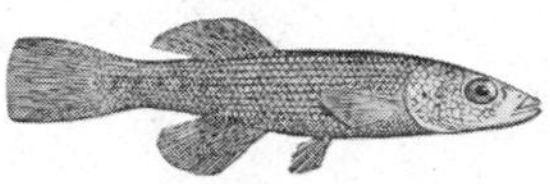
studfish
Fundulus catenatus

stum·ble (stŭm′bəl) *v.* **-bled, -bling, -bles.** *—intr.* **1. a.** To miss one's step in walking or running; to trip and almost fall. **b.** To proceed unsteadily or falteringly; to flounder. **c.** To act or speak falteringly or clumsily. **2.** To make a mistake; to blunder. **3.** To fall into evil ways; err. **4.** To come upon accidentally or unexpectedly: *"The urge to wider voyages . . . caused men to stumble upon new America"* (Kenneth Cragg). *—tr.* To cause to stumble. *—n.* **1.** The act of stumbling. **2.** A mistake, blunder, or sin. [Middle English *stumblen,* perhaps from Old Norse *stumla* (unattested). See **stam-** in Appendix.*] **—stum′bler** *n.* **—stum′bling·ly** *adv.*

stum·ble·bum (stŭm′bəl-bŭm′) *n. Slang.* **1.** A punch-drunk or second-rate prize fighter. **2.** A blundering or inept person.

stumbling block. An obstacle or impediment.

stump (stŭmp) *n.* **1.** The part of a tree trunk left protruding from the ground after the tree has fallen or been felled. **2.** Any part, as of a branch, limb, or tooth, remaining after the main part has been cut away, broken off, or worn down. **3. a.** *Plural. Informal.* The legs. **b.** An artificial leg. **4.** A short, thickset person. **5.** A heavy footfall. **6.** A platform or other place used for political or campaign oratory. **7.** A short, pointed roll of leather or paper or wad of rubber for rubbing on a charcoal or pencil drawing to shade or soften it. **8.** In cricket, any one of the three upright sticks in a wicket. **—be up a stump.** To be in a quandary. *—tr.v.* **stumped, stumping, stumps. 1.** To reduce to a stump; lop; truncate. **2.** To clear stumps from: *stump a field.* **3.** To stub (a toe or foot). **4.** To traverse (a district) making political speeches. **5.** To shade (a drawing) with a stump. **6.** *Informal.* To challenge (someone); defy; dare. **7.** *Informal.* To bring to a halt; perplex; baffle. [Middle English *stumpe,* from Middle Low German *stump.* See **stebh-** in Appendix.*] **—stump′er** *n.* **—stump′i·ness** *n.* **—stump′y** *adj.*

stump·age (stŭm′pĭj) *n.* **1.** Standing timber regarded as a commodity. **2.** The value of standing timber. **3.** The right to cut such timber.

stun (stŭn) *tr.v.* **stunned, stunning, stuns. 1.** To daze or render senseless, as by a blow. **2.** To overwhelm or daze with a loud noise. **3.** To stupefy, as with the emotional impact of an experience; astound; overwhelm. *—n.* A blow or shock that stupefies. [Middle English *stonen,* from Old French *estoner,* from Vulgar Latin *extonāre* (unattested) : Latin *ex-* (intensive) + *tonāre,* to thunder (see **stenə-** in Appendix*).]

stung. Past tense and past participle of **sting.**

stunk. Past participle and alternate past tense of **stink.**

stun·ner (stŭn′ər) *n.* **1.** One that stuns. **2.** *Informal.* An exceptionally good-looking person.

stun·ning (stŭn′ĭng) *adj.* **1.** Causing or capable of causing loss of consciousness or emotional shock. **2.** *Informal.* Of a strikingly attractive appearance. **—stun′ning·ly** *adv.*

stunt[1] (stŭnt) *tr.v.* **stunted, stunting, stunts. 1.** To check the growth or development of. **2.** To check (growth or development). *—n.* **1.** One that stunts. **2.** One that is stunted. **3.** A plant disease that causes dwarfing. [Perhaps from Middle English *stont,* short in duration (but influenced in sense by Old Norse cognate *stuttr,* short, dwarfish), Old English *stunt,* dull, half-witted. See **steu-** in Appendix.*] **—stunt′ed·ness** *n.*

stunt[2] (stŭnt) *n.* **1.** A feat displaying unusual strength, skill, or daring. **2.** Something of an unusual nature done for publicity. *—intr.v.* **stunted, stunting, stunts.** To perform a stunt or stunts. [Origin unknown.]

stunt man. In motion-picture production, one who substitutes for an actor in scenes requiring physical prowess or involving physical risk.

stu·pa (sto͞o′pə) *n.* A shrine, **tope** *(see).* [Sanskrit *stūpa,* "tuft of hair," "crown of head." See **stewə-** in Appendix.*]

stupe (sto͞op, styo͞op) *n.* A hot medicated compress. [Middle English, from Latin *stuppa,* tow, plug, from Greek *stuppē.* See **stewə-** in Appendix.*]

stu·pe·fa·cient (sto͞o′pə-fā′shənt, styo͞o′-) *adj.* Also **stu·pe·fac·tive** (-făk′tĭv). Inducing stupor; stupefying. *—n.* A drug that induces stupor, as a narcotic. [Latin *stupefaciēns,* present participle of *stupefacere,* STUPEFY.]

stu·pe·fac·tion (sto͞o′pə-făk′shən, styo͞o′-) *n.* **1.** The act of stupefying. **2.** The state of being stupefied. **3.** Great astonishment or consternation.

stu·pe·fy (sto͞o′pə-fī′, styo͞o′-) *tr.v.* **-fied, -fying, -fies. 1.** To dull the senses of; put into a stupor. **2.** To amaze; astonish. [Old French *stupefier*, from Latin *stupefacere* : *stupēre*, to be stunned (see **steu-** in Appendix*) + *facere*, to make (see **dhē-**[1] in Appendix*).] —**stu′pe·fi′er** *n.*

stu·pen·dous (sto͞o-pĕn′dəs, styo͞o-) *adj.* **1.** Of astounding force, volume, degree, or excellence; amazing; marvelous. **2.** Of tremendous size; huge; immense. —See Synonyms at **enormous.** [Latin *stupendus*, from *stupēre*, to be stunned. See **steu-** in Appendix.*] —**stu·pen′dous·ly** *adv.* —**stu·pen′dous·ness** *n.*

stu·pid (sto͞o′pĭd, styo͞o′-) *adj.* **-pider, -pidest. 1.** In a stupor; stupefied. **2.** Slow to apprehend; dull; obtuse. **3.** Showing a lack of sense or intelligence. **4.** *Informal.* Uninteresting; trite or dull: *a stupid job.* —*n. Informal.* A stupid person. [French *stupide*, from Latin *stupidus*, from *stupēre*, to be stunned. See **steu-** in Appendix.*] —**stu′pid·ly** *adv.* —**stu′pid·ness** *n.*

Synonyms: *slow, dumb, stupid, dull, obtuse, dense, crass.* These adjectives mean lacking in mental acuity. *Slow* and the informal *dumb* imply chronic sluggishness of perception or understanding; *stupid* and *dull* occasionally suggest a mere temporary state. *Stupid* and *dumb* also can refer to individual actions that are extremely foolish. *Obtuse* implies insensitivity or unreceptiveness to instruction. *Dense* suggests a mind that is virtually impenetrable or incapable of grasping even elementary ideas. *Crass* refers especially to stupidity marked by coarseness or tastelessness.

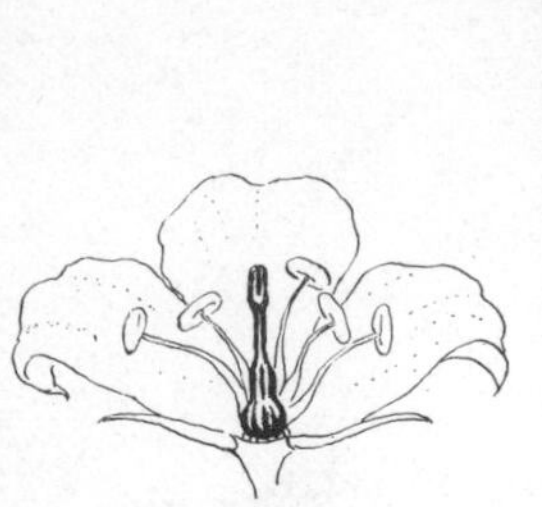

style

stu·pid·i·ty (sto͞o-pĭd′ə-tē, styo͞o-) *n., pl.* **-ties. 1.** The quality or fact of being stupid: *"the elegant stupidity of private parties"* (Jane Austen). **2.** A stupid act, remark, or idea.

stu·por (sto͞o′pər, styo͞o′-) *n.* **1.** A state of reduced sensibility; lethargy; torpor. **2.** Mental confusion; daze. —See Synonyms at **lethargy.** [Middle English, from Latin, from *stupēre*, to be stunned. See **stupid.**] —**stu′por·ous** *adj.*

stur·dy[1] (stûr′dē) *adj.* **-dier, -diest. 1.** Substantially built; durable; strong. **2.** Stalwart; robust. **3.** Vigorous or lusty: *"We admire Chaucer for his sturdy English wit"* (Thoreau). —See Synonyms at **strong.** [Middle English, giddy, rash, impetuous, from Old French *estourdi*, past participle of *estourir*, to stun, daze, from Vulgar Latin *exturdīre* (unattested), probably "to be stunned like a thrush drunk with grapes" : perhaps Latin *ex-*, completely + *turdus*, thrush (see **trozdos-** in Appendix*).] —**stur′di·ly** *adv.* —**stur′di·ness** *n.*

stur·dy[2] (stûr′dē) *n.* A disease of sheep, **gid** *(see).* [From STURDY (in earlier sense "giddy").] —**stur′died** *adj.*

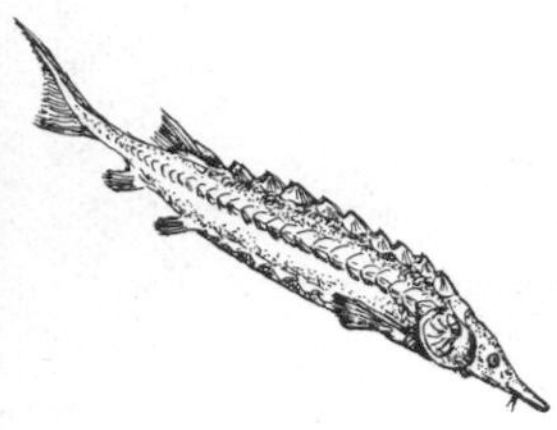

sturgeon
Acipenser oxyrhynchus

stur·geon (stûr′jən) *n.* Any of various large freshwater and marine fishes of the family Acipenseridae, of the Northern Hemisphere, having edible flesh and roe valued as a source of caviar. [Middle English, from Norman French, from Vulgar Latin *sturiō* (unattested), from Germanic *sturjōn* (unattested). See also **sterlet.**]

Stur·gis (stûr′jĭs), **Russell.** 1836–1909. American architect, author, and editor.

Sturm·ab·teil·ung (shto͝orm′äp′tī′lo͝ongk) *n., pl.* **-teilungen** (-lo͝ong-ən). *Abbr.* **S.A.** A Nazi German militia organized about 1924 and notorious for its violent and terroristic methods. Also called "Brown Shirts," "storm troopers." [German, "storm division."]

Sturm und Drang (shto͝orm′ o͝ont dräng′). A German romantic literary movement of the late 18th century, the works of which typically depicted the impulsive man struggling against conventional society. [German, "storm and stress," originally the title of a romantic play (1776) by Friedrich Maximilian von Klinger (1752–1831), German poet and dramatist.]

stut·ter (stŭt′ər) *v.* **-tered, -tering, -ters.** —*intr.* To speak with a spasmodic hesitation, prolongation, or repetition of sounds. —*tr.* To utter or say with or as if with a stutter. —See Synonyms at **stammer.** —*n.* The act or habit of stuttering. [Frequentative of obsolete *stut*, from Middle English *stutten*, perhaps of Low German origin, akin to Middle Low German *stōtern*, to stutter. See **steu-** in Appendix.*] —**stut′ter·er** *n.* —**stut′ter·ing·ly** *adv.*

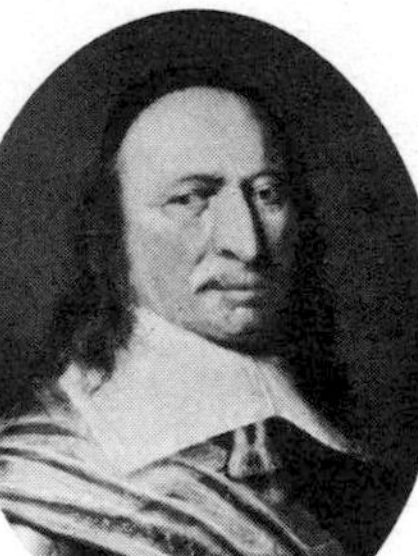

Peter Stuyvesant
Contemporary portrait by an unknown artist

Stutt·gart (stŭt′gärt; *German* shto͝ot′gärt). The capital of Baden-Württemberg, West Germany, on the Neckar in the central part of the state. Population, 632,000.

Stuy·ve·sant (stī′və-sənt), **Peter.** Originally, Petrus. 1592–1672. Dutch colonial administrator; director-general of New Netherlands (1646–64).

St. Vincent (sānt′ vĭn′sənt). An island, 133 square miles in area, in the West Indies; a former British colony, with internal self-government as one of the West Indies Associated States since 1968. Population, 80,000. Capital, Kingstown.

St. Vincent, Cape (sānt′ vĭn′sənt). The southwestern extremity of Portugal and of continental Europe.

St. Vi·tus' dance (sānt′ vī′təs-ĭz). Also **St. Vitus's dance.** *Pathology.* **Chorea** *(see).* [After St. *Vitus*, third-century Christian child martyr, venerated by sufferers of the disease.]

sty[1] (stī) *n., pl.* **sties. 1.** An enclosure for swine. **2.** Any filthy place. —*v.* **stied, stying, sties.** —*tr.* To shut up in a sty. —*intr.* To live in a sty. [Middle English *sty*, Old English *stī*, *stig*, from Germanic *stijam* (unattested).]

sty[2] (stī) *n., pl.* **sties** or **styes.** Inflammation of one or more sebaceous glands of an eyelid. [Obsolete *styany* (taken as *sty-on-eye*), Middle English *styanye* : *styan* (unattested), sty, "swelling," from Old English *stīgend*, present participle of *stīgan*, to rise (see **steigh-** in Appendix*) + EYE.]

Styg·i·an (stĭj′ē-ən) *adj.* Also **Styg·i·an.** **1.** Of or pertaining to the river Styx. **2. a.** Gloomy and dark. **b.** Infernal; hellish. **3.** Inviolable. [Latin *Stygius*, from Greek *Stugios*, from *Stux*, Styx. See **steu-** in Appendix.*]

sty·lar (stī′lər) *adj.* **1.** Of, pertaining to, or resembling a stylus. **2.** *Biology.* Of or pertaining to a style.

sty·late (stī′lāt′) *n. Biology.* Having a style or styles.

style (stīl) *n.* **1.** The way in which something is said or done, as distinguished from its substance. **2.** The combination of distinctive features of literary or artistic expression, execution, or performance characterizing a particular person, people, school, or era. **3.** Sort; kind; type: *a style of furniture.* **4.** A quality of imagination and individuality expressed in one's actions and tastes. **5. a.** A comfortable and elegant mode of existence: *living in style.* **b.** A particular mode of living: *the style of a gentleman.* **6. a.** The fashion of the moment, especially of dress; vogue: *out of* (or *in*) *style.* **b.** A particular fashion. **7.** A customary manner of presenting printed material, including usage, punctuation, spelling, typography, and arrangement. **8.** *Rare.* A name, title, or descriptive term. **9.** A slender, pointed writing instrument used by the ancients on wax tablets. **10.** An implement used for etching or engraving. **11.** The needle of a phonograph. **12.** The gnomon of a sundial. **13.** *Botany.* The usually slender part of a pistil, rising from the ovary and tipped by the stigma. **14.** *Zoology.* Any slender, tubular, or bristlelike process. **15.** *Obsolete.* A pen. **16.** A surgical probing instrument; stylet. —See Synonyms at **fashion.** —*tr.v.* **styled, styling, styles. 1.** To call or name; designate: *"whatever is mine, you may style, and think, yours"* (Sterne). **2.** To make consistent with rules of style. **3.** To design; give style to: *style hair.* [Middle English, from Old French, from Latin *stilus*†, writing instrument, style.] —**styl′er** *n.*

style book. A book giving rules and examples of usage, punctuation, and typography, used in the preparation of copy for publication.

sty·let (stī′lĭt) *n.* **1.** A slender, pointed instrument or weapon, such as a stiletto. **2.** A surgical probe; style. **3.** *Zoology.* A small, stiff, needlelike process in some invertebrates. [French, from Italian *stiletto*, STILETTO.]

sty·li·form (stī′lə-fôrm′) *adj.* Having the shape of a style; bristlelike. [*Stylis*, variant of STYLO- + -FORM.]

styl·ish (stī′lĭsh) *adj.* In step with current fashion; modish. —**styl′ish·ly** *adv.* —**styl′ish·ness** *n.*

styl·ist (stī′lĭst) *n.* **1.** A writer or speaker who cultivates an artful literary style. **2.** A designer of or consultant on styles in decorating, dress, or beauty.

sty·lis·tic (stī-lĭs′tĭk) *adj.* Of or relating to style, especially literary style. —**sty·lis′ti·cal·ly** *adv.*

sty·lite (stī′līt′) *n.* One of a number of early Christian ascetics who lived unsheltered on the tops of high pillars. [Late Greek *stulitēs* : Greek *stulos*, pillar (see **stā-** in Appendix*) + -ITE.] —**sty·lit′ic** (-lĭt′ĭk) *adj.* —**sty′lit′ism′** (stī′lĭt′ĭz′əm) *n.*

styl·ize (stī′līz′) *tr.v.* **-ized, -izing, -izes. 1.** To subordinate verisimilitude to principles of design in the representation of. **2.** To represent conventionally; conventionalize: *"An air of fastidious, stylized melancholy"* (Elizabeth Bowen). —**styl′i·za′tion** *n.* —**styl′iz′er** *n.*

stylo–. Indicates: **1.** *Biology.* A style; for example, **stylopodium. 2.** A point or styloid process; for example, **stylograph.** [From Latin *stilus*, stalk, STYLE.]

sty·lo·bate (stī′lə-bāt′) *n. Classical Architecture.* The immediate foundation of a row of columns. See **stereobate.** [Latin *stylobata*, from Greek *stulobatēs*, column base : *stulos*, column (see **stā-** in Appendix*) + *-bates*, "one that is based" (see **gwā-** in Appendix*).]

sty·lo·graph (stī′lə-grăf′, -gräf′) *n.* A fountain pen having a tubular writing point instead of a nib. Also called "stylographic pen." [STYLO- + -GRAPH.]

sty·log·ra·phy (stī-lŏg′rə-fē) *n.* The art or a method of etching, engraving, or writing with a style. [STYLO- + -GRAPHY.] —**sty′lo·graph′ic** (-lə-grăf′ĭk), **sty′lo·graph′i·cal** *adj.*

sty·loid (stī′loid′) *adj.* Slender and pointed. [New Latin *styloides*, resembling a style (after Greek *styloeidēs*, pillarlike) : STYL(O)- + -OID.]

sty·lo·lite (stī′lə-līt′) *n.* A small columnar rock development in limestone and other calcareous rocks that is at right angles to the bed, is of irregular cross-section, and has striated sides. [Greek *stulos*, pillar (see **stylite**) + -LITE.]

sty·lo·po·di·um (stī′lə-pō′dē-əm) *n., pl.* **-dia** (-dē-ə). *Botany.* An enlargement at the base of the style of certain flowers. [New Latin : STYLO- + -PODIUM.]

sty·lus (stī′ləs) *n., pl.* **-luses** or **-li** (-lī′). **1.** A sharp, pointed instrument used for writing, marking, or engraving. **2.** A phonograph needle. **3.** The sharp, pointed tool used for cutting record grooves. [Latin *stilus*, STYLE.]

sty·mie (stī′mē) *n.* Also **sty·my. 1.** A golfing situation in which an opponent's ball obstructs the line of play of one's own ball on the putting green. **2.** An impasse; quandary. —*tr.v.* **stymied, -mieing** or **-mying, -mies.** Also **sty·my, -mied, -mying, -mies.** To block; thwart. [Origin unknown.]

styp·sis (stĭp′sĭs) *n.* The action or application of a styptic. [Late Latin *stypsis*, from Greek *stupsis*, contraction, astringency, from *stuphein*, to contract. See **styptic.**]

styp·tic (stĭp′tĭk) *adj.* Also **styp·ti·cal** (-tĭ-kəl). **1.** Contracting the tissues or blood vessels; astringent. **2.** Tending to check bleeding; hemostatic. —*n.* A styptic drug or substance. [Middle English *stiptik*, from Late Latin *stypticus*, from Greek *stuptikos*, from *stuphein*, to contract. See **stewe-** in Appendix.*] —**styp′tic′i·ty** (-tĭs′ə-tē) *n.*

sty·rax (stī′răks) *n.* A resin, **storax** *(see).*

sty·rene (stī′rēn′) *n.* A colorless oily liquid, C_8H_8, the monomer for **polystyrene** *(see).* [Latin *styrax*, *storax*, STORAX (from which styrene is obtained by distillation) + -ENE.]

ă pat/ā pay/âr care/ä father/b bib/ch church/d deed/ĕ pet/ē be/f fife/g gag/h hat/hw which/ĭ pit/ī pie/îr pier/j judge/k kick/l lid, needle/m mum/n no, sudden/ng thing/ŏ pot/ō toe/ô paw, for/oi noise/ou out/o͝o took/o͞o boot/p pop/r roar/s sauce/sh ship, dish/

Styr·i·a (stîr′ē-ə). *German* **Stei·er·mark** (shtī′ər-märk). A province of Austria, occupying 6,326 square miles in the southeast. Population, 1,138,000. Capital, Graz.

Sty·ro·foam (stī′rə-fōm′) *n.* A trademark for a light, resilient polystyrene plastic. [Probably STYR(ENE) + FOAM.]

Styx (stĭks) *n. Greek Mythology.* One of the rivers of Hades, across which Charon ferried the souls of the dead. [Latin, from Greek *stux*. See **steu-** in Appendix.*]

su·a·ble (sōō′ə-bəl) *adj.* Legally subject to a court suit; capable of being sued. —**su′a·bil′i·ty** *n.*

sua·sion (swā′zhən) *n.* Persuasion. Used chiefly in the phrase *moral suasion.* [Middle English, from Latin *suāsiō*, from *suādēre* (past participle *suāsus*), to persuade. See **swād-** in Appendix.*] —**sua′sive** (-sĭv) *adj.*

suave (swäv, swāv) *adj.* Smoothly gracious in social manner; urbane. [Old French *soef, suave,* earlier *souef,* from Latin *suāvis,* delightful. See **swād-** in Appendix.*] —**suave′ly** *adv.* —**suav′i·ty, suave′ness** *n.*

Synonyms: *suave, smooth, urbane, diplomatic, politic.* These adjectives refer to a controlled or refined manner. *Suave* suggests a polished exterior and outward sophistication. *Smooth* stresses conscious, sometimes excessive effort to avoid conflict with others. *Urbane* implies a high degree of refinement together with the assurance that comes from wide social experience. *Diplomatic* especially suggests tact in handling difficult situations, and *politic* adds to this the implication of artful management, sagacity, or shrewdness in gaining an end.

sub[1] (sŭb) *n. Informal.* **1.** A submarine. **2.** A substitute. —*intr.v.* **subbed, subbing, subs.** To act as a substitute.

sub[2] (sŭb) *n. Slang.* A sandwich, the **hero** *(see).*

sub-. Indicates: **1.** Under or beneath; for example, **submarine. 2.** Inferior or secondary in rank; for example, **subprincipal. 3.** Somewhat short of or less than; for example, **subhuman, subtropical. 4.** Forming a subordinate or constituent part of a whole; for example, **subdivision, subset.** ***Note:*** Many compounds other than those entered here may be formed with *sub-*. In forming compounds, *sub-* is normally joined with the following element without space or hyphen: *subbasement.* [In borrowed Latin compounds, *sub-* indicates: 1. Under, as in **suppose.** 2. Below, beneath, as in **subaltern.** 3. Down, as in **supplicate.** 4. Up from under, from below, as in **supplant.** 5. Up, toward, as in **support.** 6. Subordinate, as in **subdeacon.** 7. Secretly, as in **suborn.** 8. In place of, as in **substitute.** Before *c, f, g, m, p,* and *r, sub-* becomes, respectively, *suc-, suf-, sug-, sum-, sup-,* and *sur-*. Sometimes it also becomes *sus-* before *c, p,* and *t.* Latin *sub-*, from *sub,* under, from below. See **upo** in Appendix.*]

sub. **1.** *Logic.* subaltern. **2.** subscription. **3.** substitute. **4.** suburb; suburban.

sub·a·cute (sŭb′ə-kyōōt′) *adj.* Somewhat acute. Said of a disease. —**sub′a·cute′ly** *adv.*

sub·aer·i·al (sŭb′âr′ē-əl) *adj.* Located or occurring on or near the surface of the earth.

sub·al·pine (sŭb′ăl′pīn′) *adj.* **1.** Of or pertaining to regions at or near the foot of the Alps. **2.** Of, designating, or growing or living in mountainous regions just below the timber line.

sub·al·tern (sŭb′ôl′tərn; *British* sŭb′əl-tûrn′) *adj.* **1.** Lower in position or rank; secondary. **2.** *Chiefly British.* Holding a military rank just below that of captain. **3.** *Logic.* In the relation of a particular proposition to a universal with the same subject, predicate, and quality. —*n.* **1.** A subordinate. **2.** *Chiefly British.* A subaltern officer. **3.** *Abbr.* **sub.** *Logic.* A subaltern proposition. [Late Latin *subalternus* : Latin *sub-*, below + *alternus,* alternate, from *alter,* other (see **al-**[1] in Appendix*).]

sub·al·ter·nate (sŭb′ôl′tər-nĭt) *adj.* **1.** Subordinate. **2.** Arranged in an alternating pattern but tending to become opposite. Said of leaves. —**sub·al′ter·na′tion** (sə-bôl′tər-nā′shən) *n.*

sub·ant·arc·tic (sŭb′ănt-ärk′tĭk, -ärt′ĭk) *adj.* Of or like regions just north of the Antarctic Circle.

sub·ap·i·cal (sŭb′ăp′ĭ-kəl) *adj.* Located below or near an apex. —**sub′ap′i·cal·ly** *adv.*

sub·a·que·ous (sŭb′ā′kwē-əs, -ăk′wē-əs) *adj.* **1.** Formed or adapted for underwater use or operation; submarine. **2.** Found or occurring under water.

sub·arc·tic (sŭb′ärk′tĭk, -ärt′ĭk) *adj.* Of or like regions just south of the Arctic Circle.

sub·ar·id (sŭb′ăr′ĭd) *adj.* Somewhat arid; moderately dry.

sub·a·tom·ic (sŭb′ə-tŏm′ĭk) *adj.* **1.** Of or pertaining to the constituents of the atom. **2.** Having dimensions or participating in reactions characteristic of these constituents.

sub·au·di·tion (sŭb′ô-dĭsh′ən) *n.* **1.** The act of understanding and mentally supplying a word or thought that has been implied but not expressed. **2.** A word or thought thus supplied. [Late Latin *subaudītiō,* from *subaudīre,* to supply an omitted word : *sub-*, secretly + *audīre,* to hear (see **aw-**[2] in Appendix*).]

sub·base (sŭb′bās′) *n. Architecture.* The lowermost front strip or molding of a baseboard.

sub·base·ment (sŭb′bās′mənt) *n.* Any story or floor beneath the main basement of a building.

sub·bass, sub·base (sŭb′bās′) *n. Music.* A pedal stop on an organ that produces the lowest tones, having 16 or 32 feet.

sub·cal·i·ber (sŭb′kăl′ə-bər) *adj.* **1.** Smaller in caliber than the barrel of the gun from which it was fired. Said of projectiles. **2.** Of or pertaining to such projectiles.

sub·car·ti·lag·i·nous (sŭb′kär′tə-lăj′ə-nəs) *adj.* **1.** Located beneath a cartilage. **2.** Partly cartilaginous.

sub·ce·les·tial (sŭb′sĭ-lĕs′chəl) *adj.* **1.** Lower than celestial; terrestrial. **2.** Mundane.

sub·chas·er (sŭb′chā′sər) *n. Naval.* A submarine chaser.

sub·class (sŭb′klăs′, -kläs′) *n.* **1.** A subdivision of a class. **2.** A taxonomic category ranking between a class and an order.

sub·cla·vi·an (sŭb′klā′vē-ən) *adj. Anatomy.* **1.** Situated beneath the clavicle. **2.** Of or relating to a subclavian part. **3.** Of or pertaining to the subclavian artery or vein. —*n.* A subclavian structure, such as a vein, nerve, or muscle. [From New Latin *subclavius* : SUB- + Latin *clāvis,* key (see **clavicle**).]

subclavian artery. A short part of a major artery originating under the clavicle and continuous with the axillary artery extending to the upper extremities or forelimbs.

subclavian vein. A part of a major vein of the upper extremities or forelimbs that is continuous with the axillary vein and is situated beneath the clavicle.

sub·cli·max (sŭb′klī′măks′) *n.* A stage in the ecological succession of a plant or animal community immediately preceding a climax, and often persisting because of the effects of fire, flood, or other conditions. —**sub′cli·mac′tic** (-klī-măk′tĭk) *adj.*

sub·com·mit·tee (sŭb′kə-mĭt′ē) *n.* A subordinate committee composed of members appointed from the main committee.

sub·con·scious (sŭb′kŏn′shəs) *adj.* Not wholly conscious but capable of being made conscious. —**sub′con′scious·ly** *adv.* —**sub′con′scious·ness** *n.*

sub·con·ti·nent (sŭb′kŏn′tə-nənt) *n.* A large land mass on a continent, but in some geographical respect independent of it, as India or southern Africa.

sub·con·tract (sŭb′kŏn′trăkt′) *n.* A contract that assigns some of the obligations of a prior contract to another party. —*v.* (sŭb′kŏn′trăkt′, sŭb′kən-trăkt′) **subcontracted, -tracting, -tracts.** —*tr.* To make a subcontract for. —*intr.* To make a subcontract.

sub·con·trac·tor (sŭb′kən-trăk′tər, sŭb′kŏn′trăk′tər) *n.* A person who enters into a subcontract and assumes some of the obligations of the primary contractor.

sub·cor·tex (sŭb′kôr′tĕks) *n., pl.* **-tices** (-tə-sēz′). The portion of the brain immediately below the cerebral cortex. —**sub′cor′ti·cal** (-tĭ-kəl) *adj.* —**sub′cor′ti·cal·ly** *adv.*

sub·cul·ture (sŭb′kŭl′chər) *n.* **1.** One culture of microorganisms derived from another. **2.** A cultural subgroup, especially of a nation, differentiated by status, ethnic background, residence, religion, or other factors that functionally unify the group and act collectively on each member.

sub·cu·ta·ne·ous (sŭb′kyōō-tā′nē-əs) *adj.* Located or found just beneath the skin. —**sub′cu·ta′ne·ous·ly** *adv.*

sub·dea·con (sŭb′dē′kən) *n.* **1.** A clergyman with rank just below that of deacon. **2.** A cleric who acts as assistant to the deacon at High Mass. [Middle English *subde(a)con,* from Late Latin *subdiaconus,* partial translation of Late Greek *hupodiakonos* : Greek *hupo-*, below, subordinate + *diakonos,* DEACON.]

sub·deb (sŭb′dĕb′) *n. Informal.* **1.** A subdebutante. **2.** A girl in her middle teens.

sub·deb·u·tante (sŭb′dĕb′yə-tänt′) *n.* **1.** A teen-age girl approaching her debut. **2.** A girl in her middle teens.

sub·di·ac·o·nate (sŭb′dī-ăk′ə-nĭt, -nāt′) *n.* The office, order, or rank of subdeacon. [Late Latin *subdiaconātus,* from *subdiaconus,* SUBDEACON.] —**sub′di·ac′o·nal** *adj.*

sub·di·vide (sŭb′də-vīd′) *v.* **-vided, -viding, -vides.** —*tr.* **1.** To divide a part or parts of into smaller parts. **2.** To divide into a number of parts; especially, to divide (land) into lots. —*intr.* To form into subdivisions. [Middle English *subdividen,* from Late Latin *subdīvidere* : Latin *sub-*, secondary, smaller + *dīvidere,* to DIVIDE.] —**sub′di·vid′er** *n.*

sub·di·vi·sion (sŭb′də-vĭzh′ən) *n.* **1.** The act or process of subdividing. **2.** One of the subdivided parts. **3.** An area composed of subdivided lots. —**sub′di·vi′sion·al** *adj.*

sub·dom·i·nant (sŭb′dŏm′ə-nənt) *n. Music.* The fourth tone of a diatonic scale, next below the dominant. —*adj.* Influential but not quite dominant.

sub·due (səb-dōō′, -dyōō′) *tr.v.* **-dued, -duing, -dues. 1.** To conquer and subjugate; put down; vanquish. **2.** To quiet or bring under control by physical force or persuasion; make tractable. **3.** To make less intense or prominent; tone down: *A vote of approval subdued his anger.* **4.** To bring (land) under cultivation. —See Synonyms at **defeat.** [Middle English *subduen,* from Latin *subdūcere,* to lead away, withdraw (but influenced in sense by Latin *subdere,* to put under, subdue) : *sub-*, from under, away + *dūcere,* to lead (see **deuk-** in Appendix*).] —**sub·du′a·ble** *adj.* —**sub·du′er** *n.*

sub·e·qua·to·ri·al (sŭb′ē-kwə-tôr′ē-əl, -tōr′ē-əl, sŭb′ĕk-wə-) *adj.* Belonging to a region adjacent to the equatorial area.

su·ber·ic acid (sōō-bĕr′ĭk). A colorless crystalline dibasic acid, $C_8H_{14}O_4$, used in drug synthesis and plastics manufacture. [French *subérique,* from Latin *sūber,* cork (from which the acid is obtained), perhaps akin to Greek *suphar*†, wrinkled skin.]

su·ber·in (sōō′bər-ən) *n.* A waxy waterproof substance present in the cell walls of cork tissue in plants. [French *subérine* : Latin *sūber,* cork (see **suberic acid**) + -IN.]

su·ber·i·za·tion (sōō′bər-ĭ-zā′shən) *n. Botany.* Formation of suberin in the walls of plant cells, thus converting them into cork tissue.

su·ber·ize (sōō′bə-rīz′) *tr.v.* **-ized, -izing, -izes.** To cause to undergo suberization. [From Latin *sūber,* cork. See **suberic acid.**]

su·ber·ose (sōō′bə-rōs′) *adj.* Also **su·ber·ous** (-rəs). Of, pertaining to, or resembling cork or cork tissue; corky. [New Latin *sūberosus,* from Latin *sūber,* cork. See **suberic acid.**]

sub·fam·i·ly (sŭb′făm′ə-lē) *n., pl.* **-lies. 1.** *Biology.* A taxonomic category ranking between a family and a genus. **2.** *Linguistics.* A division of languages below a family and above a branch.

sub·ge·nus (sŭb′jē′nəs) *n., pl.* **-genera** (-jĕn′ər-ə). *Biology.* An occasionally used taxonomic category ranking between a genus and a species. —**sub′ge·ner′ic** (-jə-nĕr′ĭk) *adj.*

sub·gla·cial (sŭb′glā′shəl) *adj.* Formed or deposited beneath a glacier. —**sub′gla′cial·ly** *adv.*

sub·group (sŭb′gro͞op′) *n.* **1.** A distinct group within a group. **2.** *Algebra.* A nonempty subset of a group. **3.** A subordinate group. **4.** *Biology.* One of the taxonomic divisions of an order.

sub·head (sŭb′hĕd′) *n.* Also **sub·head·ing** (-ĭng) (for sense 1). **1.** The heading or title of a subdivision of a printed subject. **2.** A subordinate heading or title.

sub·hu·man (sŭb′hyo͞o′mən) *adj.* **1.** Below the human race in evolutionary development. **2.** Not fully human.

Su·bic Bay (so͞o′bĭk). An inlet of the South China Sea, extending about seven miles into west-central Luzon, Republic of the Philippines, north of Bataan.

sub·in·dex (sŭb′ĭn′dĕks) *n., pl.* **-dices** (-də-sēz′). *Mathematics.* A **subscript** *(see).*

sub·in·feu·date (sŭb′ĭn-fyo͞o′dāt′) *tr.v.* **-dated, -dating, -dates.** Also **sub·in·feud** (-fyo͞od′), **-feuded, -feuding, -feuds.** To lease (lands) by subinfeudation.

sub·in·feu·da·tion (sŭb′ĭn-fyo͞o-dā′shən) *n.* **1.** The sublease of a portion of a feudal estate by a vassal to a subtenant who pays fealty to the vassal. **2.** The tenure established. **3.** The lands so leased. —**sub′in·feu′da·to′ry** (-də-tôr′ē, -tōr′ē) *adj.*

sub·ir·ri·gate (sŭb′ĭr′ə-gāt′) *tr.v.* **-gated, -gating, -gates.** To irrigate from beneath, as by means of underground pipes. —**sub′ir·ri·ga′tion** *n.*

su·bi·to (so͞o′bē-tō′) *adv.* Quickly; suddenly. Used as a musical direction. [Italian, from Latin *subitō*, suddenly, from *subire*, to come secretly, steal upon : *sub-*, secretly + *īre*, to go (see **ei-**[1] in Appendix*).]

subj. 1. subject. **2.** subjective. **3.** subjunctive.

sub·ja·cent (sŭb′jā′sənt) *adj.* **1.** Located beneath or below; underlying. **2.** Lying at a lower level but not directly beneath. [Latin *subjacēns*, present participle of *subjacēre*, to lie under : *sub-*, under + *jacēre*, to lie, from *jacere*, to throw (see **yē-** in Appendix*).] —**sub′ja′cen·cy** *n.*

sub·ject (sŭb′jĭkt) *adj.* **1.** Under the power or authority of another; owing obedience or allegiance to another. **2.** Prone; disposed. Used with *to.* **3.** Liable to incur or receive; exposed. Used with *to: subject to misinterpretation.* **4.** Contingent or dependent. Used with *to.* —*n. Abbr.* **subj. 1.** A person under the rule of another; especially, one who owes allegiance to a government or ruler: *a subject of the Crown.* **2. a.** A person or thing concerning which something is said or done; topic. **b.** That which is treated or indicated in a work of art. **3.** A course or area of study. **4.** A basis for action; cause. **5. a.** One that experiences or is subjected to something. **b.** One that is the object of clinical study. **c.** A corpse intended for study and dissection. **6.** *Grammar.* A word or phrase in a sentence that denotes the doer of the action, the receiver of the action in passive constructions, or that which is described or identified. **7.** *Logic.* The term of a proposition about which something is affirmed or denied. **8.** *Philosophy.* **a.** The essential nature or substance of something as distinguished from its attributes. **b.** The mind or thinking part as distinguished from the object of thought. —*tr.v.* (sŭb-jĕkt′) **subjected, -jecting, -jects. 1.** To subjugate; subdue. **2.** To submit for consideration. **3.** To submit to the discipline or authority of; make amenable. **4.** To render liable to something; expose. **5.** To cause to experience or undergo. [Middle English *su(b)get, subject*, from Old French *su(b)get*, from Latin *subicere* (past participle *subjectus*), to bring under : *sub-*, under + *jacere*, to throw (see **yē-** in Appendix*).] —**sub·jec′tion** (-jĕk′shən) *n.*

Synonyms: *subject, matter, topic, theme.* These nouns relate to the principal idea of any discourse or creative work. *Subject* denotes the thing represented, discussed, or otherwise treated. *Matter* refers somewhat less specifically to the material involved in the work. *Topic* is either interchangeable with *subject* or else denotes a division of it. *Theme* is sometimes used in the sense of any of the foregoing terms but often refers specifically to a basic idea that underlies or unifies the material treated and either summarizes or interprets it.

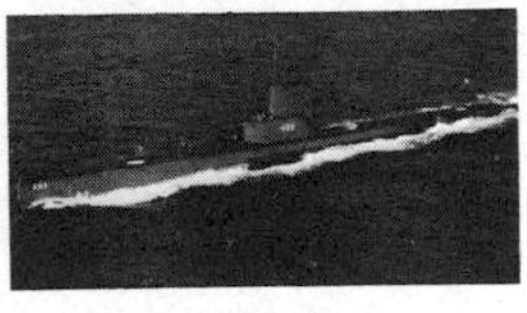

submarine

sub·jec·tive (səb-jĕk′tĭv) *adj. Abbr.* **subj. 1.** Pertaining to the real nature of something; essential. **2. a.** Proceeding from or taking place within an individual's mind such as to be unaffected by the external world. **b.** Particular to a given individual; personal. **3.** Moodily introspective. **4.** Existing only in the mind; illusory. **5.** *Psychology.* Existing only within the experiencer's mind and incapable of external verification. **6.** *Medicine.* Designating a symptom or condition perceived by the patient and not by the examiner. **7.** Expressing or bringing into prominence the individuality of the artist or author. **8.** *Grammar.* Designating the nominative case. —**sub·jec′tive·ly** *adv.* —**sub·jec′tive·ness, sub′jec·tiv′i·ty** *n.*

sub·jec·tiv·ism (səb-jĕk′tə-vĭz′əm) *n.* **1.** The quality of being subjective. **2. a.** The doctrine that all knowledge is restricted to the conscious self and its sensory states. **b.** Any theory or doctrine that emphasizes the subjective elements in experience. **3.** The theory that individual conscience is the only valid standard of moral judgment. —**sub·jec′tiv·ist** *n.* —**sub·jec′tiv·is′tic** *adj.*

subject matter. Matter under consideration in a written work or speech; theme. [Translation of Latin *subjecta materia*, translation of Greek *hupokeimenē hulē*, "underlying matter."]

sub·join (sŭb-join′) *tr.v.* **-joined, -joining, -joins.** To add at the end; append; annex. [Old French *subjoindre*, from Latin *subjungere* : *sub-*, in addition + *jungere*, to join (see **yeug-** in Appendix*).]

sub·join·der (sŭb-join′dər) *n.* Something subjoined. [From SUBJOIN (after REJOINDER).]

sub ju·di·ce (sŭb jo͞o′də-sē′, yo͞o′dē-kā′). *Law.* Under judicial deliberation; before a judge or court of law. [Latin, "under a judge."]

sub·ju·gate (sŭb′jə-gāt′) *tr.v.* **-gated, -gating, -gates. 1.** To bring under dominion; conquer; subdue. **2.** To make subservient; enslave. —See Synonyms at **defeat.** [Middle English *subjugaten*, from Latin *subjugāre*, to place under a yoke : *sub-*, under + *jugum*, yoke (see **yeug-** in Appendix*).] —**sub′ju·ga′tion** *n.* —**sub′ju·ga′tor** (-gā′tər) *n.*

sub·junc·tion (sŭb-jŭngk′shən) *n.* **1.** The act of subjoining or the condition of being subjoined. **2.** Something that is subjoined. [Late Latin *subjunctiō*, from *subjungere* (past participle *subjunctus*), SUBJOIN.]

sub·junc·tive (sŭb-jŭngk′tĭv) *adj. Abbr.* **subj.** Designating a verb form or set of forms used in English to express a contingent or hypothetical action. Compare **indicative.** —*n. Abbr.* **subj. 1.** The subjunctive mood. **2.** A subjunctive construction. [Late Latin *(mōdus) subjunctīvus*, translation of Greek *hupotaktikē enklisis*, "mood of subordination" (originally regarded as proper to subordinate clauses), from Latin *subjungere*, SUBJOIN.]

sub·king·dom (sŭb′kĭng′dəm) *n. Biology.* A former taxonomic category constituting a major division of a kingdom.

sub·lap·sar·i·an·ism (sŭb′lăp-săr′ē-ən-ĭz′əm) *n. Theology.* **Infralapsarianism** *(see).* [From New Latin *sublapsarius* : SUB- + LAPSE.] —**sub′lap·sar′i·an** *adj. & n.*

sub·lease (sŭb′lēs′) *tr.v.* **-leased, -leasing, -leases. 1.** To sublet (property). **2.** To rent (property) under a sublease. —*n.* (sŭb′lēs′). A lease of property granted by a lessee.

sub·let (sŭb′lĕt′) *tr.v.* **-let, -letting, -lets. 1.** To rent (property one holds by lease) to another. **2.** To subcontract (work). —*n. Informal.* Property, especially an apartment, rented by a tenant to another party.

Sub·lette (sŭb′lĕt′), **William Lewis.** 1799?–1845. American fur trader and frontiersman.

sub·li·mate (sŭb′lə-māt′) *v.* **-mated, -mating, -mates.** —*tr.* **1.** *Chemistry.* To cause (a solid or a gas) to change state without becoming a liquid. **2.** *Psychology.* To modify the natural expression of (an instinctual impulse) in a socially acceptable manner. —*intr.* To transform directly from the solid to the gaseous state or from the gaseous to the solid state without becoming a liquid. [Latin *sublīmāre*, to raise, from *sublīmis*, uplifted, SUBLIME.]

sub·li·ma·tion (sŭb′lə-mā′shən) *n.* **1.** The act or process of sublimating. **2.** That which has been sublimated.

sub·lime (sə-blīm′) *adj.* **1.** Characterized by nobility; grand; majestic. **2. a.** Of high spiritual, moral, or intellectual worth. **b.** Not to be excelled; supreme. **3.** Inspiring awe; impressive; moving. **4.** *Poetic.* Of lofty appearance or bearing; proud. **5.** *Archaic.* Raised aloft; set high. —*n.* **1.** Something that is sublime. Preceded by *the.* **2.** *Rare.* The ultimate example of something. Preceded by *the.* —*v.* **sublimed, -liming, -limes.** —*tr.* **1.** To render sublime; elevate; ennoble. **2.** *Chemistry.* To cause to sublimate. —*intr. Chemistry.* To sublimate. [Latin *sublīmis*. See **limen.**] —**sub·lime′ly** *adv.* —**sub·lim′er** *n.* —**sub·lim′i·ty** (sə-blĭm′ə-tē), **sub·lime′ness** *n.*

sub·lim·i·nal (sŭb-lĭm′ə-nəl) *adj. Psychology.* **1.** Below the threshold of conscious perception. Said of stimuli. **2.** Inadequate to produce conscious awareness. [SUB- + Latin *līmen* (stem *līmin-*), threshold (see **limen**).] —**sub·lim′i·nal·ly** *adv.*

sub·lin·gual (sŭb′lĭng′gwəl) *adj.* Situated beneath or on the underside of the tongue.

sub·lit·to·ral (sŭb′lĭt′ər-əl) *adj.* **1.** Near the seashore. **2.** Shallow and lying between the shoreline and the edge of the continental shelf or ranging in depth to about 50 fathoms.

sub·lu·nar·y (sŭb′lo͞o′nə-rē) *adj.* Also **sub·lu·nar** (-nər). **1.** Situated beneath the moon. **2.** Of this world; earthly; mundane: *"The princess thought, that of all sublunary things, knowledge was the best"* (Samuel Johnson). [Late Latin *sublūnāris* : Latin *sub-*, beneath + *lūna*, moon (see **leuk-** in Appendix*).]

sub·ma·chine gun (sŭb′mə-shēn′). A lightweight automatic or semiautomatic gun fired from the shoulder or hip. Compare **machine gun.**

sub·mar·gin·al (sŭb′mär′jə-nəl) *adj.* **1.** Beneath a margin. **2.** Of low productivity; infertile.

sub·ma·rine (sŭb′mə-rēn′, sŭb′mə-rēn′) *adj.* Beneath the surface of the water; undersea. —*n.* **1.** A ship capable of operating submerged. **2.** *Slang.* A sandwich, the **hero** *(see).*

submarine chaser. A small, fast boat equipped to pursue and attack submarines.

sub·mar·i·ner (sŭb′măr′ə-nər, -mə-rē′nər) *n.* A member of the crew of a submarine.

sub·max·il·lar·y (sŭb′măk′sə-lăr′ē, sŭb′măk′-) *adj.* **1.** Of or relating to the lower jaw. **2.** Situated beneath the maxilla. —*n., pl.* **submaxillaries.** An anatomical part situated beneath the maxilla, as a gland or nerve.

sub·me·di·ant (sŭb′mē′dē-ənt) *n. Music.* The sixth tone of a diatonic scale. [SUB- + MEDIANT.]

sub·merge (səb-mûrj′) *v.* **-merged, -merging, -merges.** —*tr.* **1.** To place or plunge under water or other liquid. **2.** To cover with water; inundate. **3.** To hide from view; obscure. —*intr.* To go under or as if under water. [Latin *submergere* : *sub-*, under + *mergere*, to immerse, plunge (see **mezg-**[1] in Appendix*).] —**sub·mer′gence** *n.*

sub·merged (səb-mûrjd′) *adj.* Also **sub·mersed** (-mûrst) (for sense 1). **1.** *Botany.* Growing or remaining under water: *submerged leaves.* **2.** Living in poverty or misery. **3.** Hidden.

sub·mer·gi·ble (səb-mûrj′ə-bəl) *adj.* Able to be plunged into or to remain under water. —**sub·mer′gi·bil′i·ty** *n.*

sub·merse (səb-mûrs′) *tr.v.* **-mersed, -mersing, -merses.** To submerge. [Latin *submergere* (past participle *submersus*), SUBMERGE.] —**sub·mer′sion** *n.*

sub·mers·i·ble (səb-mûr′sə-bəl) *adj.* Submergible. —*n.* A vessel capable of operating or remaining under water.

sub·mi·cro·scop·ic (sŭb′mī′krə-skŏp′ĭk) *adj.* Too small to be resolved by an optical microscope.

sub·min·i·a·ture (sŭb′mĭn′ē-ə-choor′, -chər) *adj.* Smaller than miniature; exceedingly small.

sub·min·i·a·tur·ize (sŭb′mĭn′ē-ə-chə-rīz′) *tr.v.* **-ized, -izing, -izes.** To make subminiature; especially, to manufacture or design (electronic equipment) in subminiature size. —**sub′min′i·a·tur·i·za′tion** *n.*

sub·miss (səb-mĭs′) *adj. Archaic.* **1.** Submissive. **2.** Soft in tone. [Latin *submissus,* past participle of *submittere,* SUBMIT.]

sub·mis·sion (səb-mĭsh′ən) *n.* **1. a.** The act of submitting to the power of another. **b.** The state of having submitted. **2.** The state of being submissive or compliant; meekness. **3. a.** The act of submitting something for consideration. **b.** Something thus submitted. —See Synonyms at **surrender.**

sub·mis·sive (səb-mĭs′ĭv) *adj.* Disposed to submit; docile. See Synonyms at **obedient.** —**sub·mis′sive·ly** *adv.* —**sub·mis′sive·ness** *n.*

sub·mit (səb-mĭt′) *v.* **-mitted, -mitting, -mits.** —*tr.* **1.** To yield or surrender (oneself) to the will or authority of another or others. **2.** To subject to some condition or process. **3.** To commit (something) to the consideration or judgment of another. **4.** To offer as a proposition or contention. Used with *that: I submit that the terms are entirely unreasonable.* —*intr.* **1.** To yield to the opinion or authority of another; give in. **2.** To allow oneself to be subjected to; acquiesce. —See Synonyms at **yield.** [Middle English *submitten,* from Latin *submittere,* to place under : *sub-,* under + *mittere,* to throw (see **smeit-** in Appendix*).] —**sub·mit′tal** *n.* —**sub·mit′ter** *n.*

sub·mon·tane (sŭb′mŏn′tān′, -mŏn-tān′) *adj.* Located under or at the base of a mountain or mountain range. [Late Latin *submontānus* : Latin *sub-,* under + *montānus,* mountainous, from *mōns,* mountain (see **men-**[2] in Appendix*).] —**sub′mon′tane·ly** *adv.*

sub·mul·ti·ple (sŭb′mŭl′tə-pəl) *n.* A number that is an exact divisor of another number: *2 is a submultiple of 10.*

sub·nor·mal (sŭb′nôr′məl) *adj.* Less than normal; below the average. —*n.* A person who is subnormal in some respect, as in intelligence or coordination. —**sub′nor·mal′i·ty** *n.*

sub·o·ce·an·ic (sŭb′ō′shē-ăn′ĭk) *adj.* Formed, situated, or occurring beneath the ocean or the ocean bed.

sub·or·der (sŭb′ôr′dər) *n.* **1.** *Biology.* A taxonomic category ranking after an order and before a family. **2.** A subdivision of any category termed an order.

sub·or·di·nate (sə-bôr′də-nĭt) *adj.* **1.** Belonging to a lower or inferior class or rank; minor; secondary. **2.** Subject to the authority or control of another. —*n.* One that is subordinate. —*tr.v.* (sə-bôr′də-nāt′) **subordinated, -nating, -nates. 1.** To put in a lower or inferior rank or class. **2.** To make subservient; subdue. [Medieval Latin *subōrdinātus,* past participle of *subōrdināre,* to put in a lower rank : Latin *sub-,* below + *ōrdināre,* to arrange in order, from *ōrdō,* order (see **ar-** in Appendix*).] —**sub·or′di·nate·ly** *adv.* —**sub·or′di·nate·ness, sub·or′di·na′tion** *n.* —**sub·or′di·na′tive** *adj.*

subordinate clause. *Grammar.* A **dependent clause** *(see).*

subordinate conjunction. *Grammar.* A conjunction that introduces a dependent clause, as *that, who, which,* and *where.* Compare **coordinate conjunction.**

sub·or·di·na·tion·ism (sə-bôr′də-nā′shən-ĭz′əm) *n. Theology.* The doctrine that the second and third persons of the Trinity are subordinate to the first person. —**sub·or′di·na′tion·ist** *n.*

sub·orn (sə-bôrn′) *tr.v.* **-orned, -orning, -orns. 1. a.** To induce (a person) to commit a wrong or unlawful act. **b.** To induce (a person) to commit perjury. **2.** To procure (perjured testimony). [Latin *subōrnāre* : *sub-,* secretly + *ōrnāre,* to equip (see **ar-** in Appendix*).] —**sub′or·na′tion** *n.* —**sub·orn′er** *n.*

Su·bo·ti·ca (sōō′bə-tēt′sə). Also **Su·bo·ti·tsa.** A city and industrial center of Yugoslavia, in the northeast near the Hungarian border. Population, 122,000.

sub·ox·ide (sŭb′ŏk′sīd′) *n.* An oxide containing a relatively small amount of oxygen.

sub·phy·lum (sŭb′fī′ləm) *n., pl.* **-la** (-lə). *Biology.* A taxonomic category ranking between a phylum and a class.

sub·plot (sŭb′plŏt′) *n.* A subordinate literary plot.

sub·poe·na (sə-pē′nə) *n.* Also **sub·pe·na.** A legal writ requiring appearance in court to give testimony. —*tr.v.* **subpoenaed, -naing, -nas.** To serve or summon with such a writ. [From Latin *sub poenā,* under penalty (first words in the writ) : *sub-,* under + *poenā,* penalty, from Greek *poinē* (see **kwei-**[1] in Appendix*).]

sub·prin·ci·pal (sŭb′prĭn′sə-pəl) *n.* **1.** An assistant school principal. **2.** An auxiliary or bracing rafter in a frame. **3.** *Music.* An open diapason subbass in an organ.

sub·re·gion (sŭb′rē′jən) *n.* A subdivision of a region, especially of an ecological region. —**sub′re′gion·al** *adj.*

sub·rep·tion (sŭb-rĕp′shən) *n.* **1.** A calculated misrepresentation through concealment of the facts. **2.** An inference drawn from such a misrepresentation. [Latin *subreptiō,* theft, from *subrepere* (past participle *subreptus*), to creep under, steal upon : *sub-,* under + *repere,* to creep (see **rēp-**[1] in Appendix*).] —**sub′rep′ti′tious** (-tĭ′shəs) *adj.*

sub·ro·gate (sŭb′rə-gāt′) *tr.v.* **-gated, -gating, -gates.** To substitute (one person) for another. [Latin *subrogāre,* "to nominate an alternative candidate" : *sub-,* instead of + *rogāre,* ask, propose as candidate (see **reg-**[1] in Appendix*).]

sub·ro·ga·tion (sŭb′rə-gā′shən) *n.* The substitution of one person for another; especially, the legal doctrine of substituting one creditor for another.

sub ro·sa (sŭb rō′zə). In secret; privately; confidentially. [Latin, "under the rose," from the practice of hanging a rose over a meeting as a symbol of secrecy, from the legend that Cupid once gave Harpocrates, the god of silence, a rose to make him keep the secrets of Venus.]

subs. subscription.

sub·scap·u·lar (sŭb′skăp′yə-lər) *adj. Anatomy.* Situated below or on the underside of the scapula. —*n.* A subscapular part, such as an artery or nerve.

sub·scribe (səb-scrīb′) *v.* **-scribed, -scribing, -scribes.** —*tr.* **1.** To sign (one's name) at the end of a document. **2.** To sign one's name to in attestation, testimony, or consent: *subscribe a will.* **3.** To pledge or contribute (a sum of money). —*intr.* **1.** To sign one's name. **2.** To affix one's signature to a document as a witness or to show consent. **3.** To express concurrence or approval; assent. Used with *to: "I haven't subscribed to the possibility of it as yet."* (Ben Ray Redman). **4.** To promise to pay or contribute money. **5.** To contract to receive and pay for a certain number of issues of a newspaper or periodical. Used with *to.* —See Synonyms at **assent.** [Middle English *subscriben,* from Latin *subscrībere* : *sub-,* under + *scrībere,* to write (see **skeri-** in Appendix*).] —**sub·scrib′er** *n.*

sub·script (sŭb′skrĭpt′) *adj.* Written beneath. —*n.* A distinguishing character or symbol written directly beneath or next to and slightly below a letter or number. Also called "subindex." Compare **superscript.** [Latin *subscriptus,* past participle of *subscrībere,* SUBSCRIBE.]

sub·scrip·tion (səb-skrĭp′shən) *n. Abbr.* **sub., subs. 1.** The signing of one's name, as to a document. **2.** That which has been subscribed. **3.** A purchase made by signed order, as for a periodical for a specified period of time or for a series of theatrical performances. **4.** Acceptance, as of articles of faith, demonstrated by the signing of one's name. **5. a.** The raising of money from subscribers. **b.** A sum of money subscribed. —**sub·scrip′tive** *adj.* —**sub·scrip′tive·ly** *adv.*

sub·se·quence (sŭb′sə-kwəns′) *n.* **1.** That which is subsequent; a sequel. **2.** The fact or quality of being subsequent.

sub·se·quent (sŭb′sə-kwənt) *adj.* Following in time or order; succeeding. [Middle English, from Old French, from Latin *subsequēns,* present participle of *subsequī,* to follow close after : *sub-,* close to, after + *sequī,* to follow (see **sekw-**[1] in Appendix*).] —**sub′se·quent·ly** *adv.* —**sub′se·quent·ness** *n.*

Usage: *Subsequent, subsequent to* (used prepositionally), and *subsequently* are employed, in the sense of *later,* in the following typical constructions: *a subsequent discussion; a discussion held subsequent to the meeting; a discussion held subsequently.*

sub·serve (səb-sûrv′) *tr.v.* **-served, -serving, -serves.** To serve to promote (some end); be useful to; to further. [Latin *subservīre,* to serve, be subject to : *sub-,* under + *servīre,* SERVE.]

sub·ser·vi·ent (səb-sûr′vē-ənt) *adj.* **1.** Useful as a means or instrument; serving to promote some end. **2.** Subordinate in capacity or function. **3.** Obsequious; servile. [Latin *subserviēns,* present participle of *subservīre,* SUBSERVE.] —**sub·ser′vi·ent·ly** *adv.* —**sub·ser′vi·ence, sub·ser′vi·en·cy** *n.*

sub·set (sŭb′sĕt′) *n.* A mathematical set contained within a set.

sub·shrub (sŭb′shrŭb′) *n.* **1.** A herbaceous plant having a woody lower stem. **2.** A low shrub; undershrub.

sub·side (səb-sīd′) *intr.v.* **-sided, -siding, -sides. 1.** To sink to a lower or normal level. **2.** To sink or settle down, as into a sofa. **3.** To sink to the bottom; settle, as sediment. **4.** To become less agitated or active; abate. —See Synonyms at **decrease.** [Latin *subsīdere,* to sink down : *sub-,* down + *sīdere,* to settle (see **sed-**[1] in Appendix*).] —**sub·si′dence** *n.*

sub·sid·i·ar·y (səb-sĭd′ē-ăr′ē) *adj.* **1.** Serving to assist or supplement; auxiliary. **2.** Secondary in importance; subordinate. **3.** Of, pertaining to, or of the nature of a subsidy. —*n., pl.* **subsidiaries. 1.** One that is subsidiary. **2.** A **subsidiary company** *(see).* **3.** *Music.* A theme subordinate to a main theme or subject. [Latin *subsidiārius,* in reserve, supporting, from *subsidium,* support, SUBSIDY.] —**sub·sid′i·ar′i·ly** *adv.*

subsidiary company. A company having more than half of its stock owned by another company. Also called "subsidiary."

sub·si·dize (sŭb′sə-dīz′) *tr.v.* **-dized, -dizing, -dizes. 1.** To assist or support with a subsidy. **2.** To secure the assistance of by granting a subsidy. —**sub′si·di·za′tion** *n.* —**sub′si·diz′er** *n.*

sub·si·dy (sŭb′sə-dē) *n., pl.* **-dies. 1.** Monetary assistance granted by a government to a person or a private commercial enterprise. **2.** Financial assistance given by one person or government to another. **3.** Formerly, money granted to the British Crown by Parliament. —See Synonyms at **bonus.** [Middle English *subsidie,* aid, assistance, from Norman French, from Latin *subsidium,* reserve troops, hence support, help, from *subsidēre,* to sit down, remain, be placed in reserve : *sub-,* down + *sedēre,* to sit (see **sed-**[1] in Appendix*).]

sub·sist (səb-sĭst′) *v.* **-sisted, -sisting, -sists.** —*intr.* **1. a.** To exist; be. **b.** To remain or continue in existence. **2.** To be sustained; live. Used with *on* or *by.* **3.** To reside or inhere. Used with *in.* **4.** To be logically conceivable. —*tr. Obsolete.* To maintain. [Latin *subsistere,* to stand still, stand up, remain standing : *sub-,* from below, up + *sistere,* to cause to stand (see **stā-** in Appendix*).] —**sub·sist′er** *n.*

sub·sis·tence (səb-sĭs′təns) *n.* **1.** The act or state of subsisting. **2.** A means of subsisting; sustenance. **3.** That which has real or

t tight/th thin, path/*th* this, bathe/ŭ cut/ûr urge/v valve/w with/y yes/z zebra, size/zh vision/ə about, item, edible, gallop, circus/
à *Fr.* ami/œ *Fr.* feu, *Ger.* schön/ü *Fr.* tu, *Ger.* über/KH *Ger.* ich, *Scot.* loch/N *Fr.* bon. ***Follows main vocabulary. †Of obscure origin.**

substantial existence. **4.** *Theology.* Hypostasis. —See Synonyms at **livelihood.** —**sub·sis'tent** *adj.*

sub·soil (sŭb'soil') *n.* The layer or bed of earth beneath the surface soil. —*tr.v.* **subsoiled, -soiling, -soils.** To plow or turn up the subsoil of. —**sub'soil'er** *n.*

sub·so·lar (sŭb'sō'lər) *adj.* **1.** Situated directly beneath the sun. **2.** Located between the tropics; equatorial.

sub·son·ic (sŭb'sŏn'ĭk) *adj.* **1.** Of less than audible frequency. Also "infrasonic." **2.** Having a speed less than that of sound in a designated medium.

sub·spe·cies (sŭb'spē'shēz, -sēz) *n., pl.* **subspecies.** A subdivision of a taxonomic species, usually based on geographical distribution. —**sub'spe·cif'ic** (-spə-sĭf'ĭk) *adj.*

subst. 1. substantive. **2.** substitute.

sub·stance (sŭb'stəns) *n.* **1.** *Philosophy.* The essential nature of anything, as considered apart from its form or attributes; the primary or basic element that receives modifications. **2.** *Chemistry & Physics.* **a.** Matter. **b.** Material of specified, especially complex, constitution. **3.** The essence of what is said or written; gist. **4. a.** That which is solid or real; reality as opposed to appearance. **b.** A solid or substantial quality or character. **5.** Density; body: *Air has little substance.* **6.** Material possessions; goods; wealth. [Middle English, essence, from Old French, from Latin *substantia*, from *substāns*, present participle of *substāre*, to be present, stand up : *sub-*, from below, up + *stāre*, to stand (see **stā-** in Appendix*).]

sub·stan·dard (sŭb'stăn'dərd) *adj.* **1.** Failing to meet a standard; below standard. **2.** Considered unacceptable usage by the educated members of a speech community.

sub·stan·tial (səb-stăn'shəl) *adj.* **1.** Of, pertaining to, or having substance; material. **2.** Not imaginary; true; real. **3.** Solidly built; strong. **4.** Ample; sustaining: *a substantial breakfast.* **5.** Considerable in importance, value, degree, amount, or extent: *won by a substantial margin.* **6.** Possessing wealth or property; well-to-do. —*n.* **1.** *Plural.* The essentials. **2.** *Plural.* Solid things. [Middle English *substancial*, from Late Latin *substantiālis*, from Latin *substantia*, SUBSTANCE.] —**sub·stan'ti·al'i·ty, sub·stan'tial·ness** *n.* —**sub·stan'tial·ly** *adv.*

sub·stan·ti·ate (səb-stăn'shē-āt') *tr.v.* **-ated, -ating, -ates. 1.** To support with proof or evidence; verify. **2. a.** To give material form to; embody. **b.** To make firm or solid. **3.** To give substance to; make real or actual. —See Synonyms at **confirm.** [New Latin *substantiare*, from Latin *substantia*, SUBSTANCE.] —**sub·stan'ti·a'tion** *n.*

sub·stan·ti·val (sŭb'stən-tī'vəl) *adj. Grammar.* Of, pertaining to, or of the nature of a substantive. —**sub'stan·ti'val·ly** *adv.*

sub·stan·tive (sŭb'stən-tĭv) *adj. Abbr.* **s., sb., subst. 1.** Independent in existence or function; not subordinate. **2.** Not imaginary; actual; real. **3.** Of or pertaining to the essence or substance of something; essential. **4.** Of substantial amount; considerable. **5.** Having a solid basis; firm. **6.** Expressing or denoting existence; for example, the verb *to be.* **7.** Denoting a noun or noun equivalent. —*n. Abbr.* **s., sb., subst.** A word or group of words functioning as a noun. [Middle English *substantif*, from Old French, from Late Latin *substantīvus*, self-existent, from Latin *substantia*, "thing that exists," SUBSTANCE.] —**sub'stan·tive·ly** *adv.* —**sub'stan·tive·ness** *n.*

sub·sta·tion (sŭb'stā'shən) *n.* A subsidiary or branch station, as of a post office.

sub·stit·u·ent (səb-stĭch'ŏŏ-ənt) *n.* An atom, radical, or group substituted for another in a compound. —*adj.* Of such an atom or group. [Latin *substituēns*, present participle of *substituere*, to SUBSTITUTE.]

sub·sti·tute (sŭb'stə-tōōt', -tyōōt') *n. Abbr.* **sub., subst. 1.** One that takes the place of another; a replacement. **2.** *Grammar.* A word or construction used in place of another word, phrase, or clause. —*v.* **substituted, -tuting, -tutes.** —*tr.* To put or use (a person or thing) in place of another. —*intr.* To take the place of another: *"only art can substitute for nature"* (Leonard Bernstein). [Latin *substitūtus*, a replacement, from the past participle of *substituere*, to substitute : *sub-*, in place of + *statuere*, to cause to stand (see **stā-** in Appendix*).] —**sub'sti·tut'a·bil'i·ty** *n.* —**sub'sti·tut'a·ble** *adj.*

sub·sti·tu·tion (sŭb'stə-tōō'shən, -tyōō'shən) *n.* **1. a.** The act of substituting. **b.** The state of being substituted. **2.** That which is substituted. —**sub'sti·tu'tion·al** *adj.* —**sub'sti·tu'tion·al·ly** *adv.*

sub·sti·tu·tive (sŭb'stə-tōō'tĭv, -tyōō'tĭv) *adj.* Serving or capable of serving as a substitute.

sub·strate (sŭb'strāt') *n.* **1.** The material or substance upon which an enzyme acts. **2.** *Biology.* A surface on which a plant or animal grows or is attached. **3.** A substratum. [From SUBSTRATUM.]

sub·stra·tum (sŭb'strā'təm, -străt'əm) *n., pl.* **-ta** (-tə) or **-tums. 1. a.** An underlying layer. **b.** A layer of earth beneath the surface soil; subsoil. **2.** The foundation or groundwork for something. **3.** *Philosophy.* The characterless substance that supports attributes of reality. **4.** *Biology.* A substrate. [Medieval Latin *substrātum*, from Latin, neuter past participle of *substernere*, to lie under : *sub-*, under + *sternere*, to spread out flat (see **ster-²** in Appendix*).] —**sub'stra'tive** *adj.*

sub·struc·tion (sŭb'strŭk'shən) *n.* A foundation; substructure. [Latin *substructiō*, from *substruere* (past participle *substructus*), to build beneath : *sub-*, beneath + *struere*, to build (see **ster-²** in Appendix*).] —**sub'struc'tion·al** *adj.*

sub·struc·ture (sŭb'strŭk'chər) *n.* **1.** The supporting part of a structure; a foundation. **2.** The earth bank or bed supporting railroad tracks. —**sub'struc'tur·al** *adj.*

sub·sume (sŭb-sōōm', -syōōm') *tr.v.* **-sumed, -suming, -sumes.** To place in a more comprehensive category or under a general principle. [New Latin *subsumere* : Latin *sub-*, under + *sūmere*, to take up (see **em-** in Appendix*).] —**sub·sum'a·ble** *adj.*

sub·sump·tion (səb-sŭmp'shən) *n.* **1. a.** The act or an instance of subsuming. **b.** Something that is subsumed. **2.** *Logic.* The minor premise of a syllogism. [New Latin *subsumptio*, from *subsumere*, SUBSUME.] —**sub·sump'tive** *adj.*

sub·tem·per·ate (sŭb'tĕm'pə-rĭt) *adj.* Of, pertaining to, or occurring within the colder regions of the Temperate Zones.

sub·ten·ant (sŭb'tĕn'ənt) *n.* One who rents land, a house, or the like from a tenant. —**sub'ten'an·cy** *n.*

sub·tend (səb-tĕnd') *tr.v.* **-tended, -tending, -tends. 1.** *Geometry.* To be opposite to and delimit: *The side of a triangle subtends the opposite angle.* **2.** To underlie so as to enclose or surround: *flowers subtended by leafy bracts.* [Latin *subtendere*, to extend beneath : *sub-*, beneath + *tendere*, to extend (see **ten-** in Appendix*).]

sub·ter·fuge (sŭb'tər-fyōōj') *n.* An evasive tactic used to avoid censure or other awkward confrontation: *"the paltry subterfuge of an anonymous signature"* (R.S. Surtees). See Synonyms at **artifice.** [French, from Late Latin *subterfugium*, from Latin *subterfugere*, to flee secretly : *subter*, secretly (see **upo** in Appendix*) + *fugere*, to flee (see **bheug-¹** in Appendix*).]

sub·ter·ra·ne·an (sŭb'tə-rā'nē-ən) *adj.* **1.** Situated or operating beneath the earth's surface; underground. **2.** Hidden; secret. [From Latin *subterrāneus* : *sub-*, under + *terra*, earth (see **ters-** in Appendix*).] —**sub'ter·ra'ne·an·ly** *adv.*

sub·ter·res·tri·al (sŭb'tə-rĕs'trē-əl) *adj.* Subterranean. —*n.* An animal that lives underground.

sub·tile (sŭt'l) *adj.* Subtle. —**sub'tile·ly** *adv.* —**sub·til'i·ty** (-tĭl'ə-tē), **sub'tile·ness, sub'til·ty** *n.*

sub·til·ize (sŭt'l-īz') *v.* **-ized, -izing, -izes.** —*tr.* To render subtle. —*intr.* To argue or discuss with subtlety; make fine distinctions. [Medieval Latin *subtīlizāre*, from Latin *subtīlis*, SUBTLE.] —**sub'til·i·za'tion** *n.*

sub·ti·tle (sŭb'tīt'l) *n.* **1.** A secondary and usually explanatory title, as of a literary work. **2. a.** A printed narration or portion of dialogue flashed on the screen between the scenes of a silent film. **b.** A printed translation of the dialogue of a foreign-language film shown at the bottom of the screen.

sub·tle (sŭt'l) *adj.* **-tler, -tlest. 1. a.** So slight as to be difficult to detect or analyze; elusive. **b.** Not immediately obvious; abstruse. **2.** Able to make fine distinctions; keen. **3. a.** Characterized by skill or ingenuity; clever. **b.** Characterized by craft or slyness; devious. **c.** Operating in a hidden and usually injurious way; insidious. [Middle English *sutil, subtil*, thin, fine, clever, ingenious, from Old French, from Latin *subtīlis*, thin, fine. See **teks-** in Appendix.*] —**sub'tle·ness** *n.* —**sub'tly** *adv.*

sub·tle·ty (sŭt'l-tē) *n., pl.* **-ties. 1.** The quality or state of being subtle. **2.** Something subtle; especially, a nicety of thought or a fine distinction. —See Synonyms at **tact.**

sub·ton·ic (sŭb'tŏn'ĭk) *n. Music.* The seventh tone of a diatonic scale, immediately below the tonic.

sub·tor·rid (sŭb'tôr'ĭd, -tŏr'ĭd) *adj.* Subtropical.

sub·to·tal (sŭb'tōt'l) *adj.* Less than total; incomplete. —*n.* The total of part of a series of numbers. —*v.* **subtotaled, -taling, -tals.** —*tr.* To total part of (a series of numbers). —*intr.* To arrive at a subtotal.

sub·tract (səb-trăkt') *v.* **-tracted, -tracting, -tracts.** —*tr.* To take away; deduct. —*intr.* To perform the arithmetic operation of subtraction. [Latin *substrahere* (past participle *substractus*), to draw away : *sub-*, away + *trahere*, to draw (see **tragh-** in Appendix*).] —**sub·tract'er** *n.*

sub·trac·tion (səb-trăk'shən) *n.* **1.** The act or process of subtracting; deduction. **2.** The arithmetic process or operation of finding a quantity that when added to one of two quantities produces the other.

sub·trac·tive (səb-trăk'tĭv) *adj.* **1.** Producing or involving subtraction. **2.** *Color Technology.* Designating a color produced by light passing through more than one colorant, each of which inhibits certain wavelengths, as in mixtures of pigments. See **primary color.** Compare **additive. 3.** Designating a photographic process that produces a positive image by superposition or mixing of substances that selectively absorb colored light.

sub·tra·hend (sŭb'trə-hĕnd') *n.* A quantity or number to be subtracted from another. [Latin *subtrahendum*, gerundive of *subtrahere*, SUBTRACT.]

sub·trop·i·cal (sŭb'trŏp'ĭ-kəl) *adj.* Of, relating to, or being the geographical areas adjacent to the tropics.

sub·trop·ics (sŭb'trŏp'ĭks) *pl.n.* Subtropical regions.

su·bu·late (sŭb'yə-lĭt) *adj. Biology.* Awl-shaped; tapering to a point. [New Latin *subulatus*, from Latin *sūbula*, awl. See **syū-** in Appendix.*]

sub·urb (sŭb'ərb') *n. Abbr.* **sub. 1.** A usually residential area or community outlying a city. **2.** *Plural.* The perimeter of country around a major city; environs. Used with *the.* [Middle English, from Old French *suburbe*, from Latin *suburbium* : *sub-*, near + *urbs*, city (see **urban**).]

sub·ur·ban (sə-bûr'bən) *adj. Abbr.* **sub. 1.** Of, pertaining to, or characteristic of a suburb or life in a suburb. **2.** Located or residing in a suburb. **3.** The culture, manners, and customs typical of life in the suburbs. —*n.* A suburbanite.

sub·ur·ban·ite (sə-bûr'bə-nīt') *n.* One who lives in a suburb.

sub·ur·bi·a (sə-bûr'bē-ə) *n.* **1.** Suburbs or suburbanites collectively. **2.** Suburbanites as a cultural class.

sub·ur·bi·car·i·an (sə-bûr'bĭ-kâr'ē-ən) *adj.* Designating any of the six dioceses surrounding Rome of which the pope is metropolitan. [From Late Latin *suburbicārius*, situated near Rome : *sub-*, near + *urbicārius*, of the city (especially Rome), from Latin *urbicus*, from *urbs*, city (see **urban**).]

sub·ven·tion (səb-vĕn′shən) *n.* **1.** The provision of help, aid, or support. **2.** A grant of financial aid; an endowment or subsidy, as that given by a government to an institution for research. [Middle English *subvencioun,* from Old French *subvention,* from Late Latin *subventiō,* from Latin *subvenīre* (past participle *subventus*), to come to help : *sub-,* from below, up + *venīre,* to come (see **gwā-** in Appendix*).] —**sub·ven′tion·ar′y** *adj.*

sub·ver·sion (səb-vûr′zhən, -shən) *n.* **1.** The act of subverting or the condition of being subverted. **2.** *Obsolete.* One that subverts. [Middle English *subversioun,* from Old French *subversion,* from Late Latin *subversiō,* from Latin *subvertere* (past participle *subversus*), SUBVERT.] —**sub·ver′sion·ar′y** *adj.*

sub·ver·sive (səb-vûr′sĭv, -zĭv) *adj.* Intended or serving to undermine or overthrow, such as an established government. —*n.* One who advocates or is regarded as advocating subversive means or policies. —**sub·ver′sive·ly** *adv.* —**sub·ver′sive·ness** *n.*

sub·vert (səb-vûrt′) *tr.v.* **-verted, -verting, -verts. 1.** To destroy completely; ruin: *"schemes to subvert the liberties of a great community"* (Alexander Hamilton). **2.** To undermine the character, morals, or allegiance of; to corrupt. **3.** To overthrow completely: *"economic assistance . . . must subvert the existing . . . feudal or tribal order"* (Henry A. Kissinger). [Middle English *subverten,* from Old French *subvertir,* from Latin *subvertere,* to turn upside down : *sub-,* from below, up + *vertere,* to turn (see **wer-**^{3} in Appendix*).] —**sub·vert′er** *n.*

sub·way (sŭb′wā′) *n.* **1. a.** An underground urban railroad, usually operated by electricity. **b.** A passage for such a railroad. **2.** Any underground tunnel or passage, as for a water main.

Su·car·yl (sōō′kə-rĭl) *n.* A trademark for either of two compounds used as low-calorie sweeteners.

suc·ce·da·ne·um (sŭk′sĕ-dā′nē-əm) *n., pl.* **-nea** (-nē-ə). A substitute. [New Latin, from Latin *succēdāneus,* substituted, "following," from *succēdere,* SUCCEED.]

suc·ceed (sək-sēd′) *v.* **-ceeded, -ceeding, -ceeds.** —*intr.* **1.** To come next in time or succession; follow after; especially, to replace another in an office or position. Often used with *to*: *"The beloved son of Marcus succeeded to his father"* (Gibbon). **2.** To accomplish something desired or intended. **3.** *Archaic.* To have a specific kind of success: *We have succeeded badly.* **4.** *Obsolete.* To devolve: *His estate succeeded to his heirs.* —*tr.* **1.** To follow in time or order; come after. **2.** To replace; follow in office. —See Synonyms at **follow.** [Middle English *succeden,* from Old French *succeder,* from Latin *succēdere,* to follow closely, go after : *sub-,* toward, next to + *cēdere,* to go (see **ked-**^{1} in Appendix*).] —**suc·ce′dent** *adj.* —**suc·ceed′er** *n.*

suc·cès d'es·time (sük-sĕ′ dĕs′tēm′). A critical but not popular success or achievement. [French, "success of respect."]

suc·cess (sək-sĕs′) *n.* **1.** The achievement of something desired, planned, or attempted. **2. a.** The gaining of fame or prosperity: *"Success is counted sweetest/By those who ne'er succeed."* (Emily Dickinson). **b.** The extent of such gain. **3.** One that is successful. **4.** *Obsolete.* Any result or outcome. [Latin *successus,* from the past participle of *succēdere,* SUCCEED.]

suc·cess·ful (sək-sĕs′fəl) *adj.* **1.** Having a favorable outcome. **2.** Having obtained something desired or intended. **3.** Having achieved wealth or eminence. —**suc·cess′ful·ly** *adv.*

suc·ces·sion (sək-sĕsh′ən) *n.* **1.** The act or process of following in order or sequence. **2.** A group of persons or things arranged or following in order; sequence: *"A succession of one-man stalls offered soft drinks"* (Alec Waugh). **3. a.** The sequence in which one person after another succeeds to a title, throne, dignity, or estate. **b.** The right of a person or line of persons to so succeed. **c.** The person or line vested with such a right. **4. a.** The act or process of succeeding to the rights or duties of another. **b.** The act or process of becoming entitled as a legal beneficiary to the property of a deceased person. —See Synonyms at **series.** —**suc·ces′sion·al** *adj.* —**suc·ces′sion·al·ly** *adv.*

suc·ces·sive (sək-sĕs′ĭv) *adj.* **1.** Following in uninterrupted order or sequence. **2.** Of, characterized by, or involving succession. —**suc·ces′sive·ly** *adv.* —**suc·ces′sive·ness** *n.*

suc·ces·sor (sək-sĕs′ər) *n.* One that succeeds another.

suc·cinct (sək-sĭngkt′) *adj.* **1.** Clearly expressed in few words; concise; terse. **2.** Characterized by brevity and clarity in speech or writing: *a succinct style.* **3.** *Archaic.* Encircled as if by a girdle; girded. —See Synonyms at **concise.** [Latin *succinctus,* girded, concise, from the past participle of *succingere,* to gird below, tuck up : *sub-,* below + *cingere,* to gird (see **kenk-**^{1} in Appendix*).] —**suc·cinct′ly** *adv.* —**suc·cinct′ness** *n.*

suc·cin·ic acid (sək-sĭn′ĭk). A colorless crystalline compound, $C_4H_6O_4$, occurring naturally in amber and synthesized for use in pharmaceuticals and perfumes. [From French *succinique,* from Latin *succinum*†, amber.]

suc·cor (sŭk′ər) *n.* Also *British* **suc·cour. 1.** Assistance or help in time of distress; relief. **2.** One that affords assistance or relief. —*tr.v.* **succored, -coring, -cors.** To render assistance to in time of distress. See Synonyms at **help.** [Middle English *sucurs* (taken as plural), from Old French, from Medieval Latin *succursus,* from Latin, past participle of *succurrere,* to run to the aid of, run under : *sub-,* under + *currere,* to run (see **kers-**^{2} in Appendix*).] —**suc′cor·a·ble** *adj.* —**suc′cor·er** *n.*

suc·co·ry (sŭk′ə-rē) *n., pl.* **-ries.** A plant, **chicory** *(see).* [Alteration (influenced by Middle Dutch *sūkerie,* succory) of Middle English *cicoree,* CHICORY.]

suc·co·tash (sŭk′ə-tăsh′) *n.* Kernels of corn and lima beans cooked together. [Narraganset *msíckquatash,* "boiled whole-grain corn (off the cob)" : Proto-Algonquian *mes-* (unattested), whole + *-inkw-* (unattested), grain + *-etē-* (unattested), heated, cooked + *-wali* (unattested), inanimate plural suffix.]

Suc·coth (sŏŏk′ōt, -əs) *n.* Also **Suk·koth.** A Jewish harvest festival celebrated for nine days beginning on the eve of the 15th of Tishri. [Hebrew *sukkōth,* "(feast of) booths" (commemorating the temporary shelter of the Jews in the wilderness), from *sukkāh,* booth.]

suc·cu·bus (sŭk′yə-bəs) *n., pl.* **-buses** or **-bi** (-bī′, -bē′). Also **suc·cu·ba** (sŭk′yə-bə) *pl.* **-bae** (-bē′, -bī′). **1.** A female demon supposed to descend upon and have sexual intercourse with a man while he sleeps. Compare **incubus. 2.** Any evil spirit; demon. [Medieval Latin, from Late Latin *succuba,* prostitute, from Latin *succubāre,* to lie under : Latin *sub-,* under + *cubāre,* to lie (see **keu-**^{2} in Appendix*).]

suc·cu·lent (sŭk′yə-lənt) *adj.* **1.** Full of juice or sap; juicy. **2.** *Botany.* Having thick, fleshy leaves or stems that conserve moisture. **3.** Interesting or absorbing; not dull or dry. —*n.* A succulent plant, a sedum or a cactus. [Latin *succulentus,* from *succus,* juice. See **seu-**^{4} in Appendix.*] —**suc′cu·lence, suc′cu·len·cy** *n.* —**suc′cu·lent·ly** *adv.*

suc·cumb (sə-kŭm′) *intr.v.* **-cumbed, -cumbing, -cumbs. 1.** To yield or submit to an overpowering force or overwhelming desire; give in or give up. Often used with *to*: *"Meanwhile I had succumbed to the disease of scepticism"* (Cyril Connolly). **2.** To die. [Middle English *succomben,* from Old French *succomber,* from Latin *succumbere,* to lie down under : *sub-,* under + *-cumbere,* to lie (see **keu-**^{2} in Appendix*).]

suc·cus·sion (sə-kŭsh′ən) *n.* **1.** The act or process of shaking violently. **2.** The condition of being so shaken. [Latin *succussiō,* from *succutere* (past participle *succussus*), to shake from beneath : *sub-,* beneath + *quatere,* to shake (see **kwēt-** in Appendix.*] —**suc·cus′sa·to′ry** (sə-kŭs′ə-tôr′ē, -tōr′ē) *adj.*

such (sŭch) *adj.* **1.** Of this or that kind: *We haven't had such fun as this in years!* **2.** Being the same as that which has been last mentioned or implied. Sometimes interpreted as a pronoun: *The weather was such that we could not go out.* **3.** Being the same in quality or kind: *pins, needles, and other such trivia.* **4.** Being the same as something implied but left undefined or unsaid: *Such people are never satisfied.* **5.** Of so extreme or great a degree or quality: *Such luck!* —**as such. 1.** As being the person or thing implied or previously mentioned: *A diplomat as such must negotiate.* **2.** In itself or by itself: *Money as such will seldom bring happiness.* —**such as. 1.** For example. **2.** Of the stated or implied kind or degree; similar; like: *a statement such as this.* —*pron.* **1.** Such a person or persons or thing or things. **2.** A person or persons or thing or things implied or indicated: *Such were the results of that war.* **3.** One of such kind: *pencils and papers and such.* —*adv.* **1.** To such an extent or degree: *such long paragraphs.* **2.** Very: *She has not been in such good health lately.* **3.** In such a manner or way. [Middle English *su(c)ch, swulc,* Old English *swylc, swelc.* See **swo-** in Appendix.*]

such and such. Not yet specified; undetermined: *They agreed to meet at such and such an hour.*

such·like (sŭch′līk′) *adj.* Of a similar kind; like. —*pron.* Persons or things of such a kind.

Sü·chow (shü′jō′). Formerly **Tung·shan** (tûng′shän′). A transportation center of eastern China, in Kiangsu Province, about 320 miles northwest of Shanghai. Population, 751,000.

suck (sŭk) *v.* **sucked, sucking, sucks.** —*tr.* **1.** To draw (liquid) into the mouth by inhalation. **2. a.** To draw in by establishing a partial vacuum. **b.** To draw in by or as if by a current in a fluid. **3.** To draw nourishment through or from. **4.** To hold, moisten, or maneuver (a sweet, for example) in the mouth. —*intr.* **1.** To draw in by or as if by suction. **2.** To draw nourishment; suckle. **3.** To make a sucking sound. —**suck in.** *Slang.* To take advantage of; cheat; swindle. —*n.* **1.** The act of sucking. **2.** Suction. **3.** Something drawn in by sucking. [Middle English *s(o)uken,* Old English *sūcan.* See **seu-**^{4} in Appendix.*]

suck·er (sŭk′ər) *n.* **1.** One that sucks. **2.** *Slang.* One who is easily deceived; a gullible person; dupe. **3.** A lollipop. **4. a.** A piston or piston valve, as in a suction pump or syringe. **b.** A tube or pipe, such as a siphon, through which anything is sucked. **5.** Any of numerous chiefly North American freshwater fishes of the family Catostomidae, having a thick-lipped mouth adapted for feeding by suction. **6.** A structure or part adapted for clinging by suction. **7.** *Botany.* A secondary shoot arising from the base of a tree trunk or from the lower part of some shrubs. —*v.* **suckered, -ering, -ers.** —*tr.* To strip suckers or shoots from. —*intr.* To send out suckers or shoots.

suck·er·fish (sŭk′ər-fĭsh′) *n., pl.* **suckerfish** or **-fishes.** Also **suck·fish** (sŭk′fĭsh′). The **remora** *(see).*

suck·ing (sŭk′ĭng) *adj.* Too young to be weaned.

suck·le (sŭk′əl) *v.* **-led, -ling, -les.** —*tr.* **1.** To cause or allow to take milk at the breast or udder; to nurse. **2.** To take in as sustenance; have as nourishment. **3.** To bring up; rear; nourish; foster: *"I'd rather be a pagan suckled in a creed outworn"* (Wordsworth). —*intr.* To suck at the breast. [Probably back-formation from SUCKLING.] —**suck′ler** *n.*

suck·ling (sŭk′lĭng) *n.* A young mammal that has not been weaned. [Middle English *sokelyng* : *s(o)uken,* SUCK + -LING.]

Suck·ling (sŭk′lĭng), Sir **John.** 1609–1642. English poet.

su·crase (sōō′krās′) *n. Chemistry.* **Invertase** *(see).* [French *sucre,* SUGAR + -ASE.]

su·cre (sōō′krā) *n.* **1.** The basic monetary unit of Ecuador, equal to 100 centavos. See table of exchange rates at **currency. 2.** A coin worth one sucre. [Spanish, after Antonio José de SUCRE.]

Su·cre (sōō′krā). The constitutional capital of Bolivia, in the center of the country, 260 miles southeast of La Paz, the administrative capital. Population, 541,000.

Su·cre (sōō′krā), **Antonio José de.** 1795–1830. South American military leader and liberator.

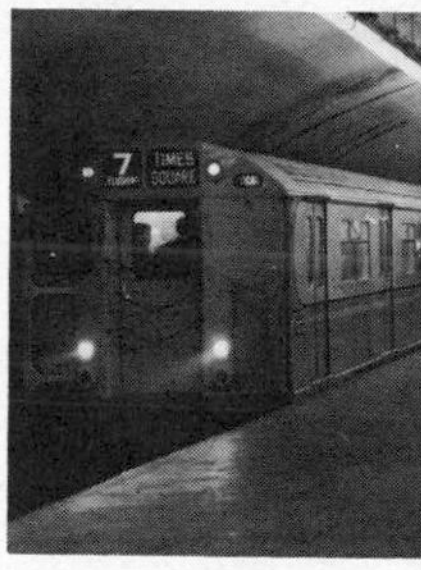

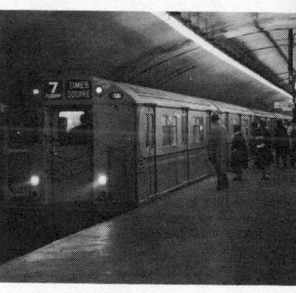

subway
New York City

su·crose (so͞o′krōs′) *n.* A crystalline disaccharide carbohydrate, $C_{12}H_{22}O_{11}$, found in many plants, mainly sugar cane, sugar beet, and maple, and used widely as a sweetener, preservative, and in the manufacture of plastics and cellulose. Also called "cane sugar," "saccharose." [French *sucre*, SUGAR + -OSE.]

suc·tion (sŭk′shən) *n.* **1.** The act or process of sucking. **2.** A force that causes a fluid or solid to be drawn into an interior space or to adhere to a surface because of the difference between the external and internal pressures. —*adj.* **1.** Creating suction. **2.** Operating by suction. [Late Latin *suctiō*, from Latin *sūgere* (past participle *sūctus*), to suck. See **seu-**[4] in Appendix.*]

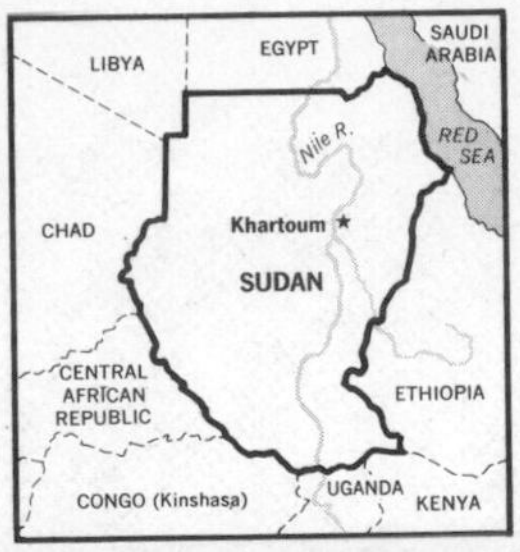

Republic of the Sudan

suction pump. A pump for drawing up a liquid by means of suction produced by a piston being drawn through a cylinder.

suction stop. *Phonetics.* A **click** *(see).*

suc·to·ri·al (sŭk′tôr′ē-əl, -tōr′ē-əl) *adj.* **1.** Adapted for sucking or clinging by suction: *a suctorial organ.* **2.** Having suctorial organs or parts. [From New Latin *sūctōrius*, from Latin *sūgere*, to suck. See **suction.**]

Su·dan (so͞o-dăn′). *French* **Sou·dan** (so͞o′däɴ′). A region lying across Africa, south of the Sahara and north of the equator. —**Su·da·nese′** (-də-nēz′, -nēs′) *adj.* & *n.*

Su·dan, Republic of the (so͞o-dăn′). A country occupying 967,500 square miles in northeastern Africa. Population, 13,011,000. Capital, Khartoum.

Su·dan·ic (so͞o-dăn′ĭk) *adj.* **1.** Of or pertaining to the Sudan. **2.** Of or pertaining to the languages of the region, chiefly Niger-Congo and Chari-Nile. —**Su·dan′ic** *n.*

su·da·to·ri·um (so͞o′də-tôr′ē-əm, -tōr′ē-əm) *n., pl.* **-ia** (-ē-ə). A hot-air room used for sweat baths. [Latin *sūdātōrium*, from *sūdāre*, to sweat. See **sweid-**[2] in Appendix.*]

su·da·to·ry (so͞o′də-tôr′ē, -tōr′ē) *adj.* Sudorific. —*n., pl.* **sudatories. 1.** A sudatorium. **2.** A sudorific.

sudd (sŭd) *n.* Floating masses of vegetation that often obstruct navigation on the White Nile. [Arabic, obstruction, from *sadda*, to obstruct.]

sud·den (sŭd′n) *adj.* **1.** Happening without warning; unforeseen. **2.** Characterized by hastiness; abrupt; rash. **3.** Characterized by rapidity; quick; swift. —See Synonyms at **impetuous.** —**all of a sudden.** Very quickly and unexpectedly; suddenly. [Middle English *sodan(e)*, from Norman French *sodein, sudein*, from Late Latin *subitānus*, variant of Latin *subitāneus*, from *subitus*, sudden, past participle of *subīre*, to approach secretly, steal upon : *sub-*, secretly + *īre*, to go (see **ei-**[1] in Appendix*).] —**sud′den·ly** *adv.* —**sud′den·ness** *n.*

sudden death. 1. A death that is not preceded by any condition that would appear fatal. **2.** *Sports.* **a.** A game played to break a tie. **b.** Extra minutes of play added to a tied game, the winning team being the first team to score.

Su·de·ten·land (so͞o-dāt′n-lănd′; *German* zo͞o-dā′tən-länt′). A border region of Bohemia, Moravia, and Silesia, in Czechoslovakia.

Su·de·tes (so͞o-dā′tēz). Also **Su·de·ten Mountains** (so͞o-dāt′n). A mountain system extending 170 miles along the border between Czechoslovakia and East Germany and Czechoslovakia and Poland. Highest elevation, 5,259 feet.

su·dor·if·er·ous (so͞o′də-rĭf′ər-əs) *adj.* Producing or secreting sweat. [Late Latin *sūdōrifer* : Latin *sūdor*, sweat (see **sweid-**[2] in Appendix*) + -FEROUS.]

su·dor·if·ic (so͞o′də-rĭf′ĭk) *adj.* Causing or increasing sweat. —*n.* A sudorific medicine. [New Latin *sūdōrificus* : Latin *sūdor*, sweat (see **sweid-**[2] in Appendix*) + -FIC.]

Su·dra (so͞o′drə) *n.* **1.** The lowest of the major Hindu castes, the members of which were originally menials but are now largely artisans and laborers. **2.** A member of this caste. [Sanskrit *śūdra.*]

suds (sŭdz) *pl.n.* **1.** Soapy water. **2.** Foam; lather. **3.** *Slang.* Beer. [Originally, dregs, muddy water, probably from Middle Dutch *sudde, sudse*, marsh, swamp. See **seu-**[1] in Appendix.*]

suds·y (sŭd′zē) *adj.* **-ier, -iest.** Full of or resembling suds.

sue (so͞o) *v.* **sued, suing, sues.** —*tr.* **1.** To make a petition to; appeal to; beseech. **2.** *Law.* **a.** To petition (a court) for redress of grievances or recovery of a right. **b.** To institute legal proceedings against (a person) for redress of grievances. **c.** To carry (an action) through to a final decision. **3.** *Archaic.* To court; woo. —*intr.* **1.** To institute legal proceedings; bring suit. **2.** To make an appeal or entreaty: *"And yet I sue for grace, and thou deny'st me"* (Francis Quarles). **3.** *Archaic.* To woo. [Middle English *sewen*, to pursue, prosecute, from Norman French *suer, suire*, from Vulgar Latin *sequere* (unattested), to follow, from Latin *sequī*. See **sekw-**[1] in Appendix.*] —**su′er** *n.*

Sue (sü), **Eugène.** Pen name of Marie Joseph Sue. 1804–1857. French novelist of Parisian life.

suede (swād) *n.* Also **suède. 1.** Leather with a soft napped surface. **2.** Fabric made to resemble this leather. In this sense, also called "suede cloth." [From *suède gloves*, partial translation of French *gants de suède*, "gloves of Sweden," from *Suède*, Sweden.]

su·et (so͞o′ĭt) *n.* The hard fatty tissues around the kidneys of cattle and sheep, used in cooking and making tallow. [Middle English *sewet*, from Norman French *sewet* (unattested), diminutive of *sue, seu*, from Latin *sēbum*, tallow, suet. See **sebum.**]

Sue·to·ni·us (swĭ-tō′nē-əs). In full, Gaius Suetonius Tranquillus. Roman historian of the second century A.D.

Su·ez (so͞o-ĕz′, so͞o′ĕz). A city and port of Egypt, at the head of the Gulf of Suez. Population, 219,000.

Su·ez, Isthmus of (so͞o-ĕz′, so͞o′ĕz). The strip of land in northeastern Egypt connecting Asia and Africa and traversed by the Suez Canal.

Su·ez Canal (so͞o-ĕz′, so͞o′ĕz). A waterway 107 miles long in northeastern Egypt, connecting the Mediterranean and the Gulf of Suez; built (1859–1869) by Ferdinand de Lesseps.

suf. suffix.

suff. 1. sufficient. **2.** suffix.

Suff. 1. Suffolk. **2.** suffragan.

suf·fer (sŭf′ər) *v.* **-fered, -fering, -fers.** —*intr.* **1.** To feel pain or distress; sustain loss, injury, harm, or punishment. **2.** To tolerate or endure evil, injury, pain, or death. **3.** To appear at a disadvantage: *"he suffers by comparison with his greater contemporary"* (Albert C. Baugh). —*tr.* **1.** To undergo or sustain (something painful, injurious, or unpleasant): *"ordinary men have always had to suffer the history their leaders were making"* (Herbert J. Muller). **2.** To experience: *suffer a change in staff.* **3.** To endure or bear; stand: *He cannot suffer boredom.* **4.** To permit; allow: *"Rulers must not be suffered thus to absolve themselves of their solemn responsibility."* (Macaulay). —See Synonyms at **bear.** [Middle English *suff(e)ren*, to undergo, endure, allow, from Norman French *suffrir*, from Vulgar Latin *sufferīre* (unattested), from Latin *sufferre*, to sustain, "to bear up" : *sub-*, up from under + *ferre*, to bear (see **bher-**[1] in Appendix*).] —**suf′fer·er** *n.* —**suf′fer·ing·ly** *adv.*

Usage: *Suffer*, in general usage, is preferably used with *from*, rather than *with*, in constructions such as *He suffered from hypertension.* According to 94 per cent of the Usage Panel, *suffered with* would be unacceptable in the preceding example. (In medical usage *suffer with* is sometimes employed with reference to experiencing actual pain or discomfort caused by a condition; *suffer from* applies more broadly to having a condition, such as anemia, that is detrimental but not necessarily painful.)

suf·fer·a·ble (sŭf′ər-ə-bəl, sŭf′rə-) *adj.* Capable of being suffered, endured, or permitted; tolerable. —**suf′fer·a·bly** *adv.*

suf·fer·ance (sŭf′ər-əns, sŭf′rəns) *n.* **1.** The capacity to tolerate pain or distress. **2.** Sanction or permission implied or given by failure to prohibit; tacit assent; tolerance. **3.** *Archaic.* Suffering; misery. **4.** *Archaic.* Patient endurance. [Middle English *suffrance*, from Old French, from Late Latin *sufferentia*, from Latin *sufferre*, to bear up, SUFFER.]

suf·fer·ing (sŭf′ər-ĭng, sŭf′rĭng) *n.* **1.** The act or condition of one who suffers. **2.** Something that causes pain or distress.

suf·fice (sə-fīs′) *v.* **-ficed, -ficing, -fices.** —*intr.* **1.** To meet present needs or requirements; be sufficient or adequate: *These rations will suffice until next week.* **2.** To be capable or competent; be equal to a specified task: *No words will suffice to convey his grief.* —*tr.* To be enough or sufficient for; satisfy the needs or requirements of. [Middle English *suffisen*, from Old French *suffire* (present stem *suffis-*), from Latin *sufficere*, to put under, substitute, suffice : *sub-*, under + *facere*, to do, make (see **dhē-**[1] in Appendix*).] —**suf·fic′er** *n.*

suf·fi·cien·cy (sə-fĭsh′ən-sē) *n.* **1.** The state or quality of being sufficient. **2.** Adequate supplies, ability, numbers, or resources; especially, an adequate but not luxurious scale of living.

suf·fi·cient (sə-fĭsh′ənt) *adj.* **1.** *Abbr.* **suff.** As much as is needed; enough; adequate: *"People can be trusted to work out useful solutions when they have sufficient education"* (Walter R. Agard). **2.** *Archaic.* Capable; competent; efficient. [Middle English, from Old French, from Latin *sufficiēns*, present participle of *sufficere*, SUFFICE.] —**suf·fi′cient·ly** *adv.*

Synonyms: *sufficient, enough, adequate.* These adjectives mean capable of fulfilling a need or requirement. *Sufficient* and *enough* refer to quantity and usually imply equality with the required amount or a slight excess. *Enough* can also be used ironically to indicate a quantity well in excess of what is desired. *Adequate* refers to both quantity and quality. With respect to quantity, it is approximately equivalent to *sufficient* and *enough* in their primary sense. With reference to quality, *adequate* implies capacity for meeting a modest standard and sometimes for barely meeting it.

suf·fix (sŭf′ĭks′) *n. Abbr.* **suf., suff.** *Grammar.* An affix added to the end of a word or stem, serving to form a new word or to form an inflectional ending, as *-ness* in *gentleness*, *-ing* in *walking*, or *-s* in *sits.* —*tr.v* **suffixed, -fixing, -fixes.** To add as a suffix. [New Latin *suffixum*, from Latin *suffixus*, neuter past participle of *suffigere*, to affix, fasten beneath : *sub-*, beneath + *figere*, to fix (see **dhīgw-** in Appendix*).] —**suf′fix′al** *adj.* —**suf·fix′ion** (sə-fĭk′shən) *n.*

suf·fo·cate (sŭf′ə-kāt′) *v.* **-cated, -cating, -cates.** —*tr.* **1.** To kill or destroy by preventing access of oxygen to (an animal or fire, for example). **2.** To impair the respiration of; to choke; asphyxiate. **3.** To cause discomfort by or as if by cutting off the supply of air. **4.** To suppress the development, imagination, or creativity of; stifle: *"The rigid formality of the place suffocated her"* (Thackeray). —*intr.* **1.** To die from suffocation. **2.** To be stifled; smother. [Latin *suffocāre* : *sub-*, under, down + *faucēs*, throat, FAUCES.] —**suf′fo·cat′ing·ly** *adv.* —**suf′fo·ca′tive** *adj.*

Suf·folk[1] (sŭf′ək). *Abbr.* **Suff.** A county occupying 1,482 square miles in southeastern England, divided administratively into East Suffolk (871 square miles; population, 343,056) with the county seat at Ipswich, and West Suffolk (611 square miles; population, 129,000) with the county seat at Bury St. Edmunds.

Suf·folk[2] (sŭf′ək) *n.* **1.** Any of an English breed of hornless sheep producing high-quality mutton. **2.** Any of a breed of English draft horses having short legs and a thickset, heavy body. [Originated in Suffolk County, England.]

suf·fra·gan (sŭf′rə-gən) *n. Abbr.* **Suff., Suffr. 1.** A bishop elected or appointed as an assistant to the bishop or ordinary of a diocese, having administrative and episcopal responsibilities but no jurisdictional functions. **2.** Any bishop regarded in his position as subordinate to his archbishop or metropolitan. Also

ă pat/ā pay/âr care/ä father/b bib/ch church/d deed/ĕ pet/ē be/f fife/g gag/h hat/hw which/ĭ pit/ī pie/îr pier/j judge/k kick/l lid, needle/m mum/n no, sudden/ng thing/ŏ pot/ō toe/ô paw, for/oi noise/ou out/o͝o took/o͞o boot/p pop/r roar/s sauce/sh ship, dish/

called "suffragan bishop." —*adj.* Of, being, or pertaining to a suffragan; auxiliary; subordinate. [Middle English, from Old French, from Medieval Latin *suffrāgāneus*, from *suffrāgium*, SUFFRAGE.] —**suf′fra·gan·ship′** *n.*

suf·frage (sŭf′rĭj) *n.* **1.** A vote cast in the procedure used in deciding a disputed question or in electing a person to office. **2.** The right or privilege of voting; franchise. **3.** The exercise of such a right. **4.** A short intercessory prayer. [Middle English, intercessory prayer, from Old French *suffrage, suffragies*, from Medieval Latin *suffrāgium*, vote, support, prayer, from Latin, ballot, right of voting. See **bhreg-** in Appendix.*]

suf·fra·gette (sŭf′rə-jĕt′) *n.* A female advocate of suffrage for women. —**suf′fra·get′tism′** *n.*

suf·fra·gist (sŭf′rə-jĭst) *n.* An advocate of the extension of political voting rights, especially to women.

suf·fru·tes·cent (sŭf′ro͞o-tĕs′ənt) *adj.* Also **suf·fru·ti·cose** (-ro͞o′tĭ-kōs′). *Botany.* Having a woody stem or base; somewhat shrubby. [New Latin *suffrutescens* : SUB- + FRUTESCENT.]

suf·fuse (sə-fyo͞oz′) *tr.v.* **-fused, -fusing, -fuses.** To spread through or over, as with liquid, color, or light: *"The sky above the roof is suffused with deep colors"* (O'Neill). [Latin *suffundere* (past participle *suffūsus*), to pour underneath or into : *sub-*, underneath + *fundere*, to pour (see **gheu-** in Appendix*).] —**suf·fu′sion** *n.* —**suf·fu′sive** (sə-fyo͞o′sĭv) *adj.*

Su·fi (so͞o′fē) *n.* A member of a Moslem mystic sect. [Arabic *sūfīy*, "(man) of wool," from *sūf*, wool (probably from their woolen garments).] —**Su′fic** (-fĭk), **Su′fis′tic** (-fĭs′tĭk) *adj.*

Su·fism (so͞o′fĭz′əm) *n.* A sect of Islamic mysticism, dating from the eighth century A.D. and developed chiefly in Persia.

sug·ar (sho͝og′ər) *n.* **1.** A sweet crystalline carbohydrate, **sucrose** *(see)*. **2.** Any of a class of water-soluble crystalline carbohydrates, including sucrose and lactose, having a characteristically sweet taste. **3.** A particular amount of sugar, as a cube. **4.** *Slang.* Sweetheart. Used as a form of endearment. —*v.* **sugared, -aring, -ars.** —*tr.* **1.** To coat, cover, or sweeten with sugar. **2.** To make less distasteful or more appealing. —*intr.* To form sugar; granulate. [Middle English *suker, sugre*, from Old French *sukere, zuchre*, from Old Italian *zucchero*, from Medieval Latin *zuccarum, succarum*, from Arabic *sukkar*, from Persian *shakar*, from Prakrit *sakkara*, from Sanskrit *śarkarā*†, pebble, gravel, sugar.]

sugar apple. A tree, the **sweetsop** *(see)*, or its fruit.

sugar beet. A form of the common beet, *Beta vulgaris*, having white roots from which sugar is obtained.

sug·ar·ber·ry (sho͝og′ər-bĕr′ē) *n., pl.* **-ries.** The **hackberry** *(see)*.

sugar bush. A grove of sugar maples used as a source of maple syrup or maple sugar. Also called "sugar orchard."

sugar cane. A tall grass, *Saccharum officinarum*, native to the East Indies, having thick, tough stems that are one of the chief commercial sources of sugar.

sug·ar-coat (sho͝og′ər-kōt′) *tr.v.* **-coated, -coating, -coats.** **1.** To coat with sugar: *sugar-coat a pill.* **2.** To cause to seem more appealing or pleasant.

sugar corn. Sweet corn *(see)*.

sug·ar-cured (sho͝og′ər-kyo͝ord′) *adj.* Cured with a preparation of sugar, salt, and nitrate. Said of meats.

sugar daddy. *Slang.* A wealthy, usually older man who gives expensive gifts to a young woman in return for her sexual favors or her companionship.

sug·ared (sho͝og′ərd) *adj.* **1.** Sweetened with sugar. **2.** Made more appealing or pleasant.

sug·ar·house (sho͝og′ər-hous′) *n.* A sugar refinery or processing plant; especially, a building in which maple sap is boiled down to yield maple syrup and maple sugar.

sugaring off. **1.** The process of boiling down maple sap to yield maple syrup and maple sugar. **2.** An informal social gathering in which the guests help make maple sugar.

sugar loaf. **1.** A large conical loaf of pure concentrated sugar. **2.** Something resembling the shape of this. —**sug′ar-loaf′** (sho͝og′ər-lōf′) *adj.*

Sugar Loaf Mountain. A peak 1,296 feet high, on Guanabara Bay, in Rio de Janeiro, Brazil.

sugar maple. A maple tree, *Acer saccharum*, of eastern North America, having sap that is the source of maple syrup and maple sugar and hard variously grained wood used in cabinetmaking. Also called "hard maple," "rock maple."

sugar of lead. Lead acetate *(see)*.

sugar of milk. Lactose *(see)*.

sugar pine. A tall evergreen timber tree, *Pinus lambertiana*, of the Pacific coast of North America.

sug·ar·plum (sho͝og′ər-plŭm′) *n.* A small piece of sugary candy.

sug·ar·y (sho͝og′ə-rē) *adj.* **-ier, -iest.** **1.** Composed of, tasting like, resembling, or containing sugar. **2.** Deceitfully or cloyingly sweet. —**sug′ar·i·ness** *n.*

sug·gest (səg-jĕst′, sə-jĕst′) *tr.v.* **-gested, -gesting, -gests.** **1.** To offer for consideration or action; propose. **2.** To bring or call to mind by logic or association; evoke. **3.** To make evident indirectly; intimate; imply. **4.** To serve as or provide a motive for; prompt; demand: *Such a crime suggests apt punishment.* [Latin *suggerere* (past participle *suggestus*), to carry or put underneath, furnish, suggest : *sub-*, underneath + *gerere*, to carry (see **gerere** in Appendix*).] —**sug·gest′er** *n.*

Synonyms: suggest, imply, hint, intimate, insinuate. These verbs mean to impart thoughts or ideas by indirection. *Suggest*, in this context, usually refers to a process whereby something is called to mind by a listener or viewer as the result of an association of ideas or train of thought. *Imply* refers to conveying an unstated or indirectly stated thought as part of something otherwise more explicit. The implied, or secondary, part is deduced as a seemingly logical consequence of the whole. *Hint* refers to expression that is indirect but contains rather pointed clues. *Intimate* applies to veiled expression that may be the result of discretion or reserve. *Insinuate* refers to covert expression of something, usually unpleasant, in a manner that suggests underhandedness.

sug·gest·i·bil·i·ty (səg-jĕs′tə-bĭl′ə-tē, sə-jĕs′-) *n.* Responsiveness or susceptibility to suggestion.

sug·gest·i·ble (səg-jĕs′tə-bəl, sə-jĕs′-) *adj.* Readily influenced by suggestion.

sug·ges·tion (səg-jĕs′chən, sə-jĕs′-) *n.* **1.** The act of suggesting. **2.** Something suggested. **3.** The sequential thought process by which one idea or concept leads to another. **4. a.** The psychological process by which an idea is induced in or adopted by an individual without argument, command, or coercion. **b.** Any idea or response so induced.

sug·ges·tive (səg-jĕs′tĭv, sə-jĕs′-) *adj.* **1. a.** Tending to suggest thoughts or ideas. **b.** Conveying a hint or suggestion; indicative. **2.** Tending to suggest something improper or indecent. —**sug·ges′tive·ly** *adv.* —**sug·ges′tive·ness** *n.*

su·i·ci·dal (so͞o′ə-sīd′l, syo͞o′-) *adj.* **1.** Pertaining to, involving, or related to suicide. **2.** Dangerous to oneself or to one's interests; self-destructive; ruinous. —**su′i·ci′dal·ly** *adv.*

su·i·cide (so͞o′ə-sīd′, syo͞o′-) *n.* **1.** The act or an instance of intentionally killing oneself. **2.** The destruction or ruin of one's own interests. **3.** One who commits suicide. —*intr.v.* **suicided, -ciding, -cides.** *Informal.* To commit suicide. [New Latin *suicida* (person), *suicidium* (act) : Latin *suī*, of oneself (see **seu-**[2] in Appendix*) + -CIDE.]

su·i gen·e·ris (so͞o′ī jĕn′ər-ĭs, syo͞o′ī). Unique; individual. [Latin, "of one's own kind."]

su·i ju·ris (so͞o′ī jo͝or′ĭs, syo͞o′ī-). *Law.* Capable of managing one's own affairs. [Latin, "of one's own right."]

su·int (so͞o′ĭnt, syo͞o′-, swĭnt) *n.* A natural grease formed from dried perspiration found in the fleece of sheep, used as a source of potash. [French, from Old French *suer*, to sweat, from Latin *sūdāre*. See **sweid-**[2] in Appendix.*]

Suisse. The French name for **Switzerland.**

Sui·sun Bay (sə-so͞on′). The eastern arm of San Francisco Bay, in western California.

suit (so͞ot) *n.* **1.** A set of outer garments consisting of a coat and trousers or skirt that match in color or fabric. **2.** Any group of things united into a set or series by having a common form or function. **3.** Any of the four sets of playing cards, each with similar pips, that constitute a deck. **4. a.** Attendance required of a vassal at his feudal lord's court or manor. **b.** *Law.* Any proceeding in court to recover a right or claim. **5.** The act or an instance of courting a woman. —**follow suit.** **1.** To play a card of the same suit as the one led. **2.** To do as another has done; follow an example. —*v.* **suited, suiting, suits.** —*tr.* **1.** To meet the requirements of; accommodate: *This candidate does not suit our qualifications.* **2.** To make appropriate or suitable; adapt: *We can suit the building to your specifications.* **3.** To please; satisfy. **4.** *Archaic.* To provide with clothing; dress. —*intr.* To be suitable or acceptable. [Middle English *su(i)te*, attendance at a sheriff's court, litigation, uniform, garb, from Old French *siute, suite*, from Vulgar Latin *sequita* (unattested), pursuit, from *sequere* (unattested), to follow. See **sue.**]

suit·a·ble (so͞o′tə-bəl, syo͞o′-) *adj.* Appropriate to a given purpose or occasion. See Synonyms at **fit.** —**suit′a·bil′ity** (-bĭl′ə-tē), **suit′a·ble·ness** *n.* —**suit′a·bly** *adv.*

suit·case (so͞ot′kās′, syo͞ot′-) *n.* A usually rectangular and flat piece of luggage for carrying clothing.

suite (swēt; *also* so͞ot *for sense 4*) *n.* **1.** A staff of attendants or a train of followers; retinue. **2.** Any succession of related things intended to be used together. **3.** A series of connected rooms used as a living unit. **4.** A set of matched furniture pieces intended for use in the same room. **5.** *Music.* An instrumental composition consisting of a succession of dances in the same or related keys. [French, from Old French *sieute*, following, retinue, from Vulgar Latin *sequita* (unattested). See **suit.**]

suit·ing (so͞o′tĭng) *n.* Fabric from which suits are made.

suit·or (so͞o′tər) *n.* **1.** A person who makes a petition or request. **2.** A person who sues in a court of law; plaintiff; petitioner. **3.** A man who is in the process of courting a woman. [Middle English *suitor*, from Norman French, follower, from Latin *secūtor*, from *sequī* (past participle *secūtus*), to follow. See **sekw-**[1] in Appendix.*]

Su·kar·no (so͞o-kär′nō), **(Achmed).** Born 1901. Indonesian statesman; president of the Republic of Indonesia (1945–67).

Su·khu·mi (so͝ok′ə-mē). A city of the Soviet Union on the Black Sea, the capital of the Abkhazian A.S.S.R. Population, 65,000.

su·ki·ya·ki (so͞o′kē-yä′kē) *n.* A Japanese dish of sliced meat, vegetables, and seasoning fried together. [Japanese.]

Suk·koth. Variant of **Succoth.**

Su·la·we·si (so͞o′lə-wā′sē). Formerly **Cel·e·bes** (sĕl′ə-bēz, sə-lē′-bēz). An island and province of Indonesia, 69,277 square miles in area, on the equator east of Borneo. Population, 6,000,000. Capital, Makassar.

sul·cate (sŭl′kāt′) *adj. Biology.* Having narrow longitudinal indentations; grooved. [Latin *sulcātus*, past participle of *sulcāre*, to furrow, from *sulcus*, furrow, SULCUS.]

sul·cus (sŭl′kŭs) *n., pl.* **-ci** (-kī′). **1.** A narrow, deep furrow or groove. **2.** *Anatomy.* Any of the narrow fissures separating adjacent cerebral convolutions. [Latin *sulcus*, furrow, groove. See **selk-** in Appendix.*]

Su·lei·man I (so͞o′lā-män). Also **So·ly·man** (sŏl′ĭ-mən). Known as Suleiman the Magnificent. 1490?–1566. Sultan of Turkey (1520–66).

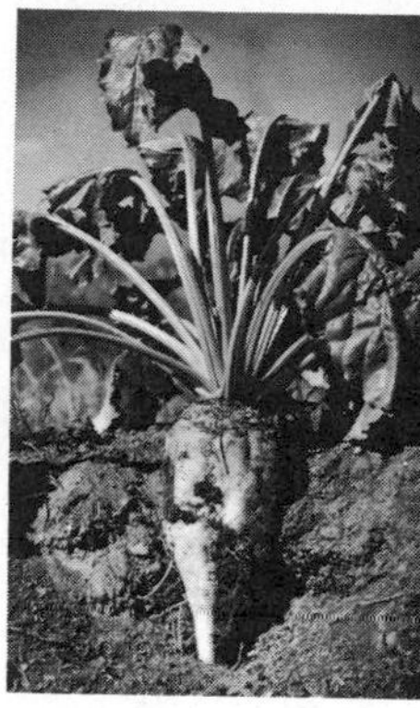

sugar beet

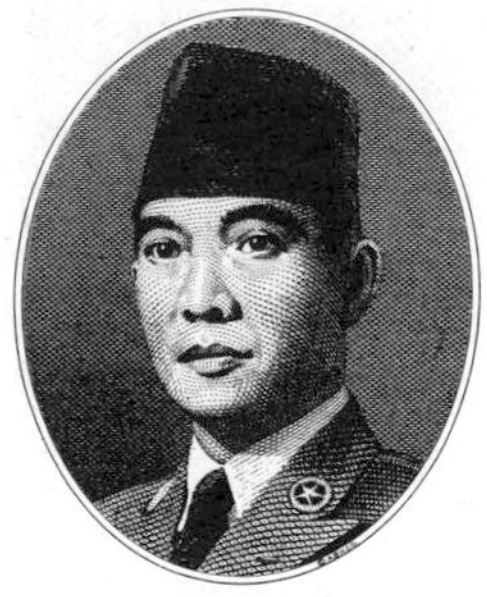

Sukarno

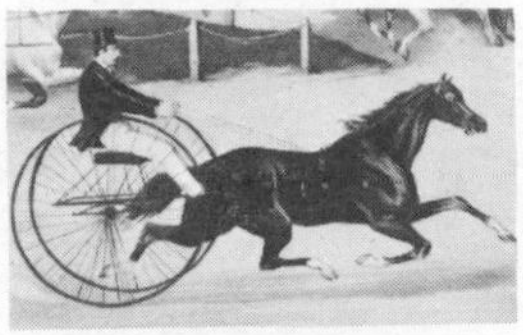

sulky²
Detail from an 1869 print by Currier and Ives

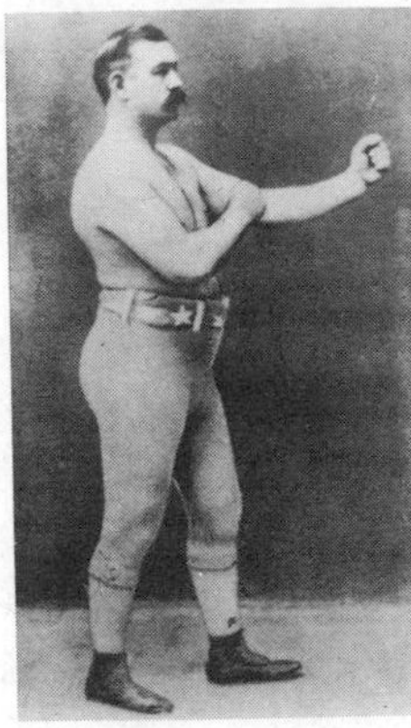

John L. Sullivan

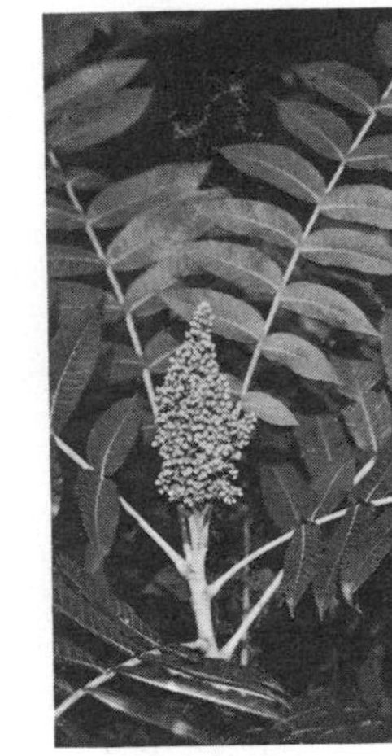

sumac
Rhus glabra

sulf–. Indicates sulfur; for example, **sulfide, sulfone.** ***Note:*** The spelling *sulph-* is no longer admitted by scientific publications. [From SULFUR.]

sul·fa drug (sŭl′fə). Any of a group of synthetic organic compounds, such as sulfathiazole and sulfadiazine, chemically similar to sulfonamide and capable of inhibiting bacterial growth and activity. [SULFA(NILAMIDE) + DRUG.]

sul·fa·nil·a·mide (sŭl′fə-nĭl′ə-mīd′) *n.* A white, odorless crystalline sulfonamide, $C_6H_8N_2SO_2$, used in the treatment of various bacterial infections. [SULF- + ANIL(INE) + AMIDE.]

sul·fate (sŭl′fāt′) *n.* A chemical compound containing the bivalent group SO_4. —*v.* **sulfated, -fating, -fates.** —*tr.* **1.** To treat or react with sulfuric acid or a sulfate. **2.** *Electricity.* To cause lead sulfate to accumulate on (the plates of a lead-acid storage battery). —*intr.* To become sulfated. [French : SULF- + -ATE.]

sul·fide (sŭl′fīd′) *n.* A compound of bivalent sulfur with an electropositive element or group; especially, a binary compound of sulfur with a metal. [SULF- + -IDE.]

sul·fi·nyl (sŭl′fə-nĭl′) *n.* The bivalent group SO. Also called "thionyl." [SULF- + -IN + -YL.]

sul·fite (sŭl′fīt′) *n.* A salt or ester of sulfurous acid. [French, variant of SULFATE.] —**sul·fit′ic** (sŭl′fĭt′ĭk) *adj.*

sulfon–. Indicates: **1.** Sulfonic; for example, **sulfonamide. 2.** Sulfonyl; for example, **sulfonmethane.** ***Note:*** The spelling *sulphon-* is no longer admitted by scientific publications. [From SULFONE.]

sul·fon·a·mide (sŭl′fŏn′ə-mīd′, -mĭd) *n.* Any of a group of organic sulfur compounds having the general formula RSO_2NH_2. [SULFON- + AMIDE.]

sul·fo·nate (sŭl′fə-nāt′) *n.* A compound in which a hydrogen atom is replaced by the sulfonic acid group SO_2OH. —*tr.v.* **sulfonated, -nating, -nates. 1.** To introduce into (an organic compound) one or more sulfonic-acid groups. **2.** To treat with sulfonic acid. [SULFON- + -ATE.] —**sul′fo·na′tion** *n.*

sul·fone (sŭl′fōn′) *n.* Any of various organic sulfur compounds having a sulfonyl group attached to two carbon atoms; especially, such a compound used to treat leprosy or tuberculosis. [SULF- + -ONE.]

sul·fon·ic acid (sŭl′fŏn′ĭk). Any of several organic acids containing one or more sulfonic groups, SO_2OH.

sul·fo·ni·um (sŭl′fō′nē-əm) *n.* The univalent cation H_3S. [New Latin : SULF(UR) + (AMM)ONIUM.]

sul·fon·meth·ane (sŭl′fŏn′mĕth′ān) *n.* A colorless crystalline or powdered compound, $C_7H_{16}S_2O_4$, used medicinally as a hypnotic. [SULFON- + METHANE.]

sul·fo·nyl (sŭl′fə-nĭl′) *n.* The bivalent radical SO_2. Also called "sulfuryl." [SULFON- + -YL.]

sul·fur (sŭl′fər) *n.* Also **sul·phur.** *Symbol* **S** A pale-yellow nonmetallic element occurring widely in nature both free and combined in several allotropic forms. It is used in black gunpowder, rubber vulcanization, the manufacture of insecticides and pharmaceuticals, and in the preparation of important sulfur compounds, such as hydrogen sulfide and sulfuric acid. Atomic number 16, atomic weight 32.064, melting point (rhombic) 112.8°C, (monoclinic) 119.0°C, boiling point 444.6°C, specific gravity (rhombic) 2.07, (monoclinic) 1.957, valences 2, 4, 6. Also *obsolete* "brimstone." See **element.** ***Note:*** The spelling *sulphur* is no longer admitted by scientific publications. However, it may occur in nonscientific contexts, especially when the reference is not directly to the element. See the entries beginning **sulphur.** —*tr.v.* **sulfured, -furing, -furs.** Also **sul·phur, -phured, -phuring, -phurs.** To treat with sulfur or a compound of sulfur. [Middle English *sulfur, sulphur(e),* from Norman French *sulf(e)re,* from Latin *sulfur*†, *sulphur.*]

sul·fu·rate (sŭl′fə-rāt′) *tr.v.* **-rated, -rating, -rates.** To treat or react with sulfur. [Late Latin *sulfurāre,* from Latin *sulfur,* SULFUR.] —**sul′fu·ra′tion** *n.*

sulfur dioxide. A colorless, extremely irritating gas or liquid, SO_2, used in many industrial processes, especially the manufacture of sulfuric acid.

sul·fu·re·ous (sŭl-fyŏŏr′ē-əs) *adj.* Of or pertaining to sulfur; sulfurous.

sul·fu·ret (sŭl′fyə-rĕt′) *tr.v.* **-reted** or **-retted, -reting** or **-retting, -rets.** To sulfurize. —*n.* A sulfide. [New Latin *sulfuretum,* sulfide, from Latin *sulfur,* SULFUR.]

sul·fu·ric (sŭl′fyŏŏr′ĭk) *adj.* Of, relating to, or containing sulfur, especially with valence 6.

sulfuric acid. A highly corrosive, dense oily liquid, H_2SO_4, colorless to dark brown depending on purity and used to manufacture a wide variety of chemicals and materials including fertilizers, paints, detergents, and explosives. Also called "oil of vitriol."

sul·fur·ize (sŭl′fə-rīz′, -fyə-rīz′) *tr.v.* **-ized, -izing, -izes. 1.** To treat or impregnate with sulfur; sulfuret. **2.** To bleach or fumigate with sulfur or sulfur dioxide. —**sul′fur·i·za′tion** *n.*

sul·fur·ous (sŭl′fə-rəs, sŭl′fyŏŏr′əs) *adj.* Also **sul·phur·ous** (for sense 3). **1.** Of, relating to, derived from, or containing sulfur, especially in its lower valence. **2.** Characteristic of or emanating from burning sulfur. **3.** Fiery; hellish.

sulfurous acid. A colorless solution of sulfur dioxide in water, H_2SO_3, characterized by a suffocating sulfurous odor, used as a bleaching agent, preservative, and disinfectant.

sulfur trioxide. A corrosive compound, SO_3, having three solid forms that may coexist in a given sample, used in the sulfonation of organic compounds.

sul·fur·y (sŭl′fə-rē) *adj.* Also **sul·phur·y** (for sense 2). **1.** Similar to or suggesting sulfur. **2.** Fiery; hellish.

sul·fur·yl (sŭl′fər-ĭl′) *n.* **Sulfonyl** *(see).* [SULFUR + -YL.]

sulfuryl chloride. A colorless liquid, SO_2Cl_2, having a pungent odor, used as a chlorinating and dehydrating agent and in the manufacture of pharmaceuticals, dyestuffs, and poison gases.

sulk (sŭlk) *intr.v.* **sulked, sulking, sulks.** To be sullenly aloof or withdrawn, as in silent resentment or protest. —*n.* A mood or display of sulking. Used in the phrase *the sulks.* [Back-formation from SULKY.]

sulk·y¹ (sŭl′kē) *adj.* **-ier, -iest. 1.** Sullenly aloof or withdrawn. **2.** Gloomy; dismal: *sulky weather.* [Perhaps from obsolete *sulke,* sluggish, perhaps ultimately from Old English *asolcen,* past participle of *āseolcan,* to be lazy, become slack. See **selg-** in Appendix.*] —**sulk′i·ly** *adv.* —**sulk′i·ness** *n.*

sulk·y² (sŭl′kē) *n., pl.* **-ies.** A light two-wheeled vehicle accommodating one person and drawn by one horse. —*adj.* Resembling a sulky: *a sulky sleigh.* [From SULKY (because it has only one seat for the driver).]

Sul·la (sŭl′ə), **Lucius Cornelius.** Surnamed, Felix. 138?–78 B.C. Roman general; dictator of Rome (82–79 B.C.).

sul·lage (sŭl′ĭj) *n.* **1.** Silt deposited by a current of water. **2.** Waste materials or refuse; sewage. [Probably from Old French *souiller,* to SOIL.]

sul·len (sŭl′ən) *adj.* **1.** Showing a brooding ill humor or resentment; morose; sulky. **2.** Gloomy or somber in tone, color, or portent: *"the surly sullen bell"* (Shakespeare). **3.** Sluggish; slow: *a sullen march.* [Middle English *solein, solain,* from Norman French *solein* (unattested), alone, sullen, from Old French *seul, sol,* alone, single, from Latin *sōlus.* See **seu-**² in Appendix.*] —**sul′len·ly** *adv.* —**sul′len·ness** *n.*

Sul·li·van (sŭl′ə-vən), Sir **Arthur (Seymour).** 1842–1900. British composer of comic operas in collaboration with W.S. Gilbert.

Sul·li·van (sŭl′ə-vən), **Frank.** In full, Francis John. Born 1892. American author and humorist.

Sul·li·van (sŭl′ə-vən), **John L(awrence).** 1858–1918. American athlete; heavyweight boxing champion (1882–92).

Sul·li·van (sŭl′ə-vən), **Louis Henri.** 1856–1924. American architect; a pioneer in skyscraper construction.

sul·ly (sŭl′ē) *tr.v.* **-lied, -lying, -lies. 1.** To mar the cleanness or luster of; soil; stain. **2.** To defile; taint. —*n., pl.* **sullies.** *Archaic.* Something that sullies; a stain or spot. [Probably from Old French *souiller,* to SOIL.]

Sul·ly (sü-lē′), **Duc de.** Title of Maximilien de Béthune. 1560–1641. French statesman; chief minister of Henry IV.

Sul·ly (sŭl′ē), **Thomas.** 1783–1872. British-born American painter of portraits and historical scenes.

Sul·ly-Prud·homme (sü′lē′prü′dôm′), **René François Armand.** 1839–1907. French poet.

sul·phur¹ (sŭl′fər) *n.* Any of various butterflies of the genus *Colias* and related genera, having yellow or orange wings marked with black. Also called "sulphur butterfly."

sul·phur². Variant of **sulfur.** ***Note:*** This spelling is no longer admitted by scientific publications. However, it may occur in nonscientific contexts, especially when the reference is not directly to the element as in the entry below.

sul·phur-bot·tom (sŭl′fər-bŏt′əm) *n.* The **blue whale** *(see).*

sul·tan (sŭl′tən) *n.* The ruler of a Moslem country, especially of the former Ottoman Empire. [Old French, from Medieval Latin *sultānus,* from Arabic *sulṭān,* ruler, from Aramaic *shulṭānā,* "power," from *shəlēṭ,* to have power.]

sul·tan·a (sŭl-tăn′ə, -tä′nə) *n.* **1.** The wife, mother, sister, or daughter of a sultan. Also called "sultaness." **2.** The mistress of a sultan, king, or prince. **3.** A small, sweet, seedless raisin of a kind originally produced in Asia Minor. [Italian, feminine of *sultano,* sultan, from Arabic *sulṭān,* SULTAN.]

sul·tan·ate (sŭl′tən-āt′, -ĭt) *n.* **1.** The office, power, or reign of a sultan. **2.** The domain of a sultan.

sul·try (sŭl′trē) *adj.* **-trier, -triest. 1.** Very hot and humid. **2.** Extremely hot; torrid. **3.** Sensual; voluptuous: *a sultry Spanish dance.* [From obsolete *sulter,* variant of SWELTER.] —**sul′tri·ly** *adv.* —**sul′tri·ness** *n.*

Su·lu (sōō′lōō) *n., pl.* **-lus** or **Sulu. 1.** A Moro people inhabiting the Sulu Archipelago. **2.** A member of this people. **3.** The Austronesian language spoken by this people. [Sulu *sulug,* "current."] —**Su′lu·an** *adj.* & *n.*

Su·lu Archipelago (sōō′lōō). A group of islands, 1,086 square miles in area, in the western Pacific Ocean, constituting the extreme southern province of the Republic of the Philippines. Population, 301,000. Capital, Jolo.

Su·lu Sea (sōō′lōō). The section of the western Pacific Ocean between the central Philippines and Borneo.

sum (sŭm) *n.* **1.** The amount obtained as a result of adding. **2.** The whole amount, quantity, or number; aggregate: *the sum of our knowledge.* **3.** The highest point or degree; summit. **4.** An amount of money: *They paid an enormous sum for their house.* **5.** An arithmetic problem: *a child good at sums.* **6.** A summary; gist. —*v.* **summed, summing, sums.** —*tr.* **1.** To summarize. Used with *up.* **2.** To add. Often used with *up.* —*intr.* To give a brief review or summary. Used with *up.* [Middle English *summe, somme,* from Old French, from Latin *(res) summa,* the highest thing, sum, total (from the Greek and Roman habit of counting upward and writing the total at the top), from *summus,* highest, topmost. See **uper** in Appendix.*]

su·mac (sōō′măk′, shōō′-) *n.* Also **su·mach.** Any of various shrubs or small trees of the genus *Rhus,* having compound leaves and clusters of small greenish flowers followed by usually red, hairy fruits. Some species cause an acute itching rash on contact. [Middle English, from Old French, from Arabic *summaq,* sumac tree, probably from Aramaic, "red."]

Su·ma·tra (sōō-mä′trə). The second-largest island of Indonesia

(163,557 square miles), lying in the Indian Ocean west of Malaysia and Borneo. Population, 15,700,000.

Sum·ba (soōm′bä). *Dutch* **Soem·ba.** Formerly **San·dal·wood Island** (săn′dəl-woŏd′). An island of south-central Indonesia, 4,306 square miles in area, west of Timor. Population, 251,000.

Sum·ba·wa (soōm-bä′wä). *Dutch* **Soem·ba·wa.** An island of south-central Indonesia, 5,965 square miles in area, between Java and Flores. Population, 508,000.

Su·mer (soō′mər). An ancient country of Mesopotamia in a region now part of southern Iraq.

Su·me·ri·an (soō-mîr′ē-ən, -mĕr′ē-ən) *adj.* Of or pertaining to ancient Sumer, its people, culture, or language. —*n.* **1.** A member of an ancient Babylonian people, probably of non-Semitic origin, who established one of the earliest historic civilizations in Sumer in the fourth millennium B.C. **2.** The unclassified language used by these people, preserved in cuneiform on clay tablets. See **Japhetic.**

sum·ma cum lau·de (soōm′ə koōm lou′dā, sŭm′ə kŭm lô′dē). *Latin.* With the greatest praise. Used to designate a university degree awarded with the highest honors or the recipient of such a degree. Compare **cum laude, magna cum laude.**

sum·ma·rize (sŭm′ə-rīz′) *tr.v.* **-rized, -rizing, -rizes.** To make a summary of; restate briefly; abstract. —**sum′ma·rist** (-ə-rĭst) *n.* —**sum′ma·ri·za′tion** *n.*

sum·ma·ry (sŭm′ə-rē) *adj.* **1.** Presenting the substance in a condensed form; concise. **2.** Performed speedily and without ceremony: *summary justice.* —See Synonyms at **concise.** —*n., pl.* **summaries.** A condensation of the substance of a larger work; an abstract or abridgment. [Middle English, from Medieval Latin *summārius,* comprising the principal parts, from Latin *summa,* SUM.] —**sum·ma′ri·ly** (sə-mâr′ə-lē, sŭm′ər-ə-lē) *adv.* —**sum′ma·ri·ness** *n.*

summary court-martial. A court-martial consisting of one officer for trying relatively minor offenses.

sum·ma·tion (sə-mā′shən) *n.* **1.** The act or process of adding or totaling; addition. **2.** A sum or aggregate. **3.** A concluding statement containing a summary of principal points, especially of a case before a court of law. [Medieval Latin *summātiō,* from *summāre,* to sum up, from Latin *summa,* SUM.]

sum·mer[1] (sŭm′ər) *n.* **1.** The usually warmest season of the year occurring between spring and autumn. In the Northern Hemisphere it extends from the summer solstice to the autumnal equinox and is popularly considered to comprise June, July, and August, while in the Southern Hemisphere it falls between the winter solstice and the vernal equinox or, popularly, December, January, and February. **2.** Any period regarded as a time of fruition, fulfillment, happiness, or beauty. —*adj.* Pertaining to, characteristic of, or occurring in summer. —*v.* **summered, -mering, -mers.** —*tr.* To lodge or keep during the summer: *summering the herd in the south meadow.* —*intr.* To pass the summer: *They summered at the beach.* [Middle English *somer, sumer,* Old English *sumor.* See **sem-**[3] in Appendix.*] —**sum′mer·ly** *adj. & adv.*

sum·mer[2] (sŭm′ər) *n. Architecture.* **1.** A heavy horizontal timber that serves as a supporting beam, especially for the floor above. **2.** A lintel. **3.** A large, heavy stone usually set on the top of a column or pilaster to support an arch or lintel. [Middle English *summer, somer,* from Norman French *sumer, somer,* "pack animal," from Vulgar Latin *saumārius* (unattested), variant of Late Latin *sagmārius,* from *sagma,* packsaddle, from Greek. See **sumpter.**]

summer cypress. A plant, *Kochia scoparia,* native to Eurasia, having dense foliage that turns bright red. Also called "burning bush."

sum·mer·house (sŭm′ər-hous′) *n.* A small, roofed structure in a park or garden affording shade and rest; a gazebo.

summer savory. See **savory** (plant).

summer school. An academic session held during the summer.

sum·mer·set. Variant of **somersault.**

summer solstice. *Astronomy.* A solstice *(see).*

summer squash. Any of several varieties of squash, such as the crookneck or the cymling, that are eaten shortly after being picked rather than kept for storage.

sum·mer·time (sŭm′ər-tīm′) *n.* The summer season.

sum·mer·wood (sŭm′ər-woŏd′) *n.* Wood that develops during the latter part of the growing season and is harder and less porous than springwood.

sum·mer·y (sŭm′ə-rē) *adj.* Pertaining to or suggesting summer.

sum·mit (sŭm′ĭt) *n.* **1.** The highest point or part; the top, especially of a mountain. **2.** The highest degree of achievement or status. **3.** The highest level of government official. Usually used attributively: *summit conferences.* [Middle English *somette,* from Old French *sommette, sumet,* diminutive of *som, sum,* top, from Latin *summum,* neuter of *summus,* highest, topmost. See **uper** in Appendix.*] —**sum′mit·al** *adj.*

Synonyms: *summit, peak, pinnacle, acme, apex, zenith, climax.* Each of these nouns is applicable to the highest point of a thing, physically or figuratively. *Summit* and *peak* refer literally to the top, as of a hill or mountain. Figuratively *summit* suggests the highest level attainable, and *peak* the highest point of achievement. *Pinnacle* refers to a tall, slender mass, such as a spire, that tapers to a point or, figuratively, to a height reached by spectacular achievement. *Acme* is used figuratively, for the most part, to represent perfection. *Apex* is applied to the pointed tip or top of a figure, such as a cone, and figuratively to the focal point or culmination of any concerted effort. *Zenith* is that point in the heavens directly overhead or, by extension, the point of highest achievement, development, or power. *Climax*

usually refers to the point of greatest development or intensity, marking the end of an ascending process.

sum·mon (sŭm′ən) *tr.v.* **-moned, -moning, -mons. 1.** To call together; convene. **2.** To send for; request to appear. **3.** To order (a person) to appear in court by the issuance of a summons. **4.** To order to do a specific act: *summon the captain to surrender.* **5.** To call forth; rouse; muster. Often used with *up:* "*He summoned up a smile, though it seemed to take all his strength*" (Colin Turnbull). [Middle English *somo(u)nen,* from Old French *somondre,* from Vulgar Latin *summonere* (unattested), from Latin *summonēre,* to remind secretly : *sub-,* secretly + *monēre,* to remind, warn (see **men-**[1] in Appendix*).]

sum·mon·er (sŭm′ən-ər) *n.* **1.** A person who summons. **2.** Formerly, a court official who served summonses.

sum·mons (sŭm′ənz) *n., pl.* **-monses. 1.** A call or order to appear, come, or do something. **2.** *Law.* **a.** A notice summoning a defendant to report to a court. **b.** A notice issued to a person summoning him to report to court as a juror or witness. —*tr.v.* **summonsed, -monsing, -monses.** To serve a court summons to. [Middle English *somo(u)ns,* from Old French *som(o)unse,* from Gallo-Roman *summonsa* (unattested), from Latin *summonita,* from the feminine past participle of *summonēre,* to remind secretly, SUMMON.]

sum·mum bo·num (soōm′əm bō′nəm). *Latin.* The greatest or supreme good.

Sum·ner (sŭm′nər), **Charles.** 1811–1874. American political leader; member of U.S. Senate (1851–74).

Sum·ner (sŭm′nər), **James Batcheller.** 1887–1955. American biochemist; demonstrated enzyme crystallization.

Sum·ner (sŭm′nər), **William Graham.** 1840–1910. American economist, sociologist, and author.

sump (sŭmp) *n.* **a.** Any low area which receives drainage. **b.** A cesspool. **2.** A hole at the lowest point of a mine shaft into which water is drained in order to be pumped out. **3.** The crankcase or oil reservoir of an internal-combustion engine. [Middle English *sompe,* a swamp, morass, from Middle Low German or Middle Dutch *sump.* See **swombho-** in Appendix.*]

sump·ter (sŭmp′tər) *n.* A pack animal, such as a horse or mule. [Middle English *sum(p)ter, sometour,* driver of a pack animal, from Old French *som(m)etier,* from Vulgar Latin *saumatārius* (unattested), from Late Latin *sagma,* packsaddle, from Greek, from *satteinǂ,* to pack.]

sump·tu·ar·y (sŭmp′choō-ĕr′ē) *adj.* **1.** Pertaining to expenditure; regulating or limiting expenses. **2.** Regulating personal behavior on moral or religious grounds: *sumptuary laws.* [Latin *sumptuārius,* from *sumptus,* expense, from the past participle of *sūmere,* to consume, spend, take. See **em-** in Appendix.*]

sump·tu·ous (sŭmp′choō-əs) *adj.* Of a size or splendor suggesting great expense; lavish: "*He likes big meals, so I cook sumptuous ones.*" (Anaïs Nin). [Middle English, from Old French *sumptueux,* from Latin *sumptuōsus,* from *sumptus,* expense. See **sumptuary.**] —**sump′tu·ous·ly** *adv.* —**sump′tu·ous·ness** *n.*

sun (sŭn) *n.* **1.** A star that is the basis of the solar system and that sustains life on Earth, being the source of heat and light. It has a mean distance from Earth of about 93 million miles, a diameter of approximately 864,000 miles, and a mass about 330,000 times that of Earth. **2.** Any star that is the center of a planetary system. **3.** The radiant energy, especially heat and visible light, emitted by the sun; sunshine. —**a place in the sun.** A dominant or favorable position or situation. —*v.* **sunned, sunning, suns.** —*tr.* To expose to the sun's rays. **2.** To warm, dry, or tan (something) in the sun. —*intr.* To bask in the sun. [Middle English *sonne, sunne,* Old English *sunne.* See **sāwel-** in Appendix.*]

Sun. Sunday.

sun bath. Exposure of the body to the rays of the sun.

sun·bathe (sŭn′bāth′) *intr.v.* **-bathed, -bathing, -bathes.** To expose the body to the direct rays of the sun. —**sun′-bath′er** *n.*

sun·beam (sŭn′bēm′) *n.* A ray of sunlight.

sun·bird (sŭn′bûrd′) *n.* Any of various small, tropical Old World birds of the family Nectariniidae, having a slender, downward-curving bill and often brightly colored plumage in the male.

sun bittern. A cranelike tropical American bird, *Eurypyga helias,* having mottled brownish plumage and often spreading its wings and tail in a showy display.

sun·bon·net (sŭn′bŏn′ĭt) *n.* A woman's wide-brimmed bonnet with a flap at the back for protecting the neck from the sun.

sun·bow (sŭn′bō′) *n.* A rainbowlike display of colors resulting from the refraction of sunlight through a spray of water.

sun·burn (sŭn′bûrn′) *n.* An inflammation or blistering of the skin caused by overexposure to direct sunlight. —*v.* **sunburned** or **-burnt** (-bûrnt′), **-burning, -burns.** To afflict with sunburn. —*intr.* To be afflicted with sunburn.

sun·burst (sŭn′bûrst′) *n.* **1.** A sudden burst of sunlight, as through broken clouds. **2.** A pattern or design consisting of a central disk with radiating spires projecting in the manner of sunbeams. **3.** A jeweled brooch with such a design.

sun·dae (sŭn′dē, -dā′) *n.* A dish of ice cream with toppings such as syrup, fruits, nuts, and whipped cream. [Origin uncertain.]

Sun·da Islands (sŭn′də, soōn′də). The western section of the Malay Archipelago, between the South China Sea and the Indian Ocean, including most of Indonesia.

sun dance. A ritual dance performed by the North American Plains Indians at the summer solstice.

Sun·da Strait (sŭn′də, soōn′də). A channel between Sumatra and Java, connecting the Java Sea with the Indian Ocean.

sunburst
Diamond brooch

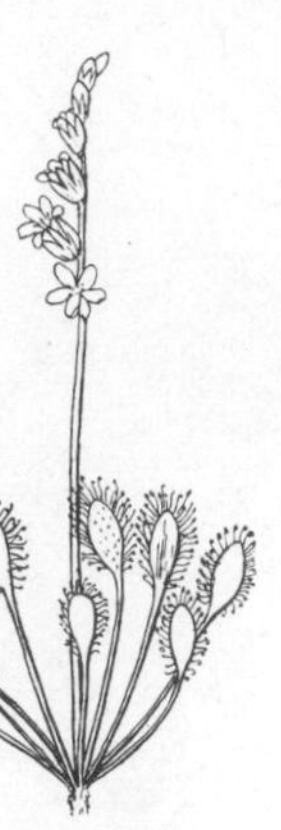
sundew
Drosera intermedia

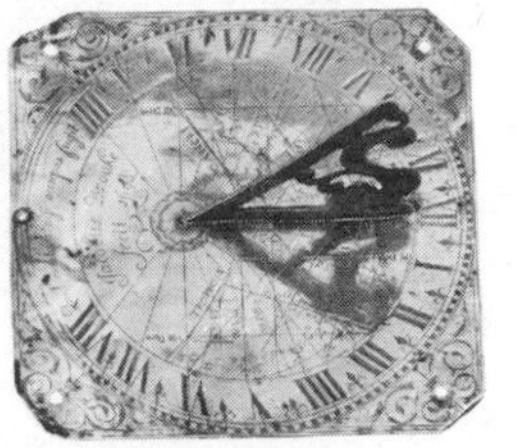
sundial

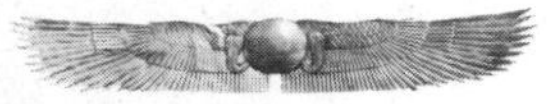
sun disk

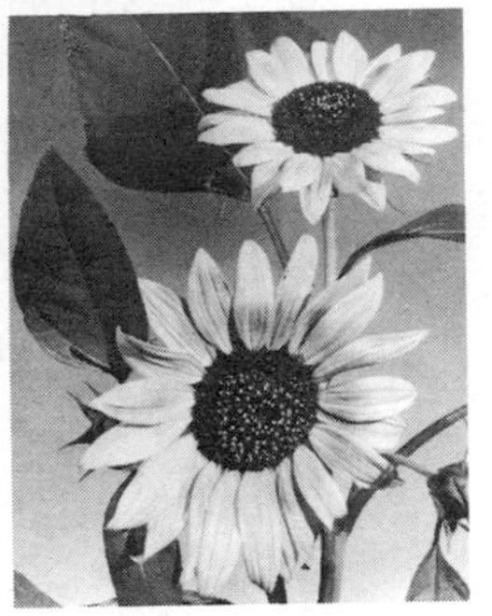
sunflower
Helianthus annuus

Sun·day (sŭn′dē, -dā′) *n. Abbr.* **Sun., S.** The first day of the week and the Christian Sabbath. See **Sabbath.** [Middle English *sone(n)day, sun(en)day,* Old English *sunnandæg,* "day of the sun." See **sāwel-** in Appendix.*]
Sun·day (sŭn′dē, -dā′), **William Ashley ("Billy").** 1862–1935. American evangelist.
Sunday school. *Abbr.* **S.S. 1.** A school, generally affiliated with a church, that offers religious instruction for children on Sundays. **2.** The teachers and pupils of a Sunday school.
sun deck. A roof, balcony, or terrace used for sun-bathing.
sun·der (sŭn′dər) *v.* **-dered, -dering, -ders.** *—tr.* To break (something) apart; divide; sever: *"an island, not widely sundered from the continent"* (Winston Churchill). *—intr.* To break into parts. —See Synonyms at **separate.** *—n.* A division or separation. [Middle English *sund(e)ren,* Old English *syndrian, sundrian.* See **sen-**[2] in Appendix.*] **—sun′der·ance** *n.*
Sun·der·land (sŭn′dər-lənd). A port and shipbuilding center of England, in northeastern Durham on the North Sea. Population, 188,000.
sun·dew (sŭn′dōō, -dyōō) *n.* Any of several insectivorous plants of the genus *Drosera,* growing in wet ground and having leaves covered with sticky hairs. [Translation of Latin *rōs sōlis.*]
sun·di·al (sŭn′dī′əl) *n.* An instrument that indicates local apparent solar time by measuring the hour angle of the sun with a style that casts a shadow on a calibrated dial.
sun disk. A symbol in Egyptian art consisting of a disk set between outspread wings, representing the sun god.
sun·dog (sŭn′dôg′, -dŏg′) *n. Meteorology.* **1.** A **parhelion** *(see).* **2.** A small halo or rainbow near the horizon just off the parhelic circle.
sun·down (sŭn′doun′) *n.* The time of sunset.
sun·down·er (sŭn′dou′nər) *n. Slang.* **1.** In Australia, a tramp who looks for a place to sleep at sundown. **2.** A ship's officer who imposes strict rules, such as the return of the crew on board at sundown. **3.** A drink taken at sundown.
sun·dries (sŭn′drēz) *pl.n.* Articles too small or numerous to be specified; miscellaneous items. [From SUNDRY.]
sun·drops (sŭn′drŏps′) *n.* Plural in form, used with a singular or plural verb. Any of several New World plants of the genus *Oenothera,* having four-petaled yellow flowers. [So called because the flowers remain open during the hours of sunlight.]
sun·dry (sŭn′drē) *adj.* Various; several; miscellaneous: *sundry items of clothing.* [Middle English *sundri, sondri,* Old English *syndrig,* apart, separate. See **sen-**[2] in Appendix.*]
sun·fish (sŭn′fĭsh′) *n., pl.* **sunfish** or **-fishes. 1.** Any of various small North American freshwater fishes of the family Centrarchidae, having laterally compressed, often brightly colored bodies. See **bluegill, pumpkinseed. 2.** Any of several large marine fishes of the family Molidae; especially, the **ocean sunfish** *(see).* [From its roundish body and bright colors.]
sun·flow·er (sŭn′flou′ər) *n.* **1.** Any of several plants of the genus *Helianthus;* especially, *H. annuus,* having tall, coarse stems and large yellow-rayed flowers that produce edible seeds rich in oil. **2.** Brilliant yellow to strong or vivid orange yellow. See **color. —sun′flow′er** *adj.*
Sunflower State. The nickname for Kansas.
sung. Past participle and alternate past tense of **sing.**
Sung (sōōng). A Chinese dynasty (A.D. 960–1280) noted for its accomplishments in painting, ceramics, and literature.
Sun·ga·ri (sōōng′gä′rē′). The major river of Manchuria, rising near the North Korean border and flowing 1,150 miles northwest, east, and finally northeast to the Amur at the Siberian border.
sun·glass (sŭn′glăs′, -gläs′) *n.* A **burning glass** *(see).*
sun·glass·es (sŭn′glăs′ĭz, -glä′sĭz) *pl.n.* Eyeglasses with tinted or polarizing lenses to protect the eyes from the sun's glare.
sun·glow (sŭn′glō′) *n.* A rose or yellow glow in the sky preceding sunrise or following sunset.
sun god. A god that personifies the sun.
sunk. Past participle and alternate past tense of **sink.** See Usage note at **sink.**
sunk·en (sŭng′kən). Alternate past participle of **sink.** *—adj.* **1.** Depressed, fallen in, or hollowed: *sunken cheeks.* **2.** Situated beneath the surface of the water or ground; submerged. **3.** Below the surrounding level: *a sunken meadow.*
sunk fence. A ditch with a retaining wall set in it to divide lands without marring the landscape.
sun lamp. 1. A lamp that radiates over a wide range of the spectrum from ultraviolet to infrared and is used in therapeutic and cosmetic treatments. **2.** A high-intensity lamp with parabolic mirrors, used in photography.
sun·less (sŭn′lĭs) *adj.* **1.** Without sunlight; dark or overcast. **2.** Gloomy; cheerless. **—sun′less·ness** *n.*
sun·light (sŭn′līt′) *n.* The light of the sun; sunshine.
sun·lit (sŭn′lĭt′) *adj.* Illuminated by the sun.
sunn (sŭn) *n.* **1.** A plant, *Crotalaria juncea,* of tropical Asia, having clusters of yellow flowers. **2.** A tough fiber from the stems of this plant, used for cordage. Also called "Bombay hemp," "Madras hemp." [Hindi *san,* from Sanskrit *śaṇaṭ,* hempen.]
Sun·na (sōōn′ə) *n.* Also **Sun·nah.** The body of traditional Moslem law, observed by the orthodox Moslems and based on the teachings and practices of Mohammed. [Arabic *sunnah,* form, course, rule.]
Sun·ni (sōōn′ē) *n.* The great branch of Islam following orthodox tradition and accepting the first four caliphs as rightful successors of Mohammed. Compare **Shiah.** [Arabic *sunnīy,* "adherent of the Sunna," from *sunnah,* SUNNA.]
Sun·nite (sōōn′īt′) *n.* A Moslem of the Sunni. [From SUNNI.]
sun·ny (sŭn′ē) *adj.* **-nier, -niest. 1.** Exposed to or abounding in sunshine: *a sunny room.* **2.** Cheerful; genial: *a sunny smile.* **—sun′ni·ly** *adv.* **—sun′ni·ness** *n.*
sun·ny-side up (sŭn′ē-sīd′). Fried only on one side. Said of eggs.
sun·rise (sŭn′rīz′) *n.* **1.** The event or time of the daily first appearance of the sun above the eastern horizon. **2.** An outset or emergence, as of civilization.
sun·set (sŭn′sĕt′) *n.* **1.** The event or time of the daily disappearance of the sun below the western horizon. **2.** The decline or final phase, as of life.
sun·shade (sŭn′shād′) *n.* Anything used as a protection from the sun's rays, as an awning or a parasol.
sun·shine (sŭn′shīn′) *n.* **1.** The light of the sun; the direct rays from the sun. **2. a.** Happiness or cheerfulness. **b.** A source of happiness or cheerfulness. **—sun′shin′y** *adj.*
sun·spot (sŭn′spŏt′) *n.* Any of the relatively dark spots that appear in groups on the surface of the sun, that have an approximate 11-year cycle, and are associated with strong magnetic fields.
sun·stone (sŭn′stōn′) *n.* A type of feldspar, **aventurine** *(see).*
sun·stroke (sŭn′strōk′) *n.* Heat stroke caused by exposure to the sun and characterized by a rise in temperature, convulsions, and coma. Also called "insolation." [Translation of French *coup de soleil.*] **—sun′struck′** (-strŭk′) *adj.*
sun tan. Also **sun·tan** (sŭn′tăn′) *n.* A tan color on the skin resulting from exposure to the sun. **—sun′tanned′** (-tănd′) *adj.*
sun·up (sŭn′ŭp′) *n.* The time of sunrise.
Sun Valley. A winter sports center in south-central Idaho.
sun·ward (sŭn′wərd) *adj.* Facing or directed toward the sun. *—adv.* Also **sun·wards** (-wərdz). Toward the sun.
sun·wise (sŭn′wīz′) *adv.* From left to right, like the sun's course as viewed in the Northern Hemisphere.
Sun Yat-sen (sōōn′ yät′sĕn′). Known as Sun Wen and Sun Chung Shan. 1866–1925. Chinese statesman and revolutionary leader; founder (1911) of the Republic of China.
Suo·mi. The Finnish name for **Finland.**
sup[1] (sŭp) *v.* **supped, supping, sups.** *—tr.* To take (a liquid) into the mouth by sips. *—intr.* To take liquid into the mouth in small amounts. *—n.* A mouthful or taste of liquid. [Middle English *s(o)upen,* Old English *sūpan.* See **seu-**[4] in Appendix.*]
sup[2] (sŭp) *intr.v.* **supped, supping, sups.** To eat the evening meal; dine. [Middle English *soupen, suppen,* from Old French *s(o)uper,* from *soup,* piece of bread dipped in broth, soup, from Germanic. See **seu-**[4] in Appendix.*]
sup. 1. above (Latin *supra*). **2.** superior. **3.** *Grammar.* superlative. **4.** supine (noun). **5.** supplement. **6.** supply.
supe (sōōp) *n. Slang.* A supernumerary actor; an extra. [Short for SUPERNUMERARY.]
su·per (sōō′pər) *n.* **1.** *Informal.* A superintendent in an apartment or office building. **2.** *Informal.* An extra person, especially a **supernumerary** *(see).* **3.** An article or product of superior size, quality, or grade. **4.** *Bookbinding.* A thin starched cotton mesh used to reinforce books. *—adj. Slang.* Ideal; first-rate. *—tr.v.* **supered, -pering, -pers.** *Bookbinding.* To reinforce or strengthen (a book) with super.
super-. Indicates: **1.** Placement above, over, or outside; for example, **supercolumnar, superimpose. 2.** Superiority in size, quality, number, or degree; for example, **superfine, supermarket. 3.** A degree exceeding a norm; for example, **supersonic. 4.** *Chemistry.* Presence of an ingredient in a high proportion; for example, **superphosphate.** ***Note:*** Many compounds other than those entered here may be formed with *super-.* In forming compounds, *super-* is normally joined with the following element without space or hyphen: *superrefined.* However, if the second element begins with a capital letter, it is separated with a hyphen: *super-American.* [From Latin *super,* above, over. See **uper** in Appendix.*]
super. 1. superintendent. **2.** superior. **3.** supernumerary.
su·per·a·ble (sōō′pər-ə-bəl) *adj.* Susceptible of being overcome or surmounted. [Latin *superābilis,* from *superāre,* to go over, overcome, from *super,* above, over. See **uper** in Appendix.*] **—su′per·a·bly** *adv.* **—su′per·a·ble·ness** *n.*
su·per·a·bound (sōō′pər-ə-bound′) *intr.v.* **-bounded, -bounding, -bounds.** To be unusually or excessively abundant. [Middle English *superabounden,* from Late Latin *superabundāre* : Latin *super-,* excessively + *abundāre,* ABOUND.]
su·per·a·bun·dant (sōō′pər-ə-bŭn′dənt) *adj.* Abundant to excess; more than ample. [Middle English, from Late Latin *superabundāns,* present participle of *superabundāre,* SUPERABOUND.] **—su′per·a·bun′dance** *n.* **—su′per·a·bun′dant·ly** *adv.*
su·per·an·nu·ate (sōō′pər-ăn′yōō-āt′) *tr.v.* **-ated, -ating, -ates. 1.** To allow to retire on a pension because of age or infirmity. **2.** To set aside or discard as old-fashioned or obsolete. [Back-formation from SUPERANNUATED.]
su·per·an·nu·at·ed (sōō′pər-ăn′yōō-ā′tĭd) *adj.* **1.** Retired or discharged because of age or infirmity. **2.** Persisting ineffectively despite advanced age: *"Nothing is more tiresome than a superannuated pedagogue."* (Henry Adams). **3.** Obsolete; antiquated. —See Synonyms at **old.** [Medieval Latin *superannuātus,* past participle of *superannuārī,* to be too old : Latin *super,* above + *annus,* year, time of life (see **at-** in Appendix*).]
su·perb (sōō-pûrb′, sə-) *adj.* **1.** Of unusually high quality. **2.** Majestic; imposing. **3.** Rich; luxurious. [Old French *superbe,* from Latin *superbus,* superior, proud, arrogant. See **uper** in Appendix.*] **—su·perb′ly** *adv.* **—su·perb′ness** *n.*
su·per·cal·en·der (sōō′pər-kăl′ən-dər) *n.* A calender with a number of rollers for giving a high finish or gloss to paper. *—tr.v.* **supercalendered, -dering, -ders.** To give high finish to.

ă pat/ā pay/âr care/ä father/b bib/ch church/d deed/ĕ pet/ē be/f fife/g gag/h hat/hw which/ĭ pit/ī pie/îr pier/j judge/k kick/l lid, needle/m mum/n no, sudden/ng thing/ŏ pot/ō toe/ô paw, for/oi noise/ou out/ŏŏ took/ōō boot/p pop/r roar/s sauce/sh ship, dish/

su·per·car·go (so͞o′pər-kär′gō) *n., pl.* **-goes** or **-gos.** An officer on board a merchant ship who has charge of the cargo and its sale and purchase. [Variant of earlier *supracargo,* from Spanish *sobrecargo* : *sobre-,* over, from Latin *super-* + CARGO.]

su·per·charge (so͞o′pər-chärj′) *tr.v.* **-charged, -charging, -charges. 1.** To increase the power of (an engine), as by fitting with a supercharger. **2.** To charge or load excessively; to overload. *—n.* An excess or extra charge.

su·per·charg·er (so͞o′pər-chär′jər) *n.* A blower or compressor, usually driven by the engine, for supplying air under high pressure to the cylinders of an internal-combustion engine.

su·per·cil·i·ar·y (so͞o′pər-sĭl′ē-ĕr′ē) *adj.* **1.** Of or pertaining to the eyebrow. **2.** Located over the eyebrow. [New Latin *superciliaris,* from Latin *supercilium,* eyebrow. See **supercilious.**]

su·per·cil·i·ous (so͞o′pər-sĭl′ē-əs) *adj.* Characterized by haughty scorn; disdainful. See Synonyms at **proud.** [Latin *superciliōsus,* from Latin *supercilium,* "upper eyelid," eyebrow, pride : *super-,* above + *cilium,* (lower) eyelid (see **kel-⁴** in Appendix*).] **—su′per·cil′i·ous·ly** *adv.* **—su′per·cil′i·ous·ness** *n.*

su·per·class (so͞o′pər-klăs′, -kläs′) *n. Biology.* A taxonomic category ranking between a phylum and a class.

su·per·co·lum·nar (so͞o′pər-kə-lŭm′nər) *adj. Architecture.* **1.** Having one order of columns above another. **2.** Situated above a colonnade or column.

su·per·con·duc·tiv·i·ty (so͞o′pər-kŏn′dŭk′tĭv′ə-tē) *n.* The flow of electric current without resistance in certain metals and alloys at temperatures near absolute zero. **—su′per·con·duc′tive** (-kən-dŭk′tĭv) *adj.* **—su′per·con·duc′tor** (-tər) *n.*

su·per·cool (so͞o′pər-ko͞ol′) *v.* **-cooled, -cooling, -cools.** *—tr.* To cool (a liquid) below a transition temperature without the transition occurring; especially, to cool below the freezing point without solidification. *—intr.* To become supercooled. Used of a liquid. Also "undercool."

su·per·dom·i·nant (so͞o′pər-dŏm′ə-nənt) *n. Music.* The tone immediately above the dominant; the submediant.

su·per·du·per (so͞o′pər-do͞o′pər, -dyo͞o′pər) *adj. Slang.* Great; marvelous. [Reduplication of SUPER (superior).]

su·per·e·go (so͞o′pər-ē′gō, -ĕg′ō) *n. Psychoanalysis.* The division of the psyche that develops by the incorporation of the perceived moral standards of the community, is mainly unconscious, and includes the conscience.

su·per·em·i·nent (so͞o′pər-ĕm′ə-nənt) *adj.* Eminent beyond all others; pre-eminent. [Late Latin *superēminēns,* from Latin, present participle of *superēminēre,* to rise above : *super-,* above + *ēminēre,* to stand out (see **eminent**).] **—su′per·em′i·nence** *n.* **—su′per·em′i·nent·ly** *adv.*

su·per·er·o·gate (so͞o′pər-ĕr′ə-gāt′) *intr.v.* **-gated, -gating, -gates.** To do more than is required, ordered, or expected. [Late Latin *superērogāre,* to spend more : Latin *super-,* excessively + *ērogāre,* to spend, pay out money from the public treasury (after asking the people's consent) : *ex-,* out of + *rogāre,* to ask (see **reg-¹** in Appendix*).]

su·per·er·o·ga·tion (so͞o′pər-ĕr′ə-gā′shən) *n.* The performance of more than is required, demanded, or expected.

su·per·e·rog·a·to·ry (so͞o′pər-ə-rŏg′ə-tôr′ē, -tōr′ē) *adj.* Also **su·per·e·rog·a·tive** (-tĭv). **1.** Performed or observed beyond the degree required or expected. **2.** Superfluous; unnecessary: *"It was supererogatory for her to gloat."* (Mary McCarthy).

su·per·fam·i·ly (so͞o′pər-făm′ə-lē) *n., pl.* **-lies.** *Biology.* A taxonomic category ranking between an order or its subdivisions and a family.

su·per·fe·cun·da·tion (so͞o′pər-fē′kən-dā′shən, -fĕk′ən-dā′shən) *n.* The impregnation of more than one ovum within a single menstrual cycle by separate acts of coitus, especially by different males.

su·per·fe·tate (so͞o′pər-fē′tāt′) *intr.v.* **-tated, -tating, -tates.** To conceive when a fetus is already present in the uterus. [Latin *superfētāre* : *super-,* over, in addition to + *fētāre,* to breed, impregnate, from *fētus,* young, fetus (see **dhēi-** in Appendix*).]

su·per·fe·ta·tion (so͞o′pər-fē-tā′shən) *n.* The presence of fetuses of different ages resulting from the fertilization and development of two or more ova liberated at different periods of ovulation in the same uterus.

su·per·fi·cial (so͞o′pər-fĭsh′əl) *adj.* **1.** Of, affecting, or being on or near the surface: *a superficial wound.* **2.** Concerned with or comprehending only what is apparent or obvious; shallow. **3. a.** Apparent rather than actual or substantial. **b.** Trivial; insignificant. [Middle English, from Late Latin *superficiālis,* from Latin *superficiēs,* surface, SUPERFICIES.] **—su′per·fi′ci·al′i·ty, su′per·fi′cial·ness** *n.* **—su′per·fi′cial·ly** *adv.*

Synonyms: *superficial, shallow, cursory.* These adjectives mean lacking in depth or thoroughness. *Superficial* applies to thought and action concerned largely with the obvious, sometimes implying lack of genuine interest or sincerity. *Shallow* emphasizes lack of intellectual or emotional depth in persons or their works; more strongly than *superficial,* it implies lack of capacity for something better. *Cursory* principally describes action performed speedily and without thoroughness.

su·per·fi·ci·es (so͞o′pər-fĭsh′ĭ-ēz, -fĭsh′ēz) *n., pl.* **superficies. 1.** The surface of an area or body. **2.** The external appearance or aspect of a thing. [Latin *superficiēs,* surface : *super-,* above, over + *faciēs,* FACE.]

su·per·fine (so͞o′pər-fīn′) *adj.* **1.** Of exceptional quality or refinement. **2.** Overdelicate or refined. **3.** Of extra fine texture. **—su′per·fine′ness** *n.*

su·per·flu·id (so͞o′pər-flo͞o′ĭd) *n.* A fluid, as an electric current or a form of helium, exhibiting frictionless flow at temperatures close to absolute zero. **—su′per·flu·id′i·ty** *n.*

su·per·flu·i·ty (so͞o′pər-flo͞o′ə-tē) *n., pl.* **-ties. 1.** The quality or condition of being superfluous. **2.** Something that is superfluous. **3.** Overabundance; excess.

su·per·flu·ous (so͞o-pûr′flo͞o-əs) *adj.* Beyond what is required or sufficient; extra. [Middle English, from Latin *superfluus,* overflowing, from *superfluere,* to overflow : *super-,* over + *fluere,* to flow (see **bhleu-** in Appendix*).] **—su·per′flu·ous·ly** *adv.* **—su·per′flu·ous·ness** *n.*

su·per·heat (so͞o′pər-hēt′) *tr.v.* **-heated, -heating, -heats. 1.** To heat excessively; overheat. **2.** To heat (steam or other vapor not in contact with its own liquid) beyond its saturation point at a given pressure. **3.** To heat (a liquid) above its boiling point at a given pressure without causing vaporization. *—n.* (so͞o′pər-hēt′). **1.** The amount that a vapor is superheated. **2.** The heat imparted in the process. **—su′per·heat′er** *n.*

su·per·het·er·o·dyne (so͞o′pər-hĕt′ər-ə-dīn′) *adj.* Indicating or pertaining to a form of radio reception in which the frequency of an incoming radio signal is converted to an intermediate frequency, by mixing with a locally generated signal, to facilitate amplification and the rejection of unwanted signals. *—n.* A superheterodyne radio receiver. [SUPER(SONIC) + HETERODYNE.]

su·per·high frequency (so͞o′pər-hī′). *Abbr.* **shf, SHF** Any radio frequency between 3,000 and 30,000 megacycles per second.

su·per·high·way (so͞o′pər-hī′wā′) *n.* A broad highway for high-speed traffic, usually with six or more traffic lanes.

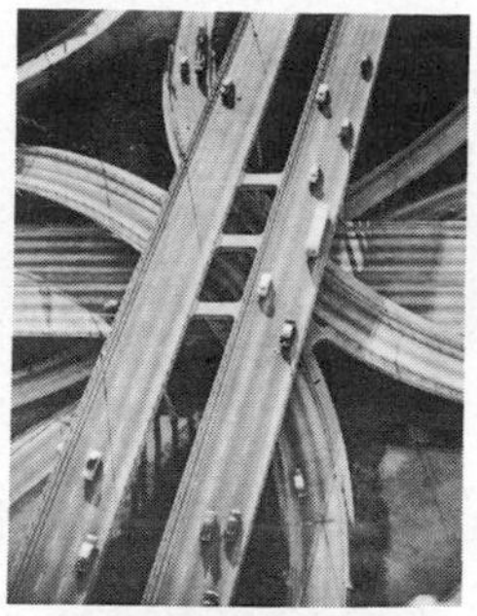

superhighway
Crossing of superhighways at Los Angeles, California

su·per·hu·man (so͞o′pər-hyo͞o′mən) *adj.* **1.** Above or beyond the human; divine; supernatural. **2.** Beyond ordinary or normal human ability, power, or experience: *"soldiers driven mad by superhuman misery"* (John Reed). **—su′per·hu·man′i·ty** (-măn′ə-tē) *n.* **—su′per·hu′man·ly** *adv.*

su·per·im·pose (so͞o′pər-ĭm-pōz′) *tr.v.* **-posed, -posing, -poses.** To lay or place upon or over something else. **—su′per·im′po·si′tion** *n.*

su·per·in·cum·bent (so͞o′pər-ĭn-kŭm′bənt) *adj.* Lying or resting on or above something else. [Latin *superincumbēns,* present participle of *superincumbere,* to lie down on or above : *super-,* above + *incumbere,* to lie down (see **incumbent**).] **—su′per·in·cum′bence, su′per·in·cum′ben·cy** *n.*

su·per·in·duce (so͞o′pər-ĭn-do͞os′, -dyo͞os′) *tr.v.* **-duced, -ducing, -duces.** To introduce as an addition. [Latin *superindūcere,* to bring upon : *super-,* on, over, in addition + *indūcere,* to lead in, INDUCE.] **—su′per·in·duc′tion** (-dŭk′shən) *n.*

su·per·in·tend (so͞o′pər-ĭn-tĕnd′) *tr.v.* **-tended, -tending, -tends.** To have charge of; exercise supervision over; manage. [Late Latin *superintendere,* to oversee : *super-,* over + *intendere,* to direct one's attention to, INTEND.] **—su′per·in·ten′dence** *n.*

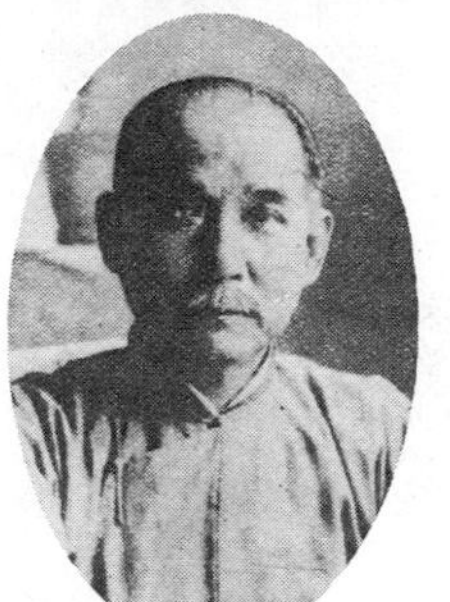

Sun Yat-sen

su·per·in·ten·dent (so͞o′pər-ĭn-tĕn′dənt) *n. Abbr.* **super., supt., Supt.** A person who supervises or directs some undertaking, institution, building, or the like; manager. *—adj.* Superintending.

su·pe·ri·or (sə-pîr′ē-ər) *adj. Abbr.* **sup., super. 1.** Higher in rank, station, or authority: *a superior officer.* **2.** Of a higher nature or kind; far above average in comparison. **3.** Of great value or excellence; extraordinary. **4.** Greater in number or amount. **5.** Affecting an attitude of disdain or conceit; haughty; supercilious. **6.** Above being affected or influenced; indifferent or immune: *"Trust magnates were superior to law"* (Gustavus Myers). **7.** Located higher; upper. **8.** *Botany.* Located above and not in contact with the calyx and corolla. Said of an ovary. **9.** *Printing.* Set above the main line of type. **10.** *Logic.* Of wider or more comprehensive application; generic. Said of a term or proposition. *—n. Abbr.* **sup., super. 1.** One who surpasses another in rank or quality. **2.** The head of a monastery, abbey, convent, or other ecclesiastical order or house. **3.** *Printing.* A superior character or letter. [Middle English, from Old French, from Latin, comparative of *superus,* situated above, upper, from *super,* above, over. See **uper** in Appendix.*] **—su·pe′ri·or′i·ty** (-pîr′ē-ôr′ə-tē, -ŏr′ə-tē) *n.* **—su·pe′ri·or·ly** *adv.*

Usage: *Superior* (adjective) and *inferior* are idiomatically followed by *to* in typical constructions such as *His first novel is superior to his latest.*

Superior, Lake. The westernmost and largest (31,820 square miles) of the Great Lakes of North America, and the largest freshwater lake in the world, situated between the United States and Canada.

superior conjunction. The position of a celestial body when it is on the opposite side of the sun from Earth.

superior court. A court of general jurisdiction, above the inferior courts and below those of last resort.

superiority complex. 1. A feeling of being superior to others. **2.** A psychological defense in which such feelings counter feelings of inferiority.

superior planet. Any planet whose mean distance from the sun is greater than that of Earth.

su·per·ja·cent (so͞o′pər-jā′sənt) *adj.* Resting or lying immediately above or upon something else. [Latin *superjacēns,* present participle of *superjacēre,* to lie above or upon : *super-,* over + *jacēre,* to lie, from *jacere,* to throw, lay (see **ye-** in Appendix*).]

su·per·la·tive (so͞o-pûr′lə-tĭv) *adj.* **1.** Of the highest order, quality, or degree; surpassing or superior to all other or others. **2.** Excessive or exaggerated. **3.** *Grammar. Abbr.* **sup., superl.** Expressing or involving the extreme degree of comparison of an adjective or adverb. *—n.* **1.** Something of the highest possible excellence. **2.** The highest degree; acme. **3.** *Grammar. Abbr.* **sup., superl. a.** The superlative degree. **b.** An adjective or adverb expressing the superlative degree; for example, *brightest* is the superlative of *bright; most brightly* is the superlative of *brightly.* [Middle English *superlatyf,* from Old French *super-*

lative, from Late Latin *superlātīvus*, from *superlātus* (past participle of *superferre*, to carry over) : *super-*, over + *-lātus*, "carried" (see **tel-**[1] in Appendix*).] **—su·per'la·tive·ly** *adv.* **—su·per'la·tive·ness** *n.*

su·per·lu·nar (so͞o'pər-lo͞o'nər) *adj.* Also **su·per·lu·na·ry** (-nə-rē). Situated beyond the moon.

su·per·man (so͞o'pər-măn') *n., pl.* **-men** (-mĕn'). **1.** A man with more than human powers. **2.** In the philosophy of Nietzsche, an ideal superior man who, through the exercise of creative power and his ability to forgo transient pleasure, would live at a level of experience beyond the standards of good and evil and would represent the goal of human evolution. [Translation of German *Übermensch*.]

su·per·mar·ket (so͞o'pər-mär'kĭt) *n.* A large self-service retail food and household-goods store.

su·per·nal (so͞o-pûr'nəl) *adj.* **1.** Celestial; heavenly. **2.** Of, coming from, or being in the sky or high above. [Middle English, from Old French, from Latin *supernus*. See **uper** in Appendix.*] **—su·per'nal·ly** *adv.*

su·per·na·tant (so͞o'pər-nā'tənt) *adj.* Floating on the surface. [Latin *supernatāns*, present participle of *supernatāre*, to swim above, float : *super-*, above + *natāre*, to swim (see **snā-** in Appendix*).] **—su'per·na'tant** *n.*

su·per·nat·u·ral (so͞o'pər-năch'ər-əl) *adj.* **1.** Of or pertaining to existence outside the natural world; especially, not attributable to natural forces. **2.** Attributed to the immediate exercise of divine power; miraculous. **3.** Of or pertaining to the miraculous. *—n.* That which is supernatural. **—su'per·nat'u·ral·ly** *adv.* **—su'per·nat'u·ral·ness** *n.*

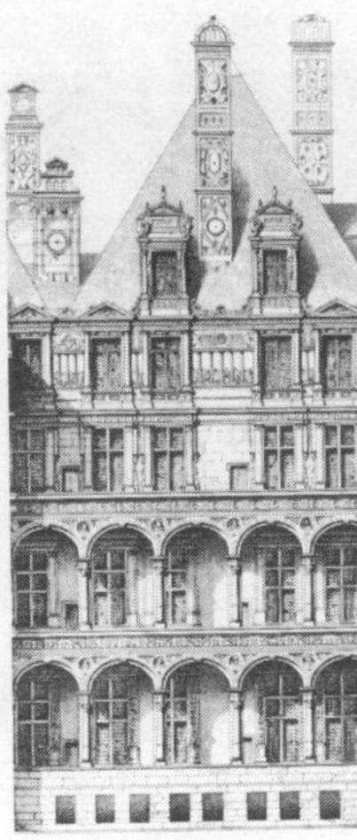

superstructure
Part of the Château de Boulogne, Paris

su·per·nat·u·ral·ism (so͞o'pər-năch'ər-əl-ĭz'əm) *n.* **1.** The quality of being supernatural. **2.** Belief in a supernatural agency that intervenes in the course of natural laws. **—su'per·nat'u·ral·ist** *adj.* & *n.* **—su'per·nat'u·ral·is'tic** *adj.*

su·per·nor·mal (so͞o'pər-nôr'məl) *adj.* Greatly exceeding the normal or average but still obeying natural laws.

su·per·no·va (so͞o'pər-nō'və) *n., pl.* **-vae** (-vē'). A rare celestial phenomenon involving the explosion of most of the material in a star, resulting in an extremely bright, short-lived object that emits vast amounts of energy. Compare **nova**.

su·per·nu·mer·ar·y (so͞o'pər-no͞o'mər-ăr'ē, so͞o'pər-nyo͞o'-) *adj.* **1.** Exceeding a fixed, prescribed, or standard number; extra. **2.** Beyond the required or desired number; superfluous. *—n., pl.* **supernumeraries**. *Abbr.* **super. 1.** Someone or something in excess of the regular, necessary, or usual number. **2.** *Theater.* A performer without a speaking part, as one who appears in a mob scene. In this sense, also informally called "super." [Late Latin *supernumerārius*, (a soldier) added to a legion in excess of its fixed number, from Latin *super numerum*, over the number : *super*, over + *numerus*, number, division of an army (see **nem-**[2] in Appendix*).]

su·per·or·der (so͞o'pər-ôr'dər) *n. Biology.* A taxonomic category ranking between a class or one of its subdivisions and an order.

su·per·phos·phate (so͞o'pər-fŏs'fāt') *n.* **1.** An acid phosphate. **2.** A fertilizer made by the action of sulfuric acid on phosphate rock, consisting chiefly of tribasic calcium phosphate, to form a mixture of gypsum and monobasic calcium phosphate.

su·per·phys·i·cal (so͞o'pər-fĭz'ĭ-kəl) *adj.* Exceeding or beyond the purely physical.

su·per·pose (so͞o'pər-pōz') *tr.v.* **-posed, -posing, -poses. 1.** To set or place over, upon, or above something else. **2.** To place (one geometrical figure) on top of another so that all the parts of both coincide. **—su'per·pos'a·ble** *adj.* **—su'per·po·si'tion** (-pə-zĭsh'ən) *n.*

su·per·sat·u·rate (so͞o'pər-săch'ər-āt') *tr.v.* **-rated, -rating, -rates.** To cause (a chemical solution) to be more highly concentrated than is normally possible under given conditions of temperature and pressure. **—su'per·sat'u·ra'tion** *n.*

su·per·scribe (so͞o'pər-skrīb') *tr.v.* **-scribed, -scribing, -scribes. 1.** To write on the outside or upper part of (a letter, for example). **2.** To write (a name or address, for example) on the top or outside. [Latin *superscrībere*, to write over : *super-*, over + *scrībere*, to write (see **skeri-** in Appendix*).]

su·per·script (so͞o'pər-skrĭpt') *adj.* Written above, as a diacritical mark. *—n.* A character set, printed, or written above and immediately to one side of another. For example, *2* is the superscript in x^2. Compare **subscript.** [Latin *superscriptus*, past participle of *superscrībere*, SUPERSCRIBE.]

su·per·scrip·tion (so͞o'pər-skrĭp'shən) *n.* **1.** Something written above or outside something; particularly, an address on a letter or package. **2.** The part of a prescription that bears the Latin word *recipe* or the symbol ℞ in a prescription.

su·per·sede (so͞o'pər-sēd') *tr.v.* **-seded, -seding, -sedes. 1.** To take the place of; replace or succeed. **2.** To cause to be set aside or displaced. —See Synonyms at **replace.** [Middle English *superceden*, to postpone, from Old French *superseder*, from Latin *supersedēre*, to sit above, desist from : *super-*, above + *sedēre*, to sit (see **sed-**[1] in Appendix*).] **—su'per·sed'er** *n.* **—su'per·se'dure** (-sē'jər), **su'per·ses'sion** (-sĕsh'ən) *n.*

su·per·se·de·as (so͞o'pər-sē'dē-əs) *n. Law.* A writ containing a command to stay legal proceedings, as in the halting or delaying of the execution of a sentence. [Medieval Latin, from Latin (first word in the writ), "you shall desist," from *supersedēre*, to desist from, SUPERSEDE.]

su·per·sen·si·ble (so͞o'pər-sĕn'sə-bəl) *adj.* Beyond or above perception by the senses. **—su'per·sen'si·bly** *adv.*

su·per·son·ic (so͞o'pər-sŏn'ĭk) *adj.* Having, caused by, or related to a speed greater than the speed of sound in a specified medium. **—su'per·son'ic** *n.*

su·per·son·ics (so͞o'pər-sŏn'ĭks) *n.* Plural in form, used with a singular verb. The study of phenomena produced by the motion of a body through a medium at velocities greater than that of sound.

su·per·sti·tion (so͞o'pər-stĭsh'ən) *n.* **1.** A belief that some action or circumstance not logically related to a course of events influences its outcome. **2.** Any belief, practice, or rite unreasoningly upheld by faith in magic, chance, or dogma. **3. a.** Fearful or abject dependence upon such beliefs. **b.** Idolatry. [Middle English *supersticion*, from Old French *superstition*, from Latin *superstitiō*, probably "a standing over something (in amazement and awe)," excessive fear, superstition, from *superstāre*, to stand over : *super-*, over + *stāre*, to stand (see **stā-** in Appendix*).]

su·per·sti·tious (so͞o'pər-stĭsh'əs) *adj.* **1.** Inclined to believe in superstitions. **2.** Of, characterized by, or proceeding from superstition. **—su'per·sti'tious·ly** *adv.* **—su'per·sti'tious·ness** *n.*

su·per·stra·tum (so͞o'pər-strā'təm, -străt'əm) *n., pl.* **-ta** (-tə). A layer superimposed upon another.

su·per·struc·ture (so͞o'pər-strŭk'chər) *n.* **1.** Any structure built on top of something else. **2.** That part of a building or other structure above the foundation. **3.** The rails, sleepers, and other parts of a railway as distinguished from the roadbed. **4.** The parts of a ship's structure above the main deck. **5.** The ideational institutions of a society as distinct from the processes and direct social relations of material production.

su·per·ton·ic (so͞o'pər-tŏn'ĭk) *n.* The second tone of the diatonic scale.

su·per·vene (so͞o'pər-vēn') *intr.v.* **-vened, -vening, -venes. 1.** To come or occur as something extraneous, additional, or unexpected. **2.** To follow immediately after; ensue. —See Synonyms at **follow, happen.** [Latin *supervenīre* : *super-*, in addition + *venīre*, to come (see **gwā-** in Appendix*).] **—su'per·ven'ient** (-yənt) *adj.* **—su'per·ven'tion** (-vĕn'shən) *n.*

su·per·vise (so͞o'pər-vīz') *tr.v.* **-vised, -vising, -vises.** To direct and inspect the performance of (workers or work); oversee; superintend. See Synonyms at **conduct.** [Medieval Latin *supervidēre* (past participle *supervīsus*), to look over : Latin *super-*, over + *vidēre*, to see (see **weid-** in Appendix*).] **—su'per·vi'sion** (-vĭzh'ən) *n.* **—su'per·vi'so·ry** (-vī'zə-rē) *adj.*

su·per·vi·sor (so͞o'pər-vī'zər) *n.* **1.** A person who supervises. **2.** An elected administrative officer in certain U.S. townships. **3.** A person in charge of the courses of study and the teachers in a particular department in some school systems.

su·pi·nate (so͞o'pə-nāt') *v.* **-nated, -nating, -nates.** *—tr.* To turn or place (the hand or forearm) so that the palm is upward. *—intr.* To assume a position with the palm or forearm upward. [Latin *supīnāre*, to bend backward, from *supīnus*, SUPINE.] **—su'pi·na'tion** *n.*

su·pi·na·tor (so͞o'pə-nā'tər) *n.* A muscle in the forearm that makes supination possible.

su·pine[1] (so͞o'pīn', so͞o'pīn') *adj.* **1.** Lying on the back or having the face upward. **2.** Having the palm upward. Said of the hand. **3.** Indisposed to act or object; lethargic; passive. **4.** Inclined; sloping. —See Synonyms at **inactive, prone.** [Latin *supīnus*. See **upo** in Appendix.*] **—su'pine'ly** *adv.* **—su'pine'ness** *n.*

su·pine[2] (so͞o'pīn') *n. Abbr.* **sup.** A Latin verbal noun having an accusative in *-um* and an ablative in *-ū*, cited as the fourth of the principal parts. [Latin *(verbum) supīnum*, from *supīnus*, SUPINE. The reason for naming is uncertain.]

supp. supplement; supplementary.

sup·per (sŭp'ər) *n.* **1.** An evening meal; especially, a light evening meal when dinner is taken at midday. **2.** A dance or social affair where supper is served. [Middle English *suppere*, from Old French *so(u)per*, from *so(u)per*, SUP.]

suppl. supplement; supplementary.

sup·plant (sə-plănt') *tr.v.* **-planted, -planting, -plants. 1.** To take the place of; supersede or displace. **2.** To usurp the position of; oust. —See Synonyms at **follow, replace.** [Middle English *supplanten*, from Old French *supplanter*, from Latin *supplantāre*, to trip up one's heel : *sub-*, up from under + *planta*, sole of the foot (see **plat-** in Appendix*).] **—sup'plan·ta'tion** *n.* **—sup·plant'er** *n.*

sup·ple (sŭp'əl) *adj.* **-pler, -plest. 1.** Readily bent; pliant. **2.** Moving and bending with agility; limber. **3.** Yielding or changing readily; compliant or adaptable. —See Synonyms at **flexible.** *—v.* **suppled, -pling, -ples.** *—tr.* To make supple. *—intr.* To become supple. [Middle English *souple*, from Old French, from Latin *supplex*, beseeching, submissive. See **plek-** in Appendix.*] **—sup'ply, sup'ple·ly** *adv.* **—sup'ple·ness** *n.*

sup·ple·jack (sŭp'əl-jăk') *n.* **1.** Any of various climbing woody vines having tough, flexible stems; especially, *Berchemia scandens*, of the southern United States. **2.** A walking stick made from the stem of such a vine. [SUPPLE + JACK (given name).]

sup·ple·ment (sŭp'lə-mənt) *n. Abbr.* **sup., supp., suppl. 1.** Something added to complete a thing, make up for a deficiency, or extend or strengthen the whole. **2.** A section added to a book or document to give further information or to correct errors. **3.** A separate section devoted to a special subject inserted into a newspaper or other periodical. **4.** *Geometry.* The angle or arc that when added to a given angle or arc makes 180 degrees or a semicircle. *—tr.v.* (sŭp'lə-mĕnt') **supplemented, -menting, -ments.** To provide or form a supplement to. [Middle English, from Latin *supplēmentum*, from *supplēre*, to complete, SUPPLY.] **—sup'ple·men'ta·ry** (-tə-rē, -trē), **sup'ple·men'tal** *adj.*

sup·pli·ant (sŭp'lī-ənt) *adj.* Asking humbly and earnestly; beseeching. *—n.* One who supplicates. [Middle English, from Old French, present participle of *supplier*, to entreat, from Latin *supplicāre*, SUPPLICATE.] **—sup'pli·ant·ly** *adv.*

ă pat/ā pay/âr care/ä father/b bib/ch church/d deed/ĕ pet/ē be/f fife/g gag/h hat/hw which/ĭ pit/ī pie/îr pier/j judge/k kick/l lid, needle/m mum/n no, sudden/ng thing/ŏ pot/ō toe/ô paw, for/oi noise/ou out/o͝o took/o͞o boot/p pop/r roar/s sauce/sh ship, dish/

sup·pli·cant (sŭp′lĭ-kənt) *n.* One who entreats or supplicates; a suppliant. —*adj.* Supplicating.

sup·pli·cate (sŭp′lĭ-kāt′) *v.* **-cated, -cating, -cates.** —*tr.* **1.** To ask for humbly or earnestly, as by praying. **2.** To make a humble entreaty to; beseech. —*intr.* To make a humble and earnest petition; beg. [Middle English *supplicaten,* from Latin *supplicāre,* to kneel down, beg humbly : *sub-,* down, underneath + *plicāre,* to fold up (see **plek-** in Appendix*).] —**sup′pli·ca′tion** *n.* —**sup′pli·ca·to′ry** (-kə-tôr′ē, -tōr′ē) *adj.*

sup·ply (sə-plī′) *v.* **-plied, -plying, -plies.** —*tr.* **1.** To make (something needed, desired, or lacking) available for use; provide. **2.** To furnish or equip with what is needed or lacking. **3.** To fill sufficiently; satisfy: *supply a need.* **4.** To make up for (a deficiency, for example); compensate for. **5.** To serve temporarily in (the position or office of another); occupy as a substitute. —*intr.* To fill a position as a substitute. —*n., pl.* **supplies.** *Abbr.* **sup. 1.** The act of supplying. **2.** Something that is or can be supplied. **3.** An amount available or sufficient for a given use; store; stock. **4.** *Usually plural.* Materials or provisions stored and dispensed when needed. **5.** *Economics.* The amount of a commodity available for meeting a demand or for purchase at a given price. **6.** A clergyman serving as a substitute or temporary pastor. [Middle English *suppl(y)en,* from Old French *so(u)pleer, soup(p)leier,* from Latin *supplēre,* to fill up, complete : *sub-,* from below, up + *plēre,* to fill (see **pel-**[8] in Appendix*).] —**sup·pli′er** *n.*

sup·port (sə-pôrt′, -pōrt′) *tr.v.* **-ported, -porting, -ports. 1.** To bear the weight of, especially from below. **2.** To hold in position; prevent from falling, sinking, or slipping. **3.** To be capable of bearing; withstand. **4.** To keep (one's spirits, for example) from failing during stress; lend strength to. **5.** To provide for or maintain by supplying with money or other necessities. **6.** To furnish evidence for; corroborate or substantiate. **7.** To aid the cause of by approving, favoring, or advocating. **8.** To endure; tolerate. **9. a.** To act (a part or role). **b.** To act in a secondary or subordinate role to (a leading actor). —*n.* **1. a.** The act of supporting. **b.** The state of being supported. **2.** Someone or something that supports. **3.** Maintenance or subsistence. —See Synonyms at **livelihood.** [Middle English *supporten,* from Old French *supporter,* from Latin *supportāre,* to carry, convey : *sub-,* up, toward + *portāre,* to carry (see **per-**[2] in Appendix*).]

Synonyms: *support, uphold, sustain, maintain, advocate, champion.* These verbs are compared in the sense of giving aid, encouragement, or the like to a person or cause. *Support* refers nonspecifically to any such aid. *Uphold* often implies aid to someone or something faced with strong opposition or a challenge. *Sustain* and *maintain* can refer to material or financial aid or support. In this comparison, however, *sustain* more often suggests keeping up a person's spirits in time of stress, whereas *maintain* applies to the defense of personal rights or a position or cause. *Advocate* implies verbal support, usually in the sense of pleading or arguing. *Champion* suggests aid in the form of defense of what is under attack or protection of what is unable to act in its own behalf.

sup·port·a·ble (sə-pôr′tə-bəl, sə-pōr′-) *adj.* Bearable; endurable. —**sup·port′a·bly** *adv.*

sup·port·er (sə-pôr′tər, sə-pōr′-) *n.* **1.** A person or thing that supports. **2.** One who promotes or advocates; a partisan; an adherent. **3.** A support or binding for some part of the body; especially, a jockstrap.

sup·por·tive (sə-pôr′tĭv, sə-pōr′-) *adj.* Furnishing support or assistance.

sup·pos·a·ble (sə-pō′zə-bəl) *adj.* That can be supposed or conjectured. —**sup·pos′a·bly** *adv.*

sup·pose (sə-pōz′) *v.* **-posed, -posing, -poses.** —*tr.* **1.** To assume (something) to be true or real for the sake of an argument or explanation. **2.** To believe, especially on uncertain or tentative grounds; be inclined to think. **3.** To imply as an antecedent condition; presuppose. **4.** To consider as a suggestion: *Suppose we dine together.* **5.** To expect or require. Used in the passive: *He is supposed to go to the store.* —*intr.* To make an assumption; to conjecture. —See Synonyms at **presume.** [Middle English *supposen,* to believe, assume, from Old French *supposer,* from Latin *suppōnere* (past participle *suppositus*), to put under, substitute, forge : *sub-,* under + *pōnere,* to place (see **apo** in Appendix*).]

sup·posed (sə-pōzd′, -pō′zĭd) *adj.* Presumed to be true, real, or genuine, especially on dubious grounds. —**sup·pos′ed·ly** (-pō′zĭd-lē) *adv.*

sup·po·si·tion (sŭp′ə-zĭsh′ən) *n.* **1.** The act of supposing. **2.** An unproven statement or assumption, especially one tentatively accepted. —**sup′po·si′tion·al** *adj.* —**sup′po·si′tion·al·ly** *adv.*

sup·pos·i·ti·tious (sə-pŏz′ə-tĭsh′əs) *adj.* **1.** Substituted with fraudulent intent; spurious; counterfeit. **2.** Hypothetical; supposed. —See Synonyms at **artificial.** [Latin *suppositīcius,* substituted, from *suppōnere* (past participle *suppositus*), to place under, substitute, SUPPOSE.] —**sup·pos′i·ti′tious·ly** *adv.* —**sup·pos′i·ti′tious·ness** *n.*

sup·pos·i·tive (sə-pŏz′ə-tĭv) *adj.* Of the nature of, including, or involving supposition. —*n. Grammar.* A conjunction introducing a supposition, such as *if* or *providing.* —**sup·pos′i·tive·ly** *adv.*

sup·pos·i·to·ry (sə-pŏz′ə-tôr′ē, -tōr′ē) *n., pl.* **-ries.** A solid medication designed to melt within a body cavity other than the mouth. [Medieval Latin *suppositōrium,* "something placed underneath," from Latin *suppositōrius,* "placed under," from Latin *suppōnere,* to place under, SUPPOSE.]

sup·press (sə-prĕs′) *tr.v.* **-pressed, -pressing, -presses. 1.** To put an end to forcibly; subdue; crush. **2.** To curtail or prohibit the activities of (a political party, for example). **3.** To keep from being revealed, published, or circulated; withhold from the public. **4.** To hold back (an impulse, for example); to check. **5.** To reduce the incidence or severity of (a hemorrhage, for example); arrest. [Middle English *suppressen,* from Latin *supprimere* (past participle *suppressus*), to press down : *sub-,* down + *premere,* to press (see **per-**[6] in Appendix*).] —**sup·press′er, sup·pres′sor** (-sər) *n.* —**sup·press′i·ble** *adj.*

Synonyms: *suppress, stifle.* These verbs refer to the exercise of power or control that either brings about extinction or severely limits force or function. *Suppress* implies crushing or restricting drastically in effectiveness. *Stifle* can refer to physical attack on a person but more often applies to restraining or smothering, as emotions, coughs, or cries.

sup·pres·sion (sə-prĕsh′ən) *n.* **1.** The act of suppressing. **2.** The state of being suppressed. **3.** *Psychoanalysis.* The conscious exclusion of painful desires or thoughts from awareness.

sup·pres·sive (sə-prĕs′ĭv) *adj.* Tending to suppress; subduing.

sup·pu·rate (sŭp′yə-rāt′) *intr.v.* **-rated, -rating, -rates.** To form pus, as a wound; fester or maturate. [Latin *suppūrāre* : *sub-,* under + *pūs* (stem *pūr-*), pus (see **pu-**[2] in Appendix*).]

sup·pu·ra·tion (sŭp′yə-rā′shən) *n.* **1.** The formation or discharge of pus. Also called "maturation." **2.** Pus. —**sup′pu·ra′tive** *adj.*

supr. supreme.

supra–. Indicates: **1.** Above or over; for example, **suprarenal. 2.** Greater than; for example, **supramolecular. 3.** Preceding; for example, **supralapsarian.** [Latin, from *suprā,* above, beyond, earlier. See **uper** in Appendix.*]

su·pra·glot·tal (so͞o′prə-glŏt′l) *adj.* **1.** Above or anterior to the glottis. **2.** *Linguistics.* Designating a phone or phoneme produced by the speech organs anterior to the glottis.

su·pra·lap·sar·i·an (so͞o′prə-lăp-săr′ē-ən) *n.* Any of the Calvinists who believe that God's determination of the elect preceded the fall of man from grace and that the fall itself had been predestined. [From SUPRA- + Latin *lapsus,* fall, from the past participle of *lābī,* to slide (see **leb-**[1] in Appendix*).] —**su′pra·lap·sar′i·an** *adj.* —**su′pra·lap·sar′i·an·ism′** *n.*

su·pra·lim·i·nal (so͞o′prə-lĭm′ə-nəl) *adj.* Above the threshold of consciousness or of sensation.

su·pra·mo·lec·u·lar (so͞o′prə-mə-lĕk′yə-lər) *adj.* **1.** Consisting of more than one molecule. **2.** Of greater complexity than a molecule.

su·pra·or·bi·tal (so͞o′prə-ôr′bĭ-təl) *adj.* Located above the orbit of the eye.

su·pra·re·nal (so͞o′prə-rē′nəl) *adj.* Located on or above the kidney. —*n.* A suprarenal gland. [New Latin *suprarenalis* : SUPRA- + Latin *rēnēs,* the kidneys (see **renal**).]

suprarenal gland. An **adrenal gland** *(see).*

su·prem·a·cy (sə-prĕm′ə-sē) *n., pl.* **-cies. 1.** The condition or quality of being supreme. **2.** Supreme power or authority.

su·preme (sə-prēm′) *adj. Abbr.* **supr. 1.** Greatest in power, authority, or rank; paramount; dominant. **2.** Greatest in importance, degree, significance, character, or achievement; utmost; extreme. **3.** Ultimate; final. [Latin *suprēmus,* superlative of *superus,* situated above, upper, from *super,* above. See **uper** in Appendix.*] —**su·preme′ly** *adv.* —**su·preme′ness** *n.*

Supreme Court. *Abbr.* **S.C. 1.** The highest Federal court in the United States, consisting of nine justices and having jurisdiction over all other courts in the nation. **2.** The highest court in a state within the United States.

Supreme Soviet. The legislature of the Soviet Union, consisting of two equal houses, the *Soviet of the Union,* whose members are elected on the basis of population, and the *Soviet of the Nationalities,* whose members are elected by the various national groups and which assures legislative voice to even the smallest national representation.

supt., Supt. superintendent.

Su·qua·mish (sə-kwä′mĭsh) *n., pl.* **Suquamish** or **-mishes.** Also **Squa·mish** (skwä′-). **1.** A Salish-speaking tribe of North American Indians of the northwestern Pacific coast, west of Puget Sound. **2.** A member of this tribe. **3.** The language of this tribe.

sur–. Indicates: **1.** Over, beyond, or above; for example, **surtax. 2.** Excessively; extremely; for example, **surbased.** [Middle English, from Old French *s(o)ur-,* from Latin *super-,* from *super,* above, over. See **uper** in Appendix.*]

sur. 1. surface. **2.** surplus.

Sur. Surrey.

su·ra (so͝or′ə) *n.* One of the chapters or sections of the Koran. [Arabic *sūrah,* "a step," from Hebrew *shūrāh,* row, line.]

Su·ra (so͞o-rä′). A river of the Soviet Union, rising in the southwestern Russian S.F.S.R. and flowing 537 miles north to the Volga east of Gorkiy.

Su·ra·ba·ya (so͝or′ə-bī′ə). Also **Su·ra·ba·ja.** *Dutch* **Soe·ra·ba·ja** (so͝or′ä-bä′yä). A seaport and industrial and commercial center of Indonesia, in northeastern Java. Population, 1,008,000.

su·rah (so͝or′ə) *n.* A soft twilled fabric of silk or of a blend of silk and rayon. Also called "surah silk." [French *surat,* originally made at SURAT.]

Su·ra·kar·ta (so͝or′ə-kär′tə). *Dutch* **Soe·ra·kar·ta** (-ä-kär′tä). A city of Java, Indonesia, in the south-central part of the island on the Solo River. Also called "Solo." Population, 368,000.

su·ral (so͝or′əl) *adj.* Of or relating to the calf of the leg. [New Latin *suralis,* from Latin *sūra*†, calf of the leg.]

Su·rat (so͝or′ət, sə-rät′). A seaport of the Republic of India, in southeastern Gujarat, 150 miles north of Bombay; site of the first British settlement in India (1612). Population, 288,000.

t tight/th thin, path/*th* this, bathe/ŭ cut/ûr urge/v valve/w with/y yes/z zebra, size/zh vision/ə about, item, edible, gallop, circus/ à *Fr.* ami/œ *Fr.* feu, *Ger.* schön/ü *Fr.* tu, *Ger.* über/KH *Ger.* ich, *Scot.* loch/N *Fr.* bon. ***Follows main vocabulary.** †**Of obscure origin.**

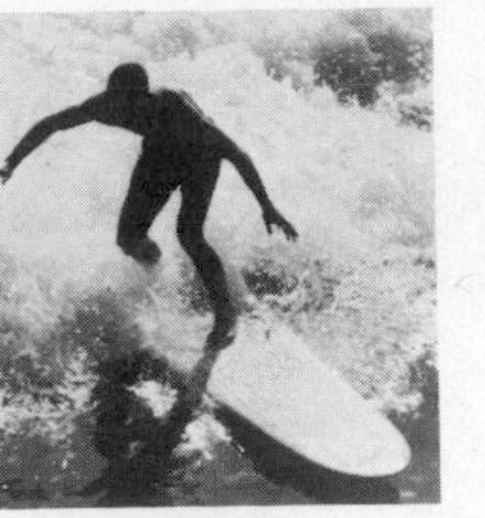

surfboard

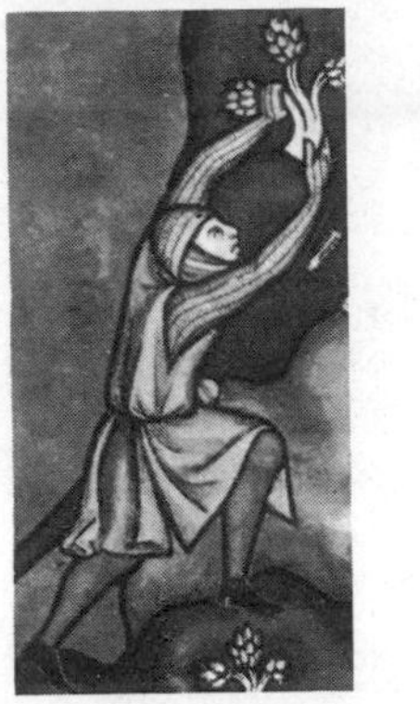

surcoat
Detail of a 13th-century manuscript illumination

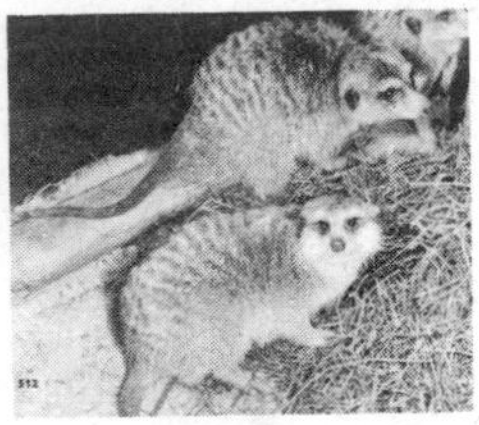

suricate

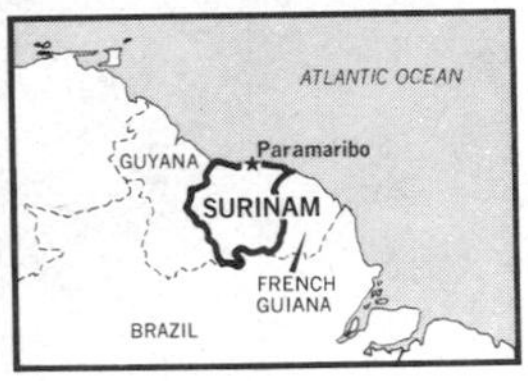

Surinam

sur·base (sûr′bās′) *n. Architecture.* A molding or border above the base of a structure, such as a pedestal or baseboard. [SUR- + BASE.]

sur·based (sûr′bāst′) *adj. Architecture.* **1.** Having a surbase. **2.** Pertaining to an arch with a rise less than half its span. [French *surbaissé*, flattened (said of an arch), from the past participle of *surbaisser*, to depress, flatten : *sur-*, extremely + *baisser*, to lower, from *bas*, low, from Old French, low, BASE.]

sur·cease (sûr′sēs′, sər-sēs′) *v.* **-ceased, -ceasing, -ceases.** *Archaic.* —*tr.* To put an end to; stop. —*intr.* To cease; stop. —*n. Archaic.* Cessation; end. [Middle English *sursesen*, from Old French *surseoir* (past participle *sursis*), to refrain, delay, from Latin *supersedēre*, to desist from, SUPERSEDE.]

sur·charge (sûr′chärj′) *n.* **1.** An additional sum added to the usual amount or cost. **2.** An overcharge, especially when unlawful. **3.** An additional or excessive burden; an overload. **4. a.** A new value or denomination overprinted on a postage or revenue stamp. **b.** The stamp to which it has been applied. **5.** *Law.* The act of surcharging. —*tr.v.* **surcharged, -charging, -charges. 1.** To overcharge (a person). **2.** To place an excessive burden upon; overload. **3.** To fill beyond usual capacity; overfill. **4.** To print a surcharge on (a postage or revenue stamp). **5.** *Law.* To show an omission of a credit in (an account). [Middle English *surchargen*, from Old French *surcharger* : *sur-*, excessively + *charg(i)er*, CHARGE.]

sur·cin·gle (sûr′sĭng′gəl) *n.* **1.** A girth that binds a saddle, pack, or blanket to the body of a horse. **2.** The fastening belt on a clerical cassock. —*tr.v.* **surcingled, -gling, -gles.** To bind or fasten with a surcingle. [Middle English *sursengle*, from Old French *so(u)rcengle* : *sur-*, over + *cengle*, belt, from Latin *cingula*, from *cingere*, to gird (see **kenk-**[1] in Appendix*).]

sur·coat (sûr′kōt′) *n.* **1.** A loose outer coat or gown. **2.** A tunic worn in the Middle Ages by a knight over his armor. [Middle English *surcote*, "overcoat," from Old French : SUR- + COAT.]

sur·cu·lose (sûr′kyə-lōs′) *adj. Botany.* Producing suckers: *a surculose shrub.* [Latin *surculōsus*, woody, ligneous, from *surculus*, diminutive of *surus*, branch. See **swer-**[3] in Appendix.*]

surd (sûrd) *n.* **1.** A sum, as $\sqrt{2} + \sqrt{3}$, containing one or more irrational roots of numbers. **2.** *Phonetics.* A voiceless sound in speech. —*adj. Phonetics.* Voiceless, as a sound. [Latin *surdus*, deaf, mute (used in mathematics to translate Arabic *jadhr aṣámm*, "deaf root," translation of Greek *alogos*, "speechless," "irrational"). See **swer-**[2] in Appendix.*]

sure (shŏŏr) *adj.* **surer, surest. 1.** Incapable of being doubted or disputed; completely true; certain: *sure proof of his innocence.* **2.** Not hesitating or wavering; stable; steady; firm: *sure convictions.* **3.** Confident of some future possibility; certain in some expectation. Used with *of*: *sure of victory.* **4. a.** Bound to come about or to happen; inevitable. **b.** Having one's course directed; destined; bound: *sure to succeed.* **5.** Certain not to miss or err; steady. **6.** Worthy of being trusted or depended upon; reliable. **7.** *Obsolete.* Free from harm or danger; safe; secure. —**make sure.** To establish without doubt; make certain. —**to be sure.** Indeed; certainly. —*adv. Informal.* Surely; certainly; indeed; undoubtedly. —**for sure.** Certainly; unquestionably: *We'll win for sure.* [Middle English *s(e)ure*, from Old French *sur*, from Latin *sēcūrus*, "free from care," safe : *sē*, without (see **seu-**[2] in Appendix*) + *cūra*, care (see **cūra** in Appendix*).] —**sure′ness** *n.*

Synonyms: *sure, certain, confident, assured.* These adjectives are compared as they apply to persons who do not doubt their own abilities. *Sure* and *certain* are frequently used interchangeably. *Sure*, however, is the more subjective term, whereas *certain* may imply belief based on experience or established evidence. *Confident* suggests belief founded on faith or reliance in oneself or in others. *Assured* suggests confidence or certainty based on knowledge that doubt has been removed.

sure-fire (shŏŏr′fīr′) *adj. Informal.* Bound to be successful or perform as expected: *a sure-fire plan.*

sure-foot·ed (shŏŏr′fŏŏt′ĭd) *adj.* Not liable to stumble or fall.

sure·ly (shŏŏr′lē) *adv.* **1.** Firmly and with confidence; unhesitatingly. **2.** Undoubtedly; certainly. Often used as an intensive: *You surely can't be serious.* **3.** Without fail: *Slowly but surely spring returns.*

sure·ty (shŏŏr′ə-tē) *n., pl.* **-ties. 1.** The condition of being sure, especially of oneself; self-assurance: *"He had no surety within himself"* (Edith Hamilton). **2.** Something beyond doubt; a certainty. **3.** A pledge or formal promise made to secure against loss, damage, or default; a guarantee or security. **4.** A person who has contracted to be responsible for another; especially, a person who assumes any responsibilities, debts, or obligations in the event of the default of another. —**sure′ty·ship′** *n.*

surf (sûrf) *n.* The offshore waters, waves, or wave action between the shoreline and the outermost boundaries of the breakers. —*intr.v.* **surfed, surfing, surfs.** To engage in surfing. [Possibly variant of earlier *suff*†.] —**surf′y** *adj.*

sur·face (sûr′fəs) *n. Abbr.* **sur. 1. a.** The outer or the topmost boundary of an object. **b.** A material layer constituting such a boundary. **2.** *Geometry.* **a.** The boundary of any three-dimensional figure. **b.** The two-dimensional locus of points located in three-dimensional space whose height z above each point (x,y) of a region of a coordinate plane is specified by a function $f(x,y)$ of two arguments. **3.** The superficial or outward appearance of anything as distinguished from inner substance or matter. **4.** *Aviation.* An airfoil. —*adj.* **1.** Pertaining to, on, or at a surface: *surface algae in the water.* **2.** Superficial; apparent as opposed to real. —*v.* **surfaced, -facing, -faces.** —*tr.* To form the surface of, as by smoothing or leveling; to give a surface to. —*intr.* **1.** To rise to the surface. **2.** To emerge after concealment. [French (formed after Latin *superficiēs*, surface) : *sur-*, above + FACE.]

sur·face-ac·tive (sûr′fĭs-ăk′tĭv) *adj.* Designating a substance capable of reducing the surface tension of a liquid in which it is dissolved. Said especially of detergents.

surface of revolution. A surface generated by revolving a plane curve about an axis in its plane.

surface plate. A planometer.

surface tension. *Abbr.* **T** A property of liquids arising from unbalanced molecular cohesive forces at or near the surface, as a result of which the surface tends to contract and has properties resembling those of a stretched elastic membrane.

surf·bird (sûrf′bûrd′) *n.* A shore bird, *Aphriza virgata*, of the Pacific coast of North and South America, found from Alaska to Chile, and having dark, spotted plumage.

surf·board (sûrf′bôrd′, -bōrd′) *n.* The narrow, somewhat rounded board, customarily longer than body-length, used by surfers for riding waves into shore.

surf·boat (sûrf′bōt′) *n.* A strong seaworthy boat that can be launched or landed in a heavy surf.

surf·cast·ing (sûrf′kăs′tĭng, -käs′tĭng) *n.* The sport of fishing from shore, casting one's line into the surf. —**surf′cast′er** *n.*

sur·feit (sûr′fĭt) *v.* **-feited, -feiting, -feits.** —*tr.* To feed or supply to fullness or excess; to satiate. —*intr. Archaic.* To overindulge. —See Synonyms at **satiate.** —*n.* **1.** The act or an instance of overindulging in food or drink. **2.** The result of such overindulgence; satiety; disgust. **3.** An excessive amount. [Middle English, from Old French, from Vulgar Latin *superfactum* (unattested), from the neuter past participle of *superficere* (unattested), to overdo : Latin *super-*, excessively + *facere*, to do (see **dhē-**[1] in Appendix*).] —**sur′feit·er** *n.*

surf·er (sûr′fər) *n.* One who engages in surfing.

surfer's knobs. Tumorlike overgrowths of connective tissue just below the knees, on the tops of the feet and often on the toes, common among surfers who paddle in a kneeling position. Also called "surfer's knee."

sur·fi·cial (sər-fĭsh′əl) *adj.* Of, pertaining to, or occurring on the earth's surface. [SURF(ACE) + (SUPERF)ICIAL.]

surf·ing (sûr′fĭng) *n.* A sport in which one paddles a surfboard out into the surf and, standing on the board, attempts to ride on or with a wave into shore.

surf·perch (sûrf′pûrch′) *n., pl.* **surfperch** or **-perches.** Any of various viviparous marine fishes of the family Embiotocidae, of North American Pacific coastal waters.

surg. surgeon; surgery; surgical.

surge (sûrj) *v.* **surged, surging, surges.** —*intr.* **1.** To move in a billowing or swelling manner; to rise and heave over violently, as waves. **2.** To roll or be tossed about on waves, as a boat. **3.** To increase suddenly. **4.** To slip around a windlass. Used of a rope. —*tr.* To loosen or slacken (a cable) gradually. —See Synonyms at **rise.** —*n.* **1.** A heavy, billowing, or swelling motion like that of great waves. **2. a.** A wave, ground swell, or billow. **b.** Such waves collectively. **3.** A violent rising and falling; a sudden onrush: *a surge of joy.* **4.** A sudden, transient increase in electric current. **5.** *Nautical.* The part of a windlass into which the cable surges. [Old French *sourgir*, from Old Spanish *surgir*, from Latin *surgere*, "to lead straight up," rise : *sub-*, up from below + *regere*, to lead, rule (see **reg-**[1] in Appendix*).]

sur·geon (sûr′jən) *n. Abbr.* **surg.** A physician specializing in surgery. [Middle English *surg(i)en*, from Norman French, short for Old French *serurgien*, from *serurgie*, SURGERY.]

sur·geon·cy (sûr′jən-sē) *n., pl.* **-cies.** The position, office, rank, or duties of a surgeon.

sur·geon·fish (sûr′jən-fĭsh′) *n., pl.* **surgeonfish** or **-fishes.** Any of various bright-colored tropical marine fishes of the family Acanthuridae, having a sharp, erectile spine near the base of the tail. [From its lancetlike spines, which resemble surgeons' instruments.]

Surgeon General *pl.* **Surgeons General.** *Abbr.* **Surg. Gen. 1.** The chief general officer in the medical departments of the United States Army or Navy. **2.** The chief medical officer in the United States Public Health Service.

surgeon's knot. Any of several knots used in surgery for tying ligatures or stitching incisions.

sur·ger·y (sûr′jə-rē) *n., pl.* **-ies.** *Abbr.* **surg. 1.** The medical diagnosis and treatment of injury, deformity, and disease by manual and instrumental operations. **2.** An operating room or laboratory of a surgeon or of a hospital's surgical staff. **3.** The skill or work of a surgeon. **4.** *Chiefly British.* A physician's office. [Middle English *surgerie*, from Old French, short for *serurgerie*, *cerurgerie*, from *serurgie*, *cerurgie*, from Latin *chirurgia*, from Greek *kheirurgia*, from *kheirurgos*, working by hand : *kheir*, hand (see **ghesor-** in Appendix*) + *ergon*, work (see **werg-**[1] in Appendix*).]

sur·gi·cal (sûr′jĭ-kəl) *adj. Abbr.* **surg. 1.** Pertaining to or characteristic of surgeons or surgery. **2.** Used in surgery. **3.** Resulting from or occurring after surgery. [From SURGEON.]

Su·ri·ba·chi, Mount (sŏŏr′ə-bä′chē). A volcanic hill, 546 feet high, on Iwo Jima in the western Pacific; the site of a U.S. victory over the Japanese in World War II (1945).

su·ri·cate (sŏŏr′ĭ-kāt′) *n.* A small, gregarious burrowing mammal, *Suricata suricatta*, of southern Africa, having grayish fur and a long tail. [French *suricate*, *surikate*, native name in South Africa.]

Su·ri·nam (sŏŏr′ə-năm). **1.** *Dutch* **Su·ri·na·me** (sü′rə-nä′mə). Formerly **Dutch Gui·a·na** (gē-ä′nə), **Netherlands Gui·a·na.** A Territory of the Kingdom of the Netherlands, occupying 55,155 square miles in northern South America. Population, 362,000. Capital, Paramaribo. **2.** See **Suriname.**

Su·ri·na·me (sür'rə-nä'mə). **1.** Also **Su·ri·nam** (sōōr'ə-năm'). A river of Surinam, northern South America, rising in the Guiana Highlands and flowing about 400 miles northward to the Atlantic. **2.** The Dutch name for **Surinam.**

sur·ly (sûr'lē) *adj.* **-lier, -liest. 1.** Sullenly rude and ill-humored; brazenly uncivil; gruff. **2.** *Obsolete.* Arrogant; domineering. [Earlier *sirly,* originally "lordly," masterful, imperious, from SIR.] **—sur'li·ly** *adv.* **—sur'li·ness** *n.*

sur·mise (sər-mīz') *v.* **-mised, -mising, -mises.** *—tr.* To infer (something) without sufficiently conclusive evidence. *—intr.* To make a guess or conjecture. —See Synonyms at **conjecture.** *—n.* An idea or opinion based upon insufficiently conclusive evidence; a guess; a conjecture. [Middle English *surmysen,* to charge on or against, accuse, from Old French *surmettre* (past participle *surmis*), from Medieval Latin *supermittere,* from Late Latin, to throw upon : Latin *super-,* upon + *mittere,* to send off, throw (see **smeit-** in Appendix*).]

sur·mount (sər-mount') *tr.v.* **-mounted, -mounting, -mounts. 1.** *Obsolete.* To surpass or exceed in amount. **2.** To overcome (an obstacle, for example); conquer. **3.** To ascend to the top and cross to the other side of; get above and over. **4.** To place something above; to top. **5.** To be above or on top of. [Middle English *surmonten,* from Old French *surmonter* : *sur-,* above + *monter,* to MOUNT.] **—sur·mount'a·ble** *adj.* **—sur·mount'a·ble·ness** *n.* **—sur·mount'er** *n.*

sur·mul·let (sər-mŭl'ĭt, sûr'mŭl'-) *n., pl.* **surmullet** or **-lets.** The **goatfish** *(see).* [French *surmulet,* from Old French *sormulet* : probably *sor,* reddish brown, from Germanic (see **saus-** in Appendix*) + *mulet,* MULLET.]

sur·name (sûr'nām') *n.* **1.** A person's family name as distinguished from his given name. **2.** A nickname or epithet added to a person's name. *—tr.v.* **surnamed, -naming, -names.** To give a surname to. [Middle English : SUR- + NAME.]

sur·pass (sər-păs', -päs') *tr.v.* **-passed, -passing, -passes. 1.** To go beyond the limit, powers, or extent of; transcend. **2.** To be or go beyond in quantity, degree, amount, or the like; exceed. —See Synonyms at **excel.** [Old French *surpasser* : *sur-,* over + *passer,* PASS.]

sur·pass·ing (sər-păs'ĭng, -päs'ĭng) *adj.* Exceptional; exceeding: *monuments of surpassing splendor.* **—sur·pass'ing·ly** *adv.*

sur·plice (sûr'plĭs) *n.* A loose-fitting white gown, having full flowing sleeves, worn over a cassock by some clergymen. [Middle English *surplis,* from Old French *sourpeliz,* from Medieval Latin *superpellicium* (originally worn by clergymen of northern countries over their fur coats) : *super-,* over + *pellicium,* fur coat, from Latin *pellicius,* made of skin, from *pellis,* skin (see **pel-⁴** in Appendix*).]

sur·plus (sûr'pləs) *adj. Abbr.* **s., sur.** Being more than or in excess of what is needed or required: *surplus grain.* *—n.* **1.** An amount or quantity in excess of what is needed; something remaining or left over. **2.** Total assets minus the sum of all liabilities. **3.** Excess of a corporation's net assets over the face value of its capital stock. **4.** Excess of receipts over expenditures. [Middle English, from Old French, from Medieval Latin *superplūs* : Latin *super-,* in addition + *plūs,* more (see **pel-⁸** in Appendix*).]

sur·plus·age (sûr'plŭs-ĭj) *n.* **1.** Surplus; excess. **2.** An excess of words; verbiage. **3.** Irrelevant matter in a legal pleading.

surplus value. In the Marxian analysis of capitalism, the difference between the value of the product produced by labor and the actual price of labor as paid out in wages.

sur·print (sûr'prĭnt') *tr.v.* **-printed, -printing, -prints.** *Photoengraving.* **1.** To overprint. **2.** To superimpose (a second negative) upon a previously printed image of the first negative. *—n.* That which is surprinted.

sur·pris·al (sər-prī'zəl) *n.* The act of surprising or the condition of being surprised.

sur·prise (sər-prīz') *tr.v.* **-prised, -prising, -prises.** Also *rare* **surprize. 1.** To encounter suddenly or unexpectedly; take or catch (a person) unawares. **2.** To attack or capture suddenly and without warning. **3.** To cause to feel wonder, astonishment, or amazement. **4. a.** To cause (someone) to do or say something unintended. Used with *into.* **b.** To elicit by these means. *—n.* **1.** The act of surprising; an unexpected occurrence, encounter, or attack. **2.** The condition of being surprised; a feeling of amazement or wonder. **3.** Something that surprises, as an unexpected encounter, event, or gift. **—take by surprise. 1.** To come upon suddenly and unexpectedly. **2.** To astonish or astound. [Middle English *surprysen,* to be seized with, from Old French *surprendre* (past participle *surpris*), "to overtake" : *sur-,* over + *prendre,* to take, from Latin *prehendere,* to seize (see **ghend-** in Appendix*).] **—sur·pris'er** *n.*

Synonyms: surprise, astonish, amaze, astound, dumbfound, flabbergast. These verbs mean to fill a person with wonder or disbelief. All imply a reaction to what is unexpected. *Surprise* refers to the effect of what is unexpected or unusual. The remaining terms are considerably stronger. *Astonish* implies the condition of being momentarily overwhelmed and often dazed and speechless. *Amaze* suggests wonder and, often, bewilderment. *Astound* implies shock, as from something that seems incredible or has no precedent in one's experience. *Dumbfound* adds to *astound* the implication of speechlessness. *Flabbergast* is used informally, usually in the sense of *astound* or *dumbfound* and sometimes as the equivalent of *astonish* or *amaze.*

surr. surrender.

sur·re·al (sə-rē'əl) *adj.* Having qualities attributed to surrealism. [Back-formation from SURREALISM.]

sur·re·al·ism (sə-rē'əl-ĭz'əm) *n.* A literary and artistic movement launched in 1924 by the French poet André Breton (1896–1966), proclaiming the radical transformation of all existing social, scientific, and philosophical values through the total liberation of the unconscious. [French *surréalisme* : *sur-,* beyond + *réalisme,* realism, from *réel,* real, from Old French, from Late Latin *reālis,* REAL.] **—sur·re'al·ist** *adj. & n.* **—sur·re'al·is'tic** *adj.* **—sur·re'al·is'ti·cal·ly** *adv.*

sur·re·but·ter (sûr'rĭ-bŭt'ər) *n.* Also **sur·re·but·tal** (-bŭt'əl). *Law.* The plaintiff's reply to the defendant's rebutter.

sur·re·join·der (sûr'rĭ-join'dər) *n. Law.* The plaintiff's reply to the defendant's rejoinder.

sur·ren·der (sə-rĕn'dər) *v.* **-dered, -dering, -ders.** *—tr.* **1.** To relinquish possession or control of to another because of demand or compulsion. **2.** To give up in favor of another. **3.** To give up or give back that which has been granted: *surrender a contractual right.* **4.** To give up or abandon: *surrender all hope.* **5.** To give over or resign (oneself) to something, as to capture or an emotion or influence. *—intr.* To give oneself up, as to an enemy. —See Synonyms at **relinquish.** *—n. Abbr.* **surr. 1.** The act of surrendering. **2.** The delivery of a prisoner, fugitive from justice, or other principal in a legal suit into legal custody. [Middle English *sorendren,* from Old French *surrendre* : *sur-,* over + *rendre,* to deliver, RENDER.]

Synonyms: surrender, submission, capitulation. These nouns refer to the act of giving up one's person or possessions into the authority of another or others or of relinquishing one's power, aims, or goals. *Surrender* is the most general. *Submission* makes more explicit the resultant subordination of one side to the other. *Capitulation* involves *surrender* under prearranged conditions.

surrender value. The value of an insurance policy either to the owner or to the beneficiary upon its expiration.

sur·rep·ti·tious (sûr'əp-tish'əs) *adj.* Performed, made, or acquired by secret, clandestine, or stealthy means. See Synonyms at **secret.** [Latin *surreptīcius,* from *surripere* (past participle *surreptus*), to seize or take away secretly : *sub-,* under, secretly + *rapere,* to seize (see **rep-** in Appendix*).] **—sur'rep·ti'tious·ly** *adv.* **—sur'rep·ti'tious·ness** *n.*

sur·rey (sûr'ē) *n., pl.* **-reys.** A horse-drawn four-wheeled pleasure vehicle having two seats. [Short for *Surrey cart,* first built in SURREY (county).]

Sur·rey (sûr'ē). *Abbr.* **Sur.** A county occupying 722 square miles in southern England. Population, 1,731,000. County seat, Kingston.

Sur·rey (sûr'ē), **Earl of.** The courtesy title of Henry Howard. 1517?–1547. English soldier and poet.

sur·ro·gate (sûr'ə-gĭt, -gāt') *n.* **1.** A person or thing that is substituted for another; a substitute. **2.** In New York and some other states, a judge having jurisdiction over the probate of wills and the settlement of estates. *—adj.* Substitute. *—tr.v.* (sûr'ə-gāt') **surrogated, -gating, -gates. 1.** To put in the place of another, especially as a successor; replace. **2.** To appoint (another) as a replacement for oneself. [Latin *surrogāre, subrogāre,* to substitute, SUBROGATE.]

sur·round (sə-round') *tr.v.* **-rounded, -rounding, -rounds. 1.** To extend on all sides of simultaneously; encircle; ring. **2.** To enclose or confine on all sides so as to bar escape or outside communication. [Middle English *sourrounden,* to submerge, overflow, from Old French *s(o)uronder,* from Late Latin *superundāre* : Latin *super-,* over + *undāre,* to rise in waves, from *unda,* wave (see **wed-¹** in Appendix*).]

sur·round·ings (sə-roun'dĭngz) *pl.n.* The external circumstances, conditions, and objects that affect the existence and development of something; environment.

sur·sum cor·da (sûr'səm côr'də). *Latin.* **1.** *Often capital* **S,** *capital* **C.** An ecclesiastical versicle offering praise and thanksgiving to God. **2.** An incitement to fervor, spirit, or courage. Literally, lift up your hearts.

sur·tax (sûr'tăks') *n.* **1.** An additional tax. **2.** A graduated income tax added to the normal income tax levied on the amount by which a person's net income exceeds a certain sum. *—tr.v.* **surtaxed, -taxing, -taxes.** To levy a surtax on.

sur·veil·lance (sər-vā'ləns) *n.* **1.** Close observation of a person or group, especially of one under suspicion. **2.** The act of observing or the condition of being observed.

sur·veil·lant (sər-vā'lənt) *adj.* Exercising surveillance. *—n.* One that keeps close watch. [French, present participle of *surveiller,* to watch over : *sur-,* over + *veiller,* to watch, from Latin *vigilāre,* from *vigil,* awake, watchful (see **weg-²** in Appendix*).]

sur·vey (sər-vā', sûr'vā) *v.* **-veyed, -veying, -veys.** *—tr.* **1.** To examine or look at in a comprehensive way. **2.** To inspect carefully; scrutinize: *"two women were surveying the other people on the platform"* (Thomas Wolfe). **3.** To determine the boundaries, the area, or the elevations of (land or structures on the earth's surface) by means of measuring angles and distances, using the techniques of geometry and trigonometry. *—intr.* To make a survey. —See Synonyms at **see.** *—n.* (sûr'vā). **1.** A detailed inspection or investigation. **2.** A general or comprehensive view. **3. a.** The process of surveying. **b.** A report on or map of that which is surveyed. [Middle English *surveyen,* from Old French *surve(i)r,* from Medieval Latin *supervidēre,* to look over : Latin *super-,* over + *vidēre,* to look, see (see **weid-** in Appendix*).] **—sur·vey'or** (-ər) *n.*

sur·vey·ing (sər-vā'ĭng) *n.* The measurement of dimensional relationships, as of horizontal distances, elevations, directions, and angles, on the earth's surface, especially for use in locating property boundaries, construction layout, and mapmaking.

surrealism
"The Mystery and Melancholy of a Street," painted by surrealist Giorgio di Chirico in 1914

surrey

surplice
Anglican surplice

ă pat/ā pay/â care/ä father/b bib/ch church/d deed/ĕ pet/ē be/f fife/g gag/h hat/hw which/ĭ pit/ī pie/îr pier/j judge/k kick/l lid, needle/m mum/n no, sudden/ng thing/ŏ pot/ō toe/ô paw, for/oi noise/ou out/ŏŏ took/ōō boot/p pop/r roar/s sauce/sh ship, dish/t tight/th thin, path/th this, bathe/ŭ cut/ûr urge/v valve/w with/y yes/z zebra, size/zh vision/ə about, item, edible, gallop, circus/ à *Fr.* ami/œ *Fr.* feu, *Ger.* schön/ü *Fr.* tu, *Ger.* über/KH *Ger.* ich, *Scot.* loch/N *Fr.* bon. *Follows main vocabulary. †Of obscure origin.

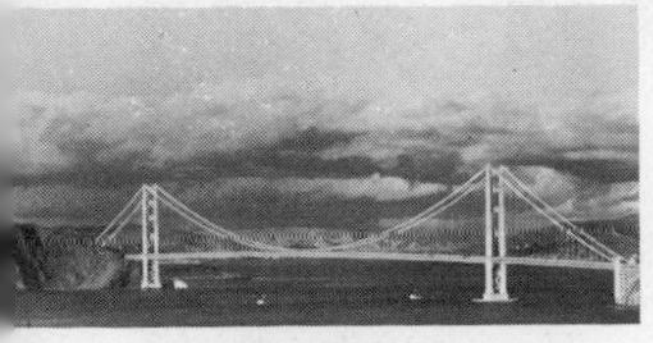

suspension bridge
The Golden Gate
Bridge at San Francisco

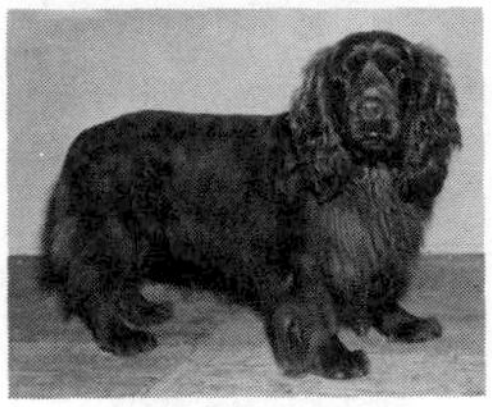

Sussex spaniel

surveyor's level. A level having a telescope and attached spirit level mounted on a tripod and rotating around a vertical axis.
surveyor's measure. A system of measurement used by surveyors, based on the chain as a unit.
sur·viv·al (sər-vī′vəl) *n.* Also **sur·viv·ance** (-vəns). **1.** The act of surviving or the fact of having survived. **2.** Something that survives, as an ancient custom or belief.
survival kit. A compact package of necessities designed to sustain a disaster victim.
survival of the fittest. Natural selection conceived of as a struggle in which only those organisms best adapted to existing conditions survive.
survival value. Usefulness in the struggle for survival. Said of a quality possessed by an organism: *"emotional activation most clearly has survival value"* (Norman L. Munn).
sur·vive (sər-vīv′) *v.* **-vived, -viving, -vives.** *—intr.* To remain alive or in existence; continue life or activity. *—tr.* To live, exist, or remain active beyond the extent of; outlive: *"The plum survives its poems."* (Wallace Stevens). —See Synonyms at **outlive.** [Middle English *surviven,* from Old French *so(u)rvivre,* from Late Latin *supervīvere* : *super-,* over + *vīvere,* to live (see **gwei-** in Appendix*).] **—sur·vi′vor** (-vər) *n.*
sur·vi·vor·ship (sər-vī′vər-shĭp′) *n.* **1.** *Law.* The right of a person who survives a partner or joint owner to the entire ownership of that which was previously owned jointly. **2.** The condition of being a survivor.
Sus. Sussex.
Su·sa (so͞o′sə, -zə). Biblical name **Shu·shan** (sho͞o′shăn). A ruined city in southwestern Iran, the capital of ancient Elam.
Su·san (so͞o′zən). A feminine given name. [Late Latin *Susanna,* from Greek *Sousanna,* from Hebrew *shōshannāh,* lily.]
Su·san·na¹ (so͞o-zăn′ə). In the Apocrypha, a captive in Babylon falsely accused of adultery and saved from death by Daniel.
Su·san·na² (so͞o-zăn′ə) *n.* The book of the Apocrypha containing the story of Susanna.
sus·cep·tance (sə-sĕp′təns) *n. Electricity.* The imaginary part of the complex representation of **admittance** *(see).* [SUSCEPT(IBILITY) + (CONDUCT)ANCE.]
sus·cep·ti·bil·i·ty (sə-sĕp′tə-bĭl′ə-tē) *n., pl.* **-ties. 1.** The condition or quality of being susceptible. **2.** The capacity to be affected by deep emotions or strong feelings; sensitivity. **3.** *Plural.* Sensibilities; sensitive feelings.
sus·cep·ti·ble (sə-sĕp′tə-bəl) *adj.* **1.** Readily subject to an influence, agency, or force; unresistant; yielding. Usually used with *of* or *to.* **2.** Liable to be stricken with or by: *susceptible to colds.* **3.** Especially sensitive; highly impressionable. [Late Latin *susceptibilis,* capable of receiving, from Latin *suscipere* (past participle *susceptus*), to take up, receive : *sub-,* up from under + *capere,* to take (see **kap-** in Appendix*).] **—sus·cep′ti·ble·ness** *n.* **—sus·cep′ti·bly** *adv.*
sus·cep·tive (sə-sĕp′tĭv) *adj.* **1.** Receptive. **2.** Susceptible. **—sus·cep′tive·ness, sus·cep′tiv′i·ty** *n.*
Su·si·an (so͞o′zē-ən) *n.* An unclassified language, **Elamite** *(see).*
Su·si·a·na. See **Elam.**
sus·pect (sə-spĕkt′) *v.* **-pected, -pecting, -pects.** *—tr.* **1.** To surmise to be true or probable; imagine. **2.** To have doubt about or distrust of. **3.** To think (a person) guilty without proof. *—intr.* To have suspicion. *—n.* (sŭs′pĕkt′). One who is suspected, especially of committing a crime. *—adj.* (sŭs′pĕkt′). Open to or viewed with suspicion. [Latin *suspectāre,* intensive of *suspicere* (past participle *suspectus*), to look up at, watch : *sub-,* up from under + *specere,* to look at (see **spek-** in Appendix*).]
sus·pend (sə-spĕnd′) *v.* **-pended, -pending, -pends.** *—tr.* **1.** To bar for a period from a privilege, office, or position, usually as a punishment: *suspend a student from school.* **2.** To cause to stop for a period; interrupt: *"He now suspended his labors and reached for the tobacco jar."* (Edmund C. Bentley). **3. a.** To maintain in an undecided state; hold in abeyance: *suspend judgment.* **b.** To render ineffective temporarily under certain conditions: *suspend a sentence; suspend parking regulations.* **4.** To hang so as to allow free movement. **5.** To support or keep from falling without apparent attachment, as by buoyancy. *—intr.* **1.** To cease for a period; to delay. **2.** To fail to make payments or meet obligations. [Middle English *suspenden,* from Old French *suspendre,* from Latin *suspendere,* to hang up : *sub-,* up from under + *pendere,* to hang (see **spen-** in Appendix*).]
suspended animation. A dormant condition resembling death, induced by reversible cessation of the vital functions.
sus·pend·er (sə-spĕn′dər) *n.* **1.** *Plural.* A pair of straps, often elastic, worn over the shoulders to support trousers or a skirt. **2.** *British.* A garter.
sus·pense (sə-spĕns′) *n.* **1.** The condition of being suspended. **2.** The state or quality of being undecided, uncertain, or doubtful. **3.** Anxiety or apprehension resulting from an uncertain, undecided, or mysterious situation. [Middle English, from Old French, from the feminine of *suspens,* suspended, from Latin *suspensus,* past participle of *suspendere,* SUSPEND.] **—sus·pense′ful** *adj.*
suspense account. A temporary account in which entries of credits or charges are made until their proper disposition can be determined.
sus·pen·sion (sə-spĕn′shən) *n.* **1.** The act of suspending or the condition of being suspended, especially: **a.** A temporary abrogation or deferment. **b.** A debarment, as from office or privilege. **c.** A postponement of judgment, opinion, or decision. **2.** *Music.* **a.** The prolonging of one or more tones of a chord into a following chord to create a temporary dissonance. **b.** The tone so prolonged. **3.** A device from which a mechanical part is suspended. **4.** The system of springs and other devices that insulates the chassis of a vehicle from shocks transmitted through the wheels. **5.** *Chemistry.* A relatively coarse, noncolloidal dispersion of solid particles in a liquid. See **colloid.**
suspension bridge. A bridge having the roadway suspended from cables that are supported by two or more towers and are firmly anchored at both ends.
suspension points. A series of dots, usually three, used to indicate the omission of a word or words.
sus·pen·sive (sə-spĕn′sĭv) *adj.* **1.** Serving or tending to suspend or temporarily stop something. **2.** Characterized by or causing suspense. **—sus·pen′sive·ly** *adv.* **—sus·pen′sive·ness** *n.*
sus·pen·sor (sə-spĕn′sər) *n.* **1.** *Botany.* A cell or cellular structure developed from a zygote in seed-bearing plants and connecting the embryo to the embryo sac. **2.** Variant of **suspensory.** [New Latin, from Medieval Latin, one that suspends, from Latin *suspendere* (past participle *suspensus*), SUSPEND.]
sus·pen·so·ry (sə-spĕn′sə-rē) *adj.* **1.** Supporting or suspending: *a suspensory bandage.* **2.** Delaying the completion of something. *—n., pl.* **suspensories.** Also **sus·pen·sor** (sə-spĕn′sər). **1.** A support or truss. **2.** An athletic supporter.
suspensory ligament. A ligament that supports an organ or bodily part.
sus·pi·cion (sə-spĭsh′ən) *n.* **1.** The act of suspecting the existence of something, especially of something wrong, without sufficient evidence or proof. **2.** A minute amount; hint; trace. —See Synonyms at **uncertainty.** *—tr.v.* **suspicioned, -cioning, -cions.** *Nonstandard.* To suspect. [Middle English *suspicio(u)n,* from Old French *suspicion,* from Latin *suspīciō,* from Latin *suspicere* (past participle *suspectus*), to look at secretly, SUSPECT.] **—sus·pi′cion·al** *adj.*
sus·pi·cious (sə-spĭsh′əs) *adj.* **1.** Arousing or apt to arouse suspicion; questionable: *suspicious behavior.* **2.** Tending to suspect; distrustful: *a suspicious nature.* **—sus·pi′cious·ly** *adv.* **—sus·pi′cious·ness** *n.*
sus·pire (sə-spīr′) *intr.v.* **-pired, -piring, -pires.** *Poetic.* **1.** To breathe: *"And from that one intake of fire/All creatures still warmly suspire."* (Robert Frost). **2.** To sigh. [Middle English *suspiren,* from Latin *suspīrāre,* to draw a deep breath : *sub-,* up from below + *spīrāre,* to breathe (see **spīrāre** in Appendix*).] **—sus′pi·ra′tion** *n.*
Sus·que·han·na (sŭs′kwə-hăn′ə). A river of the northeastern United States, rising in central New York State and flowing 444 miles south through eastern Pennsylvania and northeastern Maryland to the head of Chesapeake Bay.
Sus·sex (sŭs′ĭks). *Abbr.* **Sus., Suss.** A county occupying 1,457 square miles in southern England, divided administratively into East Sussex (829 square miles; population, 666,000; county seat, Lewes) and West Sussex (628 square miles; population, 412,000; county seat, Chichester). [Middle English *Sussex,* Old English *Sūth Seaxna lond,* "land of the South Saxons" : SOUTH + *Seaxe, Seaxan,* SAXON(S).]
Sussex spaniel. A dog of a breed developed in Sussex, England, having long ears, short legs, and a silky golden-brown coat.
sus·tain (sə-stān′) *tr.v.* **-tained, -taining, -tains. 1.** To keep in existence; maintain; prolong: *"The historical process is sustained by man's desire to become other than what he is"* (Norman O. Brown). **2.** To supply with necessities or nourishment; provide for. **3.** To support from below; keep from falling or sinking; to prop. **4.** To support the spirits, vitality, or resolution of; inspirit; encourage: *"Pride of profession, scorn of competitors, devotion to his trade sustained him."* (Mark Van Doren). **5.** To endure or withstand; bear up under: *sustain hardships.* **6.** To experience or suffer (loss or injury). See Usage note below. **7.** To affirm the validity or justice of. **8.** To prove or corroborate; confirm. —See Synonyms at **support.** [Middle English *suste(y)nen,* from Old French *sustenir,* from Latin *sustinēre,* to hold up : *sub-,* up from under + *tenēre,* to hold (see **ten-** in Appendix*).] **—sus·tain′a·ble** *adj.* **—sus·tain′er** *n.* **—sus·tain′ment** *n.*

Usage: *Sustain,* meaning to experience loss or injury, is widely employed on all levels, though held by some writers on usage to be an imprecise substitute for *suffer* or *receive.* It is acceptable to 56 per cent of the Usage Panel in typical examples, such as *sustain a fractured skull* and *sustain losses in the stock market.* Some panel members feel that *sustain* in this sense is more appropriate to loss than to physical injury and especially appropriate to the implication of enduring.

sustaining program. A radio or television program that is supported by the station or network on which it appears and has no commercial announcements.
sus·te·nance (sŭs′tə-nəns) *n.* **1.** The act of sustaining or the condition of being sustained. **2.** The supporting of life or health; maintenance: *"to deliver in every morning six beeves, forty sheep, and other victuals for my sustenance"* (Swift). **3.** One that sustains life or health; especially, food. **4.** Means of livelihood. —See Synonyms at **livelihood.** [Middle English *sustena(u)nce,* from Old French *so(u)stenance,* from *so(u)stenir, sustenir,* SUSTAIN.]
sus·ten·tac·u·lar (sŭs′tən-tăk′yə-lər) *adj. Anatomy.* Supporting. [From Latin *sustentāculum,* a support, from *sustentāre,* frequentative of *sustinēre,* SUSTAIN.]
sus·ten·ta·tion (sŭs′tən-tā′shən) *n. Rare.* Support; sustenance; food. [Middle English *sustentacion,* from Old French, from Latin *sustentātiō,* from *sustentāre,* frequentative of *sustinēre,* SUSTAIN.] **—sus′ten·ta′tive** *adj.*
Su·su (so͞o′so͞o) *n., pl.* **Susu** or **Susus. 1.** A West African people residing in Guinea, the Sudan, and along the northern border of

ă pat/ā pay/âr care/ä father/b bib/ch church/d deed/ĕ pet/ē be/f fife/g gag/h hat/hw which/ĭ pit/ī pie/îr pier/j judge/k kick/l lid, needle/m mum/n no, sudden/ng thing/ŏ pot/ō toe/ô paw, for/oi noise/ou out/o͝o took/o͞o boot/p pop/r roar/s sauce/sh ship, dish/

Sierra Leone. **2.** A member of this people. **3.** The Mande language spoken by the Susu.

su·sur·ra·tion (sōō'sə-rā'shən) *n.* Also **su·sur·rus** (sōō-sûr'əs). A soft, whispering or rustling sound; a murmur; a whisper: *"There was a low susurration of relief among all the rest."* (John C. Powys). [Middle English, from Late Latin *susurrātiō*, from Latin *susurāre*, to whisper, from *susurrus*, whisper. See **swer-**[2] in Appendix.*] —**su·sur'rant** (sōō-sûr'ənt), **su·sur'rous** (-sûr'əs) *adj.*

Suth·er·land (sûth'ər-lənd). A county occupying 2,027 square miles in northern Scotland. Population, 13,000.

Suth·er·land Falls (sŭth'ər-lənd). A waterfall, 1,904 feet high, in southwestern South Island, New Zealand.

Sut·lej (sŭt'lĕj). A river rising in southwestern Tibet and flowing about 850 miles generally southwest across India to join the Chenab in West Pakistan.

sut·ler (sŭt'lər) *n.* Formerly, a camp follower who peddled provisions to the soldiers. [Middle Dutch *soeteler*, bad cook, camp cook, probably from Middle High German *sudelen*, to do sloppy work. See **seu-**[1] in Appendix.*]

su·tra (sōō'trə) *n.* Also **sut·ta** (sōō'tə). **1.** *Hinduism.* Any of various aphoristic doctrinal summaries produced generally between 500 and 200 B.C. and later incorporated into Hindu and Buddhist literature. **2.** *Buddhism.* Any scriptural narrative; especially, any text traditionally regarded as a discourse of the Buddha. [Sanskrit *sūtra*, thread, string, collection of aphorisms or rules. See **syū-** in Appendix.*]

sut·tee (sŭ'tē', sŭt'ē') *n.* **1.** The act or practice, now forbidden by law, of a Hindu widow cremating herself on her husband's funeral pyre. **2.** A widow so cremated. [Sanskrit *satī*, good woman, faithful wife, from *sat*, "existing," virtuous. See **es-** in Appendix.*]

Sut·ter's Mill (sŭt'ərz). A site in eastern California where gold was found in 1848 on the property of John August Sutter, a Swiss pioneer, thus precipitating the gold rush of 1849.

Sut·ton (sŭt'n). A borough of London, England, comprising the former administrative divisions of Beddington and Wallington, Carshalton, and Sutton and Cheam. Population, 169,000.

su·ture (sōō'chər) *n.* **1. a.** The process of joining two surfaces or edges together along a line by or as if by sewing. **b.** The material used in this procedure, as thread, gut, or wire. **2.** The line so formed. **3.** *Anatomy.* The line of junction or an immovable joint between two bones, particularly of the skull. **4.** *Biology.* A seamlike joint or line of articulation, such as the line of dehiscence in a seed or fruit or the spiral seam marking the junction of whorls of a gastropod shell. —*tr.v.* **sutured, -turing, -tures.** *Surgery.* To join by means of sutures; sew up. [Old French, from Latin *sūtūra*, a sewing together, seam, suture, from *suere* (past participle *sūtus*), to sew. See **syū-** in Appendix.*] —**su'tur·al** *adj.* —**su'tur·al·ly** *adv.*

Su·va (sōō'vä). The capital of Fiji, a seaport on the southeastern coast of Viti Levu. Population, 37,000.

Su·wan·nee (sə-wä'nē). Also **Swa·nee** (swä'nē). A river rising in the Okefenokee Swamp of southeastern Georgia and meandering 250 miles across northern Florida to the Gulf of Mexico.

su·ze·rain (sōō'zə-rən, -rān') *n.* **1.** Formerly, a feudal lord to whom fealty was due. **2.** A nation that controls another nation in international affairs but allows it domestic sovereignty. —*adj.* Characteristic of a suzerain; sovereign. [French *suzerain* : *sus*, up, above, from Latin *sūsum*, *sursum*, (turned) upward, up : *sub-*, up + *versum*, neuter past participle of *vertere*, to turn (see **wer-**[3] in Appendix*) + *(souv)erain*, from Old French *so(u)verein*, SOVEREIGN.]

su·ze·rain·ty (sōō'zə-rən-tē, -rān'tē) *n., pl.* **-ties.** The power or domain of a suzerain.

s.v. sailing vessel.

Sval·bard (sfäl'bär). A territory of Norway comprising Spitsbergen and other island groups in the Arctic Ocean.

Sved·berg (sfād'bĕr-y'), **Theodor.** Born 1884. Swedish chemist; studied colloids.

svelte (svĕlt) *adj.* **svelter, sveltest.** Slender or graceful in figure or outline; willowy; slim. [French, from Italian *svelto*, "stretched," slender, from *svellere*, to pull out, stretch out, from Vulgar Latin *exvellere* (unattested), from Latin *evellere* : *ex-*, out + *vellere*, to pull (see **wei-**[4] in Appendix*).]

Sverd·lovsk (sfĕrd'lôfsk'). Formerly **E·kat·er·in·burg** (ĕ-kä'tər-ĭn-bûrg'). A city of the Soviet Union, in the west-central Russian S.F.S.R.; the site of the execution of Nicholas II and his family (1918). Population, 919,000.

Sver·drup (sfĕr'drəp), **Otto Neumann.** 1855–1930. Norwegian Arctic explorer.

Sver·drup Islands (sfĕr'drəp). A group of islands in the Arctic Ocean west of Ellesmere Island, part of the Northwest Territories, Canada.

Sve·rige. The Swedish name for **Sweden.**

svgs. savings.

Sviz·ze·ra. The Italian name for **Switzerland.**

sw short wave; short-wave.

SW southwest.

sw. switch.

Sw. Sweden; Swedish.

S.W.A. South-West Africa.

swab (swŏb) *n.* Also **swob.** **1.** A small piece of cotton or other absorbent material attached to the end of a stick or wire and used for cleansing or applying medicine. **2.** A specimen of mucus or other material removed with such an instrument. **3.** A mop, especially of yarn, for cleaning decks, floors, or other large areas. **4.** A person who uses such a mop, especially on a ship. Also called "swabby." **5.** A lout. —*tr.v.* **swabbed, swabbing, swabs.** Also **swob.** To use a swab on; clean or treat with a swab. [Probably from Middle Dutch *swabbe*, mop. See **swep-**[2] in Appendix.*]

Swa·bi·a (swā'bē-ə). *German* **Schwa·ben** (shvä'bən). **1.** A historic region of southwestern Germany. **2.** A duchy of southern Germany from the 10th to the mid-13th century. —**Swa'bi·an** *adj.* & *n.*

swad·dle (swŏd'l) *tr.v.* **-dled, -dling, -dles.** **1.** To wrap or bind in bandages; swathe. **2.** To wrap (a baby) in swaddling clothes. **3.** To restrain or restrict; smother. —*n.* A band or cloth used for swaddling. [Middle English *swadlen*, *swethelen*, from *swethel*, swaddling clothes, Old English *swæthel*, probably from *swathian*, to SWATHE.]

swaddling clothes. **1.** Formerly, strips of linen or other cloth wound about a newborn infant. **2.** Any restrictions imposed upon the immature. Also called "swaddling bands."

swag (swăg) *n.* **1.** Goods or property obtained by forcible or illicit means. **2.** *Australian.* The pack or bundle of a swagman. —*intr.v.* **swagged, swagging, swags.** *Chiefly British.* To lurch or sway. [Probably from Scandinavian, akin to Norwegian *swagga*, to sway. See **sweng-** in Appendix.*]

swage (swāj) *n.* **1.** A tool used in bending or shaping cold metal. **2.** A stamp or die for marking or shaping metal with a hammer. **3.** A swage block. —*tr.v.* **swaged, swaging, swages.** To bend or shape by using a swage. [Middle English, from Old French *soua(i)ge*, possibly from Vulgar Latin *sōca* (unattested), rope, from Celtic *sōg* (unattested).]

swage block. A metal block having holes or grooves for shaping metal objects.

swag·ger (swăg'ər) *v.* **-gered, -gering, -gers.** —*intr.* **1.** To walk or conduct oneself with an insolent air; to strut. **2.** To brag; bluster. —*tr.* To influence or affect by swaggering. —*n.* **1.** A swaggering movement or gait. **2.** Boastful or conceited expression; braggadocio. [Probably from SWAG.] —**swag'ger·er** *n.* —**swag'ger·ing·ly** *adv.*

swagger stick. A short metal-tipped cane typically carried by military officers.

swag·man (swăg'măn') *n., pl.* **-men** (-mĕn'). *Australian.* A man who seeks work while traveling about carrying his pack or swag; a migrant or itinerant worker.

Swa·hi·li (swä-hē'lē) *n., pl.* **Swahili** or **-lis.** **1.** A Bantu language of eastern and central Africa, widely used as a lingua franca. **2.** One of the original speakers of this language, a Bantu people of Zanzibar and the neighboring mainland. [Swahili, "(people) belonging to the coasts" : Arabic *sawāḥil*, plural of *sāḥil*, coast + *-īy*, belonging to.] —**Swa·hi'li·an** *adj.*

swain (swān) *n.* **1.** A country youth; especially, a young shepherd. **2.** A lover. [Middle English *swein*, *swayne*, from Old Norse *sveinn*, a boy, herdsman. See **seu-**[2] in Appendix.*]

swale (swāl) *n.* Also **swail.** **1.** A low tract of land, especially moist or marshy ground. **2.** Shade. [Middle English, a shade, shady place, perhaps from Scandinavian, akin to Old Norse *svalr*, cool. See **swel-**[2] in Appendix.*]

swal·low[1] (swä'lō) *v.* **-lowed, -lowing, -lows.** —*tr.* **1.** To cause (food, for example) to pass from the mouth via the throat and the esophagus into the stomach by muscular action; ingest. **2.** To consume or destroy as if by ingestion; devour. Often used with *up*: *"the final monopoly in which all previous and lesser monopolies were swallowed up"* (Edward Bellamy). **3.** To ingest (something unpleasant) reluctantly. Often used with *down.* **4. a.** To bear humbly; tolerate: *swallow an insult.* **b.** To believe without question. **5. a.** To refrain from expressing; suppress: *swallow one's feelings.* **b.** To take back; retract: *swallow one's words.* —*intr.* To perform the act of swallowing. —*n.* **1.** The act of swallowing; a gulp. **2.** The amount that is swallowed at any one time. **3.** *Nautical.* The channel through which a rope runs in a block or a mooring chock. [Middle English *swalowen*, *swolwen*, Old English *swelgan.* See **swel-**[1] in Appendix.*] —**swal'low·er** *n.*

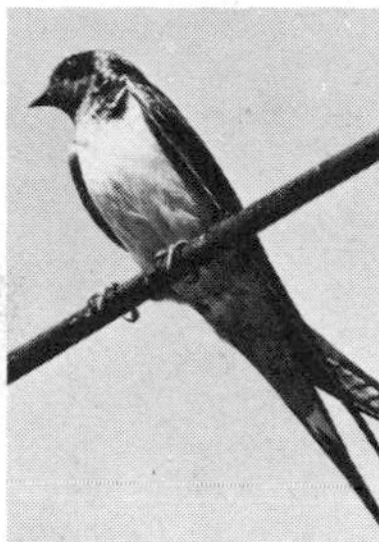
swallow[2]
Hirundo rustica
Barn swallow

swal·low[2] (swä'lō) *n.* **1.** Any of various birds of the family Hirundinidae, having long, pointed wings and a usually notched or forked tail. **2.** Broadly, any of various similar birds, such as a swift. [Middle English *swal(o)we*, *swalu*, Old English *sweal(e)we*, from Germanic *swalwō* (unattested).]

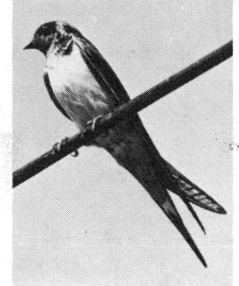

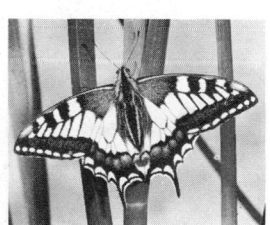

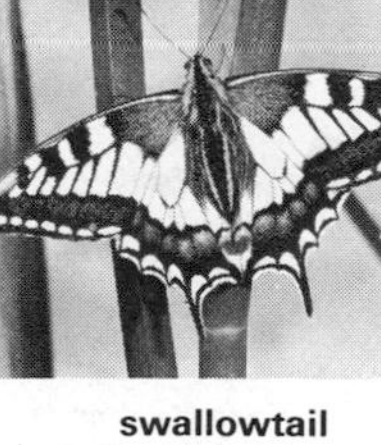
swallowtail
Papilio machaon

swal·low·tail (swä'lō-tāl') *n.* **1. a.** The deeply forked tail of a swallow. **b.** Something similar to it. **2.** *Informal.* A swallow-tailed coat. **3.** Any of various butterflies of the family Papilionidae, usually having a taillike extension at the end of each hind wing.

swal·low-tailed (swä'lō-tāld') *adj.* **1.** Having a deeply forked tail. Said of various birds. **2.** Resembling the tail of a swallow: *a swallow-tailed kite.*

swallow-tailed coat. A man's black coat worn for formal daytime occasions and having a long rounded and split tail.

swal·low·wort (swä'lō-wûrt', -wôrt') *n.* **1.** A plant, the **celandine** *(see).* **2.** Any of several vines of the genus *Cynanchum*, native to Europe; especially, *C. nigrum*, having clusters of small brownish-purple flowers. [Translation of Dutch *zwaluwenkruid* and German *Schwalbenwurz* (from the shape of its pod).]

swam. Past tense of **swim.**

swa·mi (swä'mē) *n., pl.* **-mis.** Also **swa·my** *pl.* **-mies.** **1.** Lord; master. A Hindu title of respect. **2.** A Hindu religious teacher. **3.** Loosely, a mystic; yogi. [Hindi *svāmī*, master, from Sanskrit *svāmin*, owner, prince, "one's own master." See **seu-**[2] in Appendix.*]

Swam·mer·dam (svä'mər-däm'), **Jan.** 1637–1680. Dutch naturalist; discovered the red corpuscle.

swamp (swämp, swômp) *n.* A lowland region saturated with

t tight/th thin, path/*th* this, bathe/ŭ cut/ûr urge/v valve/w with/y yes/z zebra, size/zh vision/ə about, item, edible, gallop, circus/ à *Fr.* ami/œ *Fr.* feu, *Ger.* schön/ü *Fr.* tu, *Ger.* über/KH *Ger.* ich, *Scot.* loch/N *Fr.* bon. ***Follows main vocabulary. †Of obscure origin.**

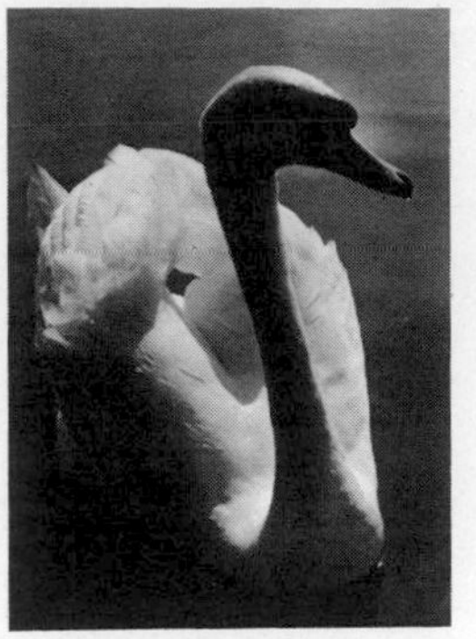

swan
Cygnus olor
Mute swan

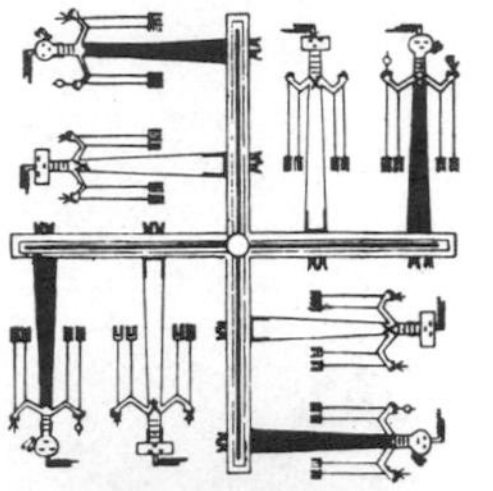

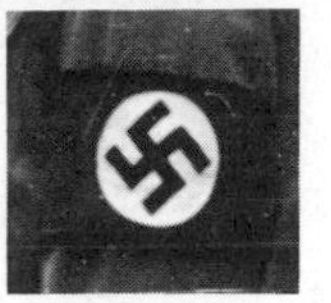

swastika
Above: Navaho Indian swastika with gods of rivers, mountains, rains
Below: Nazi swastika on a soldier's armband

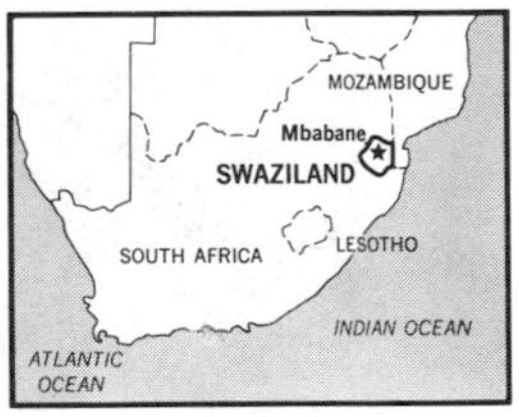

Swaziland

water; marsh. —*v.* **swamped, swamping, swamps.** —*tr.* **1.** To drench in or cover with water or other liquid. **2.** To inundate or burden; overwhelm: *swamped with work.* **3.** To fill or sink (a ship) with water. —*intr.* To become full of water or sink, as a ship. [Perhaps of Low German origin, akin to Low German *zwamp,* swamp. See **swombho-** in Appendix.*]

swamp boat. A flat-bottomed boat, powered by an airplane propeller projecting above the stern, and used in swamps or shallow waters. Also called "airboat."

swamp·er (swäm′pər, swôm′-) *n.* **1.** One who lives in or close to a swamp. **2.** One who clears a swamp or forest. **3. a.** A menial helper, as in a restaurant. **b.** A truck driver's assistant.

swamp fever. 1. Malaria *(see).* **2.** A viral disease in horses, marked by progressive anemia, a staggering gait, and fever.

swamp·land (swämp′lănd′, swômp′-) *n.* Land of swampy consistency; land having many swamps on it; marshland.

swamp law. Lynch law *(see).*

swamp·y (swäm′pē, swôm′-) *adj.* **-ier, -iest.** Of, pertaining to, or characterized by swamps; boggy; marshy. —**swamp′i·ness** *n.*

swan (swän) *n.* **1.** Any of various large aquatic birds, chiefly of the genera *Cygnus* and *Olor,* having webbed feet, a long slender neck, and usually white plumage. **2.** *Capital* **S.** A constellation, **Cygnus** *(see).* [Middle English *swan(ne), suan,* Old English *swan, suan.* See **swen-** in Appendix.*]

Swan (swän), Sir **Joseph Wilson.** 1828–1914. British physicist, chemist, and inventor; developed incandescent electric light (1879).

swan dive. A dive performed with the legs straight together, the back arched, and the arms stretched out from the sides.

Swa·nee. See **Suwannee.**

swang. *Rare.* Past tense of **swing.**

swank (swăngk) *adj.* **swanker, swankest.** Also **swank·y** (swăng′kē), **-ier, -iest. 1.** Imposingly fashionable or elegant; grand. **2.** Ostentatious; pretentious. —*n.* **1.** Smartness in style or bearing; elegance. **2.** Swagger. —*intr.v.* **swanked, swanking, swanks.** To act in an ostentatious or pretentious way; swagger. [Perhaps from Middle High German *swanken,* to swing, swag, from *swank,* a turn. See **sweng-** in Appendix.*] —**swank′i·ly** *adv.* —**swank′i·ness** *n.*

swan·ner·y (swän′ə-rē) *n., pl.* **-ies.** A place where swans are raised.

Swan River. A river in southwestern Australia, flowing 240 miles northwest and then southwest to the Indian Ocean near Perth.

Swan River daisy. An Australian plant, *Brachycome iberidifolia,* cultivated for its showy blue or white flower heads.

swan's-down (swänz′doun′) *n.* Also **swans·down. 1.** The soft down of a swan. **2.** A soft woolen fabric used especially for baby clothes. **3. Canton flannel** *(see).*

Swan·sea (swän′sē). A port of Glamorgan, Wales, in the south on the Bristol Channel. Population, 171,000.

swan·skin (swän′skĭn′) *n.* **1.** The skin of a swan with the feathers attached. **2.** Any of several flannel or cotton fabrics with a soft nap.

swan song. 1. The legendary last utterance of a dying swan. **2.** A farewell or terminal appearance, declaration, or work. [Translation of German *Schwanenlied.*]

swap (swäp) *v.* **swapped, swapping, swaps.** Also **swop.** *Informal.* —*intr.* To trade one thing for another. —*tr.* To exchange. —*n.* Also **swop.** *Informal.* An exchange of one thing for another. [Literally, "to strike hands in closing a bargain," Middle English *swappen,* to strike, hit, from Germanic, akin to German *schwappen,* to splash, whack. See **swei-[2]** in Appendix.*] —**swap′per** *n.*

sward (swôrd) *n.* Also **swarth** (swôrth). Land covered with grassy turf; a lawn or meadow. [Middle English *swerd, swarthe,* Old English *sweard, swearth,* skin of the body, rind of bacon, akin to Old Norse *svörthr,* skin.]

sware. *Archaic.* Past tense of **swear.**

swarf (swärf, swôrf) *n.* Fine metallic filings or shavings removed by a cutting tool. [Probably from Scandinavian, akin to Old Norse *svarf,* filings. See **swerbh-** in Appendix.*]

swarm[1] (swôrm) *n.* **1.** A large number of insects or other small organisms, especially when in motion. **2.** A group of bees, with a queen bee, in migration to establish a new colony. **3.** An aggregation of persons or animals, especially when in turmoil or moving in mass: *"a swarm of squealing puppies"* (Emily Brontë). —See Synonyms at **flock.** —*v.* **swarmed, swarming, swarms.** —*intr.* **1. a.** To move or emerge in a swarm. **b.** To leave a hive as a swarm. Used of bees. **2.** To move as a large group or mass of creatures; congregate; thrive: *"Alas, the devils they swarm about us, like the frogs of Egypt"* (Cotton Mather). **3.** To be overrun or filled. —*tr.* To fill with a crowd; to throng. [Middle English *swarm,* Old English *swearm.* See **swer-[2]** in Appendix.*] —**swarm′er** *n.*

swarm[2] (swôrm) *v.* **swarmed, swarming, swarms.** —*tr.* To climb by gripping with the arms and legs. —*intr.* To climb something in this way. [Origin unknown.]

swarm spore. *Biology.* A **zoospore** *(see).*

swart (swôrt) *adj. Archaic.* Swarthy. [Middle English *swarte, swe(o)rt,* Old English *sweart.* See **swordo-** in Appendix.*] —**swart′ness** *n.*

swarth·y (swôr′thē) *adj.* **-ier, -iest.** Having a dark or sunburned complexion. [Earlier *swarty,* from SWART.] —**swarth′i·ly** *adv.* —**swarth′i·ness** *n.*

swash (swäsh, swôsh) *n.* **1.** A splash of liquid or the sound of such a splash. **2.** A narrow channel through which tides flow. **3.** A bar over which waves wash freely. **4. a.** Swagger or bluster. **b.** A swaggering or blustering fellow. —*v.* **swashed, swashing, swashes.** —*intr.* **1.** To strike, move, or wash with a splashing sound. **2.** To swagger. —*tr.* **1.** To splash (a liquid). **2.** To splash a liquid against. [Probably imitative.]

swash·buck·ler (swäsh′bŭk′lər) *n.* **1.** A flamboyant swordsman or adventurer. **2.** Any sword-wielding bully or ruffian. Also called "swasher." [From the striking of bucklers in fighting.] —**swash′buck′ling** *adj.*

swash letter. An ornamental italic letter formed with fancy flourishes and tails designed to fill up space between adjacent letters. [Perhaps a specialized use of SWASH (rare sense, "angle of a blow").]

swas·ti·ka (swäs′tĭ-kə, swä-stē′kə) *n.* Also **swas·ti·ca. 1.** An ancient cosmic or religious symbol, formed by a Greek cross with the ends of the arms bent at right angles in either a clockwise or counterclockwise direction. **2.** The emblem of Nazi Germany, officially adopted in 1935. [Sanskrit *svastika,* a sign of good luck, from *svasti,* well-being, good luck : *su-,* well (see **su-[2]** in Appendix*) + *asti,* "is," being (see **es-** in Appendix*).]

swat (swät) *tr.v.* **swatted, swatting, swats.** To deal a sharp blow to; to slap. —*n.* A quick, sharp, or violent blow. [Variant of SQUAT (obsolete sense "to lay flat with a blow").]

Swat (swät). **1.** A former princely state of India, now in West Pakistan. **2.** A river of West Pakistan, rising in the north and flowing 200 miles generally south to the Kabul.

swatch (swäch) *n.* A sample strip cut from a piece of cloth or other material. [Earlier sense, "a tag attached to cloth before dyeing" (origin unknown).]

swath (swäth, swôth) *n.* Also **swathe** (swäth, swôth). **1.** The width of a scythe stroke or a mowing-machine blade. **2. a.** A path of this width made in mowing. **b.** The mown grass or grain lying on such a path. **3.** Something likened to a swath. —**cut a (wide) swath.** To create a great stir, impression, or display. [Middle English *swathe,* Old English *swæth, swathu,* track, trace, from Germanic *swath-* (unattested).]

swathe[1] (swäth) *tr.v.* **swathed, swathing, swathes. 1.** To wrap or bind with bindings or bandages. **2.** To enfold or constrict. —*n.* A wrapping, binding, or bandage. [Middle English *swathen,* Old English *swathian*†, to wrap up.] —**swath′er** *n.*

swathe[2]. Variant of **swath.**

Swa·tow (swä′tou′). A seaport of southern China, in eastern Kwangtung Province on the South China Sea. Population, 250,000.

swat·ter (swä′tər) *n.* **1.** One that swats. **2.** A small meshed or flexible flap attached to a handle, used for killing insects. **3.** *Baseball.* A hard-hitting batter.

sway (swā) *v.* **swayed, swaying, sways.** —*intr.* **1.** To move back and forth with a swinging motion; oscillate. **2.** To incline or bend to one side; veer: *She swayed and put out a hand to steady herself.* **3. a.** To incline toward change, as in opinion or feeling; vacillate. **b.** To tend toward in outlook. —*tr.* **1.** To cause to swing from side to side. **2.** To cause to incline or bend toward one side. **3.** *Nautical.* To swing into position, as a mast or a yard. **4. a.** To deter or cause to swerve; dissuade. **b.** To exert influence on or control over: *His speech swayed the voters.* **5.** *Archaic.* **a.** To rule or govern. **b.** To wield as a weapon or scepter. —See Synonyms at **swing.** —*n.* **1.** The act of moving from side to side with a swinging motion. **2.** Power; influence: *"the love of liberty . . . is antagonistic to the sway of custom"* (John Stuart Mill). **3.** Momentum; inclination; predilection. **4.** *Archaic.* Dominion or control in governing. [Middle English *sweyen, sweghen,* to move, go down, swing, probably from Old Norse *sveigja,* to bend, yield. See **swei-[2]** in Appendix.*] —**sway′er** *n.* —**sway′ing·ly** *adv.*

sway·back (swā′băk′) *n.* An excessive inward or downward curvature of the spine. —**sway′backed′** *adj.*

Swa·zi (swä′zē) *n., pl.* **Swazi** or **-zis.** A tribesman of the Bantu people of Swaziland.

Swa·zi·land (swä′zĭ-lănd′). A kingdom occupying 6,705 square miles in southeastern Africa between South Africa and Mozambique; a former British protectorate; independent since 1968. Population, 400,000. Capital, Mbabane.

swbd, swbd. switchboard.

SWbS southwest by south.

SWbW southwest by west.

swear (swâr) *v.* **swore** (swôr) or *archaic* **sware** (swâr), **sworn** (swôrn), **swearing, swears.** —*intr.* **1.** To make a solemn declaration, invoking a deity or some person or thing held sacred, in confirmation of the honesty or truth of such a declaration: *I swear to God I spoke the truth.* **2.** To make a solemn promise; to vow. **3.** To use profane oaths; blaspheme; to curse. **4.** *Law.* To give evidence or testimony under oath. —*tr.* **1.** To declare solemnly by invoking a sacred personage or thing. **2.** To promise or pledge with a solemn oath; to vow. **3.** To utter or bind oneself to (an oath). **4.** To administer a legal oath to. **5.** To say or affirm earnestly and with great conviction. —**swear by. 1.** To name (a sacred personage or thing) as invocation in taking an oath. **2.** To have great reliance upon or confidence in. —**swear in.** To administer a legal or official oath to: *swear in the mayor.* —**swear off.** *Informal.* To pledge to renounce or give up. —**swear out.** To obtain (a warrant for someone's arrest) by making a charge under oath. [Swear, swore, sworn; Middle English *swer(i)en, swor, swor(n),* Old English *swerian, swōr* (past singular), *sworen.* See **swer-[1]** in Appendix.*] —**swear′er** *n.*

swear·word (swâr′wûrd′) *n.* A word used in an obscene, insulting, or blasphemous way.

sweat (swĕt) *v.* **sweated** or **sweat, sweating, sweats.** —*intr.* **1.** To excrete perspiration through the pores in the skin; perspire. **2.** To exude in droplets, as moisture from certain cheeses

ă pat/ā pay/âr care/ä father/b bib/ch church/d deed/ĕ pet/ē be/f fife/g gag/h hat/hw which/ĭ pit/ī pie/îr pier/j judge/k kick/l lid, needle/m mum/n no, sudden/ng thing/ŏ pot/ō toe/ô paw, for/oi noise/ou out/ŏŏ took/ōō boot/p pop/r roar/s sauce/sh ship, dish/

or sap from a tree. **3.** To condense atmospheric moisture. **4. a.** To release moisture, as hay in the swath. **b.** To ferment, as tobacco during curing. **5.** *Informal.* To work long and hard. **6.** *Informal.* To suffer much, as for a misdeed. **7.** *Informal.* To fret or worry. *—tr.* **1.** To excrete (moisture) through a porous surface. **2.** To gather and condense (moisture) on a surface. **3.** To cause to perspire, as by drugs, heat, or strenuous exercise. **4.** To make damp or wet with perspiration. **5.** To cause to work excessively; to overwork. **6.** To overwork and underpay (employees). **7.** *Informal.* **a.** To interrogate (someone under duress). **b.** To extract (information) from someone under duress. **—sweat blood.** *Slang.* To work diligently or strenuously. **—sweat out.** *Slang.* **1.** To endure anxiously. **2.** To await (something) anxiously. **3.** To attempt to cure by sweating: *sweat out a cold.* *—n.* **1.** The product of the sweat glands of the skin. **2.** Any condensation of moisture in the form of droplets on a surface. **3.** The process of sweating or the condition of being sweated. **4.** Strenuous, exhaustive labor; drudgery. **5.** An exercise run given a horse before a race. **6.** *Informal.* An anxious, fretful condition; impatience. **—no sweat.** *Slang.* Easily done or handled. [Middle English *sweten, swaten,* Old English *swǣtan.* See **sweid-²** in Appendix.*] **—sweat′i·ly** *adv.* **—sweat′i·ness** *n.* **—sweat′y** *adj.*

sweat·band (swĕt′bănd′) *n.* **1.** A band of fabric or leather sewn inside the crown of a hat as protection against sweat. **2.** A cloth tied around the forehead to absorb sweat.

sweat·box (swĕt′bŏks′) *n.* **1.** A box in which something, such as hides or fruit, is fermented by sweating. **2.** Any confined place where a person sweats, especially: **a.** An interrogation room. **b.** A prison cell used for special punishment.

sweat·er (swĕt′ər) *n.* **1.** One that sweats, especially profusely. **2.** That which induces sweating; especially, a sudorific. **3.** A garment made of knit, crocheted, or woven wool, jersey, or the like, and worn on the upper part of the body.

sweat gland. Any of the numerous small, tubular glands that in man are found nearly everywhere in the skin and that secrete perspiration externally through pores.

sweat shirt. A long-sleeved cotton-jersey pullover worn especially by athletes.

sweat·shop (swĕt′shŏp′) *n.* A shop or factory where employees work long hours for low wages under bad conditions.

sweat suit. A two-piece outfit consisting of cotton-jersey pants, tightly fitted at the ankles and waist, and a sweat shirt.

Swed. Sweden; Swedish.

swede (swēd) *n.* A vegetable, the **rutabaga** *(see).* [Introduced from Sweden.]

Swede (swēd) *n.* **1.** A native or inhabitant of Sweden. **2.** A person of Swedish descent. [Low German *Swede,* from Middle Low German *Swēde*†.]

Swe·den (swēd′n). *Swedish* **Sve·ri·ge** (svăr′yə). *Abbr.* **Sw., Swed.** A kingdom occupying 158,486 square miles on the eastern part of the Scandinavian Peninsula in northern Europe. Population, 7,495,000. Capital, Stockholm. [Middle Low German, probably from the dative plural of *Swēde,* SWEDE.]

Swe·den·borg (swēd′n-bôrg′; *Swedish* svā′dən-bôr′y′), **Emanuel.** Original surname, Svedberg. 1688–1772. Swedish scientist and theologian; followers founded religion in his name.

Swe·den·bor·gi·an·ism (swēd′n-bôr′gē-ə-nĭz′əm) *n.* Also *rare* **Swe·den·borg·ism** (-bôrg′ĭz′əm). The theological philosophy of Emanuel Swedenborg that forms the basis for the Church of the New Jerusalem, claiming direct mystical communication between the world and the spiritual realm and affirming Christ as the true God.

Swed·ish (swē′dĭsh) *adj. Abbr.* **Sw., Swed.** Of or pertaining to Sweden, the Swedes, or their culture or language. *—n.* The North Germanic language of Sweden.

Swedish massage. A system of massage and exercises for the muscles and joints.

Swedish turnip. A vegetable, the **rutabaga** *(see).*

sweep (swēp) *v.* **swept** (swĕpt), **sweeping, sweeps.** *—tr.* **1.** To clean or clear the surface of with or as if with a broom or brush. **2.** To clean or clear away (dust or dirt, for example) with or as if with a broom or brush: *sweep snow from the steps.* **3.** To clear (a space) with or as if with a broom. **4.** To touch or brush lightly with or as if with a trailing garment: *Willow branches swept the ground.* **5. a.** To move, remove, or convey with a flowing motion, as by water: *The wind swept tiles from the roof.* **b.** To move or unbalance emotionally: *Love swept him off his feet.* **6.** To cause to depart; remove or destroy: *"impossible—Unless we sweep 'em from the door with cannons"* (Shakespeare). **7.** To traverse with speed or intensity; range throughout: *Plague swept Europe.* **8.** To traverse, as when searching: *Searchlights swept the hillside.* **9.** To drag the bottom of (a body of water). **10. a.** To win all the stages of (a game or contest). **b.** To win overwhelmingly: *"The Democrats swept the nation"* (Bernard De Voto). *—intr.* **1.** To clear or clean a surface with or as if with a broom or brush. **2. a.** To move, surge, or flow with smooth and steady force: *A cool wind swept over the plain.* **b.** To move swiftly or majestically: *She swept by in silence.* **3.** To trail, as a garment: *Her veil swept to the floor.* **4.** To extend gracefully or majestically: *The hills sweep down to the sea.* *—n.* **1.** The act of sweeping; removal with or as if with a broom or brush. **2.** The motion of sweeping: *a sweep of the arm.* **3.** The range or scope encompassed by sweeping: *the sweep of a machine gun.* **4. a.** A reach or extent: *a sweep of green lawn.* **b.** A curving driveway: *"The palace steps descend to a broad gravel sweep"* (Trollope). **5.** Any curve or contour: *the sweep of her hair.* **6.** One who sweeps, especially a chimney sweep. **7.** *Usually plural.* Sweepings. **8. a.** The winning of all stages of a game or contest. **b.** A total victory or success. **9.** A long oar used to propel a boat. **10.** A long pole attached to a pivot and with a bucket at one end, used to raise water from a well. **11.** *Informal.* A sweepstakes. **12.** *Electronics.* The steady motion of an electron beam across a cathode-ray tube. [Middle English *swe(e)pen,* probably from Old English *swēop,* past singular of *swāpan,* to sweep. See **swei-²** in Appendix.*] **—sweep′er** *n.*

sweep·back (swēp′băk′) *n. Aviation.* **1.** The backward slant of the leading edge of an airfoil. **2.** The degree of this slant.

sweep·ing (swē′pĭng) *adj.* **1.** Removing with or as if with a broom or brushing movement. **2.** Influencing or extending over a great area; wide-ranging: *"The sweeping definitions could be almost indefinitely extended"* (Penelope Houston). **3.** Curvilinear in form or motion: *"She made another sweeping gesture that . . . knocked over the coffee pot"* (Patrick Dennis). *—n.* **1.** The action or occupation of one who sweeps. **2.** *Plural.* That which is swept up; debris; litter. **—sweep′ing·ly** *adv.*

sweep·stakes (swēp′stāks′) *n., pl.* **sweepstakes.** Also **sweep·stake** (-stāk′). **1.** A lottery in which the participants' contributions form a fund to be awarded as a prize to the winner or winners. **2.** Any event or contest, especially a horse race, the result of which determines the winner of such a lottery. **3.** The prize won in such a lottery.

sweet (swēt) *adj.* **sweeter, sweetest. 1. a.** Having a sugary taste. **b.** Containing or derived from a sugar. **2.** Pleasing to the senses, feelings, or the mind; gratifying: *"Sin was yet very sweet to my flesh, and I was loath to leave it"* (Bunyan). **3.** Having a pleasing disposition; lovable: *a sweet child.* **4.** Not saline; fresh: *sweet water.* **5.** Not spoiled, sour, or decaying; fresh: *This milk is still sweet.* **6.** Free of acid. **7.** *Music.* **a.** Designating jazz characterized by adherence to a melodic line and to a time signature. **b.** Performing jazz in this way: *a sweet combo.* *—n.* **1.** The quality of being sweet; sweetness. **2.** Something that is sweet or contains sugar. **3.** *Usually plural.* Candy, preserves, or confections. **4.** *British.* Anything relatively sweet served as a dessert. **5.** A dear or beloved person. [Middle English *swe(e)te,* Old English *swēte.* See **swād-** in Appendix.*] **—sweet′ly** *adv.* **—sweet′ness** *n.*

Sweet (swēt), **Henry.** 1845–1912. British philologist and phonetician.

sweet alyssum. A widely cultivated plant, *Lobularia maritima,* native to the Mediterranean region, having clusters of small, fragrant white or purplish flowers.

sweet basil. A species of **basil** *(see).*

sweet bay. A small tree, *Magnolia virginiana,* of the southeastern United States, having large, fragrant white flowers.

sweet birch. A tree, the **black birch** *(see).*

sweet·bread (swēt′brĕd′) *n.* The thymus gland of an animal, used for food. [SWEET + BREAD (euphemism for the food).]

sweet·bri·er (swēt′brī′ər) *n.* Also **sweet·bri·ar.** A rose, *Rosa eglanteria,* native to Europe, having prickly stems, fragrant leaves, and pink flowers. Also called "eglantine."

sweet cherry. **1.** A widely cultivated tree, *Prunus avium,* native to Eurasia, having white flowers and sweet, edible fruit. **2.** The fruit of this tree.

sweet cicely. **1.** Any of various plants of the genus *Osmorhiza,* having aromatic roots, compound leaves, and clusters of small white flowers. **2.** An aromatic European plant, *Myrrhis odorata,* having compound leaves and clusters of small white flowers. In this sense, also called "myrrh."

sweet cider. Unfermented cider.

sweet clover. A plant, the **melilot** *(see).*

sweet corn. A variety of corn, *Zea mays rugosa,* having kernels that are sweet when young, and that is the common edible corn. Also called "sugar corn."

sweet·en (swēt′n) *v.* **-ened, -ening, -ens.** *—tr.* **1.** To make sweet or sweeter by or as if by the addition of sugar. **2.** To make pleasurable or gratifying. **3.** To make bearable; alleviate; lighten. **4.** *Informal.* To increase the value of (collateral for a loan) by adding more securities. **5.** In poker, to increase the value of (an unwon pot) by adding stakes before reopening. *—intr.* To become sweet. **—sweet′en·er** *n.*

sweet·en·ing (swēt′n-ĭng) *n.* **1.** The act or process of making sweet. **2.** Something used to sweeten.

sweet fern. An aromatic shrub, *Myrica asplenifolia* (or *Comptonia peregrina*), of eastern North America, having narrow, shallowly lobed, fernlike foliage.

sweet flag. A plant, *Acorus calamus,* growing in moist places and having bladelike leaves, minute greenish flowers, and aromatic roots. Also called "calamus."

sweet gale. A swamp shrub, *Myrica gale,* of northern regions, having aromatic, resinous leaves.

sweet gum. **1.** A New World tree, *Liquidambar styraciflua,* having sharply lobed leaves, prickly, ball-like fruit clusters, and wood used to make furniture. Also called "bilsted." **2.** The aromatic resin obtained from this tree.

sweet·heart (swēt′härt′) *n.* **1.** One who loves and is loved by another. Often used as a term of affectionate address. **2.** A lovable, friendly, or generous person.

swee·tie (swē′tē) *n. Informal.* Sweetheart; dear.

sweet·ing (swē′tĭng) *n.* **1.** A sweet apple. **2.** *Archaic.* A sweetheart.

sweet marjoram. A species of **marjoram** *(see).*

sweet·meat (swēt′mēt′) *n.* Any delicacy made with a sweetening agent; candy. [SWEET + MEAT (food).]

sweet pea. A climbing plant, *Lathyrus odoratus,* native to southern Europe, cultivated for its variously colored, fragrant flowers.

sweet pepper. The **bell pepper** *(see).*

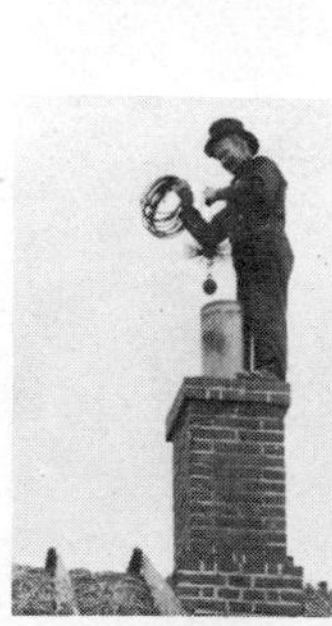

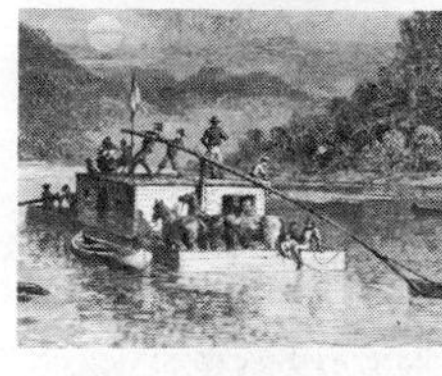

sweep
Above: A chimney sweep on a cottage roof in Denmark
Below: Emigrants descending the Ohio in a houseboat propelled by sweeps

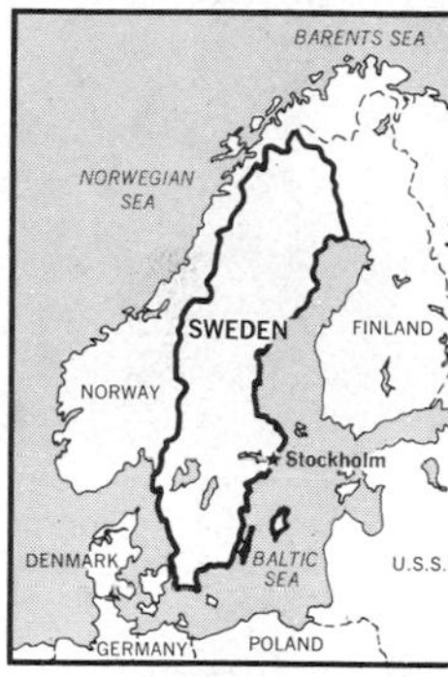

Sweden

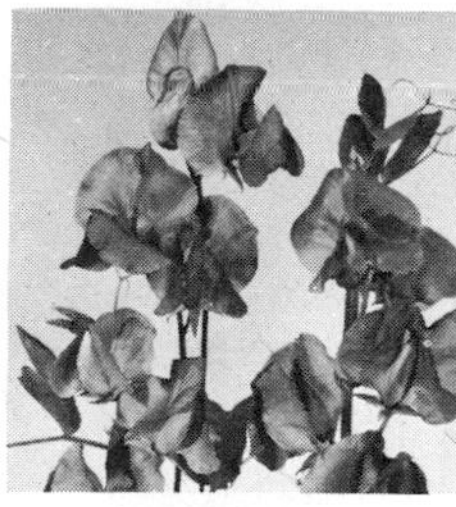

sweet pea

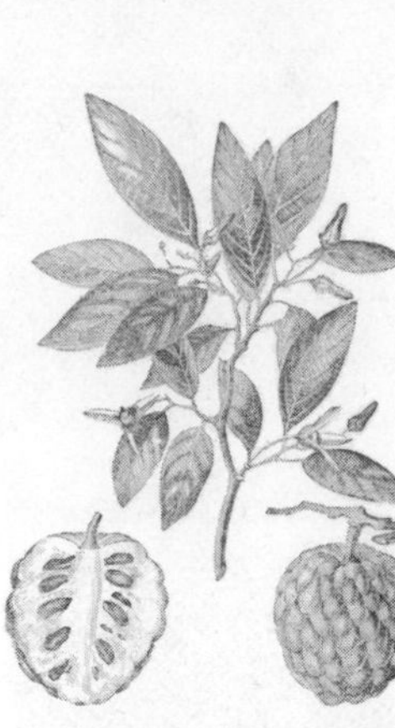

sweetsop
Left: Cross section of the fruit
Center: Leaves and flowers
Right: Fruit

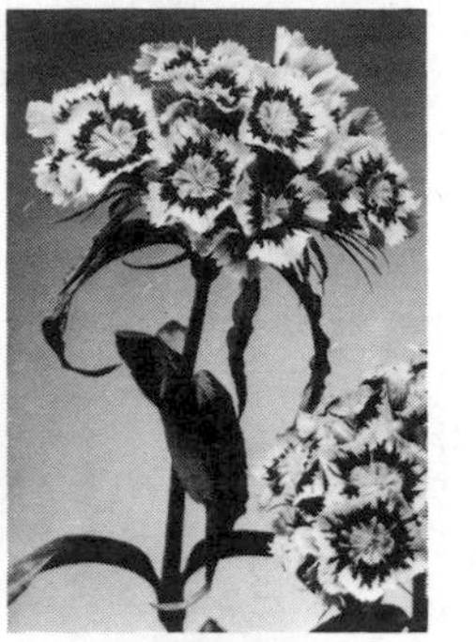

sweet William

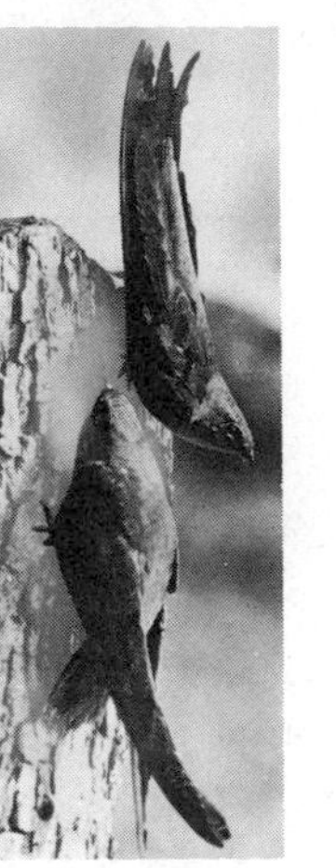

swift
Chaetura pelagica
Chimney swifts

sweet pepperbush. A North American shrub, *Clethra alnifolia,* growing in moist ground and having clusters of small, fragrant white flowers.

sweet potato. 1. A tropical American vine, *Ipomoea batatas,* cultivated for its thick, orange-colored, edible root. 2. The root of this plant, eaten cooked as a vegetable. 3. *Informal.* A musical instrument, the **ocarina** *(see).*

sweet·sop (swēt′sŏp′) *n.* 1. A tropical American tree, *Annona squamosa,* having yellowish-green fruit with sweet, edible pulp. 2. The fruit of this tree. Also called "sugar apple."

sweet sultan. An Old World plant, *Centaurea moschata,* widely cultivated for its showy, variously colored flowers.

sweet tooth. *Informal.* An inordinate fondness for sweets.

sweet William. A widely cultivated plant, *Dianthus barbatus,* native to Eurasia, having flat, dense clusters of varicolored flowers. Also called "Newport pink."

swell (swĕl) *v.* **swelled, swelled** or **swollen** (swō′lən), **swelling, swells.** —*intr.* 1. To increase in size or volume as a result of internal pressure; expand. 2. a. To increase in force, size, number, or degree. b. To grow in loudness or intensity, as a sound: *"the din in front swelled to a tremendous chorus"* (Stephen Crane). 3. To bulge out; protrude, as a sail. 4. To rise in billows above the surrounding level, as clouds. 5. To be or become filled or puffed up with an emotion, such as pride. 6. To grow within a person. —*tr.* 1. To cause to increase in volume, size, number, degree, or intensity. 2. To cause to protrude or bulge. 3. To inflate with emotion. 4. To grow gradually in volume and then decrease, as a musical note or chord. —*n.* 1. a. The act or process of swelling. b. The condition of being swollen. 2. A swollen part; a bulge or protuberance. 3. A long wave that moves continuously without breaking. 4. A rise in the land; a rounded hill. 5. *Informal.* One who is fashionably dressed or prominent in fashionable society. 6. *Music.* a. A crescendo followed by a gradual diminuendo. b. The sign indicating this. c. A device on some instruments, such as an organ or harpsichord, for regulating volume. —*adj.* **sweller, swellest.** *Informal.* 1. Fashionably elegant; smart; stylish. 2. Fine; excellent: *"It was swell out, just cool enough"* (James T. Farrell). [Swell, swollen; Middle English *swellen, swollen,* Old English *swellan, geswollen,* from Germanic *swaljan* (unattested).]

swell box. A chamber housing one or more sets of organ pipes and having shutters that can be opened or shut to regulate the volume of tone.

swell·fish (swĕl′fĭsh′) *n., pl.* **swellfish** or **-fishes.** The **puffer** *(see).*

swell·ing (swĕl′ĭng) *n.* 1. The act of swelling or expanding. 2. The state of being swollen or expanded. 3. Something that is swollen; especially, an abnormally swollen or protuberant bodily part.

swel·ter (swĕl′tər) *v.* **-tered, -tering, -ters.** —*intr.* To be affected by oppressive heat; to sweat or feel faint from heat. —*tr.* 1. To affect with oppressive heat. 2. *Archaic.* To exude. —*n.* Oppressive heat and humidity: *"All the swelter of that urban summer"* (Cyril Connolly). [Middle English *swelt(e)ren,* frequentative of *swelten,* to die, faint from heat, Old English *sweltan,* to die. See **swel-**[2] in Appendix.*]

swel·ter·ing (swĕl′tər-ĭng) *adj.* Also **swel·try** (swĕl′trē), **-trier, -triest.** 1. Oppressively hot and humid. 2. Suffering from oppressive heat. —**swel′ter·ing·ly** *adv.*

swept. Past tense and past participle of **sweep.**

swept·back (swĕpt′băk′) *adj.* Angled rearward from the points of attachment. Said especially of aircraft wings.

swerve (swûrv) *v.* **swerved, swerving, swerves.** —*intr.* To turn aside from a straight course; veer. —*tr.* To cause to veer; deflect; turn aside. —*n.* 1. A deflection or deviation. 2. Something that swerves. [Middle English *swerven,* perhaps originally "to make a circular motion in polishing," Old English *sweorfan,* to file away, scour, polish. See **swerbh-** in Appendix.*]

swift (swĭft) *adj.* **swifter, swiftest.** 1. Moving or able to move with great speed; fast; fleet. 2. Coming, occurring, or accomplished quickly; instant: *a swift retort.* 3. Ready in acting or reacting; prompt: *swift to take steps.* —See Synonyms at **fast.** —*adv.* Quickly. Often used in combination: *swift-running.* —*n.* 1. A cylinder on a carding machine. 2. A reel used to hold yarn as it is being wound off. 3. Any of various dark-colored birds of the family Apodidae, characteristically having long, narrow wings and a relatively short tail. 4. Any of various small, fast-moving North American lizards of the genera *Sceloporus* and *Uta.* [Middle English *swift(e),* Old English *swift.* See **swei-**[2] in Appendix.*] —**swift′ly** *adv.* —**swift′ness** *n.*

Swift (swĭft), **Gustavus Franklin.** 1839–1903. American industrialist and inventor; developed refrigerator car.

Swift (swĭft), **Jonathan.** 1667–1745. English satirist; dean of St. Patrick's Cathedral, Dublin.

swig (swĭg) *n. Informal.* A large swallow or draft, as of a liquid; a gulp. —*v.* **swigged, swigging, swigs.** —*tr. Informal.* To drink eagerly and with great gulps. —*intr. Informal.* To take a large swallow; gulp. [Origin unknown.] —**swig′ger** *n.*

swill (swĭl) *v.* **swilled, swilling, swills.** —*tr.* 1. To drink eagerly, greedily, or to excess: *"Unshaven horsemen swill the great wines of the Chateaux"* (W.H. Auden). 2. To flood with water, as for cleaning or washing. 3. To feed (animals) with slop. —*intr.* To drink greedily. —*n.* 1. A mixture of liquid and solid food, as table scraps, fed to animals, especially pigs. 2. Garbage; refuse. 3. A deep draft of liquor. [Middle English *swilen,* Old English *swilian,* to wash out. See **swel-**[1] in Appendix.*] —**swill′er** *n.*

swim[1] (swĭm) *v.* **swam** (swăm) or *archaic* **swum** (swŭm), **swum, swimming, swims.** —*intr.* 1. To propel oneself through water by means of movements of the body or parts of the body. 2. To move as though gliding through water. 3. To float on water or other liquid. 4. To be covered or flooded with water or other liquid; be immersed. —*tr.* 1. To propel oneself through or across (a body of water) by swimming. 2. To cause to swim or float on a body of water. —*n.* 1. The act or movements of one that swims. 2. A period or instance of swimming. —**in the swim.** *Informal.* In the current trend of affairs; participating in what is fashionable. [Swim, swam, swum; Middle English *swimmen, swam(me), swummen,* Old English *swimman, swamm* (or *swom*), *swummen.* See **swem-** in Appendix.*] —**swim′mer** *n.*

swim[2] (swĭm) *intr.v.* **swam** (swăm) or *archaic* **swum** (swŭm), **swum, swimming, swims.** 1. To be dizzy; feel faint or giddy: *"His brain still swimming with the effects of the last night's champagne"* (R.S. Surtees). 2. To appear to spin or reel hazily. —*n.* A state of dizziness; a swoon. [Middle English *swime,* dizziness, Old English *swīma.* See **swei-**[2] in Appendix.*]

swim bladder. An organ of fishes, the **air bladder** *(see).*

swim·mer·et (swĭm′ə-rĕt′) *n.* One of the paired abdominal appendages of certain aquatic crustaceans, such as shrimps, lobsters, and isopods, that function primarily as organs of respiration or locomotion. Also called "pleopod." [Diminutive of *swimmer,* "appendage used in swimming," from SWIM.]

swim·ming·ly (swĭm′ĭng-lē) *adv.* With great ease and a high degree of success: *The campaign is proceeding swimmingly.*

swimming pool. A pool constructed for swimming.

swim·suit (swĭm′so͞ot′) *n.* A garment worn while swimming.

Swin·burne (swĭn′bərn), **Algernon Charles.** 1837–1909. English poet and critic.

swin·dle (swĭnd′l) *v.* **-dled, -dling, -dles.** —*tr.* 1. To cheat or defraud (someone) of money or property. 2. To obtain (money or property, for example) by fraudulent means. —*intr.* To practice fraud as a habitual means of obtaining money. —*n.* The act or an instance of swindling; a fraud. [Back-formation from *swindler,* from German *Schwindler,* from *schwindeln,* to be dizzy, swindle, cheat, from Old High German *swintilōn,* frequentative of *swintan,* to vanish, languish, become unconscious, from Germanic *swindan* (unattested).] —**swin′dler** *n.*

swine (swīn) *n., pl.* **swine.** 1. *Usually plural.* Any of the ungulate mammals of the family Suidae, which includes pigs, hogs, and boars. 2. A contemptible, vicious, or greedy person. [Middle English *swin(e),* Old English *swīn.* See **su-**[1] in Appendix.*]

swine·herd (swīn′hûrd′) *n.* A keeper or tender of swine.

swine·pox (swīn′pŏks′) *n.* A disease of domesticated swine caused by a virus similar to that causing cowpox and smallpox and characterized by skin lesions.

swing (swĭng) *v.* **swung** (swŭng) or *rare* **swang** (swăng), **swung, swinging, swings.** —*intr.* 1. To move rhythmically back and forth suspended, or as if suspended, from above; oscillate; sway: *a rope swinging from the mast.* 2. To ride on or motivate a swing. 3. To move, walk, run, or the like with a free-swaying motion: *"They could see a cavalcade of shire horses swinging out of their own yard"* (D.H. Lawrence). 4. To turn in place, as on a hinge or other pivot. 5. To change one's attitudes, emotions, habits, or the like; vacillate. 6. *Slang.* To be executed by hanging. 7. a. To have a compulsive rhythm. Used of popular music. b. To play with a compulsive rhythm. Used of popular musicians. 8. *Slang.* a. To participate actively in youthful fads. b. To be a lively success in terms of enjoyment. —*tr.* 1. To cause to move backward and forward: *"The loud young soldier came, swinging two canteens"* (Stephen Crane). 2. To move (a person on a swing) backward and forward by pulling or pushing. 3. To move with a sweeping motion; brandish. 4. To hang or suspend (something) so as to be able to move freely. 5. a. To suspend on hinges: *swing a shutter.* b. To cause to turn hinges: *swing the door shut.* 6. To cause to change from one attitude, position, emotion, or the like to another. 7. *Slang.* To manipulate or manage successfully: *Can you swing this deal?* 8. To arrange or perform (popular music) in the style of swing. —*n.* 1. The act of swinging, especially: a. A rhythmic back-and-forth movement. b. A single movement or series of movements in one particular direction. 2. The space traversed while swinging: *The pendulum's swing is 12 inches.* 3. The manner in which a person or thing swings something, as a baseball bat or golf club. 4. Freedom and scope of movement or action. 5. a. A swaying, graceful motion. b. A sweep or swoop: *the swing of a bird across the sky.* 6. A seat suspended from above for the enjoyment of those who sit and swing thereon. 7. a. An innovation in popular dance music developed about 1935 and based on jazz but employing a larger band and simpler harmonic and rhythmic patterns. b. The rhythmic quality of this music. —**in full swing.** In action to the maximum speed, capacity, or ability. —*adj.* Pertaining to or performing swing. [Swing, swang or swung, swung; Middle English *swingen, swang* (past singular), *swungen* (past plural), *swungen,* Old English *swingan,* to whip, strike, fling oneself, *swang, swungon, geswungen.* See **sweng-** in Appendix.*]

Synonyms: *swing, oscillate, sway, rock, vibrate, fluctuate, undulate, waver.* These verbs refer to movement marked in general by a back-and-forth or up-and-down pattern. *Swing* usually applies to arclike movement of something attached at one extremity and free at the other, or to rotating or pivoting movement around an axis. *Oscillate* more specifically refers to regular back-and-forth movement, such as that of a pendulum. *Sway* suggests the movement of something unsteady, light, or flexible. *Rock* can apply both to rhythmic and rather gentle movement and to violent tilting. *Vibrate,* in general usage, usually suggests rhythmic throbbing or pulsating; thus it implies

ă pat/ā pay/âr care/ä father/b bib/ch church/d deed/ĕ pet/ē be/f fife/g gag/h hat/hw which/ĭ pit/ī pie/îr pier/j judge/k kick/l lid, needle/m mum/n no, sudden/ng thing/ŏ pot/ō toe/ô paw, for/oi noise/ou out/o͝o took/o͞o boot/p pop/r roar/s sauce/sh ship, dish/

trembling or quivering motion rather than pronounced movement. *Fluctuate* usually applies to movement of nonphysical things, such as prices, and suggests fairly constant change that follows no set course. *Undulate* implies smooth, wavelike movement. *Waver* suggests unsteady and uncertain movement, such as tottering or faltering. In figurative usage it refers to indecisiveness.

swinge (swĭnj) *tr.v.* **swinged, swinging, swinges.** *Archaic.* To strike or beat; swipe. [Middle English *swengen,* to shake, dash, beat up, Old English *swengan,* to swing, shake. See **sweng-** in Appendix.*] —**swing'er** (swĭn'jər) *n.*

swing·er (swĭng'ər) *n. Slang.* One who participates actively in youthful fads.

swin·gle·tree (swĭng'gəl-trē) *n.* A **whiffletree** *(see).* [From *swingle,* wooden instrument for beating hemp, Middle English *swingle,* from Middle Dutch *swinghel.* See **sweng-** in Appendix.*]

swing shift. *Informal.* A factory work shift between the day and night shifts, lasting from about 4 P.M. to midnight.

swin·ish (swī'nĭsh) *adj.* Resembling or befitting swine; filthy; bestial. —**swin'ish·ly** *adv.* —**swin'ish·ness** *n.*

swipe (swīp) *n.* **1.** A heavy, sweeping blow. **2.** A lever; especially, one that raises the bucket in a well. —*v.* **swiped, swiping, swipes.** —*tr.* **1.** To hit with a sweeping blow. **2.** *Slang.* To steal; filch. —*intr.* To make a sweeping blow. [Probably obscurely related to SWEEP.]

swirl (swûrl) *v.* **swirled, swirling, swirls.** —*intr.* **1.** To rotate or spin in or as if in a whirlpool or eddy. **2.** To be dizzy or faint. —*tr.* To cause to move with a whirling motion. —See Synonyms at **turn.** —*n.* **1.** The motion of whirling or spinning. **2.** Something that swirls; a whirlpool or eddy: *"A roaring swirl of white water, sweeping the valley"* (Winston Churchill). **3.** Something that is swirled, such as a line or a curl of hair; a whorl. [Middle English (Scottish dialect) *swyrl,* eddy, whirlpool, probably of Low German origin, akin to Dutch *zwirrelen,* to whirl. See **swer-²** in Appendix.*] —**swirl'y** *adj.*

swish (swĭsh) *v.* **swished, swishing, swishes.** —*intr.* **1.** To move with a sibilant whistle or hiss: *"Their brushes swished and slapped as they worked"* (James T. Farrell). **2.** To rustle, as certain fabrics: *Her silk skirt swished as she walked.* **3.** *Slang.* To move or act in the manner of an effeminate male. —*tr.* **1.** To cause to make a swishing movement or sound. **2.** To chastise with a swish or rod. —*n.* **1. a.** A sharp sibilant or rustling sound: *the swish of scythes.* **b.** A movement making such a sound. **2. a.** A rod used for flogging. **b.** A stroke made with such a rod. **3.** *Slang.* A highly effeminate male. —*adj. Slang.* **1.** *Chiefly British.* Fashionable; posh. **2.** Highly effeminate. [Probably imitative.]

swiss (swĭs) *n.* Also **Swiss.** A crisp, sheer cotton cloth used for curtains, light garments, or the like. [From SWISS (because it was first manufactured in Switzerland).]

Swiss (swĭs) *adj.* Of, pertaining to, or characteristic of Switzerland, its inhabitants, or its culture. —*n., pl.* **Swiss. 1.** A native or inhabitant of Switzerland. **2.** One of Swiss descent. [Old French *Suisse,* from Middle High German *Swīzer,* from *Swīz,* SWITZERLAND.]

Swiss chard. A vegetable, **chard** *(see).*

Swiss cheese. A firm white or pale-yellow cheese with many large holes, originally produced in Switzerland.

Swiss guards. Mercenaries from Switzerland employed as guards at the Vatican.

Swiss steak. A round or shoulder steak that is pounded with flour, braised, and usually served with a seasoned sauce.

switch (swĭch) *n. Abbr.* **sw. 1.** A slender flexible rod, stick, twig, or the like; especially, such a rod used for whipping. **2.** The bushy tip of the tail of certain animals: *a cow's switch.* **3.** A thick bunch of real or synthetic hair used by women in a coiffure. **4.** A flailing or lashing, as with a slender rod. **5.** *Electricity.* A device used to break or open an electrical circuit or to divert current from one conductor to another. **6.** A device consisting of two sections of railroad track and the accompanying apparatus, used to transfer rolling stock from one track to another. **7. a.** The act or process of operating a switching device. **b.** The result achieved by such an act. **8.** Any transference or shift, as of opinion or attention. —*v.* **switched, switching, switches.** —*tr.* **1.** To whip with or as if with a switch. **2.** To jerk or swish abruptly or sharply. **3.** To shift, transfer, change, or divert: *switch the conversation.* **4.** To exchange: *switch sides.* **5.** To connect, disconnect, or divert (an electric current) by operating a switch. **6.** To cause (an electric current or appliance) to begin or cease operation. Used with *on* or *off: switch off the radio.* **7.** To move (rolling stock) from one track to another; shunt. —*intr.* **1.** To shift or change: *"His Majesty's fleet had recently switched from coal to oil"* (John Dos Passos). **2.** To be shifted or changed. [Perhaps from Middle Dutch *swijch,* bough, twig. See **swei-²** in Appendix.*] —**switch'er** *n.*

switch·back (swĭch'băk') *n.* **1.** A road, roadbed, or trail that ascends a steep incline in a winding course. **2.** *Chiefly British.* A roller coaster.

switch·blade knife (swĭch'blād'). A pocket knife having a spring-operated blade that unsheathes when a release on the handle is pressed.

switch·board (swĭch'bôrd', -bōrd') *n. Abbr.* **swbd, swbd.** One or more panels accommodating control switches, indicators, and other apparatus for operating electric circuits.

switch hitter. *Baseball.* An ambidextrous batter.

switch·man (swĭch'mən) *n., pl.* **-men** (-mĭn). One who operates railroad switches.

switch·yard (swĭch'yärd') *n.* An area of a railroad yard where rolling stock is marshaled and trains are assembled and disassembled.

Swith·in (swĭth'ən), **Saint.** Died A.D. 862. Anglo-Saxon ecclesiastic; Bishop of Winchester (A.D. 852–862).

Switz. Switzerland.

Swit·zer (swĭt'sər) *n.* A Swiss. [Middle High German *Swīzer,* from *Swīz,* SWITZERLAND.]

Swit·zer·land (swĭt'sər-lənd). *French* **Suisse** (swēs); *German* **Schweiz** (shvīts); *Italian* **Sviz·ze·ra** (svēt-sā'rä); *Latin* **Hel·ve·tia** (hĕl-vē'shē-ə, -vā'tē-ä). *Abbr.* **Switz.** A federal republic occupying 15,944 square miles in central Europe. Population, 5,429,000. Capital, Bern. [Middle High German *Swīzer,* Swiss, from *Swīz*†, Switzerland + LAND.]

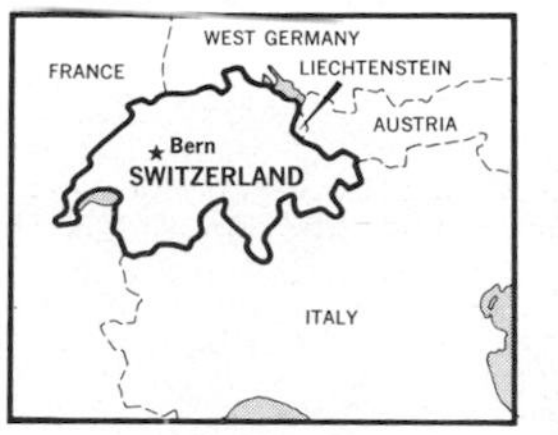

Switzerland

swive (swīv) *v.* **swived, swiving, swives.** *Archaic.* —*tr.* To copulate with. —*intr.* To copulate. [Middle English *swiven,* Old English *swīfan,* to SWIVEL.]

swiv·el (swĭv'əl) *n.* **1.** A link, pivot, or other fastening so designed that it permits free turning of attached parts. **2.** A pivoted support that allows an attached object, such as a chair or gun, to turn in a horizontal plane. **3.** A cannon that turns on a pivot. Also called "swivel gun." —*v.* **swiveled** or **-elled, -eling** or **-elling, -els.** —*tr.* **1.** To turn or rotate on or as on a swivel. **2.** To secure, fit, or support with a swivel. —*intr.* To turn on a swivel. —See Synonyms at **turn.** [Middle English *swyvel, swevill,* related to or from Old English *swīfan,* to revolve. See **swei-²** in Appendix.*]

swiz·zle (swĭz'əl) *n.* Any of various tall mixed drinks, usually made with rum. [Origin unknown.]

swizzle stick. A rod for stirring mixed drinks.

swob. Variant of **swab.**

swol·len. Alternate past participle of **swell.**

swoon (swo͞on) *intr.v.* **swooned, swooning, swoons.** To faint. —*n.* A fainting spell; syncope. [Middle English *swowenen, swounen,* probably back-formation from *swowening, swouning,* a gerund formed from *iswowen,* in a swoon, from Old English *geswōgen,* past participle of *swōgan*† (attested only in compounds), to suffocate, choke.]

swoop (swo͞op) *v.* **swooped, swooping, swoops.** —*intr.* To make a sudden sweeping movement, as a bird descending upon its prey. —*tr.* To take or snatch suddenly; scoop. Often used with *up.* —*n.* The act of swooping; a swift, sudden descent. [Middle English *swopen,* to sweep along, Old English *swāpan,* to swing, sweep, drive. See **swei-²** in Appendix.*]

swop. Variant of **swap.**

Swope (swōp), **Herbert Bayard.** 1882–1958. American journalist, foreign correspondent, and editor.

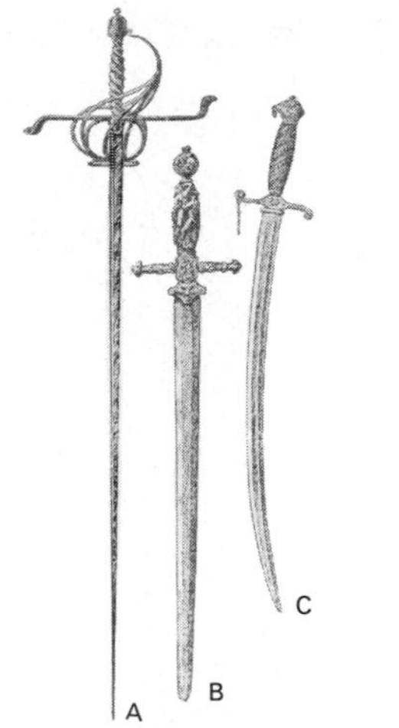

sword
A. Sixteenth-century rapier
B. Italian bronze-hilted sword
C. Eighteenth-century French hunting sword

sword (sôrd) *n.* **1.** A weapon having a long blade for cutting or thrusting, often worn ceremonially as a symbol of power or authority. **2.** Any instrument of death, combat, or destruction. **3. a.** The use of force, as in war. **b.** Power or jurisdiction. **4.** Something that resembles a sword. —**at swords' points.** Ready for combat; antagonistic. —**cross swords. 1.** To fight. **2.** To quarrel violently. —**put to the sword.** To kill with a sword. [Middle English *sw(e)ord, swerd,* Old English *sw(e)ord.* See **swer-⁴** in Appendix.*]

sword bayonet. A short swordlike bayonet.

sword·bill (sôrd'bĭl') *n.* A hummingbird, *Ensifera ensifera,* of tropical South America, having a very long, slender bill. Also called "sword-billed hummingbird."

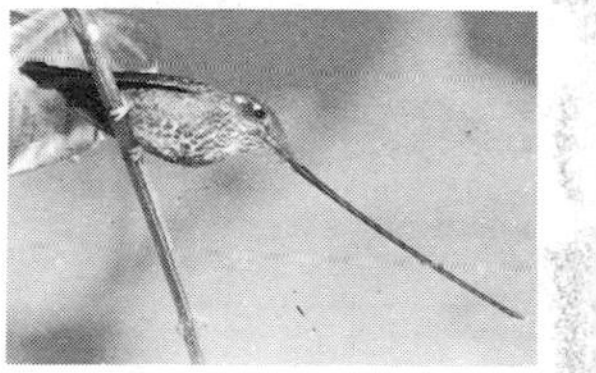
swordbill

sword cane. A cane designed to conceal a sword or dagger.

sword dance. A dance performed with swords, especially one performed around swords laid on the ground.

sword·fish (sôrd'fĭsh') *n., pl.* **swordfish** or **-fishes.** A large marine game and food fish, *Xiphias gladius,* having a long, swordlike extension of the upper jaw. Also called "broadbill."

sword grass. Any of various grasses or grasslike plants having bladelike, pointed leaves.

sword·knot (sôrd'nŏt') *n.* A decorative loop or tassle attached to the hilt of a sword.

Sword of Damocles. An impending disaster or the permanent threat of it. See **Damocles.**

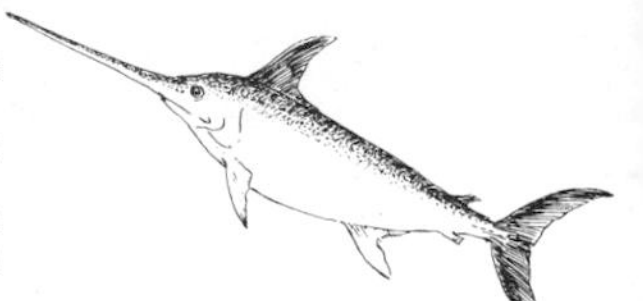
swordfish

sword·play (sôrd'plā') *n.* The action or art of using a sword; fencing. —**sword'play'er** *n.*

swords·man (sôrdz'mən) *n., pl.* **-men** (-mĭn). **1.** A person skilled in the use of the sword. **2.** A person armed with a sword. —**swords'man·ship'** *n.*

sword·tail (sôrd'tāl') *n.* A small, brightly colored freshwater fish, *Xiphophorus helleri,* of Central America, that has a long, tapering extension of the caudal fin in the male, and is popular in home aquariums.

swore. Past tense of **swear.**

sworn. Past participle of **swear.**

swounds, swouns. Variants of **zounds.**

swum. Past participle and *archaic* past tense of **swim.**

swung. Past tense and past participle of **swing.**

Syb·a·ris (sĭb'ər-ĭs). An ancient Greek city in southern Italy, on the Gulf of Taranto; founded in 720 B.C., it became a center of luxurious living before its destruction in 510 B.C.

syb·a·rite (sĭb'ər-īt) *n.* Also **Syb·a·rite.** A person devoted to pleasure and luxury; a voluptuary: *"Dressed to a sybarite's most pampered wishes"* (Byron). [Latin *Sybarita,* native of Sybaris, from Greek *Subaritēs,* from *Subaris,* SYBARIS.] —**syb'a·rit'ic** (-ə-rĭt'ĭk), **syb'a·rit'i·cal** *adj.* —**syb'a·rit'i·cal·ly** *adv.*

syc·a·mine (sĭk'ə-mĭn) *n.* A tree mentioned in the New Testament, thought to be a species of mulberry. Luke 17:6. [Latin *sȳcamīnus,* from Greek *sukaminos,* from Phoenician or Aramaic *shiqmin* (plural), akin to Hebrew *shiqmin,* plural of *shiqmāh,* mulberry tree. See also **sycamore.**]

syc·a·more (sĭk'ə-môr', -mōr') *n.* Also *obsolete* **syc·o·more** (for sense 3). **1.** A deciduous tree, *Platanus occidentalis,* of eastern North America, having lobed leaves, ball-like seed clusters, and bark that often flakes off in large patches. Also called "buttonwood" and sometimes "buttonball." **2.** A Eurasian tree, *Acer pseudoplatanus,* related to and resembling the maples. **3.** A tree, *Ficus sycomorus,* of northeastern Africa and adjacent Asia, related to the fig. This species is the sycamore of the Bible. [Middle English *sicamour,* from Old French *sicamor,* from Latin *sycomorus,* from Greek *sukamoros* : *suka-,* probably from Hebrew *shiqmāh,* mulberry tree (see **sycamine**) + *moron,* mulberry tree (see **moro-** in Appendix*).]

syce (sīs) *n.* A stableman or groom, especially in India. [Hindi *sā'is,* from Arabic *sā'is, sāyis,* from *sāsa,* to administer.]

sy·cee (sī-sē') *n.* Lumps of pure silver bearing the stamp of a banker or assayer and formerly used in China as money. Also called "sycee silver." [Cantonese *sai si,* "fine silk" (so called because the pure silver can be spun into fine threads), corresponding to Mandarin Chinese *hsi*[4] *su*[1] : *hsi*[4], thin, fine + *su*[1], silk, thread.]

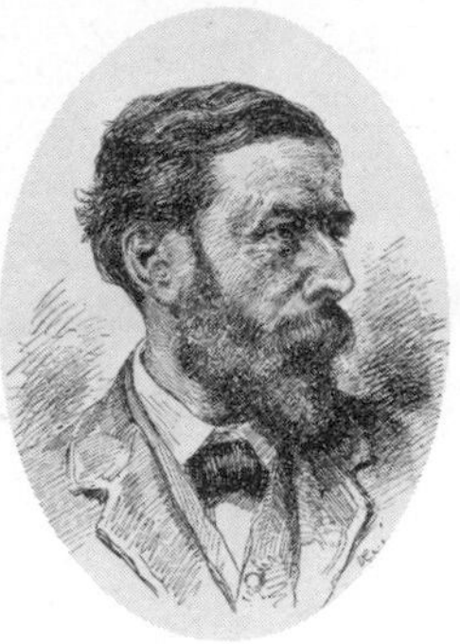

John Addington Symonds

sy·co·ni·um (sī-kō'nē-əm) *n., pl.* **-nia** (-nē-ə). The fleshy multiple fruit of the fig, consisting primarily of the enlarged floral receptacle. [New Latin, from Greek *sukon,* the fig, probably from the same Mediterranean source as Latin *ficus,* FIG.]

syc·o·phan·cy (sĭk'ə-fən-sē) *n., pl.* **-cies.** The act, practice, or behavior of a sycophant; servile flattery.

syc·o·phant (sĭk'ə-fənt) *n.* One who attempts to win favor or advance himself by flattering persons of influence; a servile self-seeker: *"the king appeared . . . with his dogs and sycophants behind him"* (Kathleen Winsor). [Latin *sycophanta,* from Greek *sukophantēs,* "fig-shower," "accuser" (from the use of the gesture of the fig in denouncing a criminal), hence an informer, flatterer : *sukon,* the fig (see **syconium**) + *-phantēs,* shower, from *phainein,* to show (see **bhā-**[1] in Appendix*).] **—syc'o·phan'tic** (-făn'tĭk), **syc'o·phan'ti·cal** *adj.* **—syc'o·phan'ti·cal·ly** *adv.*

Synonyms: *sycophant, toady, flatterer.* These nouns denote persons who lavish praise or attention on others, usually in the hope of gain. *Sycophant* and *toady* both refer to parasites of the rich or powerful and stress self-seeking motives. *Toady* especially implies truckling or adopting a menial attitude. *Flatterer,* less specific and less derogatory, does not always imply hope of gain but may suggest insincerity or servility.

sy·co·sis (sī-kō'sĭs) *n.* A chronic inflammation of the hair follicles, especially of the beard and scalp. [New Latin, from Greek *sukōsis,* eruption resembling a fig : *sukon,* fig (see **syconium**) + -OSIS.]

SYD Airport code for Sydney, Australia.

Syd·ney (sĭd'nē). The capital of New South Wales, Australia, in the east-central part of the state on the Tasman Sea. Population, 2,300,000.

Sy·e·ne. The ancient name for **Aswan.**

sy·e·nite (sī'ə-nīt') *n.* An igneous rock composed primarily of alkali feldspar together with other minerals, such as hornblende. [Latin *Syēnītēs (lapis),* "(stone) of Syene" (where it was first quarried), from *Syēnē,* Syene, from Greek *Suēnē.*] **—sy'e·nit'ic** (-nĭt'ĭk) *adj.*

syl., syll. 1. syllable. **2.** syllabus.

syl·la·bar·y (sĭl'ə-bĕr'ē) *n., pl.* **-ies.** A list of syllables; especially, a list or set of written characters, each one representing a syllable. [New Latin *syllabārium,* from Latin *syllaba,* SYLLABLE.]

syl·lab·ic (sĭ-lăb'ĭk) *adj.* **1.** Of, pertaining to, or consisting of a syllable or syllables. **2.** Designating a consonant that forms a syllable without a vowel, as the *l* in *riddle* (rĭd'l). **3.** Pronouncing every syllable distinctly: *a syllabic reading of a line of verse.* **4.** Designating a form of verse based on the number of syllables per line rather than on the arrangement of accents or quantities. **—***n.* A syllabic sound. [Medieval Latin *syllabicus,* from Greek *sullabikos,* from *sullabē,* SYLLABLE.] **—syl·lab'i·cal·ly** *adv.*

syl·lab·i·cate (sĭ-lăb'ə-kāt') *tr.v.* **-cated, -cating, -cates.** Also **syl·lab·i·fy** (-fī'), **-fied, -fying, -fies.** To form or divide into syllables. **—syl·lab'i·ca'tion** *n.*

syl·la·bism (sĭl'ə-bĭz'əm) *n.* **1.** The use of written characters that represent syllables. **2.** Division into syllables. [From Latin *syllaba,* SYLLABLE.]

syl·la·bize (sĭl'ə-bīz') *tr.v.* **-bized, -bizing, -bizes.** To syllabicate. [Medieval Latin *syllabizāre,* from Greek *sullabizein,* from *sullabē,* SYLLABLE.]

syl·la·ble (sĭl'ə-bəl) *n. Abbr.* **syl., syll. 1.** A unit of spoken language consisting of a vowel or diphthong alone, of a syllabic consonant alone, or of either with one or more consonants. **2.** One or more letters or phonetic symbols written or printed to approximate a spoken syllable. **3.** The slightest bit or expression. **—***tr.v.* **syllabled, -bling, -bles.** To pronounce (a line of verse, for example) in syllables. [Middle English *sillable,* from Old French *sillabe,* from Latin *syllaba,* from Greek *sullabē,* "a gathering (of letters)," from *sullambanein,* to gather together, spell together : *sun-,* together + *lambanein,* to take, grasp (see **slagw-** in Appendix*).]

syl·la·bub (sĭl'ə-bŭb') *n.* Also **sil·la·bub.** A drink or, with gelatin added, a dessert, consisting of wine or liquor mixed with sweetened milk or cream. [Origin unknown.]

syl·la·bus (sĭl'ə-bəs) *n., pl.* **-buses** or **-bi** (-bī'). *Abbr.* **syl., syll. 1.** An outline or brief statement of the main points of a text, lecture, or course of study. **2.** *Law.* A short statement preceding a report on an adjudged case and containing the court rulings on the legal points involved. [Medieval Latin, list, from Greek *sullabus,* a misreading (in Cicero's *Letters to Atticus*) of *silluba,* earlier *sittuba*†, book title, label, table of contents.]

syl·lep·sis (sĭ-lĕp'sĭs) *n., pl.* **-ses** (-sēz'). *Grammar.* A construction in which one word seems to be in the same relation to two or more other words but in fact is not. An example is: *He lost his coat and his temper.* Compare **zeugma.** [Latin, from Greek *sullēpsis,* "a taking together" : *sun-,* together + *lēpsis,* a taking, from *lambanein* (past participle *lēptos*), to take (see **slagw-** in Appendix*).] **—syl·lep'tic** *adj.*

syl·lo·gism (sĭl'ə-jĭz'əm) *n.* **1.** *Logic.* A form of deductive reasoning consisting of a major premise, a minor premise, and a conclusion; for example, *All men are foolish* (major premise); *Smith is a man* (minor premise); *therefore, Smith is foolish* (conclusion). **2.** Reasoning from the general to the specific; deduction. **3.** A subtle or specious piece of reasoning. [Middle English *silogisme,* from Old French, from Latin *syllogismus,* from Greek *sullogismos,* "a reckoning together," from *sullogizesthai,* to reckon together, infer : *sun-,* together + *logizesthai,* to reckon, reason, from *logos,* word, computation (see **leg-** in Appendix*).]

syl·lo·gist (sĭl'ə-jĭst) *n.* A person who uses or is skilled in syllogistic reasoning.

syl·lo·gis·tic (sĭl'ə-jĭs'tĭk) *adj.* Also **syl·lo·gis·ti·cal** (-tĭ-kəl). Of, pertaining to, resembling, or consisting of a syllogism or syllogisms. **—***n.* Also **syl·lo·gis·tics** (-tĭks) (used with a singular verb). **1.** The branch of logic dealing with syllogisms. **2.** The art of reasoning by syllogism. **—syl'lo·gis'ti·cal·ly** *adv.*

syl·lo·gize (sĭl'ə-jīz') *v.* **-gized, -gizing, -gizes. —***intr.* To reason or argue by means of syllogisms. **—***tr.* To deduce by syllogism. **—syl'lo·gi·za'tion** *n.* **—syl'lo·giz'er** *n.*

sylph (sĭlf) *n.* **1.** Any of a class of elemental beings without souls that were believed to inhabit the air. **2.** A slim, graceful woman or girl. [New Latin *sylphus,* probably coined by Paracelsus by contracting Latin *sylvestris nympha,* nymph of the woods : *sylvestris,* from *sylva,* forest (see **sylvan**) + *nympha,* NYMPH.]

sylph·id (sĭl'fĭd) *n.* A young or diminutive sylph. **—***adj.* Pertaining to or resembling a sylph. [French *sylphide,* from *sylphe,* sylph, from New Latin *sylphus,* SYLPH.]

syl·va (sĭl'və) *n.* Also **sil·va. 1.** The trees or forests of a region. **2.** A written work on such trees or forests. [Latin, forest. See **sylvan.**]

syl·van (sĭl'vən) *adj.* Also **sil·van. 1.** Pertaining to or characteristic of woods or forest regions. **2.** Located in or inhabiting a wood or forest. **3.** Abounding in trees; wooded. —See Synonyms at **rural. —***n.* One that lives in or frequents the woods. [Medieval Latin *silvānus,* from Latin *silva, sylva*†, forest.]

syl·van·ite (sĭl'və-nīt') *n.* A pale brass-yellow to silver-white gold and silver ore, chiefly (Au, Ag)Te_2. [French; found in TRANSYLVANIA.]

Syl·va·nus. See **Silvanus.**

syl·vite (sĭl'vīt') *n.* Also **syl·vin** (-vĭn), **syl·vine** (-vĭn, -vīn'), **syl·vin·ite** (-vĭn-īt'). A colorless vitreous potassium chloride mineral used as a major source of potassium compounds. [French, alteration of *sylvine,* from New Latin *(sal digestivus) Sylvii,* "(digestive salt) of Sylvius," probably after Franz de la Boë *Sylvius* (1614–1672), Dutch physician.]

sym-. Variant of **syn-.**

sym. 1. symbol. **2.** symphony.

sym·bi·ont (sĭm'bī-ŏnt', -bē-ŏnt') *n.* Also **sym·bi·ote** (sĭm'bī-ōt', -bē-ōt'). One of the organisms in a symbiotic relationship. [From Greek *sumbiōn, sumbiountos,* present participle of *sumbioun,* to live together. See **symbiosis.**]

sym·bi·o·sis (sĭm'bī-ō'sĭs, sĭm'bē-) *n. Biology.* The relationship of two or more different organisms in a close association that may be but is not necessarily of benefit to each. Compare **antibiosis.** [New Latin, from Greek *sumbiōsis,* a living together, from *sumbioun,* to live together : *sun-,* together + *bios,* life (see **gwei-** in Appendix*).] **—sym'bi·ot'ic** (-ŏt'ĭk), **sym'bi·ot'i·cal** *adj.* **—sym'bi·ot'i·cal·ly** *adv.*

sym·bol (sĭm'bəl) *n. Abbr.* **sym. 1.** Something that represents something else by association, resemblance, or convention; especially, a material object used to represent something invisible. **2.** A printed or written sign used to represent an operation, element, quantity, quality, or relation, as in mathematics or music. **—***tr.v.* **symboled, -boling, -bols.** To symbolize. [Latin *symbolum,* sign, token, from Greek *sumbolon,* token for identification (by comparing with its counterpart), from *sumballein,* to throw together, compare : *sun-,* together + *ballein,* to throw (see **gwel-**[1] in Appendix*).]

sym·bol·ic (sĭm-bŏl'ĭk) *adj.* Also **sym·bol·i·cal** (-ĭ-kəl). **1.** Of, pertaining to, or expressed by means of a symbol or symbols. **2.** Serving as a symbol. **3.** Characterized by the use of symbolism, as a work of art. **—sym·bol'i·cal·ly** *adv.* **—sym·bol'i·cal·ness** *n.*

symbolic logic. A treatment of formal logic in which a calculus or system of symbols is used to represent quantities and relationships. Also called "mathematical logic."

sym·bol·ism (sĭm'bə-lĭz'əm) *n.* **1.** The practice of representing things by means of symbols or of attributing symbolic meanings or significance to objects, events, or relationships. **2.** A system of symbols or representations. **3.** A symbolic meaning or representation. **4.** The revelation or suggestion of intangible conditions or truths by artistic invention.

sym·bol·ist (sĭm'bə-lĭst) *n.* **1.** A person who uses symbols or symbolism. **2. a.** One who interprets or represents conditions or truths by the use of symbolism. **b.** Any of a group of chiefly French artists and writers of the late 19th century who expressed their ideas and emotions indirectly through symbols. **—sym'bo·list, sym'bol·is'tic, sym'bol·is'ti·cal** *adj.*

sym·bol·ize (sĭm'bə-līz') *v.* **-ized, -izing, -izes. —***tr.* **1.** To be or serve as a symbol of: *"his whole attitude was symbolized by his* *shrug and his flippantly red carnation"* (Willa Cather). **2.** To represent or identify by a symbol or symbols. —*intr.* To use symbols. —**sym′bol·i·za′tion** *n.*

sym·bol·o·gy (sĭm·bŏl′ə-jē) *n.* **1.** The study or interpretation of symbols or symbolism. **2.** The art or practice of expression by means of symbols.

sym·met·al·ism (sĭm-mĕt′l-ĭz′əm) *n.* A system of coinage in which a unit of currency consists of a combination of two or more metals in fixed proportions. [SYM- + METAL + -ISM.]

sym·met·rics (sə-mĕt′rĭks) *pl.n.* An epigrammatic verse form invented by David McCord (1948), consisting of a quatrain beginning and ending with the same word in which the second rhyming word of the first couplet is repeated at the beginning of the second couplet, the pair forming a third line when printed, being centered between the couplets (of which they are a part) with a colon spaced equally left and right to divide them. [Irregular punning blend of SYMMETRICAL + METRICS.]

sym·me·trize (sĭm′ə-trīz′) *tr.v.* **-trized, -trizing, -trizes.** To make symmetrical; impart perfect balance to. —**sym′me·tri·za′tion** *n.*

sym·me·try (sĭm′ə-trē) *n., pl.* **-tries. 1.** A relationship of characteristic correspondence, equivalence, or identity among constituents of a system or between different systems: *electric charge symmetry; symmetry in political and religious activism.* **2.** Exact correspondence of form and constituent configuration on opposite sides of a dividing line or plane or about a center or axis. **3.** Structural or functional independence of direction; isotropy. **4.** Beauty as a result of balance or harmonious arrangement. —See Synonyms at **proportion.** [Obsolete French *symmetrie,* from Latin *symmetria,* from Greek *summetria,* from *summetros,* "of like measure," proportionable, symmetrical : *sun-,* like, same + *metron,* measure (see me-² in Appendix*).] —**sym·met′ri·cal** (sĭ-mĕt′rĭ-kəl), **sym·met′ric** *adj.* —**sym·met′ri·cal·ly** *adv.*

Sym·onds (sĭm′əndz), **John Addington.** 1840–1893. English poet, critic, and literary historian.

Sym·ons (sī′mənz), **Arthur.** 1865–1945. English poet and literary critic.

sym·pa·thec·to·my (sĭm′pə-thĕk′tə-mē) *n., pl.* **-mies.** The removal of a part of a sympathetic nerve or a number of sympathetic ganglia. [SYMPATH(ETIC) + -ECTOMY.]

sym·pa·thet·ic (sĭm′pə-thĕt′ĭk) *adj.* Also **sym·pa·thet·i·cal** (-ĭ-kəl). **1.** Of, expressing, feeling, or resulting from sympathy. **2.** In agreement; favorable; inclined. Used with *to* or *toward.* **3.** Pertaining to or acting on the sympathetic nervous system. [New Latin *sympatheticus,* from Greek *sumpathētikos,* from *sumpatheia,* SYMPATHY.] —**sym′pa·thet′i·cal·ly** *adv.*

sympathetic ink. Invisible ink *(see).*

sympathetic nervous system. A portion of the **autonomic nervous system** *(see).*

sym·pa·thin (sĭm′pə-thĭn) *n.* A hormone resembling epinephrine, thought to be formed in the muscle cells by sympathetic nerve impulses. [SYMPATH(ETIC) + -IN.]

sym·pa·thize (sĭm′pə-thīz′) *intr.v.* **-thized, -thizing, -thizes. 1.** To feel or express compassion; commiserate. Used with *with.* **2.** To share or understand another's feelings or ideas. Used with *with.* **3.** *Obsolete.* To agree in quality or disposition; correspond. —**sym′pa·thiz′er** *n.* —**sym′pa·thiz′ing·ly** *adv.*

sym·pa·tho·lyt·ic (sĭm′pə-thō-lĭt′ĭk) *adj.* Of or pertaining to an agent that opposes the activity of the sympathetic nervous system. [SYMPATH(ETIC) + -LYTIC.]

sym·pa·tho·mi·met·ic (sĭm′pə-thō-mĭ-mĕt′ĭk) *adj. Medicine.* Of or pertaining to an agent that stimulates the sympathetic nervous system. [SYMPATH(ETIC) + MIMETIC.]

sym·pa·thy (sĭm′pə-thē) *n., pl.* **-thies. 1. a.** A relationship or affinity between persons or things in which whatever affects one correspondingly affects the other. **b.** Mutual understanding or affection arising from this. **2. a.** The act of or capacity for sharing or understanding the feelings of another person. **b.** A feeling or expression of pity or sorrow for the distress of another; compassion; commiseration. **3.** Favor; agreement; accord: *He is in sympathy with their beliefs.* **4.** A feeling of loyalty; devotion; allegiance. —See Synonyms at **pity.** [Latin *sympathīa,* from Greek *sumpatheia,* from *sumpathēs,* affected by like feelings : *sun-,* like + *pathos,* emotion, feelings (see kwenth- in Appendix*).]

sympathy strike. A strike by a body of workers for the purpose of supporting a cause or another group of strikers.

sym·pat·ric (sĭm-păt′rĭk) *adj. Ecology.* Occupying the same or overlapping geographical areas without interbreeding. Said of populations of closely related species. Compare **allopatric.** [SYN- + Greek *patra, patrē,* fatherland, from *patēr,* father (see pəter in Appendix*).] —**sym·pat′ri·cal·ly** *adv.*

sym·pet·al·ous (sĭm-pĕt′ə-ləs) *adj. Botany.* **Gamopetalous** *(see).* [SYN- + PETALOUS.]

sym·phon·ic (sĭm-fŏn′ĭk) *adj.* **1.** Pertaining to or having the character or form of a symphony. **2.** Harmonious in sound.

symphonic poem. Program music based on an extramusical theme in a single, extended movement for symphony orchestra and typical chiefly of the late 19th century. Also called "tone poem."

sym·pho·ni·ous (sĭm-fō′nē-əs) *adj.* In accord; harmonious. —**sym·pho′ni·ous·ly** *adv.*

sym·pho·nist (sĭm′fə-nĭst) *n.* One who composes symphonies.

sym·pho·ny (sĭm′fə-nē) *n., pl.* **-nies. 1.** *Abbr.* **sym.** *Music.* **a.** A usually long sonata for orchestra, consisting of four related movements. **b.** An instrumental passage in a vocal or choral composition. **c.** An instrumental overture or interlude, as in early opera. **2.** *Abbr.* **sym. a.** A symphony orchestra. **b.** *Informal.* An orchestral concert. **3.** Harmony, especially of sound or

SYMBOLS AND SIGNS

The following symbols and signs are among those most commonly used by printers. The designations are also those most commonly used, and do not exhaust the meanings that may be attached to the symbols. Symbols consisting of letters of the alphabet are entered in the regular alphabetical sequence of entries. See also symbols in tables at **currency**, **element**, **measurement**, **particle**, and **proofread**, and foreign letters at **alphabet**.

Symbol	Meaning	Symbol	Meaning	Symbol	Meaning
+	plus	[ ]	brackets	◎	rain
−	minus	‖	braces	✳	snow
±	plus or minus	°	degree	⊠	snow on ground
∓	minus or plus	′	minute	←	floating ice crystals
×	multiplied by	″	second	▲	hail
÷	divided by	△	increment	△	sleet
=	equal to	ω	angular frequency; solid angle	∨	frostwork
≠ or ≠	not equal to	Ω	ohm	⊔	hoarfrost
≈ or ≐	nearly equal to	μΩ	microhm	≡	fog
≡	identical with	MΩ	megohm	∞	haze; dust haze
≢	not identical with	Φ	magnetic flux	⊤	thunder
⇔	equivalent	Ψ	dielectric flux; electrostatic flux	<	sheet lightning
∼	difference	ρ	resistivity	◑	solar corona
≅	congruent to	Λ	equivalent conductivity	⊕	solar halo
>	greater than	ℜ	reluctance	↰	thunderstorm
≯	not greater than	→	direction of flow	＼	direction
<	less than	⇄	electric current	○ or ⊙ or ①	annual
≮	not less than	◯	benzene ring	⊙⊙ or ②	biennial
≧ or ≥	greater than or equal to	→	yields	♃	perennial
≦ or ≤	less than or equal to	⇌	reversible reaction	♂ or ♂	male
‖	absolute value	↓	precipitate	♀	female
∪	logical sum or union	↑	gas	□	male (in charts)
∩	logical product or intersection	‰	salinity	○	female (in charts)
⊂	is contained in	☉ or ☼	sun	℞	take (from Latin *Recipe*)
ε	is a member of; permittivity; mean error	● or ◍	new moon	ĀĀ or Ā or āā	of each (doctor's prescription)
:	is to; ratio	☽	first quarter	℔	pound
::	as; proportion	○ or ◔	full moon	℥	ounce
≑	approaches	☾	last quarter	ʒ	dram
→	approaches limit of	☿	Mercury	℈	scruple
∾	varies as	♀	Venus	ʄʒ	fluid ounce
‖	parallel	⊖ or ⊕	Earth	ʄʒ	fluid dram
⊥	perpendicular	♂	Mars	ℳ	minim
∠	angle	♃	Jupiter	& or ⅋	and; ampersand
∟	right angle	♄	Saturn	℔	per
△	triangle	♅	Uranus	#	number
□	square	♆	Neptune	/	virgule; slash; solidus; shilling
▭	rectangle	♇	Pluto	©	copyright
▱	parallelogram	♈	Aries	%	per cent
○	circle	♉	Taurus	℅	care of
⌒	arc of circle	♊	Gemini	%	account of
⊥	equilateral	♋	Cancer	@	at
≜	equiangular	♌	Leo	*	asterisk
√	radical; root; square root	♍	Virgo	†	dagger
∛	cube root	♎	Libra	‡	double dagger
∜	fourth root	♏	Scorpius	§	section
Σ	sum	♐	Sagittarius	☞	index
! or ∟	factorial product	♑	Capricornus	´	acute
∞	infinity	≈	Aquarius	`	grave
∫	integral	♓	Pisces	˜	tilde
f	function	☌	conjunction	ˆ	circumflex
∂ or δ	differential; variation	☍	opposition	¯	macron
π	pi	△	trine	˘	breve
∴	therefore	□	quadrature	¨	dieresis
∵	because	✳	sextile	¸	cedilla
‾	vinculum (above letter)	☊	dragon's head, ascending node	˄	caret
( )	parentheses	☋	dragon's tail, descending node		

---

t tight/th thin, path/*th* this, bathe/ŭ cut/ûr urge/v valve/w with/y yes/z zebra, size/zh vision/ə about, item, edible, gallop, circus/ à *Fr.* ami/œ *Fr.* feu, *Ger.* schön/ü *Fr.* tu, *Ger.* über/KH *Ger.* ich, *Scot.* loch/N *Fr.* bon. *Follows main vocabulary. †Of obscure origin.

color. **4.** Anything characterized by a harmonious combination of elements. [Middle English *symphonie,* harmony of sound, from Old French, from Latin *symphōnia,* from Greek *sumphōnia,* from *sumphōnos,* harmonious : *sun-,* together + *phōnē,* voice, sound (see **bhā-**[2] in Appendix*).]

symphony orchestra. A large orchestra composed of string, wind, and percussion sections, designed for playing symphonic works.

sym·phy·sis (sĭm′fə-sĭs) *n., pl.* **-ses** (-sēz′). **1.** *Anatomy.* A form of bone articulation, **synarthrosis** *(see).* **2.** The coalescence of similar parts or organs. [New Latin, from Greek *sumphusis,* a growing together (especially of bones), from *sumphuein,* to cause to grow together, unite : *sun-,* together + *phuein,* to make grow (see **bheu-** in Appendix*).] —**sym′phy′se·al** (-fĭz′ē-əl), **sym′phy′si·al** *adj.*

sym·po·di·um (sĭm-pō′dē-əm) *n., pl.* **-dia** (-dē-ə). *Botany.* A primary axis that develops from a series of short lateral branches and has a zigzag or irregular form. Also called "pseudaxis." [New Latin : SYN- + Greek *podion,* small foot, base, from *pous* (stem *pod-*), foot (see **ped-**[1] in Appendix*).] —**sym·po′di·al** *adj.* —**sym·po′di·al·ly** *adv.*

sym·po·si·ac (sĭm-pō′zē-ăk′) *adj.* Of, of the nature of, appropriate to, or occurring at a symposium. —*n. Archaic.* A meeting or conference; a symposium.

sym·po·si·arch (sĭm-pō′zē-ärk′) *n.* **1.** The master or director of an ancient Greek symposium. **2.** A toastmaster. [Greek *sumposiarkhos, sumposiarkhēs* : *sumposion,* SYMPOSIUM + -ARCH.]

sym·po·si·um (sĭm-pō′zē-əm) *n., pl.* **-siums** or **-sia** (-zē-ə). **1.** A meeting or conference for discussion of some topic. **2.** A collection of writings on a particular topic, as in a magazine. **3.** A convivial meeting for drinking, music, and intellectual discussion among the ancient Greeks. [Latin, from Greek *sumposion,* drinking party : *sun-,* together + *posis,* drink (see **pōi-**[1] in Appendix*).]

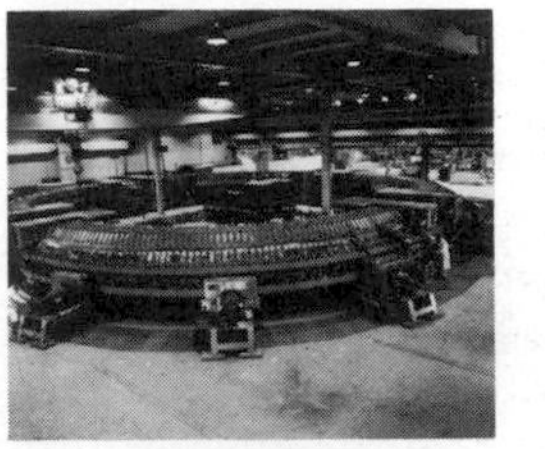

synchrotron
The Cosmotron, a synchrotron in operation since 1950 at the Brookhaven National Laboratory, Long Island, New York

symp·tom (sĭm′təm, sĭmp′-) *n.* **1.** Any circumstance or phenomenon regarded as an indication or characteristic of a condition or event. **2.** *Medicine.* Any phenomenon experienced by an individual as a departure from normal function, sensation, or appearance, generally indicating disorder or disease. —See Synonyms at **sign.** [Late Latin *symptōma,* from Greek *sumptōma,* occurrence, phenomenon, from *sumpiptein,* to fall together, fall upon, happen : *sun-,* together + *piptein,* to fall (see **pet-**[1] in Appendix*).] —**symp′to·mat′ic** *adj.* —**symp′to·mat′i·cal·ly** *adv.*

symp·tom·a·tol·o·gy (sĭm′tə-mə-tŏl′ə-jē) *n.* **1.** The medical science of disease symptoms. Also called "semiology." **2.** The complex of symptoms of a disease. [New Latin *symptomatologia* : Greek *sumptōma* (stem *sumptōmat-*), SYMPTOM + -LOGY.]

syn–, sym–. Indicates: **1.** Together or with; for example, **syndactyl, symmetalism. 2.** Same, alike, similar, or at the same time; for example, **sympatric. 3.** Union or fusion; for example, **sympetalous, syncarp.** [Greek *sun-,* from *sun, xun,* together, with. See **sem-**[1] in Appendix.* In Greek compounds, *sun-* becomes *sum-* before *b, m, p; sul-* before *l; su-* before *s* and *z,* borrowed as *sym-, syl-,* and *sy-* respectively.]

syn. synonymous; synonym; synonymy.

syn·aer·e·sis. Variant of **syneresis.**

syn·aes·the·sia. Variant of **synesthesia.**

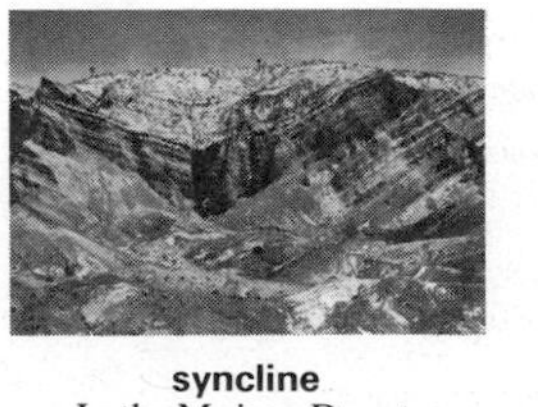

syncline
In the Mojave Desert of southern California

syn·a·gogue (sĭn′ə-gŏg′) *n.* Also **syn·a·gog. 1.** A building or place of meeting for Jewish worship and religious instruction. **2.** A congregation of Jews for worship or religious study. **3.** The Jewish religion as organized or typified in such local congregations. [Middle English *synagoge,* from Old French, from Latin *synagōga,* from Greek *sunagōgē,* assembly, from *sunagein,* to bring together : *sun-,* together + *agein,* to lead, drive (see **ag-** in Appendix*).] —**syn′a·gog′i·cal** (-gŏj′ĭ-kəl), **syn′a·gog′al** (-gŏg′əl) *adj.*

syn·a·le·pha (sĭn′ə-lē′fə) *n.* Also **syn·a·loe·pha, syn·a·le·phe, syn·a·loe·phe.** The blending into one syllable of two successive vowels of adjacent syllables; for example, *th' elite* for *the elite.* [New Latin, from Greek *sunal(o)iphē,* from *sunaleiphein,* to smear or melt together, unite two syllables : *sun-,* together + *aleiphein,* to anoint (see **leip-** in Appendix*).]

syn·apse (sĭn′ăps) *n.* Also **syn·ap·sis** (sĭ-năp′sĭs) *pl.* **-ses** (-sēz′). The point at which a nerve impulse passes from an axon of one neuron to the dendrite of another. [New Latin *synapsis,* from Greek *sunapsis,* point of contact, from *sunaptein,* to join together : *sun-,* together + *haptein*†, to fasten, connect.]

syn·ap·sis (sĭ-năp′sĭs) *n., pl.* **-ses** (-sēz′). **1.** *Biology.* The fusion of similar paternal and maternal chromosome pairs during meiosis. **2.** Variant of **synapse.** [New Latin. See **synapse.**]

syn·ar·thro·sis (sĭn′är-thrō′sĭs) *n., pl.* **-ses** (-sēz′). Also **syn·ar·thro·di·a** (-dĭ-ə) *pl.* **-diae** (-dĭ-ē). *Anatomy.* Any of several forms of bone articulation in which the bones are rigidly joined without an intervening cavity. Also called "symphysis." [New Latin, from Greek *sunarthrōsis* : *sun-,* together + *arthrōsis,* articulation, from *arthron,* a joint (see **ar-** in Appendix*).]

sync (sĭngk) *n. Informal.* Synchronization. —*v.* **synced, syncing, syncs.** *Informal.* —*intr.* To synchronize. —*tr.* To synchronize (something) with another.

syn·carp (sĭn′kärp′, sĭng′-) *n. Botany.* A fleshy fruit composed of the fruits of several flowers or several carpels of a single flower. [SYN- + -CARP.]

syn·car·pous (sĭn-kär′pəs, sĭng-) *adj. Botany.* Having or consisting of united carpels. [SYN- + -CARPOUS.]

syn·chro (sĭn′krō, sĭng′-) *n., pl.* **-chros.** *Machinery.* A **Selsyn** *(see).* [Short for SYNCHRONOUS.]

synchro–. Indicates synchronization: for example, **synchromesh.** [Shortened from SYNCHRONIZE.]

syn·chro·cy·clo·tron (sĭn′krō-sī′klə-trŏn′, sĭng′-) *n.* A proton and positive ion accelerator, the chief components and configuration of which are similar to those of a **cyclotron** *(see)* and in which the phase of the accelerating potential is synchronized with the frequency of the accelerated particles by frequency modulation to compensate for relativistic increases in particle mass at high speeds.

syn·chro·flash (sĭn′krō-flăsh′, sĭng′-) *n.* A device on a camera that synchronizes the peak of a flash created by a flash bulb with the widest opening of the shutter. —**syn′chro·flash′** *adj.*

syn·chro·mesh (sĭn′krō-mĕsh′, sĭng′-) *n.* **1.** An automotive gear-shifting system in which the gears are synchronized at the same speeds before engaging to effect a smooth change. **2.** A gear in such a system. —**syn′chro·mesh′** *adj.*

syn·chron·ic (sĭn-krŏn′ĭk, sĭng-) *adj.* Also **syn·chron·i·cal** (-ĭ-kəl). **1.** Synchronous. **2. a.** Descriptive: *synchronic linguistics.* **b.** Studying the events of a particular time or era without consideration of historical data. Compare **diachronic.** —**syn·chron′i·cal·ly** *adv.*

synchronic linguistics. **Descriptive linguistics** *(see).*

syn·chro·nism (sĭn′krə-nĭz′əm, sĭng′-) *n.* **1.** The condition of being synchronous. **2.** A chronological listing of historical personages or events so as to indicate parallel existence or occurrence. **3.** The representation in the same art work of two or more events that occurred at different times. —**syn′chro·nis′tic, syn′chro·nis′ti·cal** *adj.* —**syn′chro·nis′ti·cal·ly** *adv.*

syn·chro·nize (sĭn′krə-nīz′, sĭng′-) *v.* **-nized, -nizing, -nizes.** —*intr.* **1.** To occur at the same time; be simultaneous. **2.** To operate in unison. —*tr.* **1.** To cause to operate with exact coincidence in time or rate. **2.** To arrange (historical events) so as to indicate parallel existence or occurrence. **3.** To cause (sound effects or dialogue) to coincide with an action. [From SYNCHRONOUS.] —**syn′chro·ni·za′tion** *n.* —**syn′chro·niz′er** *n.*

syn·chro·nous (sĭn′krə-nəs, sĭng′-) *adj.* **1.** Occurring at the same time. **2.** Moving or operating at the same rate. **3. a.** Having identical periods. **b.** Having identical period and phase. —See Synonyms at **contemporary.** [Late Latin *synchronos,* from Greek *sunkhronos* : *sun-,* same + *khronos,* time (see **chronic**).] —**syn′chro·nous·ly** *adv.* —**syn′chro·nous·ness** *n.*

synchronous motor. A motor having a speed directly proportional to the frequency of the electric current that operates it.

synchronous orbit. An orbit having a period the same as the period of axial rotation of the earth and so oriented that any body in it maintains a position over one point on the earth's surface. Also called "stationary orbit."

syn·chro·ny (sĭn′krə-nē, sĭng′-) *n., pl.* **-nies.** A synchronous occurrence, movement, or arrangement. [From SYNCHRONOUS.]

syn·chro·tron (sĭn′krə-trŏn′, sĭng′-) *n.* An accelerator in which charged particles are accelerated around a fixed circular path by a radio-frequency potential and held to the path by a time-varying magnetic field. [SYNCHRO- + (ELEC)TRON.]

syn·cli·nal (sĭn-klī′nəl) *adj.* **1.** Sloping downward from opposite directions to meet in a common point or line. **2.** *Geology.* Pertaining to, formed by, or forming a syncline. —*n.* A syncline. [SYN- + Greek *klinein,* to lean (see **klei-** in Appendix*).]

syn·cline (sĭn′klīn′) *n.* A low, troughlike area in bedrock, in which rocks incline together from opposite sides. [Back-formation from SYNCLINAL.]

syn·com (sĭn′kŏm′) *n.* A communications satellite in a synchronous orbit. [SYN(CHRONOUS) + COM(MUNICATION).]

syn·co·pate (sĭn′kə-pāt′, sĭng′-) *tr.v.* **-pated, -pating, -pates. 1.** *Grammar.* **a.** To shorten (a word) by means of syncope. **b.** To drop (a letter or sound) from the spelling or pronunciation of a word. **2.** To modify (musical rhythm) by syncopation. [Medieval Latin *syncopāre,* from Late Latin *syncopē,* SYNCOPE.] —**syn′co·pa′tor** (-pā′tər) *n.*

syn·co·pa·tion (sĭn′kə-pā′shən, sĭng′-) *n.* **1.** The act of syncopating or the condition of being syncopated. **2.** Something syncopated. **3.** *Music.* A shift of accent in a passage or composition that occurs when a normally weak beat is stressed. **4.** *Grammar.* Syncope.

syn·co·pe (sĭn′kə-pē, sĭng′-) *n.* **1.** *Grammar.* The shortening of a word by the omission of a sound, letter, or syllable from the middle of the word; for example, *bos'n* for *boatswain.* **2.** *Pathology.* A brief loss of consciousness caused by transient anemia; a swoon. [Late Latin *syncopē,* from Greek *sunkopē,* from *sunkoptein,* to chop up, cut off : *sun-,* together, thoroughly + *koptein,* to strike, cut off (see **skep-** in Appendix*).] —**syn′co·pal, syn·cop′ic** (-kŏp′ĭk) *adj.*

syn·cre·tism (sĭn′krə-tĭz′əm, sĭng′-) *n.* **1.** The attempt or tendency to combine or reconcile differing beliefs, as in philosophy or religion. **2.** *Linguistics.* The fusion into one of two or more originally different inflectional forms. [New Latin *syncretismus,* from Greek *sunkrētismos,* union, from *sunkrētizein,* to unite (in the manner of the Cretan cities) against a common enemy : *sun-,* together + *Krēs* (stem *Krēt-*), CRETAN.] —**syn′cre·tist** *n.* —**syn′cre·tis′tic, syn·cret′ic** (-krĕt′ĭk) *adj.*

syn·cre·tize (sĭn′krə-tīz′, sĭng′-) *v.* **-tized, -tizing, tizes.** —*tr.* To reconcile or attempt to reconcile (differing religious beliefs, for example). —*intr.* To combine differing beliefs. [New Latin *syncretizare,* from Greek *sunkrētizein.* See **syncretism.**]

syn·cy·ti·um (sĭn-sĭ′shəm, -shĭsh′əm) *n., pl.* **-cytia** (-sĭ′shə, -shĭsh′ə). *Biology.* A mass of protoplasm with many nuclei but no clear cell boundaries. [New Latin : SYN- + CYT(O)- + -IUM.] —**syn·cy′tial** *adj.*

synd. syndicate.

syn·dac·tyl, syn·dac·tyle (sĭn-dăk′təl) *adj.* Also **syn·dac·ty·lous** (-tə-ləs). *Biology.* Having two or more wholly or partially fused digits. —*n.* A syndactyl animal. [French *syndactyle* : SYN- + Greek *daktulos,* finger, -DACTYL.] —**syn·dac′tyl·ism′** *n.*

syn·des·mo·sis (sĭn′dĕz′mō′sĭs) *n.* The articulation of bones by ligaments. [New Latin, from Greek *sundesmos,* ligament, from *sundein,* to bind together. See **syndetic.**] —**syn′des·mot′ic** (-mŏt′ĭk) *adj.*

syn·det·ic (sĭn-dĕt′ĭk) *adj.* Also **syn·det·i·cal** (-ĭ-kəl). **1.** Serving to connect, as a conjunction; copulative; conjunctive. **2.** Connected by a conjunction. [Greek *sundetikos,* from *sundetos,* bound together, from *sundein,* to bind together : *sun-,* together + *dein,* to bind (see **dē-** in Appendix*).] —**syn·det′i·cal·ly** *adv.*

syn·dic (sĭn′dĭk) *n.* **1.** One appointed to represent a corporation, university, or other organization in business transactions; business agent. **2.** A civil magistrate or similar government official. [French, from Late Latin *syndicus,* from Greek *sundikos,* assistant in a court of justice, public advocate : *sun-,* with + *dikē,* judgment (see **deik-** in Appendix*).] —**syn′di·cal** *adj.*

syn·di·cal·ism (sĭn′dĭ-kəl-ĭz′əm) *n.* A radical political movement that advocates bringing industry and government under the control of labor unions by the use of direct action, such as general strikes and sabotage. [French *syndicalisme,* from *(chambre) syndicale,* trade union : *chambre,* chamber + *syndical,* of a trade union, from *syndic,* SYNDIC.] —**syn′di·cal·ist** *adj.* & *n.* —**syn′di·cal·is′tic** *adj.*

syn·di·cate (sĭn′dĭ-kĭt) *n. Abbr.* **synd. 1. a.** An association of people authorized to undertake some duty or transact some business. **b.** An association of people formed to carry out any enterprise. **2.** An agency that sells articles for publication in a number of newspapers or periodicals simultaneously. **3.** The office, position, or jurisdiction of a syndic or body of syndics. —See Synonyms at **monopoly.** —*v.* (sĭn′dĭ-kāt′) **syndicated, -cating, -cates.** —*tr.* **1.** To organize into a syndicate. **2.** To sell (an article, for example) through a syndicate for publication. —*intr.* To organize a syndicate. [French *syndicat,* from *syndic,* SYNDIC.]

syn·drome (sĭn′drōm′) *n.* **1.** A group of signs and symptoms that collectively indicate or characterize a disease, psychological disorder, or other abnormal condition. **2.** Any complex of symptoms of the existence of an undesirable condition or quality. [New Latin, from Greek *sundromē,* a running together, concurrence (of symptoms) : *sun-,* together + *dromos,* race, racecourse (see **der-¹** in Appendix*).] —**syn·drom′ic** (-drŏm′ĭk) *adj.*

syn·ec·do·che (sĭ-nĕk′də-kē) *n. Prosody.* A figure of speech by which a more inclusive term is used for a less inclusive term or vice versa; for example, *head* for *cattle* or *the law* for *a policeman.* [Latin, from Greek *sunekdokhē,* from *sunekdekhesthai,* "to take up (or understand) with another" : *sun-,* with + *ekdekhesthai,* to take from, take or understand in a certain sense : *ex,* out of (see **eghs** in Appendix*) + *dekhesthai,* to take, receive (see **dek-¹** in Appendix*).] —**syn′ec·doch′ic** (sĭn′ĕk-dŏk′ĭk), **syn′ec·doch′i·cal** *adj.*

syn·e·col·o·gy (sĭn′ē-kŏl′ə-jē) *n.* The study of the environmental interrelationships among communities of organisms. [SYN- + ECOLOGY.] —**syn′e·co·log′ic** (-kə-lŏj′ĭk), **syn′e·co·log′i·cal** *adj.*

syn·er·e·sis (sĭ-nĕr′ə-sĭs) *n., pl.* **-ses** (-sēz′). Also **syn·aer·e·sis. 1.** The drawing together into one syllable of two consecutive vowels ordinarily pronounced separately. Compare **dieresis, synizesis. 2.** *Chemistry.* Exudation of the liquid component of a gel. [Late Latin *synaeresis,* from Greek *sunairesis,* from *sunairein,* to take or draw together, contract : *sun-,* together + *hairein,* to seize, take (see **heresy**).]

syn·er·get·ic (sĭn′ər-jĕt′ĭk) *adj.* Also **syn·er·gic** (sĭ-nûr′jĭk). *Biology.* Of or pertaining to synergism.

syn·er·gism (sĭn′ər-jĭz′əm) *n.* Also **syn·er·gy** (-ər-jē) (for sense 1). **1.** *Biology.* The action of two or more substances, organs, or organisms to achieve an effect of which each is individually incapable. **2.** *Theology.* The doctrine that regeneration is effected by a combination of human will and divine grace. [New Latin *synergismus,* from Greek *sunergos,* working together : *sun-,* together + *ergon,* work (see **werg-¹** in Appendix*).]

syn·er·gist (sĭn′ər-jĭst) *n.* **1.** *Theology.* An adherent of synergism. **2.** *Biology.* A synergetic organ, drug, or substance; an adjuvant. —**syn′er·gis′tic, syn′er·gis′ti·cal** *adj.*

syn·e·sis (sĭn′ə-sĭs) *n. Grammar.* A construction in which a form differs in number but agrees in meaning with the word governing it; for example, *If anyone arrives, tell them to wait.* [New Latin, from Greek *sunesis,* union, quick apprehension, intelligence, from *sunienai,* to bring together, understand : *sun-,* together + *hienai,* to send (see **yē-** in Appendix*).]

syn·es·the·sia (sĭn′əs-thē′zhə) *n.* Also **syn·aes·the·sia.** A phenomenon in which one type of stimulation evokes the sensation of another, as the hearing of a sound resulting in the sensation of the visualization of a color. [New Latin : SYN- + (AN)ESTHESIA.] —**syn′es·thet′ic** (-thĕt′ĭk) *adj.*

syn·ga·my (sĭng′gə-mē) *n. Biology.* The fusion of two gametes. [SYN- + -GAMY.] —**syn·gam′ic** (-găm′ĭk), **syn·gam′ous** *adj.*

Synge (sĭng), **John Millington.** 1871–1909. Irish dramatist.

syn·gen·e·sis (sĭn-jĕn′ə-sĭs) *n. Biology.* Sexual reproduction. [New Latin : SYN- + -GENESIS.] —**syn′ge·net′ic** (-jə-nĕt′ĭk) *adj.*

syn·i·ze·sis (sĭn′ə-zē′sĭs) *n., pl.* **-ses** (-sēz′). Also **syn·e·ze·sis. 1.** The contraction of two syllables into one by joining in pronunciation two adjacent vowels. Compare **syneresis. 2.** *Biology.* The phase of meiosis in which the chromatin contracts into a mass at one side of the nucleus. [Late Latin *synizēsis,* from Greek *sunizēsis,* "collapse," from *sunizein,* to collapse : *sun-,* together + *hizein,* to sit down (see **sed-¹** in Appendix*).]

syn·kar·y·on (sĭn-kăr′ē-ŏn′, -ē-ən) *n.* The nucleus of a fertilized egg immediately after the male and female nuclei have fused. [New Latin : SYN- + Greek *karuon,* nut (see **kar-¹** in Appendix*).] —**syn·kar′y·on′ic** (-ŏn′ĭk) *adj.*

syn·od (sĭn′əd) *n.* **1.** A council or assembly of churches or church officials; an ecclesiastical council. **2.** Any council or assembly. [Middle English, from Late Latin *synodus,* from Greek *sunodos,* meeting : *sun-,* together + *hodos,* road, way, journey (see **sed-²** in Appendix*).] —**syn′od·al** *adj.*

sy·nod·i·cal (sĭ-nŏd′ĭ-kəl) *adj.* Also **sy·nod·ic** (-nŏd′ĭk). **1.** Pertaining to or of the nature of a synod. **2.** Pertaining to the conjunction of celestial bodies, especially the interval between two successive conjunctions of a planet or the moon with the sun. —**sy·nod′i·cal·ly** *adv.*

sy·noe·cious (sĭ-nē′shəs) *adj.* Also **sy·ne·cious.** *Botany.* Having male and female organs in the same structure. [SYN- + (MON)OECIOUS.]

syn·o·nym (sĭn′ə-nĭm′) *n. Abbr.* **syn. 1.** A word having a meaning similar to that of another word in the same language. Compare **antonym. 2.** A word or expression accepted as a figurative or symbolic substitute for another word or expression. **3.** *Biology.* A taxonomic name of an organism that is equivalent to or has been superseded by another designation. [Middle English *sinonyme,* from Latin *synonymum,* from Greek *sunōnumon,* from *sunōnumos,* SYNONYMOUS.] —**syn′o·nym′ic, syn′o·nym′i·cal** *adj.* —**syn′o·nym′i·ty** *n.*

syn·on·y·mist (sĭ-nŏn′ə-mĭst) *n.* A person who studies or discriminates synonyms.

syn·on·y·mize (sĭ-nŏn′ə-mīz′) *tr.v.* **-mized, -mizing, -mizes.** To provide or analyze the synonyms of (a word).

syn·on·y·mous (sĭ-nŏn′ə-məs) *adj. Abbr.* **syn.** Expressing a similar meaning. Also "synonymatic." [Medieval Latin *synonymus,* from Greek *sunōnumos* : *sun-,* same + *onoma, onuma,* name (see **nomen-** in Appendix*).] —**syn·on′y·mous·ly** *adv.*

syn·on·y·my (sĭ-nŏn′ə-mē) *n., pl.* **-mies.** *Abbr.* **syn. 1.** The quality of being synonymous; equivalence of meaning. **2.** The study and classification of synonyms. **3.** A list, book, or system of synonyms. **4.** A chronological list or record of the scientific names that have been applied to a species and its subdivisions.

syn·op·sis (sĭ-nŏp′sĭs) *n., pl.* **-ses** (-sēz′). A brief statement or outline of a subject; an abstract. [Late Latin, from Greek *sunopsis,* a viewing all together, general view : *sun-,* together + *opsis,* view (see **okw-** in Appendix*).]

syn·op·size (sĭ-nŏp′sīz′) *tr.v.* **-sized, -sizing, -sizes.** To present or write a synopsis of. [Late Greek *sunopsizein,* from Greek *sunopsis,* SYNOPSIS.]

sy·nop·tic (sə-nŏp′tĭk) *adj.* Also **sy·nop·ti·cal** (-tĭ-kəl). **1.** Of or constituting a synopsis; presenting a summary. **2.** Presenting an account from the same point of view. **3.** *Often capital* **S.** Of or designating the first three Gospels of the New Testament, which correspond closely. —**sy·nop′ti·cal·ly** *adv.*

syn·os·to·sis (sĭn′ŏs-tō′sĭs) *n.* The fusion of two skeletal bones. [New Latin : SYN- + Greek *osteon,* bone (see **osth-** in Appendix*) + -OSIS.] —**syn′os·tot′ic** (-tŏt′ĭk) *adj.*

sy·no·vi·a (sə-nō′vē-ə) *n.* A clear, viscid lubricating fluid secreted by membranes in joint cavities, sheaths of tendons, and bursae. Also called "synovial fluid." [New Latin *synovia, sinovia* (coined by Paracelsus).] —**sy·no′vi·al** *adj.*

syn·tac·tics (sĭn-tăk′tĭks) *n.* Plural in form, used with a singular or plural verb. The branch of semiotics that deals with the formal properties of signs and symbols. [From syntactic, of syntax, from New Latin *syntacticus,* from Greek *suntaktikos,* putting together, from *suntassein,* to put together. See **syntax.**]

syn·tax (sĭn′tăks′) *n.* **1.** *Grammar.* **a.** The way in which words are put together to form phrases and sentences. **b.** The branch of grammar dealing with this. **2.** Systematic arrangement. [French *syntaxe,* from Late Latin *syntaxis,* from Greek *suntaxis,* from *suntassein,* to put together, arrange in order : *sun-,* together + *tassein,* to arrange (see **tāg-** in Appendix*).] —**syn·tac′tic** (-tăk′tĭk), **syn·tac′ti·cal** *adj.* —**syn·tac′ti·cal·ly** *adv.*

syn·the·sis (sĭn′thə-sĭs) *n., pl.* **-ses** (-sēz′). **1.** The combining of separate elements or substances to form a coherent whole. Compare **analysis. 2.** The whole so formed. **3.** *Chemistry.* Formation of a compound from its constituents. **4.** *Philosophy.* **a.** Reasoning from the general to the particular; logical deduction. **b.** The combination of thesis and antithesis in the dialectical process, producing a new and higher form of being. [Latin, from Greek, a putting together, from *suntithenai,* to put together : *sun-,* together + *tithenai,* to put, place (see **dhē-¹** in Appendix*).] —**syn′the·sist** *n.*

syn·the·size (sĭn′thə-sīz′) *v.* **-sized, -sizing, -sizes.** Also **syn·the·tize** (-tīz′). —*tr.* **1.** To combine so as to form a new, complex product. **2.** To produce by combining separate elements. —*intr.* To form a synthesis.

syn·the·siz·er (sĭn′thə-sī′zər) *n.* **1.** One that synthesizes. **2.** A machine having a simple keyboard and using solid-state circuitry to duplicate the sounds of musical instruments, often up to twelve instruments simultaneously.

syn·thet·ic (sĭn-thĕt′ĭk) *adj.* Also **syn·thet·i·cal** (-ĭ-kəl). **1.** Pertaining to, involving, or of the nature of a synthesis. **2.** *Chemistry.* Produced by synthesis; especially, not of natural origin; man-made. **3.** Not genuine; artificial; devised. **4.** *Linguistics.* Denoting a language such as Latin or Russian that uses inflectional affixes to express syntactic relationships. In this sense, compare **polysynthetic.** —See Synonyms at **artificial.** —*n.* A synthetic chemical compound or material. [Greek *sunthetikos,* skilled in putting together, component, from *sunthetos,* put together, compounded, composite, from *suntithenai,* to put together. See **synthesis.**] —**syn·thet′i·cal·ly** *adv.*

synthetic philosophy. Spencerism *(see).*

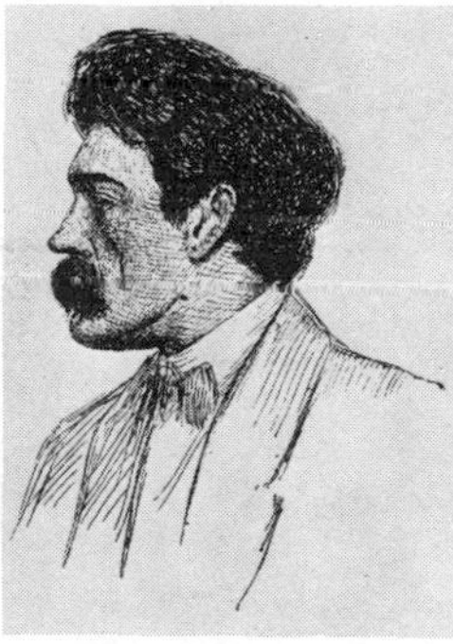
John Millington Synge

sy·pher (sī'fər) *tr.v.* **-phered, -phering, -phers.** To overlap and even (chamfered or beveled plank edges) so that they form a flush surface. [Variant of CIPHER.]

syph·i·lis (sĭf'ə-lĭs) *n.* A chronic infectious venereal disease caused by a spirochete, *Treponema pallidum*, transmitted by direct contact, usually in sexual intercourse, and progressing through three stages respectively characterized by local formation of chancres, ulcerous skin eruptions, and systemic infection leading to general paresis. [New Latin, after *Syphilis*, title character of a Latin poem (1530) by Girolamo Fracastoro, Veronese physician and poet and the supposed first victim of the disease.]

syph·i·lit·ic (sĭf'ə-lĭt'ĭk) *adj.* Of, pertaining to, or afflicted with syphilis. —*n.* A person afflicted with syphilis.

syph·i·loid (sĭf'ə-loid') *adj.* Characteristic of syphilis. [SYPHIL(IS) + -OID.]

syph·i·lol·o·gy (sĭf'ə-lŏl'ə-jē) *n.* The sum of knowledge concerning the origin, nature, course, complications, and treatment of syphilis. [SYPHIL(IS) + -LOGY.] —**syph'i·lol'o·gist** *n.*

syph·i·lo·ma (sĭf'ə-lō'mə) *n., pl.* **-mas** or **-mata** (-mə-tə). A lesion formed in an advanced stage of syphilis; a gumma. [New Latin : SYPHIL(IS) + -OMA.] —**syph'i·lom'a·tous** *adj.*

sy·phon. Variant of **siphon.**

Syr. Syria; Syriac; Syrian.

Syr·a·cuse (sîr'ə-kyōōz', -kyōōs'). **1.** A city of Italy on the southeastern coast of Sicily; in ancient times, the leading Greek city of Sicily. Population, 189,000. **2.** A city and manufacturing center of central New York State. Population, 216,000. [Greek *Surakousai*, roughly "the parts near *Surakō*" (the name of a marsh). See **suro-** in Appendix.*] —**Syr'a·cu'san** *adj. & n.*

Syr Dar·ya (sîr' där'yə). A river of the Soviet Union in Asia, rising in the Tien Shan and flowing 1,330 miles generally northwest to the Aral Sea.

Syr·ette (sĭ-rĕt') *n.* A trademark for a collapsible tube having an attached hypodermic needle containing a single dose of medicine. [SYR(INGE) + -ETTE.]

Syr·i·a (sîr'ē-ə). *Arabic* **El Sham** (ĕl shäm'). *Abbr.* **Syr. 1.** A country of southwestern Asia, occupying about 72,000 square miles on the eastern Mediterranean coast. Population, 5,067,000. Capital, Damascus. **2.** An ancient country of western Asia that included present-day Syria, Lebanon, and the Palestine region.

Syr·i·ac (sîr'ē-ăk') *n. Abbr.* **Syr.** An ancient Aramaic language spoken in Syria from the 3rd to the 13th century A.D. and surviving as the liturgical language of several eastern Christian churches.

Syr·i·an (sîr'ē-ən) *adj. Abbr.* **Syr.** Of or pertaining to Syria, its culture, or inhabitants. —*n.* **1.** A native or inhabitant of Syria. **2.** A member of a Christian church using the Syriac language.

Syrian Desert. An arid region in the northern Arabian Peninsula including parts of Syria, Iraq, Saudi Arabia, and Jordan.

sy·rin·ga (sə-rĭng'gə) *n.* A shrub, the **mock orange** *(see).* [New Latin *Syringa*, "pipe" (from the use of its hollow stems to make pipes), from Greek *surinx*, SYRINX.]

syr·inge (sə-rĭnj', sĭr'ĭnj) *n.* **1.** A medical instrument used to inject fluids into the body or draw them from it. **2.** A **hypodermic syringe** *(see).* [Middle English *syring*, from Medieval Latin *syringa*, from Greek *surinx* (stem *suring-*), SYRINX.]

sy·rin·go·my·e·li·a (sə-rĭng'gō-mī-ē'lē-ə) *n.* A chronic disease of the spinal cord characterized by the presence of liquid-filled cavities and leading to spasticity and sensory disturbances. [New Latin : Greek *surinx*, pipe, cavity (see **syrinx**) + *muelos*, marrow, from *mus*, mouse, muscle (see **mū-¹** in Appendix.*).]

syr·inx (sîr'ĭngks) *n., pl.* **syringes** (sîr'ĭn-gēz') or **syrinxes. 1.** A **panpipe** *(see).* **2.** *Zoology.* The vocal organ of a bird, consisting of thin, vibrating muscles at or close to the division of the trachea. [Latin, from Greek *surinx†*, shepherd's pipe, panpipe, pipe.] —**sy·rin'ge·al** *adj.*

Sy·ros (sī'rŏs; *Greek* sē'rôs'). Also **Si·ros.** A Greek Aegean island of the Cyclades group, 33 square miles in area.

syr·phid (sûr'fĭd) *n.* Any of numerous flies of the family Syrphidae, many of which have a form or coloration mimicking that of bees or wasps. —*adj.* Of or belonging to the Syrphidae. [New Latin *Syrphidae*, from Greek *surphos†*, gnat.]

Syr·tis Major. The ancient name for the Gulf of **Sidra.** [From Greek *Surtis.*]

Syr·tis Minor. The ancient name for the Gulf of **Gabès.**

syr·up (sûr'əp, sĭr'-) *n.* Also **sir·up. 1.** A thick, sweet, sticky liquid, consisting of a sugar base, natural or artificial flavorings, and water. **2.** The juice of a fruit or plant boiled with sugar until thick and sticky. [Middle English *sirop*, from Old French, from Medieval Latin *siropus*, from Arabic *sharāb*, beverage, syrup, from *shariba*, to drink.] —**syr'up·y** *adj.*

sys·sar·co·sis (sĭs'är-kō'sĭs) *n.* The union of bones, as the

hyoid bone and lower jaw, by muscle. [New Latin, from Greek *sussarkōsis*, a being overgrown with flesh, from *sussarkousthai*, to be also overgrown with flesh : *sun-*, likewise + *sarkousthai*, passive of *sarkoun*, to grow fleshy, from *sarx*, flesh (see **twerk-** in Appendix.*).]

sys·tal·tic (sĭs-stôl'tĭk, -stăl'tĭk) *adj.* Alternately contracting and expanding, as the heart; pulsating. [Late Latin *systalticus*, from Greek *sustaltikos*, from *sustellein*, to draw together, contract : *sun-*, together + *stellein*, to send, bind, repress, make compact (see **stel-³** in Appendix.*).]

sys·tem (sĭs'təm) *n.* **1.** A group of interacting, interrelated, or interdependent elements forming or regarded as forming a collective entity. **2.** A functionally related group of elements, as: **a.** The human body regarded as a functional physiological unit. **b.** A group of physiologically complementary organs or parts. **c.** A group of interacting mechanical or electrical components. **d.** A network of structures and channels, as for communications, travel, or distribution. **3.** A structurally or anatomically related group of elements or parts. **4.** A set of interrelated ideas, principles, rules, procedures, laws, or the like. **5.** A social, economic, or political organizational form. **6.** A naturally occurring group of objects or phenomena. **7.** A set of objects or phenomena grouped together for classification or analysis. **8.** The state or condition of harmonious, orderly interaction. —See Synonyms at **method.** [Late Latin *systēma*, from Greek *sustēma*, a composite whole, from *sunistanai*, to bring together, combine : *sun-*, together + *histanai*, to cause to stand (see **stā-** in Appendix.*).]

sys·tem·at·ic (sĭs'tə-măt'ĭk) *adj.* Also **sys·tem·at·i·cal** (-ĭ-kəl). **1.** Of, characterized by, based upon, or constituting a system. **2.** Carried on in a step-by-step procedure. **3.** Characterized by purposeful regularity; methodical. **4.** Of or pertaining to classification or taxonomy. —See Synonyms at **orderly.** —**sys'tem·at'i·cal·ly** *adv.*

sys·tem·at·ics (sĭs'tə-măt'ĭks) *n.* Plural in form, used with a singular verb. *Biology.* The classification of organisms in an ordered system designed to indicate natural relationships.

sys·tem·a·tism (sĭs'tə-mə-tĭz'əm, sĭ-stĕm'ə-) *n.* **1.** The practice of classifying or systematizing. **2.** Adherence to a system.

sys·tem·a·tist (sĭs'tə-mə-tĭst, sĭ-stĕm'ə-) *n.* **1.** A person who adheres to or formulates a system. **2.** A taxonomist.

sys·tem·a·tize (sĭs'tə-mə-tīz') *tr.v.* **-tized, -tizing, -tizes.** Also **sys·tem·ize** (-tə-mīz'). To formulate into or reduce to a system: "*The aim of science is surely to amass and systematize knowledge*" (V. Gordon Childe). —**sys'tem·a·ti·za'tion** *n.* —**sys'tem·a·tiz'er** *n.*

sys·tem·ic (sĭ-stĕm'ĭk) *adj.* **1.** Of or pertaining to a system or systems. **2.** Of, pertaining to, or affecting the entire body. —**sys·tem'i·cal·ly** *adv.*

sys·to·le (sĭs'tə-lē) *n.* The rhythmic contraction of the heart, especially of the ventricles, by which blood is driven through the aorta and pulmonary artery after each dilation or diastole. [Greek *sustolē*, contraction, from *sustellein*, to contract. See **systaltic.**] —**sys·tol'ic** (-tŏl'ĭk) *adj.*

syz·y·gy (sĭz'ə-jē) *n., pl.* **-gies. 1.** *Astronomy.* **a.** Either of two points in the orbit of a celestial body where the body is in opposition to or in conjunction with the sun. **b.** Either of two points in the orbit of the moon when the moon lies in a straight line with the sun and the earth. **c.** The configuration of the sun, the moon, and the earth lying in a straight line. **2.** In classical prosody, the combining of two feet into a single metrical unit. [Late Latin *syzygia*, from Greek *suzugia*, union, coupling, yoke of animals, from *suzugos*, yoked, paired : *sun-*, together + *zugon*, a yoke (see **yeug-** in Appendix.*).] —**sy·zyg'i·al** (sĭ-zĭj'əl) *adj.*

Szat·már·Né·me·ti. The Hungarian name for **Satu-Mare.**

Szcze·cin (shchĕ'tsēn). Formerly **Stet·tin** (shtĕ-tēn'). A city and seaport of Poland, in the northwest near the mouth of the Oder. Population, 303,000.

Sze·chwan (sŭ'chwän'). A province of China, occupying 219,691 square miles in the southwest. Population, 72,160,000. Capital, Chengtu.

Sze·ged (sĕ'gĕd). A city of Hungary in the south on the Yugoslav border. Population, 105,000.

Szent-Györ·gyi von Nagy·ra·polt (sĕnt'dyœr'dy' fən nôd'y'rô'pŏlt), **Albert.** Born 1893. Hungarian-born American biochemist; isolated vitamin C.

Szi·lard (sĕ'lärd'), **Leo.** 1898-1964. Hungarian-born American physicist.

Szold (zōld), **Henrietta.** 1860-1945. American Jewish Zionist leader; founder of Hadassah.

Szom·bat·hely (sŏm'bŏt-hā'). *German* **Stein·am·an·ger** (shtīn'äm-äng'ər). A city of Hungary, in the west near the Austrian border. Population, 57,000.

Syria

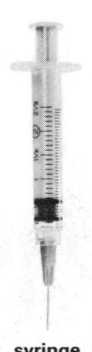

syringe

ă pat/ā pay/âr care/ä father/b bib/ch church/d deed/ĕ pet/ē be/f fife/g gag/h hat/hw which/ĭ pit/ī pie/îr pier/j judge/k kick/l lid, needle/m mum/n no, sudden/ng thing/ŏ pot/ō toe/ô paw, for/oi noise/ou out/ŏŏ took/ōō boot/p pop/r roar/s sauce/sh ship, dish/

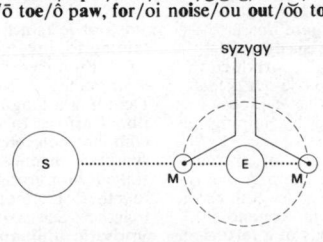

syzygy

Tt

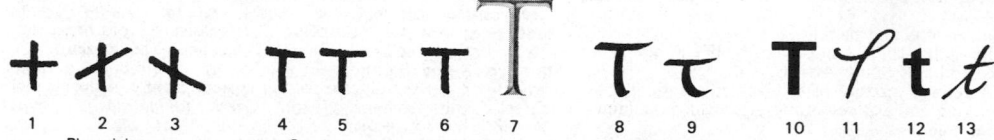

| 1 | 2 | 3 | 4 | 5 | 6 | 7 | 8 | 9 | 10 | 11 | 12 | 13 |
| Phoenician | | | Greek | | Roman | | Medieval | | | Modern | | |

Around 1000 B.C. *the Phoenicians and other Semites of Syria and Palestine began to use a graphic sign in three irregular and interchangeable forms (1,2,3). They gave it the name* tāw, *meaning "mark," and used it for the consonant* t. *After 900* B.C. *the Greeks borrowed the sign from the Phoenicians, altering its shape slightly to give it the characteristic* T *form (4,5). They also changed its name to tau. The Greek forms passed unchanged via Etruscan to the Roman alphabet (6). The Roman Monumental Capital (7) is the prototype of our modern capital, printed (10) and written (11). The written Roman form (6) developed into the late Roman and medieval Uncial (8) and Cursive (9), which are the bases of our modern small letter, printed (12) and written (13).*

t, T (tē) *n., pl.* **t's** or *rare* **ts, T's** or **Ts. 1.** The 20th letter of the modern English alphabet. See **alphabet. 2.** Any of the speech sounds represented by this letter. **3.** Anything shaped like the letter **T.** —**to a T.** Perfectly; precisely: *She fits the role to a T.*
t, T, t., T. *Note:* As an abbreviation or symbol, *t* may be a small or a capital letter, with or without a period. Established forms or those generally preferred precede the definition. When no form is given, all four forms are in general use in that sense. **1. t.** in the time of (Latin *tempore*). **2. T** *Physics.* surface tension. **3. T.** tablespoon; tablespoonful. **4. t.** *Commerce.* tare. **5. t.** teaspoon; teaspoonful. **6. T** temperature. **7. t.** tempo. **8. t., T.** *Music.* tenor. **9. t.** *Grammar.* tense. **10. T** *Physics.* tera-. **11. t.** terminal. **12. t., T.** territory. **13. T** tesla. **14. T.** Testament. **15. t., T.** time. **16. T** *Mathematics.* time reversal. **17. t** ton. **18. t., T.** town; township. **19. t.** transit. **20. t.** *Grammar.* transitive. **21. t** troy (system of weights). **22. T.** Tuesday (unofficial). **23.** The 20th in a series; 19th when *J* is omitted.
Ta The symbol for the element tantalum.
Ta·al¹ (tä-äl'). **1.** An island occupying about 15 square miles in Lake Taal, on Luzon, Republic of the Philippines. **2.** An active volcano about 1,000 feet high in the center of this island.
Taal² (täl) *n. Afrikaans (see).* [Dutch *taal,* language, speech, from Middle Dutch *tāle.* See **del-²** in Appendix.*]
Ta·al, Lake (tä-äl'). The second-largest inland lake (94 square miles) of the Republic of the Philippines, on Luzon Island.
tab (tăb) *n.* **1.** A projection, flap, or short strip attached to an object to facilitate opening, handling, or identification. **2.** A small, usually decorative, flap or tongue on a garment. **3.** A small auxiliary control surface attached to a larger one to help stabilize an airplane. **4.** A bill or a check, as for a meal in a restaurant. **5.** A tabulator, as on a typewriter. —**keep tabs** (or **a tab) on.** To account for; to watch. —*tr.v.* **tabbed, tabbing, tabs.** To supply with a tab or tabs. [Origin unknown.]
tab. table.
ta·ba·nid (tə-bā'nĭd, -băn'ĭd) *n.* Any of various blood-sucking flies of the family Tabanidae, which includes the horseflies. [New Latin *Tabanidae* : Latin *tabānus†,* horsefly + -IDAE.] —**ta·ba'nid** *adj.*
tab·ard (tăb'ərd) *n.* **1.** A short, heavy cape of coarse cloth, formerly worn outdoors. **2. a.** A tunic or capelike garment worn by a knight over his armor and emblazoned with his coat of arms. **b.** A similar garment worn by a herald and bearing his lord's coat of arms. **3.** An embroidered pennant attached to a trumpet. [Middle English, from Old French *tabart†.*]
tab·a·ret (tăb'ə-rĕt) *n.* A strong upholstery fabric having alternating stripes of satin and moiré. [Originally a trademark, probably from TABBY.]
Ta·bas·co¹ (tə-băs'kō) *n.* A trademark for a pungent sauce made from the fruit of a pepper, *Capsicum frutescens.*
Ta·bas·co² (tə-băs'kō; *Spanish* tä-väs'kō). A state of Mexico,

occupying 9,783 square miles in the southeast. Population, 546,000. Capital, Villahermosa.
tab·by (tăb'ē) *n., pl.* **-bies.** Also **tab·bis** (tăb'ĭs) (for sense 1). **1.** A rich watered silk. **2.** A plain weave fabric. **3. a.** A striped or brindled domestic cat. **b.** A female domestic cat. **4.** An old maid. **5.** A prying woman; a gossip. —*adj.* **1.** Striped or brindled. Said of domestic cats. **2.** Made of or resembling watered silk. [French *tabis,* from Old French *atabis,* from Arabic *'attābī,* originally manufactured at *Al-'attābīya,* a suburb of Baghdad, after Prince *Attāb,·* who resided in this area.]
tab·er·na·cle (tăb'ər-năk'əl) *n.* **1.** *Often capital* T. **a.** The portable sanctuary in which the Jews carried the Ark of the Covenant through the desert. **b.** The Jewish temple. **2.** *Often capital* T. A case or box on a church altar containing the consecrated host and wine of the Eucharist. **3.** A place of worship distinguished from a church; specifically, the Mormon temple. **4.** A niche for a statue or relic. **5.** *Nautical.* A boxlike support in which the heel of a mast is stepped. —*v.* **tabernacled, -cling, -cles.** —*tr.* To enshrine. —*intr.* To dwell temporarily. [Middle English, from Old French, from Late Latin *tabernaculum,* from Latin, tent, diminutive of *taberna,* hut, perhaps from Etruscan. See also **tavern.**] —**tab'er·nac'u·lar** (-năk'yə-lər) *adj.*
ta·bes (tā'bēz') *n., pl.* **tabes. 1.** Progressive bodily wasting or emaciation. **2.** Tabes dorsalis. [Latin *tābēs,* "a melting." See **tā-** in Appendix.*]
tabes dor·sa·lis (dôr-sā'lĭs, -săl'ĭs, -sä'lĭs). A syphilitic disease resulting from a hardening of the dorsal columns of the spinal cord and characterized by shooting pains, unsteadiness, and loss of the ability to coordinate voluntary movements. Also called "locomotor ataxia."
tab·la (tŭb'lə) *n.* A small hand drum of India. [Hindi, from Arabic *ṭabla,* drum.]
tab·la·ture (tăb'lə-chŏŏr') *n.* **1.** *Music.* An obsolete system of notation using letters and symbols to indicate playing directions rather than tones. **2.** An engraved tablet or surface. [French, from Medieval Latin *tabulātūra,* from *tabulātus,* tablet, from Latin, boarded, floored, from *tabula,* board. See **table.**]
ta·ble (tā'bəl) *n. Abbr.* **tab. 1.** An article of furniture supported by one or more vertical legs and having a flat horizontal surface on which objects can be placed. **2.** The objects laid out for a meal upon a table. **3.** The food and drink served at meals; fare. **4.** The company of people assembled around a table, as for a meal. **5.** *Often plural.* A gaming table, as for faro, roulette, or dice. **6. a.** Either of the leaves of a backgammon board. **b.** *Plural. Obsolete.* The game of backgammon. **7.** A plateau or tableland. **8. a.** A flat facet cut across the top of a precious stone. **b.** A stone cut in this fashion. **9.** *Music.* The front part of a stringed instrument, the **belly** *(see).* **10.** *Architecture.* **a.** A raised or sunken rectangular panel on a wall. **b.** A raised horizontal surface or continuous band on an exterior wall; stringcourse. **11.** *Geology.* A horizontal rock stratum. **12.** In palmistry, a part of the palm framed by four lines. **13.** An orderly written, typed, or printed display of data, especially a rectangular array exhibiting one or more characteristics of designated entities or categories. **14.** An abbreviated list, as of contents; a synopsis. **15.** A slab or tablet, as of stone, bearing an inscription or device. **16.** *Plural.* A system of laws or decrees; a code: *the tables of Moses.* —**on the table.** Postponed or put aside for consideration at a later date. —**turn the tables.** To reverse a situation and gain the upper hand. —*tr.v.* **tabled, -bling, -bles. 1.** To put or place on a table. **2.** To postpone consideration of (a piece of legislation, for example); shelve. **3.** *Rare.* To enter in

tabard
Woodcut of an imperial German herald of the first half of the 16th century

tabla

a list or table; tabulate. [Middle English, tablet, board, table, from Old French, from Latin *tabula*†, board, list.]

tab·leau (tăb′lō′, tă-blō′) *n., pl.* **tableaux** (tăb′lōz′, tă-blōz′) or **-leaus. 1.** A vivid or graphic description. **2.** A striking incidental scene, as of a picturesque group of people. **3.** An interlude during a scene when all the actors on stage freeze in position and then resume action as before. **4.** A tableau vivant. [French, from Old French *tablel*, diminutive of *table*, TABLE.]

ta·bleau vi·vant (tȧ-blō′ vē-väN′) *pl.* **tableaux vivants** (tȧ-blō′ vē-väN′). A scene presented on stage by costumed actors who remain silent and motionless as if in a picture. [French, "living picture."]

Table Bay. An inlet of the Atlantic in southwestern Cape of Good Hope Province, Republic of South Africa.

ta·ble·cloth (tā′bəl-klôth′, -klŏth′) *n., pl.* **-cloths** (-klôths′, -klô*thz*′, -klŏths′, -klŏ*thz*′). A cloth to cover a table, especially during a meal.

ta·ble d'hôte (tä′bəl dōt′) *pl.* **tables d'hôte** (tä′bəl dōt′). **1.** A communal table for all guests at a hotel or restaurant. **2.** A full-course meal served at a fixed price in a restaurant or hotel. In this sense, also called "prix fixe." [French, "table of (the) host."]

ta·ble-hop (tā′bəl-hŏp′) *intr.v.* **-hopped, -hopping, -hops.** To move around from table to table, greeting friends, as in a restaurant or nightclub. —**ta′ble-hop′per** *n.*

ta·ble·land (tā′bəl-lănd′) *n.* A flat, elevated region; plateau; mesa.

table linen. Tablecloths and napkins.

Table Mountain. A flat-topped mountain, 3,549 feet high, near Cape Town, Republic of South Africa.

table salt. 1. A refined mixture of salts, chiefly sodium chloride, used in cooking and as a seasoning. Also called "common salt." **2. Sodium chloride** *(see).*

ta·ble·spoon (tā′bəl-spo͞on′) *n.* **1.** A large spoon used for eating soups and serving food. **2.** *Abbr.* **T., tbs., tbsp.** A household cooking measure, three teaspoons or four liquid drams.

ta·ble·spoon·ful (tā′bəl-spo͞on′fo͝ol′) *n., pl.* **-fuls.** *Abbr.* **T., tbs., tbsp.** The amount a tablespoon will hold.

tab·let (tăb′lĭt) *n.* **1.** A slab or plaque, as of stone or ivory, with a surface intended for or bearing an inscription. **2.** A thin sheet or leaf, as of clay or ivory, used as a writing surface. **3.** A set of such leaves fastened together, as in a book. **4.** A pad of writing paper glued together along one edge. **5.** A small, flat cake of a prepared substance, such as soap. **6.** A small flat pellet of medication to be taken orally. —*tr.v.* **tableted, -leting, -lets. 1.** To inscribe on a tablet. **2.** To form into a tablet. [Middle English *tablette*, from Old French *tablete*, diminutive of *table*, TABLE.]

table talk. Casual mealtime conversation.

table tennis. A game similar to lawn tennis, played on a table with wooden paddles and a small celluloid ball. See **Ping-Pong.**

ta·ble·ware (tā′bəl-wâr′) *n.* The dishes, glassware, and silverware used in setting a table for a meal.

table wine. An unfortified wine to be served with a meal.

tab·loid (tăb′loid′) *n.* A newspaper of small format giving the news in condensed form, usually with illustrated, often sensational material. [From *Tabloid*, trademark for a tablet of condensed medicine : TABL(ET) + -OID.]

ta·boo (tə-bo͞o′, tă-) *n., pl.* **-boos.** Also **ta·bu. 1.** A prohibition excluding something from use, approach, or mention because of its sacred and inviolable nature. **2.** An object, word, or act protected by such a prohibition. **3.** A ban or inhibition attached to something by social custom or emotional aversion. **4.** Belief in or conformity to religious or social prohibitions. **5.** A proscription devised and observed by any group for its own protection. —*adj.* Excluded or forbidden from use, approach, or mention. —*tr.v.* **tabooed, -booing, -boos.** Also **ta·bu, -bued, -buing, -bus.** To exclude from use, approach, or mention; place under taboo. [Tongan *tabu*, perhaps "exceedingly marked," marked as sacred : *ta*, mark + *bu*, exceedingly.]

ta·bor (tā′bər) *n.* Also **ta·bour.** A small drum played by a fifer to accompany his fife. [Middle English *tabo(u)r*, from Old French, perhaps from Persian *tabīr*, drum. See also **tambour.**]

Ta·bor (tā′bər), **Horace Austin Warner.** 1830–1899. American silver magnate and pioneer in Colorado.

Ta·bor, Mount (tā′bər). A mountain, 1,929 feet high, in northern Israel near Nazareth.

tab·o·ret (tăb′ə-rĕt′, -rā′) *n.* Also **tab·ou·ret. 1.** A low stool without a back or arms. **2.** A low stand or cabinet. **3.** An embroidery frame. [French *tabouret*, diminutive of Old French *tabour*, TABOR.]

Ta·briz (tə-brēz′). Also **Te·briz.** Ancient name **Tau·ris** (tôr′ĭs). The capital of Eastern Azerbaijan Province, in northwestern Iran. Population, 388,000.

tab·u·lar (tăb′yə-lər) *adj.* **1.** Having a plane surface; flat. **2.** Organized as a table or list. **3.** Calculated by means of a table. [Latin *tabulāris*, from *tabula*, TABLE.] —**tab′u·lar·ly** *adv.*

tab·u·la ra·sa (tăb′yə-lə rä′sə, rä′zə). **1.** A need or opportunity to start from the beginning; a clean slate. **2.** The mind before it receives the impressions gained from experience; especially, in the philosophy of Locke, the unformed, featureless mind. [Latin, "erased tablet."]

tab·u·lar·ize (tăb′yə-lə-rīz′) *tr.v.* **-ized, -izing, -izes.** To put into tabular form; tabulate. —**tab′u·lar·i·za′tion** *n.*

tab·u·late (tăb′yə-lāt′) *tr.v.* **-lated, -lating, -lates. 1.** To arrange in tabular form; condense and list. **2.** To cut or form with a plane surface. —*adj.* (tăb′yə-lĭt, -lāt′). Having a plane surface. [From Latin *tabula*, TABLE.] —**tab′u·la′tion** *n.*

tab·u·la·tor (tăb′yə-lā′tər) *n.* **1.** A person who makes tabulations. **2.** A machine into which data can be fed for tabulation. **3.** A mechanism on a typewriter for setting automatic stops or margins for columns.

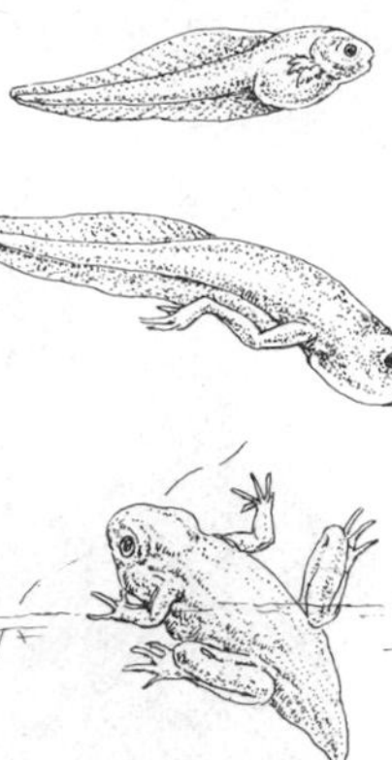

tadpole
Three stages of growth

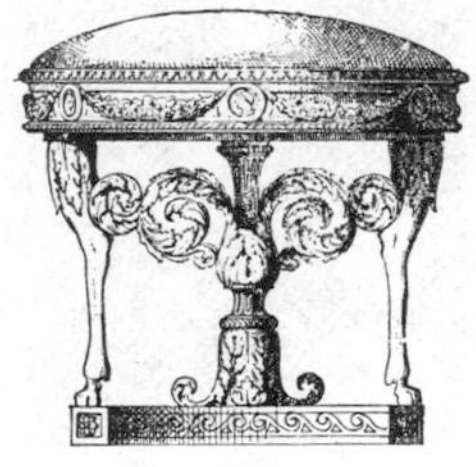

taboret
Carved gilt taboret of Empire style

tac·a·ma·hac (tăk′ə-mə-hăk′) *n.* **1.** Any of several aromatic resinous substances used in ointments and incenses. **2.** The **balsam poplar** *(see).* [Spanish *tacamahaca, tacamaca*, from Nahuatl *tecamaca.*]

ta·cet (tās′ĭt, tā′sĭt, tä′kĕt) *v. Music.* Be silent. Used only in the imperative as a direction. [Latin, it is silent, from *tacēre*, to be silent. See **tak-**[1] in Appendix.*]

tache (tăch) *n. Archaic.* A clasp or buckle. [Middle English, from Old French, nail, fastening, from Germanic. See **dek-**[2] in Appendix.*]

tach·i·na fly (tăk′ə-nə). Any of several bristly, usually grayish flies of the family Tachinidae, the larvae of which live as parasites within the bodies of other insects. [New Latin *Tachina*, type genus, from Greek *takhinos*, swift, from *takhos*, speed, akin to *takhus*, swift. See **tachy-**.]

ta·chis·to·scope (tə-kĭs′tə-skōp′) *n.* An apparatus that projects transient images onto a screen to test visual perception. [Greek *takhistos*, most swift, from *takhus*, swift (see **tachy-**) + -SCOPE.]

ta·chom·e·ter (tə-kŏm′ə-tər) *n.* An instrument used to determine speed, especially the rotational speed of a shaft. [Greek *takhos*, speed, akin to *takhus*, swift (see **tachy-**) + -METER.] —**tach′o·met′ric** (tăk′ə-mĕt′rĭk) *adj.* —**ta·chom′e·try** *n.*

tachy-. Indicates swift or accelerated; for example, **tachymeter, tachycardia.** [From Greek *takhus*†, swift.]

tach·y·car·di·a (tăk′ĭ-kär′dē-ə) *n.* Excessively rapid heartbeat. [New Latin : TACHY- + Greek *kardia*, heart (see **cardia**).]

ta·chyg·ra·phy (tă-kĭg′rə-fē) *n.* The art or practice of rapid writing or shorthand; especially, the stenography of the ancient Greeks and Romans. [From Greek *takhugraphos*, "swift writer" : TACHY- + -GRAPH.]

tach·y·lyte (tăk′ə-līt′) *n.* Also **tach·y·lite.** A black, glassy basaltic rock. [German *Tachylyt*, "that which decomposes quickly (in acids)" : TACHY- + Greek *lutos*, soluble, from *luein*, to dissolve (see **leu-**[1] in Appendix*).] —**tach′y·lyt′ic** (-lĭt′ĭk) *adj.*

ta·chym·e·ter (tă-kĭm′ə-tər) *n.* A surveying instrument used for the rapid measurement of distances, elevations, and bearings. [TACHY- + -METER.] —**ta·chym′e·try** (-ə-trē) *n.*

tac·it (tăs′ĭt) *adj.* **1.** Not spoken: *Her glance was a tacit invitation.* **2.** Implied by or inferred from actions or statements: *The argument required a tacit assumption.* **3.** *Archaic.* Silent; not speaking. [Latin *tacitus*, silent, from the past participle of *tacēre*, to be silent. See **tak-**[1] in Appendix.*] —**tac′it·ly** *adv.* —**tac′it·ness** *n.*

tac·i·turn (tăs′ə-tərn) *adj.* Habitually untalkative; laconic; uncommunicative. See Synonyms at **silent.** [French *taciturne*, from Latin *taciturnus*, from *tacitus*, silent, TACIT.] —**tac′i·tur′ni·ty** (-tûr′nə-tē) *n.* —**tac′i·turn·ly** *adv.*

Tac·i·tus (tăs′ə-təs), **Publius Cornelius.** Roman historian and orator of the late first and early second centuries A.D.

tack[1] (tăk) *n.* **1.** A short, light nail with a sharp point and a flat head. **2.** *Nautical.* **a.** A rope for holding down the weather clew of a course. **b.** A rope for hauling the outer lower corner of a studdingsail to the boom. **c.** The part of a sail to which a tack is fastened, as the weather clew of a course. **d.** The lower forward corner of a fore-and-aft sail. **3.** *Nautical.* **a.** The position of a vessel relative to the trim of its sails. **b.** The act of changing from one tack to another. **c.** The distance or leg sailed between changes of tack. **4. a.** A course of action meant to minimize opposition to the attainment of a goal. **b.** An approach, especially one of a series of changing approaches. **5.** A large, loose stitch made as a temporary binding or as a mark. **6.** Stickiness, as of a newly painted surface. —*v.* **tacked, tacking, tacks.** —*tr.* **1.** To fasten or attach with or as if with a tack. **2.** To fasten or mark (cloth or a seam, for example) with a loose basting stitch. **3.** To put together loosely and arbitrarily: *He tacked some stories together into a novel.* **4.** To append; add. Used with *on.* **5.** *Nautical.* To bring (a vessel) into the wind in order to change tack. —*intr.* **1.** *Nautical.* **a.** To change the tack of a vessel. **b.** To change tack. Used of a vessel. **2.** To change one's course of action. [Middle English *tak(ke)*, probably from Old North French *taque*, variant of Old French *tache*, nail, fastening, from Germanic. See **dek-**[2] in Appendix.*]

tack[2] (tăk) *n.* Food; especially, coarse foodstuffs. [Origin unknown.]

tack hammer. A light hammer used to drive tacks.

tack·le (tăk′əl; *also* tā′kəl *for sense 2*) *n.* **1.** The equipment used in a sport or occupation, especially in fishing; gear. **2.** *Nautical.* **a.** A system of ropes and blocks for raising and lowering weights of rigging and pulleys for applying tension. **b.** A rope and its pulley. **3.** *Football.* **a.** One of two linemen on either side of the center and between the guard and the end. **b.** The position of this player. **c.** The act of stopping another player by seizing and bringing him down. —*v.* **tackled, -ling, -les.** —*tr.* **1.** To take on and wrestle with (an opponent or problem, for example) in order to overcome permanently; come to grips with. **2.** *Football.* To seize and throw one's weight against (an opponent gaining yardage) in order to bring him to the ground and stop him. **3.** To harness (a horse). —*intr. Football.* To tackle an opponent. [Middle English *takel*, probably from Middle Low German *takel*, from *taken*, to seize. See **tak-**[2] in Appendix.*] —**tack′ler** *n.*

tack·ling (tăk′lĭng) *n. Rare.* Gear; tackle.

tack·y[1] (tăk′ē) *adj.* **-ier, -iest.** Slightly adhesive or gummy to the touch; sticky. [From TACK (to attach).] —**tack′i·ness** *n.*

tack·y[2] (tăk′ē) *adj.* **-ier, -iest.** *Informal.* **1.** Marked by neglect and disrepair; run-down; shabby. **2.** Lacking style; dowdy.

[From dialectal *tacky*†, an inferior horse.] —**tack'i·ness** *n.*
ta·co (tä'kō) *n., pl.* **-cos.** A tortilla folded around a filling, as of ground meat or cheese. [Mexican Spanish, from Spanish, wad, roll, plug, probably from Germanic. See **dek-²** in Appendix.*]
Ta·co·ma (tə-kō'mə). A city of Washington, a seaport on Puget Sound, 25 miles south of Seattle. Population, 152,000.
Ta·co·ma, Mount. The former name for Mount **Rainier.**
tac·o·nite (tăk'ə-nīt') *n.* A fine-grained sedimentary rock of magnetite, hematite, and quartz, mined as a low-grade iron ore. [Found in the *Taconic* Mountains in New England.]
tact (tăkt) *n.* **1.** The ability to appreciate the delicacy of a situation and to do or say the kindest or most fitting thing; diplomacy. **2.** *Archaic.* The sense of touch. [French, from Latin *tactus,* sense of touch, from the past participle of *tangere,* to touch. See **tag-** in Appendix.*]
Synonyms: *tact, address, diplomacy, savoir-faire, finesse, subtlety.* These nouns denote personal qualities conducive to skill in dealing with others. *Tact* involves sensitivity to what is appropriate at any given time in such relationships, together with the ability to speak or act without giving offense. More pointedly, *address* and *diplomacy* imply special talent for approaching and handling such situations adroitly and without offending. *Savoir-faire* involves saying or doing the right or graceful thing, either instinctively or, more often, as a result of social experience. *Finesse* implies artful management of difficult affairs and may suggest cunning or the use of stratagems. *Subtlety* is not limited in meaning to the context of these terms. In this comparison it is in contrast to what is obvious or direct and may imply mental acuteness or ingenuity, a tendency to indirection, or even craftiness.
tact·ful (tăkt'fəl) *adj.* Possessing or showing tact; considerate; discreet. —**tact'ful·ly** *adv.* —**tact'ful·ness** *n.*
tac·tic (tăk'tĭk) *n.* An expedient for achieving a goal; a maneuver. —*adj.* Variant of **tactical.**
tac·ti·cal (tăk'tĭ-kəl) *adj.* Also **tac·tic** (-tĭk). **1.** Of or pertaining to tactics. **2.** Characterized by adroitness in maneuvering.
tac·ti·cian (tăk'tĭsh'ən) *n.* **1.** A person skilled in the planning and execution of military tactics. **2.** A clever maneuverer.
tac·tics (tăk'tĭks) *n.* Plural in form, used with a singular verb. The technique or science of securing the objectives designated by strategy; specifically, the art of deploying and directing troops, ships, and aircraft in coefficient maneuvers against the enemy. Compare **strategy.** [New Latin *tactica,* from Greek *(ta) taktika,* "(the) matters of arrangement," from the neuter plural of *taktikos,* of order or arrangement, of tactics, from *taktos,* arranged, in order, from *tassein, tattein,* to arrange (in battle formation). See **tag-** in Appendix.*]
tac·tile (tăk'təl, -tīl') *adj.* **1.** Perceptible to the sense of touch; tangible. **2.** Used for feeling: *a tactile organ.* **3.** Of, pertaining to, or proceeding from the sense of touch: *a tactile reflex.* [Latin *tactilis,* from *tactus,* sense of touch. See **tact.**] —**tac·til'i·ty** (-tĭl'ə-tē) *n.*
tac·tion (tăk'shən) *n.* The act of touching; contact. [Latin *tactiō,* from *tangere* (past participle *tactus*), to touch. See **tact.**]
tact·less (tăkt'lĭs) *adj.* Lacking in delicacy; bluntly inconsiderate. —**tact'less·ly** *adv.* —**tact'less·ness** *n.*
tac·tu·al (tăk'chōō-əl) *adj.* Of, producing, derived from, or pertaining to the sense of touch; tactile. [From Latin *tactus,* sense of touch. See **tact.**] —**tac'tu·al·ly** *adv.*
Ta·cu·ba·ya (tä'kōō-vä'yä). A residential suburb and southwestern section of Mexico City, site of the national observatory.
tad (tăd) *n. Informal.* A small boy. [Probably from English dialectal *tad,* toad, from Middle English *tadde, tode,* TOAD.]
Tad·mor. The Biblical name for **Palmyra.**
tad·pole (tăd'pōl') *n.* The aquatic larval stage of a frog or toad, having a tail and external gills that disappear as the limbs develop and the adult stage is reached. Also called "polliwog." [Middle English *taddepol,* "toad head" (a toad with an oversized head) : *tadde, tode,* TOAD + *pol,* POLL (head).]
Ta·dzhik (tä'jĭk, -jēk') *n., pl.* **Tadzhik.** Also **Ta·jik.** One of a people of Iranian descent inhabiting the Tadzhik S.S.R., Afghanistan, and neighboring regions.
Ta·dzhik Soviet Socialist Republic (tä'jĭk, -jēk'). Also **Ta·dzhik·i·stan** (tä-jĭk'ĭ-stăn', -stän', tä-jēk'-), **Ta·jik S.S.R.** A constituent republic of the Soviet Union, 55,000 square miles in area, bordering on Afghanistan and China. Population, 2,432,000. Capital, Dushanbe.
Tae·dong (tī-dōōng'). *Japanese* **Dai·do** (dī'dō'). A river of North Korea, rising near the Manchurian border and flowing 245 miles generally southwest to Korea Bay, an inlet of the Yellow Sea, near Chinnampo.
Tae·gu (tī-gōō'). *Japanese* **Tai·kyu** (tī'kyōō'). A city of South Korea, a commercial center in the southeast, 60 miles north of Pusan. Population, 717,000.
Tae·jon (tī-jôn'). *Japanese* **Tai·den** (tī'dĕn'). A city of South Korea, a commercial and manufacturing center in the southwest, 85 miles south of Seoul. Population, 271,000.
tael (tāl) *n.* **1.** Any of various units of weight used in eastern Asia, roughly equivalent to 1⅓ ounces. Compare **liang.** **2.** A Chinese monetary unit formerly in use, equivalent in value to 1⅓ ounces of standard silver. [Portuguese *tael,* from Malay *tahil, tail,* probably from Hindi *tolā,* a weight, from Sanskrit *tulā,* balance, weight. See **tel-¹** in Appendix.*]
tae·ni·a (tē'nē-ə) *n., pl.* **-niae** (-nē-ē'). Also **te·ni·a.** **1.** A narrow band or ribbon for the hair worn in ancient Greece. **2.** *Architecture.* A band or fillet separating the Doric frieze from the architrave. **3.** Any ribbonlike anatomical structure. **4.** Any flatworm of the genus *Taenia,* which includes many tapeworms. [Latin, band, ribbon, from Greek *tainia.* See **ten-** in Appendix.*]
tae·ni·a·cide. Variant of **teniacide.**
tae·ni·a·sis. Variant of **teniasis.**
taf·fe·ta (tăf'ə-tə) *n.* A glossy, plain-woven fabric of silk, rayon, or nylon, alike on both sides and used especially for women's garments. —*adj.* Made of or resembling taffeta. [Middle English *taffeta,* from Old French *taffetas,* from Old Italian *taffettà,* from Turkish *tafta,* from Persian *tāftah,* "woven," from *tāftan,* to weave. See **temp** in Appendix.*]
taffeta weave. **Plain weave** *(see).*
taff·rail (tăf'rəl, -rāl') *n. Nautical.* **1.** The rail around the stern of a vessel. **2.** The flat upper part of the stern of a vessel, made of wood and often richly carved. [Alteration of earlier *taff(e)rel,* "carved panel," from Dutch *taffereel,* variant of *tafeleel* (unattested), diminutive of *tafel,* panel, table, from Middle Dutch *tāvele,* from Latin *tabula,* TABLE.]
taffrail log. A **screw log** *(see).*
taf·fy (tăf'ē) *n.* **1.** A sweet, chewy candy of molasses or brown sugar boiled until very thick and then pulled with the hands or by machine until the candy is glossy and holds its shape. **2.** *Informal.* Wheedling flattery. [Perhaps from TAFIA.]
taffy pull. A social gathering at which taffy is prepared.
taf·i·a (tăf'ē-ə) *n.* Also **taf·fi·a.** A cheap rum distilled from molasses and refuse sugar in the West Indies. [West Indian Creole, probably alteration of RATAFIA.]
Ta·fi·lelt (tăf'ə-lĕlt'). Also **Ta·fi·la·let** (tăf'ĭ-lə-lĕt'), **Ta·fi·lalt** (tăf'ə-lălt'). The largest oasis (200 square miles) in the Sahara, located in southern Morocco.
Taft (tăft), **Lorado.** 1860–1936. American sculptor.
Taft (tăft), **Robert Alphonso.** 1889–1953. American Republican Party leader; U.S. Senator (1939–53); son of William Howard Taft.
Taft (tăft), **William Howard.** 1857–1930. Twenty-seventh President of the United States (1909–13); Chief Justice of the United States (1921–30).
tag¹ (tăg) *n.* **1.** A strip of leather, paper, metal, or plastic attached to something or hung from a wearer's neck for the purpose of identification, classification, or labeling: *a price tag.* **2.** The plastic or metal tip with which shoelaces and some kinds of string are provided for ease in passing them through eyelets. **3.** The contrastingly colored tip of an animal's tail. **4.** A bright piece of feather, floss, or tinsel surrounding the shank of the hook on a fishing fly. **5. a.** A dirty, matted lock of wool. **b.** A loose lock of hair. **6.** A rag; a tatter. **7.** A small, loose fragment: *I have heard tags and snippets of what is being said.* **8.** An ornamental flourish at the end of a signature. **9. a.** A brief quotation, most often from the English or Latin classics or from the Bible, inserted into a discourse to lend it weight and substance: *Shakespearean tags are part of his stock in trade.* **b.** A cliché, saw, or similar short, conventional idea used as an embellishment of discourse: *These tags of wit and wisdom weary me.* **10. a.** The refrain or last lines of a song or poem. **b.** The closing lines of a speech in a play; a cue. **11.** A designation or epithet: *He did not take kindly to the tag of pauper.* —*v.* **tagged, tagging, tags.** —*tr.* **1.** To label, identify, or recognize with or as with a tag: *I tagged him as a loser.* **2.** To put a ticket on (an automobile) for a traffic or parking violation. **3.** To charge with a crime: *He was tagged for murder.* **4.** To add as an appendage to: *He tagged me with a string of insulting names.* **5.** To follow closely: *The baby tagged her mother around the house.* **6.** To cut the tags from (a sheep). —*intr.* To follow along after; accompany: *He insisted on tagging along.* [Middle English *tagge,* probably from Scandinavian, akin to Swedish *tagg,* prickle, sharp point. See **dek-²** in Appendix.*]
tag² (tăg) *n.* **1.** A children's game in which one player pursues the others until he is able to touch one of them, who then in turn becomes the pursuer. **2.** The act of touching a runner to retire him, in baseball, softball, or touch football. —*tr.v.* **tagged, tagging, tags.** **1.** To touch (another player) in the game of tag. **2. a.** *Baseball.* To touch (a runner) with the ball or the glove holding the ball in order to retire him. **b.** In touch football, to touch (the runner) as a substitute for tackling him. —**tag up.** *Baseball.* To return to and touch a base with one foot before running to the next base. [Variant of *tig,* perhaps from TICK (tapping sound, originally "a light touch").]
TAG the Adjutant General.
Ta·ga·log (tə-gä'lôg') *n., pl.* **Tagalog** or **-logs.** **1.** A member of a people native to the Philippines and inhabiting Manila and its adjacent provinces. **2.** The language of the Austronesian family spoken by this people. [Tagalog, "(people) from the (Pasig) River" : *taga,* belonging to, coming from + *ilog,* river.]
Ta·gan·rog (tăg'ən-rŏg'). A city of the Soviet Union, a major port in the southwest on the Sea of Azov. Population, 234,000.
tag day. A day on which collectors for a charitable fund solicit contributions, giving each contributor a tag.
tag·ger (tăg'ər) *n.* **1.** One that tags, especially the pursuer in the game of tag. **2.** *Plural.* A very thin sheet iron, usually plated with tin.
Ta·gore (tə-gôr', -gōr'), Sir **Rabindranath.** 1861–1941. Indian poet.
Ta·gus (tā'gəs). *Spanish* **Ta·jo** (tä'hō); *Portuguese* **Te·jo** (tā'zhōō). The longest river of the Iberian Peninsula, rising in east-central Spain and flowing 600 miles northwest and then generally southwest to the Atlantic at Lisbon, Portugal.
Ta·hi·ti (tə-hē'tē). Formerly **O·ta·hei·te** (ō'tə-hē'tē). The largest island (386 square miles) of the Society Islands in French Polynesia. Population, 52,000.
Ta·hi·tian (tə-hē'shən, -hē'tē-ən) *adj.* Of or pertaining to Tahiti

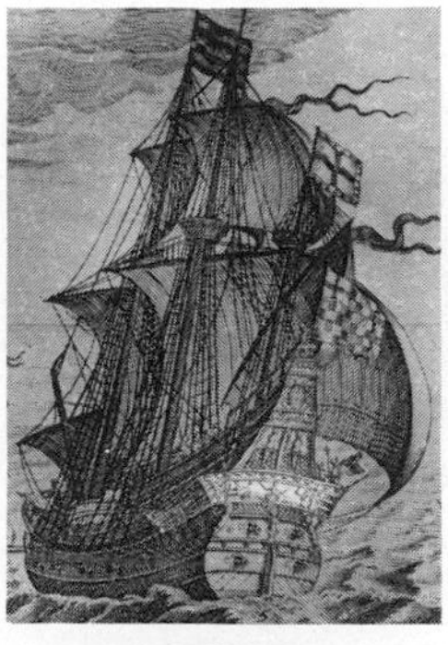

taffrail
Seventeenth-century Dutch engraving

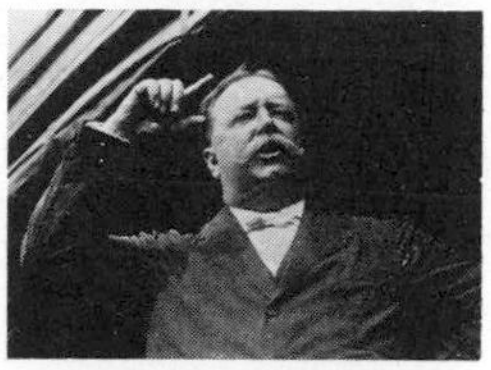

William Howard Taft
Photographed during a 1908 speech in Wisconsin

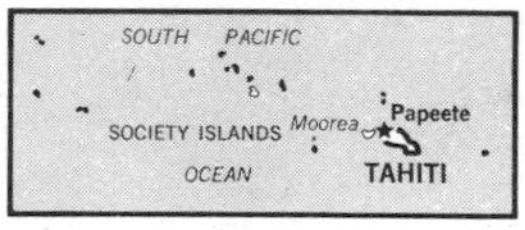

Tahiti

or its people or language. —*n.* **1.** A native or inhabitant of Tahiti. **2.** The Polynesian language of Tahiti.
Tahiti orange. A plant, the **Otaheite orange** *(see).*
Ta·hoe, Lake (tä′hō). A lake occupying about 195 square miles in eastern California and western Nevada.
tahr (tär) *n.* Any of several goatlike mammals of the genus *Hemitragus,* of mountainous regions of Asia, having curved horns and a shaggy coat. [Nepalese *thar.*]
tah·sil·dar (tə-sēl′där′) *n.* Also **tah·seel·dar.** A district official in India in charge of revenues and taxation. [Urdu *taḥsīldār,* from Persian : Arabic *taḥsīl,* collection + Persian *-dār,* holder (see **dher-**[2] in Appendix*).]
Tai[1] (tī). Also **T'ai Hu** (tī′ hōō′). A lake in east-central China, 40 miles long and 35 miles wide, lying west of Shanghai. [Mandarin Chinese *t'ai*^{4} *hu*^{2}, "great lake."]
Tai[2]. Variant of **Thai.**
Tai·chung (tī′chŏŏng′). A city in west-central Taiwan. Population, 207,000. [Mandarin Chinese *t'ai*^{2} *chung*^{1}, "(city in) central Taiwan."]
Tai·den. The Japanese name for **Taejon.**
tai·ga (tī-gä′) *n.* The subarctic evergreen forest of Siberia and of similar regions elsewhere in Eurasia and North America. [Russian *taiga,* from Turkic *taiga,* rocky mountain.]
taig·lach. Variant of **teiglach.**
Tai·kyu. The Japanese name for **Taegu.**
tail[1] (tāl) *n.* **1.** The posterior part of an animal, especially when elongated and extending beyond the trunk or main part of the body. **2.** The bottom, rear, or hindmost part of anything. **3.** The rear end of a wagon or other vehicle: *the tail of a cart.* **4.** *Aviation.* **a.** The rear portion of a fuselage. **b.** An assembly of stabilizing planes and control surfaces in this region. Also called "empennage." **5.** The vaned rear portion of any bomb or missile. **6.** Any appendage to the rear or bottom of a thing: *the tail of a kite.* **7.** A braid of hair; a pigtail. **8.** Something that follows or takes the last place: *the tail of the journey.* **9.** A retinue or train of followers. **10.** The end of a line of persons or things. **11.** *Prosody.* The short closing line of certain stanzas. **12.** The refuse or dross remaining from such processes as distilling or milling. **13.** *Printing.* The bottom of a page; bottom margin. **14.** *Plural.* The reverse of a coin: *heads or tails.* **15.** *Informal.* The trail of a person or animal in flight: *The hounds were on his tail.* **16.** *Informal.* An agent assigned to watch and report on someone's movements and actions. **17.** *Plural.* **a.** A formal evening costume worn by men. **b.** A swallow-tailed coat. **18.** *Vulgar Slang.* The female pudendum. **19.** *Vulgar Slang.* A female regarded as a sexual object. —*v.* **tailed, tailing, tails.** —*tr.* **1.** To provide with a tail: *tail a kite.* **2.** To deprive of a tail; to dock. **3.** To serve as the tail of: *The Santa Claus float tailed the parade.* **4.** To connect (objects often dissimilar or incongruous) by or as by the tail or end: *tail two ideas together.* **5.** *Architecture.* To set one end of (a beam, board, or brick) into a wall. Used with *in* or *on.* **6.** *Informal.* To follow and keep under surveillance. —*intr.* **1.** To disperse when moving in a line. Usually used with *out: The patrol tailed out in pairs.* **2.** *Architecture.* To be inserted at one end, as a floor timber or beam. **3.** *Informal.* To follow. **4.** *Nautical.* **a.** To go aground with the stern foremost. **b.** To be pointed in some direction with the stern when riding at anchor or on a mooring: *She was tailing into the wind.* —**tail down.** To ease a heavy load down a steep slope. —**tail off** (or **away**). To dwindle: *The fireworks tailed off into darkness.* —*adj.* **1.** Posterior; hindmost. **2.** Coming from behind: *a tail wind.* [Middle English *tayle,* Old English *tæg(e)l.* See **dek-**[2] in Appendix.*]
tail[2] (tāl) *n. Law.* The limitation of the inheritance of an estate to a particular person or persons. —*adj. Law.* In tail: *a tail estate.* [Middle English *taille, tayle,* from Old French *taille,* cut, division, partition, from *taillier,* to cut, from Vulgar Latin *tāl(l)iāre* (unattested). See **tailor.**]
tail·back (tāl′băk′) *n. Football.* The back on the offensive team lining up farthest from the line of scrimmage.
tail beam. A **tailpiece** *(see).*
tail·board (tāl′bôrd′, -bōrd′) *n.* A hinged board forming the rear wall of a wagon or truck that can be let down to serve as a ramp in loading or unloading.
tail end. The very end; conclusion.
tail·gate (tāl′gāt′) *n.* **1.** One of the pair of gates downstream in a canal lock. **2.** The tailboard of a vehicle. —*v.* **tailgated, -gating, -gates.** *Slang.* —*tr.* To drive so closely behind (another vehicle) that one cannot stop or swerve in an emergency. —*intr.* To follow another car at too close a distance.
tail-heav·y (tāl′hĕv′ē) *adj.* Having too much weight at the rear either by overloading or from poor design and construction.
tail·ing (tā′lĭng) *n.* **1.** *Plural.* Refuse or dross remaining after such processes as milling, distilling, or mining. **2.** *Architecture.* The portion of a tailed beam, brick, or board inside a wall. —See Synonyms at **remainder.**
taille (tä′yə, tāl) *n.* A form of direct royal taxation levied in France before 1789 on nonprivileged subjects and lands, and tending to weigh most heavily on the peasants. [French, from Old French, a cut, division, from *tailler,* to cut, from Vulgar Latin *tāl(l)iāre* (unattested). See **tailor.**]
Taille·fere (tä-y′-fâr′), **Germaine.** Born 1892. French modernist composer.
tail·light (tāl′līt′) *n.* A red light or one of a pair mounted on the rear end of a vehicle. Also called "tail lamp."
tai·lor (tā′lər) *n. Abbr.* **tlr.** A person who makes, repairs, and alters garments such as suits, coats, and dresses. —*v.* **tailored, -loring, -lors.** —*tr.* **1.** To produce (a garment). **2.** To outfit (someone) with clothes. **3.** To make, alter, or adapt for a particular end: *a speech tailored to a special audience.* —*intr.* To exercise the trade of a tailor. [Middle English *taillour,* from Norman French, variant of Old French *tailleur,* from Vulgar Latin *tāliātor* (unattested), "cutter," from *tāl(l)iāre* (unattested), to cut, from Latin *tālea*†, twig, cutting.]
tai·lor·bird (tā′lər-bûrd′) *n.* Any of several Old World tropical birds of the genus *Orthotomus,* characteristically using plant fibers or similar threads to stitch leaves together in making its nest.
tai·lored (tā′lərd) *adj.* Simple, trim, or severe in line or design, or of somewhat sturdy fabric: *a chic tailored suit.*
tai·lor-made (tā′lər-mād′) *adj.* **1.** Made by a tailor. **2.** Perfectly fitted to a condition, preference, or purpose; made or as if made to order: *a tailor-made job.* —*n.* A garment made by a tailor.
tailor's chalk. A thin piece of hard chalk used in tailoring for making temporary alteration marks on clothing.
tail·piece (tāl′pēs′) *n.* **1.** Any piece forming an end to something; an appendage. **2.** *Printing.* An engraving or design placed as an ornament at the end of a chapter or at the bottom of a page. **3.** *Architecture.* A beam tailed into a wall. Also called "tail beam." **4.** *Music.* A triangular piece of ebony to which the lower ends of the strings of a violin or cello are attached.
tail pipe. The pipe through which exhaust gases from an engine are discharged.
tail·race (tāl′rās′) *n.* **1.** The part of a millrace below the water wheel through which the spent water flows. **2.** A channel for floating away mine tailings and refuse.
tail·skid (tāl′skĭd′) *n.* A skid attached to the rear underside of certain airplanes to act as a runner.
tail·spin (tāl′spĭn′) *n.* **1.** The descent of an aircraft in a **spin** *(see),* characterized by the rapid spiral movement of the tail section. **2.** An emotional collapse; loss of emotional control.
tail·stock (tāl′stŏk′) *n.* The adjustable stock of a lathe supporting the spindle containing the dead center.
tail wind. A wind blowing in the same direction as that of the course of a vehicle.
Tai·myr Peninsula (tī-mîr′). Also **Tai·mir, Tay·myr.** A projection of Siberia, Russian S.F.S.R., extending northward some 700 miles between the Laptev and Kara seas.
tain (tān) *n.* **1.** A type of paper-thin tin plate. **2.** Tinfoil used as a backing for mirrors. [French, tinfoil, shortened from *étain,* tin, from Old French *estain,* from Latin *stagnum, stannum,* an alloy of silver and lead. See **stannic.**]
Tai·nan (tī′nän′). A city and major commercial center of southwestern Taiwan. Population, 288,000. [Mandarin Chinese *t'ai*^{2}*nan*^{2}, "(city in) southern Taiwan."]
Tai·na·ron, Cape. The Greek name for Cape **Matapan.**
Taine (tān; *French* tĕn), **Hippolyte Adolphe.** 1828–1893. French philosopher and literary historian.
Tai·no (tī′nō) *n., pl.* **Taino** or **-nos.** **1.** An extinct aboriginal Arawakan Indian people of the West Indies. **2.** The language of these people. [Spanish, from a native name in the West Indies.]
taint (tānt) *v.* **tainted, tainting, taints.** —*tr.* **1.** To stain the honor of someone or something: *Her reputation is forever tainted.* **2.** To expose to contagion; infect with or as with a disease: *"such a malady is more likely to taint a particular county or district, than an entire state"* (James Madison). **3.** To make poisonous or rotten; infect or spoil. **4.** To imbue with principles contrary to certain implicit moral or other prescriptions: *Philosophy had not tainted his innocence.* —*intr.* To become discolored; to rot. —*n.* **1.** A moral defect considered as a stain or spot. **2.** An infecting touch, influence, or tinge: *"our vices, whose deep taint/With slow perdition murders the whole man"* (Coleridge). [Middle English *taynten,* from Norman French *teinter,* from Old French *teint,* color, tint, from Latin *tinctus,* from the past participle of *tingere,* to dip in liquid, dye. See **teng-** in Appendix.*]
Tai·pei (tī′pā′). Also **Tai·peh.** The capital of the Republic of China, on Taiwan at the northern end of the island. Population, 1,028,000. [Mandarin Chinese *t'ai*^{2}*pei*^{3}, "(city in) northern Taiwan."]
Tai·wan (tī′wän′). Formerly **For·mo·sa** (fôr-mō′sə). An island off the southeastern coast of China, 13,885 square miles in area, constituting along with the Pescadores and other smaller islands the Republic of China.
Tai·yü·an (tī′yōō′än′). Formerly **Yang·ku** (yäng′kōō′). The capital of Shansi, northeastern China, a major industrial city in the center of the province. Population, 1,053,000.
Ta·iz (tä-ĭz′). Also **Ta'iz, Ta'izz.** The second capital of Yemen, in the southwestern part of the country. Population, 30,000.
taj (täzh, täj) *n.* A tall conical cap worn by Moslems as a headdress of distinction. [Arabic *tāj,* from Persian *tāj,* "crown." See **steg-**[1] in Appendix.*]
Ta·jik. **1.** Variant of **Tadzhik.** **2.** See **Tadzhik Soviet Socialist Republic.**
Taj Ma·hal (täzh′ mə-häl′, täj′). A white marble mausoleum built (1630–52) by Shah Jahan for his wife at Agra, India.
Ta·jo. The Spanish name for the **Tagus.**
Ta·ju·mul·co (tä′hōō-mōōl′kō). The highest elevation (13,816 feet) in Central America, an extinct volcano in southwestern Guatemala.
ta·ka·he (tə-kī′) *n.* An almost extinct flightless bird, *Notornis mantelli,* of New Zealand, having a large bill and brightly colored plumage. [Maori *takahe* (imitative).]

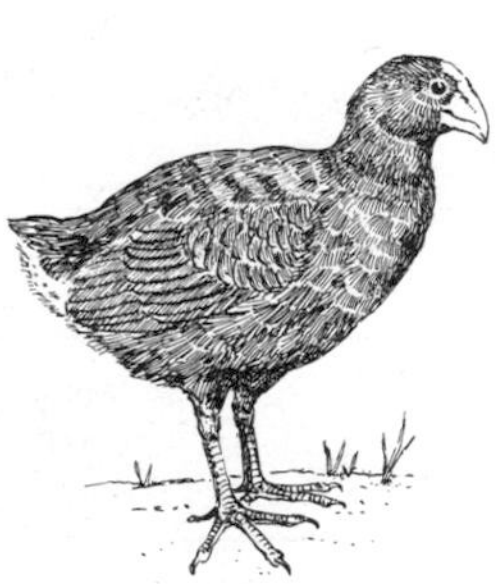
takahe

Ta·ka·mat·su (tä′kä-mät′sōō). A city of Japan, a major seaport on the northern tip of Shikoku. Population, 246,000.
Ta·ka·o·ka (tä′kä-ō′kä). A city of Japan, an industrial center

noted for its bronze ware, situated in central Honshu. Population, 139,000.

take (tāk) *v.* **took** (to͝ok), **taken** (tā′kən), **taking, takes.** —*tr.* **1.** To get into one's possession by force, skill, or artifice, especially: **a.** To capture physically; seize: *take an enemy fortress.* **b.** To kill, snare, or trap (fish or game, for example). **c.** To acquire in a game or competition; win: *take your opponent's queen.* **d.** To seize authoritatively; confiscate. **e.** To catch (a ball in play) in certain sports: *He took it at second.* **2.** To grasp with the hands; to grip: *take your partner's hand.* **3.** To be affected with; come down with; contract: *He took a cold.* **4.** To encounter or catch in a particular situation; come upon; discover: *They'll never take him unawares.* **5.** To deal a blow to; strike; hit: *He took his opponent a sharp jab to the ribs.* **6.** To affect favorably or winsomely; charm; captivate: *He was completely taken by the puppy.* **7.** To put (food or drink, for example) into the body; eat, drink, inhale, or draw in: *take a deep breath.* **8.** To expose one's body to (healthful or pleasurable treatment, for example): *take some sun.* **9.** To bring or receive into a particular relation, association, or other connection: *take a new partner into the firm.* **10.** To have sexual intercourse with: *Abraham took his slave girl.* **11.** To accept and place under one's care or keeping. **12.** To appropriate for one's own or another's use or benefit; obtain by purchase; secure; buy: *We always take season tickets.* **13. a.** To assume for or upon oneself: *I'll take the blame.* **b.** To charge or oblige oneself with the fulfillment of (a task or duty, for example); undertake; commit oneself to: *He took chairmanship of the committee.* **c.** To pledge one's obedience to; impose (a vow or promise) upon oneself. **d.** To subject oneself to: *He took extra time to do the job properly.* **e.** To accept or adopt for one's own. **f.** To put forth or adopt as a point of argument, defense, or discussion: *Your interpretation of the poem is well taken.* **g.** To require or have as a fitting or proper accompaniment: *Intransitive verbs take no direct object.* **14.** To obtain through competition: *Our candidate took Rhode Island.* **15.** To defeat: *St. Louis took Boston three to one.* **16. a.** To select; pick out; choose: *take any card.* **b.** To choose for one's own use; avail oneself of the use of: *He took a rented car.* **c.** To use as a tool or instrument for doing something: *I'm going to take scissors to that hair, son.* **d.** To use as a means of conveyance or transportation: *take a steamer to Europe.* **e.** To use as a means of safety or refuge: *take shelter in the event of an air raid.* **17.** To assume occupancy of: *take a seat.* **18.** To have as a requirement or necessity for something; require: *It takes money to live in that town.* **19.** To obtain from a source; derive; draw: *She took her domineering tone from her mother.* **20.** To obtain through certain procedures from a source or sources: *take a reading on the dial.* **21. a.** To put down in writing; write: *take a letter.* **b.** To put down an image, likeness, or representation of by or as by drawing, painting, or photography: *take a picture of us.* **22. a.** To accept (something owed, offered, or given) either reluctantly or willingly: *He takes bets on the track.* **b.** To submit to (something inflicted); endure: *He can't take criticism.* **c.** To withstand: *The dam took the heavy flood waters.* **d.** To accept or believe (something put forth) as true: *I'll take your word.* **e.** To follow (advice, a suggestion, or a lead, for example). **f.** To accept, handle, or deal with in a particular way: *He takes things in stride.* **g.** To consider in a particular relation or from a particular viewpoint: *take the bitter with the better.* **23.** To indulge in; do, perform, or accomplish: *take a bath.* **24. a.** To allow to come in; admit; give access or admission to: *The boat took in a lot of water but remained afloat.* **b.** To provide room for; accommodate: *We can't take more than 300 guests.* **c.** To become saturated or impregnated with (dye, for example). **25. a.** To understand or interpret: *"He took my silence, rightly, for disapproval."* (John Howard Griffin). **b.** To consider; assume: *"All I hope is that we may not be taken for excisemen in this whiskey country."* (Keats). **c.** To consider to be equal to; reckon: *We take their number at a thousand.* **d.** To perceive or feel; experience: *I take pleasure to inform you.* **26.** To carry along or cause to go with one to another place: *Don't forget to take your umbrella.* See Usage note at **bring.** **27.** To lead to another place: *This bus takes you past the museum.* **28.** To remove from a place: *take dishes from the left.* **29.** To secure by removing: *The dentist took two molars.* **30.** To cause to die; kill; destroy: *The blight took these tomatoes.* **31.** To subtract. **32.** To commit oneself to the study of; enroll in: *take a biology course.* **33.** To swindle; defraud; cheat: *You were taken.* **34.** *Baseball.* To refrain from swinging at (a pitched ball). —*intr.* **1.** To acquire possession. **2.** To engage or mesh; catch, as gears or other mechanical parts. **3.** To start growing; root; germinate: *Have the seeds taken?* **4.** To have the intended effect; operate; work: *The transfusion apparently took.* **5.** To gain popularity or favor: *That show will never take with the public.* **6.** To detract. Used with *from: The indiscretion takes from his public image.* **7.** To become: *He took sick.* **8.** To set out for; make one's way; go: *"Afoot and light-hearted I take to the open road"* (Walt Whitman). —**take aback.** To bewilder; astonish; nonplus. —**take a back seat.** To play a secondary or unimportant role; give way to another. —**take advantage of. 1.** To use to one's advantage; derive profit from. **2.** To impose upon a person to his detriment; exploit. —**take after. 1.** To follow as an example. **2.** To resemble in appearance, temperament, or character: *"Adam was my grandfather— And I take after him."* (Stephen Vincent Benét). —**take amiss.** To be offended by through misunderstanding. —**take apart. 1.** To divide or analyze (an object or theory, for example) into component parts; disassemble. **2.** *Informal.* To tear into violently; beat up; thrash. —**take at one's word.** To accept or believe as true. —**take back.** To retract something stated or written. —**take care.** To be careful. —**take care of.** To assume responsibility for the maintenance, support, or treatment of. —**take effect. 1.** To become operative, as under law or regulation: *The salary increase takes effect next month.* **2.** To have the intended effect, as a drug. —**take five** (or **ten**). To take a short rest or break, as of five to ten minutes. —**take for. 1.** To consider or suppose to be; regard as: *I take him for a fool.* **2.** To consider mistakenly: *We took you for dead.* —**take for granted. 1.** To consider as true, real, or forthcoming; anticipate correctly. **2.** To underestimate the value of. —**take heart.** To be confident or courageous. —**take in vain.** To use a name, especially a sacred name, profanely or blasphemously. —**take it. 1.** To understand; assume: *as I take it.* **2.** *Informal.* To endure abuse, criticism, or other harsh treatment: *You've got to learn to take it in the army.* —**take it lying down.** *Informal.* To submit to harsh treatment with no resistance. —**take it on the chin.** *Slang.* To endure punishment, suffering, or defeat. —**take it out on.** *Informal.* To abuse another person in venting one's own anger or frustration. —**take on. 1.** To hire. **2.** To undertake or begin to handle (a task, for example). **3.** To oppose in competition. **4.** *Informal.* To display violent or passionate emotion: *Don't take on so!* —**take out. 1.** To extract; remove. **2.** To secure (a license, for example) by application to an authority. **3.** *Informal.* To escort, as on a date: *He's taken me out three times.* —**take over.** To assume the control or management of. —**take place. 1.** To have as a locality. **2.** To happen. See Usage note at **occur.** —**take to. 1.** To have recourse to; go to, as for safety: *He took to the woods.* **2.** To develop as a habit or steady practice: *take to drink.* **3.** To become fond of or attracted to: *"Two keen minds that they are, they took to each other"* (Jack Kerouac). —**take to task.** To call to account for a mistake or offense; reprove. —**take up with.** *Informal.* To develop a friendship or association with: *took up with thieves.* —*n.* **1. a.** The act or process of taking. **b.** That which is taken. **2.** The number of fish, game birds, or other animals killed or captured at one time. **3.** A quantity of anything collected at one time; especially, the amount of profit or receipts taken on a business arrangement or venture. **4.** *Slang.* The amount of money collected as admission to a sporting event; the gate. **5.** The uninterrupted running of a motion picture or television camera or set of recording equipment in filming a movie or television program or cutting a record. **6. a.** A scene filmed or televised without interrupting the run of the camera. **b.** A recording made in a single session. **7. a.** Any physical reaction, as a rash, indicating a successful vaccination. **b.** A successful graft. **8.** *Slang.* Any attempt or try: *He got the answer on the third take.* [Take, took, taken; Middle English *taken, took, taken,* Old English *tacan, tōc, tacen* (unattested), from Old Norse *taka, tōk, tekinn.* See **tak-**[2] in Appendix.*]

take down. 1. To bring to a lower position from a higher. **2.** To dismantle; take apart: *take down the Christmas tree.* **3.** To lower the arrogance or self-esteem of (a person). **4.** To put down in writing.

take·down (tāk′doun′) *adj.* Capable of being taken down or apart, as certain rifles. —*n.* **1.** A takedown article. **2.** The mechanism allowing an article to be easily taken down. **3.** *Informal.* **a.** The act of humiliating a person. **b.** An instance of such mortification: *That was quite a takedown he gave you.*

take-home pay (tāk′hōm′). The amount of one's salary remaining after federal, state, and often city income taxes and other various deductions have been withheld.

take in. 1. To grant admittance to; receive as a guest or employee. **2.** To reduce in size; make smaller or shorter: *take in a sail by reefing.* **3.** To include or comprise. **4.** To understand. **5.** To deceive; to swindle. **6.** To look at thoroughly; to view: *take in the sights.*

take-in (tāk′ĭn′) *n.* An act or instance of swindling or cheating; a deception.

take off. 1. To remove, as clothing. **2.** To carry off or away. **3.** *Slang.* To go off; to start. **4.** To rise up in flight. Used of an airplane or rocket.

take-off (tāk′ôf′, -ŏf′) *n.* **1.** The act of rising in flight. Said of an aircraft or rocket. **2.** The point or place from which one takes off. **3.** *Informal.* An amusing imitative caricature or burlesque of another person. —See Synonyms at **caricature.**

tak·er (tā′kər) *n.* A person who takes or takes up something, as a wager or purchase.

take up. 1. To raise up; to lift. **2.** To reduce in size; shorten or tighten: *take up the slack in the rope.* **3.** To pay off an outstanding debt, mortgage, or note. **4.** To accept as offered, as an option, a bet, or a challenge. **5.** To begin again; resume: *Let's take up where we left off.* **6.** To use up, consume, or occupy (space or time, for example). **7.** To develop an interest in or devotion to: *take up astronomy.*

take-up (tāk′ŭp′) *n.* **1.** A device for reducing slack or taking up lost motion, as in a loom. **2.** The act of taking or tightening up.

ta·kin (tä′kēn′) *n.* A goatlike mammal, *Budorcas taxicolor,* of the mountains of central Asia, having backward-pointing horns and a shaggy coat. [Tibeto-Burman (Mishmi).]

tak·ing (tā′kĭng) *adj.* **1.** Capturing the interest; fetching; winning: *a taking smile.* **2.** Contagious; catching. Said of an infectious disease. —*n.* **1.** The act of a person or thing that takes. **2.** That which is taken, as a catch of fish. **3.** *Plural.* Receipts, especially of money.

Ta·kla·ma·kan Desert (tä′klə-mə-kän′). A vast arid area in the Sinkiang-Uigur Autonomous Region of western China.

tal·a·poin (tăl′ə-poin′) *n.* A small African monkey, *Miopithecus talapoin* (or *Cercopithecus talapoin*), having a long tail and

t tight/th thin, path/*th* this, bathe/ŭ cut/ûr urge/v valve/w with/y yes/z zebra, size/zh vision/ə about, item, edible, gallop, circus/ à *Fr.* ami/œ *Fr.* feu, *Ger.* schön/ü *Fr.* tu, *Ger.* über/KH *Ger.* ich, *Scot.* loch/N *Fr.* bon. *Follows main vocabulary. †Of obscure origin.

greenish fur. [French, "Buddhist monk" (from a fancied resemblance), from Portuguese *talapões*, plural of *talapão*, monk, from Mon *tala pōi*, "our lord" (polite address to a monk).]

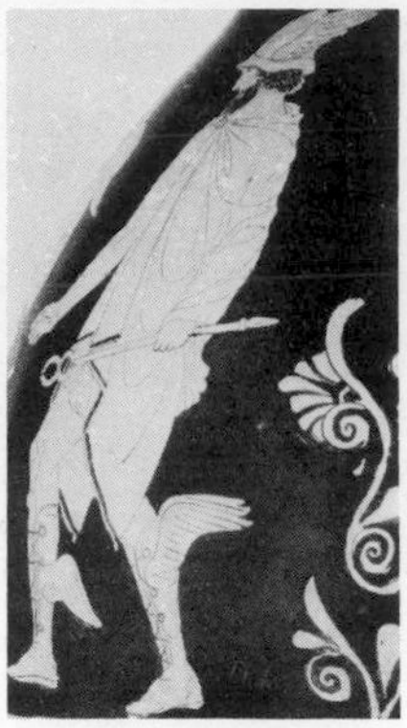

talaria

ta·lar·i·a (tə-lâr′ē-ə) *pl.n.* Winged sandals such as those worn by Hermes and Iris as represented in Greco-Roman painting and sculpture. [Latin *tālāria*, the ankles, sandals tied to the ankles, from *tālāris*, of the ankles, from *tālus*, ankle, TALUS (heel).]

Ta·laud (tä′lout′). Also **Ta·laur** (-lour′). A group of islands, 495 square miles in area, of Indonesia, in the Pacific, 180 miles northeast of Sulawesi.

Tal·bot (tôl′bət), **William Henry Fox.** 1800–1877. British inventor; pioneer in instantaneous photography.

talc (tălk) *n.* A fine-grained white, greenish, or gray mineral, essentially $Mg_3Si_4O_{10}(OH)_2$, having a soft soapy texture and used in talcum and face powder, as a paper coating, and as a filler for paint and plastics. Also called "talcum." —*tr.v.* **talcked** or **talced, talcking** or **talcing, talcs.** To apply talc to (a photographic plate, for example). [French *talc*, from Medieval Latin *talcum*, from Arabic *ṭalq*, from Persian *talk*†.]

Tal·ca (täl′kä). A city and commercial and manufacturing center of central Chile. Population, 68,000.

Tal·ca·hua·no (täl′kä-wä′nō). A city and major seaport of south-central Chile. Population, 102,000.

talc·ose (tăl′kōs′) *adj.* Also **talc·ous** (tăl′kəs), **talck·y** (tăl′kē). Made of or containing talc.

tal·cum (tăl′kəm) *n.* **1.** Soapstone or **talc** *(see).* **2.** Talcum powder. [Medieval Latin, TALC.]

talcum powder. A fine, often perfumed powder made from purified talc, for use on the skin.

tale (tāl) *n.* **1.** A report or revelation; recital of events or happenings: *She told us her tale of woe.* **2.** A malicious story; piece of gossip. **3.** A deliberate lie; falsehood. **4.** A diverting or edifying narrative of real or imaginary events. **5.** *Archaic.* A tally or reckoning; total: *the earthquake's tale of thousands dead.* [Middle English *tale*, Old English *talu*, discourse, narrative. See **del-2** in Appendix.*]

tale·bear·er (tāl′bâr′ər) *n.* One who spreads malicious stories or gossip. —**tale′bear′ing** *adj.* & *n.*

tal·ent (tăl′ənt) *n.* **1.** A mental or physical aptitude; specific natural or acquired ability. **2.** Natural endowment or ability of a superior quality. **3.** Gifted people collectively: *The company makes good use of talent.* **4.** A variable unit of weight and money used in ancient Greece, Rome, and the Middle East. —See Synonyms at **ability.** [Middle English *talent(e)*, from Old English *talente*, unit of weight or money, and Old French *talent*, inclination, aptitude, both from Latin *talentum*, unit of weight or money (in Medieval Latin, also "mental aptitude," extended sense from the parable of the talents in Matthew 25:14–30), from Greek *talanton*. See **tel-1** in Appendix.*]

talent scout. An agent sent on tour in search of talented people for acting, sports, or business.

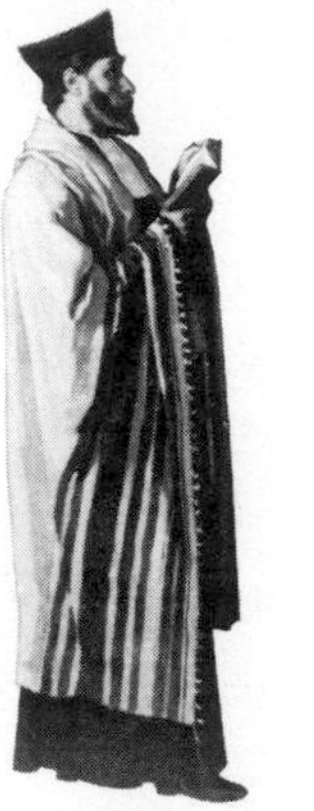

tallith

ta·ler (tä′lər) *n., pl.* **taler** or **-lers.** Also **tha·ler.** Any of numerous silver coins that served as a unit of currency in certain Germanic countries between the 15th and 19th centuries. [German *Taler*. See **dollar.**]

ta·les (tā′lēz) *n., pl.* **tales.** *Law.* **1.** A group of persons summoned to fill vacancies on a jury that has become deficient in number. **2.** The writ allowing for such a summons of jurors. [Middle English, from the Medieval Latin phrase *tales de circumstantibus*, "such (persons) from those standing about" (used in the writ), from Latin *tālēs*, plural of *tālis*, such. See **to-** in Appendix.*]

tales·man (tālz′mən, tā′lēz-) *n., pl.* **-men** (-mĭn). *Law.* A person summoned under a writ of tales.

tale·tell·er (tāl′tĕl′ər) *n.* **1.** An oral narrator. **2.** A talebearer. —**tale′tell′ing** *adj.* & *n.*

ta·li. Plural of **talus.**

Ta·lien (dä′lyĕn′). Formerly **Dai·ren** (dī′rĕn′). A city of northeastern China, constituting part of the municipal district of Lüta. Population, 766,000.

tal·i·on (tăl′ē-ən) *n.* A punishment identical to the offense, as the death penalty for murder. [Middle English *talioun*, from Old French *talion*, from Latin *tāliō*, reciprocal punishment in kind. See **tel-1** in Appendix.*]

tal·i·ped (tăl′ə-pĕd′) *adj.* Afflicted with talipes; clubfooted. —*n.* A person with a clubfoot. [See **talipes.**]

tal·i·pes (tăl′ə-pēz′) *n.* A deformity of the human foot, especially **clubfoot** *(see).* [New Latin *talipes* (stem *taliped-*), "walking on the ankles" : Latin *tālus*, ankle, TALUS + -PED.]

tal·i·pot (tăl′ə-pŏt′) *n.* A tall palm tree, *Corypha umbraculifera*, of tropical Asia, having a spreading crown of large, fanlike leaves. [Bengali *tālipōt*, palm leaf : Sanskrit *tālī*, fan palm, probably akin to *tāla* (see **toddy**) + *pattra*, feather, leaf (see **pet-1** in Appendix*).]

tal·is·man (tăl′ĭs-mən, tăl′ĭz-) *n., pl.* **-mans.** **1.** An object marked with magical signs and believed to confer on its bearer supernatural powers or protection. **2.** Anything having apparently magical power: *Her most powerful talisman was her beauty.* [French and Spanish *talisman*, from Arabic *ṭilsām* (plural *ṭilsamān*), from Late Greek *telesma*, completion, consecrated object, from *telein*, to fulfill, consecrate, from *telos*, fulfillment, result. See **kwel-1** in Appendix.*]

tal·is·man·ic (tăl′ĭs-măn′ĭk, tăl′ĭz-) *adj.* Also **tal·is·man·i·cal** (-ĭ-kəl). **1.** Of or pertaining to talismans: *talismanic formulas.* **2.** Possessing magical power: *a talismanic amulet.*

talk (tôk) *v.* **talked, talking, talks.** —*tr.* **1.** To articulate (words): *Those are real words the baby is talking.* **2.** To articulate (something) in words: *talk treason.* **3.** To speak of or discuss (something): *talk music.* **4.** To speak (an idiom): *He talks Pidgin English with the crew.* **5.** To spend (a period of time) by or as if by talking. Used with *away: talk the evening away.* —*intr.* **1.** To converse by means of spoken language: *We talked for hours.* **2.** To articulate words: *The baby can talk.* **3.** To imitate the sounds of human speech: *The parrot talks.* **4.** To manifest one's thoughts otherwise than by articulate language: *talk with the hands.* **5.** To express one's thoughts in writing: *Voltaire talks about London in this text.* **6.** To parley or negotiate with someone: *Let's talk before fighting.* **7.** To chatter incessantly: *She did nothing but talk.* **8.** To gossip: *People will talk.* **9.** To allude to something: *He knew what he was talking about.* **10.** To consult or confer with someone: *I talked with the doctor.* **11.** To yield under coercion information concerning oneself or others: *Has the prisoner talked?* **12.** To be efficacious: *Nothing talks to them but money.* —See Synonyms at **speak.** —**talk around. 1.** To persuade: *I talked him around to my position.* **2.** To speak indirectly about something: *He talked around the subject without coming to the point.* —**talk at. 1.** To say something intended for someone without addressing him directly: *He is talking at his opponent in this comment on defeatism.* **2.** To address someone without regard to his response: *She talks at people, never with them.* —**talk back. 1.** To make an impertinent reply: *His father slaps him when he talks back.* **2.** To make a belligerent response: *Our guns will talk back.* —**talk big.** *Slang.* To brag. —**talk down. 1.** To depreciate: *He talked down the importance of the move.* **2.** To silence (a person): *His boss could talk him down with one word.* **3.** To address someone with insulting condescension. —**talk (someone) into.** To persuade: *I talked him into going.* —**talk out. 1.** To discuss a matter exhaustively: *We talked out her problem.* **2.** To speak loudly and clearly. **3.** To exhaust someone by talking. **4.** *British.* To filibuster proposed legislation. —**talk (someone) out of.** To dissuade: *I talked my wife out of buying a new dress.* —**talk over. 1.** To win someone over by persuasion: *We talked him over to our side.* **2.** To discuss a subject: *Let's talk it over.* —**talk up. 1.** To make propaganda in favor of a person or thing: *talk up the candidate.* **2.** To speak up impertinently or defiantly, especially to a superior: *talking up to an officer.* —*n.* **1.** The articulation of ideas in conversation: *She knew how to make diverting and intelligent talk.* **2.** An informal speech: *give a talk.* **3.** Any hearsay, rumor, or speculation concerning something: *talk of war.* **4.** Any subject of conversation: *the talk of the town.* **5.** A conference or negotiation: *a peace talk.* **6.** Any jargon or slang: *prison talk.* **7.** Any empty speech: *much talk and no action.* **8.** A particular manner of speech: *baby talk.* [Middle English *talkien, talken*, probably frequentative formation (with *k*) from Old English *talian*, to reckon, tell, relate. See **del-2** in Appendix.*]

talk·a·tive (tô′kə-tĭv) *adj.* Having an inclination to talk; loquacious. —**talk′a·tive·ly** *adv.* —**talk′a·tive·ness** *n.*

Synonyms: *talkative, loquacious, wordy, garrulous, voluble, effusive, verbose, glib.* These adjectives describe persons or their style of speech or writing and usually imply excessive use of words. *Talkative* is the most neutral and suggests sociability more often than offensiveness. *Loquacious* stresses fluency or readiness of speech, often in a mildly derogatory sense. *Wordy* applies principally to writing in which point and clarity are dulled by needless repetition. *Garrulous* describes one who talks readily and at too great length and whose speech is usually rambling and diffuse. *Voluble* stresses fluency in speech, often unfavorably in the sense of an unending flow. *Effusive* suggests a gushing forth of oral or written expression that lacks discipline or substance. *Verbose* implies either overwriting or windy speech, characteristically marked by dullness or obscurity. *Glib* refers to one whose speech is fluent and smooth; often the term suggests shallowness, lack of sincerity, or questionable motives.

talk·er (tô′kər) *n.* A person who talks, especially a loquacious or garrulous person.

talk·ie (tô′kē) *n. Informal.* A motion-picture film with a sound track.

talking book. A phonograph record of a reading of a book, designed for use by the blind.

talking machine. A phonograph. An early usage.

talking picture. A sound film. An early usage.

talk·ing-to (tô′kĭng-to͞o′) *n., pl.* **-tos.** *Informal.* A scolding; dressing-down.

talk·y (tô′kē) *adj.* **-ier, -iest. 1.** Talkative; loquacious. **2.** Containing too much talk: *a talky, boring play.*

tall (tôl) *adj.* **taller, tallest. 1.** Having greater than ordinary height: *a tall woman.* **2.** Having a stated height: *General Tom Thumb was three feet tall.* **3.** *Informal.* Fanciful; boastful: *tall tales.* **4.** *Archaic.* Excellent; comely; fine. **5.** Long: *a tall drink.* **6.** Impressively great or difficult: *a tall order to fill.* —See Synonyms at **high.** —*adv.* Straight; with proud bearing: *stand tall.* [Middle English *tall*, seemly, handsome, valiant, probably from Old English *getæl*, swift, ready. See **del-2** in Appendix.*]

tal·lage (tăl′ĭj) *n.* An occasional tax levied by the Anglo-Norman kings on crown lands and royal towns. —*tr.v.* **tallaged, -laging, -lages.** To levy a tax on. [Middle English *ta(i)llage*, from Old French *taillage*, "a cutting," from *taillier*, to cut, from Vulgar Latin *tāl(l)iāre* (unattested). See **tailor.**]

Tal·la·has·see (tăl′ə-hăs′ē). The capital of Florida, in the northwestern part of the state. Population, 48,000.

Tal·la·hatch·ie (tăl′ə-hăch′ē). A river of Mississippi, rising in the northwest and flowing 230 miles generally south to the Yazoo.

Tal·la·poo·sa (tăl′ə-po͞o′sə). A navigable river rising in northwestern Georgia and flowing 268 miles generally southwest

ă pat/ā pay/âr care/ä father/b bib/ch church/d deed/ĕ pet/ē be/f fife/g gag/h hat/hw which/ĭ pit/ī pie/îr pier/j judge/k kick/l lid, needle/m mum/n no, sudden/ng thing/ŏ pot/ō toe/ô paw, for/oi noise/ou out/o͝o took/o͞o boot/p pop/r roar/s sauce/sh ship, dish/

through Alabama to the Coosa, with which it forms the Alabama.

tall·boy (tôl′boi′) *n. British.* A **highboy** *(see).*

tall drink. A drink served in a tall glass and consisting typically of a liquor base with any of various diluents and flavorings.

Tal·ley·rand-Pé·ri·gord (tăl′ē-rănd′pĕr′ə-gôr′; *French* tà-lĕ-räɴ′pā-rē-gôr′), **Charles Maurice de.** Prince de Bénévent. 1754–1838. French statesman and diplomat; author of *Mémoires* (published 1891–92).

Tal·linn (tăl′ĭn, täl′ĭn). *Russian* **Tal·lin** (täl′yĭn). The capital of Estonia, a seaport on the Gulf of Finland opposite Helsinki. Population, 330,000.

tal·lith (tä′lĭs, -lĭth) *n., pl.* **tallithim** (tä′lĭ-sēm′, -thēm′). A fringed prayer shawl with bands of black or blue, worn by Orthodox and Conservative Jewish men at prayer and on certain solemn occasions. [Hebrew (Mishnaic) *ṭallīth,* "cover," from Hebrew *tillēl,* he covered.]

tall oil (täl, tôl). An oily resinous liquid composed of a mixture of rosin acids and fatty acids obtained as a by-product in the treatment of pine pulp and used in soaps, emulsions, and lubricants. [Partial translation of German *Tallöl,* from Swedish *tallolja* : *tall,* pine, from Old Norse *thöll*†, young pine tree + *Öl,* oil.]

tal·low (tăl′ō) *n.* **1.** A mixture of the whitish, tasteless solid or hard fat obtained from parts of the bodies of cattle, sheep, or horses, and used in edibles or to make candles, leather dressing, soap, and lubricants. **2.** Any of various similar fats, as from plants. —*tr.v.* **tallowed, -lowing, -lows. 1.** To smear or cover with tallow. **2.** To fatten (animals) for the purpose of obtaining tallow. [Middle English *talg, talgh, talow,* from Middle Low German *talg, talch.* See **del-**[4] in Appendix.*] —**tal′low·y** *adj.*

tal·ly (tăl′ē) *n., pl.* **-lies. 1.** A stick on which notches are made to keep a count or score. **2.** The reckoning or score kept on a piece of wood, a gunstock, blackboard, or score card. **3.** A mark used in recording a number of acts or objects, most often in series of five, consisting of four vertical lines canceled diagonally or horizontally by a fifth line. **4.** A label of identification used in gardens and greenhouses. **5.** Anything that is very similar to something else; a double. **6.** A metal plate attached to a ship's machinery and bearing instructions for its use. —*v.* **tallied, -lying, -lies.** —*tr.* **1.** To record by making a mark. **2.** To reckon or count. **3.** To label with a tally. **4.** To cause to correspond or agree. —*intr.* **1.** To be alike; agree. **2.** To keep score or reckoning of a thing. [Middle English *taly, talye,* from Norman French *tallie,* from Medieval Latin *tal(l)ia,* from Latin *tālea,* twig, cutting, stick. See **tailor.**]

tal·ly·ho (tăl′ē-hō′) *interj.* Used to urge hounds in fox hunting. —*v.* **tallyhoed, -hoing, -hos.** —*tr.* To excite (hounds) on a fox hunt by shouting "tallyho" when the fox is sighted. —*intr.* To shout "tallyho" as a hunting cry. —*n., pl.* **tallyhos. 1.** The cry of "tallyho." **2.** A kind of pleasure coach drawn by four horses. [Probably from French *taïaut,* from Old French *thialau, taho,* cry used to urge hounds.]

tal·ly·man (tăl′ē-mən) *n., pl.* **-men** (-mĭn). **1.** A recorder or score keeper. **2.** *British.* A merchant whose customers pay him by the week according to a simple reckoning, without regular bookkeeping and billing.

Tal·mi gold (tăl′mē). A composite metal made of gold and brass, used in making jewelry. [German *Talmigold,* partial translation of French *Talmi-or,* contraction of *Tallois-demi-or,* "half gold (made by) Tallois (a Parisian)."]

Tal·mud (tăl′mo͝od′, tăl′məd) *n.* The collection of ancient Rabbinic writings consisting of the Mishnah and the Gemara, constituting the basis of religious authority for traditional Judaism. [Hebrew (Mishnaic) *talmūd,* learning, instruction, from *lāmadh,* he learned.] —**Tal·mu′dic** (tăl-mo͞o′dĭk, -myo͞o′dĭk, -mŭd′ĭk, -mo͝od′ĭk, tăl-), **Tal·mu′di·cal** *adj.* —**Tal′mud·ist** (tăl′mo͝od-ĭst, tăl′məd-) *n.*

tal·on (tăl′ən) *n.* **1. a.** The claw of a bird of prey. **b.** The similar claw of a predatory animal. **2.** Anything similar to or suggestive of a claw. **3.** The part of a lock which the key presses in order to shoot the bolt. **4.** The part of the deck of cards in certain card games left on the table after the deal. [Middle English, originally "heel," "hinder claw," from Old French, heel, spur, from (unattested) Vulgar Latin *tālō* (stem *tālōn-*), variant of Latin *tālus,* ankle, TALUS.]

ta·lus[1] (tā′ləs) *n., pl.* **-li** (-lī′). **1.** A tarsal bone that articulates with the tibia and fibula to form the anklebone. Also called "anklebone," "astragalus." **2.** The ankle. [New Latin, from Latin *tālus,* ankle, probably from Celtic, akin to Irish *sal*†, talon.]

ta·lus[2] (tā′ləs) *n., pl.* **-luses. 1.** A slope formed by the accumulation of debris. **2.** A sloping mass of debris at the base of a cliff. [French, from Old French, probably from Latin *talūtium,* a technical term in mining in Spain, "outcrop indicating the presence of gold-bearing topsoil," from Celtic. See **tel-**[2] in Appendix.*]

tam (tăm) *n.* A hat, a **tam-o'-shanter** *(see).*

ta·ma·le (tə-mä′lē) *n.* A Mexican dish made of fried chopped meat and crushed peppers, highly seasoned, wrapped in corn husks, and steamed. [Mexican Spanish *tamal* (plural *tamales*), from Nahuatl *tamalli.*]

Tam·al·pa·is, Mount (tăm′əl-pī′əs). A mountain rising to 2,604 feet in western California; a resort area across the Golden Gate Bridge from San Francisco.

ta·man·dua (tə-măn′də-wä′) *n.* A chiefly arboreal anteater, *Tamandua tetradactyla,* of tropical America, having a dense, furry coat. [Portuguese *tamanduá,* from Tupi, "ant-catcher" : *tacy,* ant + *monduar,* to catch.]

tam·a·rack (tăm′ə-răk′) *n.* Any of several North American larch trees; especially, *Larix laricina,* having short deciduous needles. Also called "hackmatack." [From Algonquian.]

tam·a·rau (tăm′ə-rou′) *n.* Also **ta·ma·rao.** A small, short-horned buffalo, *Anoa mindorensis,* of the island of Mindoro in the Philippines. [Tagalog *tamaráw, timaraw.*]

tam·a·rin (tăm′ə-rĭn, -răn′) *n.* Any of various small, long-tailed monkeys of the genus *Saguinus,* of tropical South America. [French, from Galibi.]

tam·a·rind (tăm′ə-rĭnd′) *n.* **1.** A tropical Old World tree, *Tamarindus indica,* having compound leaves and red-striped yellow flowers. **2.** The fruit of this tree, consisting of a long pod with seeds embedded in an edible, acid-flavored pulp. [Medieval Latin *tamarindus,* from Arabic *tamr hindī,* "date of India" : *tamr,* date + *hindī,* of India, from Persian *Hind,* India (see **Hindi**).]

tam·a·risk (tăm′ə-rĭsk′) *n.* Any of numerous shrubs or small trees of the genus *Tamarix,* native to Eurasia, having small, scalelike leaves and clusters of pink flowers. [Middle English *tamarisc, thamarike,* from Late Latin *tamariscus,* variant of Latin *tamarīx*†.]

Ta·ma·tave (tä′mä-täv′, tăm′ə-). A city and seaport on eastern Madagascar. Population, 51,000.

Ta·mau·li·pas (tä′mou-lē′päs). A state of Mexico, occupying 30,734 square miles in the east on the Gulf of Mexico. Population, 1,142,000. Capital, Ciudad Victoria.

Ta·ma·yo (tä-mä′yō), **Rufino.** Born 1899. Mexican painter.

tam·bac. Variant of **tombac.**

Tam·bo·ra, Mount (täm′bə-rä′). An active volcano in Indonesia, rising to 9,253 feet on the island of Sumbawa.

tam·bour (tăm′bo͝or′, tăm-bo͝or′) *n.* **1.** A drum or drummer. **2. a.** A small wooden embroidery frame consisting of two concentric hoops between which fabric is stretched. **b.** Embroidery made on such a frame. **3.** A rolling front or top for a desk, consisting of narrow strips of wood glued to canvas. **4. a.** The wall of a circular building surrounded with columns. **b.** The vertical part of a cupola. —*v.* **tamboured, -bouring, -bours.** —*tr.* To do (embroidery) on a tambour. —*intr.* To work at a tambour frame. [Middle English, from Old French, from Arabic *ṭanbūr,* probably alteration (by confusion with *ṭanbūr,* lute, TAMBOURA) of Persian *ṭabīr,* drum, TABOR.]

tam·bou·ra (tŭm-bo͞o′rə) *n.* Also **tam·bu·ra.** An unfretted lute of India, used as a harmonic drone. [Hindi, from Persian *ṭanbūr,* from Arabic. See also **tambour.**]

tam·bou·rin (tăm′bo͞o-rĭn; *French* täɴ-bo͞o-răɴ′) *n.* **1.** A long, narrow drum used in Provence. **2.** A player on this drum. **3.** A style of dance in lively two-beat rhythm, accompanied by the tambourin. [Provençal *tamborin,* diminutive of *tambor,* variant of Old French *tambour,* TAMBOUR.]

tam·bou·rine (tăm′bə-rēn′) *n.* A musical instrument consisting of a small drumhead with jingling disks fitted into the rim that is carried and shaken with one hand and struck with the other. [French *tambourin,* diminutive of TAMBOUR.]

Tam·bov (täm-bôf′). A city in the Russian S.F.S.R., 260 miles southeast of Moscow. Population, 203,000.

tame (tām) *adj.* **tamer, tamest. 1.** Brought from wildness into a domesticated or tractable state. **2.** Naturally gentle or unafraid; not timid. Said of animals: *"The sea otter is gentle and relatively tame,"* (Peter Matthiessen). **3.** Submissive; docile; fawning: *a tame husband.* **4.** Insipid; flat: *a tame Christmas party.* **5.** Sluggish; languid; inactive: *a tame river.* —*tr.v.* **tamed, taming, tames. 1.** To make tractable; domesticate. **2.** To subdue or curb. **3.** To soften; tone down. [Middle English *tame,* Old English *tam.* See **deme-**[2] in Appendix.*]

Tam·er·lane (tăm′ər-lān′). Also **Tam·bur·laine** (tăm′bər-lān′). Persian name **Ti·mur Lenk** (tĭ-mo͝or′ lĕngk′). Also known as Timour or Timur. 1336?–1405. Islamic conqueror of much of central Asia and eastern Europe.

Tam·il (tăm′əl, tŭm′-) *n.* **1.** A member of a Dravidian race of southern India and Ceylon. **2.** The language spoken by this race. —*adj.* Of or pertaining to the Tamils. [Tamil *Tamil, Tamir,* probably akin to Prakrit *Damiḷa, Damiḍa,* Sanskrit *Drāviḍaḥ,* DRAVIDIAN.]

Tamm (täm), **Igor Yevgenyevich.** Born 1895. Soviet physicist; worked on velocity of high-energy particles.

Tam·ma·ny (tăm′ə-nē) *n.* An organization of the Democratic Party in New York City, founded as a fraternal society in 1789. Also called "Tammany Hall." [From *Tammany* Hall, its meeting place, after *Tamanend,* "the affable," 17th-century Delaware Indian chief noted for his friendliness to white men.]

Tam·mer·fors. The Swedish name for **Tampere.**

Tam·mer·kos·ki. The Finnish name for **Tampere.**

Tam·muz (tä-mo͞oz′, tä′mo͞oz′) *n.* Also **Tham·muz.** The tenth month in the Hebrew calendar, corresponding to part of June and part of July. See **calendar.** [Hebrew *Tammūz,* from Babylonian *Du′uzu, Duzu* (name of a god), contractions of *Dumu-zi,* "the son who rises."]

tam-o'-shan·ter (tăm′ə-shăn′tər) *n.* A tight-fitting Scottish cap or braided bonnet, sometimes having a pompon, tassel, or feather in the center. Also called "tam." [After the hero of Burns's poem *Tam o'Shanter.*]

tamp (tămp) *tr.v.* **tamped, tamping, tamps. 1.** To pack down tightly by a succession of blows or taps. **2.** To pack clay, sand, or dirt into (a drill hole) above an explosive. [Probably back-formation from TAMPION.]

Tam·pa (tăm′pə). A city of west-central Florida, a seaport on Tampa Bay. Population, 302,000 (urban area).

Tam·pa Bay (tăm′pə). An inlet of the Gulf of Mexico, extending about 25 miles into west-central Florida.

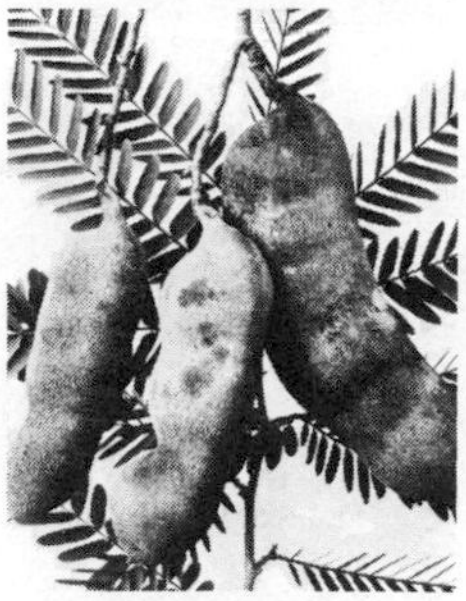

tamarind

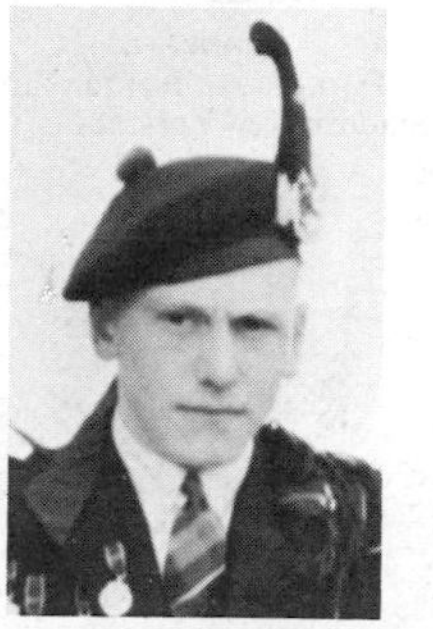

tam-o'-shanter

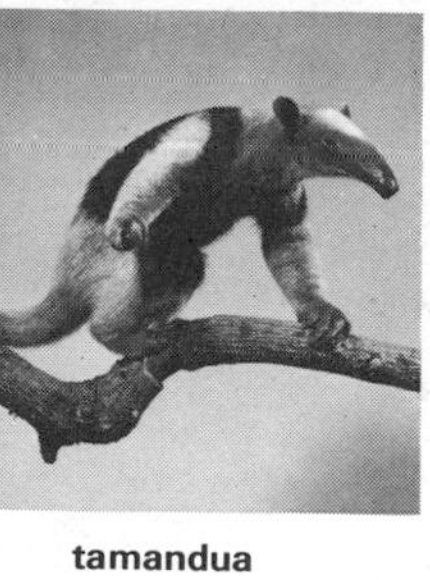

tamandua

t tight/th thin, path/*th* this, bathe/ŭ cut/ûr urge/v valve/w with/y yes/z zebra, size/zh vision/ə about, item, edible, gallop, circus/ à *Fr.* ami/œ *Fr.* feu, *Ger.* schön/ü *Fr.* tu, *Ger.* über/KH *Ger.* ich, *Scot.* loch/N *Fr.* bon. ***Follows main vocabulary. †Of obscure origin.**

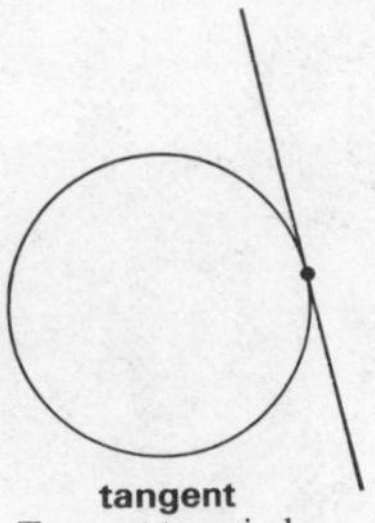
tangent
Tangent to a circle

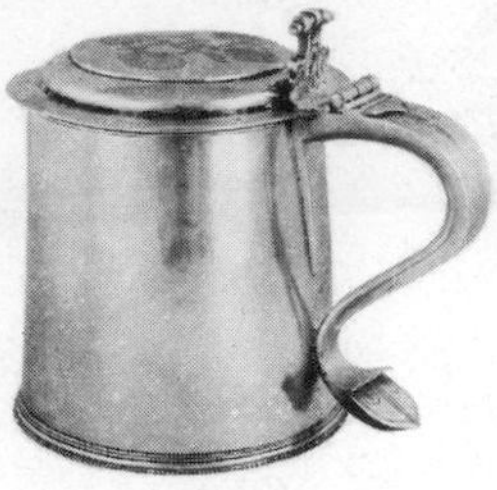
tankard
Two-quart silver tankard made in New York about 1668

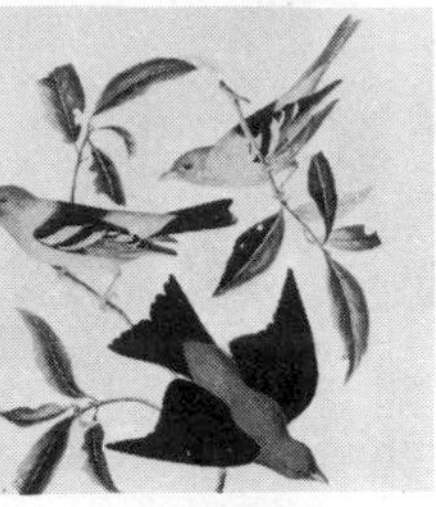
tanager
Above: Piranga ludoviciana
Below: Piranga olivacea
Painting by
John James Audubon

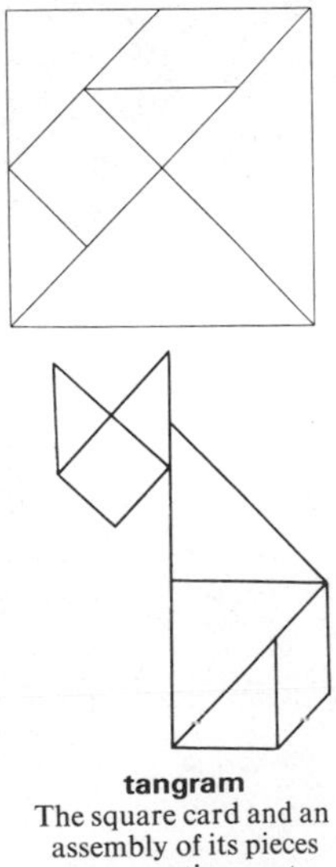
tangram
The square card and an assembly of its pieces representing a cat

tam·per[1] (tăm′pər) *v.* **-pered, -pering, -pers.** *—intr.* **1.** To interfere in a harmful manner. Used with *with: tampering with a delicate mechanism.* **2.** To meddle rashly or foolishly. Used with *with: tamper with another's feelings.* **3.** To bring about an improper situation or condition by clandestine means. Used with *with: tamper with a jury; tamper with a contract.* *—tr.* To alter improperly. See Synonyms at **interfere.** [Originally "to prepare (clay) by mixing," variant of TEMPER.] **—tam′per·er** *n.*

tamp·er[2] (tăm′pər) *n.* **1.** One that tamps. **2.** A neutron reflector in an atomic bomb that also delays the expansion of the exploding material, making possible a longer-lasting, more energetic, and more efficient explosion.

Tam·pe·re (täm′pĕ-rĕ). *Swedish* **Tam·mer·fors** (tä′mər-fôrz′); *Finnish* **Tam·mer·kos·ki** (tä′mər-kŏs′kē). A city of Finland, an industrial center in the southwest. Population, 177,000.

Tam·pi·co (tăm-pē′kō). A city of east-central Mexico, a major port and petroleum-producing center near the Gulf of Mexico. Population, 140,000.

Tampico hemp. **Pita** *(see)* or the fiber obtained from it.

tam·pi·on (tăm′pē-ən) *n.* Also **tom·pi·on** (tŏm′-). A plug or cover for the muzzle of a cannon or gun to keep out dust and moisture. [Middle English *tamp(y)on,* from Old French *tampon,* cotton plug, TAMPON.]

tam·pon (tăm′pŏn′) *n.* A plug of absorbent material inserted into a bodily cavity or wound to check a flow of blood or absorb secretions. *—tr.v.* **tamponed, -poning, -pons.** To plug or stop with a tampon. [French, from Old French, nasalized variant of *tapon,* from Frankish *tappo* (unattested), plug. See **tap-** in Appendix.*]

Tam·ri·da (tăm-rē′də). The chief town and administrative center of the island of Socotra, Southern Yemen.

tam-tam (tŭm′tŭm′, tăm′tăm′) *n.* **1.** One of a set of tuned gongs used in a gamelan orchestra. **2.** A type of drum, a **tom-tom** *(see).* [Hindi *ṭamṭam* (imitative).]

tan (tăn) *v.* **tanned, tanning, tans.** *—tr.* **1.** To convert (hide) into leather, as by treating with tannin. **2.** To make brown by exposure to the sun. **3.** *Informal.* To thrash; beat. *—intr.* To become brown or tawny from exposure to sun. *—n.* **1.** A light or moderate yellowish brown to brownish orange. See **color.** **2.** The brown color sun rays impart to the skin. **3.** **Tanbark** *(see).* **4.** **Tannin** *(see)* or a solution derived from it. *—adj.* **tanner, tannest.** **1.** Of the color tan. **2.** Having a sun tan. **3.** Used in or relating to tanning. [Middle English *tannen,* from Old English *tannian* (attested only by the past participle, *getanned* and by *tannere,* tanner) and Old French *tanner,* both from Medieval Latin *tannāre,* from *tannum,* oak bark (used in tanning), probably from Gaulish *tanno-,* oak, from Common Celtic *tann-* (unattested).]

tan tangent.

Tan (tăn) *n., pl.* **Tan** or **Tans.** A people, the **Tanka** *(see).*

Ta·na (tä′nä). **1.** A river rising in central Kenya and flowing about 500 miles first east and then south to the Indian Ocean. **2.** *Finnish* **Te·no** (tĕ′nô). A river rising in northeastern Norway and flowing 200 miles generally northeast to the Barents Sea, forming part of the Norwegian-Finnish border on its course.

Ta·na, Lake (tä′nä). Also **Tsa·na** (tsä′nä). The largest lake (1,400 square miles) of Ethiopia, in the northwestern part of the country; the source of the Blue Nile.

tan·a·ger (tăn′ĭ-jər) *n.* Any of various small New World birds of the family Thraupidae, often having brightly colored plumage in the males. [New Latin *tanagra,* from Portuguese *tangará,* from Tupi : *atá,* to walk + *carâ,* around.]

Ta·na·ka (tä-nä′kä), Baron **Giichi.** 1863–1929. Japanese militarist; prime minister (1927–29).

Tan·a·na (tăn′ə-nô′). A river rising in the Yukon Territory, Canada, near the Alaska border, and flowing 600 miles generally northwest to the Yukon River in central Alaska.

Ta·nan·a·rive (tə-năn′ə-rēv′). Also **Ta·nan·a·ri·vo** (-rē′vō). The capital of the Malagasy Republic, a city in the east-central part of the island of Madagascar. Population, 299,000.

tan·bark (tăn′bärk′) *n.* **1.** The bark of various trees, used as a source of tannin. **2.** Shredded bark from which the tannin has been extracted, used to cover circus arenas, racetracks, and the like. In this sense, also called "tan."

tan·dem (tăn′dəm) *n.* **1.** A two-wheeled carriage drawn by horses harnessed one before the other. **2.** A team of carriage horses harnessed in single file. **3.** A bicycle built for two. Also called "tandem bicycle." **4.** An arrangement of two or more persons or objects placed one behind the other. *—adv.* One behind the other. [Latin *tandem,* "exactly then," at length, finally (but jocularly taken to mean "lengthwise," "one after another") : *tam,* so, so much (see **to-** in Appendix*) + *-dem,* demonstrative suffix (see **de-** in Appendix*).] **—tan′dem** *adj.*

Tan·djung·pri·ok (tän′jŏŏng-prē′ôk). Also **Tan·jung·pri·ok.** A city of Indonesia, a seaport on the northwestern coast of Java, just east of Djakarta. Population, 141,000.

Ta·ney (tô′nē), **Roger Brooke.** 1777–1864. American jurist; Chief Justice of the United States (1836–64).

tang[1] (tăng) *n.* **1.** A sharp, often acrid taste, flavor, or odor, as that of orange juice or autumn air. **2.** A distinctive quality that adds piquancy. **3.** A trace, hint, or smattering of something. **4. a.** A sharp point, shank, tongue, or prong. **b.** A projection by which a tool, such as a chisel, sword blade, or knife, is attached to its handle or stock. In this sense, also called "shank." *—tr.v.* **tanged, tanging, tangs.** To furnish with a tang. [Middle English *tange,* serpent's tongue, insect's sting, probably from Old Norse *tangi,* a sting, point. See **denk-** in Appendix.*] **—tang′y** *adj.*

tang[2] (tăng) *n.* A loud ringing sound; a twang. *—v.* **tanged, tanging, tangs.** *—tr.* To cause to twang. *—intr.* To twang; to ring. [Imitative.]

Tang (täng). Also **T'ang.** A Chinese dynasty (A.D. 618–907).

Tan·gan·yi·ka (tăn′gən-yē′kə, tăng′-). A former nation of east-central Africa that joined with Zanzibar in 1964 to form Tanzania.

Tan·gan·yi·ka, Lake (tăn′gən-yē′kə, tăng′-). The longest (400 miles) lake in Africa, occupying 12,700 square miles between Tanzania and the Congo (Kinshasa).

tan·ge·lo (tăn′jə-lō′) *n., pl.* **-los.** **1.** A hybrid citrus tree that is a cross between certain varieties of grapefruit and tangerine. **2.** The fruit of this tree, having an acid orange pulp. [Blend of TANGE(RINE) and (POME)LO.]

tan·gen·cy (tăn′jən-sē) *n.* Also **tan·gence** (-jəns). The condition of being tangent.

tan·gent (tăn′jənt) *adj.* **1.** Making contact at a single point or along a line; touching but not intersecting. **2.** Irrelevant. *—n.* **1.** A line, curve, or surface touching but not intersecting another line, curve, or surface. **2.** *Abbr.* **tan a.** The ratio of the ordinate to the abscissa of the endpoint of an arc of a unit circle centered at the origin of a Cartesian coordinate system, the arc being of length x and measured counterclockwise from the point (1,0) if x is positive or clockwise if x is negative. **b.** The function of an acute angle in a right triangle that is the ratio of the length of the side opposite the angle to the length of the side adjacent to the angle. **3.** A sudden digression or change of course: *go off at a tangent.* [From New Latin *linea tangēns,* "touching line," from Latin *tangēns,* present participle of *tangere,* to touch. See **tag-** in Appendix.*]

tan·gen·tial (tăn-jĕn′shəl) *adj.* Also **tan·gen·tal** (-jĕnt′l). **1.** Of, pertaining to, or moving along or in the direction of a tangent. **2.** Merely touching or slightly connected. **3.** Only superficially relevant; divergent: *a tangential remark.* **—tan·gen′ti·al′i·ty** (-shē-ăl′ə-tē) *n.* **—tan·gen′tial·ly** *adv.*

tangent plane. The plane containing all the lines tangent to a specified point on a surface.

tan·ger·ine (tăn′jə-rēn′) *n.* **1.** A widely cultivated citrus tree, *Citrus nobilis deliciosa,* bearing edible fruit having an easily peeled deep-orange skin and sweet, juicy pulp. Also called "mandarin orange." **2.** The fruit of this tree. Also called "mandarin orange." **3.** Strong reddish orange to strong or vivid orange. See **color.** [Short for *tangerine orange,* "orange of Tangier," from *Tanger,* French form of TANGIER (from which such oranges were first imported).] **—tan′ger·ine′** *adj.*

Tan·ger·ine (tăn′jə-rēn′) *adj.* Of or related to Tangier, Morocco. *—n.* A native or resident of Tangier.

tan·gi·ble (tăn′jə-bəl) *adj.* **1. a.** Discernible by the touch; capable of being touched; palpable. **b.** *Law.* Visible and appraisable; corporeal: *tangible property.* **2. a.** Capable of being exactly comprehended. **b.** That can be treated as a fact; real; concrete: *tangible evidence.* —See Synonyms at **real.** *—n.* **1.** Something palpable or concrete. **2.** *Plural.* Material assets. [Old French *tangible,* from Late Latin *tangibilis,* from Latin *tangere,* to touch. See **tag-** in Appendix.*] **—tan′gi·bil′i·ty, tan′gi·ble·ness** *n.* **—tan′gi·bly** *adv.*

Tan·gier (tăn-jîr′). *French* **Tan·ger** (täN-zhā′). A city of Morocco, a major seaport in the extreme north on the Strait of Gibraltar. Population, 142,000.

tan·gle[1] (tăng′gəl) *v.* **-gled, -gling, -gles.** *—tr.* **1.** To mix together or intertwine in a confused mass; to snarl. **2.** To involve in hampering or awkward complications; entangle. **3.** To trap; ensnare. *—intr.* To be or become entangled. **—tangle with.** *Informal.* To come to grips or blows with. *—n.* **1.** A confused, intertwined mass. **2.** A jumbled or confused state or condition. **3.** A state of bewilderment. **4.** *Informal.* An argument; altercation. [Middle English *tangilen,* nasalized variant of *tagilen,* probably from Scandinavian, akin to Swedish dialectal *taggla*†, to entangle.] **—tang′ly** *adj.*

tan·gle[2] (tăng′gəl) *n.* A large seaweed of the genus *Laminaria.* [Originally Scottish, probably from Old Norse *thöngull.* See **tenk-**[2] in Appendix.*]

tan·gle·ber·ry (tăng′gəl-bĕr′ē) *n., pl.* **-ries.** The **dangleberry** *(see).*

tan·gled (tăng′gəld) *adj.* Complicated in a random way. See Synonyms at **complex.**

tan·go (tăng′gō) *n., pl.* **-gos.** **1.** A Latin-American ballroom dance in 2/4 or 4/4 time. **2.** The music for this dance. *—intr.v.* **tangoed, -going, -gos.** To dance the tango. [American Spanish, originally an Afro-American drum dance, possibly of Niger-Congo origin.]

tan·gram (tăng′grəm) *n.* A Chinese puzzle consisting of a square cut into five triangles, a square, and a rhomboid, to be reassembled into different figures. [Possibly Chinese *t'ang*[2], TANG (Chinese dynasty, hence "the Chinese") + -GRAM.]

Tang·shan (täng′shän′). A city and industrial center of northeastern China, in Hopei Province about 90 miles southeast of Peking. Population, 812,000.

Tan·guy (täN-gē′), **Yves.** 1900–1955. French-born American surrealist painter.

tanh hyperbolic tangent.

Ta·nim·bar Islands (tə-nĭm′bär′, tăn′ĭm-). A group of islands of Indonesia, 2,172 square miles in area, lying in the southern Moluccas group.

Ta·nis (tā′nĭs). Biblical name **Zo·an** (zō′ăn′). An ancient city in the Nile Delta of northern Egypt.

tan·ist (tăn′ĭst, thô′nĭst) *n.* Among the ancient Celts, the heir apparent to the chief, elected during the chief's lifetime. [Irish Gaelic *tānaiste,* "second person," from Old Irish *tānaise*†, second, next.]

tan·ist·ry (tăn′ĭ-strē, thô′nĭ-) *n.* The system of electing a tanist.
Tan·jore. See **Thanjavur.**
Tan·jung·pri·ok. See **Tandjungpriok.**
tank (tăngk) *n.* **1.** A large, often metallic container for fluids. **2.** A pool, pond, reservoir, or cistern, especially one for drinking water or irrigation. **3.** *Military.* An enclosed, heavily armored combat vehicle that is mounted with cannon and guns and moves on caterpillar treads. **4.** *Slang.* A jail or jail cell. —*tr.v.* **tanked, tanking, tanks.** To place, store, or process in a tank. [Perhaps from Gujarati *tānkh,* pond, cistern, possibly from Sanskrit *taḍāga,* pond, probably from Dravidian. *Tank* (military vehicle) was originally a British code name, from its resemblance to a benzene tank.]
tan·ka[1] (täng′kä) *n.* A Japanese verse form in five lines, the first and third composed of five syllables and the rest of seven. [Japanese, "short poem," from Ancient Chinese *tuân kâ* (Mandarin *tuan*[3] *kê*[1]) : *tuân,* short + *kâ,* song, poem.]
tan·ka[2] (tăng′kə) *n.* A Tibetan religious painting, usually mounted on fabric. [Tibetan *thanka.*]
Tan·ka (täng′kä) *n., pl.* **Tanka** or **-kas.** A people in southern China and Hong Kong who live on small boats, clustered in colonies. Also called "Tan." [Cantonese *tan ka* : *tan,* tribal name represented by the character *tan*[4], "egg" + *ka,* variant of Mandarin Chinese *chia*[1], family, people.]
tank·age (tăng′kĭj) *n.* **1.** The capacity or contents of a tank or tanks. **2.** The act or process of putting or storing in a tank. **3.** The fee for such storage. **4.** Animal residues left after rendering fat in a slaughterhouse and used for fertilizer or feed.
tank·ard (tăng′kərd) *n.* A large drinking cup having a single handle and often a hinged cover; especially, a tall pewter or silver mug. [Middle English *tankard,* probably related to Middle Dutch *tanckaert*†.]
tank destroyer. A high-speed armored vehicle equipped with antitank guns.
tank·er (tăng′kər) *n.* A ship, plane, or truck constructed to transport oil or other liquids in bulk.
tank town. **1.** A town where trains formerly refilled their boilers from a water tank. **2.** A small or unimportant town.
tank trailer. A truck trailer equipped as a tanker.
tan·nage (tăn′ĭj) *n.* **1.** The act, process, or skill of tanning. **2.** Something tanned.
Tan·nen·berg. The German name for **Stębark.**
tan·ner[1] (tăn′ər) *n.* A person who tans hides.
tan·ner[2] (tăn′ər) *n. British Slang.* A sixpence. [Origin unknown.]
tan·ner·y (tăn′ər-ē) *n., pl.* **-ies.** A place where hides are tanned.
tan·nic (tăn′ĭk) *adj.* Pertaining to or obtained from tannin.
tannic acid. A lustrous yellowish to light-brown amorphous, powdered, flaked, or spongy mass having the approximate composition $C_{76}H_{52}O_{46}$, derived from the bark and fruit of many plants and used in tanning, as a mordant, to clarify wine and beer, and as an astringent and styptic. Also called "tannin."
tan·nif·er·ous (tăn-ĭf′ər-əs) *adj.* Containing or yielding tannin. [TANNI(N) + -FEROUS.]
tan·nin (tăn′ən) *n.* **1. Tannic acid** *(see).* **2.** Any of various chemically different substances capable of promoting tanning. Also called "tan." [French *tanin,* from *tanner,* to TAN.]
tan·ning (tăn′ĭng) *n.* **1.** The art or process of making leather from rawhides. **2.** The browning of the skin by exposure to sun and weather. **3.** *Informal.* A beating; a whipping.
Ta·no·an (tä′nō-ən) *n.* A language family of several Indian peoples of New Mexico and northeastern Arizona. [From *Tano,* name of this group of peoples.] —**Ta′no·an** *adj.*
tan·rec. Variant of **tenrec.**
tan·sy (tăn′zē) *n., pl.* **-sies.** Any of several plants of the genus *Tanacetum;* especially, *T. vulgare,* native to the Old World, having clusters of buttonlike yellow flowers and pungent, aromatic juice sometimes used medicinally and as a flavoring. [Middle English, from Old French *tanesie,* perhaps from Medieval Latin *athanasia,* an elixir of life, from Greek *athanasia,* immortality : *a-,* not, without + *thanatos,* death (see **dhwene-** in Appendix*).]
Tan·ta (tän′tä). A city of Egypt, in the Nile Delta about 55 miles north of Cairo. Population, 184,000.
tan·tal·ic (tăn-tăl′ĭk) *adj.* Of, pertaining to, or containing tantalum.
tan·ta·lite (tăn′tə-līt′) *n.* A black to red-brown mineral, essentially $(Fe,Mn)(Ta,Nb)_2O_6$, distinguished from columbite by the predominance of tantalum over niobium and used as an ore of both elements. [Swedish *tantalit,* from New Latin TANTALUM.]
tan·ta·lize (tăn′tə-līz′) *tr.v.* **-lized, -lizing, -lizes.** To tease or torment by or as if by exposing to view but keeping out of reach something much desired. [From TANTALUS.] —**tan′ta·li·za′tion** *n.* —**tan′ta·liz′er** *n.* —**tan′ta·liz′ing·ly** *adv.*
tan·ta·lum (tăn′tə-ləm) *n. Symbol* **Ta** A very hard, heavy gray metallic element that is exceptionally resistant to chemical attack below 150°C. It is used to make electric-light-bulb filaments, electrolytic capacitors, lightning arresters, nuclear reactor parts, and some surgical instruments. Atomic number 73, atomic weight 180.948, melting point 2,996°C, boiling point 5,425°C, specific gravity 16.6, valences 2, 3, 4, 5. See **element.** [New Latin, after TANTALUS, from the fact that when immersed in acid it is unaltered, like Tantalus standing in the water.]
tan·ta·lus (tăn′tə-ləs) *n.* A stand in which decanters are displayed locked up. [After TANTALUS.]
Tan·ta·lus (tăn′tə-ləs). *Greek Mythology.* A king who for his crimes was condemned in Hades to stand in water that receded when he tried to drink, and with fruit hanging above him that receded when he reached for it. [Latin, from Greek *Tantalos,* "bearer," "sufferer." See **tel-**[1] in Appendix.*]
tan·ta·mount (tăn′tə-mount′) *adj.* Equivalent in effect or value. Used with *to.* [Originally a verb, "to be equal to," from Norman French *tant amunter,* to amount to so much : Old French *tant,* so much, from Latin *tantus,* from *tam,* so (see **to-** in Appendix*) + *amo(u)nter,* to AMOUNT.]
tan·ta·ra (tăn-tăr′ə, -tär′ə) *n.* **1. a.** A fanfare of a trumpet or horn. **b.** A sound resembling such a fanfare. **2.** A hunting cry. [From Latin *taratantara* (imitative).]
tan·tiv·y (tăn-tĭv′ē) *adv.* At full gallop; at top speed. —*n., pl.* **tantivies.** **1.** A hunting cry. **2.** A fast and furious gallop; top speed. [Perhaps imitative of galloping horses.]
tant mieux (täɴ myœ′). *French.* So much the better.
tant pis (täɴ pē′). *French.* So much the worse.
tan·tra (tŭn′trə) *n.* One of a comparatively recent class of Hindu or Buddhist religious writings concerned with mysticism and magic. [Sanskrit, loom, warp, hence principle, doctrine, from *tanōti,* he stretches or weaves. See **ten-** in Appendix.*]
tan·trum (tăn′trəm) *n.* A fit of bad temper. [Origin unknown.]
tan·yard (tăn′yärd′) *n.* The section in a tannery where the tanning vats are located.
Tan·za·ni·a (tăn′zə-nē′ə, tăn-zā′nē-ə). Formerly **United Republic of Tan·gan·yi·ka and Zan·zi·bar.** Officially, The United Republic of Tanzania. A republic, 362,000 square miles in area, of eastern Africa, formed in 1964 by the federation of Tanganyika and Zanzibar. Population, 10,514,000. Capital, Dar es Salaam.
tan·zan·ite (tăn′zən-īt′) *n.* A hydrated calcium aluminum silicate mineral, exhibiting blue, violet, or greenish coloration depending on the polarization of incident light, used as a gem. [TANZAN(IA) + -ITE.]
Tao·ism (tou′ĭz′əm, dou′-) *n.* A principal philosophy and system of religion of China based upon the teachings of Lao-tse in the sixth century B.C. [From Mandarin Chinese *tao*[4], "the Way."] —**Tao′ist** *adj.* & *n.* —**Tao′is′tic** *adj.*
Taos (tä′ōs). A village, noted resort, and art colony of northern New Mexico. Population, 2,000.
tap[1] (tăp) *v.* **tapped, tapping, taps.** —*tr.* **1.** To strike gently but audibly. **2.** To give a light rap with: *tap a pencil.* **3.** To produce with a succession of light blows: *tap out a rhythm.* **4. a.** To repair (shoe heels or toes) by applying a tap. **b.** To attach metal taps to. —*intr.* **1.** To deliver a gentle, light blow or blows. **2.** To walk making light clicks. —*n.* **1. a.** A gentle but audible blow. **b.** The sound made by it. **2. a.** A thin layer of leather or a substitute applied to a worn-down shoe heel or toe. **b.** A metal plate attached to the toe or heel of a shoe, as for tap-dancing. [Middle English *tappen,* from Old French *taper,* from Germanic. See **tap-** in Appendix.*]
tap[2] (tăp) *n.* **1.** A valve and spout used to regulate delivery of a fluid at the end of a pipe. **2.** A plug for a bunghole; spigot. **3. a.** Liquor drawn from a tap. **b.** Liquor of a particular brew, cask, or quality. **4.** *Surgery.* The removal of bodily fluid: *a spinal tap.* **5.** A tool for cutting an internal screw thread. **6.** A makeshift terminal in an electric circuit. —**on tap.** **1.** Ready to be drawn; in a tapped cask. Said of beer or liquor. **2.** Available for immediate use; ready. —*tr.v.* **tapped, tapping, taps.** **1.** To furnish with a spigot or tap. **2.** To pierce in order to draw off liquid: *tap a maple tree.* **3.** To draw (liquid) from a vessel or container. **4.** *Surgery.* To withdraw fluid from (a bodily cavity). **5.** To make a connection with or open outlets from: *tap a water main.* **6. a.** To wiretap (a telephone wire). **b.** To establish an electric connection in (a power line), as to divert current secretly. **7.** To cut screw threads in (a collar, socket, or other fitting). **8.** *Informal.* To ask (a person) for money. [Middle English *tappe,* Old English *tæppa.* See **tap-** in Appendix.*]
ta·pa (tä′pə) *n.* **1.** The inner bark of the **paper mulberry** *(see).* **2.** A paperlike cloth made in the Pacific islands by pounding this or similar bark. [Marquesan and Tahitian.]
tap·a·der·a (tăp′ə-dâr′ə) *n.* Also **tap·a·der·o** (-dâr′ō) *pl.* **-os.** The leather hood of the stirrup of a range saddle. Also called "bulldog." [American Spanish, from Spanish, cover, from *tapar,* to cover, from *tapa,* cover, lid, from Germanic. See **tap-** in Appendix.*]
Ta·pa·jós (tä-pä-zhôz′). Also **Ta·pa·joz.** A river of Brazil, flowing about 500 miles northeast from the southwestern border of Pará State to the Amazon.
tap dance. A dance in which the rhythm is tapped out by the heels and toes in rapid complicated steps, the sound emphasized by taps on the dancer's shoes. —**tap dancer.**
tap-dance (tăp′dăns′, -däns′) *intr.v.* **-danced, -dancing, -dances.** To perform a tap dance.
tape (tāp) *n.* **1.** A narrow strip of strong woven fabric, such as that used in sewing or bookbinding. **2.** Any continuous narrow, flexible strip of cloth, metal, paper, or plastic, such as adhesive tape, magnetic tape, or ticker tape. **3.** A string stretched across the finish line of a racetrack to be broken by the winner. **4.** A **tape recording** *(see).* —*v.* **taped, taping, tapes.** —*tr.* **1. a.** To fasten, secure, strengthen, or wrap with a tape. **b.** To bind together (the sections of a book) by applying strips of tape to. **2.** To measure with a tape measure. **3.** To record on magnetic tape. —*intr.* To measure. [Middle English *tap(p)e,* Old English *tæppa, tæppe.* See **tap-** in Appendix.*]
tape cartridge. **1.** A cartridge containing an endless loop of magnetic tape and designed for automatic use on insertion into a tape recorder or player designed to receive it. **2.** A similar but usually smaller cartridge containing unlooped tape designed for use in a cassette-type tape recorder or player. In this sense, also called "cassette."

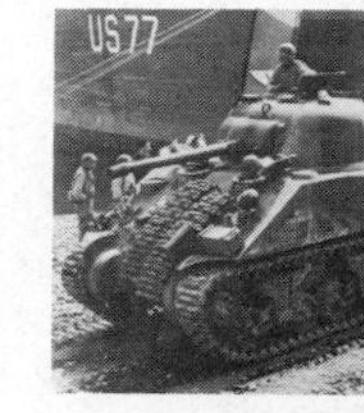

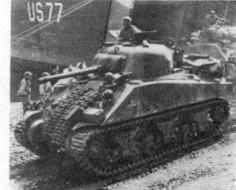

tank
World War II

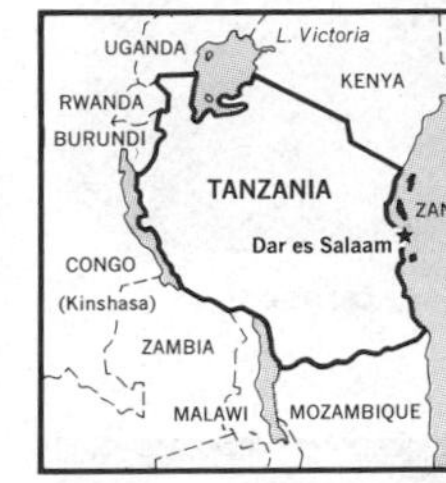

Tanzania

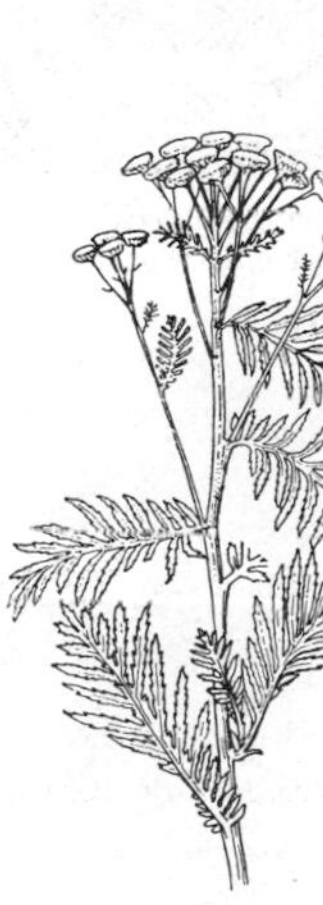
tansy
Tanacetum vulgare

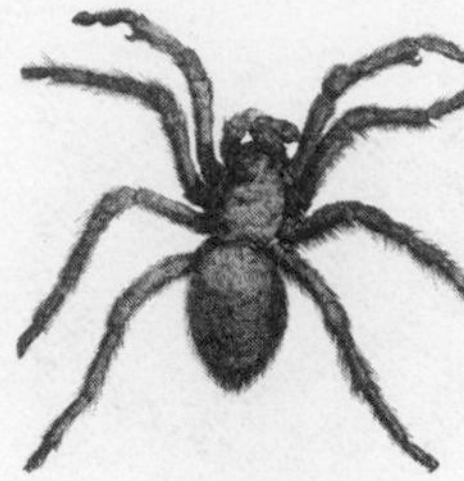
tarantula
Eurypelma californica

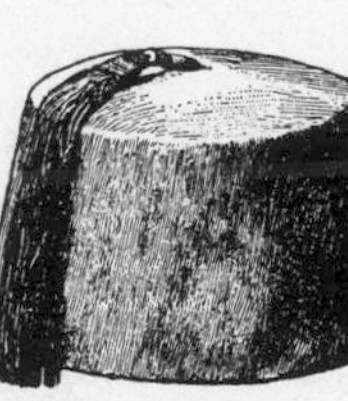
tarboosh

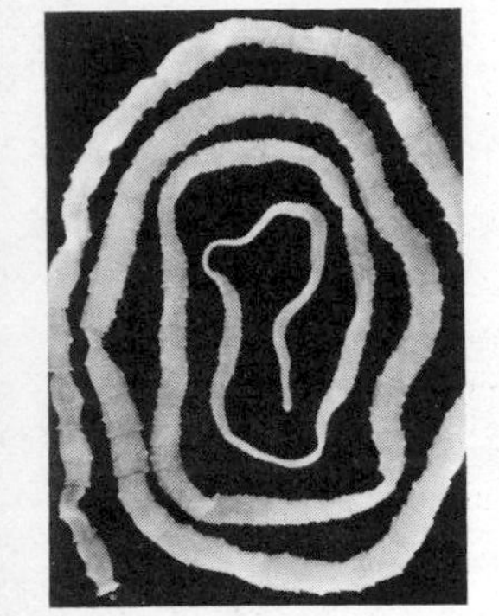
tapeworm
Taenia pisiformis

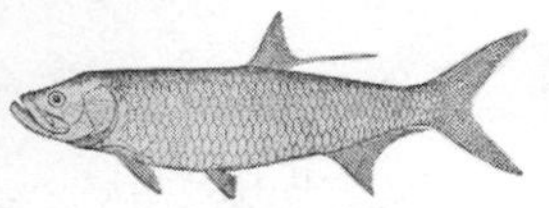
tarpon
Megalops atlantica

tape deck. A tape recorder and player having no built-in amplifiers or speakers, used as a component in a high-fidelity sound system.
tape grass. An aquatic plant, *Vallisneria spiralis,* having long, grasslike, submerged leaves. Also called "eelgrass," "wild celery."
tape measure. A tape of cloth, paper, or steel marked off in a linear scale, as inches or centimeters, for taking measurements. Also called "tapeline."
ta·per (tā′pər) *n.* **1.** A small or very slender candle. **2.** A long wax-coated wick used to light candles or gas lamps. **3.** Something that gives off a feeble light. **4.** A gradual decrease in thickness or width of an elongated object. —*v.* **tapered, -pering, -pers.** —*intr.* **1.** To become gradually narrower or thinner toward one end. **2.** To become gradually smaller or less; slacken and finally stop. Used with *off.* —*tr.* **1.** To make thinner or narrower at one end. **2.** To diminish or make smaller gradually. —*adj.* Gradually decreasing in size toward a point. [Middle English, from Old English *tapor, tapur,* probably altered from *papur* (unattested), from Latin *papȳrus,* papyrus, wick made of papyrus. See **paper.**] —**ta′per·ing·ly** *adv.*
tape-re·cord (tāp′rĭ-kôrd′) *tr.v.* **-corded, -cording, -cords.** To record on magnetic tape.
tape recorder. An apparatus used to record sound on magnetic tape and, usually, to play back sound so recorded.
tape recording. **1. a.** Magnetized tape on which sound has been recorded. **b.** The sound recorded on a magnetic tape. Also called "tape." **2.** The act of recording on magnetic tape.
tap·es·try (tăp′ĭ-strē) *n., pl.* **-tries.** **1.** A heavy textile fabric having a varicolored design woven across the warp, used for wall hangings, furniture coverings, and the like. **2.** A textile imitating this. —*tr.v.* **tapestried, -trying, -tries.** **1.** To hang or decorate with tapestry. **2.** To make, weave, or depict in a tapestry. [Middle English *tapstery,* altered from *tapissery, tapecery,* from Old French *tapisserie,* from *tapisser,* to cover with carpet, from *tapis, tapiz,* carpet, from Medieval Greek *tapition,* variant of Greek *tapētion,* diminutive of *tapēs,* carpet. See **temp-** in Appendix.*]
ta·pe·tum (tə-pē′təm) *n., pl.* **-ta** (-tə). **1.** *Botany.* A layer of nutritive cells within the sporangium of ferns and related plants or within the anther of seed plants. **2.** *Anatomy.* A membranous layer or region, especially in the choroid coat or retina. **3.** A stratum of fibers of the corpus callosum. [New Latin, from Medieval Latin, carpet, from Latin *tapēte,* from Greek *tapēs.* See **tapestry.**]
tape·worm (tāp′wûrm′) *n.* Any of various ribbonlike, often very long flatworms of the class Cestoda, that are parasitic in the intestines of vertebrates, including man.
tap house. A tavern or bar.
tap·i·o·ca (tăp′ē-ō′kə) *n.* A beady starch obtained from the root of the cassava, used for puddings and as a thickening agent in cooking. [Portuguese and Spanish, from Tupi *tipioca,* "residue."]
ta·pir (tā′pər, tə-pîr′) *n.* Any of several ungulate mammals of the genus *Tapirus,* of tropical America or southern Asia, having a heavy body, short legs, and a fleshy proboscis. [Guarani *tapiira.*]
Tap·pan Zee (tăp′ən zē′). A widening of the Hudson River in southeastern New York State.
tap·per (tăp′ər) *n.* One that taps.
tap·pet (tăp′ĭt) *n.* A lever or projecting arm that moves or is moved by contact with another part, usually to communicate a certain motion, as between a driving mechanism and a valve. [From TAP (to strike lightly).]
tap·ping (tăp′ĭng) *n.* **1.** The act of one that taps. **2.** Something that is taken or drawn by tapping.
tap·pit-hen (tăp′ĭt-hĕn′) *n. Scottish.* **1.** A crested hen. **2.** A large mug with a knobbed lid. [Scottish *tappit,* tufted, crested, from *tap,* dialectal variant of TOP.]
tap·room (tăp′ro͞om′, -ro͝om′) *n.* A bar or barroom.
tap·root (tăp′ro͞ot′, -ro͝ot′) *n. Botany.* The main root of a plant, usually stouter than the lateral roots and growing straight downward from the stem.
taps (tăps) *pl.n.* Used with a singular verb. A military bugle call or a drum signal sounded at night as an order to put out lights, and also sounded at military funerals and memorial services. [From TAP (light blow, drumbeat).]
tap·ster (tăp′stər) *n.* A person who draws and serves liquor for customers; tavernkeeper or bartender.
Ta·pu·ya (tä-po͞o′yə) *n., pl.* **Tapuya** or **-yas.** A Tapuyan Indian.
Ta·pu·yan (tä-po͞o′yən) *n.* A South American Indian linguistic stock of Brazil. —*adj.* Of or pertaining to this stock. [From Tupi *Tapua,* Tapuyan Indian, "savage."]
Ta·qua·ri (tä′kwə-rē′). A river rising in southeastern Mato Grosso, Brazil, and flowing 350 miles generally southwest to the Paraguay River near the Bolivian border.
tar[1] (tär) *n.* **1.** A dark, oily, viscid mixture, consisting mainly of hydrocarbons, produced by the destructive distillation of organic substances such as wood, coal, or peat. **2.** **Coal tar** *(see).* —*tr.v.* **tarred, tarring, tars.** To coat with tar. —**tar and feather.** To punish a person by covering with tar and feathers. —*adj.* Of, from, or like tar. [Middle English *taar, terr,* Old English *te(o)ru.* See **deru-** in Appendix.*]
tar[2] (tär) *n. Informal.* A sailor. [Short for TARPAULIN.]
Tar (tär). A river rising in north-central North Carolina and flowing 215 miles generally south to Pamlico Sound.
Tar·a (tăr′ə). A village in County Meath, Republic of Ireland, near the Hill of Tara, the historic seat of Irish kings.
Tar·a·ca·hi·tian (tăr′ə-kə-hē′shən) *adj.* Of or pertaining to a language family of the Uto-Aztecan group. [From *Tarahumara* and *Cahita,* names of two peoples in Mexico.]
tar·a·did·dle. *Informal.* Variant of **tarradiddle.**
tar·an·tel·la (tăr′ən-tĕl′ə) *n.* **1.** A lively, whirling southern Italian dance once thought to be a remedy for tarantism. **2.** The music for this dance, in 6/8 time. [Italian, diminutive formed from TARANTO, where tarantism was common.]
tar·an·tism (tăr′ən-tĭz′əm) *n.* A malady characterized by an uncontrollable urge to dance, epidemic in southern Italy from the 15th to the 17th century and believed to result from the bite of the tarantula. [New Latin *tarantismus,* after TARANTO, where tarantism was common.]
Ta·ran·to (tä′rän-tō). Ancient name **Ta·ren·tum** (tə-rĕn′təm). A city and industrial center of southern Italy, a seaport on the Gulf of Taranto. Population, 205,000.
Ta·ran·to, Gulf of (tä′rän-tō). An inlet of the Ionian Sea extending about 70 miles into southeastern Italy.
ta·ran·tu·la (tə-răn′cho͞o-lə) *n., pl.* **-las** or **-lae** (-lē′). **1.** Any of various large, hairy, chiefly tropical spiders of the family Theraphosidae, capable of inflicting a painful but not seriously poisonous bite. **2.** A similar spider, *Lycosa tarentula,* of southern Europe, once thought to cause tarantism. [Medieval Latin *tarantula,* from Italian *tarantola,* from TARANTO, where it is common.]
Ta·ra·wa (tə-rä′wə, tăr′ə-wə, tä′rä-wä′). The capital of the Gilbert and Ellice Islands, an atoll of about eight square miles in the northern Gilbert Islands; the site of a U.S. victory over the Japanese (1943). Population, 8,000.
Tarbes (tȧrb). A city of France, a commercial center in the southwest in the foothills of the Pyrenees. Population, 58,000.
tar·boosh (tär-bo͞osh′) *n.* Also **tar·bush.** A brimless, usually red, felt cap with a silk tassel, worn by Moslem men, either by itself or as the base of a turban. [Egyptian Arabic *ṭarbush,* "sweating cap" : Turkish *ter,* sweat + Persian *pūshidān*†, to cover.]
tar camphor. **Naphthalene** *(see).*
tar·di·grade (tär′də-grăd′) *n.* Any of various minute, slow-moving arthropods of the class Tardigrada, having eight legs and living in water or damp moss. —*adj.* **1.** Of or belonging to the Tardigrada. **2.** Slow in action; slow-moving. [New Latin *Tardigrada,* from Latin *tardigradus,* slow-moving : *tardus,* slow (see **tardy**) + -GRADE.]
tar·dy (tär′dē) *adj.* **-dier, -diest.** **1.** Occurring, arriving, or acting later than expected or scheduled; delayed; late. **2.** Moving slowly; sluggish. [Middle English *tardif, tardive,* slow, from Old French, from Common Romance *tardīvus* (unattested), from Latin *tardus*†, slow.] —**tar′di·ly** *adv.* —**tar′di·ness** *n.*
Synonyms: *tardy, late, overdue, dilatory, lagging.* These adjectives mean not arriving, occurring, or acting within a prescribed time. *Tardy* refers principally to persons who arrive after an appointed time, whereas *late* can apply also to the arrival or occurrence of things after a due or usual time. *Overdue,* applicable to persons and things, implies a marked violation of a scheduled time. *Dilatory* describes the habits or actions of persons who delay doing what should be done promptly. *Lagging* refers principally to persons or their actions or development and implies failure to maintain a schedule or standard of achievement.
tare[1] (târ) *n.* **1.** The common vetch, *Vicia sativa.* **2.** Any of several weedy plants that grow in grain fields. **3.** *Plural.* Noxious elements, likened to weeds growing among wheat. By allusion to Matthew 13:25: *"his enemy came and sowed tares among the wheat."* [Middle English *tare*†, seed of the vetch. (The plural *taris* was later used to render Greek *zizania,* noxious weeds, darnel.)]
tare[2] (târ) *n.* **1.** *Abbr.* **t.** The weight of a container or wrapper that is deducted from the gross weight to obtain net weight. **2.** A deduction from gross weight made to allow for the weight of a container. **3.** *Chemistry.* A counterbalance, especially an empty vessel used to counterbalance the weight of a similar container. —*tr.v.* **tared, taring, tares.** To determine, allow for, or indicate the tare. [Middle English, from Old French, waste, deficiency, from Medieval Latin *tara,* from Arabic *ṭarḥah,* thing thrown away, from *ṭaraḥa,* to reject, throw.]
Ta·ren·tum. The ancient name for **Taranto.**
targe (tärj) *n. Archaic.* A light shield or buckler. [Middle English, from Old French. See **target.**]
tar·get (tär′gĭt) *n.* **1.** An object with a marked surface that is shot at to test accuracy, as a padded disk with colored concentric circles for use in rifle or archery practice. **2.** Anything aimed or fired at. **3. a.** An object of criticism or attack. **b.** Something viewed as an object to be acted on with a view to transforming it. **4.** A desired goal. **5.** A railroad signal that indicates the position of a switch by its color, position, and shape. **6.** The sliding sight on a surveyor's leveling rod. **7.** A small, round shield. **8. a.** A structure in a camera tube with a storage surface that is scanned by an electron beam to generate a signal output current similar to the charge-density pattern stored on the surface. **b.** A usually metal part in an x-ray tube on which a beam of electrons is focused and from which x rays are emitted. [Middle English, from Old French *targette,* diminutive of *targe,* light shield, from Frankish *targa* (unattested). See **dergh-** in Appendix.*]
Tar·gum (tär′go͞om′, -go͞om′) *n., pl.* **-gums** or *Hebrew* **Targumim** (tär′go͞o-mēm′). Any of several Aramaic translations or paraphrasings of the Old Testament. [Mishnaic Hebrew *targūm,* translation, interpretation, from Hebrew *tirgēm,* he interpreted.] —**Tar′gum′ic, Tar′gum′i·cal** *adj.* —**Tar′gum·ist** *n.*
Tar Heel State. The nickname for North Carolina.
tar·iff (tăr′ĭf) *n.* **1.** A list or system of duties imposed by a

government on imported or exported goods. **2.** A duty or duties of this kind. **3.** Any schedule of prices or fees. *—tr.v.* **tariffed, -iffing, -iffs.** To fix a duty or price on. [French *tarif,* from Italian *tariffa* and Spanish *tarifa,* from Turkish *ta'rifa,* from Arabic *ta'rīf,* "information," "notification," from *'arafa,* to notify.]

Ta·rim (dä'rēm'). A river of the Sinkiang-Uigur Autonomous Region, China, formed in the west by the confluence of the Khotan and Yarkand rivers and flowing about 1,300 miles generally east to the Lop Nor Basin.

Tar·king·ton (tär'kĭng-tən), **(Newton) Booth.** 1869–1946. American novelist and playwright.

tar·la·tan (tär'lə-tən) *n.* Also **tar·le·tan.** A thin, stiffly starched open-weave muslin. [French *tarlatane,* perhaps from Portuguese *tarlatana,* irregular variant of *tiritana,* from French *tiretaine,* linsey-woolsey, TARTAN.]

tar·mac (tär'măk') *n.* **1.** *Capital* **T.** A trademark for a bituminous substance used as a binder in paving. **2.** An area paved with this substance, especially the area surrounding a hangar. **3.** A tarmacadam road or pavement. [Short for TARMACADAM.]

tar·mac·ad·am (tär'mə-kăd'əm) *n.* A pavement consisting of layers of crushed stone with a tar binder pressed to a smooth surface. [TAR + MACADAM.]

tarn (tärn) *n.* A small mountain lake. [Middle English *terne, tarne,* from Old Norse *tjörn, tjarn*†.]

Tarn (tárn). A river of southern France, rising in the Cévennes and flowing 235 miles generally west to the Garonne.

tar·nal (tär'nəl) *adj. Regional.* Damned. *—adv. Regional.* Damned; very. [From ETERNAL.] **—tar'nal·ly** *adv.*

tar·na·tion (tär-nā'shən). Euphemism for **damnation.**

tar·nish (tär'nĭsh) *v.* **-nished, -nishing, -nishes.** *—tr.* **1.** To dull the luster of; discolor, especially by exposure to air or dirt. **2.** To detract from or spoil; to taint. *—intr.* **1.** To lose luster; become discolored. **2.** To diminish or become tainted. *—n.* **1.** The condition of being tarnished. **2.** A changed or discolored luster. **3.** The condition of being spoiled or tainted; besmirchment. [Old French *ternir* (present stem *terniss-*), from Germanic *tarnjan* (unattested).] **—tar'nish·a·ble** *adj.*

Tar·nów (tär'no͞of'). A city of southern Poland, 45 miles east of Kraków. Population, 75,000.

ta·ro (tär'ō, tăr'ō) *n., pl.* **-ros. 1.** A widely cultivated tropical plant, *Colocasia esculenta,* having broad leaves and a large, starchy, edible rootstock. **2.** The rootstock of this plant. Also called "dasheen," "eddo." [Tahitian and Maori.]

tar·ok (tăr'ək) *n.* Also **tar·oc.** A card game developed in Italy in the 14th century, played with a 78-card pack consisting of four suits plus the 22 tarot cards as trumps. Also called "tarots." [Italian *tarocchi,* plural of *tarocco,* TAROT.]

tar·ot (tăr'ō) *n.* **1.** Any of a set of 22 playing cards consisting of a joker plus 21 cards depicting vices, virtues, and elemental forces, used in fortunetelling and as trump in tarok games. **2.** *Plural.* **Tarok** *(see).* [French, from Italian *tarocco*†.]

tar·pa·per (tär'pā'pər) *n.* Heavy paper impregnated or coated with tar, used as a waterproof protective material in building.

tar·pau·lin (tär-pô'lĭn, tär'pə-lĭn) *n.* **1.** Waterproof canvas used to cover and protect things from moisture. **2.** A sheet of this material. [Earlier *tarpawling* : perhaps TAR + *-pawling,* covering, from PALL (cover).]

tar·pon (tär'pən) *n., pl.* **tarpon** or **-pons.** Any of several fishes of the family Elopidae (or Megalopidae); especially, a large, silvery game fish, *Megalops atlantica,* of Atlantic coastal waters. [Origin unknown.]

Tar·quin (tär'kwĭn). Latin name, Lucius Tarquinius Superbus. Last king of Rome (534–510 B.C.).

Tar·qui·nia (tär-kwē'nyä). Ancient name **Tar·quin·i·i** (-kwĭn'ē-ī'). A town in central Italy; in ancient times, the chief city of the 12 Etruscan cities. Population, 12,000.

tar·ra·did·dle (tăr'ə-dĭd'l) *n.* Also **tar·a·did·dle.** *Informal.* A petty falsehood; fib. [Origin unknown.]

tar·ra·gon (tăr'ə-gŏn', -gən) *n.* **1.** An aromatic herb, *Artemisia dracunculus,* native to Eurasia. **2.** The leaves of this plant, used as seasoning. [Medieval Latin *tragonia, tarchon,* from Medieval Greek *tarkhōn,* from Arabic *ṭarkhūn,* possibly "dragon wort," from Greek *drakontion,* adderwort, from *drakōn,* DRAGON.]

Tar·ra·go·na (tăr'ə-gō'nə; *Spanish* tär'rä-gō'nä). Ancient name **Tar·ra·co** (tăr'ə-kō'). A city of northeastern Spain, a seaport on the Mediterranean southwest of Barcelona. Population, 46,000.

Tar·ra·sa (tär-rä'sä). A city and manufacturing center of northeastern Spain. Population, 89,000.

tar·ri·ance (tăr'ē-əns) *n. Archaic.* **1.** The act of tarrying. **2.** A temporary stay; a sojourn.

tar·ry[1] (tăr'ē) *v.* **-ried, -rying, -ries.** *—intr.* **1.** To delay or be late in going or coming; linger. **2.** To wait. **3.** To remain or stay temporarily, as in a place; sojourn. *—tr. Archaic.* To await. —See Synonyms at **stay.** *—n.* A temporary stay; a sojourn. [Middle English *tarien*†.] **—tar'ri·er** *n.*

tar·ry[2] (tär'ē) *adj.* **-rier, -riest.** Of, like, or covered with tar.

tar·sal (tär'səl) *adj.* **1.** Of, pertaining to, or situated near the tarsus of the foot. **2.** Of or pertaining to the tarsus of the eyelid. [New Latin *tarsālis,* from TARSUS.]

Tar·shish (tär'shĭsh). An ancient country on the southern coast of Spain, mentioned in the Old Testament. I Kings 10:22.

tar·si·er (tär'sē-ər, -sē-ā') *n.* Any of several small nocturnal primates of the genus *Tarsius,* of the East Indies, having large, round eyes and a long tail. [French, from *tarse,* ankle (from its elongated ankles), from New Latin *tarsus,* TARSUS.]

tar·so·met·a·tar·sus (tär'sō-mĕt'ə-tär'səs) *n., pl.* **-si** (-sī'). A compound bone between the tibia and the toes of a bird's leg, formed by fusion of the tarsal and metatarsal bones. [From TARS(US) + METATARSUS.]

tar·sus (tär'səs) *n., pl.* **-si** (-sī'). **1. a.** The section of the vertebrate foot between the leg and the metatarsus. **b.** The seven bones making up this section. **2.** A fibrous plate that supports and shapes the edge of the eyelid. Also called "tarsal plate." **3.** *Zoology.* **a.** The tarsometatarsus. **b.** The distal segmented structure on the leg of an insect or an arachnid. [New Latin, from Greek *tarsos,* frame of wickerwork, (hence) flat surface, sole of the foot, ankle. See **ters-** in Appendix.*]

Tar·sus (tär'səs). A city of Turkey, a seaport in the south on the Mediterranean; birthplace of Saint Paul. Population, 51,000.

tart[1] (tärt) *adj.* **tarter, tartest. 1.** Having a sharp, pungent taste; sour. **2.** Sharp or bitter in tone or meaning; cutting. [Middle English *tart,* Old English *teart,* sharp, severe. See **der-**[2] in Appendix.*] **—tart'ly** *adv.* **—tart'ness** *n.*

tart[2] (tärt) *n.* **1.** A small open pie with a sweet filling. **2.** A loose woman or prostitute. [Middle English *tarte,* from Old French, variant (influenced by Medieval Latin *tartarum,* TARTAR) of *torte,* from Latin *torta,* round bread, "twisted," from *torquēre,* to turn, twist. See **terkw-** in Appendix.*]

tar·tan[1] (tärt'n) *n.* **1.** Any of numerous textile patterns consisting of stripes of varying widths and colors crossed at right angles against a solid background, each forming a distinctive design worn by the members of a Scottish clan. **2.** A twilled wool fabric or garment having such a pattern. **3.** Any fabric having a similar pattern; a plaid. [Probably from Old French *tertaine, tiretaine,* linsey-woolsey, from Old Spanish *tiritaña,* a thin silk stuff, from *tiritar,* to rustle (imitative).] **—tar'tan** *adj.*

tar·tan[2] (tärt'n, tär-tăn') *n.* A small, single-masted Mediterranean ship with a large lateen sail. [French *tartane,* from Italian *tartana,* probably from Old Provençal *tartana*†, buzzard.]

tar·tar[1] (tär'tər) *n.* **1.** A reddish acid compound, chiefly potassium bitartrate, found in the juice of grapes and deposited on the sides of casks during wine-making. **2.** A hard, yellowish deposit on the teeth, consisting of organic secretions and food particles deposited in various salts, such as calcium carbonate. [Middle English *tartre, tartar,* from Old French *tartre,* from Medieval Latin *tartarum,* from Medieval Greek *tartaron*†.]

tar·tar[2] (tär'tər) *n.* Also **Tar·tar.** A ferocious or violent-tempered person. **—catch a tartar.** To grapple with an unexpectedly formidable opponent. [From *Tartar,* variant of TATAR.]

Tar·tar. Variant of **Tatar.**

Tar·tar·e·an (tär-târ'ē-ən) *adj.* Of or relating to Tartarus.

tar·tar·e·ous (tär-târ'ē-əs) *adj.* Consisting of or similar to tartar.

tartare steak. **Steak tartare** *(see).*

Tar·tar·i·an (tär-târ'ē-ən) *adj.* Of or pertaining to the Tatars or Tartary.

tar·tar·ic (tär-tăr'ĭk) *adj.* Of, relating to, or derived from tartar or tartaric acid.

tartaric acid. Any of four isomeric crystalline organic compounds, $C_4H_6O_6$, used to make cream of tartar, as a sequestrant, in tanning, and in effervescent beverages, baking powders, and photographic chemicals.

tar·tar·ize (tär'tə-rīz') *tr.v.* **-ized, -izing, -izes.** To treat, impregnate, or combine with tartar, tartar emetic, or cream of tartar. **—tar'tar·i·za'tion** *n.*

tar·tar·ous (tär'tər-əs) *adj.* Consisting of, derived from, or containing tartar.

tar·tar sauce (tär'tər). Also **tar·tare sauce.** Mayonnaise mixed with chopped onion, olives, pickles, and capers and served as a sauce with fish.

Tar·ta·rus (tär'tər-əs) *n.* **1.** *Greek Mythology.* The abysmal regions below Hades where the Titans were confined. **2.** An infernal region; hell. [Latin, from Greek *Tartaros*†.]

Tar·ta·ry (tär'tə-rē). Also **Ta·ta·ry** (tä'tə-rē). A historical region comprising the areas of eastern Europe and Asia overrun by Tatars in the 13th and 14th centuries and extending as far east as the Pacific under Genghis Khan. After his death (1227), the European section was called European or Little Tartary and the Asian section, Asiatic or Great Tartary.

tar·trate (tär'trāt') *n.* A salt or ester of tartaric acid.

tar·trat·ed (tär'trā'tĭd) *adj.* Containing, combined with, or derived from tartaric acid.

tar·tuffe (tär-to͝of', -to͞of') *n.* Also **tar·tufe.** A hypocrite; especially, one who affects religious piety. [After *Tartuffe,* title character and hypocrite in Molière's comedy (1664), from Italian *Tartufo,* from Latin *terrae tūber,* "truffle of earth," potato : *terra,* earth (see **terrace**) + *tūber,* TRUFFLE.]

Tar·vi·si·um. The ancient name for **Treviso.**

tar·weed (tär'wēd') *n.* **1.** Any of several strong-smelling, resinous western American plants of the genus *Madia,* having yellow, rayed flowers. **2.** Any of several similar or related plants.

Tas. Tasmania; Tasmanian.

Tash·kent (täsh-kĕnt'). The capital of the Uzbek S.S.R., in the eastern part of the republic. Population, 1,106,000.

task (tăsk, täsk) *n.* **1.** A piece of work assigned by a superior or done as part of one's duties. **2.** A difficult or tedious undertaking. **3.** The function that a working person, unit, or thing is expected to fill; objective. **—take to task.** To reprimand or censure. *—tr.v.* **tasked, tasking, tasks. 1.** To assign a task to or impose a task upon. **2.** To overburden with labor; to tax. [Middle English *taske, tasque,* tax, work imposed, task, from Norman French *tasque,* variant of Old French *tasche,* from Medieval Latin *tasca, taxa,* from *taxāre,* to TAX.]

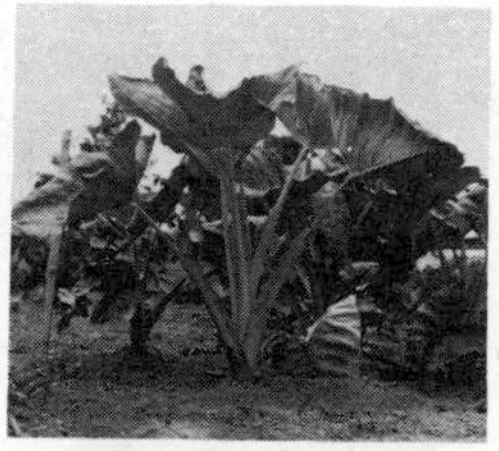
taro

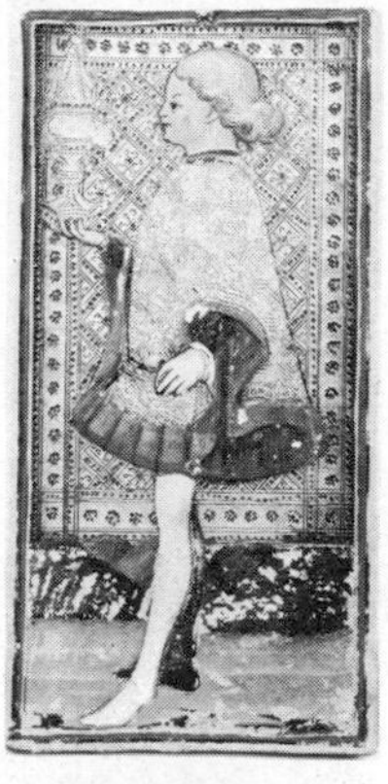
tarot
Fifteenth-century Italian playing card

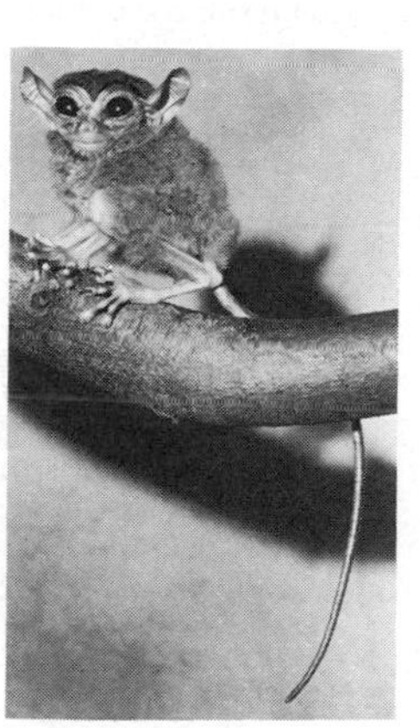
tarsier
Tarsius syrichta

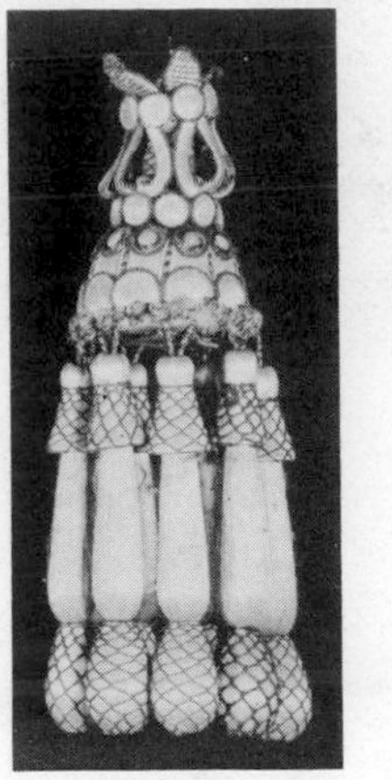

tassel
Nineteenth-century Italian

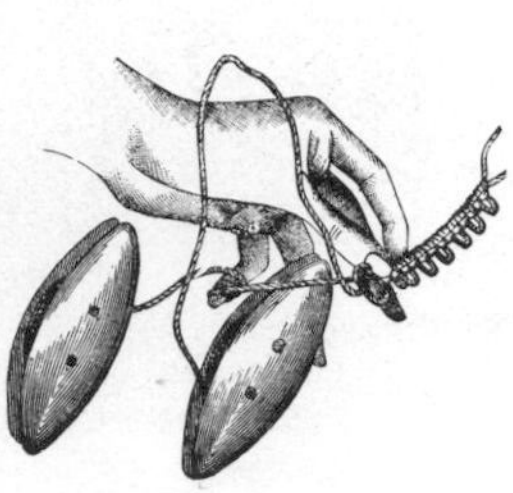

tat
Tatting with two colors requiring two shuttles

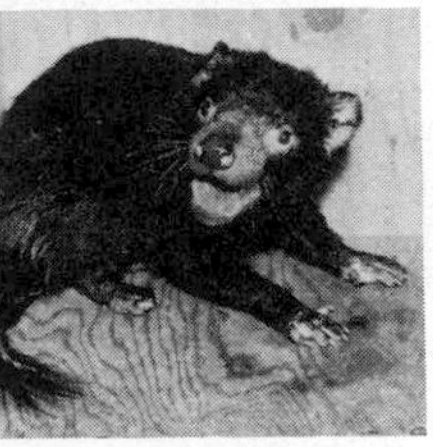

Tasmanian devil

Synonyms: *task, job, chore, stint, assignment.* These nouns refer to work considered as a specific individual undertaking. *Task* applies to a well-defined piece of work that is often imposed, of short duration, and burdensome. *Job* can refer to virtually any work, including one's regular full-time employment; in this comparison it suggests a specific short-term undertaking. *Chore* generally denotes a small, routine, or odd job; sometimes the word is applied to a specific arduous task. *Stint* usually refers to temporary work, either voluntary or one's prescribed share in a larger enterprise. *Assignment* generally denotes clearly defined short-term work given to one person or persons by another who is in authority.

task force. A temporary grouping of forces and resources, especially of military units, for the accomplishment of a specific objective.

task·mas·ter (tăsk′măs′tər, täsk′mäs′tər) *n.* One who imposes work, especially heavy work.

Tasm. Tasmania; Tasmanian.

Tas·man (tăz′mən; *Dutch* täs′män′), **Abel Janszoon.** 1603–1659. Dutch navigator; discovered Tasmania and New Zealand.

Tas·ma·ni·a (tăz-mā′nē-ə, -mān′yə). Formerly **Van Die·men's Land** (văn dē′mənz). *Abbr.* **Tas., Tasm.** A state of Australia, 26,215 square miles in area, comprising the island of Tasmania and some smaller islands lying off the southeastern coast of Australia. Population, 365,000. Capital, Hobart. —**Tas·ma′ni·an** *adj.* & *n.*

Tasmanian devil. A burrowing carnivorous marsupial, *Sarcophilus harrisii,* of Tasmania, having a predominantly blackish coat and a long, almost hairless tail.

Tasmanian wolf. A marsupial, the **thylacine** *(see).*

Tas·man Sea (tăz′mən). The part of the South Pacific between Australia and New Zealand.

Tass (tăs, täs) *n.* The chief news agency of the Soviet Union. [Russian, from *T(elegrafnoe) A(gentstvo) S(ovetskovo) S(oyuza),* Telegraphic Agency of the Soviet Union.]

tasse (tăs) *n.* Also **tas·set** (tăs′ĭt). One of a series of jointed overlapping metal splints hanging from the corselet, used as armor for the lower trunk and thighs. [Possibly from Old French *tasse,* pouch, purse, from Middle High German *tasche,* from Old High German *tasca,* from Medieval Latin *tasca,* task, payment, money pouch, from *taxa,* tax, from *taxāre,* to TAX.]

tas·sel (tăs′əl) *n.* **1.** An ornament consisting of a bunch of loose threads or cords bound at one end, hung from drapery, robes, cushions, and other articles. **2.** Something that resembles a tassel, such as the pollen-bearing inflorescence of a corn plant. —*v.* **tasseled** or **-selled, -seling** or **-selling, -sels.** —*tr.* To fringe or decorate with tassels. —*intr.* To put forth a tassellike inflorescence. Used especially of corn. [Middle English, clasp, fibula, tassel, from Old French *tassel*†.]

Tas·so (tăs′ō; *Italian* täs′sō), **Torquato.** 1544–1595. Italian epic poet.

taste (tāst) *v.* **tasted, tasting, tastes.** —*tr.* **1.** To distinguish the flavor of by taking into the mouth. **2.** To eat or drink a small quantity of. **3.** To experience or partake of, especially for the first time. **4.** *Archaic.* To like. **5.** *Obsolete.* To test by touching. —*intr.* **1.** To distinguish flavors in the mouth. **2.** To eat or drink a small amount. Often used with *of.* **3.** To have an experience; partake. Often used with *of.* **4.** To have a distinct flavor: *The stew tastes salty.* —*n.* **1. a.** The sense that distinguishes the sweet, sour, salty, and bitter qualities of dissolved substances in contact with the taste buds on the tongue. **b.** This sense in combination with the senses of smell and touch, which together receive a sensation of a substance in the mouth. **2. a.** The sensation of sweet, sour, salty, or bitter qualities produced by a substance in solution in the mouth. **b.** The unified sensation produced by any of these qualities plus a distinct smell and texture; a flavor. **3.** The act of tasting. **4.** A small quantity eaten or tasted. **5.** A limited or first experience; a sample: *"Thousands entered the war, got just a taste of it, and then stepped out"* (Mark Twain). **6.** A personal preference or liking for something; inclination. **7. a.** The faculty of discerning what is aesthetically excellent or appropriate. **b.** A manner indicative of the quality of such discernment: *furnished with superb taste.* **8. a.** The sense of what is proper, seemly, or least likely to give offense in a given social situation. **b.** A manner indicative of the quality of this sense. **9.** *Obsolete.* The act of testing; a trial. —See Synonyms at **culture.** [Middle English *tasten,* to examine by touch, test, taste, from Old French *taster,* from Vulgar Latin *tastāre, taxitāre* (unattested), frequentative of Latin *taxāre,* to touch, frequentative of *tangere.* See **tag-** in Appendix.*] —**tast′a·ble** *adj.*

taste bud. Any of numerous spherical or ovoid nests of cells distributed over the tongue embedded in the epithelium consisting of gustatory cells and supporting cells and constituting the end organs of the sense of taste.

taste·ful (tāst′fəl) *adj.* **1.** Exhibiting good taste. **2.** *Rare.* Tasty. —**taste′ful·ly** *adv.* —**taste′ful·ness** *n.*

taste·less (tāst′lĭs) *adj.* **1.** Lacking flavor; insipid. **2.** Exhibiting poor taste. **3.** *Rare.* Unable to taste. —**taste′less·ly** *adv.* —**taste′less·ness** *n.*

tast·er (tā′stər) *n.* **1.** One who tastes; specifically, one who samples a food or beverage for quality. **2.** Any of several devices or implements used in tasting.

tast·y (tā′stē) *adj.* **-ier, -iest. 1.** Having a pleasing flavor; savory. **2.** Having good taste; tasteful. —**tast′i·ly** *adv.* —**tast′i·ness** *n.*

tat (tăt) *v.* **tatted, tatting, tats.** —*intr.* To make tatting. —*tr.* To produce by tatting. [Probably back-formation from TATTING.] —**tat′ter** *n.*

Ta·tar (tä′tər) *n.* Also **Tar·tar** (tär′tər). **1. a.** A member of one of the Mongolian peoples who under Genghis Khan overran much of central and western Asia and eastern Europe in the 13th century. **b.** Broadly, a member of any of these Mongolian peoples. **2.** A descendant of these peoples, now living chiefly in parts of the Russian S.F.S.R. and Soviet Central Asia. **3.** Any of the Turkic languages of the Tatars. —*adj.* Also **Tar·tar.** Of or pertaining to the Tatars. [Middle English *Tartre, Tatar,* from Old French *Tartare,* from Medieval Latin *Tartarus* (probably influenced by Latin *Tartarus,* TARTARUS), from Persian *Tātār,* from *Tata,* Turkic ethnic name.]

Ta·tar Autonomous Soviet Socialist Republic (tä′tər). An administrative division, 26,250 square miles in area, of the west-central Russian S.F.S.R. Population, 3,069,000. Capital, Kazan.

Ta·tar Strait (tä′tər). An arm of the Pacific extending about 350 miles between Sakhalin Island and the eastern Asiatic mainland and linking the Sea of Japan with the Sea of Okhotsk. Also called "Gulf of Tatary."

Ta·ta·ry. See **Tartary.**

Tate (tāt), **Nahum.** 1652–1715. English poet and dramatist; poet laureate (1692–1715).

ta·ter (tā′tər) *n. Regional.* A potato.

Ta·tra Mountains (tä′trä). The highest range of the Carpathians, along the border between Poland and Czechoslovakia. Also called "High Tatra." Highest elevation, Gerlachova (8,737 feet).

tat·ter (tăt′ər) *n.* **1.** A torn and hanging piece of cloth; a shred. **2.** *Plural.* Torn and ragged clothing; rags. —*v.* **tattered, -tering, -ters.** —*tr.* To make ragged; reduce to shreds. —*intr.* To become ragged. [Middle English *tatter, tatar,* from Old Norse *taturr* (unattested), *tōturr,* from Germanic *tath-* (unattested).]

tat·ter·de·mal·ion (tăt′ər-də-māl′ē-ən, -măl′ē-ən) *n.* A person wearing ragged or tattered clothing; ragamuffin. —*adj.* Ragged; tattered. [TATTER + obscure second element.]

tat·tered (tăt′ərd) *adj.* **1.** Torn into shreds or tatters; ragged. **2.** Having ragged clothes; dressed in tatters.

tat·ter·sall (tăt′ər-sôl′, -səl) *adj.* Also **Tat·ter·sall.** Having a pattern of dark lines forming squares on a solid, generally light background. —*n.* Also **Tat·ter·sall. 1.** A pattern of dark lines forming squares on a light background. **2.** Cloth woven with this pattern. [Originally the pattern on blankets used at *Tattersall's* horse market in London, founded by Richard *Tattersall* (died 1795), English horseman.]

tat·ting (tăt′ĭng) *n.* **1.** Handmade lace fashioned by looping and knotting a single strand of heavy-duty thread on a small hand shuttle. **2.** The act or art of making tatting. [Perhaps related to Scottish *tate*†, tuft.]

tat·tle (tăt′l) *v.* **-tled, -tling, -tles.** —*intr.* **1.** To reveal the plans or activities of another; gossip. **2.** To chatter aimlessly; prate. —*tr.* To reveal through gossiping. —*n.* **1.** Aimless chatter; prattle. **2.** Gossip; talebearing. **3.** A tattletale. [Middle Flemish *tatelen,* to babble (imitative).] —**tat′tling·ly** *adv.*

tat·tler (tăt′lər) *n.* **1.** A person who tattles. **2.** Any of several shore birds related to and resembling the sandpipers; especially, one of the genus *Heteroscelus,* of coastal areas of the Pacific.

tat·tle·tale (tăt′l-tāl′) *n.* A person who tattles on others; an informer; a talebearer. —*adj.* Revealing; telltale.

tat·too[1] (tă-too′) *n., pl.* **-toos. 1.** A signal sounded on a drum or bugle to summon soldiers or sailors to their quarters at night. **2.** A display of military exercises offered as entertainment. **3.** A continuous even drumming or rapping. —*v.* **tattooed, -tooing, -toos.** —*intr.* To beat out an even rhythm, as with the fingers. —*tr.* To beat or tap rhythmically on; rap or drum on. [Originally *tap-too, tap-tow,* from Dutch *taptoe,* "the shutting off of the taps (at taverns at the end of the day)" : *tap,* tap, from Middle Dutch *tappe* (see **tap-** in Appendix*) + *toe,* short for *doe toe,* "do to," shut, from Middle Dutch (see **de-** in Appendix*).] —**tat·too′er** *n.*

tat·too[2] (tă-too′) *n., pl.* **-toos.** A permanent mark or design made on the skin by a process of pricking and ingraining an indelible pigment or by raising scars. —*tr.v.* **tattooed, -tooing, -toos. 1.** To mark (the skin) with a tattoo or tattoos. **2.** To form (a mark or design) on the skin. [Of Polynesian origin, akin to Tahitian *tatau,* Marquesan *ta-tu.*] —**tat·too′er** *n.*

Ta·tum (tā′təm), **Edward Lawrie.** Born 1909. American biochemist; worked on enzymes.

Ta·tung (tä′toong′). A city of northeastern China, at the northern tip of Shansi Province. Population, 243,000.

tau (tou, tô) *n.* The 19th letter of the Greek alphabet, written Τ, τ. Transliterated in English as *T, t.* See **alphabet.** [Greek, from Semitic, akin to Hebrew *tāw,* TAV.]

tau cross. A cross in the form of a T. Also called "Saint Anthony's cross."

taught. Past tense and past participle of **teach.**

Taung·gyi (toung′jē′). The capital of Shan State, Burma, a town in the southern part of the state.

taunt[1] (tônt) *tr.v.* **taunted, taunting, taunts. 1.** To deride or reproach with contempt; mock; jeer at. **2.** To drive or incite (a person) by taunting. —See Synonyms at **ridicule.** —*n.* **1.** A scornful remark or tirade; a jeer. **2.** *Archaic.* The victim of a jeer. [Perhaps from Old French *tanter, tenter,* to test, tempt, from Latin *temptāre,* TEMPT.] —**taunt′er** *n.* —**taunt′ing·ly** *adv.*

taunt[2] (tônt) *adj. Nautical.* Unusually tall. Said of masts. [Probably from *ataunt,* as much as possible, fully rigged, from Old French *autant,* as much : *al,* other, one more + *tant,* so much, from Latin *tantum,* from *tam,* so (see **to-** in Appendix*).]

taupe (tōp) *n.* Brownish gray to dark yellowish brown. See **color.** [French, "mole," from Latin *talpa*†.] —**taupe** *adj.*

Tau·po, Lake (tou′pō). The largest lake (238 square miles) of New Zealand, located in the center of North Island.

Tau·ric Cher·so·nese. An ancient name for the **Crimea.**

tau·rine¹ (tôr′ēn′) *adj.* Of or resembling a bull. [Latin *taurinus,* from *taurus,* bull. See **tauro-** in Appendix.*]

tau·rine² (tôr′ēn, -ĭn) *n.* A crystalline amino acid, $C_2H_7NO_3S$, found in bile. [TAUR(O)- + -INE (so called because first obtained from ox bile).]

Tau·ris. The ancient name for **Tabriz.**

tauro-, taur-. Indicates bull or bovine; for example, **taurocholic, taurine.** [From Latin *taurus* and Greek *tauros,* bull. See **tauro-** in Appendix.*]

tau·ro·cho·lic acid (tôr′ō-kō′lĭk, -kŏl′ĭk). A crystalline acid, $C_{26}H_{45}NO_7S$, occurring as a constituent of bile. [TAURO- + CHOLIC ACID (because first obtained from ox bile).]

tau·rom·a·chy (tô-rŏm′ə-kē) *n., pl.* **-chies.** Bullfighting or a bullfight. [Spanish *tauromaquia,* from Greek *tauromachia* : TAURO- + *makhē,* battle, from *makhesthai,* to fight (see **magh-²** in Appendix*).]

Tau·rus (tôr′əs) *n.* **1.** A constellation in the Northern Hemisphere near Orion and Aries. **2.** The second sign of the **zodiac** (*see*). Also called the "Bull." [Middle English, from Latin, bull. See **tauro-** in Appendix.*]

Tau·rus Mountains (tôr′əs). Turkish **To·ros Dağ·la·ri** (tô-ôs′ dä′lä-rĭ′). The major mountain range of southern Turkey, extending parallel to the Mediterranean coast. Highest elevation, Kaldi Dag (12,251 feet).

taut (tôt) *adj.* **tauter, tautest. 1.** Pulled or drawn tight; not slack. **2.** Strained; tense. **3.** Kept in trim shape; neat; tidy. —See Synonyms at **stiff.** [Earlier *taught, tought,* Middle English *toght, toht,* probably variant past participle of *togen, towen,* to pull, Old English *togian.* See **deuk-** in Appendix.*] —**taut′ly** *adv.* —**taut′ness** *n.*

taut·en (tôt′n) *v.* **-ened, -ening, -ens.** —*tr.* To make taut; stretch tight. —*intr.* To become taut.

tauto-, taut-. Indicates same or identical; for example, **tautomerism, tautonym.** [From Greek *tautos,* identical, from *to auto,* the same (neuter) : *to,* the (see **to-** in Appendix*) + *autos,* same (see **auto-).]

tau·tog (tô′tôg, -tŏg, tô-tôg′, -tŏg′) *n.* Also **tau·taug.** A dark-colored, edible marine fish, *Tautoga onitis,* of the North American Atlantic coast. Also called "blackfish." [Narraganset *tautauog,* plural of *taut.*]

tau·tol·o·gize (tô-tŏl′ə-jīz′) *intr.v.* **-gized, -gizing, -gizes.** To use tautology. —**tau·tol′o·gist** *n.*

tau·tol·o·gy (tô-tŏl′ə-jē) *n., pl.* **-gies. 1. a.** Needless repetition of the same sense in different words; redundancy. **b.** An instance of such repetition. **2.** *Logic.* A statement that is true because it provides for all logical possibilities; for example, *The earth is either round or it is not round.* [Late Latin *tautologia,* from Greek, from *tautologos,* repeating the same ideas : TAUTO- + *logos,* saying, word (see **-logy**).] —**tau′to·log′i·cal** (tô′tə-lŏj′ĭ-kəl), **tau′to·log′ic** *adj.* —**tau′to·log′i·cal·ly** *adv.*

tau·tom·er·ism (tô-tŏm′ə-rĭz′əm) *n.* Chemical isomerism characterized by relatively easy interconversion of isomeric forms in equilibrium. [TAUTO- + (ISO)MERISM.] —**tau′to·mer** (tô′tə-mər) *n.* —**tau′to·mer′ic** (tô′tə-měr′ĭk) *adj.*

tau·to·nym (tô′tə-nĭm′) *n.* A taxonomic designation, such as *Gorilla gorilla,* in which the genus and species names are the same. Used in zoology but no longer in botany. [TAUT(O)- + -ONYM.] —**tau′to·nym′ic, tau·ton′y·mous** (tô-tŏn′ə-məs) *adj.* —**tau·ton′y·my** *n.*

tav (täf, tôf) *n.* Also **taw.** The 23rd letter of the Hebrew alphabet, corresponding phonetically to *t* or *th* in English. See **alphabet.** [Hebrew *tāw,* probably "mark," "cross."]

tav·ern (tăv′ərn) *n.* **1.** An establishment licensed to sell liquor and beer to be drunk on the premises; saloon; bar. **2.** A public house or inn for travelers or others. [Middle English *taverne,* from Old French, from Latin *taberna,* hut, inn, possibly from Etruscan. See also **tabernacle.**]

tav·ern·er (tăv′ər-nər) *n.* One who keeps a tavern.

taw¹ (tô) *tr.v.* **tawed, tawing, taws.** To convert (skin) into white leather by mineral tanning, as by soaking in alum and salt. [Middle English *tawen,* Old English *tawian.* See **taw-** in Appendix.*] —**taw′er** *n.*

taw² (tô) *n.* **1.** A large, fancy marble used for shooting. **2.** The line from which a player shoots in marbles. **3.** A game of marbles. —*intr.v.* **tawed, tawing, taws.** To shoot a marble. [Origin unknown.]

taw³. Variant of **tav.**

taw·dry (tô′drē) *adj.* **-drier, -driest.** Gaudy and cheap; vulgarly ornamental. [From *tawdry lace,* short for *Seynt Audries lace,* cheap and gawdy lace neckties sold at fairs in honor of St. Audrey (died A.D. 679), queen of Northumbria, who died of a throat tumor regarded as punishment for her fondness for necklaces.] —**taw′dri·ly** *adv.* —**taw′dri·ness** *n.*

taw·ny (tô′nē) *n.* Also **taw·ney.** Light brown to brownish orange. See **color.** [Middle English *taune, tawny,* from Norman French *taune,* variant of Old French *tane,* tanned, from *taner, tanner,* to TAN.] —**taw′ny** *adj.*

tax (tăks) *n.* **1.** A contribution for the support of a government required of persons, groups, or businesses within the domain of that government. **2.** A fee or due levied on the members of an organization to meet its expenses. **3.** A burdensome or excessive demand; a strain. —*tr.v.* **taxed, taxing, taxes. 1.** To place a tax on (income, property, or goods). **2.** To exact a tax from. **3.** *Law.* To assess (court costs, for example). **4.** To make difficult or excessive demands upon. **5.** To make a charge against; accuse: *He was taxed with failure to appear on the day*

appointed. [Middle English *taxen,* to assess, tax, from Old French *taxer,* from Medieval Latin *taxāre,* from Latin, frequentative of *tangere,* to touch. See **tag-** in Appendix.*] —**tax′a·ble** *adj.* —**tax′a·bil′i·ty, tax′a·ble·ness** *n.* —**tax′er** *n.*

tax·a·tion (tăk-sā′shən) *n.* **1. a.** The act or practice of imposing taxes. **b.** The fact of being taxed. **2.** An assessed amount of tax.

tax·de·duct·i·ble (tăks′dĭ-dŭk′tə-bəl) *adj.* Exempt from inclusion in one's taxable income.

tax·eme (tăk′sēm′) *n.* A minimal linguistic feature, as the order or stress of words in a compound or phonemes in a word. [TAX(O)- + (PHON)EME.]

tax-ex·empt (tăks′ĭg-zěmpt′) *adj.* Not subject to taxation, as the capital or income of a philanthropic organization.

tax·i (tăk′sē) *n., pl.* **-is** or **-ies.** A taxicab (*see*). —*v.* **taxied, taxiing** or **taxying, taxies** or **taxis.** —*intr.* **1.** To be transported by taxi. **2.** To move slowly on the ground or on the surface of the water before takeoff or after landing. Used of an aircraft. —*tr.* To cause (an airplane) to taxi. [Short for TAXICAB.]

tax·i·cab (tăk′sē-kăb′) *n.* An automobile that carries passengers for a fare, usually calculated by a taximeter. Also called "taxi," "cab." [TAXI(METER) + CAB.]

taxi dancer. A girl employed by a dance hall or nightclub to dance with the patrons for a fee. [From TAXI(CAB).]

tax·i·der·mist (tăk′sə-dûr′mĭst) *n.* One whose profession is taxidermy.

tax·i·der·my (tăk′sə-dûr′mē) *n.* The art or operation of preparing, stuffing, and mounting the skins of dead animals for exhibition in a lifelike state. [*Taxi-,* variant of TAXO- + -DERM + -Y.] —**tax′i·der′mal, tax′i·der′mic** *adj.*

tax·i·me·ter (tăk′sē-mē′tər) *n.* An instrument installed in a taxicab to measure distance traveled and waiting time and to compute and indicate the fare. [French *taximètre* : *taxe,* tax, charge, from Old French *taxer,* to TAX + -METER.]

tax·ing (tăk′sĭng) *adj.* Burdensome; wearing.

tax·i·plane (tăk′sē-plān′) *n.* An airplane commercially available for short charter flights.

tax·is (tăk′sĭs) *n., pl.* **taxes** (tăk′sēz′). **1.** *Biology.* The responsive movement of an organism toward or away from an external stimulus. **2.** The moving of an organ, as in a dislocation or hernia protrusion, into normal position by manipulation. [Greek, arrangement, order, from *tattein,* to arrange. See **tag-** in Appendix.*]

-taxis, -taxy. Indicates order or arrangement; for example, **chemotaxis, phyllotaxy.** [New Latin, from Greek *taxis,* arrangement, order. See **taxis.**]

taxi stand. An area reserved for taxicabs waiting for call.

tax·i·way (tăk′sē-wā′) *n.* A strip of pavement for taxiing aircraft.

taxo-, tax-, taxi-. Indicates arrangement or order; for example, **taxonomy, taxeme, taxidermy.** [From Greek *taxis,* arrangement, order. See **taxis.**]

tax·on (tăk′sŏn′) *n., pl.* **taxa** (tăk′sə). *Biology.* A group of organisms constituting one of the categories or formal units in taxonomic classification, such as a phylum, order, family, genus, or species, and characterized by common characteristics in varying degrees of distinction. [Back-formation from TAXONOMY.]

tax·on·o·my (tăk-sŏn′ə-mē) *n. Abbr.* **taxon. 1.** The science, laws, or principles of classification. **2.** *Biology.* The theory, principles, and process of classifying organisms in established categories. See table *Taxonomic Classification* on following page. [French *taxonomie* : TAXO- + -NOMY.] —**tax′o·nom′ic** (-sə-nŏm′ĭk), **tax′o·nom′i·cal** *adj.* —**tax′o·nom′i·cal·ly** *adv.* —**tax·on′o·mist** *n.*

tax·pay·er (tăks′pā′ər) *n.* **1.** A person who pays taxes. **2.** A building intended to cover the expenses of a piece of land until it can be put to a more profitable use.

-taxy. Variant of **-taxis.**

Tay (tā). The longest river of Scotland (118 miles), rising in eastern Perthshire and flowing generally southeast to the Firth of Tay, an inlet of the North Sea.

Ta·yg·e·ta¹ (tā-ĭj′ə-tə). *Greek Mythology.* One of the Pleiades, the seven daughters of Atlas.

Ta·yg·e·ta² (tā-ĭj′ə-tə) *n.* One of the six visible stars in the Pleiades cluster.

Tay·lor (tā′lər), **Bayard.** 1825–1878. American journalist, foreign correspondent, and poet.

Tay·lor (tā′lər), **Edward.** 1644?–1729. English-born American Puritan clergyman and poet.

Tay·lor (tā′lər), **Frederick Winslow.** 1856–1915. American engineer; founder of efficiency engineering.

Tay·lor (tā′lər), **Jeremy.** 1613–1667. English religious leader and author; chaplain to Charles I.

Tay·lor (tā′lər), **(Joseph) Deems.** 1885–1966. American music critic and composer.

Tay·lor (tā′lər), **Maxwell Davenport.** Born 1901. American military leader; chairman Joint Chiefs of Staff (1962–64).

Tay·lor (tā′lər), **Tom.** 1817–1880. English playwright.

Tay·lor (tā′lər), **Zachary.** 1784–1850. Twelfth President of the United States (1849–50).

Tay·myr Peninsula. See **Taimyr Peninsula.**

Tb The symbol for the element terbium.

TB tuberculosis.

t.b. 1. trial balance. **2.** tubercle bacillus.

T.B. tubercle bacillus; tuberculosis.

T-bar lift (tē′bär′). A ski lift consisting of a bar suspended like an inverted T against which skiers lean while being towed uphill.

Tbi·li·si. The Georgian name for **Tiflis.**

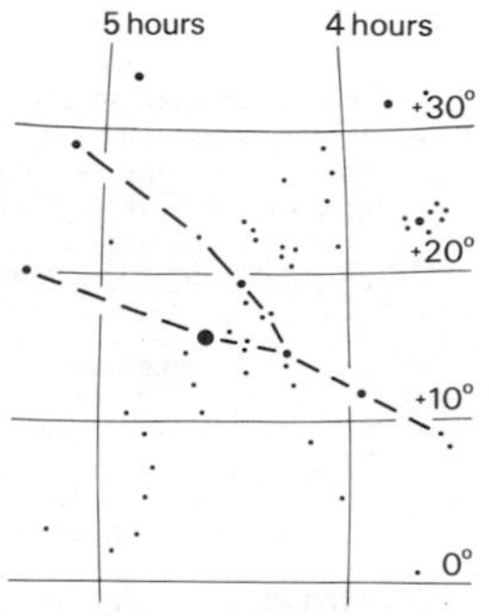

Taurus

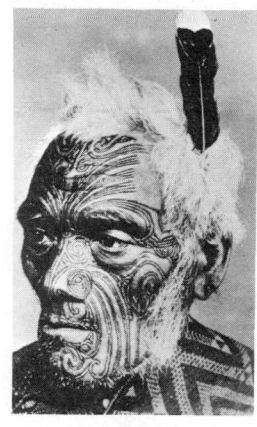

taxidermy
Man working elephant skin
into a lifelike position

tattoo²
Maori chieftain

ă pat/ā pay/âr care/ä father/b bib/ch church/d deed/ĕ pet/ē be/f fife/g gag/h hat/hw which/ĭ pit/ī pie/îr pier/j judge/k kick/l lid, needle/m mum/n no, sudden/ng thing/ŏ pot/ō toe/ô paw, for/oi noise/ou out/oo took/oo boot/p pop/r roar/s sauce/sh ship, dish/t tight/th thin, path/*th* this, bathe/ŭ cut/ûr urge/v valve/w with/y yes/z zebra, size/zh vision/ə about, item, edible, gallop, circus/ à *Fr.* ami/œ *Fr.* feu, *Ger.* schön/ü *Fr.* tu, *Ger.* über/KH *Ger.* ich, *Scot.* loch/N *Fr.* bon. *Follows main vocabulary. †Of obscure origin.

TAXONOMIC CLASSIFICATION

This table includes most of the major taxonomic categories, beginning with the broadest and most inclusive and ending with the narrowest. It is not by any means all inclusive, but consists of a representative, if arbitrary, selection intended to show the relationships between familiar groups and kinds of organisms.

The names shown are widely accepted by taxonomists, and are in general accordance with the taxonomic designations used in this Dictionary. In some instances, especially in the field of botany, there has been considerable change and difference of opinion in recent years, and the terms included in this table reflect an effort to select the most acceptable and authoritative designations.

Kingdom
Animalia* (animals)

Kingdom
Plantae* (plants)

*A more recently established third kingdom, Protista, consists of organisms not readily classified as plants or animals and includes among others such unicellular forms as amoeba and paramecium, often placed in the animal kingdom, euglena and various bacteria, often placed in the plant kingdom, as well as the slime molds, sometimes placed in the plant kingdom and sometimes in the animal kingdom.

Phylum
Porifera (sponges)
Coelenterata (coelenterates)
Mollusca (mollusks)
Annelida (segmented worms)
Arthropoda (arthropods)
Echinodermata (echinoderms)
Chordata (chordates)

Division
Thallophyta** (algae, fungi)
Bryophyta (mosses, liverworts)
Tracheophyta (vascular plants)

Subphylum
Vertebrata (vertebrates)

** An older designation now sometimes considered a subkingdom.

Superclass
Pisces (fishes)

Class
Anthozoa (corals)
Nematoda (roundworms)
Gastropoda (snails, slugs)
Crustacea (crustaceans)
Arachnida (spiders, scorpions, mites)
Insecta (insects)
Osteichthyes (bony fishes)
Amphibia (amphibians)
Reptilia (reptiles)
Aves (birds)
Mammalia (mammals)

Class
Basidiomycetes (mushrooms)
Musci (mosses)
Filicinae (or Pteridophyta) (ferns)
Gymnospermae (gymnosperms)
Angiospermae (flowering plants)

Subclass
Dicotyledonae (dicotyledons)
Monocotyledonae (monocotyledons)

Order
Lepidoptera (butterflies, moths)
Chelonia (turtles)
Rodentia (rodents)
Cetacea (whales)
Primates (monkeys, apes, man)

Order
Uredinales (rusts)
Lycopodiales (club mosses)
Coniferales (conifers)
Graminales (grasses)
Rosales (roses, related plants)

Family
Lumbricidae (earthworms)
Salmonidae (salmon, trout)
Corvidae (crows, jays)
Felidae (cats)

Family
Orchidaceae (orchids)
Fagaceae (beeches, oaks)
Cactaceae (cacti)
Compositae (asters, sunflowers)

Genus
Strombus (conchs)
Crotalus (rattlesnakes)
Perdix (partridges)
Canis (dogs)

Genus
Avena (oats)
Morus (mulberries)
Mentha (mints)
Solidago (goldenrods)

Species
Octopus vulgaris (common octopus)
Rana catesbeiana (bullfrog)
Haliaeetus leucocephalus (bald eagle)
Giraffa camelopardalis (giraffe)

Species
Zea mays (corn)
Dianthus caryophyllus (carnation)
Juglans cinerea (butternut)
Taraxacum officinale (common dandelion)

Subspecies
Panthera tigris longipilis
(Siberian tiger)

Variety
Lactuca sativa longifolia
(romaine lettuce)

The taxonomic categories in which the Siberian tiger and romaine lettuce are classified are shown below in descending order, beginning with the broadest category.

Kingdom
Animalia (animals)

Kingdom
Plantae (plants)

Phylum
Chordata (chordates)

Division
Tracheophyta (vascular plants)

Subphylum
Vertebrata (vertebrates)

Class
Angiospermae (flowering plants)

Class
Mammalia (mammals)

Subclass
Dicotyledonae (dicotyledons)

Order
Carnivora (carnivores)

Order
Campanulales (or Campanulatae)
(bellflowers, lobelias, composites)

Family
Felidae (cats)

Family
Compositae (composites)

Genus
Panthera (lion, tiger, leopard, jaguar)

Genus
Lactuca (lettuce)

Species
Panthera tigris (tiger)

Species
Lactuca sativa (cultivated lettuce)

Subspecies
Panthera tigris longipilis
(Siberian tiger)

Variety
Lactuca sativa longifolia
(romaine lettuce)

T-bone (tē′bōn′) *n.* A thick porterhouse steak taken from the small end of the loin and containing a T-shaped bone. Also called "T-bone steak."

tbs., tbsp. tablespoon; tablespoonful.

Tc The symbol for the element technetium.

Tchad. The French name for **Chad.**

Tchai·kov·sky (chī-kôf′skē, -kŏf′skē), **Peter Ilyitch.** Also **Tschai·kov·sky.** 1840–1893. Russian composer.

Tche·khov. See Chekhov.

tchr. teacher.

td, TD, td. touchdown.

T.D.N. total digestible nutrients.

Te The symbol for the element tellurium.

tea (tē) *n.* **1.** A shrub, *Thea sinensis* (or *Camellia sinensis*), of eastern Asia, having fragrant white flowers and evergreen leaves. **2.** The dried leaves of this plant, prepared by various processes and in various stages of growth, and used to make a hot beverage. **3.** An aromatic, slightly bitter beverage made by steeping tea leaves in boiling water. **4.** Any of various beverages made by steeping the leaves of certain other plants, or from beef or other extracts. **5.** Any of various plants having leaves used to make a tealike infusion. **6. a.** *Chiefly British.* An afternoon refreshment usually of cakes served with tea. **b.** A social gathering at which tea is taken. **7.** *British.* High tea. **8.** *Slang.* Marijuana *(see).* [Earlier *tay, tee* (probably via Dutch *thee* and Malay *teh*), from Amoy *te*, from Ancient Chinese *d'a* (whence Mandarin Chinese *ch'a²*).]

tea bag. A small porous sack holding sufficient tea leaves to make an individual serving of tea.

tea ball. A small perforated metal ball for immersing tea leaves in hot water.

tea·ber·ry (tē′bĕr′ē) *n., pl.* **-ries.** A plant, the **wintergreen** *(see),* or its fruit.

tea biscuit. Any of various plain cookies or biscuits often served with tea. Also called "teacake."

tea·cart (tē′kärt′) *n.* A tea wagon *(see).*

teach (tēch) *v.* **taught** (tôt), **teaching, teaches.** —*tr.* **1.** To impart knowledge or skill to; give instruction to. **2.** To provide knowledge of; instruct in. **3.** To cause to learn by example or experience: *Her rebuff taught him never to ask again.* **4.** To advocate; preach. —*intr.* To give instruction, especially as an occupation. [Teach, taught; Middle English *techen, tahte,* Old English *tǣcan, tǣhte* (past tense), *getǣht* (unattested past participle). See **deik-** in Appendix.*]

Synonyms: teach, instruct, educate, tutor, train, school, discipline, drill. These verbs mean to impart knowledge or skill. *Teach* is the most widely applicable, since it can refer to any such act of communicating. *Instruct* usually suggests methodical direction in a specific subject or area. *Educate* is comprehensive and implies a wide area of learning, achieved either by experience or, more often, by formal instruction in many subjects. *Tutor* usually refers to private instruction of one student or a small group. *Train* generally implies concentration on particular skills intended to fit a person, or sometimes an animal, for a desired role. *School* and *discipline* now usually refer to training in modes of behavior. *School* often implies indoctrination, not necessarily in an unfavorable sense, and an arduous learning process. *Discipline* usually refers to teaching of control, especially self-control. *Drill* implies rigorous instruction or training, often by repetition of a routine.

Teach (tēch), **Edward.** Also **Thach** (thăch). Known as Blackbeard. Died 1718. British pirate in the North Atlantic.

teach·a·ble (tē′chə-bəl) *adj.* Capable of or receptive to being taught. —**teach′a·bil′i·ty, teach′a·ble·ness** *n.* —**teach′a·bly** *adv.*

teach·er (tē′chər) *n. Abbr.* **tchr.** One who teaches; especially, a person hired by a school to teach.

teachers college. Also **teachers' college.** A college with a special curriculum for training teachers.

teach-in (tēch′ĭn′) *n.* An extended critical discussion of a public issue held on a college or university campus, with the participation of students, faculty, and guest speakers.

teach·ing (tē′chĭng) *n.* **1.** The work or occupation of teachers. **2.** A precept or doctrine.

teaching fellow. A graduate student in a university or college who is awarded a fellowship that provides financial aid in exchange for teaching duties. —**teaching fellowship.**

teaching machine. Any of various devices designed to teach by presenting the student with a planned sequence of statements and questions and providing an immediate response to his answers.

tea cozy. A cozy *(see).*

tea·cup (tē′kŭp′) *n.* A small cup for serving tea.

tea·cup·ful (tē′kŭp′fŏŏl′) *n., pl.* **-fuls.** The amount that a teacup will hold.

tea dance. A late-afternoon dance.

tea·house (tē′hous′) *n.* A public establishment serving tea and other refreshments.

teak (tēk) *n.* **1.** A tall evergreen tree, *Tectona grandis,* of southeastern Asia, having hard, heavy, durable wood. **2.** The yellowish-brown hard wood of this tree, used for furniture and in shipbuilding. Also called "teakwood." **3.** Olive gray or dark olive, to grayish yellowish brown or grayish to moderate brown. See color. [Portuguese *teca,* from Malayalam *tēkka.*] —**teak** *adj.*

tea·ket·tle (tē′kĕt′l) *n.* A kettle, usually with a spout, used for boiling water for tea.

teal (tēl) *n., pl.* **teal** or **teals.** **1.** Any of several small, widely distributed ducks of the genus *Anas,* many of which have brightly marked plumage. **2.** Any of various other small ducks.

ă pat/ā pay/âr care/ä father/b bib/ch church/d deed/ĕ pet/ē be/f fife/g gag/h hat/hw which/ĭ pit/ī pie/îr pier/j judge/k kick/l lid,
needle/m mum/n no, sudden/ng thing/ŏ pot/ō toe/ô paw, for/oi noise/ou out/ŏŏ took/ōō boot/p pop/r roar/s sauce/sh ship, dish/

3. Moderate or dark bluish green to greenish blue. In this sense, also called "teal blue." See **color**. [Middle English *tele*, akin to Middle Dutch *talinc*, Middle Low German *telink*†.] —**teal** *adj.*
team (tēm) *n.* **1. a.** Two or more draft animals harnessed to a vehicle or farm implement. **b.** A vehicle along with the animal or animals harnessed to it. **2.** A group of animals exhibited or performing together, as horses at an equestrian show. **3.** A group of players on the same side in a game. **4.** Any group organized to work together: *a team of engineers.* **5.** *Regional.* A brood or flock. **6.** *Obsolete.* Offspring; lineage. —*v.* **teamed, teaming, teams.** —*tr.* **1.** To harness or join together so as to form a team. **2.** To transport or haul with a draft team. —*intr.* **1.** To form a team. Often used with *up.* **2.** To drive a team. [Middle English *tem(e)*, Old English *tēam*, offspring, brood, team of animals. See **deuk-** in Appendix.*]
team·mate (tēm′māt′) *n.* A fellow member of a team.
team·ster (tēm′stər) *n.* **1.** A person who drives a team. **2.** A truck driver.
team·work (tēm′wûrk′) *n.* Cooperative effort by the members of a team to achieve a common goal.
tea·pot (tē′pŏt′) *n.* A covered pot with a spout in which tea is steeped and from which it is served.
Teapot Dome. A region near Casper, Wyoming, set aside in 1915 as a naval oil reserve; the subject of a scandal during the Harding administration (1922).
tea·poy (tē′poi′) *n.* **1.** A small table for holding a tea service. **2.** Any small, decorative three-legged table. [Alteration (influenced by TEA) of Hindi *tipāī* : Hindi *tīn*, three, from Sanskrit *tri* (see **trei-** in Appendix*) + Middle Persian *pāī*, foot (see **ped-**[1] in Appendix*).]
tear[1] (târ) *v.* **tore** (tôr, tōr), **torn** (tôrn, tōrn) (see Usage note below), **tearing, tears.** —*tr.* **1.** To pull apart or into pieces; rend. **2.** To make (an opening) by ripping. **3.** To lacerate (one's skin, for example). **4.** To extract or separate forcefully; to wrench. **5.** To divide; disunite: *torn between opposing choices.* —*intr.* **1.** To become torn. **2.** To move with heedless speed; rush headlong. —**tear down.** To demolish: *tear down old tenements.* —**tear into.** To attack with great violence or vigor. —**tear off.** To produce hurriedly and casually. —*n.* **1.** An act of tearing. **2.** The result of tearing; a rip or rent. **3.** A great rush; a hurry. **4.** *Slang.* A carousal; spree. [Tear, tore, torn; Middle English *teren, tore* (earlier *taar*), *toren*, Old English *teran, tær, toren.* See **der-**[2] in Appendix.*]
Synonyms: *tear, rip, rend, split, cleave, sever, slit, slash.* These verbs refer to the act of pulling or breaking something apart or to cutting or dividing it, usually forcibly. *Tear* involves either pulling an object apart so as to produce a breach or laceration or a complete separation of parts, or wrenching one object from another to which it has been joined. *Rip* is applicable in the senses specified for *tear* but often implies separation along a seam, joint, or other dividing line. *Rip* also is somewhat stronger in its suggestion of force. *Rend* refers to violent pulling or wrenching apart of a thing's components. *Split* refers either to dividing an object forcibly, by breaking it and thus separating its parts completely, or to producing a fracture in its entire length or breadth. *Cleave* most often refers to splitting by cutting or chopping with a sharp instrument. *Sever* usually means to cut forcibly and decisively, thus removing a part from the whole of something. *Slit* refers to cutting lengthwise and producing a narrow incision, usually methodically rather than violently. *Slash* means to cut with powerful, sweeping strokes.
Usage: *Torn,* never *tore,* is the standard past participle of the verb *to tear.*
tear[2] (tîr) *n.* **1.** A drop of the clear saline liquid that is secreted by the lachrymal gland of the eye and lubricates the surface between the eyeball and the eyelid. **2.** A drop of any liquid or hardened fluid. **3.** *Plural.* The act of weeping. Used with *in* or *to: bored to tears; The farewell party left her in tears.* —*intr.v.* **teared, tearing, tears.** To fill with tears. [Middle English *tere, tear,* Old English *tēar, tehher.* See **dakru-** in Appendix.*]
tear·drop (tîr′drŏp′) *n.* **1.** A single tear. **2.** An object having the shape of a tear.
tear·ful (tîr′fəl) *adj.* Filled with or exciting tears; piteous. —**tear′ful·ly** *adv.* —**tear′ful·ness** *n.*
tear gas. Any of various agents that on dispersal, usually from grenades or projectiles, irritate the eyes and cause blinding tears. Also called "lachrymator."
tear-jerk·er (tîr′jûr′kər) *n. Slang.* A pathetic story, drama, or performance apt to make one mawkishly weepy.
tea·room (tē′ro͞om′, -ro͝om′) *n.* A restaurant or shop serving tea and other refreshments. Also called "teashop."
tea rose. 1. Any of several cultivated roses derived from *Rosa odorata,* having fragrant yellowish or pink flowers. **2.** Pale to strong yellowish pink. See **color.** —**tea′-rose′** *adj.*
tear sheet (târ). A page taken from a periodical and used chiefly to provide evidence to an advertiser of the publication of his advertisement.
Teas·dale (tēz′dāl′), **Sara.** 1884–1933. American poet.
tease (tēz) *v.* **teased, teasing, teases.** —*tr.* **1.** To annoy; pester; vex. **2.** To make fun of; playfully mock. **3.** To arouse hope, desire, or curiosity in without affording satisfaction. **4. a.** To coax. **b.** To gain by persistent coaxing. **5.** To cut (tissue, for example) into pieces for examination. **6.** To disentangle and dress the fibers of (wool, for example). **7.** To raise the nap of (cloth) by dressing, as with a fuller's teasel. **8.** To ruffle (the hair) by combing from the ends toward the scalp for an airy, full effect. —*intr.* To annoy or make fun of someone persistently. —*n.* **1.** The act of teasing. **2.** A person or thing that teases, as: **a.** One given to playful mocking. **b.** A coquettish woman. **c.** A preliminary intended to whet the curiosity. [Middle English *tesen, teesen,* to card (wool), tear apart, Old English *tǣsan,* from West Germanic *taisan* (unattested).] —**teas′ing·ly** *adv.*
tea·sel (tē′zəl) *n.* Also **tea·zel, tea·zle. 1.** Any of several plants of the genus *Dipsacus,* native to the Old World, having thistlelike flowers surrounded by prickly bracts. **2. a.** The bristly flower head of *D. fullonum,* used to produce a napped surface on fabrics. **b.** A similar object used for the same purpose. [Middle English *tesel, tasel,* Old English *tǣsel,* from West Germanic *taisilā* (unattested), from *taisan* (unattested), TEASE.]
teas·er (tē′zər) *n.* **1.** A person or thing that teases. **2.** A device used for teasing wool.
tea service. The articles, such as matching cups and teapot, used in serving tea. Also called "tea set."
tea·shop (tē′shŏp′) *n.* **1.** A **tearoom** *(see).* **2.** *British.* A lunchroom.
tea·spoon (tē′spo͞on′) *n.* **1.** The common small spoon used especially with tea, coffee, and desserts. **2.** *Abbr.* **t., tsp.** A household cooking measure, 1/3 tablespoon or 1 1/3 drams.
tea·spoon·ful (tē′spo͞on′fo͝ol′) *n., pl.* **-fuls.** *Abbr.* **t., tsp.** The amount a teaspoon will hold.
teat (tēt, tĭt) *n.* A mammary gland or nipple; pap. [Middle English *tet(t)e,* from Old French, from West Germanic *titta* (unattested), TIT.]
tea wagon. A small table on wheels for serving tea or holding dishes. Also called "teacart."
Te·bet, Te·beth. Variants of **Tevet.**
Te·briz. See **Tabriz.**
tech. technical.
tech·ne·ti·um (tĕk′nē′shē-əm) *n. Symbol* **Tc** A silvery-gray metal, the first synthetically produced element, having 14 isotopes with masses ranging from 92 to 105 and half-lives up to 2.6×10^6 years. It is used as a tracer and to eliminate corrosion in steel. Atomic number 43, melting point 2,200°C, specific gravity 11.50, valences 3, 4, 6, 7. See **element.** [New Latin, from Greek *tekhnētos,* artificial, from *tekhnasthai,* to make by art, from *tekhnē,* art, skill. See **technical.**]
tech·nic (tĕk′nĭk) *n.* **1.** *Plural.* The theory, principles, or study of an art or process. **2.** *Plural.* Technical details, rules, methods, or the like. **3.** Variant of **technique.** —*adj.* Technical.
tech·ni·cal (tĕk′nĭ-kəl) *adj. Abbr.* **tech. 1.** Of, pertaining to, or derived from technique. **2.** Specialized: *a technical school.* **3. a.** Abstract or theoretical: *a technical analysis.* **b.** Scientific. **4.** According to principle; especially, formal rather than practical: *a technical advantage.* **5.** Industrial and mechanical; technological. **6.** *Finance.* Designating or pertaining to a market in which prices are determined or affected by internal manipulation and speculation. [Latin *technicus,* from Greek *tekhnikos,* of art or skill, from *tekhnē,* art, skill. See **teks-** in Appendix.*] —**tech′ni·cal·ly** *adv.* —**tech′ni·cal·ness** *n.*
tech·ni·cal·i·ty (tĕk′nĭ-kăl′ə-tē) *n., pl.* **-ties. 1.** The condition or quality of being technical. **2.** Something meaningful or relevant in principle only.
technical knockout. *Abbr.* **TKO** *Boxing.* A victory, with immediate termination of the match, awarded by the referee when it appears that one fighter is too badly beaten to continue.
tech·ni·cian (tĕk′nĭsh′ən) *n.* An expert in a technique, as: **a.** A person whose occupation requires training in a specific technical process: *a dental technician.* **b.** One who is known for skill in an intellectual or artistic technique: *a linguistic technician.* [TECHN(IC) + -ICIAN.]
Tech·ni·col·or (tĕk′nĭ-kŭl′ər) *n.* A trademark for a motion-picture color process.
tech·nique (tĕk-nēk′) *n.* Also **tech·nic** (tĕk′nĭk) (for sense 2). **1.** The systematic procedure by which a complex or scientific task is accomplished. **2.** The degree of skill or command of fundamentals exhibited in any performance. [French, "technical," from Greek *tekhnikos.* See **technical.**]
tech·noc·ra·cy (tĕk-nŏk′rə-sē) *n., pl.* **-cies.** A government and social system controlled by scientific technicians. [Greek *tekhnē,* art, skill (see **technology**) + -CRACY.] —**tech′no·crat′** (-nō-krăt′) *n.* —**tech′no·crat′ic** *adj.*
technol. technological; technology.
tech·no·log·i·cal (tĕk′nə-lŏj′ĭ-kəl) *adj.* Also **tech·no·log·ic** (-ĭk). *Abbr.* **technol. 1.** Pertaining to or involving technology, especially scientific technology. **2.** Affected by or resulting from scientific and industrial progress. —**tech′no·log′i·cal·ly** *adv.*
tech·nol·o·gy (tĕk-nŏl′ə-jē) *n., pl.* **-gies.** *Abbr.* **technol. 1. a.** The application of science, especially to industrial or commercial objectives. **b.** The entire body of methods and materials used to achieve such objectives. **2.** *Anthropology.* Broadly, the body of knowledge available to a civilization that is of use in fashioning implements, practicing manual arts and skills, and extracting or collecting materials. [Greek *tekhnē,* skill, art (see **teks-** in Appendix*) + -LOGY.] —**tech·nol′o·gist** *n.*
tech·y. Variant of **tetchy.**
tec·ton·ic (tĕk-tŏn′ĭk) *adj.* **1.** Pertaining to construction or building. **2.** Architectural. **3.** *Geology.* Pertaining to, causing, or resulting from structural deformation in the earth's crust. [Late Latin *tectonicus,* from Greek *tektonikos,* from *tektōn,* carpenter, builder. See **teks-** in Appendix.*]
tec·ton·ics (tĕk-tŏn′ĭks) *n.* Plural in form, used with a singular verb. **1.** The art or science of construction, especially of large buildings. **2.** The geology of the earth's structural deformation.
tec·trix (tĕk′trĭks) *n., pl.* **-trices** (-trĭ-sēz′). One of the coverts of a bird's wing. Usually used in the plural. [New Latin, feminine of Latin *tector,* coverer, from *tegere* (past participle *tectus*), to cover. See **steg-**[1] in Appendix.*]

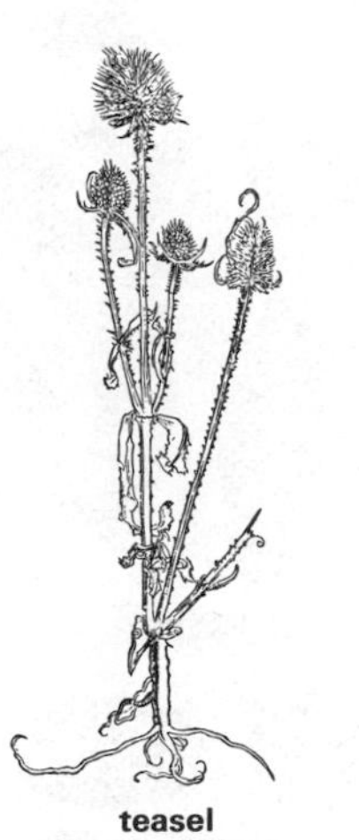
teasel
Dipsacus fullonum
Fuller's teasel

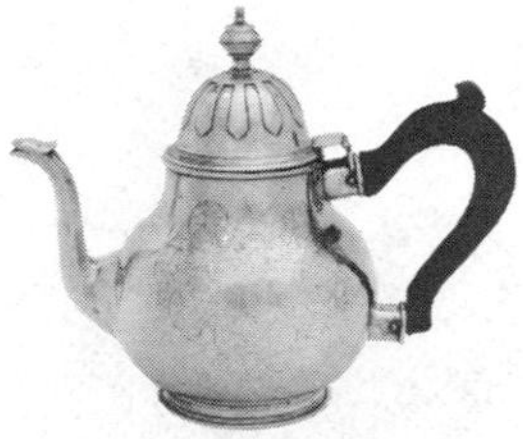
teapot
Early 18th-century American silver teapot with a wooden handle

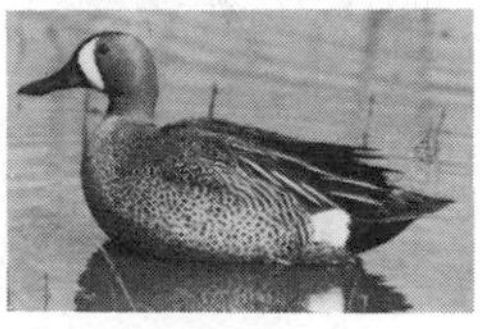
teal
Anas discors
A male of the species

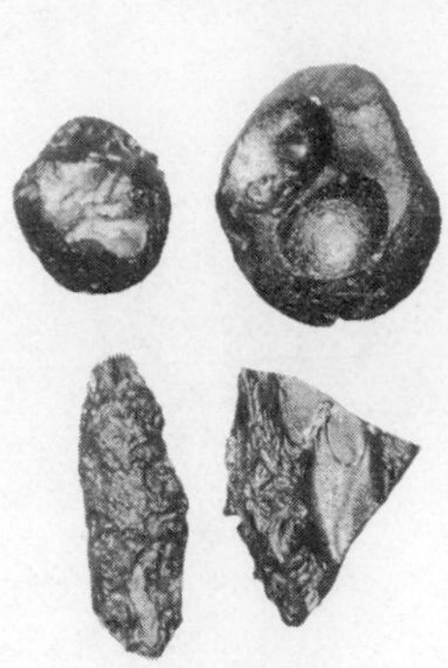

Indo-China

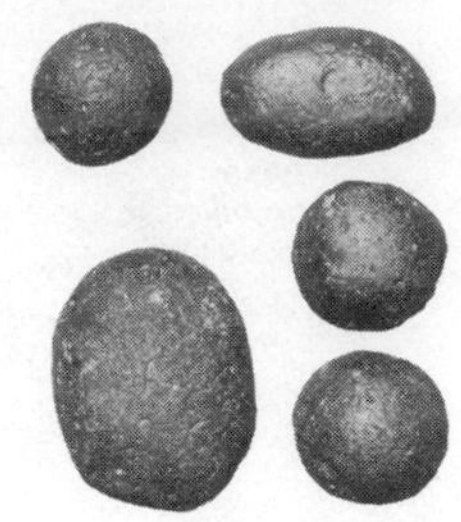

Australia

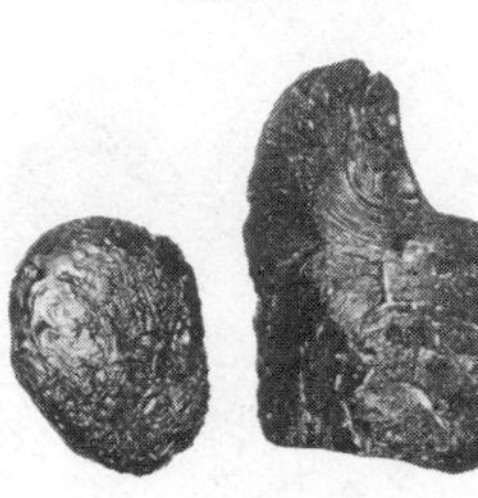

Java, Indonesia

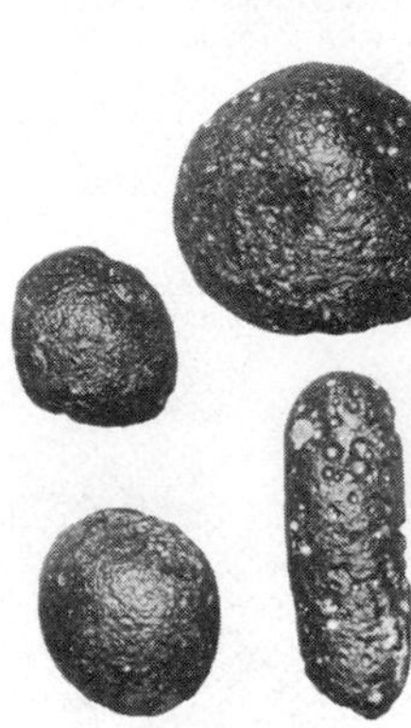

Philippines

tektite
Examples shown at approximately half size

Te·cum·seh (tĕ-kŭm′sə, -sē). 1768?–1813. American Indian leader; chief of the Shawnee; with his brother, **Tenskwatawa** (1768?–1834), tried to unite Indians against whites; defeated at Tippecanoe (1811).

ted (tĕd) *tr.v.* **tedded, tedding, teds.** To strew or spread (newly mown grass, for example) for drying. [Middle English *tedden* (attested only in the gerund *teddyng*), from Old Norse *tedhja*, to spread dung, from *tadh*, spread dung, probably related to *töturr*, TATTER.] **—ted′der** *n.*

ted·dy (tĕd′ē) *n., pl.* **-dies.** A woman's undergarment combining a shirtlike top and loose-fitting panties. [Origin unknown.]

teddy bear. Also **Teddy bear.** A child's toy bear, usually stuffed with soft material and covered with furlike plush. [After President *Theodore* Roosevelt, once depicted in a cartoon as having spared the life of a bear cub on a hunting trip.]

Teddy boy. *British.* A tough youth wearing a modified style of Edwardian clothes during the 1950's and 1960's.

Te De·um (tā′ dā′əm, tē′ dē′əm). **1.** A Latin hymn, probably written in the early fifth century A.D., beginning with the words *Te Deum laudamus*, "We praise Thee, O God," sung especially as a part of the Roman Catholic Mass. **2.** A musical setting of this text.

te·di·ous (tē′dē-əs) *adj.* **1.** Tiresome or uninteresting by reason of extreme length or slowness; wearisome; boring; monotonous: *a tedious music lesson.* **2.** *Obsolete.* Moving or progressing very slowly. —See Synonyms at **boring.** [Middle English, from Old French *tedieus*, from Late Latin *taediōsus*, from Latin *taedium*, TEDIUM.] **—te′di·ous·ly** *adv.* **—te′di·ous·ness** *n.*

te·di·um (tē′dē-əm) *n.* The quality or condition of being wearisome or monotonous; boredom; tediousness. [Latin *taedium*, from *taedēre*†, to bore, weary.]

tee¹ (tē) *n.* The letter *t.*

tee² (tē) *n.* **1.** A small peg with a concave top for holding a golf ball for an initial drive. **2.** The designated area from which a player makes his first stroke in golf. *—tr.v.* **teed, teeing, tees.** To place (a golf ball) on a tee. **—tee off. 1.** To drive a golf ball from the tee. **2.** *Slang.* To start or begin: *They teed off the fund-raising campaign with a dinner.* **—tee up.** To place or set up a ball for driving. [Earlier *teaz*†.]

tee³ (tē) *n.* A mark aimed at in certain games, such as curling or quoits. **—to a tee.** Perfectly; exactly. [Perhaps such marks were originally T-shaped.]

teem¹ (tēm) *v.* **teemed, teeming, teems.** *—intr.* **1.** To be full and, usually, in motion; abound or swarm. Used with *with: A drop of water teems with microorganisms.* **2.** *Obsolete.* To produce young; to bear. *—tr.* To give birth to; to bear. [Middle English *temen, teamen*, to give birth to, breed, Old English *tīeman, tȳman.* See **deuk-** in Appendix.*] **—teem′er** *n.*

teem² (tēm) *v.* **teemed, teeming, teems.** *—intr.* To fall heavily; pour. Used of rain. *—tr.* To pour out or empty. [Middle English *temen*, from Old Norse *tōma*, to empty, from Common Germanic *tōm-*, empty (unattested).]

teem·ing¹ (tē′mĭng) *adj.* **1.** Abounding in or swarming with. **2.** Prolific; fertile: *a teeming animal.*

teem·ing² (tē′mĭng) *adj.* Pouring, as rain.

teen (tēn) *n. Obsolete.* Injury; misery; affliction; grief. [Middle English *tene, teone*, Old English *tēona.* See **deu-³** in Appendix.*]

-teen. Used in the names of cardinal numbers **thirteen** through **nineteen.** [Middle English *-tene*, Old English *-tēne, -tȳne.* See **dekm̥** in Appendix.*]

teen-age (tēn′āj′) *adj.* Also **teen-aged** (-ājd′). Of, pertaining to, or descriptive of those of age thirteen through nineteen; adolescent.

teen-ag·er (tēn′ā′jər) *n.* A person between the ages of thirteen and nineteen inclusive; adolescent. See Synonyms at **young.**

teens (tēnz) *pl.n.* **1.** The numbers that end in *-teen.* **2.** The years of one's age between thirteen and nineteen inclusive.

tee·ny (tē′nē) *adj.* **-nier, -niest.** Also **teen·sy** (tēn′sē), **-sier, -siest.** Tiny. [Alteration of TINY.]

teen·y·bop·per (tē′nē-bŏp′ər) *n. Slang.* A girl in early adolescence held to be devoted to perpetual stylistic novelty, as in fashion or social behavior. [TEEN(-AGE) + BOP (music).]

tee·pee. Variant of **tepee.**

tee shirt. Variant of **T-shirt.**

Tees (tēz). A river of northeastern England, flowing 70 miles from eastern Cumberland to the North Sea.

tee·ter (tē′tər) *v.* **-tered, -tering, -ters.** *—intr.* **1.** To walk or move unsteadily or unsurely; to totter. **2.** To seesaw; vacillate. *—tr.* To cause to teeter or seesaw. *—n.* **1.** A **seesaw** *(see).* **2.** A teetering or seesaw motion. [Earlier *titter*, from Middle English *titeren* (attested only in the gerund *titeryng*), probably from Old Norse *titra*, to tremble. See **der-¹** in Appendix.*]

teeter board. A **seesaw** *(see).*

tee·ter-tot·ter (tē′tər-tŏt′ər) *n.* A **seesaw** *(see).*

teeth. Plural of **tooth.**

teethe (tēth) *intr.v.* **teethed, teething, teethes.** To grow teeth; cut one's teeth in infancy. [Middle English *tethen*, from *tethe*, teeth. See **tooth.**]

teething ring. A ring of hard rubber or plastic upon which a teething baby can bite.

tee·to·tal·er (tē′tōt′l-ər) *n.* Also **tee·to·tal·ler, tee·to·tal·ist** (-ĭst). A person who abstains completely from alcoholic liquors. [*Tee*, first letter in TOTAL + TOTAL (ABSTINENCE).] **—tee·to′tal·ism′** *n.*

tee·to·tum (tē′tō′təm) *n.* A kind of top spun with the fingers, usually having four lettered sides. [Earlier *T-totum*, from the letter *T* inscribed on one of the four sides, standing for Latin *tōtum*, all, and signifying "take all," from the neuter of *tōtus*, all. See **teutā-** in Appendix.*]

Tef·lon (tĕf′lŏn′) *n.* A trademark for a waxy, opaque material, polytetrafluoroethylene, used as a coating on cooking utensils and in industrial applications to prevent sticking.

t.e.g. *Library Service.* top edges gilt.

teg·men (tĕg′mən) *n., pl.* **-mina** (-mə-nə). *Biology.* A covering or integument, such as the tough, leathery forewing of certain insects or the inner coat of a seed. [New Latin, from Latin, covering, from *tegere*, to cover. See **steg-¹** in Appendix.*]

te·gua (tā′gwä, tā′wä) *n.* An ankle-high moccasin worn by Mexicans and Indians. [Native name in Mexico.]

Te·gu·ci·gal·pa (tā-gōō′sē-gäl′pä). The capital of Honduras, in the south-central part of the country. Population, 168,000.

teg·u·lar (tĕg′yə-lər) *adj.* Also **teg·u·lat·ed** (-lā′tĭd). **1.** Pertaining to or resembling a tile or tiles. **2.** Overlapping; imbricate: *tegular scales.* [From Latin *tēgula*, tile, from *tegere*, to cover. See **steg-¹** in Appendix.*] **—teg′u·lar·ly** *adv.*

teg·u·ment (tĕg′yə-mənt) *n.* An outer covering; integument. [Middle English, from Latin *tegumentum*, from *tegere*, to cover. See **steg-¹** in Appendix.*] **—teg′u·men′ta·ry** (-mĕn′tə-rē, -mĕn′trē), **teg′u·men′tal** (-mĕnt′l) *adj.*

Te·hach·a·pi (tĭ-hăch′ə-pē). A mountain range in Southern California, extending from the southern end of the Sierra Nevada to the Coast Ranges. Highest elevation, 7,950 feet.

Te·he·ran (tĕ′ə-răn′, -rän′). Also **Te·hran** (tĕ-rän′). The capital of Iran, in the north-central part of the country. Population, 2,317,000.

Te·huan·te·pec, Isthmus of (tə-wän′tə-pĕk′). The narrowest section of southern Mexico (about 125 miles), between the Gulf of Mexico in the north and the Pacific Ocean in the south.

Te·huel·che (tā-wĕl′chā) *n., pl.* **Tehuelche** or **-ches.** One of a nomadic Indian people of southern Argentina, virtually exterminated by the Spanish colonists. [Araucanian, "people of the southeast."] **—Te·huel′che·an** (-chē-ən) *adj.*

teig·lach (tāg′ləkн, -läкн′, tĭg′-) *pl.n.* Also **taig·lach.** A confection consisting of bits of dough cooked briefly in a mixture of honey, brown sugar, and nuts, then cooled and rolled into balls. [Yiddish *teyglekh*, diminutive of *teyg*, dough, from Middle High German *teig*, from Old High German *teic.* See **dheigh-** in Appendix.*]

Teil·hard de Char·din (tā-yär′ də shär-dăN′), **Pierre.** 1881–1955. French Jesuit priest, geologist, and philosopher.

Teisse·renc de Bort (tĕs-räN′ də bôr′), **Léon Phillipe.** 1855–1913. French meteorologist; discovered and named the stratosphere.

Te·jo. The Portuguese name for the **Tagus.**

Tek·a·kwith·a (tĕk′ə-kwĭth′ə), **Kateri.** 1656–1680. American Mohawk Indian Catholic nun; venerated (1943).

tek·tite (tĕk′tīt′) *n.* Any of numerous dark brown to green glass objects, generally small and rounded, thought to be of extraterrestrial origin, found chiefly in Czechoslovakia, Australia, Indonesia, the Philippines, Texas and Georgia, and having a largely silica composition with various oxides. [Greek *tēktos*, molten (from its supposed meteoric origin), from *tēkein*, to melt (see **tā-** in Appendix*) + -ITE.]

tel. 1. telegram; telegraph; telegraphic. **2.** telephone.

te·la (tē′lə) *n., pl.* **-lae** (-lē′). A weblike membrane that covers some portion of a bodily organ. [New Latin, from Latin *tēla*, web. See **teks-** in Appendix.*]

tel·aes·the·sia. Variant of **telesthesia.**

tel·a·mon (tĕl′ə-mŏn′) *n., pl.* **telamones** (tĕl′ə-mō′nēz). *Architecture.* A figure of a man used as a supporting pillar. Compare **caryatid.** [Latin, from Greek *telamōn*, bearer. See **tel-¹** in Appendix.*]

tel·an·gi·ec·ta·sia (tĕl-ăn′jē-ĕk-tā′zhə, -zhē-ə) *n.* Also **tel·an·gi·ec·ta·sis** (-ĕk′tə-sĭs). A chronic dilation of groups of capillaries of the blood vascular system causing dark-red blotches on the skin, as birthmarks. [New Latin : TEL(O)- (end) + Greek *angos*, vessel (see **angiology**) + *ectasis*, dilation, from Greek *ektasis*, expansion, stretching, from *ekteinein*, to stretch out : *ek-*, from *ex*, out + *teinein*, to stretch (see **ten-** in Appendix*).] **—tel·an′gi·ec·tat′ic** (-tăt′ĭk) *adj.*

Tel·Au·to·graph (tĕl-ô′tə-grăf′, -gräf′) *n.* A trademark for a telegraphic device having electromagnetically controlled pens at sending and receiving ends by means of which writing or drawings can be transmitted by wire.

Tel A·viv (tĕl′ ə-vēv′). The largest city of Israel, a seaport on the Mediterranean, constituting with Jaffa one municipality. Population, 394,000.

tele–, tel–. Indicates: **1.** Distance; for example, **telecommunication, telesthesia. 2.** Television; for example, **telecast.** [From Greek *tēle*, at a distance, far off. See **kwel-²** in Appendix.*]

tel·e·cast (tĕl′ə-kăst′, -käst′) *v.* **-cast** or **-casted, -casting, -casts.** *—intr.* To broadcast by television. *—tr.* To broadcast (a program) by television. *—n.* A television broadcast.

tel·e·com·mu·ni·ca·tion (tĕl′ə-kə-myōō′nĭ-kā′shən) *n.* **1.** *Often plural.* The science and technology of communication by electronic transmission of impulses, as by telegraphy, cable, telephony, radio, or television. Used with a singular verb. **2.** Any message so communicated.

tel·e·du (tĕl′ə-dōō′) *n.* A brownish-black carnivorous mammal, *Mydaus javanensis*, of the East Indies, that, like the skunk, is capable of emitting an offensive odor. [Malay *tĕledu.*]

teleg. telegram; telegraph; telegraphic; telegraphy.

te·le·ga (tə-lĕg′ə) *n. Russian.* A rough four-wheeled cart lacking springs. [Russian *telega*, from Old Russian *telĕga*, from Old Slavic *telĕga* (unattested).]

tel·e·ge·nic (tĕl′ə-jĕn′ĭk, -jē′nĭk) *adj.* Presenting a pleasing appearance on television. [TELE- + (PHOTO)GENIC.]

te·leg·o·ny (tə-lĕg′ə-nē) *n.* The supposed influence of one sire on offspring sired by subsequent males on the same female. [TELE- + -GONY.] —**tel′e·gon′ic** (tĕl′ə-gŏn′ĭk), **te·leg′o·nous** *adj.*

tel·e·gram (tĕl′ə-grăm′) *n. Abbr.* **tel., teleg.** A communication transmitted by telegraph; a wire. [TELE- + -GRAM.]

tel·e·graph (tĕl′ə-grăf′, -gräf′) *n. Abbr.* **tel., teleg. 1.** Any communications system that transmits and receives simple unmodulated electric impulses, especially one in which the transmission and reception stations are directly connected by wires. **2.** A message transmitted by such a system; a telegram. —*v.* **telegraphed, -graphing, -graphs.** —*tr.* **1.** To transmit (a message) by telegraph. **2.** To send or convey a message to (someone) by telegraph. **3.** To inform (someone) unintentionally, especially of an unexpected occurrence or event. —*intr.* To send or transmit a telegram or telegrams. [TELE- + -GRAPH.] —**te·leg′ra·pher** (tə-lĕg′rə-fər), **te·leg′ra·phist** *n.*

tel·e·graph·ic (tĕl′ə-grăf′ĭk) *adj.* Also **tel·e·graph·i·cal** (-ĭ-kəl). **1.** *Abbr.* **tel., teleg.** Pertaining to or transmitted by telegraph. **2.** Brief; concise, as a telegram. —**tel′e·graph′i·cal·ly** *adv.*

telegraph plant. A tropical Asiatic plant, *Desmodium motorium* (or *D. gyrans*), having trifoliolate compound leaves, of which the lateral leaflets move or rotate.

te·leg·ra·phy (tə-lĕg′rə-fē) *n. Abbr.* **teleg.** Communications by means of telegraph.

Tel·e·gu (tĕl′ə-gōō′) *n., pl.* **Telegu** or **-gus.** Also **Tel·u·gu. 1.** A Dravidian language spoken in Andhra Pradesh, India. **2.** A member of a Dravidian people who speak this language. —*adj.* Of or pertaining to this language or this people. [Native name.]

tel·e·ki·ne·sis (tĕl′ə-kĭ-nē′sĭs, -kī-nē′sĭs) *n.* **1.** The movement of objects by scientifically unknown or inexplicable means, as by the exercise of mystical powers. **2.** The ability to produce such movement. [New Latin : TELE- + -KINESIS.] —**tel′e·ki·net′ic** (-nĕt′ĭk) *adj.*

Te·lem·a·chus (tə-lĕm′ə-kəs). *Greek Mythology.* The son of Odysseus and Penelope who helped his father kill Penelope's suitors.

Te·le·mann (tā′lə-män), **Georg Philipp.** 1681–1767. German composer of operas, cantatas, and chamber music.

tel·e·mark (tĕl′ə-märk′) *n.* Also **Tel·e·mark.** A turn or stop in skiing executed by shifting the weight forward on the ski that will be on the outside of the turn and pulling its tip gradually inward. [Norwegian, after *Telemark,* region in southern Norway.]

te·lem·e·ter (tə-lĕm′ə-tər, tĕl′ə-mē′tər) *n.* Any of various devices used in telemetry. —*tr.v.* (tĕl′ə-mē′tər) **telemetered, -tering, -ters.** To measure and transmit (data) automatically from a distant source, as from a spacecraft or electric power grid, to a receiving station for recording or display. [TELE- + -METER.] —**tel′e·met′ric** (tĕl′ə-mĕt′rĭk), **tel′e·met′ri·cal** *adj.* —**tel′e·met′ri·cal·ly** *adv.*

te·lem·e·try (tə-lĕm′ə-trē) *n.* The science and technology of automatic measurement and transmission of data by wire, radio, or other means from remote sources, as from space vehicles, to a receiving station for recording and analysis. [TELE- + -METRY.]

tel·en·ceph·a·lon (tĕl′ĕn-sĕf′ə-lŏn′, -lən) *n.* The anterior portion of the forebrain, including the cerebral cortex and related parts. Also called "endbrain." [TEL(O)- + ENCEPHALON.] —**tel′en·ce·phal′ic** (-sə-făl′ĭk) *adj.*

tel·e·ol·o·gy (tĕl′ē-ŏl′ə-jē, tē′lē-) *n., pl.* **-gies. 1.** The philosophical study of manifestations of design or purpose in natural processes or occurrences, under the belief that natural processes are not determined by mechanism but rather by their utility in an overall natural design. Compare **dysteleology. 2.** Such ultimate purpose or design. [New Latin *teleologia* : Greek *teleos,* complete, final, from *telos,* completion, end (see **kwel-**[1] in Appendix*) + -LOGY.] —**tel′e·o·log′i·cal** (-ə-lŏj′ĭ-kəl), **tel′e·o·log′ic** *adj.* —**tel′e·o·log′i·cal·ly** *adv.* —**tel′e·ol′o·gist** *n.*

tel·e·ost (tĕl′ē-ŏst′, tē′lē-) *adj.* Also **tel·e·os·te·an** (tĕl′ē-ŏs′tē-ən, tē′lē-). Of or belonging to the Teleostei (or Teleostomi), a group consisting of numerous fishes having bony skeletons and rayed fins. —*n.* Also **tel·e·os·te·an** (-ŏs′tē-ən). A teleost fish. [New Latin *Teleostei,* "ones having complete bony skeletons," and *Teleostomi,* "ones having complete mouths" : Greek *teleos,* complete (see **teleology**) + Greek *osteon,* bone (see **osth-** in Appendix*) and *stoma,* mouth (see **stomach**).]

te·lep·a·thy (tə-lĕp′ə-thē) *n.* **1.** Communication by scientifically unknown or inexplicable means, as by the exercise of mystical powers. **2.** The ability to produce or engage in such communication. [TELE- + -PATHY.] —**tel′e·path′ic** (tĕl′ə-păth′ĭk) *adj.* —**tel′e·path′i·cal·ly** *adv.* —**te·lep′a·thist** *n.*

tel·e·phone (tĕl′ə-fōn′) *n. Abbr.* **tel. 1.** An instrument that directly modulates carrier waves with voice or other acoustic source signals to be transmitted to remote locations and that directly reconverts received waves into audible signals; especially, such an instrument connected to others by wire. **2.** A system of such instruments together with connecting and supporting equipment. —*v.* **telephoned, -phoning, -phones.** —*tr.* **1.** To communicate with (someone) by telephone. **2.** To call (someone) on the telephone. **3.** To transmit (a recorded message, television picture, or document) by telephone, using special receiving and sending equipment. —*intr.* To communicate by telephone. [TELE- + -PHONE.] —**tel′e·phon′er** *n.*

telephone book. A directory of names with corresponding addresses and telephone numbers. Also called "telephone directory."

telephone booth. A small enclosure containing a public telephone.

telephone exchange. Any of numerous central systems of switches and other equipment that establish connections between individual telephones. Also called "exchange."

telephone pole. A tall, cylindrical wooden pole several inches in diameter, used outdoors to support telephone equipment, especially wires.

telephone receiver. The part of a telephone in which incoming electrical impulses are converted into sound.

tel·e·phon·ic (tĕl′ə-fŏn′ĭk) *adj.* **1.** Of or pertaining to telephones. **2.** Transmitted or conveyed by a telephone. —**tel′e·phon′i·cal·ly** *adv.*

te·leph·o·ny (tə-lĕf′ə-nē) *n.* **1.** The electrical transmission of sound between distant stations, especially by radio or telephone. **2.** The technology and manufacture of telephone equipment.

tel·e·pho·to (tĕl′ə-fō′tō) *adj.* Of or pertaining to a photographic lens or lens system used to produce a large image of a distant object or to obtain a clear picture of a near object against a blurred background.

tel·e·pho·to·graph (tĕl′ə-fō′tə-grăf′, -gräf′) *n.* **1.** A photograph made with a telephoto lens. **2.** A photograph transmitted and reproduced by telephotography. —*tr.v.* **telephotographed, -graphing, -graphs. 1.** To photograph with a telephoto lens. **2.** To transmit by telephotography.

tel·e·pho·tog·ra·phy (tĕl′ə-fə-tŏg′rə-fē) *n.* **1.** The process or technique of photographing distant objects, using a telephoto lens or telescope on a camera. **2.** The technique or process of transmitting charts, pictures, and photographs over a distance. —**tel′e·pho′to·graph′ic** (-fō′tə-grăf′ĭk) *adj.*

tel·e·play (tĕl′ə-plā′) *n.* A play written or adapted for television.

tel·e·print·er (tĕl′ə-prĭn′tər) *n.* A **teletypewriter** *(see).*

Tel·e·promp·ter (tĕl′ə-prŏmp′tər) *n.* A trademark for a device used in television to show an actor or speaker an enlarged line-by-line reproduction of a script, unseen by the audience.

Tel·e·ran (tĕl′ə-răn′) *n.* A trademark for a system used in air traffic control in which the image of a ground-based radar unit is televised to aircraft in the vicinity so that a pilot may see his position in relation to other aircraft. [TELE- + R(ADAR) A(IR) N(AVIGATION).]

tel·e·scope (tĕl′ə-skōp′) *n.* An instrument for collecting and examining electromagnetic radiation; especially: **1.** An arrangement of lenses or mirrors or both that gathers visible light, permitting direct observation or photographic recording of distant objects. **2.** Any of various devices, such as a radio telescope, used to detect and observe distant objects by their emission, transmission, reflection, or other interaction with invisible radiation. —*v.* **telescoped, -scoping, -scopes.** —*tr.* **1.** To cause to slide inward or outward in overlapping sections, as the cylindrical sections of a small hand telescope. **2.** To crush or compress (a body) inward. **3.** To make shorter or more precise; condense. —*intr.* To slide inward or outward in or as if in overlapping cylindrical sections. [New Latin *telescopium* or Italian *telescopio,* from Greek *teleskopos,* farseeing : TELE- + *skopos,* watcher (see **spek-** in Appendix*).]

Telescope Peak. A mountain rising to 11,045 feet in the Panamint Mountains of eastern California.

tel·e·scop·ic (tĕl′ə-skŏp′ĭk) *adj.* **1.** Of or pertaining to a telescope. **2.** Seen through or obtained by means of a telescope. **3.** Visible only by means of a telescope. **4.** Able to discern distant objects; farseeing. **5.** Extensible or compressible by or as if by the successive sliding of overlapping concentric tubular sections. —**tel′e·scop′i·cal·ly** *adv.*

Tel·e·sco·pi·um (tĕl′ə-skō′pē-əm) *n.* A constellation in the Southern Hemisphere near Pavo and Sagittarius. [New Latin, from *telescopium,* TELESCOPE.]

te·les·co·py (tə-lĕs′kə-pē) *n.* The art or study of making and operating telescopes. —**te·les′co·pist** *n.*

Te·les Pi·res (tĕ′lĭs pē′rĭs). Formerly **São Ma·nuel** (souɴ mä-nōōĕl′). A river of Brazil, rising in central Mato Grosso and flowing about 600 miles generally north to the Tapajós.

tel·e·ster·e·o·scope (tĕl′ə-stĕr′ē-ə-skōp′, -stîr′ē-ə-skōp′) *n.* A binocular telescope for stereoscopic viewing of distant objects.

tel·es·the·sia (tĕl′ĭs-thē′zhə, -zhē-ə) *n.* Also **tel·aes·the·sia.** Response to or perception of distant stimuli by extrasensory, especially mystical, means. [New Latin : TEL(E)- + ESTHESIA.] —**tel′es·thet′ic** (-thĕt′ĭk) *adj.*

tel·e·ther·mo·scope (tĕl′ə-thûr′mə-skōp′) *n.* An apparatus for indicating or recording the temperatures of distant or inaccessible locations.

tel·e·thon (tĕl′ə-thŏn′) *n.* A long, continuous television program, usually to raise funds for charity. [TELE- + (MARA)-THON.]

tel·e·tran·scrip·tion (tĕl′ə-trăn-skrĭp′shən) *n.* The transcription of television programs by means of a kinescope or video tape.

Tel·e·type (tĕl′ə-tīp′) *n.* A trademark for a brand of teletypewriter. —*v.* **Teletyped, -typing, -types.** —*intr.* To operate a Teletype. —*tr.* To send a message by Teletype.

tel·e·type·writ·er (tĕl′ə-tīp′rī′tər) *n.* An electromechanical typewriter that either transmits or receives messages coded in electrical signals carried by telegraph or telephone wires. Also called "teleprinter."

te·leu·to·spore (tə-lōō′tə-spôr′, -spōr′) *n. Botany.* A **teliospore** *(see).* [Greek *teleutē,* termination, from *telos,* end, completion (see **kwel-**[1] in Appendix*) + SPORE.] —**te·leu′to·spor′ic** *adj.*

tel·e·vise (tĕl′ə-vīz′) *v.* **-vised, -vising, -vises.** —*tr.* To broadcast (a program) by television. —*intr.* To broadcast by television. [Back-formation from TELEVISION.]

tel·e·vi·sion (tĕl′ə-vĭzh′ən) *n. Abbr.* **TV 1.** The transmission of visual images of moving and stationary objects, generally with

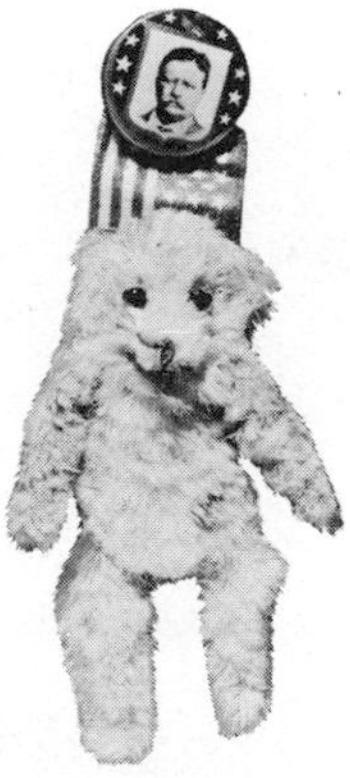

teddy bear
Campaign button used in Theodore Roosevelt's 1904 Presidential campaign

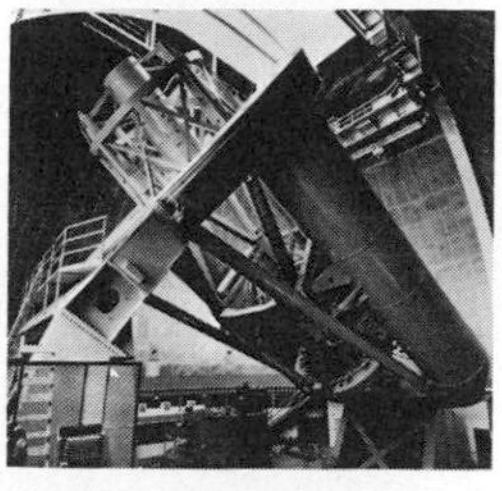

telescope
The 200-inch Hale telescope, Mount Palomar Observatory, southern California

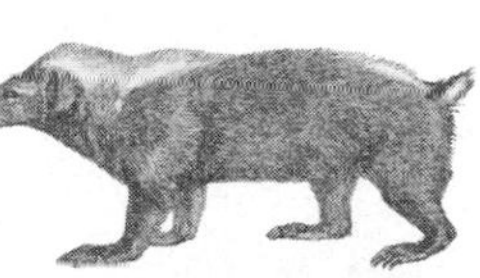

teledu

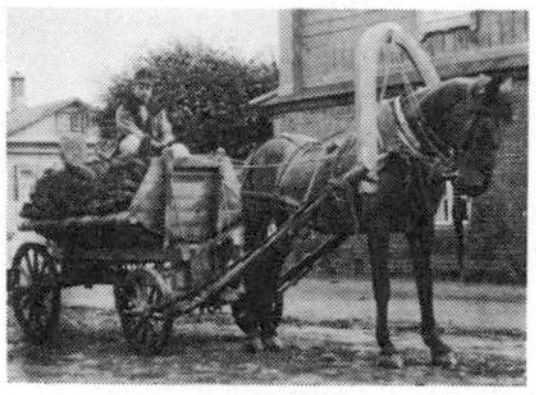

telega

accompanying sound, as electromagnetic waves and the reconversion of received waves into visual images. **2.** An electronic apparatus that receives such waves and displays the reconverted images on a screen. **3.** The integrated audible and visible content of the electromagnetic waves received and converted by such an apparatus. **4.** The industry of broadcasting television programs. [French *télévision* : TELE- + VISION.]

tel·e·vi·sor (tĕl′ə-vī′zər) *n.* A television transmitter.

tel·fer. Variant of **telpher.**

tel·ic (tĕl′ĭk, tē′lĭk) *adj.* Directed or tending toward a goal or purpose; purposeful. [Greek *telikos,* final, from *telos,* end, completion. See **kwel-**[1] in Appendix.*]

te·li·o·spore (tē′lē-ə-spôr′, -spōr′) *n.* A thick-walled, blackish resting spore of rusts and smuts, from which the basidium arises. Also called "teleutospore." [TELIUM + SPORE.]

te·li·um (tē′lē-əm) *n., pl.* **-lia** (-lē-ə). A blackish, pustulelike structure formed on the tissue of a plant infected by a rust fungus, and giving rise to teliospores. [New Latin, from Greek *teleios,* complete (formed in the final stage of the cycle of rust fungi), from *telos,* end, completion. See **kwel-**[1] in Appendix.*] —**te′li·al** *adj.*

tell (tĕl) *v.* **told** (tōld), **telling, tells.** —*tr.* **1.** To give a detailed account of; narrate; recount. **2.** To communicate by speech or writing; express with words: *"When in doubt tell the truth"* (Mark Twain). **3.** To make known to; notify; inform. **4.** To make known; reveal; disclose: *tell fortunes.* **5.** To command; order: *Do what I tell you.* **6.** *Informal.* To assure: *I tell you, he's an honest man.* Often used for emphasis. **7.** To discover by observation; discern; identify. **8.** To say (a rosary). —*intr.* **1.** To give an account, enumeration, or description. **2.** To give evidence or indication. **3.** To have an effect or impact: *In this game every move tells.* —**all told.** Including everyone or everything; in all. —**tell off. 1.** To count and set apart, especially aloud. **2.** *Informal.* To rebuke severely. —**tell on. 1.** To exhaust or tire. **2.** *Informal.* To inform against; tattle on. [Tell, told (past tense), told (past participle); Middle English *tellen, told* (or *tald*), *ytold* (or *ytald*), Old English *tellan, tealde, geteald.* See **del-**[2] in Appendix.*] —**tell′a·ble** *adj.*

Tell el A·mar·na (tĕl′ ĕl ə-mär′nə). A site containing ancient ruins in central Egypt, on the east bank of the Nile north of Asyut.

tell·er (tĕl′ər) *n.* **1.** One who tells. **2.** A bank employee who receives and pays out money. **3.** A person appointed to count votes in a legislative assembly. —**tell′er·ship′** *n.*

Tel·ler (tĕl′ər), **Edward.** Born 1908. Hungarian-born American physicist; helped develop atomic and hydrogen bombs.

tell·ing (tĕl′ĭng) *adj.* **1.** Having force or effect; striking. **2.** Full of special meaning; revealing: *"a man whose life was a telling pantomime of action, and not a tame chapter of sounds"* (Melville). —See Synonyms at **valid.** —**tell′ing·ly** *adv.*

tell·tale (tĕl′tāl′) *n.* **1.** One who informs on another person; tattler; talebearer. **2.** That which indicates or reveals information about something; a sign; token. **3.** Any of various devices that indicate or register information, specifically: **a.** A time clock. **b.** A device indicating the position of a ship's rudder. **c.** A row of strips hung above a railroad track to warn an approaching train of a low clearance ahead. —*adj.* **1.** Serving to indicate or reveal. **2.** Serving to betray what is intended to be kept secret: *a telltale blush.*

tel·lu·ri·an (tĕ-lo͝or′ē-ən) *adj.* Of, pertaining to, or inhabiting the earth. —*n.* **1.** An inhabitant of the earth; a terrestrial. **2.** Variant of **tellurion.** [From Latin *tellūs* (stem *tellūr-*), earth. See **tel-**[2] in Appendix.*]

tel·lu·ric (tĕ-lo͝or′ĭk) *adj.* **1.** Of or relating to the earth; earthly; terrestrial. **2.** Derived from or containing tellurium, especially with valence 6. [From Latin *tellūs* (stem *tellūr-*), earth. See **tel-**[2] in Appendix.*]

telluric acid. A white, crystalline inorganic acid, H_6TeO_4, that is used as a chemical reagent.

tel·lu·ride (tĕl′yə-rīd′) *n.* A binary compound of tellurium. [TELLUR(IUM) + -IDE.]

tel·lu·ri·on (tĕ-lo͝or′ē-ŏn′) *n.* Also **tel·lu·ri·an** (-ən). An instrument that shows how the movement of the earth on its axis and around the sun causes day and night and the seasons. [Latin *tellūs* (stem *tellūr-*), earth (see **tel-**[2] in Appendix*) + -ION.]

tel·lu·ri·um (tĕ-lo͝or′ē-əm) *n. Symbol* **Te** A brittle, silvery-white metallic element, occurring naturally combined with gold and other metals, produced commercially as a by-product of the electrolytic refining of copper, and used to alloy stainless steel and lead, in ceramics, and, in the form of bismuth telluride, in thermoelectric devices. Atomic number 52, atomic weight 127.60, melting point 449.5°C, boiling point 989.8°C, specific gravity 6.24, valences 2, 4, 6. See **element.** [New Latin, from Latin *tellūs* (stem *tellūr-*), earth (by analogy with URANIUM, after the planet *Uranus*). See **tel-**[2] in Appendix.*]

tel·lu·rous (tĕl′yər-əs, tĕ-lo͝or′əs) *adj.* Of, relating to, or derived from tellurium, especially with valence 4.

Tell (tĕl), **William.** A legendary hero of Swiss independence who was required to shoot an apple from his son's head with a crossbow.

tel·ly (tĕl′ē) *n., pl.* **-lies.** *Chiefly British Informal.* Television.

telo-, tel-. Indicates: **1.** Completion, perfection, or finality; for example, **telophase. 2.** End or situated at the end; for example, **telencephalon.** [From Greek *telos,* end, completion. See **kwel-**[1] in Appendix.*]

te·lo·phase (tē′lə-fāz′, tĕl′ə-) *n.* The last phase of mitosis, in which the chromosomes of daughter cells are grouped in new nuclei. [TELO- + PHASE.]

tel·pher (tĕl′fər) *n.* Also **tel·fer, tel·pher·age** (tĕl′fər-ĭj) (for sense 2). **1.** A light transportation car suspended from overhead wire cables, usually driven by electricity. **2.** A transportation system using these cars. —*tr.v.* **telphered, -phering, -phers.** Also **tel·fer.** To transport by telpher. [From TEL(E)- + Greek *pherein,* to carry (see **bher-**[1] in Appendix*).]

tel·son (tĕl′sən) *n.* A terminal structure of the posterior section of certain arthropods, such as the middle lobe of the tail fin of a lobster or shrimp or the sting of a scorpion. [New Latin, from Greek, headland, limit, from *telos,* end. See **kwel-**[1] in Appendix.*]

Tel·star (tĕl′stär′) *n.* One of two privately financed, low-altitude, active communications satellites launched by the U.S. Government in 1962 and 1963, and used commercially to transmit television pictures and telephone messages.

Tel·u·gu. Variant of **Telegu.**

tem·blor (tĕm′blər, -blôr′) *n. Regional.* An earthquake. [Spanish, from *temblar,* to shake, from Vulgar Latin *tremulāre* (unattested), TREMBLE.]

tem·er·ar·i·ous (tĕm′ə-râr′ē-əs) *adj.* Presumptuously or recklessly daring; rash. [Latin *temerārius,* rash, from *temere,* rashly. See **temerity.**] —**tem′e·rar′i·ous·ly** *adv.* —**tem′e·rar′i·ous·ness** *n.*

te·mer·i·ty (tə-mĕr′ə-tē) *n.* Foolhardy or heedless disregard of danger; foolish boldness; recklessness; rashness. [Middle English *temeryte,* from Latin *temeritās,* from *temere,* blindly, rashly. See **teme-** in Appendix.*]

Synonyms: *temerity, audacity, impetuosity, effrontery, nerve, cheek, gall.* These nouns are closely related to boldness or aggressiveness in action or speech, often in an unfavorable sense. *Temerity* implies boldness and rashness in the sense of heedlessness of danger, whereas *audacity* suggests heedlessness also of restraints imposed by prudence, propriety, or convention. *Impetuosity* implies haste or vehemence of action or speech that results from obeying impulse rather than reason. The remaining terms are more explicitly derogatory. *Effrontery* is boldness marked by impudence, arrogance, or presumptuousness; and *nerve* is an approximately equivalent informal term. *Cheek,* also informal, especially suggests impudence and brashness. *Gall* is a strong informal term that adds to *effrontery* the suggestion of brazenness, insolence, and utter lack of shame.

Te·meš. The Serbian name for the **Timiş.**

temp. 1. in the time of (Latin *tempore*). **2.** temperance. **3.** temperature. **4.** temporary.

Tem·pe, Vale of (tĕm′pē). A valley extending for about five miles between Mount Olympus and Mount Ossa in northeastern Thessaly, Greece; in ancient times considered sacred to Apollo.

tem·per (tĕm′pər) *v.* **-pered, -pering, -pers.** —*tr.* **1.** To modify by the addition of some moderating agent or quality; moderate: *"The helpless showed only their helplessness when they tempered obedience by mockery."* (Henry Adams). **2.** To bring to a specified consistency, texture, hardness, or other physical condition by or as by blending, admixture, kneading, or the like. **3.** To harden, strengthen, or toughen (a metal) by application of heat or by alternate heating and cooling. **4.** *Rare.* To adjust; to fit. **5.** *Music.* To adjust or tune (a keyboard instrument) by temperament. —*intr.* To be or become tempered. —*n.* **1.** A state of mind or emotions; mood; disposition: *"The temper of a woman is generally formed from the turn of her features"* (Goldsmith). **2.** Calmness of mind or emotions; equanimity; composure: *lose one's temper.* **3. a.** A tendency to become easily angry or irritable: *Watch out for his temper.* **b.** An outburst of rage: *a fit of temper.* **4. a.** The condition of being tempered. **b.** The degree of hardness and elasticity of a metal, chiefly steel, as a result of tempering. **5.** A substance or agent added to something to alter or modify it. **6.** *Obsolete.* The character or constitution of a man according to medieval physiology, as determined by the mixture within him of the four humors. **7.** *Archaic.* A middle course; a compromise between extremes. —See Synonyms at **mood.** [Middle English *temp(e)ren,* Old English *temprian,* to mingle, moderate, from Latin *temperāre,* "to mingle in due proportion," probably from *tempus* (stem *temper-*), time, due season. See **temporal.**] —**tem′per·a·bil′i·ty** *n.* —**tem′per·a·ble** *adj.* —**tem′per·er** *n.*

tem·per·a (tĕm′pər-ə) *n.* **1.** A painting medium in which pigment is mixed with water-soluble glutinous materials such as size or egg yolk. **2.** Painting done with this medium. [Italian, from *temperare,* to mingle, temper, from Latin *temperāre.* See **temper.**]

tem·per·a·ment (tĕm′prə-mənt, tĕm′pər-ə-) *n.* **1. a.** The manner of thinking, behaving, or reacting characteristic of a specific individual: *a nervous temperament.* **b.** The distinguishing mental and physical characteristics that established the constitution of a man according to medieval physiology, caused by the dominance of one of the four humors. See **humor. 2.** Excessive irritability or sensitiveness; temper. **3.** *Music.* **Equal temperament** *(see).* —See Synonyms at **disposition.** [Middle English *temperament,* from Latin *temperāmentum,* "a mixing (of the humors)," from *temperāre,* to mingle, TEMPER.]

tem·per·a·men·tal (tĕm′prə-mĕn′tl, tĕm′pər-ə-) *adj.* **1.** Pertaining to, caused by, or endowed with temperament or temper. **2.** Excessively sensitive or irritable; easily excited or angered; moody. —**tem′per·a·men′tal·ly** *adv.*

tem·per·ance (tĕm′pər-əns, tĕm′prəns) *n. Abbr.* **temp. 1.** The condition or quality of being temperate; moderation or self-restraint: *"that greater clearness of head and quicker apprehension which generally attend temperance in eating and drinking"* (Franklin). **2.** Total abstinence from alcoholic liquors. —See Synonyms at **abstinence.**

ă pat/ā pay/âr care/ä father/b bib/ch church/d deed/ĕ pet/ē be/f fife/g gag/h hat/hw which/ĭ pit/ī pie/îr pier/j judge/k kick/l lid, needle/m mum/n no, sudden/ng thing/ŏ pot/ō toe/ô paw, for/oi noise/ou out/o͝o took/o͞o boot/p pop/r roar/s sauce/sh ship, dish/

tem·per·ate (tĕm′pər-ĭt, tĕm′prĭt) *adj.* **1.** Exercising moderation and self-restraint. **2.** Moderate in degree or quality; tempered. **3.** Neither hot nor cold in climate; mild. —See Synonyms at **moderate.** [Middle English *temperat(e),* from Latin *temperātus,* from the past participle of *temperāre,* to moderate, TEMPER.]

Temperate Zone. Either of two middle latitude zones of the earth, the *North Temperate Zone* and the *South Temperate Zone,* lying between $23\frac{1}{2}$ degrees and $66\frac{1}{2}$ degrees north and south.

tem·per·a·ture (tĕm′pər-ə-chŏŏr′, tĕm′prə-) *n. Abbr.* **temp.** *Symbol* **T 1. a.** The degree of hotness or coldness of a body or environment. **b.** A specific degree of hotness or coldness as indicated on or referred to a standard scale; a scalar quantity that is independent of the size of the system and that determines the direction of heat flow between any two systems in thermal contact. **2.** A temperature above normal body temperature, caused by illness; fever. [Originally "a mixing," "tempering," moderate condition (of weather), temperateness, from Latin *temperātūra,* from *temperāre,* to mix, TEMPER.]

temperature gradient. The rate of change of temperature with displacement in a given direction from a given reference point.

tem·pered (tĕm′pərd) *adj.* **1.** Having a specified type of temper or disposition. Usually used in combination: *sweet-tempered.* **2.** *Music.* Tuned to temperament. Said of a scale, interval, semitone, or intonation. **3.** Moderated by the admixture of another substance, quality, or factor: *"medieval adultery . . . tempered with chivalry"* (Will Durant). **4.** Having the requisite degree of hardness or elasticity. Said of a metal.

tem·pest (tĕm′pĭst) *n.* **1.** A violent windstorm, frequently accompanied by rain, snow, or hail. **2.** A furious agitation, commotion, or tumult; uproar: *"The tempest in my mind/doth from my senses take all feeling"* (Shakespeare). —*tr.v.* **tempested, -pesting, -pests.** To disturb or agitate violently. [Middle English *tempeste,* from Old French, from Vulgar Latin *tempesta* (unattested), variant of Latin *tempestās,* storm, weather, season, from *tempus,* time, season. See **temporal.**]

tem·pes·tu·ous (tĕm-pĕs′chōō-əs) *adj.* **1.** Pertaining to or characteristic of a tempest. **2.** Tumultuous; stormy; turbulent. —**tem·pes′tu·ous·ly** *adv.* —**tem·pes′tu·ous·ness** *n.*

Tem·plar (tĕm′plər) *n.* **1.** A knight of a religious military order founded about 1118 at Jerusalem by the Crusaders. **2.** A **Knight Templar** *(see).* **3.** *Small* **t.** *British.* A lawyer or student of law having chambers in the Temple in London. [Middle English *templer,* from Norman French, variant of Old French *templier,* from Medieval Latin *(mīles) templāri(u)s,* "(soldier) of the temple," from Latin *templum,* TEMPLE.]

tem·plate (tĕm′plĭt) *n.* Also **tem·plet.** **1.** A pattern or gauge, such as a thin metal plate with a cut pattern, used as a guide in making something accurately, as in woodworking, or in replication of a standard object. **2.** A piece of stone or timber used to distribute weight or pressure, as over a door frame. [Earlier *templet* (influenced by PLATE), from French, diminutive of Old French *temple,* TEMPLE (device in a loom).]

tem·ple[1] (tĕm′pəl) *n.* **1.** A building or place dedicated to the worship or the presence of a deity. **2.** *Capital* **T.** Any of three successive buildings in ancient Jerusalem dedicated to the worship of Jehovah. **3.** A synagogue. **4.** A building in which the Mormon sacred ordinances are administered. **5.** Anything considered to contain a divine presence. **6.** The headquarters of any of several fraternal orders, especially of the Knights Templar. **7.** Any place or building serving as the focus of a special activity or of something especially valued: *a temple of learning.* **8.** *Capital* **T.** Either of the two Inns of Court in London housing England's major law societies, and formerly occupied by the Knights Templar. [Middle English *temple,* from Old English *tempel* and Old French *temple,* from Latin *templum,* sanctuary, space marked for observation by an augur. See **tem-** in Appendix.*]

tem·ple[2] (tĕm′pəl) *n.* The flat region on either side of the forehead. [Middle English, from Old French, from Vulgar Latin *tempula* (unattested), variant of Latin *tempora,* plural of *tempus,* temple of the head. See **temp-** in Appendix.*]

tem·ple[3] (tĕm′pəl) *n.* A device in a loom that keeps the cloth stretched to the correct width during weaving. [Middle English *tempylle,* from Old French *temple,* from Latin *templum,* small piece of wood. See **tem-** in Appendix.*]

tem·po (tĕm′pō) *n., pl.* **-pos** or **-pi** (-pē). **1.** *Abbr.* **t.** *Music.* The relative speed at which a composition is to be played, as indicated by a descriptive or metronomic direction to the performer. **2.** A characteristic rate or rhythm of activity; pace: *"the tempo and the feeling of modern life"* (Robert L. Heilbroner). [Italian, "time," from Latin *tempus.* See **temporal.**]

tem·po·ral[1] (tĕm′pər-əl, tĕm′prəl) *adj.* **1.** Pertaining to, concerned with, or limited by time. **2.** Pertaining to or concerned with worldly affairs. **3.** Enduring for a short time; transitory; short-lived: *the temporal dreams of youth.* **4.** Civil, secular, or lay, as distinguished from ecclesiastical. **5.** *Grammar.* Expressing time: *a temporal conjunction.* [Middle English *temporal,* from Latin *temporālis,* from *tempus*† (stem *tempor-*), time.] —**tem′po·ral·ly** *adv.*

tem·po·ral[2] (tĕm′pər-əl, tĕm′prəl) *adj.* Of, pertaining to, or near the temples of the skull. [Late Latin *temporālis,* from Latin *tempus* (stem *tempor-*), TEMPLE (of the head).]

temporal bone. Either of two complex, three-part bones forming the sides and base of the skull.

tem·po·ral·i·ty (tĕm′pə-răl′ə-tē) *n., pl.* **-ties.** **1.** The condition of being temporal or temporary. **2.** *Usually plural.* Temporal possessions, especially of the church or clergy.

tem·po·rar·y (tĕm′pə-rĕr′ē) *adj. Abbr.* **temp.** Lasting, used, or enjoyed for a limited time; impermanent; transient: *"do not allow any temporary excitement to distract you from the real business"* (C.S. Lewis). See Synonyms at **transient.** —*n. Informal.* One that serves for a limited time. [Latin *temporārius,* from *tempus* (stem *tempor-*), time. See **temporal.**] —**tem′po·rar′i·ly** *adv.* —**tem′po·rar′i·ness** *n.*

tem·po·rize (tĕm′pə-rīz′) *intr.v.* **-rized, -rizing, -rizes.** **1.** To compromise or act evasively in order to gain time, avoid argument, or postpone a decision: *"Colonial officials . . . ordered to enforce unpopular enactments, tended to temporize, to find excuses for evasion."* (J.H. Parry). **2. a.** To behave appropriately under the circumstances. **b.** To yield ostensibly to current conditions. [Old French *temporiser,* from Medieval Latin *temporizāre,* to wait one's time, from Latin *tempus* (stem *tempor-*), time. See **temporal.**] —**tem′po·ri·za′tion** *n.*

tempt (tĕmpt) *tr.v.* **tempted, tempting, tempts.** **1.** To entice (someone) to commit an unwise or immoral act, especially by a promise of reward. **2.** To be inviting or attractive to. **3.** To provoke or to risk provoking: *"No, no, Amyras; tempt not fortune so"* (Marlowe). **4.** To incline or dispose strongly: *Her anger tempted him to leave.* —See Synonyms at **lure.** [Middle English *tempten,* from Old French *tempter,* from Latin *temptāre*†, to try, test, tempt.] —**tempt′a·ble** *adj.* —**tempt′er, tempt′ress** (tĕmp′trĭs) *n.*

temp·ta·tion (tĕmp-tā′shən) *n.* **1.** The act of tempting or the condition of being tempted. **2.** That which tempts or entices.

tempt·ing (tĕmp′tĭng) *adj.* Alluring, enticing, or seductive. —**tempt′ing·ly** *adv.* —**tempt′ing·ness** *n.*

tem·pu·ra (tĕm′pōō-rə, tĕm-pōōr′ə) *n.* A Japanese dish of vegetables and shrimp or other seafood dipped in batter and fried in deep fat. [Japanese, "fried food."]

Te·mu·co (tā-mōō′kō). A city and trade center of south-central Chile. Population, 112,000.

ten (tĕn) *n.* **1.** The cardinal number written 10 or in Roman numerals X. See **number.** **2.** A playing card marked with ten pips. **3.** A ten-dollar bill. [Middle English *ten,* Old English *tien, tēne, tӯn.* See **dekm̥-** in Appendix.*] —**ten** *adj.* & *pron.*

ten. **1.** tenor. **2.** *Music.* tenuto.

ten·a·ble (tĕn′ə-bəl) *adj.* **1.** Capable of being defended or sustained; logical: *a tenable theory.* **2.** *Military.* Defensible: *a tenable outpost.* [Old French *tenable,* from *tenir,* to hold, from Latin *tenēre.* See **ten-** in Appendix.*] —**ten′a·bil′i·ty, ten′a·ble·ness** *n.* —**ten′a·bly** *adv.*

ten·ace (tĕn′ās′, tĕ-nās′, tĕn′ĭs) *n.* A combination of two high cards, such as the king and jack, held in a player's hand, especially in bridge and whist. [French, from Spanish *tenaza,* "forceps," "tongs," from Latin *tenāx* (stem *tenāc-*), TENACIOUS.]

te·na·cious (tə-nā′shəs) *adj.* **1.** Holding or tending to hold firmly; persistent; stubborn. **2.** Holding together firmly; cohesive. **3.** Clinging to another object or surface; adhesive. **4.** Tending to retain; retentive: *a tenacious memory.* —See Synonyms at **strong.** [Latin *tenāx* (stem *tenāc-*), from *tenēre,* to hold. See **ten-** in Appendix.*] —**te·na′cious·ly** *adv.* —**te·na′cious·ness** *n.*

te·nac·i·ty (tə-năs′ə-tē) *n.* The condition or quality of being tenacious. See Synonyms at **courage, perseverance.**

te·nac·u·lum (tə-năk′yə-ləm) *n., pl.* **-la** (-lə). A long-handled, slender, hooked instrument for lifting and holding parts, such as blood vessels, during surgery. [New Latin, from Late Latin, holder, from Latin *tenēre,* to hold. See **ten-** in Appendix.*]

ten·an·cy (tĕn′ən-sē) *n., pl.* **-cies.** **1.** The possession or occupancy of lands or tenements by title, under a lease, or on payment of rent. **2.** The period of a tenant's occupancy or possession. **3.** A habitation or other property held or occupied by a tenant. [From TENANT.]

ten·ant (tĕn′ənt) *n.* **1.** One who temporarily holds or occupies land, a building, or other property owned by another. **2.** *Law.* One who holds or possesses lands, tenements, and sometimes personal property by any kind of title. **3.** An occupant, inhabitant, or dweller in any place. —*v.* **tenanted, -anting, -ants.** —*tr.* To hold as a tenant; occupy; inhabit. —*intr.* To be a tenant. [Middle English *tena(u)nt,* from Old French *tenant,* from the present participle of *tenir,* to hold, from Latin *tenēre,* to hold. See **ten-** in Appendix.*]

tenant farmer. One who farms land owned by another and pays rent in cash or in kind.

ten·ant·ry (tĕn′ən-trē) *n., pl.* **-ries.** **1.** Tenants collectively. **2.** The state or condition of being a tenant; tenancy.

Te·nas·ser·im (tə-năs′ər-ĭm). An administrative division of Burma, occupying 31,588 square miles in the southeast. Capital, Moulmein.

ten-cent store (tĕn′sĕnt′). A **five-and-ten-cent store** *(see).*

tench (tĕnch) *n., pl.* **tench** or **tenches.** An edible Eurasian freshwater fish, *Tinca tinca,* having small scales and two barbels near the mouth. [Middle English *tenche,* from Old French, from Late Latin *tinca,* perhaps from Gaulish.]

Ten Commandments. The ten injunctions given by God to Moses on Mount Sinai, the basis of Mosaic Law. Exodus 20:1–17. Also called "Decalogue."

tend[1] (tĕnd) *intr.v.* **tended, tending, tends.** **1.** To move or extend in a certain direction: *Our course tended toward the north.* **2.** To be likely: *War tends to defeat its purposes.* **3.** To be disposed or inclined: *He tends toward sarcasm.* [Middle English *tenden,* from Old French *tendre,* from Latin *tendere,* to stretch, direct one's course, be inclined. See **ten-** in Appendix.*]

tend[2] (tĕnd) *v.* **tended, tending, tends.** —*tr.* **1.** To minister to the needs of; look after: *tend a child.* **2.** To take care of; serve

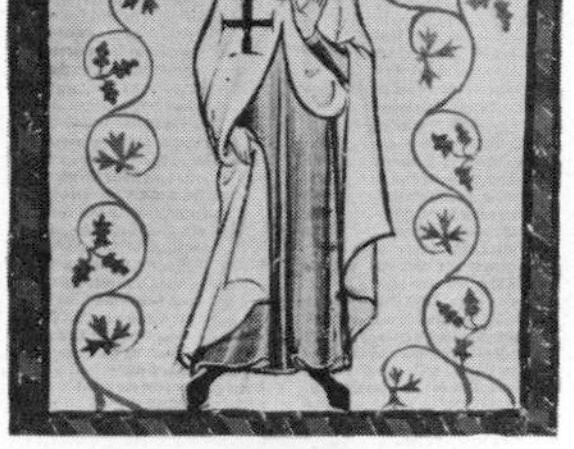

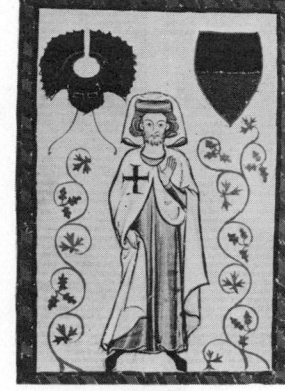

Templar
Illustration in a 12th-century manuscript

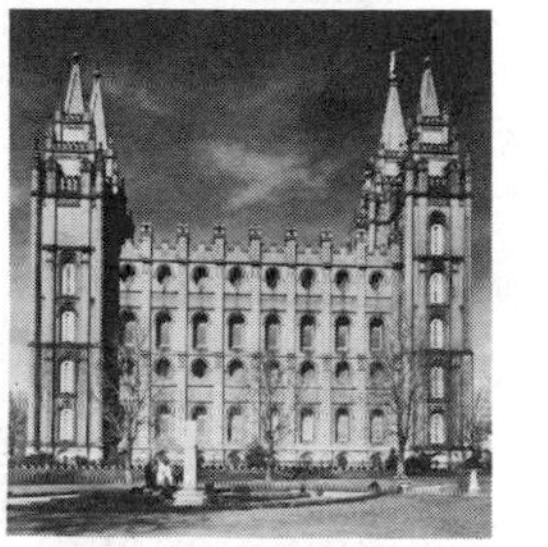

temple[1]
Mormon Temple in Salt Lake City

at: *tend bar; tend store.* —*intr.* **1.** To serve or wait. Used with *on* or *upon.* **2.** *Informal.* To apply one's attention. Used with *to: He tended to his homework.* See Usage note. [Middle English *tenden,* short for *attenden,* ATTEND.]

Usage: *Tend,* used intransitively with *to* and meaning to apply attention, is informal for *attend to.* As an example in writing not expressly informal, the following is unacceptable to 80 per cent of the Usage Panel: *A special session of the legislature has been called to tend to the problem of redistricting.*

ten·den·cy (tĕn′dən-sē) *n., pl.* **-cies. 1.** A demonstrated inclination to think, act, or behave in a certain way; propensity: *a tendency to panic.* **2.** The drift or purport of a literary work. [Medieval Latin *tendentia,* from Latin *tendēns,* present participle of *tendere,* to stretch, TEND.]

Synonyms: *tendency, trend, current, drift, tenor, inclination.* These nouns are compared as they relate to the direction or course of action or thought. *Tendency* implies a definite proneness or predisposition of a person or thing to behave in a certain way. *Trend* is usually applied to the prevailing direction of thought or practice within a given sphere, such as literature or politics. Like *current* and *drift, trend* specifies a course that reflects the thought or action of relatively large numbers of persons. *Current* suggests a course, as of thought or opinion, closely related to a given time or place. *Drift* often refers to the long-range course of institutions, such as government or law, that exert broad influence or control. *Tenor* implies a continuous course, as of a person's life, and a procedure or practice that is usually unvarying. *Inclination* usually refers to an individual's propensity or bent for behaving in a certain way at a given time. As a motivating force, an *inclination* is not as strong or consistent as a *tendency.*

ten·den·tious (tĕn-dĕn′shəs) *adj.* Also **ten·den·cious.** Written or said to promote some cause; not impartial; biased. [From TENDENCY.] —**ten·den′tious·ly** *adv.* —**ten·den′tious·ness** *n.*

ten·der[1] (tĕn′dər) *adj.* **-derer, -derest. 1. a.** Easily crushed or bruised; soft; fragile: *a tender petal.* **b.** Having a delicate quality: *a tender song.* **c.** Easily chewed or cut: *tender beef.* **2.** Young and vulnerable: *of tender age.* **3.** Frail; weakly; delicate. **4.** *Horticulture.* Sensitive to frost or severe cold; not hardy. **5. a.** Easily hurt; sensitive: *a tender skin.* **b.** Painful; sore: *a tender tooth.* **6. a.** Gentle and solicitous: *a tender mother.* **b.** Expressing gentle emotions; loving: *a tender glance.* **c.** Given to sympathy or sentimentality; soft: *a tender heart.* **7. a.** Considerate and protective; sparing. Used with *of: tender of her reputation.* **b.** Scrupulous; chary. Used with *of: tender of making false promises.* **8.** *Nautical.* Apt to lean under sail; crank. —*tr.v.* **tendered, -dering, -ders. 1.** *Rare.* To make tender. **2.** *Archaic.* To treat with tender regard. [Middle English *tender, tendre,* from Old French *tendre,* from Latin *tener,* tender, delicate. See **ten-** in Appendix.*] —**ten′der·ly** *adv.* —**ten′der·ness** *n.*

ten·der[2] (tĕn′dər) *n.* **1.** A formal offer, as: **a.** *Law.* An offer of money or service in payment of an obligation. **b.** *Commerce.* A written offer to contract goods or services at a specified cost or rate; a bid. **2.** Something tendered, especially money: *legal tender.* —*tr.v.* **tendered, -dering, -ders.** To offer formally: *tender a letter of resignation.* See Synonyms at **offer.** [From Old French *tendre,* to offer, stretch out, from Latin *tendere,* to stretch. See **ten-** in Appendix.*] —**ten′der·er** *n.*

tend·er[3] (tĕn′dər) *n.* **1.** One who tends something: *a lathe tender.* **2.** *Nautical.* A vessel attendant on another vessel or vessels, especially one that ferries supplies between ship and shore. **3.** A railroad car attached to the rear of a locomotive and designed to carry fuel and water.

ten·der·foot (tĕn′dər-fo͝ot′) *n., pl.* **-foots** or **-feet. 1.** A newcomer not yet hardened to Western ranch or mining life; a greenhorn. **2.** An inexperienced person; a novice. **3.** A beginner in the ranks of the Boy Scouts.

ten·der·heart·ed (tĕn′dər-här′tĭd) *adj.* Easily moved by another's distress; compassionate. —**ten′der·heart′ed·ly** *adv.* —**ten′der·heart′ed·ness** *n.*

ten·der·ize (tĕn′də-rīz′) *tr.v.* **-ized, -izing, -izes.** To make (meat) tender, as by marinating, pounding, or applying a tenderizer. —**ten′der·i·za′tion** *n.*

ten·der·iz·er (tĕn′də-rī′zər) *n.* A substance, such as a plant enzyme, applied to meat to make it tender.

ten·der·loin (tĕn′dər-loin′) *n.* **1.** The tenderest part of a loin of beef, pork, or the like; a fillet. **2. a.** A city district notorious for its vice and graft. **b.** *Capital* **T.** Formerly an area south of 42nd Street on the west side of Manhattan, having many brothels and theaters, and considered a choice assignment by corrupt policemen.

ten·der-mind·ed (tĕn′dər-mīn′dĭd) *adj.* Idealistic; resisting harsh facts.

ten·di·nous (tĕn′də-nəs) *adj.* **1.** Of, having, or resembling a tendon or tendons. **2.** Sinewy. [New Latin *tendinosus,* from *tendo* (stem *tendin-*), from Medieval Latin *tendō,* TENDON.]

ten·don (tĕn′dən) *n.* A band of tough, inelastic fibrous tissue that connects a muscle with its bony attachment; a sinew. [From Medieval Latin *tendō* (stem *tendon-*), from Latin *tendere,* to stretch. See **ten-** in Appendix.*]

ten·dril (tĕn′drəl) *n.* **1.** A long, slender, coiling extension, as of a stem, serving as an organ of attachment for certain climbing plants, such as the grape. **2.** Something resembling this. [Probably from obsolete French *tendrillon,* diminutive of Old French *tendron,* cartilage, young shoot, from Vulgar Latin *tenerūmen* (unattested), from Latin *tener,* tender, delicate. See **ten-** in Appendix.*]

Ten·e·brae (tĕn′ə-brā′) *n.* Plural in form, used with a singular or plural verb. *Roman Catholic Church.* The office of matins and lauds sung on the last three days of Holy Week, with a ceremony of candles. [Medieval Latin, from Latin, darkness. See **teme-** in Appendix.*]

ten·e·brif·ic (tĕn′ə-brĭf′ĭk) *adj.* **1.** Serving to obscure or darken. **2.** Gloomy; dark; dismal. [Latin *tenebrae,* darkness (see **Tenebrae**) + -FIC.]

ten·e·brous (tĕn′ə-brəs) *adj.* Also **te·neb·ri·ous** (tə-nĕb′rē-əs). Dark and gloomy. [From Latin *tenebrae,* darkness. See **Tenebrae.**] —**ten′e·bros′i·ty** (-brŏs′ə-tē) *n.*

ten·e·ment (tĕn′ə-mənt) *n.* **1.** A building to live in, especially one intended for rent; a residence. **2.** A run-down low-rental apartment building or rooming house whose facilities and maintenance barely meet minimum standards. Also called "tenement house." **3.** *Chiefly British.* An apartment or room leased to a tenant. **4.** *Law.* Real property held by one person of another. [Middle English *tenement,* from Old French, from Medieval Latin *tenementum,* feudal holding, house, from Latin *tenēre,* to hold. See **ten-** in Appendix.*] —**ten′e·men′tal** (-mĕnt′l), **ten′e·men′ta·ry** (-mĕn′tə-rē) *adj.*

Ten·er·ife (tĕn′ə-rĭf′, -rēf′). Also **Ten·er·iffe.** The largest (795 square miles) of the Canary Islands.

te·nes·mus (tə-nĕz′məs) *n.* A painfully urgent but ineffectual attempt to urinate or defecate. [Medieval Latin, variant of Latin *tenesmos,* from Greek *teinesmos,* "a straining," from *teinein,* to stretch, strain. See **ten-** in Appendix.*]

ten·et (tĕn′ĭt) *n.* An opinion, doctrine, principle, or dogma held by a person or, more especially, an organization. [Latin, he holds, from *tenēre,* to hold. See **ten-** in Appendix.*]

ten·fold (tĕn′fōld′) *adj.* **1.** Being of ten parts or members: *His reasons were tenfold.* **2.** Being ten times as great or as many. —*adv.* Ten times (in extent or number). —*n.* A number or degree ten times as great as something given.

ten-gal·lon hat (tĕn′găl′ən). A felt hat having an exceptionally tall crown and wide brim, popular in Texas.

Ten·gri Khan (tĕng′rē kän′). The second-highest elevation (22,949 feet) in the Tien Shan Range, on the border between the Kirgiz S.S.R. and the Sinkiang-Uigur Autonomous Region of western China.

Ten·gri Nor. The Mongolian name for **Nam Tso.**

te·ni·a. Variant of **taenia.**

te·ni·a·cide (tē′nē-ə-sīd′) *n.* Also **tae·ni·a·cide.** An agent that destroys tapeworms. [TAENIA + -CIDE.]

te·ni·a·sis (tē-nī′ə-sĭs) *n.* Also **tae·ni·a·sis.** Infestation with tapeworms. [TAEN(IA) + -IASIS.]

Te·niers (tə-nîrz′, tĕn′yərz). A family of Flemish painters, including **David** (1582–1649), known as the Elder, and his son **David** (1610–1690), known as the Younger.

Tenn. Tennessee.

Ten·nant (tĕn′ənt), **Smithson.** 1761–1815. British chemist; discovered the elements osmium and iridium.

Ten·nes·see (tĕn′ə-sē′). *Abbr.* **Tenn.** A Southern state of the United States, 42,246 square miles in area, extending 430 miles east from the Mississippi; the 16th state to enter the Union (1796). Population, 3,719,000. Capital, Nashville. See map at **United States of America.** —**Ten′nes·se′an** *n.* & *adj.*

Ten·nes·see River (tĕn′ə-sē′). A river of the southeastern United States, flowing about 652 miles from eastern Tennessee near Knoxville, through northern Alabama, western Tennessee, and western Kentucky to the Ohio River.

Tennessee Valley Authority. *Abbr.* **TVA, T.V.A.** A U.S. government corporation set up in 1933 to construct and operate dams, hydroelectric plants, and flood-control works throughout the Tennessee Valley.

Ten·niel (tĕn′yəl), Sir **John.** 1820–1914. British cartoonist and illustrator of *Alice's Adventures in Wonderland.*

ten·nis (tĕn′ĭs) *n.* **1.** A game played with rackets and a light ball by two players *(singles)* or two pairs of players *(doubles)* on a court divided by a net. **2. Lawn tennis** *(see).* **3. Court tennis** *(see).* [Middle English *tenetz, tennys,* probably from Old French *tenez,* imperative of *tenir,* to hold (probably from the call of the server to his opponent in the game), from Latin *tenēre,* to hold. See **ten-** in Appendix.*]

tennis shoes. Sneakers *(see).*

Ten·no (tĕn′ō) *n., pl.* **Tenno** or **-nos.** An emperor of Japan who is a religious leader and held to be divine. [Japanese *tennō,* from Ancient Chinese *t'ien gwâng* (Mandarin *t'ien*[1] *huang*[2]), "celestial emperor" : *t'ien,* heaven + *gwâng,* emperor.]

Ten·ny·son (tĕn′ə-sən), **Alfred.** First Baron Tennyson. 1809–1892. English poet; poet laureate (1850–92).

teno–. Indicates tendon; for example, **tenotomy.** [From Greek *tenōn,* tendon. See **ten-** in Appendix.*]

Te·no. The Finnish name for the **Tana.**

Te·noch·ti·tlán (tā-nŏch′tēt-län′). The ancient capital of the Aztec empire, on the site now occupied by Mexico City.

ten·on (tĕn′ən) *n.* A projection on the end of a piece of wood shaped for insertion into a mortise. —*tr.v.* **tenoned, -oning, -ons. 1.** To provide with a tenon. **2.** To join with a tenon. [Middle English, from Old French, from *tenir,* to hold, from Latin *tenēre.* See **ten-** in Appendix.*]

ten·or (tĕn′ər) *n.* **1. a.** The flow of meaning apparent in something written or spoken. **b.** General sense; purport. **2. a.** *Law.* The exact meaning or actual wording of a document as distinct from its effect. **b.** An exact copy or transcript of a document. **3.** *Abbr.* **ten., T., t.** *Music.* **a.** The highest natural adult male voice. **b.** A part for this voice. **c.** One who sings this part. —See Synonyms at **tendency.** —*adj.* Of, pertaining to, or having the range of a tenor: *a tenor sax.* [Middle English, general meaning, from Old French, from Latin *tenor,* uninter-

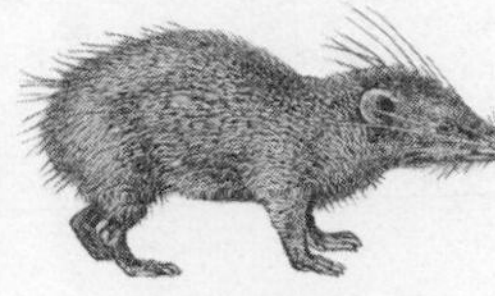

tenrec
Tenrec ecaudatus

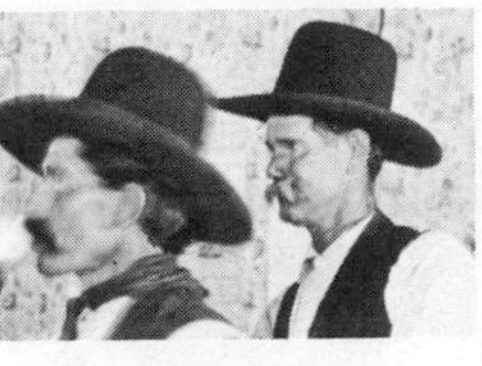

ten-gallon hat
Texas cowboys wearing ten-gallon hats in a 1908 photograph

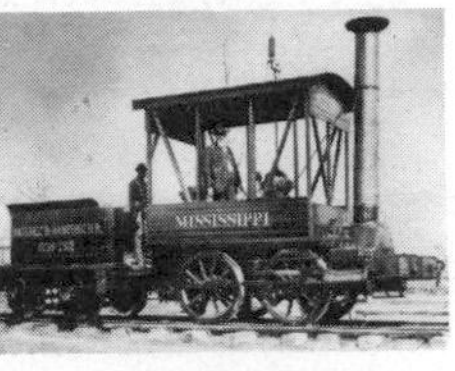

tender[3]
Engine and tender of first train to be operated in Mississippi

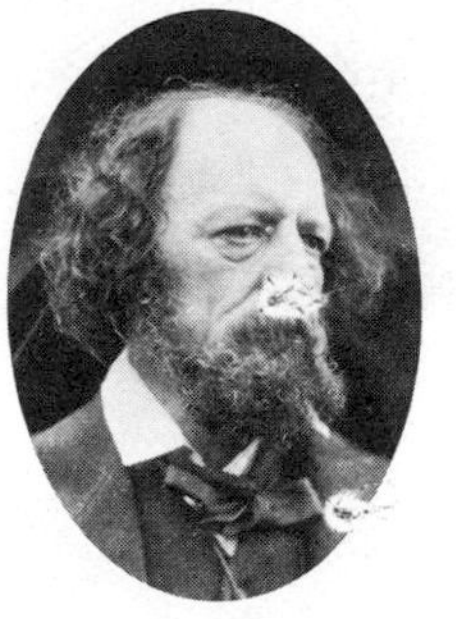

Alfred Tennyson

ă pat/ā pay/âr care/ä father/b bib/ch church/d deed/ĕ pet/ē be/f fife/g gag/h hat/hw which/ĭ pit/ī pie/îr pier/j judge/k kick/l lid, needle/m mum/n no, sudden/ng thing/ŏ pot/ō toe/ô paw, for/oi noise/ou out/o͝o took/o͞o boot/p pop/r roar/s sauce/sh ship, dish/

rupted course, a holding on, from *tenēre*, to hold. See **ten-** in Appendix.*]

te·nor·rha·phy (tĕ-nôr′ə-fē) *n., pl.* **-phies.** The surgical uniting of divided tendons with sutures. [TENO- + Greek *-rrhaphia*, from *rhaptein*, to sew (see **wer-**[3] in Appendix*).]

Te·nos (tē′nôs). Also **Ti·nos.** An island of Greece, 74 square miles in area, in the Cyclades southeast of Andros.

te·no·sy·no·vi·tis (tĕn′ō-sĭ′nō-vī′tĭs, tē′nō-) *n.* Inflammation of a tendon sheath. [TENO- + SYNOV(IA) + -ITIS.]

te·not·o·my (tə-nŏt′ə-mē) *n., pl.* **-mies.** The surgical division of a tendon for the relief of deformities caused by shortening of a muscle. [TENO- + -TOMY.]

ten·pence (tĕn′pəns) *n. British.* A sum of money equal to ten pennies.

ten·pen·ny (tĕn′pĕn′ē) *adj. British.* Valued at or costing tenpence.

tenpenny nail. A nail three inches long. [Originally sold at tenpence a hundred.]

ten·pin (tĕn′pĭn′) *n.* **1.** A bowling pin used in playing tenpins. **2.** *Plural.* A game, **bowling** *(see).*

ten·rec (tĕn′rĕk′) *n.* Also **tan·rec** (tăn′-). Any of various insectivorous, often hedgehoglike mammals of the family Tenrecidae, of Madagascar and adjacent islands. [French, from Malagasy *tàndraka.*]

tense[1] (tĕns) *adj.* **tenser, tensest. 1.** Tightly stretched; taut; strained. **2.** In a state of mental or nervous tension. **3.** Nerve-racking; suspenseful: *a tense situation.* **4.** *Phonetics.* Enunciated with taut muscles, as the consonant *t.* Compare **lax.** —See Synonyms at **stiff.** —*v.* **tensed, tensing, tenses.** —*tr.* To make tense. —*intr.* To become tense. [Latin *tensus*, past participle of *tendere*, to stretch out. See **ten-** in Appendix.*]

tense[2] (tĕns) *n. Abbr.* **t. 1.** Any of the inflected forms in the conjugation of a verb that indicate the time (past, present, or future) as well as the continuance (imperfect) or completion (perfect) of the action or state. **2.** A set of such forms indicating a particular time: *the future tense.* [Middle English *tens*, tense, time, from Old French, from Latin *tempus*, time. See **temporal.**]

ten·sile (tĕn′səl, -sĭl′) *adj.* **1.** Of or pertaining to tension. **2.** Capable of being stretched or extended; ductile. [New Latin *tensilis*, from Latin *tensus*, "stretched," TENSE.] —**ten·sil′i·ty** (tĕn-sĭl′ə-tē) *n.*

tensile strength. *Abbr.* **T.S.** The resistance of a material to a force tending to tear it apart.

ten·sim·e·ter (tĕn-sĭm′ə-tər) *n.* An apparatus used to measure differences in vapor pressure. [TENSI(ON) + -METER.]

ten·si·om·e·ter (tĕn′sē-ŏm′ə-tər) *n.* **1.** An instrument for measuring tensile strength. **2.** *Capital* **T.** A trademark for a torsion-balance apparatus used to measure the surface tension of a liquid. [TENSIO(N) + -METER.]

ten·sion (tĕn′shən) *n.* **1.** The act of stretching or the condition of being stretched. **2.** A force tending to produce elongation or extension. **3. a.** Mental, emotional, or nervous strain. **b.** A strained relation or barely controlled hostility between persons or groups. **c.** Uneasy suspense. **4.** A device for regulating tautness; especially, a device regulating the tautness of thread on a sewing machine. **5.** *Electricity.* Voltage or potential; electromotive force. —*tr.v.* **tensioned, -sioning, -sions.** To subject to tension; make taut. [Old French, from Latin *tensiō*, from *tensus*, TENSE.] —**ten′sion·al** *adj.*

ten·si·ty (tĕn′sə-tē) *n.* The state of being tense; tenseness.

ten·sive (tĕn′sĭv) *adj.* Of or causing tension.

ten·sor (tĕn′sər, -sôr′) *n.* **1.** *Anatomy.* Any muscle that tenses a part, making it firm. **2.** *Mathematics.* An element of an abstract system used to denote position determined within the context of more than one coordinate system, a special case of which is a **vector** *(see)* that is determined in a single coordinate system. —**ten·so′ri·al** (-sôr′ē-əl, -sōr′ē-əl) *adj.*

Tensor lamp. A trademark for a high-intensity electric lamp.

ten-strike (tĕn′strīk′) *n. Informal.* **1.** A strike in the game of tenpins. **2.** A remarkably successful stroke or action.

tent[1] (tĕnt) *n.* **1.** A portable shelter usually of canvas or skins stretched over a supporting framework of poles, ropes, and pegs. **2.** Something resembling this in construction or outline. —*v.* **tented, tenting, tents.** —*intr.* To encamp in a tent. —*tr.* **1.** To form a tent over. **2.** To put up in tents. [Middle English *tente*, from Old French, from Vulgar Latin *tenta* (unattested), from the feminine past participle of *tendere*, to stretch. See **ten-** in Appendix.*]

tent[2] (tĕnt) *n. Surgery.* A small roll or plug, usually of lint or gauze, for placing in a wound or orifice to keep it open or for probing. —*tr.v.* **tented, tenting, tents.** *Surgery.* To keep (a wound or cut) open with a tent. [Middle English, a probe, from Old French *tente*, from *tenter*, to probe, test, from Latin *tentāre*, variant of *temptāre*, to feel, try, TEMPT.]

tent[3] (tĕnt) *tr.v.* **tented, tenting, tents.** *Scottish.* **1.** To pay heed to. **2.** To attend; wait upon. [Middle English *tenten*, from *tent*, attention, short for *attent*, from Old French *attente*, from Latin *attenta*, feminine past participle of *attendere*, ATTEND.]

ten·ta·cle (tĕn′tə-kəl) *n.* **1.** *Zoology.* An elongated, flexible, unsegmented protrusion, such as one of those surrounding the mouth or oral cavity of the hydra, sea anemone, or squid. **2.** *Botany.* One of the hairs on the leaves of insectivorous plants, such as the sundew. **3.** Something resembling a tentacle, especially in ability to grasp or hold. [New Latin *tentaculum*, from Latin *tentāre*, variant of *temptāre*, to touch, feel, TEMPT.] —**ten·tac′u·lar** (-tăk′yə-lər) *adj.*

tent·age (tĕn′tĭj) *n.* **1.** Tents collectively. **2.** A supply of tents available for accommodation. **3.** Tent equipment.

ten·ta·tive (tĕn′tə-tĭv) *adj.* **1.** Of an experimental nature; provisional. **2.** Uncertain: *a tentative smile.* —*n.* An experiment. [Medieval Latin *tentātīvus*, from Latin *tentātus*, past participle of *tentāre*, variant of *temptāre*, to feel, try, TEMPT.] —**ten′ta·tive·ly** *adv.* —**ten′ta·tive·ness** *n.*

tent caterpillar. Any of several destructive caterpillars, especially the hairy larva of a North American moth, *Malacosoma americanum*, that live in colonies in tentlike webs constructed in deciduous trees.

tent·ed (tĕn′tĭd) *adj.* **1.** Covered with tents: *a tented shoreline.* **2.** Sheltered in tents. **3.** Resembling a tent in shape.

ten·ter (tĕn′tər) *n.* **1.** A framework upon which milled cloth is stretched for drying without shrinkage. **2.** *Obsolete.* A tenterhook. —*tr.v.* **tentered, -tering, -ters.** To stretch (cloth) on a tenter or tenters. [Middle English *teyntur*, from Norman French *tentur* (unattested), from Medieval Latin *tentōrium*, from Latin *tentus*, past participle of *tendere*, to stretch. See **ten-** in Appendix.*]

ten·ter·hook (tĕn′tər-ho͝ok′) *n.* A hooked nail for securing cloth on a tenter. —**on tenterhooks.** In a state of uneasiness, suspense, or anxiety.

tenth (tĕnth) *n.* **1.** The ordinal number ten in a series. Also written 10th. **2.** One of ten equal parts. See **number.** [Middle English *tenthe*, variant of earlier *tethe*, Old English *tēotha*, *teogetha*. See **dekm̥** in Appendix.*] —**tenth** *adj.* & *adv.*

tent stitch. A short diagonal embroidery stitch that forms close even, parallel rows to fill in a pattern or a background.

ten·u·is (tĕn′yo͞o-ĭs) *n., pl.* **-ues** (-yo͞o-ēz′). *Phonetics.* A voiceless stop in Greek. [New Latin (translation of Greek *psilos*, plain, bare), from Latin, TENUOUS.]

te·nu·i·ty (tə-no͞o′ə-tē, tə-nyo͞o′-) *n.* **1.** Lack of firmness or mettle. **2.** Delicate fragility. [Latin *tenuitās*, from *tenuis*, thin, TENUOUS.]

ten·u·ous (tĕn′yo͞o-əs) *adj.* **1.** Having a thin or slender form. **2.** Having a thin consistency; dilute; rarefied. **3.** Of little significance; weak; unsubstantial; flimsy: *a tenuous argument.* [Earlier *tenuious*, from Latin *tenuis*, thin, rare, fine. See **ten-** in Appendix.*] —**ten′u·ous·ly** *adv.* —**ten′u·ous·ness** *n.*

ten·ure (tĕn′yər, -yo͝or′) *n.* **1.** The holding of something, such as real estate or an office; occupation. **2.** The terms under which something is held. **3. a.** The period of holding. **b.** Permanence of position, often granted an employee after a specified number of years: *academic tenure.* [Middle English, from Old French, earlier *teneüre*, from *tenir*, to hold, from Latin *tenēre*. See **ten-** in Appendix.*] —**ten·u′ri·al** *adj.* —**ten·u′ri·al·ly** *adv.*

te·nu·to (tə-no͞o′tō) *adj. Abbr.* **ten.** *Music.* Held for the full time value; sustained. [Italian, from the past participle of *tenere*, to hold, from Latin *tenēre*. See **ten-** in Appendix.*]

te·o·cal·li (tē′ə-kăl′ē; *Spanish* tā′ō-kä′yē) *n., pl.* **-lis.** Also **te·o·pan** (tē′ə-păn′; *Spanish* tā′ō-pän′). **1.** A temple of ancient Mexico and Central America, usually built upon a mound of a truncated pyramidal shape. **2.** The mound itself. [Nahuatl : *teotl*, god + *calli*, house.]

te·o·sin·te (tē′ə-sĭn′tē, tā′-) *n.* A tall Central American grass, *Euchlaena mexicana*, related to corn and cultivated for fodder. [Mexican Spanish, from Nahuatl *teocentli* : *teotl*, god + *centli*, dried ear of corn.]

Te·o·ti·hua·cán (tā′ō-tē′wä-kän′). The site of an ancient city of Mexico, about 30 miles northeast of Mexico City, built some centuries before Christ, and containing the Pyramid of the Sun, the Pyramid of the Moon, and the Temple of Quetzalcoatl.

te·pal (tē′pəl, tĕp′əl) *n. Botany.* A division of the perianth of a flower having petals and sepals that are virtually indistinguishable. [French *tépale*, perhaps a blend of PETAL and SEPAL.]

tep·a·ry bean (tĕp′ə-rē). **1.** A vine, *Phaseolus acutifolius latifolius*, of the southwestern United States and adjacent Mexico, bearing edible beans. **2.** The bean borne by this plant. [Origin unknown.]

te·pee (tē′pē) *n.* Also **tee·pee, ti·pi.** A cone-shaped tent of skins or bark used by North American Indians, especially the Plains Indians. Compare **wigwam.** [Dakota *tipi*, dwelling : *ti-*, dwell + *-pi* (third person plural).]

tep·e·fy (tĕp′ə-fī′) *v.* **-fied, -fying, -fies.** —*tr.* To make tepid. —*intr.* To become tepid. [Latin *tepēre* (see **tepid**) + -FY.] —**tep′e·fac′tion** (-făk′shən) *n.*

Te·pic (tā-pēk′). The capital of Nayarit, western Mexico, in the south-central part of the state. Population, 54,000.

tep·id (tĕp′ĭd) *adj.* Moderately warm; lukewarm. [Latin *tepidus*, from *tepēre*, to be lukewarm. See **tep-** in Appendix.*] —**te·pid′i·ty** (tĕ-pĭd′ə-tē), **tep′id·ness** *n.* —**tep′id·ly** *adv.*

Te·quen·da·ma Falls (tā′kān-dä′mä). A waterfall with a drop of 482 feet on the Bogotá River in central Colombia.

te·qui·la (tə-kē′lə) *n.* An alcoholic liquor distilled from a Central American century plant, *Agave tequilana.* [Mexican Spanish, from *Tequila*, district in Mexico.]

ter-. Indicates three, third, or threefold; for example, **tercentenary.** [Latin *ter*, thrice. See **trei-** in Appendix.*]

ter. 1. terrace. **2.** territorial; territory.

tera-. Symbol **T** Indicates a trillion (10^{12}); for example, **terahertz.** [From Greek *teras*, monster. See **teratoid.**]

ter·a·hertz (tĕr′ə-hûrts′) *n. Abbr.* **THz** One trillion (10^{12}) hertz.

ter·a·ohm (tĕr′ə-ōm′) *n. Symbol* **TΩ** One trillion (10^{12}) ohms.

ter·a·phim (tĕr′ə-fĭm′) *pl.n.* Small domestic images or idols revered by ancient Semitic peoples. [Hebrew *tərāphīm*, a pejorative appellation of these idols, perhaps from *rəpha'im*, "shades."]

ter·a·toid (tĕr′ə-toid′) *adj.* Like a monster; monstrous. [New Latin *teras* (stem *terat-*), abnormality, from Greek, monster (see **kwer-**[1] in Appendix*) + -OID.]

ter·a·tol·o·gy (tĕr′ə-tŏl′ə-jē) *n.* The biological study of the

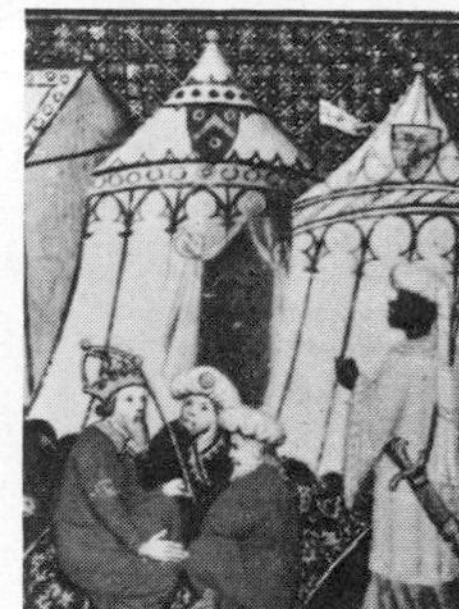

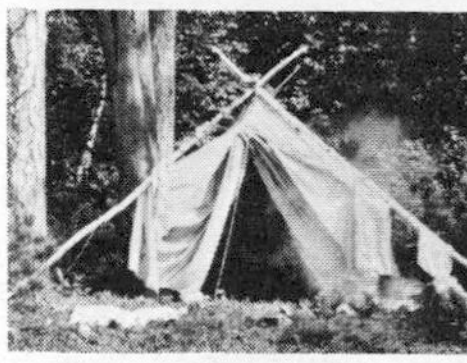

tent[1]
Above: Detail from a 14th-century French manuscript
Below: Camping tent

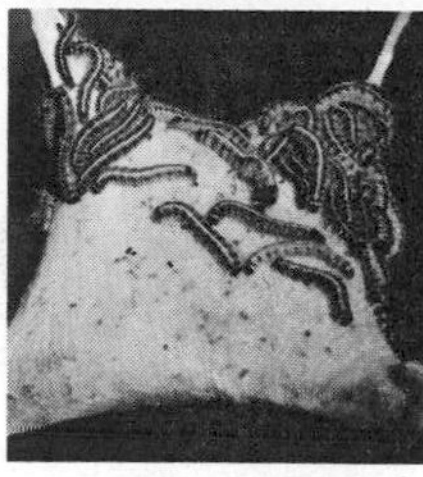

tent caterpillar
Larvae of *Malacosoma americanum*

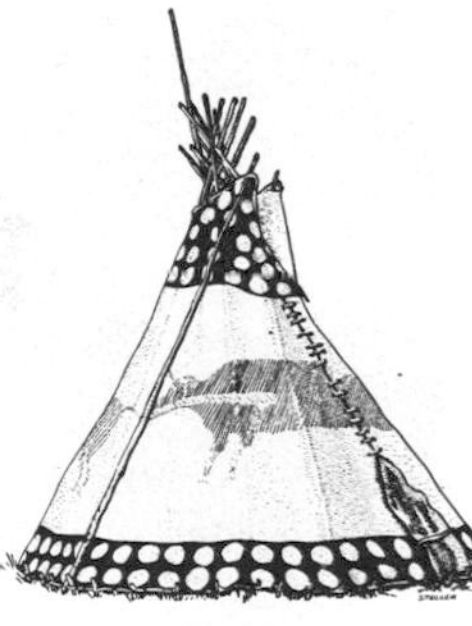

tepee
Plains tepee of poles and buffalo hides

production, development, anatomy, and classification of monsters. [Greek *teras* (stem *terat-*), marvel, monster (see **teratoid**) + -LOGY.] —**ter′a·to·log′i·cal** (-tə-lŏj′ĭ-kəl) *adj.*

ter·a·to·ma (tĕr′ə-tō′mə) *n., pl.* **-mas** or **-mata** (-mə-tə). A tumor consisting of different types of tissue, caused by the development of independent germ cells. [New Latin : Greek *teras* (stem *terat-*), monster (see **teratoid**) + -OMA.] —**ter′a·tom′a·tous** (-tŏm′ə-təs, -tō′mə-təs) *adj.*

ter·bi·um (tûr′bē-əm) *n. Symbol* **Tb** A soft, silvery-gray metallic rare-earth element, used as a solid-state dopant and as a laser material. Atomic number 65, atomic weight 158.924, melting point 1,356°C, boiling point 2,800°C, specific gravity 8.272, valences 3, 4. See **element.** [Discovered in *Ytterby,* a village in Sweden.]

terbium metal. Any of several rare-earth metals separable from other metals as a group and including europium, terbium, and gadolinium.

Ter Borch (tər bôrKH′), **Gerard.** Also **Ter·borch.** 1617–1681. Dutch portrait and genre painter.

terce. Variant of **tierce.**

Ter·cei·ra (tər-sā′rə). An island of Portugal, 153 square miles in area, lying in the central Azores. Population, 72,000.

ter·cel (tûr′səl) *n.* Also **tier·cel** (tîr′səl). A male hawk used in falconry. [Middle English, from Old French, from Vulgar Latin *tertiōlus* (unattested), from Latin *tertius,* third (from the belief that the third egg of a brood was a male). See **trei-** in Appendix.*]

ter·cen·te·nar·y (tûr′sĕn-tĕn′ə-rē, tûr-sĕn′tə-nĕr′ē) *n., pl.* **-ies.** Also **ter·cen·ten·ni·al** (tûr′sĕn-tĕn′ē-əl). A 300th anniversary or its celebration. —*adj.* Of or pertaining to a span of 300 years or to a 300th anniversary.

ter·cet (tûr′sĭt) *n.* **1.** *Prosody.* A triplet of lines that rhyme together or that are connected with adjacent rhymes. **2.** *Music.* A **triplet** *(see).* [Italian *terzetto,* diminutive of *terzo,* third, from Latin *tertius.* See **trei-** in Appendix.*]

ter·e·bene (tĕr′ə-bēn′) *n.* A mixture of terpenes prepared from oil of turpentine, used as an expectorant and antiseptic. [French *térébène,* from *térébinthe,* from Old French *terebinte,* TEREBINTH.]

te·reb·ic acid (tə-rĕb′ĭk, -rē′bĭk). A white crystalline compound, $C_7H_{10}O_4$, resulting from the action of nitric acid on turpentine. [*Terebic,* from TEREBINTH.]

ter·e·binth (tĕr′ə-bĭnth′) *n.* A small tree, *Pistachia terebinthus,* of the Mediterranean region, that yields a resinous liquid. [Middle English *therebinthe,* from Old French *t(h)erebinte,* from Latin *terebinthus,* from Greek *terebinthos, terminthos,* of Aegean origin.]

ter·e·bin·thine (tĕr′ə-bĭn′thĭn, -thīn′) *adj.* Also **ter·e·bin·thic** (-thĭk). **1.** Of or pertaining to the terebinth. **2.** Pertaining to, consisting of, or resembling turpentine.

te·re·do (tə-rē′dō, -rā′dō) *n., pl.* **-dos.** Any marine mollusk of the genus *Teredo;* a **shipworm** *(see).* [New Latin *Teredo,* from Latin *terēdō,* a kind of worm, from Greek *terēdōn.* See **ter-**[2] in Appendix.*]

Te·rek (tĕr′ək). A river of the Soviet Union, rising in the north-central Georgian S.S.R. and flowing 367 miles north and then east to a wide delta on the northwestern shore of the Caspian Sea.

Ter·ence[1] (tĕr′əns). A masculine given name. [Irish, from Latin *Terentius*†, the name of a gens.]

Ter·ence[2] (tĕr′əns). Latin name, Publius Terentius Afer. 185–159 B.C. Roman author of comedies.

Te·re·sa (tə-rē′sə, -rā′sə, -rā′zə). Also **The·re·sa.** A feminine given name. [Spanish, from Late Latin *Therasia,* from Greek *Therasia*†.]

Te·re·sa, Saint. See Saint **Theresa.**

Te·resh·ko·va (tĕ-rĕsh-kô′və), **Valentina Vladimirovna.** Born 1937. Soviet cosmonaut; first woman in space (1963).

Te·re·si·na (tā′rĕ-zē′nä). The capital of Piauí, Brazil, a city on the Parnaíba River in the northwestern part of the state. Population, 100,000.

te·rete (tə-rēt′, tĕ-rēt′) *adj.* Cylindrical but usually slightly tapering at both ends, circular in cross section, and smooth-surfaced. [Latin *teres* (stem *teret-*), rounded, smooth. See **ter-**[2] in Appendix.*]

Te·reus (tē′ro͞os′, tîr′ē-əs). *Greek Mythology.* A king of Thrace who raped Philomela and who was changed into a hoopoe.

ter·gal (tûr′gəl) *adj.* Of or pertaining to the tergum; dorsal.

ter·gi·ver·sate (tûr′jĭ-vər-sāt′) *intr.v.* **-sated, -sating, -sates.** **1.** To use evasions or ambiguities; equivocate. **2.** To change sides; to defect; apostatize. [Latin *tergiversārī,* "to turn the back," shift : *tergum,* back, TERGUM + *versus,* past participle of *vertere,* to turn (see **wer-**[3] in Appendix*).] —**ter′gi·ver·sa′tion** *n.* —**ter′gi·ver·sa′tor** (-sā′tər) *n.*

ter·gum (tûr′gəm) *n., pl.* **-ga** (-gə). *Zoology.* The upper or dorsal surface, especially of a body segment of an insect or other arthropod. [Latin *tergum*†, the back.]

ter·i·ya·ki (tĕr′ē-yä′kē) *n.* A Japanese dish consisting of skewered and broiled slices of marinated meat or shellfish. [Japanese : *teri,* sunshine, "flame" + *yaki,* to broil.]

term (tûrm) *n.* **1. a.** A limited period of time. **b.** A space of time assigned a person to serve: *a six-year term as senator.* **c.** A period when a school or a court is in session. **2. a.** A point of time beginning or ending a period. **b.** A deadline, as for making a payment. **c.** The end of a normal gestation period. **3.** *Law.* **a.** A fixed period of time during which an estate may be held. **b.** The estate to be granted. **c.** A period of time allowed a debtor to meet an obligation. **4. a.** A word having a precise meaning; especially, one that is part of the jargon of a particular group or activity: *a medical term.* **b.** *Plural.* Language or manner of expression employed: *He spoke in no uncertain terms.* **5.** *Plural.* **a.** Conditions or stipulations that define the nature and limits of an agreement: *peace terms.* **b.** The relation between two persons or groups; footing. Preceded by *on: on speaking terms.* **6.** *Mathematics.* **a.** Each of the quantities composing a ratio or a fraction or forming a series. **b.** Each of the quantities connected by addition or subtraction signs in an equation; member. **7.** *Logic.* Each of the two concepts being compared or related in a proposition; specifically, each of the words or phrases constituting the subject and the predicate. **8.** A statue of Terminus, the Roman god of boundaries, rising from a square tapering pillar, sometimes marking a boundary. —See Synonyms at **period.** —**bring to terms.** To force to submit or agree. —**come to terms.** To reach an agreement. —**reduce to its lowest terms.** To put in its simplest form. —**terms of reference.** **1.** The points a committee is charged to decide. **2.** The factors defining the scope of an inquiry. —*tr.v.* **termed, terming, terms.** To designate; to call. [Middle English *terme,* from Old French, from Latin *terminus,* boundary line, boundary, limit. See **ter-**[1] in Appendix.*] —**term′ly** *adv.*

term. **1.** terminal. **2.** termination.

ter·ma·gant (tûr′mə-gənt) *n.* A quarrelsome or scolding woman; a shrew. —*adj.* Abusive; shrewish. [Middle English *Termagaunt, Tervagaunt,* imaginary Moslem deity who appeared as such a character in Medieval mystery plays, from Old French *Tervagan(t),* from Italian *Trivigante*†.]

term·er (tûr′mər) *n.* **1.** A person serving a specified term, especially in prison: *in Sing Sing as a second termer.* **2.** *Law.* Variant of **termor.**

ter·mi·na·ble (tûr′mə-nə-bəl) *adj.* **1.** Capable of being terminated. **2.** Terminating after a designated date: *a terminable annuity.* —**ter′mi·na·bil′i·ty, ter′mi·na·ble·ness** *n.* —**ter′mi·na·bly** *adv.*

ter·mi·nal (tûr′mə-nəl) *adj. Abbr.* **term., t.** **1.** Pertaining to, situated at, or forming the end or boundary of something. **2.** *Biology.* Growing or appearing at the end of a stem, branch, stalk, or similar part. **3.** Pertaining to or occurring at the end of a section or series; concluding; final. **4.** Pertaining to or occurring in a term or each term; appearing regularly or periodically. —See Synonyms at **last.** —*n. Abbr.* **term., t.** **1.** A terminating point, limit, or part; an end; extremity. **2.** Any ornamental figure or object situated at the end of something, as a finial of a lamp. **3.** *Electricity.* **a.** A position in an electric circuit or device at which an electric connection is normally established or broken. **b.** A passive conductor at such a position used to facilitate the connection. **4. a.** Either end of a railroad or other transportation line; a terminus. **b.** A station at such a point or at a major junction on such a line. **c.** A town at the end of a carrier line. [Latin *terminālis,* from *terminus,* boundary, TERMINUS.] —**ter′mi·nal·ly** *adv.*

terminal leave. Final leave equal to accumulated unused leave granted to a member of the armed forces immediately prior to his separation or discharge from service.

ter·mi·nate (tûr′mə-nāt′) *v.* **-nated, -nating, -nates.** —*tr.* **1.** To bring to an end or halt: *"his action terminated the most hopeful period of reform in Prussian history"* (Gordon A. Craig). **2.** To occur at or form the end of; conclude; finish. —*intr.* **1.** To come to an end: *Negotiations terminated yesterday.* **2.** To have as an end or result. Often used with *in: "the Peloponnesian war . . . terminated in the ruin of the Athenian commonwealth"* (Alexander Hamilton). —See Synonyms at **complete.** [Latin *termināre,* to limit, to terminate, from *terminus,* TERMINUS.]

ter·mi·na·tion (tûr′mə-nā′shən) *n. Abbr.* **term.** **1.** The act of terminating or the condition of being terminated. **2.** The spatial or temporal end of something; a limit or boundary; conclusion or cessation. **3.** A result or outcome of something. **4.** The end of a word, as an inflectional ending, suffix, or final morpheme. —**ter′mi·na′tion·al** *adj.*

ter·mi·na·tive (tûr′mə-nā′tĭv) *adj.* Also **ter·mi·na·to·ry** (-nə-tôr′ē, -tōr′ē). Serving, designed, or tending to terminate; conclusive. —**ter′mi·na′tive·ly** *adv.*

ter·mi·na·tor (tûr′mə-nā′tər) *n.* **1.** A person or thing that terminates. **2.** The dividing line between the bright and shaded regions of the disk of the moon or an inner planet.

ter·mi·nol·o·gy (tûr′mə-nŏl′ə-jē) *n., pl.* **-gies.** **1.** The vocabulary of technical terms and usages appropriate to a particular trade, science, or art; nomenclature. **2.** The study of nomenclature. [Medieval Latin *terminus,* expression, from Latin, limit, TERMINUS + -LOGY.] —**ter′mi·no·log′i·cal** (-nə-lŏj′ĭ-kəl) *adj.* —**ter′mi·no·log′i·cal·ly** *adv.* —**ter′mi·nol′o·gist** *n.*

term insurance. Insurance for a specifically stated period providing coverage for losses to the insured during that period but becoming void upon its expiration.

ter·mi·nus (tûr′mə-nəs) *n., pl.* **-nuses** or **-ni** (-nī′). **1.** The end of something; final point or goal. **2.** A terminal on a transportation line or the town in which it is located. **3.** *Rare.* **a.** A boundary or border. **b.** A stone or post marking such a border. [Latin, boundary line, boundary, limit. See **ter-**[1] in Appendix.*]

ter·mite (tûr′mīt′) *n.* Any of numerous superficially antlike social insects of the order Isoptera, many species of which feed on wood and are highly destructive to living trees and wooden structures. Also called "white ant." [Latin *termes* (stem *termit-*), variant of *tarmes*†, wood-eating worm.]

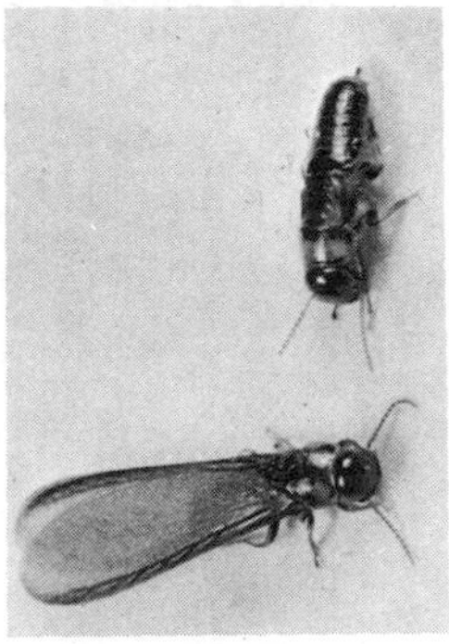

termite
Winged and wingless specimens

term·less (tûrm′lĭs) *adj.* **1.** Having no bounds or limits; unending. **2.** Unconditional.

term·or (tûr′mər) *n.* Also **term·er.** *Law.* A person who holds an estate for a certain term or for life.

term paper. A student essay on a topic drawn from the subject matter covered during a school term.

tern[1] (tûrn) *n.* Any of various sea birds of the genus *Sterna* and related genera, related to and resembling the gulls but characteristically smaller and having a forked tail. [From Scandinavian, akin to Old Norse *therna*†.]

tern[2] (tûrn) *n.* **1.** A set of three; especially, a combination of three numbers that wins a lottery prize. **2.** A three-masted schooner. [Latin *ternī*, three each, from *ter*, thrice. See **trei-** in Appendix.*]

ter·na·ry (tûr′nə-rē) *adj.* **1.** Composed of three or arranged in threes. **2.** *Mathematics.* **a.** Having the base three. **b.** Involving three variables. —*n., pl.* **ternaries.** A set or group of three. [Middle English, from Latin *ternārius*, from *ternī*, three each. See **tern.**]

ter·nate (tûr′nāt′, -nĭt) *adj.* Arranged in or consisting of sets or groups of three, as a compound leaf with three leaflets. [New Latin *ternatus*, from Medieval Latin *ternātus*, past participle of *ternāre*, multiply by three, from *ternī*, three each. See **tern.**] —**ter′nate′ly** *adv.*

Ter·na·te (tər-nä′tē). A volcanic island of Indonesia, 41 square miles in area, lying in the northern Moluccas.

terne·plate (tûrn′plāt′) *n.* Sheet iron or steel plated with an alloy of three or four parts of lead to one part of tin, used as a roofing material. Also called "terne." [French *terne*, dull, from Old French, from *ternir*, to TARNISH + PLATE.]

Ter·ni (tĕr′nē). A city of central Italy, north of Rome; the birthplace of Tacitus. Population, 101,000.

ter·pene (tûr′pēn′) *n.* Any of various unsaturated hydrocarbons, $C_{10}H_{16}$, found in essential oils and oleoresins of plants such as conifers and used in organic syntheses. [*Terp(entine)*, obsolete form of TURPENTINE + -ENE.]

ter·pin·e·ol (tər-pĭn′ē-ôl′, -ōl′) *n.* Any of three isomeric alcohols, $C_{10}H_{17}OH$, occurring naturally in the essential oils of certain plants and used as a solvent, in perfumes, soaps, and medicine. [TERP(ENE) + -INE + -OL.]

Terp·sich·o·re (tûrp-sĭk′ə-rē). The Muse of dancing and choral singing. [Greek *Terpsikhorē* : *terpein*, to delight, cheer (see **terp-** in Appendix*) + *khoros*, dance (see **gher-**[2] in Appendix*).]

terp·si·cho·re·an (tûrp′sĭk-ə-rē′ən, tûrp′sə-kôr′ē-ən, -kōr′ē-ən) *adj.* Also **terp·si·cho·re·al** (-əl). Of or pertaining to dancing. —*n.* A dancer. [From TERPSICHORE.]

terr. **1.** terrace. **2.** territorial; territory.

ter·ra al·ba (tĕr′ə ăl′bə, ôl′bə). **1.** Finely pulverized gypsum used in making paper, paints, and plastics. **2.** A clay, **kaolin** *(see).* [New Latin, "white earth."]

ter·race (tĕr′ĭs) *n. Abbr.* **ter., terr.** **1. a.** An open colonnaded platform, as a porch or promenade. **b.** A platform extending outdoors from a floor of a house or apartment building; balcony; deck. **2.** An open, often paved area adjacent to a house, serving as an outdoor living area; patio. **3.** A raised bank of earth having vertical or sloping sides and a flat top: *descending terraces on the lawn.* **4.** A flat, narrow stretch of ground, often having a steep slope facing a river or sea. **5. a.** A row of buildings erected on raised ground or on a sloping site. **b.** A section of row houses. **6.** A narrow strip of landscaped earth in the middle of a street. **7.** A street, especially one having such a terrace. —*tr.v.* **terraced, -racing, -races.** To make into or supply with a terrace. [Old French *terrasse*, terrace, pile of earth, from Old Provençal *terrassa*, from *terra*, earth, from Latin. See **ters-** in Appendix.*]

ter·ra cot·ta (tĕr′ə kŏt′ə). **1.** A hard, semifired, waterproof ceramic clay used in pottery and building construction. **2.** Ceramic wares made of this material. **3.** Grayish to dark reddish orange, light to medium reddish brown, or strong brown to brownish or deep orange. See **color.** [Italian, "cooked earth."] —**ter′ra-cot′ta** *adj.*

ter·ra fir·ma (tĕr′ə fûr′mə). Solid ground; dry land: *"For a ship is a bit of terra firma cut off from the main"* (Melville). [Latin, "firm land."]

ter·rain (tə-rān′, tĕ-) *n.* **1.** A tract of land; ground. **2.** The character of land; topography. **3.** A particular geographical area; region. **4.** Variant of **terrane.** [French, from Latin *terrēnum*, from *terrēnus*, TERRENE.]

Ter·ra·my·cin (tĕr′ə-mī′sən) *n.* A trademark for **oxytetracycline** *(see).*

ter·rane (tə-rān′, tĕ-) *n.* Also **ter·rain.** **1.** A series of related rock formations. **2.** An area having a preponderance of a particular rock or rock groups. [Variant of TERRAIN.]

ter·ra·pin (tĕr′ə-pən) *n.* **1.** Any of various aquatic North American turtles of the genus *Malaclemys* and related genera; especially, the **diamondback** *(see).* **2.** *British.* Any partly terrestrial freshwater turtle. [Algonquian (Virginia), from Eastern Algonquian *toolepeiwa* (unattested).]

ter·ra·que·ous (tĕr′ăk′wē-əs) *adj.* Composed of both land and water. [Medieval Latin *terraqueus* : *terra*, earth, from Latin (see **ters-** in Appendix*) + *aqueus*, AQUEOUS.]

ter·rar·i·um (tə-răr′ē-əm) *n., pl.* **-ums** or **-ia** (-ē-ə). A small enclosure or closed container in which small plants are grown or small animals, such as turtles or lizards, are kept. [New Latin : Latin *terra*, earth (see **ters-** in Appendix*) + -ARIUM.]

ter·raz·zo (tĕ-rät′sō) *n.* A flooring material of marble or other stone chips set in mortar and polished when dry. [Italian, "terrace," probably from Old Provençal *terrassa*, TERRACE.]

Ter·re Haute (tĕr′ə hōt′, hŭt′, hôt′). A city of western Indiana, on the Wabash River. Population, 73,000.

ter·rene (tĕr′ēn′, tə-rēn′) *adj.* Of or pertaining to the earth; earthly. [Middle English, from Latin *terrēnus*, from *terra*, earth. See **ters-** in Appendix.*]

terre·plein (tĕr′ə-plān′) *n.* The horizontal platform behind a parapet where heavy guns are mounted. [French *terre-plein*, from Italian *terrapieno*, from *terrapienare*, to fill with earth, terrace : *terra*, earth, from Latin (see **ters-** in Appendix*) + *pieno*, full, from Latin *plēnus* (see **pel-**[8] in Appendix*).]

ter·res·tri·al (tə-rĕs′trē-əl) *adj.* **1.** Of or pertaining to the earth or its inhabitants. **2.** Having a worldly, mundane character or quality. **3.** Of, pertaining to, or composed of land as distinct from water or air. **4.** *Biology.* Living or growing on land; not aquatic. —See Synonyms at **earthly.** —*n.* An inhabitant of the earth. [Middle English, from Latin *terrestris*, from *terra*, earth. See **ters-** in Appendix.*] —**ter·res′tri·al·ly** *adv.* —**ter·res′tri·al·ness** *n.*

ter·ret (tĕr′ĭt) *n.* **1.** One of the metal rings on a harness through which the reins pass. **2.** A similar ring on an animal's collar, used for attaching a leash. [Middle English *tyret, toret*, from Old French *to(u)ret*, diminutive of *tour*, "circular movement," from *tourner*, to TURN.]

terre-verte (tĕr′vĕrt′) *n.* An olive-green pigment used by artists and commonly made from **glauconite** *(see).* [French, "green earth" : *terre*, earth, from Latin *terra* (see **ters-** in Appendix*) + *verte*, green, VERT.]

ter·ri·ble (tĕr′ə-bəl) *adj.* **1.** Causing terror or fear; dreadful. **2.** Eliciting awe. **3.** Extreme in extent or degree; intense; severe; excessive: *"the life for which he had paid so terrible a price"* (Leslie Fiedler). **4.** Unpleasant; disagreeable: *a terrible time at the party.* [Middle English, from Old French, from Latin *terribilis*, from *terrēre*, to frighten. See **tres-** in Appendix.*] —**ter′ri·ble·ness** *n.* —**ter′ri·bly** *adv.*

ter·ric·o·lous (tĕ-rĭk′ə-ləs) *adj. Biology.* Living on or in the ground. [From Latin *terricola*, land dweller : *terra*, earth (see **ters-** in Appendix*) + -COLOUS.]

ter·ri·er[1] (tĕr′ē-ər) *n.* Any of various usually small, active dogs originally bred for hunting animals that live in burrows. [French *(chien) terrier*, from *terrier*, burrow, from *terre*, earth, from Latin *terra*. See **ters-** in Appendix.*]

ter·ri·er[2] (tĕr′ē-ər) *n. Law.* A document or book enumerating boundaries, acreage, and the condition of the landholdings of corporations and persons. [Old French *terrier*, from *terre*, land. See **terrier** (dog).]

ter·rif·ic (tə-rĭf′ĭk) *adj.* **1.** Causing terror or great fear; dreadful; terrifying: *a terrific wail.* **2.** Very bad or unpleasant; frightful: *a terrific headache.* **3.** Very good or fine; splendid; magnificent: *a terrific chef.* **4.** Awesome; astounding: *a terrific speed.* [Latin *terrificus* : *terrēre*, to frighten (see **tres-** in Appendix*) + -FIC.] —**ter·rif′i·cal·ly** *adv.*

ter·ri·fy (tĕr′ə-fī′) *tr.v.* **-fied, -fying, -fies.** **1.** To fill with terror; make deeply afraid; to alarm. **2.** To menace or threaten; intimidate. —See Synonyms at **frighten.** [Latin *terrificāre*, from *terrificus*, TERRIFIC.]

ter·rig·e·nous (tĕ-rĭj′ə-nəs) *adj.* Derived from the land, especially by erosive action. Said primarily of sediments. [From Latin *terrigena*, born of the earth : *terra*, earth (see **ters-** in Appendix*) + -GENOUS.]

ter·ri·to·ri·al (tĕr′ə-tôr′ē-əl, -tōr′ē-əl) *adj. Abbr.* **ter., terr.** **1.** Of or pertaining to a territory or to its powers of jurisdiction. **2.** Pertaining or restricted to a particular territory; regional; local. **3.** *Capital* **T.** Organized for national or home defense: *the British Territorial Army.* —*n.* **1.** A member of a territorial army. **2.** *Capital* **T.** A member of the Territorial Army of Great Britain. —**ter′ri·to′ri·al·ly** *adv.*

ter·ri·to·ri·al·ism (tĕr′ə-tôr′ē-əl-ĭz′əm, tĕr′ə-tōr′-) *n.* **1.** A social system that gives authority and influence in a state to the landowners; landlordism. **2.** A system of church government based on primacy of civil power. In this sense, also called "territorial system." —**ter′ri·to′ri·al·ist** *n.*

ter·ri·to·ri·al·i·ty (tĕr′ə-tôr-ē-ăl′ə-tē, tĕr′ə-tōr′-) *n.* The status of a territory.

ter·ri·to·ri·al·ize (tĕr′ə-tôr′ē-ə-līz′, tĕr′ə-tōr′-) *tr.v.* **-ized, -izing, -izes.** **1.** To add to by the acquisition of territory. **2.** To reduce to the status of a territory. **3.** To distribute among particular territories. —**ter′ri·to′ri·al·i·za′tion** *n.*

territorial waters. Inland and coastal waters under the jurisdiction of a state; especially, the ocean waters within three miles of the shoreline.

ter·ri·to·ry (tĕr′ə-tôr′ē, -tōr′ē) *n., pl.* **-ries.** *Abbr.* **t., T., ter., terr.** **1.** An area of land; a district; region. **2.** The land and waters under the jurisdiction of a state, nation, or sovereign. **3.** *Capital* **T.** **a.** A part of the United States not admitted as a state, which has a governor and other officers appointed by the President and confirmed by the Senate and which has its own legislature. **b.** A part of Canada or Australia not accorded statehood or provincial status. **4.** The area for which a person is responsible as representative or agent: *a salesman's territory.* **5.** The area of a sports field defended by a team. **6.** *Biology.* An area inhabited by an individual animal or a mating pair or group of animals, and often vigorously defended against intruders. **7.** A sphere of action or interest; province; domain. [Middle English, from Latin *territōrium*, from *terra*, land. See **ters-** in Appendix.*]

ter·ror (tĕr′ər) *n.* **1.** Intense, overpowering fear. **2.** Anything that instills such fear; a terrifying object or occurrence. **3.** The ability to instill such fear; terribleness: *the terror of the haunted house.* **4.** Violence toward private citizens, public property, and political enemies promoted by a political group to achieve or maintain supremacy. **5.** *Informal.* An annoying or intolerable pest; nuisance. Often used in the phrase *a holy terror.* [Middle English *terrour*, from Old French, from Latin *terror*, from *terrēre*, to frighten. See **tres-** in Appendix.*]

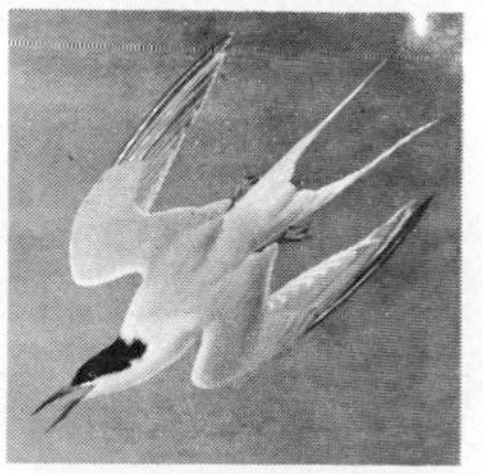

tern[1]
Sterna dougallii
Painting by
John James Audubon

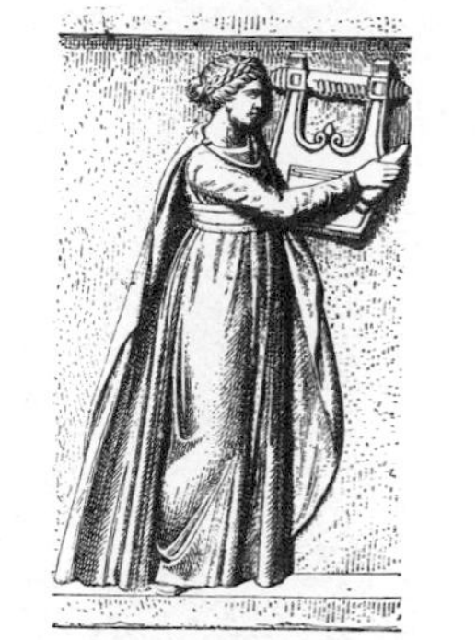

Terpsichore

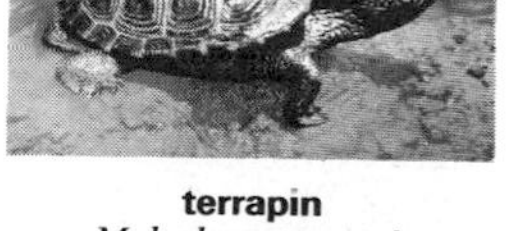

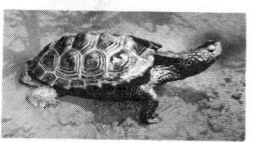

terrapin
Malaclemys terrapin
Diamondback terrapin

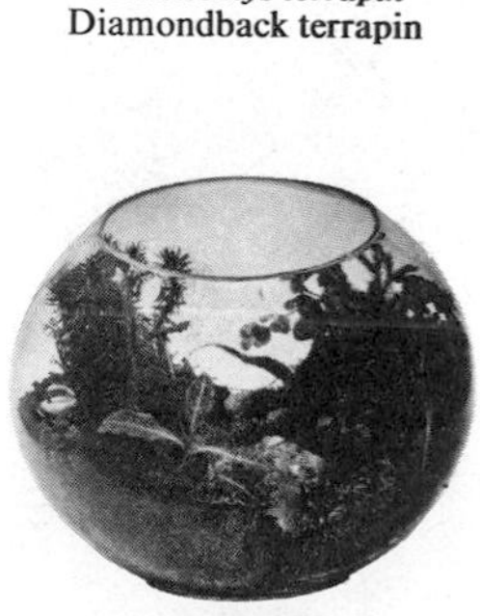

terrarium
Glass terrarium with plants

ter·ror·ism (tĕr′ər-ĭz′əm) *n.* **1.** The use of terror, violence, and intimidation to achieve an end. **2.** Fear and subjugation produced by this. **3.** A system of government that uses terror to rule. —**ter′ror·ist** *n.* —**ter′ror·is′tic** *adj.*

ter·ror·ize (tĕr′ər-īz′) *tr.v.* **-ized, -izing, -izes. 1.** To fill or overpower with terror; terrify. **2.** To coerce by intimidation or fear. —**ter′ror·i·za′tion** *n.* —**ter′ror·iz′er** *n.*

ter·ry (tĕr′ē) *n., pl.* **-ries. 1.** Any of the uncut loops that form the pile of a fabric. **2.** A pile fabric, usually woven of cotton, with uncut loops on both sides, used for such articles as bath towels and robes. In this sense, also called "terry cloth." [Origin unknown.]

Ter·ry (tĕr′ē), Dame **Ellen (Alice).** 1847–1928. British actress.

terse (tûrs) *adj.* **terser, tersest.** Effectively concise; free of superfluity. See Synonyms at **concise.** [Originally "polished," "refined," from Latin *tersus*, past participle of *tergēre*, to wipe off, polish. See **deterge.**] —**terse′ly** *adv.* —**terse′ness** *n.*

ter·tian (tûr′shən) *adj.* Recurring every other day or, when considered inclusively, every third day. —*n. Pathology.* **Tertian fever** *(see).* [Latin *tertiānus*, of the third, from *tertius*, third. See **trei-** in Appendix.*]

tertian fever. A form of malaria caused by the invasion of *Plasmodium vivax* into new red blood cells, characterized by a 48-hour life cycle in the human body with a recurrence of fever paroxysms at the end of each such period. Also called "tertian," "tertian malaria."

ter·ti·ar·y (tûr′shē-ĕr′ē) *adj.* Also **ter·tial** (-shəl) (for sense 2). **1.** Third in place, order, degree, or rank. **2.** *Ornithology.* Of, pertaining to, or designating the short flight feathers nearest the body on the inner edge of a bird's wing. **3.** *Chemistry.* **a.** Pertaining to salts of acids containing three replaceable hydrogen atoms. **b.** Pertaining to organic compounds in which a group, such as an alcohol or amine, is bound to three nonelementary radicals. **4.** *Ecclesiastical.* Of or pertaining to the third order of a monastic system. —*n., pl.* **tertiaries.** Also **ter·tial** (for sense 1). **1.** *Ornithology.* A tertiary feather. **2.** *Ecclesiastical.* A member of a tertiary order. [Latin *tertiārius*, from *tertius*, third. See **trei-** in Appendix.*]

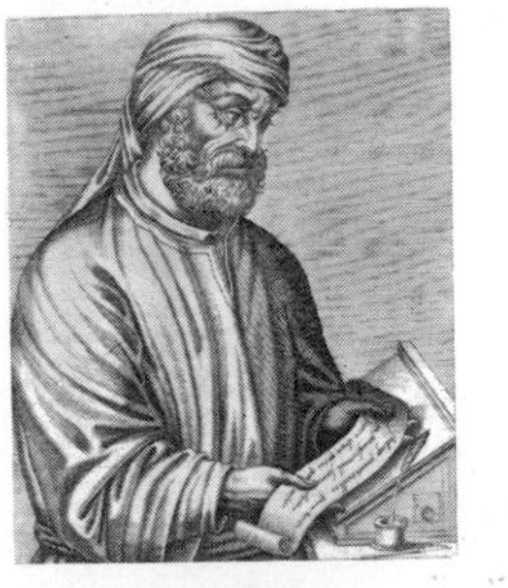

Tertullian
Sixteenth-century French engraving

Ter·ti·ar·y (tûr′shē-ĕr′ē) *adj.* Of, belonging to, or designating the geologic time, system of rocks, and sedimentary deposits of the first period of the Cenozoic era, extending from the Cretaceous period of the Mesozoic era to the Quarternary period of the Cenozoic era, characterized by the appearance of modern flora and of apes and other large mammals. See **geology.** —*n.* The Tertiary period or system of deposits. Preceded by *the.*

tertiary color. A color resulting from the mixture of two secondary colors.

ter·ti·um quid (tûr′shē-əm kwĭd′). Something that cannot be classified into either of two groups considered to be exhaustive; an intermediate thing or factor. [Late Latin, "third something" (translation of Greek *triton ti*).]

Ter·tul·lian (tər-tŭl′ē-ən). Latin name, Quintus Septimius Florens Tertullianus. A.D. 160?–230? Carthaginian theologian.

ter·va·lent. Variant of **trivalent.**

ter·za ri·ma (tĕr′tsə rē′mə) *pl.* **terze rime** (tĕr′tsā rē′mā). A verse form consisting of a series of triplets having 10-syllable or 11-syllable lines of which the middle line of one triplet rhymes with the first and third lines of the following triplet. [Italian, "third rhyme."]

tes·la (tĕs′lə) *n. Abbr.* **T** The unit of magnetic flux density in the International System, equal to one weber per square meter. See **measurement.** [After Nikola TESLA.]

Tes·la (tĕs′lə), **Nikola.** 1857–1943. Croatian-born American electrical engineer; made alternating current practical.

tesla coil. A transformer with an air-core primary and a capacitor-tuned secondary, used as a source of high-frequency power, as for x-ray tubes.

Tes·lin Lake (tĕz′lĭn). A lake of Canada, occupying about 200 square miles in northwestern British Columbia and the southern Yukon Territory.

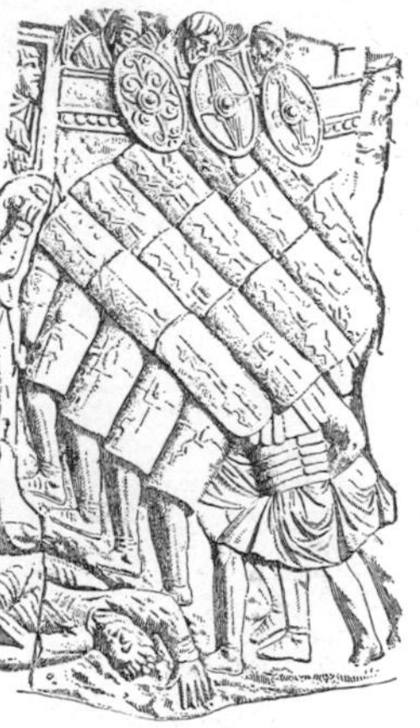

testudo
Detail from Trajan's Column in Rome

tes·sel·late (tĕs′ə-lāt′) *tr.v.* **-lated, -lating, -lates.** To form into a mosaic pattern, as by using small squares of stone or glass. [Latin *tessellātus*, from *tessella*, a small cube, diminutive of *tessera*, TESSERA.] —**tes′sel·la′tion** *n.*

tes·ser·a (tĕs′ər-ə) *n., pl.* **tesserae** (tĕs′ə-rē′). One of the small squares of stone or glass used in making mosaic patterns. [Latin, "a square," from Greek *tesseres, tessares*, four. See **kwetwer-** in Appendix.*]

test[1] (tĕst) *n.* **1.** A means of examination, trial, or proof. **2.** A series of questions or problems designed to determine knowledge or intelligence. **3.** A criterion; standard. **4.** *Chemistry.* **a.** A physical or chemical reaction by which a substance may be detected or its properties ascertained. **b.** The reagent used in such determination. **c.** A positive result obtained. **5.** A cupel. —*v.* **tested, testing, tests.** —*tr.* **1.** To subject to a test; examine. **2. a.** To determine the presence or properties of (a substance). **b.** To assay (metal) in a cupel. —*intr.* **1.** To undergo a test. **2.** To achieve as a score or rating through testing. **3.** To exhibit certain properties under test conditions. **4.** To administer a test in order to diagnose. Used with *for: test for acid content.* [Middle English, cupel for treating ores, from Old French, pot, from Latin *testum*†, earthen vessel.]

test[2] (tĕst) *n.* A hard external covering, such as that of certain insects and other invertebrates. [Latin *testa*, shell. See **testa.**]

test. 1. testator. **2.** testatrix. **3.** testimony.

Test. Testament.

tes·ta (tĕs′tə) *n., pl.* **-tae** (-tē′). The often thick or hard outer coat of a seed. [Latin *testa*†, clay, brick, tile, shell.]

tes·ta·ceous (tĕs-tā′shəs) *adj.* **1.** *Biology.* Of, pertaining to, or having a shell or shell-like outer covering. **2.** Having the characteristic reddish-brown or brownish-yellow color of bricks. [Latin *testāceus*, from *testa*, shell. See **test** (shell).]

tes·ta·cy (tĕs′tə-sē) *n. Law.* The condition of being testate or having left a will at death.

tes·ta·ment (tĕs′tə-mənt) *n.* **1.** *Law.* **a.** A written document providing for the disposition of one's personal property after death. **b.** A will. Used chiefly in the phrase *last will and testament.* **2. a.** Any proof or tribute that testifies to or serves as evidence of something. **b.** A statement of belief or conviction; credo. **3. a.** A covenant between man and God. **b.** *Capital* **T.** *Abbr.* **T., Test.** Either of the two main divisions of the Bible, the Old Testament and the New Testament. **c.** *Capital* **T.** The New Testament. [Middle English, from Late Latin *testāmentum* (translation of Greek *diathēkē*, scripture), from Latin, will, from *testārī*, to be a witness, assert, make a will, from *testis*, witness. See **trei-** in Appendix.*]

tes·tate (tĕs′tāt′) *adj.* Having made a legally valid will before death. [Middle English, from Latin *testātus*, past participle of *testārī*, to make a will. See **testament.**]

tes·ta·tor (tĕs′tā′tər, tĕs-tā′tər) *n. Abbr.* **test.** A person who has made a legally valid will before death. [Middle English *testatour*, from Norman French, from Latin *testātor*, from *testārī*, to make a will. See **testament.**]

tes·ta·trix (tĕs-tā′trĭks) *n. Abbr.* **test.** A woman who has made a legally valid will before death. [Latin *testātrix*, feminine of *testātor*, TESTATOR.]

test case. A legal action whose outcome is likely to set a precedent or test the constitutionality of a statute.

tes·ter[1] (tĕs′tər) *n.* A canopy over a bed. [Middle English, from Medieval Latin *testerium*, headpiece, from Late Latin *testa*, skull, head, from Latin, shell. See **testa.**]

tes·ter[2] (tĕs′tər) *n.* A former English coin, the **teston** *(see).* [Variant of TESTON.]

test·er[3] (tĕs′tər) *n.* One that tests.

tes·tes. Plural of **testis.**

tes·ti·cle (tĕs′tĭ-kəl) *n.* A **testis** *(see).* [Middle English *testicule*, from Latin *testiculus*, diminutive of *testis*, TESTIS.]

tes·tic·u·late (tĕs-tĭk′yə-lĭt) *adj.* Also **tes·tic·u·lar** (-lər). Having the shape of a testicle; ovoid.

tes·ti·fy (tĕs′tə-fī′) *v.* **-fied, -fying, -fies.** —*intr.* **1.** To make a declaration of truth or fact under oath. **2.** To make a serious or solemn statement in support of an argument, position, or asserted fact. **3.** *Law.* To bear witness; submit testimony. **4.** To serve as witness or evidence. Used with *to.* —*tr.* **1.** To bear witness to; provide evidence for; affirm as true. **2.** To state or affirm under oath. **3.** To declare publicly; make known. [Middle English *testifien*, from Latin *testificārī* : *testis*, witness (see **trei-** in Appendix*) + *facere*, to make (see **dhē-**[1] in Appendix*).] —**tes′ti·fi·ca′tion** *n.* —**tes′ti·fi′er** *n.*

tes·ti·mo·ni·al (tĕs′tə-mō′nē-əl) *n.* **1.** A formal or written statement testifying to a particular truth or fact. **2.** A written affirmation of another's character or worth. **3.** Something given as a tribute for a person's service or achievement. —*adj.* Relating to or constituting a testimony or testimonial. [Middle English, noun and adjective, from Old French, from Late Latin *testimōniālis*, from Latin *testimōnium*, TESTIMONY.]

tes·ti·mo·ny (tĕs′tə-mō′nē) *n., pl.* **-nies.** *Abbr.* **test. 1.** A declaration or affirmation of fact or truth, such as that given before a court. **2.** Any evidence in support of a fact or assertion; proof. **3.** The collective written and spoken testimony offered in a legal case. **4.** A public declaration regarding a religious experience. **5. a.** The law of Moses, inscribed on the tablets of stone. Exodus 25:16. **b.** *Often capital* **T.** The ark containing these. Exodus 16:34. [Middle English, from Latin *testimōnium*, from *testis*, witness. See **trei-** in Appendix.*]

tes·tis (tĕs′tĭs) *n., pl.* **-tes** (-tēz′). The male reproductive gland, the source of spermatozoa and of the androgens, normally occurring paired in an external scrotum in man and certain other mammals. Also called "testicle." [Latin, "witness" (to virility). See **trei-** in Appendix.*]

tes·ton (tĕs′tŏn′) *n.* Also **tes·toon** (tĕs-to͞on′). Any of various coins with the image of a head on one side, specifically: **1.** A 16th-century silver coin of France. **2.** An English coin stamped with the head of Henry VIII, originally worth a shilling and later sixpence. In this sense, also called "tester." [Middle English, from Old French *teste* and Italian *testa*, head, both from Late Latin *testa*, skull, from Latin, shell. See **testa.**]

tes·tos·ter·one (tĕs-tŏs′tə-rōn′) *n.* A male sex hormone, $C_{19}H_{28}O_2$, produced in the testes and functioning to control secondary sex characteristics. [TEST(IS) + STER(OL) + -ONE.]

test paper. 1. A paper saturated with a reagent, such as litmus, used in making chemical tests. **2.** A paper or booklet bearing a student's work for an examination.

test pilot. A pilot who flies aircraft of new or experimental design to test them for conformity to planned standards.

test stand. A facility for static test firing of rocket engines to determine performance characteristics.

test tube. A cylindrical clear glass tube usually open at one end and rounded at the other, used in laboratory experimentation.

tes·tu·di·nate (tĕs-to͞od′n-ĭt, -tyo͞od′n-ĭt, -āt′) *adj.* Of or pertaining to a turtle or tortoise. —*n.* A turtle or tortoise. [New Latin *Testudinata* (order), from Latin *testūdo* (stem *testūdin-*), tortoise. See **testudo.**]

tes·tu·do (tĕs-to͞o′dō, -tyo͞o′dō) *n., pl.* **-dines** (-də-nēz′). A siege device used by the Romans, consisting of a movable arched screen protecting the besiegers' approach to a wall. [Latin *testūdo*, "tortoise," a covering, from *testa*, shell. See **testa.**]

tes·ty (tĕs′tē) *adj.* **-tier, -tiest. 1.** Irritable; touchy; peevish.

2. Characterized by irritability, impatience, or exasperation: *a testy remark.* [Middle English *testif,* headstrong, from Norman French, from Old French *teste,* head. See **teston.**] —**tes′ti·ly** *adv.* —**tes′ti·ness** *n.*

Tet (tĕt) *n.* The lunar New Year as celebrated in Southeast Asia. [Vietnamese *tết,* from Ancient Chinese *tsiet,* "festival" (Mandarin Chinese *chieh²*).]

te·tan·ic (tə-tăn′ĭk) *adj.* **1.** Of or pertaining to tetanus. **2.** Of or pertaining to tetany.

tet·a·nize (tĕt′n-īz′) *tr.v.* **-nized, -nizing, -nizes.** To affect with tetanic convulsions; produce or induce tetanus in. —**tet′a·ni·za′tion** *n.*

tet·a·nus (tĕt′n-əs) *n.* **1.** An acute, often fatal infectious disease caused by a bacillus, *Clostridium tetani,* that generally enters the body through wounds, and is characterized by rigidity and spasmodic contraction of the voluntary muscles. Also called "lockjaw." **2.** A state of continuous muscular contraction caused by reaction to rapidly repeated stimuli. [Learned re-spelling of Middle English *tetane,* from Latin *tetanus,* from Greek *tetanos,* from adjective, "stretched," from *teinein,* to stretch. See **ten-** in Appendix.*] —**tet′a·nal** (tĕt′n-əl) *adj.*

tet·a·ny (tĕt′n-ē) *n.* An abnormal condition, occurring chiefly in children and young adults, characterized by periodic painful muscular spasms caused by faulty calcium metabolism. [From TETANUS.]

tetch·y (tĕch′ē) *adj.* **-ier, -iest.** Also **tech·y.** Peevish; testy. [Probably from obsolete *tecche, tache,* blemish, fault (of character), from Old French *tache, teche,* blemish, from Late Latin *tacca* (unattested), from Gothic *taikns,* sign. See **deik-** in Appendix.*] —**tetch′i·ly** *adv.* —**tetch′i·ness** *n.*

tête-à-tête (tāt′ə-tāt′; *French* tĕ-tä-tĕt′) *adv.* Together without the intrusion of a third person; in intimate privacy: *talk tête-à-tête.* —*n.* **1.** A private conversation between two people. **2.** A sofa for two, especially an S-shaped one allowing the occupants to face each other. —*adj.* For or between two only; private; intimate. [French, "head to head."]

tête-bêche (tĕt′bĕsh′) *adj.* Of, pertaining to, or characteristic of postage stamps printed upside-down in relation to one another. [French : *tête,* head + *bechevet,* "double-headed" : *bes,* twice, from Latin *bis* (see **bi-**) + *chevet,* head (of a bed), from Latin *capitium,* head covering, from *caput,* head (see **kaput** in Appendix*).]

teth (tĕt, tĕs) *n.* The ninth letter in the Hebrew alphabet. See **alphabet.** [Hebrew *ṭēth.*]

teth·er (tĕth′ər) *n.* **1.** A rope, chain, or halter for an animal, allowing it a short radius to move about in. **2.** The range or scope of one's resources or abilities. —**at the end of one's tether.** At the extreme limit of one's endurance or powers. —*tr.v.* **tethered, -ering, -ers.** To restrict or bind with or as with a tether. [Middle English *tethir,* from Old Norse *tjōthr*†.]

teth·er·ball (tĕth′ər-bôl′) *n.* A game played by two people with paddles and a ball hung by a cord from an upright post, the objective being to wind the cord around the post.

Te·thys (tē′thĭs). *Greek Mythology.* A Titaness and sea goddess who was both sister and wife of Oceanus.

Te·ton Range (tē′tŏn′). A range of the Rocky Mountains in southeastern Idaho and northwestern Wyoming. Highest elevation, Grand Teton (13,766 feet).

tet·ra (tĕt′rə) *n.* Any of various small, colorful tropical freshwater fishes of the family Characidae, popular in home aquariums. [Short for New Latin *Tetragonopterus* (former classification of tetras) : TETRAGON (from their squared-off dorsal fins) + -PTER.]

tetra–, tetr–. Indicates four; for example, **tetrachloride, tetracid.** [Greek. See **kwetwer-** in Appendix.*]

tet·ra·ba·sic (tĕt′rə-bā′sĭk) *adj.* **1.** Containing four replaceable hydrogen atoms in a molecule. Said of acids. **2.** Containing four univalent basic atoms or radicals. Said of bases or salts. —**tet′ra·ba·sic′i·ty** (-sĭs′ə-tē) *n.*

tet·ra·chlo·ride (tĕt′rə-klôr′īd′, -klōr′īd′) *n.* A chemical compound containing four chlorine atoms per molecule.

tet·ra·chord (tĕt′rə-kôrd′) *n. Music.* A series of four diatonic tones encompassing the interval of a perfect fourth. [Greek *tetrakhordon,* from *tetrakhordos* : TETRA- + *khordē,* string (see **gher-¹** in Appendix*).] —**tet′ra·chor′dal** *adj.*

te·trac·id (tĕ-trăs′ĭd) *adj.* **1.** Able to react with four molecules of a monobasic acid. Said of a base. **2.** Containing four replaceable hydrogen atoms. Said of an acid or acid salt. —*n.* An acid containing four replaceable hydrogen atoms. [TETR(A)- + ACID.]

tet·ra·cy·cline (tĕt′rə-sī′klēn′) *n.* A yellow crystalline compound, $C_{22}H_{24}N_2O_8$, synthesized or derived from certain microorganisms of the genus *Streptomyces* and used as an antibiotic. [TETRA- + CYCL(IC) + -INE.]

tet·rad (tĕt′răd′) *n.* **1.** A group or set of four. **2.** A tetravalent atom, radical, or element. **3.** *Biology.* **a.** A group of four chromatids formed at meiosis by synapsis of two chromatids from each of a pair of homologous chromosomes. **b.** A body formed of four cells, as pollen grains from one mother cell. [Greek *tetras* (stem *tetrad-*). See **kwetwer-** in Appendix.*]

te·trad·y·mite (tĕ-trăd′ə-mīt′) *n.* A steel-gray bismuth ore, chiefly Bi_2Te_2S. [From Late Greek *tetradumos,* fourfold (since it occurs in compound twin crystals) : TETRA- + Greek *didumos,* double (see **dwō** in Appendix*).]

tet·ra·dy·na·mous (tĕt′rə-dī′nə-məs) *adj. Botany.* Having six stamens, of which two are shorter than the others. [TETRA- + Greek *dynamis,* power (see **dynamic**) + -OUS.]

tet·ra·eth·yl lead (tĕt′rə-ĕth′əl). Also **tet·ra·eth·yl·lead** (tĕt′rə-ĕth′əl-lĕd). A colorless, poisonous, oily liquid, $Pb(C_2H_5)_4$, used in gasoline for internal combustion engines as an antiknock agent. Also called "lead tetraethyl."

tet·ra·gon (tĕt′rə-gŏn′) *n.* A four-sided polygon; a quadrilateral. [Late Latin *tetragōnum,* from Greek *tetragōnon* : TETRA- + -GON.] —**te·trag′o·nal** (tĕ-trăg′ə-nəl) *adj.*

Tet·ra·gram·ma·ton (tĕt′rə-grăm′ə-tŏn′) *n.* The four Hebrew letters usually transliterated as YHWH or JHVH (Yahweh or Jehovah) and used as a symbol or substitute for the ineffable name of God. [Middle English *Tetragramaton,* from Greek *tetragrammaton,* four-letter word : TETRA- + *gramma* (stem *grammat-*), letter (see **gerebh-** in Appendix*).]

tet·ra·he·dral (tĕt′rə-hē′drəl) *adj.* **1.** Pertaining to a tetrahedron. **2.** Having four faces. —**tet′ra·he′dral·ly** *adv.*

tet·ra·he·drite (tĕt′rə-hē′drīt′) *n.* A grayish-black copper ore, essentially $(CuFe)_{12}Sb_4S_{13}$, often containing other elements and sometimes used as an ore of silver. [German *Tetraëdrit,* from Greek *tetraedros,* four-faced (it occurs in tetrahedral crystals). See **tetrahedron.**]

tet·ra·he·dron (tĕt′rə-hē′drən) *n., pl.* **-drons** or **-dra** (-drə). A polyhedron with four faces. [New Latin, from Late Greek *tetraedron,* from Greek *tetraedros,* four-faced : TETRA- + *hedra,* face (see **sed-¹** in Appendix*).]

te·tral·o·gy (tĕ-trăl′ə-jē, -trŏl′ə-jē) *n., pl.* **-gies. 1.** In ancient Athens, a series of four dramas, three tragic, one satiric, performed at the festivals dedicated to Dionysus. **2.** Any series of four related dramatic, operatic, or literary works. [Greek *tetralogia* : TETRA- + -LOGY.]

te·tram·er·ous (tĕ-trăm′ər-əs) *adj.* **1.** Having or consisting of four similar parts. **2.** *Botany.* Having flower parts, such as sepals, petals, and stamens, in sets of four. Also written *4-merous.* [New Latin *tetramerus,* from Greek *tetramerēs* : TETRA- + -MEROUS.] —**te·tram′er·ism′** *n.*

te·tram·e·ter (tĕ-trăm′ə-tər) *n. Prosody.* **1.** A line of verse consisting of four metrical feet. **2.** A verse composed of such lines. [Late Latin *tetrametrus,* from Greek *tetrametros,* having four measures : TETRA- + -METER.] —**te·tram′e·ter** *adj.*

tet·ra·ploid (tĕt′rə-ploid′) *adj. Genetics.* Having four haploid sets of chromosomes. —*n. Genetics.* A tetraploid individual. [TETRA- + -PLOID.]

tet·ra·pod (tĕt′rə-pŏd′) *adj.* Having four feet, legs, or leglike appendages. [Greek *tetrapous* (stem *tetrapod-*) : TETRA- + -POD.]

te·trap·ter·ous (tĕ-trăp′tər-əs) *adj.* Having four wings, as certain insects. [Greek *tetrapteros* : TETRA- + -PTEROUS.]

tet·rarch (tĕt′rärk′, tē′trärk′) *n.* **1.** A governor of one of the four divisions of a country or province, especially under the ancient Roman Empire. **2. a.** A subordinate ruler. **b.** One of four joint rulers. **3.** In ancient Greece, the commander of a subdivision of a phalanx. [Middle English, from Late Latin *tetrarcha,* from Latin *tetrarchēs,* from Greek *tetrarkhēs* : TETRA- + -ARCH.] —**te·trar′chic** (tĕ-trär′kĭk, tē-) *adj.*

tet·rar·chy (tĕt′rär′kē, tē′trär′-) *n., pl.* **-chies.** Also **tet·rar·chate** (-kāt′, -kĭt). **1.** The area or jurisdiction of a tetrarch. **2. a.** Rule by four governors jointly. **b.** The four governors ruling jointly.

tet·ra·spore (tĕt′rə-spôr′, -spōr′) *n. Botany.* One of four spores produced in a group from a sporangium, as in red algae. —**tet′ra·spor′ic** *adj.*

te·tras·ti·chous (tĕ-trăs′tĭ-kəs) *adj. Botany.* Arranged in four vertical rows, as leaves or flowers on a stalk. [Late Latin *tetrastichus,* having four lines, from Greek *tetrastikhos* : TETRA- + -STICHOUS.]

tet·ra·tom·ic (tĕt′rə-tŏm′ĭk) *adj.* **1.** Having four atoms per molecule. **2.** Having four replaceable univalent atoms or radicals. [TETR(A)- + ATOMIC.]

tet·ra·va·lent (tĕt′rə-vā′lənt) *adj.* Having valence 4.

tet·rode (tĕt′rōd′) *n.* A four-element electron tube containing a cathode, a control grid, a screen grid, and an anode. [TETR(A)- + -ODE (path).]

te·trox·ide (tĕ-trŏk′sīd′) *n.* A chemical compound containing four oxygen atoms per molecule. [TETR(A)- + OXIDE.]

tet·ryl (tĕt′rəl) *n.* A yellow crystalline explosive, $C_7H_5N_5O_8$, used chiefly as a primer or detonator. [TETR(A)- + -YL.]

tet·ter (tĕt′ər) *n.* Any of various skin diseases such as psoriasis, herpes, and, especially, eczema, characterized by eruptions and itching. [Middle English *teter,* Old English *tet(e)r.* See **der-²** in Appendix.*]

Te·tuán (tĕ-twän′). A city of Morocco, a seaport in the northeast on the Mediterranean; the former capital of Spanish Morocco. Population, 100,000.

Tet·zel (tĕt′səl), **Johann.** Also **Te·zel.** 1465?–1519. German Dominican monk; opponent of Martin Luther.

Teu·co. See **Bermejo.**

Teut. Teuton; Teutonic.

Teu·to·bur·ger Wald (toi′tō-bo͝or′gər vält′). A range of hills in North Rhine-Westphalia, West Germany.

Teu·ton (to͞ot′n, tyo͞ot′n) *n. Abbr.* **Teut. 1.** *Plural.* An ancient people, probably of Germanic or Celtic origin, who lived in Jutland until about 100 B.C. **2.** One of the peoples speaking a Germanic language; especially, a German. [Latin *Teutonī.* See **teutā-** in Appendix.*]

Teu·ton·ic (to͞o-tŏn′ĭk, tyo͞o-) *adj. Abbr.* **Teut. 1.** Of or relating to the Teutons. **2.** Of or relating to the Germanic languages. —*n.* The subfamily of Germanic languages.

Teu·ton·ism (to͞ot′n-ĭz′əm, tyo͞ot′-) *n.* Also **Teu·ton·i·cism** (to͞o-tŏn′ə-sĭz′əm, tyo͞o-). **1.** A German practice or idiom. **2.** German character or civilization. —**Teu′ton·ist** *n.*

Teu·ton·ize (to͞ot′n-īz′, tyo͞ot′-) *tr.v.* **-ized, -izing, -izes.** To make German; Germanize. —**Teu′ton·i·za′tion** *n.*

Te·ve·re. The Italian name for the **Tiber.**

יהוה

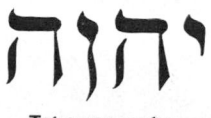

Tetragrammaton

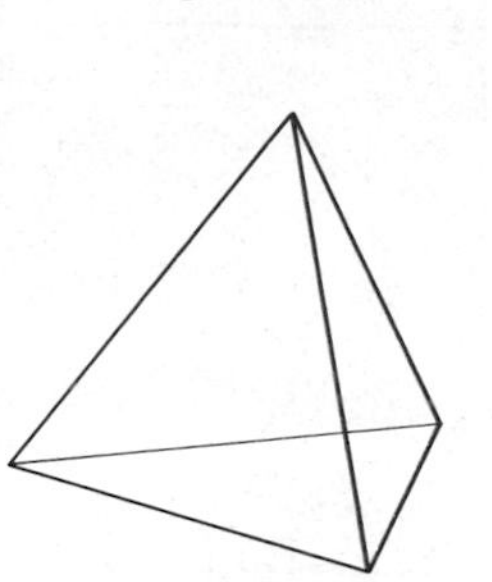

tetrahedron

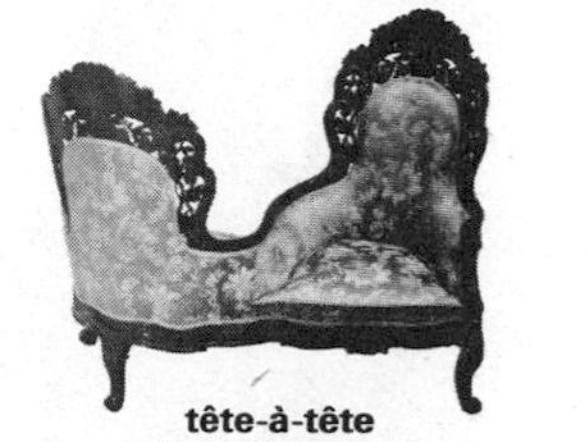

tête-à-tête
Mid-19th-century American

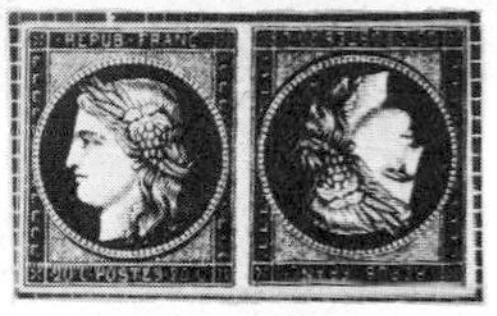

tête-bêche
"Head of Ceres" stamp issued in France between 1849 and 1870

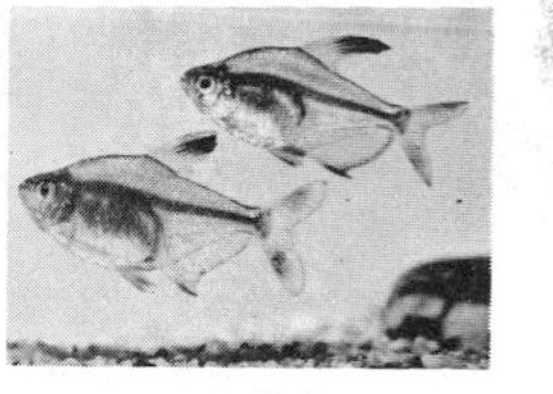

tetra
Hyphessobrycon rosaceus
Rosy tetra

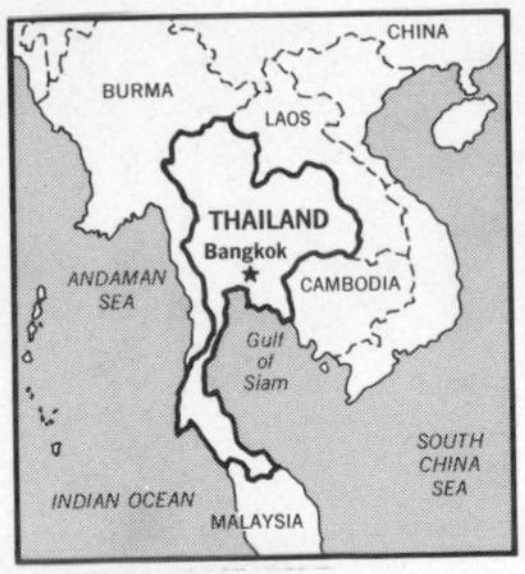

Thailand

Te·vet (tā′vəs, tā-vāt′) *n.* Also **Te·bet, Te·beth.** The fourth month of the Hebrew year. See **calendar.** [Hebrew *tēbhēth,* from Akkadian *ṭebētu,* perhaps "month of sinking in," "muddy month," from *ṭebū,* to sink in.]

Te·wa (tā′wə, tē′wə) *n., pl.* **Tewa** or **-was. 1.** A Tanoan-speaking North American Indian tribe of New Mexico and northeastern Arizona. **2.** A member of this tribe. **3.** The language of this tribe.

Tewkes·bu·ry (tōōks′bĕr′ē, -bə-rē, tyōōks′-). A town on the Severn in northern Gloucestershire, England; the site of the final defeat of the Lancastrians in the Wars of the Roses (1471). Population, 6,000.

Tex. Texas.

Tex·ar·kan·a (tĕk′sär-kăn′ə). A city lying on both sides of the border between northeastern Texas and southwestern Arkansas, with two municipal governments. Population, 30,000.

tex·as (tĕk′səs) *n.* The structure on a river steamboat containing the pilothouse and the officers' quarters. [From TEXAS.]

Tex·as (tĕk′səs). *Abbr.* **Tex.** A state of the south-central United States, the second-largest of the states (267,339 square miles), bordered on the west by Mexico and on the southeast by the Gulf of Mexico; admitted to the Union in 1845. Population, 10,551,000. Capital, Austin. See map at **United States of America.** —**Tex′an** *adj. & n.*

Tex·as City (tĕk′səs). A resort city of Texas, in the southeast on Galveston Bay. Population, 32,000.

Texas fever. An infectious disease of cattle and related animals, caused by a parasitic microorganism, *Babesia bigemina,* and transmitted by ticks.

Texas leaguer. *Baseball.* A fly ball that drops between the infielder and the outfielder for a hit. [From *Texas League,* a minor baseball league.]

Texas Ranger. 1. A member of the Texas mounted police force. **2.** A member of a band of men originally organized in Texas to fight Indians and maintain order.

Texas tower. A radar tower built offshore. [So named for its resemblance to the oil derricks off the Texas coast.]

Tex·co·co (tās-kō′kō). A town in Mexico State, central Mexico; a prominent center of the Aztec Empire and the base of Cortes' operations against Tenochtitlán. Population, 11,000.

text (tĕkst) *n.* **1. a.** The wording or words of something written or printed. **b.** The words of a speech appearing in print. **2.** The body of a printed work as distinct from a preface, footnote, or appendix; the formal content. **3.** The exact wording and word sequence of an author as opposed to a translation, revision, or condensation. **4.** A Scriptural passage to be read and expounded upon in a sermon. **5. a.** A reference used as the starting point of a discussion. **b.** The subject matter of a discourse. **6.** A textbook. [Middle English *texte,* from Old French *texte,* from Medieval Latin *textus,* (Scriptural) text, from Latin, literary composition, "woven thing," from the past participle of *texere,* to weave. See **teks-** in Appendix.*]

text·book (tĕkst′bŏŏk′) *n.* A book used as a standard work for the formal study of a particular subject.

tex·tile (tĕks′tīl′, -tĭl) *n.* **1.** Cloth; fabric, especially one that is woven or knitted. **2.** Fiber or yarn for weaving or knitting into fabric. —*adj.* Pertaining to textiles or their manufacture. [French, from Latin *textilis,* from *textus,* "woven thing." See **text.**]

tex·tu·al (tĕks′chōō-əl) *adj.* **1.** Of, pertaining to, or contained in a text. **2.** Based on or conforming to a text. **3.** Word for word; literal. —**tex′tu·al·ly** *adv.*

textual criticism. 1. A study of a written work that seeks to establish the original text. **2.** Literary criticism stressing scholarly study and analysis of the text.

tex·tu·al·ism (tĕks′chōō-ə-lĭz′əm) *n.* **1.** Strict adherence to a text, especially of the Scriptures. **2.** Textual criticism, especially of the Scriptures. —**tex′tu·al·ist** *n.*

tex·tu·ar·y (tĕks′chōō-ĕr′ē) *adj.* Of, pertaining to, or contained in a text; textual. —*n., pl.* **textuaries.** A specialist in the study of the Scriptures.

tex·ture (tĕks′chər) *n.* **1. a.** The appearance of a fabric resulting from the woven arrangement of its yarns or fibers. **b.** A surface appearance suggesting the weave of a fabric: *the rough texture of plowed fields.* **2.** A grainy, fibrous, woven, or dimensional quality as opposed to a uniformly flat, smooth aspect; surface interest: *Brick walls give a room texture.* **3.** *Fine Arts.* The representation of the structure of a surface as distinct from color or form. **4.** The composition or structure of a substance; grain: *the smooth texture of ivory.* **5.** Distinctive or identifying character: *the texture of suburban life.* [Originally, "weaving," from Latin *textūra,* from *textus,* woven thing. See **text.**] —**tex′tur·al** *adj.* —**tex′tur·al·ly** *adv.*

tex·tured (tĕks′chərd) *adj.* **1.** Having a particular kind of texture. Used in combination: *a rough-textured tweed.* **2.** Having marked texture: *a textured wall of stucco.*

tex·tus re·cep·tus (tĕks′təs rĭ-sĕp′təs). *Latin.* Received text; specifically, the received text of the Greek New Testament.

Te·zel. See Johann **Tetzel.**

T.F. *British.* Territorial Force.

tfr. transfer.

-th[1]. Indicates: **1.** The act or result of the act expressed in the verb root; for example, **spilth. 2.** The quality suggested by the adjective root; for example, **width.** [Middle English *-th(e),* Old English *-thu, -tho,* from Common Germanic *-ithō* (unattested).]

-th[2], **-eth.** Indicates ordinal numbers; for example, **millionth.** [Middle English *-the, -te,* Old English *-(o)tha, -(o)the.*]

-th[3]. See **-eth.**

Th The symbol for the element thorium.

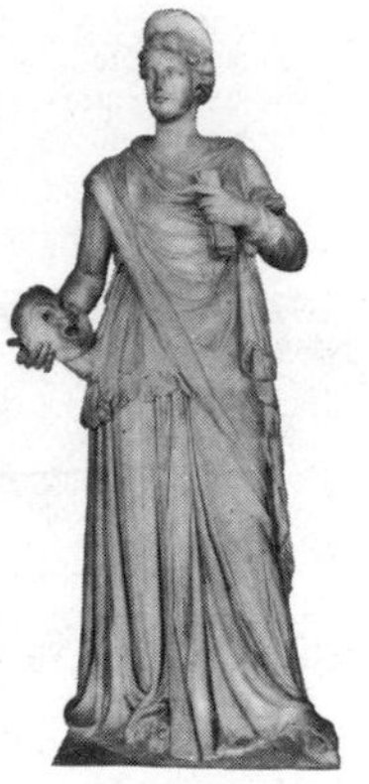
Thalia
Ancient Greek sculpture, the Louvre, Paris

Tha·ban·tsho·nya·na (tä′bän-chōn-yä′nä). The highest of the Drakensberg Mountains (11,425 feet) in Lesotho in southern Africa.

Thach, Edward. See Edward **Teach.**

Thack·er·ay (thăk′ə-rē, thăk′rē), **William Makepeace.** 1811–1863. English novelist.

Thad·de·us (thăd′ē-əs). A masculine given name. [Latin *Thaddaeus,* from Greek *Thaddaios,* from Hebrew *Taddáy.*]

Thai (tī) *n., pl.* **Thai.** Also **Tai. 1. a.** A native or citizen of Thailand. **b.** A member of the predominant ethnic group of Thailand, a people with both Mongoloid and Indonesian characteristics. **2. a.** A branch of the Sino-Tibetan family of languages, including several languages spoken throughout southeastern Asia. **b.** One of these languages, spoken as the official language of Thailand. Also called "Siamese." —*adj.* Also **Tai.** Of or pertaining to Thailand, its people, or its language. Also "Siamese."

Thai·land (tī′lănd′). Formerly **Si·am** (sī-ăm′). A kingdom of southeastern Asia, occupying 198,247 square miles between Burma and Cambodia and having a southern coastline on the Gulf of Siam. Population, 26,258,000. Capital, Bangkok.

thal·a·men·ceph·a·lon (thăl′ə-mĕn′sĕf′ə-lŏn′) *n. Anatomy.* The **diencephalon** *(see).* [THALAM(US) + ENCEPHALON.]

thal·a·mus (thăl′ə-məs) *n., pl.* **-mi** (-mī′). **1.** *Anatomy.* A large ovoid mass of gray matter that relays sensory stimuli to the cerebral cortex and acts in integrative and nonspecific functions. **2.** *Botany.* The receptacle of a flower. [New Latin, from Greek *thalamos,* inner chamber, possibly akin to *tholos*†, round building with a conical roof.] —**tha·lam′ic** (thə-lăm′ĭk) *adj.* —**tha·lam′i·cal·ly** *adv.*

tha·las·sic (thə-lăs′ĭk) *adj.* **1.** Of or pertaining to seas or oceans; pelagic. **2.** Of or pertaining to seas and gulfs as distinguished from the oceans. [French *thalassique,* from Greek *thalassa*†, sea.]

thal·as·soc·ra·cy (thăl′ə-sŏk′rə-sē) *n., pl.* **-cies.** Supremacy on the seas. [Greek *thalassokratia* : *thalassa,* sea (see **thalassic**) + -CRACY.] —**thal·as′so·crat′** (thə-lăs′ə-krăt′) *n.*

tha·ler. Variant of **taler.**

Tha·les (thā′lēz′). Called "Thales of Miletus." 640?–546? B.C. Greek philosopher and geometrician.

Tha·li·a (thə-lī′ə, thā′lē-ə, thāl′yə). **1.** The Greek Muse of comedy and pastoral poetry. **2.** One of the three Graces. [Greek *Thaleia,* "the blooming one," from *thallein,* to flourish. See **dhal-** in Appendix.*]

tha·lid·o·mide (thə-lĭd′ə-mīd′) *n.* A sedative and hypnotic drug, $C_{13}H_{10}N_2O_4$, withdrawn from sale because of association with fetal abnormalities. [(PH)THAL(IC ACID) + (IM)ID(E) + (I)MIDE.]

thal·lic (thăl′ĭk) *adj.* Of, pertaining to, or containing thallium, especially with valence 3.

thal·li·um (thăl′ē-əm) *n. Symbol* **Tl** A soft, malleable, highly toxic metallic element, used in rodent and ant poisons, in photocells, infrared detectors, and low-melting glass. Atomic number 81, atomic weight 204.37, melting point 303.5°C, boiling point 1,457°C, specific gravity 11.85, valences 1, 3. See **element.** [New Latin : Latin *thallus,* green shoot, THALLUS (from its green spectral line) + -IUM.]

thal·loid (thăl′oid′) *adj.* Also **thal·loi·dal** (thə-loid′l). Of, resembling, or constituting a thallus.

thal·lo·phyte (thăl′ə-fīt′) *n.* Any plant or plantlike organism of the division or subkingdom Thallophyta, which includes the algae, fungi, and bacteria. [New Latin *Thallophyta* : THALL(US) + -PHYTE.] —**thal′lo·phy′tic** (-fĭt′ĭk) *adj.*

thal·lous (thăl′əs) *adj.* Also **thal·li·ous** (thăl′ē-əs). Of, pertaining to, or containing thallium, especially with valence 1.

thal·lus (thăl′əs) *n., pl.* **thalli** (thăl′ī′, -ē′) or **-luses.** *Botany.* The undifferentiated stemless, rootless, leafless plant body characteristic of thallophytes. [New Latin, from Latin, young shoot, from Greek *thallos,* from *thallein,* to sprout. See **dhal-** in Appendix.*]

Thames (tĕmz). **1.** A river of England, rising in Gloucestershire and flowing 210 miles generally east past London to its wide estuary on the North Sea. **2.** A river of southern Ontario, flowing 160 miles southeast to Lake St. Clair; in the War of 1812, the Battle of the Thames, fought on its banks, ended in the defeat of British and Indian forces by the Americans and the death of Tecumseh (1813).

Tham·muz. Variant of **Tammuz.**

Tham·u·ga·di, Tham·u·ga·dis. Ancient names for **Timgad.**

than (*th*ăn) *conj.* **1.** Used in comparative statements to introduce the second element or clause of a comparison of inequality: *Pie is richer than cake.* **2.** Used in statements of preference to introduce the rejected alternative: *I would rather dance than eat.* **3.** Used with the sense of "beyond" with adverbs of degree or quantity: *Read more than the first paragraph.* —**other than.** Apart from; except for. [Middle English *than(ne),* Old English *thanne, thænne.* See **to-** in Appendix.*]

Usage: In sentences involving comparison, *than* is usually construed as a conjunction rather than as a preposition, especially in formal usage. Accordingly, the case of the word following *than* is felt to be governed by its function in the clause introduced by *than: He speaks better than I do.* This is true also of elliptical clauses in which the unexpressed words are clearly indicated: *He is a better speaker than I* (that is, *than I am*). *The students disliked no one more than her* (that is, *than they disliked her*). In the first example, *I* is construed as the subject of an unexpressed verb; in the second, *her* is construed as an object. In both examples, the words following *than* agree in case with their antecedents (the first members of the comparisons, *he* and *no one*).

Less formally, in some writing and especially in speech, *than* is construed as a preposition in such examples, and the word following *than* is in the objective case. Moreover, in some examples, either a nominative or objective pronoun can be justified when *than* is construed as a conjunction: *We had no more faithful friend than she* (*she* construed as the subject of the unexpressed *was*). *We had no more faithful friend than her* (*her* construed as in agreement with the object *friend*).

In the construction *than whom*, the pronoun is always objective: *Napoleon, than whom no more romantic soldier lived, is the subject of a new book.* See also Usage note at **different.**

than·age (thăn′ĭj) *n.* **1.** The rank, jurisdiction, or office of a thane; thaneship. **2.** The land held by a thane.

than·a·top·sis (thăn′ə-tŏp′sĭs) *n.* A meditation upon death. [Greek *thanatos,* death, THANATOS + -OPSIS.]

Than·a·tos (thăn′ə-tŏs′) *n.* **1.** Death as a personification or as a philosophical notion. **2.** *Small* **t.** An alleged instinct to self-destruction; the death wish. [Greek, "death." See **dhwene-** in Appendix.*] —**than′a·tot′ic** (-tŏt′ĭk) *adj.*

thane (thān) *n.* Also **thegn. 1.** In Anglo-Saxon England: **a.** A freeman granted land by the king in return for military service. **b.** A man ranking above an ordinary freeman and below a nobleman. **2.** A feudal lord or baron in Scotland. [Middle English *thayn, theyn,* Old English *theg(e)n.* See **tek-1** in Appendix.*]

thane·ship (thān′shĭp′) *n.* The position or office of a thane, especially in Scotland.

Than·ja·vur (tän′jä-vûr′). Also **Tan·jore** (tăn-jôr′, -jōr′). A city of Madras State, India. Population, 114,000.

thank (thăngk) *tr.v.* **thanked, thanking, thanks. 1.** To express gratitude to; give thanks to. Often used in the phrase *thank you,* with the subject *I* understood. **2.** To hold responsible; credit; blame. [Middle English *thanken,* Old English *thancian.* See **tong-** in Appendix.*]

thank·ful (thăngk′fəl) *adj.* **1.** Grateful. **2.** Expressive of thanks. —**thank′ful·ly** *adv.* —**thank′ful·ness** *n.*

thank·less (thăngk′lĭs) *adj.* **1.** Not feeling or showing gratitude; ungrateful. **2.** Not apt to be appreciated: *a thankless task.* —**thank′less·ly** *adv.* —**thank′less·ness** *n.*

thanks (thăngks) *pl.n.* **1.** An acknowledgment of a favor, gift, or benefit; gratitude. **2.** An expression of gratitude: *to give thanks.* —**thanks to. 1.** Thanks be given to. **2.** On account of; because of. —*interj.* Used to express thanks.

thanks·giv·er (thăngks′gĭv′ər) *n.* One who gives thanks.

thanks·giv·ing (thăngks′gĭv′ĭng) *n.* An act of giving thanks; an expression of gratitude, especially to God.

Thanksgiving Day. A national holiday set apart for giving thanks to God, celebrated in the United States on the fourth Thursday of November and in Canada on the second Monday of October. Also called "Thanksgiving."

thank·wor·thy (thăngk′wûr′thē) *adj.* Worthy of thanks.

thank-you-ma′am (thăngk′yŏŏ-măm′) *n.* A bump in a road that causes the jolted passenger to give the appearance of bowing or nodding.

Thant (thänt), **U** Born 1909. Burmese diplomat; secretary-general of the United Nations since 1961.

Thap·sus (thăp′səs). An ancient city on the eastern coast of Tunisia; the site of a battle in which Julius Caesar defeated the followers of Pompey (46 B.C.).

Thar Desert (tär). A vast sandy region occupying about 100,000 square miles in northwestern India and eastern West Pakistan. Also called "Indian Desert," "Great Indian Desert."

Tha·sos (thā′sŏs′). Also **Thá·sos** (thä′sôs′). An island of Greece, 170 square miles in area, in the northern Aegean Sea.

that (thăt; *unstressed* thət) *adj., pl.* **those** (thōz). **1.** Being the one singled out, implied, or understood. **2.** Being the one further removed or less obvious: *this card or that card.* **3.** *Archaic.* Such: *"I heard a humming,/And that a strange one too"* (Shakespeare). —*pron., pl.* **those. 1.** Used as a demonstrative pronoun with the sense of: **a.** The one designated, implied, mentioned, or understood. **b.** The further or less immediate one. **2.** Used as a relative pronoun to introduce a clause, especially a restrictive clause. See Usage note below. **3.** Something: *There is that about him which mystifies me.* —*adv.* To such an extent or degree; to that extent; so: *Is it that complicated?* —*conj.* **1.** Used chiefly to introduce a subordinate clause stating a fact, wish, consequence, or reason: *We supposed that you were lost. We arranged the party that you might come.* See Usage note below. **2.** Used to introduce an elliptical exclamation of desire: *Oh, that I were rich!* [Middle English *that,* Old English *thæt.* See **to-** in Appendix.*]

Usage: That, which, and *who* (*whom*) are the most commonly employed relative pronouns (those used to introduce clauses). *That* refers to persons, animals, and things; *which,* usually only to animals and things; and *who* (*whom*), to persons. Only *which* and *whom* are possible following prepositions. Otherwise, the choice between *that* and *which* (involving things) and between *that* and *who* or *whom* (referring to persons) is influenced by the functions of the clauses these relative pronouns introduce.

That is now largely confined to restrictive clauses, or clauses that define and limit the antecedent by providing information necessary for full comprehension of the sentence: *A law that is not supported by the public cannot be enforced.* Such clauses are never set off by commas, and sometimes the relative pronoun is not expressed or can be dropped: *a law not supported by . . . .* Contrary to popular misconception, *that* is not an informal or imprecise pronoun.

Which, who, and *whom* are particularly appropriate for introducing nonrestrictive (nondefining) clauses, or those that

provide incidental or nonessential information: *The law, which was enacted in 1867, soon came under challenge in the courts.* Such clauses are usually set off by commas and in theory are capable of being enclosed within parentheses.

Because the distinction between restrictive and nonrestrictive clauses is not always easy to make, the choice between relative pronouns often rests on personal interpretation. In addition, *who* and *whom* are used for clauses of both types. Many also employ *which* (for *that*) to introduce clauses that are clearly restrictive. Thus, in the first example (*a law that is not supported by the public . . .*), *which* is acceptable to 54 per cent of the Usage Panel, though many of that number specify *that* as the preferable choice. *Which* is invariably used for clauses of both types when the relative pronoun is preceded by *that* used as a demonstrative pronoun: *It is larger than that which you mentioned.*

In some instances, careful discrimination between *which* and *that* is essential to clarity: *The typewriter, which needs cleaning, is on the front table. The typewriter that needs cleaning is on the front table.* The second example implies that there is more than one typewriter involved. See also Usage note at **this.**

That (conjunction) is frequently omitted in speech and less often in writing, where there is no danger of ambiguity: *He said* (*that*) *he would go.* It should never be omitted at the expense of clarity. It is usually essential to clarity where *that* adjoins a reference to time and in sentences in which *that* introduces parallel clauses: *The mayor declared that on January first the fund would be exhausted. He said that most of the money has already been spent and that some of the expenditures are open to criticism.* In the latter example, the first *that* might be dispensed with without causing ambiguity, but not the second, which links its clause to the speaker.

thatch (thăch) *n.* **1.** Plant stalks or foliage, as reeds or palm fronds, used for roofing. **2.** Something resembling this, especially the hair of the head. —*tr.v.* **thatched, thatching, thatches.** To cover with or as if with thatch. [Middle English *thacche,* from *thacchen,* to thatch, cover, Old English *theccan.* See **steg-1** in Appendix.*] —**thatch′er** *n.* —**thatch′y** *adj.*

thau·ma·tol·o·gy (thô′mə-tŏl′ə-jē) *n., pl.* **-gies.** The study of or a discourse on miracles. [Greek *thauma*† (stem *thaumat-*), wonder, marvel + -LOGY.]

thau·ma·turge (thô′mə-tûrj′) *n.* Also **thau·ma·tur·gist** (-tûr′jĭst). A performer of miracles or magic feats. [Medieval Latin *thaumaturgus,* from Greek *thaumatourgos : thauma,* wonder (see **thaumatology**) + -*ergos,* "working," from *ergon,* work (see **werg-1** in Appendix*).]

thau·ma·tur·gy (thô′mə-tûr′jē) *n.* The working of miracles or wonders; magic. —**thau′ma·tur′gic, thau′ma·tur′gi·cal** *adj.*

thaw (thô) *v.* **thawed, thawing, thaws.** —*intr.* **1.** To change from a frozen solid to a liquid by gradual warming. **2.** To lose stiffness, numbness, or impermeability by being warmed. **3.** To become warm enough for snow and ice to melt. Used of the weather. **4.** To become less reserved; relax. —*tr.* To melt (a frozen solid) by gradual warming. —See Synonyms at **melt.** —*n.* **1.** The process of thawing. **2.** A period of warm weather during which ice and snow melt. **3.** A relaxation of reserve, restraints, or tensions. [Middle English *thawen,* Old English *thāwian.* See **tā-** in Appendix.*]

Thay·er (thā′ər), **Sylvanus.** 1785 1872. American military leader and educator; superintendent of U.S. Military Academy (1817–33).

Th.D. Doctor of Theology (Latin *Theologiae Doctor*).

the1 (thē *before a vowel;* thə *before a consonant*). The definite article, functioning as an adjective. It is used: **1.** Before singular or plural nouns and noun phrases that denote particular specified persons or things. **2.** Before a singular noun, making it generic: *the human arm.* **3.** Before a noun, and generally stressed, emphasizing its uniqueness or prominence: *That's* THE *show to see this year.* **4.** Before a title of rank or office, designating its holder: *The President arrives tomorrow.* **5.** Before an adjective, extending it to signify a class and giving it the function of a noun: *the rich; the beautiful.* **6.** Before an adjective used absolutely: *the finest we have to offer.* **7.** Before a present participle, signifying the action in the abstract: *the weaving of rugs.* **8.** Before a noun, with the force of *per:* *at a dollar the box.* [Middle English *the,* Old English *thĕ* (originally a demonstrative adjective, later superseding *sē,* masculine singular). See **to-** in Appendix.*]

the2 (thē *before a vowel;* thə *before a consonant*) *adv.* To that extent; by that much: *the sooner the better.* [Middle English *the, thi,* Old English *thy̆, thē,* instrumental case of *thĕ,* THE, and *thæt,* THAT.]

the·an·throp·ic (thē′ăn-thrŏp′ĭk) *adj.* Also **the·an·throp·i·cal** (-ĭ-kəl). Both divine and human in nature or quality. [From Late Greek *theanthrōpos :* THEO- + Greek *anthrōpos,* man (see **ner-2** in Appendix*).]

the·an·thro·pism (thē-ăn′thrə-pĭz′əm) *n.* **1.** The attribution of human traits to God; anthropomorphism. **2.** *Theology.* The doctrine of the union of human and divine natures in Christ. —**the·an′thro·pist** *n.*

the·ar·chy (thē′är-kē) *n., pl.* **-chies. 1.** Government or rule by God or a god; theocracy. **2.** A hierarchy or order of gods. [Late Greek *thearkhia :* THE(O)- + -ARCHY.]

the·a·ter (thē′ə-tər) *n.* Also **the·a·tre.** *Abbr.* **theat. 1.** A building, room, or, formerly, an outdoor structure for the presentation of plays, motion pictures, or other dramatic performances. **2.** Any room with tiers of seats used for lectures or demonstrations; auditorium. **3. a.** Dramatic literature or performance. **b.** The milieu of actors and playwrights. **c.** The quality or effectiveness

U Thant
Photographed in 1965

ă pat/ā pay/âr care/ä father/b bib/ch church/d deed/ĕ pet/ē be/f fife/g gag/h hat/hw which/ĭ pit/ī pie/îr pier/j judge/k kick/l lid, needle/m mum/n no, sudden/ng thing/ŏ pot/ō toe/ô paw, for/oi noise/ou out/ŏŏ took/ōō boot/p pop/r roar/s sauce/sh ship, dish/
t tight/th thin, path/th this, bathe/ŭ cut/ûr urge/v valve/w with/y yes/z zebra, size/zh vision/ə about, item, edible, gallop, circus/
à *Fr.* ami/œ *Fr.* feu, *Ger.* schön/ü *Fr.* tu, *Ger.* über/KH *Ger.* ich, *Scot.* loch/N *Fr.* bon. *Follows main vocabulary. †Of obscure origin.

of a theatrical production: *This play is good theater.* **4.** The audience assembled for a dramatic performance. **5. a.** A place that is the setting for dramatic events. **b.** A large geographical area in which military operations are coordinated. [Middle English *theatre,* from Old French, from Latin *theātrum,* from Greek *theatron,* from *theasthai,* to watch, look at, from *thea†,* a viewing.]

the·a·ter·go·er (thē′ə-tər-gō′ər) *n.* A person who often attends the theater.

the·a·ter-in-the-round (thē′ə-tər-ĭn-thə-round′) *n., pl.* **theaters-in-the-round** (thē′ə-tərz-). An arena theater *(see).*

the·at·ri·cal (thē-ăt′rĭ-kəl) *adj.* Also **the·at·ric** (-ăt′rĭk). **1.** Of, relating to, or suitable for the theater or dramatic performance. **2.** Marked by the self-display or the exaggerated manner associated with actors; affectedly dramatic. —*n.* A dramatic performance, especially by amateurs. Usually used in the plural. —**the·at′ri·cal·ly** *adv.* —**the·at′ri·cal′i·ty,** **the·at′ri·cal·ness** *n.*

the·at·ri·cal·ism (thē-ăt′rĭ-kə-lĭz′əm) *n.* Theatrical manner or style; showiness; exhibitionism.

the·at·rics (thē-ăt′rĭks) *pl.n.* **1.** The art of the theater. Used with a singular verb. **2.** Theatrical effects or mannerisms; histrionics.

the·ba·ine (thē′bə-ēn′, thə-bā′ēn′) *n.* A poisonous alkaloid, $C_{19}H_{21}NO_3$, obtained from opium. Also called "paramorphine." [New Latin *thebaia,* (herb of) Thebes, Egyptian opium + -INE.]

Thebes (thēbz). **1.** An ancient religious and political capital of Upper Egypt, on the Nile about 450 miles south of present-day Cairo. **2.** An ancient city of east-central Greece, the chief city of ancient Boeotia until destroyed by Alexander the Great in 336 B.C. —**The′ban** *adj. & n.*

the·ca (thē′kə) *n., pl.* **-cae** (-kē′, -kī′). *Biology.* A case, covering, or sheath, such as the spore case of a moss capsule or the outer covering of the pupa of certain insects. [New Latin, from Latin *thēca,* a case, sheath, from Greek *thēkē.* See dhē-¹ in Appendix.*] —**the′cal** *adj.*

the·cate (thē′kāt′) *adj.* Having a theca; encased or sheathed.

thee (thē) *pron. Archaic & Poetic.* The objective case of the second person pronoun thou. It is used: **1.** As the direct object of a verb: *He smote thee.* **2.** As the indirect object of a verb: *He gave thee hope.* **3.** As the object of a preposition: *This he gave to thee.* **4.** After *than* or *as* in comparisons in which the first term is in the objective case: *He gave us more than thee.* See Usage note at **than. 5.** *Nonstandard.* Used in the nominative as well as the objective case in certain religious communities, especially in the Society of Friends in the 19th century.

thee·lin (thē′lĭn) *n.* A female sex hormone, **estrone** *(see).* [Greek *thēlus,* female (see dhēi- in Appendix*) + -IN.]

theft (thĕft) *n.* **1.** The act or an instance of stealing; larceny. **2.** *Obsolete.* That which is stolen. [Middle English *theft(he),* Old English *thēofth,* from Common Germanic *thiufith* (unattested), from *thiuf* (unattested), THIEF.]

thegn. Variant of **thane.**

Thei·ler (tī′lər), **Max.** Born 1899. South African-born American microbiologist; developed yellow-fever vaccine.

their (thâr) *adj.* The possessive form of the pronoun *they.* Used attributively to indicate possession, agency, or reception of an action by the speaker: *their house; pursuing their tasks; suffered their first defeat.* [Middle English, from Old Norse *their(r)a* (genitive plural). See **to-** in Appendix.*]

theirs (thârz). Possessive pronoun, absolute form of *their.* **1.** Belonging to them; their own. Used predicatively: *The choice ought to be theirs.* **2.** The one or ones that belong or pertain to them. Used substantively: *Mine is here, and theirs is the one on the stairs.* —**of theirs.** Belonging to them. [Middle English, from THEIR.]

the·ism (thē′ĭz′əm) *n.* Belief in the existence of a god or gods; especially, belief in a personal God as creator and ruler of the world. Compare **deism, pantheism.** [THE(O)- + -ISM.] —**the′ist** *n.* —**the·is′tic, the·is′ti·cal** *adj.* —**the·is′ti·cal·ly** *adv.*

Theiss. The German name for **Tisza.**

Thel·ma (thĕl′mə). A feminine given name. [Origin uncertain.]

The·lon (thē′lŏn). A river of the Northwest Territories, Canada, rising in southeastern Mackenzie District and flowing 550 miles generally north and then east to Baker Lake.

them (thĕm) *pron.* The objective case of the third person pronoun *they.* It is used: **1.** As the direct object of a verb: *She accompanied them.* **2.** As the indirect object of a verb: *He offered them a new contract.* **3.** As the object of a preposition: *It was ruined by them.* **4.** After *than* or *as* in comparisons in which the first term is in the objective case: *She liked us more than them.* See Usage note at **than.** [Middle English *the(i)m,* partly from Old Norse *theim,* partly from Old English *thǣm.* See **to-** in Appendix.*]

the·mat·ic (thĭ-măt′ĭk) *adj.* **1.** Of, constituting, or relating to a theme or themes. **2.** *Linguistics.* Constituting the theme or stem of a word. [Greek *thematikos,* from *thema* (stem *themat-*), proposition, THEME.] —**the·mat′i·cal·ly** *adv.*

theme (thēm) *n.* **1.** A topic of discourse or discussion, often expressible as a phrase, proposition, or question. **2.** An idea, point of view, or perception embodied and expanded upon in a work of art; an underlying or essential subject of artistic representation: *the theme of the noble savage traced through British and American poetry.* **3.** A short composition assigned to a student as a writing exercise. **4.** *Music.* A melody forming the basis of variations or other development in a composition. **5.** *Linguistics.* A stem. —See Synonyms at **subject.** [Middle English *t(h)eme,* theme (of a discussion), from Old French *teme,* from Latin *thema,* from Greek, "thing placed," proposition. See dhē-¹ in Appendix.*]

theme song. 1. A melody or song played throughout a dramatic performance and often intended to convey a mood. **2.** A song that is identified with a performer, group, or radio or television program; a signature.

The·mis·to·cles (thə-mĭs′tə-klēz′). 527?–460? B.C. Athenian military and political leader; commanded victorious fleet at Salamis; exiled.

them·selves (thĕm′sĕlvz′, thəm′-) *pron.* A specialized form of the third person plural pronoun. It is used: **1.** As a reflexive pronoun forming the direct or indirect object of a verb or the object of a preposition. **2.** As an intensifying or emphasizing addition to the third person plural. **3.** As an indication of (their) accustomed or normal state: *The members of the cast were themselves again after the crisis passed.*

then (thĕn) *adv.* **1.** At that time in the past: *I was younger then.* **2.** Next in time, space, or order; immediately afterward. **3.** At another time in the future: *"now we see through a glass, darkly; but then face to face"* (I Corinthians 13:12). **4.** In that case; accordingly. **5.** In addition; moreover; besides. **6.** Yet; on the other hand. —*n.* A particular time or moment: *Until then let's remain here.* —*adj.* Being so at that time: *the then headmistress.* [Middle English *thenne, thann,* Old English *thanne, thænne.* See **to-** in Appendix.*]

the·nar (thē′när) *n.* The fleshy mass on the palm of the hand at the base of the thumb. —*adj.* Of, pertaining to, or related to the thenar. [Greek *thenar,* palm of the hand. See dhen-² in Appendix.*]

thence (thĕns, thĕns) *adv.* **1.** From that place; from there. **2.** From that time; thenceforth. **3.** From that circumstance or source; therefrom. [Middle English *thannes,* from *thanne,* from there, Old English *thanon.* See **to-** in Appendix.*]

thence·forth (thĕns-fôrth′, thĕns-) *adv.* From that time forward; thereafter.

thence·for·ward (thĕns-fôr′wərd, thĕns-) *adv.* Also **thence·for·wards** (-wərdz). **1.** Thenceforth. **2.** From that time or place onward.

theo-, the-. Indicates a god or gods; for example, **theism, theobromine.** [From Greek *theos,* god. See dhēs- in Appendix.*]

the·o·bro·mine (thē′ō-brō′mēn′) *n.* A bitter, colorless alkaloid, $C_7H_8N_4O_2$, that occurs in chocolate products, is derived principally from the cacao bean, and is used as a diuretic and a nerve stimulant. [New Latin *Theobroma,* "food of the gods," genus including the cacao tree : THEO- + Greek *brōma,* food (see gwere-² in Appendix*) + -INE.]

the·o·cen·tric (thē′ō-sĕn′trĭk) *adj.* Centering on God as the prime concern: *a theocentric cosmology.*

the·oc·ra·cy (thē-ŏk′rə-sē) *n., pl.* **-cies. 1.** Government by a god regarded as the ruling power or by priests or officials claiming divine sanction. **2.** A state so governed. [Greek *theokratia* : THEO- + -CRACY.]

the·o·crat (thē′ə-krăt′) *n.* **1.** A ruler of a theocracy. **2.** A believer in theocracy. —**the′o·crat′ic, the′o·crat′i·cal** *adj.* —**the′o·crat′i·cal·ly** *adv.*

The·oc·ri·tus (thē-ŏk′rə-təs). Greek pastoral poet of the third century B.C.

the·od·i·cy (thē-ŏd′ə-sē) *n., pl.* **-cies.** A vindication of divine justice in the face of the existence of evil. [French *Théodicée,* title of a work (1710) by Leibnitz : THEO- + Greek *dikē,* judgment (see deik- in Appendix*).]

the·od·o·lite (thē-ŏd′ə-līt′) *n.* A surveying instrument used to measure horizontal and vertical angles with a small telescope that can move in horizontal and vertical planes. [New Latin *theodelitus†.*]

The·o·do·ra (thē′ə-dôr′ə). A.D. 508?–548. Empress of the Eastern Roman Empire; wife and adviser of Justinian I.

The·o·dore (thē′ə-dôr′). A masculine given name. [Greek *theodoros,* gift of God : THEO- + *dōron,* gift (see dō- in Appendix*).]

The·od·o·ric (thē-ŏd′ər-ĭk). Called "the Great." A.D. 454?–526. King of the Ostrogoths (A.D. 474–526); founded Ostrogothic Kingdom in Italy (A.D. 493).

The·o·do·si·op·o·lis (thē-ō-dō′sī-ŏp′ə-lĭs). The ancient name for **Erzurum.**

The·o·do·sius I (thē′ə-dō′shəs). Called "the Great." A.D. 346?–395. Roman Emperor (A.D. 379–395); made peace with Goths; ruled jointly with Valentinian II (A.D. 372–392) and Gratian *(see).*

the·og·o·ny (thē-ŏg′ə-nē) *n., pl.* **-nies.** A recitation of the origin and genealogy of the gods, especially as in ancient epic poetry. [Greek *theogonia* : THEO- + -GONY.] —**the′o·gon′ic** (-ə-gŏn′ĭk) *adj.* —**the·og′o·nist** *n.*

theol. theologian; theological; theology.

the·o·lo·gi·an (thē′ə-lō′jən) *n. Abbr.* **theol.** One versed in theology, especially Christian theology.

the·o·log·i·cal (thē′ə-lŏj′ĭ-kəl) *adj.* Also **the·o·log·ic** (-lŏj′ĭk). *Abbr.* **theol.** Of or pertaining to a theology or religious philosophy. —**the′o·log′i·cal·ly** *adv.*

the·ol·o·gize (thē-ŏl′ə-jīz′) *v.* **-gized, -gizing, -gizes.** —*tr.* To make theological in form or significance. —*intr.* To speculate about theology. —**the·ol′o·giz′er** *n.*

the·ol·o·gy (thē-ŏl′ə-jē) *n., pl.* **-gies.** *Abbr.* **theol. 1.** The study of the nature of God and religious truth; rational inquiry into religious questions, especially those posed by Christianity. **2.** An organized, often formalized body of opinions concerning God and man's relationship to God. [Middle English *theologie,* from Old French, from Latin *theologia,* from Greek : THEO- + -LOGY.]

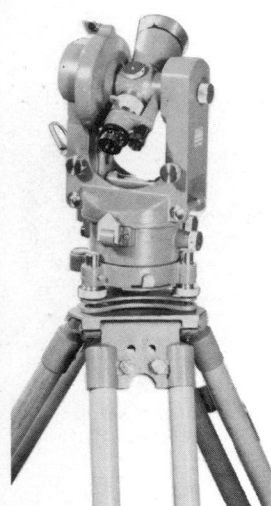

theodolite

the·om·a·chy (thē-ŏm′ə-kē) *n., pl.* **-chies.** Strife or battle among gods, as in the Homeric poems. [Late Latin *theomachia,* from Greek *theomakhia* : THEO- + *makhē,* battle, from *makhesthai,* to battle (see **magh-²** in Appendix*).]

the·o·mor·phism (thē′ō-môr′fĭz′əm) *n.* The depiction or conception of man as having the form of a god. [THEO- + MORPH(O)- + -ISM.] —**the′o·mor′phic** *adj.*

the·oph·a·ny (thē-ŏf′ə-nē) *n., pl.* **-nies.** An appearance of God or of a god to a man; a divine manifestation. [Medieval Latin *theophania,* from Late Greek *theophaneia* : THEO- + Greek *phainein,* to show (see **bhā-¹** in Appendix*).]

The·o·phras·tus (thē′ə-frăs′təs). Greek philosopher, botanist, and author of the late fourth and early third centuries B.C.

the·o·phyl·line (thē′ə-fĭl′ēn′, -fĭ′lēn′) *n.* A colorless crystalline alkaloid, $C_7H_8N_4O_2.H_2O$, derived from tea leaves and also made synthetically, used as a diuretic and cardiac stimulant. [THEO-(BROMINE) + PHYLL(O)- + -INE.]

the·or·bo (thē-ôr′bō) *n., pl.* **-bos.** A 17th-century lute having two sets of strings and an S-shaped neck with two sets of pegs, one set above and somewhat to the side of the other. [Italian *tiorba*†.]

the·o·rem (thē′ə-rəm, thîr′əm) *n.* **1.** An idea that is demonstrably true or is assumed to be so. **2.** *Mathematics.* **a.** A proposition that is provable on the basis of explicit assumptions. **b.** A proven proposition. [Late Latin *theōrēma,* from Greek, spectacle, intuition, theorem, from *theōrein,* to observe, look at, from *theōros,* spectator, from *thea,* a looking at. See **theater.**]

the·o·ret·i·cal (thē′ə-rĕt′ĭ-kəl) *adj.* Also **the·o·ret·ic** (-rĕt′ĭk). **1.** Pertaining to or based on theory. **2.** Restricted to theory; lacking verification or practical application. Compare **applied. 3.** Broadly, hypothetical or speculative; unproved or uncertain. [Late Latin *theōrēticus,* from Greek *theōrētikos,* able to perceive, from *theōretos,* observable, from *theōrein,* to observe. See **theorem.**] —**the′o·ret′i·cal·ly** *adv.*

the·o·re·ti·cian (thē′ər-ə-tĭsh′ən) *n.* A student of theory in an art or science.

the·o·ret·ics (thē′ə-rĕt′ĭks) *n.* Plural in form, used with a singular verb. The theoretical part of a science or art; principles.

the·o·rist (thē′ər-ĭst) *n.* A person who theorizes; a theoretician.

the·o·rize (thē′ə-rīz′) *intr.v.* **-rized, -rizing, -rizes. 1.** To formulate or analyze theories. **2.** To analyze by means of theory. **3.** To speculate. —**the′o·ri·za′tion** *n.* —**the′o·riz′er** *n.*

the·o·ry (thē′ə-rē, thîr′ē) *n., pl.* **-ries. 1. a.** Systematically organized knowledge applicable in a relatively wide variety of circumstances; especially, a system of assumptions, accepted principles, and rules of procedure devised to analyze, predict, or otherwise explain the nature or behavior of a specified set of phenomena. **b.** Such knowledge or such a system distinguished from experiment or practice. **2.** Abstract reasoning; speculation. **3.** Broadly, hypothesis or supposition. [Late Latin *theōria,* from Greek, contemplation, theory, from *theōros,* spectator, from *theasthai,* to observe, from *thea,* a viewing. See **theater.**]

theory of games. *Mathematics.* **Game theory** *(see).*

the·os·o·phy (thē-ŏs′ə-fē) *n., pl.* **-phies. 1.** Religious speculation dealing with the mystical apprehension of God, associated with various occult systems. **2.** *Often capital* **T.** The doctrines and beliefs of a modern religious sect, the Theosophical Society, incorporating aspects of Buddhism and Brahmanism. [Medieval Latin *theosophia,* from Late Greek *theosophia* : THEO- + -SOPHY.] —**the′o·soph′ic** (-ə-sŏf′ĭk), **the′o·soph′i·cal** *adj.* —**the′o·soph′i·cal·ly** *adv.* —**the·os′o·phist** *n.*

The·ra. See **Thira.**

therap. therapeutic; therapeutics.

ther·a·peu·tic (thĕr′ə-pyōō′tĭk) *adj.* Also **ther·a·peu·ti·cal** (-tĭ-kəl). *Abbr.* **therap. 1.** Having healing or curative powers; gradually or methodically ameliorative. **2.** Of or pertaining to therapeutics. [Greek *therapeutikos,* from *therapeutēs,* one who administers, from *therapeuein,* to administer to (medically). See **therapy.**] —**ther′a·peu′ti·cal·ly** *adv.*

ther·a·peu·tics (thĕr′ə-pyōō′tĭks) *n.* Plural in form, usually used with a singular verb. *Abbr.* **therap.** The medical treatment of disease. —**ther′a·peu′tist** *n.*

ther·a·pist (thĕr′ə-pĭst) *n.* A specialist in conducting therapy, as in physical therapy or psychotherapy.

ther·a·py (thĕr′ə-pē) *n., pl.* **-pies. 1.** The treatment of illness or disability. Often used in combination: *hydrotherapy.* **2.** Healing power or quality. **3. Psychotherapy** *(see).* [New Latin *therapia,* from Greek *therapeia,* service, from *therapeuein,* to be an attendant, from *theraps* (stem *therap-*), attendant, from Anatolian.]

Ther·a·va·da (thĕr′ə-vä′dä) *n.* A branch of Buddhism, **Hinayana** *(see).* [Pali *theravāda,* "doctrine of the elders" : *thera,* old, elder, from Sanskrit *sthavira,* thick, stout, old (see **stā-** in Appendix*) + *vāda,* speech, doctrine, from Sanskrit, sound, statement (see **wed-²** in Appendix*).]

there (*th*âr) *adv.* **1.** At or in that place. Often used as an intensifier: *Arthur there is our best writer.* **2.** To, into, or toward that place; thither: *run there.* **3.** At a point of action or time: *Start the tenors there.* **4.** Used as an introductory expletive: *There exist ten survivors here.* See Usage note below. —*n.* That place: *There is where I should like to live.* —*interj.* Used to express emotion, as relief, satisfaction, or consolation: *There, now I can have some peace!* [Middle English *ther(e),* Old English *thǣr, thēr.* See **to-** in Appendix.*]

Usage: *There* frequently precedes a linking verb such as *be, seem,* or *appear* in beginning a sentence or clause: *There has been much trouble.* The number of the verb is governed by the subject, which in such constructions follows the verb: *There is a garage across the street. There seem to be many good candidates.* But a singular verb is also possible before a compound subject whose parts are joined by a conjunction or conjunctions, especially when the parts are singular: *There is much pain and toil involved. There appears to be a man and a wagon in the distance.* When the first element of such a subject is singular, a singular verb is also possible even though the other elements are plural: *There was* (or *were*) *a man and two children in the car.* But: *There were two children and a man. There* (adverb), meaning *in that place,* comes after the noun, not before it, in constructions introduced by the demonstrative *that: That boy there is to blame* (not *that there boy*).

-there. Indicates an extinct mammalian form; for example, **megathere.** [New Latin *-therium,* from Greek *thērion,* diminutive of *thēr,* beast. See **ghwer-** in Appendix.*]

there·a·bout (*th*âr′ə-bout′) *adv.* Also **there·a·bouts** (-bouts′). Approximately: *She was thirty or thereabout.*

there·af·ter (*th*âr′ăf′tər, -äf′tər) *adv.* From a specified time onward; from then on: *an apprentice for three years, an assistant thereafter.*

there·a·gainst (*th*âr′ə-gĕnst′) *adv.* Against or in opposition to; contrary to.

there·at (*th*âr′ăt′) *adv.* **1.** At a specified place; there. **2.** At such time; on that occasion. **3.** By reason of that: *He was acclaimed victor and was pleased thereat.*

there·by (*th*âr′bī′) *adv.* **1.** Through or with the agency of; by that means; as a result. **2.** In a specified connection or relation wherein.

there·for (*th*âr′fôr′) *adv. Archaic.* For that, this, or it.

there·fore (*th*âr′fôr′, -fōr′) *adv.* For that reason; consequently; hence: *Your information is inaccurate and your conclusion therefore wrong.* Often used as a conjunction: *I lost my money; therefore, I could not buy a ticket.*

there·from (*th*âr′frŏm′, -frŭm′) *adv.* From that, this, or it; coming from that time, location, or thing.

there·in (*th*âr′ĭn′, *th*âr′ĭn′) *adv.* In that place or context.

there·in·af·ter (*th*âr′ĭn-ăf′tər, -äf′tər) *adv.* In a later or subsequent portion, as of a speech or book.

Ther·e·min (thĕr′ə-mĭn) *n.* Also **ther·e·min.** The trademark for an electronic consolelike musical instrument often used for high tremolo effects. Pitch and volume are "space-controlled" by movement of the player's hands over and between the two antennal oscillators. [Invented by Leo *Theremin* (born 1896), Russian engineer.]

there·of (*th*âr′ŏv′, -ŭv′) *adv.* **1.** Of or concerning this, that, or it. **2.** From or because of a stated cause or origin; therefrom.

there·on (*th*âr′ŏn′, -ôn′) *adv.* **1.** On or upon this, that, or it. **2.** Following that immediately; thereupon.

The·re·sa. Variant of **Teresa.**

The·re·sa (tə-rē′sə, -rēs′ə), **Saint.** Also **Te·re·sa.** Known as Theresa of Ávila. 1515–1582. Spanish Carmelite nun; founded reformed order of Carmelites; canonized in 1622.

Thé·rèse de Li·sieux (tā-rĕz′ də lē-zyœ′), **Saint.** Original name, Marie Françoise Thérèse Martin. 1873–1897. French Carmelite nun; canonized in 1925.

there·to (*th*âr′tōō′) *adv.* **1.** To that, this, or it; thereunto. **2.** *Archaic.* In addition to that; furthermore.

there·to·fore (*th*âr′tə-fôr′, -fōr′) *adv.* Until or prior to a specified time; before that.

there·un·der (*th*âr′ŭn′dər) *adv.* Under this, that, or it.

there·un·to (*th*âr′ŭn-tōō′) *adv.* To that, this, or it.

there·up·on (*th*âr′ə-pŏn′, -ə-pôn′) *adv.* **1.** Upon this, that, or it; concerning a specified subject or object. **2.** Directly following that.

there·with (*th*âr′wĭth′, -wĭ*th*′) *adv.* **1.** With that, this, or it. **2.** In addition to that. **3.** Immediately thereafter.

there·with·al (*th*âr′wĭth-ôl′) *adv.* **1.** With all that, this, or it; besides. **2.** *Obsolete.* Therewith; with that, this, or it.

the·ri·o·mor·phic (thîr′ē-ə-môr′fĭk) *adj.* Also **the·ri·o·mor·phous** (-fəs). Having the form of a beast. [Greek *thērion,* wild beast (see **-there**) + -MORPHIC.]

therm (thûrm) *n.* Also **therme.** A unit of heat equal to: **a.** One hundred thousand British thermal units. **b.** One thousand large calories. **c.** The large calorie. **d.** The small calorie. [From Greek *thermē,* heat, from *thermos,* hot. See **gwher-** in Appendix.*]

-therm. Indicates heat; for example, **poikilotherm.** [From Greek *thermē,* heat. See **therm.**]

ther·mal (thûr′məl) *adj.* Also **ther·mic** (-mĭk). Of, pertaining to, using, producing, or caused by heat. [French, from Greek *thermē,* heat. See **therm.**] —**ther′mal·ly** *adv.*

therm·i·on (thûr′mī′ən) *n.* An electrically charged particle or ion emitted by a conducting material at high temperatures. [THERM(O)- + ION.] —**therm′i·on′ic** (-mī-ŏn′ĭk) *adj.*

thermionic current. A flow of thermions.

thermionic emission. The emission of thermions from a conducting material at high temperatures.

therm·i·on·ics (thûr′mī-ŏn′ĭks) *n.* Plural in form, usually used with a singular verb. The physics of thermionic phenomena.

thermionic tube. An electron tube in which the source of electrons is a heated electrode.

therm·is·tor (thər-mĭs′tər) *n.* A resistor made of semiconductors having resistance that varies rapidly and predictably with temperature. [THERM(AL) + (RES)ISTOR.]

Ther·mit (thûr′mĭt′) *n.* A trademark for a welding and incendiary mixture of fine aluminum powder with a metallic oxide, as of iron or chromium, which when ignited yields an intense heat.

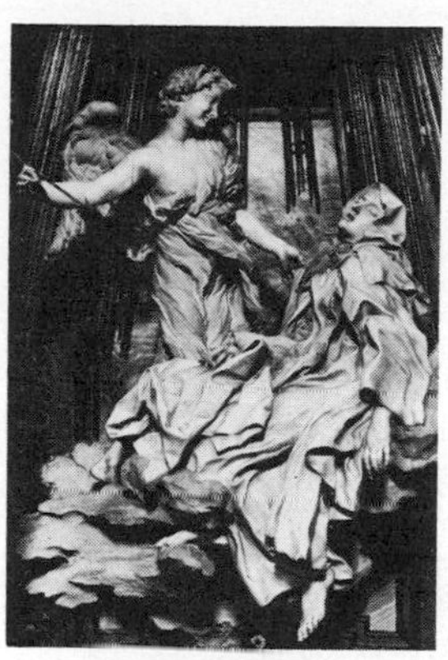

Saint Theresa
"Ecstasy of Saint Theresa," by Bernini

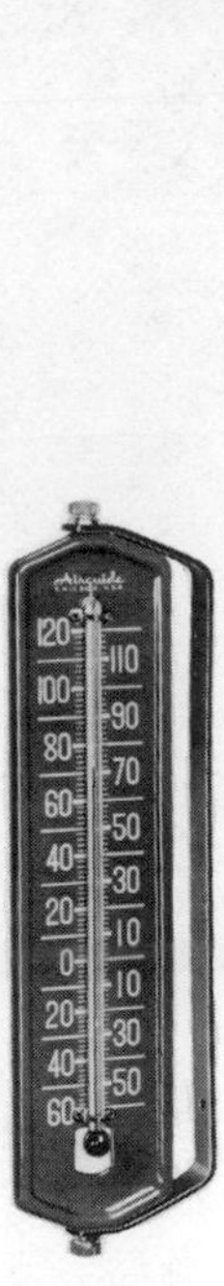

thermometer
Outdoor Fahrenheit thermometer

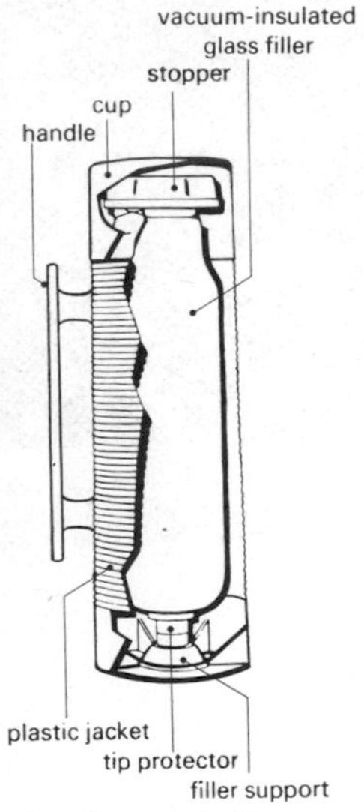
vacuum-insulated glass filler
stopper
cup
handle
plastic jacket
tip protector
filler support

thermos bottle

thermo-, therm-. Indicates pertaining to or caused by heat; for example, **thermogram, thermion.** [From Greek *thermē,* heat, from *thermos,* hot. See **gwher-** in Appendix.*]

thermochemical calorie. A unit of heat, a **calorie** *(see).*

ther·mo·chem·is·try (thûr′mō-kĕm′ĭ-strē) *n.* The chemistry of heat and heat-associated chemical phenomena. **—ther′mo·chem′i·cal** (-kĕm′ĭ-kəl) *adj.* **—ther′mo·chem′ist** *n.*

ther·mo·cou·ple (thûr′mə-kŭp′əl) *n.* A thermoelectric device used to measure temperatures accurately, especially one consisting of two dissimilar metals joined so that a potential difference generated between the points of contact is a measure of the temperature difference between the points.

ther·mo·dy·nam·ics (thûr′mō-dī-năm′ĭks) *n.* Plural in form, usually used with a singular verb. The physics of the relationships between heat and other forms of energy. **—ther′mo·dy·nam′ic** *adj.*

ther·mo·e·lec·tric (thûr′mō-ĭ-lĕk′trĭk) *adj.* Also **ther·mo·e·lec·tri·cal** (-trĭ-kəl). Characteristic of or resulting from electrical phenomena occurring in conjunction with a flow of heat. **—ther′mo·e·lec′tri·cal·ly** *adv.*

ther·mo·e·lec·tric·i·ty (thûr′mō-ĭ-lĕk′trĭs′ə-tē) *n.* Electricity generated by a flow of heat, as in a thermocouple.

ther·mo·gram (thûr′mə-grăm′) *n.* A record made by a thermograph. [THERMO- + -GRAM.]

ther·mo·graph (thûr′mə-grăf′, -gräf′) *n.* A thermometer that records the temperature it indicates. [THERMO- + -GRAPH.]

ther·mog·ra·phy (thər-mŏg′rə-fē) *n. Printing.* A process for producing raised lettering, as on stationery or calling cards, by transferring the inked lines on a plate to the paper by pressure and suction. [THERMO- + -GRAPHY.]

ther·mo·junc·tion (thûr′mō-jŭngk′shən) *n.* A point of contact between two dissimilar metals at which a thermoelectric current is produced.

ther·mo·la·bile (thûr′mō-lā′bəl, -bīl′) *adj.* Subject to destruction, decomposition, or great change by moderate heating. Said especially of certain biochemicals. Compare **thermostable.** [THERMO- + LABILE.]

ther·mo·lu·mi·nes·cence (thûr′mō-lo͞o′mə-nĕs′əns) *n.* A phenomenon in which certain minerals release previously absorbed radiation upon being moderately heated.

ther·mol·y·sis (thər-mŏl′ə-sĭs) *n.* **1.** *Physiology.* The loss of heat from the body. **2.** *Chemistry.* The dissociation or decomposition of compounds by heat. [THERMO- + -LYSIS.]

ther·mom·e·ter (thər-mŏm′ə-tər) *n.* An instrument for measuring temperature, especially one consisting of a graduated glass tube with a bulb containing a liquid, typically mercury, that expands and rises in the tube as the temperature increases. [French *thermomètre* : THERMO- + -METER.]

ther·mom·e·try (thər-mŏm′ə-trē) *n.* **1.** The measurement of temperature. **2.** The technology of temperature measurement. [THERMO- + -METRY.] **—ther′mo·met′ric** (thûr′mō-mĕt′rĭk) *adj.*

ther·mo·mo·tor (thûr′mō-mō′tər) *n.* An engine operated by heat, especially by the expansion of heated air.

ther·mo·nu·cle·ar (thûr′mō-no͞o′klē-ər, -nyo͞o′klē-ər) *adj.* **1.** Of, pertaining to, or derived from the fusion of atomic nuclei at high temperatures. **2.** Pertaining to atomic weapons based on fusion, especially as distinguished from those based on fission.

ther·mo·pe·ri·od·ism (thûr′mō-pîr′ē-ə-dĭz′əm) *n.* Also **ther·mo·pe·ri·o·dic·i·ty** (-dĭs′ə-tē). The effect of the rhythmic fluctuation of temperature upon an organism, including responses corresponding to thermal changes due to alternation of day and night.

ther·mo·phil·ic (thûr′mə-fĭl′ĭk) *n. Biology.* Requiring high temperatures for normal development, as certain bacteria. [THERMO- + -PHILIC.]

ther·mo·pile (thûr′mə-pīl′) *n.* A device to measure temperature, consisting of a number of thermocouples connected in series. [THERMO- + PILE (a heap, "series").]

ther·mo·plas·tic (thûr′mə-plăs′tĭk) *adj.* Becoming soft when heated and hardening when cooled. *—n.* A thermoplastic resin, such as polystyrene or polyethylene.

Ther·mop·y·lae (thər-mŏp′ə-lē). A locality in eastern Greece, near Lamia, an invasion route since ancient times; most famous as the site of a heroic but unsuccessful defense by the Spartans against the Persians (480 B.C.).

ther·mos bottle (thûr′məs). A commercially produced Dewar flask. Also called "thermos." [Trademark, from THERMO-.]

ther·mo·set·ting (thûr′mō-sĕt′ĭng) *adj.* Permanently hardening or solidifying on being heated. Said of certain synthetic resins.

ther·mo·sphere (thûr′mə-sfîr′) *n.* The outermost shell of the atmosphere, between the mesosphere and outer space, where temperatures increase steadily with altitude.

ther·mo·sta·ble (thûr′mō-stā′bəl) *adj.* Also **ther·mo·sta·bile** (-bəl, -bīl′). Unaffected by relatively high temperatures. Compare **thermolabile.** **—ther′mo·sta·bil′i·ty** (-stə-bĭl′ə-tē) *n.*

ther·mo·stat (thûr′mə-stăt′) *n.* A device that automatically responds to temperature changes and activates switches controlling equipment such as furnaces, refrigerators, and air conditioners. [THERMO- + -STAT.]

ther·mo·tax·is (thûr′mə-tăk′sĭs) *n.* **1.** The movement of a living organism in response to heat. **2.** The normal regulation or adjustment of body temperature. [New Latin : THERMO- + -TAXIS.] **—ther′mo·tac′tic** (-tăk′tĭk) *adj.*

ther·mo·ther·a·py (thûr′mō-thĕr′ə-pē) *n.* Therapy by application of heat.

ther·mot·ro·pism (thər-mŏt′rə-pĭz′əm) *n. Biology.* Growth or movement of plants or other organisms in response to heat. [THERMO- + -TROPISM.] **—ther′mo·trop′ic** (thûr′mə-trŏp′ĭk) *adj.*

-thermy. Indicates heat; for example, **diathermy.** [New Latin *-thermia,* from Greek *thermē,* heat, from *thermos,* hot. See **gwher-** in Appendix.*]

the·ro·pod (thîr′ə-pŏd′) *n.* Any of various carnivorous dinosaurs of the suborder Theropoda, of the Jurassic and Cretaceous periods, characteristically having small forelimbs. [New Latin *Theropoda* : Greek *thēr,* beast (see **ghwer-** in Appendix*) + -POD.] **—the·rop′o·dan** (thĭ-rŏp′ə-dən) *adj.* & *n.*

Ther·si·tes (thər-sī′tēz). An ugly, abusive Greek soldier killed by Achilles in the Trojan War.

the·sau·rus (thĭ-sôr′əs) *n., pl.* **-sauri** (-sôr′ī′) or **-ruses. 1.** A book of selected words or concepts, as a specialized vocabulary for music, medicine, or the like. **2.** A book of synonyms and antonyms. [Latin *thēsaurus,* TREASURE.]

these. Plural of **this.**

The·se·us (thē′sē-əs, -syo͞os′). *Greek Mythology.* A hero of Attica who slew the Minotaur and conquered the Amazons and married their queen. **—The·se′an** (thĭ-sē′ən) *adj.*

the·sis (thē′sĭs) *n., pl.* **-ses** (-sēz′). **1.** A proposition, as one advanced by a candidate for an academic degree, that is maintained by argument. **2.** A dissertation advancing an original point of view as a result of research, especially as a requirement for an academic degree. **3.** A hypothetical proposition, especially one put forth for the sake of argument or one to be accepted without proof. **4.** The first stage of **dialectic** *(see).* **5.** *Prosody.* The unstressed part of a foot. Compare **arsis. 6.** *Music.* The accented section of a measure. Compare **arsis.** [Late Latin, from Greek, a placing, a laying down, position, affirmation, from *tithenai,* to put, place. See **dhē-¹** in Appendix.*]

Thes·pi·an (thĕs′pē-ən) *adj.* **1.** Of or pertaining to Thespis. **2.** *Often small* **t.** Of or pertaining to drama; dramatic. *—n.* Also **thes·pi·an.** An actor or actress.

Thes·pis (thĕs′pĭs). Greek poet of the sixth century B.C.; reputed originator of tragic drama.

Thess. Thessalonians (New Testament).

Thes·sa·lo·ni·an (thĕs′ə-lō′nē-ən) *n.* A native or inhabitant of ancient Thessalonica or modern Salonika. *—adj.* Of or pertaining to ancient Thessalonica or modern Salonika.

Thes·sa·lo·ni·ans (thĕs′ə-lō′nē-ənz) *n.* Plural in form, used with a singular verb. *Abbr.* **Thess.** Either of two books of the New Testament consisting of Epistles from the Apostle Paul to the Christians of Thessalonica.

Thes·sa·lo·ni·ca. The ancient name for **Salonika.**

Thes·sa·ly (thĕs′ə-lē). *Modern Greek* **Thes·sa·li·a** (thĕ-sä′lē-ə, -säl′yə). A division of Greece, occupying 5,907 square miles in the central part of the country along the Aegean Sea. Population, 698,000. Chief city, Larisa. **—Thes′sa·li·an** *adj.* & *n.*

the·ta (thā′tə, thē′-) *n.* The eighth letter in the Greek alphabet, written Θ, θ. Transliterated in English as *th.* See **alphabet.** [Greek *thēta,* from a Phoenician cognate of Hebrew *ṭēth,* TETH.]

thet·ic (thĕt′ĭk, thē′tĭk) *adj.* Also **thet·i·cal** (thĕt′ĭ-kəl, thē′tĭ-). **1.** *Prosody.* Beginning with, constituting, or relating to the thesis. **2.** Presented dogmatically; arbitrarily prescribed. [Greek *thetikos,* fit for placing, from *thetos,* placed, from *tithenai,* to place. See **dhē-¹** in Appendix.*] **—thet′i·cal·ly** *adv.*

The·tis (thē′tĭs). *Greek Mythology.* One of the Nereids, the wife of Peleus and mother of Achilles.

the·ur·gy (thē′ûr-jē) *n., pl.* **-gies. 1.** Divine or supernatural intervention in the affairs of man. **2.** The performance of miracles with supernatural assistance. **3.** Magic performed supposedly with aid of beneficent spirits, as practiced by Neo-Platonists. [Late Latin *theurgia,* from Greek *theourgia,* sacramental rite, "mystery" : THEO- + -URGY.] **—the·ur′gic** (-jĭk), **the·ur′gi·cal** *adj.* **—the·ur′gi·cal·ly** *adv.* **—the′ur·gist** *n.*

thew (thyo͞o) *n.* **1.** A well-developed sinew or muscle. **2.** *Plural.* Muscular power or strength. [Middle English, habit, characteristic, good physical quality, Old English *thēaw,* usage, custom, characteristic. See **teu-** in Appendix.*] **—thew′y** *adj.*

they (*th*ā) *pron.* The third person plural pronoun in the nominative case. **1.** Used to represent persons or things last mentioned or implied: *There are three parts. They fit perfectly.* **2.** Used of persons as a demonstrative pronoun in the sense of *those:* "*Blessed are they which are persecuted*" (Matthew 5:10). **3.** Used to represent unspecified persons or people in general: *Whatever they say, I'll do it. He's as tough as they come.* [Middle English *thei,* partly from Old Norse *their,* partly from Old English *thā.* See **to-** in Appendix.*]

they'd (*th*ād). Contraction of *they had* or *they would.*

they'll (*th*āl). Contraction of *they will.*

they're (*th*âr). Contraction of *they are.*

they've (*th*āv). Contraction of *they have.*

thi·a·mine (thī′ə-mĭn, -mēn′) *n.* Also **thi·a·min** (-mĭn). A B-complex vitamin, $C_{12}H_{17}ClN_4OS$, produced synthetically and occurring naturally in the bran coat of grains, in yeast, and in meat, that is necessary for carbohydrate metabolism, maintenance of normal neural activity, and the prevention of beriberi. Also called "vitamin B_1." [THI(O)- + (VIT)AMIN.]

thi·a·zine (thī′ə-zēn′) *n.* Any of a class of organic chemical compounds containing a ring composed of one sulfur atom, one nitrogen atom, and four carbon atoms. [THI(O)- + AZINE.]

thi·a·zole (thī′ə-zōl′) *n.* **1.** A colorless or pale-yellow liquid, C_3H_3NS, containing a five-member ring composed of a nitrogen atom, a sulfur atom, and three carbon atoms, used in making dyes and fungicides. **2.** Any of various derivatives of this compound. [THI(O)- + AZOLE.]

thick (thĭk) *adj.* **thicker, thickest. 1.** Relatively great in depth or in extent from one surface to the opposite; not thin: *a thick board.* **2.** Measuring in this dimension: *two inches thick.* **3.** Heavy in build or stature; thickset, as a person. **4.** Having component parts in a close, compact arrangement; dense; concentrated. **5.** Having a viscous consistency; not transparent or fluid: *"so thick a mist and fog that people lost their way"* (Evelyn). **6.** Having a great number of; abounding: *a room thick with flies.* **7.** Impenetrable by the eyes; deep; profound: *a thick, gloomy blackness.* **8.** Not easy to hear; indistinctly articulated: *the thick slurrings of a drunkard.* **9.** Pronounced; heavy: *a thick brogue.* **10.** Speaking inarticulately: *a voice thick with sleep.* **11.** Lacking mental agility; stupid: *Get that through your thick head.* **12.** *Informal.* Very friendly; intimate. **13.** *Informal.* Going beyond what is tolerable; excessive. —*adv.* So as to be thick; thickly: *Slice it thick.* **—lay it on thick.** To overstate or give an exaggerated account of (one's feelings, for example). —*n.* **1.** The thickest part of something. **2.** The most active or intense part: *in the thick of the fighting.* **—through thick and thin.** Through both good and bad times; faithfully; unwaveringly. [Middle English *thikke,* Old English *thicce.* See **tegu-** in Appendix.*] **—thick'ly** *adv.*

thick·en (thĭk'ən) *v.* **-ened, -ening, -ens.** —*tr.* **1.** To make thick or thicker. **2.** To make more intense, intricate, or complex. —*intr.* To become thickened. **—thick'en·er** *n.*

thick·en·ing (thĭk'ən-ĭng) *n.* **1.** The act or process of making or becoming thick. **2.** Any material used to thicken liquid: *stir in a thickening of flour and water.* **3.** A thickened part of something.

thick·et (thĭk'ĭt) *n.* **1.** A dense growth of shrubs or underbrush; copse. **2.** Something suggestive of a thicket in impenetrability or thickness: *"the thicket of unreality which stands between us and the facts of life"* (Daniel J. Boorstin). [Middle English *thikket* (unattested), Old English *thiccet,* from *thicce,* THICK.]

thick·head (thĭk'hĕd') *n.* A stupid person; blockhead; numbskull. **—thick'head'ed** *adj.*

thick·ness (thĭk'nĭs) *n.* **1.** The state or condition of being thick. **2.** The dimension between two of an object's surfaces, usually taken to be the dimension of least measure. **3.** A layer, sheet, stratum, or ply: *a single thickness.*

thick·set (thĭk'sĕt') *adj.* **1.** Having a short, stocky body; stout. **2.** Positioned or placed closely together: *thickset rose bushes.*

thick-skinned (thĭk'skĭnd') *adj.* **1.** Having a thick skin. **2.** Not easily offended; insensitive to criticism; callous.

thick-wit·ted (thĭk'wĭt'ĭd) *adj.* Stupid; dull.

thief (thēf) *n., pl.* **thieves** (thēvz). **1.** A person who steals property. **2.** One who embezzles or commits larceny. [Middle English *thefe,* Old English *thīof, thēof,* from Common Germanic *thiuf* (unattested).]

Thiers (tyâr), **Louis Adolphe.** 1797–1877. French statesman and historian; first president of the Third Republic (1871–73).

Thieu (tyo͞o), **Nguyen Van.** Born 1923. Vietnamese military and political leader; president of South Vietnam (since 1967).

thieve (thēv) *v.* **thieved, thieving, thieves.** —*tr.* To take by theft; steal. —*intr.* To act as or be a thief; commit theft. —See Synonyms at **rob.** [Probably a back-formation from THIEF.]

thiev·er·y (thē'və-rē) *n., pl.* **-ies.** The act or practice of thieving.

thiev·ish (thē'vĭsh) *adj.* **1.** Given to thieving or stealing. **2.** Of, similar to, or characteristic of a thief; stealthy; furtive.

thigh (thī) *n.* **1. a.** The portion of the human leg between the hip and the knee. **b.** A homologous structure in animals. **2.** The femur of an insect's leg. [Middle English *thih,* Old English *thēoh.* See **teue-** in Appendix.*]

thigh·bone (thī'bōn') *n.* The **femur** *(see).*

thig·mo·tax·is (thĭg'mə-tăk'sĭs) *n.* Movement of an organism in response to a direct tactile stimulus. Also called "stereotaxis." [New Latin : Greek *thigma,* touch, from *thinganein,* to touch (see **dheigh-** in Appendix*) + -TAXIS.] **—thig'mo·tac'tic** (-tăk'tĭk) *adj.* **—thig'mo·tac'ti·cal·ly** *adv.*

thig·mot·ro·pism (thĭg-mŏt'rə-pĭz'əm) *n.* The response or motion of an organism to direct contact with a surface or object. Also called "stereotropism." [Greek *thigma,* touch (see **thigmotaxis**) + -TROPISM.]

thill (thĭl) *n.* Either of the two long shafts between which an animal is fastened when pulling a wagon. [Middle English *thille*†.]

thim·ble (thĭm'bəl) *n.* **1.** A small metal or plastic cup worn to protect the finger that pushes the needle in sewing. **2.** Any of various tubular sockets or sleeves in machinery. **3.** *Nautical.* **a.** A metal ring fitted in an eye of a sail to prevent chafing. **b.** A metal ring around which a rope splice is passed. [Middle English *thymbyl,* Old English *thȳmel,* from *thūma,* THUMB.]

thim·ble·ber·ry (thĭm'bəl-bĕr'ē) *n., pl.* **-ries.** Any of several raspberries or related plants having thimble-shaped fruit; especially, *Rubus parviflora,* of western and central North America.

thim·ble·ful (thĭm'bəl-fəl) *n.* A very small quantity.

thim·ble·rig (thĭm'bəl-rĭg') *n.* **1.** A gambling game, usually a swindle, in which the operator shuffles three inverted shells or thimbles, under one of which he has placed a marker, and spectators bet on the location of the marker. Also called "shell game." **2.** A person who operates such a game. —*tr.v.* **thimblerigged, -rigging, -rigs.** To swindle with or as if with a thimblerig. **—thim'ble·rig'ger** *n.*

thim·ble·weed (thĭm'bəl-wēd') *n.* **1.** Any of several North American plants of the genus *Anemone,* having cylindrical, thimblelike fruiting heads. **2.** Any of several coneflowers.

thi·mer·o·sal (thī-mĕr'ə-sŏl') *n.* A crystalline powder, $C_9H_9HgNaO_2S$, used as an antiseptic for surface tissues. Also known by the trademark "Merthiolate." [THI(O)- + MER(CURY) + SAL(ICYLATE).]

Thim·phu (thĭm'po͞o'). Also **Thim·bu** (-bo͞o'). The capital city of the Himalayan principality of Bhutan.

thin (thĭn) *adj.* **thinner, thinnest.** **1.** Having a relatively small distance between opposite sides or surfaces. **2.** Not great in diameter or cross section; fine: *a thin strand of hair.* **3.** Lean or slender of figure. **4.** Not dense or concentrated; sparse. **5.** Not rich or heavy in consistency: *thin gravy.* **6.** Sparsely supplied or provided; scanty: *a thin menu.* **7.** Lacking force or substance; flimsy: *a thin attempt.* **8.** Lacking resonance or fullness; tinny. Said of sound or tone. **9.** Lacking radiance or intensity. Said of light or color. **10.** *Photography.* Not having enough contrast to make satisfactory prints. Said of a negative. —*adv.* So as to be thin; thinly. —*v.* **thinned, thinning, thins.** —*intr.* To become thin or thinner. —*tr.* To make thin or thinner. [Middle English *thinne,* Old English *thynne.* See **ten-** in Appendix.*] **—thin'ness** *n.*

thine (thīn). Possessive pronoun, absolute form of *thy. Archaic & Poetic.* **1.** Belonging to thee. Used predicatively. **2.** The one or ones that belong to thee. Used substantively. **3.** Used instead of *thy* before an initial vowel or *h: thine enemy.* [Middle English *thin,* Old English *thīn.* See **tu-** in Appendix.*]

thing (thĭng) *n.* **1.** Whatever can be perceived, known, or thought to have a separate existence; an entity. **2.** The real substance of that which is indicated as distinguished from its appearances or from the name, word, or symbol denoting it. **3.** An entity existing in space or time; an object or fact. **4.** An inanimate object: *"Her enthusiasms are more for things than for people."* (Edgar Z. Friedenberg). **5.** A creature. Used to emphasize an attitude of pity, affection, contempt, or reproach: *the poor thing.* **6. a.** *Law.* That which can be possessed or owned as distinguished from a person. **b.** *Plural.* Possessions; belongings. **7.** An article of clothing. **8.** *Plural.* The equipment needed for an activity or purpose: *Where are my sewing things?* **9.** An object or entity that cannot or need not be named specifically: *What's this thing for?* **10.** An act, deed, or work. **11.** A thought, notion, or utterance. **12.** A piece of information. **13.** A means; device; recourse. **14.** A matter to be dealt with. **15.** A characteristic. **16.** A turn of events; circumstance. **17.** *Plural.* The general state of affairs; conditions. **18.** A persistent illogical feeling; obsession. **19.** The latest fashion; the rage. Preceded by *the: Chain belts were the thing last year.* **20.** *Slang.* An activity uniquely suitable and satisfying to one: *doing his thing.* **—first thing.** Right away; before anything else. **—see** (or **hear**) **things.** To have hallucinations. **—sure thing.** *Informal.* **1.** A certainty. **2.** Of course; certainly. [Middle English *thing,* Old English *thing,* creature, thing, deed, assembly. See **tenk-**[1] in Appendix.*]

thing·a·ma·bob (thĭng'ə-mə-bŏb') *n.* Also **thing·um·a·bob.** *Informal.* Something for which the exact name has been forgotten or is not known. Also called "thingamajig." [Whimsical formation.]

T-hinge (tē'hĭnj') *n.* A hinge, the two parts of which shape the letter T.

thing-in-itself (thĭng'ĭn-ĭt-sĕlf') *n., pl.* **things-in-themselves** (thĭngz'ĭn-*th*ĕm-sĕlvz'). An ultimate metaphysical reality conceived by Kant as beyond the perception of human senses and thought; a noumenon.

think (thĭngk) *v.* **thought** (thôt), **thinking, thinks.** —*tr.* **1.** To have as a thought; formulate in the mind: *He thought he would win.* **2. a.** To reason about or reflect on; ponder: *Think how complex language is.* Often used with *through* or *over: Think the matter through.* **b.** To decide by thinking: *He was thinking what he would have to do.* Often used with *out: He had to think out what to do.* **3.** To judge or regard; look upon: *I think it only fair.* **4.** To believe; suppose. **5.** To expect; anticipate; hope: *I thought to arrive early but couldn't.* **6.** To remember; call to mind: *I can't think now what his name was.* **7.** To visualize; imagine. **8.** To devise or evolve; invent. Often used with *up.* **9.** To bring into a given condition by mental preoccupation: *She thought herself into a terror of going.* —*intr.* **1.** To exercise the power of reason; to conceive of ideas, draw inferences, and use judgment. **2.** To weigh the idea; consider the matter: *They are thinking of moving.* **3.** To recall a thought or image to mind. Used with *of.* **4.** To believe; suppose: *Do you think so?* **5.** To have formed an impression: *I think of him as easygoing.* **6.** To have care or consideration. Used with *of.* **7.** To dispose the mind in a given way: *Think rich.* **—think aloud.** To say what one is thinking. **—think better of.** To decide against after reconsidering. **—think nothing of.** To regard as routine or usual. **—think twice.** To weigh something carefully. [Think, thought, thought; Middle English *thenken, thoughte, thought,* Old English *thencan, thōhte, gethōht.* See **tong-** in Appendix.*]

think·a·ble (thĭng'kə-bəl) *adj.* Fit to be considered; conceivable; possible. **—think'a·bly** *adv.*

think·er (thĭng'kər) *n.* **1.** A person who devotes his time to thought or meditation. **2.** A person who thinks or reasons in a given way: *a careful thinker.*

think·ing (thĭng'kĭng) *n.* **1.** Thought. **2.** A way of reasoning; judgment: *not to my thinking a good idea.* —*adj.* Characterized by thoughtfulness; rational: *Man is a thinking animal.*

thin·ner (thĭn'ər) *n.* A liquid, such as turpentine, mixed with paint to reduce viscosity for ease in application.

thin-skinned (thĭn'skĭnd') *adj.* **1.** Having a thin rind or skin. **2.** Oversensitive, especially to reproach or insult.

thio–, thi–. *Chemistry.* Indicates a compound containing a divalent sulfur atom, especially one in which sulfur has replaced oxygen; for example, **thiophene, thiol.** [From Greek *theion,* sulfur. See **dheu-**[1] in Appendix.*]

thi·o·car·bam·ide (thī'ō-kär'bə-mīd') *n.* **Thiourea** *(see).*

Thi·o·kol (thī'ə-kŏl', -kōl') *n.* A trademark for any of various polysulfide polymers in the form of liquids, water dispersions, and rubbers used in seals and sealants.

thi·ol (thī'ŏl, -ôl) *n.* **Mercaptan** *(see).* [THI(O)- + -OL.]

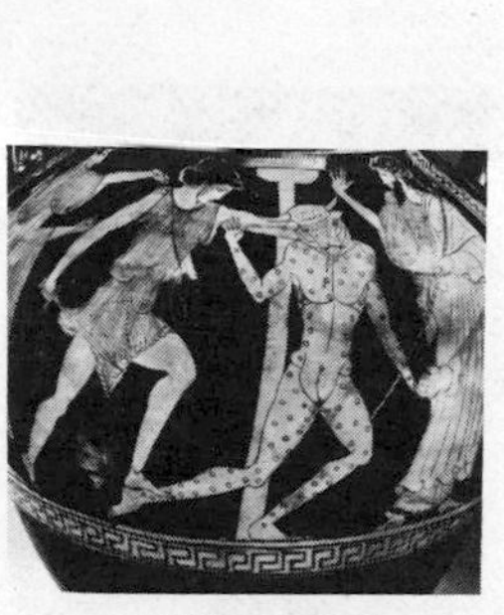

Theseus
Detail from a fifth-century B.C. Greek vase painting of Theseus killing the Minotaur

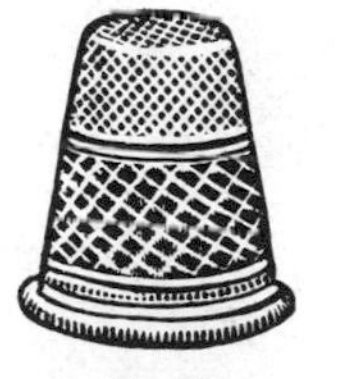

thimble

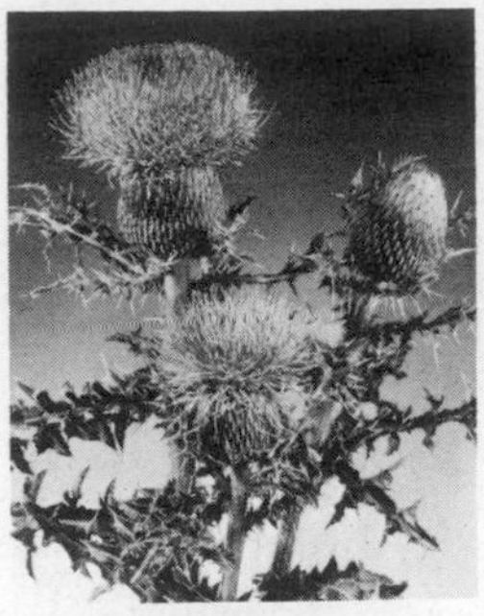
thistle
Cirsium pumilum

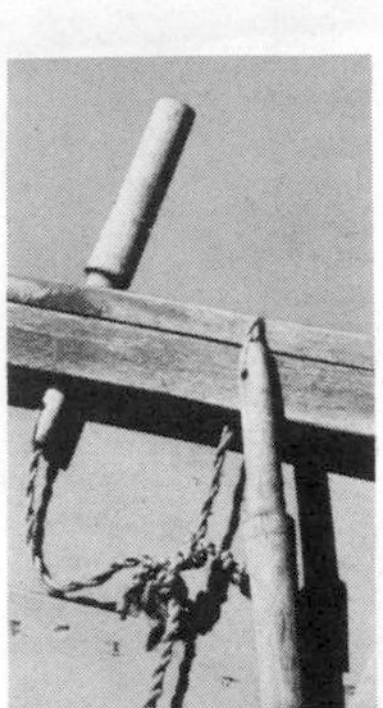
thole pin
Pair of thole pins, one in its socket and the other hanging by its lanyard

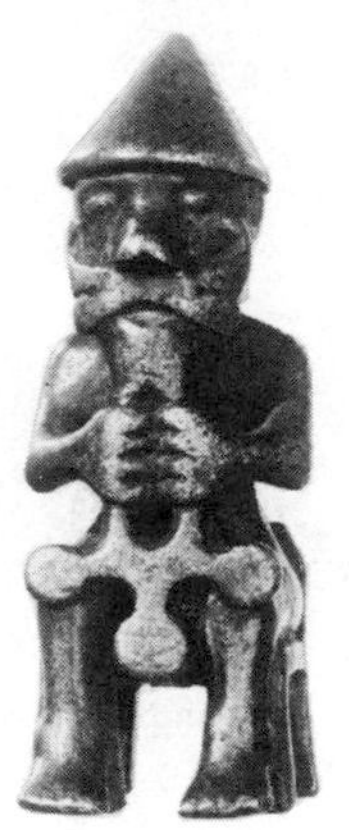
Thor
Icelandic statuette

thion–. Indicates sulfur; for example, **thionic.** [From Greek *theion,* sulfur. See **thio-**.]

thi·on·ic (thī-ŏn′ĭk) *adj.* Of, pertaining to, containing, or derived from sulfur. [THION- + -IC.]

thi·o·nyl (thī′ə-nĭl′) *n.* **Sulfinyl** *(see).* [THION- + -YL.]

thi·o·pen·tal sodium (thī-ō-pĕn′tăl′, -tôl′). A yellowish-white hygroscopic powder, $C_{11}H_{17}N_2O_2SNa$, injected intravenously as a general anesthetic. Also called "sodium pentothal," and "Pentothal Sodium," a trademark. [From THIO- + PENTA-.]

thi·o·phene (thī′ə-fēn′) *n.* A colorless liquid, C_4H_4S, used as a solvent. [THIO- + PHEN(O)- + -ENE.]

thi·o·sul·fate (thī′ō-sŭl′fāt′) *n.* A salt of thiosulfuric acid.

thi·o·sul·fu·ric acid (thī′ō-sŭl-fyo͝or′ĭk). An acid, $H_2S_2O_3$, formed by the replacement of an oxygen atom by a sulfur atom in sulfuric acid, known only in solution or by its salts and esters.

thi·o·u·re·a (thī′ō-yo͞o-rē′ə) *n.* A white, lustrous crystalline compound, $(NH_2)_2CS$, used in photography, photocopying paper, and various organic syntheses. Also called "thiocarbamide." [THIO- + UREA.]

Thi·ra (thîr′ə). Also **The·ra.** An island of Greece, 31 square miles in area; the southernmost of the Cyclades group.

third (thûrd) *n.* **1.** The ordinal number three in a series. Also written 3rd. **2.** One of three equal parts. See **number. 3.** One-sixtieth of a second, as a measure of time or of the arc of an angle. **4.** *Music.* **a.** An interval of three degrees in a diatonic scale. **b.** A tone separated by three degrees from a given tone; especially, the third tone of a scale. **5.** The gear next higher after second in an automobile transmission. *—adj.* **1.** Being number three in a series; next after second. **2.** Being one of three equal parts. *—adv.* Also **third·ly** (thûrd′lē). In the third place, rank, or order. [Middle English *thride, thirde,* Old English *third(d)a, thridda.* See **trei-** in Appendix.*]

third base. *Baseball.* **1.** The third base to be reached by a runner, up the left-field foul line from home plate. **2.** The position played by the third baseman.

third baseman. *Baseball.* The infielder stationed near third base.

third class. 1. A class of mail in the U.S. postal system including all printed matter, except newspapers and magazines, that weighs less than 16 ounces and is unsealed. **2.** Accommodations, as on a ship or train, of the third and usually lowest order of luxury and price. **—third′-class′** *adj. & adv.*

third degree. Mental or physical torture to obtain information or a confession from a prisoner.

third-degree burn (thûrd′dĭ-grē′). A severe burn in which the epidermis is destroyed and sensitive nerve endings are exposed.

third estate. The third class of a threefold political division of a kingdom; specifically, the commons in France or England. See **Estates of the Realm.**

Third International. See **International.**

Third Order. A confraternity of laymen associated with a religious order of the Roman Catholic Church.

third party. A political party organized as opposition to the existing parties in a two-party system. Compare **major party.**

third person. A set of grammatical forms used in referring to a person or thing other than the speaker or the one spoken to.

third rail. The rail through which the current runs to power the train on an electric railway. **—third′-rail′** *adj.*

Third Reich. See **Reich.**

Third Republic. The French republic from the fall of the Commune (1871) until the German occupation (1940).

thirst (thûrst) *n.* **1. a.** A sensation of dryness in the mouth related to a need or desire to drink. **b.** The desire to drink. **2.** A craving for alcoholic liquor. **3.** An insistent desire; craving. *—intr.v.* **thirsted, thirsting, thirsts. 1.** To feel a need to drink. **2.** To have a strong craving; yearn. —See Synonyms at **yearn.** [Middle English *thurst, thirst,* Old English *thurst.* See **ters-** in Appendix.*] **—thirst′er** *n.*

thirst·y (thûr′stē) *adj.* **-ier, -iest. 1.** Desiring to drink. **2.** Arid; parched. **3.** Craving. **—thirst′i·ly** *adv.* **—thirst′i·ness** *n.*

thir·teen (thûr′tēn′) *n.* The cardinal number written 13 or in Roman numerals XIII. See **number.** [Middle English *thrittene,* Old English *thrēotīne.* See **trei-** in Appendix.*] **—thir′teen′** *adj. & pron.*

thir·teenth (thûr′tēnth′) *n.* **1.** The ordinal number 13 in a series. Also written 13th. **2.** One of 13 equal parts. See **number. —thir′teenth′** *adj. & adv.*

Thirteenth Amendment. An amendment to the U.S. Constitution, ratified in 1865, abolishing slavery.

thir·ti·eth (thûr′tē-ĭth) *n.* **1.** The ordinal number 30 in a series. Also written 30th. **2.** One of 30 equal parts. See **number. —thir′ti·eth** *adj. & adv.*

thir·ty (thûr′tē) *n.* The cardinal number written 30 or in Roman numerals XXX. See **number.** [Middle English *thritty,* Old English *thrītig.* See **trei-** in Appendix.*] **—thir′ty** *adj. & pron.*

thir·ty-sec·ond note (thûr′tē-sĕk′ənd). A musical note with a time value equivalent to 1/32 of a whole note. Also *chiefly British* "demisemiquaver."

thir·ty-two·mo (thûr′tē-to͞o′mō) *n., pl.* **-mos. 1.** The page size (3½ by 5½ inches) that results when a printers' sheet is folded into 32 equal sections. **2.** A book composed of pages of this size. Also written 32mo.

Thirty Years' War. A series of religious wars fought in Europe (1618–48).

this (*th*ĭs) *pron., pl.* **these** (*th*ēz). **1.** The person or thing present or nearby in space, time, or thought. **2.** The person, thing, or idea just mentioned. **3.** What is about to be said. **4.** The one that is nearer than another or the one compared with the other: *this one and that.* **5.** The present occasion or time. *—adj., pl.* **these. 1.** Being just mentioned or present in space, time, or thought. **2.** Being nearer than another or compared with another: *this side and that.* **3.** Being about to be stated or described. *—adv.* To this extent; so. [This, these; Middle English *this, thes,* Old English *thes* or *thēs, thēos, this* (masculine, feminine, neuter singular). See **to-** in Appendix.*]

Usage: *That* and *this* are both used, as demonstrative pronouns, to represent in single summarizing words a thought expressed earlier: *Seventy witnesses testified. That* (or *this*) *is an unusually large number, even for an important hearing. The letter was unopened; that* (or *this*) *in itself casts doubt on the inspector's theory. That* is sometimes prescribed as the better choice in referring to what has gone before (as in the preceding examples), and *this* in referring to what is about to be stated. But *this* is also acceptable to 72 per cent of the Usage Panel in these examples. When such pronouns are sufficiently distant from what they represent to make their reference uncertain, the original thought should be restated in the interest of clarity. A personal pronoun is clearly preferable to *this* in referring to human beings: *The young novelist once again displays exceptional talent. He* (preferable to *this*) *is a writer with a future.*

this·tle (thĭs′əl) *n.* **1.** Any of numerous weedy plants, chiefly of the genera *Cirsium, Carduus,* or *Onopordum,* having prickly leaves and usually purplish flowers surrounded by prickly bracts. **2.** Any of various similar or related plants. [Middle English *thistel,* Old English *thistel,* from Germanic *thistilaz* (unattested).]

thistle butterfly. The **painted lady** *(see).* [So called because its larvae eat thistles.]

this·tle·down (thĭs′əl-doun′) *n.* The silky down attached to the seeds of a thistle.

thith·er (thĭ*th*′ər, thĭ*th*′-) *adv.* **1.** To or toward that place; in that direction; there: *hither and thither.* **2.** *Archaic.* To or toward that end or result. *—adj.* Located or being on the more distant side; farther: *the thither side of the pond.* [Middle English *thither, thider,* Old English *thider, thæder.* See **to-** in Appendix.*]

thith·er·to (thĭ*th*′ər-to͞o′, thĭ*th*′-) *adv.* Up to that time; until then.

thith·er·ward (thĭ*th*′ər-wərd, thĭ*th*′-) *adv.* In that direction; thither.

thix·ot·ro·py (thĭk-sŏt′rə-pē) *n.* The property exhibited by certain gels of liquefying when stirred or shaken and returning to the hardened state upon standing. [Greek *thixis,* "touching," from *thinganein,* to touch (see **dheigh-** in Appendix*) + -TROPY.] **—thix′o·trop′ic** (thĭk′sə-trŏp′ĭk) *adj.*

tho (*th*ō). *Informal.* **Though** *(see).*

thole (thōl) *tr.v.* **tholed, tholing, tholes.** *Regional.* To endure; to bear. [Middle English *tholen,* Old English *tholian,* to endure. See **tel-¹** in Appendix.*]

thole pin (thōl). *Nautical.* A wooden peg set in pairs in the gunwale of a boat to serve as an oarlock. [Middle English *tholle,* Old English *thol(l).* See **teue-** in Appendix.*]

Thom·as (tŏm′əs). *Abbr.* **Thos.** A masculine given name. [Middle English, from Norman French, from Late Latin *Thōmās,* from Greek *Thōmas,* from Aramaic *t'ōmə,* "a twin."]

Thom·as (tŏm′əs), **Dylan (Marlais).** 1914–1953. Welsh poet.

Thom·as (tŏm′əs), **Norman (Mattoon).** 1884–1968. American socialist.

Thom·as (tŏm′əs), **Saint.** Known as Didymus. One of the Twelve Apostles.

Thom·as (tŏm′əs), **Seth.** 1785–1859. American clockmaker.

Thomas à Beck·et. See **Becket.**

Thomas à Kem·pis. See **Kempis.**

Thomas A·qui·nas, Saint. See **Aquinas.**

Tho·mism (tō′mĭz′əm) *n.* The theological and philosophical system of Saint Thomas Aquinas, which became the basis of scholasticism. **—Tho′mist** (tō′mĭst) *n. & adj.* **—Tho·mis′tic** (tō-mĭs′tĭk) *adj.*

Thomp·son (tŏmp′sən), **Benjamin.** Count Rumford. 1753–1814. American physicist and philanthropist.

Thomp·son (tŏmp′sən), **Francis.** 1859–1907. English poet.

Thomp·son River (tŏmp′sən). A river of Canada, rising in the Rocky Mountains of southeastern British Columbia and flowing 270 miles south and then southwest to the Fraser River.

Thompson submachine gun. A type of .45-caliber submachine gun. Also informally called "Tommy gun." [After its co-inventor, John *Thompson* (died 1940), American army officer.]

Thom·son (tŏm′sən), **Elihu.** 1853–1937. British-born American electrical engineer and inventor.

Thom·son (tŏm′sən), Sir **George Paget.** Born 1892. British physicist; son of Sir Joseph John Thomson; worked on diffraction of electrons.

Thom·son (tŏm′sən), **James¹.** 1700–1748. Scottish poet.

Thom·son (tŏm′sən), **James².** Pen name, B.V. 1834–1882. English poet.

Thom·son (tŏm′sən), Sir **Joseph John.** 1856–1940. British physicist; father of Sir George Paget Thomson; demonstrated existence of the electron.

Thom·son (tŏm′sən), **Virgil.** Born 1896. American composer and critic.

Thom·son, William. See Baron **Kelvin.**

thong (thông, thŏng) *n.* **1.** A narrow strip of leather or other material used for binding or lashing. **2.** A whiplash of plaited leather or cord. [Middle English *thong,* Old English *thwong, thwang.* See **twengh-** in Appendix.*]

Thor (thôr). *Norse Mythology.* The god of thunder. [Old Norse *thōrr,* thunder. See **stene-** in Appendix.*]

ă pat/ā pay/âr care/ä father/b bib/ch church/d deed/ĕ pet/ē be/f fife/g gag/h hat/hw which/ĭ pit/ī pie/îr pier/j judge/k kick/l lid, needle/m mum/n no, sudden/ng thing/ŏ pot/ō toe/ô paw, for/oi noise/ou out/o͝o took/o͞o boot/p pop/r roar/s sauce/sh ship, dish/

tho·rac·ic (thə-răs′ĭk) *adj.* Of, relating to, or situated in or near the thorax.

thoracic duct. The main duct of the lymphatic system, ascending along the spinal cord and discharging into the venous system.

tho·ra·cot·o·my (thôr′ə-kŏt′ə-mē, thōr′-) *n., pl.* **-mies.** Surgical incision of the chest wall. [Latin *thōrāx* (stem *thōrāc-*), THORAX + -TOMY.]

tho·rax (thôr′ăks′, thōr′-) *n., pl.* **-raxes** or **thoraces** (thôr′ə-sēz′, thōr′-, thô-rā′-). **1.** *Anatomy.* The part of the human body between the neck and the diaphragm, partially encased by the ribs; the chest. **2.** A corresponding part in other animals. **3.** The second or middle region of the body of an arthropod, in insects bearing the true legs and wings. [Latin *thōrāx,* from Greek *thōrax*†, breastplate, coat of mail, chest covering.]

Tho·reau (thôr′ō, thə-rō′), **Henry David.** 1817–1862. American essayist and poet.

Tho·rez (tô-rĕz′), **Maurice.** 1900–1964. Secretary-General of the French Communist Party (1930–64).

tho·ri·a (thôr′ē-ə, thōr′-) *n. Chemistry.* **Thorium dioxide** *(see).* [From THORIUM.]

tho·rite (thôr′īt′, thōr′-) *n.* A vitreous brownish-yellow to black thorium ore, essentially $ThSiO_4$. [THOR(IUM) + -ITE.]

tho·ri·um (thôr′ē-əm, thōr′-) *n. Symbol* **Th** A silvery-white metallic element with 13 radioactive isotopes only one of which, thorium 232, occurs naturally. It is used in magnesium alloys and isotope 232 is a source of nuclear energy. Atomic number 90, atomic weight 232.038, approximate melting point 1,700°C, approximate boiling point 4,000°C, approximate specific gravity 11.66, valence 4. See **element.** [New Latin, after THOR.]

thorium dioxide. A heavy white powder, ThO_2, used mainly in ceramics, gas mantles, and nuclear fuels. Also called "thoria."

thorn (thôrn) *n.* **1.** *Botany.* A modified branch in the form of a sharp, woody spine. **2.** Any of various shrubs, trees, or woody plants bearing such spines, such as the hawthorn. **3.** Any of various sharp, spiny protuberances; a prickle. **4.** A person or thing that causes sharp pain, irritation, or discomfort. **5.** The name of the runic letter originally representing the sound of *th* in both *the* and *thin,* adapted into the Roman alphabet and used in writing early Germanic languages, including Old English. It now survives only in Icelandic, representing the sound of *th* in *thin.* [Middle English *thorn,* Old English *thorn,* thorn, thornbush. See **stern-** in Appendix.*]

Thorn. The German name for **Toruń.**

thorn apple. Any of various plants of the genus *Datura,* especially the **jimsonweed** *(see).*

thorn·back (thôrn′băk′) *n.* Either of two rays, *Raja clavata,* of European waters, or *Platyrhinoidis triseriata,* of Pacific waters, having spines along the back.

thorn·y (thôr′nē) *adj.* **-ier, -iest. 1.** Full of or covered with thorns. **2.** Thornlike; spiny. **3.** Painfully controversial; vexatious. **—thorn′i·ness** *n.*

tho·ron (thôr′ŏn′, thōr′-) *n.* A radioactive isotope of radon having a half-life of 54.5 seconds and produced by the disintegration of thorium. [THOR(IUM) + -ON.]

thor·ough (thûr′ō) *adj.* **1.** Fully done; finished. **2.** Completely as described; absolute; utter. **3.** Painstakingly accurate or careful. [Middle English *thorow,* from *thorugh* (adverb), through, Old English *thuruh,* from *thurh,* THROUGH.] **—thor′ough·ly** *adv.* **—thor′ough·ness** *n.*

thorough brace. One of several leather bands passed from front to back of a carriage, supporting it and serving as a spring. **—thor′ough-braced′** *adj.*

thor·ough·bred (thûr′ō-brĕd′, thûr′ə-) *adj.* **1.** Bred of pure stock; purebred; unmixed. **2.** *Capital* **T.** Pertaining or belonging to the Thoroughbred breed of horses. **3.** Thoroughly trained or educated; well-bred. **—n. 1.** A purebred or pedigreed animal. **2.** *Capital* **T.** Any of a breed of horse originating from a cross of Arabian stallions with English mares. **3.** A well-bred person.

thor·ough·fare (thûr′ō-fâr′, thûr′ə-) *n.* **1.** A main road or public highway. **2. a.** Any place of passage from one location to another. **b.** Right to such passage: *no thoroughfare.* **3.** A heavily traveled passage, such as a waterway, strait, or channel. [Middle English *thurghfare* : *thurgh,* THROUGH + FARE (passage).]

thor·ough·go·ing (thûr′ō-gō′ĭng, thûr′ə-) *adj.* **1.** Very thorough; complete. **2.** Unmitigated; unqualified.

thor·ough·paced (thûr′ō-pāst′, thûr′ə-) *adj.* **1.** Trained in all paces or gaits, as a horse. **2.** Thoroughgoing; complete.

thor·ough·pin (thûr′ō-pĭn′, thûr′ə-) *n.* An abnormal swelling on either side of the hock joint of horses and related animals. [From THOROUGH (passing through); it appears as if a pin were piercing the joint.]

thor·ough·wort (thûr′ō-wûrt′, -wôrt′, thûr′ə-) *n.* A plant, the **boneset** *(see).*

thorp (thôrp) *n. Obsolete.* A hamlet. [Middle English *thorp,* Old English *throp, thorp, throp.* See **treb-** in Appendix.*]

Thorpe (thôrp), **James Francis ("Jim").** 1888–1953. American Indian athlete.

Thors·havn (tôrs-houn′). The capital of the Faeroe Islands, a seaport on Stromo, northernmost island. Population, 7,000.

Thos. Thomas.

those. Plural of **that.**

Thoth (thōth, tōt). *Egyptian Mythology.* The god of the moon and of wisdom and learning, whose sacred bird was the ibis. He is represented with the head and neck of an ibis and carries a pen, tablet, and palm branch.

thou[1] (*thou*) *pron. Archaic & Poetic.* The second person singular pronoun in the nominative case. **1.** Used to represent the person or personal being who is spoken to: *"Thou wilt never get thee a husband."* (Shakespeare). **2.** Used in apposition before a noun to indicate address: *"Thou drone, thou snail, thou slug, thou sot!"* (Shakespeare). [Thou, thee, thy or thine; Middle English *thu, the(e), thi* (before a consonant) and *thin* (before a vowel), Old English *thu* (or *thū*), *the* (or *thē*), *thin.* See **tu-** in Appendix.*]

Usage: Beginning in Middle English, *you,* originally a plural of *thou,* came to be used in the singular as a mark of respect for the person being addressed. More and more the use of *thou* was limited to addressing intimates, children, social inferiors, and God. This distinction persisted into the 18th century in general writing and appears in the 20th century in a few dialects.

thou[2] (thou) *n. Slang.* Shortened form of *thousand.*

though (*thō*) *conj.* **1.** Despite the fact that; while; although. **2.** Conceding or supposing that; even if. **3.** However; yet. Also informally respelled "tho." —See Usage note at **although.** —*adv.* However; nevertheless. Also informally respelled "tho." See Usage note below. **—as though.** As if: *"as though in a dream I heard my father calling"* (Oscar Lewis). [Middle English *thoh, though,* from Old Norse *thō.* See **to-** in Appendix.*]

Usage: *Though* (adverb) appears at the end of a sentence or clause: *He said he wouldn't come; he did, though.* The construction is common in speech and is most appropriate to informal contexts and dialogue, according to 61 per cent of the Usage Panel, who find it unacceptable in the following example of more formal written usage: *We are not seeking special privilege; legitimate concessions would be welcome, though. However, nevertheless,* and *all the same* are more formal substitutes for *though* here.

thought (thôt). Past tense and past participle of **think.** —*n.* **1.** The act or process of thinking; cogitation. **2.** A product of thinking; idea; notion. **3.** The intellectual activity or production of a particular time or social class. **4.** Consideration; attention; concern. **5.** Intent; purpose. **6.** Expectation; hope; anticipation. **7.** A trifle; a bit: *a thought more considerate.* —See Synonyms at **idea.** [Middle English *thought,* a thought, Old English *(ge)thōht.* See **tong-** in Appendix.*]

thought·ful (thôt′fəl) *adj.* **1.** Contemplative; meditative. **2.** Well thought-out: *a thoughtful essay.* **3.** Showing regard for others; considerate. **—thought′ful·ly** *adv.* **—thought′ful·ness** *n.*

Synonyms: *thoughtful, considerate, indulgent, solicitous.* These adjectives mean showing concern for the well-being of others. *Thoughtful* and *considerate* can often be used interchangeably. *Thoughtful* sometimes implies a tendency to anticipate needs and act accordingly, whereas *considerate* is especially appropriate to situations that stress sensitivity to another's feelings. *Indulgent* suggests willingness to gratify wishes that may be unreasonable and thus to pamper or humor another. *Solicitous,* the strongest of these terms, implies concern for another's welfare that verges on anxiety or expresses itself in extremely close attention to his wishes.

thought·less (thôt′lĭs) *adj.* **1.** Careless; unthinking. **2.** Reckless; rash. **3.** Inconsiderate; inattentive. —See Synonyms at **careless. —thought′less·ly** *adv.* **—thought′less·ness** *n.*

thought reading. Mind reading *(see).*

thou·sand (thou′zənd) *n.* The cardinal number written 1,000 or in Roman numerals M. See **number.** [Middle English *thousande,* Old English *thūsend.* See **teue-** in Appendix.*] **—thou′sand** *adj. & pron.*

Thousand Islands. A group of over 1,500 islands in the St. Lawrence at the outlet of Lake Ontario; a resort area partly in Ontario, Canada, and partly in New York State.

thou·sandth (thou′zəndth, -zənth) *n.* **1.** The ordinal number thousand in a series. Also written 1,000th. **2.** One of a thousand equal parts. See **number. —thou′sandth** *adj. & adv.*

thp thrust horsepower.

THR Airport code for Teheran, Iran.

Thrace (thrās). Ancient name **Thra·cia** (thrā′shə, -shē-ə). **1.** An ancient country in the southeastern part of the Balkan Peninsula, reaching as far north as the Danube at its greatest extent and comprising modern Bulgaria and parts of Greece and Turkey. **2.** A modern region in the southern part of this province, divided into Western Thrace in Greece and Eastern Thrace in Turkey.

Thra·cian (thrā′shən) *adj.* Of or pertaining to Thrace or its people. —*n.* **1.** A native or inhabitant of Thrace. **2.** The Indo-European language related to Phrygian spoken by the ancient inhabitants of Thrace.

Thrale, Mrs. See Hester Lynch **Piozzi.**

thrall (thrôl) *n.* **1.** One who is in bondage, as a slave, serf, or bondman. **2.** One who is a slave (to something or someone). **3.** Servitude; bondage. —*tr.v.* **thralled, thralling, thralls.** *Archaic.* To enslave (a person); make a thrall of. [Middle English *thral(l),* Old English *thrǣl,* from Old Norse *thræll,* from Common Germanic *thrakh-* (unattested), to run.] **—thrall′dom** (-dəm), **thral′dom** *n.*

thrash (thrăsh) *v.* **thrashed, thrashing, thrashes.** —*tr.* **1.** To beat or flog with or as with a flail; punish, as by whipping. **2.** To swing or strike in a manner suggestive of the action of a flail. **3.** To defeat utterly; vanquish. **4.** To thresh. **5.** *Nautical.* To sail (a boat) against opposing winds or tides. —*intr.* **1.** To move the body or a bodily part wildly or violently; lash out. **2.** To strike or flail; strike out. **3.** To thresh. **4.** To move against opposing tides or winds. **—thrash out.** To discuss fully; bring to a conclusion. —*n.* **1.** The act of thrashing. **2.** A swimming kick in the backstroke and crawl. [Originally a variant of THRESH.] **—thrash′er** *n.*

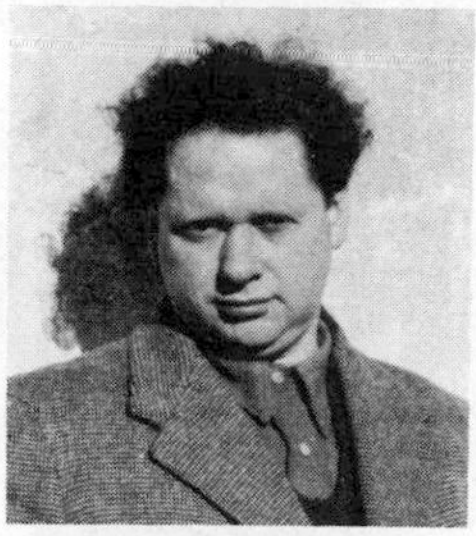

Dylan Thomas
Photograph taken in 1953

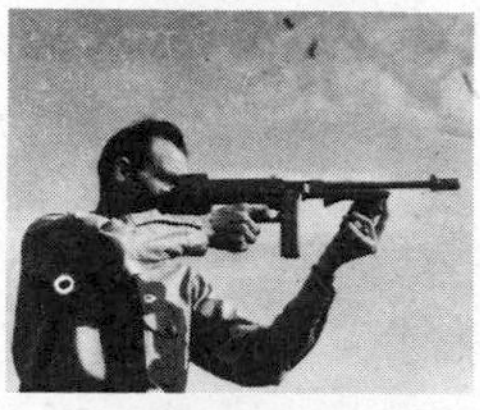

Thompson submachine gun
Being fired by a special agent of the FBI

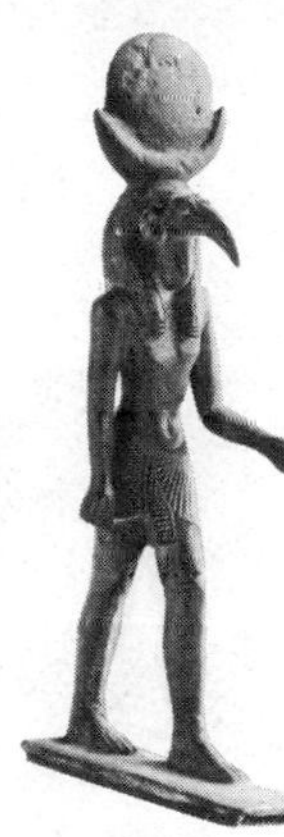

Thoth

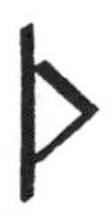

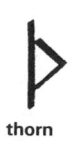

thorn
Runic letter

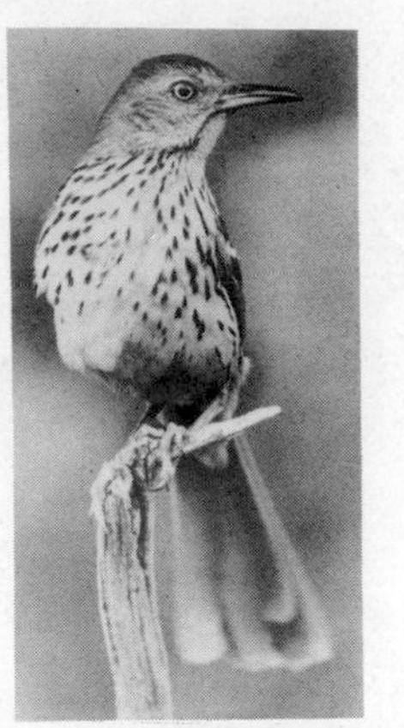

thrasher
Toxostoma rufum
Brown thrasher

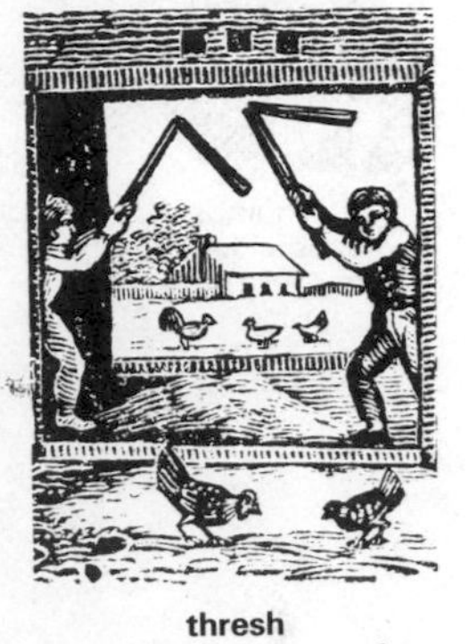

thresh
Early 19th-century woodcut

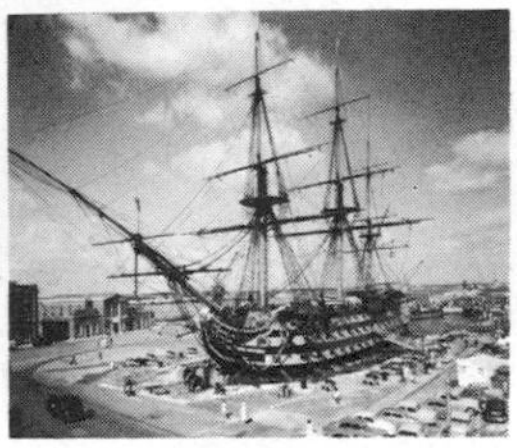

three-decker

thrash·er (thrăsh′ər) *n.* Any of various New World songbirds of the genus *Toxostoma,* having a long tail, a long, curved beak, and, in several species, a spotted breast. [Perhaps a variant of dialectal *thrusher,* from THRUSH (songbird).]

thrash·ing (thrăsh′ĭng) *n.* A severe beating; a whipping.

thra·son·i·cal (thrā-sŏn′ĭ-kəl) *adj.* Boastful. [From Latin *Thrasō* (stem *thrasōn-*), a bragging character in Terence's comedy *Eunuchus,* from Greek *Thrasōn,* from *thrasus,* bold, brave. See **dhers-** in Appendix.*] —**thra·son′i·cal·ly** *adv.*

thread (thrĕd) *n.* **1. a.** A fine cord of a fibrous material, such as cotton or flax, made of two or more filaments twisted together, and used in needlework and the weaving of cloth. **b.** A piece of this material. **2.** A strand, fiber, or filament of natural or manufactured material. **3.** Anything suggestive of the fineness or thinness of thread. **4.** Anything suggestive of the continuousness and sequence of thread. **5.** A helical or spiral ridge on a screw, nut, or bolt. —*v.* **threaded, threading, threads.** —*tr.* **1.** To pass one end of a thread through the eye of (a needle or similar device). **2.** To string (beads or similar objects) onto a thread. **3.** To pass cautiously through: *"we have to now thread our way through this greater density"* (William Barrett). **4.** To occur throughout; pervade. **5.** To machine a thread on (a screw, nut, or bolt). —*intr.* **1.** To wind cautiously through obstacles or a slender path. **2.** To proceed by a winding course. **3.** To form a thread when dropped from a spoon, as boiling sugar syrup. [Middle English *thre(e)d,* Old English *thrǣd.* See **ter-**[2] in Appendix.*] —**thread′er** *n.*

thread·bare (thrĕd′bâr′) *adj.* **1.** Having the nap worn down so that the filling or warp threads show through; frayed or shabby. **2.** Wearing old, shabby clothing. **3.** Hackneyed; stale. —See Synonyms at **trite.**

thread·fin (thrĕd′fĭn′) *n.* Any of various chiefly tropical marine fishes of the family Polynemidae, having threadlike rays extending from the lower part of the pectoral fin.

thread mark. A marking made in paper currency by a threading of colored silk fibers to make counterfeiting difficult.

Thread·nee·dle Street (thrĕd′nēd′l). A street in London, England, site of the Bank of England. —**the Old Lady of Threadneedle Street.** The Bank of England.

thread·worm (thrĕd′wûrm′) *n.* Any of various threadlike nematode worms, especially the **pinworm** *(see).*

thread·y (thrĕd′ē) *adj.* **-ier, -iest. 1.** Consisting of or resembling thread; fibrous; filamentous. **2.** Able to form threads, as a syrupy liquid; viscid. **3.** *Medicine.* Weak and shallow, as a pulse. **4.** Lacking fullness of tone; thin; weak: *a thready voice.* —**thread′i·ness** *n.*

threat (thrĕt) *n.* **1.** An expression of an intention to inflict pain, injury, evil, or punishment on a person or thing. **2.** An indication of impending danger or harm. **3.** A person, thing, or idea regarded as a possible danger; a menace. —*tr.v.* **threated, threating, threats.** *Archaic.* To threaten. [Middle English *thret,* Old English *thrēat,* oppression, use of force, threat. See **treud-** in Appendix.*]

threat·en (thrĕt′n) *v.* **-ened, -ening, -ens.** —*tr.* **1.** To express a threat against. **2.** To serve as a threat to; endanger; menace. **3.** To give signs or warning of; portend. **4.** To express threats of danger or other harm. —*intr.* **1.** To express or use threats. **2.** To indicate danger or other harm. —**threat′en·er** *n.* —**threat′en·ing·ly** *adv.*

Synonyms: *threaten, menace, intimidate.* These verbs mean to foretell danger, promise evil or injury, or inspire fear. *Threaten,* the most widely applicable, can refer to verbal promise of harm; to forewarning, as *dark skies threaten rain;* to appearance or overt action calculated or serving to make a person fearful; or to having a character that puts someone or something in danger, as *inflation threatens purchasing power. Menace* is limited principally to the last two of the foregoing senses. *Intimidate* refers to inspiring fear in a person, and often to inhibiting speech or action, by a show or promise of force.

three (thrē) *n.* The cardinal number written 3 or in Roman numerals III. See **number.** [Middle English *three,* Old English *thrī(e), thrēo.* See **trei-** in Appendix.*] —**three** *adj* & *pron.*

three-base hit (thrē′bās′). *Baseball.* A base hit that allows the batter to reach third base without being put out; a triple. Also called "three-bagger."

three birds. A plant, the **nodding pogonia** *(see).*

three-card mon·te (thrē′kärd′ mŏn′tē). A gambling card game in which each player is dealt and shown three cards, which are then placed face down on the table, the players betting they can identify a particular card.

three-col·or (thrē′kŭl′ər) *adj.* Designating a color printing or photographic process in which three primary colors are transferred by three different plates or filters to a surface, reproducing all the colors of the subject matter.

three-D (thrē′dē′) *adj.* Three-dimensional. Also written 3-D. —*n.* A three-dimensional medium, display, or performance, especially a cinematic or graphic display in three dimensions. Also written 3-D.

three-deck·er (thrē′dĕk′ər) *n.* **1.** A ship having three decks; especially, one of a class of sail-powered warships with guns on three decks. **2.** Anything with three layers; especially, a sandwich having three slices of bread.

three-di·men·sion·al (thrē′dĭ-mĕn′shən-əl) *adj.* **1.** Of, pertaining to, having, or existing in three dimensions. **2.** Having or appearing to have extension in depth.

three·fold (thrē′fōld′) *adj.* **1.** Having or consisting of three parts. **2.** Three times as many or as much; treble. —*adv.* Three times as much or as great; trebly. —*n.* An amount or number three times more than a specified unit.

three-gait·ed (thrē′gā′tĭd) *adj.* Trained in three gaits, the walk, trot, and canter. Said of a horse.

Three Graces. The **Graces** *(see).*

three-mile limit (thrē′mīl′). *International Law.* The outer limit of the area extending three miles out to sea from the coast of a land that constitutes that land's **territorial waters** *(see).*

three·pence (thrĭp′əns, thrŭp′-, thrĕp′-) *n., pl.* **threepence** or **-pences.** Also **thru·pence** (thrŭp′-). *British.* **1.** A coin worth three pennies. **2.** The sum of three pennies.

three·pen·ny (thrĭp′ə-nē, thrŭp′-, thrĕp′-) *adj. British.* **1.** Worth or priced at threepence. **2.** Very small; trifling.

three-piece (thrē′pēs′) *adj.* Made in or consisting of three parts or pieces: *a three-piece suit.*

three-ply (thrē′plī′) *adj.* Consisting of three layers or strands.

three-point landing (thrē′point′). **1.** An airplane landing in which the tailskid or tail wheel and the two forward wheels all touch the ground simultaneously; a perfect landing. **2.** *Informal.* Anything done perfectly or successfully.

three-quar·ter (thrē′kwôr′tər) *adj.* Pertaining to, consisting of, or showing three-fourths of something.

three-quarter binding. A type of bookbinding in which the leather or fabric covering the spine extends onto the covers for one third of their width.

three-ring circus (thrē′rĭng′). **1.** A circus having simultaneous performances in three separate rings. **2.** A situation characterized by a plethora of bewildering activity.

three R's. Reading, writing, and arithmetic, considered as the fundamentals of elementary education. [From the facetious spelling *reading, 'riting, and 'rithmetic.*]

three·score (thrē′skôr′, -skōr′) *adj.* Sixty; three times twenty. —**three′score′** *n.*

three·some (thrē′səm) *adj.* Consisting of or performed by three. —*n.* **1.** A group of three persons. **2.** Any activity involving three persons; especially, a golf match in which one player competes against two others who alternate their play.

three-square (thrē′skwâr′) *adj.* Having an equilateral triangular cross section: *a three-square file.*

three wood. A golf club, a **spoon** *(see).*

threm·ma·tol·o·gy (thrĕm′ə-tŏl′ə-jē) *n.* The scientific breeding of domestic plants and animals. [Greek *thremma* (stem *thremmat-*), creature (see **threph-** in Appendix*) + -LOGY.]

thren·o·dy (thrĕn′ə-dē) *n., pl.* **-dies.** A song of lamentation: *"the hermit bee / Drones a quiet threnody"* (Walter de la Mare). [Greek *thrēnōidia* : *thrēnos,* dirge, lament (see **dher-**[3] in Appendix*) + *ōidē,* song, ODE.] —**thre·no′di·al** (thrĭ-nō′dē-əl), **thre·nod′ic** (thrĭ-nŏd′ĭk) *adj.* —**thren′o·dist** *n.*

thre·o·nine (thrē′ə-nēn′) *n.* A colorless crystalline amino acid, $C_4H_9NO_3$, derived from the hydrolysis of protein, and an essential component of human nutrition. [Origin uncertain.]

thresh (thrĕsh) *v.* **threshed, threshing, threshes.** —*tr.* **1. a.** To beat the stems and husks of (grain or cereal plants) with a machine or flail to separate the grain or seeds from the straw. **b.** To separate (grain or seed) in this manner. **2.** To discuss or go over (an issue, for example) repeatedly. Often used with *over.* **3.** *Rare.* To beat severely; thrash. —*intr.* **1.** To thresh grain. **2.** To thrash about; to toss. —**thresh out.** To resolve by intensive discussion: *thresh out our differences.* —*n.* The act of threshing. [Middle English *thresshen,* Old English *therscan.* See **ter-**[2] in Appendix.*]

thresh·er (thrĕsh′ər) *n.* **1.** One who threshes. **2.** A **threshing machine** *(see).* **3.** Any of various sharks of the genus *Alopias,* having a tail with a long, whiplike upper lobe.

threshing machine. A farm machine used in threshing grain or seed plants. Also called "thresher."

thresh·old (thrĕsh′ōld′, thrĕsh′hōld′) *n.* **1.** The piece of wood or stone placed beneath a door; doorsill. **2.** An entrance or doorway. **3.** The outset; verge; beginning. **4.** The intensity below which a mental or physical stimulus cannot be perceived and can produce no response: *low threshold of pain.* [Middle English *thresshold,* Old English *therscold, threscold.* See **ter-**[2] in Appendix.*]

threw. Past tense of **throw.**

thrice (thrīs) *adv.* **1.** Three times. **2.** In a threefold quantity or degree. **3.** *Archaic.* Extremely; greatly. [Middle English *thries,* adverbial genitive of *thrie,* Old English *thriga, thriwa.* See **trei-** in Appendix.*]

thrift (thrĭft) *n.* **1.** Wise economy in the management of money and other resources; frugality. **2.** *Rare.* Vigorous growth of plants or other living things; thriving. **3.** Any of several densely tufted, chiefly European plants of the genus *Armeria;* especially, *A. maritima,* having rounded clusters of pink flowers. [Middle English, prosperity, a flourishing, profit, savings, from Old Norse, prosperity, from *thrīfask,* to THRIVE.]

thrift·y (thrĭf′tē) *adj.* **-ier, -iest. 1.** Wisely economical; frugal. **2.** Industrious and thriving; prosperous. **3.** Growing vigorously; thriving, as a plant. —See Synonyms at **sparing.** —**thrift′i·ly** *adv.* —**thrift′i·ness** *n.*

thrill (thrĭl) *v.* **thrilled, thrilling, thrills.** —*tr.* **1.** To cause to feel a sudden intense sensation; excite greatly. **2.** To give great pleasure to; to delight. **3.** To cause to quiver or vibrate. —*intr.* **1.** To feel a sudden quiver of emotion. **2.** To quiver, tremble, or vibrate. —*n.* **1.** A quivering or trembling passing through the body as a result of sudden emotion. **2.** That which produces such excitement. **3.** *Pathology.* A slight vibration that accompanies a cardiac or vascular murmur. [Middle English *thrillen,* variant of *thirlen,* to pierce, Old English *thyrlian,* from *thyr(e)l,* hole. See **ter-**[3] in Appendix.*] —**thrill′ing·ly** *adv.*

thrill·er (thrĭl′ər) *n.* **1.** One that thrills. **2.** *Informal.* A sensational or suspenseful story or motion picture.

ă pat/ā pay/âr care/ä father/b bib/ch church/d deed/ĕ pet/ē be/f fife/g gag/h hat/hw which/ĭ pit/ī pie/îr pier/j judge/k kick/l lid, needle/m mum/n no, sudden/ng thing/ŏ pot/ō toe/ô paw, for/oi noise/ou out/ŏŏ took/ōō boot/p pop/r roar/s sauce/sh ship, dish/

thrips (thrĭps) *n., pl.* **thrips.** Any of various small, often wingless insects of the order Thysanoptera, many of which are destructive to plants. [Latin, woodworm, from Greek *thrips*†.]

thrive (thrīv) *intr.v.* **throve** (thrōv) or **thrived, thrived** or **thriven** (thrĭv′ən), **thriving, thrives. 1.** To improve steadily, as in wealth or position; prosper. **2.** To grow vigorously; flourish. [Thrive, throve, thriven; Middle English *thrīven, throfe, thriven,* to increase, flourish, from Old Norse *thrīfask,* "to grasp for oneself," reflexive of *thrīfa*†, to seize.] **—thriv′er** *n.*

throat (thrōt) *n.* **1.** *Anatomy.* **a.** The portion of the digestive tract that lies between the rear of the mouth and the esophagus and includes the fauces and the pharynx. **b.** The anterior portion of the neck. **2.** *Botany.* The outer, expanded part of a tubular corolla. **3.** Any narrow passage or part suggestive of the human throat: *the throat of a tennis racket.* **—lump in the throat.** *Informal.* A choking feeling in the throat resulting from intense emotion. **—stick in one's throat.** *Informal.* To be difficult to express because of one's reluctance to do so. *—tr.v.* **throated, throating, throats.** To pronounce with a harsh or guttural voice. [Middle English *throte,* Old English *throte, throtu,* from Germanic *thrut-* (unattested).]

throat·latch (thrōt′lăch′) *n.* A strap passing under the neck of a horse or other animal for holding a bridle or halter in place.

throat·y (thrō′tē) *adj.* **-ier, -iest.** Uttered or sounding as if uttered deep in the throat; guttural, hoarse, or husky. **—throat′i·ly** *adv.* **—throat′i·ness** *n.*

throb (thrŏb) *intr.v.* **throbbed, throbbing, throbs. 1.** To beat rapidly or violently; to pound: *"Her heart throbs, and with very shame would break."* (Marvell). **2.** To vibrate, pulsate, or sound with a steady, pronounced rhythm. —See Synonyms at **pulsate.** *—n.* The act of throbbing; a beat, palpitation, or vibration. [Middle English *throbben* (attested only in the present participle); imitative.] **—throb′bing·ly** *adv.*

throe (thrō) *n.* **1.** *Often plural.* A violent pang or spasm of pain, as in childbirth or at the crisis of an illness. **2.** *Plural.* A condition of agonizing struggle or effort. [Middle English *throwe,* Old English *thrawe*†, paroxysm.]

throm·bin (thrŏm′bən) *n.* An enzyme in blood that facilitates blood clotting by reacting with fibrinogen to form fibrin. [THROMB(O)- + -IN.]

thrombo-, thromb-. Indicates a blood clot; for example, **thromboplastin, thrombin.** [From Greek *thrombos,* THROMBUS.]

throm·bo·cyte (thrŏm′bə-sīt′) *n.* A blood platelet. [THROMB(O)- + -CYTE.]

throm·bo·em·bo·lism (thrŏm′bō-ĕm′bə-lĭz′əm) *n.* The blocking of a blood vessel by a thrombus dislodged from a vein.

throm·bo·plas·tic (thrŏm′bō-plăs′tĭk) *adj.* **1.** Causing or promoting blood clotting. **2.** Of or pertaining to thromboplastin. [THROMBO- + -PLASTIC.]

throm·bo·plas·tin (thrŏm′bō-plăs′tən) *n.* A protein complex essential for thrombin formation and blood clotting. [THROMB(O)- + -PLAST + -IN.]

throm·bo·sis (thrŏm-bō′sĭs) *n., pl.* **-ses** (-sēz′). The formation, presence, or development of a thrombus. [New Latin, from Greek *thrombōsis,* a clotting, from *thrombousthai,* to clot, from *thrombos,* THROMBUS.]

throm·bus (thrŏm′bəs) *n., pl.* **-bi** (-bī′). A clot occluding a blood vessel or formed in a heart cavity, produced by coagulation of the blood. [New Latin, from Greek *thrombos*†, lump, clot.]

throne (thrōn) *n.* **1.** The chair occupied by a sovereign, bishop, or other exalted personage on state or ceremonial occasions. **2.** A personage who occupies a throne: *a decree from the throne.* **3.** The power, dignity, or rank of such a personage; sovereignty. **4.** *Plural. Theology.* The third of the nine orders of angels. *—v.* **throned, throning, thrones.** *—tr.* To enthrone. *—intr.* To occupy a throne; to reign. [Middle English, learned respelling of earlier *trone,* from Old French, from Latin *thronus,* from Greek *thronos.* See **dher-**[2] in Appendix.*]

throne room. The room in which an enthroned monarch or church dignitary holds audiences.

throng (thrŏng) *n.* **1.** A large group of people gathered or crowded closely together; a multitude. **2.** Any large group of things; a host. *—v.* **thronged, thronging, throngs.** *—tr.* **1.** To crowd into; fill utterly. **2.** To press in upon; surround with large numbers. *—intr.* To gather, press, or move in a throng: *"A thousand fantasies/Begin to throng into my memory"* (Milton). [Middle English *throng, thrang,* Old English *thrang,* probably from Common Germanic *thring-* (unattested), to press, crowd.]

thros·tle (thrŏs′əl) *n.* **1.** *Poetic.* Any of various Old World thrushes. **2.** A machine formerly used for spinning cotton, wool, or other fiber. [Middle English *throstle,* Old English *throstle.* See **trozdos-** in Appendix.*]

throt·tle (thrŏt′l) *n.* **1. a.** A valve in an internal-combustion engine that regulates the amount of vaporized fuel entering the cylinders. **b.** A similar valve in a steam engine regulating the amount of steam. **2.** A lever or pedal controlling this valve. **3.** *Rare.* The throat or windpipe. *—tr.v.* **throttled, -tling, -tles. 1. a.** To regulate the flow of (fuel) in an engine. **b.** To regulate the speed of (an engine) with a throttle. **2.** To strangle; to choke. **3.** To suppress. [Sense 1, perhaps diminutive of THROAT; sense 3, Middle English *throtelen,* to throttle, perhaps from *throte,* THROAT.] **—throt′tler** *n.*

through (thrōō) *prep.* **1.** In one side and out the opposite or another side of. **2.** Among or between; in the midst of: *a walk through the flowers.* **3.** By way of. **4.** By the means or agency of: *"they preserved their individuality through men and not by opposition to them"* (F. Scott Fitzgerald). **5.** Here and there in; around: *a tour through France.* **6.** From the beginning to the end of: *stayed up through the night.* **7.** At or to the end of; done or finished with, especially successfully: *We are through the initial testing period.* **8.** Without stopping for: *drove through a red light.* **9.** Because of. Also informally respelled "thru." —See Synonyms at **by.** *—adv.* **1.** From one end or side to another or opposite end or side. **2.** From beginning to end; completely; thoroughly. **3.** To a conclusion or accomplishment: *see the matter through.* **4.** Out into the open. **—through and through. 1.** In every part of; throughout. **2.** In every respect; completely. Also informally respelled "thru." *—adj.* **1.** Passing or extending from one end, side, or surface to another: *a through beam.* **2.** Allowing continuous passage; unobstructed: *a through street.* **3.** Affording transportation to a destination with few or no stops and no transfers. **4.** Finished; done. See Usage note below. **5.** At the end of one's effectiveness or resources: *He's through financially.* See Usage note below. Also informally respelled "thru." [Middle English *thru(g)h, thurh,* Old English *thurh, thurȝh.* See **ter-**[3] in Appendix.*]

Usage: *Through* (adjective) is employed on all levels in the sense of "arrived at completion; finished": *When you are through with this book, please return it* (acceptable to 75 per cent of the Usage Panel as an example in writing). It is used more informally in extended senses meaning "having no further relationship": *You and I are through* and "having no further usefulness": *As a serious contender, he's through.*

through·ly (thrōō′lē) *adv. Archaic.* Thoroughly.

through·out (thrōō-out′) *prep.* In, to, through, or during every part of; all through. *—adv.* **1.** In or through all parts; everywhere. **2.** During the entire time or extent.

through·way. Variant of **thruway.**

throve. Past tense of **thrive.**

throw (thrō) *v.* **threw** (thrōō), **thrown** (thrōn), **throwing, throws.** *—tr.* **1.** To propel through the air with a swift motion of the arm; to hurl. **2.** To discharge into the air by any means. **3.** To hurl with great force, as in anger: *He threw himself at his opponent.* **4.** To hurl to the ground or floor. **5.** To perplex or mislead. **6. a.** To put on or off hastily or carelessly: *throw on a cape.* **b.** To put quickly into use or place: *throw in extra troops.* **7.** To put abruptly or forcibly into a specified condition: *threw him into a fit of laughter.* **8.** To form on a potter's wheel: *throw a vase.* **9.** To twist (fibers) into thread. **10. a.** To roll (dice). **b.** To roll (a particular combination) with dice. **11.** *Card Games.* To discard or play (a card). **12.** To cast (a shadow). **13.** To bear (young), as cows or horses. **14.** *Slang.* To arrange or give (a party, for example). **15.** To move (a controlling lever or switch). **16.** *Informal.* To lose (a contest) purposely. *—intr.* To cast, fling, or hurl something. **—throw in. 1.** To engage (a clutch or gears, for example). **2.** To add (an extra amount) with no additional charge. **—throw in with.** To join company with. **—throw off. 1.** To cast out; to reject; spurn. **2.** To give off; emit. **3.** To rid oneself of; evade. **—throw out. 1.** To give off; emit. **2.** To reject or discard. **3.** To offer, as a suggestion or plan. **4.** To disengage (a clutch or gears). **5.** *Baseball.* To put out (a base runner) by throwing the ball to the player guarding the base to which he is running. —See Synonyms at **eject. —throw over. 1.** To overturn. **2.** To abandon. **—throw up. 1.** To abandon; relinquish. **2.** To construct hurriedly. **3.** To vomit. *—n.* **1.** The act of throwing; a cast; a fling. **2.** The distance, height, or direction of something thrown: *a low throw.* **3. a.** A roll or cast of dice. **b.** The combination of numbers so obtained. **4.** A chance; venture. **5.** *Wrestling.* The technique used to throw an opponent. **6. a.** A light coverlet, such as an afghan. **b.** A scarf or shawl. **7.** *Machinery.* **a.** The length of the radius of a circle described by a crank, cam, or similar part. **b.** The maximum displacement of a part moved by a crank, cam, or the like. **8.** *Geology.* **a.** The amount of vertical displacement of a fault. **b.** The vertical component of the net slip. [Middle English *throwen, thrawen,* to turn, twist, hence to hurl, cast (presumably "to turn the body in the act of throwing"), Old English *thrāwan,* to turn, twist. See **ter-**[2] in Appendix.*] **—throw′er** *n.*

Synonyms: *throw, cast, hurl, fling, pitch, toss, sling, heave.* These verbs mean to propel an object, usually with a movement of the arm. *Throw* is the general, nonspecific term. Especially in earlier usage, *cast* was often interchangeable with *throw. Cast* now usually refers to propelling with great force or to propelling something light with a quick, skillful movement of the arm that culminates in sudden release. In the latter sense it implies careful aim. *Hurl* and *fling* mean to throw with great force. Both terms, like *pitch,* can imply impetuous or even haphazard action; but *pitch* more often means to propel something with a set aim or purpose in mind. *Toss,* in contrast, usually means to throw a light object in a leisurely or offhand manner. *Sling* stresses force of propulsion. *Heave* generally refers to lifting and throwing a ponderous object.

throw away. 1. To discard as useless. **2.** To fail to use.

throw·a·way (thrō′ə-wā′) *n.* Something that is or may be thrown away; especially, a handbill distributed on the street.

throw back. To revert to a type or stage in one's ancestral past.

throw·back (thrō′băk′) *n.* **1.** A reversion to a former type or ancestral characteristic. **2.** Loosely, an **atavism** *(see).*

thrown. Past participle of **throw.**

throw rug. A **scatter rug** *(see).*

thru (thrōō). *Informal.* **Through** *(see).*

thrum[1] (thrŭm) *v.* **thrummed, thrumming, thrums.** *—tr.* **1.** To play (a stringed instrument) idly or monotonously. **2.** To repeat or recite in a monotonous tone of voice. *—intr.* **1.** To strum

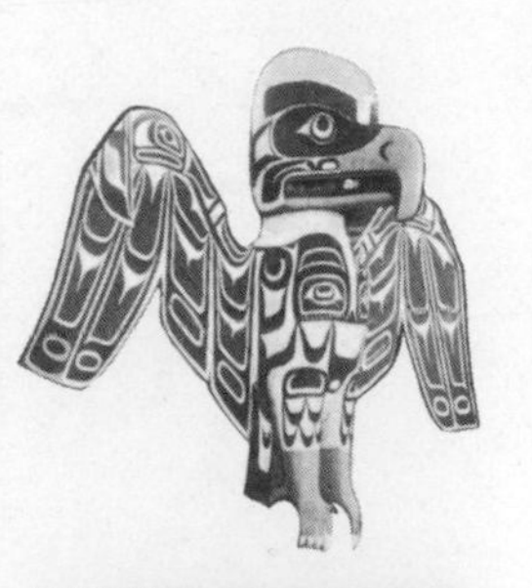

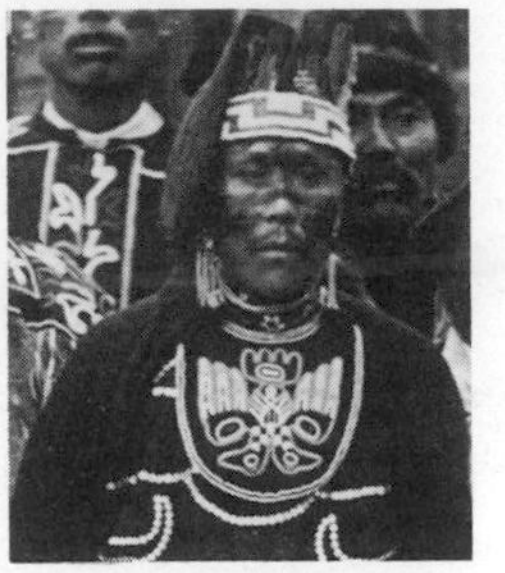

thunderbird
Above: At the top of a Kwakiutl totem pole
Below: Represented on a Tlingit Indian costume

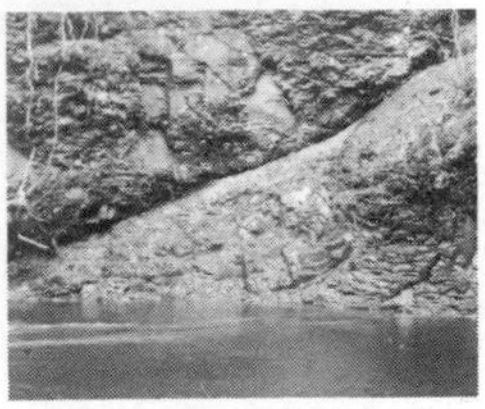

thrust fault
In shale rock strata in west-central New York State

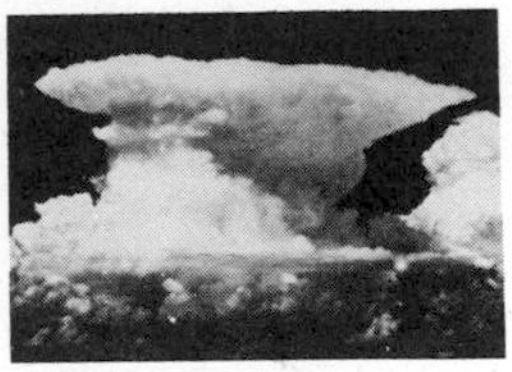

thunderhead

idly on a stringed instrument. **2.** To speak in a monotonous voice; to drone. —*n.* A thrumming sound. [Imitative.]

thrum[2] (thrŭm) *n.* **1. a.** The fringe of warp threads left on a loom after the cloth has been cut off. **b.** One of these threads. **2.** Any loose end, fringe, or tuft of thread. **3.** *Plural. Nautical.* Short bits of rope yarn inserted into canvas for the purpose of roughening the surface. —*tr.v.* **thrummed, thrumming, thrums. 1.** To cover or trim with thrums; to fringe. **2.** *Nautical.* To sew thrums in (canvas). [Middle English *thrum*, Old English *thrum* (attested only in *tungethrum*, ligament of the tongue). See **ter-**[1] in Appendix.*]

thru·pence. Variant of **threepence.**

thrush[1] (thrŭsh) *n.* **1.** Any of various songbirds of the family Turdidae, characteristically having brownish upper plumage and a spotted breast. **2.** Any of various similar or related birds. [Middle English *thrusch(e)*, Old English *thrysce.* See **trozdos-** in Appendix.*]

thrush[2] (thrŭsh) *n.* **1.** An oral infection with a fungus, *Candida albicans*, characterized by white eruptions in the mouth. **2.** A suppurative infection of a horse's foot caused by standing in a wet, unhygienic stall. [Obscurely akin to Swedish and Old Danish *tørsk*†.]

thrust (thrŭst) *v.* **thrust, thrusting, thrusts.** —*tr.* **1. a.** To push or drive quickly and forcibly. **b.** To stab; pierce. **2.** To force (oneself or another) into a specified condition or situation. **3.** To put in; interject. —*intr.* **1.** To shove into something; to push. **2.** To pierce or stab with a pointed weapon. **3.** To force one's way. —*n.* **1.** A forceful shove or push; a lunge. **2. a.** A driving force or pressure. **b.** The forward-directed force developed in a jet or rocket engine as a reaction to the rearward ejection of fuel gases at high velocities. **3.** A stab. **4.** The general direction or tendency: *"the whole thrust and purpose of their lives was forced under scrutiny"* (Hannah Green). **5.** *Architecture.* Outward or lateral stress in a structure, such as an arch. [Middle English *thrusten*, from Old Norse *thrȳsta*, to thrust, compress. See **treud-** in Appendix.*]

thrust fault. *Geology.* A reverse fault having a low angle of inclination in relation to the horizontal plane.

thru·way (thro͞o′wā′) *n.* Also **through·way.** An express highway; an expressway.

Thu·cyd·i·des (tho͞o-sĭd′ə-dēz′). Greek historian of the fifth century B.C.; author of *History of the Peloponnesian War.*

thud (thŭd) *n.* **1.** A dull sound, as that of a heavy object striking a solid surface. **2.** A blow or fall causing such a sound. —*intr.v.* **thudded, thudding, thuds.** To make such a sound. [Middle English *thudden*, Old English *thyddan* (imitative).]

thug (thŭg) *n.* **1.** A cutthroat or ruffian; hoodlum; a tough. **2.** One of a former band of professional assassins in northern India. [Hindi *ṭhag*, cheat, thief, from Sanskrit *sthaga*, robber, from *sthagati*, to cover, hide. See **steg-**[1] in Appendix.*] —**thug′ger·y** *n.* —**thug′gish** *adj.*

thug·gee (thŭg′ē′) *n.* The murderous practices or methods of the thugs in India. [Hindi *ṭhagī*, robbery, from *ṭhag*, THUG.]

Thu·le (tho͞o′lē *for sense 1;* to͞o′lē *for sense 2*). **1.** The most northerly region of the ancient habitable world, conceived as an island north of Britain by Ptolemy and other ancient geographers. See **ultima Thule. 2.** A settlement on the northwestern coast of Greenland, the site of a U.S. air base. Population, 600.

thu·li·um (tho͞o′lē-əm) *n. Symbol* **Tm** A bright silvery rare-earth element having 16 known isotopes with mass numbers ranging from 161 to 176. The x-ray emitting isotope Tm 170 is used in small portable medical x-ray units. Atomic number 69, atomic weight 168.934, melting point 1,545°C, boiling point 1,727°C, specific gravity 9.332, valences 2, 3. See **element.** [From THULE.]

thumb (thŭm) *n.* **1.** The short first digit of the human hand, apposable to each of the other four digits. **2.** A corresponding digit in other animals, especially primates. **3.** The part of a glove or mitten that covers the thumb. **4.** *Architecture.* An **ovolo** *(see).* —**all thumbs.** Clumsy; awkward. —**thumbs down.** Used to indicate rejection, refusal, or prohibition. Often used in the phrase *turn thumbs down (on).* —**thumbs up.** An expression intended to raise one's hopes. —**under the thumb of.** Under the influence, authority, or power of. —*v.* **thumbed, thumbing, thumbs.** —*tr.* **1.** To disarrange, soil, or wear by careless or frequent handling. **2.** *Informal.* To solicit (a ride) from a passing automobile by pointing one's thumb in the direction one is traveling. —*intr.* To hitchhike. —**thumb one's nose.** To express scorn or derision by or as if by placing the thumb on the nose and wiggling the fingers. —**thumb through.** To browse rapidly through (the pages of a book or magazine). [Middle English *thom(b)e*, Old English *thūma.* See **teuə-** in Appendix.*]

Thumb, General Tom. See **Stratton.**

thumb·hole (thŭm′hōl′) *n.* The hole on a wind instrument that is opened or closed with the thumb.

thumb index. A series of rounded indentations cut into the front edge of a reference book, each labeled, as with a letter, to indicate a section of the book.

thumb-in·dex (thŭm′ĭn′dĕks) *tr.v.* **-dexed, -dexing, -dexes.** To furnish with a thumb index.

thumb·nail (thŭm′nāl′) *n.* The nail of the thumb. —*adj.* **1.** Of the size of a thumbnail. **2.** Brief: *a thumbnail sketch.*

thumb·nut (thŭm′nŭt′) *n.* A **wing nut** *(see).*

thumb·screw (thŭm′skro͞o′) *n.* **1.** A screw so designed that it can be turned with the thumb and fingers. **2.** An instrument of torture formerly used to compress the thumb or thumbs.

thumb·stall (thŭm′stôl′) *n.* A sheath or cap worn on the thumb in certain manual tasks or to protect it when injured.

thumb·tack (thŭm′tăk′) *n.* A tack with a smooth, rounded head that can be pressed into place with the thumb. —*tr.v.* **thumbtacked, -tacking, -tacks.** To affix with a thumbtack.

Thum·mim. See **Urim and Thummim.**

thump (thŭmp) *n.* **1.** A blow with a blunt instrument. **2.** The muffled sound produced by such a blow or by a similarly muted noise; thud. —*v.* **thumped, thumping, thumps.** —*tr.* **1.** To beat with a blunt or dull instrument, or with the hand or foot, so as to produce a muffled sound or thud. **2.** To beat soundly or thoroughly; to drub. —*intr.* **1.** To hit or fall in such a way as to produce a thump; to pound. **2.** To walk with heavy steps; to stump. **3.** To throb audibly. [Imitative.] —**thump′er** *n.*

thump·ing (thŭm′pĭng) *adj.* **1.** Of or pertaining to something that thumps. **2.** *Informal.* **a.** Large; whopping. **b.** Thoroughly enjoyable. —**thump′ing·ly** *adv.*

Thun, Lake of (to͞on). A lake occupying about 18 square miles in central Switzerland, southeast of Bern, formed by a widening of the Aar River.

thun·der (thŭn′dər) *n.* **1.** The sound emitted by rapidly expanding gases along the path of the electrical discharge of lightning. **2.** Any similar sound. —**steal the thunder (from).** To anticipate or adopt another's idea or practice for one's own credit. —*v.* **thundered, -dering, -ders.** —*intr.* **1.** To produce thunder. **2.** To produce sounds like thunder. **3.** To utter loud, vociferous remarks or threats. —*tr.* To express violently, commandingly, or angrily; to roar. [Middle English *thunder*, *thon(d)re*, Old English *thunor.* See **stene-** in Appendix.*] —**thun′der·er** *n.*

thun·der·bird (thŭn′dər-bûrd′) *n.* In the mythology of some North American Indians, thunder, lightning, and rain personified as a huge bird.

thun·der·bolt (thŭn′dər-bōlt′) *n.* **1.** The discharge of lightning that accompanies thunder. **2.** A flash of lightning imagined as a bolt or dart hurled from the heavens. **3.** Someone or something that acts with sudden and destructive fury.

thun·der·clap (thŭn′dər-klăp′) *n.* **1.** A single sharp crash of thunder. **2.** Anything of similar violence, as a startling or shocking piece of news; a bombshell.

thun·der·cloud (thŭn′dər-kloud′) *n.* **1.** A large, dark cloud charged with electricity and producing thunder and lightning; a cumulonimbus. **2.** Anything of dread or menacing aspect.

thun·der·head (thŭn′dər-hĕd′) *n.* The swollen upper portion of a thundercloud, often associated with the coming of a thunderstorm; a cumulonimbus.

thun·der·ous (thŭn′dər-əs) *adj.* Also **thun·drous** (-drəs). **1.** Producing thunder or a similar sound. **2.** Loud and unrestrained: *thunderous applause.* —**thun′der·ous·ly** *adv.*

thun·der·show·er (thŭn′dər-shou′ər) *n.* A brief rainstorm accompanied by thunder and lightning.

thun·der·stone (thŭn′dər-stōn′) *n.* **1.** Any of various mineral concretions formerly supposed to be thunderbolts, such as a **belemnite** *(see).* **2.** *Archaic.* A flash of lightning conceived as a stone; thunderbolt.

thun·der·storm (thŭn′dər-stôrm′) *n.* An electrical storm accompanied by heavy rain.

thun·der·struck (thŭn′dər-strŭk′) *adj.* Also **thun·der·strick·en** (-strĭk′ən). Struck with sudden astonishment or amazement.

Thur·ber (thûr′bər), **James (Grover).** 1894–1961. American artist and writer.

thu·ri·ble (tho͝or′ə-bəl) *n.* A vessel, a **censer** *(see).* [Middle English *thoryble*, from Old French *thurible*, from Latin *t(h)ūribulum*, from *t(h)ūs* (stem *t(h)ūr-*), incense, from Greek *thuos*, (sacrificial) incense, burnt offering, offering. See **dheu-**[1] in Appendix.*]

thu·ri·fer (tho͝or′ə-fər) *n.* An altar boy or acolyte who carries a thurible. [New Latin, from Latin *thūrifer*, "incense bearing" : *thūs* (stem *thūr-*), incense (see **thurible**) + -FER.]

Thu·rin·gi·a (tho͝o-rĭn′jē-ə). *German* **Thü·rin·gen** (tü′rĭng′ən). A former state of central Germany and, for a time, of East Germany; now divided among three East German states.

Thu·rin·gi·an (tho͝o-rĭn′jē-ən, -jən) *adj.* Of or pertaining to Thuringia or its people. —*n.* **1.** One of an ancient tribe inhabiting central Germany until the sixth century A.D. **2.** An inhabitant or native of Thuringia.

Thuringian Forest. *German* **Thü·rin·ger Wald** (tü′rĭng′ər vält′). A mountainous and forested region extending southeastward through southern East Germany to the border with Czechoslovakia. Highest elevation, 3,222 feet.

Thur·rock (thûr′ək). An urban district in southeastern England, 20 miles east of London. Population, 118,000.

Thurs·day (thûrz′dē, -dā′) *n. Abbr.* **Thurs.** The fifth day of the week. [Middle English *thur(e)sday*, Old English *thūr(e)s dæg* (influenced by Old Norse *thōrsdagr*, "Thor's day"), from earlier *thunresdæg*, "Thor's day" (translation of Late Latin *Jovis diēs*, "Jupiter's day") : *thunres*, genitive of *thunor*, THUNDER + *dæg*, DAY.]

Thursday Island. A small island (about one square mile) off Queensland, Australia; a pearl-fishing center in Torres Strait northwest of Cape York.

Thurs·ton Island (thûrs′tən). An island adjacent to the Walgreen coast of Antarctica.

thus (thŭs) *adv.* Also *nonstandard* **thus·ly** (thŭs′lē) (for sense 1). **1.** In a manner previously stated or to be stated; in this manner. See Usage note below. **2.** To a stated degree or extent; so: *thus far.* **3.** Therefore; consequently. [Middle English *thus*, Old English *thus.* See **to-** in Appendix.*]

Usage: *Thusly* is occasionally employed humorously, for mock-stylish effects. Otherwise, as a variant of *thus* (itself an adverb), *thusly* is termed unacceptable by 97 per cent of the Usage Panel.

ă pat/ā pay/âr care/ä father/b bib/ch church/d deed/ĕ pet/ē be/f fife/g gag/h hat/hw which/ĭ pit/ī pie/îr pier/j judge/k kick/l lid, needle/m mum/n no, sudden/ng thing/ŏ pot/ō toe/ô paw, for/oi noise/ou out/o͝o took/o͞o boot/p pop/r roar/s sauce/sh ship, dish/

thwack (thwăk) *tr.v.* **thwacked, thwacking, thwacks.** To strike or hit with something flat; to whack: *"We'll thwack him hence with distaffs"* (Shakespeare). —*n.* A hard blow with something flat; a whack. [Imitative.]

thwart (thwôrt) *tr.v.* **thwarted, thwarting, thwarts. 1.** To prevent from taking place; frustrate; block. **2.** To challenge, oppose, or offend; antagonize. —See Synonyms at **frustrate.** —*n.* A seat across a boat, on which the oarsman sits. —*adj.* **1.** Extending, lying, or passing across something; transverse. **2.** Perverse; stubborn. —*adv. Archaic.* Athwart; across. —*prep. Archaic.* Athwart; across. [From Middle English *thwert,* athwart, across, perverse, from Old Norse *thvert,* neuter of *thverr,* transverse. See **terkw-** in Appendix.*] —**thwart′ed·ly** *adv.* —**thwart′er** *n.*

thy (*th*ī) *adj.* The possessive form of the pronoun *thou. Archaic & Poetic.* Used attributively to indicate possession, agency, or reception of an action by the person or persons spoken to: *"He sees his brood about thy knee."* (Tennyson). [Middle English *thy, thin,* Old English *thīn,* thine. See **tu-** in Appendix.*]

thy·la·cine (thī′lə-sīn′) *n.* A wolflike marsupial, *Thylacinus cynocephalus,* of forest areas of Tasmania, having dark transverse bands across its back. Also called "Tasmanian wolf." [New Latin *thylacinus,* from Greek *thulakos*†, a sack.]

thyme (tīm) *n.* **1.** Any of several aromatic herbs or low shrubs of the genus *Thymus;* especially, *T. vulgaris,* of southern Europe, having small purplish flowers. **2.** The leaves of this plant, used as seasoning. [Middle English *t(h)yme,* from Old French *thym,* from Latin *thymum,* from Greek *thumon,* thyme. See **dheu-**[1] in Appendix.*]

-thymia. Indicates state of mind or temperament; for example, **schizothymia.** [New Latin, from Greek *thumos,* soul, spirit, mind, temper. See **dheu-**[1] in Appendix.*]

thym·ic[1] (tī′mĭk) *adj.* Of or pertaining to thyme.

thy·mic[2] (thī′mĭk) *adj.* Of or pertaining to the thymus.

thy·mol (thī′môl′, -mōl′) *n.* A white, crystalline, aromatic compound, $C_{10}H_{14}O$, derived from thyme oil and other oils and used as an antiseptic, in perfumery, and as a preservative. [THYM(E) + -OL.]

thy·mus (thī′məs) *n.* A ductless glandlike structure, situated just behind the top of the sternum, that plays some part in building resistance to disease but is usually vestigial in adults after reaching its maximum development during early childhood. [New Latin, from Greek *thumos*†.]

thy·roid (thī′roid′) *adj.* Of or relating to the thyroid gland or the thyroid cartilage. —*n.* **1.** The **thyroid gland** *(see).* **2.** The **thyroid cartilage** *(see).* **3.** A dried and powdered preparation of the thyroid gland of certain domestic animals, used in the treatment of hypothyroid conditions, as cretinism. [Obsolete French *thyroide,* from Greek *thuroidēs, thureoeidēs,* shaped like a door or oblong shield, from *thureos,* door-shaped : *thura,* door (see **dhwer-** in Appendix*) + -OID.]

thyroid cartilage. The largest cartilage of the larynx, having two broad processes that join anteriorly to form the Adam's apple. Also called "thyroid."

thy·roid·ec·to·my (thī′roi′dĕk′tə-mē) *n., pl.* **-mies.** Surgical removal of the thyroid gland. [THYROID + -ECTOMY.]

thyroid gland. A two-lobed endocrine gland found in all vertebrates, located in front of and on either side of the trachea in humans, and producing the hormone thyroxin. Also called "thyroid."

thy·roid·i·tis (thī′roi-dī′tĭs) *n.* Inflammation of the thyroid gland. [New Latin : THYROID + -ITIS.]

thy·ro·tox·i·co·sis (thī′rō-tŏk′sĭ-kō′sĭs) *n.* Poisoning from hyperthyroidism. [New Latin : THYRO(ID) + TOXICOSIS.]

thy·rot·ro·pin (thī-rŏt′rə-pĭn, thī′rə-trō′pĭn) *n.* Also **thy·rot·ro·phin** (-fĭn). A hormone of the anterior pituitary that stimulates and regulates the development and secretion of the thyroid gland hormone. [THYRO(ID) + -TROP(E) + -IN.]

thy·rox·in (thī-rŏk′sĭn) *n.* Also **thy·rox·ine** (thī-rŏk′sēn′, -sĭn). An iodine-containing hormone, $C_{15}H_{11}I_4NO_4$, produced by the thyroid gland to regulate metabolism and made synthetically for treatment of thyroid disorders. [THYR(OID) + OX(Y)- + -IN.]

thyrse (thûrs) *n. Botany.* A branched flower cluster, as of the lilac, of which the main axis does not terminate in a flower. Also called "thyrsus." [New Latin *thyrsus,* THYRSUS.]

thyr·soid (thûr′soid′) *adj.* Also **thyr·soi·dal** (thûr′soid′l). *Botany.* Shaped like or similar to a thyrse.

thyr·sus (thûr′səs) *n., pl.* **-si** (-sī′). **1.** A staff tipped with a pine cone and twined with ivy, represented as carried by Dionysius, Dionysian revelers, or satyrs. **2.** *Botany.* A **thyrse** *(see).* [New Latin, from Latin, from Greek *thursos*†.]

thy·self (*th*ī-sĕlf′) *pron. Archaic.* Yourself. Used as the reflexive or emphatic form of *thee* or *thou.*

THz terahertz.

ti[1] (tē) *n. Music.* A syllable representing the seventh tone of the diatonic scale in solmization. Formerly called "si." [Alteration of *si,* short for Latin *Sancte Iohannes,* "Saint John," from a stanza sung in a hymn to Saint John the Baptist. See **gamut.**]

ti[2] (tē) *n.* Any of several trees or shrubs of the genus *Cordyline,* of tropical Asia and adjacent Pacific regions; especially, *C. australis,* having a terminal tuft of long, narrow leaves. [Tahitian and Maori.]

Ti The symbol for the element titanium.

Ti·a Jua·na. See **Tijuana.**

ti·ar·a (tē-ăr′ə, -âr′ə, -är′ə) *n.* **1.** The triple crown worn by the pope. **2.** An ornamental crownlike headpiece, often decorated with jewels, worn by women on formal occasions. **3.** The headdress worn by ancient Persian kings. [Originally a turbanlike headdress worn among the Persians, from Latin *tiāra,* from Greek *tiara(s),* of Oriental origin.]

Ti·ber (tī′bər). *Italian* **Te·ve·re** (tā′vā-rā). Ancient name **Ti·ber·is** (tī′bər-ĭs). A river of central Italy, rising in the Apennines and flowing 251 miles south past Rome to the Tyrrhenian Sea.

Ti·be·ri·as (tī-bîr′ĭ-əs). A town of Israel, in the northeast on the Sea of Galilee; the capital of Galilee and center of Jewish learning in Palestine under the Romans. Population, 22,000.

Ti·be·ri·as, Lake. See Sea of **Galilee.**

Ti·be·ri·us (tī-bîr′ĭ-əs). In full, Tiberius Claudius Nero Caesar. 42 B.C.–A.D. 37. Second Roman Emperor (A.D. 14–37); stepson and successor of Augustus.

Ti·bes·ti Mas·sif (tĭ-bĕs′tĭ mă-sēf′). A Saharan mountain group in northern Chad. Highest elevation, Emi Koussi (11,204 feet).

Ti·bet (tĭ-bĕt′). *Chinese* **Si·tsang** (shē′tsäng′). A former theocratic state occupying 560,000 square miles in southern Asia, constituting the Tibetan Autonomous Region of southern China since 1957. Population, 1,270,000. Capital, Lhasa.

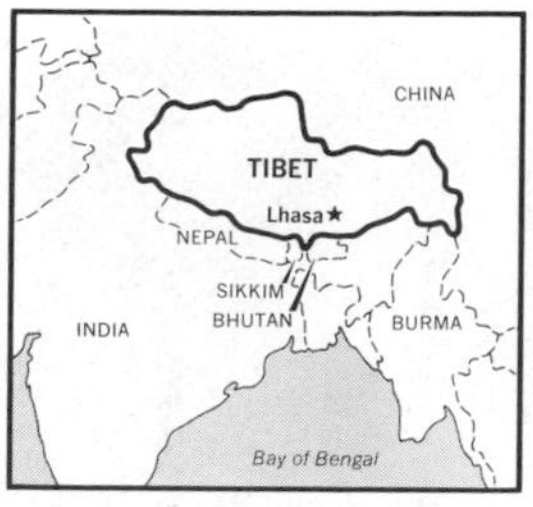

Tibet

Ti·bet·an (tĭ-bĕt′n) *adj.* Of or pertaining to Tibet, its people, or their language or culture. —*n.* **1.** One of the Mongoloid people of Tibet. **2.** The Tibeto-Burman language of Tibet.

Ti·bet·o-Bur·man (tĭ-bĕt′ō-bûr′mən) *n.* Also **Ti·bet·o-Bur·mese** (tĭ-bĕt′ō-bər-mēz′, -mēs′). A language family including principally Tibetan, Burmese, Lolo, and Balti, usually classed as a subgroup of Sino-Tibetan. —**Ti·bet′o-Bur′man, Ti·bet′o-Bur′mese′** *adj.*

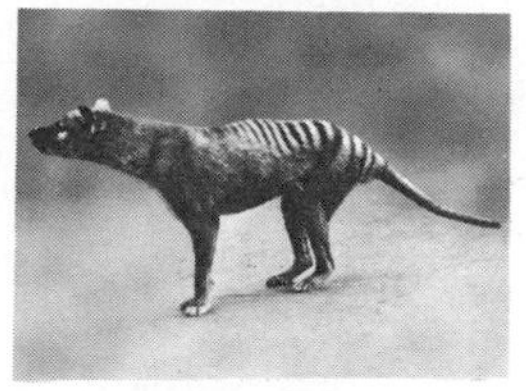
thylacine

tib·i·a (tĭb′ē-ə) *n., pl.* **-iae** (-ē-ē′) or **-ias. 1.** The inner and larger of the two bones of the lower human leg from the knee to the ankle. Also called "shin," "shinbone." **2.** A homologous bone in animals. **3.** The fourth division of an insect's leg, between the femur and the tarsi. **4.** A kind of ancient flute originally made from an animal's leg bone. [Latin *tībia*†, shinbone, pipe.] —**tib′i·al** *adj.*

Ti·bur. The ancient name for **Tivoli.**

Ti·bu·rón (tē′vo͞o-rôn′). An island of Mexico, occupying 458 square miles in the Gulf of California.

tic (tĭk) *n.* **1.** A habitual spasmodic muscular contraction, usually in the face or extremities, and often of neurotic origin. **2.** Tic douloureux. [French, originally a veterinary term (perhaps imitative).]

tic dou·lou·reux (tĭk′ do͞o′lo͞o-ro͞o′). **Trigeminal neuralgia** *(see).* [French, "painful tic."]

Ti·ci·no (tē-chē′nō). **1.** Ancient name **Ti·ci·nus** (tĭ-sī′nəs). A river rising in southern Switzerland and flowing 154 miles generally south to the Po in northern Italy. **2.** A canton occupying 1,086 square miles in southern Switzerland. Population, 196,000. Capital, Bellinzona.

tick[1] (tĭk) *n.* **1.** The recurring sharp, clicking sound made by a machine, especially by a clock. **2.** *British Informal.* An instant; a moment. **3.** A light mark such as a dot or dash used to check off or call attention to an item. —*v.* **ticked, ticking, ticks.** —*intr.* To emit recurring sharp, clicking sounds, as a clock. —*tr.* To mark or check off (a listed item) with a tick. [Middle English *tek* (perhaps imitative).]

tick[2] (tĭk) *n.* **1.** Any of numerous bloodsucking parasitic arachnids of the family Ixodidae within the order Acarina, many of which transmit infectious diseases. **2.** Any of various usually wingless, louselike insects of the family Hippoboscidae, that are parasitic on sheep, goats, and other animals. [Middle English *tyke, teke,* Old English *ticia.* See **deigh-** in Appendix.*]

tick[3] (tĭk) *n.* **1. a.** The cloth case of a mattress or pillow. **b.** A light mattress without inner springs. **2.** Ticking. [Middle English *tikke,* probably from Middle Dutch *tike,* from West Germanic *tēka* (unattested), from Latin *thēca,* cover, case, from Greek *thēkē.* See **dhē-**[1] in Appendix.*]

tick[4] (tĭk) *n. British Informal.* Credit; trust: *on tick.* [Short for TICKET.]

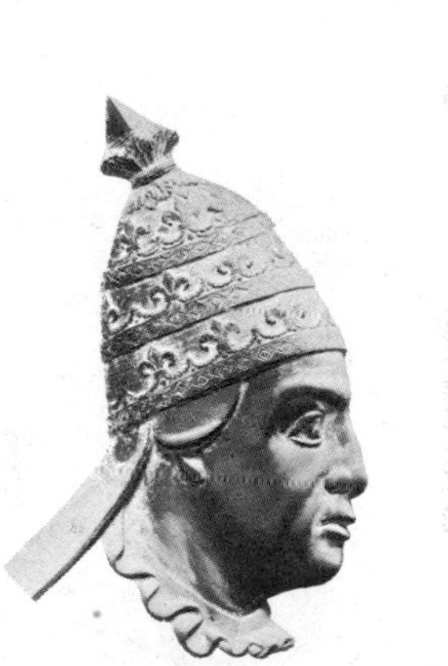
tiara
Detail of a bronze door of St. Peter's Basilica, showing Pope Eugene IV wearing a tiara

tick·er (tĭk′ər) *n.* **1. a.** A former telegraphic instrument that receives and records stock-market quotations on a paper tape. **b.** Any of various devices in current use that record similar information by electronic means rather than paper tape. **2.** *Slang.* A watch. **3.** *Slang.* The heart.

ticker tape. The paper strip on which a ticker prints.

tick·er-tape parade (tĭk′ər-tāp′). A traditional hero's welcome to New York City in which ribbons of paper are strewn from buildings as the hero parades by.

tick·et (tĭk′ĭt) *n.* **1.** *Abbr.* **tkt.** A paper slip or card indicating that its holder has paid for or is entitled to a specified service, right, or consideration: *a bus ticket.* **2.** A certifying document; especially, a captain's or pilot's license. **3.** An identifying or descriptive tag attached to merchandise; a label. **4.** *Rare.* A short notice or memorandum. **5.** A list of candidates proposed or endorsed by a political party; a slate. **6.** A legal summons, especially for a traffic violation. **7.** *Slang.* The proper thing: *A change of scene would be just the ticket for her.* —*tr.v.* **ticketed, -eting, -ets. 1.** To provide with a ticket or tickets for admission or passage. **2.** To attach a tag to; to label. **3.** To designate for a specified use or end; destine. **4.** To serve (an offender) with a legal summons. [Obsolete French *etiquet,* ticket, label, from Old French *estiquet(te),* from *estiquier,* to stick, from Middle Dutch *steken.* See **steig-** in Appendix.*]

ticket scalper. A profiteer who buys up desirable admission tickets and resells them at higher prices.

tick fever. Any of various diseases, such as Rocky Mountain spotted fever, transmitted by ticks.

tick·ing (tĭk′ĭng) *n.* A strong, tightly woven fabric of cotton or linen used to make ticks.

tick·le (tĭk′əl) *v.* **-led, -ling, -les.** —*tr.* **1.** To touch (the body)

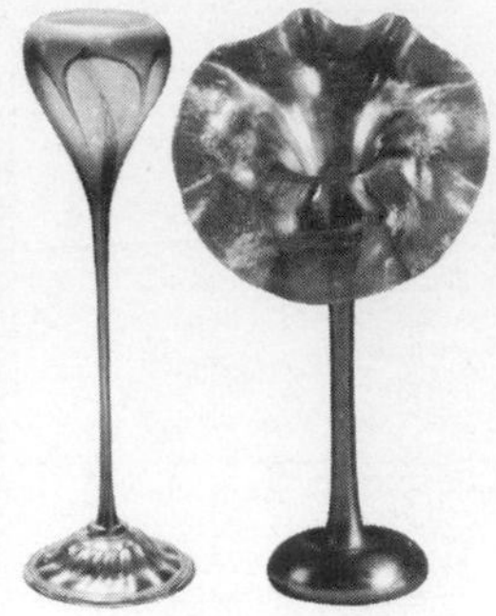

Tiffany glass
Two flower-shaped vases of Tiffany glass

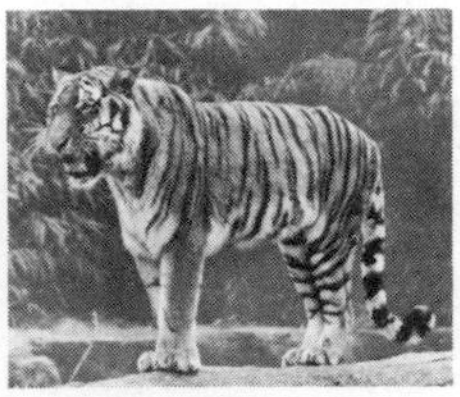

tiger
Panthera tigris

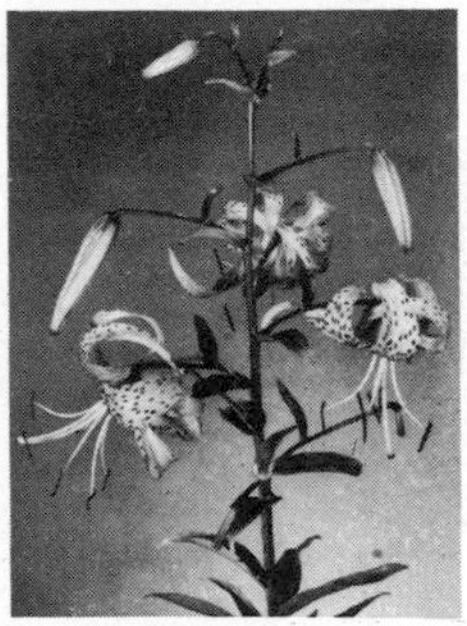

tiger lily

lightly with a tingling sensation causing laughter or twitching movements. **2. a.** To tease or excite pleasurably; titillate. **b.** To fill with mirth or pleasure; to delight. —*intr.* To feel or cause a tingling sensation on the skin. —**tickle pink.** *Informal.* To please; delight. Usually used in the passive: *She was tickled pink by the gift.* —*n.* **1.** The act of tickling. **2.** A tickling sensation. [Middle English *tikelen,* probably from *tiken, ticken*†, to touch lightly.]

tick·ler (tĭk′lər) *n.* **1.** One that tickles. **2.** A memorandum book or file to aid the memory.

tick·lish (tĭk′lĭsh) *adj.* **1.** Sensitive to tickling. **2.** Easily offended or upset; touchy. **3.** Requiring skillful or tactful handling; delicate. —**tick′lish·ly** *adv.* —**tick′lish·ness** *n.*

tick·seed (tĭk′sēd′) *n.* A plant, the **coreopsis** *(see).* [So called from its shape.]

tick·tack (tĭk′tăk′) *n.* Also **tic-tac.** **1.** A steady ticking sound, as of a clock. **2.** A prankster's device for tapping on a door or window from a distance. [Imitative.]

tick·tack·toe (tĭk′tăk′tō′) *n.* Also **tick-tack-toe.** A game played with a figure made by two horizontal lines crossing two vertical lines. Two players take turns marking squares, the winner being the first to mark a row of three in any direction. Also called "crisscross." [Probably TICKTACK (from the sounds made on slates on which the earlier form of the game was played) + TOE.]

tick·tock (tĭk′tŏk′) *n.* The ticking sound made by a clock, especially a pendulum clock. —*intr.v.* **ticktocked, -tocking, -tocks.** To make this sound. [Imitative.]

tick trefoil. Any of various plants of the genus *Desmodium,* having compound leaves with three leaflets, clusters of small purplish or white flowers, and jointed seed pods with easily separable, sticky segments. [Its seed pods adhere like ticks to animals.]

Ti·con·der·o·ga (tī′kŏn-də-rō′gə, tī-kŏn′-). A village and resort in northeastern New York State; the site of Fort Ticonderoga, a strategic point in the Revolutionary War.

tid·al (tīd′l) *adj.* **1.** Pertaining to, affected by, or having tides: *a tidal river.* **2.** Dependent upon or scheduled by the time of high tide: *a tidal ship.*

tidal wave. **1.** An unusual rise or incursion of water along the seashore, as from a storm or a combination of wind and spring tide. **2.** Loosely, a **tsunami** *(see).*

tid·bit (tĭd′bĭt′) *n.* Also **tit·bit** (tĭt′-). A choice morsel, as of food or gossip. [Perhaps dialectal *tid*†, tender, fanciful + BIT.]

tid·dly·winks (tĭd′lē-wĭngks′) *n.* Also **tid·dle·dy·winks** (tĭd′l-dē-). Plural in form, used with a singular verb. A game in which players try to snap small disks into a cup by pressing them on the edge with a larger disk. [Earlier *tiddlywink*†.]

tide¹ (tīd) *n.* **1. a.** The periodic variation in the surface level of the oceans and of bays, gulfs, inlets, and tidal regions of rivers, caused by the gravitational attraction of the sun and moon, the lunar effect being the more powerful. **b.** A specific occurrence of such a variation. **c.** The waters in such a variation. See **flood tide, ebb tide, neap tide, spring tide.** **2.** Any stress exerted on a body or part of a body by the gravitational attraction of another: *atmospheric tide.* **3.** A tendency, as of fortune, regarded as alternating and inexorable: *The tide has turned at the roulette table.* **4.** A time or season. Usually used in combination: *eventide; Christmastide.* **5.** *Archaic.* A favorable occasion; opportunity. —*v.* **tided, tiding, tides.** —*intr.* **1.** To rise and fall like the tide. **2.** To drift or ride with the tide. —*tr.* **1.** To carry along with or as if with the tide. **2.** To support through a difficult period. Used with *over: The five dollars tided him over until payday.* [Middle English *tid(e),* season, time, tide, Old English *tīd,* season, time. See **dā-** in Appendix.*]

tide² (tīd) *intr.v.* **tided, tiding, tides.** *Archaic.* To betide; befall. [Middle English *tiden,* Old English *tīdan,* "to fall as one's lot." See **dā-** in Appendix.*]

tide·land (tīd′lănd′) *n.* Coastal land submerged during high tide.

tide·mark (tīd′märk′) *n.* A line or artificial indicator marking the high-water or low-water limit of the tides.

tide·rip (tīd′rĭp′) *n.* A stretch of water roughened by the meeting of opposing tides or currents.

tide·wait·er (tīd′wā′tər) *n.* A customs officer who boards incoming ships at a harbor.

tide·wa·ter (tīd′wô′tər, -wŏt′ər) *n.* **1.** Water that inundates land at flood tide. **2.** Water affected by the tides; especially, tidal streams. **3.** Low coastal land drained by tidal streams. Often used attributively: *tidewater Virginia.*

tide·way (tīd′wā′) *n.* A channel in which a tidal current runs.

tid·ings (tī′dĭngz) *pl.n.* Information; news: *tidings of great joy.* [Plural of *tiding,* an event, Middle English *tiding,* perhaps from Old Norse *tidhendi,* events, from *tidhr,* occurring. See **dā-** in Appendix.*]

ti·dy (tī′dē) *adj.* **-dier, -diest.** **1.** Orderly and neat in appearance or procedure. **2.** *Informal.* **a.** Adequate; satisfactory. **b.** Substantial; considerable: *a tidy nest egg.* —See Synonyms at **neat.** —*v.* **tidied, -dying, -dies.** —*tr.* To make tidy; put in order. —*intr.* To put things in order. Used with *up.* —*n., pl.* **tidies.** A fancy protective covering for the arms or headrest of a chair. [Middle English, timely, seasonable, fair, excellent, from *tid,* season, TIDE.] —**ti′di·ly** *adv.* —**ti′di·ness** *n.*

ti·dy·tips (tī′dē-tĭps′) *n.* Plural in form, used with a singular or plural verb. A plant, *Layia elegans,* of California, having daisylike flowers with yellow, white-tipped rays.

tie (tī) *v.* **tied, tying, ties.** —*tr.* **1.** To fasten or secure with a cord, rope, strap, or similar means. **2.** To fasten by drawing together the parts or sides with strings or laces and knotting them: *tie one's shoes.* **3. a.** To make (a knot or bow). **b.** To put a knot or bow in: *tie a necktie.* **4.** To confine or restrict as if with cord. **5.** To bring together closely; bind; unite. **6.** To equal (an opponent or his score) in a contest. **7.** *Music.* To join (notes) by a tie. —*intr.* **1.** To be fastened with strings. **2.** To achieve equal scores in a contest. —**tie one on.** *Slang.* To get drunk. —*n.* **1.** A cord, string, or other means by which something is tied. **2.** That which unites; a bond: *marital ties.* **3.** A necktie. **4.** A beam or rod that joins parts and gives support. **5.** One of the timbers laid across a railroad bed to support the tracks; a sleeper. **6. a.** An equality of scores, votes, or performance in a contest. **b.** A contest resulting in this; a draw. **7.** *Music.* A curved line put either above or below two notes of the same pitch, indicating that the tone is to be sustained for their combined duration. [Middle English *t(e)yen,* Old English *tīgan.* See **deuk-** in Appendix.*]

tie·back (tī′băk′) *n.* **1.** A decorative loop of fabric, cord, or metal for parting and draping curtains to the sides. **2.** *Plural.* A pair of curtains meant to be tied back at about midlength.

tie beam. A horizontal beam that connects the rafters in a roof.

tie clasp. An ornamental device that holds the ends of a necktie to the shirt front. Also called "tie clip."

tie in. **1.** To be or make consistent or concomitant; to coordinate. **2.** To arrange a tie-in sale of.

tie-in (tī′ĭn′) *n.* **1.** A connection or relation. **2. a.** The sale of two (occasionally more) products or services so that a minor item is expected to be purchased with the major one. **b.** One of the products or services so offered, usually the minor one.

Tien Shan (tĭ-ĕn′ shän′). A major mountain system of Asia, extending 1,500 miles from the Kirghiz S.S.R. into the Sinkiang-Uigur Autonomous Region of western China. Highest elevation, Pobeda Peak (24,406 ft.).

Tien·tsin (tĭn′tsĭn′). A city of China, a port on the Yellow Sea, 70 miles southeast of Peking. Population, 3,320,000.

Tie·po·lo (tē-ā′pə-lō), **Giovanni Battista.** 1696–1770. Italian rococo painter and graphic artist.

tier¹ (tîr) *n.* One of a series of rows placed one above another. —*v.* **tiered, tiering, tiers.** —*tr.* To arrange in tiers. —*intr.* To rise in tiers. [Old French *tire,* sequence, rank, from *tirer,* to draw out, from Vulgar Latin *tīrāre*† (unattested).]

ti·er² (tī′ər) *n.* One that ties.

tierce (tîrs) *n.* Also **terce** (tûrs) (for sense 1). **1. a.** The third of the seven **canonical hours** *(see).* **b.** The time of day set aside for this prayer, usually the third hour after sunrise. **2.** A former measure of liquid capacity, equal to a third of a pipe, or 42 gallons. **3.** *Card Games.* A sequence of three cards of the same suit. **4.** *Fencing.* The third position from which a parry or thrust can be made. **5.** *Music.* An interval of a third. [Middle English, one third, the third canonical hour, from Old French, from the feminine of *t(i)ers,* third, from Latin *tertius.* See **trei-** in Appendix.*]

tier·cel. Variant of **tercel.**

Ti·er·ra del Fu·e·go (tĭ-ĕr′ə dĕl fōō-ā′gō, fyōō-). **1.** An archipelago at the extreme southern tip of South America. **2.** The main island of this archipelago, divided between Chile (10,250 square miles) and Argentina (7,750 square miles).

tier table. A table with two or more successive tops.

tie tack. A short pin with a decorative head used to attach a tie to a shirt front by means of a snap or chain.

Tie·tê River (tyə-tā′). A river of southern Brazil, flowing about 500 miles northwest through São Paulo State to the Paraná.

tie up. **1.** To bring to a standstill; immobilize. **2.** To detain or preoccupy; make unavailable.

tie-up (tī′ŭp′) *n.* A congested or immobilized condition, especially: **a.** Such a condition of automobile traffic. **b.** The halting of an activity by trade-union action.

tiff (tĭf) *n.* **1.** A fit of irritation; a huff. **2.** A petty quarrel. —*intr.v.* **tiffed, tiffing, tiffs.** To have a tiff. [Origin unknown.]

tif·fa·ny (tĭf′ə-nē) *n., pl.* **-nies.** A thin, transparent gauze of silk or cotton muslin. [Literally, "a material which shows the wearer naked," possibly originally "manifestation," from Old French *tifanie,* Epiphany, from Medieval Latin *theophania,* THEOPHANY.]

Tif·fa·ny (tĭf′ə-nē), **Louis Comfort.** 1848–1933. American painter, stained-glass artist, and glass manufacturer.

Tiffany glass. Stained or iridescent glass of a kind popular in the early 1900's for decorative objects or lamps.

tif·fin (tĭf′ĭn) *n.* *Anglo-Indian.* Luncheon. —*intr.v.* **tiffined, -fining, -fins.** *Anglo-Indian.* To eat lunch. [Short for obsolete *tiffing,* gerund of *tiff*†, to sip.]

Tif·lis (tĭf′lĭs; *Russian* tə-flēs′). *Georgian* **Tbi·li·si** (tə-bĭl′ə-sē, tə-pĭl′-). The capital of the Georgian S.S.R., in the southeast on the Kura River. Population, 812,000.

ti·ger (tī′gər) *n.* **1.** A large carnivorous feline mammal, *Panthera tigris,* of Asia, having a tawny coat with transverse black stripes. **2.** Broadly, any of various other similar felines. **3.** A fierce, aggressive, or audacious person. [Middle English *tigre,* from Old French, from Latin *tigris,* from Greek. See **steig-** in Appendix.*]

tiger beetle. Any of numerous active, often varicolored beetles of the family Cicindelidae, chiefly of warm, sandy regions.

tiger cat. Broadly, any of various small felines resembling the tiger in either appearance or behavior.

ti·ger-eye (tī′gər-ī′) *n.* Also **ti·ger's-eye** (tī′gərz-). A yellow-brown, semiprecious chatoyant gemstone, made of silicified crocidolite.

ti·ger·ish (tī′gər-ĭsh) *adj.* Of or characteristic of a tiger. —**ti′ger·ish·ly** *adv.* —**ti′ger·ish·ness** *n.*

tiger lily. A plant, *Lilium tigrinum,* native to Asia, having large, black-spotted reddish-orange flowers with reflexed petals.

tiger moth. Any of numerous often brightly colored moths of the family Arctiidae, characteristically having wings marked with spots or lines.

tight (tīt) *adj.* **tighter, tightest. 1. a.** Of such close construction, texture, or organization as to be impermeable, especially by water or air. **b.** Closely reasoned or worded. **2.** Fastened, held, or closed securely. **3.** Compressed, leaving few or no intervening spaces; compact. **4.** Drawn out to the fullest extent; taut. **5.** Cramped; constrained; rigid. **6.** Snug, often uncomfortably so: *a tight fit.* **7.** Constricted: *a tight feeling in the chest.* **8.** Close-fisted; stingy. **9. a.** Difficult to obtain: *tight money.* **b.** Affected by scarcity: *a tight market.* **10.** Difficult to deal with or get out of: *a tight spot.* **11.** Barely profitable: *a tight bargain.* **12.** Closely contested: *a tight match.* **13.** *Regional.* Neat and trim. **14.** *Slang.* Drunk. —*adv.* **1.** Firmly; securely. **2.** Soundly: *sleep tight.* —**sit tight.** To make no further move; watch and wait. [Middle English, probably variant of *thyght,* thickset, dense, from Old Norse *thēttr,* watertight, dense. See **tenk-²** in Appendix.*] —**tight′ly** *adv.* —**tight′ness** *n.*

tight·en (tīt′n) *v.* **-ened, -ening, -ens.** —*tr.* To make tight or tighter. —*intr.* To become tight or tighter. —**tight′en·er** *n.*

tight end. *Football.* The player at the right end of the offensive team in the modern T-formation; so called because he is stationed close to the adjoining tackle.

tight·fist·ed (tīt′fĭs′tĭd) *adj.* Stingy; parsimonious.

tight·lipped (tīt′lĭpt′) *adj.* **1.** Having the lips pressed together, as when grim. **2.** Reticent. —See Synonyms at **silent.**

tight·rope (tīt′rōp′) *n.* A tightly stretched rope, usually of wire, on which acrobats perform high above the ground.

tights (tīts) *pl.n.* A snug stretchable garment covering the body from the waist down or from the shoulders, worn by acrobats and dancers and for general wear by women and girls.

tight·wad (tīt′wŏd′) *n. Slang.* One who hates to spend money; a miser. [TIGHT + WAD (money).]

tig·lic acid (tĭg′lĭk). A thick, syrupy poisonous liquid, $C_5H_8O_2$, derived from croton oil, with a spicy odor and used in making perfumes and flavoring agents. [From New Latin *(Croton) tiglium,* a seed of the (Croton) species, perhaps from Greek *tilos†,* liquid feces (from the use of the seeds as a purgative).]

ti·glon (tī′glŏn) *n.* Also **ti·gon** (tī′gŏn). The hybrid offspring of a male tiger and a female lion. [Blend of TIGER and LION.]

Ti·gré (tē-grā′) *n.* A Semitic language of northern Ethiopia.

ti·gress (tī′grĭs) *n.* **1.** A female tiger. **2.** A fierce, aggressive, or audacious woman.

Ti·gri·nya (tē-grē′nyä) *n.* Also **Ti·gri·ña.** A Semitic language of northern Ethiopia.

Ti·gris (tī′grĭs). A river of southwestern Asia, rising in the Taurus Mountains of Turkey and flowing about 1,150 miles generally southeast to join the Euphrates in southern Iraq and form the Shatt-al-Arab.

Ti·hwa. The Chinese name for **Urumchi.**

Ti·jua·na (tē-wä′nə; *Spanish* tē-hwä′nä). Also **Ti·a Jua·na** (tē′ə wä′nə; *Spanish* tē′ä hwä′nä). A city of northwestern Mexico, on the U.S. border. Population, 244,000.

tike (tīk). Variant of **tyke.**

ti·ki (tē′kē) *n.* **1.** *Capital* **T.** A male figure in Polynesian mythology, sometimes identified as the first man. **2.** A wood or stone image of a Polynesian god. **3.** A Maori figurine representing an ancestor, often intricately carved from greenstone and worn about the neck as a talisman. [Maori.]

til (tĭl) *n.* The sesame plant, especially as used in India as a source of food and oil. [Hindi *til,* from Sanskrit *tila†.*]

Til·burg (tĭl′bûrg′). An industrial city of the south-central Netherlands. Population, 145,000.

til·bur·y (tĭl′bĕr′ē, -bə-rē) *n., pl.* **-ies.** A light open gig seating two persons, popular in the early 19th century. [Invented by *Tilbury,* a 19th-century London coach maker.]

til·de (tĭl′də) *n.* The diacritical mark (˜) placed over the letter *n* in Spanish to indicate the palatal nasal sound (ny) as in *cañon,* or over a vowel in Portuguese to indicate nasalization as in *lã, pão.* [Spanish, from Latin *titulus,* superscription, TITLE.]

Til·den (tĭl′dən), **Samuel Jones.** 1814–1886. American political leader; Democratic candidate for President (1876).

Til·den (tĭl′dən), **William Tatem, Jr. ("Big Bill")** 1893–1953. American athlete; world tennis champion (1920–25).

tile (tīl) *n.* **1.** A thin, flat, or convex slab of baked clay, plastic, concrete, or other material, laid in rows to cover walls, floors, and roofs. **2.** A short length of pipe made of clay or concrete, used in sewers and drains. **3.** A hollow fired clay or concrete block used for building walls. **4.** Tiles collectively. **5.** One of the marked playing pieces, as in mahjong. —*tr.v.* **tiled, tiling, tiles.** To cover or provide with tiles. [Middle English *til(e),* *teyele,* Old English *tigele, tigule,* from West Germanic *tegala* (unattested), from Latin *tēgula,* from *tegere,* to cover. See **steg-¹** in Appendix.*] —**til′er** *n.*

tile·fish (tīl′fĭsh′) *n., pl.* **tilefish** or **-fishes.** Any of several marine food fishes of the family Branchiostegidae; especially, *Lopholatilus chamaeleonticeps,* of deep Atlantic waters, having varicolored markings. [Tile-, short for New Latin *Lopholatilus* (influenced by TILE, from its tilelike spots).]

til·ing (tī′lĭng) *n.* **1.** The laying of tiles. **2.** Tiles collectively. **3.** A tiled surface.

till¹ (tĭl) *tr.v.* **tilled, tilling, tills.** To prepare (land) for the raising of crops by plowing, harrowing, and fertilizing. [Middle English *tilien, til(l)en,* Old English *tilian,* to work at, labor, cultivate, from Germanic *tilōjan* (unattested), from *tilam* (unattested), aim, fixed point.] —**till′a·ble** *adj.*

till² (tĭl) *prep.* Until. —*conj.* Until. [Middle English *till,* Old

English *til,* probably from Common Germanic *tilam* (unattested), fixed point. See **till** (cultivate).]

Usage: Till and *until* are generally interchangeable, and each is appropriate to the highest level of usage. In formal writing, *until* is the more common as the first word of a sentence. *'Til* is a possible variant form of *until,* though most authorities now consider it a needless one; *'till* is nonstandard. As conjunctions, *till* and *until* are used in the approximate sense of *before* to introduce conditions in negative constructions: *She can't go till she finishes her work. Until injustice is ended, peace will never be realized.* In the following typical constructions, *till* or *until* sometimes appear, but are preferably replaced by *before* or *when* in formal usage: *It was not long before he noticed the change. She had scarcely arrived when it began to storm.*

till³ (tĭl) *n.* A drawer, small chest, or compartment for money, especially in a store. [Middle English *tylle†.*]

till⁴ (tĭl) *n.* Glacial drift composed of an unconsolidated, heterogeneous mixture of clay, sand, gravel, and boulders. [Origin unknown.]

till·age (tĭl′ĭj) *n.* **1.** The cultivation of land. **2.** The state of being tilled. **3.** Land that is tilled for crops.

til·land·si·a (tĭ-lănd′zē-ə) *n.* Any of various usually epiphytic plants of the genus *Tillandsia,* such as Spanish moss, of tropical and subtropical America. [New Latin, after Elias *Tillands* (died 1693), Swedish botanist.]

till·er¹ (tĭl′ər) *n.* One that tills land.

till·er² (tĭl′ər) *n.* A lever used to turn a rudder and steer a boat. [Middle English *tiler, telor,* beam of a crossbow, from Norman French *telier,* weaver's beam, from Medieval Latin *tēlārium,* web, warp of a fabric, also weaver's beam. See **teks-** in Appendix.*]

till·er³ (tĭl′ər) *n.* A shoot, especially one that sprouts from the base of a grass. —*intr.v.* **tillered, -ering, -ers.** To send forth tillers. [Middle English *tiller* (unattested), Old English *telgor, telgra.* See **del-³** in Appendix.*]

Til·lich (tĭl′ĭk), **Paul Johannes.** 1886–1965. German-born American theologian and educator.

Till·man (tĭl′mən), **Benjamin Ryan.** 1847–1918. American political leader and U.S. Senator (1895–1918).

tilt¹ (tĭlt) *v.* **tilted, tilting, tilts.** —*tr.* **1.** To cause to slope, as by raising one end; to incline; to tip. **2. a.** To aim or thrust (a lance) in a joust. **b.** To charge (an opponent). **3.** To forge with a tilt hammer. —*intr.* **1.** To slope; incline. **2.** To joust. **3.** To quarrel. —*n.* **1. a.** An inclination from the horizontal or vertical; a slant. **b.** A sloping surface, as of the ground. **2.** The act of tilting. **3. a.** A medieval sport in which two mounted knights with lances charged together and attempted to unhorse one another. **b.** A thrust or blow with a lance. **4.** A verbal duel. **5.** A tilt hammer *(see).* —**at full tilt.** At full speed. —*adj.* **1.** Tilted. **2.** Designed for tilting: *a tilt cart.* [Middle English *tylten, tilten,* to cause to fall, overthrow, perhaps from Scandinavian, akin to Swedish *tulta†.*]

tilt² (tĭlt) *n.* A canopy or awning for a boat, wagon, or cart. —*tr.v.* **tilted, tilting, tilts.** To cover with a tilt. [Middle English *tild, teld,* Old English *teld,* a tent. See **del-³** in Appendix.*]

tilth (tĭlth) *n.* **1.** The cultivation of land; tillage. **2.** Tilled earth. [Middle English *tilth,* Old English *tilth,* from *tilian,* to TILL (cultivate).]

tilt hammer. A heavy forge hammer having a pivoted lever by which it is tilted up and then allowed to drop.

tilt·yard (tĭlt′yärd′) *n.* An enclosed yard for tilting contests.

Tim. Timothy (New Testament).

tim·bal (tĭm′bəl) *n.* Also **tym·bal.** A kettledrum. [French *timbale,* variant (influenced by *cymbale,* cymbal) of obsolete *tamballe,* variant (influenced by *tambour,* tambour) of Old Spanish *atabal,* a kettledrum, from Arabic *aṭ-ṭabl,* the drum.]

tim·bale (tĭm′bəl) *n.* **1.** A bland, custardlike dish of cheese, chicken, fish, or vegetables baked in a drum-shaped pastry mold. **2.** Such a mold. [French, "kettledrum," TIMBAL.]

tim·ber (tĭm′bər) *n.* **1.** Trees or wooded land considered as a source of wood. **2. a.** Wood as a building material; lumber. **b.** A dressed piece of wood; especially, a beam in a structure. **c.** A rib in a ship's frame. **3.** Material: *He's executive timber.* —*tr.v.* **timbered, -bering, -bers.** To support or shore up with timbers. —*interj.* Used to warn of a falling tree. [Middle English *timber,* building, building material, Old English *timber.* See **dem-¹** in Appendix.*]

tim·bered (tĭm′bərd) *adj.* **1. a.** Constructed of or covered with timber. **b.** Built with exposed timbers. **2.** Wooded.

tim·ber·head (tĭm′bər-hĕd′) *n. Nautical.* A timber end that projects above the deck and is used as a bollard.

timber hitch. *Nautical.* A knot used for fastening a rope around a spar or log to be hoisted or towed.

tim·ber·ing (tĭm′bər-ĭng) *n.* Timber or work made of it.

tim·ber·land (tĭm′bər-lănd′) *n.* Forested land considered commercially.

tim·ber·line (tĭm′bər-līn′) *n.* Also **timber line.** The limit of altitude in mountainous regions beyond which trees do not grow. Also called "tree line."

timber right. A claim to the trees on property belonging to another.

timber wolf. A grayish or whitish wolf, *Canis lupus,* of forested northern regions. Also called "gray wolf."

tim·ber·work (tĭm′bər-wûrk′) *n.* The part of a structure made with timbers, as the framework of a boat or house.

tim·bre (tĭm′bər, tăm′-; *French* tăn′br′) *n.* The quality of a sound that distinguishes it from other sounds of the same pitch and volume; especially, the distinctive tone of a musical instrument, a voice, or a voiced speech sound. [French, from

tiller²

tilefish
Lopholatilus chamaeleonticeps

timber wolf

ă pat/ā pay/âr care/ä father/b bib/ch church/d deed/ĕ pet/ē be/f fife/g gag/h hat/hw which/ĭ pit/ī pie/îr pier/j judge/k kick/l lid, needle/m mum/
t tight/th thin, path/th this, bathe/ŭ cut/ûr urge/v valve/w with/y yes/z zebra, size/zh vision/ə about, item, edible, gallop, circus/
à Fr. ami/œ Fr. feu, Ger. schön/ü Fr. tu, Ger. über/KH Ger. ich, Scot. loch/N Fr. bon. *Follows main vocabulary. †Of obscure origin.

Old French, a bell struck with a hammer, timbrel, timbre, from Vulgar Latin *timbano* (unattested), a drum, from Medieval Greek *timbanon,* from Greek *tumpanon.* See **tympanum.**]

tim·brel (tĭm′brəl) *n.* An ancient percussion instrument similar to a tambourine. [From Middle English *timbre,* from Old French, a drum, TIMBRE.]

Tim·buk·tu (tĭm′bŭk-to͞o′, tĭm-bŭk′to͞o). A town in central Mali, near the Niger River; in the 16th century, a seat of Islamic learning and a flourishing trade center. Population, 9,000.

time (tīm) *n.* **1.** A nonspatial continuum in which events occur in apparently irreversible succession from the past through the present to the future. **2.** An interval separating two points on this continuum, measured essentially by selecting a regularly recurring event, such as the sunrise, and counting the number of its occurrences during the interval; duration. **3.** *Abbr.* **t., T.** A number, as of years, days, or minutes, representing such an interval. **4.** *Abbr.* **t., T.** A similar number representing a specific point, such as the present, as reckoned from an arbitrary past point on the continuum. **5.** A system by which such intervals are measured or such numbers are reckoned. **6.** *Often plural.* An interval marked by similar events, conditions, or phenomena; especially, a span of years; era: *Edwardian times; a time of troubles.* **7.** One's heyday. **8.** A suitable or opportune moment or season. **9.** A moment or period designated, as by custom, for a given activity: *harvest time; bedtime.* **10.** An appointed or fated moment, especially of death: *died before his time.* **11.** One of several instances. **12.** An occasion. **13.** *Informal.* A prison sentence. **14. a.** The customary period of work: *hired for full time.* **b.** The period spent working. **15.** The rate of speed of a measured activity: *marching in double time.* **16.** The characteristic beat of musical rhythm: *three-quarter time.* —See Synonyms at **period.** —**against time.** With a quickly approaching time limit. —**at one time. 1.** Simultaneously. **2.** At a period or moment in the past. —**at the same time.** However; nonetheless. —**at times.** On occasion; sometimes. —**behind the times.** Out-of-date; old-fashioned. —**for the time being.** Temporarily. —**from time to time.** Once in a while; at intervals. —**gain time.** To run too fast. Said of a timepiece. —**high time.** Long overdue. —**in good time. 1.** In a reasonable length of time. **2.** When or before due. **3.** Quickly. —**in no time.** Almost instantly; immediately. —**in time. 1.** Before the time limit expires. **2.** Within an indefinite amount of passing time. **3.** In tempo; keeping the rhythm. —**keep time. 1.** To indicate the correct time. **2.** To maintain the tempo or rhythm. —**lose time. 1.** To operate too slowly. Said of a timepiece. **2.** To delay advancement. —**make time. 1.** To make progress; proceed quickly. **2.** *Slang.* To make progress in pursuit of a girl's favors. —**on time. 1.** Promptly; according to schedule. **2.** By paying in installments. —*adj.* **1.** Of or relating to time. **2.** Constructed so as to operate at a particular moment: *time bomb.* **3.** Payable on a future date or dates: *time loan.* **4.** Of or relating to installment buying. —*tr.v.* **timed, timing, times. 1.** To set the time for (an event or occasion). **2.** To adjust to keep accurate time. **3.** To regulate for the orderly sequence of movements or events: *timed his leap beautifully.* **4.** To record the speed or duration of. **5.** To set or maintain the tempo, speed, or duration of. [Middle English *time,* Old English *tīma.* See **dā-** in Appendix.*]

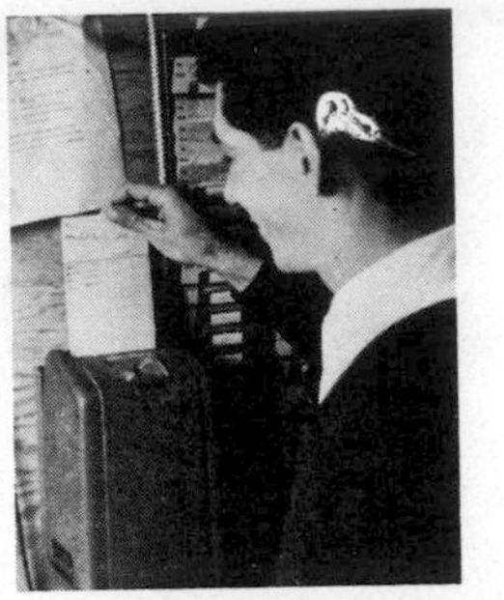

time clock
Employee punching a timecard

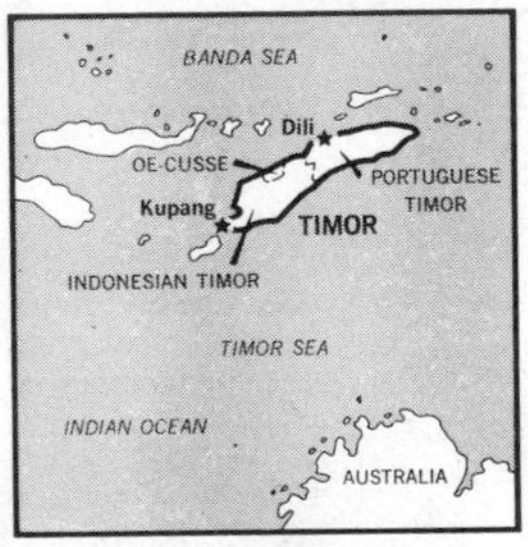

Timor

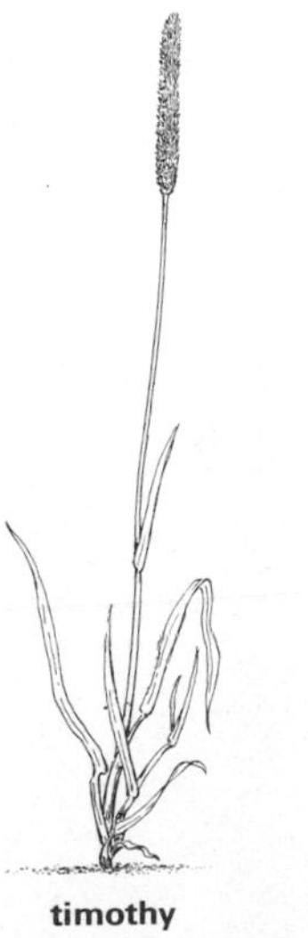

timothy

time and a half. A rate of pay that is one and a half times the regular rate, as for overtime work.

time and motion study. An analysis of the efficiency with which an industrial operation is performed. Also called "time study," "motion study."

time bill. A bill of exchange payable at an indicated future time.

time bomb. A bomb with a detonating mechanism that can be set for a particular time.

time capsule. A sealed container preserving articles and records of contemporary culture for perusal by scientists and scholars of the distant future.

time·card (tīm′kärd′) *n.* A card, either maintained by the employee or stamped by a time clock, recording an employee's arrival and departure time each day.

time clock. A clock that records the arrival and departure times of employees, usually by punching timecards.

time deposit. A bank deposit that cannot be withdrawn before a date specified at the time of deposit.

time dilatation. Also **time dilation.** The relativistic slowing of a clock that moves with respect to a stationary observer.

time exposure. 1. A photographic exposure made for a relatively long period of time. **2.** An image made by such an exposure.

time-hon·ored (tīm′ŏn′ərd) *adj.* Honored because of age or age-old observance.

time immemorial. 1. Time long past, beyond memory or record. **2.** *Law.* Time antedating legal records.

time·keep·er (tīm′kē′pər) *n.* **1.** A timepiece. **2.** The person who keeps track of time, as in a sports event or in a place of employment. **3.** A railroad dispatcher.

time-lapse (tīm′lăps′) *adj.* Of or using a motion-picture technique for filming a naturally slow process, as the unfolding of a leaf, by photographing it at intervals so that the continuous projection of the frames gives an accelerated view of it.

time·less (tīm′lĭs) *adj.* **1.** Independent of time; unending; eternal. **2.** Unaffected by time; ageless. **3.** *Obsolete.* Untimely. —**time′less·ly** *adv.* —**time′less·ness** *n.*

time loan. A loan to be paid within or by a specified time.

time lock. A lock set to open at a specific time.

time·ly (tīm′lē) *adj.* **-lier, -liest. 1.** Occurring at a suitable or opportune time; well-timed. **2.** *Archaic.* Early; premature. —*adv.* **1.** Opportunely; in time. **2.** *Archaic.* Early; soon. —**time′li·ness** *n.*

time note. A promissory note or similar instrument specifying a date or dates of payment.

time·ous (tī′məs) *adj. Scottish.* Timely. —**time′ous·ly** *adv.*

time-out (tīm′out′) *n.* Also **time out. 1.** A brief cessation of play at the request of a sports team for rest or consultation. **2.** Any short break from work or play.

time·piece (tīm′pēs′) *n.* An instrument that measures, registers, or records time.

tim·er (tī′mər) *n.* **1.** A person who keeps track of time; timekeeper. **2.** A timepiece, especially one used for measuring intervals of time. **3.** A switch or regulator that controls or activates another mechanism at fixed intervals.

time reversal. *Symbol* **T** A mathematical operation representing a transformation from a given physical system undergoing a given sequence of events (states) to a system in which the exact reverse sequence of states is undergone.

times (tīmz) *prep.* Multiplied by: *Five times two is ten.*

time·sav·ing (tīm′sā′vĭng) *adj.* Saving time through an efficient method or a shorter route; expeditious. —**time′sav′er** *n.*

time·serv·er (tīm′sûr′vər) *n.* A person who conforms to the prevailing ways and opinions of his time or condition for personal advantage; an opportunist. —**time′serv′ing** *adj.* & *n.*

time signature. *Music.* A symbol, commonly in the form of a numerical fraction, placed on a staff to indicate the meter.

Times Square. An area of New York City extending from 42nd to 47th Street between Broadway and Seventh Avenue; the center of a neighborhood containing many places of entertainment.

time study. Time and motion study *(see).*

time·ta·ble (tīm′tā′bəl) *n.* A schedule listing the times at which certain events, such as arrivals and departures at a transportation station, are expected to take place.

time·work (tīm′wûrk′) *n.* Work paid for in specified time units, as by the hour. —**time′work′er** *n.*

time·worn (tīm′wôrn′, -wōrn′) *adj.* **1.** Showing the effects of long use or wear. **2.** Used too often; trite.

time zone. Any of the 24 longitudinal divisions of the earth's surface in which a standard time is kept, the primary division being that bisected by the Greenwich meridian. Each zone is 15 degrees of longitude in width, with local variations, and observes a clock time one hour earlier than the zone immediately to the east.

Tim·gad (tĭm′găd′). Ancient names **Tham·u·ga·di** (thăm′yə-gä′dē), **Tham·u·ga·dis** (-dĭs). A site in northeastern Algeria of ruins of an ancient city founded by Trajan in A.D. 100.

tim·id (tĭm′ĭd) *adj.* **-ider, -idest. 1.** Shrinking from dangerous or difficult circumstances; hesitant or fearful. **2.** Shrinking from public attention; shy. [Latin *timidus,* from *timēre*†, to fear.] —**ti·mid′i·ty, tim′id·ness** *n.* —**tim′id·ly** *adv.*

tim·ing (tī′mĭng) *n.* The art or operation of regulating occurrence, pace, or coordination to achieve the most desirable effects, as in music, the theater, athletics, or in a machine.

Ti·miş (tē′mēsh). *Serbian* **Te·meš** (tĕ′mĕsh). A river rising in western Rumania and flowing 270 miles west and then south to the Danube near Belgrade, Yugoslavia.

Ti·mi·soa·ra (tē′mē-shwä′rä). A city of Rumania, near the border with Yugoslavia. Population, 152,000.

ti·moc·ra·cy (tī-mŏk′rə-sē) *n., pl.* **-cies. 1.** A state described by Plato as being governed on principles of honor and military glory. **2.** An Aristotelian state in which civic honor or political power is proportional to the property one owns. [Old French *tymocracie,* from Medieval Latin *tīmocratia,* from Greek *timokratia* : *timē,* honor, value, worth (see **kwei-**[1] in Appendix*) + -CRACY.] —**ti′mo·crat′ic** (tī′mə-krăt′ĭk) *adj.*

Ti·mor (tē′môr, tē-môr′). An island at the eastern end of the Indonesian Archipelago, covering about 13,100 square miles and divided politically between Indonesian Timor and Portuguese Timor.

tim·or·ous (tĭm′ər-əs) *adj.* Full of apprehensiveness; timid. [Middle English, from Old French *timoureus,* from Medieval Latin *timorōsus,* from Latin *timor,* fear, from *timēre,* to fear. See **timid.**] —**tim′or·ous·ly** *adv.* —**tim′or·ous·ness** *n.*

Ti·mor Sea (tē′môr, tē-môr′). An arm of the Indian Ocean, about 300 miles wide, between Timor and Australia.

tim·o·thy (tĭm′ə-thē) *n.* A grass, *Phleum pratense,* native to Eurasia, having narrow, cylindrical flower spikes, and widely cultivated for hay. [Said to have been taken from New York to the Carolinas in 1720 by *Timothy* Hanson, American farmer.]

Tim·o·thy[1] (tĭm′ə-thē). A masculine given name. [Latin *Timotheus,* from Greek *Timotheos,* "God-honoring" : *timē,* honor, worth (see **kwei-**[1] in Appendix*) + *theos,* a god, God (see **dhēs-** in Appendix*).]

Tim·o·thy[2] (tĭm′ə-thē) *n. Abbr.* **Tim.** Either of two books of the New Testament, each an epistle to Saint Timothy attributed to Saint Paul.

Tim·o·thy (tĭm′ə-thē), **Saint.** Also **Ti·moth·e·us** (tĭ-mŏth′ē-əs, tī-). Christian leader of first century A.D.; convert and companion of Saint Paul; legendary martyr.

tim·pa·ni (tĭm′pə-nē) *pl.n.* Also **tym·pa·ni.** A set of kettledrums. [Italian, plural of *timpano,* kettledrum, from Latin *tympanum,* TYMPANUM.] —**tim′pa·nist** *n.*

Tim·pa·no·gos (tĭm′pə-nō′gəs). The highest (12,008 feet) of the Wasatch Mountains, in north-central Utah.

tim·pa·num. Variant of **tympanum.**

Ti·mur Lenk. Persian name of **Tamerlane** *(see).*

tin (tĭn) *n.* **1.** *Symbol* **Sn** A malleable, silvery metallic element obtained chiefly from cassiterite. It is used to coat other metals to prevent corrosion, and forms part of numerous alloys, such as soft solder, pewter, type metal, and bronze. Atomic number 50, atomic weight 118.69, melting point 231.89°C, boiling point 2,270°C, specific gravity 7.31, valences 2, 4. See **element.** **2.** Tin plate. **3.** A tin container or box. **4.** *Chiefly British.* A container for preserved foodstuff; a can. —*tr.v.* **tinned, tinning, tins. 1.** To plate or coat with tin. **2.** *Chiefly British.* To preserve or pack in tins; to can. [Middle English *tin*, Old English *tin*, from Germanic *tinam* (unattested).]

tin·a·mou (tĭn′ə-mo͞o′) *n.* Any of various chickenlike or quail-like birds of the family Tinamidae, of Central and South America. [French, from Galibi *tinamu*.]

tin·cal (tĭng′kəl) *n.* Crude borax. [Malay *tingkal*, from Sanskrit *ṭankaṇa*†.]

tin can. 1. A container of tin-plated sheet steel used especially for preserving food. **2.** *Navy Slang.* A destroyer.

tinct (tĭngkt) *n.* *Archaic.* A color or tint. —*adj.* *Archaic.* Tinged. [Latin *tinctus*, past participle of *tingere*, TINGE.]

tinct. tincture.

tinc·to·ri·al (tĭngk-tôr′ē-əl, -tōr′ē-əl) *adj.* Pertaining to the processes of dyeing or coloring. [From Latin *tinctōrius*, from *tinctus*, past participle of *tingere*, TINGE.]

tinc·ture (tĭngk′chər) *n.* *Abbr.* **tinct. 1.** A dyeing substance; pigment. **2.** An imparted color; a stain; a tint. **3.** A quality that colors, pervades, or distinguishes. **4.** A trace; vestige. **5.** A component of a substance extracted by means of a solvent. **6.** *Pharmacology.* An alcohol solution of a nonvolatile medicine: *tincture of iodine.* **7.** A heraldic metal, color, or fur. —*tr.v.* **tinctured, -turing, -tures. 1.** To stain or tint with a color. **2.** To infuse, as with a quality; impregnate. [Middle English, from Latin *tinctūra*, a dyeing, from *tinctus*, past participle of *tingere*, TINGE.]

Tin·dal or **Tin·dale, William.** See **Tyndale.**

tin·der (tĭn′dər) *n.* Readily combustible material, such as dry twigs, used to kindle fires. [Middle English *tinder*, Old English *tynder*, from Common Germanic *tund-* (unattested), past participle form of *tend-* (unattested), to burn, kindle.]

tin·der·box (tĭn′dər-bŏks′) *n.* **1.** A metal box for holding tinder. **2.** A potentially explosive place or situation.

tine (tīn) *n.* **1.** A branch of a deer's antlers. **2.** A prong on a fork, pitchfork, or similar implement. [Middle English *tind*, *tene*, Old English *tind*, from Common Germanic *tind-* (unattested), point.]

tin·e·a (tĭn′ē-ə) *n.* Any of several fungous skin diseases, such as ringworm. [Latin *tinea*†, a gnawing worm, moth.]

tin·foil (tĭn′foil′) *n.* Also **tin foil.** A thin, pliable sheet of tin or of tin-lead alloy, used as a protective wrapping.

ting (tĭng) *n.* A single light metallic sound, as of a small bell. —*intr.v.* **tinged** (tĭngd), **tinging, tings.** To give forth such a sound. [From Middle English *tyngen*, to produce a ringing sound (imitative).]

tinge (tĭnj) *tr.v.* **tinged** (tĭnjd), **tingeing** or **tinging, tinges. 1.** To apply a trace of color to; to tint. **2.** To affect slightly, as with a contrasting quality: *comedy tinged with tragedy.* —*n.* **1.** A faint trace of a color incorporated or added. **2.** Any slight admixture. [Middle English *tyngen*, from Latin *tingere*, to moisten, plunge, dye. See **teng-** in Appendix.*]

tin·gle (tĭng′gəl) *v.* **-gled, -gling, -gles.** —*intr.* **1.** To have a prickling, stinging sensation as from the cold, a sharp slap, or excitement: *tingle all over with joy.* **2.** To cause such a sensation or feeling. —*tr.* To cause to tingle. —*n.* A prickly or stinging sensation. [Middle English *tinglen*, originally, to be affected with a ringing sound in the ears, perhaps variant of *tynclen*, TINKLE.] —**tin′gler** *n.* —**tin′gly** *adj.*

tin·horn (tĭn′hôrn′) *n.* *Slang.* A petty braggart, especially a gambler, who pretends to be wealthier than he is.

tink·er (tĭng′kər) *n.* **1.** A traveling mender of metal household utensils. **2.** A person who enjoys repairing and experimenting with machine parts. **3.** One who is clumsy at his work; a bungler. —*v.* **tinkered, -ering, -ers.** —*intr.* **1.** To work as a tinker. **2.** To play with machine parts experimentally. —*tr.* To mend as a tinker. [Middle English *tyn(e)kere*, probably from *tynken*, to TINKLE (perhaps from the sounds made by a tinker at work).]

tinker's damn. Also **tinker's dam.** *Slang.* Something of the smallest value: *not worth a tinker's damn.* [From the tinkers' reputed habit of cursing.]

tin·kle (tĭng′kəl) *v.* **-kled, -kling, -kles.** —*intr.* To make light metallic sounds, such as those of a small bell. —*tr.* **1.** To cause to tinkle. **2.** To signal or call by tinkling. —*n.* **1.** A light, clear metallic sound or a sound suggestive of it. **2.** The act of tinkling. [Middle English *tynclen*, frequentative of *tynken* (imitative).] —**tin′kly** *adj.*

tin lizzie. *Slang.* **1.** An automobile, the **Model T** *(see).* **2.** Any dilapidated or cheap car. [TIN (by analogy with the common food can) + *Lizzie*, pet form of ELIZABETH.]

tin·ner (tĭn′ər) *n.* **1.** A tin miner. **2.** A person who makes or deals in tinware; tinsmith.

tin·ni·tus (tĭ-nī′təs) *n.* A sound in the ears, such as buzzing, ringing, or whistling, caused by a defect in the auditory nerve. [Latin *tinnītus*, from the past participle of *tinnīre*, to ring, tinkle (imitative).]

tin·ny (tĭn′ē) *adj.* **-nier, -niest. 1.** Of, containing, or yielding tin. **2.** Shiny and attractive but cheap. **3.** Having a thin metallic sound. **4.** Tasting or smelling of tin, as food from a tin can. —**tin′ni·ly** *adv.* —**tin′ni·ness** *n.*

Ti·nos. See **Tenos.**

Tin Pan Alley. Also **tin-pan alley. 1.** A district associated with musicians, composers, and publishers of popular music. **2.** The publishers and composers of popular music as a group. [From earlier *tin-pan*, noisy, tinny.]

tin plate. Thin sheet iron or steel coated with tin.

tin-plate (tĭn′plāt′) *tr.v.* **-plated, -plating, -plates.** To coat with tin. —**tin′-plat′er** *n.*

tin pyrites. A mineral, **stannite** *(see).*

tin·sel (tĭn′səl) *n.* **1.** Very thin sheets, strips, or threads of a glittering material used as a decoration. **2.** A yarn or fabric interwoven with gold or silver thread. **3.** Anything superficially sparkling or showy but basically valueless. —*adj.* **1.** Made of or decorated or covered with tinsel. **2.** Gaudy and showy but basically valueless. —*tr.v.* **tinseled** or **-selled, -seling** or **-selling, -sels. 1.** To decorate with or as if with tinsel. **2.** To give a showy appearance to. **3.** To cover defects with or as if with tinsel. [Earlier *tinselle*, adorned with metallic threads, probably from Old French *estincelle*, past participle of *e(s)tinceller*, to sparkle, from *estincelle*, a spark, from Vulgar Latin *stincilla* (unattested), variant of Latin *scintilla*. See **skī-** in Appendix.*]

tin·smith (tĭn′smĭth′) *n.* One who makes and repairs things made of light metal, such as tin.

tin·stone (tĭn′stōn′) *n.* A mineral, **cassiterite** *(see).*

tint (tĭnt) *n.* **1.** A shade of a color, especially a pale or delicate variation; a tinge. **2.** A gradation of a color made by adding white to it to lessen its saturation. **3.** A slight coloration; a hue. **4.** A barely detectable evidence of something; a trace. **5.** In engraving, a shaded effect produced by hatching. **6.** *Printing.* A panel of color on which matter in another color, as an illustration, may be printed. **7.** A dye for the hair. —*v.* **tinted, tinting, tints.** —*tr.* To imbue with a tint; to color. —*intr.* To take or acquire a tint. [Variant (probably influenced by Italian *tinto*, tint) of earlier *tinct*, from Latin *tinctus*, a dipping or dyeing, from the past participle of *tingere*, to wet, dip, dye. See **teng-** in Appendix.*]

Tin·tag·el Head (tĭn-tăj′əl). A promontory in western Cornwall, England; the site of Tintagel Castle, according to tradition the birthplace of King Arthur.

tin·tin·nab·u·lar (tĭn′tĭ-năb′yə-lər) *adj.* Also **tin·tin·nab·u·lar·y** (-lĕr′ē), **tin·tin·nab·u·lous** (-ləs). Of or relating to bells or the ringing of bells. [From TINTINNABULUM.]

tin·tin·nab·u·la·tion (tĭn′tĭ-năb′yə-lā′shən) *n.* The ringing or sounding of bells. [From TINTINNABULUM.]

tin·tin·nab·u·lum (tĭn′tĭ-năb′yə-ləm) *n.*, *pl.* **-la** (-lə). A small, tinkling bell. [Latin, from *tintinnāre*, *tintinnīre*, to jingle, reduplication of *tinnīre*, to ring. See **tinnitus.**]

Tin·to·ret·to (tĭn′tə-rĕt′ō; *Italian* tēn′tō-rāt′tō), **Il.** Original name, Jacopo Robusti. 1518–1594. Italian painter.

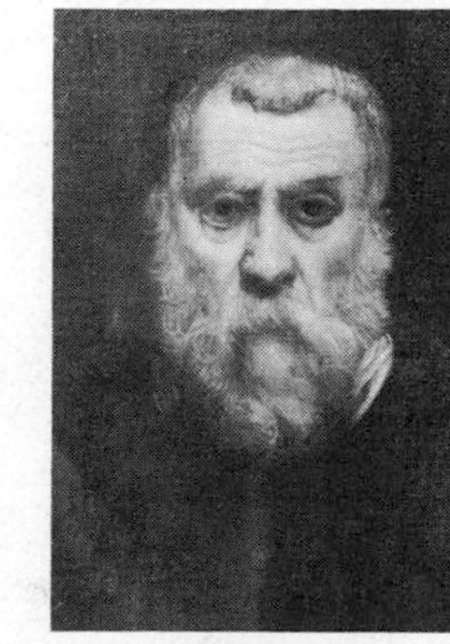

Tintoretto
A self-portrait

tin·type (tĭn′tīp′) *n.* A **ferrotype** *(see).*

tin·work (tĭn′wûrk′) *n.* **1.** Work in tin. **2.** *Plural.* A place where tin is smelted and rolled. Used with a singular or plural verb.

ti·ny (tī′nē) *adj.* **-nier, -niest.** Extremely small; minute. See Synonyms at **small.** [From Middle English *tine*†.]

-tion. Indicates action or process involved with; for example, **adsorption.** [Middle English *-cioun*, from Old French *-tion*, from Latin *-tiō* (stem *-tiōn*) : *-t-*, of the past participial stem + *-iōn*, -ION.]

tip¹ (tĭp) *n.* **1.** The end or extremity of something, especially of something pointed or projecting. **2.** A piece or attachment meant to be fitted to the end of something, as a cap or ferrule. —*tr.v.* **tipped, tipping, tips. 1.** To furnish with a tip. **2.** To cover, decorate, or remove the tip of. **3.** *Bookbinding.* To attach (an insert) in a book by gluing along the binding edge. Often used with *in.* **4.** To stain strands or ends of hair, as of furs, with dye so as to give a different appearance. [Middle English *tip(pe)*, probably from Old Norse *typpi*. See **tap-** in Appendix.*]

tip² (tĭp) *v.* **tipped, tipping, tips.** —*tr.* **1.** To knock over or upset. Usually used with *over.* **2.** To move to a slanting position; to tilt. **3.** To touch or raise (one's hat) in greeting. —*intr.* **1.** To topple over; overturn. Usually used with *over.* **2.** To become tilted; to slant. **3.** *British.* To empty by overturning; to dump. —*n.* **1.** A tilt or slant; an incline. **2.** *British.* An area or place for dumping something, as rubbish or refuse from a mine. [Middle English *typen*, *tipen*†.]

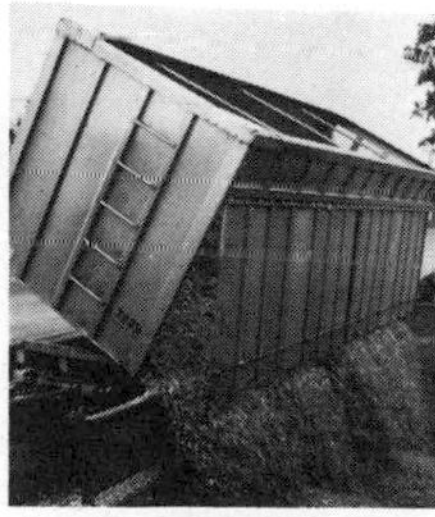

tipcart
Truck trailer being unloaded from the side

tip³ (tĭp) *tr.v.* **tipped, tipping, tips. 1.** To strike gently; to tap. **2.** *Baseball.* To hit (the ball) with the side of the bat so that it glances off. —*n.* A light blow; a tap. [Middle English *tippen*, perhaps from Low German. See **tap-** in Appendix.*]

tip⁴ (tĭp) *n.* **1.** A small sum of money given as an acknowledgment of services rendered; gratuity. **2. a.** Advance or inside information given as a guide to action, as in speculating on the stock market or betting on a race. **b.** A helpful hint. —*v.* **tipped, tipping, tips.** —*tr.* **1.** To give a tip or gratuity to. **2.** To provide advance or inside information to. Often used with *off.* —*intr.* To give a tip or tips. [Originally a slang word meaning "to give," "to pass to," from TIP (to tap).] —**tip′per** *n.*

tip·cart (tĭp′kärt′) *n.* A cart having a body that can be tilted to facilitate unloading.

ti·pi. Variant of **tepee.**

tip-off (tĭp′ôf′, -ŏf′) *n.* *Informal.* An item of advance or inside information; a hint or warning.

Tip·pe·ca·noe (tĭp′ē-kə-no͞o′). A river rising in northern Indiana and flowing 166 miles west and then south to the Wabash River in the west-central part of the state, near the site of the Battle of Tippecanoe in which General William Henry Harrison defeated the Indians under Tecumseh (1811).

Tip·per·ar·y (tĭp′ə-râr′ē). A county of the Republic of Ireland, occupying 1,642 square miles in the south-central part of the country. Population, 124,000. County seat, Clonmel.

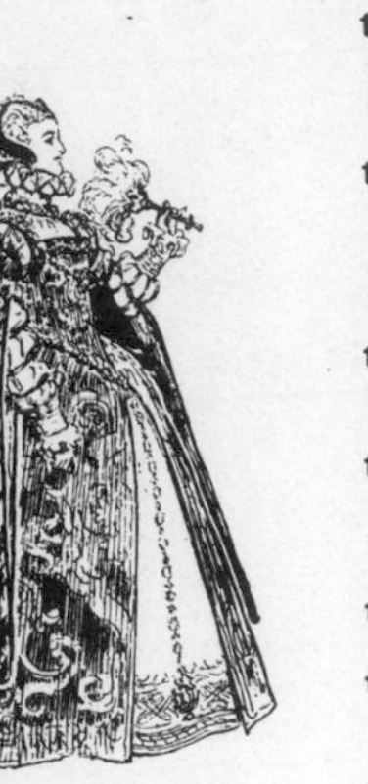

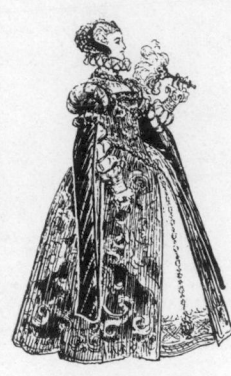

tippet
Sixteenth-century French court dress with tippets on the sleeves

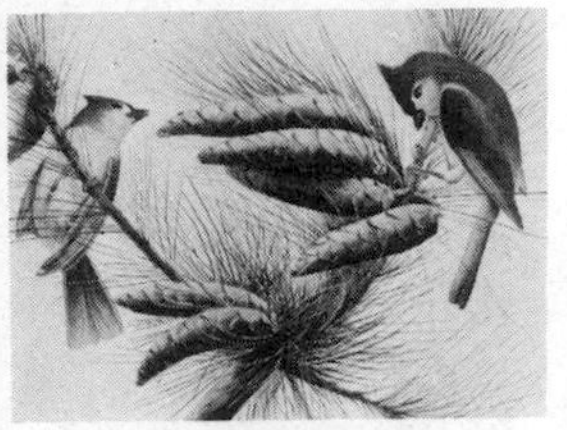

titmouse
Parus bicolor
Tufted titmouse
Painting by
John James Audubon

tip·pet (tĭp′ĭt) *n.* **1.** A covering for the shoulders, as of fur, with long ends that hang in front. **2.** A long stole worn by clergymen of the Anglican Church. **3.** A long, hanging part, as of a sleeve, hood, or cape. [Middle English *tipet*†.]

tip·ple[1] (tĭp′əl) *v.* **-pled, -pling, -ples.** —*intr.* To drink alcoholic liquor, especially habitually or intemperately. —*tr.* To drink (alcoholic liquor), especially habitually. —*n.* Alcoholic liquor. [Back-formation from *tippler*, a tapster, bartender, from Middle English *tipler*†.] —**tip′pler** *n.*

tip·ple[2] (tĭp′əl) *n.* **1.** An apparatus for unloading freight cars by tipping them. **2.** A place where this is done. [From dialectal *tipple*, to tip, overturn, frequentative of TIP.]

tip·staff (tĭp′stăf′, -stäf′) *n., pl.* **-staves** (-stāvz′, -stăvz′, -stävz′) or **-staffs. 1.** A staff with a metal tip, carried as a sign of office. **2.** An officer who carries such a staff, as a bailiff or constable. [Short for *tipped staff.*]

tip·ster (tĭp′stər) *n. Informal.* A person who sells tips or information to bettors or speculators.

tip·sy (tĭp′sē) *adj.* **-sier, -siest. 1.** Slightly drunk. **2.** Likely to tip over; unsteady; crooked. [From TIP (to tilt, be unsteady).] —**tip′si·ly** *adv.* —**tip′si·ness** *n.*

tip·toe (tĭp′tō′) *intr.v.* **-toed, -toeing, -toes.** To walk or move on or as if on the tips of one's toes; walk stealthily or quietly. —*n.* The tip of a toe. —**on tiptoe. 1.** Standing or walking on the tips of one's toes. **2.** Full of anticipation; eager. **3.** Silently; stealthily. —*adj.* **1.** Standing or walking on or as if on the tips of one's toes. **2.** Stealthy; wary. —*adv.* On tiptoe.

tip·top (tĭp′tŏp′) *n.* **1.** The highest point or summit. **2.** The highest degree of quality or excellence. —*adj.* Excellent; first-rate. —*adv.* At the highest point of excellence.

ti·rade (tī′răd′, tī-răd′) *n.* A long violent or blustering speech, especially when censorious or denouncing; a diatribe. [French, "a stretching" (as in *tout d'une tirade*, all at one stretch), from Italian *tirata*, act of drawing, from *tirare*, to draw, from Vulgar Latin *tīrāre* (unattested). See **tier** (layer).]

Ti·ran, Strait of (tē-rän′). A strait off the tip of the Sinai Peninsula, connecting the Red Sea and the Gulf of Aqaba.

Ti·ra·na (tĭ-rä′nə). Also **Ti·ra·në.** The capital of Albania, in the center of the country. Population, 153,000.

tire[1] (tīr) *v.* **tired, tiring, tires.** —*intr.* **1.** To grow weary or fatigued. **2.** To grow bored or impatient; lose interest. Often used with *of: He tired of reading.* —*tr.* **1.** To diminish the strength or energy of; to weary; to fatigue. **2.** To exhaust the interest or patience of; to bore. —**tire out.** To fatigue; to exhaust. [Middle English *tyren*, to stop, to tire, Old English *tēorian*. See **deu-[1]** in Appendix.*]

tire[2] (tīr) *n.* Also *British* **tyre. 1.** A solid or air-filled covering for a wheel, typically of rubber or a similarly elastic synthetic material, fitted around the wheel's rim to absorb shock and provide traction. **2.** A hoop of iron or heavy rubber fitted about the rim of a wheel. [Probably from TIRE (attire).]

tire[3] (tīr) *tr.v.* **tired, tiring, tires.** *Archaic.* To adorn or attire. —*n. Archaic.* **1.** Attire. **2.** A headband or headdress. [Middle English *tiren*, short for *attiren*, to ATTIRE.]

tired (tīrd) *adj.* **1. a.** Worn-out; fatigued. **b.** Impatient; bored. **2.** Overused; hackneyed.

Synonyms: *tired, weary, exhausted, fatigued, jaded, bushed.* These adjectives apply to conditions in which physical strength or strength of spirit is depleted, usually as the result of exertion or tribulation. *Tired* is the general, nonspecific term. *Weary,* like *tired,* is applicable to deficiency of strength or spirit, but often carries a stronger implication of discontent resulting from what is burdensome, irksome, boring, or the like. *Exhausted* and *fatigued* are much stronger terms. *Exhausted* specifies complete or nearly complete expenditure of physical strength. *Fatigued* implies great, though not necessarily complete, expenditure of physical or mental power. *Jaded* refers largely to dullness of spirit, often resulting from overindulgence. *Bushed* informally suggests temporary deficiency of strength resulting usually from physical exertion.

tire·less (tīr′lĭs) *adj.* Untiring; indefatigable. —**tire′less·ly** *adv.* —**tire′less·ness** *n.*

Ti·re·si·as (tī-rē′sē-əs, -zē-əs). A blind prophet of Thebes prominent in many Greek myths and tragedies.

tire·some (tīr′səm) *adj.* Causing fatigue or boredom; wearisome; tedious. See Synonyms at **boring.** —**tire′some·ly** *adv.* —**tire′some·ness** *n.*

tire·wom·an (tīr′wo͝om′ən) *n., pl.* **-women** (-wĭm′ĭn). **1.** A dressing assistant, as in a theater. **2.** *Archaic.* A lady's maid. [From TIRE (attire).]

Ti·rich Mir (tē′rĭch mēr′). The highest elevation (25,263 feet) of the Hindu Kush, situated in northern West Pakistan.

ti·ro. Variant of **tyro.**

Ti·rol. See **Tyrol.**

Tir·pitz (tĭr′pĭts), **Alfred von.** 1849–1930. German admiral; organized German Navy of World War I.

Tir·so de Mo·li·na (tēr′sō dā mō-lē′nä). Pen name of Gabriel Tellez. 1571?–1648. Spanish dramatist.

Ti·ruch·i·rap·al·li (tĭ-ro͞och′ĭ-räp′ə-lĭ). Also **Trich·i·nop·o·ly** (trĭch′ə-nŏp′ō-lĭ). A city of India, on the Cauvery River in south-central Madras. Population, 280,000.

'tis (tĭz). *Archaic & Poetic.* Contraction of *it is.*

ti·sane (tĭ-zăn′, -zän′) *n.* A herbal infusion or similar preparation, drunk as a beverage or for its mildly medicinal effect. [French, from Latin *ptisana*, barley, PTISAN.]

Tish·ri (tĭsh′rē) *n.* The first month of the civil year in the Hebrew calendar. See **calendar.** [Hebrew *Tishrī*, from Akkadian *Tashrītu*, from *shurrū*, to begin.]

Ti·siph·o·ne (tĭ-sĭf′ə-nē). One of the three **Furies** *(see).*

tis·sue (tĭsh′o͞o) *n.* **1.** *Biology.* **a.** An aggregation of morphologically and functionally similar cells. **b.** Cellular matter regarded as a collective entity. **2.** A soft, very absorbent piece of paper, generally made up of two thin layers, and used as a disposable handkerchief or towel. **3.** Unsized thin, translucent paper used for packing, wrapping, or protecting delicate articles. Also called "tissue paper." **4.** A fine sheer cloth, such as gauze. **5.** An interwoven or interrelated number of things; a web; network: *"The text is a tissue of mocking echoes."* (Richard Kain). [Middle English *tissu*, a rich cloth, fine gauze, from Old French, from the past participle of *tistre*, to weave, from Latin *texere*. See **teks-** in Appendix.*]

Ti·sza (tē′sô). *German* **Theiss** (tīs); *Czech, Rumanian, Serbo-Croatian* **Ti·sa** (tē′sə). A river of Europe, rising in the Carpathian Mountains and flowing 800 miles generally south through Czechoslovakia, Hungary, and Yugoslavia to the Danube above Belgrade.

tit[1] (tĭt) *n.* **1.** Any of various small Old World birds of the family Paridae, related to and resembling the New World chickadees. Sometimes called "titmouse." **2.** Any of various similar or related birds. [Short for TITMOUSE.]

tit[2] (tĭt) *n.* **1.** A teat or nipple. **2.** *Vulgar.* A breast. [Middle English *titte*, Old English *titt*, from West Germanic *titta* (unattested).]

tit. title.

Tit. Titus (New Testament).

ti·tan (tīt′n) *n.* A person of colossal size, strength, or achievement: *a titan of American literature.* —*adj.* Gigantic; titanic. [From TITAN.]

Ti·tan[1] (tīt′n). *Greek Mythology.* One of a family of primordial gods, the children of Uranus and Gaea, overthrown and succeeded by the Olympian gods. [Middle English, the sun god, from Latin *Tītan*, elder brother of Kronos and ancestor of the Titans, from Greek *Titan*, from *titō*, day, sun, from a source in Asia Minor.]

Ti·tan[2] (tīt′n) *n. Astronomy.* The largest satellite of Saturn. [After TITAN.]

ti·tan·ate (tīt′n-āt′) *n.* A salt of titanic acid. [TITAN(IUM) + -ATE (salt).]

Ti·tan·ess (tīt′n-ĭs). *Greek Mythology.* A female Titan.

Ti·ta·ni·a (tĭ-tā′nē-ə, tī-). *Medieval Folklore.* The queen of the fairies, wife of Oberon.

ti·tan·ic[1] (tī-tăn′ĭk) *adj.* **1. a.** Having great stature or enormous strength; huge; colossal. **b.** Of enormous scope, power, or influence. **2.** *Capital* **T.** Of or pertaining to the Titans. [After TITAN.] —**ti·tan′i·cal·ly** *adv.*

ti·tan·ic[2] (tī-tăn′ĭk, tĭ-) *adj.* Pertaining to or containing titanium, especially with valence 4. [TITAN(IUM) + -IC.]

titanic acid. 1. A white, powdered inorganic acid, H_2TiO_3, derived from an acid solution of titanates and used as a mordant. **2. Titanium dioxide** *(see).*

ti·tan·if·er·ous (tīt′n-ĭf′ər-əs) *adj.* Containing or yielding titanium. [TITANI(UM) + -FEROUS.]

Ti·tan·ism (tīt′n-ĭz′əm) *n.* The spirit of rebellion; defiance of and revolt against the established order or authority. [After TITAN.]

ti·tan·ite (tīt′n-īt′) *n. Mineralogy.* **Sphene** *(see).* [German *Titanit* : TITAN(IUM) + -ITE.]

ti·ta·ni·um (tī-tā′nē-əm, tĭ-) *n. Symbol* **Ti** A strong, low-density, highly corrosion-resistant, lustrous white metallic element that occurs widely in igneous rocks and is used to alloy aircraft metals for low weight, strength, and high-temperature stability. Atomic number 22, atomic weight 47.90, melting point 1,675°C, boiling point 3,260°C, specific gravity 4.54, valences 2, 3, 4. See **element.** [New Latin, from Greek *Titan*, TITAN. So named by Klaproth who had also named uranium after the planet Uranus. Uranus, in Greek mythology, is the father of the Titans.]

titanium dioxide. A white powder, TiO_2, used as an exceptionally opaque white pigment. Also called "titanic acid."

titanium white. Titanium dioxide used as a paint pigment with great covering power and durability.

ti·tan·o·there (tī-tăn′ə-thîr′) *n.* Any of various extinct herbivorous mammals of the genus *Brontotherium* and related genera, of the Eocene and Oligocene epochs, resembling the rhinoceros. [New Latin *Titanotherium*, "gigantic beast" : TITAN + -THERE.]

ti·tan·ous (tī-tăn′əs, tĭ-) *adj.* Pertaining to or containing titanium, especially with valence 3.

tit·bit. Variant of **tidbit.**

ti·ter (tī′tər) *n.* Also **ti·tre. 1.** The concentration of a substance in solution or the strength of such a substance determined by titration. **2.** The minimum volume needed to cause a particular result in titration. [French *titre*, a title, qualification, fineness of gold or silver in an alloy, from Old French *titre*, *title*, TITLE.]

tit for tat. Repayment in kind, as for an injury; retaliation. [Variant of earlier *tip for tap.*]

tithe (tīth) *n.* **1.** A tenth part of one's annual income, either in kind or money, contributed voluntarily for charitable purposes or due as a tax for the support of the clergy or church. **2.** Any tax or assessment of one tenth. **3. a.** The tenth part of something. **b.** Any very small part. —*v.* **tithed, tithing, tithes.** —*tr.* **1.** To contribute or pay a tenth part of (one's annual income). **2.** To levy a tithe upon. —*intr.* To pay a tithe. [Middle English *tithe*, Old English *tēotha*, *teogetha*, TENTH.] —**tith′a·ble** (tī′thə-bəl) *adj.* —**tith′er** (tī′thər) *n.*

tith·ing (tī′thĭng) *n.* **1.** The act of levying or paying tithes. **2.** A tithe. **3.** An administrative division consisting of ten householders in the old English system of frankpledge.

ti·ti[1] (tī′tī′, tē′tē′) *n.* Any of several New World shrubs of the genus *Cyrilla* and related genera; especially, *C. racemiflora,* of warm, swampy areas, having leathery leaves, clusters of white flowers, and yellow fruit. Also called "leatherwood." [Origin uncertain.]

ti·ti[2] (tē-tē′) *n.* Any of various small, long-tailed South American monkeys of the genus *Callicebus.* [Spanish, perhaps of Tupian origin.]

ti·tian (tĭsh′ən) *n.* Brownish orange. See **color.** [Often used as a hair color in paintings by TITIAN.] —**ti′tian** *adj.*

Ti·tian (tĭsh′ən). Original name, Tiziano Vecelli or Vecellio. 1477–1576. Italian painter; leader of the Venetian school.

Ti·ti·ca·ca (tē′tē-kä′kä). A lake of South America, occupying 3,200 square miles in the Andes between Peru and Bolivia, at an altitude of 12,507 feet.

tit·il·late (tĭt′ə-lāt′) *tr.v.* **-lated, -lating, -lates. 1.** To stimulate by tickling or touching lightly. **2.** To excite agreeably. [Latin *tītillāre.* See **tit-** in Appendix.*] —**tit′il·lat′ing·ly** *adv.* —**tit′il·la′tion** *n.* —**tit′il·la′tive** *adj.*

tit·i·vate (tĭt′ə-vāt′) *tr.v.* **-vated, -vating, -vates.** To make decorative additions to; spruce up. [Earlier *tidivate* : perhaps TIDY + (CULTI)VATE.] —**tit′i·va′tion** *n.*

tit·lark (tĭt′lärk′) *n.* A bird, the **pipit** *(see).* [TIT(MOUSE) + LARK.]

ti·tle (tīt′l) *n. Abbr.* **tit. 1.** An identifying name given to a book, play, motion picture, musical composition, work of art, or the like. **2. a.** All the material that appears on the title page of a book. **b.** A general or descriptive heading, as of a book chapter. **3. a.** Written matter included in a motion picture or television show to give credits. **b.** The subtitle in a motion picture. **4. a.** The heading that names a legal document or statute. **b.** The heading of a document or declaration giving the names of the parties and of the court and the number of the case. **5.** A division of a law book, declaration, or bill, generally larger than a section or article. **6.** *Law.* **a.** The coincidence of all the elements that constitute the fullest legal right to control and dispose of property or a claim. **b.** The aggregate means or body of events giving rise to this right; just cause of possession or control. **c.** The evidence of such means. **d.** The instrument constituting this evidence, such as a deed. **7. a.** Anything that provides ground for or justifies a claim. **b.** An acknowledged or alleged right. **8.** A formal appellation attached to a person or family by virtue of office, rank, hereditary privilege, attainment, or as a mark of respect; especially, such an appellation as an indication of nobility. **9.** A descriptive appellation; epithet. **10.** *Sports.* A championship. **11.** *Ecclesiastical.* **a.** A source of income or area of work required of a candidate for ordination in the Church of England. **b.** A Roman Catholic church in or near Rome having a cardinal for its nominal head. —See Synonyms at **name, right.** —*tr.v.* **titled, -tling, -tles.** To give a title to; confer a name upon. [Middle English, from Old French, from Latin *titulus,* superscription, label, title. See **tel-**[2] in Appendix.*]

ti·tled (tīt′əld) *adj.* Having a title, especially of nobility.

title page. *Abbr.* **t.p.** A page at the front of a book giving the complete title, the names of the author and publisher, and the place of publication.

tit·man (tĭt′mən) *n., pl.* **-men** (-mĭn). **1.** The runt in a litter of pigs. **2.** A man who has been either mentally or physically stunted. [Perhaps TIT(MOUSE) + MAN.]

tit·mouse (tĭt′mous′) *n., pl.* **-mice** (-mīs′). **1.** Any of several small North American birds of the genus *Parus,* having grayish plumage and a pointed crest. **2.** A related Old World bird, a **tit** *(see).* [Perhaps dialectal *tit,* a small object (see **tit,** girl) + MOUSE.]

Ti·to (tē′tō), **Marshal.** Original name, Josip Broz. Born 1892. Yugoslav statesman; prime minister (1945–53); president (since 1953).

Ti·to·grad (tē′tō-grăd′). Formerly **Pod·go·ri·ca** or **Pod·go·ri·tsa** (pŏd′gə-rē′tsə). The capital of Montenegro, Yugoslavia, in the southern part of the republic. Population, 37,000.

Ti·to·ism (tē′tō-ĭz′əm) *n.* The Communist policies and practices associated with Marshal Tito of Yugoslavia; especially, the assertion by a Communist state of its national interests independently of and often in opposition to Soviet policy.

ti·trate (tī′trāt′) *v.* **-trated, -trating, -trates.** —*tr.* To determine the concentration of (a solution) by titration. —*intr.* To perform the operation of titration. [From French *titrer,* from *titre,* TITER.]

ti·tra·tion (tī-trā′shən) *n.* The process or method of determining the concentration of a substance in solution by adding to it a standard reagent of known concentration in carefully measured amounts until a reaction of definite and known proportion is completed, as shown by a color change or by electrical measurement, and then calculating the unknown concentration.

ti·tre. Variant of **titer.**

tit·ter (tĭt′ər) *intr.v.* **-tered, -tering, -ters.** To utter a restrained, nervous giggle, as in ridicule or childish amusement. —*n.* A nervous giggle. [Imitative.] —**tit′ter·er** *n.* —**tit′ter·ing·ly** *adv.*

tit·tle (tĭt′l) *n.* **1.** A small diacritical mark, such as an accent, vowel mark, or dot over an *i.* **2.** The tiniest bit; an iota. [Middle English *titel,* a diacritical mark, from Medieval Latin *titulus,* from Latin, TITLE.]

tit·tle-tat·tle (tĭt′l-tăt′l) *n.* Petty gossip; trivial talk. —*intr.v.* **tittle-tattled, -tling, -tles.** To talk idly or foolishly; to gossip. [Reduplication of TATTLE.]

tit·tup (tĭt′əp) *intr.v.* **-tuped** or **-tupped, -tuping** or **-tupping, tups.** To move in an affected, lively manner; to prance or caper. —*n.* A lively, affected manner of moving or walking; a prance or caper. [Imitative of the sounds of a horse's hoofs.]

tit·u·ba·tion (tĭch′o͞o-bā′shən) *n.* A staggering or stumbling gait characteristic of certain nervous disorders. [Latin *titubātiō,* from *titubātus,* past participle of *titubāre*†, to reel, stagger.]

tit·u·lar (tĭch′o͞o-lər) *adj.* **1.** Pertaining to, having the nature of, or constituting a title. **2.** Existing as such in name only; nominal: *the titular head of the company.* **3. a.** Bearing a title. **b.** Related to or arising from a title, as honors. **4.** From whom or from the name of which the title is derived: *the titular role in a play.* **5.** Of or designating one of the ancient churches in or near Rome from which a cardinal takes his title. —*n.* Also **tit·u·lar·y** (tĭch′o͞o-lĕr′ē) *pl.* **-ies.** A person who holds a title. [From Latin *titulus,* TITLE.] —**tit′u·lar·ly** *adv.*

Ti·tus[1] (tī′təs) *n. Abbr.* **Tit.** An epistle in the New Testament attributed to Saint Paul and addressed to Titus, his disciple.

Ti·tus[2] (tī′təs). Full name, Titus Flavius Sabinus Vespasianus. A.D. 40?–81. Emperor of Rome (A.D. 79–81); son and successor of Vespasian.

Ti·tus (tī′təs), **Saint.** Christian leader of the first century A.D.; convert and companion of Saint Paul.

Ti·u (tē′o͞o). *Germanic Mythology.* The god of war and the sky, identified with the Norse god Tyr. [Old English *Tīw.* See **deiw-** in Appendix.*]

Ti·vo·li (tĭv′ə-lē; *Italian* tē′vō-lē). Ancient name **Ti·bur** (tī′bər). A city in central Italy, noted for its ruins of ancient villas, particularly that of Hadrian. Population, 34,000.

tiz·zy (tĭz′ē) *n., pl.* **-zies.** *Slang.* A state of nervous confusion; a dither. [Origin unknown.]

Tji·re·bon (chĭr′ə-bôn′). Also **Cher·i·bon** (chĕr′-). A port of Indonesia on the Java Sea; the site of the drafting of the agreement by which the Dutch recognized Indonesian independence (1946). Population, 158,000.

tk. truck.

TKO technical knockout.

tkt. ticket.

Tl The symbol for the element thallium.

Tlax·ca·la (tläs-kä′lä). **1.** The smallest state (1,555 square miles) of Mexico, situated in the south-central part of the country. Population, 368,000. **2.** The capital of this state, near its southern border. Population, 8,000.

TLC tender loving care.

Tlin·git (tlĭng′gĭt) *n., pl.* **Tlingit** or **-gits. 1.** A group of North American Indian seafaring tribes inhabiting the coastal areas of southern Alaska and northern British Columbia. **2.** A member of any of these tribes. **3.** A linguistic family of the Na-Dene phylum constituting only the language of the Tlingit.

t.l.o. total loss only.

tlr. tailor.

TLV Airport code for Tel Aviv/Jaffa, Israel.

Tm The symbol for the element thulium.

t.m. true mean.

tme·sis (tmē′sĭs, mē′-) *n.* The separation of the parts of a compound word by one or more intervening words; for example, *where I go ever* instead of *wherever I go.* [Late Latin *tmēsis,* "a cutting," from Greek, from *temnein,* to cut. See **tem-** in Appendix.*]

TN Tennessee (with Zip Code).

tn. 1. town. **2.** train.

tng. training.

tnpk. turnpike.

TNR Airport code for Tananarive, Malagasy Republic.

TNT (tē′ĕn-tē′) *n.* An explosive compound, **trinitrotoluene** *(see).*

to (to͞o; *unstressed* tə) *prep.* **1.** In a direction toward; so as to approach or come near: *going to Paris; bear to the right.* **2.** In the direction of; so as to reach or terminate in: *a trip to Paris.* **3.** Reaching as far as; through and terminating in: *rotten to the core.* **4.** Toward or reaching the condition or state of: *a rise to power.* **5.** To the extent of: *starved to death.* **6.** In contact with: *dancing cheek to cheek; apply polish to the shoes.* **7.** In front of: *face to face.* **8.** Through and including; until: *at home from three to five.* **9.** For the attention, benefit, or possession of: *Tell it to me.* **10.** For the purpose of; for: *She worked to that end.* **11.** Pertaining to; for or of: *the belt to this dress.* **12.** Concerning or regarding; in response to: *deaf to her pleas.* **13.** In relation to: *parallel to the road.* **14.** With the resulting condition of: *a flag torn to shreds.* **15.** As an accompaniment or addition for: *Sing to the music.* **16.** With regard to: *the secret to his success.* **17.** Composing or constituting; in: *two pints to the quart.* **18.** In correspondence or accord with: *not to my liking.* **19.** As compared with: *a score of four to three.* **20.** Before: *ten to five.* **21.** In honor of: *a toast to his success.* **22.** *Regional.* With: *an acre planted to wheat.* **23.** *Regional.* At or in (a specified location): *He's to town.* —*adv.* **1.** Into a position or condition, especially shut or closed: *He slammed the door to.* **2.** Into consciousness: *He came to.* **3.** Into a state of application to the matter, action, or work at hand: *We sat down for lunch and fell to.* **4.** *Nautical.* Turned into the wind. Used of a sailing vessel. [Middle English *to,* Old English *tō, te.* See **de-** in Appendix.*]

Usage: *To* is also used before a verb to indicate the infinitive: *He came to conquer,* and may appear alone in place of the infinitive: *You may leave if you want to.*

t.o. turnover.

toad (tōd) *n.* **1.** Any of numerous tailless amphibians chiefly of the family Bufonidae, related to and resembling the frogs but characteristically more terrestrial and having rougher, drier skin. **2.** A lizard, the **horned toad** *(see).* **3.** A repulsive person. [Middle English *tadde, tode,* Old English *tādi(g)e*†.]

toad·eat·er (tōd′ē′tər) *n.* A toady. [Originally, a charlatan's

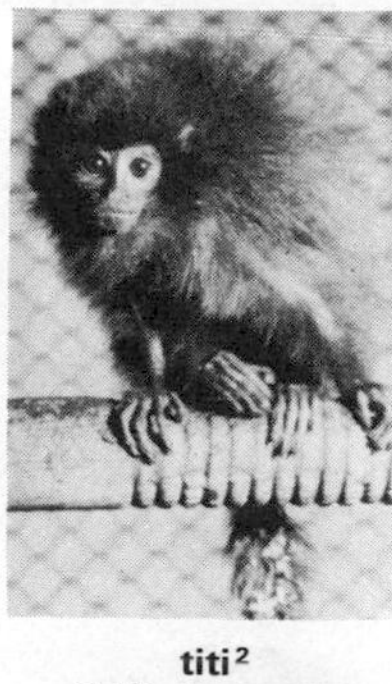

titi[2]
Callicebus cupreus

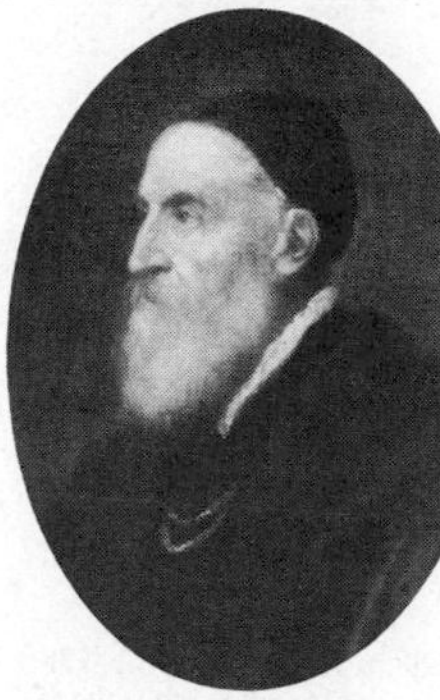

Titian
A self-portrait

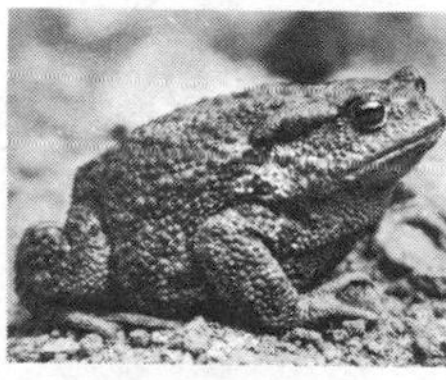

toad
Bufo bufo

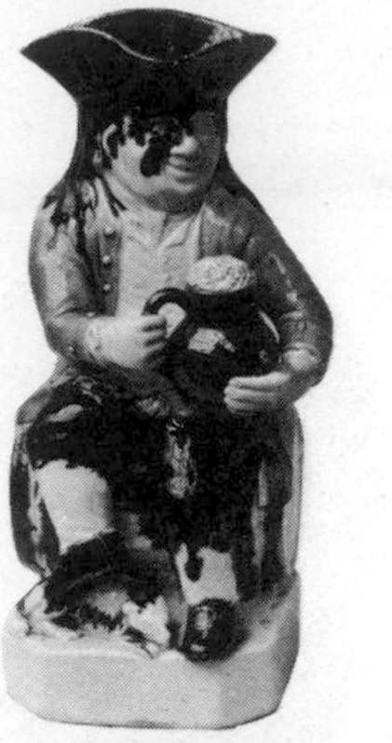

toby
Made in England about 1780 of lead-glazed earthenware

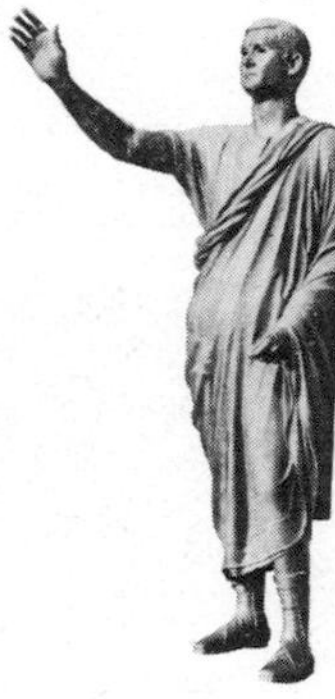

toga
Etruscan statue of an orator wearing a toga

attendant who was hired to pretend to eat toads (thought to be poisonous) to prove that the charlatan could easily expel the poison.]

toad·fish (tōd′fĭsh′) *n., pl.* **toadfish** or **-fishes.** Any of various bottom-dwelling, chiefly marine fishes of the family Batrachoididae, having a broad, flattened head and a wide mouth.

toad·flax (tōd′flăks′) *n.* Any of various plants of the genus *Linaria,* having narrow leaves and spurred, two-lipped flowers; especially, the common wildflower **butter-and-eggs** *(see).*

toad spit. An insect secretion, **cuckoo spit** *(see).*

toad·stone (tōd′stōn′) *n.* A stone formerly believed to be formed in the body of a toad and worn as a charm.

toad·stool (tōd′stōōl′) *n.* An inedible fungus with an umbrella-shaped fruiting body, as distinguished from an edible mushroom. [Middle English *todestool* : *tode,* TOAD + STOOL (from its stoollike shape and the popular association of it with toads, which were thought to be poisonous).]

toad·y (tō′dē) *n., pl.* **-ies.** One who panders to the wealthy or influential; a servile flatterer. See Synonyms at **sycophant.** —*v.* **toadied, -ying, -ies.** —*tr.* To be a toady to. —*intr.* To be a toady. [From TOADEATER.]

to and fro. In one direction and the opposite; back and forth. —**to′-and-fro′** (tōō′ən-frō′) *adj.*

toast[1] (tōst) *v.* **toasted, toasting, toasts.** —*tr.* **1.** To heat and brown (bread, for example) by placing close to a fire or in a toaster. **2.** To warm thoroughly, as before a fire: *toast one's feet.* —*intr.* To become toasted. —*n.* Sliced bread heated and browned. [Middle English *tosten,* from Old French *toster,* from Vulgar Latin *tostāre* (unattested), from Latin *torrēre* (past participle *tostus*), to dry, parch. See **ters-** in Appendix.*]

toast[2] (tōst) *n.* **1.** A person, institution, sentiment, or the like to whose health or in whose honor a company drinks. **2.** The act of proposing the health or honor of a person or thing as a toast. **3.** *Archaic.* A lady to whose beauty or charms toasts are frequently proposed. **4.** One receiving much acclaim. —*v.* **toasted, toasting, toasts.** —*tr.* To drink to the health or honor of. —*intr.* To propose or drink a toast. [From TOAST (from the notion that the name of a celebrated lady could flavor the drink like a piece of spiced toast).]

toast·er (tō′stər) *n.* A device used to toast bread by exposure to electrically heated wire coils.

toast·mas·ter (tōst′măs′tər, -mäs′tər) *n.* One who proposes the toasts and introduces the guests or speakers at a banquet.

to·bac·co (tə-băk′ō) *n., pl.* **-cos** or **-coes. 1.** Any of various plants of the genus *Nicotiana;* especially, *N. tabacum,* native to tropical America, widely cultivated for its leaves, which are used primarily for smoking. **2.** The leaves of cultivated tobacco, dried and processed chiefly for use in cigarettes, snuff, or cigars, or for smoking in pipes. **3.** Products made from tobacco. **4.** The habit of smoking tobacco: *I gave up tobacco.* **5.** A crop of tobacco. [Earlier *tabac(c)o,* from Spanish *tabaco,* probably from Arabic *ṭabāq,* euphoria-causing herb.]

to·bac·co·nist (tə-băk′ə-nĭst) *n.* A dealer in tobacco.

To·ba·go (tə-bā′gō). An island, 116 square miles in area, in the Atlantic Ocean off Venezuela; part of the independent state of **Trinidad and Tobago** *(see).*

To·ba·ta (tō-bä′tä). **Kita Kyushu** *(see).*

To·bi·as[1] (tō-bī′əs). A masculine given name. [Late Latin *Tōbiās,* from Greek *Tōbias,* from Hebrew *ṭōbhīyyāh,* "the Lord is good," from *ṭōbh,* good, akin to Aramaic *ṭabh,* Akkadian *ṭābu,* to be good.]

To·bi·as[2] (tō-bī′əs) *n.* **Tobit** *(see).*

To·bit (tō′bĭt) *n.* A book of the Old Testament Apocrypha, named after its hero, a Hebrew captive in Nineveh. Also called "Tobias."

to·bog·gan (tə-bŏg′ən) *n.* A long, narrow, runnerless sled constructed of thin boards curled upward at the front and used for transporting goods over snow and ice or for coasting down slopes. —*intr.v.* **tobogganed, -ganing, -gans. 1.** To coast, ride, or travel on a toboggan. **2.** To decline or fall rapidly: *His good fortune tobogganed.* [Canadian French *tobagan,* from Micmac *tobăkan.*] —**to·bog′gan·er, to·bog′gan·ist** *n.*

To·bol (tə-bôl′). A river of the Soviet Union, rising in the Ural Mountains in the Kazakh S.S.R. and flowing about 1,000 miles generally northwest to the Irtish.

To·bruk (tō′brŏŏk). *Italian* **To·bruch** (tō′brŏŏk). A town of Libya, a seaport in the northeast on the Mediterranean; the scene of heavy fighting in World War II (1941–42).

to·by (tō′bē) *n., pl.* **-bies.** Also **To·by. 1.** A drinking mug usually in the shape of a stout man wearing a large three-cornered hat. Also called "Toby jug." **2.** *Slang.* A type of long cigar made of inferior tobacco. [From TOBY (name).]

To·by (tō′bē). A masculine given name. [Pet form of TOBIAS.]

To·can·tins (tō′kăɴ-tēɴs′). A river of Brazil, rising in south-central Goiás State and flowing 1,648 miles generally north to the Pará southwest of Belém.

toc·ca·ta (tə-kä′tə) *n.* A composition, usually for organ or other keyboard instrument, in free style. [Italian, "a touching" (originally a piece intended to show touch technique), from the feminine past participle of *toccare,* to touch, from Vulgar Latin *toccāre* (unattested), to strike, TOUCH.]

To·char·i·an (tō-kâr′ē-ən, -kär′ē-ən) *n.* Also **To·khar·i·an. 1.** A member of a people of possible European origin, with an advanced culture, living in Asia until about the tenth century A.D. **2.** An Indo-European language with eastern and western dialects, *Tocharian A* and *Tocharian B* respectively, known from documents of the seventh century A.D. [French *Tocharien,* from Latin *Tochari,* from Greek *Tokharoi*† (mentioned by Strabo).]

to·col·o·gy (tō-kŏl′ə-jē) *n.* Also **to·kol·o·gy.** The practice of obstetrics or midwifery. [Greek *tokos,* childbirth, from *tiktein,* to beget (see **tek-**[1] in Appendix*) + -LOGY.]

to·coph·er·ol (tō-kŏf′ə-rôl′, -rōl′) *n.* Any of a group of four chemically related compounds, differing slightly in structure, that together constitute vitamin E. [Greek *tokos,* childbirth (see **tocology**) + Greek *pherein,* to carry, bear (see **bher-**[1] in Appendix*) + -OL.]

Tocque·ville (tōk′vĭl; *French* tôk-vēl′), **Alexis Charles Henri Maurice Clérel de.** 1805–1859. French political figure, traveler, and historian.

toc·sin (tŏk′sĭn) *n.* **1.** An alarm sounded on a bell. **2.** A warning; omen. [French, from Old French *toquesain,* from Old Provençal *tocasenh* : *tocar,* to strike (a bell), touch, from Vulgar Latin *toccāre* (unattested), to ring a bell, TOUCH + *senh,* bell, from Latin *signum,* token, SIGN.]

tod (tŏd) *n.* **1.** *Chiefly British.* A unit of weight used especially for wool, equivalent to about 28 pounds. **2.** *British.* A bushy clump, as of ivy. [Middle English *todd(e),* a unit of weight, probably akin to Middle Low German *toddelen,* to fall apart into bunches, and Old High German *zot(t)a,* a tuft, from Germanic *toddōn* (unattested).]

to·day (tə-dā′) *adv.* Also **to-day. 1.** During or on the present day. **2.** During or at the present time. —*n.* Also **to-day.** The present day, time, or age. [Middle English *to day,* Old English *tōdæg(e),* on this day : TO + *dæge,* dative of *dæg,* DAY.]

Todd (tŏd), Sir **Alexander Robertus.** Born 1907. British chemist; studied nucleic acid and nucleotide structure.

tod·dle (tŏd′l) *intr.v.* **-dled, -dling, -dles.** To walk with short, unsteady steps, as a small child. —*n.* The act of toddling; a slow, uncertain gait. [Origin unknown.]

tod·dler (tŏd′lər) *n.* **1.** A child who has learned to walk but not yet perfectly. **2.** A size of clothing for children between the ages of about one to three.

tod·dy (tŏd′ē) *n., pl.* **-dies. 1.** A drink consisting of brandy or other liquor combined with hot water, sugar, spices, and a slice of lemon. Also called "hot toddy." **2. a.** The sweet sap of several tropical Asian palm trees, especially *Caryota urens,* used as a beverage. **b.** A liquor fermented from this sap. [Earlier *tarry,* from Hindi *tāṛī,* sap of a palm, from *tāṛ,* palm yielding toddy, from Sanskrit *tāla, tāra,* probably from Dravidian, akin to Kannada *taṛ,* Telegu *tāḍu.*]

to-do (tə-dōō′) *n., pl.* **-dos** (-dōōz′). *Informal.* Commotion or bustle; a stir; a fuss. [From the infinitive *to do* (as in phrases *much to do, more to do,* but in sense influenced by ADO).]

to·dy (tō′dē) *n., pl.* **-dies.** Any of various small, colorful birds of the family Todidae, of the West Indies. [French *todier,* from Latin *todī*† (unattested), name of certain small birds.]

toe (tō) *n.* **1.** One of the digits of the foot, especially of a vertebrate animal. **2.** The forward part of something worn on the foot, as a shoe or sock. **3. a.** The base or lower tip of something, as the end of the head on a golf club. **b.** Anything suggestive of a toe in form, function, or location. —**on one's toes.** Alert; ready to act. —**tread on someone's toes.** To hurt, offend, or interfere with the feelings, actions, or province of another, especially accidentally. —*v.* **toed, toeing, toes.** —*tr.* **1.** To touch, kick, follow, or trace with the toe. **2.** To drive (a golf ball) with the toe of the club. **3.** *Carpentry.* **a.** To drive (a nail or spike, for example) obliquely. **b.** To secure (beams, for example) with nails driven obliquely. —*intr.* To walk or move with the toes pointed in a specified direction: *He toes out.* —**toe the mark** (or **line**). **1.** To touch a mark or line with the toe or hands in readiness for the start of a race or competition. **2.** To obey rules conscientiously; conform. [Middle English *ta, to,* Old English *tā.* See **deik-** in Appendix.*]

toe·cap (tō′kăp′) *n.* A reinforced covering of leather or metal for the toe of a shoe or boot.

toed (tōd) *adj.* **1.** Driven obliquely. Said of a nail. **2.** Secured by obliquely driven nails. **3.** Having a specified number of toes. Used in combination: *a two-toed sloth.*

toe dance. A dance performed on the toes. —**toe dancer.**

toe·hold (tō′hōld′) *n.* **1.** A small indentation or ledge on which the toe can find support in climbing. **2.** Any slight or initial advantage useful for future progress: *Family connections gave him a toehold in politics.* **3.** A wrestling hold in which one competitor wrenches the other's foot.

toe·nail (tō′nāl′) *n.* **1.** The nail on a toe. **2.** *Carpentry.* Any nail driven obliquely, as to join vertical and horizontal beams. —*tr.v.* **toenailed, -nailing, -nails.** *Carpentry.* To secure (beams) with obliquely driven nails.

toff (tŏf) *n. British Slang.* A gentleman or dandy. [Probably variant of TUFT (a tassel, hence a titled student at Oxford or Cambridge).]

tof·fee (tŏf′ē, tô′fē) *n.* Also **tof·fy** *pl.* **-fies.** A hard or chewy candy of brown sugar and butter. [Variant of TAFFY.]

toft (tôft, tŏft) *n. British.* **1.** A homestead. **2.** A hillock. [Middle English *toft,* Old English *toft,* site of a building, homestead, from Old Norse *topt.* See **demə-**[1] in Appendix.*]

tog (tŏg) *n. Informal.* **1.** A coat or cloak. **2.** *Plural.* Clothes: *gardening togs.* —*tr.v.* **togged, togging, togs.** *Informal.* To dress or clothe. Often used with *up* or *out.* [Short for cant *togeman(s), togman* : probably obsolete *toge,* cloak, from Middle English, from Old French *tog(u)e,* from Latin *toga,* TOGA + *-mans*†, a cant noun suffix.]

to·ga (tō′gə) *n., pl.* **-gas** or **-gae** (-jē). **1.** A draped one-piece outer garment worn in public by citizens of ancient Rome. **2.** Any robe or gown characteristic of a profession: *the judge's toga.* [Latin, from *tegere,* to cover. See **steg-**[1] in Appendix.*] —**to′gaed** (tō′gəd) *adj.*

to·geth·er (tə-gĕth′ər) *adv.* **1.** In or into a single group, company, gathering, mass, or place: *We gather together.* **2.** Against or in relationship to one another; mutually or reciprocally: *He rubbed his hands together.* **3.** Regarded collectively; in total: *He is worth more than all of us together.* **4.** Simultaneously: *The bells rang out together.* **5.** In harmony, accord, or cooperation: *We stand together on this question.* [Middle English *togeder(e)*, Old English *tōgædere*. See **ghedh-** in Appendix.*]

Usage: *Together with* is often employed following the subject of a sentence or clause to introduce an addition. The addition, however, does not alter the number of the verb, which is governed by the subject: *The king* (singular), *together with two aides, is expected in an hour.* The same is true of *along with, as well as, besides, in addition to,* and *like.* For example: *Common sense as well as training is a requisite for a good job.*

to·geth·er·ness (tə-gĕth′ər-nĭs) *n.* The quality of being in close relationship or harmony; comradeship or intimacy.

tog·ger·y (tŏg′ə-rē) *n., pl.* **-ies.** *Informal.* **1.** Clothing; togs. **2.** A clothing store.

tog·gle (tŏg′əl) *n.* **1.** A device used to secure or hold something, especially: **a.** A pin inserted in a nautical knot to keep it from slipping. **b.** A device attached to the end of or inserted in a loop in a rope, chain, or strap to prevent slipping, to tighten, or to hold an attached object. **2.** An apparatus having a toggle joint. —*tr.v.* **toggled, -gling, -gles.** To furnish or fasten with a toggle or toggles. [Origin unknown.]

toggle bolt. A fastener consisting of a threaded bolt and a mated toggle.

toggle iron. A hinged harpoon head that turns at right angles to its shaft when pulled. Also called "toggle harpoon."

toggle joint. An elbowlike joint composed of two arms pivoted so that a force applied to their hinge to straighten them produces an outward force at the ends.

toggle switch. A switch in which a projecting lever employing a toggle joint with a spring is used to open or close an electric circuit.

To·go (tō′gō). Officially, Republic of Togo. A republic of Africa, independent since 1960, occupying 20,733 square miles in the west on the Gulf of Guinea. Population, 1,500,000. Capital, Lomé.

To·go·land (tō′gō-lănd′). A former German protectorate in western Africa, divided after World War I into the British western sector, which became part of independent Ghana in 1957, and the French eastern sector, which achieved independence as Togo in 1960.

togue (tōg) *n.* The **lake trout** *(see).* [Canadian French, probably from a native American Indian name.]

toil¹ (toil) *intr.v.* **toiled, toiling, toils. 1.** To labor continuously and untiringly; work strenuously. **2.** To proceed or make one's way with difficulty, pain, or exhaustion: *toiling over the mountains.* —*n.* **1.** Exhausting labor or effort. **2.** *Obsolete.* Strife; contention. —See Synonyms at **work.** [Middle English *toilen*, to struggle, to battle, from Norman French *toiler*, from Old French *tooillier*, to stir, to agitate, from Latin *tudiculāre*, to stir about, from *tudicula*, a mill for crushing olives, diminutive of *tudes*, a hammer. See **steu-** in Appendix.*]

toil² (toil) *n.* **1.** *Obsolete.* A long net or a series of nets for trapping game. **2.** *Usually plural.* Any entrapment: *in the toils of despair.* [Old French *toile*, a web, net, from Latin *tēla*. See **teks-** in Appendix.*]

toile (twäl) *n.* **1.** A sheer linen fabric. **2.** A fine, monochromatic cretonne. [French, cloth, net. See **toil** (net).]

toi·let (toi′lĭt) *n.* **1.** A disposal apparatus consisting of a hopper, fitted with a flushing device, used for urination and defecation. **2.** A room or booth containing such an apparatus and often a washbowl. **3.** The act or process of grooming and dressing oneself. **4.** A dressing table. **5. a.** Dress; attire. **b.** A costume or gown. —**make one's toilet.** To groom oneself. [French *toilette*, lavatory, dressing table, from Old French, cloth cover for a dressing table, a dressing table, diminutive of *toile*, cloth, net. See **toil** (net).]

toilet paper. Thin, absorbent paper, usually in rolls, used for cleansing oneself after defecation or urination.

toi·let·ry (toi′lĭ-trē) *n., pl.* **-ries.** Any article or cosmetic used in dressing or grooming oneself.

toi·lette (twä-lĕt′) *n.* **1.** The act or process of dressing or grooming oneself; toilet. **2.** A person's dress or style of dress. **3.** A gown or costume. [French, TOILET.]

toilet water. Cologne or mild perfume.

toil·some (toil′səm) *adj.* Characterized by or requiring toil; done with difficulty. —**toil′some·ly** *adv.* —**toil′some·ness** *n.*

To·jo (tō′jō), **Hideki.** 1885–1948. Japanese military and political leader; prime minister and dictator (1941–44); executed.

To·ka·ra (tō-kä′rə). A chain of small islands between the East China Sea and the Pacific Ocean, the northernmost islands of the Ryukyu group.

To·kay (tō-kā′) *n.* **1.** A sweet, reddish variety of grape originally grown near Tokay, Hungary. **2.** A sweet, rich wine made from these grapes.

to·ken (tō′kən) *n.* **1.** Something that serves as an indication or representation of some fact, event, emotion, or the like; a sign; symbol: *"Tears are queer tokens of happiness"* (O'Neill). **2.** Something that tangibly signifies authority, validity, identity, or the like: *The scepter is a token of kingship.* **3.** A keepsake or souvenir. **4.** A piece of stamped metal used as a substitute for currency. —See Synonyms at **sign.** —**by the same token.** In the same manner; likewise. —**in token of.** As indication or evidence of. —*tr.v.* **tokened, -kening, -kens.** To betoken or symbolize; portend. —*adj.* Done as an indication or pledge: *a token payment.* [Middle English *taken, token*, Old English *tāc(e)n*. See **deik-** in Appendix.*]

To·khar·i·an. Variant of **Tocharian.**

To·klas (tō′kləs), **Alice B.** 1877–1967. American author; resident in France; companion of Gertrude Stein.

to·kol·o·gy. Variant of **tocology.**

To·ku·shi·ma (tō′ko͞o-shē′mə). A city of Japan, a seaport on the eastern coast of Shikoku Island. Population, 190,000.

To·ky·o (tō′kē-ō). Also **To·ki·o.** Formerly **E·do** (ĕ′dō′), **Ye·do** (yĕ′dō′). The capital of Japan, a seaport on Honshu on the northwestern shore of Tokyo Bay. Population, 8,527,000; metropolitan area, 11,022,000. [Japanese *Tōkyō*, "Eastern Capital" : *tō*, east, from Ancient Chinese *tung* (Mandarin *tung¹*) + *kyō*, capital city, from Ancient Chinese *kiang* (Mandarin *ching¹*).]

To·ky·o Bay (tō′kē-ō). An inlet of the Pacific Ocean extending about 30 miles into east-central Honshu, Japan.

TOL Airport code for Toledo, Ohio.

to·la (tō′lə, tō-lä′) *n.* A unit of weight used in India, equal to the weight of one silver rupee, or 180 troy grains. [Hindi *tolā*, from Sanskrit *tulā*, balance, weight. See **tel-¹** in Appendix.*]

tol·booth (tōl′bo͞oth′) *n.* Also **toll·booth.** *Scottish.* A prison; jail. [Middle English *tolbothe*, toll station, tax-collection booth, town hall (beneath which there were jail cells) : TOLL + BOOTH.]

tol·bu·ta·mide (tŏl-byo͞o′tə-mīd′) *n.* A white powder, $C_{12}H_{18}N_2O_3S$, used in the treatment of diabetes. [TOL(U) + BUT(YRIC ACID) + AMIDE.]

told. Past tense and past participle of **tell.**

tole (tōl) *n.* Also **tôle.** Lacquered or enameled metalware, usually gilded, popular in the 18th century. [French *tôle*, sheet metal, sheet iron, from French dialect, a slab, table, variant of *table*, from Latin *tabula*, a board. See **table.**]

To·le·do¹ (tə-lē′dō; *Spanish* tō-lā′thō). **1.** A city of central Spain, 40 miles south of Madrid and bordered on three sides by the Tagus. Population, 29,000. **2.** A city of Ohio, a port in the northwest on Lake Erie. Population, 363,000.

To·le·do² (tə-lē′dō) *n., pl.* **-dos.** Also **to·le·do.** A sword made in Toledo, Spain, a city noted for its manufacture of fine-tempered steel blades.

tol·er·a·ble (tŏl′ər-ə-bəl) *adj.* **1.** Able to be tolerated; endurable. **2.** That can be allowed; permissible. **3.** Fair or adequate; passable. —See Synonyms at **average.** —**tol′er·a·bil′i·ty, tol′er·a·ble·ness** *n.* —**tol′er·a·bly** *adv.*

tol·er·ance (tŏl′ər-əns) *n.* **1.** The capacity for or practice of allowing or respecting the nature, beliefs, or behavior of others. **2. a.** Leeway for variation from a standard. **b.** The permissible deviation from a specified value of a structural dimension. **3.** The capacity to endure; especially, the ability to endure hardship or pain. **4. a.** Physiological resistance to poison. **b.** The capacity to absorb a drug continuously or in large doses without adverse effect.

tol·er·ant (tŏl′ər-ənt) *adj.* **1.** Inclined to tolerate the beliefs, practices, or traits of others; forbearing. **2.** Able to withstand or endure an adverse environmental condition: *plants tolerant of extreme heat.* —**tol′er·ant·ly** *adv.*

tol·er·ate (tŏl′ə-rāt′) *tr.v.* **-ated, -ating, -ates. 1.** To allow without prohibiting or opposing; permit. **2.** To recognize and respect, as the rights, opinions, or practices of others, whether agreeing with them or not. **3.** To put up with; to bear; endure. **4.** *Medicine.* To have tolerance for (a drug or poison). —See Synonyms at **bear.** [Latin *tolerāre*, to bear, tolerate. See **tel-¹** in Appendix.*] —**tol′er·a′tive** *adj.* —**tol′er·a′tor** (-ə-rā′tər) *n.*

tol·er·a·tion (tŏl′ə-rā′shən) *n.* **1.** Tolerance. **2.** Official recognition of the rights of individuals and groups to hold dissenting opinions; especially, the sufferance by a government of religious freedom. —**tol′er·a′tion·ism′** *n.* —**tol′er·a′tion·ist** *n.*

tol·i·dine (tŏl′ə-dēn′) *n.* Any of several isomeric bases, $C_{14}H_{16}N_2$, derived from toluene, one of which is used as a reagent for gold and for chlorine in water. [TOL(UENE) + -ID(E) + -INE.]

To·li·ma (tō-lē′mä). Also **Ne·va·da del To·li·ma** (nā-vä′thä dĕl). A volcanic mountain rising to 18,438 feet in west-central Colombia.

Tol·kien (tŏl′kēn′), **J(ohn) R(onald) R(euel).** Born 1892. English philologist and author of novels of fantasy.

toll¹ (tōl) *n.* **1.** A fixed charge or tax for an access or privilege, especially for passage across a bridge or along a road. **2.** A charge for services, as for shipping goods or for long-distance telephoning. **3.** A quantity of people or things destroyed or adversely affected, as in a natural disaster or in war; price: *The drought took a heavy toll in cattle.* —*tr.v.* **tolled, tolling, tolls.** *Rare.* To exact as a toll. [Middle English *tol(le)*, Old English *toll*, from West Germanic *toln-* (unattested), from Late Latin *tolonium, telōnium*, a tollbooth, customhouse, from Greek *telōnion*, from *telōnēs*, a tax collector, from *telos*, tax. See **tel-¹** in Appendix.*]

toll² (tōl) *v.* **tolled, tolling, tolls.** —*tr.* **1.** To sound (a large bell) slowly at regular intervals. **2.** To announce or summon by tolling. —*intr.* To sound in slowly repeated single tones. Used of a bell. —*n.* **1.** The act of tolling. **2.** The sound of a tolling bell. [Middle English *tollen*, probably special use of *tollen, tullen*, to entice, lure, perhaps Old English *tollian* (unattested), perhaps from Germanic *tull* (unattested).]

toll·booth (tōl′bo͞oth′) *n.* **1.** A booth at a tollgate, where a toll is collected. Also called "tollhouse." **2.** *Scottish.* Variant of **tolbooth.**

toll call. Any telephone call for which a higher rate is charged than that standard for a local call.

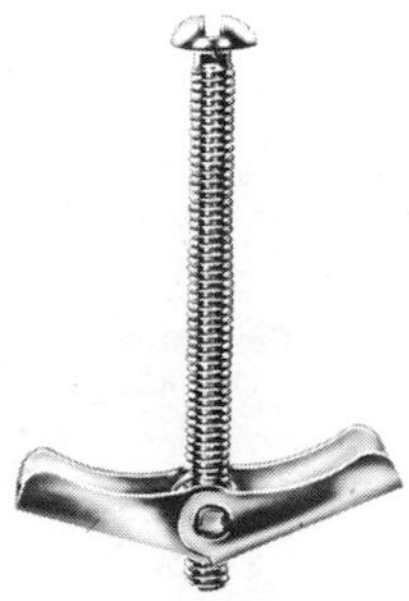

toggle bolt

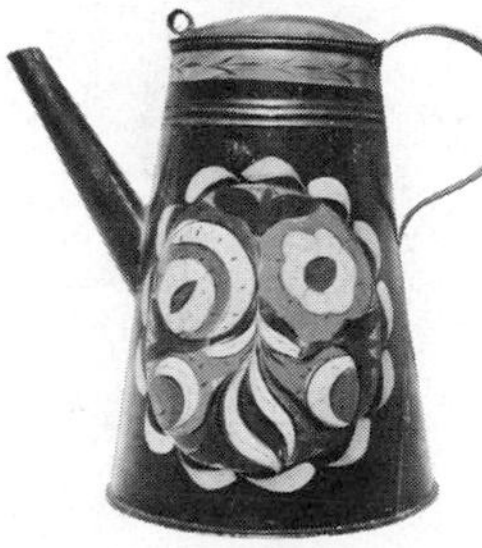

tole
Coffeepot of lacquered tin

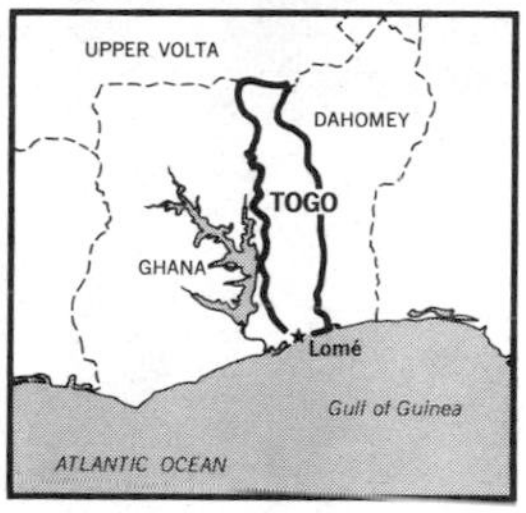

Togo

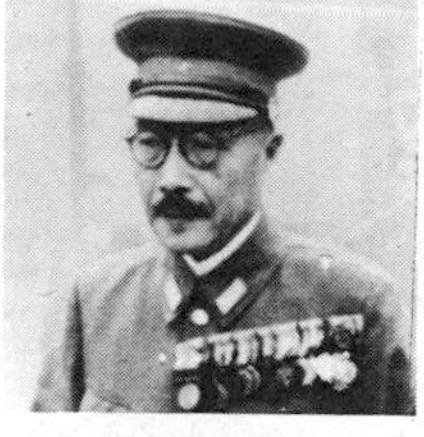

Hideki Tojo
Photographed in 1943

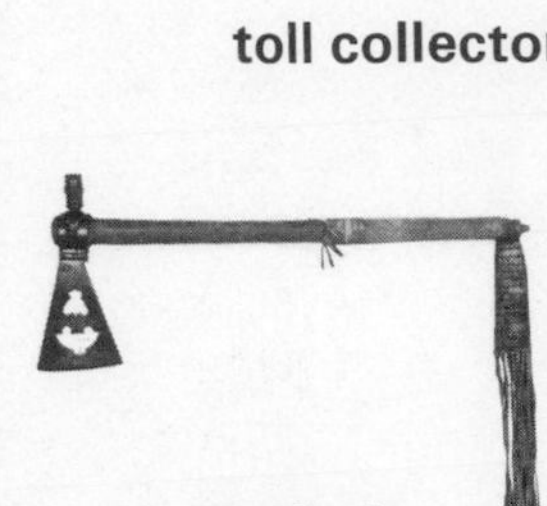

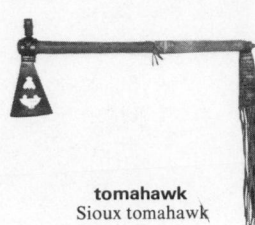

tomahawk
Sioux tomahawk

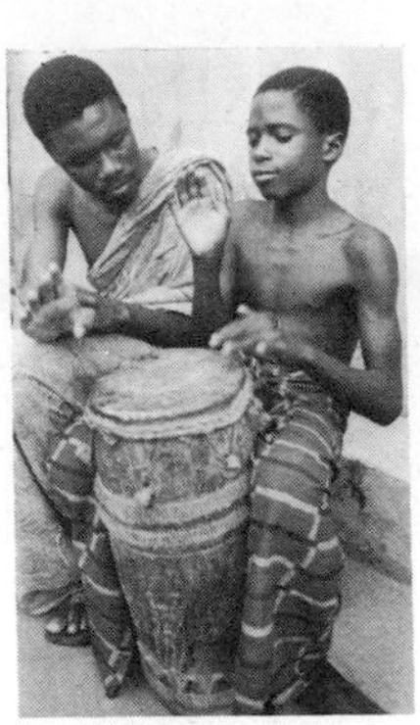

tom-tom
Ivory Coast boy being taught to play a tom-tom

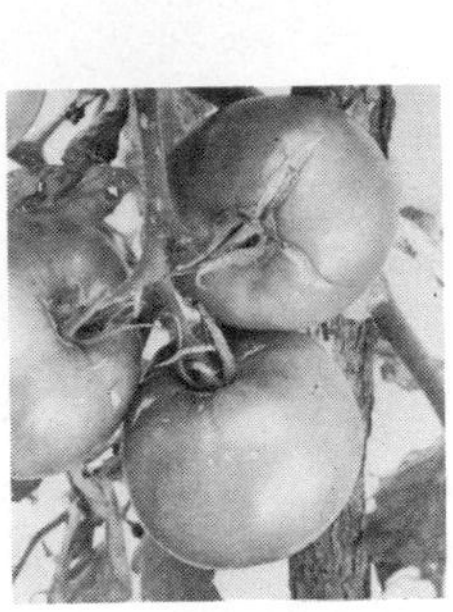

tomato

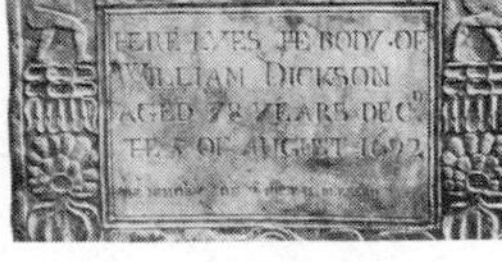

tombstone
Cambridge, Massachusetts

toll collector. One employed to receive toll payments. Also called "tollkeeper."

toll·er (tō′lər) *n.* **1.** One who tolls a bell. **2.** A bell used for tolling.

toll·gate (tōl′gāt′) *n.* A gate barring passage to a road, tunnel, or bridge until a toll is collected. Also called "tollbar."

toll·house (tōl′hous′) *n.* **1.** A house occupied by the toll collector adjoining a tollgate. **2.** A **tollbooth** *(see).*

toll line. A long-distance telephone line or circuit.

Tol·stoi (tōl′stoi′, tŏl′-), Count **Lev Nikolaevich.** English name, Leo Tolstoy. 1828–1910. Russian novelist and philosopher; author of *War and Peace* (1866).

Tol·tec (tōl′tĕk′, tŏl′-) *n.* One of an ancient Nahuatl people of central and southern Mexico whose culture flourished in about A.D. 1000. *—adj.* Also **Tol·tec·an** (tōl-tĕk′ən, tŏl-). Of or pertaining to the Toltecs or their culture. [Spanish *Tolteca,* from Nahuatl.]

to·lu (tə-lo͞o′) *n.* A resin, **balsam of Tolu** *(see).* [Spanish *tolú,* from Santiago de *Tolú,* Colombia, its place of origin.]

To·lu·ca (tō-lo͞o′kä). Officially **To·lu·ca de Ler·do** (dā lĕr′*th*ō). The capital of Mexico State in central Mexico. Population, 77,000.

tol·u·ene (tŏl′yo͞o-ēn′) *n.* A colorless flammable liquid, $CH_3C_6H_5$, obtained from coal tar or petroleum and used in aviation and other high-octane fuels, in dyestuffs, explosives, and as a solvent for gums and lacquers. [TOLU (from which it was originally obtained) + -ENE.]

to·lu·i·dine (tə-lo͞o′ə-dēn′) *n.* Any of three isomeric compounds, C_7H_9N, used to make dyes. [TOLU(ENE) + -ID(E) + -INE.]

tol·u·ol (tŏl′yo͞o-ôl′, -ōl′) *n.* Toluene. [TOLU + -OL.]

tol·yl (tŏl′əl) *n.* The univalent organic radical $CH_3C_6H_4$. [TOL(U) + -YL.]

tom (tŏm) *n.* The male of various animals; especially, a male cat. *—adj.* Male. [From TOM (name).]

Tom[1] (tŏm). A masculine given name. [Pet form of THOMAS.]

Tom[2] (tŏm, tôm). A river of the Soviet Union, rising in the Altai Mountains and flowing 440 miles generally northwest to the Ob near Tomsk.

Tom[3] (tŏm) *n. Slang.* An **Uncle Tom** *(see).*

tom·a·hawk (tŏm′ə-hôk′) *n.* **1.** A light ax used as a tool or weapon by North American Indians. **2.** Any similar implement or weapon. *—tr.v.* **tomahawked, -hawking, -hawks.** To strike with a tomahawk. [Virginia Algonquian *tamahaac, tamohake* : Proto-Algonquian *temah-* (unattested), to cut off by tool + *-aakan* (unattested), noun suffix.]

tom·al·ley (tŏ-măl′ē, tŏm′ăl′ē) *n., pl.* **-leys.** The liver of a lobster, esteemed as a culinary delicacy. [Of Cariban origin, akin to Carib *tumali,* sauce of lobster or crab liver.]

Tom and Jer·ry (jĕr′ē). A hot drink consisting of rum, a beaten egg, milk or water, sugar, and spices. [Arbitrarily adopted from names of two chief characters, Corinthian *Tom* and *Jerry* Hawthorn, in *Life in London* (1821), by Pierce Egan (1772–1849), English sportswriter.]

to·ma·to (tə-mā′tō, -mä′tō) *n., pl.* **-toes. 1.** A plant, *Lycopersicon esculentum,* native to South America, widely cultivated for its edible, fleshy, usually red fruit. **2.** The fruit of this plant. **3.** *Slang.* An attractive girl. [Variant of earlier *tomate,* from Spanish, from Nahuatl *tomatl.*]

tomb (to͞om) *n.* **1.** A vault or chamber serving as a repository for the dead. **2.** Any grave or place of burial. **3.** A monument commemorating the dead. [Middle English *t(o)umbe,* from Norman French *tumbe,* from Late Latin *tumba,* sepulchral mound, from Greek *tumbos.* See **teue-** in Appendix.*]

tom·bac (tŏm′băk′) *n.* Also **tam·bac, tom·back, tom·bak.** Any one of several alloys of copper and zinc, used in making inexpensive jewelry. [French, from Dutch *tombak,* from Malay *tĕmbaga,* copper.]

Tom·baugh (tŏm′bô′), **Clyde William.** Born 1906. American astronomer; discovered the planet Pluto.

Tom·big·bee (tŏm-bĭg′bē). A river rising in northeastern Mississippi and flowing over 500 miles generally south to the Mobile River in southern Alabama.

tom·boy (tŏm′boi′) *n.* A girl, especially a young girl, who behaves like a spirited boy. [TOM + BOY.] **—tom′boy′ish** *adj.*

tomb·stone (to͞om′stōn′) *n.* A stone or monument, usually inscribed, marking a grave; gravestone.

Tomb·stone (to͞om′stōn′). A town in southeastern Arizona, once a prosperous gold-mining center. Population, 1,300.

tom·cat (tŏm′kăt′) *n.* A male cat. [After *Tom,* hero of the anonymous work *The Life and Adventures of a Cat* (1760).]

tom·cod (tŏm′kŏd′) *n., pl.* **tomcod** or **-cods.** Either of two edible marine fishes, *Microgadus tomcod,* of North American Atlantic waters, or *M. proximus,* of northern Pacific waters, related to and resembling the cod.

Tom Col·lins (kŏl′ĭnz). A beverage consisting of gin, lemon or lime juice, carbonated water, and sugar. [Said to be the name of the bartender who invented it.]

Tom, Dick, and Harry. Anybody at all; everyone: *Every Tom, Dick, and Harry came to the party.*

tome (tōm) *n.* **1.** One of the books in a work of several volumes. **2.** Any book; especially, a large or scholarly book. [Old French, from Latin *tomus,* cut, tome, roll of paper, from Greek *tomos,* from *temnein,* to cut, slice. See **tem-** in Appendix.*]

-tome. Indicates a cutting instrument; for example, **microtome.** [New Latin *-tomus,* from Greek *-tomos,* a cutting, from *temnein,* to cut. See **tome.**]

to·men·tose (tō-mĕn′tōs′, tō′mən-tōs′) *adj. Biology.* Covered with dense, short, matted hairs. [New Latin *tomentosus,* from Latin *tōmentum,* cushion stuffing. See **tomentum.**]

to·men·tum (tō-mĕn′təm) *n., pl.* **-ta** (-tə). **1.** *Anatomy.* A network of extremely small blood vessels passing between the pia mater and cerebral cortex. **2.** *Biology.* A covering of closely matted woolly hairs. [New Latin, from Latin *tōmentum*†, cushion stuffing.]

tom·fool (tŏm′fo͞ol′) *n.* A stupid or foolish person; blockhead. *—adj.* Extremely foolish or stupid. [Middle English *Thome Fole,* name given to half-witted persons : *Thome,* pet form of THOMAS (personal name) + *fole,* FOOL.]

tom·fool·er·y (tŏm′fo͞o′lə-rē) *n., pl.* **-ies. 1.** Foolish behavior. **2.** Something trivial or foolish; nonsense.

tom·my (tŏm′ē) *n., pl.* **-mies.** *British Informal.* **1.** A loaf or piece of bread. **2.** Food; victuals; provisions. **3.** *Often capital* **T.** A Tommy Atkins. [From *Tommy,* pet form of TOM.]

Tommy At·kins (ăt′kĭnz). A private of the regular British army; a British soldier. [Originally a fictitious name used in sample forms for privates in the British army.]

Tommy gun. *Informal.* A **Thompson submachine gun** *(see).*

tom·my·rot (tŏm′ē-rŏt′) *n. Informal.* Utter foolishness; nonsense. [*Tommy,* pet form of TOM + ROT.]

to·mog·ra·phy (tō-mŏg′rə-fē) *n.* Any of several techniques for making x-ray pictures of a predetermined plane section of a solid object by blurring out the images of other planes. [Greek *tomos,* a cut, section (see **tome**) + -GRAPHY.]

To·mo·na·ga (tō′mō-nä′gä), **Shinichiro.** Born 1906. Japanese physicist; worked on quantum mechanics.

to·mor·row (tə-môr′ō, -mŏr′ō) *n.* Also **to-mor·row. 1.** The day following today. **2.** The near future. *—adv.* Also **to-mor·row.** On or for the day following today. [Middle English *to morge, to mor(o)we,* Old English *tō morgen(ne)* : TO (at, on) + *morgenne,* dative of *morgen,* MORROW.]

tom·pi·on. Variant of **tampion.**

Tomp·kins (tŏmp′kənz), **Daniel D.** 1774–1825. Vice President of the United States (1817–25) under James Monroe.

Tomsk (tômsk). A city of the Soviet Union, in western Siberia near the junction of the Tom and Ob rivers. Population, 302,000.

Tom Thumb. 1. A diminutive hero of English folklore. **2.** A tiny person; midget. **3.** Stage name of Charles **Stratton** *(see).*

tom·tit (tŏm′tĭt′) *n. British.* A tit or other small bird. [Perhaps TOM + TIT(MOUSE).]

tom-tom (tŏm′tŏm′) *n.* **1.** Any of various small-headed drums, usually long and narrow, that are beaten with the hands. Also called "tam-tam." **2.** A type of gong having a metal disk struck with a felt-covered hammer or stick. **3.** A monotonous rhythmical drumbeat or similar sound. [Hindi *ṭamṭam* (imitative). See **tam-tam.**]

-tomy. Indicates a cutting of (a specified part or tissue); for example, **craniotomy.** [New Latin *-tomia,* from Greek *-tomos,* -TOME.]

ton (tŭn) *n.* **1.** *Abbr.* **t a.** A unit of weight in the U.S. Customary System, an avoirdupois unit equal to 2,240 pounds. Also called "long ton." **b.** A unit of weight in the U.S. Customary System, an avoirdupois unit equal to 2,000 pounds. Also called "short ton," "net ton." See **measurement, metric ton. 2.** Loosely, a very large quantity of anything. [Middle English *tonne,* a measure of wine, TUN.]

to·nal (tō′nəl) *adj.* Of or pertaining to a tone, tones, or tonality. **—to′nal·ly** *adv.*

to·nal·i·ty (tō-năl′ə-tē) *n., pl.* **-ties. 1.** *Music.* **a.** A system or arrangement of seven tones built upon a tonic key. **b.** The arrangement of all the tones and chords of a musical composition in relation to a tonic. **2.** The scheme or interrelation of the tones in a painting.

tone (tōn) *n.* **1. a.** A sound of distinct pitch, quality, and duration. **b.** Quality of sound: *sweet, clear tones of a lute.* **2.** *Music.* **a.** The interval of a major second; a whole step. **b.** The characteristic quality or timbre of a particular instrument or voice. **3.** The pitch of a word used to determine its meaning, as in Mandarin Chinese. **4.** The particular or relative pitch of a word, phrase, or sentence. **5.** Manner of expression in speech or writing: *an angry tone of voice.* **6.** A general quality, effect, or atmosphere: *The tone of the debate was antagonistic.* **7. a.** A color or shade of color. **b.** Quality of color. **8.** *Physiology.* **a.** The tension in resting muscles. **b.** Normal firmness of tissue. *—v.* **toned, toning, tones.** *—tr.* **1.** To give a particular tone or inflection to. **2.** To soften or change the color of, as a photographic negative. **3.** *Rare.* To intone; sound monotonously. *—intr.* **1.** To assume a particular color quality. **2.** To harmonize in color. **—tone down. 1.** To reduce the tone of. **2.** To lessen or soften in degree or effect; subdue. **—tone up. 1.** To increase the tone of. **2.** To strengthen the state or vitality of. [Middle English *ton,* from Old French, from Latin *tonus,* a stretching, tone, sound, from Greek *tonos.* See **ten-** in Appendix.*]

tone arm. The pivoted arm of a record player that holds the cartridge and stylus.

tone color. The timbre of a singing voice or instrument. [Translation of German *Klangfarbe.*]

tone language. A language that distinguishes meanings among words of similar form by variations in pitch and tone.

tone·less (tōn′lĭs) *adj.* **1.** Lacking tone. **2.** Lacking vitality; listless. **—tone′less·ly** *adv.* **—tone′less·ness** *n.*

tone poem. A **symphonic poem** *(see).*

tong[1] (tông, tŏng) *tr.v.* **tonged, tonging, tongs.** To seize, hold, collect, or manipulate with tongs. [Back-formation from TONGS.]

tong[2] (tông, tŏng) *n.* **1.** A Chinese association, clan, or fraternity. **2.** Formerly, a secret society of Chinese in the United

ă pat/ā pay/âr care/ä father/b bib/ch church/d deed/ĕ pet/ē be/f fife/g gag/h hat/hw which/ĭ pit/ī pie/îr pier/j judge/k kick/l lid, needle/m mum/n no, sudden/ng thing/ŏ pot/ō toe/ô paw, for/oi noise/ou out/o͝o took/o͞o boot/p pop/r roar/s sauce/sh ship, dish/

States. [Cantonese *t'ong*, a hall, auditorium, assembly hall, from Mandarin Chinese *t'ang²*.]

Ton·ga (tŏng'gə). An island group occupying 270 square miles in the South Pacific, about 500 miles south of Western Samoa; an independent constitutional monarchy under British protection. Population, 71,000. Capital, Nukualofa, on Tongatabu Island. Also called "Friendly Islands."

Ton·gan (tŏng'gən) *n.* A Polynesian language spoken in Tonga.

Tong·king. See **Tonkin.**

tongs (tôngz, tŏngz) *n.* Plural in form, sometimes used with a singular verb. A grasping device consisting of two arms joined at one end by a pivot or hinge. [Middle English *tang(e)s*, variant of *tangen, tongen*, Old English *tangan*, plural of *tang(e)*. See **denk-** in Appendix.*]

tongue (tŭng) *n.* **1.** The fleshy muscular organ, attached in most vertebrates to the floor of the mouth, that is the principal organ of taste, an important organ of speech, and moves to aid chewing and swallowing. **2.** A homologous invertebrate structure, as in insects or certain mollusks. **3.** The tongue of an animal, such as a cow, used as food. **4.** A spoken language or dialect. **5.** Style or quality of utterance: *her sharp tongue.* **6.** The flap of material under the laces or buckles of a shoe. **7.** A spit of land; promontory. **8.** Anything resembling the shape of a tongue, as a flame. **9.** A bell clapper. **10.** The harnessing pole attached to the front axle of a horse-drawn vehicle. **11.** A protruding strip along the edge of a board that fits into a matching groove on the edge of another board. —**on the tip of one's tongue.** On the verge of being recalled or expressed. —*v.* **tongued, tonguing, tongues.** —*tr.* **1.** To separate or articulate (musical notes) by tonguing. **2.** To touch or lick with the tongue. **3. a.** To provide (a board) with a tongue. **b.** To join by means of a tongue and groove. **4.** *Archaic.* To scold. —*intr.* **1.** To separate notes on a wind instrument. **2.** To project, as a promontory. [Middle English *t(o)unge*, Old English *tunge*. See **dṇghū** in Appendix.*]

tongue and groove. A joint made by fitting a tongue on the edge of a board into a matching groove on another board.

tongue·fish (tŭng'fĭsh') *n., pl.* **tonguefish** or **-fishes.** Any of various marine flatfishes of the family Cynoglossidae, having the posterior part of the body tapering to a point. [From its tongue-shaped body.]

tongue-in-cheek (tŭng'ən-chēk') *adj.* Meant or expressed ironically or facetiously.

tongue-lash·ing (tŭng'lăsh'ĭng) *n. Informal.* A scolding.

tongue-tie (tŭng'tī') *n.* Restricted mobility of the tongue resulting from abnormal shortness of the frenum. —*tr.v.* **tongue-tied, -tying, -ties.** To make tongue-tied.

tongue-tied (tŭng'tīd') *adj.* **1.** Affected with tongue-tie. **2.** Speechless or confused in expression, as from shyness, embarrassment, or astonishment.

tongue twister. **1.** A word or words difficult to articulate rapidly, usually because of a succession of similar consonantal sounds; for example: *Shall she sell seashells?* **2.** Anything difficult to pronounce.

tongu·ing (tŭng'ĭng) *n. Music.* An interruption of the wind stream through an instrument by a movement of the tongue.

-tonia. Indicates tonicity; for example, **myotonia.** [New Latin, from TONUS.]

ton·ic (tŏn'ĭk) *n.* **1.** Anything that invigorates, refreshes, or restores. **2.** A medicine or other agent that restores or increases bodily tone. **3.** *Music.* The primary tone of a diatonic scale; a keynote. **4. a.** Quinine water. **b.** *Regional.* A flavored carbonated beverage. **5.** *Linguistics.* **a.** A **tonic accent** *(see).* **b.** *Obsolete.* A voiced sound. —*adj.* **1.** Producing or stimulating physical, mental, or emotional vigor. **2.** *Music.* Pertaining to or based on the tonic. **3.** *Linguistics.* **a.** Stressed, as a syllable; accented. **b.** *Obsolete.* Voiced. **4.** *Physiology.* Of or pertaining to tissue or muscular tension. [From New Latin *tonicus*, of tension or tone, from Greek *tonikos*, from *tonos*, a stretching, TONE.]

tonic accent. A stress produced by rising pitch as distinguished from increased volume. Also called "pitch accent," "tonic."

to·nic·i·ty (tō-nĭs'ə-tē) *n.* **1.** Normal functional readiness in bodily tissues. **2.** Active resistance to stretching in muscles. Also called "tonus."

tonic sol-fa. *Music.* A system of notation that is based on key relationships and that replaces usual staff notation with solmization syllables or their abbreviations.

to·night (tə-nīt') *adv.* Also **to-night.** On or during the present or coming night. —*n.* Also **to-night.** This night or the night of this day. [Middle English *to night*, Old English *tōniht* : TO (at, on) + *niht*, NIGHT.]

ton·ka bean (tŏng'kə). **1.** Any of several South American trees of the genus *Dipteryx;* especially, *D. odorata*, having seeds that yield the fragrant compound coumarin. **2.** The seed of any of these trees. [Perhaps from Galibi *tonka.*]

Ton·kin (tŏn'kĭn', tŏng'kĭn'). Also **Tong·king** (tŏng'kĭng'). A former French protectorate in northern Indochina, now part of North Vietnam.

Ton·kin, Gulf of (tŏn'kĭn', tŏng'kĭn'). An arm of the South China Sea extending for about 300 miles between North Vietnam and Hainan Island, China.

Ton·kin·ese (tŏn'kə-nēz', tŏng'-) *n.* A Vietnamese dialect spoken in Tonkin.

Ton·le Sap (tŏn'lā' săp'). A lake occupying 1,000 to 2,500 square miles, depending on the seasons, in central Cambodia.

ton·nage (tŭn'ĭj) *n.* Also **tun·nage.** *Abbr.* **tonn.** **1.** The number of tons of water a ship displaces afloat. See **displacement.** **2.** The capacity of a merchant ship in units of 100 cubic feet. **3.** A duty or charge per ton on cargo, as at a port or canal. **4.** The total shipping of a country or port, figured in tons, with reference to carrying capacity. **5.** Weight, measured in tons.

ton·neau (tŭn-ō') *n.* The rear seating compartment of an early type of automobile. [French, "barrel," "cask," from Old French *tonnel.* See **tunnel.**]

to·nom·e·ter (tō-nŏm'ə-tər) *n.* **1.** Any of various instruments for measuring fluid or vapor pressure. **2.** *Music.* An instrument or device, such as a graduated set of tuning forks, used to determine the pitch or vibration rate of tones. [Greek *tonos*, tension, TONE + -METER.] —**to'no·met'ric** (tō'nə-mĕt'rĭk) *adj.* —**to·nom'e·try** *n.*

ton·sil (tŏn'səl) *n.* A mass of lymphoid tissue, especially either of two such masses, embedded in the lateral walls of the aperture between the mouth and the pharynx. [Latin *tonsillae* (plural), probably from *tōlēs*†, goiter.] —**ton'sil·ar** *adj.*

ton·sil·lec·to·my (tŏn'sə-lĕk'tə-mē) *n., pl.* **-mies.** The surgical removal of a tonsil. [Latin *tonsillae*, TONSIL(S) + -ECTOMY.]

ton·sil·li·tis (tŏn'sə-lī'tĭs) *n.* Tonsil inflammation. [New Latin : Latin *tonsillae*, TONSIL(S) + -ITIS.] —**ton'sil·lit'ic** (-lĭt'ĭk) *adj.*

ton·sil·lot·o·my (tŏn'sə-lŏt'ə-mē) *n.* The surgical incision of a tonsil. [Latin *tonsillae*, TONSIL(S) + -TOMY.]

ton·so·ri·al (tŏn-sôr'ē-əl, -sōr'ē-əl) *adj.* Of or pertaining to a barber or to barbering. Often used humorously. [From Latin *tonsōrius*, from *tonsor*, a barber, from *tonsus*, past participle of *tondēre*, to shear. See **tonsure.**]

ton·sure (tŏn'shər) *n.* **1.** The act of shaving the top or crown of the head, especially as a preliminary to becoming a priest or a member of a monastic order. **2.** The part of a monk's or priest's head so shaven. —*tr.v.* **tonsured, -suring, -sures.** To shave the head of. [Middle English, from Old French, from Medieval Latin *tonsūra*, from Latin, a shearing, from *tonsus*, past participle of *tondēre*, to shear, shave. See **tem-** in Appendix.*]

Ton·ti (tŏn'tē; *French* tôN-tē'), **Henry de.** Also **Ton·ty.** 1650–1704. French explorer, trader, and colonizer of the Mississippi Valley.

ton·tine (tŏn'tēn', tŏn-tēn') *n.* **1.** An insurance plan whereby a group of participants allow the annuities to accumulate as each participant dies, the final survivor receiving the whole. **2.** Each member's share of this. **3.** The subscribers to such a plan, collectively. [French, after Lorenzo *Tonti*, Neapolitan banker, who introduced this scheme in France in about 1653.]

to·nus (tō'nəs) *n.* **Tonicity** *(see).* [New Latin, from Latin, tension, TONE.]

too (tōō) *adv.* **1.** In addition; also; as well: *He's coming too.* **2.** More than sufficient; excessively: *He studied too much.* **3.** Very; extremely; immensely: *He's only too willing to be of service.* **4.** *Informal.* Indeed; so. Used for emphasis: *You will too do it!* —See Synonyms at **also.** [Emphatic form of Middle English *to*, in addition to, TO.]

Usage: *Too*, preceded by *not* or another form of negative, is frequently employed as a form of understatement to convey humor or sarcasm: *He was not too pleased when she ignored him. He is not too bright.* Used knowingly, it is employed on all levels. *Not too*, meaning approximately not very, is less defensible, though common in casual usage: *Passage of the bill is not now considered too likely* (termed unacceptable, as an example in writing, by 80 per cent of the Usage Panel). *Too* can often be eliminated from such sentences without loss, but if such deletion gives undue stress to the negative sense, the writer may find *not very* or *none too* preferable choices. *Not too* is even less defensible when it creates ambiguity by making unclear whether *too* means excessively or very: *One cannot say too much for his style. Her background is not too good for this work.*

took. Past tense of **take.**

Tooke (tŏŏk), **(John) Horne.** 1736–1812. British radical political leader and philologist.

tool (tōōl) *n.* **1.** An instrument, such as a hammer or rake, used or worked by hand. **2. a.** A machine, such as a lathe, used to cut and shape machinery parts; machine tool. **b.** The cutting part of such a machine. **3.** Anything used in the performance of an operation; an instrument: *"modern democracies have the fiscal and monetary tools . . . to end chronic slumps and galloping inflations"* (Paul A. Samuelson). **4.** Anything regarded as necessary to the carrying out of one's occupation or profession: *Words are the tools of his trade.* **5.** A person utilized to carry out the designs of another; a dupe. **6. a.** A bookbinder's hand stamp. **b.** A design impressed on a book cover by this means. —*v.* **tooled, tooling, tools.** —*tr.* **1.** To form, work, or decorate with a tool or tools. **2.** To furnish tools or machinery for (a factory, industry, or shop). **3.** To ornament (a book cover) with a bookbinder's tool. **4.** *Informal.* To drive (a vehicle). —*intr.* **1.** To work with a tool or tools. **2.** *Informal.* To travel in a vehicle. —**tool up.** To prepare for production, as a factory, by providing machinery and tools suitable for a particular job. [Middle English *to(o)l*, Old English *tōl.* See **taw-** in Appendix.*]

Synonyms: *tool, instrument, implement, utensil, appliance, gadget.* These nouns refer to devices or aids for performing work. *Tool* can apply broadly to any device for doing or facilitating work. Specifically, it refers to a small manually operated device of the kind employed by carpenters and plumbers, to a power-driven machine tool such as a lathe, or to the part of a machine that cuts or shapes. *Instrument* refers to any of the relatively small precision tools used by specially trained professionals such as doctors, technicians, and draftsmen. *Implement* is the preferred term for tools used in agriculture and certain building trades, or it can mean any device essential for performing work. *Utensil* usually refers to a device for house-

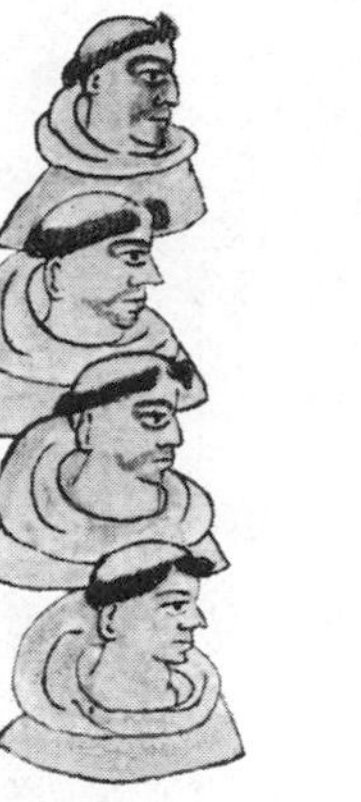

tonsure
Tonsured monks, detail from an illustration in an Aztec manuscript

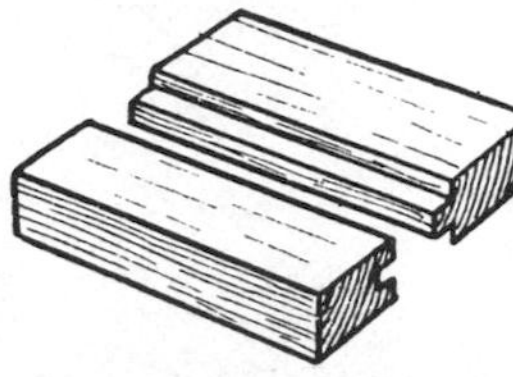

tongue and groove

hold work, such as a pot, pan, or vessel. *Appliance* denotes a power-driven machine or tool, such as a device for household cleaning. *Gadget* refers informally to a small contrivance, or accessory of a machine, that performs a specific function.

tool·box (to͞ol′bŏks′) *n.* A case for carrying or storing hand tools.

tool·ing (to͞o′lĭng) *n.* **1.** Work or ornamentation done with tools; especially, stamped or gilded designs on leather. **2.** The process of providing a factory with machinery in preparation for production.

tool·ma·ker (to͞ol′mā′kər) *n.* A master machinist skilled in making tools and parts.

toon (to͞on) *n.* **1.** A tall tree, *Cedrela toona* (or *Toona ciliata*), of tropical Asia and Australia, having reddish, aromatic wood. **2.** The wood of this tree. [Hindi *tūn,* from Sanskrit *tunna*†.]

toot (to͞ot) *v.* **tooted, tooting, toots.** —*intr.* **1.** To sound a horn or whistle in short blasts. **2.** To make this sound or a sound resembling this. —*tr.* **1.** To blow or sound (a horn or whistle). **2.** To sound (a blast or series of blasts) on a horn or whistle. —*n.* The act or sound of tooting. [Probably from Middle Dutch *tūten* (imitative).] —**toot′er** *n.*

tooth (to͞oth) *n., pl.* **teeth** (tēth). **1.** In most vertebrates, one of a set of hard, bonelike structures rooted in sockets in the jaws, typically composed of a core of soft pulp surrounded by a layer of hard dentine that is coated with cement or enamel at the crown, and used to seize, hold, or masticate. **2.** A similar structure in invertebrates, such as one of the pointed denticles or ridges on the exoskeleton of an arthropod or the shell of a mollusk. **3.** Any usually small projection resembling a tooth in shape or function, as on a comb, gear, or saw. **4.** A small, notched projection along a margin, especially of a leaf. **5.** *Plural.* Something that injures or destroys as if by biting or gnawing: *the teeth of the blizzard.* **6.** Taste or appetite for something: *She always had a sweet tooth.* —**get one's teeth into.** To be actively involved in; get a firm grasp of. —**in the teeth of. 1.** Directly and forcefully against. **2.** In defiance of. —**put teeth into.** To make effective or forceful, as a law. —**show one's teeth.** To express a readiness to fight; threaten defiantly. —**to the teeth.** Completely; lacking nothing: *armed to the teeth; dressed to the teeth.* —*v.* (to͞oth, to͞o*th*) **toothed, toothing, tooths.** —*tr.* **1.** To furnish (a tool, for example) with teeth. **2.** To make a jagged edge on. —*intr.* To mesh; become interlocked. [Tooth, teeth; Middle English *to(o)th, te(e)th,* Old English *tōth, tēth.* See **dent-** in Appendix.*]

tooth·ache (to͞oth′āk′) *n.* An aching pain in or near a tooth.

toothache tree. The **prickly ash** *(see).*

tooth and nail. With great ferocity; as hard as possible.

tooth·brush (to͞oth′brŭsh′) *n.* A brush used for cleaning teeth.

toothed (to͞otht, to͞o*th*d) *adj.* **1.** Having teeth. **2.** Having a certain number or type of teeth. Used in combination: *saw-toothed.*

tooth·less (to͞oth′lĭs) *adj.* **1.** Lacking teeth. **2.** Lacking force; ineffectual. —**tooth′less·ly** *adv.* —**tooth′less·ness** *n.*

tooth·paste (to͞oth′pāst′) *n.* A paste dentifrice.

tooth·pick (to͞oth′pĭk′) *n.* A small piece of wood or other material, for removing food particles from between the teeth.

tooth·pow·der (to͞oth′pou′dər) *n.* A powdered dentifrice.

tooth shell. Any of various burrowing marine mollusks of the class Scaphopoda, having a long, tapering, slightly curved tubular shell. Also called "tusk shell."

tooth·some (to͞oth′səm) *adj.* **1.** Delicious; savory: *a toothsome morsel of pie.* **2.** Pleasant; attractive: *a toothsome offer.* **3.** Voluptuous; sexually attractive. —**tooth′some·ly** *adv.* —**tooth′some·ness** *n.*

tooth·wort (to͞oth′wûrt′, -wôrt′) *n.* **1.** Any of several plants of the genus *Dentaria,* such as the **crinkleroot** *(see).* **2.** A parasitic European plant, *Lathraea squamaria,* having scaly cream-colored or pink stems and pinkish flowers.

tooth·y (to͞o′thē) *adj.* **-ier, -iest.** Having or showing prominent teeth. —**tooth′i·ly** *adv.*

too·tle (to͞ot′l) *intr.v.* **-tled, -tling, -tles.** To toot softly and repeatedly, as on a flute. —*n.* The act or sound of tootling. [Frequentative of TOOT.]

toots (to͞ots) *n.* Also **toot·sy** (to͞ot′sē). *Slang.* Dear; sweetheart. Used affectionately or humorously. [Origin obscure.]

toot·sy (to͞ot′sē) *n., pl.* **-sies.** Also **toot·sie. 1.** A person's foot. Used affectionately or humorously. **2.** Variant of **toots.** [Variant of *footsy,* from FOOT.]

top¹ (tŏp) *n.* **1.** The uppermost part, point, surface, or end of anything. **2.** The crown of the head. **3.** The part of a plant, such as a rutabaga, that is above the ground. **4.** Something that covers or forms the uppermost part of something, as a lid or cap. **5.** *Nautical.* A platform enclosing the head of each mast of a sailing ship, to which the topmast rigging is attached. **6. a.** In various sports and games, a stroke that lands above the center of the ball, giving it forward spin. **b.** A forward spin on a ball resulting from this. **7.** The highest degree, pitch, or point; a peak; acme; zenith. **8. a.** The highest position or rank. **b.** A person in this position. **9.** *Card Games.* The highest card or cards in a suit or a hand. **10.** The best part; the pick; the cream. **11.** The earliest part or beginning: *the top of the first inning.* —**blow one's top.** *Slang.* **1.** To lose one's temper. **2.** To lose one's mind; become insane. —**on top. 1.** At the highest point or peak. **2.** In a dominant, controlling, or successful position. —**on top of. 1.** On or at the uppermost part or side of. **2.** *Informal.* **a.** In control of. **b.** Fully informed about. **3.** Besides; in addition to. **4.** Following closely upon; coming immediately after. —**over the top. 1.** Over the breastwork, as an attack in trench warfare. **2.** Surpassing a goal or quota. —*adj.* Of, pertaining to, situated on, or forming the top; uppermost; highest. —*v.* **topped, topping, tops.** —*tr.* **1. a.** To remove the top from. **b.** To prune the upper branches from. **2.** To furnish, form, or serve as a top. **3.** To reach the top of. **4.** To go over the top of. **5.** To exceed or surpass. **6.** To be at the head or top of; to lead: *He topped his class.* **7. a.** In various sports and games, to strike the upper part of (a ball), giving it forward spin. **b.** To make (a stroke) in this way. —*intr.* To top a person or thing. —**top off.** To finish up. —**top out.** To put the framework for the top story on (a building). [Middle English *top(pe),* Old English *topp.* See **tap-** in Appendix.*]

top² (tŏp) *n.* A toy consisting of a symmetrical rigid body spun on a pointed end about the axis of symmetry. [Middle English *to(o)p,* Old English *topp.* See **tap-** in Appendix.*]

to·paz (tō′păz′) *n.* **1.** A colorless, blue, yellow, brown, or pink aluminum silicate mineral, often found in association with granitic rocks and valued as a gemstone, especially in the brown and pink varieties. **2.** Any of various yellow gemstones, especially a yellow variety of sapphire or corundum. **3.** A light-yellow variety of quartz. **4.** Either of two colorful South American hummingbirds, *Topaza pyra* or *T. pella.* [Middle English *topace,* from Old French *topace, topaze,* from Latin *topazus,* from Greek *topazos*†.]

top boot. A high boot usually having its upper part trimmed with a contrasting color or texture of leather.

top·coat (tŏp′kōt′) *n.* A lightweight overcoat.

top dog. *Informal.* A person or group considered to have the highest authority, especially as a result of victory in some variety of competition. —**top′-dog′** *adj.*

top-drawer (tŏp′drôr′) *adj. Informal.* Of the highest importance, rank, privilege, or merit.

top-dress (tŏp′drĕs′) *tr.v.* **-dressed, -dressing, -dresses.** To cover (land or a road surface) with loose material that is not worked in; especially, to cover (farmland) with fertilizer.

top dressing. 1. A covering of manure or other fertilizer spread on soil without being plowed under. **2.** A covering of loose gravel on a road.

tope¹ (tōp) *v.* **toped, toping, topes.** *Archaic.* —*tr.* To drink (alcoholic liquors) habitually and excessively. —*intr.* To drink to excess habitually. [Originally an interjection used in proposing a toast, perhaps from French *tope!* agreed! from *toper,* to accept a bet, agree, from Spanish *topar* (perhaps imitative of the striking of hands of two adversaries as a sign of agreement to a bet).]

tope² (tōp) *n.* Any of several small sharks, especially one of the genus *Galeorhinus.* [Origin unknown.]

tope³ (tōp) *n.* A dome-shaped Buddhist shrine with a cupola on top. Also called "stupa." [Hindi *tōp,* probably from Prakrit *thūpo,* from Sanskrit *stūpa,* a tuft of hair, crown. See **stewe-** in Appendix.*]

To·pe·ka (tə-pē′kə). The capital of Kansas, a city in the northeast on the Kansas River. Population, 119,000.

top·er (tō′pər) *n.* A chronic drinker; drunkard. [From TOPE (to drink).]

top·flight (tŏp′flīt′) *adj.* First-rate; superior.

top·full (tŏp′fo͝ol′) *adj.* Also **top·ful.** Full to the brim.

top·gal·lant (tə-găl′ənt, tŏp-) *adj. Nautical.* Designating the mast above the topmast, its sails, or rigging.

top·ham·per (tŏp′hăm′pər) *n.* Also **top hamper. 1.** *Nautical.* Any rigging, cables, spars, or other materials or weight not immediately necessary and stored either aloft or on the upper decks. **2.** Cumbersome and unnecessary or meaningless matter.

top hat. A man's hat having a narrow brim and a tall cylindrical crown, usually made of silk.

top-heav·y (tŏp′hĕv′ē) *adj.* **-ier, -iest. 1.** Likely to topple because overloaded at the top. **2.** *Finance.* Overcapitalized. —**top′-heav′i·ness** *n.*

To·phet (tō′fĕt, -fĭt) *n.* **1.** A place near Gehenna where human sacrifices were made. Jeremiah 19:4. **2.** Hell or a hellish place. [Middle English *Tophet(h),* from Hebrew *tōpheth,* (probably) "altar," place where children were burned, from the root *t-ph-th,* to burn.]

to·phus (tō′fəs) *n., pl.* **-phi** (-fī′). **1.** A urate deposit found in tissue, such as cartilage, around the joints. Also called "chalkstone." **2.** A concretion of mineral salts and organic matter deposited on the surface of the teeth. [Latin *tōphus,* TUFA.]

to·pi (tō-pē′, tō′pē) *n., pl.* **-pis.** Also **to·pee.** A pith helmet worn for protection against sun and heat. [Hindi *topī*†, hat.]

to·pi·ar·y (tō′pē-ĕr′ē) *adj.* Of, designating, or characterized by the clipping or trimming of shrubs or trees into decorative shapes, such as those of animals, birds, or geometric forms. —*n., pl.* **topiaries. 1.** Topiary work or art. **2.** A topiary garden. [Latin *topiārius,* of gardening, from *topia,* landscape gardening, from Greek *topia,* plural of *topion,* a field, small place, diminutive of *topos,* a place. See **topic.**]

top·ic (tŏp′ĭk) *n.* **1.** A subject treated in a speech, essay, thesis, or portion of a discourse; a theme. **2.** A subject of discussion or conversation. **3.** A subdivision of a theme, thesis, or outline. —See Synonyms at **subject.** [Originally "matter for rhetoricians," an argument, from Aristotle's *Topics,* which contains commonplace arguments, from Latin *Topica,* from Greek *(Ta) Topika,* from *topikos,* of a place, commonplace, from *topos*†, a place.]

top·i·cal (tŏp′ĭ-kəl) *adj.* **1.** Pertaining or belonging to a particular location or place; local. **2.** *Medicine.* Applied or pertaining to a local part of the body. **3.** Contemporary in reference or allusion. **4.** Of or pertaining to a particular topic or topics. [From Greek *topikos,* of a place. See **topic.**] —**top′i·cal′i·ty** (-kăl′ə-tē) *n.* —**top′i·cal·ly** *adv.*

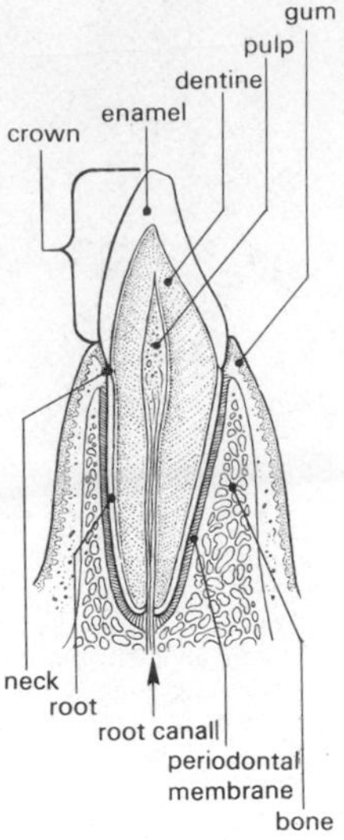
gum
pulp
dentine
enamel
crown
neck
root
root canal
periodontal membrane
bone

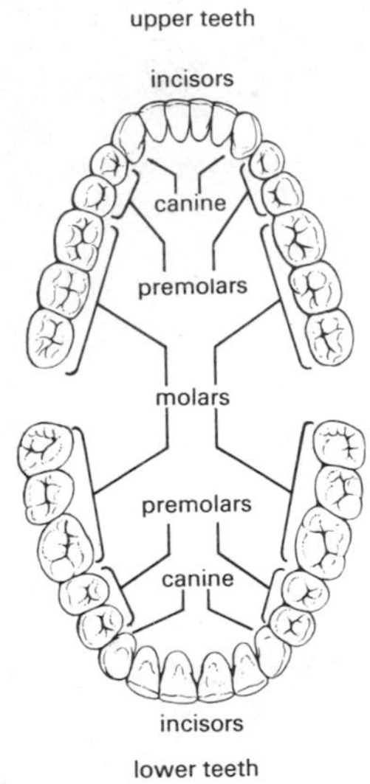
upper teeth
incisors
canine
premolars
molars
premolars
canine
incisors
lower teeth

tooth
Above: Cross section of a human incisor
Below: The upper and lower teeth of an adult human

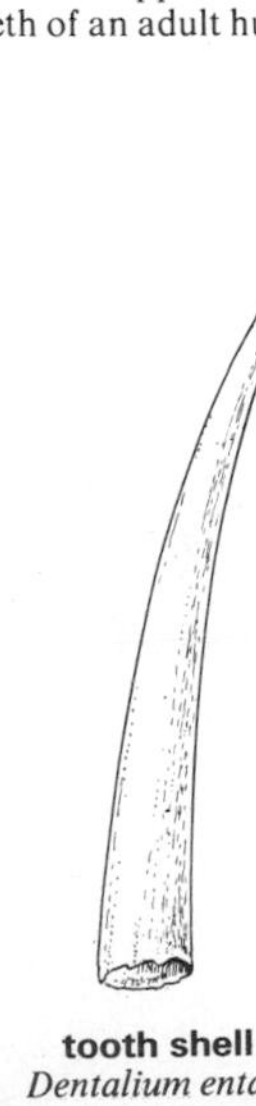

tooth shell
Dentalium entale

topic sentence. The sentence within a paragraph that states the main thought, and is usually placed at the beginning.
top kick. *Slang.* A first sergeant.
top·knot (tŏp′nŏt′) *n.* **1.** A crest or knot of hair or feathers on the crown of the head. **2.** Any decorative ribbon, bow, or the like, worn as a headdress.
top·less (tŏp′lĭs) *adj.* **1. a.** Having no top. **b.** Having no part covering the breasts: *a topless bathing suit.* **c.** Wearing a topless garment: *a topless waitress.* **2.** So high as to appear to extend out of sight: *the topless Alps.*
top·loft·y (tŏp′lôf′tē, -lŏf′tē) *adj.* **-ier, -iest.** *Informal.* Haughty; pretentious. **—top′loft′i·ness** *n.*
top·mast (tŏp′məst, -măst′, -mäst′) *n. Nautical.* The mast that is below the topgallant mast in a square-rigged ship and next above the lower mast in a fore-and-aft-rigged ship.
top·min·now (tŏp′mĭn′ō) *n.* **1.** Any of several small New World freshwater fishes of the genus *Fundulus,* related to the killifishes. **2.** Any of various small, viviparous New World fishes of the family Poeciliidae, of fresh or brackish waters. [So called because it swims near the surface of water.]
top·most (tŏp′mōst′) *adj.* Highest; uppermost.
top·notch (tŏp′nŏch′) *adj. Informal.* First-rate; excellent.
topo–, top–. Indicates place or region; for example, **topology, toponymy.** [From Greek *topos,* a place. See **topic.**]
topog. topographical; topography.
to·pog·ra·pher (tə-pŏg′rə-fər) *n.* **1.** A person skilled in topography. **2.** A person who describes and maps the surface features of geographical regions.
to·pog·ra·phy (tə-pŏg′rə-fē) *n., pl.* **-phies.** *Abbr.* **topog. 1.** The detailed and accurate description of a place or region. **2.** The art of graphically representing on a map the exact physical configuration of a place or region. **3.** The features of a place or region. **4.** The surveying of the features of a region or place. [Middle English *topographie,* from Late Latin *topographia,* from Greek, from *topographein,* to describe a place : TOPO- + *graphein,* to write (see **-graphy**).] **—top′o·graph′ic** (tŏp′ə-grăf′ĭk), **top′o·graph′i·cal** *adj.* **—top′o·graph′i·cal·ly** *adv.*
to·pol·o·gy (tə-pŏl′ə-jē) *n.* **1.** The topographical study of a given place in relation to its history. **2.** The anatomy of specific areas of the body. **3.** *Mathematics.* The study of the properties of geometric configurations invariant under transformation by continuous mappings. In this sense, also formerly called "analysis situs." [TOPO- + -LOGY.] **—top′o·log′ic** (tŏp′ə-lŏj′ĭk), **top′o·log′i·cal** *adj.* **—to·pol′o·gist** *n.*
top·o·nym (tŏp′ə-nĭm′) *n.* Any name derived from a place or region. [Back-formation from TOPONYMY.] **—top′o·nym′ic, top′o·nym′i·cal** *adj.*
to·pon·y·my (tə-pŏn′ə-mē, tō-) *n., pl.* **-mies. 1.** *Anatomy.* Nomenclature with respect to a region of the body rather than to organs or structures. **2.** The study of place names. [TOP(O)- + -ONYMY.]
top·o·type (tŏp′ə-tīp′) *n. Biology.* A specimen of an organism taken from the area typical for that species. [TOPO- + -TYPE.]
top·per (tŏp′ər) *n.* **1.** One that takes off tops: *a carrot topper.* **2.** A short, lightweight topcoat for a woman. **3.** *Slang.* A top hat. **4.** *Slang.* Something that outdoes or climaxes that which has gone before, especially a bantering remark.
top·ping (tŏp′ĭng) *n.* A sauce, frosting, or garnish for food. *—adj.* **1.** Held in very high opinion; outstanding. **2.** *British Informal.* First-rate; excellent.
top·ple (tŏp′əl) *v.* **-pled, -pling, -ples.** *—tr.* To push over; overturn. *—intr.* **1.** To totter and fall. **2.** To lean over as if about to fall. [Frequentative of TOP (to remove the top of).]
top round. A cut of meat, as a roast or steak, cut from the inner section of the round.
tops (tŏps) *adj. Slang.* First-rate; excellent; topmost.
top·sail (tŏp′səl, -sāl′) *n. Nautical.* **1.** A square sail set above the lowest sail on the mast of a square-rigged ship. **2.** A triangular or square sail set above the gaff of a lower sail on a fore-and-aft-rigged ship.
topsail schooner. A schooner carrying two or more square topsails on her foremast.
top-se·cret (tŏp′sē′krĭt) *adj.* Designating materials or information of the highest level of security classification.
top sergeant. *Informal.* A first sergeant.
top·side (tŏp′sīd′) *n.* The upper parts of a ship that are above the main deck. Often used in the plural. *—adv.* On or to the upper parts of a ship; on deck.
top·soil (tŏp′soil′) *n.* The surface layer of soil. *—tr.v.* **topsoiled, -soiling, -soils.** To remove the surface layer of soil from (land).
top·stitch (tŏp′stĭch′) *tr.v.* **-stitched, -stitching, -stitches.** To sew a line of stitching close to the seam or edge of (a garment) on the right side of the fabric.
top·sy-tur·vy (tŏp′sē-tûr′vē) *adv.* **1.** With the top downward and the bottom up; upside-down. **2.** In a state of utter disorder or confusion. *—adj.* In a confused or disordered condition. *—n.* Confusion; chaos. [Earlier *topsy-tervy, topsy-tirvy* : probably from the plural of TOP + obsolete *tervy,* to turn, Middle English *turven,* to wallow, probably from Old English *tierfan* (unattested), to roll (see **derbh-** in Appendix*).] **—top′sy-tur′vi·ly** *adv.* **—top′sy-tur′vi·ness** *n.*
toque (tōk) *n.* **1.** A small brimless, close-fitting woman's hat. **2.** A plumed velvet cap with a full crown and small rolled brim, worn by men and women in 16th-century France. [French, from Spanish *toca*†.]
tor (tôr) *n.* A high rock or pile of rocks on the top of a hill. [Middle English *torre,* Old English *torr,* probably from Old Welsh *turr,* from Old Celtic *tur-* (unattested), a heap.]
to·rah (tôr′ə, tōr′ə) *n.* **1.** The body of Jewish literature and oral tradition as a whole, containing the laws, teachings, and divine knowledge of the religion. **2.** *Capital* **T. a.** The Pentateuch. **b.** The scroll of parchment or leather on which the Pentateuch is written, used in a synagogue during services. [Hebrew *tōrāh,* a law, instruction, from *yārāh,* to teach, to instruct.]
tor·bern·ite (tôr′bər-nīt′) *n.* An emerald or grass-green hydrous crystalline phosphate of uranium and copper. [German *Torbernit,* after *Torbern* O. Bergman (1735–1784), Swedish chemist.]
torch (tôrch) *n.* **1.** A portable light produced by the flame of an inflammable material wound about the end of a stick of wood and ignited; a flambeau. **2.** A portable apparatus that produces a very hot flame by the combustion of gases, used in welding and construction. **3.** Anything that serves to illuminate, enlighten, or guide. **4.** *British.* A flashlight. **—carry a** (or **the**) **torch for.** To love (someone) who does not reciprocate. [Middle English *torche,* from Old French, a torch originally made of twisted straw dipped in wax, from Vulgar Latin *torca* (unattested), from Latin *torquēs,* a twisted necklace, wreath, from *torquēre,* to twist. See **terkw-** in Appendix.*]
torch·bear·er (tôrch′bâr′ər) *n.* **1.** A person who carries a torch. **2.** A person who imparts knowledge, truth, or inspiration to others, as a leader of a movement.
tor·chon lace (tôr′shŏn′; *French* tôr-shôɴ′). A lace made of coarse linen or cotton thread twisted in simple geometric patterns. [French *torchon,* duster, dishcloth, from Old French, twisted straw, from *torche,* TORCH.]
torch song. A typically sentimental popular song: *"a torch song, . . . one of those forlorn and touching ballads"* (John Cheever). [From the phrase *to carry a torch for.*]
torch·wood (tôrch′wo͝od′) *n.* **1.** Any of several tropical American trees of the genus *Amyris;* especially, *A. balsamifera,* having resinous wood that burns with a torchlike flame. **2.** The wood of such a tree.
tore[1]. Past tense of **tear.**
tore[2] (tôr) *n. Geometry & Architecture.* A **torus** *(see).* [French, from Latin TORUS.]
tor·e·a·dor (tôr′ē-ə-dôr′) *n.* A bullfighter. [Spanish, from *torear* (past participle *toreado*), to fight bulls, from *toro,* a bull, from Latin *taurus.* See **tauro-** in Appendix.*]
to·re·ro (tə-râr′ō; *Spanish* tō-rā′rō) *n., pl.* **toreros** (tə-râr′ōz; *Spanish* tō-rā′rōs). A matador or one of his team. [Spanish, from Late Latin *taurārius,* from Latin *taurus,* a bull. See **tauro-** in Appendix.*]
to·reu·tics (tə-ro͞o′tĭks) *n.* Plural in form, used with a singular verb. The art of working metal or other materials by the use of embossing and chasing to form minute detailed reliefs. [From toreutic, from Greek *toreutikos,* from *toreutos,* worked in relief, from *toreuein,* to bore through, from *toreus,* a boring tool. See **ter-**[2] in Appendix.*] **—to·reu′tic** *adj.*
tor·ic (tôr′ĭk, tŏr′-) *adj.* Of, pertaining to, or shaped like a torus or a part of a torus.
to·ri·i (tôr′ē-ē′, tōr′-) *n., pl.* **torii.** The gateway of a Shinto temple, consisting of two uprights with a straight crosspiece at the top and a concave lintel above the crosspiece. [Japanese, "bird residence" : *tori,* bird + *i-,* from *iru,* to dwell.]
To·ri·no. The Italian name for **Turin.**
tor·ment (tôr′mĕnt′) *n.* **1.** Great physical pain or mental anguish. **2.** A source of harassment, annoyance, or pain. **3.** The torture inflicted on prisoners put to the question, as in the proceedings of the Inquisition. *—tr.v.* (tôr-mĕnt′, tôr′mĕnt′) **tormented, -menting, -ments. 1.** To cause to undergo great physical pain or mental anguish. **2.** To agitate or upset greatly. **3.** To annoy, pester, or harass. —See Synonyms at **harass.** [Middle English, instrument of torture, torment, from Old French, from Latin *tormentum, torquementum* (unattested), a twisted rope, (instrument of) torture, from *torquēre,* to twist. See **terkw-** in Appendix.*] **—tor·ment′ing·ly** *adv.*
tor·men·til (tôr′mən-tĭl′) *n.* A Eurasian plant, *Potentilla tormentilla* (or *P. erecta*), having yellow flowers and astringent roots. [Middle English *tormentille,* from Medieval Latin *tormentilla*†.]
tor·men·tor (tôr-mĕn′tər, tôr′mĕn′tər) *n.* Also **tor·ment·er. 1.** One that torments. **2.** A hanging used at each side of the stage in a theater directly behind the proscenium to block the wing area and sidelights from the audience. **3.** A sound-absorbent screen used on a motion-picture set to prevent echo.
torn. Past participle of **tear.**
tor·na·do (tôr-nā′dō) *n., pl.* **-does** or **-dos. 1.** A rotating column of air usually accompanied by a funnel-shaped downward extension of a cumulonimbus cloud and having a vortex several hundred yards in diameter whirling destructively at speeds of up to 300 miles per hour. Also called "cyclone," "twister." Compare **waterspout. 2.** A violent thunderstorm in West Africa and nearby Atlantic waters. **3.** Any whirlwind or hurricane. —See Synonyms at **wind.** [Variant (influenced by Spanish *tornado,* turned) of Spanish *tronada,* thunderstorm, from the feminine past participle of *tronar,* to thunder, from Latin *tonāre.* See **stene-** in Appendix.*] **—tor·na′dic** (-nā′dĭk, -năd′ĭk) *adj.*
Tor·ne (tôr′nə). A river rising in northeastern Sweden and flowing 250 miles generally southeast to the Gulf of Bothnia, forming part of the border between Sweden and Finland.
Tor·ne, Lake (tôr′nə). A lake occupying 124 square miles in northern Sweden near the Norwegian border.
to·roid (tôr′oid′, tōr′-) *n.* **1.** *Geometry.* **a.** A surface generated by a closed curve rotating about, but not intersecting or containing, an axis in its own plane. **b.** A solid having such a surface. **2.** An object having the shape of such a figure. [TOR(US) + -OID.] **—to·roi′dal** (tô-roid′l) *adj.*

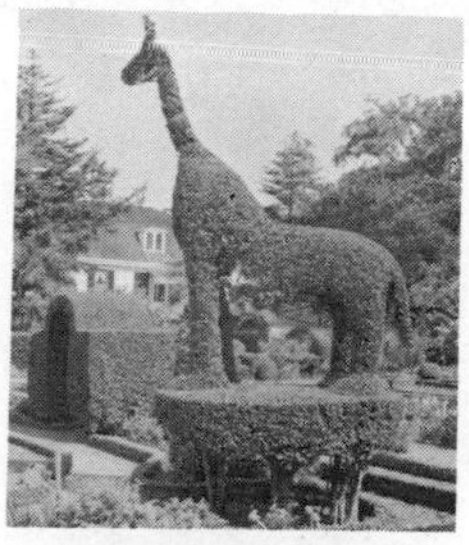

topiary

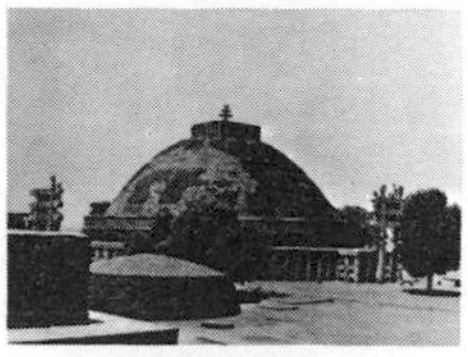

tope[3]
The Great Tope at Sanchi, central India, built about 250 B.C.

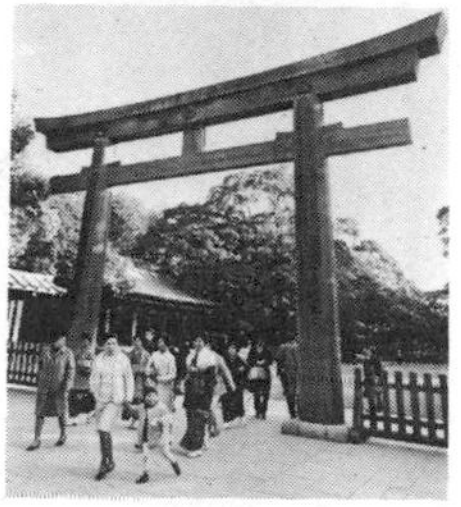

torii
At the Meiji shrine in Tokyo

To·ron·to (tə-rŏn′tō). The capital of Ontario, Canada, on the northern shore of Lake Ontario. Population, 1,824,000.

To·ros Dağ·la·ri. The Turkish name for the **Taurus Mountains.**

to·rose (tôr′ōs′, tōr′-) *adj.* Cylindrical and having ridges or swellings. [Latin *torōsus,* from *torus,* a protuberance, TORUS.]

tor·pe·do (tôr-pē′dō) *n., pl.* **-does. 1.** A cigar-shaped, self-propelled underwater projectile launched from a plane, ship, or submarine, and designed to detonate on contact with or in the vicinity of a target. **2.** Any of various submarine explosive devices, especially a submarine mine. **3.** A small explosive placed on a railroad track that is fired by the weight of the train to sound a warning of an approaching hazard. **4.** An explosive fired in an oil or gas well to begin or increase the flow. **5.** A small firework consisting of some gravel wrapped in tissue paper with a percussion cap that explodes when thrown against a hard surface. **6.** Any of several cartilaginous fishes of the genus *Torpedo,* related to the skates and rays. See **electric ray.** —*tr.v.* **torpedoed, -doing, -does.** To attack, explode, or destroy with or as if with a torpedo or torpedoes. [New Latin *Torpedo,* genus of fish that give electric shocks, from Latin *torpēdō,* stiffness, numbness, the torpedo (fish), from *torpēre,* to be stiff. See **ster-**[1] in Appendix.*]

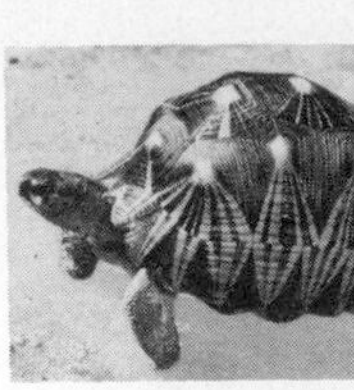

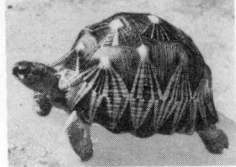

tortoise
Testudo radiata

torpedo boat. A fast, thinly plated boat equipped with heavy machine guns and torpedo tubes.

tor·pe·do-boat destroyer (tôr-pē′dō-bōt′). A fast vessel, larger and more heavily armed than a torpedo boat, designed to destroy the latter, but often serving the same purpose.

torpedo tube. The torpedo-launching tube in the hull of certain war vessels.

tor·pid (tôr′pĭd) *adj.* **1.** Deprived of the power of motion or feeling; benumbed. **2.** Dormant; hibernating. **3.** Lethargic; apathetic. —See Synonyms at **inactive.** [Latin *torpidus,* from *torpēre,* to be stiff. See **torpedo.**] —**tor′pid·ly** *adv.*

tor·por (tôr′pər) *n.* **1.** A condition of mental or physical inactivity or insensibility: *"opium does not of necessity produce inactivity or torpor"* (De Quincey). **2.** Lethargy; apathy. —See Synonyms at **lethargy.** [Latin, from *torpēre,* to be stiff. See **torpedo.**] —**tor′po·rif′ic** (-pə-rĭf′ĭk) *adj.*

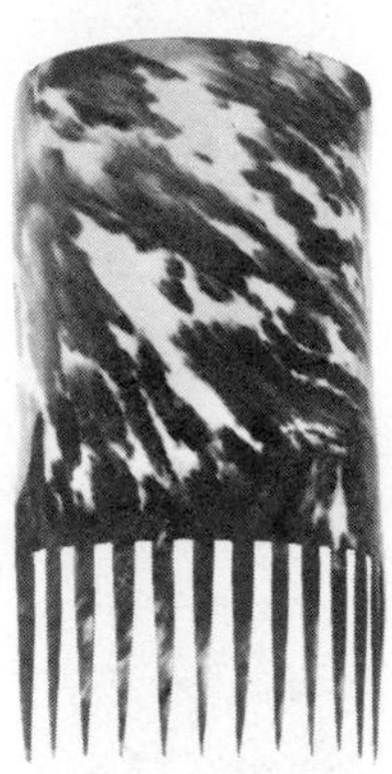

tortoiseshell
Tortoiseshell comb made in 1825

tor·quate (tôr′kwāt′) *adj. Zoology.* Having a ringlike or collarlike band or marking about the neck. [Latin *torquātus,* having a collar, from *torquēs,* TORQUE (collar).]

Tor·quay (tôr-kē′). A city in Devonshire, England, a resort in the south on the English Channel. Population, 52,000.

torque[1] (tôrk) *n.* **a.** The moment of a force, a measure of its tendency to produce torsion and rotation about an axis, equal to the vector product of the radius vector from the axis of rotation to the point of application of the force by the force applied. **b.** Broadly, a turning or twisting force. [From Latin *torquēre,* to twist. See **terkw-** in Appendix.*]

torque[2] (tôrk) *n.* A collar, necklace, or armband made of a strip of twisted metal, worn by the ancient Gauls, Germans, and Britons. [French, from Latin *torquis, torquēs,* a twisted neck chain, from *torquēre,* to twist. See **terkw-** in Appendix.*]

torque converter. A mechanical or hydraulic device for changing the ratio of torque to speed between the input and output shafts of a mechanism.

Tor·que·ma·da (tôr′kā-mä′*thä*), **Tomás de.** 1420?–1498. Spanish grand inquisitor.

tor·ques (tôr′kwēz) *n. Zoology.* A band of feathers, hair, or coloration around the neck. [Latin *torquēs,* TORQUE (collar).]

torr (tôr) *n.* A unit of pressure equal to 1.316×10^{-3} atmosphere. See **measurement.** [After Evangelista TORRICELLI.]

Tor·rance (tôr′əns, tŏr′-). A manufacturing city of California, in the southwest near Los Angeles. Population, 101,000.

Tor·rens, Lake (tôr′ənz, tŏr′-). A lake of Australia, occupying 2,230 square miles in south-central South Australia.

tor·rent (tôr′ənt, tŏr′-) *n.* **1.** A turbulent, swift-flowing stream. **2.** A raging flood; deluge. **3.** Any turbulent or overwhelming flow: *"When the first torrent of tenderness was over . . . reason began to open the eyes of the lady"* (Fielding). [French, from Italian *torrente,* from Latin *torrēns,* a burning, a torrent, from the present participle of *torrēre,* to dry, burn. See **ters-** in Appendix.*]

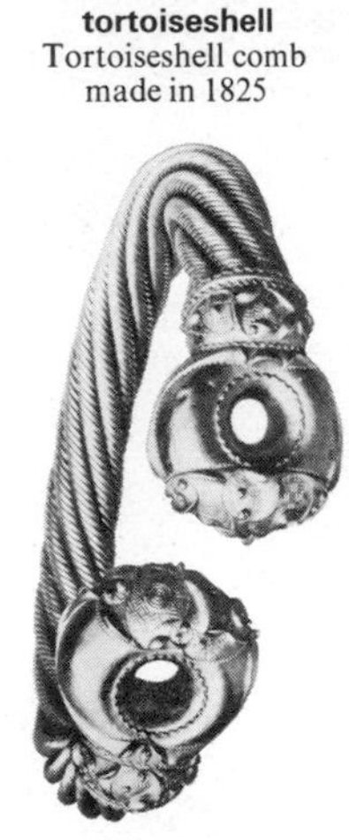

torque[2]
First-century B.C. armband

tor·ren·tial (tô-rĕn′shəl, tə-) *adj.* **1.** Of or pertaining to a torrent. **2.** Resembling a torrent; turbulent; wild: *torrential applause.* **3.** Resulting from the action of a torrent or torrents: *torrential erosion.* —**tor·ren′tial·ly** *adv.*

Tor·re·ón (tôr′rĕ-ôn′). A city of Mexico, in southeastern Coahuila State. Population, 212,000.

Tor·res Strait (tôr′ĭs). A strait 95 miles wide between Cape York Peninsula, Australia, and southern New Guinea.

Tor·ri·cel·li (tôr′rē-chĕl′lē), **Evangelista.** 1608–1647. Italian mathematician and physicist; invented mercury barometer.

tor·rid (tôr′ĭd, tŏr′-) *adj.* **1.** Parched with the heat of the sun. **2.** Scorching; burning. **3.** Passionate; ardent. [Latin *torridus,* from *torrēre,* to dry, parch. See **ters-** in Appendix.*] —**tor·rid′i·ty, tor′rid·ness** *n.* —**tor′rid·ly** *adv.*

Torrid Zone. The region of the earth's surface between the tropics of Cancer and Capricorn.

tor·sade (tôr-säd′, -sād′) *n.* A decorative trimming for hats of twisted ribbon or cord. [French, from (obsolete) *tors,* twisted, from Late Latin *torsus,* from the past participle of Latin *torquēre,* to twist. See **terkw-** in Appendix.*]

tor·sion (tôr′shən) *n.* **1. a.** The act of twisting or turning. **b.** The condition of being twisted or turned. **2.** The stress caused when one end of an object is twisted in one direction and the other end is held motionless or twisted in the opposite direction. [Late Latin *torsiō,* from *torsus,* "twisted." See **torsade.**] —**tor′sion·al** *adj.* —**tor′sion·al·ly** *adv.*

torsion balance. An instrument with which small forces, as of electricity or magnetism, are measured by means of the torsion they produce in a wire or slender rod.

torsion bar. A part of an automobile suspension consisting of a bar that twists to maintain stability.

tor·so (tôr′sō) *n., pl.* **-sos** or **-si** (-sē′). **1.** The trunk of the human body. **2.** A statue of the trunk of the human body, especially with the head and limbs truncated. **3.** Any truncated or unfinished thing. [Italian, a stalk, trunk of a statue, from Latin *thyrsus,* THYRSUS.]

tort (tôrt) *n. Law.* Any wrongful act, damage, or injury done willfully, negligently, or in circumstances involving strict liability, but not involving breach of contract, for which a civil suit can be brought. [Middle English, from Old French, from Medieval Latin *tortum,* from Latin, twisted, distorted, from the neuter past participle of *torquēre,* to twist. See **terkw-** in Appendix.*]

torte (tôrt; *German* tôr′tə) *n.* A kind of rich layer cake made with many eggs and little flour and usually containing chopped nuts. [German *Torte,* perhaps from Italian *torta,* from Late Latin *tōrta*†, a kind of bread.]

tor·ti·col·lis (tôr′tə-kŏl′ĭs) *n.* A contracted state of the neck muscles producing an unnatural position of the head. Also called "wryneck." [New Latin : Latin *tortus,* past participle of *torquēre,* to twist (see **tort**) + *collum,* the neck (see **kwel-**[1] in Appendix*).] —**tor′ti·col′lar** *adj.*

tor·til·la (tôr-tē′yə) *n.* A thin unleavened pancake characteristic of Mexican cookery, served hot with various fillings. [American Spanish, diminutive of Spanish *torta,* a round cake, from Late Latin *tōrta,* TORTE.]

tor·toise (tôr′təs) *n.* **1. a.** Any of various terrestrial turtles; especially, one of the family Testudinidae, characteristically having thick, scaly limbs and a high, rounded carapace. **b.** *Chiefly British.* Any terrestrial or freshwater chelonian. **2.** One that moves slowly. [Middle English *tortuce, tortu,* from Old French *tortue,* probably from Medieval Latin *tortūca*†.]

tor·toise·shell (tôr′təs-shĕl′) *n.* Also **tor·toise-shell, tortoise shell. 1.** The mottled, horny, translucent brownish covering of the carapace of certain of the sea turtles, especially the hawksbill, used to make combs, jewelry, and other articles. **2.** A domestic cat having fur with brown, black, and yellowish markings. **3.** Any of several butterflies, chiefly of the genus *Nymphalis,* having wings with orange, black, and brown markings. —**tor′toise·shell′** *adj.*

Tor·to·la (tôr-tō′lə). An island, 21 square miles in area, in the British Virgin Islands; the principal island of the group.

Tor·tu·ga (tôr-to͞o′gə). *French* **La Tor·tue** (là tôr-tü′). An island of Haiti, 70 square miles in area, lying off the northern coast; a base and stronghold of pirates in the 17th century.

tor·tu·os·i·ty (tôr′cho͞o-ŏs′ə-tē) *n., pl.* **-ties. 1.** The state of being tortuous; twistedness; crookedness. **2.** A bent or twisted part, passage, or thing; a twist; turn; winding.

tor·tu·ous (tôr′cho͞o-əs) *adj.* **1.** Having or marked by repeated turns or bends; winding; twisting. **2.** Not straightforward; deceitful; devious. **3.** Highly involved; circuitous; complex. [Middle English, from Old French, from Latin *tortuōsus,* from *tortus,* a twist, from the past participle of *torquēre,* to twist. See **terkw-** in Appendix.*] —**tor′tu·ous·ly** *adv.* —**tor′tu·ous·ness** *n.*

Usage: *Tortuous* and *torturous* are often confused. Though they are related, careful usage tends to prescribe *tortuous* for the senses listed above and to restrict *torturous* to senses directly related to pain or torture.

tor·ture (tôr′chər) *n.* **1.** The infliction of severe physical pain as a means of punishment or coercion. **2.** The experience of this. **3.** Mental anguish. **4.** Any method or thing that causes such pain or anguish. —*tr.v.* **tortured, -turing, -tures. 1.** To subject (a person or animal) to torture. **2.** To afflict with great physical or mental pain. **3.** To twist or turn abnormally; distort. [French, from Late Latin *tortūra,* a twisting, torment, from Latin *tortus,* "twisted." See **tortuous.**] —**tor′tur·er** *n.* —**tor′tur·ous** *adj.* (See Usage note at **tortuous.**) —**tor′tur·ous·ly** *adv.*

To·ruń (tô′ro͞on′y′). *German* **Thorn** (tôrn). A city in north-central Poland, a river port on the Vistula; the birthplace of Copernicus. Population, 112,000.

to·rus (tôr′əs, tōr′-) *n., pl.* **tori** (tôr′ī′, tōr′ī′). **1.** *Architecture.* A large molding of convex semicircular cross section, usually found just above the plinth of the base of a classical column. Also called "tore." **2.** *Anatomy.* A bulging or rounded projection or swelling. **3.** *Biology.* A moundlike or rounded structure, as the receptacle of a flower. **4.** *Geometry.* A toroid generated by a circle; a surface having the shape of a doughnut. In this sense, also called "anchor ring," "tore." [New Latin, from Latin *torus*†, a protuberance, round swelling.]

To·ry (tôr′ē, tōr′ē) *n., pl.* **-ries. 1.** A member of a British political party, founded in 1689, that was the opposition party to the Whigs, and has been known as the Conservative Party since about 1832. **2.** Any American who during the period of the American Revolution favored the English side. **3.** *Sometimes small* **t.** A member of a Conservative Party, as in Canada. [From Irish *tōraige* (unattested), runaway, from Old Irish *tōir,* pursuit. See **ret-** in Appendix.* The name originally denoted an Irishman who, dispossessed by the English in the mid-17th century, became a bandit; it then became a term for any marauder, and was subsequently applied as a term of abuse to Irish Catholic royalists, then to supporters of James II, and after 1689 to the English party that initially opposed the Glorious Revolution.] —**To′ry** *adj.* —**To′ry·ism′** *n.*

Tos·ca·na. The Italian name for **Tuscany.**

Tos·ca·ni·ni (tŏs′kə-nē′nē; *Italian* tôs′kä-nē′nē), **Arturo.** 1867–

ă pat/ā pay/âr care/ä father/b bib/ch church/d deed/ĕ pet/ē be/f fife/g gag/h hat/hw which/ĭ pit/ī pie/îr pier/j judge/k kick/l lid, needle/m mum/n no, sudden/ng thing/ŏ pot/ō toe/ô paw, for/oi noise/ou out/o͝o took/o͞o boot/p pop/r roar/s sauce/sh ship, dish/

1957. Italian conductor of opera and symphony orchestras.

toss (tôs, tŏs) *v.* **tossed, tossing, tosses.** —*tr.* **1.** To throw, fling, or heave continuously about; pitch to and fro. **2.** To throw lightly with or as with the hand or hands; pitch gently or with a sudden slight jerk. **3.** *Informal.* To discuss informally; bandy about. **4.** To move or lift (the head) with rapidity: *"'Idiot!' said the Queen, tossing her head impatiently"* (Lewis Carroll). **5.** To disturb or agitate; to upset. **6.** To throw to the ground. **7.** To flip a coin with (someone) in order to decide something. **8.** To mix (a salad) lightly so as to cover with dressing. —*intr.* **1.** To be thrown here and there; be flung to and fro. **2.** To move oneself about vigorously; throw oneself from side to side: *toss in one's sleep.* **3.** To flip a coin. —See Synonyms at **throw.** —**toss down.** To empty a drinking glass by suddenly tilting it and drinking in one draft: *He tossed down one right after another.* —**toss off. 1.** To drink up in one draft. **2.** To do, finish, accomplish, or perform in a casual, easy manner: *He tossed off a few appropriate jokes.* —*n.* **1.** The act of tossing or the condition of being tossed. **2.** The distance something can be tossed. **3.** A rapid movement or lift, as of the head. **4.** An even chance. [Origin obscure.] —**toss'er** *n.*

toss up. To flip a coin.

toss·up (tôs'ŭp', tŏs'-) *n. Informal.* **1.** The flipping of a coin to decide an issue between two persons or groups according to which side of the coin falls face up. **2.** An even chance or choice.

tot¹ (tŏt) *n.* **1.** A small child. **2.** A small amount of something, as of liquor. [Origin obscure.]

tot² (tŏt) *tr.v.* **totted, totting, tots.** To total. Usually used with *up.* [Short for TOTAL.]

to·tal (tōt'l) *n.* **1.** The amount or quantity obtained by addition; a sum. **2.** A whole quantity; an entirety. —*adj.* **1.** Constituting or pertaining to the whole; entire. **2.** Complete; utter; absolute. —*v.* **totaled** or **-talled, -taling** or **-talling, -tals.** —*tr.* **1.** To determine the sum or total of. **2.** To equal a total of; amount to. **3.** *Slang.* To demolish (a vehicle) completely. —*intr.* To add up; to amount. Often used with *to: It totals to three dollars.* [From Middle English, of the whole, from Old French, from Medieval Latin *tōtālis,* from Latin *tōtus,* whole. See **teutā-** in Appendix.*]

to·tal·i·tar·i·an (tō-tăl'ə-târ'ē-ən) *adj.* Of or designating a polity whose main characteristic is considered to be monolithic unity upheld by authoritarian means: *"Medieval science could be termed 'totalitarian'; it was designed to corroborate the credo of the regime"* (Fritz Kahn). [TOTAL + (AUTHOR)ITARIAN.] —**to·tal'i·tar'i·an·ism'** *n.*

to·tal·i·ty (tō-tăl'ə-tē) *n., pl.* **-ties. 1.** The state or condition of being total. **2.** The aggregate amount; a sum. **3.** The state of an eclipse when it is total.

to·tal·i·za·tor (tōt'l-ə-zā'tər) *n.* A machine for computing and showing totals; especially, a pari-mutuel machine showing the total number and amounts of bets at a racetrack.

to·tal·ize (tōt'l-īz') *tr.v.* **-ized, -izing, -izes.** To make or combine into a total. —**to'tal·i·za'tion** *n.*

to·tal·iz·er (tōt'l-īz'ər) *n.* **1.** A pari-mutuel machine. **2.** An adding machine.

to·tal·ly (tōt'l-ē) *adv.* Entirely; wholly; completely.

to·ta·quine (tō'tə-kwīn', -kwēn', -kwĭn) *n.* A powdered yellowish, bitter mixture of quinine and alkaloids from cinchona bark, used as an antimalarial. [New Latin *totaquina* : TOTA(L) + Spanish *quina,* cinchona bark (see **quinine**).]

tote¹ (tōt) *tr.v.* **toted, toting, totes.** *Informal.* **1.** To haul; lug. **2.** To have on one's person; pack: *toting guns.* —*n. Informal.* A load; burden. [Origin unknown.] —**tot'er** *n.*

tote² (tōt) *n. Informal.* A pari-mutuel machine. [Short for TOTALIZATOR.]

tote bag. *Informal.* A large handbag or shopping bag.

to·tem (tō'təm) *n.* **1.** An animal, plant, or natural object serving among certain primitive peoples as the emblem of a clan or family by virtue of an asserted ancestral relationship. **2.** A representation of this being. **3.** A social group having a common totemic affiliation. **4.** Any venerated emblem or symbol. [Ojibwa *nintōtēm,* "my family mark," from a stem *ōtē-* (unattested), "to be from a local group."] —**to·tem'ic** (tō-tĕm'ĭk) *adj.*

to·tem·ism (tō'təm-ĭz'əm) *n.* **1.** The belief in kinship through common totemic affiliation or the identification of an individual or group with a totem. **2.** The primitive kinship system of which this is a reflection. —**to'tem·ist** *n.* —**to'tem·is'tic** *adj.*

totem pole. 1. A post carved and painted with a series of totemic symbols and erected before a dwelling, as among certain Indian peoples of the northwestern coast of North America. **2.** *Slang.* A hierarchy: *low man on the totem pole.*

toth·er, t'oth·er (tŭth'ər) *pron. Informal.* The other. [Middle English *the tother,* mistaken division of *thet other* : *thet,* the, Old English *thæt,* THAT + OTHER.]

to·ti·pal·mate (tō'tī-păl'māt') *adj.* Having webbing that connects each of the four toes, as in water birds such as pelicans and gannets. [Latin *tōtus,* whole (see **total**) + PALMATE.]

to·tip·o·ten·cy (tō-tĭp'ə-tən-sē, tō'tĭ-pōt'ən-sē) *n.* Also **to·tip·o·tence** (tō-tĭp'ə-təns, tō'tĭ-pōt'əns). The ability of a cell, such as an egg, to give rise to unlike cells and thus to form a new individual or part. [Latin *tōtus,* whole (see **total**) + POTENCY.] —**to·tip'o·tent** *adj.*

Tot·ten·ham (tŏt'n-əm). A former administrative division of London, England, now part of **Harringay** *(see).*

tot·ter (tŏt'ər) *intr.v.* **-tered, -tering, -ters. 1. a.** To sway as if about to fall. **b.** To appear about to collapse: *a tottering empire.* **2.** To walk unsteadily or feebly. **3.** To waver; vacillate: *"His extreme oddness still tottered this side of lunacy."* (Evelyn Waugh). —*n.* The act or condition of tottering. [Middle English *tot(e)ren,* from Middle Dutch *touteren,* to stagger, perhaps akin to Swedish *tulta.* See **tilt.**] —**tot'ter·er** *n.* —**tot'ter·y** *adj.*

tou·can (to͞o'kăn', -kän') *n.* Any of various tropical American birds of the family Ramphastidae, having brightly colored plumage and a very large bill. [French, from Portuguese *tucano,* from Tupi *tucana.*]

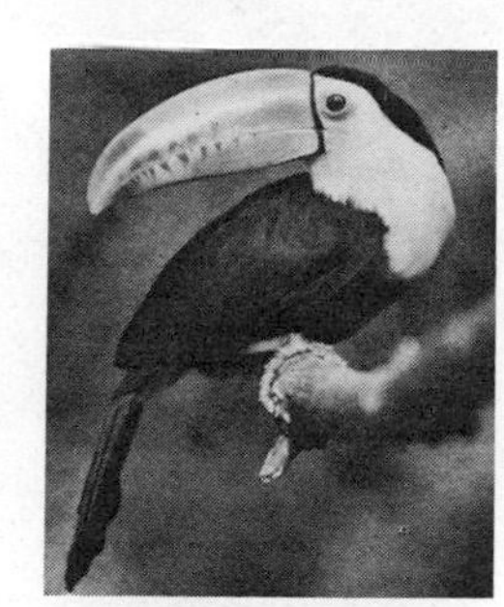

toucan
Ramphastos discolorus

touch (tŭch) *v.* **touched, touching, touches.** —*tr.* **1.** To cause or permit a part of the body to come in contact with so as to feel. **2. a.** To bring something into contact with: *touch the contact with a wire.* **b.** To bring (something) into contact with something else: *touch a wire to the contact.* **3.** To cause (something) to be in contact with something else: *He touched the control and the plane leveled off.* **4.** To tap or nudge very lightly. **5.** To strike or lay hands on in violence. Usually with a negative: *Don't dare touch her!* **6.** To use or partake of. Usually with a negative: *She didn't touch her food.* **7.** To disturb or move by handling. **8. a.** To meet; adjoin; border. **b.** *Geometry.* To be tangent to. **9.** To come up to; to equal: *His work couldn't touch his master's.* **10.** To treat of; deal with as a subject. **11.** To be pertinent to; concern. **12.** To have an effect upon; act on; change: *"She barely touched him with her smile."* (James Thurber). **13.** To injure or spoil slightly. **14.** To color slightly; to tinge. **15.** To affect the emotions of; move to tender response. **16.** To draw with light strokes. **17.** To change or improve by adding fine lines or strokes. **18.** To strike or pluck the keys or strings of (a musical instrument). **19.** To play (a musical piece). **20.** To stamp (tested metal). **21.** *Slang.* To wheedle a loan from. —*intr.* **1.** To touch someone or something. **2.** To be or come into contact. —See Synonyms at **affect.** —**touch at.** To stop briefly at (a port, for example). —**touch off. 1.** To cause to explode; to fire. **2.** To initiate (a chain of events, for example); to trigger. —**touch on** (or **upon**). **1.** To deal with (a topic) in passing. **2.** To pertain to; to concern. **3.** To approach being; verge on. —*n.* **1.** The act or instance of touching. **2.** The physiological sense by which external objects or forces are perceived through contact with the body. **3.** A sensation experienced in touching something with a characteristic texture. **4.** A mild tap or shove. **5.** A discernible mark or effect left by contact with something. **6.** A subtle effect wrought by a small change or addition. **7.** A suggestion; a hint; a tinge. **8.** A mild attack: *a touch of the flu.* **9.** A small amount; a trace; a dash: *a touch of paprika.* **10. a.** A manner or technique of striking the keys of a keyboard instrument, such as a piano or typewriter. **b.** The resistance to being struck by the fingers characteristic of a keyboard. **11.** A characteristic manner in one's personal relationships. **12.** A facility; knack: *lose one's touch.* **13.** The state of being in contact with a specified or unspecified reality: *getting out of touch.* **14.** A test or trial, as to establish quality. **15.** The official stamp indicating the quality of a metal product. **16.** *Slang.* **a.** The act of approaching someone to wheedle a loan. **b.** A sum of money borrowed. **c.** A person liable to be the victim of an approach for a loan. Often used in the phrases *soft touch, easy touch.* **17.** *Rugby & Soccer.* The area just outside the sidelines. [Middle English *to(u)chen,* from Old French *tochier,* from Vulgar Latin *toccāre* (unattested), to strike, ring a bell, touch (probably imitative).] —**touch'a·ble** *adj.* —**touch'a·ble·ness** *n.* —**touch'er** *n.*

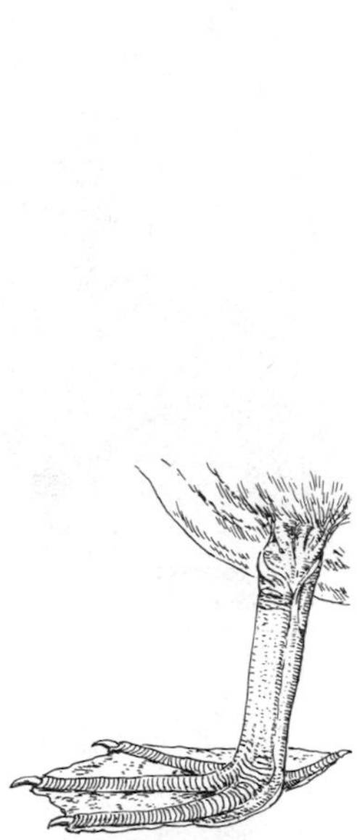

totipalmate
Totipalmate foot of a pelican

touch and go. A precarious state of affairs.

touch-and-go (tŭch'ən-gō') *adj.* **1.** Of insecure future; uncertain. **2.** Of or performed without attention; casual.

touch·back (tŭch'băk') *n. Football.* The act of touching the ball to the ground behind one's own goal line, the ball having been impelled over the line by an opponent. Compare **safety.**

touch down. To land, especially briefly, as for repairs. Used of aircraft or spacecraft.

touch·down (tŭch'doun') *n. Abbr.* **TD, td., td 1.** *Football.* A play worth six points, accomplished by being in possession of the ball when it is declared dead on or behind the opponent's goal line. **2.** The contact, or moment of contact, of a landing aircraft or spacecraft with the landing surface.

tou·ché (to͞o-shā') *interj.* Used to express concession to an opponent for a point well made, as in an argument. [French, "touched," indicating that one has been touched by the opponent's foil in fencing.]

touched (tŭcht) *adj.* **1.** Emotionally affected or moved. **2.** Somewhat demented or mentally unbalanced.

touch football. A variety of football for playing on an improvised field and without protective equipment, involving the substitution of touching for tackling.

touch·hole (tŭch'hōl') *n.* The opening in early firearms and cannons through which the powder was ignited.

touch·ing (tŭch'ĭng) *adj.* Eliciting a tender reaction; affecting. See Synonyms at **moving.** —*prep. Archaic.* Concerning; about. —**touch'ing·ly** *adv.* —**touch'ing·ness** *n.*

touch·line (tŭch'līn') *n. Rugby.* Either of the sidelines bordering the playing field.

touch-me-not (tŭch'mē-nŏt') *n.* Any of several plants of the genus *Impatiens;* especially, the **jewelweed** *(see).* [Its seed pods burst open at the slightest touch when ripe.]

touch paper. A type of paper impregnated with saltpeter so that it burns slowly and without a flame. [From TOUCH (in the rare sense of "to kindle").]

touch·stone (tŭch'stōn') *n.* **1.** A hard black stone, such as jasper or basalt, formerly used to test the quality of gold or silver by comparing the streak left on the stone by one of these metals with that of a standard alloy. **2.** A criterion; a standard:

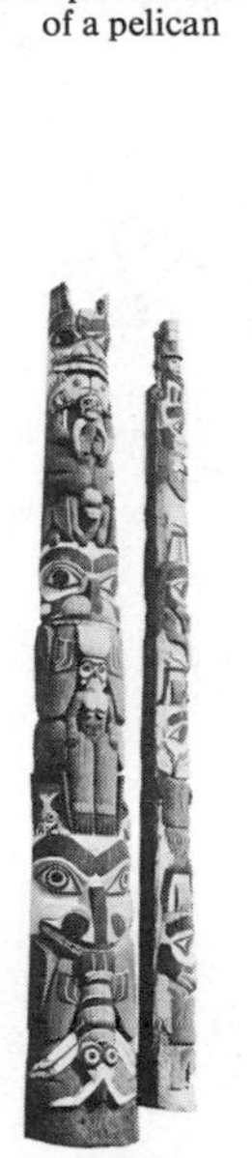

totem pole
Poles carved by Haida Indians

t tight/th thin, path/*th* this, bathe/ŭ cut/ûr urge/v valve/w with/y yes/z zebra, size/zh vision/ə about, item, edible, gallop, circus/ à *Fr.* ami/œ *Fr.* feu, *Ger.* schön/ü *Fr.* tu, *Ger.* über/KH *Ger.* ich, *Scot.* loch/N *Fr.* bon. ***Follows main vocabulary. †Of obscure origin.**

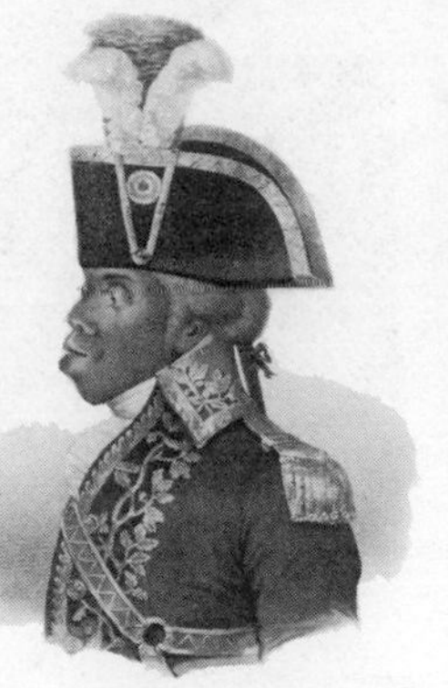

Toussaint L'Ouverture

"The touchstone of an art is its precision." (Ezra Pound).

touch-type (tŭch′tīp′) *intr.v.* **-typed, -typing, -types.** To type without having to look at the keyboard, the fingers being trained to locate the keys by position.

touch up. To make minor changes, additions, or improvements in (a work, for example).

touch·up (tŭch′ŭp′) *n.* The act or process of finishing or improving by small alterations and additions.

touch·wood (tŭch′wŏŏd′) *n.* Decayed wood or similar material used as tinder; punk. [From TOUCH (in the rare sense of "to kindle").]

touch·y (tŭch′ē) *adj.* **-ier, -iest. 1.** Apt to take offense with very slight cause; oversensitive; irritable. **2.** Requiring tact or skill; precarious; risky: *a touchy situation.* **3.** Sensitive to touch. Said of a bodily part. **4.** Easily ignited; flammable. **—touch′i·ly** *adv.* **—touch′i·ness** *n.*

tough (tŭf) *adj.* **tougher, toughest. 1.** Strong and resilient; able to withstand great strain without tearing or breaking. **2.** Hard to cut or chew. **3.** Physically hardy; rugged. **4.** Severe; harsh. **5.** Aggressive; pugnacious. **6.** Demanding or troubling; difficult. **7.** Strong-minded; resolute. **8.** Vicious; rough. **9.** *Informal.* Unfortunate; too bad. —See Synonyms at **strong.** *—n.* A hoodlum; thug. [Middle English *togh,* Old English *tōh.* See **denk-** in Appendix.*] **—tough′ly** *adv.* **—tough′ness** *n.*

tough·en (tŭf′ən) *v.* **-ened, -ening, -ens.** *—tr.* To make tough. *—intr.* To become tough. **—tough′en·er** *n.*

tough-mind·ed (tŭf′mīn′dĭd) *adj.* Not sentimental or timorous. **—tough′-mind′ed·ly** *adv.* **—tough′-mind′ed·ness** *n.*

Tou·lon (tōō-lôɴ′). A city of southeastern France, a seaport and major naval base on the Mediterranean. Population, 221,000.

Tou·louse (tōō-lōōz′). A city of southwestern France, a cultural and industrial center on the Garonne. Population, 329,000.

Tou·louse-Lau·trec (tōō-lōōz′lō-trĕk′). Full name, Henri Marie Raymond de Toulouse-Lautrec Monfa. 1864–1901. French painter and lithographer.

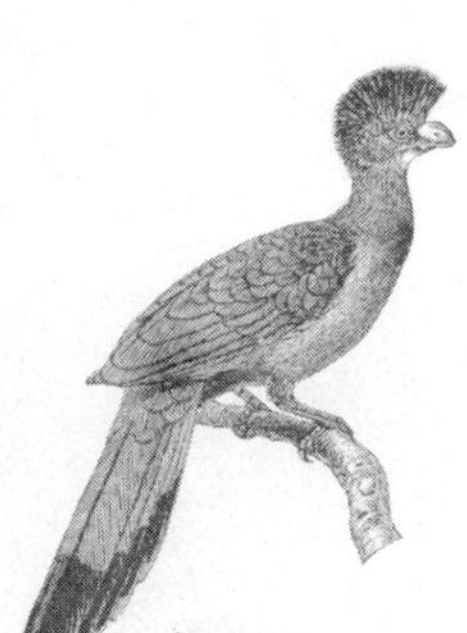

touraco
Corythaeola cristata

tou·pee (tōō-pā′) *n.* **1.** A partial wig or hair piece worn to cover a bald spot. **2.** A curl or lock of hair worn during the 18th century as a topknot on a periwig. [French *toupet,* a tuft of hair, forelock, from Old French, from *top, toup,* top, summit, from Frankish *topp-* (unattested). See **tap-** in Appendix.*]

tour (tŏŏr) *n.* **1.** A comprehensive trip with visits to places of established interest. **2.** A group organized for such a trip or for a shorter sightseeing excursion. **3.** A brief trip to or through a place for the purpose of seeing it: *a tour of the house.* **4.** A journey to fulfill a round of engagements in several places: *a concert tour.* **5.** A shift, as in a factory. **6.** A period of duty at a single place or job. *—v.* **toured, touring, tours.** *—intr.* To go on a tour. *—tr.* **1.** To make a tour of. **2.** To present (a theatrical performance) on a tour. [Middle English, one's turn, a turning, from Old French *tour, to(u)rn,* turn, circuit, from Latin *tornus,* tool for drawing a circle, lathe. See **turn.**]

tou·ra·co (tŏŏr′ə-kō′) *n., pl.* **-cos.** Also **tu·ra·co.** Any of various African birds of the family Musophagidae, many of which have brightly colored plumage. [French, from a native West African name.]

Tou·raine (tōō-rĕn′). A region and former province of west-central France.

Tou·rane. The former name for **Da Nang.**

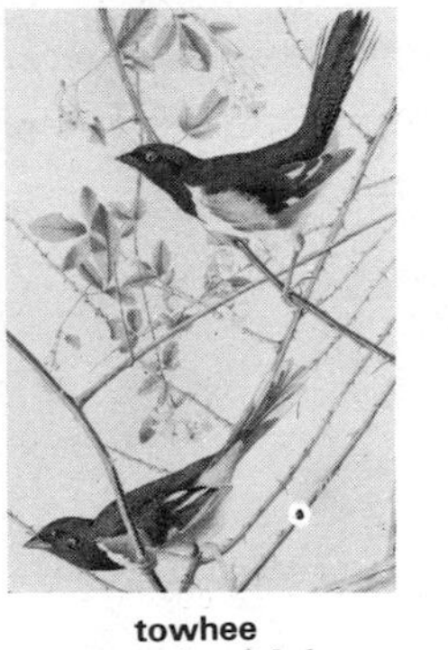

towhee
Pipilo erythrophthalmus
Painting by
John James Audubon

tour·bil·lion (tŏŏr-bĭl′yən) *n.* **1. a.** A whirlwind. **b.** A vortex, as of a whirlwind or whirlpool. **2.** A skyrocket that has a spiral flight. [Old French *tourbillon,* from Latin *turbō* (stem *turbin-*), whirlwind, circular movement. See **turbine.**]

Tour·coing (tŏŏr-kwăɴ′). A city of France, in the north near the Belgian border. Population, 89,000.

tour de force (tŏŏr′ də fôrs′). *French.* A feat of strength or virtuosity.

Tou·ré (tōō-rā′), **Sékou.** Born 1922. Guinean statesman; president (since 1958).

touring car. A large open automobile for five or more persons, popular in the 1920's.

tour·ism (tŏŏr′ĭz′əm) *n.* Also **tour·is·try** (tŏŏr′ĭ-strē) (for sense 1). **1.** The practice of traveling for pleasure. **2.** The business of providing tours and services for tourists.

tour·ist (tŏŏr′ĭst) *n.* A person who is traveling for pleasure. *—adj.* Also **tour·is·tic** (tŏŏ-rĭs′tĭk). Of or for tourists.

tourist class. A grade of travel accommodations less luxurious than first class or cabin class.

tour·ma·line (tŏŏr′mə-lĭn, -lēn′) *n.* Also **tur·ma·line.** A complex crystalline silicate containing aluminum, boron, and other elements, used in electronic instrumentation and, especially in its green, clear, and blue varieties, as a gemstone. [French, from Singhalese *toramalli,* carnelian.]

tour·na·ment (tŏŏr′nə-mənt, tûr′-) *n.* **1.** A contest involving a number of contestants who compete in a series of elimination games or trials. **2.** A medieval sport in which mounted contestants endeavored to unseat one another with blunted lances or swords; jousting match. [Middle English *tornement,* from Old French *torneiement,* from *torneier,* to TOURNEY.]

tour·ne·dos (tŏŏr′nə-dō′; *French* tŏŏr′nə-dō′) *n., pl.* **-dos.** A fillet of beef cut from the tenderloin, often bound in bacon or suet for cooking. [French : *tourner,* to TURN + *dos,* back, from Latin *dorsum* (see **dorsal**).]

Tour·neur (tûr′nər), **Cyril.** 1575?–1626. English dramatist.

tour·ney (tŏŏr′nē, tûr′-) *intr.v.* **-neyed, -neying, -neys.** To compete in a tournament. *—n., pl.* **tourneys.** A tournament. [Middle English *torneyen,* from Old French *torneier,* "to turn around" (from the combatants' turning around for each attack), from Vulgar Latin *tornidiāre* (unattested), to wheel, turn, from Latin *tornus,* a lathe, TURN.]

tour·ni·quet (tŏŏr′nĭ-kĭt, -kā′, tûr′-) *n.* Any device used to stop temporarily the flow of blood through a large artery in a limb; especially, a cloth band tightened around a limb, often over a pad placed to focus pressure on the artery. [French, "a turning instrument," swivel, perhaps from *tourner,* to TURN.]

Tours (tŏŏr). A city of west-central France on the Loire; the site of the defeat of the Saracens by Charles Martel (A.D. 732). Population, 91,000.

tou·sle (tou′zəl) *tr.v.* **-sled, -sling, -sles.** Also **tou·zle.** To disarrange or rumple; dishevel. *—n.* Also **tou·zle.** A disheveled mass, as of hair. [Middle English *touselen,* frequentative of *-tusen†,* to pull about.]

Tous·saint L'Ou·ver·ture (tōō-săɴ′ lōō-vĕr-tür′), **Pierre Dominique.** 1743–1803. Haitian general, liberator, and administrator (1801–02).

tout (tout) *v.* **touted, touting, touts.** *Informal.* *—intr.* **1.** To solicit customers, votes, or patronage, especially in a brazen way. **2.** To obtain and deal in horseracing information. *—tr.* **1.** To solicit or importune. **2.** To obtain or sell information on (a racing horse or stable) for the guidance of bettors. **3.** To publicize as being of great worth; praise as if peddling: *a rookie highly touted by the press.* *—n. Informal.* **1.** A person who obtains information on racehorses and their prospects and sells it to bettors. **2.** A person who solicits customers persistently or brazenly. [Middle English *tuten,* to peep, watch, Old English *tūtian* (unattested), from Germanic *tūt-* (unattested), to stick out, protrude.] **—tout′er** *n.*

to·va·risch (tə-vär′ĭsh) *n.* Also **to·va·rish, to·va·rich.** *Russian.* Comrade. Used in direct address.

tow¹ (tō) *tr.v.* **towed, towing, tows.** To draw or pull along behind by a chain or line. *—n.* **1. a.** An act of towing. **b.** The condition of being towed. **2.** Something being towed, as a barge or car. **3.** Something that tows, as a tugboat. **4.** A rope or cable used in towing. **—in tow. 1.** Being towed or drawn along. **2.** Under one's sway or control; in one's charge. [Middle English *togen, towen,* Old English *togian.* See **deuk-** in Appendix.*]

tow² (tō) *n.* Coarse broken flax or hemp fiber prepared for spinning. [Middle English *towe,* probably Old English *tow-,* "spinning." See **taw-** in Appendix.*]

tow·age (tō′ĭj) *n.* **1.** The act or service of towing. **2.** A charge for towing.

to·ward (tôrd, tōrd, tə-wôrd′) *prep.* Also **to·wards** (tôrdz, tōrdz, tə-wôrdz′). **1.** In the direction of. **2.** In a position facing. **3.** Somewhat before in time; approaching: *It began to rain toward morning.* **4.** With regard to; in relation to. **5.** In furtherance or partial fulfillment of. **6.** By way of achieving; with a view to: *efforts toward peace.* *—adj.* (tôrd, tōrd). *Rare.* **1.** Favorable. **2.** In progress or imminent. **3.** Tractable; docile. [Middle English *toward,* Old English *tōweard,* coming, favorable, future : TO + -WARD.]

to·ward·ly (tôrd′lē, tōrd′-) *adj. Rare.* **1.** Promising. **2.** Advantageous; favorable. **—to′ward·li·ness** *n.*

tow·boat (tō′bōt′) *n.* A **tugboat** *(see).*

tow·el (tou′əl) *n.* A piece of absorbent cloth or paper used for wiping or drying. **—throw in the towel.** To give up; quit in defeat. *—v.* **toweled** or **-elled, -eling** or **-elling, -els.** *—tr.* To wipe or rub dry with a towel. *—intr.* To dry oneself with a towel. [Middle English *towelle,* from Old French *toail(l)e,* from Frankish *thwahliō* (unattested), from Common Germanic *thwahan* (unattested), to bathe. See also **twaddle.**]

tow·el·ing (tou′əl-ĭng) *n.* Any of various fabrics of cotton or linen used for making towels.

tow·er (tou′ər) *n.* **1. a.** An exceptionally tall building. **b.** An exceptionally tall part of a building. **2.** A tall framework or structure, the elevation of which is functional, as for observation, signaling, or pumping. *—intr.v.* **towered, -ering, -ers. 1.** To rise to a conspicuous height; to loom: *"There he stood, grown suddenly tall, towering above them."* (J.R.R. Tolkien). **2.** To fly directly upward before swooping or falling. Used of certain birds. —See Synonyms at **rise.** [Middle English *to(u)r,* from Old English *torr* and Old French *tor, tur,* both from Latin *turris,* from Greek, probably of Mediterranean origin.]

Tower Hamlets. A borough of London, England, comprising the former boroughs of Bethnal Green, Poplar, and Stepney. Population, 205,000.

tow·er·ing (tou′ər-ĭng) *adj.* **1.** Of imposing height. **2.** Outstanding; pre-eminent. **3.** Awesomely intense; furious: *a towering rage.* —See Synonyms at **high.**

Tower of London. A group of buildings on the Thames, in London, that served first as a palace, later as a prison for political prisoners, and is now a museum.

tow·head (tō′hĕd′) *n.* **1.** A head of white-blond hair. **2.** One with such hair. [From TOW (hemp).] **—tow′head′ed** *adj.*

tow·hee (tō′hē, tō-hē′) *n.* Any of several North American birds of the genera *Pipilo* or *Chlorura;* especially, *P. erythrophthalmus,* having black, white, and rust-colored plumage in the male. Also called "chewink," "ground robin." [Imitative of the cry of some of the birds.]

tow·line (tō′līn′) *n.* A line, cable, or chain used in towing a vessel or vehicle. Also called "towrope."

town (toun) *n. Abbr.* **T., t., tn. 1.** A population center, often incorporated, larger than a village and smaller than a city. **2.** *Informal.* A city. **3.** *British.* A rural village that has a market or fair periodically. **4.** The commercial district or center of an area: *I'm going into town.* **5.** The residents of a town. **—go to town.** *Slang.* To do something with no inhibitions or restrictions; go all out. **—on the town.** *Slang.* On a spree. **—paint the town red.** *Slang.* To go on an elaborate or wild spree. [Middle

English *t(o)un, town,* Old English *tūn,* an enclosed place, homestead, village. See **dhūno-** in Appendix.*]
Town (toun), **Ithiel.** 1784–1844. American architect; designed and constructed public buildings, churches, and bridges.
town clerk. A public official in charge of keeping the records of a town.
town crier. A person formerly employed by a town to walk the streets proclaiming announcements. Also called "bellman."
town hall. The building that contains the offices of the public officials of a town and houses the town council and courts.
town house. **1.** A house or other residence in the city as distinguished from one in the country. **2.** One of a row of houses connected by common side walls.
town·ie (tou′nē) *n.* Also **town·y** *pl.* **-nies.** *Slang.* A resident of a college town as opposed to a student.
town meeting. A legislative assembly of townspeople.
Town·send (toun′zənd), **Francis Everett.** 1867–1960. American physician and social reformer.
town·ship (toun′shĭp′) *n. Abbr.* **twp., tp., t., T.** **1.** A subdivision of a county in most Northeastern and Midwestern states, having the status of a unit of local government with varying governmental powers. **2.** A public land surveying unit of 36 sections or 36 square miles. **3.** An ancient administrative division of a large parish in England.
towns·man (tounz′mən) *n., pl.* **-men** (-mĭn). **1.** A resident of a town. **2.** A fellow resident of one's town.
towns·peo·ple (tounz′pē′pəl) *pl.n.* The inhabitants or citizens of a town or city. Also called "townsfolk."
towns·wom·an (tounz′wo͝om′ən) *n., pl.* **-women** (-wĭm′ĭn). **1.** A woman resident of a town. **2.** A woman residing in one's own town.
tow·path (tō′păth′, -päth′) *n., pl.* **-paths** (-păthz′, -päthz′). A path along a canal or river used by animals towing boats.
tow·rope (tō′rōp′) *n.* A **towline** *(see).*
tox–. Indicates poison; for example, **toxemia.** [From Latin *toxicum,* poison. See **toxic.**]
tox·al·bu·min (tŏk′săl-byo͞o′mən) *n.* Any of various toxic proteins. [TOX- + ALBUMIN.]
tox·e·mi·a (tŏk-sē′mē-ə) *n.* A condition in which toxins produced by body cells at a local source of infection or derived from the growth of microorganisms are contained in the blood. Also called "blood poisoning." [New Latin : TOX- + -EMIA.] **—tox·e′mic** *adj.*
tox·ic (tŏk′sĭk) *adj.* **1.** Of or pertaining to a toxin. **2.** Harmful, destructive, or deadly; poisonous. [Late Latin *toxicus,* from Latin *toxicum,* poison for arrows, from Greek *toxikon,* from *toxikos,* of or for a bow, from *toxon,* a bow. See **tekw-** in Appendix.*] **—tox′i·cal·ly** *adv.*
tox·i·cant (tŏk′sĭ-kənt) *n.* A poison or poisonous agent. *—adj.* Poisonous; toxic. [Medieval Latin *toxicāns,* present participle of *toxicāre,* to poison, from Latin *toxicum,* poison. See **toxic.**]
tox·ic·i·ty (tŏk-sĭs′ə-tē) *n., pl.* **-ties.** **1.** The quality or condition of being toxic. **2.** The degree to which a poison is toxic.
tox·i·co·gen·ic (tŏk′sĭ-kō-jĕn′ĭk) *adj.* **1.** Producing poison or toxic substances. **2.** Derived from toxic matter. [From TOXIC + -GENIC.]
tox·i·col·o·gy (tŏk′sĭ-kŏl′ə-jē) *n.* The study of the nature, effects, and detection of poisons and the treatment of poisoning. [From TOXIC + -LOGY.] **—tox′i·co·log′i·cal** (-kə-lŏj′ĭ-kəl) *adj.* **—tox′i·co·log′i·cal·ly** *adv.* **—tox′i·col′o·gist** *n.*
tox·i·co·sis (tŏk′sĭ-kō′sĭs) *n., pl.* **-ses** (-sēz′). Any pathological condition resulting from poisoning. [New Latin : TOXIC + -OSIS.]
tox·in (tŏk′sĭn) *n.* Also **tox·ine** (-sēn′). A poisonous substance, having a protein structure, secreted by certain organisms and capable of causing toxicosis when introduced into the body tissues but also capable of inducing a counteragent or an antitoxin. [TOX- + -IN.]
tox·in-an·ti·tox·in (tŏk′sĭn-ăn′tĭ-tŏk′sĭn) *n.* A mixture of a toxin, as from diphtheria, and its antitoxin with a slight excess of toxin, formerly used as a vaccine.
tox·oid (tŏk′soid′) *n.* A toxin that has lost toxicity but has retained the capacity to stimulate the production of or combine with antitoxins, used in immunization. [TOX- + -OID.]
tox·o·plas·mo·sis (tŏk′sō-plăz′mō′sĭs) *n.* A disease caused by infection with a microorganism, *Toxoplasma gondii,* and characterized by lesions, especially, in the case of infants, in the brain and eye. [New Latin : *Toxoplasma* : Latin *toxicum,* poison (see **toxic**) + PLASMA + -OSIS.]
toy (toi) *n.* **1.** An object for children to play with. **2.** Something of little importance; a trifle. **3.** A small ornament; bauble; trinket. **4.** A diminutive thing or person. **5.** A dog of a very small breed or one much smaller than is characteristic of its breed, usually kept as a pet. **6.** *Scottish.* A loose covering for the head, formerly worn by women. *—intr.v.* **toyed, toying, toys.** To amuse oneself idly; to trifle. Used with *with.* *—adj.* **1.** Designed as a toy. **2.** Smaller than normal; miniature. [Middle English *toye*†, dallying, amorous sport.]
To·ya·ma (tō-yä′mä). A seaport of west-central Honshu, Japan. Population, 218,000.
Toyn·bee (toin′bē), **Arnold Joseph.** Born 1889. British historian and educator.
To·yo·ha·shi (tō-yō-hä′shē). A seaport of southern Honshu, Japan. Population, 237,000.
toy·on (toi′ŏn′) *n.* An evergreen shrub, *Heteromeles arbutifolia* (or *Photinia arbutifolia*), of the Pacific coast of southern North America, having clusters of fragrant white flowers and red, berrylike fruit. Also called "Christmas berry." [American Spanish *tollon,* probably of Mexican Indian origin.]
tp. township.
t.p. title page.
TPE Airport code for Taipei, Taiwan.
tpk. turnpike.
tr. **1.** *Grammar.* transitive. **2.** translated; translation; translator. **3.** transpose; transposition. **4.** treasurer. **5.** *Law.* trust; trustee.
tra·be·at·ed (trā′bē-ā′tĭd) *adj.* Also **tra·be·ate** (-bē-ĭt, -āt′). *Architecture.* Having horizontal beams or lintels rather than arches. [From Latin *trabs* (stem *trabe-*), a beam, timber. See **treb-** in Appendix.*] **—tra′be·a′tion** *n.*
tra·bec·u·la (trə-bĕk′yə-lə) *n., pl.* **-lae** (-lē′). **1.** A small supporting beam or bar. **2.** *Anatomy.* Any of the supporting strands of connective tissue projecting into an organ and constituting part of the framework of that organ. **3.** *Botany.* A transverse rodlike or platelike structure, often extending across a cavity. [New Latin, from Latin, diminutive of *trabs,* a beam. See **treb-** in Appendix.*] **—tra·bec′u·lar** *adj.*
Trab·zon. The Turkish name for **Trebizond.**
trace[1] (trās) *n.* **1.** A visible mark or sign of the former presence or passage of some person, thing, or event. **2.** A barely perceivable indication of something; a touch. **3. a.** A minute quantity. **b.** A constituent, as a chemical compound or element, present in quantities less than a standard limit. **4.** A path or trail through a wilderness that has been beaten out by the passage of animals or people. **5.** *Archaic.* A way or route followed. **6.** A line drawn by a recording instrument, such as a cardiograph. **7.** *Mathematics.* **a.** The point at which a line, or the curve in which a surface, intersects a coordinate plane. **b.** The sum of the elements of the principal diagonal of a matrix. *—v.* **traced, tracing, traces.** *—tr.* **1.** To follow the course or trail of. **2.** To ascertain the successive stages in the development or progress of. **3.** To locate or discover (a cause, for example) by searching or researching evidence. **4.** To delineate or sketch (a figure). **5.** To imprint (a design) on something. **6.** To form (letters) with special concentration or care. **7.** To copy by following lines seen through a sheet of transparent paper. **8.** To make a design or series of markings on (a surface). **9.** To record (a variable), as on a graph. *—intr.* **1.** To make one's way; follow a path. **2.** To have origins; be traceable. Used with *to.* [Middle English, a path, a course, from Old French, from *tracier,* to make one's way, from Vulgar Latin *tractiāre* (unattested), to drag, from Latin *tractus,* a dragging. See **tract** (expanse).] **—trace′a·bil′i·ty, trace′a·ble·ness** *n.* **—trace′a·ble** *adj.* **—trace′a·bly** *adv.*
Synonyms: *trace, vestige, track, trail, spoor.* These nouns refer to indications of something that has gone before. *Trace* applies broadly to any such evidence, such as a footprint, a fragment, or a slight indication of something intangible. *Vestige* refers to a perceptible mark of what is past or no longer existent, or to an existing biological form of something that was once more fully developed. *Track* usually denotes a single mark or, more often, a succession of marks left by something that has passed through. *Trail* can refer to such a succession of marks or to the scent of a person or animal. *Spoor* is applied most often to sensible evidence of the passage of a wild animal.
trace[2] (trās) *n.* **1.** One of two side straps or chains connecting a harnessed draft animal to the vehicle it is pulling. **2.** A bar or rod, hinged at either end to another part, that transfers movement from one part of a machine to another. [Middle English *trais,* a pair of traces, from Old French, plural of *trait,* a pulling, a strap, from Latin *tractus,* a dragging. See **tract** (expanse).]
trac·er (trā′sər) *n.* **1.** A person employed to locate missing goods or persons. **2.** An investigation or inquiry organized to trace missing goods or persons. **3.** Any of several instruments used in making tracings or other drawings. **4.** *Military.* A tracer bullet. **5.** An identifiable substance, as a dye or radioactive isotope, that can be followed through the course of a mechanical or biological process, providing information on the pattern of events in the process or on the redistribution of the parts or elements involved.
tracer bullet. A bullet that leaves a luminous or smoky trail.
trac·er·y (trā′sə-rē) *n., pl.* **-ies.** Ornamental work of interlaced and ramified lines; specifically, the lacy openwork in a Gothic window. [From TRACE (draw).]
tra·che·a (trā′kē-ə) *n., pl.* **-cheae** (-kē-ē′) or **-as.** **1.** *Anatomy.* A thin-walled tube of cartilaginous and membranous tissue descending from the larynx to the bronchi and carrying air to the lungs. Also called "windpipe." **2.** *Zoology.* One of the internal respiratory tubes of insects and some other terrestrial arthropods. **3.** *Botany.* One of the tubular conductive vessels in the xylem of plants. [Middle English *trache,* from Medieval Latin *trăchēa,* from Late Latin *trāchīa,* from Greek *(artēria) trakheia,* "rough (artery)," from the feminine of *trakhus,* rough. See **dher-[1]** in Appendix.*] **—tra′che·al** *adj.*
tra·che·id (trā′kē-ĭd) *n.* One of the elongated, tapering, supporting and conductive cells in woody tissue. [TRACHE(O)- + -ID.]
tra·che·i·tis (trā′kē-ī′tĭs) *n.* Inflammation of the trachea. [New Latin : TRACHE(O)- + -ITIS.]
tracheo–, trache–. Indicates the trachea; for example, **tracheotomy, tracheid.** [New Latin, from Medieval Latin *trăchēa,* TRACHEA.]
tra·che·ot·o·my (trā′kē-ŏt′ə-mē) *n., pl.* **-mies.** The act or procedure of cutting into the trachea through the neck. [TRACHEO- + -TOMY.]
tra·cho·ma (trə-kō′mə) *n.* A contagious viral disease of the conjunctiva of the eye characterized by inflammation, hypertrophy, and granules of adenoid tissue. [New Latin, from

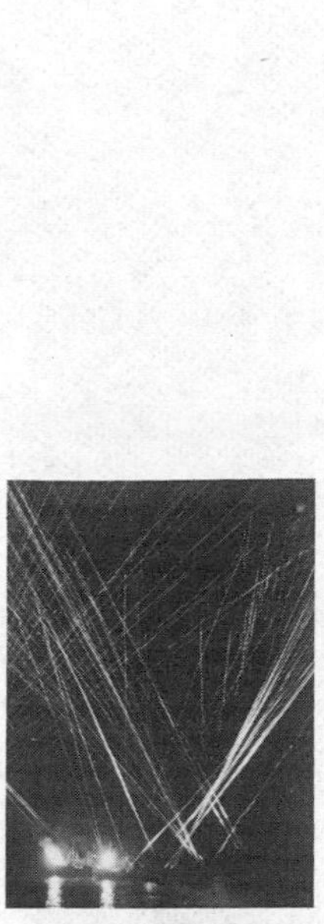
tracer bullet
U.S. ships repelling a Nazi air attack off Salerno, Italy, during World War II

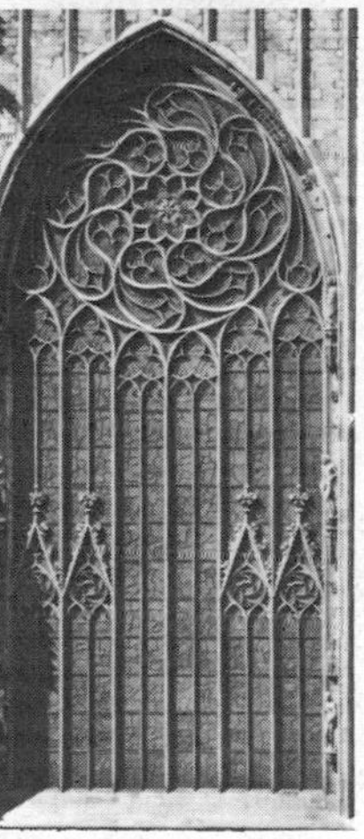
tracery
Cathedral of Milan

Greek *trakhōma* : *trakhus,* rough (see **dher-**[1] in Appendix*) + -OMA.] —**tra·cho′ma·tous** *adj.*

tra·chyte (trā′kīt′, trăk′īt′) *n.* A light-colored igneous rock consisting essentially of alkalic feldspar. [French, "rough stone" : Greek *trakhus,* rough (see **trachea**) + -ITE.] —**tra·chyt′ic** (trə-kĭt′ĭk) *adj.*

trac·ing (trā′sĭng) *n.* **1.** A reproduction made by superimposing a transparent sheet and tracing the original upon it. **2.** A graphic record made by a recording instrument, such as a cardiograph.

track (trăk) *n.* **1. a.** A mark, as a footprint, left by the passage of a person, animal, or thing; a trace. **b.** The path, route, or course indicated by such marks; a trail. **2.** A course of action; method of proceeding. **3. a.** A road or course, as of cinder or dirt, laid out for running or racing. **b.** Athletic competition on such a course; track events. **c. Track and field** *(see).* **4.** A rail or set of parallel rails upon which a train or trolley runs. —See Synonyms at **trace.** —**in one's tracks.** Exactly where one is standing. —**keep track of.** To remain in touch with. —**lose track of.** To fail to remain in touch with. —**make tracks.** *Informal.* To move or go hurriedly. —*v.* **tracked, tracking, tracks.** —*tr.* **1.** To follow the footprints or traces of; to trail. **2.** To pursue successfully; seek and overtake. Often used with *down: "When, like a running grave, time tracks you down"* (Dylan Thomas). **3.** To move over or along; to traverse. **4.** To carry on the shoes and deposit as footprints. **5.** To observe or monitor the course of (aircraft, for example), as by radar. **6.** To equip with a track or tracks. —*intr.* **1.** To keep a constant distance apart. Used of a pair of wheels. **2.** To be in alignment. **3.** To pursue a track; to trail. [Middle English *trak,* trace, trail, footprints, from Old French *trac,* perhaps Middle Dutch *trek,* a drawing, from *trekken,* to draw, pull. See **trek.**] —**track′a·ble** *adj.* —**track′er** *n.*

track·age (trăk′ĭj) *n.* **1.** Railway tracks. **2. a.** The right of one railroad company to use the track system of another. **b.** The charge for this.

track and field. Athletic events performed on a running track and the field associated with it. Also called "track." —**track′-and-field′** *adj.*

track events. The running events at a track meet as distinguished from the field events.

tracking station. An observing station for maintaining contact by means of radar or radio with an object in the atmosphere or in space.

track·less (trăk′lĭs) *adj.* **1.** Not running on tracks or rails. **2.** Unmarked by trails or paths.

track·man (trăk′mən) *n., pl.* **-men** (-mĭn). A workman employed to maintain or inspect railroad tracks.

track meet. An athletic competition of track-and-field events.

track·walk·er (trăk′wô′kər) *n.* A workman employed to inspect a section of track.

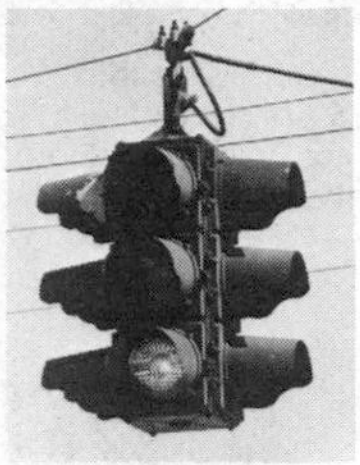

traffic light

tract[1] (trăkt) *n.* **1.** An expanse of land; a region. **2.** *Anatomy.* **a.** A system of organs and tissues that together perform one specialized function: *the alimentary tract.* **b.** A bundle of nerve fibers having a common origin, termination, and function. **3.** *Archaic.* A stretch or lapse of time. [Latin *tractus,* "a drawing," course, tract, region, from *trahere* (past participle *tractus*), to draw. See **tragh-** in Appendix.*]

tract[2] (trăkt) *n.* A distributed paper or pamphlet containing a declaration or appeal, especially one put out by a religious or political group. [Middle English *tracte,* shortened from Latin *tractātus,* a discussion, treatise, from the past participle of *tractāre,* to pull violently, discuss. See **tractable.**]

tract[3] (trăkt) *n.* The verses from Scripture sung during Lent or on Ember days after the gradual in the Roman Catholic Mass. [Middle English *tracte,* from Medieval Latin *tractus,* from Latin, "a drawing out" (the verses are sung without a break by one voice). See **tract** (area).]

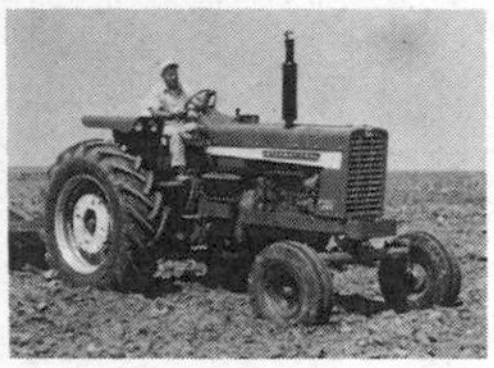

tractor

tract·a·ble (trăk′tə-bəl) *adj.* **1.** Easily managed or controlled; governable. **2.** Easily handled or worked; malleable. —See Synonyms at **obedient.** [Latin *tractābilis,* from *tractāre,* to pull violently, to take in hand, manage, frequentative of *trahere* (past participle *tractus*), to draw, pull. See **tragh-** in Appendix.*] —**tract′a·bil′i·ty, tract′a·ble·ness** *n.* —**tract′a·bly** *adv.*

Trac·tar·i·an·ism (trăk-târ′ē-ə-nĭz′əm) *n.* The religious opinions and principles of the founders of the Oxford movement, put forth in a series of 90 pamphlets entitled *Tracts for the Times,* published at Oxford, England (1833–41). Also called "Puseyism." —**Trac·tar′i·an** *adj.* & *n.*

trac·tate (trăk′tāt′) *n.* A treatise; essay. [Latin *tractātus,* TRACT.]

trac·tile (trăk′tĭl, -tīl′) *adj.* Capable of being drawn out in length, as certain metals; ductile. [From Latin *tractus.* See **traction.**] —**trac·til′i·ty** *n.*

trac·tion (trăk′shən) *n.* **1.** The act of drawing or pulling, as a load over a surface by motor power. **2.** The condition of being drawn or pulled. **3.** Adhesive friction, as of a wheel on a track. **4.** The pulling power of a railroad engine. [Medieval Latin *tractiō,* from Latin *tractus,* past participle of *trahere,* to draw, pull. See **tragh-** in Appendix.*] —**trac′tion·al** *adj.*

traction engine. A locomotive used on roads or fields rather than on tracks.

trac·tive (trăk′tĭv) *adj.* Serving to pull or draw; exerting traction. [From Latin *tractus.* See **traction.**]

trac·tor (trăk′tər) *n.* **1.** A small vehicle, powered by a gasoline or diesel motor, having large, heavily treaded tires, and used in farming for pulling machinery. **2.** A truck having a cab and no body, used for pulling large vehicles such as vans or trailers. **3.** An airplane having a propeller mounted in front of the supporting surfaces. In this sense, also called "tractor airplane." [New Latin, from Latin *tractus.* See **traction.**]

trade (trād) *n.* **1.** An occupation, especially one requiring skilled labor; a craft. **2.** The business of buying and selling commodities; commerce. **3.** The persons working in or associated with a specified business or industry. **4.** The customers, collectively, of a specified business or industry. **5.** An instance of buying or selling; transaction. **6.** An exchange of one thing for another. **7.** *Plural.* The trade winds. —See Synonyms at **business.** —*v.* **traded, trading, trades.** —*intr.* **1.** To engage in buying and selling for profit. **2.** To make an exchange of one thing for another. **3.** To shop or buy regularly at a given store. —*tr.* **1.** To give in exchange for something else. **2.** To buy and sell (stock, for example). **3.** To pass back and forth: *We traded anecdotes.* —**trade on.** To put to advantage; utilize. [Middle English *tra(i)d, trade,* a course, way, track, from Middle Low German *trade,* a track, path. See **der-**[1] in Appendix.*]

trade acceptance. A bill of exchange for the amount of a purchase drawn by the seller on the purchaser, bearing the purchaser's signature and specifying time and place of payment.

trade book. A book published for distribution to the general public through booksellers, as distinguished from a textbook or a limited edition.

trade discount. A discount on the list price granted by a manufacturer or wholesaler to buyers in the same trade.

trade dollar. A U.S. silver dollar of 420 grains issued (1873–85) for trade in the Orient.

trade in. To turn (an old item) in to a dealer as partial payment for a new purchase.

trade-in (trād′ĭn′) *n.* **1.** A piece of merchandise accepted as partial payment for a new purchase. **2.** A transaction involving such an item.

trade-last (trād′lăst′, -läst′) *n. Informal.* A favorable remark that one has overheard about another person and offers to repeat to that person when he can come forward with a similar compliment overheard.

trade magazine. A magazine published regularly by a particular business or industry to give pertinent news and developments.

trade·mark (trād′märk′) *n.* **1.** A name, symbol, or other device identifying a product, officially registered and legally restricted to the use of the owner or manufacturer. **2.** A distinctive sign by which a person or thing comes to be known. —*tr.v.* **trademarked, -marking, -marks. 1.** To label (a product) with a trademark. **2.** To register as a trademark.

trade name. 1. The name by which a commodity, service, process, or the like is known to the trade. **2.** The name under which a business firm operates.

trad·er (trā′dər) *n.* **1.** A person who trades; dealer. **2.** A ship employed in foreign trade. **3.** A member of a stock exchange who trades for himself and not as a broker for customers.

trade rat. The **pack rat** *(see).* [Perhaps from its habit of dropping whatever it is carrying upon encountering a more attractive item.]

trade route. A sea lane used by trading ships.

trade school. A secondary school that offers instruction in skilled trades; vocational school.

trade secret. A secret formula, method, or device that gives one an advantage over competitors.

trades·man (trādz′mən) *n., pl.* **-men** (-mĭn). **1.** A man engaged in the retail trade, especially a shopkeeper; dealer. **2.** A skilled worker; craftsman.

trade union. Also *chiefly British* **trades union.** *Abbr.* **T.U.** A labor union; specifically, one limited in membership to people in the same trade, as distinguished from people in the same company or industry. —**trade unionism.** —**trade unionist.**

trade wind. An extremely consistent system of winds occupying most of the tropics, constituting the major component of the general circulation of the atmosphere, blowing northeasterly in the Northern Hemisphere and southeasterly in the Southern Hemisphere. [From the phrase *to blow trade,* to blow in a regular course, from TRADE (in the obsolete sense of a course).]

trading cards. Picture cards or playing cards with designs on the backs, collected and traded by children.

trading post. A station or store in a sparsely settled area established by traders to barter supplies for local products.

trading stamp. A stamp given by a retailer to a buyer for a purchase of a specified amount and intended to be redeemed in quantity for merchandise.

tra·di·tion (trə-dĭsh′ən) *n.* **1.** The passing down of elements of a culture from generation to generation, especially by oral communication. **2. a.** A mode of thought or behavior followed by a people continuously from generation to generation; a cultural custom or usage. **b.** A set of such customs and usages viewed as a coherent body of precedents influencing the present. **3.** A body of unwritten religious precepts. **4.** Any time-honored practice or a set of such practices. **5.** *Law.* The transfer of property to another. [Middle English *tradicion,* a handing down, a surrender, from Old French, from Latin *trāditiō,* from *trādere,* to hand over : *trāns-,* over + *dare,* to give (see **dō-** in Appendix*).]

tra·di·tion·al (trə-dĭsh′ən-əl) *adj.* Also **tra·di·tion·ar·y** (trə-dĭsh′ə-nĕr′ē). Pertaining to or in accord with tradition. —**tra·di′tion·al·ly** *adv.*

tra·di·tion·al·ism (trə-dĭsh′ən-əl-ĭz′əm) *n.* **1.** Adherence to tradition; especially, excessive reverence for religious tradition. **2.** A philosophical system holding that all knowledge is derived from original divine revelation and is transmitted by tradition. —**tra·di′tion·al·ist** *n.* & *adj.* —**tra·di′tion·al·is′tic** *adj.*

tra·di·tion·al·ize (trə-dĭsh′ən-əl-īz′) *tr.v.* **-ized, -izing, -izes.** To make traditional.

trad·i·tor (trăd′ə-tər) *n., pl.* **traditores** (trăd′ə-tôr′ēz, -tōr′ēz). One of the early Christians who betrayed fellow Christians during the Roman persecutions. [Middle English *traditour,* from Latin *trāditor,* traitor, from *trādere,* to hand over, betray. See **tradition.**]

tra·duce (trə-dōōs′, -dyōōs′) *tr.v.* **-duced, -ducing, -duces.** To speak falsely or maliciously of; to slander; defame. See Synonyms at **malign.** [Latin *trādūcere,* to lead across, make public, expose to ridicule : *trāns-,* across + *dūcere,* to lead (see **deuk-** in Appendix*).] —**tra·duce′ment** *n.* —**tra·duc′er** *n.* —**tra·duc′i·ble** *adj.* —**tra·duc′ing·ly** *adv.*

tra·du·cian·ism (trə-dōō′shə-nĭz′əm, trə-dyōō′-) *n. Theology.* The belief that the soul is inherited from the parents along with the body. [From Medieval Latin *trāduciānus,* believer in this doctrine, from *trādux,* inheritance, from Latin *trādūcere,* to lead across, TRADUCE.] —**tra·du′cian·ist** *n.* —**tra·du′cian·is′tic** *adj.*

Tra·fal·gar, Cape (trə-făl′gər; *Spanish* trä′fäl-gär′). A cape on the Atlantic coast of southern Spain; site of naval battle in which Nelson defeated the French and Spanish fleets (1805).

traf·fic (trăf′ĭk) *n.* **1.** The commercial exchange of goods; trade. **2. a.** The business of moving passengers and cargo through a system of transportation. **b.** The amount of cargo or number of passengers conveyed. **3. a.** The passage of persons, vehicles, or messages through routes of transportation or communication. **b.** The amount, as of vehicles, in transit: *heavy traffic on the turnpike.* **4.** Connections; dealings. —See Synonyms at **business.** —*intr.v.* **trafficked, -ficking, -fics.** To carry on trade; have dealings. [Old French *traffique,* from Old Italian *traffico,* from *trafficare*†, to trade.] —**traf′fick·er** *n.*

traf·fi·ca·tor (trăf′ĭ-kā′tər) *n.* A vehicular direction signal. [TRAFFIC + (INDIC)ATOR.]

traffic circle. A circular one-way road at a junction of thoroughfares, facilitating uninterrupted traffic. Also called "rotary."

traffic island. A raised area over which cars may not pass, placed at a junction of thoroughfares or between opposing traffic lanes.

traffic light. A road signal that beams a red or green light or an amber warning light to direct traffic to stop or proceed. Also called "traffic signal."

trag·a·canth (trăg′ə-kănth′, trăj′-) *n.* **1.** Any of various thorny shrubs of the genus *Astragalus;* especially, *A. gummifer,* of southwestern Asia, yielding a gum used in pharmacy, adhesives, and textile printing. **2.** The gum of such a shrub. [Latin *tragacantha,* from Greek *tragakantha,* "goat's thorn" : *tragos,* goat (see **tragedy**) + *akantha,* thorn (see **ak-** in Appendix*).]

tra·ge·di·an (trə-jē′dē-ən) *n.* **1.** A writer of tragedies. **2.** An actor of tragic roles. [Middle English *tragedien,* from Old French, from *tragedie,* TRAGEDY.]

tra·ge·di·enne (trə-jē′dē-ĕn′) *n.* An actress of tragedy. [French, from Old French, feminine of *tragedien,* TRAGEDIAN.]

trag·e·dy (trăj′ə-dē) *n., pl.* **-dies.** **1.** A dramatic or literary work depicting a protagonist engaged in a morally significant struggle ending in ruin or profound disappointment, specifically: **a.** A classical verse drama in which a noble protagonist is brought to ruin essentially as a consequence of some extreme quality which is both his greatness and his downfall. **b.** A Renaissance or modern drama like the classical model in representing terrible struggle and calamity, but freer in style and choice of protagonist. **c.** Any play or narrative that seriously treats of calamitous events and has an unhappy but meaningful ending. **2.** Any dramatic, disastrous event, especially one of some moral significance. **3.** The tragic aspect or element of something. [Middle English *tragedie,* from Old French, from Latin *tragoedia,* from Greek *tragōidia,* "goat-song" (probably the name of a form of choric ceremony associated with goat-satyr plays) : *tragos*†, goat + *ōidē,* song, from *aeidein,* to sing (see **wed-**[2] in Appendix*).]

trag·ic (trăj′ĭk) *adj.* Also **trag·i·cal** (trăj′ĭ-kəl). **1.** Pertaining to, in the style of, or having the character of tragedy. **2.** Writing or performing in tragedy: *a tragic poet.* **3.** Having the elements of tragedy; calamitous; disastrous: *a tragic accident.* [French *tragique,* from Latin *tragicus,* from Greek *tragikos,* from *tragos,* goat. See **tragedy.**] —**trag′i·cal·ly** *adv.* —**trag′i·cal·ness** *n.*

trag·i·com·e·dy (trăj′ĭ-kŏm′ə-dē) *n., pl.* **-dies.** A drama that combines elements of both tragedy and comedy. [French *tragicomédie,* from Old French, from Late Latin *tragicōmoedia,* from Latin *tragicocōmoedia* : TRAGIC + COMEDY.] —**trag′i·com′ic, trag′i·com′i·cal** *adj.* —**trag′i·com′i·cal·ly** *adv.*

trag·o·pan (trăg′ə-păn′) *n.* Any of several Asian pheasants of the genus *Tragopan,* of which the male has brightly colored plumage and two hornlike appendages on the head. [Latin *tragopān,* fabulous bird in Ethiopia, from Greek *tragopan,* "goat of Pan" : *tragos,* goat (see **tragedy**) + *Pan,* PAN.]

tra·gus (trā′gəs) *n., pl.* **-gi** (-gī′, -jī′). **1.** The projection of skin-covered cartilage in front of the meatus of the external ear. **2.** Any of the hairs growing at the entrance to the meatus of the external ear. [New Latin, from Greek *tragos,* "goat" (from the resemblance of the hair to a goat's beard). See **tragedy.**]

trail (trāl) *v.* **trailed, trailing, trails.** —*tr.* **1.** To allow to drag or stream behind, as along the ground. **2. a.** To form (a course, path, or track); to blaze. **b.** To make a path or track through. **3.** To follow the traces or scent of, as in hunting; to track. **4. a.** To follow slowly. **b.** To lag behind (an opponent). —*intr.* **1.** To drag or be dragged along, brushing the ground. **2.** To extend, grow, or droop along the ground or over a surface, as a vine or plant. **3.** To drift in a tenuous stream, as smoke from a cigarette. **4.** To become gradually fainter: *Her voice trailed off in confusion.* **5. a.** To walk with dragging steps; to trudge. **b.** To fall behind in competition; to lag. —*n.* **1.** Something that hangs loose and long: *trails of ticker tape.* **2.** That which is drawn along or follows behind; a train. **3.** The part of a gun carriage that rests or slides on the ground. **4. a.** A mark, trace, course, or path left by a moving body. **b.** The scent of a person or animal. **c.** A blazed path or beaten track, as through woods or wilderness. **5.** The act or action of trailing. —See Synonyms at **trace, way.** [Middle English *trailen,* probably from Old North French *trailler* and Middle Low German *treilen,* to tow (a boat), both from Vulgar Latin *tragulāre* (unattested), to drag, from Latin *trāgula,* dragnet, from *trahere,* to pull. See **tragh-** in Appendix.*]

trail·blaz·er (trāl′blā′zər) *n.* **1.** One who blazes a trail. **2.** A leader in any field; a pioneer. —**trail′blaz′ing** *n. & adj.*

trail boss. The man in charge of a cattle drive in the West.

trail·er (trā′lər) *n.* **1.** One that trails. **2.** A large transport vehicle designed to be hauled by a truck or tractor. **3.** A furnished van drawn by a truck or automobile and used as a house or office when parked. **4.** A short filmed advertisement for a motion picture.

trailer camp. A campsite for house trailers.

trailing arbutus. A low-growing plant, *Epigaea repens,* of eastern North America, having evergreen leaves and clusters of fragrant pink or white flowers. Also called "mayflower."

trailing edge. The rearmost edge of a structure, especially of an airfoil.

trail rope. A rope for guiding or dragging, as on a dirigible or gun carriage.

train (trān) *n.* **1.** Something that follows or is drawn along behind, as the part of a gown that trails behind the wearer. **2.** A staff of persons following behind in attendance; retinue. **3.** A service unit of men, vehicles, and equipment following and attending an army. **4.** A long line of moving persons, animals, or vehicles. **5.** *Abbr.* **tn.** A string of connected railroad cars. **6.** An orderly succession of related events or thoughts; sequence. **7.** A set of linked mechanical parts: *a train of gears.* **8.** A string of gunpowder that acts as a fuse for exploding a charge. —See Synonyms at **series.** —*v.* **trained, training, trains.** —*tr.* **1.** To coach in or accustom to some mode of behavior or performance. **2.** To make proficient with specialized instruction and practice. **3.** To prepare physically, as with a regimen; make fit: *train a long-distance runner.* **4.** To cause (a plant or one's hair) to take a desired course or shape, as by manipulating. **5.** To focus or direct; to aim. Usually used with *on* or *upon: Train your sights upon the hilltop.* **6.** *Rare.* To draw, drag, or trail. —*intr.* To give or undergo a course of training. —See Synonyms at **teach.** [Middle English *trayne,* from Old French *train,* from *tra(h)iner,* to drag, from Vulgar Latin *trāgināre* (unattested), from *tragere* (unattested), variant of Latin *trahere.* See **tragh-** in Appendix.*] —**train′a·ble** *adj.*

train·band (trān′bănd′) *n.* A militia trained as a supplement to the army in England from the 16th to the 18th century. [Originally *trained band.*]

train·bear·er (trān′bâr′ər) *n.* An attendant who holds up the train of a robe or gown, as in a procession.

train·ee (trā-nē′) *n.* A person who is being trained.

train·er (trā′nər) *n.* **1.** One who trains, especially one who coaches athletes, racehorses, or show animals. **2.** A contrivance or apparatus used in training. **3.** *U.S. Navy.* The member of a gun crew who trains the cannon horizontally.

train·ing (trā′nĭng) *n. Abbr.* **tng.** **1.** The act, process, or routine of one who trains. **2.** The state of being trained.

training school. **1.** A school that gives practical vocational and technical instruction. **2.** A detention house for juvenile delinquents that offers vocational training.

training table. A table, as in a mess hall, providing carefully planned meals for athletes in training.

train·load (trān′lōd′) *n.* The full capacity of a freight or passenger train.

train·man (trān′mən) *n., pl.* **-men** (-mĭn). A member of the operating crew on a railroad train, especially the brakeman.

train·mas·ter (trān′măs′tər, -mäs′tər) *n.* A railroad official who supervises a division of a rail line.

train oil. *Rare.* Oil obtained from the blubber of a whale or other marine animal. [Middle English *trane,* from Middle Dutch *traen,* drop, tear (see **dakru-** in Appendix*) + OIL.]

traipse (trāps) *intr.v.* **traipsed, traipsing, traipses.** *Informal.* To walk about idly or intrusively. [Origin unknown.]

trait (trāt) *n.* **1.** A distinguishing feature, as of the character. **2.** *Rare.* A stroke; a touch. —See Synonyms at **quality.** [French, from Old French, pencil mark, stroke, from Latin *tractus,* a pulling, a drawing, from the past participle of *trahere,* to pull, drag. See **tragh-** in Appendix.*]

trai·tor (trā′tər) *n.* A person who betrays his country, a cause, or a trust; especially, one who has committed treason. [Middle English *traitour,* from Old French, from Latin *trāditor,* from *trādere,* to hand over, betray. See **tradition.**]

trai·tor·ous (trā′tər-əs) *adj.* **1.** Having the character of a traitor; disloyal. **2.** Constituting treason: *a traitorous act.* —See Synonyms at **faithless.** —**trai′tor·ous·ly** *adv.* —**trai′tor·ous·ness** *n.*

trai·tress (trā′trĭs) *n.* A female traitor.

Tra·jan (trā′jən). Latin name, Marcus Ulpius Trajanus. A.D. 52–117. Roman Emperor (A.D. 98–117).

tra·ject (trə-jĕkt′) *tr.v.* **-jected, -jecting, -jects.** To transmit (light or color). [Latin *trājicere* (past participle *trājectus*), to throw across : *trāns-,* across + *jacere,* to throw (see **yē-** in Appendix*).] —**tra·jec′tion** *n.*

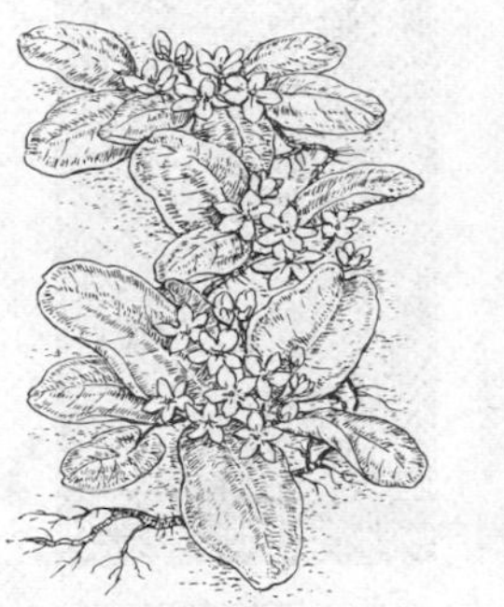

trailing arbutus

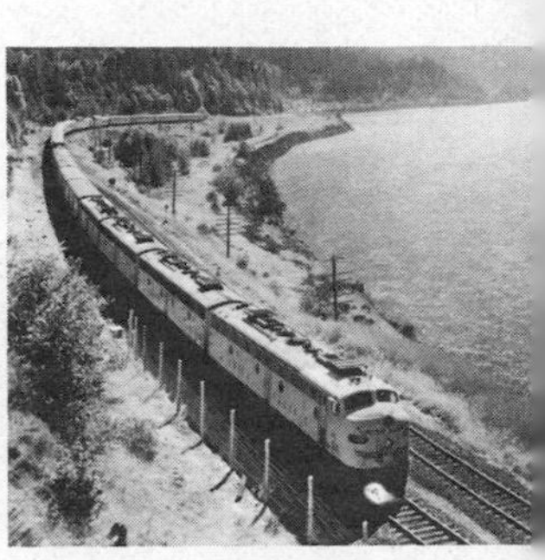

train

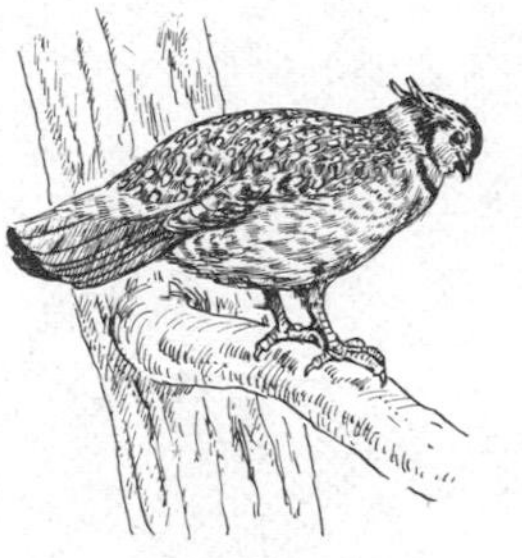

tragopan
Tragopan satyra
A male of the species

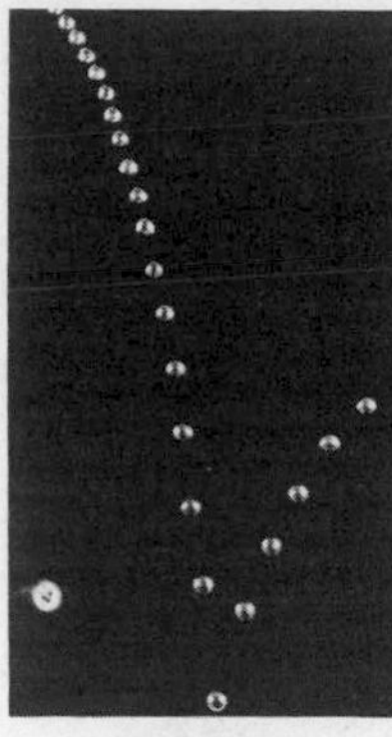

trajectory
Steel ball bouncing off a steel plate

tra·jec·to·ry (trə-jĕk′tə-rē) *n., pl.* **-ries. 1.** The path of a moving particle or body, especially such a path in three dimensions. **2.** *Geometry.* A curve that cuts all of a given family of curves or surfaces at the same angle. [Medieval Latin *trājectōrius,* from Latin *trājectus.* See **traject.**]

Tra·lee (trä-lē′). The county seat of County Kerry, southwestern Republic of Ireland. Population, 11,000.

tram¹ (trăm) *n.* **1.** *Chiefly British.* **a.** A **streetcar** *(see).* **b.** A tramway. **c.** A cable car. **2.** A four-wheeled, open box-shaped wagon or iron car run on tracks in a coal mine. *—tr.v.* **trammed, tramming, trams.** To move or convey in a tram. [Originally "shaft or frame of a truck," perhaps from Scandinavian, akin to Old Norse *thrömr, thram-,* beam, and Old High German *drâm*†, beam.]

tram² (trăm) *n.* **1.** A machine gauge, a **trammel** *(see).* **2.** Accurate mechanical adjustment: *The device is in tram.* *—tr.v.* **trammed, tramming, trams.** To adjust or align (mechanical parts) with a trammel. [Short for TRAMMEL.]

tram³ (trăm) *n.* A heavy silk thread used for the weft, or cross threads, in fine velvet or silk. [French *trame,* from Old French *traime,* woof, from Latin *trāma*†.]

tram·car (trăm′kär′) *n.* **1.** *Chiefly British.* A **streetcar** *(see).* **2.** A coal car in a mine.

tram·line (trăm′līn′) *n. British.* A streetcar line.

tram·mel (trăm′əl) *n.* Also **tram·el, tram·ell. 1.** A shackle used to teach a horse to amble. **2.** *Usually plural.* Something that restricts activity or free movement; a hindrance. **3.** A vertically set fishing net of three layers, consisting of a finely meshed net between two nets of coarse mesh. Also called "trammel net." **4. a.** An instrument for describing ellipses. **b.** The pivoted beam of a beam compass. **5.** An instrument for gauging and adjusting parts of a machine. Also called "tram." **6.** An arrangement of links and a hook in a fireplace for raising or lowering a kettle. *—tr.v.* **trammeled** or **-melled, -meling** or **-melling, -mels.** Also **tram·el, tram·ell. 1.** To confine or hinder. **2.** To entrap. Sometimes used with *up.* [Middle English *tramale,* trammel net, from Old French *tramail,* from Late Latin *tremaculum* : *trēs,* three (see **trei-** in Appendix*) + *macula,* mesh, spot (see **macula** in Appendix*).] **—tram′mel·er** *n.*

tra·mon·tane (trăm′ən-tān′, trə-mŏn′-) *adj.* **1. a.** Dwelling beyond or coming from the far side of the mountains, especially the Alps as viewed from Italy. **b.** Foreign. **c.** Barbarous. **2.** Sweeping down from the mountains. Said of a wind. *—n.* **1.** A person who lives beyond the mountains; an outsider; foreigner. **2.** In Italy, a north or cold wind. [Italian *tramontano,* from Latin *trānsmontānus* : *trāns-,* beyond + *montānus,* mountainous (see **mountain**).]

tramp (trămp) *v.* **tramped, tramping, tramps.** *—intr.* **1.** To walk with a firm, heavy step; to trudge. **2. a.** To go on foot; to hike. **b.** To wander about aimlessly, as a tramp. *—tr.* **1.** To traverse on foot: *tramp the fields.* **2.** To tread down; trample: *tramp down snow.* *—n.* **1. a.** A heavy footfall; a stamp. **b.** A heavy rhythmic tread, as of a marching army. **c.** The sound produced by heavy walking or marching. **2.** A walking trip; a hike. **3.** A person who travels aimlessly about on foot, doing odd jobs or begging for a living, as a vagrant. **4. a.** A prostitute. **b.** A promiscuous girl or woman. **5.** A cargo vessel that has no regular schedule but takes on freight wherever it may be found and discharges it wherever required. Also called "tramp steamer." **6.** A metal plate attached to the sole of a shoe for protection, as when spading ground. [Middle English *trampen,* probably from Middle Low German. See **der-¹** in Appendix.*] **—tramp′er** *n.*

tram·ple (trăm′pəl) *v.* **-pled, -pling, -ples.** *—tr.* **1.** To beat down with the feet so as to crush, bruise, violate, or destroy; tramp upon. **2.** To treat harshly or ruthlessly, as if tramping upon. *—intr.* To tread heavily or contemptuously. *—n.* The action or sound of treading underfoot. [Middle English *tramp(e)len,* frequentative of *trampen,* to TRAMP.] **—tram′pler** *n.*

tram·po·line (trăm′pə-lēn′) *n.* Also **tram·po·lin** (-lən). A sheet of strong, taut canvas attached with springs to a metal frame and used for acrobatic tumbling. [Spanish *trampolin,* from Italian *trampolino,* "performance on stilts," from *trampoli,* stilts, from Germanic. See **der-¹** in Appendix.*] **—tram′po·lin′er, tram′po·lin′ist** *n.*

tram·way (trăm′wā′) *n. British.* **1. a.** A street track or railway for trams. **b.** A streetcar line. **2.** A cable or system of cables for a cablecar.

trance (trăns) *n.* **1.** A hypnotic, cataleptic, or ecstatic state. **2.** A state of detachment from one's physical surroundings, as in contemplation or daydreaming. **3.** A dazed state, as between sleeping and waking; stupor. *—tr.v.* **tranced, trancing, trances.** To put into a trance. [Middle English *traunce,* from Old French *transe,* from *transir,* "to pass (from life to death)," depart, from Latin *transīre,* to go across. See **transit.**]

tran·quil (trăn′kwəl) *adj.* **-quiler** or **-quiller, -quilest** or **-quillest. 1.** Free from agitation or other disturbance; calm; unruffled; serene: *a tranquil rural life.* **2.** Steady; even: *a tranquil flame.* —See Synonyms at **calm, still.** [Latin *tranquillus.* See **kweyə-** in Appendix.*] **—tran′quil·ly** *adv.* **—tran′quil·ness** *n.*

tran·quil·ize (trăn′kwə-līz′) *v.* **-ized, -izing, -izes.** Also **tran·quil·lize.** *—tr.* To make tranquil; to quiet. *—intr.* To become tranquil. **—tran′quil·i·za′tion** *n.*

tran·quil·iz·er (trăn′kwə-līz′ər) *n.* **1.** Something that tranquilizes, as music or liquor. **2.** Any of various drugs that are used to calm or pacify.

tran·quil·li·ty, tran·quil·i·ty (trăn-kwĭl′ə-tē) *n.* The state or quality of being tranquil; serenity.

trans–. Indicates: **1.** Across or over; for example, **transpolar. 2.** Beyond or above; for example, **transpontine. 3.** From one place to another; for example, **translocate. 4.** Transferring or transporting; for example, **transship. 5.** Changing; for example, **transliterate. 6.** Having a greater atomic number; for example, **transuranic.** ***Note:*** Many compounds other than those entered here may be formed with *trans-.* In forming compounds, *trans-* is normally joined with the following element without space or hyphen: *transculturation.* If the second element begins with a capital letter, it is usually separated with a hyphen: *trans-Canadian.* Note, however, that certain compounds have become one word: *transatlantic, transalpine, Transcaucasia.* All such forms are entered in this Dictionary. [From Latin *trāns,* across, over, beyond, through, through and through. See **ter-³** in Appendix.*]

trans. 1. transaction. **2.** *Grammar.* transitive. **3.** translated; translation; translator. **4.** transportation. **5.** transpose; transposition. **6.** transverse.

trans·act (trăn-săkt′, -zăkt′) *v.* **-acted, -acting, -acts.** *—tr.* To do, carry out, perform, manage, or conduct (business or affairs, for example). *—intr.* To do business with; negotiate. [Latin *transigere* (past participle *transactus*), to drive or carry through, complete : *trāns-,* through + *agere,* to drive, do (see **ag-** in Appendix*).] **—trans·ac′tor** (trăn-săk′tər, -zăk′tər) *n.*

trans·ac·tion (trăn-săk′shən, -zăk′shən) *n. Abbr.* **trans. 1.** The act of transacting or the fact of being transacted. **2.** Something transacted; especially, a piece of business. **3.** *Plural.* The proceedings, as of a convention. **—trans·ac′tion·al** *adj.*

Trans A·lai (trăns ä-lī′, trănz). A mountain range of the Soviet Union, a branch of the Pamirs, extending between the Kirghiz and Tadzhik Soviet republics. Highest elevation, Lenin Peak (23,382 feet).

trans·al·pine (trăns-ăl′pīn′, trănz-) *adj.* Pertaining to, living on, or coming from the other side of the Alps, especially as seen from Italy. *—n.* One who lives beyond the Alps.

Transalpine Gaul. The section of Gaul that lay northwest of the Alps.

trans·at·lan·tic (trăns′ət-lăn′tĭk, trănz′ət-) *adj.* **1.** On the other side of the Atlantic. **2.** Spanning or crossing the Atlantic.

Trans·cau·ca·sia (trăns′kô-kā′zhə, -shə, trănz′-). A region of the Soviet Union, in the southeast between the Caucasus Mountains and the borders with Turkey and Iran, and including the Soviet republics of Azerbaijan, Georgia, and Armenia; formerly (1922–36) constituting the Transcaucasian S.F.S.R.

trans·ceiv·er (trăn-sē′vər) *n.* A module consisting of a radio receiver and transmitter. [TRANS(MITTER) + (RE)CEIVER.]

tran·scend (trăn-sĕnd′) *v.* **-scended, -scending, -scends.** *—tr.* **1. a.** To pass beyond (a human limit): *an emotion that transcends understanding.* **b.** To exist above and independent of (material experience or the universe): *"one never can see the thing in itself, because the mind does not transcend phenomena"* (Hilaire Belloc). **2.** To rise above or across; surpass; exceed: *"He not only transcends himself in various ways, he also transcends his culture."* (Abraham H. Maslow). *—intr.* To surpass. —See Synonyms at **excel.** [Middle English *transcenden,* from Old French *transcendre,* from Latin *transcendere,* "to climb over" : *trāns-,* over + *scandere,* to climb (see **skand-** in Appendix*).]

tran·scen·dent (trăn-sĕn′dənt) *adj.* **1.** Surpassing others of the same kind; pre-eminent. **2. a.** *Philosophy.* Transcending the Aristotelian categories. **b.** In Kant's theory of knowledge, designating knowledge that is beyond the limits of experience. **3.** Above and independent of the material universe. Said of the Deity. **4.** *Mathematics.* Designating a number not formed by the fundamental arithmetic operations, each performed only a finite number of times. **—tran·scen′dence, tran·scen′den·cy, tran·scen′dent·ness** *n.* **—tran·scen′dent·ly** *adv.*

tran·scen·den·tal (trăn′sĕn-dĕnt′l) *adj.* **1.** *Philosophy.* **a.** Concerned with the a priori basis of knowledge; minimizing the importance or denying the reality of sense experience. **b.** Asserting a fundamental irrationality or supernatural element in experience. **2.** Rising above common thought or ideas; exalted; mystical. **3.** *Mathematics.* **a.** Not capable of being determined by any combination of a finite number of equations with rational integral coefficients. **b.** Not expressible as an integer or quotient of integers. Said of numbers, especially nonrepeating infinite decimals. **—tran′scen·den′tal·ly** *adv.*

tran·scen·den·tal·ism (trăn′sən-dĕnt′l-ĭz′əm) *n.* **1.** *Philosophy.* **a.** The belief that knowledge of reality is derived from intuitive sources rather than from objective experience. **b.** Any doctrine based on this belief, as the philosophy of Kant. **2.** The quality or condition of being transcendental. **—tran′scen·den′tal·ist** *n.*

trans·con·ti·nen·tal (trăns′kŏn′tə-nĕn′təl, trănz′-) *adj.* Spanning or crossing a continent.

tran·scribe (trăn-skrīb′) *tr.v.* **-scribed, -scribing, -scribes. 1. a.** To write or type a copy of; write out fully, as from shorthand notes: *transcribe a letter.* **b.** To transfer (information) from one recording and storing system to another. **2.** To adapt or arrange (a musical composition) for a voice or instrument other than the original. **3.** To record, usually on tape, for broadcasting at a later date. **4.** To represent (speech sounds) by phonetic symbols. [Latin *transcrībere,* to copy, "write over" : *trāns-,* from one place to another, across + *scrībere,* to write (see **skeri-** in Appendix*).] **—tran·scrib′a·ble** *adj.* **—tran·scrib′er** *n.*

tran·script (trăn′skrĭpt′) *n.* Something transcribed; a written, typewritten, or printed copy, especially of a legal record or a student's school record. [Middle English *transcri(p)t,* from Old French *transcrit,* from Latin *transcriptum,* from the neuter past participle of *transcrībere,* TRANSCRIBE.]

tran·scrip·tion (trăn-skrĭp′shən) *n.* **1.** The act or process of transcribing. **2.** Something that has been transcribed, especially: **a.** An adaptation of a musical composition. **b.** A recorded radio or television program. —**tran·scrip′tion·al, tran·scrip′tive** *adj.* —**tran·scrip′tion·al·ly, tran·scrip′tive·ly** *adv.*

trans·cul·tu·ra·tion (trăns-kŭl′chər-ā′shən, trănz-) *n.* Cultural change induced by the introduction of elements of a foreign culture. [TRANS- + CULTURE + -ATION.]

trans·cur·rent (trăns-kûr′ənt, trănz-) *adj.* Extending, passing, or running transversely.

trans·duc·er (trăns-dōō′sər, -dyōō′sər, trănz-) *n.* Any of various substances or devices, as a piezoelectric crystal or a photoelectric cell, that convert input energy of one form into output energy of another. [From Latin *transdūcere,* to lead across, transfer : *trāns-,* across + *dūcere,* to lead (see **deuk-** in Appendix*).]

trans·duc·tion (trăns-dŭk′shən, trănz-) *n.* The transfer of genetic material from one bacterial cell to another by a bacteriophage. [Latin *transductiō,* a transfer, from *transductus,* past participle of *transdūcere,* to transfer. See **transducer.**]

tran·sect (trăn-sĕkt′) *tr.v.* **-sected, -secting, -sects.** To divide by cutting transversely. [TRANS- + Latin *secāre* (past participle *sectus*), to cut (see **sek-** in Appendix*).] —**tran·sec′tion** *n.*

tran·sept (trăn′sĕpt′) *n. Architecture.* Either of the two lateral arms of a cruciform church. [New Latin *transeptum* : TRANS- + SEPTUM (partition).]

trans·e·unt (trăn′sē-ənt) *adj. Philosophy.* Productive of effects outside of the mind. Compare **immanent.** [Latin *transiēns* (oblique stem *transeunt-*), going over, TRANSIENT.]

trans·fer (trăns-fûr′, trăns′fər) *v.* **-ferred, -ferring, -fers.** —*tr.* **1.** To convey or shift from one person or place to another. **2.** To make over the possession or legal title of to another. **3.** To convey (a drawing, pattern, mural, or design) from one surface to another. —*intr.* **1.** To move oneself, as from one location, job, or school to another. **2.** To change from one train, airplane, bus, or other carrier to another. —See Synonyms at **convey.** —*n.* (trăns′fər). Also **trans·fer·al** (trăns-fûr′əl), **trans·fer·ral** (for senses 1, 2). *Abbr.* **tfr., transf. 1.** The conveyance or removal of something from one person or place to another. **2. a.** Any person or object that has or has been transferred, as a student enrolled in a new school. **b.** A design conveyed or to be conveyed from one surface, usually paper, to another. **3. a.** A ticket entitling a passenger to change from one carrier to another. **b.** A place where such changes are permitted or required. **4.** *Law.* **a.** The conveyance of title or property from one person to another. **b.** The document effecting such conveyance. [Middle English *transferren,* from Old French *transferer,* from Latin *transferre,* to bear across : *trāns-,* across + *ferre,* to bear (see **bher-¹** in Appendix*).] —**trans·fer′a·bil′i·ty** *n.* —**trans·fer′a·ble** *adj.*

trans·fer·ase (trăns′fər-ās′, -āz′) *n.* Any of various enzymes that catalyze the transfer of atoms or groups of atoms from one molecule to another. [TRANSFER + -ASE.]

trans·fer·ee (trăns′fər-ē′) *n.* **1.** *Law.* One to whom a transfer of title or property is made. **2.** One who is transferred.

trans·fer·ence (trăns-fûr′əns, trăns′fər-əns) *n.* **1. a.** An act or process of transferring. **b.** The condition of being transferred. **2.** *Psychoanalysis.* The process in and by which an individual's feelings, thoughts, and wishes shift from one person to another; especially, this process in psychoanalysis with the analyst made the object of the shift. —**trans·fer·en′tial** (trăns′fə-rĕn′shəl) *adj.*

trans·fer·or (trăns-fûr′ər) *n. Law.* A person who makes a transfer of title or property.

trans·fer·rer (trăns-fər′ər) *n.* One that transfers.

trans·fer·rin (trăns-fûr′ĭn) *n.* A blood globulin that can combine reversibly with and transport iron ions in the body. [TRANS- + FERR(O)- + -IN.]

trans·fig·u·ra·tion (trăns-fĭg′yə-rā′shən) *n.* **1.** A radical transformation of figure or appearance; metamorphosis. **2.** *Capital* **T. a.** The sudden emanation of radiance from Jesus' person that occurred on the mountain. Matthew 17:2; Mark 9:2. **b.** The Christian commemoration of this, observed on August 6.

trans·fig·ure (trăns-fĭg′yər) *tr.v.* **-ured, -uring, -ures. 1.** To transform the figure or appearance of; alter radically. **2.** To exalt; glorify. [Middle English, from Latin *trānsfigūrāre* : *trāns-,* change + *figūra,* FIGURE.] —**trans·fig′ure·ment** *n.*

trans·fi·nite (trăns-fī′nĭt′) *adj.* Beyond the finite.

transfinite number. A cardinal or ordinal number that is not an integer.

trans·fix (trăns-fĭks′) *tr.v.* **-fixed, -fixing, -fixes. 1.** To pierce through with or as if with a pointed weapon. **2.** To fix fast; impale. **3.** To render motionless, as with terror, amazement, or awe. [Latin *trānsfigere* (past participle *trānsfixus*) : *trāns-,* through + *figere,* to pierce, fix (see **dhīgw-** in Appendix*).] —**trans·fix′ion** (-fĭk′shən) *adj.*

trans·form (trăns-fôrm′) *v.* **-formed, -forming, -forms.** —*tr.* **1.** To change markedly the form or appearance of. **2.** To change the nature, function, or condition of; to convert. **3.** *Mathematics.* To subject to a mathematical transformation. **4.** *Linguistics.* A construction derived by transformation. **5.** *Electricity.* To subject to the action of a transformer. —*intr.* To undergo a transformation. —See Synonyms at **change.** —*n.* The result, especially a mathematical quantity, of a transformation. —**trans·form′a·ble** *adj.*

trans·for·ma·tion (trăns′fər-mā′shən) *n.* **1. a.** The act of transforming. **b.** The state or an instance of being transformed. **c.** Something that has been transformed. **2.** A woman's hair piece or wig. **3.** *Mathematics.* **a** The replacement of the variables in an algebraic expression by their values in terms of

another set of variables. **b.** A mapping of one space onto another or onto itself. **4.** *Linguistics.* **a.** The process of converting a syntactic construction into a semantically equivalent construction according to the rules shown to generate the syntax of the language. **b.** A construction derived by such transformation; a transform. —**trans·for′ma·tive** (-fôr′mə-tĭv) *adj.*

transformational grammar. A grammar that accounts for the constructions of a language by linguistic transformations and phrase structures, especially **generative transformational grammar** *(see).*

trans·form·er (trăns-fôr′mər) *n.* **1.** One that transforms. **2.** A device used to transfer electric energy, usually that of an alternating current, from one circuit to another; especially, a pair of multiply wound, inductively coupled wire coils that effect such a transfer with a change in voltage, current, phase, or other electric characteristic. See **step-down transformer, step-up transformer.**

trans·fuse (trăns-fyōōz′) *tr.v.* **-fused, -fusing, -fuses. 1.** To transfer (liquid) by pouring from one vessel into another. **2.** To permeate; instill. **3.** *Medicine.* To administer a transfusion of or to. [Middle English *transfusen,* from Latin *trānsfundere* (past participle *trānsfūsus*) : *trāns-,* from one place to another + *fundere,* to pour (see **gheu-** in Appendix*).] —**trans·fus′er** *n.* —**trans·fus′i·ble** *adj.* —**trans·fu′sive** (-fyōō′sĭv, -zĭv) *adj.*

trans·fu·sion (trăns-fyōō′zhən) *n.* **1.** The act or process of transfusing. **2.** *Medicine.* The direct injection of whole blood, plasma, or another solution into the bloodstream.

trans·gress (trăns-grĕs′, trănz-) *v.* **-gressed, -gressing, -gresses.** —*tr.* **1.** To go beyond or over (a limit or boundary). **2.** To act in violation of (the law, for example). —*intr.* To trespass; to sin. [Latin *trānsgredī* (past participle *trānsgressus*), to step across : *trāns-,* across + *gradī,* to step (see **ghredh-** in Appendix*).] —**trans·gress′i·ble** *adj.* —**trans·gres′sive** *adj.* —**trans·gres′sive·ly** *adv.* —**trans·gres′sor** (-grĕs′ər) *n.*

trans·gres·sion (trăns-grĕsh′ən, trănz-) *n.* **1.** The violation of a law, command, or duty. **2.** The exceeding of due bounds or limits. —See Synonyms at **breach.**

tran·ship. Variant of **transship.**

trans·hu·mance (trăns-hyōō′məns, trănz-) *n.* The movement of livestock and herders to different grazing grounds with the changing of the seasons. [French, from *transhumer,* to make seasonal movement of livestock, from Spanish *transhumar* : Latin *trāns-,* from one place to another + *humus,* earth, ground (see **dhghem-** in Appendix*).] —**trans·hu′mant** *adj. & n.*

tran·si·ence (trăn′shəns, -zhəns, -zē-əns) *n.* Also **tran·sien·cy** (-shən-sē, -zhən-sē, -zē-ən-sē). The state or quality of being transient.

tran·sient (trăn′shənt, -zhənt, -zē-ənt) *adj.* **1.** Passing away with time; transitory; fleeting. **2.** Passing through from one place to another; stopping only briefly or overnight: *transient laborers.* **3.** *Physics.* Decaying with time, especially as a simple exponential function of time. —*n.* **1.** One that is transient; especially, a person staying a single night at a hotel. **2.** *Physics.* A transient phenomenon or property, especially a transient electric current. [Latin *transiēns,* present participle of *transīre,* to go over : *trāns-,* over, across + *īre,* to go (see **ei-¹** in Appendix*).] —**tran′siont·ly** *adv.* —**tran′sient·ness** *n.*

Synonyms: *transient, transitory, ephemeral, fleeting, fugitive, momentary, evanescent, temporary, provisional.* These adjectives mean being present or having existence for a short or limited time. In modern usage *transient* usually refers to what literally remains only a short time, such as a guest at a hotel. It can also mean inherently short-lived or impermanent, but the latter sense is more often expressed by *transitory. Ephemeral, fleeting, fugitive, momentary,* and *evanescent* all underscore the idea of very brief existence. *Ephemeral* often implies lack of enduring quality or appeal. *Fleeting,* in contrast, is often applied to what passes more swiftly than one would wish. *Fugitive* especially suggests what passes but leaves a distinct impression. *Momentary* stresses mere brevity, and *evanescent* suggests that which has the substance and lasting power of a vapor. *Temporary* usually describes what is meant to last for a limited period pending establishment of something intended as long-range. *Provisional* refers to what is adapted to a present necessity and consequently may be a stopgap.

tran·sis·tor (trăn-zĭs′tər, trăn-sĭs′-) *n.* **1.** A three-terminal semiconductor device used for amplification, switching, and detection, typically containing two rectifying junctions and characteristically operating so that the current between one pair of terminals controls the current between the other pair, one terminal being common to input and output. **2.** A radio equipped with transistors. In this sense, also called "transistor radio." [Originally a trademark : TRAN(SFER) + (RE)SISTOR (it transfers electric signals across a resistor).]

tran·sis·tor·ize (trăn-zĭs′tə-rīz′, trăn-sĭs′-) *tr.v.* **-ized, -izing, -izes.** To equip (an electronic circuit or device) with transistors.

tran·sit (trăn′sĭt, -zĭt) *n. Abbr.* **t. 1. a.** The act of passing over, across, or through; passage. **b.** The conveyance of persons or goods from one place to another, especially on a local public transportation system. **2.** A transition or change, especially from one life to another at death. **3.** *Astronomy.* **a.** The passage of a celestial body across the observer's meridian. **b.** The passage of a smaller celestial body across the disk of a larger celestial body. **4.** A surveying instrument similar to a theodolite that measures horizontal and vertical angles. —*v.* **transited, -siting, -sits.** —*tr.* **1.** To pass over, across, or through. **2.** To revolve (the telescope of a surveying transit) about its horizontal transverse axis in order to reverse its direction. —*intr.*

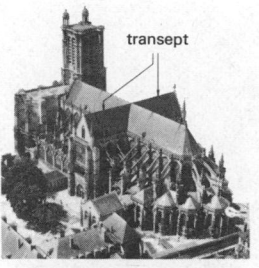

transept

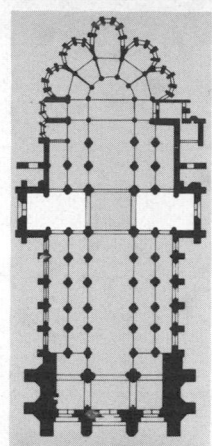

transept
Exterior and plan of
Troyes Cathedral, France

Astronomy. To make a transit. [Latin *transitus,* from the past participle of *transire,* to go across. See **transient.**]

tran·si·tion (trăn-zĭsh′ən, -sĭsh′ən) *n.* **1.** The process or an instance of changing from one form, state, activity, or place to another. **2.** Passage from one subject to another, as in discourse. **3.** *Music.* **a.** A modulation, especially a brief one. **b.** A passage connecting two themes. **—tran·si′tion·al, tran·si′tion·ar′y** (-ĕr′ē) *adj.* **—tran·si′tion·al·ly** *adv.*

transition element. **1.** Any of the elements that serve as transitional links between the most and the least electropositive in a series of elements, and that are characterized by high melting points, densities, magnetic moments, multiple valences, and the ability to form stable complex ions. **2.** Any of the elements in which an inner electron shell rather than an outer shell is only partially filled, generally taken to include elements 21–29, 38–46, and 71–78. Also called "transition metal." See **element.**

transition metal. A **transition element** *(see).*

tran·si·tive (trăn′sə-tĭv, trăn′zə-) *adj.* **1.** *Abbr.* **t., tr., trans.** *Grammar.* Expressing an action that is carried from the subject to the object; requiring a direct object to complete its meaning. Said of a verb or verb construction. **2.** Characterized by or effecting transition. —*n. Abbr.* **t., tr., trans.** *Grammar.* A transitive verb. [Late Latin *transitīvus,* passing over (as from the subject to the object), from Latin *transitus,* TRANSIT.] **—tran′si·tive·ly** *adv.* **—tran′si·tive·ness, tran′si·tiv′i·ty** *n.*

tran·si·to·ry (trăn′sə-tôr′ē, -tōr′ē, trăn′zə-) *adj.* Existing or occurring only briefly; short-lived; passing. See Synonyms at **transient.** [Middle English *transitorie,* from Norman French, from Late Latin *transitōrius,* from Latin, adapted for passing through, from *transitus,* TRANSIT.] **—tran′si·to′ri·ly** *adv.* **—tran′si·to′ri·ness** *n.*

Trans-Jor·dan (trăns-jôrd′n, trănz-). Also **Trans·jor·dan.** Formerly **Trans·jor·dan·ia** (trăns′jôr-dā′nē-ə, trănz′-). A section of Palestine between the Jordan River and the Syrian Desert, formerly a kingdom under the British mandate for Palestine that achieved full independence in 1946; now, officially, the Hashemite Kingdom of Jordan.

Trans·kei, The (trăns-kā′, -kī′). A semiautonomous Bantu homeland occupying 15,780 square miles in eastern Cape of Good Hope Province, South Africa; formed in 1963 of the former United Transkei Territories. Population, 1,200,000. Capital, Umtata.

transl. translated; translation.

trans·late (trăns-lāt′, trănz-, trăns′lāt′, trănz′-) *v.* **-lated, -lating, -lates.** —*tr.* **1.** To express in another language, systematically retaining the original sense. **2.** To put in simpler terms; explain. **3.** To convey from one form or style to another; convert. **4.** To transfer (a bishop) to another see. **5.** To forward or retransmit (a telegraphic message). **6.** *Theology.* To convey to heaven without natural death. **7.** *Physics.* To subject (a body) to translation. **8.** *Archaic.* To transport; enrapture. —*intr.* **1. a.** To make a translation. **b.** To work as a translator. **2.** To admit of translation. **3.** *Aerospace.* To move from one place to another in space by means of reaction power. [Middle English *translaten,* to transport, to translate, from Latin *translātus* (past participle of *transferre,* to carry across, transfer, translate) : *trāns-,* across + *-lātus,* "carried" (see **tel-**[1] in Appendix*).] **—trans·lat′a·bil′i·ty, trans·lat′a·ble·ness** *n.* **—trans·lat′a·ble** *adj.*

trans·la·tion (trăns-lā′shən, trănz-) *n. Abbr.* **transl., trans., tr.** **1. a.** The act or process of translating, especially from one language to another. **b.** The condition of being translated. **2.** A translated version of a text. **3.** *Physics.* Motion of a body in which every point of the body moves parallel to, and the same distance as, every other point of the body; nonrotational displacement. **—trans·la′tion·al** *adj.*

trans·la·tor (trăns-lā′tər, trănz-, trăns′lā′tər, trănz′-) *n. Abbr.* **tr., trans.** **1.** One who translates; especially, one professionally employed to translate written works. **2.** An interpreter. **—trans′la·to′ri·al** (trăns′lə-tôr′ē-əl, -tōr′ē-əl, trănz′-) *adj.*

trans·lit·er·ate (trăns-lĭt′ə-rāt′, trănz-) *tr.v.* **-ated, -ating, -ates.** To represent (letters or words) in the corresponding characters of another alphabet. [TRANS- + Latin *littera,* LETTER + -ATE.] **—trans·lit′er·a′tion** *n.*

trans·lo·cate (trăns′lō-kāt′, trănz′-) *tr.v.* **-cated, -cating, -cates.** To cause to change from one position to another; displace.

trans·lo·ca·tion (trăns′lō-kā′shən, trănz′-) *n.* **1.** A change in location. **2.** *Genetics.* A chromosomal aberration in which different nonhomologous genes are interchanged.

trans·lu·cent (trăns-lo͞o′sənt, trănz-) *adj.* Transmitting light but causing sufficient diffusion to eliminate perception of distinct images. Compare **transparent, opaque.** [Latin *translūcēns,* present participle of *translūcēre,* to shine through : *trāns-,* through + *lūcēre,* to shine (see **leuk-** in Appendix*).] **—trans·lu′cence, trans·lu′cen·cy** *n.* **—trans·lu′cent·ly** *adv.*

trans·ma·rine (trăns′mə-rēn′, trănz′-) *adj.* **1.** Crossing the sea. **2.** Being beyond or coming from across the sea. [Latin *transmarīnus* : *trāns-,* across, beyond + *mare,* sea (see **mori-** in Appendix*).]

trans·mi·grant (trăns-mī′grənt, trănz-) *n.* **1.** One who transmigrates; an immigrant. **2.** An immigrant in transit through a country on his way to the country in which he intends to settle.

trans·mi·grate (trăns-mī′grāt′, trănz-) *intr.v.* **-grated, -grating, -grates.** **1.** To migrate. **2.** To pass into another body after death. Used of the soul. **—trans·mi′gra′tor** (-grā′tər) *n.* **—trans·mi′gra·to′ry** (-mī′grə-tôr′ē, -tōr′ē) *adj.*

trans·mi·gra·tion (trăns′mī-grā′shən, trănz′-) *n.* **1.** The act or process of transmigrating. **2.** The passing of a soul into another body after death; metempsychosis. Also called "transmigration of souls." **—trans′mi·gra′tion·ism′** *n.*

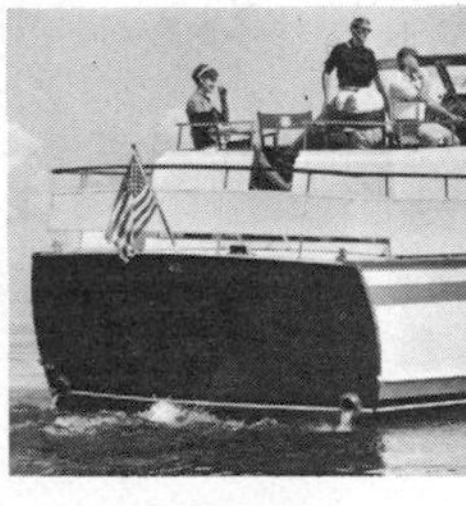
transom
On a modern cabin cruiser

trans·mis·si·ble (trăns-mĭs′ə-bəl, trănz-) *adj.* Capable of being transmitted. **—trans′mis′si·bil′i·ty** *n.*

trans·mis·sion (trăns-mĭsh′ən, trănz-) *n.* **1. a.** The act or process of transmitting. **b.** The state of being transmitted. **2.** Something transmitted, such as a voice or message. **3. a.** An automotive assembly of gears and associated parts by which power is transmitted from the engine to a driving axle. **b.** A system of gears. **4.** *Radio.* The sending of modulated carrier waves from a transmitter; a broadcasting. [Latin *transmissiō,* from *transmissus,* past participle of *transmittere,* TRANSMIT.] **—trans·mis′sive** (-mĭs′ĭv) *adj.*

trans·mit (trăns-mĭt′, trănz-) *v.* **-mitted, -mitting, -mits.** —*tr.* **1.** To send from one person, thing, or place to another; convey. **2.** To cause to spread; pass on: *transmit an infection.* **3.** To impart or convey to others by heredity; hand down. **4.** *Electronics.* To send (a signal), as by wire or radio. **5.** *Physics.* To cause (a disturbance) to propagate through a medium. **6.** To convey (force or energy) from one part of a mechanism to another. —*intr.* To send out a signal. —See Synonyms at **convey.** [Middle English *transmitten,* from Latin *transmittere,* to send across : *trāns-,* across + *mittere,* to send (see **smeit-** in Appendix*).] **—trans·mit′ta·ble, trans·mit′ti·ble** *adj.*

trans·mit·tal (trăns-mĭt′l, trănz-) *n.* The act or process of transmitting; a transmission.

trans·mit·tance (trăns-mĭt′əns, trănz-) *n.* **1.** A transmittal. **2.** *Physics.* The ratio of the radiant energy transmitted to the total radiant energy incident on a given body. Compare **absorptance.**

trans·mit·ter (trăns-mĭt′ər, trănz-) *n.* **1.** One that transmits. **2.** A telegraphic sending instrument. **3.** The portion of a telephone that converts the incident sounds into electrical impulses that are conveyed to a remote receiver. **4.** Electronic equipment that generates and amplifies a carrier wave, modulates it with a meaningful signal, as derived from speech or other sources, and radiates the resulting signal from an antenna.

trans·mog·ri·fy (trăns-mŏg′rə-fī′, trănz-) *tr.v.* **-fied, -fying, -fies.** To change into a different shape or form, especially one that is fantastic or bizarre. [Origin obscure.] **—trans·mog′ri·fi·ca′tion** *n.*

trans·mon·tane (trăns-mŏn′tān′, trănz-, trăns′mŏn-tān′, trănz′-) *adj.* Located beyond a mountain or mountain range; tramontane. [Latin *trānsmontānus,* TRAMONTANE.]

trans·mu·ta·tion (trăns′myo͞o-tā′shən, trănz′-) *n.* **1.** The act of transmuting. **2.** The state of being transmuted. **3.** *Alchemy.* The alleged conversion of base metals into gold or silver. **4.** *Physics.* The transformation of one element into another by one or a series of nuclear reactions. **—trans′mu·ta′tion·al, trans·mut′a·tive** (-myo͞o′tə-tĭv) *adj.*

trans·mute (trăns-myo͞ot′, trănz-) *tr.v.* **-muted, -muting, -mutes.** To change from one form, nature, substance, or state into another; transform. See Synonyms at **change.** [Middle English *transmuten,* from Latin *transmūtāre* : *trāns-,* from one to another + *mūtāre,* to change (see **mei-**[1] in Appendix*).] **—trans·mut′a·bil′i·ty, trans·mut′a·ble·ness** *n.* **—trans·mut′a·ble** *adj.* **—trans·mut′a·bly** *adv.* **—trans·mut′er** *n.*

trans·o·ce·an·ic (trăns′ō-shē-ăn′ĭk, trănz′-) *adj.* **1.** Situated beyond or on the other side of the ocean. **2.** Spanning or crossing the ocean.

tran·som (trăn′səm) *n.* **1. a.** A small hinged window above a door or another window. **b.** The horizontal crosspiece to which such a window is hinged. **2.** A horizontal dividing piece of wood or stone in a window. **3.** *Nautical.* **a.** A transverse beam affixed to the sternpost of a wooden ship and forming part of the stern. **b.** In steel ships, the aftermost transverse structural member including the floor, frame, and beam assembly at the sternpost. **c.** The stern of a square-sterned boat when it is a structural member. **4.** The horizontal beam on a cross or gallows. [Middle English *traunson,* crossbeam, lintel, perhaps from Latin *transtrum* : *trāns,* across (see **ter-**[3] in Appendix*) + *-trum,* suffix denoting an instrument.] **—tran′somed** *adj.*

tran·son·ic (trăn-sŏn′ĭk) *adj.* Of or pertaining to aerodynamic flow or flight conditions at speeds close to the speed of sound. [TRANS- + (SUPER)SONIC.]

Trans·ox·i·an·a. The modern name for **Sogdiana.**

transp. transportation.

trans·pa·cif·ic (trăns′pə-sĭf′ĭk) *adj.* **1.** Crossing the Pacific Ocean. **2.** Situated across or beyond the Pacific Ocean.

trans·par·en·cy (trăns-pâr′ən-sē, -păr′ən-sē) *n., pl.* **-cies.** Also **trans·par·ence** (-pâr′əns, -păr′əns) (for sense 1). **1.** The quality or state of being transparent. **2.** A transparent object; especially, a photographic slide.

trans·par·ent (trăns-pâr′ənt, -păr′ənt) *adj.* **1.** Capable of transmitting light so that objects or images can be seen as if there were no intervening material. Compare **translucent, opaque.** **2.** Permeable to electromagnetic radiation of specified frequencies, as to visible light or radio waves. **3.** Of such fine or open texture that objects may be easily seen on the other side; diaphanous; sheer. **4.** Easily understood or detected; flimsy or obvious: *transparent lies.* **5.** Guileless; candid; open. **6.** *Obsolete.* Shining through; luminous. [Middle English, from Old French, from Medieval Latin *trānspārēns,* present participle of *trānspārēre,* to be seen through : Latin *trāns-,* through + *pārēre,* to show (see **appear.**)] **—trans·par′ent·ly** *adv.* **—trans·par′ent·ness** *n.*

tran·spi·ra·tion (trăn′spə-rā′shən) *n.* The act or process of transpiring, especially through the stomata of plant tissue or the pores of the skin.

tran·spire (trăn-spīr′) *v.* **-spired, -spiring, -spires.** —*tr.* To give off (vapor containing waste products) through the pores of the

skin or the stomata of plant tissue. —*intr.* **1.** To give off vapor containing waste products through animal or plant pores. **2.** To become known; come to light. **3.** To happen; occur. See Usage note. [French *transpirer,* from Old French : Latin *trāns-,* out + *spīrāre,* to breathe (see **spīrāre** in Appendix*).]
Usage: *Transpire,* in the sense of happen, come to pass, or occur, is widely employed but still disputed. It is not acceptable in that sense to 62 per cent of the Usage Panel.

trans·plant (trăns-plănt′, -plänt′) *v.* **-planted, -planting, -plants.** —*tr.* **1.** To uproot and replant (a growing plant). **2.** To transfer from one place or residence to another; resettle; relocate. **3.** *Surgery.* To transfer (tissue or an organ) from one body, or body part, to another. —*intr.* **1.** To engage in transplanting. **2.** To withstand transplanting. —*n.* (trăns′plănt′, -plänt′). **1.** Something transplanted. **2.** The act or process of transplanting. [Middle English *transplaunten,* from Late Latin *trānsplantāre* : Latin *trāns-,* across + *plantāre,* to plant (see **plant**).] —**trans′plan·ta′tion** *n.* —**trans·plant′er** *n.*

trans·po·lar (trăns-pō′lər) *adj.* Extending across or crossing over either of the geographic polar regions.

tran·spond·er (trăn-spŏn′dər) *n.* A radio or radar receiver-transmitter activated for transmission by reception of a predetermined signal. [TRAN(SMITTER) + (RE)SPONDER.]

trans·pon·tine (trăns-pŏn′tīn′) *adj.* **1.** Situated across or beyond a bridge. **2.** Pertaining to the part of London on the south side of the Thames. [TRANS- + Latin *pōns* (stem *pont-*), bridge (see **pent-** in Appendix*) + -INE.]

trans·port (trăns-pôrt′, -pōrt′) *tr.v.* **-ported, -porting, -ports.** **1.** To carry from one place to another; convey. **2.** To move to strong emotion; enrapture; carry away. **3.** To send abroad to a penal colony; deport. —See Synonyms at **banish, convey.** —*n.* (trăns′pôrt′, -pōrt′). **1.** The act of transporting; conveyance. **2.** The state or condition of being transported by emotion; rapture. **3.** A ship used to transport troops or military equipment. **4.** A vehicle, such as an aircraft, used to transport passengers, mail, or freight. **5.** A deported convict. —See Synonyms at **ecstasy.** [Middle English *transporten,* from Old French *transporter,* from Latin *trānsportāre* : *trāns-,* from one place to another + *portāre,* to carry (see **per-**[2] in Appendix*).] —**trans·port′a·bil′i·ty** *n.* —**trans·port′a·ble** *adj.* —**trans·port′er** *n.* —**trans·port′ive** *adj.*

trans·por·ta·tion (trăns′pər-tā′shən) *n. Abbr.* **trans., transp.** **1.** The act of transporting. **2.** The state of being transported. **3. a.** A means of transport; a conveyance. **b.** The business of transporting passengers, goods, materials, or the like. **4.** A charge for transporting; a fare.

trans·pose (trăns-pōz′) *v.* **-posed, -posing, -poses.** —*tr.* **1.** To reverse or transfer the order or place of; to interchange. **2.** To put into a different place or order. **3.** *Mathematics.* To move (a term) from one side of an algebraic equation to the other side, reversing its sign to maintain equality. **4.** *Music.* To write or perform (a composition) in a key other than the original or given key. **5.** *Obsolete.* To transform. —*intr.* **1.** *Music.* To write or perform music in a different key. **2.** To admit of being transposed. —See Synonyms at **reverse.** [Middle English *transposen,* from Old French *transposer* : *trans,* from Latin *trāns-,* from one place to another + *poser,* to place, POSE.] —**trans·pos′a·ble** *adj.* —**trans·pos′er** *n.*

trans·po·si·tion (trăns′pə-zĭsh′ən) *n.* Also **trans·pos·al** (trăns-pō′zəl). *Abbr.* **tr., transp.** **1.** The act of transposing. **2.** The state of being transposed. **3.** Something that has been transposed. —**trans′po·si′tion·al** *adj.*

trans·sex·u·al (trăns-sĕk′shōō-əl) *n.* **1.** A person with an overwhelming desire to become the other sex. **2.** A person whose sex has been changed externally through surgery. —**trans·sex′u·al** *adj.* —**trans·sex′u·al·ism′** *n.*

trans·ship (trăns-shĭp′) *v.* **-shipped, -shipping, -ships.** Also **tran·ship.** —*tr.* To transfer from one vessel or vehicle to another for reshipment. —*intr.* To transfer cargo from one vessel or conveyance to another. —**trans·ship′ment** *n.*

Trans-Si·be·ri·an Railroad (trăns′sī-bîr′ē-ən). A railroad of the Soviet Union, constructed by the Russian government (1891–98) and extending about 4,600 miles from Chelyabinsk in the Ural Mountains to Vladivostok on the Pacific.

tran·sub·stan·ti·ate (trăn′səb-stăn′shē-āt′) *tr.v.* **-ated, -ating, -ates.** **1.** To change (one substance) into another; transmute; transform. **2.** *Theology.* To change the substance of (the Eucharistic bread and wine) into the true presence of Christ. [Medieval Latin *transubstantiāre* : Latin *trāns-,* change + *substantia,* SUBSTANCE.]

tran·sub·stan·ti·a·tion (trăn′səb-stăn′shē-ā′shən) *n.* **1.** *Theology.* The doctrine that the bread and wine of the Eucharist are transformed into the true presence of Christ, although their appearance remains the same. Compare **consubstantiation.** **2.** The conversion of one substance into another; transformation. —**tran′sub·stan′ti·a′tion·al·ist** *n.*

tran·su·date (trăn-sōō′dāt′,-syōō′dāt′, trăn′sōō-dāt′, trăn′syōō-) *n.* Also **tran·su·da·tion** (trăn′sōō-dā′shən, trăn′syōō-) **1.** A substance that transudes. **2.** The act of transuding.

tran·sude (trăn-syōōd′, -sōōd′) *intr.v.* **-suded, -suding, -sudes.** To exude or pass through pores or interstices, in the manner of perspiration. [New Latin *transudare* : Latin *trāns-,* through + *sūdāre,* to sweat (see **sweid-**[2] in Appendix*).] —**tran·su′da·to′ry** (trăn-sōō′də-tôr′ē, -tōr′ē, trăn-syōō′-) *adj.*

trans·u·ran·ic (trăns′yōō-răn′ĭk, trănz′-) *adj.* Also **trans·u·ra·ni·an** (-rā′nē-ən), **trans·u·ra·ni·um** (-nē-ŭm). Having an atomic number greater than 92. [TRANS- + URAN(IUM) + -IC.]

Trans·vaal (trăns-väl′, trănz-). Formerly **South African Republic.** A province of the Republic of South Africa, occupying 110,450 square miles in the northeast. Population, 6,273,000. Capital, Pretoria.

trans·val·ue (trăns-văl′yōō, trănz-) *tr.v.* **-ued, -uing, -ues.** To evaluate by a new standard or principle, especially one that varies from conventional standards. —**trans′val·u·a′tion** *n.*

trans·ver·sal (trăns-vûr′səl, trănz-) *adj.* Transverse. —*n. Geometry.* A line that intercepts a system of lines. Also called "traverse."

trans·verse (trăns-vûrs′, trănz-, trăns′vûrs′, trănz′-) *adj. Abbr.* **trans.** Situated or lying across; athwart; crosswise. —*n. Abbr.* **trans.** Something transverse, such as a part or beam. [Latin *trānsversus,* from the past participle of *trānsvertere,* to turn or direct across : *trāns-,* across + *vertere,* to turn (see **wer-**[3] in Appendix*).] —**trans·verse′ly** *adv.* —**trans·verse′ness** *n.*

transverse colon. The part of the colon that lies across the upper part of the abdominal cavity.

transverse process. A lateral projection from the side of a vertebra.

trans·ves·tism (trăns-vĕs′tĭz′əm, trănz-) *n.* Also **trans·ves·ti·tism** (-vĕs′tə-tĭz′əm). **1.** The abnormal desire to dress in the clothing of the opposite sex. **2.** The act or state of being so dressed.

trans·ves·tite (trăns-vĕs′tīt′, trănz-) *n.* One who experiences transvestism. [German *Transvestit* : Latin *trāns-,* over, across + *vestītus,* past participle of *vestīre,* to dress, from *vestis,* garment (see **wes-**[4] in Appendix*).]

Tran·syl·va·ni·a (trăn′sĭl-vā′nē-ə, -vān′yə). A historic region and former province of central Rumania. —**Tran′syl·va′ni·an** *adj.* & *n.*

Transylvanian Alps. The southern section of the Carpathian Mountains extending about 170 miles in central and southwestern Rumania. Highest elevation, 8,361 feet.

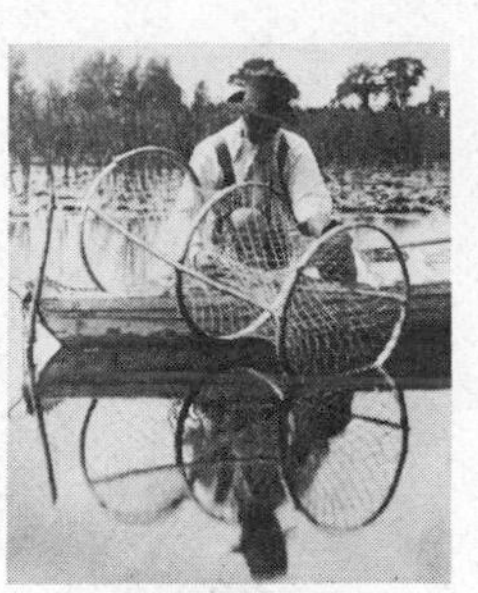

trap[1]
Man with fish trap

trap[1] (trăp) *n.* **1.** A device for catching and holding animals, such as a net, a pitfall, or a clamplike apparatus that springs shut suddenly. **2.** Any stratagem or device for betraying, tricking, or exposing an unsuspecting person. **3. a.** Any receptacle for collecting waste or other materials, as a grease trap; a strainer for residue. **b.** A device for sealing a passage against the escape of gases; especially, a U-shaped or S-shaped bend in a drainpipe that prevents the return flow of sewer gas. **4.** A device that hurls clay pigeons, balls, or disks into the air to be shot at. **5.** *Golf.* A land hazard or bunker; sand trap. **6.** A light two-wheeled carriage with springs. **7.** A **trap door** *(see).* **8.** *Usually plural.* Percussion instruments, such as snare drums, cymbals, or bells. **9.** *Slang.* The mouth. —*v.* **trapped, trapping, traps.** —*tr.* **1.** To catch in or as if in a trap; ensnare. **2.** To place in a confining or embarrassing position. **3.** To seal off (gases) by a trap. **4.** To furnish (a drain) with a trap. —*intr.* **1.** To set traps for game. **2.** To trap fur-bearing animals, especially as a business. [Middle English *trappe,* Old English *træppe.* See **der-**[1] in Appendix.*]

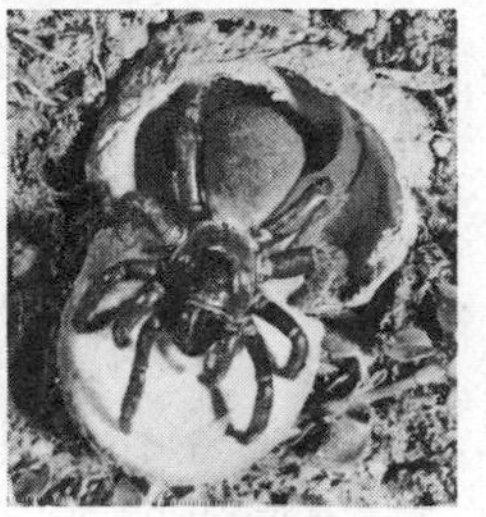

trap-door spider

trap[2] (trăp) *n.* **1.** *Plural. Informal.* Personal belongings or household goods; baggage. **2.** *Usually plural. Obsolete.* Trappings; a caparison. —*tr.v.* **trapped, trapping, traps.** To furnish with trappings. [Middle English *trappe,* probably from Old French *drap,* cloth, from Late Latin *drappus,* from Celtic. See **der-**[2] in Appendix.*]

trap[3] (trăp) *n.* A steplike configuration in igneous rocks, as in basalt. Also called "trap rock," "traprock." [Swedish *trapp,* from *trappa,* step, stair, from Middle Low German *trappe.* See **der-**[1] in Appendix.*]

tra·pan. Variant of **trepan** (to trick).

Tra·pa·ni (trä′pä-nē). Ancient name **Drep·a·num** (drĕp′ə-nəm). A city of Italy, a seaport on the northwestern tip of Sicily. Population, 77,000.

trap door. A hinged or sliding door in a floor, roof, or ceiling.

trap-door spider (trăp′dôr′, -dōr′). Any of various spiders of the family Ctenizidae, that construct a silk-lined burrow concealed by a hinged lid.

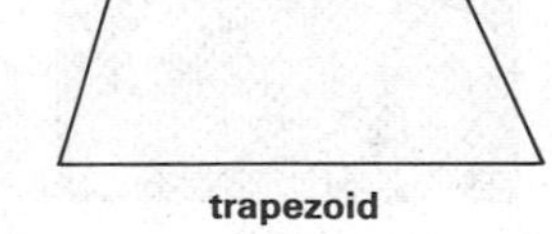

trapezoid

tra·peze (tră-pēz′) *n.* A short horizontal bar suspended from the ends of two parallel ropes, used for exercises or for acrobatic stunts. [French *trapèze,* from Late Latin *trapezium,* TRAPEZIUM.]

tra·pe·zi·form (trə-pē′zə-fôrm′) *adj.* Formed in the shape of a trapezium. [TRAPEZI(UM) + -FORM.]

tra·pe·zi·um (trə-pē′zē-əm) *n., pl.* **-ums** or **-zia** (-zē-ə). **1. a.** A quadrilateral having no parallel sides. **b.** *British.* A **trapezoid** *(see).* **2.** A bone in the wrist at the base of the thumb. [Late Latin, from Greek *trapezion,* small table, diminutive of *trapeza,* table, "four-footed" : *tra-,* four (see **kwetwer-** in Appendix*) + *peza,* foot (see **ped-**[1] in Appendix*).]

tra·pe·zi·us (trə-pē′zē-əs) *n.* Either of two large, flat muscles running from the base of the occiput to the middle of the back that support, and make it possible to raise, the head and shoulders. [New Latin *(musculus) trapezius,* "trapezium-shaped (pair of muscles)," from TRAPEZIUM.]

tra·pe·zo·he·dron (trə-pē′zō-hē′drən, trăp′ə-zō-) *n., pl.* **-drons** or **-dra** (-drə). Any of several forms of crystal with trapeziums as faces. Also called "trisoctahedron." [TRAPEZ(IUM) + -HEDRON.]

trap·e·zoid (trăp′ə-zoid′) *n.* **1.** A quadrilateral having two parallel sides. In British usage, also called "trapezium." **2.** A small bone in the wrist, situated near the base of the index finger. [New Latin *trapezoides,* from Greek *trapezoeidēs,* trapezium-shaped : *trapeza,* table (see **trapezium**) + -OID.] —**trap′e·zoid′,** **trap′e·zoi′dal** *adj.*

trap·pe·an (trăp′ē-ən, trə-pē′ən) *adj.* Also **trap·pous** (trăp′əs), **trap·pose** (-ōs′). *Geology.* Of, pertaining to, resembling, or consisting of trap.

trap·per (trăp′ər) *n.* One whose occupation is trapping animals for their furs.

trap·pings (trăp′ĭngz) *pl.n.* **1.** An ornamental covering or harness for a horse; a caparison. **2.** Articles of dress or adornment.

Trap·pist (trăp′ĭst) *n.* A member of a branch of the Cistercian order of monks, known for austerity and absolute silence, established in 1664 in La Trappe, Normandy. *—adj.* Of or pertaining to the Trappists.

trap·shoot·ing (trăp′sho͞o′tĭng) *n.* The sport of shooting at clay pigeons or glass balls hurled into the air from spring traps. **—trap′shoot′er** *n.*

tra·pun·to (trə-po͝on′tō) *n., pl.* **-tos.** Quilting having a raised effect made by outlining the design with running stitches and then filling it with cotton. [Italian, from the past participle of *trapungere,* to embroider : Latin *trāns-,* through + *pungere,* to prick, pierce (see **peuk-** in Appendix*).]

trash (trăsh) *n.* **1.** Worthless or discarded material or objects; refuse; garbage. **2. a.** Cheap or empty expressions or ideas. **b.** Worthless literary or artistic material. **3.** Something broken off or removed to be discarded; especially, plant trimmings. **4.** A person or group of persons regarded as ignorant or contemptible. *—tr.v.* **trashed, trashing, trashes.** To cut off leaves or branches from; especially, to lop off the outer leaves from (growing sugar cane). [Origin obscure.]

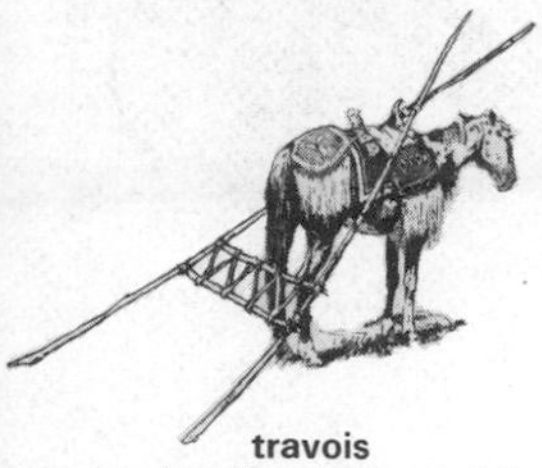

travois
Frederic Remington sketch

trash·y (trăsh′ē) *adj.* **-ier, -iest.** Resembling or of the nature of trash; worthless; inferior. **—trash′i·ly** *adv.* **—trash′i·ness** *n.*

Tra·si·me·no, Lake (trä′zē-mâ′nō). Ancient name **Tras·i·me·nus** (trăs′ə-mē′nəs). A lake occupying 50 square miles in central Italy. On its shores, Hannibal defeated the Romans (217 B.C.). Also called "Lake of Perugia."

trass (trăs) *n.* A light-colored tuff used in hydraulic cement. [Earlier Dutch *terras,* from French *terrasse,* pile of earth, from Old French *terrasse, terrace,* TERRACE.]

trau·ma (trou′mə, trô′-) *n., pl.* **-mas** or **-mata** (-mə-tə). **1.** *Pathology.* A wound, especially one produced by sudden physical injury. **2.** *Psychiatry.* An emotional shock that creates substantial and lasting damage to the psychological development of the individual, generally leading to neurosis. [Greek, wound, hurt. See **ter-**[2] in Appendix.*] **—trau·mat′ic** (-măt′ĭk) *adj.* **—trau·mat′i·cal·ly** *adv.*

trau·ma·tism (trou′mə-tĭz′əm, trô′-) *n.* **1.** An injury. **2.** A wound produced by injury; trauma.

trau·ma·tize (trou′mə-tīz′, trô′-) *tr.v.* **-tized, -tizing, -tizes. 1.** To wound or injure. **2.** To damage the psychological development of (an individual).

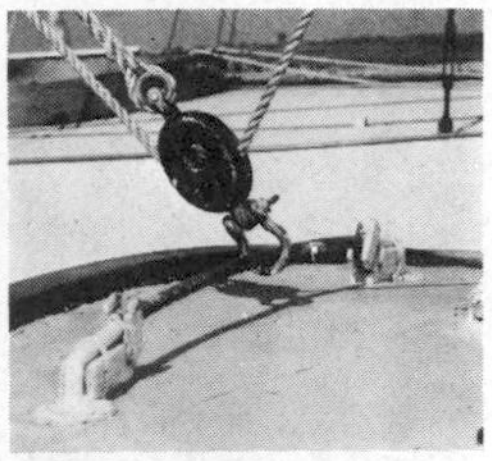

traveler

trav. traveler; travels.

tra·vail[1] (trə-vāl′, trăv′āl′) *n.* **1.** Strenuous mental or physical exertion; labor; toil. **2.** Tribulation or agony; anguish. **3.** The labor of childbirth. —See Synonyms at **work.** *—intr.v.* **travailed, -vailing, -vails. 1.** To labor strenuously; to toil. **2.** To be in the labor of childbirth. [Middle English, from Old French, from *travailler,* to work hard, from Vulgar Latin *tripāliāre* (unattested), to torture, from *tripālium* (unattested), torture instrument (made of three stakes), from Latin *tripālis,* having three stakes : *tri-,* three + *pālus,* stake (see **pag-** in Appendix*).]

tra·vail[2] (trə-vāl′) *n.* A primitive sledge, a **travois** *(see).*

Trav·an·core (trăv′ən-kôr′, -kōr′). A former princely state, later part of Travancore-Cochin State, India.

Trav·an·core-Co·chin (trăv′ən-kôr′kō′chĭn, trăv′ən-kōr′-, -kŏch′ĭn). A former state of southwestern India, mostly in Kerala since 1956.

trave (trāv) *n.* **1.** A wooden frame for confining a horse being shod. **2.** *Architecture.* **a.** A crossbeam. **b.** A section, as of a ceiling, formed by crossbeams. [Middle English, from Old French, stake, beam, from Latin *trabs.* See **treb-** in Appendix.*]

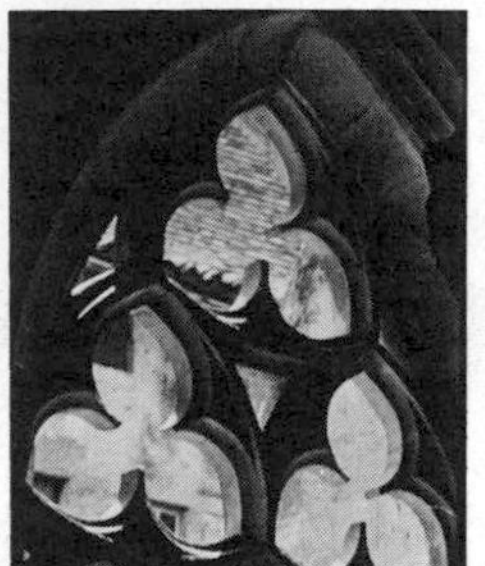

trefoil
In a window of the cloister of Chartreuse de Villefranche de Rouergue, southern France

trav·el (trăv′əl) *v.* **-eled** or **-elled, -eling** or **-elling, -els.** *—intr.* **1.** To go from one place to another; to journey. **2.** To journey from one place to another as a traveling salesman. **3.** To be transmitted; move, as light. **4.** To keep or be in company; to associate: *travel in wealthy circles.* **5.** To admit of being transported: *Some wines travel poorly.* **6.** *Informal.* To move swiftly. **7.** *Basketball.* To walk or run illegally while holding the ball. After two steps, the player must remain in position unless the ball is dribbled. *—tr.* To pass or journey over or through; to traverse. *—n.* **1.** The act or process of traveling. **2.** *Plural. Abbr.* **trav. a.** A series of journeys. **b.** A written account of these. **3.** Activity or traffic along a route or through a given point. [Middle English *travailen,* to toil, make a (toilsome) journey, from Old French *travailler,* to TRAVAIL.]

trav·eled (trăv′əld) *adj.* **1.** Having traveled widely; experienced in travel. **2.** Much frequented by travelers.

trav·el·er (trăv′əl-ər, trăv′lər) *n. Abbr.* **trav. 1. a.** A person who is traveling. **b.** One who has traveled or who customarily travels. **2.** *Chiefly British.* A traveling salesman. **3.** *Nautical.* **a.** A metal ring that moves freely back and forth on a rope, rod, or spar. **b.** The rope, rod, or spar on which such a ring moves.

traveler's check. An internationally redeemable draft purchasable from a bank, express company, or travel agency, in various denominations, valid only with the holder's own endorsement against his original signature.

trav·el·er's-joy (trăv′əl-ərz-joi′, trăv′lərz-) *n.* Any of several climbing vines of the genus *Clematis;* especially, *C. vitalba,* of the Old World, having clusters of white flowers.

traveling salesman. A salesman who solicits business orders or sells merchandise through personal dealings with potential customers within a given territory.

trav·e·logue (trăv′ə-lôg′, -lŏg′) *n.* Also **trav·e·log. 1.** A lecture illustrated by travel slides or films. **2.** A narrated motion picture about travels. [TRAVEL + -LOGUE.]

Trav·ers (trăv′ərz), **P(amela) L.** Born 1904. Australian-born English author; creator of Mary Poppins.

trav·erse (trăv′ərs, trə-vûrs′) *v.* **-ersed, -ersing, -erses.** *—tr.* **1.** To travel across, over, or through. **2.** To move forward and backward over; cross and recross. **3.** To go up, down, or across (a hill, for example) at an angle. **4.** To move (a gun, for example) laterally; cause to swivel. **5.** To extend across; to cross. **6.** To look over carefully; examine. **7.** To go counter to; thwart. **8.** *Law.* **a.** To deny formally (an allegation of fact by the opposition) in a suit. **b.** To join issue upon (an indictment). **9.** To make a traverse survey of. **10.** *Nautical.* To brace (a yard) fore and aft. *—intr.* **1.** To move or go along, across, or back and forth. **2.** To turn laterally; swivel. **3.** To descend a slope in a zigzag manner, as in skiing. **4.** *Fencing.* To glide or pressure one's blade toward the hilt of the opponent's weapon. *—n.* **1. a.** The act of traversing; a passing across, over, or through. **b.** A route or path across. **2.** Something lying across something else, especially: **a.** An intersecting line, a **transversal** *(see).* **b.** *Architecture.* A structural crosspiece; transom. **c.** *Architecture.* A gallery, deck, or loft crossing from one side of a building to the other. **d.** A railing, curtain, or screen. **e.** A defensive barrier across a rampart or trench, as a bank of earth thrown up for protection from enfilade fire. **3.** Something that obstructs and thwarts; an obstacle. **4. a.** *Nautical.* The zigzag route of a vessel forced by contrary winds to sail on different courses. **b.** The zigzag course made by a skier on a steep slope. **5.** The horizontal swivel of a mounted gun. **6. a.** A lateral movement, as of a lathe tool across a piece of work. **b.** A part of a mechanism that moves in this manner. **7.** *Surveying.* A line established by sighting in the measurement of a tract of land. **8.** *Law.* The formal denial of an allegation of fact in a suit. *—adj.* **1.** Lying or extending across; transverse. **2.** Relating to the installation or operation of draperies that can be drawn: *a traverse rod; a traverse cord.* *—adv. Obsolete.* Crosswise; transversely. [Middle English *traversen,* from Old French *traverser,* from Late Latin *trā(ns)versāre,* from Latin *trānsversus,* TRANSVERSE.] **—trav′ers·a·ble** *adj.* **—tra·vers′al** (trə-vûr′səl) *n.* **—trav′ers·er** *n.*

trav·er·tine (trăv′ər-tēn′, -tĭn) *n.* **1.** A light-colored, porous calcite, $CaCO_3$, deposited from solution in ground or surface waters and forming, among other deposits, the stalactites and stalagmites of caverns. **2.** A compact type of calcium carbonate, creamy-colored and similarly formed, used as a facing material in construction. [Italian *travertino,* earlier *tibertino,* from Latin *(lapis) Tīburtīnus,* "(stone) of Tibur."]

trav·es·ty (trăv′ĭ-stē) *n., pl.* **-ties. 1.** An exaggerated or grotesque imitation with intent to ridicule; a burlesque. **2.** *Literature.* A broad and grotesque parody on a lofty work or theme. —See Synonyms at **caricature.** *—tr.v.* **travestied, -tying, -ties.** To make a travesty on or of; to ridicule. [French *travesti,* past participle of *travestir,* to ridicule, from Italian *travestire,* "to disguise" : *tra-,* across, from Latin *trāns-,* indicates change + *vestire,* to dress, from Latin *vestīre,* from *vestis,* garment (see **wes-**[4] in Appendix*).]

Trav·is (trăv′ĭs), **William Barret.** 1809–1836. American military leader; commander at the Alamo.

tra·vois (trə-voi′, trăv′oi′) *n., pl.* **travois** (trə-voiz′, trăv′oiz′) or **travoises** (trə-voi′zĭz, trăv′oi′zĭz). Also **tra·voise** (trə-voiz′, trăv′oiz′). A primitive sledge formerly used by Plains Indians and consisting of a platform or netting supported by two long trailing poles, the forward ends of which are fastened to a dog or horse. Also called "travail." [Canadian French, variant of French *travail,* perhaps from *travail,* frame to restrain restive horses for shodding, from Vulgar Latin *tripālium* (unattested). See **travail.**]

trawl (trôl) *n.* **1.** A large, tapered fishing net of flattened conical shape, towed along the sea bottom. Also called "trawl net." **2.** A multiple fishing line, a **setline** *(see).* Also called "trawl line." *—v.* **trawled, trawling, trawls.** *—tr.* To catch (fish) by means of a trawl. *—intr.* **1.** To fish with a trawl net or line. **2.** To troll. [Perhaps from Dutch *tragel,* dragnet, from Middle Dutch *traghel,* from Latin *trāgula,* from *trahere,* to pull, draw. See **tragh-** in Appendix.*]

trawl·er (trô′lər) *n.* **1.** A boat used for trawling. **2.** One who trawls.

tray (trā) *n.* A flat, shallow receptacle of wood, metal, or the like, with a raised edge or rim, used for carrying, holding, or displaying articles. [Middle English *tray,* Old English *trīg, trēg.* See **deru-** in Appendix.*]

treach·er·ous (trĕch′ər-əs) *adj.* **1.** Betraying a trust; traitorous; disloyal. **2. a.** Not to be relied upon; not dependable. **b.** Not to be trusted; deceptive; dangerous: *treacherous waters.* **—treach′er·ous·ly** *adv.* **—treach′er·ous·ness** *n.*

treach·er·y (trĕch′ə-rē) *n., pl.* **-ies. 1.** Willful betrayal of fidelity, confidence, or trust; perfidy; treason. **2.** An act or instance of this. [Middle English *trecherie, tricherie,* from Old French, from *trichier,* to TRICK.]

trea·cle (trē′kəl) *n.* **1. a.** *British.* Molasses. **b.** A kind of syrup. **2.** A medicinal compound formerly used as an antidote for poison. **3.** Cloying speech or sentiment. [Middle English *triacle,* antidote for poison, from Old French, from Latin *thēriaca,* from Greek *(antidotos) thēriakē,* from *thērion,* poisonous beast, diminutive of *thēr,* beast. See **ghwer-** in Appendix.*] **—trea′cly** (-klē) *adj.*

tread (trĕd) *v.* **trod** (trŏd) or *archaic* **trode** (trōd), **trodden** (trŏd′n) or **trod, treading, treads.** *—tr.* **1.** To walk on, over, or along. **2.** To press beneath the foot; trample. **3.** To treat or put down harshly or cruelly; crush forcibly; oppress; subdue. **4.** To make by walking or trampling, as a path. **5.** To execute by walking or dancing: *tread a measure.* **6.** To copulate with. Used of male birds. *—intr.* **1.** To go on foot; walk; step. **2.** To trample so as to press, crush, or injure. Used with *on* or *upon.* **3.** To copulate. Used of birds. **—tread on (someone's) toes.** To offend someone. **—tread water.** *Past tense* **treaded water.** *Swimming.* To maintain one's head above water while in an upright position by moving the feet up and down as if walking. *—n.* **1. a.** The act, manner, or sound of treading. **b.** An instance of treading; a step. **2.** The horizontal part of a step in a staircase. **3.** The part of a wheel that makes contact with the ground or rails. **4.** The grooved face of an automobile tire. **5.** The part of a sole of a shoe that touches the ground. [Tread, trod (or trode), trodden; Middle English *treden, trode* (or *trade*), *troden,* Old English *tredan, træd* (plural *trǣdon*), *treden.* See **der-**[1] in Appendix.*] **—tread′er** *n.*

tread·le (trĕd′l) *n.* A pedal or lever operated by the foot for circular drive, as in a potter's wheel or sewing machine. *—intr.v.* **treadled, -ling, -les.** To work a treadle. [Middle English *tredel,* Old English *tredel,* step of a stair, from *tredan,* TREAD.] **—tread′ler** (trĕd′lər) *n.*

tread·mill (trĕd′mĭl′) *n.* **1.** A mechanism operated by one or more persons walking on the moving steps of a wheel, or treading an endless sloping belt, used formerly as a prisoner's punishment. **2.** A similar device operated by an animal. **3.** Any monotonous task or routine.

treas. treasurer; treasury.

trea·son (trē′zən) *n.* **1.** Violation of allegiance toward one's sovereign or country; especially, the betrayal of one's own country by waging war against it or by consciously and purposely acting to aid its enemies. **2.** *Rare.* Any betrayal of trust or confidence; treachery. [Middle English *treison,* from Norman French *tre(i)soun,* from Medieval Latin *trāditiō,* from Latin, a handing over. See **tradition.**]

trea·son·a·ble (trē′zən-ə-bəl) *adj.* Pertaining to or involving treason. **—trea′son·a·ble·ness** *n.* **—trea′son·a·bly** *adv.*

trea·son·ous (trē′zən-əs) *adj.* Treasonable; treacherous. **—trea′son·ous·ly** *adv.*

treas·ure (trĕzh′ər) *n.* **1.** Accumulated, stored, or cached wealth in the form of valuables, such as money or jewels. **2.** A person or thing considered especially precious or valuable. *—tr.v.* **treasured, -uring, -ures. 1.** To accumulate and save for future use; to hoard. **2.** To value highly. —See Synonyms at **appreciate.** [Middle English *tresor,* from Old French, from Vulgar Latin *tresaurus* (unattested), variant of Latin *thēsaurus,* from Greek *thēsauros*†.] **—treas′ure·a·ble** *adj.*

Treasure Island. An artificial island in San Francisco Bay, used as a U.S. naval base.

treas·ur·er (trĕzh′ər-ər) *n. Abbr.* **tr., treas.** A person having charge of funds or revenues; especially, a financial officer or recorder for a government, corporation, or society. [Middle English *tresourer,* from Old French *tresorier,* from *tresor,* TREASURE.] **—treas′ur·er·ship′** *n.*

treas·ure-trove (trĕzh′ər-trōv′) *n.* **1.** *Law.* Any treasure found hidden and not claimed by its owner. **2.** Any discovery of great value. [Norman French *tresor trove,* "discovered treasure" : Old French *tresor,* TREASURE + *trove,* past participle of *trover,* to find, compose (see **trouvère**).]

treas·ur·y (trĕzh′ə-rē) *n., pl.* **-ies.** *Abbr.* **treas. 1.** A place where treasure is kept or stored. **2.** A place where private or public funds are received, kept, managed, and disbursed. **3.** Such funds or revenues. **4.** Any collection of valuables or things considered as valuable. **5.** *Capital* **T.** The executive department of a government in charge of the collection, management, and expenditure of the public revenue. [Middle English *tresorie,* from Old French, from *tresor,* TREASURE.]

treasury note. A note or bill issued by the U.S. Treasury as legal tender for all debts.

treat (trēt) *v.* **treated, treating, treats.** *—tr.* **1.** To act or behave in a specified manner toward. **2.** To regard or consider in a certain way. Usually used with *as.* **3.** To deal with in writing or speech; expound: *treat astronomical questions.* **4.** To deal with or represent in a specified manner or style, as in art or literature: *treat a subject poetically.* **5.** To entertain at one's own expense: *treat her to the theater.* **6.** To subject to some process, action, or change, especially: **a.** To give medical aid to. **b.** To subject to a chemical or physical process or application. *—intr.* **1.** To deal with a subject or topic in writing, speaking, or thought. Usually used with *of: The essay treats of courtly love.* **2.** To pay for another's entertainment, food, or the like. **3.** To negotiate; bargain. Used with *with.* *—n.* **1.** Something, as food or entertainment, generously paid for by someone else. **2.** The act of providing a treat, especially in return: *It's my turn to treat today.* **3.** Anything considered a special delight or pleasure. [Middle English *treten,* from Old French *traitier* (French *traiter*), from Latin *tractāre,* to drag, handle, treat, frequentative of *trahere* (past participle *tractus*), to draw, drag. See **tragh-** in Appendix.*] **—treat′a·ble** *adj.* **—treat′er** *n.*

trea·tise (trē′tĭs) *n.* **1.** A formal account in writing treating systematically of some subject. **2.** *Obsolete.* A tale; narrative. [Middle English *tretis,* from Norman French, from Old French *traitier,* TREAT.]

treat·ment (trēt′mənt) *n.* **1.** The act or manner of treating something, such as a person or a subject. **2.** The application of remedies with the object of effecting a cure; therapy.

trea·ty (trē′tē) *n., pl.* **-ties. 1. a.** A formal agreement between two or more states containing terms of trade, peace, alliance, or the like; a pact. **b.** A document embodying this. **2.** Any contract or agreement. **3.** *Obsolete.* Negotiation for the purpose of reaching an agreement. **4.** *Obsolete.* An entreaty. [Middle English *tretee,* from Old French *traite,* from Medieval Latin *tractātus,* from Latin, past participle of *tractāre,* TREAT.]

treaty port. Formerly, a port kept open for trade according to the terms of a treaty; especially, in China, any of several such ports open to foreign commerce.

Treb·bia (trĕb′byä). Ancient name **Tre·bi·a** (trē′bē-ə). A river of northwestern Italy, rising near Genoa and flowing 70 miles generally northeast to the Po; the site of a battle in which Hannibal defeated the Romans (218 B.C.).

Treb·i·zond (trĕb′ə-zŏnd′). *Turkish* **Trab·zon** (träb-zôn′). **1.** A province occupying 1,753 square miles in northeastern Turkey, that was an independent Byzantine state from 1204 to 1461. Population, 532,000. **2.** The capital of this province, a seaport on the Black Sea. Population, 53,000.

treb·le (trĕb′əl) *adj.* **1.** Triple; threefold. **2.** *Music.* Of, having, or performing the highest part, voice, or range. **3.** High-pitched; shrill. *—n.* **1.** *Music.* **a.** The highest part, voice, instrument, or range; soprano. **b.** A singer or player that performs this part. **2.** A high, shrill sound or voice. *—v.* **trebled, -ling, -les.** *—tr.* To make triple. *—intr.* To become triple. [Middle English, from Old French, from Latin *triplus,* TRIPLE.] **—treb′le·ness** *n.* **—treb′ly** (trĕb′lē) *adv.*

treble clef. *Music.* A symbol centered on the second line of the staff to indicate the position of G above middle C. Also called "G clef."

treb·u·chet (trĕb′yə-shĕt′) *n.* Also **treb·uc·ket** (trĕb′ə-kĕt′). A medieval catapult for throwing heavy stones. [Middle English, from Old French, trap, pitfall, from *trebucher,* to stumble, overturn : *tre-,* over, from Latin *trāns-* + *buc,* trunk of the body, from (unattested) Frankish *būk* (see **beu-**[1] in Appendix*).]

tre·cen·to (trā-chĕn′tō) *n.* The 14th century, with reference especially to Italian art and literature. [Italian, "three hundred," short for *(mil) trecento,* (one thousand) three hundred : *tre,* three, from Latin *trēs* (see **trei-** in Appendix*) + *cento,* hundred, from Latin *centum* (see **dekm̥** in Appendix*).]

tree (trē) *n.* **1.** A usually tall woody plant, distinguished from a shrub by having comparatively greater height and, characteristically, a single trunk rather than several stems. **2.** Broadly, a plant or shrub resembling a tree in form or size. **3.** A wooden beam, post, stake, or bar used as a part of a framework or structure. **4.** *Archaic.* A gallows; gibbet. **5.** *Often capital* **T.** *Archaic.* The cross on which Jesus was crucified. **6.** A **saddletree** *(see).* **7.** Something suggestive of a tree: *a clothes tree.* **8.** A diagram showing a family lineage; family tree. **9.** A **Christmas tree** *(see).* **—up a tree.** *Informal.* In a situation of confusion or embarrassment from which there is no retreat. *—tr.v.* **treed, treeing, trees. 1.** To force to climb a tree in evasion of pursuit. **2.** *Informal.* To force into a difficult position; to corner. **3.** To stretch (shoes) on a shoetree. [Middle English *tree,* Old English *treo(w).* See **deru-** in Appendix.*]

Tree (trē), Sir **Herbert Beerbohm.** Original name, Herbert Beerbohm. 1853–1917. British actor and theatrical producer.

tree fern. Any of various treelike tropical ferns, especially of the family Cyatheaceae, having a woody, trunklike stem and a terminal crown of large, divided fronds.

tree frog. Any of various small, arboreal frogs of the genus *Hyla* and related genera, having long toes terminating in adhesive disks. Also called "tree toad."

tree heath. A shrub or tree, the **briar** *(see).*

tree·hop·per (trē′hŏp′ər) *n.* Any of various diversely shaped insects of the family Membracidae, that are sometimes damaging to plants.

tree line. 1. The limit of northern or southern latitude beyond which trees do not grow except as stunted forms. **2.** The **timberline** *(see).*

tree·nail (trē′nāl′, trĕn′əl, trŭn′əl) *n.* Also **tre·nail, trun·nel** (trŭn′əl). A wooden peg which swells when wet, used to fasten timbers, especially in shipbuilding.

tree of heaven. A tree, the **ailanthus** *(see).*

tree of knowledge. The tree in the Garden of Eden whose forbidden fruit Adam and Eve ate, causing loss of innocence. Genesis 2:9, 17; 3:6. Also called "tree of knowledge of good and evil."

tree of life. 1. The **arborvitae** *(see).* **2.** A tree in the Garden of Eden whose fruit, if eaten, gave man immortality. Genesis 3:22.

tree poppy. A shrub, *Dendromecon rigidum,* of southern California, having evergreen foliage and showy, golden-yellow flowers. Also called "bush poppy."

tree shrew. Any of various primates of the family Tupaiidae, of eastern Asia, generally resembling squirrels in habit and appearance.

tree surgery. The treatment of diseased or damaged trees by filling cavities, pruning, and bracing branches. **—tree surgeon.**

tref (trāf) *adj.* Unclean and unfit for consumption according to Jewish dietary law, as pork, lobster, or venison. Compare **kosher.** [Yiddish *treyf,* from Hebrew *terēphāh,* "torn," flesh of an animal torn by wild beasts, from *táraf,* to tear.]

tre·foil (trē′foil′, trĕf′oil′) *n.* **1.** Any of various plants of the genera *Trifolium, Lotus,* and related genera, having compound leaves with three leaflets. **2.** Any ornament, symbol, or architectural form having the appearance of a trifoliate leaf. [Middle English, from Norman French *trifoil,* from Latin *trifolium,* three-leaved grass : *tri-,* three + *folium,* leaf (see **bhel-**[3] in Appendix*).]

tre·ha·la (trĭ-hä′lə) *n.* A sugarlike, edible substance obtained from the pupal case of an Old World beetle, *Larinus maculatus.* [New Latin, from Turkish *tīgāla,* from Persian *tīghāl*†.]

tre·ha·lose (trĭ-hä′lōs′, -lōz′) *n.* A sweet-tasting, crystalline disaccharide, $C_{12}H_{22}O_{11} \cdot 2H_2O$, found in trehala and in many

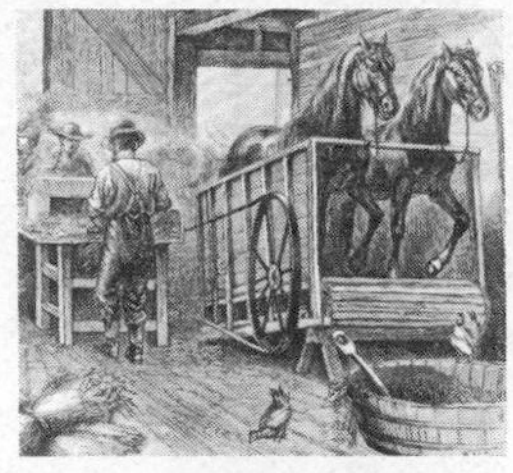

treadmill
Horse-powered treadmill

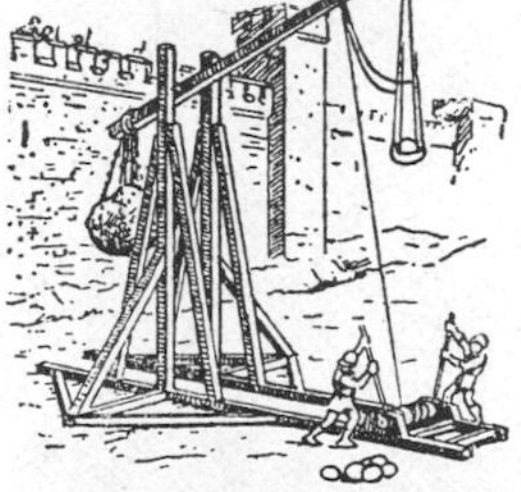

trebuchet

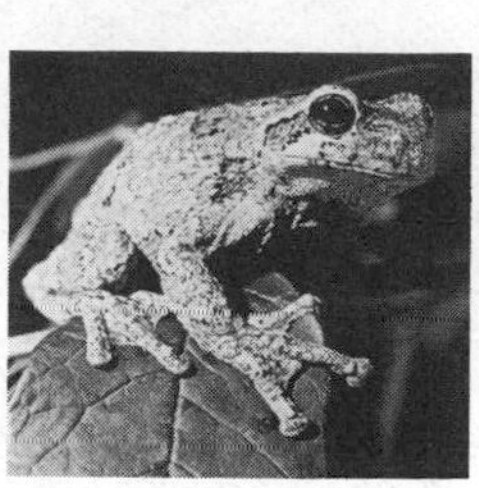

tree frog

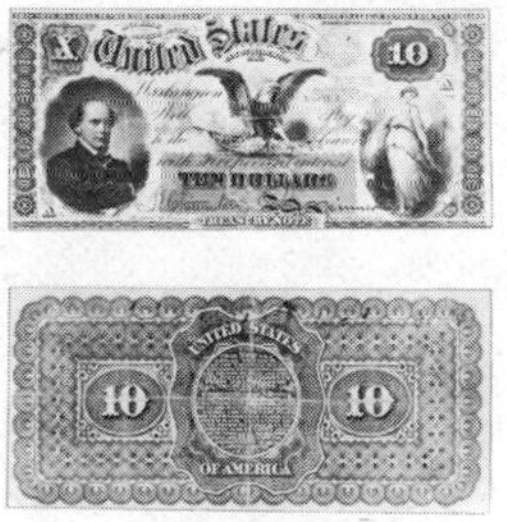

treasury note
The two sides of the 1863 ten-dollar treasury note

fungi that store it instead of starch. [TREHAL(A) + -OSE.]

treil·lage (trĕ-yäzh′, trā′lĭj) n. Latticework, especially, a trellis for vines. [French, from Old French, from *treille*, arbor, from Latin *trichila*†, bower, arbor.]

trek (trĕk) intr.v. **trekked, trekking, treks. 1.** To make a slow or arduous journey: *"trekking with camera and microphone through the darkest TV networks"* (Jack Paar). **2.** In South Africa, to travel by ox wagon. —n. **1.** A journey or leg of a journey, especially when slow or difficult. **2.** A migration. **3.** A journey by ox wagon in South Africa. [Afrikaans, from Middle Dutch *trekken*, to pull, draw, travel, akin to Old High German *trechan*†.] —**trek′ker** n.

Usage: Trek, as noun and verb, is widely used on all levels in the general sense of travel involving slow, difficult going. It is acceptable in that sense to 78 per cent of the Usage Panel in the following, as an example in writing: *The daily trek to midtown Manhattan takes about an hour and a half.* The usage is often employed humorously. Even so, *trek* is used loosely when it refers to any trip or travel, or as the equivalent of *go.*

Tre·law·ny (trĭ-lô′nē), **Edward John.** 1792–1881. British adventurer; companion of Shelley and Byron.

trel·lis (trĕl′ĭs) n. **1.** A frame supporting open latticework, used for training vines and other creeping plants. **2.** An arbor or arch made with this structure. —tr.v. **trellised, -lising, -lises. 1.** To provide with a trellis; especially, to train (a plant) on a trellis. **2.** To make in the form of a trellis. [Middle English *trelis*, from Old French *treliz*, a coarse fabric, later (influenced by *treillage*, TREILLAGE) trellis, from Vulgar Latin *trilīcius* (unattested), from Latin *trilix*, triple-twilled : *tri-*, three + *līcium*†, thread.]

trel·lis·work (trĕl′ĭs-wûrk′) n. Latticework.

trem·a·tode (trĕm′ə-tōd′) n. Any of numerous parasitic flatworms of the class Trematoda, having a thick outer cuticle, and one or more suckers for attaching to host tissue. Also called "fluke." —adj. Of or belonging to the Trematoda. [New Latin *Trematoda*, from Greek *trēmatōdēs*, having a vent to the intestinal canal (taken to mean "having holes," perhaps from the cavity of the suckers) : *trēma*, perforation (see ter-² in Appendix*) + -ODE (like).]

trem·ble (trĕm′bəl) intr.v. **-bled, -bling, -bles. 1.** To shake involuntarily, as from fear, cold, or sickness; to quake; shiver; shake. **2.** To feel or express fear or anxiety: *I tremble to think of it.* **3.** To vibrate; to quiver: *The leaves trembled in the wind.* —See Synonyms at **shake.** —n. **1.** The act or state of trembling. **2.** *Sometimes plural.* A convulsive fit of trembling. **3.** *Plural. Veterinary Medicine.* **a.** A viral encephalomyelitis of sheep. Also called "louping ill." Usually used with a singular verb. **b.** Poisoning of domestic animals, especially cattle and sheep, caused by eating white snakeroot. Also called "milk sickness." Usually used with a singular verb. [Middle English *trem(b)len*, from Old French *trembler*, from Vulgar Latin *tremulāre* (unattested), from Latin *tremulus*, TREMULOUS.] —**trem′bler** n. —**trem′bling·ly** adv. —**trem′bly** adj.

tre·men·dous (trĭ-mĕn′dəs) adj. **1.** Capable of making one tremble; terrible: *the tremendous tragedy of war.* **2. a.** Extremely large in amount, extent, or degree; enormous: *a tremendous task.* **b.** *Informal.* Marvelous; wonderful: *We had a tremendous time.* —See Synonyms at **enormous.** [Latin *tremendus*, gerundive of *tremere*, to tremble. See trem- in Appendix.*] —**tre·men′dous·ly** adv. —**tre·men′dous·ness** n.

trem·o·lite (trĕm′ə-līt′) n. A white to dark-gray calcium magnesium amphibole, $Ca_2Mg_5Si_8O_{22}(OH)_2$, usually occurring in aggregates, used as a substitute for asbestos and in paints and ceramics. [French *trémolite*, first found in *Tremola*, valley in southern Switzerland.]

trem·o·lo (trĕm′ə-lō′) n., pl. **-los.** *Music.* **1. a.** A tremulous effect produced by the rapid repetition of a single tone. **b.** A similar effect produced by the rapid alternation of two tones. **2.** A device on an organ for producing this tone. Also called "tremolant," "tremulant." **3.** A vibrato in singing, used for emotional effect or resulting from poor vocal control. Compare **trill, vibrato.** [Italian, "tremulous," from Latin *tremulus*, TREMULOUS.]

trem·or (trĕm′ər) n. **1.** A quick shaking or vibrating movement: *an earth tremor.* **2.** An involuntary trembling motion of the body: *He suffered from a nervous tremor.* **3.** A nervous quiver or shiver; a thrill: *"A tremor ran through him, like a shudder passing over the sea"* (J.M. Barrie). **4.** A state of nervous agitation or tension: *all in a tremor.* **5.** A tremulous sound; a quaver. [Middle English *tremour*, from Old French, from Latin *tremor*, from *tremere*, to tremble. See trem- in Appendix.*]

trem·u·lous (trĕm′yə-ləs) adj. Also **trem·u·lant** (-lənt), **trem·u·lent** (for sense 1). **1.** Vibrating or quivering; trembling. **2.** Timid; fearful; timorous. [Latin *tremulus*, from *tremere*, to tremble. See trem- in Appendix.*] —**trem′u·lous·ly** adv. —**trem′u·lous·ness** n.

tre·nail. Variant of **treenail.**

trench (trĕnch) n. **1.** A deep furrow. **2.** A ditch. **3.** A long, narrow, crooked ditch embanked with its own soil and used for concealment and protection in warfare. —v. **trenched, trenching, trenches.** —tr. **1.** To cut or dig a trench or trenches in. **2.** To fortify with a trench or trenches. **3.** To put into a trench. **4.** To cut. **5.** To slash, sever, slice, or gash by cutting. —intr. **1.** To dig a trench or ditch: *Torrents trenched the mountain.* **2.** To cut, carve, or slash. **3.** To verge or encroach. Used with *on* or *upon.* [Middle English *trenche*, long narrow ditch, path cut through, from Old French, from *trenchier*, to cut, dig, probably from Vulgar Latin *trincāre* (unattested), from Latin

truncāre, to mutilate, from *truncus*, torso. See ter-³ in Appendix.*]

trench·ant (trĕn′chənt) adj. **1.** Keen; incisive; penetrating: *a trenchant comment.* **2.** Forceful; effective; vigorous: *a trenchant argument.* **3.** Distinct; sharply defined; clear-cut. —See Synonyms at **incisive.** [Middle English, cutting, from Old French, present participle of *trenchier*, to cut. See **trench.**] —**trench′an·cy** n. —**trench′ant·ly** adv.

trench coat. A loose-fitting, belted raincoat having many pockets and flaps, suggesting a military style.

trench·er¹ (trĕn′chər) n. **1.** A wooden board or plate on which food is cut or served. **2.** *Obsolete.* One who carves meat. [Middle English *trenchour*, cutting board, from Norman French, from Old French *trenchier*, to cut. See **trench.**]

trench·er² (trĕn′chər) n. One that digs trenches.

trench·er·man (trĕn′chər-mən) n., pl. **-men** (-mĭn). **1.** A hearty eater. **2.** *Archaic.* One who frequents another's table; hanger-on. [From TRENCHER (board).]

trench fever. An acute infectious relapsing fever caused by a microorganism, *Rickettsia quintana*, and transmitted by a louse, *Pediculus humanus humanus.* [From its occurrence among soldiers living in trenches.]

trench foot. Frostbite of the feet, often afflicting soldiers obliged to stand in cold water over long periods of time. [From its occurrence among soldiers living in trenches.]

trench knife. A knife, used in warfare, having a short, double-edged blade.

trench mortar. *Military.* A mortar (see).

trench mouth. A form of gingivitis characterized by pain, foul odor, and the formation of a gray film over the diseased area. Also called "Vincent's disease." [From its occurrence among soldiers living in trenches.]

trend (trĕnd) n. **1.** A direction of movement; a course; flow: *a trend of thought.* **2.** A general inclination or tendency: *"A noticeable trend away from narrow 'laws of learning' "* (Gertrude Hildreth). —See Synonyms at **tendency.** —intr.v. **trended, trending, trends. 1.** To extend, bend, turn, or move in a specified direction: *The prevailing wind trends east-northeast.* **2.** To have a general tendency; tend. [From Middle English *trenden*, to turn, roll, revolve, Old English *trendan*, from Germanic *trand-* (unattested).]

Treng·ga·nu (trĕng-gä′nōō). A state of Malaysia, occupying 5,050 square miles along the eastern coast of the Malay Peninsula. Population, 346,000. Capital, Kuala Trengganu.

Trent¹ (trĕnt). The third-longest river of England (170 miles), rising in Staffordshire and flowing generally northeast to the Ouse with which it forms the Humber.

Trent² (trĕnt). *Italian* **Tren·to** (trĕn′tō). The capital of Trentino-Alto Adige, northern Italy, on the Adige River in the south-central part of the region. Population, 50,000.

Trent, Council of. A council of the Roman Catholic Church at Trent, Italy, held discontinuously between 1545 and 1563, which attempted to find a political solution to the Reformation, clarified Catholic doctrine, and initiated reform within the Church.

trente et qua·rante (tränt′ ā′ kä-ränt′). A gambling game, *rouge et noir* (see).

Tren·ti·no-Al·to A·di·ge (trĕn-tē′nō-äl′tō ä′dē-jä). A region of Italy, occupying 5,252 square miles in the northeast. Population, 785,000. Capital, Trent.

Tren·ton (trĕn′tən). The capital of New Jersey, on the Delaware River in the western part of the state. Population, 116,000.

tre·pan¹ (trĭ-păn′) n. **1.** *Mining.* A rock-boring tool used for sinking shafts. **2.** *Surgery.* A trephine (see). —tr.v. **trepanned, -panning, -pans. 1.** *Mining.* To bore (a shaft) with a trepan. **2.** *Surgery.* To trephine. [Middle English *trepane*, from Medieval Latin *trepanum*, from Greek *trupanon*, auger, borer, from *trupan*, to pierce, from *trupē*, hole. See ter-² in Appendix.*] —**trep′a·na′tion** (trĕp′ə-nā′shən, trĭ-păn′ā′shən) n. —**tre·pan′ner** n.

tre·pan² (trĭ-păn′) tr.v. **-panned, -panning, -pans.** Also **tra·pan** (trə-păn′). *Archaic.* To trap; ensnare; trick. —n. *Archaic.* **1.** A prankster; trickster. **2.** A trick; stratagem. [Origin unknown.]

tre·pang (trĭ-păng′) n. **1.** Any of several sea cucumbers of the genus *Holothuria*, of the southern Pacific and Indian oceans. **2.** The eviscerated, dried or smoked body of any of these animals, used as food in the Orient. Also called "bêche-de-mer." [Malay *tĕripang*.]

tre·phine (trĭ-fīn′, -fēn′) n. A surgical instrument having circular, sawlike edges, used to cut out disks of bone, usually from the skull. Also called "trepan." —tr.v. **trephined, -phining, -phines.** *Surgery.* To operate on with a trephine. [Earlier *trafine*, from Latin *três fines*, three ends : *três*, three (see trei- in Appendix*) + *finis*, end (see final).] —**treph′i·na′tion** (trĕf′ə-nā′shən, trĭ-fī′-, trĭ-fē′-) n.

trep·id (trĕp′ĭd) adj. Timid; timorous. [Latin *trepidus*. See trep-¹ in Appendix.*]

trep·i·da·tion (trĕp′ə-dā′shən) n. **1.** A state of alarm or dread; apprehension. **2.** A quivering movement; a trembling. —See Synonyms at **fear.** [Latin *trepidātiō*, from *trepidāre*, to hurry with alarm, tremble at, from *trepidus*, alarmed, TREPID.]

trep·o·neme (trĕp′ə-nēm′) n. Any of a group of spirochetes of the genus *Treponema*, including those that cause syphilis and yaws. [New Latin *Treponema*, "twisted thread" (from its shape) : Greek *trepein*, to turn (see trep-² in Appendix*) + *nēma*, thread (see snē-¹ in Appendix*).]

tres·pass (trĕs′pəs, -păs′) intr.v. **-passed, -passing, -passes. 1.** To commit an offense or sin; err; transgress. **2.** To infringe upon the privacy, time, or attention of another. Used with *on* or *upon: "I must . . . not trespass too far on the patience of a good-natured critic."* (Fielding). **3.** *Law.* To invade the property, rights, or person of another without his consent and with the actual or implied commission of violence; especially, to enter onto another's land illegally. —*n.* **1.** The transgression of a law, code, or duty. **2.** A transgression against another. **3.** *Law.* **a.** The act of trespassing. **b.** A legal suit brought for this. —See Synonyms at **breach.** [Middle English *trespassen,* from Old French *trespasser,* from Medieval Latin *transpassāre* : Latin *trāns-,* across + Medieval Latin *passāre,* to cross, pass, from Latin *passus,* step, pace (see **pass**).] —**tres'pass·er** *n.*

tress (trĕs) *n.* **1.** A lock of a woman's hair: *"Fasten your hair with a golden pin,/And bind up every wandering tress"* (Yeats). **2.** A plait or braid of hair. **3.** *Plural.* A woman's long hair. [Middle English *tresse,* from Old French *tresse, trece*†.]

tres·tle (trĕs'əl) *n.* **1.** A horizontal beam or bar held up by two pairs of divergent legs and used as a support. **2.** A framework consisting of vertical, slanted supports and horizontal crosspieces supporting a bridge. [Middle English *trestel,* from Old French, from Vulgar Latin *transtellum* (unattested), diminutive of Latin *transtrum,* crossbeam. See **transom.**]

tres·tle·tree (trĕs'əl-trē') *n. Nautical.* One of a pair of horizontal beams set into a masthead to support the crosstrees.

tres·tle·work (trĕs'əl-wûrk') *n.* A trestle or system of trestles, as that supporting a bridge.

tret (trĕt) *n.* An allowance formerly paid to purchasers of goods for waste or deterioration incurred in transit. [Old French, a pulling, turn of the scale, perhaps variant of *trait,* TRAIT.]

Trèves. The French name for **Trier.**

Tre·vi·so (trā-vē'zō). Ancient name **Tar·vi·si·um** (tär-vĭzh'ē-əm). A city of Italy, in the northeast, 16 miles north of Venice. Population, 75,000.

Trev·i·thick (trĕv'ə-thĭk'), **Richard.** 1771–1833. British inventor of practical steam locomotives.

trews (tro͞oz) *n.* Plural in form, used with a singular verb. Close-fitting trousers, usually of tartan. [Scottish Gaelic *triubhas,* TROUSERS.]

trey (trā) *n.* A card, die, or domino with three pips; a three. [Middle English *treis, treye,* from Old French *treis,* from Latin *trēs,* three. See **trei-** in Appendix.*]

t.r.f. tuned radio frequency.

tri–. Indicates: **1.** Three, as in number of parts or elements; for example, **trioxide. 2.** Every three or every third; thrice; for example, **trimonthly.** [Latin and Greek, three. See **trei-** in Appendix.*]

tri·a·ble (trī'ə-bəl) *adj.* **1.** Capable of being tried or tested. **2.** *Law.* Subject to judicial examination. —**tri'a·ble·ness** *n.*

tri·ac·id (trī-ăs'ĭd) *adj.* **1.** Able to react with three molecules of a monobasic acid. Said of a base. **2.** Containing three replaceable hydrogen atoms. Said of an acid or an acid salt. —*n.* An acid containing three replaceable hydrogen atoms.

tri·ad (trī'ăd', -əd) *n.* **1.** A group of three persons or things; trinity. **2.** *Music.* A chord of three tones; especially, one built on a given root tone plus a major or minor third and a perfect fifth. [Late Latin *trias* (stem *triad-*), the number three, group of three, from Greek. See **trei-** in Appendix.*] —**tri·ad'ic** *adj.*

tri·al (trī'əl, trīl) *n.* **1.** *Law.* The examination of evidence and applicable law by a competent tribunal to determine the issue of specified charges or claims. **2. a.** The act or process of testing, trying, or putting to the proof by actual or simulated use and experience: *a trial of one's faith.* **b.** A single complete instance of such testing, especially as part of an experimental series: *negative on the first trial.* **3.** An effort or attempt: *He succeeded on his fourth trial.* **4.** A state of pain or anguish caused by a difficult situation or condition: *"The fiery trial through which we pass"* (Lincoln). **5.** A test of patience or endurance: *He was a trial to his parents.* —**on trial.** In the state or process of being tested or tried. —*adj.* **1.** Of or pertaining to a trial or trials. **2.** Made, done, used, or performed during the course of a trial or trials: *a trial run at Daytona.* [Norman French *trial, triel,* from Old French *trier,* TRY.]

trial and error. An empirical method of establishing a satisfactory solution to a problem for which there is no existing or conveniently applicable theory, consisting of repeating experimental trials of various hypotheses until error is sufficiently reduced or eliminated. —**tri'al-and-er'ror** *adj.*

trial balance. *Abbr.* **t.b.** *Bookkeeping.* A statement of all the open debit and credit items in a double-entry ledger made to test their equality.

trial balloon. A preliminary statement or campaign released on a small scale to test public reaction. [Originally applied to a balloon for testing weather conditions.]

trial jury. A **petit jury** *(see).*

tri·an·gle (trī'ăng'gəl) *n.* **1.** The plane figure formed by connecting three points not in a straight line by straight line segments; a three-sided polygon. **2.** Something having the shape of this figure. **3.** Any of various flat, three-sided drawing and drafting guides, used especially to draw straight lines at specified angles. **4.** *Music.* A percussion instrument consisting of a piece of metal in the shape of a triangle open at one angle. **5.** A relationship among three persons, two of whom are in love with the third, especially two men in love with the same woman. [Middle English, from Old French, from Latin *triangulum,* from *triangulus,* three-angled : *tri-,* three + *angulus,* ANGLE.]

tri·an·gu·lar (trī-ăng'gyə-lər) *adj.* **1.** Of, pertaining to, or shaped like a triangle; three-cornered; three-sided. **2.** Having a triangle for a base. **3.** Pertaining to, involving, or consisting of three interrelated entities, as three persons, objects, or ideas. —**tri·an'gu·lar'i·ty** (-lăr'ə-tē) *n.* —**tri·an'gu·lar·ly** *adv.*

tri·an·gu·late (trī-ăng'gyə-lāt') *tr.v.* **-lated, -lating, -lates. 1.** To divide into triangles. **2.** To survey by the method of triangulation. **3.** To make triangular. **4.** To measure by using trigonometry. —*adj.* (trī-ăng'gyə-lĭt). **1.** Of or pertaining to triangles; triangular. **2.** Made up of or marked with triangles.

tri·an·gu·la·tion (trī-ăng'gyə-lā'shən) *n.* **1.** A surveying technique in which a region is divided into a series of triangular elements based on a line of known length so that accurate measurements of distances and directions may be made by the application of trigonometry. **2.** The network of triangles so laid out. **3.** The location of an unknown point, as in navigation, by forming a triangle having the unknown point and two known points as the vertices.

Tri·an·gu·lum (trī-ăng'gyə-ləm) *n.* A constellation in the northern sky near Aries and Andromeda. [From Latin *triangulum,* TRIANGLE.]

Triangulum Aus·tra·le (ô-strā'lē). A constellation in the polar region of the southern sky near Apus and Norma. [New Latin, "southern triangle."]

tri·ar·chy (trī'är'kē) *n., pl.* **-chies. 1.** Government by three persons; a triumvirate. **2.** A country governed by three rulers. [Greek *triarkhia* : *tri-,* three + -ARCHY.]

Tri·as·sic (trī-ăs'ĭk) *adj.* Of, belonging to, or designating the geologic time, system of rocks, and sedimentary deposits of the first period of the Mesozoic era, after the Permian period of the Paleozoic era and before the Jurassic period of the Mesozoic era. See **geology.** —*n. Geology.* The Triassic period or system of deposits. Preceded by *the.* [From Late Latin *trias,* TRIAD (from the subdivision of the geologic strata beneath the Jurassic into three groups).]

tri·at·ic stay (trī-ăt'ĭk). *Nautical.* A rope attached to the mainmast from the foremast to which tackles are attached for hoisting cargo. [Perhaps from TRI- + -ATE + -IC.]

tri·a·tom·ic (trī'ə-tŏm'ĭk) *adj.* **1.** Containing three atoms per molecule. **2.** Containing three replaceable atoms or radicals.

tri·ax·i·al (trī-ăk'sē-əl) *adj.* Having three axes.

tri·a·zine (trī'ə-zēn', trī-ăz'ēn') *n.* **1.** Any of three isomeric compounds, $C_3H_3N_3$, each having three carbon and three nitrogen atoms in a six-membered ring. **2.** Any compound derived from these isomers. [TRI- + AZINE.]

tri·a·zole (trī'ə-zōl', trī-ăz'ōl') *n.* Any of several compounds with composition $C_2H_3N_3$ having a five-membered ring of two carbon atoms and three nitrogen atoms. [TRI- + AZOLE.]

trib. tributary.

trib·ade (trĭb'əd) *n.* A lesbian. [French, from Latin *tribas,* from Greek, "she who rubs," from *tribein,* to rub. See **ter-**[2] in Appendix.*] —**trib'a·dism'** (trĭb'ə-dĭz'əm) *n.*

trib·al (trī'bəl) *adj.* Pertaining to or of the nature of a tribe or tribes. —**trib'al·ly** *adv.*

trib·al·ism (trī'bə-lĭz'əm) *n.* **1.** The organization, culture, or beliefs of a tribe. **2.** The sense of entity of a tribe.

tri·ba·sic (trī-bā'sĭk) *adj.* **1.** Containing three replaceable hydrogen atoms per molecule. Said of acids. **2.** Containing three univalent basic atoms or radicals per molecule. Said of bases or salts.

tribe (trīb) *n.* **1.** Any of various systems of social organization comprising several local villages, bands, districts, lineages, or other groups and sharing a common ancestry, language, culture, and name. ***Note:*** In this Dictionary, *tribe* is used for convenience to designate all North American Indian peoples, even though only about half of them actually had tribal organization. **2.** A political, ethnic, or ancestral division of ancient states and cultures, specifically: **a.** Any of the three divisions of the ancient Romans, namely, the Latin, Sabine, and Etruscan. **b.** Any of the 12 divisions of ancient Israel. **c.** A phyle of ancient Greece. **3.** A group of persons with a common occupation, interest, or habit: *a tribe of beggars.* **4.** *Informal.* A large family. **5.** *Biology.* A taxonomic category sometimes placed between a family and a genus. [Middle English *tribu, tribe,* from Old French *tribu,* from Latin *tribus,* division of the Roman people, from Etruscan.]

tribes·man (trībz'mən) *n., pl.* **-men** (-mĭn). A member of a tribe.

tri·brach (trī'brăk') *n. Prosody.* A foot of three short or unstressed syllables. [Latin *tribrachys,* from Greek *tribrakhus* : *tri-,* three + *brakhus,* short (see **mreghu-** in Appendix*).]

tri·bro·mo·eth·a·nol (trī'brō'mō-ĕth'ə-nôl', -nōl') *n.* A white crystalline compound, CBr_3CH_2OH, having a slight aromatic odor and taste, and used as a basal anesthetic. [TRI- + BROMO- + ETHANOL.]

trib·u·la·tion (trĭb'yə-lā'shən) *n.* **1.** Great affliction, trial, or distress; suffering: *the tribulations of the persecuted.* **2.** An experience or condition that causes such distress. [Middle English *tribulacioun,* from Old French *tribulation,* from Late Latin *trībulātiō,* from *trībulāre,* to oppress, from Latin, to press, from *trībulum,* threshing sledge. See **ter-**[2] in Appendix.*]

tri·bu·nal (trī-byo͞o'nəl, trĭ-) *n.* **1.** A seat or court of justice. **2.** The platform or seat upon which a judge or other presiding officer sits in court. **3.** Anything having the power of determining or judging: *the tribunal of public opinion.* [Latin *tribūnāl(e),* court of the tribunes, tribunal, from *tribūnālis,* of a tribune, from *tribūnus,* TRIBUNE.]

trib·u·nate (trĭb'yə-nāt', trĭ-byo͞o'nĭt) *n.* The rank, office, dignity, or authority of a tribune. Also called "tribuneship."

trib·une[1] (trĭb'yo͞on', trĭ-byo͞on') *n.* **1.** An official of ancient Rome chosen by the plebs to protect their rights against the patricians. **2.** Any protector or champion of the people. [Middle English, from Latin *tribūnus,* "head of the tribe," tribune, from *tribus,* TRIBE.] —**trib'u·nar'y** (trĭb'yə-nĕr'ē) *adj.*

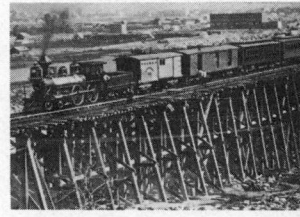

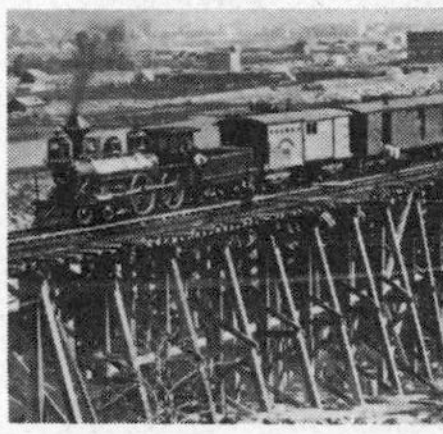
trestle

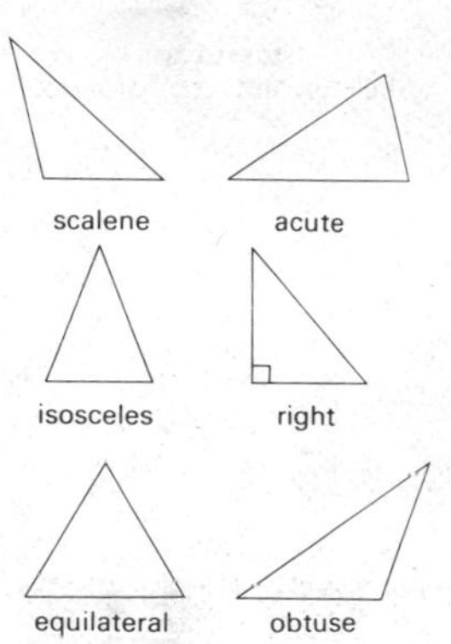
scalene
acute
isosceles
right
equilateral
obtuse
triangle

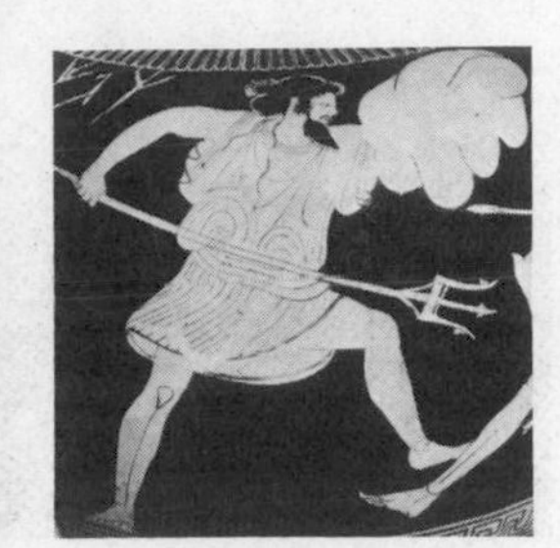

trident
Ancient Greek vase
painting of Poseidon

trib·une[2] (trĭb′yo͞on′, trĭ-byo͞on′) *n.* A raised platform or dais from which a speaker addresses an assembly. [French, from Italian *tribuna*, from Medieval Latin *tribūna*, variant of Latin *tribūnal*, TRIBUNAL.]

trib·u·tar·y (trĭb′yə-tĕr′ē) *adj.* **1.** Making additions or offering supplies; contributory; subsidiary. **2.** Having the nature of tribute: *a tributary payment.* **3.** Paying tribute: *a tributary colony.* —*n., pl.* **tributaries. 1.** One that pays tribute. **2.** *Abbr.* **trib.** A stream or river flowing into a larger stream or river. In this sense, compare **distributary.** [Middle English *tributarie*, from Latin *tribūtārius*, of a tribute, from *tribūtum*, TRIBUTE.] —**trib′u·tar′i·ly** *adv.* —**trib′u·tar′i·ness** *n.*

trib·ute (trĭb′yo͞ot) *n.* **1.** A gift, payment, declaration, or other acknowledgment of gratitude, respect, or admiration: *"To love and grief tribute of verse belongs"* (Donne). **2. a.** A sum of money or other valuables paid by one ruler or nation to another as acknowledgment of submission or as the price for protection by that nation. **b.** Any payment made for protection. **3. a.** In feudal times, any payment or tax given by a vassal to his overlord. **b.** The obligation involved in such a payment. [Middle English *tribut*, from Latin *tribūtum*, from the neuter past participle of *tribuere*, to give, distribute (as among the Roman tribes), from *tribus*, TRIBE.]

Usage: *Tribute* is well established in a rather special sense in the idiom "a tribute to": *The verdict is a tribute to their fairness* (that is, illustrative of, attributable to, and reflecting credit on their sense of fairness). The idiom is restricted to contexts involving things that merit praise. It has been disputed by some writers on usage as a misapplication of *tribute*, but is acceptable to 69 per cent of the Usage Panel on the basis of the representative example quoted.

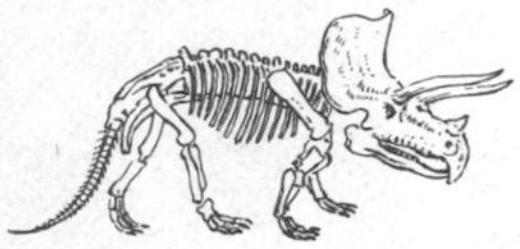

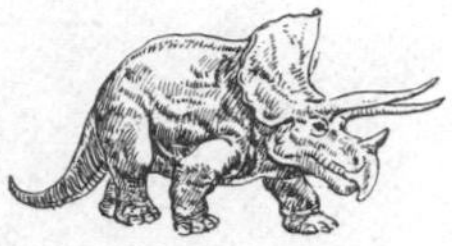

triceratops
Skeleton and reconstruction

trice (trīs) *tr.v.* **triced, tricing, trices.** To hoist and secure (a sail, for example); to lash. Usually used with *up.* —*n.* A very short period of time; moment; an instant. Used chiefly in the phrase *in a trice: "And all the waiters in a trice/His summons did obey"* (Suckling). See Synonyms at **moment.** [Middle English *trisen*, from Middle Dutch, akin to Middle Dutch *trise*†, pulley; noun sense, Middle English *at a tryse*, "at a pull," immediately, from *trisen*, to hoist.]

tri·cen·ten·ni·al (trī′sĕn-tĕn′ē-əl) *adj.* Tercentenary. —*n.* A tercentenary event or celebration.

tri·ceps (trī′sĕps′) *n.* A large three-headed muscle running along the back of the upper arm and serving to extend the forearm. [Latin, three-headed : *tri-*, three + *caput*, head (see **kaput** in Appendix*).]

tri·cer·a·tops (trī-sĕr′ə-tŏps′) *n.* A horned herbivorous dinosaur of the genus *Triceratops*, of the Cretaceous period, having a bony plate covering the neck. [New Latin *Triceratops* : TRI- + Greek *keras* (stem *kerat-*), horn (see **ker-**[1] in Appendix*) + *ōps*, eye, face (see **okw-** in Appendix*).]

tri·chi·a·sis (trĭ-kī′ə-sĭs) *n.* A condition of ingrowing hairs about an orifice, especially of ingrowing eyelashes. [Late Latin, from Greek *trikhiasis* : TRICH(O)- + -IASIS.]

tri·chi·na (trĭ-kī′nə) *n., pl.* **-nae** (-nē) or **-nas.** A parasitic nematode worm, *Trichinella spiralis*, infesting the intestines of various mammals, and having larvae that move through the blood vessels and become encysted in the muscles. [New Latin, from Greek *trikhinos*, hairy, from *thrix*, hair. See **thrix** in Appendix.*]

trich·i·nize (trĭk′ə-nīz′) *tr.v.* **-nized, -nizing, -nizes.** To infect with trichinae. —**trich′i·ni·za′tion** *n.*

Trich·i·no·po·ly. See **Tiruchirapalli.**

trich·i·no·sis (trĭk′ə-nō′sĭs) *n.* A disease caused by eating inadequately cooked pork containing trichinae, and characterized by intestinal disorders, fever, muscular swelling, pain, and insomnia. [New Latin : TRICHIN(A) + -OSIS.]

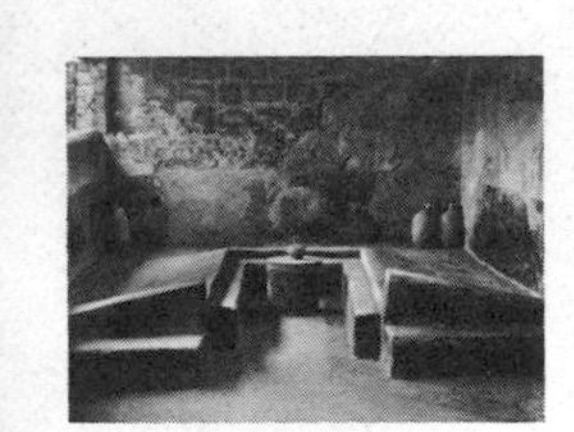

triclinium
Dining room in a house
in Pompeii

tri·chi·nous (trĭ-kī′nəs, trĭk′ə-nəs) *adj.* **1.** Containing trichinae: *trichinous pork.* **2.** Of or relating to trichinae or trichinosis: *a trichinous infection.*

trich·ite (trĭk′īt′) *n.* A small needle-shaped filament or crystal. [German *Trichit* : TRICH(O)- + -ITE.] —**tri·chit′ic** (trĭ-kĭt′ĭk) *adj.*

tri·chlo·ride (trī-klôr′īd′, -klōr′īd′) *n.* Also **tri·chlo·rid** (-klôr′ĭd, -klōr′ĭd). A compound containing three chlorine atoms per molecule.

tri·chlo·ro·a·ce·tic acid (trī-klôr′ō-ə-sē′tĭk, trī-klōr′ō-). A colorless, deliquescent, corrosive, crystalline compound, CCl_3COOH, used as a herbicide and topically as an astringent and antiseptic. [TRI- + CHLORO- + ACETIC ACID.]

tri·chlo·ro·eth·yl·ene (trī-klôr′ō-ĕth′ə-lēn′, trī-klōr′ō-) *n.* Also **tri·chlor·eth·yl·ene** (trī-klôr′-, trī-klōr′-). A heavy, colorless, toxic liquid, $CHCl{:}CCl_2$, used to degrease metals, as an extraction solvent for oils and waxes, as a refrigerant, in dry cleaning, and as a fumigant. [TRI- + CHLORO- + ETHYLENE.]

tricho–. Indicates hair or hairlike part; for example, **trichopteran, trichogyne.** [Greek *trikho-*, from *thrix* (stem *trikh-*), hair. See **thrix** in Appendix.*]

trich·o·cyst (trĭk′ə-sĭst′) *n.* One of the minute capsulelike bodies in the outer cytoplasm of certain protozoans, capable of ejecting a threadlike or bristlelike extension. [TRICHO- + CYST.] —**trich′o·cys′tic** *adj.*

trich·o·gyne (trĭk′ə-jīn′, -gīn′) *n.* A receptive filament of the female reproductive structure of certain fungi or algae. [TRICHO- + -GYNE.]

trich·oid (trĭk′oid′, trī′koid′) *adj.* Resembling hair; hairlike. [Greek *trikhoeidēs* : TRICH(O)- + -OID.]

trich·ome (trĭk′ōm′, trī′kōm′) *n.* A hairlike or bristlelike outgrowth, as from the epidermis of a plant. [German *Trichom*, from Greek *trikhōma*, hair growth, from *trikhoun*, to furnish with hair, from *thrix* (stem *trikh-*), hair. See **thrix** in Appendix.*] —**tri·chom′ic** (trĭ-kŏm′ĭk, -kō′mĭk, trī-) *adj.*

trich·o·mon·ad (trĭk′ə-mŏn′ăd′, -mō′năd′) *n.* Any of various flagellate protozoans of the genus *Trichomonas*, occurring in the digestive and urogenital tracts of vertebrates. [New Latin *Trichomonas* (stem *Trichomonad-*) : TRICHO- + MONAD.]

trich·o·mo·ni·a·sis (trĭk′ə-mə-nī′ə-sĭs) *n.* **1.** A vaginal infection caused by a protozoan, *Trichomonas vaginalis*, and resulting in inflammation and discomfort. **2.** Any infection caused by trichomonads. [New Latin : *Trichomonas*, TRICHOMON(AD) + -IASIS.]

tri·chop·ter·an (trī-kŏp′tər-ən) *n.* Any insect of the order Trichoptera, which includes the caddis flies. [New Latin *Trichoptera*, "hairy winged" : TRICHO- + -PTER.]

tri·cho·sis (trĭ-kō′sĭs) *n.* Disease of the hair. [New Latin, from Greek *trikhōsis*, growth of hair, from *trikhoun*, to furnish with hair. See **trichome.**]

tri·chot·o·my (trī-kŏt′ə-mē) *n., pl.* **-mies.** Division into three parts; specifically, the theological division of man into body, soul, and spirit. [Greek *trikha*, in three parts (see **trei-** in Appendix*) + -TOMY.] —**trich′o·tom′ic** (trĭk′ə-tŏm′ĭk), **tri·chot′o·mous** *adj.* —**tri·chot′o·mous·ly** *adv.*

–trichous. Indicates a specific kind of hair; for example, **amphitrichous.** [Greek *-trikhos*, from *thrix* (stem *trikh-*), hair. See **thrix** in Appendix.*]

tri·chro·ism (trī′krō-ĭz′əm) *n.* The property possessed by certain minerals of exhibiting three different colors when illuminated by white light and viewed from three different directions. [Greek *trikhroos*, "tricolored" : TRI- + -CHRO(OUS) + -ISM.] —**tri·chro′ic** (trī-krō′ĭk) *adj.*

tri·chro·mat·ic (trī′krō-măt′ĭk) *adj.* Also **tri·chrome** (trī′krōm′), **tri·chro·mic** (trī-krō′mĭk). **1.** Of, relating to, or having three colors, as in photography or printing. **2.** Having visual perception of the three primary colors, as in normal vision. [TRI- + CHROMATIC.] —**tri·chro′ma·tism′** (trī-krō′mə-tĭz′əm) *n.*

trick (trĭk) *n.* **1.** A device or action designed to achieve an end by deceptive or fraudulent means; stratagem; ruse. **2.** A mischievous action; practical joke; prank. **3.** A stupid, disgraceful, or childish act or performance. **4.** A peculiar trait or characteristic; mannerism: *"Mimicry is the trick by which a moth or other defenseless insect comes to look like a wasp"* (Marston Bates). **5.** The quality necessary to accomplish something with facility: *Patience is the trick in doing a job well.* **6.** A feat of magic or legerdemain. **7.** A difficult, dexterous, or clever act, designed to amuse. **8.** *Card Games.* All the cards played in a single round. **9.** A period or turn of duty. **10.** *Informal.* An attractive girl. **11.** *Slang.* A prostitute's customer. —See Synonyms at **artifice.** —**do** (or **turn**) **the trick.** To bring about the desired result. —*v.* **tricked, tricking, tricks.** —*tr.* **1.** To swindle or cheat; deceive; delude. **2.** To ornament or adorn. Used with *up* or *out.* —*intr.* To practice deception or trickery. —*adj.* **1.** Of, pertaining to, or involving tricks. **2.** Capable of doing tricks: *a trick dog.* **3.** Weak, defective, or liable to fail: *a trick knee.* [Middle English *trik*, from Old North French *trique*, variant of Old French *triche*, from *trichier*, to deceive, possibly from Vulgar Latin *triccāre* (unattested), from Latin *trīcārī*, to start difficulties, dally, play tricks, from *trīcae*†, trifles, tricks. See also **intricate, extricate.**] —**trick′er** *n.*

trick·er·y (trĭk′ə-rē) *n., pl.* **-ies.** The practice or use of tricks; deception by stratagem; artifice.

trick·ish (trĭk′ĭsh) *adj.* Characterized by or tending to use tricks or trickery. —**trick′ish·ly** *adv.* —**trick′ish·ness** *n.*

trick·le (trĭk′əl) *v.* **-led, -ling, -les.** —*intr.* **1.** To flow or fall in drops or in a thin, intermittent stream; drip gently but steadily. **2.** To move or proceed slowly or bit by bit: *The audience trickled in.* —*tr.* To cause to trickle. —*n.* **1.** The act or condition of trickling. **2.** Any slow, small, or irregular quantity of something that moves, proceeds, or occurs intermittently. [Middle English *triklen* (perhaps imitative).]

trick·ster (trĭk′stər) *n.* One who tricks; a cheater.

trick·y (trĭk′ē) *adj.* **-ier, -iest. 1.** Given to or characterized by deception or trickery; crafty; sly; wily. **2.** Requiring caution or skill: *a tricky recipe.* —See Synonyms at **dishonest, sly.** —**trick′i·ly** *adv.* —**trick′i·ness** *n.*

tri·clin·ic (trī-klĭn′ĭk) *adj. Abbr.* **tricl.** Having three unequal axes intersecting at oblique angles. Said of certain crystals. [TRI- + -CLINIC.]

tri·clin·i·um (trī-klĭn′ē-əm) *n., pl.* **-ia** (-ē-ə). **1.** A couch surrounding three sides of a table, used by the ancient Romans for reclining at meals. **2.** A room containing such a couch. [Latin *triclīnium*, from Greek *triklinion*, diminutive of *triklinos*, room with three couches : *tri-*, three (see **trei-** in Appendix*) + *klinē*, couch (see **klei-** in Appendix*).]

tri·col·or (trī′kŭl′ər) *adj.* Also **tri·col·ored** (-ərd). Having three colors. —*n.* **1.** A tricolor flag. **2.** *Sometimes capital* **T.** The French flag.

tri·corn (trī′kôrn′) *n.* Also **tri·corne.** A hat having the brim turned up on three sides. —*adj.* Having three projections, horns, or corners. [French *tricorne*, from Latin *tricornis*, three-horned : *tri-*, three + *cornū*, horn (see **ker-**[1] in Appendix*).]

tri·cor·nered (trī′kôr′nərd) *adj.* Having three corners.

tri·cos·tate (trī-kŏs′tāt′) *adj.* Having three costae or riblike ridges. [TRI- + COSTATE.]

tri·cot (trē′kō) *n.* **1.** A plain, warp-knitted cloth of any of various yarns. **2.** A soft ribbed cloth of wool or a wool blend, usually used for dresses. [French, from *tricoter*, to knit, from *tricot*, short stick, from Old French *(es)trique*, from *estriquer*, "to pass a stick over a measure for removing excessive grain," probably from Middle Dutch *striken*, to pass one thing over another, strike. See **streig-** in Appendix.*]

ă pat/ā pay/âr care/ä father/b bib/ch church/d deed/ĕ pet/ē be/f fife/g gag/h hat/hw which/ĭ pit/ī pie/îr pier/j judge/k kick/l lid, needle/m mum/n no, sudden/ng thing/ŏ pot/ō toe/ô paw, for/oi noise/ou out/o͝o took/o͞o boot/p pop/r roar/s sauce/sh ship, dish/

tric·o·tine (trĭk′ə-tēn′, trē′kə-) *n.* A sturdy worsted fabric with a double twill, used for dresses and suits. [French, from TRICOT.]

tri·crot·ic (trī-krŏt′ĭk) *adj. Medicine.* Having three waves or elevations to one beat of the pulse. [From Greek *trikrotos,* having a triple beat : *tri-,* three (see **trei-** in Appendix*) + *krotein,* to beat (see **kret-**[2] in Appendix*).] —**tri′cro·tism′** (-krə-tĭz′əm) *n.*

tri·cus·pid (trī-kŭs′pĭd) *adj.* Also **tri·cus·pi·dal** (-pə-dəl), **tri·cus·pi·date** (-pə-dāt′). **1.** Having three points or cusps, as a molar tooth. **2.** *Anatomy.* Pertaining to the tricuspid valve of the heart. —*n. Anatomy.* A tricuspid organ or part, especially a tooth. [Latin *tricuspis* (stem *tricuspid-*) : *tri-,* three + *cuspis,* point, CUSP.]

tricuspid valve. The three-segmented valve of the heart that keeps the blood from flowing back from the right ventricle into the right atrium.

tri·cy·cle (trī′sĭk′əl, -sĭ-kəl) *n.* A vehicle with three wheels usually propelled by pedals. Also called "velocipede." [TRI- + CYCLE.]

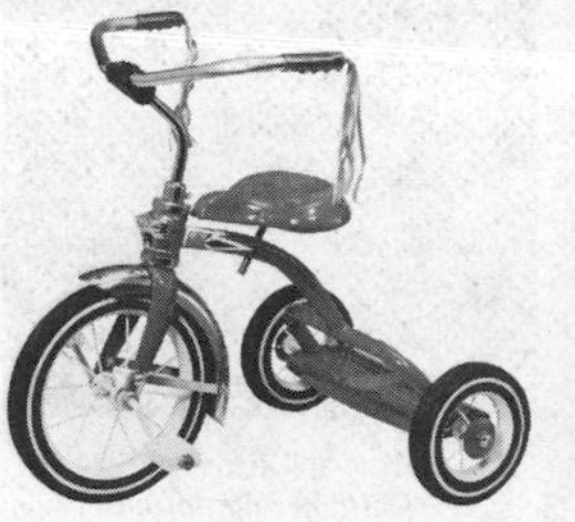

tricycle

tri·dac·tyl (trī-dăk′təl) *adj.* Also **tri·dac·ty·lous** (-tə-ləs). *Zoology.* Having three toes, claws, or similar parts. [Greek *tridaktulos,* three-fingered : *tri-,* three (see **trei-** in Appendix*) + *daktulos,* finger (see **dactyl**).]

tri·dent (trīd′ənt) *n.* A long, three-pronged fork or weapon; especially, the three-pronged spear carried by the classical god of the sea, Neptune or Poseidon. —*adj.* Also **tri·den·tate** (trī-dĕn′tāt′). Having three teeth, prongs, or similar protrusions. [Latin *tridēns,* three-toothed : *tri-,* three + *dēns,* tooth (see **dent-** in Appendix*).]

Tri·den·tine (trī-dĕn′tīn, -tēn′) *adj.* Of or relating to the Council of Trent or to the results or decrees of that Council. —*n.* A Roman Catholic who conforms to the Tridentine Creed formulated at the Council of Trent. [Medieval Latin *Tridentīnus,* from *Tridentum,* ancient form of TRENT.]

tri·e·cious. Variant of **trioecious.**

tried (trīd) *adj.* Thoroughly tested and proved to be good or trustworthy.

tri·en·ni·al (trī-ĕn′ē-əl) *adj.* **1.** Occurring every third year. **2.** Lasting three years. —*n.* **1.** A third anniversary. **2.** A celebration or other ceremony occurring every three years. [From TRIENNIUM.] —**tri·en′ni·al·ly** *adv.*

tri·en·ni·um (trī-ĕn′ē-əm) *n., pl.* **-ums** or **-ennia** (-ĕn′ē-ə). A period of three years. [Latin *triennium* : *tri-,* three + Latin *annus,* year (see **at-** in Appendix*).]

Trier (trēr). *French* **Trèves** (trĕv). A city in West Germany, on the Moselle near the Luxembourg border; site of Roman ruins. Population, 87,000.

tri·er·arch (trī′ə-rärk′) *n.* **1.** The captain of a Greek trireme. **2.** An Athenian who outfitted and maintained a trireme as a part of his civic duties. [Latin *triērarchus,* from Greek *triērarkhos* : *triērēs,* trireme (see **trei-** in Appendix*) + -ARCH.]

tri·er·ar·chy (trī′ə-rär′kē) *n., pl.* **-chies.** **1.** The authority or office of the commander of a trierarch. **2.** The ancient Athenian system whereby individual citizens furnished and maintained triremes as a part of their public duty.

Tri·este (trē-ĕst′). A seaport in northeast Italy on the Gulf of Trieste, an inlet of the Gulf of Venice. Population, 280,000.

Tri·este, Free Territory of (trē-ĕst′). A former territory occupying 285 square miles north of the northern tip of the Adriatic, and including the city of Trieste and parts of Istria; established by the United Nations in 1947, and divided between Italy and Yugoslavia in 1954.

tri·fa·cial (trī-fā′shəl) *adj. Anatomy.* **Trigeminal** *(see).*

tri·fid (trī′fĭd) *adj.* Divided or cleft into three narrow parts or lobes. [Latin *trifidus* : *tri-,* three + -FID.]

tri·fle (trī′fəl) *n.* **1.** Something of slight importance or very little value. **2.** A small amount of something; a little. **3.** A dessert consisting of sponge cake spread with jam, soaked in wine, sprinkled with crushed macaroons, and topped with custard and whipped cream. **4. a.** A moderately hard variety of pewter. **b.** *Plural.* Utensils made from this. —**a trifle.** Very little; somewhat: *a trifle stingy.* —*v.* **trifled, -fling, -fles.** —*intr.* **1.** To deal with something as if it were of little significance or value. Usually used with *with.* **2.** To act, perform, or speak with little seriousness or purpose; to jest. **3.** To play or toy with something; handle things idly. —*tr.* To waste (time or money, for example). [Middle English *trifle, truf(f)le,* from Old French *truf(f)le*†, trickery.] —**tri′fler** (trī′flər) *n.*

tri·fling (trī′flĭng) *adj.* **1.** Of slight importance; insignificant: *"he had come to know every trifling feature that bordered the great river"* (Mark Twain). **2.** Characterized by frivolity or idleness. —See Synonyms at **trivial.** —**tri′fling·ly** *adv.*

tri·fo·cal (trī-fō′kəl) *adj.* Having three focal lengths. —*n.* Eyeglasses having trifocal lenses. Used in the plural.

tri·fold (trī′fōld′) *adj.* Triple; having three parts. [TRI- + -FOLD.]

tri·fo·li·ate (trī-fō′lē-ĭt) *adj.* Also **tri·fo·li·at·ed** (-fō′lē-ā′tĭd). Having three leaves, leaflets, or leaflike parts: *a trifoliate compound leaf.*

tri·fo·li·o·late (trī-fō′lē-ə-lāt′) *adj. Botany.* Having three leaflets.

tri·fo·ri·um (trī-fôr′ē-əm, -fōr′ē-əm) *n., pl.* **-foria** (-fôr′ē-ə, -fōr′ē-ə). *Architecture.* A gallery of arches above the side-aisle vaulting in the nave of a church. [Medieval Latin *triforium*†, special name of the gallery in Canterbury Cathedral, but subsequently taken to mean "structure with three openings" (Latin *tri-,* three + *fores,* doors) and thus applied to the elevated gallery characteristic of Gothic architecture, sometimes having three arches or openings.]

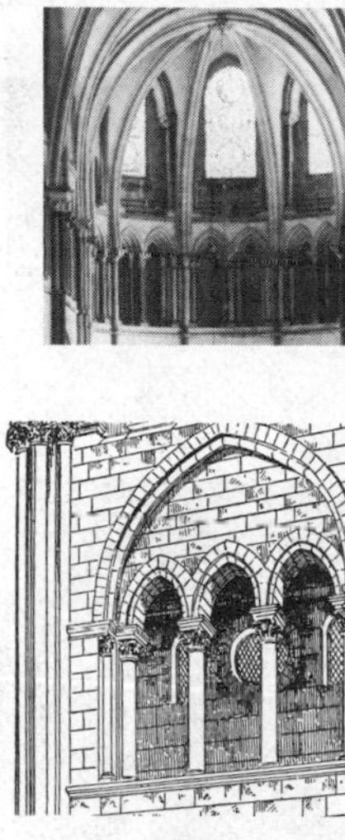

triforium
Above: The gallery in Canterbury Cathedral
Below: Triple arch of a typical triforium

tri·formed (trī′fôrmd′) *adj.* Also **tri·form** (-fôrm′). Having three different forms or parts. —**tri·form′i·ty** *n.*

tri·fur·cate (trī-fûr′kĭt, -kāt′, trī′fər-kāt′) *adj.* Also **tri·fur·cat·ed** (trī′fər-kā′tĭd). Having three forks or branches. [TRI- + FURCATE.] —**tri′fur·ca′tion** *n.*

trig[1] (trĭg) *adj.* **1.** Trim; neat; tidy. **2.** In good condition; firm; strong. —*tr.v.* **trigged, trigging, trigs.** To make trim or neat, especially in dress. Often used with *up* or *out.* [Middle English, true, active, from Old Norse *tryggr.* See **deru-** in Appendix.*] —**trig′ly** *adv.* —**trig′ness** *n.*

trig[2] (trĭg) *tr.v.* **trigged, trigging, trigs.** **1.** To stop (a wheel) from rolling, as with a wedge. **2.** To prop up; support. —*n.* A wedge or other braking device. [Perhaps from Scandinavian, akin to Old Norse *tryggr,* true, firm. See **trig** (trim).]

trig. trigonometric; trigonometry.

tri·gem·i·nal (trī-jĕm′ə-nəl) *adj. Anatomy.* Pertaining to the trigeminus. Also "trifacial."

trigeminal neuralgia. An intensely painful inflammation of the facial area around the trigeminal nerve. Also called "tic douloureux."

tri·gem·i·nus (trī-jĕm′ə-nəs) *n., pl.* **-ni** (-nī′). The chief facial sensory nerve and the motor nerve of the masticatory muscles. [New Latin, from Latin, three born at a birth, threefold (probably from its three branches) : *tri-,* three + *geminus,* twin-born, twin (see **yem-** in Appendix*).]

trig·ger (trĭg′ər) *n.* **1.** The lever pressed by the finger to discharge a firearm. **2.** Any similar device used to release or activate a mechanism. **3.** An event that precipitates others; a stimulus. —*tr.v.* **triggered, -gering, -gers.** To initiate; activate; set off. See Usage note. [Earlier *tricker,* from Dutch *trekker,* something pulled, from Middle Dutch *trecker,* from *trecken,* to pull, travel. See **trek.**]

Usage: *Trigger* (verb), in earlier usage largely restricted to the literal sense of pressing a trigger, is now chiefly employed in the figurative sense of initiating or setting off something, such as a celebration. It is acceptable in that sense, according to 77 per cent of the Usage Panel, but is most appropriate to what is not expressly formal.

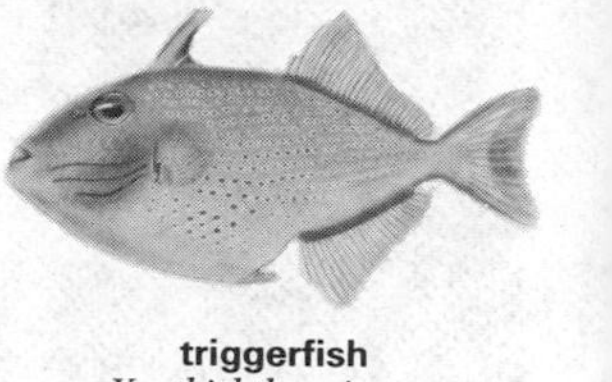

triggerfish
Xanthichthys ringens

trig·ger·fish (trĭg′ər-fĭsh′) *n., pl.* **triggerfish** or **-fishes.** Any of various brightly colored fishes of the family Balistidae, of warm coastal seas, characteristically having a sharp, erectile dorsal spine.

trig·ger-hap·py (trĭg′ər-hăp′ē). *Slang.* Inclined to react violently at the slightest provocation, as by shooting a gun.

Tri·glav (trē′gläv′). The highest mountain (9,395 feet) of the Julian Alps, in northwestern Yugoslavia.

tri·glyph (trī′glĭf′) *adj. Architecture.* An ornament in a Doric frieze, consisting of a projecting block having three parallel vertical channels on its face. [Latin *trīglyphus,* from Greek *trigluphos* : *tri-,* three (see **trei-** in Appendix*) + *gluphē,* carving, GLYPH.] —**tri·glyph′ic** *adj.*

tri·gon (trī′gŏn′) *n.* **1.** A triangular lyre or harp of Roman and Greek antiquity. **2.** *Astrology.* A **triplicity** *(see).* **3.** *Obsolete.* A triangle. [Latin *trigonum,* triangle, from Greek *trigōnon,* from *trigōnos,* triangular : *tri-,* three + -GON.]

trigonometric function. A function of an angle expressed as the ratio of two of the sides of a right triangle that contains the angle; in general, for any angle formed in a coordinate plane by the intersection of the abscissal axis with the radius vector from the origin to a point in the plane, the ratio of any two of the values abscissa, ordinate, and radius vector of that point.

trig·o·nom·e·try (trĭg′ə-nŏm′ə-trē) *n. Abbr.* **trig.** The study of the properties and applications of trigonometric functions. [New Latin *trigonometria* : Greek *trigōnon,* triangle, TRIGON + -METRY.] —**trig′o·no·met′ric** (-nə-mĕt′rĭk), **trig′o·no·met′ri·cal** *adj.* —**trig′o·no·met′ri·cal·ly** *adv.*

tri·he·dral (trī-hē′drəl) *adj.* Formed by the plane surfaces of a trihedron. —*n.* A **trihedron** *(see).*

tri·he·dron (trī-hē′drən) *n., pl.* **-drons** or **-dra** (-drə). A figure formed by the intersection of three noncoplanar lines. Also called "trihedral." [New Latin : TRI- + -HEDRON.]

tri·lat·er·al (trī-lăt′ər-əl) *adj.* Having three sides. [From Latin *trilaterus* : *tri-,* three + *latus* (stem *later-*), side (see **lateral**).] —**tri·lat′er·al·ly** *adv.*

tri·lin·e·ar (trī-lĭn′ē-ər) *adj.* Relating to, having, or bounded by three lines.

tri·lin·gual (trī-lĭng′gwəl) *adj.* Having or expressed in three languages.

tri·lit·er·al (trī-lĭt′ər-əl) *adj.* Consisting of three letters. Used chiefly of consonantal roots in Semitic languages. —*n.* A three-letter word or word element.

trill (trĭl) *n.* **1.** A fluttering or tremulous sound, such as that made by certain birds; a warble. **2.** *Music.* **a.** The rapid alternation of two tones either a whole or a half tone apart. **b.** A vibrato. Compare **tremolo.** **3.** *Linguistics.* **a.** A rapid vibration of one speech organ against another, as of the tongue against the alveolar ridge in Spanish *rr.* **b.** A speech sound pronounced with such a vibration. —*v.* **trilled, trilling, trills.** —*tr.* **1.** To sound, sing, or play with a trill. **2.** *Phonetics.* To articulate with a trill. —*intr.* To produce or give forth a trill. [Italian *trillo,* from *trillare*†, to trill.]

tril·lion (trĭl′yən) *n.* **1.** The cardinal number represented by 1 followed by 12 zeros, usually written 10^{12}. Called in British usage "billion." See **number.** **2.** In Great Britain, the cardinal number represented by 1 followed by 18 zeros, usually written 10^{18}. See **number.** [French : TRI- + (M)ILLION.] —**tril′lion** *adj.*

tril·lionth (trĭl′yənth) *n.* **1.** The ordinal number one trillion in a series. **2.** One of a trillion equal parts. See **number.** —**tril′lionth** *adj.* & *adv.*

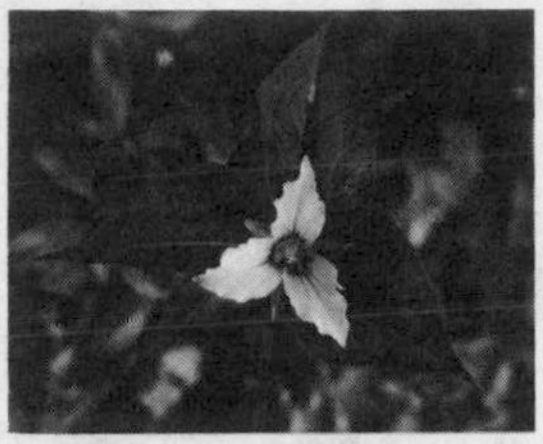

trillium
Trillium undulatum
Painted trillium

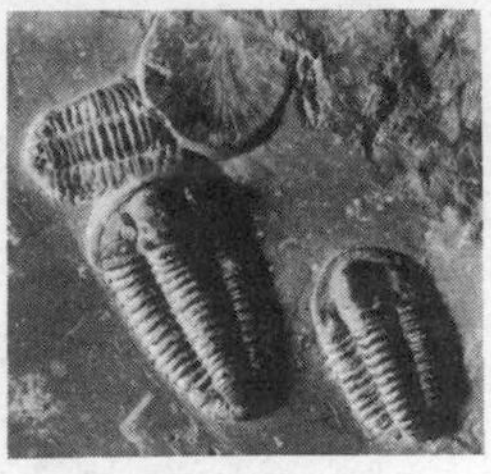

trilobite
Fossilized trilobites, genus *Calymene*

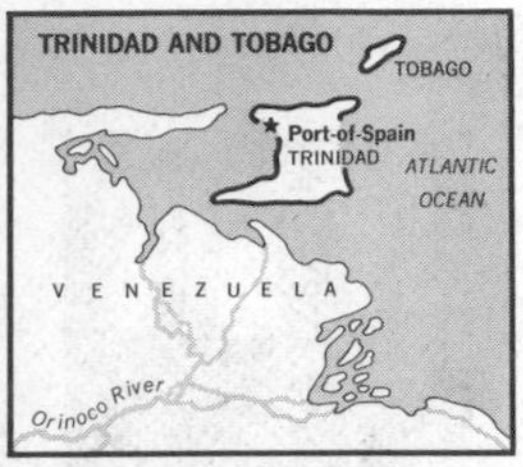

Trinidad and Tobago

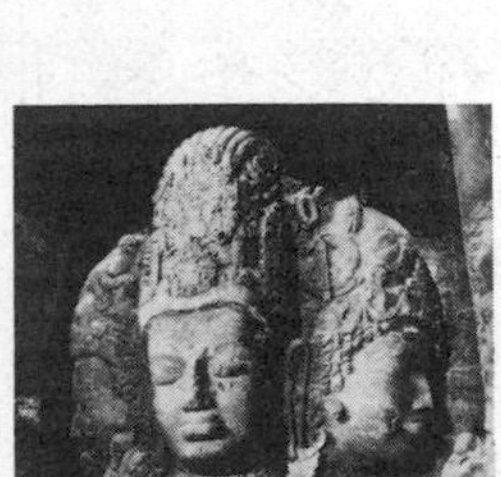

Trimurti
Eighth-century A.D. sculpture

tril·li·um (trĭl′ē-əm) *n.* Any of various plants of the genus *Trillium,* of North America and eastern Asia, usually having a single whorl of three leaves, and a variously colored, three-petaled flower. Also called "wake-robin." [New Latin : TRI- + *(vertic)illium* : Latin *(vertic)illus,* whorl, VERTICIL + -IUM.]

tri·lo·bate (trī-lō′bāt′) *adj.* Also **tri·lo·bal** (-lō′bəl), **tri·lo·bat·ed** (-lō′bā′tĭd), **tri·lobed** (trī′lōbd′). Having three lobes, as certain leaves.

tri·lo·bite (trī′lə-bīt′) *n.* Any of numerous extinct marine arthropods of the class Trilobita, of the Paleozoic era, having a segmented exoskeleton divided by grooves or furrows into three longitudinal lobes. [New Latin *Trilobites* (division), from Greek *trilobos,* "three-lobed" : *tri-,* three + *lobos,* LOBE.] —**tri′lo·bit′ic** (-bĭt′ĭk) *adj.*

tri·loc·u·lar (trī-lŏk′yə-lər) *adj.* Having three chamberlike divisions or cavities. [TRI- + LOCULAR.]

tril·o·gy (trĭl′ə-jē) *n., pl.* **-gies.** A group of three dramatic or literary works related in subject or theme. [Greek *trilogia* : TRI- + -LOGY.]

trim (trĭm) *v.* **trimmed, trimming, trims.** —*tr.* **1.** To make neat or tidy by clipping, smoothing, or pruning. **2. a.** To rid (a budget, for example) of excess by cutting. **b.** To remove (excess) by cutting: *trim off the rotten bark.* **3.** To ornament; decorate. **4.** *Informal.* **a.** To thrash. **b.** To defeat soundly. **c.** To cheat. **5.** *Nautical.* **a.** To adjust (the sails and yards) so that they receive the wind properly. **b.** To balance (a ship) by shifting its cargo or contents. **6.** To balance (an airplane) in flight by regulating the control surfaces and tabs. **7.** *Obsolete.* To furnish or equip. —*intr.* **1.** *Nautical.* **a.** To be in or retain equilibrium. **b.** To make sails and yards ready for sailing. **2. a.** To affect cautious neutrality. **b.** To fashion one's views for momentary popularity or advantage. —*n.* **1.** State of order, arrangement, or appearance; condition. **2. a.** Moldings, framework, or other exterior ornamentation. **b.** Ornamentation, as for clothing. **3.** Material used in commercial window displays. **4.** Excised or rejected material. **5.** Personal quality; character. **6.** *Nautical.* **a.** The readiness of a vessel for sailing, with regard to ballast, sails, and yards. **b.** The balance of a ship. **c.** The difference between the draft at the bow and at the stern. **7.** The position of an aircraft relative to its horizontal axis. —*adj.* **trimmer, trimmest. 1.** In good or neat order. **2.** Having lines, edges, or forms of neat and pleasing simplicity. —See Synonyms at **neat.** —*adv.* In a trim manner. [Perhaps from Middle English *trimmen* (unattested), Old English *trymman, trymian,* to strengthen, arrange. See **deru-** in Appendix.*] —**trim′ly** *adv.* —**trim′ness** *n.*

tri·mer (trī′mər) *n. Chemistry.* A polymeric compound consisting of three identical monomeric molecules. [TRI- + Greek *meros,* part (see **-merous**).]

trim·er·ous (trĭm′ər-əs) *adj.* **1.** Having three similar segments or parts. **2.** *Botany.* Having flower parts, such as petals, sepals, and stamens, in sets of three. Also written *3-merous.* [New Latin *trimerus,* from Greek *trimerēs* : *tri-,* three + -MEROUS.] —**trim′er·ism′** *n.*

tri·mes·ter (trī-mĕs′tər) *n.* **1.** A period or term of three months. **2.** One of three equal academic terms in some universities. Compare **semester.** —*adj.* Also **tri·mes·tral** (-trəl), **tri·mes·tri·al** (-trē-əl). Of or pertaining to periods of three months. [French *trimestre,* from Latin *trimestris,* "of three months" : *tri-,* three + *mēnsis,* month (see **mē-**[2] in Appendix*).]

trim·e·ter (trĭm′ə-tər) *n. Prosody.* A verse line of three metrical feet. [Latin *trimetrus,* from Greek *trimetros* : TRI- + METER.]

tri·meth·a·di·one (trī′mĕth-ə-dī′ōn′) *n.* A granular, crystalline substance, $C_6H_9NO_3$, used in treating epilepsy. [TRI- + METH(YL) + DI- + -ONE.]

tri·met·ric (trī-mĕt′rĭk) *adj.* Also **tri·met·ri·cal** (-rĭ-kəl). *Prosody.* Consisting of three feet, or of lines of three feet.

tri·met·ro·gon (trī-mĕt′rə-gŏn′) *n.* A system of aerial photography in which one vertical and two oblique photographs are simultaneously taken for use in topographic mapping. [TRI- + Greek *metron,* measure, METER + -GON.]

trim·mer (trĭm′ər) *n.* **1.** One that trims, especially any of various devices used for trimming, as a lumber trimmer. **2.** A person who changes his opinions to suit the needs of the moment; a timeserver.

trim·ming (trĭm′ĭng) *n.* **1.** That which is added as decoration; an ornament. **2.** *Plural.* Accessories; extras: *roast turkey with all the trimmings.* **3.** *Plural.* That which is removed when something is trimmed; excess. **4.** *Informal.* A sound defeat, beating, or punishment.

tri·mo·lec·u·lar (trī′mə-lĕk′yə-lər) *adj.* Pertaining to or formed from three molecules.

tri·month·ly (trī-mŭnth′lē) *adj.* Done, occurring, or appearing every three months. —**tri·month′ly** *adv.*

tri·morph (trī′môrf′) *n.* **1.** A substance that occurs in three distinct forms. **2.** One of the forms in which such a substance occurs. [Back-formation from TRIMORPHIC.]

tri·mor·phic (trī-môr′fĭk) *adj.* Also **tri·mor·phous** (-fəs). **1.** *Biology.* Having or occurring in three differing forms. **2.** *Chemistry.* Crystallizing in three distinct forms. [From Greek *trimorphos,* having three forms : *tri-,* three + -MORPHOUS.] —**tri·mor′phi·cal·ly** *adv.* —**tri·mor′phism′** *n.*

Tri·mur·ti (trĭ-mŏŏr′tē) *n. Hindu Mythology.* The Vedaic triad of Brahma, Vishnu, and Shiva. [Sanskrit *trimūrti* : *tri,* three (see **trei-** in Appendix*) + *mūrti*†, form.]

Tri·na·cri·a. The ancient name for **Sicily.**

tri·nal (trī′nəl) *adj.* Having three parts; threefold; triple. [Latin *trīnālis,* from Latin *trīnus,* TRINE.]

tri·na·ry (trī′nə-rē) *adj.* Consisting of three parts or proceeding by threes; ternary. [Late Latin *trīnārius,* from Latin *trīnus,* TRINE.]

trine (trīn) *adj.* **1.** Threefold; triple. **2.** *Astrology.* **a.** Situated in trine. **b.** Of or relating to a favorable positioning of two planets. —*n.* **1.** A group of three. **2.** *Astrology.* The aspect of two planets when 120 degrees apart. [Middle English, from Old French, from Latin *trīnus,* from *trīnī,* three each. See **trei-** in Appendix.*]

Trine (trīn) *n.* The Trinity. [From TRINE.]

Trin·i·dad (trĭn′ə-dăd′). An island, 1,864 square miles in area, in the Atlantic Ocean off Venezuela; part of the independent state of Trinidad and Tobago. —**Trin′i·dad′i·an** *adj. & n.*

Trin·i·dad and To·ba·go (trĭn′ə-dăd′; tə-bā′gō). A state, independent since 1962, and member of the Commonwealth of Nations, comprising the islands and former British colonies of Trinidad and Tobago. Population, 932,000. Capital, Port-of-Spain.

Tri·nil man (trē′nĭl′). **Pithecanthropus** *(see).* [From *Trinil,* village in Java, where remains were found.]

Trin·i·tar·i·an (trĭn′ə-târ′ē-ən) *adj.* **1.** Describing or relating to the Trinity. **2.** Believing or professing belief in the Trinity or the doctrine of the Trinity. Compare **Unitarian. 3.** Pertaining to the Order of the Holy Trinity. —*n.* **1.** A person who believes in the doctrine of the Trinity. **2.** A member of the Order of the Holy Trinity, founded in 1198 for the ransoming of Christian captives. —**Trin′i·tar′i·an·ism′** *n.*

tri·ni·tro·ben·zene (trī′nī′trō-bĕn′zēn′, -bĕn-zēn′) *n.* A yellow crystalline compound, $C_6H_3N_3O_6$, derived from trinitrotoluene and used as an explosive. [TRI- + NITRO- + BENZENE.]

tri·ni·tro·cre·sol (trī′nī′trō-krē′sôl′, -sōl′) *n.* A yellow crystalline compound, $C_7H_5N_3O_7$, used in high explosives. [TRI- + NITRO- + CRESOL.]

tri·ni·tro·glyc·er·in (trī′nī′trō-glĭs′ə-rĭn) *n. Chemistry.* **Nitroglycerin** *(see).*

tri·ni·tro·phe·nol (trī′nī′trō-fē′nōl′, -nôl′) *n. Chemistry.* **Picric acid** *(see).* [TRI- + NITRO- + PHENOL.]

tri·ni·tro·tol·u·ene (trī′nī′trō-tŏl′yŏŏ-ēn′) *n.* A yellow crystalline compound, $C_7H_5N_3O_6$, used mainly as a high explosive. Also called "TNT," "trinitrotoluol." [TRI- + NITRO- + TOLUENE.]

trin·i·ty (trĭn′ə-tē) *n., pl.* **-ties. 1.** The state or condition of being three. **2.** Any three parts in union; a triad. Also called "triunity." [Middle English *trinite,* from Old French, from Latin *trīnitās,* from *trīnus,* TRINE.]

Trin·i·ty (trĭn′ə-tē) *n.* **1.** *Theology.* The union of three divine figures, the Father, Son, and Holy Ghost, in one Godhead. **2. Trinity Sunday** *(see).*

Trinity River. A river of Texas, rising northwest of Fort Worth and flowing 360 miles generally southeast to Galveston Bay.

Trinity Sunday. The first Sunday after Pentecost, or Whitsunday, dedicated to the Trinity. Also called "Trinity."

trin·ket (trĭng′kĭt) *n.* **1.** Any small ornament, such as a piece of jewelry. **2.** A trivial thing; a trifle. [Origin unknown.]

tri·no·mi·al (trī-nō′mē-əl) *adj.* **1.** Consisting of three names or terms, as a taxonomic designation. **2.** *Mathematics.* Having three algebraic terms connected by plus or minus signs. —*n.* **1.** *Mathematics.* A trinomial algebraic expression. **2.** A three-part taxonomic designation indicating genus, species, and subspecies or variety, such as *Brassica oleracea botrytis,* the cauliflower. [TRI- + (BI)NOMIAL.]

tri·o (trē′ō) *n., pl.* **-os. 1.** Any three people or things joined or associated. See Usage note below. **2.** *Music.* **a.** A composition for three performers. **b.** The people (collectively) who perform this composition. **c.** The middle section of a minuet or scherzo, a march, or of various dance forms. [Italian, variant (influenced by *duo*) of Latin *tria,* neuter of *trēs,* three. See **trei-** in Appendix.*]

Usage: *Trio,* applied to persons, implies common action or at least close association. In careful usage it is not merely a synonym for any three.

tri·ode (trī′ōd′) *n.* A highly evacuated electron tube containing an anode, a cathode, and a control grid. [TRI- + -ODE (path).]

tri·oe·cious (trī-ē′shəs) *adj.* Also **tri·e·cious.** *Botany.* Having male, female, and bisexual flowers borne on separate plants. [From New Latin *Trioecia,* former order of such plants : TRI- + Greek *oikia,* dwelling, from *oikos,* house (see **weik-**[1] in Appendix*).] —**tri·oe′cious·ly** *adv.*

tri·o·let (trē′ə-lā′, trī′ə-lĭt) *n.* A poem or stanza of eight lines constructed on two rhymes, the scheme being *abaaabab.* [French, diminutive of *trio,* trio, from Italian, TRIO.]

tri·ox·ide (trī-ŏk′sīd′) *n.* Also **tri·ox·id** (-ŏk′sĭd). A chemical compound containing three oxygen atoms per molecule.

trip (trĭp) *n.* **1.** A going from one place to another; journey. **2.** *Slang.* **a.** A protracted hallucination induced by a hallucinogen. **b.** Any experience regarded as similar to such a hallucination. **3.** A light or nimble step or tread. **4.** A stumble or fall caused by an obstacle or loss of balance. **5.** A maneuver causing someone to stumble or fall. **6.** A mistake; blunder. **7. a.** A device, such as a pawl, for tripping a mechanism. **b.** The action of such a device. —*v.* **tripped, tripping, trips.** —*intr.* **1.** To stumble; make a false step. **2.** To move quickly or nimbly with light, rapid steps; skip. **3.** To make a mistake; err. **4.** To be released, as a tooth on an escapement wheel in a watch. **5.** *Rare.* To make a trip or a journey. —*tr.* **1.** To cause to stumble or fall. Often used with *up.* **2.** To trap or catch in an error or inconsistency. **3.** *Archaic.* To perform (a dance) nimbly or lightly. **4.** To release a catch, trigger, or switch, setting something in operation. **5.** *Nautical.* **a.** To raise (an anchor) from the bottom. **b.** To tip or turn (a yardarm) into a position for lowering. **c.** To lift (an upper mast) in order to remove the fid before lowering. [Middle English, short journey, light movement, from *trippen*, to move nimbly, cause to stumble, from Old French *trip(p)er*, from Middle Dutch *trippen*, to hop. See der-¹ in Appendix.*]

tri·pal·mi·tin (trī-păl′mə-tĭn) *n. Chemistry.* **Palmitin** (*see*).

tri·par·tite (trī-pär′tīt′) *adj.* **1.** Composed of or divided into three parts. **2.** Relating to or executed by three parties.

tri·par·ti·tion (trī′pär-tĭsh′ən) *n.* Division into three parts or among three parties: *the tripartition of a defeated nation.*

tripe (trīp) *n.* **1.** The light-colored, rubbery lining of the stomach of cattle or other ruminants, used as food. **2.** *Informal.* Anything with no value; rubbish. [Middle English, from Old French *tripe*.]

tri·ped·al (trī-pĕd′l) *adj.* Having three feet or legs; tripodal. [Latin *tripedālis* : *tri-*, three + *pēs* (stem *ped-*), foot (see ped-¹ in Appendix*).]

tri·pet·al·ous (trī-pĕt′l-ĕs) *adj. Botany.* Having three petals.

trip hammer. Also **trip·ham·mer** (trĭp′hăm′ər), **trip-ham·mer.** A heavy, power-operated hammer that is lifted by a cam or lever and then dropped.

tri·phen·yl·meth·ane (trī′fĕn′əl-mĕth′ān′, trī′fē′nəl-) *n.* A colorless, crystalline hydrocarbon, $(C_6H_5)_3CH$, from which a large number of synthetic dyes are derived by substitution. [TRI- + PHENYL + METHANE.]

triph·thong (trĭf′thông′, -thŏng′, trĭp′-) *n.* A compound vowel sound resulting from the combination of three simple ones and functioning as a unit. [TRI- + (DI)PHTHONG.] —**triph·thon′gal** (trĭf-thôn′gəl, -thŏn′gəl, trĭp-) *adj.*

triph·y·lite (trĭf′ə-līt′) *n.* Also **triph·y·line** (-lēn′). Any of a vitreous bluish-gray mineral series of lithium, iron, and manganese phosphates. [TRI- + Greek *phulon*, tribe (see phyletic) + -ITE (from its three bases).]

tri·pin·nate (trī-pĭn′āt′) *adj. Botany.* Divided into leaflets that are subdivided into smaller, further subdivided leaflets or lobes, as the fronds of some ferns. —**tri·pin′nate·ly** *adv.*

tripl. triplicate.

tri·plane (trī′plān′) *n.* An airplane with wings placed above each other in three levels.

tri·ple (trĭp′əl) *adj.* **1.** Consisting of three parts; threefold. **2.** Three times as many or as much; thrice multiplied. —*n.* **1.** A number or quantity three times as great as another. **2.** A group or set of three; triad. **3.** *Baseball.* A three-base hit. —*v.* **tripled, -ling, -les.** —*tr.* To make three times as great in number or amount. —*intr.* **1.** To be or become three times as great in number or amount. **2.** *Baseball.* To make a three-base hit. [Middle English, from Old French, from Latin *triplus* : *tri-*, three + *-plus*, "-fold" (see pel-³ in Appendix*).] —**trip′ly** *adv.*

Triple Alliance. 1. The alliance of England, Sweden, and the Netherlands against France in 1668. **2.** The alliance of England, France, and the Netherlands against Spain in 1717, called the Quadruple Alliance when joined by Austria in 1718. **3.** The alliance of Great Britain, Austria, and Russia against France in 1795. **4.** The Dreibund formed by Germany, Austria, and Italy in 1882.

Triple Entente. The military alliance formed by Great Britain, France, and Russia prior to World War I as a means of counterbalancing the Dreibund.

triple play. *Baseball.* A rare defensive play in which three putouts, as two base runners and the batter, are executed during one turn at bat, thereby ending suddenly the offensive threat and the inning.

trip·let (trĭp′lĭt) *n.* **1.** A group or set of three of one kind. **2.** One of three children born at one birth. **3.** *Prosody.* A group of three rhyming lines. **4.** A group of three musical notes having the time value of two notes of the same kind. Also called "tercet." **5.** *Physics.* A **multiplet** (*see*) with three components. [TRIPL(E) + (DOUBL)ET.]

trip·le·tail (trĭp′əl-tāl′) *n.* Any of several chiefly marine fishes of the family Lobotidae; especially, *Lobotes surinamensis,* having prominent dorsal and anal fins that resemble extra tails.

triple time. A musical time or rhythm having three beats to the measure, with the accent on the first beat. Also called "triple measure."

trip·lex (trĭp′lĕks′, trī′plĕks′) *adj.* Composed of three parts; threefold; triple. —*n.* Something triplex. [Latin, threefold, triple. See trei- in Appendix*.]

trip·li·cate (trĭp′lĭ-kĭt) *adj. Abbr.* **tripl. 1.** Made with three identical copies; threefold; triple. **2.** Third. —*n.* One of a set of three identical objects or copies. —*tr.v.* (trĭp′lĭ-kāt′) **triplicated, -cating, -cates. 1.** To increase threefold; to triple. **2.** To make three identical copies of. [Middle English, from Latin *triplicātus*, past participle of *triplicāre*, to triple, from *triplex* (stem *triplic-*), TRIPLEX.] —**trip′li·cate·ly** *adv.* —**trip′li·ca′tion** *n.*

tri·plic·i·ty (trĭ-plĭs′ĭ-tē) *n., pl.* **-ties. 1.** The condition or quality of being triple. **2.** A group or set of three. **3.** *Astrology.* One of four groups of the zodiac, each consisting of three signs. In this sense, also called "trigon." [Middle English *triplicite*, a trigon, from Late Latin *triplicitās*, quality of being triple, from *triplex*, TRIPLEX.]

trip·loid (trĭp′loid′) *adj.* Having three haploid sets of chromosomes in each nucleus. —*n.* An organism having such sets of chromosomes. [Greek *triploos*, triple (see trei- in Appendix*) + (HAPL)OID.]

tri·pod (trī′pŏd′) *n.* **1.** A three-legged utensil, stool, table, or the like. **2.** An adjustable three-legged stand for supporting a transit, camera, or the like. [Latin *tripūs* (stem *tripod-*), from Greek *tripous*, three-tooted : *tri-*, three + *-pous*, -POD.] —**trip′o·dal** (trĭp′ə-dəl, trī′pŏd′l) *adj.*

trip·o·li (trĭp′ə-lē) *n.* A porous, lightweight, siliceous rock of various colors, derived from weathering of chert and siliceous limestone. [Found in TRIPOLI, Libya.]

Trip·o·li (trĭp′ə-lē). **1.** Ancient name **Trip·o·lis** (trĭp′ə-lĭs). A city of Lebanon, a seaport in the north on the Mediterranean. Population, 100,000. **2.** A capital of Libya, a seaport in the northwest on the Mediterranean. Population, 376,000.

Trip·o·li·ta·ni·a (trĭp′ō-lĭ-tā′nē-ə). Ancient name **Trip·o·lis** (trĭp′-ə-lĭs). A region of Libya occupying about 136,000 square miles in the northwest; established as a Phoenician colony in the seventh century B.C. and later one of the Barbary States. Capital, Tripoli.

tri·pos (trī′pŏs) *n., pl.* **-poses.** At Cambridge University in England, any of the examinations for the B.A. degree with honors. [Variant of Latin *tripūs*, TRIPOD, formerly someone who humorously disputed with the candidates while sitting on a three-legged stool.]

trip·pet (trĭp′ĭt) *n. Machinery.* A cam or projection in a mechanism designed to strike another part at regular intervals. [Middle English *tripet*, piece of wood used in the game of tipcat, from *trippen*, to TRIP.]

trip·ping (trĭp′ĭng) *adj.* Moving or stepping lightly and briskly; easy; nimble. —**trip′ping·ly** *adv.*

trip·tane (trĭp′tān′) *n.* A colorless liquid antiknock additive, C_7H_{16}, used in aviation fuels. [Short for *trimethylbutane*.]

trip·tych (trĭp′tĭk) *n.* **1.** A hinged writing tablet consisting of three leaves, used in antiquity. **2.** A tableau of three hinged or folding panels bearing a religious story in painting, used as an altarpiece. [Greek *triptukhos*, threefold : *tri-*, three + *ptukhē*, fold (see **diptych**).]

triptych
Fourteenth-century French

Tri·pu·ra (trĭp′ə-rə). A territory of India occupying 4,032 square miles in the northeast, adjoining eastern East Pakistan. Population, 1,142,000. Capital, Agartala.

tri·reme (trī′rēm′) *n.* An ancient Greek or Roman galley or warship, having three tiers of oars on each side. [Latin *trirēmis*, having three tiers of oars : *tri-*, three + *rēmus*, oar (see ere-¹ in Appendix*).]

tri·sac·cha·ride (trī-săk′ə-rīd′, -rĭd) *n. Chemistry.* A carbohydrate that upon hydrolysis yields three monosaccharides.

tri·sect (trī′sĕkt′, trī-sĕkt′) *tr.v.* **-sected, -secting, -sects.** To divide into three equal parts. [TRI- + -SECT.] —**tri′sec′tion** (trī′sĕk′shən, trī-sĕk′-) *n.* —**tri′sec′tor** (trī′sĕk′tər, trī-sĕk′-) *n.*

tri·sep·al·ous (trī-sĕp′ə-ləs) *adj.* Having three sepals.

tri·skel·i·on (trī-skĕl′ē-ən, trĭs-kĕl′-) *n., pl.* **-ia** (-ē-ə). Also **tri·skele** (trī′skēl′, trĭs′kēl′), **tri·scele.** A figure consisting of three curved lines or branches, or three stylized human arms or legs, radiating from a common center. [New Latin, from Greek *triskelēs*, three-legged : *tri-*, three + *skelos*, leg (see skel-³ in Appendix*).]

tris·mus (trĭz′məs) *n. Pathology.* **Lockjaw** (*see*). [New Latin, from Greek *trismos, trigmos*, a scream, a grating, a rasping. See strei- in Appendix.*] —**tris′mic** *adj.*

tris·oc·ta·he·dron (trĭs-ŏk′tə-hē′drən) *n., pl.* **-drons** or **-dra** (-drə). **1.** *Geometry.* A solid figure having 24 congruent triangular faces and an octahedron as a base. **2.** *Crystallography.* A **trapezohedron** (*see*). [Greek *tris*, thrice (see trei- in Appendix*) + OCTAHEDRON.] —**tris·oc′ta·he′dral** *adj.*

tri·so·mic (trī-sō′mĭk) *adj. Genetics.* Having at least one triploid chromosome in an otherwise diploid set. [TRI- + (CHROMO)SOM(E) + -IC.] —**tri′some**′ (trī′sōm′) *n.*

Tris·tan (trĭs′tən, -tän′, -tăn′). Also **Tris·tram** (trĭs′trəm). *Arthurian Legend.* A prince who fell in love with the Irish princess Iseult and died with her.

tri·ste·a·rin (trī-stē′ə-rĭn, -stîr′ĭn) *n. Chemistry.* **Stearin** (*see*).

trist·ful (trĭst′fəl) *adj. Archaic.* Sorrowful; gloomy. [From Middle English *trist*, from Old French *triste*, from Latin *trīstis†*, gloomy.] —**trist′ful·ly** *adv.*

tris·tich (trĭs′tĭk) *n.* A stanza or strophic unit of three lines. [TRI- + (DI)STICH.]

tri·sul·fide (trī-sŭl′fīd′) *n.* Also **tri·sul·phide, tri·sul·fid** (-fĭd), **tri·sul·phid.** A sulfide containing three sulfur atoms per molecule.

tri·syl·la·ble (trī′sĭl′ə-bəl) *n.* A three-syllable word. —**tri′syl·lab′ic** (-sĭ-lăb′ĭk), **tri′syl·lab′i·cal** *adj.* —**tri′syl·lab′i·cal·ly** *adv.*

trit. triturate.

tri·tan·o·pi·a (trī′tə-nō′pē-ə) *n.* A rare visual defect involving an inability to distinguish the color blue. [New Latin, "ability to see only one third (of the colors of the spectrum)" : Greek *tritos*, a third (see trei- in Appendix*) + *anopia*, blindness : AN- (not) + -OPIA.]

trite (trīt) *adj.* **triter, tritest. 1.** Overused and commonplace; lacking interest or originality. **2.** *Archaic.* Frayed or worn by use. [Latin *trītus*, past participle of *terere*, to rub (away), wear out. See ter-² in Appendix*.] —**trite′ly** *adv.* —**trite′ness** *n.*

Synonyms: *trite, hackneyed, shopworn, stereotyped, commonplace, threadbare, stale, banal.* These adjectives describe writing and speech that is without freshness of expression and consequently without appeal. *Trite, hackneyed,* and *shopworn* all imply overfamiliarity resulting from overuse of combinations of words or overworking of a theme; *hackneyed* is strongest in suggesting reduction of a once forceful expression or idea to an empty verbal formula or cliché. *Stereotyped* can refer to a theme or treatment of theme so lacking in originality or creative force that it seems a mechanical reproduction of timeworn generalizations or clichés. *Commonplace* applies to speech or writing that is pedestrian through its stress on what is obvious, conventional, or platitudinous. *Threadbare* describes a theme or topic or an individual expression that has been overworked to the point where its further employment with profit is extremely

triplane

triskelion

ă pat/ā pay/âr care/ä father/b bib/ch church/d deed/ĕ pet/ē be/f fife/g gag/h hat/hw which/ĭ pit/ī pie/îr pier/j judge/k kick/l lid, needle/m mum/n no, sudden/ng thing/ŏ pot/ō toe/ô paw, for/oi noise/ou out/oo took/oo boot/p pop/r roar/s sauce/sh ship, dish/t tight/th thin, path/th this, bathe/ŭ cut/ûr urge/v valve/w with/y yes/z zebra, size/zh vision/ə about, item, edible, gallop, circus/ à Fr. ami/œ Fr. feu, Ger. schön/ü Fr. tu, Ger. über/KH Ger. ich, Scot. loch/N Fr. bon. *Follows main vocabulary. †Of obscure origin.

unlikely. *Stale* can imply loss of taste or appeal through overuse or through mere age. *Banal* often adds to lack of freshness the implication of inanity or of lack of good taste.

tri·the·ism (trī′thē-ĭz′əm) *n.* Belief in three gods; specifically, the belief that the Father, Son, and Holy Ghost are three separate and distinct gods. [TRI- + THEISM.] —**tri′the·ist** *n.* —**tri′the·is′tic, tri′the·is′ti·cal** *adj.*

trit·i·um (trĭt′ē-əm, trĭsh′ē-) *n.* A rare radioactive hydrogen isotope with atomic mass 3 and half-life 12.5 years, prepared artificially for use as a tracer and as a constituent of hydrogen bombs. [New Latin, from Greek *tritos,* third. See **trei-** in Appendix.*]

tri·ton¹ (trīt′n) *n.* Any of various chiefly tropical marine gastropod mollusks of the genus *Cymatium* and related genera, having a pointed, spirally twisted, often colorfully marked shell. [After TRITON, whose trumpet is a shell.]

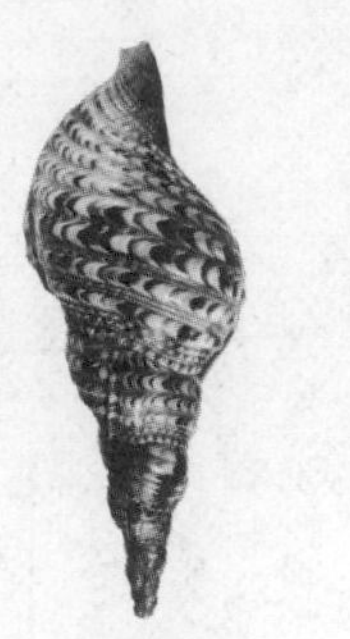

triton¹
Charonia tritonis

tri·ton² (trī′tŏn′) *n.* The nucleus of a tritium atom consisting of two neutrons and one proton. [TRIT(IUM) + -ON.]

Tri·ton (trīt′n). *Greek Mythology.* **1.** A god of the sea, son of Poseidon and Amphitrite, portrayed as having the head and trunk of a man and the tail of a fish. **2.** One of a race of lesser sea deities. [Latin, from Greek *Tritōn*†.]

tri·tone (trī′tōn′) *n. Music.* An interval composed of three whole tones. [Greek *tritonos,* having three tones : TRI- + TONE.]

trit·u·rate (trĭch′ə-rāt′) *tr.v.* **-rated, -rating, -rates.** To rub, crush, grind, or pound into fine particles or a powder; pulverize. —*n.* (trĭch′ər-ĭt). *Abbr.* **trit.** A triturated substance, especially a powdered drug. [Late Latin *trītūrāre,* to pulverize corn, from Latin *trītūra,* a rubbing or chafing, from *trītus,* past participle of *terere,* to rub. See **ter-²** in Appendix.*] —**trit′u·ra·ble** (trĭch′ər-ə-bəl) *adj.* —**trit′u·ra′tor** (-rā′tər) *n.*

trit·u·ra·tion (trĭch′ə-rā′shən) *n.* **1.** The act or process of triturating. **2.** The composing of a dental amalgam by mortar and pestle.

tri·umph (trī′əmf) *intr.v.* **-umphed, -umphing, -umphs. 1.** To be victorious or successful; to win; prevail. **2.** To rejoice over a success or victory; exult. **3.** In ancient Rome, to receive honors upon return from a victory. —*n.* **1.** The instance or fact of being victorious; success. **2.** Exultation or merriment derived from victory. **3.** A public celebration in ancient Rome to welcome a returning victorious commander and his army. **4.** *Obsolete.* Any public celebration or spectacular pageant. —See Synonyms at **victory.** [Latin *triumphāre,* from *triumphus,* a triumph, variant of Old Latin *triumpus,* akin to or possibly from Greek *thriambos,* hymn to Bacchus, of Aegean origin.] —**tri′umph·er** *n.*

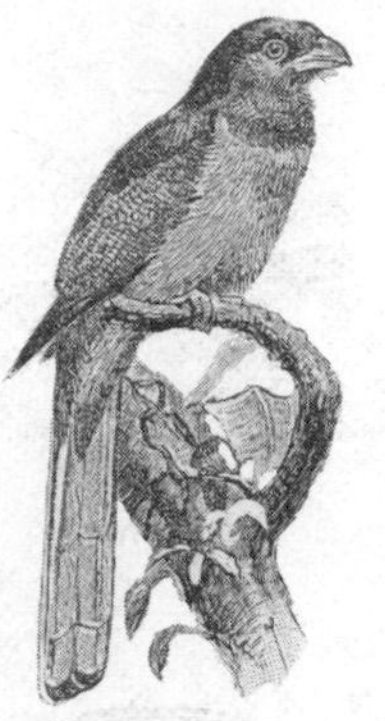

trogon
Apaloderma narina

tri·um·phal (trī-ŭm′fəl) *adj.* **1.** Pertaining to or having the nature of a triumph. **2.** Celebrating or commemorating a victory or triumph.

tri·um·phant (trī-ŭm′fənt) *adj.* **1.** Exulting in success or victory. **2.** Victorious; conquering; successful. **3.** *Obsolete.* Triumphal. **4.** *Obsolete.* Magnificent; splendid. —**tri·um′phant·ly** *adv.*

tri·um·vir (trī-ŭm′vər) *n., pl.* **-virs** or **-viri** (-və-rī′). One of three men sharing public administration or civil authority, as in ancient Rome. [Latin, singular of *triumvirī,* from *trium virōrum,* "(one) of three men," genitive of *trēs virī,* three men : *trēs,* three (see **trei-** in Appendix*) + *virī,* plural of *vir,* man (see **wiros** in Appendix*).] —**tri·um′vi·ral** *adj.*

tri·um·vi·rate (trī-ŭm′vər-ĭt) *n.* **1.** A group of three men jointly governing a realm. **2. a.** The office or term of a triumvir. **b.** Government by triumvirs. **3.** Any association or group of three. [Latin *triumvirātus,* from *triumvir,* TRIUMVIR.]

tri·une (trī′yo͞on′) *adj.* Being three in one. Said especially of the single Godhead of the Trinity. —*n.* A trinity. [TRI- + Latin *ūnus,* one (see **oino-** in Appendix*).]

tri·u·ni·ty (trī-yo͞o′nə-tē) *n., pl.* **-ties.** A **trinity** *(see).* [TRI- + UNITY.]

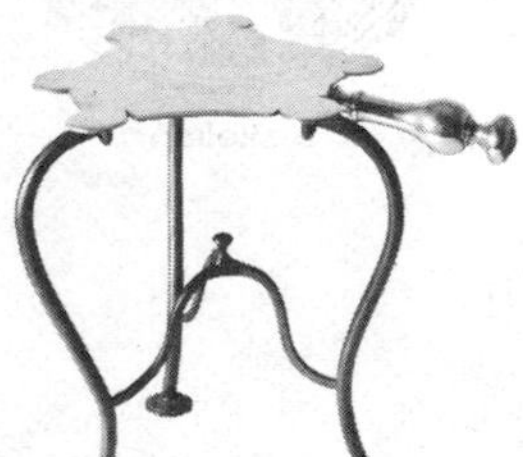

trivet
Eighteenth-century trivet of iron and brass

tri·va·lent (trī-vā′lənt) *adj.* Also **ter·va·lent** (tûr′və-lənt, tər-vā′lənt). *Chemistry.* Having valence 3. —**tri·va′lence, tri·va′len·cy** *n.*

tri·valve (trī′vălv′) *adj.* Having three valves.

Tri·van·drum (trĭ-văn′drəm). The capital of Kerala, Republic of India, in the extreme southern part of the state on the Arabian Sea. Population, 257,000.

triv·et (trĭv′ĭt) *n.* **1.** A three-legged stand made of iron or the like, used for supporting cooking vessels in a fireplace. **2.** A metal stand with short feet, used under a hot dish on a table. [Middle English *trevet,* probably Old English *trefet,* from Latin *tripēs,* "three-footed" : *tri-,* three + *pēs,* foot (see **ped-¹** in Appendix*).]

triv·i·a¹ (trĭv′ē-ə) *pl.n.* Insignificant or inessential matters; trivialities; trifles: *the trivia that deprive such meetings of any real value.* [New Latin, trivia, "that which comes from the street," from Latin, plural of *trivium,* place where three roads meet, public square. See **trivium.**]

triv·i·a². Plural of **trivium.**

triv·i·al (trĭv′ē-əl) *adj.* **1.** Of little importance or significance; trifling. **2.** Ordinary; commonplace. **3.** Concerned with or involving trivia. —**triv′i·al·ly** *adv.*

Synonyms: trivial, trifling, paltry, petty, picayune. These adjectives all apply to what is small or unimportant, but they are not always interchangeable. *Trivial* refers principally to things that have little importance or significance in themselves or that require no intellectual depth on the part of persons concerned with them. *Trifling* describes things so unimportant or so small in size or value as to be scarcely worth notice. *Paltry* describes things, especially sums of money, whose size or value arouses contempt; thus the term implies marked insufficiency in relation to what is required or desired. *Petty* can refer to insignificant things or to persons who have subordinate rank or who are small-minded or mean. *Picayune* describes things of little significance or value, in the sense of paltriness; or it can apply figuratively to persons totally lacking in stature, capacity, breadth of outlook, or fineness of temperament.

triv·i·al·i·ty (trĭv′ē-ăl′ə-tē) *n., pl.* **-ties. 1.** The condition or quality of being trivial. **2.** A trivial matter, idea, occurrence, or the like.

trivial name. 1. In taxonomic nomenclature, the term following the genus name and designating the species, as *troglodytes* in *Pan troglodytes,* the chimpanzee. **2.** A vernacular name as distinguished from a taxonomic designation.

triv·i·um (trĭv′ē-əm) *n., pl.* **-ia** (-ē-ə). The elementary division of the seven liberal arts in medieval schools, consisting of grammar, logic, and rhetoric. Compare **quadrivium.** [Medieval Latin, from Latin, place where three roads meet, public square : *tri-,* three + *via,* road, way (see **wei-²** in Appendix*).]

tri·week·ly (trī-wēk′lē) *adj.* **1.** Happening, done, or appearing three times a week. **2.** Happening, done, or appearing every three weeks. —*adv.* **1.** Three times a week. **2.** Every three weeks. —*n., pl.* **triweeklies.** A periodical published triweekly.

Tro·as (trō′ăs′). Also **the Tro·ad** (trō′ăd′). The region along the Aegean in northwestern Asia Minor of which ancient Troy was the center.

Tro·bri·and Islands (trō′brē-änd′). A group of small islands, about 170 square miles in area, off eastern New Guinea in the southwestern Pacific; part of the Territory of Papua.

tro·car (trō′kär′) *n.* A sharp-pointed surgical instrument, used with a cannula to puncture a body cavity for fluid aspiration. [French *trocart,* from Old French, "three-sided instrument" : *trois,* three, from Latin *trēs* (see **trei-** in Appendix*) + *carre,* side, from *carrer,* to square, from Latin *quadrāre,* from *quadrus,* a square (see **kwetwer-** in Appendix*).]

tro·cha·ic (trō-kā′ĭk) *adj.* Of, pertaining to, or consisting of trochees. —*n.* A trochaic foot, line, or verse. [French *trochaïque,* from Latin *trochaicus,* from Greek *trokhaikos,* from *trokhaios.* See **trochee.**]

tro·chal (trō′kəl) *adj.* Shaped like a wheel. [From Greek *trokhos,* wheel, from *trekhein,* to run. See **dhregh-** in Appendix.*]

tro·chan·ter (trō-kăn′tər) *n.* **1.** Any of several bony processes on the upper part of the femur of many vertebrates. **2.** The second proximal segment of the leg of an insect. [Greek *trokhantēr,* from *trekhein,* to run. See **trochal.**]

tro·che (trō′kē) *n.* A small circular medicinal lozenge; pastille. [Earlier *trochies* (plural), from Middle English *trociske* (singular), from Late Latin *trochiscus,* from Greek *trokhiskos,* diminutive of *trokhos,* wheel. See **trochal.**]

tro·chee (trō′kē) *n. Prosody.* A metrical foot consisting of one long or stressed syllable followed by one short or unstressed syllable. [French *trochée,* from Latin *trochaeus,* from Greek *trokhaios (pous),* "running (foot)," from *trokhos,* running, from *trekhein,* to run. See **dhregh-** in Appendix.*]

troch·le·a (trŏk′lē-ə) *n., pl.* **-leae** (-lē-ē′). An anatomical structure that resembles a pulley, as the part of the distal end of the humerus that articulates with the ulna. [Latin, system of pulleys, from Greek *trokhileia.* See **dhregh-** in Appendix.*]

troch·le·ar (trŏk′lē-ər) *adj.* **1.** Of, resembling, or situated near a trochlea. **2.** Of or pertaining to the trochlear, or fourth, cranial nerve. **3.** *Botany.* Shaped like a pulley.

tro·choid (trō′koid′, trŏk′oid′) *adj.* Also **tro·choi·dal** (trō-koid′l, trŏk-oid′l). Capable of or exhibiting rotation about a central axis. —*n.* The plane locus of a point on the radius or on an extension of the radius of a circle, as the circle rolls along a fixed straight line. [Greek *trokhoeidēs,* resembling a wheel, wheellike, circular : *trokhos,* wheel (see **troche**) + -OID.] —**tro·choi′dal·ly** *adv.*

troch·o·phore (trŏk′ə-fôr′, -fōr′) *n.* The small aquatic larva of various invertebrates, including certain mollusks and annelids. [Greek *trokhos,* wheel (see **troche**) + -PHORE (from its spheroidal body and ring of cilia).]

trod. Past tense and alternate past participle of **tread.**

trod·den. Past participle of **tread.**

trode. *Archaic.* Past tense of **tread.**

trof·fer (trŏf′ər, trô′fər) *n.* An inverted, usually metal trough suspended from a ceiling as a fixture for fluorescent lighting tubes. [From *troff-,* variant of TROUGH.]

trog·lo·dyte (trŏg′lə-dīt′) *n.* **1.** A prehistoric cave dweller. **2.** A person likened to a cave man, as in reclusiveness or brutishness. [Latin *Trōglodyta,* from Greek *Trōglodutēs,* singular of *Trōglodutai,* variant (influenced by *trōglos,* cave, and *-dutai,* those who enter) of *Trōgodutai*†, name of an Ethiopian people.] —**trog′lo·dyt′ic** (-dĭt′ĭk), **trog′lo·dyt′i·cal** *adj.*

tro·gon (trō′gŏn′) *n.* Any of various colorful tropical birds of the family Trogonidae, which includes the quetzal. [New Latin, "gnawer," from Greek *trōgōn,* present participle of *trōgein,* gnaw. See **ter-²** in Appendix.*]

troi·ka (troi′kə) *n.* **1.** A kind of small Russian carriage drawn by a team of three horses abreast. **2.** A triumvirate. [Russian *troyka,* from *troje,* three. See **trei-** in Appendix.*]

Troi·lus (troi′ləs, trō′ə-ləs). *Greek Mythology.* A son of Priam of Troy, killed by Achilles. He is depicted as Cressida's lover in medieval romance.

Trois Ri·vières (trwä′ rē-vyâr′). *English* **Three Rivers.** A city on the St. Lawrence in southern Quebec. Population, 53,000.

Tro·jan (trō′jən) *n.* **1.** A native or inhabitant of ancient Troy. **2.** A person of courageous determination or energy. —*adj.* Of or pertaining to ancient Troy or its residents. [Middle English, from Latin *Trōjānus,* from *Trōjā,* TROY.]

ă pat/ā pay/âr care/ä father/b bib/ch church/d deed/ĕ pet/ē be/f fife/g gag/h hat/hw which/ĭ pit/ī pie/îr pier/j judge/k kick/l lid, needle/m mum/n no, sudden/ng thing/ŏ pot/ō toe/ô paw, for/oi noise/ou out/o͝o took/o͞o boot/p pop/r roar/s sauce/sh ship, dish/

Trojan horse. **1.** The hollow wooden horse in which, according to Virgil, Greeks hid and gained entrance to Troy, later opening the gates to their army. **2.** Any subversive group or device insinuated within enemy ranks.

Trojan War. The prehistoric ten-year war waged against Troy by the confederated Greeks, ending in the burning of Troy. It is known chiefly through Homeric legend, which gives the cause as the abduction of the Spartan queen, Helen, by Paris, a Trojan prince.

troll[1] (trōl) *v.* **trolled, trolling, trolls.** —*tr.* **1.** To fish for by trailing a baited line from behind a slowly moving boat. **2.** To trail (a baited line) in fishing. **3.** To sing in succession the parts of (a round, for example). **4.** To sing heartily: *troll a carol.* **5.** To roll or revolve. —*intr.* **1.** To fish by trailing a line, as from a moving boat. **2.** To sing heartily or gaily. **3.** To be sung or uttered in a rolling, hearty manner: *The tune trolled on.* **4.** To roll or spin around. **5.** *Obsolete.* To wander about; to ramble. —*n.* **1.** *Obsolete.* A vocal composition in successive parts; a round. **2.** The act of trolling for fish. **3.** A lure used for trolling, as a spoon or spinner. [Middle English *trollen*†, to ramble, roll.] —**troll'er** *n.*

troll[2] (trōl) *n.* A supernatural creature of Scandinavian folklore variously portrayed as a friendly or mischievous dwarf, or sometimes a giant, that lives in caves, in the hills, or under bridges. [Norwegian, from Old Norse *troll*†, monster, demon.]

trol·ley (trŏl'ē) *n., pl.* **-leys.** Also **trol·ly** *pl.* **-lies. 1.** An electric car, a **streetcar** *(see).* **2.** A wheeled carriage, cage, or basket that is suspended from and travels on an overhead track. **3.** A device that collects electric current from an underground conductor, an overhead wire, or a third rail, and transmits it to the motor of an electric vehicle. **4.** A small truck or car operating on a track and used in a mine, quarry, or factory for conveying materials. **5.** *British.* A cart. —*v.* **trolleyed, -leying, -leys.** Also **trol·ly, -lied, -lying, -lies.** —*tr.* To convey by trolley. —*intr.* To travel by trolley. [Probably from TROLL (to move about).]

trolley bus. An electric bus that does not run on tracks and is powered by electricity from an overhead wire.

trolley car. A **streetcar** *(see).*

trol·lop (trŏl'əp) *n.* **1.** A slovenly, untidy woman; a slattern. **2.** A loose woman; strumpet. [Perhaps from TROLL (to roll, "move back and forth").]

Trol·lope (trŏl'əp), **Anthony.** 1815–1882. English novelist.

Trom·be·tas (trōN-bā'täs). A river of Brazil, rising in northwestern Pará State near the Guyana border and flowing 470 miles generally south to the Amazon River.

trom·bic·u·li·a·sis (trŏm-bĭk'yə-lī'ə-sĭs) *n.* Also **trom·bic·u·lo·sis** (-lō'sĭs), **trom·bi·di·a·sis** (trŏm'bə-dī'ə-sĭs). *Pathology.* Infestation with chiggers. [New Latin : *Trombicula,* genus of mites, diminutive of *Trombidium*† + -IASIS.]

trom·bone (trŏm-bōn', trəm-, trŏm'bōn') *n.* A brass musical instrument consisting of a long cylindrical tube bent upon itself twice and ending in a bell-shaped mouth. [French, from Italian, augmentative of *tromba,* trumpet, from Old High German *trumpa,* TRUMP.] —**trom·bon'ist** *n.*

trom·mel (trŏm'əl) *n.* A revolving cylindrical sieve used for sizing rock and ore. [German *Trommel,* barrel, drum, from Middle High German *trummel,* from *trumme,* drum, akin to Middle Dutch *tromme,* DRUM.]

tromp (trŏmp) *v.* **tromped, tromping, tromps.** *Informal.* —*intr.* To walk heavily and noisily; to tramp. —*tr.* **1.** To trample underfoot. **2.** To defeat soundly; trounce. —**tromp on.** *Informal.* To abuse verbally. [Blend of TRAMP and STOMP.]

trompe (trŏmp) *n.* An apparatus in which water falling through a perforated pipe entrains air into and down the pipe to produce an air blast for a furnace or forge. [French, "trumpet," from Old French. See **trump** (trumpet).]

Trom·sø (trŏm'sō, -sœ). A city of Norway, a seaport in the northern part of the country. Population, 33,000.

–tron. Indicates: **1.** Vacuum tube; for example, **dynatron. 2.** Device for manipulating subatomic particles; for example, **cyclotron.** [Greek, suffix denoting instrument.]

tro·na (trō'nə) *n.* A natural vitreous gray or white mineral, $Na_2CO_3 \cdot NaHCO_3 \cdot 2H_2O$, used as a source of sodium compounds. [Swedish, probably from Arabic *trōn,* short for *natrūn,* **natron.** See **nitron** in Appendix.*]

Trond·heim (trôn'hām', trŏn'-). Also **Trond·hjem** (trôn'yĕm', trŏn'-). Formerly **Ni·dar·os** (nē'dä-rōs'). A city of Norway, a major seaport in the west on Trondheim Fjord, an 80-mile-long inlet of the Norwegian Sea. Population, 114,000.

Tro·o·dos Mountain (trô'ô-*th*ôs). The highest elevation (6,400 feet) on Cyprus, and a mountain in the center of the island.

troop (tro͞op) *n. Abbr.* **trp. 1.** A group or company of people, animals, or things. **2.** A group of soldiers. **3.** *Plural.* Military units; soldiers. **4.** A unit of at least five Boy Scouts or Girl Scouts under the guidance of an adult leader. **5.** *Informal.* A great many; a lot. —See Synonyms at **flock.** —*intr.v.* **trooped, trooping, troops. 1.** To move or go as a throng. **2.** To proceed; move along: *children trooping home.* **3.** To consort; associate. Used with *with.* [French *troupe,* back-formation from *troupeau,* herd, from Medieval Latin *troppus*†.]

troop·er (tro͞o'pər) *n.* **1. a.** A cavalryman. **b.** A cavalry horse. **2.** A mounted policeman. **3.** A state policeman.

troop·ship (tro͞op'shĭp') *n.* A transport ship designed for carrying troops.

troost·ite (tro͞o'stīt') *n.* A reddish crystalline mineral, a variety of **willemite** *(see),* in which the zinc is partly replaced by manganese. [After Gerald *Troost* (1776–1850), American geologist.]

trop. tropic; tropical.

trope (trōp) *n.* **1.** The figurative use of a word or expression; a figure of speech. **2.** A word or phrase interpolated as an embellishment in the sung parts of certain medieval liturgies. [Latin *tropus,* from Greek *tropos,* a turn, way, manner. See **trep-**[2] in Appendix.*]

troph·ic (trŏf'ĭk, trō'fĭk) *adj.* Of or pertaining to nutrition or to the nutritive processes. [Greek *trophikos,* nursing, from *trophē,* food, from *trephein,* to nourish. See **thrch-** in Appendix.*] —**troph'i·cal·ly** *adv.*

tropho–. Indicates nutrition; for example, **trophoblast.** [From Greek *trophē,* food, from *trephein,* to nourish. See **threph-** in Appendix.*]

troph·o·blast (trŏf'ə-blăst', trō'fə-) *n.* The outermost layer of cells of the morula that attaches the fertilized ovum to the uterine wall and acts as a nutritive pathway. Also called "trophoderm." [TROPHO- + -BLAST.] —**troph'o·blas'tic** *adj.*

troph·o·zo·ite (trŏf'ə-zō'īt', trō'fə-) *n.* A protozoan of the class Sporozoa in the active stage. [TROPHO- + ZO(O)- + -ITE.]

tro·phy (trō'fē) *n., pl.* **-phies. 1.** A prize or memento received as a symbol of victory. **2.** An accumulation of captured arms or other spoils kept as a memorial of victory. **3.** A specimen or part, often mounted, preserved as a token of successful hunting. **4.** The monument of an enemy's defeat, consisting of captured arms and spoils, customary in antiquity. **5.** *Architecture.* A marble carving or bronze cast depicting a group of weapons, armor, and the like placed upon a four-sided or circular base as an ornament. **6.** Any memento, as of one's personal achievements. [Old French *trophee,* from Latin *trophaeum,* from Greek *tropaion,* "monument of the enemy's defeat," from *tropaios,* of turning, of defeat, from *tropē,* a turn, repulse of the enemy. See **trep-**[2] in Appendix.*]

–trophy. Indicates a specified type of nutrition or growth; for example, **hypertrophy.** [New Latin *-trophia,* from Greek, from *trophē,* food. See **tropho-.**]

trop·ic (trŏp'ĭk) *n. Abbr.* **trop. 1.** *Astronomy.* Either of two circles on the celestial sphere parallel to and at an angular distance of 23 degrees 27 minutes from the equator that are the limits of the apparent northern and southern passages of the sun. **2.** *Geography.* Either of the two corresponding parallels of latitude on the earth that constitute the boundaries of the Torrid Zone. See **tropic of Cancer, tropic of Capricorn. 3.** *Plural.* The region of the earth's surface lying between these latitudes; the Torrid Zone. Usually preceded by *the.* —*adj.* Of or relating to the tropics; tropical. [Middle English *tropik,* solstice point at which the sun "turns" back and moves toward the earth, from Late Latin *tropicus,* from Greek *tropikos,* of turning, from *tropē,* a turn. See **trep-**[2] in Appendix.*]

–tropic. Indicates turning in response to a specified stimulus; for example, **orthotropic.** [From Greek *tropos,* a turn, TROPE.]

trop·i·cal (trŏp'ĭ-kəl) *adj. Abbr.* **trop. 1.** Of, indigenous to, or characteristic of the tropics. **2.** Hot and humid; sultry; torrid. —**trop'i·cal·ly** *adv.*

tropical cyclone. A very low pressure area 50 to 100 miles in radius that originates in tropical regions and is frequently marked by winds of hurricane strength circulating around the calm eye in the center of the region.

tropical fish. Any of various small or brightly colored fishes native to tropical waters and often kept in home aquariums.

tropical storm. A tropical cyclone having winds ranging from 30 miles to 75 miles per hour.

tropical year. The time interval between two successive passages of the sun through the vernal equinox; the calendar year, or 365.2422 mean solar days. Also called "solar year." See **year.**

trop·ic·bird (trŏp'ĭk-bûrd') *n.* Any of several predominantly white sea birds of the genus *Phaethon,* of warm regions, having a pair of long, slender, projecting tail feathers.

tropic of Cancer. The parallel of latitude 23 degrees 27 minutes north of the equator, the northern boundary of the Torrid Zone, and the most northerly latitude at which the sun reaches an altitude of 90 degrees.

tropic of Capricorn. The parallel of latitude 23 degrees 27 minutes south of the equator, the southern boundary of the Torrid Zone, and the most southerly latitude at which the sun reaches an altitude of 90 degrees.

tro·pine (trō'pēn', -pĭn) *n.* Also **tro·pin** (-pĭn). A white, crystalline, poisonous alkaloid, $C_8H_{15}NO$, having a tobacco odor and used as a medicine. [Short for ATROPINE.]

tro·pism (trō'pĭz'əm) *n. Biology.* The responsive growth or movement of an organism toward or away from an external stimulus. [From -TROPISM.]

–tropism. Indicates the growth or movement of an organism or part in response to a specified stimulus; for example, **phototropism.** [From Greek *tropos,* turn. See **tropo-.**]

tropo–. Indicates turning or change, especially change of temperature or condition; for example, **troposphere.** [From Greek *tropos,* a turn, change. See **trep-**[2] in Appendix.*]

tro·pol·o·gy (trō-pŏl'ə-jē) *n., pl.* **-gies.** A mode of Biblical interpretation insisting on the morally edifying sense of tropes in Scripture. [Late Latin *tropologia,* from Late Greek : Greek *tropos,* TROPE + -LOGY.] —**tro'po·log'ic** (trō'pə-lŏj'ĭk, trŏp'ə-), **tro'po·log'i·cal** *adj.* —**tro'po·log'i·cal·ly** *adv.*

tro·po·pause (trō'pə-pôz', trŏp'ə-) *n.* The boundary between the upper troposphere and the lower stratosphere that varies in altitude from 5 miles at the poles to 11 miles at the equator. [TROPO- + PAUSE.]

tro·po·phyte (trō'pə-fīt', trŏp'ə-) *n.* A plant adapted to climatic conditions in which periods of heavy rainfall alternate with periods of drought. [TROPO- + -PHYTE.] —**tro'po·phyt'ic** (-fĭt'ĭk) *adj.*

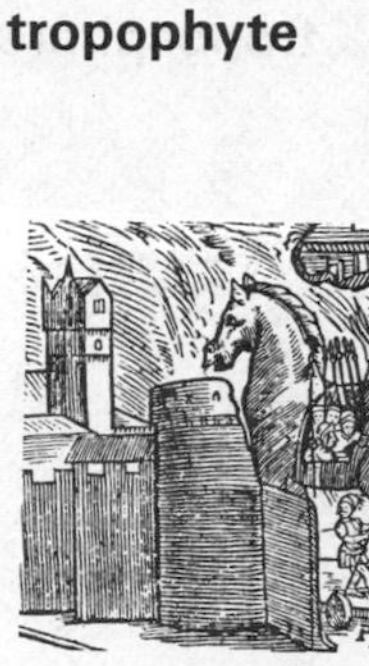

Trojan horse

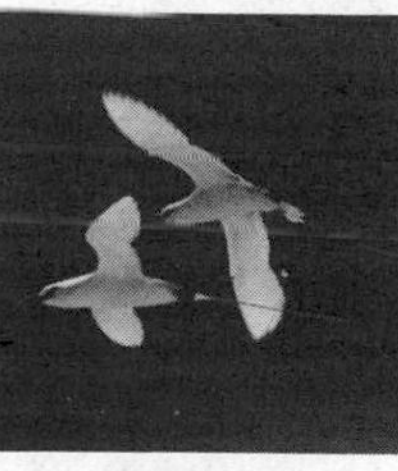
tropicbird
Phaethon rubricauda

t tight/th thin, path/*th* this, bathe/ŭ cut/ûr urge/v valve/w with/y yes/z zebra, size/zh vision/ə about, item, edible, gallop, circus/ à *Fr.* ami/œ *Fr.* feu, *Ger.* schön/ü *Fr.* tu, *Ger.* über/KH *Ger.* ich, *Scot.* loch/N *Fr.* bon. ***Follows main vocabulary.** **†Of obscure origin.**

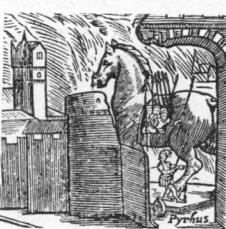

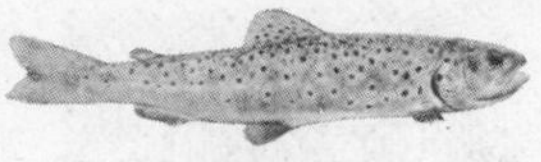

trout
Salmo trutta
Brown trout

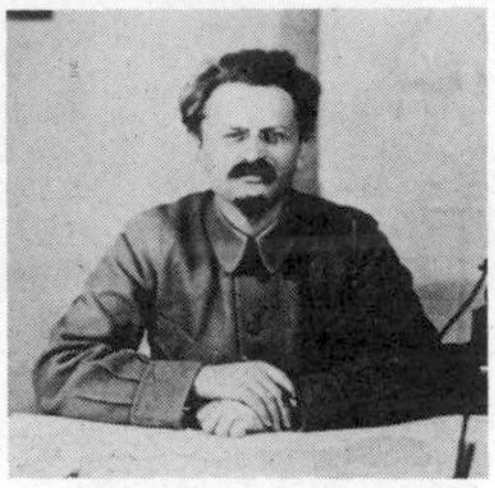

Leon Trotsky

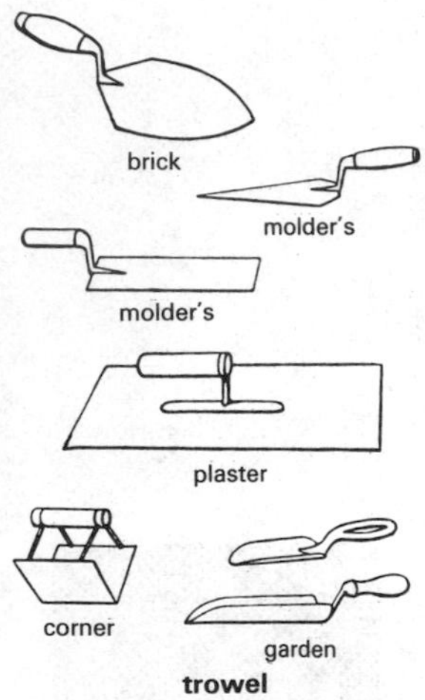
brick
molder's
molder's
plaster
corner
garden

trowel

tro·po·sphere (trō′pə-sfîr′, trŏp′ə-) *n.* The lowest region of the atmosphere between the earth's surface and the tropopause, characterized by decreasing temperature with increasing altitude. [TROPO- + SPHERE.]

–tropous. Indicates a turning from a stimulus; for example, **amphitropous, anatropous.** [Greek *-tropos,* of turning, from *trepein,* to turn. See **trep-**[2] in Appendix.*]

–tropy. Indicates the condition of turning; for example, **allotropy, thixotropy.** [Greek *-tropia,* from *-tropos,* -TROPOUS.]

trot (trŏt) *n.* **1.** A gait of a four-footed animal, between a walk and a run in speed, in which diagonal pairs of legs move forward together. **2.** A gait of a person, faster than a walk; a jog. **3.** A race for trotters. **4.** *Informal.* A literal translation, a **pony** *(see).* **5.** *Rare.* A toddler. **6.** *Archaic.* An old woman; crone. **—the trots.** *Slang.* Diarrhea. *—v.* **trotted, trotting, trots.** *—intr.* **1.** To go or move at a trot. **2.** To proceed rapidly; to hurry. *—tr.* To cause to move at a trot. **—trot out.** *Informal.* To bring out and show for inspection or admiration. [Middle English, from Old French, from *troter,* to trot, from Vulgar Latin *trottāre* (unattested), from Frankish *trottōn* (unattested). See **der-**[1] in Appendix.*]

troth (trôth, trŏth, trōth) *n.* **1.** Good faith; fidelity. **2.** One's pledged fidelity; betrothal. *—tr.v.* **trothed, trothing, troths.** *Archaic.* To pledge or betroth. [Middle English *trouth(e),* Old English *trēowth,* TRUTH.]

troth·plight (trôth′plīt′, trŏth′-, trōth′-) *n. Archaic.* A betrothal. *—tr.v.* **trothplighted, -plighting, -plights.** *Archaic.* To betroth. [Middle English *trouth plight* : TROTH + PLIGHT (pledge).]

trot·line (trŏt′līn′) *n.* A fishing line, a **setline** *(see).* [Perhaps TROT (run) + LINE.]

Trots·ky (trŏt′skē), **Leon.** Also **Trots·ki.** Original name, Lev Davidovich Bronstein. 1877–1940. Russian revolutionist and Soviet statesman; banished (1929); assassinated in Mexico.

Trots·ky·ism (trŏt′skē-ĭz′əm) *n.* The theories of Communism advocated by Leon Trotsky and his followers, who argued for worldwide revolution and bitterly opposed the leadership of Stalin. **—Trots′ky·ist, Trots′ky·ite′** *adj.* & *n.*

trot·ter (trŏt′ər) *n.* **1.** A horse that trots; especially, one trained for harness racing. **2.** *Informal.* A foot; especially, the foot of a pig or sheep prepared as food.

trou·ba·dour (trōō′bə-dôr′, -dōr′, -dŏŏr′) *n.* **1.** One of a class of lyric poets of the 12th and 13th centuries attached to the courts of Provence and northern Italy, who composed songs in complex metrical forms. Compare **trouvère. 2.** A strolling minstrel. [French, from Old French, from Old Provençal *trobador,* from *trobar,* to invent, find, compose poetry, variant of Old French *trover.* See **trouvère.**]

troub·le (trŭb′əl) *n.* **1.** A state of distress, affliction, danger, or need. Often used in the phrase *in trouble.* **2.** Something that contributes to such a state; a difficulty or problem: *One trouble after another delayed the job.* **3.** Exertion; effort; pains. **4.** A condition of pain, disease, or malfunction: *heart trouble.* *—v.* **troubled, -ling, -les.** *—tr.* **1.** To agitate; stir up. **2.** To afflict with pain or discomfort. **3.** To cause distress or confusion in; vex; perturb. **4.** To inconvenience; to bother: *May I trouble you to close the window.* *—intr.* To take pains: *trouble over every detail.* [Middle English, from Old French, from *troubler,* to trouble, from Vulgar Latin *turbulāre* (unattested), from *turbulus* (unattested), confused, from Latin *turbidus,* TURBID.] **—troub′ler** *n.* **—troub′ling·ly** *adv.*

troub·le·mak·er (trŭb′əl-mā′kər) *n.* A person who habitually stirs up trouble or strife.

troub·le·shoot·er (trŭb′əl-shōō′tər) *n.* A person who locates and eliminates sources of trouble, as in mechanical operations or diplomatic affairs.

troub·le·some (trŭb′əl-səm) *adj.* **1.** Causing trouble, especially repeatedly; worrisome. **2.** Difficult; trying. —See Synonyms at **hard. —troub′le·some·ly** *adv.* **—troub′le·some·ness** *n.*

troub·lous (trŭb′ləs) *adj.* **1.** Attended with trouble; uneasy; troubled. **2.** *Obsolete.* Causing trouble; troublesome.

trou-de-loup (trōō′də-lōō′) *n., pl.* **trous-de-loup** (trōō′də-lōō′). *Military.* Any of a series of conical pits having pointed stakes set upright in their centers, formerly used as an obstacle to enemy cavalry. [French, "wolf's pit."]

trough (trôf, trŏf) *n.* **1.** A long, narrow, generally shallow receptacle, especially one for holding water or feed for animals. **2.** A gutter under the eaves of a roof. **3.** A long, narrow depression, as between waves or ridges. **4.** A low point in a business cycle or on a statistical graph. **5.** *Meteorology.* An elongated region of low atmospheric pressure, often associated with a front. [Middle English *trough,* Old English *trog.* See **deru-** in Appendix.*]

trounce (trouns) *tr.v.* **trounced, trouncing, trounces. 1.** To thrash; beat. **2.** To defeat decisively. [Origin unknown.]

troupe (trōōp) *n.* A company or group, especially of touring actors, singers, or dancers. *—intr.v.* **trouped, trouping, troupes.** To tour with a theatrical company. [French, TROOP.]

troup·er (trōō′pər) *n.* **1.** A member of a theatrical company. **2.** A veteran actor or performer. **3.** *Informal.* A faithful and good-natured worker.

troup·i·al (trōō′pē-əl) *n.* Any of several tropical American birds of the genus *Icterus,* related to the orioles and New World blackbirds; especially, *I. icterus,* having orange and black plumage. [French *troupiale,* from *troupe,* flock, TROOP (from its living in flocks).]

trou·ser (trou′zər) *adj.* Of, for, or on trousers. [Back-formation from TROUSERS.]

trou·sers (trou′zərz) *pl.n.* Also **trow·sers.** An outer garment for covering the body from the waist to the ankles, divided into sections to fit each leg separately, worn especially by men and boys. [Variant (influenced by DRAWERS) of earlier *trouse,* from Scottish Gaelic *triubhas,* perhaps from Old French *trebus*†.]

trous·seau (trōō′sō, trōō-sō′) *n., pl.* **-seaux** (-sōz, -sōz′) or **-seaus.** The special wardrobe that a bride assembles for her marriage. [French, from Old French, diminutive of *trusse,* a bundle. See **truss.**]

trout (trout) *n., pl.* **trout** (for senses 1, 2) or **trouts** (for all senses). **1.** Any of various freshwater or anadromous food and game fishes of the genera *Salvelinus* and *Salmo,* usually having a speckled body. **2.** Broadly, any of various similar fishes. **3.** *British Slang.* A silly old woman. [Middle English *troute,* Old English *trūht,* from Late Latin *tructa*†.]

trout lily. The **dogtooth violet** *(see).* [From the spots on its leaves, resembling the speckles on a trout.]

trou·vère (trōō-vâr′) *n.* Also **trou·veur** (-vûr′). Any of a school of poets flourishing in northern France in the 12th and 13th centuries, who chiefly wrote narrative works, such as the chansons de geste. Compare **troubadour.** [French, from Old French *trovere,* from *trover,* to invent, find, compose poetry, from Vulgar Latin *tropāre* (unattested), to use tropes, from Latin *tropus,* TROPE.]

trove (trōv) *n.* Something of value discovered or found; a find. [Short for TREASURE-TROVE.]

tro·ver (trō′vər) *n.* A common-law action to recover damages for personal property illegally withheld or converted to use by another. [From Old French, to compose, find. See **trouvère.**]

trow (trō) *intr.v.* **trowed, trowing, trows.** *Archaic.* To think; suppose. [Middle English *trowen, trewen,* Old English *trēowian* and *trūwian.* See **deru-** in Appendix.*]

trow·el (trou′əl) *n.* **1.** A flat-bladed hand tool for leveling, spreading, or shaping substances such as cement or mortar. **2.** A small implement with a pointed, scoop-shaped blade used for digging, as in setting plants. *—tr.v.* **troweled** or **-elled, -eling** or **-elling, -els.** To spread, smooth, form, or scoop with a trowel. [Middle English *trowell,* from Old French *truelle,* from Late Latin *truella,* variant of Latin *trulla,* diminutive of *trua*†, stirring spoon, ladle.] **—trow′el·er** *n.*

troy (troi) *adj. Abbr.* **t** Of or expressed in troy weight. [Middle English *troye,* from Norman French, probably first used at a fair in *Troyes,* France.]

Troy (troi). **1.** *Latin* **Il·i·um** (ĭl′ē-əm). An ancient city in Troas, northwestern Asia Minor, the site of the Trojan War. **2.** A city of New York State, in the east on the Hudson River. Population, 67,000.

troy weight. *Abbr.* **t** A system of units of weight in which the grain is the same as in the avoirdupois system and the pound contains 12 ounces, 240 pennyweights, or 5,760 grains. See **measurement.**

trp. troop.

tru·an·cy (trōō′ən-sē) *n., pl.* **-cies.** Also **tru·ant·ry** (-ən-trē). **1.** An act of being truant. **2.** The condition of being truant.

tru·ant (trōō′ənt) *n.* **1.** A person who is absent without permission, especially from school. **2.** A person who shirks his work or duty. *—adj.* **1.** Absent without permission, especially from school. **2.** Idle, lazy, or neglectful. *—intr.v.* **truanted, -anting, -ants.** To be truant. [Middle English, beggar, idle rogue, from Old French, from Gaulish *trugant-* (unattested). See **ter-**[2] in Appendix.*]

truant officer. An official who investigates unauthorized absences from school.

truce (trōōs) *n.* A temporary cessation or suspension of hostilities by agreement of the contending forces; an armistice. [Middle English *trewes,* plural of *trewe,* truce, peace, Old English *trēow,* faith, pledge. See **deru-** in Appendix.*]

Tru·cial O·man (trōō′shəl ō-măn′, ō-män′). A region occupying about 12,000 square miles on the eastern coast of the Arabian Peninsula, divided among seven British-protected sheikdoms. Population, 111,000. Capital, Dubai.

truck[1] (trŭk) *n. Abbr.* **tk. 1.** Any of various heavy automotive vehicles designed for transporting loads. **2.** A two-wheeled barrow for moving heavy objects by hand. Also called "hand truck." **3.** A wheeled platform, sometimes equipped with a motor, for conveying loads in a warehouse or freight yard. **4.** *British.* A railroad freight car without a top. **5.** One of the swiveling frames of wheels under each end of a railroad car, trolley car, or the like. *—v.* **trucked, trucking, trucks.** *—tr.* To transport by truck. *—intr.* **1.** To carry goods by truck. **2.** To drive a truck. [Perhaps either short for TRUCKLE or from Latin *trochus,* a wheel, from Greek *trokhos,* from *trekhein,* to run. See **dhregh-** in Appendix.*]

truck[2] (trŭk) *v.* **trucked, trucking, trucks.** *—tr.* **1.** To exchange; barter. **2.** *Rare.* To peddle. *—intr.* To have dealings or commerce; to traffic. *—n.* **1.** Trade goods; articles of commerce. **2.** Garden produce raised for the market. **3.** *Informal.* Worthless articles; rubbish. **4.** Barter; exchange. **5.** *Informal.* Dealings; business. [Middle English *trukken,* from Old French *troquer,* akin to Spanish *trocar*†.]

truck·age (trŭk′ĭj) *n.* **1.** Transportation of goods by truck. **2.** A charge for this.

truck·er (trŭk′ər) *n.* **1.** A truck driver. **2.** A person or company engaged in trucking goods.

truck farm. A farm producing vegetables for the market. Also called "truck garden." **—truck farmer. —truck farming.**

truck·le (trŭk′əl) *n.* **1.** A small wheel or roller; caster. **2.** A **trundle bed** *(see).* *—intr.v.* **truckled, -ling, -les.** To be servile or submissive; yield weakly. [Middle English *trocle,* pulley, from Norman French, from Latin *trochlea,* system of pulleys. See **trochlea.**] **—truck′ler** *n.*

ă pat/ā pay/âr care/ä father/b bib/ch church/d deed/ĕ pet/ē be/f fife/g gag/h hat/hw which/ĭ pit/ī pie/îr pier/j judge/k kick/l lid, needle/m mum/n no, sudden/ng thing/ŏ pot/ō toe/ô paw, for/oi noise/ou out/ŏŏ took/ōō boot/p pop/r roar/s sauce/sh ship, dish/

truck·load (trŭk′lōd′) *n.* The quantity or weight that a truck carries.

truck·man (trŭk′mən) *n., pl.* **-men** (-mĭn). **1.** A truck driver. **2.** A person engaged in the trucking business; trucker.

truck system. The practice of paying wages in goods instead of money.

truc·u·lence (trŭk′yə-ləns) *n.* Also **truc·u·len·cy** (-lən-sē). **1.** Savagery. **2.** Pugnacity; belligerence.

truc·u·lent (trŭk′yə-lənt) *adj.* **1.** Savage and cruel; fierce. **2.** Vitriolic; scathing. **3.** Disposed to fight; pugnacious; defiant. See Usage note. [Latin *truculentus,* from *trux* (stem *truc-*), fierce. See **ter-**[3] in Appendix.*] —**truc′u·lent·ly** *adv.*

Usage: *Truculent* is well established, and now principally occurs, in a newer and milder sense synonymous with *pugnacious, defiant,* or *surly.* It is acceptable in that sense to 86 per cent of the Usage Panel. Earlier, the term was largely confined to the senses pertaining to savagery.

Tru·deau (trōō-dō′), **Pierre Elliott.** Born 1919. Prime Minister of Canada (since 1968).

trudge (trŭj) *intr.v.* **trudged, trudging, trudges.** To walk in a laborious, heavy-footed way; to plod. —*n.* A long, tedious walk. [Origin unknown.] —**trudg′er** *n.*

trudg·en (trŭj′ən) *n.* Also **trudg·eon.** A swimming stroke in which a double overarm movement is combined with a scissors kick. Also called "trudgen stroke." [Introduced from Argentina by John *Trudgen,* 19th-century English swimmer.]

true (trōō) *adj.* **truer, truest. 1.** Consistent with fact or reality; not false or erroneous. **2.** Exactly conforming to a rule, standard, or pattern: *trying to sing true B.* **3.** Reliable; accurate: *a true prophecy.* **4.** Real; genuine. **5.** Faithful, as to a friend, vow, or cause; steadfast; loyal. **6.** *Archaic.* Honorable; upright. **7.** Sincerely felt or expressed; unfeigned. **8.** Fundamental; essential: *his true motive.* **9.** Rightful; legitimate: *the true heir.* **10.** Accurately shaped or fitted. **11.** Accurately placed, delivered, or thrown. **12.** Quick and exact in sensing and responding. **13.** Determined with reference to the earth's axis, not the magnetic poles: *true north.* **14.** Conforming to the definitive criteria of the designation; properly or accurately so called: *The horseshoe crab is not a true crab.* —See Synonyms at **real, faithful.** —**come true.** To become fact; conform to expectation or prediction. —*adv.* **1.** Rightly; truthfully. **2.** Unswervingly; exactly: *He aimed true.* **3.** So as to conform to the ancestral type or stock: *breed true.* —*tr.v.* **trued, truing** or **trueing, trues.** To adjust or fit so as to conform with a standard. —*n.* **1.** Truth. **2.** Proper alignment or adjustment: *in or out of true.* [Middle English *trewe,* Old English *trēowe,* loyal, trustworthy. See **deru-** in Appendix.*] —**true′ness** *n.*

true bill. *Law.* A bill of indictment endorsed by a grand jury.

true-blue (trōō′blōō′) *n.* Also **true blue.** A person of unswerving loyalty. [Originally a 17th-century Scottish Presbyterian or Covenanter, from the color blue adopted in opposition to the Royalists' red.] —**true′-blue′** *adj.*

true·born (trōō′bôrn′) *adj.* Being authentically or genuinely such by birth.

true·love (trōō′lŭv′) *n.* One's beloved; a sweetheart.

true lovers' knot. A stylized knot, generally a form of bowknot, used as an emblem of love. Also called "lovers' knot."

true·pen·ny (trōō′pĕn′ē) *n., pl.* **-nies.** *Archaic.* An honest fellow; a trusty person. [From an association with a genuine coin.]

true rhyme. **Perfect rhyme** *(see).*

true rib. Any of the ribs, in man any of the upper seven, that are attached to the sternum by a costal cartilage.

truf·fle (trŭf′əl) *n.* Any of various fleshy subterranean fungi, chiefly of the genus *Tuber,* often esteemed as food. [Obsolete French, variant of Old French *truffe,* from Old Provençal *trufa,* from Vulgar Latin *tūfera* (unattested), from Latin *tūber,* tuber, truffle. See **teue-** in Appendix.*]

tru·ism (trōō′ĭz′əm) *n.* A statement of an obvious truth. See Synonyms at **cliché.** —**tru·is′tic** (-ĭs′tĭk) *adj.*

Tru·jil·lo Mo·li·na (trōō-hē′yō mō-lē′nä), **Rafael Leonidas.** 1891–1961. Dictator of the Dominican Republic (1930–38 and 1942–52); assassinated.

Truk (trŭk, trŏŏk). An island group, about 39 square miles in area, in the Caroline Islands in the western Pacific; site of a major Japanese naval base in World War II.

trull (trŭl) *n. Archaic.* A strumpet; harlot. [Perhaps from German *Trulle,* from Middle High German *trolle,* clumsy person, akin to Old Norse *troll,* creature, TROLL.]

tru·ly (trōō′lē) *adv.* **1.** Sincerely; genuinely. **2.** Truthfully; accurately. **3.** Indeed; verily: *truly ugly.*

Tru·man (trōō′mən), **Harry S** Born 1884. Thirty-third President of the United States (1945–53).

Trum·bull (trŭm′bəl), **John.** 1756–1843. American historical and portrait painter; son of Jonathan Trumbull.

Trum·bull (trŭm′bəl), **Jonathan.** 1710–1785. American statesman; Colonial governor of Connecticut (1769–84); supported Revolutionary War; father of John Trumbull.

trump[1] (trŭmp) *n.* **1.** *Card Games.* **a.** *Often plural.* A suit the cards of which are declared as outranking all other cards for the duration of a hand. **b.** A card of such a suit. **2.** A key resource to be used at the opportune moment. **3.** *Informal.* A reliable or admirable person. —*v.* **trumped, trumping, trumps.** *Card Games.* —*tr.* To take (a card or trick) with a trump. —*intr.* To play a trump card. —**trump up.** To devise fraudulently; concoct; counterfeit. [Variant of TRIUMPH.]

trump[2] (trŭmp) *n. Archaic.* A trumpet. [Middle English *trompe,* from Old French, from Old High German *trumpa,* akin to Old Norse *trumba*†.]

trump·er·y (trŭm′pə-rē) *n., pl.* **-ies. 1.** Showy but worthless finery; bric-a-brac. **2.** Nonsense; rubbish. **3.** Deception; trickery; fraud. —*adj.* Showy but valueless. [Middle English *trompery,* from Old French *tromperie,* from *tromper*†, to cheat.]

trum·pet (trŭm′pĭt) *n.* **1.** A soprano brass wind instrument consisting of a long metal tube looped once and ending in a flared bell, the modern type being equipped with three valves for producing variations in pitch. **2.** Something shaped like or sounding like a trumpet. **3.** An organ stop that produces a tone like that of the trumpet. **4.** A resounding call, as that of the elephant. —*v.* **trumpeted, -peting, -pets.** —*intr.* **1.** To play a trumpet. **2.** To give forth a resounding call. —*tr.* To sound or proclaim loudly. [Middle English *trumpette,* from Old French, diminutive of *trompe,* TRUMP (trumpet).]

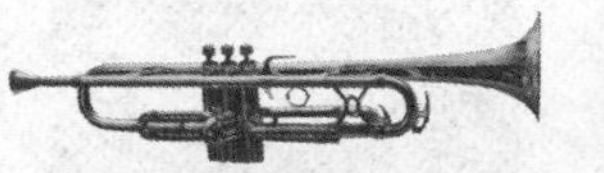

trumpet

trumpet creeper. A woody vine, *Campsis radicans,* of the eastern United States, having compound leaves and trumpet-shaped reddish-orange flowers.

trum·pet·er (trŭm′pĭt-ər) *n.* **1.** A trumpet player. **2.** A person who announces something, as on a trumpet; a herald. **3.** Any of several large birds of the genus *Psophia,* of tropical South America, having a loud, resonant call. **4.** The trumpeter swan.

trumpeter swan. A large white swan, *Olor buccinator,* of western North America, having a loud, buglelike call.

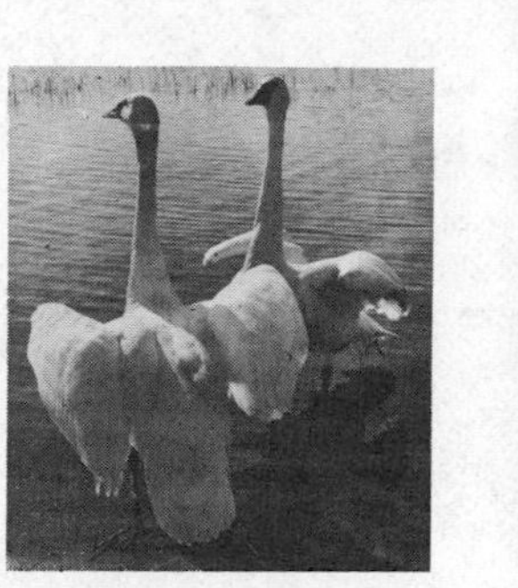

trumpeter swan

trumpet honeysuckle. A vine, *Lonicera sempervirens,* of the eastern United States, having tubular reddish flowers.

trun·cate (trŭng′kāt′) *tr.v.* **-cated, -cating, -cates. 1.** To shorten by or as if by cutting off the end or top; to lop. **2.** To replace (the edge of a crystal) with a plane face. —*adj.* **1.** Appearing to terminate abruptly, as a leaf or a coiled gastropod shell that lacks a spire. **2.** Truncated. [Latin *truncāre,* from *truncus,* torso, TRUNK.] —**trun·ca′tion** *n.* —**trun′cate′ly** *adv.*

trun·ca·ted (trŭng′kā′tĭd) *adj.* **1.** Having the apex cut off and replaced by a plane, especially one parallel to the base. Said of a cone or pyramid. **2.** Truncate.

trun·cheon (trŭn′chən) *n.* **1.** A staff carried as a symbol of office or authority; baton. **2.** A short stick carried by policemen; billy. **3.** *Obsolete.* A heavy club; a cudgel. **4.** *Obsolete.* A fragment of a spear shaft. **5.** A thick cutting from a plant, as for grafting. —*tr.v.* **truncheoned, -cheoning, -cheons.** *Archaic.* To beat with a club; to bludgeon. [Middle English *tronchon,* fragment, club, from Old French, from Vulgar Latin *tronciō* (unattested), from Latin *truncus,* torso, TRUNK.]

trun·dle (trŭnd′l) *n.* **1.** A small wheel or roller. **2.** The motion or noise of rolling. **3.** A trundle bed. **4.** *Obsolete.* A low-wheeled cart; dolly. —*v.* **trundled, -dling, -dles.** —*tr.* **1.** To push or propel on wheels or rollers: *"I doubt if Emerson could trundle a wheelbarrow through the streets."* (Thoreau). **2.** To spin; twirl. —*intr.* To move along by or as if by rolling. [Variant of dialectal *trendle,* wheel, from Middle English *trendil,* Old English *trendel,* circle, from Germanic *trand-* (unattested). See **trend.**] —**trun′dler** *n.*

trundle bed. A low bed on casters that can be rolled under another bed when not in use. Also called "truckle."

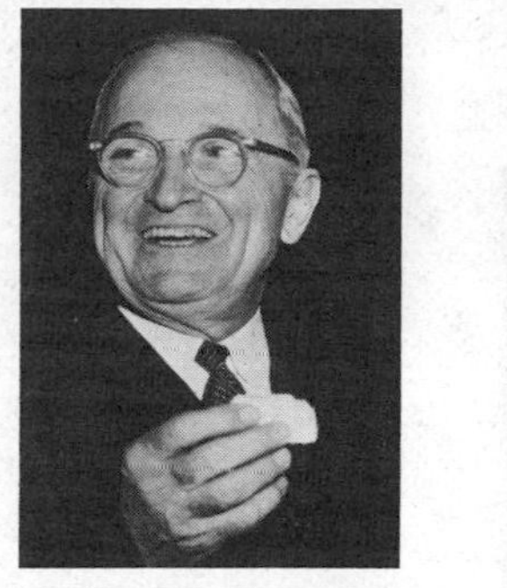

Harry S Truman
Photographed on his seventieth birthday

trunk (trŭngk) *n.* **1.** The main woody axis of a tree. **2. a.** The human body excluding the head and limbs; torso. **b.** An analogous part of an organism, as the thorax of an insect. **3.** A main body, apart from tributaries or appendages. **4.** A **trunk line** *(see).* **5.** A large packing case or box that clasps shut, used as luggage or for storage. **6.** A covered compartment for luggage and storage, generally at the rear of an automobile. **7.** A proboscis, especially the long, prehensile proboscis of an elephant. **8.** A chute or conduit. **9.** *Nautical.* A shaft connecting two or more decks. **10.** The housing for the centerboard of a vessel. **11.** *Nautical.* Any of certain structures projecting above part of a main deck, as: **a.** A covering over a ship's hatches. **b.** An expansion chamber on a tanker. **c.** A cabin on a small boat. **12.** *Architecture.* The shaft of a column. **13.** *Plural.* Men's shorts worn for swimming or athletics. **14.** *Plural. Obsolete.* Trunk hose. —*adj.* Of or designating the main body or line of a system: *a trunk route.* [Middle English *trunke,* from Old French *tronc,* a tree trunk, from Latin *truncus.* See **ter-**[3] in Appendix.*]

trunk·fish (trŭngk′fĭsh′) *n., pl.* **trunkfish** or **-fishes.** Any of various tropical marine fishes of the family Ostraciidae, having boxlike armor enclosing the body. Also called "boxfish."

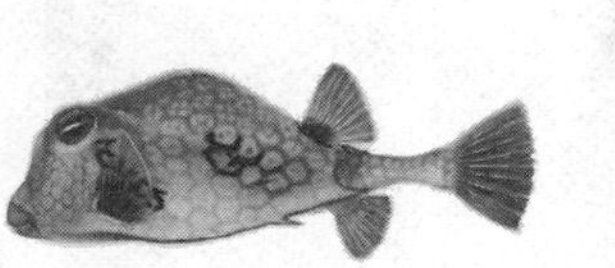

trunkfish
Lactophrys trigonus

trunk hose. Short, ballooning breeches, extending from the waist to midthigh, worn by men in the 16th and 17th centuries. Also called "trunk breeches." [Probably from obsolete *trunk,* to cut short, from Latin *truncāre,* to TRUNCATE.]

trunk line. 1. A direct line between two telephone switchboards. **2.** The main line of a communication or transportation system.

trun·nel. Variant of **treenail.**

trun·nion (trŭn′yən) *n.* A pin or gudgeon; especially, either of two small cylindrical projections on a cannon forming an axis on which it pivots. [French *trognon,* core of fruit, tree trunk, from Old French, from *estrongner,* to cut off the branches, variant of *estronchier* : *es-,* from Latin *ex-,* off + *tronchier,* to cut, from Latin *truncāre,* to TRUNCATE.]

truss (trŭs) *n.* **1.** *Medicine.* A supportive device worn to prevent enlargement of a hernia or the return of a reduced hernia. **2.** *Engineering.* A framework of wooden beams or metal bars, often arranged in triangles, to support a roof, bridge, or similar structure. **3.** *Architecture.* A bracket. **4.** Something gathered into a bundle; a pack. **5.** *British.* A bundle of a set weight of straw or hay, generally 60 pounds of new hay, 56 pounds of old hay, or 36 pounds of straw. **6.** *Nautical.* An iron fitting by which a lower yard is secured to a mast. **7.** A compact cluster of flowers at the end of a stalk. —*tr.v.* **trussed, trussing, trusses. 1.** To tie up or bind. Often used with *up.* **2.** To bind or skewer

the wings or legs of (a fowl) before cooking. **3. a.** To enclose or confine (the body) in tight-fitting clothes. **b.** To fasten (laces or strings). **4.** To support or brace with a truss. [Middle English *trusse,* a bundle, from Old French *tr(o)usse,* from *tr(o)usser,* to tie in a bundle, perhaps from Vulgar Latin *torsāre* (unattested), from *torsus* (unattested), past participle of Latin *torquēre,* to twist. See **terkw-** in Appendix.*]

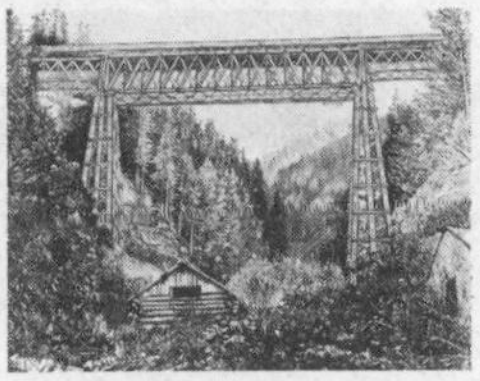
truss bridge

truss bridge. A bridge supported by trusses.

truss·ing (trŭs′ĭng) *n.* **1.** The parts forming a truss. **2.** A system of trusses supporting a structure.

trust (trŭst) *n.* **1.** Firm reliance on the integrity, ability, or character of a person or thing; confident belief; faith. **2.** The person or thing in which confidence is placed. **3.** Custody; care. **4.** Something committed into the care of another; a charge. **5.** The condition and resulting obligation of having confidence placed in one: *"He has violated his public trust."* (John F. Kennedy). **6.** Reliance on something in the future; hope. **7.** Reliance on the intention and ability of a purchaser to pay in the future; credit. **8.** *Abbr.* **tr.** *Law.* **a.** A legal title to property held by one party (the trustee) for the benefit of another (the beneficiary). **b.** The confidence reposed in a trustee in giving him legal title to property to administer for another, and his obligation with respect to the property and the beneficiary. **c.** The property so held. **d.** The right of the beneficiary to the property. **9.** A combination of firms or corporations for the purpose of reducing competition and controlling prices throughout a business or industry. —See Synonyms at **monopoly.** —*v.* **trusted, trusting, trusts.** —*intr.* **1.** To rely; depend. Used with *in* or *to.* **2.** To be confident; hope. **3.** To sell on credit. —*tr.* **1.** To have confidence in; feel sure of. **2.** To expect with assurance; assume. **3.** To believe. **4.** To place in the care of another; entrust. **5.** To grant discretion to confidently: *Shall I trust him with the boat?* **6.** To extend credit to. —See Synonyms at **rely.** —*adj.* Maintained in trust. [Middle English *truste,* probably from Old Norse *traust,* confidence, firmness. See **deru-** in Appendix.*] —**trust′er** *n.*

Synonyms: *trust, faith, confidence, reliance, dependence.* These nouns refer to a feeling that a person or thing will not fail in performance. *Trust* implies depth and assurance of such feeling, which may not always be supported by proof. When acceptance of someone or something is unquestioning and emotionally charged, *faith* is the more appropriate term. *Confidence* suggests less intensity of feeling but, frequently, good evidence for being sure. *Reliance* implies a decision to commit oneself to another and to accept the consequences in case of failure; with *dependence* the commitment is not a free choice.

trust·bust·er (trŭst′bŭs′tər) *n. Informal.* A government official who works to dissolve illegal business combinations.

trust company. A commercial bank or other corporation that manages trusts.

trus·tee (trŭs′tē′) *n. Abbr.* **tr.** **1.** A person or agent, such as a bank, holding legal title to property in order to administer it for a beneficiary. **2.** A member of a board elected or appointed to direct the funds and policy of an institution. **3.** A garnishee. —*tr.v.* **trusteed, -teeing, -tees.** **1.** To place (property) in the care of a trustee. **2.** To garnishee (property).

trustee process. **Garnishment** *(see).*

trus·tee·ship (trŭs′tē′shĭp′) *n.* **1.** The position or function of a trustee. **2. a.** The administration of a territory by a country or countries so commissioned by the United Nations. **b.** A region so administered, a **trust territory** *(see).* Compare **mandate.**

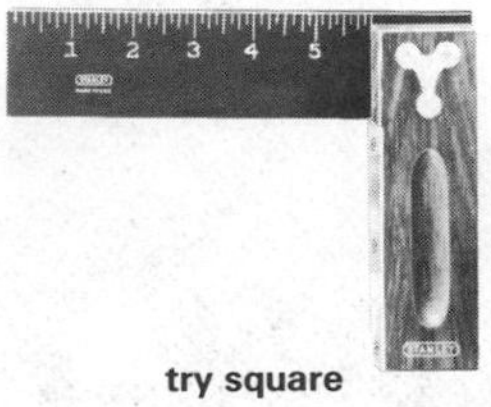
try square

trust·ful (trŭst′fəl) *adj.* Inclined to believe or confide readily; full of trust. —**trust′ful·ly** *adv.* —**trust′ful·ness** *n.*

trust fund. An estate, especially money and securities, held or settled in trust.

trust territory. A colony or territory placed under the administration of a country or countries by commission of the United Nations. Compare **mandate.**

trust·wor·thy (trŭst′wûr′*th*ē) *adj.* Warranting trust; dependable; reliable. See Synonyms at **faithful.** —**trust′wor′thi·ly** *adv.* —**trust′wor′thi·ness** *n.*

trust·y (trŭs′tē) *adj.* **-ier, -iest.** **1.** Dependable; faithful; reliable. **2.** *Obsolete.* Trustful. —*n., pl.* **trusties.** A trusted person; specifically, a convict granted special privileges. —**trust′i·ly** *adv.* —**trust′i·ness** *n.*

truth (trōōth) *n., pl.* **truths** (trōō*th*z, trōōths). **1.** Conformity to knowledge, fact, actuality, or logic. **2.** Fidelity to an original or standard. **3.** Reality; actuality. **4.** A statement proven to be or accepted as true. **5.** Sincerity; integrity; honesty. **6.** *Capital* **T.** *Christian Science.* God. [Middle English *trewthe, treothe,* Old English *trēowth, trīewth.* See **deru-** in Appendix.*]

Synonyms: *truth, veracity, verity, verisimilitude, candor, frankness.* These nouns name qualities of being in accordance with reality. *Truth* is most commonly used to mean correspondence with facts or with what actually occurred. *Veracity* implies factual accuracy and honesty, principally with respect to spoken or written expression. *Verity* applies principally to an enduring or repeatedly demonstrated truth. *Verisimilitude,* the quality of having the appearance of truth or reality, is often applied to effective artistic representation. *Candor* and *frankness* both refer to forthrightness, openness, and outspokenness.

truth·ful (trōōth′fəl) *adj.* **1.** Consistently telling the truth; honest. **2.** Corresponding to reality; true. —**truth′ful·ly** *adv.* —**truth′ful·ness** *n.*

truth-val·ue (trōōth′văl′yōō) *n. Logic.* Either the truth or the falsehood of a proposition.

try (trī) *v.* **tried, trying, tries.** —*tr.* **1.** To taste, sample, or otherwise test in order to determine strength, effect, worth, or desirability. Sometimes used with *out.* **2. a.** To examine or hear (evidence or a case) by judicial process. **b.** To put (an accused person) on trial. **3.** To subject to great strain or hardship; to tax: *The last steep ascent tried his every muscle.* **4.** To melt (lard, for example) to separate out impurities; render. Often used with *out.* **5.** To make an effort (to do or accomplish something); to attempt. Used chiefly with an infinitive: *Try to do it.* See Usage note below. **6.** To smooth, fit, or align accurately. —*intr.* To make an effort; strive. See Usage note below. —*n., pl.* **tries.** An attempt; effort. See Usage note below. [Middle English *trien,* to separate, pick out, sift, from Old French *trier*†.]

Usage: *Try and* is common in speech for *try to,* especially in such established combinations as *try and stop me* or *try and make me* (defiance) and *try and get some rest* (exhortation). In most contexts, however, it is usually not interchangeable with *try to* unless the level is expressly informal. As an example in writing, the following is unacceptable to 79 per cent of the Usage Panel: *It is a mistake to try and force compliance with something so unpopular* (preferably *try to force*). *Try,* as a noun equivalent to the more formal *attempt,* has a wider acceptance, though it too is especially appropriate to certain phrases in speech: *a nice try; the old college try; give it a try.* The following example is acceptable in written usage to 59 per cent of the Panel: *The speech was a good try at restoring unity.*

try·ing (trī′ĭng) *adj.* Causing severe strain, hardship, or distress.

try·ma (trī′mə) *n., pl.* **-mata** (-mə-tə). A nut, such as a pecan or walnut, having an outer husk or rind that separates from the shell of the fruit. [New Latin, from Greek *truma, trumē,* a hole (from the hollow drupe). See **ter-**[2] in Appendix.*]

try out. To undergo a competitive qualifying test, as for a job.

try·out (trī′out′) *n. Informal.* A test to ascertain the qualifications of applicants, as for an athletic team or for a theatrical role.

try·pan·o·some (trĭ-păn′ə-sōm′, trĭp′ə-nə-) *n.* Any of various parasitic protozoans of the genus *Trypanosoma,* transmitted to the vertebrate bloodstream by certain insects, and often causing diseases such as sleeping sickness. [New Latin *Trypanosoma* "auger-bodied" (from its shape) : Greek *trupanon,* an auger, borer, from *trupan,* to bore, from *trupa, trupē,* a hole (see **ter-**[2] in Appendix*) + -SOME (body).]

try·pan·o·so·mi·a·sis (trĭ-păn′ə-sō-mī′ə-sĭs, trĭp′ə-nō-sō-) *n.* Any disease caused by a trypanosome. [New Latin : TRYPANOSOM(E) + -IASIS.]

try·pars·am·ide (trĭ-pär′sə-mīd′) *n.* A white crystalline powder, $C_8H_{10}AsN_2O_4Na \cdot \frac{1}{2}H_2O$, used in the treatment of spirochetal and trypanosomic diseases. [Originally a trade name : TRYP(ANOSOME) + ARS(ENIC) + AMIDE.]

tryp·sin (trĭp′sĭn) *n.* One of the proteolytic enzymes of the pancreatic juice, important in the digestive processes. [Perhaps Greek *tripsis,* a rubbing (first obtained by rubbing the pancreas with glycerin), from *tribein,* to rub (see **ter-**[2] in Appendix*) + (PEPS)IN.] —**tryp′tic** (-tĭk) *adj.*

tryp·sin·o·gen (trĭp-sĭn′ə-jən) *n.* The substance produced by the pancreas that is converted into trypsin when acted upon by certain enzymes. [From TRYPSIN + -GEN.]

tryp·to·phan (trĭp′tə-făn′) *n.* Also **tryp·to·phane** (-fān′). An amino acid, $C_{11}H_{12}N_2O_2$, that is produced in the digestive process and is essential in human nutrition. [TRYP(SIN) + (PEP)T(IC) + -PHAN(E).]

try·sail (trī′səl, -sāl′) *n. Nautical.* A small fore-and-aft sail hoisted abaft the foremast and mainmast in a storm to keep a ship's bow to the wind. Also called "spencer." [From TRY (noun, in the obsolete nautical sense of "lying to in a storm").]

try square. A carpenter's tool consisting of a ruled metal straightedge set at right angles to a wooden straight piece, used for measuring and marking square work.

tryst (trĭst) *n.* **1.** An agreement between lovers to meet at a certain time and place. **2.** The meeting or meeting place so arranged: *"She comes home very late one night from a tryst, bleary and lipstick-smeared"* (J.D. Salinger). —*intr.v.* **trysted, trysting, trysts.** To keep a tryst. [Middle English, from Old French *triste,* an appointed station in hunting, perhaps from Scandinavian, akin to Old Norse *treysta,* to trust, make firm. See **deru-** in Appendix.*] —**tryst′er** *n.*

T.S. *Physics.* tensile strength.

tsa·de. Variant of **sade.**

Tsa·na, Lake. See Lake **Tana.**

tsar. Variant of **czar.**

Tsa·ri·tsyn. A former name for **Volgograd.**

Tschai·kov·sky. See **Tchaikovsky.**

tset·se disease (tsĕt′sē, tsēt′sē). **Nagana** *(see).*

tset·se fly (tsĕt′sē, tsēt′sē). Also **tzet·ze fly.** Any of several bloodsucking African flies of the genus *Glossina,* often carrying and transmitting pathogenic trypanosomes to human beings and livestock. [Afrikaans, from Tswana.]

Tshi. Variant of **Twi.**

T-shirt (tē′shûrt′) *n.* Also **tee shirt.** **1.** A short-sleeved, collarless undershirt worn by men. **2.** An outer shirt of similar design. [So called from its shape.]

Tshom·be (chŏm′bā′), **Moise-Kapenda.** Born 1919. Congolese political leader; premier of Katanga Province (1960–63); premier of Congo (Kinshasa) (1964–65).

tsim·mes (tsĭm′ĭs) *n.* Also **tzim·mes.** **1.** A stew of vegetables or fruits cooked slowly over very low heat. **2.** The overcomplication of a relatively simple situation; a state of confusion: *She made a whole tsimmes out of planning the birthday party.* [Yiddish, "vegetable or fruit stew."]

Tsi·nan (jē′nän′). Also **Chi·nan.** The capital of Shantung, eastern China, a commercial center on the Yellow River in the central part of the province. Population, 882,000.

ă pat/ā pay/âr care/ä father/b bib/ch church/d deed/ĕ pet/ē be/f fife/g gag/h hat/hw which/ĭ pit/ī pie/îr pier/j judge/k kick/l lid, needle/m mum/n no, sudden/ng thing/ŏ pot/ō toe/ô paw, for/oi noise/ou out/ŏŏ took/ōō boot/p pop/r roar/s sauce/sh ship, dish/

Tsing·hai (chĭng′hī′). Also **Ch'ing·hai, Ching·hai.** A province of west-central China, occupying 278,378 square miles. Population, 2,050,000. Capital, Sining.
Tsing·tao (chĭng′dou′). A city of eastern China, a port on the Yellow Sea in Shantung Province. Population, 1,121,000.
Tsing·yuan. The former name for **Paoting.**
Tsi·tsi·har (chē′chē′här′, tsē′tsē′-). A city of northeastern China in Heilungkiang Province, of which it is the former capital. Population, 704,000.
tsp. teaspoon; teaspoonful.
T-square (tē′skwâr′) *n.* A rule having a short, sometimes sliding, perpendicular crosspiece at one end, used by draftsmen for establishing and drawing parallel lines.
Tsu·ga·ru Strait (tso͞o′gä-ro͞o′). A strait between northern Honshu and southern Hokkaido, Japan, linking the Pacific with the Sea of Japan.
tsu·na·mi (tso͞o-nä′mē) *n.* A very large ocean wave caused by an underwater earthquake or volcanic eruption. Also loosely called "tidal wave." [Japanese : *tsu,* port, harbor + *nami,* wave.]
tsu·ris (tso͝or′ĭs, tsôr′-) *n.* Also **tzu·ris.** A series of misfortunes; a state or period of suffering; problems: *tsuris with his wife, his landlord, and his boss.* [Yiddish, "trouble," "distress."]
Tsu·shi·ma (tso͞o-shē′mə). An island, 271 square miles in area, in Korea Strait between southern South Korea and Kyushu, Japan; near the site of a naval battle of the Russo-Japanese War in which the Russians were defeated (1905).
tsu·tsu·ga·mu·shi disease (tso͞o′tsə-gə-mo͞o′shē). *Pathology.* **Scrub typhus** *(see).* [Japanese *tsutsugamushi* : *tsutsuga,* illness + *mushi,* an insect, mite.]
Tswa·na (tswä′nə, sä′-) *n.* The Sotho language of Botswana.
Tu. Tuesday (unofficial).
T.U. trade union.
Tu·a·mo·tu Archipelago (to͞o′ə-mō′to͞o). A group of islands, 330 square miles in area, in French Polynesia in the South Pacific. Also called "Low Archipelago."
Tuan (twän) *n.* A Malayan form of respectful address, equivalent to the English "Sir" or "Mister." [Malay, master, lord.]
Tua·reg (twä′rĕg′) *n., pl.* **Tuareg** or **-regs.** A member of one of the tall, nomadic, Hamitic-speaking peoples who occupy western and central Sahara and an area along the Niger and who have adopted the Moslem religion. [Arabic *Tawāriq.*]
tu·a·ta·ra (to͞o′ə-tär′ə) *n.* A lizardlike reptile, *Sphenodon punctatus,* of New Zealand, the only surviving representative of the order Rhynchocephalia that flourished during the Mesozoic era. [Maori *tuatàra.*]
tub (tŭb) *n.* **1. a.** A round, open, flat-bottomed vessel, usually wider than it is tall, originally made of staves held together with hoops, and used for packing, storing, or washing. **b.** The amount held by such a vessel. **c.** The contents of such a vessel: *a tub of butter.* **2. a.** A **bathtub** *(see).* **b.** *Chiefly British Informal.* A bath taken in a bathtub. **3.** *Informal.* Something resembling a tub in shape or size, especially a wide, clumsy, slow-moving boat or a stout person. **4. a.** A bucket used for conveying ore or coal up a mine shaft. **b.** A coal car used in a mine. —*v.* **tubbed, tubbing, tubs.** —*tr.* **1.** To pack or store in a tub. **2.** To wash or bathe in a tub. —*intr.* To take a bath. [Middle English *tubbe, tobbe,* from Middle Dutch and Middle Low German *tubbe*†.] —**tub′ba·ble** *adj.* —**tub′ber** *n.*
tu·ba (to͞o′bə, tyo͞o′-) *n., pl.* **-bas** or **-bae** (-bē) (for sense 3). **1.** A large brass musical wind instrument with a bass pitch and several valves. Also called "bass horn." **2.** A powerful reed stop in an organ, having eight-foot pitch. **3.** An ancient Roman war trumpet. [Italian, from Latin, a trumpet, akin to Latin *tubus,* TUBE.]
tu·bal (to͞o′bəl, tyo͞o′-) *adj.* Of, pertaining to, or occurring in a tube, especially the Fallopian tube.
tu·bate (to͞o′bāt′, tyo͞o′-) *adj.* Forming or having a tube.
tub·by (tŭb′ē) *adj.* **-bier, -biest. 1.** Short and fat. **2.** Having a dull sound; lacking resonance. —**tub′bi·ness** *n.*
tube (to͞ob, tyo͞ob) *n.* **1.** A hollow cylinder that conveys a fluid or functions as a passage. **2.** An organic structure so shaped or so functioning; a duct. **3.** A small, flexible cylindrical container sealed at one end and having a screw cap at the other, for pigments, toothpaste, mustard, or other pastelike substances. **4.** The cylindrical part of a wind instrument. **5. a.** An **electron tube** *(see).* **b.** A **vacuum tube** *(see).* **6.** *Botany.* The lower, joined part of a gamopetalous corolla or a gamosepalous calyx. **7. a.** A subway tunnel. **b.** The subway. —*tr.v.* **tubed, tubing, tubes. 1.** To provide with a tube or tubes; insert a tube in: *tube a tire.* **2.** To place in or enclose in a tube. [French, from Latin *tubus*†. See also **tuba.**]
tube foot. One of the numerous external, fluid-filled muscular tubes of echinoderms, such as the starfish, serving primarily as organs of locomotion.
tube·less tire (to͞ob′lĭs, tyo͞ob′-). A pneumatic vehicular tire in which the air is held in the assembly of casing and rim without an inner tube.
tu·ber (to͞o′bər, tyo͞o′-) *n.* **1.** *Botany.* A swollen, usually underground stem, such as the potato, bearing buds from which new plant shoots arise. **2.** *Anatomy.* A swelling; tubercle. [Latin *tūber,* a lump, swelling, tumor. See **teuə-** in Appendix.*]
tu·ber·cle (to͞o′bər-kəl, tyo͞o′-) *n.* **1.** A small, rounded prominence or process, such as a wartlike excrescence on the roots of some leguminous plants or a knoblike process in the skin or on a bone. **2.** *Pathology.* **a.** A nodule or swelling. **b.** The characteristic lesion of tuberculosis. [Latin *tūberculum,* diminutive of *tūber,* a lump, TUBER.]
tubercle bacillus. *Abbr.* **t.b., T.B.** A rod-shaped bacterium, *Mycobacterium tuberculosis,* that causes tuberculosis.
tu·ber·cu·lar (to͞o-bûr′kyə-lər, tyo͞o-) *adj.* **1.** Of, relating to, or covered with tubercles; tuberculate. **2.** Of, relating to, or afflicted with tuberculosis. —*n.* A person having tuberculosis.
tu·ber·cu·late (to͞o-bûr′kyə-lĭt, tyo͞o-) *adj.* Also **tu·ber·cu·la·ted** (-lā′tĭd). **1.** Having tubercles. **2.** Tubercular. —**tu·ber′cu·late·ly** *adv.* —**tu·ber′cu·la′tion** *n.*
tu·ber·cu·lin (to͞o-bûr′kyə-lĭn, tyo͞o-) *n.* A substance derived from cultures of tubercle bacilli, used in the diagnosis and treatment of tuberculosis. [Latin *tūberculum,* TUBERCLE + -IN.]
tu·ber·cu·loid (to͞o-bûr′kyə-loid′, tyo͞o-) *adj.* **1.** Resembling tuberculosis. **2.** Resembling a tubercle.
tu·ber·cu·lo·sis (to͞o-bûr′kyə-lō′sĭs, tyo͞o-) *n. Abbr.* **TB, T.B. 1.** A communicable disease of man and animals, caused by a microorganism, *Mycobacterium tuberculosis,* and manifesting itself in lesions of the lung, bone, and other parts of the body. **2.** Tuberculosis of the lungs. In this sense, also called "consumption," "pulmonary tuberculosis." [New Latin : Latin *tūberculum,* TUBERCLE + -OSIS.]
tu·ber·cu·lous (to͞o-bûr′kyə-ləs, tyo͞o-) *adj.* **1.** Of, relating to, or having tuberculosis. **2.** Of, affected with, or caused by tubercles. [New Latin *tuberculosus,* from Latin *tūberculum,* TUBERCLE.]
tube·rose¹ (to͞ob′rōz′, tyo͞ob′-, to͞o′bə-rōz′, tyo͞o′-, -rōs′) *n.* A tuberous plant, *Polianthes tuberosa,* native to Mexico, cultivated for its fragrant white flowers. [New Latin *(Polianthes) tuberosa,* from the feminine of Latin *tūberōsus,* TUBEROUS.]
tu·ber·ose². Variant of **tuberous.**
tu·ber·os·i·ty (to͞o′bə-rŏs′ə-tē, tyo͞o′-) *n., pl.* **-ties.** A projection or protuberance, especially one at the end of a bone for the attachment of a muscle or tendon.
tu·ber·ous (to͞o′bər-əs, tyo͞o′-) *adj.* Also **tu·ber·ose** (-bə-rōs′). **1.** *Botany.* **a.** Producing or bearing tubers. **b.** Resembling a tuber: *a tuberous root.* **2.** *Rare.* Covered with small, rounded projections; knobby. [Latin *tūberōsus,* full of lumps, from *tūber,* a lump, TUBER.]
tu·bi·fex (to͞o′bə-fĕks′, tyo͞o′-) *n., pl.* **tubifex** or **-fexes.** Any of various small, slender, reddish freshwater worms of the genus *Tubifex,* often used as food for tropical aquarium fish. [New Latin *Tubifex* : Latin *tubus,* TUBE (each one is partially enclosed in a tube) + *-fex,* "maker" (see **dhē-**¹ in Appendix*).]
tub·ing (to͞o′bĭng, tyo͞o′-) *n.* **1.** Tubes collectively. **2.** A system of tubes. **3.** A piece or length of tube. **4.** Tubular fabric, such as that used for making pillowcases.
Tub·man (tŭb′mən), **Harriet.** 1820?–1913. American Negro abolitionist leader.
Tub·man (tŭb′mən), **William Vacanarat Shadrach.** Born 1895. Liberian statesman; president of Liberia (since 1944).
tub thumper. *Informal.* A ranter; soapbox orator.
Tu·bu·ai Islands (to͞o′bo͞o-ī′). An island group, 115 square miles in area, of southern French Polynesia in the South Pacific. Also called "Austral Islands."
tu·bu·lar (to͞o′byə-lər, tyo͞o′-) *adj.* **1.** Of or pertaining to a tube or tubes. **2.** Having the form of a tube. **3.** Constituting or consisting of a tube or tubes.
tu·bu·late (to͞o′byə-lĭt, tyo͞o′-, -lāt′) *adj.* Also **tu·bu·lat·ed** (-lā′tĭd). **1.** Formed into or resembling a tube; tubular. **2.** Having a tube. [Latin *tubulātus,* from *tubulus,* diminutive of *tubus,* TUBE.] —**tu′bu·la′tion** *n.* —**tu′bu·la′tor** (-lā′tər) *n.*
tu·bule (to͞o′byo͞ol, tyo͞o′-) *n.* A very small tube or tubular structure. [Latin *tubulus,* diminutive of *tubus,* TUBE.]
tu·bu·lif·er·ous (to͞o′byə-lĭf′ər-əs, tyo͞o′-) *adj.* Having or consisting of tubules. [TUBULE + -FEROUS.]
tu·bu·li·flo·rous (to͞o′byə-lə-flôr′əs, tyo͞o′-, -flōr′əs) *adj.* Having flowers or florets with tubular corollas. [From TUBUL(E) + -FLOROUS.]
tu·bu·lous (to͞o′byə-ləs, tyo͞o′-) *adj.* **1.** Tubular. **2.** Composed of tubes or having tubular parts. [New Latin *tubulosus,* from Latin *tubulus,* TUBULE.] —**tu′bu·lous·ly** *adv.*
T.U.C. *British.* Trades Union Congress.
Tu·ca·na (to͞o-kā′nə, tyo͞o-, -kä′nə) *n.* A constellation in the polar region of the Southern Hemisphere near Indus and Hydrus, containing the smaller **Magellanic cloud** *(see).* [Probably Tupi *tucana,* TOUCAN.]
tu·chun (do͞o′jün′) *n., pl.* **-chuns** or **tuchun.** A Chinese military governor of a province. [Chinese *tu¹chün¹* : *tu¹,* to supervise + *chün¹,* army, troops.] —**tu′chun·ate′** *n.* —**tu′chun·ism′** *n.*
tuck¹ (tŭk) *v.* **tucked, tucking, tucks.** —*tr.* **1.** To make one or more folds in. **2.** To gather up and fold, thrust, or turn in in order to secure or confine: *tuck a scarf into a shirt.* **3. a.** To put in a snug spot. **b.** To put in an out-of-the-way and snug place: *a cabin tucked among the pines.* **c.** To store in a safe spot; save. Used with *away: tuck away a bit of lace; tuck away millions.* **4.** To draw in; contract. —*intr.* **1.** To make tucks. **2.** To submit readily to being tucked. —**tuck in** (or **away**). *Chiefly British Informal.* To consume (food) heartily or greedily; to gorge. —**tuck in** (or **into**) **bed.** To put to bed and cover snugly. —*n.* **1.** A flattened pleat or fold, especially a very narrow one stitched in place. **2.** A thrusting, wrapping, or folding in of an edge. **3.** *Nautical.* The part of a ship's hull under the stern where the ends of the bottom planks come together. **4.** *British Slang.* Food, especially sweets and pastry. [Middle English *tukken, tucken,* to punish, tug at, pull, Old English *tūcian*†, to punish, torment.]
tuck² (tŭk) *n. Scottish.* A beat or tap, especially on a drum. [From obsolete *t(o)uk,* to beat the drum, sound the trumpet, from Middle English *tukken,* from Old North French *toquer,* to strike, touch, from Vulgar Latin *toccāre* (unattested), to TOUCH.]

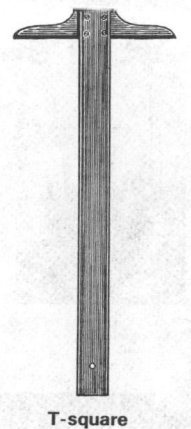

T-square

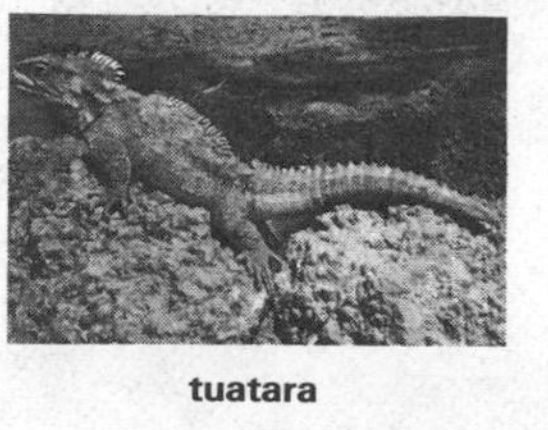

tuatara

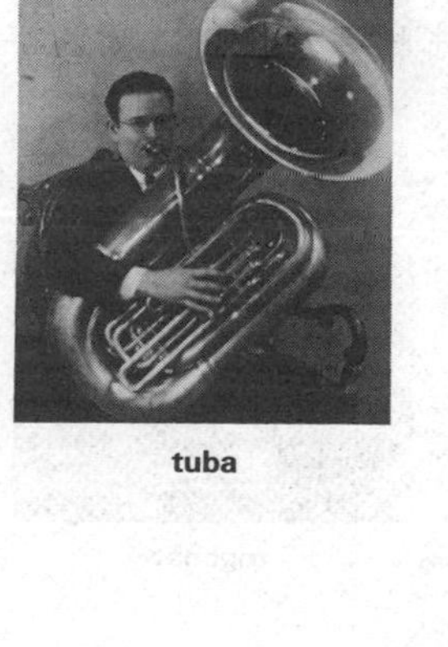

tuba

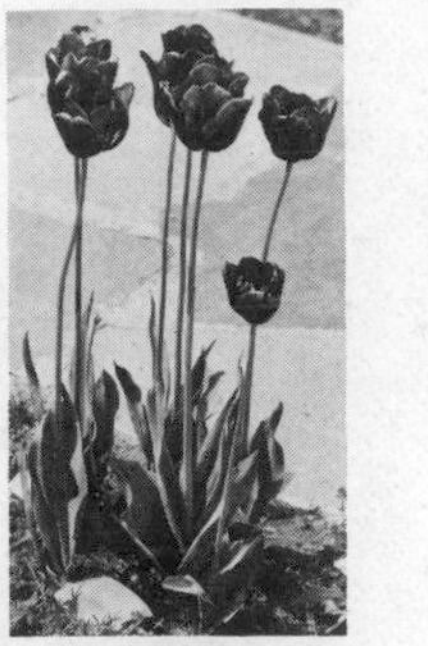

tulip

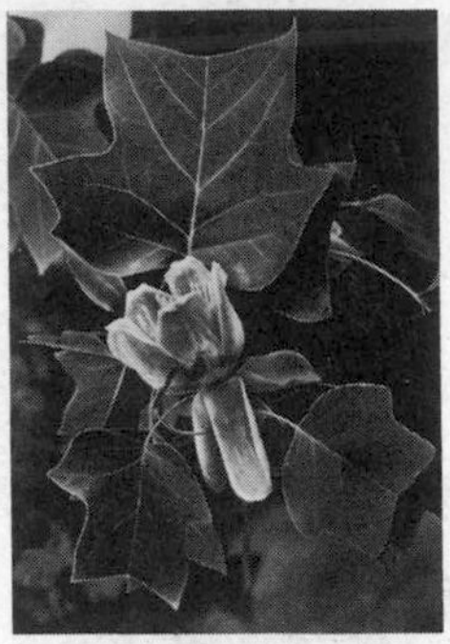

tulip tree

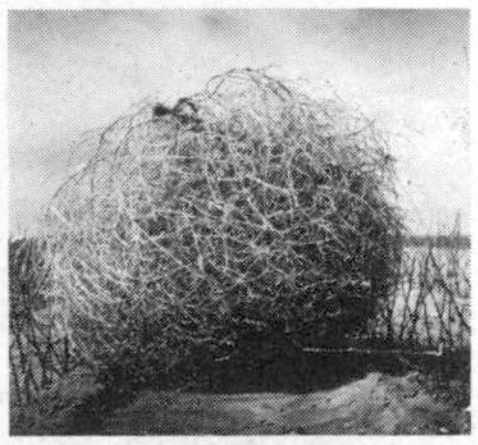

tumbleweed
Amaranthus albus

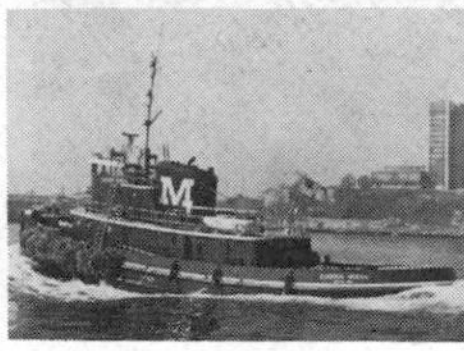

tugboat

tuck[3] (tŭk) *n. Archaic.* A slender sword; rapier. [Earlier *to(c)ke*, from French (Normandy dialect) *étoc*, from Old French *estoc*, "a tree trunk," sword, sword point, from Frankish *stok* (unattested). See **steu-** in Appendix.*]
tuck·a·hoe (tŭk'ə-hō') *n.* Any of various plants or plant parts used by American Indians as food; especially, the edible root of certain arums or the sclerotium of certain fungi. [From Algonquian (Virginia) *taccaho*.]
tuck·er[1] (tŭk'ər) *n.* **1.** One that tucks; especially, a sewing-machine attachment that makes tucks. **2.** A piece of linen or frill of lace formerly worn by women around the neck and shoulders. **3.** *Obsolete.* A fuller.
tuck·er[2] (tŭk'ər) *tr.v.* **-ered, -ering, -ers.** *Informal.* To weary; to exhaust. Usually used with *out.* [Frequentative of TUCK (to pull under).]
tuck·er-bag (tŭk'ər-băg') *n. Australian Informal.* A bag for carrying food, used by a traveler in the bush or by a swagman.
tuck·et (tŭk'ĭt) *n.* A trumpet fanfare. [From obsolete *t(o)uk*, to sound the trumpet. See **tuck** (drumbeat).]
tuck pointing. *Masonry.* The pointing of grooved mortar joints with a thin ridge of fine lime mortar or putty.
tuck-shop (tŭk'shŏp') *n. British Slang.* A confectionery. [From TUCK (food).]
Tuc·son (tōō'sŏn'). A city of Arizona, a noted winter health resort in the southern part of the state. Population, 213,000.
Tu·cu·mán (tōō'kōō-män'). A city of northwestern Argentina, in the center of a sugar-producing region. Population, 287,000.
-tude. Indicates a condition or state of being; for example, **exactitude.** [Old French, from Latin *-tūdō*.]
Tu·dor[1] (tōō'dər, tyōō'-). Surname of the English royal family from Henry VII (1485) through Elizabeth I (1603).
Tu·dor[2] (tōō'dər, tyōō'-) *adj.* **1.** Of or pertaining to the Tudor family. **2. a.** Of, pertaining to, or characteristic of the Tudor period, especially in architecture. **b.** Of, pertaining to, or characteristic of an architectural style derived from the Tudor period, having exposed beams as a typical feature.
Tues·day (tōōz'dē, tyōōz'-, -dā') *n. Abbr.* **Tues.** The third day of the week, following Monday and preceding Wednesday. [Middle English *tiwesday, tuesdai*, Old English *tīwesdæg*, "day of Tiu" : *Tīw*, TIU + *dæg*, DAY.]
tu·fa (tōō'fə, tyōō'-) *n.* **1.** The calcareous and siliceous rock deposits of springs, lakes, or ground water. **2. Tuff** *(see).* [Obsolete Italian *tufa, tufo*, from Latin *tōphus, tōfus*†.] —**tu·fa'ceous** (-fā'shəs) *adj.*
tuff (tŭf) *n.* A rock composed of compacted volcanic ash varying in size from fine sand to coarse gravel. Also called "tufa." [French *tuf, tuffe*, from obsolete Italian *tufo*, TUFA.] —**tuff·a'ceous** (tŭ-fā'shəs) *adj.*
tuf·fet (tŭf'ĭt) *n.* **1.** A clump or tuft of grass. **2.** A stool or other low seat. [Perhaps variant of TUFT.]
tuft (tŭft) *n.* **1.** A short cluster of yarn, hair, feathers, grass, or the like, attached at the base or growing close together. **2.** A dense clump of trees or bushes. **3.** A goatee. —*v.* **tufted, tufting, tufts.** —*tr.* **1.** To furnish or ornament with a tuft or tufts. **2.** To pass threads through the layers of (a quilt, mattress, or upholstery), securing the thread ends with a knot or button in the depressions thus created. —*intr.* To separate or form into tufts; grow in a tuft. [Middle English *tuft, toft*, from Old French *tof(f)e*, from Germanic. See **tap-** in Appendix.*] —**tuft'er** *n.* —**tuft'y** *adj.*
tug (tŭg) *v.* **tugged, tugging, tugs.** —*tr.* **1.** To pull at vigorously; strain at. **2.** To move by pulling with great effort or exertion; to haul; drag: *tug a person out of bed.* **3.** To tow by tugboat. —*intr.* **1.** To pull hard: *She tugged at her boots.* **2.** To toil or struggle; to strain. **3.** To vie; contend. —*n.* **1.** A strong pull or pulling force: *the tug of the sea.* **2.** A contest; struggle: *a tug between loyalty and desire.* **3.** A **tugboat** *(see).* **4.** A rope, chain, or strap used in hauling; especially, a harness trace. [Middle English *tuggen, toggen*, intensive form of Old English *tēon.* See **deuk-** in Appendix.*] —**tug'ger** *n.*
tug·boat (tŭg'bōt') *n.* A powerful small boat designed for towing larger vessels. Also called "towboat," "tug."
Tu·ge·la (tōō-gā'lə). A river of South Africa, rising in the Drakensberg range in Natal and flowing about 300 miles generally east to the Indian Ocean.
tug of war. 1. A contest of strength in which two teams tug on opposite ends of a rope, each trying to pull the other across a dividing line. **2.** A struggle for supremacy.
Tui·le·ries (twē'lə-rēz'; *French* twēl-rē'). A royal residence in Paris, France, begun in 1564 by Catherine de Médicis and burned in 1871; now the site of the Tuileries Gardens, a park near the Louvre.
tuille (twēl) *n.* A steel plate used in medieval armor for protecting the thigh. [Middle English *toile*, from Old French *tuille*, tuille, tile, from Latin *tēgula*, tile, from *tegere*, to cover. See **steg-**[1] in Appendix.*]
tu·i·tion (tōō-ĭsh'ən, tyōō-) *n.* **1.** A fee for instruction, especially at a formal institution of learning. **2.** Instruction; teaching. **3.** *Archaic.* Guardianship. [Middle English, protection, tutelage, from Old French, from Latin *tuitiō*, protection, a watching, from *tuērī*, to look at, watch, protect. See **teu-** in Appendix.*] —**tu·i'tion·al, tu·i'tion·ar'y** (-ĕr'ē) *adj.*
Tu·la (tōō'lə). A city of the Soviet Union, a major industrial center about 120 miles south of Moscow. Population, 336,000.
tu·la·re·mi·a (tōō'lə-rē'mē-ə, tyōō'-) *n.* An infectious disease caused by the bacterium *Pasteurella tularensis*, transmitted from infected rodents to man by insect vectors or by handling infected animals, and characterized by fever and swelling of the lymph nodes. Also called "rabbit fever." [New Latin : *Tulare*, a county in California where it was discovered + -EMIA.]
tu·le (tōō'lē) *n.* Any of several bulrushes of the genus *Scirpus*, growing in marshy lowlands of the southwestern United States. [Spanish, from Nahuatl *tollin, tullin.*]
tu·lip (tōō'lĭp, tyōō'-) *n.* **1.** Any of several bulbous plants of the genus *Tulipa*, native to Asia, widely cultivated for their showy, variously colored flowers. **2.** The flower of this plant. [New Latin *Tulipa*, from Turkish *tül(i)bend*, TURBAN (from its turban-shaped flower).]
tulip tree. A tall deciduous tree, *Liriodendron tulipifera*, having large, tuliplike green and orange flowers and yellowish, easily worked wood. Also called "yellow poplar," "tulip poplar."
tu·lip·wood (tōō'lĭp-wŏŏd', tyōō'-) *n.* **1.** The wood of the tulip tree. **2.** The irregularly striped, ornamental wood of any of several other trees; especially, that of *Dalbergia variabilis*, of tropical South America.
tulle (tōōl) *n.* A fine starched net of silk, rayon, or nylon, used for veils, tutus, or bouffant gowns. [French, originally produced in *Tulle*, city in central France.]
Tul·sa (tŭl'sə). A city of Oklahoma, in the northeast on the Arkansas River. Population, 262,000.
Tu·ma·ca·co·ri National Monument (tōō'mə-kä'kə-rē). A ten-acre site in Arizona, south of Tucson, containing ruins of a 17th-century Spanish mission.
tum·ble (tŭm'bəl) *v.* **-bled, -bling, -bles.** —*intr.* **1.** To perform acrobatic feats, such as somersaults, rolls, or twists. **2. a.** To fall or roll end over end: *The kittens tumbled over each other.* **b.** To spill or roll out in confusion or disorder: *Schoolchildren tumbled out of the bus.* **c.** To pitch headlong; stumble; fall. **d.** To proceed haphazardly: *tumble into clothes.* **3. a.** To topple, as from power or high position; to fall. **b.** To collapse: *and the walls came tumbling down.* **c.** To drop: *Prices tumbled.* **4.** To come upon accidentally; happen upon: *We tumbled upon a first-rate restaurant.* **5.** *Slang.* To come to a sudden understanding; catch on. —*tr.* **1.** To cause to fall; bring down. **2.** To put, spill, or toss haphazardly. **3.** To toss or whirl in a drum or tumbler; treat in a tumbling box. —*n.* **1.** An act of tumbling; a fall. **2.** A condition of confusion or disorder. **3.** *Informal.* A sign of recognition or encouragement. [Middle English *tumblen*, frequentative of *tumben*, to tumble, leap, dance, Old English *tumbian*, perhaps from Germanic *tumōjan-* (unattested).]
tum·ble·bug (tŭm'bəl-bŭg') *n.* Any of various beetles of the family Scarabaeidae, that roll up balls of dung to protect their eggs and serve as food for the newly hatched larvae.
tum·ble·down (tŭm'bəl-doun') *adj.* Dilapidated; rickety.
tum·ble-home (tŭm'bəl-hōm') *n.* The inward curve of a ship's topsides.
tum·bler (tŭm'blər) *n.* **1.** One that tumbles; especially, an acrobat or gymnast. **2. a.** A drinking glass, originally with a rounded bottom. **b.** A flat-bottomed glass having no handle, foot, or stem. **c.** The contents of a drinking glass. **3.** A toy made with a weighted, rounded base so that it can rock over and then right itself. **4.** One of a breed of domestic pigeons characteristically tumbling or somersaulting in flight. **5.** A piece in a gunlock that forces the hammer forward by action of the mainspring. **6.** The part in a lock that releases the bolt when moved by a key. **7. a.** The drum of a clothes dryer. **b.** A **tumbling box** *(see).* **8. a.** A projecting piece on a revolving or rocking part in a mechanism that transmits motion to the part it engages. **b.** The rocking frame that moves a gear into place in a selective transmission, as in an automobile.
tum·ble·weed (tŭm'bəl-wēd') *n.* Any of various densely branched New World plants, chiefly of the genus *Amaranthus*, that when withered break off and are rolled about by the wind; especially, *A. albus*, of western prairies.
tum·bling (tŭm'blĭng) *n.* The skill or practice of gymnastic falling, rolling, or somersaulting.
tumbling box. A revolving drum in which objects are reduced in size, polished, or cleaned by tumbling with abrasives. Also called "tumbler," "tumbling barrel," "rumble."
tum·brel, tum·bril (tŭm'brəl) *n.* **1.** A two-wheeled cart; especially, a farmer's cart that can be tilted to dump a load. **2.** A crude cart used to carry condemned prisoners to their place of execution, as during the French Revolution. [Middle English *tomberel*, cucking stool, a dung cart, from Old French, a dumpcart, from *tomber, tumer*, to leap, overturn, from Frankish *tūmon* (unattested), perhaps from Germanic *tumōjan-* (unattested), to leap. See **tumble.**]
tu·me·fa·cient (tōō'mə-fā'shənt, tyōō'-) *adj.* Producing or tending to produce swelling or tumefaction. [Latin *tumefaciēns*, present participle of *tumefacere*, to cause to swell : *tumēre*, to swell (see **teue-** in Appendix*) + *facere*, to make (see **dhē-**[1] in Appendix*).]
tu·me·fac·tion (tōō'mə-făk'shən, tyōō'-) *n.* **1. a.** The action or process of puffing or swelling. **b.** A swollen condition. **2.** A puffy or swollen part. [Old French, from Latin *tumefactus*, past participle of *tumefacere*, to cause to swell. See **tumefacient.**] —**tu'me·fac'tive** *adj.*
tu·me·fy (tōō'mə-fī', tyōō'-) *v.* **-fied, -fying, -fies.** —*tr.* To cause to swell. —*intr.* To swell; become tumid. [Old French *tumefier* : Latin *tumēre*, to swell (see **teue-** in Appendix*) + -FY.]
Tu·men (tōō'mŭn'). A river rising in northern North Korea and flowing 324 miles northeast and then southeast to the Sea of Japan, forming part of the Korea-China border and the Korea-U.S.S.R. border on its course.
tu·mes·cence (tōō-mĕs'əns) *n.* **1. a.** A swelling or enlarging. **b.** A swollen condition. **2.** A swollen part or organ.
tu·mes·cent (tōō-mĕs'ənt) *adj.* Swelling; somewhat tumid.

[Latin *tumēscēns,* present participle of *tumēscere,* to begin to swell, from *tumēre,* to swell. See **teuə-** in Appendix.*]

tu·mid (tōō′mĭd, tyōō′-) *adj.* **1.** Swollen; distended. Said of a bodily part or organ. **2.** Of a bulging shape; protuberant. **3.** Overblown; bombastic: *tumid political prose.* [Latin *tumidus,* from *tumēre,* to swell. See **teuə-** in Appendix.*] —**tu·mid′i·ty, tu′mid·ness** *n.* —**tu′mid·ly** *adv.*

tum·my (tŭm′ē) *n., pl.* **-mies.** *Informal.* The stomach. [Baby-talk variant of STOMACH.]

tu·mor (tōō′mər, tyōō′-) *n.* **1.** A circumscribed, noninflammatory growth arising from existing tissue but growing independently of the normal rate or structural development of such tissue and serving no physiological function. **2.** Any swollen part. [Latin *tumor,* from *tumēre,* to swell. See **teuə-** in Appendix.*]

tump·line (tŭmp′līn′) *n.* A strap slung across the forehead or the chest to support a load carried on the back. Also called "tump." [*Tump,* perhaps of Algonquian origin + LINE.]

Tu·muc-Hu·mac Mountains (tōō-mōōk′ōō-mäk′). A range of South America, extending about 180 miles through northeastern Brazil along the borders of Surinam and French Guiana. Highest elevation, 2,800 feet.

tu·mu·lar (tōō′myə-lər, tyōō′-) *adj.* Pertaining to or having the shape of a tumulus.

tu·mu·lose (tōō′myə-lōs′, tyōō′-) *adj.* Also **tu·mu·lous** (-ləs). Having many mounds or small hills. [Latin *tumulōsus,* from *tumulus,* TUMULUS.] —**tu′mu·los′i·ty** (-lŏs′ə-tē) *n.*

tu·mult (tōō′məlt, tyōō′-) *n.* **1.** The din and commotion of a great crowd: *the tumult of a marketplace.* **2.** A disorderly commotion or disturbance; a tempestuous act, as an uprising. **3.** Agitation of the mind or emotions. [Middle English *tumulte,* from Old French, from Latin *tumultus.* See **teuə-** in Appendix.*]

tu·mul·tu·ar·y (tə-mŭl′chōō-ĕr′ē) *adj.* Marked by haste, disorder, and irregularity; showing haste and confusion. [Latin *tumultuārius,* from *tumultus,* TUMULT.]

tu·mul·tu·ous (tə-mŭl′chōō-əs) *adj.* **1.** Noisy and disorderly; riotous: *a tumultuous political convention.* **2.** Making a tumult; tending to incite: *a tumultuous group of malcontents.* **3.** Confusedly or violently agitated: *a tumultuous heart.* —**tu·mul′tu·ous·ly** *adv.* —**tu·mul′tu·ous·ness** *n.*

tu·mu·lus (tōō′myə-ləs, tyōō′-) *n., pl.* **-li** (-lī′). An ancient grave mound; barrow. [Latin, a raised heap of earth, hillock, tumulus. See **teuə-** in Appendix.*]

tun (tŭn) *n.* **1.** A large cask for liquids, especially wine. **2.** A measure of liquid capacity, especially one equivalent to 252 gallons. [Middle English *tunne, tonne,* a measure of wine, Old English *tunne,* cask, vat, from Medieval Latin *tunna,* from Celtic, akin to Middle Irish *tunna*†.]

TUN Airport code for Tunis, Tunisia.

tu·na¹ (tōō′nə, tyōō′-) *n., pl.* **tuna** or **-nas. 1. a.** Any of various, often large marine and food fishes of the genus *Thunnus* and related genera, many of which, including *T. thynnus* and the albacore, are commercially important sources of canned fish. Also called "tunny." **b.** Any of several related fishes, such as the bonito. **2.** The canned or commercially processed flesh of any of these fishes. In this sense, also called "tuna fish." [American Spanish, ultimately from Latin *thunnus,* TUNNY.]

tu·na² (tōō′nə, tyōō′-) *n.* **1.** Any of several tropical American cacti of the genus *Opuntia,* which includes the prickly pears; especially, *O. tuna,* bearing edible red fruit. **2.** The fruit of such a plant. [Spanish, from Taino.]

tun·a·ble (tōō′nə-bəl, tyōō′-) *adj.* Also **tune·a·ble. 1.** Able to be tuned. **2.** *Archaic.* Tuneful. —**tun′a·ble·ness** *n.* —**tun′a·bly** *adv.*

tun·dra (tŭn′drə) *n.* A treeless area between the ice cap and the tree line of arctic regions, having a permanently frozen subsoil and supporting low-growing vegetation such as lichens, mosses, and stunted shrubs. [Russian, from Lapp *tundar,* akin to Finnish *tunturi,* an arctic hill, a bare hill.]

tune (tōōn, tyōōn) *n.* **1.** A melody, especially of simple and easily remembered character. **2. a.** Correct musical pitch. **b.** The state of being properly adjusted for pitch: *a piano out of tune.* **3. a.** Agreement in pitch: *play in tune with the piano.* **b.** Concord or agreement; harmony: *in tune with the times.* **c.** *Archaic.* Frame of mind; disposition. **4.** *Electronics.* Adjustment of a receiver or circuit for maximum response to a given signal or frequency. **5.** *Obsolete.* A musical tone. —**change one's tune.** To change one's approach or attitude. —**to the tune of.** To the sum or amount of. —*v.* **tuned, tuning, tunes.** —*tr.* **1.** To put in proper pitch with mechanical adjustments. **2. a.** To adjust in order to bring into harmony. **b.** To adapt; adjust; attune: *tune oneself to life in the tropics.* **3.** To adjust (an engine) for maximum performance. **4.** *Archaic.* To utter musically; sing. —*intr.* To become attuned. —**tune in.** To adjust a radio or television receiver to receive signals at a particular frequency. —**tune out.** To adjust a radio receiver so as not to receive a particular signal. [Middle English, variant of *ton(e),* TONE.]

tune·ful (tōōn′fəl, tyōōn′-) *adj.* **1.** Full of tune; melodious; musical. **2.** Producing musical sounds. —**tune′ful·ly** *adv.* —**tune′ful·ness** *n.*

tune·less (tōōn′lĭs, tyōōn′-) *adj.* **1.** Deficient in melody; not tuneful; unmusical. **2.** Giving no music; silent. —**tune′less·ly** *adv.* —**tune′less·ness** *n.*

tun·er (tōō′nər, tyōō′-) *n.* **1.** One that tunes: *a piano tuner.* **2.** A device for tuning; especially, an electronic circuit or device used to select signals at a specific radio frequency for amplification and conversion to sound.

tune up. 1. To bring (a musical instrument) up to pitch. **2.** To adjust (a motor or engine) to efficient working order.

tune-up (tōōn′ŭp′, tyōōn′-) *n.* **1.** An adjustment of a motor or engine to put it in efficient working order. **2.** An engine warm-up.

Tung·chow. The former name for **Nantung.**

Tung·hai. The former name for **Sinhailien.**

tung oil (tŭng). A yellow or brownish oil extracted from the seeds of the **tung tree** *(see)* and used as a drying agent in varnishes and paints and for waterproofing. Also called "Chinese wood oil."

Tung·shan. The former name for **Süchow.**

tung·state (tŭng′stāt′) *n.* A chemical compound derived from tungstic acid and containing tungsten with valence 6. [TUNGST(EN) + -ATE.]

tung·sten (tŭng′stən) *n. Symbol* **W** A hard, brittle, corrosion-resistant gray to white metallic element extracted from wolframite, scheelite, and other minerals, having the highest melting point and lowest vapor pressure of any metal. Tungsten and its alloys are used in high-temperature structural materials, electrical elements, notably lamp filaments, and instruments requiring thermally compatible glass-to-metal seals. Atomic number 74, atomic weight 183.85, melting point 3,410°C, boiling point 5,927°C, specific gravity 19.3 (20°C), valences 2, 3, 4, 5, 6. Also *rare* "wolfram." See **element.** [Swedish, "heavy stone" : *tung,* heavy, from Old Norse *thungr* (see **tengh-** in Appendix*) + *sten,* stone, from Old Norse *steinn* (see **stei-** in Appendix*).] —**tung·sten′ic** *adj.*

tungsten carbide. An extremely hard, fine gray powder with composition WC, used in tools, dies, wear-resistant machine parts, and abrasives.

tungsten lamp. An incandescent electric lamp with a tungsten filament.

tungsten steel. A very hard, heat-resistant steel containing tungsten.

tung·stic (tŭng′stĭk) *adj.* Of, pertaining to, or containing tungsten, especially with valence 6. [From TUNGSTEN.]

tungstic acid. A yellow powder, H_2WO_4, used in textiles and plastics.

tung·stite (tŭng′stīt′) *n.* A yellow or yellowish-green mineral, essentially WO_3, often occurring with tungsten ores. [TUNGST(EN) + -ITE.]

Tung·ting, Lake (tŭng′tĭng′). A shallow lake occupying 1,450 square miles in northern Hunan Province, China.

tung tree. Any of several Asian trees of the genus *Aleurites;* especially, *A. fordii,* cultivated for its seeds that yield a commercially valuable drying oil. Also called "tung-oil tree." [Mandarin Chinese *t'ung²* + TREE.]

Tun·gus (tōōng-gōōz′) *n., pl.* **-guses** or **Tungus.** Also **Tun·gese** (tŭng-gēz′) (for sense 2). **1.** A Mongoloid people inhabiting eastern Siberia. **2.** The Tungusic language of these people. [Russian *Tunguz,* a Tungus, from Yakut *tungus,* from Turkic *tungus* (unattested), "pig" (probably because many Tungus tribes were pig breeders).]

Tun·gus·ic (tōōng-gōō′zĭk) *n.* A subgroup of the Altaic family of languages, including the Tungus and Manchu languages, spoken in eastern Siberia and northern Manchuria. —*adj.* Of or pertaining to the Tungus peoples or to Tungusic.

Tun·gus·ka (tōōng-gōōz′kä). Any of three rivers of the Soviet Union, in central Siberia; the Upper Tunguska, the lower course of the **Angara** *(see);* the Lower Tunguska, rising in the Irkutsk Region and flowing about 2,000 miles first north and then west to the Yenisei; and the Stony Tunguska, flowing about 1,000 miles generally northwest to the Yenisei.

tu·nic (tōō′nĭk, tyōō′-) *n.* **1. a.** A loose-fitting garment, sleeved or sleeveless, extending to the knees and worn by men and women especially in ancient Greece and Rome. **b.** A medieval surcoat. **2. a.** A long plain close-fitting military jacket, usually with a high stiff collar. **b.** A long plain sleeved or sleeveless blouse worn over a skirt by women. **c.** A short pleated and belted dress worn by women for some sports. **3.** *Anatomy.* A coat or layer enveloping an organ or part. **4.** *Botany.* A membranous outer covering, as of a seed. **5.** A tunicle. [Latin *tunica,* a sheath, tunic, from a Phoenician source, from Aramaic *kittūnā,* akin to Hebrew *kəthōnet.* See also **chiton.**]

tu·ni·ca (tōō′nĭ-kə, tyōō′-) *n., pl.* **-cae** (-kē′, -kī′, -sē′). *Anatomy.* An integument; a tunic. [New Latin, from Latin, TUNIC.]

tu·ni·cate (tōō′nĭ-kĭt, -nĭ-kāt′, tyōō′-) *n.* Any of various chordate marine animals of the subphylum Urochordata (or Tunicata), having a cylindrical or globular body enclosed in a tough outer covering, or tunic, and including the sea squirts and salps. —*adj.* **1.** Of or pertaining to the tunicates. **2.** *Anatomy.* Having a tunic. **3.** *Botany.* Having concentric layers, as the bulb of an onion. [Latin *tunicātus,* past participle of *tunicāre,* to clothe with a tunic, from *tunica,* TUNIC.]

tu·ni·cle (tōō′nĭk-əl, tyōō′-) *n.* A short vestment worn over the alb by a subdeacon or with the dalmatic by a bishop or cardinal. [Middle English, from Latin *tunicula,* diminutive of *tunica,* TUNIC.]

tuning fork. A small two-pronged instrument that when struck produces a sound of fixed pitch, now 440 cycles per second in standard international use.

Tu·nis (tōō′nĭs, tyōō′-). **1.** The capital of Tunisia, a seaport in the north on the Mediterranean. Population, 714,000. **2.** A former Barbary state on the northern coast of Africa.

Tu·ni·sia (tōō-nē′zhə, -nĭzh′ə, -nĭsh′ə, tyōō-). A republic occupying 48,300 square miles in northern Africa; a former French protectorate, independent since 1956. Population, 4,030,000. Capital, Tunis.

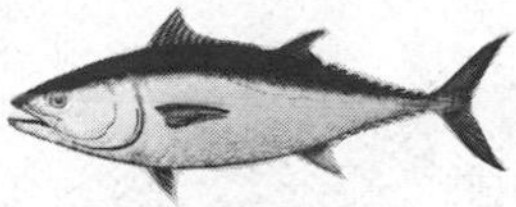

tuna¹
Thunnus thynnus

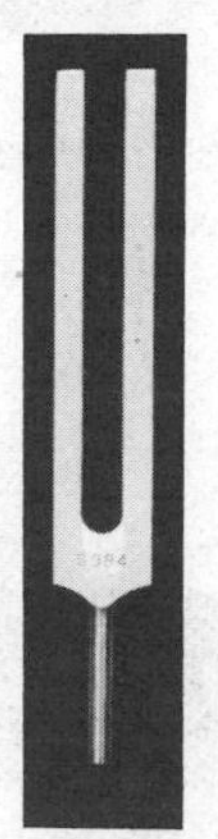

tuning fork

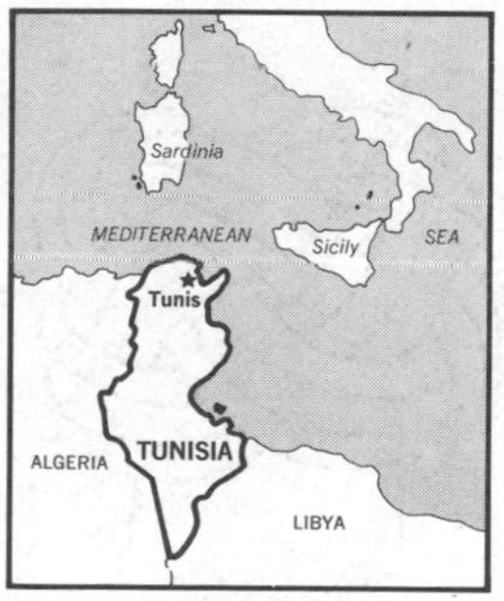

Tunisia

Tu·ni·sian (tōō-nē′zhən, -nĭzh′ən, -nĭsh′ən, tyōō-) *adj.* Of or pertaining to Tunisia, its capital city, people, or language. —*n.* A native or inhabitant of Tunisia or Tunis.
tun·nage. Variant of **tonnage.**
tun·nel (tŭn′əl) *n.* **1.** An underground or underwater passage. **2.** A passage through any extended barrier. **3.** *Regional.* A funnel. **4.** *Obsolete.* The main flue on a chimney. —*v.* **tunneled** or **-nelled, -neling** or **-nelling, -nels.** —*tr.* **1.** To make a tunnel under or through. **2.** To shape or dig in the form of a tunnel: *tunnel a passage.* —*intr.* To make a tunnel. [Middle English *tonel,* a pipelike net for catching birds, from Old French *ton(n)el,* a cask, from *tonne,* a tun, from Medieval Latin *tunna, tonna,* TUN.] —**tun′nel·er, tun′nel·ler** *n.*
tunnel disease. *Pathology.* **Caisson disease** *(see).*
tun·ny (tŭn′ē) *n., pl.* **-nies** or **tunny.** A fish, the **tuna** *(see).* [Old French *thon,* from Old Provençal *ton,* from Latin *thunnus, thynnus,* from Greek *thunnos,* akin to Hebrew *tannīn,* "great sea monster."]
tup (tŭp) *n.* **1.** *Chiefly British.* A male sheep; a ram. **2.** A heavy metal body, especially the head of a power hammer. —*v.* **tupped, tupping, tups.** —*tr.* To copulate with (a ewe). Used of a ram. —*intr.* To copulate with a ewe. [Middle English *toupe, tup(pe)*†, a ram.]

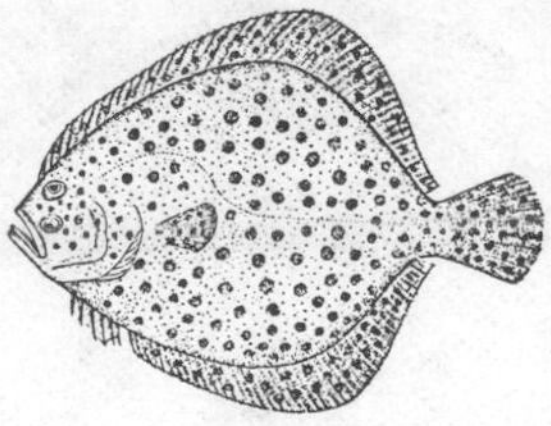
turbot
Psetta maxima

tu·pe·lo (tōō′pə-lō′, tyōō′-) *n., pl.* **-los.** **1.** Any of several trees of the genus *Nyssa;* especially, *N. aquatica,* of the southeastern United States, having soft, light wood. **2.** The wood of any of these trees. [Creek *ito opilwa,* "swamp tree" : *ito,* tree + *opilwa,* swamp.]
Tu·pi (tōō′pē, tōō-pē′) *n., pl.* **Tupi** or **-pis.** **1.** A member of any of a group of peoples living along the coast of Brazil, in the Amazon River valley, and in Paraguay. **2.** The Tupian language of these peoples.
Tu·pi·an (tōō′pē-ən, tōō-pē′ən) *adj.* Of or pertaining to the Tupi. —*n.* A major division of Tupi-Guarani that includes Tupi.
Tu·pi-Gua·ra·ni (tōō-pē′gwär′ən-ē′, tōō′pē′-) *n.* A family of languages, of which the chief divisions are Tupian and Guarani, spread throughout large areas of coastal Brazil, the Amazon River valley, and northeastern South America. —**Tu·pi′-Gua′ra·ni′, Tu·pi′-Gua′ra·ni′an** *adj.*
Tu·po·lev (tōō-pō′ləf), **Andrei Nikolayevich.** Born 1888. Soviet aeronautical engineer; designed pioneer aircraft.
tup·pence. *British Informal.* Variant of **twopence.**
tup·pen·ny. *Chiefly British Informal.* Variant of **twopenny.**
Tu·pun·ga·to (tōō′pōōn-gä′tō). A mountain rising to 21,490 feet in the Andes on the border between Chile and Argentina.
tuque (tōōk, tyōōk) *n.* A knitted woolen cap in the form of a cylindrical bag with tapered ends that is worn with one end tucked into the other. [Canadian French, from French *toque,* TOQUE.]

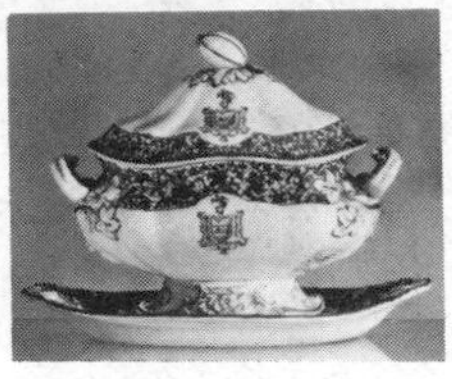
tureen

tu quo·que (tōō kwō′kwē, tyōō). *Latin.* Likewise you; you, too. A retort accusing an accuser of a similar offense.
tu·ra·co. Variant of **touraco.**
Tu·ra·ni·an (tōō-rā′nē-ən, tyōō-) *adj.* Of or pertaining to the Ural-Altaic languages or to the peoples who speak them. —*n.* **1.** A language group, **Ural-Altaic** *(see).* **2.** A member of any of the peoples who speak languages of this group. [From Persian *Tūrān,* region north of the Oxus River.]
tur·ban (tûr′bən) *n.* **1.** A headdress of Moslem origin, consisting of a long scarf of linen, cotton, or silk wound around the head or a cap. **2.** Any of various hats worn by women and children, either brimless or with a very short brim turned up close against the crown. **3.** Any headdress resembling these. [Old French *turbant, tolliban,* from Old Italian *turbante, tolipante,* from Turkish *tül(i)bend,* from Persian *dulband*†.]

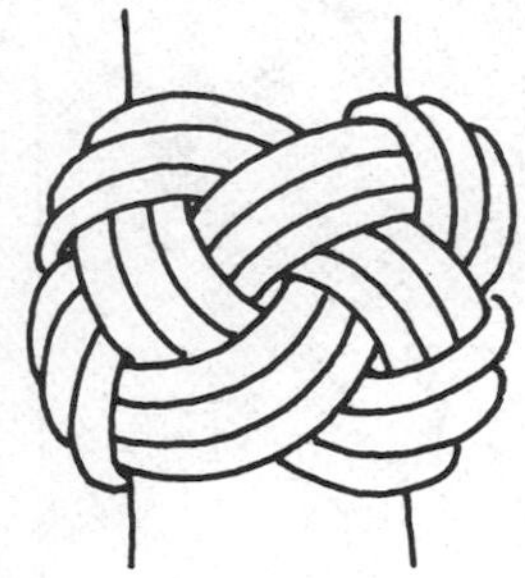
Turk's-head

tur·ba·ry (tûr′bə-rē) *n., pl.* **-ries.** **1.** A place where peat can be dug; a peat bog. **2.** *British Law.* The right to dig peat or turf on someone else's ground. [Middle English *turbary(e),* turf land, peat bog, from Norman French *turberie,* from Old French *t(o)urberie,* from Medieval Latin *turbāria,* from *turba,* turf, from Germanic. See **derbh-** in Appendix.*]
tur·bel·lar·i·an (tûr′bə-lâr′ē-ən) *n.* Any of various chiefly aquatic ciliate flatworms of the class Turbellaria. —*adj.* Of or belonging to the Turbellaria. [From New Latin *Turbellaria,* from Latin *turbellae* (plural), bustle, stir (their cilia vibrate and produce little whirls in the water), from *turba,* turmoil, uproar. See **turbid.**]
tur·bid (tûr′bĭd) *adj.* **1.** Having sediment or foreign particles stirred up or suspended; muddy; cloudy: *turbid water.* **2.** Heavy, dark, or dense, as smoke or fog. **3.** In turmoil; muddled: *"the turbid life of Dublin"* (Stanislaus Joyce). [Latin *turbidus,* wild, confused, muddy, from *turba,* turmoil, uproar, probably from Greek *turbē,* disorder. See **twer-**[1] in Appendix.*] —**tur′bid·ly** *adv.* —**tur′bid·ness, tur′bid′i·ty** *n.*
tur·bi·nal (tûr′bə-nəl) *adj.* Having the shape of a cone resting on its apex. —*n. Anatomy.* A turbinate bone. [From Latin *turbō* (stem *turbin-*), a spinning thing. See **turbine.**]
tur·bi·nate (tûr′bə-nĭt, -nāt′) *adj.* Also **tur·bi·nat·ed** (-nā′tĭd). **1.** Shaped like a top. **2.** Spinning like a top. **3.** *Zoology.* Spiral and decreasing sharply in diameter from base to apex. Said of shells. **4.** *Anatomy.* Designating a small curved bone that extends horizontally along the lateral wall of the nasal passage. [Latin *turbinātus,* from *turbō* (stem *turbin-*), a top. See **turbine.**]
tur·bi·na·tion (tûr′bə-nā′shən) *n.* A turbinate formation.
tur·bine (tûr′bĭn, -bīn′) *n.* Any of various machines in which the kinetic energy of a moving fluid is converted to mechanical power by the impulse or reaction of the fluid with a series of buckets, paddles, or blades arrayed about the circumference of a wheel or cylinder. See **gas turbine.** [French, from Latin *turbō* (stem *turbin-*), a spinning thing, top, whirlwind, perhaps from Greek *turbē,* disorder. See **twer-**[1] in Appendix.*]
tur·bit (tûr′bĭt) *n.* One of a breed of domestic pigeons having a small crested head and a ruffled breast. [Origin obscure.]
turbo–. Indicates turbine, or pertaining to or driven by a turbine; for example, **turbojet.** [From TURBINE.]
tur·bo·fan (tûr′bō-făn′) *n.* **1.** A turbojet engine in which a fan supplements the total thrust by forcing air diverted from the main engine directly into the hot turbine exhaust. **2.** An aircraft in which such an engine is used.
tur·bo·jet (tûr′bō-jĕt′) *n.* **1.** A jet engine having a turbine-driven compressor and developing thrust from the exhaust of hot gases. **2.** An aircraft in which such an engine is used.
tur·bo·prop (tûr′bō-prŏp′) *n.* **1.** A turbojet engine used to drive an external propeller. **2.** An aircraft in which such an engine is used. [Short for *turbopropeller.*]
tur·bo·ram·jet (tûr′bō-răm′jĕt′) *n.* **1.** A turbojet engine that at high speeds compresses air taken in as a ramjet and increases exhaust velocities with an afterburner. **2.** An aircraft in which such an engine is used.
tur·bo·su·per·charg·er (tûr′bō-sōō′pər-chär′jər) *n.* A supercharger that uses an exhaust-driven turbine to maintain air-intake pressure in high-altitude aircraft.
tur·bot (tûr′bət) *n., pl.* **turbot** or **-bots.** **1.** A European flatfish, *Psetta maxima* (or *Scophthalmus maximus*), esteemed as food. **2.** Any of various similar or related flatfishes. [Middle English, from Old French, probably from Old Swedish *törnbut,* turbot, "thorn-flatfish" (presumably referring to its shape in profile) : *törn,* thorn (see **stern-** in Appendix*) + *but,* flat fish (see **bhau-** in Appendix*).]
tur·bu·la·tor (tûr′byə-lā′tər) *n.* Any device designed to cause turbulence in fluids. [From TURBULENT.]
tur·bu·lence (tûr′byə-ləns) *n.* **1.** The state or quality of being agitated, violently disturbed, or in commotion. **2. Turbulent flow** *(see).*
tur·bu·lent (tûr′byə-lənt) *adj.* **1.** Violently agitated or disturbed; tumultuous: *turbulent rapids.* **2.** Having a chaotic or restless character or tendency: *a turbulent period of history.* **3.** Causing unrest or disturbance; unruly. [Latin *turbulentus,* from *turba,* confusion. See **turbid.**] —**tur′bu·lent·ly** *adv.*
turbulent flow. The motion of a fluid having local velocities and pressures that fluctuate randomly. Also called "turbulence."
Tur·co·man. Variant of **Turkoman.**
turd (tûrd) *n.* **1. a.** *Vulgar.* A piece of dung. **b.** *Obsolete.* Excrement. **2.** *Vulgar Slang.* A worthless or contemptible person. [Middle English *tord, turd,* Old English *tord.* See **der-**[2] in Appendix.*]
tu·reen (tōō-rēn′, tyōō-) *n.* A broad, deep dish with a cover used for serving soups, stews, or the like. [Earlier *ter(r)ene,* from French *terrine,* "earthen vessel," from Old French, feminine of *terrin,* earthen, from Vulgar Latin *terrīnus* (unattested), from Latin *terra,* earth. See **ters-** in Appendix.*]
Tu·renne (tü-rĕn′), **Vicomte de.** Title of Henri de la Tour d'Auvergne. 1611–1675. French military leader in Thirty Years' War and the Fronde.
turf (tûrf) *n., pl.* **turfs** or *archaic* **turves** (tûrvz). **1.** A surface layer of earth containing a dense growth of grass and its matted roots; sod. **2.** A piece cut from such a layer of earth or sod. **3.** A piece of peat that is burned for use as fuel. **4.** *Slang.* The area claimed by a juvenile gang as its personal territory. —**the turf.** **1.** A racetrack, either of grass or dirt. **2.** The sport or business of racing horses. [Middle English *turf,* Old English *turf.* See **derbh-** in Appendix.*] —**turf′y** *adj.*
Tur·fan (tōōr′fän′). The lowest point in Asia (over 900 feet below sea level), a depression in the northeastern part of the Sinkiang-Uigur Autonomous Region, China.
Tur·ge·nev (tōōr-gā′nyəf), **Ivan Sergeyevich.** 1818–1883. Russian novelist.
tur·ges·cence (tûr′jĕs′əns) *n.* Also **tur·ges·cen·cy** (-ən-sē). **1.** The process of swelling up, or the condition of being swollen. **2.** Pomposity; self-importance. [Latin *turgēscens,* present participle of *turgēscere,* to begin to swell, inceptive of *turgēre,* to be swollen. See **turgid.**] —**tur′ges′cent** *adj.*
tur·gid (tûr′jĭd) *adj.* **1.** Overdistended; swollen; bloated: *"a sort of thick, turgid darkness full of menace"* (D.H. Lawrence). **2.** Overornate in style or language; grandiloquent. [Latin *turgidus,* from *turgēre*†, to be swollen, to swell.] —**tur·gid′i·ty, tur′gid·ness** *n.* —**tur′gid·ly** *adv.*
tur·gor (tûr′gôr, -gər) *n.* **1.** The state of being turgid. **2.** *Biology.* The normal fullness or tension produced by the fluid content of blood vessels, capillaries, and plant or animal cells. [Late Latin, from Latin *turgēre,* to be swollen. See **turgid.**]
Tur·got (tōōr-gō′), **Anne Robert Jacques.** Baron de l'Aulne. 1727–1781. French statesman and economic reformer.
Tu·rin (tōō′rĭn, tyōō′-). *Italian* **To·ri·no** (tō-rē′nō). The capital of Piedmont, Italy, an industrial center in the northwestern part of the country. Population, 1,117,000.
tu·ri·on (tōōr′ē-ən) *n. Botany.* A scaly shoot, as of asparagus, that rises from the ground. [New Latin *turio* (stem *turion-*), from Latin *turiō*†, shoot, sprout, tendril.]
Turk (tûrk) *n.* **1.** A native or inhabitant of Turkey. **2.** A person speaking a Turkic language. **3.** A Moslem. **4.** Formerly, an Ottoman. **5.** A brutal or tyrannical person. **6.** Turkic. [Middle English, from Old French *Turc,* from Medieval Latin *Turcus,* from Turkish *Türk.*]
Turk. Turkey; Turkish.
Tur·ke·stan (tûr′kə-stän′, -stăn′). Also **Tur·ki·stan.** A region of central Asia extending from the Caspian Sea to the Gobi

Desert, including parts of the Soviet Union (Russian Turkestan) and China (Chinese Turkestan).

tur·key (tûr′kē) *n., pl.* **-keys.** **1. a.** A large North American bird, *Meleagris gallopavo,* that has brownish plumage and a bare, wattled head and neck and is widely domesticated for food. **b.** A related bird, *Agriocharis ocellata,* of Mexico and Central America. **2.** *Slang.* A stage play or other production that fails. **3.** *Slang.* A person regarded as continually inept; a misfit. **—talk turkey.** To discuss in a straightforward and direct manner. [Short for TURKEY COCK.]

Tur·key (tûr′kē). *Abbr.* **Turk.** A republic occupying 296,185 square miles, mainly in Asia Minor and partly, across the Dardanelles and the Bosporus, in southeastern Europe. Population, 31,391,000. Capital, Ankara. [Middle English *Turkye,* from Old French *Turquie,* from Medieval Latin *Turchia,* from *Turcus,* TURK.]

turkey buzzard. A New World vulture, *Cathartes aura,* having dark plumage and bare red head and neck similar to that of the turkey. Also called "turkey vulture."

turkey cock. **1.** A male turkey. **2.** A strutting, conceited person. [Originally applied to the guinea fowl (with which the American bird was later mistakenly identified), first imported by the Portuguese from Africa by way of Turkey.]

Turkey red. Moderate red. See **color.** [The color often used in cotton cloth manufactured in Turkey.] **—Tur′key-red′** *adj.*

turkey trot. A ragtime dance of the early 20th century, characterized by a springy walk with the feet well apart and a swinging up-and-down movement of the shoulders.

Tur·ki (tûr′kē′) *adj.* **1.** Of or pertaining to Turkic. **2.** Of or pertaining to the Turks, especially those speaking an Eastern Turkic language. *—n.* **1.** Any Turkic language. **2.** A member of a people speaking a Turkic language. [Persian *turkī,* from *Turk,* a Turk, from Turkish *Türk,* TURK.]

Tur·kic (tûr′kĭk) *n.* A subdivision of Altaic including Turkish, Turkoman, Azerbaijani, Tatar, Uzbek, Uigur, Kirghiz, Karakalpak, Chuvash, Chagatai, and Yakut. *—adj.* **1.** Of or pertaining to the Turks. **2.** Of or pertaining to Turkic.

Turk·ish (tûr′kĭsh) *adj. Abbr.* **Turk.** **1.** Of or relating to Turkey or the Turks. **2.** Of or relating to the Turkic language of Turkey. *—n.* The Turkic language of Turkey. When written in the Arabic script, as it was until 1930, it is generally referred to as Ottoman Turkish or Osmanli.

Turkish bath. **1.** A steam bath inducing heavy perspiration in the bather, followed by a shower and massage. **2.** An establishment where such bathing facilities are available.

Turkish coffee. Pulverized coffee in a thin sugar syrup.

Turkish delight. A candy of Turkish origin, usually consisting of jellylike cubes covered with powdered sugar.

Turkish Empire. See **Ottoman Empire.**

Turkish towel. Also **turkish towel.** A thick rough towel with a nap of uncut pile.

Turk·ism (tûr′kĭz′əm) *n.* **1.** The cultural, religious, or social system of the Turks. **2.** Any characteristic of Turkish language.

Turk·men Soviet Socialist Republic (tûrk′mĕn, -mən). Also **Turk·men·i·stan** (tûrk′mĕ-nĭ-stăn′, -stän′). A constituent republic of the Soviet Union, occupying 187,200 square miles in central Asia between the Caspian Sea and Afghanistan. Population, 1,802,000. Capital, Ashkhabad.

Tur·ko·man (tûr′kə-mən) *adj.* Also **Turk·men** (tûrk′mən), **Tur·co·man** (tûr′kə-mən). **1.** Of or pertaining to Turkoman. **2.** Of or pertaining to the Turkomans. *—n., pl.* **Turkomans.** Also **Tur·co·man.** **1.** Any of a formerly nomadic people inhabiting the Turkmen, Uzbek, Kazakh, and Kara-Kalpak republics of the U.S.S.R. **2.** The Turkic language of these people. [Medieval Latin *Turcomannus,* from Persian *Turkuman, Turkmēn,* from *turkmān, turkmēn,* like a Turk, from *Turk,* a Turk, from Turkish *Türk,* TURK.]

Turks and Cai·cos Islands (tûrks; kī′kōs). Two island groups in the West Indies, lying southeast of the Bahamas, and having a combined area of about 202 square miles; administered by Jamaica. Population, 6,000.

Turk's-cap lily (tûrks′kăp′). **1.** A North American lily, *Lilium superbum,* having orange-red, spotted flowers with reflexed petals. **2.** A plant, the **martagon** *(see).* [From the shape of its flower.]

Turk's-head (tûrks′hĕd′) *n. Nautical.* A turban-shaped knot made by winding a smaller rope around a larger one.

Tur·ku (tŏŏr′kōō′). *Swedish* **Å·bo** (ō′bōō). A city of Finland, a major seaport in the southwest on the Gulf of Bothnia. Population, 178,000.

Turk·ut. See **Old Turkic.**

tur·ma·line. Variant of **tourmaline.**

tur·mer·ic (tûr′mər-ĭk) *n.* **1.** A plant, *Curcuma longa,* of India, having yellow flowers and an aromatic rootstock. **2.** The powdered rootstock of this plant, used as a condiment and as a yellow dye. **3.** Any of several other plants having similar roots. [Earlier *tarmaret,* from Old French *terre mérite,* from Medieval Latin *terra merita,* "meritorious earth."]

turmeric paper. Paper saturated with turmeric and used as an indicator for the presence of alkalis, which turn the paper brown, or for boric acid, which turns it red-brown.

tur·moil (tûr′moil) *n.* Utter confusion; extreme agitation; commotion; tumult: *"and from this cavern, with ceaseless turmoil seething, / A mighty fountain momently was forced"* (Coleridge). [Origin unknown.]

turn (tûrn) *v.* **turned, turning, turns.** *—tr.* **1.** To cause to execute an angular displacement; move around; rotate; revolve. **2.** To cause to move around in order to achieve a desired result; change the position of by rotating: *turn a window plant frequently so that it keeps its shape.* **3.** To alter or control the functioning of (a mechanical device, for example) by the use of a rotating or similar movement: *turn the volume down on the radio.* **4.** To perform or accomplish by rotating or revolving: *turn a somersault.* **5. a.** To change the position of so that the underside becomes the upperside: *turn the steak.* **b.** To spade or plow (soil) to bring the undersoil to the surface. **c.** To reverse and resew the material of (a collar or cuffs, for example). **6. a.** To produce a rounded shape in (wood or metal, for example) by applying a cutting tool. **b.** To produce a rounded form in by any means: *turn a heel in knitting a sock.* **c.** To shape or form: *turn a vase on a potter's wheel.* **d.** To give distinctive, artistic, or graceful form to: *turn a phrase.* **7.** To revolve in the mind; think over; consider; examine. Often used with *over: turn an idea over for several days.* **8. a.** To change the position of by traversing an arc of a circle; to pivot: *He turned his chair to the speaker.* **b.** To change the position of by folding, twisting, or bending: *turn the blankets down.* **c.** To change the position of so as to show another side of: *turn the page.* **d.** To injure by twisting: *turn an ankle.* **e.** To upset or make nauseated: *That turns my stomach.* **9.** To change the direction or course of: *turn the car left.* **10.** To divert or deflect: *turn a stampede.* **11.** To reverse the course of; cause to retreat: *turn an enemy.* **12.** To make a course around or about: *turn the corner.* **13.** To change the purpose, intention, or content of by persuasion or influence: *His speech turned my thinking.* **14.** To change the order or disposition of; unsettle; upset: *"Sudden prosperity had turned Garrick's head."* (Macaulay). **15.** To set in a specified way or direction; to direct; to point. **16.** To aim or focus; train: *turn one's gaze to the sky.* **17.** To direct (the attention, interest, or mind, for example) toward or away from something: *"To all his supplications, the captain turned a deaf ear."* (Melville). **18.** To devote or apply (oneself, for example) to something: *He turned himself to music.* **19.** To become, reach, or surpass (a certain age, time, or amount): *The price had turned ten dollars by the next bid.* **20.** To cause to act or go against; make antagonistic. **21.** To cause to go in any direction; to direct: *They turned their way back.* **22.** To send, drive, or let go: *turn the braggart out of the bar; turn the dog loose.* **23.** To pour, let fall, or otherwise release (contents) from a receptacle: *turn the dough onto a floured board.* **24.** To make sour; ferment: *Lack of refrigeration turned the milk.* **25.** To affect or change the color of: *Autumn turns the foliage.* **26.** To change; transform: *turn a molehill into a mountain.* **27.** To exchange; convert. Used with *into: She turns her singing talent into extra money.* **28.** To cause to take on a specified character, nature, or appearance. **29. a.** To fold, bend, or curve (something). **b.** To make a bend or curve in: *He could turn a bar of steel.* **c.** To blunt or dull (the edge of a cutting instrument). **30.** To keep in circulation; sell and restock: *We turned a great deal of merchandise during the holidays.* **31.** To get by buying and selling: *turn a fair profit.* *—intr.* **1.** To execute an angular displacement; move around an axis or center; rotate; revolve. **2.** To appear to revolve or whirl, as in dizziness or giddiness: *After the fall, my head kept turning.* **3.** To roll from side to side or back and forth: *I tossed and turned all night.* **4. a.** To operate a lathe. **b.** To be formed on a lathe. **5.** To direct one's way or course. **6.** To change or reverse one's way, course, or direction. **7.** To have a specific reaction or effect, especially when adverse. **8.** To change one's actions or attitudes adversely; become hostile or antagonistic: *All the world has turned against him.* **9.** To attack suddenly and violently with no apparent motive: *The animal turned on the children.* **10.** To channel one's attention, interest, or thought toward or away from something. **11.** To convert from one religion to another. **12.** To switch one's loyalty from one side or party to another. **13.** To have recourse to a person or thing for help, support, or information. **14.** To devote or apply oneself to something, as to a field of study. **15.** To depend upon for success, failure, or other result; rely: *The game turned on the play of the quarterback.* **16.** To change; become transformed. **17.** To change color. **18.** To be stocked and easily sold: *This merchandise will turn easily.* **19.** To become dull or blunt after bending back. Used of the edge of a cutting instrument. **—turn down.** **1.** To diminish the speed, volume, intensity, or flow of. **2.** *Informal.* To reject or refuse, as a person, advice, or a suggestion. **—turn in.** **1.** To turn or go into; enter. **2.** To hand in; give over; to return: *turn in an income-tax return.* **3.** To bend inward. **4.** *Informal.* To go to bed. **—turn on.** **1.** To cause to begin the operation, activity, or flow of: *turn on the light bulb; turn on the charm.* **2.** *Slang.* **a.** To affect with great pleasure: *Shakespeare turns me on.* **b.** To smoke or ingest a drug for the purpose of experiencing a heightened sensual response to given stimuli. **—turn tail.** To run away; flee. **—turn to.** **1.** To begin work on. **2.** To refer to, as for information or support. *—n.* **1.** The act of turning or the condition of being turned; a rotation; revolution. **2.** A change of direction, motion, or position: *a right turn.* **3.** A departure or deviation, as in a trend: *a turn of events.* **4.** A point of change in time: *at the turn of the century.* **5. a.** A chance or opportunity to do something. **b.** One of a series of such opportunities accorded individuals in succession or in scheduled order: *waiting his turn at bat.* **6.** A period of participation in something: *a turn at creative writing.* **7.** A characteristic mood, style, or habit; natural inclination: *"persons of a curious and speculative turn of mind"* (Lamb). **8.** A propensity or adeptness: *a turn for carpentry.* **9.** A movement in the direction of. Usually used with *for: a turn for the worse.* **10.** A deed or action having a specified effect on another: *"He thought some friend had done him an ill turn"* (Stephen Crane). **11.** Advantage or purpose: *It*

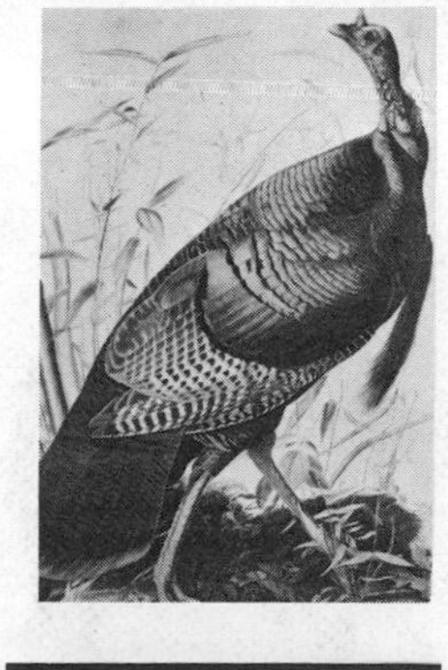

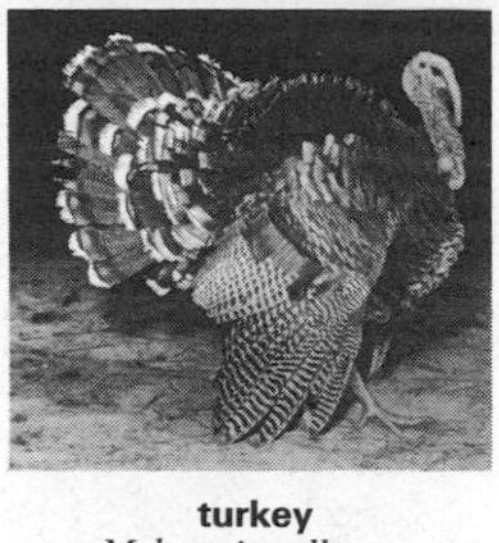

turkey
Meleagris gallopavo
Above: Wild form
Painting by
John James Audubon
Below: Domesticated form

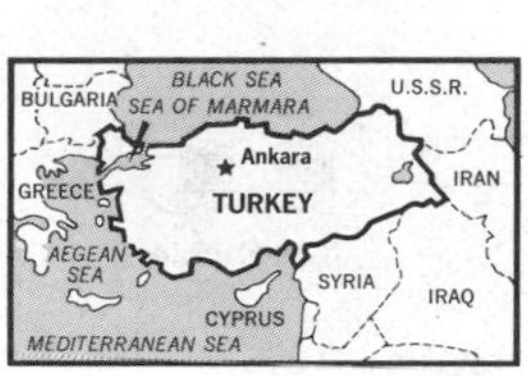

Turkey

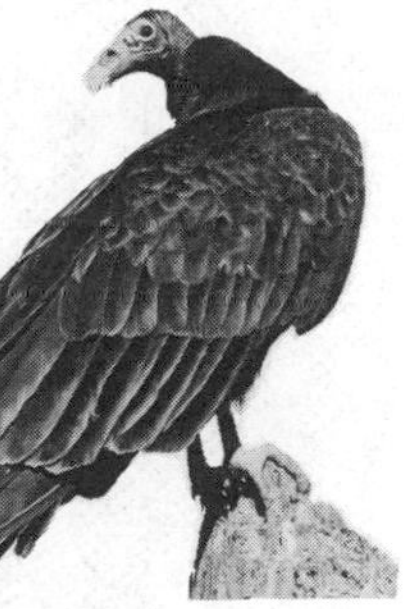

turkey buzzard

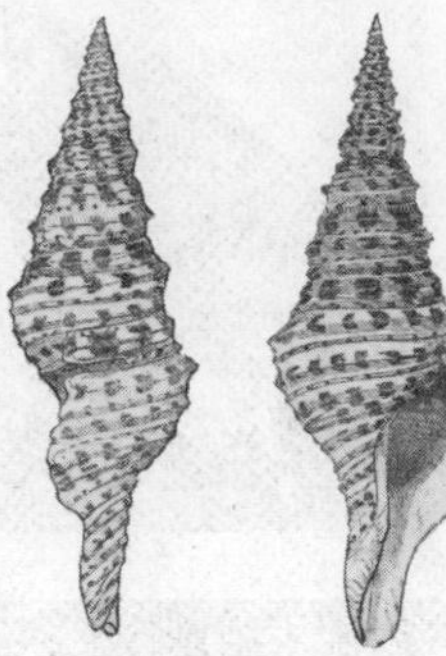

turreted
Turreted shells

served his turn. **12.** A short tour or excursion: *a turn in the park.* **13.** A twist or other distortion in shape. **14.** The condition of being twisted or wound. **15. a.** A winding of one thing about another. **b.** A single wind or convolution, as of wire upon a spool. **16.** *Music.* A figure or ornament consisting of four notes in rapid succession, the second and fourth of which are identical, the first is a degree above, and the third is a degree below. **17.** An attack of illness or severe nervousness; a fit; a spell. **18.** *Informal.* A momentary shock or scare: *I had quite a turn when I first heard the news.* **19.** A variation of kind or type: *"his muse occasionally takes a humorous and satirical turn"* (Albert C. Baugh). **20. a.** A brief theatrical act: *the turns of a vaudeville show.* **b.** A performer in such an act. **c.** Any histrionic or overdramatic performance. **21. a.** A transaction on the stock market involving both a sale and a purchase. **b.** Any similar commercial transaction. **—at every turn.** In every place; at every moment. **—by turns.** Alternately; one after another. **—in turn.** In the proper order or sequence. **—out of turn. 1.** Not in the proper order or sequence. **2.** At an inappropriate time or in an inappropriate manner. **—take turns.** To take part or do in order, one after another. **—to a turn.** To a precise degree; perfectly: *The roast was done to a turn.* [Middle English *turnen, tornen,* from Old English *tyrnan, turnian* and Old French *to(u)rner,* both from Latin *tornāre,* to turn in a lathe, to round off, from *tornus,* a lathe, from Greek *tornos,* tool for drawing a circle, circle, lathe. See **ter-**[2] in Appendix.*]

Synonyms: *turn, rotate, revolve, gyrate, spin, whirl, circle, eddy, swirl, swivel, roll.* These verbs all refer to movement in a pattern that is circular or approximately so. *Turn* can mean to move around an axis or pivot or to travel around a relatively fixed object in the way that planets move around the sun. In either case a complete or partial circular course is indicated. *Rotate* and *revolve,* which generally imply repeated movement in a complete course, are narrower. *Rotate* involves movement around an object's own axis or center: *The earth rotates. A wheel rotates on its axle. Revolve* primarily involves the other sense of turning, that of orbital movement, as of the earth around the sun; less often the term applies to rotation. *Gyrate* can refer to either revolving or rotating movement on a spiral course. *Spin* refers to rapid, continuous rotating movement, usually within a narrow compass: *A top spins. Automobile wheels spin on ice. Whirl* applies to continuous revolving or rotating movement at high speed. *Circle* can refer to any circular movement, including that which encompasses something. *Eddy* usually refers to rapid movement of water or air in a circular course contrary to the main current; a whirlpool is a product of such action. *Swirl* is interchangeable with either *whirl* or *eddy,* depending on the context involved. *Swivel* usually refers to circular movement in a horizontal plane from a fixed position or pivot. *Roll,* in this comparison, specifies movement of a curved object, such as a wheel, over a surface with which the object's circumference is in continuous contact.

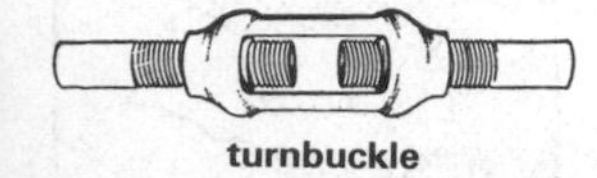

turnbuckle

turn·a·bout (tûrn′ə-bout′) *n.* **1.** The act of turning about and facing or moving in the opposite direction. **2.** A shift or change in opinion, loyalty, or allegiance. **3.** *Regional.* A dance or party to which girls invite boys.

turn·buck·le (tûrn′bŭk′əl) *n.* A metal coupling device consisting of an oblong piece internally threaded at both ends, into each end of which a threaded rod is screwed. It is used for tightening a rod or wire rope.

turn·coat (tûrn′kōt′) *n.* One who traitorously switches allegiance.

turn·er[1] (tûr′nər) *n.* One who or that which turns; especially, a person who works a lathe.

turn·er[2] (tûr′nər) *n.* A tumbler or gymnast; especially, a member of a turnverein. [German *Turner,* from *turnen,* to do gymnastics, from Old High German *turnēn,* to turn, from Latin *tornāre,* to TURN.]

Tur·ner (tûr′nər), **Frederick Jackson.** 1861–1932. American historian.

Tur·ner (tûr′nər), **Joseph Mallord William.** 1775–1851. British painter.

Tur·ner (tûr′nər), **Nat.** 1800–1831. American leader of a slave rebellion; executed.

turn·er·y (tûr′nə-rē) *n., pl.* **-ies.** The work or workshop of a lathe operator.

turn·hall (tûrn′hôl′) *n.* A hall in which gymnasts practice; gymnasium. [German *Turnhalle* : *turnen,* to do gymnastics (see **turner**) + *Halle,* a hall, from Old High German *halla* (see **kel-**[4] in Appendix*).]

turn·ing (tûr′nĭng) *n.* **1.** A deviation from a straight course; a turn. **2.** The shaping of metal or wood on a lathe.

turning point. 1. A point at which something turns, changes, or reverses in direction or motion. **2.** *Mathematics.* A maximum or minimum point on a curve. **3.** A point at which a crucial decision must be made; decisive moment.

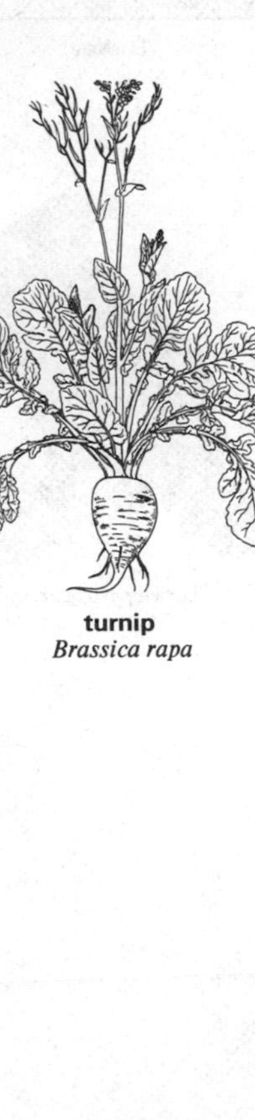

turnip
Brassica rapa

tur·nip (tûr′nĭp) *n.* **1.** A widely cultivated plant, *Brassica rapa,* native to the Old World, having a large, edible yellow or white root. **2.** The root of this plant, eaten as a vegetable. **3.** Any of several similar or related plants. **4.** A large, rounded pocket watch. [Earlier *turnepe* : *tur-* (origin and meaning unknown) + *nepe,* turnip, from Middle English *nepe,* Old English *nǣp,* from Latin *nāpus* (see **napiform**).]

turnip cabbage. A vegetable, **kohlrabi** *(see).*

turn·key (tûrn′kē′) *n., pl.* **-keys.** The keeper of the keys in a prison; a jailer.

turn off. 1. To stop the operation, activity, or flow of; shut off. **2.** To leave a path or road at a point and enter another; change direction. **3.** To divert or deflect. **4.** *British.* To discharge (an employee). **5.** *Slang.* To affect with dislike, displeasure, or revulsion: *Her continuous chatter turns me off.*

turn·off (tûrn′ôf′, -ŏf′) *n.* A branch of a road or path leading from the main thoroughfare; especially, an exit on a highway.

turn out. 1. To shut off, as a light. **2.** To arrive or assemble, as for a public event or entertainment. **3.** To produce by some process; make. **4.** To be found to be, as after experience or trial: *The machine turned out to be in perfect repair.* **5.** To result; end up: *The cake turned out beautifully.* **6.** To equip; dress; outfit. **7.** *Informal.* To get out of bed.

turn·out (tûrn′out′) *n.* **1.** The act of turning out. **2.** The number of people at a gathering; attendance. **3.** A number of things produced; output. **4.** *British.* **a.** A labor strike. **b.** A laborer on strike. **5.** An array of equipment; an outfit. **6.** An outfit of a carriage with its horse or horses; equipage. **7.** A railroad siding. **8.** A widening in a highway to allow vehicles to pass.

turn over. 1. To bring the bottom to the top, or vice versa; reverse in position. **2.** To shift the position of, as by rolling from one side to the other. **3.** To go through at least one cycle. Used of an internal-combustion engine: *The car won't turn over in cold weather.* **4.** To think about; consider. **5. a.** To transfer to another; give over. **b.** To give up. **6.** To do business to the extent or amount of: *turn over a million dollars a year.*

turn·o·ver (tûrn′ō′vər) *n. Abbr.* **t.o. 1.** The act of turning over; an upset or overthrow. **2.** An abrupt change; reversal. **3.** A small pastry made by covering one half of a circular piece of dough with fruit, preserves, or other filling, and turning the other half over on top. **4.** The number of times a particular stock of goods is sold and restocked during a given period of time. **5.** The amount of business transacted during a given period of time. Also called "overturn." **6.** The number of shares of stock sold on the market during a given period of time. **7.** The amount of capital loaned on call during a given period of time. **8. a.** The number of workers hired by a given establishment to replace those who have left. **b.** The ratio of this number to the number of employed workers. *—adj.* Capable of being turned or folded down or over, as a collar.

turn·pike (tûrn′pīk′) *n. Abbr.* **tpk., tnpk. 1.** A road; especially, a wide, modern highway with tollgates. **2.** A tollgate. [Middle English *turnepike,* a revolving barrier furnished with spikes used to block a road : *turnen,* to TURN + PIKE.]

turn·sole (tûrn′sōl′) *n.* Any of various plants, such as the heliotrope, that move or are believed to move in response to the sun. [Middle English *turnesole,* from Old French *tournesol,* from Old Italian *tornasole* : *tornare,* to turn, from Latin *tornāre,* TURN + *sole,* the sun, from Latin *sōl* (see **sāwel-** in Appendix*).]

turn·spit (tûrn′spĭt′) *n.* **1.** A person who turns a roasting spit. **2.** A dog formerly used in a treadmill to turn a roasting spit.

turn·stile (tûrn′stīl′) *n.* **1.** A mechanical device used to control passage from one public area to another, typically consisting of several horizontal arms supported by and radially projecting from a central vertical post. **2.** A similar structure that permits the passage of persons, but not of horses or cattle.

turn·stone (tûrn′stōn′) *n.* Either of two wading birds, *Arenaria interpres,* having predominantly reddish and white plumage, or *A. melanocephala,* having black and white plumage. [From its habit of turning over stones in search of food.]

turn·ta·ble (tûrn′tā′bəl) *n.* **1.** A circular horizontal rotating platform equipped with a railway track, used for turning locomotives, as in a roundhouse. **2. a.** The circular horizontal rotating platform of a phonograph on which the record is placed. **b.** A phonograph exclusive of amplifying circuitry and speakers. **3.** Any similar rotating platform or disk, as on a microscope.

turn up. 1. a. To find: *He turned up the missing papers under his blotter.* **b.** To be found: *It will turn up sooner or later.* **2.** To make an appearance; arrive.

turn·up (tûrn′ŭp′) *n.* Something that is turned up or turns up, as the cuffs on trousers. *—adj.* Turned up or capable of being turned up.

turn·ver·ein (tûrn′və-rīn′, to͝orn′-) *n.* A club of turners or gymnasts. [German *Turnverein* : *turnen,* to do gymnastics (see **turner**) + *Verein,* union, from *vereinen,* to unite : *ver-,* completely, from Old High German *far-* (see **per**[1] in Appendix*) + *ein,* one, from Old High German (see **oino-** in Appendix*).]

tur·pen·tine (tûr′pən-tīn′) *n. Abbr.* **turp. 1.** A thin volatile essential oil, $C_{10}H_{16}$, obtained by steam distillation or other means from the wood or the exudate of certain pine trees, and used as a paint thinner, solvent, and medicinally as a liniment. Also called "spirits of turpentine." **2.** The sticky mixture of resin and volatile oil from which this oil is distilled. **3.** A similar resinous liquid obtained from the terebinth. *—tr.v.* **turpentined, -tining, -tines. 1.** To apply turpentine to or mix turpentine with. **2.** To extract turpentine from (a tree). [Middle English *ter(e)bentyne, turpentyne,* resin of the terebinth, from Old French *ter(e)bentine,* from Latin *terebinthina,* from *terebinthus,* TEREBINTH.]

tur·peth (tûr′pĭth) *n.* **1.** A vine, *Ipomoea turpethum* (or *Operculina turpethum*), of tropical Asia and Australia, having roots that yield a resinous substance used medicinally as a purgative. **2.** The root of this plant. [Middle English *turbit,* from Old French, from Medieval Latin *turbit(h)um, turpetum,* from Arabic *turbid, turbed.*]

Tur·pin (tûr′pĭn), **Dick.** 1706–1739. English highwayman; subject of legends.

tur·pi·tude (tûr′pə-to͞od′, -tyo͞od′) *n.* **1.** Baseness; depravity. **2.** A base act. [Latin *turpitūdō,* from *turpis*†, ugly, vile.]

turps (tûrps) *n.* Plural in form, used with a singular verb. *Informal.* Turpentine. [Colloquial shortening of TURPENTINE.]

ă pat/ā pay/âr care/ä father/b bib/ch church/d deed/ĕ pet/ē be/f fife/g gag/h hat/hw which/ĭ pit/ī pie/îr pier/j judge/k kick/l lid, needle/m mum/n no, sudden/ng thing/ŏ pot/ō toe/ô paw, for/oi noise/ou out/o͝o took/o͞o boot/p pop/r roar/s sauce/sh ship, dish/

tur·quoise (tûr′kwoiz′, -koiz′) *n.* **1.** A blue to blue-green mineral of aluminum and copper, mainly $CuAl_6(PO_4)_4(OH)_8 \cdot 4H_2O$, esteemed as a gemstone in its polished blue form. **2.** Light to brilliant bluish green. See **color.** [Middle English *turkeis,* from Old French *(pierre) turqueise,* "Turkish (stone)," from *turqueis,* Turkish (it was first found in Turkestan), from *Turc,* TURK.] —**tur′quoise′** *adj.*

tur·ret (tûr′ĭt) *n.* **1.** A small ornamented tower or tower-shaped projection on a building. **2.** *Military.* A low, heavily armored structure, usually rotating horizontally, containing mounted guns and their gunners or crew, as on a warship or tank. **3.** A domelike gunner's enclosure projecting from the fuselage of a military aircraft. **4.** A tall wooden structure mounted on wheels and used in ancient warfare by besiegers to scale the walls of an enemy fortress. **5.** An attachment for a lathe consisting of a rotating, cylindrical block holding various cutting tools. [Middle English *t(o)uret,* from Old French *t(o)urete,* diminutive of *t(o)ur,* a TOWER.]

tur·ret·ed (tûr′ĭt-ĭd) *adj.* **1.** Furnished with a turret or turrets. **2.** Having the shape or form of a turret, as certain long-spired gastropod shells.

tur·tle[1] (tûrt′l) *n.* **1.** Any of various reptiles of the order Chelonia, having horny, toothless jaws and the body enclosed in a bony or leathery shell into which the head, limbs, and tail can be withdrawn in most species. **2.** *Chiefly British.* Any marine chelonian. —*intr.v.* **turtled, -tling, -tles.** To hunt for turtles, especially as an occupation. [Perhaps variant of French *tortue,* TORTOISE.]

tur·tle[2] (tûrt′l) *n. Archaic.* A turtledove: "*the voice of the turtle is heard in our land*" (Song of Solomon 2:12). [Middle English *turtle,* Old English *turtla, turtle,* from Latin *turtur*†.]

tur·tle·back (tûrt′l-băk′) *n.* An arched, dome-shaped structure built over the bow or stern of a ship to protect it against heavy seas. Also called "turtle deck."

tur·tle·dove (tûrt′l-dŭv′) *n.* **1.** A slender European dove, *Streptopelia turtur,* having a white-edged tail and a soft, purring voice. **2.** Loosely, the **mourning dove** *(see).* [TURTLE (dove) + DOVE.]

turtle grass. A grasslike aquatic plant, *Thalassia testudinum,* of warm Atlantic waters, often forming extensive submerged beds.

tur·tle·head (tûrt′l-hĕd′) *n.* Any of several plants of the genus *Chelone;* especially, *C. glabra,* of eastern North America, having white or pink flowers. Also called "snakehead." [From the shape of its flower.]

tur·tle·neck (tûrt′l-nĕk′) *n.* **1.** A high, turned-down collar that fits closely about the neck. **2.** A sweater or other garment having this collar.

turves. *Archaic.* Plural of **turf.**

Tus·ca·loo·sa (tŭs′kə-lo͞o′sə). A city in west-central Alabama; formerly, the state capital (1826–46). Population, 63,000.

Tus·can (tŭs′kən) *adj.* **1.** Of or pertaining to Tuscany or to its people. **2.** *Architecture.* Of or pertaining to the Tuscan order. —*n.* **1.** A native or inhabitant of Tuscany. **2.** Any of the Italian dialects spoken in Tuscany, especially the dialect of Florence. [Latin *Tuscānus,* from *Tuscus,* a Tuscan, probably from Etruscan.]

Tuscan order. *Architecture.* A classical order similar to Roman Doric, but having an unfluted shaft with a simplified base, capital, and entablature.

Tus·ca·ny (tŭs′kə-nē). *Italian* **Tos·ca·na** (tôs-kä′nä). A region of Italy occupying 8,876 square miles in the northwest. Population, 3,286,000. Capital, Florence.

Tus·ca·ro·ra (tŭs′kə-rôr′ə, -rōr′ə) *n., pl.* **Tuscarora** or **-ras. 1.** A tribe of Iroquoian-speaking North American Indians formerly inhabiting North Carolina, and now living in New York and Ontario. **2.** A member of this tribe. **3.** The language of this tribe. [From Tuscarora *Skărūreⁿ,* "hemp gatherers."]

tu·sche (to͝osh′ə) *n.* A substance used for drawing in lithography and as a resist in etching and silk-screen work. [German *Tusche,* from *tuschen,* to ink up, from French *toucher,* to touch, from Old French *tochier,* TOUCH.]

Tus·cu·lum (tŭs′kyə-ləm). An ancient city, now in ruins, in Latium, Italy, southeast of Rome of which it was once a rival.

tush[1] (tŭsh) *interj.* Used to express mild reproof, disapproval, or admonition: *Tush, tush, my dear, it's nothing.* [Middle English *tussch* (expressive formation).]

tush[2] (tŭsh) *n.* A tusk. —*tr.v.* **tushed, tushing, tushes.** To tusk. [Middle English *tusche,* Old English *tūsc,* TUSK.]

tusk (tŭsk) *n.* **1.** An elongated, pointed tooth, usually one of a pair, extending outside of the mouth in certain animals, such as the walrus, elephant, or wild boar. **2.** Any long, projecting tooth or toothlike part. —*tr.v.* **tusked, tusking, tusks.** To dig or gore with the tusks or a tusk. [Middle English *tux, tuske,* Old English *tūx, tūsc.* See **dent-** in Appendix.*]

tusk·er (tŭs′kər) *n.* An animal bearing tusks, as a wild boar.

tusk shell. A **tooth shell** *(see).*

tus·sah (tŭs′ə, tŭs′ô′) *n.* Also **tus·sore** (tŭs′ôr′, -ōr′). **1.** An undomesticated Asian silkworm, *Antheraea paphia,* that produces a coarse brownish or yellowish silk. **2.** The silk itself, or a fabric woven from it. [Hindi *tasar,* from Sanskrit *tasara,* a shuttle (probably from the shape of its cocoon). See **tens-** in Appendix.*]

tus·sis (tŭs′ĭs) *n.* A cough. [Latin *tussis.* See **steu-** in Appendix.*] —**tus′sal, tus′sive** *adj.*

tus·sle (tŭs′əl) *intr.v.* **-sled, -sling, -sles.** To struggle; to scuffle. —*n.* A rough-and-tumble struggle; a scuffle. [Middle English *tussillen,* probably from *-t(o)usen,* TOUSLE.]

tus·sock (tŭs′ək) *n.* Also **tus·suck. 1.** A clump or tuft of growing grass or a similar plant. **2.** A tuft of hair, feathers, or the like. [Probably variant of dialectal *tusk*†, a tuft of hair, rushes.] —**tus′sock·y** *adj.*

tussock moth. Any of various moths of the family Lymantriidae, having hairy caterpillars that are often destructive to deciduous trees.

tut (tŭt) *interj.* Also **tut tut.** Used to express annoyance, impatience, or mild reproof. [Expressive formation.]

Tut·ankh·a·men (to͞ot′täng-kä′mən). Also **Tut·ankh·a·mon.** King of Egypt during the late 14th century B.C.

tu·te·lage (to͞ot′tə-lĭj, tyo͞o′-) *n.* **1.** The function or capacity of a guardian; guardianship. **2.** The act or capacity of a tutor; instruction; teaching. **3.** The state of being under a guardian or tutor. [From Latin *tūtēla,* a watching, from *tūtor,* TUTOR.] —**tu′te·lar** (-lər), **tu′te·lar′y** (-lĕr′ē) *adj.*

tu·tor (to͞o′tər, tyo͞o′-) *n.* **1. a.** A private instructor. **b.** One who gives additional, special, or remedial instruction. **2.** In some universities and colleges, a teacher or teaching assistant with a rank lower than that of an instructor. **3.** A graduate responsible for the special supervision of an undergraduate at some British universities. **4.** *Law.* The guardian of a minor and of his property. —*v.* **tutored, -toring, -tors.** —*tr.* **1.** To act as a tutor to; instruct or teach privately. **2.** To discipline or treat sternly, as a tutor might. **3.** To act as the guardian to; have the care of. —*intr.* **1.** To function as a tutor or private instructor. **2.** To be instructed by or study under a tutor. —See Synonyms at **teach.** [Middle English *tutour,* from Old French, from Latin *tūtor,* a guardian, tutor, from *tūtus,* past participle of *tuērī,* to watch, protect. See **teu-** in Appendix.*] —**tu·to′ri·al** (to͞o-tôr′ē-əl, -tōr′ē-əl, tyo͞o-) *adj.*

tutorial system. An instructional system in which college or university tutors are responsible for the special supervision of students individually or in small groups.

tu·tor·ship (to͞o′tər-shĭp′, tyo͞o′-) *n.* **1.** The office or functions of a tutor. **2.** Tutelage.

tut·ti (to͞o′tē; *Italian* to͞ot′tē) *adj. Music.* All. Used to indicate that all performers are to take part. —*n., pl.* **tuttis. 1.** A passage of ensemble music intended to be executed by all the performers simultaneously. **2.** The tonal effect thus produced. [Italian, plural of *tutto,* all, from Latin *tōtus.* See **teutā-** in Appendix.*] —**tut′ti** *adv.*

tut·ti-frut·ti (to͞o′tē-fro͞o′tē) *n.* **1.** A confection, especially ice cream, containing a variety of chopped candied fruits. **2.** A flavoring simulating the flavor of many fruits. —*adj.* Having a combination of fruit flavors. [Italian, "all fruits."]

tut·ty (tŭt′ē) *n.* An impure zinc oxide obtained as a sublimate from the flues of zinc-smelting furnaces and used as a polishing powder. [Middle English *tutie,* from Old French, from Arabic *tūtiyā.*]

tu·tu (to͞o′to͞o) *n. French.* A very short ballet skirt consisting of many layers of gathered sheer fabric.

Tu·tu·i·la (to͞o′to͞o-ē′lə). The largest island, 40 square miles in area, of American Samoa in the South Pacific.

Tu·va Autonomous Soviet Socialist Republic (to͞o′və). Also **Tu·vin·i·an A.S.S.R.** (to͞o-vĭn′ē-ən). Formerly **Tu·va Autonomous Region.** An administrative division, 65,810 square miles in area, of the south-central Russian S.F.S.R. Population, 208,000. Capital, Kyzyl.

tux·e·do (tŭk-sē′dō) *n., pl.* **-dos.** Also **Tux·e·do. 1.** A man's jacket, usually black, with satin or grosgrain lapels worn for formal or semiformal occasions. Also called "dinner jacket." **2.** A complete outfit including this jacket, black trousers with a stripe down the side, and a black bowtie. [From the name of a country club in *Tuxedo* Park, New York, where it became popular.]

Tux·tla Gu·tiér·rez (to͞os′tlä go͞o-tyĕr′rĕs). Also **Tux·tla** (to͞os′tlä). The capital of Chiapas, Mexico, in the west-central part of the state. Population, 41,000.

tu·yère (twē-yâr′) *n.* The pipe, nozzle, or other opening through which air is forced into a blast furnace or forge to facilitate combustion. [French, from Old French *tuyere,* from *tuyau,* a pipe, probably from (unattested) Frankish *thūta* (imitative).]

Tu·zi·goot National Monument (to͞o′zĭ-go͞ot′). An area of 43 acres in central Arizona, reserved to protect the ruins of a prehistoric village.

TV television.

TV dinner (tē′ vē′). Also **T.V. dinner.** A packaged ready-to-serve meal, usually frozen in an aluminum tray, that can be heated in an oven.

TVA, T.V.A. Tennessee Valley Authority.

Tver. The former name for **Kalinin.**

twad·dle (twŏd′l) *intr.v.* **-dled, -dling, -dles.** Also **twat·tle** (twŏt′l). To talk foolishly; prate. —*n.* Also **twat·tle. 1.** Foolish, trivial, or idle talk or chatter. **2.** Silly pretentious speech or writing. [Probably from Scandinavian, akin to Old Norse *thvætta,* to wash, "babble," iterative of *thvā,* to wash, from Common Germanic *thwahan* (unattested), to bathe. See also **towel.**] —**twad′dler** *n.*

twain (twān) *adj. Archaic.* Two. —*n. Poetic.* **1.** A set of two: "*Oh, East is East, and West is West, and never the twain shall meet*" (Kipling). **2.** The two-fathom mark on a sounding line used on riverboats. [Middle English *tweien, tweyen,* Old English *twēgen* (nominative and accusative masculine), two. See **dwō** in Appendix.*]

Twain (twān), **Mark.** Pen name of Samuel Langhorne **Clemens** *(see).* [From the expression *mark twain,* "by the mark two fathoms," used by Mississippi riverboat pilots in sounding shallows for minimum navigable depths.]

twang (twăng) *v.* **twanged, twanging, twangs.** —*intr.* **1.** To emit a sharp, vibrating sound, as the string of a musical in-

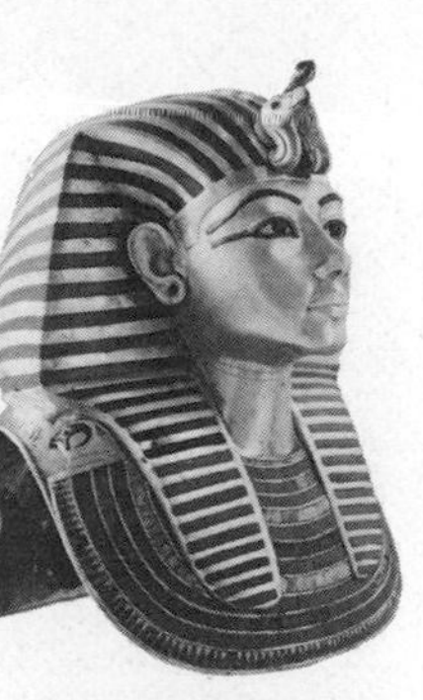

Tutankhamen
Mask of the king from his tomb at Thebes

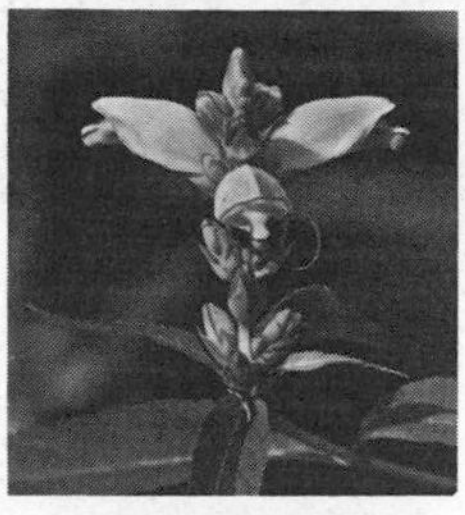

turtlehead
Chelone glabra

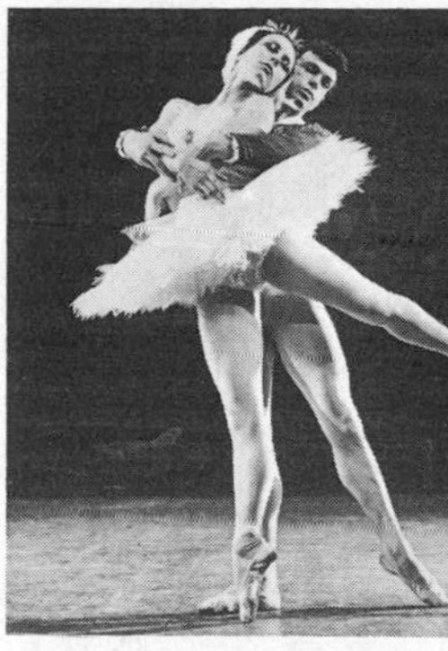

tutu

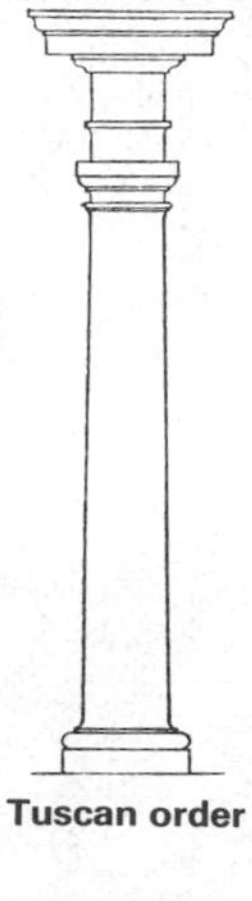

Tuscan order

t tight/th thin, path/*th* this, bathe/ŭ cut/ûr urge/v valve/w with/y yes/z zebra, size/zh vision/ə about, item, edible, gallop, circus/ à *Fr.* ami/œ *Fr.* feu, *Ger.* schön/ü *Fr.* tu, *Ger.* über/KH *Ger.* ich, *Scot.* loch/N *Fr.* bon. ***Follows main vocabulary.** †**Of obscure origin.**

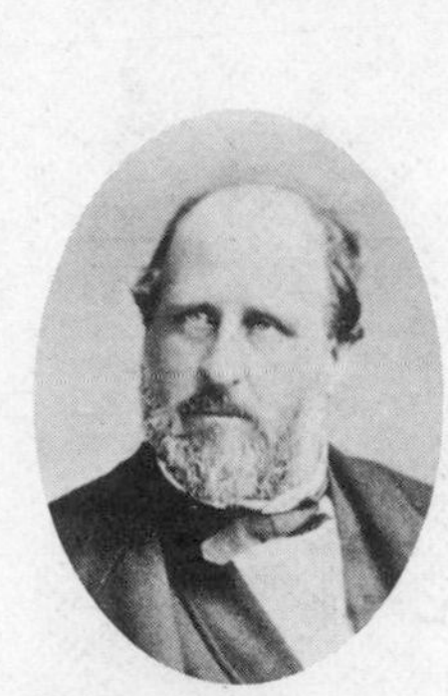

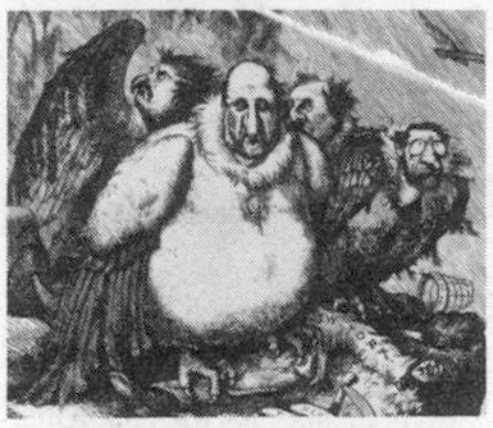

"Boss Tweed"
Above: Photograph
Below: Cartoon drawn by Thomas Nast in 1871

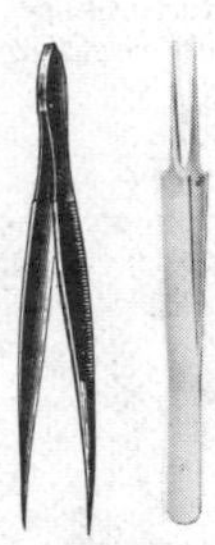

tweezers

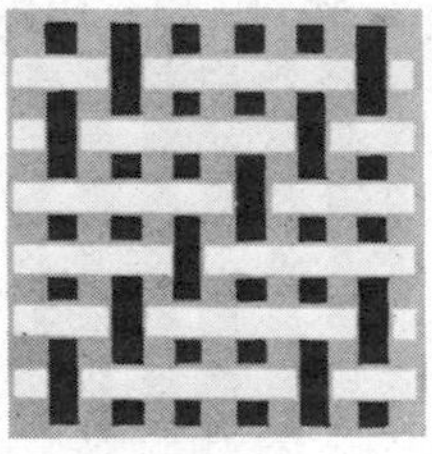

twill
Diagram of a right-hand twill weave

strument when plucked: *"bull-frogs twanging like guitars"* (Richard Hughes). **2.** To be released or to resound with a sharp, vibrating sound. Used of an arrow. —*tr.* **1.** To cause to make a sharp, vibrating sound. **2.** To utter with a twang. —*n.* **1.** A sharp, vibrating sound, as that of a plucked string. **2.** An excessively nasal tone of voice, especially as a peculiarity of certain regional dialects. **3.** Any sound resembling either of these. [Imitative.] —**twang'y** *adj.*

tway·blade (twā'blād') *n.* Any of various small terrestrial orchids of the genera *Liparis* and *Listera,* having two basal leaves and a terminal cluster of greenish or purplish flowers. [Translation of Medieval Latin *bifolium,* "two-leaved" : obsolete English *tway,* two, Middle English *twei,* Old English *twēge,* short for *twēgen,* TWAIN + BLADE.]

tweak (twēk) *tr.v.* **tweaked, tweaking, tweaks.** To pinch, pluck, or twist sharply. —*n.* A sharp, twisting pinch. [Probably variant of dialectal *twick,* Middle English *twikken,* Old English *twiccian.* See **twik-** in Appendix.*] —**tweak'y** *adj.*

tweed (twēd) *n.* **1.** A coarse, rugged, often nubby woolen fabric made in any of various twill weaves, and used chiefly for suits and coats for casual wear. **2.** *Plural.* Clothing made of this fabric: *wear tweeds to the races.* [Originally a trademark, a misspelling (influenced by the river TWEED) of *tweel, tweeled,* Scottish variants of TWILL.] —**tweed'i·ness** *n.* —**tweed'y** *adj.*

Tweed (twēd). A river rising in southern Peebles County, Scotland, flowing 97 miles east and then northeast to the North Sea, and forming part of the Scottish-English border.

Tweed (twēd), **William Marcy.** Called "Boss Tweed." 1823–1878. American political boss; developed machine system in New York City (1859–71).

Tweed·dale. See **Peebles.**

twee·dle·dum and twee·dle·dee (twēd'l-dŭm'; twēd'l-dē'). Two persons or groups resembling each other so closely that they are practically indistinguishable. [After *Tweedledum and Tweedledee,* proverbial rival fiddlers supposedly representative of Handel and G.B. Bononcini, who had a musical rivalry.]

Tweeds·muir, Baron. See Sir John **Buchan.**

'tween. *Poetic.* Between.

tweet (twēt) *intr.v.* **tweeted, tweeting, tweets.** To utter a weak, chirping sound, as a young or small bird. —*n.* A weak, chirping sound. [Imitative.]

tweet·er (twē'tər) *n.* A loud-speaker designed to reproduce high-pitched sounds in a high-fidelity audio system. Compare **woofer.** [From TWEET.]

tweeze (twēz) *tr.v.* **tweezed, tweezing, tweezes.** To handle or extract with tweezers. [Back-formation from TWEEZERS.]

tweez·ers (twē'zərz) *pl.n.* Any small, usually metal, pincerlike tool used for plucking or handling small objects. Often called "pair of tweezers." [Originally "a set or case of small instruments," from obsolete *tweezes,* plural of *tweeze, etweese,* from the plural of *etwee,* from French *étui,* ÉTUI.]

twelfth (twĕlfth) *n.* **1.** The ordinal number 12 in a series. Also written 12th. **2.** One of 12 equal parts. See **number.** **3.** *Music.* **a.** A 12-degree interval in a diatonic scale. **b.** A tone 12 degrees below or above a given tone. [Middle English *twelfthe,* Old English *twelfta.* See **dwō** in Appendix.*] —**twelfth** *adj.* & *adv.*

Twelfth-day (twĕlfth'dā') *n.* The day of Epiphany, January 6, 12 days after Christmas.

Twelfth-night (twĕlfth'nīt') *n.* The evening of January 5, before Twelfth-day. —*adj.* Of or pertaining to Twelfth-night.

Twelfth·tide (twĕlfth'tīd') *n.* The season of Epiphany.

twelve (twĕlv) *n.* The cardinal number written 12 or in Roman numerals XII. See **number.** [Middle English *twelfe, twelve,* Old English *twelf.* See **dwō** in Appendix.*] —**twelve** *adj.* & *pron.*

Twelve Apostles. 1. The 12 disciples chosen by Jesus. Also called "the Twelve." **2.** A high governing body in the Mormon Church, composed of 12 officials.

twelve·mo (twĕlv'mō') *n., pl.* **-mos. Duodecimo** *(see).*

twelve·month (twĕlv'mŭnth') *n.* A year.

twelve-tone (twĕlv'tōn') *adj. Music.* Relating to, consisting of, or based on an atonal arrangement of the traditional 12 chromatic tones.

twen·ti·eth (twĕn'tē-ĭth) *n.* **1.** The ordinal number 20 in a series. Also written 20th. **2.** One of 20 equal parts. See **number.** —**twen'ti·eth** *adj.* & *adv.*

twen·ty (twĕn'tē) *n.* The cardinal number written 20 or in Roman numerals XX. See **number.** [Middle English *twenty,* Old English *twēntig.* See **dwō** in Appendix.*] —**twen'ty** *adj.* & *pron.*

twen·ty-one (twĕn'tē-wŭn') *n.* A card game, **blackjack** *(see).*

twerp (twûrp) *n.* Also **twirp.** *Slang.* A small or contemptible person. [Origin unknown.]

Twi (chwē, chē). Also **Tshi.** A language spoken in western Africa, especially by the Ashanti.

twi·bil (twī'bĭl') *n.* Also **twi·bill. 1.** A battle-ax with two cutting edges. **2.** A mattock with one arm like an ax and the other like an adz. [Middle English *twibil,* Old English *twibil(l)* : *twi-,* two (see **dwō** in Appendix*) + BILL (instrument).]

twice (twīs) *adv.* **1.** In two cases or on two occasions; two times. **2.** In doubled degree or amount: *twice as many.* [Middle English *twice, twiges,* Old English *twiges,* from *twige, twiga,* twice. See **dwō** in Appendix.*]

twice-laid (twīs'lād') *adj.* Made from strands of old or used rope.

Twick·en·ham (twĭk'ən-əm). A former administrative division of London, England, now part of **Richmond-on-Thames** *(see).*

twid·dle (twĭd'l) *v.* **-dled, -dling, -dles.** —*tr.* To turn over or around idly or lightly; fiddle with. —*intr.* **1.** To trifle with something. **2.** To be busy about trifles. **3.** To twirl or rotate without purpose. —**twiddle one's thumbs. 1.** To twirl one's thumbs idly around each other. **2.** To do little or nothing; be idle. —*n.* The act of twiddling; an idle, twirling motion. [Probably a blend of TWIRL and FIDDLE.] —**twid'dler** *n.*

twig[1] (twĭg) *n.* A small branch or slender shoot, as of a tree or shrub. [Middle English *twig(ge),* Old English *twigge.* See **dwō** in Appendix.*]

twig[2] (twĭg) *v.* **twigged, twigging, twigs.** *British Slang.* —*tr.* **1.** To observe or watch; to notice. **2.** To understand. —*intr.* To be aware of the situation; understand. [Irish Gaelic *tuigim,* I understand, from Old Irish *tuicse,* variant of *to-ucc-,* to understand. See **euk-** in Appendix.*]

twig·gen (twĭg'ən) *adj.* Constructed of twigs; wicker.

twig·gy (twĭg'ē) *adj.* **-gier, -giest. 1.** Resembling a twig or twigs; slender; fragile. **2.** Abounding in twigs.

twi·light (twī'līt') *n.* **1.** The time interval during which the sun is below the horizon at an angle less than any of several standard angular distances. **2.** The state of illumination of the atmosphere during this interval, especially after a sunset. **3.** Any dim or faint illumination. **4.** Any period or condition of decline following growth, glory, success, or the like; a waning: *in the twilight of his life.* —*adj.* Pertaining to or characteristic of twilight. [Middle English *twilight,* "light between (night and day)," half-light : *twi-,* half, two, Old English *twi-* (see **dwō** in Appendix*) + LIGHT.]

twilight sleep. An analgesic and amnesic condition induced by an injection of morphine and scopolamine, characterized by the absence of sensibility to pain without loss of consciousness, and administered during labor in childbirth.

twill (twĭl) *n.* **1.** A fabric with diagonal parallel ribs. **2.** The weave used to produce such cloth. —*tr.v.* **twilled, twilling, twills.** To weave (cloth) so as to produce the pattern of twill. [Middle English *twyl(l), twyle,* Old English *twilic,* "two-threaded" : *twi-,* two (see **twilight**) + Latin *(bi)līx,* "two-threaded" : BI- + *līcium,* a thread (see **trellis**).]

twilled (twĭld) *adj.* Woven so as to have diagonal parallel ribs.

twin (twĭn) *n.* **1.** One of two offspring born at the same birth. **2.** One of two identical or similar persons, animals, or things; a counterpart. **3.** *Capital* **T.** *Plural.* The constellation and sign of the zodiac, **Gemini** *(see).* **4.** *Plural. Crystallography.* Two interwoven crystals in which unlike faces are parallel. Also called "macle." —*adj.* **1.** Being two or one of two offspring born at the same birth. **2.** Being one of two identical or similar persons, animals, or things: *a twin bed.* **3.** Consisting of two identical or similar related or connected parts. —*v.* **twinned, twinning, twins.** —*intr.* **1.** To give birth to twins. **2.** *Archaic.* To be one of twin offspring. **3.** To be paired or coupled. —*tr.* **1.** To give birth to, as twins. **2.** To provide a match or counterpart to. [Middle English *twin, twyn* (adjective and noun), Old English *twinn* (adjective only), *getwinn.* See **dwō** in Appendix.*]

twin·ber·ry (twĭn'bĕr'ē) *n., pl.* **-ries.** The **partridgeberry** *(see).* [From the single berry formed from a pair of flowers.]

Twin Cities. Minneapolis and St. Paul, Minnesota.

twine (twīn) *v.* **twined, twining, twines.** —*tr.* **1.** To twist together; intertwine, as threads. **2.** To form by twisting, intertwining, or interlacing. **3.** To encircle or coil about: *A vine twined the fencepost.* **4.** To wind, coil, or wrap around something. —*intr.* **1.** To become twisted, interlaced, or interwoven. **2.** To go in a winding course; twist about: *a stream twining through the forest.* —*n.* **1.** A strong string or cord formed of two or more threads twisted together. **2.** Any thing or part formed by twining: *a twine of bread dough.* **3.** A tangle; a knot. [Middle English *twinen,* from *twin,* a rope of two strands, Old English *twin.* See **dwō** in Appendix.*] —**twin'er** *n.*

Twin Falls. A city of Idaho, in the south near the Snake River. Population, 33,000.

twin·flow·er (twĭn'flou'ər) *n.* A creeping evergreen plant, *Linnaea borealis,* of northern regions, having roundish, evergreen leaves and paired, bell-shaped, pinkish flowers.

twinge (twĭnj) *n.* **1.** A sharp, sudden physical pain. **2.** A mental or emotional pain: *a twinge of conscience.* —*v.* **twinged, twinging, twinges.** —*tr.* **1.** To cause to feel a sharp pain. **2.** *Obsolete.* To tweak; to pinch. —*intr.* To feel a twinge or twinges. [Middle English *twengen, twynchen,* to pinch, wring, Old English *twengan.* See **twengh-** in Appendix.*]

twi-night (twī'nīt') *adj. Baseball.* Designating a double-header in which the first game begins in late afternoon. [TWI(LIGHT) + NIGHT.]

twin·kle (twĭng'kəl) *intr.v.* **-kled, -kling, -kles. 1.** To shine with slight, intermittent gleams, as distant lights or stars; flicker or glimmer. **2.** To be bright or sparkling, as with delight. Used of the eyes. **3.** *Archaic.* To blink or wink. —See Synonyms at **flash.** —*n.* **1.** A slight, intermittent gleam of light; a glimmer; a sparkling flash. **2.** A sparkle of merriment or delight in the eye. **3.** A brief interval; a twinkling. [Middle English *twynklen,* Old English *twinclian,* frequentative of *twincan* (unattested), to wink, from West Germanic *twink-* (unattested).] —**twin'kler** *n.*

twin·kling (twĭng'klĭng) *n.* **1.** An act of blinking. **2.** A blink or twinkle. **3.** The time it takes to blink once; an instant.

twin-leaf (twĭn'lēf') *n., pl.* **-leaves** (-lēvz'). A woodland plant, *Jeffersonia diphylla,* of eastern North America, having leaves deeply cleft into two lobes, and a solitary white flower.

twinned (twĭnd) *adj.* **1.** Born at a single birth. **2.** Paired or coupled with something identical or similar. **3.** Formed of crystals by the process of twinning.

twin·ning (twĭn'ĭng) *n.* **1.** The bearing of twins. **2.** A pairing or union of two similar or identical objects. **3.** The formation of twin crystals.

twin-screw (twĭn'skrōō') *adj.* Having two propellers, one on

ă pat/ā pay/âr care/ä father/b bib/ch church/d deed/ĕ pet/ē be/f fife/g gag/h hat/hw which/ĭ pit/ī pie/îr pier/j judge/k kick/l lid, needle/m mum/n no, sudden/ng thing/ŏ pot/ō toe/ô paw, for/oi noise/ou out/ŏŏ took/ōō boot/p pop/r roar/s sauce/sh ship, dish/

either side of the keel, that usually revolve in opposite directions. Said of a ship.

twirl (twûrl) *v.* **twirled, twirling, twirls.** —*tr.* **1.** To rotate or revolve briskly; swing in a circle; to spin. **2.** To twist or wind around: *twirl thread on a spindle.* **3.** *Baseball Slang.* To pitch. —*intr.* **1.** To move or spin around rapidly, suddenly, or repeatedly. **2.** To whirl or turn suddenly; make an about-face. —*n.* **1.** A twirling or being twirled; a quick spinning or twisting. **2.** Something twirled; a twist: *a twirl of cotton candy.* [Possibly a blend of TRILL or TWIST and WHIRL.]

twirp. Variant of **twerp.**

twist (twĭst) *v.* **twisted, twisting, twists.** —*tr.* **1. a.** To entwine (two or more threads) so as to produce a single strand. **b.** To form in this manner: *twist a length of rope.* **2.** To wind or coil (vines, rope, or the like) about something. **3.** To interlock or interlace: *twist flowers in one's hair.* **4.** To impart a coiling or spiral shape to. **5. a.** To turn or open by turning. **b.** To pull, break, or snap by turning. Used with *off: twist off a dead branch.* **6.** To wrench or sprain: *twist one's wrist.* **7.** To alter the normal aspect of; contort: *twist one's mouth into a wry smile.* **8.** To alter or distort the intended meaning of. —*intr.* **1.** To be or become twisted. **2.** To move or progress in a winding course; meander. **3.** To squirm; writhe: *twist with pain.* **4.** To rotate or revolve. **5.** To dance the twist. —See Synonyms at **distort.** —*n.* **1.** Something twisted or formed by winding, especially: **a.** A length of yarn, cord, or thread, especially a strong silk thread used mainly to bind the edges of buttonholes. **b.** Tobacco leaves processed into the form of a rope or roll. **c.** Bread or other bakery products for which the dough was twisted before baking. **d.** A sliver of citrus peel twisted over or dropped into a beverage to impart flavor. **2.** The act of twisting or the condition of being twisted; a spin or twirl; rotation. **3.** A spinning motion given to a ball when thrown or struck in a specific way. **4. a.** The state of being twisted into a spiral; torsional stress or strain. **b.** The degree or angle of such stress. **5.** A sprain or wrench, as of a muscle. **6.** An unexpected change in a process or a departure from a pattern, often producing a distortion or perversion: *a twist of fate; a twist in his character led him to crime.* **7.** A contortion or distortion, as of the face. **8.** A personal inclination or eccentricity; penchant or flaw: *a twist in his character.* **9.** A dance characterized by vigorous arm and hip motions. [Middle English *twysten,* from Old English *-twist,* a rope. See **dwō** in Appendix.*] —**twist'a·bil'i·ty** *n.* —**twist'a·ble** *adj.* —**twist'ing·ly** *adv.*

twist drill. A drill having deep helical grooves along the shank from the point.

twist·er (twĭs'tər) *n.* **1.** One that twists. **2.** A ball thrown or batted with a twist. **3.** *Informal.* A cyclone or a **tornado** *(see).* —See Synonyms at **wind.**

twit (twĭt) *tr.v.* **twitted, twitting, twits.** To taunt, ridicule, or tease, especially for embarrassing mistakes or faults. See Synonyms at **ridicule.** —*n.* **1.** The act of twitting. **2.** A reproach, gibe, or taunt. **3.** *Chiefly British Slang.* An idiot. [Earlier *(a)twite,* Middle English *atwiten,* Old English *ætwitan,* to reproach with : *æt-* (indicating opposition), from *æt,* from, AT + *witan,* to reproach, ascribe to (see **weid-** in Appendix*).]

twitch (twĭch) *v.* **twitched, twitching, twitches.** —*tr.* To draw, pull, or move suddenly and sharply; to jerk: *The fisherman twitched his line.* —*intr.* **1.** To move jerkily or spasmodically. **2.** To ache sharply from time to time; to twinge. —*n.* **1.** A sudden involuntary or spasmodic muscular movement: *a twitch in the eye.* **2.** A sudden pulling; a jerk or tug. **3.** *Western U.S.* A looped cord used to restrain a horse by tightening it around the animal's upper lip. [Middle English *twicchen,* perhaps of Low German origin, akin to Low German *twikken.* See **twik-** in Appendix.*] —**twitch'ing·ly** *adv.*

twitch grass. Couch grass *(see).*

twit·ter[1] (twĭt'ər) *v.* **-tered, -tering, -ters.** —*intr.* **1.** To utter a succession of light chirping or tremulous sounds, as a bird; to chirrup. **2.** To titter. **3.** To tremble with nervous agitation, excitement, or the like. —*tr.* To utter or say with a twitter: *She twittered her greeting.* —*n.* **1.** The light chirping sounds made by certain birds. **2.** Light, tremulous speech or laughter. **3.** A state of agitation or excitement; a flutter. [Middle English *twiteren,* akin to Old High German *zwizzirōn,* from (unattested) West Germanic *twittwirōjan* (imitative).] —**twit'ter·er** *n.* —**twit'ter·y** *adj.*

twit·ter[2] (twĭt'ər) *n.* One who twits.

twixt (twĭkst) *prep.* Also **'twixt.** *Archaic & Poetic.* Betwixt.

two (to͞o) *n.* **1.** The cardinal number written 2 or in Roman numerals II. See **number.** **2.** Something representing two units, as a playing card, die, or domino with two pips. —**in two.** So as to be in two separate units: *He split the log in two.* —**put two and two together.** To reach a correct conclusion after considering a given set of circumstances. [Middle English *two,* Old English *twā, tū.* See **dwō** in Appendix.*] —**two** *adj. & pron.*

two-base hit (to͞o'bās'). *Baseball.* A hit enabling the batter to reach second base; a double. Also called "two-bagger."

two-bit (to͞o'bĭt') *adj. Slang.* Worth very little; cheap; insignificant. [From TWO BITS.]

two bits. *Informal.* **1.** Twenty-five cents. **2.** A petty sum.

two-by-four (to͞o'bī-fôr', -fōr', to͞o'bə-) *adj.* **1.** Measuring two by four inches, or in the same ratio in other units. **2.** *Informal.* Small in size; boxed-in; cramped: *a two-by-four apartment.* —*n.* Any length of lumber measuring 1 5/8 inches in thickness and 3 3/8 inches in width.

two-di·men·sion·al (to͞o'dĭ-mĕn'shə-nəl) *adj.* **1.** Having only two dimensions, especially length and width; planar; flat. **2.** Lacking dimension or completion; limited in range or depth.

two-edged (to͞o'ĕjd') *adj.* **1.** Having a keen edge on both sides, as a razor or sword blade. **2.** Having two contrasting effects, meanings, or interpretations.

two-faced (to͞o'fāst') *adj.* **1.** Having two faces or surfaces. **2.** Hypocritical or double-dealing; deceitful. —**two'-fac'ed·ly** (to͞o'fā'sĭd-lē, -fāst'lē) *adv.* —**two'-fac'ed·ness** *n.*

two-fer (to͞o'fər) *n.* Also **two·fer.** *Informal.* **1.** A special offer of two tickets, as for a play or show, for the price of one. **2.** Loosely, any discounted ticket.

two-fisted (to͞o'fĭs'tĭd) *adj. Informal.* Aggressive; virile; vigorous: *a two-fisted drinker.*

two·fold (to͞o'fōld', -fōld') *adj.* **1.** Having two components. **2.** Having twice as much or twice as many; double. —*adv.* Two times as much or as many; doubly.

two-hand·ed (to͞o'hăn'dĭd) *adj.* **1.** Requiring the use of two hands at once: *a two-handed sledgehammer.* **2.** Made to be operated by two people. **3.** Able to use both hands with equal facility; ambidextrous. **4.** Having two hands.

two iron. A **midiron** *(see).*

two-mast·er (to͞o'măs'tər, -mäs'tər) *n.* A sailing vessel rigged with two masts.

two-name (to͞o'nām') *adj. Finance.* Pertaining to or designating a commercial paper bearing the signatures of two persons liable to the obligation.

two·pence (tŭp'əns) *n.* Also *informal* **tup·pence.** *British.* **1.** Two pennies regarded as a monetary unit. **2.** A silver coin worth two pennies, since 1662 minted only for distribution on Maundy Thursday. **3.** A copper coin of this value minted during the reign of George III. **4.** A very small amount; a whit: *He didn't care twopence about politics.*

two·pen·ny (to͞o'pĕn'ē; *British* tŭp'ə-nē) *adj.* Also *British informal* **tup·pen·ny** (tŭp'ə-nē). **1.** Worth or costing twopence: *twopenny candy.* **2.** Cheap; worthless.

two-phase (to͞o'fāz') *adj.* Pertaining to two alternating electrical currents with phases at 90 degrees. Also "quarter-phase."

two-ply (to͞o'plī') *adj.* **1.** Made of two interwoven layers. **2.** Consisting of two thicknesses or strands: *two-ply yarn.*

Two Sic·i·lies, The (sĭs'ə-lēz). A former kingdom of southern Italy consisting of the kingdoms of Sicily and Naples (1061–1860).

two·some (to͞o'səm) *n.* **1.** Two people together; a pair or couple; a duo. **2.** A game played by two people, as a round of golf.

two-spot (to͞o'spŏt') *n.* **1.** A playing card bearing two spots or pips; deuce. **2.** *Slang.* **a.** A two-dollar bill. **b.** Two dollars.

two-step (to͞o'stĕp') *n.* **1.** A ballroom dance in 2/4 time and characterized by long, sliding steps. **2.** The music to which such a dance is done.

two-time (to͞o'tīm') *tr.v.* **-timed, -timing, -times.** *Slang.* To be unfaithful or deceitful to (a loved one). —**two'-tim'er** *n.*

two-way (to͞o'wā') *adj.* **1.** Affording passage to vehicular traffic in two directions: *a two-way street.* **2.** Permitting communication in two directions, as a telephone connection; reciprocal or mutual. **3. a.** Expressive of or involving mutual action, relationship, or responsibility. **b.** Involving two participants, as a treaty. **4.** Permitting the flow in either of two directions: *a two-way valve.*

twp. township.

TX Texas (with Zip Code).

-ty[1]. Indicates a condition or quality; for example, **realty.** [Middle English *-te(e), -tie,* from Old French *-te, -tet,* from Latin *-tās* (stem *-tāt-*), akin to Greek *-tēs,* Sanskrit *-tat, -tati.*]

-ty[2]. Indicates a multiple of ten; for example, **forty, fifty, sixty.** [Middle English *-ty, -ti,* Old English *-tig.* See **dekm̥** in Appendix.*]

ty·coon (tī-ko͞on') *n.* **1.** *Informal.* A wealthy and powerful businessman or industrialist; magnate. See Usage note below. **2.** A title formerly applied to the Japanese shogun. [Japanese *taikun,* title of a shogun, from Ancient Chinese *t'ai kiuən,* emperor : *t'ai,* great (Mandarin *ta*[4]) + *kiuən,* prince, sovereign (Mandarin *chün*[1]).]

Usage: *Tycoon* is well established in its more recent sense of wealthy and powerful businessman or industrialist, and appears frequently in writing on all but a scholarly or otherwise expressly formal level. It is acceptable to 90 per cent of the Usage Panel in the following, as an example in writing: *He was the last of the tycoons worthy of the name.*

tyke (tīk) *n.* Also **tike.** **1.** *Informal.* A small child, especially a mischievous one. **2.** A mongrel or cur. **3.** *Scottish.* A mean or uncouth fellow; boor. [Middle English, from Old Norse *tīk,* a bitch. See **digh-** in Appendix.*]

Ty·ler (tī'lər). A city and industrial center in northeastern Texas. Population, 51,000.

Ty·ler (tī'lər), **John.** 1790–1862. Tenth President of the United States (1841–45).

Ty·ler (tī'lər), **Royall.** 1757–1826. American jurist.

Ty·ler (tī'lər), **Wat.** Died 1381. A leader of the peasants' revolt in England (1381).

tym·bal. Variant of **timbal.**

tym·pan (tĭm'pən) *n.* **1.** *Printing.* A padding of paper or cloth placed over the platen of a printing press to provide support for the sheet being printed. **2.** *Architecture.* A **tympanum** *(see).* **3.** A tightly stretched sheet or membrane, as on the head of a drum. [Middle English *tympan, timpan,* a drum, Old English *timpana,* from Latin *tympanum.* See **tympanum.**]

tym·pa·ni. Variant of **timpani.**

tym·pan·ic (tĭm-păn'ĭk) *adj.* Also **tym·pa·nal** (tĭm'pə-nəl) (for sense 2). **1.** Pertaining to or resembling a drum. **2.** *Anatomy.* Of or pertaining to the tympanum. [From TYMPANUM.]

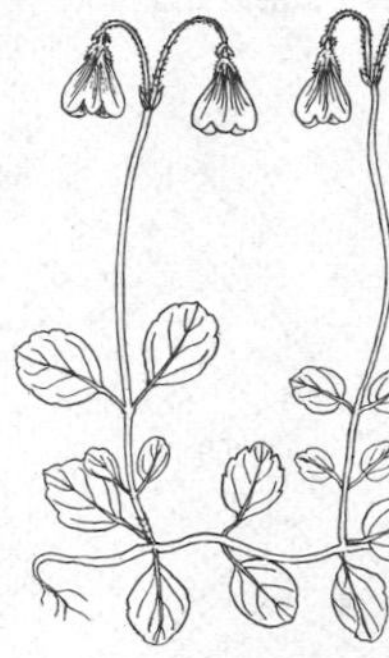

twinflower

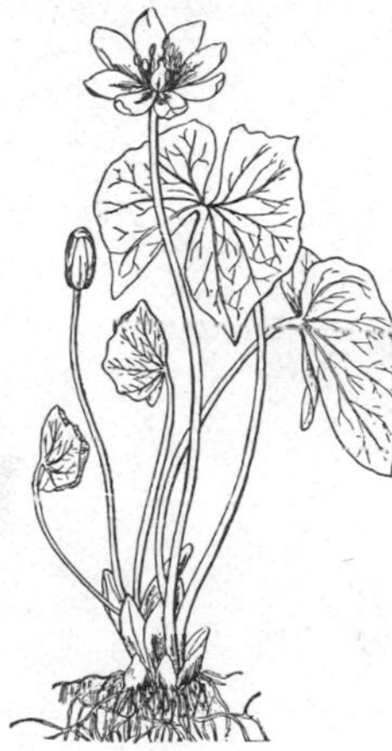

twin-leaf

t tight/th thin, path/*th* this, bathe/ŭ cut/ûr urge/v valve/w with/y yes/z zebra, size/zh vision/ə about, item, edible, gallop, circus/ à *Fr.* ami/œ *Fr.* feu, *Ger.* schön/ü *Fr.* tu, *Ger.* über/KH *Ger.* ich, *Scot.* loch/N *Fr.* bon. ***Follows main vocabulary. †Of obscure origin.**

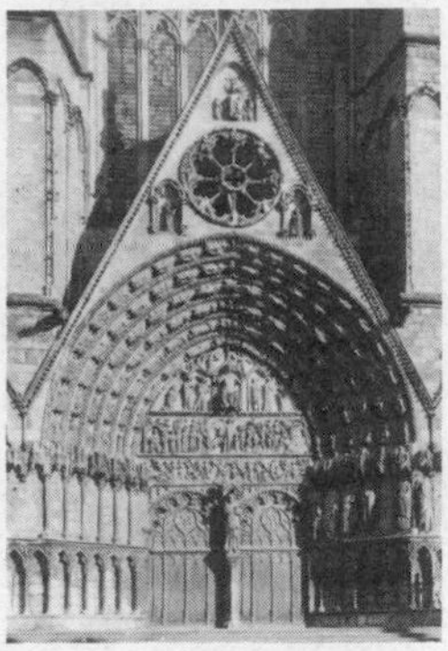

tympanum
Bourges Cathedral, France

tympanic bone. The part of the temporal bone of the skull that partially encloses the auditory canal and supports the tympanic membrane.

tympanic membrane. The thin, semitransparent, oval-shaped membrane separating the middle ear from the external ear. Also called "eardrum."

tym·pa·nist (tĭm′pə-nĭst) *n.* The member of an orchestra who plays the kettledrums and other percussion instruments. [Latin *tympanista,* from Greek *tumpanistēs,* from *tumpanizein,* to beat a drum, from *tumpanon,* a drum. See **tympanum.**]

tym·pa·ni·tes (tĭm′pə-nī′tēz) *n.* A distention of the abdomen resulting from the accumulation of gas or air in the intestine or peritoneal cavity. [Middle English, from Late Latin *tympanitēs,* from Greek *tumpanitēs,* from *tumpanon,* a drum. See **tympanum.**]

tym·pa·num (tĭm′pə-nəm) *n., pl.* **-na** (-nə) or **-nums.** Also **tim·pa·num. 1. a.** The **middle ear** *(see).* **b.** The tympanic membrane; eardrum. **2.** *Zoology.* A membranous external auditory structure, as in certain insects. **3.** *Architecture.* **a.** The recessed, ornamental space or panel enclosed by the cornices of a triangular pediment. **b.** A similar space between an arch and the lintel of a portal. Also called "tympan." **4.** The diaphragm of a telephone. [Medieval Latin, the eardrum, from Latin, a drum, from Greek *tumpanon.* See **steu-** in Appendix.*]

tym·pa·ny (tĭm′pə-nē) *n., pl.* **-nies. 1.** *Archaic.* An inflated manner or style; bombast. **2.** A low-pitched resonance obtained by percussion. [Medieval Latin *tympanias,* "a drumlike swelling," from Greek *tumpanias,* from *tumpanon,* a drum. See **tympanum.**]

Tyn·dale (tĭn′dəl), **William.** Also **Tin·dal, Tin·dale.** 1492?–1536. English religious reformer and martyr; translated the Pentateuch and New Testament.

Tyn·dall (tĭn′dəl), **John.** 1820–1893. Irish physicist.

Tyn·dall, Mount (tĭn′dəl). A mountain rising to 14,025 feet in the Sierra Nevada of southern California.

Tyne (tīn). A river of northern England, rising in eastern Cumberland and flowing 80 miles east to the North Sea.

TYO Airport code for Tokyo, Japan.

typ. typographer; typographical; typography.

typ·al (tī′pəl) *adj.* Pertaining to or serving as a type; typical.

type (tīp) *n.* **1.** A group of persons or things sharing common traits or characteristics that distinguish them as an identifiable group or class; a kind; category. **2.** A person or thing having the features of a group or class. **3.** An example or model; embodiment: *"He was the perfect type of a military dandy"* (Joyce Cary). **4.** *Informal.* A person regarded as exemplifying a certain profession, rank, social group, or the like: *a group of executive types.* **5.** A figure, representation, or symbol of something to come, as an event in the Old Testament that foreshadows another in the New Testament. **6. a.** A taxonomic designation, such as the name of a species or genus, used as the basis of ascription to or characterization of the next highest taxonomic category. **b.** A specimen or sample used as the basis of description of a species. **7.** *Printing.* **a.** A small block of metal or wood bearing a raised letter or character on the upper end, that, when inked and pressed upon paper, leaves a printed impression. **b.** Such pieces collectively. **8.** Printed or typewritten characters; print. **9.** A pattern, design, or image impressed or stamped upon the face of a coin: *Morgan type.* —*v.* **typed, typing, types.** —*tr.* **1.** To write (something) with a typewriter; to typewrite. **2.** To determine the type of (a blood sample). **3.** To classify according to a particular type: *typed him a hero.* **4.** To represent or typify. **5.** To prefigure. —*intr.* To write with a typewriter; to typewrite. [Late Latin *typus,* a form, type, from Latin, figure, image, from Greek *tupos,* a blow, impression. See **steu-** in Appendix.*]

Synonyms: *type, kind, sort, nature, character, ilk.* These nouns refer to groups of persons or things whose members show resemblance and consequently are regarded as constituting a class. In precise usage, *type* implies such close resemblance that the distinction between the group in question and other groups is clear-cut. Less formally, *type* can refer to a group whose members' resemblance is not so marked; in this sense it does not imply such rigid classification. *Kind* can refer to a natural class in which the resemblance of members is innate, or to a group of less precisely related members. *Sort* is generally applied when the resemblance or relationship is not precisely definable; when a close relationship is implied, the term generally refers to persons, often disparagingly: *men of his sort. Nature,* in this context, is approximately equivalent to essence; hence close resemblance and distinctness of class are indicated. *Character* implies resemblance based on qualities peculiar to members of the group. *Ilk,* in a sense that is widespread but sometimes disputed, refers to persons considered as a particular class or breed; often the reference is disparaging.

Usage: *Type* (noun) is followed by *of* in constructions such as *that type of leather.* The variant form omitting *of, that type leather,* is termed unacceptable by 94 per cent of the Usage Panel. As the accompanying synonymy indicates, *type* is generally most appropriate when it refers to a specific, clearly definable category or group, whereas *kind* and *sort* are the better choices when the reference is more general. Less strictly, *type* is often used where *kind* or *sort* would be preferable: *He is not the type of person one can trust.* In this example, *type* is acceptably used, according to 67 per cent of the Panel, though many members state a preference for *kind.* —See Usage notes at **a** (article) and **noun.**

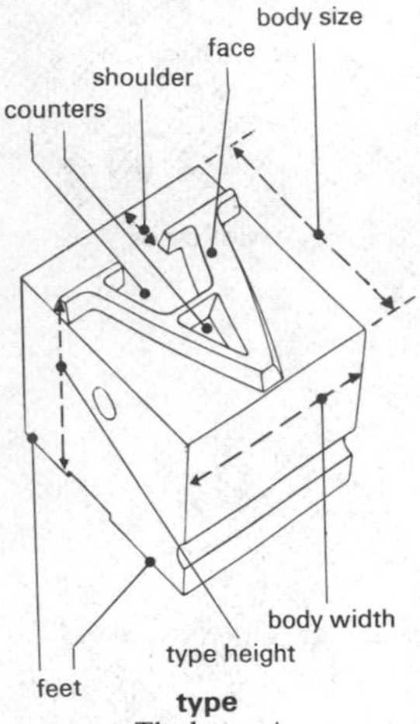

type
The letter *A*

-type. Indicates: **1.** Type or representative form; for example, **monotype. 2.** Stamping or printing type, or photographic process; for example, **collotype.** [French; from Latin *-typus,* from Greek *-tupos,* from *tupos,* TYPE.]

type·cast (tīp′kăst′, -käst′) *tr.v.* **-cast, -casting, -casts. 1.** To cast in an acting role akin or natural to one's own personality or fitted to one's physical appearance. **2.** To assign (an actor or actress) repeatedly to the same kind of part.

type·face (tīp′fās′) *n. Printing.* **1.** The surface of a body of type that makes the impression. **2.** The impression itself. **3.** The size or style of the letter or character on the type. **4.** The full range of type of the same design. Also called "face."

type foundry. A factory where type metal is cast. —**type founder.**

type genus. The name of a taxonomic genus that is designated as representative of the family to which it belongs; for example, the genus *Canis,* which includes dogs and wolves, is the type genus of the family Canidae.

type-high (tīp′hī′) *adj.* As high as the standard height of type, 0.9186 of an inch. Also called "letter-high."

type metal. *Printing.* An alloy used for making metal types, consisting mainly of tin, lead, and antimony.

type·script (tīp′skrĭpt′) *n.* **1.** A typewritten copy, as of a book. **2.** Typewritten matter.

type·set·ter (tīp′sĕt′ər) *n.* **1.** A person who sets type; compositor. **2.** A machine used for setting type. —**type′set′ting** *n.*

type species. The name of a taxonomic species that is designated as representative of the genus to which it belongs; for example, *Panthera pardus,* the leopard, is the type species of the genus *Panthera.*

type specimen. The individual specimen used as a basis for determining the characteristics of a species.

type·write (tīp′rīt′) *v.* **-wrote** (-rōt′), **-written** (-rĭt′n), **-writing, -writes.** —*tr.* To write (something) with a typewriter; to type. —*intr.* To write with a typewriter; to type. [Back-formation from TYPEWRITER.]

type·writ·er (tīp′rī′tər) *n. Abbr.* **typw. 1.** A keyboard machine that prints characters and numerals by means of a set of metal hammers bearing raised, inked type that strike the paper when actuated by manually pressed keys. **2.** *Archaic.* A typist. **3.** *Printing.* A type style like that of typewritten copy.

type·writ·ing (tīp′rī′tĭng) *n.* **1.** The act, process, or skill of using a typewriter. **2.** Copy produced by typewriting; typescript.

Ty·phoe·us (tī-fē′əs, -fō′yo͞os). *Greek Mythology.* A monster having 100 snakelike heads, killed by Zeus and buried under Mt. Etna. —**Ty·phoe′an** (-fē′ən, -fō′ən) *adj.*

ty·pho·gen·ic (tī′fə-jĕn′ĭk) *adj.* Causing typhus. [TYPH(US) + -GENIC.]

ty·phoid (tī′foid′) *n.* Typhoid fever. —*adj.* Also **ty·phoi·dal** (tī-foid′l). Of, relating to, or resembling typhoid fever. [TYPH(US) + -OID.]

typhoid fever. An acute, highly infectious disease caused by the typhoid bacillus, *Salmonella typhosa,* transmitted by contaminated food or water and characterized by red rashes, high fever, bronchitis, and intestinal hemorrhaging. Also called "enteric fever."

Typhoid Mary. A person from whom something undesirable or deadly spreads to those around him. [From the name given to *Mary* Mallon (died 1938), Irish cook in U.S., who was found to be a typhoid carrier.]

Ty·phon (tī′fŏn′). *Greek Mythology.* A monster called by Hesiod the son of Typhoeus; father of the Winds.

ty·phoon (tī-fo͞on′) *n.* A severe tropical hurricane occurring in the western Pacific or the China Sea. See Synonyms at **wind.** [Cantonese *tai fung,* "great wind," corresponding to Chinese (Mandarin) *ta⁴fêng¹* : *ta⁴,* great + *fêng,* wind (but in form influenced by Greek *Tuphōn,* TYPHON).]

ty·phus (tī′fəs) *n.* Any of several forms of an infectious disease caused by microorganisms of the genus *Rickettsia,* especially when flea-borne as in *endemic typhus,* louse-borne as in *epidemic typhus,* or mite-borne as in *scrub typhus,* and characterized generally by severe headache, sustained high fever, depression, delirium, and red rashes. Also called "typhus fever," "prison fever." [New Latin, from Greek *tuphos,* (fever causing) delusion, from *tuphein,* to make smoke. See **dheu-¹** in Appendix.*] —**ty′phous** (-fəs) *adj.*

typ·i·cal (tĭp′ĭ-kəl) *adj.* Also **typ·ic** (-ĭk). **1.** Exhibiting the traits or characteristics peculiar to its kind, class, group, or the like; representative of a whole group: *a typical suburban community.* **2.** Of or pertaining to a representative specimen; characteristic; distinctive. **3.** Conforming to a type, as a species. **4.** Of the nature of, constituting, or serving as a type; emblematic. —See Synonyms at **normal, characteristic, usual.** [Late Latin *typicālis,* from *typicus,* typical, from Greek *tupikos,* impressionable, from *tupos,* impression, TYPE.] —**typ′i·cal·ly** *adv.* —**typ′i·cal·ness, typ′i·cal′i·ty** *n.*

typ·i·fy (tĭp′ə-fī′) *tr.v.* **-fied, -fying, -fies. 1.** To serve as a typical example of; embody the essential characteristics of. **2.** To represent by an image, form, or model; symbolize; prefigure. [From TYP(E) + -FY.] —**typ′i·fi·ca′tion** *n.* —**typ′i·fi′er** *n.*

typ·ist (tī′pĭst) *n.* One who operates a typewriter.

ty·po (tī′pō) *n., pl.* **-os.** *Informal.* A typographical error.

typo., typog. typographer; typographical; typography.

ty·pog·ra·pher (tī-pŏg′rə-fər) *n. Abbr.* **typ., typo., typog.** A printer or compositor.

typographical error. A mistake in printing, typing, or writing.

ty·pog·ra·phy (tī-pŏg′rə-fē) *n., pl.* **-phies.** *Abbr.* **typ., typo., typog. 1. a.** The composition of printed material from movable type. **b.** The art and technique of this. **2.** The arrangement and appearance of such matter. [Medieval Latin *typographia* : Greek *tupos,* impression, TYPE + -GRAPHY.] —**ty′po·graph′i·cal**

(tĭ′pə-grăf′ĭ-kəl), **ty′po·graph′ic** *adj.* —**ty′po·graph′i·cal·ly** *adv*
ty·pol·o·gy (tī-pŏl′ə-jē) *n., pl.* **-gies. 1.** The study of types, as in a systematic classification. **2.** A theory or doctrine of types, as in scriptural studies. [Greek *tupos*, impression, TYPE + -LOGY.] —**ty′po·log′i·cal** (tī′pə-lŏj′ĭ-kəl) *adj.* —**ty·pol′o·gist** *n.*
typw. typewriter; typewritten.
Tyr (tîr). Also **Tyrr.** *Norse Mythology.* A god of war, son of Odin. [Old Norse *Tȳr.* See **deiw-** in Appendix.*]
ty·ra·mine (tī′rə-mēn′) *n.* A colorless, crystalline amine, C₈H₁₁-NO, found in mistletoe, putrefied animal tissue, certain cheeses, and ergot, and also produced synthetically, used in medicine. [TYR(OSINE) + AMINE.]
ty·ran·ni·cal (tĭ-răn′ĭ-kəl, tī-) *adj.* Also **ty·ran·nic** (-răn′ĭk). Of, pertaining to, or characteristic of a tyrant; despotic; arbitrary; oppressive. —**ty·ran′ni·cal·ly** *adv.* —**ty·ran′ni·cal·ness** *n.*
tyr·an·nize (tĭr′ə-nīz′) *v.* **-nized, -nizing, -nizes.** —*intr.* **1.** To exercise absolute power, especially arbitrarily: *"So it is the nature of such persons to insult and tyrannize over little people"* (Fielding). **2.** To rule as a tyrant. —*tr.* To treat tyrannically; to crush; oppress. [Old French *tyranniser,* from Late Latin *tyrannizāre,* from Latin *tyrannus,* TYRANT.] —**tyr′an·niz′er** *n.* —**tyr′an·niz′ing·ly** *adv.*
ty·ran·no·saur (tĭ-răn′ə-sôr′, tī-) *n.* Also **ty·ran·no·saur·us** (tĭ-răn′ə-sôr′əs, tī-). A large carnivorous dinosaur of the genus *Tyrannosaurus,* of the Cretaceous period, having small forelimbs and a large head. [New Latin : Greek *turannos,* TYRANT + -SAUR.]
tyr·an·nous (tĭr′ə-nəs) *adj.* Characterized by tyranny; despotic; tyrannical. —**tyr′an·nous·ly** *adv.*
tyr·an·ny (tĭr′ə-nē) *n., pl.* **-nies. 1.** A government in which a single ruler is vested with absolute power. **2.** The office, authority, or jurisdiction of such a ruler. **3.** Absolute power, especially when exercised unjustly or cruelly: *"I have sworn eternal hostility to every form of tyranny over the mind of man."* (Jefferson). **4.** The arbitrary use of such power; a tyrannical act. **5.** Extreme harshness or severity; rigor. [Middle English *tyrannye,* from Old French *tyrannie,* from Late Latin *tyrannia,* from Greek *turannia,* from *turannos,* TYRANT.]
ty·rant (tī′rənt) *n.* **1.** An absolute ruler who governs arbitrarily without constitutional or other restrictions, especially one in ancient Greece. **2.** A ruler who exercises power in a harsh, cruel manner; an oppressor. **3.** Any tyrannical or despotic person. [Middle English *tyra(u)nt,* from Old French *tyran(t),* from Latin *tyrannus,* from Greek *turannos,* probably from a source in Asia Minor.]
tyre. *British.* Variant of **tire** (wheel part).
Tyre (tīr). The capital of ancient Phoenicia, a seaport on the Mediterranean, the site of which is in southern Lebanon. —**Tyr′i·an** (tîr′ē-ən) *adj. & n.*
Tyrian purple. A reddish dyestuff obtained from the bodies of

certain mollusks of the genus *Murex,* and highly prized in ancient times.
ty·ro (tī′rō) *n., pl.* **-ros.** Also **ti·ro.** An inexperienced person; a beginner; neophyte. [Medieval Latin *tȳro,* from Latin *tīrō†,* a young soldier, recruit.]
Ty·rol (tĭ-rōl′, tī′rōl′, tîr′ōl′). Also **Ti·rol. 1.** A region and former Austrian crown territory in western Austria and northern Italy. Often called "The Tyrol." **2.** A province of Austria, occupying 4,883 square miles in the western part of the country. Population, 463,000. Capital, Innsbruck.
Tyr·o·lese (tîr′ə-lēz′, -lēs′, tī′rə-) *n., pl.* **Tyrolese.** Also **Ty·ro·le·an** (tĭ-rō′lē-ən, tī-). A native or inhabitant of Tyrol. —*adj.* Also **Ty·ro·le·an.** Of or pertaining to Tyrol.
Ty·rone (tĭ-rōn′). A county of Northern Ireland, occupying 1,218 square miles in the west. Population, 136,000. County seat, Omagh.
ty·ro·sin·ase (tī′rō-sĭ-nās′, tĭ-rŏs′ə-nās′, -nāz′) *n.* A copper-containing enzyme of plant and animal tissues that catalyzes the production of melanin from tyrosine, as in the blackening of a potato exposed to air. [TYROSIN(E) + -ASE.]
ty·ro·sine (tī′rə-sēn′) *n.* A white crystalline amino acid, C₉H₁₁-NO₃, derived from the hydrolysis of protein, used as a growth factor in nutrition and as a dietary supplement. [Greek *turos,* cheese (see **teue-** in Appendix*) + -INE.]
ty·ro·thri·cin (tī′rō-thrī′sĭn) *n.* A grayish to brown mixture of antibiotics obtained from cultures of soil bacteria, especially *Bacillus brevis,* and used topically in treating infections caused by Gram-positive bacteria. [New Latin *Tyrotrix* (stem *Tyrothric-*), generic name for certain spore-forming bacteria, "cheese-haired" : Greek *turos,* cheese (see **teue-** in Appendix*) + *thrix,* hair (see **thrix** in Appendix*) + -IN.]
Tyrr. Variant of **Tyr.**
Tyr·rhe·ni·an Sea (tĭ-rē′nē-ən). The section of the Mediterranean Sea lying between Italy and the islands of Corsica, Sardinia, and Sicily.
Tyu·men (tyōō-mĕn′). A city of the Soviet Union, in the west-central Russian S.F.S.R. Population, 201,000.
tzar. Variant of **czar.**
Tze·kung (dzŭ′gŏŏng′). A city of south-central China, in south-eastern Szechwan Province. Population, 291,000.
Tze·po (dzŭ′pō′). A city of eastern China, in central Shantung Province. Population, 875,000.
tzet·ze fly. Variant of **tsetse fly.**
Tzi·gane (tsē-gän′) *n.* A Gypsy. —*adj.* Of or pertaining to Gypsies or their music. [French, from Hungarian *cigány.*]
tzim·mes. Variant of **tsimmes.**
Tz'u Hsi (tsōō′ shē′). 1835–1908. Dowager Empress of China (1862–73, 1875–89, and 1898–1908); reign led to Boxer Rebellion.
tzu·ris. Variant of **tsuris.**

typewriter

---

t tight/th thin, path/*th* this, bathe/ŭ cut/ûr urge/v valve/w with/y yes/z zebra, size/zh vision/ə about, item, edible, gallop, circus/ à *Fr.* ami/œ *Fr.* feu, *Ger.* schön/ü *Fr.* tu, *Ger.* über/KH *Ger.* ich, *Scot.* loch/N *Fr.* bon. ***Follows main vocabulary. †Of obscure origin.**

tyrannosaur

Uu

YY YΚΥV VV Uu U𝒰u𝑢

1	2	3	4	5	6	7	8	9	10	11	12	13	14
Phoenician		Greek				Roman		Medieval			Modern		

The letter U is a descendant of the letter V (see). Around 1000 B.C. the Phoenicians and other Semites of Syria and Palestine began to use a graphic sign in the forms (1,2). They gave it the name wāw and used it for a semiconsonant w, as in English know, knows. After 900 B.C., when the Greeks borrowed the alphabet from the Phoenicians, they developed two signs from wāw. The first sign, which they called upsilon, "bare u," they used for the vowel u (3,4,5,6). (For the other sign, see F.) The Greek form without the tail passed via Etruscan to the Roman alphabet (7,8), in which it was used for two sounds, semiconsonantal w and vocalic u, as in the writing of VENIO and IVLIVS. In later Roman times the sound w became v. In late Roman Uncial (9) the sounds v, w, and u were not systematically distinguished. Gradually, as in the Cursive (10), a characteristic tailed form was used for the u. Eventually in modern times a curved shape was formalized for the upper-case printed letter (11), while the lower-case (13) and the written forms (12,14) followed the Cursive.

Uganda

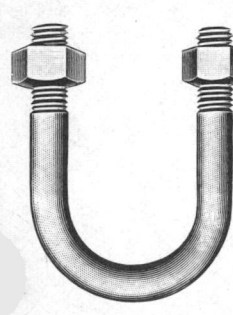

U-bolt

u, U (yōō) *n., pl.* **u's** or *rare* **us, U's** or **Us. 1.** The 21st letter of the modern English alphabet. See **alphabet. 2.** Any of the speech sounds represented by this letter. **3.** Anything shaped like the letter **U.**

u, U, u., U. *Note:* As an abbreviation or symbol, *u* may be a capital or a small letter, with or without a period. Established forms or those generally preferred precede the definition. When no form is given, all four forms are in general use in that sense. **1. u., U.** uncle. **2. U** *Mathematics.* union. **3. u.** unit. **4. U.** university. **5. u., U.** upper. **6. U** The symbol for the element uranium. **7.** The 21st in a series; 20th when *J* is omitted.

U (yōō) *adj. British Informal.* Of or appropriate to the upper class, especially in language usage. Compare **non-U.**

UAR, U.A.R. United Arab Republic.

Uau·pés (wou-pās′). A river of South America, rising as the Vaupés in south-central Colombia and flowing about 500 miles generally southeast to the Río Negro in Brazil.

UAW, U.A.W. 1. United Auto, Aircraft and Agricultural Implements Workers. **2.** United Automobile Workers.

U·ban·gi (yōō-băng′gē, ōō-bäng′gē). A river of Africa, formed by the confluence of the Bomu and Uele on the Central African Republic-Congo (Kinshasa) border and flowing about 600 miles generally southwest to the Congo River.

U·ban·gi-Sha·ri. Former name for **Central African Republic.**

U·be (ōō′bě). A city of Japan, on southwestern Honshu at the western end of the Inland Sea. Population, 168,000.

u·biq·ui·tous (yōō-bĭk′wə-təs) *adj.* Being or seeming to be everywhere at the same time; omnipresent: *"he plodded through the shadows fruitlessly like an ubiquitous spook"* (Joseph Heller). [From UBIQUITY.] **—u·biq′ui·tous·ly** *adv.* **—u·biq′ui·tous·ness** *n.*

u·biq·ui·ty (yōō-bĭk′wə-tē) *n.* Existence everywhere at the same time; omnipresence. [New Latin *ubiquitas,* from Latin *ubīque,* everywhere : *ubī,* where (see **kwo-** in Appendix*) + *-que,* generalizing particle (see **kwe** in Appendix*).]

u·bi su·pra (ōō′bē sōō′prä). *Abbr.* **u.s.** *Latin* Where (mentioned) above.

U-boat (yōō′bōt′) *n.* A German submarine. [German *U-boot,* short for *Unterseeboot,* "undersea boat."]

U-bolt (yōō′bōlt′) *n.* A bolt shaped like the letter U, fitted with threads and a nut at each end.

u.c. *Printing.* upper case.

U·ca·ya·li (ōō′kä-yä′lē). A river of Peru, flowing over 1,000 miles from the east-central part of the country north to the Marañón, with which it forms the Amazon.

Uc·cel·lo (ōōt-chěl′lō), **Paolo.** Original surname, di Dono. 1397–1475. Italian painter of the Florentine school.

U·chee, U·che·an. Variants of **Yuchi.**

UCMJ Uniform Code of Military Justice.

U·dai·pur (ōō-dī′pōōr, ōō′dī-pōōr′). A city in south-central Rajasthan, Republic of India. Population, 118,000.

U·dall (yōō′dôl′, yōōd′l), **Nicholas.** 1505–1556. English schoolmaster; author of first English comedy, *Ralph Roister Doister.*

UDC Universal Decimal Classification.

ud·der (ŭd′ər) *n.* The baglike mammary organ characteristic of cows, sheep, and goats, having two or more teats. [Middle English *udder,* Old English *ūder.* See **eudh-** in Appendix.*]

U·di·ne (ōō′dē-nā). A city of Italy, in the northeast about 60 miles northeast of Venice. Population, 86,000.

Ud·murt Autonomous Soviet Socialist Republic (ōōd′-mōōrt). An administrative division, 16,250 square miles in area, of the west-central Russian S.F.S.R. Population, 1,376,000. Capital, Izhevsk.

u·do (ōō′dō) *n.* A Japanese plant, *Aralia cordata,* of which the young shoots are cooked and eaten as a vegetable. [Japanese.]

U.E.L. United Empire Loyalists.

Ue·le (wě′lā). A river of Africa, rising in the northeastern Democratic Republic of the Congo and flowing 700 miles generally west to the Bomu, with which it forms the Ubangi.

U·fa (ōō-fä′). **1.** The capital of the Bashkir A.S.S.R., an industrial city at the junction of the Ufa and Byelaya rivers. Population, 665,000. **2.** A river of the Soviet Union, rising in the southern Ural Mountains and flowing 600 miles southwest to the Byelaya.

UFO, U.F.O. unidentified flying object.

U·gan·da (yōō-găn′də, ōō-gän′dä). A country occupying 93,981 square miles in east-central Africa; a former British protectorate, independent since 1962. Population, 7,190,000. Capital, Kampala.

U·ga·rit·ic (ōō′gə-rĭt′ĭk) *n.* The Semitic language of the ancient city-state of Ugarit in Syria. **—U′ga·rit′ic** *adj.*

ugh (ŭκн, ŏōκн, ŭg) *interj.* Used to express horror, disgust, or repugnance.

ug·li (ŭg′lē) *n., pl.* **-lis** or **-lies.** A citrus fruit indigenous to Jamaica, produced by a cross between a grapefruit and a tangerine and having a loose, wrinkled yellowish rind. [Perhaps from UGLY (from its ugly wrinkled rind).]

ug·li·fy (ŭg′lə-fī′) *tr.v.* **-fied, -fying, -fies.** To make ugly; disfigure. **—ug′li·fi·ca′tion** *n.*

ug·ly (ŭg′lē) *adj.* **-lier, -liest. 1.** Displeasing to the eye; unsightly. **2.** Repulsive or offensive in any way; objectionable; unpleasant. **3.** Morally reprehensible; bad. **4.** Threatening; ominous: *ugly weather.* **5.** *Informal.* Cross; disagreeable: *an ugly temper.* [Middle English *ugli(c),* frightful, repulsive, from Old Norse *uggligr,* from *uggr†,* fear.] **—ug′li·ness** *n.*

ugly duckling. One considered ugly or unpromising at first but having the potential of becoming beautiful or admirable in maturity. [From the story by Hans Christian Andersen.]

U·gri·an (ōō′grē-ən, yōō′-) *n.* **1.** A member of a group of Finno-Ugric peoples of western Siberia and Hungary, including the Magyars. **2.** Ugric. [From Old Russian *Ugrin′* (plural *Ugre*), from Common Slavic *Og′rin′* (unattested), from Turkic *Onogouroi.* See also **Hungary.**] **—U′gri·an** *adj.*

U·gric (ōō′grĭk, yōō′-) *n.* A branch of the Finno-Ugric subfamily of languages consisting of Magyar (Hungarian), Ostyak, and Vogul. **—U′gric** *adj.*

ug·some (ŭg′səm) *adj. Archaic.* Disgusting; loathsome. [Middle English *ugsom : uggen,* to inspire dread or disgust, from Old

---

ă pat/ā pay/âr care/ä father/b bib/ch church/d deed/ĕ pet/ē be/f fife/g gag/h hat/hw which/ĭ pit/ī pie/îr pier/j judge/k kick/l lid, needle/m mum/n no, sudden/ng thing/ŏ pot/ō toe/ô paw, for/oi noise/ou out/ŏŏ took/ōō boot/p pop/r roar/s sauce/sh ship, dish/

Norse *ugga,* to fear, akin to *uggr,* fear (see **ugly**) + -SOME.]

UGT urgent (telegram).

uhf, UHF ultrahigh frequency.

uh·lan (o͞o′län′, yo͞o′lən) *n.* Also **u·lan.** One of a body of cavalry armed with lances that formed part of the former Polish and, later, German armies. [German *u(h)lan,* from Polish *ułan,* from Turkish *oğlan,* "youth," from *oğul,* son.]

Ui·gur (wē′go͝or) *n.* Also **Ui·ghur. 1.** One of a Turkic people dominant in Mongolia and eastern Turkestan from the 8th to the 12th century, now inhabiting northwestern China. **2.** The East Turkic language of this people. [Uigur *Uighur.*] —**Ui·gu′ri·an** (wē-go͝or′ē-ən), **Ui·gu′ric** (wē-go͝or′ĭk) *adj.*

U·in·ta·ite (yo͞o-ĭn′tə-īt′) *n.* An asphalt, **gilsonite** *(see).* [After the UINTA MOUNTAINS, where it was discovered.]

U·in·ta Mountains (yo͞o-ĭn′tə). A range of the Rocky Mountains in northeastern Utah and southwestern Wyoming. Highest elevation, Kings Peak (13,498 feet).

UIO Airport code for Quito, Ecuador.

uit·land·er (oit′lăn′dər, īt′-) *n. Afrikaans.* **1.** An outlander; a foreigner. **2.** *Capital* **U.** A native of Great Britain residing in the former republics of the Orange Free State or Transvaal. [Afrikaans, from Middle Dutch *utelander,* from *utelant,* foreign land : *ute,* out (see **ud-** in Appendix*) + *land,* land (see **lendh-**[2] in Appendix*).]

U·ji·ji (o͞o-jē′jē). A small port town on Lake Tanganyika; site of the meeting of Stanley and Livingston (1871).

Uj·jain (o͞o′jīn). A city of the Republic of India, in northwestern Madhya Pradesh; one of the seven cities sacred to Hindus. Population, 140,000.

Uj·pest (o͞o′ē-pĕsht′). A city of Hungary, on the Danube near Budapest, of which it is a suburb. Population, 80,000.

U.K. United Kingdom.

u·kase (yo͞o-kās′, -kāz′, yo͞o′kās′, -kāz′) *n.* **1.** A proclamation of the czar having the force of law in imperial Russia. **2.** Any authoritative order or decree; an edict. [French, from Russian *ukaz,* decree, from *ukazat′,* to order, direct : *u-,* intensive prefix, "away" (see **au-**[3] in Appendix*) + *-kazat′,* to show (see **kwek-** in Appendix*).]

uke (yo͞ok) *n.* Shortened form of **ukulele.**

U·krain·i·an (yo͞o-krā′nē-ən) *n.* **1.** An inhabitant or native of the Ukraine. **2.** A Slavic language, similar to but distinct from Russian, that is spoken by most natives of the Ukraine. Also called "Little Russian." [Ukrainian *Ukrayina,* from Old Russian *Ukraina,* "borderland" : *u-,* away from, at (see **au-**[3] in Appendix*) + *kraĭ,* edge, brink, end (see **skeri-** in Appendix*).] —**U·krain′i·an** *adj.*

Ukrainian Soviet Socialist Republic. Also **U·kraine** (yo͞o-krān′, yo͞o-krīn′, yo͞o′krān). A constituent republic of the Soviet Union, occupying 222,600 square miles in the southwest. Population, 45,100,000. Capital, Kiev.

u·ku·le·le (yo͞o′kə-lā′lē, o͞o′kə-) *n.* A small four-stringed guitar popularized in Hawaii. [Hawaiian *'ukulele,* "jumping little flea" (said to be nickname of Edward Putvis, 19th-century British officer, who popularized the instrument) : *'uku,* flea + *lele,* jumping.]

u·lan. Variant of **uhlan.**

U·lan Ba·tor (o͞o′län bä′tôr). Formerly **Ur·ga** (o͞or′gə). The capital of the Mongolian People's Republic, situated in the north-central part of the country. Population, 250,000. [Mongolian *ulaan baatar,* "red hero."]

U·lan-U·de (o͞o′län′o͞o-dā′). The capital of Buryat A.S.S.R., situated east of Lake Baikal. Population, 213,000.

-ular. Indicates a relationship or resemblance; for example, **tubular.** [Latin *-ulāris,* from *-ulus,* -ULE.]

Ul·bricht (o͝ol′brĭKHt), **Walter.** Born 1893. East German political leader; chairman of the council of state of the German Democratic Republic (since 1960).

ul·cer (ŭl′sər) *n.* **1. a.** An inflammatory, often suppurating lesion on the skin or an internal mucous surface of the body, resulting in necrosis of the tissue. **b.** A necrotic lesion of the stomach and duodenum. **2.** Any corrupting condition or influence. [Middle English, from Old French *ulcere,* from Latin *ulcus* (stem *ulcer-*), a sore, ulcer. See **elkos-** in Appendix.*]

ul·cer·ate (ŭl′sə-rāt′) *v.* **-ated, -ating, -ates.** —*intr.* To become affected with or as if with an ulcer. —*tr.* To affect with ulcers. —**ul′cer·a′tive** (ŭl′sə-rā′tĭv, ŭl′sər-ə-tĭv) *adj.*

ul·cer·a·tion (ŭl′sə-rā′shən) *n.* **1.** The development of an ulcer. **2.** An ulcer or ulcerous condition.

ul·cer·ous (ŭl′sər-əs) *adj.* Pertaining to or exhibiting ulcers.

-ule. Indicates smallness of size; for example, **disseminule, valvule.** [French *-ule,* from Latin *-ulus* (masculine), *-ula* (feminine), *-ulum* (neuter), diminutive suffixes.]

u·le·ma (o͞o′lə-mä′) *n., pl.* **ulema** or **-mas.** Also **u·la·ma. 1.** The scholars or priests trained in traditional Moslem religion and law. Used with a singular verb. **2.** A Moslem scholar or religious leader. [Turkish *'ulemā,* from Arabic *'ulamā',* "wise men," plural of *'ālim,* wise, learned, from *'alimā,* to know.]

-ulent. Indicates abundance or fullness; for example, **flatulent.** [Old French, from Latin *-ulentus.*]

ul·lage (ŭl′ĭj) *n.* The amount of liquid within a container that is lost during shipment or storage, as through leakage. [Middle English *oylage,* from Old French *auoillage,* from *auoiller,* to fill up a cask to the bunghole, from *oeil,* eye, bunghole, from Latin *oculus.* See **okw-** in Appendix.*]

Ulm (o͝olm). A city of West Germany, on the Danube in eastern Baden-Württemberg. Population, 93,000.

ul·na (ŭl′nə) *n., pl.* **-nae** (-nē′) or **-nas.** *Anatomy.* **1.** The bone extending from the elbow to the wrist on the side opposite to the thumb. **2.** A homologous bone in the vertebrate forelimb. [New Latin, from Latin, elbow, arm. See **el-**[1] in Appendix.*] —**ul′nar** *adj.*

u·lot·ri·chous (yo͞o-lŏt′rĭ-kəs) *adj.* Having wiry or woolly hair. [New Latin, "woolly-haired," from Greek *oulothrix* (stem *oulotrikh-*) : *oulos,* woolly, curly (see **wel-**[3] in Appendix*) + *thrix,* hair (see **thrix** in Appendix*).] —**u·lot′ri·chy** (-kē) *n.*

ul·ster (ŭl′stər) *n.* A loose, long overcoat made of heavy, rugged fabric. [After ULSTER, Ireland.]

Ul·ster (ŭl′stər). **1.** A former province of Ireland, of which the northern part is now officially Northern Ireland. **2.** A province of the Republic of Ireland, occupying 3,393 square miles in the north. Population, 217,000.

ult. 1. ultimate; ultimately. **2.** ultimo.

ul·te·ri·or (ŭl-tîr′ē-ər) *adj.* **1.** Lying beyond or outside the area of immediate interest. **2.** Lying beyond what is evident or avowed; especially, concealed intentionally so as to deceive: *an ulterior motive.* **3.** Occurring later; subsequent. [Latin, farther, comparative of *ulter,* on the other side, from *uls,* beyond. See **al-**[1] in Appendix.*]

ul·ti·ma (ŭl′tə-mə) *n.* The last syllable of a word. [Latin, feminine of *ultimus,* farthest, last. See **ultimate.**]

ul·ti·mate (ŭl′tə-mĭt) *adj. Abbr.* **ult. 1.** Completing a series or process; final; conclusive. **2.** Representing the farthest possible extent of analysis or division into parts: *ultimate particle.* **3.** Fundamental; elemental. **4.** Of the greatest possible size or significance; maximum: *"Socrates' death is the ultimate proof of his sincerity."* (Karl Popper). **5.** Farthest; most remote. —See Synonyms at **last.** —*n.* **1.** The basic or fundamental fact. **2.** The final point; conclusive result; conclusion. **3.** The maximum; greatest extreme. [Medieval Latin *ultimātus,* past participle of *ultimāre,* to come to an end, from Latin *ultimus,* farthest, last, superlative degree of *ulter,* on the other side, from *uls,* beyond. See **al-**[1] in Appendix.*] —**ul′ti·mate·ly** *adv.* —**ul′ti·mate·ness** *n.*

ultima Thu·le (tho͞o′lē). **1.** The northernmost region of the habitable world as thought of by ancient geographers. **2.** A remote goal or ideal. [Latin.]

ul·ti·ma·tum (ŭl′tə-mā′təm, -mä′təm) *n., pl.* **-tums** or **-ta** (-tə). A final statement of terms made by one party to another; especially, in diplomatic negotiations, a statement that expresses or implies the threat of serious penalties if the terms are not accepted. [New Latin, from Medieval Latin, neuter of *ultimātus,* last, ULTIMATE.]

ul·ti·mo (ŭl′tə-mō′) *adv. Abbr.* **ult.** In or of the month before the present one. Compare **proximo.** [Latin *ultimo (mense),* in last (month), from *ultimus,* last, ULTIMATE.]

ul·tra (ŭl′trə) *adj.* Immoderately adhering to a belief, fashion, or course of action; extreme. —*n.* An extremist. [From ULTRA-.]

ultra-. Indicates: **1.** A surpassing of a specified limit, range, scope, or beyond; for example, **ultramicroscopic, ultrasonic. 2.** An exceeding of what is common, moderate, or proper or of an extreme degree; for example, **ultraconservative.** ***Note:*** Many compounds other than those entered here may be formed with *ultra-.* In forming compounds, *ultra-* is normally joined with the following element without space or a hyphen: *ultramodern; ultrafashionable.* However, if the second element begins with a capital letter or with the letter *a,* it is separated with a hyphen: *ultra-British, ultra-atomic.* [Latin, from *ultrā,* beyond, from *ulter* (unattested), on the other side, from *uls,* beyond. See **al-**[1] in Appendix.*]

ul·tra·cen·tri·fuge (ŭl′trə-sĕn′trə-fyo͞oj′) *n.* A convection-free high-velocity centrifuge used in the separation of colloidal or submicroscopic particles. —**ul′tra·cen·trif′u·gal** (-sĕn-trĭf′yə-gəl, -trĭf′ə-gəl) *adj.* —**ul′tra·cen·trif′u·ga′tion** (-gā′shən) *n.*

ul·tra·con·ser·va·tive (ŭl′trə-kən-sûr′və-tĭv) *adj.* Conservative to an extreme, especially in political beliefs; reactionary. —*n.* One who is extremely conservative.

ul·tra·high frequency (ŭl′trə-hī′). *Abbr.* **uhf, UHF** A band of radio frequencies from 300 to 3,000 megacycles per second.

ul·tra·ism (ŭl′trə-ĭz′əm) *n.* Extremism, especially in politics or government; radicalism. —**ul′tra·ist** *adj.* & *n.*

ul·tra·ma·rine (ŭl′trə-mə-rēn′) *n.* **1.** A blue pigment made from powdered lapis lazuli. **2.** Any similar pigment made from other substances. **3.** Vivid or strong blue to purplish blue. See **color.** —*adj.* **1.** Having a deep-blue purplish color. **2.** Of or from some place beyond the sea. [Medieval Latin *ultrāmarīnus,* "(coming from) beyond the sea" (because lapis lazuli was imported from Asia by sea) : Latin *ultrā-,* beyond + *mare,* sea (see **mori-** in Appendix*).]

ul·tra·mi·crom·e·ter (ŭl′trə-mī-krŏm′ə-tər) *n.* An extremely accurate micrometer.

ul·tra·mi·cro·scope (ŭl′trə-mī′krə-skōp′) *n.* A microscope with high-intensity illumination used to study very minute objects, such as colloidal particles, by means of their diffraction system, which appears as a bright spot against a black background. Also called "dark-field microscope."

ul·tra·mi·cro·scop·ic (ŭl′trə-mī′krə-skŏp′ĭk) *adj.* **1.** Too small to be seen with an ordinary microscope. **2.** Of or relating to an ultramicroscope.

ul·tra·mod·ern (ŭl′trə-mŏd′ərn) *adj.* Suggestive of a style or period beyond the contemporary; futuristic. —**ul′tra·mod′ern·ism′** *n.* —**ul′tra·mod′ern·ist** *n.* —**ul′tra·mod′ern·is′tic** *adj.*

ul·tra·mon·tane (ŭl′trə-mŏn′tān′, -mŏn-tān′) *adj.* **1.** Of or pertaining to peoples or regions lying south of the Alps. **2.** Supporting the authority of the papal court over national or diocesan authority in the Roman Catholic Church. **3.** Pertaining to or supporting the doctrine of papal supremacy. —*n.* **1.** A person living beyond the mountains, especially, south of the Alps. **2.** *Often capital* **U.** A Roman Catholic who advocates

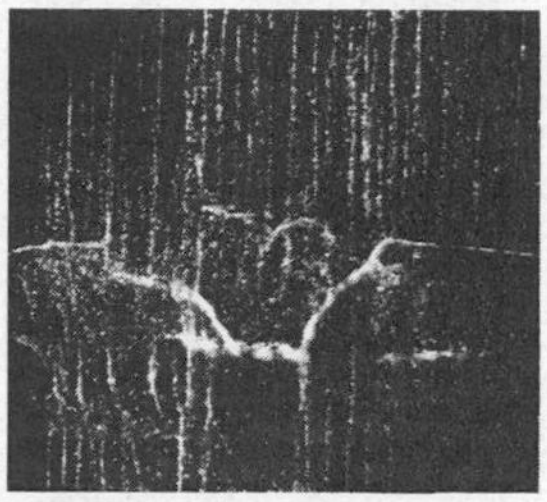

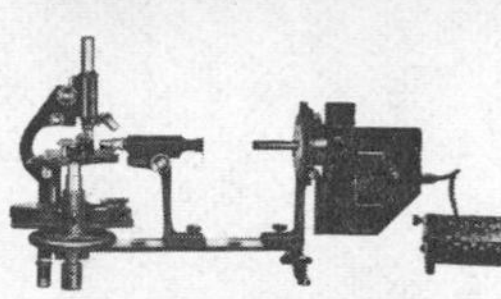

ultramicroscope
Above: Detail from an ultramicroscopic photograph of a single ruby crystal
Below: The instrument

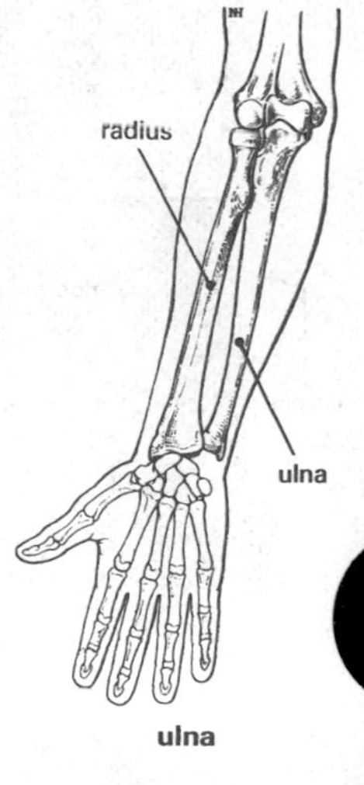

ulna

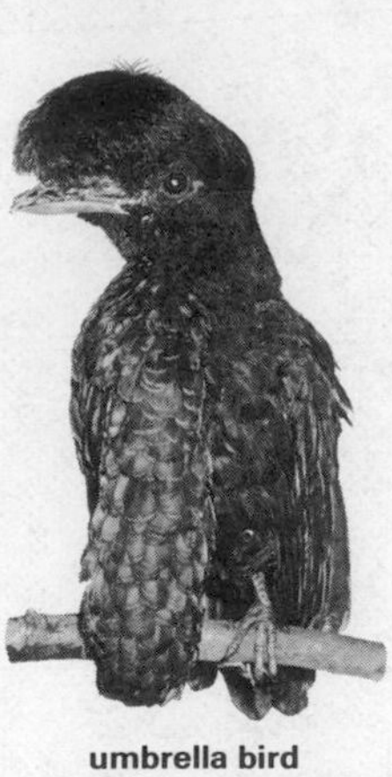

umbrella bird
Cephalopterus ornatus

support of papal policy in ecclesiastical and political matters. [Medieval Latin *ultrāmontānus,* beyond the mountain (applied by the French to the papal court at Rome) : Latin *ultrā-,* beyond + *mōns* (stem *mont-*), mountain (see **men-²** in Appendix*).]
Ul·tra·mon·ta·nism (ŭl′trə-mŏn′tə-nĭz′əm) *n.* The policy that absolute authority in the Roman Catholic Church should be vested in the pope. Compare **Gallicanism.**
ul·tra·mun·dane (ŭl′trə-mŭn′dān′, -mŭn′dān′) *adj.* Extending or being beyond the world or the limits of the universe. [Latin *ultrāmundānus* : *ultrā-,* beyond + *mundus,* the world (see **mundus** in Appendix*).]
ul·tra·na·tion·al·ism (ŭl′trə-năsh′ən-əl-ĭz′əm) *n.* Extreme nationalism, especially when opposed to international cooperation. —**ul′tra·na′tion·al** *adj.* —**ul′tra·na′tion·al·ist** *n.* & *adj.* —**ul′tra·na′tion·al·is′tic** *adj.*
ul·tra·son·ic (ŭl′trə-sŏn′ĭk) *adj.* Pertaining to acoustic frequencies above the range audible to the human ear, or above approximately 20,000 cycles per second.
ul·tra·son·ics (ŭl′trə-sŏn′ĭks) *n.* Plural in form, used with a singular verb. **1.** The acoustics of ultrasonic sound. **2.** A technology using ultrasonic sound, as for medical therapy.
ul·tra·sound (ŭl′trə-sound′) *n.* Ultrasonic sound.
ul·tra·vi·o·let (ŭl′trə-vī′ə-lĭt) *adj.* Of or pertaining to the range of radiation wavelengths from about 4,000 angstroms, just beyond the violet in the visible spectrum, to about 40 angstroms, on the border of the x-ray region. —**ul′tra·vi′o·let** *n.*
ultraviolet lamp. A mercury-vapor lamp that produces ultraviolet light.
ul·tra·vi·rus (ŭl′trə-vī′rəs) *n.* A virus small enough to pass through the finest bacterial filter; a filterable virus.
U·lugh Muz·tagh (o͞o′lə məz-tä′, məz-täg′). The highest elevation (25,340 feet) of the Kunlun range, China, on the border between Tibet and the Sinkiang-Uigur Autonomous Region.
ul·u·late (ŭl′yə-lāt′, yo͞ol′-) *intr.v.* **-lated, -lating, -lates.** To howl, hoot, wail, or lament loudly. [Latin *ululāre,* to howl. See **ul-** in Appendix.*] —**ul′u·la′tion** *n.*
Ul·ya·novsk (o͞ol-yä′nəfsk). Formerly **Sim·birsk** (sĭm-bîrsk′). A city of the Soviet Union, a river port on the Volga in the western Russian S.F.S.R. Population, 265,000.
U·lys·ses. The Latin name for **Odysseus.**
U·may·yad (o͞o-mī′yăd′). Also **Om·mi·ad** (ə-mī′ăd′). A dynasty of rulers of the Moslem Empire (A.D. 661–750) and Moslem Spain (A.D. 756–1031). [From *Ummayah,* its founder.]
um·bel (ŭm′bəl) *n. Botany.* A flat-topped or rounded flower cluster in which the individual flower stalks arise from about the same point as in the carrot and related plants. [New Latin *umbella,* from Latin, an umbrella, diminutive of *umbra,* shadow. See **andho-** in Appendix.*]
um·bel·late (ŭm′bə-lāt′, ŭm′bĕl′ĭt) *adj.* Having, forming, or of the nature of an umbel.
um·bel·lif·er·ous (ŭm′bə-lĭf′ər-əs) *adj. Botany.* Bearing umbels. [New Latin *umbellifer* : *umbella,* UMBEL + -FEROUS.]
um·bel·lule (ŭm′bəl-yo͞ol′, ŭm′bĕl′yo͞ol) *n.* Also **um·bel·let** (ŭm′bə-lĭt). *Botany.* One of the smaller secondary umbels forming a compound umbel. [New Latin *umbellula,* diminutive of *umbella,* UMBEL.]
um·ber (ŭm′bər) *n.* **1.** A natural brown earth composed of ferric oxide, silica, alumina, lime, and manganese oxides and used as pigment. **2.** Any of the shades of brown produced by umber in its various states. —*adj.* **1.** Of or related to umber. **2.** Having a brownish hue. —*tr.v.* **umbered, -bering, -bers.** To cover with or as with umber. [Old French *umbre,* short for *terre d'Umbre,* "earth of Umbria."]
um·bil·i·cal (ŭm′bĭl′ĭ-kəl) *adj.* **1.** Of, pertaining to, or resembling an umbilicus. **2.** Pertaining to or located near the central area of the abdomen. —*n. Aerospace.* An **umbilical cord** *(see).*
umbilical cord. 1. *Anatomy.* The flexible, cordlike structure connecting the fetus at the navel with the placenta and containing two umbilical arteries and one vein that nourish the fetus and remove its wastes. **2.** *Aerospace.* **a.** Any of various external electrical lines or fluid tubes supplying a rocket before launch. **b.** The line that supplies an astronaut with oxygen and in some cases with communications while he is outside the spacecraft. Often shortened to "umbilical" in aerospace use.
um·bil·i·cate (ŭm′bĭl′ĭ-kĭt, -kāt′) *adj.* Also **um·bil·i·cat·ed** (-kā′tĭd). **1.** Having a central mark or depression resembling a navel. **2.** Having an umbilicus. —**um′bil′i·ca′tion** *n.*
um·bil·i·cus (ŭm′bĭl′ĭ-kəs, ŭm′bə-lī′kəs) *n., pl.* **-ci** (-sī′). **1.** The navel. **2.** *Biology.* Any similar small opening or depression, such as the hollow at the base of the shell of some gastropod mollusks or one of the openings in the shaft of a feather. [Latin *umbilīcus.* See **nobh-** in Appendix.*]
um·bo (ŭm′bō) *n., pl.* **umbones** (ŭm-bō′nēz) or **-bos. 1.** The boss or knob at the center of a shield. **2.** *Biology.* A similar knoblike protuberance, such as a prominence near the hinge of a bivalve shell. **3.** *Anatomy.* A small projection at the center of the outer surface of the tympanic membrane of the ear. [Latin *umbō* (stem *umbōn-*). See **nobh-** in Appendix.*] —**um′bo·nal** (ŭm′bə-nəl, ŭm′bō′nəl), **um′bon′ic** (ŭm′bŏn′ĭk) *adj.*
um·bo·nate (ŭm′bə-nāt′, -nĭt) *adj.* Having or resembling a knob or knoblike protuberance.

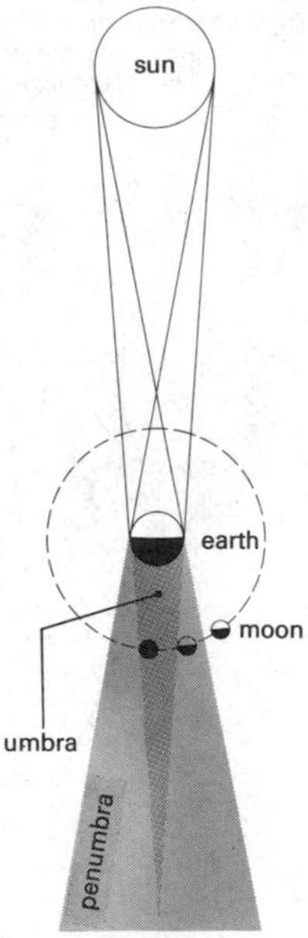

umbra

um·bra (ŭm′brə) *n., pl.* **-brae** (-brē). **1.** A dark area; specifically, the blackest part of a shadow from which all light is cut off. **2.** *Astronomy.* **a.** The shadow region over an area of the earth where a solar eclipse is total. **b.** The darkest region of a sunspot. [Latin *umbra,* shadow. See **andho-** in Appendix.*]
um·brage (ŭm′brĭj) *n.* **1.** Offense; resentment: *took umbrage at their rudeness.* **2.** *Archaic.* **a.** Something that affords shade: *"A chesnut [sic] spread its umbrage wide"* (Coleridge). **b.** Shadow or shade. **3.** *Obsolete.* A shadowy or indistinct indication; hint. [Middle English, shade, from Old French, from Vulgar Latin *umbrāticum* (unattested), neuter of Latin *umbrāticus,* of a shadow, from *umbra,* shadow, UMBRA.]
um·bra·geous (ŭm′brā′jəs) *adj.* **1.** Affording or forming shade; shady or shading. **2.** Easily offended; irritable. —**um′bra′geous·ly** *adv.* —**um′bra′geous·ness** *n.*
um·brel·la (ŭm′brĕl′ə) *n.* **1.** A device for protection from the weather consisting of a collapsible canopy mounted on a central rod. **2.** *Military.* An **air cover** *(see).* **3.** *Zoology.* The contractile gelatinous, rounded mass constituting the major part of the body of most jellyfishes. [Italian *ombrella,* diminutive of *ombra,* shade, from Latin *umbra.* See **andho-** in Appendix.*]
umbrella bird. Any of several tropical American birds of the genus *Cephalopterus;* especially, *C. ornatus,* having a retractile black crest and a long, feathered wattle hanging from the throat.
umbrella leaf. A plant, *Diphylleia cymosa,* of the southeastern United States, having a broad, rounded basal leaf and a terminal cluster of white flowers.
umbrella palm. A palm tree, *Hedyscepe canterburyana,* of the South Pacific, cultivated for its feathery, drooping foliage.
umbrella pine. An evergreen tree, *Sciadopitya vaticillata,* native to Japan, having umbrellalike tufts of narrow leaves.
umbrella tree. 1. Any of several trees of the genus *Magnolia,* of the southeastern United States; especially, *M. tripetala,* having large leaves clustered in an umbrellalike form at the ends of the branches. **2.** A tree, *Schefflera actinophylla,* native to Australia, having compound leaves and widely cultivated in its smaller forms as a house plant.
Um·bri·a (ŭm′brē-ə). A region of Italy, occupying 3,270 square miles in the center of the country. Population, 795,000. Capital, Perugia.
Um·bri·an (ŭm′brē-ən) *adj.* Of or pertaining to Umbria or its people. —*n.* **1.** An inhabitant or native of ancient or modern Umbria. **2.** The extinct Italic language of ancient Umbria.
u·mi·ak (o͞o′mē-ăk′) *n.* Also **oo·mi·ak.** A large open Eskimo boat made of skins stretched on a wooden frame, usually propelled by paddles. Compare **kayak.** [Eskimo.]
um·laut (o͝om′lout′) *n. Linguistics.* **1.** A change in a vowel sound caused by partial assimilation to a vowel or semivowel, originally occurring in the following syllable, now usually lost. An example is English *bed,* produced by umlaut from the earlier Germanic form in Gothic *badi.* Compare **ablaut. 2.** A vowel sound changed in this manner, such as the German *ä, ö,* or *ü.* **3.** The diacritical mark (¨) placed over a vowel to indicate an umlaut, especially in German. —*tr.v.* **umlauted, -lauting, -lauts. 1.** To modify a vowel sound by umlaut. **2.** To write or print a vowel with an umlaut. [German *Umlaut* : *um-,* prefix indicating alteration, "around," from Middle High German *um(b)-,* from *umbe,* from Old High German *umbi* (see **ambhi** in Appendix*) + *Laut,* sound, from Middle High German *lūt,* from Old High German *hlūt* (see **kleu-¹** in Appendix*).]
Um·nak (o͞om′năk). An island about 83 miles long and 2 to 15 miles wide in the Aleutians off southwestern Alaska.
um·pir·age (ŭm′pī′rĭj, -pə-rĭj) *n.* Also **um·pire·ship** (ŭm′pīr-shĭp′). **1.** The position, function, or authority of an umpire. **2.** A ruling or decision of an umpire.
um·pire (ŭm′pīr′) *n.* **1.** A person appointed to rule on plays in various sports, especially baseball. **2.** A person selected or empowered to settle a dispute between other persons or groups. **3.** A judge: *"Those who are esteemed umpires of taste are often persons who have acquired some knowledge"* (Emerson). —See Synonyms at **judge.** —*v.* **umpired, -piring, -pires.** —*tr.* To act as umpire in or of; referee; arbitrate. —*intr.* To be or act as an umpire. [Middle English *(an) oumpere,* originally *(a) noumpere,* (an) umpire, from Old French *nomper, nonper,* "not one of a pair (of contestants)" : *non-,* not + *per,* match. PEER.]
ump·teen (ŭmp-tēn′, ŭm-) *adj. Informal.* Large but indefinite in number: *umpteen reasons; umpteen guests.* [*Umpty,* Morse code term for "dash," hence a great number : *ump-,* expressive element + -TY + -TEEN.] —**ump·teenth′** *adj.*
UMT Universal Military Training.
Um·ta·ta (o͞om-tä′tə). The capital of The Transkei in eastern Cape of Good Hope Province, South Africa. Population, 12,000.
UMTS Universal Military Training Service (or System).
UMW United Mine Workers.
un-¹. Indicates not or contrary to; for example, **unhappy.** ***Note:*** Many compounds other than those entered here may be formed with *un-.* In forming compounds, *un-* is normally joined with the following element without space or a hyphen: *unnamed.* However, if the second element begins with a capital letter, it is separated with a hyphen: *un-American.* See Usage note at **un-².** [Middle English *un-,* Old English *un-.* See **ne** in Appendix.*]
un-². Indicates: **1.** Reversal of an action; for example, **unlock, unmake. 2.** Deprivation; for example, **unman, unsex, untrock. 3.** Release or removal from; for example, **unearth, unyoke, unhorse. 4.** Intensified action; for example, **unloose.** [Middle English *un-,* Old English *un-,* variant of *ond-, and-,* against. See **anti** in Appendix.*]
Usage: *Un-,* used in combination to indicate negation, is distinguished from *in-* (and its assimilated forms *il-, im-, ir-*) in the following general sense: *un-* is frequently confined to stressing mere lack and is consequently rather neutral and literal; *in-* and its variants more often give the original term a more strongly negative sense or one contrary to the meaning of the original. Thus *unhuman* and *unartistic* primarily apply to what is outside

ă pat/ā pay/âr care/ä father/b bib/ch church/d deed/ĕ pet/ē be/f fife/g gag/h hat/hw which/ĭ pit/ī pie/îr pier/j judge/k kick/l lid, needle/m mum/n no, sudden/ng thing/ŏ pot/ō toe/ô paw, for/oi noise/ou out/o͝o took/o͞o boot/p pop/r roar/s sauce/sh ship, dish/

the realm of the human and artistic. *Inhuman* and *inartistic* imply the contrary of what is human and artistic, such as cruelty and lack of taste or talent. This applies, however, only where the *un-* and *in-* forms of words are both in current usage. See Usage note at **non-**.

UN, U.N. United Nations.

un·a·bashed (ŭn'ə-băsht') *adj.* Not disconcerted or embarrassed; poised. **—un'a·bash'ed·ly** (-băsh'ĭd-lē) *adv.*

un·a·bat·ed (ŭn'ə-bā'tĭd) *adj.* At original full force; as strong as before: *They fought with unabated violence.*

un·a·ble (ŭn-ā'bəl) *adj.* **1.** Lacking the necessary power, authority, or means; not able. **2.** Lacking mental capability or efficiency; incompetent.

un·a·bridged (ŭn'ə-brĭjd') *adj. Abbr.* **unabr.** Having the original content; not condensed. Said of books and other documents.

un·ac·cent·ed (ŭn'ăk'sĕn-tĭd) *adj.* **1.** Having no diacritical mark. Said of a word, syllable, or letter. **2.** Having weak or no stress, or lacking some other specified phonological feature. Said of a speech segment.

un·ac·com·mo·dat·ed (ŭn'ə-kŏm'ə-dā'tĭd) *adj.* **1.** Not adapted or accommodated. **2.** Lacking accommodations; unprovided.

un·ac·com·pa·nied (ŭn'ə-kŭm'pə-nēd) *adj.* **1.** Going or acting without a companion or companions. **2.** *Music.* Performed or scored without accompaniment.

un·ac·com·plished (ŭn'ə-kŏm'plĭsht) *adj.* **1.** Not completed or done; unfinished. **2.** Lacking special skills or abilities; unpolished, as in the social graces.

un·ac·count·a·ble (ŭn'ə-koun'tə-bəl) *adj.* **1.** Not able to be accounted for; inexplicable; mysterious. **2.** Free from being held to account; not responsible. **—un'ac·count'a·ble·ness** *n.* **—un'ac·count'a·bly** *adv.*

un·ac·cus·tomed (ŭn'ə-kŭs'təmd) *adj.* **1.** Not used to; not accustomed. **2.** Unfamiliar: *unaccustomed surroundings.*

u·na cor·da (ōō'nə kôr'də) With the soft pedal depressed. Used as a direction in music for piano. [Italian, "one string."]

un·a·dorned (ŭn'ə-dôrnd') *adj.* Without embellishment or artificiality; simple; genuine; pure.

un·a·dul·ter·at·ed (ŭn'ə-dŭl'tə-rā'tĭd) *adj.* Not mingled or diluted with extraneous matter; pure: *"They had real courage: the unadulterated liking of danger"* (Isak Dinesen).

un·ad·vised (ŭn'əd-vīzd') *adj.* **1.** Having received no advice; not informed. **2.** Ill-advised; rash; imprudent. **—un'ad·vis'ed·ly** (-vī'zĭd-lē) *adv.* **—un'ad·vis'ed·ness** *n.*

un·af·fect·ed (ŭn'ə-fĕk'tĭd) *adj.* **1.** Not changed, modified, or affected. **2.** Natural; sincere; genuine. **—See Synonyms at naive, sincere. —un'af·fect'ed·ly** *adv.* **—un'af·fect'ed·ness** *n.*

u·nai (yōō'nī, -nou, ōō'-) *n.* Also **u·nau.** A two-toed sloth of the genus *Choloepus.* See **sloth.** [French *unau*, from Tupi *unáu.*]

Un·a·las·ka Island (ŭn'ə-lăs'kə, ōō'nə-). An island 30 miles long and 6 to 30 miles wide in the Aleutians off southwestern Alaska.

un·al·ien·a·ble (ŭn-āl'yə-nə-bəl) *adj. Archaic.* Not to be separated; inalienable: *"that all men are endowed by their Creator with certain unalienable rights"* (Declaration of Independence).

un·al·loyed (ŭn'ə-loid') *adj.* **1.** Not in mixture with other metals; pure. **2.** Complete; unqualified: *an unalloyed success.*

un-A·mer·i·can (ŭn'ə-mĕr'ĭ-kən) *adj.* Considered contrary or threatening to the institutions or interests of the United States.

U·na·mu·no y Ju·go (ōō'nä-mōō'nō ē hōō'gō), **Miguel de.** 1864–1936. Spanish philosopher, essayist, and poet.

unan. unanimous.

un·a·neled (ŭn'ə-nēld') *adj. Archaic.* Not having received extreme unction.

u·na·nim·i·ty (yōō'nə-nĭm'ə-tē) *n.* The condition of being unanimous; complete agreement or accord.

u·nan·i·mous (yōō-năn'ə-məs) *adj. Abbr.* **unan.** **1.** Sharing the same opinions or views; being in complete harmony or accord. **2.** Based on or characterized by complete assent or agreement. [Latin *ūnanimus*, "of one mind" : *ūnus*, one (see **oino-** in Appendix*) + *animus*, soul, mind (see **ane-** in Appendix*).] **—u·nan'i·mous·ly** *adv.* **—u·nan'i·mous·ness** *n.*

un·an·swer·a·ble (ŭn-ăn'sər-ə-bəl, -än'sər-ə-bəl) *adj.* Impossible to answer; irrefutable; incontrovertible.

un·ap·peal·a·ble (ŭn'ə-pē'lə-bəl) *adj.* Not subject to appeal.

un·ap·proach·a·ble (ŭn'ə-prō'chə-bəl) *adj.* **1.** Not friendly; aloof; distant. **2.** Not accessible; inapproachable. **—un'ap·proach'a·ble·ness** *n.* **—un'ap·proach'a·bly** *adv.*

un·ap·pro·pri·at·ed (ŭn'ə-prō'prē-ā'tĭd) *adj.* **1.** Not designated for a specific use. **2.** Not possessed by or formally assigned to a particular person or organization.

un·arm (ŭn-ärm') *tr.v.* **-armed, -arming, -arms.** *Archaic.* To divest of armor or arms; disarm.

un·armed (ŭn'ärmd') *adj.* **1.** Lacking weapons or armor; defenseless. **2.** *Biology.* Having no thorns or spines.

un·as·sail·a·ble (ŭn'ə-sā'lə-bəl) *adj.* **1.** Not capable of being disputed or disproven; undeniable; unquestionable. **2.** Not capable of being attacked or seized successfully; impregnable. **—un'as·sail'a·ble·ness** *n.* **—un'as·sail'a·bly** *adv.*

un·as·sist·ed (ŭn'ə-sĭs'tĭd) *adj.* **1.** Not assisted; unaided. **2.** *Baseball.* Designating a play handled by only one fielder.

un·as·sum·ing (ŭn'ə-sōō'mĭng) *adj.* Not pretentious, boastful, or ostentatious; modest. **—un'as·sum'ing·ly** *adv.*

un·at·tached (ŭn'ə-tăcht') *adj.* **1.** Not attached or joined, especially to surrounding tissue: *unattached earlobes.* **2. a.** Not committed to or dependent upon a person, group, or organization. **b.** Not engaged or married. **3.** *Law.* Not possessed or seized as security.

un·at·test·ed (ŭn'ə-tĕs'tĭd) *adj.* Not attested. Used in linguistic descriptions, as in the etymologies of this Dictionary, to des-

ignate a form whose existence is not established by documentary evidence but is reliably inferred from comparative evidence.

u·na vo·ce (yōō'nə vō'sē). *Latin.* With one voice; unanimously.

un·a·void·a·ble (ŭn'ə-voi'də-bəl) *adj.* **1.** Not able to be avoided; inevitable. **2.** Not able to be voided or nullified. **—un'a·void'a·bil'i·ty, un'a·void'a·ble·ness** *n.* **—un'a·void'a·bly** *adv.*

un·a·ware (ŭn'ə-wâr') *adj.* Not aware or cognizant. **—adv.** Unawares.

Usage: **Unaware,** followed by *of* (expressed or implied), is the adjectival form modifying a noun or pronoun or following a linking verb: *Unaware of the difficulty, I went ahead. He was unaware of my presence.* The adverb *unawares* occurs in these typical examples: *The rain caught them unawares* (without warning). *They came upon it unawares* (without design or plan).

un·a·wares (ŭn'ə-wârz') *adv.* **1.** By surprise; unexpectedly: *"Sorrow comes to all, and to the young it comes with bittered agony because it takes them unawares"* (Lincoln). **2.** Without forethought or plan. **—See Usage note at unaware.**

unb. *Bookbinding.* unbound.

un·backed (ŭn'băkt') *adj.* **1.** Lacking backing or support. **2.** Not having a back, as a bench. **3.** Never ridden, as a horse.

un·bal·ance (ŭn'băl'əns) *tr.v.* **-anced, -ancing, -ances. 1.** To upset the balance, stability, or equilibrium of. **2.** To derange (the mind). **—n.** The condition of being unbalanced.

un·bal·anced (ŭn'băl'ənst) *adj.* **1.** Not in balance or in proper balance. **2. a.** Mentally deranged. **b.** Not of sound judgment; erratic; irrational. **3.** *Bookkeeping.* Not adjusted so that debit and credit correspond.

un·bal·last·ed (ŭn'băl'ə-stĭd) *adj.* **1.** Not stabilized or properly stabilized by ballast. **2.** Unsteady; wavering.

un·bar (ŭn'bär') *v.* **-barred, -barring, -bars. —tr.** To remove the bar or bars from. **—intr.** To become unbarred; open.

un·bat·ed (ŭn'bā'tĭd) *adj.* **1.** Unabated. **2.** *Archaic.* Not blunted by a guard on the tip, as a fencing foil.

unbd. *Bookbinding.* unbound.

un·bear·a·ble (ŭn'bâr'ə-bəl) *adj.* Unendurable; intolerable. **—un'bear'a·bly** *adv.*

un·beat·a·ble (ŭn'bē'tə-bəl) *adj.* Impossible to surpass or defeat. **—un'beat'a·bly** *adv.*

un·beat·en (ŭn'bēt'n) *adj.* **1.** Undefeated. **2.** Untrod. **3.** Not beaten or pounded.

un·be·com·ing (ŭn'bĭ-kŭm'ĭng) *adj.* **1.** Not appropriate, attractive, or flattering: *an unbecoming dress.* **2.** Not seemly; indecorous; improper: *an unbecoming remark.* **—See Synonyms at improper. —un'be·com'ing·ly** *adv.*

un·be·got·ten (ŭn'bĭ-gŏt'ən) *adj.* **1.** Not yet begotten; as yet unborn. **2.** Self-existent; eternal.

un·be·known (ŭn'bĭ-nōn') *adj.* Occurring or existing without the knowledge of; unknown. Usually used with *to.* [UN- + obsolete *beknown,* known, Middle English *beknowen,* past participle of *beknowen,* to get to know, Old English *becnāwan* : BE- + *cnāwan,* KNOW.]

un·be·knownst (ŭn'bĭ-nōnst') *adj.* Unbeknown. **—adv.** Without the knowledge of. Used with *to:* *"a haunted castle which ... unbeknownst to anyone, is still occupied"* (Patrick Dennis). [UNBEKNOWN + -*st* as in *amongst, amidst.*]

un·be·lief (ŭn'bĭ-lēf') *n.* Lack of belief or faith, especially in religious matters. **—un'be·liev'er** *n.*

un·be·liev·a·ble (ŭn'bĭ-lē'və-bəl) *adj.* Not to be believed; incredible. **—un'be·liev'a·bly** *adv.*

un·bend (ŭn'bĕnd') *v.* **-bent** (-bĕnt'), **-bending, -bends. —tr. 1.** To relax; unwind, as from mental tension. **2.** To release (a bow, for example) from flexure or tension. **3.** *Nautical.* To untie or loosen (a rope or sail). **4.** To straighten (something crooked or bent). **—intr. 1.** To become less tense; relax. **2.** To become less strict. **3.** To become straight.

un·bend·ing (ŭn'bĕn'dĭng) *adj.* Resolute; uncompromising.

un·bi·ased (ŭn'bī'əst) *adj.* Also **un·bi·assed.** Without bias or prejudice; impartial. See Synonyms at **fair.** **—un'bi'ased·ly** *adv.* **—un'bi'ased·ness** *n.*

un·bid·den (ŭn'bĭd'n) *adj.* Also **un·bid** (-bĭd'). Not invited; unasked: *unbidden company.*

un·bind (ŭn'bīnd') *tr.v.* **-bound** (-bound'), **-binding, -binds. 1.** To untie or unfasten, as wrappings or bindings. **2.** To release from restraints or bonds; to free.

un·blenched (ŭn'blĕncht') *adj.* Undaunted.

un·blessed (ŭn'blĕst') *adj.* Also **un·blest. 1.** Deprived of a blessing. **2.** Unholy; evil.

un·blink·ing (ŭn'blĭng'kĭng) *adj.* **1.** Without blinking. **2.** Without visible emotion. **3.** Fearless in facing reality: *His self-analysis was unblinking.* **—un'blink'ing·ly** *adv.*

un·blush·ing (ŭn'blŭsh'ĭng) *adj.* **1.** Without shame or remorse. **2.** Not blushing. **—See Synonyms at shameless.**

un·bod·ied (ŭn'bŏd'ēd) *adj.* **1.** Without body or form; incorporeal. **2.** Disembodied.

un·bolt (ŭn'bōlt') *tr.v.* **-bolted, -bolting, -bolts.** To release the bolts of (a door or gate); unlock.

un·bolt·ed (ŭn'bōl'tĭd) *adj.* Not sifted, as flour.

un·born (ŭn'bôrn') *adj.* Not yet in existence; not born.

un·bos·om (ŭn'bōōz'əm, -bōō'zəm) *v.* **-omed, -oming, -oms. —tr.** To confide, as one's thoughts or feelings. **—intr.** To reveal one's thoughts or feelings. **—un'bos'om·er** *n.*

un·bound (ŭn'bound') *adj.* **1.** *Abbr.* **unb., unbd.** Not bound, as a book. **2.** Freed from bonds or shackles; released.

un·bound·ed (ŭn'boun'dĭd) *adj.* **1.** Having no boundaries or limits. **2.** Not kept within bounds; uncontrolled; unrestrained: *unbounded enthusiasm.* **—un'bound'ed·ly** *adv.*

un·bowed (ŭn'boud') *adj.* **1.** Not bowed; unbent. **2.** Not subdued; unyielding: *"My head is bloody but unbowed."* (W.E. Henley).
un·brace (ŭn'brās') *tr.v.* **-braced, -bracing, -braces.** **1.** To set free by removing bands or braces. **2.** To release from tension; relax. **3.** To weaken; make slack.
un·bred (ŭn'brĕd') *adj.* **1.** Ill-bred; impolite. **2.** Not taught or instructed; untaught. **3.** *Obsolete.* Not begotten.
un·bri·dled (ŭn'brī'dəld) *adj.* **1.** Not wearing or fitted with a bridle. **2.** Unrestrained; uncontrolled. **—un'bri'dled·ly** *adv.*
un·bro·ken (ŭn'brō'kən) *adj.* Also **un·broke** (-brōk'). **1.** Not broken or tampered with; intact. **2.** Not violated or breached. **3.** Uninterrupted; continuous; even. **4.** Not tamed or broken to harness, as a horse. **5.** Not disordered or disorganized. **—un'bro'ken·ly** *adv.* **—un'bro'ken·ness** *n.*
un·buck·le (ŭn'bŭk'əl) *tr.v.* **-led, -ling, -les.** To loosen or undo the buckle or buckles of.
un·bur·den (ŭn'bûrd'n) *tr.v.* **-dened, -dening, -dens.** To free or relieve from a burden or trouble: *unburden one's mind.*
un·but·ton (ŭn'bŭt'n) *v.* **-toned, -toning, -tons.** *—tr.* **1.** To unfasten the button or buttons of. **2.** To free or remove (a button) from a buttonhole. **3.** To open as if by unbuttoning: *unbutton the hatches.* **4.** To expose or air: *unbutton one's secret thoughts.* *—intr.* To undo a button or buttons.
un·caged (ŭn'kājd') *adj.* **1.** Not confined in or as if in a cage. **2.** Released from a cage.
un·called-for (ŭn'kôld'fôr') *adj.* **1.** Not required or requested. **2.** Out of place; impertinent; unnecessary.
un·can·ny (ŭn'kăn'ē) *adj.* **-nier, -niest.** **1.** Exciting wonder and fear; inexplicable; strange: *an uncanny laugh.* **2.** So keen and perceptive as to seem preternatural: *uncanny insight.* —See Synonyms at **weird.** **—un'can'ni·ly** *adv.* **—un'can'ni·ness** *n.*
un·cap (ŭn'kăp') *v.* **-capped, -capping, -caps.** *—tr.* To remove the cap or covering of. *—intr.* To remove one's head covering as a sign of deference.
Un·cas (ŭng'kəs). 1588?–1683. American Indian leader; a chief of the Mohegan Pequots.
un·caused (ŭn'kôzd') *adj.* Existing without having been caused; spontaneous.
un·ceas·ing (ŭn'sē'sĭng) *adj.* Not ceasing or letting up; continuous. **—un'ceas'ing·ly** *adv.*
un·cer·e·mo·ni·ous (ŭn'sĕr'ə-mō'nē-əs) *adj.* **1.** Not ceremonious; informal. **2.** Without the due formalities; abrupt. **—un'cer'e·mo'ni·ous·ly** *adv.*
un·cer·tain (ŭn'sûrt'n) *adj.* **1.** Not known or established; questionable; doubtful: *an uncertain outcome.* **2.** Not determined; vague; undecided: *uncertain plans.* **3.** Not having sure knowledge. **4.** Subject to change; variable: *uncertain weather.* **5.** Unsteady; fitful: *uncertain light.* **—un'cer'tain·ly** *adv.*
un·cer·tain·ty (ŭn'sûrt'n-tē) *n., pl.* **-ties.** Also **un·cer·tain·ness** (-nĭs) (for sense 1). **1.** The condition of being in doubt; lack of certainty. **2.** Something that is uncertain.
Synonyms: *uncertainty, doubt, dubiety, skepticism, suspicion, mistrust.* These nouns all involve the condition of being unsure about something or someone. *Uncertainty, doubt,* and *dubiety* are interchangeable in this sense in many contexts. Usually they imply a questioning state of mind that causes a person to hesitate in accepting some premise or in making a decision. *Skepticism* generally suggests a habitual tendency to question and demand proof of truth, merit, or the like before committing oneself. More than the preceding terms, *suspicion* and *mistrust* imply rather intense resistance to belief or acceptance, arising more from a specific lack of trust than from mere tentativeness of feeling. *Mistrust,* the stronger of the two terms, especially suggests a feeling that the person or thing in question is wrong, evil, or otherwise unworthy of confidence.
uncertainty principle. The quantum mechanical principle that the product of the uncertainties in the values of certain related variables, as of the position and momentum of a particle, is greater than or equal to Planck's constant. Also called "Heisenberg uncertainty principle," "principle of indeterminacy."
un·chain (ŭn'chān') *tr.v.* **-chained, -chaining, -chains.** To release from a chain or bond; set free.
un·change·a·ble (ŭn'chān'jə-bəl) *adj.* Not capable of being altered; immutable.
un·charged (ŭn'chärjd') *adj.* **1.** Not loaded. Said of weapons. **2.** *Law.* Not formally accused. **3.** Lacking electric charge.
un·char·i·ta·ble (ŭn'chăr'ə-tə-bəl) *adj.* Not charitable or generous; unkind. **—un'char'i·ta·ble·ness** *n.* **—un'char'i·ta·bly** *adv.*
un·chart·ed (ŭn'chär'tĭd) *adj.* Not charted or recorded on a map or plan; unexplored; unknown.
un·chaste (ŭn'chāst') *adj.* Not chaste or modest. **—un'chaste'ly** *adv.* **—un'chaste'ness, un'chas'ti·ty** (-chăs'tə-tē) *n.*
un·chris·tian (ŭn'krĭs'chən) *adj.* **1.** Not Christian. **2.** Not in accordance with the Christian spirit. **3.** Uncivilized.
un·church (ŭn'chûrch') *tr.v.* **-churched, -churching, -churches.** **1.** To expel from a church or from church membership. **2.** To deprive (a congregation or sect) of the status of a church.
un·cial (ŭn'shəl, -shē-əl) *adj.* Also **Un·cial.** Of or pertaining to a style of writing characterized by somewhat rounded capital letters and found especially in Greek and Latin manuscripts of the fourth to the eighth centuries A.D. *—n.* Also **Un·cial.** **1.** The uncial style or hand. **2.** An uncial letter. [Late Latin *unciāles (litterae),* "letters of an inch long" (applied loosely by Saint Jerome to uncial letters), plural of Latin *unciālis,* of an inch, from *uncia,* a 12th part, ounce, inch, from *ūnus,* one. See **oino-** in Appendix.*]
un·ci·form (ŭn'sə-fôrm') *adj.* Hook-shaped. [New Latin *unciformis* : Latin *uncus,* hook (see **uncinus**) + -FORM.]

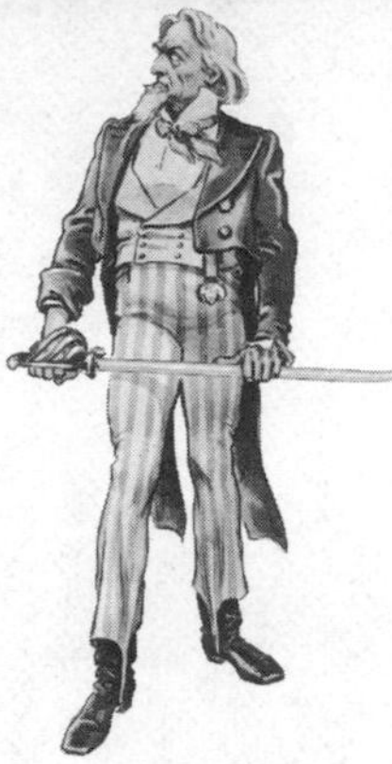
Uncle Sam
As depicted in an 1898 cartoon by Joseph Keppler

un·ci·nate (ŭn'sə-nāt', -nĭt) *adj.* Hooked at the tip. [Latin *uncīnātus,* from *uncīnus,* hook, UNCINUS.]
un·ci·nus (ŭn'sī'nəs) *n., pl.* **-ni** (-nī'). A small hooklike structure, such as one of the setae of certain annelid worms. [New Latin, from Latin, hook, barb, from *uncus,* hook. See **ank-** in Appendix.*]
un·cir·cum·cised (ŭn'sûr'kəm-sīzd') *adj.* **1.** Not circumcised. **2.** Not Jewish; Gentile. **3.** Heathen.
un·cir·cum·ci·sion (ŭn'sûr'kəm-sĭzh'ən) *n.* **1.** The state of not being circumcised. **2.** Those who have not been circumcised; in the Scriptures, the Gentiles.
un·civ·il (ŭn'sĭv'əl) *adj.* **1.** Impolite; discourteous; rude. **2.** Uncivilized; barbarous. **—un'civ'il·ly** *adv.*
un·civ·i·lized (ŭn'sĭv'ə-līzd') *adj.* Not civilized; barbarous.
un·clad (ŭn'klăd') *adj.* Not wearing clothes; naked.
un·clasp (ŭn'klăsp', -kläsp') *v.* **-clasped, -clasping, -clasps.** *—tr.* **1.** To release or loosen the clasp of. **2.** To release or loosen from a clasp or embrace. *—intr.* **1.** To become unfastened. **2.** To let go; release or relax a clasp or grasp.
un·class·i·fied (ŭn'klăs'ə-fīd') *adj.* Not placed or included in a class or category.
un·cle (ŭng'kəl) *n.* **1.** *Abbr.* **u., U. a.** The brother of one's mother or father. **b.** The husband of one's aunt. **2.** A form of respectful address to an older man, used especially by children. **3.** One who counsels. **4.** *Slang.* A pawnbroker. *—interj. Slang.* Used to express surrender: *They beat him until he cried uncle.* [Middle English *uncle,* from Old French *oncle,* from Late Latin *aunculus,* variant of Latin *avunculus,* maternal uncle. See **awo-** in Appendix.*]
un·clean (ŭn'klēn') *adj.* **-cleaner, -cleanest.** **1.** Not clean; foul or dirty. **2.** Morally defiled; unchaste. **3.** Ceremonially impure.
un·clean·ly (ŭn'klĕn'lē) *adj.* **-lier, -liest.** Unclean. *—adv.* (ŭn'klēn'lē). In an unclean manner. **—un'clean'li·ness** (ŭn'klĕn'lē-nĭs) *n.*
un·clear (ŭn'klîr') *adj.* **-clearer, -clearest.** Not clearly defined; not sharp or explicit.
un·clench (ŭn'klĕnch') *v.* **-clenched, -clenching, -clenches.** *—tr.* To loosen from a clenched position; relax; open: *unclench one's fists.* *—intr.* To become unclenched.
Uncle Sam. *Abbr.* **U.S.** A personification of the U.S. Government, represented as a tall, thin man with a white beard and wearing a blue swallow-tailed coat, red-and-white-striped trousers, and a tall hat with a band of stars. [Extension from *U.S.* (for *U*nited *S*tates); said to be a jocular interpretation of this abbreviation (stamped on U.S. Army supply packages during the War of 1812) as initials of the inspector Samuel Wilson, nicknamed Uncle Sam.]
Uncle Tom. A Negro who is held to be humiliatingly subservient or deferential to whites. [After the Negro slave in *Uncle Tom's Cabin* (1851–52), novel by Harriet Beecher Stowe.]
un·cloak (ŭn'klōk') *tr.v.* **-cloaked, -cloaking, -cloaks.** **1.** To remove a cloak or cover from. **2.** To expose; reveal.
un·close (ŭn'klōz') *v.* **-closed, -closing, -closes.** *—tr.* To open or disclose. *—intr.* To become opened or disclosed.
un·clothe (ŭn'klōth') *tr.v.* **-clothed** or **-clad** (-klăd'), **-clothing, -clothes.** To remove the clothing or cover from; to strip.
un·co (ŭng'kō) *adj. Scottish.* So unusual as to be surprising; uncanny. *—n., pl.* **uncos.** *Scottish.* **1.** An unusual or amazing person. **2.** A stranger. **3.** *Plural.* News. *—adv. Scottish.* To an excessive degree; remarkably. [Middle English (Scottish) *unkow,* variant of UNCOUTH.]
un·coil (ŭn'koil') *v.* **-coiled, -coiling, -coils.** *—tr.* To unwind; untwist. *—intr.* To become unwound or untwisted.
un·coined (ŭn'koind') *adj.* **1.** Not minted. **2.** Not artificial or counterfeit.
un·com·fort·a·ble (ŭn'kŭmf'tə-bəl, -kŭm'fər-tə-bəl) *adj.* **1.** Experiencing discomfort; uneasy. **2.** Causing discomfort; disquieting. **—un'com'fort·a·ble·ness** *n.* **—un'com'fort·a·bly** *adv.*
un·com·mer·cial (ŭn'kə-mûr'shəl) *adj.* **1.** Not engaged in or involving trade or commerce. **2.** Not in accordance with the spirit or methods of commerce; not businesslike.
un·com·mit·ted (ŭn'kə-mĭt'ĭd) *adj.* Not pledged to a specific cause or course of action.
un·com·mon (ŭn'kŏm'ən) *adj.* **-moner, -monest.** **1.** Not common; unusual; rare. **2.** Wonderful; remarkable. **—un'com'mon·ly** *adv.* **—un'com'mon·ness** *n.*
un·com·mu·ni·ca·tive (ŭn'kə-myōō'nĭ-kā'tĭv, -nĭ-kə-tĭv) *adj.* Not disposed to be communicative; taciturn; reserved. See Synonyms at **silent.** **—un'com·mu'ni·ca'tive·ly** *adv.* **—un'com·mu'ni·ca'tive·ness** *n.*
Un·com·pah·gre Peak (ŭn'kəm-pä'grē). The highest (14,306 feet) of the San Juan Mountains in southwest-central Colorado.
un·com·pli·men·ta·ry (ŭn'kŏm-plə-mĕn'trē, -mĕn'tə-rē) *adj.* Rather insulting; derogatory.
un·com·pro·mis·ing (ŭn'kŏm'prə-mī'zĭng) *adj.* Not granting concessions; inflexible; rigid. **—un'com'pro·mis'ing·ly** *adv.*
un·con·cern (ŭn'kən-sûrn') *n.* **1.** Lack of interest; indifference; apathy. **2.** Lack of worry or apprehensiveness.
un·con·cerned (ŭn'kən-sûrnd') *adj.* **1.** Not interested; indifferent. **2.** Not anxious or apprehensive; unworried. —See Synonyms at **indifferent.** **—un'con·cern'ed·ly** (-kən-sûr'nĭd-lē) *adv.* **—un'con·cern'ed·ness** (-kən-sûr'nĭd-nĭs) *n.*
un·con·di·tion·al (ŭn'kən-dĭsh'ən-əl) *adj.* Without conditions or limitations; absolute. **—un'con·di'tion·al·ly** *adv.*
un·con·di·tioned (ŭn'kən-dĭsh'ənd) *adj.* **1.** Unconditional; unrestricted. **2.** *Psychology.* Not the result of conditioning.
unconditioned response. A response evoked by a stimulus before the initiation of a learning or conditioning process. Formerly called "unconditioned reflex."

ă pat/ā pay/âr care/ä father/b bib/ch church/d deed/ĕ pet/ē be/f fife/g gag/h hat/hw which/ĭ pit/ī pie/îr pier/j judge/k kick/l lid, needle/m mum/n no, sudden/ng thing/ŏ pot/ō toe/ô paw, for/oi noise/ou out/ŏŏ took/ōō boot/p pop/r roar/s sauce/sh ship, dish/

unconditioned stimulus. A stimulus that evokes a certain response before the initiation of a conditioning process.

un·con·form·a·ble (ŭn'kən-fôr'mə-bəl) *adj.* **1.** Not conforming or capable of conforming. **2.** *Geology.* Showing unconformity. —**un'con·form'a·bil'i·ty, un'con·form'a·ble·ness** *n.* —**un'con·form'a·bly** *adv.*

un·con·for·mi·ty (ŭn'kən-fôr'mə-tē) *n., pl.* **-ties. 1.** Lack of conformity; nonconformity. **2.** *Geology.* An eroded space, or space caused by lack of deposit that separates younger strata from older rocks.

un·con·nect·ed (ŭn'kə-nĕk'tĭd) *adj.* **1.** Not joined or connected. **2.** Not coherent; disconnected. —**un'con·nect'ed·ly** *adv.* —**un'con·nect'ed·ness** *n.*

un·con·quer·a·ble (ŭn'kŏng'kər-ə-bəl) *adj.* Incapable of being overcome or defeated.

un·con·scion·a·ble (ŭn'kŏn'shən-ə-bəl) *adj.* **1.** Not restrained by conscience; unscrupulous. **2.** Beyond prudence or reason; immoderate; excessive. —**un'con'scion·a·ble·ness** *n.* —**un'con'scion·a·bly** *adv.*

un·con·scious (ŭn'kŏn'shəs) *adj.* **1.** Without conscious awareness; especially, psychological rather than physiological, and unavailable for direct conscious scrutiny: *unconscious resentment.* **2.** Temporarily lacking full awareness, as in a coma or deep sleep. **3.** Without conscious control; involuntary. —*n.* The division of the psyche not subject to direct conscious observation but inferred from its effects on conscious processes and behavior. —**un'con'scious·ly** *adv.* —**un'con'scious·ness** *n.*

un·con·sid·ered (ŭn'kən-sĭd'ərd) *adj.* Not reasoned or considered; unpremeditated; rash: *an unconsidered remark.*

un·con·sti·tu·tion·al (ŭn'kŏn-stə-to͞o'shən-əl, -tyo͞o'shən-əl) *adj.* Not in accord with the principles set forth in the constitution of a country; specifically, contrary to the U.S. Constitution. —**un'con·sti·tu'tion·al'i·ty** *n.* —**un'con·sti·tu'tion·al·ly** *adv.*

un·con·trol·la·ble (ŭn'kən-trō'lə-bəl) *adj.* Not able to be controlled or governed. —**un'con·trol'la·bil'i·ty, un'con·trol'la·ble·ness** *n.* —**un'con·trol'la·bly** *adv.*

un·con·ven·tion·al (ŭn'kən-vĕn'shən-əl) *adj.* Not adhering to convention; out of the ordinary. —**un'con·ven'tion·al'i·ty** *n.* —**un'con·ven'tion·al·ly** *adv.*

un·cork (ŭn'kôrk') *tr.v.* **-corked, -corking, -corks. 1.** To draw the cork from. **2.** To free from a sealed or constrained state: *uncork a secret.*

un·count·ed (ŭn'koun'tĭd) *adj.* **1.** Not counted. **2.** Unable to be counted; innumerable: *uncounted hosts of angels.*

un·coup·le (ŭn'kŭp'əl) *v.* **-led, -ling, -les.** —*tr.* **1.** To disconnect (something coupled): *uncouple railroad cars.* **2.** To set loose; release; unleash. —*intr.* To come or break loose.

un·couth (ŭn'ko͞oth') *adj.* **1.** Crude; unrefined; rude. **2.** Awkward or clumsy; ungraceful: *an uncouth gait.* **3.** *Archaic.* Foreign; unfamiliar. [Middle English *unc(o)uth,* unknown, strange, Old English *uncūth* : *un-,* not + *cūth,* known (see **gnō-** in Appendix*).] —**un'couth'ly** *adv.* —**un'couth'ness** *n.*

un·cov·e·nant·ed (ŭn'kŭv'ə-nən-tĭd) *adj.* **1.** Not bound by a covenant. **2.** Not promised or guaranteed by a covenant.

un·cov·er (ŭn'kŭv'ər) *v.* **-ered, -ering, -ers.** —*tr.* **1.** To remove the cover from; to unveil, uncap, or the like. **2.** To manifest or disclose; reveal. **3.** To remove the hat from (one's head) in respect or reverence. —*intr.* **1.** To remove a cover. **2.** To bare the head in respect or reverence.

un·cov·ered (ŭn'kŭv'ərd) *adj.* **1.** Having no cover or protection. **2.** Lacking the protection of insurance or collateral security. **3.** Bareheaded.

un·cre·at·ed (ŭn'krē-ā'tĭd) *adj.* **1.** Not created; not yet existing. **2.** Existing of itself; uncaused.

un·cross (ŭn'krôs', -krŏs') *tr.v.* **-crossed, -crossing, -crosses.** To move (one's legs, for example) from a crossed position.

unc·tion (ŭngk'shən) *n.* **1.** The act of anointing as part of a religious, ceremonial, or healing ritual. See **extreme unction. 2.** An ointment or oil; salve. **3.** Something that serves to soothe or restore; a balm. **4.** Affected or exaggerated earnestness, especially in language; unctuousness. [Middle English, from Latin *unctiō,* from *unguere* (past participle *unctus*), to anoint (see **ongw-** in Appendix*).]

unc·tu·ous (ŭngk'cho͞o-əs) *adj.* **1.** Having the quality or characteristics of oil or ointment; greasy; slippery to the touch. **2.** Containing or composed of oil or fat. **3.** Abundant in organic materials; soft and rich: *unctuous soil.* **4.** Characterized by affected, exaggerated, or insincere earnestness: *unctuous flattery.* [Middle English, from Medieval Latin *unctuōsus,* from Latin *unctum,* ointment, from *unctus,* past participle of *unguere,* to anoint. See **ongw-** in Appendix.*] —**unc'tu·ous·ly** *adv.* —**unc'tu·ous·ness, unc'tu·os'i·ty** (-ŏs'ə-tē) *n.*

un·cus (ŭng'kəs) *n., pl.* **unci** (ŭn'sī'). *Biology.* A hook-shaped part or process. [New Latin, from Latin, hook. See **ank-** in Appendix.*]

un·cut (ŭn'kŭt') *adj.* **1.** Not cut. **2.** *Bookbinding.* Having the page edge not slit or trimmed. **3.** Not ground to a specific shape. Said of a gemstone. **4.** Not made concise; unabridged.

un·damped (ŭn'dămpt') *adj.* **1.** Not tending toward a state of rest; not damped. Said of oscillations. **2.** Not stifled or discouraged; unchecked: *His ardor was undamped.*

un·daunt·ed (ŭn'dôn'tĭd, -dän'tĭd) *adj.* Not discouraged or disheartened; resolute; fearless. See Synonyms at **brave.** —**un'daunt'ed·ly** *adv.* —**un'daunt'ed·ness** *n.*

un·de·ceive (ŭn'dĭ-sēv') *tr.v.* **-ceived, -ceiving, -ceives.** To disabuse; to free from illusion or deception.

un·de·cid·ed (ŭn'dĭ-sī'dĭd) *adj.* **1.** Not yet determined or settled; open. **2.** Not having reached a decision; uncommitted. —**un'de·cid'ed·ly** *adv.* —**un'de·cid'ed·ness** *n.*

un·decked (ŭn'dĕkt') *adj.* **1.** Not decorated; unornamented. **2.** Having no deck. Said of a vessel.

un·de·mon·stra·tive (ŭn'dĭ-mŏn'strə-tĭv) *adj.* Not disposed to expressions of feeling; reserved. —**un'de·mon'stra·tive·ly** *adv.* —**un'de·mon'stra·tive·ness** *n.*

un·de·ni·a·ble (ŭn'dĭ-nī'ə-bəl) *adj.* **1.** Not able to be denied; irrefutable. **2.** Unquestionably good; outstanding; excellent. —**un'de·ni'a·bly** *adv.*

un·der (ŭn'dər) *prep.* **1.** In a lower position or place than: *a signature under a painting.* **2.** Beneath the surface of: *under the ground.* **3.** Beneath the assumed surface or guise of: *under a false name.* **4.** Less than; smaller than. **5.** Less than the required amount or degree of: *under voting age.* **6.** Inferior to in status or rank. **7.** Subject to the authority, rule, or control of: *under a dictatorship.* **8.** Subject to the supervision, instruction, or influence of: *under parental guidance.* **9.** Undergoing or receiving the effects of: *under intensive care.* **10.** Subject to the restraint or obligation of: *under contract.* **11.** Within the group or classification of: *listed under biology.* **12.** In the process of: *under discussion.* **13.** In view of; because of: *under these conditions.* **14.** With the authorization of; attested by; by virtue of: *under the king's seal.* **15.** Sowed or planted with: *an acre under oats.* —See Synonyms at **below.** —*adv.* **1.** In or into a place below or beneath. **2.** In or into a subordinate or inferior condition or position. **3.** So as to be covered or enveloped by. **4.** So as to be less than the required amount or degree. —**go under. 1.** To give oneself over to; yield, as to fatigue or a sedative. **2.** To fail or fall through, as a business deal. —*adj.* **1.** Located or moving beneath something else or on a lower level. **2.** Lower in rank, power, or authority; subordinate; inferior. **3.** Less than is required or customary; substandard. **4.** Lower in amount or degree. Used predicatively: *Keep your prices under.* **5.** Lower in strength or intensity; held in restraint or check. [Middle English *under,* Old English *under.* See **ṇdher** in Appendix.*]

under-. Indicates: **1.** Location below or under; for example, **underground, underclothes. 2.** Inferiority in rank or importance; for example, **undersecretary, underclassman. 3.** Degree, rate, or quantity that is lower or less than normal or proper; for example, **underdo, underestimate. 4.** Secrecy or treachery; for example, **undermine, underhand.** ***Note:*** Many compounds other than those entered here may be formed with *under-.* In forming compounds, *under-* is joined with the following element without space or a hyphen: *underrate; undergrow.* Note, however, that the adjective *under* may combine with other words as a unit modifier. In such cases, the words are joined by hyphens: *an under-the-table deal.* [Middle English *under-,* Old English *under-,* from *under,* UNDER.]

un·der·a·chieve (ŭn'dər-ə-chēv') *intr.v.* **-chieved, -chieving, -chieves.** To perform below the level indicated by tests of intelligence, aptitude, or ability, especially in schoolwork. —**un'der·a·chiev'er** *n.*

un·der·act (ŭn'dər-ăkt') *v.* **-acted, -acting, -acts.** —*tr.* **1.** To perform (a role) weakly. **2.** To understate (a role) intentionally. —*intr.* To perform in an understated way.

un·der·age (ŭn'dər-āj') *adj.* Below the customary or required age; especially, below the legal age, as for drinking or voting.

un·der·arm¹ (ŭn'dər-ärm') *adj.* Located, placed, or used under the arm. —*n.* The armpit.

un·der·arm² (ŭn'dər-ärm') *adj. Sports.* Executed with the hand kept below the level of the shoulder, as in bowling, tennis, baseball, or cricket. Also "underhand." —*adv.* With an underarm motion or delivery.

un·der·bel·ly (ŭn'dər-bĕl'ē) *n., pl.* **-lies. 1.** The lowest part of an animal's body. **2.** The vulnerable or weak part of something: *"the soft underbelly of Europe"* (Winston Churchill).

un·der·bid (ŭn'dər-bĭd') *v.* **-bid, -bidding, -bids.** —*tr.* **1.** To bid lower than (a competitor). **2.** *Bridge.* To bid less than the full value of (one's hand). —*intr.* To make an unnecessarily low bid. —**un'der·bid'der** *n.*

un·der·brush (ŭn'dər-brŭsh') *n.* Small trees, shrubs, or similar plants growing beneath the taller trees in a forest.

un·der·car·riage (ŭn'dər-kăr'ĭj) *n.* **1.** A supporting framework or structure, as for the body of an automobile. **2.** The landing gear of an aircraft.

un·der·charge (ŭn'dər-chärj') *tr.v.* **-charged, -charging, -charges. 1.** To charge (someone) less than is customary or required. **2.** To load (a firearm) with an insufficient charge. —*n.* (ŭn'dər-chärj'). An insufficient or improper charge.

un·der·class·man (ŭn'dər-klăs'mən, -kläs'mən) *n., pl.* **-men** (-mĭn). A student in the freshman or sophomore class at a secondary school or college.

un·der·clothes (ŭn'dər-klōz', -klōthz') *pl.n.* Also **un·der·cloth·ing** (-klō'thĭng). Clothes worn next to the skin, beneath one's outer clothing; underwear.

un·der·coat (ŭn'dər-kōt') *n.* Also **un·der·coat·ing** (-ĭng) (for sense 3). **1.** A coat worn beneath another coat. **2.** A covering of short hairs or fur concealed by the longer outer hairs of an animal's coat. **3. a.** A coat of sealing material applied to a surface before the topcoat is applied. **b.** A tarlike substance sprayed on the underside of an automobile to prevent rusting. —*tr.v.* **undercoated, -coating, -coats.** To apply an undercoat.

un·der·cool (ŭn'dər-ko͞ol') *tr.v.* **-cooled, -cooling, -cools.** To **supercool** *(see).*

un·der·cov·er (ŭn'dər-kŭv'ər) *adj.* Performed or occurring in secret: *an undercover investigation.*

un·der·croft (ŭn'dər-krôft', -krŏft') *n.* A crypt. [Middle English *under croft* : UNDER + *croft(e),* vault, from Medieval Latin *crupta,* variant of Latin *crypta,* CRYPT.]

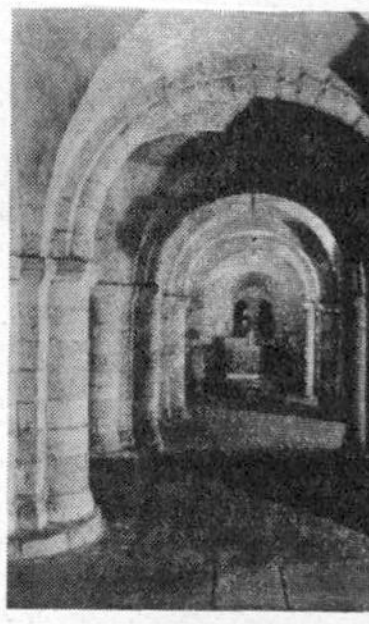

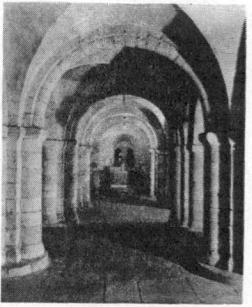

undercroft

un·der·cur·rent (ŭn′dər-kûr′ənt) *n.* **1.** A current, as of air or water, below another current or beneath a surface. **2.** An underlying tendency, force, or influence often contrary to what is superficially evident; intimation: *"the Gaucho began to talk, calmly but with an undercurrent of passion"* (Thomas Pynchon).

un·der·cut (ŭn′dər-kŭt′) *v.* **-cut, -cutting, -cuts.** —*tr.* **1.** To make a cut under or below. **2.** To create an overhang by cutting material away from, as in carving. **3.** To sell at a lower price than or to work for lower wages or fees than (a competitor). **4.** To anticipate or pre-empt the province or effectiveness of (a rival) by swift or unexpected action; undermine. **5.** *Sports.* **a.** To impart backspin to (a ball) by striking downward as well as forward, as in golf and baseball. **b.** To cut or slice (a ball) with an underarm stroke, as in tennis. —*intr.* To undercut someone or something. —*n.* **1.** A cut made in the under part to remove material. **2.** The material so removed. **3.** A notch cut in a tree to direct its fall and insure a clean break. **4.** *Chiefly British.* The tenderloin of beef; fillet. **5.** *Sports.* **a.** A spin given to a ball opposite to its direction of flight, a **backspin** *(see).* **b.** A cut or slice made with an underarm motion. —*adj.* Having undercuts in, as a sculpture or a relief.

un·der·de·vel·oped (ŭn′dər-dĭ-vĕl′əpt) *adj.* **1.** Not adequately or normally developed; immature; deficient: *an underdeveloped mind in an underdeveloped body.* **2.** *Photography.* Left in a developing solution for too short a time to produce a normal degree of contrast. **3.** Industrially or economically backward; having potential but not yet self-sufficient.

un·der·do (ŭn′dər-do͞o′) *tr.v.* **-did** (-dĭd′), **-done** (-dŭn′), **doing, -does** (-dŭz′). **1.** To do or effect to an insufficient degree. **2.** To cook inadequately or lightly: *She underdid the roast.*

un·der·dog (ŭn′dər-dôg′, -dŏg′) *n.* **1.** One who is expected to lose a contest or struggle, as in sports or politics. **2.** One who is at a disadvantage.

un·der·draw·ers (ŭn′dər-drôrz′) *pl.n.* Shorts or briefs worn as undergarments, especially those for a man; underpants.

un·der·dress (ŭn′dər-drĕs′) *n.* **1.** Apparel worn beneath outer garments; underclothing. **2.** An outer garment worn as part of a costume or suit, such as a dress beneath a tunic or coat.

un·der·dressed (ŭn′dər-drĕst′) *adj.* Too informally dressed.

un·der·drive (ŭn′dər-drīv′) *n.* A gearing device causing the output drive shaft to rotate at a slower rate than the engine input shaft.

un·der·es·ti·mate (ŭn′dər-ĕs′tə-māt′) *tr.v.* **-mated, -mating, -mates.** To estimate too low the quantity, degree, or worth of. —*n.* (ŭn′dər-ĕs′tə-mĭt). An estimate that is or proves to be too low. —**un′der·es′ti·ma′tion** *n.*

Usage: *Underestimate,* like *minimize,* is sometimes misused in ways that can convey the opposite of the sense intended: *His great value to the firm cannot be underestimated* (intended sense, "cannot be overestimated" or "should not be underestimated"). *The threat of forest fires in the dry season can never be underestimated* (properly, *should never be*).

un·der·ex·pose (ŭn′dər-ĭk-spōz′) *tr.v.* **-posed, -posing, -poses.** To expose (film) to light for too short a time to produce normal image contrast. —**un′der·ex·po′sure** (-ĭk-spō′zhər) *n.*

un·der·feed (ŭn′dər-fēd′) *tr.v.* **-fed** (-fĕd′), **-feeding, -feeds.** **1.** To feed insufficiently. **2.** To supply (an engine) with or channel fuel from below.

un·der·foot (ŭn′dər-fo͝ot′) *adv.* **1.** Below or under the foot or feet; on the ground; directly below. **2.** In the way. —*adj.* **1.** Under the feet; on the ground. **2.** Low; base; downtrodden.

un·der·fur (ŭn′dər-fûr′) *n.* The dense, soft, fine fur beneath the coarse outer hairs of certain mammals.

un·der·gar·ment (ŭn′dər-gär′mənt) *n.* A garment that is worn under outer garments; especially, one worn next to the skin.

un·der·gird (ŭn′dər-gûrd′) *tr.v.* **-girt** (-gûrt′) or **-girded, -girding, -girds.** To gird, support, or strengthen from beneath.

un·der·glaze (ŭn′dər-glāz′) *n.* Coloring applied to pottery before it is glazed. —**un′der·glaze′** *adj.*

un·der·go (ŭn′dər-gō′) *tr.v.* **-went** (-wĕnt′), **-gone** (-gôn′, -gŏn′), **-going, -goes** (-gōz′). **1.** To experience; be subjected to. **2.** To endure; suffer; sustain. [Middle English *undergon,* to submit to, go through : *under,* UNDER + *gon,* GO.]

un·der·grad·u·ate (ŭn′dər-grăj′o͞o-ĭt) *n.* A college or university student who has not yet received a degree. —*adj.* **1.** Of, pertaining to, or characteristic of undergraduates. **2.** Having undergraduate standing.

un·der·ground (ŭn′dər-ground′) *adj.* **1.** Occurring, operating, or situated below the surface of the earth. **2.** Hidden or concealed; clandestine. **3.** Of or pertaining to an organization involved in secret or illegal activity. **4.** Of, pertaining to, or describing an avant-garde movement or its films, publications, and art, usually privately produced and of special appeal and often concerned with social or artistic experiment. —*n.* (ŭn′dər-ground′). **1.** A covert, often nationalist, organization fostering or planning hostile activities against, or the overthrow of, a government in power, such as an occupying military government. **2.** *British.* A subway system. Usually preceded by *the.* —*adv.* (ŭn′dər-ground′). **1.** Below the surface of the earth. **2.** In secret; stealthily.

underground railroad. **1.** A tunneled railroad system below the surface of the earth; subway. Also called "underground railway." **2.** *Capital* **U**, *capital* **R**. Before 1861 in the United States, a secret network of cooperation aiding fugitive slaves in reaching sanctuary in the free states or Canada.

un·der·grown (ŭn′dər-grōn′) *adj.* Not fully grown; puny.

un·der·growth (ŭn′dər-grōth′) *n.* **1. a.** Low-growing plants, saplings, and shrubs beneath trees in a forest: *"the baroque tangle of luxurious forest undergrowth"* (William Meyers). **b.** Something resembling this, as a growth of short, fine hairs beneath longer ones. **2.** The condition of being undergrown.

un·der·hand (ŭn′dər-hănd′) *adj.* **1.** Done in a treacherous or deceitful manner; sneaky; disreputable; base. **2. Underarm** *(see).* —See Synonyms at **dishonest, secret.** —*adv.* **1.** With an underhand movement. **2.** Slyly; secretly; clandestinely.

un·der·hand·ed (ŭn′dər-hăn′dĭd) *adj.* **1.** Underhand. **2.** Lacking the required number of workers or players; short-handed. —**un′der·hand′ed·ly** *adv.* —**un′der·hand′ed·ness** *n.*

un·der·hung (ŭn′dər-hŭng′) *adj.* **1. a.** Protruding from beneath. **b.** Supported by or lying over something that projects. **2.** Resting on or mounted along a supporting track, as a sliding door on rollers. **3.** *Machinery.* Underslung.

un·der·laid (ŭn′dər-lād′) *adj.* **1.** Placed or laid underneath. **2.** Supported or raised by something from beneath; having an underlay.

un·der·lay (ŭn′dər-lā′) *tr.v.* **-laid, -laying, -lays.** **1.** To put (one thing) under another. **2.** To provide with a base or sublining. **3.** *Printing.* To raise or support by underlays. —*n.* (ŭn′dər-lā′). **1.** Something underlaid, as felt under a carpet. **2.** *Printing.* A piece of paper or other material used under type to raise the level of a printing bed.

un·der·let (ŭn′dər-lĕt′) *tr.v.* **-let, -letting, -lets.** **1.** To lease for less than the proper value. **2.** To sublet.

un·der·lie (ŭn′dər-lī′) *tr.v.* **-lay** (-lā′), **-lain** (-lān′), **-lying, -lies.** **1.** To be located under or below. **2.** To be the support or basis of; account for: *Many facts underlie my decision.* **3.** *Finance.* To comprise a prior claim over: *Dividends for preferred stock underlie those of common stock.*

un·der·line (ŭn′dər-līn′, ŭn′dər-līn′) *tr.v.* **-lined, -lining, -lines.** **1.** To draw a line under; underscore, especially for distinguishing or emphasizing certain writing. **2.** To emphasize or stress. —*n.* (ŭn′dər-līn′). A line drawn under writing to indicate emphasis or italic type.

un·der·ling (ŭn′dər-lĭng) *n.* A subordinate; lackey.

un·der·lin·ing (ŭn′dər-lī′nĭng) *n.* **1.** The act of drawing a line or lines under; underscoring. **2.** Emphasis or stress, as in instruction or argument.

un·der·ly·ing (ŭn′dər-lī′ĭng) *adj.* **1.** Lying under or beneath something: *underlying strata.* **2.** Basic; fundamental. **3.** Implicit; hidden: *an underlying meaning.* **4.** *Finance.* Taking precedence; prior: *an underlying claim.*

un·der·mine (ŭn′dər-mīn′) *tr.v.* **-mined, -mining, -mines.** **1.** To dig a mine or tunnel beneath. **2.** To weaken by wearing away a base or foundation: *Water undermined the stone foundations.* **3.** To weaken, injure, or impair, often by degrees or imperceptibly; to sap: *Late hours undermine one's health.*

un·der·most (ŭn′dər-mōst′) *adj.* Lowest in position, rank, or place; bottom. —*adv.* Lowest.

un·der·neath (ŭn′dər-nēth′) *adv.* **1.** In a place beneath; below. **2.** On the lower face or underside. —*prep.* **1.** Under; below; beneath. **2.** Under the power or control of. —See Synonyms at **below.** —*adj.* Lower; under. —*n.* The part or side below or under. [Middle English *undernethe,* from Old English *underneothan* : UNDER + *neothan,* below (see **ni** in Appendix*).]

un·der·nour·ish (ŭn′dər-nûr′ĭsh) *tr.v.* **-ished, -ishing, -ishes.** To provide with insufficient quantity or quality of nourishment to sustain proper health and growth. —**un′der·nour′ish·ment** *n.*

un·der·pants (ŭn′dər-pănts′) *pl.n.* An undergarment worn over the loins and sometimes over the thighs; drawers; shorts.

un·der·pass (ŭn′dər-păs′, -päs′) *n.* A passage underneath something, especially a section of road that passes under another road or railroad.

un·der·pay (ŭn′dər-pā′) *tr.v.* **-paid, -paying, -pays.** To pay insufficiently or less than deserved.

un·der·pin (ŭn′dər-pĭn′) *tr.v.* **-pinned, -pinning, -pins.** **1.** To support from below, as with props, girders, masonry, or the like. **2.** To corroborate or substantiate.

un·der·pin·ning (ŭn′dər-pĭn′ĭng) *n.* **1.** Material or masonry used to support a structure, such as a wall. **2.** *Usually plural.* Undergarments or stays worn to support the shape of an outer garment, to enhance one's figure, or for activity such as sports. **3.** *Usually plural. Informal.* The legs.

un·der·play (ŭn′dər-plā′, ŭn′dər-plā′) *v.* **-played, -playing, -plays.** —*tr.* To act (a role) subtly or with restraint. —*intr.* To act a role subtly or with restraint.

un·der·price (ŭn′dər-prīs′) *tr.v.* **-priced, -pricing, -prices.** **1.** To price lower than the value. **2.** To undercut in price: *underprice a competitor.*

un·der·priv·i·leged (ŭn′dər-prĭv′ə-lĭjd) *adj.* Not having opportunities or advantages enjoyed by other members of one's community; deprived.

un·der·pro·duc·tion (ŭn′dər-prə-dŭk′shən) *n.* **1.** Production below full capacity. **2.** Production below demand.

un·der·proof (ŭn′dər-pro͞of′) *adj.* Having a smaller proportion of alcohol than **proof spirit** *(see).*

un·der·prop (ŭn′dər-prŏp′) *tr.v.* **-propped, -propping, -props.** To prop (something) from below; to support.

un·der·quote (ŭn′dər-kwōt′) *tr.v.* **-quoted, -quoting, -quotes.** **1.** To sell (goods) at a price lower than the official list or market price; undersell. **2.** To quote a lower price than (another).

un·der·rate (ŭn′dər-rāt′) *tr.v.* **-rated, -rating, -rates.** To rate too low; underestimate.

un·der·run (ŭn′dər-rŭn′) *tr.v.* **-ran** (-răn′), **-run, -running, -runs.** **1.** To run, pass, or go beneath. **2.** *Nautical.* To haul (a line or cable) up to a boat and examine or repair it.

un·der·score (ŭn′dər-skôr′, -skōr′) *tr.v.* **-scored, -scoring, -scores.** **1.** To underline. **2.** To emphasize or stress. —*n.* A line drawn under writing to indicate emphasis or italic type.

ă pat/ā pay/âr care/ä father/b bib/ch church/d deed/ĕ pet/ē be/f fife/g gag/h hat/hw which/ĭ pit/ī pie/îr pier/j judge/k kick/l lid, needle/m mum/n no, sudden/ng thing/ŏ pot/ō toe/ô paw, for/oi noise/ou out/o͝o took/o͞o boot/p pop/r roar/s sauce/sh ship, dish/

un·der·sea (ŭn′dər-sē′) *adj.* Pertaining to, existing, or created for use beneath the surface of the sea. —*adv.* (ŭn′dər-sē′). Also **un·der·seas** (-sēz′). Beneath the surface of the sea.
un·der·sec·re·tar·y (ŭn′dər-sĕk′rə-tĕr′ē) *n., pl.* **-ies.** An official directly subordinate to a Cabinet member.
un·der·sell (ŭn′dər-sĕl′) *tr.v.* **-sold** (-sōld′), **-selling, -sells. 1.** To sell for a lower price than. **2.** To sell at a price less than the actual value. —**un′der·sell′er** *n.*
un·der·set (ŭn′dər-sĕt′) *n.* An ocean undercurrent.
un·der·sexed (ŭn′dər-sĕkst′) *adj.* Having less sexual potency or desire than normal.
un·der·shirt (ŭn′dər-shûrt′) *n.* An upper undergarment, usually having short sleeves, worn next to the skin under a shirt.
un·der·shoot (ŭn′dər-sho͞ot′) *v.* **-shot** (-shŏt′), **-shooting, -shoots.** —*tr.* **1.** To shoot a missile short of (a target). **2.** *Aviation.* **a.** To start one's final approach to (a landing area) too low or too soon. **b.** To land an aircraft short of (a landing area). —*intr.* To shoot or to land short of a target or a landing area.
un·der·shot (ŭn′dər-shŏt′) *adj.* **1.** Driven by water passing from below, as a water wheel. **2.** Projecting from below.
un·der·shrub (ŭn′dər-shrŭb′) *n.* A low-growing shrub.
un·der·side (ŭn′dər-sīd′) *n.* The side or surface that is underneath; bottom side.
un·der·sign (ŭn′dər-sīn′) *tr.v.* **-signed, -signing, -signs.** To sign one's name at the bottom of (a letter or document).
un·der·signed (ŭn′dər-sīnd′) *adj.* **1.** Having placed one's signature at the bottom of a document. **2.** Having a signature at the bottom or the end. Said of documents. —*n.* The person or persons who have signed at the bottom of a document.
un·der·sized (ŭn′dər-sīzd′) *adj.* Also **un·der·size** (-sīz′). Being of subnormal or insufficient size.
un·der·skirt (ŭn′dər-skûrt′) *n.* **1.** A skirt worn under another; a petticoat. **2.** One skirt of a layered gown over which outer skirts are formed and draped.
un·der·sleeve (ŭn′dər-slēv′) *n.* **1.** A sleeve worn under another. **2.** An ornamental sleeve worn under another, designed to extend below or show through slashes in the outer sleeve.
un·der·slung (ŭn′dər-slŭng′) *adj.* Having springs attached to the axles from below. Said of a vehicle.
un·der·soil (ŭn′dər-soil′) *n.* Soil below the ground surface.
un·der·staffed (ŭn′dər-stăft′) *adj.* Having too small a staff; having insufficient personnel: *an understaffed hospital.*
un·der·stand (ŭn′dər-stănd′) *v.* **-stood** (-sto͝od′), **-standing, -stands.** —*tr.* **1.** To perceive and comprehend the nature and significance of; know: *"I don't pretend to understand the Universe—it's a great deal bigger than I am"* (Carlyle). **2.** To know thoroughly by close contact with or long experience of. **3. a.** To grasp or comprehend the meaning intended or expressed by (another): *"for thank God I can read and perhaps understand Shakespeare to his depths"* (Keats). **b.** To comprehend the language, sounds, form, or symbols of (any kind of expression): *"Understandest thou what thou readest?"* (Acts 8:30). **4.** To know and be tolerant or sympathetic toward (the needs, feelings, or views of another): *"For a man he must go with a woman, which women don't understand"* (Kipling). **5.** To learn indirectly, as by hearsay; gather; assume. **6.** To conclude; infer: *Am I to understand that you are staying the night?* **7.** To accept as an agreed fact; regard as definite: *It is understood that the fee will be five dollars.* —*intr.* **1.** To have understanding, knowledge, or comprehension: *"Hear and understand."* (Matthew 15:10). **2.** To learn indirectly or at secondhand; gather: *They were just married, or so I understand.* —See Synonyms at **apprehend.** [Middle English *understanden,* Old English *understandan.* See **stā-** in Appendix.*] —**un′der·stand′a·ble** *adj.* —**un′der·stand′a·bly** *adv.*
un·der·stand·ing (ŭn′dər-stăn′dĭng) *n.* **1.** The quality or condition of one who understands; comprehension; discernment. **2.** The faculty by which one understands; intelligence. **3.** Individual or specified judgment or outlook in a matter; opinion; interpretation. **4. a.** A compact implicit between two or more persons or groups. **b.** The matter implicit in such a compact. **5.** A reconciliation of differences; an agreement: *They finally reached an understanding.* —See Synonyms at **reason.** —*adj.* **1.** Having or characterized by comprehension, good sense, or discernment. **2.** Compassionate and sympathetic: *"Women liked him; he was so strong, and good, and understanding"* (Gertrude Stein). —**un′der·stand′ing·ly** *adv.*
un·der·state (ŭn′dər-stāt′) *v.* **-stated, -stating, -states.** —*tr.* **1.** To state with less completeness or truth than seems warranted by the facts. **2.** To express with restraint or lack of emphasis, especially ironically or for dramatic impact. **3.** To state (a number, quantity, or the like) that is too low: *understate one's age.* —*intr.* To give an understatement.
un·der·state·ment (ŭn′dər-stāt′mənt) *n.* **1.** A disclosure or statement that is less than complete. **2.** Intentional lack of emphasis in expression, as in irony.
un·der·stood (ŭn′dər-sto͝od′) *adj.* **1.** Agreed upon; assumed. **2.** Not expressed in writing; implied.
un·der·stra·tum (ŭn′dər-strā′təm, -străt′əm) *n., pl.* **-strata** (-strā′tə, -străt′ə) or **-tums.** A substratum.
un·der·stud·y (ŭn′dər-stŭd′ē) *v.* **-ied, -ying, -ies.** —*tr.* **1.** To study or know (a role) so as to be able to replace the regular actor or actress when required. **2.** To act as an understudy to. —*intr.* To be engaged in studying a role so as to be able to replace the regular actor or actress when required. —*n., pl.* **understudies. 1.** An actor or actress who understudies. **2.** Any person trained to do the work of another.
un·der·take (ŭn′dər-tāk′) *v.* **-took** (-to͝ok′), **-taken, -taking, -takes.** —*tr.* **1.** To take upon oneself; decide or agree to do: *undertake a task.* **2.** To pledge or commit oneself to: *"What I had undertaken was the whole care of her"* (Henry James). **3.** *Obsolete.* To accept combat with; take on. —*intr. Archaic.* To make oneself responsible. Used with *for.* [Middle English *undertaken,* to accept, take in hand : UNDER + TAKE.]
un·der·tak·er (ŭn′dər-tā′kər *for sense 1;* ŭn′dər-tā′kər *for sense 2*) *n.* **1.** One who undertakes a task or job; especially, an entrepreneur. **2.** One whose business it is to arrange for the burial or cremation of the dead and to assist at funeral rites; a mortician.
un·der·tak·ing (ŭn′dər-tā′kĭng) *n.* **1.** A task or assignment undertaken; an enterprise or venture. **2.** A guaranty, engagement, or promise. **3.** The profession or duties of an undertaker.
un·der-the-count·er (ŭn′dər-*th*ə-koun′tər) *adj.* Transacted or sold illicitly. Said especially of scarce or rationed goods.
un·der-the-ta·ble (ŭn′dər-*th*ə-tā′bəl) *adj.* Under-the-counter.
un·der·tint (ŭn′dər-tĭnt′) *n.* A slight or subtle tint.
un·der·tone (ŭn′dər-tōn′) *n.* **1.** A tone of low pitch or volume, especially of spoken sound. **2. a.** A pale or subdued color. **b.** A color applied under or seen through another color. **3.** An underlying or implied tendency or meaning; undercurrent.
un·der·tow (ŭn′dər-tō′) *n.* The seaward pull of receding waves breaking on a shore.
un·der·trick (ŭn′dər-trĭk′) *n. Card Games.* A trick, especially in bridge, the loss of which prevents a declarer from making his contract.
un·der·trump (ŭn′dər-trŭmp′) *intr.v.* **-trumped, -trumping, -trumps.** *Card Games.* To play a trump lower than another player's trump when trump has not been led.
un·der·val·ue (ŭn′dər-văl′yo͞o) *tr.v.* **-ued, -uing, -ues. 1.** To assign too low a value to; underestimate. **2.** To have too little regard or esteem for. —**un′der·val′u·a′tion** *n.*
un·der·vest (ŭn′dər-vĕst′) *n. British.* An undershirt.
un·der·wa·ter (ŭn′dər-wô′tər, -wŏt′ər) *adj.* Pertaining to, occurring, used, or performed beneath the surface of water. —**un′der·wa′ter** *adv.*
under way. 1. In motion or operation; started. **2.** Already commenced or initiated; in progress; afoot. **3.** *Nautical.* Not anchored and not moored to a fixed object.
un·der·wear (ŭn′dər-wâr′) *n.* Clothing worn under the outer clothes and next to the skin; underclothes.
un·der·weight (ŭn′dər-wāt′) *adj.* Weighing less than is normal, healthy, or required. —*n.* Insufficiency of weight.
un·der·went. Past tense of **undergo.**
un·der·wing (ŭn′dər-wĭng′) *n.* **1.** One of a pair of hind wings partially or wholly covered by the forewings, as in certain moths. **2.** Any of various moths of the genus *Calocala,* having brightly colored underwings.
un·der·wood (ŭn′dər-wo͝od′) *n.* Shrubs and small trees growing beneath taller trees; underbrush; undergrowth.
un·der·world (ŭn′dər-wûrld′) *n.* **1.** Any region, realm, or dwelling place conceived to be below the surface of the earth. **2.** The opposite side of the earth; the antipodes. **3.** *Greek & Roman Mythology.* The world of the dead, said to be below and separate from the world of the living; Hades. **4.** The part of society that is engaged in and organized for the purpose of crime and vice. **5.** *Archaic.* The world beneath the heavens; the earth.
un·der·write (ŭn′dər-rīt′) *v.* **-wrote** (-rōt′), **-written** (-rĭt′n), **-writing, -writes.** —*tr.* **1.** To write under; subscribe; especially, to sign or endorse (a document). **2.** To assume financial responsibility for; guarantee (an enterprise) against failure: *underwrite a theatrical production.* **3.** *Insurance.* **a.** To sign an insurance policy, thus assuming liability in case of specified losses. **b.** To insure. **c.** To insure against losses totaling (a given amount). **4.** *Finance.* To guarantee the purchase of (a full issue of stock or bonds); specifically, to agree to buy (the stock in a new enterprise not yet sold publicly) at a fixed time and price. —*intr.* To act as an underwriter; especially, to issue an insurance policy.
un·der·writ·er (ŭn′dər-rī′tər) *n. Abbr.* **UW 1.** *Insurance.* A person or firm engaged in an insurance business; specifically, an insurance agent who assesses the risk of enrolling an applicant for coverage or a policy. **2.** A person or company that guarantees the purchase of a full issue of stocks or bonds.
undescended testicle. A testicle that has remained within the inguinal canal and has not descended to the scrotum.
un·de·serv·ed·ly (ŭn′dĭ-zûr′vĭd-lē) *adv.* Unfairly or unjustifiably; regrettably; wrongly.
un·de·sign·ing (ŭn′dĭ-zī′nĭng) *adj.* Without ulterior motives; straightforward.
un·de·sir·a·ble (ŭn′dĭ-zīr′ə-bəl) *adj.* Not desirable; objectionable. —**un′de·sir′a·bil′i·ty** *n.* —**un′de·sir′a·bly** *adv.*
un·de·ter·mined (ŭn′dĭ-tûr′mĭnd) *adj.* **1.** Not yet determined; undecided. **2.** Not specifically known or ascertained.
un·dies (ŭn′dēz) *pl.n. Informal.* Underwear.
un·dine (ŭn-dēn′, ŭn′dēn′) *n.* A female water spirit who, according to Paracelsus, could earn a soul by marrying a mortal and bearing his child. [New Latin *Undīna,* from Latin *unda,* wave. See **wed-**[1] in Appendix.*]
un·di·rect·ed (ŭn′dĭ-rĕk′tĭd, -dī′rĕk′tĭd) *adj.* **1.** Not guided; without object or purpose. **2.** Having no prescribed destination, as an unaddressed letter.
un·dis·crim·i·nat·ing (ŭn′dĭs-krĭm′ə-nā′tĭng) *adj.* **1.** Indiscriminate. **2.** Lacking sensitivity, taste, or judgment.
un·dis·posed (ŭn′dĭs-pōzd′) *adj.* **1.** Not settled, removed, or resolved. Often used with *of.* **2.** Disinclined; unwilling.
un·do (ŭn′do͞o′) *v.* **-did** (-dĭd′), **-done** (-dŭn′), **-doing, -does** (-dŭz′). —*tr.* **1.** To reverse or erase; cancel; annul: *"The injury*

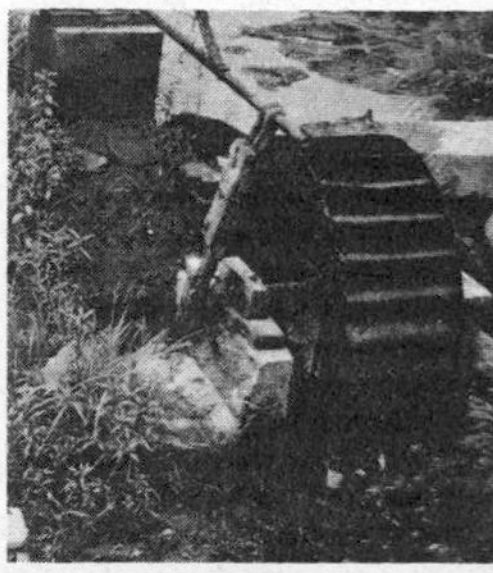

undershot
Water wheel on an Amish farm in Pennsylvania

of this . . . could never be undone" (Sterne). **2.** To untie, disassemble, or loosen: *undo a shoelace.* **3.** To open (a parcel, for example); unwrap. **4.** *Obsolete.* To solve or interpret; unravel. **5. a.** To cause the ruin or downfall of; destroy. **b.** To throw into confusion; unsettle. *—intr.* To come open or undone. [Middle English *undon,* from Old English *undōn,* to unfasten, untie, annul, destroy : UN- + *dōn,* to DO.] **—un·do'er** *n.*

un·do·ing (ŭn'dōō'ĭng) *n.* **1.** The act of reversing or annulling something accomplished; cancellation. **2.** The act of unfastening or loosening. **3. a.** The act of bringing to ruin. **b.** The cause or source of ruin; downfall: *"Kluck's undoing was his adherence to the principles of Klausewitz"* (Reginald Pound).

un·doubt·ed (ŭn'dou'tĭd) *adj.* Accepted as beyond question; undisputed. See Usage note at **doubtless.** **—un·doubt'ed·ly** *adv.*

un·draw (ŭn'drô') *tr.v.* **-drew** (-drōō'), **-drawn** (-drôn'), **-drawing, -draws.** To draw to one side, as a curtain.

un·dress (ŭn'drĕs') *v.* **-dressed, -dressing, -dresses.** *—tr.* **1.** To remove the clothing of; disrobe; strip: *"By this time all were stolen aside/To counsel and undress the Bride"* (Suckling). **2.** To remove the bandages from (a wound or burn, for example). *—intr.* To take off one's clothing; to strip. *—n.* **1.** Informal attire as distinguished from formal attire. **2.** Nakedness.

un·dressed (ŭn-drĕst') *adj.* **1. a.** Naked. **b.** Not fully dressed. **2.** Not specially treated or processed: *undressed leather.*

un·due (ŭn'dōō', -dyōō') *adj.* **1.** Exceeding what is appropriate or normal; excessive: *"I was grateful, without showing undue excitement"* (Katherine Mansfield). **2.** Not just, proper, or legal: *undue use of power.* **3.** Not yet payable or due.

un·du·lant (ŭn'jōō-lənt, ŭn'dyə-, ŭn'də-) *adj.* Resembling waves in occurrence, appearance, or motion.

undulant fever. A persistent and recurrent fever caused by bacteria of the genus *Brucella,* transmitted by contact with infected animals or by consuming infected meat or milk and marked by weakness and painful joints. Also called "brucellosis," "Malta fever," "Mediterranean fever."

un·du·late (ŭn'jōō-lāt', ŭn'dyə-, ŭn'də-) *v.* **-lated, -lating, -lates.** *—tr.* **1.** To cause to move in a smooth wavelike motion. **2.** To give a wavelike appearance or form to. *—intr.* **1.** To move in waves or with a wavelike or sinuous motion; to ripple. **2.** To have a wavelike appearance or form. —See Synonyms at **swing.** *—adj.* (ŭn'jōō-lĭt, -lāt', ŭn'dyə-, ŭn'də-). Also **un·du·la·ted** (-lā'tĭd). Having a wavy outline or appearance: *leaves with undulate margins.* [Late Latin *undulāre,* from *undula,* diminutive of Latin *unda,* wave. See **wed-**[1] in Appendix.*]

un·du·la·tion (ŭn'jōō-lā'shən, ŭn'dyə-, ŭn'də-) *n.* **1.** A regular rising and falling or movement to alternating sides; movement in waves. **2.** A wavelike form, outline, or appearance. **3.** One of a series of waves or wavelike segments; a pulsation.

un·du·ly (ŭn'dōō'lē, ŭn'dyōō'-) *adv.* **1.** Excessively; immoderately. **2.** In disregard of a legal or moral precept.

un·du·ti·ful (ŭn'dōō'tĭ-fəl, ŭn'dyōō'-) *adj.* Lacking a sense of duty; unreliable; disobedient.

un·dy·ing (ŭn'dī'ĭng) *adj.* Endless; everlasting; immortal.

un·earned (ŭn'ûrnd') *adj.* **1.** Not gained by work or service. **2.** Not deserved. **3.** Not yet earned: *unearned interest.*

unearned increment. The increase in property value resulting from factors independent of the owner, such as a general rise in demand for land, as opposed to increase of value earned directly by the efforts of the owner.

un·earth (ŭn'ûrth') *tr.v.* **-earthed, -earthing, -earths.** **1.** To bring up out of the earth; dig up; uproot. **2.** To bring to public notice; uncover.

un·earth·ly (ŭn'ûrth'lē) *adj.* **-lier, -liest.** **1.** Not of the earth; supernatural. **2.** Frighteningly weird and unaccountable; unnatural: *"a shriek so loud, piercing and unearthly . . . that the blood seemed to freeze in my veins"* (W.H. Hudson). **3.** Ridiculously unreasonable or uncustomary; absurd: *out of bed at an unearthly hour.* —See Synonyms at **weird.** **—un'earth'li·ness** *n.*

un·eas·y (ŭn'ē'zē) *adj.* **-ier, -iest.** **1.** Lacking ease, comfort, or a sense of security: *The farmers were uneasy until the crop was in.* **2.** Affording no ease or reassurance; difficult; delicate: *an uneasy calm.* **3.** Awkward or unsure in manner; constrained: *uneasy with strangers.* **—un'eas'i·ly** *adv.* **—un'eas'i·ness** *n.*

un·ed·u·cat·ed (ŭn'ĕj'ōō-kā'tĭd) *adj.* Not educated; especially, lacking in literacy. See Synonyms at **ignorant.**

un·em·ploy·a·ble (ŭn'ĭm-ploi'ə-bəl) *adj.* Not able to find or hold a job. *—n.* One who cannot be employed.

un·em·ployed (ŭn'ĭm-ploid') *adj.* **1.** Out of work; jobless. **2.** Not being used; idle. *—n.* A person who does not have a job. **—un'em·ploy'ment** *n.*

un·e·qual (ŭn'ē'kwəl) *adj.* **1.** Not the same in any measurable aspect, as extent or quantity. **2.** Not the same as another in rank or social position. **3.** Consisting of ill-matched opponents: *an unequal race.* **4.** Having unbalanced sides or parts; asymmetric. **5.** Not even or consistent; variable; irregular. **6.** Not having the required abilities; inadequate. Used with *to: "It was maddening to be unequal to many enterprises"* (D.H. Lawrence). *—n.* One that is unequal. **—un'e'qual·ly** *adv.*

un·e·qualed (ŭn'ē'kwəld) *adj.* Also **un·e·qualled.** Not matched or paralleled by others of its kind; unrivaled.

un·e·quiv·o·cal (ŭn'ĭ-kwĭv'ə-kəl) *adj.* Undisguised or unobscured; admitting of no doubt or misunderstanding; clear. **—un'e·quiv'o·cal·ly** *adv.*

un·err·ing (ŭn'ûr'ĭng, -ĕr'ĭng) *adj.* Committing no mistakes; consistently accurate; errorless. **—un'err'ing·ly** *adv.*

UNESCO (yōō-nĕs'kō) United Nations Educational, Scientific, and Cultural Organization.

un·es·sen·tial (ŭn'ə-sĕn'shəl) *adj.* Not necessary; not of importance; dispensable. *—n.* A nonessential.

un·e·ven (ŭn'ē'vən) *adj.* **-vener, -venest.** **1.** Not equal, as in size, length, or quality. **2.** Not consistent or uniform: *an uneven color.* **3.** Not smooth or level: *uneven surface of a cobblestone road.* **4.** Not straight or parallel: *uneven margins.* **5.** *Archaic.* Not fair or equitable. **6.** Designating an odd number. —See Synonyms at **rough.** **—un'e'ven·ly** *adv.* **—un'e'ven·ness** *n.*

un·e·vent·ful (ŭn'ĭ-vĕnt'fəl) *adj.* Lacking in significant events; without incident. **—un'e·vent'ful·ly** *adv.* **—un'e·vent'ful·ness** *n.*

un·ex·am·pled (ŭn'ĭg-zăm'pəld, -zäm'pəld) *adj.* Without precedent; unparalleled: *"Witchcraft blazed forth with unexampled virulence"* (Montague Summers).

un·ex·cep·tion·a·ble (ŭn'ĭk-sĕp'shən-ə-bəl) *adj.* Beyond the least reasonable objection; irreproachable. **—un'ex·cep'tion·a·ble·ness** *n.* **—un'ex·cep'tion·a·bly** *adv.*

un·ex·cep·tion·al (ŭn'ĭk-sĕp'shən-əl) *adj.* **1.** Not varying from a norm; usual; ordinary. **2.** Not subject to exceptions; absolute. **—un'ex·cep'tion·al·ly** *adv.*

Usage: *Unexceptional* is often confused with *unexceptionable,* for which it cannot be substituted except loosely. When the desired meaning is "not open to objection" or "above reproach," the term is *unexceptionable. Unexceptional* is not acceptable in that sense, according to 87 per cent of the Usage Panel.

un·ex·pect·ed (ŭn'ĭk-spĕk'tĭd) *adj.* Coming without warning; unforeseen. **—un'ex·pect'ed·ly** *adv.* **—un'ex·pect'ed·ness** *n.*

un·ex·pres·sive (ŭn'ĭk-sprĕs'ĭv) *adj.* **1.** Not conveying the meaning intended or the emotion felt. **2.** *Obsolete.* Inexpressible. **—un'ex·pres'sive·ly** *adv.* **—un'ex·pres'sive·ness** *n.*

un·fail·ing (ŭn'fā'lĭng) *adj.* **1.** Inexhaustible. **2.** Constant; unflagging. **3.** Incapable of error; infallible. **—un'fail'ing·ly** *adv.* **—un'fail'ing·ness** *n.*

un·fair (ŭn'fâr') *adj.* **-fairer, -fairest.** **1.** Not just or evenhanded; biased. **2.** Contrary to laws or conventions, especially in commerce; unethical. **—un'fair'ly** *adv.* **—un'fair'ness** *n.*

un·faith·ful (ŭn'fāth'fəl) *adj.* **1.** Not adhering to a pledge or contract; disloyal. **2.** Not true or constant to a sexual partner; specifically, guilty of adultery. **3.** Not justly representing or reflecting the original; inaccurate. **4.** *Obsolete.* Without or deficient in religious faith; unbelieving. —See Synonyms at **faithless.** **—un'faith'ful·ly** *adv.* **—un'faith'ful·ness** *n.*

un·fa·mil·iar (ŭn'fə-mĭl'yər) *adj.* **1.** Not within one's knowledge; strange. **2.** Not being acquainted; not conversant. Used with *with.* **—un'fa·mil'i·ar'i·ty** (-mĭl'yăr'ə-tē, -mĭl'ē-ăr'ə-tē) *n.* **—un'fa·mil'iar·ly** *adv.*

un·fas·ten (ŭn'făs'ən, -fä'sən) *v.* **-tened, -tening, -tens.** *—tr.* To separate the connected parts of; to unloose or open. *—intr.* To become loosened or separated.

un·fa·thered (ŭn'fä'*th*ərd) *adj.* **1.** Having no known father; illegitimate; bastard. **2.** Of uncertain origin or authenticity.

un·fa·vor·a·ble (ŭn'fā'vər-ə-bəl, -fā'vrə-bəl) *adj.* **1.** Not propitious. **2.** Adverse; opposed. **3.** Undesirable; disadvantageous. **—un'fa'vor·a·ble·ness** *n.* **—un'fa'vor·a·bly** *adv.*

un·feel·ing (ŭn'fē'lĭng) *adj.* **1.** Having no feeling or sensation; insentient. **2.** Not sympathetic; callous. **—un'feel'ing·ly** *adv.* **—un'feel'ing·ness** *n.*

un·feigned (ŭn'fānd') *adj.* Not simulated; genuine. See Synonyms at **sincere.** **—un'feign'ed·ly** (ŭn'fā'nĭd-lē) *adv.*

un·fin·ished (ŭn'fĭn'ĭsht) *adj.* **1.** Not brought to an end; incomplete: *unfinished business.* **2.** Not having received special processing; natural: *unfinished wood.*

un·fit (ŭn'fĭt') *adj.* **1.** Not meant or adapted for a given purpose; inappropriate. **2.** Below the required standard; unqualified. **3.** Not in good physical or mental health. *—tr.v.* **unfitted, -fitting, -fits.** To cause to be unsuited or unqualified; disqualify. **—un'fit'ly** *adv.* **—un'fit'ness** *n.*

un·fix (ŭn'fĭks') *tr.v.* **-fixed, -fixing, -fixes.** **1.** To detach from what secures; unfasten. **2.** To unsettle; disturb.

un·fledged (ŭn'flĕjd') *adj.* **1.** Not yet sufficiently developed to fly, as an immature bird still lacking flight feathers. **2.** Inexperienced, immature, or untried.

un·flinch·ing (ŭn'flĭn'chĭng) *adj.* Not betraying fear or indecision; unshrinking; resolute: *"He combines the steady unflinching aim . . . with the most supple adaptability of approach"* (Gilbert Highet). **—un'flinch'ing·ly** *adv.*

un·fold (ŭn'fōld') *v.* **-folded, -folding, -folds.** *—tr.* **1.** To open and spread out; extend (something folded). **2.** To remove the coverings from; disclose to view. **3.** To reveal gradually by written or spoken explanation; make known. *—intr.* **1.** To become spread out; open out. **2.** To be revealed gradually to the understanding.

un·for·get·ta·ble (ŭn'fər-gĕt'ə-bəl) *adj.* Earning a permanent place in the memory; memorable. **—un'for·get'ta·bly** *adv.*

un·formed (ŭn'fôrmd') *adj.* **1.** Having no definite shape or structure; unorganized. **2.** Not yet developed to maturity. **3.** Not yet given a physical existence; uncreated.

un·for·tu·nate (ŭn'fôr'chə-nĭt) *adj.* **1.** Characterized by undeserved lack of good fortune; unlucky. **2.** Causing misfortune; disastrous. **3.** Regrettable; deplorable: *an unfortunate lack of good manners.* *—n.* A victim of bad luck, disaster, poverty, or the like. **—un'for'tu·nate·ly** *adv.* **—un'for'tu·nate·ness** *n.*

un·found·ed (ŭn'foun'dĭd) *adj.* **1.** Not yet established. **2.** Not based on fact or sound observation; groundless. **—un'found'ed·ly** *adv.* **—un'found'ed·ness** *n.*

un·fre·quent·ed (ŭn'frĭ-kwĕn'tĭd, ŭn'frē'kwən-tĭd) *adj.* Receiving few or no visitors; unpatronized.

un·friend·ed (ŭn'frĕn'dĭd) *adj.* Having no friends.

un·friend·ly (ŭn'frĕnd'lē) *adj.* **-lier, -liest.** **1.** Not disposed to friendship; hostile; disagreeable. **2.** Indicating a bad prospect; unfavorable. **—un'friend'li·ness** *n.*

un·frock (ŭn'frŏk') *tr.v.* **-frocked, -frocking, -frocks. 1.** To strip of priestly privileges and functions. **2.** To deprive of the right to practice a profession. Also "defrock."

un·fruit·ful (ŭn'fro͞ot'fəl) *adj.* **1.** Not bearing fruit or offspring; barren. **2.** Not productive of good results; unprofitable or unsuccessful. —See Synonyms at **sterile.** —**un'fruit'ful·ly** *adv.* —**un'fruit'ful·ness** *n.*

un·furl (ŭn'fûrl') *v.* **-furled, -furling, -furls.** —*tr.* To spread or open out; unroll: *"Grandmother, unfurling an immense cloak of dove-colored cut velvet"* (Katherine Anne Porter). —*intr.* To become spread or opened out.

un·gain·ly (ŭn'gān'lē) *adj.* **-lier, -liest. 1.** Without grace or ease of movement; clumsy. **2.** Difficult to move or use; unwieldy. —See Synonyms at **awkward.** —**un'gain'li·ness** *n.*

Un·ga·va (ŭng-gā'və, -gä'və). The name sometimes used for the region of northern Quebec Province, Canada, roughly coextensive with New Quebec.

Un·ga·va Bay (ŭng-gā'və, -gä'və). An inlet of Hudson Strait extending 200 miles into northern Quebec, Canada.

Un·ga·va Peninsula (ŭng-gā'və, -gä'və). A peninsula of northern Quebec, Canada, extending northward for 400 miles between Hudson and Ungava bays.

un·gen·er·ous (ŭn'jĕn'ər-əs) *adj.* **1.** Not generous; stingy. **2.** Harsh in judgment; unkind. —**un'gen'er·ous·ly** *adv.*

un·girt (ŭn'gûrt') *adj.* **1.** Having the belt, girdle, or other restraining or supporting garment removed or loosened. **2.** Loose or free; slack.

un·god·ly (ŭn'gŏd'lē) *adj.* **-lier, -liest. 1.** Not revering God; impious. **2.** Sinful; wicked. **3.** *Informal.* Outrageous: *He called at an ungodly hour.* —**un'god'li·ness** *n.*

un·gov·ern·a·ble (ŭn'gŭv'ər-nə-bəl) *adj.* Not able to be governed; not controllable. See Synonyms at **unruly.** —**un'gov'ern·a·ble·ness** *n.* —**un'gov'ern·a·bly** *adv.*

un·gra·cious (ŭn'grā'shəs) *adj.* **1.** Lacking social grace or graciousness; rude. **2.** Not welcome or acceptable; unattractive. —**un'gra'cious·ly** *adv.* —**un'gra'cious·ness** *n.*

un·gram·mat·i·cal (ŭn'grə-măt'ĭ-kəl) *adj.* **1.** Not in accord with a normative prescriptive grammar. **2.** Not in accord with any observable pattern of syntax of a language.

un·grate·ful (ŭn'grāt'fəl) *adj.* **1.** Without a feeling or expression of gratitude, thanks, or appreciation. **2.** Not agreeable or pleasant; repellent: *"I will not perform the ungrateful task of comparing cases of failure"* (Lincoln). —**un'grate'ful·ly** *adv.* —**un'grate'ful·ness** *n.*

un·gual (ŭng'gwəl) *adj. Zoology.* Of, resembling, or bearing a hoof, nail, or claw. [From Latin *unguis,* UNGUIS.]

un·guard·ed (ŭn'gär'dĭd) *adj.* **1.** Without guard or protection; vulnerable. **2.** Without discretion; imprudent; incautious. —**un'guard'ed·ness** *n.*

un·guent (ŭng'gwənt) *n.* A salve for soothing or healing; an ointment. [Middle English, from Latin *unguentum,* from *unguere,* to anoint. See **ongw-** in Appendix.*]

un·guic·u·late (ŭng-gwĭk'yə-lĭt, -lāt') *adj.* **1.** *Zoology.* Having nails or claws. **2.** *Botany.* Having a claw-shaped base, as a petal. —*n.* A mammal having nails or claws. [New Latin *unguiculatus,* from Latin *unguiculus,* fingernail, diminutive of *unguis,* UNGUIS.]

un·guis (ŭng'gwĭs) *n., pl.* **-gues** (-gwēz'). A nail, claw, hoof, or clawlike structure. [Latin *unguis,* claw, nail. See **nogh-** in Appendix.*]

un·gu·late (ŭng'gyə-lĭt, -lāt') *adj.* **1.** Having hoofs. **2.** Of or belonging to the former order Ungulata, now divided into the orders Perissodactyla and Artiodactyla, and including hoofed mammals such as horses, cattle, deer, swine, and elephants. —*n.* An ungulate mammal. [Late Latin *ungulātus,* from Latin *ungula,* diminutive of *unguis,* UNGUIS.]

un·hal·low (ŭn'hăl'ō) *tr.v.* **-lowed, -lowing, -lows.** *Archaic.* To profane; desecrate.

un·hal·lowed (ŭn'hăl'ōd) *adj.* **1.** Not hallowed or consecrated. **2. a.** Impious; profane; irreligious. **b.** Not pure or moral; immoral; wicked.

un·hand (ŭn'hănd') *tr.v.* **-handed, -handing, -hands.** To remove one's hand or hands from; let go: *"Unhand me, you villain."*

un·hand·some (ŭn'hăn'səm) *adj.* **1.** Not attractive or beautiful; homely. **2.** Not courteous or in good taste; ungracious. —**un'hand'some·ly** *adv.* —**un'hand'some·ness** *n.*

un·hand·y (ŭn'hăn'dē) *adj.* **-ier, -iest. 1.** Difficult to handle or manage; unwieldy; cumbersome. **2.** Lacking manual skill or dexterity. —**un'hand'i·ly** *adv.* —**un'hand'i·ness** *n.*

un·hap·py (ŭn'hăp'ē) *adj.* **-pier, -piest. 1.** Not happy or joyful; sad. **2.** Not bringing good fortune; unlucky. **3.** Not suitable or tactful; inappropriate. —**un'hap'pi·ly** (-hăp'ə-lē) *adv.* —**un'hap'pi·ness** *n.*

un·har·ness (ŭn'här'nĭs) *tr.v.* **-nessed, -nessing, -nesses. 1.** To remove the harness from. **2.** To release or liberate, as energy or emotions.

un·health·y (ŭn'hĕl'thē) *adj.* **-ier, -iest. 1.** In a state of ill health; sick. **2.** Characterizing or symptomatic of ill health: *an unhealthy pallor.* **3.** Causing or conducive to poor health; unwholesome. **4.** Harmful to character or moral health; corruptive. **5.** Of a risky nature; dangerous. —**un'health'i·ly** (-hĕl'thə-lē) *adv.* —**un'health'i·ness** *n.*

un·heard (ŭn'hûrd') *adj.* **1.** Not sensed by the ear. **2.** Not given a hearing; not listened to. **3.** *Archaic.* Not heard of; obscure; unknown.

un·heard-of (ŭn'hûrd'ŭv', -ŏv') *adj.* **1.** Not previously known; unknown. **2.** Without precedent.

un·hes·i·tat·ing (ŭn'hĕz'ə-tā'tĭng) *adj.* **1.** Prompt; ready. **2.** Unfaltering; steadfast. —**un'hes'i·tat'ing·ly** *adv.*

un·hinge (ŭn'hĭnj') *tr.v.* **-hinged, -hinging, -hinges. 1.** To remove from hinges. **2.** To remove the hinges from. **3.** To confuse; disrupt.

un·hitch (ŭn'hĭch') *tr.v.* **-hitched, -hitching, -hitches.** To release from or as if from a hitch; unfasten.

un·ho·ly (ŭn'hō'lē) *adj.* **-lier, -liest. 1.** Not hallowed or consecrated. **2.** Wicked; immoral. **3.** *Informal.* Outrageous: *"We take unholy risks to prove/We are what we cannot be"* (LeRoi Jones). —**un'ho'li·ly** (-hō'lə-lē) *adv.* —**un'ho'li·ness** *n.*

un·hook (ŭn'ho͝ok') *tr.v.* **-hooked, -hooking, -hooks. 1.** To release or remove from a hook. **2.** To unfasten the hooks of.

un·hoped (ŭn'hōpt') *adj. Archaic.* Unexpected; not hoped or looked for.

un·hoped-for (ŭn'hōpt'fôr') *adj.* Not expected; unanticipated.

un·horse (ŭn'hôrs') *tr.v.* **-horsed, -horsing, -horses. 1.** To cause to fall from a horse. **2.** To overthrow or dislodge; to upset.

un·hou·seled (ŭn'hou'zəld) *adj. Obsolete.* Not having received the Eucharist. [UN- (not) + HOUSEL.]

uni–. Indicates the state of being single or of having or consisting of only one; for example, **unicameral, unicostate.** [Latin, from *ūnus,* one. See **oino-** in Appendix.*]

U·ni·at (yo͞o'nē-ăt') *n.* Also **U·ni·ate** (yo͞o'nē-ĭt, -āt'). A member of a Uniat Church. —*adj.* Of or pertaining to the Uniat Church or its members, practices, or doctrines. [Russian *uniyat,* from Polish *uniat,* from *unja,* "church-union" (of the Greek and the Roman Catholic Churches), from Late Latin *ūniō,* UNION.]

Uniat Church. Also **Uniate Church.** Any Eastern Christian church that acknowledges the supremacy of the pope but retains its own distinctive liturgy.

u·ni·ax·i·al (yo͞o'nē-ăk'sē-əl) *adj.* **1.** Having only one axis. **2.** Of or along a single axis. Also "monaxial."

u·ni·cam·er·al (yo͞o'nĭ-kăm'ər-əl) *adj.* Having or consisting of a single legislative chamber. [UNI- + CAMERA (chamber).]

UNICEF (yo͞o'nĭ-sĕf') United Nations Children's Fund.

u·ni·cel·lu·lar (yo͞o'nĭ-sĕl'yə-lər) *adj.* Consisting of one cell; one-celled: *unicellular organisms.*

u·ni·col·or (yo͞o'nĭ-kŭl'ər) *adj.* Monochromatic.

u·ni·corn (yo͞o'nə-kôrn') *n.* **1.** A fabled creature usually represented as a horse with a single spiraled horn projecting from its forehead and often with a goat's beard and a lion's tail. **2.** *Capital* **U.** *Astronomy.* The constellation **Monoceros** *(see).* [Middle English, from Old French, from Latin *ūnicornis* : UNI- + *cornū,* horn (see **ker-**[1] in Appendix*).]

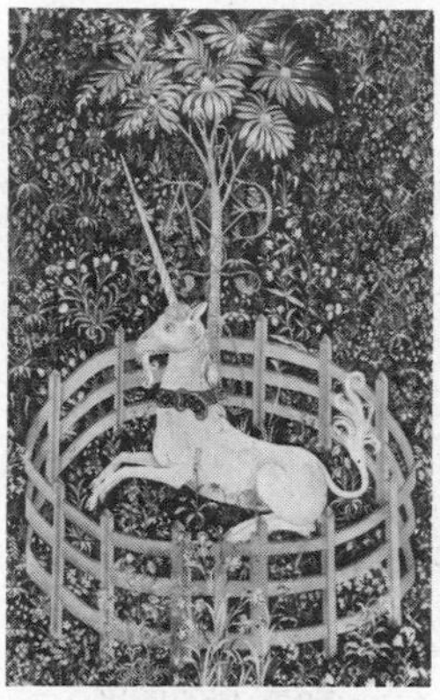

unicorn
Early 16th-century
French tapestry,
"The Unicorn in Captivity"

unicorn plant. A plant, *Proboscidea louisiana,* of the southern United States, having yellowish-purple flowers and a beaked, woody pod.

u·ni·cos·tate (yo͞o'nĭ-kŏs'tāt') *adj.* Having a single main costa, rib, or riblike part. [UNI- + COSTA + -ATE.]

u·ni·cy·cle (yo͞o'nĭ-sī'kəl) *n.* A vehicle consisting of a frame mounted over a single wheel and usually propelled by pedals. Also called "monocycle." —**u'ni·cy'clist** (-klĭst) *n.*

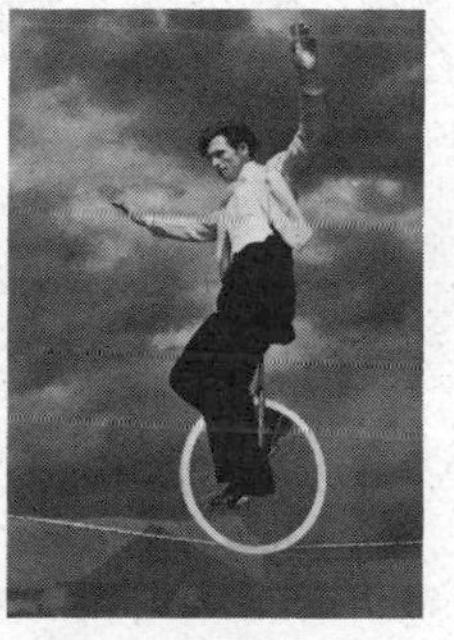

unicycle

unidentified flying object. *Abbr.* **UFO, U.F.O. 1.** A flying or apparently flying object of an unknown nature. **2.** A **flying saucer** *(see).*

u·ni·di·rec·tion·al (yo͞o'nĭ-dĭ-rĕk'shən-əl, -dī-rĕk'shən-əl) *adj.* Having, operating, or moving in one direction only.

u·ni·fi·a·ble (yo͞o'nə-fī'ə-bəl) *adj.* Capable of unification.

unified field theory. A physical theory that combines the treatment of two or more types of fields in order to deduce previously unrecognized interrelationships; especially, such a theory unifying the theories of nuclear, electromagnetic, and gravitational forces.

u·ni·fi·lar (yo͞o'nĭ-fī'lər) *adj.* Having or utilizing only one thread, wire, or the like.

u·ni·fo·li·ate (yo͞o'nĭ-fō'lē-ĭt, -āt') *adj.* Having a single leaf.

u·ni·fo·li·o·late (yo͞o'nĭ-fō'lē-ə-lāt') *adj.* Compound in structure, but having a single leaflet, and often a winglike extension along the leafstalk.

u·ni·form (yo͞o'nə-fôrm') *adj.* **1. a.** Always the same; unchanging; unvarying: *a uniform gait.* **b.** Without fluctuation or variation; consistent; regular. **2.** Being the same as another or others; identical; consonant: *"Language was not uniform throughout the country but fell into dialects"* (Kemp Malone). **3.** Consistent in appearance; having an unvaried texture, color, or design. —See Synonyms at **steady.** —*n.* **1.** A distinctive outfit intended to identify those who wear it as members of a specific group. **2.** A single outfit of such apparel. —*tr.v.* **uniformed, -forming, -forms. 1.** To make uniform. **2.** To provide or dress with a uniform. [Old French *uniforme,* from Latin *ūniformis,* of one form : UNI- + -FORM.] —**u'ni·for'mi·ty, u'ni·form'ness** *n.* —**u'ni·form'ly** *adv.*

u·ni·for·mi·tar·i·an·ism (yo͞o'nə-fôr'mə-târ'ē-ə-nĭz'əm) *n. Geology.* The theory that all geological phenomena may be explained as the result of existing forces having operated uniformly from the origin of the earth to the present time. —**u'ni·for'mi·tar'i·an** *adj. & n.*

u·ni·fy (yo͞o'nə-fī') *v.* **-fied, -fying, -fies.** —*tr.* To make into a unit; consolidate. —*intr.* To become unified. [Old French *unifier,* from Late Latin *ūnificāre* : UNI- + Latin *facere,* to make (see **dhē-**[1] in Appendix*).] —**u'ni·fi·ca'tion** *n.* —**u'ni·fi'er** *n.*

u·ni·lat·er·al (yo͞o'nĭ-lăt'ər-əl) *adj.* **1.** Of, on, pertaining to, involving, or affecting only one side. **2.** Obligating only one of two or more parties, nations, or persons, as a contract or agreement. **3.** Emphasizing or recognizing only one side of a subject. **4.** Having only one side. **5.** Tracing the lineage of one parent only: *a unilateral genealogy.* —**u'ni·lat'er·al·ly** *adv.*

u·ni·loc·u·lar (yo͞o'nĭ-lŏk'yə-lər) *adj. Botany.* Having a single compartment or chamber. [UNI- + LOCULUS.]

U·ni·mak Island (yōō′nə-măk′). An island 70 miles long and 17 to 30 miles wide in the Aleutian chain off southwestern Alaska.

un·im·peach·a·ble (ŭn′ĭm-pē′chə-bəl) *adj.* Beyond doubt or reproach; unquestionable. —**un′im·peach′a·bly** *adv.*

un·im·proved (ŭn′ĭm-prōōvd′) *adj.* 1. Not improved; not bettered. 2. Not made use of or put to advantage. 3. Not built upon or cultivated so as to increase in value. Said of land.

un·in·hib·i·ted (ŭn′ĭn-hĭb′ə-tĭd) *adj.* 1. Not inhibited; open: *uninhibited laughter.* 2. Free from the expected social or moral constraints. —**un′in·hib′i·ted·ly** *adv.*

un·in·spired (ŭn′ĭn-spīrd′) *adj.* Having no intellectual or spiritual excitement; dull.

un·in·tel·li·gent (ŭn′ĭn-tĕl′ə-jənt) *adj.* 1. Lacking intelligence; stupid. 2. Uneducated; ignorant. —**un′in·tel′li·gence** *n.* —**un′·in·tel′li·gent·ly** *adv.*

un·in·ter·est·ed (ŭn-ĭn′trĭs-tĭd, -ĭn′tə-rĕs′tĭd) *adj.* 1. Without an interest; especially, not having a financial interest. 2. Not paying attention; indifferent; unconcerned. See Usage note at **disinterested.**

un·ion (yōōn′yən) *n.* 1. The act of uniting or the state of being united. 2. A combination so formed; especially, an alliance or confederation of persons, parties, or political entities for mutual interest or benefit: *"I projected and drew a plan for the union of all the colonies under one government"* (Franklin). 3. *Symbol* **U** *Mathematics.* A set, every member of which is an element of one or another of two or more given sets. Compare **intersection.** 4. Agreement resulting from an alliance; concord; harmony. 5. a. The state of matrimony; marriage. b. Sexual congress; intercourse. 6. a. Formerly, a combination of parishes for joint administration of relief for the poor in Britain. b. A workhouse maintained by such a union. 7. A **labor union** *(see).* 8. A coupling device for connecting parts, as pipes or rods. 9. A device on a flag or ensign, occupying the upper inner corner or the entire field, that signifies the union of two or more sovereignties. 10. *Capital* **U.** a. An organization at a college or university that provides facilities for recreation. b. A building housing such facilities. —See Synonyms at **unity.** —**the Union.** 1. The United States of America, especially during the Civil War. 2. The former Union of South Africa. —*adj.* 1. Of or pertaining to a labor union. 2. *Capital* **U.** Supporting the Federal Government in the Civil War. [Middle English, from Old French, from Late Latin *ūniō,* unity, from Latin *ūnus,* one. See oino- in Appendix.*]

Un·ion (yōōn′yən). A city of northeastern New Jersey. Population, 51,000.

union catalog. A library catalog combining in alphabetical sequence the contents of a number of catalogs or the contents of more than one library.

Union City. A city of New Jersey, in the northeast on the Hudson. Population, 52,000.

un·ion·ism (yōōn′yə-nĭz′əm) *n.* 1. The principle or theory of forming a union. 2. The principles, theory, or system of a union, especially a trade union. 3. *Capital* **U.** Loyalty to the Federal Government during the Civil War. —**un′ion·ist** *n.*

un·ion·ize (yōōn′yə-nīz′) *v.* -ized, -izing, -izes. —*tr.* 1. To organize into a labor union. 2. To cause to join such a union. —*intr.* To organize or join a labor union. —**un′ion·i·za′tion** *n.*

union jack. 1. Any flag consisting entirely of a union. 2. *Usually capital* **U,** *capital* **J.** The flag of the United Kingdom.

union label. An identifying mark attached to a product indicating it has been produced by members of a trade union.

Union of Soviet Socialist Republics. *Abbr.* **U.S.S.R.** A country comprising 15 constituent republics and occupying 8,570,000 square miles in northern Eurasia, bordered by the Pacific on the east, the Arctic Ocean on the north, and the Black and Caspian seas in the southwest. Also called "Soviet Union," "Soviet Russia," "Russia." Population, 226,253,000. Capital, Moscow.

union shop. A business or industrial establishment whose employees are required to be union members or agree to join the union within a specified time after being hired. Also called "closed shop." Compare **open shop.**

union suit. Undershirt and underdrawers combined in a single garment.

u·nip·a·rous (yōō-nĭp′ər-əs) *adj.* 1. Producing only one offspring at a time. 2. Having produced only one offspring. 3. *Botany.* Forming a single axis at each branching, as certain flower clusters. [UNI- + -PAROUS.]

u·ni·per·son·al (yōō′nĭ-pûr′sən-əl) *adj.* 1. Being manifested as or existent in the form of only one person: *a unipersonal spirit.* 2. *Grammar.* Used only in one person; specifically, the third person singular. Said of certain verbs; for example, *meseems.*

u·ni·pla·nar (yōō′nĭ-plā′nər, -när′) *adj.* Situated or occurring in one plane.

u·ni·po·lar (yōō′nĭ-pō′lər) *n.* Having, acting by means of, or produced by a single pole.

u·nique (yōō-nēk′) *adj.* 1. Being the only one of its kind; solitary; sole: *"Man's language is unique in consisting of words"* (Julian Huxley). 2. Being without an equal or equivalent; unparalleled: *"Your crisis is by no means unique"* (William Demby). —See Synonyms at **single.** [French, from Latin *ūnicus,* only, sole. See oino- in Appendix.*] —**u·nique′ly** *adv.* —**u·nique′ness** *n.*

Usage: *Unique,* in careful usage, is not preceded by adverbs that qualify it with respect to degree. Examples such as *rather unique,* with reference to a book, and *the most unique,* referring to the most unusual of a rare species of animals, are termed unacceptable by 94 per cent of the Usage Panel, on the ground that the quality described by *unique* cannot be said to vary in

degree or intensity and is therefore not capable of comparison. The same objection is raised about examples in which *unique* is preceded by *more, somewhat,* and *very.* In such examples an appropriate substitute for *unique* can usually be found from among *unusual, remarkable, rare, exceptional,* or the like, which are weaker and can be qualified freely. However, *unique* can be modified by terms that do not imply degree in the sense noted: *almost* (or *nearly*) *unique; really* (or *quite,* meaning *truly*) *unique; more* (or *most*) *nearly unique.*

u·ni·sex·u·al (yōō′nĭ-sĕk′shōō-əl) *adj.* 1. Of only one sex. 2. Having only one type of sexual organ. 3. *Botany.* Having either stamens or pistils but not both. —**u′ni·sex′u·al′i·ty** *n.* —**u′ni·sex′u·al′ly** *adv.*

u·ni·son (yōō′nə-sən, -zən) *n.* 1. a. Identity of musical pitch; the interval of a perfect prime. b. The combination of musical parts at the same pitch or in octaves. 2. Any speaking of the same words simultaneously by two or more speakers. 3. Any instance of agreement; concord; harmony. [Old French, from Medieval Latin *ūnisonus,* of the same sound : UNI- + Latin *sonus,* sound (see swen- in Appendix*).]

u·nis·o·nous (yōō-nĭs′ə-nəs) *adj.* Also **u·nis·o·nal** (-nəl), **u·nis·o·nant** (-nənt). 1. Sounding in unison. 2. Being in harmony; concordant.

u·nit (yōō′nĭt) *n. Abbr.* **u.** 1. An individual, group, structure, or other entity regarded as an elementary structural or functional constituent of a whole. 2. A group regarded as a distinct entity within a larger group. 3. a. A mechanical part or module. b. An entire apparatus or the equipment that performs a specific function. 4. *Measurement.* A precisely specified quantity in terms of which the magnitudes of other quantities of the same kind can be stated. 5. A fixed amount of scholastic study used as a basis for calculating academic credits, usually measured in hours of classroom instruction or laboratory work. 6. The number immediately to the left of the decimal point in the Arabic numeral system. [Back-formation from UNITY (used to translate Greek *monas,* MONAD.)]

Unit. Unitarian; Unitarianism.

U·ni·tar·i·an (yōō′nə-târ′ē-ən) *n.* 1. A monotheist who rejects the doctrine of the Trinity. Compare **Trinitarian.** 2. *Abbr.* **Unit.** A member of a Christian denomination that rejects the doctrine of the Trinity and emphasizes freedom and tolerance in religious belief and the autonomy of each congregation. See **Universalist.** —*adj. Abbr.* **Unit.** Of, pertaining to, or supporting the Unitarians or their beliefs. [From New Latin *unitarius,* from Latin *ūnitās,* UNITY.] —**U′ni·tar′i·an·ism′** *n.*

u·ni·tar·y (yōō′nə-tĕr′ē) *adj.* 1. Of or pertaining to a unit. 2. Having the nature of a unit; whole. 3. Based on or characterized by one or more units.

u·nite (yōō-nīt′) *v.* -nited, -niting, -nites. —*tr.* 1. To bring together so as to form a whole. 2. To combine (people) in interest, attitude, or action: *"The ancient schools of philosophy were bodies of men united by a common spirit"* (W.D. Ross). 3. To join (a couple) in marriage. 4. To cause to adhere; to bond. 5. To have or demonstrate in combination: *He unites common sense with vision.* —*intr.* 1. To become or seem to become joined, formed, or combined into a unit. 2. To join and act together in a common purpose or endeavor. 3. To be or become bound together by adhesion. —See Synonyms at **join.** [Middle English *uniten,* from Late Latin *ūnīre* (past participle *ūnītus*), from Latin *ūnus,* one. See oino- in Appendix.*]

United Arab Republic. *Abbr.* **UAR, U.A.R.** The official name for Egypt.

United Church of Christ. A Protestant denomination founded in 1957 by a merger of the Congregational Christian Church and the Evangelical and Reformed Church.

United Kingdom. *Abbr.* **U.K.** 1. In full, United Kingdom of Great Britain and Northern Ireland. A kingdom of western Europe, consisting of England, Scotland, Wales, and Northern Ireland, with a combined area of 94,212 square miles. Population, 54,068,000. Capital, London. 2. In full, United Kingdom of Great Britain and Ireland. A former kingdom comprising England, Scotland, Wales, and all of Ireland.

United Methodist Church. A Protestant church formed in 1968 by the union of the Methodist Church and the Evangelical United Brethren.

United Nations. 1. *Abbr.* **UN, U.N.** An international organization of 126 independent countries, with headquarters in New York City, formed in 1945 to promote peace and international security and cooperation. 2. A coalition of 26 countries formed in 1942 to combat the Axis powers in World War II.

United Nations Trust Territory. A trust territory *(see).*

United Provinces of A·gra and Oudh (ä′grə; oud). A former British political unit in north-central India; since 1950, the Indian state of Uttar Pradesh.

United States of A·mer·i·ca (ə-mĕr′ə-kə). *Abbr.* **USA, U.S.A.** A federal republic composed of 50 states (48 of them in central North America, Alaska in northwestern North America, and Hawaii, an archipelago in the Pacific Ocean) and the District of Columbia, with a combined area of 3,615,211 square miles. Population, 200,000,000. Capital, Washington, coextensive with the District of Columbia.

u·ni·tive (yōō′nə-tĭv, yōō-nī′-) *adj.* Tending to promote unity or serving to unite.

unit magnetic pole. A magnetic pole that repels an identical magnetic pole with a force of one dyne at a distance of one centimeter.

unit rule. In a Democratic Party national convention, a rule that a state's entire vote must go to the candidate preferred by the majority of that state's delegates.

United Kingdom

Union Jack

Union of Soviet Socialist Republics

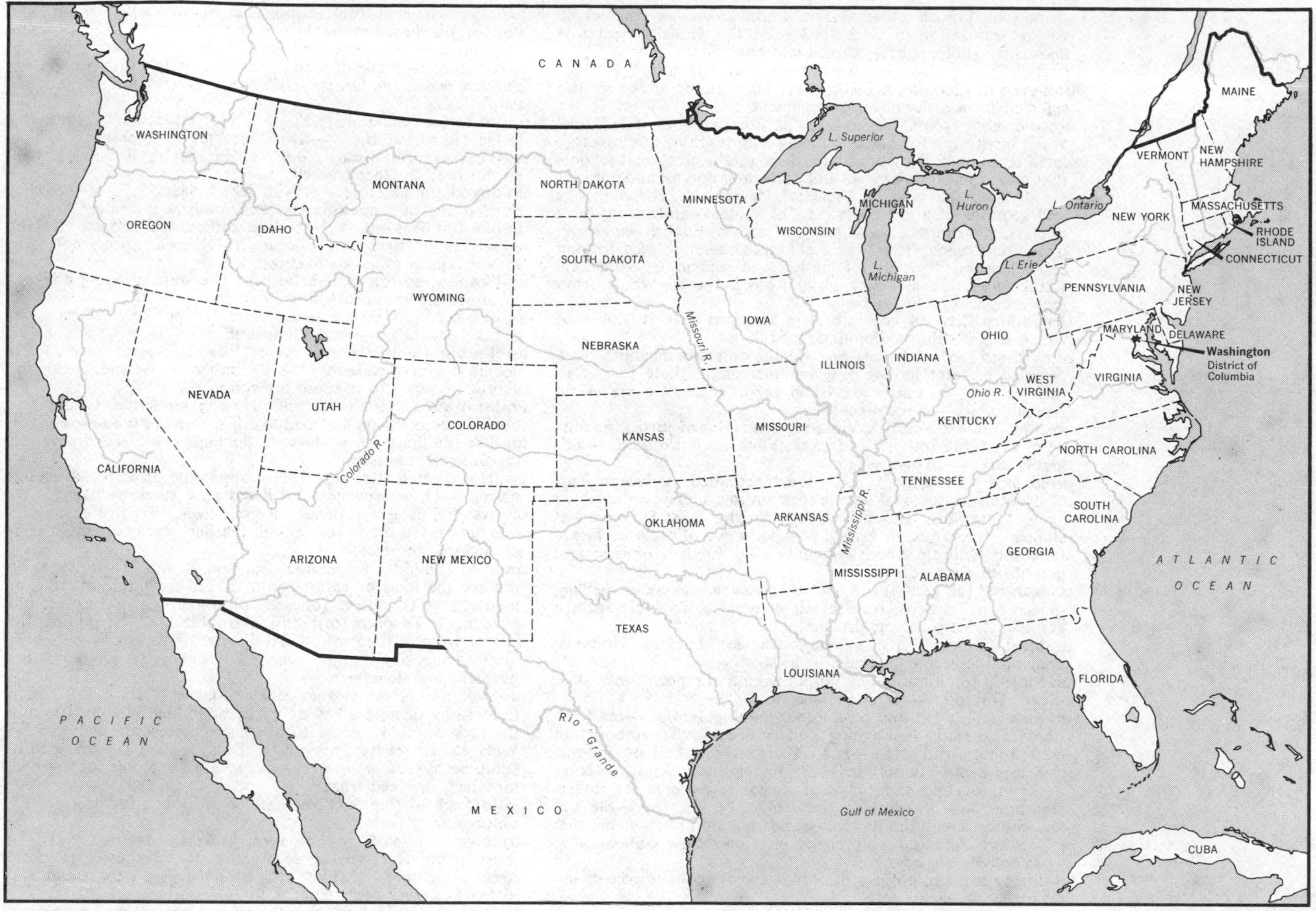

United States of America

t tight/th thin, path/*th* this, bathe/ŭ cut/ûr urge/v valve/w with/y yes/z zebra, size/zh vision/ə about, item, ědible, gallop, circus/
à *Fr.* ami/œ *Fr.* feu, *Ger.* schön/ü *Fr.* tu, *Ger.* über/кн *Ger.* ich, *Scot.* loch/N *Fr.* bon. *Follows main vocabulary. †Of obscure origin.

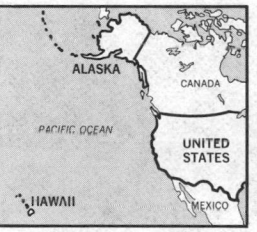

United States of America
The states of
Alaska and Hawaii

u·ni·ty (yōō′nə-tē) *n., pl.* **-ties. 1.** The state of being one; singleness. **2.** The state, quality, or condition of accord or agreement; concord. **3.** The combination or arrangement of parts into a whole; unification. **4.** A combination or union thus formed. **5. a.** An ordering of all elements in a work of art or literature so that each contributes to a unified aesthetic effect. **b.** The effect thus produced. **6.** Singleness or constancy of purpose or action; continuity. **7.** *Mathematics.* **a.** The number 1. **b.** An element *I* in a groupoid satisfying *x·I* = *x* = *I·x* for each *x* in the groupoid. Also called "identity." **—the unities.** Three principles of dramatic composition, derived from Aristotle's *Poetics,* based upon unity of time, action, and place. They state that a drama should have but one plot, the action of which should be contained within one day and confined to one locality. [Middle English *unite,* from Old French, from Latin *ūnitās,* from *ūnus,* one. See **oino-** in Appendix.*]

Synonyms: unity, union, solidarity, homogeneity. These nouns refer to the condition of oneness in some sense; they are not always interchangeable, however. *Unity* is the fact or condition of being one; in most contexts it implies fundamental agreement of interdependent and usually varied components, which in turn produces harmony, as of thought, purpose, or artistic quality. *Union* is interchangeable with the preceding term when both refer to harmony or concord; but *union* more often refers to the act of joining persons or things and to the product that results, such as an organization of persons, a political body, or a marriage. In its most common application, *solidarity* is an intensification of *unity,* for it refers to the identity or likeness of interests, objectives, and responsibilities that enables a group of persons to think and act as one. *Homogeneity* involves oneness in the sense of uniformity of overall structure or character, resulting from likeness or compatibility of components.

Unity of Science Movement. Scientific empiricism (*see*).
univ. 1. universal. **2.** university.
Univ. 1. Universalist. **2.** university.
U·ni·vac (yōō′nə-văk′) *n.* A trademark for a general-purpose digital computer.
u·ni·va·lent (yōō′nĭ-vā′lənt) *adj.* **1.** *Chemistry.* **a.** Having valence 1. **b.** Having only one valence. **2.** *Genetics.* An unpaired chromosome.
u·ni·valve (yōō′nĭ-vălv′) *n.* **1.** A mollusk, especially a gastropod, having a single shell. **2.** The shell of such a mollusk. **—***adj.* Pertaining to or having such a shell.
u·ni·ver·sal (yōō′nə-vûr′səl) *adj. Abbr.* **univ. 1.** Of, pertaining to, extending to, or affecting the entire world or all within the world, worldwide. **2.** Including, pertaining to, or affecting all

members of the class or group under consideration: *the universal skepticism of philosophers.* **3.** Applicable or common to all purposes, conditions, or situations. **4.** Of or pertaining to the universe or cosmos; cosmic. **5.** Comprising all or many subjects; comprehensively broad: *"Maury was a universal genius but his deepest passion was the movement of tides."* (Bernard De Voto). **6.** *Mechanics.* Adapted or adjustable to many sizes or uses. **7.** *Logic.* Predicable of all the members of a class or genus denoted by the subject. Said of a proposition. Compare **particular. —***n.* **1.** *Logic.* **a.** A universal proposition. **b.** A general or abstract concept or term considered absolute or axiomatic. **2.** Any general or widely held principle, concept, or notion. **3.** A trait or pattern of behavior characteristic of all the members of a particular culture or of all human beings. **—u′ni·ver′sal·ly** *adv.* **—u′ni·ver′sal·ness** *n.*
universal coupling. A universal joint (*see*).
Universal Decimal Classification. *Abbr.* **UDC** A system of arranging materials in libraries or information centers based on the Dewey decimal system.
universal donor. A person of blood type O.
u·ni·ver·sal·ism (yōō′nə-vûr′sə-lĭz′əm) *n.* **1.** *Capital* **U.** *Theology.* The doctrine of universal salvation. **2.** Universality.
U·ni·ver·sal·ist (yōō′nə-vûr′sə-list) *n. Abbr.* **Univ.** One who believes that salvation is extended to all mankind; especially, a member of a Christian denomination that adheres to this doctrine. In 1961, the Universalists merged with the Unitarians, forming the Unitarian Universalist Association. **—***adj.* Of or pertaining to Universalism or Universalists.
u·ni·ver·sal·i·ty (yōō′nə-vər-săl′ə-tē) *n., pl.* **-ties. 1.** The quality, fact, or condition of being universal. **2.** Great or unbounded versatility of the mind.
u·ni·ver·sal·ize (yōō′nə-vûr′sə-līz′) *tr.v.* **-ized, -izing, -izes.** To make universal; generalize. **—u′ni·ver′sal·i·za′tion** *n.*
universal joint. A joint or coupling that allows parts of a machine not collinear with each other limited freedom of movement in any direction while transmitting rotary motion. Also called "universal coupling."
Universal Military Training. *Abbr.* **UMT** A system in which every qualified male receives military training when he reaches a certain age.
u·ni·verse (yōō′nə-vûrs′) *n.* **1.** All existing things, including the earth, the heavens, the galaxies, and all therein, regarded as a whole; the cosmos; macrocosm. **2. a.** The earth together with all its inhabitants and created things. **b.** All mankind. **3.** The sphere or realm in which something exists or takes place. **4.** *Logic.* The **universe of discourse** (*see*). [Middle English,

from Old French *univers,* from Latin *ūniversum,* the whole world (translation of Greek *to holon,* "the whole"), neuter of *ūniversus,* whole, entire, "turned into one" : UNI- + *versus,* past participle of *vertere,* to turn (see **wer-**³ in Appendix*).]

universe of discourse. *Logic.* A class containing all the entities referred to in a discourse or argument.

u·ni·ver·si·ty (yoo͞′nə-vûr′sə-tē) *n., pl.* **-ties.** *Abbr.* **U., univ., Univ. 1.** An institution for higher learning with teaching and research facilities comprising a graduate school and professional schools that award master's degrees and doctorates and an undergraduate division that awards bachelor's degrees. **2.** The buildings and grounds of a university. **3.** The students and faculty of a university, regarded as a body. [Middle English *universite,* from Old French, from Medieval Latin *ūniversitās (magistrorum et scholarium),* "society (of masters and students)," from Late Latin *ūniversitās,* a society, guild, from Latin, the whole, from *ūniversus,* whole. See **universe.**]

University City. A city in eastern Missouri near St. Louis, of which it is a suburb. Population, 51,000.

u·niv·o·cal (yoo͞-nĭv′ə-kəl) *adj.* Having only one meaning. *—n.* A word or term having only one meaning. [Late Latin *ūnivōcus* : UNI- + Latin *vōx* (stem *vōc-*), voice (see **wekw-** in Appendix*).] **—u·niv′o·cal·ly** *adv.*

un·just (ŭn′jŭst′) *adj.* **1.** Violating principles of justice or fairness; wrongful; unfair. **2.** *Archaic.* Faithless; dishonest. **—un′just′ly** *adv.* **—un′just′ness** *n.*

un·kempt (ŭn′kĕmpt′) *adj.* **1. a.** Uncombed: *unkempt hair.* **b.** Lacking neatness of appearance; untidy; messy: *an unkempt lawn.* **2.** *Archaic.* Unpolished; rude; rough. —See Synonyms at **sloppy.** [UN- (not) + *kempt,* past participle of dialectal *kemb,* to comb, Middle English *kemben,* Old English *cemban* (see **gembh-** in Appendix*).]

un·ken·nel (ŭn′kĕn′əl) *tr.v.* **-neled** or **-nelled, -neling** or **-nelling, -nels. 1. a.** To drive from a lair or den. **b.** To loose from a kennel. **2.** To uncover; disclose.

un·kind (ŭn′kīnd′) *adj.* **-kinder, -kindest.** Lacking kindness; unsympathetic; harsh; cruel. **—un′kind′ness** *n.*

un·kind·ly (ŭn′kīnd′lē) *adv.* In an unkind manner. *—adj.* **-lier, -liest.** Unkind. **—un′kind′li·ness** *n.*

un·knit (ŭn′nĭt′) *v.* **-knit** or **-knitted, -knitting, -knits.** *—tr.* **1.** To unravel or undo (something knit or tied). **2.** To smooth out (something wrinkled). *—intr.* To become unknit or undone.

un·know·a·ble (ŭn′nō′ə-bəl) *adj.* Impossible to know or comprehend; beyond the range of human experience or understanding. *—n.* Something that cannot be known. **—the Unknowable.** The ultimate reality underlying all phenomena that is beyond human comprehension. **—un′know′a·ble·ness** *n.* **—un′know′a·bly** *adv.*

un·know·ing (ŭn′nō′ĭng) *adj.* Not knowing; uninformed; unaware. **—un′know′ing·ly** *adv.*

un·known (ŭn′nōn′) *adj.* **1.** Not known; unfamiliar; strange. **2. a.** Not identified or ascertained. **b.** Not established or verified. *—n.* **1.** One that is unknown. **2.** *Mathematics.* **a.** A quantity of unknown numerical value. **b.** The symbol for this quantity.

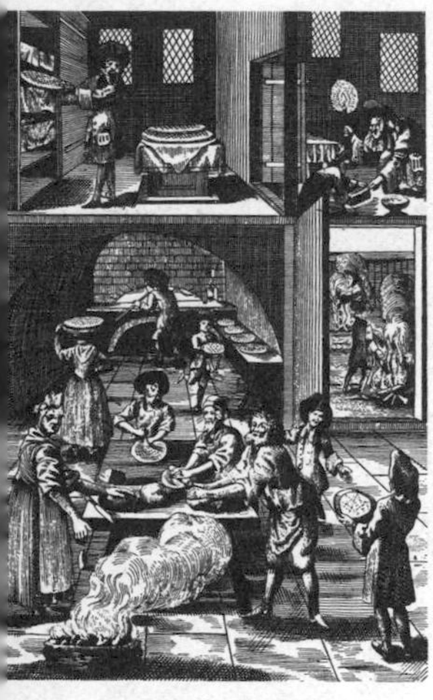

unleavened
Early 18th-century engraving showing the preparation of unleavened bread for the Passover

un·la·bored (ŭn′lā′bərd) *adj.* **1.** Done with or requiring little effort; effortless. **2.** Not tilled; uncultivated.

un·lace (ŭn′lās′) *tr.v.* **-laced, -lacing, -laces. 1. a.** To loosen or undo the lace or laces of. **b.** To remove or loosen the clothing of. **2.** *Obsolete.* To disgrace.

un·lade (ŭn′lād′) *v.* **-laded, -lading, -lades.** *—tr.* **1.** To unload (a cargo) from a ship. **2.** To unload (a ship). *—intr.* To discharge a cargo.

un·laid (ŭn′lād′) *adj.* **1.** Not fixed or placed. **2.** Not allayed or pacified. **3.** Not twisted, as a rope. **4.** *Obsolete.* Not laid out for burial, as a corpse.

un·lash (ŭn′lăsh′) *tr.v.* **-lashed, -lashing, -lashes.** To untie the lashing of; to loose.

un·latch (ŭn′lăch′) *v.* **-latched, -latching, -latches.** *—tr.* To unfasten or open by releasing the latch. *—intr.* To become unfastened or opened.

un·law·ful (ŭn′lô′fəl) *adj.* **1.** Not lawful; in violation of law; illegal. **2.** Illegitimate. Said of offspring. **—un′law′ful·ly** *adv.* **—un′law′ful·ness** *n.*

un·lay (ŭn′lā′) *v.* **-laid** (-lād′), **-laying, -lays.** *Nautical. —tr.* To untwist the strands of (a rope). *—intr.* To untwist.

un·lead (ŭn′lĕd′) *tr.v.* **-leaded, -leading, -leads. 1.** To remove the lead from. **2.** *Printing.* To extricate the leads from between (lines of type).

un·lead·ed (ŭn′lĕd′ĭd) *adj.* **1.** Not provided with or weighted with lead. **2.** *Printing.* Not spaced or separated with lead, as lines of type; set solid.

un·learn (ŭn′lûrn′) *tr.v.* **-learned** or **-learnt** (-lûrnt′), **-learning, -learns.** To put (something learned) out of the mind; forget.

un·learn·ed (ŭn′lûr′nĭd *for senses 1, 3;* ŭn′lûrnd′ *for sense 2*) *adj.* **1.** Not educated; ignorant or illiterate. **2.** Not acquired by training or studying: *an unlearned response.* **3.** Not skilled or versed in a specified discipline. —See Synonyms at **ignorant.** **—un′learn′ed·ly** (-lûr′nĭd-lē) *adv.*

un·leash (ŭn′lēsh′) *tr.v.* **-leashed, -leashing, -leashes.** To release or loose from or as if from a leash: *"the malignant death instinct can unleash those hydrogen bombs"* (Norman O. Brown).

un·leav·ened (ŭn′lĕv′ənd) *adj.* Made without leavening. Said especially of the bread of the Passover.

un·less (ŭn-lĕs′) *conj.* Except on the condition that; except under the circumstances that. *—prep. Rare.* Except; except for. [Middle English *unlesse,* alteration of *onlesse (than* or *that),* originally *(up)on less than,* "on a less condition than," hence except, if . . . not : ON + LESS.]

Usage: The expressions *unless and until* and *unless or until* are undesirable because the principal components overlap when combined. Either *unless* or *until,* used singly and chosen in accordance with the desired sense, is usually sufficient: *Unless this sum is paid, no further credit can be extended* (not *unless and until*).

un·let·tered (ŭn′lĕt′ərd) *adj.* **1. a.** Not educated. **b.** Illiterate. **2.** Devoid of lettering. —See Synonyms at **ignorant.**

un·li·censed (ŭn′lī′sənst) *adj.* **1.** Having no license. **2.** Unauthorized. **3.** Unrestrained.

un·licked (ŭn′lĭkt′) *adj.* **1.** Not licked clean. Said of the newborn young of some animals. **2.** Unpolished; crude.

un·like (ŭn′līk′) *adj.* **1.** Not alike; different; dissimilar. **2.** Not equal, as in strength. *—prep.* **1.** Different from; not like. **2.** Not typical of. **—un′like′ness** *n.*

un·like·li·hood (ŭn′līk′lē-hoo͝d′) *n.* The state of being unlikely or improbable; improbability.

un·like·ly (ŭn′līk′lē) *adj.* **-lier, -liest. 1.** Not likely; improbable. **2.** Likely to fail. **—un′like′li·ness** *n.*

un·lim·ber (ŭn′lĭm′bər) *v.* **-bered, -bering, -bers.** *—tr.* **1.** To detach (a gun or caisson) from its limber. **2.** To make ready for action. *—intr.* To prepare for action.

un·lim·it·ed (ŭn′lĭm′ĭ-tĭd) *adj.* Having no limits, bounds, or qualifications. **—un′lim′it·ed·ly** *adv.* **—un′lim′it·ed·ness** *n.*

un·link (ŭn′lĭngk′) *tr.v.* **-linked, -linking, -links.** To disconnect the links of; unfasten.

un·list·ed (ŭn′lĭs′tĭd) *adj.* **1.** Not appearing on a list. **2.** Designating stock or securities not listed on a stock exchange.

un·live (ŭn′lĭv′) *tr.v.* **-lived, -living, -lives.** To live in such a manner as to undo or annul (earlier years or their consequences); reverse.

un·load (ŭn′lōd′) *v.* **-loaded, -loading, -loads.** *—tr.* **1. a.** To remove the load or cargo from. **b.** To discharge (a cargo or load). **2. a.** To relieve (oneself) of something oppressive; unburden. **b.** To pour forth (one's troubles). **3.** To remove the charge from (a firearm). **4.** To dispose of, especially by selling in great quantity; dump. *—intr.* To discharge a cargo or other burden. **—un′load′er** *n.*

un·lock (ŭn′lŏk′) *v.* **-locked, -locking, -locks.** *—tr.* **1. a.** To undo (a lock) by turning a key or a corresponding part. **b.** To undo the lock of. **2.** To cause to open; give access to: *unlocked her heart.* **3.** To set free; release. **4.** To provide a key to; open to solution: *unlock a mystery.* *—intr.* To become unfastened, loosened, or freed from.

un·looked-for (ŭn′lo͝okt′fôr′) *adj.* Not looked for or expected; unforeseen.

un·loose (ŭn′lo͞os′) *tr.v.* **-loosed, -loosing, -looses. 1.** To let loose or unfasten; release; set free. **2.** To relax; ease, as a hold upon something. [Middle English *unlo(o)sen* : UN- (intensive) + *lo(o)sen,* to loosen, from *lo(o)s,* LOOSE.]

un·loos·en (ŭn′lo͞o′sən) *tr.v.* **-ened, -ening, -ens.** To unloose.

un·love·ly (ŭn′lŭv′lē) *adj.* **-lier, -liest.** Not beautiful or pleasant; disagreeable; repugnant.

un·luck·y (ŭn′lŭk′ē) *adj.* **-ier, -iest. 1.** Subjected to or marked by misfortune. **2.** Forecasting bad luck; inauspicious. **3.** Not producing the desired outcome; disappointing. **—un′luck′i·ly** *adv.* **—un′luck′i·ness** *n.*

unm. unmarried.

un·make (ŭn′māk′) *tr.v.* **-made** (-mād′), **-making, -makes. 1.** To deprive of position, rank, or authority; depose. **2.** To ruin; destroy. **3.** To alter the characteristics of.

un·man (ŭn′măn′) *tr.v.* **-manned, -manning, -mans. 1.** To cause to lose courage: *"The idea of the grisly occupant unmanned him"* (R.L. Stevenson). **2.** To deprive of virility; emasculate.

un·man·ly (ŭn′măn′lē) *adj.* **-lier, -liest. 1. a.** Dishonorable; degrading. **b.** Cowardly. **2.** Effeminate. **—un′man′li·ness** *n.*

un·manned (ŭn′mănd′) *adj.* **1.** Without crew: *an unmanned ship.* **2.** *Obsolete.* Untrained. Said of a hawk.

un·man·nered (ŭn′măn′ərd) *adj.* Without manners; rude.

un·man·ner·ly (ŭn′măn′ər-lē) *adj.* Rude; ill-mannered. **—un′man′ner·li·ness** *n.*

un·marked (ŭn′märkt′) *adj.* **1.** Not bearing a mark. **2.** Not observed or noticed. **3.** Not marked with a grade, corrections, price, or the like.

un·mask (ŭn′măsk′, -mäsk′) *v.* **-masked, -masking, -masks.** *—tr.* **1.** To remove a mask from. **2.** To disclose the true character of; expose. *—intr.* To remove one's mask.

un·mean·ing (ŭn′mē′nĭng) *adj.* **1.** Meaningless; senseless. **2.** Expressionless; vacant. **—un′mean′ing·ly** *adv.*

un·meant (ŭn′mĕnt′) *adj.* Not meant or intentional.

un·meet (ŭn′mēt′) *adj.* Improper; unseemly.

un·men·tion·a·ble (ŭn′mĕn′shən-ə-bəl) *adj.* **1.** Not fit to be mentioned. **2.** Unspeakable. **—un′men′tion·a·ble·ness** *n.* **—un′men′tion·a·bly** *adv.*

un·men·tion·a·bles (ŭn′mĕn′shən-ə-bəlz) *pl.n.* Underwear.

un·mer·ci·ful (ŭn′mûr′sĭ-fəl) *adj.* **1.** Having no mercy; merciless. **2.** Excessive: *unmerciful heat.* **—un′mer′ci·ful·ly** *adv.* **—un′mer′ci·ful·ness** *n.*

un·mind·ful (ŭn′mīnd′fəl) *adj.* Careless, forgetful; oblivious. Used with *of: unmindful of the time.* See Synonyms at **forgetful.** **—un′mind′ful·ly** *adv.* **—un′mind′ful·ness** *n.*

un·mis·tak·a·ble (ŭn′mĭ-stā′kə-bəl) *adj.* Obvious; evident. **—un′mis·tak′a·bly** *adv.*

un·mit·i·gat·ed (ŭn′mĭt′ə-gā′tĭd) *adj.* **1.** Not diminished or moderated in intensity or severity; unrelieved. **2.** Absolute; unqualified; unconscionable: *an unmitigated lie.* **—un′mit′i·gat′ed·ly** *adv.*

un·mod·u·lat·ed (ŭn′mŏj′o͞o-lā′tĭd) *adj.* Not modulated.

un·moor (ŭn′mo͝or′) *v.* **-moored, -mooring, -moors.** *—tr.* **1.** To

ă pat/ā pay/âr care/ä father/b bib/ch church/d deed/ĕ pet/ē be/f fife/g gag/h hat/hw which/ĭ pit/ī pie/îr pier/j judge/k kick/l lid, needle/m mum/n no, sudden/ng thing/ŏ pot/ō toe/ô paw, for/oi noise/ou out/o͝o took/o͞o boot/p pop/r roar/s sauce/sh ship, dish/

release from or as if from moorings. **2.** To release (a ship) from all but one anchor. —*intr.* To cast off moorings.

un·mor·al (ŭn′môr′əl, -mŏr′əl) *adj.* Having no moral quality; amoral. —**un′mor′al·ly** *adv.*

un·mor·tise (ŭn′môr′tĭs) *tr.v.* **-tised, -tising, -tises. 1.** To loosen the joints of (something mortised). **2.** To separate.

un·muf·fle (ŭn′mŭf′əl) *v.* **-fled, -fling, -fles.** —*tr.* To remove from (the face) something that muffles or conceals it. —*intr.* To remove or cast off something that muffles.

un·nat·u·ral (ŭn′năch′ər-əl) *adj.* **1.** Violating natural law. **2.** Inconsistent with an individual pattern or custom. **3.** Deviating from a behavioral, ethical, or social norm: *an unnatural attachment.* **4.** Contrived or constrained; artificial: *an unnatural manner.* **5.** Outrageously violating natural feelings; inhuman. —**un′nat′u·ral·ly** *adv.* —**un′nat′u·ral·ness** *n.*

un·nec·es·sar·y (ŭn′nĕs′ə-sĕr′ē) *adj.* Not necessary; needless. —**un′nec′es·sar′i·ly** (-sâr′ə-lē) *adv.* —**un′nec′es·sar′i·ness** *n.*

un·nerve (ŭn′nûrv′) *tr.v.* **-nerved, -nerving, -nerves.** To deprive of composure, energy, or firmness.

un·num·bered (ŭn′nŭm′bərd) *adj.* **1.** Not numbered; countless. **2.** Not marked with an identifying number.

un·ob·tru·sive (ŭn′əb-trōō′sĭv) *adj.* Not readily noticeable. —**un′ob·tru′sive·ly** *adv.* —**un′ob·tru′sive·ness** *n.*

un·oc·cu·pied (ŭn′ŏk′yə-pīd′) *adj.* **1.** Not occupied; vacant. **2.** Not occupied by foreign troops. **3.** Unemployed; idle.

un·of·fi·cial (ŭn′ə-fĭsh′əl) *adj.* **1.** Not official. **2.** Not acting officially. —**un′of·fi′cial·ly** *adv.*

un·or·gan·ized (ŭn′ôr′gə-nīzd′) *adj.* **1.** Lacking order, system, or unity. **2.** Having no organic qualities; not living; inorganic. **3.** Not unionized.

un·o·rig·i·nal (ŭn′ə-rĭj′ən-əl) *adj.* Lacking originality; trite.

un·or·tho·dox (ŭn′ôr′thə-dŏks′) *adj.* Not orthodox; breaking with convention or tradition. —**un′or′tho·dox′ly** *adv.*

unp. *Library Service.* unpaged.

un·pack (ŭn′păk′) *v.* **-packed, -packing, -packs.** —*tr.* **1.** To remove the contents of (a suitcase, for example). **2.** To remove from a container or from packaging. **3.** To remove a pack from (a pack animal). —*intr.* To unpack goods, a trunk, or the like.

un·paged (ŭn′pājd′) *adj. Abbr.* **unp.** *Library Service.* Having no page numbers.

un·paid (ŭn′pād′) *adj.* **1.** Not yet paid: *an unpaid bill.* **2.** Serving without pay; contributing one's time; unsalaried.

un·par·al·leled (ŭn′păr′ə-lĕld′) *adj.* Without parallel; unmatched; unequal.

un·par·lia·men·ta·ry (ŭn′pär-lə-mĕn′tə-rē, -mĕn′trē) *adj.* Not in accordance with parliamentary procedure.

un·peg (ŭn′pĕg′) *tr.v.* **-pegged, -pegging, -pegs. 1.** To remove the peg or pegs from. **2.** To open, unfasten, or detach by or as if by the removal of pegs.

un·peo·ple (ŭn′pē′pəl) *tr.v.* **-pled, -pling, -ples.** To depopulate (an area).

un·peo·pled (ŭn′pē′pəld) *adj.* Uninhabited.

un·per·fo·rat·ed (ŭn′pûr′fə-rā′tĭd) *adj.* **1.** Lacking perforations. **2.** *Philately.* Imperforate.

un·pick (ŭn′pĭk′) *tr.v.* **-picked, -picking, -picks.** To undo (sewing) by removing stitches: *unpick a seam.*

un·pin (ŭn′pĭn′) *tr.v.* **-pinned, -pinning, -pins. 1.** To remove a pin or pins from. **2. a.** To open or unfasten by removing pins. **b.** To free.

un·pleas·ant (ŭn′plĕz′ənt) *adj.* **-anter, -antest.** Not pleasing; offensive; disagreeable. —**un′pleas′ant·ly** *adv.*

un·pleas·ant·ness (ŭn′plĕz′ənt-nĭs) *n.* **1.** The condition or quality of being unpleasant. **2. a.** An unpleasant experience or situation. **b.** An argument or quarrel.

un·plug (ŭn′plŭg′) *tr.v.* **-plugged, -plugging, -plugs. 1.** To remove a plug, stopper, or obstruction from. **2. a.** To remove (an electric plug). **b.** To disconnect (an electric appliance) by removing its plug from an outlet.

un·plumbed (ŭn′plŭmd′) *adj.* Not explored as to depth or signification; not fathomed: *unplumbed waters; an unplumbed theory.*

un·po·lit·i·cal (ŭn′pə-lĭt′ĭ-kəl) *adj.* Not political.

un·polled (ŭn′pōld′) *adj.* **1.** Not interviewed in a poll. **2.** Not registered at the polls.

un·pop·u·lar (ŭn′pŏp′yə-lər) *adj.* Lacking general approval or acceptance. —**un′pop′u·lar′i·ty** (-lâr′ə-tē) *n.*

un·prac·ticed (ŭn′prăk′tĭst) *adj.* **1.** Not yet tested or tried. **2.** Without benefit of experience; unskilled.

un·prec·e·dent·ed (ŭn′prĕs′ə-dĕn′tĭd) *adj.* Without precedent. —**un′prec′e·dent′ed·ly** *adv.*

un·pre·dict·a·ble (ŭn′prĭ-dĭk′tə-bəl) *adj.* Not predictable. —**un′pre·dict′a·bly** *adv.*

un·prej·u·diced (ŭn′prĕj′ŏō-dĭst) *adj.* Free from prejudice; impartial. See Synonyms at **fair**.

un·pre·med·i·tat·ed (ŭn′prĭ-mĕd′ə-tā′tĭd) *adj.* Not premeditated; not planned: *"His one act of rebellion was quite unpremeditated"* (R. Prawer Jhabvala). See Synonyms at **extemporaneous**. —**un′pre·med′i·tat′ed·ly** *adv.* —**un′pre·med′i·ta′tion** *n.*

un·pre·pared (ŭn′prĭ-pârd′) *adj.* **1.** Having made no preparations. **2.** Not equipped to meet a contingency. **3.** Not steeled, as to face a shock. **4.** Impromptu. —**un′pre·par′ed·ly** (-pâr′ĭd-lē) *adv.* —**un′pre·par′ed·ness** (-pâr′ĭd-nĭs, -pârd′nĭs) *n.*

un·pre·pos·sess·ing (ŭn′prē-pə-zĕs′ĭng) *adj.* Failing to impress favorably; unattractive; nondescript: *"The small company entered the yellow unprepossessing door and disappeared."* (Dreiser). —**un′pre·pos·sess′ing·ly** *adv.*

un·pre·ten·tious (ŭn′prĭ-tĕn′shəs) *adj.* Lacking pretention; unostentatious; modest. —**un′pre·ten′tious·ness** *n.*

un·priced (ŭn′prīst′) *adj.* Having no fixed or attached price.

un·prin·ci·pled (ŭn′prĭn′sə-pəld) *adj.* Lacking principles or moral scruples; unscrupulous: *unprincipled behavior.*

un·print·a·ble (ŭn′prĭn′tə-bəl) *adj.* Not proper for publication for legal or moral reasons.

un·pro·duc·tive (ŭn′prə-dŭk′tĭv) *adj.* **1.** Producing or yielding little or nothing. **2.** *Economics.* Adding nothing to exchangeable value. —**un′pro·duc′tive·ly** *adv.* —**un′pro·duc′tive·ness** *n.*

un·pro·fes·sion·al (ŭn′prə-fĕsh′ən-əl) *adj.* **1. a.** Not in a profession. **b.** Not a qualified member of a professional group. **2.** Not conforming to the standards of a profession. **3.** Amateurish. —**un′pro·fes′sion·al·ly** *adv.*

un·prof·it·a·ble (ŭn′prŏf′ĭ-tə-bəl) *adj.* Not profitable; serving no purpose; without gain; useless.

un·pro·nounce·a·ble (ŭn′prə-noun′sə-bəl) *adj.* **1.** Difficult to pronounce correctly. **2.** Not fit to be mentioned.

un·pro·vid·ed (ŭn′prə-vī′dĭd) *adj.* Not supplied, furnished, or equipped. Used with *with.* —**unprovided for.** Not provided with an adequate means of support: *He left his children unprovided for.* —**un′pro·vid′ed·ly** *adv.*

un·pro·voked (ŭn′prə-vōkt′) *adj.* Not provoked or prompted: *"a small book . . . which he'd bought that morning as a completely unprovoked gift to Margaret"* (Kingsley Amis).

un·qual·i·fied (ŭn′kwŏl′ə-fīd′) *adj.* **1.** Lacking the proper or required qualifications. **2.** Without reservations; unconditioned.

un·ques·tion·a·ble (ŭn′kwĕs′chən-ə-bəl) *adj.* Beyond question or doubt; indisputable; certain. —**un′ques′tion·a·bil′i·ty, un′ques′tion·a·ble·ness** *n.* —**un′ques′tion·a·bly** *adv.*

un·ques·tioned (ŭn′kwĕs′chənd) *adj.* **1.** Not subjected to questioning; not interrogated. **2.** Not able to be questioned or doubted; indisputable. **3.** Not called into question or examination; not doubted.

un·qui·et (ŭn′kwī′ĭt) *adj.* **-eter, -etest. 1.** Emotionally or mentally uneasy; agitated; disturbed; distraught. **2.** Characterized by unrest or disorder; turbulent: *unquiet times.* **3.** Noisy. —**un′qui′et·ly** *adv.* —**un′qui′et·ness** *n.*

un·quote (ŭn′kwōt′) *v.* **-quoted, -quoting, -quotes.** —*tr.* To close (a quotation). —*intr.* To close a quotation. Used by a speaker to indicate the termination of a quotation.

un·rav·el (ŭn′răv′əl) *v.* **-eled** or **-elled, -eling** or **-elling, -els.** —*tr.* **1. a.** To undo or ravel the knitted fabric of; reduce to yarn. **b.** To separate (entangled threads). **2.** To separate and clarify the elements of (something mysterious or baffling); solve; clear up: *"set himself to unravel Hugh's mechanical paradox"* (Lewis Carroll). —*intr.* To become unraveled.

un·read (ŭn′rĕd′) *adj.* **1.** Not read, studied, or perused. **2.** Having read little; ignorant.

un·read·a·ble (ŭn′rē′də-bəl) *adj.* **1.** Illegible. **2.** Not interesting; dull. **3.** Incomprehensible; obscure. **4.** Unsuitable for or not worth reading.

un·read·y (ŭn′rĕd′ē) *adj.* **-ier, -iest. 1.** Not ready or prepared. **2.** Slow to see or respond; not prompt. —**un′read′i·ly** *adv.* —**un′read′i·ness** *n.*

un·re·al (ŭn′rē′əl, -rēl′) *adj.* Not real or substantial; imaginary; artificial; illusory.

un·rea·son (ŭn′rē′zən) *n. Rare.* **1.** Absence or lack of reason; irrationality. **2.** Nonsense; absurdity.

un·rea·son·a·ble (ŭn′rē′zə-nə-bəl) *adj.* **1.** Not governed by or predicated upon reason. **2.** Exceeding reasonable limits; exorbitant; immoderate. —See Synonyms at **excessive**. —**un′rea′son·a·ble·ness** *n.* —**un′rea′son·a·bly** *adv.*

un·rea·son·ing (ŭn′rē′zə-nĭng) *adj.* Not governed by reason; unchecked by reason. —**un′rea′son·ing·ly** *adv.*

un·reck·on·a·ble (ŭn′rĕk′ə-nə-bəl) *adj.* Incalculable.

un·re·con·struct·ed (ŭn′rē-kən-strŭk′tĭd) *adj.* Unreconciled to social and economic change.

un·reel (ŭn′rēl′) *v.* **-reeled, -reeling, -reels.** —*tr.* To unwind from or as if from a reel. —*intr.* To unwind.

un·reeve (ŭn′rēv′) *v.* **-reeved** or **-rove** (-rōv′), **-reeved** or **-roven** (-rō′vən), **-reeving, -reeves.** *Nautical.* —*tr.* To withdraw (a rope, cable, or line) from a block, thimble, deadeye, or other opening. —*intr.* **1.** To become unreeved. **2.** To unreeve a rope.

un·re·flec·tive (ŭn′rĭ-flĕk′tĭv) *adj.* Not reflective. —**un′re·flec′tive·ly** *adv.*

un·re·gen·er·ate (ŭn′rĭ-jĕn′ər-ĭt) *adj.* **1.** Not regenerated; unrepentant: *"chivalrous for the instant even though still unregenerate"* (Faulkner). **2.** Unreconstructed. —**un′re·gen′er·a·cy** (-jĕn′ər-ə-sē) *n.* —**un′re·gen′er·ate·ly** *adv.*

un·re·hearsed (ŭn′rĭ-hûrst′) *adj.* Not rehearsed. See Synonyms at **extemporaneous**.

un·re·lent·ing (ŭn′rĭ-lĕn′tĭng) *adj.* **1.** Inexorable: *"Oedipus and Jocasta . . . the victims of an unrelenting fate"* (Thomas Bulfinch). **2.** Not diminishing in intensity, speed, or effort.

un·re·li·a·ble (ŭn′rĭ-lī′ə-bəl) *adj.* Not reliable. —**un′re·li′a·bil′i·ty, un′re·li′a·ble·ness** *n.* —**un′re·li′a·bly** *adv.*

un·re·li·gious (ŭn′rĭ-lĭj′əs) *adj.* **1.** Irreligious. **2.** Having no connection with religion.

un·re·mit·ting (ŭn′rĭ-mĭt′ĭng) *adj.* Never slackening; incessant; persistent. —**un′re·mit′ting·ly** *adv.* —**un′re·mit′ting·ness** *n.*

un·re·proved (ŭn′rĭ-prōōvd′) *adj.* Not reproved; uncensured.

un·re·serve (ŭn′rĭ-zûrv′) *n.* Frankness of manner; candor.

un·re·served (ŭn′rĭ-zûrvd′) *adj.* **1.** Given without reservation; unqualified; unlimited; unstinted: *unreserved praise.* **2.** Not reserved in manner; frank; candid. —**un′re·serv′ed·ly** (-zûr′vĭd-lē) *adv.* —**un′re·serv′ed·ness** (-zûr′vĭd-nĭs, -zûrvd′nĭs) *n.*

un·re·spon·sive (ŭn′rĭ-spŏn′sĭv) *adj.* Not responsive. —**un′re·spon′sive·ly** *adv.* —**un′re·spon′sive·ness** *n.*

un·rest (ŭn′rĕst′) *n.* Uneasiness; disquiet: *social unrest.*

---

un·re·strained (ŭn'rĭ-strānd') *adj.* **1. a.** Unchecked. **b.** Not given to restraint. **2.** Not constrained; natural. —**un're·strain'-ed·ly** (-strā'nĭd-lē) *adv.*

un·rid·dle (ŭn'rĭd'l) *tr.v.* **-dled, -dling, -dles.** To solve or explain (a riddle or mystery).

un·ri·fled[1] (ŭn'rī'fəld) *adj.* Having a smooth bore, as a gun.

un·ri·fled[2] (ŭn'rī'fəld) *adj.* Not rifled or ransacked.

un·rig (ŭn'rĭg') *tr.v.* **-rigged, -rigging, -rigs.** *Nautical.* To strip (a vessel) of rigging.

un·right·eous (ŭn'rī'chəs) *adj.* **1.** Not righteous; wicked: *an unrighteous man.* **2.** Not right or fair; unjust: *an unrighteous law.* —**un'right'eous·ly** *adv.* —**un'right'eous·ness** *n.*

un·rip (ŭn'rĭp') *tr.v.* **-ripped, -ripping, -rips.** To rip open; separate or detach by ripping. [UN- (intensive) + RIP.]

un·ripe (ŭn'rīp') *adj.* **-riper, -ripest. 1.** Not matured. **2.** Immature. **3.** Not ready. —**un'ripe'ness** *n.*

un·ri·valed (ŭn'rī'vəld) *adj.* Unequaled; peerless; supreme.

un·roll (ŭn'rōl') *v.* **-rolled, -rolling, -rolls.** —*tr.* **1.** To unwind and open out (something rolled up). **2.** To unfold; reveal. —*intr.* To become unrolled.

un·root (ŭn'rōōt', -rŏŏt') *tr.v.* **-rooted, -rooting, -roots.** To uproot.

un·round (ŭn'round') *tr.v.* **-rounded, -rounding, -rounds.** *Phonetics.* To pronounce (a vowel sound) with the lips in a flattened or neutral position.

UNRRA United Nations Relief and Rehabilitation Administration.

un·ruf·fled (ŭn'rŭf'əld) *adj.* Not ruffled or agitated; calm. See Synonyms at **cool.**

un·ru·ly (ŭn'rōō'lē) *adj.* **-lier, -liest.** Difficult or impossible to govern; not amenable to discipline. [Middle English *unreuly* : UN- + *reuly,* easy to govern, from *reule,* RULE.]

Synonyms: unruly, ungovernable, intractable, refractory, recalcitrant, willful, headstrong, wayward. These adjectives all mean difficult to control. *Unruly* usually refers to disorderly human conduct. *Ungovernable,* which is stronger, applies to what defies handling or restraint, to things made insuperable by sheer size, nature, or complexity, and to persons and their attributes that are beyond discipline. *Intractable* implies unyieldingness in persons who resist authority or guidance and in things that resist human efforts to control, adapt, or manipulate them. *Refractory* applies to things in this same sense; more often it and *recalcitrant,* which is stronger, describe persons who not only resist authority but rebel openly against it. *Willful* and *headstrong* describe the attitude and behavior of persons bent on having their own way, regardless of counsel to the contrary. *Wayward* implies insistence on taking a course in violation of established authority or of a sense of responsibility or virtue.

UNRWA United Nations Relief and Works Agency.

un·sad·dle (ŭn'săd'l) *v.* **-dled, -dling, -dles.** —*tr.* **1.** To remove the saddle from. **2.** To throw from the saddle; unhorse. —*intr.* To remove the saddle from a horse.

un·sat·u·rat·ed (ŭn'săch'ə-rā'tĭd) *adj.* **1.** Of or pertaining to a compound, especially of carbon, containing atoms that share more than one valence bond. **2.** Capable of dissolving more of a solute at a given temperature.

un·saved (ŭn'sāvd') *adj.* Not saved; especially, not redeemed from sin.

un·sa·vor·y (ŭn'sā'və-rē) *adj.* **1.** Not savory; tasteless; insipid. **2.** Distasteful or disagreeable. **3.** Morally offensive: *an unsavory scandal.* —**un'sa'vor·i·ly** *adv.* —**un'sa'vor·i·ness** *n.*

un·say (ŭn'sā') *tr.v.* **-said** (-sĕd'), **-saying, -says.** To retract (something said): *"What he did say, he would always unsay the next minute."* (Trollope).

un·scathed (ŭn'skāthd') *adj.* Unharmed; uninjured.

un·schooled (ŭn'skōōld') *adj.* **1.** Not schooled; uninstructed. **2.** Not the result of training; natural.

un·sci·en·tif·ic (ŭn'sī-ən-tĭf'ĭk) *adj.* **1.** Not in accord with the principles of science; especially, lacking in objectivity. **2.** Not knowledgeable of science. —**un'sci·en·tif'i·cal·ly** *adv.*

un·scram·ble (ŭn'skrăm'bəl) *tr.v.* **-bled, -bling, -bles. 1.** To disentangle; straighten out; resolve. **2.** To restore (a scrambled message) to intelligible form.

un·screw (ŭn'skrōō') *v.* **-screwed, -screwing, -screws.** —*tr.* **1.** To take out the screw or screws from. **2.** To loosen, adjust, or detach by rotating. —*intr.* To become or admit of being unscrewed.

un·scru·pu·lous (ŭn'skrōō'pyə-ləs) *adj.* Without scruples; contemptuous of what is right or honorable: *"A woman seeking a husband is the most unscrupulous of all the beasts of prey."* (G.B. Shaw). —**un'scru'pu·lous·ly** *adv.* —**un'scru'pu·lous·ness** *n.*

un·seal (ŭn'sēl') *tr.v.* **-sealed, -sealing, -seals.** To break or remove the seal of; to open.

un·seam (ŭn'sēm') *tr.v.* **-seamed, -seaming, -seams.** To undo the seam or seams of.

un·search·a·ble (ŭn'sûr'chə-bəl) *adj.* Beyond research; inscrutable; imponderable.

un·sea·son·a·ble (ŭn'sē'zə-nə-bəl) *adj.* **1.** Not suitable to or appropriate for the season. **2.** Not characteristic of the time of year. **3.** Poorly timed; inopportune: *"husbands who caught him in their houses at unseasonable hours"* (Macaulay). —**un'sea'son·a·ble·ness** *n.* —**un'sea'son·a·bly** *adv.*

un·sea·soned (ŭn'sē'zənd) *adj.* **1.** Not made savory with seasoning. **2.** Inadequately aged or seasoned; not ripe or mature: *unseasoned wood.* **3.** Inexperienced. —**un'sea'soned·ness** *n.*

un·seat (ŭn'sēt') *tr.v.* **-seated, -seating, -seats. 1.** To remove from a seat, especially from a saddle. **2.** To dislodge from a position or office.

un·seem·ly (ŭn'sēm'lē) *adj.* **-lier, -liest.** Not in good taste;

indecorous; unbecoming. See Synonyms at **improper.** —*adv.* In an unseemly manner. —**un'seem'li·ness** *n.*

un·seen (ŭn'sēn') *adj.* Not directly evident; invisible.

un·sel·fish (ŭn'sĕl'fĭsh) *adj.* Not selfish; generous. —**un'sel'-fish·ly** *adv.* —**un'sel'fish·ness** *n.*

un·set (ŭn'sĕt') *adj.* **1.** Not yet firm, stiff, or solidified, as glue or concrete. **2.** Unmounted, as a precious stone.

un·set·tle (ŭn'sĕt'l) *v.* **-tled, -tling, -tles.** —*tr.* **1.** To displace from a settled condition; render unstable; disrupt. **2.** To render uneasy; disturb; discompose. —*intr.* To become unsettled.

un·set·tled (ŭn'sĕt'əld) *adj.* **1.** Disordered; disturbed: *unsettled times.* **2.** Variable; uncertain: *unsettled weather.* **3.** Not determined or resolved: *an unsettled issue.* **4.** Not paid or adjusted: *an unsettled bill.* **5.** Unpopulated. **6.** Not fixed or established, as in a residence or routine. —**un'set'tled·ness** *n.*

un·sex (ŭn'sĕks') *tr.v.* **-sexed, -sexing, -sexes. 1.** To deprive of sexual capacity or sexual attributes. **2.** To castrate.

un·shack·le (ŭn'shăk'əl) *tr.v.* **-led, -ling, -les.** To release from or as if from confinement or shackles; set free.

un·shap·en (ŭn'shā'pən) *adj.* Also **un·shaped** (-shāpt') (for sense 1). **1.** Not shaped or formed. **2.** Misshapen.

un·sheathe (ŭn'shēth') *tr.v.* **-sheathed, -sheathing, -sheathes.** To draw from or as if from a sheath or scabbard.

un·ship (ŭn'shĭp') *v.* **-shipped, -shipping, -ships.** —*tr.* **1.** To unload from a ship; discharge. **2.** To remove (a tiller or other piece of nautical gear) from its proper place. —*intr.* To be removable or detachable.

un·sight·ed (ŭn'sī'tĭd) *adj.* **1.** Not sighted or examined. **2.** Not equipped with or assisted by a sight for aiming.

un·sight·ly (ŭn'sīt'lē) *adj.* **-lier, -liest.** Unpleasant or offensive to look at; unattractive. —**un'sight'li·ness** *n.*

un·skilled (ŭn'skĭld') *adj.* **1.** Lacking skill or technical training: *unskilled labor.* **2.** Requiring no training or skill. **3.** Showing no skill; crude.

un·skill·ful (ŭn'skĭl'fəl) *adj.* **1.** Without skill or proficiency; not adroit; inexpert; clumsy. **2.** *Obsolete.* Ignorant. —**un'skill'ful·ly** *adv.* —**un'skill'ful·ness** *n.*

un·slaked lime (ŭn'slākt'). Calcium oxide (see).

un·sling (ŭn'slĭng') *tr.v.* **-slung** (-slŭng'), **-slinging, -slings. 1.** To remove from a sling or a slung position. **2.** *Nautical.* To remove the slings of (a yard, for example).

un·snap (ŭn'snăp') *tr.v.* **-snapped, -snapping, -snaps.** To undo the snaps of; unfasten.

un·snarl (ŭn'snärl') *tr.v.* **-snarled, -snarling, -snarls.** To free of snarls; disentangle.

un·so·cia·ble (ŭn'sō'shə-bəl) *adj.* **1.** Not disposed to seek the company of others; not companionable; reserved. **2.** Not congenial; incompatible. **3.** Not conducive to social exchange: *an unsociable atmosphere.* —**un'so·cia·bil'i·ty, un'so·cia·ble·ness** *n.* —**un'so'cia·bly** *adv.*

un·so·phis·ti·cat·ed (ŭn'sə-fĭs'tĭ-kā'tĭd) *adj.* Not sophisticated. See Synonyms at **naive.** —**un'so·phis'ti·cat·ed·ly** *adv.* —**un'so·phis'ti·cat·ed·ness** *n.*

un·sound (ŭn'sound') *adj.* **-sounder, -soundest. 1.** Not dependably strong or solid. **2.** Not physically healthy; diseased. **3.** Not logically founded; fallacious; invalid. —**un'sound'ly** *adv.* —**un'sound'ness** *n.*

un·spar·ing (ŭn'spâr'ĭng) *adj.* **1.** Not frugal. **2.** Unmerciful; severe. —**un'spar'ing·ly** *adv.* —**un'spar'ing·ness** *n.*

un·speak (ŭn'spēk') *tr.v.* **-spoke** (-spōk'), **-spoken** (-spō'kən), **-speaking, -speaks.** *Obsolete.* To retract; unsay.

un·speak·a·ble (ŭn'spē'kə-bəl) *adj.* **1.** Beyond description; inexpressible: *unspeakable happiness.* **2.** Inexpressibly bad or objectionable. **3.** Not to be spoken: *an unspeakable word.* —**un'speak'a·ble·ness** *n.* —**un'speak'a·bly** *adv.*

un·spe·cial·ized (ŭn'spĕsh'ə-līzd') *adj.* Having no special function; without specialty or specialization.

un·sphere (ŭn'sfîr') *tr.v.* **-sphered, -sphering, -spheres.** *Rare.* To remove from a sphere or place in the heavens.

un·spot·ted (ŭn'spŏt'ĭd) *adj.* **1.** Not spotted. **2.** Morally unblemished. —**un'spot'ted·ness** *n.*

un·sta·ble (ŭn'stā'bəl) *adj.* **-bler, -blest. 1. a.** Tending strongly to change. **b.** Not constant; fluctuating. **2. a.** Of fickle temperament; irresponsible; flighty. **b.** Psychologically maladjusted. **3.** Not firmly placed; unsteady; not balanced. **4.** *Chemistry.* **a.** Decomposing readily. **b.** Highly or violently reactive. **5.** *Physics.* **a.** Decaying with relatively short lifetime. Said of subatomic particles. **b.** Radioactive. —**un'sta'ble·ness** *n.* —**un'sta'bly** *adv.*

un·stead·y (ŭn'stĕd'ē) *adj.* **-ier, -iest. 1.** Not securely in place; unstable. **2.** Fluctuating; inconstant. **3.** Wavering; uneven: *an unsteady voice.* —*tr.v.* **unsteadied, -ying, -ies.** To cause to become unsteady. —**un'stead'i·ly** *adv.* —**un'stead'i·ness** *n.*

un·steel (ŭn'stēl') *tr.v.* **-steeled, -steeling, -steels.** To make soft; disarm: *Their pleas unsteeled his heart.*

un·step (ŭn'stĕp') *tr.v.* **-stepped, -stepping, -steps.** *Nautical.* To remove (a mast) from a step.

un·stick (ŭn'stĭk') *tr.v.* **-stuck** (-stŭk'), **-sticking, -sticks.** To free from being stuck.

un·stop (ŭn'stŏp') *tr.v.* **-stopped, -stopping, -stops. 1.** To remove a stopper or stop from. **2.** To remove an obstruction from; open.

un·stopped (ŭn'stŏpt') *adj.* **1.** Not stopped. **2.** *Phonetics.* Capable of being prolonged, as the consonants *z* and *l.*

un·strap (ŭn'străp') *tr.v.* **-strapped, -strapping, -straps.** To remove or loosen the strap or straps of.

un·strat·i·fied (ŭn'străt'ə-fīd') *adj.* Lacking definite layers.

un·stressed (ŭn'strĕst') *adj.* **1.** Not stressed or having the weakest stress. Said of a segment of speech. **2.** Not emphasized.

un·stri·at·ed (ŭn'strī'ā'tĭd) *adj.* Lacking striations; smooth-textured.
un·string (ŭn'strĭng') *tr.v.* **-strung** (-strŭng'), **-stringing, -strings.** **1.** To remove from a string. **2.** To unfasten the strings of. **3.** To weaken the nerves of; unnerve.
un·striped (ŭn'strīpt') *adj.* Not striped.
un·struc·tured (ŭn'strŭk'chərd) *adj.* **1.** Lacking structure. **2.** *Psychology.* **a.** Having no intrinsic or objective meaning; meaningful by subjective interpretation only. Said of items, such as inkblots or incomplete sentences, on projective tests. Compare **structured.** **b.** Not regulated or regimented: *an unstructured environment.*
un·strung (ŭn'strŭng') *adj.* **1.** Having a string or strings loosened or removed. **2.** Emotionally upset; unnerved.
un·stud·ied (ŭn'stŭd'ēd) *adj.* **1.** Not contrived for effect; natural. **2.** Not having been instructed; unversed.
un·sub·stan·tial (ŭn'səb-stăn'shəl) *adj.* **1.** Lacking material substance; insubstantial. **2.** Lacking firmness or strength; flimsy. **3.** Lacking basis in fact; insubstantial. —**un'sub·stan'ti·al'i·ty** *n.* —**un'sub·stan'tial·ly** *adv.*
un·suc·cess·ful (ŭn'sək-sĕs'fəl) *adj.* Not succeeding; without success. —**un'suc·cess'ful·ly** *adv.* —**un'suc·cess'ful·ness** *n.*
un·suit·a·ble (ŭn'so͞o'tə-bəl) *adj.* Not suitable; unfitting. —**un'suit'a·bil'i·ty, un'suit'a·ble·ness** *n.* —**un'suit'a·bly** *adv.*
un·sung (ŭn'sŭng') *adj.* **1.** Not sung. **2.** Not honored or praised in song; uncelebrated: *unsung heroes of battle.*
un·sus·pect·ed (ŭn'sə-spĕk'tĭd) *adj.* **1.** Not under suspicion. **2.** Not known to exist. —**un'sus·pect'ed·ly** *adv.*
un·sus·pect·ing (ŭn'sə-spĕk'tĭng) *adj.* Not suspicious; trusting. —**un'sus·pect'ing·ly** *adv.*
un·swathe (ŭn'swŏ*th*', -swô*th*', -swā*th*') *tr.v.* **-swathed, -swathing, -swathes.** To remove the swathings from; unbind.
un·swear (ŭn'swâr') *v.* **-swore** (-swôr', -swōr'), **-sworn** (-swôrn', -swōrn'), **-swearing, -swears.** —*tr.* To retract (an oath), often by swearing another oath. —*intr.* To recant or retract something sworn.
un·sym·met·ri·cal (ŭn'sĭ-mĕt'rĭ-kəl) *adj.* Asymmetric. —**un'sym·met'ri·cal·ly** *adv.*
un·tan·gle (ŭn'tăng'gəl) *tr.v.* **-gled, -gling, -gles.** **1.** To free from a tangle; disentangle. **2.** To clarify; resolve.
un·taught (ŭn'tôt') *adj.* **1.** Not instructed; ignorant. **2.** Not acquired by instruction; natural; untutored. —See Synonyms at **ignorant.**
un·teach (ŭn'tēch') *tr.v.* **-taught** (-tôt'), **-teaching, -teaches.** **1.** To cause to forget or unlearn something. **2.** To negate (what has been taught) with contradictory information.
un·ten·a·ble (ŭn'tĕn'ə-bəl) *adj.* **1.** Not defendable. **2.** Not suitable for occupation. —**un'ten'a·bil'i·ty, un'ten'a·ble·ness** *n.* —**un'ten'a·bly** *adv.*
Un·ter den Lin·den (o͝on'tər dĕn lĭn'dən). The main street of East Berlin, extending from the Brandenburg Gate to the center of the city.
Un·ter·mey·er (ŭn'tər-mī'ər), **Louis.** Born 1885. American poet and anthologist.
un·thank·ful (ŭn'thăngk'fəl) *adj.* **1.** Not thankful; ungrateful. **2.** Not drawing thanks; unwelcome; thankless. —**un'thank'ful·ly** *adv.* —**un'thank'ful·ness** *n.*
un·think (ŭn'thĭngk') *tr.v.* **-thought** (-thôt'), **-thinking, -thinks.** To dismiss from the mind; disregard.
un·think·a·ble (ŭn'thĭng'kə-bəl) *adj.* **1.** Not thinkable; inconceivable. **2.** Not to be thought of or considered; out of the question. **3.** Contrary to what is reasonable or probable.
un·think·ing (ŭn'thĭng'kĭng) *adj.* **1.** Not thinking or mindful; inattentive; heedless. **2.** Not deliberate; inadvertent. —**un'think'ing·ly** *adv.* —**un'think'ing·ness** *n.*
un·thread (ŭn'thrĕd') *tr.v.* **-threaded, -threading, -threads.** **1.** To draw out the thread from. **2.** To find one's way out of (a labyrinth, for example).
un·ti·dy (ŭn'tī'dē) *adj.* **-dier, -diest.** **1.** Not neat and tidy; slovenly. **2.** Lacking orderliness or organization. —See Synonyms at **sloppy.** —**un'ti'di·ly** *adv.* —**un'ti'di·ness** *n.*
un·tie (ŭn'tī') *v.* **-tied, -tying, -ties.** —*tr.* **1.** To undo or loosen (a knot or something knotted). **2.** To free from something that binds or restrains. **3.** To straighten out (difficulties or perplexities). —*intr.* To become untied.
un·til (ŭn-tĭl') *prep.* **1.** Up to the time of: *We danced until dawn.* **2.** Before a specified time. Used with a negative: *not until Friday.* **3.** *Chiefly Scottish.* Unto; to. —*conj.* **1.** Up to the time that. **2.** Before. See Usage note at **till.** **3.** To the point or extent that. [Middle English *until(l)*, to, toward, up to, till : *un-*, from Old Norse *und*, unto (see **anti** in Appendix*) + *til*, TILL.]
un·time·ly (ŭn'tīm'lē) *adj.* **-lier, -liest.** **1.** Occurring or done at an inappropriate time; inopportune. **2.** Occurring too soon; premature. —*adv.* **1.** Inopportunely. **2.** Prematurely. —**un'time'li·ness** *n.*
un·tir·ing (ŭn'tīr'ĭng) *adj.* **1.** Not tiring. **2.** Not ceasing despite fatigue or frustration; persistent; indefatigable: *untiring efforts in his friend's behalf.* —**un'tir'ing·ly** *adv.*
un·ti·tled (ŭn'tī'təld) *adj.* **1.** Having no right or claim. **2.** Having no title: *an untitled novel; untitled nobility.*
un·to (ŭn'to͞o) *prep. Poetic & Archaic.* To. [Middle English *un-*, to (see **until**) + TO.]
un·told (ŭn'tōld') *adj.* **1.** Not told or revealed: *untold secrets.* **2.** Beyond description or enumeration: *untold suffering.*
un·touch·a·ble (ŭn'tŭch'ə-bəl) *adj.* **1.** Not to be touched. **2.** Out of reach; unobtainable. **3.** Beyond the reach of criticism, impeachment, or attack. **4.** Loathsome, unpleasant, or defiling to the touch. —*n* Also **Un·touch·a·ble.** A Hindu, usually of the Sudra caste, who is considered unclean and with whom physical contact has been considered defiling by Hindus of higher castes. —**un'touch'a·bil'i·ty** *n.*
un·to·ward (ŭn'tôrd', -tōrd') *adj.* **1.** Unfavorable; unpropitious. **2.** Hard to control; refractory. **3.** *Archaic.* Awkward. —**un'to'ward·ly** *adv.* —**un'to'ward·ness** *n.*
un·trav·eled (ŭn'trăv'əld) *adj.* **1.** Not traversed, as a road. **2. a.** Not having traveled. **b.** Provincial; narrow-minded.
un·tread (ŭn'trĕd') *tr.v.* **-trod** (-trŏd'), **-trodden** (-trŏd'n) or **-trod, -treading, -treads.** To retrace (one's course).
un·tried (ŭn'trīd') *adj.* **1.** Not attempted, tested, or proved. **2.** Not tried in court.
un·true (ŭn'tro͞o') *adj.* **-truer, -truest.** **1.** Contrary to fact; false. **2.** Deviating from a standard; not straight, even, level, or exact. **3.** Disloyal; unfaithful. —**un'tru'ly** *adv.*
un·truss (ŭn'trŭs') *v.* **-trussed, -trussing, -trusses.** *Archaic.* —*tr.* **1.** To unfasten; undo: *untrussed the points of his breeches.* **2.** To undress. —*intr.* To remove one's clothes, especially one's breeches.
un·truth (ŭn'tro͞oth') *n.* **1.** A lie. **2.** The state or quality of being a lie. **3.** *Obsolete.* Unfaithfulness.
un·truth·ful (ŭn'tro͞oth'fəl) *adj.* **1.** Contrary to truth. **2.** Given to falsehood; mendacious. —See Synonyms at **dishonest.** —**un'truth'ful·ly** *adv.* —**un'truth'ful·ness** *n.*
un·tu·tored (ŭn'to͞o'tərd, -tyo͞o'tərd) *adj.* **1.** Having had no formal education or instruction: *an untutored genius.* **2.** Unsophisticated; unrefined: *"What could bind, tame or civilize . . . that wild, generous, untutored intelligence?"* (Virginia Woolf). —See Synonyms at **ignorant.**
un·twine (ŭn'twīn') *v.* **-twined, -twining, -twines.** —*tr.* **1.** To loosen or separate, as strands of twisted fiber. **2.** To disentangle. —*intr.* To become untwined.
un·twist (ŭn'twĭst') *v.* **-twisted, -twisting, -twists.** —*tr.* To loosen or separate (that which is twisted together) by turning in the opposite direction; unwind. —*intr.* To become untwisted.
un·used (ŭn'yo͞ozd' *for senses 1, 2;* ŭn'yo͞ost' *for sense 3*) *adj.* **1.** Not in use or put to use. **2.** Never having been used. **3.** Not accustomed. Used with *to: unused to city traffic.*
un·u·su·al (ŭn'yo͞o'zho͞o-əl) *adj.* Not usual, common, or ordinary. —**un'u'su·al·ly** *adv.* —**un'u'su·al·ness** *n.*
un·ut·ter·a·ble (ŭn'ŭt'ər-ə-bəl) *adj.* **1.** Not capable of being uttered or expressed; too profound for oral expression: *"I burned in the unutterable beauty of being alive"* (John Peale Bishop). **2.** Not capable of being pronounced. —**un'ut'ter·a·ble·ness** *n.* —**un'ut'ter·a·bly** *adv.*
un·val·ued (ŭn'văl'yo͞od) *adj.* **1.** Not prized or valued; unappreciated. **2.** Not appraised or assayed: *an unvalued gemstone.* **3.** *Obsolete.* Inestimable; invaluable.
un·var·nished (ŭn'vär'nĭsht) *adj.* **1.** Not varnished. **2.** Stated or otherwise presented without any effort to soften, disguise, or obfuscate: *The unvarnished truth dissipated his subterfuge.*
un·veil (ŭn'vāl') *v.* **-veiled, -veiling, -veils.** —*tr.* **1.** To remove a veil or other covering from. **2.** To disclose; reveal. —*intr.* To take off one's veil; reveal oneself.
un·voice (ŭn'vois') *tr.v.* **-voiced, -voicing, -voices.** *Phonetics.* To utter without vibrating the vocal cords; devoice.
un·voiced (ŭn'voist') *adj.* **1.** Not expressed or uttered. **2.** *Phonetics.* Voiceless.
un·war·rant·a·ble (ŭn'wôr'ən-tə-bəl, ŭn'wŏr'-) *adj.* Not justifiable; inexcusable. —**un'war'rant·a·bly** *adv.*
un·war·rant·ed (ŭn'wôr'ən-tĭd, ŭn'wŏr'-) *adj.* Having no justification; groundless: *"A judgment is unwarranted whenever it lacks basis in fact"* (Gordon W. Allport).
un·war·y (ŭn'wâr'ē) *adj.* **-ier, -iest.** Not alert to danger or deception; unguarded. —**un'war'i·ly** *adv.* —**un'war'i·ness** *n.*
un·washed (ŭn'wŏsht', -wôsht') *adj.* **1.** Not washed; unclean. **2.** *Informal.* Of the lower classes; plebeian.
un·wea·ried (ŭn'wîr'ēd) *adj.* **1.** Not tired; fresh. **2.** Never wearying; tireless. —**un'wea'ried·ly** *adv.*
un·well (ŭn'wĕl') *adj.* **1.** Not well; ailing; ill. **2.** Menstruating. —See Synonyms at **sick.**
un·wept (ŭn'wĕpt') *adj.* **1.** Not mourned or wept for: *the unwept dead.* **2.** Not shed. Said of tears.
un·whole·some (ŭn'hōl'səm) *adj.* **1.** Injurious to physical, mental, or moral health. **2.** Suggestive of disease or degeneracy. **3.** Offensive or loathsome: *"What was unwholesome to him, he regarded as unfit for anybody"* (Jane Austen). —**un'whole'some·ly** *adv.* —**un'whole'some·ness** *n.*
un·wield·y (ŭn'wēl'dē) *adj.* **-ier, -iest.** **1.** Difficult to carry or manage because of bulk or shape. **2.** Clumsy; ungainly. —See Synonyms at **heavy, awkward.**
un·willed (ŭn'wĭld') *adj.* Involuntary; spontaneous.
un·will·ing (ŭn'wĭl'ĭng) *adj.* **1.** Hesitant; loath. **2.** Done, given, or said reluctantly: *unwilling consent.* —**un'will'ing·ly** *adv.* —**un'will'ing·ness** *n.*
un·wind (ŭn'wīnd') *v.* **-wound** (-wound'), **-winding, -winds.** —*tr.* **1.** To reverse the winding or twisting direction of; unroll; uncoil. **2.** To separate the tangled parts of; disentangle. —*intr.* **1.** To become unwound. **2.** To become less tense; relax.
un·wise (ŭn'wīz') *adj.* **-wiser, -wisest.** Lacking wisdom; foolish or imprudent: *an unwise decision.* —**un'wise'ly** *adv.*
un·wish (ŭn'wĭsh') *tr.v.* **-wished, -wishing, -wishes.** **1.** To cease to wish for. **2.** *Rare.* To wish out of existence.
un·wit·ting (ŭn'wĭt'ĭng) *adj.* **1.** Not knowing; unaware: *an unwitting victim of fraud.* **2.** Not intended; unintentional. [Middle English *un-*, not + *witting*, present participle of *wit(t)en*, to know, Old English *witan* (see **weid-** in Appendix*).] —**un'wit'ting·ly** *adv.*
un·wont·ed (ŭn'wôn'tĭd, -wōn'tĭd, -wŭn'tĭd) *adj.* **1.** Not habitual or ordinary; unusual: *"Her unwonted breach of deli-*

cacy . . .perplexed him" (Meredith). **2.** *Obsolete.* Not accustomed. —**un'wont'ed·ly** *adv.* —**un'wont'ed·ness** *n.*

un·world·ly (ŭn'wûrld'lē) *adj.* **-lier, -liest. 1.** Not of this world; extraterrestrial; spiritual. **2.** Concerned with matters of the spirit or soul. **3.** Not worldly-wise; naive. —**un'world'li·ness** *n.*

un·wor·thy (ŭn'wûr'*th*ē) *adj.* **-thier, -thiest. 1.** Insufficient in worth; undeserving. Usually used with *of.* **2.** Not suiting or befitting. Usually used with *of: "The acquaintances she had already formed were unworthy of her"* (Jane Austen). **3.** Lacking value or merit; worthless. **4.** Vile; despicable. —**un'wor'thi·ly** *adv.* —**un'wor'thi·ness** *n.*

un·wrap (ŭn'răp') *v.* **-wrapped, -wrapping, -wraps.** —*tr.* To remove the wrappings from; to open. —*intr.* To become unwrapped.

un·writ·ten (ŭn'rĭt'n) *adj.* **1.** Not written or recorded. **2.** Not formulated; forceful or effective through custom; traditional. **3.** Not written upon; blank.

unwritten law. A code, rule, or law of morality, conduct, procedure, or the like whose authority lies in custom, tradition, or general usage rather than in documentation.

un·yoke (ŭn'yōk') *v.* **-yoked, -yoking, -yokes.** —*tr.* **1.** To release (a draft animal) from a yoke. **2.** To separate or disjoin. —*intr.* **1.** To remove a yoke. **2.** *Archaic.* To stop working.

un·zip (ŭn'zĭp') *v.* **-zipped, -zipping, -zips.** —*tr.* To open or unfasten (a zipper or something held by a zipper). —*intr.* To become unzipped.

up (ŭp) *adv.* **1.** From a lower to a higher position. **2.** In or toward a higher position: *looking up.* **3.** From a reclining to an upright position: *setting up the chessmen.* **4. a.** Above a surface: *coming up for air.* **b.** Above the horizon. **5.** Into view, existence, or consideration. **6.** In or toward a position conventionally regarded as higher, as on a scale, chart, or map. **7.** To or at a higher price. **8.** So as to advance, increase, or improve. **9.** With or to a greater pitch or volume. **10.** Into a state of excitement or turbulence. **11.** So as to detach or unearth: *pulling up weeds.* **12.** To a stop. **13.** Apart; into pieces: *tore it up.* **14.** *Nautical.* To windward. **15.** Each; apiece: *The score was eight up.* **16.** Completely; entirely. **17.** Suggesting thoroughness or conclusiveness. Used as an intensifier of verbs: *cleaning up; typing up a list.* —See Usage note at **on.** —*adj.* **1.** High or relatively high. **2. a.** Standing; erect. **b.** Out of bed. **3.** Moving or directed upward: *an up elevator.* **4.** Actively functioning; healthy: *up and around; up and doing.* **5.** Rising toward the flood level. **6.** Marked by agitation or acceleration: *The winds are up.* **7.** *Informal.* Taking place; going on: *What's up?* **8.** Being considered; under study: *a contract up for renewal.* **9.** Running as a candidate. **10.** Charged; on trial. **11.** Finished; over: *His time was up.* **12.** *Informal.* Well-informed: *not up on sports.* **13.** Being ahead of the opponent: *up two holes in a golf match.* **14.** *Baseball.* At bat. **15.** As a bet; at stake. Often used in the phrase *put up.* **16.** *Nautical.* Bound for a specified place. —**up against.** Confronted with; facing. —**up to. 1.** Occupied with; especially, devising or scheming: *idlers up to no good.* **2.** Primed or prepared for. **3.** Dependent upon: *It's up to us.* —*prep.* **1.** From a lower to or toward a higher point on. **2.** Toward or at a point farther along: *up the road.* **3.** In a direction toward the source of: *up the Hudson.* **4.** Against: *up the wind.* —*n.* **1.** An upward slope; a rise or ascent. **2.** An upward movement or trend. —**on the up and up.** *Slang.* Open and honest. —*v.* **upped, upping, ups.** —*tr.* **1.** To increase or improve. **2.** To raise. —*intr.* **1.** To get up; rise. **2.** *Informal.* To act suddenly or unexpectedly. Usually used with *and* plus a verb: *"She upped and perjured her immortal soul"* (Margery Allingham). [Middle English *up,* upward, and *uppe,* on high, Old English *ūp* and *uppe.* See **upo** in Appendix.*]

up–. Indicates: **1.** Up; for example, **uplift. 2.** Upper; for example, **upmost. 3.** Upward; for example, **upsweep.** [Middle English *up-,* Old English *ūp-, upp-,* upward, on high. See **upo** in Appendix.*]

up. upper.

up-and-com·ing (ŭp'ən-kŭm'ĭng) *adj.* Marked for future success; promising and enterprising: *an up-and-coming ingenue.*

up-and-down (ŭp'ən-doun') *adj.* **1.** Consisting of alternating upward and downward movement; fluctuating. **2.** Vertical.

U·pan·i·shad (ōō-păn'ə-shăd') *n.* Any of a group of philosophical treatises contributing to the theology of ancient Hinduism, elaborating upon the earlier Vedas. [Sanskrit *upanisad,* "a sitting down near to," "secret session" : *úpa,* near to (see **upo** in Appendix*) + *ni,* down (see **ni** in Appendix*) + *sad-,* to sit (see **sed-**[1] in Appendix*).]

u·pas (yōō'pəs) *n.* **1.** A tree, *Antiaris toxicaria,* of tropical Asia, that yields a juice used as an arrow poison. Also called "ordeal tree." **2.** The poison obtained from this tree or similar trees or plants. [Javanese, poison, dart poison.]

up·beat (ŭp'bēt') *n. Music.* An unaccented beat, upon which the conductor's hand is raised; especially, the last beat of a measure. —*adj. Informal.* Optimistic; happy; cheerful.

up-bow (ŭp'bō') *n. Music.* A stroke executed toward the heel of the bow on a violin or similar stringed instrument.

up·braid (ŭp'brād') *tr.v.* **-braided, -braiding, -braids.** To reprove sharply; scold or chide vehemently; censure. See Synonyms at **scold.** [Middle English *upbreyden,* Old English *ūpbrēdan,* "to throw up against," reproach : *ūp-,* up + *bregdan,* to move quickly, throw, weave (see **bherek-** in Appendix*).] —**up'braid'er** *n.* —**up'braid'ing·ly** *adv.*

up·bring·ing (ŭp'brĭng'ĭng) *n.* The rearing and training received during childhood.

up·build (ŭp'bĭld') *tr.v.* **-built** (-bĭlt'), **-building, -builds.** To build up; enlarge or enhance. —**up'build'er** *n.*

up·cast (ŭp'kăst', -käst') *adj.* Directed or thrown upward. —*n.* **1.** Something cast upward. **2.** A ventilating shaft, as in a mine.

up·chuck (ŭp'chŭk') *v.* **-chucked, -chucking, -chucks.** *Slang.* —*intr.* To vomit. —*tr.* To vomit (stomach contents).

up·com·ing (ŭp'kŭm'ĭng) *adj.* Anticipated; forthcoming.

Usage: *Upcoming* has considerably less standing than its synonyms *coming, forthcoming,* and *approaching,* especially on a formal level. As an example in writing, *the upcoming election* is termed unacceptable by 71 per cent of the Usage Panel.

up·coun·try (ŭp'kŭn'trē) *n.* The inland or interior region of a country. —*adj.* (ŭp'kŭn'trē). Located, originating from, or characteristic of the upcountry. —*adv.* (ŭp'kŭn'trē). In, to, or toward the upcountry.

up·date (ŭp'dāt') *tr.v.* **-dated, -dating, -dates.** To bring up to date: *update a textbook.*

Up·dike (ŭp'dīk), **John (Hoyer).** Born 1932. American author of novels and short stories.

up·draft (ŭp'drăft', -dräft') *n.* An upward current of air.

up·end (ŭp'ĕnd') *v.* **-ended, -ending, -ends.** —*tr.* **1.** To stand, set, or turn on one end. **2.** To overturn or overthrow. —*intr.* To be upended.

up·grade (ŭp'grād') *tr.v.* **-graded, -grading, -grades. 1.** To raise to a higher grade or standard. **2.** To improve the quality of (livestock) by selective breeding for desired characteristics. —*n.* An incline leading uphill. —**on the upgrade. 1.** Rising. **2.** Improving or progressing. —*adj.* Uphill. —*adv.* Uphill.

up·growth (ŭp'grōth') *n.* **1.** The process of growing upward. **2.** Upward growth or development.

up·heav·al (ŭp'hē'vəl) *n.* **1.** The process or an instance of being heaved upward. **2.** A sudden and violent disruption or upset: *"The psychic upheaval caused by war"* (Wallace Fowlie). **3.** *Geology.* A lifting up of the earth's crust by the movement of stratified or other rocks.

up·heave (ŭp'hēv') *v.* **-heaved** or **-hove** (-hōv'), **-heaving, -heaves.** —*tr.* To heave upward; lift forcefully from beneath. —*intr.* To be lifted or thrust upward.

up·hill (ŭp'hĭl') *adj.* **1.** Going up a hill or slope. **2.** Prolonged and laborious. —*n.* (ŭp'hĭl'). An upward slope or incline. —*adv.* (ŭp'hĭl'). **1.** To or toward higher ground; upward. **2.** Against adversity; with difficulty.

up·hold (ŭp-hōld') *tr.v.* **-held** (-hĕld'), **-holding, -holds. 1.** To hold aloft; to raise. **2.** To prevent from falling or sinking; support. **3.** To maintain or affirm in the face of a challenge: *"The Declaration of Right upheld the principle of hereditary monarchy."* (Burke). —See Synonyms at **support.** [Middle English *upholden* : UP- + HOLD.] —**up·hold'er** *n.*

up·hol·ster (ŭp-hōl'stər) *tr.v.* **-stered, -stering, -sters. 1.** To furnish (chairs, sofas, or similar soft furniture) with stuffing, springs, cushions, and covering fabric. **2.** To furnish or adorn (rooms) with drapes, carpets, and similar accessories. [Back-formation from UPHOLSTERER.]

up·hol·ster·er (ŭp-hōl'stər-ər) *n.* A person who upholsters furniture as an occupation. [From obsolete *upholster,* a dealer in or repairer of small wares, Middle English *upholdester,* one who upholds or repairs, from *upholden,* UPHOLD.]

up·hol·ster·y (ŭp-hōl'stər-ē, -strē) *n., pl.* **-ies. 1.** The fabrics and other materials used in upholstering. **2.** The act, craft, or business of upholstering.

u·phroe. Variant of **euphroe.**

UPI, U.P.I. United Press International.

up·keep (ŭp'kēp') *n.* **1.** Maintenance in proper operation, condition, and repair. **2.** The cost of such maintenance.

up·land (ŭp'lənd, -lănd') *n.* **1.** The higher parts of a region or tract of land. **2.** Inland country; upcountry. —*adj.* Of, pertaining to, or located in an upland.

upland cotton. A plant, *Gossypium hirsutum,* native to tropical America and widely cultivated for its fiber.

upland plover. A brownish, long-necked New World bird, *Bartramia longicauda,* of fields and prairies.

up·lift (ŭp-lĭft') *tr.v.* **-lifted, -lifting, -lifts. 1.** To raise up or aloft; elevate. **2.** To raise to a higher social, intellectual, or moral level or condition. **3.** To raise to spiritual or emotional heights; exalt. —*adj.* (ŭp'lĭft'). Uplifted. —*n.* (ŭp'lĭft'). **1.** The act, process, or result of raising or lifting up. **2.** A movement to improve social, moral, or intellectual standards. **3.** Any agent or influence causing upward movement or lifting. **4.** *Geology.* An upheaval.

up·most (ŭp'mōst') *adj.* Uppermost.

U·po·lu (ōō-pō'lōō). The principal island of Western Samoa, 430 square miles in area. Population, 82,000.

up·on (ə-pŏn', ə-pôn') *prep.* On. See Usage note at **on.** [Middle English (formed after Old Norse *upp ā*) : UP + ON.]

up·per (ŭp'ər) *adj. Abbr.* **up., u., U. 1.** Higher in place, position, or rank. **2. a.** Situated on higher ground. **b.** Lying farther inland. **c.** Northern. **3.** *Capital* **U.** *Geology & Archaeology.* Being a later division of the period named. —*n.* **1.** That part of a shoe or boot above the sole. **2.** *Informal.* An upper berth. **3.** *Plural. Informal.* The upper teeth or a set of upper dentures. —**on one's uppers.** *Informal.* **1.** Wearing shoes with worn-out soles. **2.** Impoverished; destitute.

Upper Aus·tri·a (ôs'trē-ə). A province of Austria, occupying 4,625 square miles in the north. Population, 1,132,000. Capital, Linz.

upper bound. A number that is not exceeded by any number in a given set.

Upper Bur·ma (bûr'mə). The inland districts of northern Burma, incorporated with Lower Burma in 1886 to form the Burma province of India.

Upper Ca·na·da (kăn'ə-də). A former administrative division

of Canada (1791–1841), coextensive with modern Ontario.
Upper Carboniferous. *Geology.* **Pennsylvanian** *(see).*
upper case. *Abbr.* **u.c.** The case of printing type containing the capital letters and special characters.
up·per-case (ŭp′ər-kās′) *adj.* Pertaining to or printed in capital letters; capital. —*tr.v.* **upper-cased, -casing, -cases.** To print in upper-case letters.
up·per-class (ŭp′ər-klăs′, -kläs′) *adj.* **1.** Pertaining or belonging to an upper social class. **2.** Belonging to or characteristic of the junior and senior classes in a school or college.
up·per·class·man (ŭp′ər-klăs′mən, -kläs′mən) *n., pl.* **-men** (-mĭn). A student in the junior or senior class of a secondary school or college.
upper crust. *Informal.* The highest social class or group.
up·per·cut (ŭp′ər-kŭt′) *n. Boxing.* A short swinging blow directed upward, as to the opponent's chin. —*v.* **uppercut, -cutting, -cuts.** To punch with an uppercut.
Upper Dar·by (där′bē). A residential district of southeastern Pennsylvania near Philadelphia. Population, 93,000.
Upper E·gypt (ē′jĭpt). The southern section of Egypt, extending from south of Cairo to the Sudan border.
upper hand. A position of control or advantage.
Upper House. Also **upper house.** The branch of a bicameral legislature that is smaller and less broadly representative of the population, as the House of Lords in the British Parliament.
Upper Kar·roo. See **Karroo.**
up·per·most (ŭp′ər-mōst′) *adj.* Highest in position, place, rank, or influence; topmost; foremost. —*adv.* In the first or highest rank, position, or place; first.
Upper Pa·lat·i·nate. See the **Palatinate.**
Upper Peninsula. The northern section of Michigan, separated from the Lower Peninsula by the Straits of Mackinac.
Upper Vol·ta (vŏl′tə). *French* **Haute-Vol·ta** (ōt-vôl-tȧ′). A landlocked republic of western Africa, occupying 106,011 square miles south of Mali. Population, 4,600,000. Capital, Ouagadougou.
up·pi·ty (ŭp′ə-tē) *adj. Informal.* Tending to be snobbish or arrogant. Also "uppish." [From UP.]
Upp·sa·la (ŭp′sə-lä′, ŭp-sä′lə; *Swedish* o͝op′sä′lä). Also **Up·sa·la.** A city and cultural center of Sweden, in the east, 40 miles north of Stockholm. Population, 84,000.
up·raise (ŭp-rāz′) *tr.v.* **-raised, -raising, -raises.** To raise or lift up; elevate.
up·rear (ŭp-rîr′) *v.* **-reared, -rearing, -rears.** —*tr.* To raise or lift up. —*intr.* To be raised up; to rise.
up·right (ŭp′rīt′) *adj.* **1. a.** In a vertical position, direction, or stance. **b.** Erect in posture or carriage: *"She sat with grim determination, upright as a darning needle stuck in a board"* (Harriet Beecher Stowe). **2.** Morally respectable; honorable. —See Synonyms at **vertical.** —*n.* **1.** A perpendicular position; verticality. **2.** Something standing upright, as a beam. **3.** An **upright piano** *(see).* [Middle English *upright,* Old English *ūpriht* : UP- + RIGHT.] —**up′right′ly** *adv.* —**up′right′ness** *n.*
upright piano. A piano having the strings mounted vertically in a rectangular case with the keyboard at a right angle to the case. Also called "upright."
up·rise (ŭp′rīz′) *intr.v.* **-rose** (-rōz′), **-risen** (-rĭz′ən), **-rising, -rises. 1.** To get up or stand up; rise. **2.** To go, move, or incline upward; ascend. **3.** To rise into view, especially from below the horizon. **4.** To increase in size; swell. —*n.* (ŭp′rīz′). **1.** The act or process of rising up. **2.** An upward slope; ascent.
up·ris·ing (ŭp′rī′zĭng) *n.* **1.** The act of rising up. **2.** An ascent; upward slope. **3.** A revolt; insurrection. —See Synonyms at **rebellion.**
up·riv·er (ŭp′rĭv′ər) *adj.* Toward or near the source of a river; in the direction opposite to that of the flow of water. —*n.* A region lying upriver. —**up′riv′er** *adv.*
up·roar (ŭp′rôr′, -rōr′) *n.* **1.** A condition of noisy excitement and confusion; a tumult. **2.** A heated controversy. —See Synonyms at **noise.** [Alteration (influenced by ROAR) of Dutch *oproer,* from Middle Dutch : *op,* up (see **upo** in Appendix*) + *roer,* motion (see **kerə-** in Appendix*).]
up·roar·i·ous (ŭp′rôr′ē-əs, ŭp′rōr′-) *adj.* **1.** Causing or accompanied by an uproar. **2.** Loud and full, as laughter; boisterous. **3.** Causing hearty laughter; hilarious. —**up′roar′i·ous·ly** *adv.* —**up′roar′i·ous·ness** *n.*
up·root (ŭp-ro͞ot′, -ro͝ot′) *tr.v.* **-rooted, -rooting, -roots. 1.** To tear or remove (a plant and its roots) from the ground. **2.** To destroy or remove completely; eradicate. **3.** To force to leave an accustomed or native location. —**up·root′er** *n.*
ups and downs. Alternating periods of good and bad fortune or spirits.
up·set (ŭp-sĕt′) *v.* **-set, -setting, -sets.** —*tr.* **1.** To overturn or capsize; tip over. **2.** To disturb in usual or normal functioning, order, or course. **3.** To distress or perturb mentally or emotionally. **4.** To defeat unexpectedly. **5.** To make shorter and thicker by hammering on the end, to swage. —*intr.* **1.** To become overturned; tip over; capsize. **2.** To become disturbed. —*n.* (ŭp′sĕt′). **1. a.** An act of upsetting. **b.** The condition of being upset. **2.** A disturbance, disorder, or agitation. **3.** A game or contest in which the favorite is defeated. **4. a.** A tool used for upsetting; a swage. **b.** An upset part or piece. —*adj.* (ŭp-sĕt′). **1.** Overturned; capsized. **2.** Disordered; disturbed. **3.** Distressed; distraught; agitated. [Originally "to set up," "erect," later "to overset," Middle English *upsetten* : UP- + *setten,* SET.] —**up·set′ter** *n.*
upset price. The lowest price at which merchandise or property will be auctioned or sold at public sale.
up·shot (ŭp′shŏt′) *n.* The final result; outcome. See Synonyms at **effect.** [Originally the last shot at an archery contest, hence an outcome or decision.]
up·side-down (ŭp′sīd′doun′) *adj.* **1.** Overturned completely so that the upper side is down. **2.** In great disorder or confusion; topsy-turvy. —*adv.* Also **upside down.** Topsy-turvy. [Alteration (influenced by obsolete *upside*) of earlier *upsedown,* Middle English *up so doun,* "up as if down" : UP + SO + DOWN.]
upside-down cake. A single-layer cake baked with sliced fruit at the bottom, then served with the fruit side up.
up·si·lon (ŭp′sə-lŏn′) *n.* The 20th letter in the Greek alphabet, written Υ, υ. Transliterated in English as *U, u,* often also as *y.* See **alphabet.** [Medieval Greek *u psilon,* "simple upsilon" (name adopted for graphic *u* as distinguished from graphic *oi,* both of which were pronounced identically as /ī/ in Late Greek) : Greek *u,* upsilon + *psilon,* neuter of *psilos,* bare, simple, mere (see **bhes-**[1] in Appendix*).]
up·spring (ŭp′sprĭng′) *n.* A leap or spring upward. —*intr.v.* (ŭp′sprĭng′) **upsprang** (-sprăng′) or **-sprung** (-sprŭng′), **-sprung, -springing, -springs. 1.** To spring up, as from the soil. **2.** To come into being; arise.
up·stage (ŭp′stāj′) *adj.* **1.** Pertaining to or involving the rear of a stage. **2.** *Informal.* Haughty; aloof. —*adv.* Toward, to, on, or at the back part of the stage. —*tr.v.* (ŭp′stāj′) **upstaged, -staging, -stages. 1.** To distract audience attention from (another actor), as by standing in front of him or forcing him to face away from the audience. **2.** *Informal.* To steal the show from; force out of the spotlight. **3.** *Informal.* To treat haughtily.
up·stairs (ŭp′stârz′) *adv.* In, on, or to an upper floor or story; up the stairs. —*adj.* (ŭp′stârz′). Of or pertaining to an upper floor or floors: *an upstairs maid.* —*n.* (ŭp′stârz′). Plural in form, used with a singular or plural verb. A floor or story above ground level. —**kick upstairs.** *Informal.* To dispose of by promotion to an ineffectual position.
up·stand·ing (ŭp′stăn′dĭng, ŭp′-) *adj.* **1.** Standing erect or upright. **2.** Morally upright; honest.
up·start (ŭp′stärt′) *n.* **1.** One that springs up suddenly; specifically, a person of humble origin who attains sudden wealth or consequence; a parvenu. **2.** A person having an exaggerated sense of his own importance or ability. —*adj.* **1.** Suddenly raised to a position of consequence. **2.** Characteristic of an upstart; self-important; presumptuous. —*intr.v.* (ŭp′stärt′) **upstarted, -starting, -starts.** To spring or start up suddenly.
up·state (ŭp′stāt′) *adj.* Pertaining to or designating that part of a state lying inland or farther north of a large city. —*n.* The upstate region. —**up′state′** *adv.* —**up′stat′er** *n.*
up·stream (ŭp′strēm′) *adv.* In, at, or toward the source of a stream or current.
up·stroke (ŭp′strōk′) *n.* An upward stroke, as of a brush.
up·surge (ŭp′sûrj′) *intr.v.* **-surged, -surging, -surges.** To surge up. —*n.* (ŭp′sûrj′). A rapid upward swell or rise.
up·sweep (ŭp′swēp′) *n.* A curve or sweep upward; especially, a hairdo that is smoothed upward in the back and piled on top of the head. —*tr.v.* (ŭp′swēp′) **upswept** (-swĕpt′), **-sweeping, -sweeps.** To brush, curve, or sweep upward.
up·swing (ŭp′swĭng′) *n.* An upward swing or trend; an increase as in movement or activity: *an upswing of the stock market.*
up·take (ŭp′tāk′) *n.* **1.** A passage for drawing up smoke or air; a flue or ventilating shaft. **2.** Understanding; comprehension: *very quick on the uptake.*
up·throw (ŭp′thrō′) *n.* **1.** A throwing upward. **2.** *Geology.* An upward displacement of rock on one side of a fault.
up tight. Also **up·tight** (ŭp′tīt′). *Slang.* **1.** Tense; nervous. **2.** Destitute. **3.** On intimate terms with another person. **4.** Conforming rigidly to convention.
up-to-date (ŭp′tə-dāt′) *adj.* Informed of or reflecting the latest improvements, facts, or style; modern. —**up′-to-date′ness** *n.*
up·town (ŭp′toun′) *adv.* In or toward the upper part of a town or city. —*n.* The upper part of a town or city. —**up′town′** *adj.*
up·turn (ŭp′tûrn′, ŭp′tûrn′) *v.* **-turned, -turning, -turns.** —*tr.* **1.** To turn up or over, as soil. **2.** To upset; overturn. **3.** To direct upward. —*intr.* To turn over or up. —*n.* (ŭp′tûrn′). An upward movement, curve, or trend.
UPU Universal Postal Union.
up·ward (ŭp′wərd) *adv.* Also **up·wards** (-wərdz). **1.** In, to, or toward a higher place, level, or position. **2.** To or toward the source, origin, or interior. **3.** Toward the head or upper parts. **4.** Toward a higher amount, degree, or rank: *Prices soared upward.* **5.** Toward a later time or greater age. **6.** Toward something greater or better. —**upward** (or **upwards**) **of.** More than; in excess of: *"The onslaught of upwards of seventy divisions"* (Winston Churchill). See Usage note below. —*adj.* Directed toward a higher place or position. [Middle English *upward,* Old English *ūpweard* : UP- + -WARD.] —**up′ward·ly** *adv.*
Usage: *Upward* (or *upwards*) *of* is confined in careful usage to what is in excess of a given quantity. It is sometimes employed as the equivalent of *a bit less than, about,* or *almost,* but is unacceptable in all of those senses, according to 82 per cent of the Usage Panel.
up·wind (ŭp′wĭnd′) *adv.* In or toward the direction from which the wind blows. —**up′wind′** *adj.*
Ur (ûr, o͝or). An ancient city in Sumer, on a site now in southeastern Iraq. In the Old Testament, called "Ur of the Chaldees."
URA Urban Renewal Administration.
u·ra·cil (yo͝or′ə-sĭl) *n.* A pyrimidine, $C_4H_4N_2O_2$, a constituent of ribonucleic acids. [UR(O)- + AC(ETIC) + -IL(E).]
u·rae·mi·a. Variant of **uremia.**
u·rae·us (yo͞o-rē′əs) *n.* The figure of the sacred serpent, depicted on the headdress of ancient Egyptian rulers and deities as an

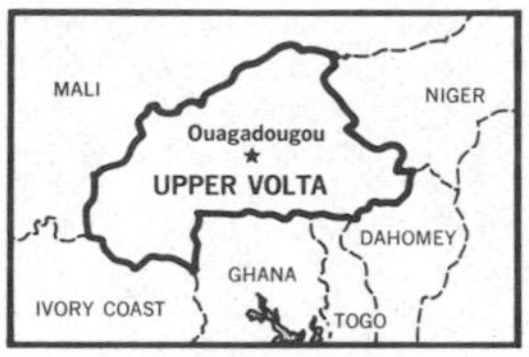

Upper Volta

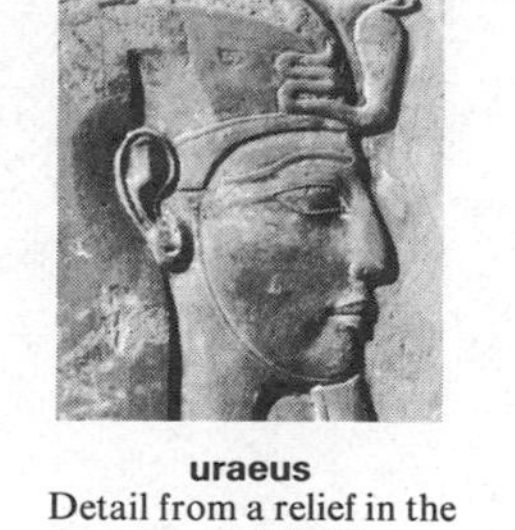
uraeus
Detail from a relief in the tomb of Seti I

emblem of sovereignty. [New Latin, from Late Greek *ouraios*, from Egyptian *uro*, asp.]

U·ral (yo͝or′əl). A river of the Soviet Union, rising in the Ural Mountains and flowing 1,574 miles west and then south to the Caspian Sea.

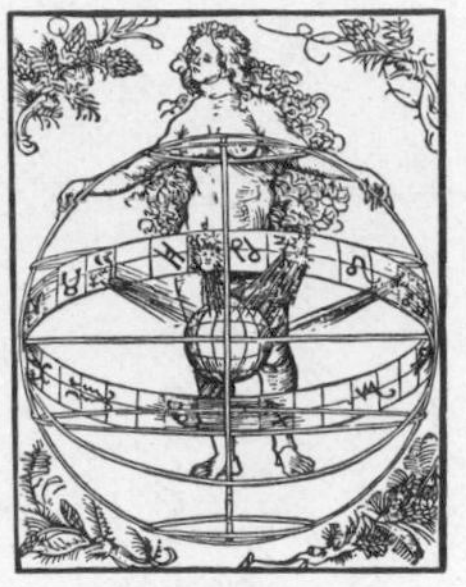

Urania
Shown holding an armillary sphere in a woodcut by Albrecht Dürer

U·ral-Al·ta·ic (yo͝or′əl-ăl-tā′ĭk) *n.* A hypothetical group of languages including the Uralic and Altaic families. Also called "Turanian." —*adj.* **1.** Pertaining to or designating this language group. **2.** Of or pertaining to the Ural and Altaic mountain ranges.

U·ral·ic (yo͞o-răl′ĭk) *n.* Also **U·ra·li·an** (yo͞o-rā′lē-ən). A family of languages including the Finno-Ugric and Samoyedic subfamilies. —*adj.* Of or designating this language family.

U·ral Mountains (yo͝or′əl). A mountain system of the Soviet Union, extending 1,300 miles across the Russian S.F.S.R. from the Arctic Ocean to the Kazakh S.S.R. and constituting the traditional boundary between Europe and Asia. Highest elevation, 6,184 feet.

U·ra·ni·a (yo͞o-rā′nē-ə, -rān′yə). *Greek Mythology.* The Muse of astronomy. [Latin, from Greek *Ourania*, "the heavenly one," from *ouranos*, heaven. See **Uranus.**]

u·ran·ic (yo͞o-răn′ĭk, -rā′nĭk) *adj.* **1.** Of or relating to the heavens; celestial. **2.** *Chemistry.* Of, pertaining to, or derived from uranium, especially with valence higher than in comparable uranous compounds. [Sense 1, from Latin *ūranus*, heaven, from Greek *ouranos*. See **Uranus.** Sense 2, from URANIUM.]

u·ra·ni·nite (yo͞o-rā′nə-nīt′) *n.* A complex brownish-black mineral, chiefly UO_2 partially oxidized to UO_3 and containing variable amounts of radium, lead, thorium, rare-earth metals, helium, argon, and nitrogen. [From German *Uranin*, uraninite : URAN(IUM) + -IN.]

u·ra·ni·um (yo͞o-rā′nē-əm) *n. Symbol* **U** A heavy silvery-white metallic element, radioactive, easily oxidized, and having 14 known isotopes of which U 238 is the most abundant in nature. The element occurs in several minerals, including pitchblende and carnotite, from which it is extracted and processed for use in research, nuclear fuels, and nuclear weapons. Atomic number 92, atomic weight 283.03, melting point 1,132°C, boiling point 3,818°C, specific gravity 18.95, valences 3, 4, 5, 6. See **element.** [New Latin, after the planet URANUS.]

uranium 235. The uranium isotope with mass number 235 and half-life 7.13×10^8 years, fissionable with slow neutrons and capable in a critical mass of sustaining a chain reaction that can proceed explosively with appropriate mechanical arrangements.

uranium 238. The most common isotope of uranium, having mass number 238 and half-life 4.51×10^9 years, nonfissionable but irradiated with neutrons to produce fissionable plutonium 239.

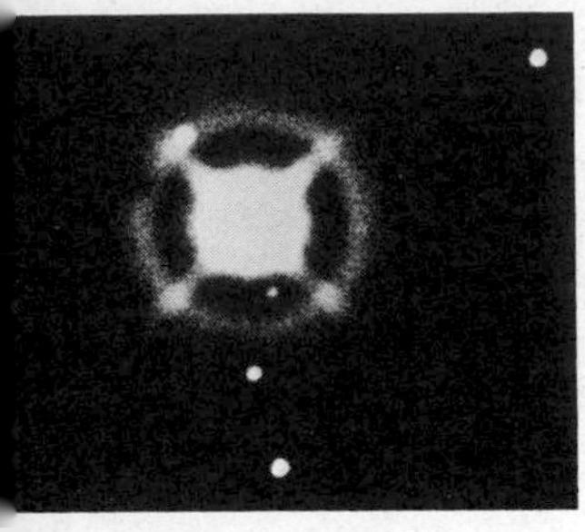

Uranus[2]
The planet and its satellite system of five known moons

u·ra·nous (yo͞o-rā′nəs, yo͝or′ə-nəs) *adj. Chemistry.* Of or pertaining to uranium, especially with valence lower than in comparable uranic compounds.

U·ra·nus[1] (yo͝or′ə-nəs, yo͞o-rā′nəs). *Greek Mythology.* The earliest supreme god, a personification of the sky, who was the son and consort of Gaea and the father of the Cyclopes and Titans. [Latin *Ūranus*, from Greek *Ouranos*, personification of *ouranos*†, heaven.]

U·ra·nus[2] (yo͝or′ə-nəs, yo͞o-rā′nəs) *n.* The seventh planet from the sun, revolving about it every 84.02 years at a distance of approximately 1,790,000,000 miles. It has an equatorial diameter of 30,000 miles, a mass 14.6 times that of Earth, and five satellites. See **solar system.** [After the god URANUS.] —**U·ra′ni·an** (yo͞o-rā′nē-ən, -rān′yən) *adj.*

u·ra·nyl (yo͝or′ə-nĭl, yo͞o-rā′nəl) *n.* The divalent radical UO_2. [URAN(IUM) + -YL.]

u·ra·ri. Variant of **curare.**

u·rase. Variant of **urease.**

u·rate (yo͝or′āt′) *n.* A salt of uric acid. [UR(IC ACID) + -ATE.]

U·ra·wa (o͞o-rä′wä). A city of Japan, a suburb of Tokyo on east-central Honshu. Population, 203,000.

Ur·bain (o͞or-băN′), **Georges.** 1872–1938. French chemist; worked with rare-earth elements.

ur·ban (ûr′bən) *adj.* **1.** Pertaining to, located in, or constituting a city. **2.** Characteristic of the city or city life. Compare **rural.** [Latin *urbānus*, from *urbs*†, city.]

Ur·ban II (ûr′bən). Original name, Odo or Udo. 1042?–1099. Pope (1088–99); promoted First Crusade.

urban district. An administrative district of England, Wales, and Northern Ireland, usually composed of several densely populated communities, resembling a borough but lacking a borough charter.

ur·bane (ûr′bān′) *adj.* Having or showing the refined manners of polite society; elegant: *"Urbane and pliant . . . he was at ease even in the drawing rooms of Paris"* (R.R. Palmer). See Synonyms at **suave.** [French *urbain, urbaine*, from Latin *urbānus*, characteristic of city life, URBAN.] —**ur′bane′ly** *adv.*

ur·ban·ism (ûr′bə-nĭz′əm) *n.* **1.** The culture or life style of city dwellers. **2.** Urbanization.

ur·ban·ite (ûr′bə-nīt′) *n.* A city dweller.

ur·ban·i·ty (ûr′băn′ə-tē) *n., pl.* **-ties. 1.** Refinement and elegance of manner; polished courtesy. **2.** *Plural.* Courtesies; civilities.

ur·ban·ize (ûr′bə-nīz′) *tr.v.* **-ized, -izing, -izes.** To make urban in nature or character. —**ur′ban·i·za′tion** *n.*

urban renewal. The state-sponsored destruction of slum neighborhoods with a view to the construction of new housing.

ur·ce·o·late (ûr′sē′ə-lĭt, ûr′sē-ə-lāt′) *adj.* Urn-shaped: *an urceolate corolla.* [New Latin *urceolatus*, from Latin *urceolus*, diminutive of *urceus*, jug, pitcher, akin to *urna*, URN.]

ur·chin (ûr′chĭn) *n.* **1.** A small, mischievous boy; a scamp: *"Those urchins who pencil mustaches on the faces of girls in advertisements"* (W.H. Auden). **2.** A **sea urchin** *(see).* **3.** *Archaic.* A hedgehog. [Middle English variant of *(h)irchon*, hedgehog, from Norman French *herichon*, from Latin *(h)ēricius*, from *(h)ēr*, hedgehog. See **ghers-** in Appendix.*]

Ur·du (o͝or′do͞o, ûr′-) *n.* **1.** A Hindustani language spoken in West Pakistan, where it is the principal language, and by Moslems in India. **2.** Hindustani. [Hindi *urdū*, short for *zabān-i-urdū*, "language of the camp" : Persian *zabān*, language + *urdū*, army, camp, from Turkish *ordū*, HORDE.]

-ure. Indicates: **1.** An act or process; for example, **erasure. 2.** A function or office or a body performing a function; for example, **legislature.** [Middle English, from Old French, from Latin *-ūra*.]

u·re·a (yo͞o-rē′ə) *n.* A white crystalline or powdery compound, $CO(NH_2)_2$, found in mammalian urine and other body fluids, synthesized from ammonia and carbon dioxide, and used as fertilizer, in animal feed, and in resins. [New Latin, from French *urée*, formed from *urine*, URINE.]

u·re·a-for·mal·de·hyde resin (yo͞o-rē′ə-fôr-măl′də-hīd′). Any of various thermosetting resins made by combining urea and formaldehyde and widely used to make molded household and mechanical objects.

u·re·ase (yo͝or′ē-ās′, -āz′) *n.* Also **u·rase** (yo͝or′ās′, -āz′). An enzyme occurring in urine, jack beans, soy beans, and as a secretion of certain microorganisms that is used to determine the urea content of blood and urine. [URE(A) + -ASE.]

u·re·din·i·um (yo͝or′ə-dĭn′ē-əm) *n., pl.* **-ia** (-ē-ə). Also **u·re·di·um** (yo͞o-rē′dē-əm) *pl.* **-dia** (-dē-ə). A reddish, pustulelike structure formed on the tissue of a plant infected by a rust fungus, having hyphae that produce uredospores. [New Latin, from Latin *ūrēdo* (stem *ūrēdin-*), blight, burning itch, UREDO.]

u·re·do (yo͞o-rē′dō) *n. Pathology.* **Urticaria** *(see).* [Latin *ūrēdo*, blight, burning itch, from *ūrere*, to burn. See **eus-** in Appendix.*]

u·re·do·spore (yo͞o-rē′də-spôr′, -spōr′) *n.* Also **u·re·din·i·o·spore** (yo͝or′ə-dĭn′ē-ə-spôr′, -spōr′). A reddish spore that is produced in the uredinium of a rust fungus and that spreads to and infects other plants.

u·re·ide (yo͝or′ē-īd′) *n. Chemistry.* Any of various derivatives of urea. [URE(A) + -IDE.]

u·re·mi·a (yo͞o-rē′mē-ə) *n.* Also **u·rae·mi·a. 1.** An excess of urea in the blood. **2.** A condition usually accompanying kidney disease and characterized by headache, nausea, vomiting, and coma. Also called "azotemia." [New Latin : UR(O)- + -EMIA.]

u·re·ter (yo͞o-rē′tər) *n.* The long, narrow duct that conveys urine from the kidney to the urinary bladder. [New Latin, from Greek *ourētēr*, from *ourein*, to urinate, from *ouron*, urine. See **wer-**[7] in Appendix.*]

u·re·thane (yo͝or′ə-thān′) *n.* **1.** A colorless crystalline or white granular compound, $C_3H_7NO_2$, used in palliative treatment for leukemia and as a solvent. **2.** Any of several esters, other than the ethyl ester, of carbamic acid. [French *uréthane* : UR(O)- (urine) + ETH(YL) + -AN(E).]

u·re·thra (yo͞o-rē′thrə) *n., pl.* **-thras** or **thrae** (-thrē). The canal through which urine is discharged in most mammals and which serves as the male genital duct. [Late Latin *ūrēthra*, from Greek *ourēthra*, from *ourein*, to urinate, from *ouron*, urine. See **wer-**[7] in Appendix.*] —**u·re′thral** *adj.*

u·re·thri·tis (yo͝or′ə-thrī′tĭs) *n.* Inflammation of the urethra. [New Latin : URETHR(A) + -ITIS.]

u·re·thro·scope (yo͞o-rē′thrə-skōp′) *n.* An instrument for examining the interior of the urethra. [URETHR(A) + -SCOPE.]

u·ret·ic (yo͞o-rĕt′ĭk) *adj.* Of or relating to urine; urinary. [Late Latin *ūrēticus*, from Greek *ourētikos*, from *ourein*, to urinate, from *ouron*, urine. See **wer-**[7] in Appendix.*]

U·rey (yo͝or′ē), **Harold Clayton.** Born 1893. American chemist and cosmogonist; discovered heavy hydrogen.

Ur·fa (o͝or-fä′). Ancient name **E·des·sa** (ĭ-dĕs′ə). A city in southern Turkey; a stronghold of the Crusaders (1097–1144). Population, 60,000.

Ur·fé (do͝or-fā′), **Honoré d′.** 1568–1625. French author of pastoral novels.

Ur·ga. The former name for **Ulan Bator.**

urge (ûrj) *v.* **urged, urging, urges.** —*tr.* **1.** To drive forward or onward forcefully; impel; spur. **2.** To entreat earnestly and repeatedly; plead with; exhort: *The board was urged to approve the budget.* **3.** To advocate persistently the doing, consideration, or approval of; press emphatically: *urge passage of the bill.* **4.** To stimulate; excite: *"It urged him to an intensity like madness"* (D.H. Lawrence). **5.** To persuade, force, or otherwise move to some course of action. —*intr.* **1.** To present a forceful argument, claim, or case. **2.** To exert an impelling force; push vigorously. —*n.* **1.** The act of urging. **2.** An irresistible or impelling force, influence, or instinct: *"There is a human urge to clarify, rationalize, justify"* (Leonard Bernstein). [Latin *urgēre*, to push, press. See **wreg-** in Appendix.*]

Synonyms: *urge, press, exhort, plead, coax.* These verbs mean to request or pressure a person to do something that one advocates. *Urge* suggests making an earnest appeal for such action. *Press* implies a somewhat more forceful act of urging or soliciting or repeated acts of this sort. *Exhort* suggests a stirring, eloquent appeal; *plead*, a humble but fervent one; and *coax*, an attempt to persuade through persistent application of courtesy, flattery, or blandishment.

ur·gen·cy (ûr′jən-sē) *n., pl.* **-cies. 1.** The quality or condition of being urgent; imperativeness; pressing importance: *"His work has the urgency of personal creation"* (John R. Taylor). **2.** A pressing necessity.

ur·gent (ûr′jənt) *adj.* **1.** Compelling immediate action; imperative; pressing: *a crisis of an urgent nature.* **2.** Insistent or importunate; earnest: *urgent pleas.* **3.** Conveying or relating a sense of urgency, as a message. [Middle English, from Old French, from Latin *urgēns,* present participle of *urgēre,* to push, press, URGE.]

Synonyms: *urgent, pressing, imperative.* These adjectives are compared as they refer to degrees of importance or order of priority. *Urgent* and *pressing* are applied to what requires or demands immediate attention. The terms are often interchangeable, though *urgent* sometimes conveys a stronger sense of need. *Imperative,* which is stronger than either, specifies a need or demand that cannot be deferred or evaded and from which, in most instances, no appeal is possible.

-urgy. Indicates a technology; for example, **metallurgy, zymurgy.** [New Latin *-urgia,* from Greek *-ourgos,* "worker," from *ergon,* work. See **werg-**[1] in Appendix.*]

-uria. *Pathology.* Indicates: **1.** A diseased condition of the urine; for example, **pyuria. 2.** A substance in the urine; for example, **albuminuria.** [New Latin, from Greek *-ouria,* from *ouron,* urine. See **wer-**[7] in Appendix.*]

U·ri·ah (yo͞o-rī′ə). The husband of Bathsheba and a Hittite officer in the Israelite army, whose death was contrived by David in order that he might marry his wife. II Samuel 11:3–27. [Hebrew *ūriyāh,* probably "Yahweh is my light."]

u·ric (yo͝or′ĭk) *adj.* Pertaining to, contained in, or obtained from urine. [UR(O)- + -IC.]

uric acid. A white crystalline compound, $C_5H_4N_4O_3$, the end product of purine metabolism in man and other primates, birds, terrestrial reptiles, and most insects.

ur·i·dine (yo͝or′ə-dēn′) *n.* A white, odorless powder, $C_9H_{12}N_2O_6$, that is the nucleoside of uracil, important in carbohydrate metabolism and used in biochemical experiments. [UR(O)- + -ID(E) + -INE.]

U·ri·el (yo͝or′ē-əl). One of the archangels. [Hebrew *ūrī'ēl,* probably "God is my light."]

U·rim and Thum·mim (yo͝or′ĭm; thŭm′ĭm). Objects carried inside the breastplate of the chief priests of ancient Israel and used as oracular media to divine the will of God. Exodus 28:30; Leviticus 8:8.

u·ri·nal (yo͝or′ə-nəl) *n.* **1. a.** An upright wall fixture used by men for urinating. **b.** A room or other place containing such a fixture or fixtures. **2.** A receptacle for urine used by a bedridden patient. [Middle English, chamber pot, from Old French *urinal,* from Late Latin *ūrīnal,* from *ūrīna,* URINE.]

u·ri·nal·y·sis (yo͝or′ə-năl′ə-sĭs) *n.* The chemical analysis of urine. [New Latin : URIN(O)- + (AN)ALYSIS.]

u·ri·nar·y (yo͝or′ə-nĕr′ē) *adj.* Of or relating to urine, its production, function, or excretion. *—n., pl.* **urinaries.** A reservoir for keeping animal urine for use as fertilizer.

urinary bladder. A muscular membrane-lined sac situated in the anterior part of the pelvic cavity and used as a urine reservoir prior to excretion.

urinary calculus. A solid concretion of mineral and organic substances in the urinary system. Also called "urolith."

u·ri·nate (yo͝or′ə-nāt′) *intr.v.* **-nated, -nating, -nates.** To excrete urine. [Medieval Latin *ūrīnāre,* from Latin *ūrīna,* URINE.]

u·rine (yo͝or′ĭn) *n.* The fluid and dissolved substances secreted by the kidneys, stored in the bladder, and excreted from the body through the urethra. [Middle English, from Old French, from Latin *ūrīna.* See **wer-**[7] in Appendix.*]

u·ri·nif·er·ous (yo͝or′ə-nĭf′ər-əs) *adj.* Conveying urine. [URIN(O)- + -FEROUS.]

urino–, urin–. Indicates urine; for example, **urinalysis, urinogenital.** [From Latin *ūrīna,* URINE.]

u·ri·no·gen·i·tal. Variant of **urogenital.**

u·ri·nous (yo͝or′ə-nəs) *adj.* Also **u·ri·nose** (-nōs′). Of, resembling, or containing urine.

Ur·mi·a, Lake (o͝or′mē-ə). The largest lake (1,500 to 2,300 square miles, depending on the season) in Iran, in the northwest between Tabriz and the Turkish border.

urn (ûrn) *n.* **1.** A vase of varying size and shape, usually having a footed base or pedestal and used especially as a receptacle for the ashes of the cremated dead: *"I go between birth and the urn, a bright ash"* (George Barker). **2.** A closed metal vessel having a spigot and used for warming or serving tea or coffee; a samovar. **3.** *Botany.* The spore-bearing part of a moss capsule. [Middle English *urne,* a vessel containing the ashes of the dead, burial urn, from Latin *urna.* See **urceus** in Appendix.*]

uro-[1]**, ur-.** Indicates urine or the urinary tract; for example, **urogenital, uridine.** [New Latin, from Greek *ouro-,* from *ouron,* urine. See **wer-**[7] in Appendix.*]

uro-[2]**, ur-.** Indicates a tail; for example, **uropod.** [New Latin, from Greek *oura,* tail. See **ors-** in Appendix.*]

u·ro·chord (yo͝or′ə-kôrd′) *n. Zoology.* A notochord limited to the caudal region, as in tunicates. [URO- (tail) + CHORD.]

u·ro·chrome (yo͝or′ə-krōm′) *n.* The pigment responsible for the normal yellow color of urine. [URO- + -CHROME.]

u·ro·gen·i·tal (yo͝or′ō-jĕn′ə-təl) *adj.* Also **u·ri·no·gen·i·tal** (yo͝or′ə-nō-). Of, pertaining to, or involving both the urinary and genital functions.

u·ro·lith (yo͝or′ə-lĭth′) *n. Pathology.* A **urinary calculus** *(see).* [URO- + -LITH.] —**u′ro·lith′ic** *adj.*

u·rol·o·gy (yo͞o-rŏl′ə-jē) *n.* The medical study of the physiology and pathology of the urogenital tract. [URO- + -LOGY.]

-uronic. Indicates a connection with urine; for example, **hyaluronic.** [From Greek *ouron,* urine. See **wer-**[7] in Appendix.*]

u·ro·pod (yo͝or′ə-pŏd′) *n.* One of a pair of posterior abdominal appendages of certain crustaceans, such as the lobster or shrimp. [URO- (tail) + -POD.]

uropygial gland. An oil-secreting gland at the base of a bird's tail. Also called "oil gland."

u·ro·pyg·i·um (yo͝or′ə-pĭj′ē-əm) *n.* The posterior part of a bird's body, from which the tail feathers grow; rump. [New Latin, from Greek *ouropugion* : URO- (tail) + *pugē,* rump (see **pygidium**).] —**u′ro·pyg′i·al** *adj.*

u·ros·co·py (yo͞o-rŏs′kə-pē) *n., pl.* **-pies.** *Medicine.* The examination of urine with a microscope. [URO- + -SCOPY.]

-urous. Indicates a tail or type of tail; for example, **anurous.** [New Latin *-urus,* from Greek *-ouros,* from *oura,* tail. See **ors-** in Appendix.*]

Ur·quhart (ûr′kərt), Sir **Thomas.** 1611–1660. Scottish author and translator of Rabelais.

Ur·sa Major (ûr′sə). A constellation in the region of the north celestial pole, near Draco and Leo, containing the seven stars that form the Big Dipper. Also called the "Great Bear." [From Latin *ursa,* feminine of *ursus,* bear. See **ursine.**]

Ursa Minor. A constellation having the shape of a ladle with **Polaris** *(see)* at the tip of its handle. Also called "Little Bear," "Little Dipper."

ur·sine (ûr′sīn′) *adj.* Of or characteristic of a bear. [Latin *ursīnus,* from *ursus,* bear. See **ṛkso-** in Appendix.*]

Ur·spra·che (o͞or′shprä′KHə) *n.* A reconstructed language set up as the parent of groups of related languages, as, for example, the Indo-European *Ursprache,* the hypothetical ancestor of Latin, Greek, Slavic, Celtic, and Germanic. Compare **protolanguage.** [German, "protolanguage."]

Ur·su·la (ûr′sə-lə, -syə-lə), **Saint.** A legendary British princess of the Christian faith who was reputedly killed, with her 11,000 virgin handmaidens, by the Huns at Cologne in the fourth or fifth century A.D.

Ur·su·line (ûr′sə-lĭn, -līn′, -lēn′, ûr′syə-) *n.* A member of an order of nuns of the Roman Catholic Church, founded in about 1537 and devoted to the education of girls. *—adj.* Of or belonging to this order. [After Saint URSULA.]

Ur·text (o͞or′tĕkst′) *n.* A reconstructed proto-text set up as the basis of variants in extant later texts. [German, "proto-text."]

ur·ti·cant (ûr′tĭ-kənt) *adj.* Causing itching or stinging. *—n.* A substance that causes itching or stinging.

ur·ti·car·i·a (ûr′tĭ-kâr′ē-ə) *n.* A skin condition characterized by intensely itching welts and caused by allergic reactions to internal or external agents, by foci of infection, or by psychic stimuli. Also called "hives," "nettle rash," "uredo." [New Latin, from Latin *urtīca,* nettle. See **urticate.**]

ur·ti·cate (ûr′tĭ-kāt′) *intr.v.* **-cated, -cating, -cates.** To sting or whip with or as with nettles. *—adj.* (ûr′tĭ-kĭt, -kāt′). *Pathology.* Characterized by the presence of itching or stinging wheals. [Medieval Latin *urtīcāre,* from Latin *urtīca*†, nettle.]

ur·ti·ca·tion (ûr′tĭ-kā′shən) *n.* **1.** *Medicine.* Formerly, a lashing with nettles as treatment of a paralyzed part of the body. **2.** The sensation of having been stung by nettles. **3.** Urticaria.

U·ru·bam·ba (o͞o′ro͞o-väm′bä). A river of Peru, rising in the Andes and flowing 450 miles first northeast and then northwest to the Apurímac, with which it forms the Ucayali.

U·ru·guay (yo͝or′ə-gwā′, -gwī′; *Spanish* o͞o′ro͞o-gwī′). **1.** Formerly **Ban·da O·ri·en·tal** (bän′dä ō′rē-ĕn-täl′). A republic of South America, occupying 72,152 square miles in the southeast on the Atlantic. Population, 2,590,000. Capital, Montevideo. **2.** A river of South America, rising in southern Brazil and flowing about 1,000 miles generally south to the Río de la Plata.

U·rum·chi (o͞o-ro͝om′chē). *Chinese* **Ti·hwa** (dē′hwä′). The capital of the Sinkiang-Uigur Autonomous Region, China, in the central part of the region. Population, 320,000.

U·run·di (o͞o-ro͞on′dē). The southern portion of the former U.N. Trust Territory of Ruanda-Urundi, in central Africa.

u·rus (yo͝or′əs) *n.* An extinct bovine mammal, the **aurochs** *(see).* [Latin *ūrus,* from Germanic. See **wer-**[12] in Appendix.*]

u·ru·shi·ol (ə-ro͞o′shē-ôl′, -ōl′) *n.* A toxic substance present in the resin of plants of the genus *Rhus,* which includes poison ivy and the lacquer tree, *R. verniciflua,* from which a black Japanese lacquer is obtained. [Japanese *urushi,* lacquer + -OL.]

us (ŭs) *pron.* The objective case of the first person plural pronoun *we.* It is used: **1.** As the direct object of a verb: *He assisted us.* **2.** As the indirect object of a verb: *They offered us a ride.* **3.** As the object of a preposition: *They came to us first.* **4.** After *than* or *as* in comparisons in which the first term is in the objective case: *They gave you more than us.* **5.** *Informal.* In place of the reflexive pronoun *ourselves,* as the indirect object of a verb: *We'll get us some dinner.* **6.** In various elliptical, absolute, or interjectional phrases in which it is neither subject nor object: *Who, us? Lucky us!* See Usage note at **we.** [Middle English *us,* Old English *ūs.* See **nes-**[2] in Appendix.*]

US United States.

u.s. 1. ubi supra. **2.** ut supra.

U.S. 1. Uncle Sam. **2.** *Photography.* Uniform system (of lens aperture). **3.** United States.

USA, U.S.A. 1. Union of South Africa. **2.** United States Army. **3.** United States of America.

us·a·ble (yo͞o′zə-bəl) *adj.* Also **use·a·ble. 1.** Capable of being used. **2.** In a fit condition for use; intact or operative. —**us′a·ble·ness** *n.* —**us′a·bly** *adv.*

USAF, U.S.A.F. United States Air Force.

USAFI, U.S.A.F.I. United States Armed Forces Institute.

us·age (yo͞o′sĭj, -zĭj) *n.* **1. a.** The act or manner of using or treating; use or employment. See Usage note below. **b.** The act of using. **2.** Customary practice; habitual use. **3.** The actual or expressed way in which a language or its elements are used, interrelated, or pronounced in expression: *contemporary English*

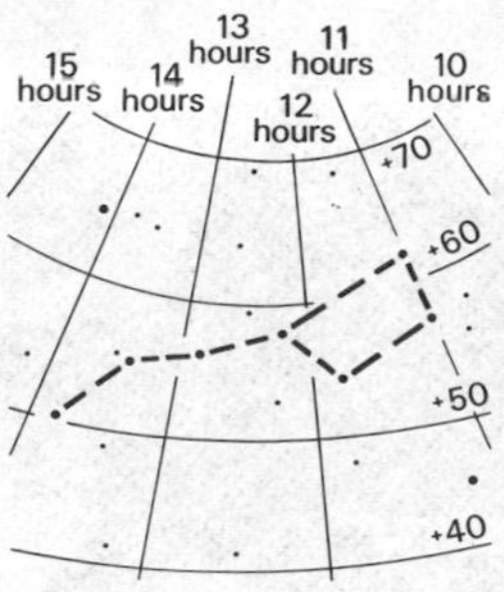

Ursa Major

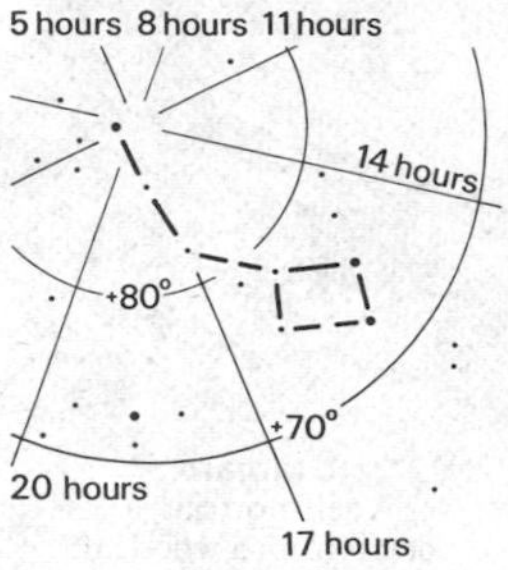

Ursa Minor

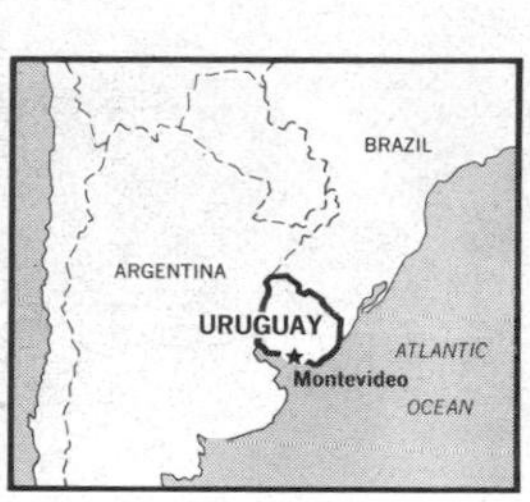

Uruguay

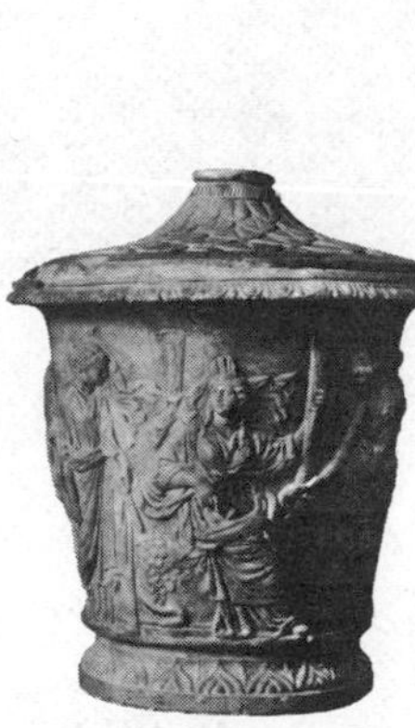
urn
Roman cinerary urn

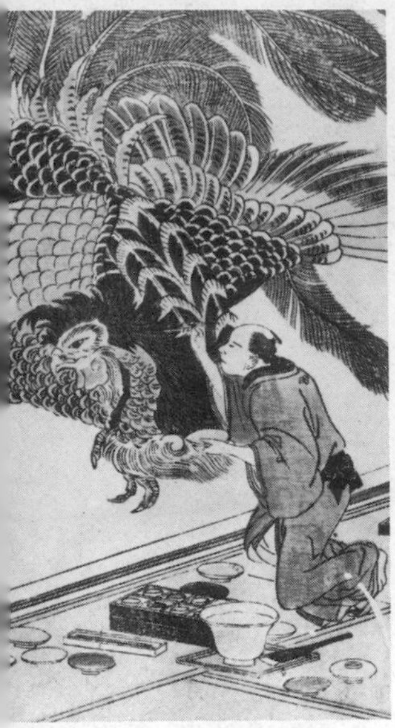

Utamaro
A self-portrait, a detail from a woodcut

usage. **4.** An instance of this; a particular expression in speech or writing: *a nonce usage.* —See Synonyms at **habit.** [Middle English, from Old French, from *user,* to USE.]

Usage: *Usage* is a more specialized term than *use.* Though the two nouns have some overlapping senses, *use* is clearly preferable to *usage* when the desired meaning relates broadly to employment or usefulness: *Use of such drugs is restricted by law. Synthetic materials have wide use in modern dress.*

us·ance (yo͞o′zəns) *n.* Also *obsolete* **us·aunce. 1.** *Commerce.* The length of time, established by custom and varying between countries, that is allowed for payment of a foreign bill of exchange. **2.** *Obsolete.* Use. **3.** *Obsolete.* Usage; custom. **4.** *Obsolete.* Interest paid on money. [Middle English *usaunce,* custom, usage, from Old French *usance,* from Vulgar Latin *ūsantia* (unattested), from *ūsāre* (unattested), to USE.]

USAR United States Army Reserve.

USAREUR United States Army, Europe.

Us·beg, Us·bek. Variants of **Uzbek.**

U.S.C. United States Code.

U.S.C.A. United States Code Annotated.

USCG, U.S.C.G. United States Coast Guard.

USDA, U.S.D.A. United States Department of Agriculture.

use (yo͞oz) *v.* **used, using, uses.** —*tr.* **1.** To bring or put into service; employ for some purpose: *use soap for washing.* **2.** To make a practice of; make a habit of employing. **3.** To conduct oneself toward in treating or handling: *"the peace-offering of a man who once used you unkindly"* (Sterne). **4.** To consume or expend the whole of; deplete or exhaust. Often used with *up.* **5.** *Informal.* To exploit for one's own advantage or gain: *He gave nothing to his friends; he merely used them.* **6.** To take or partake of, as tobacco, alcohol, or the like. —*intr.* To be accustomed to doing something as a habitual practice or custom. Now used only in the past tense with an expressed or implied infinitive. See Usage note below. —**used to.** Accustomed to or familiar with: *He was used to working a long day.* —*n.* (yo͞os). **1. a.** The act of using; the application or employment of something for some purpose: *the use of a pencil for writing.* **b.** The condition or fact of being used. **2.** The manner of using; usage: *the proper use of power tools.* **3. a.** The permission, privilege, or benefit of using something: *have use of the car.* **b.** The power or ability to use something: *lose the use of one arm.* **4.** The need or occasion to use or employ: *Do you still have any use for this book?* **5.** The quality of being suitable or adaptable to an end; usefulness. **6.** The goal, object, or purpose for which something is used. **7.** Accustomed or usual procedure; habitual practice; custom. **8.** *Law.* **a.** The enjoyment of property, as by occupying or exercising it. **b.** The benefit or profit of lands and tenements of which the legal title and possession are vested in another who holds them in trust for the beneficiary. **c.** The arrangement establishing the equitable right to such benefits and profits. **9.** The special or distinctive form of ritual, ceremony, or public worship practiced in a particular church, ecclesiastical district, or community. **10.** *Obsolete.* Usual occurrence or experience. —See Synonyms at **habit.** —**have no use for. 1.** To have no need of or occasion to use. **2.** To have no tolerance for or patience with; to dislike. —**in use.** In the process of being used; occupied; not presently available. —**make use of.** To find occasion to use; put to use. —**put to use.** To use or employ. [Middle English *usen,* from Old French *user,* from Vulgar Latin *ūsāre* (unattested), frequentative of Latin *ūtī*† (past participle *ūsus*), to use.]

Synonyms: *use, employ, utilize.* These verbs mean to avail oneself of something or to turn it to one's service. *Use* can apply to any such act, taking as its object either a person or thing. In a related but narrower sense, *use* refers to taking advantage of another person as a means of achieving an end: *He used his glamorous sister to advance his political career. Employ* is generally interchangeable with *use* in a broad sense; moreover, *employ* applies to the hiring of persons. *Utilize* is especially appropriate in the narrower sense of making useful or productive what has been otherwise or of expanding productivity by finding new uses for the thing or person involved.

Usage: The following examples illustrate *use* as an auxiliary verb in positive, negative, and interrogative constructions: *He used to go there. He used not to go* (or *did not use to go*). *Did* (or *didn't*) *he use to go?*

used (yo͞ozd) *adj.* Not new; secondhand: *a used car.*

use·ful (yo͞os′fəl) *adj.* Capable of being used advantageously or beneficially; serviceable. —**use′ful·ly** *adv.* —**use′ful·ness** *n.*

use·less (yo͞os′lĭs) *adj.* **1.** Having no beneficial purpose or use; of little or no worth; meaningless: *"a useless thing, incapable of serving their interest"* (Charlotte Brontë). **2.** Futile; to no avail. —**use′less·ly** *adv.* —**use′less·ness** *n.*

us·er (yo͞o′zər) *n.* **1.** One that uses. **2.** *Law.* The exercise or enjoyment of any right or property. **3.** *Slang.* A drug addict.

USES United States Employment Service.

ush·er (ŭsh′ər) *n.* **1.** One who serves as official doorkeeper, as in a courtroom or legislative chamber. See **sergeant at arms. 2.** A person employed to escort people to their seats in a theater, church, stadium, or the like. **3.** A male attendant at a wedding. **4.** An official whose duty is to make introductions between unacquainted persons or to precede persons of rank in a procession or the like. **5.** *British. Obsolete.* An assistant teacher in a school. —*tr.v.* **ushered, -ering, -ers. 1.** To serve as an usher to; to escort. **2.** To lead or conduct; cause to enter. Used with *through* or *into: "though she started to protest he swiftly ushered her through the door and closed it"* (Kathleen Winsor). **3.** To precede and introduce; serve as the beginning of. Usually used with *in.* [Middle English, from Norman French *usser,* variant of Old French *ussier,* from Medieval Latin *ūstiārius,* variant of Latin *ōstiārius,* doorkeeper, from *ōstium,* entrance, river mouth, from *ōs,* mouth, orifice. See **ōs-** in Appendix.*]

ush·er·ette (ŭsh′ə-rĕt′) *n.* A female usher, as in a theater.

Us·hua·ia (o͞os-wä′yä). The capital of the Tierra del Fuego territory of Argentina, the world's southernmost settlement. Population, about 3,000.

USIA United States Information Agency.

Usk (ŭsk). A river rising in southern Wales and flowing 60 miles generally southeast to the Severn estuary.

Üs·küb. The Turkish name for **Skoplje.**

U.S.M. United States Mail.

USMA, U.S.M.A. United States Military Academy.

USMC, U.S.M.C. United States Marine Corps.

USN, U.S.N. United States Navy.

USNA, U.S.N.A. United States Naval Academy.

USNR United States Naval Reserve.

USO, U.S.O. United Service Organizations.

U.S.P. United States Pharmacopoeia.

U.S.P.O. United States Post Office.

us·que·baugh (ŭs′kwĭ-bô′, -bä′) *n.* Also **us·qua·bae** (-kwə-bā′), **us·que·bae** (-kwĭ-bā′). *Irish & Scottish.* Whisky. [Irish Gaelic *uisce beathadh,* "water of life" : Old Irish *uisce,* water (see **wed-¹** in Appendix*) + *bethad,* genitive of *bethu,* life (see **gwei-** in Appendix*).]

U.S.S. 1. United States Senate. **2.** United States Ship.

Ussh·er (ŭsh′ər), **James.** 1581–1656. Irish Archbishop of Armagh; propounded Biblical chronology.

U.S.S.R. Union of Soviet Socialist Republics.

Us·su·ri (o͞o-so͝or′ē). A river rising north of Vladivostok, in the Soviet Union, and flowing about 365 miles generally north to the Amur, forming part of the Manchuria-Soviet border.

u·su·al (yo͞o′zho͞o-əl) *adj.: Abbr.* **usu. 1.** Such as is commonly or frequently encountered, experienced, observed, or used; ordinary; normal. **2.** Habitual or customary; particular. [Middle English, from Old French, from Late Latin *ūsuālis,* ordinary, from Latin *ūsus,* use, custom, from the past participle of *ūtī,* to USE.] —**u′su·al·ly** *adv.* —**u′su·al·ness** *n.*

Synonyms: *usual, typical, habitual, customary, accustomed.* These adjectives apply to what is frequent in occurrence and consequently considered regular or expected. *Usual* refers to what accords with normal or ordinary practice or procedure and is therefore common and familiar. It is closely related to, but somewhat broader than, *typical,* which implies conformity with a well-established, clearly defined pattern. *Habitual* implies almost unfailing repetition of practice and suggests force of habit or addiction. *Customary* can refer to conformity with prevailing custom or convention or with an individual's own established practice. *Accustomed* applies principally to what an individual is familiar with, or used to, through regular experience, or to something considered as a distinguishing quality: *her accustomed optimism.* In the latter sense, *accustomed* is interchangeable with *customary.*

u·su·fruct (yo͞o′zə-frŭkt′, yo͞o′zyo͞o-) *n. Law.* The right to utilize and enjoy the profits and advantages of something belonging to another so long as the property is not damaged or altered in any way. [From Latin *ūsusfrūctus,* "use (and) enjoyment" : *ūsus,* use (see **usual**) + *frūctus,* enjoyment, FRUIT.]

u·su·fruc·tu·ar·y (yo͞o′zə-frŭk′cho͞o-ĕr′ē, yo͞o′zyo͞o-) *n., pl.* **-ies.** A person who holds property by usufruct. —*adj.* Of or of the nature of a usufruct.

U·sum·bu·ra. The former name for **Bujumbura.**

u·su·rer (yo͞o′zhər-ər) *n.* A person who lends money at an exorbitant or unlawful rate of interest. [Middle English, from Norman French, from Medieval Latin *ūsūrārius,* from Latin *ūsūra,* interest, USURY.]

u·su·ri·ous (yo͞o-zho͝or′ē-əs) *adj.* **1.** Practicing usury. **2.** Of, pertaining to, or constituting usury: *a usurious rate of interest.* —**u·su′ri·ous·ly** *adv.* —**u·su′ri·ous·ness** *n.*

u·surp (yo͞o-sûrp′, -zûrp′) *v.* **-surped, -surping, -surps.** —*tr.* **1.** To seize and hold, as the power, position, or rights of another, by force and without legal right or authority. **2.** To take over or occupy physically, as territory or possessions; to appropriate. —*intr.* To commit such illegal seizure; encroach. [Middle English *usurpen,* from Old French *usurper,* from Latin *ūsūrpāre,* to take into use. See **reup-** in Appendix.*] —**u·surp′er** *n.* —**u·surp′ing·ly** *adv.*

u·sur·pa·tion (yo͞o′sər-pā′shən, yo͞o′zər-) *n.* **1.** The act of usurping; especially, the illegal seizure of royal sovereignty. **2.** *Law.* The illegal encroachment upon or exercise of authority or privilege belonging to another: *"in our own day, gross usurpations upon the liberty of private life"* (John Stuart Mill).

u·su·ry (yo͞o′zhə-rē) *n., pl.* **-ries. 1.** The act or practice of lending money at an exorbitant or illegal rate of interest. **2.** Such an excessive rate of interest. **3.** *Archaic.* The act or practice of lending money at any rate of interest. **4.** *Obsolete.* Interest charged or paid on such a loan. [Middle English, from Norman French *usurie* (unattested), from Medieval Latin *ūsūria,* from Latin *ūsūra,* use of money lent, interest, from *ūsus,* use. See **usual.**]

ut (ŭt, o͞ot) *n. Music.* A syllable representing the tone *C,* otherwise represented by *do,* in the French system of solmization. See **gamut.** [Latin *ut,* that (first word of a hymn to Saint John the Baptist). See **kwo-** in Appendix.*]

UT Utah (with Zip Code).

U·tah (yo͞o′tô, -tä). A mountain state of the United States, occupying 84,916 square miles in the west-central part of the country; admitted to the Union in 1896. Population, 992,000.

ă pat/ā pay/âr care/ä father/b bib/ch church/d deed/ĕ pet/ē be/f fife/g gag/h hat/hw which/ĭ pit/ī pie/îr pier/j judge/k kick/l lid, needle/m mum/n no, sudden/ng thing/ŏ pot/ō toe/ô paw, for/oi noise/ou out/o͝o took/o͞o boot/p pop/r roar/s sauce/sh ship, dish/

Capital, Salt Lake City. See map at **United States of America.** [Spanish *Yutta,* from Ute *Yutu,* UTE.]

U·ta·ma·ro (ōō'tä-mä'rō), **Kitagawa.** 1763–1806. Japanese wood-block engraver.

Ute (yōōt) *n., pl.* **Ute** or **Utes. 1.** A tribe of Uto-Aztecan-speaking North American Indians formerly inhabiting Utah, Colorado, and New Mexico and now living on reservations in Utah and Colorado. **2.** A member of this tribe. **3.** The language of this tribe. [Ute *Yuta.*]

u·ten·sil (yōō-těn'səl) *n.* **1.** Any instrument or container, especially one used domestically, as in a kitchen or on a farm. **2.** Any instrument or tool; implement. —See Synonyms at **tool.** [Middle English *utensele,* from Old French *utensile,* from Latin *ūtēnsilia,* "things for use," from the neuter plural of *ūtēnsilis,* fit for use, from *ūtī,* to USE.]

u·ter·ine (yōō'tər-ĭn, -tə-rīn') *adj.* **1.** Of or pertaining to the uterus. **2.** Having the same mother but different fathers. [Late Latin *uterinus,* from *uterus,* UTERUS.]

u·ter·us (yōō'tər-əs) *n.* **1.** A pear-shaped muscular organ of gestation that is located in the pelvic cavity of female mammals and receives and holds the fertilized ovum during the development of the fetus and is the principal agent in its expulsion at birth. Also called "womb." **2.** A similar part of the female reproductive tract in many invertebrates, serving as a repository for the storage or development of eggs or embryos. [Latin *uterus.* See udero- in Appendix.*]

Ut·gard (ōōt'gärd'). *Norse Mythology.* The home of Utgard-Loki. Also called "Jotunheim."

Ut·gard-Lo·ki (ōōt'gärd'lō'kē). *Norse Mythology.* An invincible giant.

U Thant (ōō thänt). See **Thant.**

U·ther (yōō'thər). Called "Uther Pendragon." A legendary king of Britain and father of Arthur.

U·ti·ca (yōō'tĭ-kə). **1.** An ancient city of northern Africa, 18 miles north of modern Tunis. **2.** A city on the Mohawk River in central New York State. Population, 100,000.

u·tile (yōō'tĭl, -tīl') *adj. Rare.* Useful. [Middle English *utyle,* from Old French *utile,* from Latin *ūtilis.* See **utility.**]

u·til·i·tar·i·an (yōō-tĭl'ə-târ'ē-ən) *adj.* **1.** Pertaining to or associated with utility. **2.** Stressing the value of practical over aesthetic qualities. **3.** Intended or made for the purposes of utility. **4.** Believing in or advocating utility. —*n.* An advocate or adherent of utilitarianism. [UTILIT(Y) + -ARIAN.]

u·til·i·tar·i·an·ism (yōō-tĭl'ə-târ'ē-ə-nĭz'əm) *n.* **1.** The philosophical doctrine that considers utility as the criterion of action and the useful as good or worthwhile. **2.** The ethical theory proposed by Jeremy Bentham and John Stuart Mill that all moral, social, or political action should be directed toward achieving the greatest good for the greatest number of people.

u·til·i·ty (yōō-tĭl'ə-tē) *n., pl.* **-ties.** **1.** The condition or quality of being useful; usefulness: *"I have always doubted the utility of these conferences on disarmament"* (Winston Churchill). **2.** A useful article or device. **3.** A public service, such as gas, electricity, water, or transportation. **4.** *Plural.* Shares of stock in a public service company. **5.** In utilitarianism, the principle of the greatest good for the greatest number. —*adj.* Of the lowest U.S. Government grade of meat. [Middle English *utilite,* usefulness, from Old French, from Latin *utilitās,* from *utilis,* useful, from *ūtī,* to USE.]

utility man. 1. A member of a theatrical cast who must be prepared to play any of the smaller roles on short notice. **2.** *Baseball.* A reserve player capable of playing several positions. **3.** Any worker expected to serve in several capacities.

u·til·ize (yōō'tə-līz') *tr.v.* **-ized, -izing, -izes.** To put to use for a certain purpose. See Synonyms at **use.** [French *utiliser,* from Italian *utilizzare,* from *utile,* useful, from Latin *ūtilis.* See **utility.**] —**u'til·iz'a·ble** *adj.* —**u'til·i·za'tion** *n.* —**u'til·iz'er** *n.*

ut in·fra (ŭt ĭn'frə, ōōt ĭn'frä). *Latin.* As below.

u·ti pos·si·de·tis (yōō'tī pŏs'ə-dē'tĭs). A principle of international law providing that a belligerent is entitled to absolute possession and control of the territory occupied by it at the end of a war. [Latin, as you possess.]

ut·most (ŭt'mōst') *adj.* **1.** Being or situated at the farthest limit or point; most extreme. **2.** Of the highest or greatest degree, amount, intensity, or the like: *a matter of the utmost secrecy.* —*n.* The greatest amount, degree, or extent; maximum. [Middle English *utmost, ut(te)mast,* Old English *ūt(e)-mest,* outermost : *ūt(e),* out (see ud- in Appendix*) + -*mest,* -MOST.]

U·to-Az·tec·an (yōō'tō-ăz'těk'ən) *n.* **1.** A large language family of North and Central American Indians, including Ute, Pima, Hopi, Shoshone, Nahuatl, and other languages. **2.** A tribe speaking a Uto-Aztecan language. **3.** A member of such a tribe. —*adj.* Of or pertaining to the Uto-Aztecans or to the languages spoken by them. [UTE + AZTEC.]

u·to·pi·a (yōō-tō'pē-ə) *n.* **1.** Any condition, place, or situation of social or political perfection. **2.** Any idealistic goal or concept for social and political reform. [From UTOPIA.]

U·to·pi·a (yōō-tō'pē-ə). An imaginary island that served as the subject and title of a book by Sir Thomas More in 1516 and that was described as a seat of perfection in moral, social, and political life. [New Latin, "no-place" : Greek *ou†,* not, no + *topos,* place (see topic).]

u·to·pi·an (yōō-tō'pē-ən) *adj.* Excellent or ideal but existing only in visionary or impractical thought or theory. —*n.* A zealous but impractical reformer of human society.

u·to·pi·an·ism (yōō-tō'pē-ə-nĭz'əm) *n.* The ideals or principles of a utopian; idealistic and impractical social theory.

U·trecht (yōō'ŭckt'). **1.** A province of the Netherlands, occupying 501 square miles in the center of the country. Population, 734,000. **2.** The capital of this province; site of the signing of the treaty that ended the War of the Spanish Succession (1713). Population, 267,000.

u·tri·cle (yōō'trĭ-kəl) *n.* Also **u·tric·u·lus** (yōō-trĭk'yə-ləs) *pl.* -**li** (-lī'). **1.** A small, delicate membranous sac connecting with the semicircular canals of the inner ear and functioning in the maintenance of bodily equilibrium and coordination. **2.** *Botany.* A small, bladderlike one-seeded fruit. [French *utricule,* from Latin *ūtriculus,* diminutive of *ūter,* leather bag or bottle, possibly from Greek *hudria,* water pot, pitcher, from *hudōr,* water. See wed-¹ in Appendix.*]

u·tric·u·lar (yōō-trĭk'yə-lər) *adj.* **1.** Of, pertaining to, or resembling a utricle. **2.** Having one or more utricles. **3.** Pertaining to the uterus.

U·tril·lo (ü-trē-yō'), **Maurice.** 1883–1955. French painter.

U·tsu·no·mi·ya (ōō'tsōō-nō'mē-yä). A city of Japan, on central Honshu, 60 miles north of Tokyo. Population, 254,000.

ut su·pra (ŭt sōō'prä, ōōt sōō'prä). *Abbr.* **u.s., ut sup.** *Latin.* As above.

Ut·tar Pra·desh (ōōt'ər prə-dāsh'). A state of the Republic of India, occupying 112,523 square miles in the north. Population, 73,746,000. Capital, Lucknow.

ut·ter¹ (ŭt'ər) *tr.v.* **-tered, -tering, -ters. 1.** To express audibly; pronounce; speak. **2.** *Obsolete.* To express or make known in any way: *utter fear by trembling.* **3. a.** To put (counterfeit money or the like) into circulation. **b.** To deliver (something counterfeit) to another. **4.** *Obsolete.* To publish (a book or the like). **5.** *Obsolete.* To sell or deliver (merchandise) in trading. —See Synonyms at **vent.** [Middle English *utt(e)ren, outren,* from Middle Dutch *ūteren,* to drive away, announce, speak. See ud- in Appendix.*] —**ut'ter·a·ble** *adj.* —**ut'ter·er** *n.*

ut·ter² (ŭt'ər) *adj.* Complete; absolute; entire. [Middle English *utter,* Old English *ūtera, ūttra,* outer, external. See ud- in Appendix.*]

ut·ter·ance¹ (ŭt'ər-əns) *n.* **1. a.** The act of uttering or expressing vocally. **b.** The power of speaking. **2.** Something that is uttered or expressed.

ut·ter·ance² (ŭt'ər-əns) *n. Obsolete.* The uttermost end or extremity; bitter end; death: *fight to the utterance.* [Middle English *utt(e)raunce,* from Old French *outrance,* from *outrer,* to go beyond limits, from Vulgar Latin *ultrāre* (unattested), from Latin *ultrā,* beyond, from *uls,* beyond. See al-¹ in Appendix.*]

ut·ter·ly (ŭt'ər-lē) *adv.* Completely; absolutely; entirely.

ut·ter·most (ŭt'ər-mōst') *adj.* **1.** Utmost. **2.** Outermost. —*n.* Utmost. [Middle English *uttermost, uttermest* : UTTER (outer, complete) + -MOST.]

U-turn (yōō'tûrn') *n.* A turn, as by a vehicle, completely reversing the direction of travel.

u·va·rov·ite (yōō-vär'ə-vīt', ōō-) *n.* An emerald-green garnet, $Ca_3Cr_2(SiO_4)_3$, found in chromium deposits. [German *Uvarovit;* discovered by Count Sergei S. *Uvarov* (1785–1855), Russian statesman and writer.]

u·ve·a (yōō'vē-ə) *n.* The pigmented vascular layer of the eye including the iris, ciliary body, and choroid. [Medieval Latin *ūvea,* from Latin *uva,* grape, bunch of grapes (from its round shape). See og- in Appendix.*] —**u've·al** *adj.*

u·ve·i·tis (yōō'vē-ī'tĭs) *n.* Inflammation of the uvea. [New Latin : UVE(A) + -ITIS.]

u·vu·la (yōō'vyə-lə) *n.* The small, conical, fleshy mass of tissue suspended from the center of the soft palate above the back of the tongue. [Middle English, from Late Latin, "small grape" (from the shape of the uvula), diminutive of Latin *ūva,* a grape. See og- in Appendix.*]

u·vu·lar (yōō'vyə-lər) *adj.* **1.** Pertaining to or associated with the uvula. **2.** *Phonetics.* Articulated by vibration of the uvula or with the back of the tongue near or touching the uvula.

u·vu·li·tis (yōō'vyə-lī'tĭs) *n.* Inflammation of the uvula. [New Latin : UVUL(A) + -ITIS.]

UW underwriter.

Ux·bridge (ŭks'brĭj). A former administrative division of London, England, now part of **Hillingdon** (see).

Ux·mal (ōōz-mäl'). An ancient ruined Mayan city in Yucatán, Mexico.

ux·o·ri·al (ŭk·sôr'ē-əl, ŭk'sōr'-, ŭg'zôr'-, ŭg'zōr'-) *adj.* Pertaining to, characteristic of, or befitting a wife. [From Latin *uxōrius,* of a wife, UXORIOUS.]

ux·o·ri·cide (ŭk'sôr'ə-sīd', ŭk'sōr'-, ŭg'zôr'-, ŭg'zōr'-) *n.* **1.** The killing of a wife by her husband. **2.** A man who kills his wife. [Medieval Latin *uxōricīdium,* the murder of one's wife : Latin *uxor,* wife (see euk- in Appendix*) + -CIDE.]

ux·o·ri·ous (ŭk'sôr'ē-əs, ŭk'sōr'-, ŭg'zôr'-, ŭg'zōr'-) *adj.* Excessively or irrationally submissive or devoted to one's wife. [Latin *uxōrius,* from *uxor,* wife. See euk- in Appendix.*] —**ux'o'ri·ous·ly** *adv.* —**ux'o'ri·ous·ness** *n.*

Uz·bek (ōōz'běk, ŭz'-). Also **Uz·beg** (-běg), **Us·bek** (ōōs'běk, ŭs'-), **Us·beg** (-běg). **1.** A member of a group of Turkic people inhabiting the Uzbek region of the S.S.R. **2.** The Turkic language spoken by the Uzbeks.

Uz·bek Soviet Socialist Republic (ōōz'běk, ŭz'-). Also **Uz·bek·i·stan** (ōōz-běk'ə-stän', -stän', ŭz-). A constituent republic of the Soviet Union, occupying 157,300 square miles in central Asia. Population, 10,130,000. Capital, Tashkent.

Maurice Utrillo

ĭ tight/th thin, path/*th* this, bathe/ŭ cut/ûr urge/v valve/w with/y yes/z zebra, size/zh vision/ə about, item, edible, gallop, circus/ à *Fr.* ami/œ *Fr.* feu, *Ger.* schön/ü *Fr.* tu, *Ger.* über/кн *Ger.* ich, *Scot.* loch/N *Fr.* bon. *Follows main vocabulary. †Of obscure origin.

Vv

Ψ Y   Y ⲕ Y V   ᴠ V   U υ   V V v v

1	2		3	4	5	6		7	8		9	10		11	12	13	14
Phoenician				Greek					Roman			Medieval				Modern	

The letter V *is ancestral to the letters* U, W, Y, *and* F. *Around 1000* B.C. *the Phoenicians and other Semites of Syria and Palestine began to use a graphic sign in the forms (1,2). They gave it the name* wāw *and used it for a semiconsonant* w, *as in English know, knows. After 900* B.C., *when the Greeks borrowed the alphabet from the Phoenicians, they developed two signs from wāw. One sign, which they called upsilon, "bare* u," *they used for the vowel* u (3,4,5,6). (*For the other sign, see* F.) *The Greek form without the tail (6) passed via Etruscan to the Roman alphabet (7,8), in which it was used for two sounds, semiconsonantal* w *and vocalic* u, *as in the writing of* VENIO *and* IVLIVS. *In later Roman times the sound* w *became* v. *In late Roman Uncial (9) the sounds* v, w, *and* u *were not systematically distinguished. Gradually, as in the Cursive (10), a characteristic tailless form was used for the sound* v. *Eventually in modern times the angular form was adopted for* v *in printed letters, capital (11) and lower-case (13), while in writing (12,14), the angularity is not usually so distinct.*

v, V (vē) *n., pl.* **v's** *or rare* **vs, V's** *or* **Vs. 1.** The 22nd letter of the modern English alphabet. See **alphabet. 2.** Any of the speech sounds represented by this letter. **3.** Anything shaped like the letter **v**.

v, V, v., V. *Note:* As an abbreviation or symbol, *v* may be a small or a capital letter, with or without a period. Established forms or those generally preferred precede the definition. When no form is given, all four forms are in general use in that sense. **1. V** The symbol for the element vanadium. **2. V** *Physics.* velocity. **3. V** venerable (in titles). **4. v.** verb. **5. v.** verse. **6. v.** version. **7. v.** verso. **8. v.** versus. **9. v.** very (in titles). **10. v., V.** vice (in titles). **11. V** victory (used by the Allies in World War II). **12. v.** vide. **13. v., V.** village. **14. v.** violin. **15. V.** viscount; viscountess. **16. v.** vocative. **17. v.** voice. **18. V** *Electricity.* volt. **19. V** volume. **20. v.** volume (book). **21. v.** von. **22. v.** vowel. **23. v, V** The Roman numeral for five. **24.** The 22nd in a series; 21st when *J* is omitted.

V-1. A robot bomb *(see).* [German *Vergeltungswaffe eins,* "retaliation weapon (number) one."]

V-2. A long-range liquid-fuel rocket used by the Germans as a ballistic missile in World War II. [German *Vergeltungswaffe zwei,* "retaliation weapon (number) two."]

VA 1. Veterans' Administration. **2.** Virginia (with Zip Code).

Va. Virginia.

v.a. *Grammar.* active verb.

V.A. 1. Veterans' Administration. **2.** vicar apostolic. **3.** vice admiral.

Vaal (väl). A river of South Africa, rising in eastern Transvaal and flowing 750 miles southwest to the Orange River.

vac. vacuum.

va·can·cy (vā'kən-sē) *n., pl.* **-cies. 1.** The state or condition of being vacant or unoccupied; emptiness. **2.** An empty or unoccupied space; a gap. **3.** A position, office, or accommodation that is unfilled or unoccupied. **4.** Emptiness of mind; inanity; blankness. **5.** *Archaic.* A period of leisure; idleness.

va·cant (vā'kənt) *adj.* **1.** Containing nothing; empty; unfilled. **2.** Without an incumbent or occupant: *a vacant chair.* **3.** Not occupied or put to use: *a vacant lot.* **4.** *Law.* Not claimed, as by an heir: *a vacant estate.* **5. a.** Lacking intelligence or knowledge: *"Then gay ideas crowd the vacant brain"* (Pope). **b.** Expressionless; blank; unresponsive: *a vacant stare.* **6.** Unfilled by any activity: *vacant hours.* —See Synonyms at **empty.** [Middle English *vaca(u)nt,* from Old French *vacant,* from Latin *vacāns,* present participle of *vacāre,* to be empty. See **vacate.**] —**va'cant·ly** *adv.* —**va'cant·ness** *n.*

va·cate (vā'kāt') *v.* **-cated, -cating, -cates.** —*tr.* **1. a.** To cease to occupy or hold; give up; leave. **b.** To empty of occupants or incumbents. **2.** *Law.* To make void; countermand; annul. —*intr.* To leave a job, office, lodging, or the like. [Latin *vacāre,* to be empty. See **eu-²** in Appendix.*]

va·ca·tion (vā-kā'shən) *n.* **1.** A period of time devoted to pleasure, rest, or relaxation; especially, such a period during which a working person is exempt from work but collects his pay. **2. a.** A holiday. **b.** A fixed period of holidays; especially, one during which a school, court, business, or the like suspends activities; a recess. **3.** *Archaic.* An act or instance of vacating. —*intr.v.* **vacationed, -tioning, -tions.** To take or spend a vacation. [Middle English *vacacioun,* from Old French *vacation,* from Latin *vacātiō,* freedom, release from occupation, from *vacāre,* to be empty, be free. See **vacate.**] —**va·ca'tion·er** *n.*

va·ca·tion·ist (vā-kā'shə-nĭst) *n.* A person on vacation.

vacation land. A place with special attractions for vacationists.

vac·ci·nal (văk'sə-nəl) *adj.* Caused by or relating to vaccine or vaccination.

vac·ci·nate (văk'sə-nāt') *v.* **-nated, -nating, -nates.** *Medicine.* —*tr.* To inoculate with a vaccine in order to produce immunity against smallpox, diphtheria, typhoid fever, poliomyelitis, cholera, typhus, and other infectious diseases. —*intr.* To perform a vaccination. [From VACCINE.]

vac·ci·na·tion (văk'sə-nā'shən) *n.* **1.** Inoculation with a vaccine in order to protect against a given disease. **2.** A scar left on the skin by such an inoculation.

vac·ci·na·tor (văk'sə-nā'tər) *n.* One that vaccinates.

vac·cine (văk-sēn') *n.* **1.** A suspension of attenuated or killed microorganisms, as of viruses or bacteria, incapable of inducing severe infection but capable, when inoculated, of counteracting the unmodified species. **2.** Such a suspension prepared from the cowpox virus and inoculated against smallpox. —*adj.* **1.** Of or derived from cows, especially from cows infected with cowpox. **2.** Of or relating to cowpox. **3.** Of or relating to vaccination. [French *(virus) vaccine,* (virus) of cowpox, from Latin *vaccīnus,* pertaining to cows, from *vacca,* cow. See **wak-** in Appendix.*]

vac·cin·i·a (văk-sĭn'ē-ə) *n.* Cowpox *(see).* [New Latin, from Latin *vaccīnus,* of cows. See **vaccine.**]

vac·il·lant (văs'ə-lənt) *adj.* Vacillating.

vac·il·late (văs'ə-lāt') *intr.v.* **-lated, -lating, -lates. 1.** To sway from one side to the other; fluctuate; oscillate. **2.** To swing indecisively from one course of action or opinion to another; be irresolute; waver. —See Synonyms at **hesitate.** [Latin *vacillāre†,* to waver.] —**vac'il·la'tion** *n.* —**vac'il·la'tor** (-lā'tər) *n.*

vac·il·lat·ing (văs'ə-lā'tĭng) *adj.* Also **vac·il·la·to·ry** (-lə-tôr'ē, -tōr'ē). Inclined to waver; irresolute. —**va'cil·lat'ing·ly** *adv.*

va·cu·i·ty (vă-kyōō'ĭ-tē) *n., pl.* **-ties. 1.** Total absence of matter; emptiness. **2.** An empty space; vacuum. **3.** Total lack of ideas; emptiness of mind: *"Perhaps some infatuated swain has ere this mistaken . . . dullness for maiden reserve, mere vacuity for sweet bashfulness"* (Thackeray). **4.** Absence of meaningful occupation; idleness: *"the crew, being patient people, much given to slumber and vacuity"* (Washington Irving). **5.** The quality or fact of being devoid of something specified: *a vacuity of taste.* **6.** Something, especially a remark, utterly without substance or point; an inanity. [Old French *vacuite,* from Latin *vacuitās,* from *vacuus,* empty. See **vacuum.**]

vac·u·o·lat·ed (văk'yōō-ə-lā'tĭd) *adj.* Also **vac·u·o·late** (văk'-yōō-ə-lāt', -lĭt). Containing a vacuole or vacuoles.

vac·u·ole (văk'yōō-ōl') *n.* Any small cavity in the protoplasm of a cell. [French, "little vacuum," from Latin *vacuum,* VACUUM.] —**vac'u·o'lar** *adj.* —**vac'u·o·la'tion** (-ə-lā'shən) *n.*

ă pat/ā **pay**/âr care/ä father/b **bib**/ch **church**/d **deed**/ĕ pet/ē be/f fife/g gag/h hat/hw **which**/ĭ pit/ī pie/îr **pier**/j **judge**/k **kick**/l lid,
needle/m **mum**/n no, sudden/ng thing/ŏ pot/ō toe/ô paw, for/oi noise/ou **out**/ŏŏ took/ōō **boot**/p pop/r roar/s sauce/sh ship, dish/

vac·u·ous (văk′yo͞o-əs) *adj.* **1.** Devoid of matter; empty. **2. a.** Stupid; dull. **b.** Expressionless. **3.** Devoid of substance or meaning; inane. **4.** Purposeless; unoccupied; idle. —See Synonyms at **empty.** [Latin *vacuus,* empty. See **vacuum.**] —**vac′u·ous·ly** *adv.* —**vac′u·ous·ness** *n.*

vac·u·um (văk′yo͞o-əm, -yo͞om) *n., pl.* **-ums** or **vacua** (văk′yo͞o-ə) (except for sense 4). *Abbr.* **vac. 1. a.** The absence of matter. **b.** A space empty of matter. **c.** A space relatively empty of matter. **2.** A state or feeling of emptiness; a void. **3.** A state of being sealed off from external or environmental influences; isolation. **4.** A vacuum cleaner. —*adj.* **1.** Pertaining to or used to create a vacuum. **2.** Containing air or other gas at a reduced pressure. **3.** Working by means of suction or by maintaining of a partial vacuum. —*v.* **vacuumed, -uming, -ums.** —*tr.* To clean with a vacuum cleaner. —*intr.* To use a vacuum cleaner. [Latin, neuter of *vacuus,* empty, from *vacāre,* to be empty. See **eu-**² in Appendix.*]

vacuum bottle. A bottle or flask having a partial vacuum between its inner and outer walls, designed to maintain the desired temperature of the contents.

vacuum cleaner. An electrical appliance that draws light dirt from surfaces by suction.

vacuum coffee maker. A coffee maker consisting of two bowls, the upper one having a tubular part that fits into the lower one. As the water in the lower chamber boils, it rises, blends with the ground coffee in the upper chamber, and then is drawn back down by suction.

vacuum gauge. A device for determining the pressure in a partial vacuum.

vac·u·um-packed (văk′yo͞o-əm-păkt′, văk′yo͞om-păkt′) *adj.* **1.** Packed in a container with little or no air. **2.** Packed in a vacuum.

vacuum pump. 1. A pump used to evacuate an enclosure. **2.** A **pulsometer** *(see).*

vacuum tube. An electron tube having an internal vacuum sufficiently high to permit electrons to move with low interaction with any remaining gas molecules. Also called in England, "vacuum valve."

va·de me·cum (vā′dē mē′kəm) *pl.* **vade mecums. 1.** A useful thing that a person constantly carries with him. **2.** A guidebook or other ready reference book. [Latin, "go with me."]

V. Adm. vice admiral.

Va·duz (fä-do͞ots′). The capital of the principality of Liechtenstein, on the upper Rhine. Population, 4,000.

vag·a·bond (văg′ə-bŏnd′) *n.* **1.** A person without a fixed home who moves from place to place and has no apparent means of support; wanderer. **2.** An itinerant beggar or thief; a vagrant; a tramp. **3.** A wandering rogue; drifter. —*adj.* **1.** Of, relating to, or characteristic of a wanderer; nomadic. **2.** Aimless; drifting; unstable. **3.** Irregular in course or behavior; unpredictable. —*intr.v.* **vagabonded, -bonding, -bonds.** To lead a vagabond's life; roam about. [Middle English *vagabound,* from Old French *vagabond,* from Latin *vagābundus,* wandering, from *vagāri,* to wander, from *vagus,* wandering, undecided, VAGUE.] —**vag′a·bond′age** *n.* —**vag′a·bond′ism′** *n.*

va·gal (vā′gəl) *adj.* Of or pertaining to the vagus nerve.

Va·gar·sha·pat. The former name for **Echmiadzin.**

va·gar·y (vā′gə-rē, və-gâr′ē) *n., pl.* **-ies.** An extravagant or erratic notion or action; flight of fancy. See Synonyms at **caprice.** [Originally "a roaming tour," ramble, from Latin *vagāri,* to wander, from *vagus,* wandering, undecided, VAGUE.]

va·gil·i·ty (və-jĭl′ə-tē) *n.* The capacity or tendency of an organism to become widely dispersed. [From obsolete *vagile,* wandering, roaming, from Latin *vagus.* See **vague.**]

va·gi·na (və-jī′nə) *n., pl.* **-nas** or **-nae** (-nē). **1.** *Anatomy.* **a.** The passage leading from the external genital orifice to the uterus in female mammals. **b.** A similar structure in some invertebrates. **2.** *Biology.* A sheathlike structure or part, such as that formed by the base of a leaf enclosing a stem. [Latin *vāgīna,* sheath. See **wag-** in Appendix.*]

vag·i·nal (văj′ə-nəl) *adj.* **1.** Of or pertaining to the vagina. **2.** Pertaining to or resembling a sheath.

vag·i·nate (văj′ə-nĭt, -nāt′) *adj.* Also **vag·i·nat·ed** (-nā′tĭd). Forming or enclosed in a sheath.

vag·i·nec·to·my (văj′ə-nĕk′tə-mē) *n., pl.* **-mies. 1.** Surgical excision of all or part of the vagina. **2.** Surgical excision of the serous membrane covering the testis and epididymus. [VAGIN(O)- + -ECTOMY.]

vag·i·nis·mus (văj′ə-nĭz′məs, -nĭs′məs) *n.* A painful contractional spasm of the vagina. [New Latin : VAGIN(O)- + -ISM.]

vag·i·ni·tis (văj′ə-nī′tĭs) *n.* Inflammation of the vagina. [New Latin : VAGIN(O)- + -ITIS.]

vagino-, vagin-. Indicates the vagina; for example, **vaginectomy.** [From Latin *vāgīna,* sheath. See **wag-** in Appendix.*]

va·got·o·my (vā-gŏt′ə-mē) *n., pl.* **-mies.** Surgical division of the lower thoracic or upper abdominal fibers of the vagus nerve, used to diminish acid secretion of the stomach and control a duodenal ulcer. [VAG(US) + -TOMY.]

va·go·to·ni·a (vā′gə-tō′nē-ə) *n.* Pathological overactivity of the vagus nerve. [New Latin : VAG(US) + -TONIA.]

va·go·trop·ic (vā′gə-trŏp′ĭk) *adj.* Affecting or acting on the vagus nerve. Said chiefly of drugs. [VAG(US) + -TROPIC.]

va·gran·cy (vā′grən-sē) *n., pl.* **-cies. 1.** The state of being a vagrant. **2.** The conduct or mode of existence of a vagrant. **3.** A wandering in mind or thought.

va·grant (vā′grənt) *n.* **1.** A person who wanders from place to place without a fixed home or livelihood and ekes out a living by begging or stealing; a tramp; vagabond. **2.** A wanderer; rover. **3.** One who lives on the streets and constitutes a public nuisance, as a drunkard or a prostitute. —*adj.* **1.** Wandering from place to place; homeless and without work; roving. **2.** Wayward; unrestrained. **3.** Moving in a random fashion; not fixed in place. [Middle English *vag(a)raunt,* from Norman French, probably from Latin *vagārī,* to wander, from *vagus,* wandering, undecided, VAGUE.] —**va′grant·ly** *adv.*

vague (vāg) *adj.* **vaguer, vaguest. 1.** Not clearly expressed or outlined; inexplicit; indefinite: *vague instructions.* **2.** Uncertain or indefinite in thought or expression: *She was vague about her future.* **3.** Lacking definite shape, form, or character; not clearly defined: *vague plans.* **4.** Ambiguous in meaning or application: *"The word* spiritual *seems vague nowadays."* (Edward Conze). **5.** Indistinctly felt, perceived, understood, or recalled; hazy: *a vague uneasiness.* —See Synonyms at **ambiguous.** [Old French, from Latin *vagus*†, wandering, undecided, vague. See also **extravagant.**] —**vague′ly** *adv.* —**vague′ness** *n.*

va·gus (vā′gəs) *n., pl.* **-gi** (-gī′). The tenth and longest of the cranial nerves, passing through the neck and thorax into the abdomen and supplying sensation to part of the ear, the larynx, and the pharynx, motor impulses to the vocal-cord muscles, and motor and secretory impulses to the abdominal and thoracic viscera. Also called "vagus nerve," "pneumogastric nerve." [New Latin *vagus (nervus),* "wandering (nerve)," from Latin *vagus,* wandering, VAGUE.]

Váh (väKH). A river of Czechoslovakia, rising in the northeast and flowing 245 miles west and then south to the Danube.

va·hi·ne. Variant of **wahine.**

Vai·gach Island (vī′gəch). An island of the Soviet Union, 1,430 square miles in area, in the Kara Sea southeast of Novaya Zemlya.

vail¹ (vāl) *v.* **vailed, vailing, vails.** *Archaic.* —*tr.* **1.** To lower, as a banner. **2.** To doff (a hat or headpiece) as a token of respect or submission. —*intr.* **1.** To descend; to lower. **2.** To doff one's hat. [Middle English *valen,* short for *avalen,* to let fall, from Old French *avaler,* to lower, from Vulgar Latin *advallāre* (unattested), from Latin *ad vallem,* "to the valley" : *ad,* to + *vallis, vallēs,* valley (see **wel-**³ in Appendix*).]

vail². *Obsolete.* Variant of **veil.**

vain (vān) *adj.* **vainer, vainest. 1.** Not yielding the desired outcome; unsuccessful; futile; fruitless: *a vain attempt.* **2.** Lacking substance or worth; hollow; idle: *vain talk.* **3.** Showing undue preoccupation with or pride in one's appearance or accomplishments; conceited: *"Whistler was not just immodest, he was shamelessly vain."* (Kenneth Rexroth). **4.** *Archaic.* Foolish. —**in vain. 1.** Without effect or avail; to no use or purpose: *Our labor was in vain.* **2.** Without due respect or piety; profanely. Used chiefly in the phrase *take the name of God in vain.* [Middle English, from Old French, from Latin *vānus,* empty. See **eu-**² in Appendix.*] —**vain′ly** *adv.* —**vain′ness** *n.*

vain·glo·ri·ous (vān-glôr′ē-əs, -glōr′ē-əs) *adj.* **1.** Showing excessive vanity; boastful. **2.** Characterized by or proceeding from vainglory. —**vain·glo′ri·ous·ly** *adv.* —**vain·glo′ri·ous·ness** *n.*

vain·glo·ry (vān′glôr′ē, -glōr′ē) *n., pl.* **-ries. 1.** Boastful and unwarranted celebration of one's accomplishments or qualities. **2.** Vain and ostentatious display. [Middle English *vein glory, waynglori,* from Old French *vaine glorie,* from Latin *vānus glōria,* empty pride : *vānus,* VAIN + *glōria,* pride, GLORY.]

vair (vâr) *n.* **1.** A fur, probably squirrel, much used in medieval times to line and trim robes. **2.** *Heraldry.* A heraldic representation of fur. [Middle English *veir, vaire,* variegated fur, from Old French *vair,* from Latin *varius,* variegated, VARIOUS.]

Vaish·na·va (vīsh′nə-və) *n.* A Hindu sect that worships Vishnu. [Sanskrit *viṣṇava,* of Vishnu, from *Viṣṇu,* VISHNU.] —**Vaish′na·vism′** *n.*

Vais·ya (vīs′yə, vī′shə) *n.* **1.** A Hindu caste originally composed of farmers and herders but now largely made up of merchants and businessmen. **2.** A member of this caste. See **caste.** [Sanskrit *vaisya,* "settler." See **weik-**¹ in Appendix.*]

val. valuation; value.

val·ance (văl′əns) *n.* **1.** A short ornamental drapery hung across the top of a window or along a bed, shelf, canopy, or the like, often to conceal structural detail. **2.** A decorative board or metal strip similar to this. —*tr.v.* **valanced, -ancing, -ances.** To supply with a valance. [Middle English *valaunce,* perhaps after *Valence,* textile town in southeastern France where the material for such drapery was made.]

Val·dai (väl-dī′). A hilly plateau area of the Soviet Union, in the northwestern Russian S.F.S.R.

Val·di·vi·a (văl-dē′vē-ə; *Spanish* väl-dē′vyä), **Pedro de.** 1500?–1553. Spanish soldier; conqueror of Chile.

vale¹ (vāl) *n.* **1.** A valley, often coursed by a stream; dale. **2.** The world as a scene of sorrow: *this vale of dross and tears.* [Middle English *vale, vaal,* from Old French *val,* from Latin *vallēs, vallis.* See **wel-**³ in Appendix.*]

va·le² (vā′lē, wä′lā) *interj.* Used to express leave-taking or farewell. —*n.* A good-by. [Latin *valē,* imperative of *valēre,* to be strong or well. See **wal-** in Appendix.*]

val·e·dic·tion (văl′ə-dĭk′shən) *n.* **1.** A bidding farewell; a leave-taking. **2.** A speech or statement made at a time of leaving. [From Latin *valedīcere,* to say farewell : *valē,* VALE (farewell) + *dīcere,* to say (see **deik-** in Appendix*).]

val·e·dic·to·ri·an (văl′ə-dĭk-tôr′ē-ən, -tōr′ē-ən) *n.* A student, usually of the highest scholastic standing, who delivers the farewell oration at commencement.

val·e·dic·to·ry (văl′ə-dĭk′tə-rē) *adj.* Pertaining to or by way of a farewell. —*n., pl.* **valedictories.** A farewell address, especially one delivered by a valedictorian.

va·lence (vā′ləns) *n.* Also **va·len·cy** (vā′lən-sē) *pl.* **-cies. 1.** *Chemistry* **a.** The capacity of an atom or group of atoms to

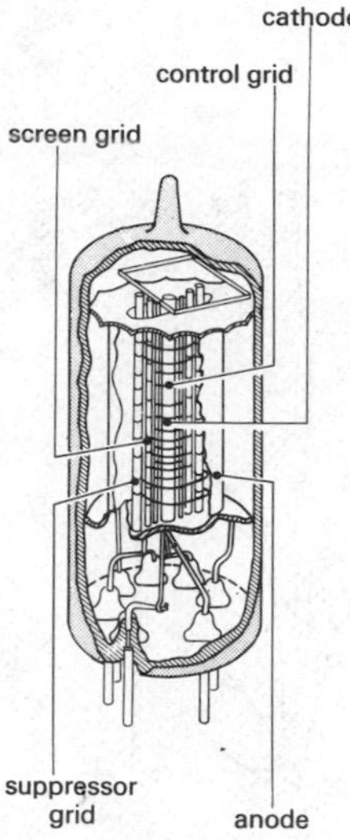

vacuum tube

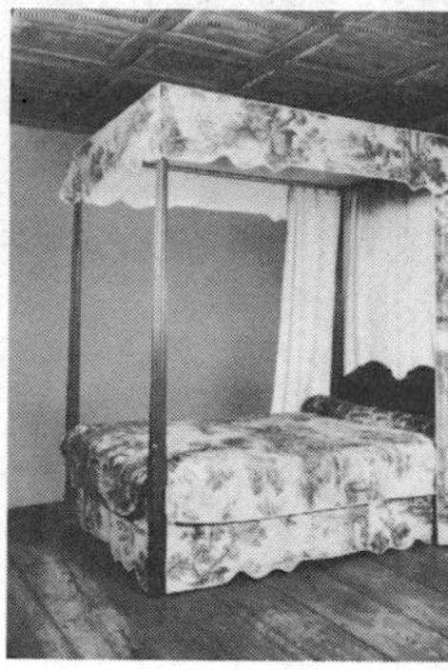
valance

combine in specific proportions with other atoms or groups of atoms. **b.** An integer, often one of several for any given element, used to represent this capacity in terms of an arbitrary assignment of 1 to an atom or group capable of forming a single bond with chlorine and of −1 to an atom or group capable of forming a single bond with hydrogen. **2.** Broadly, the capacity of something to unite, react, or interact with something else. [Late Latin *valentia*, strength, capacity, from Latin *valēns*, present participle of *valēre*, to be strong. See **wal-** in Appendix.*]

valence electron. An electron in an outer or next outer shell of an atom that can participate in forming chemical bonds with other atoms.

valence shell. A shell of an atom that contains the valence electrons.

Va·len·ci·a (və-lĕn′shē-ə, -shə; *Spanish* vä-lĕn′thyä). **1.** A region and former kingdom of Spain, in the east on the Mediterranean. **2.** A province of Spain occupying 8,998 square miles in this region. Population, 1,429,000. **3.** The capital of this province, a seaport on the Mediterranean. Population, 583,000. **4.** A city of Venezuela, in the north on the western shore of Lake Valencia. Population, 161,000.

Va·len·ci·a, Lake (və-lĕn′shē-ə, -shə; *Spanish* vä-lĕn′thyä). A freshwater lake of Venezuela, occupying 125 square miles in the north.

Va·len·ci·ennes[1] (və-lĕn′sē-ĕnz′; *French* và-läɴ-syĕn′) *n.* A fine type of lace with a floral pattern originally manufactured at Valenciennes. Also called "Valenciennes lace."

Va·len·ci·ennes[2] (và-läɴ-syĕn′). A city and manufacturing center of north-central France, near the Belgian border. Population, 46,000.

val·en·tine (văl′ən-tīn′) *n.* **1. a.** A greeting card of a sentimental or satirical nature sent, usually, to one of the opposite sex on Saint Valentine's Day. **b.** A card or gift sent as a token of love to one's sweetheart on Saint Valentine's Day. **2.** A person singled out as one's sweetheart on Saint Valentine's Day.

Val·en·tine (văl′ən-tīn′), **Saint.** Roman Christian martyr of the third century A.D.

Valentine's Day, Valentines Day. Saint Valentine's Day *(see).*

Va·le·ra, Eamon de. See **de Valera.**

va·le·ri·an (və-lîr′ē-ən) *n.* **1.** Any of various plants of the genus *Valeriana*, having dense clusters of small white or pinkish flowers; especially, *V. officinalis*, native to Eurasia and widely cultivated. This species is also called "garden heliotrope." **2.** The dried roots of *V. officinalis*, used medicinally as a sedative. [Middle English, from Old French *valeriane*, from Medieval Latin *valeriāna*, from Latin *Valeriānus*, of Valeria, Roman province where the plant originated, from *Valerius*, name of a Roman gens, from *valēre*, to be strong. See **wal-** in Appendix.*]

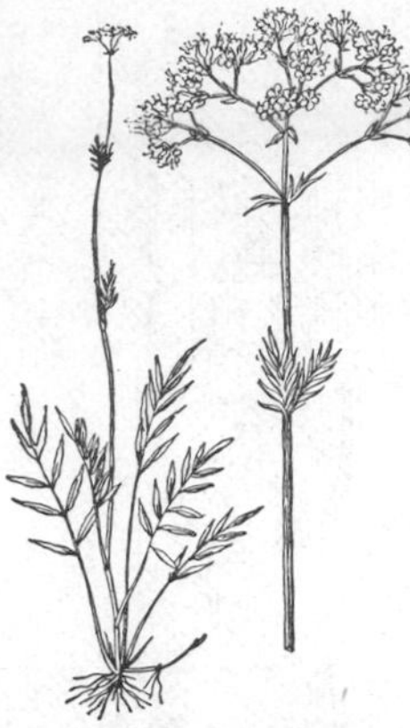

valerian
Valeriana officinalis
Left: Flowering plant
Right: Detail of flowers

va·le·ric acid (və-lĕr′ĭk, -lîr′ĭk). A colorless liquid, $C_5H_{10}O_2$, used in flavorings, perfumes, plasticizers, and pharmaceuticals. [Obtained from the root of VALERIAN.]

Va·le·rie (văl′ə-rē). Also **Va·le·ri·a** (və-lîr′ē-ə). A feminine given name. [French, from Latin *Valeria*, feminine of *Valerius*. See **valerian.**]

Va·lé·ry (và-lā-rē′), **Paul.** 1871–1945. French poet.

val·et (văl′ĭt, vă-lā′) *n.* **1.** A man's personal attendant. **2.** A hotel employee who performs personal services for patrons. —*v.* **valeted** (văl′ə-tĭd, vă-lād′), **-eting, -ets.** —*tr.* To act as a personal servant to; attend. —*intr.* To work as a valet. [French, from Old French *vaslet*, *varlet*, originally "young nobleman," "squire," from Medieval Latin *vassellitus* (unattested), from Celtic *wasso-* (unattested). See **upo** in Appendix.*]

va·let de cham·bre (và-lā′ də shäɴ′br′) *pl.* **valets de chambre** (và-lā′ də shäɴ′br′). *French.* A man's valet.

Va·let·ta. See **Valletta.**

val·e·tu·di·nar·i·an (văl′ə-to͞od′n-âr′ē-ən, văl′ə-tyo͞od′-) *n.* A chronic invalid; especially, one constantly and morbidly concerned with his health. —*adj.* **1.** Chronically ailing; sickly; infirm. **2.** Endeavoring to recover health. [Latin *valētūdinārius*, in poor health, from *valētūdō*, state of health, from *valēre*, to be strong. See **wal-** in Appendix.*] —**val′e·tu′di·nar′i·an·ism′** *n.*

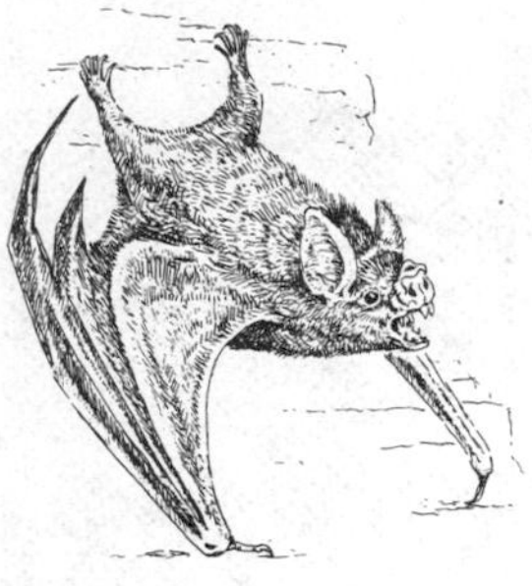

vampire
Desmodus rotundus

val·e·tu·di·nar·y (văl′ə-to͞o′də-nĕr′ē, văl′ə-tyo͞o′-) *adj.* Valetudinarian. —*n.* A valetudinarian.

val·gus (văl′gəs) *n., pl.* **-guses.** *Pathology.* **1.** A knock-kneed person. **2.** *Archaic.* A bowlegged person. See **varus.** [Latin *valgus*†, bowlegged.] —**val′goid′** (-goid′) *adj.*

Val·hal·la (văl-hăl′ə) *n.* Also **Wal·hal·la** (văl-, wŏl-). *Norse Mythology.* The great hall of immortality in which the souls of warriors slain heroically were received by Odin and enshrined. [Old Norse *Valhöll* : *valr*, those slain in battle (see **wel-**[4] in Appendix*) + *höll*, hall (see **kel-**[4] in Appendix*).]

val·iant (văl′yənt) *adj.* **1.** Possessing or acting with valor; brave; courageous; stouthearted. **2.** Showing valor: *"In a valiant suffering for others . . . did nobleness ever lie."* (Carlyle). —See Synonyms at **brave.** —*n.* A valiant person. [Middle English *valiaunt*, from Norman French, from Vulgar Latin *valente* (unattested), from Latin *valēns*, present participle of *valēre*, to be strong. See **wal-** in Appendix.*] —**val′ian·cy, val′iance, val′iant·ness** *n.* —**val′iant·ly** *adv.*

val·id (văl′ĭd) *adj.* **1.** Well-grounded; sound; supportable: *a valid objection.* **2.** Producing the desired results; efficacious: *valid methods.* **3.** Legally sound and effective; incontestable; binding: *a valid title.* **4.** *Logic.* **a.** Containing premises from which the conclusion may logically be derived: *a valid argument.* **b.** Correctly inferred or deduced from a premise: *a valid conclusion.* **5.** *Archaic.* Of sound health; robust. [French *valide*, from Old French, from Latin *validus*, strong, effective, from *valēre*, to be strong. See **wal-** in Appendix.*] —**va′lid·ly** *adv.* —**va′lid·ness** *n.*

Synonyms: *valid, sound, convincing, telling, conclusive.* These adjectives are applied, not always interchangeably, to such things as statements, arguments, and reasoning; in each case they greatly heighten the effectiveness or force of what they describe. *Valid* and *sound* both refer to qualities that give inner strength and capacity to resist challenge or attack. What is *valid* is justifiable because it is based on truth or fact or has legal force. What is *sound* has a firm basis in truth, right, or wisdom. *Convincing* and *telling* more often refer to assertiveness. *Convincing* implies power to assure, allay doubt, or silence opposition. *Telling* means having a marked effect, sometimes suddenly produced. *Conclusive* means decisive and thus capable of putting an end to doubt or debate.

val·i·date (văl′ə-dāt′) *tr.v.* **-dated, -dating, -dates. 1.** To declare or make legally valid. **2.** To mark with an indication of official sanction. **3.** To substantiate; verify. —See Synonyms at **confirm.** —**val′i·da′tion** *n.*

va·lid·i·ty (və-lĭd′ə-tē) *n.* The state or quality of being valid.

val·ine (văl′ēn′, vā′lēn′) *n.* A crystalline amino acid, $C_5H_{11}NO_2$, essential for normal human growth. [VAL(ERIC ACID) + -INE.]

va·lise (və-lēs′) *n.* A small piece of hand luggage. [French, from Italian *valigia*, akin to Medieval Latin *valisia*†.]

Val·kyr·ie (văl-kîr′ē, -kī′rē, văl′kîr′ē, -kī′rē) *n.* Also **Wal·kyr·ie** (văl-, wŏl-). *Norse Mythology.* Any of Odin's handmaidens who hover over battlefields, choosing warriors to be victorious and conducting the souls of slain heroes to Valhalla. [Old Norse *valkyrja*, "chooser of the slain." See **wel-**[4] in Appendix.*]

Va·lla·do·lid (bä′lyä-*th*ō-lē*th*′). A city of north-central Spain, about 98 miles northwest of Madrid; the capital of Castile (1454–1598). Population, 172,000.

val·la·tion (vă-lā′shən) *n.* **1.** An earthwork wall used for military defense; a rampart. **2.** The art or process of planning or erecting such fortifications. [Late Latin *vallātiō*, from Latin *vallāre*, to surround with a rampart, from *vallum*, palisade, rampart, from *vallus*, stake. See **walso-** in Appendix.*] —**val′la·to′ry** (văl′ə-tôr′ē, -tōr′ē) *adj.*

val·lec·u·la (vă-lĕk′yə-lə) *n., pl.* **-lae** (-lē′). *Biology.* A shallow groove, depression, or furrow. [Late Latin, variant of Latin *vallicula*, diminutive of *vallēs*, VALLEY.] —**val·lec′u·lar** (-lər), **val·lec′u·late** (-lĭt, -lāt′) *adj.*

Val·le·jo (və-lā′ō, -lā′hō). A city of California, on San Pablo Bay northeast of San Francisco. Population, 61,000.

Val·le·jo (və-lā′ō, -lā′hō; *Spanish* bä-yā′hō), **Mariano Guadalupe.** 1808–1890. Mexican-born California pioneer.

Val·let·ta (və-lĕt′ə). Also **Va·let·ta.** The capital of Malta, a seaport on the northeastern coast. Population, 18,000.

val·ley (văl′ē) *n., pl.* **-leys. 1.** An elongated lowland between ranges of mountains or hills, or other uplands, often having a river or stream running along the bottom. **2.** The extensive land area drained or irrigated by a river system. **3.** Any depression or hollow resembling or suggesting a valley, as where two slopes of a roof meet. [Middle English *valey*, from Norman French, from Vulgar Latin *vallāta* (unattested), from Latin *vallis*, *vallēs*. See **wel-**[3] in Appendix.*]

Valley Forge. A village in southeastern Pennsylvania; the site of George Washington's winter headquarters (1777–78).

Va·lois[1] (và-lwà′). A royal house that held the French throne from 1328 to 1589.

Va·lois[2] (và-lwà′). A historic region and former duchy of northern France.

va·lo·ni·a (və-lō′nē-ə, -lōn′yə) *n.* An extract from the dried acorn cups of an oak tree, *Quercus aegilops*, of eastern Europe and Asia Minor, used chiefly in tanning and dyeing. [Italian *vallonia*, from Modern Greek *balania*, plural of *balani*, acorn, from Greek *balanos*. See **gwel-**[3] in Appendix.*]

val·or (văl′ər) *n.* Also *chiefly British* **val·our.** Courage and boldness, as in battle; bravery. [Middle English *valour*, value, worth, from Old French, from Latin *valor*, from *valēre*, to be strong, be of value. See **wal-** in Appendix.*]

val·or·ize (văl′ə-rīz′) *tr.v.* **-ized, -izing, -izes.** To establish and maintain the price of (a commodity) by governmental action. [Portuguese *valorizar*, from *valor*, value, price, from Latin. See **valor.**] —**val′or·i·za′tion** *n.*

val·or·ous (văl′ər-əs) *adj.* Possessing or marked by personal bravery; valiant. See Synonyms at **brave.** —**val′or·ous·ly** *adv.* —**val′or·ous·ness** *n.*

Val·pa·rai·so (văl′pə-rī′zō, -rā′zō). *Spanish* **Val·pa·ra·í·so** (väl′pä-rä-ē′sō). A city of west-central Chile, a major seaport on the Pacific. Population, 259,000.

val·u·a·ble (văl′yo͞o-ə-bəl, văl′yə-) *adj.* **1.** Having high monetary or material value for use or exchange. **2.** Highly useful for a specific purpose. **3.** Having admirable or esteemed qualities or characteristics. —See Synonyms at **costly.** —*n.* A valuable personal possession, such as a piece of jewelry. Usually used in the plural. —**val′u·a·ble·ness** *n.* —**val′u·a·bly** *adv.*

val·u·a·tion (văl′yo͞o-ā′shən) *n. Abbr.* **val. 1.** The act or process of assessing the value or price of something; an appraisal. **2.** The assessed value or price of something. **3.** An estimation or appreciation of the worth, merit, or character of something: *"The African does not adopt the valuation which a European sets on saving money."* (Michael Banton). —**val′u·a′tion·al** *adj.*

val·u·a·tor (văl′yo͞o-ā′tər) *n.* One who estimates values; an appraiser.

val·ue (văl′yo͞o) *n. Abbr.* **val. 1.** An amount considered to be a suitable equivalent for something else; a fair price or return for goods or services. **2.** Monetary or material worth. **3.** Worth in usefulness or importance to the possessor; utility or merit. **4.** A principle, standard, or quality considered worthwhile or desirable. **5.** Precise meaning or import, as of a carefully considered word. **6.** *Mathematics.* An assigned or calculated numerical quantity. **7.** *Music.* The relative duration of a tone or rest. **8. a.** The relative darkness or lightness of a color in a picture. **b.** That aspect of color in the Munsell color system by which a sample appears to reflect more or less of the incident light. Value corresponds to **lightness** *(see)* of the perceived color. See **color.** **9.** *Phonetics.* The sound quality of a letter or diphthong. —See Synonyms at **worth.** —*tr.v.* **valued, -uing, -ues.** **1.** To determine or estimate the worth or value of; appraise. **2.** To regard highly; prize; esteem. **3.** To rate according to relative estimate of worth or desirability; evaluate. **4.** To assign a value to (a unit of currency, for example). —See Synonyms at **appreciate.** [Middle English, from Old French, from the feminine past participle of *valoir,* to be worth, from Latin *valēre,* to be strong, be of value. See **wal-** in Appendix.*] —**val'u·er** *n.*

val·ued (văl'yo͞od) *adj.* Highly regarded; much esteemed.

valued policy. An insurance policy requiring the insurer to pay the insured the full face value of the policy in the event of total loss, regardless of the actual value of the lost property.

value judgment. A judgment based upon or reflecting one's personal or class values.

val·ue·less (văl'yo͞o-lĭs) *adj.* Having no value; worthless.

val·vate (văl'vāt') *adj.* **1.** Having or characterized by valves or valvelike parts. **2.** *Botany.* Meeting at the edges without overlapping, as petals or sepals.

valve (vălv) *n.* **1.** *Anatomy.* A membranous structure in a hollow organ or passage, as in an artery or vein, that retards or prevents the return flow of a bodily fluid. **2. a.** Any of various devices that regulate the flow of gases, liquids, or loose materials through structures, such as piping, or through apertures by opening, closing, or obstructing ports or passageways. **b.** The movable control element of such a device. **c.** *Music.* A device in a brass wind instrument that permits change in pitch by allowing a rapid varying of the air column in a tube. **3.** *Biology.* **a.** One of the paired, hinged shells of many mollusks and of brachiopods. **b.** A similar paired part, as of the cell wall of a diatom. **4.** *Botany.* **a.** One of the sections into which a seed pod or other dehiscent fruit splits. **b.** A lidlike covering of an anther. **5.** *Chiefly British.* An electron tube or vacuum tube. **6.** *Archaic.* Either half of a double or folding door. —*tr.v.* **valved, valving, valves.** **1.** To provide with a valve or valves. **2.** To control by means of a valve or valves. [Middle English, leaf of a door, from Latin *valva.* See **wel-**³ in Appendix.*]

valve-in-head engine (vălv'ĭn-hĕd'). An internal-combustion engine having the inlet and exhaust valves in the cylinder head instead of in the engine block, as in some automobiles.

val·vu·lar (văl'vyə-lər) *adj.* Pertaining to, having, or operating by means of valves or valvelike parts.

val·vule (văl'vyo͞ol) *n.* Also **val·vu·la** (văl'vyə-lə) *pl.* **-lae** (-lē'). A small valve or valvelike structure. [New Latin *valvula,* diminutive of Latin *valva,* leaf of a door, VALVE.]

val·vu·li·tis (văl'vyə-lī'tĭs) *n.* Inflammation of a valve, especially of a cardiac valve. [New Latin : *valvula,* VALVULE + -ITIS.]

vam·brace (văm'brās') *n.* Armor used to protect the forearm. [Middle English *va(u)mbras,* from Norman French *vauntbras,* short for Old French *avauntbras,* "forearm" : *avant,* before (see **vanguard**) + *bras,* arm, from Latin *bracchium,* from Greek *brakhiōn* (see **mreghu-** in Appendix*).] —**vam'braced'** *adj.*

va·moose (vă-mo͞os', və-) *intr.v.* **-moosed, -moosing, -mooses.** Also **va·mose** (-mōs'), **-mosed, -mosing, -moses.** *Slang.* To leave hurriedly; go away hastily. [Spanish *vamos,* "let's go," from Latin *vādāmus,* from *vādere,* to go. See **wādh-** in Appendix.*]

vamp¹ (vămp) *n.* **1.** The part of a boot or shoe covering the instep and sometimes extending over the toe. **2.** Something patched up or refurbished; patchwork, as a book based on old material. **3.** An improvised musical accompaniment. —*v.* **vamped, vamping, vamps.** —*tr.* **1.** To provide (a shoe) with a new vamp. **2.** To patch up; refurbish. **3.** To fabricate; improvise. Usually used with *up.* **4.** *Music.* To improvise (a simple accompaniment or the like) for a solo. —*intr.* To improvise simple accompaniments, variations of tunes, or the like. [Middle English *vampe,* from Old French *avantpie* : *avant,* before (see **vanguard**) + *pie(d),* foot, from Latin *pēs* (stem *ped-*) (see **ped-**¹ in Appendix*).] —**vamp'er** *n.*

vamp² (vămp) *n. Informal.* An unscrupulously seductive woman; especially, one who assumes an air of exotic mystery and sexuality to entice men. —*v.* **vamped, vamping, vamps.** *Informal.* —*tr.* To seduce or exploit (a man) in the manner of a vamp. —*intr.* To play the part of a vamp. [Short for VAMPIRE.]

vam·pire (văm'pīr') *n.* **1.** In folklore, a reanimated corpse that rises from the grave at night to suck the blood of sleeping persons. **2.** One who preys upon others, as: **a.** An extortionist. **b.** A woman who uses sexual attraction to exploit men. **3. a.** Any of various tropical American bats of the family Desmodontidae, that feed on the blood of living mammals. **b.** Any of various other bats, as those of the family Megadermatidae, erroneously believed to feed on blood. In senses 3a and 3b, also called "vampire bat." [French, from German *Vampir,* from Magyar *vampir,* probably from Russian *upyr',* from Kazan Tatar *ubyr,* witch.] —**vam·pir'ic** (văm-pĭr'ĭk) *adj.*

vam·pir·ism (văm'pī-rĭz'əm) *n.* **1.** Belief in the vampires of folklore. **2.** The practice of a vampire; bloodsucking.

van¹ (văn) *n.* **1.** A large covered truck or wagon for transporting goods or livestock. **2.** *Chiefly British.* A closed railroad car used for carrying baggage or freight. [Short for CARAVAN.]

van² (văn) *n.* The vanguard; forefront. [Short for VANGUARD.]

van³ (văn) *n.* **1.** *Archaic.* Any winnowing device, as a fan. **2.** *Poetic.* A wing. [Middle English *van(ne),* fan, from Old English *fann* and Old French *van,* both from Latin *vannus.* See **wē-** in Appendix.*]

van·a·date (văn'ə-dāt') *n.* Any of three anions, VO_3, VO_4, or V_2O_7. [From VANADIUM.]

va·nad·ic acid (və-năd'ĭk). **1.** An acid containing a vanadate group, especially HVO_3, H_3VO_4, or $H_4V_2O_7$, not existing in a pure state. **2. Vanadium pentoxide** *(see).*

va·nad·i·nite (və-năd'n-īt') *n.* A deep ruby-red or yellow to brown vanadium and lead ore, essentially $Pb_5(VO_4)_3Cl$. [VANAD(IUM) + -IN + -ITE.]

va·na·di·um (və-nā'dē-əm) *n. Symbol* **V** A bright white soft ductile metallic element found in several minerals, notably vanadinite and carnotite, having good structural strength and used in rust-resistant high-speed tools, as a carbon stabilizer in some steels, as a titanium-steel bonding agent, and as a catalyst. Atomic number 23, atomic weight 50.942, melting point 1,890°C, boiling point 3,000°C, specific gravity 6.11, valences 2, 3, 4, 5. See **element.** [New Latin, after Old Norse *Vanadīs,* name of the goddess Freya : *vana-,* akin to *Vanr,* fertility god (see **wen-** in Appendix*) + *dis*†, woman, goddess.]

vanadium pentoxide. A yellow to red crystalline powder, V_2O_5, used as a catalyst in various organic reactions and as a starting material for other vanadium salts. Also called "vanadic acid."

vanadium steel. Steel alloyed with vanadium for added strength, hardness, and high-temperature stability.

Van Al·len (văn ăl'ən), **James Alfred.** Born 1914. American physicist; predicted radiation belt around the earth.

Van Allen belt. Either of two zones of high-intensity particulate radiation trapped in the earth's magnetic field and surrounding the planet, beginning at an altitude of approximately 800 kilometers and extending several tens of thousands of kilometers into space.

Van·brugh (văn-bro͞o', văn'brə), Sir **John.** 1664–1726. English dramatist and architect.

Van Bu·ren (văn byo͞or'ən), **Martin.** 1782–1862. Eighth President of the United States (1837–41).

Van·cou·ver (văn-ko͞o'vər). A port city of British Columbia, Canada, on the western mainland coast opposite Vancouver Island. Population, 385,000.

Van·cou·ver (văn-ko͞o'vər), **George.** 1757–1798. British navigator; explorer of the Pacific Ocean.

Van·cou·ver, Mount (văn-ko͞o'vər). A mountain 15,700 feet high in the St. Elias range in southwestern Yukon Territory, Canada, near the Alaskan border.

Van·cou·ver Island (văn-ko͞o'vər). An island of British Columbia, Canada, 13,049 square miles in area, lying off the southwestern coast of the province.

van·dal (vănd'l) *n.* A person who willfully or maliciously defaces or destroys public or private property. —*adj.* Willfully or maliciously destructive. [From VANDAL.] —**van·dal'ic** (văn-dăl'ĭk) *adj.*

Van·dal (vănd'l) *n.* A member of a Germanic people that overran Gaul, Spain, and northern Africa in the fourth and fifth centuries A.D. and sacked Rome in A.D. 455. [Latin *Vandalus,* "wanderer," from Germanic. See **wendh-** in Appendix.*] —**Van·dal'ic** (văn-dăl'ĭk) *adj.*

van·dal·ism (vănd'l-ĭz'əm) *n.* The willful or malicious destruction of public or private property, especially of anything beautiful or artistic.

Van de Graaff (văn' də grăf'), **Robert Jemison.** 1901–1967. American physicist; invented the Van de Graaff generator.

Van de Graaff generator (văn' də grăf'). An electrostatic generator in which electric charge is either removed from or transferred to a large hollow spherical electrode by a rapidly moving belt, in some configurations producing potentials over a million volts, and used with an acceleration tube as an electron or ion accelerator.

Van·den·berg (văn'dən-bûrg'), **Arthur Hendrick.** 1844–1951. American diplomat and political leader; U.S. senator from Michigan (1928–51).

Van·der·bilt (văn'dər-bĭlt'), **Cornelius.** 1794–1877. American financier and philanthropist.

van der Ro·he, Ludwig Mies. See **Mies van der Rohe.**

Van Die·men's Land. The former name for **Tasmania.**

van Dong·en (văn dŏng'ən, vän), **Kees.** 1877–1968. Dutch painter.

Van Do·ren (văn dôr'ən, dōr'ən), **Carl Clinton.** 1885–1950. American critic, biographer, and historian; brother of Mark Van Doren.

Van Do·ren (văn dôr'ən, dōr'ən), **Mark Albert.** Born 1894. American poet and critic; brother of Carl Van Doren.

Van·dyke (văn-dīk') *adj.* Pertaining to or suggesting the style of Sir Anthony Vandyke, his paintings, or the mode of dress depicted in his paintings. —*n.* **1.** A painting by Vandyke. **2.** A Vandyke beard or collar.

Van·dyke (văn-dīk'), Sir **Anthony.** Also **Van Dyck.** 1599–1641. Flemish baroque portrait painter; court painter to Charles I of England.

Van Dyke (văn dīk'), **Henry.** 1852–1933. American Presbyterian clergyman, educator, and author.

Vandyke beard. A short, pointed beard.

vandyke brown. Moderate to grayish brown. See **color.** [From its frequent use by VANDYKE.] —**van·dyke'-brown'** *adj.*

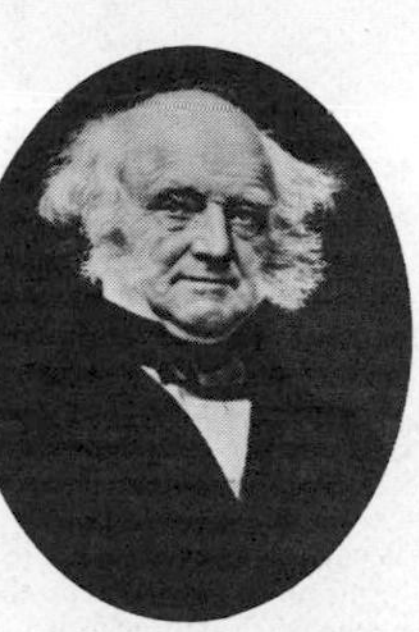

Martin Van Buren
Photograph by Mathew Brady

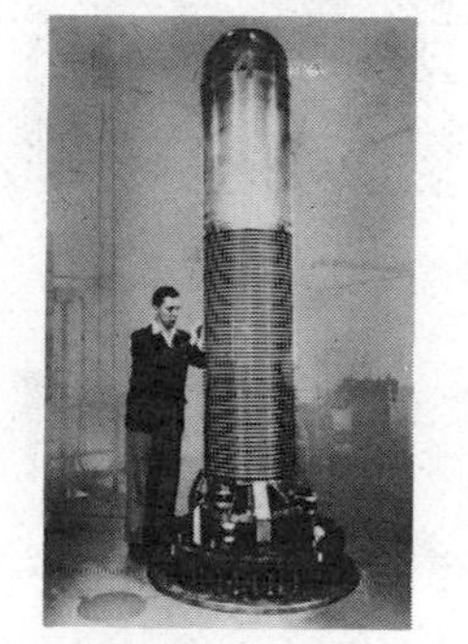

Van de Graaff generator

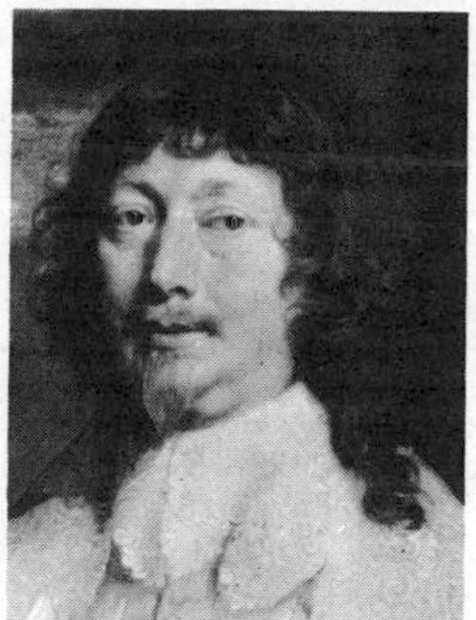

Vandyke
Detail of a self-portrait showing a Vandyke beard and collar

t tight/th thin, path/*th* this, bathe/ŭ cut/ûr urge/v valve/w with/y yes/z zebra, size/zh vision/ə about, item, edible, gallop, circus/ à *Fr.* ami/œ *Fr.* feu, *Ger.* schön/ü *Fr.* tu, *Ger.* über/KH *Ger.* ich, *Scot.* loch/N *Fr.* bon. ***Follows main vocabulary.** **†Of obscure origin.**

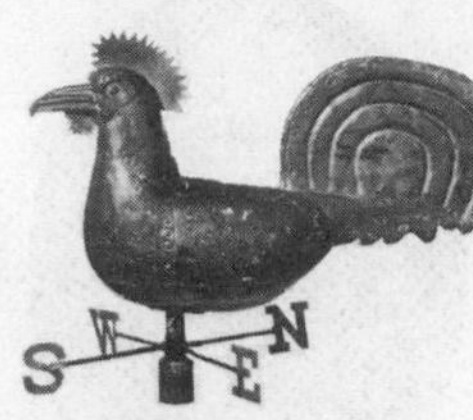

vane
Weather vane made in 1836 and once mounted on the home of Washington Irving

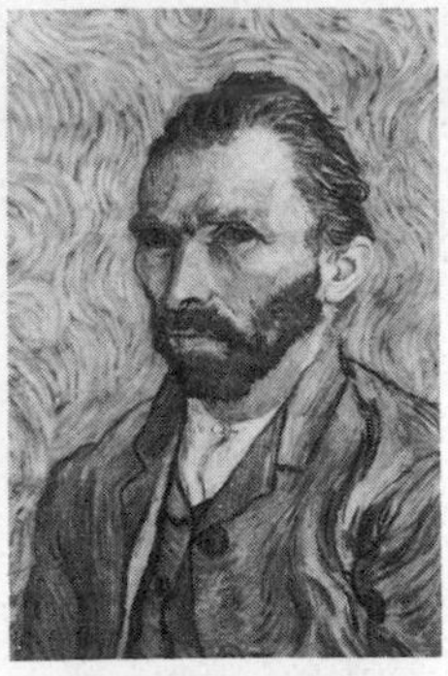

Vincent van Gogh
A self-portrait

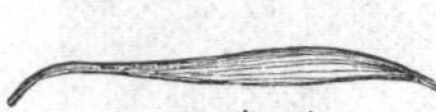

seed pod

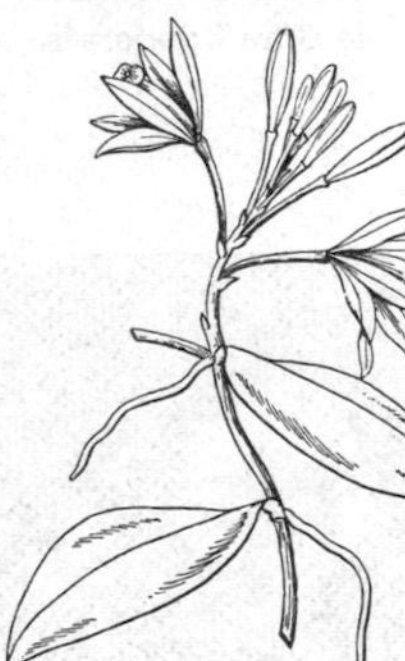

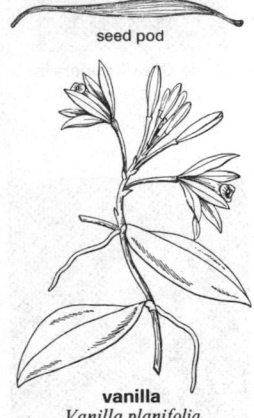

vanilla
Vanilla planifolia

Vandyke collar. A large collar of linen or lace having a deeply indented or scalloped edge.

vane (vān) *n.* **1.** A thin plate of wood or metal, often having the shape of a rooster or an arrow, that pivots on an elevated vertical spindle to indicate the direction of the wind; weather vane; weathercock. **2.** One of several usually relatively thin, rigid, flat, or sometimes curved surfaces radially mounted along an axis that is turned by or used to turn a fluid. **3.** The flattened, weblike part of a feather, consisting of a series of barbs on either side of the shaft. **4. a.** The movable target on a leveling rod. **b.** A sight on a quadrant or compass. **5.** One of the metal guidance or stabilizing fins attached to the tail of a bomb or other missile. [Middle English *vane, fane,* Old English *fana,* banner. See **pan-** in Appendix.*]

Vane (vān), Sir **Henry.** 1613–1662. English Puritan; colonial administrator in America (1635–37); executed for treason.

Vä·nern, Lake (vā'nərn). The largest lake of Sweden, occupying 2,141 square miles in the southwest.

van Eyck (văn īk'), **Jan.** 1370?–1440? Flemish painter; originator of Flemish school.

vang (văng) *n. Nautical.* A guy rope running from the peak of a gaff or derrick to the deck. [Dutch, "a catch," "seizure," from *vangen,* to catch. See **pag-** in Appendix.*]

van Gogh (văn gō', gôKH'; *Dutch* vän KHôKH'), **Vincent.** 1853–1890. Dutch postimpressionist painter.

van·guard (văn'gärd') *n.* **1.** The foremost position in an army or fleet; the van. **2. a.** The foremost or leading position in a trend or movement. **b.** Those occupying such a position. [Middle English *vantgard,* short for *avaunt garde,* from Old French *avant-garde* : *avant,* before, from Latin *abante* : *ab-,* from + *ante,* before, in front of (see **anti-** in Appendix*) + *garde,* guard, from *garder,* to GUARD.]

va·nil·la (və-nĭl'ə) *n.* **1.** Any of various tropical American orchids of the genus *Vanilla;* especially, *V. planifolia,* cultivated for its long, narrow seed pods from which a flavoring agent is obtained. **2.** The aromatic seed pod of this plant. Also called "vanilla bean." **3.** A flavoring extract prepared from these seed pods or produced synthetically. [Spanish *vainilla,* "little sheath" (from its elongated fruit), from *vaina,* sheath, from Latin *vāgīna.* See **wag-** in Appendix.*]

va·nil·lic (və-nĭl'ĭk) *adj.* Of, relating to, or derived from vanilla or vanillin.

va·nil·lin (və-nĭl'ĭn, văn'əl-ĭn) *n.* A white or yellowish crystalline compound, $C_8H_8O_3$, found in vanilla beans and certain balsams and resins and used in perfumes, flavorings, and pharmaceuticals. [VANILL(A) + -IN.]

Va·nir (vä'nîr) *pl.n. Norse Mythology.* An early race of gods who dwelt with the Aesir in Asgard. [From Old Norse *Vanr,* fertility god. See **wen-** in Appendix.*]

van·ish (văn'ĭsh) *intr.v.* **-ished, -ishing, -ishes. 1.** To disappear or become invisible, especially quickly or in an unexplained manner: *"She vanished like a discontented fairy"* (Dickens). **2.** To fade or decay to nothing; pass out of existence: *"Her voice would not cease, it would just vanish"* (Faulkner). **3.** *Mathematics.* To become zero. Used of a function or variable. [Middle English *vanisshen,* from Old French *esvanir* (present stem *esvaniss-*), from Vulgar Latin *exvānīre* (unattested), variant of Latin *ēvānēscere* : *ex-,* away from + *vānēscere,* to disappear, "become empty," from *vānus,* empty (see **eu-²** in Appendix*).] **—van'ish·er** *n.*

vanishing cream. A cosmetic preparation containing less oil than cold cream, used as a powder base and night cream.

vanishing point. 1. A point in a drawing at which parallel lines drawn in perspective converge or seem to converge. **2.** A point at which a thing disappears or ceases to exist.

van·i·ty (văn'ə-tē) *n., pl.* **-ties. 1.** The quality or condition of being vain; excessive pride in one's appearance or accomplishments; conceit. **2.** Lack of usefulness, worth, or effect; hollowness; futility; worthlessness. **3. a.** Something that is vain, futile, or worthless. **b.** Something about which one is vain or conceited: *"He caught himself having vanity about his wool shirt"* (Carl Sandburg). **4.** A vanity case. **5.** A **dressing table** *(see).* [Middle English *vanite,* from Old French, from Latin *vānitās,* from *vānus,* empty, vain. See **eu-²** in Appendix.*]

vanity case. 1. A woman's compact. **2.** A small handbag or case used by women for carrying cosmetics or toiletries.

Vanity Fair. Also **vanity fair.** Any place or scene of ostentation or empty, idle amusement and frivolity, as the social world. [From the fair in Bunyan's *Pilgrim's Progress.*]

vanity press. A publisher that publishes a book at the expense of the author. Also called "vanity publisher."

van Loon (văn lōōn', lōn'), **Hendrik Willem.** 1882–1944. Dutch-born American author.

van·quish (văng'kwĭsh, văn'-) *tr.v.* **-quished, -quishing, -quishes. 1. a.** To defeat or conquer in battle; subjugate. **b.** To defeat in any contest, conflict, or competition. **2.** To overcome or subdue (an emotion, for example); suppress: *His success vanquished his fears.* —See Synonyms at **defeat.** [Middle English *vencusen, vaynquysshen,* from Old French *vainquir* (present stem *vanquiss-*), variant of *vaincre,* from Latin *vincere.* See **weik-⁵** in Appendix.*] **—van'quish·a·ble** *adj.* **—van'quish·er** *n.*

Van Rens·se·laer (văn rĕn'sə-lîr', rĕn'sə-lər), **Kiliaen.** 1595–1644. Dutch merchant; a founder of Dutch West India Company; colonized a large area of upstate New York; ancestor of Stephen Van Rensselaer.

Van Rens·se·laer (văn rĕn'sə-lîr', rĕn'sə-lər), **Stephen.** 1764–1839. American military and political leader and educator; descendant of Kiliaen Van Rensselaer.

van·tage (văn'tĭj) *n.* **1. a.** An advantage in a competition or conflict; superiority. **b.** A position, condition, or opportunity likely to provide superiority or advantage. **2.** A position that affords a wide or commanding view or outlook. Often used in the phrase *vantage point.* **3.** *Tennis.* **Advantage** *(see).* [Middle English, from Norman French, short for Old French *avantage,* ADVANTAGE.]

van't Hoff (vänt hôf'), **Jacobus Henricus.** 1852–1911. Dutch physical chemist; worked on stereochemistry and thermodynamics.

Van Vech·ten (văn vĕk'tən), **Carl.** 1880–1964. American author, critic, and photographer.

van·ward (văn'wərd) *adj.* Located in the van or front; advanced. *—adv.* Toward or to the van or front; forward.

Van·zet·ti (văn-zĕt'ē; *Italian* vän-dzĕt'tē), **Bartolomeo.** 1888–1927. Italian-born political activist; with his friend Nicola **Sacco** *(see)* executed after a controversial murder trial.

vap·id (văp'ĭd) *adj.* **1.** Lacking taste, zest, or flavor; flat; stale: *vapid beer.* **2.** Lacking life, spirit, or animation; dull; tedious: *vapid conversation.* [Latin *vapidus.* See **kwēp-** in Appendix.*] **—va·pid'i·ty, vap'id·ness** *n.* **—vap'id·ly** *adv.*

va·por (vā'pər) *n.* Also *chiefly British* **va·pour. 1.** Any barely visible or cloudy diffused matter, such as mist, fumes, or smoke, suspended in the air. **2. a.** The state of a substance that exists below its critical temperature and that may be liquefied by application of sufficient pressure. **b.** Broadly, the gaseous state of any substance that is liquid or solid under ordinary conditions. **3. a.** The vaporized form of a substance for use in industrial, military, or medical processes. **b.** A mixture of a vapor and air, as the explosive gasoline-air mixture burned in an internal-combustion engine. **4.** *Archaic.* **a.** Something unsubstantial, worthless, or fleeting. **b.** A fantastic or foolish idea. **5.** *Plural.* **a.** *Archaic.* Exhalations within a body organ, especially the stomach, supposed to affect the mental or physical condition. **b.** A depressed condition; hysteria. *—v.* **vapored, -poring, -pors.** Also *chiefly British* **va·pour.** *—tr.* To vaporize. *—intr.* **1.** To give off vapor. **2.** To evaporate. **3.** To engage in boastful talk. [Middle English *vapour,* from Old French *vapeur, vapour,* from Latin *vapor,* steam. See **kwēp-** in Appendix.*]

va·por·es·cence (vā'pə-rĕs'əns) *n.* The formation of vapor.

va·por·if·ic (vā'pə-rĭf'ĭk) *adj.* **1.** Producing or turning to vapor. **2.** Having the nature of vapor; vaporous. [VAPOR + -FIC.]

va·por·ing (vā'pə-rĭng) *adj.* Foolishly bombastic; boastful. *—n.* Boastful or bombastic talk or behavior: *"all his . . . dreams of fame were the vaporings of a shoddy aesthete without talent"* (Thomas Wolfe). **—va'por·ing·ly** *adv.*

va·por·ish (vā'pər-ĭsh) *adj.* **1.** Suggestive of or like vapor. **2.** *Archaic.* Affected by the vapors; inclined toward low spirits.

va·por·i·za·tion (vā'pər-ə-zā'shən) *n.* The act or process of vaporizing or the condition of being vaporized.

va·por·ize (vā'pə-rīz') *v.* **-ized, -izing, -izes.** *—tr.* To convert (a solid or liquid) to vapor, especially by heating. *—intr.* To be converted into vapor. **—va'por·iz'a·ble** *adj.*

va·por·iz·er (vā'pə-rī'zər) *n.* One that vaporizes, especially a device used to vaporize medicine for inhalation.

vapor lock. A pocket of vaporized gasoline in the fuel line of an internal-combustion engine that obstructs normal flow of fuel.

va·por·ous (vā'pər-əs) *adj.* Also **va·por·y** (vā'pə-rē). **1.** Pertaining to or resembling vapor. **2. a.** Producing vapors; volatile. **b.** Giving off or full of vapors. **3.** Insubstantial, vague, or ethereal: *"the imponderable mysterious and vaporous illusions of twilight"* (John C. Powys). **4.** Extravagantly fanciful; high-flown: *vaporous conjecture.* **—va'por·os'i·ty** (vā'pə-rŏs'ə-tē), **va'por·ous·ness** *n.* **—va'por·ous·ly** *adv.*

vapor pressure. The pressure exerted by a vapor in equilibrium with its solid or liquid phase.

vapor trail. A **contrail** *(see).*

va·que·ro (vä-kâr'ō) *n., pl.* **-ros.** *Southwestern U.S.* A cowboy; herdsman. [Spanish, from *vaca,* cow, from Latin *vacca.* See **wak-** in Appendix.*]

var. 1. variable. **2.** variant. **3.** variation. **4.** variety. **5.** various.

va·ra (vä'rä) *n.* **1.** A Spanish, Portuguese, and Latin American unit of linear measure, varying from 32 to 43 inches. **2.** A square vara. [Spanish and Portuguese, "rod," "yardstick," from Latin *vāra,* forked pole, from *vārus,* bent inward. See **wā-¹** in Appendix.*]

Va·ra·na·si (vä-rä'nə-sē). Formerly **Be·na·res** (bə-när'əs, -ēz), **Ba·na·ras** (bə-när'əs). A city in southeastern Uttar Pradesh, India, on the Ganges; a sacred city of the Hindus. Population, 514,000.

Va·rang·er Fjord (vä-räng'ər). An inlet of the Barents Sea, extending 42 miles into extreme northeastern Norway.

Va·ran·gi·an (və-răn'jē-ən) *n.* One of a group of Scandinavian seafarers who established a dynasty in Russia in the ninth century. [Medieval Latin *Varangus,* from Medieval Greek *Barangos,* from Old Norse *Væringi,* probably "confederate," from *vār,* agreement, pledge. See **wēros** in Appendix.*]

Var·dar (vär'där). A river rising in southern Yugoslavia near the Albanian border and flowing 230 miles south to the Gulf of Salonika.

Va·rèse (və-rāz', -rĕz'), **Edgard.** 1885–1965. French-born American composer.

Var·gas (vär'gəs), **Getulio Dornelles.** 1883–1954. Brazilian statesman; president of Brazil (1930–45 and 1951–54).

va·ri·a (vâr'ē-ə) *n.* A miscellany, especially of literary works. [Latin, neuter plural of *varius,* VARIOUS.]

var·i·a·ble (vâr'ē-ə-bəl) *adj. Abbr.* **var. 1. a.** Liable or likely to change or vary; subject to variation; changeable. **b.** Inconstant; fickle. **2.** *Biology.* Tending to deviate from an established type;

aberrant. 3. *Mathematics.* Having no fixed quantitative value. —*n. Abbr.* **var.** 1. Anything that varies or is prone to variation. 2. *Astronomy.* A variable star. 3. *Mathematics.* a. A quantity capable of assuming any of a set of values. b. A symbol representing such a quantity. —**var′i·a·bil′i·ty, var′i·a·ble·ness** *n.* —**var′i·a·bly** *adv.*

variable cost. Cost that fluctuates directly with output changes.

variable star. A star whose brightness varies because of internal changes or periodic eclipsing of component stars.

Var·i·an (vâr′ē-ən), **Russell Harrison.** 1898–1959. American physicist; with his brother, **Sigurd** (1901–1961), invented the klystron.

var·i·ance (vâr′ē-əns) *n.* 1. a. The act of varying. b. The state or quality of being variant or variable; variation; difference. c. A difference between what is expected and what actually occurs. 2. A difference of opinion; dissension; a dispute. 3. *Law.* a. A discrepancy between two statements or documents in a legal proceeding. b. The license to engage in an act contrary to a usual rule. 4. *Statistics.* The mean of the squares of the variations from the mean of a frequency distribution. 5. *Chemistry.* The number of thermodynamic variables required to specify a state of equilibrium of a system, given by the phase rule. —See Synonyms at **discord.** —**at variance.** 1. In a state of discrepancy; differing; conflicting. Said of things: *The facts are at variance.* 2. In a state of discord or dissension; quarreling. Said of persons: *Two factions of the party are at variance.*

var·i·ant (vâr′ē-ənt) *adj. Abbr.* **var.** 1. Having or exhibiting variation; differing. 2. Tending or liable to vary; variable; changeable. 3. Deviating from a standard; exhibiting slight difference. —*n.* Something that differs only slightly from another in form, as a different spelling or pronunciation of the same word. [Middle English, from Old French, from Latin *variāns,* present participle of *variāre,* VARY.]

var·i·ate (vâr′ē-ĭt, -āt′) *n.* 1. Something that varies; a variable. 2. *Statistics.* A random variable with a numerical value that is defined on a given sample space. [From Latin *variāre,* VARY.]

var·i·a·tion (vâr′ē-ā′shən) *n. Abbr.* **var.** 1. a. The act, process, or result of varying; change or deviation. b. The state or fact of being varied. 2. The extent or degree of such deviation: *a variation of ten pounds in weight.* 3. A natural compass error, **magnetic declination** *(see).* 4. Something that is slightly different from another of the same type. 5. *Biology.* Marked difference or deviation from characteristic form, function, or structure. 6. *Mathematics.* A function that relates the values of one variable to those of other variables. 7. a. A musical form that is an altered version of some given theme, diverging from it by melodic ornamentation and by changes in harmony, rhythm, or key. b. One of a series of such forms based on a single theme. 8. *Ballet.* A solo dance, especially one forming part of a larger work. —See Synonyms at **difference.** —**var′i·a′tion·al** *adj.*

var·i·cel·la (văr′ə-sĕl′ə) *n.* **Chicken pox** *(see).* [New Latin, irregular diminutive of VARIOLA.] —**var′i·cel′loid′** *adj.*

var·i·ces. Plural of **varix.**

varico-, varic-. Indicates varix or varicose veins; for example, **varicocele, varicosis.** [From Latin *varix* (stem *varic-*), VARIX.]

var·i·co·cele (văr′ə-kō-sēl′) *n.* A varicose condition of veins of the spermatic cord or the ovaries, forming a soft tumor. [VARICO- + -CELE (tumor).]

var·i·col·ored (vâr′ĭ-kŭl′ərd) *adj.* Having a variety of colors; variegated; motley.

var·i·cose (văr′ə-kōs′) *adj.* 1. Designating blood or lymph vessels that are abnormally dilated, knotted, and tortuous. 2. Causing unusual swelling. [Latin *varicōsus,* from *varix,* VARIX.]

var·i·co·sis (văr′ə-kō′sĭs) *n.* The state of being varicose. [VARIC(O)- + -OSIS.]

var·i·cos·i·ty (văr′ə-kŏs′ə-tē) *n., pl.* **-ties.** 1. Varicosis. 2. a. A varicose distention or swelling. b. The state of having varicose veins.

var·i·cot·o·my (văr′ə-kŏt′ə-mē) *n., pl.* **-mies.** Subcutaneous incision to cure varicose veins. [VARICO- + -TOMY.]

var·ied (vâr′ēd) *adj.* 1. Having various kinds or forms; marked by variety. 2. Modified or altered. 3. Varicolored; variegated. —See Synonyms at **miscellaneous.** —**var′ied·ly** *adv.*

varied thrush. A bird, *Ixoreus naevius,* of western North America, resembling the robin but having a black transverse stripe on the breast.

var·i·e·gate (vâr′ē-ə-gāt′) *tr.v.* **-gated, -gating, -gates.** 1. To change the appearance of, especially by marking with different colors; to streak. 2. To give variety to; make varied. [Late Latin *variēgāre,* from Latin *varius,* VARIOUS.]

var·i·e·gat·ed (vâr′ē-ə-gā′tĭd) *adj.* 1. Having streaks, marks, or patches of a different color or colors. 2. Distinguished or characterized by variety; diversified.

var·i·e·ga·tion (vâr′ē-ə-gā′shən) *n.* The state of being variegated; diversified coloration.

va·ri·e·tal (və-rī′ə-təl) *adj.* Of, indicating, or named for a biological variety. [From VARIETY.] —**va·ri′e·tal·ly** *adv.*

va·ri·e·ty (və-rī′ə-tē) *n., pl.* **-ties.** *Abbr.* **var.** 1. The condition or quality of being various or varied; a lack of monotony; diversity. 2. A number or collection of varied things, especially of a particular group; an assortment: *"Here are also a great variety of birds throughout the seasons, inhabiting both sea and land"* (William Bartram). 3. A different kind, sort, or form of something of the same general classification. 4. *Biology.* a. A taxonomic category forming a subdivision of a species and consisting of naturally occurring or selectively bred individuals having varying characteristics. b. An organism, especially a plant, belonging to such a category. [Old French *variete,* from Latin *varietās,* from *varius,* VARIOUS.]

variety meat. Meat taken from a part other than skeletal muscles, as liver or sweetbreads, or processed, as sausage.

variety show. A theatrical entertainment consisting of successive unrelated acts, such as songs, dances, and comedy skits.

variety store. A retail store carrying a large variety of usually low-cost merchandise. Also called "variety shop."

var·i·form (vâr′ə-fôrm′) *adj.* Having a variety of forms; diversiform. [VARI(O)- + -FORM.]

vario-, vari-. Indicates variety or difference; for example, **variometer, variform.** [From Latin *varius,* VARIOUS.]

va·ri·o·la (və-rī′ə-lə) *n.* Smallpox. [New Latin, from Medieval Latin, pustule, from Latin *varius,* speckled, VARIOUS.]

var·i·o·late (vâr-ē′ə-lāt′, -lĭt′) *adj.* Having pustules or marks like those of smallpox. —*tr.v.* **variolated, -lating, -lates.** To inoculate with smallpox.

var·i·o·lite (vâr′ē-ə-līt′) *n.* A basic rock with a pock-marked appearance due to numerous white, rounded spherules embedded in it. [Medieval Latin *variola,* smallpox, VARIOLA + -ITE.]

var·i·o·loid (vâr′ē-ə-loid′) *n.* A mild form of smallpox in persons who have previously been vaccinated or who have previously had the disease. [VARIOL(A) + -OID.]

var·i·om·e·ter (vâr′ē-ŏm′ə-tər) *n.* A variable inductor used to measure variations in terrestrial magnetism. [VARIO- + -METER.]

var·i·o·rum (vâr′ē-ôr′əm, -ōr′əm) *n.* 1. An edition particularly of the complete works of a classical author, with notes by various scholars or editors. 2. An edition containing various versions of a text. —*adj.* Designating or pertaining to such an edition or text. [Short for Latin *editiō cum notīs variōrium,* edition with the notes of various (commentators), from *variōrum,* genitive plural of *varius,* VARIOUS.]

var·i·ous (vâr′ē-əs) *adj. Abbr.* **var.** 1. a. Of diverse kinds. b. Unlike; different. 2. More than one; numerous; several. 3. Many-sided; varying; versatile. 4. Having a variegated nature or appearance. 5. Being one of a class or group; individual and separate: *The various reports all agreed.* 6. *Archaic.* Changeable; variable. [Latin *varius,* speckled, variegated, changeable. See **wā-**[1] in Appendix.*] —**var′i·ous·ly** *adv.* —**var′i·ous·ness** *n.*

Usage: *Various* sometimes appears as a plural collective pronoun followed by *of* rather than by a noun, but the usage is widely condemned: *He spoke to various of the members* (or *spoke to various of them*). The preceding example is termed unacceptable by 91 per cent of the Usage Panel. *Various* has its proper function as an adjective in *He spoke to various members.*

var·i·sized (vâr′ĭ-sīzd′) *adj.* Of different sizes.

Var·i·typ·er (vâr′ĭ-tī′pər) *n.* A trademark for a typewriter used to prepare copy in a variety of type styles.

var·ix (vâr′ĭks) *n., pl.* **-ices** (-ə-sēz′). 1. A vein, artery, or lymph vessel that is abnormally dilated and twisted. 2. One of the longitudinal ridges marking a resting stage in the development of the lip of a gastropod shell. [Latin, swollen vein. See **wā-**[1] in Appendix.*]

var·let (vär′lĭt) *n. Archaic.* 1. An attendant or servant. 2. A knight's page. 3. A rascal; knave. [Middle English, from Old French, variant of *vaslet, valet,* VALET.]

var·let·ry (vär′lĭt-rē) *n. Archaic.* A crowd of attendants or menials, especially when disorderly; the rabble.

var·mint (vär′mənt) *n. Regional.* A person or animal considered undesirable, obnoxious, or troublesome. [Variant of VERMIN.]

Var·na (vär′nä). Formerly **Sta·lin** (stä′lĭn). A city of eastern Bulgaria, a port on the Black Sea. Population, 175,000.

var·nish (vär′nĭsh) *n.* 1. An oil-based paint containing a solvent and an oxidizing or an evaporating binder, used to coat a surface with a hard, glossy, thin film. 2. a. The smooth coating or gloss resulting from the application of varnish. b. Something resembling or likened to varnish. 3. Any deceptively attractive external appearance; an outward show. —*tr.v.* **varnished, -nishing, -nishes.** 1. To cover with varnish. 2. To give a smooth and glossy finish to. 3. To give a deceptively nice appearance to; gloss over. [Middle English *vernisch,* from Old French *vernis,* from Medieval Latin *veronix,* sandarac, from Medieval Greek *berenikē,* perhaps from Greek *Berenikē,* Berenice, city in Cyrenaica, Libya, where varnishes were first used.] —**var′nish·er** *n.*

varnish tree. Any of several trees having milky juice used to make varnish.

Var·ro (văr′ō), **Marcus Terentius.** 116–27 B.C. Roman scholar and encyclopedist.

var·si·ty (vär′sə-tē) *n., pl.* **-ties.** 1. The principal team representing a university, college, or school in sports or other competitions. 2. *Chiefly British Informal.* A university. [Shortened and altered from UNIVERSITY.] —**var′si·ty** *adj.*

Var·u·na (văr′ōō-nə, vûr′-). *Hinduism.* The Vedic god of the skies and seas. [Sanskrit *Varuṇa.* See **wel-**[1] in Appendix.*]

var·us (vâr′əs) *n., pl.* **-uses.** An abnormal positioning of a bone of the leg or foot. [From Latin *vārus,* crooked, bent inward. See **wā-**[1] in Appendix.*]

varve (värv) *n. Geology.* 1. A layer of sediment deposited in one year. 2. A pair of distinct layers of sediment, indicating seasonal deposits. [Swedish *varv,* layer, turn, from *varva,* to bend, turn, from Old Norse *hverfa.* See **kwerp-** in Appendix.*]

var·y (vâr′ē) *v.* **-ied, -ying, -ies.** —*tr.* 1. To make or cause changes in characteristics or attributes; modify or alter. 2. To make varied; give variety to: *"Using the preceding recipe, you may vary the sauce in a number of ways"* (Julia Child). 3. To introduce under new aspects; express in a different manner.

- -*intr.* **1.** To undergo or show change: *a varying society.* **2.** To be different; deviate or depart. Used with *from.* **3.** To undergo successive or alternate changes in attributes or qualities. —See Synonyms at **change.** [Middle English *varien,* from Old French *varier,* from Latin *variāre,* from *varius,* speckled, changeable. See **wā-**[1] in Appendix.*] —**var'i·er** *n.*
varying hare. The **snowshoe rabbit** *(see).*
vas (văs) *n., pl.* **vasa** (vā'sə). An organic vessel or duct. [Latin *vās,* vessel, probably akin to Umbrian *vasor*†, vessels.]
Va·sa·ri (vä-zä'rē), **Giorgio.** 1511–1574. Italian painter, architect, and art historian.
Vas·co da Ga·ma. See **Gama.**
vas·cu·lar (văs'kyə-lər) *adj.* **1.** *Biology.* Of, characterized by, or containing vessels for the transmission or circulation of plant or animal fluids such as blood, lymph, or sap. **2.** Characterized by vigor and ardor; passionate. [From Latin *vāsculum,* diminutive of *vās,* vessel, VAS.]
vascular bundle. A strand of supportive and conductive plant tissue consisting essentially of xylem and phloem.
vascular plant. Any plant of the division Tracheophyta, which includes the ferns and seed-bearing plants characterized by a system of specialized conductive and supportive tissue.
vascular tissue. Plant tissue consisting of vascular bundles.
vas·cu·lum (văs'kyə-ləm) *n., pl.* **-la** (-lə). A small box or case used for carrying newly collected plant specimens. [Latin *vāsculum,* small vessel. See **vascular.**]
vas def·er·ens (văs' dĕf'ər-ənz, -ə-rĕnz'). The vertebrate duct that carries sperm from the epididymal duct to the ejaculatory duct. [New Latin, "carrying-off vessel."]
vase (vās, vāz, väz) *n.* An open vessel, usually tall and circular, made of glass, crystal, earthenware, or the like, used chiefly for holding and displaying flowers or for ornamentation. [French, from Latin *vās,* vessel, VAS.]
va·sec·to·my (vă-sĕk'tə-mē) *n., pl.* **-mies.** Surgical excision of a part of the vas deferens.
Vas·e·line (văs'ə-lēn', -lĭn) *n.* A trademark for a petroleum jelly used primarily as a vehicle for external applications of medicinal agents and as a protective coating for metal surfaces. [Arbitrarily from German *Wasser,* water, from Old High German *wazzar* (see **wed-**[1] in Appendix*) + Greek *elaion,* OIL + -INE.]

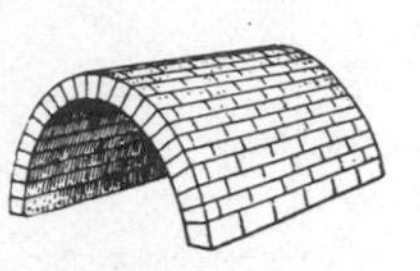

barrel vault

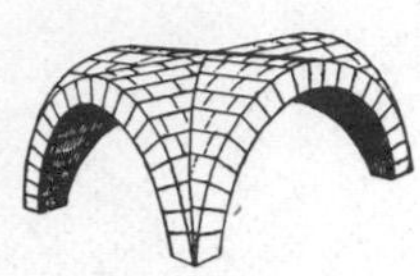

intersecting vault

vault[1]

vaso-, vas-. Indicates: **1.** A blood vessel; for example, **vasomotor.** **2.** The vas deferens; for example, **vasectomy.** [From Latin *vās,* vessel, VAS.]
vas·o·con·stric·tion (văs'ō-kən-strĭk'shən) *n.* Constriction of a blood vessel.
vas·o·con·stric·tor (văs'ō-kən-strĭk'tər) *n.* An agent, as a nerve or a drug, that causes vasoconstriction.
vas·o·dil·a·ta·tion (văs'ō-dĭl'ə-tā'shən, -dī'lə-tā'shən) *n.* Dilatation of a blood vessel.
vas·o·di·la·tor (văs'ō-dī-lā'tər, -dĭ-lā'tər) *n.* An agent, as a nerve or drug, that causes vasodilatation.
vas·o·mo·tor (văs'ō-mō'tər, vā'sō-) *adj.* Causing or regulating vasoconstriction or vasodilatation.
vas·sal (văs'əl) *n.* **1.** A person who holds land from a feudal lord and receives protection in return for homage and allegiance. **2.** One subject or subservient to another; a subordinate or dependent. **3.** A bondman; slave. —*adj.* Being or pertaining to a vassal. [Middle English, from Old French, from Medieval Latin *vassallus,* from *vassus,* servant, valet, from Celtic *wasso-* (unattested), young man, squire. See **upo** in Appendix.*]
vas·sal·age (văs'ə-lĭj) *n.* **1.** The condition of being a vassal. **2.** The service, homage, and fealty required of a vassal. **3.** A position of subordination or subjection; servitude: *"Am I the man to reproach Coleridge with this vassalage to opium?"* (De Quincey). **4.** The land held by a vassal; a fief. **5.** Vassals collectively or the vassals of a particular lord.
vast (văst, väst) *adj.* **vaster, vastest.** **1.** Very great in size, number, amount, or quantity. **2.** Very great in area or extent; immense. **3.** Very great in degree or intensity. —See Synonyms at **enormous.** —*n. Archaic.* An immense space. [Latin *vastus,* immense, vast. See **eu-**[2] in Appendix.*] —**vast'ly** *adv.* —**vast'ness** *n.*

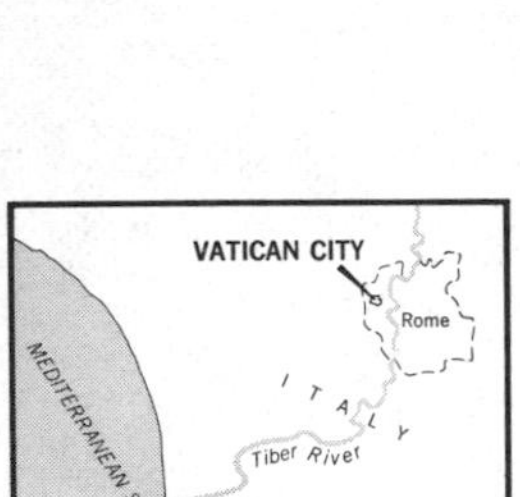

Vatican City

vas·ti·tude (văs'tə-tōōd', -tyōōd', väs'-) *n.* Also **vas·ti·ty** (-tē). The state or quality of being vast; immensity. [Latin *vastitās,* from *vastus,* VAST.]
vast·y (văs'tē, väs'-) *adj.* **-ier, -iest.** *Archaic.* Vast.
vat (văt) *n.* A large vessel, such as a tub, cistern, or barrel, used to store or hold liquids. —*tr.v.* **vatted, vatting, vats.** To place into or treat in a vat. [Middle English *vat, fat,* Old English *fæt.* See **ped-**[2] in Appendix.*]
Vat. Vatican.
vat dye. Any of a series of dyes that produce a fast color by impregnating the fiber with a reduced soluble form that is then oxidized to an insoluble form.
vat·ic (văt'ĭk) *adj.* Also **vat·i·cal** (-ĭ-kəl). Of or characteristic of a prophet; oracular. [From Latin *vātēs,* prophet. See **wāt-** in Appendix.*]
Vat·i·can (văt'ĭ-kən) *n. Abbr.* **Vat.** **1.** The official residence of the pope in Vatican City, Italy. Preceded by *the.* **2.** The papal government; the papacy. —*adj.* Of or relating to the Vatican: *a Vatican decree.* [French, from Latin *Vāticānus (mōns),* the Vatican (Hill), of Etruscan origin.]
Vatican City. *Italian* **Cit·tà del Va·ti·ca·no** (chē-tä' dĕl vä'tē-kä'nō). A sovereign papal state, established in 1929, in an enclave of about 108 acres in the city of Rome, Italy. Population, 900.
Vat·i·can·ism (văt'ĭ-kə-nĭz'əm) *n.* The policies and authority of the Vatican, especially in regard to papal infallibility. Often used derogatorily.
va·tic·i·nal (və-tĭs'ə-nəl) *adj.* Prophetic.
va·tic·i·nate (və-tĭs'ə-nāt') *v.* **-nated, -nating, -nates.** —*tr.* To prophesy; foretell. —*intr.* To be a prophet. [Latin *vāticinārī,* from *vātēs,* prophet. See **vatic.**] —**va·tic'i·na'tor** (-nā'tər) *n.*
va·tic·i·na·tion (və-tĭs'ə-nā'shən) *n.* **1.** The act of prophesying. **2.** A prediction or prophecy.
Vät·ter, Lake (vĕt'ər). A lake occupying 733 square miles in south-central Sweden.
vau. Variant of **vav.**
Vau·ban (vō-bäN'), **Marquis de.** Title of Sébastien le Prestre. 1633–1707. French military engineer.
vaude·ville (vôd'vĭl, vōd'-, vô'də-vĭl') *n.* **1. a.** Stage entertainment, especially popular in the early 20th century, offering a variety of short acts such as slapstick turns, song-and-dance routines, juggling performances, animal acts, and impersonations. **b.** A theatrical performance of this kind; variety show. **2.** A light comic play that often includes songs, pantomime, and dances. **3.** A popular, often satirical, song. —See Synonyms at **musical comedy.** [French, from Old French *vaudevire,* short for *chanson du Vau de Vire,* type of satirical song popularized in the Valley of Vire, a region in Normandy, from *vau, val,* VALE.]
vaude·vil·lian (vôd'vĭl'yən, vōd'-, vô'də-vĭl'-) *n.* One who works in vaudeville, especially as a performer.
Vau·dois (vō-dwä') *pl.n.* The **Waldenses** *(see).*
Vaughan (vôn), **Henry.** 1622–1695. English metaphysical poet.
Vaughan Williams (vôn wĭl'yəmz), **Ralph.** 1872–1958. British composer.
vault[1] (vôlt) *n.* **1. a.** An arched structure, usually of stone, brick, or concrete, forming a ceiling or roof. **b.** Any arched covering resembling a vault, as the sky. **2.** A room or space with arched walls and ceiling, especially when underground, as a cellar or storeroom. **3.** A room or compartment, often built of steel, for the safekeeping of valuables: *a bank vault.* **4.** A burial chamber, especially when underground. **5.** *Anatomy.* An arched anatomical part. —*tr.v.* **vaulted, vaulting, vaults.** **1.** To construct or supply with an arched ceiling; cover with a vault. **2.** To build in the shape of a vault; to arch. [Middle English *vaute, voute,* from Old French, from Vulgar Latin *vol(vi)ta* (unattested), a turn, vault, variant of Latin *volūta,* feminine past participle of *volvere,* to turn. See **wel-**[3] in Appendix.*]
vault[2] (vôlt) *v.* **vaulted, vaulting, vaults.** —*tr.* To jump or leap over, especially with the aid of a support, such as the hands or a pole. —*intr.* **1.** To jump or leap, especially with the use of the hands or a pole. **2.** To achieve or surmount something, as if by bounding vigorously: *vault into a position of wealth.* —*n.* The act of vaulting; a jump. [Old French *volter,* from Italian *voltare,* to turn (a horse), leap, gambol, from Vulgar Latin *volvitāre* (unattested), frequentative of Latin *volvere,* to turn. See **wel-**[3] in Appendix.*] —**vault'er** *n.*
vault·ing[1] (vôl'tĭng) *n.* **1.** The practice or craft of building vaults. **2.** Vaults collectively.
vault·ing[2] (vôl'tĭng) *adj.* **1.** Leaping upward or over. **2.** Reaching too far; exaggerated: *vaulting ambition.* **3.** Used for leaping over: *a vaulting pole.*
vaunt (vônt, vänt) *v.* **vaunted, vaunting, vaunts.** —*tr.* To describe in boastful terms; brag about. —*intr.* To boast; brag. —See Synonyms at **boast.** —*n.* A boastful remark or speech of extravagant self-praise. [Middle English *va(u)nten,* from Old French *vanter,* from Late Latin *vānitāre* (attested only in the present participle *vānitāns*), to be vain, from Latin *vānus,* empty, vain. See **eu-**[2] in Appendix.*] —**vaunt'er** *n.* —**vaunt'ing·ly** *adv.*
vaunt-cour·i·er (vônt'kŏŏr'ē-ər, -kûr'ē-ər, vänt'-) *n.* **1.** *Obsolete.* A member of an advance guard of an army. **2.** One sent in advance, as a herald. [Old French *avant-cour(r)ier* : *avant,* in front of (see **vanguard**) + COURIER.]
Vau·pés. See **Uaupés.**
Vau·quelin (vō-klăN'), **Louis Nicolas.** 1763–1829. French chemist; discovered the elements chromium and beryllium.
vav (väv, vôv) *n.* Also **vau, waw.** The sixth letter of the Hebrew alphabet. See **alphabet.**
vav·a·sor (văv'ə-sôr', -sōr') *n.* Also **vav·a·sour, vav·as·sor.** In the feudal system, a tenant who ranks directly below a baron or peer. [Middle English *vavasour,* from Old French, from Medieval Latin *vavassor,* perhaps contraction of *vassus vassōrum,* "vassal of vassals," from Latin *vassus,* servant, VASSAL.]
vb. verb; verbal.
V.C. **1.** vice chairman. **2.** vice chancellor. **3.** vice consul. **4.** Victoria Cross. **5.** Vietcong.
VD venereal disease.
v.d. **1.** vapor density. **2.** various dates.
V.D. venereal disease.
Ve·a·dar (vā'ä-där') *n.* Also **Ve·a·dar.** An extra month of the Hebrew year, having 29 days, added in leap years after the regular month of Adar. Also called "Adar Sheni." See **calendar.** [Hebrew *va'adhar,* "and Adar."]
veal (vēl) *n.* Also **veal·er** (vē'lər) (for sense 2). **1.** The meat of a calf. **2.** A calf raised to be slaughtered for food. [Middle English *veel,* from Old French, from Latin *vitellus,* diminutive of *vitulus,* calf, "yearling." See **wet-** in Appendix.*]
Veb·len (vĕb'lən), **Thorstein Bunde.** 1857–1929. American sociologist and economist.
vec·tor (vĕk'tər) *n.* **1.** *Mathematics.* A quantity completely specified by a magnitude and a direction. Compare **scalar.** **2.** *Pathology.* An organism that carries pathogens from one host to another. **3.** Broadly, any force or influence. [Latin *vector,* carrier, from *vehere* (past participle *vectus*), to carry. See **wegh-** in Appendix.*] —**vec·to'ri·al** (vĕk-tôr'ē-əl, -tōr'ē-əl) *adj.*

vector product. A vector, **C**, that has magnitude equal to the product of the magnitudes of two vectors, **A** and **B**, and the sine of the angle between **A** and **B**, and that is perpendicular to the plane of **A** and **B** and in a right-handed coordinate system directed so that a right-handed rotation about **C** carries **A** into **B** through an angle not greater than 180 degrees. Compare **scalar product.**

Ve·da (vā′də, vē′-) *n.* Any of the oldest sacred writings of Hinduism, including the psalms, incantations, hymns, and formulas of worship incorporated in four collections called the Rig-Veda, the Yajur-Veda, the Sama-Veda, and the Atharva-Veda. [Sanskrit *veda,* "knowledge." See **weid-** in Appendix.*] —**Ve′dic** (vā′dĭk, vē′-) *adj.*

Ve·dan·ta (vĭ-dän′tə, -dăn′tə) *n.* The system of Hindu philosophy that further develops the implications in the Upanishads that all reality is a single principle, Brahman, and teaches that the believer's goal is to transcend the limitations of self-identity and realize his unity with Brahman. [Sanskrit *vedanta,* "complete knowledge of the Veda" : *veda,* VEDA + *anta,* end (see **anti-** in Appendix*).] —**Ve·dan′tic** *adj.* —**Ve·dan′tism′** *n.* —**Ve·dan′tist** *n.*

V-E Day (vē′ē′). The day of victory for the Allied forces in Europe during World War II; officially, May 8, 1945. [Short for *Victory in Europe Day.*]

Ved·da (vĕd′ə) *n.* Also **Ved·dah.** One of a small, dark-skinned, wavy-haired aboriginal people of Ceylon. [Singhalese, "hunter," from Dravidian, akin to Tamil *vēṭṭam,* hunting.]

ve·dette (vĭ-dĕt′) *n.* Also **vi·dette.** **1.** A mounted sentinel stationed in advance of an outpost. **2.** A small scouting boat used to observe and report on an opposing naval force. In this sense, also called "vedette boat." [French, from Italian *vedetta,* variant (influenced by *vedere,* to see) of *veletta,* from Spanish *vela,* a watch, from *velar,* to watch, from Latin *vigilāre,* from *vigil,* awake. See **weg-**[2] in Appendix.*]

Ve·dic (vā′dĭk, vē′-) *adj.* Of or pertaining to the Veda or Vedas or to the Hindu culture that produced them. —*n.* The early Sanskrit in which the Vedas are written.

vee (vē) *n.* The letter *v.*

veep (vēp) *n. Slang.* **1.** A vice president. **2.** *Capital* **V.** The Vice President of the United States. [From the abbreviation V.P.]

veer[1] (vîr) *v.* **veered, veering, veers.** —*intr.* **1.** To turn aside from a course, direction, or purpose; swerve; shift. **2.** To shift in direction by a clockwise motion. Used of the wind. Compare **back. 3.** *Nautical.* To change the direction of a ship by turning away from the direction of the wind; wear ship. —*tr.* **1.** To alter the direction of; turn. **2.** *Nautical.* To change the course of (a ship) by turning away from the direction of the wind. —*n.* A change in direction; a swerve. [Old French *virer,* from Vulgar Latin *vīrāre* (unattested), perhaps variant (influenced by Latin *vibrāre,* VIBRATE) of Latin *gȳrāre,* GYRATE.]

veer[2] (vîr) *tr.v.* **veered, veering, veers.** *Nautical.* To let out or release (an anchor chain or line, for example). [Middle English *veren,* from Middle Dutch *vieren.* See **per**[1] in Appendix.*]

veer·y (vîr′ē) *n., pl.* **-ies.** A thrush, *Hylocichla fuscescens,* of the New World, having a reddish-brown back and an indistinctly spotted breast. [Perhaps imitative of its notes.]

Ve·ga (vē′gə, vā′-) *n.* The brightest star in the constellation Lyra. [Medieval Latin, from Arabic *(al nasr) al wāqi',* the constellation Lyra, "the falling (vulture)."]

Ve·ga (vā′gə; *Spanish* vĕ′gä), **Lope de.** Full name, Lope Félix de Vega Carpio. 1562–1635. Spanish dramatist and poet.

veg·e·ta·ble (vĕj′tə-bəl, vĕj′ə-tə-) *n.* **1. a.** A plant cultivated for an edible part or parts, as roots, stems, leaves, or flowers. **b.** The edible part of such a plant. **2.** An organism classified as a plant; a member of the vegetable kingdom. **3.** A person who leads a monotonous, passive, or merely physical existence. —*adj.* **1.** Of, pertaining to, or derived from a plant or plants. **2. a.** Suggesting or like a vegetable, as in passivity or dullness of existence; monotonous; inactive. **b.** Boundlessly growing or multiplying. [Middle English, living, growing, from Old French, from Medieval Latin *vegetābilis,* from Late Latin, enlivening, from Latin *vegetāre,* to enliven, from *vegetus,* lively, from *vegēre,* to be lively. See **weg-**[2] in Appendix.*]

vegetable ivory. A hard, ivorylike material obtained from the **ivory nut** *(see)* and used in making small objects such as buttons.

vegetable kingdom. The category of living organisms that includes all plants. Compare **animal kingdom, mineral kingdom.**

vegetable marrow. *Chiefly British.* An edible squash having very large, elongated greenish fruit. Also called "marrow squash."

vegetable oil. Any of various oils obtained from plants, used in food products and industrially.

vegetable oyster. A plant, **salsify** *(see).*

vegetable silk. Any of several silky fibers from the seed pods of certain plants.

vegetable sponge. A **loofa** *(see).*

vegetable tallow. Any of various waxy fats obtained from certain plants, such as the bayberry, and used in making soap and candles.

vegetable wax. A waxy substance of plant origin, as that obtained from certain palm trees.

veg·e·tal (vĕj′ə-təl) *adj.* **1.** Of, pertaining to, or characteristic of a plant or plants. **2.** Pertaining to growth rather than to sexual reproduction; vegetative. [French, from Old French *vegeter,* to grow, from Late Latin *vegetāre,* from Latin, to enliven. See **vegetable.**]

veg·e·tar·i·an (vĕj′ə-târ′ē-ən) *n.* One who practices or advocates vegetarianism. —*adj.* **1.** Pertaining to, practicing, or advocating vegetarianism. **2.** Consisting of vegetables: *a vegetarian diet.* [From VEGETABLE (coined in 1847 by the Vegetarian Society at Ramsgate, England).]

veg·e·tar·i·an·ism (vĕj′ə-târ′ē-ə-nĭz′əm) *n.* The practice of or belief in eating only vegetables and plant products, usually for health or moral reasons.

veg·e·tate (vĕj′ə-tāt′) *intr.v.* **-tated, -tating, -tates. 1.** To grow or sprout as a plant does. **2.** *Pathology.* To grow or spread abnormally. **3.** To lead a monotonous, passive, or merely physical existence. [Late Latin *vegetāre,* to grow, from Latin, to enliven. See **vegetable.**]

veg·e·ta·tion (vĕj′ə-tā′shən) *n.* **1.** The act or process of vegetating. **2.** The plants of an area or region; plant life collectively. **3.** *Pathology.* Any abnormal growth on the body.

veg·e·ta·tive (vĕj′ə-tā′tĭv) *adj.* Also **veg·e·tive** (vĕj′ə-tĭv). **1.** Of, pertaining to, or characteristic of plants or plant growth. **2.** *Biology.* **a.** Of, pertaining to, or capable of growth. **b.** Of, pertaining to, or functioning in processes such as growth or nutrition, rather than sexual reproduction. **c.** Of or pertaining to asexual reproduction, as fission or budding.

ve·he·ment (vē′ə-mənt) *adj.* **1.** Characterized by forcefulness of expression or intensity of emotion, passion, or conviction; ardent; emphatic: *vehement denial.* **2.** Marked by or full of vigor or energy; strong; violent. [Old French *vehement,* from Latin *vehemēns*†.] —**ve′he·mence, ve′he·men·cy** *n.* —**ve′he·ment·ly** *adv.*

ve·hi·cle (vē′ĭ-kəl) *n.* **1.** Any device for carrying passengers, goods, or equipment, usually one moving on wheels or runners, as a car or sled; a conveyance. **2.** Anything through or by which something, as thought, power, information, or the like, is conveyed, transmitted, expressed, or achieved: *"We may regard fiction . . . as the vehicle of a certain philosophy of life"* (J.B. Priestley). **3.** A play, role, or piece of music used to display the special talents of one performer or company. **4.** *Pharmacology.* A substance of no therapeutic value used as the medium in which active medicines are administered. **5.** *Painting.* A substance, as oil, in which pigments are mixed for application. [French *véhicule,* from Latin *vehiculum,* from *vehere,* to carry. See **wegh-** in Appendix.*] —**ve·hic′u·lar** (vē-hĭk′yə-lər) *adj.*

Ve·ii (vē′ī′). An ancient Etruscan town north of Rome, destroyed by the Romans in 396 B.C.

veil (vāl) *n.* Also *obsolete* **vail. 1. a.** A piece of cloth, often wide-meshed and transparent, worn by women over the head, shoulders, and often part of the face for concealment, protection, or as a token of modesty. **b.** A length of netting attached to a woman's hat or headdress for decoration, hanging before all or part of the face. **2.** The part of a nun's headdress that frames the face and falls over the shoulders. **3. a.** The life of a nun. **b.** The vows of a nun. Preceded by *the.* **4.** A piece of light fabric hung to separate or conceal what is behind it; a curtain. **5.** Anything that conceals, separates, or screens like a curtain: *a veil of secrecy.* **6.** *Biology.* A membranous covering, such as that partially or completely enveloping the developing fruiting body of certain mushrooms; a velum. —*tr.v.* **veiled, veiling, veils.** Also *obsolete* **vail.** To cover, conceal, mask, or disguise with or as if with a veil: *"veiling cruelty under apparent harmony"* (Johan Huizinga). [Middle English *veile,* from Norman French, from Latin *vēla,* neuter plural of *vēlum,* covering, veil. See **weg-**[1] in Appendix.*]

veil·ing (vā′lĭng) *n.* **1.** A veil. **2.** Gauzy material used for veils.

vein (vān) *n.* **1.** *Anatomy.* A vessel that transports blood toward the heart. **2.** Loosely, any blood vessel. **3.** *Botany.* One of the vascular bundles that form the branching framework and support of a leaf. **4.** *Zoology.* One of the chitinous, usually longitudinal ribs that stiffen and support the wing of an insect. **5.** *Geology.* A regularly shaped and lengthy occurrence of an ore; a lode. **6.** A long, wavy strip of color, as in wood or marble. **7.** Any fissure, crack, or cleft. **8.** Inherent character, quality, or tendency; a strain or streak: *"all through the interminable narrative there ran a vein of impressive earnestness"* (Mark Twain). **9.** A transient or temporary attitude or mood; turn of mind: *a talk in a serious vein.* —*tr.v.* **veined, veining, veins. 1.** To supply or fill with veins. **2.** To mark or decorate with veins. [Middle English *veine,* from Old French, from Latin *vēna*†, vein.] —**vein′al** *adj.*

veined (vānd) *adj.* Exhibiting veins; having veinlike features or markings.

vein·let (vān′lĭt) *n.* A small or secondary vein, as of an insect's wing.

vein·stone (vān′stōn′) *n.* Mineral matter in a vein exclusive of the ore; gangue.

vel. *Bookbinding.* vellum.

Ve·la (vē′lə) *n.* A constellation of the Southern Hemisphere in the Milky Way, near Antlia and Carina. [Latin *vēla,* sail, VEIL (from the saillike shape of the constellation).]

ve·la·men (vĭ-lā′mən) *n., pl.* **velamina** (və-lăm′ə-nə). **1.** *Anatomy.* Any membranous covering or integument; a velum. **2.** *Botany.* The spongy outer covering of the aerial roots of epiphytic orchids and certain other plants, capable of absorbing atmospheric moisture. [Latin *vēlamen,* covering, from *vēlāre,* to cover, from *vēlum,* covering. See **velum.**]

ve·lar (vē′lər) *adj.* **1. a.** Of or pertaining to a velum. **b.** Concerning or using the soft palate. **2.** *Phonetics.* Formed with the back of the tongue on or near the soft palate, as (g) in *good* and (k) in *cup.* —*n.* A velar sound. Also called "guttural." [New Latin *velaris,* from Latin *vēlum,* VELUM.]

ve·lar·ize (vē′lə-rīz′) *tr.v.* **-ized, -izing, izes.** *Phonetics.* To articulate (a sound) by retracting the back of the tongue toward the soft palate.

ve·late (vē′lĭt, -lāt′) *adj. Biology.* Having or covered by a velum

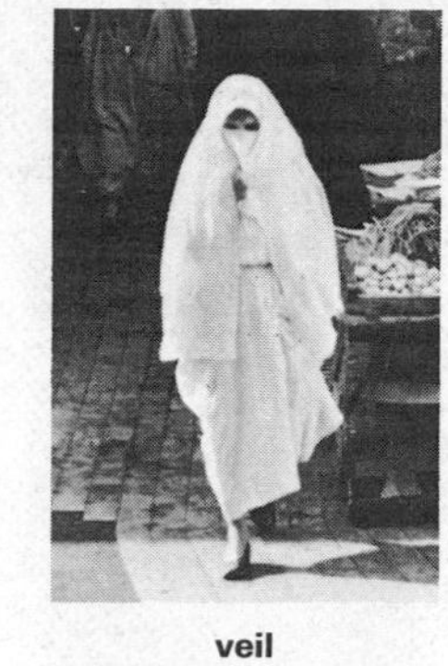

veil
Veiled Moslem woman in the Casbah of Algiers

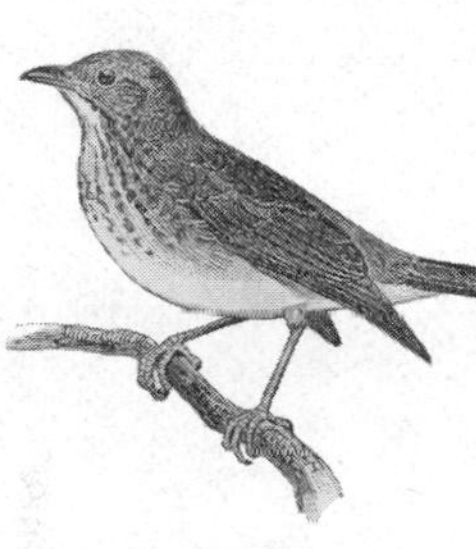

veery

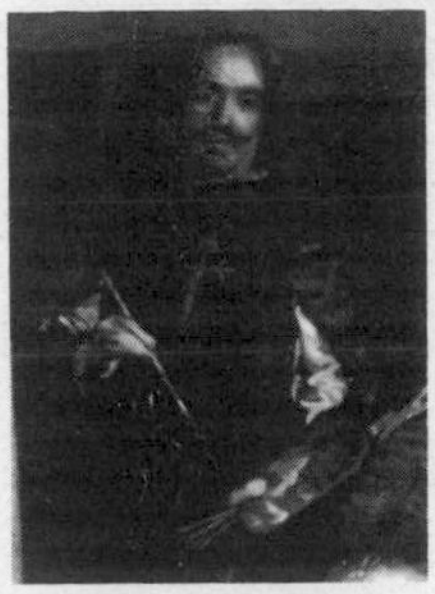

Diego Velázquez
Self-portrait in a detail from "Maids of Honor," painted in 1656

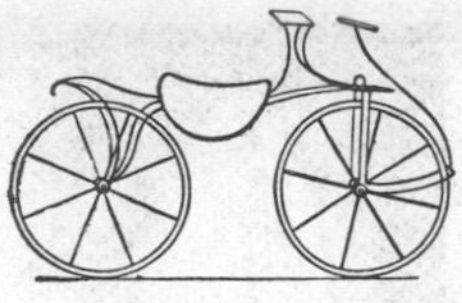

velocipede

Venezuela

or veil. [Latin *vēlātus,* past participle of *vēlāre,* to cover, from *vēlum,* veil, covering. See **velum**.]

Ve·láz·quez (və-läs′kĭs, -kās, və-lăs′-; *Spanish* vā-läth′kāth), **Diego Rodriguez de Silva y.** Also **Ve·lás·quez.** 1599–1660. Spanish painter.

veldt (fĕlt, vĕlt) *n.* Also **veld.** Any of the open grazing areas of southern Africa. [Afrikaans *veld,* from Middle Dutch *velt, veld,* field. See **pele-¹** in Appendix.*]

vel·le·i·ty (vĕ-lē′ə-tē) *n., pl.* **-ties. 1.** The lowest level of volition. **2.** A mere wish not accompanied by action or effort to obtain it. [Medieval Latin *velleitās,* from Latin *velle,* to wish. See **wel-²** in Appendix.*]

vel·lum (vĕl′əm) *n. Abbr.* **vel. 1.** A fine parchment made from the skins of calf, lamb, or kid and used for the pages and binding of fine books. **2.** A work written or printed on vellum. **3.** A heavy off-white fine-quality paper resembling vellum. [Middle English *velim,* from Old French *velin,* from *veel,* calf, VEAL.]

ve·lo·ce (vā-lō′chā) *adv. Music.* Rapidly. Used as a direction. [Italian, from Latin *vēlōx* (stem *vēlōc-*), fast. See **velocity**.]

ve·loc·i·pede (və-lŏs′ə-pēd′) *n.* **1.** An early bicycle propelled by pushing the feet along the ground while straddling the vehicle. **2.** Any of several early bicycles having pedals attached to the front wheel. **3.** A **tricycle** *(see).* [French *vélocipède,* "swift-footed" : Latin *vēlōx,* fast (see **velocity**) + -PED.]

ve·loc·i·ty (və-lŏs′ə-tē) *n., pl.* **-ties. 1.** Broadly, rapidity or speed. **2.** *Abbr.* **V** *Physics.* A vector quantity, the magnitude of which is a body's speed and the direction of which is the body's direction of motion. **3.** Distance traveled in a specified amount of time. [French *vélocité,* from Latin *vēlōcitās,* from *vēlōx* (stem *vēlōc-*), fast. See **weg-²** in Appendix.*]

ve·lours, ve·lour (və-lo͝or′) *n., pl.* **-lours** (-lo͝or′). **1.** A closely napped, velvetlike fabric, used chiefly for clothing and upholstery. **2.** A felt resembling velvet, used in making hats. [French, from Old French *velo(u)s,* from Latin *villōsus,* hairy, from *villus,* shaggy hair, wool. See **wel-⁵** in Appendix.*]

ve·lou·té (və-lo͞o-tā′) *n.* A white sauce made with flour, butter, and a chicken or veal stock. [French, "velvety."]

ve·lum (vē′ləm) *n., pl.* **-la** (-lə). **1.** *Biology.* A covering or partition of thin membranous tissue, such as the veil of mushroom. **2.** *Anatomy.* The soft palate. [New Latin, from Latin *vēlum,* veil, covering, sail. See **weg-¹** in Appendix.*]

ve·lure (və-lo͝or′) *n. Obsolete.* Velvet or a velvetlike fabric. [Variant of French *velours,* VELOURS.]

ve·lu·ti·nous (və-loot′n-əs) *adj.* Covered with dense, soft, silky hairs; velvety. [New Latin *velutinus,* from Medieval Latin *velūtum,* velvet, from *villūtus,* velvety, shaggy. See **velvet**.]

vel·vet (vĕl′vĭt) *n.* **1. a.** A fabric made usually of silk or a synthetic fiber such as rayon or nylon, and having a smooth, dense pile and a plain back. **b.** Anything likened to the surface of this fabric. **2.** Smoothness; softness. **3.** The soft covering on the newly developing antlers of deer and related animals. —*adj.* **1.** Made of or covered with velvet. **2.** Resembling velvet. [Middle English *veluet,* from Old French *veluotte,* from *velu,* shaggy, from Medieval Latin *villūtus,* from Latin *villus,* shaggy hair, wool. See **wel-⁵** in Appendix.*] —**vel′vet·y** *adj.*

velvet ant. Any of various wasps of the family Mutillidae, having a dense, hairy, often brightly colored covering. Sometimes called "cow killer."

vel·vet·een (vĕl′və-tēn′) *n.* A velvetlike fabric made of cotton. [From VELVET.]

velvet plant. A species of **mullein** *(see).*

Ven. venerable.

ve·na (vē′nə, vā′-) *n., pl.* **venae** (vē′nē′, vā′nī′). *Anatomy.* A vein. [Latin *vēna,* VEIN.]

ve·na ca·va (vē′nə kā′və, vā′nə kä′və) *pl.* **venae cavae** (vē′nē′ kā′vē′, vā′nī′ kä′vī′). Either of the two large veins in air-breathing vertebrates that enter into and return blood to the right atrium of the heart. [Latin, "hollow vein."]

ve·nal (vē′nəl) *adj.* **1. a.** Open or susceptible to bribery. **b.** Capable of betraying one's honor, duty, or scruples for a price; corruptible. **2.** Marked by corrupt or unscrupulous dealings: *a venal era.* **3.** Obtainable by purchase or bribery rather than by merit. [Latin *vēnālis,* for sale, from *vēnum,* sale. See **wes-¹** in Appendix.*] —**ve′nal·ly** *adv.*

ve·nal·i·ty (vē-năl′ə-tē, vĭ-) *n., pl.* **-ties. 1.** The quality of being open to bribery or corruption. **2.** The use of a position of trust for dishonest gain.

ve·nat·ic (vē-năt′ĭk) *adj.* Also **ve·nat·i·cal** (-ĭ-kəl). **1.** Pertaining to or used in hunting. **2.** Given to hunting for sport or livelihood. [Latin *vēnāticus,* from *vēnārī,* to hunt. See **wen-** in Appendix.*]

ve·na·tion (vē-nā′shən, vā-) *n.* The distribution or arrangement of veins. Also called "nervation." [From VENA.]

vend (vĕnd) *v.* **vended, vending, vends.** —*tr.* **1.** To sell. **2.** To offer (an idea, for example) for public consideration. —*intr.* **1.** To sell goods; be a vender. **2.** To have a market. [French *vendre,* from Latin *vēndere* : *vēnum,* sale (see **wes-¹** in Appendix*) + *dare,* to give (see **dō-** in Appendix*).]

vend·ee (vĕn-dē′) *n.* A buyer.

ven·der (vĕn′dər) *n.* Also **ven·dor. 1.** A person who sells or vends; a peddler or salesman. **2.** A vending machine.

ven·det·ta (vĕn-dĕt′ə) *n.* **1.** A hereditary blood feud between two families, perpetuated by retaliatory acts of revenge. **2.** Any act or attitude motivated by vengeance. [Italian, revenge, from Latin *vindicta,* from the feminine past participle of *vindicāre,* to revenge, VINDICATE.]

vend·i·ble (vĕn′də-bəl) *adj.* **1.** Capable of being sold; suitable for sale. **2.** Venal. —*n.* Something that can be sold.

vending machine. A machine that dispenses small goods upon the deposit of a coin or coins in a slot.

ven·due (vĕn-do͞o′, -dyo͞o′) *n.* A public sale; auction. [Dutch *vendu,* from Old French *vendue,* from *vendre,* VEND.]

ve·neer (və-nîr′) *n.* **1.** A thin finishing or surface layer of fine wood, laminated plastic, formica, or the like, bonded to an inferior substratum such as an inexpensive wood. **2.** Any of the thin layers glued together in making plywood. **3.** An outward show that enhances but misrepresents what lies beneath: *"The erotic . . . demanded for him a veneer of the poetic"* (Leslie Fiedler). —*tr.v.* **veneered, -neering, -neers. 1.** To overlay (a surface) with a decorative or fine material. **2.** To glue together (layers of wood) in making plywood. **3.** To conceal (something common or crude) with an attractive but superficial appearance; gloss over. [German *Furnier,* from *furniren,* to furnish, veneer, from Old French *furnir,* from Common Romance *fornir* (unattested). See **per¹** in Appendix.*] —**ve·neer′er** *n.*

ve·neer·ing (və-nîr′ĭng) *n.* **1.** Material used as a veneer. **2.** A surface of veneer.

ven·er·a·ble (vĕn′ər-ə-bəl) *adj.* **1.** Worthy of reverence or respect by virtue of dignity, character, position, or age: *"Parliament and the courts . . . are venerable to me"* (Carlyle). **2.** Commanding respect or reverence by association: *venerable relics.* **3.** *Abbr.* **V., Ven.** *Ecclesiastic.* Honored above others. Used in titles of respect given to an Anglican archdeacon or to a Roman Catholic who has attained the first degree of sanctity. —See Synonyms at **old.** [Middle English, from Old French, from Latin *venerābilis,* from *venerārī,* VENERATE.] —**ven′er·a·ble·ness, ven′er·a·bil′i·ty** *n.* —**ven′er·a·bly** *adv.*

ven·er·ate (vĕn′ə-rāt′) *tr.v.* **-ated, -ating, -ates.** To regard with respect, reverence, or heartfelt deference. See Synonyms at **revere.** [Latin *venerārī,* from *venus* (stem *vener-*), love. See **wen-** in Appendix.*] —**ven′er·a′tor** (-tər) *n.*

ven·er·a·tion (vĕn′ə-rā′shən) *n.* **1.** The act of venerating. **2.** Profound respect or reverence: *"They have not suffered a blind veneration to overrule the suggestions of their own good sense"* (James Madison). **3.** The condition or status of one who is venerated. —See Synonyms at **honor.**

ve·ne·re·al (və-nîr′ē-əl) *adj.* **1.** Of or pertaining to sexual intercourse. **2. a.** Transmitted by sexual intercourse. **b.** Of or pertaining to venereal disease. **3.** Of or pertaining to the genitals. [Middle English *venerealle,* from Latin *venereus,* from *venus* (stem *vener-*), love, lust. See **wen-** in Appendix.*]

venereal disease. *Abbr.* **V.D., VD** Any of several contagious diseases, such as syphilis and gonorrhea, contracted through sexual intercourse.

ve·ne·re·ol·o·gy (və-nîr′ē-ŏl′ə-jē) *n.* The study of venereal disease. [VENERE(AL) + -LOGY.] —**ve·ne′re·ol′o·gist** *n.*

ven·er·y¹ (vĕn′ər-ē) *n. Archaic.* Indulgence in or the pursuit of sexual activity. [Middle English *venerie,* from Medieval Latin *veneria,* from Latin *venus* (stem *vener-*), love. See **wen-** in Appendix.*]

ven·er·y² (vĕn′ər-ē) *n. Archaic.* The act, art, or sport of hunting; the chase. [Middle English *venerie,* from Old French, from *vener,* to hunt, from Latin *vēnārī.* See **wen-** in Appendix.*]

ven·e·sec·tion (vĕn′ə-sĕk′shən) *n. Surgery.* **Phlebotomy** *(see).* [Medieval Latin *vēnae sectiō,* cutting of a vein : Latin *vēnae,* genitive of *vēna,* vein, VENA + *sectiō,* SECTION.]

Ve·ne·ti·a (və-nē′shē-ə, -shə). **1.** A historical region of northern Italy, now divided into the modern regions of Trentino-Alto Adige, Friuli-Venezia Giulia, and Venetia. **2.** Also **Ve·ne·to** (vā′nā-tō). A region of Italy occupying 7,098 square miles in the northeast. Population, 3,247,000. Capital, Venice.

Ve·ne·tian (və-nē′shən) *adj.* Of or pertaining to Venice, its culture, or its inhabitants. —*n.* A native or inhabitant of Venice. [Middle English *Venecien,* from Old French, from Medieval Latin *Venetiānus,* from Latin *Venetia,* VENICE.]

Venetian blind. A window screen consisting of a number of thin horizontal slats that may be raised and lowered with one cord and all set at a desired angle with another cord, thus regulating the amount of light admitted.

venetian blue. Strong blue to greenish blue. See **color.**

venetian red. Deep to strong reddish brown. See **color.**

Venetian school. A school of painting originating in Venice in the 15th century and climaxing in the 16th century, notable for its mastery of color and perspective.

Venez. Venezuela.

Ve·ne·zia. The Italian name for **Venice.**

Ve·ne·zia Giu·lia (vā-nā′tsyä jo͞o′lyä). A former region of northeastern Italy, divided between Yugoslavia, Italy, and the Free Territory of Trieste since 1947.

Ven·e·zue·la (vĕn′ə-zwā′lə, -zwē′lə). *Abbr.* **Venez.** A republic, 352,141 square miles in area, in northern South America. Population, 8,722,000. Capital, Caracas.

Ven·e·zue·la, Gulf of (vĕn′ə-zwā′lə, -zwē′lə). An inlet of the Caribbean extending about 75 miles into northwestern Venezuela and touching on northern Colombia.

venge (vĕnj) *tr.v.* **venged, venging, venges.** *Archaic.* To avenge. [Middle English *vengen,* from Old French *venger.* See **vengeance.**]

venge·ance (vĕn′jəns) *n.* The act or motive of punishing another in payment for a wrong or injury he has committed; retribution: *"The black man in our midst carried murder in his heart, he wanted vengeance"* (James Baldwin). —**with a vengeance. 1.** With great violence or fury. **2.** Excessively. [Middle English, from Old French, from *venger,* to revenge, from Latin *vindicāre,* to revenge, VINDICATE.]

venge·ful (vĕnj′fəl) *adj.* **1.** Desiring vengeance; vindictive. **2.** Indicating or proceeding from a desire for revenge. **3.** In-

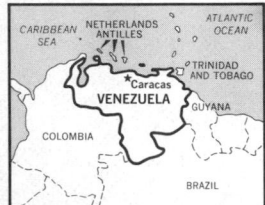

flicting or serving to inflict vengeance. —See Synonyms at **vindictive**.

V-en·gine (vē′ĕn′jən) *n.* An internal-combustion engine having cylinders arranged so that pairs form V shapes.

ve·ni·al (vē′nē-əl, vēn′yəl) *adj.* **1.** Easily excused or forgiven; pardonable: *a venial offense.* **2.** *Roman Catholic Church.* Minor in nature and warranting only temporal punishment: *a venial sin.* Compare **mortal.** [Middle English, from Old French, from Late Latin *veniālis,* from *venia,* forgiveness. See **wen-** in Appendix.*] —**ve′ni·al′i·ty** (vē′nē-ăl′ə-tē, vēn′yăl′-), **ve′ni·al·ness** *n.* —**ve′ni·al·ly** *adv.*

Ven·ice (vĕn′ĭs). *Italian* **Ve·ne·zia** (vā-nā′tsyä). The capital of Venetia, Italy, a port city at the head of the Adriatic, located on 118 islands in the Lagoon of Venice, the northwestern part of the Gulf of Venice. Population, 360,000. [Latin *Venetia,* from *Venetī,* a people in northern Italy. See **wen-** in Appendix.*]

ven·i·punc·ture (vĕn′ə-pŭngk′chər) *n.* Puncture of a vein, as for drawing blood, intravenous feeding, or administration of medicine. [VENA + PUNCTURE.]

ve·ni·re (vĭ-nī′rē) *n. Law.* **1.** A writ issued by a judge to a sheriff, ordering him to summon prospective jurors. Also called "venire facias." **2.** The panel of prospective jurors from which a jury is selected. [Medieval Latin *venīre (facias),* "(you are to cause) to come" (words used in the writ), from Latin *venīre,* to come. See **gwā-** in Appendix.*]

ve·ni·re·man (və-nī′rē-mən) *n., pl.* **-men** (-mĭn). A person summoned to jury duty under a venire.

ven·i·son (vĕn′ə-sən, -zən; *British* vĕn′zən) *n.* **1.** The flesh of a deer, used for food. **2.** *Archaic.* The flesh of any game animal thus used. [Middle English *veneso(u)n,* from Old French, from Latin *vēnātiō,* hunting, game, from *vēnārī,* to hunt. See **wen-** in Appendix.*]

ven·om (vĕn′əm) *n.* **1.** A poisonous secretion of some animals, such as certain snakes, spiders, scorpions, or insects, usually transmitted by a bite or sting. **2.** *Rare.* Any poison. **3.** Malice; evil; spite. [Middle English *venim,* from Old French, from Vulgar Latin *venīmen* (unattested), variant of Latin *venēnum.* See **wen-** in Appendix.*]

ven·om·ous (vĕn′ə-məs) *adj.* **1.** Secreting and transmitting venom: *a venomous snake.* **2.** Full of or containing venom. **3.** Malicious; malignant; spiteful: *a venomous utterance.* —**ven′om·ous·ly** *adv.* —**ven′om·ous·ness** *n.*

ve·nose (vē′nōs′) *adj.* **1.** Having noticeable veins or veinlike markings. **2.** Venous. [Latin *vēnōsus,* VENOUS.]

ve·nos·i·ty (vĭ-nŏs′ə-tē) *n.* The condition or quality of being venous or venose.

ve·nous (vē′nəs) *adj.* **1.** Of or pertaining to a vein or veins. **2.** *Physiology.* Returning to the heart through the great veins. [Latin *vēnōsus,* from *vēna,* vein, VENA.] —**ve′nous·ly** *adv.* —**ve′nous·ness** *n.*

vent (vĕnt) *n.* **1.** A means of escaping or leaving a confined space; an exit. **2.** An opening permitting the passage or escape of liquids, gases, fumes, steam, or the like: *a vent above the kitchen stove.* **3.** The small hole at the breech of a gun through which the charge is ignited. **4.** *Zoology.* The cloacal or anal excretory opening in animals such as birds, reptiles, amphibians, and fish. —**give vent to.** To give utterance or expression to: *"People gave vent to their unutterable relief that the slaughter was over"* (Walter Lippmann). —*tr.v.* **vented, venting, vents. 1.** To give expression or utterance to; express: *"So he gave some ease to his oppressed heart by thus venting his sorrows"* (Walton). **2.** To relieve through the expression of emotion. **3.** To discharge through a vent. **4.** To provide with a vent. [Middle English *venten,* to provide with an outlet, Old French *esventer,* to let out air, from Vulgar Latin *exventāre* (unattested) : Latin *ex-,* out + *ventus,* wind (see **wē-** in Appendix*).] —**ven′ter** *n.*

Synonyms: *vent, express, utter, voice, air, broach.* These verbs mean to give an outlet to thought or emotion. *Vent* is applied to speech, writing, or other action by which a person unburdens himself of a strong, hitherto pent-up emotion such as anger or grief. *Express,* a more comprehensive word, can refer to communication by any means, including the nonverbal. *Utter* involves vocal expression, either words or inarticulate sounds; with reference to speech it often implies forthright or even bold public statement. *Voice* generally refers to the public expression, in speech or writing, of ideas, opinions, or beliefs. *Air* especially suggests public discussion of such ideas or opinions. *Broach* refers to introducing a subject, usually after careful thought, as a topic of discussion or written discourse.

vent·age (vĕn′tĭj) *n.* A small opening; vent. [From VENT.]

ven·tail (vĕn′tāl′) *n.* The lower front part of a medieval helmet, fitting over the neck. [Middle English, from Old French *ventail,* leaf of a window, from *vent,* wind, air, from Latin *ventus.* See **wē-** in Appendix.*]

ven·ter (vĕn′tər) *n.* **1. a.** *Anatomy.* The abdomen or belly. **b.** The uterus. **c.** The wide swelling portion of a muscle. **2.** *Biology.* A similar swollen structure or part. **3.** *Law.* The womb as the source of offspring. [Norman French, from Latin, belly, womb. See **udero-** in Appendix.*]

ven·ti·late (vĕnt′l-āt′) *tr.v.* **-lated, -lating, -lates. 1.** To admit fresh air into in order to replace stale air. **2.** To circulate within (a room or mine, for example) in order to freshen. Used of air. **3.** To provide with a vent or a similar means of airing. **4.** To expose (a substance) to the circulation of fresh air for the purpose of retarding spoilage or the like. **5.** To expose to public discussion or examination: *The workers ventilated their grievances.* **6.** To aerate or oxygenate (blood). [Middle English *ventilaten,* to blow away, from Latin *ventilāre,* to fan, from *ventus,* wind. See **wē-** in Appendix.*] —**ven′ti·la′tion** *n.*

ven·ti·la·tor (vĕnt′l-ā′tər) *n.* One that ventilates; especially, a device, such as an exhaust fan, that expels stale air and circulates fresh air. —**ven′ti·la·to′ry** (vĕnt′l-ə-tôr′ē, -tōr′ē) *adj.*

ven·tral (vĕn′trəl) *adj.* **1.** *Anatomy.* **a.** Pertaining to or situated on or close to the belly; abdominal. **b.** Pertaining to the anterior aspect of the human body or the lower surface of the body of an animal. **2.** *Botany.* Of or on the lower or inner surface of an organ. [French, from Latin *ventrālis,* from *venter,* VENTER.]

ventral fin. *Zoology.* A **pelvic fin** *(see).*

ven·tri·cle (vĕn′trĭ-kəl) *n.* A small anatomical cavity or chamber, as of the brain or heart, especially: **a.** The chamber on the left side of the heart that receives arterial blood from the left atrium and contracts to drive it into the aorta. **b.** The chamber on the right side of the heart that receives venous blood from the right atrium and drives it into the pulmonary artery. [Middle English, from Old French, from Latin *ventriculus,* diminutive of *venter,* VENTER.] —**ven·tric′u·lar** (vĕn-trĭk′yə-lər) *adj.*

ven·tri·cose (vĕn′trĭ-kōs′) *adj.* Also **ven·tri·cous** (-kəs). Inflated; swollen; distended. [New Latin *ventricosus,* from Latin *venter,* VENTER.] —**ven′tri·cos′i·ty** (-kŏs′ə-tē) *n.*

ven·tric·u·lus (vĕn-trĭk′yə-ləs) *n., pl.* **-li** (-lī′). A hollow digestive organ; especially, the stomach of an insect or the gizzard of a bird. [Latin, VENTRICLE.]

ven·tri·lo·qui·al (vĕn′trə-lō′kwē-əl) *adj.* Of, pertaining to, or practicing ventriloquism. —**ven′tri·lo′qui·al·ly** *adv.*

ven·tril·o·quism (vĕn-trĭl′ə-kwĭz′əm) *n.* Also **ven·tril·o·quy** (-kwē) *pl.* **-quies.** A method of producing vocal sounds so that they seem to originate in a source other than the speaker, as from a mechanical dummy. [From Late Latin *ventriloquus,* "speaking from the belly" : Latin *venter,* VENTER + *loquī,* to speak (see **tolkw-** in Appendix*).] —**ven·tril′o·quist** (-ə-kwĭst) *n.* —**ven·tril′o·quis′tic** *adj.*

ven·tril·o·quize (vĕn-trĭl′ə-kwīz′) *intr.v.* **-quized, -quizing, -quizes.** To practice ventriloquism.

ven·ture (vĕn′chər) *n.* **1.** An undertaking that is dangerous, daring, or of doubtful outcome. **2.** Something at hazard in such an undertaking; a stake. —**at a venture.** By mere chance or fortune; at hazard; at random. —*v.* **ventured, -turing, -tures.** —*tr.* **1.** To expose to danger or risk; to stake: *"Her face took on the expression of an inexperienced gambler about to venture all"* (Nathanael West). **2.** To brave the dangers of: *ventured the high seas in a light boat.* **3.** To express at the risk of denial, criticism, or censure; to dare: *"Ernest ventured a little mild dissent"* (Samuel Butler). —*intr.* To take a risk or dare; make a venture. [Middle English *venturen, venteren,* short for *aventuren,* from *aventure,* ADVENTURE.] —**ven′tur·er** *n.*

ven·ture·some (vĕn′chər-səm) *adj.* **1.** Disposed to venture or to take risks; daring; bold. **2.** Involving risk or danger; hazardous. —See Synonyms at **reckless.** —**ven′ture·some·ly** *adv.* —**ven′ture·some·ness** *n.*

ven·tu·ri (vĕn-to͝or′ē) *n.* **1.** A short tube with a constricted throat that is used to determine fluid pressures and velocities by measurement of differential pressures generated at the throat as a fluid traverses the tube. **2.** A constricted throat in the air passage of a carburetor, causing a reduction in pressure by means of which fuel vapor is drawn out of the carburetor bowl. [After G.B. *Venturi* (1746–1822), Italian physicist, whose study inspired its invention.]

ven·tur·ous (vĕn′chər-əs) *adj.* **1.** Courageous and daring; adventurous; bold: *"And yet men are so foolishly venturous as to set out lightly on pilgrimage"* (Bunyan). **2.** Hazardous, dangerous, or risky. —See Synonyms at **reckless.** —**ven′tur·ous·ly** *adv.* —**ven′tur·ous·ness** *n.*

ven·ue (vĕn′yo͞o) *n. Law.* **1.** The locality where a crime is committed or a cause of action occurs. **2.** The locality or political division from which a jury must be called and in which a trial must be held. **3.** The clause within a declaration naming the locality in which the trial is occurring or will occur. **4.** The clause in an affidavit naming the locality where it was made and sworn to. —**change of venue.** The change of the place of a trial, as when the court is liable to be prejudiced. [Middle English, arrival, assault, from Old French, from the feminine past participle of *venir,* to come, from Latin *venīre.* See **gwā-** in Appendix.*]

ven·ule (vĕn′yo͞ol) *n.* A minute vein, as one joining with a capillary or branching from a vein in an insect's wing. [Latin *vēnula,* diminutive of *vēna,* VEIN.] —**ven′u·lar** (-yə-lər) *adj.*

Ve·nus[1] (vē′nəs). *Roman Mythology.* The goddess of love and beauty, identified with the Greek goddess Aphrodite. [Middle English *Venus,* Old English *Venus,* from Latin, personification of *venus,* love. See **wen-** in Appendix.*]

Ve·nus[2] (vē′nəs) *n.* The second planet from the sun, having an average radius of 3,800 miles, a mass 0.816 times that of the earth, and a sidereal period of revolution about the sun of 224.7 days at a mean distance of approximately 67.2 million miles. See **solar system.** [After the goddess VENUS.]

Ve·nu·sian (vĭ-no͞o′zhən, -nyo͞o′zhən) *adj.* Pertaining to or characteristic of the planet Venus. —*n.* A hypothetical inhabitant of the planet Venus.

Venus's flower basket. A sponge of the genus *Euplectella,* of deep marine waters, having a cylindrical skeleton of glassy, intricately interlaced latticework.

Ve·nus's-fly·trap (vē′nə-sĭz-flī′trăp′) *n.* An insectivorous plant, *Dionaea muscipula,* of boggy areas of the southeastern United States, having marginally spined, hinged leaf blades that close and entrap insects.

Venus's girdle. A ribbon-shaped marine animal, *Cestum veneris,* having a jellylike bluish-green, iridescent body.

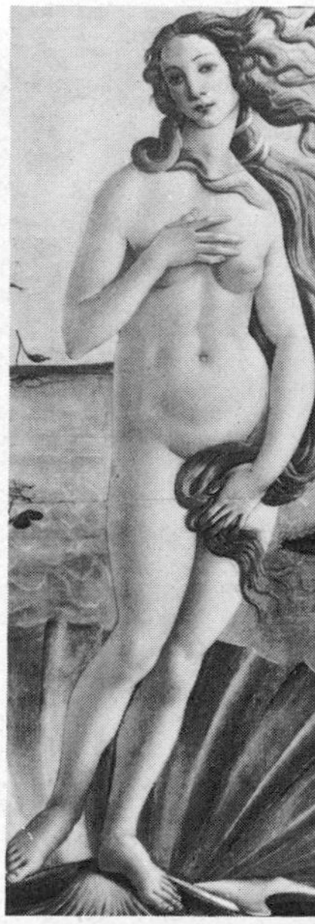

Venus[1]
Detail from Botticelli's "Birth of Venus"

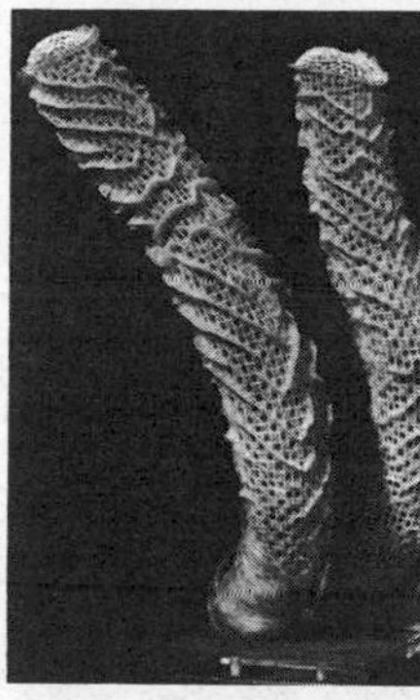

Venus's flower basket
Euplectella speciosissima

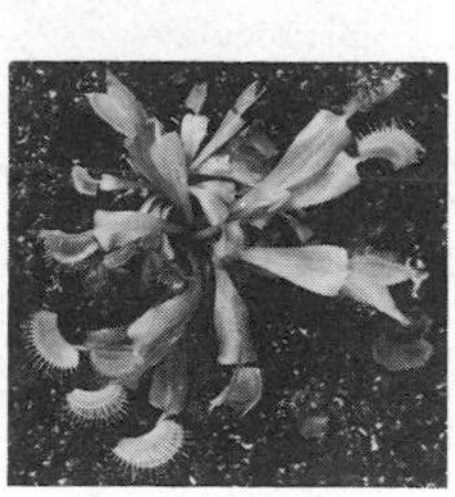

Venus's-flytrap

Venus's-hair (vē′nə-sĭz-hâr′) *n.* A maidenhair fern, *Adiantum capillus-veneris,* of moist warm regions, having slender blackish stalks.

Ve·nus's-look·ing-glass (vē′nə-sĭz-lo͝ok′ĭng-glăs′, -gläs′) *n.* Any of several plants of the genus *Specularia;* especially, *S. speculum-veneris,* native to Europe, and *S. perfoliata,* of North America, having small blue or white star-shaped flowers.

ver. 1. verse. 2. version.

Ve·ra (vîr′ə). A feminine given name. [Russian *vjera,* faith. See **wēros** in Appendix.*]

ve·ra·cious (və-rā′shəs) *adj.* 1. Honest; truthful. 2. Accurate; precise. [From Latin *vērāx* (stem *vērāc-*), truth. See **wēros** in Appendix.*] —**ve·ra′cious·ly** *adv.* —**ve·ra′cious·ness** *n.*

ve·rac·i·ty (və-răs′ə-tē) *n., pl.* **-ties.** 1. Habitual adherence to the truth. 2. Conformity to truth or fact; accuracy; precision: *"There was no question about the veracity of these doctrines"* (Fritz Kahn). 3. Something that is true. —See Synonyms at **honesty, truth.** [Medieval Latin *vērācitās,* from Latin *vērāx,* truth. See **veracious.**]

Ve·ra·cruz (vĕr′ə-kro͞oz′; *Spanish* vä′rä-kro͞os′). 1. A state of Mexico, occupying 27,758 square miles in the east on the Gulf of Mexico. Population, 2,982,000. Capital, Jalapa. 2. Also **Ve·ra·cruz Lla·ve** (yä′vā). A leading port city in the east-central part of this state. Population, 173,000.

ve·ran·dah, ve·ran·da (və-răn′də) *n.* A porch or balcony, usually roofed and often partly enclosed, extending along the outside of a building; piazza; gallery. [Hindi, from Portuguese, from *varare* (unattested), to surround with poles, from *vara,* pole, from Latin *vāra,* forked pole, from *vārus,* bent inward. See **wā-**[1] in Appendix.*]

ve·rat·ri·dine (və-răt′rə-dēn′, -dĭn) *n.* A yellowish-white, amorphous powdered alkaloid, $C_{36}H_{51}NO_{11}$, obtained from sabadilla seeds and from the rhizome of a species of hellebore, *Veratrum album.* [VERATR(INE) + -ID + -INE.]

ver·a·trine (vĕr′ə-trēn′, -trĭn) *n.* A poisonous mixture of colorless crystalline alkaloids extracted from sabadilla seeds and formerly used medicinally as a counterirritant. [French *vératrine,* from New Latin *Veratrum,* genus name of a hellebore, from Latin *vērātrum,* hellebore, perhaps from *veru,* spit. See **gweru-** in Appendix.*]

verb (vûrb) *n. Abbr.* **v., vb.** 1. In most languages, that part of speech that expresses existence, action, or occurrence. 2. Any of the words within this part of speech; for example, *be, run,* or *conceive.* 3. Any phrase or other construction used as a verb. —*adj.* Pertaining to or having the character or function of a verb: *a verb phrase.* [Middle English *verbe,* from Old French, from Latin *verbum,* word. See **wer-**[6] in Appendix.*]

ver·bal (vûr′bəl) *adj. Abbr.* **vb.** 1. Of, pertaining to, or associated with words: *a verbal symbol.* 2. Concerned with words rather than with the facts or ideas they represent. 3. Expressed or transmitted in speech; unwritten: *a verbal contract.* 4. Literal; word for word: *a verbal translation.* 5. *Grammar.* a. Pertaining to, having the nature or function of, or derived from a verb. b. Used to form verbs: *a verbal suffix.* —*n. Grammar.* A verbal noun, adjective, or other word derived from a verb and preserving some of the verb's characteristics. [Old French, from Late Latin *verbālis,* from Latin *verbum,* word, VERB.] —**ver′bal·ly** *adv.*

Usage: *Verbal* (adjective) is less precise than *oral* in expressing the sense of "by word of mouth." *Verbal* can also refer to what is written; *oral* cannot. The distinction has special bearing when one of these adjectives is applied to terms such as *agreement, promise, commitment,* or *understanding.* If the agreement or the like is not in writing, *oral* makes that sense explicit.

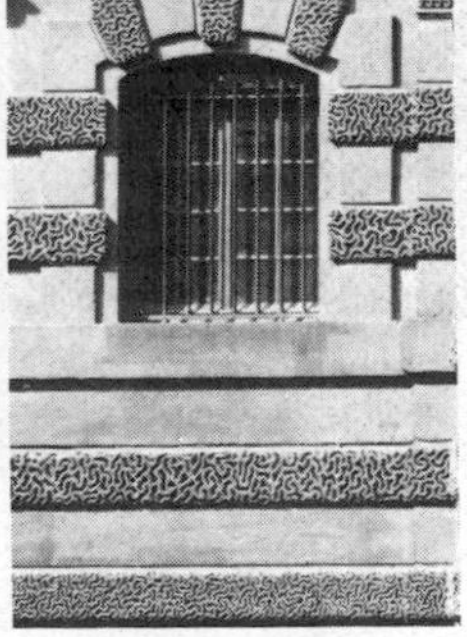

vermiculate
Vermiculate masonry around a window of the Louvre, Paris

ver·bal·ism (vûr′bə-lĭz′əm) *n.* 1. An expression in words; a word or phrase. 2. A meaningless phrase or sentence. 3. An expression, sentence, or other construction emphasizing words over content or idea.

ver·bal·ist (vûr′bə-lĭst) *n.* 1. One skilled in the employment of words. 2. One who favors words over ideas or facts. —**ver′bal·is′tic** *adj.*

ver·bal·ize (vûr′bə-līz′) *v.* **-ized, -izing, -izes.** —*tr.* 1. To express in words: *"Ties of feeling and understanding that were seldom verbalized"* (Haakon Chevalier). 2. To convert (a noun, for example) to verbal use. —*intr.* 1. To express oneself in words. 2. To be verbose. —**ver′bal·i·za′tion** *n.* —**ver′bal·i′zer** *n.*

verbal noun. A noun derived from a verb; in English, either a gerund or an infinitive; for example, *smoking causes cancer* or *to think is to be.*

ver·ba·tim (vûr-bā′tĭm) *adj.* Using exactly the same words; word for word. —*adv.* In exactly the same words. [Middle English, from Medieval Latin, from Latin *verbum,* word, VERB.]

ver·be·na (vər-bē′nə) *n.* 1. Any of various New World plants of the genus *Verbena;* especially, one of several species cultivated for their showy clusters of variously colored flowers. 2. Any of several similar or related plants, such as the **lemon verbena** *(see).* [New Latin *Verbena,* from Latin *verbēna,* usually in plural *verbēnae,* sacred boughs of olive or myrtle. See **vervain.**]

ver·bi·age (vûr′bē-ĭj) *n.* 1. Words in excess of those needed for clarity or precision; wordiness. 2. The manner in which one expresses oneself in words; diction. [French, from Latin *verbum,* word, VERB.]

verb·i·fy (vûr′bə-fī′) *tr.v.* **-fied, -fying, -fies.** To use (a noun, for example) as a verb; to form into a verb.

ver·bose (vər-bōs′) *adj.* Using or containing an excessive number of words; wordy; prolix. See Synonyms at **talkative.** [Latin *verbōsus,* from *verbum,* word, VERB.] —**ver·bose′ly** *adv.* —**ver·bose′ness, ver·bos′i·ty** (-bŏs′ə-tē) *n.*

ver·bo·ten (fĕr-bōt′n) *adj.* Rigorously forbidden. [German, from Old High German *farboten,* past participle of *farbiotan,* to forbid. See **bheudh-** in Appendix.*]

ver·dant (vûr′dənt) *adj.* 1. Green with vegetation; covered with a green growth: *"the land not covered by forest or marsh was verdant and fertile"* (Winston Churchill). 2. Green in color. 3. Inexperienced or unsophisticated. [Old French *verdeant,* present participle of *verdoier, verdier,* to become green, from *verd, vert,* green, from Latin *viridis,* from *virēre,* to be green. See **virēre** in Appendix.*] —**ver′dan·cy** *n.* —**ver′dant·ly** *adv.*

verd antique (vûrd). Also **verde antique.** 1. A dull-green mottled or veined serpentine marble used in interior decoration. 2. Verdigris. [French, "ancient green."]

Verde, Cape (vûrd). The westernmost point of the African continent, a peninsula on the coast of Senegal.

ver·der·er (vûr′dər-ər) *n.* Also **ver·de·ror** (-dər-ər). The official in charge of the royal forests of England. [Norman French, from Old French *verdier,* from *verde, verte,* green, "forest." See **verdant.**]

Ver·di (vâr′dē), **Giuseppe.** 1813–1901. Italian composer known primarily for his many celebrated operas.

ver·dict (vûr′dĭkt) *n.* 1. The decision reached by a jury at the conclusion of a legal proceeding: *"He set to work to secure a verdict of not guilty for a poor girl"* (Ford Madox Ford). 2. An expressed conclusion; a judgment: *"I do not intend to pronounce the verdicts of history"* (Edgar Snow). [Middle English *verdit,* from Norman French, variant of Old French *veirdit, voirdit,* "true saying" : *veir,* true, from Latin *vērus* (see **wēros** in Appendix*) + *dit,* saying, from Latin *dictum,* from the neuter past participle of *dīcere,* to speak, say (see **deik-** in Appendix*).]

ver·di·gris (vûr′də-grēs, -grĭs) *n.* 1. A blue or green basic copper acetate, used as a paint pigment, fungicide, and insecticide. 2. A green patina or crust of copper sulfate or copper chloride formed on copper, brass, and bronze exposed to air or sea water for long periods of time. Compare **patina.** [Middle English *vertegres,* from Old French *vertegrez, vert-de-Grice,* "green of Greece" : *vert,* green (see **verdant**) + *Grece, Grice,* Greece, from Latin *Graecia,* GREEK.]

Ver·di·gris (vûr′də-grĭs). A river rising in east-central Kansas and flowing 280 miles generally south to the Arkansas River in northeastern Oklahoma.

ver·din (vûr′dĭn) *n.* A small grayish bird, *Auriparus flaviceps,* of the southwestern United States and adjacent Mexico, having a yellowish head and throat. [French *verdin*†, yellowhammer.]

ver·di·ter (vûr′də-tər) *n.* Either of two basic carbonates of copper, used as a blue or green pigment. [Old French *verd de terre,* "green of earth" : *verd,* green (see **verdant**) + *de,* of, from Latin *de* + *terre,* earth, from Latin *terra* (see **ters-** in Appendix*).]

Ver·dun (vər-dŭn′; *French* vĕr-dœN′). A city in northeastern France, on the Meuse; the site of a prolonged World War I battle in which nearly one million lives were lost (1916). Population, 21,000.

ver·dure (vûr′jər) *n.* 1. The fresh, vibrant greenness of flourishing vegetation. 2. Such vegetation itself: *"Deciduous trees seem to burst into radiant verdure"* (Havelock Ellis). 3. Any fresh or flourishing condition: *the verdure of childhood.* [Middle English, from Old French, from *verd,* green. See **verdant.**] —**ver′dur·ous** *adj.* —**ver′dur·ous·ness** *n.*

Ve·ree·ni·ging (fə-rē′nə-KHĭng). A city of South Africa, in southern Transvaal; the site of the signing of the treaty that ended the Boer War (1902). Population, 120,000.

Ver·ein (fĕr-īn′) *n.* A society, association, or club. [German, "union."]

Vé·ren·drye, Sieur de La. See **La Vérendrye.**

verge[1] (vûrj) *n.* 1. The extreme edge, rim, or margin of something; brink: *the verge of a stream.* 2. a. An enclosing boundary. b. The space enclosed by such a boundary. 3. The point beyond which an action, state, or condition is likely to begin or occur: *"The whole book had thrilled me to the verge of spiritual exhaustion"* (Stephen Leacock). 4. *Architecture.* The edge of the tiling that projects over a roof gable. 5. A rod, wand, or staff carried as an emblem of authority or office. 6. *Feudalism.* The rod held by a tenant swearing fealty to his lord. 7. The spindle of a balance wheel in a clock or watch; especially, such a spindle in a clock with vertical escapement. 8. The male organ of an invertebrate. —See Synonyms at **border.** —*intr.v.* **verged, verging, verges.** 1. To approach the verge or limit; come near. Usually used with *on* or *upon: "He had a rich complexion / Which verged on swarthiness"* (Hardy). 2. To constitute the verge or limit of; to border: *tracks verging on the slum area.* [Middle English, margin, from Old French, from Latin *virga*†, rod, strip.]

verge[2] (vûrj) *intr.v.* **verged, verging, verges.** 1. To slope or incline. Used with *to* or *toward.* 2. To be in the process of becoming something else. Used with *into* or *on: "Doesn't that verge rather on shop?"* (Evelyn Waugh). [Latin *vergere,* to tend toward. See **wer-**[3] in Appendix.*]

verg·er (vûr′jər) *n.* 1. A person who carries the verge before a scholastic, legal, or religious dignitary in a procession. 2. *Chiefly British.* A person who has charge of the interior of a church.

Ver·gil. See **Virgil.**

ve·rid·i·cal (və-rĭd′ĭ-kəl) *adj.* Also **ve·rid·ic** (və-rĭd′ĭk). Expressing the truth; accurate; veracious. [Latin *vēridicus* : *vērus,* true (see **wēros** in Appendix*) + *dicere,* to say (see **deik-** in Appendix*).] —**ve·rid′i·cal′i·ty** *n.* —**ve·rid′i·cal·ly** *adv.*

ver·i·fi·ca·tion (vĕr′ə-fə-kā′shən) *n.* 1. The act of verifying or condition of being verified. 2. a. A confirmation of the truth of a theory or fact. b. A formal statement of such a confirmation. 3. *Law.* A short formulaic oath concluding a pleading and affirming that the pleader is ready to prove his allegations. —**ver′i·fi·ca′tive** (vĕr′ə-fə-kā′tĭv) *adj.*

ver·i·fy (vĕr′ə-fī′) *tr.v.* **-fied, -fying, -fies. 1.** To prove the truth of by the presentation of evidence or testimony; substantiate. **2.** To determine or test the truth or accuracy of, as by comparison, investigation, or reference: *"Findings are not accepted by scientists unless they can be verified"* (Norman L. Munn). **3.** *Law.* **a.** To affirm formally or under oath. **b.** To append a verification to (a pleading); conclude with a verification. —See Synonyms at **confirm.** [Middle English *verifien,* from Old French *verifier,* from Medieval Latin *vērificāre* : Latin *vērus,* true (see **wēros** in Appendix*) + *facere,* to make (see **dhē-**[1] in Appendix*).] —**ver′i·fi′a·ble** *adj.* —**ver′i·fi′er** *n.*

ver·i·ly (vĕr′ə-lē) *adv. Archaic.* **1.** In truth; in fact; of a certainty. **2.** With confidence; assuredly. [Middle English *verraily,* from *verray,* true, VERY.]

ver·i·sim·i·lar (vĕr′ə-sĭm′ə-lər) *adj.* Appearing to be true or real; probable; likely. [From Latin *vērisimilis* : *vēri,* of truth, from *vērum,* truth, from *vērus,* true (see **wēros** in Appendix*) + *similis,* SIMILAR.] —**ver′i·sim′i·lar·ly** *adv.*

ver·i·si·mil·i·tude (vĕr′ə-sĭm-ĭl′ə-to͞od′, -tyo͞od′) *n.* **1.** The quality of appearing to be true or real; likelihood. **2.** Something that has the appearance of being true or real. —See Synonyms at **truth.** [Latin *vērisimilitūdō,* from *vērisimilis,* VERISIMILAR.]

ver·ism (vĕr′ĭz′əm) *n.* Realism in art and literature. [Italian *verismo,* from *vero,* true, from Latin *vērus.* See **wēros** in Appendix.*] —**ver′ist** *n.* & *adj.* —**ve·ris′tic** (və-rĭs′tĭk) *adj.*

ver·i·ta·ble (vĕr′ə-tə-bəl) *adj.* Unquestionable; actual; true. See Synonyms at **real.** [Middle English, from Old French, from *verite,* VERITY.] —**ver′i·ta·ble·ness** *n.* —**ver′i·ta·bly** *adv.*

ver·i·tas (vĕr′ə-təs) *n.* Truth. [Latin *vēritās.* See **verity.**]

ver·i·ty (vĕr′ə-tē) *n., pl.* **-ties. 1.** The condition or quality of being real, accurate, or correct. **2.** A statement, principle, or belief considered to be established and permanent truth: *"the verities that the church proclaims are not verifiable"* (Theodor Reik). —See Synonyms at **truth.** [Middle English *verite,* from Old French, from Latin *vēritās,* from *vērus,* true. See **wēros** in Appendix.*]

ver·juice (vûr′jo͞os′) *n.* The acidic juice of sour or unripe fruit, such as grapes or crab apples. [Middle English *verjus,* from Old French *vertjus* : *vert,* green (see **verdant**) + *jus,* JUICE.]

Ver·laine (vĕr-lĕn′), **Paul.** 1844–1896. French symbolist poet.

Ver·meer (vər-mâr′, -mîr′), **Jan.** Also known as Jan van der Meer van Delft. 1632–1675. Dutch painter.

ver·meil (vûr′mĭl) *n.* **1.** *Poetic.* Vermilion or a similar bright-red color. **2.** Gilded metal, such as silver, bronze, or copper. —*adj.* Bright red in color. [Middle English *vermayl,* from Old French *vermeil,* from Late Latin *vermiculus,* from Latin, small worm, cochineal (which yields a red dye), from *vermis,* worm. See **wer-**[3] in Appendix.*]

vermi–. Indicates worm; for example, **vermicide.** [From Latin *vermis,* worm. See **wer-**[3] in Appendix.*]

ver·mi·cel·li (vûr′mə-chĕl′ē, -sĕl′ē) *n.* A food consisting of wheat flour paste made into long threads, thinner than spaghetti. [Italian, plural of *vermicello,* diminutive of *verme,* worm, from Latin *vermis.* See **wer-**[3] in Appendix.*]

ver·mi·cide (vûr′mə-sīd′) *n.* Anything used to kill worms. [VERMI- + -CIDE.] —**ver′mi·cid′al** (-sīd′l) *adj.*

ver·mic·u·lar (vər-mĭk′yə-lər) *adj.* **1.** Having the shape or motion of a worm. **2.** Having wormlike markings; vermiculate. **3.** Caused by or relating to worms. [Medieval Latin *vermiculāris,* from Latin *vermiculus,* diminutive of *vermis,* worm. See **wer-**[3] in Appendix.*] —**ver·mic′u·lar·ly** *adv.*

ver·mic·u·late (vər-mĭk′yə-lāt′) *tr.v.* **-lated, -lating, -lates.** To adorn or decorate with wavy or winding lines: *vermiculate a pottery jar.* —*adj.* (vər-mĭk′yə-lĭt, -lāt′). **1.** Bearing wormlike wavy lines. **2.** Having a wormlike motion; twisting or wriggling. **3.** Sinuous; tortuous; devious. **4.** Infested with worms; worm-eaten. [Latin *vermiculārī,* to be full of worms, from *vermiculus,* small worm. See **vermeil.**]

ver·mic·u·la·tion (vər-mĭk′yə-lā′shən) *n.* **1.** Motion resembling that of a worm; especially, the wavelike contractions of the intestine; peristalsis. **2.** Wormlike marks or carvings, as in mosaic or masonry. **3.** The condition of being worm-eaten.

ver·mic·u·lite (vər-mĭk′yə-līt′) *n.* Any of a group of micaceous hydrated silicates of varying composition, related to the chlorites and used as heat insulation and for starting plant seeds and cuttings. [Latin *vermiculus,* small worm (see **vermeil**) + -ITE (from the wormlike projections it forms when subjected to the blowpipe).]

ver·mi·form (vûr′mə-fôrm′) *adj.* Resembling or having the shape of a worm. [New Latin *vermiformis* : VERMI- + -FORM.]

vermiform appendix. The wormlike blind vestigial process of the cecum found in man and some other mammals. Also called "appendix," "vermiform process."

ver·mi·fuge (vûr′mə-fyo͞oj′) *n.* Any agent that expels or destroys intestinal worms. [VERMI- + -FUGE.]

ver·mil·ion (vər-mĭl′yən) *n.* Also **ver·mil·lion. 1.** A bright red **mercuric sulfide** *(see),* used as a pigment. **2.** Vivid red to reddish orange. Also called "Chinese red," "cinnabar." See **color.** —*adj.* Also **ver·mil·lion.** Of a vivid red to reddish orange. —*tr.v.* **vermilioned, -ioning, -ions.** Also **ver·mil·lion.** To color or dye vermilion. [Middle English *vermelyon,* from Old French *vermeillon,* from *vermeil,* VERMEIL.]

ver·min (vûr′mĭn) *n., pl.* **vermin. 1.** Any of various small animals or insects that are destructive, annoying, or injurious to health, as cockroaches or rats. **2.** Any of various animals that prey on game, as the fox or weasel. **3. a.** A person having verminous traits. **b.** Such persons collectively: *"the most pernicious race of little odious vermin that nature ever suffered to crawl upon the surface of the earth"* (Swift). [Middle English, from Old French, from Vulgar Latin *vermīnum* (unattested), from Latin *vermis* (stem *vermin-*), worm. See **wer-**[3] in Appendix.*]

ver·mi·na·tion (vûr′mə-nā′shən) *n.* **1.** The condition of being infested with vermin or worms. **2.** The breeding of worms, larvae, or vermin.

ver·min·ous (vûr′mə-nəs) *adj.* **1.** Of, pertaining to, or infested with vermin. **2.** Of the nature of vermin; repulsive; noxious. —**ver′mi·nous·ly** *adv.*

ver·miv·o·rous (vər-mĭv′ər-əs) *adj.* Feeding on worms. [VERMI- + -VOROUS.]

Ver·mont (vər-mŏnt′). *Abbr.* **Vt.** A New England state of the United States, occupying 9,609 square miles; admitted to the Union in 1791. Population, 409,000. Capital, Montpelier. See map at **United States of America.** —**Ver·mont′er** *n.*

ver·mouth (vər-mo͞oth′) *n.* Also **ver·muth.** A white wine flavored with aromatic herbs and spices, either sweet or dry, used chiefly as an ingredient in cocktails. [French *vermout,* from German *Wermut,* wormwood, from Middle High German *wermuot,* from Old High German *wermuōta,* from Germanic *wer(i)mōda* (unattested). See also **wormwood.**]

ver·nac·u·lar (vər-năk′yə-lər) *n.* **1.** The standard native language of a country or locality. **2.** The nonstandard or substandard everyday speech of a country or locality. **3.** The idiom of a particular trade or profession: *in the legal vernacular.* **4.** An idiomatic word, phrase, or expression. **5.** The commonly used name of a plant or animal as distinguished from the taxonomic designation. —See Synonyms at **dialect.** —*adj.* **1.** Native to or commonly spoken by the members of a particular country or locality. Said of a language or dialect. **2.** Using the native language of a locality as distinct from literary language. Said of a writer. **3.** Pertaining to, spoken in, or written in the native language or dialect. **4.** Pertaining to the style of architecture and decoration peculiar to a specific culture. **5.** *Rare.* Occurring or existing in a particular locality; endemic: *a vernacular disease.* **6.** Designating or pertaining to the commonly used nonscientific name of a plant or animal. [From Latin *vernāculus,* domestic, from *verna,* native slave, probably from Etruscan.] —**ver·nac′u·lar·ly** *adv.*

ver·nac·u·lar·ism (vər-năk′yə-lə-rĭz′əm) *n.* A vernacular word, phrase, or expression.

ver·nal (vûr′nəl) *adj.* **1.** Of, pertaining to, or occurring in the spring: *"rising suns that gild the vernal morn"* (Darwin). **2.** Characteristic of or resembling spring. **3.** Fresh and young; youthful. [Latin *vernālis,* from *vernus,* of spring, from *vēr,* spring. See **wesr̥** in Appendix.*] —**ver′nal·ly** *adv.*

vernal equinox. 1. The point at which the ecliptic intersects the celestial equator, the sun having a northerly motion. **2.** The moment at which the sun passes through this point, about March 21, marking the beginning of spring. Compare **autumnal equinox.**

ver·nal·i·za·tion (vûr′nə-lə-zā′shən) *n.* The subjection of seeds or seedlings to low temperature in order to hasten plant development.

ver·na·tion (vər-nā′shən) *n. Botany.* The arrangement of the folded leaves in a bud. [New Latin *vernatio,* from Latin *vernāre,* to flourish, from *vernus,* VERNAL.]

Verne (vûrn; *French* vĕrn), **Jules.** 1828–1905. French author of science-fiction romances.

Ver·ner's Law (vûr′nərz, vâr′-). *Linguistics.* A law stating essentially that Proto-Germanic noninitial voiceless fricatives in voiced environments became voiced when the previous syllable was unstressed in Proto-Indo-European. [Formulated by Karl Adolph *Verner* (1846–1896), Danish philologist.]

ver·ni·er (vûr′nē-ər) *n.* **1.** A small, movable auxiliary graduated scale attached parallel to a main graduated scale, calibrated to indicate fractional parts of the subdivisions of the larger scale, and used on certain precision instruments to increase accuracy in measurement. **2.** Any auxiliary device designed to facilitate fine adjustments or measurements on precision instruments. Also called "vernier scale." —*adj.* Of a vernier. [Invented by Pierre *Vernier* (1580–1637), French mathematician.]

vernier caliper. A measuring instrument consisting of an L-shaped frame with a linear scale along its longer arm and an L-shaped sliding attachment with a vernier scale, used to read directly the dimension of an object represented by the separation between the inner or outer edges of the two shorter arms. Also called "caliper."

vernier rocket. A small rocket engine used primarily to make fine adjustments in velocity and trajectory. Also called "vernier engine."

Ver·no·le·ninsk. The former name for **Nikolaev.**

Ver·nyi. The former name for **Alma-Ata.**

Ve·ro·na (və-rō′nə; *Italian* vā-rō′nä). A city of northeastern Italy, on the Adige River in western Venetia. Population, 240,000. —**Ver′o·nese′** (vĕr′ə-nēz′, -nēs′) *adj.* & *n.*

Ver·o·nal (vĕr′ə-nôl′, -nəl) *n.* A trademark for a type of barbital. [German, coined by two German chemists from the name VERONA (probably in allusion to the sleeping potion in the Romeo and Juliet legend).]

Ve·ro·ne·se (vā′rō-nā′zā), **Paolo.** 1528–1588. Italian painter of the Venetian school.

ve·ron·i·ca[1] (və-rŏn′ĭ-kə) *n.* Any of various plants of the genus *Veronica,* which includes the speedwells. [Perhaps from the name VERONICA.]

ve·ron·i·ca[2] (və-rŏn′ĭ-kə) *n.* **1.** The representation or image of the face of Jesus, which, according to legend, was impressed upon the handkerchief offered to him by Saint Veronica on the

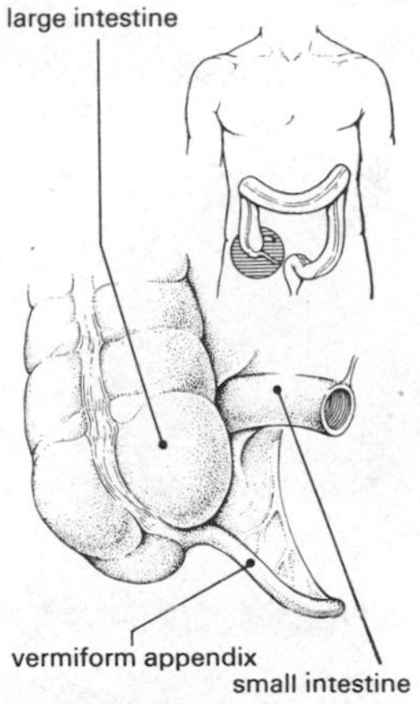

vermiform appendix

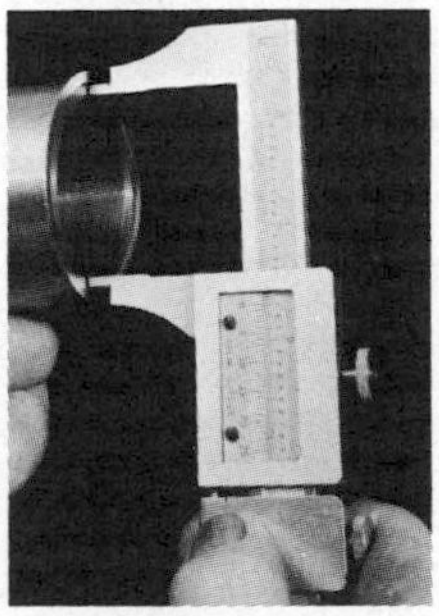
vernier

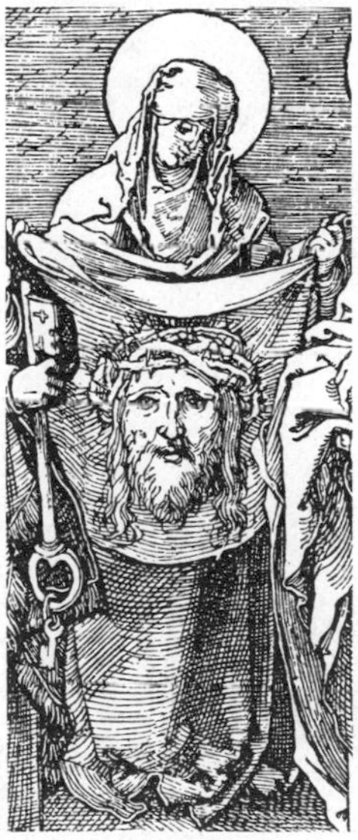
veronica[2]
Detail from a woodcut by Albrecht Dürer

road to Calvary. **2.** The handkerchief itself. **3.** Any similar representation of Jesus' face on a textile fabric.

ve·ron·i·ca[3] (və-rŏn′ĭ-kə) *n.* In bullfighting, a maneuver in which the matador stands immobile and passes the cape slowly before the charging bull. [Spanish, from the name VERONICA.]

Ve·ron·i·ca (və-rŏn′ĭ-kə). A feminine given name. [Medieval Latin, from Late Latin *Veraiconica*, Saint Veronica, whose handkerchief preserves the true image of Jesus' face : Latin *vērus*, true (see **wēros** in Appendix*) + *iconicus*, of an image, from *icon*, image, ICON.]

Ver·ra·za·no (vĕr′ə-zä′nō; *Italian* vār′rä-tsä′nō), **Giovanni da.** Also **Ver·raz·za·no.** 1485?–1528? Florentine explorer of Atlantic coast of America.

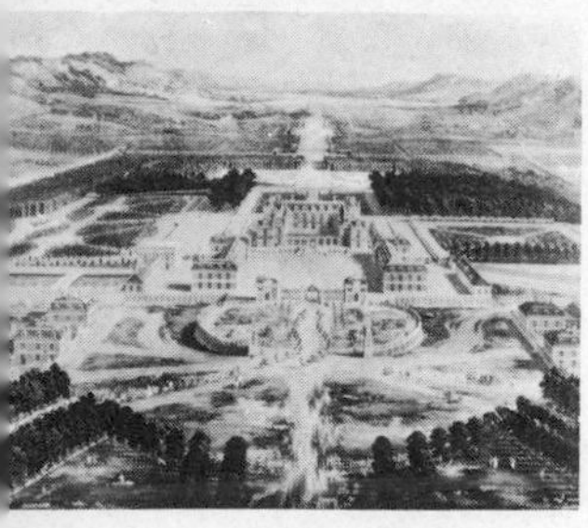

Versailles
The palace and gardens at Versailles

Ver·roc·chio (və-rō′kē-ō′; *Italian* vār-rôk′kyō), **Andrea del.** Also **Ve·roc·chio** (və-rō′kē-ō′; *Italian* vā-rôk′kyō). 1435–1488. Florentine sculptor and painter.

ver·ru·ca (və-rōō′kə) *n., pl.* **-cae** (-sē). **1.** *Medicine.* A wart. **2.** *Biology.* A wartlike projection, as on the back of a toad or on some leaves. [Latin *verrūca*. See **wer-**[1] in Appendix.*]

ver·ru·cose (və-rōō′kōs′, vĕr′ə-kōs′) *adj.* Also **ver·ru·cous** (-kəs). Covered with warts or wartlike projections. [Latin *verrucōsus*, from *verrūca*, VERRUCA.]

vers versed sine.

Ver·sailles (vər-sī′, vĕr-). A city of France, about 14 miles southwest of Paris; the site of the palace of Louis XIV and of the signing of the treaty between the Allies and Germany after World War I (1919). Population, 95,000.

ver·sant (vûr′sənt) *n.* **1.** The slope of one side of a mountain or mountain range. **2.** The general slope of any region. [French, from Latin *versāns*, present participle of *versārī*, to turn frequently. See **versatile.**]

ver·sa·tile (vûr′sə-təl; *chiefly British* vûr′sə-tīl′) *adj.* **1.** Capable of turning competently from one task, subject, or occupation to another; having a generalized aptitude. **2.** Having varied uses or serving many functions: *"The most versatile of vegetables is the tomato"* (Craig Claiborne). **3.** Inconstant or variable; changeable. **4.** *Biology.* Capable of moving freely in all directions, as the antenna of an insect or the loosely attached anther of a flower. [French, from Latin *versātilis*, from *versārī*, frequentative of *vertere*, to turn. See **wer-**[3] in Appendix.*] —**ver′sa·tile·ly** *adv.* —**ver′sa·til′i·ty, ver′sa·tile·ness** *n.*

verse[1] (vûrs) *n. Abbr.* **v., ver. 1. a.** A line of words arranged in accordance with the principles of prosody; one line of poetry. **b.** A subdivision of any metrical composition, as a stanza of a hymn or of a long poem. **2.** Metrical or rhymed composition; poetry. **3.** Light metrical composition seen as distinct from serious poetry. **4.** A specific type of metrical composition, such as *elegiac verse, blank verse,* or *free verse.* **5.** One of the numbered subdivisions of a chapter in the Bible. —*v.* **versed, versing, verses.** *Rare.* —*tr.* To versify (something). —*intr.* To versify; to write poetry. [Middle English *vers*, from Old English *fers* and Old French *vers*, from Latin *versus*, "a turning of the plow," furrow, line, verse, from the past participle of *vertere*, to turn. See **wer-**[3] in Appendix.*]

verse[2] (vûrs) *tr.v.* **versed, versing, verses.** To make familiar, knowledgeable, or skilled; to school. Used with *in.* Usually used in the passive: *He is well versed in history.* [From *versed*, acquainted with, from Latin *versātus*, past participle of *versārī*, to turn, occupy oneself with. See **versatile.**]

versed cosine. *Abbr.* **covers** A trigonometric function of an angle equal to one minus the sine of that angle. Also called "coversine."

versed sine. *Abbr.* **vers** A trigonometric function of an angle equal to one minus the cosine of that angle. Also called "versine." [New Latin *sinus versus*, "inverse-order sine," from Latin *versus*, turned. See **verse** (poetry).]

ver·si·cle (vûr′sĭ-kəl) *n.* **1.** A short verse. **2.** A short sentence spoken or chanted by a priest and followed by a response from the congregation. [Middle English, from Old French *versicule*, from Latin *versiculus*, diminutive of *versus*, VERSE.]

ver·si·col·or (vûr′sĭ-kŭl′ər) *adj.* Also **ver·si·col·ored** (-kŭl′ərd). **1.** Having a variety of colors; variegated. **2.** Changing in color; iridescent. [Latin : *versus*, turned, changed (see **verse**) + COLOR.]

ver·si·fi·er (vûr′sə-fī′ər) *n.* One who versifies. See Synonyms at **poet.**

ver·si·fy (vûr′sə-fī′) *v.* **-fied, -fying, -fies.** —*tr.* **1.** To change from prose into metrical form. **2.** To treat or tell in verse; write a poem about: *"Narrative poets liked to versify Bible stories"* (George Sherburn). —*intr.* To write verses. [Middle English *versifien*, from Old French *versifier*, from Latin *versificāre* : *versus*, VERSE + -FY.] —**ver′si·fi·ca′tion** *n.* —**ver′si·fi′er** *n.*

ver·sine (vûr′sīn′) *n. Trigonometry.* A **versed sine** *(see).* [Contraction of VERSED SINE.]

ver·sion (vûr′zhən, -shən) *n. Abbr.* **v., ver. 1.** A description, narration, or account related from the specific or subjective viewpoint of the narrator: *Her version of the accident differed from his.* **2. a.** A translation. **b.** *Usually capital* **V.** A translation of the entire Bible or of a part of it: *the King James Version.* **3.** A variation of any prototype; variant: *"At home we played soccer . . . and sometimes a version of hurling"* (Brendan Behan). **4.** An adaptation of a work of art or literature into another medium or style: *Lamb's version of Shakespeare.* **5.** *Medicine.* **a.** Manipulation of a fetus in the uterus to bring it into a favorable position for delivery. **b.** A deflection of an organ, such as the uterus, from its normal position. [Old French, from Medieval Latin *versiō*, conversion, translation, Latin *vertere*, to turn, change. See **wer-**[3] in Appendix.*] —**ver′sion·al** *adj.*

vers li·bre (vĕr lē′br′). Free verse.

ver·so (vûr′sō) *n., pl.* **-sos.** *Abbr.* **v., vo. 1.** *Printing.* The left-hand page of a book or the reverse side of a leaf as opposed to the **recto** *(see).* **2.** The back of a coin or medal. Compare **obverse.** [Latin *versō (folio)*, "(the page) being turned," the page one sees when the leaf is turned over, ablative of *versus*, turned. See **versus.**]

verst (vûrst) *n.* A Russian measure of linear distance, equivalent to about two-thirds of a mile. [French *verste*, from Russian *versta*, "line." See **wer-**[3] in Appendix.*]

ver·sus (vûr′səs) *prep. Abbr.* **v., vs. 1.** Against. Used in law and in sports: *the plaintiff versus the defendant; the Mets versus the Giants at Shea Stadium.* **2.** As an alternative to; in contrast with: *death versus dishonor.* [Medieval Latin, from Latin, turned toward, from the past participle of *vertere*, to turn. See **wer-**[3] in Appendix.*]

vert (vûrt) *n.* **1. a.** In English forest law, any green vegetation that can serve as cover for deer. **b.** The right to cut such vegetation. **2.** The color green, especially in heraldry. [Middle English *verte*, from Old French *vert*, green. See **verdant.**]

vert. vertical.

ver·te·bra (vûr′tə-brə) *n., pl.* **-brae** (-brē) or **-bras.** Any of the bones or cartilaginous segments forming the spinal column. [Latin, joint, vertebra, "something to turn on," from *vertere*, to turn. See **wer-**[3] in Appendix.*]

ver·te·bral (vûr′tə-brəl) *adj.* **1.** Relating to or of the nature of a vertebra. **2.** Having or consisting of vertebrae.

vertebral canal. *Anatomy.* The **spinal canal** *(see).*

vertebral column. *Anatomy.* The **spinal column** *(see).*

ver·te·brate (vûr′tə-brāt′, -brĭt) *adj.* **1.** Having a backbone or spinal column. **2.** Of or characteristic of a vertebrate or vertebrates. —*n.* Any member of the subphylum Vertebrata, a primary division of the phylum Chordata that includes the fishes, amphibians, reptiles, birds, and mammals, all of which are characterized by a segmented bony or cartilaginous spinal column. [Latin *vertebrātus*, from *vertebra*, VERTEBRA.]

ver·tex (vûr′tĕks′) *n., pl.* **-texes** or **-tices** (-tə-sēz′). **1.** The highest point of anything; apex; summit. **2.** *Anatomy.* **a.** The highest point of the skull. **b.** The top of the head. **3.** *Astronomy.* The highest point reached in the apparent motion of a celestial body. **4.** *Geometry.* **a.** The point at which the sides of an angle intersect. **b.** The point on a triangle opposite to and farthest away from its base. **c.** A point on a polyhedron common to three or more sides. **d.** The fixed point that is one of the three generating characteristics of a conic section. [Latin, whirl, crown of the head, highest point, from *vertere*, to turn. See **wer-**[3] in Appendix.*]

ver·ti·cal (vûr′tĭ-kəl) *adj. Abbr.* **vert. 1.** At right angles to the horizon; extending perpendicularly from a plane; upright. Compare **horizontal. 2.** Pertaining to or situated at the vertex or highest point; directly overhead. **3.** *Anatomy.* Of or pertaining to the vertex of the head. **4.** *Economics.* Pertaining to, composed of, or controlling all the grades or levels in the manufacture and sale of a product. —*n. Abbr.* **vert. 1.** A vertical line, plane, circle, or the like. **2.** A vertical position. [French, from Late Latin *verticālis*, from Latin *vertex*, VERTEX.] —**ver′ti·cal′i·ty, ver′ti·cal·ness** *n.* —**ver′ti·cal·ly** *adv.*

Synonyms: *vertical, upright, perpendicular, plumb.* These adjectives are compared as they mean at right angles, or approximately so, to the plane of the horizon or to the plane of a supporting surface. *Vertical* and especially *upright* are often used to signify contradistinction to what is horizontal or situated crosswise. In such a general sense they do not always imply a strictly right angle but an approximation instead. *Perpendicular* and *plumb* are generally used with precision and thus specify an angle of 90 degrees.

vertical circle. Any great circle on the celestial sphere, passing through the zenith and the nadir, and thus perpendicular to the horizon.

vertical file. Ephemeras, such as pamphlets, sheets of paper, and mounted photographs, that have been collected and arranged for ready reference, as in a library.

vertical union. A labor union in which workers are organized according to the industry for which they work instead of by their particular skill or craft.

ver·ti·ces. Alternate plural of **vertex.**

ver·ti·cil (vûr′tə-səl) *n. Biology.* A circular arrangement, as of flowers or leaves, about a point on an axis; a whorl. [Latin *verticillus*, the whirl of a spindle, diminutive of *vertex*, whirl, VERTEX.]

ver·ti·cil·las·ter (vûr′tə-sə-lăs′tər) *n. Botany.* An inflorescence resembling a whorl but actually arising in the axils of opposite leaves. [VERTICIL + -ASTER.] —**ver′ti·cil·las′trate′** (-trāt′) *adj.*

ver·ti·cil·late (vûr′tə-sĭl′ĭt, -āt′) *adj.* Also **ver·ti·cil·lat·ed** (-sĭl′ā′tĭd). Arranged in or forming a whorl or whorls. —**ver′ti·cil′late·ly** *adv.* —**ver′ti·cil·la′tion** *n.*

ver·tig·i·nous (vər-tĭj′ə-nəs) *adj.* **1.** Revolving; whirling; rotary. **2.** Affected by vertigo; dizzy. **3.** Tending to produce vertigo: *vertiginous speed.* **4.** Liable to quick change; unstable; inconstant. [Latin *vertīginōsus*, from *vertīgō* (stem *vertigin-*), VERTIGO.] —**ver·tig′i·nous·ly** *adv.* —**ver·tig′i·nous·ness** *n.*

ver·ti·go (vûr′tĭ-gō′) *n., pl.* **-goes** or **vertigines** (vər-tĭj′ə-nēz′). **1.** The sensation of dizziness and the feeling that oneself or one's environment is whirling about. **2.** A confused, disoriented state of mind. [Latin *vertīgō*, "a whirling," from *vertere*, to turn. See **wer-**[3] in Appendix.*]

ver·tu. Variant of **virtu.**

ver·vain (vûr′vān′) *n.* Any of several plants of the genus *Verbena*, having slender spikes of small blue, purplish, or white flowers. [Middle English *verveine*, from Old French, from

Latin *verbēna*, often in plural *verbēnae*, sacred leaves or twigs of olive, myrtle, or laurel. See **wer-**[3] in Appendix.*]

verve (vûrv) *n.* **1.** Energy and enthusiasm in the expression of ideas and especially in artistic endeavor: *The play lacks verve.* **2.** Vitality; liveliness; vigor. **3.** *Rare.* Aptitude; talent. [French, from Old French, fancy, fanciful expression, from Latin *verba*, plural of *verbum*, word. See **wer-**[6] in Appendix.*]

ver·vet (vûr′vĭt) *n.* A small, long-tailed African monkey, *Cercopithecus pygerythrus*, having a yellowish-brown or greenish coat. [French, short for *vert grivet* : *vert*, green (see **verdant**) + GRIVET.]

Ver·woerd (fər-vo͝ort′), **Hendrik Frensch.** 1901–1966. Prime Minister of South Africa (1958–66); assassinated.

ver·y (vĕr′ē) *adv. Abbr.* **v., V. 1.** In a high degree; extremely; exceedingly: *very happy.* **2.** Truly. Used as an intensive with superlatives: *the very best way to proceed.* **3.** Precisely: *the very same one.* —*adj.* **verier, -iest. 1.** Complete; absolute; utter: *at the very end of his career.* **2.** Identical; selfsame: *"These very characteristics were out of tune with the party intrigues . . . of the day"* (John F. Kennedy). **3.** Used as an intensive to emphasize the importance of the thing described: *The very mountains crumbled.* **4.** Particular; precise: *the very center of town.* **5.** Mere: *The very mention of the name was frightening.* **6.** Actual: *caught in the very act.* **7.** *Archaic.* **a.** Genuine; real; true: *"Like very sanctity she did approach"* (Shakespeare). **b.** Lawful; rightful: *the very vengeance of the gods.* [Middle English *verray*, from Old French *ver(r)ai*, true, real, from Vulgar Latin *vērāius* (unattested), from Latin *vērus*, true. See **wēros** in Appendix.*]

Usage: *Very* (adverb) is sometimes employed to qualify directly a past participle used predicatively in passive constructions: *He was very tired* (or *very discouraged*). This usage is now generally acceptable when the participle is felt to have the nature of an adjective, as in the foregoing example. In general, if the participle is defined separately as an adjective or if it functions readily as an adjective in other contexts, it may usually be preceded by *very*. When the participle in question does not meet such tests and consequently remains essentially a verb form, it is generally preferable to replace *very* with *very much, much, greatly*, or a like term that fits the sentence at hand. As an example in writing, the following is accepted by 86 per cent of the Usage Panel: *He seemed very worried.* The remaining examples, however, are termed unacceptable in writing by the percentages indicated: *She was very disliked by her students* (by 87 per cent). *Call us if you are very delayed* (by 85 per cent). *We were very inconvenienced by it* (by 80 per cent). Preferable phrasings include *much* (or *greatly*) *disliked; delayed much* or *seriously delayed; much* (or *very much*) *inconvenienced.*

very high frequency. *Abbr.* **VHF, vhf** A band of radio frequencies falling between 30 and 300 megacycles per second.

very low frequency. *Abbr.* **VLF, vlf** A band of radio frequencies falling between 3 and 30 kilocycles per second.

Ver·y pistol (vĕr′ē). A pistol used for firing colored signal flares. [Invented by Edward W. *Very* (died 1910), American naval officer.]

Ve·sa·li·us (vĭ-sā′lē-əs), **Andreas.** 1514–1564. Flemish anatomist and surgeon; regarded as father of modern anatomy.

ve·si·ca (və-sī′kə, -sē′kə) *n., pl.* **-cae** (-sē). A bladder; especially, the urinary bladder or the gallbladder. [Latin *vēsīca*, bladder, blister. See **udero-** in Appendix.*] —**ves′i·cal** (vĕs′ĭ-kəl) *adj.*

ves·i·cant (vĕs′ĭ-kənt) *n.* A blistering agent; especially, such an agent, as mustard gas, used in chemical warfare. —*adj.* Causing blisters.

ves·i·cate (vĕs′ĭ-kāt′) *v.* **-cated, -cating, -cates.** —*tr.* To blister. —*intr.* To be or become blistered. [Late Latin *vēsīcāre*, from Latin *vēsīca*, bladder, blister, VESICA.]

ves·i·ca·to·ry (vĕs′ĭ-kə-tôr′ē, -tōr′ē) *adj.* Vesicant. —*n., pl.* **vesicatories.** A vesicant.

ves·i·cle (vĕs′ĭ-kəl) *n.* **1.** A small bladderlike cell or cavity. **2.** *Anatomy.* A small bladder or sac, especially one containing fluid. **3.** *Pathology.* A serum-filled blister formed in or beneath the skin. **4.** *Geology.* A small air pocket or cavity formed in volcanic rock during solidification. [French *vésicule*, from Latin *vēsīcula*, diminutive of *vēsīca*, VESICA.]

ve·sic·u·lar (və-sĭk′yə-lər) *adj.* **1.** Of or pertaining to vesicles. **2.** Composed of or containing vesicles. **3.** Having the form of a vesicle. —**ve·sic′u·lar·ly** *adv.*

ve·sic·u·late (və-sĭk′yə-lāt′) *v.* **-lated, -lating, -lates.** —*tr.* To make vesicular. —*intr.* To become vesicular. —*adj.* (və-sĭk′yə-lĭt, -lāt). Full of or bearing vesicles; vesicular. —**ve·sic′u·la′tion** *n.*

Ves·pa·sian (vĕs-pā′zhən). Latin name, Titus Flavius Sabinus Vespasianus. A.D. 9–79. Emperor of Rome (69–79).

ves·per (vĕs′pər) *n.* **1.** A bell used to summon persons to vespers. Also called "vesper bell." **2.** *Archaic.* Evening. —*adj.* Pertaining to, appearing in, or appropriate for the evening: *a vesper serenade.* [From VESPER.]

Ves·per (vĕs′pər) *n.* Formerly, the **evening star** *(see).* [Middle English, from Latin, evening, the evening star. See **wespero-** in Appendix.*]

ves·per·al (vĕs′pər-əl) *n.* **1.** A book containing the words and hymns to be used at vespers. **2.** A covering used to protect the altar cloth between services.

ves·pers (vĕs′pərz) *pl.n.* Also **Ves·pers. 1. a.** The sixth of the seven **canonical hours** *(see).* **b.** The time of day set aside for this prayer, in the late afternoon or evening. **2.** Any worship service held in the late afternoon or evening. **3.** *Anglican Church.* **Evening Prayer** *(see).* **4.** *Roman Catholic Church.* A service held on Sundays or holy days which includes the office of vespers.

vesper sparrow. A North American sparrow, *Pooecetes gramineus*, having white markings on its outer tail feathers. [From its singing in the evening.]

ves·per·tine (vĕs′pər-tĭn, -tīn′) *adj.* Also **ves·per·ti·nal** (vĕs′pər-tī′nəl). **1.** Pertaining to or appearing in the evening. **2.** *Botany.* Opening or blooming in the evening. **3.** *Zoology.* Becoming active in the evening; crepuscular. [Latin *vespertīnus*, from *vesper*, evening, VESPER.]

ves·pi·ar·y (vĕs′pē-ĕr′ē) *n., pl.* **-ies.** A nest or colony of wasps or hornets. [Latin *vespa*, wasp (see **wopsā** in Appendix*) + (AP)IARY.]

ves·pid (vĕs′pĭd) *n.* Any of various insects of the family Vespidae, which includes certain wasps, hornets, and yellow jackets. —*adj.* Of or belonging to the Vespidae. [New Latin *Vespidae*, from Latin *vespa*, wasp. See **vespiary.**]

ves·pine (vĕs′pīn′, -pĭn) *adj.* Of, pertaining to, or resembling a wasp. [From Latin *vespa*, wasp. See **vespiary.**]

Ves·puc·ci (vĕs-po͞ot′chē), **Amerigo.** Latin name, Americus Vespucius. 1451–1512. Italian navigator for whom America was named; explored New World coastline after Columbus.

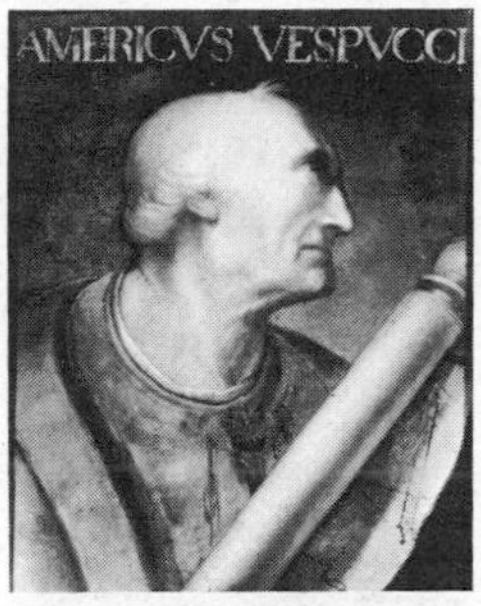

Amerigo Vespucci

ves·sel (vĕs′əl) *n.* **1. a.** A hollow utensil used as a container, especially for liquids. **b.** A person considered as a receptacle or agent of some quality: *a vessel of mercy.* **2.** A craft, especially one larger than a rowboat, designed to navigate on water. **3.** An airship. **4.** *Anatomy.* A duct, canal, or other tube for containing or circulating a bodily fluid: *a blood vessel.* **5.** *Botany.* One of the tubular conductive structures of woody tissue, consisting of cylindrical, often dead cells that are attached end to end. [Middle English, from Old French *vaissel, vessel*, from Late Latin *vascellum*, diminutive of Latin *vās*, vessel, VAS.]

vest (vĕst) *n.* **1.** A short, close-fitting sleeveless garment, buttoning in front, worn typically by men over a shirt and under a suit coat. Also *chiefly British* "waistcoat." **2.** A fabric trimming or decoration worn by women to cover the bosom. **3.** *Chiefly British.* An undershirt. **4.** *Archaic.* Clothing; raiment; dress. **5.** *Obsolete.* An ecclesiastical vestment. —*v.* **vested, vesting, vests.** —*tr.* **1.** To clothe or dress, as with ecclesiastical vestments. **2.** To place (authority or ownership, for example) in the control of. Used with *in: He vested his estate in his son.* **3.** To place (authority or power, for example). Used with *with: "these corporations were vested with enormous powers"* (Gustavus Myers). —*intr.* **1.** To dress oneself, especially in ecclesiastical vestments. **2.** To be or become legally vested in or possessed by a person or persons. [French *veste*, from Italian, from Latin *vestis*, garment. See **wes-**[4] in Appendix.*]

ves·ta (vĕs′tə) *n.* A short friction match made of wax or wood. [After the goddess VESTA.]

Ves·ta[1] (vĕs′tə). *Roman Mythology.* The goddess of the hearth, identified with the Greek goddess Hestia and worshiped in a temple containing the sacred fire tended by the vestal virgins. [Latin. See **wes-**[3] in Appendix.*]

Ves·ta[2] (vĕs′tə) *n.* The third-largest asteroid in the solar system, having a diameter of approximately 240 miles. [After the goddess VESTA.]

ves·tal (vĕs′təl) *adj.* **1.** Pertaining to or sacred to Vesta. **2.** Pertaining to or characteristic of the vestal virgins; chaste; pure. —*n.* **1.** A vestal virgin. **2.** A virgin woman. **3.** A nun.

vestal virgin. One of the six virgin priestesses who tended the sacred fire in the temple of Vesta in ancient Rome.

vest·ed (vĕs′tĭd) *adj.* **1.** *Law.* Settled, complete, or absolute; without contingency. **2.** Dressed or clothed, especially in ecclesiastical vestments.

vested interest. 1. *Law.* A right or title that can be conveyed to another. **2.** A strong concern for something, such as an institution, from which one expects private benefit. **3.** A group that has a vested interest.

vest·ee (vĕ-stē′) *n.* A decorative garment worn by women to cover the bosom. [From VEST.]

Ves·ter·a·len (vĕs′tə-rô′lən). An archipelago of Norway, about 1,200 square miles in area, in the Norwegian Sea off the northwestern coast.

ves·ti·ar·y (vĕs′tē-ĕr′ē) *adj.* Of or pertaining to clothes. —*n., pl.* **vestiaries.** A dressing room, cloakroom, or vestry. [Middle English *vestiarie*, from Old French, from Medieval Latin *vestiārium*, from Latin, wardrobe, from *vestiārius*, of clothes, from *vestis*, garment. See **vest.**]

vestibular nerve. A division of the **acoustic nerve** *(see).*

ves·ti·bule (vĕs′tə-byo͞ol′) *n.* **1.** A small entrance hall or antechamber between two doors of a house or building; a lobby. **2.** An enclosed area at the end of a passenger car on a railroad train. **3.** *Anatomy.* Any cavity, chamber, or channel that serves as an approach or entrance to another cavity. —*tr.v.* **vestibuled, -buling, -bules.** To furnish with a vestibule. [French, from Latin *vestibulum*†.] —**ves·tib′u·lar** (vĕ-stĭb′yə-lər) *adj.*

ves·tige (vĕs′tĭj) *n.* **1.** A visible trace, evidence, or sign of something that has once existed but exists or appears no more. **2.** *Biology.* A small, degenerate, or rudimentary organ or part existing in an organism as a usually nonfunctioning remnant of an organ or part fully developed and functional in a preceding generation or earlier developmental stage. —See Synonyms at **trace.** [French, from Latin *vestīgium*†, footprint, trace.]

ves·tig·i·al (vĕ-stĭj′ē-əl) *adj.* **1.** Of, pertaining to, or constituting a vestige. **2.** *Biology.* Occurring or persisting as a rudimentary or degenerate structure. —**ves·tig′i·al·ly** *adv.*

vest·ment (vĕst′mənt) *n.* **1.** A garment; especially, a robe or gown worn as an indication of office or state. **2.** *Ecclesiastical.* Any of the ritual robes worn by clergymen, altar boys, or other assistants at services or rites; especially, a garment worn at the celebration of the Eucharist. [Middle English *vestiment*, from

Old French, from Latin *vestimentum,* from *vestīre,* to dress, from *vestis,* garment. See **vest.**] —**vest·ment′al** *adj.*

vest-pock·et (vĕst′pŏk′ĭt) *adj.* **1.** Designed to fit into a vest pocket: *a vest-pocket book.* **2.** Relatively small; diminutive.

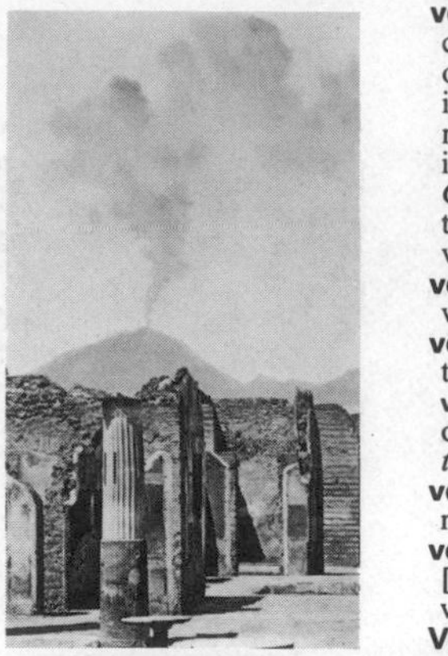

Vesuvius
Seen from the ruins of Pompeii

ves·try (vĕs′trē) *n., pl.* **-tries. 1.** A room in a church where the clergymen put on their vestments and where these robes and other sacred objects are stored; a sacristy. **2.** A meeting room in a church. **3.** In the Anglican and Episcopal churches, a committee of members of the parish or congregation that administers the affairs of the parish or congregation. **4.** *Anglican Church.* A meeting of this group or of the entire congregation or the place in which the meeting is held. [Middle English *vestrie,* variant of *vestiarie,* VESTIARY.]

ves·try·man (vĕs′trē-mən) *n., pl.* **-men** (-mĭn). A member of a vestry.

ves·ture (vĕs′chər) *n. Archaic.* **1.** Clothing; apparel. **2.** Anything that covers or cloaks: *hills in a vesture of mist.* —*tr.v.* **vestured, -turing, -tures.** To cover with vesture; clothe. [Middle English, clothes, from Old French, from Late Latin *vestītūra,* from Latin *vestīre,* to clothe. See **vestment.**]

ve·su·vi·an (və-so͞o′vē-ən) *n.* **1.** A mineral, **idocrase** *(see).* **2.** A match used for lighting cigars; a fusee. [From VESUVIUS.]

ve·su·vi·an·ite (və-so͞o′vē-ə-nīt′) *n.* A mineral, **idocrase** *(see).* [*Vesuvian,* of VESUVIUS (because first found in the lava of the volcano) + -ITE.]

Ve·su·vi·us (və-so͞o′vē-əs). *Italian* **Ve·su·vi·o** (vā-zo͞o′vyō). An active volcano, 3,891 feet high, in western Italy near Naples.

vet (vĕt) *n. Informal.* A veterinarian. —*v.* **vetted, vetting, vets.** *Informal.* —*tr.* **1.** To practice veterinary medicine upon. **2.** *Chiefly British.* To examine or appraise expertly: *vet a manuscript.* —*intr.* To be or become a veterinarian.

vet. 1. veteran. **2.** veterinarian; veterinary.

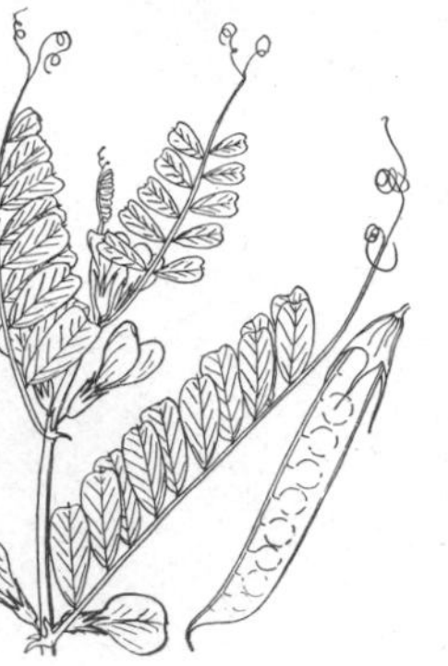

vetch
Vicia sativa

vetch (vĕch) *n.* Any of various climbing or twining plants of the genus *Vicia,* having pinnate leaves and small, usually purplish flowers. [Middle English *fecche,* from Old North French *veche,* from Latin *vicia.* See **weik-**[4] in Appendix.*]

vetch·ling (vĕch′lĭng) *n.* Any of several plants of the genus *Lathyrus,* having pinnate leaves, slender tendrils, and small, variously colored flowers. [VETCH + -LING.]

veter. veterinary.

vet·er·an (vĕt′ər-ən, vĕt′rən) *n. Abbr.* **vet. 1.** One who has a long record of service in a given activity or capacity. **2.** One who has been a member of the armed forces. —*adj.* **1.** Experienced because of long service: *a veteran politician.* **2.** Pertaining to or suggestive of a veteran or veterans. [French *vétéran,* from Latin *veterānus,* from *vetus* (stem *veter-*), old. See **wet-** in Appendix.*]

Veterans' Administration. *Abbr.* **VA, V.A.** A Federal agency concerned with the welfare of veterans of the armed forces.

Veterans Day. November 11, observed as a national holiday in the United States, commemorating the armistice in World War I (1918). Formerly called "Armistice Day."

Veterans of Foreign Wars. *Abbr.* **VFW, V.F.W.** A society founded in 1899 composed of veterans of the United States Armed Forces who have fought in a foreign country.

vet·er·i·nar·i·an (vĕt′ər-ə-nâr′ē-ən, vĕt′rə-) *n. Abbr.* **vet.** A person trained and authorized to treat animals medically.

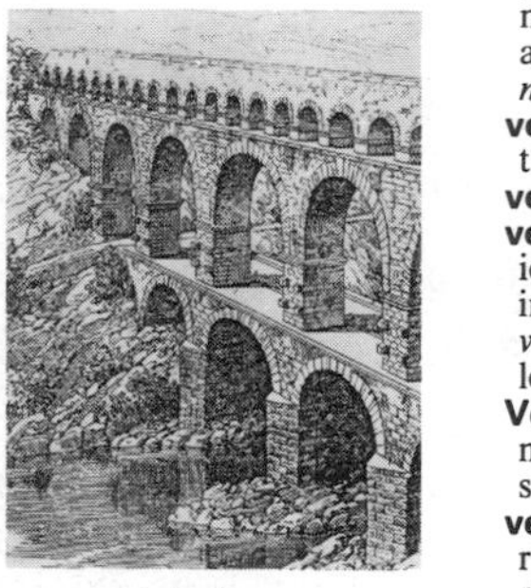

viaduct
The Pont du Gard, near Nîmes, France, a Roman aqueduct now used as a viaduct

vet·er·i·nar·y (vĕt′ər-ə-nĕr′ē, vĕt′rə-) *adj. Abbr.* **vet., veter.** Of, pertaining to, or being the science of the diagnosis and treatment of diseases and injuries of animals, especially domestic animals. —*n., pl.* **veterinaries.** A veterinarian. [Latin *veterīnārius,* from *veterīnus,* of cattle. See **wet-** in Appendix.*]

veterinary medicine. The medical science of the diagnosis and treatment of animal diseases and injuries.

veterinary surgeon. *Abbr.* **V.S.** A veterinarian.

vet·i·ver (vĕt′ə-vər) *n.* **1.** A grass, *Vetiveria zizanioides,* of tropical Asia, cultivated for its aromatic roots that yield an oil used in perfumery. **2.** The roots of this plant. [French *vetiver, vetyver,* from Tamil *veṭṭivēru* : *veṭṭi,* worthlessness + *vēru,* useless.]

Vet·lu·ga (vĕt-lo͞o′gə). A river of the Soviet Union, rising in the northern Urals and flowing 500 miles north, west, and then south to the Volga.

ve·to (vē′tō) *n., pl.* **-toes. 1.** The vested power or constitutional right of one branch or department of government, especially the right of a chief executive, to reject a bill passed by a legislative body and thus prevent or delay its enactment into law. **2.** The exercise of this right. **3.** The official document communicating the rejection and the reasons for it. Also called "veto message." **4.** Any authoritative prohibition or rejection of a proposed or intended act. —*tr.v.* **vetoed, -toing, -toes. 1.** To prevent (a legislative bill) from becoming law by exercising the power of veto. **2.** To forbid or prevent authoritatively; prohibit. [Latin *vetō,* I forbid, from *vetāre*†, to forbid.] —**ve′to′er** *n.*

vex (vĕks) *tr.v.* **vexed, vexing, vexes. 1.** To irritate or annoy, as with petty importunities; bother; pester: *"The beauties she so truly sees,/She thinks I have no eye for these,/And vexes me for reason why"* (Robert Frost). **2.** To confuse; baffle; puzzle. **3.** To debate (a problem) at length; bring up repeatedly for discussion: *Let us not vex the question.* **4.** To toss about or stir up; agitate. —See Synonyms at **annoy.** [Middle English *vexen,* from Old French *vexer,* from Latin *vexāre.* See **wegh-** in Appendix.*] —**vex′er** *n.* —**vex′ing·ly** *adv.*

vex·a·tion (vĕk-sā′shən) *n.* **1.** The act of vexing. **2.** The state or condition of being vexed; annoyance: *"The chauffeur, furious, kicks the car with a groan of vexation"* (G.B. Shaw). **3.** One that vexes; a source of irritation or annoyance.

vex·a·tious (vĕk-sā′shəs) *adj.* **1.** Causing or creating vexation; annoying; irksome. **2.** Full of vexation; disturbed; annoyed. **3.** *Law.* Instituted without sufficient grounds, to serve solely as an annoyance to a defendant. Said of legal actions. —**vex·a′tious·ly** *adv.* —**vex·a′tious·ness** *n.*

vexed (vĕkst) *adj.* **1.** Irritated; annoyed; troubled. **2.** Much discussed or debated; brought up repeatedly. —**vex′ed·ly** (vĕk′sĭd-lē) *adv.* —**vex′ed·ness** *n.*

vex·il·lar·y (vĕk′sə-lĕr′ē) *n., pl.* **-ies. 1.** A member of the oldest class of army veterans who served under a special standard in ancient Rome. **2.** A standard-bearer. —*adj.* Also **vex·il·lar** (vĕk′sə-lər). Of or pertaining to a banner or standard. [Latin *vexillārius,* from *vexillum,* flag. See **vexillum.**]

vex·il·late (vĕk′sə-lāt′, vĕk-sĭl′ĭt) *adj.* Having a vexillum or vexilla.

vex·il·lum (vĕk-sĭl′əm) *n., pl.* **vexilla** (vĕk-sĭl′ə). **1.** *Botany.* A usually enlarged upper petal of certain flowers; a standard. **2.** *Zoology.* The weblike part of a feather; the vane. [Latin, flag, diminutive of *vēlum,* cloth, veil, sail. See **weg-**[1] in Appendix.*]

V.F. 1. vicar forane. **2.** video frequency. **3.** visual field.

VFW, V.F.W. Veterans of Foreign Wars.

V.G. vicar general.

vhf, VHF very high frequency.

VI Virgin Islands (with Zip Code).

v.i. vide infra.

V.I. 1. Virgin Islands. **2.** volume indicator.

vi·a (vī′ə, vē′ə) *prep.* By way of. [Latin *viā,* ablative of *via,* road, way. See **wei-**[2] in Appendix.*]

vi·a·ble (vī′ə-bəl) *adj.* **1.** Capable of living, as a newborn infant or fetus reaching a stage of development that will permit it to survive and develop under normal conditions. **2.** Capable of living, developing, or germinating under favorable conditions, as seeds, spores, or eggs. **3.** Capable of actualization, as a project; practicable: *"How viable are the ancient legends as vehicles for modern literary themes?"* (Richard Kain). —See Synonyms at **possible.** [French, from Old French, from *vie,* life, from Latin *vīta.* See **gwei-** in Appendix.*] —**vi′a·bil′i·ty** *n.*

Vi·a Do·lo·ro·sa (vī′ə dŏl′ə-rō′sə, vē′ə dō′lə-rō′sə). **1.** Jesus' route from Pilate's judgment hall to Golgotha. **2.** A difficult course or experience. [Latin, "sad road."]

vi·a·duct (vī′ə-dŭkt′) *n.* A series of spans or arches used to carry a road or railroad over a wide valley or over other roads or railroads. [Latin *via,* road, way (see **via**) + (AQUA)DUCT.]

vi·al (vī′əl) *n.* A small container, usually glass, for liquids. Also called "phial." —*tr.v.* **vialed** or **vialled, -aling** or **-alling, -als.** To put or keep in or as if in a vial. [Middle English *viole,* variant of *fiole,* PHIAL.]

vi·a me·di·a (vī′ə mē′dē-ə, vē′ə mā′dē-ə). *Latin.* A middle way; mean between two extremes.

vi·and (vī′ənd) *n.* **1.** An article of food. **2.** *Plural.* Provisions; victuals. [Middle English *viaunde,* from Old French *viande,* from Vulgar Latin *vī(v)anda* (unattested), variant of Latin *vīvenda,* gerundive of *vīvere,* to live. See **gwei-** in Appendix.*]

vi·at·ic (vī-ăt′ĭk) *adj.* Also **vi·at·i·cal** (-ĭ-kəl). Of or pertaining to traveling, a road, or a way. [Latin *viāticus.* See **viaticum.**]

vi·at·i·cum (vī-ăt′ĭ-kəm, vē-) *n., pl.* **-ca** (-kə) or **-cums. 1.** *Ecclesiastical.* The Eucharist, as given to a dying person or one in danger of death: *"Pope, Cardinal, or washerwoman, they would all take their viaticum with gratitude from the lowest country priest"* (Morris L. West). **2.** Supplies for a journey. [Latin *viāticum,* traveling provisions, from *viāticus,* of a road or journey, from *via,* way, road. See **via.**]

vi·a·tor (vī-ā′tər, vē-ä′tôr′) *n., pl.* **viatores** (vī′ə-tôr′ēz, -tōr′ēz, vē′ä-tôr′ās′). A traveler; wayfarer. [Latin *viātor,* from *via,* way. See **via.**]

Vi·borg. The Swedish name for **Vyborg.**

vi·brac·u·lum (vī-brăk′yə-ləm) *n., pl.* **-la** (-lə). *Zoology.* One of the long, whiplike filaments on the surface of certain bryozoan colonies. [New Latin, diminutive formation from Latin *vibrāre,* to shake, brandish, VIBRATE.] —**vi·brac′u·lar** (-lər) *adj.* —**vi·brac′u·loid′** (-loid′) *adj.*

vi·brant (vī′brənt) *adj.* **1.** Exhibiting, characterized by, or resulting from vibration; vibrating. **2.** Pulsing or throbbing with energy or activity: *"his verse . . . is alive, vibrant"* (D.B. Wyndham Lewis). **3.** *Phonetics.* Voiced. —*n. Phonetics.* A voiced sound. —**vi′bran·cy** *n.* —**vi′brant·ly** *adv.*

vi·bra·phone (vī′brə-fōn′) *n.* A musical instrument similar to a marimba but having metal bars and rotating disks in the resonators to produce a vibrato. Also called "vibra-harp." [VIBRA(TE) + -PHONE.] —**vi′bra·phon′ist** (-fō′nĭst) *n.*

vi·brate (vī′brāt′) *v.* **-brated, -brating, -brates.** —*intr.* **1.** To move back and forth rapidly. **2.** To produce a sound; resonate. **3.** To be moved emotionally; thrill: *vibrate with excitement.* **4.** To fluctuate or waver in making choices; vacillate. —*tr.* **1.** To cause to tremble or quiver. **2.** To cause to move back and forth rapidly. **3.** To produce (sound) by vibration. —See Synonyms at **swing.** [Latin *vibrāre.* See **weip-** in Appendix.*]

vi·bra·tile (vī′brə-tĭl, -tīl′) *adj.* **1.** Characterized by vibration. **2.** Capable of or adapted to vibratory motion. [French, from Latin *vibrāre,* VIBRATE.] —**vi′bra·til′i·ty** (-tĭl′ə-tē) *n.*

vi·bra·tion (vī-brā′shən) *n.* **1.** The act of vibrating. **2.** The condition of being vibrated. **3.** *Physics.* **a.** A rapid linear motion of a particle or of an elastic solid about an equilibrium position. **b.** Any periodic process. **4.** A single complete vibrating motion; quiver; tremor. —**vi·bra′tion·al** *adj.*

vi·bra·to (vĭ-brä′tō, vē-) *n., pl.* **-tos.** *Music.* A tremulous or pulsating effect produced in an instrumental or vocal tone by barely perceptible minute and rapid variations in pitch. Compare **tremolo.** [Italian, from Latin *vibrātus,* past participle of *vibrāre,* VIBRATE.]

vi·bra·tor (vī′brā′tər) *n.* **1.** Something that vibrates. **2.** An electrically operated device used for massage. **3.** An electrical device consisting basically of a vibrating conductor interrupting a current.

vi·bra·to·ry (vī′brə-tôr′ē, -tōr′ē) *adj.* Also **vi·bra·tive** (vī′brā′tĭv, vī′brə-). **1.** Of, characterized by, or consisting of vibration. **2.** Causing vibration. **3.** Vibrating or capable of vibration.

vib·ri·o (vĭb′rē-ō′) *n., pl.* **-os.** Any of various S-shaped or comma-shaped microorganisms of the genus *Vibrio*, especially *V. comma*, which causes cholera. [New Latin *Vibrio*, arbitrarily from Latin *vibrāre*, VIBRATE (from their vibratory motion).] —**vib′ri·oid′** (-oid′) *adj.*

vi·bris·sa (vī-brĭs′ə, vĭ-) *n., pl.* **-brissae** (-brĭs′ē). A stiff hair or hairlike projection, as a nostril hair, one of the whiskers of a cat, or one of the modified feathers near the beak of an insectivorous bird. [Latin *vibrissae* (plural), from *vibrāre*, VIBRATE.]

vi·bur·num (vī-bûr′nəm) *n.* Any of various shrubs or trees of the genus *Viburnum*, characteristically having clusters of small white flowers and berrylike red or black fruit. [New Latin *Viburnum*, from Latin *viburnum†*, wayfaring tree.]

vic. **1.** vicar. **2.** vicinity.

vic·ar (vĭk′ər) *n. Abbr.* **vic. 1.** In the Church of England, the priest of a parish who receives a stipend or salary from a layman or religious corporation responsible for impropriating the principal revenues. **2.** In the Episcopal Church of the United States, a clergyman in charge of a chapel. **3.** In the Anglican Communion generally, a clergyman acting in the place of a rector or bishop. **4. a.** In the Roman Catholic Church, a deputy or representative for an ecclesiastic. **b.** The pope as the earthly deputy of Christ. Also called "Vicar of Christ." **5.** One who fulfills the duties of another; a substitute; deputy. [Middle English, from Old French *vicaire*, from Latin *vicārius*, a substitute, from *vicārius*, substituting, acting for, from *vicis*, change, turn, office. See **weik**⁴ in Appendix.*]

vic·ar·age (vĭk′ər-ĭj) *n.* **1.** The residence of a vicar. **2.** The benefice of a vicar. **3.** The duties or office of a vicar; vicariate.

vicar apostolic. *Abbr.* **V.A.** *Roman Catholic Church.* **1. a.** A titular bishop who administers a region that is not yet a diocese as a representative of the Holy See. **b.** A titular bishop appointed to administer to a vacant see in which the succession of bishops has been interrupted. **2.** Formerly, a bishop or archbishop delegated by the pope to act in his stead in a particular region.

vicar fo·rane (vĭk′ər fô-rān′, fō-). *Abbr.* **V.F.** *Roman Catholic Church.* A priest who by a bishop's appointment exercises limited jurisdiction over the clergy in a district of a diocese. [From Late Latin *forānus*, FOREIGN.]

vicar general *pl.* **vicars general.** *Abbr.* **V.G. 1.** *Roman Catholic Church.* A priest acting as deputy to a bishop to assist him in the administration of his diocese. **2.** An ecclesiastical, usually lay official, in the Church of England who assists an archbishop or bishop in administrative and judicial duties.

vi·car·i·al (vī-kâr′ē-əl, vĭ-) *adj.* **1.** Of or relating to a vicar or vicars. **2.** Acting as or having the position of a vicar. **3.** Vicarious or delegated, as powers of an office or position.

vi·car·i·ate (vī-kâr′ē-ĭt, -āt′, vĭ-) *n.* Also **vic·ar·ate** (vĭk′ər-ĭt). **1.** The office or authority of a vicar. **2.** The district under a vicar's jurisdiction. [Medieval Latin *vicāriātus*, from Late Latin *vicārius*, vicar, VICARIOUS.]

vi·car·i·ous (vī-kâr′ē-əs, vĭ-) *adj.* **1.** Performed or endured by one person substituting for another; fulfilled by the substitution of the actual offender with some other person or thing: *vicarious punishment.* **2.** Acting in place of someone or something else; delegated; substituted. **3.** Experienced or enjoyed through sympathetic or imaginative participation in the experiences of another: *a vicarious thrill.* **4.** *Physiology.* Occurring in or performed by a part of the body not normally associated with a certain function. [Latin *vicārius*, substituting, from *vicis*, change, turn, office. See **weik**⁴ in Appendix.*] —**vi·car′i·ous·ly** *adv.* —**vi·car′i·ous·ness** *n.*

Vicar of Christ. *Roman Catholic Church.* A vicar *(see).*

vic·ar·ship (vĭk′ər-shĭp′) *n.* The office or tenure of a vicar.

vice¹ (vīs) *n.* **1.** An evil, degrading, or immoral practice or habit; a serious moral failing. **2.** Wicked or evil conduct or habits; indulgence in degrading practices; depravity; corruption. **3.** Sexual immorality; especially, prostitution. **4.** A slight personal failing; foible. **5.** A flaw or imperfection; blemish; defect; fault: *"The radical vice of his theory of life was that he confounded physical with spiritual remoteness"* (James Russell Lowell). **6.** A physical defect or weakness. **7.** An abnormal behavior in a domestic animal. **8.** *Capital* **V. a.** A character representing generalized or particular vice in English morality plays. **b.** A jester; buffoon. —See Synonyms at **fault.** [Middle English, from Old French, from Latin *vitium*, blemish, offense, vice. See **wei**⁴ in Appendix.*]

vice². Variant of **vise.**

vice³ (vīs) *adj. Abbr.* **v., V.** Substituting for; acting in place of; deputy: *vice chairman.* —*n.* One who acts in the place of another; a deputy. —*prep.* In place of; replacing. [Latin *vice*, ablative of *vicis*, change. See **weik**⁴ in Appendix.*]

vice-. Indicates one substituting for another; for example, **viceregal.** [Middle English *vis-*, from Old French, from Late Latin *vice-*, from Latin *vice*, in place of, VICE.]

vice admiral. *Abbr.* **V.A., V. Adm.** A naval officer ranking next below an admiral.

vice-ad·mir·al·ty (vīs-ăd′mə-rəl-tē) *n., pl.* **-ties.** The office, rank, or command of a vice admiral.

vice chancellor. *Abbr.* **V.C. 1.** *Law.* A judge in equity courts ranking below a chancellor. **2.** A deputy or assistant chancellor in a university. **3.** A deputy or substitute for a head of state or official bearing the title chancellor. —**vice′-chan′cel·lor·ship′** *n.*

vice consul. *Abbr.* **V.C.** A consular officer who is subordinate to and a deputy of a consul or consul general. —**vice′-con′su·lar** *adj.* —**vice′-con′su·late** *n.* —**vice′-con′sul·ship′** *n.*

vice·ge·ren·cy (vīs-jîr′ən-sē) *n., pl.* **-cies. 1.** The position, function, or authority of a vicegerent. **2.** A district under a vicegerent's jurisdiction.

vice·ge·rent (vīs-jîr′ənt) *n.* A person appointed by a ruler or head of state to act as an administrative deputy. [Medieval Latin *vicegerēns* : VICE- + GERENT.] —**vice·ge′ral** *adj.*

vic·e·nar·y (vĭs′ə-nĕr′ē) *adj.* **1.** Consisting of or pertaining to 20. **2.** Designating a notation system based on 20. [Latin *vicēnārius*, from *vicēnī*, 20 each, from *vīginti*, 20. See **wĭkmtī** in Appendix.*]

vi·cen·ni·al (vī-sĕn′ē-əl) *adj.* **1.** Happening once every 20 years. **2.** Existing or lasting for 20 years. [From Late Latin *vicennium*, period of 20 years : Latin *viciēs*, 20 times, from *vīginti*, 20 (see **wĭkmtī** in Appendix*) + *annus*, year (see **at-** in Appendix*).]

Vi·cen·za (vē-chĕn′tsä). A city of northeastern Italy, in Venetia northeast of Verona. Population, 105,000.

vice president. *Abbr.* **V.P., V. Pres. 1.** An officer ranking next below a president, usually empowered to assume the president's duties under such conditions as absence, illness, or death. **2.** A deputy of a president, especially in a corporation, in charge of a separate department or location: *vice president in charge of sales.* —**vice′-pres′i·den·cy** *n.* —**vice′-pres·i·den′tial** *adj.*

vice-re·gal (vīs-rē′gəl) *adj.* Of or pertaining to a viceroy. [VICE- + REGAL.] —**vice·re′gal·ly** *adv.*

vice regent. One who acts as a regent's deputy. —**vice-re′gen·cy** *n.* —**vice-re′gent** *adj.*

vice-reine (vīs′rān′) *n.* **1.** The wife of a viceroy. **2.** *Rare.* A woman viceroy. [French : VICE- + *reine*, queen, from Latin *rēgina*, feminine of *rēx*, king (see **reg-**¹ in Appendix*).]

vice·roy (vīs′roi′) *n., pl.* **-roys. 1.** A governor of a country, province, or colony, ruling as the representative of a sovereign or king. **2.** An orange and black North American butterfly, *Limenitis archippus*, resembling but somewhat smaller than the monarch. [French : *vice-* + *roi*, king, from Latin *rēx* (see **reg-**¹ in Appendix*).]

vice·roy·al·ty (vīs′roi′əl-tē) *n., pl.* **-ties. 1.** The office, authority, or term of service of a viceroy. **2.** A district or province governed by a viceroy. Also called "viceroyship."

vice squad. A police division charged with the control of vice.

vi·ce ver·sa (vī′sē vûr′sə, vīs′, vī′sə). *Abbr.* **v.v.** The order or meaning being reversed; with principal items transposed; conversely. Said of a preceding statement. [Latin, "the position being changed" : *vice*, ablative singular of *vicis*, change, office, position (see **weik**⁴ in Appendix*) + *versā*, ablative feminine singular of *versus*, past participle of *vertere*, to turn, change (see **wer-**³ in Appendix*).]

Vi·cha·da (vē-chä′thä). A river of Colombia, rising in the east-central part of the country and flowing 400 miles east to the Orinoco on the Venezuelan border.

Vi·chy (vĭsh′ē; French vē-shē′). A city of central France, a health resort since Roman times; the seat of the French government during World War II (1940–44). Population, 31,000.

vi·chy·soisse (vĭsh′ē-swäz′, vē′shē-) *n.* A thick, creamy potato soup flavored with leeks or onions and usually served cold. [French, "(cream) of Vichy."]

Vichy water. 1. A naturally effervescent mineral water from the springs at Vichy, France, reputed to have medicinal benefits. **2.** A sparkling mineral water resembling this. Also called "Vichy," "vichy."

vic·i·nage (vĭs′ə-nĭj) *n.* **1. a.** A limited region around a particular area; neighborhood; vicinity. **b.** A number of places situated near each other taken collectively. **2.** The residents of a particular neighborhood. **3.** The state of living in a neighborhood; proximity; nearness. [Middle English *vesinage*, from Old French *visenage*, from Vulgar Latin *vīcīnāticum* (unattested), from *vīcīnus*, neighbor. See **vicinity**.]

vic·i·nal (vĭs′ə-nəl) *adj.* **1.** Of, belonging to, or restricted to a limited area or neighborhood; nearby; adjacent. **2.** Designating a local road as opposed to a highway. **3.** *Crystallography.* Approximating, resembling, or taking the place of a fundamental form or face. **4.** *Chemistry.* Designating the consecutive positions of substituted elements or radicals on a benzene ring. [Latin *vīcīnālis*, from *vīcīnus*, neighbor. See **vicinity**.]

vi·cin·i·ty (vī-sĭn′ə-tē) *n., pl.* **-ties.** *Abbr.* **vic. 1.** The state of being near in space or relationship; proximity; propinquity: *two restaurants in close vicinity.* **2.** A nearby, surrounding, or adjoining region; neighborhood; locality. [Latin *vīcīnitās*, from *vīcīnus*, neighbor, from *vīcus*, village. See **weik-**¹ in Appendix.*]

vi·cious (vĭsh′əs) *adj.* **1.** Having the nature of vice, evil, or immorality; depraved; debased. **2.** Addicted to vice, immorality, or depravity; malicious; reprobate; evil. **3.** Characterized by spite or malice: *vicious gossip.* **4.** Failing to meet a standard or criterion; having a fault, flaw, or defect: *a vicious syllogism.* **5.** Impure; foul; diseased. **6.** Disposed to or characterized by violence or destructive behavior. **7.** Behaving in an unruly or potentially dangerous manner: *a vicious animal.* **8.** Being of an extreme or intense degree: *a vicious hurricane.* —See Synonyms at **cruel.** [Middle English, from Old French, from Latin *vitiōsus*, from *vitium*, VICE.] —**vi′cious·ly** *adv.* —**vi′cious·ness** *n.*

vicious circle. 1. A situation in which the solution of one problem in a chain of circumstances creates a new problem, and increases the difficulty of solving the original problem. **2.** A

viburnum
Viburnum carlesii

viceroy

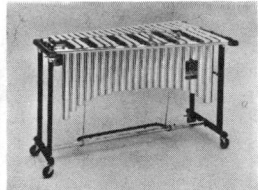

vibraphone

ă pat/ā pay/âr care/ä father/b bib/ch church/d deed/ĕ pet/ē be/f fife/g gag/h hat/hw which/ĭ pit/ī pie/îr pier/j judge/k kick/l lid, needle/m mum/n no, sudden/ng thing/ŏ pot/ō toe/ô paw, for/oi noise/ou out/o͞o took/o͞o boot/p pop/r roar/s sauce/sh ship, dish/t tight/th thin, path/th this, bathe/ŭ cut/ûr urge/v valve/w with/y yes/z zebra, size/zh vision/ə about, item, edible, gallop, circus/ä Fr. ami/œ Fr. feu, Ger. schön/ü Fr. tu, Ger. über/KH Ger. ich, Scot. loch/N Fr. bon. *Follows main vocabulary. †Of obscure origin.

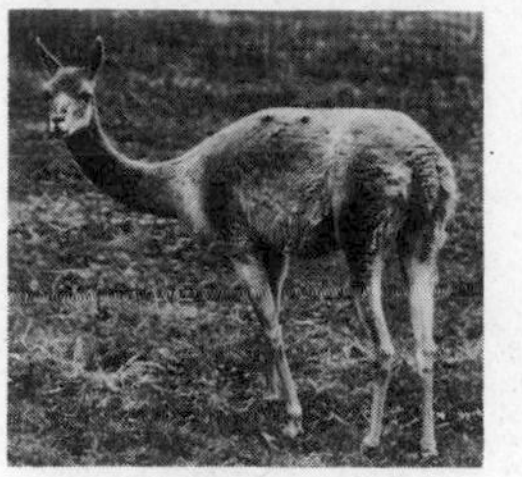
vicuña

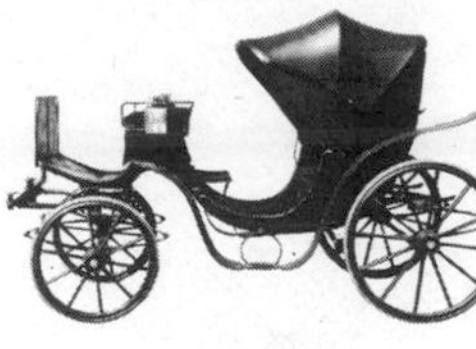
victoria
Carriage built
about 1905

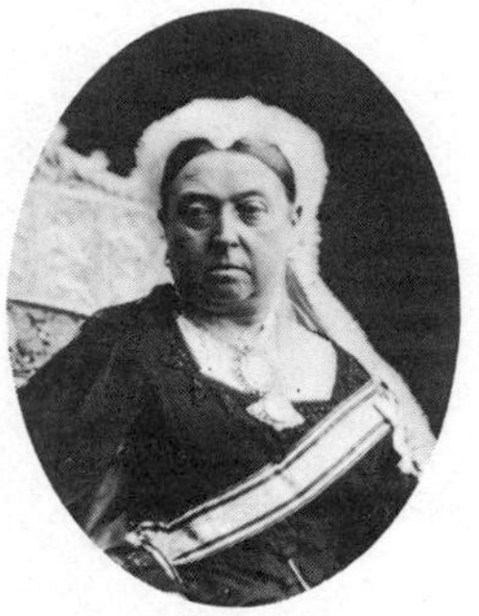
Victoria[1]
Photographed in 1876

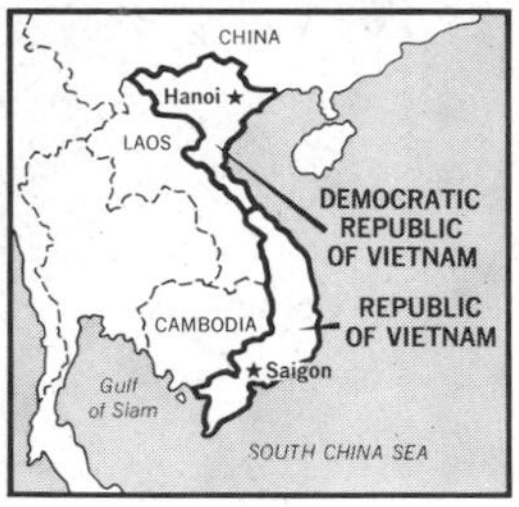

Vietnam

condition in which a disorder or disease gives rise to another which subsequently affects the first. **3.** *Logic.* A **circle** *(see).*

vi·cis·si·tude (vĭ-sĭs′ə-to͞od′, -tyo͞od′) *n.* **1.** *Usually plural.* Any change or variation in something; mutability. **2.** Natural change or variation; alterations manifested in nature and human affairs. **3. a.** An alteration or variation in fortune. **b.** An alternating change; a succession. [Old French, from Latin *vicissitūdō,* from *vicissim,* in turn, from *vicis,* change, turn. See **weik-**[4] in Appendix.*]

vi·cis·si·tu·di·nar·y (vĭ-sĭs′ə-to͞od′n-ĕr′ē, -tyo͞od′n-ĕr′ē) *adj.* Also **vi·cis·si·tu·di·nous** (-əs). Characterized by or subject to vicissitudes.

Vicks·burg (vĭks′bûrg). A city of Mississippi, in the west at the confluence of the Yazoo and Mississippi rivers; captured by Union forces in the Civil War (1863). Population, 29,000.

vic·tim (vĭk′tĭm) *n.* **1.** Someone who is put to death or subjected to torture or suffering by another. **2.** A living creature slain and offered as a sacrifice to a deity or as part of a religious rite. **3.** One who is harmed by or made to suffer from an act, circumstance, agency, or condition: *victims of war.* **4.** A person who suffers injury, loss, or death as a result of a voluntary undertaking: *a victim of his own scheming.* **5.** A person who is tricked, swindled, or taken advantage of; a dupe. [Latin *victima.* See **weik-**[2] in Appendix.*]

vic·tim·ize (vĭk′tə-mīz′) *tr.v.* **-ized, -izing, -izes. 1.** To subject to swindle or fraud; to cause discomfort and suffering to. **2.** To make a victim of by or as if by slaying. —**vic′tim·i·za′tion** *n.* —**vic′tim·iz′er** *n.*

vic·tor (vĭk′tər) *n.* **1.** One who defeats or vanquishes an adversary; the winner in a fight, battle, or war. **2.** A winner of a contest or struggle. [Middle English, from Latin, from *vincere* (past participle *victus*), to conquer. See **weik-**[5] in Appendix.*]

Vic·tor Em·man·u·el II (vĭk′tər ĭ-măn′yo͞o-əl). 1820–1878. First king of Italy (1861–78).

vic·to·ri·a (vĭk-tôr′ē-ə, -tōr′ē-ə) *n.* **1.** A low, light four-wheeled carriage for two with a folding top and an elevated driver's seat in front. **2.** A touring car with a folding top usually covering only the rear seat. [After Queen VICTORIA.]

Vic·to·ri·a[1] (vĭk-tôr′ē-ə, -tōr′ē-ə). In full, Victoria Alexandrina. 1819–1901. Queen of the United Kingdom of Great Britain and Ireland (1837–1901); Empress of India (1876–1901).

Vic·to·ri·a[2] (vĭk-tôr′ē-ə, -tōr′ē-ə). **1.** A state of southeastern Australia occupying 87,884 square miles. Population, 2,930,000. Capital, Melbourne. **2.** The capital of British Columbia, a seaport on the southern tip of Vancouver Island. Population, 55,000. **3.** The capital of Hong Kong, a port on the island of Hong Kong. Population, 1,005,000 (metropolitan area).

Vic·to·ri·a, Lake (vĭk-tôr′ē-ə, -tōr′ē-ə). Also **Victoria Ny·an·za** (nī-ăn′zə, nyăn′zä). The largest lake in Africa, occupying 26,828 square miles in the east-central part of the continent and bordered by Uganda, Kenya, and Tanzania.

Vic·to·ri·a, Mount (vĭk-tôr′ē-ə, -tōr′ē-ə). **1.** The highest elevation (10,018 feet) of the Chin Hills in northwestern Burma. **2.** The highest elevation (13,240 feet) of the Owen Stanley Range, Papua, New Guinea.

Victoria Cross. *Abbr.* **V.C.** A bronze Maltese cross, Britain's highest military award for conspicuous valor.

Vic·to·ri·a Falls (vĭk-tôr′ē-ə, -tōr′ē-ə). A waterfall on the Zambezi river in southeastern Africa, extending over a mile between Zambia and Rhodesia and having a drop of about 400 feet; discovered by Livingston (1855).

Vic·to·ri·a Island (vĭk-tôr′ē-ə, -tōr′ē-ə). An island, 80,340 square miles in area, of the Northwest Territories, Canada, lying in the Arctic Ocean.

Vic·to·ri·a Land (vĭk-tôr′ē-ə, -tōr′ē-ə). A section of Antarctica south of New Zealand and largely in the Ross Dependency.

Vic·to·ri·an (vĭk-tôr′ē-ən, -tōr′ē-ən) *adj.* **1.** Pertaining or belonging to the period of Queen Victoria's reign: *a Victorian novel.* **2.** Exhibiting qualities usually associated with the time of Queen Victoria, as moral severity or hypocrisy, middle-class stuffiness, and pompous conservatism. **3.** Being in the highly ornamented, massive style of architecture, decor, and furnishings popular in 19th-century England. —*n.* A person belonging to or exhibiting characteristics typical of the period of Queen Victoria.

Vic·to·ri·a Nile. See **Nile.**

Vic·to·ri·an·ism (vĭk-tôr′ē-ə-nĭz′əm, vĭk-tōr′-) *n.* **1.** The state of exhibiting Victorian characteristics, as in attitude, style, or taste. **2.** Something exhibiting Victorian characteristics.

Vic·to·ri·a River (vĭk-tôr′ē-ə, -tōr′ē-ə). A river of Australia, rising in the northwestern Northern Territory and flowing 240 miles northeast and then northwest to the Timor Sea.

vic·to·ri·ous (vĭk-tôr′ē-əs, -tōr′ē-əs) *adj.* **1.** Having overcome an enemy; triumphant; conquering. **2.** Characteristic of or expressing a sense of victory or fulfillment: *a victorious smile.* [Middle English, from Latin *victōriōsus,* from *victōria,* VICTORY.] —**vic·to′ri·ous·ly** *adv.* —**vic·to′ri·ous·ness** *n.*

vic·to·ry (vĭk′tə-rē) *n., pl.* **-ries.** *Abbr.* **V 1.** Final and complete defeat of the enemy in a military engagement. **2.** Any successful struggle against an opponent or obstacle. **3.** The state of having triumphed. [Middle English, from Old French *victorie,* from Latin *victōria,* from *victor,* VICTOR.]

Synonyms: *victory, conquest, triumph.* These nouns refer to the fact of winning, as in war or in a competition. *Victory,* the general term, is broadly interchangeable with the others but lacks their overtones. *Conquest* connotes physically subjugating or harnessing something, such as an enemy nation or a rampaging river, or it can refer to surmounting (a mountain peak) or overcoming barriers to knowledge, understanding, and control: *conquest of yellow fever. Triumph* refers to a victory or success that is especially noteworthy because it is decisive, significant, or spectacular.

Victory Medal. A bronze medal awarded with the Victory Ribbon to anyone who served in the armed forces of the United States during World War I or World War II.

vic·tress (vĭk′trĭs) *n.* A female victor.

Vic·tro·la (vĭk-trō′lə) *n.* A trademark for a phonograph.

vict·ual (vĭt′l) *n.* Also *nonstandard* **vit·tle. 1.** Food fit for human consumption. **2.** *Usually plural.* Provisions; food supplies. —*v.* **victualed** or **-ualled, -ualing** or **-ualling, -uals.** Also *nonstandard* **vit·tle, -tled, -tling, -tles.** —*tr.* To provide with food. —*intr.* **1.** To lay in food supplies. **2.** *Rare.* To eat. [Middle English *vitaille,* from Old French, from Late Latin *victūālia,* plural of *victūālis,* provision, from Latin *vīctus,* sustenance, from the past participle of *vīvere,* to live. See **gwei-** in Appendix.*]

vict·ual·er (vĭt′l-ər) *n.* Also **vict·ual·ler. 1.** A supplier of victuals; a sutler. **2.** A supply ship. **3.** *Chiefly British.* An innkeeper.

vi·cu·ña (və-ko͞on′yə, -ko͞o′nə, -kyo͞o′nə, vī-) *n.* Also **vi·cu·na. 1.** A llamalike ruminant mammal, *Vicugna vicugna,* of the central Andes, having fine, silky fleece. **2. a.** The fleece of this animal. **b.** Fabric made from this fleece. [Spanish, from Quechua *wikuña.*]

vi·de (vī′dē) *v. Abbr.* **v., vid.** See. Used to direct a reader's attention; for example, *vide page 64.* [Latin *vidē,* imperative of *vidēre,* to see. See **weid-** in Appendix.*]

vi·de an·te (vī′dē ăn′tē). *Latin.* See before.

vi·de in·fra (vī′dē ĭn′frə). *Abbr.* **v.i.** *Latin.* See below.

vi·de·li·cet (vĭ-dĕl′ə-sĭt) *adv. Abbr.* **viz.** That is; namely. Used to introduce examples, lists, or items. [Latin *vidēlicet,* it is easy (literally, permissible) to see, plainly, namely : *vidēre,* to see (see **vide**) + *licet,* it is permitted, from *licēre,* to be permitted. See **leisure.**]

vid·e·o (vĭd′ē-ō′) *adj.* Of or pertaining to television, especially to televised images. —*n.* **1.** The visual portion of a televised broadcast, as distinguished from **audio** *(see).* **2.** Television: *a star of stage, screen, and video.* [From Latin *vidēre,* to see. See **vide.**]

vid·e·o·gen·ic (vĭd′ē-ō-jĕn′ĭk) *adj.* Appearing to advantage on television; telegenic. [VIDEO + (PHOTO)GENIC.]

video tape. A relatively wide **magnetic tape** *(see)* used to record television images, usually together with the associated sound, for subsequent playback and broadcasting.

vi·de post (vī′dē pōst′). *Latin.* See below; see after.

vi·de su·pra (vī′dē so͞o′prə). *Abbr.* **v.s.** *Latin.* See above.

vi·dette. Variant of **vedette.**

vid·i·con (vĭd′ə-kŏn′) *n.* A small television camera tube that forms a charge-density image on a photoconductive surface for subsequent electron-beam scanning. [VID(EO) + ICON(OSCOPE).]

vie (vī) *v.* **vied, vying, vies.** —*intr.* To strive for victory or superiority; contend; compete, as in an athletic contest. Used with *for* or *with.* —*tr.* **1.** To offer in competition; to match. **2.** To wager; to bet. —See Synonyms at **rival.** [Shortened from Middle English *envien,* from Old French *envier,* to challenge, bid, from Latin *invītāre,* INVITE.]

VIE Airport code for Vienna, Austria.

Vi·en·na (vē-ĕn′ə). *German* **Wien** (vēn). The capital of Austria, in the northeast on the Danube. Population, 1,628,000.

Vienna sausage. A small sausage resembling a frankfurter, often served as an hors d'oeuvre.

Vi·en·nese (vē′ə-nēz′, -nēs′) *adj.* Of the city of Vienna. —*n., pl.* **Viennese.** An inhabitant or native of Vienna.

Vien·tiane (vyăN-tyăn′). The administrative capital of Laos, in the northwest on the Mekong River. Population, 100,000.

Vie·ques Island (vyā′kās′). An island of Puerto Rico, 51 square miles in area, lying nine miles southeast of the main island. Also called "Crab Island."

Vi·et·cong (vē-ĕt′kŏng′, vyĕt′-) *n., pl.* **Vietcong.** Also **Vi·et Cong.** *Abbr.* **V.C. 1.** A Vietnamese belonging to or supporting the National Liberation Front of South Vietnam. **2.** The Front itself; especially, its armed forces. —*adj.* Of or pertaining to the Vietcong. [Short for Vietnamese *Viet Nam Cong Sam,* Vietnamese Communist : VIETNAM + *Cong Sam,* Communism, Communist, from Mandarin Chinese *kung*[4] *ch'an*[3] : *kung*[4], to share + *ch'an*[3], property.]

Vi·et·minh (vē-ĕt′mĭn′, vyĕt′-) *n., pl.* **Vietminh.** Also **Vi·et Minh. 1.** The Vietnamese league for national independence formed by an alliance of patriotic and revolutionary forces under the leadership of Ho Chi Minh that defeated the Japanese and the French between 1941 and 1954. **2.** A member or members of this front, especially of its armed forces. —*adj.* Of or pertaining to the Vietminh. [Vietnamese, short for *Viet Nam Doc Lap Dong Minh Hoi,* Vietnam Federation of Independence : VIETNAM + *doc lap,* independence + *dong minh,* federation, pact + *hoi,* association (corresponding to Mandarin Chinese *tu*[2] *li*[4] *t'ung*[2] *mêng*[2] *hui*[4]), respectively from Ancient Chinese *duk,* alone + *liəp,* to stand + *d'ung,* together + *miwang,* pact, federation + *ẏwâi,* association.]

Viet·nam (vē-ĕt′näm′, -năm′, vyĕt′-). Also **Viet Nam.** A country on the eastern coast of the Southeast Asia peninsula, divided since 1954 into two political entities: the Democratic Republic of Vietnam (unofficially, North Vietnam), 63,344 square miles in area, with a population of 15,917,000 and its capital at Hanoi; and the Republic of Vietnam (unofficially, South Vietnam), 66,263 square miles in area, with a population of 14,200,000 and its capital at Saigon. [Vietnamese, from Ancient Chinese *ywet nam* (Mandarin Chinese *yüeh⁴ nan²*), "(territory) south of Yüeh" : *ywet*, Yüeh, an area in southern China identified with the provinces of Kwangtung, Fukien, Chekiang, and Kiangsi + *nam*, south.]

Vi·et·nam·ese (vē-ĕt'nə-mēz', -mēs', vyĕt'-) *n.* **1.** A native or inhabitant of Vietnam. **2.** The language of Vietnam, commonly considered as belonging to the Mon-Khmer subfamily of Austro-Asiatic languages and including Tonkinese and Cochin Chinese dialects. Formerly called "Annamese."

Viet·nik (vĕt'nĭk, vē-ĕt'-, vyĕt'-) *n. Slang.* An American actively opposed to the U.S. intervention in Vietnam during the years following 1954. Used derogatorily. [VIET(NAM) + (BEAT)NIK.]

view (vyo͞o) *n.* **1.** An examination or inspection. **2.** A systematic survey; coverage. **3.** *Often plural.* A specific perception, observation, or interpretation; a thought: *Her views on the situation are likely to be of no special help.* **4.** *Often plural.* A personal opinion. **5.** The field of vision. **6. a.** A prospect or vista. **b.** Visual access or vantage: *a room with a view.* **c.** A picture of a landscape. **d.** An aspect, as of something seen from a given vantage point. **7.** An aim; intention. **8.** Expectation; chance: *The measure has no view of success.* —See Synonyms at **opinion.** —**in view of.** Taking into account; in consideration of. —**on view.** Being exhibited; placed so as to be seen. —**with a view to.** With the intention or hope of. —*tr.v.* **viewed, viewing, views. 1.** To see; behold; be present at a showing of. **2. a.** To examine; inspect. **b.** To survey or study mentally; consider. —See Synonyms at **see.** [Middle English *vewe*, from Old French *veue*, from the feminine past participle of *veoir*, to see, from Latin *vidēre*. See **weid-** in Appendix.*]

view·er (vyo͞o'ər) *n.* **1.** One who views. **2.** Any of various optical devices used to facilitate the viewing of photographic transparencies by illuminating or magnifying them.

view finder. *Photography.* A **finder** *(see).*

view hal·loo (hŏl'ər *for sense 1;* hə-lo͞o', hŏl'ər *for sense 2*). Also **view hal·loa. 1.** A strident call given during a fox hunt by a servant or a follower to inform the huntsman that a fox has been viewed. **2.** A loud cry or clarion call announcing a sudden appearance or advent: *"Old Gabriel's/ Final view halloo"* (Ormonde de Kay, Jr.).

view·less (vyo͞o'lĭs) *adj. Poetic.* Invisible.

view·point (vyo͞o'point') *n.* A point of view.

Usage: *Viewpoint,* although well established, is considered inferior to *point of view* by some writers and grammarians. *Viewpoint* is acceptable on a formal level to 76 per cent of the Usage Panel.

view·y (vyo͞o'ē) *adj.* **-ier, -iest. 1.** Exhibiting extravagant or visionary opinions. **2.** Showy.

vi·ges·i·mal (vī-jĕs'ə-məl) *adj.* **1.** Twentieth. **2.** Proceeding or occurring in intervals of 20. **3.** Based on or pertaining to 20. [From Latin *vīgēsimus, vīcēsimus,* twentieth, from *vīcēnī,* twenty each, from *vīgintī,* twenty. See **wīkmtī** in Appendix.*]

vig·il (vĭj'əl) *n.* **1.** A watch kept during normal sleeping hours. **2.** The eve of a religious festival as observed by devotional watching. **3.** *Usually plural.* Ritual devotions observed on the eve of a holy day. [Middle English *vigile,* from Old French, from Latin *vigilia,* from *vigil,* alert. See **weg-²** in Appendix.*]

vig·i·lance (vĭj'ə-ləns) *n.* The state or quality of being vigilant; watchfulness: *"the cold vigilance of a sentry whose rounds are not without apprehension"* (Djuna Barnes).

vigilance committee. In the 19th-century South and West, an informal council exercising police power for the capture, speedy trial, and summary punishment of criminal offenders, and later for joint action with the police in labor disputes.

vig·i·lant (vĭj'ə-lənt) *adj.* On the alert; watchful. See Synonyms at **aware.** [Middle English, from Old French, from Latin *vigilāns,* present participle of *vigilāre,* to be alert, from *vigil,* alert. See **weg-²** in Appendix.*]

vig·i·lan·te (vĭj'ə-lăn'tē) *n.* One belonging to a vigilance committee. [Spanish, from Latin *vigilāns,* VIGILANT.]

vigil light. 1. A small candle kept burning in the chancel of Christian churches to symbolize the presence of the Holy Sacrament; altar light. **2.** A candle lighted by a worshiper for a special devotional purpose. **3.** Any light or candle kept burning at a shrine.

vi·gnette (vĭn-yĕt') *n.* **1. a.** An unenclosed decorative design placed at the beginning or end of a book or a chapter of a book. **b.** Decorative tracery along the border of a page. **2.** An unbordered portrait that shades off into the surrounding color at the edges. **3.** A literary sketch having the intimate charm and subtlety attributed to vignette portraits: *"nobody . . . has given us a more robust, more tenderly destructive vignette"* (Kenneth Tynan). —*tr.v.* **vignetted, -gnetting, -gnettes.** To soften the edges of (a picture) in vignette style. [French, from Old French, "young vine," diminutive of *vigne,* VINE.]

vi·gnet·ter (vĭn-yĕt'ər) *n.* Also **vi·gnet·tist** (-ĭst) (for sense 2). **1.** A device used to print borderless illustrations and photographs. **2.** A person who makes or specializes in vignettes.

Vi·gny (vē-nyē'), Comte **Alfred de.** 1797–1863. French poet.

Vi·go (vē'gō). A city of Spain, a seaport in the northwest on the Atlantic. Population, 166,000.

vig·or (vĭg'ər) *n.* Also *chiefly British* **vig·our. 1. a.** Active physical or mental strength. **b.** The prime or height, as of life: *in the vigor of manhood.* **2.** The capacity for natural growth and survival, as of plants or animals. **3.** Expressive power or forcefulness, as of language. **4.** Legal effectiveness or validity. **5.** Energetic and rigorous exercise of power: *measures effected with vigor and resolution.* [Middle English *vigour,* from Old French, from Latin *vigor,* from *vigēre,* to be lively or vigorous. See **weg-²** in Appendix.*]

vi·go·ro·so (vē'gō-rō'sō) *adj. Music.* Vigorous; with emphasis and spirit. [Italian, from Medieval Latin *vigōrōsus,* from Latin *vigor,* VIGOR.]

vig·or·ous (vĭg'ər-əs) *adj.* **1.** Robust; hardy. **2.** Energetic; lively. —See Synonyms at **active, healthy.** —**vig'or·ous·ly** *adv.* —**vig'or·ous·ness** *n.*

Vii·pu·ri. The Finnish name for **Vyborg.**

Vi·ja·ya·va·da (vĭj'ə-yə-wä'də, -vä'də). Formerly **Bez·wa·da** (bĕz-wä'də). A city of India, in east-central Andhra Pradesh. Population, 253,000.

vi·king (vī'kĭng) *n.* Also **Vi·king.** One of the Scandinavian mariners whose pirate bands attacked and pillaged coastal settlements of northern and western Europe from the eighth through the tenth century. [Old Norse *víkingr*†.]

vil. village.

Vi·la (vē'lə). The capital of the New Hebrides, on Efate.

vi·la·yet (vē'lä-yĕt') *n.* An administrative division of Turkey. [Turkish *vilāyet,* from Arabic *wilāyah,* province, from *wālī,* governor.]

vile (vīl) *adj.* **viler, vilest. 1.** Miserably poor; wretched: *a vile existence.* **2.** Depraved; ignoble. **3.** Loathsome; disgusting: *vile language.* **4.** Unpleasant or objectionable: *vile weather.* **5.** Having an abominable taste; unpalatable: *vile food.* [Middle English *vyle,* from Old French *vil,* from Latin *vīlis*†.] —**vile'ly** *adv.* —**vile'ness** *n.*

vil·i·fy (vĭl'ə-fī') *tr.v.* **-fied, -fying, -fies.** To defame; denigrate. See Synonyms at **malign.** [Middle English *vilifien,* from Late Latin *vīlificāre* : Latin *vīlis,* VILE + *facere,* to make (see **dhē-¹** in Appendix*).] —**vil'i·fi·ca'tion** *n.* —**vil'i·fi'er** *n.*

vil·i·pend (vĭl'ə-pĕnd') *tr.v.* **-pended, -pending, -pends. 1.** To view or treat with contempt; despise. **2.** To disparage or abuse. [Middle English *vilipenden,* from Old French *vilipender,* from Latin *vilipendere* : *vīlis,* VILE + *pendere,* to weigh, consider (see **spen-** in Appendix*).]

vil·la (vĭl'ə) *n.* **1.** A country or resort residence. **2.** A Roman country estate with a substantial house. **3.** *Chiefly British.* A middle-class house in the suburbs. [Italian, from Latin *villa,* country home. See **weik-¹** in Appendix.*]

Vil·la (vē'yä), **Francisco ("Pancho").** Original name, Doroteo Arango. 1877–1923. Mexican revolutionary leader.

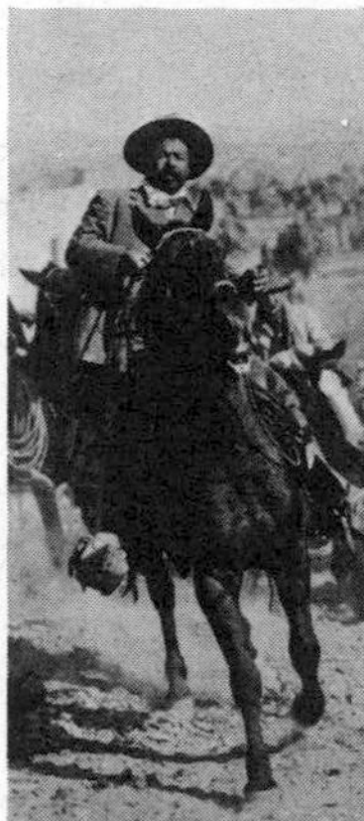

"Pancho" Villa

vil·lage (vĭl'ĭj) *n. Abbr.* **v., V., vil. 1.** A small group of dwellings in a rural area, usually ranking in size between a hamlet and a town. **2.** In some U.S. states, an incorporated community smaller in population than a town. **3.** The inhabitants of a village; villagers. —*adj.* **1.** Of or pertaining to a village. **2.** Characteristic of villages; rustic. [Middle English, from Old French, from *ville,* village, farm, from Latin *vīlla,* VILLA.]

vil·lag·er (vĭl'ĭ-jər) *n.* An inhabitant of a village.

Vi·lla·her·mo·sa (vē'yä-ĕr-mō'sä). The capital of Tabasco, Mexico, in the north-central part of the state. Population, 52,000.

vil·lain (vĭl'ən) *n.* **1.** A depraved, base-minded scoundrel. **2.** A dramatic or fictional character who is typically at cross-purposes with the hero. **3.** *Obsolete.* A vile, brutish peasant. **4.** Variant of **villein.** [Middle English *vilain,* from Old French, originally "feudal serf," from Medieval Latin *villānus,* from Latin *villa,* country house. See **weik-¹** in Appendix.*]

vil·lain·ess (vĭl'ə-nĭs) *n.* A female villain.

vil·lain·ous (vĭl'ə-nəs) *adj.* **1.** Viciously wicked or criminal. **2.** Obnoxious. —**vil'lain·ous·ly** *adv.* —**vil'lain·ous·ness** *n.*

vil·lain·y (vĭl'ə-nē) *n., pl.* **-ies. 1.** Viciousness of conduct or action. **2.** Baseness of mind or character: *"The next transition of his soul was to exquisite villainy."* (Horace Walpole). **3.** A treacherous or vicious act.

Vil·la-Lo·bos (vē'lə-lō'bo͝osh, -bo͞os), **Heitor.** 1887–1959. Brazilian composer.

vil·la·nelle (vĭl'ə-nĕl') *n.* A 19-line poem of fixed form consisting of five tercets and a final quatrain on two rhymes, with the first and third lines of the first tercet repeated alternately as a refrain closing the succeeding stanzas and joined as the final couplet of the quatrain. [French, from Italian *villanella,* an old rustic Italian song, from *villanello,* rustic, from *villano,* peasant, from Medieval Latin *villānus.* See **villain.**]

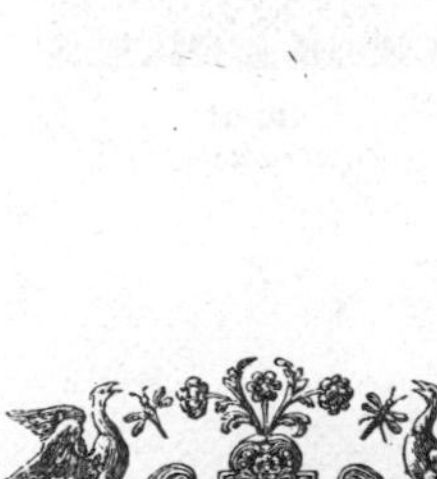

vignette

vil·lat·ic (vĭ-lăt'ĭk) *adj.* Rustic; rural. [Latin *villāticus,* from *villa,* VILLA.]

vil·lein (vĭl'ən) *n.* Also **vil·lain.** One of a class of feudal serfs who held the legal status of freemen in their dealings with all persons except their lord. [Middle English *villein,* variant of *vilain,* VILLAIN.]

vil·lein·age (vĭl'ə-nĭj) *n.* Also **vil·lain·age. 1.** The legal status or condition of a villein. **2.** The legal tenure by which a villein held his land. Also called "bondage."

Vil·liers, George. See **Buckingham.**

vil·li·form (vĭl'ə-fôrm') *adj.* Having the form of a villus or the appearance of villi.

Vil·lon (vē-yôɴ'), **François.** 1431–1463? French poet.

vil·los·i·ty (vĭ-lŏs'ə-tē) *n., pl.* **-ties. 1.** The condition of being villous. **2.** A villous surface or coating. **3.** A villus.

vil·lous (vĭl'əs) *adj.* Also **vil·lose** (-ōs'). **1.** Of, pertaining to, resembling, or covered with villi. **2.** *Botany.* Covered with fine, unmatted hairs. [Middle English, from Latin *villōsus,* from *villus,* shaggy hair, VILLUS.] —**vil'lous·ly** *adv.*

vil·lus (vĭl'əs) *n., pl.* **villi** (vĭl'ī'). **1.** *Anatomy.* Any minute projection arising from a mucous membrane. **2.** *Botany.* A fine, hairlike epidermal outgrowth. [Latin, shaggy hair. See **wel-⁵** in Appendix.*]

Vil·ni·us (vĭl'nē-əs, vēl'-). Also **Vil·na** (vĭl'nə, vēl'-). The capital of Lithuania, in the southeastern part of the republic. Population, 271,000.

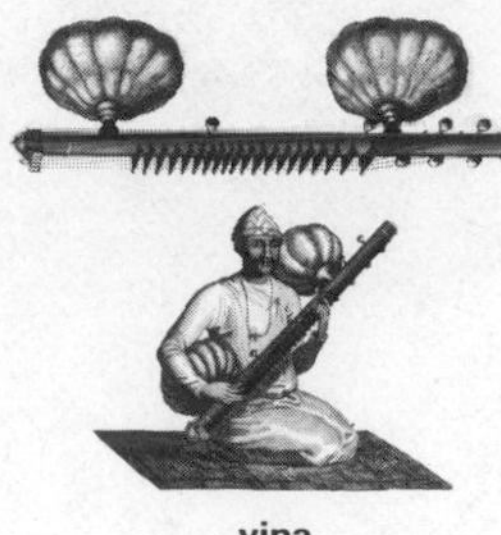

vina

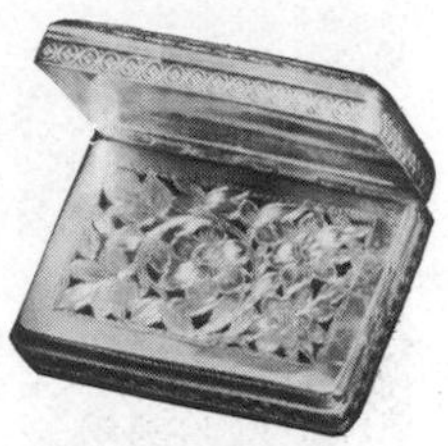

vinaigrette

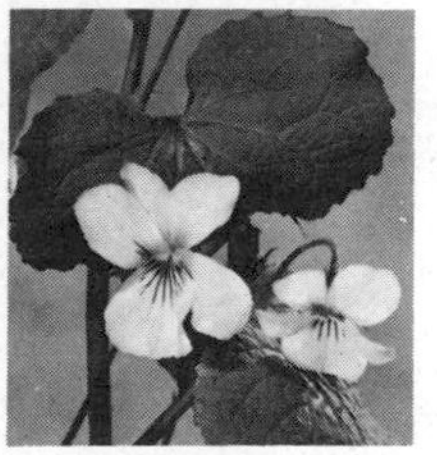

violet
Viola canadensis

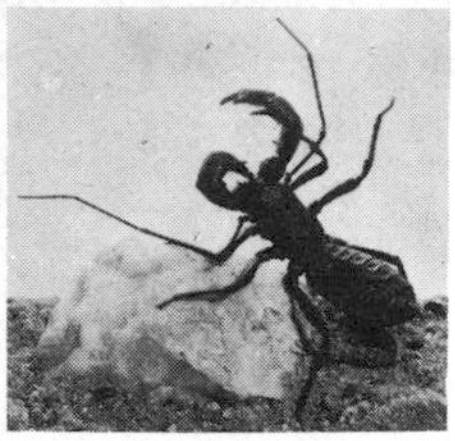

vinegarroon

Vi·lyui (vĭl′yo͞o′ē). A river of the Soviet Union, rising in central Siberia and flowing 1,512 miles generally east to the Lena.
vim (vĭm) *n.* Ebullient vitality and energy. [Latin *vim,* accusative of *vīs,* power. See **wei-**[5] in Appendix.*]
Vim·i·nal (vĭm′ə-nəl). One of the Seven Hills of Rome. [Latin *Vīminālis (collis),* "(hill) of osiers" (from the willow copse on the hill), from *vīmen,* osier. See **wei-**[1] in Appendix.*]
vi·na (vē′nä) *n.* A stringed musical instrument of India that has a long, fretted finger board with resonating gourds at each end. [Hindi *vīṇā,* from Sanskrit *vīṇāh*†.]
vi·na·ceous (vī-nā′shəs) *adj.* Having the color of red wine; wine-colored. [Latin *vīnāceus,* of wine, from *vīnum,* wine. See **vīnum** in Appendix.*]
Vi·ña del Mar (vē′nyä *th*ĕl mär′). A city and seaside resort in west-central Chile. Population, 136,000.
vin·ai·grette (vĭn′ə-grĕt′) *n.* **1.** A small decorative bottle or container with a perforated top, used for holding an aromatic restorative, such as smelling salts. **2.** Vinaigrette sauce. [French, from Old French *vinaigre,* VINEGAR.]
vinaigrette sauce. A cold sauce or dressing made of vinegar and oil flavored with finely chopped onions, herbs, and other seasonings.
vi·nasse (vĭ-năs′) *n.* The residue left in a still after the process of distillation. [French, from Latin *vīnācea,* feminine of *vīnāceus,* of wine, VINACEOUS.]
Vin·cennes (văN-sĕn′ *for sense 1;* vĭn-sĕnz′ *for sense 2*). **1.** A city in north-central France, near Paris; a former royal residence. Population, 50,000. **2.** A city of Indiana, on the Wabash in the southwest; the capital of the Indiana Territory (1800–13). Population, 18,000.
Vin·cent (vĭn′sənt). A masculine given name. [Middle English, from Latin *Vincentius,* from *vincēns,* present participle of *vincere,* to conquer. See **weik-**[5] in Appendix.*]
Vin·cent de Paul (vĭn′sənt də pôl′), **Saint.** 1581?–1660. French priest and author; founded two Roman Catholic orders.
Vincent's disease. *Pathology.* **Trench mouth** *(see).* Also called "Vincent's infection." [Discovered by Jean Hyacinthe *Vincent* (1862–1950), French physician.]
Vin·ci, Leonardo da. See **Leonardo da Vinci.**
vin·ci·ble (vĭn′sə-bəl) *adj. Rare.* Capable of being overcome or defeated. [Latin *vincibilis,* from *vincere,* to conquer. See **weik-**[5] in Appendix.*] —**vin′ci·bil′i·ty** *n.*
vin·cu·lum (vĭng′kyə-ləm) *n., pl.* **-la** (-lə). **1.** *Mathematics.* A bar drawn over two or more algebraic terms to indicate that they are to be treated as a single term. See table at **symbol. 2.** *Anatomy.* A ligament that limits the movement of an organ or part. **3.** A bond or tie. [Latin, band, cord, from *vincīre*†, to tie.]
Vind·hya Pra·desh (vĭn′dyə prə-dāsh′). A former state of India, now part of Madhya Pradesh, Republic of India.
vin·di·ca·ble (vĭn′dĭ-kə-bəl) *adj.* Justifiable.
vin·di·cate (vĭn′dĭ-kāt′) *tr.v.* **-cated, -cating, -cates. 1.** To clear of accusation, blame, suspicion, or doubt with supporting arguments or proof. **2.** To justify or support: *vindicate one's claim.* **3.** To justify or prove the worth of, especially in light of later developments. [Latin *vindicāre,* to claim, defend, revenge, from *vindex,* claimant, defender, avenger. See **deik-** in Appendix.*] —**vin′di·ca′tor** (-kā′tər) *n.*
vin·di·ca·tion (vĭn′dĭ-kā′shən) *n.* **1.** The act or condition of being vindicated. **2.** The evidence, argument, event, or the like, that serves to justify a claim or deed.
vin·di·ca·to·ry (vĭn′dĭ-kə-tôr′ē, -tōr′ē) *adj.* **1.** Vindicating; justifying. **2.** Exacting retribution; punitive.
vin·dic·tive (vĭn-dĭk′tĭv) *adj.* **1.** Disposed to seek revenge; revengeful. **2.** Unforgiving; bitter; spiteful. [From Latin *vindicta,* vengeance, from *vindicāre,* to revenge, VINDICATE.] —**vin·dic′tive·ly** *adv.* —**vin·dic′tive·ness** *n.*
Synonyms: *vindictive, spiteful, vengeful, revengeful.* These adjectives describe the attitudes and, in some cases, the actions of persons filled with ill will, usually as a result of the infliction on them of a real or imagined wrong. *Vindictive* and *spiteful* both imply abundance of rancor and resentment and disposition to do harm, but *vindictive* is more specific in its suggestion of desire for revenge. *Vengeful* and *revengeful* can refer both to the attitude of one seeking to pay back another and to an act that effects such a desire.
vine (vīn) *n.* **1.** Any plant having a flexible stem supported by climbing, twining, or creeping along a surface. **2.** The stem of such a plant. **3. a.** A grapevine. **b.** Grapevines collectively: *products of the vine.* [Middle English, from Old French *vine, vigne,* from Latin *vīnea,* from the feminine of *vīneus,* of wine, from *vīnum,* wine. See **vīnum** in Appendix.*]
vine·dress·er (vīn′drĕs′ər) *n.* A person who cultivates grapevines.
vin·e·gar (vĭn′ĭ-gər) *n.* An impure dilute solution of acetic acid obtained by fermentation beyond the alcohol stage and used as a condiment and preservative. [Middle English *vinegre,* from Old French *vinaigre, vyn egre* : *vin,* wine, from Latin *vīnum* (see **vīnum** in Appendix*) + *aigre,* sour, from Latin *acer,* sharp (see **ak-** in Appendix*).]
vinegar eel. A small nematode worm, *Anguillula aceti,* that feeds on the organisms that cause fermentation in vinegar. Also called "eelworm," "vinegar worm."
vin·e·gar·roon (vĭn′ĭ-gə-ro͞on′) *n.* Also **vin·e·ga·rone** (-rōn′). A large, nonvenomous scorpionlike arachnid, *Mastigoproctus giganteus,* of the southern United States and Mexico, that emits a strong odor of vinegar when disturbed. [Mexican Spanish *vinagrón,* augmentative of Spanish *vinagre,* vinegar, from Old French *vinaigre.* See **vinegar.**]
vin·e·gar·y (vĭn′ĭ-gə-rē) *adj.* Also **vin·e·gar·ish** (-gər-ĭsh). **1.** Having the nature of vinegar; sour; acid: *a vinegary taste.* **2.** Sour in disposition or speech; crabbed.
vin·er·y (vī′nə-rē) *n., pl.* **-ies.** An area or greenhouse for growing vines.
vine·yard (vĭn′yərd) *n.* **1.** Ground planted with cultivated grapevines. **2.** *Informal.* A sphere of spiritual, mental, or physical endeavor.
vini-, vino-, vin-. Indicates wine; for example, **viniculture, vinometer, vinyl.** [From Latin *vīnum,* wine. See **vīnum** in Appendix.*]
vi·nic (vī′nĭk) *adj.* Of, contained in, or derived from wine. [From Latin *vīnum,* wine. See **vine.**]
vin·i·cul·ture (vĭn′ĭ-kŭl′chər, vī′nĭ-) *n.* The cultivation of grapes; viticulture. —**vin′i·cul′tur·al** *adj.* —**vin′i·cul′tur·ist** *n.*
Vin·land (vĭn′lənd). Also **Vine·land** (vīn′lənd). The name given to the area of northeastern North America, possibly Nova Scotia, visited by early Norse voyagers.
vi·no (vē′nō) *n., pl.* **-nos.** Wine. [Italian and Spanish, from Latin *vīnum,* wine. See **vine.**]
vi·nom·e·ter (vĭ-nŏm′ə-tər, vī-) *n.* A hydrometer used to determine the percentage of alcohol in a wine. [*Vino-,* variant of VINI- + -METER.]
vin or·di·naire (văN ôr-dē-nâr′) *pl.* **vins ordinaires** (văN ôr-dē-nâr′). *French.* An ordinary inexpensive red wine; table wine.
vi·nous (vī′nəs) *adj.* **1.** Of or pertaining to wine or its consumption: *"it was good to have a large vinous night"* (Anthony Burgess). **2.** Affected or caused by the consumption of wine: *vinous laughter.* **3.** Having the color of wine. [Latin *vinōsus,* from *vīnum,* wine. See **vine.**] —**vi·nos′i·ty** (vī-nŏs′ə-tē) *n.*
vin·tage (vĭn′tĭj) *n.* **1.** The yield of wine or grapes from a particular vineyard or district during one season. **2.** Wine, usually of high quality, identified as to year and vineyard or district of origin. Also called "vintage wine." **3.** The year in which or place where a particular wine was bottled. **4.** The harvesting of a grape crop or the initial stages of winemaking. **5.** *Informal.* **a.** Any group or collection of persons or things sharing certain characteristics. **b.** A year or period of origin: *a car of 1942 vintage.* —*adj.* **1.** Characterized by excellence, maturity, and enduring appeal; venerable; classic. **2.** Old or outmoded. [Middle English *vyntage,* variant (influenced by *vineter,* VINTNER) of *vendage,* from Old French, from Latin *vindēmia,* grape gathering : *vīnum,* wine (see **vine**) + *dēmere,* to take off : *dē-,* off + *emere,* to take (see **em-** in Appendix*).]
vin·tag·er (vĭn′tĭ-jər) *n.* A harvester of wine grapes.
vintage year. 1. The year in which a vintage wine is produced. **2.** Any year of outstanding achievement or success.
vint·ner (vĭnt′nər) *n.* A wine merchant. [Middle English *vineter,* from Old French *vinetier,* from Medieval Latin *vīnātārius,* from Latin *vīnētum,* vineyard, from *vīnum,* wine. See **vine.**]
vin·y (vī′nē) *adj.* **-ier, -iest. 1.** Of, pertaining to, or of the nature of a vine or vines. **2.** Overgrown with or abounding in vines.
vi·nyl (vī′nəl) *n.* **1.** The univalent chemical radical CH_2CH, derived from ethylene. **2.** Any of various compounds containing this group, typically highly reactive, easily polymerized, and used as basic materials for plastics. **3.** Any of various plastics, typically tough, flexible, and shiny, often used for coverings and clothing. [VIN(I)- + -YL.] —**vi′nyl** *adj.*
vi·ol (vī′əl) *n.* **1.** Any of a family of stringed instruments, chiefly of the 16th and 17th centuries, having a fretted fingerboard, usually six strings, a flat back, and played with a curved bow. **2.** A bass viol, **viola da gamba** *(see).* [Old French *viole,* from Old Provençal *viola,* VIOLA (instrument).]
vi·o·la[1] (vē-ō′lə, vī-) *n.* **1.** A stringed musical instrument of the violin family, slightly larger than a violin, tuned a fifth lower, and having a deeper, more sonorous tone; the tenor violin. **2.** An organ stop usually of eight-foot or four-foot pitch yielding stringlike tones. [Italian, from Old Provençal *viola, viula,* perhaps from *violar,* to play the viola (imitative).]
vi·o·la[2] (vī-ō′lə, vē-, vī′ə-lə) *n.* Any plant of the genus *Viola,* which includes the violets and pansies; especially, a variety having flowers resembling violets in size and shape and pansies in coloration. [New Latin *Viola,* from Latin *viola,* VIOLET.]
vi·o·la·ble (vī′ə-lə-bəl) *adj.* Capable of being violated or easily broken. —**vi′o·la·bil′i·ty, vi′o·la·ble·ness** *n.* —**vi′o·la·bly** *adv.*
vi·o·la·ceous (vī′ə-lā′shəs) *adj.* **1.** *Botany.* Of or belonging to the family Violaceae, which includes the violets. **2.** Having a violet color. [Latin *violāceus* : *viola,* VIOLET + -ACEOUS.]
vi·o·la da brac·cio (vē-ō′lə də brä′chō). A stringed instrument of the viol family with approximately the range of the viola. [Italian, "viola of the arm."]
vi·o·la da gam·ba (vē-ō′lə də gäm′bə). **1.** A stringed instrument, the bass of the viol family, with approximately the range of the cello. Also called "viol," "bass viol." **2.** An organ stop of eight-foot pitch yielding tones similar to those of the viola da gamba. [Italian, "viola of the leg."]
vi·o·la d'a·mo·re (vē-ō′lə dä-môr′ā). A stringed instrument, the tenor of the viol family, having six or seven stopped strings and an equal number of sympathetic strings that produce a characteristic silvery tone. [Italian, "viola of love."]
vi·o·late (vī′ə-lāt′) *tr.v.* **-lated, -lating, -lates. 1.** To break (a law or regulation, for example) intentionally or unintentionally; fail to keep; transgress; disregard: *violate a promise.* **2.** To injure the person or property of; especially, to rape. **3.** To do harm to (property or qualities considered sacred); to profane; desecrate. **4.** To disturb rudely or improperly; break in upon without right: *violate the peace.* [Middle English *violaten,* from Latin *violāre,* from *vīs,* force. See **wei-**[5] in Appendix.*] —**vi′o·la′tive** (-lā′tĭv) *adj.* —**vi′o·la′tor** (-lā′tər) *n.*
vi·o·la·tion (vī′ə-lā′shən) *n.* **1.** The act of violating or the con-

dition of being violated. **2.** An instance of violation; a transgression; desecration; infraction: *"dead men, troubled in their graves by the violation of their last wishes"* (Charlotte Brontë). —See Synonyms at **breach.**

vi·o·lence (vī′ə-ləns) *n.* **1.** Physical force exerted for the purpose of violating, damaging, or abusing: *"The essence of war is violence"* (Macaulay). **2.** An act or instance of violent action or behavior. **3.** Intensity or severity, as in natural phenomena; untamed force: *the violence of a hurricane.* **4.** The abusive or unjust exercise of power; an outrage; a wrong. **5.** Abuse or injury to meaning, content, or intent: *do violence to a text.* **6.** Vehemence of feeling or expression; fervor; fanaticism.

vi·o·lent (vī′ə-lənt) *adj.* **1.** Displaying or proceeding from extreme physical force or rough action. **2.** Exhibiting intense force or effect; extreme; severe: *violent contrast.* **3.** Caused by or displaying undue mental or emotional force: *"I'm always afraid of any kind of violence, even violent emotions"* (John Barth). **4.** Characterized by the immoderate use of force; severe; harsh. **5.** Caused by unexpected force or injury rather than by natural causes: *a violent death.* **6.** Tending to distort or injure meaning, phrasing, or intent: *violent editing.* [Middle English, from Old French, from Latin *violentus.* See **wei-**⁵ in Appendix.*] —**vi′o·lent·ly** *adv.*

vi·o·let (vī′ə-lĭt) *n.* **1.** Any of various low-growing plants of the genus *Viola,* having spurred, irregular flowers that are characteristically purplish-blue but sometimes yellow or white. **2.** Any of several similar plants, such as the **African violet** *(see).* **3.** Any of a group of colors, reddish blue in hue, that may vary in lightness and saturation; the hue of that portion of the spectrum that may be evoked in the normal observer by radiant energy of wavelengths approximately 420 nanometers. See **color. 4.** *Informal.* A **shrinking violet** *(see).* [Middle English, from Old French *violete,* diminutive of *viole,* from Latin *viola,* from the same Mediterranean origin as Greek *ion,* violet. See **iodine.**] —**vi′o·let** *adj.*

vi·o·lin (vī′ə-lĭn′) *n. Abbr.* **v. 1.** A stringed instrument played with a bow, having four strings tuned at intervals of a fifth, an unfretted fingerboard, and a shallower body than the viol, and capable of great flexibility in range, tone, and dynamics. Also informally called "fiddle." **2.** A violinist. [Italian *violino,* diminutive of *viola,* VIOLA (instrument).]

vi·o·lin·ist (vī′ə-lĭn′ĭst) *n.* A person who plays the violin.

vi·o·list (vē-ō′lĭst) *n.* **1.** A person who plays the viola. **2.** A person who plays a viol.

vi·o·lon·cel·list (vē′ə-lən-chĕl′ĭst) *n.* A cellist.

vi·o·lon·cel·lo (vē′ə-lən-chĕl′ō) *n., pl.* **-los.** A cello *(see).* [Italian, diminutive of *violone,* VIOLONE.]

vio·lo·ne (vyō-lō′nā) *n.* **1.** A 16-foot organ stop yielding string-like tones similar to a cello. **2.** A double bass. [Italian, augmentative of *viola,* VIOLA (instrument).]

vi·os·ter·ol (vī-ŏs′tə-rōl′) *n.* Ultraviolet irradiated ergosterol, **vitamin D₂** *(see).* [(ULTRA)VIO(LET) + STEROL.]

VIP *Informal.* very important person.

vi·per (vī′pər) *n.* **1.** Any of various venomous Old World snakes of the family Viperidae; especially, a common Eurasian species, *Vipera berus,* which is also called "adder." **2.** A **pit viper** *(see).* **3.** Broadly, any venomous or supposedly venomous snake. **4.** A treacherous or malicious person. [Old French *vipere,* from Latin *vipera,* snake, contracted from *vivipara* (unattested), "that which produces living young" (from the ancient belief that vipers were viviparous) : *vivus,* alive (see **gwei-** in Appendix*) + *parere,* to produce (see **per-**⁴ in Appendix*).]

vi·per·ine (vī′pər-in, -pə-rīn′) *adj.* Of, resembling, or characteristic of a viper.

vi·per·ous (vī′pər-əs) *adj.* **1.** Suggestive of a viper or venomous snake. **2.** Venomous; spiteful; malicious.

viper's bugloss. A bristly plant, *Echium vulgare,* native to Eurasia, having bright blue flowers. Also called "blueweed."

vir·a·gin·i·ty (vîr′ə-jĭn′ə-tē) *n.* Masculine mentality and psychology in a woman. [From Latin *virāgō* (stem *virāgin-*), manlike woman, VIRAGO.] —**vir·a′gin·ous** (vĭ-răj′ə-nəs) *adj.*

vi·ra·go (vĭ-rä′gō, -rā′gō, vĭ-) *n., pl.* **-goes** or **-gos. 1.** A noisy, domineering woman; a scold. **2.** *Archaic.* A large, strong, or courageous woman; an Amazon. [Latin *virāgō,* from *vir,* man. See **wiros** in Appendix.*]

vi·ral (vī′rəl) *adj.* Of, pertaining to, or caused by a virus. [From VIRUS.]

vir·e·lay (vîr′ə-lā′) *n.* Also *French* **vir·e·lai** (vēr-lĕ′). Any of several medieval French verse and song forms, especially one in which each stanza has two rhymes, the end rhyme recurring as the first rhyme of the following stanza. [Middle English *virelai,* from Old French, variant (influenced by *lai,* LAY) of *vireli,* perhaps originally a meaningless refrain.]

vir·e·o (vîr′ē-ō′) *n., pl.* **-os.** Any of various small New World birds of the genus *Vireo,* having grayish or greenish plumage. [Latin *vireo,* greenfinch, from *virēre,* to be green. See **virēre** in Appendix.*]

vi·res·cence (vĭ-rĕs′əns) *n.* The state or process of becoming green; specifically, the abnormal development of green coloration in plant parts normally not green.

vi·res·cent (vĭ-rĕs′ənt) *adj.* Becoming green; greenish. [Latin *virēscēns,* present participle of *virēscere,* to become green, from *virēre,* to be green. See **virēre** in Appendix.*]

vir·ga (vûr′gə) *n.* Wisps of precipitation streaming from a cloud but evaporating before reaching the earth. [Latin, twig, stripe. See **verge.**]

vir·gate¹ (vûr′gĭt, -gāt′) *adj.* Shaped like a wand or rod; straight, long, and slender. [Latin *virgātus,* made of twigs, from *virga,* twig. See **virga.**]

vir·gate² (vûr′gĭt, -gāt′) *n.* An early English measure of land area of varying value, often equivalent to about 30 acres. [Medieval Latin *virgāta,* from *virga,* a measure, yard, from Latin, twig. See **virga.**]

Vir·gil (vûr′jəl). Also **Ver·gil.** Full name, Publius Vergilius Maro. 70–19 B.C. Roman poet; author of the epic poem *Aeneid.* —**Vir·gil′i·an** *adj.*

vir·gin (vûr′jĭn) *n.* **1.** A person who has not experienced sexual intercourse. **2.** A chaste or unmarried woman; a maiden. **3.** An unmarried woman who has taken religious vows of chastity. **4.** *Capital* **V.** Mary, the mother of Jesus. Preceded by *the.* Also called "the Blessed Virgin." **5.** Any female animal that has not mated. **6.** *Capital* **V.** The constellation and the sign of the zodiac, Virgo *(see).* —*adj.* **1.** Characteristic of or appropriate to a virgin; chaste; maidenly. **2.** In a pure or natural state; untouched; unsullied: *virgin snow.* **3.** Unused, uncultivated, or unexplored: *"The North American drive had been towards the virgin west"* (Gordon K. Lewis). **4.** Existing in native or raw form; not processed or refined. **5.** Happening for the first time; initial: *"guiding my virgin steps on the hard road of letters"* (Maugham). **6.** Obtained directly from the first pressing. Said of vegetable oils. [Middle English, from Old French *virgine,* from Latin *virgō*† (stem *virgin-*).]

vir·gin·al¹ (vûr′jə-nəl) *adj.* **1.** Pertaining to, characteristic of, or befitting a virgin; chaste; pure: *"Virgins are not so virginal as they used to be."* (Sinclair Lewis). **2.** Remaining in a state of virginity. **3.** Untouched or unsullied; fresh.

vir·gin·al² (vûr′jə-nəl) *n.* A small, legless rectangular harpsichord popular in the 16th and 17th centuries. Often used in the plural: *a pair of virginals.* [From VIRGIN (because it was played by young girls).]

virgin birth. *Theology.* The doctrine that Jesus was miraculously begotten by God and born of Mary, who was a virgin.

Vir·gin·ia¹ (vər-jĭn′yə). A feminine given name. [French, from Latin, feminine of *Virginius,* name of a Roman gens.]

Vir·gin·ia² (vər-jĭn′yə). *Abbr.* **Va.** A Southern state of the United States, occupying 40,815 square miles in the east on the Atlantic; one of the original 13 states. Population, 4,400,000. Capital, Richmond. See map at **United States of America.** [From Latin *virgō* (stem *virgin-*), VIRGIN (after Queen Elizabeth I of England, the "virgin queen").] —**Vir·gin′ian** *adj. & n.*

Vir·gin·ia City (vər-jĭn′yə). A village of western Nevada, a flourishing city in the late 19th century after the discovery of the nearby Comstock Lode (1859). Population, 500.

Virginia cowslip. A plant, *Mertensia virginica,* of eastern North America, having clusters of nodding blue flowers.

Virginia creeper. A North American climbing vine, *Parthenocissus quinquefolia,* having compound leaves with five leaflets and bluish-black, berrylike fruit. Sometimes called "American ivy," "woodbine."

Virginia deer. The **white-tailed deer** *(see).*

Virginia fence. A **worm fence** *(see).* Also called "Virginia rail fence."

Virginia reel. A country dance in which couples, initially facing each other from two parallel lines, perform various figures to the instructions of a caller.

Virgin Islands. *Abbr.* **V.I.** A group of about 100 islands lying east of Puerto Rico in the West Indies and divided into: **a.** The **British Virgin Islands** *(see).* **b.** The **Virgin Islands of the United States,** formerly Danish West Indies, including the islands of St. Thomas, St. John, and St. Croix, and several islets, with a combined area of 133 square miles; population, 32,000; capital, Charlotte Amalie on St. Thomas.

vir·gin·i·ty (vər-jĭn′ə-tē) *n., pl.* **-ties. 1.** The condition of being a virgin; virginal chastity; maidenhood. **2.** The state of being pure, unsullied, or untouched.

Virgin Mary. The mother of Jesus. Usually preceded by *the.*

vir·gin's-bow·er (vûr′jĭnz-bou′ər) *n.* Any of several plants of the genus *Clematis;* especially, *C. virginiana,* of eastern North America, having clusters of white flowers and plumed seeds. Also called "old-man's-beard."

virgin wool. Wool that has not yet been processed.

Vir·go (vûr′gō) *n.* **1.** A constellation in the region of the celestial equator near Leo and Libra. **2.** The sixth sign of the **zodiac** *(see).* Also called the "Virgin." [Latin *virgō,* VIRGIN.]

vir·gu·late (vûr′gyə-lĭt, -lāt′) *adj.* Shaped like a small rod. [From Latin *virgula,* small rod. See **virgule.**]

vir·gule (vûr′gyōōl) *n.* A diagonal mark (/) used especially to separate alternatives, as in *and/or,* to represent the word *per,* as in *miles/hour,* and to indicate the ends of verse lines printed continuously, as in *Candy/Is dandy.* Also called "slash," "shilling," "solidus." [French, comma, from Latin *virgula,* small rod, from *virga,* rod, twig. See **verge.**]

vir·id (vîr′ĭd) *adj.* Bright green with or as if with vegetation; verdant. [Latin *viridis,* green, from *virēre,* to be green. See **virēre** in Appendix.*]

vir·i·des·cent (vîr′ĭ-dĕs′ənt) *adj.* Green or slightly green. [Latin *viridis,* green, VIRID + -ESCENT.] —**vir′i·des′cence** *n.*

vir·id·i·an (və-rĭd′ē-ən) *n.* A durable bluish-green pigment. [From Latin *viridis,* green, VIRID.]

vi·rid·i·ty (və-rĭd′ə-tē) *n., pl.* **-ties.** Greenness; verdancy.

vir·ile (vîr′əl) *adj.* **1.** Of or having the characteristics of an adult male. **2.** Having masculine strength, vigor, force, or the like. **3.** Of or pertaining to male sexual functions. —See Synonyms at **male.** [Old French *viril,* from Latin *virīlis,* from *vir,* man. See **wiros** in Appendix.*]

vir·il·ism (vîr′ə-lĭz′əm) *n.* The development of male secondary sexual characteristics in a woman.

vi·ril·i·ty (və-rĭl′ə-tē) *n., pl.* **-ties. 1.** Masculine vigor; potency:

virginal²
Engraving by
Wenceslaus Hollar

Virginia creeper

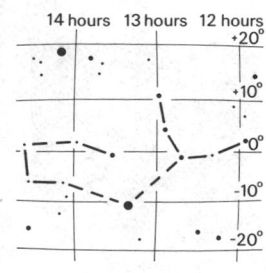
virgin's-bower
Clematis virginiana
Seed clusters

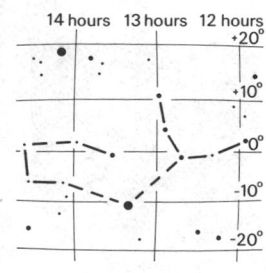
Virgo

ă pat/ā pay/âr care/ä father/b bib/ch church/d deed/ĕ pet/ē be/f fife/g gag/h hat/hw which/ĭ pit/ī pie/îr pier/j judge/k kick/l lid, needle/m mum/n no, sudden/ng thing/ŏ pot/ō toe/ô paw, for/oi noise/ou out/ŏŏ took/ōō boot/p pop/r roar/s sauce/sh ship, dish/
t tight/th thin, path/th this, bathe/ŭ cut/ûr urge/v valve/w with/y yes/z zebra, size/zh vision/ə about, item, edible, gallop, circus/
à *Fr.* ami/œ *Fr.* feu, *Ger.* schön/ü *Fr.* tu, *Ger.* über/KH *Ger.* ich, *Scot.* loch/N *Fr.* bon. *Follows main vocabulary. †Of obscure origin.

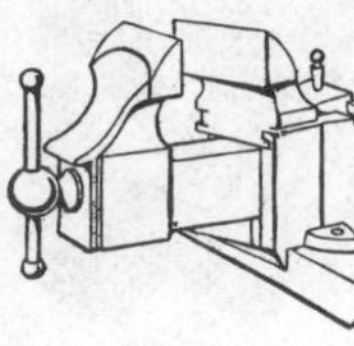

vise

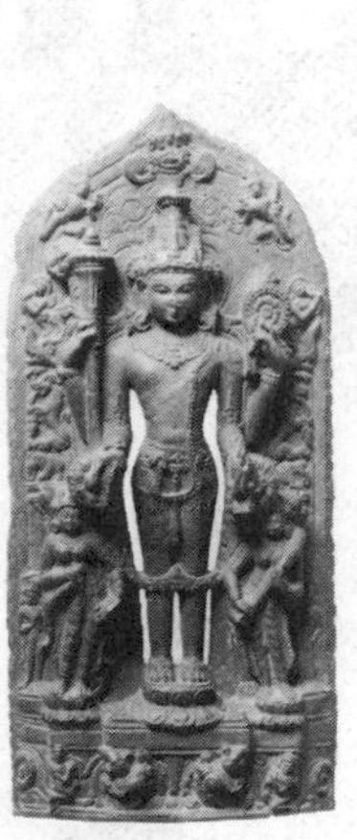

Vishnu
Eleventh-century sculpture

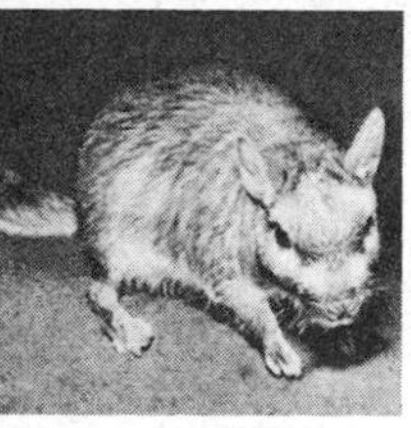

viscacha
Lagostomus maximus

"virility has now become self-conscious—men . . . are now writing only with the male side of their brains" (Virginia Woolf). **2.** Manliness of thought or action.

vi·rol·o·gy (vī-rŏl′ə-jē) *n.* The study of viruses and viral diseases. [VIR(US) + -LOGY.] **—vi·rol′o·gist** *n.*

vir·tu (vər-tōō′, vûr′tōō) *n.* Also **ver·tu. 1.** A knowledge of or taste for the fine arts. **2.** The quality of being beautiful, rare, or otherwise interesting to a collector. Used in the phrases *articles of virtu* and *objects of virtu.* **3.** Such articles or objects collectively. [Italian *virtù,* taste, virtue, from Latin *virtūs,* VIRTUE.]

vir·tu·al (vûr′chōō-əl) *adj.* Existing or resulting in essence or effect though not in actual fact, form, or name. [Middle English *virtuall,* effective, powerful, from Medieval Latin *virtuālis,* from Latin *virtūs,* capacity, VIRTUE.] **—vir′tu·al′i·ty** (-ăl′ə-tē) *n.*

virtual focus. The point from which divergent rays of reflected or refracted light seem to have emanated, as from the image of a point in a plane mirror.

virtual image. An image from which rays of reflected or refracted light appear to diverge, as from an image seen in a plane mirror.

vir·tu·al·ly (vûr′chōō-ə-lē) *adv.* In fact or to all purposes; essentially; practically. See Usage note at **practically.**

vir·tue (vûr′chōō) *n.* **1.** The quality of moral excellence, righteousness, and responsibility; probity; goodness. **2.** Conformity to standard morality or mores, as by abstention from vices; rectitude: *"what is virtue but the Trade Unionism of the married?"* (G.B. Shaw). **3. a.** A specific type of moral excellence or other exemplary quality considered meritorious; a worthy practice or ideal. **b.** Any of the particular moral excellences considered exemplary in philosophy and theology. See **cardinal virtues. 4.** Chastity. **5. a.** A particular efficacious or beneficial quality: *"A stone or a flower each has its virtue, its combination of specific qualities"* (Erich Fromm). **b.** A preferable quality; an advantage: *This plan has the virtue of being practical.* **6.** Effective force or power; efficacy. **7.** *Obsolete.* Manly courage; valor. **8.** *Plural. Theology.* One of the orders of angels. See **angel. —by** (or **in**) **virtue of.** On the grounds or basis of; by reason of: *By virtue of the authority vested in me, I pronounce you man and wife.* **—make a virtue of necessity.** To appear to do freely or by inclination what one must do necessarily. [Middle English *vertu,* from Old French, from Latin *virtūs,* manliness, strength, capacity, from *vir,* man. See **wiros** in Appendix.*]

vir·tu·os·i·ty (vûr′chōō-ŏs′ə-tē) *n., pl.* **-ties.** The technical skill, fluency, or style exhibited by a virtuoso.

vir·tu·o·so (vûr′chōō-ō′sō) *n., pl.* **-sos** or **-si** (-sē). **1.** A musician with masterly ability, technique, or personal style; a brilliant performer. **2.** One with masterly skill or technique in any field, especially in the arts. **3.** A connoisseur or dilettante. [Italian, from Late Latin *virtuōsus,* virtuous, skillful, from Latin *virtūs,* VIRTUE.] **—vir′tu·os′ic** (-ŏs′ĭk) *adj.*

vir·tu·ous (vûr′chōō-əs) *adj.* **1.** Exhibiting virtue; righteous: *virtuous conduct.* **2.** Possessing or characterized by chastity; pure: *a virtuous woman.* —See Synonyms at **moral. —vir′tu·ous·ly** *adv.* **—vir′tu·ous·ness** *n.*

vir·u·lent (vîr′yə-lənt, vîr′ə-) *adj.* **1.** Extremely poisonous or pathogenic. Said of a disease, toxin, or microorganism. **2.** Bitterly hostile or antagonistic; venomously spiteful; full of hate. **3.** Intensely irritating, obnoxious, or harsh: *virulent antirationalism.* [Middle English, from Latin *vīrulentus,* from *vīrus,* VIRUS.] **—vir′u·lence** (-ləns) *n.* **—vir′u·lent·ly** *adv.*

vi·rus (vī′rəs) *n., pl.* **-ruses. 1.** Any of various submicroscopic pathogens consisting essentially of a core of a single nucleic acid surrounded by a protein coat, having the ability to replicate only inside a living cell. **2.** Any specific pathogen. **3.** *Rare.* Venom, as of a snake or other animal. —See Synonyms at **germ.** [Latin *vīrus,* poison, slime. See **weis-¹** in Appendix.*]

vis. 1. visibility. **2.** visual.

Vis. viscount; viscountess.

vi·sa (vē′zə) *n.* An official authorization appended to a passport, permitting entry into and travel within a particular country or region. *—tr.v.* **visaed, -saing, -sas. 1.** To endorse or ratify (a passport). **2.** To give a visa to. [French, from Latin *vīsa,* "things seen," neuter plural of *vīsus,* past participle of *vidēre,* to see. See **weid-** in Appendix.*]

vis·age (vĭz′ĭj) *n.* **1.** The face or facial expression of a person; countenance: *"On his bold visage middle age/ Had slightly press'd its signet sage"* (Scott). **2.** Appearance; aspect: *the visage of winter.* [Middle English, from Old French, from *vis,* face, from Latin *vīsus,* from the past participle of *vidēre,* to see. See **weid-** in Appendix.*]

vis·aged (vĭz′ĭjd) *adj.* Having a (specified kind of) visage. Used in combination: *square-visaged.*

vis·ard. Variant of **vizard.**

vis-à-vis (vē′zə-vē′; *French* vē-zȧ-vē′) *n., pl.* **vis-à-vis.** One of two persons or things opposite or corresponding to each other. *—adv.* Face to face. *—prep.* Compared with; in relation to. [French, "face to face."] **—vis′-à-vis′** *adj.*

Vi·sa·yan (vē-sä′yən) *n.* Also **Bi·sa·yan** (bē-). **1.** A member of the largest native group of the Philippines, found in the Visayan Islands. **2.** The Malay language spoken by these people. *—adj.* Also **Bi·sa·yan.** Of or pertaining to the Visayans, their culture, or their language.

Vi·sa·yan Islands (vē-sä′yən). Also **Bi·sa·yan Islands** (bē-). An island group of the Republic of the Philippines, 23,621 square miles in area, lying between Luzon and Mindanao. Also called "Visayans."

Visc. viscount; viscountess.

vis·ca·cha (vĭs-kä′chə) *n.* Any of several gregarious, burrowing South American rodents of the genera *Lagostomus* and *Lagidium,* related to and resembling the chinchilla. [Spanish, from Quechua *wiscacha.*]

vis·cer·a (vĭs′ər-ə) *pl.n. Singular* **viscus** (vĭs′kəs). **1.** The internal organs of the body, especially those contained within the abdominal and thoracic cavities. **2.** Broadly, the intestines. [Latin *vīscera,* plural of *vīscus*†, body organ.]

vis·cer·al (vĭs′ər-əl) *adj.* **1.** Pertaining to, situated in, or affecting the viscera. **2.** Intensely emotional: *"The scientific approach to life is not really appropriate to states of visceral anguish"* (Anthony Burgess).

vis·cer·o·mo·tor (vĭs′ə-rō-mō′tər) *adj.* Producing or related to movements of the viscera. [VISCER(A) + MOTOR.]

vis·cid (vĭs′ĭd) *adj.* **1.** Thick and adhesive. Said of a fluid. **2.** Covered with a sticky or clammy coating. [Late Latin *viscidus,* from Latin *viscum,* mistletoe, birdlime (made from mistletoe berries). See **weis-¹** in Appendix.*] **—vis·cid′i·ty, vis′cid·ness** *n.* **—vis′cid·ly** *adv.*

vis·com·e·ter (vĭs-kŏm′ə-tər) *n.* An instrument used to measure viscosity. [VISCO(US) + -METER.] **—vis′co·met′ric** (vĭs′kō-mĕt′rĭk) *adj.*

vis·cose (vĭs′kōs′) *n.* **1.** A thick, golden-brown viscous solution of cellulose xanthate, used in the manufacture of rayon and cellophane. **2.** Viscose rayon. *—adj.* **1.** Viscous. **2.** Of, relating to, or made from viscose. [Middle English, sticky, viscid, from Late Latin *viscōsus,* VISCOUS.]

viscose rayon. A rayon made by reconverting cellulose from a soluble xanthate form to tough fibers by washing in acid.

vis·co·sim·e·ter (vĭs′kə-sĭm′ə-tər) *n.* A viscometer.

vis·cos·i·ty (vĭs-kŏs′ə-tē) *n., pl.* **-ties. 1.** The condition or property of being viscous. **2.** *Physics.* The degree to which a fluid resists flow under an applied force.

vis·count (vī′kount′) *n. Abbr.* **V., Vis., Visc., Visct.** A peer ranking below an earl and above a baron. [Middle English, from Old French *visconte,* from Medieval Latin *vicecomes* : VICE (substitute) + *comes,* COUNT.]

vis·count·cy (vī′kount′sē) *n., pl.* **-cies.** The rank, title, or dignity of a viscount. Also called "viscounty."

vis·count·ess (vī′koun′tĭs) *n. Abbr.* **V., Vis., Visc., Visct.** The wife of a viscount.

Viscount Mel·ville Sound (mĕl′vĭl). A sound located between Victoria Island and Melville Island, Northwest Territories, Canada.

vis·cous (vĭs′kəs) *adj.* **1.** Having relatively high resistance to flow. **2.** Viscid. [Middle English *viscouse,* from Norman French *viscous,* from Late Latin *viscōsus,* from Latin *viscum,* mistletoe, birdlime (made from mistletoe berries). See **weis-¹** in Appendix.*] **—vis′cous·ly** *adv.* **—vis′cous·ness** *n.*

Visct. viscount; viscountess.

vis·cus. Singular of **viscera.**

vise (vīs) *n.* Also **vice.** A clamping device of metal or wood, usually consisting of two jaws closed or opened by a screw or lever, used in carpentry or metalworking to hold a piece in position. *—tr.v.* **vised, vising, vises.** Also **vice.** To hold in or as in a vise. [Middle English *vis,* winding staircase, screw, from Latin *vītis,* (winding) vine. See **wei-¹** in Appendix.*]

Vish·nu (vĭsh′nōō) *n. Hinduism.* The chief deity worshiped by the Vaishnava, and the second member of the trinity including also Brahma and Shiva. [Sanskrit *Viṣṇu*†.]

vis·i·bil·i·ty (vĭz′ə-bĭl′ə-tē) *n., pl.* **-ties. 1.** The fact, state, or degree of being visible. **2.** *Abbr.* **vis.** The greatest distance under given weather conditions to which it is possible to see without instrumental assistance.

vis·i·ble (vĭz′ə-bəl) *adj.* **1.** Capable of being seen; perceptible to the eye: *a visible object.* **2.** Obvious to the eye: *a visible change of expression.* **3.** Manifest; apparent: *no visible solution.* **4.** Available; on hand: *a visible supply.* **5.** Constructed or designed to keep important parts in easily accessible view: *a visible file.* **6.** Represented visually, as by symbols. [Middle English, from Old French, from Latin *vīsibilis,* from *vīsus,* sight, VISION.] **—vis′i·ble·ness** *n.* **—vis′i·bly** *adv.*

visible speech. A system of phonetic notation used as an aid for teaching speech to the deaf and consisting of diagrams of the organs of speech in the various positions required to articulate sounds.

Vis·i·goth (vĭz′ə-gŏth′) *n.* A member of the western Goths that invaded the Roman Empire in the fourth century A.D. and settled in France and Spain, establishing a monarchy that lasted until the early eighth century A.D. Compare **Ostrogoth.** [From Late Latin *Visigothi* (plural), probably "West Goths." See **wesperos** in Appendix.*] **—Vis′i·goth′ic** *adj.*

vi·sion (vĭzh′ən) *n.* **1. a.** The faculty of sight: *poor vision.* **b.** That which is or has been seen. **2.** Unusual competence in discernment or perception; intelligent foresight: *a man of vision.* **3.** The manner in which one sees or conceives of something. **4.** A mental image produced by the imagination: *"In visions he had seen himself in many struggles."* (Stephen Crane). **5.** The mystical experience of seeing as if with the eyes the supernatural or a supernatural being. **6.** A person or thing of extraordinary beauty. *—tr.v.* **visioned, -sioning, -sions.** To see in or as if in a vision. [Middle English, from Old French, from Latin *vīsiō,* from *vīsus,* sight, from the past participle of *vidēre,* to see. See **weid-** in Appendix.*] **—vi′sion·al** *adj.* **—vi′sion·al·ly** *adv.*

vi·sion·ar·y (vĭzh′ən-ĕr′ē) *adj.* **1.** Characterized by vision or foresight. **2.** Having the nature of fantasies or dreams. **3.** Characterized by or given to apparitions, prophecies, or revelations. **4.** Not practicable at present; idealistic; utopian. *—n., pl.* **visionaries. 1.** One who has visions; a seer; prophet. **2.** One who is given to impractical or speculative ideas; a dreamer.

vis·it (vĭz′ĭt) *v.* **-ited, -iting, -its.** *—tr.* **1.** To go or come to see (a person), as by way of friendship or duty; call on: *visit Aunt Martha.* **2.** To go or come to see (a place), as on a tour: *visit a museum.* **3.** To stay with as a guest. **4.** To go or come to see in an official or professional capacity. **5.** To go or come to generally: *I visit the bank on Fridays.* **6.** To go or come to in order to aid: *visit the wounded.* **7.** To afflict; assail: *A plague visited the village.* **8.** To inflict punishment upon or for; avenge: *"I shall visit their sin upon them."* (Exodus 32:34). **9.** *Archaic.* To come to in order to comfort or bless. Said of the Deity. —*intr.* **1.** To pay a call or calls. **2.** To inflict punishment; avenge. **3.** *Informal.* To converse or chat: *Stay and visit with me for a while.* —*n.* **1.** An act or instance of visiting a person, place, or thing. **2.** A stay or sojourn as a guest. **3.** An act of visiting in a professional capacity. **4.** An act of visiting in an official capacity, as an inspection or examination. [Middle English *visiten,* from Old French *visiter,* from Latin *visitāre,* to go to see, from *vīsāre,* to view, from *vīsus,* sight, VISION.]

vis·it·a·ble (vĭz′ə-tə-bəl) *adj.* **1.** Capable of or suitable for a visit. **2.** Subject to or allowing official visit, as for inspection.

vis·i·tant (vĭz′ə-tənt) *n.* **1.** A visitor; guest; a transient. **2.** A supernatural being; a ghost or specter. **3.** A migratory animal or bird that stops in a particular place for a limited period of time. —*adj. Archaic.* Visiting. [Latin *visitāns,* present participle of *visitāre,* to VISIT.]

vis·i·ta·tion (vĭz′ə-tā′shən) *n.* **1.** The act of visiting or being visited; a visit. **2.** A visit for the purpose of making an official inspection or examination, as of a bishop to his diocese. **3.** The right of a parent to visit a child as specified in a divorce or separation order. **4. a.** A visit of punishment or affliction or of comfort and blessing, regarded as being ordained by God. **b.** A calamitous event or experience; grave misfortune. **5.** The appearance or arrival of a supernatural being. **6.** *Capital* V. **a.** The visit of the Virgin Mary to her cousin Elizabeth. Luke 1:39–56. **b.** The Roman Catholic Church festival held July 2 in commemoration of this visit. —**vis′i·ta′tion·al** *adj.*

vis·i·ta·to·ri·al (vĭz′ə-tə-tôr′ē-əl, -tōr′ē-əl) *adj.* Also **vis·i·to·ri·al** (vĭz′ə-tôr′ē-əl, -tōr′ē-əl). **1.** Of or pertaining to an official visitor or visit. **2.** Having the right or power of visitation.

visiting card. A calling card.

visiting fireman. *Informal.* **1.** An influential visitor who is entertained impressively. **2.** A visitor to a city who is welcomed because he is thought to be a free spender.

visiting professor. A professor on leave invited to serve as a member of the faculty of another college or university for a limited period of time, often an academic year.

visiting teacher. A teacher affiliated with a public school system who visits sick or handicapped children in the area for the purpose of instruction.

vis·i·tor (vĭz′ə-tər) *n.* **1.** One who pays a visit; a guest; caller. **2.** A sightseer or tourist.

vis ma·jor (vĭs mā′jər) *pl.* **vires majores** (vī′rēz′ mə-jôr′ēz′, -jōr′ēz′). *Law.* An overwhelming force of nature having unavoidable consequences that under certain circumstances can exempt one from the obligations of a contract. [Latin, "greater force."]

Vi·so, Mount (vē′zō). The highest (12,002 feet) of the Cottian Alps, in northwestern Italy near the border with France.

vi·sor (vī′zər, vĭz′ər) *n.* Also **vi·zor. 1.** A piece projecting from the front of a cap to shade the eyes or protect against wind or rain. **2.** A fixed or movable shield against glare above the windshield of an automobile. **3.** The front piece of the helmet of a suit of armor, capable of being raised and lowered and designed to protect the eyes, nose, and forehead. **4.** Any means of concealment or disguise; a mask. —*tr.v.* **visored** (vī′zərd), **-soring, -sors.** Also **vi·zor.** To mask or protect with a visor. [Middle English *viser,* from Norman French, from Old French *vis,* face, from Latin *vīsus,* sight, VISION.]

vis·ta (vĭs′tə) *n.* **1.** A distant view seen through a passage, as between buildings or rows of trees; scene; prospect. **2.** The passage framing the approach to such a scene; an avenue. **3.** A comprehensive awareness of a series of remembered, present, or anticipated events: *"He opened a vista into a mean life."* (Rebecca West). [Italian, from *visto,* past participle of *vedere,* to see, from Latin *vidēre.* See **weid-** in Appendix.*]

VISTA (vĭs′tə) An organization sponsored by the U.S. Office of Economic Opportunity composed of volunteer members devoted to educating and teaching skills to the poor. [V(OLUNTEERS) I(N) S(ERVICE) T(O) A(MERICA).]

Vis·tu·la (vĭs′chŏŏ-lə). *Polish* **Wis·ła** (vēs′lä). A river of Poland, rising in the Carpathians in the south and flowing 678 miles northeast, northwest, and then north to the Gulf of Danzig.

vis·u·al (vĭzh′ōō-əl) *adj. Abbr.* **vis. 1.** Serving, resulting from, or pertaining to the sense of sight. **2.** Capable of being seen by the eye; visible. **3.** *Optics.* Optical. **4.** Done, maintained, or executed by the sight only: *visual navigation.* **5.** Having the nature of or producing an image in the mind. **6.** Designating a method of instruction involving sight. [Middle English, from Late Latin *vīsuālis,* from Latin *vīsus,* VISION.] —**vis′u·al·ly** *adv.*

visual aid. Graphic material used in education to impart instruction by visual means. Often used in the plural.

visual field. *Abbr.* **V.F.** The entire area visible to the immobile eye or eyes at a given moment; the field of vision.

vis·u·al·ize (vĭzh′ōō-ə-līz′) *v.* **-ized, -izing, -izes.** —*tr.* To form a mental image or vision of; envisage. —*intr.* To form a mental image or images. —**vis′u·al·i·za′tion** *n.*

vis·u·al·iz·er (vĭzh′ōō-ə-lī′zər) *n.* One who visualizes; especially, one whose mental images are predominantly visual.

visual purple. A red-light-sensitive pigment of the retina, **rhodopsin** *(see).*

vi·tal (vī′təl, vīt′l) *adj.* **1.** Of or characteristic of life: *vital processes.* **2.** Necessary to the continuation of life; life-sustaining: *vital functions.* **3.** Full of life; energetic; vigorous; animated: *"The sky was blue, and young and vital, there were no clouds in it"* (Thomas Wolfe). **4.** *Poetic.* Imparting life or animation; invigorating. **5.** Having immediate importance; essential; indispensable: *"Irrigation was vital to early civilization"* (William H. McNeill). **6.** Concerned with or recording data pertinent to lives. **7.** *Archaic.* Destructive to life; fatal; deadly: *a vital wound.* —See Synonyms at **necessary.** [Middle English, from Old French, from Latin *vitālis,* from *vīta,* life. See **gwei-** in Appendix.*] —**vi′tal·ly** *adv.* —**vi′tal·ness** *n.*

vi·tal·ism (vīt′l-ĭz′əm) *n.* The philosophical doctrine that life processes possess a unique character radically different from physiochemical phenomena. —**vi′tal·ist** *n.* —**vi′tal·is′tic** *adj.*

vi·tal·i·ty (vī-tăl′ə-tē) *n., pl.* **-ties. 1.** That which distinguishes the living from the nonliving; an energy, force, or principle characteristic of life. **2.** The capacity to live, grow, or develop. **3.** Vigor; energy; exuberance: *"to combine the experience of an old hand with the vitality of a young one"* (G.B. Shaw). **4.** The power to survive.

vi·tal·ize (vīt′l-īz′) *tr.v.* **-ized, -izing, -izes. 1.** To endow with life. **2.** To invigorate or animate. —**vi′tal·i·za′tion** *n.* —**vi′tal·iz′er** *n.*

vi·tals (vī′təlz) *pl.n.* **1.** Any bodily parts or organs regarded as the center or source of life: *"the overmastering chill seized my own vitals"* (Edward Bellamy). **2.** Those elements essential to continued functioning, as of a system.

vital statistics. Data that record significant events and dates in human life, as births, deaths, and marriages.

vi·ta·mer (vī′tə-mər) *n.* One of two or more similar chemical compounds capable of fulfilling a specific vitamin function. [VITA(MIN) + (ISO)MER.]

vi·ta·min (vī′tə-mən) *n.* Also *rare* **vi·ta·mine** (-mēn, -mĭn). Any of various relatively complex organic substances occurring naturally in plant and animal tissue and essential in small amounts for the control of metabolic processes. [German *Vitamine* : Latin *vīta,* life (see **gwei-** in Appendix*) + AMINE (so called because it was once thought to be an amine).] —**vi′ta·min′ic** *adj.*

vitamin A. A vitamin or a mixture of vitamins, especially vitamin A₁ or a mixture of vitamins A₁ and A₂, occurring principally in fish-liver oils and some yellow and dark-green vegetables, functioning in normal cell growth and development, and responsible in deficiency for hardening and roughening of the skin, night blindness, and degeneration of mucous membranes.

vitamin A₁. A yellow crystalline compound, $C_{20}H_{30}O$, extracted from fish-liver oils. See **vitamin A.**

vitamin A₂. A golden-yellow oil, $C_{20}H_{28}O$, occurring in pike-liver oils and having approximately 40 per cent of the biological activity of vitamin A₁. See **vitamin A.**

vitamin B. 1. Vitamin B complex. **2.** A member of the vitamin B complex, especially thiamine.

vitamin Bₑ. Folic acid *(see).*

vitamin B₁. Thiamine *(see).*

vitamin B₂. Riboflavin *(see).*

vitamin B₆. Pyridoxine *(see).*

vitamin B₁₂. A complex, cobalt-containing coordination compound produced in the normal growth of certain microorganisms, found in liver, and widely used to treat pernicious anemia.

vitamin B complex. A group of vitamins originally thought to be a single substance, generally regarded as including thiamine, riboflavin, niacin, pantothenic acid, biotin, pyridoxine, folic acid, inositol, and vitamin B₁₂, and occurring chiefly in yeast, liver, eggs, and some vegetables.

vitamin C. Ascorbic acid *(see).*

vitamin D. Any of several chemically similar activated sterols, especially vitamin D₂ or vitamin D₃, produced in general by ultraviolet irradiation of sterols, obtained from milk, fish, and eggs, required for normal bone growth, and used to treat rickets in children and osteomalacia in adults.

vitamin D₂. A white crystalline compound, $C_{28}H_{44}O$, produced by ultraviolet irradiation of ergosterol. Also called "calciferol," "ergocalciferol," "viosterol." See **vitamin D.**

vitamin D₃. A colorless crystalline compound, $C_{27}H_{44}O$, with essentially the same biological activity as vitamin D₂ but significantly more potent in poultry. See **vitamin D.**

vitamin E. Any of several chemically related viscous oils, especially $C_{29}H_{50}O_2$, found chiefly in grains and vegetable oils and used to treat sterility and various abnormalities of the muscles, red blood cells, liver, and brain.

vitamin G. Riboflavin *(see).*

vitamin H. Biotin *(see).*

vitamin K. Any of several natural and synthetic substances essential for the promotion of blood clotting and prevention of hemorrhage, occurring naturally in leafy green vegetables, tomatoes, and vegetable oils.

vitamin P. A crystalline fraction of citrus juices used to treat certain conditions involving hemorrhage into the skin.

vi·ta·scope (vī′tə-skōp′) *n.* An early type of motion-picture projector. [Latin *vīta,* life (see **gwei-** in Appendix*) + -SCOPE.]

Vi·tebsk (vē′tĕpsk′, vē-tĕpsk′). A city of the Soviet Union, in northeastern Byelorussia. Population, 187,000.

vi·tel·lin (vī-tĕl′ĭn, vĭ-) *n.* A protein found in egg yolk. [VITELL(US) + -IN.]

vi·tel·line (vī-tĕl′ĭn, vĭ-) *adj.* **1.** Pertaining to or associated with the yolk of an egg: *the vitelline membrane.* **2.** Having the yellow color of an egg yolk; dull-yellow. —*n.* The yolk of an egg. [VITELL(US) + -INE.]

visor
Fifteenth-century French helmet with visor

ă pat/ā pay/âr care/ä father/b bib/ch church/d deed/ĕ pet/ē be/f fife/g gag/h hat/hw which/ĭ pit/ī pie/îr pier/j judge/k kick/l lid, needle/m mum/n no, sudden/ng thing/ŏ pot/ō toe/ô paw, for/oi noise/ou out/ŏŏ took/ōō boot/p pop/r roar/s sauce/sh ship, dish/t tight/th thin, path/*th* this, bathe/ŭ cut/ûr urge/v valve/w with/y yes/z zebra, size/zh vision/ə about, item, edible, gallop, circus/à *Fr.* ami/œ *Fr.* feu, *Ger.* schön/ü *Fr.* tu, *Ger.* über/KH *Ger.* ich, *Scot.* loch/N *Fr.* bon. *Follows main vocabulary. †Of obscure origin.

vi·tel·lus (vĭ-tĕl′əs, vĭ-) n. Rare. The yolk of an egg. [Latin, "little calf," from vitulus, calf. See wet- in Appendix.*]

vi·ti·ate (vĭsh′ē-āt′) tr.v. -ated, -ating, -ates. 1. To impair the value or quality of; make faulty or impure; spoil. 2. To corrupt morally; debase; pervert. 3. To invalidate or render legally ineffective, as a contract. [Latin vitiāre, from vitium, defect, fault. See wei-⁴ in Appendix.*] —vi′ti·a·ble (-ē-ə-bəl) adj. —vi′ti·a′tion n. —vi′ti·a′tor (-ā′tər) n.

vit·i·cul·ture (vĭt′ĭ-kŭl′chər, vī′tĭ-) n. The cultivation of grapes. [Latin vītis, vine (see wei-¹ in Appendix*) + CULTURE.] —vit′i·cul′tur·al adj. —vit′i·cul′tur·ist n.

Vi·ti Le·vu (vē′tē lā′voo). The principal island of the Fiji Islands, 4,010 square miles in area; the site of Suva, the capital of the colony.

vit·i·li·go (vĭt′l-ī′gō) n. A skin disease characterized by the occurrence of whitish nonpigmented areas surrounded by hyperpigmented borders. [Latin vitilīgō, cutaneous eruption, tetter. See wei-⁴ in Appendix.*]

Vi·tim (vē-tēm′). A river of the Soviet Union, rising in the south-central Buryat A.S.S.R. and flowing 1,192 miles generally north to the Lena.

Vi·to·ri·a (vĭ-tôr′ē-ə, -tōr′ē-ə; Spanish vē-tō′ryä). A city of north-central Spain; the site of a battle (1813) in which Wellington defeated the French. Population, 66,000.

Vi·tó·ria (vĭ-tôr′ē-ə, -tōr′ē-ə; Portuguese vē-tôr′ryä). The capital of Espírito Santo, eastern Brazil, a seaport on the Atlantic Coast. Population, 83,000.

vit·re·ous (vĭt′rē-əs) adj. 1. Pertaining to, resembling, or having the nature of glass; glassy. 2. Obtained or made from glass. 3. Of or pertaining to the vitreous humor. [Latin vitreus, from vitrum†, glass.] —vit′re·os′i·ty (-ŏs′ə-tē), vit′re·ous·ness n.

vitreous body. A gelatinous body of matter composed mainly of vitreous humor that fills the part of the eyeball between the retina and the lens.

vitreous enamel. Porcelain enamel (see).

vitreous humor. A watery fluid that is a major component of a vitreous body.

vi·tres·cence (vĭ-trĕs′əns) n. 1. Transformation into glass. 2. The state of becoming vitreous or like glass.

vi·tres·cent (vĭ-trĕs′ənt) adj. 1. Tending to become glass or like glass. 2. Capable of being turned into glass. [Latin vitrum, glass (see vitreous) + -ESCENT.]

vit·ri·fi·ca·tion (vĭt′rə-fə-kā′shən) n. 1. The act or process of vitrifying or the state of being vitrified. 2. Something vitrified.

vit·ri·fy (vĭt′rə-fī′) v. -fied, -fying, -fies. —tr. To change or make into glass or a similar substance, especially through heat fusion. —intr. To become vitreous. [French vitrifier, from Old French : Latin vitrum, glass (see vitreous) + -FY.] —vit′ri·fi′a·bil′i·ty n. —vit′ri·fi′a·ble adj.

vit·ri·ol (vĭt′rē-ōl′) n. 1. Chemistry. a. Sulfuric acid. b. Any of various sulfates of metals, such as ferrous sulfate (green vitriol), zinc sulfate (white vitriol), or copper sulfate (blue vitriol). 2. Vituperative feeling or utterance. —tr.v. vitrioled or -olled, -oling or -olling, -ols. To expose or subject to vitriol. [Middle English, from Old French, from Medieval Latin vitriolum, from Latin vitrum, glass (from the glassy appearance of its sulfates). See vitreous.]

vit·ri·ol·ic (vĭt′rē-ōl′ĭk) adj. 1. Of, similar to, or derived from a vitriol. 2. Bitterly scathing; caustic.

Vi·tru·vi·us Pol·li·o (vĭ-trōō′vē-əs pŏl′ē-ō′), **Marcus.** Roman writer on architecture of the first century B.C.

vit·ta (vĭt′ə) n., pl. vitae (vĭt′ē). 1. Biology. A streak or band of color. 2. Botany. An oil tube in the fruit of certain plants, as the carrot or parsley. [Latin, headband. See wei-¹ in Appendix.*] —vit′tate′ (vĭt′āt′) adj.

vit·tle. Nonstandard. Variant of victual.

vi·tu·per·ate (vī-tōō′pə-rāt′, vĭ-tyōō′-, vĭ-) tr.v. -ated, -ating, -ates. To rail against severely or abusively; revile; berate. See Synonyms at malign. [Latin vituperāre. See wei-⁴ in Appendix.*] —vi·tu′per·a′tor (-pə-rā′tər) n.

vi·tu·per·a·tion (vī-tōō′pə-rā′shən, vī-tyōō′-, vĭ-) n. 1. Censure; blame. 2. Invective; railing.

vi·tu·per·a·tive (vī-tōō′pər-ə-tĭv, vī-tyōō′-, vĭ-) adj. Harshly abusive; acrimonious: "Five minutes won't be ample time for a vituperative phone call" (Kingsley Amis). —vi·tu′per·a·tive·ly adv.

vi·va (vē′vä) interj. Used to express acclamation, salute, or applause. —n. A shout of "viva." [Italian, from vivere, to live, from Latin vīvere. See gwei- in Appendix.*]

vi·va·ce (vē-vä′chā) adv. Music. Lively; vivaciously; briskly. Used as direction. [Italian, from Latin vīvāx, VIVACIOUS.]

vi·va·cious (vĭ-vā′shəs, vī-) adj. Animated; sprightly; spirited. [Latin vīvāx (stem vīvāci-), lively, from vīvere, to live. See gwei- in Appendix.*] —vi·va′cious·ly adv. —vi·va′cious·ness n.

vi·vac·i·ty (vĭ-văs′ə-tē, vī-) n. The condition or quality of being vivacious; liveliness.

Vi·val·di (vē-väl′dē), **Antonio.** 1680?-1743. Italian composer.

vi·van·diè·re (vē-vän-dyâr′) n. Formerly, especially in France, a woman who accompanied troops to sell them food, supplies, and liquor. [French, feminine of vivandier, provisioner, from Old French, from viande, VIAND.]

vi·var·i·um (vī-vâr′ē-əm) n., pl. -ums or -ia (-ē-ə). A place or enclosure for keeping and raising living animals for observation or research. [Latin : vīvus, alive (see vivify) + -ARIUM.]

vi·va vo·ce (vī′və vō′sē). By word of mouth; spoken; oral. [Middle Latin, "with the living voice."]

vive (vēv) interj. French. Used to acclaim, salute, or applaud a person or personification specified: Vive la France!

Vi·ve·ka·nan·da (vē′və-kə-nŭn′də). Original name, Narend-

ranath Datta. 1863-1902. Hindu Vedantist leader and educator.

vi·ver·rine (vī-vĕr′ĭn, -ĭn′, vĭ-) adj. Of or belonging to the family Viverridae, which includes carnivorous mammals such as the civets and mongooses. —n. A member of the Viverridae. [From Latin viverra, ferret. See wer-¹⁰ in Appendix.*]

Viv·i·an (vĭv′ē-ən). Also **Viv·i·en.** A feminine or masculine given name. [Middle English Vivian, from Late Latin Vīviānus, "lively," from Latin vīvus, alive. See vivify.]

viv·id (vĭv′ĭd) adj. 1. Perceived as bright and distinct; brilliant: the vivid evening star. 2. a. Having intensely bright colors: a vivid tapestry. b. Very strong. Said of color. 3. Full of the vigor and freshness of immediate experience. 4. a. Evoking lifelike images within the mind; heard, seen, or felt as if real: a vivid description. b. Active in forming lifelike images: a vivid imagination. [Latin vīvidus, full of life, lifelike, from vīvere, to live. See gwei- in Appendix.*] —viv′id·ly adv. —viv′id·ness n.

viv·i·fy (vĭv′ə-fī′) tr.v. -fied, -fying, -fies. 1. To give or bring life to; to animate. 2. To make more lively, intense, or striking; enliven. [Old French vivifier, from Late Latin vīvificāre : Latin vīvus, alive (see gwei- in Appendix*) + facere, to do (see dhē-¹ in Appendix*).] —viv′i·fi·ca′tion n. —viv′i·fi′er n.

vi·vip·a·rous (vī-vĭp′ər-əs) adj. 1. Zoology. Giving birth to living offspring that develop within the mother's body. Compare oviparous, ovoviviparous. 2. Botany. a. Germinating or producing seeds that germinate before becoming detached from the parent plant. b. Producing bulbils or new plants rather than seed. [Latin vīviparus : vīvus, alive (see vivify) + -PAROUS.] —viv′i·par′i·ty (vī′və-păr′ə-tē) n. —vi·vip′a·rous·ly adv.

viv·i·sect (vĭv′ə-sĕkt′) v. -sected, -secting, -sects. —tr. To perform vivisection on (a living animal). —intr. To practice vivisection. [Back-formation from VIVISECTION.] —viv′i·sec′tor (-sĕk′tər) n.

viv·i·sec·tion (vĭv′ə-sĕk′shən) n. The act of cutting into or dissecting the body of a living animal, especially for scientific research. [Latin vīvus, alive (see vivify) + -SECTION.] —viv′i·sec′tion·al adj. —viv′i·sec′tion·ist n.

vix·en (vĭk′sən) n. 1. A female fox. 2. A quarrelsome, shrewish, or malicious woman. [Middle English fixene, Old English fyxe, she-fox. See puk-² in Appendix.*] —vix′en·ish adj. —vix′en·ly adj. & adv.

viz. videlicet.

viz·ard (vĭz′ərd) n. Also **vis·ard.** 1. A visor. 2. A mask. [Earlier vizar, viser, variants of VISOR.]

Viz·ca·í·no (vēz-kä-ē′nō; Spanish vēth-kä-ē′nō), **Sebastián.** 1550?-1615. Spanish explorer of the Pacific Coast of North America.

vi·zier (vĭ-zîr′, vĭz′yər) n. Also **vi·zir** (vĭ-zîr′). A high officer in a Moslem government, especially in the old Turkish Empire. [French vizir, from Turkish vezîr, from Arabic wazîr, porter, from wazara, to bear, carry.] —vi·zier′i·al adj.

vi·zier·ate (vĭ-zîr′ĭt, -āt′, vĭz′yər-ĭt, -yə-rāt′) n. The office, authority, or term of office of a vizier. Also called "vizieralty," "viziership."

vi·zor. Variant of visor.

V-J Day (vē′jā′). The day of victory for the Allied forces over Japan in World War II; officially, September 2, 1945. [Short for Victory in Japan Day.]

Vlaan·de·ren. The Flemish name for Flanders.

Vlad·i·mir (vlăd′ə-mîr′; Russian vlä-dē′mĭr). A city of the Soviet Union, 110 miles northeast of Moscow. Population, 181,000.

Vla·di·vos·tok (vlăd′ə-vŏs-tŏk′, -vŏs′tŏk). A city of the Soviet Union, a seaport in extreme southeastern Russian S.F.S.R. on the Sea of Japan. Population, 367,000.

Vla·minck (vlä-măNK′), **Maurice de.** 1876-1958. French painter; noted for his landscapes.

vlf, VLF very low frequency.

Vl·ta·va (vl′tä-vä). A river of Czechoslovakia, rising on the eastern slopes of the Bohemian Forest and flowing 267 miles generally north to the Elbe.

V-mail (vē′māl′) n. A postal service used during World War II in which letters were reduced photographically, transmitted overseas, and there enlarged and delivered. [From V(ICTORY).]

V.M.D. Doctor of Veterinary Medicine (Latin Veterinariae Medicinae Doctor).

vo. verso.

voc. vocative.

vocab. vocabulary.

vo·ca·ble (vō′kə-bəl) n. A word considered only as a sequence of sounds or letters rather than as a unit of meaning. —adj. Capable of being voiced or spoken. [French, from Old French, from Latin vocābulum, an appellation, from vocāre, to call. See wekw- in Appendix.*]

vo·cab·u·lar·y (vō-kăb′yə-lĕr′ē) n., pl. -ies. Abbr. vocab. 1. A list of words and often phrases, usually arranged alphabetically and defined or translated; a lexicon or glossary. 2. All the words of a language. 3. The sum of words used by, understood by, or at the command of a particular person, social group, profession, trade, or the like. 4. A command or reserve of expressive techniques; repertoire: a dancer's vocabulary of movement. —See Synonyms at diction. [Medieval Latin vōcābulārium, from vocābulārius, of words, from Latin vocābulum, an appellation, name. See vocable.]

vo·cal (vō′kəl) adj. 1. Of or pertaining to the voice. 2. Uttered or produced by the voice: a vocal prayer. 3. Having a voice; capable of emitting sound or speech. 4. Full of voices; resounding with speech. 5. Quick to speak or criticize; outspoken. 6. Phonetics. a. Vocalic. b. Voiced. —n. 1. Phonetics. A vocal sound. 2. A popular piece of music for a singer, often with instrumental accompaniment. [Middle English, from Latin

Maurice de Vlaminck

vōcālis, speaking, talking, from *vōx,* voice. See **wekw-** in Appendix.*] —**vo′cal·ly** *adv.* —**vo′cal·ness** *n.*

vocal cords. The lower of two pairs of bands or folds in the larynx that vibrate when pulled together and when air is passed up from the lungs, thereby producing vocal sounds.

vo·cal·ic (vō-kăl′ĭk) *adj.* **1.** Containing many vowel sounds. **2.** Pertaining to or having the nature of a vowel or vowels.

vo·cal·ism (vō′kə-lĭz′əm) *n.* **1.** The use of the voice in speaking or singing. **2.** The act, technique, or art of singing. **3.** A vowel or vocalic sound. **4.** A system of vowels, as within a specific language.

vo·cal·ist (vō′kə-lĭst) *n.* A singer.

vo·cal·ize (vō′kə-līz′) *v.* **-ized, -izing, -izes.** —*tr.* **1.** To make vocal; produce with the voice. **2.** To give voice to; to articulate. **3.** To mark (a vowelless Hebrew text, for example) with diacritical vowel points. **4.** *Phonetics.* **a.** To change (a consonant) into a vowel during articulation. **b.** To voice. —*intr.* **1.** To use the voice; especially, to sing. **2.** *Phonetics.* To be changed into a vowel. —**vo′cal·i·za′tion** *n.* —**vo′cal·iz′er** *n.*

vo·ca·tion (vō-kā′shən) *n.* **1.** A regular occupation or profession; especially, one for which one is specially suited or qualified. **2.** An urge or predisposition to undertake a certain kind of work, especially a religious career; a calling. [Middle English *vocacioun,* divine call to a religious life, from Old French *vocation,* from Latin *vōcātiō,* a calling, summoning, from *vōcāre,* to call. See **wekw-** in Appendix.*]

vo·ca·tion·al (vō-kā′shən-əl) *adj.* **1.** Of or pertaining to vocations or one's vocation. **2.** Pertaining to, providing, or undergoing training in a special skill to be pursued as a trade. —**vo·ca′tion·al·ly** *adv.*

vocational school. A school, especially one on a secondary level, that trains persons with special aptitudes for qualification in specific trades or occupations, such as mechanics, stenography, or the like.

voc·a·tive (vŏk′ə-tĭv) *adj.* **1.** Pertaining to, characteristic of, or used in calling. **2.** *Abbr.* **v., voc.** Pertaining to or designating a grammatical case used in Latin and certain other languages to indicate the person or thing being addressed. —*n. Abbr.* **v., voc. 1.** The vocative case. **2.** A word in this case. [Middle English *vocatif,* from Old French, from Latin *vocātivus,* from *vōcāre,* to call. See **vocation.**] —**voc′a·tive·ly** *adv.*

vo·cif·er·ate (vō-sĭf′ə-rāt′) *v.* **-ated, -ating, -ates.** —*intr.* To cry out vehemently, especially in protest; to clamor. —*tr.* To exclaim loudly and insistently. [Latin *vōciferārī* : *vōx* (stem *vōci-*), voice (see **vocal**) + *ferre,* to bear (see **bher-**[1] in Appendix*).] —**vo·cif′er·a′tion** *n.* —**vo·cif′er·a′tor** (-ə-rā′tər) *n.*

vo·cif·er·ous (vō-sĭf′ər-əs) *adj.* Also **vo·cif·er·ant** (-ənt). **1.** Making an outcry; clamorous. **2.** Characterized by loudness and vehemence. [From VOCIFERATE.] —**vo·cif′er·ous·ly** *adv.* —**vo·cif′er·ous·ness** *n.*

Synonyms: *vociferous, blatant, boisterous, strident, clamorous.* These adjectives describe what is conspicuously loud, usually offensively so. *Vociferous* suggests the noise of an outcry, as of vehement demanding or protesting. *Blatant* suggests noise associated with coarseness, vulgarity, or obtrusive behavior. *Boisterous* is even stronger in implying a combination of noise and rowdy behavior, caused usually by unruliness or high spirits. *Strident* describes noise that is offensively harsh, shrill, or discordant. *Clamorous* adds to *vociferous* the idea of long duration; or the term can refer to any combination of loud, distracting sounds.

vod·ka (vŏd′kə) *n.* An alcoholic liquor originally distilled from fermented wheat mash but now also made from a mash of rye, corn, or potatoes. [Russian *vodka,* diminutive of *voda,* water. See **wed-**[1] in Appendix.*]

vogue (vōg) *n.* **1.** The prevailing fashion, practice, or style. Often used with *in: Hoop skirts were once in vogue.* **2.** Popular acceptance or favor; popularity. —See Synonyms at **fashion.** [French, fashion, "rowing," from *voguer,* to row, go along smoothly, from Old French, from Old Low German *wogon* (unattested). See **wegh-** in Appendix.*]

Vo·gul (vō′go͝ol) *n.* **1.** One of a people living in western Siberia. **2.** The Ugric language of these people. [Russian, from Ostyak *Uogal′, Uogat′.*]

voice (vois) *n. Abbr.* **v. 1.** The sound or sounds produced by the vocal organs of a vertebrate, especially by those of a human being. **2.** The ability to produce such sounds. **3.** Any sound resembling or reminiscent of vocal utterance. **4.** The specified quality, condition, or timbre of vocal sound: *a hoarse voice.* **5. a.** A medium or agency of expression: *give voice to one's anger.* **b.** The right or opportunity to express a choice or opinion. **6.** *Obsolete.* **a.** Rumor or report. **b.** Reputation or fame. **7.** *Grammar.* A verb form indicating the relation between the subject and the action expressed by the verb. See **active, passive. 8.** *Phonetics.* The expiration of air through vibrating vocal cords, used in the production of the vowels and voiced consonants. Compare **breath. 9. a.** Musical tone produced by the vibration of vocal cords and resonated within the throat and head cavities. **b.** The quality or condition of a person's singing: *a baritone in excellent voice.* **c.** A singer: *a choir of excellent voices.* **10.** Any of the melodic parts for a musical composition. In this sense, also called "voice part." —**with one voice.** In unison; unanimously. —*tr.v.* **voiced, voicing, voices. 1.** To express or utter; give voice to. **2.** *Phonetics.* To utter with voice. **3.** *Music.* To regulate the tone of (the pipes of an organ, for example). —See Synonyms at **vent.** [Middle English, from Old French *vois, voix,* from Latin *vōx.* See **wekw-** in Appendix.*]

voice box. The larynx.

voiced (voist) *adj.* **1.** Having a voice or having a specified kind of voice. Often used in combination: *harsh-voiced.* **2.** Expressed by means of the voice: *a voiced opinion.* **3.** *Phonetics.* Uttered with vibration of the vocal cords, as the consonants *d* and *b.* Compare **voiceless.**

voice·ful (vois′fəl) *adj.* Having a voice; especially, having a loud voice; resounding. —**voice′ful·ness** *n.*

voice·less (vois′lĭs) *adj.* **1.** Having no voice; mute; silent. **2.** *Phonetics.* Uttered without vibration of the vocal cords, as the consonants *t* and *p.* Compare **voiced.** —See Synonyms at **dumb.** —**voice′less·ly** *adv.* —**voice′less·ness** *n.*

voice part. *Music.* A **voice** *(see).*

voice·print (vois′prĭnt′) *n.* An electronically recorded graphic representation of voice, typically with time plotted on the horizontal axis, frequency on the vertical, and amplitude exhibited in a series of contour lines, the configuration being characteristic of an individual speaker's articulation of any given word.

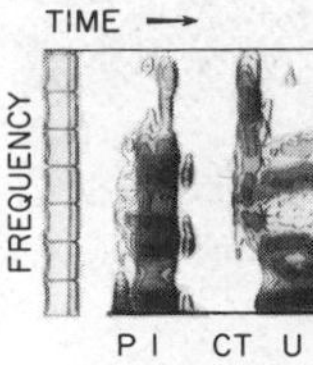

voiceprint
A contour spectrogram of the word "pictures"

void (void) *adj.* **1.** Containing no matter; empty. **2.** Unoccupied; unfilled, as a position. **3.** Devoid; lacking. Used with *of: void of understanding.* **4.** Ineffective; useless. **5.** Having no legal force or validity; null. —See Synonyms at **empty.** —*n.* **1.** Something that is void; an empty space; a vacuum. **2.** An open space or break in continuity; a gap: *"hanging in a kind of void between my mother's fried chicken and the cold prison floor"* (James Baldwin). **3.** A feeling or state of emptiness, loneliness, or loss. —*tr.v.* **voided, voiding, voids. 1.** To make void or of no effect; invalidate. **2. a.** To empty or take out (the contents of something). **b.** To evacuate (body wastes). **3.** *Archaic.* To leave; vacate. —See Synonyms at **nullify.** [Middle English, from Old French *voide, vuide,* from Vulgar Latin *vocitus* (unattested), from *vocāre,* to be empty. See **eu-**[2] in Appendix.*] —**void′er** *n.*

void·a·ble (voi′də-bəl) *adj.* Capable of being voided; especially, capable of being annulled. —**void′a·ble·ness** *n.*

void·ance (voi′dəns) *n.* **1.** The act of voiding, emptying, or evacuating. **2.** The condition of being vacant; emptiness.

void·ed (voi′dĭd) *adj. Heraldry.* Having the central area cut out or left vacant, leaving a narrow border or outline.

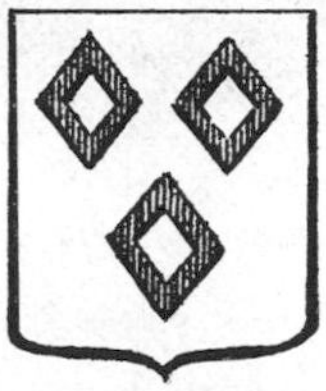

voided
Voided lozenges

voi·là (vwä-lä′) *interj. French.* There it is! There you are!

voile (voil; *French* vwäl) *n.* A sheer fabric of cotton, rayon, silk, or wool used for making dresses, curtains, or the like. [French, from Latin *vēla,* neuter of *vēlum,* cloth, veil. See **weg-**[1] in Appendix.*]

voir dire (vwär dēr′). *Law.* A preliminary examination concerning the competence of a prospective witness or juror. [Norman French, from Old French, "to speak the truth" : *voir,* truth, from Latin *vērus* (see **wēros** in Appendix*) + *dire,* to say, from Latin *dīcere* (see **deik-** in Appendix*).]

Voit (foit), **Karl von.** 1831–1908. German physiologist.

voix cé·leste (vwä sā-lĕst′). An organ stop that produces a gentle tremolo effect. Also called "vox angelica." [French, "celestial voice."]

Voj·vo·di·na (voi′vô-dĭ-nä). Also **Voi·vo·di·na, Voy·vo·di·na.** An autonomous province of Yugoslavia, occupying 8,683 square miles in Serbia. Population, 1,855,000. Capital, Novi Sad.

vol. 1. volcano. **2.** volume. **3.** volunteer.

Vo·lans (vō′lănz) *n.* Also **Vo·lan** (-län). A constellation in the polar region of the Southern Hemisphere near Carina and Dorado. [Latin *volāns,* flying, VOLANT.]

vo·lant (vō′lənt) *adj.* **1.** Flying or capable of flying. **2.** Moving quickly or nimbly; agile. **3.** *Heraldry.* Depicted with the wings extended as in flying. [Latin *volāns,* present participle of *volāre,* to fly. See **gwel-**[4] in Appendix.*]

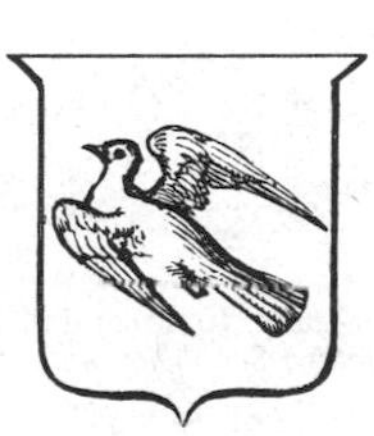

volant
A martlet volant

Vo·la·pük (vō′lə-pük′) *n.* An international language invented in 1879. [*Vol,* from English WORLD + *pük,* from English SPEECH: coined by Johann Schleyer (1831–1912), German linguist.] —**Vo′la·pük′ist** *n.*

vo·lar (vō′lər) *adj.* Of or pertaining to the sole of the foot or the palm of the hand. [From Latin *vola,* palm, sole. See **wel-**[3] in Appendix.*]

vol·a·tile (vŏl′ə-tĭl) *adj.* **1.** Evaporating readily at normal temperatures and pressures. **2.** Capable of being readily vaporized. **3.** Changeable, as: **a.** Inconstant; fickle. **b.** Tending to violence; explosive. **c.** Lighthearted; flighty. **d.** Ephemeral; fleeting. **4.** *Obsolete.* Flying or capable of flying; volant. [Middle English *volatil,* flying, fleeting, from Old French, from Latin *volātilis,* from *volāre,* to fly. See **volant.**]

volatile oil. A rapidly evaporating oil, especially an essential oil, that does not leave a stain.

vol·a·til·i·ty (vŏl′ə-tĭl′ə-tē) *n.* The quality or state of being volatile.

vol·a·til·ize (vŏl′ə-tə-līz′) *v.* **-ized, -izing, -izes.** —*intr.* **1.** To become volatile. **2.** To pass off in vapor; evaporate. —*tr.* **1.** To make volatile. **2.** To cause to evaporate. —**vol′a·til·iz′a·ble** *adj.* —**vol′a·til·i·za′tion** *n.* —**vol′a·til·iz′er** *n.*

vol-au-vent (vô-lō-vän′) *n.* A light pastry shell filled with a ragout of meat or fish. [French, "flight in the wind."]

vol·can·ic (vŏl-kăn′ĭk) *adj.* **1.** Pertaining to, characteristic of, or resembling an erupting volcano. **2.** Produced by or discharged from a volcano. **3.** Tending to violent eruption; powerfully explosive: *a volcanic temper.* —**vol′can·i′ci·ty** (-kə-nĭs′ə-tē) *n.* —**vol·can′i·cal·ly** *adv.*

volcanic glass. A volcanic igneous rock of vitreous or glassy texture, such as obsidian or pitchstone.

vol·can·ism (vŏl′kə-nĭz′əm) *n.* Also **vul·can·ism** (vŭl′-). Volcanic force or activity.

vol·can·ize (vŏl′kə-nīz′) *tr.v.* **-ized, -izing, -izes.** To subject to or change by the effects of volcanic heat. —**vol′can·i·za′tion** *n.*

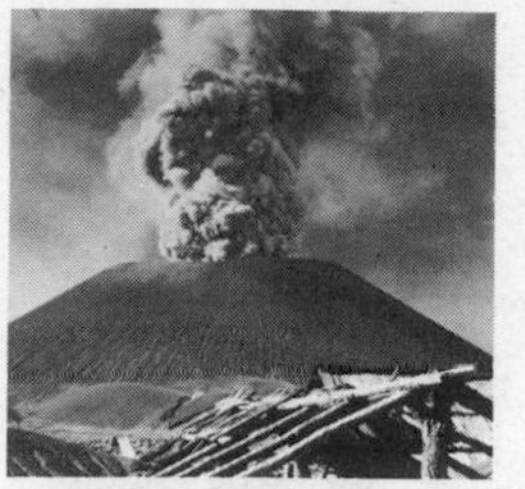

volcano
Paricutín, Mexico

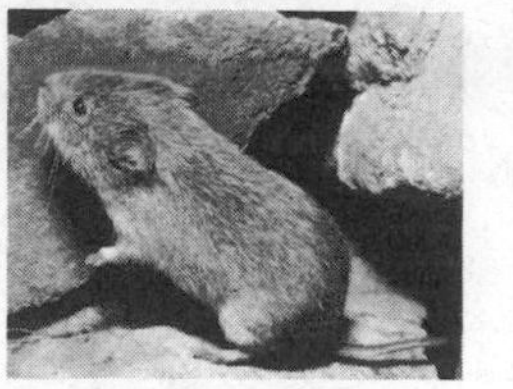

vole[1]
Genus *Microtus*

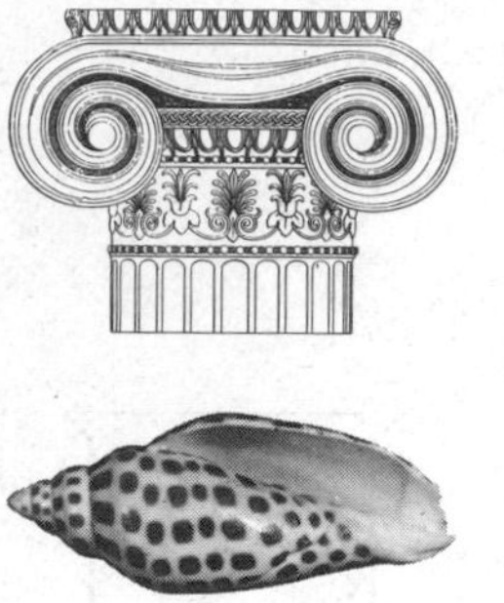

volute
Above: Ionic capital
Below: *Scaphella junonia*

vol·ca·no (vŏl-kā′nō) *n., pl.* **-noes** or **-nos.** *Abbr.* **vol. 1.** A vent in the earth's crust through which molten lava and gases are ejected. **2.** A mountain formed by the materials so ejected. [Italian, from Latin *Volcānus,* VULCAN.]
Volcano Islands. Three small islands (about 11 square miles) in the western Pacific, among them Iwo Jima, administered by the United States from 1945 to 1968, when they were restored to Japan.
vol·can·ol·o·gy (vŏl′kə-nŏl′ə-jē) *n.* Also **vul·can·ol·o·gy** (vŭl′-). The science concerned with volcanic phenomena. **—vol′can·o·log′i·cal** (-nə-lŏj′ĭ-kəl) *adj.* **—vol′can·ol′o·gist** *n.*
vole[1] (vōl) *n.* Any of various rodents of the genus *Microtus* and related genera, resembling rats or mice but having a relatively short tail. [Earlier *volemouse,* "field mouse," from Norwegian *voll,* field, from Old Norse *vǫllr.* See **welt-** in Appendix.*]
vole[2] (vōl) *n.* The winning of all the tricks in a card game; a grand slam. **—go the vole.** To risk everything in the hope of great profit. *—intr.v.* **voled, voling, voles.** To win all the tricks in a game. [French, from *voler,* to fly, from Old French, from Latin *volāre.* See **volant.**]
Vol·ga (vŏl′gə). The longest river of Europe, rising in the Valdai Hills of the northwestern Russian S.F.S.R. and flowing 2,290 miles in a winding course to the Caspian Sea in the south.
Vol·go·grad (vŏl′gə-grăd′; *Russian* vəl-gŏ-grät′). Formerly **Sta·lin·grad** (stäl′ĭn-grăd), **Tsa·ri·tsyn** (tsə-rē′tsĭn). A city of the Soviet Union, on the Volga in the southwestern Russian S.F.S.R. Population, 663,000.
vol·i·tant (vŏl′ə-tənt) *adj.* **1.** Flying or capable of flying. **2.** Moving about rapidly. [Latin *volitāns,* present participle of *volitāre,* frequentative of *volāre,* to fly. See **volant.**]
vol·i·ta·tion (vŏl′ə-tā′shən) *n.* The act of flying or the ability to fly; flight. **—vol′i·ta′tion·al** *adj.*
vo·li·tion (və-lĭsh′ən) *n.* **1.** An act of willing, choosing, or deciding. **2.** A conscious choice; decision. **3.** The power or capability of choosing; the will. [French, from Medieval Latin *volitiō,* from Latin *velle* (present stem *vol-*), to wish. See **wel-[2]** in Appendix.*] **—vo·li′tion·al** *adj.* **—vo·li′tion·al·ly** *adv.*
vol·i·tive (vŏl′ə-tĭv) *adj.* **1.** Pertaining to or originating in the will. **2.** Expressing a wish or permission.
vol·ley (vŏl′ē) *n., pl.* **-leys. 1. a.** The simultaneous discharge of a number of missiles. **b.** The missiles thus discharged. **2.** A bursting forth of a number of things simultaneously: *a volley of oaths.* **3.** A shot, especially in tennis, made by striking the ball before it touches the ground. *—v.* **volleyed, -leying, -leys.** *—tr.* **1.** To discharge in or as if in a volley. **2.** To strike (a tennis ball, for example) before it touches the ground. *—intr.* To be discharged in or as if in a volley. [Old French *volee,* from Vulgar Latin *volāta* (unattested), flight, from Latin *volātus,* past participle of *volāre,* to fly. See **volant.**] **—vol′ley·er** *n.*
vol·ley·ball (vŏl′ē-bôl′) *n.* **1.** A court game in which one team attempts to score by grounding a ball on the opposing team's side of a high net. **2.** The large inflated ball used in this game.
Vo·log·da (vô′ləg-də). A city of the Soviet Union, in the Russian S.F.S.R. 250 miles north of Moscow. Population, 159,000.
vol·plane (vŏl′plān′) *intr.v.* **-planed, -planing, -planes.** To glide toward the earth with the engine cut off. Used of an airplane or winged missile. *—n.* The glide of an airplane. [French *vol plané* : *vol,* flight, from *voler,* to fly, from Latin *volāre* (see **volant**) + *plané,* past participle of *planer,* to PLANE (to soar).]
Vol·sci (vŏl′sē) *pl.n. Singular* **Volscian** (vŏl′shən). A people of ancient Italy whose territory was conquered by the Romans in the fourth century B.C.
Vol·scian (vŏl′shən) *adj.* Of or pertaining to the Volsci or their language. *—n.* The Italic language of the Volsci.
Vol·stead Act (vŏl′stĕd′). The act of Congress (1919) that provided for Federal enforcement of prohibition. [Introduced by Andrew *Volstead* (1860–1947), American legislator.]
volt[1] (vōlt) *n. Abbr.* **V 1.** The International System unit of electric potential and electromotive force, equal to the difference of electric potential between two points on a conducting wire carrying a constant current of one ampere when the power dissipated between the points is one watt. See **measurement. 2.** A unit of electric potential and electromotive force equal to 1.00034 times the International System unit. In this sense, also called "international volt." [After Count VOLTA.]
volt[2] (vōlt) *n.* Also **volte. 1.** A circular movement executed by a horse in manège. **2.** *Fencing.* A sudden movement made in avoiding a thrust. [French *volte,* a turn, from Italian *volta,* from Vulgar Latin *volvita* (unattested), from *volvitāre* (unattested), frequentative of Latin *volvere,* to turn. See **wel-[3]** in Appendix.*]
Vol·ta (vŏl′tə). A river of western Africa, flowing about 300 miles generally south through Ghana to the Gulf of Guinea.
Vol·ta (vôl′tä), Count **Alessandro.** 1745–1827. Italian physicist; pioneer in study of electricity.
volt·age (vōl′tĭj) *n.* Electromotive force or potential difference, usually expressed in volts.
voltage divider. A number of resistors in series provided with taps at certain points to make available a fixed or variable fraction of the applied voltage.
vol·ta·ic (vŏl-tā′ĭk) *adj.* **1.** Pertaining to or denoting electricity or electric current produced by chemical action; galvanic. **2.** Producing electricity by chemical action. [After Count VOLTA.]
voltaic battery. An electric battery composed of a primary cell or cells.
voltaic cell. *Electricity.* A **primary cell** *(see).*
voltaic couple. Two dissimilar conductors in contact or in the same electrolytic solution, resulting in a difference of potential between them. Also called "galvanic couple."
voltaic pile. A source of electricity consisting of a number of alternating disks of two different metals separated by acid-moistened pads, forming primary cells connected in series.
Vol·taire (vŏl-târ′, vōl-; *French* vôl-târ′). Pen name of François Marie Arouet. 1694–1778. French poet, dramatist, satirist, and historian.
vol·ta·ism (vŏl′tə-ĭz′əm) *n. Electricity.* **Galvanism** *(see).* [VOLTA(IC) + -ISM.]
Vol·ta, Lake (vŏl′tə). An expansion of the Volta River extending for 250 miles in southeastern Ghana, formed by a dam completed in 1966.
volt·am·me·ter (vōlt′ăm′mē′tər) *n.* An instrument designed to measure current or potential. [VOLT-AM(PERE) + -METER.]
volt-am·pere (vōlt′ăm′pîr′) *n.* A unit of electric power equal to the product of one volt and one ampere, equivalent to one watt.
volte. Variant of **volt** (movement).
volte-face (vōlt-fäs′; *French* vôlt-fȧs′) *n. French.* An about-face; a reversal, as in policy.
volt·me·ter (vōlt′mē′tər) *n.* An instrument, such as a galvanometer, for measuring potential differences in volts.
Vol·tur·no (vôl-to͞or′nō). The principal river of southern Italy, rising in the Apennines and flowing 109 miles generally southwest to the Tyrrhenian Sea.
vol·u·ble (vŏl′yə-bəl) *adj.* **1.** Characterized by a ready flow of words in speaking; garrulous; fluent; loquacious. **2.** *Rare.* Turning easily on an axis; rotating. **3.** Twining or twisting, as a plant. —See Synonyms at **talkative.** [Old French, from Latin *volūbilis,* from *volvere* (past participle *volūtus*), to turn. See **wel-[3]** in Appendix.*] **—vol′u·bil′i·ty, vol′u·ble·ness** *n.* **—vol′u·bly** *adv.*
vol·ume (vŏl′yo͞om, -yəm) *n.* **1.** *Abbr.* **v., vol.** A collection of written or printed sheets bound together; a book. **2.** *Abbr.* **v., vol.** One of the books within a complete set. **3.** Any written material in a library that has been assembled and cataloged as an individual unit. **4.** A roll of parchment; a scroll. **5.** *Abbr.* **V a.** The size or extent of a three-dimensional object or region of space. **b.** Broadly, the capacity of such a region or of a specified container. **6.** A large amount: *volumes of praise.* **7. a.** The amplitude or loudness of a sound. **b.** A control, as on a radio, for adjusting loudness. **—speak volumes.** To be informative or deeply significant. [Middle English, roll of parchment, from Old French, from Latin *volūmen,* from *volvere,* to roll, turn. See **wel-[3]** in Appendix.*]
vo·lu·me·ter (və-lo͞o′mə-tər) *n.* Any of several instruments for measuring the volume of liquids, solids, and gases. [VOLU(ME) + -METER.]
vol·u·met·ric (vŏl′yə-mĕt′rĭk) *adj.* Of or pertaining to measurement of volume. [VOLU(ME) + METRIC.] **—vol′u·met′ri·cal·ly** (-mĕt′rĭk-ə-lē) *adv.*
volumetric analysis. 1. Quantitative analysis using accurately measured, especially titrated, volumes of standard chemical solutions. **2.** The analysis of a gas by volume.
vo·lu·mi·nous (və-lo͞o′mə-nəs) *adj.* **1.** Having great volume, fullness, size, or number. **2. a.** Filling or capable of filling volumes. **b.** Prolific in speech or writing. **3.** *Rare.* Having many coils; winding: *the voluminous labyrinth.* [Late Latin *volūminōsus,* having many folds, from Latin *volūmen,* roll of writing, VOLUME.] **—vo·lu′mi·nos′i·ty** (-nŏs′ə-tē), **vo·lu′mi·nous·ness** *n.* **—vo·lu′mi·nous·ly** *adv.*
vol·un·ta·rism (vŏl′ən-tə-rĭz′əm) *n.* Belief in the primacy of will. **—vol′un·ta·rist** *n.* **—vol′un·ta·ris′tic** *adj.*
vol·un·tar·y (vŏl′ən-tĕr′ē) *adj.* **1.** Arising from one's own free will; acting on one's own initiative: *"Ignorance, when it is voluntary, is criminal"* (Samuel Johnson). **2.** Acting or serving in a specified capacity willingly and without constraint or guarantee of reward. **3.** Normally controlled by or subject to individual volition. **4.** Capable of exercising will; volitional. **5.** Proceeding from impulse; spontaneous. **6.** *Law.* **a.** Acting or performed without external persuasion or compulsion. **b.** Without legal obligation, payment, or valuable consideration: *a voluntary conveyance.* **c.** Not accidental; intentional: *voluntary manslaughter.* *—n., pl.* **voluntaries. 1.** Any act or work not imposed or demanded by another. **2.** *Music.* Solo organ music, occasionally improvised, that is played usually before and sometimes during or after a church service. **3.** *Obsolete.* A volunteer. [Middle English, from Latin *voluntārius,* from *voluntās,* will, free will, from *velle* (present stem *vol-*), to wish. See **wel-[2]** in Appendix.*] **—vol′un·tar′i·ly** *adv.* **—vol′un·tar′i·ness** *n.*
Synonyms: *voluntary, intentional, deliberate, willful, willing, spontaneous.* These adjectives mean unforced. *Voluntary* is applied in several related senses to what is done by choice, to physical movement subject to regulation by the will, and less often to action that is not only of one's choice but premeditated. The last-named sense is more basic to *intentional* and *deliberate;* in addition, *deliberate* stresses the idea of action taken with full awareness of the consequences. *Willful* can mean merely in accordance with one's will but often implies headstrong persistence in a self-determined course of action. *Willing* suggests acceding to a course proposed by another, without reluctance or even eagerly. *Spontaneous* refers to behavior that seems wholly unpremeditated, a natural response and a true reflection of one's feelings.
vol·un·tar·y·ism (vŏl′ən-tĕr′ē-ĭz′əm) *n.* The principle of reliance on voluntary contributions rather than government funds, as for churches or schools. **—vol′un·tar′y·ist** *n.*
voluntary muscle. Muscle normally controlled by individual volition.

ă pat/ā pay/âr care/ä father/b bib/ch church/d deed/ĕ pet/ē be/f fife/g gag/h hat/hw which/ĭ pit/ī pie/îr pier/j judge/k kick/l lid, needle/m mum/n no, sudden/ng thing/ŏ pot/ō toe/ô paw, for/oi noise/ou out/o͝o took/o͞o boot/p pop/r roar/s sauce/sh ship, dish/

vol·un·teer (vŏl′ən-tîr′) *n. Abbr.* **vol. 1.** A person who performs or gives his services of his own free will. **2.** *Law.* **a.** A person who renders aid, performs a service, or assumes an obligation voluntarily. **b.** A person who holds property under a deed made without valuable consideration. **3.** A cultivated plant growing from self-sown or accidentally dropped seed. —*adj.* **1.** Pertaining to or consisting of volunteers: *a volunteer militia.* **2.** Enlisted or serving as a volunteer. **3.** Growing from self-sown or accidentally dropped seed. Said of a cultivated plant or crop that has reseeded itself. —*v.* **volunteered, -teering, -teers.** —*tr.* To give or offer to give on one's own initiative. —*intr.* To enter into or offer to enter into any undertaking of one's own free will. [French *volontaire,* from Latin *voluntārius,* VOLUNTARY.]

vo·lup·tu·ar·y (və-lŭp′cho͞o-ĕr′ē) *n., pl.* **-ies.** A person whose life is given over to luxury and sensual pleasures; a sensualist: *"an adventurous voluptuary, angling in all streams for variety of pleasures"* (De Quincey). [Late Latin *voluptuārius,* from Latin *voluptārius,* from *voluptās,* pleasure. See **voluptuous.**] —**vo·lup′tu·ar′y** *adj.*

vo·lup·tu·ous (və-lŭp′cho͞o-əs) *adj.* **1.** Consisting of or characterized by strong visual and tactile delights: *"my plays are built to induce not voluptuous but intellectual interest"* (G.B. Shaw). **2.** Devoted to or frequently indulging in sensual gratifications. **3. a.** Full and appealing in form: *a voluptuous mouth.* **b.** Directed toward or anticipating sensuous gratification: *voluptuous thoughts.* **c.** Arising from the satisfying of luxurious or sensual desires. —See Synonyms at **sensuous.** [Middle English, from Old French *voluptueux,* from Latin *voluptuōsus,* from *voluptās,* pleasure. See **wel-**[2] in Appendix.*] —**vo·lup′tu·ous·ly** *adv.* —**vo·lup′tu·ous·ness** *n.*

vo·lute (və-lo͞ot′) *n.* **1.** A spiral, scroll-like ornament such as that used on an Ionic capital. **2.** A twisted or spiral formation, such as one of the whorls of a gastropod shell. **3.** Any of various marine gastropod mollusks of the family Volutidae, having a spiral, often colorfully marked shell. —*adj.* Also **vo·lut·ed** (və-lo͞o′tĭd). Having a spiral form; spirally twisted or rolled. [French, from Latin *volūta,* scroll, from the feminine past participle of *volvere,* to turn. See **wel-**[3] in Appendix.*]

vo·lu·tion (və-lo͞o′shən) *n.* **1.** A turn or twist about a center; a spiral. **2.** *Zoology.* One of the whorls of a spiral shell. [From Latin *volvere* (past participle *volūtus*), to turn. See **volute.**]

vol·va (vŏl′və) *n.* A cuplike structure around the base of the stalk of certain fungi, a remnant of the veil. [Latin *volva, vulva,* covering. See **wel-**[3] in Appendix.*] —**vol′vate′** *adj.*

vol·vox (vŏl′vŏks′) *n.* Any of various flagellate protozoans of the genus *Volvox,* that form hollow, spherical multicellular colonies. [New Latin, from Latin *volvere,* to turn, roll. See **volute.**]

vol·vu·lus (vŏl′vyə-ləs) *n.* Obstruction in the intestine caused by abnormal twisting. [New Latin, from Latin *volvere,* to turn. See **volute.**]

vo·mer (vō′mər) *n.* The flat bone forming the inferior and posterior part of the nasal septum. [Latin *vōmer,* plowshare. See **wogwhni-** in Appendix.*] —**vo′mer·ine** (vō′mər-īn, vŏm′-) *adj.*

vom·i·ca (vŏm′ĭ-kə) *n., pl.* **-cae** (-sē). **1.** The profuse expectoration of putrid matter. **2. a.** An abnormal pus-containing cavity in a lung, caused by the deterioration of tissue. **b.** The purulent matter contained in such a cavity. [Latin, boil, ulcer, from *vomere,* to VOMIT.]

vom·it (vŏm′ĭt) *v.* **-ited, -iting, -its.** —*intr.* **1.** To eject part or all of the contents of the stomach through the mouth, usually in a series of involuntary spasmic movements. **2.** To be discharged forcefully and abundantly; spew forth. —*tr.* **1.** To eject from the stomach through the mouth. **2.** To eject or discharge in a gush; spew out. —*n.* **1.** The act of ejecting matter from the stomach. **2.** Matter ejected from the stomach. **3.** An emetic. [Middle English *vomiten,* from Latin *vomere* (past participle *vomitus*). See **wem-** in Appendix.*] —**vom′it·er** *n.*

vomiting gas. *Chemistry.* **Chloropicrin** *(see).*

vom·i·tive (vŏm′ə-tĭv) *adj.* Pertaining to or causing vomiting. —*n.* An emetic.

vom·i·to·ry (vŏm′ə-tôr′ē, -tōr′ē) *adj.* Inducing vomiting; vomitive. —*n., pl.* **vomitories. 1.** Something that induces vomiting. **2.** An aperture through which matter is discharged. **3.** One of the passageways of a Roman amphitheater leading from the outside wall to the foot of the banked seats.

vom·i·tu·ri·tion (vŏm′ə-cho͞o-rĭsh′ən) *n.* Forceful but ineffectual attempts at vomiting; retching. [VOMIT + (MICT)URITION.]

vom·i·tus (vŏm′ə-təs) *n.* Vomited matter. [Latin, past participle of *vomere,* to VOMIT.]

von Bé·ké·sy, Georg. See Georg von **Békésy.**

von Braun, Wernher. See Wernher von **Braun.**

von Kár·mán, Theodor. See Theodor von **Kármán.**

von Neu·mann, John. See John von **Neumann.**

von Stro·heim, Erich. See Erich von **Stroheim.**

voo·doo (vo͞o′do͞o) *n., pl.* **-doos. 1.** A religious cult of African origin practiced in the Western Hemisphere mainly by the Negroes of Haiti and characterized by a belief in sorcery and fetishes and rituals in which participants communicate by trance with ancestors, saints, or animistic deities. **2.** A charm, fetish, spell, or curse believed by adherents of this cult to hold magic power. **3.** One who performs rites at a meeting of adherents of this cult. —See Synonyms at **magic.** —*adj.* Of, pertaining to, or used in voodoo. —*tr.v.* **voodooed, -dooing, -doos.** To place under the influence of a voodoo spell; put a hex on. [Louisiana French *voudou,* from Ewe *vodu.*]

voo·doo·ism (vo͞o′do͞o-ĭz′əm) *n.* **1.** The view of life and death embodied in the voodoo cult. **2.** The practice of voodoo. —**voo′doo·ist** *n.* —**voo′doo·is′tic** *adj.*

vo·ra·cious (vô-rā′shəs, vō-, və-) *adj.* **1.** Consuming or eager to consume great amounts of food; ravenous. **2.** Having an insatiable appetite for some activity or pursuit; greedy: *"I continued to spend many hours of each day in rapid voracious reading"* (Susan Sontag). [Latin *vorax* (stem *vorāci-*), from *vorāre,* to devour. See **gwerə-**[2] in Appendix.*] —**vo·ra′cious·ly** *adv.* —**vo·ra′ci·ty** (vô-răs′ə-tē, vō-, və-), **vo·ra′cious·ness** *n.*

vor·la·ge (fôr′lä′gə, fōr′-) *n.* A posture assumed in skiing in which the skier leans forward from the ankles, usually without lifting the heels. [German *Vorlage* : *vor,* before, from Old High German *fora* (see **per**[1] in Appendix*) + *Lage,* stance, from Old High German *lāga* (see **legh-** in Appendix*).]

Vo·ro·nezh (vŏ-rô′nĭsh). A city of the Soviet Union, on the Don in the western Russian S.F.S.R. Population, 576,000.

Vo·ro·shi·lov (və-rŏ-shē′lôf), **Kliment Efremovich.** Born 1881. Soviet military and political leader; Chairman of the Presidium of the Supreme Soviet (1953–60).

Vo·ro·shi·lov·grad. The former name for **Lugansk.**

Vo·ro·shi·lovsk. The former name for **Stavropol.**

-vorous. Indicates eating or feeding on; for example, **herbivorous, piscivorous.** [Latin *-vorus,* from *vorāre,* to devour. See **gwerə-**[2] in Appendix.*]

vor·tex (vôr′tĕks) *n., pl.* **-texes** or **-tices** (-tə-sēz′). **1.** Fluid flow involving rotation about an axis; a whirlwind; whirlpool. **2.** A situation regarded as drawing into its center all that surrounds it: *"As happened with so many theater actors, he was swept up in the vortex of Hollywood."* (New York Times). [Latin *vortex, vertex,* from *vertere,* to turn. See **wer-**[3] in Appendix.*]

vor·ti·cal (vôr′tĭ-kəl) *adj.* Also **vor·ti·cose** (-kōs′). Pertaining to or resembling a vortex; whirling. [From Latin *vortex* (stem *vortic-*), VORTEX.] —**vor′ti·cal·ly** *adv.*

vor·ti·cel·la (vôr′tə-sĕl′ə) *n.* Any of various bell-shaped, ciliated, stalked protozoans of the genus *Vorticella.* [New Latin *Vorticella,* from Latin *vortex* (stem *vortic-*), VORTEX.]

vor·tig·i·nous (vôr-tĭj′ə-nəs) *adj.* Whirling; vortical. [From Latin *vortīgō* (stem *vortīgin-*), variant of *vertīgō,* a whirling, from *vertere,* to turn. See **vortex.**]

Vosges Mountains (vōzh). A range of mountains in eastern France, along the Rhine opposite the Black Forest of West Germany. Highest elevation, Grand Ballon (4,672 feet).

vo·ta·ry (vō′tə-rē) *n., pl.* **-ries. 1.** A person bound by vows to live a life of religious worship or service; a monk or nun. **2.** Any person fervently devoted to a religion, activity, leader, or ideal. Also called "votarist." —*adj.* **1.** Consecrated by a vow. **2.** Like or pertaining to a vow. [From Latin *vōtus,* past participle of *vovēre,* to vow. See **wegwh-** in Appendix.*]

Synonyms: *votary, devotee, habitué, fan.* These nouns mean an adherent of a person, cause, or activity. *Votary* and *devotee* imply strong personal commitment to the service of a person or thing, usually in a favorable sense. Both can refer to religious dedication or, by extension, to attachment to a branch of learning, a hobby, or a cultural pursuit. *Habitué* refers to one in regular attendance at a place offering a certain kind of activity. *Fan* is an informal term for an ardent enthusiast or admirer.

vote (vōt) *n.* **1.** A formal expression of preference for a candidate for office or for a proposed resolution of an issue. **2.** That by which such a preference is made known, as a raised hand or a ballot. **3.** The number of votes cast in an election or to resolve an issue: *a heavy vote in his favor.* **4.** A group of voters: *the labor vote.* **5.** The result of an election, referendum, or the like. **6.** The right to participate as a voter; suffrage. —*v.* **voted, voting, votes.** —*intr.* To express one's preference by a vote; cast one's vote. —*tr.* **1.** To express one's preference for; endorse by a vote. **2.** To bring into existence or make available by vote: *vote new funds for a program.* **3.** To declare or pronounce by general consent: *voted the play a success.* —**vote down.** To defeat by casting a negative vote. —**vote in.** To elect. —**vote out.** To remove from elective office by supporting the opposition. [Latin *vōtum,* vow, from *vōtus,* past participle of *vovēre,* to vow. See **wegwh-** in Appendix.*] —**vot′a·ble, vote′a·ble** *adj.* —**vot′er** *n.*

vote getter. 1. A candidate with abilities and qualities that attract votes in his favor. **2.** A means of drawing votes.

voting machine. An apparatus for use in polling places that mechanically records and counts votes.

vo·tive (vō′tĭv) *adj.* **1.** Given or dedicated in fulfillment of a vow or pledge: *a votive offering.* **2.** Expressing a wish, desire, or vow: *a votive prayer.* [Latin *vōtīvus,* from *vōtum,* vow, VOTE.]

votive Mass. *Roman Catholic Church.* A Mass differing from one prescribed for a certain day in that it is celebrated at the direction of authority, because of special circumstances, or at the decision of the priest.

vou. voucher.

vouch (vouch) *v.* **vouched, vouching, vouches.** —*tr.* **1.** To substantiate by supplying evidence; verify. **2.** *Law.* To summon as a witness to give warranty of title. **3.** *Archaic.* To cite (an authority, doctrine, or principle, for example) as supporting evidence for one's statements, opinions, or actions. **4.** *Obsolete.* To assert; declare. —*intr.* **1.** To furnish a guarantee; give personal assurance. Used with *for.* **2.** To function or serve as a guarantee; furnish supporting evidence. Used with *for: a deed that vouched for his courage.* —*n. Obsolete.* A declaration of opinion; an assertion. [Middle English *vouchen,* to summon (as a witness), from Old French *voucher,* from Latin *vōcāre,* to call. See **wekw-** in Appendix.*]

vouch·er (vou′chər) *n.* **1.** A person who vouches; a supporter, sponsor, or witness. **2.** *Abbr.* **vou.** A signed or stamped doc-

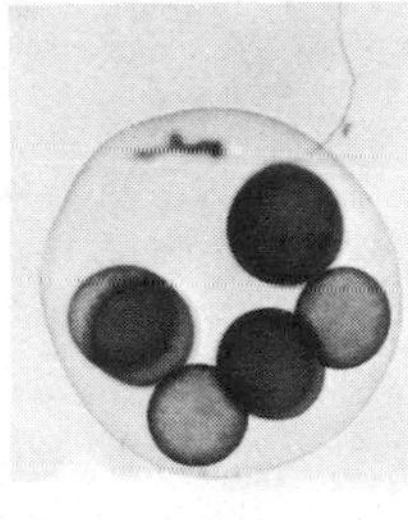

volvox
Photomicrograph of volvox colony

ument that serves as proof that the terms of a transaction have been met.

vouch·safe (vouch′sāf′) *tr.v.* **-safed, -safing, -safes.** To condescend to grant or bestow (a reply, favor, or privilege, for example); to deign: *"The only display of emotion that she had ever known him to vouchsafe"* (Ford Madox Ford). See Synonyms at **grant.** [Middle English *vouchen sauf,* "to warrant as safe" : VOUCH (obsolete sense "to warrant") + SAFE.]

vous·soir (vo͞o-swär′) *n.* Any of the wedge-shaped stones that form the curved parts of an arch or vaulted ceiling. [French, from Old French *vossoir,* from Vulgar Latin *volsōrium* (unattested), from *volsus* (unattested), variant of Latin *volutus,* past participle of *volvere,* to roll, turn. See **wel-³** in Appendix.*]

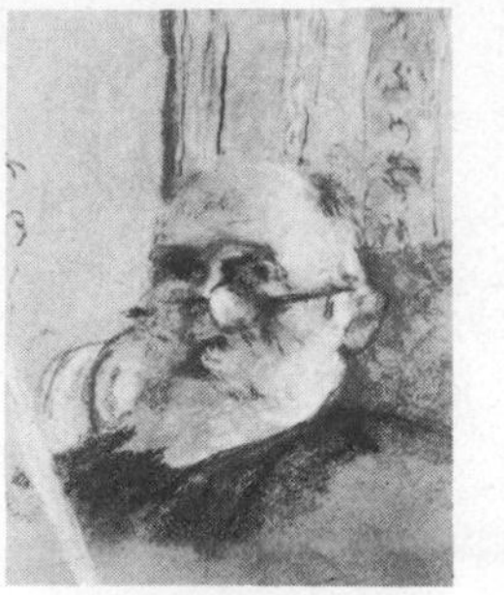

Jean Édouard Vuillard
A self-portrait

vow (vou) *n.* **1.** An earnest promise or pledge that binds one to perform a specified act or behave in a certain manner; especially, a solemn promise to live and act in accordance with the prescriptions of a religious body: *a nun's vows.* **2.** A formal declaration or assertion. **—take vows.** To enter a religious order. *—v.* **vowed, vowing, vows.** *—tr.* **1.** To promise or pledge solemnly. **2.** To make a pledge or threat to undertake: *vowing revenge on their persecutors.* **3.** To declare or assert formally: *"Well, I vow it is as fine a boy as ever was seen!"* (Fielding). *—intr.* To express a promise or pledge; make a vow. [Middle English *vowe,* from Old French, from Latin *vōtum,* from the neuter past participle of *vovēre,* to pledge, promise. See **wegwh-** in Appendix.*] **—vow′er** *n.*

vow·el (vou′əl) *n. Abbr.* **v. 1.** *Phonetics.* A speech sound created by the relatively free passage of breath through the larynx and oral cavity, usually forming the most prominent and central sound of a syllable. Compare **consonant. 2.** A letter that represents such a sound, as, in the English alphabet, *a, e, i, o, u,* and sometimes *y.* *—adj.* Of or constituting a vowel or vowels. [Middle English *vowelle,* from Old French *vouel,* from Latin *(littera) vōcālis,* "sounding (letter)," from *vōx* (stem *vōc-*), voice. See **wekw-** in Appendix.*]

vowel fracture. *Linguistics.* **Breaking** *(see).*

vow·el·ize (vou′ə-līz′) *tr.v.* **-ized, -izing, -izes.** To provide with vowel points. **—vow′el·i·za′tion** (-ĭ-zā′shən) *n.*

vowel point. Any of a number of diacritical marks written above or below consonants to indicate a preceding or following vowel in languages such as Hebrew and Arabic that are usually written without vowel letters.

vox an·gel·i·ca (vŏks ăn-jĕl′ĭ-kə). An organ stop, the **voix céleste** *(see).* [Latin, "angelic voice."]

vox hu·ma·na (hyo͞o-mā′nə, -mä′nə). An organ reed stop that produces tones imitative of the human voice. [Latin, "human voice."]

vox po·pu·li (pŏp′yə-lī′, -lē). Popular opinion or sentiment. [Latin, "voice of the people."]

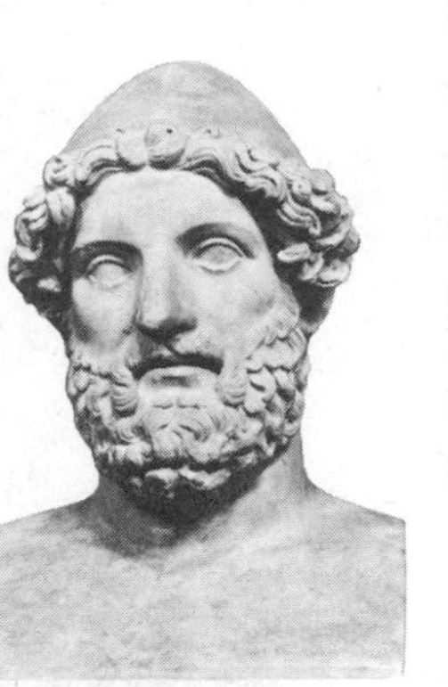

Vulcan

voy·age (voi′ĭj) *n.* **1.** A long journey, usually to a foreign or distant land; especially, a journey across an open sea or ocean. **2.** A record or account of a journey of exploration or discovery. **3.** *Obsolete.* An ambitious project or undertaking. *—v.* **voyaged, -aging, -ages.** *—intr.* To make a voyage. *—tr.* To travel over in a journey; sail across. [Middle English, from Old French *veiyage,* from Latin *viāticum,* provisions for a journey, from *viāticus,* of a journey, from *via,* road, way. See **wei-²** in Appendix.*] **—voy′ag·er** *n.*

vo·ya·geur (vwä-yä-zhœr′) *n., pl.* **-geurs** (-zhœr′). A woodsman, boatman, or guide, especially one employed by fur companies to transport furs and supplies between remote stations in the U.S. and Canadian northwest. [French, "voyager."]

vo·yeur (vwä-yûr′) *n.* A person who derives sexual gratification from observing the sex organs or sexual acts of others, usually from a secret vantage point. [French, from Old French, "one who sees," from *voir,* to see, from Latin *vidēre.* See **weid-** in Appendix.*] **—vo·yeur′ism′** *n.* **—vo′yeur·is′tic** (vwä′yə-rĭs′tĭk) *adj.* **—vo′yeur·is′ti·cal·ly** *adv.*

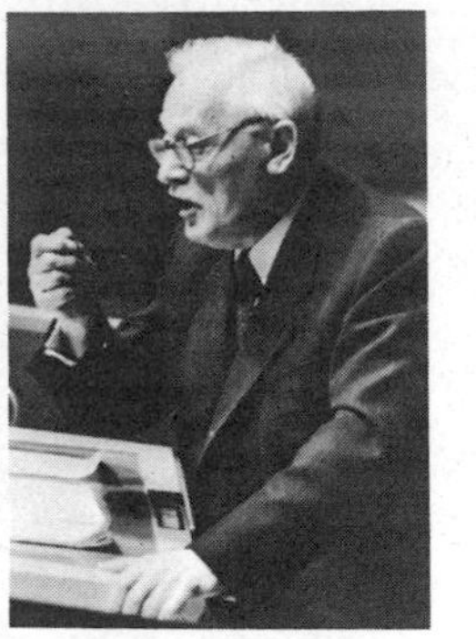

Andrei Vyshinsky
Addressing the United Nations General Assembly in 1953

Voy·vo·di·na. See **Vojvodina.**

Voz·ne·sen·sky (vŏz-nə-sĕn′skē), **Andreĭ Andreyevich.** Born 1933. Soviet poet.

V.P. vice president.

V-par·ti·cle (vē′pär′tĭ-kəl) *n.* Any of several subatomic particles with half-lives in the range of 10^{-10} to 10^{-6} second. [From the V-shaped tracks left by their decay products in a cloud chamber.]

V. Pres. vice president.

vs. versus.

v.s. vide supra.

V.S. veterinary surgeon.

VT Vermont (with Zip Code).

Vt. Vermont.

VT fuze. *Military.* A **proximity fuze** *(see).* [V(ARIABLE) T(IME) FUZE.]

VTOL vertical takeoff and landing.

Vuil·lard (vwē-yär′), **Jean Édouard.** 1868–1940. French painter; noted for still-life and flower paintings.

Vul. Vulgate.

Vul·can (vŭl′kən). *Roman Mythology.* The god of fire and craftsmanship, especially metalworking, identified with the Greek god Hephaestus. [Latin *Vulcānus, Volcānus,* perhaps obscurely related to Cretan *Welkhanoc,* from Hittite *Valhanasses*†.]

vul·ca·ni·an (vŭl′kā′nē-ən) *adj.* Also **Vul·ca·ni·an, Vul·can·ic** (-kăn′ĭk) (for sense 2). **1.** *Geology.* Pertaining to or from a volcano or volcanic eruption. **2. a.** Pertaining to the god Vulcan. **b.** Pertaining to craftsmanship or metalworking.

vul·can·ism. Variant of **volcanism.**

vul·can·ite (vŭl′kə-nīt′) *n.* A hard rubber produced by vulcanization.

vul·can·ize (vŭl′kə-nīz′) *tr.v.* **-ized, -izing, -izes. 1.** To improve the strength, resiliency, and freedom from stickiness and odor of (rubber) by combining with sulfur or other additives in the presence of heat and pressure. **2.** To treat (other substances) similarly. [From VULCAN.] **—vul′can·iz′a·ble** *adj.* **—vul′can·i·za′tion** *n.* **—vul′can·iz′er** *n.*

vul·can·ol·o·gy (vŭl′kə-nŏl′ə-jē) *n.* **Volcanology** *(see).*

vulg. vulgar.

Vulg. Vulgate.

vul·gar (vŭl′gər) *adj.* **1.** Of or associated with the great masses of people as distinguished from the educated or cultivated classes; common: *"It is a vulgar error that thunder never kills any who are asleep"* (Cotton Mather). **2.** *Abbr.* **vulg.** Spoken by, or expressed in language spoken by, the common people; vernacular. **3. a.** Deficient in taste, delicacy, or refinement. **b.** Ill-bred; boorish; crude. **c.** Tasteless in appearance or quality; garish: *a vulgar display of wealth.* **4.** *Abbr.* **vulg.** Obscene or indecent; offensive; coarse or bawdy: *a vulgar joke.* —See Synonyms at **coarse, common.** *—n.* **1.** The common people; especially, the ignorant and uncultivated: *"The vulgar thus through imitation err."* (Pope). **2.** *Obsolete.* The vernacular. [Middle English, from Latin *vulgāris,* from *vulgus*†, the common people.] **—vul′gar·ly** *adv.* **—vul′gar·ness** *n.*

vul·gar·i·an (vŭl′gâr′ē-ən) *n.* A vulgar person; especially, one who makes a conspicuous display of his money: *"Curse the whole pack of money-grubbing vulgarians!"* (Thackeray).

vul·gar·ism (vŭl′gə-rĭz′əm) *n.* **1.** Vulgarity. **2.** A word, phrase, or manner of expression used mainly by uncultivated people.

vul·gar·i·ty (vŭl′găr′ə-tē) *n., pl.* **-ties. 1.** The condition or quality of being vulgar; tastelessness; coarseness. **2.** Something, as an act or expression, that offends good taste or propriety.

vul·gar·ize (vŭl′gə-rīz′) *tr.v.* **-ized, -izing, -izes. 1.** To render vulgar; debase; cheapen. **2.** To popularize. **—vul′gar·i·za′tion** *n.* **—vul′gar·iz′er** *n.*

Vulgar Latin. The common speech of ancient Rome, differing from the literary or standard Latin used by Roman aristocrats and forming the basis for the development of the Romance languages. Compare **Classical Latin.**

vul·gate (vŭl′gāt′, -gĭt) *n.* **1.** The common speech of a people; vernacular. **2.** A widely accepted text or version of a work. *—adj.* Widely distributed and accepted; popular. [From Latin *vulgātus,* common. See **Vulgate.**]

Vul·gate (vŭl′gāt′, -gĭt) *n. Abbr.* **Vul., Vulg.** The Latin translation of the Bible made by Saint Jerome at the end of the fourth century A.D., now used in a revised form as the Roman Catholic authorized version. See **Bible.** *—adj.* Of or taken from the Vulgate. [Late Latin *vulgāta (ēditiō),* "the popular (edition)," from Latin *vulgātus,* common, popular, from *vulgāre,* to make commonly known, from *vulgus,* common people. See **vulgar.**]

vul·ner·a·ble (vŭl′nər-ə-bəl) *adj.* **1.** Susceptible to injury; unprotected from danger. **2.** Susceptible to physical attack; insufficiently defended: *"We are vulnerable both by water and land, without either fleet or army."* (Alexander Hamilton). **3. a.** Liable to censure or criticism; assailable. **b.** Liable to succumb to persuasion or temptation. **4.** *Bridge.* In a position to receive greater penalties or bonuses. Said of the partners of a team that has won one game of a rubber. [Late Latin *vulnerābilis,* from Latin *vulnerāre,* to wound, from *vulnus* (stem *vulner-*), wound. See **wel-⁴** in Appendix.*] **—vul′ner·a·bil′i·ty, vul′ner·a·ble·ness** *n.* **—vul′ner·a·bly** *adv.*

vul·ner·ar·y (vŭl′nə-rĕr′ē) *adj. Rare.* Used in the healing or treating of wounds. *—n. Rare.* A remedy so used. [Latin *vulnerārius,* from *vulnus* (stem *vulner-*), wound. See **vulnerable.**]

Vul·pec·u·la (vŭl-pĕk′yə-lə) *n.* A constellation in the Northern Hemisphere near Cygnus and Sagitta. [Latin *vulpēcula,* small fox, from *vulpēs,* fox. See **vulpine.**]

vul·pine (vŭl′pīn, -pĭn′) *adj.* **1.** Of, resembling, or characteristic of a fox. **2.** Clever; devious; cunning. [Latin *vulpīnus,* from *vulpēs,* fox. See **wlp-** in Appendix.*]

vul·ture (vŭl′chər) *n.* **1.** Any of various large birds of the family Cathartidae, of the New World, or the family Accipitridae, of the Old World, characteristically having dark plumage, a naked head and neck, and feeding on carrion. **2.** A person of a rapacious or predatory nature. [Middle English, from Old French *voltour,* from Latin *vultur.* See **gwltur-** in Appendix.*]

vul·tur·ine (vŭl′chə-rīn′, -chər-ĭn) *adj.* Also **vul·tur·ous** (-chər-əs). **1.** Pertaining to or characteristic of a vulture. **2.** Suggestive of a vulture; rapacious; predatory.

vul·va (vŭl′və) *n., pl.* **-vae** (-vē). The external female genitalia including the labia majora, labia minora, clitoris, and vestibule of the vagina. [Latin *vulva, volva,* womb, covering. See **wel-³** in Appendix.*] **—vul′val, vul′var, vul′vate′** (-vāt′, -vĭt) *adj.* **—vul′vi·form′** (vŭl′və-fôrm′) *adj.*

vul·vi·tis (vŭl-vī′tĭs) *n. Pathology.* Inflammation of the vulva. [New Latin : VULV(A) + -ITIS.]

vul·vo·vag·i·ni·tis (vŭl′vō-văj′ə-nī′tĭs) *n. Pathology.* Simultaneous inflammation of the vulva and vagina.

vv. verses.

v.v. vice versa.

Vy·borg (vē′bôrg′). *Finnish* **Vii·pu·ri** (vē′po͞o-rĭ); *Swedish* **Vi·borg** (vē′bôr′). A city of the Soviet Union, a seaport in the northwest near the Finnish border. Population, 51,000.

vy·ing (vī′ĭng) *adj.* Competing; contending. **—vy′ing·ly** *adv.*

Vy·shin·sky (vĭ-shĭn′skē), **Andrei Yanuarievich.** 1883–1954. Soviet jurist and diplomat; foreign minister (1949–53).

ă pat/ā pay/âr care/ä father/b bib/ch church/d deed/ĕ pet/ē be/f fife/g gag/h hat/hw which/ĭ pit/ī pie/îr pier/j judge/k kick/l lid, needle/m mum/n no, sudden/ng thing/ŏ pot/ō toe/ô paw, for/oi noise/ou out/o͝o took/o͞o boot/p pop/r roar/s sauce/sh ship, dish/

Ww

Ψ Υ ΥΚΥΥ ∨ W U ω W 𝒲 w 𝓌

1 2   3 4 5 6   7 8   9 10   11 12 13 14
Phoenician   Greek   Roman   Medieval   Modern

The letter W is a descendant of the letter V (see). Around 1000 B.C. the Phoenicians and other Semites of Syria and Palestine began to use a graphic sign in the forms (1,2). They gave it the name wāw and used it for a semiconsonant w, as in English know, knows. *After 900 B.C., when the Greeks borrowed the alphabet from the Phoenicians, they developed two signs from wāw. The first sign, which they called* upsilon, *"bare u," they used for the vowel u (3,4,5,6). (For the other sign, see* F.) *The Greek form without the tail (6) passed via Etruscan to the Roman alphabet (7,8), in which it was used for two sounds, semiconsonantal w and vocalic u, as in the writing of* VENIO *and* IVLIVS. *In later Roman times the sound w became v. Before the Norman Conquest of England the Anglo-Saxons used the Latin letter V, as in the Uncial form (9), for the sounds u, v, and w. Later the habit developed to use V for u and v, but to write V doubly for the sound w. Gradually the two separate letters were linked to make a new character, as in the Cursive form (10). Our modern printed letters, capital (11) and lower-case (13), are formally constructed by analogy with the printed V, while the written forms (12,14) revert to the Cursive.*

w, W (dŭb′əl-yōō, -yŏŏ) *n., pl.* **w's** or *rare* **ws, W's** or **Ws. 1.** The 23rd letter of the modern English alphabet. See **alphabet. 2.** Any of the speech sounds represented by this letter.

w, W, w., W. *Note:* As an abbreviation or symbol, *w* may be a small or a capital letter, with or without a period. Established forms or those generally preferred precede the definition. When no form is given, all four forms are in general use in that sense. **1. W** The symbol for the element tungsten. **2. W** *Electricity.* watt. **3. W.** Wednesday. **4. w.** week. **5. W.** Welsh. **6.** west; western. **7. w.** width. **8. w.** wife. **9. w.** with. **10. w, W** *Physics.* work. **11. W** *Broadcasting.* A letter prefixed to the call letters of some radio and television stations within the United States. **12.** The 23rd in a series; 22nd when *J* is omitted.

WA Washington (with Zip Code).

WAAC Women's Army Auxiliary Corps.

WAAF Women's Auxiliary Air Force.

Waal (väl). The southern branch of the Lower Rhine flowing through the Netherlands to the Meuse.

Waals (wôlz), **Johannes Diderik van der.** 1837–1923. Dutch physicist; worked on gas equations.

Wa·bash (wô′băsh). A river in western Ohio and Indiana, flowing 475 miles west and then south to the Ohio River.

wab·ble. Variant of **wobble.**

Wac (wăk) *n.* A member of the Women's Army Corps of the U.S. Army, organized during World War II. [W(OMEN'S) A(RMY) C(ORPS).]

WAC, W.A.C. Women's Army Corps.

wack·y (wăk′ē) *adj.* **-ier, -iest.** Also **whack·y.** *Slang.* Highly irrational or erratic; crazy; silly. [Probably variant of dialectal *whacky,* a fool, from *whack-head,* "one stunned by a heavy blow on the head," from WHACK.]

Wa·co (wā′kō). A city of central Texas, about 80 miles south of Fort Worth. Population, 98,000.

wad (wŏd) *n.* **1.** A small mass of soft material, often folded or rolled, used for padding, stuffing, packing, stopping holes, or the like. **2.** A compressed ball, roll, or lump of something, as of tobacco. **3. a.** A plug, as of cloth or paper, used to hold in a powder charge in a muzzleloading gun or cannon. **b.** A disk, as of felt or paper, to keep the powder and shot in place in a shotgun cartridge. **4.** *Informal.* A large amount. **5.** *Informal.* **a.** A sizable roll of paper money. **b.** A considerable amount of money. —*v.* **wadded, wadding, wads.** —*tr.* **1.** To compress into a wad. **2.** To pad, pack, line, or plug with wadding. **3.** To hold (shot or powder) in place with a wad; insert a wad in (a gun). —*intr.* To form into a wad. [Origin obscure.]

Wad·den·zee (väd′n-zā′, vä′dən-). A body of water lying between the Netherlands mainland and the West Frisian Islands; the remaining portion of the former Zuyder Zee.

wad·ding (wŏd′ĭng) *n.* **1.** A wad or wads collectively. **2.** A soft layer of fibrous cotton or wool used for padding or stuffing. **3.** Material for gun wads.

wad·dle (wŏd′l) *intr.v.* **-dled, -dling, -dles. 1.** To walk with short steps that tilt the body from side to side, as a duck does. **2.** To walk heavily and clumsily with a pronounced sway. —*n.* A waddling gait. [Probably frequentative of WADE.]

wad·dy¹ (wŏd′ē) *n., pl.* **-dies.** *Australian.* A heavy straight stick or club thrown as a weapon by Australian aborigines. —*tr.v.* **waddied, -dying, -dies.** To strike with a waddy. [An Australian native name, perhaps corruption of English WOOD.]

wad·dy² (wŏd′ē) *n., pl.* **-dies.** Also **wad·die.** *Western U.S.* **1.** A cowboy. **2.** Formerly, a cattle rustler. [Origin unknown.]

wade (wād) *v.* **waded, wading, wades.** —*intr.* **1.** To walk in or through water or something that similarly impedes normal movement. **2.** To make one's way arduously. —*tr.* To cross or pass through by wading. —**wade in** (or **into**). To plunge into, begin, or attack resolutely and energetically. —*n.* The act of wading. [Middle English *waden,* to go, walk through (water), Old English *wadan,* to go, wade. See **wādh-** in Appendix.*]

wad·er (wā′dər) *n.* **1.** One that wades. **2.** A long-legged bird that frequents shallow water. **3.** *Plural.* Waterproof hip boots or trousers worn especially by fishermen or hunters.

wa·di (wä′dē) *n., pl.* **-dis.** Also **wa·dy** *pl.* **-dies. 1.** In northern Africa and southwestern Asia, a valley, gully, or riverbed that remains dry except during the rainy season. **2.** A stream that flows through such a channel. **3.** An oasis. [Arabic *wādī.*]

Waf (wäf, wăf) *n.* A member of the women's branch of the U.S. Air Force, organized after World War II. [W(OMEN in the) A(IR) F(ORCE).]

WAF, W.A.F. Women in the Air Force.

wa·fer (wā′fər) *n.* **1.** A small, thin, crisp cake, biscuit, or candy. **2.** *Ecclesiastical.* A small, thin disk of unleavened bread used in the sacrament of the Eucharist. **3.** *Pharmacology.* A flat tablet of dried flour paste encasing a powdered drug. **4.** A small disk of adhesive material used as a seal for papers. **5.** *Electronics.* A small, thin, flat circular disk of a semiconducting material, such as pure silicon, that is masked, oxide-coated, doped, and otherwise processed for ultimate separation into numerous individual electronic devices or for packaging as an integrated circuit. —*tr.v.* **wafered, -fering, -fers.** To seal or fasten together with a wafer. [Middle English *wafre,* from Norman French, from Old North French *waufre,* from Middle Low German *wāfel.* See **webh-** in Appendix.*]

waff (wäf, wăf) *v.* **waffed, waffing, waffs.** *Scottish & British Regional.* —*intr.* To wave; flutter. —*tr.* To cause to wave or flutter. —*n. Scottish & British Regional.* **1.** A waving motion. **2.** A waft; a gust of air. **3.** A glimpse. [Middle English (northern) *waffen,* variant of *waven,* to WAVE.]

waf·fle (wŏf′əl) *n.* A light, crisp batter cake baked in a waffle iron. [Dutch *wafel,* from earlier *waefel.* See **webh-** in Appendix.*]

waffle iron. An appliance having hinged, indented metal plates that impress a grid pattern into waffle batter as it bakes.

waft (wäft, wăft) *v.* **wafted, wafting, wafts.** —*tr.* **1.** To carry or cause to go gently and smoothly through the air or over water. **2.** To convey or send floating through the air or over water: *"flowers brighter than love wafting the odour of spices"* (Ronald

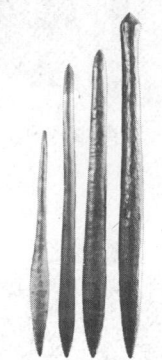

waddy¹
Several types of waddy

waffle iron
Early 19th-century
Pennsylvania Dutch

---

t tight/th thin, path/*th* this, bathe/ŭ cut/ûr urge/v valve/w with/y yes/z zebra, size/zh vision/ə about, item, edible, gallop, circus/ à *Fr.* ami/œ *Fr.* feu, *Ger.* schön/ü *Fr.* tu, *Ger.* über/KH *Ger.* ich, *Scot.* loch/N *Fr.* bon. *Follows main vocabulary. †Of obscure origin.

Firbank). —*intr.* To float easily and gently, as on the air; to drift. —*n.* **1.** Something, as an odor, carried through the air. **2.** A light breeze; rush of air. **3.** The act of wafting or waving. **4.** *Nautical.* **a.** A flag used for signaling or indicating wind direction. **b.** A signal with a flag. [Originally "to convoy (ships)," back-formation from obsolete *wafter,* a convoy, Middle English *waughter,* from Middle Dutch *wachter,* a guard, from *wachten,* to watch, guard. See **weg-²** in Appendix.*]

waft·age (wăf'tĭj, wäf'-) *n.* The act or state of being wafted.

waf·ture (wăf'chər, wäf'-) *n.* **1.** The act or action of waving; a waving movement. **2.** The action of wafting.

wag¹ (wăg) *v.* **wagged, wagging, wags.** —*intr.* **1. a.** To move briskly and repeatedly from side to side, to and fro, or up and down. **b.** To be incessantly active. **2.** To walk with a clumsy sway; waddle. **3.** *Archaic.* To be on one's way; depart. —*tr.* To wag (a part of the body) as in playfulness, agreement, admonition, or chatter: *"Carrados wagged his head in good-natured resignation."* (Ernest Bramah). —*n.* The act or motion of wagging. [Middle English *waggen,* ultimately from Old English *wagian,* to totter. See **wegh-** in Appendix.*]

wag² (wăg) *n.* A mischievous person. [Origin uncertain.]

wage (wāj) *n.* **1.** *Sometimes plural.* Payment for services to a workman; usually, remuneration on an hourly, daily, or weekly basis or by the piece. Compare **salary. 2.** *Plural. Economics.* The portion of the national product that represents the aggregate paid for all contributing labor and services as distinguished from the portion retained by management or reinvested in capital goods. **3.** *Usually plural.* A fitting return; recompense; requital. Used with a singular or plural verb: *"For the wages of sin is death"* (Romans 6:23). —*tr.v.* **waged, waging, wages.** To engage in (a war or campaign). [Middle English, a pledge, wage, soldier's pay, from Old North French, from Frankish *wadi* (unattested). See **wadh-** in Appendix.*]

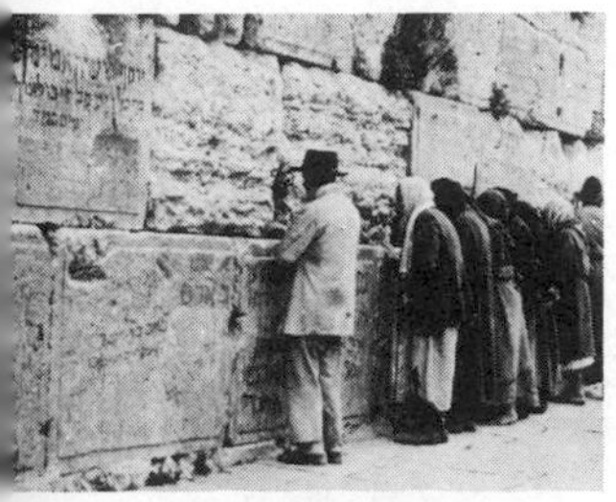

Wailing Wall

wage earner. 1. A person who works for wages. **2.** One whose earnings support a household.

wa·ger (wā'jər) *n.* **1.** An agreement under which each bettor pledges a certain amount to the other depending upon the outcome of an unsettled matter. **2.** The matter betted on; a gamble. **3.** Something staked on an uncertain outcome; a bet. **4.** *Archaic.* A pledge of personal combat to resolve an issue or case. —*v.* **wagered, -gering, -gers.** —*tr.* To risk or stake (an amount or possession) on an uncertain outcome; to bet. —*intr.* To make a wager; to bet. [Middle English, a pledge, prize at a contest, from Norman French *wageure,* from Old North French *wagier,* to pledge, from *wage,* a pledge, WAGE.] —**wa'ger·er** *n.*

wage scale. The scale of wages paid to employees for the various jobs within an industry, factory, or company.

wage·work·er (wāj'wûr'kər) *n.* A wage earner.

wag·ger·y (wăg'ə-rē) *n., pl.* **-ies. 1.** Waggish behavior or spirit; drollery. **2.** A droll remark or act. [From WAG (joker).]

wag·gish (wăg'ĭsh) *adj.* Characteristic of a wag; playfully humorous. See Synonyms at **playful.** —**wag'gish·ly** *adv.* —**wag'gish·ness** *n.*

wag·gle (wăg'əl) *v.* **-gled, -gling, -gles.** —*tr.* To move (an attached part) with short, quick motions: *She waggled her foot impatiently.* —*intr.* To move shakily; to wobble. —*n.* A waggling motion. [Frequentative of WAG.] —**wag'gly** *adj.*

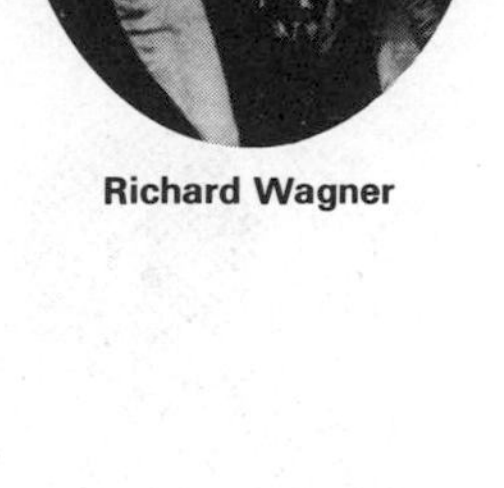

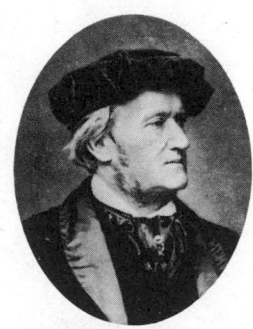

Richard Wagner

Wag·ner (wăg'nər), **John Peter ("Honus").** 1874–1955. American baseball player.

Wag·ner (väg'nər), **(Wilhelm) Richard.** 1813–1883. German poet and composer.

Wag·ne·ri·an (väg-nîr'ē-ən) *adj.* Of, pertaining to, or characteristic of Wagner, his music, or his theories. —*n.* An admirer or disciple of Wagner.

Wag·ner von Jau·regg (väg'nər fôn you'rĕk'), **Julius.** 1857–1940. Austrian neurologist and psychiatrist.

wag·on (wăg'ən) *n.* Also *chiefly British* **wag·gon. 1.** A four-wheeled, usually horse-drawn vehicle having a large rectangular body for transporting loads and often a detachable cover. **2. a.** A light automotive transport or delivery vehicle. **b.** A station wagon. **c.** A police patrol wagon. **3.** A child's low four-wheeled cart hauled by a long handle that governs the direction of the front wheels. **4.** A small table or tray on wheels for serving drinks or food: *a dessert wagon.* **5.** *British.* An open railway freight car. **6.** *Capital* **W.** *Astronomy.* An asterism, the **Big Dipper** *(see).* **7.** *Obsolete.* A chariot. —**off the wagon.** *Slang.* No longer abstaining from liquor. —**on the wagon.** *Slang.* Abstaining from liquor. —*v.* **wagoned, -oning, -ons.** Also *chiefly British* **wag·gon.** —*tr.* To transport by wagon. —*intr.* To travel or transport goods by wagon. [Earlier *wagen, waghen,* from Dutch, from Middle Dutch. See **wegh-** in Appendix.*]

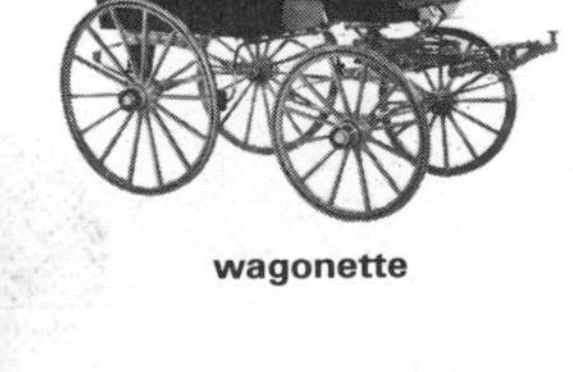

wagonette

wag·on·age (wăg'ə-nĭj) *n. Archaic.* **1.** Conveyance by wagon. **2.** The cost of such conveyance.

wag·on·er (wăg'ə-nər) *n.* **1.** A wagon driver. **2.** *Obsolete.* A charioteer. **3.** *Capital* **W. a.** The constellation Ursa Major. **b.** The constellation Auriga.

wag·on·ette (wăg'ə-nĕt') *n.* A light horse-drawn wagon with two facing lengthwise seats placed behind the driver's seat.

wa·gon-lit (vä-gôN-lē') *n., pl.* **wagons-lits** or **wagon-lits** (vä-gôN-lē'). A railroad sleeping car. [French : *wagon,* railway car, from English WAGON + *lit,* bed, from Latin *lectus* (see **legh-** in Appendix*).]

wag·on·load (wăg'ən-lōd') *n.* The load held by one wagon.

wagon train. A line or train of wagons traveling cross-country.

Wa·gram (vä'gräm). A village of Austria, ten miles north of Vienna; the site of Napoleon's defeat of the Austrians (1809).

wag·tail (wăg'tāl') *n.* Any of various birds of the genus *Motacilla* and related genera, having a long, constantly wagging tail.

Wah·ha·bi, Wa·ha·bi (wä-hä'bē) *n.* Also **Wah·ha·bee, Wah·ha·bite** (wä-hä'bīt'). A member of a Moslem sect founded by Abdul Wahhab in the 18th century, known for its strict observance of the Koran and flourishing mainly in Arabia. —**Wah·ha'bism', Wa·ha'bism'** (wä-hä'bĭz'əm) *n.*

wa·hi·ne (wä-hē'nē, -nā') *n.* Also **va·hi·ne** (vä-). A woman. [Hawaiian and Maori.]

wa·hoo¹ (wä-ho͞o', wä'ho͞o) *n., pl.* **-hoos.** A shrub or small tree, *Euonymus atropurpureus,* of eastern North America, having small purplish flowers and red fruit. Also called "burning bush." [Dakota *wāhu.*]

wa·hoo² (wä-ho͞o', wä'ho͞o) *n., pl.* **-hoos. 1.** An elm, *Ulmus alata,* of the southeastern United States, having twigs with winged, corky edges. **2.** Any of several similar trees. [Creek *ūhawhu.*]

wa·hoo³ (wä-ho͞o', wä'ho͞o) *n., pl.* **wahoo** or **-hoos.** A tropical marine game fish, *Acanthocybium solanderi.* [Origin unknown.]

wa·hoo⁴ (wä'ho͞o) *interj. Chiefly Western U.S.* Used to express exuberance. [Expressive formation.]

waif¹ (wāf) *n.* **1. a.** A stray homeless person, especially a forsaken or orphaned child. **b.** An abandoned young animal. **2.** Something found and unclaimed, such as an object cast up by the sea. [Middle English *waife, wayf,* ownerless property, from Norman French *waif, weif,* variant of Old North French *gaif,* from Scandinavian. See **weip-** in Appendix.*]

waif² (wāf) *n.* A small flag for signaling; a waft. [Probably from Scandinavian, akin to Old Norse *veif,* a waving thing. See **weip-** in Appendix.*]

Wai·ki·ki (wī'kē-kē', wī'kē-kē'). A famous beach and resort area of Honolulu, Hawaii, on the southern shore of Oahu.

wail (wāl) *v.* **wailed, wailing, wails.** —*intr.* **1.** To grieve or protest audibly; to lament. **2.** To make a prolonged, high-pitched sound suggestive of a cry: *The wind wailed through the trees.* —*tr.* **1.** *Archaic.* To lament over; bewail. **2.** To cry out plaintively. —See Synonyms at **cry.** —*n.* **1.** A long, loud, high-pitched cry as of grief or pain. **2.** Any similar sound. [Middle English *wailen, weilen,* probably from Old Norse *veila* (unattested), to moan, lament. See **wai** in Appendix.*] —**wail'er** *n.* —**wail'ing·ly** *adv.*

wail·ful (wāl'fəl) *adj.* **1.** Resembling a wail; mournful; plaintive. **2.** Issuing a sound like a wail.

Wailing Wall. A wall in the old city of Jerusalem believed to be a remnant of the temple of Solomon and revered by Jews as a place of pilgrimage, lamentation, and prayer.

wain (wān) *n.* **1.** A large open farm wagon. **2.** *Capital* **W.** *Astronomy.* An asterism, the **Big Dipper** *(see).* [Middle English *wain,* Old English *wæg(e)n, wǣn.* See **wegh-** in Appendix.*]

wain·scot (wān'skət, -skŏt', -skōt') *n.* **1.** A facing or paneling, usually of wood, applied to the walls of a room. **2.** The lower part of an interior wall when finished in a material different from that of the upper part. —*tr.v.* **wainscoted** or **-scotted, -scoting** or **-scotting, -scots.** To line or panel (a room or wall) with wainscot. [Middle English *waynscot(te), weynshet,* from Middle Dutch *wagenschot,* perhaps "timber for wagons" : *wagen,* WAGON + *schot,* wooden partition, planking (see **skeud-** in Appendix*).]

wain·scot·ing (wān'skə-tĭng, -skŏt'ĭng, -skō'tĭng) *n.* Also **wain·scot·ting. 1.** A wainscoted wall or walls; paneling. **2.** Wood or other material for such paneling.

wain·wright (wān'rīt') *n.* A builder and repairer of wagons.

waist (wāst) *n.* **1.** The part of the human trunk between the bottom of the rib cage and the pelvis. **2. a.** The part of a garment that encircles the waist of the body. **b.** The upper part of a garment, extending from the shoulders to the waistline; especially, the bodice of a woman's dress. **c.** A blouse. **d.** A child's undershirt. **3.** The middle section or part of an object, especially when narrower than the rest. **4.** *Nautical.* The middle part of the deck of a ship between the forecastle and the quarter-deck. [Middle English *wa(a)st,* Old English *wæst* (unattested), growth, size of body. See **aug-¹** in Appendix.*]

waist·band (wāst'bănd', -bənd) *n.* **1.** A garment band encircling and fitting the waist, as on trousers or a skirt. **2.** A sash.

waist·cloth (wāst'klôth', -klŏth') *n., pl.* **-cloths** (-klôths', -klôthz', -klŏths', -klŏthz'). A loincloth.

waist·coat (wĕs'kĭt, wāst'kōt') *n.* **1.** *Chiefly British.* A vest. **2.** A garment formerly worn by men under a doublet.

waist·line (wāst'līn') *n.* **1. a.** The natural indentation of the body at the waist; the place at which the circumference of the waist is smallest. **b.** The measurement of this circumference. **2.** The point or line at which the skirt and bodice of a dress join.

wait (wāt) *v.* **waited, waiting, waits.** —*intr.* **1. a.** To remain inactive or stay in one spot until something anticipated occurs. **b.** To tarry until another catches up. **2.** To remain or be in readiness or expectation. **3.** To remain temporarily neglected, unattended to, or postponed: *The trip will have to wait.* **4.** To work as a waiter or waitress. —*tr.* **1.** To remain or stay in expectation of; await: *wait one's turn.* **2.** *Informal.* To delay (a meal or event); postpone: *They waited lunch.* **3.** To be a waiter at: *wait table.* —See Synonyms at **stay.** —**wait on** (or **upon**). **1.** To serve the needs of; be in attendance upon. **2.** To make a formal call upon; to visit. **3.** To follow as a result; depend upon. —See Usage note below. —**wait out.** To delay until the termination of: *wait out a war.* —**wait up. 1.** To postpone going to bed in anticipation of something or someone. **2.** *Informal.* To stop or pause so that another can catch up. —*n.* **1.** The act of waiting or the time spent waiting. **2.** *British.* **a.** One of a group of musicians employed, usually by a city, to play in parades, public ceremonies, or the like. **b.** One of a

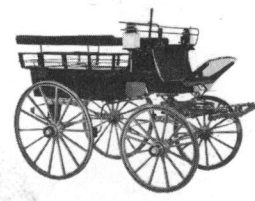

group of musicians or carolers who perform in the streets at Christmastime. **—lie in wait.** To be on the watch for; await a chance to ambush. [Middle English *waiten, wayten,* to watch, lie in wait, wait, from Old North French *waitier,* from Frankish *wahtōn* (unattested), to watch. See **weg-**[2] in Appendix.*]

Usage: *Wait on* is restricted to the senses specified above, in formal usage. It is not acceptable on that level as the equivalent of *wait for,* as in *They will wait for* (not *on*) *you if you hurry.*

wait-a-bit (wāt′ə-bĭt′) *n.* Any of several plants having sharp, often hooked thorns. [Translation of obsolete Afrikaans *wacht-en-bitje* (because the thorns catch hold of passers-by).]

wait·er (wā′tər) *n.* **1.** A man who waits on table, as in a restaurant. **2.** A tray or salver.

wait·ing (wā′tĭng) *n.* **1.** The act of a person who waits. **2.** The period of time spent waiting. **—in waiting.** In attendance.

waiting game. The stratagem of allowing the passage of time to work in one's favor by deferring action.

waiting list. A list of persons waiting, as for an appointment.

waiting room. A room, as in a railroad station or doctor's office, for the use of persons waiting.

wait·ress (wā′trĭs) *n.* A woman or girl who waits on table.

waive (wāv) *tr.v.* **waived, waiving, waives. 1.** To relinquish or give up (a claim or right) voluntarily. **2.** To refrain from insisting upon or enforcing; dispense with: *"The original ban on private trading had long since been waived"* (William L. Schurz). **3.** To put aside or off for the time. —See Synonyms at **relinquish.** [Middle English *weiven,* to outlaw, abandon, relinquish, from Norman French *weyver,* variant of Old North French *gaiver,* from *gaif,* ownerless property. See **waif.**]

waiv·er (wā′vər) *n.* **1.** The intentional relinquishment of a right, claim, or privilege. **2.** The document that evidences such an act. [Norman French *weyver,* from *weyver,* to WAIVE.]

Wa·ka·ma·tsu (wä′kä-mä′tsōō). A city of Japan, now part of Kita Kyushu.

Wa·kash·an (wô′kə-shăn′, wä-kăsh′ən) *n.* A family of North American Indian languages spoken by the Nootka and other tribes of Washington and British Columbia. [From Wakashan *waukash,* good.] **—Wa′kash·an** *adj.*

Wa·ka·ya·ma (wä′kä-yä′mä). A city of Japan, a seaport on southern Honshu. Population, 318,000.

wake[1] (wāk) *v.* **woke** (wōk) or *rare* **waked** (wākt), **waked** or *chiefly British & regional* **woke** or **woken** (wō′kən), **waking, wakes.** *—intr.* **1. a.** To cease to sleep; become awake; awaken. Often used with *up.* **b.** To be brought into a state of awareness or alertness. **2.** *Regional.* To keep watch or guard, especially over a corpse. **3.** To be or remain awake. *—tr.* **1.** To rouse from sleep; awaken. Often used with *up.* **2.** To stir, as from a dormant or inactive condition; rouse: *wake old animosities.* **3.** To make aware of; to alert. Often used with *to: It waked him to the facts.* **4.** *Regional.* **a.** To keep a vigil over. **b.** To hold a wake over. *—n.* **1. a.** A watch; vigil. **b.** A watch over the body of a deceased person before burial, sometimes accompanied by festivity. **2.** *British.* A parish festival held annually, often in honor of the patron saint. **3.** The condition of being awake: *between wake and sleep.* [Middle English *wakien* and *waken,* Old English *wacian,* to be awake and *wacan* (unattested), to rouse. See **weg-**[2] in Appendix.*]

Usage: The verbs *wake, waken, awake,* and *awaken* are alike in meaning but differentiated in usage. Each has transitive and intransitive senses, but *awake* is used largely intransitively and *waken* transitively. In the passive voice, *awaken* and *waken* are the more frequent: *I was awakened* (or *wakened*) *by his call.* In figurative usage, *awake* and *awaken* are the more prevalent: *He awoke to the danger; his suspicions were awakened. Wake* is frequently used with *up;* the others do not take a preposition. The preferred past participle of *wake* is *waked,* not *woke* or *woken: When I had waked him, I discovered that the danger was past.* The preferred past participle of *awake* is *awaked,* not *awoke: He had awaked several times earlier in the night.*

wake[2] (wāk) *n.* **1.** The visible track of turbulence left by something moving through water: *the wake of a ship.* **2.** The track or course left behind anything that has passed: *"Every revolutionary law has naturally left in its wake defection, resentment, and counterrevolutionary sentiment."* (C. Wright Mills). **—in the wake of. 1.** Following directly upon. **2.** In the aftermath of; as a consequence of. [Probably Middle Low German *wake,* from Old Norse *vök,* a hole or crack in ice. See **wegw-** in Appendix.*]

Wake·field (wāk′fēld). **1.** A city of southern Yorkshire, England, the administrative center of the West Riding. Population, 60,000. **2.** An estate on the Potomac in southeastern Virginia; the birthplace of George Washington. Also called "Bridges Creek."

wake·ful (wāk′fəl) *adj.* **1. a.** Not sleeping or able to sleep. **b.** Without sleep; sleepless. **2.** Watchful; alert; vigilant. **—wake′ful·ly** *adv.* **—wake′ful·ness** *n.*

Wake Island (wāk). An atoll in the Pacific, between Hawaii and the Marianas; held by Japanese forces in World War II (1941–45); administered by the United States and site of a U.S. naval and air base.

wake·less (wāk′lĭs) *adj.* Unbroken. Said of sleep.

wak·en (wā′kən) *v.* **-ened, -ening, -ens.** *—tr.* **1.** To rouse from sleep; awake. **2.** To rouse from a quiescent or inactive state; stir. *—intr.* To become awake; wake up. —See Usage note at **wake.** [Middle English *wak(e)nen,* Old English *wæcn(i)an.* See **weg-**[2] in Appendix.*] **—wak′en·er** *n.*

wake-rob·in (wāk′rŏb′ĭn) *n.* **1.** A plant, the **trillium** *(see).* **2.** Any of several other plants that bloom early in the spring. [Origin uncertain.]

Waks·man (wăks′mən), **Selman Abraham.** Born 1888. Russian-born American microbiologist; discovered streptomycin.

Wa·la·chi·a. See **Wallachia.**

Wał·brzych (väw′bzhĭkh). *German* **Wal·den·burg** (väl′dən-bŏŏrk). A city of Poland, a mining center in the southwest near the Czechoslovak border. Population, 123,000.

Wal·che·ren (väl′kHər-ən). An island, 80 square miles in area, off the southwestern coast of the Netherlands at the mouth of the Scheldt.

Wald (wôld), **George.** Born 1906. American biologist.

Wal·deck (väl′dĕk). A former principality and province of west-central Germany, now incorporated in northern Hesse, West Germany.

Wal·den Pond (wôl′dən). A pond in northeastern Massachusetts near Concord; the site of Henry David Thoreau's cabin.

Wal·den·ses (wŏl-dĕn′sēz) *pl.n.* A Christian sect of dissenters originating in southern France in the late 12th century under the leadership of Peter Waldo, a Lyon merchant, and adopting Calvinist doctrines in the 16th century. Also called "Vaudois." **—Wal·den′sian** (-chən, -sē-ən) *adj & n.*

wald·grave (wôld′grāv′) *n.* **1.** Formerly, a king's officer in charge of a royal forest. **2.** A former German title of nobility. [German *Waldgraf* : *Wald,* forest, from Old High German (see **wel-**[5] in Appendix*) + *Graf,* count, ruler, from Middle High German *grāve,* from Old High German *grāvo* (see **gravo-** in Appendix*).]

Wal·dorf salad (wôl′dôrf′). A salad of diced raw apples, celery, and walnuts mixed with mayonnaise. [Originally served in the *Waldorf*-Astoria Hotel, New York City.]

wale (wāl) *n.* **1.** A **welt** *(see).* **2. a.** One of the parallel ribs or ridges in the surface of a fabric, such as corduroy. **b.** The texture or weave of such a fabric: *a wide wale.* **3.** *Nautical.* **a.** The gunwale. **b.** One of the heavy planks or strakes extending along the sides of a wooden ship. *—tr.v.* **waled, waling, wales.** To mark (the skin) with wales. [Middle English *wale,* a ridge, gunwale, Old English *walu,* a ridge of earth or stone, weal. See **wel-**[3] in Appendix.*]

Wal·er (wā′lər) *n. Anglo-Indian.* A rugged cavalry horse imported to British India from New South Wales.

Wales (wālz). A principality comprising part of the United Kingdom of Great Britain and Northern Ireland, occupying 8,016 square miles in Great Britain west of England. Population, 2,676,000. [Middle English *Wales,* Old English *Wealas,* Welshmen, Wales, plural of *wealh,* foreigner, Roman, Celt, Welshman. See **Volcae** in Appendix.*]

Wal·fish Bay. See **Walvis Bay.**

Wal·green Coast (wôl′grēn′). A region of Antarctica bordering on Amundsen Sea and including part of Byrd Land.

Wal·hal·la. Variant of **Valhalla.**

walk (wôk) *v.* **walked, walking, walks.** *—intr.* **1.** To go or advance on foot; move by steps. **2.** To roam about in visible form, as a ghost; appear. **3.** To go on foot for pleasure or exercise; stroll. **4.** To move in a manner suggestive of walking. Used of inanimate objects. **5.** To conduct oneself or behave in a particular manner; to live: *"Of him who walked in glory and in joy"* (Coleridge). **6. a.** *Baseball.* To go to first base after the pitcher has thrown four balls. **b.** *Basketball.* To travel. **7.** *Obsolete.* To be in constant motion. *—tr.* **1.** To go or pass over, on, or through by walking: *walk the streets.* **2.** To bring to a specified condition or state by walking: *walk someone to exhaustion.* **3.** To cause to walk or proceed at a walk: *walk a horse uphill.* **4.** To accompany in walking; escort on foot: *walk her home.* **5.** To assist or force to walk. **6.** To traverse on foot in order to survey or measure; pace off. **7.** To move (a heavy or cumbersome object) in a manner suggestive of walking. **8.** *Baseball.* To allow (a batter) to go to first base by pitching four balls. **—walk away from. 1.** To outdo, outrun, or defeat with little difficulty. **2.** To survive (an accident) with very little injury. **—walk off with. 1.** To win easily or unexpectedly. **2.** To steal. **—walk out on.** *Informal.* To desert; abandon. **—walk the plank.** To be executed at sea by walking the length of a plank and falling into the water. **—walk through.** To perform (a play, acting role, or dance, for example) in a perfunctory fashion, as at a first rehearsal. *—n.* **1. a.** The act or an instance of walking; especially, a stroll for pleasure or exercise. **b.** The gait of a human being or other biped in which the feet are lifted alternately with one part of a foot always on the ground. **c.** The gait of a quadruped in which at least two feet are always touching the ground; specifically, in a horse, the gait in which the feet touch the ground in the four-beat sequence of near hind foot, near forefoot, off hind foot, off forefoot. **d.** The self-controlled movement in space of an astronaut or cosmonaut. **2. a.** The rate at which one walks; walking pace. **b.** The characteristic way in which one walks. **3.** The distance covered or to be covered in walking. **4.** A place on which one may walk, as a sidewalk or promenade. **5. a.** *Baseball.* The taking of first base after four balls have been pitched to the batter. **b.** *Track.* An event in which contestants compete in walking a specified distance: *the 1,000-meter walk.* **6.** An enclosed area designated for the exercise or pasture of livestock. **7.** An arrangement of or space between trees or shrubs planted in widely spaced rows. **—walk of life.** Social class or occupation. [Middle English *walken* and *walkien,* respectively from Old English *wealcan,* to roll, toss, and *wealcian,* to roll up, muffle up. See **wel-**[3] in Appendix.*] **—walk′er** *n.*

walk·a·way (wôk′ə-wā′) *n.* A contest or victory easily won. Also called "walkover."

Walk·er (wô′kər), **James John ("Jimmy").** 1881–1946. American political leader; mayor of New York City (1926–32).

Walk·er (wô′kər), **William.** 1824–1860. American adventurer;

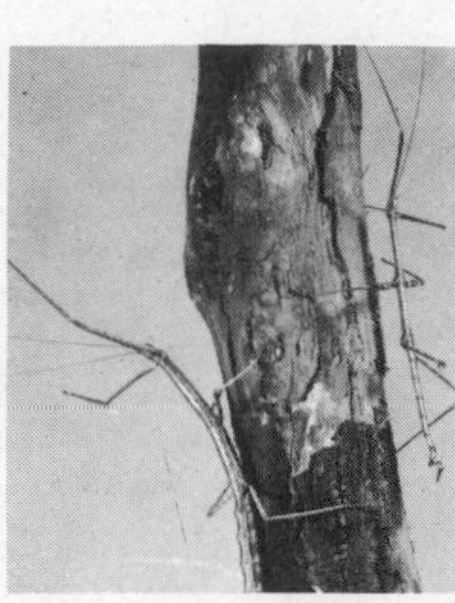

walking stick
Diapheromera femorata

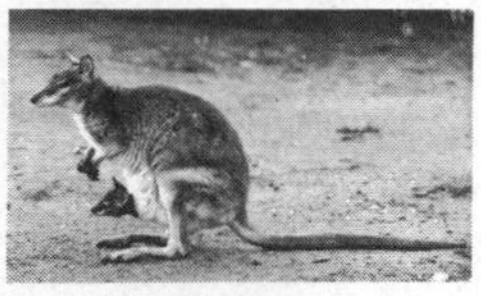

wallaby
Thylogale stigmatica

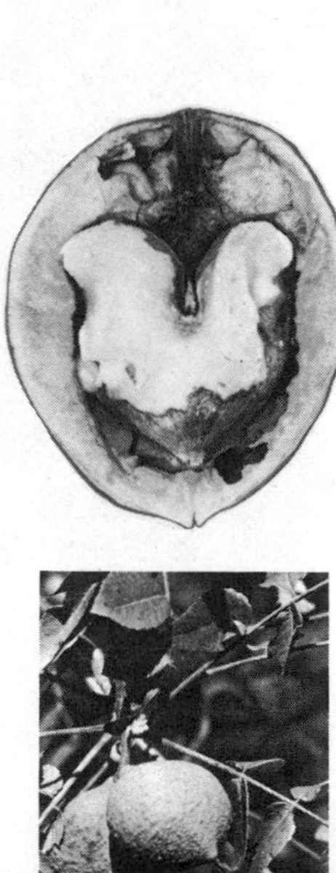

walnut
Above: Nut of *Juglans regia*
Below: Fruit and foliage of *Juglans nigra*

revolutionary in Lower California, Mexico, and Nicaragua (1853–57).

walk·ie-talk·ie (wô′kē-tô′kē) *n.* Also **walk·y-talk·y** *pl.* **-ies.** A battery-powered portable sending and receiving radio set.

walk-in (wôk′ĭn′) *adj.* **1.** Large enough to admit entrance, as a closet. **2.** Located so as to be entered directly from the street, as an apartment. **—walk′-in′** *n.*

walking bass. A repetitive bass figure composed of nonsyncopated eighth notes, used in jazz.

walking delegate. A trade-union official appointed to inspect and confer with the local unions or to serve as a representative of the union in dealings with an employer.

walking fern. A North American fern, *Camptosorus rhizophyllus,* having leaflike fronds with slender tips that often take root.

walking papers. *Informal.* Notice of discharge or dismissal.

walking stick. **1.** A cane or staff used as an aid in walking. **2.** Any of various insects of the family Phasmidae, having the appearance of twigs or sticks. Also called "stick insect."

walk-on (wôk′ŏn′, -ôn′) *n.* A minor role in a theatrical production, usually having no speaking lines.

walk out. **1.** To go on strike. **2.** To leave or quit as a sign of disagreement.

walk·out (wôk′out′) *n.* **1.** A strike of workmen. **2.** The act of leaving or quitting a meeting, company, or organization, especially as a sign of protest.

walk over. **1.** *Informal.* To treat badly or contemptuously. **2.** To gain an easy or uncontested victory.

walk·o·ver (wôk′ō′vər) *n.* **1.** A horse race with only one horse entered, won by the mere formality of walking the length of the track. **2.** A **walkaway** *(see).*

walk·up (wôk′ŭp′) *n.* Also **walk-up.** **1.** An apartment house or office building with no elevator. **2.** An apartment or office in such a building. **—walk′up′** *adj.*

walk·way (wôk′wā′) *n.* A passage for walking.

Wal·kyr·ie. Variant of **Valkyrie.**

wall (wôl) *n.* **1.** An upright structure of masonry, wood, plaster, or other building material serving to enclose, divide, or protect an area; specifically, a vertical construction forming an inner partition or exterior siding of a building. **2.** *Usually plural.* A continuous structure of masonry or other material forming a rampart and built for defensive purposes. **3.** A structure of stonework, cement, or other material built to retain a flow of water; a dam, levee, or dike. **4.** Something resembling a wall in appearance, function, or construction, as the exterior surface of a bodily organ or part: *the abdominal wall.* **5.** *Surfing.* The vertical surface of a wave. **6.** Something resembling a wall in impenetrability or strength: *a wall of silence.* **7.** An extreme or desperate condition or position, such as defeat or ruin. Used in the phrase *to the wall.* *—tr.v.* **walled, walling, walls.** **1.** To enclose, surround, or fortify with or as if with a wall. **2.** To divide or separate with or as if with a wall: *wall off half a room.* **3.** To enclose within a wall; immure. **4.** To block or close (an opening or passage, for example) with or as if with a wall. [Middle English *wal(le),* Old English *weall,* from Latin *vallum,* palisade, wall, from *vallus,* stake. See **walso-** in Appendix.*]

wal·la·by (wŏl′ə-bē) *n., pl.* **-bies.** Any of various marsupials of the genus *Wallabia* and related genera, of Australia and adjacent islands, related to and resembling the kangaroos but generally smaller. [Australian native name *wolabā.*]

Wal·lace (wŏl′ĭs), **Alfred Russel.** 1823–1913. British naturalist.

Wal·lace (wŏl′ĭs), **George Corley.** Born 1919. American political leader; governor of Alabama (1963–67).

Wal·lace (wŏl′ĭs), **Henry Agard.** 1888–1965. Vice President of the United States under Franklin D. Roosevelt (1941-45); Progressive Party Presidential candidate (1948).

Wal·lace (wŏl′ĭs), **Lew(is).** 1827–1905. American military and political leader; author of *Ben Hur.*

Wal·lace (wŏl′ĭs), Sir **William.** 1272?–1305. Scottish patriot and military leader; executed by the English.

Wal·lach (wŏl′ək; *German* väl′əKH), **Otto.** 1847–1931. German organic chemist.

Wal·la·chia (wŏ-lā′kē-ə). Also **Wa·la·chi·a.** A region and former principality of southeastern Rumania.

wal·lah (wä′lä) *n.* Also **wal·la.** *Anglo-Indian.* One employed in a particular occupation or activity. Used in combination: *a kitchen wallah.* [Hindi *-wālā,* adjectival suffix, mistaken by Europeans for a suffix indicating a man.]

wal·la·roo (wŏl′ə-ro͞o′) *n., pl.* **-roos.** A kangaroo, *Macropus robustus* (or *Osphranter robustus*), of hilly regions of Australia. Also called "euro." [Australian native name *wolàrū.*]

Wal·la·sey (wŏl′ə-sē). An industrial city of western England, in Cheshire county across the Mersey from Liverpool. Population, 103,000.

Wal·la Wal·la (wŏl′ə wŏl′ə). **1.** A city in southeastern Washington, on the Walla Walla River near the Oregon border. Population, 25,000. **2.** A river rising in northeastern Oregon and flowing 60 miles generally northwest to the Columbia.

wall·board (wôl′bôrd′, -bōrd′) *n.* Any of several structural boards or sheets of various materials, such as gypsum plaster encased in paper or compressed wood fibers and chips, used in construction as a substitute for plaster or wood panels.

wall creeper. A long-billed crimson and grayish bird, *Tichodroma muraria,* of alpine regions of the Old World, characteristically seeking food on rocky cliffs or walls.

Wal·ler (wŏl′ər), **Edmund.** 1606–1687. English poet.

wal·let (wŏl′ĭt) *n.* A small, flat folding case, usually made of leather, for holding paper money, cards, photographs, or the like; billfold. [Middle English *walet,* a pilgrim's knapsack or provisions bag, probably from Norman French *walet* (unattested), from Germanic. See **wel-**^{3} in Appendix.*]

wall·eye (wôl′ī′) *n.* **1.** An eye in which the cornea is white or opaque. **2.** *Pathology.* **a.** Leukoma of the cornea. **b.** A divergent strabismus. **3.** A freshwater food and game fish, *Stizostedium vitreum,* of North America, having large, conspicuous eyes. Also called "walleyed pike" and sometimes "pickerel," "pike perch," and "dory." [Back-formation from WALLEYED.]

wall·eyed (wôl′īd′) *adj.* **1.** Having a whitish or grayish eye or eyes. **2. a.** Having leukoma of the cornea. **b.** Having divergent strabismus. **3. a.** Having large bulging or staring eyes. **b.** *Slang.* Having eyes with greatly distended pupils. **4.** *Slang.* Drunk. [Variant (influenced by WALL) of Middle English *wawil-eghed,* from Old Norse *vagleygr* : *vagl,* a wooden beam, perhaps film over the eye (see **wegh-** in Appendix*) + *-eygr,* -eyed, from *auga,* an eye (see **okw-** in Appendix*).]

wall·flow·er (wôl′flou′ər) *n.* **1.** A widely cultivated plant, *Cheiranthus cheiri,* native to Europe, having fragrant yellow, orange, or brownish flowers. **2.** A similar, related plant, *Erysimum asperum,* of the western United States. **3.** *Informal.* A person, especially a woman, who does not participate in the activity at a social event because of shyness or unpopularity.

Wal·lis (wŏl′ĭs), **John.** 1616–1703. English mathematician.

Wal·lis and Fu·tu·na Islands (wŏl′ĭs; fo͞o-to͞o′nä). Two island groups with an area of about 75 square miles in the southwestern Pacific, administered by France.

Wal·loon (wŏ-lo͞on′) *n.* **1.** One of a French-speaking people of Celtic descent inhabiting southern and southeastern Belgium and adjacent regions of France. Compare **Fleming.** **2.** The French dialect of this people. *—adj.* Of or pertaining to the Walloons or their language. [Old French *Wallon,* from Medieval Latin *Wallō* (stem *Wallōn-*), a foreigner, Welshman, from Germanic. See **Volcae** in Appendix.*]

wal·lop (wŏl′əp) *v.* **-loped, -loping, -lops.** *Informal.* *—tr.* **1.** To beat soundly; thrash. **2.** To strike with a hard blow. **3.** To defeat thoroughly. *—intr.* **1.** To move in a rolling, clumsy manner; to waddle. **2.** To boil noisily. Used of a liquid. *—n.* *Informal.* **1.** A hard or severe blow. **2. a.** The ability to strike such a blow: *a punch that packs a wallop.* **b.** The capacity to create a forceful effect; impact. [Earlier "to make violent, heavy motions," from Middle English *walopen,* to gallop, from Old North French *waloper,* from Frankish *walahlaupan* (unattested), "to jump well" : *wala* (unattested), well (see **wel-**^{2} in Appendix*) + *hlaupan* (unattested), to jump, run (see **klou-** in Appendix*).] **—wal′lop·er** *n.*

wal·lop·ing (wŏl′ə-pĭng) *adj.* *Informal.* Very large; huge: *a walloping fish.* *—adv.* To an exaggerated degree: *a walloping huge lie.* *—n.* *Informal.* A sound thrashing or defeat.

wal·low (wŏl′ō) *intr.v.* **-lowed, -lowing, -lows.** **1.** To roll the body about indolently or clumsily in water, snow, or mud. **2.** To luxuriate; revel: *wallow in self-righteousness.* **3.** To be or become abundantly supplied with something: *wallowing in money.* **4.** To move with difficulty in a clumsy or rolling manner; to flounder: *"The little ship wallowed in a heavy long swell"* (Evelyn Waugh). **5.** To swell or surge forth; billow. *—n.* **1.** An act of wallowing. **2.** A pool of water, mud, or the like where animals go to wallow. **3.** The depression, pool, or pit produced by wallowing animals. **4.** A condition of degradation or baseness. [Middle English *walowen,* Old English *wealwian.* See **wel-**^{3} in Appendix.*] **—wal′low·er** *n.*

wall·pa·per (wôl′pā′pər) *n.* Paper printed with designs or colors, used as a decorative wall covering. *—v.* **wallpapered, -pering, -pers.** *—tr.* To cover with wallpaper. *—intr.* To decorate a wall or room with wallpaper.

wall plate. **1.** A horizontal timber situated along the top of a wall at eaves level for bearing the ends of joists or rafters. **2.** *Machinery.* A plate used to attach a bracket or similar device to a wall.

wall plug. An electric socket, usually located in a wall, that is connected to and used as a source of electric power.

wall rock. The rock that forms the walls of a vein or lode.

wall rue. A small, delicate fern, *Asplenium ruta-muraria,* growing on rocks or in rocky crevices.

Wall Street. The controlling financial interests of the United States. [From the name of the main street of the financial district of New York City.]

wall-to-wall (wôl′tə-wôl′) *adj.* Covering a floor completely: *wall-to-wall carpeting.*

wal·nut (wôl′nŭt′, -nət) *n.* **1.** Any of several trees of the genus *Juglans,* having round, sticky fruit enclosing an edible nut. **2.** The ridged or corrugated nut of such a tree. **3.** The hard, dark-brown wood of such a tree, used for gunstocks and in cabinetwork. [Middle English *walnot,* Old English *wealhhnutu* (translation of Latin *nux gallia,* "Gaulish or foreign nut"). See **Volcae** in Appendix.*]

Walnut Canyon National Monument. An area of 1,641 acres in central Arizona, reserved to protect its cliff dwellings.

Wal·pole (wôl′pōl′, wŏl′-), **Horace.** 1717–1797. Fourth Earl of Orford. English man of letters.

Wal·pole (wôl′pōl′, wŏl′-), Sir **Robert.** 1676–1745. First Earl of Orford. British statesman; prime minister (1721–42); father of Horace Walpole.

Wal·pur·gis Night (väl-po͝or′gĭs). Also *German* **Wal·pur·gis·nacht** (väl-po͝or′gĭs-näKHt′). **1.** The eve of May Day, believed in medieval Europe to be the occasion of a witches' Sabbath. **2.** An episode or situation having the quality of nightmarish wildness associated with this Sabbath. [Partial translation of German *Walpurgisnacht* : *Walpurgis,* St. *Walpurga* (died 777),

ă pat/ā pay/âr care/ä father/b bib/ch church/d deed/ĕ pet/ē be/f fife/g gag/h hat/hw which/ĭ pit/ī pie/îr pier/j judge/k kick/l lid, needle/m mum/n no, sudden/ng thing/ŏ pot/ō toe/ô paw, for/oi noise/ou out/o͝o took/o͞o boot/p pop/r roar/s sauce/sh ship, dish/

English nun and missionary active in Germany, whose feast day falls on May Day + NIGHT.]

wal·rus (wôl′rəs, wŏl′-) *n., pl.* **-ruses** or **walrus**. A large marine mammal, *Odobenus rosmarus*, of Arctic regions, having tough, wrinkled skin and large tusks. [Dutch, from Scandinavian, akin to Danish *hvalros*. See **skwalo-** in Appendix.*]

walrus mustache. A bushy, drooping mustache.

Wal·sall (wôl′sôl, -səl). A city of England, an industrial center in southern Staffordshire. Population, 120,000.

Wal·ter (wôl′tər). A masculine given name. [Middle English, from Norman French *Waltier*, probably from Old High German *Walthari*, "army commander" : *waltan*, to rule (see ... **koro-** in Ap-

... astern Massa-
... lation, 55,000.
... h of London,
... divisions of
... on, 248,000.
... rmer adminis-
... of **Waltham**

... n 1903. Irish
... an of letters;

... strong accent
... —*v.* **waltzed**,
... **2.** To move
... nplish a task,
... with *through*:
... he waltz with.
... ly; to march:
... *Walzer*, from
... e, from Old
... Appendix.*]

... l. An inlet of
... An exclave
... a, occupying
... d seaport on

... bles. *Chiefly*
... g, or rolling
... —*n.* **1.** A
... lish *wam(e)-*
... akin to Old
... **bling·ly** *adv.*

... ag or -ags.
... an Indians.
... cent parts of
... language of
... he) eastern
... vampum) +

... trical beads
... h American
... eag." **2.** In-

... shell beads
... m. [From
... *npumpeage,*
... ted), white
... unattested),

... le, as from
... l *wan fond*
... ariness, ill-
... *expression.*
... ome pale,
... *n*†, dusky,

wa... A slender
ro... pter. **3.** A
m... sed by a
m... o foot slat
us...), *wond(e)*,
fr...

Wa... n *Wanda*,
po... to Polish
W...

wa... . To move
ab... roam aimlessly. **2.** To go by an indirect route or at no set pace; to amble; stroll: *wander towards town.* **3.** To proceed in an irregular course or action; to meander. **4.** To go astray: *wander from the path of righteousness.* **5.** To think or express oneself unclearly or incoherently. —*tr.* To wander across or through: *wander the forests and fields.* —*n.* The act of wandering; a stroll; amble. [Middle English *wand(e)ren*, Old English *wandrian*. See **wendh-** in Appendix.*] —**wan′der·er** *n.* —**wan′der·ing·ly** *adv.*

Synonyms: wander, ramble, roam, rove, range, meander, stray, gallivant, gad. These verbs all mean to move or travel about freely. *Wander* and *ramble* stress the absence of a fixed course or goal; figuratively they apply to writers or speakers who digress freely. *Roam* and *rove* emphasize freedom of movement over a wide area but do not necessarily imply aimlessness. *Range* also suggests a wide radius and does not rule out the

possibility of a clear purpose; especially in figurative usage, the term can stress inclusiveness of coverage: *The speech ranged over a broad area of social problems. Meander* suggests leisurely and sometimes aimless progression over a course as irregular as that of a winding river. *Stray* refers to movement, physical or figurative, away from a direct course; figuratively it can also apply to deviation from proper behavior. *Gallivant* refers to traveling about in search of pleasure, and *gad*, to thoughtless, idle travel.

wandering albatross. A white and black sea bird, *Diomedea exulans*, having a very wide wingspread.

wandering Jew. Either of two trailing plants, *Tradescantia fluminensis* or *Zebrina pendula*, native to tropical America, having usually variegated foliage and popular as house plants. [Fancifully named after the WANDERING JEW.]

Wandering Jew. The subject of a medieval legend, condemned to wander until the Day of Judgment for having mocked Christ on the day of Crucifixion.

wan·der·lust (wŏn′dər-lŭst′) *n.* A strong or irresistible impulse to travel. [German *Wanderlust* : *wandern*, to wander, from Old High German (see **wendh-** in Appendix*) + *Lust*, desire, delight, from Old High German *lust* (see **las-** in Appendix*).]

wan·der·oo (wŏn′də-rōō′) *n.* A monkey, *Macaca silenus*, of south-central Asia, having a glossy black coat and a ruff of gray hair about the face. [Singhalese *vanduru*, plural of *vandurā*, "forest-dweller," monkey, from Sanskrit *vānara*, from *vana*, a forest. See **wen-** in Appendix.*]

Wands·worth (wŏndz′wûrth). **1.** A borough of London, England, comprising the former administrative division of Battersea and part of the former administrative division of Wandsworth. Population, 335,000. **2.** A former administrative division, a portion of which is now part of **Lambeth** (*see*).

wane (wān) *intr.v.* **waned**, **waning**, **wanes**. **1.** To decrease gradually in size, amount, intensity, or degree; dwindle; decline: *"In the nineteenth century the general influence of mathematics waned."* (A.N. Whitehead). **2.** To show decreasing illuminated area from full moon to new moon. Used of the moon. Compare **wax. 3.** To approach an end. —*n.* **1.** The act or process of waning; a gradual declining or diminishing. **2.** A period or phase of waning; specifically, the period of the decrease of the moon's illuminated visible surface. **3.** A defective edge of a board caused by remaining bark or a beveled end. —**on the wane.** In a period of decline; waning: *"The tide was near the turn and already the day was on the wane."* (Joyce). [Middle English *wan(i)en*, Old English *wanian*, to lessen. In the sense "defective edge of a log," from Middle English *wane*, defect, shortage, Old English *wana*. See **eu-²** in Appendix.*]

wan·gle (wăng′gəl) *v.* **-gled**, **-gling**, **-gles**. *Informal.* —*tr.* **1.** To make, achieve, or get by contrivance: *"Not yet eighteen, he wangled a reporting job on the Kansas City Star"* (A.E. Hotchner). **2.** To manipulate or juggle, especially fraudulently. **3.** To extricate (oneself) from difficulty. —*intr.* **1.** To use indirect, tricky, or fraudulent methods. **2.** To extricate oneself by subtle or indirect means, as from difficulty; wriggle. —*n. Informal.* An act of wangling. [Originally a printer's term, "to manipulate or devise a substitute for," perhaps blend of WAGGLE and dialectal *wankle*, unsteady, wavering, Middle English *wankel*, Old English *wancol* (see **weng-** in Appendix*).] —**wang′ler** *n.*

wan·i·gan (wŏn′ə-gən) *n.* Also **wan·ni·gan**, **wan·gan** (wŏng′gən, wăng′-). **1.** A supply chest used in a logging camp. **2.** A shack on wheels or a movable platform, used in a logging camp for shelter or by workmen. [Ojibwa *wanikkan*, "man-made hole."]

Wanks. A former name for the **Coco.**

Wan·ne-Eick·el (vä′nə-i′kəl). A city and industrial center of West Germany, in west central North Rhine-Westphalia. Population, 109,000.

Wan·stead and Wood·ford (wŏn′stĕd, -stĭd; wŏŏd′fərd). A former administrative division of London, England, now part of **Redbridge** (*see*).

want (wŏnt, wônt) *v.* **wanted**, **wanting**, **wants**. —*tr.* **1.** To fail to have; be without; lack. **2.** To desire greatly; wish for. Often used with the infinitive: *He wants to leave.* **3.** To need or require: *" 'Your hair wants cutting,' said the Hatter."* (Lewis Carroll). **4. a.** To request the presence of. **b.** To seek with intent to capture: *The fugitive is wanted by the police.* **5.** To feel an inclination toward; like. —*intr.* **1.** To have need. Used with *for.* See Usage note below. **2.** To be destitute or needy. **3.** To be disposed; like; wish: *Call her if you want.* —See Synonyms at **lack.** —**want in** (or **out**). *Informal.* **1.** To desire greatly to come (or go). **2.** To wish to join (or leave) a project, business, or other undertaking. —*n.* **1.** The condition or quality of lacking a usual or necessary amount: *"there was no want of respect in the young man's address"* (Jane Austen). **2.** Pressing need; destitution: *live in want.* **3.** Something needed or desired; a need: *moderate wants.* **4.** A defect of character; a fault. [Middle English *wanten*, from Old Norse *vanta*, to be lacking. See **eu-²** in Appendix.*]

Usage: Want (verb) is used with *for* only when *want* means *have need: He does not want for money.* It is not used with *for*, in acceptable usage, in the sense of *wish, desire: I want you to go* (not *want for you to go* or *want you should go*). The constructions *want out* (elliptical for *want to get out*) and *want in* are informal.

want ad. *Informal.* A classified advertisement (*see*).

want·ing (wŏn′tĭng, wôn′-) *adj.* **1.** Absent; missing; lacking. **2.** Not up to standards or expectations; deficient. —*prep.* **1.** Lacking; without. **2.** Minus; less: *an hour wanting fifteen minutes.*

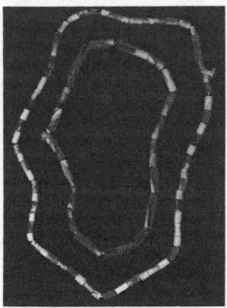

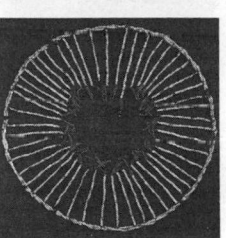

wampum
Above: From Long Island
Below: Iroquois

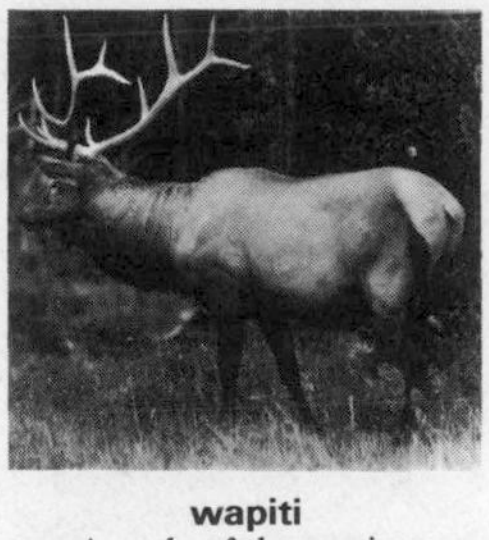

wapiti
A male of the species

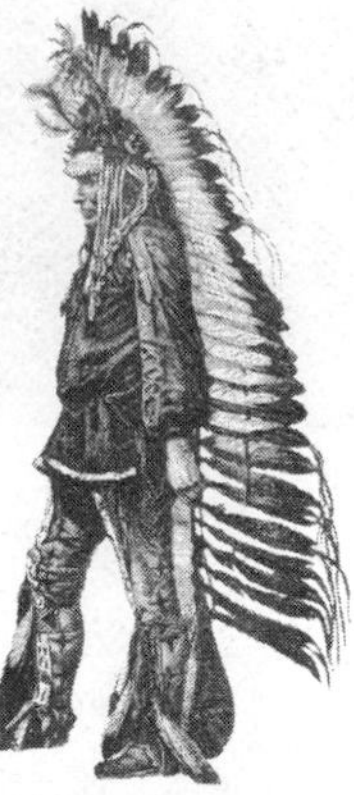

war bonnet
Sioux chief
wearing war bonnet

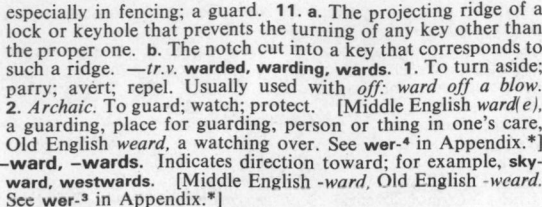

wan·ton (wŏn′tən) *adj.* **1.** Immoral or unchaste; lewd. **2. a.** Maliciously cruel; merciless: *"The wanton troopers riding by/Have shot my Faun and it will die"* (Marvell). **b.** Characterized by such mercilessness; unjust. **3.** Freely extravagant; excessive: *wanton spending.* **4.** Luxuriant; overabundant: *wanton tresses.* **5.** *Archaic.* Frolicsome; playful. **6.** *Obsolete.* Rebellious; refractory. —*v.* **wantoned, -toning, -tons.** —*intr.* To act, grow, or move in a wanton manner; be wanton. —*tr.* To waste or squander wantonly. —*n.* **1.** An immoral, lewd, or licentious person, especially a woman. **2.** One that is playful or frolicsome. **3.** One that is undisciplined or spoiled. [Middle English *wantowen,* lacking discipline, lewd : *wan-, un-,* lacking, Old English *wan-* (see **eu-**[2] in Appendix*) + *towen,* Old English *togen,* past participle of *tēon,* to draw, bring up (see **deuk-** in Appendix*).] —**wan′ton·ly** *adv.* —**wan′ton·ness** *n.*

wap·en·take (wŏp′ən-tāk′, wăp′-) *n.* A historical subdivision of some northern counties in England, corresponding roughly to the hundred. [Middle English *wapentake,* subdivision, court of each division, Old English *wǣpengetæc,* from Old Norse *vāpnatak,* "taking of weapons" (vote by an assembly by brandishing of weapons, hence assembly) : *vāpna,* genitive plural of *vāpn,* a weapon (see **wēpnam** in Appendix*) + *tak,* a taking, from *taka,* to take (see **tak-**[2] in Appendix*).]

wap·i·ti (wŏp′ə-tē) *n., pl.* **-tis** or **wapiti.** A large North American deer, *Cervus canadensis.* Also called "elk," "American elk." [Shawnee *wapiti,* "white rump" : Proto-Algonquian *wap-* (unattested), white + *-itwiy-* (unattested), rump.]

Wap·si·pin·i·con (wŏp′sĭ-pĭn′ĭ-kən). A river rising in southeastern Minnesota and flowing 255 miles southeast to the Mississippi in east-central Iowa.

war (wôr) *n.* **1. a.** A state of open, armed, often prolonged conflict carried on between nations, states, or parties. **b.** The period of such conflict. **2.** Any condition of active antagonism or contention: *"O, what a war of looks there was between them!"* (Shakespeare). **3.** The techniques or procedures of war; military science; strategy. —**at war.** In an active state of conflict or contention: *"Life and death are at war within us"* (Thomas Merton). —**declare war on.** To state formally the intention to carry on hostilities against. —*intr.v.* **warred, warring, wars. 1.** To wage or carry on war. **2.** To be in a state of hostility; contend. —*adj.* Of, resulting from, or used in war. [Middle English *werre, warre,* from Old North French *werre,* from Old High German *werra,* confusion, strife. See **wers-** in Appendix.*]

War Warwickshire.

war. warrant.

Wa·ran·gal (wûr′əng-gəl). A city of India, in north-central Andhra Pradesh. Population, 164,000.

war baby. A child born during wartime, especially during World War I or World War II.

War·beck (wôr′bĕk′), **Perkin.** 1474–1499. Flemish pretender to the English throne.

War Between the States. The **Civil War** *(see).*

war·ble[1] (wôr′bəl) *v.* **-bled, -bling, -bles.** —*tr.* To sing with trills, runs, or other melodic embellishments. —*intr.* **1.** To sing with trills, runs, or quavers. **2.** To be sounded in a trilling or quavering manner. —*n.* **1.** The act of warbling. **2.** A song, especially one that is warbled. [Old North French *werbler,* from *werble,* a warbling, melody, from Frankish *hwirbilōn* (unattested), to whirl, trill. See **kwerp-** in Appendix.*]

war·ble[2] (wôr′bəl) *n.* **1.** An abscessed swelling under the hide of the back of cattle or other animals, caused by the larva of a warble fly. **2.** The warble fly, especially in its larval stage. [Probably from a Scandinavian compound corresponding to obsolete Swedish *varbulde.* See **wer-**[1] in Appendix.*] —**war′-bled** *adj.*

warble fly. Any of several flies of the family Oestridae, whose larvae form warbles within the bodies of cattle and other animals.

war·bler (wôr′blər) *n.* **1.** Any of various small New World birds of the family Parulidae, many of which have yellowish plumage or markings. **2.** Any of various small, brownish or grayish Old World birds of the subfamily Silviinae.

war bonnet. A ceremonial headdress used by some North American Plains Indians consisting of a cap or band and a trailing extension decorated with erect feathers.

War·burg (vär′bŏŏrk′), **Otto Heinrich.** Born 1883. German biochemist; worked on respiration.

war club. A weapon consisting of a weight of iron or stone fixed to a handle, widely used by American Indians.

war correspondent. A journalist, reporter, or commentator assigned to report directly from a war or combat area.

war crime. Any of various crimes committed during a war and considered to be in violation of the customs of warfare, as mistreatment of prisoners of war or genocide. —**war criminal.**

war cry. 1. A cry uttered by combatants as they attack; battle cry. **2.** A phrase or slogan used to rally people to a cause.

ward (wôrd) *n.* **1.** A division of a city or town for administrative and representative purposes. **2.** A district of some English and Scottish counties corresponding roughly to the hundred or wapentake. **3. a.** A large room in a hospital usually holding six or more patients. **b.** A division in a hospital for the care of a particular group of patients. **4.** One of the divisions of a jail or other penal institution. **5.** An open court or area of a castle or fortification enclosed by walls. **6. a.** *Law.* A child or incompetent person placed under the care or protection of a guardian or court. **b.** Any person under the protection or care of another. **7.** The state of being under guard; custody. **8.** The act of guarding or protecting someone; guardianship. **9.** A means of protection; a defense. **10.** A defensive movement or attitude, especially in fencing; a guard. **11. a.** The projecting ridge of a lock or keyhole that prevents the turning of any key other than the proper one. **b.** The notch cut into a key that corresponds to such a ridge. —*tr.v.* **warded, warding, wards. 1.** To turn aside; parry; avert; repel. Usually used with *off: ward off a blow.* **2.** *Archaic.* To guard; watch; protect. [Middle English *ward(e),* a guarding, place for guarding, person or thing in one's care, Old English *weard,* a watching over. See **wer-**[4] in Appendix.*]

-ward, -wards. Indicates direction toward; for example, **skyward, westwards.** [Middle English *-ward,* Old English *-weard.* See **wer-**[3] in Appendix.*]

Ward (wôrd), **Artemas.** 1727–1800. American general; second in command of Continental Army (1775–76).

Ward (wôrd), **Artemus.** Pen name of Charles F. **Browne** *(see).*

Ward (wôrd), **Mary Augusta (Arnold).** Known as Mrs. Humphry Ward. 1851–1920. English novelist.

war dance. A tribal dance performed before a battle or as a celebration after a victory.

ward·ed (wôr′dĭd) *adj.* Having notches or wards, as keys.

war·den (wôrd′n) *n.* **1.** The chief administrative official of a prison. **2.** An official charged with the enforcement of certain laws and regulations, as an air-raid warden. **3.** *British.* **a.** The chief executive official in charge of a port or market. **b.** Any of various crown officers having administrative duties. **4.** The chief executive of a borough in certain states. **5.** *British.* One of the governing officials of certain colleges, schools, guilds, or hospitals; a trustee. **6.** A churchwarden. [Middle English *wardein,* from Old North French, from *warder,* to guard, from Germanic. See **wer-**[4] in Appendix.*]

war·den·ry (wôrd′n-rē) *n., pl.* **-ries.** Also **war·den·ship** (-shĭp′). The office, duties, or jurisdiction of a warden.

ward·er[1] (wôr′dər) *n.* **1.** A guard, porter, or watchman of a gate or tower. **2.** *British.* A prison guard. [Middle English, from Norman French *wardere,* from Old North French *warder,* to guard, keep. See **warden.**] —**war′der·ship′** *n.*

ward·er[2] (wôr′dər) *n.* A baton formerly used by a ruler or commander to signal orders. [Short for Middle English *warderer,* perhaps a jocular use of obsolete *warderere,* "look out behind" : Norman French *ware,* beware, from Germanic (see **wer-**[4] in Appendix*) + *derere,* behind, from Vulgar Latin *dē retrō* (unattested) : Latin *dē,* from + *retrō,* behind (see **retro-**).]

ward heel·er (hē′lər). *Slang.* A worker for the ward organization of a political machine.

ward·ress (wôrd′rĭs) *n. Chiefly British.* A prison matron.

ward·robe (wôrd′rōb′) *n.* **1.** A tall cabinet, closet, or small room designed to hold clothes. **2.** Garments collectively; especially, all the articles of clothing belonging to one person. **3. a.** The costumes belonging to a theater or theatrical troupe. **b.** The place in which they are kept. **4.** The department in charge of wearing apparel, jewelry, or the like in a royal or noble household. [Middle English *warderobe,* from Old North French : *warder,* to guard, keep, from Germanic (see **wer-**[4] in Appendix*) + *robe,* ROBE.]

ward·room (wôrd′rōōm′, -rŏŏm′) *n.* **1.** The common recreation area and dining room for the commissioned officers on a warship. **2.** These officers collectively.

-wards. Variant of **-ward.**

ward·ship (wôrd′shĭp′) *n.* **1.** The state of being a ward or in the charge of a guardian. **2.** Guardianship; custody.

ware[1] (wâr) *n.* **1.** Articles of the same general kind. Often used in combination: *glassware.* **2.** Pottery or ceramics or a special kind of pottery. Often used in combination: *earthenware.* **3.** *Plural.* **a.** Articles of commerce; goods. **b.** Any incorporeal asset or benefit, as a service or personal accomplishment, that is regarded as an article of commerce. [Middle English *ware,* Old English *waru.* See **wer-**[4] in Appendix.*]

ware[2] (wâr) *tr.v.* **wared, waring, wares.** *Archaic.* To beware of. Used chiefly in the imperative. —*adj. Obsolete.* Watchful; wary. [Middle English *waren,* Old English *warian.* See **wer-**[4] in Appendix.*]

ware·house (wâr′hous′) *n.* **1.** *Abbr.* **whs.** A place in which goods or merchandise are stored; storehouse. **2.** *British.* A large shop, usually wholesale. —*tr.v.* **warehoused, -housing, -houses.** To place or store in a warehouse, especially in a bonded or government warehouse.

ware·room (wâr′rōōm′, -rŏŏm′) *n.* A room used for the storage or display of goods or wares.

war·fare (wôr′fâr′) *n.* **1.** The waging of war; armed conflict. **2.** Conflict of any kind; struggle; strife. [Middle English *werrefare,* a going to war : *warre, werre,* WAR + *fare,* a journey, Old English *faru* and *fær* (see **per-**[2] in Appendix*).]

war·fa·rin (wôr′fər-ən) *n.* A colorless crystalline compound, $C_{19}H_{16}O_4$, used as a rodenticide and medicinally as an anticoagulant. [Patented by *W(isconsin) A(lumni) R(esearch) F(oundation)* + (COUM)ARIN.]

war game. Also **war games.** A simulated battle in military training maneuvers.

war hawk. A member of the Twelfth U.S. Congress (1811–13) who advocated war with Great Britain.

war·head (wôr′hĕd′) *n.* A part of the armament system in the forward part of a projectile, such as a guided missile, torpedo, or bomb, containing the explosive charge.

war·horse (wôr′hôrs′) *n.* Also **war horse. 1.** A horse used in combat; a charger. **2.** *Informal.* A person who has been through many battles, struggles, or fights. **3.** *Informal.* A musical or dramatic work that has become hackneyed.

war·like (wôr′līk′) *adj.* **1.** Belligerent; hostile. **2.** Of or pertaining to war; martial. **3.** Threatening or indicative of war.

war·lock (wôr′lŏk′) *n.* A male witch, sorcerer, wizard, or demon. [Middle English *warloghe,* Old English *wǣrloga,* "oath-breaker" : *wǣr,* faith, pledge (see **wēros** in Appendix*) + *-loga,* liar, from *lēogan,* to lie (see **leugh-** in Appendix*).]

war·lord (wôrʹlôrdʹ) *n.* A military commander exercising civil power in a given region, whether in nominal allegiance to the national government or in defiance of it.

warm (wôrm) *adj.* **warmer, warmest. 1.** Somewhat hotter than temperate; moderately hot: *a warm climate.* **2.** Having the natural heat of living beings. **3.** Preserving or imparting heat: *a warm overcoat.* **4.** Having a sensation of unusually high bodily heat, as from exercise or hard work; overheated. **5.** Marked by enthusiasm; fervent; ardent: *warm support.* **6.** Characterized by liveliness, excitement, disagreement, or the like: *a warm debate.* **7.** Marked by or revealing friendliness or sincerity; sympathetic; cordial: *warm greetings.* **8.** Loving; passionate; amorous: *a warm embrace.* **9.** Quick to be aroused; fiery: *a warm temper.* **10.** Predominantly red or yellow in color: *a warm sunset.* **11.** Recently made; fresh: *a warm trail.* **12.** Close to discovering, guessing, or finding something, as in certain games. **13.** *Informal.* Uncomfortable because of danger or annoyance: *Things are getting warm for the bookies.* —*v.* **warmed, warming, warms.** —*tr.* **1.** To raise slightly in temperature; make warm. **2.** To make zealous or ardent; inspire with life, zest, or color; enliven. **3.** To fill with pleasant emotions: *"I was chilled by thin merriment even though it was meant to warm me"* (James Baldwin). —*intr.* **1.** To become warm. **2.** To become ardent, enthusiastic, or animated. Usually used with *to.* **3.** To become kindly disposed or friendly. Usually used with *to* or *toward: "I warmed to the room at once, I liked its fly-by-night look"* (Truman Capote). —*n. Informal.* A warming or heating. [Middle English *warm,* Old English *wearm.* See **wer-**[9] in Appendix.*] —**warmʹer** *n.* —**warmʹish** *adj.* —**warmʹly** *adv.* —**warmʹness** *n.*

warm-blood·ed (wôrmʹblŭdʹĭd) *adj.* **1.** *Zoology.* Maintaining a relatively constant and warm body temperature independent of environmental temperature; homoiothermous. **2.** Ardent; impetuous; passionate.

warmed-o·ver (wôrmdʹōʹvər) *adj. Informal.* **1.** Reheated: *warmed-over tidbits.* **2.** Not new, fresh, or spontaneous.

warm front. A front along which an advancing mass of warm air rises over a mass of cold air.

warm-heart·ed (wôrmʹhärʹtĭd) *adj.* Kind; friendly; sympathetic. —**warmʹheartʹed·ly** *adv.* —**warmʹheartʹed·ness** *n.*

warming pan. A metal pan with a cover and a long handle, designed to hold hot liquids or coals and used to warm a bed. Sometimes called "bedpan."

war·mon·ger (wôrʹmŭngʹgər, -mŏngʹər) *n.* One who advocates or attempts to stir up war. —**warʹmonʹger·ing** *adj.* & *n.*

warmth (wôrmth) *n.* **1.** The state, sensation, or quality of producing or having a moderate degree of heat. **2.** Excitement or intensity, as of love or passion; ardor; zeal. **3.** The glowing effect produced by using predominantly red or yellow colors. [Middle English *warmth,* Old English *wiermthu* (unattested). See **wer-**[9] in Appendix.*]

warm up. 1. To warm. **2.** To exercise or practice, as in preparation for an athletic event. **3.** To make or become ready for operation, as an engine. **4.** To enter a phase of violently intensified contradictions.

warm-up (wôrmʹŭpʹ) *n.* The act, procedure, or period of warming up.

warn (wôrn) *v.* **warned, warning, warns.** —*tr.* **1.** To make aware of potential or probable harm, danger, or evil; to caution. **2.** To admonish as to action or manners. **3.** To notify (a person) to go or stay away. Usually used with *off* or *away.* **4.** To notify or apprise in advance. —*intr.* To give a warning. [Middle English *warnen,* Old English *w(e)arnian,* to take heed, warn. See **wer-**[5] in Appendix.*] —**warnʹer** *n.*

Synonyms: *warn, admonish, caution, forewarn.* These verbs mean to give a person advance notice of actual danger or of the possibility of danger, risk, or error. *Warn,* the most comprehensive, can refer either to giving specific word of impending danger or to counseling about something, such as a fault, trait, or circumstance, that could have dangerous or unpleasant consequences. The latter sense is basic to *admonish* and *caution.* However, *caution* is the stronger of these two in implying the act of alerting to danger or risk; *admonish* primarily suggests reproving for a shortcoming. *Forewarn* intensifies the sense of notice in advance and usually implies the presence of, or strong probability of, real danger.

warn·ing (wôrʹnĭng) *n.* **1.** An intimation, threat, or sign of impending danger or evil. **2. a.** Advice to beware, as of a person or thing. **b.** Counsel to desist from a specified undesirable course of action. **3.** A cautionary or deterrent example. —*adj.* Acting or serving as a warning. —**warnʹing·ly** *adv.*

War of 1812. A war between the United States and Great Britain (1812–15), fought over the rights of neutrals on the high seas and issues related to American westward expansion.

War of American Independence. *British.* The **American Revolution** *(see).*

War of Independence. The **American Revolution** *(see).*

War of Secession. The **Civil War** *(see).*

War of the Spanish Succession. A war fought by Austria, England, the Netherlands, and Prussia against France and Spain (1701–14), over the succession in Spain after the death of Charles II. The North American phase, between English and French colonists, is also called "Queen Anne's War."

warp (wôrp) *v.* **warped, warping, warps.** —*tr.* **1.** To turn or twist out of shape. **2.** To turn from a correct, healthy, or true course; to pervert; to corrupt. **3.** In weaving, to arrange (yarn or thread) so as to form a warp. **4.** *Nautical.* To move (a vessel) by hauling on a line that is fastened to or around a piling, anchor, or pier. —*intr.* **1.** To become bent or twisted out of shape, as wood. **2.** To turn aside from a true, correct, or natural course; go astray; deviate. **3.** *Nautical.* To move a vessel by hauling on a line that is fastened to or around a piling, anchor, or pier. —See Synonyms at **distort.** —*n.* **1.** The state of being twisted or bent out of shape. **2.** A distortion or twist, especially in a piece of wood. **3.** A mental or moral twist, aberration, or deviation. **4.** The threads that run lengthwise in a fabric, crossed at right angles by the woof. **5.** *Nautical.* A towline used in warping a vessel. [Middle English *werpen,* to warp, throw, Old English *weorpan,* to throw (away). See **wer-**[3] in Appendix.*] —**warpʹer** *n.*

war paint. 1. Pigments applied to the face or body by certain tribes, as the Indians of North America, preparatory to going to war. **2.** *Informal.* Cosmetics such as lipstick, rouge, or mascara. **3.** *Informal.* Official dress; regalia.

warp and woof. The underlying structure upon which something is built; a foundation; base.

war·path (wôrʹpăthʹ, -päthʹ) *n., pl.* **-paths** (-păthzʹ, -päthzʹ, -păthsʹ, -päthsʹ). **1.** The route taken by a party of North American Indians on the attack. **2.** A hostile course or mood. Used in the phrase *on the warpath.*

war·plane (wôrʹplānʹ) *n.* A combat aircraft.

war·rant (wôrʹənt, wŏrʹ-) *n. Abbr.* **war., wrnt. 1.** Authorization or certification; sanction, as given by a superior. **2.** Justification for some action; right; grounds. **3.** Something that assures, attests to, or guarantees some event or result; evidence; proof. **4.** A writing, writ, or other order that serves as authorization for something, specifically: **a.** A voucher authorizing payment or receipt of money. **b.** *British.* A warehouse receipt for goods received for storage. **c.** *Law.* A judicial writ authorizing an officer to make a search, seizure, or arrest or to execute a judgment. **d.** *Military.* A certificate of appointment given to warrant officers. —*tr.v.* **warranted, -ranting, -rants. 1.** To guarantee or attest to the quality, accuracy, or condition of. **2.** To guarantee or attest to the character or reliability of; vouch for. **3. a.** To guarantee (a product). **b.** To guarantee (a purchaser) indemnification against damage or loss. **4.** To guarantee the immunity or security of. **5.** To justify or call for; deserve. **6.** To grant authorization or sanction to (someone); authorize or empower. **7.** *Law.* To guarantee clear title to (real property, for example). [Middle English *war(r)ant,* protector, protection, authorization, from Old North French *warant,* probably from Medieval Latin *warantus,* from Old High German *werenti,* "the one protecting," present participle of *werren, weren, werien,* to protect, guarantee. See **wer-**[5] in Appendix.*] —**warʹrant·a·ble** *adj.* —**warʹrant·a·ble·ness** *n.* —**warʹrant·a·bly** *adv.* —**warʹrant·er** *n.*

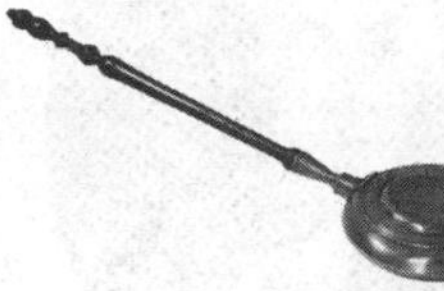
warming pan

war·ran·tee (wôrʹən-tēʹ, wŏrʹ-) *n. Law.* A person to whom a warranty is made.

warrant officer. *Abbr.* **WO, W.O.** *Military.* An officer, usually a skilled technician, intermediate in rank between a noncommissioned officer and a commissioned officer, having authority by virtue of a warrant.

war·ran·tor (wôrʹən-tər, -tôrʹ, wŏrʹ-) *n. Law.* A person who makes a warrant or gives a warranty to another.

war·ran·ty (wôrʹən-tē, wŏrʹ-) *n., pl.* **-ties. 1.** Official authorization, sanction, or warrant. **2.** Justification or valid grounds for an act or course of action. **3.** *Law.* **a.** An assurance by the seller of property that the goods or property are as represented or will be as promised. **b.** The insured's guarantee that the facts are as stated in reference to an insurance risk or that specified conditions will be fulfilled to keep the contract effective. **c.** A covenant by which the seller of land binds himself and his heirs to defend the security of the estate conveyed. **d.** A judicial writ; warrant. [Middle English *warantie,* from Old North French, from the feminine past participle of *warantir,* to guarantee, from *warant,* protection, WARRANT.]

war·ren (wôrʹən, wŏrʹ-) *n.* **1. a.** An area where rabbits live in burrows. **b.** A colony of rabbits. **2.** An enclosure for small game animals. **3.** Any overcrowded place of habitation. —See Synonyms at **flock.** [Middle English *warenne,* from Old North French, from Germanic. See **wer-**[5] in Appendix.*]

War·ren (wôrʹən, wŏrʹ-). **1.** A city of Michigan, north of Detroit, of which it is a suburb. Population, 89,000. **2.** A city of northeastern Ohio. Population, 60,000.

War·ren (wôrʹən, wŏrʹ-), **Earl.** Born 1891. Chief Justice of the United States (1953–69).

war·ren·er (wôrʹə-nər, wŏrʹ-) *n.* One who keeps a warren.

war·ri·or (wôrʹē-ər, -yər, wŏrʹ-) *n.* One engaged or experienced in battle. [Middle English *werreour,* from Old North French *werreieor,* from *werreier,* to make war, from *werre,* WAR.]

war·saw (wôrʹsô) *n.* A large grouper, *Epinephelus nigritus,* of warm Atlantic waters. Also called "warsaw grouper." [Variant (influenced by WARSAW, the city) of Spanish *guasa,* probably from a native name in the West Indies.]

War·saw (wôrʹsô). *Polish* **War·sza·wa** (vär-shäʹvä). The capital of Poland, a city on the Vistula in the central part of the country. Population, 1,241,000.

war·ship (wôrʹshĭpʹ) *n.* Any ship constructed or equipped for use in battle.

Wars of the Roses. See **Roses, Wars of the.**

wart (wôrt) *n.* **1.** A circumscribed hypertrophy of the outer region of the corium, caused by a virus, covered with a keratinous layer, and occurring typically on the hands or feet. **2.** Any similar protuberance, as on a plant. [Middle English *werte, wart,* Old English *wearte.* See **wer-**[1] in Appendix.*]

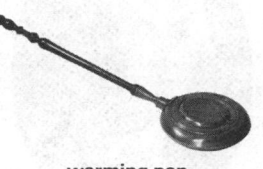

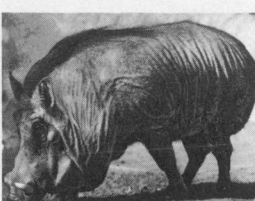

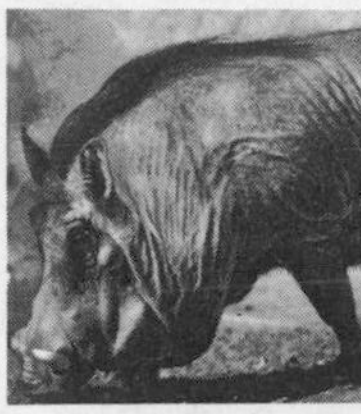
wart hog

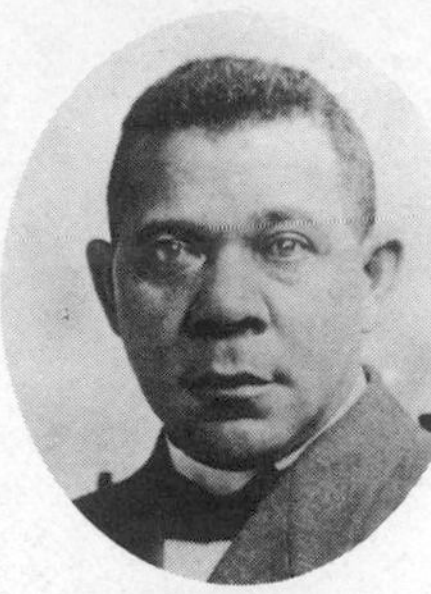
Booker T. Washington

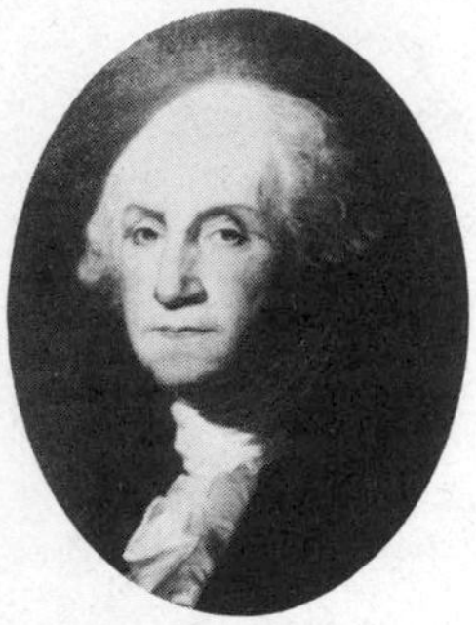
George Washington
Portrait by
Rembrandt Peale

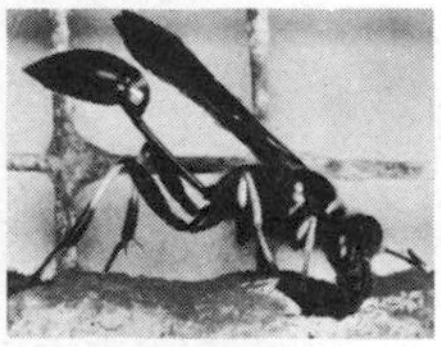
wasp
Sceliphron cementarium

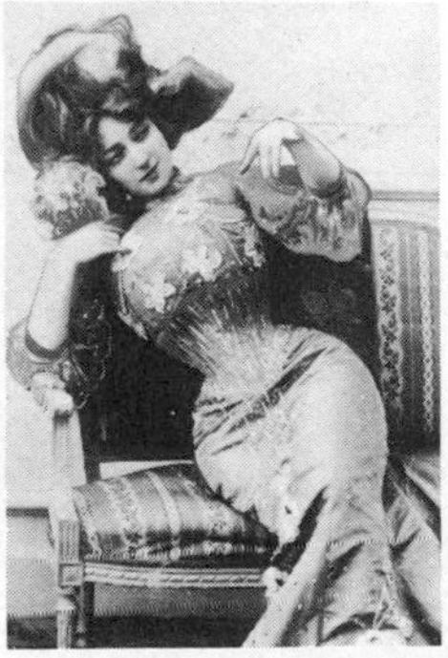
wasp waist

War·ta (vär′tä). A river of Poland, rising in the southeast and flowing 492 miles generally northwest to the Oder.

wart hog. A wild African hog, *Phacochoerus aethiopicus,* having tusks and wartlike protuberances on the face.

war·time (wôr′tīm′) *n.* A period or time of war.

wart·y (wôr′tē) *adj.* **-ier, -iest. 1.** Having or covered with warts or wartlike protuberances. **2.** Of or resembling a wart or warts.

war whoop. A war cry, especially of North American Indians.

War·wick (wôr′ĭk, wŏr′-; wôr′wĭk, wŏr′- *for sense 3*). **1.** Also **War·wick·shire** (wôr′ĭk-shîr, -shər, wŏr′-). *Abbr.* **War** A county occupying 985 square miles in central England. Population, 2,082,000. **2.** The county seat of this county. Population, 16,000. **3.** A textile manufacturing city in east-central Rhode Island. Population, 78,000.

War·wick (wôr′ĭk, wŏr′-), **Earl of.** Title of Richard Neville. 1428–1471. English military and political leader.

war·y (wâr′ē) *adj.* **-ier, -iest. 1.** On one's guard; cautious; watchful. **2.** Characterized by caution: *a wary glance.* [From obsolete *ware,* wary, from Middle English *ware,* Old English *wær.* See **wer-**[4] in Appendix.*] —**war′i·ly** *adv.* —**war′i·ness** *n.*

was (wŏz, wŭz; *unstressed* wəz). First and third person singular past indicative mood of **be.** See Usage note at **were.**

Wa·satch Range (wô′săch). A range of the Rocky Mountains, extending from southeastern Idaho into northern Utah. Highest elevation, Mount Timpanogos (12,008 feet).

wash (wŏsh, wôsh) *v.* **washed, washing, washes.** —*tr.* **1.** To cleanse, using water or other liquid, usually with soap, detergent, bleach, or the like, by immersing, dipping, rubbing, or scrubbing. **2.** To rid of corruption, defilement, or guilt; cleanse or purify: *"Unto him that loved us, and washed us from our sins"* (Revelation 1:5). **3.** To make moist or wet; dampen; drench: *Tears washed her cheeks.* **4.** To flow over, against, or past: *shores washed by ocean tides.* **5.** To soak, rinse out, and remove (dirt or stain) with or as with water. Used with *off, out,* or *away.* **6.** To sweep or carry away. Used with *off, out,* or *away: "The beetles had disappeared: the rain had apparently washed them away"* (Graham Greene). **7.** To erode, remove, damage, or destroy by moving water. Used with *out* or *away: The roads were washed out.* **8.** To serve as an effective cleaning agent for: *This soap washes wool.* **9.** To cover or coat with a watery layer of paint or other coloring substance. **10.** *Chemistry.* **a.** To purify (a gas) by passing through or over a liquid, as to remove soluble matter. **b.** To pass a solvent, such as distilled water, through (a precipitate). **11.** *Mining.* To remove particulate constituents from (an ore) by immersion in or agitation with water. —*intr.* **1.** To wash oneself. Sometimes used with *up: wash for dinner.* **2.** To wash clothes, dishes, or the like in or by means of water or other liquid. **3.** To undergo washing without fading or other damage: *This fabric will wash.* **4.** *British Informal.* To hold up under examination; be convincing: *Your excuse won't wash!* **5.** To be cleaned or removed by washing. Usually used with *out: The colors washed out.* **6.** To be carried away, removed, or drawn by the action of water. Used with *out* or *away: washed out to sea; washed away from the river bank.* **7.** To flow, sweep, or beat with a characteristic lapping sound. Used with *against, along,* or *over: The waves washed over the pilings.* —**wash down. 1.** To clean by washing with water from top to bottom, as a wall, a car, or the like. **2.** To follow the ingestion of (food, for example) with the ingestion of a liquid. —**wash one's hands of. 1.** To refuse to accept responsibility for. **2.** To abandon or renounce. —*n.* **1.** The act or process of washing or cleansing. **2.** A quantity of articles washed or intended for washing. **3.** Waste liquid; swill. **4.** Fermented liquid from which liquor is distilled. **5.** Any preparation or product used in washing or coating. **6.** A cosmetic or medicinal liquid, such as a mouthwash. **7. a.** A thin layer of water color or India ink spread on a drawing. **b.** Any light tint or hue: *"When old Godolphin awoke it was to a wash of red sunset through the window"* (Thomas Pynchon). **8. a.** The rush or surge of water or waves. **b.** The sound of this. **9. a.** The removal or erosion of soil, subsoil, or the like by the action of moving water. **b.** A deposit of recently eroded debris. **10. a.** Low or marshy ground washed by tidal waters. **b.** A stretch of shallow water. **11.** *Western U.S.* The dry bed of a stream. **12.** A turbulence in air or water caused by the motion or action of an oar, propeller, jet, or airfoil. —*adj.* **1.** Used for washing. **2.** Capable of being washed; washable. [Middle English *waschen, wasshen,* Old English *wæscan, wacsan.* See **wed-**[1] in Appendix.*]

Wash. Washington.

Wash, The (wŏsh, wôsh). An inlet of the North Sea in eastern England between Lincolnshire and Norfolk.

wash·a·ble (wŏsh′ə-bəl, wôsh′-) *adj.* Capable of being washed without fading or other injury.

wash-and-wear (wŏsh′ən-wâr′, wôsh′-) *adj.* Treated so as to be easily or quickly washed or rinsed clean and to require little or no ironing: *a wash-and-wear shirt.*

wash·board (wŏsh′bôrd′, -bōrd′, wôsh′-) *n.* **1. a.** A board having a corrugated surface of metal, wood, or the like, upon which clothes can be rubbed in the process of laundering. **b.** A similar board used as a percussion instrument. **2.** A board fastened to a wall at the floor, a baseboard. **3.** *Nautical.* A thin plank fastened to the side of a boat or to the sill of a port to keep out the sea and the spray.

wash·bowl (wŏsh′bōl′, wôsh′-) *n.* A basin that can be filled with water for use in washing oneself. Also called "washbasin."

wash·cloth (wŏsh′klôth′, -klŏth′, wôsh′-) *n., pl.* **-cloths** (-klô*thz*′, -klôths′, -klŏ*thz*′, -klŏths′). A small, usually square cloth of absorbent material used for washing the face or body. Also called "face cloth," "washrag."

wash·day (wŏsh′dā′, wôsh′-) *n.* A day, often the same day of every week, set aside for doing the household washing.

washed-out (wŏsht′out′, wôsht′-) *adj.* **1.** Lacking color or intensity; pale; faded. **2.** *Informal.* Exhausted; tired-looking.

washed-up (wŏsht′ŭp′, wôsht′-) *adj.* **1.** No longer successful or needed; finished. **2.** Ready to give up in disgust.

wash·er (wŏsh′ər, wôsh′-) *n.* **1.** One that washes. **2.** *Machinery.* A small perforated disk, as of metal, rubber, leather, or plastic, placed beneath a nut or at an axle bearing or joint to relieve friction, prevent leakage, or distribute pressure. **3.** A machine or apparatus for washing; especially, one for washing clothes or dishes.

wash·er·wom·an (wŏsh′ər-wo͝om′ən, wô′shər-) *n., pl.* **-women** (-wĭm′ĭn). Also **wash·wom·an** (wŏsh′wo͝om′ən, wôsh′-). A woman who washes clothes as a means of livelihood; a laundress.

wash·ing (wŏsh′ĭng, wôsh′-) *n.* **1.** The act or process of one that washes. **2.** A quantity of articles washed or intended to be washed at one time: *the week's washing.* **3.** The residue after an ore or other material has been washed. **4.** The liquid that is used to wash something. Sometimes used in the plural.

washing soda. A hydrated **sodium carbonate** *(see),* used as a general cleanser.

Wash·ing·ton (wŏsh′ĭng-tən, wôsh′-). **1.** *Abbr.* **Wash.** A Pacific state of the United States, occupying 68,192 square miles in the northwest; admitted to the Union in 1889. Population, 3,037,000. Capital, Olympia. See map at **United States of America.** **2.** The capital of the United States of America, a city in and coextensive with the District of Columbia, in the east, on the Maryland shore of the Potomac. Population, 784,000. See map at **United States of America.** —**Wash′ing·to′ni·an** (-tō′nē-ən) *adj.* & *n.*

Wash·ing·ton (wŏsh′ĭng-tən, wôsh′-), **Booker T(aliaferro).** 1856–1915. American Negro educator.

Wash·ing·ton (wŏsh′ĭng-tən, wôsh′-), **George.** 1732–1799. First President of the United States (1789–97).

Washington, Lake (wŏsh′ĭng-tən, wôsh′-). A lake about 20 miles long and 4 miles wide in west-central Washington.

Washington, Mount (wŏsh′ĭng-tən, wôsh′-). The highest (6,288 feet) of the White Mountains in New Hampshire.

Washington's Birthday. February 22, observed as a legal holiday in most states of the United States in honor of the birthday of George Washington.

Wash·i·ta (wŏsh′ə-tô, wôsh′-). **1.** A river rising in northern Texas and flowing 450 miles generally southeast through Oklahoma to Lake Texoma. **2.** See **Ouachita.**

wash·out (wŏsh′out′, wôsh′-) *n.* **1. a.** The erosion of a relatively soft surface, such as a roadbed, by a transient stream of water. **b.** A channel produced by washout. **2.** A total failure or disappointment.

wash·room (wŏsh′ro͞om′, -ro͝om′, wôsh′-) *n.* A bathroom, rest room, or lavatory, especially in a public place.

wash sale. The illegal buying of stock by a seller's agents to give the impression of an active market.

wash·stand (wŏsh′stănd′, wôsh′-) *n.* **1.** A stand designed to hold a basin and pitcher of water for washing. **2.** A stationary bathroom sink.

wash·tub (wŏsh′tŭb′, wôsh′-) *n.* A tub used for washing clothes.

wash·y (wŏsh′ē, wôsh′ē) *adj.* **-ier, -iest. 1.** Watery; diluted: *washy tea.* **2.** Lacking intensity or strength. —**wash′i·ness** *n.*

was·n't (wŏz′ənt, wŭz′-). Contraction of *was not.*

wasp (wŏsp, wôsp) *n.* Any of numerous social or solitary insects, chiefly of the superfamilies Vespoidea and Sphecoidea, having a slender body with a constricted abdomen, membranous wings, and in the females an ovipositor often modified as a sting. [Middle English *waspe,* Old English *wæsp, wæps.* See **wopsā** in Appendix.*]

Wasp, WASP, wasp (wŏsp, wôsp) *n.* A person of Caucasoid, northern European, largely Protestant stock whose members are held by some to constitute the most privileged and influential group in U.S. society; broadly, a white U.S. citizen of nonspecific ethnic or religious identity: *"The Wasp had come to take power."* (Norman Mailer). [W(HITE) A(NGLO)-S(AXON) P(ROTESTANT).] —**Wasp′ish, Wasp′y** *adj.*

wasp·ish (wŏs′pĭsh, wôs′-) *adj.* **1.** Pertaining to or suggestive of a wasp. **2.** Easily irritated or annoyed; irascible; snappish. —**wasp′ish·ly** *adv.* —**wasp′ish·ness** *n.*

wasp waist. A very slender or tightly corseted waist. —**wasp′-waist′ed** (wŏsp′wās′tĭd, wôsp′-) *adj.*

wasp·y (wŏs′pē, wôs′-) *adj.* **-ier, -iest.** Characteristic of a wasp; wasplike.

was·sail (wŏs′əl, wăs′-, wŏ-sāl′) *n.* **1.** A salutation or toast formerly given in drinking someone's health or as an expression of good will at a festivity. **2.** The drink used in such toasting, commonly ale or wine spiced with roasted apples and sugar. **3.** A festivity characterized by much drinking. —*v.* **wassailed, -sailing, -sails.** —*tr.* To drink to the health of; to toast. —*intr.* To engage in or drink a wassail. [Middle English *wassayl,* contraction of *wæs hæil,* from Old Norse *ves heill,* be in good health : *ves,* imperative singular of *vesa, vera,* to be (see **wes-**[3] in Appendix*) + *heill,* hale, healthy (see **kailo-** in Appendix*).] —**was′sail·er** *n.*

Was·ser·mann test (wä′sər-mən). A diagnostic test for syphilis involving the fixation or inactivation of a complement by an antibody in a blood serum sample. Also called "Wassermann reaction." [Discovered by August von *Wassermann* (1866–1925), German bacteriologist.]

wast. *Archaic.* Second person singular past tense of *be.*

ă pat/ā pay/âr care/ä father/b bib/ch church/d deed/ĕ pet/ē be/f fife/g gag/h hat/hw which/ĭ pit/ī pie/îr pier/j judge/k kick/l lid, needle/m mum/n no, sudden/ng thing/ŏ pot/ō toe/ô paw, for/oi noise/ou out/o͝o took/o͞o boot/p pop/r roar/s sauce/sh ship, dish/

wast·age (wā′stĭj) *n.* **1.** Loss by deterioration, wear, destruction, or the like: *"Disease and desertion still caused much greater wastage than battle"* (Theodore Ropp). **2.** The gradual process of wasting. **3.** That which is wasted or lost by wear.

waste (wāst) *v.* **wasted, wasting, wastes.** *—tr.* **1.** To use, consume, or expend thoughtlessly or carelessly; use to no avail; squander. **2.** To cause to lose energy, strength, or vigor; exhaust, tire, or enfeeble. **3.** To fail to take advantage of or use for profit; lose: *waste an opportunity.* *—intr.* **1.** To lose energy, strength, or vigor; become weak or enfeebled. Often used with *away.* **2.** To pass: *Time is wasting.* *—n.* **1.** The act of wasting or the condition of being wasted; thoughtless or careless expenditure, consumption, or use: *a waste of talent.* **2.** A place, region, or land that is uninhabited or uncultivated; a desert or wilderness. **3.** A devastated or destroyed region, town, building, or the like; a ruin. **4. a.** Any useless or worthless by-product of a process or the like; refuse or excess material. **b.** Something that escapes without being used, such as steam. **5.** Garbage; trash. **6.** The undigested residue of food eliminated from the body. *—adj.* **1.** Regarded or discarded as worthless or useless: *waste paper.* **2.** Used as a conveyance or container for refuse: *a waste can.* **3.** Not cultivated or inhabited: *The land lay waste.* **4.** Excreted from the body as useless. [Middle English *wasten,* from Old North French *waster,* from Common Romance *wāstāre* (unattested), from Latin *vāstāre,* to make empty, from *vāstus,* empty. See **eu-**[2] in Appendix.*]

waste·bas·ket (wāst′băs′kĭt, -bäs′kĭt) *n.* An open-topped container for rubbish. Also called "wastepaper basket."

wast·ed (wā′stĭd) *adj.* **1.** Not profitably used or maintained. **2.** Needless or superfluous: *wasted words.* **3.** Deteriorated; ravaged. **4.** Physically haggard, as from disease or dissipation: *"their wasted bodies and shrunken, skeletal faces"* (J.R. Salamanca). **5.** *Obsolete.* Elapsed. —See Synonyms at **haggard.**

waste·ful (wāst′fəl) *adj.* **1.** Characterized by heedless wasting; extravagant. **2.** Causing waste or devastation; neglectful; needlessly destructive. **—waste′ful·ly** *adv.* **—waste′ful·ness** *n.*

waste·land (wāst′lănd′) *n.* **1.** Uncultivated or desolate country; a barren, ruined, or ravaged land. **2.** Any place, era, or aspect of life considered humanistically, spiritually, or culturally barren; a hopeless or stagnant society; vacuum.

wast·er (wā′stər) *n.* A person who wastes; a spendthrift or prodigal; wastrel.

wast·ing (wā′stĭng) *adj.* **1.** Gradually deteriorating; declining: *the wasting countryside of America.* **2.** Sapping the strength, energy, or substance of the body; emaciating: *a wasting disease.*

wast·rel (wā′strəl) *n.* **1.** A person who wastes; especially, one who wastes money. **2.** An idler or loafer; a good-for-nothing. [WAST(E + SCOUND)REL.]

wa·tap (wă-täp′, wä-) *n.* Also **wa·ta·pe** (-tä′pē). A stringy thread made from the roots of various conifers and used by American Indians in sewing and weaving. [Cree *watapiy.*]

watch (wŏch) *v.* **watched, watching, watches.** *—intr.* **1.** To look or observe attentively or carefully; be closely observant. **2.** To look and wait expectantly or in anticipation. Used with *for: watch for an opportunity.* **3.** To be on the lookout or alert; be constantly observant or vigilant. **4.** To stay awake at night while serving as a guard, sentinel, or watchman. **5.** To stay alert as a devotional or religious exercise; keep vigil. *—tr.* **1.** To look at steadily; observe carefully or continuously. **2.** To guard; keep a watchful eye on. **3.** To observe the course of mentally; keep up on or informed about: *watch the election returns.* **4.** To tend, as flocks. **—watch out.** To be careful or on the alert; take care. *—n.* **1.** The act or process of keeping awake or mentally alert, as for the purpose of guarding. **2.** Formerly, any of the periods into which the night was divided; a part of the night. **3.** A period of close observation, often in order to discover something: *a watch during the child's illness.* **4.** A person or group of persons serving, especially at night, to guard or protect. **5.** The post or period of duty of a guard, sentinel, or watchman. **6.** A small, portable timepiece, especially one worn on the wrist or carried in the pocket. **7. a.** A period of wakefulness, especially one observed as a religious vigil. **b.** A wake. **8.** *Nautical.* **a.** Any of the periods of time into which the day aboard ship is divided and during which a part of the crew is assigned to duty. **b.** The members of a ship's crew on duty during a specific watch. **c.** A chronometer on a ship. **9.** *Obsolete.* A candle marked into equal sections and used for keeping time. **10.** *Obsolete.* The cry of a watchman or sentinel. **11.** Wakefulness. **12.** A flock of nightingales. —See Synonyms at **flock.** **—on the watch.** On the lookout; waiting for something or someone expectantly. [Middle English *wa(c)chen, wecchen,* Old English *wæccan,* to be or stay awake, keep vigil. See **weg-**[2] in Appendix.*]

watch cap. *U.S. Navy.* A small woolen cap of navy blue worn for cold-weather duty by enlisted men.

watch·case (wŏch′kās′) *n.* The casing for the mechanism of a watch.

watch·dog (wŏch′dôg′, -dŏg′) *n.* **1.** A dog trained to guard property. **2.** A person who serves as a guardian or protector against waste, loss, or illegal practices.

watch·er (wŏch′ər) *n.* **1.** One that watches. **2.** A person keeping vigil, as at a sick person's bedside.

watch·ful (wŏch′fəl) *adj.* **1.** Closely observant or alert; vigilant. **2.** *Archaic.* Awake; not sleeping. —See Synonyms at **aware.** **—watch′ful·ly** *adv.* **—watch′ful·ness** *n.*

watch glass. A shallow glass dish used as a beaker cover or evaporating surface.

watch·mak·er (wŏch′mā′kər) *n.* One whose occupation is making or repairing watches. **—watch′mak′ing** *n.*

watch·man (wŏch′mən) *n., pl.* **-men** (-mĭn). A man employed to stand guard or keep watch.

watch night. 1. New Year's Eve. **2.** A religious service held on New Year's Eve. Also called "watch meeting."

watch·tow·er (wŏch′tou′ər) *n.* An observation tower upon which a guard or lookout is stationed to keep watch, as for enemies or forest fires or over prisoners.

watch·word (wŏch′wûrd′) *n.* **1.** A prearranged reply to a challenge, as from a guard or sentry; password; countersign. **2.** A rallying cry: *Let our watchword be freedom.*

wa·ter (wô′tər, wŏt′ər) *n.* **1.** A clear, colorless, nearly odorless and tasteless liquid, H_2O, essential for most plant and animal life and the most widely used of all solvents. Melting point 0°C (32°F), boiling point 100°C (212°F), specific gravity (4°C) 1.0000, weight per gallon (15°C) 8.337 pounds. **2.** Any of various forms of water, such as rain. **3.** Any body of water, such as a sea, lake, river, or stream. **4.** Any one of the liquids passed out of the body, such as urine, perspiration, tears, or the like. **5.** The fluid surrounding the fetus in the uterus; amniotic fluid. **6.** An aqueous solution of any substance, especially a gas: *ammonia water.* **7.** A wavy finish or sheen, as of a fabric. **8.** *Finance.* **a.** The valuation of the assets of a business firm beyond their real value. **b.** Stock issued in excess of paid-in capital. **—above water.** Out of trouble. **—by water.** By boat. **—hold water.** To be logical or consistent: *His story holds water.* **—in deep water.** In great difficulty. **—make** (or **pass**) **water.** To urinate. *—v.* **watered, -tering, -ters.** *—tr.* **1.** To pour water upon; make wet. **2. a.** To give drinking water to. **b.** To lead (an animal) to drinking water. **3.** To dilute or weaken by adding water to. Often used with *down.* **4.** To give a sheen to the surface of (silk, linen, or metal). **5.** To increase (the number of shares of stock) without increasing the value of the assets they represent. **6.** To irrigate (land). *—intr.* **1.** To produce or discharge fluid, as from the eyes. **2.** To salivate in anticipation of food. **3.** To take on a supply of water, as a ship. **4.** To drink water, as an animal. **—make one's mouth water.** To cause to anticipate with relish. [Middle English *water,* Old English *wæter.* See **wed-**[1] in Appendix.*] **—wa′ter** *adj.* **—wa′ter·er** *n.*

wa·ter·age (wô′tər-ĭj, wŏt′ər-) *n. British.* **1.** The movement of goods or merchandise by water. **2.** The fee paid for this.

water arum. A species of **calla** *(see).*

water back. A tank for heating water in a coal stove.

water ballet. 1. The art of dancelike movement in water; synchronized swimming. **2.** Any performance of this kind.

Water Bearer. The constellation and sign of the zodiac, **Aquarius** *(see).*

water beetle. Any of various aquatic beetles, especially of the family Dytiscidae, characteristically having a smooth, oval body and flattened hind legs especially adapted for swimming.

water bird. Any swimming or wading bird.

water biscuit. A biscuit made of flour and water.

water blister. A blister having a nonpurulent watery content.

water boatman. Any of various aquatic insects of the family Corixidae, having long, oarlike hind legs adapted for swimming.

wa·ter·borne (wô′tər-bôrn′, -bōrn′, wŏt′ər-) *adj.* **1.** Floating on or supported by water; afloat. **2.** Transported by water, as freight. **3.** Transmitted in water, as a disease germ.

water boy. One who keeps a group, as a work team, supplied with drinking water.

water brash. Regurgitation of watery acid from the stomach.

wa·ter·buck (wô′tər-bŭk′, wŏt′ər-) *n.* Any of several African antelopes of the genus *Kobus,* having curved, ridged horns and frequenting swamps or bodies of water.

water buffalo. A large buffalo, *Bubalus bubalis,* of Asia and Africa, having large, spreading horns and often domesticated, especially as a draft animal. Also called "carabao."

water bug. Any of various insects of wet places; especially, a large aquatic insect of the family Belostomatidae.

Wa·ter·bur·y (wô′tər-bĕr′ē, wŏt′ər-). A city and industrial center of Connecticut, in the west-central part of the state. Population, 142,000.

water chestnut. 1. A floating aquatic plant, *Trapa natans,* native to Asia, bearing four-pronged, nutlike fruit. Also called "water caltrop." **2.** A Chinese sedge, *Eleocharis tuberosa,* having an edible corm. **3.** The succulent corm of this plant, used in Oriental cookery.

water chinquapin. A North American aquatic plant, *Nelumbo lutea,* related to the lotus and the water lilies, having large, cup-shaped leaves, large, pale-yellow flowers, and edible, nutlike seeds.

water clock. Any of various time-keeping or time-measuring devices, such as a **clepsydra** *(see),* based on the motion of running water.

water closet. *Abbr.* **w.c.** A room or booth containing a toilet and often a washbowl.

water color. Also **wa·ter·col·or** (wô′tər-kŭl′ər, wŏt′ər-), **wa·ter·col·or.** **1.** A paint composed of a water-soluble pigment. **2.** A work done in water colors. **3.** The art of using water colors. **—wa′ter·col′or** *adj.* **—water colorist.**

wa·ter-cool (wô′tər-ko͞ol′, wŏt′ər-) *tr.v.* **-cooled, -cooling, -cools.** To cool (an engine) with water, especially with circulating water.

water cooler. A vessel, device, or apparatus for cooling, storing, and dispensing drinking water.

wa·ter·course (wô′tər-kôrs′, -kōrs′, wŏt′ər-) *n.* **1.** A **waterway** *(see).* **2.** The bed or channel of a waterway.

wa·ter·cress (wô′tər-krĕs′, wŏt′ər-) *n.* **1.** A plant, *Nasturtium officinale,* native to Eurasia, growing in freshwater ponds and

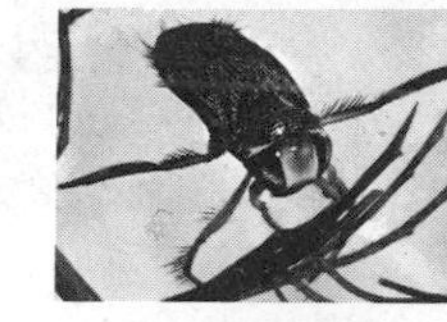

water boatman
Genus *Corixa*

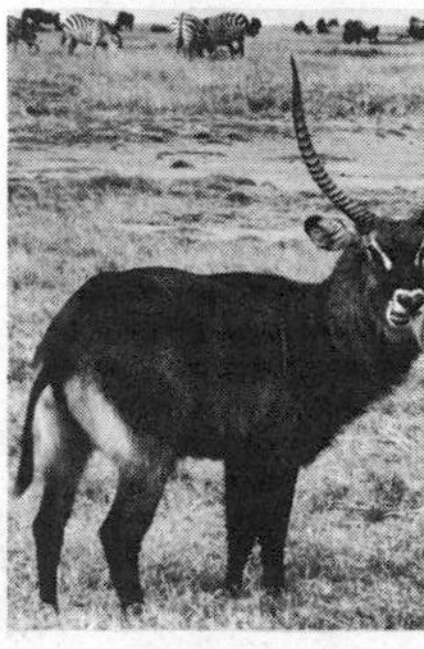

waterbuck
Kobus ellipsiprymnus

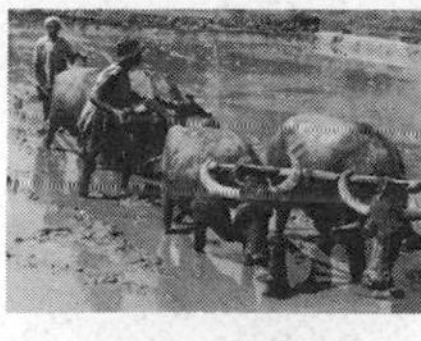

water buffalo

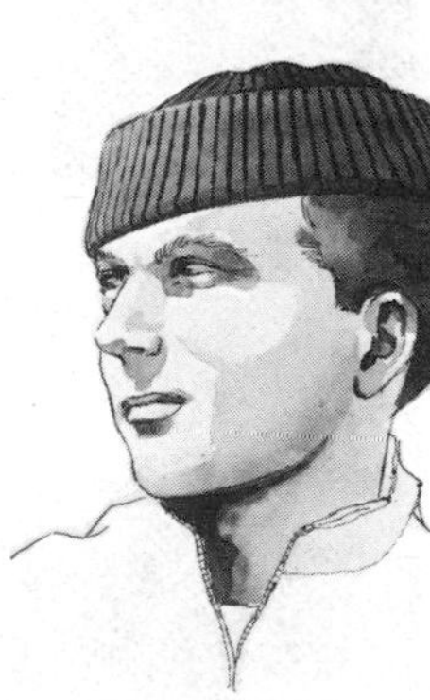

watch cap

streams and having pungent leaves used in salads as a garnish. **2.** Any of several similar, related plants.

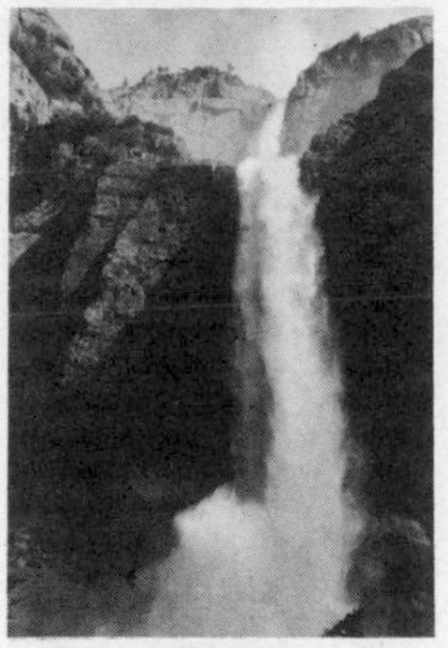

waterfall
Yosemite Falls,
Yosemite National Park

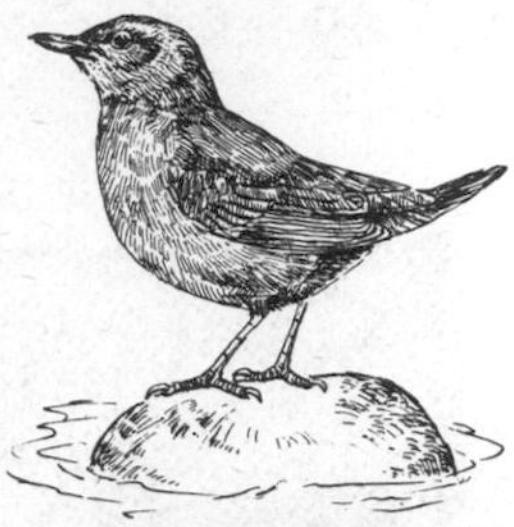

water ouzel
Cinclus mexicanus

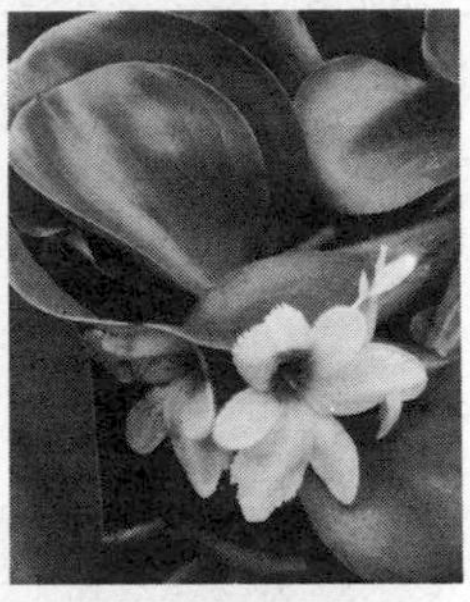

water hyacinth

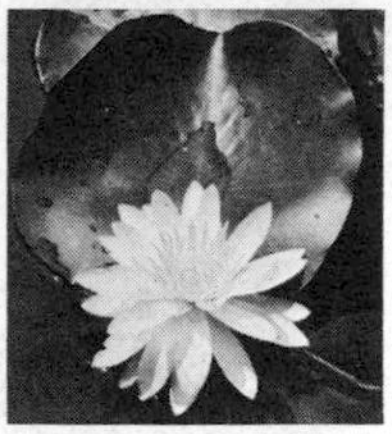

water lily
Nymphaea odorata

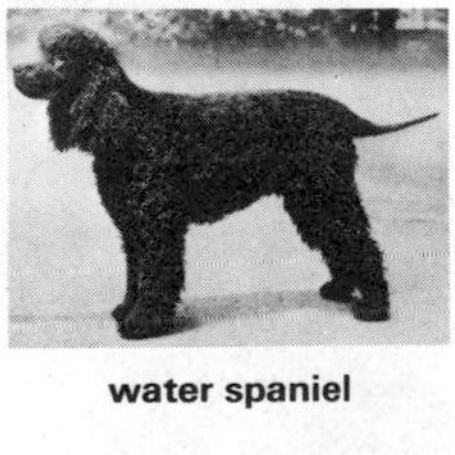

water spaniel

water cure. *Medicine.* Hydropathy or hydrotherapy.

water dog. **1.** A dog that is at home in water, especially one trained for hunting waterfowl. **2.** One who is at home in or on the water. **3.** A salamander, a **mud puppy** *(see).*

water elm. The **planer tree** *(see).*

wa·ter·fall (wô′tər-fôl′, wŏt′ər-) *n.* A steep descent of water from a height; a cascade.

wa·ter·find·er (wô′tər-fīn′dər, wŏt′ər-) *n.* A dowser.

water flea. Any of various small aquatic crustaceans of the order Cladocera, characteristically swimming with jerking, flea-like motions.

Wa·ter·ford (wô′tər-fərd, wŏt′ər-). **1.** A county occupying 710 square miles in southern Ireland. Population, 71,000. **2.** The county seat of this county. Population, 28,000.

wa·ter·fowl (wô′tər-foul′, wŏt′ər-) *n., pl.* **waterfowl** or **-fowls.** **1.** A swimming bird, as a duck or goose, usually frequenting freshwater areas. **2.** Such birds collectively.

wa·ter·front (wô′tər-frŭnt′, wŏt′ər-) *n.* Improved or unimproved land abutting on a body of water, such as a lake, harbor, or the like. *—adj.* Of or pertaining to a waterfront.

water gap. A transverse cleft in a mountain ridge through which a stream flows.

water gas. A fuel gas containing about 50 per cent carbon monoxide, 40 per cent hydrogen, and small amounts of carbon dioxide and nitrogen, made by passing steam over heated coke.

water gate. A **floodgate** *(see).*

water gauge. Also **water gage.** An instrument indicating the level of water, as in a boiler, tank, reservoir, or stream.

water glass. **1.** A drinking glass or goblet. **2.** A tube or similar structure having a glass bottom for making observations below the surface of the water. **3. Sodium silicate** *(see).* **4.** A water gauge made of glass. **5.** A clepsydra.

water gum. A gum tree, as a tupelo, growing in wet places.

water hammer. **1.** A banging noise heard in a water pipe following an abrupt alteration of the flow with resulting pressure surges. **2.** A similar noise in steam pipes, caused by steam bubbles entering a cold pipe partially filled with water.

water hemlock. Any of several poisonous plants of the genus *Cicuta;* especially, *C. maculata,* of marshy areas, having clusters of small white flowers. Also called "cowbane."

water hen. Any of various chickenlike birds of marshy areas, as a rail or coot.

water hole. A small natural depression in which water collects; especially, a pool used by animals as a watering place.

water horehound. A plant, the **bugleweed** *(see).*

water hyacinth. A floating aquatic plant, *Eichhornia crassipes,* native to tropical America, having bluish-purple flowers and often forming dense masses in ponds and streams.

water ice. A dessert made from sweetened, flavored, finely crushed ice.

wa·ter-inch (wô′tər-ĭnch′, wŏt′ər-) *n.* A former unit of hydraulic measure based on the discharge of water through a circular one-inch opening, commonly estimated at 14 pints per minute.

watering place. **1.** A place where animals find water. **2.** A health resort featuring water activities or mineral springs; spa.

watering pot. A vessel, often with a spout and a perforated nozzle, used to water plants. Also called "watering can."

wa·ter·ish (wô′tər-ĭsh, wŏt′ər-) *adj.* Watery.

wa·ter-jack·et (wô′tər-jăk′ĭt, wŏt′ər-) *tr.v.* **-eted, -eting, -ets.** To encase in or provide with a water jacket.

water jacket. A casing containing water circulated by a pump, used around a part to be cooled, especially in water-cooled internal-combustion engines.

water jump. An obstacle in a steeplechase course or horse-show ring consisting of a ditch of water and, usually, a fence on the takeoff side.

wa·ter·leaf (wô′tər-lēf′, wŏt′ər-) *n., pl.* **-leafs.** Any of various North American plants of the genus *Hydrophyllum,* having clusters of white or purplish flowers.

wa·ter·less (wô′tər-lĭs, wŏt′ər-) *adj.* **1.** Without water; dry. **2.** Not requiring water, as a cooling system.

water level. **1.** The height of the surface of a body of water. **2.** *Geology.* A **water table** *(see).* **3.** The water line of a ship.

water lily *pl.* **water lilies.** **1.** Any of various aquatic plants of the genus *Nymphaea,* having floating leaves and showy, variously colored flowers; especially, *N. odorata,* having fragrant, many-petaled white or pinkish flowers. **2.** Any of various similar or related plants. Also called "pond lily."

water line. *Abbr.* **WL, w.l.** **1.** *Nautical.* **a.** The line on the hull of a ship to which the water surface rises. **b.** Any of several lines parallel to this marked on the hull of a ship, indicating the depth to which the ship sinks under various loads. **2.** A line or stain, as that left on a sea wall, indicating the height to which water has risen or may rise.

wa·ter·log (wô′tər-lôg′, -lŏg′, wŏt′ər-) *tr.v.* **-logged, -logging, -logs.** To soak or saturate with water; cause to lose buoyancy.

wa·ter-logged (wô′tər-lôgd′, -lŏgd′, wŏt′ər-) *adj.* **1.** Heavy and sluggish in the water because of flooding in the hold. Said of a ship. **2.** Soaked or saturated with water: *water-logged fields.* [WATER + *-logged,* probably "made (unmanageable) like a log in water," from LOG.]

Wa·ter·loo[1] (wô′tər-lo͞o′). **1.** A town in Brabant, central Belgium, near the site of a decisive defeat of Napoleon by Wellington and Blücher (1815). Population, 12,000. **2.** A city of Iowa, northwest of Cedar Rapids. Population, 72,000.

Wa·ter·loo[2] (wô′tər-lo͞o′) *n.* A disastrous or crushing defeat. Usually used in the phrase *meet one's Waterloo.*

water main. A principal pipe in a system of pipes for conveying water, especially one installed underground.

wa·ter·man (wô′tər-mən, wŏt′ər-) *n., pl.* **-men** (-mĭn). A boatman. **—wa′ter·man·ship′** *n.*

wa·ter·mark (wô′tər-märk′, wŏt′ər-) *n.* **1.** A mark showing the height to which water has risen; especially, a line indicating the heights of high and low tide. **2.** *Abbr.* **wmk.** A translucent design impressed on paper during manufacture and visible when the finished paper is held to the light. **3.** The metal pattern that produces this design. *—tr.v.* **watermarked, -marking, -marks.** **1.** To mark (paper) with a watermark. **2.** To impress (a pattern or design) as a watermark.

wa·ter·mel·on (wô′tər-mĕl′ən, wŏt′ər-) *n.* **1.** A vine, *Citrullus vulgaris,* native to Africa, cultivated for its large, edible fruit. **2.** The fruit of this plant, having a hard green rind and sweet, watery pink or reddish flesh.

water meter. An instrument that records the quantity of water passing through a pipe.

water milfoil. Any of various aquatic plants of the genus *Myriophyllum,* having feathery, finely dissected leaves.

water mill. A mill with water-driven machinery.

water moccasin. A venomous snake, *Agkistrodon piscivorus* (or *Ancistrodon piscivorus*), of lowlands and swampy regions of the southern United States. Also called "cottonmouth."

water of crystallization. Water in chemical combination with a crystal and necessary for the maintenance of crystalline properties but capable of being removed by sufficient heat.

water of hydration. Water chemically combined with a substance so that it can be removed, as by heating, without substantially changing the chemical composition of the substance.

water ouzel. Any of several small birds of the genus *Cinclus,* that dive into swift-moving streams and feed along the bottom. Also called "dipper."

water parting. A **watershed** *(see).*

water pepper. A marsh plant, *Polygonum hydropiper* (or *Persicaria hydropiper*), having reddish stems, clusters of small, greenish flowers, and acrid-tasting leaves.

water pimpernel. A plant, the **brookweed** *(see).*

water pipe. **1.** A water conduit. **2.** A **hookah** *(see).*

water plantain. Any of various aquatic plants of the genus *Alisma,* having branching clusters of small white or pinkish flowers.

water polo. A water sport with two teams, each of which tries to pass a ball into the other's goal.

wa·ter·pow·er (wô′tər-pou′ər, wŏt′ər-) *n.* **1.** The energy of running or falling water as used for driving machinery, especially for generating electricity. **2.** A source of such power, as a waterfall. **3.** A water right owned by a mill.

wa·ter·proof (wô′tər-pro͞of′, wŏt′ər-) *adj.* **1.** Impenetrable to or unaffected by water. **2.** Made of or treated with rubber, plastic, or a sealing agent to resist water penetration. *—n.* **1.** A waterproof material or fabric. **2.** *Chiefly British.* A raincoat or other waterproof garment. *—tr.v.* **waterproofed, -proofing, -proofs.** To make waterproof. [WATER + -PROOF.]

water purslane. **1.** An aquatic plant, *Didiplis diandra,* having small greenish flowers. **2.** A marsh plant, *Ludwigia palustris,* having reddish stems and small reddish flowers.

water rat. **1.** Any of various semiaquatic rodents, as one of the genus *Hydromis,* of Australia and adjacent islands, or *Neofiber alleni,* of Florida and southern Georgia, resembling the muskrat. **2.** *Slang.* A waterfront thief, ruffian, or habitué.

wa·ter-re·pel·lent (wô′tər-rĭ-pĕl′ənt, wŏt′ər-) *adj.* Resisting penetration by but not entirely impervious to water.

wa·ter-re·sis·tant (wô′tər-rĭ-zĭs′tənt, wŏt′ər-) *adj.* Resistant to wetting but not waterproof.

water right. **1.** The right to draw water from a particular source, such as a lake, irrigation canal, or stream. **2.** The right to navigate on particular waters.

water sapphire. A deep-blue cordierite often used as a gemstone.

wa·ter·scape (wô′tər-skāp′, wŏt′ər-) *n.* A seascape.

water scorpion. Any of various aquatic insects of the family Nepidae, having a respiratory tube projecting from the posterior part of the abdomen and inflicting a painful sting.

wa·ter·shed (wô′tər-shĕd′, wŏt′ər-) *n.* **1.** A ridge of high land dividing two areas that are drained by different river systems. Also called "water parting." **2.** The region draining into a river, river system, or body of water. **3.** A crucially important or divisive factor, time, or event. [Probably translation of German *Wasserscheide.*]

water shield. **1.** An aquatic plant, *Brasenia schreberi,* having floating oval leaves and purplish flowers. **2.** Any of several related plants of the genus *Cabomba.*

wa·ter-sick (wô′tər-sĭk′, wŏt′ər-) *adj.* Not productive owing to the results of excessive irrigation. Said of land.

wa·ter·side (wô′tər-sīd′, wŏt′ər-) *n.* Land bordering any body of water; a bank; shore. *—adj.* **1.** Of, pertaining to, or situated at the waterside. **2.** Living or working along the waterside.

wa·ter-ski (wô′tər-skē′, wŏt′ər-) *intr.v.* **skied, -skiing, -skis.** To ski on water while being towed by a power boat. *—n., pl.* **water-skis** or **-ski.** Also **water ski.** A broad ski used in water-skiing. **—wa′ter-ski′er** *n.*

water snake. **1.** Any of various nonvenomous snakes of the genus *Natrix,* frequenting freshwater streams and ponds. **2.** Any of various other aquatic or semiaquatic snakes.

wa·ter-soak (wô′tər-sōk′, wŏt′ər-) *tr.v.* **-soaked, -soaking, -soaks.** To soak or saturate with water.

water spaniel. A spaniel of a breed characterized by a curly, water-resistant coat, often used for retrieving waterfowl.

wa·ter·spout (wô′tər-spout′, wŏt′ər-) *n.* **1.** A tornado or lesser whirlwind occurring over water and resulting in a whirling column of spray and mist. Compare **tornado**. **2.** A hole or pipe from which water is discharged. —See Synonyms at **wind**.
water sprite. A sprite or nymph living in or near the water.
water strider. Any of various insects of the family Gerridae, having long, slender legs with which they support themselves on the surface of water. Also called "skater," "water skater."
water supply. **1.** The water available for a community or region. **2.** The sources and delivery system of such water.
water system. **1.** A river and all its tributaries. **2.** A water supply.
water table. **1.** A projecting ledge, molding, or stringcourse along the side of a building, designed to throw off rainwater. **2.** The surface in a permeable body of rock of a zone saturated with water. Also called "water level."
water thrush. Either of two brownish New World birds, *Seiurus noveboracensis* or *S. motacilla*, characteristically walking along the edges of streams or ponds.
water tiger. The predacious larva of a **diving beetle** *(see)*.
wa·ter·tight (wô′tər-tīt′, wŏt′ər-) *adj.* **1.** So assembled or constructed that water cannot enter or escape; waterproof. **2.** Having no flaws or loopholes; incapable of being misconstrued: *"a very irregular will, but watertight"* (Patrick Dennis).
water tower. **1.** A standpipe or tank used as a reservoir or for maintaining equal pressure on a water system. **2.** A vehicular towerlike fire-fighting apparatus for raising hoses to the upper levels of a burning structure.
water turkey. A blackish New World bird, *Anhinga anhinga*, of swampy regions, having a long, slender, flexible neck. Also called "anhinga," "darter," "snakebird."
water vapor. Water diffused as a vapor in the atmosphere, especially at a temperature below the boiling point.
Wa·ter·vliet (wô′tər-vlēt′, wŏt′ər-). A city of New York State, on the Hudson opposite Troy; the site of the first American Shaker community (established 1775). Population, 14,000.
wa·ter·way (wô′tər-wā′, wŏt′ər-) *n.* A river, channel, canal, or other navigable body of water used for travel or transport. Also called "watercourse."
wa·ter·weed (wô′tər-wēd′, wŏt′ər-) *n.* Any of various aquatic plants; especially, one of the genus *Anacharis* (or *Elodea*), having submerged stems with densely crowded, narrow leaves.
water wheel. **1.** A wheel propelled by falling or running water, primarily for use as a source of power. **2.** A wheel, with buckets attached to its rim, used for raising water.
water wings. An inflatable device used to support the body in learning to swim.
water witch. One who professes the ability to find underground water by means of a divining rod or other device.
wa·ter·works (wô′tər-wûrks′, wŏt′ər-) *pl.n.* **1. a.** The water system, including reservoirs, tanks, buildings, pumps, pipes, and other apparatus, of a city or town. **b.** A single unit, as a pumping station, within such a system. Often used with a singular verb. **2.** An exhibition of moving water, as artificial fountains or waterfalls. **3.** *Slang.* Tears.
wa·ter·y (wô′tə-rē, wŏt′ə-) *adj.* **-ier, -iest.** **1.** Filled with, consisting of, or containing water; moist; wet: *watery soil.* **2.** Resembling or suggestive of water; liquid. **3.** Diluted: *watery soup.* **4.** Without force; insipid: *watery prose.* **5.** Secreting or discharging water, especially as a symptom of disease. —**wa′ter·i·ness** *n.*
Wat·ling Street (wŏt′lĭng). A Roman road in Britain that ran from Dover, through London, to a point near Shrewsbury.
Wat·son (wŏt′sən), **James Dewey.** Born 1928. American biologist; discovered molecular structure of DNA with F.H.C. **Crick** *(see)*.
Wat·son (wŏt′sən), **John Broadus.** 1878–1958. American behavioral psychologist.
Wat·son-Watt (wŏt′sən-wŏt′), Sir **Robert Alexander.** Born 1892. British physicist; a developer of radar.
watt (wŏt) *n. Abbr.* **W** A unit of power in the International System equal to one joule per second. See **measurement**. [After James WATT.]
Watt (wŏt), **James.** 1736–1819. Scottish engineer and inventor; invented modern condensing steam engine and the centrifugal governor.
wat·tage (wŏt′ĭj) *n.* **1.** An amount of power, especially electric power, expressed in watts. **2.** The electric power required by an appliance or device.
Wat·teau (wä-tō′, vä-), **Jean Antoine.** 1684–1721. French painter.
watt-hour (wŏt′our′) *n. Abbr.* **W-hr** A unit of energy, especially electrical energy, equal to the energy of one watt acting for one hour and equivalent to 3,600 joules.
wat·tle (wŏt′l) *n.* **1.** Poles intertwined with twigs, reeds, or branches for use in construction, as of walls or fences. **2.** Materials thus used. **3.** A fleshy, often brightly colored fold of skin hanging from the neck or throat, characteristic of certain birds and some lizards. **4.** Any of various Australian trees or shrubs of the genus *Acacia.* —*tr.v.* **wattled, -tling, -tles.** **1.** To construct from wattle. **2.** To weave into wattle. —*adj.* Constructed, woven, or covered with wattle. [Middle English *wattel*, Old English *watel, watul.* See **aw-**[1] in Appendix.*]
wat·tle·bird (wŏt′l-bûrd′) *n.* Any of several birds of the genus *Anthochaera*, of Australia and adjacent regions, having pendent wattles on each side of the head.
wat·tled (wŏt′əld) *adj.* Constructed with or having wattles.
watt·me·ter (wŏt′mē′tər) *n.* An instrument for measuring in watts the power flowing in a circuit.
Wa·tu·si (wä-tōō′sē) *n., pl.* **Watusi** or **-sis.** **1.** A member of a pastoral people of Rwanda and Burundi in central equatorial Africa, distinguished by their tall stature. **2.** A dance supposedly imitative of Watusi tribal dances. —*intr.v.* **Watusied, -siing, -sis.** To dance the Watusi.
Wau·ke·gan (wô-kē′gən). A city of Illinois, a resort center in the northeast on Lake Michigan. Population, 55,000.
Wau·wa·to·sa (wô′wə-tō′sə). A city of southeastern Wisconsin west of Milwaukee. Population, 57,000.
wave (wāv) *v.* **waved, waving, waves.** —*intr.* **1.** To move back and forth or up and down in the air: *branches waving in the wind.* **2.** To make a signal with an up-and-down or back-and-forth movement with the hand or with an object in the hand: *He waved in salute.* **3.** To curve or curl; undulate: *Her hair waves.* —*tr.* **1.** To move back and forth or up and down; cause to flutter: *She waved her fan.* **2. a.** To move or swing as in giving a signal: *wave one's hand.* **b.** To signal or express by such movement: *He waved good-by.* **3.** To arrange into curves, curls, or undulations: *wave one's hair.* —*n.* **1. a.** A ridge or swell moving along the surface of a large body of water and generated by the action of gravity or the wind. **b.** A small ridge or swell moving across the interface of two fluids and dependent on the surface tension. **2.** *Often plural.* The sea or seas. **3.** A moving curve or a succession of curves in or upon a surface; an undulation: *waves of wheat in the wind.* **4. a.** A curve or curl, or a succession of curves, as in the hair. **b.** Any curved shape, outline, or pattern. **5.** A movement up and down or back and forth: *a wave of the hand.* **6.** Something resembling a wave or waves; a surge: *a wave of indignation.* **7.** A widespread, persistent meteorological condition, especially of temperature: *a cold wave.* **8.** A group of people, animals, or events that advance in a body: *a wave of pioneers heading west.* **9.** *Physics.* **a.** A disturbance or oscillation propagated from point to point in a medium or in space and described, in general, by mathematical specification of its amplitude, velocity, frequency, and phase. **b.** A graphic representation of the variation of such a disturbance with time. [As verb, Middle English *waven*, Old English *wafian*, to move back and forth (especially with the hands). See **webh-** in Appendix.* As noun, perhaps variant (influenced by the verb WAVE) of Middle English *wawe, waghe*, probably Old English *wǣg*, motion, wave. See **wegh-** in Appendix.*] —**wav′er** *n.*
Wave (wāv) *n.* A member of the WAVES.
wave·band (wāv′bănd′) *n.* A range of frequencies, especially of radio frequencies such as those assigned to communication transmissions.
wave equation. **1.** A partial differential equation in one, two, or three dimensions, the solution of which represents the propagation of a wave with constant velocity. **2.** The fundamental equation of wave mechanics, a partial differential equation formulated by Erwin Schrödinger in 1926, the solutions of which specify the possible dynamic states of any atomic system. In this sense, also called "Schrödinger equation," "Schrödinger wave equation."
wave·form (wāv′fôrm′) *n.* The mathematical representation of a wave, especially a graph of deviation at a fixed point versus time.
wave front. A surface of a propagating wave that is the locus of all points having identical phase, the surface being usually, but not always, perpendicular to the direction of propagation.
wave function. A mathematical function used in wave mechanics to describe a specified state of a quantum system, the square of the amplitude of the function at a given point being representative of the probability of the system in that state being found at that point.
wave-guide (wāv′gīd′) *n.* A system of material boundaries in the form of a solid dielectric rod or dielectric-filled tubular conductor, capable of guiding high-frequency electromagnetic waves.
wave·length (wāv′lĕngth′) *n.* In a periodic wave, the distance between two points of corresponding phase in consecutive cycles.
wave·let (wāv′lĭt) *n.* A small wave or ripple.
wave mechanics. The formulation of **quantum mechanics** *(see)*, based on the wave equation of Schrödinger.
wave number. A frequency of a wave divided by its velocity of propagation; the reciprocal of the wavelength.
wave-particle duality (wāv′pär′tĭ-kəl). *Physics.* The exhibition of both wavelike and particlelike properties by a single entity, as of both diffraction and linear propagation by light.
wa·ver (wā′vər) *intr.v.* **-vered, -vering, -vers.** **1.** To swing or move back and forth; to sway. **2.** To show irresolution or indecision; vacillate: *"Men's minds may waver, but reality is always reliable"* (Lionel Trilling). **3.** To become unsteady or unsure; falter: *"This belief in the goodness of the child has never wavered"* (A.S. Neill). **4.** To tremble, quaver, or shake. Used of a sound, as a voice or a musical tone. **5.** To flicker, flash, or gleam. Used of light. —See Synonyms at **hesitate, swing.** —*n.* A wavering. [Middle English *waveren*, to wander, stray, fluctuate, possibly from Old Norse *vafra*, to move unsteadily, hover. See **webh-** in Appendix.*] —**wa′ver·ing·ly** *adv.*
WAVES (wāvz). The women's reserve of the U.S. Navy. [W(OMEN) A(CCEPTED for) V(OLUNTEER) E(MERGENCY) S(ERVICE).]
wave train. *Physics.* A succession of similar wave pulses.
wave trap. An electronic filtering device designed to exclude unwanted signals or interference from a receiver.
wa·vy (wā′vē) *adj.* **-vier, -viest.** **1.** Abounding in, having, or rising in waves: *a wavy sea.* **2.** Proceeding in a wavelike form or

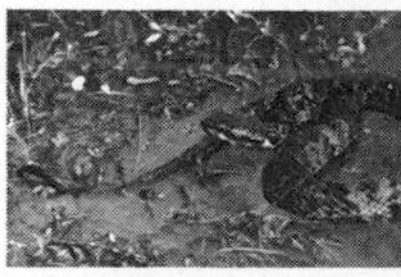

water moccasin

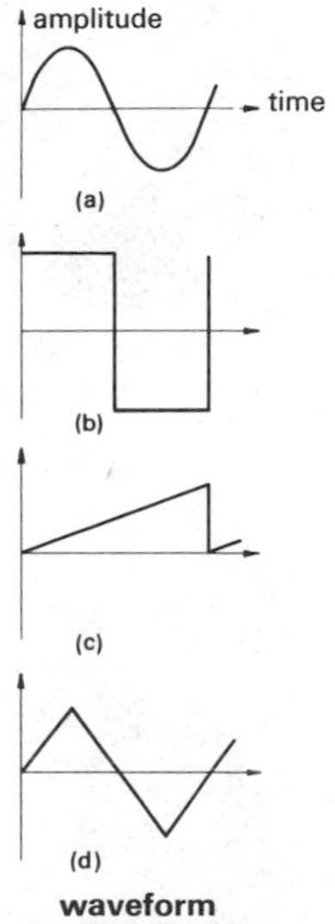

waveform
Single period of common electrical waveforms: (a) sine wave; (b) square wave; (c) saw-tooth wave; (d) triangular wave

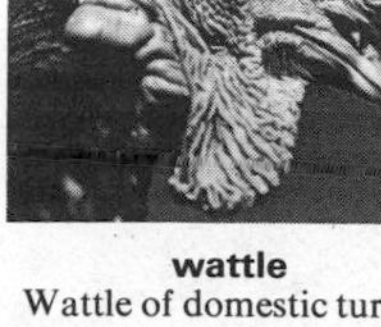

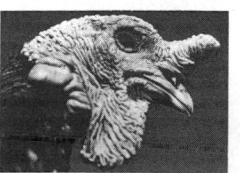

wattle
Wattle of domestic turkey

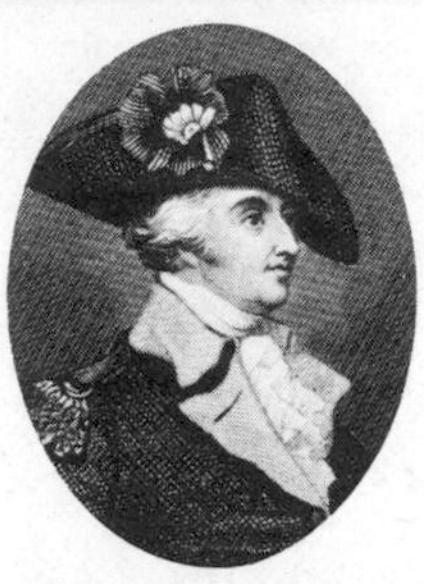
Anthony Wayne

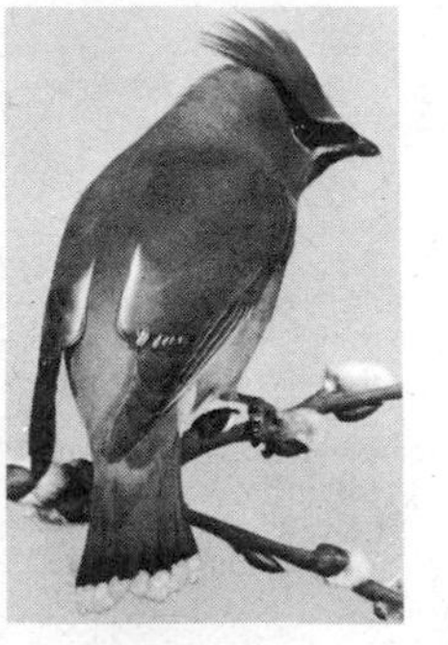
waxwing
Bombycilla cedrorum
Cedar waxwing

motion; sinuous. **3.** Having curls, curves, or undulations: *wavy hair.* **4.** Characteristic of, resembling, or suggestive of waves. **5.** Wavering; unstable. —**wav'i·ly** *adv.* —**wav'i·ness** *n.*

waw. Variant of **vav.**

WAW Airport code for Warsaw, Poland.

wax[1] (wăks) *n.* **1. a.** Any of various natural unctuous, viscous or solid heat-sensitive substances, consisting essentially of high molecular weight hydrocarbons or esters of fatty acids, characteristically insoluble in water but soluble in most organic solvents. **b.** A substance secreted by bees; beeswax. **c.** A waxy substance found in the ears; cerumen. **2.** A solid plastic or pliable liquid substance of mineral origin, primarily petroleum, such as ozocerite or paraffin, used in paper coating, as insulation, in crayons, and often in medicinal preparations. **3.** A resinous mixture used by shoemakers to wax their thread. **4.** Any waxlike substance that is readily molded and impressionable. —*tr.v.* **waxed, waxing, waxes.** To coat or treat with wax. —*adj.* Made of or relating to wax. [Middle English *wax, wexe,* Old English *weax, wæx,* beeswax. See **wokso-** in Appendix.*]

wax[2] (wăks) *intr.v.* **waxed, waxing, waxes. 1.** To become gradually larger, more numerous, stronger, or more intense. **2.** To increase in illumination or progress toward being full. Used of the moon. Compare **wane. 3.** To grow or become as specified: *the seas wax calm.* [Middle English *wexen, waxen,* Old English *weaxan.* See **aug-**[1] in Appendix.*]

wax bean. A variety of string bean having yellow pods. Also called "butter bean."

wax·ber·ry (wăks'bĕr'ē) *n., pl.* **-ries.** The waxy fruit of the wax myrtle or the snowberry.

wax·bill (wăks'bĭl') *n.* Any of various tropical Old World birds of the genus *Estrilda* and related genera, having a short, often brightly colored waxy beak.

wax·en (wăk'sən) *adj.* **1.** Consisting of or covered with wax. **2.** Suggestive of wax, as: **a.** Pale. **b.** Smooth and lustrous.

wax moth. A **bee moth** *(see).*

wax myrtle. A shrub, *Myrica cerifera,* of the southeastern United States, having evergreen leaves and small, berrylike fruit with a waxy coating. Also called "candleberry."

wax palm. Any of several palm trees that yield wax, such as *Copernica cerifera,* the source of carnauba wax, or *Ceroxylon andicola,* of South America.

wax paper. Also **waxed paper.** Paper that has been made moistureproof by treatment with wax.

wax plant. A tropical Old World vine, *Hoya carnosa,* having waxy white or pinkish flowers.

wax·wing (wăks'wĭng') *n.* Any of several birds of the genus *Bombycilla,* having crested heads, predominantly brown plumage, and waxy red tips on the secondary wing feathers.

wax·work (wăks'wûrk') *n.* **1. a.** Figures or ornaments made of wax; especially, life-size wax representations of famous persons. **b.** One such work. **2.** *Plural.* An exhibition of waxwork in a museum. —**wax'work'er** *n.*

wax·y (wăk'sē) *adj.* **-ier, -iest. 1.** Resembling wax, as: **a.** Pale. **b.** Smooth and lustrous. **c.** Pliable or impressionable. **2.** Consisting of, abounding in, or covered with wax. **3.** *Pathology.* Containing white, insoluble deposits of a waxlike protein in certain portions of the body; amyloid.

way (wā) *n.* Also *regional* **ways** (for sense 9). **1.** A course affording passage from one place to another; a road, path, or highway. **2.** Room or space to proceed with any action or course of action: *clear the way for a parade.* **3.** A course that is or may be used in going from one place to another: *Show me the way to go home.* **4.** Progress or travel along a certain route or in a specific direction: *on my way north.* **5.** A course of experience, life, or conduct; a path of life: *follow the straight and narrow way.* **6.** The manner of doing something or a course of action: *several ways of baking cakes.* **7.** A usual or habitual manner or mode of being, living, or acting: *the American way of life.* **8. a.** An individual or personal manner of behaving, acting, or doing: *Have it your own way.* **b.** Freedom to do as one prefers: *have one's way.* **9.** Distance in general: *a good way off.* **10.** A specific direction: *He glanced my way.* **11.** An aspect, particular, or feature: *You're correct in several ways.* **12.** Wish or will: *if I had my way.* **13.** The range or scope of one's observation or experience: *Wealth never came his way.* **14.** *Informal.* A state or condition; especially, a state of health or prosperity: *in a bad way financially.* **15.** *Informal.* A district, neighborhood, or area: *Drop in our way soon.* **16.** *Often plural. Machinery.* A longitudinal strip on a surface that serves to guide a moving part. **17.** *Plural. Nautical.* The timbered structure upon which a ship is built and from which it slides when launched. Sometimes used with a singular verb. —See Synonyms at **method.** —**by the way.** Incidentally; in passing. —**by way of. 1.** Through; by route of. **2.** As a means of; in order to serve as: *He made no comment by way of apology.* —**give way. 1.** To yield, submit, or agree. **2.** To fall or break down under pressure. —**give way to.** To yield or give in to. —**go out of one's** (or **the**) **way.** To inconvenience oneself in doing something beyond that which is required. —**have a way with.** To have the ability to handle or deal with: *He has a way with horses.* —**in the way.** Having such a nature or position as to obstruct, hinder, or interfere. —**out of the way. 1.** Having such a position as not to obstruct, interfere or hinder. **2.** In an inconvenient or unusual location. **3.** Of an unusual character; particular. **4.** Illegal or immoral; wrong; amiss. **5.** Misplaced; lost. —**pave the way for.** To prepare for by making things easier or convenient. —**see one's way (clear) to.** To be willing or find it possible to do something. —**under way.** Making progress or headway. —*adv.* Also **'way.** *Regional.* **1.** At a great distance; far: *way off yonder.* **2.** Away: *go way.* [Middle English *wey(e), wei(e), way,* Old English *weg,* a road, path. See **wegh-** in Appendix.*]

Synonyms: *way, path, route, course, passage, pass, artery, trail.* These nouns refer in various ways to movement or travel. *Way, path, route, course,* and *passage* are all used in the general sense of direction followed: *the way home; the path of a missile; the route of a voyage; the course of a satellite; the passage to the Northwest Territory. Passage* also denotes the act or condition of going: *grant them safe passage.* In a narrower sense, *route* frequently refers to a planned, well-established, or regularly traveled way or course, and *passage,* to a water route. Some of the terms also specify that over which, or through which, a person or thing travels. *Path* refers to a footway, especially to one worn by frequent travel, and *passage,* to a corridor of a building or similar enclosed area that connects buildings. *Pass* denotes a narrow opening between mountains; *artery,* a main route, such as a highway; and *trail,* a track or path worn by travel or marked for guidance through a wilderness.

Usage: *Way* (noun), not *ways,* is the only acceptable form in formal usage, especially in writing, when the term means distance in general: *a long way to go.* The construction *under way* (meaning in motion or in progress) is written thus in all contexts, including nautical (not as *under weigh*). Note, however, that an anchor is *weighed* and when off the bottom is *aweigh,* not *away.*

way·bill (wā'bĭl') *n. Abbr.* **w.b., W.B.** A document containing a list of goods and shipping instructions relative to a shipment, prepared and transported by a common carrier.

way·far·er (wā'fâr'ər) *n.* One who travels; especially, one who travels by foot. [Middle English *weyfarere* : *wey,* WAY + *fare,* a journey, traveling, Old English *faru* (see **per-**[2] in Appendix*).]

way·far·ing (wā'fâr'ĭng) *n.* Traveling; especially, traveling on foot. [Middle English *wayfaringe, weyfarende,* Old English *wegfarende* : *weg,* WAY + *farende,* present participle of *faran,* to go (see **per-**[2] in Appendix*).] —**way'far'ing** *adj.*

wayfaring tree. A shrub, *Viburnum lantana,* having clusters of white flowers and berries that turn from red to black.

way·lay (wā'lā') *tr.v.* **-laid** (-lād'), **-laying, -lays. 1.** To lie in wait for and assail from ambush. **2.** To accost unexpectedly. **3.** To intercept or delay the progress or movement of. —**way'lay'er** *n.*

Wayne (wān), **Anthony.** Known as Mad Anthony. 1745–1796. American general in the Revolutionary War.

-ways. Indicates manner, direction, or position; for example, **sideways.** [Middle English *-ways, -weys,* from *way(e)s, wey(e)s,* in (such) a way, Old English *weges,* adverbial genitive of *weg,* WAY.]

ways and means. The financial resources or methods for increasing the financial resources available to a person or group for accomplishing a specific end.

way·side (wā'sīd') *n.* The side or edge of a road. —**go** (or **let go**) **by the wayside.** To postpone or be postponed because of a more worthy or urgent consideration. —*adj.* Near or at the edge of a road: *a wayside inn.*

way station. A station between major stops on a route.

way·ward (wā'wərd) *adj.* **1.** Wanting one's own way in spite of the advice or wishes of another; willful; headstrong. **2.** Swayed by caprice; erratic; unpredictable. —See Synonyms at **contrary, unruly.** [Middle English, short for *awayward,* turned away : AWAY + -WARD.] —**way'ward·ly** *adv.* —**way'ward·ness** *n.*

way·worn (wā'wôrn', -wōrn') *adj.* Wearied from traveling.

Wa·zir·i·stan (wä-zîr'ĭ-stän'). A tribal region of West Pakistan, occupying 5,214 square miles in the northwest along the Afghanistan border.

Wb *Physics.* weber.

w.b. 1. *Shipping.* water ballast. **2.** waybill. **3.** westbound.

W.B. 1. waybill. **2.** Weather Bureau.

WBC *Medicine.* white blood count.

WbN west by north.

WbS west by south.

w.c. 1. water closet. **2.** without charge.

W.C.T.U. Women's Christian Temperance Union.

WD War Department.

wd. 1. wood. **2.** word.

W.D. War Department.

we (wē) *pron.* The first person plural pronoun in the nominative case. **1.** Used to represent the speaker and one or more others that share in the action of a verb. **2.** Sometimes used for *I* by a monarch or by an editor who purports to speak for a publication. **3.** *Informal.* Sometimes used for *you* in playful intimacy, especially with children: *Are we going to eat our cereal?* **4.** Often used to represent people in general: *We cannot see beyond the grave.* [Middle English *we,* Old English *wē.* See **we-** in Appendix.*]

Usage: The choice between *we* (nominative) and *us* (objective) is determined by the function served by these pronouns, and this is equally true when the terms are followed by nouns: *We students are entitled to a hearing. For us teachers, the choice is not easy. Let us visitors show respect for their customs.*

weak (wēk) *adj.* **weaker, weakest. 1.** Lacking physical strength, energy, or vigor; feeble. **2.** Liable to fail under pressure, stress, or strain; lacking resistance: *a weak link in a chain.* **3.** Lacking firmness of character or strength of will. **4.** Lacking effectiveness or force; inadequate: *a weak defense.* **5.** Lacking the usual, proper, or full strength of some component or ingredient. **6.** Lacking the capacity to function well or in a normal manner; unsound: *a weak stomach.* **7.** Lacking capacity or capability: *a weak student.* **8.** Resulting from a lack of intelligence; not persuasive or convincing. **9.** Lacking authority, influence, or power to rule: *a weak monarchy.* **10.** Lacking or deficient in a specified thing, as a quality or component. **11.** *Linguistics.* **a.** Designating those verbs in Germanic languages that form a past tense by means of a dental suffix; for example, *start, started; have, had; bring, brought.* Compare **strong. b.** Inflected by the addition of a suffix originally appropriate to stems ending in *-n.* Said of Germanic nouns and adjectives. **12.** *Phonetics.* Unstressed or unaccented. **13.** *Prosody.* Being a verse ending in which the stress falls on a word or syllable that is normally unstressed, such as a preposition. **14.** Tending downward in price. Said of the stock market. [Middle English *waike, we(i)ke,* from Old Norse *veikr,* pliant, flexible. See **weik-**[4] in Appendix.*] **—weak'ly** *adv.* **—weak'ness** *n.*

Synonyms: *weak, feeble, frail, infirm, decrepit, debilitated.* These adjectives mean deficient in strength. *Weak,* the most widely applicable, can refer to things or persons; with respect to persons, it may imply lack of physical, mental, or moral strength, deficiency of will or purpose, or general ineptitude. Applied to things, it indicates relative lack of force or effect. *Feeble,* said of persons, suggests either marked physical weakness or mental incompetence; with respect to things, it usually means hopelessly inadequate to a specified requirement. *Frail* primarily suggests slightness of physique or structure. *Infirm* generally implies lack of physical or mental soundness in persons, caused by advanced age or illness; or it can imply lack of firm will or purpose. *Decrepit* describes things or persons worn out or broken down by age. *Debilitated* suggests more gradual impairment of strength, as through strenuous use.

weak·en (wē'kən) *v.* **-ened, -ening, -ens.** *—tr.* To make weak or weaker. *—intr.* To become weak or weaker. **—weak'en·er** *n.*

weak·fish (wēk'fĭsh') *n., pl.* **weakfish** or **-fishes.** Any of several marine food and game fishes of the genus *Cynoscion;* especially, *C. regalis,* of North American Atlantic waters. Also called "sea trout," "squeteague." [Obsolete Dutch *weekvische, weekvis* : *week,* soft, weak (probably from its soft, fleshy mouth, which pulls very weakly on a line when caught), from Middle Dutch *weec* (see **weik-**[4] in Appendix*) + Middle Dutch *visch, vis,* fish (see **peisk-** in Appendix*).]

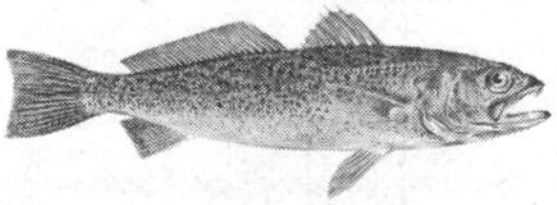

weakfish
Cynoscion regalis

weak-kneed (wēk'nēd') *adj.* Irresolute; timid.

weak·ling (wēk'lĭng) *n.* A person of weak constitution or character. *—adj.* Weak; feeble.

weak·ly (wēk'lē) *adj.* **-lier, -liest.** Sickly; delicate; feeble. *—adv.* **1.** With little strength or force. **2.** With little strength of character.

weak-mind·ed (wēk'mīn'dĭd) *adj.* **1. a.** Irresolute; indecisive. **b.** Foolish. **2.** Feeble-minded. **—weak'-mind'ed·ness** *n.*

weak·ness (wēk'nĭs) *n.* **1. a.** The state or quality of being weak. **b.** An instance or display of this. **2.** A personal defect or failing. **3. a.** A special fondness; foible: *a weakness for chocolates.* **b.** Something for which one has an irresistible desire. —See Synonyms at **fault.**

weak sister. *Slang.* A member of a group who is considered a weakling or an incompetent.

weal[1] (wēl) *n.* **1.** Prosperity; happiness: *in weal and woe.* **2.** The welfare of the community; the general good: *"educated, intelligent men, zealous for the public weal"* (W.H. Hudson). [Middle English *we(o)le,* Old English *we(o)la,* wealth, well-being. See **wel-**[2] in Appendix.*]

weal[2] (wēl) *n.* A ridge on the flesh raised by a blow; a welt: *"The weals where the whips stripped me at my shoulder"* (George Barker). [Variant (influenced by WHEAL) of WALE (ridge).]

weald (wēld) *n. Chiefly British.* **1.** A woodland. **2.** An area of open rolling upland. [From *The Weald,* once-forested area of Kent, Surrey, and Sussex, from Middle English *weld(e), weeld,* a woodland, Old English *weald,* a forest. See **wel-**[5] in Appendix.*]

wealth (wĕlth) *n.* **1.** A great quantity of valuable material possessions or resources; riches. **2.** The state of being rich; affluence. **3.** A profusion or abundance. **4.** *Economics.* All goods and resources having economic value. [Middle English *welthe,* well-being, riches, from *wele,* WEAL (welfare).]

wealth·y (wĕl'thē) *adj.* **-ier, -iest. 1.** Prosperous; affluent. **2.** Abundant. **—wealth'i·ly** *adv.* **—wealth'i·ness** *n.*

wean (wēn) *tr.v.* **weaned, weaning, weans. 1.** To withhold mother's milk from (the young of a mammal) and substitute other nourishment. **2.** To detach (a person) from that to which he is accustomed or devoted: *"To wean us from the love of the World, and all earthly things."* (Thomas Cooper). [Middle English *wenen, wa(i)nen,* Old English *wenian,* to accustom, train, wean. See **wen-** in Appendix.*]

wean·ling (wēn'lĭng) *n.* A recently weaned child or animal. *—adj.* Recently weaned.

weap·on (wĕp'ən) *n.* **1. a.** Any instrument used in combat. **b.** Any part of the body used in attack or defense, such as an animal's horns or claws. **2.** Any means employed to get the better of another: *Her smile was her most effective weapon.* *—tr.v.* **weaponed, -oning, -ons.** To supply with a weapon; to arm. [Middle English *wepen, wepne,* Old English *wǣp(e)n.* See **wēpnam** in Appendix.*]

weap·on·eer (wĕp'ən-îr') *n.* **1.** An individual who arms and otherwise prepares a nuclear weapon for release onto a target. **2.** An individual who designs or devises nuclear weapons.

weap·on·ry (wĕp'ən-rē) *n.* Weapons collectively.

wear[1] (wâr) *v.* **wore** (wôr, wōr), **worn** (wôrn, wōrn), **wearing, wears.** *—tr.* **1.** To be clothed in; have on. **2.** To have or carry habitually on one's person. **3.** To affect or exhibit: *wear a smile.* **4.** To bear, carry, or maintain in a particular manner: *She wears her hair long.* **5.** To fly or display (colors), as a ship, jockey, or knight. **6.** To impair, consume, waste, efface, or erode by or as by long or hard use, friction, or exposure to elements: *"women that passion has worn/as the tide wears the dove-gray sands"* (Yeats). **7. a.** To produce by constant use, rubbing, or exposure: *They eventually wore hollows in the steps.* **b.** To bring to a specific state by use or exposure: *"We wear our fingers rough with handling them."* (Robert Frost). **8. a.** To fatigue; weary: *The effort wore him.* **b.** To diminish; exhaust: *His incessant criticism wore her patience.* *—intr.* **1.** To stand continual or hard use: *That fabric will wear badly.* **2.** To withstand the effects of activity or use; to last: *Those tweeds will wear forever.* **3.** To react to use, strain, or the like, in a specified way: *The gold band wore thin.* **4.** To pass gradually or tediously: *The hours wore on endlessly.* **—wear down.** To break down the resistance of by relentless pressure. **—wear off. 1.** To diminish gradually and vanish: *The headache wore off.* **2.** To become effaced; rub off: *The gilt soon wore off.* **—wear out. 1.** To make or become unusable through heavy use. **2.** To use up; to consume: *She is wearing out her welcome.* **3.** To exhaust; to tire. *—n.* **1.** The act of wearing or state of being worn; use: *The coat has had heavy wear.* **2.** Clothing, especially of a particular kind or for a particular use. Often used in combination: *footwear.* **3.** Gradual impairment, waste, or diminution from use or attrition. **4.** The capacity to withstand use; durability: *The engine has plenty of wear left.* [Middle English *wer(i)en,* Old English *werian,* wear, carry. See **wes-**[5] in Appendix.*] **—wear'er** *n.*

wear[2] (wâr) *v.* **wore** (wôr, wōr), **worn** (wôrn, wōrn), **wearing, wears.** *Nautical.* *—tr.* To make (a sailing ship) come about with the wind aft: *wear ship.* *—intr.* To come about with the stern to windward. [Earlier *weare*†.]

wear·a·ble (wâr'ə-bəl) *adj.* Suitable for wear. *—pl.n.* Garments. **—wear'a·bil'i·ty** *n.*

wear and tear. Loss, damage, or depreciation resulting from ordinary use or exposure.

wea·ri·ful (wîr'ē-fəl) *adj.* Wearisome; tedious. **—wea'ri·ful·ly** *adv.* **—wea'ri·ful·ness** *n.*

wea·ri·less (wîr'ē-lĭs) *adj.* Tireless. **—wea'ri·less·ly** *adv.*

wear·ing (wâr'ĭng) *adj.* **1.** Designating articles of clothing: *wearing apparel.* **2.** Causing wear; tiring; exhausting: *a wearing experience.* **—wear'ing·ly** *adv.*

wea·ri·some (wîr'ē-səm) *adj.* Causing mental or physical fatigue. **—wea'ri·some·ly** *adv.* **—wea'ri·some·ness** *n.*

wea·ry (wîr'ē) *adj.* **-rier, -riest. 1.** Tired; fatigued. **2.** Expressive of or prompted by fatigue or resignation: *"With a weary sound that was not a sigh, nor a groan, he bent to work"* (Dickens). **3.** Causing fatigue; wearisome: *a weary task.* —See Synonyms at **tired.** *—v.* **wearied, -rying, -ries.** *—tr.* To make weary; to fatigue. *—intr.* To become weary; grow tired: *"She wearied of perpetual ecstasies."* (Edith Hamilton). [Middle English *wery, weri(e),* Old English *wērig,* from Germanic *wōriga* (unattested).] **—wear'i·ly** *adv.* **—wear'i·ness** *n.*

wea·sand (wē'zənd) *n.* The gullet or throat. Also called "wizen." [Middle English *wesa(u)nt, wesand, wosen,* Old English *wāsend, wǣsend* (unattested), gullet, from West Germanic *wāsand-* (unattested).]

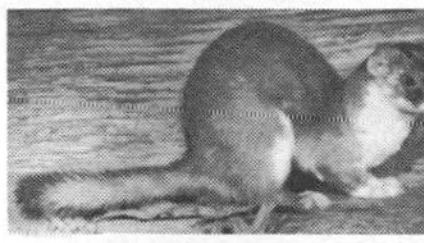

weasel
Mustela frenata

wea·sel (wē'zəl) *n.* **1.** Any of various carnivorous mammals of the genus *Mustela,* having a long, slender body, a long tail, and brownish fur that in many species turns white in winter. **2.** A treacherous or sneaky person. *—intr.v.* **weaseled, -seling, -sels.** To be evasive; equivocate. **—weasel out.** *Informal.* To back out of a situation or commitment in a sneaky or cowardly manner. [Middle English *wesele, wesill,* Old English *we(o)sule, wesle.* See **weis-**[1] in Appendix.*]

weasel word. A word of an equivocal nature used to deprive a statement of its force or to evade a direct commitment. [An allusion to the weasel's ability to suck up the contents of an egg without doing obvious damage to the shell.]

weath·er (wĕth'ər) *n.* **1.** The state of the atmosphere at a given time and place, described by specification of variables such as temperature, moisture, wind velocity, and pressure. **2. a.** Unpleasant or destructive atmospheric conditions: *The house must be protected from the weather.* **b.** Violent conditions such as high winds and heavy rain on the seas and in the air: *We flew into weather over the Azores.* **—make heavy weather of.** To exaggerate the difficulty of something to be done. **—under the weather.** *Informal.* **1.** Slightly indisposed; unwell. **2. a.** Drunk. **b.** Suffering from a hangover. *—v.* **weathered, -ering, -ers.** *—tr.* **1.** To expose to the action of the weather, as for drying, seasoning, or coloring. **2.** To discolor, disintegrate, wear, or otherwise affect adversely by exposure. **3.** To pass through safely; survive; outride: *"I weathered some merry snow-storms"* (Thoreau). **4.** To slope (a roof or the like) so as to shed water. **5.** *Nautical.* To pass to windward of, despite bad weather. *—intr.* **1.** To become discolored, disintegrated, or otherwise show the effects of exposure to the weather: *The barn walls had weathered and mellowed.* **2.** To resist or withstand the effects of weather or adverse conditions. *—adj.* Of or pertaining to the side of a ship toward the wind; windward. [Middle English *weder, wethyr,* Old English *weder.* See **wē-** in Appendix.*]

weather balloon. A balloon used to carry instruments aloft to gather meteorological data in the atmosphere.

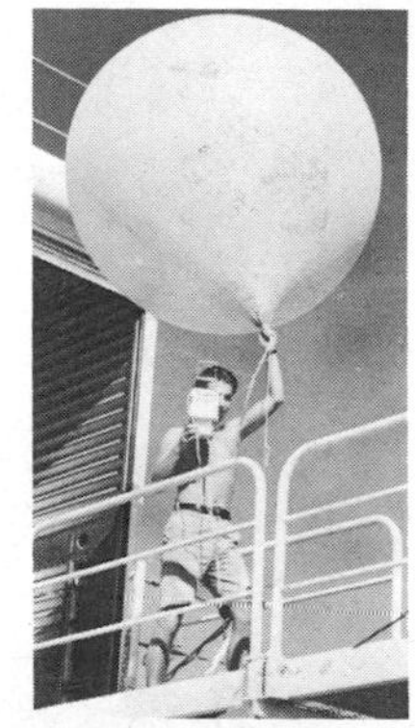

weather balloon
Release of weather balloon from aboard ship

weath·er-beat·en (wĕth'ər-bēt'n) *adj.* **1.** Worn by exposure to the weather. **2.** Tanned and leathery from being outdoors.

weath·er·board (wĕth'ər-bôrd', -bōrd') *n.* Clapboard; siding.

weath·er·board·ing (wĕth'ər-bôr'dĭng, -bōr'dĭng) *n.* Weatherboards collectively; siding.

weath·er-bound (wĕth'ər-bound') *adj.* Delayed, halted, or kept indoors by bad weather.

Weather Bureau. *Abbr.* **W.B.** A bureau of the U.S. Department of Commerce responsible for the gathering of meteorological data for weather forecasts and weather study.

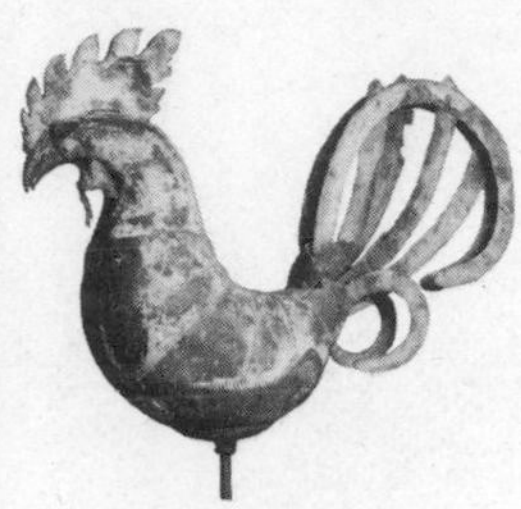
weathercock
Seventeenth-century French

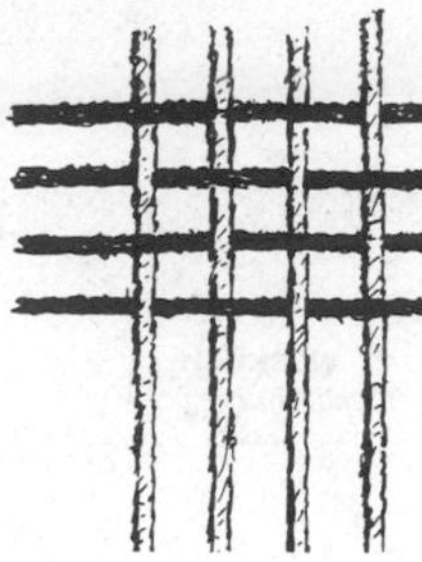
weave
Diagram of plain-weave fabric showing warp (vertical strands) and woof (horizontal strands)

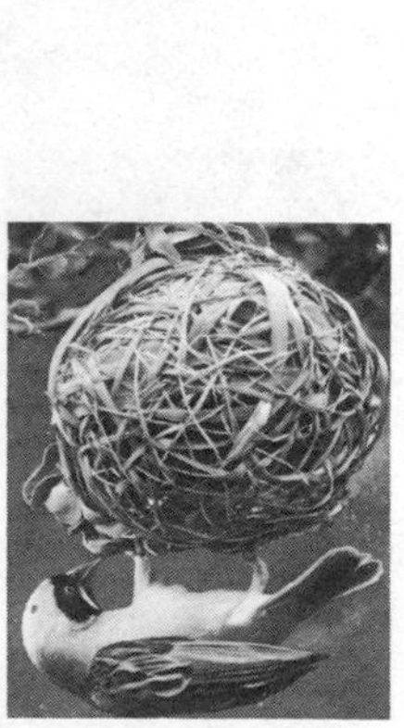
weaverbird
Ploceus intermedius

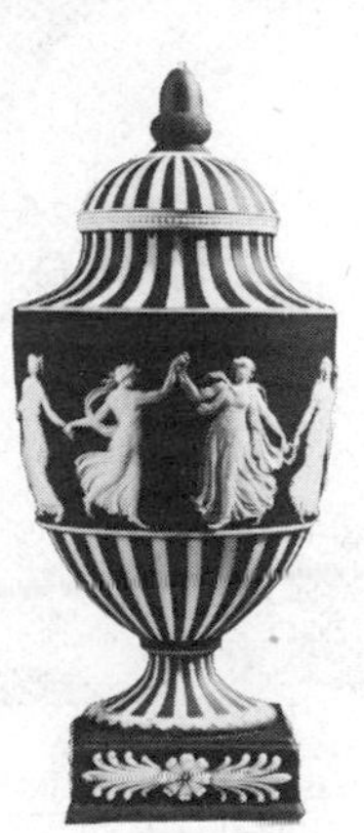
Wedgwood
Covered vase

weath·er·cast (wĕth′ər-kăst′, -käst′) *n.* A broadcast of weather conditions. **—weath′er·cast′er** *n.*

weath·er·cock (wĕth′ər-kŏk′) *n.* **1.** A weather vane, especially one in the form of a cock. **2.** One that is fickle. *—intr.v.* **weathercocked, -cocking, -cocks.** To have a tendency to veer in the direction of the wind. Used of an aircraft or a missile.

weath·ered (wĕth′ərd) *adj.* **1.** Seasoned; worn, stained, or warped by or as by exposure to weather. **2.** *Architecture.* Sloped to allow water to run off: *a weathered masonry joint.* **—weathered in.** Having weather conditions that prevent flying.

weather eye. An eye trained to recognize indications of weather changes.

weath·er·glass (wĕth′ər-glăs′, -gläs′) *n.* A barometer.

weath·er·ing (wĕth′ər-ĭng) *n.* Any of the chemical or mechanical processes by which rocks exposed to the weather decay to soil.

weath·er·ly (wĕth′ər-lē) *adj. Nautical.* Capable of sailing close to the wind with little drift to leeward. **—weath′er·li·ness** *n.*

weath·er·man (wĕth′ər-măn′) *n., pl.* **-men** (-mĕn′). A person who reports weather conditions.

weather map. A map or chart depicting the meteorological conditions over a specific geographical area at a specific time.

weath·er·proof (wĕth′ər-prōōf′) *adj.* Able to withstand exposure to weather without damage. *—tr.v.* **weatherproofed, -proofing, -proofs.** To render weatherproof.

weather ship. An oceangoing vessel equipped to make meteorological observations.

weather station. A station at which meteorological data are gathered, recorded, and released.

weath·er-strip (wĕth′ər-strĭp′) *tr.v.* **-stripped, -stripping, -strips.** To fit or equip with weather stripping.

weather stripping. **1.** A narrow piece of material, such as rubber, felt, or metal, installed around doors and windows to protect an interior from external extremes of temperature. Also called "weather strip." **2.** Such pieces collectively.

weather vane. A vane for indicating wind direction.

weath·er-wise (wĕth′ər-wīz′) *adj.* Experienced or expert in predicting shifts in the weather, public opinion, or the like.

weath·er·worn (wĕth′ər-wôrn′, -wōrn′) *adj.* Weather-beaten.

weave (wēv) *v.* **wove** (wōv) or **weaved** (only form for transitive sense 6 and intransitive sense 2), **woven** (wō′vən) or *rare* **wove** (wōv), **weaving, weaves.** *—tr.* **1. a.** To make (cloth) by interlacing the threads of the weft and the warp on a loom. **b.** To interlace (yarns) into cloth. **2.** To construct by interlacing or interweaving the materials or components of: *weave a basket.* **3.** To interweave or combine (elements) into a whole: *He wove the incidents into a story.* **4.** To run (something) in and out through some material or composition. **5.** To spin, as a web. **6.** To make (a course, for example) by winding in and out or shuttling from side to side: *weave one's way through traffic.* *—intr.* **1. a.** To engage in weaving an article. **b.** To work at a loom. **2.** To sway or move from side to side: *"I could see the black, sweat-washed forms weaving in the smoky-blue atmosphere"* (Ralph Ellison). *—n.* The pattern, method of weaving, or construction of a fabric: *a twill weave; a loose weave.* [Weave, wove, woven; Middle English *weven, wo(o)f, woven* or *weven,* Old English *wefan, wæf, wefen.* See **webh-** in Appendix.*]

weav·er (wē′vər) *n.* **1.** One who weaves. **2.** A weaverbird.

Wea·ver (wē′vər), **James Baird.** 1833–1912. American Populist political leader.

weav·er·bird (wē′vər-bûrd′) *n.* Any of various chiefly tropical Old World birds of the family Ploceidae, many of which build complex communal nests of intricately woven vegetation.

weaver's hitch. *Nautical.* A sheet bend. Also called "weaver's knot."

web (wĕb) *n.* **1. a.** A textile fabric, especially one being woven on a loom or in the process of being removed from it. **b.** The structural part of cloth as distinguished from its pile or pattern. **2.** A latticed or woven structure; an interlacing of materials. **3.** A structure of threadlike filaments characteristically spun by spiders or certain insect larvae. **4.** Something intricately constructed; especially, something that ensnares or entangles. **5.** A complex network. **6.** A fold of skin or membranous tissue; especially, the membrane connecting the toes of certain water birds. **7.** The vane of a feather. **8.** *Architecture.* The surface between the ribs of a ribbed vault. **9.** A metal sheet or plate connecting the heavier sections, ribs, or flanges of any structural element. **10.** A thin metal plate or strip, as the bit of a key, the blade of a saw, or the like. **11.** A continuous roll of paper, as newsprint, in the process of manufacture in a paper machine or as it comes from the mill. *—tr.v.* **webbed, webbing, webs.** **1.** To provide with a web. **2.** To cover or envelop with a web. **3.** To ensnare in a web. [Middle English *web(be),* Old English *web(b).* See **webh-** in Appendix.*]

Webb (wĕb), **Sidney James.** 1859–1947. English economist; with his wife, **Beatrice Potter** (1858–1943), writer and social reformer.

webbed (wĕbd) *adj.* Having or connected by a web.

web·bing (wĕb′ĭng) *n.* **1.** Sturdy cotton or nylon fabric woven in widths generally of from one to six inches, for use where strength is required, as for seat belts, brake lining, or upholstering. **2.** Anything forming a web.

Web·bi She·be·li (wā′bē shĕ-bā′lē). Also **We·bi Shi·be·li** (shĭ-bā′lē). A river, about 1,200 miles long, rising in central Ethiopia and flowing generally southeastward to the Indian Ocean coast of Somalia, to which it flows parallel before ending in coastal swamps.

web·by (wĕb′ē) *adj.* **-bier, -biest.** Having, resembling, or consisting of a web.

we·ber (wĕb′ər) *n. Abbr.* **Wb** The International System unit of magnetic flux equal to the magnetic flux that in linking a circuit of one turn produces in it an electromotive force of one volt as it is uniformly reduced to zero within one second. [After Wilhelm E. WEBER.]

We·ber (vā′bər), Baron **Carl Maria Friedrich Ernst von.** 1786–1826. German composer and conductor.

We·ber (vā′bər), **Ernst Heinrich.** 1795–1878. German physiologist and psychologist; brother of W.E. Weber.

We·ber (vā′bər), **Wilhelm Eduard.** 1804–1891. German physicist; studied electricity; brother of E.H. Weber.

We·bern (vā′bərn), **Anton von.** 1883–1945. Austrian composer of twelve-tone music.

web-foot·ed (wĕb′fōōt′ĭd) *adj.* Having feet with webbed toes.

web member. One of the structural elements connecting the top and bottom flanges of a lattice girder or the outside members of a truss.

web press. A printing press that prints on a continuous roll of paper.

web·ster (wĕb′stər) *n. Obsolete.* A weaver. [Middle English *web(e)ster,* Old English *webbestre,* feminine of *webba,* a weaver, from *webb,* a WEB.]

Web·ster (wĕb′stər), **Daniel.** 1782–1852. American political leader, administrator, and diplomat.

Web·ster (wĕb′stər), **John.** 1580?–1625? English dramatist.

Web·ster (wĕb′stər), **Noah.** 1758–1843. American lexicographer.

web·worm (wĕb′wûrm′) *n.* Any of various usually destructive caterpillars that construct webs.

wed (wĕd) *v.* **wedded, wed** or **wedded, wedding, weds.** *—tr.* **1.** To take as husband or wife; marry. **2.** To perform the marriage ceremony for; join in matrimony. **3.** To bind or join; unite. *—intr.* To take a husband or wife; to marry. [Middle English *wedden,* Old English *weddian,* to engage (to do something), marry. See **wadh-** in Appendix.*]

we'd (wēd). Contraction of *we had, we should,* or *we would.*

Wed. Wednesday.

Wed·dell Sea (wĕd′l). An inlet of the South Atlantic in Antarctica, between Coats Land and the Antarctic Peninsula.

wed·ding (wĕd′ĭng) *n.* **1.** The act of marrying; the ceremony or celebration of a marriage. **2.** The anniversary of a marriage: *a silver wedding.* **3.** A close association or union. —See Synonyms at **marriage.**

wedding ring. **1.** A ring, usually a plain gold or platinum band, given by the groom to his bride during the wedding ceremony. **2.** A similar ring sometimes given by the bride to the groom.

We·de·kind (vā′də-kĭnt′), **Frank.** 1864–1918. German playwright and poet.

wedge (wĕj) *n.* **1.** A piece of metal or wood tapered for insertion in a narrow crevice and used for splitting, tightening, securing, or levering. **2.** Anything in the shape of a wedge: *a wedge of cheese.* **3.** A wedge-shaped formation, as in football or ground warfare. **4.** Any tactic, event, policy, or idea that tends to divide or split associations of people. **5.** *Meteorology.* An elongated, V-shaped region of relatively high atmospheric pressure. **6.** *Golf.* An iron with a very slanted face, used to lift the ball from sand or the like. **7.** One of the triangular characters of cuneiform writing. *—v.* **wedged, wedging, wedges.** *—tr.* **1.** To split or force apart with or as with a wedge. **2.** To fix in place with a wedge. **3.** To crowd, push, or force into a limited space. *—intr.* To become lodged like a wedge. [Middle English *wegge,* Old English *wecg,* a wedge, ingot of metal. See **wogwhni-** in Appendix.*]

wedg·ie (wĕj′ē) *n. Informal.* A woman's shoe or mule having a wedge-shaped sole that incorporates the heel.

Wedg·wood (wĕj′wŏŏd′) *n.* A type of pottery or china made by Josiah Wedgwood (1730–1795) and his successors; especially, a fine ware with classical figures in white cameo relief on an unglazed blue or black background.

wed·lock (wĕd′lŏk′) *n.* The state of being married; matrimony. See Synonyms at **marriage.** **—out of wedlock.** Born of parents not married to one another. [Middle English *wedlo(c)ke,* Old English *wedlāc,* "pledge-giving," marriage vow : *wedd,* a pledge (see **wadh-** in Appendix*) + *-lāc,* suffix denoting activity (see **leig-**[3] in Appendix*).]

Wednes·day (wĕnz′dē, -dā′) *n. Abbr.* **Wed.** The fourth day of the week, occurring after Tuesday and before Thursday. [Middle English *Wodnesday, Wednesday,* Old English *Wōdnesdæg,* "Woden's day" (translation of Latin *Mercurii diēs,* "day of Mercury"). See **wāt-** in Appendix.*]

wee (wē) *adj.* **weer, weest.** **1.** Very small; tiny. **2.** Very early: *the wee hours.* —See Synonyms at **small.** *—n. Scottish.* A short time; a little bit: *bide a wee.* [Middle English *we,* from *we(i),* a little, a small amount, Old English *wǣge,* a weight. See **wegh-** in Appendix.*]

weed[1] (wēd) *n.* **1. a.** A plant considered undesirable, unattractive, or troublesome; especially, one growing where it is not wanted in cultivated ground. **b.** A rank growth of such plants. **2.** Any of various usually common or abundantly growing plants. Usually used in combination: *seaweed; chickweed.* **3.** The leaves or stems of a plant as distinguished from the seeds: *dill weed.* **4.** *Informal.* Tobacco. Often preceded by *the.* **5.** *Slang.* **Marijuana** *(see).* **6.** *Informal.* A cigarette. **7.** Something useless, detrimental, or worthless; especially, an animal unfit for breeding. *—v.* **weeded, weeding, weeds.** *—tr.* **1.** To remove weeds from; clear of weeds: *weed a flower bed.* **2. a.** To remove (weeds). Used with *out: weed out dandelions.* **b.** To eliminate as unsuitable or unwanted. Used with *out: weed out unqualified applicants.* *—intr.* To remove weeds from a plot.

ă pat/ā pay/âr care/ä father/b bib/ch church/d deed/ĕ pet/ē be/f fife/g gag/h hat/hw which/ĭ pit/ī pie/îr pier/j judge/k kick/l lid, needle/m mum/n no, sudden/ng thing/ŏ pot/ō toe/ô paw, for/oi noise/ou out/ŏŏ took/ōō boot/p pop/r roar/s sauce/sh ship, dish/

[Middle English *weed,* Old English *wēod,* from West Germanic *wiudha* (unattested).]

weed² (wēd) *n.* **1.** A token of mourning, as a black band worn usually on the sleeve. **2.** *Plural.* A widow's mourning clothes. **3.** Any garment. Often used in the plural. [Middle English *wede,* a garment, armor, Old English *wǣd* and *wǣde,* a garment. See **aw-¹** in Appendix.*]

weed·er (wē′dər) *n.* **1.** A person who weeds. **2.** A device for removing weeds.

weed·y (wē′dē) *adj.* **-ier, -iest. 1.** Full of or consisting of weeds. **2.** Resembling or characteristic of a weed. **3.** Of a scrawny build; spindly; gawky. **—weed′i·ly** *adv.* **—weed′i·ness** *n.*

wee folk. Fairies; elves.

week (wēk) *n.* *Abbr.* **w., wk. 1. a.** A period of seven days: *a week of rain.* **b.** A seven-day calendar period, especially one starting with Sunday and continuing through Saturday: *this week.* **2. a.** A week designated by an event or holiday occurring within it: *commencement week.* **b.** A week set aside for the honoring of some cause or institution. **3.** The part of a calendar week devoted to work. **4. a.** One week from a specified day: *I'll see you Friday week.* **b.** One week ago from a specified day: *It was Friday week that we last met.* [Middle English *wike, weke,* Old English *wice, wicu.* See **weik-⁴** in Appendix.*]

week·day (wēk′dā′) *n.* **1.** Any day of the week except Sunday. **2.** Any day exclusive of the days of the weekend.

week·end (wēk′ĕnd′) *n.* The end of the week; usually, the period from Friday evening through Sunday evening. *—intr.v.* **weekended, -ending, -ends.** To spend the weekend.

week·end·er (wēk′ĕn′dər) *n.* **1.** A person who vacations or visits, especially habitually, on weekends. **2.** A small suitcase or bag for carrying clothing and toiletries for a weekend.

week·ly (wēk′lē) *adv.* **1.** Once a week. **2.** Every week. **3.** By the week. *—adj.* **1.** Of or pertaining to a week. **2.** Occurring once a week or each week. **3.** Computed by the week. *—n., pl.* **weeklies.** *Abbr.* **wkly.** A publication issued once a week.

ween (wēn) *v.* **weened, weening, weens.** *Archaic.* *—tr.* To think; suppose. *—intr.* To think it possible. [Middle English *wenen,* Old English *wēnan.* See **wen-** in Appendix.*]

ween·ie (wē′nē) *n.* *Informal.* A **wienerwurst** *(see).*

wee·ny (wē′nē) *adj.* **-nier, -niest.** *Informal.* Very small; tiny; wee. [Blend of WEE and TINY or TEENY.]

weep (wēp) *v.* **wept** (wĕpt), **weeping, weeps.** *—tr.* **1.** To mourn; lament; bewail. **2.** To shed (tears). **3.** To bring or wear to a specified condition by weeping: *She wept herself into a state of exhaustion.* **4.** To ooze, exude, or let fall drops of liquid. *—intr.* **1.** To express emotion by shedding tears; shed tears. **2.** To mourn or grieve. Used with *for.* **3.** To emit or run with drops of moisture. —See Synonyms at **cry.** *—n.* A period or fit of weeping. Often used in the plural. [Middle English *we(o)pen,* Old English *wēpan.* See **wāb-** in Appendix.*]

weep·er (wē′pər) *n.* **1.** One that weeps. **2.** A hired mourner. **3.** A badge of mourning formerly worn by men. **4.** A hole or pipe in a wall to allow water to run off.

weep·ing (wē′pĭng) *adj.* **1.** Tearful. **2.** Dropping rain: *weeping clouds.* **3.** Having slender, drooping branches.

weeping willow. A widely cultivated tree, *Salix babylonica,* native to China, having long, slender, drooping branches and narrow leaves.

weep·y (wē′pē) *adj.* **-ier, -iest.** Lachrymose; tearful.

wee·ver (wē′vər) *n.* Any of several marine fishes of the family Trachinidae, having venomous spines. [Old North French *wivre,* a serpent, viper, from Latin *vīpera,* VIPER.]

wee·vil (wē′vəl) *n.* Any of numerous beetles, chiefly of the family Curculionidae, characteristically having a downward-curving snout and destructive to plants and stored plant products. [Middle English *wevel,* Old English *wifel,* a beetle. See **webh-** in Appendix.*] **—wee′vil·y, wee′vil·ly** *adj.*

weft (wĕft) *n.* **1. a.** The horizontal threads interlaced through the warp in a woven fabric; filling; woof. **b.** Yarn to be used for the weft. **2.** Woven fabric. [Middle English *wefte, weft,* Old English *wefta, weft.* See **webh-** in Appendix.*]

We·ge·ner (vā′gə-nər), **Alfred Lothar.** 1880–1930. German geologist; devised theory of continental drift.

Wei·er·strass (vī′ər-shträs′), **Karl Wilhelm Theodor.** 1815–1897. German mathematician.

Wei·fang (wā′fäng′). A city of eastern China, in north-central Shantung Province. Population, 200,000.

wei·ge·la (wī-gē′lə, -jē′lə, wī′jə-lə) *n.* Any of various shrubs of the genus *Weigela;* especially, *W. florida,* widely cultivated for its pink, white, or red flowers. [New Latin, after Christian E. *Weigel* (1748–1831), German physician.]

weigh¹ (wā) *v.* **weighed, weighing, weighs.** *—tr.* **1.** To determine the weight of by or as if by using a scale or balance. **2.** To measure off an amount equal in weight to. Usually used with *out: weigh out a pound of cheese.* **3.** To balance in one's mind to determine the worth of; to ponder; evaluate: *"weigh the present enjoyment of your pleasures against the necessary consequences of them"* (Lord Chesterfield). **4.** To cause to sag by the addition of weights or burdens; oppress; force down. Used with *down.* **5.** *Nautical.* To raise (anchor). *—intr.* **1.** To have or be of a specific weight. **2.** To carry weight; be considered important; have influence. **3.** To be a burden or weight; bear down. Used with *on* or *upon: "Jack Potter was beginning to find the shadow of a deed weigh upon him like a leaden slab."* (Stephen Crane). **4.** *Nautical.* **a.** To raise anchor. **b.** To sail out of port. **—weigh in. 1.** To weigh or be weighed before entering a sports contest. **2.** To have one's baggage weighed. **—weigh (one's) words.** To choose one's words with great care; express oneself with deliberation. [Middle English *weghen, weien,* Old English *wegan,* to carry, balance in the scale, weigh. See **wegh-** in Appendix.*] **—weigh′er** *n.*

weigh² (wā) *n.* *Nautical.* Way. Used only in the phrase *under weigh.* See Usage note at **way.** [Variant (erroneously from the phrase *to weigh anchor*) of WAY.]

weight (wāt) *n.* *Abbr.* **wt. 1.** A measure of the heaviness or mass of an object. **2.** The gravitational force exerted by the earth or another celestial body on an object, equal to the product of the object's mass and the local value of gravitational acceleration. **3. a.** A unit measure of this force. **b.** A system of such measures. See **measurement. 4.** The measured heaviness of a specific object. **5.** Any object used principally to exert a force by virtue of its gravitational attraction to the earth, especially: **a.** A metallic solid used as a standard of comparison in weighing. **b.** An object used to hold something down. **c.** A counterbalance in a machine. **d.** A dumbbell or a solid metallic disk balanced on a crossbar, lifted for exercise or in athletic competition. **6.** *Mathematics.* One of a set of numbers assigned as multipliers to quantities to be averaged to indicate the relative importance of each quantity's contribution to the average. **7.** Burden; oppressiveness: *the weight of responsibilities.* **8.** The greatest part or stress; preponderance: *the weight of evidence.* **9. a.** Influence; importance; authority: *"Carrie thought of this doubtfully; but coming from him, it had weight with her."* (Dreiser). **b.** Ponderous quality: *the weight of his words.* **10.** A classification according to comparative lightness or heaviness. Usually used in combination: *a heavyweight iron.* —See Synonyms at **importance. —by weight.** According to weight rather than volume or other measure. **—carry weight.** To have influence or authority. **—pull one's weight.** To do one's job or share. **—throw one's weight around.** To make a show of one's importance. *—tr.v.* **weighted, weighting, weights. 1.** To add heaviness or weight to; make heavy or heavier. **2.** To load down; burden. **3.** To treat (fabric) with chemical substances in order to give it body or extra weight. **4.** *Mathematics.* To assign a weight or weights to. [Middle English *wighte, weit(e),* Old English *wiht, gewiht.* See **wegh-** in Appendix.*]

weight·less (wāt′lĭs) *adj.* **1.** Having little or no weight. **2.** Experiencing little or no gravitational force. **—weight′less·ly** *adv.* **—weight′less·ness** *n.*

weight·lift·ing (wāt′lĭf′tĭng) *n.* The lifting of heavy weights in a prescribed manner as an exercise or in athletic competition.

weight·y (wā′tē) *adj.* **-ier, -iest. 1.** Heavy; ponderous. **2.** Burdensome; oppressive. **3.** Of great consequence; momentous: *the weighty matters before the peace delegates.* **4.** Carrying weight; efficacious: *a weighty argument.* **5.** Solemn; serious. —See Synonyms at **heavy. —weight′i·ly** *adv.* **—weight′i·ness** *n.*

Wei Ho (wā′ hō′). A river of China, rising in southeastern Kansu Province and flowing 540 miles generally east to the Yellow River in Shensi. Also called "Wek River."

Weill (wīl), **Kurt.** 1900–1950. German composer in United States (from 1935).

Wei·mar (vī′mär′, wī′-). A city of southwestern East Germany. Population, 66,700.

Wei·mar·an·er (vī′mä-rä′nər, wī′-) *n.* A large dog of a breed originating in Germany, having a smooth grayish coat.

Weimar Republic. The German Republic founded at Weimar in 1919 by a constitutional assembly and dissolved in 1933.

weir (wîr) *n.* **1.** A fence or wattle placed in a stream to catch or retain fish. **2.** A dam placed across a river or canal to raise or divert the water, as for a millrace, or to regulate the flow. [Middle English *wer(r)e,* Old English *wer.* See **wer-⁵** in Appendix.*]

weird (wîrd) *adj.* **weirder, weirdest. 1.** Suggestive of or concerned with the supernatural; unearthly; eerie; uncanny. **2.** Of an odd and inexplicable character; unusual; strange, fantastic. **3.** *Archaic.* Of or pertaining to fate or the Fates. *—n.* *Scottish & Archaic.* **1. a.** Fate; destiny. **b.** One's assigned lot or fortune; kismet. **2.** *Usually capital* **W.** One of the Fates. [Middle English *werde, wirde,* having power to control fate, from *wird, werd,* fate, destiny, Old English *wyrd.* See **wer-³** in Appendix.*] **—weird′ly** *adv.* **—weird′ness** *n.*

Synonyms: *weird, eerie, uncanny, unearthly.* These adjectives refer to what is inexplicably strange and, sometimes, frightening. *Weird* can mean mysterious in the sense of occult, but is also applied to what is bizarre, grotesque, eccentric, or markedly unconventional. *Eerie* describes what inspires fear, uneasiness, or wonder that cannot be explained rationally and therefore may suggest the preternatural or a sinister influence. *Uncanny* refers to what is extremely puzzling as a source of wonder or fascination, such as a talent or knack. *Unearthly* literally means so strange as to suggest what is not of this world; in popular usage it is sometimes applied, like *weird,* to what is merely very odd or far-fetched.

weird·ie (wîr′dē) *n.* Also **weird·y** *pl.* **-ies, weird·o** (wîr′dō) *pl.* **-oes.** *Slang.* An unusually strange person, thing, or event.

weis·en·hei·mer. Variant of **wisenheimer.**

Weis·mann (vīs′män′), **August.** 1834–1914. German biologist; asserted that hereditary characteristics were transmitted by a germinal plasm and that acquired characteristics were nontransmissible.

Weiss·horn (vīs′hôrn′). A mountain rising to 14,792 feet in the Alps of southern Switzerland.

Weiz·mann (vīts′män′, wīts′mən), **Chaim.** 1874–1952. Russian-born chemist, educator, and first president of Israel (1949–52).

Weiz·säck·er (vīts′zĕk′ər), **Karl Friedrich von.** Born 1912. German astronomer, cosmologist, and physicist.

we·ka (wē′kə, wā′-) *n.* A flightless bird, *Gallirallus australis,* of

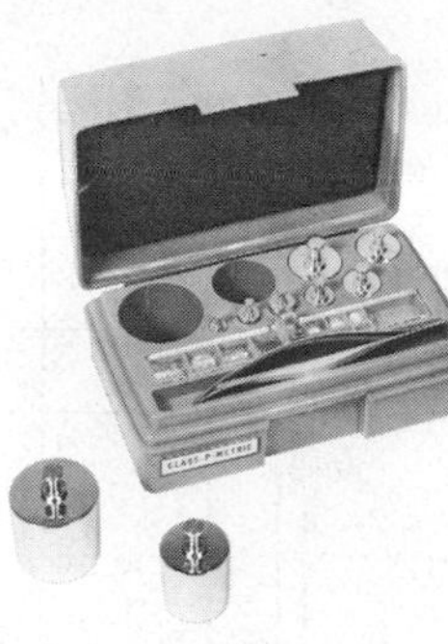

weight
Set of analytical weights for use in making scientific measurements

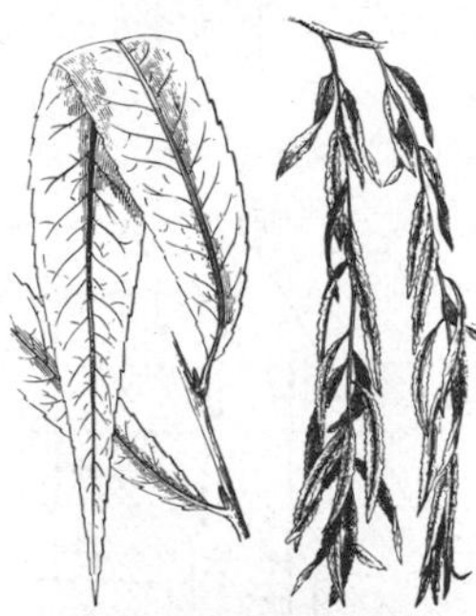

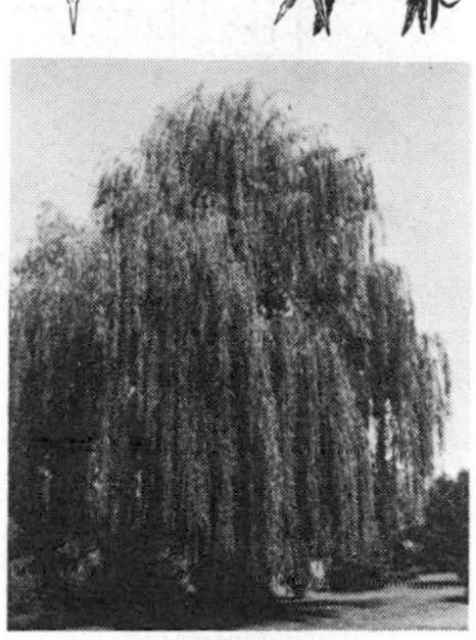

weeping willow
Above: Foliage

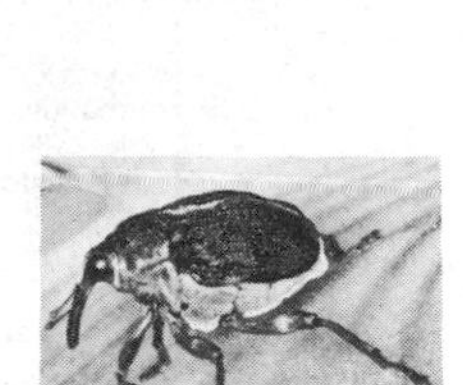

weevil

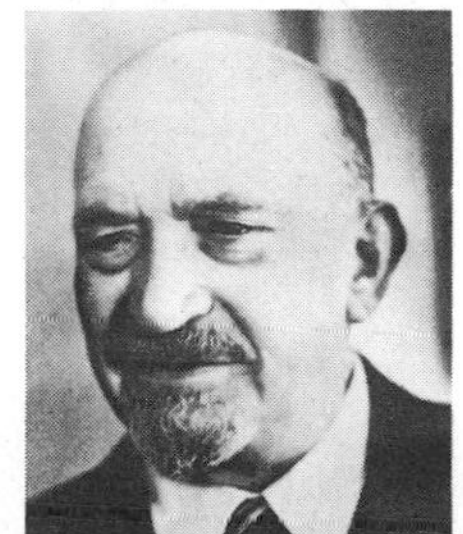

Chaim Weizmann

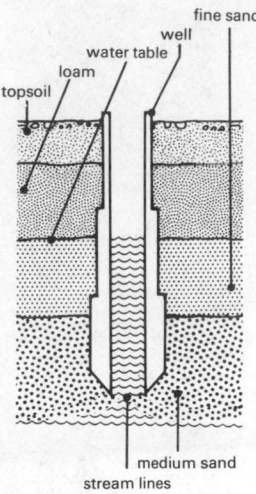

fine sand
well
water table
loam
topsoil
medium sand
stream lines

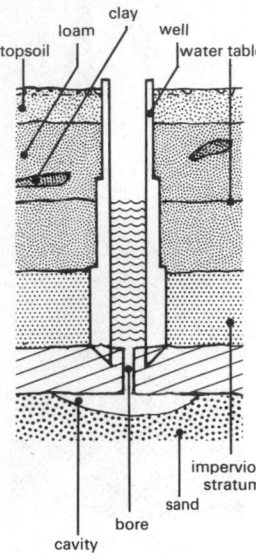

clay
loam
well
topsoil
water table
impervious stratum
sand
bore
cavity

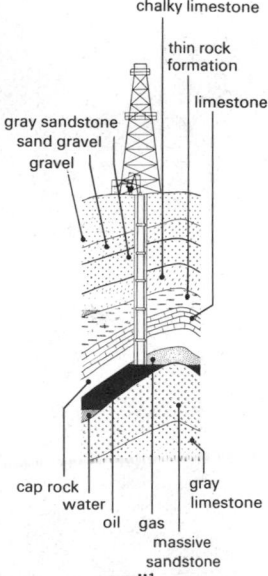

chalky limestone
thin rock formation
limestone
gray sandstone
sand gravel
gravel
cap rock
water
oil
gas
gray limestone
massive sandstone

well¹
Above: Shallow well
Center: Deep well
Below: Oil well

New Zealand, having brown, mottled plumage. [Maori.]

welch. Variant of **welsh.**

Welch. *Rare.* Variant of **Welsh.**

wel·come (wĕl′kəm) *adj.* **1.** Received with pleasure and hospitality into one's company or home: *a welcome guest.* **2.** Gratifying: *a welcome respite.* **3.** Cordially permitted or invited, as to do or enjoy. **4.** Freely granted one's courtesy. Used to acknowledge an expression of gratitude, usually in the exchange "Thank you!" "You're welcome!" —*n.* **1.** A cordial greeting to or reception of an arriving person. **2.** The state of being welcome; hospitable reception. **3.** The act of welcoming; willing or glad acceptance. —*tr.v.* **welcomed, -coming, -comes. 1.** To greet, receive, or entertain cordially or hospitably. **2.** To receive or accept gladly: *welcome a little privacy.* —*interj.* Used to greet cordially a visitor or recent arrival. [Middle English *welcume,* alteration (by influence by *wel,* WELL) of Old English *wilcuma,* a welcome guest, and *wilcume,* the greeting of welcome. See **gwā-** in Appendix.*] —**wel′come·ly** *adv.* —**wel′come·ness** *n.* —**wel′com·er** *n.*

weld¹ (wĕld) *v.* **welded, welding, welds.** —*tr.* **1.** To join (metals) by applying heat, sometimes with pressure and sometimes with an intermediate or filler metal having a high melting point. **2.** To bring into close association; bring together as a unit. —*intr.* To be capable of being welded. —*n.* **1.** The union of two metal parts by welding. **2.** The joint so formed. [Variant (influenced by past tense and past participle *welded*) of WELL (to pour forth, in the obsolete sense of to weld).]

weld² (wĕld) *n.* Also **wold** (wōld). **1.** A plant, the **dyer's rocket** (*see*). **2.** The yellow dye obtained from this plant. [Middle English *welde, wold,* Old English *wealde, walde* (both unattested). See **wel-⁵** in Appendix.*]

weld·ment (wĕld′mənt) *n.* A unit composed of an assemblage of pieces welded together.

wel·fare (wĕl′fâr′) *n.* **1. a.** Health, happiness, and general well-being. **b.** Prosperity. **2.** Welfare work. **3.** Public relief. —**on welfare.** Dependent on public relief. [Middle English *welfare,* well-being, good cheer, from the phrase *wel faren,* to fare well, Old English *wel faran* : *wel,* WELL + *faran,* to go, FARE.]

Welfare Island. Formerly **Black·wells Island** (blăk′wĕlz′). An island occupying 139 acres in the East River, New York City, the site of two municipal hospitals.

welfare state. 1. A social system whereby the state assumes primary responsibility for the welfare of citizens. **2.** A nation characterized by its adoption of this system.

welfare work. Organized efforts by a community or an organization for the betterment of the poor.

wel·far·ism (wĕl′fâr-iz′əm) *n.* The set of policies, practices, and social attitudes associated with the welfare state.

wel·kin (wĕl′kĭn) *n. Archaic.* **1.** The vault of heaven; sky: *make the welkin ring.* **2.** The upper air. [Middle English *w(e)olcne, welken,* a cloud, the sky, firmament, Old English *wolc(e)n.* See **welk-** in Appendix.*]

well¹ (wĕl) *n.* **1.** A deep hole or shaft dug or drilled to obtain water, oil, gas, or brine. **2.** A cavity or space resembling this in shape or function, as an inkwell. **3.** An opening cut vertically through the floors of a building, as for stairs or ventilation. **4.** An enclosure in a ship's hold for the pumps. **5.** A cistern with a perforated bottom in the hold of a fishing vessel for keeping fish alive. **6.** *British.* The space in a law court where the counsel or solicitor sits. **7.** A spring or fountain. **8.** A source to be drawn upon: *a well of information.* —*v.* **welled, welling, wells.** —*intr.* **1.** To rise to the surface, ready to flow. **2.** To rise or surge from some inner source: *"she felt welling up in her mind some peculiar imagination"* (Glenway Wescott). —*tr.* To pour forth. [Middle English *well(e), walle,* Old English *wælla, well, wiella.* See **wel-³** in Appendix.*]

well² (wĕl) *adv.* **better** (bĕt′ər), **best** (bĕst). **1.** Satisfactorily. **2.** In a good or proper manner; with skill: *sing well.* **3.** In a comfortable or affluent manner: *live well.* **4.** Advantageously: *married well.* **5.** With reason or propriety; properly; reasonably: *I can't very well say no.* **6.** Prudently: *You would do well to say nothing.* **7.** On close or familiar terms: *I know him well.* **8.** In a kindly manner; graciously; favorably: *speak well of him.* **9.** Thoroughly; completely: *well cooked.* **10.** Entirely; fully: *well worth seeing.* **11.** To a considerable or suitable extent or degree: *I'm well pleased.* **12.** Far: *well in advance.* **Note:** The adverb *well* combines with many adjectives, usually derived from the participles of verbs, to form attributive modifiers before nouns: *a well-regulated life; a well-deserving woman.* In such use the elements are joined with a hyphen. However, when *well* modifies a predicate adjective, the two words are written separately: *His life was well regulated. The woman is well deserving.* —**as well. 1.** In addition; also. **2.** With equal or better effect: *I might as well go.* —**as well as, 1,** In addition to; moreover. See Usage note below. **2.** As satisfactorily as: *He did as well as you.* **3.** As much as: *He would like to go as well as you.* —*adj.* **1.** In a satisfactory state or circumstances; right; proper. Usually used predicatively: *All is well.* **2. a.** In good health; not ailing or diseased. **b.** Cured or healed, as a wound. **3. a.** Advisable; prudent: *It would be well not to ask.* **b.** Fortunate; good: *It is well that you stayed.* —See Synonyms at **healthy.** —**in well with.** *Informal.* In a position to have the ear of; in favor with: *He's in well with the management.* —*interj.* **1.** Used to express surprise. **2.** Used to introduce a remark or simply to gain time to collect one's thoughts. [Middle English *well(e), well,* Old English *wel.* See **wel-²** in Appendix.*]

Usage: As well as, in the sense of in addition to, does not have the conjunctive force of *and.* Consequently, in the following examples, the singular subjects remain singular and govern

singular verbs: *The parent company as well as its affiliate was named in the indictment. Harris, as well as Lewis, has announced his candidacy.* As well as is not used in combination with *both:* *Both in theory and in practice, the idea is unsound.* Alternative construction: *In theory as well as in practice, the idea is unsound.*

we'll (wĕl). Contraction of *we will* and *we shall.*

Wel·land Ship Canal (wĕl′ənd). A waterway of Canada, connecting Lakes Ontario and Erie in southern Ontario.

well·a·way (wĕl′ə-wā′) *interj.* Also **well·a·day** (-dā′). *Archaic.* Alas! Woe is me! —*n., pl.* **wellaways.** Also **well·a·day.** A lamentation. [Middle English *weilawey, wellaway,* Old English *wei lā wei,* variant (influenced by Old Norse *vei,* woe) of *wā lā wā* : *wā,* woe (see **wai** in Appendix*) + *lā,* LO + *wā,* woe.]

well-bal·anced (wĕl′băl′ənst) *adj.* **1.** Evenly proportioned, balanced, or regulated. **2.** Mentally stable; sensible; sound.

well-be·ing (wĕl′bē′ĭng) *n.* The state of being healthy, happy, or prosperous; welfare.

well-born (wĕl′bôrn′) *adj.* Of good lineage or stock.

well-bred (wĕl′brĕd′) *adj.* **1.** Of good upbringing; well-mannered; refined. **2.** Of good breed. Said of animals.

well-dis·posed (wĕl′dĭs-pōzd′) *adj.* Disposed to be kindly, friendly, or sympathetic.

well-done (wĕl′dŭn′) *adj.* **1.** Cooked all the way through: *a well-done steak.* **2.** Satisfactorily or properly accomplished.

Wel·ler (wĕl′ər), **Thomas Huckle.** Born 1915. American microbiologist.

well-fa·vored (wĕl′fā′vərd) *adj.* Attractive; comely; handsome.

well-fed (wĕl′fĕd′) *adj.* **1.** Adequately or properly nourished. **2.** Overfed; fat.

well-fixed (wĕl′fĭkst′) *adj. Informal.* Financially secure; well-to-do.

well-found (wĕl′found′) *adj.* Properly furnished or equipped.

well-found·ed (wĕl′foun′dĭd) *adj.* Well-substantiated; based on sound judgment, reasoning, or evidence.

well-groomed (wĕl′grōōmd′) *adj.* **1.** Attentive to details of dress; meticulously neat. **2.** Carefully tended or curried: *a well-groomed horse.* **3.** Trim and tidy: *a well-groomed lawn.*

well-ground·ed (wĕl′groun′dĭd) *adj.* **1.** Adequately versed in a subject. **2.** Having a sound basis; well-founded.

well-han·dled (wĕl′hănd′əld) *adj.* **1.** Managed well. **2.** Showing the signs of much handling.

well·head (wĕl′hĕd′) *n.* **1.** The source of a well or stream. **2.** A principal source or fountainhead.

well-heeled (wĕl′hēld′) *adj. Slang.* Having plenty of money.

Wel·ling·ton (wĕl′ĭng-tən). The capital of New Zealand, a seaport at the southern end of North Island. Population, 127,000.

Wel·ling·ton (wĕl′ĭng-tən), **First Duke of.** Title of Arthur Wellesley. Known as the Iron Duke. 1769–1852. British soldier and statesman; defeated Napoleon at Waterloo (1815); prime minister (1828–30).

Wellington boot. A boot extending to the top of the knee in front but cut low in back. [Popularized by Arthur Wellesley, First Duke of WELLINGTON.]

well-in·ten·tioned (wĕl′ĭn-tĕn′shənd) *adj.* Having or marked by good intentions; meant to be helpful.

well-known (wĕl′nōn′) *adj.* **1.** Widely known; familiar or famous. **2.** Fully known.

well-man·nered (wĕl′măn′ərd) *adj.* Polite; courteous.

well-mean·ing (wĕl′mē′nĭng) *adj.* Having or prompted by good intentions.

well-meant (wĕl′mĕnt′) *adj.* Kindly or honestly intended.

well-nigh (wĕl′nī′) *adv.* Nearly; almost.

well-off (wĕl′ôf′, -ŏf′) *adj.* **1.** In fortunate circumstances. **2.** Wealthy; prosperous.

well-read (wĕl′rĕd′) *adj.* Knowledgeable through having read extensively.

Wells (wĕlz), **H(erbert) G(eorge).** 1866–1946. English author.

well-spo·ken (wĕl′spō′kən) *adj.* **1.** Chosen or expressed with aptness or propriety. **2.** Courteous in speech.

well·spring (wĕl′sprĭng′) *n.* **1.** The source of a stream or spring; fountainhead. **2.** A source of supply: *a wellspring of ideas.*

well-thought-of (wĕl-thôt′ŭv′, -ŏv′) *adj.* Respected; esteemed.

well-tim·bered (wĕl′tĭm′bərd) *adj.* **1.** Having a good framework or structure. **2.** Covered with a good growth of timber.

well-timed (wĕl′tīmd′) *adj.* Occurring or done at an opportune time: *a well-timed remark.*

well-to-do (wĕl′tə-dōō′) *adj.* Prosperous; affluent; well-off. [From the phrase *to do well.*]

well-turned (wĕl′tûrnd′) *adj.* **1.** Expertly turned: *a well-turned tower.* **2.** Shapely: *a well-turned ankle.* **3.** Concisely or aptly expressed: *a well-turned phrase.*

well-wish·er (wĕl′wĭsh′ər) *n.* A person who wishes another well; one who extends good wishes. —**well′-wish′ing** *adj.* & *n.*

well-worn (wĕl′wôrn′, -wōrn′) *adj.* **1.** Showing signs of much wear or use. **2.** Repeated too often; trite; hackneyed. **3.** Carried or worn in a becoming manner: *well-worn fame.*

Wels·bach burner (wĕlz′băk′, -bäk′). A trademark for a gauze mantle impregnated with cerium and thorium compounds and used with a gas burner that becomes incandescent when heated, producing light. Also called "gas mantle." [Designed by Baron Carl Auer von *Welsbach* (1858–1929), Austrian chemist.]

welsh (wĕlsh, wĕlch) *intr.v.* **welshed, welshing, welshes.** Also **welch** (wĕlch). *Slang.* **1.** To swindle a person by not paying a debt or wager. **2.** To fail to fulfill an obligation. [Origin obscure.] —**welsh′er** *n.*

Welsh (wĕlsh) *adj.* Also *rare* **Welch.** *Abbr.* **W.** Of or pertaining to Wales, its people, its language, or its culture. —*n.* **1.** The natives or inhabitants of Wales. Used with *the.* **2.** The Celtic language of Wales. [Middle English *Wal(i)sche,* Old English

Wælisc, Wel(i)sc, from *W(e)alh,* a Welshman. See **Volcae** in Appendix.*]

Welsh cor·gi (kôr′gē). A dog of a breed originating in Wales, having a long body, short legs, and a foxlike head.

Welsh·man (wĕlsh′mən) *n., pl.* **-men** (-mĭn). A native of Wales.

Welsh rabbit. A dish made of melted cheese, milk or cream, seasonings, and sometimes ale, served hot over toast or crackers. Also called "Welsh rarebit." [A fanciful culinary term.]

Welsh terrier. A terrier of a breed originating in Wales, having a wiry black-and-tan coat and resembling a small Airedale.

welt (wĕlt) *n.* **1.** A strip of leather or other material stitched into a shoe between the sole and the upper. **2.** A tape or covered cord sewn into a seam as reinforcement or trimming; welting. **3. a.** A ridge or bump raised on the skin by a lash or blow or sometimes by an allergic disorder. Also called "wale." **b.** *Informal.* A lash or blow producing such a mark. —*tr.v.* **welted, welting, welts. 1.** To reinforce or trim with a welt or welting. **2.** To beat severely; flog. **3.** To raise a welt or welts on: *"Stones thrown at him in the street had welted his head and body."* (Carl Sandburg). [Middle English *welte, walt,* perhaps Old English *wealt†, waelt* (both unattested).]

Welt·an·schau·ung (vĕlt′än′shou′ŏŏng) *n., pl.* **-ungs** or **-ungen** (-ŏŏng-ən). A comprehensive world view, especially from a specified standpoint. [German, "world view."]

wel·ter (wĕl′tər) *intr.v.* **-tered, -tering, -ters. 1.** To writhe, roll, or wallow. **2.** To lie soaked in blood. **3.** To roll and surge, as the sea. —*n.* **1.** Turbulence; tossing: *"bright welter of wavecords"* (Ezra Pound). **2. a.** Confusion; turmoil: *"the welter of workaday annoyances which all of us meet with"* (James Thurber). **b.** A confused mass; a jumble: *a welter of papers and magazines.* [Middle English *welteren,* perhaps from Middle Dutch. See **wel-³** in Appendix.*]

wel·ter·weight (wĕl′tər-wāt′) *n.* A boxer or wrestler who weighs between 136 and 147 pounds. [Perhaps **WELTER** + **WEIGHT**.]

welt·ing (wĕl′tĭng) *n.* A cord or strip used to welt a seam.

Welt·schmerz (vĕlt′shmĕrts′) *n.* Sadness over the evils of the world, especially as an expression of romantic pessimism. [German, "world pain."]

Wem·bley (wĕm′blē) **1.** A former administrative division of London, England, now part of **Brent** *(see).* **2.** A residential suburb of London, England. Population, 125,000.

wen¹ (wĕn) *n.* A cyst containing sebaceous matter. [Middle English *wenne, wen,* Old English *wen(n), wæn(n).* See **wâ-²** in Appendix.*]

wen² (wĕn) *n.* An Old English runic letter represented by the Modern English *w.* [Old English *wen,* probably variant of *wyn(n),* pleasure, joy. See **wen-** in Appendix.*]

wench (wĕnch) *n. Archaic.* **1.** A young woman or girl; especially, a peasant girl. Now used familiarly or humorously: *"and brawny country wenches, laughing, draw near to bandy ale-house jest"* (Jerome K. Jerome). **2.** A female servant. **3.** A wanton woman; a prostitute. —*intr.v.* **wenched, wenching, wenches.** *Archaic.* To consort with prostitutes. [Middle English *wenche,* short for *wenchel,* a girl, maid, Old English *wencel,* a child of either sex, maid. See **weng-** in Appendix.*] —**wench′er** *n.*

Wen·chow (wŭn′jō′). A city of China, a port in Chekiang Province in the southeast. Population, 210,000.

wend (wĕnd) *v.* **wended** or *archaic* **went** (wĕnt), **wending, wends.** —*tr.* To proceed on or along; go. Used chiefly in the phrase *wend one's way.* —*intr. Archaic.* To go one's way; proceed. [Middle English *wenden,* Old English *wendan,* to turn around or away, direct, happen. See **wendh-** in Appendix.*]

Wend (wĕnd) *n.* One of a Slavic people inhabiting Saxony and Brandenburg. Also called "Sorb," "Sorbian." [German *Wende,* from Old High German *Winida.* See **wen-** in Appendix.*]

Wend·ish (wĕn′dĭsh) *adj.* Of or pertaining to the Wends or their language. —*n.* The West Slavic language of the Wends. Also called "Lusatian," "Sorbian."

went. 1. Past tense of **go. 2.** *Archaic.* Past tense and past participle of **wend.**

wen·tle·trap (wĕnt′l-trăp′) *n.* Any of various marine snails of the family Epitoniidae, having a tapering spiral shell with numerous raised longitudinal ridges. [Dutch *wenteltrap,* from Middle Dutch *wendeltrappe,* "winding stair," spiral shell : *wendel,* winding, from *wenden,* to wind (see **wendh-** in Appendix*) + *trappe,* a step, stairs (see **der-¹** in Appendix*).]

Went·worth (wĕnt′wûrth′), **William Charles.** 1792–1872. Australian nationalist statesman.

wept. Past tense and past participle of **weep.**

were. 1. Plural and second person singular of the past indicative of **be. 2.** Past subjunctive of **be.** See Usage note.

Usage: Were, as a past subjunctive form, occurs principally in clauses expressing conditions that are clearly hypothetical or contrary to fact, as in *if I were you.* Often such clauses are introduced by *if, as if,* or *as though.* Sometimes they express a wish or desire. Typical examples are: *I wish that it were completed. It is only rumor, but suppose that it were fact. If the situation were more favorable, we could begin. He spoke as though everything were settled.* The singular indicative *was* often appears in such sentences, especially in speech. However, in the four examples cited, only *were* is acceptable on a formal level, according to substantial majorities of the Usage Panel. *Was* is acceptable to only 26 per cent in the first example, to 22 per cent in the second, to 19 per cent in the third, and to 31 per cent in the last, which involves a less clear-cut example of what is hypothetical or contrary to fact. When the clause expresses a mere condition that is neither purely hypothetical nor contrary

to fact, however, *was* is the choice. It is also the choice in indirect questions. In each of the following, *was* (not *were*) is proper: *He said that if Smith were elected, he would resign. I peered out to see whether the way was clear. They sent an inspector to see whether the charge was true. He inquired whether I was satisfied with the outcome.*

we're (wîr). Contraction of *we are.*

wer·en't (wûrnt, wûr′ənt). Contraction of *were not.*

were·wolf (wîr′wŏŏlf′, wûr′-, wâr′-) *n., pl.* **-wolves** (-wŏŏlvz′). Also **wer·wolf.** A person transformed into a wolf or capable of assuming the form of a wolf at will; lycanthrope. [Middle English *wer(e)wolf,* Old English *wer(e)wulf* : probably *wer,* a man (see **wiros** in Appendix*) + *wulf,* a WOLF.]

wer·geld (wûr′gĕld′) *n.* Also **wer·gild** (-gĭld′), **were·gild.** In Anglo-Saxon and Germanic law, a price set upon a man's life on the basis of his rank and paid as compensation by the family of a slayer to the kindred or lord of a slain man to free the culprit of further punishment or obligation. [Middle English (Scottish) *weregehelde,* Old English *wergeld,* "man-payment" : *wer,* a man (see **wiros** in Appendix*) + *geld, gield,* service, payment (see **ghelt-** in Appendix*).]

Wer·ner (vĕr′nər), **Alfred.** 1866–1919. German-born Swiss chemist; developed coordination theory of valence.

wer·ner·ite (wûr′nə-rīt′) *n. Mineralogy.* **Scapolite** *(see).* [French, after A.G. *Werner* (1750–1817), German mineralogist.]

wert. *Archaic.* Second person singular past indicative and past subjunctive of **be.**

We·ser (vā′zər). A river of West Germany, flowing about 300 miles northwest to the North Sea.

wes·kit (wĕs′kĭt) *n.* A waistcoat or vest. [Variant of **WAISTCOAT.**]

Wes·ley (wĕs′lē, wĕz′-), **Charles.** 1707–1788. British Methodist preacher and author of 6,500 hymns; brother of John Wesley.

Wes·ley (wĕs′lē, wĕz′-), **John.** 1703–1791. British founder of Methodism; brother of Charles Wesley.

Wes·ley·an (wĕs′lē-ən, wĕz′-) *adj.* Of or pertaining to John or Charles Wesley or to Methodism. —*n.* A Methodist. —**Wes′·ley·an·ism′** *n.*

Wes·sex (wĕs′ĭks). An Anglo-Saxon kingdom established in the fifth century in southern England. [Middle English *Wessex,* Old English *West Seaxe, Wesseax,* "West Saxons" : **WEST** + **SAXON(s).**]

west (wĕst) *n. Abbr.* **w, W, w., W. 1. a.** The direction opposite that of the earth's axial rotation; the general direction of the sunset. **b.** The cardinal point on the mariner's compass 270 degrees clockwise from north and directly opposite east. See **compass card. 2.** Any area or region lying in this direction. **3.** *Often capital* **W. a.** The part of the earth west of Asia and Asia Minor, especially Europe and the Western Hemisphere; the Occident. **b.** The Western Hemisphere. **c.** The western part of any country or region. **d.** The noncommunist countries of Europe and the Americas. —**the West.** In the United States: **1.** Formerly, the region lying west of the Alleghenies. **2.** The region west of the Mississippi. —*adj.* **1.** To, toward, of, facing, or in the west. **2.** Coming from or originating in the west, as a wind. **3.** *Capital* **W.** Officially designating the western part of a country, continent, or other geographical area: *West Bengal.* —*adv.* In, from, or toward the west. —**go west. 1.** *Informal.* To die. **2.** To move to the Western Hemisphere or to the western part of the United States or Canada. [Middle English *west,* Old English *west.* See **wespero-** in Appendix.*]

West (wĕst), **Benjamin.** 1738–1820. American painter, resident in England.

West Al·lis (ăl′ĭs). A city of southeastern Wisconsin, just west of Milwaukee. Population, 68,000.

West Ben·gal (bĕn-gäl′). A state of the Republic of India, occupying 33,839 square miles in the northeast, formerly part of **Bengal** *(see).* Population, 34,926,000. Capital, Calcutta.

West Ber·lin. See **Berlin.**

west·bound (wĕst′bound′) *adj. Abbr.* **w.b.** Going toward the west.

west by north. *Abbr.* **WbN** The direction or point on the mariner's compass halfway between due west and west-north-west; 78 degrees 45 minutes west of due north. See **compass card.**

west by south. *Abbr.* **WbS** The direction or point on the mariner's compass halfway between due west and west-south-west; 101 degrees 15 minutes west of due north. See **compass card.**

West Co·vi·na (kō-vē′nə). A city of southern California, east of Los Angeles. Population, 51,000.

West Dray·ton (drāt′n). A former administrative division of London, England, now part of **Hillingdon** *(see).*

West End. A section of western London, England, noted for its theaters, parks, and fashionable shops.

west·er (wĕs′tər) *intr.v.* **-ered, -ering, -ers. 1.** To move westward. Used of the sun, moon, or a star. **2.** To shift to the west. Used of the wind. —*n.* A storm or wind coming from the west. [Middle English *west(e)ren,* from **WEST.**]

west·er·ing (wĕs′tər-ĭng) *adj.* Moving westward and declining toward the horizon.

west·er·ly (wĕs′tər-lē) *adj.* **1.** Situated toward the west. **2.** From the west. Said of wind. —*n., pl.* **westerlies.** A storm or wind from the west. [From obsolete *wester,* western, from Middle English *wester,* Old English *westra.* See **wespero-** in Appendix.*] —**west′er·ly** *adv.*

west·ern (wĕs′tərn) *adj. Abbr.* **w, W, w., W. 1.** Situated toward, in, or facing the west. **2.** Coming from the west. Said of wind.

Welsh corgi

Welsh terrier

John Wesley

wentletrap
Epitonium angulatum

ă pat/ā pay/âr care/ä father/b bib/ch church/d deed/ĕ pet/ē be... t tight/th thin, path/th this, bathe/ŭ cut/ûr urge/v valve/w with/y yes/z zebra, size/zh vision/ə about, item, edible, gallop, circus/ à Fr. ami/œ Fr. feu, Ger. schön/ü Fr. tu, Ger. über/KH Ger. ich, Scot. loch/N Fr. bon. *Follows main vocabulary. †Of obscure origin.

3. Growing in the west. **4.** *Often capital* **W.** Of, pertaining to, or characteristic of western regions or the West. **5.** *Capital* **W.** Of, pertaining to, or characteristic of Europe and the Western Hemisphere; Occidental: *Western technology.* **6.** *Often capital* **W.** Of, pertaining to, or characteristic of the American West. **7.** *Capital* **W.** Of or pertaining to the Roman Catholic Church as distinguished from the Eastern Orthodox Church. —*n.* **1.** A westerner. **2.** *Often capital* **W.** A novel or film dealing with frontier or cowboy life. [Middle English *west(e)ren,* Old English *westerne.* See **wespero-** in Appendix.*]

Western Aus·tral·ia (ô-strāl′yə). The largest state (975,920 square miles) of Australia, occupying almost one-third of the continent in the west. Population, 804,000. Capital, Perth.

Western A·zer·bai·jan. See Azerbaijan.

Western Dvi·na. See Dvina.

west·ern·er (wĕs′tər-nər) *n.* **1.** A native or inhabitant of the west. **2.** *Often capital* **W.** A native or inhabitant of the western United States.

Western Ghats. See Ghats.

Western Hemisphere. The half of the earth that includes all of North and South America, the surrounding waters, and all neighboring islands.

Western Islands. See Hebrides.

west·ern·ize (wĕs′tər-nīz′) *tr.v.* **-ized, -izing, -izes.** To convert to the ways of Western civilization. —**west′ern·i·za′tion** *n.*

Western Ocean. In ancient times, the North Atlantic Ocean.

western omelet. An omelet cooked with diced ham, chopped green pepper, and onion.

Western Region. A federal region of Nigeria, occupying 45,376 square miles in the southwest. Population, 10,279,000. Capital, Ibadan.

Western Reserve. A section of northeastern modern Ohio on the southern shore of Lake Erie, held by Connecticut out of western lands ceded to the Federal government in 1776 and relinquished in 1800.

Western Sa·mo·a (sə-mō′ə). The western section of the Samoa island group in the Pacific, a state independent since 1962, with an area of 1,133 square miles; formerly a United Nations Trust Territory. Population, 122,000. Capital, Apia.

western sandwich. A sandwich having a western omelet as a filling.

Western Thrace. See Thrace.

West Flan·ders (flăn′dərz). A province of Belgium, occupying 1,249 square miles in the west. Population, 1,021,000. Capital, Bruges.

West Fris·ians. See Frisian Islands.

West Germanic. A subdivision of the Germanic languages that includes High German, Low German, Dutch, Afrikaans, Flemish, Frisian, English, and Yiddish.

West Ger·ma·ny. The unofficial name for the German Federal Republic. See **Germany.**

West Greek. A principal dialectal division of Ancient Greek, comprising Doric and Northwest Greek.

West Hart·ford (härt′fərd). A city of Connecticut, a residential center just west of Hartford. Population, 70,000.

West In·dies (ĭn′dēz). *Abbr.* **W.I.** An island chain extending in an eastward arc between the southeastern United States and the northern shore of South America, separating the Caribbean Sea from the Atlantic Ocean and including the Bahamas, the Greater Antilles, and the Lesser Antilles. —**West Indian.**

West In·dies, Federation of (ĭn′dēz). A federation of former British colonies in the West Indies, established in 1958 and dissolved in 1962. Also called "West Indies Federation."

West Indies Associated States. A group of former British colonies in the West Indies, became independent in 1967 in association with Great Britain and including Antigua, Dominica, Grenada, St. Lucia, St. Kitts-Nevis-Anguilla, and St. Vincent.

west·ing (wĕs′tĭng) *n.* **1.** *Nautical.* **a.** The distance sailed by a ship on a westerly course. **b.** The longitudinal distance from a given meridian on a westward course. **2.** A westward direction or movement. [From WEST.]

West·ing·house (wĕs′tĭng-hous′), **George.** 1846–1914. American engineer and manufacturer; awarded 400 patents.

West I·ri·an (ĭr′ē-än). Formerly **Dutch New Guin·ea** (gĭn′ē), **Netherlands New Guin·ea.** A province of Indonesia, comprising the western half of the island of New Guinea and several offshore islands, with a combined area of 159,375 square miles. Population, about 700,000. Capital, Sukarnapura.

West Lo·thi·an (lō′thē-ən). A county of Scotland, occupying 120 square miles in the southeast, on the Firth of Forth. Population, 101,000. County seat, Linlithgow.

Westm. Westmorland.

West·meath (wĕst′mēth′). A county, 680 square miles in area, of north-central Republic of Ireland. Population, 53,000. County seat, Mullingar.

West·min·ster (wĕst′mĭn′stər). A borough of London, England, comprising the former administrative divisions of Westminster, Paddington, and St. Marylebone. Population, 269,000.

Westminster Abbey. A Gothic church in Westminster, London, the scene of coronations of English monarchs and the burial place of many famous Englishmen.

West·mor·land (wĕst′mər-lənd). *Abbr.* **Westm.** A county occupying 789 square miles in the Lake District of northwestern England. Population, 67,000. County seat, Appleby.

west-north-west (wĕst′nôrth′wĕst′; *Nautical* -nôr′wĕst′) *n. Abbr.* **WNW** The direction or point on the mariner's compass halfway between west and northwest; 67 degrees 30 minutes west of due north. See **compass card.** —*adj.* Situated toward,

facing, or in this direction. —*adv.* In, from, or toward this direction.

West Pa·ki·stan (păk′ĭ-stăn′, pä′kĭ-stän′). A province of Pakistan, occupying 309,424 square miles northwest of the Republic of India. Population, 42,880,000. Capital, Lahore.

West Palm Beach. A city and resort center of southeastern Florida. Population, 56,000.

West·pha·lia (wĕst-fāl′yə, -fā′lē-ə). A former Prussian province, incorporated into West Germany in 1945.

West Point. A U.S. military reservation on the Hudson in southeastern New York State; the site of the U.S. Military Academy since 1802.

West Prus·sia (prŭsh′ə). A former Prussian province incorporated into Poland in 1945.

West Pun·jab (pŭn-jäb′, -jäb′, pŭn′jäb, -jäb). That part of the former British province of Punjab incorporated into West Pakistan in 1947.

West Ri·ding (rī′dĭng). An administrative division occupying 2,936 square miles in southwestern Yorkshire, England. Population, 3,704,000. Administrative center, Wakefield.

West River. See Si Kiang.

West Saxon. **1.** An Old English dialect spoken in Wessex, the chief literary dialect of England before the Norman Conquest. **2.** One of the Saxons inhabiting Wessex during the centuries before the Norman Conquest.

West Slavic. The western division of the Slavic languages, consisting of Czech and Polish.

west-south-west (wĕst′south′wĕst′; *Nautical* -sou-wĕst′) *n. Abbr.* **WSW** The direction or point on the mariner's compass halfway between west and southwest; 112 degrees 30 minutes west of due north. See **compass card.** —*adj.* Situated toward, facing, or in this direction. —*adv.* In, from, or toward this direction.

West Spits·ber·gen (spĭts′bûr′gən). The largest (15,000 square miles) of the Spitsbergen island group in the Arctic Ocean.

West Vir·gin·ia (vûr-jĭn′yə). *Abbr.* **W.Va.** A state of the United States, occupying 24,181 square miles in the east-central part of the country; admitted to the Union in 1863. Population, 1,860,000. Capital, Charleston. See map at **United States of America.** —**West Virginian.**

west·ward (wĕst′wərd) *adv.* Also **west·wards** (-wərdz). Toward the west. —*adj.* Situated toward, facing, or in the west. —*n.* **1.** A direction or point toward the west. **2.** A region situated in or toward the west. —**west′ward·ly** *adj. & adv.*

wet (wĕt) *adj.* **wetter, wettest. 1.** Covered or saturated with a liquid, especially water; moistened; damp. **2.** Not yet dry or firm: *wet plaster.* **3.** Stored or preserved in liquid. **4.** Used or prepared with water or other liquids. **5. a.** Rainy, humid, or foggy: *wet weather.* **b.** Characterized by frequent or heavy rainfall or snowfall: *a wet climate.* **6.** *Informal.* Allowing alcoholic beverages to be produced and sold or supporting the legalization of their production and sale: *a wet county.* —**all wet.** *Slang.* Entirely mistaken. —**wet behind the ears.** Inexperienced; green. —*n.* **1.** That which makes wet; moisture. **2.** Rainy or snowy weather: *go out into the wet.* **3.** *Informal.* One who supports the legality of the production and sale of alcoholic beverages. —*v.* **wetted, wetting, wets.** —*tr.* **1.** To make wet; moisten or dampen: *wet a sponge.* **2.** To make (a bed or one's clothes) wet by urinating. —*intr.* To become wet. —**wet one's whistle.** To take a drink. [Middle English *wet,* Old English *wæt, wēt.* See **wed-**[1] in Appendix.*]

Synonyms: wet, damp, moist, dank, humid. These adjectives refer to the presence of a liquid, usually water. *Wet* generally describes what is soaked or saturated or has a surface covered with liquid, as *a wet sidewalk,* or what is not yet dry, as *wet paint. Damp* and *moist* both mean slightly wet, but *damp* often implies an unpleasant sensation. *Dank* suggests the odorous and perhaps injurious atmosphere of marshes or enclosed spaces. *Humid* refers to moisture in the atmosphere; when used without qualification, it implies unpleasantly high saturation.

We·tar (wĕ′tär). An island of Indonesia, 1,400 square miles in area, in the southern Moluccas.

wet·back (wĕt′băk′) *n.* A Mexican laborer who illegally crosses the U.S. border, as by crossing the Rio Grande. Compare **bracero.**

wet blanket. *Informal.* One that discourages enjoyment, enthusiasm, or the like. [Originally a soaked blanket used in putting out fires.]

wet cell. A primary cell having an electrolyte in the form of a liquid bath. Compare **dry cell.**

wet dream. An erotic dream accompanied by sexual climax.

weth·er (wĕth′ər) *n.* A gelded male sheep. [Middle English *wether,* wether, a ram, Old English *wether.* See **wet-** in Appendix.*]

wet monsoon. *Meteorology.* A monsoon (see).

wet nurse. 1. A woman who suckles another woman's child. **2.** One who treats another with excessive care or solicitude.

wet-nurse (wĕt′nûrs′) *tr.v.* **-nursed, -nursing, -nurses. 1.** To serve as wet nurse for. **2.** To treat with excessive care.

wet pack. The usual form of a therapeutic pack (see), wrung out of hot or cold water.

Wet·ter·horn (vĕt′ər-hôrn′). **1.** A mountain rising to 14,020 feet in the San Juan Mountains of southwestern Colorado. **2.** A mountain, 12,153 feet high, in the Bernese Alps, central Switzerland.

wetting agent. Any compound that causes a liquid to spread more easily across or penetrate into the surface of a solid by reducing the surface tension of the liquid.

we've (wēv). Contraction of *we have.*

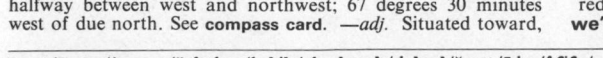

WESTERN SAMOA map showing SOLOMON ISLANDS, NEW GUINEA, AUSTRALIA, PACIFIC OCEAN, NEW ZEALAND, WESTERN SAMOA·Apia, FIJI

Western Samoa

Wex·ford (wĕks'fərd). **1.** A county of the Republic of Ireland, occupying 907 square miles in the southeast. Population, 83,000. **2.** The county seat of this county. Population, 11,000.
Wey·den (vīd'n), **Rogier van der**. 1400–1464. Flemish painter.
wf *Printing.* wrong font.
WFTU World Federation of Trade Unions.
w.g. wire gauge.
wh. white.
whack (hwăk) *v.* **whacked, whacking, whacks.** —*tr.* To strike with a sharp blow; to slap. —*intr.* To deal a sharp, resounding blow. —*n.* **1.** A sharp, swift blow. **2.** The sound made by such a blow. —**have** (or **take**) **a whack at.** *Informal.* To attempt; try out. —**out of whack.** *Informal.* Improperly ordered or balanced; not functioning correctly. [Perhaps variant of THWACK.]
whack·ing (hwăk'ĭng) *adj. Chiefly British Informal.* Superlative. —*adv. Chiefly British Informal.* Superlatively.
whack·y. Variant of **wacky.**
whale[1] (hwāl) *n.* **1.** Any of various marine mammals of the order Cetacea, having a generally fishlike form with forelimbs modified to form flippers and a tail with horizontal flukes; especially, one of the very large species as distinguished from the smaller dolphins, porpoises, and others. **2.** *Informal.* A superlative example of a thing specified. Used with *of: a whale of a game.* —*intr.v.* **whaled, whaling, whales.** To engage in the hunting of whales. [Middle English *whale,* Old English *hwæl.* See skwalo- in Appendix.*]
whale[2] (hwāl) *v.* **whaled, whaling, whales.** —*tr.* To strike repeatedly with a whip, stick, or the like; thrash; flog. —*intr.* To attack vehemently. Often used with *away: The poet whaled away at his critics.* [Origin uncertain.]
whale·back (hwāl'băk') *n.* A steamship with the bow and upper deck rounded so as to shed water.
whale·boat (hwāl'bōt') *n.* **1.** A long rowboat, pointed at both ends and designed to move and turn swiftly, formerly used in the pursuit and harpooning of whales. **2.** Any boat of similar size and shape. Also called "whaler."
whale·bone (hwāl'bōn') *n.* **1.** The durable, elastic, hornlike material forming plates or strips in the upper jaw of whalebone whales. Also called "baleen." **2.** An object made of this material, as a corset stay.
whalebone whale. Any of various whales of the suborder Mysticeti, lacking teeth and characteristically filtering plankton through plates of whalebone.
whale oil. A yellowish oil obtained from whale blubber, used in making soap and candles and as a lubricating oil.
whal·er (hwā'lər) *n.* **1.** One who hunts or processes whales. **2.** A whaling ship. **3.** A whaleboat (*see*).
Whales, Bay of. An inlet of the Ross Sea in the Ross Shelf Ice, Antarctica.
whale shark. A large shark, *Rhincodon typus,* of warm marine waters, having a spotted body and feeding chiefly on plankton.
whal·ing (hwā'lĭng) *n.* The business or practice of hunting, killing, and processing whales.
wham (hwăm) *n.* **1.** A forceful, resounding blow. **2.** The sound of such a blow; a thud. —*v.* **whammed, whamming, whams.** —*tr.* To strike or smash into with resounding impact. —*intr.* To smash with great force. [Imitative.]
wham·my (hwăm'ē) *n., pl.* **-mies.** *Slang.* A supernatural spell capable of subduing an adversary; hex: *put the whammy on someone.* [Perhaps from WHAM.]
whang[1] (hwăng) *n. Informal.* **1.** A thong or whip of hide or leather. **2. a.** A lashing blow, as by a whip. **b.** The sound of such a blow. —*tr.v.* **whanged, whanging, whangs.** *Informal.* **1.** To beat or whip with a thong. **2.** To beat with a sharp blow or blows. [Variant of Middle English *thwang,* THONG.]
whang[2] (hwăng) *v.* **whanged, whanging, whangs.** *Informal.* —*tr.* To strike so as to produce a loud, reverberant noise. —*intr.* To produce a loud, reverberant noise. —*n. Informal.* A loud, reverberant noise. [Imitative.]
whang·ee (hwăng-gē') *n.* **1.** Any of several bamboolike Asian grasses of the genus *Phyllostachys.* **2.** A walking stick made from the woody stem of such a plant. [Chinese (Mandarin) *huang²li²: huang²,* yellow + *li²,* a kind of bramble.]
Whang·poo. The former name for the **Hwangpoo.**
wharf (hwôrf) *n., pl.* **wharves** (hwôrvz) or **wharfs.** **1.** *Abbr.* **whf.** A landing place at which vessels may tie up and load or unload. **2.** *Obsolete.* A shore or river bank. —*v.* **wharfed, wharfing, wharfs.** **1.** To moor (a vessel) at a wharf. **2.** To take to or store (cargo) on a wharf. **3.** To furnish, equip, or protect with a wharf or wharves. —*intr.* To berth at a wharf. [Middle English *wharfe, werf,* Old English *hwearf.* See kwerp- in Appendix.*]
wharf·age (hwôr'fĭj) *n.* **1.** The use of a wharf or wharves. **2.** The charges for this. **3.** Wharves collectively.
wharf·in·ger (hwôr'fĭn-jər) *n.* The owner or manager of a wharf. [WHARF + the ending of words like HARBINGER and PASSENGER.]
wharf rat. 1. A rat that infests wharves and shipping. **2.** *Slang.* An undesirable person who frequents wharves.
Whar·ton (hwôrt'n), **Edith (Newbold Jones).** 1862–1937. American author.
what (hwŏt, hwŭt; *unstressed* hwət) *pron.* **1.** Which thing. Used as an interrogative pronoun in questions that ask for a specification or identification of something inanimate or abstract: **a.** Which particular one of many: *What are you having for dinner?* Also used in this sense in requests for repetition or explanation: *What did you say?* **b.** Which kind, character, or designation: *What are these objects?* **c.** A person or thing of

how much value or significance: *What are possessions to a dying man?* **2.** That which. Used as a relative pronoun in phrases in which something is left unidentified: **a.** The thing that: *Listen to what I tell you.* **b.** Whatever thing that: *come what may.* **3. a.** *Nonstandard.* Which, who, or that: *It's the poor what gets the blame.* **b.** *Informal.* Something: *I'll tell you what.* —**and what not.** And other less prominent or unspecified things; and so on. —**what have you.** What remains and need not be mentioned; all the rest. —**what if.** What would occur if; suppose that. —**what of it?** How is it important; what does it matter? —**what's what.** *Informal.* The fundamentals and details of a situation or process; the true state or condition. —**what with.** Taking into consideration; in view of; because of: *What with the heat and humidity, we really suffered.* — *adj.* **1.** Which one or ones of many. Used both interrogatively and relatively: *What college are you attending? You should know what musical that song is from.* **2.** Whatever; as much or many as: *They soon repaired what damage had been done.* **3.** *Archaic.* How much; which degree of: *What love do you bear for her?* **4.** How great; how astonishing. Used in exclamations: *What a fool!* —*adv.* **1.** How; how much; in what respect: *What does it matter?* **2.** Why; which reason. Used with *for: What are you hurrying for?* —*conj. Nonstandard.* That. Usually used with *but.* See Usage note at **but.** —*interj.* **1.** Used to express surprise, incredulity, or other strong and sudden excitement. **2.** *British Informal.* Used to express agreement: *A fine evening, what?* [Middle English *what,* Old English *hwæt.* See kwo- in Appendix.*]
Usage: What (relative pronoun), used as the subject of a clause, can be either singular or plural in construction, depending on the sense involved. It is construed as singular when it is the equivalent of *that which* or a (or the) *thing that,* and plural when it stands for *things that* or *those which.* The number of the verb or verbs governed by *what* depends on how it is construed: *He is involved in what seems to be an outright fraud. They are making what appear to be signs of welcome. What impresses me most is his sincerity. What were intended as gestures of friendship seem to have aroused suspicion instead.* In the third and fourth examples, involving two verbs after *what,* note that the verbs agree in number. In some sentences, either a singular or plural interpretation of *what* is possible, especially when the elements following the second verb can be construed collectively or abstractly in the sense of *that which: Sometimes what really commands respect is power and the willingness to use it. What is most revealing in the pictures is the varied contrasts of light and shadow.* Or two plural verbs could be used.
what·ev·er (hwŏt-ĕv'ər, hwŭt-) *pron.* Also poetic **what·e'er** (-âr'). **1.** Everything or anything that: *Do whatever you please.* **2.** What amount that; the whole of what: *Whatever is left over is yours.* **3.** No matter what; regardless of what: *Whatever happens, we'll meet here tonight.* **4.** *Informal.* What; which thing or things. Used in questions expressing surprise or puzzlement: *Whatever does he mean?* —*adj.* **1.** Of any number or kind; any: *Whatever requests you make will be granted.* **2.** All of; the whole of: *He applied whatever strength he had left to the task.* **3.** No matter what: *"blown oblivious and without destination upon whatever wind"* (Faulkner). **4.** Of any kind at all. Used emphatically following the noun modified: *No campers whatever may use the lake before noon.*
what·not (hwŏt'nŏt', hwŭt'-) *n.* **1.** A minor or unspecified object or article; a trivial item. **2.** A set of light, open shelves for ornaments.
what·so·ev·er (hwŏt'sō-ĕv'ər, hwŭt'-) *pron.* Also poetic **what·so·e'er** (-sō-âr'). Whatever. —*adj.* Whatever. Used for emphasis: *no power whatsoever.*
wheal (hwēl) *n.* A small acute swelling on the skin. [Variant (influenced by obsolete *wheal,* to suppurate) of WALE (ridge).]
wheat (hwēt) *n.* **1.** Any of various cereal grasses of the genus *Triticum;* especially, *T. aestivum,* widely cultivated in many varieties for its commercially important edible grain. **2.** The grain of such a plant, ground to produce flour used in breadstuffs and pasta products such as spaghetti and macaroni. [Middle English *whet(e),* Old English *hwǣte.* See kweit- in Appendix.*]
wheat·ear (hwēt'îr') *n.* A brown, black, and white bird, *Oenanthe oenanthe,* of northern regions. [Back-formation from *wheatears* (taken as plural), "white-rumped (bird)" : probably WHITE + Middle English *ers,* ASS.]
wheat·en (hwēt'n) *adj.* Of, pertaining to, or derived from wheat.
wheat germ. The vitamin-rich embryo of the wheat kernel, separated during or after milling for use as a cereal or food supplement.
Whea·ton (hwēt'n). An urban area of west-central Maryland, just north of Washington, D.C. Population, 55,000.
Wheat·stone bridge (hwēt'stōn'). Also **Wheat·stone's bridge** (-stōnz'). An instrument or circuit consisting of four resistors, or their equivalent, in series, with a galvanometer linking the junction between one pair and the other, used to determine the value of an unknown resistance when the other three resistances are known. [After Sir Charles *Wheatstone* (died 1875), English physicist.]
wheat·worm (hwēt'wûrm') *n.* A nematode worm, *Anguina tritici,* that is parasitic on and destructive to wheat.
whee·dle (hwēd'l) *v.* **-dled, -dling, -dles.** —*tr.* **1.** To persuade or attempt to persuade by flattery or guile; cajole: *"many a tradesman had she coaxed and wheedled into good humour"* (Thackeray). **2.** To obtain through the use of flattery or guile. —*intr.* To use flattery or cajolery to achieve one's ends. [Perhaps from German *wedeln,* "to wag the tail," from Middle High

whaleback

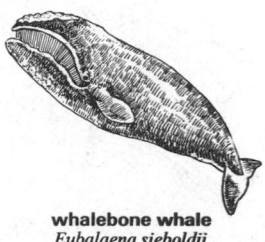
whalebone whale
Eubalaena sieboldii

wheat
Triticum aestivum

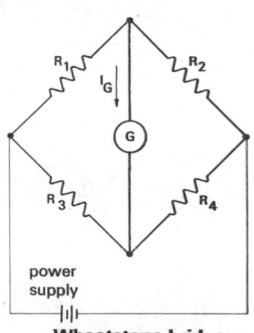

$$R_1 \times R_3 = R_2 \times R_4$$

Wheatstone bridge
The current I_G, measured
by detector G, is zero
when $R_1 \times R_3 = R_2 \times R_4$

ă pat/ā pay/âr care/ä father/b bib/ch church/d deed/ĕ pet/ē be/f fife/g gag/h hat/hw which/ĭ pit/ī pie/îr pier/j judge/k kick/l lid, needle/m mum/n no, sudden/ng thing/ŏ pot/ō toe/ô paw, for/oi noise/ou out/ŏŏ took/ōō boot/p pop/r roar/s sauce/sh ship, dish/t tight/th thin, path/th this, bathe/ŭ cut/ûr urge/v valve/w with/y yes/z zebra, size/zh vision/ə about, item, edible, gallop, circus/à Fr. ami/œ Fr. feu, Ger. schön/ü Fr. tu, Ger. über/KH Ger. ich, Scot. loch/N Fr. bon. *Follows main vocabulary. †Of obscure origin.

German *wadelen,* from Old High German *wadal,* tail. See **wē-** in Appendix.*] —**whee'dler** *n.* —**whee'dling·ly** *adv.*

wheel (hwēl) *n.* **1.** A solid disk or a rigid circular ring connected by spokes to a hub, designed to turn around an axle passed through the center. **2.** Anything resembling such a device in appearance or movement or having such a device as its principal part or characteristic, as: **a.** In the Middle Ages, an instrument to which a victim was bound for torture. **b.** A type of firework that rotates while burning. **c.** The steering device on a vehicle. **d.** *Informal.* A bicycle. **e.** A spinning wheel. **f.** A water wheel. **g.** A potter's wheel. **h.** A device used in roulette and other games of chance. **3.** *Plural.* Forces that provide energy, movement, or direction: *the wheels of commerce.* **4.** The act or process of turning; a revolution or rotation. **5.** *Military.* A maneuver to change the direction of movement of a formation of troops, ships, or the like, in which the formation is maintained while the outer unit describes an arc and the inner unit remains stationary as a pivot. **6.** *Plural. Slang.* An automobile or access thereto. **7.** *Slang.* One with a great deal of power or influence. —**at** (or **behind**) **the wheel. 1.** Operating the steering mechanism of a vehicle; driving. **2.** In charge; directing or controlling. —**wheels within wheels.** A complex series of actions and interactions. —*v.* **wheeled, wheeling, wheels.** —*tr.* **1.** To roll, move, or transport on a wheel or wheels. **2.** To cause to turn around or as if around a central axis; revolve; rotate. **3.** To provide with a wheel or wheels. —*intr.* **1.** To turn around or as if around a central axis; revolve; rotate. **2.** To roll or move on or as if on a wheel or wheels. **3.** To fly in a curving or circular course: *"nine-and-fifty swans . . . scatter wheeling in great broken rings"* (Yeats). **4.** To turn or whirl around in place; to pivot: *"the boy wheeled and the fried eggs leaped from his tray"* (Ivan Gold). **5.** To reverse one's opinion or practice. Often used with *about.* **6.** *Informal.* To engage in the advancement of one's own interests. Used in the phrase *wheel and deal.* [Middle English *wheel(e),* Old English *hwēol, hweogol.* See **kwel-**[1] in Appendix.*]

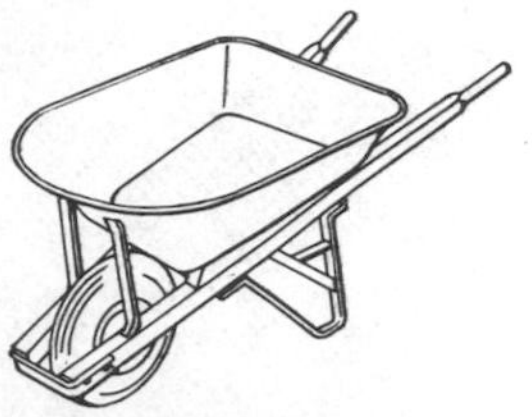
wheelbarrow

wheel and axle. A mechanical device, analogous to the lever, consisting of two coaxial wheels of different diameter conjoined so that the effort applied by a cord to the larger wheel in the form of a torque is transmitted as an action by a cord around the circumference of the smaller, yielding a mechanical advantage equal to the ratio of the diameters of the wheels.

wheel animalcule. A microorganism, a **rotifer** *(see).*

wheel·bar·row (hwēl'băr'ō) *n.* A one- or two-wheeled vehicle with handles, used to convey small, heavy loads by hand.

wheel·base (hwēl'bās') *n.* The distance from front to rear axle in a motor vehicle, usually expressed in inches.

wheel bug. A large predatory insect, *Arilus cristatus,* having a notched, wheellike projection on the thorax.

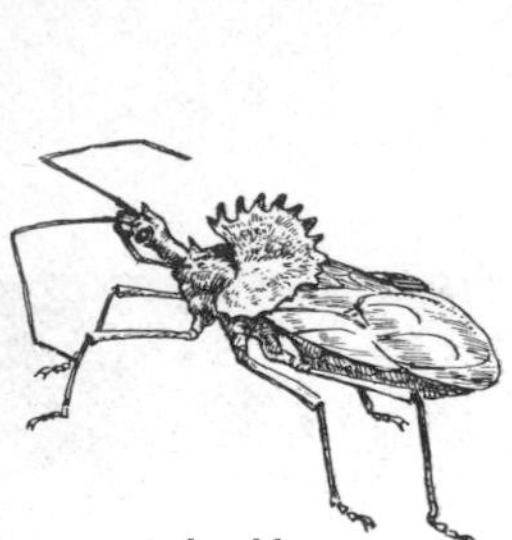
wheel bug

wheel·chair (hwēl'chār') *n.* Also **wheel chair.** A chair mounted on large wheels for the use of the sick or disabled.

wheeled (hwēld) *adj.* Having a wheel or wheels. Often used in combination: *four-wheeled.*

wheel·er (hwē'lər) *n.* **1.** One that wheels. **2.** A thing that moves on or is equipped with a wheel or wheels. Often used in combination: *a three-wheeler.* **3.** A **wheel horse** *(see).*

Wheel·er (hwē'lər), **William Almon.** 1819–1887. Vice President of the United States under Rutherford B. Hayes (1877–81).

wheel·er-deal·er (hwē'lər-dē'lər) *n. Informal.* A person who wheels and deals; a sharp operator.

Wheel·er Peak (hwē'lər). A mountain, 13,160 feet high, in north-central New Mexico; the highest point in the state.

wheel horse. 1. In a team, the horse that follows the leader and is harnessed nearest to the front wheels. **2.** Any diligent, dependable worker, especially in a political organization. Also called "wheeler."

wheel house. A **pilothouse** *(see).*

Wheel·ing (hwē'lĭng). A city of northern West Virginia, a river port on the Ohio. Population, 51,000.

wheel lock. A firing mechanism in certain obsolete small arms, in which a small wheel produces sparks by revolving against a flint.

wheel·man (hwēl'mən) *n., pl.* **-men** (-mĭn). **1.** One who steers a ship; a helmsman. Also called "wheelsman." **2.** A bicyclist.

wheel·work (hwēl'wûrk') *n.* An arrangement of gears or wheels in a mechanical device.

wheel·wright (hwēl'rīt') *n.* One whose trade is the building and repairing of wheels.

wheeze (hwēz) *v.* **wheezed, wheezing, wheezes.** —*intr.* **1.** To breathe with difficulty, producing a hoarse whistling sound. **2.** To make a sound suggestive of laborious breathing. —*tr.* To produce or utter with a hoarse whistling sound: *"A tugboat, wheezing wreathes of steam, / Lunged past"* (Hart Crane). —*n.* **1.** A wheezing sound. **2.** *Informal.* An old joke. [Middle English *whesen,* probably from Old Norse *hvæsa,* to hiss. See **kwes-** in Appendix.*] —**wheez'er** *n.* —**wheez'ing·ly** *adv.*

whelk[1]
Left: Busycon canalicalatum
Right. Busycon contrarium

wheez·y (hwē'zē) *adj.* **-ier, -iest. 1.** Given to wheezing. **2.** Producing a wheezing sound. —**wheez'i·ly** *adv.* —**wheez'i·ness** *n.*

whelk[1] (hwĕlk) *n.* Any of various large, sometimes edible marine snails of the family Buccinidae, having pointed, turreted shells. [Middle English *w(h)elke,* Old English *weoloc, wioloc.* See **wel-**[3] in Appendix.*]

whelk[2] (hwĕlk) *n. Pathology.* A swelling, protuberance, or pustule; a wheal. [Middle English *whelke,* Old English *hwylca†.*] —**whelk'y** *adj.*

whelm (hwĕlm) *tr.v.* **whelmed, whelming, whelms. 1.** To cover with water; submerge. **2.** To overwhelm. [Middle English *whelmen,* to turn over, Old English *hwelman* (unattested). See **kwelp-**[1] in Appendix.*]

whelp (hwĕlp) *n.* **1.** A young offspring of a dog, wolf, or similar animal. **2. a.** A mere child or youth. **b.** An impudent young fellow. **3. a.** A tooth of a sprocket wheel. **b.** Any of the ridges on the barrel of a windlass or capstan. —*v.* **whelped, whelping, whelps.** —*intr.* To give birth to a whelp or whelps. —*tr.* To give birth to (a whelp or whelps). [Middle English *w(h)elpe,* Old English *hwelp,* from Germanic.]

when (hwĕn) *adv.* **1.** At what time. Used interrogatively: *When will we leave?* **2.** At which time: *I know when to leave.* —*conj.* **1.** At the time that: *in the spring, when the snow melts.* **2.** At the time at which; as soon as: *We will try when the wind is stronger.* **3.** At the times at which; whenever: *When the wind blows, all the doors rattle.* **4.** During the time at which; while: *when I was younger.* **5.** Whereas: *He sleeps when he should be working.* **6.** Considering that; since; if: *How can he succeed when he won't work?* —*pron.* What or which time: *Since when has this been going on?* —*n.* The time or date: *Have they decided the where and when?* [Middle English *when, wane,* Old English *hwanne, hwenne.* See **kwo-** in Appendix.*]

Usage: *When* and *where* are not acceptably used in definitions of terms when they occur immediately after *is,* as in *A summit conference is when* (or *where*) *heads of major powers meet.*

when·as (hwĕn-ăz') *conj. Archaic.* **1.** When. **2.** Whereas.

whence (hwĕns) *adv.* **1.** From where; from what place: *Whence came this man?* **2.** From what origin or source: *Whence came his pride?* **3.** Out of which place; out of which: *He longed for the land whence he came.* —*conj.* By reason of which; from which; wherefore: *He was not dead, whence we derived some comfort.* [Middle English *whennes,* from *whenne,* whence, Old English *hwanon.* See **kwo-** in Appendix.*]

Usage: *Whence* contains the sense of from; consequently, the construction *from whence* is redundant, though it has literary precedent, and *whence* is preferably used alone. The example *injustices from whence revolts spring* is termed unacceptable by 64 per cent of the Usage Panel.

whence·so·ev·er (hwĕns'sō-ĕv'ər) *adv.* From whatever place or source. —*conj.* From any place or source that.

when·ev·er (hwĕn-ĕv'ər) *adv.* Also **when ever** (for sense 2), *poetic* **when·e'er** (-âr'). **1.** At whatever time. **2.** When. Used as an intensive. —*conj.* Also *poetic* **when·e'er. 1.** At whatever time that: *We can leave whenever you're ready.* **2.** Every time that: *He smiles whenever he sees her.*

when·so·ev·er (hwĕn'sō-ĕv'ər) *adv.* At whatever time at all; whenever. —*conj.* Whenever.

where (hwâr) *adv.* **1.** At or in what place: *Where is the telephone?* **2.** In what situation or position: *Where would we be without your help?* **3.** From what place or source: *Where did you get this idea?* **4.** To what place; toward what end: *Where is this argument leading?* —*conj.* **1.** At what or which place: *He moved to the city, where jobs are available.* **2. a.** In a place in which: *He lives where the climate is mild.* **b.** In any place or situation in which; wherever: *Where there's smoke, there's fire.* **3. a.** To a place in which: *We should go where it is quieter.* **b.** To any place or situation in which: *He will go where he is happy.* —*pron.* Which place: *Where did they come from?* —*n.* The place or occasion: *We know the when but not the where of it.* [Middle English *wher(e),* Old English *hwǣr.* See **kwo-** in Appendix.*]

Usage: *Where* is used with *from* to indicate motion from a place: *Where did they come from?* A preposition is not needed to indicate direction or motion to a place in a corresponding construction such as *Where did they go?* (*go to* is redundant); nor is a preposition used to indicate location or position of rest in *Where are they?* (not *Where are they at?*). *Where* is not acceptably used as a conjunction equivalent to *that* in constructions such as: *I see that* (not *where*) *the schedule has been changed.* —See Usage note at **when.**

where·a·bouts (hwâr'ə-bouts') *adv.* About where; in, at, or near what location: *Whereabouts do you live?* —*n.* The approximate location of someone or something. Used with a singular or plural verb.

where·as (hwâr-ăz') *conj.* **1.** It being the fact that; inasmuch as. Often used to introduce a formal document. **2.** While at the same time. **3.** While on the contrary. —*n., pl.* **whereases.** A document, statement, clause, or argument prefaced with the word *whereas.*

where·at (hwâr-ăt') *adv. Archaic.* **1.** At which place. **2.** At which time or event; whereupon.

where·by (hwâr-bī') *adv. Archaic.* **1.** In accordance with or by means of which. **2.** By what means; how: *"Whereby shall I know this?"* (Luke 1:18).

where·fore (hwâr'fôr', -fōr') *adv. Archaic.* For what purpose or reason; why. —*conj. Archaic.* For which reason; because of which: *"And the thing which he did displeased the Lord: wherefore he slew him also."* (Genesis 38:10). —*n.* A purpose or cause. Now used chiefly in the phrase *whys and wherefores.* [Middle English *wherfor* : WHERE + FOR.]

where·from (hwâr'frŏm', -frŭm') *adv. Archaic.* From what or where; whence.

where·in (hwâr-ĭn') *adv.* **1.** In what; how: *Wherein have we sinned?* **2.** In which thing, place, or situation: *the bed wherein he slept.*

where·in·to (hwâr-ĭn'tōō) *adv. Archaic.* Into what or which.

where·of (hwâr-ŏv', -ŭv') *adv. Archaic.* **1.** Of what or which. **2.** Of whom.

where·on (hwâr-ŏn', -ôn') *adv. Archaic.* On which or what.

where·so·ev·er (hwâr'sō-ĕv'ər) *conj.* Also *poetic* **where·so·e'er** (-âr'). In, to, or from whatever place at all; wherever.

where·through (hwâr'thrōō') *conj. Rare.* Through, because of, or during which.

ă pat/ā pay/âr care/ä father/b bib/ch church/d deed/ĕ pet/ē be/f fife/g gag/h hat/hw which/ĭ pit/ī pie/îr pier/j judge/k kick/l lid, needle/m mum/n no, sudden/ng thing/ŏ pot/ō toe/ô paw, for/oi noise/ou out/ŏŏ took/ōō boot/p pop/r roar/s sauce/sh ship, dish/

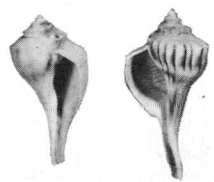

where·to (hwâr′to͞o′) *adv.* Also *archaic* **where·un·to** (hwâr′ŭn-to͞o′). **1.** To what place; toward what end. **2.** To which.
where·up·on (hwâr′ə-pŏn′, -pôn′) *adv.* **1.** *Archaic.* Upon what. **2.** On top of which. **3.** *Archaic.* Because of which. **4.** At which time; after which.
wher·ev·er (hwâr-ĕv′ər) *adv.* Also **where ever** (for sense 2), *poetic* **wher·e'er** (-âr′). **1.** In or to whatever place. **2.** Where. Used as an intensive. —*conj.* Also *poetic* **where·e'er**. In or to whichever place or situation. [Middle English *wherever* : WHERE + EVER.]
where·with (hwâr′wĭth′, -wĭth′) *adv.* With what or which: *"The fingers of this hand wherewith I write"* (Elizabeth Barrett Browning). —*pron. Archaic.* The thing or things with which: *"Make ready wherewith I may sup"* (Luke 17:8).
where·with·al (hwâr′wĭth-ôl′, -wĭth-ôl′) *adv. Archaic.* Wherewith. —*pron. Archaic.* Wherewith. —*n.* The necessary means, especially financial means: *to have the wherewithal for war.*
wher·ry (hwĕr′ē) *n., pl.* **-ries.** **1.** A light, swift rowboat built for one person and often used in racing. **2.** A kind of sailing barge used in East Anglia. [Middle English *whery*†.]
whet (hwĕt) *tr.v.* **whetted, whetting, whets.** **1.** To sharpen (a knife or other tool); to hone. **2.** To make more keen; stimulate; heighten: *"the raw morning air whetted his resolute piety"* (Joyce). —*n.* **1.** The act of whetting. **2.** That which whets. **3.** *Informal.* An appetizer or aperitif. [Middle English *whetten,* Old English *hwettan.* See **kwed-** in Appendix.*]
wheth·er (hwĕth′ər) *conj.* **1.** If it is so that; if the case is that. Used in indirect questions to introduce one alternative: *We should find out whether the museum is open.* **2.** If it happens that; in case. Used to introduce the first of a set of possibilities and sometimes a following possibility: *Whether he wins or (whether he) loses, this is his last fight.* **3.** Either: *He passed the test, whether by skill or luck.* —*pron. Obsolete.* Which. —**whether or no.** Regardless of circumstances. [Middle English *whether,* Old English *hwæther, hwether.* See **kwo-** in Appendix.*]
whet·stone (hwĕt′stōn′) *n.* A stone for honing tools.
whew (hwo͞o, hwyo͞o) *interj.* Used to express relief, amazement, or the like. Usually partially unvoiced in imitation of a whistle. [Middle English *whewe* (imitative).]
whey (hwā) *n.* The watery part of milk that separates from the curds, as in the process of making cheese. Also called "serum." [Middle English *whey,* Old English *hwæg,* from Germanic *khwuja-* (unattested).] —**whey′ey** *adj.*
whey-face (hwā′fās′) *n.* A person with a pallid face.
whf. wharf.
which (hwĭch) *pron.* **1.** What particular one or ones: *Which of these is yours?* **2.** The particular one or ones: *Take those which are yours.* **3.** The thing, animal, group of people, or event previously designated or implied, specifically: **a.** Used as a relative pronoun in a clause that provides additional information about the antecedent: *my house, which is small and old.* See Usage note below. **b.** Used as a relative pronoun preceded by *that* or a preposition in a clause that defines or restricts the antecedent: *the subject on which he spoke.* **c.** Used instead of *that* as a relative pronoun in a clause that defines or restricts the antecedent: *The movie which was shown later was better.* **4.** *Archaic.* The person designated or implied. **5.** Any of the things, events, or persons designated or implied; whichever: *Choose which you like best.* **6.** A thing or circumstance that: *He left early, which was wise.* —*adj.* **1.** What particular one or ones of a number of things or persons: *Which part of town?* **2.** Any one or any number of; whichever: *Use which door you please.* **3.** Being the one or ones previously designated: *It started to rain, at which point we ran.* [Middle English *which, wilke,* Old English *hwilc, hwelc.* See **kwo-** in Appendix.*]
Usage: *Which* sometimes functions like a relative pronoun but refers to an entire preceding statement rather than to a single word: *She ignored him, which proved unwise.* The usage is well established when the reference is clear, as in the preceding sentence, which is acceptable to 85 per cent of the Usage Panel. The construction is undesirable when the reference is unclear; especially when *which* follows a noun, the antecedent may be in doubt and ambiguity may result: *We learned that Edna had made the complaint, which came as a shock.* If *which* is intended to refer to the entire first clause rather than to *complaint,* the desired sense would be expressed more clearly by: *We learned that Edna had made the complaint, and the discovery came as a shock.* —See also Usage note at **that.**
which·ev·er (hwĭch-ĕv′ər) *pron.* **1.** Any one or ones. **2.** No matter which; regardless of what one or ones. —*adj.* **1.** Any one or any number of a group of things or persons: *Read whichever books you please.* **2.** No matter what; regardless of which: *It's a long trip whichever road you take.*
which·so·ever (hwĭch′sō-ĕv′ər) *pron.* Whichever. —*adj.* Whichever. Used for emphasis.
whick·er (hwĭk′ər) *intr.v.* **-ered, -ering, -ers.** To whinny. Used of a horse. —*n.* A whinny. [Imitative.]
whid·ah. Variant of **whydah.**
Whid·by Island (hwĭd′bē). An island 40 miles long in Puget Sound, northwestern Washington.
whiff (hwĭf) *n.* **1.** A slight, gentle gust of air; a waft: *a whiff of cool air.* **2.** A brief, passing odor carried in the air; a momentary smell: *"a whiff of lilac drifted across the room"* (Elizabeth Bowen). **3.** An inhalation of air, perfume, tobacco smoke, or the like: *Take a whiff of this pipe.* —*v.* **whiffed, whiffing, whiffs.** —*intr.* **1.** To be carried in brief gusts; to waft. **2.** To draw in or breathe out air, smoke, or the like. —*tr.* **1.** To blow or convey in whiffs. **2.** To inhale through the nose; to smell; sniff. **3.** To draw in or breathe out (air or tobacco smoke, for example). [Imitative.] —**whiff′er** *n.*
whif·fle (hwĭf′əl) *v.* **-fled, -fling, -fles.** —*intr.* **1.** To move or think erratically; vacillate. **2.** To blow in fitful gusts; to puff. Used of the wind. **3.** To whistle lightly. —*tr.* To blow, displace, or scatter with gusts of air. [From WHIFF (to blow).]
whif·fle·tree (hwĭf′əl-trē) *n.* The pivoted horizontal crossbar to which the harness traces of a draft animal are attached and which is in turn attached to a vehicle or an implement. Also called "whippletree," "singletree," "swingletree." [Variant of WHIPPLETREE.]
Whig (hwĭg) *n.* **1.** In England, a member of a political party of the 18th and 19th centuries, opposed to the Tories. **2.** In the American Revolution, one who supported the war against England. **3.** In the United States, a political party (1834–55) formed to oppose the Democratic Party, succeeded by the Republican Party, and favoring high tariffs and a loose interpretation of the Constitution. —*adj.* Belonging to, composed of, supported by, or characteristic of the Whigs. [Probably short for *Whiggamore,* one of a body of 17th-century Scottish insurgents : perhaps *whig*†, to drive + Middle English *mere,* horse, MARE.] —**Whig′gish** *adj.*
Whig·ger·y (hwĭg′ə-rē) *n., pl.* **-ies.** Also **Whig·gism** (hwĭg′ĭz′əm). The principles or practices of Whigs.
while (hwīl) *n.* **1.** A period of time. Usually used in adverbial phrases: *stay for a while; sang (all) the while.* **2.** The time, effort, or trouble taken in doing something: *"It is not worth the while to go round the world to count the cats in Zanzibar"* (Thoreau). —*conj.* **1.** As long as; during the time that: *It was lovely while it lasted.* **2.** Although; at the same time that: *While he loves his wife, he is strict with her.* **3.** Whereas; and: *The soles are leather, while the uppers are canvas.* —*tr.v.* **whiled, whiling, whiles.** To spend (time) idly or pleasantly. Usually used with *away: "At ease/in light frocks they walk the streets/to while the time away"* (William Carlos Williams). [Middle English *while, qwile,* Old English *hwīl.* See **kweye-** in Appendix.*]
Usage: *While* (conjunction) is employed most precisely with reference to time. In its other senses, the term is less well established, though it is widely used and acceptable to many, especially in contexts that do not involve ambiguity. In the sense of *although,* it is acceptably used in the following sentence, as an example in writing, according to 68 per cent of the Usage Panel: *While we hate force, we recognize the need for law and order.* In the sense of *whereas* or *but,* implying contrast or opposition, *while* is acceptably used in the following, again as an example in writing, according to 59 per cent: *The colonists imported their weapons, while the Indians produced their own. While* is least justifiably used when it is intended to have only the sense and force of *and: John is English, his wife is French, while his business associate is German* (accepted by only 37 per cent). Sometimes, when *while* is used as a substitute for *whereas* or *but,* the sense related to time is suggested inadvertently, as in the last example cited or in the example: *He spent his youth in Ohio, while his father grew up in England.* In such sentences, a semicolon is often a desirable substitute for *while.* The unintentional suggestion of time can also produce ambiguity in sentences in which *while* is intended to mean *although,* and in which *although* would be clearer: *While he had several hunting rifles, he believed strongly in control of firearms.*
whiles (hwīlz) *conj. Obsolete.* While. [Middle English, adverbial genitive of WHILE.]
whi·lom (hwī′ləm) *adj.* Former; having once been: *She is the whilom Miss Smith.* —*adv. Archaic.* Formerly. [Middle English *whilom,* Old English *hwīlum.* See **kweye-** in Appendix.*]
whilst (hwīlst) *conj. Chiefly British.* While: *"There was a dead silence in the court, whilst the White Rabbit read out these verses"* (Lewis Carroll). [Middle English *whylst,* from WHILES.]
whim (hwĭm) *n.* **1.** A sudden or capricious idea; a passing fancy. **2.** Arbitrary thought or impulse: *governed by whim.* **3.** *Mining.* A vertical horse-powered drum used as a hoist. —See Synonyms at **caprice.** [Short for earlier *whim-wham*†.]
whim·brel (hwĭm′brəl) *n.* A grayish-brown wading bird, *Numenius phaeopus,* having long legs and a long, downward-curving bill. [Imitative of its cry.]
whim·per (hwĭm′pər) *v.* **-pered, -pering, -pers.** —*intr.* **1.** To cry or sob with soft intermittent sounds; to whine. **2.** To complain. —*tr.* To utter in a whimper. —See Synonyms at **cry.** —*n.* A low, broken, whining sound; a whine. [Dialectal *whimp* (imitative).] —**whim′per·er** *n.* —**whim′per·ing·ly** *adv.*
whim·si·cal (hwĭm′zĭ-kəl) *adj.* **1.** Capricious; playful; arbitrary: *"Ichabod became the object of whimsical persecution to Bones and his gang of rough riders"* (Washington Irving). **2.** Unusual; fantastic; odd. [From WHIMSY.] —**whim′si·cal·ly** *adv.*
whim·si·cal·i·ty (hwĭm′zĭ-kăl′ə-tē) *n., pl.* **-ties.** **1.** The state of being whimsical. **2.** A whimsical idea or its expression; caprice.
whim·sy (hwĭm′zē) *n., pl.* **-sies.** Also **whim·sey** *pl.* **-seys.** **1.** An odd or capricious idea; idle fancy. **2.** Anything quaint, fanciful, or odd. —See Synonyms at **caprice.** [Probably from WHIM.]
whin[1] (hwĭn) *n.* A spiny shrub, **gorse** *(see).* [Middle English *whynne*†.]
whin[2] (hwĭn) *n.* **Whinstone** *(see).* [Middle English *quin*†.]
whin·chat (hwĭn′chăt′) *n.* A brownish Old World bird, *Saxicola rubetra,* frequenting open country. [From WHIN (gorse) (the bird is often found around gorse bushes).]
whine (hwīn) *v.* **whined, whining, whines.** —*intr.* **1.** To utter a plaintive, high-pitched, protracted sound, as in pain, fear, supplication, or complaint. **2.** To complain or protest in a childish, annoying fashion. **3.** To produce a sustained noise of relatively high pitch. Used of a machine. —*tr.* To utter with a whine.

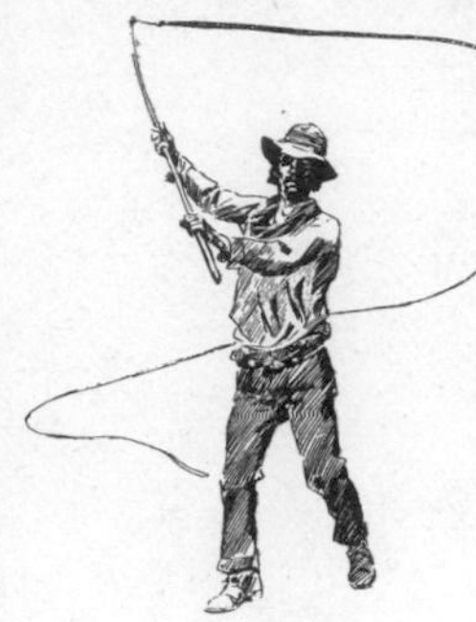

whip
Drawing by
Charles M. Russell

—*n.* 1. A whining sound. 2. The act of whining. 3. A complaint uttered in a plaintive tone. [Middle English *whinen*, Old English *hwīnan*. See **kwei-**⁴ in Appendix.*] —**whin'er** *n.* —**whin'ing·ly** *adv.* —**whin'y** *adj.*

whin·ny (hwĭn'ē) *v.* **-nied, -nying, -nies.** —*intr.* To neigh, as a horse, especially in a gentle tone. —*tr.* To express in a whinny. —*n., pl.* **whinnies.** The sound made in whinnying; a neigh. [Probably from WHINE.]

whin·stone (hwĭn'stōn') *n.* Any of various hard, dark-colored rocks, especially basalt and chert. Also called "whin."

whip (hwĭp) *v.* **whipped** or **whipt, whipping, whips.** —*tr.* 1. To strike with repeated strokes, as of a strap or rod; lash; beat. 2. a. To punish or chastise in this manner; flog; thrash. b. To afflict, castigate, or reprove severely: *"For nonconformity the world whips you with its displeasure"* (Emerson). 3. To drive, force, or compel by flogging, lashing, or other means of coercion. Usually used with *on, up,* or *in.* 4. To strike or effect in a manner similar to whipping or lashing: *Icy winds whipped his face.* 5. To beat (cream or eggs, for example) into a froth or foam. 6. To move or remove in a sudden, rapid manner. Usually used with *away, out,* or *off: He whipped off his cap.* 7. To sew with a loose overcast or overhand stitch. 8. To wrap or bind (a rope, for example) with twine to prevent unraveling or fraying. 9. *Nautical.* To hoist by means of a rope passing through an overhead pulley. 10. *Informal.* To defeat; outdo; beat: *Our team can whip your team.* —*intr.* 1. To move in a sudden, quick manner; to dart. 2. To move in a manner similar to a whip; thrash or snap about: *Branches whipped against the windows.* —*n.* 1. An instrument, either a flexible rod or a flexible thong or lash attached to a handle, used for driving animals or administering corporal punishment. 2. A whipping or lashing motion or stroke; whiplash. 3. A blow, wound, or cut made by or as by whipping. 4. Anything similar to a whip in form or flexibility, as an automobile radio antenna. 5. Flexibility, as in the shaft of a golf club. 6. A **whipper-in** *(see).* 7. *Politics.* a. A member of a legislative body, such as the U.S. Congress or the British Parliament, charged by his party with enforcing party discipline and insuring attendance. Also formerly called "whipper-in." b. A call issued to party members in a lawmaking body to insure attendance at a particular time. 8. A dish made of sugar and stiffly beaten egg whites or cream, often with fruit or fruit flavoring: *prune whip.* 9. A windmill arm. 10. *Nautical.* A hoist consisting of a single rope passing through an overhead pulley. 11. A ride in an amusement park, consisting of small cars that move in a rapid, whipping motion. —**whip in.** To keep together, as members of a political party or hounds in a pack. —**whip up.** 1. To arouse; excite: *whip up a crowd; whip up enthusiasm.* 2. *Informal.* To prepare quickly, as a meal. [Middle English *wippen,* perhaps from Middle Low German or Middle Dutch, to vacillate, swing. See **weip-** in Appendix.*] —**whip'per** *n.*

whip·cord (hwĭp'kôrd') *n.* 1. A worsted fabric with a distinct diagonal rib. 2. A strong twisted or braided cord sometimes used in making whiplashes. 3. Catgut.

whip hand. 1. The hand in which a driver holds his whip. 2. A dominating position; advantage.

whip·lash (hwĭp'lăsh') *n.* 1. The lash of a whip. 2. An injury to the cervical spine caused by an abrupt jerking motion of the head, either backward or forward. —**whip'lash'** *adj.*

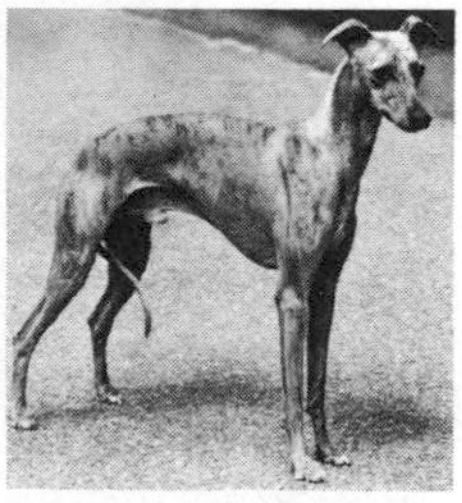

whippet

whip·per-in (hwĭp'ər-ĭn') *n., pl.* **whippers-in.** 1. In foxhunting, one who assists the huntsman in handling a pack of hounds. Also called "whip." 2. *Politics.* Formerly, a **whip** *(see).*

whip·per·snap·per (hwĭp'ər-snăp'ər) *n.* An insignificant and pretentious person. [Variant of *snippersnapper*†.]

whip·pet (hwĭp'ĭt) *n.* A short-haired, swift-running dog of a breed developed in England, resembling the greyhound but smaller. [Origin uncertain.]

whip·ping (hwĭp'ĭng) *n.* 1. The act of one that whips. 2. A thrashing administered especially as punishment. 3. Material, as cord or thread, used to lash or bind parts.

whipping boy. 1. A scapegoat. 2. A boy formerly raised with a prince or other young nobleman and whipped for the latter's misdeeds.

Whip·ple (hwĭp'əl), **George Hoyt.** Born 1878. American pathologist; studied anemia.

whip·ple·tree (hwĭp'əl-trē) *n.* A **whiffletree** *(see).*

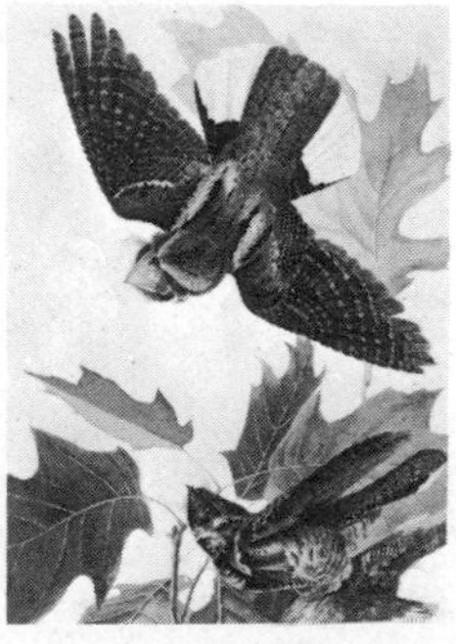

whippoorwill
Painting by
John James Audubon

whip·poor·will (hwĭp'ər-wĭl', hwĭp'ər-wĭl') *n.* Also **whip-poorwill.** A brownish nocturnal North American bird, *Caprimulgus vociferus,* having a distinctive call of which its name is imitative.

whip·saw (hwĭp'sô') *n.* A narrow two-man crosscut saw. —*tr.v.* **whipsawed** or **-sawn** (-sôn'), **-sawing, -saws.** 1. To cut with a whipsaw. 2. To win two bets from (a person) at one time, as in faro. 3. To defeat or best in two ways at once.

whip scorpion. Any of various nonvenomous scorpionlike arachnids of the order Pedipalpi, such as the vinegarroon.

whip snake. 1. Any of several slender nonvenomous snakes of the genus *Masticophis,* of the New World. 2. Any of several similar or related snakes.

whip·stall (hwĭp'stôl') *n.* A usually intentional stall in which a small aircraft enters a vertical climb, pauses, slips backward momentarily, then drops nose downward.

whip·stitch (hwĭp'stĭch') *tr.v.* **-stitched, -stitching, -stitches.** To sew with overcast stitches, as in finishing a fabric edge or binding two pieces of fabric together. —*n.* A stitch or stitches made in this manner.

whip·stock (hwĭp'stŏk') *n.* The handle of a whip.

whipt. Alternate past tense and past participle of **whip.**

whip·tail (hwĭp'tāl') *n.* Any of various New World lizards of the genus *Cnemidophorus,* having a long, slender tail.

whip·worm (hwĭp'wûrm') *n.* A slender, whiplike parasitic roundworm, *Trichuris trichiura,* that infests the large intestine in man.

whir (hwûr) *v.* **whirred, whirring, whirs.** Also *chiefly British* **whirr.** —*intr.* To move so as to produce a vibrating or buzzing sound, as might the wings of certain birds or a dynamo. —*tr.* To cause to make a vibratory sound. —*n.* 1. A sound of buzzing or vibration. 2. A bustle; a hurry. [Middle English *whirren,* from Scandinavian, akin to Danish *hvirre.* See **kwerp-** in Appendix.*]

whirl (hwûrl) *v.* **whirled, whirling, whirls.** —*intr.* 1. To revolve rapidly about a center or axis. 2. To rotate or spin rapidly. 3. To turn aside or away rapidly; to wheel. 4. To have the sensation of spinning; to reel. 5. To move or drive rapidly. —*tr.* 1. To cause to rotate or turn rapidly. 2. To move or drive in a circular or curving course. 3. To drive at high speed. 4. *Obsolete.* To hurl. —See Synonyms at **turn.** —*n.* 1. The act of rotating or revolving rapidly. 2. Something that whirls or is whirled, as a cloud of dust. 3. A state of confusion; tumult; turmoil. 4. A swift succession or round of events: *the social whirl.* 5. A state of mental confusion or giddiness; dizziness: *My head is in a whirl.* 6. *Informal.* A short trip. 7. *Informal.* A brief try. Usually used in the phrase *give it a whirl.* [Middle English *whirlen,* from Old Norse *hvirfla.* See **kwerp-** in Appendix.*] —**whirl'er** *n.*

whirl·a·bout (hwûrl'ə-bout') *n.* 1. The act of whirling around. 2. Anything that turns or whirls around; a whirligig.

whirl·i·gig (hwûr'lĭ-gĭg') *n.* 1. Any of various spinning toys. 2. A carousel or merry-go-round. 3. Something that continuously whirls. 4. The whirligig beetle. [Middle English *whirlegigge* : *whirlen,* WHIRL + *gigg(e),* GIG (coach).]

whirligig beetle. Any of various beetles of the family Gyrinidae that circle about rapidly on the surface of quiet water.

whirl·pool (hwûrl'po͞ol') *n.* 1. Water in rapid rotating movement, as from the converging of two tides; an eddy or vortex. 2. Anything suggesting the rapid motion of whirling water.

whirl·wind (hwûrl'wĭnd') *n.* 1. A column of air centered on an area of low atmospheric pressure, rotating violently around a more or less vertical axis and moving forward; a tornado. 2. A small, momentary current of such whirling air over dusty flat land; a dust devil. 3. Anything moving forward or whirling with violence and force. —See Synonyms at **wind.** —*adj.* Hard-driving: *a whirlwind campaign.*

whirl·y·bird (hwûr'lē-bûrd') *n. Slang.* A helicopter. [From WHIRL + BIRD.]

whisk (hwĭsk) *v.* **whisked, whisking, whisks.** —*tr.* 1. To move or cause to move with quick light sweeping motions. Usually used with *away, off,* or *out.* 2. To whip (eggs or cream). —*intr.* To move lightly, nimbly, and rapidly. —*n.* 1. A quick light sweeping motion. 2. A small broom. 3. A small bunch, as of twigs or hair. 4. A kitchen utensil for whipping foodstuffs. [Middle English (Scottish) *quhisken,* from Scandinavian, akin to Swedish *viska*†.]

whisk·broom (hwĭsk'bro͞om', -bro͝om') *n.* A small short-handled broom used especially to brush clothes.

whisk·er (hwĭs'kər) *n.* 1. *Plural.* The unshaven hair on a man's face; the beard or any portion of the beard. 2. *Plural. Informal.* The moustache. 3. One hair from the beard. 4. One of the long stiff bristles or hairs growing near the mouth of certain animals. 5. *Informal.* A narrow margin; hairbreadth: *He lost by a whisker.* 6. Anything that whisks. 7. *Nautical.* One of two spars or booms projecting from the side of a bowsprit for spreading the jib or flying-jib guys. Also called "whisker boom." 8. *Chemistry.* Any of the extremely fine filamentary crystals that can be grown from supersaturated solutions of certain minerals and metals and that possess extraordinary shear strength and unusual electrical or surface properties. [From WHISK.] —**whisk'ered, whisk'er·y** *adj.*

whis·key (hwĭs'kē) *n., pl.* **-keys.** Also **whis·ky** *pl.* **-kies.** 1. An alcoholic liquor distilled from grain, such as corn, rye, or barley, and containing approximately 40 to 50 per cent ethyl alcohol by volume. 2. A drink of whiskey. —*adj.* Also **whis·ky.** Pertaining to, resembling, or made from whiskey. [Short for earlier *whiskybae,* variant of USQUEBAUGH.]

Usage: *Whiskey* is the usual American spelling, especially with reference to U.S. and Irish liquor. *Whisky* is the spelling used in *Scotch whisky* and *Canadian whisky.*

whiskey jack. The **Canada jay** *(see).* [From obsolete *whiskyjohn,* by folk etymology, from Cree *wiskačan(is),* "gray jay."]

whiskey sour. A cocktail made with whiskey, lemon juice, and sugar.

whis·per (hwĭs'pər) *n.* 1. Soft speech produced without full voice. 2. Something uttered in this manner. 3. A secretly or surreptitiously expressed belief, rumor, or hint. 4. A low rustling sound. —*v.* **whispered, -pering, -pers.** —*intr.* 1. To speak softly, without full voice. 2. To speak quietly, as by way of gossip, slander, or intrigue. 3. To make a soft rustling sound, as surf or leaves. —*tr.* 1. To utter very softly. 2. To say or tell privately or secretly. [Middle English *whisperen,* Old English *hwisprian.* See **kwei-**⁴ in Appendix.*] —**whis'per·er** *n.*

whist (hwĭst) *n.* A game of cards played with 52 cards by two teams of two players each. It is a forerunner of bridge. [Perhaps variant of WHISK, from the whisking up of the tricks.]

whis·tle (hwĭs'əl) *v.* **-tled, -tling, -tles.** —*intr.* 1. To produce a clear musical sound or series of sounds by forcing air through the teeth or through an aperture formed by pursing the lips. 2. To produce a clear, shrill, sharp musical sound or series of sounds by some other method, as by blowing on or through a device. 3. To produce a high-pitched sound when moving swiftly through the air: *"The whisky bottle whistled past the bartender's head, splattering in a mass of glass and gin"* (J.P. Donleavy). **4.** To emit a shrill, sharp, high-pitched cry, as some birds and animals. **5.** To summon by whistling. *—tr.* **1.** To produce by whistling: *whistle a tune.* **2.** To summon, signal, or direct by whistling. **3.** To cause to move with a whistling noise. *—n.* **1.** A device or instrument for making whistling sounds by means of the breath, air, or steam. **2.** A sound produced by such a device or by whistling through the lips. **3.** Any whistling sound, as of an animal or projectile. **4.** The act of whistling. **5.** A whistling sound used to summon or command. **6.** *Informal.* The mouth and throat. **—whistle in the dark.** To attempt to keep one's courage up. [Middle English *whist(e)len,* Old English *hwistlian.* See **kwei-**[4] in Appendix.*]

whis·tler (hwĭs′lər) *n.* **1.** One that whistles. **2.** A marmot, *Marmota caligata,* of the mountains of northwestern North America, having a grayish coat and a shrill, whistling cry. **3.** Any of various birds that produce a whistling sound. **4.** *Physics.* An electromagnetic wave of audio frequency produced by atmospheric disturbances such as lightning, having a characteristically decreasing frequency responsible for a whistling sound of descending pitch in detection equipment. **5.** A horse having a respiratory disease characterized by wheezing.

Whis·tler (hwĭs′lər), **James Abbott McNeill.** 1834–1903. American artist.

whistle stop. **1.** A town at which a train stops only if signaled. **2.** A brief appearance of a political candidate in a small town, traditionally on the observation platform of a train.

whis·tle-stop (hwĭs′əl-stŏp′) *intr.v.* **-stopped, -stopping, -stops.** To conduct a political campaign by making brief appearances or speeches in a series of small towns.

whistling swan. A North American swan, *Olor columbianus,* having a black beak marked with yellow at the base.

whit (hwĭt) *n.* A particle; least bit; iota. Usually used with a negative: *"And so mistake you not a whit, my Lord"* (Marlowe). [Variant of Middle English *wi(g)ht,* thing, creature, WIGHT.]

white (hwīt) *n. Abbr.* **wh.** **1.** An achromatic color of maximum lightness, the complement or antagonist of black, the other extreme of the neutral gray series. Although typically a response to maximum stimulation, white appears always to depend upon contrast. See **color.** **2.** The white or nearly white part of something, as: **a.** The albumen of an egg. **b.** The white part of an eyeball. **c.** A blank unprinted area, as of an advertisement. **3.** Something or somebody white or nearly white, as: **a.** *Plural.* White trousers or a white outfit of a special nature: *tennis whites.* **b.** A white wine. **c.** A white pigment: *titanium white.* **d.** A white breed of animal. **e.** A Caucasoid. **f.** *Usually plural.* Products of a white color, as flour, salt, and sugar. **4.** *Chess & Checkers.* **a.** The white or light-colored pieces. **b.** The player using these pieces. **5.** *Archery.* **a.** The outermost ring of a target. **b.** A hit in this ring. **6.** *Plural. Pathology.* Leukorrhea. **7.** In some European countries, a royalist or a counterrevolutionary. *—adj.* **whiter, whitest.** **1.** Being of the color white; devoid of hue, as new snow. **2.** Approaching this color, as: **a.** Pale; weakly colored; almost colorless: *white wine.* **b.** Pale gray; silvery and lustrous, as silver or tin or objects made of such metals. **c.** Hoary with age: *white hair.* **d.** Bloodless; blanched. **3.** Light or whitish in color or having light or whitish parts. Used with animal and plant names: *white whale; white clover.* **4. a.** Having the comparatively pale complexion typical of Caucasoids. **b.** Of, pertaining to, characteristic of, or dominated by Caucasians. **c.** *Slang.* Fair or generous; decent. Usually used ironically: *That was very white of you!* **5.** Not written or printed upon; blank. **6.** Unsullied; pure. **7.** Habited in white: *white nuns.* **8.** Accompanied by or mantled with snow: *a white Christmas.* **9. a.** Incandescent: *white heat.* **b.** Intensely heated; impassioned: *white with fury.* **10.** In some countries of Europe, reactionary or counterrevolutionary. **11.** *Chiefly British.* With milk added. Said of tea or coffee. *—tr.v.* **whited, whiting, whites.** **1.** *Printing.* To create or leave blank spaces in (printed or illustrated matter). Often used with *out: white out a line.* **2.** *Obsolete.* **a.** To whiten; whitewash. **b.** To blanch. [Middle English *white,* Old English *hwīt,* white, white of an egg. See **kweit-** in Appendix.*]

White (hwīt), **Stanford.** 1853–1906. American architect.

White (hwīt), **William Allen.** 1868–1944. American journalist.

white ant. A **termite** *(see).*

white·bait (hwīt′bāt′) *n.* **1.** The young of various fishes, such as the herring, considered a delicacy when fried. **2.** Any of various other small edible fishes.

white birch. Any of several birch trees having white bark, such as *Betula pendula,* of Europe, or the **paper birch** *(see).*

white blood cell. A **leukocyte** *(see).*

white book. An official publication of a national government. [So called because it was formerly bound in white.]

white bryony. A climbing European vine, *Bryonia dioica,* having lobed leaves, greenish-white flowers, and scarlet berries.

white·cap (hwīt′kăp′) *n.* A wave with a crest of foam.

white cedar. Any of several North American evergreen trees, chiefly of the genus *Chamaecyparis,* having light-colored wood.

white cloud. A small, brightly colored freshwater fish, *Tanichthys albonubes,* native to China and popular in home aquariums.

white clover. A common clover, *Trifolium repens,* native to Eurasia, having rounded white flower heads. Also called "Dutch clover."

white coal. Water regarded as a source of power.

white-col·lar (hwīt′kŏl′ər) *adj.* Of or pertaining to workers, salaried or professional, whose work usually does not involve manual labor and who are expected to dress with some degree of formality. Often regarded as designating a social class. Compare **blue-collar.**

white corpuscle. A **leukocyte** *(see).*

white crappie. See **crappie.**

white daisy. See **daisy.**

whited sepulcher. A hypocrite; an evil person who pretends to be holy or good. Matthew 23:27.

white elephant. **1.** A rare whitish or light-gray form of the Asian elephant, often regarded with special veneration in regions of southeastern Asia. **2. a.** A rare and expensive possession that is financially a burden to maintain. **b.** A thing or gift regarded with reservations; something dubious or limited in value: *"My friend Fred Perlès is just being given a sort of white elephant in the way of a lousy magazine"* (Henry Miller). **3.** An article, ornament, or household utensil no longer wanted by its owner. **4.** An endeavor or venture that proves to be a conspicuous failure.

white-eye (hwīt′ī′) *n.* Any of various small greenish birds of the genus *Zosterops,* of Africa, southern Asia, and the Pacific islands, having a narrow ring of white feathers around each eye.

white-faced (hwīt′fāst′) *adj.* **1.** Pale; pallid. **2.** Having a white patch extending from the muzzle to the forehead.

white feather. A sign of cowardice. **—show the white feather.** To act like a coward. [A gamecock with a white feather is regarded as a poor fighter.]

White·field (hwīt′fēld′, hwĭt′-), **George.** 1714–1770. English evangelist; founder of Calvinistic Methodism.

white·fish (hwīt′fĭsh′) *n., pl.* **whitefish** or **-fishes.** **1.** Any of various chiefly North American freshwater food fishes of the genus *Coregonus,* having a generally silvery color. **2.** Any of various similar or related fishes.

white flag. A white cloth or flag signaling surrender or truce.

white·fly (hwīt′flī′) *n., pl.* **-flies.** Any of various small whitish insects of the family Aleyrodidae, often injurious to plants.

white-foot·ed mouse (hwīt′fo͝ot′ĭd). The **deer mouse** *(see).*

white fox. The **arctic fox** *(see)* in its winter color phase.

White Friar. A **Carmelite** *(see).* [After the color of his habit.]

white frost. **Hoarfrost** *(see).*

white gasoline. Gasoline that contains no tetraethyl lead. Also called "white gas."

white gold. An alloy of gold and nickel, and sometimes palladium or zinc, having a platinumlike color.

White·hall (hwīt′hôl′). The British civil-service administration as distinct from the party government. [From *Whitehall,* a street in London where many departments of the government are located.]

White·head (hwīt′hĕd′), **Alfred North.** 1861–1947. British mathematician and philosopher.

white-head·ed (hwīt′hĕd′ĭd) *adj.* **1.** Having white hair or plumage on the head, as a bird or animal. **2. a.** White-haired, as from old age. **b.** Flaxen-haired. **3.** *Chiefly Irish.* Favorite; darling: *the white-headed boy.*

white heat. **1. a.** The temperature of a white-hot substance. **b.** The physical condition of a white-hot substance. **2.** A state of intense emotion or excitement.

white horse. A wave capped with foam; whitecap.

White·horse (hwīt′hôrs′). The capital of the Yukon Territory, Canada, on the Yukon River. Population, 5,000.

white-hot (hwīt′hŏt′) *adj.* So hot as to glow with a bright white light; broadly, hotter than red-hot.

White House, The. **1.** The executive mansion of the President of the United States in Washington, D.C. **2.** The supreme executive authority of the United States Government.

white iron pyrites. A mineral, **marcasite** *(see).*

white lead. A heavy white poisonous compound of basic lead carbonate, lead silicate, or lead sulfate, used in paint pigments. Also called "ceruse."

white leather. Also **whit·leath·er** (hwĭt′lĕth′ər). A specially treated leather that is white.

white lie. A diplomatic or well-intentioned untruth.

white magic. Magic or incantation that is practiced for good purposes or as a counter to evil.

white mahogany. A wood, **primavera** *(see).*

white man's burden. The gratuitously assumed duty of the Caucasoid race to govern the nonwhite peoples of the world. [From "The White Man's Burden" (1899), a poem by Rudyard Kipling.]

white matter. White brain and spinal-cord tissue, consisting mostly of myelinated nerve fibers. Compare **gray matter.**

white meat. Light-colored meat, especially of poultry.

white metal. Any of various whitish alloys containing high percentages of tin or lead, such as pewter.

white mica. A mineral, **muscovite** *(see).*

White Mountains. A range of the Appalachians in northern New Hampshire. Highest elevation, Mount Washington (6,288 feet).

white mulberry. A tree, *Morus alba,* native to China, having whitish or purplish fruit.

whit·en (hwīt′n) *v.* **-ened, -ening, -ens.** *—tr.* To make (something) white, especially by bleaching. *—intr.* To become white. **—whit′en·er** *n.*

white·ness (hwīt′nĭs) *n.* **1.** The condition or quality of being white. **2.** Paleness or pallor. **3.** Moral purity; innocence. **4.** A white substance or area.

White Nile. The section of the **Nile** *(see)* that flows north from Lake No, in Sudan, to the Blue Nile at Khartoum.

white noise. Acoustical or electrical noise in which the intensity is the same at all frequencies within a given band.

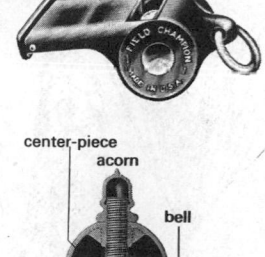

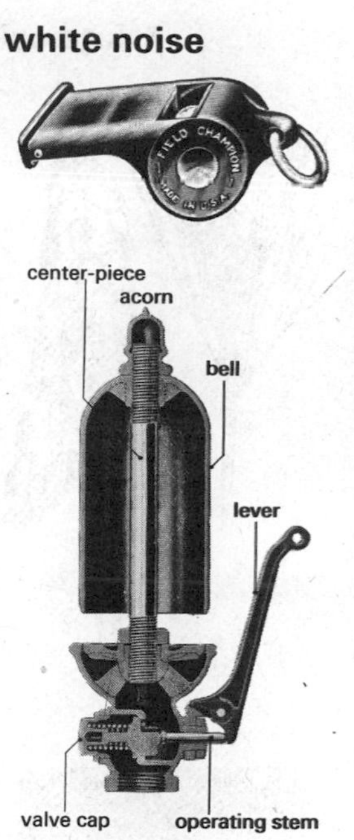
FIELD CHAMPION
center-piece
acorn
bell
lever
valve cap
operating stem
whistle
Above: Police whistle
Below: Steam whistle

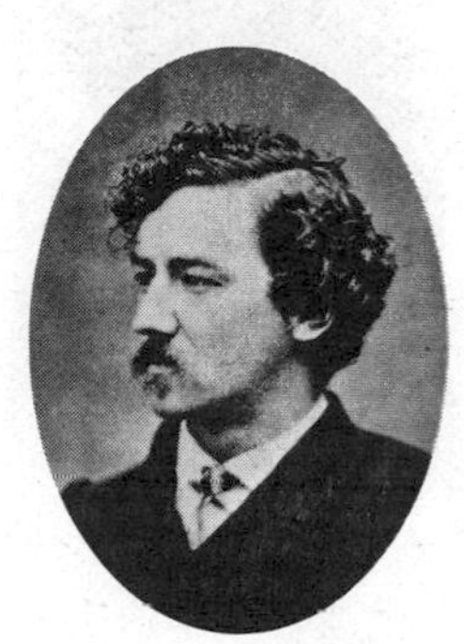
James Whistler

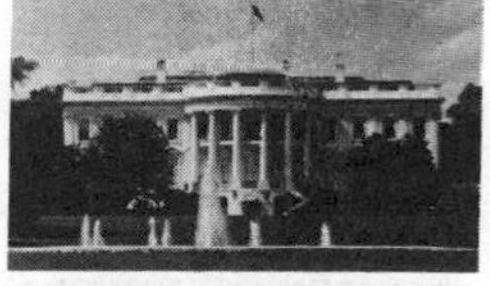
The White House
View from the south lawn

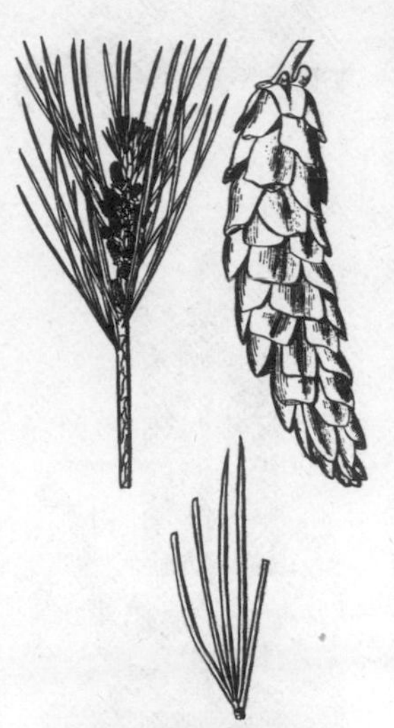

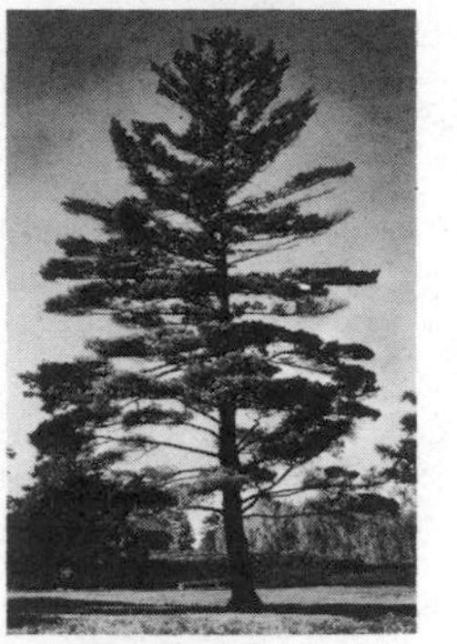

white pine
Pinus strobus
Above: Needles and cone

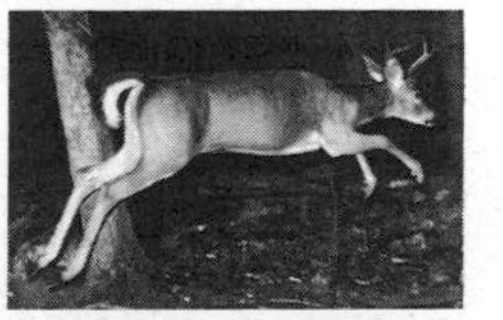

white-tailed deer

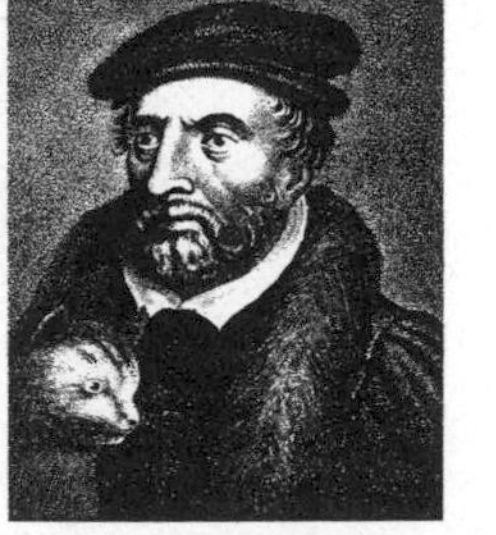

Richard Whittington

white oak. 1. A large oak, *Quercus alba,* of eastern North America, having heavy, hard, light-colored wood. 2. Any of various other oaks, such as the **roble** *(see).*
white·out (hwīt′out′) *n.* A polar weather condition caused by a heavy cloud cover over the snow, in which the light coming from above is approximately equal to the light reflected from below, and which is characterized by the absence of shadow, the invisibility of the horizon, and the discernibility of only very dark objects.
white paper. A paper published by a government to justify its position in some matter of international interest.
White Pass. A pass reaching an altitude of 2,888 feet through the Coast Mountains between southeastern Alaska and northwestern British Columbia, Canada.
white pepper. See **pepper.**
white perch. A small food fish, *Roccus americanus,* of the Atlantic coast and freshwater ponds of North America.
white pine. 1. A timber tree, *Pinus strobus,* of eastern North America, having needles in clusters of five and durable, easily worked wood. 2. Any of several other pines having needles in clusters of five. 3. The wood of any of these trees.
white plague. Tuberculosis of the lungs.
White Plains. A city of southeastern New York State, about 25 miles northeast of New York City; the site of the ratification of the Declaration of Independence (1776). Population, 50,000.
white poplar. A tree, *Populus alba,* native to Eurasia, having leaves with whitish undersides. Also called "abele."
white·print (hwīt′prĭnt′) *n.* A photomechanical copy, usually of line drawings, in which black or colored lines appear on a white background.
White River. 1. A river rising in northwestern Arkansas and flowing 690 miles first north into Missouri and then southeast through Arkansas to the Mississippi River. 2. A river rising in northwestern Nebraska and flowing 325 miles northeast and east through South Dakota to the Missouri River.
White Russia. See **Byelorussian S.S.R.**
White Russian. Byelorussian *(see).*
White Sands National Monument. An area of 219 square miles in south-central New Mexico, containing the world's largest surface gypsum deposit and lying south of the White Sands Proving Grounds, a missile-testing range and the site of the explosion of the first atomic bomb (1945).
white sauce. A sauce made with butter, flour, and milk, cream, or stock, used as a basis for other sauces.
White Sea. An inlet of the Barents Sea occupying 36,680 square miles in the extreme northwestern Soviet Union.
white slave. A woman held unwillingly for purposes of prostitution. —**white′-slave′** *adj.*
white slaver. A procurer of white slaves.
white slavery. Imposed prostitution.
white snakeroot. A poisonous North American plant, *Eupatorium rugosum,* having heart-shaped leaves and flat-topped clusters of small white flowers.
white squall. A sudden squall occurring in tropical or subtropical waters, characterized by the absence of a dark cloud and the presence of white-capped waves or broken water.
white-tailed deer (hwīt′tāld′). A North American deer, *Odocoileus virginianus,* having a grayish coat that turns reddish brown in summer and a tail that is white on the underside. Also called "whitetail," "Virginia deer."
white·throat (hwīt′thrōt′) *n.* Either of two Old World songbirds, *Sylvia communis* or *S. curruca,* having brownish plumage and a white throat.
white-throat·ed sparrow (hwīt′thrō′tĭd). A North American sparrow, *Zonotrichia albicollis,* having a white throat and a distinctive song. Also called "peabody bird."
white tie. 1. A white bow tie worn as a part of men's formal evening dress. 2. Men's formal evening dress.
white trash. *Southern U.S.* A poor white or poor whites as a class. Used contemptuously.
white vitriol. *Chemistry.* **Zinc sulfate** *(see).*
White Vol·ta (vŏl′tä). A river rising in northern Upper Volta and flowing 550 miles southward through Ghana, joining the Black Volta to form the Volta.
white-wall tire (hwīt′wôl′). A vehicular tire having a white band on the visible side. Often shortened to "whitewall."
white walnut. A tree, the **butternut** *(see).*
white·wash (hwīt′wŏsh′, -wôsh′) *n.* 1. A mixture of lime and water, often with whiting, size, or glue added, that is used to whiten walls, concrete, or the like. 2. A cosmetic application for whitening the skin. 3. A concealing or glossing over of flaws or failures. 4. *Informal.* A defeat in a game in which the loser scores no points. —*tr.v.* **whitewashed, -washing, -washes.** 1. To paint or coat with or as if with whitewash. 2. To gloss over (a flaw, for example). —**white′wash′er** *n.*
white water. Turbulent or frothy water, as in rapids.
white whale. A small whale, *Delphinapterus leucas,* chiefly of northern waters, that is white when full-grown. Also called "beluga."
white·wood (hwīt′wo͝od′) *n.* The soft, light-colored wood of any of various trees such as the tulip tree, basswood, or cottonwood.
whit·ey (hwī′tē) *n., pl.* **-eys.** 1. *Slang.* A blond man or boy. Used in familiar address. 2. a. The white man, especially the American white community. An offensive term used derogatorily. b. Used in contemptuous address to a white person.
whith·er (hwĭth′ər) *adv.* 1. To what place, result, or condition: *Whither are we wandering?* 2. To which specified place, position, or the like. Used relatively: *the shores whither the storm tossed them.* 3. To whatever place, result, or condition: *"whither thou goest, I will go"* (Ruth 1:16). [Middle English *whider, whither,* Old English *hwider.* See **kwo-** in Appendix.*]
whith·er·so·ev·er (hwĭth′ər-sō-ĕv′ər) *adv.* To whatever place; to any place whatsoever.
whit·ing¹ (hwī′tĭng) *n.* A pure white grade of chalk that has been ground and washed for use in paints, ink, and putty. [Middle English *whityng,* from *whiten,* to white, from WHITE.]
whit·ing² (hwī′tĭng) *n.* 1. A food fish, *Gadus merlangus,* of European Atlantic waters, related to the cod. 2. Any of several marine fishes of the genera *Menticirrhus* and *Merluccius,* of North American coastal waters. [Middle English *whitynge,* from Middle Dutch *wijting.* See **kweit-** in Appendix.*]
whit·ish (hwī′tĭsh) *adj.* Somewhat or almost white.
whit·leath·er. Variant of **white leather.**
whit·low (hwĭt′lō) *n. Pathology.* Any inflammation of the area of a finger or toe around the nail. [Middle English *whitflawe, whit(f)lowe* : WHITE + *flawe,* fissure, FLAW.]
Whit·man (hwĭt′mən), **Marcus.** 1802–1847. American Protestant missionary and pioneer in Oregon country.
Whit·man (hwĭt′mən), **Walt.** 1819–1892. American poet.
Whit·mon·day (hwĭt′mŭn′dē, -dā′) *n.* Also **Whit-Mon·day, Whit·sun-Mon·day** (hwĭt′sən-). The Monday following Whitsunday, observed in England as a holiday.
Whit·ney (hwĭt′nē), **Eli.** 1765–1825. American inventor of the cotton gin.
Whit·ney, Mount (hwĭt′nē). The highest elevation (14,495 feet) in the United States, excluding Alaska, in the Sierra Nevada of eastern California.
Whit·sun (hwĭt′sən) *adj.* Of, pertaining to, or observed on Whitsunday or at Whitsuntide. [Middle English *whitsone,* short for *whitsonday,* WHITSUNDAY.]
Whit·sun·day (hwĭt′sən-dē, -dā′) *n.* **Pentecost** *(see).* [Middle English *whitsonday,* Old English *hwīta sunnandæg,* "white Sunday" (from a tradition of clothing the newly baptized in white baptismal robes on Whitsunday).]
Whit·sun·tide (hwĭt′sən-tīd′) *n.* Also **Whit·sun Tide.** The week beginning with Whitsunday or Pentecost, especially the first three days of this week.
Whit·ti·er (hwĭt′ē-ər), **John Greenleaf.** 1807–1892. American poet; author of *Snow-Bound* (1886).
Whit·ting·ton (hwĭt′ĭng-tən), **Richard.** 1358?–1423. English merchant; three times lord mayor of London.
whit·tle (hwĭt′l) *v.* **-tled, -tling, -tles.** —*tr.* 1. To cut small bits or pare shavings from (a piece of wood). 2. To fashion or shape in this way. 3. To reduce or eliminate gradually by or as if by whittling with a knife. Usually used with *down, away,* or *off: He whittled down his expenditures by 60 dollars.* —*intr.* To whittle wood with a knife. [From Middle English *whyttel,* knife, variant of *thwitel,* from *thwiten,* to whittle down, Old English *thwītan.* See **twei-** in Appendix.*] —**whit′tler** *n.*
whit·tlings (hwĭt′lĭngz) *pl.n.* The chips and shavings from a piece of wood being whittled.
whiz (hwĭz) *v.* **whizzed, whizzing, whizzes.** Also **whizz.** —*intr.* 1. To make a whirring, buzzing, or hissing sound, as of something rushing through air. 2. To rush past. —*tr.* To cause to whiz: *The pitcher whizzed the ball to first.* —*n., pl.* **whizzes.** 1. The sound or passage of something that whizzes. 2. A quick trip. 3. *Slang.* One who has remarkable skill: *a whiz at tennis.* [Imitative.]
whizz-bang (hwĭz′băng′) *n.* A small-caliber high-speed shell of World War I that, fired in a flat trajectory, was heard only an instant before landing and exploding.
who (ho͞o) *pron.* The interrogative pronoun in the nominative case. 1. What or which person or persons: *Who left?* 2. That. Used as a relative pronoun to introduce a clause when the antecedent is a human: *The boy who came yesterday.* 3. The person or persons that; whoever. [Who, whose, whom; Middle English *who* or *qwa, whoos, whom(e),* Old English *hwā, hwæs, hwǣm.* See **kwo-** in Appendix.*]
Usage: *Who* and *whoever* are nominative forms employed when the pronoun in question functions as subject or as predicate after a form of the verb *be. Whom* and *whomever,* the corresponding objective forms, are used when the pronoun is an object of a verb or preposition or a subject of a complementary infinitive, as in *the boy whom I took to be your brother.* These grammatical distinctions in case are supported by a substantial majority of the Usage Panel with respect to formal usage, especially writing. With respect to spoken language, a smaller majority of the Panel recognizes that many persons consider *whom* less natural in speech than *who,* regardless of grammatical requirements. The first two of the following examples reflect this standard of judgment. In formal written usage, *whom,* as object of a verb, is the only acceptable choice in the first example, according to 87 per cent of the Panel: *Whom did you meet?* In speech, however, *who* is acceptable to 66 per cent. Especially when such an interrogative pronoun occurs in the first position in a sentence, *who* is the more common form in speech. When the pronoun comes directly after a preposition and thus serves as object, the grammatical form *whom* occurs both in speech and in writing. When the preposition and pronoun are separated by other words, however, *who* often occurs in speech: *He wants to know who he should speak to.* Here *who* is acceptable in speech to 59 per cent of the Panel, but *whom* is the only acceptable form in written usage, according to 92 per cent. In certain constructions involving a choice between *who* and *whom,* the pronoun is often misconstrued as the object of a verb when in fact it is the subject of a clause: *He interviewed a girl who he thinks will be excellent in the role.* Here *who* is the only

acceptable choice in written usage, according to 89 per cent, and the only acceptable form in speech to 83 per cent. The remaining examples illustrate typical uses of such pronouns in clauses: *Who shall I say is inquiring? We must offer it to whoever applies first. He has pledged to support whoever is nominated. Each candidate should support whomever the convention chooses.* —See also Usage notes at **than, that** (relative pronoun).

WHO World Health Organization.

whoa (hwō) *interj.* Used in commanding a horse to stop. [Middle English *whoo,* variant of HO! (halt).]

who·dun·it (hōō-dŭn′ĭt) *n. Informal.* A mystery story. [WHO + DONE + IT.]

who·ev·er (hōō-ĕv′ər) *pron.* An interrogative pronoun in the nominative case. **1.** Anyone that; any person who. **2.** No matter who; no matter what person. **3.** What person ever; who.

whole (hōl) *adj.* **1.** Containing all component parts; complete: *a whole formal wardrobe.* **2.** Not divided or disjoined; in one unit: *a whole acre.* **3. a.** Sound; healthy: *a whole organism.* **b.** Restored; healed. **4.** Constituting the full amount, extent, or duration: *He cried the whole trip home.* **5.** Having the same parents: *a whole sister.* **6.** *Mathematics.* Integral; not fractional. —*n.* **1.** All of the component parts or elements of a thing. **2.** A complete entity or system. —**as a whole.** Altogether; all things considered. —**on the whole.** Considering everything; in general; as a rule. [Middle English *hool, (w)holle,* sound, unharmed, Old English *hāl.* See **kailo-** in Appendix.*]

whole blood. 1. Blood drawn directly from a living human being and prepared for use in transfusion. **2.** Loosely, blood from which no constituent has been removed.

whole gale. A wind with a speed from 55 to 63 miles per hour.

whole·heart·ed (hōl′här′tĭd) *adj.* Undertaken with sincerity and energy. See Synonyms at **sincere.** —**whole′heart′ed·ly** *adv.* —**whole′heart′ed·ness** *n.*

whole hog. *Slang.* The whole way or the fullest extent.

whole life insurance. A type of insurance that provides death protection for the insured's entire lifetime.

whole milk. Milk from which no constituent has been removed.

whole·ness (hōl′nĭs) *n.* The state or quality of being whole.

whole note. *Music.* A note having, in common time, the value of four beats.

whole number. An integer.

whole·sale (hōl′sāl′) *n. Abbr.* **whsle.** The sale of goods in large quantities, as for resale by a retailer. —*adj.* **1.** Pertaining to or engaged in the sale of goods at wholesale. **2.** Sold in large bulk or quantity, usually at a lower cost. **3.** Made or accomplished extensively and indiscriminately; blanket: *the wholesale elimination of life by nuclear weapons.* —*adv.* **1.** In large bulk or quantity; on wholesale terms. **2.** Extensively and indiscriminately. —*v.* **wholesaled, -saling, -sales.** —*tr.* To sell at wholesale. —*intr.* **1.** To engage in wholesale selling. **2.** To be sold wholesale. [From the phrase *by (the) whole sale.*] —**whole′sal′er** *n.*

whole·some (hōl′səm) *adj.* **1.** Conducive to sound health or well-being; salutary. **2.** Morally or socially salubrious. **3.** Healthy. —See Synonyms at **healthy.** [Middle English *holsom,* Old English *hālsum* (unattested). See **kailo-** in Appendix.*] —**whole′some·ly** *adv.* —**whole′some·ness** *n.*

whole-wheat (hōl′hwēt′) *adj.* **1.** Made from the entire grain of wheat, including the bran: *whole-wheat flour.* **2.** Made with whole-wheat flour, as bread.

who'll (hōōl). Contraction of *who will* or *who shall.*

whol·ly (hō′lē, hōl′lē) *adv.* **1.** Entirely: *"The old American purposes are still wholly relevant"* (John F. Kennedy). **2.** Exclusively.

whom. The objective case of **who.** See Usage notes at **than, who, that.**

whom·ev·er. The objective case of **whoever.**

whom·so·ev·er. The objective case of **whosoever.**

whoop (hōōp, hwōōp) *n.* **1. a.** A cry of exultation or excitement. **b.** A battle cry or hunter's halloo. **2.** A hooting cry, as of a bird. **3.** The paroxysmal gasp characteristic of whooping cough. —*v.* **whooped, whooping, whoops.** —*intr.* **1.** To utter a loud shout or cry. **2.** To utter a hooting cry. **3.** To make the paroxysmal gasp characteristic of whooping cough. —*tr.* **1.** To utter with a whoop. **2.** To chase, call, urge on, or drive with a whoop or whoops: *whooping the horses on down the road.* —**whoop it up.** *Slang.* **1.** To have a jolly time. **2.** To arouse interest or enthusiasm. [Middle English *whope* (interjection); imitative.]

whoop·ee (hwōō′pē, hwōō′pē) *interj. Slang.* Used to express jubilance. —**make whoopee. 1.** To celebrate noisily. **2.** To make love. [From WHOOP.]

whoop·er (hōō′pər, hwōō′-) *n.* **1.** One that whoops. **2.** An Old World swan, *Cygnus cygnus* (or *Olor cygnus*), having a loud cry. Also called "whooper swan."

whoop·ing cough (hōō′pĭng, hōōp′ĭng). An infectious disease involving catarrh of the respiratory passages and characterized by spasms of coughing interspersed with deep, noisy inspiration. Also called "pertussis," "chincough."

whooping crane. A large, long-legged North American bird, *Grus americana,* now very rare, having black and white plumage and a shrill, trumpeting cry.

whoops (hwōōps, hwōōps) *interj.* Used to express mild surprise or apology. [From WHOOP.]

whoosh (hwōōsh, hwōōsh) *intr.v.* **whooshed, whooshing, whooshes. 1.** To hurtle or gush rapidly. **2.** To make a gushing or rushing sound. —*n.* A whooshing sound. [Imitative.]

whop (hwŏp) *tr.v.* **whopped, whopping, whops.** To thrash; defeat. —*n.* A sharp thud. —*adv.* With a sudden thud. [Middle English *whappen,* variant of *wappen* (perhaps imitative).]

whop·per (hwŏp′ər) *n.* **1.** Something exceptionally big or remarkable. **2.** A gross untruth.

whop·ping (hwŏp′ĭng) *adj.* Exceptionally big or remarkable. —*adv.* Thoroughly; resoundingly: *a whopping good joke.*

whore (hôr, hōr) *n.* A prostitute. —*intr.v.* **whored, whoring, whores. 1.** To have sexual intercourse or consort with whores. **2.** To be or act as a whore. [Middle English *ho(o)re,* Old English *hōre.* See **kā-** in Appendix.*]

whore·dom (hôr′dəm, hōr′-) *n.* **1.** Fornication; harlotry. **2.** In Biblical use, idolatry. [Middle English *hordom,* from Old Norse *hōrdōmr.* See **kā-** in Appendix.*]

whore·house (hôr′hous′, hōr′-) *n.* A brothel.

whore·mas·ter (hôr′măs′tər, -mäs′tər, hōr′-) *n.* One who consorts with whores; a fornicator.

whore·mong·er (hôr′mŭng′gər, -mŏng′gər, hōr′-) *n.* A fornicator.

whore·son (hôr′sən, hōr′-). *n. Archaic.* A bastard. Used as a term of abuse. —*adj. Archaic.* Abominable; bastardly.

whor·ish (hôr′ĭsh, hōr′-) *adj.* Characteristic of a whore; lewd. —**whor′ish·ly** *adv.* —**whor′ish·ness** *n.*

whorl (hwôrl, hwûrl) *n.* **1.** A small flywheel that regulates the speed of a spinning wheel. **2.** *Botany.* An arrangement of three or more parts, as leaves or petals, radiating from a single organ or node. **3.** *Zoology.* A single turn or volution of a spiral shell. **4.** One of the circular ridges or convolutions of a fingerprint. **5.** *Architecture.* An ornamental device consisting of stylized vine leaves and tendrils. **6.** A coil, curl, or convolution: *"their hair curled into wild whorls and peaks"* (Ray Bradbury). [Middle English *whorle,* perhaps variant of *whirle,* a whirl, from *whirlen,* to WHIRL.]

whorled (hwôrld, hwurld) *adj.* **1.** Having or forming a whorl or whorls. **2.** Having convolutions, as of vine leaves: *"halls, giddy with plush and whorled designs in gold."* (Djuna Barnes).

whort (hwûrt) *n.* Also **whor·tle** (hwûrt′l). The whortleberry or its fruit. [Variant of dialectal *hurt*†.]

whor·tle·ber·ry (hwûrt′l-bĕr′ē) *n., pl.* **-ries. 1.** A small European shrub, *Vaccinium myrtillus,* having edible blackish berries. **2.** The fruit of this shrub. Also called "bilberry." [Variant of dialectal *hurtleberry* : *hurt,* WHORT + BERRY.]

whose (hōōz). The possessive form of the interrogative pronoun *who* and, less commonly, *which.* [Middle English *whos, whas, hwas,* Old English *hwæs.* See **kwo-** in Appendix.*]

Usage: *Whose,* as the possessive form of a relative pronoun, can refer to both persons and things. Thus it functions as the possessive of both *who* and *which.* The following example, in which *whose* refers to an inanimate object, is acceptable on all levels to 74 per cent of the Usage Panel: *The play, whose style is rigidly formal, is typical of the period.* The alternative possessive form *of which* is also possible in referring to things but is often cumbersome in application.

who·so (hōō′sō) *pron.* Who; whoever; whatever person.

who·so·ev·er (hōō′sō-ĕv′ər) *pron.* Whoever.

W-hr *Electricity.* watt-hour.

whs. warehouse.

whsle. wholesale.

why (hwī) *adv.* **1.** For what purpose, reason, or cause; with what intention, justification, or motive. **2.** The purpose, reason, or cause for which. **3.** For which; because of which. —*n., pl.* **whys. 1.** The cause or intention underlying a given action or situation. **2.** A difficult problem or question. —*interj.* Used to express indignation, surprise, or impatience. [Middle English *why,* Old English *hwȳ.* See **kwo-** in Appendix.*]

Usage: *Why* is redundant in *the reason why;* consequently the construction is frowned on despite the frequency of its occurrence. The following typical sentence is termed unacceptable in writing by 65 per cent of the Usage Panel: *The reason why he opposed the nomination is not clear.* Alternative phrasings include: *Why he opposed the nomination is not clear. His reason for opposing the nomination is not clear.*

whyd·ah (hwĭd′ə) *n.* Also **whid·ah.** Any of several African birds of the genus *Vidua,* the breeding plumage of the male being predominantly black with long tail feathers. Also called "widow bird." [Perhaps variant of WIDOW (BIRD).]

WI Wisconsin (with Zip Code).

w.i. when issued (financial stock).

W.I. West Indian; West Indies.

Wich·i·ta[1] (wĭch′ə-tô′) *n., pl.* **Wichita** or **-tas. 1.** A confederacy of Caddoan-speaking North American Indians, formerly living between the Arkansas River and central Texas. **2.** A member of this confederacy. **3.** The language of these Indians. [Perhaps ultimately from Caddo *Wic'ita.*]

Wich·i·ta[2] (wĭch′ə-tô). **1.** A city of Kansas, in the south on the Arkansas River. Population, 255,000. **2.** A river of Texas rising east of Lubbock and flowing 250 miles east to the Red River.

Wich·i·ta Falls (wĭch′ə-tô). A city of north-central Texas, on the Wichita River. Population, 102,000.

wick[1] (wĭk) *n.* **1.** A cord or strand of loosely woven, twisted or braided fibers, as on a candle or oil lamp, that draws up fuel to the flame by capillary action. **2.** Any similar device that conveys liquid by capillary action. [Middle English *wike,* Old English *wēoce,* akin to Middle Low German *wēke* and Old High German *wiohha*†.]

wick[2] (wĭk) *n. Obsolete.* A village or town. Now surviving only in place names such as Warwick. [Middle English *wik(e),* Old English *wīc,* from West Germanic *wīka* (unattested), from Latin *vīcus.* See **weik-**[1] in Appendix.*]

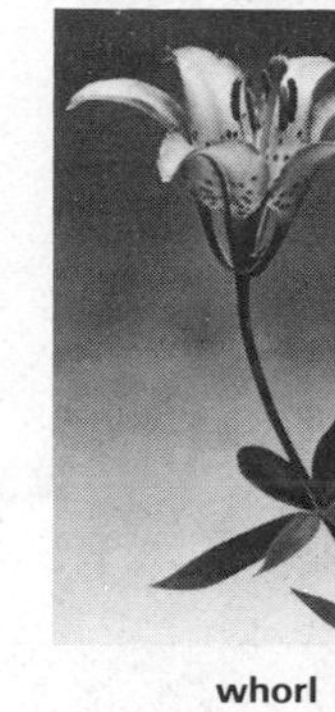

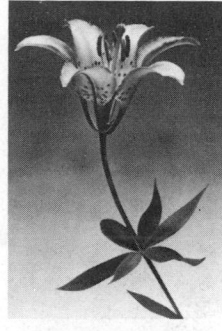

whorl
Whorled leaves and flower parts of *Lilium philadelphicum*

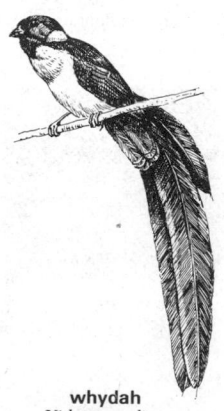

whydah
Vidua paradisea

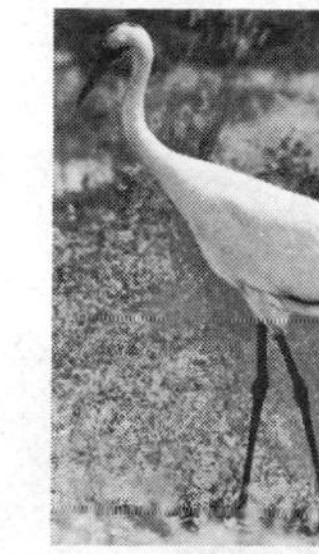

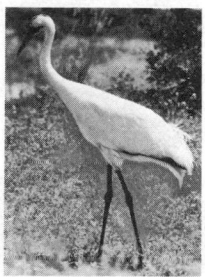

whooping crane

t tight/th thin, path/*th* this, bathe/ŭ cut/ûr urge/v valve/w with/y yes/z zebra, size/zh vision/ə about, item, edible, gallop, circus/ à *Fr.* ami/œ *Fr.* feu, *Ger.* schön/ü *Fr.* tu, *Ger.* über/KH *Ger.* ich, *Scot.* loch/N *Fr.* bon. *Follows main vocabulary. †Of obscure origin.

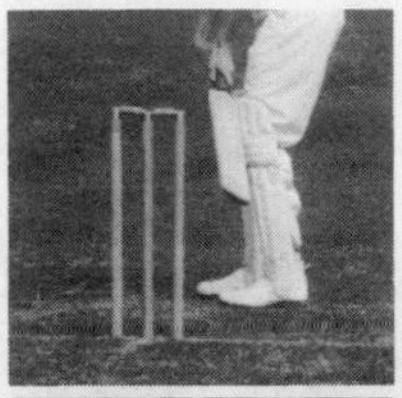

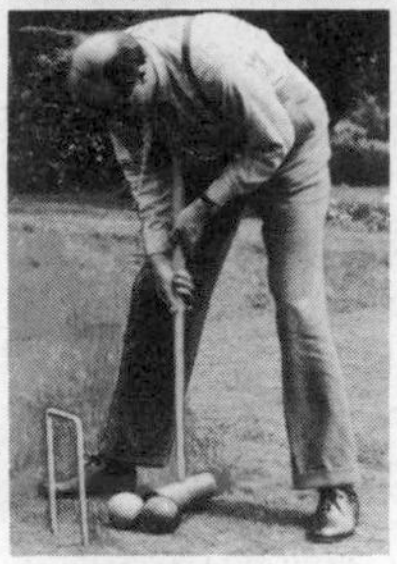

wicket
Above: Cricket wicket
Below: Croquet wicket

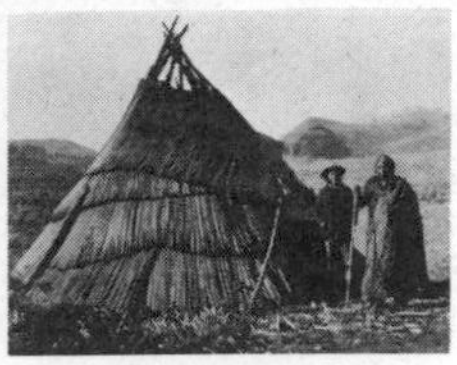

wickiup
Mat-covered Paiute wickiup

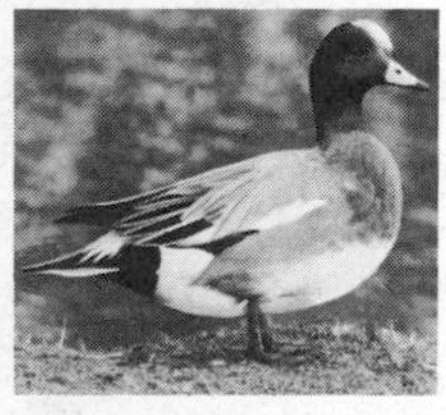

widgeon
Mareca penelope

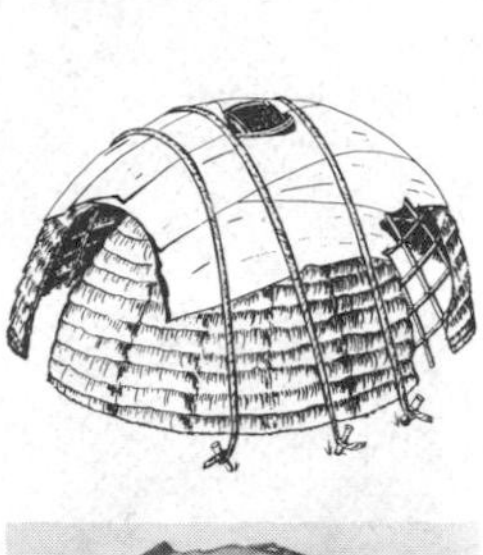

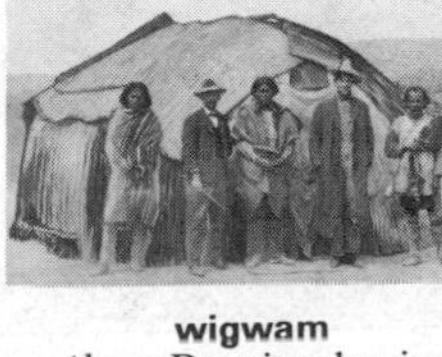

wigwam
Above: Drawing showing structural details

wick·ed (wĭk′ĭd) *adj.* **-eder, -edest. 1.** Vicious; depraved: *wicked habits.* **2.** Mischievous or playfully malicious: *a wicked joke.* **3.** Harmful; pernicious: *a wicked cough.* **4.** Obnoxious; offensive: *a wicked stench.* **5.** Formidable; excellent: *a wicked set of tennis.* —See Synonyms at **bad.** [Middle English, from *wicke,* wicked, Old English *wicca,* wizard. See **weik-**[2] in Appendix.*] **—wick′ed·ly** *adv.* **—wick′ed·ness** *n.*

wick·er (wĭk′ər) *n.* **1.** A flexible shoot, as of a willow, used in weaving baskets or certain articles of furniture. **2.** Wickerwork. —*adj.* Constructed, consisting of, or covered with wicker. [Middle English *wiker,* from Scandinavian, akin to Swedish *viker.* See **weik-**[4] in Appendix.*]

wick·er·work (wĭk′ər-wûrk′) *n.* Woven wicker.

wick·et (wĭk′ĭt) *n.* **1.** A small door or gate, especially one built into or near a larger one. **2.** A small window or opening, often fitted with glass or a grating. **3.** A sluice gate for regulating the amount of water in a millrace or a canal or for emptying a lock. **4.** *Cricket.* **a.** Either of the two sets of three stumps, topped by bails, that forms the target of the bowler and is defended by the batsman. **b.** A batsman's innings, which may be terminated by the ball knocking the bails off the stumps. **c.** The termination of a batsman's innings. **d.** The period during which two batsmen are in together. **e.** The pitch, especially with respect to wetness or other conditions. **5.** *Croquet.* Any of the small arches, usually made of wire, through which one tries to direct the ball. [Middle English, from Old North French *wiket,* from Germanic. See **weik-**[4] in Appendix.*]

wick·et·keep·er (wĭk′ĭt-kē′pər) *n. Cricket.* The player positioned immediately behind the wicket in play.

wick·i·up (wĭk′ē-ŭp′) *n.* Also **wik·i·up.** A frame hut covered with matting, bark, brush, or the like, used by the nomadic Indians of North America. [Fox *wikiyapi,* "house," from Proto-Algonquian *wikiwahmi* (unattested), WIGWAM.]

Wick·liffe, John. See **Wycliffe.**

Wick·low (wĭk′lō). A county of the Republic of Ireland, occupying 782 square miles in the east on the Irish Sea. Population, 51,000.

Wic·lif, John. See **Wycliffe.**

wic·o·py (wĭk′ə-pē) *n., pl.* **-pies.** Any of several North American trees, shrubs, or plants, especially the **leatherwood** *(see).* [Cree *wikopiy,* willow bark, from Proto-Algonquian *wikwepyi* (unattested), wicopy bark.]

wid·der·shins. Variant of **withershins.**

wide (wīd) *adj.* **wider, widest. 1.** Extending over a large area from side to side; broad. **2.** Having a specified extent from side to side; in width: *a ribbon two inches wide.* **3.** Having great range or scope: *a wide selection.* **4.** Full or ample, as clothing. **5.** Fully open or extended: *look with wide eyes.* **6.** Landing or located away from the desired goal or point: *wide of the mark.* **7.** Apart from the truth or pertinent issue: *"Tilley finds that Faulkner is just as wide of the legal facts"* (Cleanth Brooks). **8.** *Phonetics.* Lax. —See Usage note at **broad.** —*adv.* **1.** Over a large area; extensively: *journey far and wide.* **2.** To the full extent; completely: *the door was open wide.* **3.** So as to miss the target; astray. —*n. Cricket.* A ball bowled outside of the batsman's reach, counting as a run for the batting team. [Middle English *wide,* Old English *wīd.* See **wi-** in Appendix.*] **—wide′ly** *adv.* **—wide′ness** *n.*

wide-an·gle lens (wīd′ăng′gəl). A lens that has a relatively short focal length and permits an angle of view wider than approximately 70 degrees.

wide-a·wake (wīd′ə-wāk′) *adj.* **1.** Completely awake. **2.** Alert; watchful. —*n.* A soft felt hat with a wide brim.

wide-eyed (wīd′īd′) *adj.* **1.** With the eyes completely opened, as in wonder. **2.** Innocent; credulous.

wid·en (wīd′n) *v.* **-ened, -ening, -ens.** —*tr.* To make wider. —*intr.* To be or become wide or wider. **—wid′en·er** *n.*

wide-o·pen (wīd′ō′pən) *adj.* **1.** Opened completely: *a wide-open door.* **2.** Without laws or law enforcement: *a wide-open town.*

wide·spread (wīd′sprĕd′) *adj.* Also **wide-spread, wide-spreading** (-sprĕd′ĭng). **1.** Spread or scattered over a considerable extent. **2.** Occurring or accepted widely.

wid·geon (wĭj′ən) *n., pl.* **widgeon** or **-geons.** Also *British* **wigeon.** Either of two ducks, *Mareca americana,* of North America, or *M. penelope,* of Europe, having brownish plumage. The former species is also called "baldpate." [Origin uncertain.]

wid·ow (wĭd′ō) *n.* **1.** A woman whose husband has died and who has not remarried. **2.** *Card Games.* An additional hand dealt to the table. **3.** *Printing.* **a.** An incomplete line of type, as one ending a paragraph, carried over to the top of the next page or column. **b.** A short line at the bottom of a page or column. —*tr.v.* **widowed, -owing, -ows.** To make a widow of. Used chiefly in the past participle. [Middle English *wid(e)we,* Old English *widuwe.* See **weidh-** in Appendix.*]

widow bird. The **whydah** *(see).* [From its black plumage.]

wid·ow·er (wĭd′ō-ər) *n.* A man whose wife has died and who has not remarried. [Middle English *widewer,* from *widewe,* WIDOW.]

wid·ow·hood (wĭd′ō-hŏŏd′) *n.* The condition or period of being a widow.

widow's mite. A small contribution made by one who has little. [By allusion to Mark 12:42.]

widow's peak. A hairline having a V-shaped point at the middle of the forehead. Also called "peak." [From the superstition that it is a sign of early widowhood.]

widow's walk. A railed, rooftop gallery on a dwelling, designed to observe vessels at sea.

width (wĭdth, wĭth) *n. Abbr.* **w. 1.** The state, quality, or fact of being wide. **2.** The measurement of the extent of something from side to side; the size of something in terms of its wideness. **3.** Something that has a specified width; especially, in sewing, a piece of fabric measured from selvage to selvage: *a skirt having four widths.* [From WIDE.]

width·wise (wĭdth′wīz′, wĭth′-) *adv.* From side to side; in terms of width.

Wie·land (vē′länt′), **Christoph Martin.** 1733–1813. German poet and translator.

Wie·land (vē′länt′), **Heinrich.** 1877–1957. German chemist.

wield (wēld) *tr.v.* **wielded, wielding, wields. 1.** To handle (a weapon or tool, for example). **2.** To exercise or exert (power or influence). —See Synonyms at **handle.** [Middle English *welden,* Old English *wealdan* and *wieldan.* See **wal-** in Appendix.*] **—wield′a·ble** *adj.* **—wield′er** *n.*

wield·y (wēl′dē) *adj.* **-ier, -iest.** Easily wielded or managed.

Wien. The German name for **Vienna.**

Wien (vēn), **Wilhelm.** 1864–1928. German physicist; studied blackbody radiation.

wie·ner (wē′nər) *n.* A **wienerwurst** *(see).* [German, short for WIENERWURST.]

Wie·ner (wē′nər), **Norbert.** 1894–1964. American mathematician; developed cybernetics.

Wie·ner schnit·zel (vē′nər shnĭt′səl). A breaded veal cutlet. [German, "Vienna cutlet."]

wie·ner·wurst (wē′nər-wûrst′; *German* vē′nĕr-vŏŏrsht′) *n.* A type of smoked pork or beef sausage, similar to a frankfurter. Also called "wiener," and informally "weenie." [German, "Vienna sausage."]

Wies·ba·den (vēs′bäd′n). The capital of Hesse, West Germany, on the Rhine in the southwest. Population, 260,000.

wife (wīf) *n., pl.* **wives** (wīvz). *Abbr.* **w. 1.** A woman married to a man. **2.** *Archaic.* A woman. Now used chiefly in certain phrases: *old wives' tales.* **—take to wife.** To marry. [Middle English *wif(e),* Old English *wīf,* from Germanic *wīf* (unattested), woman.] **—wife′hood′, wife′dom** *n.* **—wife′ly** *adj.*

wig (wĭg) *n.* A headpiece of artificial or human hair worn as personal adornment, part of a costume, or to conceal baldness. —*tr.v.* **wigged, wigging, wigs.** *British Informal.* To scold or censure. [Shortened from PERIWIG.]

wig·an (wĭg′ən) *n.* A stiff fabric used for stiffening. [First made in *Wigan,* Lancashire, England.]

wi·geon. *British.* Variant of **widgeon.**

wigged (wĭgd) *adj.* Wearing a wig.

wig·ger·y (wĭg′ə-rē) *n., pl.* **-ies. 1.** A wig or wigs collectively. **2.** The practice of wearing wigs.

wig·gle (wĭg′əl) *v.* **-gled, -gling, -gles.** —*intr.* To move, twist, or proceed with short irregular motions from side to side. —*tr.* To cause to move in such a fashion: *wiggle one's toes.* —*n.* The act of wiggling; a wiggling movement or course. **—get a wiggle on.** *Slang.* To hurry or hurry up. [Middle English *wiglen,* from Middle Dutch or Middle Low German *wiggelen.* See **wegh-** in Appendix.*] **—wig′gly** *adj.*

wig·gler (wĭg′lər) *n.* **1.** One that wiggles. **2.** The larva or pupa of a mosquito.

wight[1] (wīt) *n. Archaic.* A human being; creature: *"What wailing wight/Calls the watchman of the night?"* (Blake). [Middle English *wight,* Old English *wiht.* See **wekti-** in Appendix.*]

wight[2] (wīt) *adj. Obsolete.* Valorous; brave. [Middle English *wiht,* from Old Norse *vīgt,* neuter of *vīgr,* able in battle. See **weik-**[5] in Appendix.*]

Wight, Isle of (wīt). An island of 147 square miles in the English Channel off south-central England, an administrative county of Hampshire. Population, 96,000. County seat, Newport.

Wig·ner (wĭg′nər), **Eugene Paul.** Born 1902. Hungarian-born American theoretical physicist.

Wig·town (wĭg′tən, ′-toun). **1.** Also **Wig·town·shire** (-shîr, -shər). A county occupying 487 square miles in southwestern Scotland. Population, 29,000. **2.** The county seat of this county. Population, 1,000.

wig·wag (wĭg′wăg′) *v.* **-wagged, -wagging, -wags.** —*tr.* **1.** To move back and forth, especially as a means of signaling. **2.** To signal by such motions. —*intr.* **1.** To move back and forth; to wag. **2.** To wave the hand or a device in signaling. —*n.* **1.** The act or practice of giving signals by wigwagging. **2.** A message so relayed. [Dialectal *wig,* perhaps from WIGGLE + WAG.] **—wig′wag′ger** *n.*

wig·wam (wĭg′wŏm′) *n.* **1.** A North American Indian dwelling, commonly having an arched or conical framework overlaid with bark, hides, or mats. Compare **tepee. 2.** *Informal.* A large building, often temporary, used for public gatherings or meetings. [Eastern Abnaki *wikəwam,* from Proto-Algonquian *wikiwahmi* (unattested), perhaps from root *wik-* (unattested), to dwell.]

wik·i·up. Variant of **wickiup.**

Wil·ber·force (wĭl′bər-fôrs′, -fōrs′) **William.** 1759–1833. English philanthropist and abolitionist.

wild (wīld) *adj.* **wilder, wildest. 1.** Occurring, growing, or living in a natural state; not domesticated, cultivated, or tamed. **2.** Not inhabited; desolate. **3.** Uncivilized or barbarous; savage. **4.** Lacking discipline, restraint, or control; unruly: *"Never did I hear/Of any prince so wild a libertine."* (Shakespeare). **5.** Disorderly; disarranged. **6.** Incoherent or chaotic; frenzied: *wild talk.* **7.** Full of intense, ungovernable emotion: *wild with jealousy.* **8. a.** Eccentric; notoriously odd or amusing: *a wild character.* **b.** Extravagant; fantastic: *a wild idea.* **9.** Furiously disturbed or turbulent; stormy. **10.** Reckless; risky. **11.** Random or spontaneous; whimsical: *make a wild guess.* **12.** Deviating widely; erratic: *a wild bullet.* **13.** *Card Games.* Having an arbitrary equivalence or value determined by the holder's needs or choice: *playing poker with deuces wild.* —*adv.* In a wild manner. —*n.* An uninhabited or uncultivated region. —**the wild.** A natural, unrestrained life or state; nature. [Middle English *wilde,* Old English *wilde.* See **wel-**[5] in Appendix.*] —**wild′ly** *adv.* —**wild′ness** *n.*

wild basil. See **basil.**

wild bergamot. An aromatic plant, *Monarda fistulosa,* of eastern North America, having clusters of lilac-purple flowers.

wild boar. See **boar.**

wild carrot. A plant; **Queen Anne's lace** *(see).*

wild·cat (wīld′kăt′) *n.* **1.** Any of various wild felines of small to medium size; especially, one of the genus *Lynx.* **2.** A quick-tempered or fierce person, especially a woman. **3.** An oil well drilled in an area not known to yield oil. —*adj.* **1.** Risky or unsound, especially financially. **2.** Accomplished or operating without official sanction or authority. —*v.* **wildcatted, -catting, -cats.** —*tr.* To prospect for (oil, for example) in an area supposed to be unproductive. —*intr.* To prospect in an untapped or questionable area.

wildcat strike. A strike unauthorized by a labor union.

wild·cat·ter (wīld′kăt′ər) *n.* **1.** A person engaged in mining or oil-drilling in untapped or doubtful areas. **2.** A promoter of speculative or fraudulent enterprises.

wild celery. A plant, the **tape grass** *(see).*

Wilde (wīld), **Oscar (Fingal O'Flahertie Wills).** 1854–1900. Irish poet, dramatist, and wit.

wil·de·beest (wĭl′də-bēst′, vĭl′-) *n.* A mammal, the **gnu** *(see).* [Obsolete Afrikaans : Dutch *wild,* wild, from Middle Dutch *wilt, wilde* (see **wel-**[5] in Appendix*) + *beest,* beast, from Middle Dutch *beeste,* from Old French *beste,* BEAST.]

wil·der (wĭl′dər) *v.* **-dered, -dering, -ders.** *Archaic.* —*tr.* **1.** To lead astray; mislead. **2.** To bewilder; confuse; perplex. —*intr.* **1.** To lose one's way. **2.** To become bewildered. [Perhaps a back-formation from WILDERNESS.] —**wil′der·ment** *n.*

Wil·der (wīl′dər), **Thornton (Niven).** Born 1897. American author of novels and plays.

wil·der·ness (wĭl′dər-nĭs) *n.* **1.** Any unsettled, uncultivated region left in its natural condition, especially: **a.** A large wild tract of land covered with dense vegetation or forests. **b.** An extensive area that is barren or empty, as a desert or ocean; a waste. **c.** A piece of land set aside to grow wild. **2.** Something likened to a wild region in bewildering vastness, perilousness, or unchecked profusion: *a wilderness of voices.* [Middle English *wildernesse,* Old English *wildēornes,* from *wildēor,* wild beast. See **wel-**[5] in Appendix.*]

Wil·der·ness, The (wĭl′dər-nĭs). A region in north-central Virginia; the site of a major Civil War battle in May 1864 between the armies of Grant and Lee.

wild-eyed (wīld′īd′) *adj.* Glaring in or as if in anger, terror, or madness.

wild·fire (wīld′fīr′) *n.* **1.** A highly flammable material formerly used in warfare. **2.** A raging fire that travels and spreads rapidly. **3.** Lightning occurring without thunder being heard. **4.** A luminosity that appears at night hovering over swamps or marshes; ignis fatuus.

wild·flow·er (wīld′flou′ər) *n.* Also **wild flower. 1.** A flowering plant that grows in a natural, uncultivated state. **2.** The flower of such a plant.

wild·fowl (wīld′foul′) *n., pl.* **wildfowl** or **-fowls.** A wild bird, such as a duck, goose, or quail, hunted as game.

wild geranium. A North American woodland plant, *Geranium maculatum,* having rose-purple flowers. Also called "spotted cranesbill" and sometimes "alumroot."

wild ginger. A North American plant, *Asarum canadense,* having broad leaves, a solitary brownish flower, and an aromatic root.

wild-goose chase (wīld′go͞os′). A hopeless pursuit of an unattainable or imaginary object. [Originally a race similar to the flight of geese, where the object was to follow accurately and at a definite interval.]

wild hyacinth. A plant, *Camassia scilloides,* of the central United States, having narrow leaves and a cluster of pale-blue or white flowers.

wild indigo. Any of several North American plants of the genus *Baptisia;* especially, *B. tinctoria,* having compound leaves with three leaflets and yellow flowers.

wild·ing (wīl′dĭng) *n.* **1.** A plant that grows wild or has escaped from cultivation; especially, a wild apple tree or its fruit. **2. a.** A wild animal. **b.** An untamed or unconventional person. —*adj.* **1.** Growing wild; not cultivated. **2.** Undomesticated; unrestrained. [From WILD.]

wild·life (wīld′līf′) *n.* Wild animals and vegetation; especially, animals living in a natural, undomesticated state.

wild lily of the valley. A woodland plant, *Maianthemum canadense,* of eastern North America, having a terminal cluster of small white flowers. Also called "Canada mayflower."

wild·ling (wīld′lĭng) *n.* A wild plant or animal; especially, a wild plant transplanted to a cultivated spot.

wild marjoram. See **marjoram.**

wild oat. 1. *Usually plural.* A grass, *Avena fatua,* native to Eurasia, related to the cultivated oat. **2.** *Plural.* The indiscretions of youth. Used in the phrase *sow one's wild oats.*

wild olive. Any of various trees resembling the olive.

wild pansy. Any of several pansylike plants of the genus *Viola;* especially, the **heartsease** *(see).*

wild pink. Any of several North American plants of the genus *Silene;* especially, *S. caroliniana,* having pink or white flowers.

wild pitch. *Baseball.* An erratic pitch that the catcher cannot be expected to catch and that enables a runner to advance. Compare **passed ball.**

wild rice. 1. A tall aquatic grass, *Zizania aquatica,* of northern North America, bearing edible grain. **2.** The grain of this plant.

wild rye. Any of various grasses of the genus *Elymus.*

wild type. The typical form of an organism as it occurs in nature, as distinguished from mutant specimens that may result from selective breeding.

wild vanilla. A plant, *Trilisa odoratissima,* of the southeastern United States, having vanilla-scented leaves.

Wild West. The western United States during the period of its settlement, especially with reference to its lawlessness.

wild·wood (wīld′wo͝od′) *n.* A forest or wooded area in its natural state.

wile (wīl) *n.* **1.** A deceitful stratagem or trick. **2.** A disarming or seductive manner, device, or procedure. **3.** Trickery; cunning; deceit. —See Synonyms at **artifice.** —*tr.v.* **wiled, wiling, wiles. 1.** To influence or lead by means of wiles; entice; lure. **2.** To pass (time) agreeably. Used with *away: wile away a Sunday afternoon.* [Middle English *wil,* perhaps from Old Norse *wihl-* (unattested). See **weik-**[2] in Appendix.*]

wil·ful. Variant of **willful.**

Wil·helm, Mount (vĭl′hĕlm). The highest peak (14,107 feet) of the Bismarck Mountains in northeastern New Guinea.

Wil·hel·mi·na (wĭl′hĕl-mē′nə). 1880–1962. Queen of the Netherlands (1890–1948); abdicated.

Wil·helms·ha·ven (vĭl′hĕlms-hä′fən). A city of West Germany, a port on the North Sea. Population, 101,000.

Wilkes (wĭlks), **Charles.** 1798–1877. American naval officer; explorer of Antarctica and Pacific Coast of North America.

Wilkes (wĭlks), **John.** 1727–1797. British political reformer.

Wilkes-Bar·re (wĭlks′băr′ē, -băr′ə). A city and industrial center in north-central Pennsylvania. Population, 64,000.

Wilkes Land (wĭlks). A section of Antarctica bordering on the Indian Ocean, south of Australia.

Wil·kins (wĭl′kĭnz), Sir **George Hubert.** 1888–1958. Australian aviator and explorer of the Arctic and Antarctic.

Wil·kins (wĭl′kĭnz), **Maurice Hugh Frederick.** Born 1916. British physicist; investigated the structure of DNA.

Wil·kins (wĭl′kĭnz), **Roy.** Born 1901. American social reformer; executive secretary of the NAACP (since 1955).

will[1] (wĭl) *n.* **1.** The mental faculty by which one deliberately chooses or decides upon a course of action; volition: *"Will is the sustaining, coercive, and ministerial power—the police officer* [in man]." (Emerson). **2.** An instance of the exercising of this faculty; a deliberate decision or conclusion; choice. **3.** Something desired or decided upon by a person of authority or supremacy. **4.** Deliberate intention or wish: *against his will.* **5.** Free discretion; pleasure; inclination: *wandered about at will.* **6.** Bearing or attitude toward others; disposition: *full of good will.* **7.** The power to arrive at one's own decision and to act upon it independently in spite of opposition. **8.** Determination; diligent purposefulness: *the will to win.* **9. a.** A legal declaration of how a person wishes his possessions to be disposed of after his death. **b.** The document containing this declaration. —*v.* **willed, willing, wills.** —*tr.* **1.** To decide upon; choose. **2.** To desire; yearn for: *"she makes you will your own destruction"* (G.B. Shaw). **3.** To decree; dictate; order. **4.** To resolve with a forceful will; determine. **5.** To influence or induce by sheer force of will or by supernatural power: *We willed the sun to come out.* **6.** To bequeath; grant in a legal will. —*intr.* **1.** To exercise the will; use the power of the will. **2.** To decree or make a firm choice. [Middle English *will(e),* Old English *will, willa.* See **wel-**[2] in Appendix.*]

will[2] (wĭl) *v.* past **would** (wo͝od) also *archaic* **wouldest** (wo͝od′ĭst) or **wouldst** (wo͝odst) for second person singular, present **will** (also *archaic* **wilt** (wĭlt) for second person singular). Used as an auxiliary followed by a simple infinitive or, in reply to a question or suggestion, with the infinitive understood. It can indicate: **1.** Simple futurity: *They will appear later.* **2.** Likelihood or certainty: *You will regret this.* **3.** Willingness: *Will you help me with this package?* **4.** Requirement or command: *You will report to me afterward.* **5.** Customary or habitual action: *She would spend hours in the kitchen.* **6.** Capacity or ability: *This metal will not crack under heavy pressure.* **7.** *Informal.* Probability or expectation: *That will be the postman ringing.* —See Usage note below. —*intr.* To have a desire: *Sit here, if you will.* —*tr.* To desire; wish: *Do what you will.* [Will, would, wouldest; Middle English *willen, wolde, woldest,* Old English *wyllan, wolde, woldest.* See **wel-**[2] in Appendix.*]

Usage: *Would have,* as an auxiliary verb form, is often misused for *had* in conditional clauses introduced by *if.* The following examples illustrate the proper forms: *He could have helped if he had wanted to* (not *if he would have wanted to*). *If she had listened, this would not have happened* (not *If she would have listened*). *Had* is also the auxiliary in clauses following *wish,* as in *I wish that we had known* (not *I wish that we would have known*). —See also Usage notes at **shall, should.**

Wil·lam·ette (wĭl-ăm′ĭt). A river of central Oregon flowing 190 miles north to the Columbia near Portland.

Wil·lard (wĭl′ərd), **Emma (Hart).** 1787–1870. American educator and poet.

willed (wĭld) *adj.* Having a will of a specified kind: *weak-willed.*

wil·lem·ite (wĭl′ə-mīt′) *n.* A colorless vitreous to resinous silicate of zinc, Zn_2SiO_4, often fluorescent and a minor ore of zinc. [Dutch *willemit,* from *Willem,* William, after *William* I (died 1834), king of the Netherlands.]

Wil·lem·stad (vĭl′əm-stät). The capital of the Netherlands Antilles, on the south coast of Curaçao. Population, 44,000.

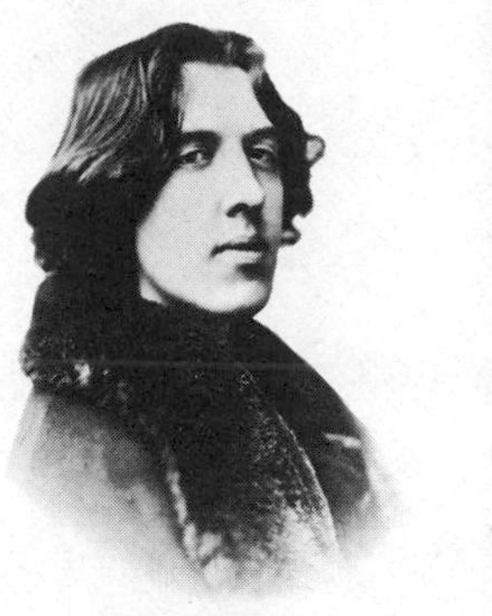

Oscar Wilde

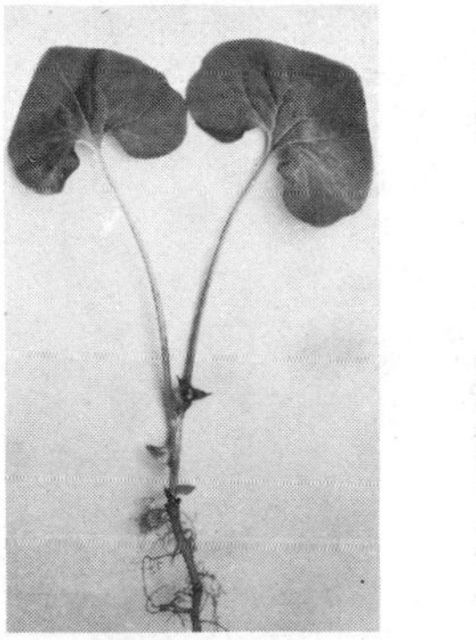

wild ginger

ā pat/ā pay/âr care/ä father/b bib/ch church/d deed/ĕ pet/ē be/f fife/g gag/h hat/hw which/ĭ pit/ī pie/îr pier/j judge/k kick/l lid, needle/m mum/n no, sudden/ng thing/ŏ pot/ō toe/ô paw, for/oi noise/ou out/o͝o took/o͞o boot/p pop/r roar/s sauce/sh ship, dish/

t tight/th thin, path/*th* this, bathe/ŭ cut/ûr urge/v valve/w with/y yes/z zebra, size/zh vision/ə about, item, edible, gallop, circus/ à *Fr.* ami/œ *Fr.* feu, *Ger.* schön/ü *Fr.* tu, *Ger.* über/KH *Ger.* ich, *Scot.* loch/N *Fr.* bon. ***Follows main vocabulary.** †**Of obscure origin.**

Willes·den (wĭlz′dən). A former administrative division of London, England, now part of **Brent** *(see).*
wil·let (wĭl′ĭt) *n.* A long-billed New World shore bird, *Catoptrophorus semipalmatus.* [Imitative of its cry.]
will·ful (wĭl′fəl) *adj.* Also **wil·ful. 1.** Said or done in accordance with one's will; deliberate. **2.** Inclined to impose one's will; unreasoningly obstinate. —See Synonyms at **contrary, voluntary, unruly.** —**will′ful·ly** *adv.* —**will′ful·ness** *n.*
Wil·liam (wĭl′yəm). *Abbr.* **Wm.** A masculine given name. [Middle English, from Norman French *Guillaume,* from Old High German *Willahelm* : *willo,* will (see **wel-**[2] in Appendix*) + *helm,* helmet (see **kel-**[4] in Appendix*).]
Wil·liam I[1] (wĭl′yəm). Known as the Conqueror. 1027–1087. King of England (1066–87); led Norman Conquest (1066).
Wil·liam I[2] (wĭl′yəm). Known as the Silent. 1533–1584. Prince of Orange; founder of the Dutch Republic and first stadholder (1579–84).
Wil·liam I[3] (wĭl′yəm). 1797–1888. King of Prussia (1861–88) and emperor of Germany (1871–88).
Wil·liam II[1] (wĭl′yəm). Known as William Rufus. 1056?–1100. King of England (1087–1100); son of William the Conqueror.
Wil·liam II[2] (wĭl′yəm). 1859–1941. Emperor of Germany and king of Prussia (1888–1918); abdicated.
Wil·liam III (wĭl′yəm). 1650–1702. Stadholder of Holland (1672–1702); King of England (1689–1702) as joint sovereign with **Mary II** *(see).*
Wil·liam IV (wĭl′yəm). 1765–1837. King of Great Britain and Ireland and king of Hanover (1830–37); son of George III.
Wil·liams, Ralph Vaughan. See **Vaughan Williams.**
Wil·liams (wĭl′yəmz), **Roger.** 1603?–1683. English clergyman in America; founder of Rhode Island.
Wil·liams (wĭl′yəmz), **Tennessee.** Original name, Thomas Lanier Williams. Born 1914. American dramatist.
Wil·liams (wĭl′yəmz), **William Carlos.** 1883–1963. American poet and physician.
Wil·liams·burg (wĭl′yəmz-bûrg). A town in east-central Virginia; the capital of colonial Virginia (1699–1779), restored after 1927 as a town of the colonial period. Population, 7,000.
William Tell. See **Tell.**
wil·lies (wĭl′ēz) *pl.n. Slang.* Feelings of uneasiness: *This place gives me the willies.* [Origin unknown.]
will·ing (wĭl′ĭng) *adj.* **1.** Of or resulting from the process of choosing; volitional. **2.** Disposed to accept or tolerate; consenting; acquiescent. **3.** Acting or ready to act gladly; eagerly compliant: *"the spirit indeed is willing, but the flesh is weak"* (Matthew 26:41). **4.** Done, given, accepted, or offered freely and heartily. —See Synonyms at **voluntary.** —**will′ing·ly** *adv.* —**will′ing·ness** *n.*
wil·li·waw (wĭl′ē-wô′) *n.* **1.** A violent gust of cold wind blowing seaward from a mountainous coast. **2.** Any sudden gust of wind; a squall. [Origin unknown.]
Will·kie (wĭl′kē), **Wendell L(ewis).** 1892–1944. American lawyer; Republican Presidential candidate (1940).
will-o′-the-wisp (wĭl′ə-*thə*-wĭsp′) *n.* **1. Ignis fatuus** *(see).* **2.** A delusive or misleading goal. [Origin uncertain.]
wil·low (wĭl′ō) *n.* **1.** Any of various deciduous trees or shrubs of the genus *Salix,* having usually narrow leaves, flowers borne in catkins, and strong, lightweight wood. **2.** The wood of any of these trees. **3.** Something made from willow, as a cricket bat. **4.** A textile machine consisting of a spiked drum revolving inside a chamber fitted internally with spikes, used to open and clean unprocessed cotton or wool. —*tr.v.* **willowed, -lowing, -lows.** To open and clean (textile fibers) with a willow. [Middle English *wilowe,* Old English *welig.* See **wel-**[3] in Appendix.*]
willow herb. Any of various plants of the genus *Epilobium,* having narrow leaves and terminal clusters of pink, purplish, or white flowers. Sometimes called "rosebay." See **fireweed.**
willow oak. A timber tree, *Quercus phellos,* of the southern and central United States, having narrow, willowlike leaves.
wil·low·ware (wĭl′ō-wâr′) *n.* Household china decorated with a blue-on-white design depicting a willow tree and often a river.
wil·low·y (wĭl′ō-ē) *adj.* **-ier, -iest. 1.** Planted with or abounding in willows. **2.** Resembling or suggestive of a willow tree, especially: **a.** Flexible; pliant. **b.** Slender and graceful.
will power. The ability to carry out one's decisions, wishes, or plans; strength of mind; self-control.
wil·ly-nil·ly (wĭl′ē-nĭl′ē) *adv.* Whether desired or not. —*adj.* Being or occurring whether desired or not. [Variant of *will I nill I,* "be I willing, be I unwilling."]
Wil·ming·ton (wĭl′mĭng-tən). A city of Delaware, a port in the north on the Delaware River. Population, 96,000.
Wil·son (wĭl′sən), **Alexander.** 1766–1813. Scottish-born American ornithologist.
Wil·son (wĭl′sən), **Charles Thomson Rees.** 1869–1959. British physicist; devised the cloud chamber.
Wil·son (wĭl′sən), **Henry.** Original name, Jeremiah Jones Colbath. 1812–1875. Vice President of the United States under Ulysses S. Grant (1873–75).
Wil·son (wĭl′sən), **(James) Harold.** Born 1917. Prime Minister of the United Kingdom (since 1964).
Wil·son, Mount (wĭl′sən). A mountain, 5,710 feet high, in the San Gabriel Mountains of southern California; the site of Mount Wilson Observatory.
Wil·son (wĭl′sən), **(Thomas) Woodrow.** 1856–1924. Twenty-eighth President of the United States (1913–21).
Wil·son Dam (wĭl′sən). A dam on the Tennessee River in northwestern Alabama, forming the 25-square-mile Lake Wilson at Muscle Shoals.
wilt[1] (wĭlt) *v.* **wilted, wilting, wilts.** —*intr.* **1.** To become limp or flaccid; droop. **2.** To become less active or energetic; weaken: *"his brain wilted from hitherto unprecedented weariness"* (Vladimir Nabokov). —*tr.* **1.** To cause to droop or lose freshness. **2.** To deprive of energy or courage; enervate. —*n.* **1.** The act of wilting or the state of being wilted. **2.** Any of various plant diseases characterized by slow or rapid collapse of terminal shoots, branches, or entire plants. [Variant of dialectal *wilk, welk,* from Middle English *welken,* perhaps from Middle Low German or Middle Dutch. See **welk-** in Appendix.*]
wilt[2]. *Archaic.* Second person singular present tense of **will.**
Wil·ton (wĭl′tən) *n.* A kind of carpet woven on a Jacquard loom and having a velvety surface formed by the cut loops of a pile. Also called "Wilton carpet," "Wilton rug." [From *Wilton,* carpet-weaving center in southern Wiltshire.]
Wilts. Wiltshire (county).
Wilt·shire[1] (wĭlt′shĭr, -shər) *n.* A sheep of a breed originating in England, characterized by a long head and pure white fleece.
Wilt·shire[2] (wĭlt′shĭr, -shər). *Abbr.* **Wilts.** A county of England, occupying 1,345 square miles in the southwest. Population, 423,000. County seat, Salisbury.
wi·ly (wī′lē) *adj.* **-lier, -liest.** Full of wiles; guileful; calculating. See Synonyms at **sly.** —**wi′li·ly** *adv.* —**wi′li·ness** *n.*
wim·ble (wĭm′bəl) *n.* Any of numerous hand tools for the boring of holes, as a brace and bit or a gimlet. —*tr.v.* **wimbled, -bling, -bles.** To bore with a wimble. [Middle English, from Norman French, perhaps from Middle Dutch *wimmel.* See **weip-** in Appendix.*]
Wim·ble·don (wĭm′bəl-dən). A former administrative division of London, England, now part of **Merton** *(see);* the site of annual international lawn tennis matches.
wim·ple (wĭm′pəl) *n.* **1.** A cloth wound around the head, framing the face, and drawn into folds beneath the chin, worn by women in medieval times and as part of the habit of certain orders of nuns. **2. a.** A fold or pleat in cloth. **b.** A ripple, as on the surface of water. **c.** A curve or bend. —*v.* **wimpled, -pling, -ples.** —*tr.* **1.** To cover or furnish with a wimple. **2.** To cause to form folds, pleats, or ripples. —*intr.* **1.** To form or lie in folds. **2.** To ripple. [Middle English *wimpel,* Old English *wimpel.* See **weip-** in Appendix.*]
Wims·hurst machine (wĭmz′hûrst′). An electrostatic generator having oppositely rotating mica or glass disks with metal carriers on which charges are produced by induction, used chiefly as a demonstration apparatus. [After James *Wimshurst* (1832–1903), British engineer.]
win (wĭn) *v.* **won** (wŭn), **winning, wins.** —*intr.* **1.** To achieve victory over others in a competition. **2.** To achieve success in an effort or venture. **3.** To struggle through to a desired place or condition: *He won loose and escaped.* **4.** To finish first in a race. Compare **place, show.** —*tr.* **1.** To achieve victory in. **2.** To receive as a prize or reward for performance. **3.** To achieve by effort; earn: *win fame.* **4.** To reach with difficulty: *The ship won a safe port.* **5.** To take in battle; capture. **6.** To succeed in gaining the favor or support of; prevail upon: *His eloquence won his audience.* **7. a.** To gain the affection or loyalty of. **b.** To appeal successfully to (someone's loyalty, sympathy, or other emotion). **c.** To persuade (someone) to marry one. **8.** To make (one's way) with effort. **9.** *Mining.* **a.** To discover and open (a vein or deposit); render fit for mining. **b.** To extract from a mine. —**win out.** To succeed or prevail. —*n.* **1.** A victory; a triumph, especially in a competition. See Usage note below. **2.** An amount won or earned; a profit. [Win, won, won; Middle English *winnen,* to win, strive, Old English *winnan,* to strive. See **wen-** in Appendix.*]
Usage: *Win* (noun), in the sense of victory or success, is principally appropriate to sports reporting or other informal contexts. As an example in writing on a more serious level, the following is termed unacceptable by 67 per cent of the Usage Panel: *An impressive win in the primary would strengthen his position greatly.*
wince (wĭns) *intr.v.* **winced, wincing, winces.** To shrink or start involuntarily, as in pain or distress; to flinch. —*n.* A wincing movement or gesture. [Middle English *wincen,* to kick, wince, from Norman French *wencir* (unattested), from Germanic. See **weng-** in Appendix.*] —**winc′er** *n.*
winch (wĭnch) *n.* **1.** A stationary motor-driven or hand-powered hoisting machine having a drum around which a rope or chain winds as the load is lifted. **2.** The crank used to give motion to a grindstone or similar device. —*tr.v.* **winched, winching, winches.** To hoist or move with or as if with a winch. [Middle English *winche,* a pulley, Old English *wince.* See **weng-** in Appendix.*] —**winch′er** *n.*
Win·ches·ter[1] (wĭn′chĕs′tər, -chə-stər). **1.** The county seat of Hampshire, southern England. Population, 30,000. **2.** A city of Virginia, in the north near the northern end of the Shenandoah Valley; the site of two Civil War battles (1862 and 1864). Population, 15,000.
Win·ches·ter[2] (wĭn′chĕs′tər, -chə-stər) *n.* A trademark for a breechloading repeating rifle with lever action and a magazine attached horizontally under the barrel, first issued in 1866. [After Oliver *Winchester* (1810–1880), American manufacturer.]
wind[1] (wĭnd) *n.* **1.** Moving air; especially, a natural and perceptible movement of air parallel to or along the ground. **2. a.** A movement or current of air blowing from one of the four cardinal points of the compass: *the four winds.* **b.** The direction from which a strong or prevailing current of air comes: *The wind is northeast.* **3.** A blast of air that disrupts or destroys; a gale. **4.** *Nautical.* The direction from which the wind is blowing. **5.** Moving air carrying an odor, scent, or sound. **6.** A

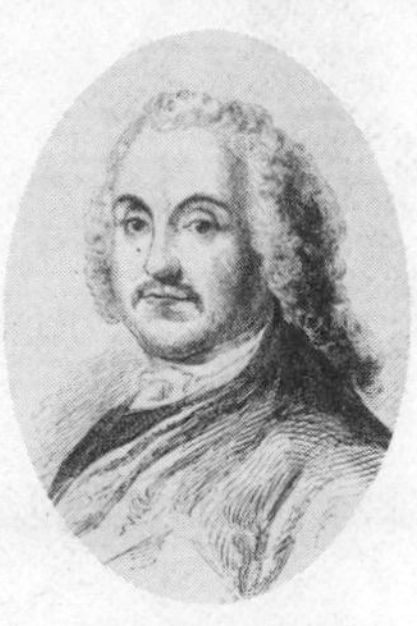
Roger Williams

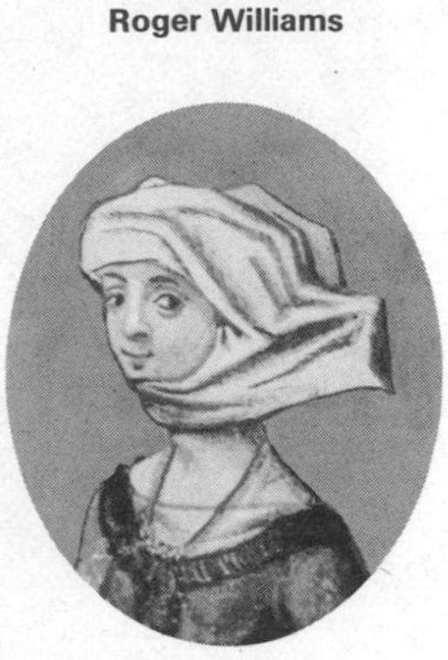
wimple
Detail of a 16th-century German painting

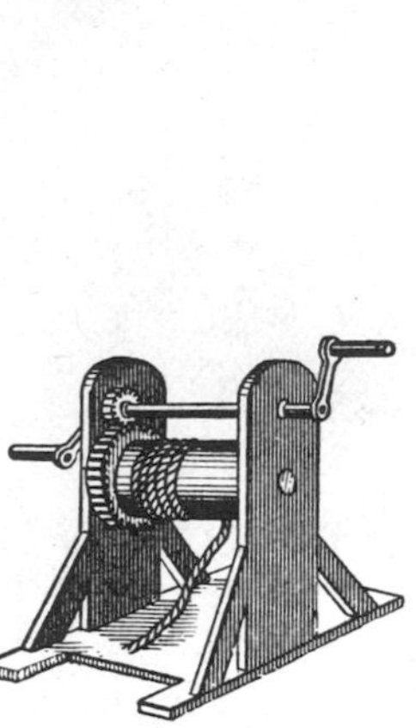
winch

current or stream of air generated by a fan, bellows, or other artificial means. **7.** *Plural.* **a.** The wind instruments in an orchestra or band. **b.** Players of wind instruments. **8.** Gas produced in the body during digestion; flatulence. **9.** Respiration; breath; especially, normal or adequate breathing. **10. a.** Utterance empty of meaning; verbiage. **b.** Futile or idle labor or thought. —**break wind.** To eject intestinal gas. —**get wind of.** To receive hints or intimations of. —**have the wind of.** To hold an advantage over (an opponent). —**in the wind.** Likely to occur; in the offing. —**on** (or **into** or **down**) **the wind.** In the same or nearly the same direction as the wind. —**sail close to the wind. 1.** To sail or travel as directly against the wind as possible. **2.** To live frugally or economically. **3.** To approach near to a limit; verge on excess or danger. —**up the wind.** In a direction opposite or nearly opposite to the wind. —*tr.v.* **winded, winding, winds. 1.** To expose to the free movement of air; ventilate or dry. **2. a.** To catch a scent or trace of. **b.** To pursue by following a scent. **3.** To cause to be out of or short of breath. **4.** To afford a recovery of breath. [Middle English *wind,* Old English *wind.* See **wē-** in Appendix.*]

Synonyms: *wind, breeze, zephyr, blast, gust, gale, whirlwind, tornado, twister, cyclone, hurricane, typhoon, waterspout.* These nouns refer to the movement of air by the forces of nature. *Wind* is any such movement. *Breeze* and *zephyr,* which is chiefly a literary term, refer to light, gentle winds. *Blast* and *gust* are names for sudden, brief, and strong movements. *Gale* applies to a strong, sustained, and potentially destructive wind. The remaining terms all refer to wind that whirls in a circular or spiral course around a central axis, at the same time moving forward over land or at sea. *Whirlwind* is applied to such a rotating windstorm on a small scale. Sometimes *whirlwind* is used interchangeably with *tornado,* which is the precise term for a violent windstorm that has a small diameter and consequently follows a narrow path for many miles, accompanied by a funnel-shaped cloud. *Twister* is generally used as a less formal term for *tornado. Cyclone* is the general term for a system of rotating wind, often hundreds of miles in diameter, that travels widely, bringing driving rain and often great destruction. Such a storm originating in the vicinity of the West Indies is a *hurricane.* The corresponding term for a cyclone originating in the tropical regions of the western Pacific Ocean and the China Sea is *typhoon. Waterspout* refers to a column of rotating wind, enclosing mist and sometimes masses of water, that originates on and travels over a large body of water.

wind² (wīnd) *v.* **wound** (wound) or *rare* **winded, winding, winds.** —*tr.* **1.** To wrap (something) around an object or center once or repeatedly. **2.** To wrap or encircle (an object) in a series of coils; entwine. **3.** To set on a curving or twisting course. **4.** To proceed on (one's way) with a curving or twisting course. **5.** To present or introduce in a disguised or devious manner: *He wound a plea for money into his letter.* **6.** To turn in a series of circular motions, as a crank or handle. **7.** To coil the spring of (a clock or other mechanism) by turning a stem, cord, or the like. **8.** To lift or haul by means of a windlass or winch. —*intr.* **1.** To move in or as if in a bending or coiling course. **2. a.** To move in or have a spiral or circular course. **b.** To be coiled or spiraled about something. **3.** To be twisted or whorled into curved forms. **4.** To proceed misleadingly or insidiously in discourse or conduct. **5.** To become wound. —*n.* **1.** The act of winding. **2.** A single turn, twist, or curve. [Wind, wound, wound; Middle English *winden, wond, wonden,* Old English *windan, wond, wunden.* See **wendh-** in Appendix.*]

wind³ (wīnd, wĭnd) *tr.v.* **winded** (wīn′dĭd, wĭn′-) or **wound** (wound), **winding, winds. 1.** To blow (a wind instrument). **2.** To sound by blowing. [From WIND (air).] —**wind′or** *n.*

wind·age (wĭn′dĭj) *n.* **1. a.** The effect of wind on the course of a projectile. **b.** The point or degree at which the wind gauge or sight of a rifle or gun must be set to compensate for the effect of the wind. **2.** *Ballistics.* The difference, in a given firearm, between the diameter of the projectile fired and the diameter of the bore of the firearm. **3.** The disturbance of air caused by the passage of a fast-moving object, such as a railway train or missile. **4.** *Nautical.* The part of the surface of a ship that is left exposed to the wind.

wind·bag (wĭnd′băg′) *n. Slang.* A talkative person who communicates nothing of substance or interest.

wind-blown (wĭnd′blōn′) *adj.* **1.** Blown or dispersed by the wind. **2.** Growing or shaped in a manner governed by the prevailing winds. **3.** Cut short and curled or combed toward the front of the head. Said of a woman's hair style.

wind-borne (wĭnd′bôrn′, -bōrn′) *adj.* Carried by the wind.

wind-bound (wĭnd′bound′) *adj.* Forced to remain in port because of high winds.

wind·break (wĭnd′brāk′) *n.* A hedge, row of trees, or fence serving to lessen or break the force of the wind.

Wind·break·er (wĭnd′brā′kər) *n.* A trademark for a warm jacket having close-fitting, often elastic, cuffs and waistband.

wind-bro·ken (wĭnd′brō′kən) *adj.* Suffering from the heaves or other impairment of respiration. Said of horses.

wind·burn (wĭnd′bûrn′) *n.* Skin irritation or discoloration caused by exposure to wind.

wind cone (wĭnd). A wind indicator, **windsock** *(see).*

wind·ed (wĭn′dĭd) *adj.* **1.** Having breath or respiratory power. Used in combination: *short-winded.* **2.** Out of breath.

wind·er (wīn′dər) *n.* **1.** One that winds; especially, a person who winds cloth or materials in a textile factory. **2.** A spool, barrel, or other object around which material is wound. **3.** A device such as a key for winding up a spring-driven mechanism. **4.** One of the steps of a winding staircase.

Win·der·mere, Lake (wĭn′dər-mîr). The largest lake in England, ten miles long, in Westmorland and Lancashire.

wind·fall (wĭnd′fôl′) *n.* **1.** Something that has been blown down by the wind, as a ripened fruit. **2.** A sudden and unexpected piece of good fortune or personal gain.

wind·flaw (wĭnd′flô′) *n.* A sudden gust or blast of wind.

wind·flow·er (wĭnd′flou′ər) *n.* An **anemone** *(see).*

wind·gall (wĭnd′gôl′) *n.* A soft swelling near the fetlock joint of a horse.

wind gap (wĭnd). A shallow notch or ravine on the side of a deep mountain ridge.

wind harp (wĭnd). An **Aeolian harp** *(see).*

Wind·hoek (vĭnt′ho͝ok). The capital of South-West Africa, located in the center of the territory. Population, 48,000.

wind·ing (wīn′dĭng) *n.* **1. a.** The act of one that winds. **b.** One complete turn of something wound. **2.** A thing in a wound condition; a spiral. **3.** A curve or bend, as of a road. **4.** *Electricity.* **a.** Wire wound into a coil. **b.** The manner in which such a coil is wound. **c.** A single loop of such a coil. —*adj.* **1.** Twisting or turning; sinuous. **2.** Spiral. —**wind′ing·ly** *adv.*

winding sheet (wīn′dĭng). A sheet for wrapping a dead body; a shroud.

wind instrument (wĭnd). Any musical instrument sounded by wind, especially by the breath, as a clarinet, trumpet, or harmonica.

wind·jam·mer (wĭnd′jăm′ər) *n.* **1.** A large sailing ship. **2.** A crew member of a sailing ship. [From WIND + JAM (verb).]

wind·lass (wĭnd′ləs) *n.* Any of numerous hauling or lifting machines consisting essentially of a drum or cylinder wound with rope and turned by a crank. Compare **capstan.** —*tr.v.* **windlassed, -lassing, -lasses.** To raise with a windlass. [Middle English *wyndlas,* variant of *windas,* from Norman French, from Old Norse *vindāss* : *vinda,* to wind (see **wendh-** in Appendix*) + *āss*†, pole.]

win·dle·straw (wĭn′dəl-strô′) *n. Scottish & British Regional.* A dried grass stalk, or such dried stalks collectively. [Middle English *windlestraw* (unattested), Old English *windelstrēaw* : *windel,* basket, from *windan,* to WIND + *strēaw,* STRAW.]

wind·mill (wĭnd′mĭl′) *n.* **1.** A mill or other machine that runs on the energy generated by a wheel of adjustable blades or slats rotated by the wind. **2.** Anything similar to a windmill in appearance or operation, as a toy pinwheel. **3.** A person or thing imagined to be threatening or evil. Used chiefly in the phrase *tilting at windmills.* [Sense 3 is a reference to Cervantes' Don Quixote who imagined windmills were evil giants.]

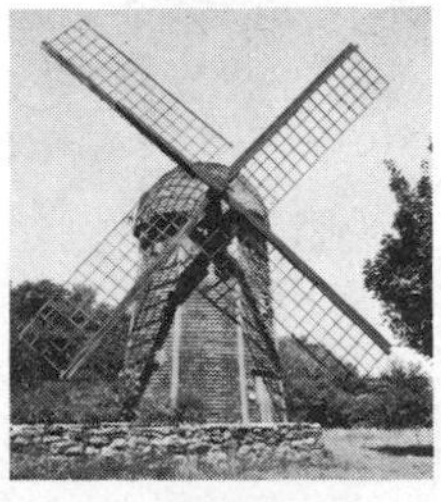

windmill

win·dow (wĭn′dō) *n.* **1.** An opening constructed in a wall or roof and functioning to admit light or air to an enclosure, usually framed and spanned with glass mounted to permit opening and closing. **2. a.** A framework enclosing a pane of glass; a sash. **b.** A pane of glass, clear plastic, or the like; windowpane. **3.** Any opening that resembles a window in function or appearance, as the transparent space on an envelope that reveals the address printed on the enclosure. **4.** A code name for strips of metal foil dropped from aircraft as a radar countermeasure; chaff. —*tr.v.* **windowed, -dowing, -dows.** To provide with or as if with a window. [Middle English *window(e),* from Old Norse *vindauga* : *vindr,* wind, air (see **wē-** in Appendix*) + *auga,* eye (see **okw-** in Appendix*).]

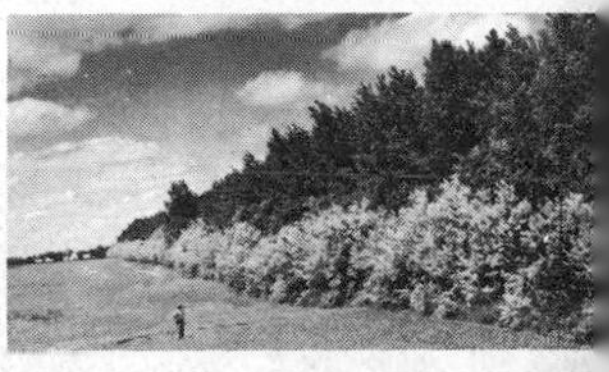

windbreak

window box. 1. A usually long and narrow box for growing plants, placed on a windowsill or ledge. **2.** One of the vertical grooves on the inner sides of a window frame for the weights that counterbalance the sash.

win·dow-dress·ing (wĭn′dō-drĕs′ĭng) *n.* Also **window dressing. 1. a.** The decorative exhibition of retail merchandise in store windows. **b.** Goods and trimmings used in such displays. **2.** A report, statement, or the like, that gives emphasis to favorable conditions. —**win′dow-dress′er** *n.*

win·dow·pane (wĭn′dō-pān′) *n.* A plate of glass in a window.

window shade. An opaque fabric mounted to cover or expose a window.

win·dow-shop (wĭn′dō-shŏp′) *intr.v.* **-shopped, -shopping, -shops.** To look at merchandise in store windows or showcases without making purchases. —**win′dow-shop′per** *n.*

win·dow·sill (wĭn′dō-sĭl′) *n.* The horizontal ledge at the base of a window opening.

wind·pipe (wĭnd′pīp′) *n. Anatomy.* The **trachea** *(see).*

Wind River Range (wĭnd). A mountain range in west-central Wyoming, part of the Rocky Mountain system. Highest elevation, Gannett Peak (13,785 feet).

wind rose (wĭnd). Any of a class of meteorological diagrams depicting the distribution of wind direction over a period of time. [German *Windrose,* "a rose of winds," compass card.]

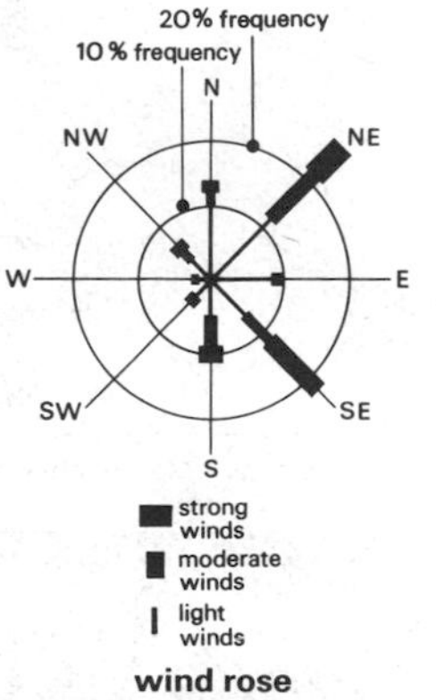

wind rose
Strength of winds indicated by thickness of radial segment; frequency of winds in a given direction indicated by length of segment

wind·row (wĭnd′rō′) *n.* **1.** A row, as of leaves or snow, heaped up by the wind. **2.** A long row of cut hay or grain left to dry in a field before being bundled. —*tr.v.* **windrowed, -rowing, -rows.** To shape or arrange into a windrow. —**wind′row′er** *n.*

wind·shake (wĭnd′shāk′) *n.* A crack or separation between growth rings in timber, attributed to the straining of tree trunks in high winds.

wind·shield (wĭnd′shēld′) *n.* **1.** A framed pane of usually curved glass or other transparent shielding located in front of the occupants of a vehicle to protect them from the wind. **2.** Any shield placed to protect an object from the wind.

wind·sock (wĭnd′sŏk′) *n.* A large, tapered, open-ended sleeve, pivotally attached to a standard, that indicates the direction of the wind blowing through it. Also called "air sock," "drogue," "wind cone," "wind sleeve."

Wind·sor (wĭn′zər). Family name of rulers of Great Britain since 1917.

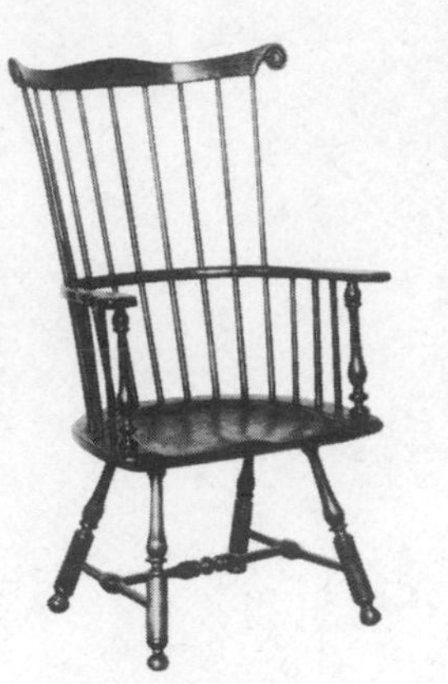

Windsor chair

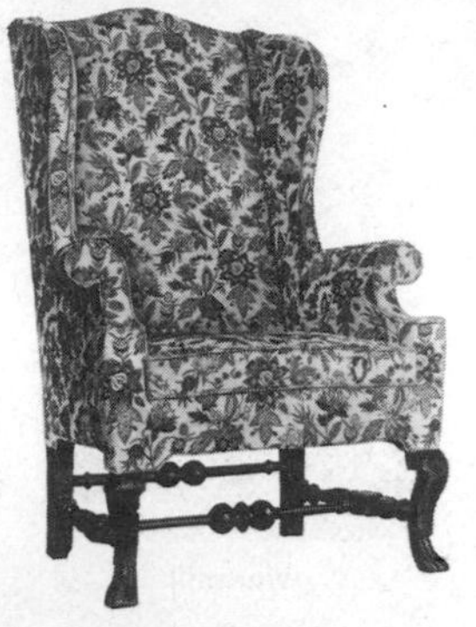

wing chair
Early 18th-century
New England

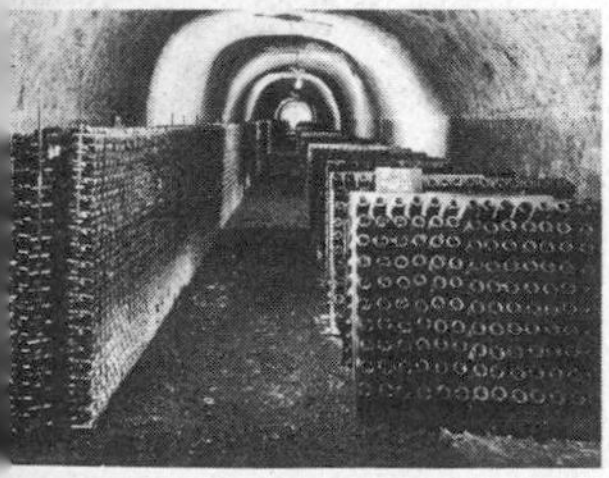

wine cellar

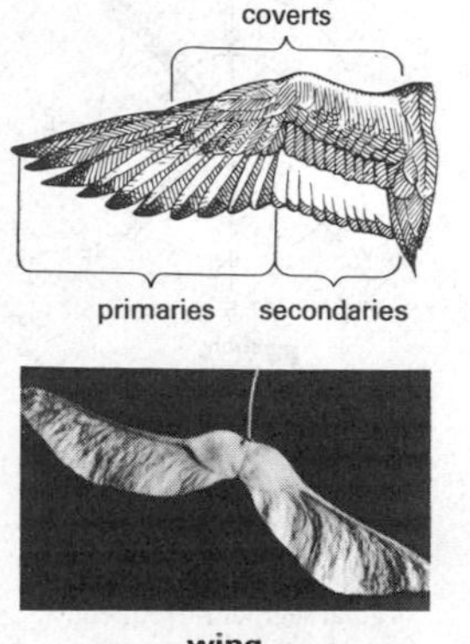
coverts
primaries
secondaries

wing
Above: Upper surface of a bird's wing
Below: Wings of maple samara

Wind·sor (wĭn′zər). **1.** Officially, New Windsor. A town in Berkshire, England, 23 miles west of London. Population, 29,000. **2.** A city of Ontario, Canada, across the Detroit River from Detroit, Michigan. Population, 193,000.
Wind·sor, Duke of. See **Edward VIII.**
Windsor chair. A wooden chair widely used in 18th-century England and America, typically having a high spoked back and outward-slanting legs connected by a crossbar.
Windsor tie. A wide silk necktie tied in a loose bow.
wind sprint (wĭnd). A sprint run to develop the breath.
wind·storm (wĭnd′stôrm′) *n.* A storm with high winds or violent gusts but little or no rain.
wind·suck·er (wĭnd′sŭk′ər) *n.* A horse given to swallowing quantities of air.
wind·swept (wĭnd′swĕpt′) *adj.* Exposed to or moved by the force of wind.
wind tee (wĭnd). A large weather vane with a horizontal T-shaped wind indicator, commonly found at airfields.
wind tunnel (wĭnd). A chamber through which air is forced at controllable velocities in order to study the aerodynamic flow around and effects on airfoils, scale models, or other objects mounted within.
wind up (wīnd). **1.** To come to an end; to finish. **2.** To bring to an end; settle. **3.** To make anxious or expectant. **4.** *Baseball.* To swing back the arm and raise the front foot in preparation for pitching the ball.
wind-up (wīnd′ŭp′) *n.* **1. a.** The act of bringing something to a conclusion. **b.** The concluding part of an action, presentation, speech, or the like. **2.** *Baseball.* The coordinated movements of a pitcher's arm, body, and legs preparatory to pitching the ball.
wind·ward (wĭnd′wərd) *n.* The direction from which the wind blows. **—to (the) windward of.** Favorably situated with respect to. *—adj.* **1.** Of or moving toward the quarter from which the wind blows. **2.** Of or on the side exposed to the wind or to prevailing winds. *—adv.* In a direction from which the wind blows; against the wind. Compare **leeward.**
Windward Islands. **1.** A group of islands in the eastern Caribbean, comprising the southern Lesser Antilles. **2.** A former British colony formed of the islands of Dominica, Grenada, St. Lucia, St. Vincent, and their dependencies.
Windward Passage. A strait about 50 miles wide between eastern Cuba and northwestern Haiti.
wind·y (wĭn′dē) *adj.* **-ier, -iest.** **1.** Characterized by or abounding in wind. **2.** Open to the wind; unsheltered. **3.** Resembling wind in swiftness, force, or variability. **4. a.** Characterized by lack of substance; empty. **b.** Characterized by or given to prolonged talk. **5.** Flatulent. **—wind′i·ly** *adv.* **—wind′i·ness** *n.*
wine (wīn) *n.* **1.** The fermented juice of any of various kinds of grapes, usually containing from 10 to 15 per cent alcohol by volume. **2.** The fermented juice of any of various other fruits or plants. **3.** Something that intoxicates or exhilarates. **4.** The color of red wine. *—v.* **wined, wining, wines.** *—tr.* To provide or entertain with wines: *The guests were wined and dined.* *—intr.* To drink wine. [Middle English *win(e)*, Old English *wīn*, from West Germanic *wīna-* (unattested), from Latin *vīnum*. See **vīnum** in Appendix.*]
wine·bib·bing (wīn′bĭb′ĭng) *adj.* Given to much drinking of wine. *—n.* The habitual drinking of wine. **—wine′bib′ber** *n.*
wine cellar. **1.** A place for storing wine. **2.** A stock of wines.
wine·glass (wīn′glăs′, -gläs′) *n.* A glass, usually with a stem, from which wine is drunk.
wine·glass·ful (wīn′glăs′fo͝ol′, -gläs′fo͝ol′) *n., pl.* **-fuls.** The amount held by a wineglass, usually two fluid ounces.
wine·grow·er (wīn′grō′ər) *n.* One who owns a vineyard and produces wine. **—wine′grow′ing** *adj.* & *n.*
wine palm. Any of various palm trees having sap or juice from which wine is prepared.
wine·press (wīn′prĕs′) *n.* Also **wine presser.** A vat in which the juice is pressed from grapes.
win·er·y (wī′nə-rē) *n., pl.* **-ies.** A wine-making establishment.
Wine·sap (wīn′săp′) *n.* A variety of apple having fruit with dark-red skin.
wine·skin (wīn′skĭn′) *n.* A bag for holding and dispensing wine, made from goatskin or other animal skin.
wing (wĭng) *n.* **1.** One of a pair of specialized organs of flight, as: **a.** The feather-covered modified forelimb of a bird. **b.** The membranous tissue supported by the elongated digits of the forelimb of a bat. **c.** A reticulated, membranous structure extending from the thorax of an insect. **d.** The enlarged pectoral fin of a flying fish. **2.** Any organ or structure homologous to or resembling a wing. **3.** *Botany.* **a.** A thin or membranous extension, as of the fruit of the maple or ash or along a twig or stem. **b.** One of the lateral petals of the flower of a pea or related plant. **4.** *Informal.* An arm of a human being. **5.** *Aviation.* An airfoil whose principal function is providing lift; especially, either of two such airfoils symmetrically positioned on each side of the fuselage. **6.** Anything that resembles a wing in appearance, function, or position relative to a main body. **7.** A means of flight or of rapid ascent. **8.** Something that is moved by or moves against the air, as a weather vane. **9.** *British.* The fender of an automobile. **10.** A folding section, as of a double door or of a movable partition. **11.** Either of the two side projections on the back of a wing chair. **12.** *Theater.* **a.** A flat of scenery projecting onto the stage from the side. **b.** *Theater.* The unseen backstage area on either side of the stage of a proscenium theater. **13.** A structure attached to the side of a house, building, or fortification. **14.** A section of a large building devoted to a specific purpose: *the children's wing of the hospital.* **15.** A group affiliated with or subordinate to an older or larger organization. **16.** A section of a party, legislature, or community holding distinct, especially dissenting, political views: *the conservative wing.* **17.** *Military.* Either the left or right flank of an army or a naval fleet. **18.** *Sports.* Either of the forward positions played near the sideline, as in hockey. **19.** *U.S. Air Force.* A unit larger than a group but smaller than a division or command. **—on the wing.** In flight; flying. **—take wing.** To fly off; soar away. **—under one's wing.** Under one's protection; in one's care. *—v.* **winged, winging, wings.** *—intr.* To move on or as if on wings; fly. *—tr.* **1.** To furnish with wings. **2.** To feather (an arrow). **3.** To carry or transport by or as if by flying; speed along. **4.** To wound superficially, as in the wing or arm. **5.** To furnish with side or subordinate extensions, as a building or altarpiece. **—wing it.** *Theater.* To improvise or adlib. [From Middle English *wenge(n)*, from Old Norse *vængi*, accusative plural of *vængr*, bird's wing. See **wē-** in Appendix.*]
wing and wing. *Nautical.* With sails extended on both sides.
wing·back (wĭng′băk′) *n.* *Football.* **1.** A back positioned on offense behind or outside of an end. **2.** The position itself.
wing·bow (wĭng′bō′) *n.* A mark of color on the bend of the wing in a domestic fowl.
wing chair. An armchair with a high back from which project large, enclosing sidepieces or wings.
wing·ding (wĭng′dĭng′) *n.* *Slang.* A lavish or lively party or celebration. [Origin unknown.]
winged (wĭngd; *poetic* wĭng′ĭd) *adj.* **1.** Having wings or winglike appendages. **2.** Moving on or as if on wings; flying. **3.** Soaring; elevated; sublime. **4.** Swift; fleet.
wing-foot·ed (wĭng′fo͝ot′ĭd) *adj.* Swift; fleet of foot.
wing·less (wĭng′lĭs) *adj.* Having no wings or having only rudimentary wings.
wing·let (wĭng′lĭt) *n.* A small or rudimentary wing.
wing loading. *Aviation.* The gross weight of an airplane divided by the wing area. Used in stress analysis.
wing nut. A nut with winglike projections for thumb and forefinger leverage in turning. Also called "thumbnut."
wing·o·ver (wĭng′ō′vər) *n.* A flight maneuver or stunt in which a plane enters a climbing turn until almost stalled and is allowed to fall while the turn is continued until normal flight is attained in a direction opposite the original heading.
wing·span (wĭng′spăn′) *n.* **1.** The linear distance between the extremities of an airfoil. **2.** The linear distance from wing tip to wing tip of an aircraft or bird; wingspread.
wing·spread (wĭng′sprĕd′) *n.* The distance between the tips of the wings when fully extended, as of an airplane, bird, or insect.
wing tip. **1.** A shoe part, often perforated, which covers the toe and extends backward along the sides of the shoe from a point at the center. **2.** A style of shoe having such a toe.
wink (wĭngk) *v.* **winked, winking, winks.** *—intr.* **1.** To close and open the eyelid of one eye deliberately, as to convey a message, signal, or suggestion. **2.** To close and open the eyelids of both eyes; blink. **3.** To shine fitfully; twinkle. *—tr.* **1.** To close and open (an eye or the eyes) rapidly. **2.** To signal or express by winking. *—n.* **1.** The act of winking. **2.** The time required for a wink. **3.** A signal or hint conveyed by winking. **4.** A gleam; twinkle. **5.** *Informal.* A brief moment of sleep. **—wink at.** To pretend not to see: *winked at corruption in his ministry.* See Usage note at **blink.** [Middle English *winken*, Old English *wincian*, to close one's eyes. See **weng-** in Appendix.*]
win·kle (wĭng′kəl) *n.* A mollusk, the **periwinkle** *(see).*
Win·ne·ba·go (wĭn′ə-bā′gō) *n., pl.* **Winnebago** or **-gos** or **-goes.** **1.** A Siouan-speaking tribe of North American Indians, inhabiting eastern Wisconsin. **2.** A member of this tribe. **3.** The language of this tribe.
Win·ne·ba·go, Lake (wĭn′ə-bā′gō). The largest lake in Wisconsin, occupying 215 square miles in the east-central part of the state.
Win·ne·pe·sau·kee, Lake (wĭn′ə-pə-sô′kē). The largest lake of New Hampshire, occupying 71 square miles in the east-central part of the state.
win·ner (wĭn′ər) *n.* One that wins; especially, a successful person or a victor in sports.
win·ning (wĭn′ĭng) *adj.* **1.** Successful; victorious. **2.** Charming: *a winning personality.* *—n.* **1.** The act of one that wins; victory. **2.** *Usually plural.* That which has been won, especially money. **3.** A section of a mine that has been recently prepared or opened for working. **—win′ning·ly** *adv.* **—win′ning·ness** *n.*
winning gallery. In court tennis, an opening below the side penthouse. A ball played into this opening is counted as a win.
winning post. The post at the end of a racecourse.
Win·ni·peg (wĭn′ə-pĕg). The capital of Manitoba, Canada, in the south. Population, 476,000 (metropolitan area).
Win·ni·peg, Lake (wĭn′ə-pĕg). A lake of Canada, occupying 9,396 square miles in south-central Manitoba.
Win·ni·pe·go·sis, Lake (wĭn′ə-pə-gō′sĭs). A lake occupying 2,086 square miles west of Lake Winnipeg in western Manitoba, Canada.
Win·ni·peg River (wĭn′ə-pĕg). A river of Canada, rising in the Lake of the Woods, southeastern Ontario, and flowing 200 miles northwest to Lake Winnipeg in Manitoba.
win·now (wĭn′ō) *v.* **-nowed, -nowing, -nows.** *—tr.* **1.** To separate the chaff from (grain) by means of a current of air. **2.** To blow (chaff) off or away. **3.** To blow away; scatter; disperse. **4.** To blow upon; cause to flutter or fly. **5.** To examine closely in order to separate the good from the bad; analyze; sift. **6.** To separate (a desirable or undesirable part); to sort or eliminate. Often used with *out.* *—intr.* **1.** To separate grain from chaff. **2.** To separate the good from the bad. *—n.* **1.** A device for winnowing grain. **2.** An act of winnowing. [Middle English

windowen, wynwen, Old English *windwian,* from *wind,* WIND.] —**win′now·er** *n.*

win·o (wī′nō) *n., pl.* **winoes** or **winos.** *Slang.* One who is habitually drunk on wine.

Wins·low (wĭnz′lō), **Edward.** 1595–1655. English Puritan colonist in America; three times governor of Plymouth Colony (1633–44).

win·some (wĭn′səm) *adj.* Winning; charming; engaging. [Middle English *winsum,* Old English *wynsum.* See **wen-** in Appendix.*] —**win′some·ly** *adv.* —**win′some·ness** *n.*

Win·ston-Sa·lem (wĭn′stən-sā′ləm). A city of North Carolina, in the north-central part of the state. Population, 111,000.

win·ter (wĭn′tər) *n.* **1.** The usually coldest season of the year, occurring between autumn and spring. In the Northern Hemisphere it extends from the winter solstice to the vernal equinox and is popularly considered to comprise December, January, and February; in the Southern Hemisphere it falls between the summer solstice and the autumnal equinox, or, popularly, June, July, and August. **2.** A year as expressed through the recurrence of this season. **3.** Any period of time characterized by coldness, misery, barrenness, or death. —*v.* **wintered, -tering, -ters.** —*intr.* To spend the winter. —*tr.* To lodge, keep, or care for during the winter: *wintering the sheep in the stable.* —*adj.* **1.** Pertaining to, characteristic of, or occurring in winter. **2. a.** Capable of being stored for use during the winter. Said of fruits or vegetables. **b.** Planted in the autumn and harvested in the spring or summer: *winter wheat.* [Middle English *winter,* Old English *winter.* See **wed-**[1] in Appendix.*] —**win′ter·er** *n.* —**win′ter·less** *adj.*

winter aconite. A frequently cultivated European plant, *Eranthis hyemalis,* having a solitary yellow flower that blooms in winter or early spring. Also called "New Year's gift."

win·ter·ber·ry (wĭn′tər-bĕr′ē) *n., pl.* **-ries.** Any of several North American shrubs of the genus *Ilex,* having showy red berries.

winter cherry. A frequently cultivated Eurasian plant, *Physalis alkekengi,* having red berries enclosed in inflated papery, orange-red seed cases. Also called "Chinese lantern plant."

win·ter-feed (wĭn′tər-fēd′) *tr.v.* **-fed** (-fĕd′), **-feeding, -feeds.** To feed (livestock) when grazing is not possible.

win·ter·green (wĭn′tər-grēn′) *n.* **1.** A low-growing plant, *Gaultheria procumbens,* of eastern North America, having white or pinkish flowers, aromatic evergreen leaves, and spicy, edible red berries. Also called "checkerberry," "teaberry." **2.** Any of several similar or related plants, such as the **pipsissewa** *(see).* [Translation of Dutch *wintergroen.*]

win·ter·ize (wĭn′tə-rīz′) *tr.v.* **-ized, -izing, -izes.** To prepare or equip for winter weather, as an automobile or house.

win·ter·kill (wĭn′tər-kĭl′) *v.* **-killed, -killing, -kills.** —*tr.* To kill (plants, for example) by exposing to extremely cold winter weather. —*intr.* To die from exposure to cold winter weather. Used especially of plants. —*n.* Death, as of plants, resulting from exposure to winter weather.

win·ter·ly (wĭn′tər-lē) *adj.* Wintry.

winter melon. A variety of melon, *Cucumis melo inodorus,* having fruit with sweet, usually light-colored flesh. [Translation of Chinese *tung*[1] *kua*[1].]

winter purslane. A plant, *Montia perfoliata,* of western North America, having small white flowers and leaves sometimes eaten in salads. Also called "miner's lettuce."

winter rose. A plant, the **Christmas rose** *(see).*

winter savory. See **savory** (plant).

winter solstice. *Astronomy.* A **solstice** *(see).*

winter squash. Any of several thick-rinded varieties of squash, such as the acorn squash, that can be stored for long periods.

Win·ter·thur (vĭn′tər-to͝or′). A city of Switzerland, in the north, northeast of Zurich. Population, 86,000.

win·ter·time (wĭn′tər-tīm′) *n.* The winter season.

winter wheat. Wheat planted in the autumn and harvested the following spring or early summer.

Win·throp (wĭn′thrəp). Family of English colonial administrators in America, including **John** (1588–1649), first and seven times governor of Massachusetts Bay colony (1629–49); his son, **John** (1606–1676), three times governor of Connecticut (1636; 1657; 1659–76); and his grandson, **John** (1638–1707), governor of Connecticut (1698–1707).

win·try (wĭn′trē) *adj.* **-trier, -triest.** Also **win·ter·y** (wĭn′tə-rē) **-ier, -iest. 1.** Belonging to or characteristic of winter; cold. **2.** Suggestive of winter; cheerless. —**win′tri·ly** *adv.* —**win′tri·ness** *n.*

win·y (wī′nē) *adj.* **-ier, -iest.** Having the qualities or taste of wine; intoxicating; heady.

Win·yah Bay (wĭn′yô). An inlet of the Atlantic Ocean in eastern South Carolina.

winze (wĭnz) *n. Mining.* An inclined or vertical shaft or passage between levels. [Variant of earlier *winds,* probably from Middle English *wynde,* windlass, perhaps from Middle Dutch or Middle Low German *winde.* See **wendh-** in Appendix.*]

wipe (wīp) *tr.v.* **wiped, wiping, wipes. 1.** To subject to light rubbing or friction, as of a cloth or paper, in order to clean or dry. **2.** To remove by rubbing; to brush. Usually used with *off* or *away.* **3.** To rub, move, or pass over something. **4.** *Plumbing.* To form (a joint) by spreading solder with a piece of cloth or leather. —**wipe out. 1.** To destroy; annihilate. **2.** *Informal.* To murder. **3.** In surfing, to lose balance and fall or jump off a surfboard. —*n.* **1.** The act of wiping. **2.** A wiper. **3.** A blow; swipe. **4.** *Informal.* A jeer; gibe. [Middle English *wipen,* Old English *wīpian.* See **weip-** in Appendix.*]

wip·er (wī′pər) *n.* **1.** One that wipes. **2.** A device designed for wiping, as for a windshield. **3.** *Machinery.* A cam that projects from a rotating horizontal shaft to activate another part. **4.** *Electricity.* A movable electrical contact, as in a rheostat.

wire (wīr) *n.* **1.** A usually pliable metallic strand or rod made in many lengths and diameters, sometimes clad and often electrically insulated, used chiefly for structural support or to conduct electricity. **2.** A group of such strands bundled or twisted together as a functional unit; a cable. **3.** Something resembling a wire, as in slenderness or stiffness. **4.** The telegraph service. **5.** A telegram. **6.** An open telephone connection. **7.** The screen on which sheets of paper are formed in a papermaking machine. **8.** The finish line of a racetrack. —**get (in) under the wire.** To arrive somewhere or finish something just in the nick of time. —**lay wires for.** To make preparations for. —**pull wires.** To use secret or underhand means to accomplish something, as if manipulating puppets. —*adj.* Made of or resembling a wire or wires. —*v.* **wired, wiring, wires.** —*tr.* **1.** To bind, connect, or attach with a wire or wires. **2.** To string on wire, as beads. **3.** To equip with a system of electrical wires. **4.** To send by telegraph: *wire congratulations.* **5.** To send a telegram to. —*intr.* To send a telegram; to telegraph. [Middle English *wir(e),* Old English *wīr.* See **wei-**[1] in Appendix.*]

wire cloth. A mesh woven of fine wire.

wire-draw (wīr′drô′) *tr.v.* **-drew** (-dro͞o′), **-drawn** (-drôn′), **-drawing, -draws. 1.** To draw (metal) into wire. **2.** To treat (a subject, for example) with great length, excessive detail, or overrefinement; spin out. —**wire′draw′er** *n.*

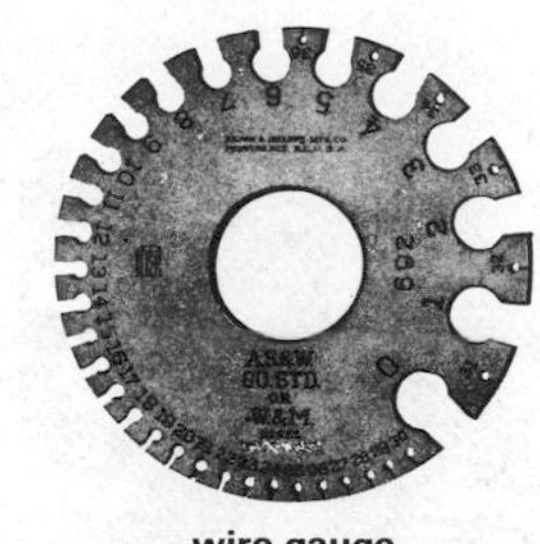

wire gauge

wire gauge. *Abbr.* **w.g. 1.** A gauge for measuring the diameter of wire, usually in the form of a disk having variously sized slots in its periphery or a long graduated plate with similar slots along its edge. **2.** A standardized system of wire sizes.

wire gauze. A material woven of very fine wires.

wire glass. Sheet glass reinforced with wire netting.

wire·grass (wīr′grăs′, -gräs′) *n.* Any of various grasses having tough, wiry roots or rootstocks, such as **Bermuda grass** *(see).*

wire-haired (wīr′hârd′) *adj.* Having a coat of stiff, wiry hair.

wire-haired terrier. A dog, a variety of **terrier** *(see).*

wire·less (wīr′lĭs) *adj.* **1.** Without wires. **2.** *British.* Radio. —*n.* **1.** A radio telegraph or telephone system. **2.** A message transmitted by wireless telegraph or telephone. **3.** *British.* Radio. —*v.* **wirelessed, -lessing, -lesses.** —*tr.* To communicate with by wireless. —*intr.* To communicate by wireless.

wireless telegraphy. Telegraphy by radio rather than by long-distance transmission lines. Also called "wireless telegraph."

wireless telephone. **Radiotelephone** *(see).*

wire·man (wīr′mən) *n., pl.* **-men** (-mĭn). One who works with electric wiring; a lineman.

wire netting. Netting made of woven wire, as for fences.

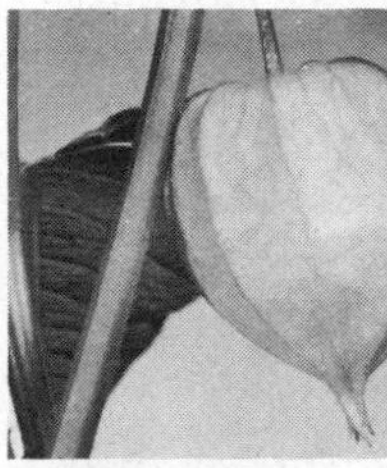

winter cherry
Seed case

wire·pull·er (wīr′po͝ol′ər) *n.* **1.** One who pulls wires or strings, as of puppets. **2.** One who uses subterfuge, private influence, or underhand means in order to further his own or another's interests. —**wire′pull′ing** *n.*

wir·er (wīr′ər) *n.* **1.** A trapper who uses wire traps to snare game. **2.** One who wires.

wire recorder. A forerunner of the tape recorder that recorded sound on a spool of wire rather than on magnetic tape.

wire rope. A rope composed of twisted strands of wire.

wire·tap (wīr′tăp′) *n.* **1.** A concealed listening or recording device connected to a communications circuit. **2.** The installation of such a device. —*v.* **wiretapped, -tapping, -taps.** —*tr.* **1.** To connect a wiretap to. **2.** To monitor (a telephone line) by means of a wiretap. —*intr.* To install or monitor by a wiretap. —*adj.* Of or pertaining to a wiretap. —**wire′tap′per** *n.*

wire·work (wīr′wûrk′) *n.* **1.** Wire fabric. **2.** Articles made of wire or wire fabric.

wire·worm (wīr′wûrm′) *n.* **1.** The wirelike larva of various click beetles, causing severe damage by boring into the roots of many kinds of plants. **2.** Any of various millipedes.

wire-wove (wīr′wōv′) *adj.* **1.** Denoting a high grade of writing paper with a smooth finish. **2.** Made of woven wire.

wir·ing (wīr′ĭng) *n.* **1.** The act of attaching, connecting, or installing electric wires. **2.** A system of electric wires.

wir·ra (wĭr′ə) *interj. Irish.* Used to express sorrow. [Short for Irish Gaelic *a Muire,* "Oh, Mary."]

wir·y (wīr′ē) *adj.* **-ier, -iest. 1.** Of wire. **2.** Wirelike; stiff; kinky: *wiry hair.* **3.** Sinewy and lean; slender but tough. Said of animals and persons. —**wir′i·ly** *adv.* —**wir′i·ness** *n.*

Wis·con·sin (wĭs-kŏn′sən). *Abbr.* **Wis.** A state of the United States, occupying 56,154 square miles in the north on Lake Superior and Lake Michigan; admitted to the Union in 1848. Population, 4,107,000. Capital, Madison. See map at **United States of America.**

Wis·con·sin River (wĭs-kŏn′sən). A river rising in north-central Wisconsin and flowing 430 miles south to the Mississippi.

wis·dom (wĭz′dəm) *n.* **1.** Understanding of what is true, right, or lasting. **2.** Common sense; sagacity; good judgment: *"it is a characteristic of wisdom not to do desperate things"* (Thoreau). **3.** Learning; erudition. —See Synonyms at **knowledge.** [Middle English *wisedom,* Old English *wīsdōm.* See **weid-** in Appendix.*]

Wisdom of Jesus, the Son of Si·rach (sī′răk′). A book of the Apocrypha, **Ecclesiasticus** *(see).*

Wisdom of Solomon. A book of the Apocrypha.

wisdom tooth. One of four molars, the last on each side of both jaws, usually erupting much later than the others. [Translation of New Latin *dentes sapientiae* (plural).]

wise[1] (wīz) *adj.* **wiser, wisest. 1.** Having wisdom or discernment for what is true, right, or lasting; judicious. **2.** Possessed of common sense; prudent; sensible. **3.** Having great learning; highly educated; erudite. **4.** Shrewd; crafty; cunning: *a wise*

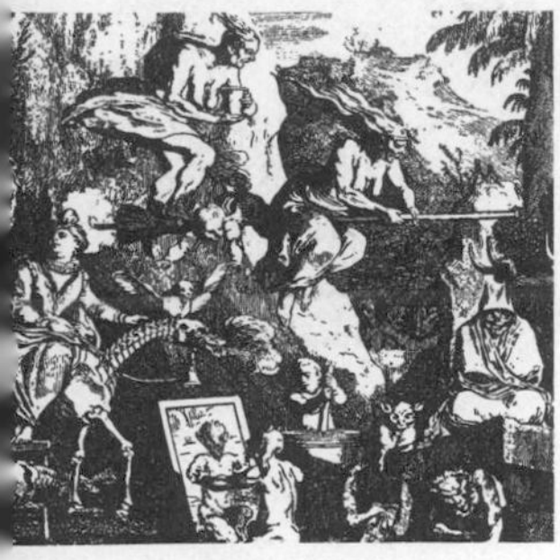

witches' Sabbath

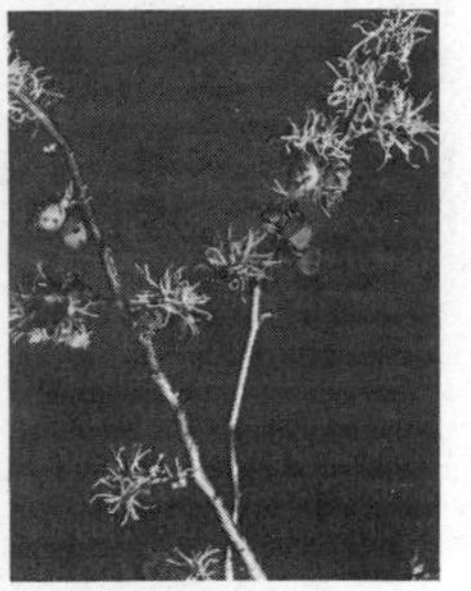

witch hazel
Hamamelis virginiana
Flowers and seed capsules

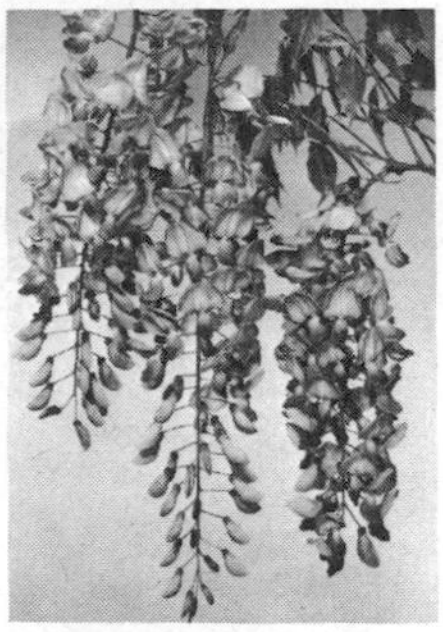

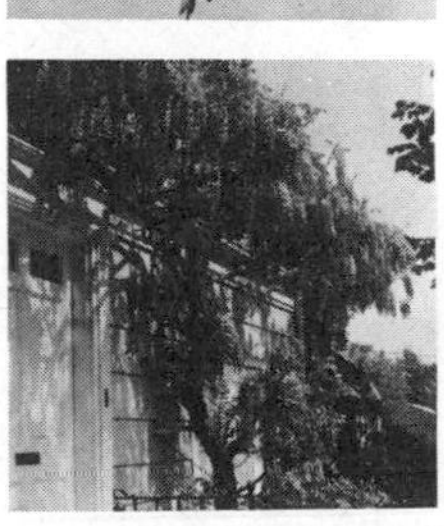

wisteria
Wisteria sinensis
Above: Flower clusters

move. **5.** Having knowledge or information; informed; aware of. **6.** *Slang.* Offensively self-assured; arrogant. **—get wise.** *Slang.* **1.** To learn the facts or become aware of. Usually used with *to.* **2.** To become provocatively insolent. **—wise up.** *Slang.* To become or make aware or sophisticated. Often used with *to.* [Middle English *wis(e),* Old English *wīs.* See **weid-** in Appendix.*] **—wise'ly** *adv.*

wise[2] (wīz) *n.* Method or manner of doing; fashion; way. Usually used in the phrases *in no wise; in this wise; in any wise.* [Middle English *wise,* Old English *wīse, wīs,* manner, condition. See **weid-** in Appendix.*]

-wise. Used to form adverbs from nouns or adjectives to indicate: **1.** Manner, direction, or position; for example, **clockwise. 2.** *Informal.* With reference to. See Usage note. [Middle English *-wise,* in a certain manner, Old English *-wisan,* from *wīse,* WISE (manner).]

Usage: The practice of attaching *-wise* to nouns, in the sense of *with reference to,* has become so closely associated with commercial jargon in the minds of many writers and speakers that it is dubious usage on any higher level. Resistance to such combinations is also strengthened by the tendency of some persons to form them indiscriminately and to overuse them. The following typical examples, often found in business writing and speech as an aid to conciseness, are termed unacceptable in general usage by 84 per cent of the Usage Panel: *Taxwise, it is an attractive arrangement. The report is not encouraging saleswise.*

wise·a·cre (wīz'ā'kər) *n. Informal.* An offensively self-assured person. [Middle Dutch *wijsseggher,* soothsayer, variant (influenced by *segghen,* to say) of Old High German *wīssago, wīzago,* seer. See **weid-** in Appendix.*]

wise·crack (wīz'krăk') *n. Slang.* A flippant, commonly sardonic remark or retort; a joke or gibe. See Synonyms at **joke.** *—intr.v.* **wisecracked, -cracking, -cracks.** *Slang.* To make or utter a wisecrack. **—wise'crack'er** *n.*

wise guy. *Slang.* An offensively self-assured person.

wis·en·heim·er (wīz'ən-hī'mər) *n.* Also **weis·en·heim·er.** *Informal.* An offensively self-assured person. [Pseudo-German, from WISE.]

wi·sent (vē'zĕnt') *n.* The European bison, *Bison bonasus.* See **bison.** [German *Wisent,* from Old High German *wisunt.* See **weis-**[1] in Appendix.*]

wish (wĭsh) *n.* **1.** A desire, longing, or strong inclination for some specific thing. **2.** An expression or confession of such a desire, longing, or strong inclination; petition; prayer. **3.** Something desired or longed for; a goal. *—v.* **wished, wishing, wishes.** *—tr.* **1.** To desire or long for; to want: *I wish to know.* **2.** To desire (a person or thing) to be in a specified state or condition: *I wish this rug were green.* **3.** To entertain or express wishes for; to bid: *He wished her good night.* **4.** To call or invoke upon: *I wish him luck.* **5.** To order or entreat: *I wish you to go.* **6.** To impose or force; foist. Used with *on: They wished a hard job on him.* *—intr.* **1.** To have or feel a desire. Usually used with *for: wish for the moon.* **2.** To express a wish. [Middle English *wisshen,* Old English *wȳscan.* See **wen-** in Appendix.*] **—wish'er** *n.*

Usage: *Wish,* as a transitive verb meaning *want, desire,* or *wish for,* is usually followed by an object in the form of an infinitive or clause, by an object with an infinitive, or by an object in combination with an indirect object, as in *wish him success.* In modern usage *want* is preferable to *wish* in this sense when the verb is followed merely by a simple object: *Do you want coffee?* In the example just cited, *wish* is acceptable to only 39 per cent of the Usage Panel, and is considered a genteelism by most of those who prefer *want.*

wish·bone (wĭsh'bōn') *n.* The forked bone, or furcula, anterior to the breastbone of most birds, formed by the fusion of the clavicles. [So called from its use as a wish token. When it is snapped apart by two people, the person getting the longer piece will supposedly have his wish fulfilled.]

wish·ful (wĭsh'fəl) *adj.* Having or expressing a wish or longing. **—wish'ful·ly** *adv.* **—wish'ful·ness** *n.*

wish fulfillment. **1.** The gratification of a desire. **2.** *Psychoanalysis.* The satisfaction of a desire or the release of tension by the exercise of imagination.

wishful thinking. Erroneous identification of one's own wishes with reality.

wish-wash (wĭsh'wŏsh', -wôsh') *n. Informal.* A thin, watery drink; slops. [Reduplication of WASH.]

wish·y-wash·y (wĭsh'ē-wŏsh'ē, -wô'shē) *adj.* **-ier, -iest.** *Informal.* **1.** Watery; thin; weak. **2.** Lacking in strength or purpose; feeble. [Reduplication of *washy,* from WASH.]

Wis·la. The Polish name for the **Vistula.**

wisp (wĭsp) *n.* **1.** A small bunch or bundle, as of straw, hair, or grass. **2. a.** Someone or something thin, frail, or slight. **b.** A thin or faint streak or fragment, as of smoke or clouds. **3.** A fleeting trace or indication; a hint; suggestion: *a wisp of a smile.* **4.** A flock of birds, especially of snipe. **5.** A will-o'-the-wisp, **ignis fatuus** *(see).* —See Synonyms at **flock.** *—tr.v.* **wisped, wisping, wisps.** To twist into a wisp. [Middle English *wisp, wips*†.] **—wisp'y** *adj.*

wist. *Archaic.* Past tense and past participle of **wit** (to know).

wis·ter·i·a (wĭ-stîr'ē-ə) *n.* Also **wis·tar·i·a** (wĭ-stâr'ē-ə). Any of several climbing woody vines of the genus *Wisteria,* having compound leaves and drooping clusters of showy purplish or white flowers. [New Latin *Wisteria,* after Caspar *Wistar* or *Wister* (1761–1818), American anatomist.]

wist·ful (wĭst'fəl) *adj.* Full of a melancholy yearning; longing pensively; wishful. [Originally "attentive," from obsolete *wistly*†.] **—wist'ful·ly** *adv.* **—wist'ful·ness** *n.*

wit[1] (wĭt) *n.* **1.** The natural ability to perceive or know; understanding; intelligence; good sense. **2.** *Usually plural.* **a.** Keenness of perception or discernment; ingenuity; resourcefulness: *using one's wits.* **b.** Sound mental faculties; sanity: *scared out of one's wits.* **3. a.** The ability to perceive and express in an ingeniously humorous manner the relationship or similarity between seemingly incongruous or disparate things: *"Humor is, as it were, the growth of nature and accident; wit is the product of art and fancy."* (Hazlitt). **b.** One noted for this ability; especially, one skilled in repartee. —See Synonyms at **mind. —at one's wits' end.** At the limit of one's mental resources; utterly at a loss. **—have** (or **keep**) **one's wits about one.** To remain alert or calm, especially in a crisis. [Middle English *wit,* Old English *wit.* See **weid-** in Appendix.*]

Synonyms: *wit, humor, repartee, sarcasm, irony.* These nouns, related but not always interchangeable, are compared as they denote forms of expression. *Wit* especially implies mental keenness, ability to discern those elements of a situation or condition that relate to what is comic, and talent for making an effective comment on them. *Humor,* closely related, suggests the ability to recognize the incongruity and absurdity inherent in life and to use them as the basis of expression in some medium. Both *wit* and *humor* are associated with amusement or laughter, but *wit* often implies brilliant, pointed, or cutting statement, whereas *humor* is also applicable to what is kindly or broadly funny. *Repartee,* or the exchange of wit, generally in conversation, implies facility in answering quickly and cleverly. *Sarcasm* is usually a form of wit intended to taunt, wound, or subject another to ridicule or contempt. Often it involves *irony,* a form of statement whose witty intent is contrary to, and sometimes the opposite of, the literal meaning of the words employed. In this sense *irony* is often employed to point up mockingly the discrepancies between reality, with its shortcomings, and a more desirable state.

wit[2] (wĭt) *v.* **wist** (wĭst), **witting** or **witing,** present indicative **I wot** (wŏt), **thou wost** (wŏst) or **wostteth** (wŏs'təth), **he wot** or **wotteth** (wŏt'əth), **we, you, they wite** (wĭt) or **witen** (wĭt'n). *Archaic.* *—tr.* To be or become aware of; know; learn. *—intr.* To know. **—to wit.** That is to say; namely. [Middle English *witen,* Old English *witan.* See **weid-** in Appendix.*]

wit·an (wĭt'än) *pl.n.* **1.** The members of the **witenagemot** *(see)* in Anglo-Saxon England. **2.** The **witenagemot** *(see).* [Old English *witan,* plural of *wita,* councilor. See **weid-** in Appendix.*]

witch (wĭch) *n.* **1.** A woman who practices sorcery or is believed to have dealings with the devil. **2.** An ugly, vicious old woman; a hag. **3.** *Informal.* A bewitching young woman or girl. *—tr.v.* **witched, witching, witches. 1.** To work or cast a spell upon; bewitch. **2.** To cause, bring, or effect by witchcraft. [Middle English *wicche,* Old English *wicce* (feminine), witch, and *wicca* (masculine), wizard. See **weik-**[2] in Appendix.*]

witch·craft (wĭch'krăft', -kräft') *n.* **1.** Black magic; sorcery. **2.** A magical or irresistible influence, attraction, or charm. —See Synonyms at **magic.**

witch doctor. A medicine man or shaman among primitive peoples.

witch elm. Variant of **wych elm.**

witch·er·y (wĭch'ə-rē) *n., pl.* **-ies. 1.** Sorcery; witchcraft. **2.** Power to charm or fascinate.

witch·es-broom (wĭch'ĭz-brōōm', -brŏŏm') *n.* An abnormal, brushlike growth of weak, closely clustered shoots or branches on a tree or woody plant, caused by fungi or viruses.

witches' Sabbath. An orgy of demons, witches, and sorcerers. Also called "sabbat."

witch grass. 1. A North American grass, *Panicum capillare,* having branching, purplish panicles. **2. Couch grass** *(see).*

witch hazel. 1. Any of several shrubs of the genus *Hamamelis;* especially, *H. virginiana,* of eastern North America, having yellow flowers that bloom in late autumn or winter. **2.** An alcoholic solution containing an extract of the bark and leaves of this shrub, applied externally as a mild astringent. [From Middle English *wyche,* WYCH (ELM) + HAZEL.]

witch hunt. A political campaign launched on the pretext of investigating activities subversive to the state. **—witch'-hunt'er** *n.* **—witch'-hunt'ing** *adj.* & *n.*

witch·ing (wĭch'ĭng) *adj.* **1.** Pertaining to or appropriate for witchcraft: *the witching hour.* **2.** Having power to charm or enchant; bewitching. *—n.* Witchcraft. **—witch'ing·ly** *adv.*

witch moth. Any of several large moths of the genus *Erebus,* of the southern United States and tropical America. [From its nocturnal habits.]

wite[1] (wīt) *n. Scottish.* Blame; fault. [Middle English *wite,* Old English *wīte,* fine, penalty. See **weid-** in Appendix.*]

wite[2]. *Archaic.* First, second, and third person plural present indicative of **wit** (to know).

wit·en. *Archaic.* Alternate first, second, and third person plural present indicative of **wit** (to know).

wit·e·na·ge·mot (wĭt'n-ə-gə-mōt') *n.* An Anglo-Saxon advisory council to the king, composed of about 100 nobles, prelates, and other officials, convened at intervals to discuss administrative and judicial affairs. Also called "witan." [Old English *witena gemōt* : *witena,* genitive plural of *wita,* councilor (see **weid-** in Appendix*) + *gemōt,* meeting, assembly (see **mōd-** in Appendix*).]

with (wĭth, wĭth) *prep. Abbr.* **w. 1.** As a companion of; accompanying: *Who went with him?* **2.** Next to: *Walk with him.* **3.** Having as a possession, attribute, or characteristic: *a man with a moustache.* **4.** In a manner characterized by: *perform with skill.* **5.** In the charge or keeping of: *She left the letter with* *the doorman.* **6.** In the opinion or estimation of: *if it's all right with you.* **7.** In support of; on the side of: *Are you with me or against me?* **8.** Of the same opinion or belief as: *He is with us on that.* **9.** In the same group or mixture as; among: *Mix the roses with the fern.* **10.** In the membership or employment of: *He is with a publishing company.* **11.** By the means or agency of: *eat with a fork.* **12.** In spite of: *With all his talent, he could not get a job.* **13.** In the same direction as: *bend with the wind.* **14.** At the same time as: *rise with the sun.* **15.** In regard to: *I am pleased with her.* **16.** In comparison or contrast to: *a dress identical with the one she has just bought.* **17.** Having received: *With her permission, he left.* **18.** And; plus; added to. See Usage note below. **19.** In opposition to; against: *wrestling with an opponent.* **20.** As a result or consequence of; under the influence of: *trembling with fear.* **21.** To; onto: *Couple the first car with the second.* **22.** So as to be free of or separated from: *part with a friend.* **23.** In the course of: *We grow older with the hours.* **24.** In proportion to: *wines that improve with age.* **25.** In relationship to: *at ease with his peers.* **26.** As well as; in favorable comparison to: *She sings with the best of them.* —See Synonyms at **by.** —**be** (or **get**) **with it.** *Informal.* To be or become aware, sophisticated, or up-to-date. —**in with.** In league or association with: *He is in with the wrong crowd.* [Middle English *with,* with, against, by means of, Old English *with,* against or in opposition to, together with. See **wi-** in Appendix.*]

Usage: *With* does not have the conjunctive force of *and.* Consequently, when *with* introduces a phrase following a singular subject, it does not affect the number of the verb, which remains singular: *The governor, with two of his aides, is expected at the fair on Monday.* Inexperienced writers often use *with* loosely as a means of attaching to a sentence an additional thought that would be treated more clearly and grammatically as an independent clause either following a semicolon or introduced by *and: English and history are his major subjects with economics as his first elective* (preferably *English and history are his major subjects; economics is his first elective*).

with·al (wĭth-ôl′) *adv.* **1.** Besides; in addition: *"And, withal, a wider publicity was given to thought-provoking ideas"* (Holbrook Jackson). **2.** Despite that; nevertheless: *"the boys* [were] *mettlesome and dangerous but, withal, sweet-tempered to those who knew how to handle them"* (Margaret Mitchell). **3.** *Archaic.* Therewith: *a maid for him to marry withal.* —*prep. Archaic.* With. [Middle English *with al(le)* : WITH + ALL.]

with·draw (wĭth-drô′, wĭth-) *v.* **-drew** (-dro͞o′), **-drawn** (-drôn′), **-drawing, -draws.** —*tr.* **1.** To take back or away; remove. **2.** To recall; retract. —*intr.* **1.** To move or draw back; retreat; retire. **2.** To remove oneself from activity or a social or emotional environment. [Middle English *withdrawen* : *with,* away from, WITH + *drawen,* to pull, DRAW.]

with·draw·al (wĭth-drô′əl, wĭth-) *n.* Also **with·draw·ment** (-drô′mənt). **1.** The act or process of withdrawing, as: **a.** A retreat or retirement. **b.** A detachment, as from emotional involvement. **c.** A removal from a place or position of something that has been deposited. **2. a.** Termination of the administration of a habit-forming substance. **b.** The physiological readjustment that takes place upon such discontinuation.

with·drawn (wĭth-drôn′, wĭth-). Past participle of **withdraw.** —*adj.* **1.** Not readily approached; remote; isolated. **2.** Socially retiring; modest; shy. **3.** Emotionally unresponsive.

with·drew. Past tense of **withdraw.**

withe (wĭth, wĭth, wīth) *n.* A tough, supple twig, especially a willow twig, used for binding things together; withy. —*tr.v.* **withed, withing, withes.** To bind with withes. [Middle English *witthe, withe,* Old English *withthe.* See **wei-¹** in Appendix.*]

with·er (wĭth′ər) *v.* **-ered, -ering, -ers.** —*intr.* **1.** To dry up or shrivel from or as if from loss of moisture. **2.** To lose freshness; fade; droop. —*tr.* **1.** To cause to shrivel or fade. **2.** To cause to feel belittled; cut down; abash: *withered her with a glance.* [Middle English *widderen,* perhaps variant of *wederen,* to weather, from *weder,* WEATHER.]

with·er·ite (wĭth′ə-rīt′) *n.* A white, yellow, or gray vitreous mineral, chiefly $BaCO_3$. [First described and analyzed by William *Withering* (1741–1799), English physician.]

withe rod. A shrub, *Viburnum cassinoides,* of eastern North America, having clusters of small white flowers and bluish-black fruit. Sometimes called "Appalachian tea."

with·ers (wĭth′ərz) *pl.n.* The high point of the back of a horse, or of a similar or related animal, located at the base of the neck and between the shoulder blades. [Perhaps from obsolete *wither-,* denoting opposition (the withers resist or "oppose" a horse's load), from Middle English *wither-,* Old English *wither-,* from *wither,* against. See **wi-** in Appendix.*]

with·er·shins (wĭth′ər-shĭnz′) *adv.* Also **wid·der·shins** (wĭd′-). *Scottish.* **1.** In the opposite direction; in reverse; counterclockwise. **2.** In a direction opposite to the course of the sun. [Middle Low German *weddersin(ne)s,* from Middle High German *widersinnes,* "counter-course" : *wider,* against, from Old High German *widar* (see **wi-** in Appendix*) + *sinnes,* genitive of *sin,* journey (see **sent-** in Appendix*).]

with·hold (wĭth-hōld′, wĭth-) *v.* **-held** (-hĕld′), **-holding, -holds.** —*tr.* **1.** To keep in check; restrain. **2.** To refrain from giving, granting, or permitting. —*intr.* To refrain; forbear. —See Synonyms at **keep.** [Middle English *withholden* : *with,* back, away from, WITH + *holden,* to HOLD.] —**with·hold′er** *n.*

withholding tax. A portion of an employee's wages or salary withheld by his employer as partial payment of his income tax.

with·in (wĭth-ĭn′, wĭth-) *adv.* **1.** In or into the inner part; inside. **2.** Not outside; indoors. **3.** Inside the body, mind, heart, or soul; inwardly. —*prep.* **1.** In the inner part or parts of; inside: *"it's there/within you/though the key's missing"* (Denise Levertov). **2.** Inside the limits or extent in time, degree or distance: *within ten miles of home.* **3.** Inside the fixed limits of; not exceeding or transgressing: *within the laws of the land.* **4.** In the scope or sphere of: *within the medical profession.*

with·in·doors (wĭth-ĭn′dôrz′, -dōrz′, wĭth-) *adv.* Into or inside a building; indoors.

with·out (wĭth-out′, wĭth-) *adv.* **1.** In or on the outside. **2.** Outdoors. —**do without.** To get along although lacking: *do without money.* —*prep.* **1.** Not having; lacking: *a family without a car.* **2. a.** With no or none of; in the absence of: *without help.* **b.** Not accompanied by: *smoke without fire.* **3.** Free from: *without doubt.* **4.** At, on, to, or toward the outside or exterior of. **5.** With neglect or avoidance of: *went by without speaking to us.* —*conj. Regional.* Unless. [Middle English *withouten,* Old English *withūtan* : *with,* not together with, separated, WITH + *ūtan,* outside of, from *ūt,* OUT.]

with·out·doors (wĭth-out′dôrz′, -dōrz′, wĭth-) *adv.* Outside of a house or shelter; outdoors.

with·stand (wĭth-stănd′, wĭth-) *v.* **-stood** (-sto͝od′), **-standing, -stands.** —*tr.* To oppose (something) with force; resist. —*intr.* To resist or endure successfully. —See Synonyms at **oppose.** [Middle English *withstanden,* Old English *withstandan* : *with,* against, WITH + *standan,* to STAND.] —**with·stand′er** *n.*

with·y (wĭth′ē, wĭth′ē) *adj.* **1.** Made of or as flexible as withes; tough. **2.** Wiry and agile. Said of people. —*n., pl.* **withies.** **1.** A rope or band made of withes. **2.** A long, flexible twig, as that of an osier. **3.** A tree or shrub having such twigs. [Middle English *wythy,* flexible twig, willow wand, Old English *wīthig.* See **wei-¹** in Appendix.*]

wit·ing. *Archaic.* Alternate present participle of **wit** (to know).

wit·less (wĭt′lĭs) *adj.* Lacking intelligence or wit; stupid. —**wit′less·ly** *adv.* —**wit′less·ness** *n.*

wit·ling (wĭt′lĭng) *n. Archaic.* One who thinks himself a wit.

wit·loof (wĭt′lōf′) *n.* A salad plant, **endive** *(see).* [Dutch, "white leaf."]

wit·ness (wĭt′nĭs) *n.* **1. a.** One who has seen or heard something. **b.** One who furnishes evidence. **2.** Anything that serves as evidence; a sign. **3.** *Law.* **a.** One who is called upon to testify before a court. **b.** One who is called upon to be present at a transaction in order to attest to what took place. **c.** One who signs his name to a document for the purpose of attesting to its authenticity. **4.** An attestation to a fact, statement, or event. —*v.* **witnessed, -nessing, -nesses.** —*tr.* **1.** To be present at or have personal knowledge of. **2.** To provide or serve as evidence of. **3.** To testify to; bear witness. **4.** To be the setting or site of: *This auditorium witnesses many ceremonies.* **5.** To attest to the legality or authenticity of by signing one's name. —*intr.* To furnish or serve as evidence; testify. [Middle English *witnes(se),* Old English *witnes,* witness, knowledge, from *wit,* knowledge, WIT.] —**wit′ness·er** *n.*

witness stand. The place in a courtroom from which a witness presents testimony. Also *chiefly British* "witness box."

Wit·ten·berg (wĭt′n-bûrg; *German* vĭt′n-bĕrk). A city of East Germany; the site of Luther's public challenge of the Roman Catholic Church. Population, 46,000.

wit·ti·cism (wĭt′ĭ-sĭz′əm) *n.* A witty remark or saying. See Synonyms at **joke.** [From WITTY (influenced by CRITICISM).]

wit·ting (wĭt′ĭng). *Archaic.* Present participle of **wit** (to know). —*adj.* **1.** Aware or conscious. **2.** Done intentionally or with premeditation; deliberate. —**wit′ting·ly** *adv.*

wit·tol (wĭt′l) *n. Obsolete.* A man who tolerates his wife's infidelity. [Middle English *wetewold* : *weten, witen,* to WIT (know) + *(coke)wold,* (CUCK)OLD.]

wit·ty (wĭt′ē) *adj.* **-tier, -tiest.** **1.** Possessing or demonstrating wit in speech or writing; very clever and humorous. **2.** Characterized by or having the nature of wit: *a witty saying.* **3.** *British Regional.* Intelligent. —**wit′ti·ly** *adv.* —**wit′ti·ness** *n.*

Wit·wa·ters·rand (wĭt-wô′tərz-rănd, wĭt-wôt′ərz-). A region of South Africa, in southern Transvaal, noted for its rich deposits of gold and other minerals; the site of several industrial cities, including Johannesburg. Also informally called "The Rand."

wive (wīv) *v.* **wived, wiving, wives.** *Archaic.* —*tr.* **1.** To marry (a woman); take as a wife. **2.** To provide a wife for. —*intr.* To marry a woman. [Middle English *wiven,* Old English *wīfian,* from *wīf,* WIFE.]

wi·vern, wy·vern (wī′vərn) *n.* Also **wi·ver** (wī′vər). *Heraldry.* A two-legged dragon having wings and a barbed and knotted tail. [Middle English *wiver, guivre,* viper, from Old French *wivre, guivre,* from Latin *vipera,* VIPER.]

wives. Plural of **wife.**

wiz (wĭz) *n. Informal.* A person considered exceptionally gifted or skilled. [Short for WIZARD.]

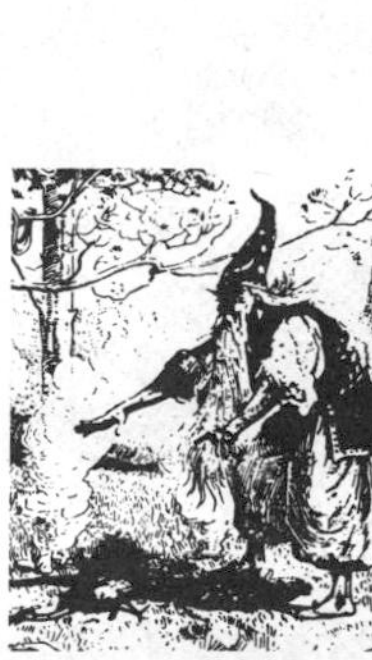

wizard

wiz·ard (wĭz′ərd) *n.* **1.** A male witch; a sorcerer or magician. **2.** A skillful or clever person. **3.** *Obsolete.* A wise man or sage. —*adj.* **1.** Of or pertaining to wizards or wizardry. **2.** *Chiefly British Slang.* Excellent. [Middle English *wysard* : *wys, wis,* WISE (smart) + -ARD.]

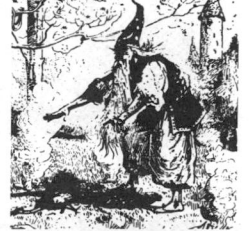

wiz·ard·ry (wĭz′ər-drē) *n.* The art, skill, or practice of a wizard; witchcraft; sorcery.

wiz·en¹ (wĭz′ən) *v.* **-ened, -ening, -ens.** —*intr.* To wither or sear; dry up; shrivel. —*tr.* To cause to wither or dry up. —*adj.* Shriveled or dried up; withered: *"There would be a day when his face would be wrinkled and wizen"* (Oscar Wilde). [Middle English *wisenen,* Old English *wisnian.* See **wei-³** in Appendix.*]

wiz·en² (wē′zən) *n.* The gullet, **weasand** *(see).*

wiz·ened (wĭz′ənd) *adj.* Shriveled; wizen.

wk. **1.** weak. **2.** week. **3.** work.

wkly. weekly.

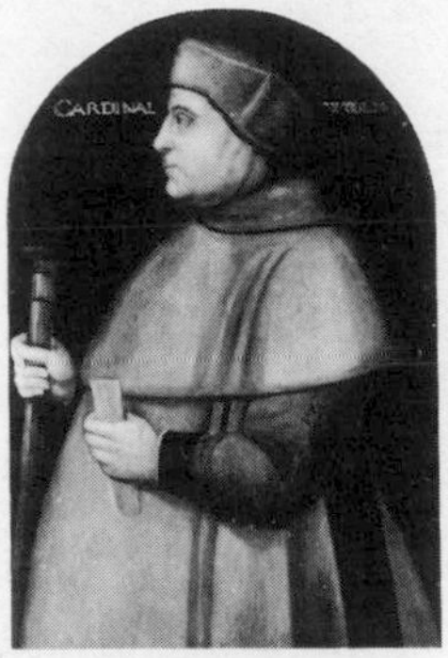

Thomas Wolsey

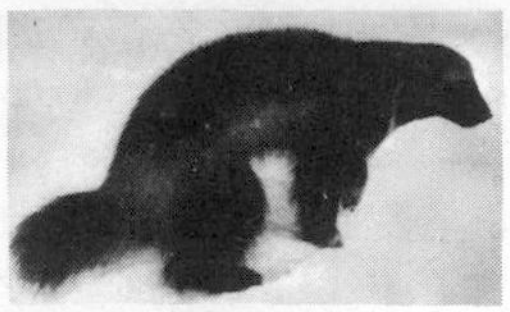
wolverine

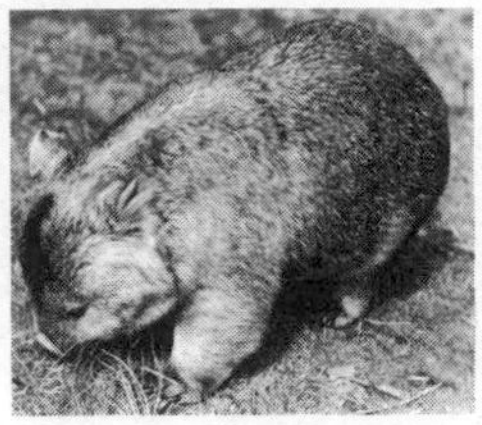
wombat
Phascolomis ursinus

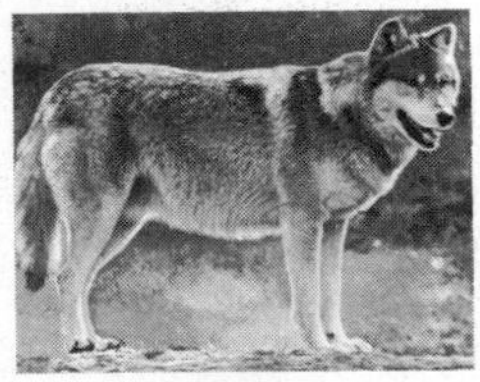
wolf
Canis lupus
Timber wolf

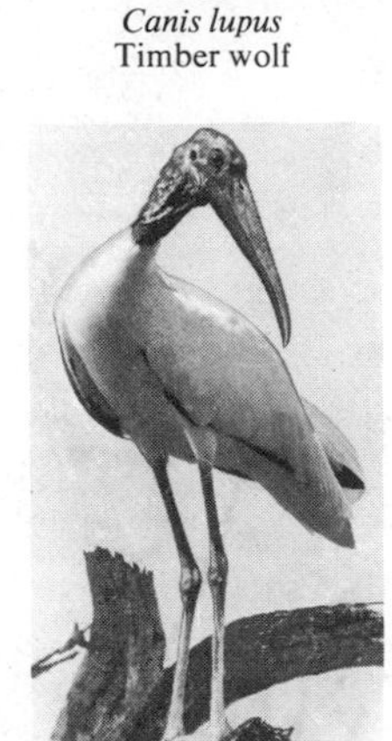
wood ibis
Mycteria americana

WL, w.l. water line.
Wm. William.
WMC War Manpower Commission.
wmk. watermark.
WMO World Meteorological Organization.
WNW west-northwest.
WO, W.O. warrant officer.
woad (wōd) *n.* **1.** An Old World plant, *Isatis tinctoria,* formerly cultivated for its leaves that yield a blue dye. **2.** The dye obtained from this plant. [Middle English *wod(e),* Old English *wād*.]
woad·wax·en (wōd′wăk′sən) *n.* A shrub, **dyer's greenweed** *(see).* [Variant (influenced by WOAD) of WOODWAXEN.]
wob·ble (wŏb′əl) *v.* **-bled, -bling, -bles.** Also **wab·ble.** —*intr.* **1.** To move erratically from side to side. **2.** To tremble or quaver; to shake, as a voice. **3.** To waver or vacillate in one's opinions, feelings, or the like. —*tr.* To cause to wobble. —*n.* Also **wab·ble. 1.** The act or an instance of wobbling; an unsteady motion. **2.** A tremulous and uncertain tone or sound: *a vocal wobble.* —See Synonyms at **shake.** [Perhaps from Low German *wabbeln.* See **webh-** in Appendix.*] —**wob′bler** *n.* —**wob′bling·ly** *adv.*
wob·bly[1] (wŏb′lē) *adj.* **-blier, -bliest.** Tending to wobble; unsteady; shaky.
wob·bly[2] (wŏb′lē) *n., pl.* **-blies.** Also **Wob·bly.** *Slang.* A member of the Industrial Workers of the World (I.W.W.). [Origin unknown.]
w.o.c. without compensation.
Wo·den (wōd′n). Also **Wo·dan.** The chief Teutonic god, often identified with the Norse god Odin. [Old English *Wōden.* See **wāt-** in Appendix.*]
woe (wō) *n.* Also *archaic* **wo. 1.** Deep sorrow; grief. **2.** Misfortune; calamity: *"Woe to the inhabiters of the earth and of the sea!"* (Revelation 12:12). —See Synonyms at **regret.** —*interj.* Used to express sorrow or dismay. [Middle English *wo(e),* Old English *wā* (interjection). See **wai** in Appendix.*]
woe·be·gone (wō′bĭ-gôn′, -gŏn′) *adj.* Also **wo·be·gone. 1.** Mournful or sorrowful in appearance. **2.** *Archaic.* Struck by disaster; afflicted. —See Synonyms at **sad.** [Middle English *wo begon* : *wo(e),* WOE + *begon,* beset, from *begon,* to beset, go about : *be-,* about + *gon,* to GO.]
woe·ful (wō′fəl) *adj.* Also **wo·ful. 1.** Afflicted with woe; mournful. **2.** Pitiful or deplorable.
Wöh·ler (vœ′lər), **Friedrich.** 1800–1882. German organic chemist; synthesized urea.
woke. Past tense and *chiefly British & regional* past participle of **wake.**
wok·en. *Chiefly British & Regional.* Past participle of **wake.**
wold[1] (wōld) *n.* An unforested rolling plain; a moor. [Middle English *wold,* a forest, hill, plain, Old English *weald, wald.* See **wel-**[5] in Appendix.*]
wold[2]**.** Variant of **weld** (plant).
Wolds, the (wōldz). A range of chalk hills along the coasts of Lincolnshire and Yorkshire, England.
wolf (wŏŏlf) *n., pl.* **wolves** (wŏŏlvz). **1. a.** Either of two carnivorous mammals, *Canis lupus,* of northern regions, or *C. rufus* (or *C. niger*), of southwestern North America, related to and resembling the dogs. **b.** The fur of such an animal. **2.** Any of various similar or related mammals. **3.** *Rare.* The destructive larva of any of various moths, beetles, or flies. **4. a.** One that is rapacious, predatory, and fierce. **b.** *Slang.* A man given to avid amatory pursuit of women. **5.** *Music.* **a.** Dissonance produced in some tones of a bowed stringed instrument through defective vibration. **b.** Dissonance in some intervals of a keyboard instrument tuned to a system of unequal temperament. —**cry wolf.** To raise a false alarm. —*tr.v.* **wolfed, wolfing, wolfs.** To eat voraciously. Often used with *down: "the town's big shots were . . . wolfing down the buffet"* (Ralph Ellison). [Middle English *wolf(e),* Old English *wulf.* See **wḷkwo-** in Appendix.*] —**wolf′ish** *adj.* —**wolf′ish·ly** *adv.*
Wolf (vôlf), **Hugo.** 1860–1903. Austrian composer of songs.
wolf·ber·ry (wŏŏlf′bĕr′ē) *n., pl.* **-ries.** A shrub, *Symphoricarpos occidentalis,* of western North America, having white berries.
Wolf Cub. *Chiefly British.* A Cub Scout.
wolf dog. 1. A dog trained to hunt wolves. **2.** The offspring of a dog and a wolf.
Wolfe (wŏŏlf), **James.** 1727–1759. British general; mortally wounded in the capture of Quebec (1759).
Wolfe (wŏŏlf), **Thomas (Clayton).** 1900–1938. American novelist.
Wolff·i·an body (wŏŏl′fē-ən). *Embryology.* The **mesonephros** *(see).* [Described by Kasper Friedrich *Wolff* (1733–1794), German scientist.]
wolf fish. Any of several northern marine fishes of the genus *Anarhichas,* having sharp, powerful teeth.
wolf·hound (wŏŏlf′hound′) *n.* Any of various large dogs trained to hunt wolves or other large game. See **borzoi, Irish wolfhound.**
wolf pack. A group of submarines attacking a single vessel or convoy.
wolf·ram (wŏŏl′frəm) *n. Rare.* The element **tungsten** *(see).* [German *Wolfram* : perhaps Middle High German *wolf,* wolf, from Old High German (see **wḷkwo-** in Appendix*) + *rām,* dirt, black, probably akin to Sanskrit *Rāma,* RAMA.]
wolf·ram·ite (wŏŏl′frə-mīt′) *n.* Any of several red-brown to black minerals with the general formula $(Fe,Mn)WO_4$, a major source of tungsten. [German *Wolframit,* from WOLFRAM.]
wolfs·bane (wŏŏlfs′bān′) *n.* A plant, the **monkshood** *(see).*
Wol·las·ton (wŏŏl′ə-stən), **William Hyde.** 1766–1828. British chemist, physiologist, and physicist.
wol·las·ton·ite (wŏŏl′ə-stə-nīt′) *n.* A mineral, essentially $CaSiO_3$, found in metamorphic rocks and used in various ceramics, paints, plastics, and cements. [After William WOLLASTON.]
Wol·lon·gong (wŏŏl′ən-gäng, -gông). A city of Australia, a port on the Tasman Sea south of Sydney. Population, 134,000.
Wo·lof (wō′lŏf′) *n.* A West Atlantic language of Senegal.
Wol·sey (wŏŏl′zē), **Thomas.** 1475?–1530. English cardinal and statesman; adviser to Henry VIII.
Wol·ver·hamp·ton (wŏŏl′vər-hămp′tən). A city of central England, in southern Staffordshire. Population, 150,000.
wol·ver·ine (wŏŏl′və-rēn′) *n.* A carnivorous mammal, *Gulo gulo* (or *G. luscus*), of northern regions, having dark fur and a bushy tail. Also called "glutton." [Irregularly from WOLF.]
Wolverine State. The nickname for Michigan.
wolves. Plural of **wolf.**
wom·an (wŏŏm′ən) *n., pl.* **women** (wĭm′ĭn). **1.** An adult female human being. **2.** Women collectively; womankind: *Woman is fickle.* **3.** Feminine quality or aspect; womanliness. Often preceded by *the: brought out the woman in him.* **4.** A maidservant. **5.** A mistress; paramour. **6.** *Informal.* A wife. —*adj.* Female as opposed to male. [Middle English *wumman, wimman,* Old English *wīfmann* : *wīf,* WIFE + *man(n),* person, MAN.]
wom·an·hood (wŏŏm′ən-hŏŏd′) *n.* **1.** The state of being a woman. **2.** Woman's nature. **3.** Womankind.
wom·an·ish (wŏŏm′ə-nĭsh) *adj.* **1.** Characteristic of a woman; womanlike. **2.** Effeminate and weak. —See Synonyms at **feminine.** —**wom′an·ish·ly** *adv.* —**wom′an·ish·ness** *n.*
wom·an·ize (wŏŏm′ə-nīz′) *v.* **-ized, -izing, -izes.** —*tr.* To give feminine characteristics to. —*intr.* To pursue women illicitly or excessively. —**wom′an·iz′er** *n.*
wom·an·kind (wŏŏm′ən-kīnd′) *n.* Female human beings collectively; women.
wom·an·ly (wŏŏm′ən-lē) *adj.* **-lier, -liest.** Having the becoming qualities of a woman. See Synonyms at **feminine.** —**wom′an·li·ness** *n.*
woman suffrage. The right of women to vote; exercise of the franchise by women. Also called "female suffrage." —**wom′an-suf′fra·gist** *n.*
womb (wōōm) *n.* **1.** *Anatomy.* The **uterus** *(see).* **2. a.** A place where something is generated. **b.** Any protective and confining organ, receptacle, or area. **3.** *Obsolete.* The belly. [Middle English *womb(e),* Old English *wamb,* from Common Germanic *wambō* (unattested).]
wom·bat (wŏm′băt′) *n.* Either of two Australian marsupials, *Phascolomis ursinus* or *Lasiorhinus latifrons,* somewhat resembling small bears. [Native Australian name.]
wom·en. Plural of **woman.**
wom·en·folk (wĭm′ĭn-fōk′) *pl.n.* Also **wom·en·folks** (-fōks′). **1.** Women collectively. **2.** A particular group of women.
won[1] (wŭn) *intr.v.* **wonned, wonning, wons.** *Archaic.* To dwell or abide. [Middle English *won(i)en,* Old English *wunian.* See **wen-** in Appendix.*]
won[2] (wôn) *n., pl.* **won. 1.** The basic monetary unit of South Korea, equal to 100 chon. See table of exchange rates at **currency. 2.** The basic monetary unit of North Korea, equal to 100 jun. See table of exchange rates at **currency.** [Korean.]
won[3]**.** Past tense and past participle of **win.**
won·der (wŭn′dər) *n.* **1.** That which arouses awe, astonishment, surprise, or admiration; a marvel: *"the decision of one age or country is a wonder to another"* (John Stuart Mill). **2.** The emotion thus aroused. **3.** A feeling of puzzlement or doubt. **4.** *Often capital* **W.** A monumental human creation regarded with awe; especially, one of seven monuments of the ancient world that appeared on various lists of late antiquity. Most commonly they are: the Colossus of Rhodes, the Pharos at Alexandria, the Hanging Gardens (and walls) of Babylon, the temple of Artemis at Ephesus, the Egyptian pyramids, the tomb of Mausolus at Halicarnassus, and the statue of Zeus at Olympia. —**for a wonder.** Surprisingly. —*v.* **wondered, -dering, -ders.** —*intr.* **1.** To have a feeling of awe or admiration; to marvel. **2.** To be filled with curiosity or doubt. —*tr.* To have doubts or curiosity about. [Middle English *wonder,* Old English *wundor,* from Germanic *wundar-* (unattested).] —**won′der·er** *n.*
won·der·ful (wŭn′dər-fəl) *adj.* **1.** Capable of exciting wonder; astonishing: *"the Greenland whale is one of the most wonderful animals in the world"* (Darwin). **2.** Admirable; excellent. —**won′der·ful·ly** *adv.* —**won′der·ful·ness** *n.*
won·der·land (wŭn′dər-lănd′) *n.* **1.** A marvelous imaginary realm. **2.** A marvelous real place or scene.
won·der·ment (wŭn′dər-mənt) *n.* **1.** Astonishment, awe, or surprise. **2.** Something that produces wonder; a marvel. **3.** Puzzlement or curiosity.
won·der·work (wŭn′dər-wûrk′) *n.* A miracle or marvel. —**won′der·work′er** *n.* —**won′der·work′ing** *adj.*
won·drous (wŭn′drəs) *adj.* Wonderful. —*adv. Archaic.* To a wonderful or remarkable extent. —**won′drous·ly** *adv.*
won·ky (wŏng′kē) *adj.* **-kier, -kiest.** *British Slang.* Shaky; feeble. [Variant of dialectal *wanky,* from Middle English *wankel,* Old English *wancol.* See **weng-** in Appendix.*]
Won·san (wœn′sän′). *Japanese* **Gen·san** (gĕn′sän′). A city of North Korea on the eastern coast. Population, 113,000.
wont (wônt, wōnt, wŭnt) *adj.* **1.** Accustomed or used to. Usually used with an infinitive: *"The poor man is wont to complain that this is a cold world"* (Thoreau). **2.** Apt or likely. —*n.* Usage or custom: *" 'Tis not my wont to look that far ahead' "* (John Barth). See Synonyms at **habit.** —*v.* **wont, wont** or **wonted, wonting, wonts.** —*tr.* To make (someone) accustomed to. —*intr.* To be in the habit of. [Middle English *wont,* from

ă pat/ā pay/âr care/ä father/b bib/ch church/d deed/ĕ pet/ē be/f fife/g gag/h hat/hw which/ĭ pit/ī pie/îr pier/j judge/k kick/l lid, needle/m mum/n no, sudden/ng thing/ŏ pot/ō toe/ô paw, for/oi noise/ou out/ŏŏ took/ōō boot/p pop/r roar/s sauce/sh ship, dish/

the past participle of *wonen,* to be accustomed, dwell, to WON.]
won't (wōnt). Contraction of *will not.*
wont·ed (wôn′tĭd, wōn′-, wŭn′-) *adj.* Accustomed; usual: *"the successive business of the seasons continues to make its wonted revolutions"* (Samuel Johnson).
won ton (wŏn′ tŏn′). **1.** In Chinese cookery, a noodle-dough dumpling filled with spiced minced pork, usually served in soup. **2.** Soup containing such dumplings. [Cantonese *wan tan,* corresponding to Mandarin Chinese $hun^2\ t'un^2$.]
woo (wōō) *v.* **wooed, wooing, woos.** *—tr.* **1.** To seek the affection of with intent to marry. **2. a.** To seek to achieve; try to gain. **b.** To tempt or invite. **3.** To entreat, solicit, or importune. *—intr.* To court a woman. [Middle English *wowen,* Old English *wōgian*†.] **—woo′er** *n.*
wood[1] (wŏŏd) *n. Abbr.* **wd. 1. a.** The tough, fibrous cellular substance constituting the xylem of trees and shrubs, lying beneath the bark and consisting largely of cellulose and lignin. **b.** Such a substance used for any of innumerable human purposes, as for building material or fuel. **2.** *Often plural.* A dense growth of trees; a forest. **3.** An object made of wood, especially: **a.** A woodwind. **b.** A golf club having a wooden head. **—out of the woods.** *Informal.* Free of difficulties. *—adj.* **1.** Made or consisting of wood; wooden. **2.** Associated with, used on, or containing wood: *a wood screw; a wood box.* **3.** Growing or living in woods or forests. *—v.* **wooded, wooding, woods.** *—tr.* **1.** To fuel with wood. **2.** To cover with trees; to forest. *—intr.* To gather or be supplied with wood. [Middle English *wode,* Old English *wudu.* See **widhu-** in Appendix.*]
wood[2] (wōōd, wŏŏd) *adj. Obsolete.* Violently insane. [Middle English *wo(o)d,* Old English *wōd.* See **wāt-** in Appendix.*]
Wood (wŏŏd), **Grant.** 1892–1942. American painter.
Wood (wŏŏd), **Leonard.** 1860–1927. American colonial administrator and military commander in Spanish-American War.
wood alcohol. Methyl alcohol *(see).*
wood anemone. Either of two plants, *Anemone quinquefolia,* of eastern North America, or *A. nemorosa,* of Europe, having deeply divided leaves and a solitary white flower.
wood betony. A plant, the **lousewort** *(see).*
wood·bin (wŏŏd′bĭn′) *n.* A box for holding firewood.
wood·bine (wŏŏd′bīn′) *n.* Any of various climbing vines, especially: **a.** An Old World honeysuckle, *Lonicera periclymenum,* having yellowish flowers. **b.** The **Virginia creeper** *(see).* [Middle English *wodebinde,* Old English *wudubinde* : *wudu,* WOOD + *bindan,* to BIND (it climbs up around trees).]
wood·block (wŏŏd′blŏk′) *n.* Also **wood block** (for sense 2). **1.** A **woodcut** *(see).* **2.** *Music.* A hollow block of wood struck with a drumstick to produce percussive effects in an orchestra.
wood·bor·er (wŏŏd′bôr′ər, -bōr′ər) *n.* Any of various insects, insect larvae, or mollusks that bore into wood.
Wood·bridge (wŏŏd′brĭj). A residential city of northeastern New Jersey. Population, 79,000.
wood·carv·ing (wŏŏd′kär′vĭng) *n.* **1.** The art of carving in wood. **2.** An object carved from wood. **—wood′carv′er** *n.*
wood·chat (wŏŏd′chăt′) *n.* An Old World bird, *Lanius senator,* having black and white plumage with a reddish crown.
wood·chuck (wŏŏd′chŭk′) *n.* A common rodent, *Marmota monax,* of northern and eastern North America, having a short-legged, heavy-set body and grizzled brownish fur. Also called "ground hog." [Variant (by folk etymology) of Cree *oček,* from Proto-Algonquian *wečyeka* (unattested), "fisher."]
wood coal. 1. Charcoal. **2.** Lignite.
wood·cock (wŏŏd′kŏk′) *n., pl.* **woodcock** or **-cocks.** Either of two related game birds, *Scolopax rusticola,* of the Old World, or *Philohela minor,* of North America, having brownish plumage, short legs, and a long bill. [Middle English *wodecok,* Old English *wuducocc* : *wudu,* WOOD + *cocc,* COCK.]
wood·craft (wŏŏd′krăft′, -kräft′) *n.* **1.** Skill and experience in matters pertaining to the woods, as hunting, fishing, or camping. **2.** The act, process, or art of working with wood.
wood·cut (wŏŏd′kŭt′) *n.* **1.** A piece of wood upon which a design for printing is engraved, especially in the plane of the grain. **2.** A print made from such a piece of wood. Also called "woodblock," "woodprint."
wood·cut·ter (wŏŏd′kŭt′ər) *n.* A person who cuts wood or trees. **—wood′cut′ting** *n.*
wood·ed (wŏŏd′ĭd) *adj.* Having trees or woods.
wood·en (wŏŏd′n) *adj.* **1.** Made or consisting of wood. **2.** Stiff; lifeless. **3.** Clumsy. **—wood′en·ly** *adv.* **—wood′en·ness** *n.*
wood engraving. 1. A piece of wood upon which a design for printing is engraved, usually on the end grain. **2.** The art or process of making wood engravings. **3.** A print made from such a piece of wood.
wood·en·head (wŏŏd′n-hĕd′) *n.* A blockhead. **—wood′en-head′ed** *adj.*
wooden Indian. A wooden effigy of an American Indian brave holding a cluster of cigars and used formerly as the emblem of a tobacconist. Also called "cigar-store Indian."
Wood Green. A former administrative division of London, England, now part of **Harringay** *(see).*
wood ibis. Any of several large wading birds of the subfamily Mycteriinae, related to and resembling the storks; especially, *Mycteria americana,* of the New World. This species is also called "flinthead."
wood·land (wŏŏd′lənd, -lănd′) *n.* Land having a cover of trees and shrubs. *—adj.* Of or indigenous to such a wooded area. **—wood′land·er** (wŏŏd′lən-dər) *n.*
wood·lark (wŏŏd′lärk′) *n.* An Old World songbird, *Lullula arborea,* resembling but smaller than the skylark.
wood lot. An area restricted to the growing of forest trees.
wood louse. A terrestrial crustacean, the **sow bug** *(see).*
wood·note (wŏŏd′nōt′) *n.* A song or call of or characteristic of a woodland bird.
wood nymph. 1. A nymph of the forest. **2.** Any of several tropical hummingbirds of the genera *Thalurania* and *Cyanophaia.* **3.** Any of various butterflies of the family Satyridae; especially, *Cercyonis pegala,* having brownish wings with dark eyespots.
wood·peck·er (wŏŏd′pĕk′ər) *n.* Any of various birds of the family Picidae, having strong claws and a stiff tail adapted for clinging to and climbing trees, and a chisellike bill for drilling through bark and wood.
wood pigeon. A large Eurasian pigeon, *Columba palumbus,* having a white band on each wing. Also called "ringdove."
wood·pile (wŏŏd′pīl′) *n.* A pile of wood, especially when stacked for use as fuel.
wood·print (wŏŏd′prĭnt′) *n.* A **woodcut** *(see).*
wood pulp. Any of various cellulose pulps ground from wood, chemically processed, and used especially to make paper.
wood pussy. *Informal.* A skunk.
wood rat. The **pack rat** *(see).*
wood·ruff (wŏŏd′rəf, -rŭf′) *n.* Any of several plants of the genus *Asperula;* especially, *A. odorata,* native to Eurasia, having small white flowers and narrow, fragrant leaves used as flavoring and in sachets. [Middle English *woderofe,* Old English *wudurofe* : *wudu,* WOOD + *-rofe*†.]
Woods, Lake of the. A lake occupying 1,485 square miles in southwestern Ontario, Canada, and north-central Minnesota.
wood·shed (wŏŏd′shĕd′) *n.* A shed in which firewood is stored.
Woods Hole. A village in Falmouth, southeastern Massachusetts; site of a major oceanographic institute. Population, 1,000.
woods·man (wŏŏdz′mən) *n., pl.* **-men** (-mĭn). One who works or lives in the woods or is versed in woodcraft; a forester.
wood sorrel. Any of various plants of the genus *Oxalis,* having compound leaves with three leaflets and yellow, white, or pinkish flowers.
wood spirits. Methyl alcohol *(see).*
wood sugar. Xylose *(see).*
woods·y (wŏŏd′zē) *adj.* **-ier, -iest.** Of, relating to, characteristic of, or suggestive of the woods.
wood tar. A black, syruplike viscous fluid that is a by-product of the destructive distillation of wood and is used in pitch, wood preserving oils, preservatives, and medicines.
wood thrush. A North American thrush, *Hylocichla mustelina,* having a melodious song.
wood·turn·ing (wŏŏd′tûr′nĭng) *n.* The art or process of shaping wood into various forms on a lathe. **—wood′turn′er** *n.*
wood vinegar. *Chemistry.* **Pyroligneous acid** *(see).*
wood·wax·en (wŏŏd′wăk′sən) *n.* A shrub, the **dyer's greenweed** *(see).* [Middle English *wodewexen,* Old English *wudu weaxe* : *wudu,* WOOD + probably *weaxan,* to grow, WAX.]
wood·wind (wŏŏd′wĭnd′) *n.* **1.** Any of a group of musical wind instruments that includes the bassoons, clarinets, flutes, oboes, and sometimes the saxophones. **2.** *Plural.* The section of an orchestra or band composed of woodwind instruments. **—wood′wind′** *adj.*
wood·work (wŏŏd′wûrk′) *n.* Objects made of or work done in wood; especially, wooden interior fittings in a house, such as moldings, doors, staircases, or windowsills.
wood·worm (wŏŏd′wûrm′) *n.* A worm or insect larva that bores into wood.
wood·y (wŏŏd′ē) *adj.* **-ier, -iest. 1.** Forming or consisting of wood; ligneous: *woody tissue.* **2.** Characterized by the presence of wood or xylem: *woody plants.* **3.** Characteristic or suggestive of wood: *a woody smell.* **4.** Abounding in trees; wooded.
woof[1] (wōōf, wŏŏf) *n.* **1.** The threads that run crosswise in a woven fabric, at right angles to the warp threads. **2.** The texture of a fabric. [Variant (influenced by WARP) of Middle English *oof,* Old English *ōwef* : *ō-,* from *on,* ON + *wefan,* to weave (see **webh-** in Appendix*).]
woof[2] (wŏŏf) *n.* **1.** The deep, gruff bark of a dog. **2.** A sound similar to this. [Imitative.]
woof·er (wŏŏf′ər) *n.* A loud-speaker designed to reproduce bass frequencies. Compare **tweeter.** [From WOOF (sound).]
wool (wŏŏl) *n.* **1.** The dense, soft, often curly hair forming the coat of sheep and certain other mammals, valued as a textile fabric. **2.** A material or garment made of wool. **3.** Any filamentous or fibrous covering or substance suggestive of the texture of wool. *—adj.* Of, pertaining to, or consisting of wool or woolen material. [Middle English *wolle, wull,* Old English *wull.* See **wel-**[5] in Appendix.*]
wool-clip (wŏŏl′klĭp′) *n.* The annual yield of wool.
wool·en (wŏŏl′ən) *adj.* Also **wool·len.** Of, pertaining to, or consisting of wool. *—n.* Also **wool·len.** Fabric or clothing made from wool. Usually used in the plural.
Woolf (wŏŏlf), **(Adeline) Virginia (Stephen).** 1882–1941. English novelist and essayist.
wool fat. Lanolin *(see).*
wool·gath·er·ing (wŏŏl′găth′ər-ĭng) *n.* Absent-minded indulgence in fanciful daydreams. *—adj.* Indulging in fancies; absent-minded. **—wool′gath′er·er** *n.*
wool·grow·er (wŏŏl′grō′ər) *n.* A person who raises sheep or other animals for the production of wool. **—wool′grow′ing** *adj.*
wool·ly (wŏŏl′ē) *adj.* **-lier, -liest.** Also **wool·y. 1. a.** Pertaining to, consisting of, or covered with wool. **b.** Resembling wool. **2.** Lacking sharp detail or clarity; blurry; fuzzy: *woolly thinking.* **3.** Having the characteristics of the rough, generally lawless atmosphere of frontier America. Used chiefly in the phrase *wild and woolly.* *—n., pl.* **woollies.** Also **wool·y. 1.** A garment made

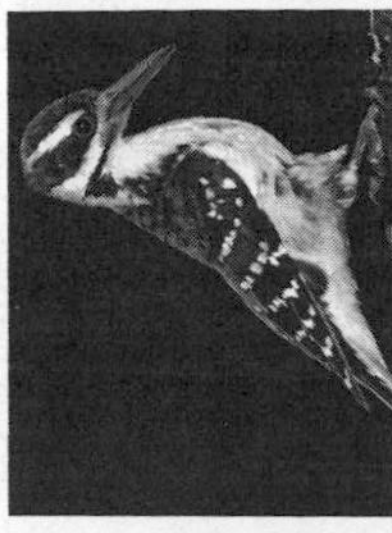

woodpecker
Dendrocopos villosus
Hairy woodpecker

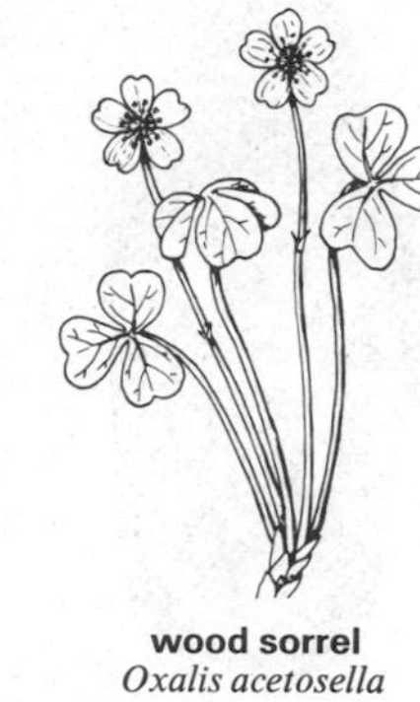

wood sorrel
Oxalis acetosella

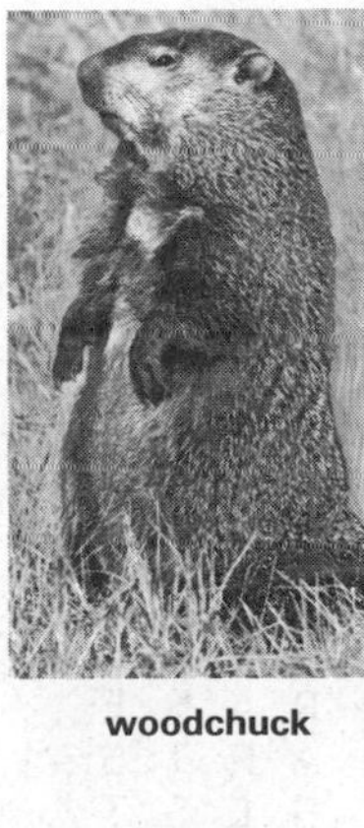

woodchuck

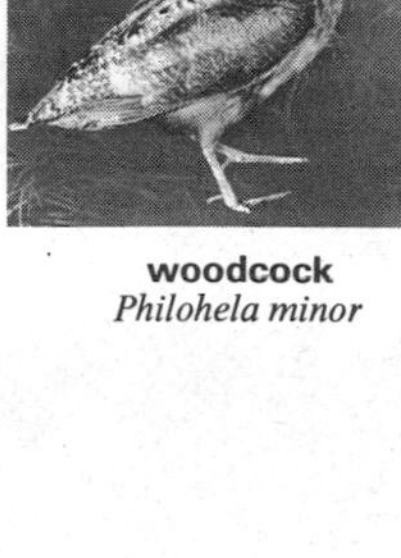

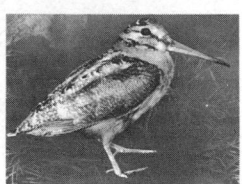

woodcock
Philohela minor

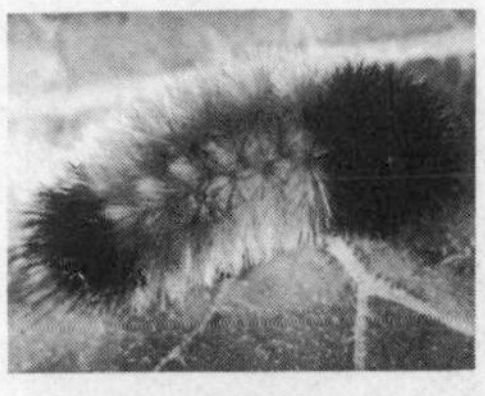

woolly bear
Caterpillar of
Isia isabella

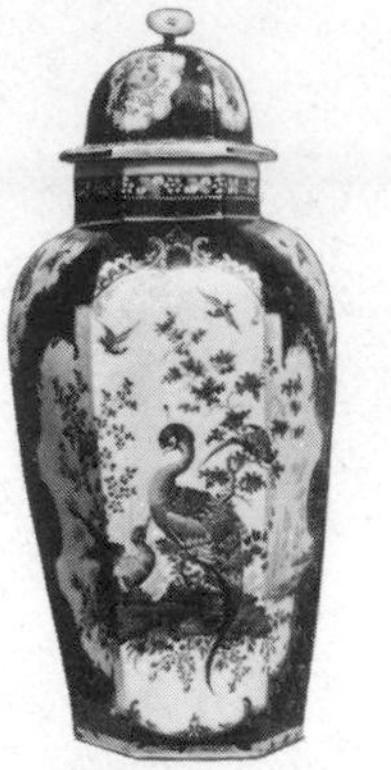

Worcester china
Covered vase
made about 1775

C R A B
R A R E
A R T S
B E S T

B R A T
R A C E
A C R E
T E E M

word square
Examples of word squares

of wool; especially, an undergarment. **2.** *Usually plural. Western U.S.* A sheep. —**wool′li·ness** *n.*
woolly bear. The hairy caterpillar of any of various tiger moths, especially that of *Isia isabella.*
wool·pack (wŏŏl′păk′) *n.* **1.** A bag used for packing a bale of wool for shipment. **2.** A cumulus cloud.
wool·sack (wŏŏl′săk′) *n.* **1.** A sack for wool. **2. a.** The official seat of the Lord Chancellor in the House of Lords. **b.** The Lord Chancellorship.
wool shed. A building or complex of buildings in which sheep are sheared and wool is prepared for shipment to market.
wool·skin (wŏŏl′skĭn′) *n.* A sheepskin with the wool still on it.
wool·sta·pler (wŏŏl′stā′plər) *n.* **1.** A dealer in wool. **2.** A person who sorts wool by quality of the staple or fiber. —**wool′-sta′pling** *adj.* & *n.*
Wool·wich (wŏŏl′ĭch, -ĭj). A former administrative division of London, England, now part of **Greenwich** *(see).*
Wool·worth (wŏŏl′wûrth′), **Frank Winfield.** 1852–1919. American merchant.
Woo·mer·a (wŏŏ′mər-ə). A town of Australia, in southeastern South Australia; the site of a rocket- and bomb-testing range. Population, 5,000.
Woon·sock·et (wŏŏn-sŏk′ĭt). A city and textile center of northern Rhode Island. Population, 47,000.
wooz·y (wōō′zē, wŏŏz′ē) *adj.* **-ier, -iest. 1.** Dazed; stunned; confused. **2.** Dizzy or queasy, as from drink. [Perhaps variant of OOZY.] —**wooz′i·ly** *adv.* —**wooz′i·ness** *n.*
wop (wŏp) *n.* An Italian. An offensive term used derogatorily. [Italian dialectal *guappo,* dandy, from Spanish *guapo*†.]
Worces·ter (wŏŏs′tər). **1.** Also **Worces·ter·shire** (wŏŏs′tər-shîr, -shər). *Abbr.* **Worcs** A county occupying 699 square miles in west-central England. Population, 570,000. **2.** The county seat of this county. Population, 68,000. **3.** A city of central Massachusetts, west of Boston. Population, 187,000.
Worcester china. A fine china or porcelain made in Worcester, England, from 1751. Also called "Worcester porcelain."
Worcestershire sauce. A piquant sauce of soy, vinegar, and spices, originally made in Worcester, England.
Worcs Worcester.
word (wûrd) *n.* **1.** *Abbr.* **wd.** A sound or a combination of sounds, or its representation in writing or printing, that symbolizes and communicates a meaning and may consist of a single morpheme or of a combination of morphemes. **2.** Something that is said; an utterance, remark, or comment: *May I say a word about that?* **3.** *Plural.* A discourse or talk; speech. **4.** *Plural.* The text of a vocal musical composition; lyrics. **5.** An assurance or promise; sworn intention: *a man of his word.* **6. a.** A command or direction; an order: *executed at the general's word.* **b.** A verbal signal; a password or watchword. **7. a.** News: *the latest word.* **b.** Rumor: *Word has it she's married.* **8. a.** *Plural.* A dispute or argument; a quarrel. **b.** A quarrelsome remark or conversation: *Words were exchanged between umpire and batter.* **9.** *Capital* **W. a.** The Logos. **b.** The Scriptures or Gospel: *the Word of God.* —**at a word.** In immediate response. —**by word of mouth.** Orally; by speech. —**have no words for.** To be unable to describe or talk about. —**in a word.** In most precise form; in short: *You are, in a word, a fool.* —**in so many words.** Precisely as stated; exactly. —**take one at one's word.** To be convinced of another's sincerity and act in accordance with his statement. —**word for word.** In the same words. —*tr.v.* **worded, wording, words.** To express in words. [Middle English *word,* Old English *word.* See **wer-**[6] in Appendix.*]
word·age (wûr′dĭj) *n.* **1.** Words collectively. **2.** The use of an excessive number of words; verbiage. **3.** The number of words used, as in a novel. **4.** Wording.
word blindness. A type of cerebral disorder, **alexia** *(see).* —**word′-blind′** *adj.*
word·book (wûrd′bŏŏk′) *n.* A lexicon; vocabulary; dictionary.
word deafness. One form of aphasia in which information in the form of speech is incomprehensible.
word·ing (wûr′dĭng) *n.* The act or style of expressing in words; phraseology; diction. See Synonyms at **diction.**
word·less (wûrd′lĭs) *adj.* Without words; unspoken; inarticulate; silent. —**word′less·ly** *adv.* —**word′less·ness** *n.*
word order. The syntactic arrangement of words in a sentence, clause, or phrase.
word play. 1. A witty or clever exchange of words; repartee. **2.** A play on words; a pun.
word square. A group of words arranged in a square that read the same vertically and horizontally. Also called "acrostic."
Words·worth (wûrdz′wûrth′), **William.** 1770–1850. English poet.
word·y (wûr′dē) *adj.* **-ier, -iest. 1.** Pertaining to, consisting of, or having the nature of words; verbal. **2.** Expressed in or using more words than are necessary to convey meaning. —See Synonyms at **talkative.** —**word′i·ly** *adv.* —**word′i·ness** *n.*
wore. 1. Past tense of **wear** (to be clothed in). **2.** Past tense of **wear** (to turn, as a ship).
work (wûrk) *n.* **1.** Physical or mental effort or activity directed toward the production or accomplishment of something; toil; labor. **2.** *Abbr.* **wk.** Employment; a job: *look for work.* **3.** *Abbr.* **wk.** The means by which one earns one's livelihood; a trade, craft, business, or profession. **4. a.** Something that one is doing, making, or performing, especially as a part of one's occupation; a duty or task: *begin the day's work.* **b.** The amount of this done or required. **5.** *Abbr.* **wk.** Something that has been done, made, or performed as a result of one's occupation, effort, or activity, especially: **a.** *Plural.* The output of an artist or artisan considered or collected as a whole: *the works of Verdi.* **b.** *Plural.* Engineering structures, such as bridges or dams. **c.** A piece of needlework or embroidery. **6.** Any material or piece being processed in a machine during manufacture. **7.** The area, office, or place where one pursues his occupation: *She called him at work.* **8.** *Plural.* A factory, plant, or similar building or system of buildings where a specific type of business or industry is carried on. Used with a singular verb. **9.** *Plural.* Machinery: *the works of a watch.* **10.** The manner or style of working or the quality of treatment; workmanship: *good work.* **11.** A froth produced during the process of fermentation, as on vinegar, cider, or other liquid. **12.** *Physics. Abbr.* **w, W** The transfer of energy from one physical system to another; especially, the transfer of energy to a body by the application of force, calculated as the line integral between any two points of the scalar product of the force and the body's displacement along the path over which the integral is taken. **13.** *Plural. Theology.* Moral or righteous acts or deeds: *salvation by faith rather than works.* —**shoot the works.** *Slang.* **1.** To risk all on one chance or attempt. **2.** To make a supreme attempt. —**the works.** *Slang.* **1.** Everything; the whole of a set: *He had the works, from appetizer to dessert.* **2.** Extreme punitive treatment. —*v.* **worked** or *archaic* **wrought** (rôt), **working, works.** —*intr.* **1.** To exert one's efforts for the purpose of doing or making something; to labor or toil. **2.** To be employed; have a job. **3.** To perform a function or act; operate: *The machine doesn't work.* **4.** To operate effectively or successfully; prove successful: *The combination seemed to work.* **5.** To have an influence, result, or effect, as on a person, the mind, or the like: *The plea for help worked on her compassion.* **6.** To be changed into a specified state, especially gradually or by repeated movement: *The stitches worked loose.* **7.** To force a passage or way: *They worked through the snow to the street.* **8.** To move or contort from emotion or pain: *Her mouth worked with fear.* **9.** To be handled or processed: *Not all metals work easily.* **10.** To ferment. **11.** *Nautical.* To be under strain in heavy seas so that seams loosen and fastenings become slack. **12.** To undergo small motions that result in friction and wear: *The gears work against each other.* —*tr.* **1.** To cause or effect; bring about: *I can't work miracles.* **2.** To cause to operate or function; handle or use: *work a power mower.* **3.** To form or shape; mold: *They work glass.* **4.** To sew, weave, knit, or the like. **5.** To solve (an arithmetic problem). **6.** To handle or manipulate for the purpose of preparing: *work the butter and sugar before adding eggs.* **7.** To achieve (a specified condition) by gradual or repeated effort: *They worked their way out of the wood.* **8.** To bring into a specified condition or place by gradual effort: *"He worked a grain of tobacco to the tip of his tongue and spat it out."* (D.H. Lawrence). **9.** To make productive; cultivate: *work a farm.* **10.** To make or force to work or to do work: *He works his laborers hard.* **11.** To excite, rouse, or provoke: *He worked the children to tears.* **12.** To influence or persuade, especially by somewhat underhand means; woo or induce: *Work him to do your bidding.* **13.** *Informal.* To use or employ for one's own ends or purposes: *work one's contacts.* **14.** *Informal.* To practice trickery or deception on; cheat. **15.** To function or operate in; to cover: *This mailman works our street.* **16.** To ferment (liquors). —**work in. 1.** To put in or introduce; insert. **2.** To be or become introduced or inserted. —**work off.** To get rid of; eliminate; dissipate: *work off extra pounds.* —**work on** (or **upon**). **1.** To persuade, influence, or affect. **2.** To attempt to persuade or influence. —**work over. 1.** To do for a second time; to repeat. **2.** *Slang.* To inflict severe physical damage upon; thrash or beat up. —**work up. 1.** To make one's or its way up; proceed up; rise. **2.** To arouse or excite, as an emotion. **3.** To develop or follow up on; formulate or elaborate. [Middle English *werke, worke,* Old English *we(o)rc,* act, deed, work. See **werg-**[1] in Appendix.*]
Synonyms: *work, labor, toil, drudgery, travail.* These nouns refer to the exertion of physical or mental faculties in order to accomplish something, contrasted with play or recreation. *Work* is the most widely applicable; it alone can refer not only to the effort of persons but also to the activity of machines and of the forces of nature. *Labor* is largely restricted to human effort, especially physical and manual. *Toil* is principally applicable to strenuous and fatiguing labor; *drudgery,* to dull, wearisome, monotonous, and sometimes demeaning labor; and *travail,* to work involving great effort and pain or suffering.
-work. Indicates: **1.** A product composed of a (specified) material; for example, **paperwork. 2.** Work produced in a (specified) way or of a (specified) kind; for example, **piecework. 3.** Work performed in a (specified) place, area, or the like; for example, **housework.** [From WORK.]
work·a·ble (wûr′kə-bəl) *adj.* **1.** Capable of being worked, dealt with, or handled. **2.** Capable of being worked conveniently; practicable or feasible. —See Synonyms at **possible.** —**work′a·bil′i·ty, work′a·ble·ness** *n.*
work·a·day (wûr′kə-dā′) *adj.* **1.** Pertaining or appropriate to working days; everyday. **2.** Mundane; commonplace: *"the practical, workaday world, of . . . ordinary undistinguished things"* (Lionel Trilling). [From Middle English *werkeday,* a workday : *werke,* WORK + DAY.]
work·bag (wûrk′băg′) *n.* A bag to hold material, as needlework, on which one is working, or implements needed for work.
work·bench (wûrk′bĕnch′) *n.* A sturdy table or bench at which an artisan, such as a machinist or carpenter, works.
work·book (wûrk′bŏŏk′) *n.* **1.** A booklet containing problems and exercises in which a student may directly write, calculate, or the like. **2.** A manual containing operating instructions, as for

an appliance or a machine. **3.** A book in which a record is kept of work proposed or accomplished.

work·box (wûrk′bŏks′) *n.* A box for implements or materials used in sewing or other work.

work·day (wûrk′dā′) *n.* **1.** Any day on which work is done. **2.** The part of the day during which one works: *an eight-hour workday.* —*adj.* Workaday.

work·er (wûr′kər) *n.* **1.** One that works. **2. a.** One who does manual or industrial labor. **b.** One who belongs to the working class. **3.** One of the sterile females of certain social insects, as the ant or bee, that performs specialized work.

work·folk (wûrk′fōk′) *pl.n.* Also **work·folks** (-fōks′). Laborers; especially, farm laborers.

work force. **1.** Those workers employed in a specific project; a staff. **2.** All workers potentially available to a nation, project, industry, or the like.

work function. The amount of work required to remove an electron from a solid; especially, the work exerted against coulomb forces in removing an electron from just inside to just outside the surface of a metal.

work hardening. The increase in strength that sometimes accompanies plastic deformation of a solid.

work·horse (wûrk′hôrs′) *n.* **1.** A horse that is used for labor rather than for racing or riding. **2.** *Informal.* A person who works tirelessly, especially at difficult tasks.

work·house (wûrk′hous′) *n.* **1.** A prison in which limited sentences (under one year in most systems) are served at manual labor. **2.** A former public institution in Britain in which the indigent were fed and forced to work.

work·ing (wûr′kĭng) *adj.* **1.** Pertaining to or designating a person or thing that works; employed: *the working wife.* **2.** Pertaining to, used for, or spent in working: *a working uniform.* **3.** Sufficient or large enough for using or being worked: *a working knowledge of Spanish.* **4.** Capable of being used as the basis of further work: *a working mode.* **5.** Contorting, as from pain. **6.** In the process of fermentation. Said of alcoholic liquors. **7. a.** Functioning, especially on a reduced scale: *a working model.* **b.** Used as a guide: *a working drawing.*

working capital. **1.** The assets of a business enterprise that can be applied to its operation. **2.** The current assets of an individual or business enterprise as opposed to the current liabilities.

working class. The part of society whose income is from wages; the proletariat. —**work′ing-class′** *adj.*

working fluid. A **working substance** *(see)* that is a fluid.

work·ing·man (wûr′kĭng-măn′) *n., pl.* **-men** (-mĕn′). A man who works for wages, especially at manual labor.

working papers. Legal documents certifying the right of an individual to employment.

working substance. A substance, such as a coolant, used to effect a thermodynamic change in a system.

work·less (wûrk′lĭs) *adj.* Unemployed.

work·load (wûrk′lōd′) *n.* The amount of work assigned to or done by a worker or unit of workers in a given time period.

work·man (wûrk′mən) *n., pl.* **-men** (-mĭn). **1.** A man who performs some form of labor. **2.** A person who works in a specified way: *a creative workman.*

work·man·like (wûrk′mən-līk′) *adj..* Also **work·man·ly** (-lē). **1.** Characteristic of or befitting a skilled workman or craftsman: *workmanlike pottery.* **2.** Without nuance or inspiration; ordinary: *a workmanlike production of* Hamlet.

work·man·ship (wûrk′mən-shĭp′) *n.* **1.** The art, skill, or technique of a workman. **2.** The quality of such art, skill, or technique: *silver of poor workmanship.* **3.** That which is produced by a workman. **4.** The product of effort or endeavor.

workmen's compensation. Payments required by law to be made to an employee who is injured in the course of his work.

work of art. A piece of superior artistic work.

work out. **1.** To come or make its way out: *a nail working out of a board.* **2.** To exhaust (a mine, soil, or the like). **3.** To accomplish by work or effort. **4.** To find a solution for; solve. **5.** To fulfill, as an obligation or debt, by working instead of paying money. **6.** To formulate or develop: *work out a plan.* **7.** To prove successful, effective, or satisfactory: *Did your job work out?* **8.** To have a specified end or result: *work out well.* **9.** To perform a series of exercises or drills.

work·out (wûrk′out′) *n.* **1.** A period of exercise or practice, especially in athletics. **2.** An exhausting task.

work·peo·ple (wûrk′pē′pəl) *pl.n.* Those who work for wages.

work·room (wûrk′ro͞om′, -ro͝om′) *n.* A room where work is done, especially manual work.

work·shop (wûrk′shŏp′) *n.* **1.** An area, room, or establishment in which manual or industrial work is done. **2.** A group of people who meet regularly for a seminar in some specialized field: *a creative-writing workshop.*

work·ta·ble (wûrk′tā′bəl) *n.* A table designed for a specific task or activity, such as needlework or graphic arts.

work·week (wûrk′wēk′) *n.* The number of hours worked or required to be worked in one week.

world (wûrld) *n.* **1.** The earth. **2.** The universe. **3.** The earth and its inhabitants collectively. **4.** The human race. **5.** Man considered as a social creature; the public: *the world's response to Lindbergh's flight.* **6.** *Often capital* **W.** A particular part of the earth: *the Western World.* **7.** A particular period in history, including its people, culture, and social order: *the Victorian world.* **8.** Any sphere, realm, domain, or kingdom: *"The social unit of life in the elephant world is the herd"* (Richard Carrington). **9.** A field or sphere of human endeavor: *the world of the arts.* **10. a.** A specified way of life or state of being: *the world of the rich.* **b.** One specified aspect of this: *the orphan's world of sorrow.* **11.** The secular life and its morality as distinguished from the religious life: *a man of the world.* **12.** Those people who are devoted to the secular life or to worldly concerns. **13.** *Often plural.* A large amount; much: *College did him worlds of good.* **14.** A planet or other celestial body: *the possibility of life on another world.* —**for all the world.** **1.** For anything or for any reason: *I wouldn't go for all the world.* **2.** Precisely; exactly: *He looked for all the world like a movie star.* —**on top of the world.** *Informal.* Elated, exultant, or blissful. —**out of this world.** *Informal.* Excellent; very fine. [Middle English *w(e)orld,* Old English *world, weorold.* See **wiros** in Appendix.*]

World Court. **1.** The Permanent Court of International Justice, established by the League of Nations (1920). **2.** The **International Court of Justice** *(see).*

world·ling (wûrld′lĭng) *n.* A person absorbed in or devoted to this world; a worldly person.

world·ly (wûrld′lē) *adj.* **-lier, -liest.** **1.** Of, pertaining to, or devoted to the temporal world; not spiritual or religious; secular. **2.** Sophisticated or cosmopolitan; worldly-wise: *"an experienced and worldly man who had been almost everywhere"* (Willa Cather). —See Synonyms at **earthly.** —*adv.* In a worldly manner. —**world′li·ness** *n.*

world·ly-wise (wûrld′lē-wīz′) *adj.* Experienced in the ways of the world; sophisticated.

world power. A political entity whose actions influence or change the course of international events.

World Series. Also **world's series.** The series of professional baseball games played each fall between the championship teams of the American League and the National League.

world-shak·ing (wûrld′shā′kĭng) *adj.* Of great significance.

world soul. A spiritual principle relating to the world as the human soul relates to a human being.

World War I. *Abbr.* **W.W.I** A war fought from 1914 to 1918, in which Great Britain, France, Russia, Belgium, Italy, Japan, the United States, and other allies defeated Germany, Austria-Hungary, Turkey, and Bulgaria. Also called "First World War," "Great War."

World War II. *Abbr.* **W.W.II** A war fought from 1939 to 1945, in which Great Britain, France, the Soviet Union, the United States, and other allies defeated Germany, Italy, and Japan. Also called "Second World War."

world-wea·ry (wûrld′wîr′ē) *adj.* **-rier, -riest.** Tired of the world and the pleasures afforded by it. —**world′-wea′ri·ness** *n.*

world·wide (wûrld′wīd′) *adj.* Reaching or extending throughout the world; universal. —**world′wide′** *adv.*

worm (wûrm) *n.* **1.** Any of various invertebrates, as those of the phyla Annelida, Nematoda, or Platyhelminthes, having a long, flexible rounded or flattened body, often without obvious appendages. **2.** Any of various insect larvae having a soft, elongated body. **3.** Any of various unrelated animals resembling a worm in habit or appearance, as the shipworm or the slowworm. **4.** An object or device that is like a worm in appearance or action, as a threaded screw or a zigzag road. **5.** An insidiously tormenting or devouring force: *"The worm of conscience still begnaw thy soul!"* (Shakespeare). **6.** A pitiable or contemptible creature; poor wretch. **7.** *Plural. Pathology.* Intestinal infestation with worms or wormlike parasites. In this sense, also called "helminthiasis." —*v.* **wormed, worming, worms.** —*tr.* **1.** To make (one's way) with or as if with the sinuous crawling motion of a worm. **2.** To elicit by artful or devious means. Used with *out of.* **3.** To cure of intestinal worms. **4.** *Nautical.* To wrap yarn or twine around (rope). —*intr.* **1.** To move in a sinuous manner suggestive of a worm. **2.** To make one's way by artful or devious means. Used with *into* or *out of.* [Middle English *worm,* Old English *wyrm,* worm, serpent. See **wer-³** in Appendix.*]

worm-eat·en (wûrm′ēt′n) *adj.* **1.** Bored through or gnawed by worms. **2.** Decayed; rotten. **3.** Antiquated; decrepit.

worm fence. A fence of crossed rails supporting one another and forming a zigzag pattern. Also called "snake fence," "Virginia fence," "Virginia rail fence."

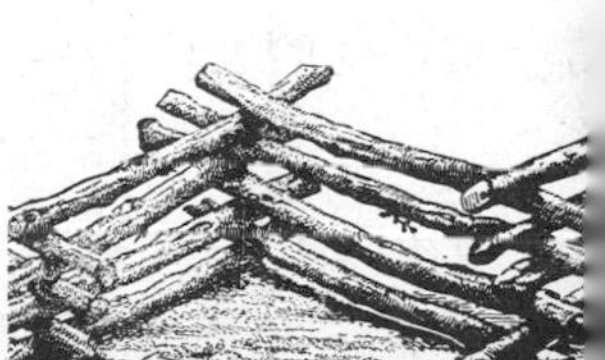

worm fence

worm gear. **1.** A gear consisting of a threaded shaft and a wheel with teeth that mesh into it. **2.** A **worm wheel** *(see).*

worm·grass (wûrm′grăs′, -gräs′) *n.* A plant, the **pinkroot** *(see).* [From the use of pinkroot as a vermifuge.]

worm·hole (wûrm′hōl′) *n.* A hole made by a burrowing worm.

Worms (wûrmz; *German* vôrms). A city of West Germany, on the Rhine in the southwest; the site of the Diet of Worms (1521), at which Luther was declared to be a heretic. Population, 62,000.

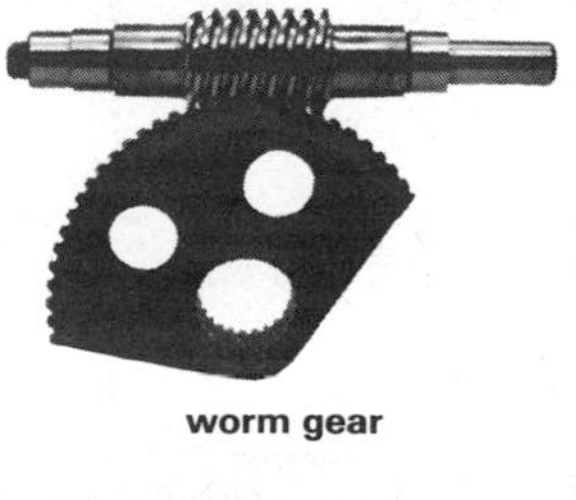

worm gear

worm screw. The threaded shaft of a worm gear.

worm·seed (wûrm′sēd′) *n.* **1.** A tropical American plant, *Chenopodium ambrosioides,* yielding an oil used as an anthelmintic. **2.** Any of several other plants similarly used.

worm wheel. The toothed wheel of a worm gear. Also called "worm gear."

worm·wood (wûrm′wo͝od′) *n.* **1.** Any of several aromatic plants of the genus *Artemisia;* especially, *A. absinthium,* native to Europe, yielding a bitter extract used in making absinthe and in flavoring certain wines. Also called "absinthe." **2.** Something harsh or embittering. [Middle English *wormwode,* variant (influenced by WORM and WOOD) of *wermode,* Old English *wermōd,* from Germanic *wer-mōd-, wor-mōd-* (unattested). See also **vermouth.**]

worm·y (wûr′mē) *adj.* **-ier, -iest.** **1.** Infested with or damaged by worms. **2.** Suggestive of a worm. —**worm′i·ness** *n.*

worn (wôrn, wōrn). Past participle of **wear.** —*adj.* **1.** Affected by wear or use. **2.** Impaired or damaged by wear or use: *worn* *pockets on a jacket.* **3. a.** Exhausted; spent. **b.** Showing exhaustion; drawn. **4.** Trite; hackneyed. —See Synonyms at **haggard.** [Middle English, past participle of *weren,* to WEAR.]

worn-out (wôrn′out′, wōrn′-) *adj.* **1.** Worn or used until no longer usable: *a worn-out suit.* **2.** Thoroughly exhausted; spent.

wor·ri·ment (wûr′ē-mənt) *n. Informal.* The act or a cause of worrying; worry.

wor·ri·some (wûr′ē-səm) *adj.* **1.** Causing worry or anxiety. **2.** Tending to worry; anxious. —**wor′ri·some·ly** *adv.*

wor·ry (wûr′ē) *v.* **-ried, -rying, -ries.** —*intr.* **1.** To feel uneasy about some uncertain or threatening matter; be troubled. **2.** To pull, bite, or tear at something. **3.** To work under difficulty or hardship; to struggle: *worried away at a problem.* —*tr.* **1.** To cause to feel anxious, distressed, or troubled. **2.** To bother; annoy: *Don't worry me with your complaints.* **3. a.** To grasp and tug at repeatedly: *a dog worrying a bone.* **b.** To touch, press, or handle idly; toy with: *worrying the sore tooth with his tongue.* —*n., pl.* **worries. 1.** The act of worrying or the condition of being worried; mental uneasiness or anxiety. **2.** A source of nagging concern or uneasiness. —See Synonyms at **anxiety.** [Middle English *worien, wirien,* to seize by the throat, harass, Old English *wyrgan,* to strangle. See **wer-**[3] in Appendix.*] —**wor′ri·er** *n.*

wor·ry·wart (wûr′ē-wôrt′) *n. Informal.* One who tends to worry excessively and needlessly.

worse (wûrs). **1.** Comparative of **bad. 2.** Comparative of **ill.** —*adj.* Also *obsolete* **wors·er. 1.** More inferior, as in quality, condition, or effect. **2.** More severe or unfavorable. **3.** Further from a standard; less desirable or satisfactory. —*n.* Something that is worse. —*adv.* In a worse way. [Middle English *wors(e),* Old English *wyrsa.* See **wers-** in Appendix.*]

wors·en (wûr′sən) *v.* **-ened, -ening, -ens.** —*intr.* To be or become worse. —*tr.* To make worse.

wor·ship (wûr′shĭp) *n.* **1.** The reverent love and allegiance accorded a deity, idol, or sacred object. **2.** A set of ceremonies, prayers, or other religious forms by which this love is expressed. **3.** Ardent, humble devotion. **4.** The object of such devotion. **5.** *Often capital* **W.** *Chiefly British.* A title of honor used in addressing magistrates, mayors, and certain other dignitaries. Used with a possessive pronoun: *Your Worship.* —*v.* **worshiped** or **worshipped, -shiping** or **-shipping, -ships.** —*tr.* **1.** To honor and love as a deity; venerate. **2.** To love or pursue devotedly. —*intr.* **1.** To participate in religious rites of worship. **2.** To perform any act of worship. —See Synonyms at **revere.** [Middle English *worschipe,* Old English *weorthscipe,* honor, dignity, reverence : *weorth,* WORTH + -SHIP.] —**wor′ship·er** *n.*

wor·ship·ful (wûr′shĭp-fəl) *adj.* **1.** Given to or expressive of worship; reverent or adoring. **2.** *Chiefly British.* Honorable by virtue of position or rank. Used in titles of respect. —**wor′ship·ful·ly** *adv.* —**wor′ship·ful·ness** *n.*

worst (wûrst). **1.** Superlative of **bad. 2.** Superlative of **ill.** —*adj.* **1.** Most inferior, as in quality, condition, or effect. **2.** Most severe or unfavorable. **3.** Furthest from an ideal or standard; least desirable or satisfactory. —**in the worst way.** *Informal.* Very much; a great deal. —*n.* Something that is worst. —**at worst.** Under the worst foreseeable circumstances; if the worst should happen. —**get the worst of it.** To suffer a defeat or disadvantage. —**if (the) worst comes to (the) worst.** At the very worst. —*adv.* In the worst manner or degree. —*tr.v.* **worsted, worsting, worsts.** To gain the advantage over; to defeat. [Middle English *worste, wurst,* Old English *wyrsta.* See **wers-** in Appendix.*]

wor·sted (wo͝os′tĭd, wûr′stĭd) *n.* **1.** Firm-textured, compactly twisted woolen yarn made from long-staple fibers. **2.** Fabric made from such yarn. —*adj.* Consisting of or made from worsted. [Middle English *worsted,* first made in *Worthstede* (now Worstead), a village in Norfolk, England.]

wort (wûrt, wôrt) *n.* **1.** A plant. Used chiefly in combination: *liverwort; milkwort.* **2.** An infusion of malt fermented to make beer. [Middle English *wort, wurt,* Old English *wyrt,* plant, herb. See **werād-** in Appendix.*]

worth[1] (wûrth) *n.* **1.** The quality of something that renders it desirable, useful, or valuable: *the worth of higher education.* **2.** The material or market value of something: *have a worth of ten million dollars.* **3.** The number or quantity of something that may be purchased for a specific sum: *two dollars' worth of gasoline.* **4.** Wealth; riches. **5.** The quality within a person that renders him deserving of respect. —*adj.* **1.** Equal in value to something specified: *worth its weight in gold.* **2.** Deserving of; meriting: *a proposal worth consideration.* **3.** Having wealth or riches amounting to: *a man not worth three cents.* —**for all one is worth.** To the utmost of one's powers or ability. [Middle English *worth,* Old English *weorth.* See **wer-**[3] in Appendix.*]

Synonyms: *worth, value.* These nouns refer to the sum of qualities that make a thing desirable and consequently may determine what it commands in an exchange. They are largely interchangeable when the reference is monetary. Otherwise, *worth* is especially appropriate in denoting qualities in persons or things that add up to moral excellence or to merit considered as an intangible apart from utility. *Value* suggests a more practical, objective scale of measurement. It is most often applied to what is demonstrably useful.

worth[2] (wûrth) *intr.v.* **worthed, worthing, worths.** *Archaic.* To befall; betide: *"Howl ye, Woe worth the day!"* (Ezekiel 30:2). [Middle English *worthen,* Old English *weorthan.* See **wer-**[3] in Appendix.*]

worth·less (wûrth′lĭs) *adj.* **1.** Without worth, use, or value. **2.** Without dignity or honor; low and despicable. —**worth′less·ly** *adv.* —**worth′less·ness** *n.*

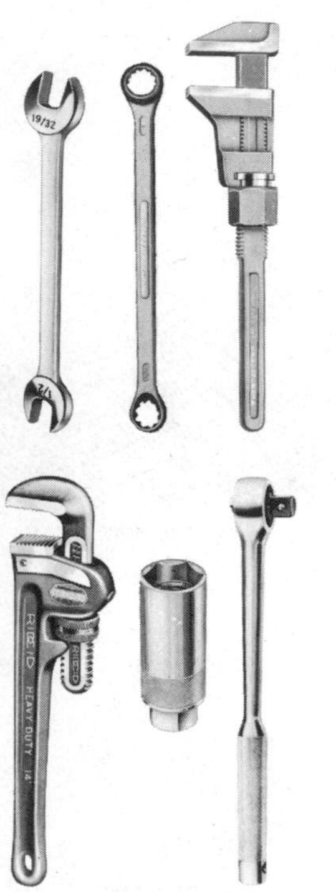

wrench
Above, from left:
Open-end wrench; long-box wrench; monkey wrench
Below, from left:
Stillson wrench; socket wrench and fixture

worth·while (wûrth′hwīl′) *adj.* Sufficiently valuable or important to justify the expenditure of time or effort.

wor·thy (wûr′thē) *adj.* **-thier, -thiest. 1.** Having worth, merit, or value; useful or valuable. **2.** Honorable; admirable: *a worthy fellow.* **3.** Having sufficient worth; deserving: *worthy to be revered; worthy of acclaim.* —*n., pl.* **worthies. 1.** A person esteemed for his worth, dignity, or importance. **2.** A figure locally renowned or respected. Often used humorously. —**wor′thi·ly** *adv.* —**wor′thi·ness** *n.*

wost. *Archaic.* Second person singular present tense of **wit** (to know).

wost·teth. *Archaic.* Alternate second person singular present tense of **wit** (to know).

wot. *Archaic.* First and third person singular present tense of **wit** (to know).

Wo·tan (vō′tän). A Teutonic god identified with Woden.

wot·teth. *Archaic.* Alternate third person singular present tense of **wit** (to know).

would. Past tense of **will** (defective verb). See Usage notes at **will, should.**

would-be (wo͝od′bē′) *adj.* Desiring or pretending to be.

would·n't (wo͝od′ənt). Contraction of *would not.*

wouldst, would·est. *Archaic.* Second person singular past tense of **will** (defective verb).

wound[1] (wo͞ond) *n.* **1.** An injury, especially one in which the skin or other external organic surface is torn, pierced, cut, or otherwise broken. **2.** An injury to the feelings. —*v.* **wounded, wounding, wounds.** —*tr.* To inflict a wound or wounds upon. —*intr.* To inflict a wound or wounds. —See Synonyms at **injure.** [Middle English *wound(e),* Old English *wund.* See **wā-**[2] in Appendix.*]

wound[2] (wound). **1.** Past tense and past participle of **wind** (to wrap). **2.** Alternate past tense and past participle of **wind** (to sound).

wound·wort (wo͞ond′wûrt′, -wôrt′) *n.* **1.** Any of several plants of the genus *Stachys,* having downy leaves formerly used to treat wounds. **2.** Any of several similarly used plants.

wove. Past tense and *rare* past participle of **weave.**

wo·ven. Past participle of **weave.**

wove paper. Paper made on a closely woven wire roller or mold and having a faint mesh pattern. Compare **laid paper.**

wow[1] (wou) *interj.* Used in expressing wonder, amazement, or the like. —*n. Informal.* An outstanding success. —*tr.v.* **wowed, wowing, wows.** *Informal.* To have a strong and usually pleasurable impact on. [Expressive formation.]

wow[2] (wou) *n.* A slow variation in the pitch of sound reproduced by a phonograph or tape recorder, usually the result of irregular movement of a mechanical part. [Imitative.]

WPA Work Projects Administration.

w.p.m. words per minute.

W.r. *Medicine.* Wassermann reaction.

wrack[1] (răk) *n.* **1.** Damage or destruction by violent means: *bring to wrack and ruin.* **2.** Wreckage, especially of a ship cast ashore. **3.** A tangled mass of seaweed or other marine vegetation, cast ashore or floating. **4.** *British Regional.* Weeds. —*v.* **wracked, wracking, wracks.** —*tr.* To cause the ruin of; wreck. —*intr.* To be wrecked. [Middle English *wrack,* Old English *wræc,* punishment, vengeance, and Middle Dutch *wrak,* wreckage, wrecked ship. See **wreg-** in Appendix.*]

wrack[2]. Variant of **rack** (clouds).

wraith (rāth) *n.* **1.** An apparition of a living person. **2.** The ghost of a dead person. [Origin unknown.]

Wran·gel Island (răng′gəl). An island, 1,740 square miles in area, off the northeastern coast of Siberia.

Wran·gell, Mount (răng′gəl). An active volcano, 14,005 feet high, at the western end of the Wrangell Mountains.

Wran·gell Mountains (răng′gəl). A range of 100 miles in southeastern Alaska. Highest elevation, 16,420 feet.

wran·gle (răng′gəl) *v.* **-gled, -gling, -gles.** —*intr.* To dispute noisily or angrily; to quarrel; bicker. —*tr.* **1.** To win or obtain by argument. **2.** *Western U.S.* To herd horses or other livestock. —See Synonyms at **argue.** —*n.* **1.** An angry, noisy argument or dispute. **2.** The act of wrangling. [Middle English *wranglen,* probably of Low German origin, akin to Low German *wrangeln.* See **wer-**[3] in Appendix.*]

wran·gler (răng′glər) *n.* **1.** One who wrangles. **2.** A cowboy, especially one who tends saddle horses. **3.** A winner of the highest honors in mathematics at Cambridge University.

wrap (răp) *v.* **wrapped** or **wrapt, wrapping, wraps.** —*tr.* **1.** To arrange or fold about in order to cover or protect something: *She wrapped her coat about her.* **2.** To cover, envelop, pack, or encase. **3.** To package, as with paper. **4.** To clasp, fold, or coil about something: *She wrapped her arms about his neck.* **5.** To envelop and obscure, often with the effect of concealing or disguising the nature of: *Fog wrapped the countryside.* **6.** To immerse in some condition: *wrapped in grief; wrapped in thought.* —*intr.* **1.** To coil, wind, or twist about or around something: *The flag wrapped around the pole.* **2.** To put on warm clothing; bundle up. Used with *up.* —*n.* **1.** A garment to be wrapped or folded about a person; especially, a robe, cloak, shawl, or coat. **2.** A blanket. **3.** A wrapping or wrapper. —**keep under wraps.** To keep secret or concealed. [Middle English *wrappen,* probably from Germanic, akin to Danish dialectal *vravle,* to wind. See **wer-**[3] in Appendix.*]

wrap·a·round (răp′ə-round′) *adj.* **1.** Designating a garment, such as a dress, skirt, or robe, that is open to the hem and that is wrapped around the body before being fastened. **2.** Having ends that curve back or that overlap the sides.

wrap·per (răp′ər) *n.* **1.** One that wraps. **2.** The paper or other material in which something is wrapped: *a candy wrapper.* **3.** The paper encircling a mailed magazine or newspaper. **4.** *Chiefly British.* A book jacket. **5.** The tobacco leaf covering a cigar. **6.** A loose robe or negligee.

wrap·ping (răp′ĭng) *n.* Also **wrap·pings** (-ĭngz). The material in which something is wrapped.

wrapt. Alternate past tense of **wrap.**

wrap up. 1. To work out and complete the details of: *wrap up a business deal.* **2.** To encompass in a few words; summarize.

wrap-up (răp′ŭp′) *n.* A brief summary of the news.

wrasse (răs) *n.* Any of numerous chiefly tropical, often brightly colored marine fishes of the family Labridae. [Cornish and Welsh *gwrach*†, "old woman."]

wrath (răth, räth) *n.* **1.** Violent, resentful anger; rage; fury: *"His mind was hot with wrath and the memory of evil."* (J.R.R. Tolkien). **2. a.** A manifestation of anger. **b.** Divine retribution for sin. —See Synonyms at **anger.** —*adj. Obsolete.* Wrathful. [Middle English *wrath(th)e,* Old English *wrǣththu,* from *wrāth,* angry. See **wer-[3]** in Appendix.*]

wrath·ful (răth′fəl, räth′-) *adj.* **1.** Full of wrath; fiercely angry. **2.** Proceeding from or expressing wrath: *wrathful vengeance.* —**wrath′ful·ly** *adv.* —**wrath′ful·ness** *n.*

wreak (rēk) *tr.v.* **wreaked, wreaking, wreaks. 1.** To inflict (vengeance or punishment) upon a person. **2.** To express or gratify (anger, malevolence, or resentment); to vent. **3.** *Archaic.* To take vengeance for; avenge: *"it was not our custom to wreak our wrongs in cold blood"* (H. Rider Haggard). [Middle English *wreken,* Old English *wrecan,* to drive, expel, vent. See **wreg-** in Appendix.*]

wreath (rēth) *n., pl.* **wreaths** (rēthz). **1. a.** A ring or circlet of flowers or leaves worn on the head, placed as a memorial, or used as a decoration. **b.** A representation of this, as in woodwork. **2.** A curling shape; ring: *"clouds of light vapor were rising in spiral wreaths"* (James Fenimore Cooper). [Middle English *wrethe,* Old English *writha.* See **wer-[3]** in Appendix.*]

wreathe (rēth) *v.* **wreathed, wreathing, wreathes.** —*tr.* **1.** To twist or entwine into a wreath. **2.** To twist or curl into a wreathlike shape or contour. **3.** To crown or decorate with or as with a wreath. **4.** To coil or curl: *"One plant had wreathed itself round a statue"* (Hawthorne). **5.** To form a wreath around. —*intr.* **1.** To assume the form of a wreath. **2.** To curl, writhe, or spiral: *"The smoke from the fire at times . . . wreathed into the room"* (Stephen Crane). [From WREATH.]

wreck (rĕk) *n.* **1. a.** The action of wrecking or the condition of being wrecked; destruction. **b.** The accidental destruction of a ship; shipwreck. **2.** The stranded hulk of a ship that has been gravely damaged, as by being driven on rocks. **3.** The remains of something that has been wrecked or ruined, as by collision. **4.** Fragments of a ship or goods cast ashore by the sea after a shipwreck; wreckage. **5.** A person, animal, or thing in a shattered, broken-down, or worn-out state: *This hat is a wreck.* —*v.* **wrecked, wrecking, wrecks.** —*tr.* **1.** To destroy accidentally, as by collision. **2.** To tear down or dismantle. **3.** To bring to a state of ruin; disable or destroy; undermine. —*intr.* **1.** To suffer destruction, ruin, or shipwreck. **2.** To engage in wrecking or tearing down. —See Synonyms at **ruin.** [Middle English *wrek,* from Norman French *wrec,* from Scandinavian, akin to Old Norse *(v)rek,* wreckage. See **wreg-** in Appendix.*]

wreck·age (rĕk′ĭj) *n.* **1.** The act of wrecking or the condition of being wrecked. **2.** The debris of anything wrecked.

wreck·er (rĕk′ər) *n.* **1. a.** One who wrecks or causes a wreck. **b.** A member of a wrecking or demolition crew. **c.** One who destroys or ruins: *a wrecker of dreams.* **2. a.** A person, piece of equipment, vehicle, railroad car, or ship employed in recovering or removing a wreck. **b.** One who salvages wrecked cargo or parts. **3. a.** One who lures a vessel to destruction, as on a rocky coastline, in order to plunder. **b.** A plunderer.

wrecking bar. A small crowbar with a claw at one end and a slight curve at the other end.

wren (rĕn) *n.* **1.** Any of various small, brownish birds of the family Troglodytidae. **2.** Any of various similar birds. [Middle English *wrenne,* Old English *wrenna,* from Germanic *wrend(il)a-* (unattested).]

Wren (rĕn) *n. British Informal.* A member of the Women's Royal Naval Service.

Wren (rĕn), Sir **Christopher.** 1632–1723. English architect.

wrench (rĕnch) *n.* **1.** A sudden sharp, forcible twist or turn. **2.** An injury produced by twisting or straining. **3.** A sudden tug at one's emotions; a surge of compassion, sorrow, anguish, or the like. **4. a.** A break or parting that causes emotional distress. **b.** The pain associated with this: *"As she left, he felt the wrench of her going in the two parents."* (Hannah Green). **5.** A distortion in the original form of a speech or the like, or a twisted interpretation. **6.** Any of various tools with fixed or adjustable jaws for gripping, especially for gripping a nut, bolt, or pipe, and a long handle for effective leverage in turning. —*v.* **wrenched, wrenching, wrenches.** —*tr.* **1. a.** To twist or turn suddenly and forcibly. **b.** To twist and sprain. **2. a.** To force free by pulling at; yank; wrest. Usually used with *off* or *away:* *"the . . . violent effort with which one wrenches one's head away from the pillow in a nightmare"* (George Orwell). **b.** To pull with a wrench. **3.** To pull at the feelings or emotions of; give pain to: *It wrenched her to say good-by.* **4.** To distort or twist the original character or import of. —*intr.* To give a wrench, twist, or turn. [From Middle English *wrenchen,* to twist, wrench, Old English *wrencan,* to twist. See **wer-[3]** in Appendix.*]

wrest (rĕst) *tr.v.* **wrested, wresting, wrests. 1.** To obtain by or as by pulling with violent twisting movements: *wrest a book out of another's hands.* **2.** To usurp forcefully: *wrest power.* **3.** To extract by extortion, guile, or persistent effort; wring: *wrest the meaning from an obscure poem.* **4. a.** To distort or twist the nature or meaning of: *"if you wrest my words beyond their fair construction, it is you, and not I, that are the April Fool."* (Lamb). **b.** To misapply. —*n.* **1.** The action of wresting. **2.** *Archaic.* A small tuning key for the pins of a harp or piano. [Middle English *wresten,* Old English *wrǣstan,* to twist. See **wer-[3]** in Appendix.*] —**wrest′er** *n.*

wres·tle (rĕs′əl) *v.* **-tled, -tling, -tles.** —*intr.* **1.** To contend by grappling and attempting to throw one's opponent, especially under certain contest rules. **2. a.** To contend; to struggle. Used with *with* or *against: city planners wrestling with budget cuts.* **b.** To strive in an effort to master: *wrestle with one's conscience.* —*tr.* **1. a.** To take part in (a wrestling match). **b.** To wrestle with. **2.** *Western U.S.* To throw (a calf or other animal) for branding. —*n.* **1.** An act of wrestling; especially, a wrestling match. **2.** A struggle. [Middle English *wrest(e)len,* Old English *wrǣstlian.* See **wer-[3]** in Appendix.*] —**wres′tler** *n.*

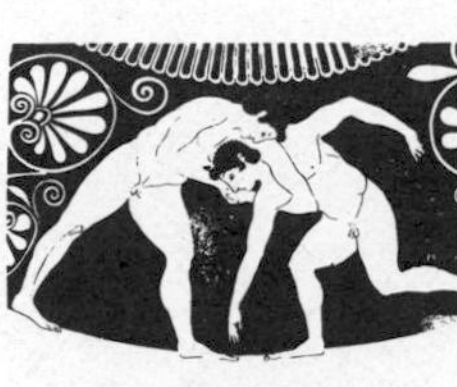
wrestling
Detail from ancient Greek vase painting

wres·tling (rĕs′lĭng) *n.* A gymnastic exercise or contest between two competitors who attempt to throw each other by grappling.

wrest pin. One of the pins to which the strings, especially of a keyboard stringed instrument, are attached and tuned.

wretch (rĕch) *n.* **1.** A miserable, unfortunate, or unhappy person. **2.** A base, mean, or despicable person: *"A stony adversary, an inhuman wretch"* (Shakespeare). [Middle English *wrecche,* Old English *wrecca,* wretch, exile. See **wreg-** in Appendix.*]

wretch·ed (rĕch′ĭd) *adj.* **-eder, -edest. 1.** Living in degradation and misery; miserable: *"The wretched prisoners huddling in the stinking cages"* (George Orwell). **2.** Attended by misery and woes: *a wretched life.* **3.** Of a poor or mean character; dismal: *a wretched building.* **4.** Contemptible; despicable. **5.** Inferior in performance or quality: *"Johnson was a wretched etymologist."* (Macaulay). **6.** Very unpleasant; deplorable. —See Synonyms at **sad.** [Middle English *wrecched,* irregularly from *wrecche,* WRETCH.] —**wretch′ed·ly** *adv.* —**wretch′ed·ness** *n.*

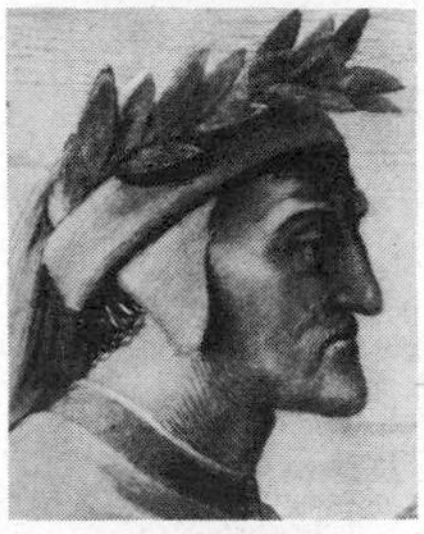
wreath
Detail from painting by Raphael

wrig·gle (rĭg′əl) *v.* **-gled, -gling, -gles.** —*intr.* **1.** To turn or twist the body with sinuous writhing motions; squirm. **2.** To proceed with writhing motions. **3.** To worm one's way into or out of a situation; insinuate or extricate oneself by sly or subtle means. —*tr.* **1.** To move with a wriggling motion: *wriggle a toe.* **2.** To make (one's way, for example) by wriggling: *He wriggled his way into favor.* —*n.* The action or movement of wriggling. [Middle English *wrigglen,* from Middle Low German *wriggeln.* See **wer-[3]** in Appendix.*] —**wrig′gly** *adj.*

wrig·gler (rĭg′lər) *n.* **1.** One that wriggles. **2.** The larva of a mosquito.

wright (rīt) *n.* A person who constructs something. Used chiefly in combination: *playwright; shipwright.* [Middle English *wright,* Old English *wryhta, wyrhta.* See **werg-[1]** in Appendix.*]

Wright (rīt), **Frank Lloyd.** 1869–1959. American architect.

Wright (rīt), **Wilbur.** 1867–1912. American aviation pioneer; with his brother, **Orville** (1871–1948), made first powered flights in heavier-than-air craft (1903) in a machine of their own invention and construction.

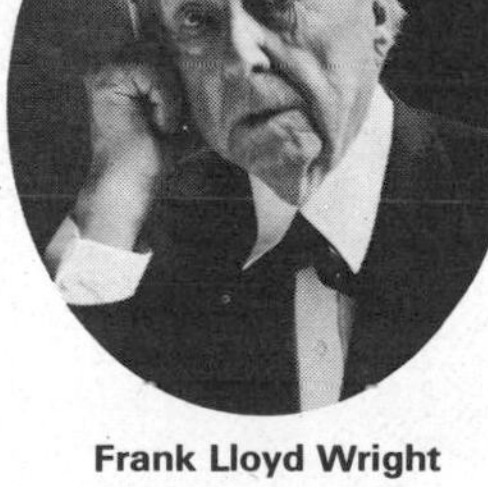
Frank Lloyd Wright

wring (rĭng) *v.* **wrung** (rŭng) or *rare* **wringed, wringing, wrings.** —*tr.* **1.** To twist and squeeze; to compress, as between the rollers of a machine, especially to extract liquid. Often used with *out.* **2.** To extract (liquid) by twisting or compressing. **3.** To wrench or twist forcibly or painfully: *wring one's neck.* **4.** To clasp and twist or squeeze, as in distress: *wring one's hands.* **5.** To cause distress to; affect with painful emotion: *wring one's heart.* **6.** To obtain by applying force or pressure to: *wring the truth out of a person.* —*intr.* To writhe or squirm, as in pain. —*n.* The act of wringing; a squeeze or twist. [Middle English *wringen,* Old English *wringan.* See **wer-[3]** in Appendix.*]

wring·er (rĭng′ər) *n.* One that wrings; especially, a device in which laundry is pressed or spun to extract water.

wrin·kle[1] (rĭng′kəl) *n.* **1.** A small furrow, ridge, or crease on a normally smooth surface, caused by crumpling, folding, or shrinking. **2.** A line or crease in the skin, as from age. —*v.* **wrinkled, -kling, -kles.** —*tr.* **1.** To make a wrinkle or wrinkles in. **2.** To draw up; to pucker: *wrinkle one's nose in disdain.* —*intr.* To form wrinkles. [Middle English, back-formation from *wrinkled,* wrinkled, probably Old English *gewrinclod,* serrated, winding, participle of *gewrinclian,* to wind. See **wer-[3]** in Appendix.*] —**wrin′kly** *adj.*

wrin·kle[2] (rĭng′kəl) *n. Informal.* An ingenious new trick or method; a clever innovation. [Middle English *wrinkel,* crooked action, trick, specialized use of *wrinkle,* WRINKLE.]

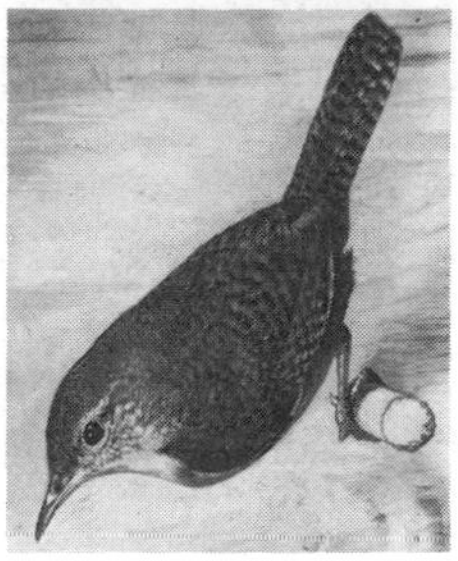
wren
Troglodytes aedon

wrist (rĭst) *n.* **1. a.** The junction between the hand and forearm. **b.** *Anatomy.* The system of bones forming this junction. Also called "carpus." **2.** The part of a sleeve or glove that encircles the wrist. [Middle English *wrist,* Old English *wrist.* See **wer-[3]** in Appendix.*]

wrist·band (rĭst′bănd′) *n.* A band, as on a long sleeve or on a wrist watch, that encircles the wrist.

wrist·let (rĭst′lĭt) *n.* **1.** A band of material worn round the wrist for warmth or additional strength. **2.** A bracelet.

wrist·lock (rĭst′lŏk′) *n.* A wrestling hold in which an opponent's wrist is gripped and twisted to immobilize him.

wrist pin. A pin that joins a piston to its connecting rod. Also called "gudgeon pin."

wrist watch. A watch worn on a band worn about the wrist.

writ[1] (rĭt) *n.* **1.** *Law.* A written order issued by a court, commanding the person to whom it is addressed to perform or cease performing some specified act. **2.** Writings. [Middle English *writ,* Old English *writ,* from Germanic *writan* (unattested), to scratch. See **write.**]

writ[2]. *Archaic.* Past tense and past participle of **write.**

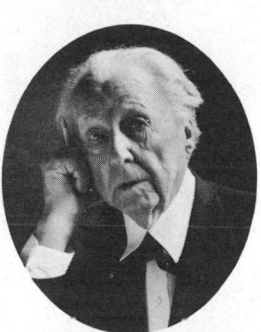

write (rīt) v. **wrote** (rōt) or archaic **writ** (rĭt), **written** (rĭt′n) or archaic **writ**, **writing**, **writes.** —tr. **1.** To form (letters, symbols, or characters) on a surface with a pen, pencil, or other tool; inscribe. **2.** To form (words, sentences, or the like) by inscribing the correct letters or symbols on paper or other material: write one's name. **3.** To compose, especially as an author or musician. **4.** To draw up in legal form; to draft: write a will. **5.** To fill in with the required information: write a check. **6.** To cover with writing: write a page. **7.** To set down; to record: write one's thoughts. **8.** To relate or communicate by writing: write the news from home. **9.** Informal. To send a letter or note to: write your aunt. **10.** To underwrite, as an insurance policy. **11.** To depict clearly; to mark: "Utter dejection was written on every face." (Winston Churchill). **12.** To ordain by fate or prophecy. —intr. **1.** To trace or form letters, words, or symbols on paper or another surface. **2.** To produce articles, books, or other matter to be read. **3. a.** To compose and send a letter or letters. **b.** To maintain a correspondence. [Middle English writen, Old English wrītan, from Germanic wrītan (unattested), to tear, scratch.]

write down. 1. To put into writing. **2.** To reduce in rank, value, or price. **3.** To disparage in writing. **4.** To write in a consciously simplified or condescending style.

write-down (rīt′doun′) n. Chiefly British. A reduction of the entered value of an asset; a write-off.

write in. 1. To apply or request by mail. **2.** To cast a vote for (one not listed on a ballot), as by inserting his name.

write-in (rīt′ĭn′) n. A vote for one not listed on a ballot, usually cast by the insertion of his name in a space provided. —adj. Of, for, or pertaining to such votes: a write-in campaign.

write off. 1. To reduce the entered value of (an asset); depreciate. **2.** To cancel from accounts as a loss. **3.** To consider as a loss or failure.

write-off (rīt′ôf′, -ŏf′) n. **1. a.** A cancellation in account books. **b.** An amount canceled or lost. **2.** A depreciation.

writ·er (rī′tər) n. **1.** A person who has written (something specified): the writer of the note. **2.** A person who writes as an occupation; an author.

writer's cramp. A cramp chiefly affecting the muscles of the thumb and two adjacent fingers after prolonged writing.

write up. 1. To write a report or description of, as for publication. **2.** To bring (a journal, for example) up to date. **3.** To overstate the value of (assets).

write-up (rīt′ŭp′) n. **1.** A published account, review, or notice, especially a favorable one. **2.** An illegal overevaluation of a corporation's assets.

writhe (rīth) v. **writhed**, **writhed** or archaic **writhen** (rĭth′ən), **writhing**, **writhes.** —intr. **1.** To twist or squirm, as in pain, struggle, or embarrassment. **2.** To move with a twisting or contorted motion. —tr. To cause to twist or squirm; contort: "He writhed himself quite off his stool in the excitement of his feelings" (Dickens). —n. An act or instance of writhing; a contortion. [Middle English writhen, Old English wrīthan. See wer-³ in Appendix.*] —writh′er n.

writ·ing (rī′tĭng) n. **1.** Written form: Put it in writing. **2.** Language symbols or characters written or imprinted on a surface; readable matter. **3.** Any written work; especially, a literary composition. **4.** The activity, art, or occupation of a writer.

writing paper. Stationery especially prepared to receive ink.

Writ·ings (rī′tĭngz) pl.n. **Hagiographa** (see).

writ of election. A writ issued by a governor or other executive authority requiring that an election be held, especially a special election to fill a vacancy.

writ of error. A writ commissioning an appellate court to review the proceedings of another court and correct the judgment given if deemed necessary.

writ of prohibition. An order issued by a higher court, commanding a lower court to cease from proceeding in some matter not within its jurisdiction.

writ of summons. A writ directing a person to appear in court to answer a complaint.

writ·ten. Past participle of **write.**

wrnt. warrant.

Wro·claw (vrô′tswäf). German **Bres·lau** (brĕs′lou). A city of southwestern Poland on the Oder. Population, 452,000.

wrong (rông, rŏng) adj. **1.** Not correct; erroneous. **2. a.** Contrary to conscience, morality, or law; wicked; immoral. **b.** Unfair or unjust. **3.** Not required, intended, or wanted: We took a wrong turn. **4.** Not fitting or suitable; inappropriate; improper: the wrong moment. **5.** Not in accordance with an established usage, method, or procedure. **6.** Not functioning properly; out of order; amiss. **7.** Unacceptable or undesirable according to social convention. —adv. **1.** In a wrong manner; mistakenly; erroneously. **2.** Immorally or unjustly: behave wrong. —**go wrong. 1.** To take a wrong turn or course. **2.** To go astray morally. **3.** To happen or turn out badly; go amiss. See Usage note below. —n. **1.** That which is wrong morally or socially; an unjust, injurious, or immoral act or circumstance. **2. a.** An invasion or violation of another's legal rights. **b.** Law. A tort. **3.** The condition of being mistaken or to blame: in the wrong. —See Synonyms at injustice. —tr.v. **wronged**, **wronging**, **wrongs. 1.** To treat unjustly, injuriously, or dishonorably. **2.** To discredit unjustly; to malign. [Middle English wrang, wrong, probably from Scandinavian, akin to Danish vrang, Old Norse rangr and vrangr (unattested). See wer-³ in Appendix.*] —wrong′er n. —wrong′ly adv.

Usage: Wrong and wrongly, as adverbs, are frequently interchangeable, especially in the sense of "erroneously." Wrong is more common in that sense except when the adverb occurs before the verb or participle that it modifies: He advised us wrong (less often wrongly). He spelled it wrong (less often wrongly). Wrongly is preferred in: a wrongly conceived plan; a wrongly arranged compartment.

wrong·do·er (rông′dōō′ər, rŏng′-) n. One who does wrong. —**wrong′do′ing** n.

wrong font. Abbr. **wf** The incorrect font. Used to designate a typeface used out of place.

wrong·ful (rông′fəl, rŏng′-) adj. **1.** Wrong; injurious; unjust. **2.** Contrary to law; unlawful; illegal. —**wrong′ful·ly** adv. —**wrong′ful·ness** n.

wrong-head·ed (rông′hĕd′ĭd, rŏng′-) adj. Persistently erroneous in judgment; wrong in stubborn defiance of the evidence. —**wrong′-head′ed·ly** adv. —**wrong′-head′ed·ness** n.

wrote. Past tense of **write.**

wroth (rôth) adj. Archaic. Wrathful; angry. [Middle English wrath, wroth, Old English wrāth. See wer-³ in Appendix.*]

wrought (rôt). Archaic. Past tense and past participle of **work.** —adj. **1.** Put together: carefully wrought. **2.** Shaped by hammering with tools. Said of metals or metalwork. **3.** Made delicately or elaborately: "wrought dice-cups in Pagan temples" (Amy Lowell). —**wrought up.** Agitated; excited.

wrought iron. An easily welded or forged iron containing approximately 0.2 per cent carbon and total impurities less than approximately 0.5 per cent.

wrung. Past tense and past participle of **wring.**

wry (rī) adj. **wrier** or **wryer**, **wriest** or **wryest. 1.** Abnormally twisted or bent to one side; crooked. Said of the features or the neck. **2.** Temporarily twisted in an expression of distaste or displeasure: "You find the wine too dry or too sweet, and you are making a wry face at it." (George Santayana). **3.** At variance with what is right or proper. **4.** Drily humorous, often with a touch of irony. [From Middle English wrien, to bend, twist, turn aside, Old English wrīgian, to proceed, turn. See wer-³ in Appendix.*] —**wry′ly** adv. —**wry′ness** n.

wry·neck (rī′nĕk′) n. **1.** Either of two Old World birds, Jynx torquilla or J. ruficollia, that are capable of twisting the neck into unusual contortions. **2.** Pathology. **Torticollis** (see).

WSA War Shipping Administration.

WSW west-southwest.

wt. weight.

Wu·han (wōō′hän′). The capital of Hupei Province, China, a city on the Yangtze including the former Han Cities of Hankow, Hanyang, and Wuchang. Population, 2,226,000.

Wu·hu (wōō′hōō′). A city of China, a port on the Yangtze in Anhwei Province. Population, 240,000.

Wu Kiang (wōō′ jyäng′). A river of central China, rising in western Kweichow and flowing about 500 miles generally north to the Yangtze in Szechwan.

wul·fen·ite (wōōl′fə-nīt′) n. A yellow to orange-red mineral, $PbMoO_4$, used as a molybdenum ore. [German Wulfenit, after Franz X. von Wulfen (1728–1805), Austrian mineralogist.]

Wu·pat·ki National Monument (wōō-pät′kē). An area of about 54 square miles in north-central Arizona, reserved to protect the ruins of prehistoric Indian dwellings.

Wup·per·tal (vŏōp′ər-täl). A city of West Germany in central North Rhine-Westphalia. Population, 422,000.

wurst (wûrst, wŏōrst) n. Sausage. [German Wurst, from Old High German wurst. See wer-³ in Appendix.*]

Würt·tem·berg (wûr′təm-bûrg; German vür′təm-bĕrk). A former state of southern West Germany, part of Baden-Württemberg since 1951.

Würz·burg (wûrts′bûrg; German vürts′bōōrk). A city of West Germany, in northwestern Bavaria. Population, 121,000.

Wu·sih (wōō′shē′). Also **Wu·hsi.** Formerly **Chang·chow** (chäng′jō′). A city of China, an inland port on the Grand Canal in southern Kiangsu Province. Population, 616,000.

WV West Virginia (with Zip Code).

W.Va. West Virginia.

WVS Women's Volunteer Service.

W.W.I World War I.

W.W.II World War II.

WY Wyoming (with Zip Code).

Wy·an·dot (wī′ən-dŏt′) n., pl. **Wyandot** or **-dots.** Also **Wy·an·dotte. 1.** A North American Indian of a tribe in the Huron confederacy. **2.** The Iroquoian language spoken by the Wyandot. [Wyandot wădát, tribal name.]

Wy·an·dotte (wī′ən-dŏt′) n. **1.** A domestic fowl of a breed developed in North America. **2.** Variant of **Wyandot.**

Wy·att (wī′ət), Sir **Thomas.** 1503–1542. English poet.

wych elm (wĭch). Also **witch elm.** An Old World elm, Ulmus glabra, often planted as a shade tree. [From Middle English wyche, Old English wice. See weik-⁴ in Appendix.*]

Wych·er·ley (wĭch′ər-lē), **William.** 1640?–1716. English Restoration playwright.

Wyc·liffe (wĭk′lĭf), **John.** Also **Wick·liffe**, **Wyc·lif**, **Wic·lif.** 1320?–1384. English theologian and religious reformer.

wye (wī) n. The letter y.

Wy·eth (wī′ĭth). Family of American painters, including **Newell Convers** (1882–1945) and his son, **Andrew Newell** (born 1917).

Wy·o·ming (wī-ō′mĭng). Abbr. **Wyo.** A Rocky Mountain state of the United States, occupying 97,914 square miles in the west-central part of the country; admitted to the Union in 1890. Population, 340,000. Capital, Cheyenne. See map at **United States of America.**

Wy·o·ming Valley (wī-ō′mĭng). A region on the Susquehanna in northeastern Pennsylvania; site of a massacre of settlers by Iroquois and British forces (1778).

wy·vern. Variant of **wivern.**

Sir Thomas Wyatt
Engraving from a drawing by
Hans Holbein the Younger

ă pat/ā pay/âr care/ä father/b bib/ch church/d deed/ĕ pet/ē be/f fife/g gag/h hat/hw which/ĭ pit/ī pie/îr pier/j judge/k kick/l lid, needle/m mum/n no, sudden/ng thing/ŏ pot/ō toe/ô paw, for/oi noise/ou out/ŏŏ took/ōō boot/p pop/r roar/s sauce/sh ship, dish/

X x

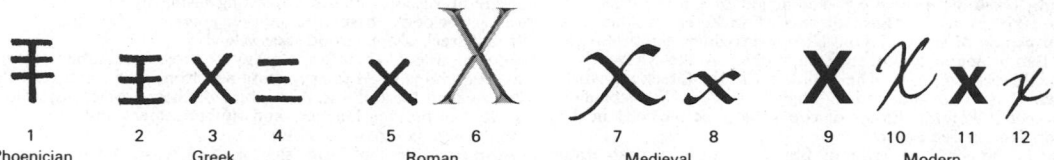

1	2	3	4	5	6	7	8	9	10	11	12
Phoenician		Greek			Roman		Medieval		Modern		

Around 1000 B.C. *the Phoenicians and other Semites of Syria and Palestine began to use a graphic sign in the form (1). They gave it the name* sāmekh, *meaning "fish," and used it for their consonant* s. *After 900* B.C. *the Greeks borrowed the sign from the Phoenicians, altering its form slightly (2,4), and in some scripts introducing a new form (3). They also changed its value to x and renamed it* xi. *The Greek form (3) passed unchanged via Etruscan to the Roman alphabet (5). The Roman Monumental Capital (6) is the prototype of our modern capital, printed (9) and written (10). The written Roman form (5) developed into the late Roman and medieval Uncial (7) and Cursive (8). These are the bases of our modern small letter, printed (11) and written (12).*

x, X (ĕks) *n., pl.* **x's** or *rare* **xs, X's** or **Xs. 1.** The 24th letter of the modern English alphabet. See **alphabet. 2.** Any of the speech sounds represented by this letter. **3.** Anything shaped like the letter **X. 4.** The mark **X** inscribed to represent the signature of an illiterate person.

x, X, x., X. *Note:* As an abbreviation or symbol, *x* may be a small or a capital letter, with or without a period. Established forms or those generally preferred precede the definition. When no form is given, all four forms are in general use in that sense. **1. X** A symbol for Christ or Christian. **2. x.** *Commerce & Finance.* ex. **3. x** A symbol used to indicate a mechanical defect in type. See table of Proofreaders' Marks at **proofread. 4. X** The symbol for a kiss. **5. X** A symbol placed on a map or diagram to mark the location or position of a point. **6. x, X** The Roman numeral for ten. **7.** *Mathematics.* The symbol for: **a.** An unknown number. **b.** An algebraic variable. **8.** Any unknown or unnamed factor, thing, or person. **9.** The 24th in a series; 23rd when *J* is omitted.

x (ĕks) *tr.v.* **x'd** or **xed, x-ing** or **x'ing, x's** or **xes. 1.** To mark or sign with an *x.* **2.** To delete, cancel, or obliterate with a series of *x's.* Usually used with *out.*

xan·thate (zăn′thāt′) *n.* A salt of a xanthic acid; especially, a simple xanthic acid salt, as of sodium or potassium, used as a flotation collector for copper, silver, and gold. [XANTH(O)- + -ATE.]

xan·thic acid (zăn′thĭk). Any of various unstable acids of the form ROC(S)SH, in which R is usually an alkyl radical. [From Greek *xanthos,* yellow (referring to the color of its salts).]

xan·thin (zăn′thĭn) *n.* A yellow plant pigment, such as xanthophyll. [XANTH(O)- + -IN.]

xan·thine (zăn′thēn′, -thĭn) *n.* A yellowish-white purine base, $C_5H_4N_4O_2$, found in blood, urine, and some plants. [French *xanthine* : XANTH(O)- + -INE.]

xantho-, xanth-. Indicates the color yellow; for example, **xanthochroid, xanthoma.** [New Latin, from Greek *xanthos†,* yellow.]

xan·tho·chroid (zăn′thə-kroid′) *adj.* Having a light complexion and light hair. —*n.* A xanthochroid individual. [New Latin *xanthochroi,* light-haired, fair-skinned people : XANTH(O)- + Greek *ōkhros,* pale, wan (see **ocher**) + -OID.]

xan·tho·ma (zăn-thō′mə) *n.* A skin disease characterized by nodular yellowish-orange patches, especially on the eyelids. [New Latin : XANTH(O)- + -OMA.]

xan·tho·phyll (zăn′thə-fĭl′) *n.* A yellow carotenoid pigment, $C_{40}H_{56}O_2$, found with chlorophyll in green plants and in egg yolk. [French *xanthophylle* : XANTHO- + -PHYLL.]

xan·thous (zăn′thəs) *adj.* **1.** Yellow. **2.** Having light-brown or yellowish skin. Compare **melanous.** [From Greek *xanthos,* yellow. See **xantho-.**]

Xan·thus (zăn′thəs). A city and the capital of ancient Lycia, in southwestern Turkey. —**Xan′thi·an** (-thē-ən) *adj.*

Xa·vi·er (zā′vē-ər, zăv′ē-; *Spanish* hä-vyĕr′), **Saint Francis.** 1506–1552. Spanish Jesuit missionary in India, Ceylon, and Japan; canonized in 1622.

x-ax·is (ĕks′ăk′sĭs) *n., pl.* **x-axes** (-sēz). **1.** The horizontal axis of a two-dimensional Cartesian coordinate system. **2.** One of three axes in a three-dimensional Cartesian coordinate system.

X-chro·mo·some (ĕks′krō′mə-sōm′) *n.* The sex chromosome associated with female characteristics, occurring paired in the female and single in the male sex-chromosome pair. Compare **Y-chromosome.**

Xe The symbol for the element xenon.

xe·bec (zē′bĕk′) *n.* Also **ze·bec, ze·beck.** A small three-masted Mediterranean vessel with both square and triangular sails, once used commonly by Arab corsairs. [Earlier *chebec,* from French, from Italian *sciabecco,* from Arabic *shabbāk.*]

xe·ni·a (zē′nē-ə) *n. Botany.* The effect on a hybrid plant produced by the transfer of pollen from one strain to the seed of a different strain. [New Latin, from Greek, hospitality, from *xenos,* a guest, stranger. See **xeno-.**]

xeno–. Indicates the presence of or a reference to that which is strange, foreign, or different; for example, **xenolith, xenophobe.** [New Latin, from Greek *xenos,* stranger. See **xenos** in Appendix.*]

xen·o·cryst (zĕn′ə-krĭst′) *n.* A crystal foreign to the igneous rock in which it occurs. [XENO- + CRYST(AL).]

xe·nog·a·my (zĭ-nŏg′ə-mē) *n. Botany.* The transfer of pollen from one plant to another; cross-pollination. [XENO- + -GAMY.] —**xe·nog′a·mous** (-məs) *adj.*

xen·o·gen·e·sis (zĕn′ə-jĕn′ə-sĭs) *n.* The supposed production of offspring markedly different from and showing no relationship to either of its parents. [XENO- + -GENESIS.] —**xen′o·ge·net′ic** (zĕn′ə-jə-nĕt′ĭk), **xen′o·gen′ic** (-jĕn′ĭk) *adj.*

xen·o·lith (zĕn′ə-lĭth′) *n.* A rock fragment foreign to the igneous mass in which it occurs. [XENO- + -LITH.]

xe·non (zē′nŏn′) *n. Symbol* **Xe** A colorless, odorless, highly unreactive gaseous element found in minute quantities in the atmosphere, extracted commercially from liquefied air, and used in stroboscopic, bactericidal, and laser-pumping lamps. Atomic number 54, atomic weight 131.30, melting point −111.9°C, boiling point −107.1°C, density 5.887 grams per liter, specific gravity (liquid) 3.52 (−109°C). See **element.** [From Greek *xenon,* neuter of *xenos,* stranger. See **xeno-.**]

xen·o·phobe (zĕn′ə-fōb′) *n.* A person unduly fearful or contemptuous of strangers or foreigners, especially as reflected in his political or cultural views. [XENO- + -PHOBE.] —**xen′o·pho′bi·a** *n.* —**xen′o·pho′bic** *adj.*

Xen·o·phon (zĕn′ə-fən). 430?–355? B.C. Greek general and writer.

Xe·res. The former name for **Jerez.**

xer·ic (zĕr′ĭk, zîr′-) *adj.* Of, characterized by, or adapted to an extremely dry habitat. [From Greek *xēros,* dry. See **xero-.**]

xero-, xer-. Indicates dryness; for example, **xerophyte, xerosis.** [New Latin, from Greek *xēros,* dry. See **ksero-** in Appendix.*]

xer·o·der·ma (zîr′ō-dûr′mə) *n.* Also **xe·ro·der·mi·a** (-mē-ə). Abnormal dryness of the skin. [XERO- + -DERMA.]

xe·rog·ra·phy (zĭ-rŏg′rə-fē) *n.* A dry photographic or photocopying process in which a negative image formed by a resinous powder on an electrically charged plate is transferred to and thermally fixed as positive on a paper or other copying surface. [XERO- + -GRAPHY.] —**xer′o·graph′ic** (zîr′ə-grăf′ĭk) *adj.* —**xe·rog′raph·er** *n.*

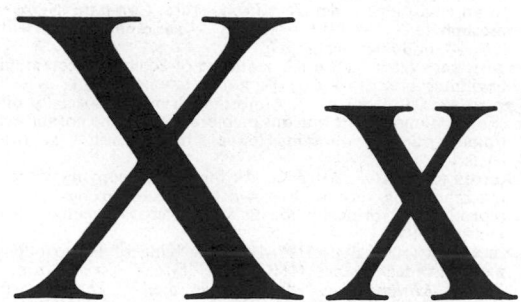

Saint Francis Xavier

X-chromosome
From human metaphase
(599-344-14)

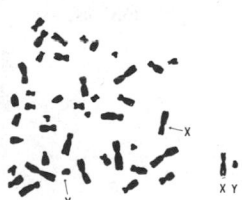

xebec

xe·roph·i·lous (zĭ-rŏf′ə-ləs) *adj.* Flourishing in or able to withstand a dry, hot environment. [XERO- + -PHILOUS.]

xer·oph·thal·mi·a (zîr′əf-thăl′mē-ə) *n.* Extreme dryness of the conjunctiva, thought to result from vitamin A deficiency. [Late Latin *xerophthalmia,* from Greek *xērophthalmia* : XER(O)- + OPHTHALMIA.]

xer·o·phyte (zîr′ə-fīt′) *n.* A plant that grows in and is adapted to an environment deficient in moisture. Compare **hydrophyte, mesophyte.** [XERO- + -PHYTE.] **—xer′o·phyt′ic** (zîr′ə-fĭt′ĭk) *adj.* **—xer′o·phyt′i·cal·ly** *adv.*

xe·ro·sere (zîr′ə-sîr′) *n.* A sequence of ecological communities beginning in a dry area. [XERO- + SERE (series).]

xe·ro·sis (zĭ-rō′sĭs) *n.* **1.** Abnormal dryness, especially of the skin, conjunctiva, or mucous membranes. **2.** The normal evolutionary sclerosis of aging tissue. [New Latin : XER(O)- + -OSIS.]

Xer·ox (zîr′ŏks) *n.* A trademark for a photocopying process or machine using xerography. **—***tr.v.* **Xeroxed, -oxing, -oxes.** To reproduce or print by means of a Xerox machine. [From XEROGRAPHY.]

Xerx·es I (zûrk′sēz). 519?–465 B.C. King of Persia (486–465 B.C.); invaded Greece (480 B.C.). [Greek *Xerxes,* from Old Persian *Khshayārshan-,* "ruling over men" : *khshaya-,* ruling (see **ksei-²** in Appendix*) + *arshan-,* man (see **ers-²** in Appendix*).]

x-height (ĕks′hīt′) *n. Printing.* The height of a lower-case *x.*

Xho·sa (kō′sä) *n., pl.* **Xhosa** or **-sas.** Also **Xo·sa. 1.** One of a Bantu people of Cape of Good Hope Province, South Africa. **2.** A Bantu language akin to Zulu spoken by the Xhosa.

xi (zī, sī; *Greek* ksē) *n.* **1.** The 14th letter in the Greek alphabet, written Ξ, ξ. Transliterated in English as *X, x.* See **alphabet. 2.** *Symbol* Ξ *Physics.* Either of two subatomic particles in the baryon family. See **particle.**

Xin·gu (shĭng-gŏo′). A river of Brazil, rising in central Mato Grosso and flowing 1,230 miles generally north to the Amazon.

xiphi–. Indicates sword; for example, **xiphisternum.** [New Latin, from Greek *xiphos,* sword, probably of Oriental origin.]

xiph·i·ster·num (zĭf′ə-stûr′nəm) *n., pl.* **-na** (-nə). The posterior and smallest of the three divisions of the sternum. Also called "xiphoid process." [New Latin : XIPHI- + STERNUM.]

xiph·oid (zĭf′oid′) *adj.* **1.** Having the shape of a sword. **2.** Of or pertaining to the xiphisternum. **—***n.* The xiphisternum. [Greek *xiphoeidēs,* "sword-shaped" : XIPHI- + -OID.]

xiph·o·su·ran (zĭf′ə-sŏor′ən) *n.* Any arthropod of the order Xiphosura, which includes the horseshoe crab and many extinct forms. **—***adj.* Of or belonging to the order Xiphosura. [New Latin *Xiphosura,* "sword-tailed ones" : Greek *xiphos,* sword (see **xiphi-**) + *-ura,* plural of *-urus,* -UROUS.]

XL extra large.

X·mas (krĭs′məs, ĕks′məs) *n. Informal.* Christmas. [From the Greek letter *X,* transliterated as *Kh* (see **chi**) and representing Greek *Khristos,* CHRIST.]

Usage: Xmas occurs principally in commercial writing and is now chiefly appropriate to that level, though the term itself has a long history. In general usage on a formal level, it is considered unacceptable by 88 per cent of the Usage Panel.

XP A monogram used to represent Christ or Christianity, composed of *chi* and *rho,* the first two letters of the Greek word for Christ.

x-ra·di·a·tion (ĕks′rā′dē-ā′shən) *n.* **1.** Treatment with or exposure to x rays. **2.** Radiation composed of x rays.

x ray. Also **X ray** (for sense 2). **1. a.** A relatively high-energy photon with wavelength in the approximate range from 0.05 angstroms to 100 angstroms. **b.** *Usually plural.* A stream of such photons, used for their penetrating power in radiography, radiology, radiotherapy, and research. Also called "Roentgen ray." **2.** A photograph taken with x rays. Also called "x-ray photograph." [Translation of German *X Strahlen* (so called because its exact nature was not known).] **—x′-ray′** *adj.*

x-ray (ĕks′rā′) *tr.v.* **x-rayed, x-raying, x-rays. 1.** To irradiate with x rays. **2.** To photograph with x rays.

x-ray crystallography. The study of crystal structure by means of x-ray diffraction.

x-ray microscope. An instrument used to render a highly magnified image of the atomic structure of a crystalline system by means of the contrasts arising from the differences in such a structure's absorption or emission of x rays.

x-ray therapy. Radiotherapy with x rays.

x-ray tube. A vacuum tube containing electrodes that accelerate electrons and direct them to a metal anode, where their impacts produce x rays.

xu (zōō) *n., pl.* **xu.** A coin equal to $\frac{1}{100}$ of the dong, the monetary unit of North Vietnam. See table of exchange rates at **currency.** [Vietnamese.]

Xu·thus (zōō′thəs). *Greek Mythology.* A son of Hellen, and the ancestor of the Ionian Greeks.

xy·lan (zī′lən) *n.* A yellow, gummy pentosan found in plant cell walls and yielding xylose upon hydrolysis. [XYL(O)- + -AN.]

xy·lem (zī′ləm) *n. Botany.* The supporting and water-conducting tissue of vascular plants, consisting primarily of tracheids and vessels; woody tissue. Compare **phloem.** [German *Xylem,* from Greek *xulon,* wood. See **xylo-**.]

xy·lene (zī-lēn′, zī′lēn′) *n.* **1.** Any of three flammable isomeric hydrocarbons, $C_6H_4(CH_3)_2$, obtained from wood and coal tar. Also called "xylol." **2.** A mixture of these isomers used as a solvent in making lacquers and rubber cement and as an aviation fuel. [XYL(O)- + -ENE.]

xy·li·dine (zī′lə-dēn′, -dĭn, zĭl′-) *n.* **1.** Any of six toxic isomers, $(CH_3)_2C_6H_3NH_2$, derived from xylene, used chiefly as dye intermediates. **2.** Any of various mixtures of these isomers. [XYL(O)- + -ID + -INE.]

xylo-, xyl–. Indicates: **1.** Wood; for example, **xylograph; xylophone. 2.** Xylene; for example, **xylidine.** [From Greek *xulon†,* wood.]

xy·lo·graph (zī′lə-grăf′, -gräf′) *n.* **1.** An engraving on wood. **2.** An impression from a wood block. **—***tr.v.* **xylographed, -graphing, -graphs.** To print from a wood engraving. **—xy·log′ra·pher** (zī-lŏg′rə-fər) *n.*

xy·log·ra·phy (zī-lŏg′rə-fē) *n.* **1.** Wood engraving, especially of an early period. **2.** The art of printing texts or illustrations, sometimes with color, from wood blocks, as distinct from typography. [French *xylographie* : XYLO- + -GRAPHY.] **—xy′lo·graph′ic** (-lə-grăf′ĭk) *adj.* **—xy′lo·graph′i·cal·ly** *adv.*

xy·loid (zī′loid′) *adj.* Of or similar to wood. [XYL(O)- + -OID.]

xy·loph·a·gous (zī-lŏf′ə-gəs) *adj.* Feeding on wood, as certain insects. [Greek *xylophagos* : XYLO- + -PHAGOUS.]

xy·lo·phone (zī′lə-fōn′) *n.* A musical percussion instrument consisting of a mounted row of wooden bars graduated in length to sound a chromatic scale, played with two small mallets. [XYLO- + -PHONE.] **—xy′lo·phon′ist** *n.*

xy·lose (zī′lōs′) *n.* A white crystalline aldose sugar, $C_5H_{10}O_5$, used in dyeing, tanning, and in diabetic diets. Also called "wood sugar." [XYL(O)- + -OSE.]

xy·lot·o·my (zī-lŏt′ə-mē) *n.* The preparation of sections of wood for microscopic study. [XYLO- + -TOMY.]

xys·ter (zĭs′tər) *n.* A surgical instrument for scraping bones. [New Latin, from Greek *xuster,* scraper, from *xuein,* to scrape. See **kes-¹** in Appendix.*]

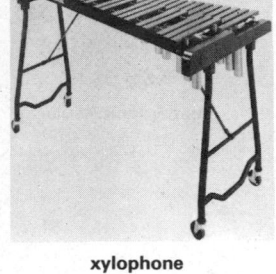

xylophone

ă pat/ā pay/âr care/ä father/b bib/ch church/d deed/ĕ pet/ē be/f fife/g gag/h hat/hw which/ĭ pit/ī pie/îr pier/j judge/k kick/l lid, needle/m mum/n no, sudden/ng thing/ŏ pot/ō toe/ô paw, for/oi noise/ou out/ŏŏ took/ōō boot/p pop/r roar/s sauce/sh ship, dish/

Xerxes I

Yy

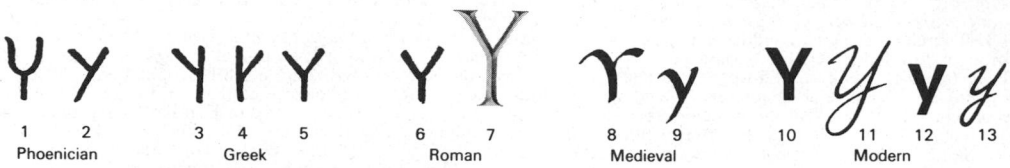

1	2	3	4	5	6	7	8	9	10	11	12	13
Phoenician		Greek			Roman		Medieval			Modern		

The letter Y is a descendant of the letter V (see). Around 1000 B.C. the Phoenicians and other Semites of Syria and Palestine began to use a graphic sign in the forms (1,2). They gave it the name wāw and used it for a semiconsonant w, as in English know, knows. *After 900 B.C., when the Greeks borrowed the alphabet from the Phoenicians, they developed two signs from wāw. The first sign, which they called upsilon, "bare u," they used for the vowel u (3,4,5,6). (For the other sign, see* F.) *The Greek form with the tail (5) passed to the Roman alphabet (6,7) when the need arose to transliterate borrowed Greek words. The Greek upsilon (and its Roman transliteration), originally pronounced u, gradually acquired the pronunciation ü (as in German* über). *In late Roman and medieval Uncial (8) and Cursive (9), the letter tended also to be interchangeable with i, both consonantal and vocalic, in many situations. In modern English it only represents consonantal i, while retaining a variety of vocalic applications. The printed forms (10,12) are modeled on the Roman Monumental Capital (7), the written forms (11,13) on the Cursive.*

y, Y (wī) *n., pl.* **y's** or *rare* **ys, Y's** or **Ys. 1.** The 25th letter of the modern English alphabet. See **alphabet. 2.** Any of the speech sounds represented by this letter. **3.** Anything shaped like the letter Y.

y, Y, y-. Y. *Note:* As an abbreviation or symbol, *y* may be a small or a capital letter, with or without a period. Established forms or those generally preferred precede the definition. When no form is given, all four forms are in general use in that sense. **1. Y** hypercharge. **2. y** ordinate. **3. y.** year. **4. Y** yen (currency). **5. Y, Y.** A shortened form of the abbreviations Y.M.C.A., Y.M.H.A., Y.W.C.A., and Y.W.H.A. **6. Y** The symbol for the element yttrium. **7.** The 25th in a series; 24th when *J* is omitted.

y-, i-. *Archaic.* Indicates the past participle; for example, **yclept.** [Middle English *i-, y-,* Old English *ge-.* See **kom** in Appendix.*]

-y¹, -ey. Indicates: **1.** The existence or possession of what is expressed in the root; for example, **curly, rainy, cloudy. 2.** A relationship or resemblance to what is expressed in the root; for example, **clayey, glassy, watery.** [Middle English *-ie, -y, -ey,* Old English *-ig, -ǣg,* from Common Germanic *-iga, -aga* (untested).]

-y². Indicates: **1.** A condition or state of being or quality; for example, **jealousy, beggary. 2.** An activity, products dealt with, or a place of business; for example, **cannery, cookery.** [Middle English *-ie,* from Old French, from Latin *-ia,* -IA.]

-y³, -ey, -ie. Indicates: **1.** Smallness or diminutiveness; for example, **kiddy, doggy. 2.** Familiarity or endearment; for example, **sweetie, daddy.** [Middle English *-ie.*]

Ya·blo·no·vyy Range (yä′blə-nə-vē′). A range in the southeastern Soviet Union, east of Lake Baikal, a section of the watershed between the Pacific and Arctic oceans.

yacht (yät) *n.* Any of various relatively small sailing or mechanically propelled vessels, generally with smart, graceful lines, used for pleasure cruises or racing. —*intr.v.* **yachted, yachting, yachts.** To race, sail, or cruise in a yacht. [Earlier *yaught,* from obsolete Dutch *jaghte,* short for *jaght(schip),* "chasing (ship)," from *jagen,* to chase, hunt, from Germanic *jagojan* (unattested). See **jaeger.**]

yacht·ing (yät′ing) *n.* The sport of sailing in yachts.

yachts·man (yäts′mən) *n., pl.* **-men** (-mĭn). A person who owns or sails a yacht. **—yachts′man·ship′** *n.*

ya·gi (yä′gē, yäg′ē) *n. Electronics.* A directional radio and television antenna consisting of a horizontal conductor with several insulated dipoles parallel to and in the plane of the conductor. Also called "yagi antenna." [Invented by Hidetsugu *Yagi* (born 1888), Japanese engineer.]

yah (yä) *adv. Informal.* Yes. [Variant of YEA.]

Ya·ha·ta (yä-hä′tä). A city of northern Kyushu, Japan, now part of Kita Kyushu.

ya·hoo (yä′hōō, yä′-, yä-hōō′) *n., pl.* **-hoos.** A crude or brutish person. [After the *Yahoos,* a race representing humanity at large in Swift's *Gulliver's Travels.*]

Yah·weh (yä′wĕ). Also **Jah·weh, Yah·veh** (-vĕ), **Jah·veh.** A name for God assumed by modern scholars to be a rendering of the pronunciation of the Tetragrammaton. Compare **Elohim.**

Yah·wist (yä′wĭst) *n.* Also **Jah·wist, Yah·vist** (-vĭst), **Jah·vist.** The author of the earliest sources of the Hexateuch, in which God is called Yahweh. Also called "Jehovist." Compare **Elohist. —Yah·wis′tic** *adj.*

yak¹ (yăk) *n.* A long-haired bovine mammal, *Bos grunniens,* of the mountains of central Asia, where it is often domesticated. [Tibetan *gyag.*]

yak¹

yak² (yăk) *intr.v.* **yakked, yakking, yaks.** Also **yack, yacked, yacking, yacks.** *Slang.* To talk or chatter persistently and meaninglessly. —*n.* Also **yack.** *Slang.* Continuous, meaningless chatter. [Imitative.]

Yak·i·ma (yăk′ə-mô′). A city of south-central Washington, on the Yakima River. Population, 45,000.

Yak·i·ma River (yăk′ə-mô′). A river of Washington, rising in the Cascade Range and flowing 200 miles generally southeast to the Columbia.

Ya·kut (yä-kōōt′) *n.* **1.** One of a people living in the Yakut Autonomous Soviet Socialist Republic. **2.** The Turkic language of the Yakuts.

Ya·kut Autonomous Soviet Socialist Republic (yä-kōōt′). Also **Ya·kutsk** (yä-kōōtsk′). An administrative division, 1,197,760 square miles in area, of the east-central Russian S.F.S.R. Population, 614,000. Capital, Yakutsk.

Ya·kutsk (yä-kōōtsk′). The capital of the Yakut A.S.S.R., a port on the Lena River. Population, 89,000.

Yale (yāl), **Elihu.** 1649–1721. American-born English merchant and benefactor of Yale College.

Yal·ta (yäl′tə, yôl′tə). A city of the Soviet Union, a port in the southern Crimea on the Black Sea; the site of a conference attended by Roosevelt, Stalin, and Churchill (1945). Population, 44,000.

Ya·lu (yä′lōō). A river rising in northern North Korea and flowing about 300 miles along the North Korea-Manchuria border to the Yellow Sea.

Ya·lung (yä′lōong′). A river of China, rising in southern Tsinghai and flowing about 800 miles generally southeast to the Yangtze.

yam (yăm) *n.* **1.** Any of various chiefly tropical vines of the genus *Dioscorea,* many of which have edible tuberous roots. **2.** The starchy root of such a vine, used in the tropics as food. **3.** A sweet potato having reddish flesh. [Portuguese *inhame,* "edible," possibly from Fulani *nyami,* to eat.]

yam
Dioscorea esculenta

Ya·mal Peninsula (yə-mäl′). A peninsula of the Soviet Union, in northwestern Siberia, extending north some 400 miles between the Kara Sea and the Gulf of Ob.

Ya·ma·sa·ki (yäm′ä-sä′kē), **Minoru.** Born 1912. American architect.

ya·men (yä′mən) *n.* The office or residence of any official in the Chinese Empire. [Mandarin Chinese *ya² mên²* : *ya²,* office of a magistrate, probably from *ya²,* tooth, flag with serrated borders (placed at the entrance of a governor's office) + *mên²,* door.]

Yam ham Me·lah. The Hebrew name for the **Dead Sea.**

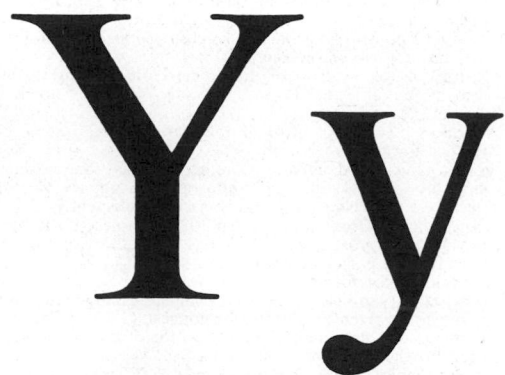

ă pat/ā pay/âr care/ä father/b bib/ch church/d deed/ĕ pet/ē be/f fife/g gag/h hat/hw which/ĭ pit/ī pie/îr pier/j judge/k kick/l lid, needle/m mum/n no, sudden/ng thing/ŏ pot/ō toe/ô paw, for/oi noise/ou out/ōō took/ōō boot/p pop/r roar/s sauce/sh ship, dish/t tight/th thin/*th* this/*ŭ* cut/ûr urge/v valve/w with/y yes/z zebra, size/zh vision/ə about, item, edible, gallop, circus/à *Fr.* ami/œ *Fr.* feu, *Ger.* schön/ü *Fr.* tu, *Ger.* über/KH *Ger.* ich, *Scot.* loch/N *Fr.* bon. *Follows main vocabulary. †Of obscure origin.

yarrow
Achillea millefolium

yashmak

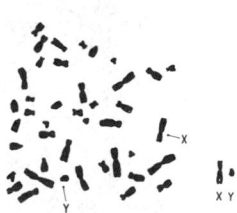

Y-chromosome
From human metaphase
(599-344-14)

yam·mer (yăm′ər) *v.* **-mered, -mering, -mers.** *Informal.* —*intr.* **1.** To complain peevishly or whimperingly; to whine: " *'It's easy to yammer,' he said. 'Why not do something for a change?'* " (Aldous Huxley). **2.** To talk volubly and loudly. —*tr.* To utter or say in a complaining or clamorous tone. —*n. Informal.* An act or instance of yammering. [Alteration of earlier *yomer,* Middle English *yomeren,* Old English *gēomrian,* from Common Germanic.] —**yam′mer·er** *n.*

Ya·na (yä′nə). A river of the Soviet Union, rising in the east-central Yakut A.S.S.R. and flowing 750 miles north to the Laptev Sea.

Ya·naon (yä-noun′). A town of eastern India, a free port of the former French India until 1954.

yang (yăng) *n.* Also **Yang.** The active, masculine cosmic principle in Chinese dualistic philosophy. Compare **yin.** [Mandarin Chinese *yang²,* the sun, masculine element.]

Yang (yăng), **Chen Ning.** Born 1922. Chinese-born American physicist; proposed, with T.D. **Lee** (see), the violation of conservation of parity in weak interactions.

Yang·ku. The former name for **Taiyüan.**

Yang·tze (yăng′tsē′). Official name, **Chang·kiang** (chăng′-jyăng′). A river of China, the longest (3,430 miles) in Asia, rising in the highlands of Tibet and flowing first southeast and then northeast to the East China Sea.

yank (yăngk) *v.* **yanked, yanking, yanks.** *Informal.* —*tr.* To pull or extract suddenly; to jerk: *"She yanked her out of the swing without a word and carried her off screaming."* (Shirley Ann Grau). —*intr.* To pull on something suddenly; to jerk. —*n.* A sudden vigorous pull; a jerk. [Origin unknown.]

Yank (yăngk) *n. Informal.* Yankee. [Short for YANKEE.]

Yan·kee (yăng′kē) *n.* **1.** A native or inhabitant of New England. **2.** A native or inhabitant of a Northern state; especially, a Union soldier during the Civil War. **3.** A native or inhabitant of the United States. [Possibly from the Dutch name *Janke,* diminutive of *Jan,* Dutch form for JOHN.]

Yan·kee·dom (yăng′kē-dəm) *n.* **1.** The Northern states or New England. **2.** The United States. **3.** Yankees collectively.

Yankee Doo·dle (do͞od′l). A Yankee. [From the title of a song popular during the Revolutionary War.]

Yan·kee·ism (yăng′kē-ĭz′əm) *n.* **1.** A Yankee custom or characteristic. **2.** A Yankee peculiarity, as of language or pronunciation.

Ya·oun·dé (yä-o͞on-dā′). The capital of Cameroun, central Africa, in the southwest. Population, 93,000.

yap (yăp) *v.* **yapped, yapping, yaps.** —*intr.* **1.** To bark sharply or shrilly; yelp. **2.** *Slang.* To talk noisily or stupidly; jabber. **3.** *Slang.* To talk abusively; scold; yell. —*tr.* To utter by yapping. —*n.* **1.** A sharp, shrill bark; yelp. **2.** *Slang.* Noisy, stupid talk; jabbering. **3.** *Slang.* A crude, loud, stupid person. **4.** *Slang.* The mouth. [Imitative.]

Yap (yäp, yăp). An island group, 80 square miles in area, in the Caroline Islands of the western Pacific.

ya·pok (yə-pŏk′) *n.* An aquatic marsupial mammal, *Chironectes minimus,* of tropical America, having dense fur, webbed hind feet, and a long tail. [After *Oyapock,* river in South America.]

Ya·qui¹ (yä′kē) *n., pl.* **Yaqui** or **-quis. 1.** A tribe of North American Indians of Uto-Aztecan linguistic stock, now living in Sonora, Mexico. **2.** A member of this tribe. **3.** The language of this tribe.

Ya·qui² (yä′kē). A river of Mexico, rising in northern Sonora and flowing about 400 miles generally south to the Gulf of California.

Yar·bor·ough (yär′bər-ō; *British* -bər-ə) *n.* A bridge or whist hand containing no card higher than a nine. [After Charles Anderson Worsley (died 1897), Second Earl of *Yarborough,* who is said to have bet 1,000 to 1 that such a hand would not occur (and it did).]

yard¹ (yärd) *n.* **1.** *Abbr.* **yd** The fundamental unit of length in both the U.S. Customary System and the British Imperial System, equal to 0.9144 meter. See **measurement. 2.** *Nautical.* A long, tapering spar slung at right angles to a mast to support and spread the head of a square sail, lugsail, or lateen. [Middle English *yerde, yarde,* Old English *gerd, gierd,* staff, twig, measuring rod. See **ghasto-** in Appendix.*]

yard² (yärd) *n.* **1.** A tract of ground adjacent to, surrounding, or surrounded by a building or group of buildings. **2.** A tract of ground, often enclosed, used for a specific work, business, or other activity. Often used in combination: *shipyard; graveyard.* **3.** An area provided with a system of tracks where railroad trains are made up and cars are switched, stored, or serviced. **4.** A winter pasture for deer or other grazing animals. **5.** An enclosed tract of ground in which animals, such as chickens or pigs, are kept. —*v.* **yarded, yarding, yards.** —*tr.* To enclose, collect, or put in or as if in a yard. —*intr.* To gather in or as if in a yard. [Middle English *yarde, yerd,* Old English *geard,* enclosure, residence. See **gher-²** in Appendix.*]

yard·age¹ (yär′dĭj) *n.* **1.** The amount or length of something measured in yards. **2.** Cloth sold by the yard.

yard·age² (yär′dĭj) *n.* **1.** The use of a livestock yard at a station in the process of transporting cattle by railroad. **2.** The fee paid for such use.

yard·arm (yärd′ärm′) *n. Nautical.* Either end of a yard of a square sail.

yard goods. Cloth sold by the yard; **piece goods** *(see).*

yard grass. Any of several weedy grasses of the genus *Eleusine.*

yard·man (yärd′mən) *n., pl.* **-men** (-mĭn). A man employed in a yard, especially a railroad yard.

yard·mas·ter (yärd′măs′tər, -mäs′tər) *n.* A railroad employee in charge of a yard.

yard·stick (yärd′stĭk′) *n.* **1.** A graduated measuring stick one yard in length. **2.** Any test or standard used in measurement, comparison, or judgment.

yare (yâr) *adj. Archaic.* **1.** Responding easily; manageable; maneuverable. Said of a vessel. **2.** Bright; lively; quick. **3.** Ready; prepared. —*adv. Obsolete.* Soon; quickly; promptly. [Middle English *yare,* Old English *gearo, gearu,* finished, ready. See **garwian** in Appendix.*] —**yare′ly** *adv.*

Yar·kand (yär-kănd′). **1.** *Chinese* **So·che** (swô′chŭ′). A city of China, in the southwestern Sinkiang-Uigur Autonomous Region. Population, 80,000. **2.** A river of China, rising in the western Sinkiang-Uigur Autonomous Region near the Soviet border and flowing about 500 miles northeast to the Khotan with which it forms the Tamir.

Yar·mouth. See **Great Yarmouth.**

yar·mul·ke (yä′məl-kə) *n.* Also **yar·mel·ke.** A skullcap worn by male Jews, especially those adhering to Orthodox or Conservative tradition. [Yiddish, from Polish and Ukrainian *yarmulka,* perhaps from Turkish *yağmurluk,* raincoat, from *yağmur,* rain.]

yarn (yärn) *n.* **1.** A continuous strand of twisted threads of natural or synthetic material, such as wool, cotton, flax, or nylon, used in weaving or knitting. **2.** *Informal.* A long, complicated story or a tale of real or fictitious adventures, often elaborated upon by the teller during the telling. —*intr.v.* **yarned, yarning, yarns.** *Informal.* To tell a long, complicated story; spin a yarn. [Middle English *yarn,* Old English *gearn.* See **gher-¹** in Appendix.*]

yarn-dyed (yärn′dīd′) *adj.* Made of yarn dyed before weaving.

Ya·ro·slavl (yə-rŏ-släv′ly′). A city of the Soviet Union, on the Volga in the western Russian S.F.S.R. Population, 478,000.

yar·row (yăr′ō) *n.* Any of several plants of the genus *Achillea;* especially, *A. millefolium,* native to Eurasia, having finely dissected foliage and flat clusters of usually white flowers. Also called "milfoil." [Middle English *yar(ro)we,* Old English *gearwe,* from West Germanic *garw-* (unattested).]

yash·mak (yäsh-mäk′, yăsh′măk) *n.* Also **yash·mac, yas·mak.** A veil worn by Moslem women to cover the face in public. [Arabic *yashmaq, yashmak.*]

yat·a·ghan (yăt′ə-găn′, -gən; *Turkish* yä′tä-gän′) *n.* Also **yat·a·gan, at·a·ghan** (ăt′ə-găn′). A Turkish sword or scimitar having a double-curved blade, an eared pommel, and lacking a handle guard. [Turkish *yatağan.*]

yau·pon (yô′pən) *n.* A holly, *Ilex vomitoria,* of the southeastern United States, having scarlet fruit and evergreen leaves, once used medicinally. [Catawba *yopun,* diminutive of *yop,* tree.]

Ya·va·rí. The Spanish name for the **Javarí.**

yaw (yô) *v.* **yawed, yawing, yaws.** —*intr.* **1.** To deviate from the intended course. Used of a ship. **2.** To move unsteadily; weave: *"The* Poseidon *pitched, yawed, and rolled in the heavy seas"* (John Barth). **3.** To turn about the vertical axis. Used of an aircraft or projectile. —*tr.* To cause to yaw. —*n.* **1.** The action of yawing. **2.** The extent of this movement, measured in degrees. [Origin unknown.]

Ya·wa·ta (yə-wät′ə). A city of Japan, now part of Kita Kyushu.

yawl (yôl) *n.* **1.** A two-masted fore-and-aft-rigged sailing vessel similar to the ketch but having a smaller jigger mast stepped abaft the rudder. Also called "dandy." **2.** A ship's small boat, manned by oarsmen. [Middle Low German *jolle†.*]

yawn (yôn) *v.* **yawned, yawning, yawns.** —*intr.* **1.** To open the mouth wide with a deep inspiration, usually involuntarily, from drowsiness, fatigue, or boredom. **2.** To open wide; to gape: *The chasm yawned at our feet.* —*tr.* To utter wearily, as if in yawning. —*n.* An act or instance of yawning. [Middle English *yonen, yenen,* Old English *geonian, ginan.* See **ghēi-** in Appendix.*] —**yawn′er** *n.*

yawn·ing (yôn′ĭng) *adj.* Gaping open; cavernous: *"They . . . overflowed down the yawning hatchways"* (Conrad).

yawp (yôp) *intr.v.* **yawped, yawping, yawps.** Also **yaup. 1.** To utter a sharp cry; to bark; yelp. **2.** *Slang.* To talk loudly and stupidly. —*n.* **1.** A bark; yelp. **2.** *Slang.* Loud, stupid talk. [Middle English *yolpen,* perhaps variant of *yelpen,* YELP.]

yaws (yôz) *pl.n.* An infectious tropical skin disease, caused by a spirochete, *Treponema pertenue,* and characterized by multiple red pimples. Also called "frambesia." [A Cariban word.]

y-ax·is (wī′ăk′sĭs) *n., pl.* **y-axes** (-sēz). **1.** The vertical axis of a two-dimensional Cartesian coordinate system. **2.** One of three axes in a three-dimensional Cartesian coordinate system.

Ya·zoo (yăz′o͞o). A river of Mississippi, rising in the northwest and flowing 189 miles generally southwest to the Mississippi River near Vicksburg.

Yb The symbol for the element ytterbium.

Y-chro·mo·some (wī′krō′mə-sōm′) *n.* The sex chromosome associated with male characteristics, occurring with one X-chromosome in the male sex-chromosome pair. Compare **X-chromosome.**

y·clept (ĭ-klĕpt′). Also **y·cleped.** *Archaic.* Past participle of **clepe.** —*adj. Archaic.* Known as; named; called. [Middle English *ycleped,* Old English *gecleopod,* past participle of *clipian, cleopian,* to speak, call, CLEPE.]

yd yard (measurement).

ye¹ (*thē*) *adj. Archaic.* The. [Incorrect transcription resulting from the close resemblance between the runic letter called thorn (properly transcribed as *th*) and the letter *y* in certain Middle English manuscripts. See **thorn.**]

ye² (yē) *pron.* **1.** *Poetic & Archaic.* You (plural). **2.** *Regional.* You (singular). [Middle English *ye,* Old English *gē.* See **yu-¹** in Appendix.*]

yea (yā) *adv.* **1.** Yes; aye. Now archaic except in recording or expressing a vote. **2.** *Archaic.* Indeed; truly: *They have spoken,* *yea, shouted their reply.* —*n.* **1.** An affirmative statement or vote. **2.** One who votes affirmatively. [Middle English *ye, ya,* Old English *gēa,* yes. See i- in Appendix.*]

yeah (yĕ′ə, yă′ə, yā′ə) *adv.* Also **yeh.** *Informal.* Yes. [Variant of YEA.]

yean (yēn) *v.* **yeaned, yeaning, yeans.** —*intr.* To bear young. Used of sheep and goats. —*tr.* To bear; give birth to. [Middle English *yenen,* Old English *geēanian* (unattested) : ge-, Y- + *ēanian,* to bear young (see agwhno in Appendix*).]

yean·ling (yēn′lĭng) *n.* The young of a sheep or goat; a lamb or kid. —*adj.* Newly born; infant. [YEAN + -LING (little).]

year (yîr) *n.* *Abbr.* **y., yr. 1.** The period of time as measured by the Gregorian calendar in which the earth completes a single revolution around the sun, consisting of 365 days, 5 hours, 49 minutes, and 12 seconds of mean solar time divided into 12 months, 52 weeks, and 365 or 366 days, and beginning on January 1 and ending on December 31. Also called "calendar year." **2. Sidereal year** (see). **3. Tropical year** (see). **4.** A period of about equal length in other calendars. **5.** Any period of approximately this duration: *We were married a year ago.* **6.** A period equal to the calendar year but beginning on a different date: *a fiscal year.* **7.** A specific period of time, usually shorter than 12 months, devoted to some special activity: *the academic year.* **8.** *Plural.* Age; especially, old age: *feeling his years.* **9.** *Plural.* Time; especially, a long time: *a great many years ago.* [Middle English *year, yere,* Old English *gēar.* See yēro- in Appendix.*]

year·book (yîr′bŏŏk′) *n.* **1.** A documentary, memorial, or historical book published every year, containing information about the previous year. **2.** A yearly record or book published by the graduating class of a high school or college.

Yeard·ley (yärd′lē), Sir George. 1587?–1627. English colonial administrator; three times governor of Virginia (1616–27).

year·ling (yîr′lĭng) *n.* **1.** An animal that is one year old or has not completed its second year. **2.** A thoroughbred racehorse, regarded as a colt or filly one year old dating from January 1 of the year that it was foaled. —*adj.* Being one year old.

year·long (yîr′lông′, -lŏng′) *adj.* Lasting through one year.

year·ly (yîr′lē) *adj.* Occurring once a year or every year; annual. —*adv.* Once a year; annually. —*n., pl.* **yearlies.** A publication issued once a year.

yearn (yûrn) *intr.v.* **yearned, yearning, yearns. 1.** To have a strong or deep desire; be filled with longing. Usually used with *for* or *to.* **2.** To feel deep pity, sympathy, or tenderness: *"he yearns after/you protectively/hopelessly wanting nothing"* (William Carlos Williams). [Middle English *yernen,* Old English *gyrnan, giernan,* to strive, desire. See gher-⁶ in Appendix.*]

Synonyms: yearn, long, pine, hanker, hunger, thirst. These verbs mean to have a strong desire. *Yearn* and *long* both stress protracted and insistent desire or craving. Sometimes *yearn* is applied to a wish for the return of something lost, and *long* to desire for the attainment of something unfulfilled. *Pine* implies lingering desire that saps strength or spirit. *Hanker* often refers to a fleeting desire, but it can also apply to an urge to satisfy a physical appetite or to a craving for fame, power, or wealth. *Hunger* and *thirst* are applied figuratively to compelling desire for the attainment or possession of something.

yearn·ing (yûr′nĭng) *n.* A deep longing.

year-round (yîr′round′) *adj.* Existing, active, or continuous throughout the year; during all seasons.

yeast (yēst) *n.* **1.** Any of various unicellular fungi of the genus *Saccharomyces* and related genera, reproducing by budding and capable of fermenting carbohydrates. **2.** Froth consisting of yeast cells together with the carbon dioxide they produce in the process of fermentation, present in or added to fruit juices and other substances in the production of alcoholic beverages. **3.** A commercial preparation, either in powdered or compressed form, containing yeast cells and inert material such as meal, and used especially as a leavening agent or as a dietary supplement. **4.** Foam; froth; spume. **5.** An agent of ferment or activity. —*intr.v.* **yeasted, yeasting, yeasts. 1.** To ferment. **2.** To froth or foam. [Middle English *yest,* Old English *gist, gyst.* See yes- in Appendix.*]

yeast·y (yē′stē) *adj.* **-ier, -iest. 1.** Of, similar to, or containing yeast. **2.** Causing or characterized by a ferment *n.* **3.** Restless; turbulent. **4.** Frothy; frivolous. —**yeast′i·ness** *n.*

Yeats (yāts), **William Butler.** 1865–1939. Irish poet and playwright.

Ye·do. A former name for Tokyo.

yegg (yĕg) *n.* *Slang.* A thief; especially, a burglar or safecracker. [Said to be after a safecracker named John *Yegg.*]

yeh. Variant of **yeah.**

Ye·ka·te·ri·no·slav. The former name for **Dnepropetrovsk.**

yel. yellow.

yell (yĕl) *v.* **yelled, yelling, yells.** —*intr.* To cry out loudly, as in pain, fright, surprise, or enthusiasm. —*tr.* To utter loudly; to shout. —See Synonyms at **scream.** —*n.* **1.** A loud cry; a shriek; shout. **2.** A rhythmic cheer uttered or chanted in unison by a group: *a college yell.* [Middle English *yellen,* Old English *giellan,* to sound, shout. See ghel-¹ in Appendix.*] —**yell′er** *n.*

yel·low (yĕl′ō) *n.* *Abbr.* **yel. 1.** Any of a group of colors of a hue resembling that of ripe lemons and varying in lightness and saturation; the hue of that portion of the spectrum lying between green and orange; one of the psychological primary hues, evoked in the normal observer by radiant energy of wavelength approximately 580 nanometers; also one of the subtractive primaries. See **color, primary color. 2.** A pigment or dye having this hue. **3.** Something that has this hue. **4.** The yolk of an egg. **5.** *Plural.* Any of various plant diseases usually caused by fungi

of the genus *Fusarium* or viruses of the genus *Chlorogenus* and characterized by yellow or yellowish discoloration. —*adj.* **1.** Of the color yellow. **2.** Designating a person or people having yellowish skin; especially, Oriental. **3.** *Slang.* Cowardly. —*v.* **yellowed, -lowing, -lows.** —*tr.* To make or render yellow. —*intr.* To become yellow. [Middle English *yelwa, yelow,* Old English *geolu.* See ghel-² in Appendix.*] —**yel′low·ly** *adv.* —**yel′low·ness** *n.*

yel·low-bark (yĕl′ō-bärk′) *n.* A kind of tree bark, **calisaya** (see).

yel·low-bel·lied (yĕl′ō-bĕl′ēd) *adj.* **1.** Having a belly yellow or yellowish in color, as certain birds. **2.** *Slang.* Cowardly.

yellow birch. A North American tree, *Betula lutea,* having yellowish bark and hard, light-colored wood used for furniture and flooring.

yel·low-bird (yĕl′ō-bûrd′) *n.* Any of various yellow or predominantly yellow birds, such as the gold finch or the yellow warbler.

yellow cypress. A tree, the **Nootka cypress** (see).

yel·low-dog contract (yĕl′ō-dôg′, -dŏg′). An employer-employee contract, no longer legal, by which the employee agrees not to join a union while employed.

yellow fever. An acute infectious disease of subtropical and tropical New World areas, caused by a filterable virus transmitted by a mosquito of the genus *Aedes* and characterized by jaundice and dark-colored vomit resulting from hemorrhages. Also called "yellow jack."

yel·low-ham·mer (yĕl′ō-hăm′ər) *n.* **1.** A bird, a species of **flicker** (see). **2.** A Eurasian bird, *Emberiza citrinella,* having brown and yellow plumage. [Earlier *yelambre* : perhaps YELLOW + *-ambre,* ultimately from Old English *amore, omer,* an unidentified bird, akin to Old High German *amero,* bunting, perhaps from *amaro†,* spelt (presumably food for the bird).]

yel·low-ish (yĕl′ō-ĭsh) *adj.* Somewhat yellow; tinged with yellow. See **color.** —**yel′low·ish·ness** *n.*

yellow jack. 1. Yellow fever (see). **2.** *Nautical.* A yellow flag hoisted to request pratique or to warn of disease on board. **3.** A silvery and yellowish food fish, *Caranx bartholomaei,* of western Atlantic and Caribbean waters.

yellow jacket. Any of several small wasps of the family *Vespidae,* having yellow and black markings and usually nesting in the ground.

yellow journalism. Journalism that exploits, distorts, or exaggerates the news to create sensations and attract readers. [Said to be short for *Yellow Kid Journalism,* an allusion to the "Yellow Kid" cartoons in the *New York World,* which was noted for sensationalism and vulgarity.]

Yel·low·knife (yĕl′ō-nīf′). The capital since 1967 of the Northwest Territories, Canada, on the northern shore of Great Slave Lake in southern Mackenzie District. Population, 3,000.

yel·low·legs (yĕl′ō-lĕgz′) *n., pl.* **yellowlegs.** Either of two North American wading birds, *Totanus melanoleucus* or *T. flavipes,* having yellow legs and a long, narrow bill.

yellow peril, Yellow Peril. The threatened expansion of the Oriental peoples as magnified in the Western imagination.

yellow pine. 1. Any of several North American evergreen trees having yellowish wood, such as *Pinus echinata,* of the southeastern United States, or the **ponderosa pine** (see). **2.** The wood of any of these trees.

yellow poplar. The **tulip tree** (see).

Yellow River. Chinese **Huang Ho** (hwäng′hō′). A river of China, rising in the highlands of Tibet and flowing 2,900 miles north, east, south, and northeast to the Gulf of Po Hai.

Yellow Sea. Chinese **Huang Hai** (hwäng′hī′). An arm of the Pacific lying between the Chinese mainland and the Korean peninsula.

yellow spot. A part of the human retina, the **macula lutea** (see).

Yel·low·stone National Park (yĕl′ō-stōn′). The oldest of the U.S. national parks (established in 1872), occupying 3,458 square miles, mostly in northwestern Wyoming, noted for its scenic beauty, wildlife, and geysers.

Yellowstone River. A river rising in northwestern Wyoming and flowing 671 miles north through Yellowstone Lake (139 square miles) and into Montana and then northeast to the Missouri on the North Dakota border.

yellow streak. A proneness to cowardice and disloyalty.

yel·low-tail (yĕl′ō-tāl′) *n.* **1.** A marine game fish, *Seriola dorsalis,* of coastal waters of southern California and Mexico. **2.** Any of several other fishes having a yellowish tail, such as the **mademoiselle** (see).

yel·low-throat (yĕl′ō-thrōt′) *n.* Any of several small New World birds of the genus *Geothlypis;* especially, *G. trichas,* having a brownish back, a yellow throat, and, in the male, a black facial mask.

yellow warbler. A small New World bird, *Dendroica petechia,* having predominantly yellow plumage.

yel·low-weed (yĕl′ō-wēd′) *n.* Any of various plants having yellow flowers, such as the **dyer's rocket** (see).

yel·low-wood (yĕl′ō-wŏŏd′) *n.* **1.** A tree, *Cladrastis lutea,* of the southeastern United States, having compound leaves, drooping clusters of white flowers, and yellow wood yielding a yellow dye. Sometimes called "gopherwood." **2.** Any of various other trees having yellow wood. **3.** The wood of any of these trees.

yel·low-y (yĕl′ō-ē) *adj.* Somewhat yellow.

yelp (yĕlp) *v.* **yelped, yelping, yelps.** —*intr.* **1.** To utter a sharp, short bark or cry. **2.** To cry out sharply, as in pain or surprise. —*tr.* To utter by yelping. —*n.* A sharp, short cry or bark. [Middle English *yelpen,* to cry aloud, Old English *gielpan,* to boast, exult. See ghel-¹ in Appendix.*] —**yelp′er** *n.*

Ye·men (yĕm′ən). A country occupying 75,000 square miles on

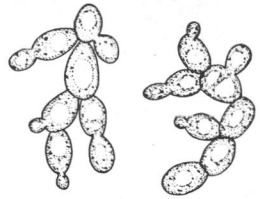

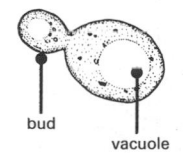

bud

vacuole
yeast
Yeast cells and buds

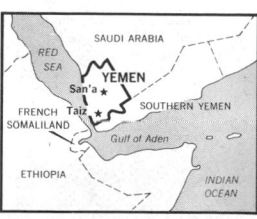

Yemen

the southern Arabian Peninsula. Population, 4,500,000. Capitals, San'a and Taiz.

yen[1] (yĕn) *intr.v.* **yenned, yenning, yens.** *Informal.* To yearn; to long. —*n.* *Informal.* A yearning; a longing. [Cantonese *yan*, corresponding to Mandarin Chinese *yin*[3], addiction.]

yen[2] (yĕn) *n., pl.* **yen.** **1.** *Symbol* **Y** The basic monetary unit of Japan, equal to 100 sen. See table of exchange rates at **currency.** **2.** A coin or note worth one yen. [Japanese *en*, from Mandarin Chinese *yüan*[2], "round (piece)," dollar.]

Ye·nan (yĕ′nän′). A city of China in northern Shensi Province, the former headquarters of the Chinese Communist Party (1937–49). Population, 50,000.

Yen·i·sei (yĭ-nyĭ-syā′). Also **E·ni·sei.** A river rising in the highlands of northern Mongolia and flowing 2,364 miles north across the central Russian S.F.S.R. to the Kara Sea.

yen·ta (yĕn′tə) *n. Slang.* A gossipy woman, especially one who pries into the affairs of others and offers unsolicited advice. [Yiddish, perhaps from Italian *gentile*, gentle, from Latin *gentilis*, GENTLE.]

Yen·tai. The official name for **Chefoo.**

yeo. yeomanry.

yeo·man (yō′mən) *n., pl.* **-men** (-mĭn). **1.** An independent farmer; especially, a member of a former class of small freeholding farmers in England. **2.** A **yeoman of the guard** *(see).* **3.** An attendant, servant, or lesser official in a royal or noble household. **4.** A petty officer performing chiefly clerical duties in the U.S. Navy. **5.** *Archaic.* An assistant or other subordinate, as of a sheriff. **6.** A diligent and dependable worker. —*adj.* Also **yeo·man·ly** (-lē). **1.** Pertaining to or ranking as a yeoman. **2.** Befitting a yeoman; sturdy, staunch, or workmanlike. [Middle English *yoman, yuman*, perhaps contraction of *yongman* : YOUNG + MAN.]

yeoman of the guard. A member of a ceremonial guard attending the British sovereign and royal family, consisting of 100 yeomen with their officers.

yeo·man·ry (yō′mən-rē) *n. Abbr.* **yeo. 1.** The class of yeomen; small farmers. **2.** *British.* A volunteer cavalry force organized in 1761 to serve as a home guard and later incorporated into the Territorial Army.

yep (yĕp) *adv. Slang.* Yes. [From YES (after NOPE).]

yer·ba ma·té (yâr′bə mä-tā′, yûr′bə; *Spanish* yâr′bä mä-tā′). A tree, the **maté** *(see).* [Spanish *yerba*, herb, from Latin *herba*, plant, HERB.]

Ye·re·van (yĭ-ryĭ-vän′). Also **E·re·van, E·ri·van.** The capital of the Armenian S.S.R. Population, 578,000.

yes (yĕs) *adv.* It is so; as you say or ask. Used to express affirmation, agreement, positive confirmation, or consent. —*n., pl.* **yeses. 1.** An affirmative or consenting reply. **2.** An affirmative vote or voter. —*tr.v.* **yessed, yessing, yeses.** To give an affirmative reply to. Usually used to indicate habitual acquiescence. [Middle English *yes*, Old English *gese* : *gēa*, YEA + *sīe*, "may it be" (see **es-** in Appendix*).]

Ye·sil Ir·mak (yĕ-shēl′ ĭr-mäk′). Ancient name **I·ris** (ī′rĭs). A river of Turkey, rising in the north and flowing 260 miles north to the Black Sea.

Ye·şil·köy. The Turkish name for **San Stefano.**

yes man. *Informal.* A person who slavishly agrees with his superior; a sycophant.

yester–. Indicates: **1.** The day before the present day; for example, **yestermorning. 2.** A previous and indeterminate period of time; for example, **yesteryear.** [Middle English *yister-*, Old English *geostra(n)*. See **gzhyes** in Appendix.*]

yes·ter·day (yĕs′tər-dā′, -dē) *n.* **1.** The day before the present day. **2.** *Sometimes plural.* Time in the immediate past. —*adv.* **1.** On the day before the present day. **2.** A short while ago. [Middle English *yesterdai*, Old English *geostran dæg* : YESTER- + DAY.]

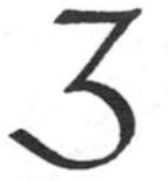

yogh

yes·ter·eve·ning (yĕs′tər-ēv′nĭng) *n.* Also **yes·ter·eve** (-ēv′), **yes·ter·e·ven** (-ē′vən), *Scottish* **yes·treen** (yĕs-trēn′). The evening of yesterday. —**yes′ter·eve′ning** *adv.*

yes·ter·morn·ing (yĕs′tər-môr′nĭng) *n.* Also **yes·ter·morn** (-môrn′). Yesterday morning. —**yes′ter·morn′ing** *adv.*

yes·ter·night (yĕs′tər-nīt′) *n.* Last night. —**yes′ter·night′** *adv.*

yes·ter·year (yĕs′tər-yîr′) *n.* **1.** The year before this one. **2.** Time past, especially as thought of nostalgically; yore. —**yes′ter·year′** *adv.*

yet (yĕt) *adv.* **1.** At this time; for the present; now: *Don't sing yet.* **2.** Up to a specified time; thus far: *The end had not yet come.* See Usage note below. **3.** In the time remaining; still: *There is yet a solution to be found.* **4.** Besides; in addition: *Play the tape yet another time.* **5.** Even; still more: *a yet sadder tale.* **6.** Nevertheless: *young yet wise.* **7.** At some future time; eventually. —**as yet.** Up to the present time; up to now. See Usage note below. —*conj.* Nevertheless; and despite this: *He said he would be late, yet he arrived on time.* —See Synonyms at **but.** [Middle English *yet, yit*, Old English *gīet, gīeta.* See **i-** in Appendix.*]

Usage: *Yet*, as an adverb of time in the sense up to the present, thus far, or in the phrase *as yet*, occurs with a perfect tense rather than with the simple past: *They have not started yet. Have you visited her yet?*

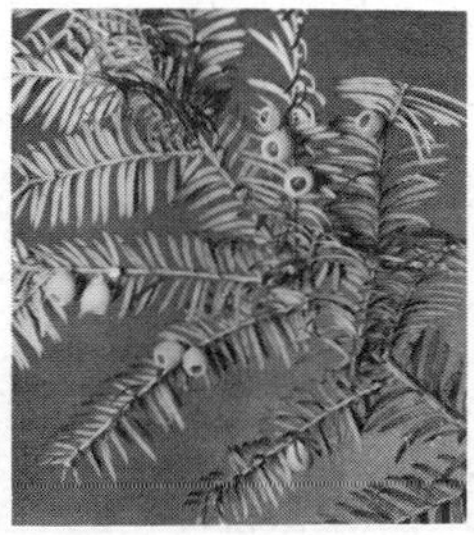

yew
Taxus cuspidata

ye·ti (yĕ′tē) *n.* The **abominable snowman** *(see).*

Yev·tu·shen·ko (yĕv′tōō-shĕng′kō), **Yevgeny Alexandrovich.** Born 1933. Soviet poet.

yew (yōō) *n.* **1.** Any of several evergreen trees or shrubs of the genus *Taxus*, of which the flat, dark-green needles and often the scarlet berries are poisonous. See **ground hemlock. 2.** The wood of a yew; especially, the durable, fine-grained wood of an Old World species, *T. baccata*, used in cabinetmaking and for archery bows. [Middle English *ew*, Old English *ēow, īw.* See **ei-**[2] in Appendix.*]

Ye·zo. The former name for **Hokkaido.**

Ygg·dra·sil (ĭg′drə-sĭl, üg′-) *n.* Also **Yg·dra·sil.** *Norse Mythology.* The great ash tree that holds together earth, heaven, and hell by its roots and branches. [Old Norse, probably "the horse of Yggr" : *Yggr*, name of Odin, from *yggr*, variant of *uggr*, frightful (see **ugly**) + *drasill*†, horse.]

YHWH, YHVH, JHWH, JHVH The Hebrew Tetragrammaton representing the name of God.

yid (yĭd) *n.* A Jew. An offensive term used derogatorily. [Yiddish, from Middle High German *Jüde.* See **Yiddish.**]

Yid·dish (yĭd′ĭsh) *n.* A language derived from High German dialects with additional vocabulary drawn from Hebrew and from Slavic languages, written in Hebrew characters and spoken chiefly as a vernacular in eastern European Jewish communities and by emigrants from these communities throughout the world. [Yiddish *Yidish*, from Middle High German *jüdisch diutsch*, "Jewish German," from *Jüde*, Jew, from Old High German *judo*, from Latin *Jūdaeus*, JEW.]

yield (yēld) *v.* **yielded, yielding, yields.** —*tr.* **1.** To give forth by or as if by a natural process, especially by cultivation: *a field that yields many bushels.* **2.** To furnish or give in return; be productive of: *an investment that yields six per cent.* **3.** To surrender (something) in deference or defeat; relinquish: *yielded the field to a rival.* **4.** To grant or concede: *yield right of way.* **5.** *Obsolete.* To pay, recompense, or reward. —*intr.* **1.** To furnish or give a return; be productive. **2.** To give up; surrender; submit. **3.** To give way to pressure, force, or persuasion. **4.** To give way to what is stronger or better; be overcome. Used with *to*: *"Wrong opinions and practices gradually yield to fact and argument"* (John Stuart Mill). —See Synonyms at **relinquish.** —*n.* **1.** The amount yielded or produced; a product. **2.** The profit obtained from investment; a return. **3.** The energy released by an explosion, especially by a nuclear explosion, expressed in units of weight of TNT required to produce an equivalent release: *a 100-megaton yield.* [Middle English *yieldan*, Old English *gieldan*, to yield, pay. See **ghelt-** in Appendix.*] —**yield′er** *n.*

Synonyms: *yield, relent, bow, defer, submit, capitulate.* These verbs all have a sense of abandoning or retreating from a position or stand. *Yield* has the widest application. It can refer to giving way for reasons ranging from recognition that one is overmatched to acknowledgment that an adversary's position is the more correct one. *Relent* refers to moderating a stand one has taken with respect to another and thus showing him clemency. *Bow* involves giving way either out of necessity or out of respect for or courtesy to another. *Defer* can mean either giving way to authority or changing one's stand as an act of courtesy, respect, or recognition of another's superior knowledge, judgment, or the like. *Submit* implies giving way out of necessity after opposing unsuccessfully. *Capitulate*, in this sense, also implies surrender but not necessarily after active opposition.

yield·ing (yēl′dĭng) *adj.* Inclined to yield; submissive; docile. —**yield′ing·ly** *adv.* —**yield′ing·ness** *n.*

Yiews·ley (yōōz′lē). A former administrative division of London, England, now part of **Hillingdon** *(see).*

yin (yĭn) *n.* The passive, female cosmic element, force, or principle that is opposite but always complementary to **yang** *(see)* in Chinese dualistic philosophy. [Mandarin Chinese *yin*[1], the moon, shade, femininity.]

Yin·chwan (yĭn′chwän′). Formerly **Ning·si·a** (nĭng′shyä′). The capital of the Ningsia Hui Autonomous Region in north-central China. Population, 91,000.

Ying·kow (yĭng′kō′). Formerly **New·chwang** (nyōō′chwäng′; *Chinese* nĭ-ü′jōō-äng′). A city and seaport of Liaoning Province, northeastern China. Population, 160,000.

yip (yĭp) *n.* A sharp, high-pitched bark; a yelp. —*intr.v.* **yipped, yipping, yips.** To make such sounds; to yelp. [Imitative.]

yipe (yīp) *interj.* Also **yipes** (yīps). Used to express surprise, fear, or dismay.

yip·pee (yĭp′ē) *interj.* Used to express joy or elation.

-yl. Indicates a radical; for example, **carbonyl, ethyl.** [French *-yle*, from Greek *hulē*, wood, matter. See **hulē** in Appendix.*]

y·lang-y·lang (ē′läng-ē′läng) *n.* Also **i·lang-i·lang. 1.** A tropical Asian tree, *Cananga odorata* (or *Canangium odoratum*), having fragrant greenish-yellow flowers that yield an oil used in perfumery. **2.** An oil or perfume obtained from the flowers of this tree. [Tagalog *ilang-ilang.*]

Y.M.C.A. Young Men's Christian Association.

Y.M.H.A. Young Men's Hebrew Association.

yod (yōd; *Hebrew* yōōd) *n.* Also **yodh.** The tenth letter of the Hebrew alphabet. See **alphabet.** [Hebrew *yōdh*, from *yādh*, hand.]

yo·del (yōd′l) *v.* **-deled** or **-delled, -deling** or **-delling, -dels.** Also **yo·dle, -dled, -dling, -dles.** —*intr.* To sing so that the voice fluctuates between the normal chest voice and a falsetto. —*tr.* To sing (a song) in this fashion. —*n.* A song or cry that is yodeled. [German *jodeln* (imitative).] —**yo′del·er** *n.*

yo·ga (yō′gə) *n.* **1.** *Often capital* **Y.** A Hindu discipline aimed at training the consciousness for a state of perfect spiritual insight and tranquillity. **2.** A system of exercises practiced as part of this discipline to promote control of the body and mind. [Sanskrit, union, yoking. See **yeug-** in Appendix.*]

yogh (yōKH) *n.* A Middle English letter representing a velar or palatal fricative, usually voiced. [Middle English *yogh, yok*, perhaps from *yok*, YOKE (from its shape).]

yo·gi (yō′gē) *n., pl.* **-gis.** Also **yo·gin** (yō′gĭn). One who practices yoga. [Hindi, from Sanskrit *yogin*, from *yoga*, YOGA.]

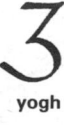

ă pat/ā pay/âr care/ä father/b bib/ch church/d deed/ĕ pet/ē be/f fife/g gag/h hat/hw which/ĭ pit/ī pie/îr pier/j judge/k kick/l lid, needle/m mum/n no, sudden/ng thing/ŏ pot/ō toe/ô paw, for/oi noise/ou out/ŏŏ took/ōō boot/p pop/r roar/s sauce/sh ship, dish/

yo·gurt (yō′gərt, -go͝ort′) *n.* Also **yo·ghurt, yo·ghourt.** A food of a custardlike consistency, prepared from milk curdled by bacteria, especially *Lactobacillus bulgaricus* and *Streptococcus thermophilus,* and often sweetened or flavored with fruit. [Turkish *yoğurt.*]

yo·him·bine (yō-hĭm′bēn′) *n.* A poisonous alkaloid, $C_{21}H_{26}N_2O_3$, derived from the bark of a tree, *Corynanthe yohimbe,* and formerly used as an aphrodisiac, local anesthetic, and mydriatic. [From New Latin *yohimbe,* the tree, from Bantu.]

yoicks (yoiks) *interj.* Also **hoicks** (hoiks). Used as a hunting cry to urge the hounds after the fox.

yoke (yōk) *n., pl.* **yokes** or **yoke** (for sense 2). **1.** A crossbar with two U-shaped pieces that encircle the necks of a pair of oxen, mules, or other draft animals working in a team. **2.** A pair of draft animals joined by such a device or trained to work together. **3.** A frame or crossbar designed to be carried across a person's shoulders with equal loads suspended from each end. **4.** A bar used with a double harness to connect the collar of each horse to the tongue of a wagon, coach, or the like. **5.** *Nautical.* A crossbar on a ship's rudder to which the steering cables are connected. **6.** *Machinery.* A clamp or vise that holds a part in place or controls its movement or that holds two parts together. **7.** A piece of a garment that is closely fitted, either around the neck and shoulders or at the hips, and from which an unfitted or gathered part of the garment is hung. **8.** Something that connects or joins together; a bond. **9.** A structure made of two upright spears with a third laid across them, under which conquered enemies of ancient Rome were forced to march in subjection. **10.** Any form or symbol of subjugation or bondage: *"Having groaned myself under that yoke, I pity, and blame him not"* (De Quincey). —See Synonyms at **couple.** —*v.* **yoked, yoking, yokes.** —*tr.* **1.** To fit or join with a yoke. **2. a.** To harness a draft animal to. **b.** To harness (a draft animal) to something. **3.** To connect, join, or bind together. **4.** *Rare.* To force into bondage or servitude. —*intr.* To become connected, joined, or bound together. [Middle English *yok,* Old English *geoc.* See **yeug-** in Appendix.*]

yoke·fel·low (yōk′fĕl′ō) *n.* A work companion; comrade. Also called "yokemate."

yo·kel (yō′kəl) *n.* A country bumpkin; a naive or gullible rustic: *"These conspirators were not all the unlettered yokels which some historians would have them to be."* (E.P. Thompson). [Perhaps from English dialectal *yokel,* green woodpecker (probably imitative of its note).]

Yok·kai·chi (yōk′kī′chē). A city of Japan, a seaport on southern Honshu. Population, 221,000.

Yo·ko·ha·ma (yō′kə-hä′mə). A city of Japan, a seaport on Tokyo Bay in central Honshu. Population, 1,619,000.

Yo·ko·su·ka (yō′kə-so͞o′kə; *Japanese* yō′kō′sə-kä′). A city and seaport of Japan, in central Honshu on the western shore of Tokyo Bay. Population, 297,000.

yolk (yōk) *n.* **1.** The nutritive material of an ovum, consisting primarily of protein and fat; especially, the yellow, usually spheroidal mass of the egg of a bird or reptile, surrounded by the albumen. **2.** A greasy substance found in unprocessed sheep's wool. [Middle English *yolke,* Old English *geoloca, geolca,* from *geolu,* YELLOW.] —**yolk′y** *adj.*

yolk sac. A membranous sac attached to the embryo and providing early nourishment in the form of yolk in bony fishes, sharks, reptiles, birds, and primitive mammals, and functioning as the circulatory system of the human embryo prior to the initiation of internal circulation by the pumping of the heart.

Yom Kip·pur (yŏm′ kĭp′ər; *Hebrew* yōm′ kĭ-po͝or′). The holiest Jewish holiday, celebrated on the tenth day of Tishri, on which fasting and prayer for the atonement of sins are prescribed. Also called "Day of Atonement." [Hebrew *yōm kippūr* : *yōm,* day + *kippūr,* atonement, from *kippēr,* they covered, they made atonement.]

yon (yŏn) *adj. Poetic.* Yonder. —*adv. Poetic.* Yonder. [Middle English *yon,* Old English *geon.* See **i-** in Appendix.*]

yond (yŏnd) *adj. Poetic.* Yonder. —*adv. Poetic.* Yonder. [Middle English *yond,* Old English *geond.* See **i-** in Appendix.*]

yon·der (yŏn′dər) *adj.* Being at an indicated distance, usually within sight. —*adv.* In or at that indicated place; over there. [Middle English *yonder,* from *yond,* YOND.]

yo·ni (yō′nē) *n.* A symbol for the vulva in Indian and Tibetan religion. [Sanskrit *yoni*†, abode, womb.]

Yon·kers (yŏng′kərz). A city of New York State, on the Hudson just north of New York City. Population, 191,000.

yoo-hoo (yo͞o′ho͞o′) *interj.* Used to hail persons.

yore (yôr, yōr) *n.* Time long past. Used usually in the phrase *days of yore.* [Middle English *yore,* Old English *gēara,* formerly, once, perhaps from the genitive plural of *gēar,* YEAR.]

York[1] (yôrk). A royal house that held the English throne from 1461 to 1485.

York[2] (yôrk). **1.** See **Yorkshire. 2.** A city and the county seat of Yorkshire, northeastern England. Population, 105,000. **3.** A city and industrial center of southern Pennsylvania. Population, 55,000.

York (yôrk), **Alvin Cullum.** 1887–1964. Known as Sergeant York. American soldier; hero of World War I.

York, Cape (yôrk). The northernmost point of Australia, on Torres Strait at the tip of Cape York Peninsula.

York·ist (yôr′kĭst) *n.* A supporter of the House of York in its contention with the House of Lancaster during the Wars of the Roses. —**York′ist** *adj.*

York·shire (yôrk′shîr, -shər). Also **York** (yôrk). *Abbr.* **Yorks.** A county occupying 6,080 square miles in northeastern England and comprising the administrative divisions of East Riding, West Riding, and North Riding. Population, 3,704,000. County seat, York.

York·shire pudding (yôrk′shîr, -shər). A pudding of popover batter, made of eggs, flour, and milk, and baked in the drippings of roast beef.

Yorkshire terrier. A toy terrier of a breed developed in Yorkshire, England, having a long, bluish-gray coat.

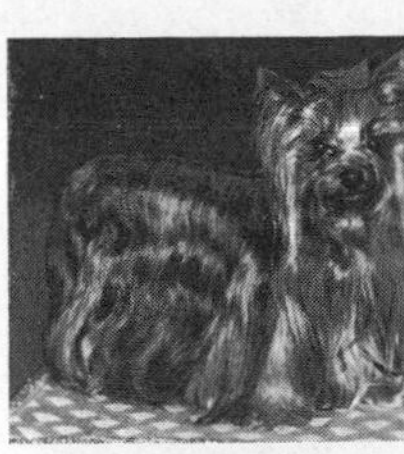

Yorkshire terrier

York·town (yôrk′toun). A village in southeastern Virginia, the site of the surrender of Cornwallis in the Revolutionary War (1781).

Yo·ru·ba (yō′ro͞o-bä) *n., pl.* **Yoruba** or **-bas. 1.** A member of a West African Negro people living chiefly in southwestern Nigeria. **2.** The West Sudanic Niger-Congo language of these people. —**Yo′ru·ban** *adj.*

Yo·sem·i·te National Park (yō-sĕm′ə-tē). An area of 1,183 square miles in east-central California, the site of Yosemite Valley, a gorge extending for seven miles and containing the Yosemite Falls (Upper Fall, 1,430 feet; Lower Fall, 320 feet).

you (yo͞o) *pron.* The second person singular or plural pronoun in the nominative or objective case. See Usage note at **thou. 1.** Used to represent the one or ones addressed by the speaker: *I tell you.* **2.** Used in apposition before a noun to indicate address: *You fool!* **3.** Used reflexively for *yourself* or *yourselves: "Which can say more than this rich praise, that you alone are you."* (Shakespeare). **4.** Often used in general statements to represent any person or persons: *You can't win them all.* In the most formal contexts, the pronoun *one* is preferred. —*n.* The individuality of the person being addressed: *Such is the real you.* [Middle English *you, eow,* Old English *ēow,* dative and accusative of *gē,* ye. See **yu-**[1] in Appendix.*]

you-all (yo͞o′ôl′) *pl.pron. Southeastern U.S.* You. Used in addressing two or more persons or referring to two or more persons, one of whom is addressed.

you'd (yo͞od). Contraction of *you had* or *you would.*

you'll (yo͞ol). Contraction of *you will* or *you shall.*

young (yŭng) *adj.* **younger, youngest. 1.** Being in the early or undeveloped period of life or growth; not old. **2.** Newly begun or formed; not advanced: *The evening is young.* **3.** Pertaining to or suggestive of youth or early life: *young for her age.* **4.** Vigorous or fresh; youthful. **5.** Lacking experience; immature; green: *a young hand at plowing.* **6.** Designating the junior of two people having the same name. **7.** *Geology.* Being of an early stage in a geological cycle. Said of bodies of water and land formations. —*n.* **1.** Young persons collectively; youth. **2.** Offspring; brood: *a lioness with her young.* —**with young.** Pregnant. [Middle English *yong,* Old English *geong.* See **yeu-**[2] in Appendix.*]

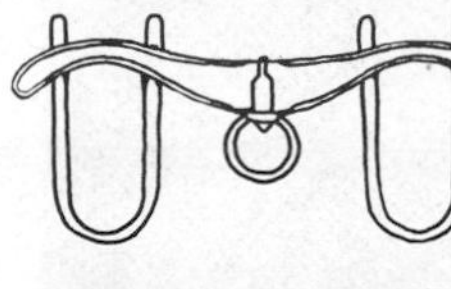

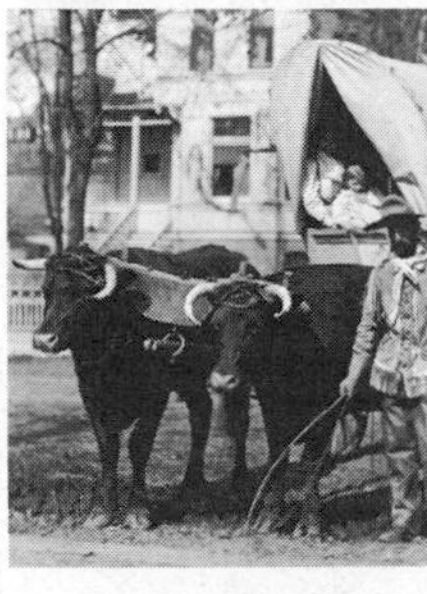

yoke

Below: Yoke of oxen with covered wagon

Synonyms: *young, youth, juvenile, adolescent, teen-ager.* These nouns refer to persons in the age group between childhood and maturity. *Young* and *youth* denote persons in that span considered collectively, and *youth* also is applied in the singular to any male of that age. Both are essentially neutral, categorizing terms, whereas *juvenile* and *adolescent* usually stress immaturity. *Adolescent* in particular suggests the difficulties of physical and emotional maturation. *Teen-ager* refers to a person between thirteen and nineteen, often considered with respect to the tastes and interests of that age group.

Young (yŭng), **Brigham.** 1801–1877. American Mormon leader and territorial governor of Utah.

Young (yŭng), **Denton True ("Cy").** 1867–1955. American baseball pitcher; holds record for most games won (511).

Young (yŭng), **Edward.** 1683–1765. English poet and playwright.

Young (yŭng), **Thomas.** 1773–1829. British physicist, physician, and Egyptologist; studied light and color.

Young (yŭng), **Whitney Moore, Jr.** Born 1921. American Negro leader; executive director of National Urban League (since 1961).

young·ber·ry (yŭng′bĕr′ē) *n., pl.* **-ries. 1.** A trailing, prickly hybrid between a blackberry and a dewberry, cultivated in the western United States. **2.** The edible, dark-red berry of this plant. [Developed by B.M. *Young,* 20th-century American fruit grower.]

young·ish (yŭng′ĭsh) *adj.* Somewhat young.

young·ling (yŭng′lĭng) *n.* **1.** A young person. **2.** A young animal. **3.** A young plant. [Middle English *yongling,* Old English *geongling* : YOUNG + -LING (noun suffix).]

Young Pretender. See Charles Edward **Stuart.**

young·ster (yŭng′stər) *n.* **1.** A young person; a child or youth. **2.** A young animal. **3.** *U.S. Navy.* A midshipman of the second-year class in the U.S. Naval Academy.

Youngs·town (yŭngz′toun). A city of Ohio, an iron- and steel-producing center in the northeast. Population, 165,000.

Young Turk. A progressive or insurgent member of a political party or other collective enterprise. [Originally a member of a Turkish revolutionary party in the early 20th century.]

youn·ker (yŭng′kər) *n.* A young man. [Dutch *jonker,* from Middle Dutch *jonckher, jonchere,* young nobleman : *jonc,* young (see **yeu-**[2] in Appendix*) + *here,* master, lord (see **kei-**[2] in Appendix*).]

your (yo͝or, yôr, yōr; *unstressed* yər) *adj.* The possessive form of the pronoun *you. Abbr.* **yr. 1.** Used attributively to indicate possession, agency, or reception of an action by the one or ones addressed by the speaker: *your wallet; pursuing your tasks; suffered your first rebuff.* **2.** Used to designate something having special significance to you: *Today is your day.* **3.** *Informal.* Used with little or no sense of possession but suggesting mutual knowledge or experience: *He is not one of your two-bit philosophers.* **4.** Used to indicate possession, agency, or reception of

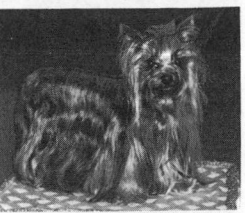

yucca
Yucca radiosa

Yugoslavia

an action by any unspecified person or persons: *The house is on your right, as you go toward town.* In the most formal contexts, the pronoun *one's* is preferred in this sense. [Middle English *your,* Old English *ēower.* See **yu-** in Appendix.*]

you're (yŏor; *unstressed* yər). Contraction of *you are.*

yours (yŏorz, yôrz, yōrz). Possessive pronoun, absolute form of *your.* **1.** Belonging to you; your own. Used predicatively: *The brown boots are yours.* **2.** The one or ones belonging to you. Used substantively: *If I can't find my hat, I'll take yours.* **3.** Used in the complimentary closing of letters: *Yours; Very truly yours.* **—of yours.** Belonging or pertaining to you: *a friend of yours.* [Middle English *youres,* genitive of YOUR.]

your·self (yŏor-sĕlf′, yôr-, yər-) *pron., pl.* **-selves** (-sĕlvz′). A specialized form of the second person pronoun. **1.** Used reflexively, forming the direct or indirect object of a verb or the object of a preposition: *hurt yourself; give yourself time; talk to yourself.* **2.** Used for emphasis: *Do it yourself.* **3.** Used as an indication of one's real, normal, or healthy identity or condition: *You have not been yourself since your illness.*
Usage: Yourself and yourselves function principally as reflexive or emphatic forms and to indicate a normal or proper state, all as defined above. In other respects, especially in written usage, they are not interchangeable with *you,* though they are sometimes heard in casual speech, especially in examples involving compound objects or subjects or enumerations: *He plans to invite Mary and yourself* (preferably *you*). *I hope that John and yourselves* (preferably *you*) *will come. Yourself* (far preferably *you*) *and the others will have to make different arrangements.*

youth (yŏoth) *n., pl.* **youths** (yŏoths, yŏo*th*z). **1.** The condition or quality of being young. **2.** An early period of development or existence. **3. a.** The time of life between childhood and maturity. **b.** Young people collectively. **c.** A young person; especially, a young man. —See Synonyms at **young.** [Middle English *youthe,* Old English *geoguth.* See **yeu-²** in Appendix.*]

youth·ful (yŏoth′fəl) *adj.* **1.** Possessing youth; still young. **2.** Characteristic of youth; vigorous; fresh; active. **3.** Of or belonging to youth. **4.** In an early stage of development; new. **5.** *Geology.* Young. **—youth′ful·ly** *adv.* **—youth′ful·ness** *n.*

youth hostel. A hostel *(see).*

you've (yŏov). Contraction of *you have.*

yow (you) *interj.* Used to express alarm, pain, or surprise.

YOW Airport code for Ottawa, Ontario.

yowl (youl) *v.* **yowled, yowling, yowls.** *—intr.* To utter a loud, long, mournful cry; to howl; wail. *—tr.* To say or utter with such a cry. *—n.* A loud, mournful cry; a wail. [Middle English *youlen* (imitative).]

yo-yo (yō′yō′) *n., pl.* **-yos.** A toy in the shape of a spool, around which a string is wound. The string is attached to the finger, and the yo-yo is spun down and reeled up by moving the hand. [Originally from a trademark.]

YQB Airport code for Quebec, Canada.

YQG Airport code for Windsor, Ontario.

Y·quem (ē-kĕm′) *n.* A variety of sauterne wine. [Made at Chateau d'*Yquem,* an estate in southwestern France.]

yr. **1.** year. **2.** younger. **3.** your.

Y.T. Yukon Territory.

yt·ter·bi·a (ĭ-tûr′bē-ə) *n.* Ytterbium oxide *(see).* [New Latin, from YTTERBIUM.]

yt·ter·bi·um (ĭ-tûr′bē-əm) *n.* *Symbol* **Yb** A soft bright silvery rare-earth element occurring in two allotropic forms and used as an x-ray source for portable irradiation devices, in some laser materials, and in some special alloys. Atomic number 70, atomic weight 173.04, melting point 824°C, boiling point 1,427°C, specific gravity 6.977 or 6.54 depending on allotropic form, valences 2, 3. See **element.** [New Latin; discovered at *Ytterby,* town in Sweden.] **—yt·ter′bic** (ĭ-tûr′bĭk) *adj.*

ytterbium oxide. A colorless hygroscopic compound, Yb_2O_3, used in certain alloys. Also called "ytterbia."

yt·tri·a (ĭt′rē-ə) *n.* Yttrium oxide *(see).* [New Latin, from *Ytterby,* town in Sweden where it was discovered.]

yt·tric (ĭt′rĭk) *adj.* Of, relating to, or derived from yttrium.

yt·tri·um (ĭt′rē-əm) *n.* *Symbol* **Y** A silvery metallic element, not a rare earth but occurring in nearly all rare-earth minerals, used in various metallurgical applications, notably to increase the strength of magnesium and aluminum alloys. Atomic number 39, atomic weight 88.905, melting point 1,495°C, boiling point 2,927°C, specific gravity 4.45, valence 3. See **element.** [New Latin, from YTTR(IA).] **—yt′tric** (ĭt′rĭk) *adj.*

yttrium oxide. A yellowish powder, Y_2O_3, used in optical glasses, ceramics, and color-television tubes. Also called "yttria."

yu·an (yü′än′) *n., pl.* **yuan** or **yuans.** **1. a.** The basic monetary unit of China, equal to 10 chiao or 100 fen. **b.** The basic monetary unit of Taiwan, equal to 100 cents. See table of exchange rates at **currency.** **2.** A coin or note worth one yuan. [Mandarin Chinese *yüan²,* round (thing), dollar.]

Yu·an (yŏo′än′). A river of China, rising in central Kweichow and flowing 540 miles northeast to Lake Tungting in Hunan.

Yü·an (yü′än′). A Mongolian dynasty (1280–1368), founded in China by Kublai Khan. [Mandarin Chinese *yüan²,* "first," "beginning."]

Yu·an Kiang. The Chinese name for the **Red River.**

Yu·ca·tán (yŏo′kə-tän′; *Spanish* yŏo-kä-tän′). A state of Mexico, occupying 14,868 square miles in the southeast on the Yucatán Peninsula. Population, 614,000. Capital, Mérida.

Yu·ca·tán Channel (yŏo′kə-tän′; *Spanish* yŏo-kä-tän′). The channel between northern Yucatán, Mexico, and western Cuba, connecting the Gulf of Mexico with the Caribbean Sea.

Yu·ca·tán Peninsula (yŏo′kə-tän′; *Spanish* yŏo-kä-tän′). A region, 70,000 square miles in area, of southern Mexico and northern British Honduras and Guatemala, with its Mexican section projecting north between the Gulf of Mexico and the Caribbean.

Yuc·a·tec (yŏo′kə-tĕk′) *n., pl.* **Yucatec** or **-tecs.** **1.** A member of an Indian people inhabiting the Yucatán Peninsula, Mexico. **2.** The Mayan language of this people.

yuc·ca (yŭk′ə) *n.* Any of various chiefly tropical New World plants of the genus *Yucca,* often tall and stout-stemmed, and having a terminal cluster of white flowers. [Spanish *yuca,* from an American Indian word.]

Yucca House National Monument. An area of about ten acres in southwestern Colorado, reserved to protect its ruins of prehistoric dwellings.

Yu·chi (yŏo′chē) *n., pl.* **Yuchi** or **-chis.** Also **U·chee** (for all senses), **Yu·chi·an** or **U·che·an** (yŏo′chē-ən) (for sense 1 only). **1.** A North American Indian language family consisting only of the language of the Yuchi tribe. **2.** A tribe of Yuchi-speaking North American Indians formerly inhabiting eastern Georgia. **3.** A member of this tribe. **4.** The language of this tribe.

Yüeh. The Chinese name for **Cantonese.**

Yu·ga (yŏog′ə) *n.* Also **Yug** (yŏog). *Hinduism.* One of the four ages constituting the cycle of history. [Sanskrit, yoke, pair, age. See **yeug-** in Appendix.*]

Yu·go·sla·vi·a (yŏo′gō-slä′vĭ-ə). Also **Ju·go·sla·vi·a.** *Serbo-Croatian* **Ju·go·sla·vi·ja** (yŏo′gō-slä′vē-yä). Formerly **Kingdom of the Serbs, Croats, and Slovenes.** Officially, **Socialist Federal Republic of Yugoslavia.** A republic of southeastern Europe, the largest (98,725 square miles) of the Balkan states, with a long shoreline on the Adriatic and composed of six constituent republics. Population, 19,279,000. Capital, Belgrade. [Serbo-Croatian *Jugoslavija* : *jug,* South, from Old Slavic *juga* (see **aug-²** in Appendix*) + Middle English *Sclave,* from Medieval Latin *S(c)lavus,* from Late Greek *Sklabos†.]

Yu·ka·wa (yŏo′kä′wä), **Hideki.** Born 1907. Japanese nuclear physicist; predicted the existence of the pion.

Yü Kiang (yü′ jĭ′äng′). Formerly **Siang** (shĭ′äng′). A river of China, rising in southeastern Yunnan and flowing 500 miles generally east to the Si Kiang in the Kwangsi Chuang Autonomous Region.

Yu·kon (yŏo′kŏn). *Abbr.* **Y.T.** A Territory of Canada, occupying 215,346 square miles in the northwest between Alaska and the Northwest Territories. Population, 15,000. Capital, Whitehorse.

Yu·kon River (yŏo′kŏn). A river flowing 1,979 miles generally northwest from southern Yukon Territory, Canada, through Alaska to the Bering Sea.

Yukon Time. Time at the 135th meridian west of Greenwich, England, and in the ninth time zone based on it in North America. It is nine hours earlier than Greenwich time.

YUL Airport code for Montreal, Quebec.

yu·lan (yŏo′län; *Chinese* yü′län′) *n.* A tree, *Magnolia denudata,* native to China and often cultivated for its large, cup-shaped, fragrant white flowers. [Mandarin Chinese *yü⁴ lan²,* "jade orchid" : *yü⁴,* jade + *lan²,* orchid.]

Yule (yŏol) *n.* Christmas or the season or feast celebrating Christmas. [Middle English *yole, yule,* Old English *gēol, geohhol,* originally a twelve-day heathen feast, from Common Germanic *jehwla-, jegwla-* (unattested).]

yule log. A large log traditionally burned in the fireplace at Christmas.

Yule·tide (yŏol′tīd′) *n.* The Christmas season.

Yu·ma (yŏo′mə) *n., pl.* **Yuma** or **-mas.** **1.** A tribe of Yuman-speaking North American Indians of southwestern Arizona and the adjacent parts of California and Mexico. **2.** A member of this tribe. **3.** The language of this tribe. [Spanish *Yuma†.]

Yu·man (yŏo′mən) *n.* A language family comprising the languages of the Yuma and Mohave Indians and other Indian languages of southwestern Arizona and the adjacent parts of California and Mexico. *—adj.* Of or pertaining to Yuman.

yum·my (yŭm′ē) *adj.* **-mier, -miest.** *Slang.* Delightful; delicious. [From *yum,* imitative of the sound made by the lips while tasting delicious food.]

Yung·ning. The former name for **Nanning.**

Yun·nan (yŏo′nän′). A province occupying 160,000 square miles in south-central China. Population, 19,100,000. Capital, Kunming.

yurt (yûrt) *n., pl.* **yurta** (yûr′tə). A circular, domed portable tent used by the nomadic Mongols of Siberia. [Russian *yurta,* from Turkic, akin to Turkish *yurt,* home.]

Yuzh·no-Sakh·a·linsk (yŏozh′nə-səкн-ə-lyēnsk′). The administrative center of Sakhalin, a seaport near the southern tip of the island. Population, 86,000.

Yu·zov·ka. The original name for **Donetsk.**

YVR Airport code for Vancouver, British Columbia.

Y.W.C.A. Young Women's Christian Association.

YWG Airport code for Winnipeg, Manitoba.

Y.W.H.A. Young Women's Hebrew Association.

y·wis. Variant of **iwis.**

YXD Airport code for Edmonton, Alberta.

YYC Airport code for Calgary, Alberta.

YYZ Airport code for Toronto, Ontario.

ă pat/ā pay/âr care/ä father/b bib/ch church/d deed/ĕ pet/ē be/f fife/g gag/h hat/hw which/ĭ pit/ī pie/îr pier/j judge/k kick/l lid,
needle/m mum/n no, sudden/ng thing/ŏ pot/ō toe/ô paw, for/oi noise/ou out/ŏo took/ōo boot/p pop/r roar/s sauce/sh ship, dish/

Zz

Around 1000 B.C. the Phoenicians and other Semites of Syria and Palestine began to use a graphic sign in the forms (1,2,3). They gave it the name zayin *and used it for the consonant* z. *After 900 B.C. the Greeks borrowed the sign from the Phoenicians (4,5) and changed its name to* zēta. *The Greek forms passed to the Roman alphabet (6). The Romans used* Z *sparingly and chiefly in words borrowed from Greek. The Roman Monumental Capital (7) is the prototype of our modern capital, printed (10) and written (11). The written Roman form (6) developed into the late Roman and medieval Uncial (8) and Cursive (9), which are the bases of our modern small letter, printed (12) and written (13).*

z, Z (zē; *British* zĕd) *n., pl.* **z's** or *rare* **zs, Z's** or **Zs. 1.** The 26th letter of the modern English alphabet. See **alphabet. 2.** Any of the speech sounds represented by this letter.

z, Z, z., Z. *Note:* As an abbreviation or symbol, *z* may be a small or a capital letter, with or without a period. Established forms or those generally preferred precede the definition. When no form is given, all four forms are in general use in that sense. **1. Z** atomic number. **2. Z** impedance. **3. z.** zero. **4. z.** zone. **5.** The 26th in a series; 25th when *J* is omitted.

za·ba·glio·ne (zä′bəl-yō′nē; *Italian* tzä-bä-lyō′nä) *n.* A dessert consisting of egg yolks, sugar, and wine beaten until thick and served hot or cold. [Italian *zaba(gl)ione.* See **sab-** in Appendix.*]

Zab·rze (zäb′zhĕ). *German* **Hin·den·burg** (hĭn′dən-bŏŏrk). A city and industrial center of Poland, located in the southwest. Population, 200,000.

Za·ca·te·cas (sä-kä-tā′käs). **1.** A state of central Mexico, occupying 28,125 square miles. Population, 871,000. **2.** The capital of this state, a silver-mining center in the southeast. Population, 32,000.

Zach·a·ri·as (zăk′ə-rī′əs). Also **Zech·a·ri·ah** (zĕk′ə-rī′ə). The husband of Elizabeth and father of John the Baptist. Luke 1:5.

Zach·a·ry (zăk′ə-rē). A masculine given name. [Late Latin *Zachariās,* from Greek *Zakharias,* from Hebrew *Zakhar′yah,* "God is renowned" : *zəkhar′,* remembrance + *Yah,* God.]

zaf·fer (zăf′ər) *n.* Also **zaf·fre.** An impure oxide of cobalt, used to produce a blue color in enamel and in the making of smalt. [Italian *zaffera,* from Old French *safre,* from Arabic *ṣufr,* yellow copper.]

zaf·tig, zof·tig (zäf′tĭk, -tĭg) *adj. Slang.* **1.** Full-bosomed. **2.** Having a comfortably ample figure. [Yiddish, "plump."]

ZAG Airport code for Zagreb, Yugoslavia.

Za·greb (zä′grĕb). The capital of Croatia, Yugoslavia, in the north-central part of the republic. Population, 481,000.

Za·gros Mountains (zăg′rəs). A mountain system of western Iran, extending for about 1,000 miles from the Iraqi border to the Persian Gulf. Highest elevation, about 15,000 feet.

zai·bat·su (zī′bät-soo′) *n., pl.* **zaibatsu.** A powerful family-controlled commercial combine of Japan. [Japanese, plutocrat, plutocracy : *zai,* wealth, from Chinese (Mandarin) *ts'ai²* + *batsu,* family, powerful person, from Chinese (Mandarin) *fa².*]

zaire (zâr) *n.* The basic monetary unit of the Democratic Republic of the Congo (Kinshasa), equal to 100 makuta. See table of exchange rates at **currency.** [Native word in the Congo.]

Za·ma (zä′mə). An ancient village in northern Africa in what is now Tunisia; the site of the defeat of Hannibal by Scipio Africanus (202 B.C.).

Zam·be·zi (zăm-bē′zē). Also **Zam·be·si.** A river of southern Africa, rising in eastern Angola and flowing 1,600 miles south through Zambia and then generally east through Mozambique to the Mozambique Channel.

Zam·bi·a (zăm′bē-ə). Formerly **Northern Rho·de·sia** (rō-dē′zhə). A republic occupying 290,323 square miles in south-central Africa; a former British colony, independent since 1964. Population, 3,733,000. Capital, Lusaka.

Zam·bo·an·ga (säm′bō-äng′gä). A city of the Republic of the Philippines, a seaport on southwestern Mindanao. Population, 131,000.

za·mi·a (zā′mē-ə) *n.* Any of various chiefly tropical American cycads of the genus *Zamia,* having a thick, usually underground trunk and palmlike terminal leaves. [New Latin *Zamia,* from a misreading of *(nūces) azāniae,* pine (nuts), probably from Greek *azainein,* to dry, to parch. See **as-** in Appendix.*]

za·min·dar (zə-mēn-där′) *n.* Also **ze·min·dar. 1.** An official in precolonial India assigned to collect the land taxes of his district. **2.** A native landholder in British colonial India, responsible for collecting and paying to the government the taxes on the land under his jurisdiction. [Persian *zamīndār : zamīn,* earth, land (see **dhghem-** in Appendix*) + *-dār,* holder, from Old Persian *dār-,* to hold (see **dher-²** in Appendix*).]

za·min·dar·i (zə-mēn-där′ē) *n., pl.* **-is.** Also **ze·min·dar·y** *pl.* **-ies. 1.** The system of tax collection by zamindars. **2.** The area administered by a zamindar. [Hindi *zamīndāri,* from Persian, from *zamīndār,* ZAMINDAR.]

za·na·na. Variant of **zenana.**

za·ny (zā′nē) *n., pl.* **-nies. 1.** A ludicrous, buffoonish character in old comedies who attempts feebly to mimic the tricks of the clown. **2.** A comical person given to extravagant or outlandish behavior. —*adj.* **zanier, -niest. 1.** Ludicrously comical; clownish; droll. **2.** Comical because of incongruity or strangeness; bizarre; absurd. [Italian *zani, zanni,* buffoon, from *Zanni,* dialectal variant of *Gianni,* pet form for *Giovanni,* Italian form of JOHN.]

Zan·zi·bar (zăn′zə-bär, zăn-zə-bär′). **1.** A region of Tanzania, a former nation consisting of the islands of Zanzibar (640 square miles) and Pemba (380 square miles) in the Indian Ocean off east-central Africa. Population, 299,000. **2.** In full **Zan·zi·bar City.** The capital of this region, on the western coast of the island of Zanzibar. Population, 58,000.

zap (zăp) *tr.v.* **zapped, zapping, zaps.** *Slang.* **1.** To destroy or kill with a burst of gunfire, flame, or electric current. **2.** To attack (an enemy in warfare) with heavy firepower; strafe or bombard. [Imitative.]

Za·pad·na·ya Dvi·na. The Russian name for the (western) Dvina.

Za·pa·ta (sä-pä′tä), **Emiliano.** 1877?–1919. Mexican revolutionist.

za·pa·te·a·do (thä-pä-tā-ä′tho) *n., pl.* **-dos.** *Spanish.* **1.** The rhythmic stamping of the heels characteristic of Spanish flamenco dances. **2.** A Spanish flamenco dance in which the performer stamps rhythmically with his heels. [Spanish, from *zapatear,* to tap with the shoe, from *zapáto,* shoe. See **sabot.**]

Za·po·ro·zhe (zə-pə-rô′zhyĕ). Formerly **A·le·ksan·drovsk** (ə-lĭk-sän′drəfsk). A city of the Soviet Union, on the Dnieper in the southern Ukrainian S.S.R. Population, 580,000.

Za·po·tec (zä′pə-tĕk′, sä′-) *n.* Any of a group of Central American languages spoken in southern Mexico. [Spanish *Zapoteca,* from Nahuatl *Tzapoteca.*] —**Za′po·tec′** *adj.*

Za·ra·go·za. The Spanish name for **Saragossa.**

Za·ra·thus·tra. See **Zoroaster.**

za·re·ba (zə-rē′bə) *n.* Also **za·ree·ba. 1.** An enclosure of bushes or stakes protecting a campsite or village in northeastern Africa. **2.** A campsite or village so protected. [Arabic *zarībah,* pen for cattle, from *zarb,* sheepfold.]

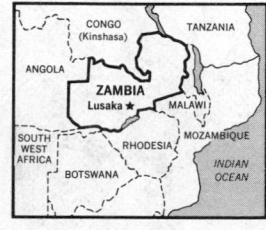

Zambia

---

zarf (zärf) *n.* A chalicelike holder for a hot coffee cup, typically made of ornamented metal, used in the Middle East. [Arabic *ẓarf,* "container."]
zas·tru·ga. Variant of **sastruga.**
zax (zăks) *n.* A hatchetlike tool for cutting and dressing roofing slates. [Variant of SAX (tool).]
za·yin (zä′yĭn) *n.* The seventh letter of the Hebrew alphabet. See **alphabet.** [Hebrew *zayin,* "weapon," from Aramaic.]
z.B. zum Beispiel (*German* for example).
zeal (zēl) *n.* Enthusiastic and diligent devotion in pursuit of a cause, ideal, or goal; fervent adherence or service; ardor; fervor: *"So he displayed the zeal of an insane sprinter in his purpose to keep them in the rear"* (Stephen Crane). See Synonyms at **passion.** [Middle English *zele,* from Late Latin *zēlus,* from Greek *zēlos.* See **yā-** in Appendix.*]
Zea·land. The English name for **Sjaelland.**
zeal·ot (zĕl′ət) *n.* One who is zealous; a fanatically committed person: *"an uncompromising zealot, a passionate seeker after truth"* (Louis Untermeyer). See Synonyms at **fanatic.**
Zeal·ot (zĕl′ət) *n.* A member of a Jewish sect that resisted Roman rule in Palestine during the first century A.D. [Late Latin *zēlōtes,* from Greek *zēlōtēs,* from *zēlos,* ZEAL.]
zeal·ot·ry (zĕl′ət-rē) *n.* Excessive zeal; fanaticism.
zeal·ous (zĕl′əs) *adj.* Filled with or motivated by zeal; ardent; enthusiastic; fervent. See Synonyms at **eager.** —**zeal′ous·ly** *adv.* —**zeal′ous·ness** *n.*
ze·bec, ze·beck. Variants of **xebec.**
Zeb·e·dee (zĕb′ə-dē). A fisherman whose sons James and John became disciples of Jesus. Matthew 4:21.
ze·bra (zē′brə) *n.* Any of several horselike African mammals of the genus *Equus,* having characteristic overall markings of conspicuous dark and whitish stripes. [Portuguese, from Old Spanish *zebra, zebro*†, wild ass.]
zebra finch. A small Australian bird, *Poephila castanotis,* having black and white striped markings, and popular as a cage bird.
zebra fish. A small freshwater tropical fish, *Brachydanio rerio,* of India, having horizontal dark-blue and silvery stripes, and popular in home aquariums. Also called "zebra danio."
ze·bra·wood (zē′brə-wŏŏd′) *n.* **1.** Any of several African or tropical American trees having striped wood. **2.** The wood of such a tree, used in cabinetmaking.
ze·bu (zē′byōō′) *n.* A domesticated bovine mammal, *Bos indicus,* of Asia and Africa, having a prominent hump on the back and a large dewlap. [French *zébu,* possibly from Tibetan *mdzo-p'o,* hybrid male offspring of the yak bull and the domestic cow : *mdzo,* name of this breed + *p'o,* masculine suffix.]
Zeb·u·lon[1] (zĕb′yə-lən). Also **Zeb·u·lun.** A son of Jacob and Leah. Genesis 30:20. [Hebrew *Zəbhūlōn,* from *zəbhūl,* dwelling, from *zābhal,* he dwelled.]
Zeb·u·lon[2] (zĕb′yə-lən) *n.* Also **Zeb·u·lun.** A tribe of Israel descended from Zebulon.
zec·chi·no (tsĕk-kē′nō) *n., pl.* **-ni** (-nē). Also **zec·chin** (zĕk′ĭn), **zech·in.** A coin, a **sequin** *(see).* [Italian, SEQUIN.]
Zech. Zechariah (Old Testament).
Zech·a·ri·ah[1] (zĕk′ə-rī′ə). A Hebrew prophet of the sixth century B.C.
Zech·a·ri·ah[2] (zĕk′ə-rī′ə) *n. Abbr.* **Zech.** A book of the Old Testament.
Zech·a·ri·ah[3]. See **Zacharias.**
zed (zĕd) *n. Chiefly British.* The letter *z.* [Middle English *zed,* from Old French *zede,* from Late Latin *zēta,* ZETA.]
Zed·e·ki·ah (zĕd′ə-kī′ə). The last king of Judah (597–586 B.C.), who died in captivity at Babylon. II Kings 24:17. [Hebrew, *Ṣidqīyāh(ū),* "the Lord is righteousness."]
zed·o·ar·y (zĕd′ō-ĕr′ē) *n.* The dried rhizome of a tropical Asian plant, *Curcuma zedoaria,* used as a stimulant and condiment. [Middle English *zeodoarye,* from Medieval Latin *zeodoaria,* from Arabic *zadwār,* from Persian *zedwār*†.]
zee (zē) *n.* The letter *z.*
Zee·brug·ge (zē′brŏŏg-ə; *Flemish* zā′brœKH-ə). A town in northwestern Belgium on the North Sea, the port for Bruges, with which it is connected by canal. Population, 3,000.
Zee·land (zē′lənd; *Dutch* zā′länt). A province of the Netherlands, occupying 651 square miles in the southwest. Population, 290,000. Capital, Middelburg.
Zee·man (zā′män), **Pieter.** 1865–1943. Dutch physicist.
Zee·man effect (zā′män). The splitting of single spectral lines of an emission spectrum into three or more polarized components when the radiation source is in a magnetic field.
ze·in (zē′ĭn) *n.* A prolamine protein derived from corn and used in the manufacture of various plastics, coatings, and lacquers. [New Latin *Zea,* genus name for corn, from Greek *zea, zeia,* one-seeded wheat (see **yewo-**[2] in Appendix*) + -IN.]
Zeit·geist (tsīt′gīst′) *n. German.* The spirit of the time; the taste and outlook characteristic of a period or generation.
ze·min·dar. Variant of **zamindar.**
ze·min·dar·y. Variant of **zamindari.**
Zem·lya Fran·tsa Io·si·fa. The Russian name for **Franz Josef Land.**
zemst·vo (zĕms′tvō) *n., pl.* **-vos.** An elective council responsible for the local administration of a provincial district in czarist Russia. [Russian, from *zemlya,* land. See **dhghem-** in Appendix.*]
ze·na·na (zə-nä′nə) *n.* Also **za·na·na.** The part of a house in India and Pakistan reserved for the women of the household. [Hindi *zenāna,* from Persian, from *zan,* woman. See **gwen-** in Appendix.*]
Zen Buddhism (zĕn). A Chinese and Japanese school of Mahayana Buddhism that asserts that enlightenment can be attained through meditation, self-contemplation, and intuition rather than through the scriptures. Also called "Zen." [Japanese *zen,* from Mandarin Chinese *ch'an*[2], short for *ch'an*[2] *na*[4], meditation, from Pali *jhāna,* from Sanskrit *dhyāna,* from *dhyāti,* he meditates. See **dheyə-** in Appendix.*] —**Zen Buddhist.**
Zend (zĕnd) *n.* **1.** The **Zend-Avesta** *(see).* **2.** Formerly, a language, **Avestan** *(see).*
Zend-A·ves·ta (zĕnd′ə-vĕs′tə) *n.* The entire body of sacred writings of the Zoroastrian religion. Also called "Zend." [Persian *zandavastā, zendastā,* from *Avesta-va-zend,* Avesta with an interpretation : Middle Persian *upastāk,* AVESTA + *va,* with + *zend*†, interpretation.] —**Zend′-A·ves·ta′ic** (-ə-vĕs′tā′ĭk) *adj.*
Zeng·er (zĕng′ər), **John Peter.** 1697–1746. German-born printer in America; central figure in trial that established a legal precedent for freedom of the press.
ze·nith (zē′nĭth) *n.* **1.** The point on the celestial sphere that is directly above the observer. **2. a.** The upper region of the sky. **b.** The highest point above the observer's horizon attained by a celestial body. **3.** The highest point of any path or course; a point of culmination; peak; summit; acme. —See Synonyms at **summit.** [Middle English, from Old French *cenith,* from Old Spanish *zenit,* from Arabic *samt,* road, in *samt ar-ra's,* road (over) the head.]
Ze·no (zē′nō). 342?–270? B.C. Greek philosopher; founder of Stoicism.
ze·o·lite (zē′ə-līt′) *n.* Any of a group of approximately 30 hydrous aluminum silicate minerals or their corresponding synthetic compounds, used chiefly as molecular filters and ion-exchange agents. [Swedish *zeolit,* "boiling stone" (because it swells and boils under the blowpipe) : Greek *zeein,* to boil (see **yes-** in Appendix*) + -LITE.]
Zeph. Zephaniah (Old Testament).
Zeph·a·ni·ah[1] (zĕf′ə-nī′ə). A Hebrew prophet of the seventh century B.C.
Zeph·a·ni·ah[2] (zĕf′ə-nī′ə) *n. Abbr.* **Zeph.** A book of the Old Testament containing the prophecies of Zephaniah.
zeph·yr (zĕf′ər) *n.* **1. a.** The west wind. **b.** A gentle breeze. **2.** Any of various light, soft fabrics, yarns, or garments. **3.** Any airy, insubstantial, or passing thing. —See Synonyms at **wind.** [Middle English *Zephirus,* from Latin *zephyrus,* from Greek *zephuros,* akin to *zophos*†, darkness, west.]
zephyr lily. Any of several plants of the genus *Zephyranthes,* native to tropical America, having grasslike leaves and variously colored flowers.
Zeph·y·rus (zĕf′ər-əs). *Greek Mythology.* A god personifying the gentle west wind. [Latin, from Greek *Zephuros,* from *zephuros,* ZEPHYR.]
zep·pe·lin (zĕp′ə-lĭn; *German* tsĕp′ə-lēn′) *n.* Also **Zep·pe·lin.** A rigid airship having a long, cylindrical body supported by internal gas cells. [Invented by Count Ferdinand von ZEPPELIN.]
Zep·pe·lin (zĕp′ə-lĭn; *German* tsĕp′ə-lēn′), Count **Ferdinand von.** 1838–1917. German military leader; designer, manufacturer, and pilot of airships.
Zer·matt (tsĕr-mät′). A village in the Alps of southern Switzerland, noted as a winter-sports resort. Population, 3,000.
Zer·ni·ke (zĕr′nĭ-kə), **Frits.** 1888–1966. Dutch physicist.
ze·ro (zîr′ō, zē′rō) *n., pl.* **-ros** or **-roes.** *Abbr.* **z. 1.** The numerical symbol "0"; a cipher; nought. **2.** *Mathematics.* **a.** An element of a set that when added to any other element in the set produces a sum identical with the element to which it is added. **b.** A cardinal number indicating the absence of any or all units under consideration. **c.** An ordinal number indicating an initial point or origin. **d.** An argument at which the value of a function vanishes. **3.** The temperature indicated by the numeral 0 on a thermometer. **4.** A sight setting that enables a firearm to shoot on target. **5.** One having no influence or importance; nonentity; nobody. **6.** The lowest point: *His prospects were set at zero.* **7.** Nothing; nil. —*adj.* **1.** Of, pertaining to, or being zero. **2. a.** Having no measurable or otherwise determinable value. **b.** Absent, inoperative, or irrelevant in specified circumstances: *zero gravity.* **3. a.** Limited by cloud cover to little or no vertical visibility. **b.** Permitting little or no horizontal visibility. —*tr.v.* **zeroed, -roing, -roes.** To adjust (an instrument or device) to zero value. —**zero in. 1.** To aim or concentrate firepower on an exact target location. **2.** To adjust the aim or sight of by repeated firings. **3.** To converge intently; move near; close in: *The children zeroed in on the toy display.* [French *zéro,* from Italian *zero,* from Medieval Latin *zephirum,* from Arabic *ṣifr,* zero, CIPHER.]
zero hour. The scheduled time for the start of an operation or action, especially a concerted military attack. Also called "H-hour."
ze·ro-point energy (zîr′ō-point′, zē′rō-). The irreducible minimum energy possessed by a substance at absolute zero temperature.
ze·ro-sum game (zîr′ō-sŭm′, zē′rō-). A game in which the sum of the winnings of all players equals the sum of the losses of all players.
zest (zĕst) *n.* **1.** Added flavor or interest; piquancy; charm. **2.** Spirited enjoyment; wholehearted interest; gusto: *"At fifty-three he retains all the heady zest of adolescence"* (Kenneth Tynan). **3.** The outermost part of the rind of an orange or lemon, used as flavoring. —*tr.v.* **zested, zesting, zests.** To give zest, charm, or spirit to. [Obsolete French *zest*†, orange or lemon peel.] —**zest′ful** *adj.*
ze·ta (zā′tə, zē′-) *n.* The sixth letter in the Greek alphabet, written Z, ζ. Transliterated in English as *Z, z.* See **alphabet.** [Late

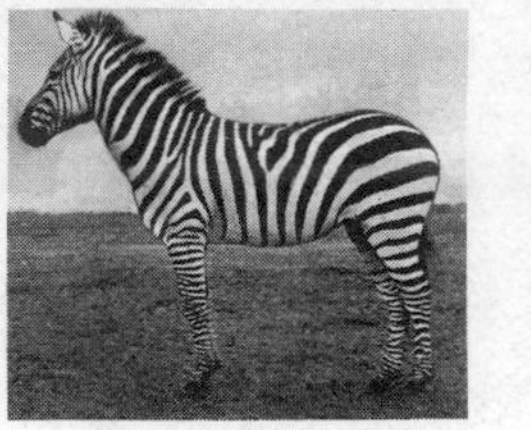
zebra
Equus burchelli

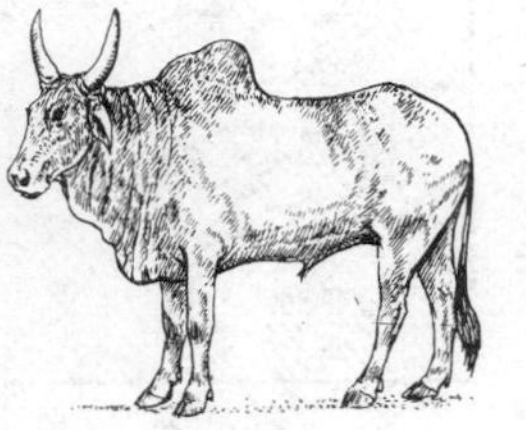
zebu

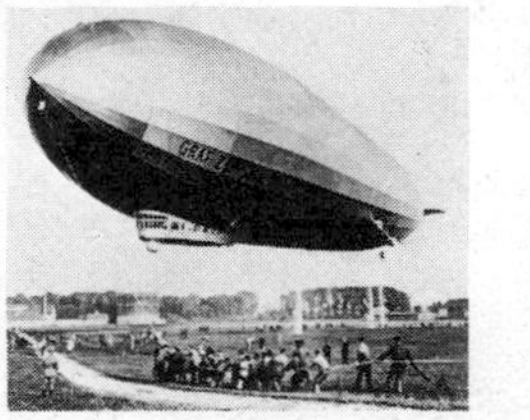
zeppelin

ă pat/ā pay/âr care/ä father/b bib/ch church/d deed/ĕ pet/ē be/f fife/g gag/h hat/hw which/ĭ pit/ī pie/îr pier/j judge/k kick/l lid, needle/m mum/n no, sudden/ng thing/ŏ pot/ō toe/ô paw, for/oi noise/ou out/ŏŏ took/ōō boot/p pop/r roar/s sauce/sh ship, dish/

Latin *zēta*, from Greek, probably from Semitic, akin to Hebrew *zayit*, Aramaic *zētā*.]

Ze·thus (zē′thəs). Also **Ze·thos**. *Greek Mythology.* The twin brother of **Amphion** (*see*).

Zet·land. See **Shetland Islands**.

zeug·ma (zoōg′mə) *n.* A rhetorical figure in which a word is used to modify or govern two or more words although its use is grammatically or logically correct with only one; for example, *She left in high spirits and a Cadillac.* Compare **syllepsis**. [Latin, from Greek *zeugma*, a joining, uniting, yoking. See **yeug-** in Appendix.*]

Zeus (zoōs). The presiding god of the Greek pantheon, ruler of the heavens and father of other gods and mortal heroes. [Greek. See **deiw-** in Appendix.*]

Zhda·nov (zhdä′nôf). Formerly **Ma·ri·u·pol** (măr′ĭ-yoō′pôl). A city of the Soviet Union, a port in the southeastern Ukraine on the Sea of Azov. Population, 361,000.

zib·e·line, zib·el·line (zĭb′ə-lēn′, -lĭn) *n.* **1.** A thick, lustrous, soft fabric of wool and other animal hair, such as mohair, having a silky nap. **2.** *Rare.* The sable or its fur. [Old French, from Old Italian *zibellino*, from Slavic, akin to Russian *sobol*†.]

zib·et (zĭb′ĭt) *n.* Also **zib·eth**. *Rare.* A civet cat, *Viverra zibetha*, of southeastern Asia. [Italian *zibetto*, from Medieval Latin *zibethum*, from Arabic *zabād*, CIVET.]

Zieg·feld (zĕg′fĕld, zĭg′-), **Florenz**. 1867–1932. American theatrical producer.

Zie·gler (tsē′glər), **Karl**. Born 1898. German chemist.

zig·gu·rat (zĭg′oō-răt′) *n.* Also **zik·ku·rat** (zĭk′-). A temple tower of the ancient Assyrians and Babylonians, having the form of a terraced pyramid of successively receding stories. [Assyrian *ziqquratu*, summit, mountain top, from *zaqaru*, to be high.]

zig·zag (zĭg′zăg′) *n.* **1.** A line or course that proceeds by sharp turns in alternating directions. **2.** One of a series of such sharp turns. **3.** Something exhibiting one or a series of sharp turns, such as a road or design. —*adj.* Having or moving in a zigzag. —*adv.* In a zigzag manner or pattern. —*v.* **zigzagged, -zagging, -zags.** —*intr.* To move in or form a zigzag. —*tr.* To cause to move in or form a zigzag. [French, from German *Zickzack*, expressive formation.]

zig·zag·ger (zĭg′zăg′ər) *n.* **1.** A person or thing that zigzags. **2.** A sewing-machine attachment for sewing zigzag stitches.

zil·lion (zĭl′yən) *n.* *Informal.* An extremely large indefinite number. Used jocosely.

Zil·pah (zĭl′pə). The servant of Leah who bore Jacob two sons, Gad and Asher. Genesis 30:9-13.

Zim·ba·bwe (zĭm-bä′bwā). An archaeological site in southeastern Rhodesia, containing the ruins of a city built in precolonial times.

zinc (zĭngk) *n.* Symbol **Zn** A bluish-white, lustrous metallic element that is brittle at room temperatures but malleable with heating. It is used to form a wide variety of alloys including brass, bronze, German silver, various solders, and nickel silver, in galvanizing iron and other metals, for electric fuses, anodes, and meter cases, and in roofing, gutters, and various household objects. Atomic number 30, atomic weight 65.37, melting point 419.4°C, boiling point 907°C, specific gravity 7.133 (25°C), valence 2. See **element**. —*tr.v.* **zinced** or **zincked, zincing** or **zincking, zincs.** To coat or treat with zinc; galvanize. [German, *Zink*, perhaps from *Zinke*, prong (so named because it becomes jagged in the furnace), from Old High German *zinko*. See **denk-** in Appendix.*]

zinc·ate (zĭngk′āt′) *n.* Any of several chemical compounds derived from the reaction of zinc or zinc oxide with certain alkali solutions.

zinc blende. A mineral, **sphalerite** (*see*).

zinc·ite (zĭngk′īt′) *n.* A red to yellow-orange zinc ore, essentially ZnO.

zin·co·graph (zĭngk′ə-grăf′, -gräf′) *n.* **1.** A prepared zinc plate used in zincography. **2.** A print or picture obtained from such a plate. [ZINC + -GRAPH.]

zin·cog·ra·phy (zĭng-kŏg′rə-fē) *n.* The process of engraving zinc printing plates. [ZINC + -GRAPHY.] —**zin·cog′ra·pher** *n.* —**zinc′o·graph′ic** (zĭng′kə-grăf′ĭk), **zinc′o·graph′i·cal** *adj.*

zinc ointment. *Medicine.* A salve consisting of about 20 per cent zinc oxide with beeswax or paraffin and petrolatum, used in the treatment of skin diseases.

zinc oxide. An amorphous white or yellowish powder, ZnO, used as a pigment, in compounding rubber, in the manufacture of plastics, and in pharmaceuticals and cosmetics. Also called "Chinese white," "zinc white."

zinc sulfate. A colorless crystalline compound, $ZnSO_4·7H_2O$, used medicinally as an emetic and astringent, as a fungicide, and in wood and skin preservatives. Also called "white vitriol."

zinc white. A paint pigment, **zinc oxide** (*see*).

zin·fan·del (zĭn′făn-dĕl′) *n.* Also **Zin·fan·del**. A dry red table wine produced from grapes grown chiefly in California. [Origin unknown.]

zing (zĭng) *n.* A brief high-pitched humming or buzzing sound, such as that made by a swiftly passing object or a taut vibrating string. —*intr.v.* **zinged, zinging, zings.** *Informal.* To make or move with such a sound. [Imitative.]

zin·ga·ro (tsēn′gä-rō′) *n.*, *pl.* **-ri** (-rē′). *Feminine* **zin·ga·ra** (-gä-rä′) *pl.* **-re** (-rā′). A Gypsy. [Italian *zingaro*, probably from Greek *Athinganoi*† (plural), name of an oriental people.]

zink·en·ite (zĭng′kən-īt′) *n.* Also **zinck·en·ite**. A steel-gray mineral, essentially $Pb_6Sb_{14}S_{27}$. [German *Zinkenit*, after J.K.L. Zinken (1790-1862), German mineralogist.]

zin·ni·a (zĭn′ē-ə) *n.* Any of various plants of the genus *Zinnia*, native to tropical America; especially, *Z. elegans*, widely cul-

Zeus
Ancient Greek statue of the god throwing a thunderbolt

tivated for its showy, variously colored flowers. [New Latin *Zinnia*, after Johann Gottfried *Zinn* (1727-1759), German botanist and physician.]

Zin·zen·dorf (tsĭn′tsən-dôrf), Count **Nicholas Ludwig von**. 1700-1760. German theologian; founder of the Moravian Church.

Zi·on (zī′ən) *n.* Also **Si·on** (sī′ən). **1. a.** The Jewish people; Israel. **b.** The Jewish homeland as a symbol of Judaism. **2.** A place or religious community regarded as sacredly devoted to God; a city of God. **3.** An idealized harmonious community; a utopia. [Middle English *Sion*, Old English *Sion*, from Late Latin *Siōn*, from Greek *Seiōn*, from Hebrew *Ṣiyōn*.]

Zi·on, Mount (zī′ən). **1.** The part of Jerusalem that constituted the City of David. **2.** The hill in Jerusalem on which Solomon's temple was built.

Zi·on·ism (zī′ən-ĭz′əm) *n.* **1.** A plan or movement of the Jewish people to return from the Diaspora to Palestine. **2.** A movement originally aimed at the re-establishment of a Jewish national homeland and state in Palestine and now concerned with development of Israel. —**Zi′on·ist** *adj. & n.* —**Zi′on·is′tic** *adj.*

Zi·on National Park (zī′ən). A scenic area occupying over 200 square miles in southwestern Utah and containing Zion Canyon, a gorge extending for 15 miles and having sides half a mile high.

zip (zĭp) *n.* **1.** A brief, sharp, hissing sound, such as that made by a flying arrow. **2.** Energetic activity; alacrity; vim. —*v.* **zipped, zipping, zips.** —*intr.* **1.** To move with a sharp, hissing sound. **2. a.** To move or act with a speed that suggests such a sound: *The cars zipped by endlessly.* **b.** To act or proceed swiftly and energetically. **3.** To become fastened or unfastened by a zipper. —*tr.* **1.** To give speed and force to. **2.** To impart life or zest to. **3.** To fasten or unfasten with a zipper. Often used with *up* or *open*. [Imitative.]

Zi·pan·gu (zĭ-păng′goō). Marco Polo's name for Japan.

Zip Code. Also **zip code, ZIP Code**. A system designed to expedite the sorting and delivery of mail by assigning a five-digit number to each delivery area in the United States. The first three digits indicate a district, often a city, and the last two the local zone. Also called "ZIP." [Z(ONE) I(MPROVEMENT) P(ROGRAM).]

zip gun. A crude homemade pistol.

zip·per (zĭp′ər) *n.* A fastening device consisting of parallel rows of metal or nylon teeth on adjacent edges of an opening which are interlocked by a sliding tab. [From a trademark *Zipper*, from ZIP.]

Zip·per (zĭp′ər) *n.* A trademark for a rubber-coated boot or overshoe fastened with a zipper.

zip·py (zĭp′ē) *adj.* **-pier, -piest.** Full of energy; brisk; lively; snappy.

zir·con (zûr′kŏn′) *n.* A brown to colorless mineral, essentially $ZrSiO_4$, which is heated, cut, and polished to form a brilliant blue-white gem. [German *Zirkon*, from French *jargon*, from Italian *giargone*, from Arabic *zarqūn*, from Persian *zargūn*, gold-colored : *zar*, gold (see **ghel-²** in Appendix*) + *gūn-*†.]

zir·con·ate (zûr′kə-nāt′) *n.* Any of several chemical compounds formed by heating zirconium oxide with a metal carbonate or oxide in the presence of an acid. [ZIRCON + -ATE.]

zir·co·ni·a (zûr-kō′nē-ə) *n.* Zirconium oxide (*see*). [New Latin, from ZIRCON.]

zir·co·ni·um (zûr-kō′nē-əm) *n.* Symbol **Zr** A lustrous, grayish-white, strong, ductile metallic element obtained primarily from zircon and used chiefly in ceramic and refractory compounds, as an alloying agent, in nuclear reactors, and in medical prosthesis. Atomic number 40, atomic weight 91.22, melting point 1,852°C, boiling point 3,578°C, specific gravity 6.53 (calculated), principal valence 4. See **element**. [New Latin, from ZIRCON.]

zirconium oxide. A hard white amorphous powder, ZrO_2, derived from zirconium and also found naturally, used chiefly in pigments, refractories, ceramics, and as an abrasive. Also called "zirconia."

zith·er (zĭth′ər) *n.* Also **zith·ern** (-ərn). A musical instrument constructed of a flat sounding box with about 30 to 40 strings stretched over it and played horizontally with the fingertips or a plectrum. [German *Zither*, from Old High German *zithera*, *cithera*, from Latin *cithara*, from Greek *kithara*, CITHARA.] —**zith′er·ist** *n.*

zither

zi·ti (zē′tē; *Italian* tsē′tē) *n.* Tubular pasta. [Italian *ziti*†.]

zi·zith (tsē-tsēt′, tsī′tsĭs) *pl.n.* The tassels or fringes of thread on the four corners of prayer shawls worn by Jewish males. [Hebrew *ṣiṣith*, tassel.]

Zla·to·ust (zlə-tŭ-ōōst′). A city of the Soviet Union, a manufacturing center in the southern Ural Mountains. Population, 175,000.

zlo·ty (zlô′tē) *n.*, *pl.* **-tys** or **zloty. 1.** The basic monetary unit of Poland, equal to 100 groszy. See table of exchange rates at **currency**. **2.** A coin worth one zloty. [Polish *zloty*, "golden," from *zloto*, gold. See **ghel-²** in Appendix.*]

Zn The symbol for the element zinc.

zo-. Variant of **zoo-**.

zo·a. Alternate plural of **zoon**.

-zoa. Indicates certain animal organisms; for example, **entozoa**. Used chiefly in names of taxonomic groups, such as Protozoa. [New Latin, from Greek *zōia*, plural of *zōion*, animal. See **gwei-** in Appendix.*]

Zo·an. The Biblical name for **Tanis**.

-zoan. *Zoology.* Indicates individuals within a taxonomic group; for example, **protozoan**. [From -ZOA.]

zinnia
Zinnia elegans

zo·di·ac (zō′dē-ăk′) *n.* **1. a.** *Astronomy.* A band of the celestial sphere, extending about eight degrees to either side of the ecliptic, that represents the path of the principal planets, the moon, and the sun. **b.** *Astrology.* This band divided into 12 equal parts called signs, each 30 degrees wide, bearing the name of a constellation for which it was originally named but with which it no longer coincides owing to the precession of the equinoxes. **2.** A diagram or figure representing the zodiac. **3.** A complete circuit; circle. [Middle English, from Old French *zodiaque,* from Latin *zōdiacus,* from Greek *zōidiakos (kuklos),* "(circle) of carved figures," from *zōidion,* carved figure, sign of the zodiac, diminutive of *zōion,* animal. See **gwei-** in Appendix.*] **—zo·di′a·cal** (zō-dī′ə-kəl) *adj.*

zodiacal light. A faint hazy cone of light, often visible in the west just after sunset or in the east just before sunrise, apparently caused by the reflection of sunlight from meteoric particles surrounding the sun.

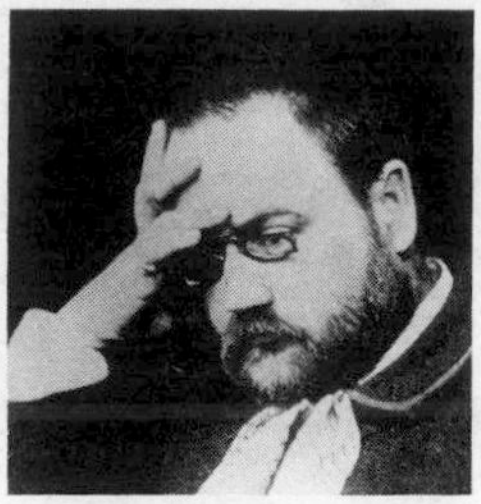
Émile Zola

Zo·e (zō′ē). A feminine given name. [Greek *zōē,* life. See **gwei-** in Appendix.*]

-zoic. Indicates: **1.** A specific kind of animal existence; for example, **holozoic. 2.** A specific geological division; for example, **Mesozoic.** [From Greek *zōikos,* of animals, from *zōion,* animal. See **gwei-** in Appendix.*]

zois·ite (zoi′sīt′) *n.* A gray, brown, or pink mineral, essentially $Ca_2Al_3(SiO_4)_3(OH)$, used in ornamental stonework. [German *Zoisit,* named after its discoverer, Baron S. *Zois* von Edelstein (1747–1819), Slovenian nobleman.]

Zo·la (zō-lä′), **Émile.** 1840–1902. French novelist.

zoll·ver·ein (tsôl′fər-īn, zōl′fə-rīn) *n.* **1.** *Often capital* **Z.** A union of German states during the 19th century that established a uniform tariff on imports from nonmembers and free trade among themselves. **2.** Any customs or tariff union. [German *Zollverein,* "custom union."]

Zom·ba (zŏm′bə). The interim capital of Malawi, pending construction of a new capital at Lilongwe. Population, 12,000.

zom·bie (zŏm′bē) *n.* Also **zom·bi** *pl.* **-bis. 1.** A snake god of voodoo cults in West Africa, Haiti, and the southern United States. **2. a.** A supernatural power or spell that according to voodoo belief can enter into and reanimate a dead body. **b.** A corpse revived in this way. **3.** One who looks or behaves like an automaton. **4.** A tall drink made of various rums, liqueur, and fruit juice. [Kongo *zumbi,* "fetish."]

zo·nal (zō′nəl) *adj.* Also **zo·na·ry** (zō′nər-ē). **1.** Of or associated with a zone or zones. **2.** Divided into zones. **—zo′nal·ly** *adv.*

zo·nate (zō′nāt′) *adj.* Also **zo·nat·ed** (zō′nā′tĭd). Having zones; belted, striped, or ringed.

zo·na·tion (zō-nā′shən) *n.* **1.** Arrangement or formation in zones; zonate structure. **2.** *Ecology.* The distribution of organisms in biogeographic zones.

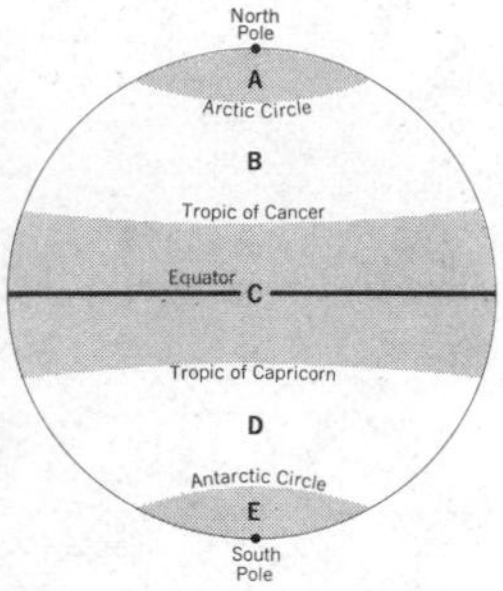

zone
Geographic zones

zone (zōn) *n. Abbr.* **z. 1.** An area, region, or division distinguished from adjacent parts by some distinctive feature or character. **2. a.** *Geography.* Any of the five regions of the surface of the earth that are loosely divided according to prevailing climate and latitude, including the Torrid Zone, the North and South Temperate Zones, and the North and South Frigid Zones. **b.** A similar division on any planet. **c.** *Geometry.* A portion of a sphere bounded by the intersections of two parallel planes with the sphere. **3.** *Ecology.* An area characterized by distinct physical conditions and populated by communities of certain kinds of organisms. **4.** *Geology.* A region or stratum distinguished by composition or content. **5. a.** A section or division of an area or territory established to distinguish it from other similar areas for a specific purpose. **b.** A municipal area in a city designated for a particular type of building, enterprise, or activity: *residential zone.* **6.** The total number of railroad stations located in a given radius from a particular shipping point. **7.** *Archaic.* A belt or girdle. —See Synonyms at **area.** —*tr.v.* **zoned, zoning, zones. 1.** To divide into zones. **2.** To designate or mark off into zones. **3.** To surround or encircle with or as if with a belt or girdle. [Latin *zōna,* girdle, zone, from Greek *zōnē.* See **yōs-** in Appendix.*]

zone·time (zōn′tīm′) *n.* Standard time used at sea according to the time zone in which a ship is located.

zo·nule (zō′nyōōl′) *n.* A small zone, belt, or band. [Latin *zōnula,* diminutive of *zōna,* belt, ZONE.]

zoo (zōō) *n., pl.* **zoos.** A public park or institution in which living animals are kept and exhibited to the public. Also called "zoological garden." [Short for ZOOLOGICAL GARDEN.]

zoo-, zo-. Indicates animals or animal forms; for example, **zoology, zoogeography, zooid.** [Greek *zōio-,* from *zōion, zōon,* living being, animal. See **gwei-** in Appendix.*]

zo·o·chore (zō′ə-kôr′, -kōr′) *n.* A plant dispersed by animals. [ZOO- + -CHORE.]

zoogeog. zoogeography.

zo·o·ge·o·graph·ic (zō′ə-jē-ə-grăf′ĭk) *adj.* Also **zo·o·ge·o·graph·i·cal** (-grăf′ĭ-kəl). Of or pertaining to zoogeography. **—zo′o·ge′o·graph′i·cal·ly** *adv.*

zoogeographic region. An ecological region characterized by the dominance of certain kinds of animal life.

zo·o·ge·og·ra·phy (zō′ə-jē-ŏg′rə-fē) *n. Abbr.* **zoogeog.** The biological study of the geographical distribution of animals. **—zo′o·ge·og′ra·pher** *n.*

zo·o·gloe·a, zo·o·gle·a (zō′ə-glē′ə) *n., pl.* **-gleae** (-glē′ə) or **-as.** Any of various bacteria of the genus *Zoogloea,* forming colonies in a jellylike secretion. [New Latin : ZOO- + Medieval Greek *glia, gloia,* glue (see **gel-**[1] in Appendix*).]

zo·og·ra·phy (zō-ŏg′rə-fē) *n.* The biological description of animals. [ZOO- + -GRAPHY.] **—zo′o·graph′ic** (zō′ə-grăf′ĭk), **zo′o·graph′ic·al** *adj.*

zo·oid (zō′oid′) *n.* **1.** *Biology.* An organic cell or organized body that has independent movement within a living organism; especially, a motile gamete such as a spermatozoon. **2.** *Zoology.* One of the usually microscopic animals forming an aggregate or colony, as of bryozoans or hydrozoans. [ZO(O)- + -OID.] **—zo·oi′dal** *adj.*

zool. zoological; zoology.

zo·ol·a·try (zō-ŏl′ə-trē) *n., pl.* **-tries.** The worship of animals. [New Latin *zoolatria* : ZOO- + -LATRY.] **—zo·ol′a·ter** *n.* **—zo·ol′a·trous** *adj.*

zo·o·log·i·cal (zō′ə-lŏj′ĭ-kəl) *adj.* Also **zo·o·log·ic** (-ə-lŏj′ĭk). *Abbr.* **zool. 1.** Of or pertaining to animals or animal life. **2.** Of or pertaining to the science of zoology. **—zo′o·log′i·cal·ly** *adv.*

zoological garden. A zoo *(see).*

zo·ol·o·gist (zō-ŏl′ə-jĭst) *n.* One who specializes in the study of animals.

zo·ol·o·gy (zō-ŏl′ə-jē) *n., pl.* **-gies.** *Abbr.* **zool. 1.** The biological science of animals. **2.** The animal life of a particular area. **3.** The characteristics of an animal group or category: *the zoology of mammals.* **4.** A book or scholarly work on zoology. [New Latin *zoologia* : ZOO- + -LOGY.]

zoom (zōōm) *v.* **zoomed, zooming, zooms.** —*intr.* **1.** To make a continuous low-pitched buzzing or humming sound. **2.** To move while making such a sound. **3.** To climb suddenly and sharply in an airplane. **4.** To move about rapidly; swoop. **5. a.** To move rapidly toward or away from a photographic subject. Used of a camera. Often used with *in* or *out.* **b.** To simulate such a movement, as by means of a zoom lens. Often used with *in* or *out.* —*tr.* To cause to zoom. —*n.* The act or sound of zooming. [Imitative.]

Usage: *Zoom* (verb), applied to aeronautics, always specifies upward movement. It is also applicable to related movement over a relatively level course, according to a majority of the Usage Panel, especially when there is a strong suggestion of accompanying sound: *The racing car zoomed around the course* (acceptable to 64 per cent of the Panel). The verb is less appropriate when downward movement is specified: *The eagle zoomed down on its prey* (acceptable to only 31 per cent).

zo·om·e·try (zō-ŏm′ə-trē) *n.* Measurement and comparison of the sizes of animals or animal parts, especially the measurement of bulk. [ZOO- + -METRY.] **—zo′o·met′ric** (zō′ə-mĕt′rĭk), **zo′o·met′ri·cal** *adj.* **—zo′o·met′ri·cal·ly** *adv.*

zoom lens. A camera lens whose focal length can be rapidly changed, allowing rapid change in the size of an image.

zo·o·mor·phism (zō′ə-môr′fĭz′əm) *n.* Also **zo·o·mor·phy** (-môr′fē). **1.** The attribution of animal characteristics or qualities to a god or gods. **2.** The use of animal forms in symbolism, literature, or graphic representation. [ZOO- + -MORPH + -ISM.] **—zo′o·mor′phic** *adj.*

zo·on (zō′ŏn′) *n., pl.* **-ons** or **zoa** (zō′ə). An animal developed from a fertilized egg. [New Latin, from Greek *zōion, zōon,* living being, animal. See **gwei-** in Appendix.*]

-zoon. Indicates an individual animal or independently moving organic unit; for example, **spermatozoon.** [New Latin, from Greek *zōion, zōon,* living being, animal. See **gwei-** in Appendix.*]

zo·on·o·sis (zō-ŏn′ə-sĭs) *n., pl.* **-ses** (-sēz). A disease such as rabies or malaria that can be transmitted from animals to man. [New Latin : ZOO- + Greek *nosos,* illness (see **noso-**).]

zo·oph·a·gous (zō-ŏf′ə-gəs) *adj.* Feeding on animal matter. [ZOO- + -PHAGOUS.]

zo·o·phile (zō′ə-fīl′, -fĭl) *n.* A lover of animals; especially, one opposed to vivisection. [ZOO- + -PHILE.]

zo·oph·i·lous (zō-ŏf′ə-ləs) *adj. Botany.* Pollinated by animals.

zo·o·pho·bi·a (zō′ə-fō′bē-ə) *n.* An irrational fear of animals. [New Latin : ZOO- + -PHOBIA.]

zo·o·phyte (zō′ə-fīt′) *n.* An invertebrate animal such as a sea anemone or sponge that remains attached to a surface and superficially resembles a plant. [Greek *zōophuton* : ZOO- + -PHYTE.] **—zo′o·phyt′ic** (zō′ə-fĭt′ĭk), **zo′o·phyt′i·cal** *adj.*

zo·o·plank·ton (zō′ə-plăngk′tən) *n.* Floating, often microscopic aquatic animals. [ZOO- + PLANKTON.]

zo·o·plas·ty (zō′ə-plăs′tē) *n.* Surgical transfer of tissue from a lower animal to man. [ZOO- + -PLASTY.] **—zo′o·plas′tic** *adj.*

zo·o·sperm (zō′ə-spûrm′) *n. Biology.* A **spermatozoon** *(see).* [ZOO- + -SPERM.]

zo·o·spo·ran·gi·um (zō′ə-spə-răn′jē-əm) *n., pl.* **-gia** (-jē-ə). *Botany.* A sporangium in which zoospores develop.

zo·o·spore (zō′ə-spôr′, -spōr′) *n.* A motile, flagellated asexual spore, as of certain algae and fungi. Also called "swarm spore." **—zo′o·spor′ic, zo′o·spor′ous** *adj.*

zo·os·ter·ol (zō-ŏs′tə-rōl′) *n. Biochemistry.* Any of several animal sterols, such as cholesterol.

zo·o·tech·nics (zō′ə-tĕk′nĭks) *n.* Plural in form, used with a singular or plural verb. Zootechny. [From ZOO- + Greek *tekhnē,* art (see **zootechny**).]

zo·o·tech·ny (zō′ə-tĕk′nē) *n.* The domestication, breeding, and improvement of animals; the technology of animal husbandry. [ZOO- + Greek *tekhnē,* art (see **teks-** in Appendix*).] **—zo′o·tech′ni·cal** *adj.* **—zo′o·tech·ni′cian** (-tĕk-nĭsh′ən) *n.*

zo·ot·o·my (zō-ŏt′ə-mē) *n.* **1.** Dissection of animals other than man. **2.** Comparative anatomy. [ZOO- + -TOMY.]

zoot suit (zōōt). *Slang.* A man's suit popular during the early 1940's, characterized by full-legged, tight-cuffed trousers and a long coat with wide lapels and wide, heavily padded shoulders. [*Zoot,* rhyming formation based on SUIT.]

Zo·rach (zō′răk), **William.** 1887–1966. Lithuanian-born American sculptor.

zor·ille (zôr′ĭl, zŏr-) *n.* Also **zor·il.** An African mammal, *Ictonyx* *striatus,* resembling the skunk in appearance and defensive action. [French, from Spanish *zorrillo, zorrilla,* "small fox," from *zorro,* fox, from Old Spanish *zorrar†,* to drag.]

Zo·ro·as·ter (zōr'ō-ăs'tər). Also **Zar·a·thus·tra** (zăr'ə-thōōs'trə, zä'rä-thōōs'trä). Persian prophet of the sixth century B.C.; founder of Zoroastrianism. [Latin *Zōroastrēs,* from Greek, from Avestan *Zarathustra,* "owner of old camels" : *zara(n)t-,* old (see **ger-²** in Appendix*) + *ustra,* camel (see **wes-²** in Appendix*).]

Zo·ro·as·tri·an·ism (zōr'ō-ăs'trē-ən-ĭz'əm) *n.* The religious system founded in Persia by Zoroaster and set forth in the Zend-Avesta, teaching the worship of Ormazd in the context of a universal struggle between the forces of light and of darkness. Also called "Mazdaism." —**Zo'ro·as'tri·an** *adj. & n.*

Zor·ril·la y Mo·ral (thôr-rē'lyä ē mō-räl'), **José.** 1817–1893. Spanish poet and dramatist.

zos·ter (zŏs'tər) *n.* **1.** A belt or girdle worn by men in ancient Greece. **2.** *Pathology.* **Herpes zoster** *(see).* [Latin, from Greek *zōstēr,* girdle. See **yòs-** in Appendix.*]

Zou·ave (zōō-äv', swäv) *n.* **1.** A member of a French infantry unit, formerly composed of Algerian recruits, characterized by colorful oriental uniforms and precision drilling. **2.** A member of any group patterned after the French Zouaves; especially, a member of such a unit of the Union Army in the Civil War. [French, from *zwāwa,* Algerian tribal name.]

zounds (zoundz) *interj.* Also **swounds** (zwoundz, zoundz), **swouns** (zwounz, zounz). Used to express anger, surprise, or indignation. [Euphemism for *God's wounds.*]

zoy·si·a (zoi'zē-ə) *n.* Any of several creeping grasses of the genus *Zoysia,* native to Asia and Australia, and widely cultivated as a lawn grass. [New Latin *Zoysia;* after Karl von *Zois* (died 1800), German botanist.]

Zr The symbol for the element zirconium.

ZRH Airport code for Zurich, Switzerland.

Zsig·mon·dy (zhĭg'mŏn-dē), **Richard Adolf.** 1865–1929. Austrian-born German chemist; worked on colloids.

zuc·chet·to (zōō-kĕt'ō; *Italian* tsōōk-kĕt'tō) *n., pl.* **-tos.** *Roman Catholic Church.* A skullcap worn by clergymen, varying in color with the rank of the wearer. [Italian, incorrect diminutive of *zucca,* gourd, head, from Late Latin *cucutia,* gourd, probably from Latin *cucurbita,* GOURD.]

zuc·chi·ni (zōō-kē'nē; *Italian* tzōōk-kē'nē) *n., pl.* **zucchini.** A variety of squash having an elongated shape and a smooth, thin dark-green rind. [Italian, plural of *zuchino,* diminutive of *zucca,* gourd. See **zucchetto.**]

Zug·spit·ze (tsōōKH'shpĭt'sə). The highest mountain (9,727 feet) of West Germany and of the Bavarian Alps.

Zu·lu (zōō'lōō) *n., pl.* **Zulu** or **-lus. 1.** A member of a large Bantu nation of southeastern Africa, situated between Natal and Lourenço Marques. **2.** The Bantu language spoken by these people. —*adj.* Of or pertaining to the Zulus, their culture, or their language.

Zu·lu·land (zōō'lōō-lǎnd'). A former kingdom in southern Africa, now a district of Natal, Republic of South Africa.

Zun·gar·i·a. See **Dzungaria.**

Zu·ñi (zōō'nyē, -nē, sōō'-) *n., pl.* **Zuñi** or **-ñis. 1.** A member of a pueblo-dwelling tribe of North American Indians of western New Mexico. **2.** The language used by this tribe.

Zu·ñi·an (zōō'nyē-ən, sōōn'yē-ən) *n.* A distinct language family made up of Zuñi alone. —**Zu'ñi·an** *adj.*

Zu·rich (zōōr'ĭk). German **Zü·rich** (tsü'rĭKH). A city of Switzerland, in the northeast at the northern tip of the Lake of Zurich (35 square miles). Population, 444,000.

Zuy·der Zee (zī'dər zā', zē', zoi'dər). Also **Zui·der Zee.** A former marshy inlet of the North Sea in the northern coast of the Netherlands, now divided by a dike into the Ijsselmeer and the Waddenzee.

Zwick·au (tsvĭk'ou). A city of south-central East Germany, 40 miles south of Leipzig. Population, 129,000.

zwie·back (zwī'bǎk', -bäk', zwē'-, swī'-) *n.* A type of usually sweetened bread baked first as a loaf and later cut into slices and toasted. [German *Zwieback,* "twice-baked (bread)" : *zwie-,* twice, from Old High German *zwi-* (see **dwó** in Appendix*) + *backen,* to bake, from Old High German *bahhan, backan* (see **bhē-** in Appendix*).]

Zwing·li (tsvĭng'lē), **Ulrich** or **Huldreich.** 1484–1531. Swiss religious reformer.

Zwing·li·an (zwĭng'lē-ən, tsvĭng'-) *adj.* Of or pertaining to Zwingli or to his theological system, especially his doctrine that the physical body of Christ is not present in the Eucharist and that the ceremony is merely a symbolic commemoration of Christ's death. —*n.* A follower of Zwingli. —**Zwing'li·an·ism'** *n.* —**Zwing'li·an·ist** *n.*

zwit·ter·i·on (tsvĭt'ər-ī'ən) *n. Physics.* An ion carrying both a positive and a negative charge, thus forming an electrically neutral molecule. [German *Zwitterion,* "mongrel ion" : *Zwitter,* mongrel, hybrid, from Old High German *zwitar(a)n,* from *zwi-,* twice (see **dwó** in Appendix*) + ION.] —**zwit'ter·i·on'ic** (-ī-ŏn'ĭk) *adj.*

Zwol·le (zvŏl'ə). The capital of Overijssel, the Netherlands, in the northwestern part of the province. Population, 58,000.

Zwor·y·kin (zwôr'ə-kĭn), **Vladimir Kosma.** Born 1889. Russian-born American physicist; developed first practical television camera.

zyg·a·poph·y·sis (zĭg'ə-pŏf'ə-sĭs, zī'gə-) *n., pl.* **-ses** (-sēz'). *Anatomy.* One of two usually paired processes of a vertebra that articulate with corresponding parts of adjacent vertebrae. [ZYG(O)- + APOPHYSIS.]

zygo-, zyg-. Indicates: **1.** Yoke or pair; for example, **zygodactyl, zygapophysis. 2.** Union or fusion; for example, **zygospore, zygomorphic.** [New Latin, from Greek *zugon,* yoke. See **yeug-** in Appendix.*]

zy·go·dac·tyl (zī'gō-dǎk'tĭl) *adj.* Having two toes projecting forward and two projecting backward, as certain birds. —*n.* A zygodactyl bird. [ZYGO- + DACTYL.]

zy·go·ma (zī-gō'mə) *n., pl.* **-mata** (-mə-tə) or **-mas. 1.** The zygomatic bone. **2.** The zygomatic arch. **3.** The zygomatic process. [New Latin, from Greek *zugōma,* bolt, bar, yoke, from *zugoun,* to yoke, connect. See **yeug-** in Appendix.*] —**zy'go·mat'ic** (zī'gə-mǎt'ĭk) *adj.*

zygomatic arch. The bony arch in vertebrates that extends along the side or front of the skull beneath the orbit.

zygomatic bone. A small quadrangular bone in vertebrates on the side of the face below the eye, forming, in mammals, part of the orbit and part of the zygomatic arch; the malar. Also called "cheekbone."

zygomatic process. Any of the three processes that articulate to make up the zygomatic arch.

zy·go·mor·phic (zī'gō-môr'fĭk) *adj.* Also **zy·go·mor·phous** (-fəs). Bilaterally symmetrical so as to be capable of being symmetrically divided only along a single longitudinal plane. Said of organisms or parts. [ZYGO- + -MORPHIC.] —**zy'go·mor'phism'** *n.*

zy·go·sis (zī-gō'sĭs) *n., pl.* **-ses** (-sēz'). The union of gametes to form a zygote; conjugation. [ZYG(O)- + -OSIS.]

zy·go·spore (zī'gō-spôr', -spōr') *n.* A thick-walled resting spore formed by conjugation of similar gametes, as in algae or fungi.

zy·gote (zī'gōt') *n.* **1.** The cell formed by the union of two gametes. **2.** The organism that develops from such a cell as characterized by its genetic constitution and subsequent development. [Greek *zugōtos,* joined, yoked, from *zugoun,* to join, to yoke. See **zygoma.**] —**zy·got'ic** (zī-gŏt'ĭk) *adj.* —**zy·got'i·cal·ly** *adv.*

–zygous. Indicates a certain zygotic constitution; for example, **heterozygous.** [Greek *-zugos,* yoked, from *zugon,* yoke. See **yeug-** in Appendix.*]

zy·mase (zī'mās', -māz') *n.* The enzyme complex found in yeast, bacteria, and higher plants and animals that acts in glycolysis. [ZYM(O)- + -ASE.]

–zyme. Indicates an enzyme; for example, **lysozyme.** [From Greek *zumē,* leaven. See **yeu-¹** in Appendix.*]

zymo-, zym-. Indicates fermentation or relation to fermentation; for example, **zymolysis, zymase.** [New Latin, from Greek *zumē,* leaven. See **yeu-¹** in Appendix.*]

zy·mo·gen (zī'mə-jən) *n.* The inactive protein precursor of an enzyme. [ZYMO- + -GEN.]

zy·mo·gen·ic (zī'mə-jĕn'ĭk) *adj.* Also **zy·mog·e·nous** (zī-mŏj'ə-nəs). **1.** Of or pertaining to a zymogen. **2.** Capable of causing fermentation. **3.** Enzyme-producing.

zy·mol·o·gy (zī-mŏl'ə-jē) *n.* The chemistry of fermentation. [New Latin *zymologia* : ZYMO- + -LOGY.] —**zy'mo·log'ic** (-mə-lŏj'ĭk), **zy'mo·log'ic·al** *adj.* —**zy·mol'o·gist** *n.*

zy·mol·y·sis (zī-mŏl'ə-sĭs) *n.* Fermentation. [ZYMO- + -LYSIS.] —**zy'mo·lyt'ic** (-mə-lĭt'ĭk) *adj.*

zy·mo·plas·tic (zī'mə-plǎs'tĭk) *adj.* Participating in enzyme production. [ZYMO- + -PLASTIC.]

zy·mo·scope (zī'mə-skōp') *n.* An instrument used to determine fermentation efficiency by measurement of carbon dioxide produced. [ZYMO- + -SCOPE.]

zy·mo·sis (zī-mō'sĭs) *n.* **1.** Fermentation. **2.** *Medicine.* The process of infection. [New Latin, from Greek *zumōsis,* fermentation, from *zumoun,* to leaven, ferment, from *zumē,* leaven. See **zymo-.**] —**zy·mot'ic** (-mŏt'ĭk) *adj.* —**zy·mot'i·cal·ly** *adv.*

zy·mur·gy (zī'mûr-jē) *n.* The manufacturing chemistry of fermentation processes in brewing. [ZYM(O)- + -URGY.]

zyz·zy·va (zĭz'ə-və) *n.* Any of various tropical American weevils of the genus *Zyzzyva,* often destructive to plants. [New Latin *Zyzzyva†.*]

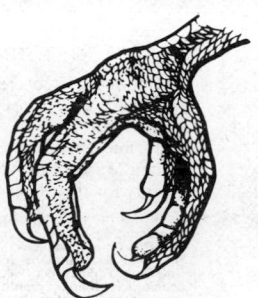

zygodactyl
Zygodactyl foot of a parrot

zucchini

zodiac

Picture Credits

The following list of credits includes the names of many of the organizations and individuals who helped secure illustrations for this Dictionary. The editors wish to thank all of them—as well as others not specifically mentioned—for their invaluable assistance. Special acknowledgment is due the staffs of The Metropolitan Museum of Art and of the Picture Collection of The New York Public Library for their help. The credits are arranged alphabetically by entry word, which is printed in boldface type. In those cases where two or more illustrations are credited for the same entry word, dashes are used to separate them sequentially from left to right and/or top to bottom. The abbreviations NAS and NYPL stand for, respectively, the National Audubon Society and The New York Public Library. Unless we have indicated to the contrary, all maps were supplied by Francis & Shaw, Inc.

aardvark Ernest Walker from NAS; **abaca** Library of the New York Botanical Gardens; **abacus** From the Collection of the IBM Corp.—After Nicholson; **abalone** John H. Gerard from NAS; **Abraham**[2] Courtesy of Parke-Bernet Galleries; **Abyssinian cat** Walter Chandoha; **acacia** T.H. Everett; **acanthus** (Corinthian capital) Epidaurus Museum; **accommodation ladder** Garelick Manufacturing Co.; **accordion** M. Hohner, Inc.; **ace** U.S. Playing Card Co.; **achene** Lynwood Chace from NAS; **Achilles** Vatican Museum, Photo Alinari; **acorn** John H. Gerard from NAS; **Acropolis** Photo Hirmer; **Actaeon** Museo Nazionale, Palermo, Photo Alinari; **Adam**[3] Copyright Country Life; **John Adams** U.S. Bureau of Engraving; **John Quincy Adams** Courtesy of the New-York Historical Society, New York City; **adjacent angle** Carl Bass; **adobe** Collection of Alfred L. Bush; **Adonis**[1] National Gallery of Art, Washington, D.C., Widener Collection; **Cyrille Adoula** Pictorial Parade; **adz** Jean Erdoes; **Aeolian harp** The Metropolitan Museum of Art, Crosby Brown Collection of Musical Instruments, 1889; **Aeolus** Photo Alinari; **aerialist** State Historical Society, Wisconsin; **aerosol bomb** Jean Erdoes; **Aesculapius, Aesop** Vatican Museum, Photo Anderson; **Afghan hound** Evelyn M. Shafer; **African violet** Roche; **Aga Khan III** United Press International Photo; **Agamemnon** Photo Giraudon; **agaric** Alexander H. Smith, University of Michigan Press; **agave** Josef Muench; **Agni** Service Photographique, Musée Guimet; **Agnus Dei** Archives Photographiques; **agrimony** Ethel H. Hausman; **aigrette** Photo from NAS; **ailanthus** Courtesy of The American Museum of Natural History—Annan Photo Features; **aircraft carrier** Official U.S. Navy Photograph; **Airedale** Evelyn M. Shafer; **airship** Nebraska State Historical Society; **Ajax**[1] Photo Alinari; **Alaric** Kunsthistorishes Museum, Vienna; **the Alamo** Hampshire Engraving Corp.; **albatross** Annan (E.F. Pollock)—M.F. Soper from NAS; **Alexander the Great** Museo Nazionale, Naples, Photo Alinari; **alfalfa** Ethel H. Hausman; **Ali Baba** Brown Brothers; **allegory** New York State Historical Association; **alligator** Allan D. Cruickshank from NAS; **alluvial fan** Courtesy of The American Museum of Natural History; **aloe** John H. Gerard from NAS; **alpenhorn** Gidal from Monkmeyer Press; **alternate** Ethel H. Hausman; **alternate angle** Carl Bass; **althorn** The Metropolitan Museum of Art, Crosby Brown Collection of Musical Instruments, 1889; **amaryllis** Roche; **Amazon**[1] The Metropolitan Museum of Art, Rogers Fund, 1906; **ambo** Photo Anderson; **ambulance** Scully-Walton, Inc.; **Amenhotep III** Courtesy of The Brooklyn Museum; **Jeffery Amherst** In the Collection of Amherst College; **amoeba** Walter Dawn; **André Marie Ampère** Bibliothèque Nationale; **amphibian** AVCO, Lycoming Division; **amphora** (with stand) The Metropolitan Museum of Art, Rogers Fund, 1906; **amulet** Photograph by Harry Burton, The Metropolitan Museum of Art—Vikram Dalal, Scientific Photographers—Picture from the Photographic Archive of the Jewish Theological Seminary of America, New York, Frank J. Darmstaedter; **Roald Amundsen** Library of Congress; **anaconda** Dade W. Thornton from NAS; **anchor** Baldt Anchor, Chain & Forge Div. of Universal Marion Corp.; **Marian Anderson** Philippe Halsman; **andiron** Princeton University Library; **Andromeda**[2] George Lindbloom; **anechoic** Bell Telephone Laboratories; **anemometer** Bendix Aviation Corp.; **anemone** Library of the New York Botanical Gardens; **angel** The Metropolitan Museum of Art; **angle**[2] Carl Bass; **animated cartoon** "How to Make Animated Cartoons" by Nat Falk; **Anne**[2] Blenheim Library, Photograph by Edwin Smith; **annual ring** Cal Sacks; **annulet** *The Doric Temple,* by Elizabeth Ayrton, Thames and Hudson Publishing Co.; **anopheles** N.E. Beck Jr. from NAS; **anteater** Annan Photo Features; **antenna** Walter Dawn from NAS—Ray Glover from NAS; **anthemion** Photo Giraudon; **anthurium** Hawaii Visitors Bureau Photo; **anticline** From *Principles of Geology,* 2nd Edition, by James Gilluly, A.C. Waters, and A.O. Woodford, W.H. Freeman and Co., Copyright © 1951; **Anubis** The Book of the Dead, British Museum; **anvil** "Steelways," Published by the American Iron and Steel Institute; **aorta** Neil Hardy; **Aphrodite** Louvre (Photo Courtesy of Shell, Ltd.); **Apis** *Egyptian Mythology,* © 1965 Paul Hamlyn Ltd., London; **Apollo** Vatican Museum, Photo Anderson; **apostle** Staatsbibliothek, Munich, Codex Monacensis Lat. 23338; **Appian Way** E.N.I.T.; **apple** Grant Heilman Photography; **appliqué** Shelburne Museum, Inc., Photographer Einars J. Mengis; **apron** National Park Service Photo by Cecil W. Stoughton; **apse** French Government Tourist Bureau—Bibliothèque Nationale; **aquaplane** Florida Cypress Gardens, Inc.; **Aquarius** George Lindbloom; **aqueduct** Spanish National Tourist Office; **Aquila** George Lindbloom; **Saint Thomas Aquinas** Vatican, Chapel of Nicholas V, Photo Alinari; **arcade** The Metropolitan Museum of Art, The Cloisters Collection; **arch**[1] The Metropolitan Museum of Art, The Cloisters Collection, Purchase 1932 and 1940; **archaeopteryx** Courtesy of The American Museum of Natural History; **archaic smile** Acropolis Museum; **archerfish** *Animate Creation,* by John George Wood, New York, Hess 1885; **architrave** After Nicholson; **arethusa** *Wild Flowers of America,* New York, Buck 1894; **argali** Matthew Kalmenoff; **argus pheasant** New York Zoological Society Photo; **Aries** George Lindbloom; **aril** Ward's Natural Science Establishment, Inc., W.H. Hodge, Photographer; **Aristophanes** Museo Nazionale, Naples; **armadillo** Leonard Lee Rue from NAS; **armillary sphere** Barsotti; **armoire** Cincinnati Art Museum; **armor** (Japanese) The Metropolitan Museum of Art, Rogers Fund, 1904; **Louis Armstrong** Culver Pictures, Inc.; **arrow arum, arrowhead** Ethel H. Hausman; **artesian well** Cal Sacks; **Artemis** Photo Giraudon; **Chester A. Arthur** U.S. Bureau of Engraving; **artichoke** Treat Davidson from NAS; **the Ascension** Bayerishes Staatsmuseum, Munich; **ash**[2] Matthew Kalmenoff; **Ashurbanipal** British Museum, London (Werner Forman); **aspergill** Herman J. Wolf Co., Inc.—Annan Photo Features; **aspidistra** John H. Gerard from NAS; **assembly line** General Electric Co.; **Astarte** O.E. Nelson, Photographer, Sculptura, Inc.; **astrolabe** The Royal Scottish Museum, Edinburgh; **asymptote** Carl Bass; **Atahualpa** Gilcrease Institute; **Atalanta** E.J. Poynter; **Athena** British Museum (Leonard Von Matt); **Atlas**[1] Museo Nazionale, Naples; **atoll** From *Principles of Geology,* 3rd Edition, by James Gilluly, A.C. Waters, and A.O. Woodford, W.H. Freeman & Co., Copyright © 1968; **atrium** Photo Alinari; **Attis** Photo Giraudon; **auctioneer** Princeton University Library; **W.H. Auden** Culver Pictures, Inc., **John James Audubon** Library of Congress; **auger** Stanley Tools; **Augustus**[2] Leonard Von Matt; **Auriga** George Lindbloom; **aurochs** Courtesy of The American Museum of Natural History; **Jane Austen** National Portrait Gallery, London; **autograph** Courtesy Charles Hamilton, Autographs; **avocado** Roche; **avocet** Annan Photo Features; **awl** Stanley Tools; **ax** Fayette R. Plumb, Inc., **axolotl** Arthur W. Ambler from NAS; **aye-aye** Zoological Society of London; **Aztec Ruins National Monument** Aztec Ruins Monument, New Mexico.

babirusa Zoological Society of London; **baboon** Annan Photo Features; **Bacchus** The Metropolitan Museum of Art, Bequest of George Blumenthal, 1941; **backgammon** Prints Division, NYPL; **bacteria** Prepared from materials in Frobisher's *Fundamentals of Microbiology,* 8th Edition, W.B. Saunders Co., Philadelphia, Pa., 1968; **badger** Matthew Kalmenoff; **bagworm** Walter S. Chansler from NAS; **balalaika** The Metropolitan Museum of Art, Gift of Mr. Ustin Smolensky, 1948; **balance** John E. Thierman; **bald cypress** Grant Heilman Photography; **bald eagle** Philip Gendreau from NAS; **ball-and-socket joint** Richard Glassman, **ballistic missile** U.S. Air Force Photo; **ball-peen hammer** Stanley Tools; **Baltimore oriole** Henry C. Johnson from NAS; **baneberry** Roche; **banjo clock** American Clock and Watch Museum, Inc., Bristol, Conn.; **banyan** Annan Photo Features; **barge** Philip Gendreau; **bark**[2] Jane Latta; **bark**[3], **barkentine** Reproduced by permission from *Sailing and Small Craft Down the Ages,* copyrighted 1940 by the U.S. Naval Institute, Annapolis, Maryland; **barometer** From *McGraw-Hill Encyclopedia of Science and Technology,* Vol. 2, Copyright © 1960, Used by permission of McGraw-Hill Book Company; **barracuda** R.C. Hermes from NAS; **bartizan** Philip Gendreau; **Béla Bartók** Culver Pictures, Inc.; **bascule** S & G from Pictorial Parade; **basenji** Evelyn M. Shafer; **basketball** Columbia University; **basset hound** Evelyn M. Shafer; **bassoon** Elsa Posell; **bat**[2] Matthew Kalmenoff; **bathysphere** New York Zoological Society Photo; **battle-ax** Bibliothèque Municipale, Angers; **battlement** Philip Gendreau; **bayonet** U.S. Army Photograph; **bay window** *Art Journal,* 1877; **beagle** Evelyn M. Shafer; **beaker** Corning Glass Works; **Aubrey Beardsley** Prints Division, NYPL; **bearskin** The British Travel Association; **the Beatles** London Daily Express; **beaver**[1] A.A. Francesconi from NAS; **Thomas à Becket** Walters Art Gallery, Baltimore; **bedbug** U.S. Department of Agriculture Photo; **Bedlington terrier** Don Bowden; **beef** Jean Erdoes; **beekeeper** Hal H. Harrison from NAS; **belfry** Culver Pictures, Inc.; **belladonna** Matthew Kalmenoff; **Bellerophon** The Metropolitan Museum of Art, Huntley Bequest, 1958; **bellows** Ronald Bowen; **bench mark** Fundamental Photographs; **David Ben-Gurion** United Nations; **bentwood** Collection, The Museum of Modern Art, New York; **benzene ring** John Keaveny; **beret** Photo Sabine Weiss from Rapho Guillumette Pictures; **Giovanni Bernini** Photo Anderson; **berth** Union Pacific Railroad Co.; **Bessemer converter** John Keaveny; **Mary McLeod Bethune** N.Y. Amsterdam News; **Bevatron** University of California Lawrence Radiation Laboratory, Berkeley; **bevel gear** Carl Bass; **bezant** American Numismatic Society—Photo by Böhm, Venice; **bicycle** Bicycle Institute of America, Inc.; **Big Ben** The British Travel Association; **bighorn** Annan Photo Features; **binnacle** *Primer of Navigation,* 3rd Edition, by George Mixter, D. Van Nostrand Co., Inc.; **binoculars** Richard Glassman; **biplane** National Archives, Photographic Records Office; **bird of paradise** Matthew Kalmenoff; **bird-of-paradise flower** Roche; **bit**[2] Stanley Tools; **bittern**[1] Courtesy of the New-York Historical Society, New York City; **bitterroot** Ernst Peterson; **bittersweet** Roche; **blackberry** Sweeney, Krist & Dimm; **black-eyed Susan** Arthur W. Ambler from NAS; **black grouse** Annan Photo Features; **black widow** Alfred Renfro from NAS; **blast furnace** United States Steel Corp.; **bleeding-heart** Roche; **Captain Bligh** National Portrait Gallery, London; **blinders** Philip Gendreau; **block** Ronald Bowen; **blockhouse** John Keaveny; **bloodhound** Evelyn M. Shafer; **bloodroot** "Common Poisonous Plants," by John M. Kingsbury, Cornell Extension Bulletin 538; **bloomer**[2] Library of Congress; **blue-eyed grass** Walter Dawn; **blue jay** Karl H. Maslowski from NAS; **bluff**[2] U.S. Coast Guard Photo; **boar** Azaria Alon from NAS; **boatbill** Arthur W. Ambler from NAS; **bobolink** Courtesy of the New-York Historical Society, New York City; **bobsled** United Press International Photo; **bobwhite** Jackson Abbott; **Boccaccio** Biblioteca Nazionale, Florence; **bola** *Centaurs of Many Lands* by Edward L. Tinker, Humanities Research Center, University of Texas, drawing by Albert Guiraldez; **bolection** *Concise Encyclopedia of Architecture,* by Martin Briggs, E. P. Dutton & Co., N.Y.; **bolt**[1] Russell, Burdsall & Ward Bolt and Nut Co.; **bomb** Richard Glassman; **boneset** Matthew Kalmenoff; **bongo drums** Charles Perry Weimer; **bonnet** National Gallery of Art, Index of American Design; **bonsai** Paul E. Genereux; **Boötes** George Lindbloom; **Edwin Thomas Booth** Culver Pictures, Inc.; **John Wilkes Booth** Collection of Mrs. Frank S. Coleman; **borzoi** Evelyn M. Shafer; **Boston rocker** Shelburne Museum, Inc., Photographer, Einars J. Mengis; **Boston terrier** Don Bowden; **bottlenosed dolphin** Allan D. Cruickshank from NAS; **bouncing Bet** "Common Poisonous Plants," by John M. Kingsbury, Cornell Extension Bulletin 538; **Bouvier des Flandres** Don Bowden; **bowerbird** John Warham, Christ Church, New Zealand; **bowfin** Gene Wolfsheimer from NAS; **bowline** From *The Ashley Book of Knots,* by Clifford W. Ashley, Copyright 1944 by Clifford W. Ashley, Reprinted by permission of Doubleday & Co., Inc.; **boxer**[3] Evelyn M. Shafer; **box kite** *Buch des Fluges,* Hermann Hoernes, Wien, G. Szelinski, 1911–12; **box turtle** John H. Gerard from NAS; **bracelet** The Metropolitan Museum of Art, Harris Brisbane Dick Fund, 1957; **bracket fungus** Hugh Spencer from NAS; **Brahma**[1] The Metropolitan Museum of Art, Eggleston Fund, 1927; **brain** Neil Hardy; **brake**[1] American Brake Shoe Company; **branding iron** Irwin E. Smith Photograph, Library of Congress; **Brazil nut** Library of the New York Botanical Gardens; **breadfruit** T.H. Everett; **breakwater, breeches buoy** U.S. Coast Guard Photos; **brewery** Miller Brewing Co.; **Leonid Brezhnev** Pictorial Parade; **bridge**[1] Airviews Ltd.; **brig**[1], **brigantine** Reproduced by permission from *Sailing and Small Craft Down the Ages,* copyrighted 1940 by the U.S. Naval Institute, Annapolis, Maryland; **broadbill** Karl Kenyon from NAS; **broadsword** New York Public Library; **brocade** The Metropolitan Museum of Art, Rogers Fund, 1920; **bronchia** Neil Hardy; **brontosaur** Matthew Kalmenoff; **brooch** The Metropolitan Museum of Art, Bequest of Edward C. Moore, 1891; **John Brown** Boston Atheneum; **Anton Bruckner** Culver Pictures, Inc.; **Brussels sprouts** Burpee Seeds; **bubble chamber** University of California Lawrence Radiation Laboratory, Berkeley; **James Buchanan** Brown Brothers; **bucksaw** Pennsylvania Saw Corp.; **budgerigar** Jeanne White from NAS; **buffalo** P.W. Hay from NAS; **Bukhara rug** The Metropolitan Museum of Art, Rogers Fund, Purchase 1906; **bulldog** Evelyn M. Shafer; **bullfinch** *Birds of Britain,* by J. Lewis Bonhote, London, Adam & Charles Black, 1907; **bullroarer** Charles C. Colley, Arizona Pioneers' Historical Society; **bull terrier** Evelyn M. Shafer; **bumblebee** Treat Davidson from NAS; **Ralph Bunche** United Nations; **Bunsen burner** Annan Photo Features; **Luther Burbank** Ken Studio; **burette** Kimble Products, Owens-Illinois; **burnoose** Brassai, from Rapho Guillumette Pictures; **Ambrose Burnside** Lloyd Ostendorf Collection; **busby** Royal Artillery Archives; **buskin** Instituto Archeologico Germanico; **bustard** Animated Museum—Photo from NAS; **bustle**[2] The Metropolitan Museum of Art, Harris Brisbane Dick Fund, 1932; **butterfly fish** *Fishes of the Bahamas and Adjacent Tropical Waters,* by James E. Böhlke and Charles C.G. Chaplin, illustrated by Steven P. Gigliotti and Fritz Janschka, published for the Academy of Natural Sciences of Philadelphia by Livingston Publishing Company, Wynnewood, Pa., 1968; **buttonhole stitch** Singer Company; **Richard Byrd** U.S. Navy Photograph.

cabbage Lewis Watson from Monkmeyer Press; **cabriole** John Brown House, Rhode Island Historical Society; **cacao** Matthew Kalmenoff; **cacomistle** Woodrow Goodpaster from NAS; **caduceus** Museo Nazionale, Florence, Photo Alinari; **Julius Caesar** Photo Alinari; **caftan** Art and Architecture Division, NYPL; **Cairn terrier** Don Bowden; **calceolaria** Burpee Seeds; **calculator** SCM Corporation; **California quail** B. Max Thompson from NAS; **caliper** Courtesy of the L.S. Starrett Co.; **calla** Josef Muench; **calumet** Library of Congress; **camellia** Roche; **camera** Fundamental Photographs; **campanile** Italian Government Travel Office; **can**[2] Can Manufacturers Institute; **Canada goose** Annan Photo Features; **Cancer** George Lindbloom; **candelabrum** Nordenfjeldske Kunstindustrimuseum, Trondheim; **candlestick** The Metropolitan Museum of Art, Bequest of A.T. Clearwater, 1933; **Canis Major, Canis Minor** George Lindbloom; **Canopic** *Egyptian Mythology,* © 1965 Paul Hamlyn Ltd., London; **cantaloupe** Burpee Seeds; **cantilever** José Antonio Torroja; **canvasback** Courtesy of the New-York Historical Society, New York City; **caparison** Universitatsbibliothek, Heidelberg; **capercaillie** Annan Photo Features; **Capricornus** George Lindbloom; **capsule** Roche; **capybara** Zoological Society of London; **caracal** Franklin Williamson from NAS; **caracara** From *Mexican Birds,* by George Miksch Sutton, Copyright 1951 by the University of Oklahoma Press; **caravel** Courtesy, The Mariners Museum, Newport News, Va.; **carburetor** Richard Glassman; **cardioid** Carl Bass; **caribou** Annan Photo Features; **caricature** Brown Brothers—Culver Pictures, Inc.; **carillon** Whitechapel Bell Foundry Ltd.; **carob** Matthew Kalmenoff; **carpal** Neil Hardy; **cartouche** *Ornamentale Vorlageblätter des 15. bis 18. Jahrhunderts,* by Rudolf Berliner, Klinkhardt & Biermann, Berlin, 1924–26; **cartridge** Remington Arms Co., Inc.; **casement** *Stagecraft and Scene Design,* by H.P. Philippi, Houghton Mifflin Co.; **cashew** Matthew Kalmenoff; **casket** Musée des Arts Décoratifs, Paris; **Cassiopeia** George Lindbloom; **castle** Aerofilms, Ltd.—Consulate General of Japan, N.Y.; **catalpa** Grant Heilman Photography—Annan Photo Features; **catamaran** Duncan Sutphen, Inc.; **catapult** Cal Sacks; **catfish** John H. Gerard from NAS; **cathedral** Archives Photographiques; **Catherine the Great** A La Vieille Russie, New York; **cathode-ray tube** Jean Erdoes; **cat's cradle** Gabriel Gély, Ottawa; **cattail** Roche; **cauliflower** U.S. Department of Agriculture Photo; **C clef** Franco Colombo Publications, New York; **cecropia moth** Gaston LePage from NAS; **celestial sphere** Francis & Shaw, Inc.; **cell** Neil Hardy; **Celtic cross** Photo Courtesy Irish Tourist Board; **censer** Musée de Cluny, Paris; **Centaurus** George Lindbloom; **century plant** Josef Muench; **Cepheus**[2] George Lindbloom; **cerebellum, cerebral cortex** Neil Hardy; **cestus**[2] Culver Pictures, Inc.; **Cetus** George Lindbloom; **Cézanne** The Phillips Collection, Washington; **chalice** The Metropolitan Museum of Art, The Cloisters Collection, Purchase, 1947; **chamois** Courtesy of The American Museum of Natural History; **Samuel de Champlain** Public Archives of Canada; **chandelier** The Metropolitan Museum of Art, Gift of James Walter Carter, 1963; **chanterelle** Alexander H. Smith, University of Michigan Press; **Charlie Chaplin** Culver Pictures, Inc.; **John Chapman** The Western Reserve Historical Society, Cleveland; **charkha** Musée Guimet; **Charon** National Museum, Athens, Photo Alison Frantz; **chase**[2] The Mead Corporation; **chastity belt** Musée Vivenel, Compiègne; **chateau** Cliché, Photothèque Française; **Chaucer** Henry Huntingdon Library, Ellesmere Chaucer, Facsimile, NYPL; **cheetah** *Drawing at the Zoo,* by Raymond Sheppard, Studio Publications, 1949; **chef** Oakland Art Museum, California, George and Lydia Clark Collection; **Chekhov** Library of Congress; **Cheshire cat** Prints Division, NYPL; **chestnut** Thomas Leigh Wood from NAS; **chestnut oak** Jack Dermid from NAS; **chiaroscuro** Louvre, Photo Giraudon; **chignon** Culver Pictures, Inc.; **Chimera** Museum of Archaeology, Florence; **chimpanzee** San Diego Zoo Photo; **chinchilla** New York Zoological Society Photo; **chipmunk** Allan D. Cruickshank from NAS; **Chippendale** Victoria and Albert Museum; **chokecherry** Paul E. Genereux—Alvin Staffan from NAS; **cholla** Josef Muench; **chopsticks** Japanese Government Railways; **chorus girl** Culver Pictures, Inc.; **chow**[1] Evelyn M. Shafer; **Christmas rose** "Common Poisonous Plants," by John M. Kingsbury, Cornell Extension Bulletin 538; **Henri Christophe** Bibliothèque Nationale; **chromosome** Oak Ridge National Laboratory; **chrysalis** (mourning cloak, monarch) Matthew Kalmenoff; **chrysanthemum** Roche; **chuck**[2] Jacobs Manufacturing Co.; **chukar** Karl H. Maslowski from NAS; **Winston Churchill** © Karsh, Ottawa; **cicada** Dade Thornton from NAS: **Circe** Louvre, Photo Giraudon; **circle** Carl Bass; **circular saw** Wen Products, Inc.; **civet** Matthew Kalmenoff; **clamp, clapboard** Jane Latta; **clarinet** Courtesy of Benny Goodman; **clavichord** Worcester Art Museum; **clavicle** Neil Hardy; **cleaver** Clyde Cutlery Corp.; **clerestory** Sturgis, *Dictionary of Architecture;* **Grover Cleveland** Library of Congress; **cliff swallow** Allan D. Cruickshank from NAS; **climbing irons** Reprinted from *Dictionary of Americanisms on Historical Principles,* by Mitford M. Mathews, by permission of The University of Chicago Press; **climbing perch** Matthew Kalmenoff; **clinometer** Keuffel & Esser Co.; **clipper** Peabody Museum of Salem; **clitellum** John H. Gerard from NAS; **cloisonné** Louvre, Photo Giraudon; **cloister** Photo Anderson; **cloverleaf** Philip Gendreau; **clown** Culver Pictures, Inc.; **club moss** Hugh Spencer from NAS; **Clumber spaniel** Annan Photo Features; **clutch**[1] Ford Motor Co.; **Clydesdale** Culver Pictures, Inc.; **coati** Leonard Lee Rue from NAS; **coaxial cable** Cal Sacks; **Cochin**[2] Matthew Kalmenoff; **cockatiel** Robert C. Hermes from NAS; **cockatoo** Alfred Baily from NAS; **cockleshell** John H. Gerard from NAS; **coconut palm** H.W. Kitchen from NAS; **codpiece** Orvieto Cathedral, Photo Alinari; **coelacanth** Courtesy of The American Museum of Natural History; **coffer** Monkmeyer Press; **cog railway** Philip Gendreau; **cold chisel** Mueller; **collar** (19th century) The Metropolitan Museum of Art, Bequest of Mrs. Maria P. James, 1911; **collie** Annan Photo Features; **colonnade** Hirmer; **Colosseum** Leonard Von Matt; **Samuel Colt** The Bettmann Archive; **columbine** Library of the New York Botanical Gardens—The Pierpont Morgan Library, The Guennol Collection; **column** The Metropolitan Museum of Art, The Cloisters Collection; **comb** (tortoiseshell) The Metropolitan Museum of Art, Gift of Emily Crane Chadbourne, 1952; **comet** Yerkes Observatory Photograph; **comic strip** © 1957 United Feature Syndicate; **commode** The Metropolitan Museum of Art, The Sylmaris Collection, Gift of George Coe Graves, 1931; **Commodus** Museo dei Conservatori, Rome, Photo Alinari; **compact**[1] Annan Photo Features; **compass** Jean Erdoes; **compass card** E.S. Ritchie & Sons, Inc.; **component** Carl Bass; **composing stick** Rand McNally & Co.; **composite** Matthew Kalmenoff; **composite order** The Metropolitan Museum of Art, Fletcher Fund, 1926; **compote** The Metropolitan Museum of Art, Rogers Fund, 1940; **compound eye** Stephen Dalton from NAS; **Anthony Comstock** Brown Brothers; **concave** Carl Bass; **concertina** Annan Photo Features; **conch** Courtesy of The American Museum of Natural History; **concrete mixer** Oshkosh Truck Corp.; **condor** Carl B. Koford from NAS; **cone** Carl Bass—John H. Gerard from NAS—Annan Photo Features; **Conestoga wagon** Reprinted from *Dictionary of Americanisms on Historical Principles,* by Mitford M. Mathews, by permission of The University of Chicago Press; **conger** Matthew Kalmenoff; **conic section** Carl Bass; **conning tower** Philip Gendreau; **Joseph Conrad** Doubleday & Co., Inc.; **conservatory** Paul E. Genereux; **Constitution** Culver Pictures, Inc.; **contortionist** Archiv Lauterbach; **contour map** U.S. Geological Survey; **control tower** Pictorial Parade; **conversation piece** Collection of the Marquess of Cholmondeley; **convex** Carl Bass; **conveyer** Annan Photo Features; **Calvin Coolidge** Library of Congress; **coot** Allan D. Cruickshank from NAS; **cope**[2] Church House, London; **copperhead** John H. Gerard from NAS; **coral snake** Jack Dermid from NAS; **corbel** Bibliothèque Nationale; **corbie-step** Princeton University Library; **cordate** Roche; **Corinthian order** After Nicholson; **cormorant** Arthur W. Ambler from NAS; **corn**[1] Grant Heilman Photography; **cornice** After Nicholson; **coronet** By permission of Ede and Ravenscroft Ltd., London; **corselet** The Metropolitan Museum of Art, Gift of William H. Riggs, 1913; **Hernando Cortéz** Biblioteca Nacional, Madrid; **corvette** Culver Pictures, Inc.; **cot**[1] The Telescope Folding Furniture Co., Inc.; **cotter pin** John Keaveny; **cotton** Watson from Monkmeyer Press; **cotton gin** Philip Gendreau; **cotyledon** Matthew Kalmenoff; **coupé** The Metropolitan Museum of Art, Gift of William Brewester, 1931; **Gustave Courbet** Musée Fabre, Montpellier, Photo Giraudon; **cowbane** Matthew Kalmenoff; **cowboy** *The Charles M. Russell Book,* by Harold McCracken; **cowry, coyote** Courtesy of The American Museum of Natural History; **crab**[1] Matthew Kalmenoff; **cradle** Princeton University Library; **crampon** Ronald Bowen; **cran-**

berry Matthew Kalmenoff; **crane** Arthur W. Ambler from NAS—Bucyrus-Erie Co.; **crankshaft** Ford Motor Co.; **crash helmet** Pictorial Parade; **crater** California Institute of Technology; **crazy quilt** Shelburne Museum, Inc., Photographer Einars J. Mengis; **creamer** The Metropolitan Museum of Art, Bequest of A.T. Clearwater, 1933; **crèche** Bavarian National Museum, Munich; **crenate** Matthew Kalmenoff; **crescent** R.C. Dickinson; **crewel** National Gallery of Art, Index of American Design; **cricket[1]** Hugh Spencer from NAS; **cricket[2]** G.R. Roberts, New Zealand; **crocodile** Annan Photo Features; **crocodile bird** Arthur W. Ambler from NAS; **crocus** Roche; **crosier** Stiftsammlungen, Klosternenberg; **crossbow** British Museum; **crosshatch** Prints Division, NYPL; **cross vault** Sturgis, *Dictionary of Architecture;* **crow's-nest** Philip Gendreau; **crucifix** Museo di Santa Croce, Photo Alinari; **George Cruikshank** British Museum—Prints Division, NYPL; **crystal** Courtesy of The American Museum of Natural History; **cube** Carl Bass; **cuckoopint** Matthew Kalmenoff; **cucumber** Roche; **cultivator** Jane Latta; **cumin** American Spice Trade Association; **cuneate** Matthew Kalmenoff; **cuneiform** Louvre; **Cupid** Museo Nazionale, Naples, Photo Alinari; **cupola** Sturgis, *Dictionary of Architecture;* **cupping** British Museum; **cup plant** Roche; **Marie Curie** Wide World Photos; **curlew** Jackson M. Abbott; **currant** Matthew Kalmenoff; **currency** (coins) American Numismatic Society, George Resch, photographer; **curule** Photographic Archives, Vatican; **cusk, custard apple** Matthew Kalmenoff; **cutlass** Collection of Hamilton Cochran; **cutter** Philip Gendreau; **cuttlefish** Matthew Kalmenoff; **cycloid** Carl Bass; **cyclotron** John Keaveny—University of California Lawrence Radiation Laboratory, Berkeley; **Cygnus** George Lindbloom; **cylinder** Carl Bass; **cypress vine** Matthew Kalmenoff.

dachshund Evelyn M. Shafer; **daisy** Matthew Kalmenoff; **Dalmatian** Evelyn M. Shafer; **dalmatic** The Metropolitan Museum of Art, Gift of Mrs. Valentine A. Blacque, 1933, in memory of Valentine A. Blacque; **damselfish** *Fishes of the Bahamas and Adjacent Tropical Waters,* by James E. Böhlke and Charles C.G. Chaplin, illustrated by Steven P. Gigliotti and Fritz Janschka, published for The Academy of Natural Sciences of Philadelphia by Livingston Publishing Company, Wynnewood, Pa., 1968; **Daphne** Museo Borghese, Rome, Photo Anderson; **Darius I** The Oriental Institute, The University of Chicago; **Clarence Darrow** Brown Brothers; **Charles Darwin** Radio Times Hulton Picture Library; **date line** Francis & Shaw, Inc.; **Honoré Daumier** Nadar, George Eastman House Collection; **Jefferson Davis** National Archives, Brady Collection; **davit** Smithsonian Institution, Cooper-Hewitt Museum of Design; **dayflower** Charles C. Johnson; **deadeye** Official Mystic Seaport Photograph by Louis S. Martel; **deadly nightshade** Matthew Kalmenoff; **Dead Sea Scrolls** Palestine Archaeological Museum; **declinometer** U.S. Department of Commerce, Coast and Geodetic Survey; **décolletage** Culver Pictures, Inc.; **decoy** Courtesy of Museum of Fine Arts, Boston, M. and M. Karolik Collection; **decurrent** Matthew Kalmenoff; **deerhound** Evelyn M. Shafer; **Daniel Defoe** Brown Brothers; **Degas** Louvre, Photo Giraudon; **Charles De Gaulle** United Press International Photo; **Delacroix** Louvre, Photo Giraudon; **delft** The Metropolitan Museum of Art, Fletcher Fund, 1927; **delphinium** Roche; **delta** NASA Photo; **Demeter** Museo Nazionale delle Terme, Photo Alinari; **demijohn** Philip Gendreau; **demoiselle** Arthur W. Ambler from NAS; **Demosthenes** Culver Pictures, Inc.; **"Jack" Dempsey** United Press International Photo; **deoxyribonucleic acid** *Molecular Biology of the Gene,* by James D. Watson, W.A. Benjamin, Inc.; **Deposition** Louvre, Archives Photographiques; **depot** David Plowden; **depth charge** Official U.S. Navy Photograph; **derrick** Standard Oil Co. of New Jersey; **dervish** *Ridpath's Universal History,* by John Clark Ridpath, Merrill & Baker, N.Y., © 1899; **desk** Courtesy of Henry Ford Museum, Dearborn, Michigan—Courtesy of Henry Francis du Pont Winterthur Museum; **desman** Matthew Kalmenoff; **Hernando de Soto** Wisconsin State Historical Society; **destroyer** National Archives, U.S. Bureau of Ships; **Eamon de Valera** Brown Brothers; **Devi** Philadelphia Museum of Art, Photograph by A.J. Wyatt, Staff Photographer; **dewlap** Grant Heilman Photography; **diamondback** William Allen Jr. from NAS—Jack Dermid from NAS; **diatom** Carl Struwe from Monkmeyer Press; **Emily Dickinson** © Photograph Harper & Brothers; **die[2]** The International Silver Company; **diesel engine** Daimler-Benz Aktiengesellschaft; **differential gear** © Dynamic Gear Company, Inc., 1966; **digestive system** Neil Hardy; **dihedral angle** Carl Bass; **dike** Philip Gendreau; **dill** N.E. Beck Jr. from NAS; **dimorphism** Matthew Kalmenoff; **Isak Dinesen** Edoardo Brofferio; **dingo** Australian News & Information Bureau; **dinothere** Courtesy of The American Museum of Natural History; **Diogenes** Brown Brothers; **diptych** Museo Nazionale, Florence, Photo Alinari; **dirigible** University of Georgia Library; **discoid** *Handbook of Plant and Floral Ornament,* by Richard G. Hatton, Dover Publications, Inc.; **dirk** The Metropolitan Museum of Art, Gift of Jean Jacques Reubell, 1926, in memory of his mother, Julia C. Coster, and of his wife, Adeline E. Post, both of New York City; **dishwasher** General Electric Co.; **disk harrow** Grant Heilman Photography; **"Walt" Disney** Culver Pictures, Inc.; **disposal** In-Sink-Erator Manufacturing Co., Racine, Wisconsin; **Disraeli** Radio Times Hulton Picture Library; **dissected** Ethel H. Hausman; **distaff** Old Sturbridge Village Photo; **diver** Official U.S. Navy Photograph; **divider** Stanley Tools; **Doberman pinscher** Evelyn M. Shafer; **dobson fly** G. Ronald Austing from NAS; **dog** Francis & Shaw, Inc.; **dogcart** The Suffolk Museum and Carriage House at Stony Brook, L.I.; **dogwood** Roche; **dolmen** Philip Gendreau; **domino[1]** Prints Division, NYPL; **donjon** Aerofilms, Ltd.; **Doric order** After Nicholson; **Don Quixote** Musée des Beaux-Arts, Reims, Photo Giraudon; **dormer** McGraw-Hill Publishing Co.; **dormouse, dory[1]** Annan Photo Features; **double bass** Elsa Z. Posell; **doublet** Victoria & Albert Museum, Crown Copyright; **doubloon** The Chase National Bank Collection of Moneys of the World, New York; **Douglas fir** (trees) West Coast Lumbermen's Association; **Frederick Douglass** Library of Congress; **douroucouli** New York Zoological Society Photo; **Draco** George Lindbloom; **drag** The Metropolitan Museum of Art, Gift of William Brewester, 1931; **dragonet** Matthew Kalmenoff; **dragon** Prints Division, NYPL; **dragonfly** Jeanne White from NAS; **drawbridge** Jane Latta; **drawknife** (standard) Stanley Tools; **dresser[2]** National Gallery of Art, Washington, D.C.; **drill press** Egyptian State Tourist Administration; **droshky** Old Print Shop; **dry cell** Cal Sacks; **dry dock** Bethlehem Steel Corp.; **duel** Library of Congress; **dugong** Matthew Kalmenoff; **dump truck** Euclid Division of General Motors Corp.; **dune** Arabian American Oil Co.; **dung beetle** John R. Clawson from NAS; **Eleuthère Irénée Du Pont** E.I. DuPont de Nemours & Co.; **Dürer** Museo del Prado, Madrid; **Dutchman's-breeches** Roche; **dynamo** General Electric Co.

eagle Philip Gendreau from NAS; **ear** Neil Hardy; **Amelia Earhart** Culver Pictures, Inc.; **earthworm** John H. Gerard from NAS; **earwig** U.S. Dept. of Agriculture; **easel** M. Grumbacher; **Easter egg** Surma Book & Music Co., NYC; **eaves** *The Gingerbread Age,* by John Maass, Rinehart & Co., Inc., 1957; **echidna** Arthur W. Ambler from NAS; **eclipse** John G. Kirk, Kitt Peak National Observatory; **Mary Baker Eddy** © 1954 The Christian Science Publishing Society; **edelweiss** Swiss National Tourist Office; **Sir Anthony Eden** Keystone Press; **edh** Alice Koeth; **Thomas Alva Edison** George Eastman House Collection; **Edward VIII** *The Windsor Years,* H.R.H. The Duke of Windsor's Collection, Photo Dorothy Wilding, Courtesy of The Viking Press, Inc.; **eel** *Ichthyology,* by Lagler, Bardach, and Miller, John Wiley & Sons, 1962; **eelpout** New York Zoological Society Photo; **eft** Jack Dermid from NAS; **egg[1]** Jack Dermid from NAS—Gordon Smith from NAS—Roche from NAS—Gordon Smith from NAS; **egret** Annan Photo Features; **eider** Paul Johnsgard from NAS; **Eiffel Tower** French Government Tourist Office; **Albert Einstein** Ernst Haas, © 1966 Magnum Photos; **Dwight David Eisenhower** Burt Glinn, © 1966 Magnum Photos; **ejection seat** Martin-Baker Aircraft Co.; **eland** Dade Thornton from NAS; **elderberry** Roche; **electric furnace** U.S. Steel Corp.; **electroencephalogram** Medcraft Electronic Corp.; **electromagnet** Ohio Magnetics Div., Howell International, Inc.; **electron microscope** Bell Telephone Laboratories; **elephant** Annan Photo Features—Cy La Tour; **elevated railway** Museum of the City of New York, J. Clarence Davies Collection; **elevator** Otis Elevator Co.; **Elizabeth I** National Portrait Gallery, London; **ellipse, ellipsoid** Carl Bass; **elm** Roche; **elytron** Matthew Kalmenoff; **emblem** Library of Congress; **embroidery** Victoria and Albert Museum; **Ralph Waldo Emerson** George Eastman House Collection; **emu** Arthur W. Ambler from NAS; **endive** U.S. Dept. of Agriculture—John H. Gerard from NAS; **endocarp** Matthew Kalmenoff; **endocrine gland** Neil Hardy; **en garde** Fencing equipment by Santelli; **English horn** Boosey & Hawkes Ltd., London; **English setter** Evelyn M. Shafer; **ensiform** Roche; **entrechat** *The Classic Ballet,* by Muriel Stuart, Knopf, 1952; **entresol** Art & Architecture Division, NYPL; **eohippus** Courtesy of The American Museum of Natural History; **Eos** Louvre, Photo Giraudon; **epergne** The Metropolitan Museum of Art, Gift of Lewis Einstein, 1952; **epicycloid** Carl Bass; **equinox** Courtesy of The American Museum of Natural History; **Erasmus** Louvre, Photo Giraudon; **ergot** U.S. Dept. of Agriculture; **Erlenmeyer flask** Scientific Glass Apparatus Co., Inc.; **ermine** Annan Photo Features; **Max Ernst** © H. Cartier-Bresson, Magnum; **escapement** The Science Museum, London; **escarole** U.S. Dept. of Agriculture; **esophagus** Neil Hardy; **espalier** Roche; **Eton collar** Hills & Saunders of Eton Ltd.; **eucalyptus** O.M. Erpenstein from NAS—Gladys Diesing from NAS; **Eugénie** Culver Pictures, Inc.; **Euripides** Carlsberg Glyptotek, Copenhagen; **Europa[1]** Museo Nazionale, Palermo, Photo Alinari; **evening primrose** Roche; **ewer** Museum of the City of New York; **excavator** Monkmeyer Press; **exhibition** Brown Brothers; **exploded view** Ford Motor Co.; **exterior angle** Carl Bass; **eye** Neil Hardy; **eyestalk** Annan Photo Features.

façade French Government Tourist Office; **fairy ring** U.S. Dept. of Agriculture; **falcon** Allan Cruickshank from NAS; **fallow deer** Annan Photo Features; **false Solomon's seal** Roche; **fang** John H. Gerard from NAS; **fanlight** Jane Latta; **fan palm** John H. Gerard from NAS; **fan vaulting** National Monuments Record; **Admiral Farragut** Library of Congress; **fasces** American Numismatic Society; **faucet** "Handbook of Building Terms and Definitions," by Herbert Waugh & Nelson Burbank, Simmons-Boardman Publishing Corp.; **feather** Cal Sacks; **feather palm** Annan Photo Features; **feather star** Matthew Kalmenoff; **featherstitch** *The Basic Stitches of Embroidery,* by N. Victoria Wade, Victoria & Albert Museum; **feedbag** Annan Photo Features; **feeder** Grant Heilman Photography; **felucca** Princeton University Library, Sinclair Hamilton Collection; **fencing** Ewing Galloway; **fender** Chevrolet Photo; **Enrico Fermi** The Bettmann Archive; **ferret[1]** New York Zoological Society Photo; **Ferris wheel** Culver Pictures, Inc.; **ferrule** Delta Brush Co.; **ferryboat** Southern Pacific Railroad; **feverfew** Matthew Kalmenoff; **fez** Philip Gendreau; **fichu** *What People Wore,* by Douglas Gorsline, Copyright 1951, 1952 by Douglas Gorsline, reprinted by permission of The Viking Press, Inc.; **fiddlehead** Sonja Bullaty from NAS; **fiddler crab** John H. Gerard from NAS; **fife** Louvre, Photo Giraudon; **fig[1]** Roche—Annan Photo Features; **figurehead** National Gallery of Art, Index of American Design; **file[2]** Cal Sacks; **filefish** *Fishes of the Bahamas,* by J.E. Böhlke and C.C.G. Chaplin, illustrated by S.P. Gigliotti, published for Academy of Natural Sciences of Philadelphia by Livingston Publishing Co., 1968; **filigree** Vestlandske Kunstindustri Museum, Bergen, Norway; **fimbriate** Matthew Kalmenoff; **finial** Editorial Photocolor Archives, Inc.; **fin keel** Ericson Yachts; **fireboat** N.Y. Fire Dept.; **fire engine** American LaFrance; **fire escape** Photo Berenice Abbott, Museum of the City of New York; **fire irons** The Metropolitan Museum of Art, Fletcher Fund, 1929; **fireplace** Jane Latta; **fish** Francis & Shaw, Inc.; **fisher** San Diego Zoo Photo; **fishing rod** L.L. Bean, Inc.; **fishnet** Jane Latta; **flabellum** The Metropolitan Museum of Art, The Cloisters Collection, 1947; **flamboyant** Photo Jean Roubier; **flatcar** Pullman-Standard; **flea** Su Zan Noguchi Swain; **flèche** Editorial Photocolor Archives, Inc.; **flicker[2]** Courtesy of The New-York Historical Society, New York City; **flight deck** Official U.S. Navy Photograph; **flintlock** The Metropolitan Museum of Art, Gift of Wilfred Wood, 1956; **floodgate** Central & Southern Florida Flood Control District; **flounce[1]** Photo Collection Georges Sirot, Paris; **flower** Matthew Kalmenoff; **flügelhorn** Courtesy of H. & A. Selmer, Inc.; **fluke[2]** (whale) Matthew Kalmenoff; **flume** Ewing Galloway; **fly agaric** Leonard Lee Rue from NAS; **flying buttress** Bibliothèque Nationale; **flying fish** H.E. Edgerton from NAS; **flying squirrel** Annan Photo Features; **flywheel** Westinghouse Electric Corp.; **foamflower** Roche; **foil[3]** Fencing equipment by Santelli; **folium** Carl Bass; **follicle** Walter Dawn; **font[1]** Copyright Poul Pedersen; **fool[1]** British Museum; **football** United Press International Photo; **forceps** *Stedman's Medical Dictionary,* 21st Edition, © 1966, The William's & Wilkins Co., Baltimore, Md.; **foreshorten** Brera, Milan; **forge[1]** Iron Works, Inc.; **forget-me-not** Roche; **Fortuna** Vatican Museum, Photo Anderson; **fossil** Annan Photo Features—Annan Photo Features—Courtesy of The American Museum of Natural History; **fountain** Photo Anderson; **fountain pen** Parker Pen Co.; **four-eyed fish** New York Zoological Society Photo; **four-in-hand** Museum of the City of New York, Harry T. Peters Collection; **four-poster** John E. Thierman; **fox** Karl H. Maslowski from NAS; **foxglove** Roche; **fox terrier** Evelyn M. Shafer—Annan Photo Features; **Jean Honoré Fragonard** California Palace of the Legion of Honor, San Francisco, Gift of Mr. & Mrs. Louis Benoist; **Francisco Franco** Paris Match; **francolin** R. Van Nostrand from NAS; **Benjamin Franklin** Historical Society of Pa.; **Franklin stove** Cal Sacks; **freesia** Roche; **freighter** Moran Towing; **French door** Photo Doisneau-Rapho; **fret[2]** Cal Sacks; **Sigmund Freud** Culver Pictures, Inc.; **frigate bird** The Peabody Museum of Salem; **fringed gentian** Harry Brevoort from NAS; **fritillary** Burpee Seeds—Dade Thornton from NAS; **frock coat** *What People Wore,* by Douglas Gorsline, copyright 1951, 1952 by Douglas Gorsline, reprinted by permission of The Viking Press, Inc.; **frontal bone** Neil Hardy; **fuchsia** Roche; **fulcrum** Frances Davies; **fuller's teasel** C.G. Maxwell from NAS; **fulmar** Courtesy of The New-York Historical Society, New York City; **Robert Fulton** New York State Historical Association, Cooperstown; **furrow** United Press International Photo; **fur seal** Karl W. Kenyon from NAS; **fuse[2]** Bussmann Mfg. Div., McGraw Edison Co. Eagle Electric Mfg. Co.; **fut tock shroud** Courtesy of The Marine Historical Association.

gable 20th Century Fox; **gadwall** Karl H. Maslowski from NAS; **gaff** Annan Photo Features; **galaxy** California Institute of Technology—Mt. Wilson and Palomar Observatories—(diagrams) *The Sourcebook on the Space Sciences,* by Samuel Glasstone, D. Van Nostrand Co., © 1965; **gall[3]** Hugh Spencer from NAS; **gallbladder** Neil Hardy; **John Galsworthy** Culver Pictures, Inc.; **gamopetalous** Roche; **Mahatma Gandhi** Information Service of India; **gannet** Gaston LePage from NAS; **gar[1]** Matthew Kalmenoff; **Greta Garbo** Brown Brothers; **gargoyle** French Government Tourist Office; **garter** The Illustrated London News, 1953; **gastropod** Annan Photo Features; **gate-leg table** The Metropolitan Museum of Art, Bequest of Mrs. J. Insley Blair, 1952; **Gatling gun** U.S. Air Force—National Archives; **Paul Gauguin** National Gallery of Art, Chester Dale Collection; **gazelle** Zoological Society of London; **gear** Fundamental Photographs; **Geiger counter** Eon Corp.; **Gemini** George Lindbloom; **generator** *The Way Things Work,* Simon & Schuster, 1967; **gentleman-at-arms** Radio Times Hulton Picture Library; **geode** Fundamental Photographs; **geodesic dome** Annan Photo Features; **geranium** Roche; **gerbil** Courtesy of The American Museum of Natural History; **gerenuk** R. Van Nostrand from NAS; **German shepherd** Evelyn M. Shafer; **Geronimo** National Archives; **geyser** Union Pacific Railroad Photo; **ghat** Lynn McLaren, Rapho-Guillumette; **Alberto Giacometti** Copyright by Ernst Scheidegger, Zurich, Agence Rapho; **Giant's Causeway** British Travel Association; **gibbon** San Diego Zoo; **Gibson girl** Prints Division, NYPL; **gig[1]** The Suffolk Museum & Carriage House at Stony Brook, L.I.; **Gila monster** Annan Photo Features; **gill[1]** Neil Hardy; **giraffe** Arthur Markowitz from NAS; **girandole** The Metropolitan Museum of Art, Rogers Fund, 1921; **girder** George Eastman House Collection; **gladiator** Museo Nazionale delle Terme, Rome, Photo Alinari; **gladiolus** Roche; **William Ewart Gladstone** National Portrait Gallery, London; **glass blowing** Steuben Glass; **Glengarry** British Travel Association; **John H. Glenn, Jr.** NASA; **glider** Charles Rotkin, P.F.I.; **glissade** *The Classic Ballet,* by Muriel Stuart, Knopf, 1952; **globe** Hammond, Inc.; **glockenspiel** J.C. Deagan; **glove** The Metropolitan Museum of Art, Gift of Mrs. Edward S. Harkness, 1928; **gloxinia** Roche; **glyptograph** Courtesy of The American Museum of Natural History; **gnu** Arthur W. Ambler from NAS; **goat** Grant Heilman Photography; **Gobelin** Archives Photographiques, Paris; **godwit** Annan Photo Features; **Johann Wolfgang von Goethe** Louvre, Photo Giraudon; **Golden Gate** Charles Rotkin, P.F.I.; **goldenrod** Jack Dermid from NAS; **goldfinch** G. Ronald Austing from NAS—Annan Photo Features; **goldfish** Annan Photo Features; **gondola** Photo by Pan American; **Charles Goodyear** Brown Brothers; **goose[1]** Annan Photo Features; **gooseberry, gopher** Matthew Kalmenoff; **gorilla** Arthur W. Ambler from NAS; **goshawk** Annan Photo Features; **gourd** John H. Gerard from NAS; **gramophone** Brown Brothers; **grampus** Matthew Kalmenoff; **Ulysses S. Grant** The GAF Historical Photo Collection; **grapefruit** Anita Este from NAS; **graptolite** Ralph Buchsbaum; **grasshopper** Leonard Lee Rue from NAS; **grater** Annan Photo Features; **grayling** Matthew Kalmenoff; **grease paint** Jane Latta; **great auk** The New-York Historical Society, New York City; **Great Dane** Evelyn M. Shafer; **grebe** Allan D. Cruickshank from NAS; **green dragon** Matthew Kalmenoff; **greyhound** Evelyn M. Shafer; **griffin** Louvre, Photo Giraudon; **D.W. Griffith** Culver Pictures, Inc.; **Jakob Grimm** Brown Brothers; **grison** Annan Photo Features; **gristmill** Greater Knoxville Chamber of Commerce; **grizzly bear** Annan Photo Features; **grosbeak** G. Ronald Austing from NAS; **George Grosz** Permission of the Estate of George Grosz, Princeton, N.J.; **ground cherry** Roche; **ground squirrel** Keith D. Henley from NAS; **grouper, grouse[1]** Annan Photo Features; **grunt** Kitchen-Kinne from NAS; **guardant** Crown Copyright; **guelder rose** Roche; **Guernsey[2]** Allan B. Lang from NAS; **guided missile** Official NORAD Photo; **guillotine** Carnavalet Museum, Bulloz; **Johann Gutenberg** Culver Pictures, Inc.; **"Woody" Guthrie** Courtesy of the Guthrie Children's Trust Fund; **gyrfalcon** The New-York Historical Society, New York City; **gyroscope** Fundamental Photographs.

hackle[1] Arthur W. Ambler from NAS; **hacksaw** Stanley Tools; **Hadrian** Vatican Museum, Photo Alinari; **Hadrian's Wall** Radio Times Hulton Picture Library; **haik** Cal Sacks; **hairspring** Fundamental Photographs; **half eagle** American Numismatic Society; **halibut** Bureau of Commercial Fisheries; **Edmund Halley** British Museum; **halo** Museo Diocesano, Cortona, Photo Alinari; **halter[1]** NASCO, Ft. Atkinson, Wisc.; **Dag Hammarskjöld** United Nations; **hammer** Stanley Tools; **hammerhead** Matthew Kalmenoff; **handcar** Culver Pictures, Inc.; **handcuff** Brown Brothers; **George Frederick Handel** J. van Rhijn-Viollet; **hand organ** Culver Pictures, Inc.; **hansom** Brown Brothers; **hanuman** San Diego Zoo; **Warren G. Harding** Library of Congress; **hare** P.W. Hay from NAS; **harebell** Roche; **Harlequin** Dance Collection, NYPL; **harmonica** M. Hohner; **harp** Philip Gendreau; **harpsichord** The Metropolitan Museum of Art, Anonymous Gift, 1945; **harquebus** Crown Copyright; **hartebeest** H.W. Kitchen from NAS; **hatchet** Stanley Tools; **havelock** Culver Pictures, Inc.; **hawk[1]** Karl H. Maslowski from NAS; **hawksbill** Lynwood Chace from NAS; **hawthorn** John H. Gerard from NAS; **Nathaniel Hawthorne** Prints Division, NYPL; **headboard** Index of American Design, National Gallery of Art; **headset** Roanwell; **hearth** Kosti Ruohomaa, Black Star; **heath hen** Matthew Kalmenoff; **Hebe** Museo Jatta, Ruvo, Italy, Photo Alinari; **Hecate** Staatliche Museum, Berlin, F.L. Kenett; **Hector** Vatican Museum, Photo Alinari; **hedgehog** Zoological Society of London; **Jascha Heifetz** Culver Pictures, Inc.; **helicon** *The History of Musical Instruments,* by Curt Sachs, copyright 1940 by W.W. Norton, renewed 1968 by Irene Sachs; **helicopter** Boeing Photo—Fairchild Hiller—Boeing Photo; **helix** Carl Bass; **hellgrammite** G. Ronald Austing from NAS; **helm[1]** Motor Boating; **Ernest Hemingway** Wide World Photos; **hemlock** Roche; **hemstitch** Courtesy, The Cooper-Hewitt Museum of Design, Smithsonian Institution; **hepatica** Roche; **Hepplewhite** The Metropolitan Museum of Art, Gift of Mrs. Russell Sage, 1909; **Hercules[1]** Museo Nazionale, Naples; **Hercules[2]** George Lindbloom; **hermaphrodite brig** *Sailing and Small Craft Down the Ages,* copyright 1940 by the U.S. Naval Institute, Annapolis; **Hermes** Louvre, Photo Giraudon; **hermit crab** Matthew Kalmenoff; **heron** Annan Photo Features; **herring gull** Allan D. Cruickshank from NAS; **heterocercal** Matthew Kalmenoff; **hexagram** Carl Bass; **hibachi** Portland Stove Foundry; **hibiscus** Annan Photo Features; **"Wild Bill" Hickok** Kansas State Historical Society; **hieroglyphic** Courtesy of The Brooklyn Museum; **highboy** Courtesy, Henry Francis du Pont Winterthur Museum; **highchair** Thomas Morley; **Sir Edmund Hillary** Mt. Everest Foundation; **Paul von Hindenburg** United Press International; **hinge** Stanley Tools; **hip[1]** Ethel H. Hausman; **Hippocrates** Museum, Cos, Hirmer; **hippopotamus, hip roof** Annan Photo Features; **Hirohito** Brown Brothers; **Adolf Hitler** Wide World Photos; **hobnail** John Keaveny; **Ho Chi Minh** Eastfoto; **hogan** Culver Pictures, Inc.; **hogfish** Matthew Kalmenoff; **Hans Holbein** Trustees of The Wallace Collection; **holly, hollyhock** Roche; **Oliver Wendell Holmes[2]** Culver Pictures, Inc.; **Holstein[2]** Grant Heilman Photography; **Winslow Homer** *Winslow Homer at Prout's Neck,* Philip C. Beam, Little, Brown & Co., Boston; **homocercal, honey badger** Matthew Kalmenoff; **honeycomb** Annan Photo Features; **honeysuckle** William J. Jahoda from NAS; **hookah** Editorial Photocolor Archives; **hoop** Chansonetta Stanley Emmons; **Herbert Hoover** Fabian Bachrach; **hop[2]** Matthew Kalmenoff; **horn** Art by Enid Kotschning from "Horns and Antlers" by Walter Modell, Copyright © April, 1969, by Scientific American, Inc., all rights reserved; **horned toad, hornet** Annan Photo Features; **horse** Francis & Shaw, Inc.; **horsecar** Brown Brothers; **horse chestnut** Roche—Lynwood Chace from NAS; **horseshoe crab** Dianon T. Smithers from NAS—Lynwood Chace from NAS; **horsetail** Grant M. Haist from NAS; **hourglass** Courtesy of The American Museum of Natural History; **houseboat** Annan Photo Features; **house sparrow** John H. Gerard from NAS—M.F. Soper from NAS; **howdah** Culver Pictures, Inc.; **howitzer** West Point Museum; **Langston Hughes** Wide World Photos; **Victor Hugo** Brown Brothers; **hull** Annan Photo Features; **hummingbird** Arthur W. Ambler from NAS—Anthony Merciera from NAS; **hurdy-gurdy** Roger-Viollet; **Aldous Huxley** Culver Pictures, Inc.; **Sir Julian Huxley, Thomas Huxley** Radio Times Hulton Picture Library; **hyacinth** Roche; **hydra[1], hydrangea** Annan Photo Features; **hydrofoil** Boeing Photo; **hydroplane** Wide World Photos; **hyena** Annan Photo Features; **hyperbola, hyperbolic paraboloid, hyperboloid** Carl Bass; **hyrax** Arthur W. Ambler from NAS.

ibex Annan Photo Features; **ibis** Allan D. Cruickshank from NAS; **ice ax** Colorado Mountain Industries; **icebreaker** U.S. Coast Guard; **ichneumon, ichneumon fly, ichthyosaur** Matthew Kalmenoff; **ideogram** Ta-tsun Chen; **igloo** Steve & Dolores McCutcheon, Alaska Pictorial Service; **Saint Ignatius Loyola** Leonard Von Matt; **ignition** *The Harper Encyclopedia of Science,* ed. by James R. Newman, Harper & Row, 1967; **iguana** Arthur W. Ambler from NAS; **imbricate** Roche; **impala** J.D. Ovington from NAS; **imperial moth** N.E. Beck, Jr., from NAS; **impost[2]** The Metropolitan Museum of Art, The Cloisters Collection; **incandescent lamp** General Electric; **incubator** Air-Shields; **incuse** National Museum, Palermo; **Indian paintbrush** Matthew Kalmenoff; **Indian pipe** Jack Dermid from NAS; **Indian tobacco** Matthew Kalmenoff; **induction coil** Prestolite; **ingot** U.S. Steel; **Ingres** Musée Condé Chantilly, Photo Giraudon; **inkstand** Philadelphia Museum of Art; **inlay** Photo Alinari; **insect, involucel** Matthew Kalmenoff; **io moth** Hal H. Harrison from NAS; **iris** Roche—Annan Photo Features; **Irish elk** Courtesy of The American Museum of Natural History; **Irish setter, Irish wolfhound** Evelyn M. Shafer; **ironwork** Delta Air Lines; **Isabella I** National Museum of Fine Arts, Madrid; **Isis[1]** Archives Photographiques; **Ivan the Terrible** Danish National Museum, Copenhagen.

jacana Arthur W. Ambler from NAS; **jack-in-the-pulpit** Roche; **jack rabbit** Karl H. Maslowski from NAS; **Andrew Jackson** The New-York Historical Society, New York City; **jaguar** R. Van Nostrand from NAS; **James I** National Portrait Gallery, London; **Jesse James** Culver Pictures, Inc.; **Janus** Museum of Fine Arts, Boston, Buffam Collection, Gift of Mrs. James P. Tolman; **Japanese beetle** U.S. Dept. of Agriculture; **jasmine** Jack Dermid from NAS; **jaunting car** Ewing Galloway; **John Jay** National Gallery of Art; **Thomas Jefferson** The New-York Historical Society, New York City; **jerboa** Gordon Smith from NAS; **Jerusalem cherry** Roche; **jet engine** Pratt & Whitney; **jetty[1]** Annan Photo Features; **jewelweed** Ethel H. Hausman; **jib[1]** *Sailing and Small Craft Down the Ages,* copyright 1940 by the U.S. Naval Institute, Annapolis; **jimsonweed** "Common Poisonous Plants," by John M. Kingsbury, Cornell Extension Bulletin 538; **Joan of Arc** Archives Nationales; **joe-pye weed** Roche; **John XXIII** United Press International; **Andrew Johnson** Library of Congress; **Lyndon Baines Johnson** Gerry Cranham, Rapho-Guillumette; **jonquil** Roche; **Joshua tree** Dade W. Thornton from NAS; **joust** Universitätsbibliothek, Heidelberg; **James Joyce** Culver Pictures, Inc.; **Benito Pablo Juárez** Library of Congress; **jug** Courtesy, Henry Francis du Pont Winterthur Museum; **juggler** *Circus,* Bertha B. Burlieth, Putnam, 1930; **jumping jack** Museum of the City of New York; **junco** Roger T. Peterson from NAS; **junk[2]** The Science Museum, London; **Juno** Vatican Museum, Photo Alinari; **Justinian I** S. Vitale, Scala.

kabuki Prints Division, NYPL; **Kamehameha I** Honolulu Academy of Arts; **kangaroo** Arthur W. Ambler from NAS; **kangaroo rat** Woodrow Goodpaster from NAS; **karabiner** Georgia Engelhard from Monkmeyer Press; **karakul** Annan Photo Features; **katydid** Alvin E. Staffan from NAS; **kayak** Steve & Dolores McCutcheon, Alaska Pictorial Service; **John Keats** National Portrait Gallery, London; **Helen Keller** Culver Pictures, Inc.; **John F. Kennedy** Ted Spiegel, Rapho-Guillumette; **Jomo Kenyatta** United Nations; **Kerry blue terrier** Evelyn M. Shafer; **key** Pencil Points, Dec., 1939; **Francis Scott Key** Culver Pictures, Inc.; **keystone** Annan Photo Features; **Nikita Khrushchev** United Nations; **Søren Kierkegaard** Ministry of Foreign Affairs, Copenhagen; **killdeer** Jerry Focht from NAS; **kiln** Philip Gendreau; **kilt**

British Travel Association; **kimono** *Japanese Costume,* H. Minnich, Charles E. Tuttle, 1963; **Martin Luther King, Jr.** Wide World; **kingfisher** Annan Photo Features; **king snake** Robert H. Wright from NAS; **kinkajou** Robert H. Hermes from NAS; **kiosk** Annan Photo Features; **Rudyard Kipling** Culver Pictures, Inc.; **koala** Pat Witherspoon from NAS; **kohlrabi** Burpee Seeds; **Komodo dragon** R. Van Nostrand from NAS; **kookaburra** Frank Stevens from NAS; **koto** Courtesy, Art Institute of Chicago; **Krishna**[1] William Rockhill Nelson Gallery of Art, Kansas City, Mo.; **Kublai Khan** Bibliothèque Nationale; **kudu** P.W. Hay from NAS; **kumquat** Vaughn Printers.

lace Cooper-Hewitt Museum of Design, Smithsonian Institution; **lacewing** NAS; **ladle** Annan Photo Features; **lady's-slipper** Roche; **Marquis de Lafayette** Prints Division, NYPL; **Fiorello H. La Guardia** Culver Pictures, Inc.; **lake trout** Treat Davidson from NAS; **lamb** Cal Sacks; **Charles Lamb** National Portrait Gallery, London; **lamprey** Bureau of Commercial Fisheries—Matthew Kalmenoff; **landau** British Travel Association; **Sidney Lanier** Culver Pictures, Inc.; **lantern fish, lantern fly** Courtesy of The American Museum of Natural History; **larch** (below) Jeanne White from NAS; **large intestine** Neil Hardy; **larva** Stephen Dalton from NAS—Lynwood Chace from NAS—Treat Davidson from NAS; **laser** Daphne Prout; **lateen** The Peabody Museum of Salem; **Latin cross** The Walters Art Gallery; **Henry Laurens** Prints Division, NYPL; **lava-lava** Philip Gendreau; **lavender** Roche; **Antoine Lavoisier** Culver Pictures, Inc.; **lawn mower** Clemson Bros.; **D.H. Lawrence, Ernest Lawrence** Culver Pictures, Inc.; **T.E. Lawrence** Lowell Thomas; **lazy tongs** Henry Francis du Pont Winterthur Museum; **leafhopper** Richard Parker from NAS; **leaf spring** *Van Nostrand's Scientific Encyclopedia,* 3rd ed., D. Van Nostrand Co., copyright 1938, 1947, 1958; **Le Corbusier** Lucien Hervé; **lectern** Florene Maine Antiques; **Huddie Ledbetter** Culver Pictures, Inc.; **leech**[1] Grant Heilman Photography; **Fernand Léger** Photo Roger-Viollet; **leghorn** Grant Heilman Photography; **leg-of-mutton** Culver Pictures, Inc.; **lei**[1] Kenneth Russell Ho; **lemming** John H. Gerard from NAS; **lemur** San Diego Zoo; **lens** Bausch & Lomb; **Lenin** Tass from Sovfoto; **Leo** George Lindbloom; **Leonardo da Vinci** Palazzo Reale, Turin, Photo Alinari; **leopard** San Diego Zoo; **levee**[1] Ewing Galloway; **level** Stanley Tools; **lever** Frances Davies; **Meriwether Lewis** Library of Congress; **Sinclair Lewis** Culver Pictures, Inc.; **Libra** George Lindbloom; **lifeboat, life jacket, life preserver** Philip Gendreau; **lighthouse** Annan Photo Features; **lightning rod** Electra Protection Co.; **Queen Liliuokalani** Brown Brothers; **lily** Grant Heilman Photography—Roche; **lily of the valley** Arthur W. Ambler from NAS; **lime**[1] Grant Heilman Photography; **limpet** Annan Photo Features; **limpkin** Dade Thornton from NAS; **Abraham Lincoln** Library of Congress; **Charles A. Lindbergh** U.S. Air Force; **line of force** *The Physics of Electricity and Magnetism,* by Scott, John Wiley & Sons; **Carolus Linnaeus** Culver Pictures, Inc.; **Lin Piao** Wide World Photos; **lion** Jeanne White from NAS; **Joseph Lister** Brown Brothers; **Franz Liszt** Georges Sirot, Paris; **litchi** Kit & Max Hunn; **live oak** Don Eckelberry from NAS—Grant Heilman Photography; **liver** Neil Hardy; **lizard** Hal H. Harrison from NAS; **llama** Arthur W. Ambler from NAS; **lobster** John H. Gerard from NAS; **lock**[1] Eaton, Yale & Towne—Panama Canal Co.; **locomotive** Association of American Railroads; **locust**[1] J.M. Conrader from NAS; **locust**[2] Roche; **loganberry** Matthew Kalmenoff; **Lombardy poplar** Grant M. Haist from NAS; **longbow** Mansell Collection; **Henry Wadsworth Longfellow** George Eastman House Collection; **longhorn** U.S. Dept. of Agriculture; **lookdown** *Fishes of the Bahamas,* by J.E. Böhlke and C.C.G. Chaplin, illustrated by S.P. Gigliotti, published for Academy of Natural Sciences of Philadelphia by Livingston Publishing Co., 1968; **Federico García Lorca** Francisco García Lorca; **loris** Zoological Society of London; **lorgnette** Lissac Frères; **lotus** Arthur W. Ambler from NAS; **Louis XIV** Versailles Museum, Photo Giraudon; **Joe Louis** Wide World Photos; **love-in-a-mist** Burpee Seeds; **loving cup** Culver Pictures, Inc.; **lowboy** Henry Francis du Pont Winterthur Museum; **Amy Lowell** Brown Brothers; **lumpfish** Courtesy of The American Museum of Natural History; **luna moth** Hugh Spencer from NAS; **lungfish** Matthew Kalmenoff; **lupine**[1] "Common Poisonous Plants," by John M. Kingsbury, Cornell Extension Bulletin 538; **lure** Fred Arbogast Co.; **Martin Luther** Uffizi Gallery, Florence, Photo Alinari; **lynx** San Diego Zoo; **Lyra** George Lindbloom; **lyre** Louvre, Archives Photographiques; **lyrebird** Matthew Kalmenoff.

macaw New York Zoological Society Photo; **Niccolò Machiavelli** Palazzo Vecchio, Florence, Photo Alinari-Giraudon; **mackerel** U.S. Fish and Wildlife Service; **Archibald MacLeish** Anthony Saris; **Dolley Madison** North Carolina News Bureau; **James Madison** U.S. Bureau of Engraving; **Madonna** The Metropolitan Museum of Art, Gift of J. Pierpont Morgan, 1917; **Ferdinand Magellan** Bibliothèque Nationale; **Magen David** Argenziano Associates; **magnetic field** Fundamental Photographs; **magpie** Philip Strowbridge from NAS; **Gustave Mahler** Brown Brothers; **Aristide Maillol** Photo G. Karguel; **Moses Maimonides** The Jewish Museum; **majolica** The Metropolitan Museum of Art, Fletcher Fund, 1946; **Makarios III** The Granger Collection; **malamute** William Brown; **Maltese cross** The Bettmann Archive; **manatee** Reprinted from *Natural History,* Jan. 1930; **mandala** *The Theory and Practice of Mandala,* by Giuseppe Tucci, Rider & Co., London, 1961; **mandible** Neil Hardy; **mandrill** R. Van Nostrand from NAS; **mangrove** U.S. Dept. of Agriculture Photo; **Thomas Mann** Conzette & Huber, Zurich; **manticore** *The Book of Beasts,* by T.H. White, Jonathan Cape Ltd.; **manual alphabet** Gallaudet College, Washington, D.C.; **Manx cat** Walter Chandoha; **maple** (Red maple) Ed McLaughlin; **Guglielmo Marconi** The Bettmann Archive; **Marduk** Louvre, Archives Photographiques; **marigold** Library of The New York Botanical Garden; **marionette** *Marionetten von Pierce Gauchat,* by Edwin Arnet, Zurich, Eugen Rentsch, 1949; **Gaius Marius** Vatican Museum, Photo Alinari; **Christopher Marlowe** Corpus Christi College, Cambridge; **marmoset** New York Zoological Society Photo; **George C. Marshall** Rapho-Guillumette; **marsh hawk** Allan D. Cruickshank from NAS; **Marx Brothers** Pictorial Parade; **mask** Harissiadis, National Museum, Athens—Courtesy of The Museum of Primitive Art—Courtesy of The American Museum of Natural History—Wilson Sporting Goods Co.—U.S. Army Photograph; **massasauga** Hugh M. Halliday from NAS; **"Bat" Masterson** Pictorial Parade; **mastiff** Evelyn M. Shafer; **mastoid process** Neil Hardy; **matchlock** (detail) Phoebe McGuire; **Henri Matisse** Helene Adant; **Saint Matthew** Bibliothèque Municipale, Autun; **W. Somerset Maugham** London Daily Express; **mausoleum** *Handbook of Greek & Roman Architecture,* 2nd Edition, by Donald Struan Robertson, Cambridge University Press, 1954; **maxilla** Neil Hardy; **May apple** Jesse Lunger from NAS—Roche; **maze** Carl Bass; **meadowlark** Ed Cesar from NAS; **meander** U.S. Geological Survey; **Medal of Honor** Official U.S. Navy Photograph; **Lorenzo de' Medici** National Gallery of Art, Washington, D.C., Samuel H. Kress Collection; **medicine man** Courtesy of The American Museum of Natural History; **medlar** Matthew Kalmenoff; **Medusa** Galleria Uffizi, Photo Brogi; **Meissen ware** The Metropolitan Museum of Art, The Michael Friedsam Collection; **Andrew Mellon** National Gallery of Art, Washington, D.C., Gift of Ailsa Mellon Bruce; **melon** Don Bowden; **melting point** Dick Morrill, Inc.; **Herman Melville** The Granger Collection; **Menander** Princeton University Art Museum; **Menorah** Jewish Theological Seminary of America, New York; **Mephistopheles** The Bettmann Archive; **Mercury** Museo Nazionale, Florence, Photo Alinari; **mercury-vapor lamp** General Electric Co.; **merino** Australian News & Information Bureau; **mesquite** Josef Muench; **metacarpus** Neil Hardy; **metacenter** Ed McLaughlin; **metamorphosis** Walter Dawn; **meteor** Official U.S. Navy Photograph; **metope** Mary Evans Picture Library, London; **Prince Metternich** Prints Division, NYPL; **mezuzah** Jewish Theological Seminary of America, New York; **micawber** Berg Collection, NYPL; **Michelangelo** Photo Alinari; **microscope** Cal Sacks; **microtome** E. Leitz, Inc.; **Ludwig Mies van der Rohe** Rapho-Guillumette—Norman McGrath; **mignonette** Burpee Seeds; **milestone** Brown Brothers; **milkweed** Grant Heilman Photography—Arthur W. Ambler from NAS; **millipede** N.E. Beck Jr. from NAS; **minaret** Donald Ferguson from Monkmeyer Press; **Ming** The Metropolitan Museum of Art, Mr. and Mrs. Isaac D. Fletcher Collection, Bequest of Isaac D. Fletcher, 1917; **miniature** The Metropolitan Museum of Art, The Cloisters Collection, Purchase, 1954; **mink** Ed Cesar from NAS; **Minorca**[2] U.S. Dept. of Agriculture Photo; **Minotaur** Courtesy Museum of Modern Art, Collection of Roland Penrose; **minuteman** U.S. Treasury Dept.; **Joan Miró** Agence Rapho, Photo Sabine Weiss; **missel thrush** Eric Hosking from NAS; **mistletoe** Field Museum of Natural History; **miter** The Metropolitan Museum of Art, Cloisters Fund, Purchase, 1953; **miter joint** Ed McLaughlin; **mitt** Spalding & Bros., Inc.; **Möbius strip** Fundamental Photographs; **moccasin** Courtesy of Museum of the American Indian, Heye Foundation; **moccasin flower** Roche; **moiré effect** Adapted from "Moiré Patterns" by Gerald Oster and Yasunori Nishijima, Copyright © 1963 by Scientific American, Inc., all rights reserved; **mold**[1] (plastic mold) Cerro Sales Corp.; **mold**[2] Phoebe McGuire; **mole**[2] Roche; **monarch** Hal H. Harrison from NAS; **Mondrian** Courtesy of Sidney Janis Gallery; **mongoose** Lewis Wayne Walker from NAS; **monkey puzzle** *An Illustrated Manual of Pacific Coast Trees,* Copyright © 1937, reprinted 1963, by University of California Press; **monkey wrench** Crescent Tool Co.; **monogram** Prints Division, NYPL; **James Monroe** The Metropolitan Museum of Art, Bequest of Seth Low, 1929; **monstrance** Walter R. Engel, Inc.; **Montezuma II** National Archives, Mexico, D.F.; **moon** NASA; **moose** Annan Photo Features; **moray** Arthur W. Ambler from NAS; **Saint Thomas More** Copyright The Frick Collection, New York; **morel** Hugh Spencer from NAS; **Morgan** Stephen Greene Press; **morion**[1] The Metropolitan Museum of Art, Rogers Fund, 1904; **morning-glory** Henry M. Mayer from NAS; **mortar** Coors Porcelain Co.; **mortise** Phoebe McGuire; **motorcycle** Harley-Davidson Motor Co.; **mountain ash** Ethel H. Hausman; **mountain goat** Ed Cesar from NAS; **mountain laurel** Roche; **mourning dove** Karl H. Maslowski from NAS; **mouth** Neil Hardy; **mucro** Walter Dawn; **mule**[1] Philip Gendreau; **mullein** Charles C. Johnson; **Müller-Lyer illusion** Carl Bass; **multifoil** Rev. F. Sumner; **mummy case** The Granger Collection; **muntjac** Arthur W. Ambler from NAS; **murex** John H. Gerard from NAS; **Muse** Vatican Museum, Photo Anderson; **Benito Mussolini** United Press International Photo; **muzzle** Lenny Ross School for Dogs, Inc., Kendra K. Ho; **Myrmidon** Istituto Italiano Arti Grafiche, Bergamo.

naiad Bibliothèque Nationale; **nail** *Popular Mechanics;* **Nanak** *The Great Humanist Guru Nanak,* by Sir Jogendra Singh and Raja Sir Daljit Singh, Unity Publishers, New Delhi, 1959; **Carry Nation** Brown Brothers; **nautch** *World Costumes,* by Angela Bradshaw, Adam and Charles Black, London, 1952; **nautilus** Courtesy of The American Museum of Natural History; **nave**[1] Roger-Viollet; **Neanderthal man** Courtesy of The American Museum of Natural History; **nebula** Yerkes Observatory Photograph; **nectarine** The Keith Thomas Co.; **needlepoint** From *Needlepoint* by Hope Hanley, used by permission of Charles Scribner's Sons and Mrs. Roman V. Mrozinski, Copyright © 1964 Hope Hanley; **needle valve** Fischer and Porter Co.; **Nefertiti** Staatliche Museum, Berlin; **Neptune**[1] Wichita City Library; **Nero** The American Numismatic Society, New York; **nerve cell** Neil Hardy; **nest** Allan D. Cruickshank from NAS—Karl H. Maslowski from NAS—*Illustrated London News,* June 19, 1948; **netsuke** The Metropolitan Museum of Art, Rogers Fund, 1913—Charles E. Tuttle Co., Inc.; **neuropteran** George Porter from NAS; **newel** The Metropolitan Museum of Art, Rogers Fund, 1932; **Newfoundland**[2] Evelyn M. Shafer; **niche** Chiesa de Or San Michelle, Florence, Photo Alinari; **night-blooming cereus** Josef Muench; **Nike** Photo Bulloz; **nimbus** The Minneapolis Institute of Arts; **Niobe** Galleria Uffizi, Florence, Photo Alinari; **Richard M. Nixon** United Press International Photo; **no**[3] The Metropolitan Museum of Art, Gift of the Kokusai Bunka Shinkokai through Setsuiche Aoki, Secretary, 1935; **Noah** Pierpont Morgan Library; **Alfred Bernhard Nobel** Swedish Information Service; **noctule** Eric Hosking from NAS; **nomograph** Carl Bass; **noose** Phoebe McGuire; **nopal** Josef Muench; **noria** Ministerio de Información y Turismo, Madrid; **normal distribution** Carl Bass; **nose** Neil Hardy; **nose cone** H.M. Johnson; **nostrum** Warshaw Collection of Business Americana; **note** Cal Sacks; **John Humphrey Noyes** Collection of George W. Noyes; **nozzle** Fundamental Photographs; **nuclear reactor** U.S. Atomic Energy Commission; **nucleus** Neil Hardy; **nut** Cal Sacks; **nutcracker** Fundamental Photographs; **nymph** Acropolis Museum, Athens.

oak John R. Terres from NAS; **oarfish** Matthew Kalmenoff; **obelisk** Hirmer Verlag, Munich; **obi**[1] *Japanese Costume,* by H. Minnick, Charles E. Tuttle Pub. Co., Inc.; **oboe** Elsa Z. Posell; **observatory** Mt. Wilson and Palomar observatories; **obtuse angle** Carl Bass; **ocean sunfish** New York Zoological Society Photo; **octagon, octahedron** Carl Bass; **octopus** Courtesy of The American Museum of Natural History; **odalisque** The Metropolitan Museum of Art, Wolfe Fund, 1938; **Odin** Statens Historiska Museum Antikvarisk-Topografiska Arkivet; **Odysseus** Photo Giraudon; **Oedipus** Vatican Museum, Photo Alinari; **Jacques Offenbach** The Granger Collection; **ogive** Photo Clarence Ward; **James Oglethorpe** National Portrait Gallery, London; **okapi** New York Zoological Society Photo; **okra** Roche; **Old English sheepdog** Evelyn M. Shafer; **oleander** T.H. Everett; **oleograph** Fundamental Photographs; **olive** Annan Photo Features—Theodore R. Sills, Inc.; **Lawrence Olivier** Pictorial Parade; **Omar Khayyám** The Free Library of Philadelphia; **onager** Zoological Society of London; **Eugene O'Neill** Erwin Blumenfeld; **onion** Matthew Kalmenoff; **onyx** The Metropolitan Museum of Art, The Milton Weil Collection, Gift of Mrs. Ethel Weil Worgelt, 1940; **opah** Matthew Kalmenoff; **open-hearth** Cal Sacks; **opera glass** The Metropolitan Museum of Art, Anonymous gift, 1939; **opera hat** George Eastman House Collection; **ophicleide** G. Shirmer Co.; **Ophiuchus** George Lindbloom; **J. Robert Oppenheimer** United Press International Photo; **opposite, orange** T.H. Everett; **orang-utan** Matthew Kalmenoff; **orb** Kunsthistorishe Museum; **orbit** Courtesy of The American Museum of Natural History; **Oregon grape** Oregon State Highway Dept. Photo; **organ** Aeolian-Skinner Organ Co.; **organ grinder** Culver Pictures, Inc.; **organ-pipe cactus** Annan Photo Features; **Orion**[2] George Lindbloom; **Ormazd** The Oriental Institute, University of Chicago; **ornithopter** Cabinet des Estampes, Bibliothèque Nationale; **Orpheus** Swedish Information Service; **orphrey** The Metropolitan Museum of Art, The Cloisters Collection, Purchase 1953; **orthogonal projection** Carl Bass; **oryx** Culver Pictures, Inc.; **oscilloscope** Tektronix, Inc.; **Osiris** *Egyptian Mythology,* © 1965 Paul Hamlyn Ltd., London; **osprey** Courtesy of The New-York Historical Society, New York City; **ossuary** The Metropolitan Museum of Art, Fletcher Fund, 1937; **ostrich** Arthur W. Ambler from NAS; **Ouija** Ouija®, Registered U.S. Trademark of Parker Brothers, Inc., Salem, Mass.; **outboard motor** The Fisher-Pierce Co., Inc.; **outcrop** Donald W. Fisher; **outrigger** Annan Photo Features; **ovate** *Pacific Coast Trees,* by Lloyd Lyman, University of California Press; **ovenbird** Courtesy of The New-York Historical Society, New York City; **overalls** Brown Brothers; **overpass** Port of New York Authority; **overshot** Bruce Roberts from Rapho Guillumette; **ovum** Neil Hardy; **Jesse Owens** Wide World Photos; **ox** Lea Wolff from Monkmeyer Press; **oyster** Lynwood Chace from NAS; **oystercatcher** Courtesy of The New-York Historical Society, New York City.

pachysandra Roche; **paddlefish** John H. Gerard from NAS; **pagoda** Bibliothèque Nationale—Ministry of Information, India—J. Allan Cash, London; **Mohammed Riza Pahlavi** Pictorial Parade; **paisley** Courtesy of the Cooper-Hewitt Museum of Design, Smithsonian Institution; **palanquin** *La foile imprimée at les indiennes de traite,* © 1941 by H.R. d'Allemagne; **palmate** Annan Photo Features; **palmette** The Metropolitan Museum of Art, Rogers Fund, 1915; **palmetto** John H. Gerard from NAS; **pampas grass** Harry M. Johnson; **Pan** Naples Museum; **pancreas** Neil Hardy; **panda** Gordon Smith from NAS; **pansy** Roche; **panther** Arthur W. Ambler from NAS; **papaya** F.E. Westlack from NAS; **papyrus** John H. Gerard from NAS—The Metropolitan Museum of Art, Rogers Fund, 1929; **parabola, paraboloid** Carl Bass; **parachute** U.S. Air Force; **paramecium** Walter Dawn; **parapet** Cal Sacks; **parasol** The Metropolitan Museum of Art, Gift of Misses Mary and Emily Gross, 1939; **Ambroise Paré** Photo Giraudon; **parbuckle** Cal Sacks; **parget** The Metropolitan Museum of Art, Gift of the Samuel H. Kress Foundation, 1958; **parietal bone** Neil Hardy; **parka** Steve and Dolores McCutcheon, Alaska Pictorial Service; **Catherine Parr** By permission of His Grace the Archbishop of Canterbury and the Church Commissioner; **parsnip** Library of the New York Botanical Gardens; **Blaise Pascal** The Pierpont Morgan Library; **passementerie** The Metropolitan Museum of Art, Rogers Fund, 1908; **passenger pigeon** Culver Pictures, Inc.; **passionflower** Library of the New York Botanical Gardens; **patchwork** The Metropolitan Museum of Art, Gift of Mr. and Mrs. Sidney Hosmer, 1948; **Saint Patrick** Irish Tourist Board; **Saint Paul** Musée des Beaux Arts, Photo Giraudon; **Linus Carl Pauling** Pictorial Parade; **pawl** Diamond Studios; **Anna Pavlova** Culver Pictures, Inc.; **peach**[1] Grant Heilman Photography; **peacock** Pierre Berger from NAS; **peanut** Matthew Kalmenoff; **pear** Courtesy of The American Museum of Natural History; **peccary** Woodrow Goodpaster from NAS; **pectoral** Neil Hardy—Photograph by Harry Burton, The Metropolitan Museum of Art; **pediment** *The Doric Temple,* by Elizabeth Ayrton, Thames and Hudson Publishing Co., 1961; **Pegasus**[2] George Lindbloom; **Pekingese** Evelyn M. Shafer; **pelican** Jeanne White from NAS; **pelvis** Neil Hardy; **pendant** A La Vieille Russie, N.Y.; **pendentive** Marcelle Barton; **pendulum** Cal Sacks; **penguin** Zoological Society of London; **William Penn** Historical Society of Pennsylvania; **pennon** Rare Book Division, NYPL; **pentacle** Carl Bass; **penumbra** Cal Sacks; **peony** Roche; **peplum** Vogue, 1936; **Samuel Pepys** Old Print Shop; **perch**[2] U.S. Fish & Wildlife Service; **peregrine falcon** G. Ronald Austing from NAS; **S.J. Perelman** The Times, London; **perfoliate** Ethel H. Hausman; **Pericles** British Museum; **periscope** Cal Sacks; **periwinkle**[1] John H. Gerard from NAS; **periwinkle**[2] Jane Latta; **Frances Perkins** Culver Pictures, Inc.; **Matthew Calbraith Perry** Library of Congress; **Perseus**[2] George Lindbloom; **Persian cat** Walter Chandoha; **persimmon** Matthew Kalmenoff; **perspective** Cal Sacks; **Saint Peter** Vatican Grottoes, Leonard Von Matt; **petroglyph** John V. Young; **petticoat narcissus** Roche; **petunia** John H. Gerard from NAS; **phaeton** The Suffolk Museum & Carriage House at Stony Brook, L.I.; **phalanger** Arthur W. Ambler from NAS; **phalanx** Neil Hardy; **Pharaoh** Musco Egizio, Turin, Photo Anderson; **Philip II of Macedonia** Bibliothèque Nationale, Photo Giraudon; **philodendron** Roche; **phlox** Library of the New York Botanical Gardens; **photoelectric cell** Cal Sacks; **Phrygian cap** Leonard Von Matt; **phylactery** The Jewish Theological Seminary of America, New York; **Picasso** Culver Pictures, Inc.; **pick**[2] (ice pick) Stanley Tools; **Mary Pickford** George Eastman House Collection; **pictograph** Garrick Mallory, NYPL; **Franklin Pierce** Library of Congress; **pig** Grant Heilman Photography; **pika** Leonard Lee Rue from NAS; **pilaster** George Eastman House Collection; **pileated woodpecker** Allan D. Cruickshank from NAS; **pillory** The Mansell Collection, London; **pimpernel** T.H. Everett; **pincers, pinion**[2] Cal Sacks; **pink**[1] Library of the New York Botanical Gardens; **pintail** Hal H. Harrison from Monkmeyer Press; **pipefish** *Fishes of the Bahamas,* by J.E. Böhlke and C.C.G. Chaplin, illustrated by S.P. Gigliotti, published for Academy of Natural Sciences of Philadelphia by Livingston Publishing Co., 1968; **pipette** Corning Glass Works; **piranha** Annan Photo Features; **pistol** Musée de l'Armée; **Pisces** George Lindbloom; **pitcher**[2] The Metropolitan Museum of Art, Rogers Fund, Purchase 1955; **pitcher plant** T.H. Everett; **pitchfork** Cal Sacks; **plain weave** Textile Museum, Washington, D.C.; **planarian** Hugh Spencer from NAS—Phoebe McGuire; **plane**[2] Stanley Tools; **plane tree** *Pacific Coast Trees,* by Howard E. McMinn and Evelyn Maino, University of California Press, 1963; **planetary nebula** Mt. Wilson and Palomar Observatories; **platypus** Matthew Kalmenoff; **playground** Thomas Morley; **playing card** U.S. Playing Card Co.; **pleat** The Metropolitan Museum of Art, Gift of Finley J. Shepard, 1939; **pliers** Stanley Tools; **plow, plum**[1] Grant Heilman Photography; **Plymouth Rock** Grant Heilman Photography; **Pocahontas** National Portrait Gallery, Smithsonian Institution, Washington, D.C.; **pocketknife** Culver Pictures, Inc.; **pod**[1] Grant Heilman Photography—Lynwood Chace from NAS; **Edgar Allan Poe** Culver Pictures, Inc.; **pointer** Evelyn M. Shafer; **poison hemlock** "Common Poisonous Plants" by J.M. Kingsbury, Cornell Extension Bulletin 538; **poison ivy** Jane Latta; **pokeweed** Henry M. Mayer from NAS; **polar bear** Annan Photo Features; **polar coordinate** Carl Bass; **pole vault** Pictorial Parade; **James K. Polk** U.S. Bureau of Engraving; **Jackson Pollock** Hans Namuth; **Marco Polo** Escorial Library, Spain; **polonaise** Art & Architecture Division, NYPL; **polygraph** Sol Mednick, Scientific American, Jan. 1967; **pomegranate** John H. Gerard from NAS; **Pompey** Museo Nazionale, Naples, Photo Alinari; **poncho** Annan Photo Features; **pontoon bridge** Army News Features; **poodle** New York Times; **poppy** Roche; **porcupine** Charles J. Ott from NAS; **porcupine fish** (top) Annan Photo Features; **porcupine fish, porgy** *Fishes of the Bahamas,* by J.E. Böhlke and C.C.G. Chaplin, illustrated by S.P. Gigliotti, published for Academy of Natural Sciences of Philadelphia by Livingston Publishing Co., 1968; **pork** Cal Sacks; **porpoise** Painting by Else Bostelmann, © National Geographic Society; **porringer** The Metropolitan Museum of Art, Bequest of A.T. Clearwater, 1933; **Portuguese man-of-war** Courtesy of The American Museum of Natural History; **poster**[1] Collection of The Museum of Modern Art, N.Y.; **potbelly stove** Shelburne Museum, Inc.; **Prince Potemkin** Slavic Division, NYPL; **Beatrix Potter** Frederick Warne & Co., Inc.; **potter's wheel** Annan Photo Features; **Nicolas Poussin** Louvre, Photo Giraudon; **Ezra Pound** Paris Match; **powder horn** John E. Thierman; **press**[1] The Shaker Museum; **pressure suit** NASA; **pricket** National Gallery of Art, Washington, D.C.; **prickly pear** Josef Muench; **Joseph Priestly** National Portrait Gallery, London; **primer** Rare Book Division, NYPL; **primrose** Roche; **princess** Art & Architecture Division, NYPL; **prism** Cal Sacks; **profile** British Museum—Scrovegni Chapel, Pauda, Photo Alinari—Musée Condé, Chantilly—Prints Division, NYPL; **Prometheus** Graphische Sammlung der Universitäts-Bibliothek Erlangen; **prominence** Mt. Wilson and Palomar Observatories; **propeller** Cessna Aircraft Co.—Bethlehem Steel Corp.; **prop root** Conzett & Huber, Zurich; **Proteus** The Bettmann Archive; **protractor** Keuffel & Esser Co.; **Marcel Proust** Collection of Madame Mante-Proust, Photo Hachette; **Psyche** Museo Capitolino, Rome, Photo Anderson; **pterodactyl** Courtesy of The American Museum of Natural History; **pteropod** William H. Amos; **Ptolemaic system** Redrawn by Phoebe McGuire; **pueblo** Collection of Alfred L. Bush, Princeton, N.J.; **puffball** Annan Photo Features; **puffin** Prentice K. Stout from NAS; **pulley** Fundamental Photographs; **pulmonary** Neil Hardy; **pumpkin** Roche; **pumpkinseed** Treat Davidson from NAS; **pug**[1] Evelyn M. Shafer; **punka** The Bettmann Archive; **punt**[1] Annan Photo Features; **pupa** John H. Gerard from NAS—Annan Photo Features; **puppet** Bibliothèque Nationale; **Purple Heart** U.S. Army Photograph; **purple loosestrife** Jeanne White from NAS; **purple martin** Allan D. Cruickshank from NAS; **Aleksander Pushkin** Brown Brothers; **pussy willow** Roche; **puttee** Philip Gendreau; **Pythagoras** Museo Capitolino, Rome, Photo Alinari; **pyrotechnics** Pictorial Parade; **pyxis** Henry Mayer from NAS.

quadrangle *Words: The New Dictionary,* Grosset & Dunlap, 1947; **quail**[1] Leonard Lee Rue from NAS; **quarrel**[2] Phoebe McGuire; **quarry**[2] G.R. Roberts, Documentary Photographs; **quartz** Courtesy of The American Museum of Natural History; **quarter-deck** *The Ship,* by Bjorn Landstrom, illustrations Copyright © 1961 by Bjorn Landstrom, reprinted by permission of Doubleday & Co., Inc.; **quetzal** Robert C. Hermes from NAS; **Queen Anne's lace** Roche; **Quetzalcoatl** Bibliothèque Nationale; **quill** Matthew Kalmenoff; **Quonset hut** U.S. Army Photograph; **quiver**[2] C.O.V. Kienbusch.

Ra John R. Freeman, British Museum; **raccoon** U.S. Fish & Wildlife Service; **raceme** Roche; **rack**[1] Cal Sacks; **radiosonde** ESSA Photo; **radish** Roche; **radius** Neil Hardy; **radome** Official NORAD Photo; **ragweed** Roche; **rail**[2] Princeton University Library; **rainbow trout** Gene Hornbeck from NAS; **ram** Charles J. Ott from NAS; **Rama** Government Museum, Madras; **Rameses** Unesco, Laurenza; **rampant** Central Office of Information, London; **randan** Salter Bros. Ltd., Boat Builders, Oxford; **Raphael**[1] Uffizi, Florence, Photo Alinari; **rapier** The Metropolitan Museum of Art, Gift of William H. Riggs, 1913; **Rasputin** Culver Pictures, Inc.; **rat** "Rats," by S.A. Barnett, Copyright © January 1967 by Scientific American, Inc., all rights reserved; **ratchet** Diamond Studios; **rattle**[1] The Metropolitan Museum of Art, Rogers Fund, 1947; **rattlesnake flag** Courtesy U.S. Naval Academy Museum; **raven**[1] Courtesy of The New-York Historical Society, New York City; **ray** R.C. Hermes from NAS; **razor-billed auk** Courtesy of The New-York Historical Society, New York City; **razor clam** Douglas P. Wilson; **reaper** Grant Heilman Photography; **rebec** Uffizi, Florence, Photo Alinari; **rebus** Collection of Mr. & Mrs. Sherman Post Haight; **recorder** The Metropolitan Museum of Art, Crosby Brown Collection of Musical Instruments, 1889; **redbud** Jack Dermid from NAS—Roche; **redingote** Art & Architecture Division, NYPL; **redwing** Allan D. Cruickshank from NAS; **reel**[1] Pflueger Corp.; **re-entrant angle** Carl Bass; **reflection, refraction** Fundamental Photographs; **relief** Smithsonian Institution—Museo Civico, Palermo, Photo Alinari; **reliquary** The Metropolitan Museum of Art, Gift of J. Pierpont Morgan, 1917; **Rembrandt** Copyrighted by Frick Collection, N.Y.; **remora** Matthew Kalmenoff; **reniform** Phoebe McGuire; **Jean Renoir** The Museum of Modern Art, Film Stills Archive; **Pierre Auguste Renoir** Culver Pictures, Inc.; **reredos** Art & Architecture Division, NYPL; **réseau** The Metropolitan Museum of Art, Gift by Subscription, 1909, Blackborne Collection; **resultant** Cal Sacks; **retable** R. Geissler, Inc.; **retort**[2] Corning Glass Works; **retriever** Evelyn M. Shafer; **Paul Revere** Courtesy, Museum of Fine Arts, Boston, gift of the Revere family; **revetment** U.S. Signal Corps; **revolver** Smith & Wesson, Inc.; **Syngman Rhee** A.F.P. from Pictorial Parade; **rhesus monkey** Lynwood Chace from NAS; **rhinoceros** Jane Latta; **Rhode Island Red** Arthur W. Ambler from NAS; **Rhodesian ridgeback** Evelyn M. Shafer; **rhododendron** Roche; **rib** Neil Hardy; **ribbon snake, ribgrass** John H. Gerard from NAS; **Baron von Richthofen** Pictorial Parade; **Edward Rickenbacker** Culver Pictures, Inc.; **ridgepole** *Words: The New Dictionary,*

Grosset & Dunlap, 1947; **rifle**[1] West Point Museum Collections, U.S. Army Signal Corps Photographs; **Jacob Riis** Culver Pictures, Inc.; **ring-necked pheasant** Annan Photo Features; **roadrunner** Matthew Kalmenoff; **Paul Robeson** Paris Match; **robin** Allan D. Cruickshank from NAS—M.F. Soper from NAS; **rockaway** The Suffolk Museum & Carriage House at Stony Brook, L.I.; **rock bass** Don Woolridge from NAS; **rocker arm** Aluminum Co. of America; **rocking horse** Philip Gendreau; **roentgenogram** Deutsches Röntgen-Museum, Remscheid-Lennep; **roller coaster** Philip Gendreau; **roller skate** Ewing Galloway; **rolling mill** *McGraw-Hill Encyclopedia of Science and Technology*, Copyright © 1966, used by permission of McGraw Hill Book Co.; **Romulus** Herschel Levit; **Franklin Delano Roosevelt** Franklin D. Roosevelt Library; **Theodore Roosevelt** The White House Collection; **rorqual** Matthew Kalmenoff; **rose**[1] Matthew Kalmenoff—Roche; **rose window** Archives Photographiques; **rosette** Roche—R. Van Nostrand from NAS; **rotisserie** International Appliance Corp.; **Georges Rouault** Collection, The Museum of Modern Art, N.Y.; **roulette** Ruth Adams from Black Star; **Round Table** Photo Giraudon; **rowan** Roche; **royal palm** Robert Hermes from NAS; **rubber plant** T.H. Everett; **rubbing** Courtesy Abby Aldrich Rockefeller Folk Art Collection; **Peter Paul Rubens** Brown Brothers; **ruby-throated hummingbird** Jackson Abbott; **rudder** New York State Historical Association, Cooperstown; **ruff**[1] The Bettmann Archive; **ruffed grouse** D. Muir from NAS; **Rugby football** United Press International Photo; **rumble seat** Courtesy of the Ford Archives, Henry Ford Museum, Dearborn, Michigan; **runcinate** Ethel H. Hausman; **rune** Alice Koeth; **Mount Rushmore** U.S. Forest Service; **Lillian Russell** Library of Congress; **Babe Ruth** United Press International Photo.

saber Fencing equipment by Santelli; **saber-toothed tiger** Courtesy of The American Museum of Natural History; **sable antelope** Bucky Reeves from NAS; **sabot** Photo Karquel; **safety pin** Risdon Manufacturing Co.; **sage grouse** Hugh M. Halliday from NAS; **Sagittarius** George Lindbloom; **saguaro** Library of the New York Botanical Gardens; **saiga** New York Zoological Society Photo; **Saint Bernard** Evelyn M. Shafer; **Jonas Salk** March of Dimes; **Salome** Bob Jones University Collection; **saltbox** Pilgrim Society, Plymouth, Mass.; **saluki** Evelyn M. Shafer; **salver** The Metropolitan Museum of Art, Rogers Fund, 1912; **samara** Leonard Lee Rue from NAS—Lynwood Chace from NAS; **samisen** Bärenreiter Bild-Archiv; **sand dollar** Walter Dawn; **sandpiper** Allan D. Cruickshank from NAS; **sandwich man** Culver Pictures, Inc.; **sansevieria** T.H. Everett; **Santa Claus** Prints Division, NYPL; **Sappho** Staatliche Antikensammlungen, Munich; **sapsucker** Gordon S. Smith from NAS; **sarcophagus** The Metropolitan Museum of Art, Rogers Fund, 1947; **sari** The Metropolitan Museum of Art, Gift of Mrs. Albert Blum, 1920; **sassafras** Hugh Spencer from NAS; **satellite** NASA; **satin** Courtesy of the Cooper-Hewitt Museum of Design, Smithsonian Institution; **Satsuma ware** The Metropolitan Museum of Art, Gift of Charles Stewart Smith, 1893; **Saturn**[2] Yerkes Observatory Photograph; **sawfish** Robert Hermes from NAS; **saxophone** Elsa Z. Posell; **scabbard** The Metropolitan Museum of Art, Gift of J. Pierpont Morgan, 1917; **scaffold, scaffolding** Philip Gendreau; **scapula** Neil Hardy; **Scaramouch** Bibliothèque Nationale; **scarab** Karl H. Maslowski from NAS—Photograph by Harry Burton, The Metropolitan Museum of Art; **scaup** Roger T. Peterson from NAS; **scepter** Louvre, Photo Alinari-Giraudon; **schnauzer** Evelyn M. Shafer; **schooner** Annan Photo Features; **Schopenhauer** Photo Giraudon; **scimitar** Wallace Kirkland, The Art Institute of Chicago; **scoop** (basswood) Eric Sloane, *Barns and Covered Bridges*; **scorpion** Annan Photo Features; **scorpion fish** *Fishes of the Bahamas*, by J.E. Böhlke and C.C.G. Chaplin, illustrated by S.P. Gigliotti, published for Academy of Natural Sciences of Philadelphia by Livingston Publishing Co., 1968; **Scorpius** George Lindbloom; **Scottish terrier** Evelyn M. Shafer; **screamer** *Introducing Birds*, Stanek, Golden Pleasure Books, London, 1963; **screech owl** New York Zoological Society Photo; **screwdriver** Stanley Tools; **scrimshaw** Seamen's Bank for Savings, N.Y.; **scroll** The Jewish Theological Seminary of America, New York—Hirmer Fotoarchiv, Munich; **scuba** Ron Church from Rapho Guillumette Pictures; **scythe** George Eastman House Collection; **sea anemone** Paul Unger, Photo Library, Inc.—C.G. Maxwell from NAS; **sea cucumber** Courtesy of The American Museum of Natural History; **sea fan** Kitchen-Kinne from NAS; **sea holly** Library of the New York Botanical Gardens; **sea lion** P. Berger from NAS; **sea otter** Matthew Kalmenoff; **secretary bird** *Introducing Birds*, Stanek, Golden Pleasure Books, London, 1963; **secund** Ethel H. Hausman; **sedilia** *A History of Architecture*, 17th Edition, by Banister Fletcher, Athlone Press, University of London; **seesaw** Ruth Orkin Engel; **seismograph** Environmental Science Services Admin.; **self-heal** Ethel H. Hausman; **semaphore** General Railway Signal Co.; **semipalmate** Matthew Kalmenoff; **Semiramis** Honolulu Academy of Arts; **sentry box** British Travel Association; **sepal** Matthew Kalmenoff; **sergeant major** *Fishes of the Bahamas*, by J.E. Böhlke and C.C.G. Chaplin, illustrated by S.P. Gigliotti, published for Academy of Natural Sciences of Philadelphia by Livingston Publishing Co., 1968; **serpent** Courtesy, Museum of Fine Arts, Boston; **serrate** Matthew Kalmenoff; **serval** New York Zoological Society Photo; **sessile** Matthew Kalmenoff; **setback** Fred F. French Co., drawn by Earl Horter; **settle** The Metropolitan Museum of Art, Gift of Mrs. J. Insley Blair, 1947; **seventeen-year locust** U.S. Dept. of Agriculture; **Sèvres** The Metropolitan Museum of Art, Gift of Mrs. Alexander Hosack, 1886; **William H. Seward** Culver Pictures, Inc.; **sexpartite** *A History of Architecture*, 17th Edition, by Banister Fletcher, Athlone Press, University of London; **sextant** Victory Museum, Portsmouth; **Jane Seymour** Kunsthistorisches Museum, Vienna; **shagbark** John H. Gerard from NAS; **shaggy mane** Alvin E. Staffan from NAS; **shako** The Smithsonian Institution; **shamrock** Frances J. Davies; **sharpie** The Smithsonian Institution; **shawl** Musée Carnavalet; **sheik** The Illustrated London News; **shepherd** University of Oregon, Moorhouse College; **shepherd's-purse** Library of the New York Botanical Gardens; **Sheraton** Victoria and Albert Museum; **shinleaf** Matthew Kalmenoff; **Shiva** Dr. & Mrs. Samuel Eilenberg; **shock**[2] State Historical Society of Wisconsin; **shoebill** The Illustrated London News; **shofar** The Jewish Theological Seminary of America, New York; **shooting star** Matthew Kalmenoff; **shrike** G. Ronald Austing from NAS; **shuffleboard** Cunard Line; **Siamese cat** Jeanne White from NAS; **Siamese fighting fish** New York Zoological Society Photo; **sickle** (Above) Dijon, *Moralia in Job*; **sideburns** The National Archives; **sidesaddle** H. Kaufman & Sons Saddlery Co., Photo by Kendra K. Ho; **side wheel** Oregon Historical Society; **silhouette** The Metropolitan Museum of Art, Bequest of Mary Martin, 1938; **silkworm** New York Zoological Society Photo; **silo** Lewis W. Hine, George Eastman House Collection; **Silvanus** British Museum; **Upton Sinclair** Brown Brothers; **sine curve** Carl Bass; **siphon** John Keaveny; **siren** British Museum; **sitar** Marilyn Silverstone, Magnum; **Sitting Bull** National Archives, U.S. Signal Corps; **ski jump** Annan Photo Features; **skimmer** Courtesy of The New-York Historical Society, New York City; **skullcap** Israeli Government Tourist Office; **skunk cabbage** Elsie M. Rodgers from NAS; **skywriting** Philip Gendreau; **slapstick** Culver Pictures, Inc.; **sled, sleigh** Princeton University Library, Sinclair Hamilton Collection; **slingshot** Philip Gendreau; **John Sloan** Art Students League of New York, Photo by Peter A. Juley & Son; **sloop** Stanley Rosenfeld; **sloth bear** San Diego Zoo Photo; **sluice** Dale Walden; **smallclothes** Bibliothèque Nationale; **small intestine** Neil Hardy; **smartweed** Library of the New York Botanical Gardens; **smocking** Victoria and Albert Museum; **snail** Annan Photo Features; **snakeroot** "Common Poisonous Plants," by John M. Kingsbury, Cornell Extension Bulletin 538; **snapdragon** Library of the New York Botanical Gardens; **snapping turtle** Isabelle Conant from NAS; **snipe** Joe Van Wormer from NAS; **snow leopard** R. Van Nostrand from NAS; **snowshoe** Public Archives of Canada; **snuffbox** The Metropolitan Museum of Art, Gift of J. Pierpont Morgan, 1917; **soda fountain** Brown Brothers; **sofa** The Metropolitan Museum of Art, Rogers Fund, 1925; **solleret** The Metropolitan Museum of Art, Rogers Fund and Gift of William H. Riggs, 1917; **Solomon's seal** Matthew Kalmenoff; **sombrero** Brown Brothers; **Sophocles** Bibliothèque Nationale, Photo Giraudon; **sorghum** Grant Heilman Photography; **sorus** Courtesy of The American Museum of Natural History; **soursop** Matthew Kalmenoff; **John Philip Sousa** Library of Congress; **sousaphone** Philip Gendreau; **space station** NASA—Lockheed; **spadefish** Annan Photo Features; **spadix** Matthew Kalmenoff; **Spanish bayonet** Hugo Schroder from NAS; **Spanish moss** Robert Ellison from NAS—Standard Oil Co., N.J.; **spanker** *Sailing and Small Craft Down the Ages*, copyrighted 1940 by the U.S. Naval Institute, Annapolis, Maryland; **spathe** Matthew Kalmenoff; **spectroheliogram** Yerkes Observatory Photograph; **Oswald Spengler** The Bettmann Archive; **sphenoid bone** Neil Hardy; **sperm whale** Matthew Kalmenoff; **sphinx** John Ross; **sphygmomanometer** Bernard Cole Photo; **spider** Jerome Wexler from NAS; **spine** Neil Hardy; **spinnaker** Philip Gendreau; **spiny lobster** Matthew Kalmenoff; **spitz** Capt. Arthur J. Haggerty; **splay** Art & Architecture Division, NYPL; **spleenwort** Roche; **spline** Cal Sacks; **spoke**[1] N.Y. Herald Tribune; **spoonbill** Dade W. Thornton from NAS; **sporran, spreader** Philip Gendreau; **springer spaniel** Evelyn M. Shafer; **squash**[1] Matthew Kalmenoff; **squid** Robert Hermes from NAS; **squirrel** Allan D. Cruickshank from NAS; **squirrelfish** *Fishes of the Bahamas*, by J.E. Böhlke and C.C.G. Chaplin, illustrated by S.P. Gigliotti, published for Academy of Natural Sciences of Philadelphia by Livingston Publishing Co., 1968; **squirrel monkey** San Diego Zoo Photo; **stadium** Mella; **stained glass** Archives Photographiques; **staircase** Charleston Museum, by Louis Schwartz; **stalactite, stalagmite** National Park Service Photos; **stamen** Matthew Kalmenoff; **stamp** Emmett Collection, NYPL; **starfish** G. Clifford Carl from NAS; **stargazer** Matthew Kalmenoff; **star-nosed mole** Lynwood Chace from NAS; **star sapphire** Courtesy of The American Museum of Natural History; **Statue of Liberty** The Port of New York Authority; **steam engine** Skinner Engine Co.—*McGraw-Hill Encyclopedia of Science and Technology*, copyright © 1960, used by permission of McGraw-Hill Book Company; **steam shovel** Bucyrus-Erie Co.; **steelyard** The Metropolitan Museum of Art Purchase, 1900; **steeple** Samuel Chamberlain; **stegosaur** Courtesy of The American Museum of Natural History; **stele** National Museum, Athens, Hirmer; **stentor** Walter Dawn; **stem**[1] Universitetets Oldsaksamling, Oslo; **stern**[2] The Science Museum, London; **stern-wheeler, Stetson** Standard Oil Co., N.J.; **stethoscope** Bernard Cole; **stile**[1] Anthony Howarth; **stingray** *Fishes of the Bahamas*, by J.E. Böhlke and C.C.G. Chaplin, illustrated by S.P. Gigliotti, published for Academy of Natural Sciences of Philadelphia by Livingston Publishing Co., 1968; **stinkhorn** Grant Haist from NAS; **stipule** Matthew Kalmenoff; **stoat** Zoological Society of London; **stole**[1] Crocker Art Gallery; **stomach** Neil Hardy; **stomacher** Louvre, Photo Giraudon; **Stonehenge** British Information Service; **stoop**[2] Museum of The City of New York; **stork** Eric Hosking from NAS; **storm center** Environmental Science Services Administration; **storm petrel** Courtesy of The New-York Historical Society, New York City; **Harriet Beecher Stowe** The Metropolitan Museum of Art, Gift of I.N. Phelps Stokes, Edward S. Hawes, Alice Mary Hawes, Marion Augusta Hawes, 1937; **straining beam** Cal Sacks; **stratocumulus** U.S. Weather Bureau; **stratum** Courtesy of The American Museum of Natural History; **strawberry** Grant Heilman Photography; **streetcar** Frank Rawsome, Jr.; **stretcher-bearer** Heeres, Museum, Vienna; **string bean** Burpee Seeds; **stroboscope** General Radio Co.; **Erich von Stroheim** Paramount Pictures, Inc.; **strut** Photo Alinari; **Gilbert Stuart** Redwood Library and Athenaeum, Newport, R.I.; **sturgeon, style** Matthew Kalmenoff; **Peter Stuyvesant** Courtesy of The New-York Historical Society, New York City; **submarine** Official U.S. Navy Photo; **sugar beet** Grant Heilman Photography; **Sukarno** American Bank Note Co.; **sulky**[2] Library of Congress; **John L. Sullivan** Brown Brothers; **sumac** Hugh Spencer from NAS; **sunburst, sundial** Courtesy of Parke-Bernet Galleries; **sun disk** Hirmer Fotoarchiv, Munich; **sunflower** Roche; **superhighway** U.S. Travel Service; **surcoat** The Pierpont Morgan Library; **surfboard** Annan Photo Features; **surrealism** The Museum of Modern Art; **surrey** George Eastman House Collection; **suspension bridge** Californians Inc.; **Sussex spaniel** C.M. Cooke & Son; **swallow**[2] Allan D. Cruickshank from NAS; **swallow-tail** Stephen Dalton from NAS; **swan** Annan Photo Features; **swastika** *Lore and Lure of Outer Space*, by Ernst and Johanna Lehner, Tudor, 1964—U.S. Army Photograph; **sweep** Jane Latta—Princeton University Library, Sinclair Hamilton Collection; **sweet William** Roche; **swift** Lynwood Chace from NAS; **swordbill** New York Zoological Society Photo; **synchrotron** Brookhaven National Laboratory; **syncline** *Geology Illustrated*, by John S. Shelton, W.H. Freeman and Co., Copyright © 1966; **John Millington Synge** Bibliothèque Nationale; **syringe** Becton, Dickinson & Co.; **syzygy** John Keaveny.

tabla Information Service of India; **tadpole** Matthew Kalmenoff; **taffrail** The Science Museum, London; **William Howard Taft** Library of Congress; **takahe** Matthew Kalmenoff; **talaria** Courtesy, Museum of Fine Arts, Boston, William Amory Gardner Fund; **tallith** The Jewish Theological Seminary of America, New York; **tamandua** Annan Photo Features; **tamarind** Smithsonian Institution; **tanager** Courtesy of The New-York Historical Society, New York City; **tangent** Carl Bass; **tangram** *Tangrams; Picture-Making Puzzle Game*, by Peter Van Note, Charles E. Tuttle Co., 1966; **tank** United Press International Photo; **tankard** Courtesy, Museum of Fine Arts, Boston; **tarantula** Princeton University Library, Sinclair Hamilton Collection; **taro** U.S. Dept. of Agriculture; **tarot** The Pierpont Morgan Library; **tarsier** Arthur W. Ambler from NAS; **Tasmanian devil** R. Van Nostrand from NAS; **tassel** Courtesy of the Cooper-Hewitt Museum of Design, Smithsonian Institution; **tattoo**[2] Philip Gendreau; **Taurus** George Lindbloom; **taxidermy** Courtesy of The American Museum of Natural History; **teal** Allan D. Cruickshank from NAS; **teapot** The Metropolitan Museum of Art, Rogers Fund, 1946; **teddy bear** Theodore Roosevelt Assoc.; **tektite** Courtesy of The American Museum of Natural History; **telega** Brown Brothers; **telescope** Photo Researchers Inc.; **Templar** Universitätsbibliothek, Heidelberg; **temple**[1] Utah Tourist & Publicity Council, Hal Rumel; **tender**[3] Illinois Central Railroad; **ten-gallon hat** Library of Congress, Courtesy Mrs. L.M. Pettis, Irwin E. Smith Photo; **Alfred Tennyson** Julia Cameron, George Eastman House Collection; **tent**[1] Bibliothèque Nationale—State of Minnesota; **tent caterpillar** Hal H. Harrison from NAS; **tepee** *Red Man's America*, by Ruth Underhill, © 1953 University of Chicago; **tern**[1] Courtesy of The New-York Historical Society, New York City; **terrapin** Jack Dermid from NAS; **terrarium** Gottscho-Schleisner, Inc.; **tête-à-tête** The Metropolitan Museum of Art, Gift of Mrs. Charles Reginald Leonard, 1957, in memory of Edgar Welch Leonard, Robert Jarvis Leonard, and Charles Reginald Leonard; **tête-bêche** The Philatelic Foundation; **tetra** Gene Wolfsheimer from NAS; **tetrahedron** Carl Bass; **Thalia** Roger-Viollet; **U Thant** United Nations; **theodolite** Wild-Heerbrugg Instruments Inc.; **Saint Theresa** S. Maria della Vittoria, Photo Anderson; **Theseus** Vatican Museum, Photo Anderson; **thistle** Roche; **thole pin** Courtesy of The Marine Historical Association; **Dylan Thomas** Rollie McKenna; **Thor** National Museum of Iceland, Photo Gestsson; **thorn** Alice Koeth; **Thoth** Louvre, Photo Agraci; **thrasher** Annan Photo Features; **three-decker** Brian Seed; **thresh** Princeton University Library, Sinclair Hamilton Collection; **thrust fault** U.S. Geological Survey, V.H. Barnett; **thunderbird** Provincial Archives, Victoria, B.C.—By Permission of the Bancroft Library, University of California, Berkeley; **thunderhead** U.S. Weather Bureau, Butler; **thylacine** Australian News & Information Bureau; **tiara** Rome, Photo Anderson; **Tiffany glass** Courtesy of Parke-Bernet Galleries; **tiger** Jane Latta; **tiger lily** Roche; **tilefish** Courtesy of The American Museum of Natural History; **tiller**[2] Courtesy of The Marine Historical Association; **timber wolf** Annan Photo Features; **time clock** Monkmeyer Press; **timothy** Matthew Kalmenoff; **Tintoretto** Louvre, Photo Giraudon; **tippet** Bibliothèque Nationale; **titi**[2] Zoological Society of London; **Titian** Museo del Prado, Madrid; **titmouse** Courtesy of The New-York Historical Society, New York City; **toby** The Metropolitan Museum of Art, Gift of R. Thornton Wilson, 1943, in memory of his wife, Florence Ellsworth Wilson; **toga** Museo Archeologico, Florence, Photo Alinari; **Hideki Tojo** Wide World Photos; **tole** Jane Latta; **tomahawk** Museum of the American Indian; **tomato** Roche; **tom-tom** Marc & Evelyne Bernheim from Rapho-Guillumette; **tonsure** Bibliothèque Nationale; **tooth** Neil Hardy; **tooth shell** Matthew Kalmenoff; **tope**[3] Agence Rapho, Louis-Frédéric; **topiary** Paul Genereux; **torii** Minoru Aoki from Rapho Guillumette; **torque**[2] British Museum; **tortoiseshell** Museum of the City of New York; **totem pole** Courtesy of The American Museum of Natural History; **totipalmate** Matthew Kalmenoff; **Toussaint L'Ouverture** The Old Print Shop; **towhee** Courtesy of The New-York Historical Society, New York City; **tracer bullet** United Press International Photo; **tracery** Photo Anderson; **traffic light** Philip Gendreau; **tragopan, trailing arbutus** Matthew Kalmenoff; **train** Union Pacific Railroad; **trajectory** Fundamental Photographs; **transept** (cathedral) Photo Pilotte et Opérateur; **trap**[1] George Eastman House Collection; **trap-door spider** Lynwood Chace from NAS; **traveler** Courtesy of The Marine Historical Association; **treadmill** Library of Congress; **treasury note** Chase Manhattan Money Museum; **tree frog** Carl Koski; **trefoil** Photo Jean Roubier; **trestle** Museum of the City of New York; **triangle** Carl Bass; **triceratops** Matthew Kalmenoff; **triclinium** Photo Alinari; **tricycle** F.A.O. Schwarz; **trident** Photo D. Widmer; **triforium** (Canterbury) Photo Boudot-Lamotte; **triggerfish** *Fishes of the Bahamas*, by J.E. Böhlke and C.C.G. Chaplin, illustrated by S.P. Gigliotti, published for Academy of Natural Sciences of Philadelphia by Livingston Publishing Co., 1968; **trillium** Earl Palmer; **trilobite** Courtesy of The American Museum of Natural History; **Trimurti** Leonard McCombe, Life Magazine © Time Inc.; **triplane** Culver Pictures, Inc.; **triptych** The Metropolitan Museum of Art, Gift of J. Pierpont Morgan, 1917; **trivet** Courtesy, Henry Francis du Pont Winterthur Museum; **tropicbird** Karl Kenyon from NAS; **Leon Trotsky** Culver Pictures, Inc.; **Harry S Truman** Wide World Photos; **trumpet** *Musical Instruments Through the Ages*, Spring Books, 1956; **trumpeter swan** Annan Photo Features; **trunkfish** *Fishes of the Bahamas*, by J.E. Böhlke and C.C.G. Chaplin, illustrated by S.P. Gigliotti, published for Academy of Natural Sciences of Philadelphia by Livingston Publishing Co., 1968; **truss bridge** The Illustrated London News; **T-square** J.L. Hammett Co.; **tuatara** Alfred M. Bailey from NAS; **tuba** Culver Pictures, Inc.; **tugboat** Moran Towing; **tulip** Roche; **tulip tree** Arthur W. Ambler from NAS; **tumbleweed** Grant Heilman Photography; **tuna**[1] U.S. Bureau of Commercial Fisheries; **tuning fork** Kitching Co.; **tureen** Courtesy of Parke-Bernet Galleries; **turkey** Courtesy of The New-York Historical Society, New York City—John H. Gerard from NAS; **turkey buzzard** Allan D. Cruickshank from NAS; **Turk's-head** *The Ashley Book of Knots*, copyright 1944 by Clifford W. Ashley, reprinted by permission of Doubleday & Co., Inc.; **turtlehead** Arthur W. Ambler from NAS; **Tutankhamen** Photograph by Harry Burton, The Metropolitan Museum of Art; **tutu** Courtesy Hurok Concerts; **"Boss Tweed"** (photo) Brown Brothers; **twill** Courtesy of the Cooper-Hewitt Museum of Design, Smithsonian Institution; **tympanum** Archives Photographiques; **typewriter** SCM Corp.; **tyrannosaur** Matthew Kalmenoff.

U-bolt Chicago Hardware & Fixture Co.; **ulna** Neil Hardy; **ultramicroscope** Pennsylvania State University—Bausch & Lomb; **umbra** Cal Sacks; **umbrella bird** Arthur W. Ambler from NAS; **undercroft** Bildarchiv Foto Marburg; **undershot** Jane Latta; **unicorn** The Metropolitan Museum, The Cloisters Collection, Gift of John D. Rockefeller, Jr., 1937; **unicycle** Brown Brothers; **uraeus** Hirmer Fotoarchiv, Munich; **Uranus**[2] Yerkes Observatory Photograph; **urn** Museo Nazionale delle Terme, Rome, Photo Alinari; **Ursa Major, Ursa Minor** George Lindbloom; **Utamaro** British Museum; **Maurice Utrillo** Culver Pictures, Inc.

valance Courtesy of The Brooklyn Museum, Dick S. Ramsay Fund; **vampire** Matthew Kalmenoff; **Martin Van Buren** Library of Congress; **Van de Graaff generator** Oak Ridge National Laboratory; **Vandyke** Prado-Scala; **vane** Courtesy of The New-York Historical Society, New York City; **Vincent van Gogh** Louvre, Photo Giraudon; **veil** Philip Gendreau; **Diego Velázquez** Prado Museum; **Venus**[1] Uffizi Gallery, Florence, Photo Alinari; **Venus's flower basket** Courtesy of The American Museum of Natural History; **Venus's-flytrap** Roche; **verniculate** Photo Viollet; **vermiform appendix** Neil Hardy; **vernier** Brown & Sharpe Mfg. Co.; **Versailles** Musée de Versailles, Photo Giraudon; **Amerigo Vespucci** Uffizi Gallery, Florence; **Vesuvius** Brogi, Pompeii; **vibraphone** Premier Drum Co., London; **viburnum** Roche; **viceroy** Gaston LePage from NAS; **victoria** The Suffolk Museum & Carriage House at Stony Brook, L.I.; **Victoria**[1] Radio Times Hulton Picture Library; **vicuña** Arthur W. Ambler from NAS; **"Pancho" Villa** Brown Brothers; **vina** Music Division, NYPL; **vinaigrette** From the collection of Eileen Ellenbogen, Courtesy of Antiques Magazine; **vinegarroon** New York Zoological Society Photo; **violet** Roche; **virginal**[2] Prints Division, NYPL; **Virginia creeper** Jane Latta; **virgin's-bower** Roche; **Virgo** George Lindbloom; **Vishnu** Courtesy, Museum of Fine Arts, Boston, Marianne Brimmer Fund; **visor** Roger-Viollet; **Maurice de Vlaminck** Culver Pictures, Inc.; **voiceprint** Bell Telephone Laboratories; **volcano** Western Ways Photo by Tad Nichols; **vole**[1] Annan Photo Features; **volvox** William H. Amos; **Jean Édouard Vuillard** Photo Giraudon; **Vulcan** Vatican Museum, Photo Anderson; **Andrei Vyshinsky** Wide World Photos.

waddy Anthropological Museum, University of Aberdeen; **waffle iron** Philadelphia Museum of Art; **Richard Wagner** Photo Roger-Viollet; **wagonette** The Suffolk Museum & Carriage House at Stony Brook, L.I.; **Wailing Wall** Zionist Archives & Library; **walking stick** Annan Photo Features; **wallaby** Zoological Society of London; **walnut** John H. Gerard from NAS—Alvin Staffan from NAS; **walrus** Matthew Kalmenoff; **wampum** Chase Manhattan Money Museum—National Museum of Canada; **wapiti** Willis Peterson; **war bonnet** Culver Pictures, Inc.; **warming pan** Philadelphia Museum of Art; **wart hog** Jeanne White from NAS; **Booker T. Washington** Chicago American's Morgue; **George Washington** Pennsylvania Academy of the Fine Arts; **wasp** Robert C. Hermes from NAS; **wasp waist** Culver Pictures, Inc.; **watch cap** Cal Sacks; **water boatman** Stephen Dalton from NAS; **waterbuck** Lynn Millar, Rapho-Guillumette; **water buffalo** UNESCO, J.P. Faure; **waterfall** Ray Atkeson; **water hyacinth, water lily** Roche; **water moccasin** Leonard Lee Rue from NAS; **water ouzel** Matthew Kalmenoff; **water spaniel** Evelyn M. Shafer; **wattle** Annan Photo Features; **waveform** Carl Bass; **waxwing** Karl H. Maslowski from NAS; **weasel** John H. Gerard from NAS; **weather balloon** ESSA Photo; **weathercock** M. Bazin, Paris; **weave** Cal Sacks; **weaverbird** Karl H. Maslowski from NAS; **wedgwood** Wedgwood Co.; **weeping willow** (photo) John H. Gerard from NAS; **weevil** Jerome Wexler from NAS; **weight** Ohaus Scale; **Chaim Weizmann** Israel Information Services; **well**[1] Cal Sacks; **Welsh corgi, Welsh terrier** Annan Photo Features; **wentletrap** John H. Gerard from NAS; **John Wesley** National Portrait Gallery, London; **whaleback** The Great Lakes Historical Society, Cleveland; **whalebone whale** Matthew Kalmenoff; **wheat** Grant Heilman Photography; **Wheatstone Bridge** Carl Bass; **wheelbarrow** Cal Sacks; **wheel bug** Matthew Kalmenoff; **whelk**[1] John H. Gerard from NAS; **whip** From The Charles M. Russell Book by Harold McCracken; **whippet** Evelyn M. Shafer; **whippoorwill** The New-York Historical Society, New York City; **whistle** Field Manufacturing Co.—Lunkenheimer; **James Whistler** Library of Congress; **The White House** Philip Gendreau; **white pine** (photo) Jeanne White from NAS; **white-tailed deer** Annan Photo Features; **whooping crane** Allan D. Cruickshank from NAS; **whorl** Roche; **whydah** Matthew Kalmenoff; **wicket** G.R. Roberts, New Zealand—Van De Poll from Monkmeyer Press; **wickiup** Smithsonian Institution, American Ethnology Collection; **widgeon** Roger T. Peterson from NAS; **wigwam** (photo) Museum of the American Indian; **Oscar Wilde** Prints Division, NYPL; **wild ginger** John H. Gerard from NAS; **wimple** Stadt Augsburg, Kunstsammlungen; **windbreak** U.S. Dept. of Agriculture; **windmill** Jane Latta; **wind rose** *McGraw-Hill Encyclopedia of Science and Technology*, Copyright © 1960, used by permission of McGraw-Hill Book Co.; **Windsor chair** Philadelphia Museum of Art; **wine cellar** Philip Gendreau; **wing** Cal Sacks; **wing chair** National Gallery of Art; **winter cherry, wisteria** Roche; **witch hazel** Gottscho-Schleisner; **wolf** Arthur W. Ambler from NAS; **Thomas Wolsey** National Portrait Gallery, London; **wolverine** Annan Photo Features; **wombat** Australian News & Information Bureau; **woodchuck** Annan Photo Features; **woodcock** Karl H. Maslowski from NAS; **wood ibis** Dade W. Thornton from NAS; **woodpecker** Annan Photo Features; **wood sorrell** Ethel H. Hausman; **woolly bear** Lynwood Chace from NAS; **Worcester china** The Metropolitan Museum of Art, Gift of Mr. & Mrs. Luke Vincent Lockwood, 1939; **worm gear** Superior Manufacturing & Instrument; **wreath** Photo Anderson-Giraudon; **wren** John H. Gerard from NAS; **wrench** (A) New Britain Machine (B) Powr-Kraft (C) Crescent Tool (D) Ridgid Tool (E) New Britain Machine (F) New Britain Machine; **Frank Lloyd Wright** Obma Studios.

Saint Francis Xavier The Folger Shakespeare Library; **X-chromosome** NYS Psychiatric Institute, Jarvik & Kato; **Xerxes I** Archaeological Museum, Teheran, Photo Joubert; **xylophone** J.C. Deagan.

yam Matthew Kalmenoff; **yarrow** Roche; **yashmak** Culver Pictures, Inc.; **Y-chromosome** NYS Psychiatric Institute, Jarvik & Kato; **yeast** *Botany*, 3rd edition, by Carl L. Wilson and Walter E. Loomis, Copyright 1952, © 1957, 1962 by Holt, Rinehart and Winston, Inc.; **yew** Roche; **yogh** Alice Koeth; **yoke** Moorhouse Collection, University of Oregon Library; **Yorkshire terrier** Annan Photo Features; **yucca** Joseph Muench.

zebra Annan Photo Features; **zebu** Matthew Kalmenoff; **zeppelin** Denver Public Library Western Collection; **Zeus** National Archaeological Museum, Athens; **zinnia** Roche; **zither** Culver Pictures, Inc.; **zodiac** Zodiac design adapted from zodiac drawn by Hans Holbein and Albrecht Dürer, reproduced with the permission of Charles Scribner's Sons from *Shakespeare's Globe Playhouse* by Irwin Smith, Copyright © 1956 Charles Scribner's Sons; **Émile Zola** Bibliothèque Nationale; **zucchini** Roche; **zygodactyl** *A New Dictionary of Birds*, ed. by A.L. Thomson, McGraw-Hill Book Co. and Thomas Nelson and Sons, Ltd., 1964.

Indo-European and the Indo-Europeans

This description of reconstructed Proto-Indo-European, together with observations of the cultural inferences that can be drawn from it, follows on from Professor Watkins' general introduction to the subject in the front of the Dictionary.

The forms given in **boldface** type are Indo-European roots that are entries in the Appendix. The words in SMALL CAPITALS are English words whose etymologies in the body of the Dictionary relate them to the roots here discussed. For fuller insight into the relationships alluded to, the reader is encouraged to pursue both of these kinds of reference. According to regular linguistic convention, an asterisk is placed before every reconstructed form (a form that is not attested in documents).

by Calvert Watkins

After the initial discovery of a prehistoric language underlying the modern Indo-European family, and the foundation of the science of comparative linguistics, the detailed reconstruction of Proto-Indo-European proceeded by stages still fascinating to observe. The main outlines of the reconstructed language were already seen by the end of the 1870's, but it is only in the twentieth century that certain of these features have received general acceptance. Though not affecting vocabulary in any serious way, many questions remain open even today, both in reconstruction and in the histories of the individual languages.

An Example of Reconstruction

We may illustrate the comparative method by a concrete case, which will serve at the same time to indicate the high degree of preciseness that the techniques of reconstruction permit.

A number of Indo-European languages show a similar word for the kinship term "daughter-in-law": Sanskrit *snuṣā́*, Old English *snoru*, Old Church Slavonic *snŭkha* (Russian *snokhá*), Latin *nurus*, Greek *nuós*, and Armenian *nu*. Albanian has *nuse* in the meaning "bride," a meaning shared by the Armenian form; in a patrilocal and patriarchal society, where the bride went to live in her husband's father's house, "daughter-in-law" and "bride" were equivalents.

All of these forms, spoken of as *cognates*, provide evidence for the phonetic shape of the prehistoric Indo-European word for "daughter-in-law" that is their common ancestor. Sanskrit, Germanic, and Slavic agree in showing an Indo-European word that began with *sn-*. We know that an Indo-European *s* was lost before *n* in other words in Latin, Greek, Armenian, and Albanian, so we can confidently assume that Latin *nurus*, Greek *nuós*, Armenian *nu*, and Albanian *nuse* go back to an Indo-European **sn-*. (Compare Latin *nix* (stem *niv-*), "snow," with English SNOW, preserving the *s*.) This principle is spoken of as the *regularity of sound correspondences;* it is basic to the sciences of etymology and comparative linguistics.

Sanskrit, Latin, Greek, Armenian, and Albanian agree in showing the first vowel as *-u-*. We know from other examples that Slavic *ŭ* regularly corresponds to Sanskrit *u* and that Ger-

manic *o* (of Old English *snoru*) in this position has been changed from an earlier *u*. It is thus justifiable to reconstruct an Indo-European word beginning **snu-*.

For the consonant originally following **snu-*, closer analysis is required. The key is furnished first by the Sanskrit form, for we know there is a rule in Sanskrit that *s* always changes to *ṣ* (a *sh*-like sound) after the vowel *u*. Hence a Sanskrit *snuṣ-* must go back to an earlier **snus-*. In the same position, after *u*, an old *s* changes to *kh* (like the *ch* in Scottish *loch* or German *ach*) in Slavic; hence the Slavic word, too, reflects **snus-*. In Latin always, and under certain conditions also in Germanic, an old *-s-* between vowels went to *-r-*. For this reason Latin *nurus* and Old English *snoru* may go back to older **snus-* (followed by a vowel) as well. In Greek and Armenian, on the other hand, an old *-s-* between vowels disappeared entirely, as we know from numerous instances. Greek *nuós* and Armenian *nu* (stem *nuo-*) thus regularly presuppose the same earlier form, **snus-* (followed by a vowel). Finally, that *-s-* between vowels is still preserved—almost accidentally, one might say—in Albanian *nuse*. All the comparative evidence agrees, then, on the Indo-European root form **snus-*.

For the ending, the final vowels of Sanskrit *snuṣā́*, Old English *snoru*, and Slavic *snŭkha* all presuppose earlier *-ā* (**snus-ā*), which is the ordinary feminine ending of these languages. On the other hand, Latin *nurus*, Greek *nuós*, and Armenian *nu* (stem *nuo-*) all regularly presuppose the earlier ending **-os* (**snus-os*). We have an apparent impasse; but the way out is given by the gender of the forms in Greek and Latin. They are feminine, even though most nouns in Latin *-us* and Greek *-os* are masculine.

Feminine nouns in Latin *-us* and Greek *-os*, since they are an abnormal type, cannot have been created afresh; they must have been inherited. This suggests that the original Indo-European form was **snusos*, of feminine gender. On the other hand, the commonplace freely formed ending for feminine nouns was **-ā*. It is reasonable to suggest that the three languages Sanskrit, Germanic, and Slavic replaced the peculiar feminine ending **-os* (because the ending was normally masculine) with the normal ordinary feminine ending **-ā*, and thus that the oldest form of the word was **snusos* (feminine).

One point remains to be ascertained: the accent. Of those

four language groups that reflect the Indo-European accent, Sanskrit, (Balto-)Slavic, Greek, and Germanic, the first three are agreed in showing a form accented on the last syllable: *snuṣá̄, snochá, nuós*. The Germanic form is equally precise, however, since the rule is that old *-s-* went to *-r-* (Old English *snoru*) only if the accented syllable came after the *-s-*.

On this basis we may add the finishing touch to our reconstruction: the full form of the word for "daughter-in-law" in Indo-European is **snusós*.

It is noteworthy that no single language in the family preserves this word intact. In every language, in every tradition in the Indo-European family, the word has been somehow altered from its original shape. It is the comparative method that permits us to explain the different forms in this variety of languages, by the reconstruction of a unitary common prototype, a common ancestor.

Phonology and Morphology

The system of sounds in Proto-Indo-European was rich in stop consonants. We have an unvoiced series, *p, t, k, kw* (like the *qu* of *quick*), a voiced series, *b, d, g, gw*, and a voiced aspirate series, *bh, dh, gh, gwh*, pronounced like the voiced series but followed by a puff of breath. Some forms suggest also the existence of an unvoiced aspirate series, *ph, th, kh*, as well, at least for the dialect of Indo-European from which Greek, Armenian, and Indo-Iranian came. If the language was rich in stop consonants, it was correspondingly poor in continuants (fricatives, like English *f, v, th, s, z*), having only *s*.

The language had two nasals, *m* and *n*, two liquids, *r* and *l*, and the glides *w, y*, and *ə*. A salient characteristic of Indo-European was that these sounds could function both as consonants and as vowels. Their consonantal value was as in English; *ə*, the "laryngeal," had an *h*-like sound, of which there may have been more than one variety. As vowels, symbolized *m̥, n̥, l̥, r̥*, the liquids and nasals sounded much like the final syllables of English *bottom, button, bottle, butter*. The vocalic counterparts of *w, y*, and *ə* were the vowels *u, i*, and *ə* (schwa).

The other vowels of Indo-European were *e, o*, and *a*. These and *i* and *u* occurred both long and short. Since we can distinguish chronological layers in Proto-Indo-European, it can be said that a number of the long vowels of later Indo-European result from contractions of early Indo-European short vowels with a following *ə*. The sound *ə* (often written H and in Hittite transliterated *ḫ*) is preserved as such only in Hittite and the other Anatolian languages in cuneiform documents from the second millennium B.C. In all the other languages of the family, its former presence in a word can only be deduced from these contractions and from other indirect evidence. The elucidation of the details of these laryngeals remains one of the most interesting problems confronting Indo-Europeanists today.

A characteristic feature of Indo-European was the system of vocalic alternations termed *apophony* or *ablaut*. This was a set of internal vowel changes expressing different morphological functions. A clear reflex of this feature is preserved in the English strong verbs, where for example the vocalic alternations between *write* and *wrote, give* and *gave* express the present and preterit tenses. Ablaut in Indo-European affected the vowels *e* and *o*. The fundamental form was *e;* this *e* could appear as *o* under certain conditions, and in other conditions both *e* and *o* could disappear entirely. On this basis we speak of given forms in Indo-European as exhibiting, respectively, the *e-grade* (or full grade), the *o-grade*, or the *zero-grade*. The *e* and the *o* might furthermore occur as long *ē* or *ō*, termed the *lengthened-grade*.

To illustrate: the Indo-European root **ped-*[1], "foot," appears in the e-grade in Latin *ped-* (PEDAL) but in the o-grade in Greek *pod-* (PODIATRIST). Germanic **fōtuz* (FOOT) reflects the lengthened o-grade **pōd-*. The zero-grade of the same root shows no vowel at all: **pd-*, a form attested in Sanskrit.

When the zero-grade involved a root with one of the sounds *m, n, r, l, w, y*, or *ə* (collectively termed *resonants*), the resonant would regularly appear in vocalic function, forming a syllable. We have the e-grade root **sengwh-* in English SING, the o-grade form **songwh-* in SANG and SONG, and the zero-grade form **sngwh-* in SUNG.

Grammar and Syntax

Proto-Indo-European was a highly inflected language. Grammatical relationships and the syntactic function of words in the sentence were indicated primarily by variations in the endings of the words. Nouns had different endings for the case of the subject of the verb, the direct object of the verb, the possessive, and for many other functions, as well as for singular, plural, and a special dual number for objects occurring in pairs. Verbs had different endings for the different persons (first, second, third) and numbers (singular, plural, dual), for the voices active and passive (or middle, a sort of reflexive), as well as special affixes for a rich variety of tenses, moods, and such categories as causative-transitive and stative-intransitive verbs. Practically none of this rich inflection is preserved in native Modern English, but it has left its trace in many formations in Germanic and in other languages such as Latin and Greek. These are noted in the Appendix where they are relevant.

With the exception of the numbers five to ten and a group of particles including certain conjunctions and quasi-adverbial forms, all Indo-European words underwent inflection. The structure of all inflected words, regardless of part of speech, was the same: *root* plus one or more *suffixes* plus *ending*. Thus the word **ker-wo-s*, "a stag," is composed of the root **ker-*[1], "horn," plus the noun suffix *-wo-*, plus the nominative singular ending *-s*. The root contained the basic semantic kernel, the underlying notion, which the suffix could modify in various ways. It was primarily the suffix that determined the part of speech of the word. Thus a single root like **prek-* (variant of **perk-*[2]) could, depending on the suffix, form a verb **prk-sko-*, "to ask" (Latin *poscere*), a noun **prek-*, "prayer" (Latin *precēs*), and an adjective **prok-o-*, "asking" (underlying Latin *procus*, "suitor"). Note that **prek-, *prok-*, and **prk-* have, respectively, e-, o-, and zero-grade.

The root could undergo certain modifications, spoken of as *extensions* or *enlargements*. These did not affect the basic meaning and simply reflect formal variations between languages.

Suffixes had more specific values. We have verbal suffixes that make nouns into verbs and others that mark different types of action, like transitive and intransitive. We have nominal suffixes that make agent nouns, abstract nouns, verbal nouns and verbal adjectives, nouns of instrument, and other functions.

The root plus suffix(es) constituted the *stem*. The stems represented the basic lexical stock of Indo-European, the separate words of its dictionary. Yet commonly a single root would furnish a large number of derivative stems with different suffixes, both nominal and verbal (much as English *love* is both noun and verb), as well as the base of such derivatives as *lovely, lover, beloved*. For this reason it is customary to group such collections of derivatives, in a variety of Indo-European languages, under the root on which they are built. The root Appendix of this Dictionary is so arranged, with derivatives exhibiting similar suffixes forming subgroups consisting of Indo-European stems, or words.

Indo-European made extensive use of suffixation in the formation of words but had very few prefixes. The use of such prefixes ("preverbs") as Latin *ad-, con-, de-, ex-* (ADVENT, CONVENTION, etc.) or Germanic *be-* (BECALM, BECLOUD) can be shown to be a development of the individual languages after the breakup of the common language. In Indo-European, such "compounds" still represented two independent words, a situation still reflected in Hittite and the older Sanskrit of the Rig-Veda (the sacred hymns of the ancient Hindus) and surviving in isolated remnants in Greek and Latin.

App.

An important technique of word formation in Indo-European was *composition,* the combining in a single word of two separate words or notions. Such forms were and continue to be built on underlying simple sentences; an example in English would be "he is someone who *cuts wood,*" whence "he is a *woodcutter.*" It is in the area of composition that English has most faithfully preserved the ancient Indo-European patterns of word formation, by continuously forming them anew, recreating them. Thus *housewife* is immediately decomposable into *house* + *wife,* a so-called descriptive compound in which the first member modifies the second; and the same elements compounded in Old English, *hūs* + *wīf,* have been preserved as an indivisible unit in HUSSY. Modern English has many different types of compound, such as *catfish, housewife, woodcutter, pickpocket,* or *blue-eyed;* exactly similar types may be found in the other Germanic languages and in Sanskrit, Greek, Latin, Celtic, and Slavic.

The comparative study of Indo-European poetics has shown that such compounds were considered particularly apt for elevated, formal styles of discourse; they are a salient characteristic especially of Indo-European poetic language. In addition, it is amply clear that in Indo-European society the names of individual persons—at least in the priestly, ruling, or warrior classes—were formed by such two-member compounds. Greek names like *Sophocles,* "famed for wisdom," Celtic names like *Vercingetorix,* "warrior-king," Slavic names like *Wenceslas,* "having greater glory," Old Persian names like *Xerxes,* "ruling men," Germanic names like *Bertram,* "bright raven," are all compounds. The type goes as far back as Proto-Indo-European, even if the individual names do not. English family names continue the same tradition, with such types as *Cartwright* and *Shakespeare,* as do those of other languages like Irish: *Kennedy,* "hideous-head."

Semantics

A word of caution should be entered about the semantics of the roots. It is perhaps more hazardous to attempt to reconstruct meaning than to reconstruct linguistic form, and the meaning of a root can only be extrapolated from the meanings of the descendants it has left. Often these diverge sharply from one another, and the scholar finds himself reduced in practice to inferring only what seems to him a reasonable, or even merely possible, semantic common denominator. The result is that reconstructed words and particularly roots are often assigned hazy, vague, or unspecific meanings. This is doubtless quite illusory; no human society from Proto-Indo-European times to the present day would be viable if conversation were limited to vague generalities. The apparent haziness in meaning of a given Indo-European root often simply reflects the fact that with the passage of several millennia the different words in divergent languages derived from this root have undergone semantic changes that are no longer recoverable in detail.

Lexicon and Culture

The reconstruction of a *protolanguage*—the common ancestor of a family of spoken or attested languages—has a further implication. Language is a social fact; languages are not spoken in a vacuum, but by human beings living in a society. When we have reconstructed a protolanguage, we have also necessarily established the existence of a prehistoric society, a speech community that used that protolanguage. The existence of Proto Indo-European presupposes the existence, in some fashion, of a society of Indo-Europeans.

Language is intimately linked to culture, in a complex fashion; it is at once the expression of culture and a part of it. Especially the lexicon of a language, its dictionary, is a face turned toward culture. Though by no means a perfect mirror,

the lexicon of a language remains the single most effective way of approaching and understanding the culture of its speakers. As such, the contents of the Indo-European lexicon provide a remarkably clear view of the whole culture of an otherwise unknown prehistoric society.

Archaeology, archaeological evidence, is limited to material remains. But human culture is not confined to material artifacts alone. The reconstruction of vocabulary can offer a fuller, more interesting view of the culture of a prehistoric people than archaeology precisely because it includes nonmaterial culture.

Consider the case of religion. To form an idea of the religion of a people, archaeologists proceed by inference, examining temples, sanctuaries, idols, votive objects, funerary offerings, and other material remains. But these may not be forthcoming; archaeology is, for example, of little or no utility in understanding the religion of the ancient Hebrews. Yet for the Indo-European-speaking society we can reconstruct with certainty the word for "god," **deiw-os,* and the two-word name of the chief deity of the pantheon, **dyeu-pəter-* (Latin *Jūpiter,* Greek *Zeus patēr,* Sanskrit *Dyaus pitar,* and Luvian *Tatis Tiwaz*). The forms **dyeu-* and **deiw-os* are both derivatives of a root **deiw-,* meaning "to shine," and appearing in the word for "day" in numerous languages (Latin *diēs;* but English DAY is not related). The notion of deity was therefore linked to the notion of the bright sky.

The second element of the name of the chief god, **dyeu-pəter-,* is the general Indo-European word for FATHER. But this word did not refer here to the physical sense of father as parent, but to the social sense of the adult male who is head of the household, the sense of Latin *pater familiās.* For the Indo-Europeans, the society of the gods was conceived, in the image of their own society, as patriarchal. The reconstructed words **deiw-os* and **dyeu-pəter-* alone tell us more about the conceptual world of the Indo-Europeans than a roomful of graven images.

The comparative method enables us to construct a basic vocabulary for the society of speakers of Proto-Indo-European that extends to virtually all aspects of their culture. This basic vocabulary is, to be sure, not uniform in its attestation. Most Indo-European "words" are found only in certain of the attested languages, not in all, which suggests that they may well have been formed only at a period posterior to the oldest common Indo-European we can reconstruct. There exist certain dialectal words that are limited in the area of their extension; such is the case of such an important sociological term as the word for tribe, **teutā-,* which is confined to the western branches Italic, Celtic, and Germanic. (It is the base of German *Deutsch* and of DUTCH and TEUTONIC.) In cases such as these, where a word is attested in several traditions, it is still customary to call it Indo-European, even though it may not date from the remotest reconstructible time. It is in this sense, universally accepted by scholars, that the term Indo-European has been used in the root Appendix.

We may examine the contents of this Indo-European lexicon, which aside from its inherent interest permits us to ascertain many characteristics of Indo-European society. It is remarkable that by far the greater part of this reconstructed vocabulary is preserved in native or borrowed derivatives in Modern English.

General Terms. It is appropriate to begin with a sampling of basic terms in the lexicon, which have no special cultural value but attest the richness of the tradition. All are widespread in the family. We have two verbs expressing existence, **es-* and **bheu-,* found in English IS, Latin *esse,* and English BE, Latin *fu-tūrus* (FUTURE), respectively. We have verbs "to sit" (**sed-¹*), "to lie" (**legh-, *kei-¹*), "to stand" (**stā-*). We have a number of verbs of motion, like **gwā-,* "to come," **ei-¹, *yā-,* "to go," **ter-³,* "to cross over," **sekw-¹,* "to follow," **kei-³,* "to set in motion," and the variants of rolling or turning motion in **wel-³, *wer-³, *kwel-¹.*

Reconstructions are by no means confined to general, imprecise meanings such as these; we have also such specific semantic values as *nes-¹, "to return home, return to a familiar place" (NOSTALGIA).

The notion of carrying is represented by the widespread root *bher-¹ (BEAR¹), found in every family except Anatolian. This root is noteworthy in that it formed a phrase *nomn̥ bher-, "to bear a name," which is reconstructible from several traditions, including English. This phrase formed a counterpart to *nomn̥ dhē-, "to give a name," with the verb *dhē-¹, "to place, put," in Sanskrit, Greek, and Slavic tradition. The persistence of these expressions attests the importance of the name-giving ritual in Indo-European society.

For the notions of eating and drinking, the roots *ed- and *pōi-¹ are most widespread. A root *swel-¹ is attested in Avestan, and survives in English both in SWALLOW¹ and in as humble a word as SWILL. For drink, a root *srebh- is found in some dialects (ABSORB). The metaphor in "drunk, intoxicated" seems to have been created independently a number of times in the history of the Indo-European languages; Latin ebrius, "drunk" (INEBRIATED), was without etymology until a cognate turned up in the Hittite verb meaning "to drink."

The verb "to live" was *gwei-; it formed an adjective *gwī-wos, "alive," which survives in English QUICK (the original sense is seen in the Biblical phrase the quick and the dead). For the notion of begetting we have two roots, *tek-¹ and the extremely widely represented *genə-, which appears not only as a verb but also in various nominal forms like *gen-os, "race," and the prototypes of English KIN and KIND.

A number of qualitative adjectives are attested that go back to the protolanguage. Some come in semantic pairs: *sen-¹, "old," and *newo-, "new"; also *sen-, "old," and *yeu-¹, "young"; *tenu-, "thin" (under ten-), and *tegu-, "thick"; *gwer-², "heavy," and *legwh-, "light." We have also the two prefixes *su-², "good, well-," and *dus-, "bad, ill-," in the Greek forms borrowed as EU- and DYS-. But normally adjectives of value judgments like good and bad are not widespread in the family and are subject to replacement; English good, Latin bonus, and Greek agathos have nothing to do with each other, and each is confined to its own branch of the family.

The personal pronouns belong to the very earliest layer of Indo-European that can be reached by reconstruction. The forms are unlike those of any other paradigms in the language; they have been called the "Devonian rocks" of Indo-European. The lack of any formal resemblance in English between the subject case (nominative) I and the object case (accusative) ME is a direct and faithful reflex of the same disparity in Proto-Indo-European, respectively *eg (*egō) and *me-¹. The other pronouns are *tu- (*te-), "thou," *nes-², *we-, "we," *yu-¹ (*wes), "you." No pronouns for the third person were in use.

The cognate languages give evidence for demonstrative and interrogative pronouns. Both have developed also into relative pronouns in different languages. The most persistent and widespread pronominal stems are *to- and *kwo-, which are preserved in the English demonstrative and interrogative-relative pronouns and adverbs beginning with th- (THIS, THEN) and wh- (WHO, WHICH, WHEN).

All the languages of the family show some or all of the Indo-European numerals. The language had a decimal system. We have complete agreement on the numerals from two to ten: *dwō (*duwō), *trei- (*treyes), *kwetwer- (*kwetwores), *penkwe, *sweks (*(k)seks), *septm̥, *oktō, *newn̥ (*newm̥), *dekm̥. For the numeral one the dialects vary. We have a root *sem-¹ in some derivatives, while the western Indo-European languages Germanic, Celtic, and Latin share the form *oino-. The word for "hundred," formed from *dekm̥, "ten," was *(d)km̥tom. No common form for "thousand" or any other higher number can be reconstructed for the protolanguage.

Man and His Physical Environment.

A large number of terms relating to time, weather, seasons, and natural surroundings can be reconstructed from the daughter languages, some of which permit certain inferences about the homeland of the Indo-European-speaking people before the period of migrations took them to the different localities where they appear historically.

We have several words for "year," words that relate to differing conceptions of the passage of time. Such are *yēro- (English YEAR), related to words denoting activity; *wet-, the year as a measure of the growth of a domestic animal (WETHER, basically "yearling"); and *at- in Latin annus (ANNUAL), from a verb meaning "to go," referring to the year as passage. The seasons were distinguished in Indo-European: *ghei-², "winter," *esr-, "spring," *sem-³, "summer," and *esen-, "fall, harvest," the latter plausibly reflected in Germanic *aznōn, "to earn," referring to harvest labor in an agricultural society.

The lunar month was a unit of time. The word for "month" (*mēns-) is in some languages identical with the word for "moon," in others a derivative of it, as in Germanic *mēnōth- from *mēnōn-. "Moon/month" in Indo-European is a derivative of the verb "to measure," *mē-². The adjective *sen-¹ (*seno), "old," was also evidently used for the waning of the moon, on the evidence of several languages.

The other celestial bodies recognized were the sun, *sāwel-, and the stars, *ster-³. There is evidence from several traditions for similar designations of the constellation Ursa Major, though these may not go back to the earliest Indo-European times. The movement of the sun dictated the names for the points of the compass. EAST is derived from a verbal root *awes- (*aus-), "to shine," as is the word for "dawn" (Latin Aurora), divinized since Indo-European times on the evidence of Greek, Lithuanian, and Sanskrit. The setting sun furnished the word for evening and for west: *wespero-. The Indo-Europeans oriented themselves by facing east. Therefore the root *deks-, "right," could also denote "south." "Right" was considered lucky; the terms for "left" vary from language to language (one Indo-European term is *laiwo-), and were evidently subject to taboo.

Indo-European is noteworthy for having a number of words for "day," but only a single form for NIGHT, *nekwt-. Words for "day" include *āmer- and *agh-² and such dialectal creations as Latin diēs; *ayer- refers to the morning. The old word for "darkness," *regwos-, shows up in Greek as a term for the underworld.

The Indo-Europeans knew snow in their homeland; the word *sneigwh- is nearly ubiquitous. Curiously enough the word for "rain," however, varies notably among the different branches; we have words of differing distribution like *seu-⁴, *ombhro-, and *reg-².

Conceptions of the sky, heaven, were varied in the different dialects. As we have seen, the root *deiw- occurs widely as the divinized bright sky. On the other hand, certain languages viewed the heavens as basically cloudy; *nebh- is "sky" in Balto-Slavic and Iranian, but "cloud" elsewhere. Germanic has a derivative of *kamer-, "a vault," with the basic sense of "the vault of heaven." Another divinized natural phenomenon is illustrated by the root *stenə-, "thunder," and the name of the Germanic god THOR.

A word for the earth can be reconstructed as *dhghem- (*dheghom). Other terms of lesser distribution designated forest or uncultivated land, like *kaito- and *welt-, surviving in English WILD. Swampy or boggy terrain was also apparently familiar, from the evidence of the roots *sel-os, *pel-⁸ (*pelu-), and *māno-. But since none of these runs through the whole family, it would not be justifiable to infer anything from them regarding the terrain of a hypothetical original homeland of the Indo-Europeans.

On the other hand, from the absence of a general word for "sea" we may deduce that the Indo-Europeans were originally an inland people. A root *mori- is attested dialectally (MERE), but may well have referred to a lake or other smaller body of water. Transportation by or across water was, however, known to the Indo-Europeans, since most of the languages attest an old word for boat or ship, *nāu-², probably propelled by oars or pole (*erə-¹, "to row").

The names for a number of different trees are widely enough attested to be viewed as Proto-Indo-European in date. The general term for tree and wood was *deru. The original meaning of the root was doubtless "to be firm, solid," and from it is derived not only the family of English TREE but also that of English TRUE. Note that the semantic evolution has here been from the general to the particular, from "solid" to "tree" (and even "oak" in some dialects), and not the other way around.

We have very widely represented words for the beech tree, *bhāgo-, and the birch, *bherəg-. Formerly these played a significant role in attempts to locate the original homeland of the Indo-Europeans, since their distribution is geographically distinct. But these ranges may have changed over several millennia, and, more important, the same word may be applied to entirely different species of tree. Thus the Greek and Latin cognates of BEECH designate a kind of oak found in the Mediterranean lands.

Of fruit trees in the usual sense, only the apple (*abel-) was known, and there are some indications that it is a loan-word into Indo-European from another, autochthonous language family whose sole survivor is Burushaski, spoken in the remote fastnesses of Kashmir. Wine was made, and the pear and the olive, as well as the grape, were cultivated in the Mediterranean basin before the arrival of the Indo-Europeans. As immigrants into Greece and Italy they adopted the names along with the fruits, and both were later widely diffused.

Indo-European had a generic term for "wild animal," *ghwer- (FERAL). The wolf was known and evidently feared; his name is subject to *taboo deformation* (conscious alteration of the form of a tabooed word, as in English *gol-derned, dad-burned*). The variant forms *wl̥p-, *wl̥kwo-, and *lupo- are all found. The name of the bear was likewise subject to a hunter's taboo; the animal could not be mentioned by his real name on the hunt. The southern Indo-European languages have the original form, *r̥kso- (Latin *ursus*, Greek *arktos*), but all the northern languages have a substitute term. In Slavic he is the "honey-eater," in Germanic the "brown one" (BEAR, and note also BRUIN).

The BEAVER was evidently known (*bhibhru-, from *bher-³), at least in Europe; and the MOUSE (*mūs-, under *mū-¹) then as now was ubiquitous. The HARE, probably named from his color (*kas-, "gray"), is also widespread. Domesticated animals are discussed below.

A generic term for "fish" existed, *gzhū- (also *peisk- in Europe). The salmon (*laks-) and the eel (*angwhi-) were known, the latter also in the meaning "snake." Several birds were known, including the crane (*ger-⁴), the eagle (*er-²), the THRUSH (*trozdos-), the STARLING (*storos), and, at least in some dialects, the SPARROW (*sper-³), FINCH (*sping-), and woodpecker (*speik-). The generic term for "bird" was *awi- (Latin *avis*), and from this was derived the well-represented word for egg, *ōwyo-.

The names for a number of insects can be reconstructed in the protolanguage, including the WASP (*wopsā), the hornet (*kr̥as-ro-, a derivative of *ker-¹, "head," from the shape of the insect), and the fly (*mu-²). The BEE (*bhei-¹) was particularly important as the producer of honey, for which we have the common Indo-European name *melit-. Honey was the only source of sugar and sweetness (*swād-, "sweet," is ancient), and notably was the base of the only certain Indo-European alcoholic beverage, MEAD, *medhu-, meaning in different dialects both "mead" (wine in Greece) and "honey." The Germanic languages have innovated, perhaps from a taboo on speaking the name while gathering wild honey; the common Germanic English word HONEY is from an old color adjective for "yellow," *kenəko-.

The Indo-Europeans were clearly also troubled by more "personal" insect pests. A root *sker-¹ is the base of a word *kori-, attested in different languages as either "bedbug" or "moth." English NIT faithfully continues Indo-European *knid-, "louse, louse egg," attested in many branches of the family. And *lūs-, "louse," has rhymed with *mūs, "mouse," since Indo-European times.

Man and Society.

For man himself, a number of terms were employed, with different nuances of meaning. The general terms for "man" and "woman" are *wiros (VIRILE) and *gwenā from *gwen- (GYNECOLOGY). For man as a human being, the oldest word was apparently *manu- (*man-¹), as preserved in English MAN and in Slavic and Sanskrit. In other dialects we find interesting metaphorical expressions, which attest a set of religious concepts opposing the gods as immortal and celestial to mankind as mortal and terrestrial. Man is either *mor-tos, "mortal" (*mer-², "to die"), or *dhghomyo-, "earthling" (*dhghem-, "earth").

The parts of the body belong to the basic layer of vocabulary, and are for the most part faithfully preserved in Indo-European languages. Such are *ker-², "head" (also *kaput- in dialects, doubtless a more colloquial word), *genu-², "chin, jaw," *dent-, "tooth," *okw-, "eye," *ous-, "ear," *nas-, "nose," *leb-², "lip," *bhrū-, "brow," *ōs-, "mouth," *dn̥ghu, "tongue," and *mon-, "neck." The word for "foot" is attested everywhere (*ped-¹), while that for the hand differs according to dialect.

Internal organs were also named in Indo-European times, including the womb (*gwelbh-), gall (*ghel-²), brain (*mreghmo-, confined to Low German and Greek), spleen (*spelgh-), and liver (*yekwr̥-). The male sexual organs, *pes- and *orghi-, are common patrimony, as is *ors-, "backside."

A large number of kinship terms have been reconstructed. They are agreed in pointing to a society that was patriarchal, patrilocal (the bride leaving her household to join that of her husband's family), and patrilineal (descent reckoned by the male line). "Father" and "head of the household" are one: *pəter-, with his spouse, the *māter-. These terms are ultimately derived from the baby-talk syllables *pa(pa)* and *ma(ma)*, but they had a sociological significance in the Indo-European family over and above this, which is marked by the kinship-term suffix *-ter-*. Related terms are found for the grandfather (*awo-) and the maternal uncle (*awon-), and correspondingly the term *nepōt- (feminine *nepti-) applied to both grandson (originally daughter's son?) and nephew (sister's son). English SON and DAUGHTER clearly reflect Indo-European *sunu- and *dhughəter-.

Male blood relations were designated as *bhrāter- (BROTHER), which doubtless extended beyond those with a common father or mother; the Greek cognate means "fellow member of a clanlike group." The female counterpart was *swesor- (SISTER), probably literally "the female member of the kin group," with a feminine suffix *-sor- and the root *swe- (from seu-²), designating the self, one's own group.

While there exist many special terms for relatives by marriage on the husband's side, like *daiwer, "husband's brother," no corresponding terms on the wife's side can be reconstructed for the protolanguage. The terms vary from dialect to dialect, providing good evidence for the patrilocal character of marriage.

The root *demə-¹ denoted both the house (Latin *domus*) and the household as a social unit. The father of the family (Latin *pater familiās*) was the "master of the house" (Greek *despotēs*) or simply "he of the house" (Latin *dominus*). A larger unit was the village, designated by the word *weik-. The community may have been grouped into divisions by location; this seems to be the basic meaning of the *dā-mo- (from *dā-) in Greek *dēmos*, people (DEMOCRACY).

A root designating a human settlement is *sel-¹. These establishments were frequently built on the top of high places fortified for defense, a practice taken by Indo-European migrants into Central and Western Europe, and Italy and Greece, as confirmed by archaeological finds. Words for such fortified high places vary; we have *pelə-², variant *poli- (ACROPOLIS), *ark-, *dhūno- (TOWN), and *bhergh-² (-*burg* in place names).

Economic Life and Technology. A characteristic of Indo-European and other archaic societies was the principle of exchange and reciprocal gift-giving. The presentation of a gift entailed the obligation of a countergift, and the acts of giving and receiving were equivalent. They were simply facets of a single process of generalized exchange, which assured the circulation of wealth throughout the society.

This principle has left clear traces in the Indo-European vocabulary. The root *dō- of Latin *dōnāre* means "to give" in most dialects but in Hittite means "to take." The root *nem-² is "to distribute" in Greek (NEMESIS), but in German it means "to take," and even cognates of English GIVE (*ghabh-) have the meaning "to take" in Irish. The notion of exchange predominates in the root *skamb- and in *gher-⁶. The root *dap- means "to apportion in exchange," which may carry a bad sense as well; Latin *damnum* is "damage entailing liability." The GUEST (*ghosti-) in Indo-European times was the person with whom one had mutual obligations of hospitality. But he was also the stranger, and the stranger in an uncertain and warring tribal society may well be hostile; the Latin cognate *hostis* means "enemy."

The Indo-Europeans practiced agriculture and the cultivation of cereals. We have several terms of Indo-European antiquity for grain: *grəno- (CORN), *yewo-, and *pūro-, which may have designated wheat or spelt. Others of more restricted distribution are *wrughyo-, "rye," and *bhares-, "barley." Two roots for grinding are attested, *al-⁴ and *melə- (MEAL², MILL). The latter is confined to the European branch of the family. Another European term is *sē-¹, "to sow," not found in Greek, Armenian, or Indo-Iranian. The verb "to plow" is *arə-, again a common European term, with the name of the plow, *arə-trom. English PLOW (British PLOUGH) is from *plōg-, a word found only in Germanic and Italic. Terms for the furrow are *perk-³ and *selk-; *wogwhni- designated the wedge-shaped plowshare. Other related roots are *yeug-, "to yoke," *serp-¹, "sickle, hook," and *kerp-, "to gather, pluck" (HARVEST). The root *gwer-², "heavy," is the probable base of *gwerən-, "hand mill" (QUERN). The term is found throughout the Indo-European-speaking world, including India.

Stockbreeding and animal husbandry were an important part of Indo-European economic life. The names for all the familiar domesticated animals are present throughout the family: *gwou-, "cow and bull," *owi-, "sheep," *agwhno-, "lamb," *aig- and *ghaido-, "goat," *su-¹, "swine," and *porko-, "farrow." The domestic dog was ancient (*kwon-); his name apparently underlies the common Indo-European word for horse, *ekwo-. The expansion and migration of the Indo-European-speaking peoples in the later third and early second millennia B.C. is intimately bound up with the diffusion of the horse. The verbal root *demə-², "to force," acquired the special sense of "to tame horses," whence English TAME. Stock was a source and measure of wealth; the original sense of *peku- was probably wealth, riches, as in Latin *pecūnia,* whence wealth in cattle and finally cattle proper. The same evolution from the general to the particular may be observed in the root *neud-, "to make use of," whence English NEAT².

The verbal roots *pā-, "protect," and *kwel-¹, "revolve, move around," are widely used for the notion of herding or watching over stock, and it is interesting to note that the metaphor of the god or priest watching over mankind like a shepherd (Latin *pāstor*) over his flock occurs in many Indo-European dialects.

Roots indicating a number of technical operations are attested in most of the languages of the family. Such is *teks-, which in some dialects means "to fabricate, especially by working with an ax," but in others means "to weave" (TEXTILE). A root *dheigh-, meaning "mold, shape," is applied both to bread (DOUGH) and to mud or clay, whence words for both pottery and mud walls (Iranian *pari-daiza,* "walled around," borrowed into Greek as the word which became English PARADISE).

The construction of the house was denoted by the root *dem-, "build in stages" (under *demə-¹). The house (*domo-) included a *dhwer- (door), which probably referred originally to the gateway into the enclosure of the household. The house would have had a central hearth, denoted in some languages by *aidh- (properly a verb, "to burn"). Fire itself was known by two words: one was of animate gender (*egnis, Latin *ignis)* and one neuter (*pūr-, Greek *pur).

Indo-European has a verb "to cook" (*pekw-, also having the notion "to ripen") and an adjective "raw" (*om-). Another operation is denoted by *peis-¹, "to crush in a mortar." Meat (*mēms-) was an established item of diet, and some sort of sauce or broth is indicated by the term *yeu-¹ (*yūs-, JUICE, from Latin).

Other household activities included spinning (*snē-¹), weaving (*webh-), and sewing (*syū-). The verb *wes-⁴, English WEAR, is ancient and everywhere attested. The Indo-European garment was probably belted: *yōs-, "to gird."

The Indo-Europeans knew metal and metallurgy, to judge from the presence of the word *ayos- (*ayes-) in Sanskrit, Germanic, and Latin. The term designated copper and perhaps already bronze. Iron is a latecomer, technologically, and the terms for it vary from dialect to dialect. Latin has *ferrum,* while the Germanic and Celtic term was *isarno-, properly "holy (metal)," doubtless so called because the first iron was derived from small meteorites. Gold was known from ancient times, though the names for it vary: *ghel-², probably "yellow (metal)," and aurum (*aus-; Latin *aurum)* are widespread. Silver was *arg-, with various suffixes, doubtless meaning "white (metal)."

It was probably only after the dispersal of the Proto-Indo-European community that the use of the wheel and wheeled transport were adopted. Despite the existence of widespread word families, most terms relating to wheeled vehicles seem to to be metaphors formed from already existing words; they are not primitives or primary vocables. So the word for AXLE (*aks-) may mean simply "a pivotlike juncture"; the NAVE or hub of the wheel (*nobh-) is the same word as NAVEL. This is clearly the case with the wheel itself, where the widespread *kw(e)-kwl-o- is an expressive derivative of a verb (*kwel-¹) meaning "to revolve or go around." Other words for wheel are dialectal and again derivative, like Latin *rota* from a verbal root *ret-, "to run." A root *wegh-, "to convey, to go in a vehicle" (WAGON), is attested quite early, though not in Hittite. This evidence for the late appearance of the wheel agrees with archaeological findings that date the distribution of the wheel in Europe to the end of the third millennium B.C., too late for the community of Proto-Indo-European proper.

Ideology. We pointed out earlier that the great advantage of lexicon as an approach to culture and history is that it is not confined to material remains. Words exist for artifacts, objects, and phenomena that can be verified in nature or from their material remains. But words also exist for ideas, abstractions, and relations. The Indo-European protolanguage is particularly rich in such vocabulary items.

A number of verbs denoting mental activity are found. The most widespread is *men-, preserved in English MIND. Other derivatives refer to remembering, warning (putting in mind), and thinking in general. A root notable for the diversity of its derivatives is *med-, which may be defined as "to take the appropriate measures." Reflexes of this verb range in meaning from "rule," through "measure" (MODICUM, from Latin), to "physician" (Latin *medicus).

The notion of government and sovereignty was well represented. The presence of the old word for tribal king, *reg- (under *reg-¹), only in the extreme east (RAJAH) and the extreme west (Latin *rēx,* Celtic *-rix*) virtually guarantees its presence in the earliest Indo-European society. (Here we have an example of the phenomenon of marginal or peripheral conservation of a form lost in the central innovating area.) Roman tradition well attests the sacral character of kingship among the Indo-

Europeans. The functions of king and priest were different aspects of a single function of sovereignty. It is this which is symbolized by the divine name *dyeu-pəter- (*deiw-), the chief of the gods.

Indo-European is particularly rich in religious vocabulary. An important form, also found only in the peripheral languages Sanskrit, Latin, and Celtic, is the two-word phrase *kred-dhə-, literally "to put (dhē-¹) trust or faith (*kerd-¹)." The two words have been joined together in the western languages: Latin crēdō, "I believe." Here a term of the most ancient pagan religion of the Indo-Europeans has been taken over by Christianity. A common word for priest, and member of the priestly class, may be preserved in BRAHMIN, from Sanskrit.

Oral prayers, requests of the deity, and other ritual utterances must have played a significant role in Indo-European religion. We have the roots *wegwh-, "to preach," and *sengwh-, "to prophesy, sing, make incantations," now secularized in SING. Another is *gwerə-¹, "to praise aloud," which in Latin grātia (GRACE) has had a considerable fortune in Christianity.

Several words apparently denoted specific ritual actions, like *tyegw-, "to retreat with awe," *ghow-ē-, "to honor, worship," and *sep-el-yo- (*sep-), with the specific notion "to venerate the dead," found in the Latin verb meaning "to bury." The root *spend- has the basic meaning of "to make an offering or perform a rite," whence "to engage oneself by a ritual act." Its Latin derivative spondēre means "to promise" (SPOUSE).

Even a hint of Indo-European metaphysics appears in the word *aiw-, "vital force," whence "long life, the eternal recreation of life, eternity" (English EON). It is noteworthy that the idea of "holy" is intimately bound up with that of "whole, healthy" in a number of forms: *kailo- (WHOLE and HOLY), *swento- (SOUND²), and *sol-, whence Latin salvus (SALVATION). An ancient root relating solely to religion is *sak- (SACRED).

Another aspect of the function of sovereignty is the sphere of the law. We have an old word, probably for "religious law," *yewo-¹ (*yewes-), in Latin jūs. Latin lēx is also ancient (*leg-), though the details of its etymology are uncertain. In a society that emphasized the principle of exchange and reciprocity, it is scarcely surprising that the notion of contractual obligation should be well represented. Several roots specify the notion of "bond": *bhendh-, *ned-, *leig-¹, all of which have derivatives with technical legal meanings in various languages. We have the word for "a pledge," *wadh-, in western Indo-European, whence the English verb for making a particular kind of contract, WED. The oath then as now was important: roots *serk- and in Germanic and Celtic *oito-. The verb *kwei-¹ meant "to pay compensation for an injury." Its derivative noun, *kwoinā, was borrowed from Doric Greek into the most ancient Roman law, Latin poena, pūnīre, whence English PUNISH and a host of legal terms. The Greek word for justice, dikē, is derived from the notion of "boundary marker" (*deik-; compare also *ter-¹, *ter-men-).

In conclusion we may add that poetry and a tradition of poetics are also common patrimony in a number of Indo-European traditions. The hymns of the Rig-Veda are written in meters related to those used by the Greek poets, and the earliest verse forms found among the Celts and the Slavs go back to the same Indo-European source.

A number of metaphorical expressions would appear to be creations of ancient, even Indo-European date. Thus the verb *dhegwh-, "to burn, warm," forms derivatives in Latin and Celtic which mean "to keep warm, to cherish," and refer especially to the duties of the pious son toward his aged parent.

Most interesting are the cases where from two or more traditions (usually including Homer and the Rig-Veda) it is possible to reconstruct a poetic phrase consisting of two members. Such are the expressions "imperishable fame," *klewos ŋgwzhitom (roots *kleu-¹, *gzwhei-); "strong (and holy) mind," *isərom menos (roots *eis-¹, *men-¹); and the "weaver (or crafter) of words," the Indo-European poet himself, *wekwōm teks- (roots *wekw-, *teks-).

Conclusion

This survey has touched on only a representative sample of the available reconstructed Indo-European lexicon and has made no attempt to cite the mass of evidence in all the languages of the family, ancient and modern, for these reconstructions.

For this essay, we have given only the information about Indo-European culture that could be derived from language and lexicon alone. Other disciplines serve to fill out and complete the picture to be gathered from the study of vocabulary: archaeology, prehistory, comparative mythology, and the history of institutions.

Archaeologists have not in fact succeeded in locating the Indo-Europeans. An artifact other than a written record is silent on the language of its user, and prehistoric Eurasia offers an abundant choice of culture areas. Archaeologists are generally agreed that the so-called Kurgan people, named after the Russian word for their characteristic "barrow" or "tumulus" grave structure, spoke an Indo-European language. Some time around the middle of the third millennium B.C., these people expanded from the steppe zone north of the Black Sea and beyond the Volga into the Balkans and adjacent areas. These Kurgan people were the bearers of a new mobile and aggressive culture into Neolithic Europe, and it is not unreasonable to associate them with the coming of the Indo-Europeans. But the time around 2500 B.C. is already too late for the common Indo-European protolanguage; one millennium is not long enough for a single language to develop forms as divergent as Mycenean Greek and Hittite as they are historically attested a thousand or so years later. We must be content to recognize the Kurgan people as speakers of certain Indo-European languages and as sharing a common Indo-European cultural patrimony. The ultimate "cradle" of the Indo-Europeans may well never be known, and language remains the best and fullest evidence for their prehistoric society.

Guide to the Appendix

This Dictionary carries the etymology of the English language to its logical and natural conclusion; if the documentary history of words is of interest and value, so is their reconstructed prehistory. The historical component is given in the etymologies after the definitions in the main body of the Dictionary. This Appendix supplies the prehistoric component.

Structure and Style of the Appendix Entry

The form given in **boldface** type at the head of each entry in the Appendix is, unless otherwise identified, an Indo-European root in a basic form. Often an equal variant or variants, also in boldface, and preceded by the word *Also,* may follow. Next, in roman type, is the basic meaning of the root. This usually takes the form of a substitutable word or phrase, like a dictionary definition, or it may be an expository description, identifying derivative meanings as well as the basic meaning.

(There are a number of entries in the Appendix that are not Indo-European roots, but Germanic roots or Greek or Latin words that have generated several or many widely separated English words. Brackets are placed around these entries, and they are explicitly identified. They are included for convenience of cross-reference. Their style is analogous to that of the entries of Indo-European roots.)

The rest of the entry describes the patterns whereby the root has generated words in Modern English. Usually more than one channel is involved, and the different sections are numbered and subdivided to whatever degree is required. If no semantic or morphological development needs to be explained, the *lemma* (the historically attested representative of the root) is immediately given at the beginning of each section.

> **ekwo-**. Horse. **1.** Latin *equus,* horse...
> **melit-**. Honey. **1.** Greek *meli,* honey...

Much more commonly, intermediate developments need to be explained. An asterisk is placed before every unattested form (except the entry forms). The descriptive terminology used covers typical morphological processes of Indo-European, as follows.

basic form. The unchanged root; so identified only for descriptive contrast, when suffixed or otherwise altered forms have previously been introduced.

suffixed form. A form with a suffix or suffixes, written with an internal hyphen.

> **mut** . Suffixed form **mut-il-*...
> **āpero-**. Suffixed form **āper-yo-*...
> **mel-⁴**. **1.** Suffixed (comparative) form **mel-yos-*...

prefixed form. A form with a prefix, written with an internal hyphen.

> **op-¹**. *1.* Prefixed form **co-op-*...

extended form. A form with an extension or enlargement, written solid.

> **pel-⁶**. **1.** Extended form **peld-*...

nasalized form. A form with a nasal infix, written with internal hyphens.

> **tag-**. **1.** Nasalized form **ta-n-g-*...

expressive form. A form with "expressive gemination," the final consonant being doubled, written solid.

> **gal-²**. **3.** Expressive form **gall-*...

compound form. A form compounded with a form of another root, written with an internal hyphen.

> **demə-¹**. **2.** Compound form **dems-pot-*...

full-grade form. A form with e-vocalism (the basic form); so identified only for descriptive contrast, when forms with other grades of apophonic vocalism have previously been introduced.

o-grade form. A form with o-vocalism.

> **nekwt-.** O-grade form **nokwt-. . .*

zero-grade form. A form with zero-vocalism.

> **men-¹.** **I.** Zero-grade form **mṇ-. . .*

lengthened-grade form. A form with lengthened vocalism.

> **ghers-.** **2.** Lengthened-grade form **ghḗrs-. . .*

shortened form. A form with shortened vocalism.

> **plāk-².** **1.** Shortened form **plak-. . .*

reduced form. A form with morphological loss, typically in final position.

> **stā-.** **V.** Reduced form **st-.*

variant form. A form altered in any way other than the above categories.

> **deru-.** **2.** Variant form **dreu-. . .*

Frequently two or more of these terms are used simultaneously.

> **bhel-³.** **I.** Suffixed o-grade form **bhol-yo-. . .*
> **dhēi-.** **1.** Suffixed reduced form **dhē-mnā. . .*
> **peig-¹.** **2.** Nasalized zero-grade form **pi-n-g-. . .*
> **pet-².** **2.** Suffixed (stative) variant form **pat-ē-. . .*
> **med-.** **7.** Perhaps lengthened o-grade form **mōd-. . .*
> **mer-².** **II. 1.** Zero-grade form **mṛ-* in. . .**d.** prefixed and suffixed form **ṇ-mṛ-to-. . .*

When the intermediate forms have been given and described, sometimes in several stages, the connective word *in* is used to indicate their representation in historically attested lemmas.

> **tag-.** To touch, handle. **1.** Nasalized form **ta-n-g-* in Latin *tangere,* to touch. . .
> **mē-³.** Big. **3.** Suffixed o-grade form **mō-ro-* in Gaelic *mōr,* big. . .

In order to give proper emphasis to the fact that English belongs to the Germanic branch of Indo-European and to give precedence to its native words, words that are *inherited* from prehistoric Germanic and thus in turn from Proto-Indo-European, as against those that are *borrowed* from other branches, the intermediate stages in Germanic etymologies are covered in fuller detail than in the other branches. The Common or Proto-Germanic (here called simply Germanic) forms underlying English words are always given.

> **māter-.** Mother. **1.** Germanic **mōthar-* in Old English *mōdor,* mother. . .
> **dher-¹.** To make muddy; darkness. **1.** Suffixed form **dher-g-* in Germanic **derk-* in Old English *deorc,* dark. . .

Furthermore, where no other considerations intervene, Germanic is given first of the Indo-European groups, and Old English is given first within Germanic. This precedence is not, however, rigidly applied. Where an extensive spread occurs or the semantic and morphological pattern of lemmas demands to be observed, it would be awkward to insist on putting na-

tive words automatically first. For example, the root **melit-,** "honey," is represented in native English only by the word MILDEW, which is a compound and far removed semantically from the original sense. The borrowed Latin and Greek derivatives are therefore placed first.

Each lemma is followed by a colon, after which the Modern English derivatives are listed in SMALL CAPITALS. If there are several or many derivatives, the simple (uncompounded) ones are listed first, in alphabetical order, and the compounds afterward, also in alphabetical order. Every word in the Dictionary that cross-refers directly to the Appendix is listed there. In addition, many words whose etymologies in the Dictionary refer to other related words that in turn refer to the Appendix are added to the lists, usually in parentheses. For example, the word NOSTRIL is a compound of Old English *nosu,* NOSE, and therefore, since it is alphabetically nearby, its etymology cross-refers to NOSE. NOSE refers to its Indo-European root, **nas-,** in the Appendix, and there NOSTRIL is listed in parentheses after NOSE, since the fact of the relationship is interesting and not entirely obvious.

It must be stressed that the English words in small capitals should be read merely as cross-references, rather than as etymological statements. For example, the root **ghwer-,** "wild beast," has a lemma, Greek *thēr,* "wild beast," after which are listed the English derivatives -THERE, THEROPOD, and TREACLE. Little information is conveyed by this until the reader turns to the definitions in the main body of the Dictionary, with their individual etymologies.

Further occasional features of the Appendix entries are cross-references to other entries in the Appendix, in cases where roots are related or associated. These are self-explanatory.

The final item in most entries is an abbreviated reference to Julius Pokorny's *Indogermanisches Etymologisches Wörterbuch* (Bern, 1959). This, the standard work of reference and synthesis in the Indo-European field, carries a full range of the actual comparative material on which the roots are reconstructed. This Appendix presents only those aspects of the material that are directly relevant to English. For example, the English word MANY refers to its root, **menegh-,** "copious." This entry in the Appendix describes the transition of the Indo-European form through Germanic **managa-* to Old English *manig, mænig,* many. It does not cite the comparative evidence upon which this assertion is based, but it refers to [Pok. *men(e)gh-* 730.]. This entry in Pokorny's dictionary cites, beside the Old English word, the forms in Sanskrit, Celtic, Gothic, Old High German, Old Norse, Slavic, and Lithuanian, from which the reconstruction of the root was made. These references are intended for the convenience of scholars. They should also serve as a reminder to the general reader that the information given in this Appendix is assertive rather than expository; the evidence and evaluation upon which its assertions are based are not presented here, as being inappropriate to a general dictionary of English. This is also the place to observe that the Appendix is the product of a program of new evaluation of the etymology of English, with particular attention to the Indo-European aspect, carried out by members of the Department of Linguistics of Harvard University under the direction of Professor Watkins. This body of work refers to but does not depend on Pokorny's work; the student will find very many instances where the material in this Appendix differs from Pokorny's account in the reconstruction of forms and meanings, in the attribution of lemmas, and in every other respect.

Indo-European Roots

abel-. Apple. Germanic *aplu-, *apal- in: **a.** Old English æppel, apple: APPLE; **b.** Old Norse apall-, apple: DAPPLE-GRAY. [Pok. abel- 1.]

ad-. To, near, at. **1.** Germanic *at in: **a.** Old English æt, near, by, at: AT; **b.** Old Norse at, to: ADO. **2.** Latin ad, to, toward: AD-, -AD, EN-CORE, PARAMOUNT. [Pok. 1. ad- 3.]

ag-. To drive. **1.** Latin agere, to do, act, drive, conduct, lead: ACT, AGENDUM, AGENT, AGILE, AGITATE, AMBAGE, AMBIGUOUS, (ASSAY), CACHE, COAGULUM, COGENT, ESSAY, EXACT, EXAMINE, EXIGENT, FUMIGATE, FUSTIGATE, INTRANSIGENT, LEVIGATE, LITIGATE, NAVIGATE, OBJURGATE, PRODIGAL, PURGE, RETROACTIVE, SQUAT, TRANSACT. **2.** Greek agein, to drive, lead: -AGOGUE, AGONY; ANAGOGE, (ANTAGONIZE), CASTIGATE, CHORAGUS, DEMAGOGUE, EPACT, HYPNAGOGIC, MYSTAGOGUE, PEDAGOGUE, PRO-TAGONIST, STRATAGEM, SYNAGOGUE. **3.** Suffixed form *ag-to- in Celtic *amb(i)-ag-to-, "one sent around" (*ambi, around; see **ambhi**), in Latin ambactus, envoy, vassal: AMBASSADOR, (EMBASSY). **4.** Suffixed form *ag-mṇ- in Latin agmen, a train, a moving forward, a marching column, group: AGMINATE. **5.** Suffixed form *ag-ti-, "weighing" (Greek agein, "to lead," has a sense "to weigh"), in Greek axios, worthy, of like value, weighing as much: AXIOM, AXIOLOGY, CHRONAXY. **6.** Possibly suffixed form *ag-ro-, driving, pursuing, grabbing, in Greek agra, a seizing: PELLAGRA, PODAGRA. Derivative agro-. [Pok. aĝ- 4.]

ages-. Fault, guilt. Possibly Old English acan, to ache (perhaps < "to cause mental pain"): ACHE. [Pok. agos- 8.]

agh-¹. To be depressed, be afraid. **1.** Suffixed form *agh-lo- in Old English eglan, to trouble, afflict: AIL. **2.** Suffixed form *agh-es- in Old Norse agi, frightened: AWE. [Pok. agh- 7.]

agh-². A day (considered as a span of time). Germanic *dagaz (with initial d- of obscure origin), day, in: **a.** Old English dæg, day: DAY, (DAISY), TODAY; **b.** Old English denominative dagian, to dawn: DAWN. [Pok. agher- 7.]

agro-. Field. Derivative of **ag-**, "to drive" (< "place to which cattle are driven"). **1.** Germanic *akraz in Old English æcer, field, acre: ACRE. **2.** Latin ager (genitive agri), district, property, field: AGRARIAN, AGRESTAL, AGRI-CULTURE, AIR, PEREGRINE, (PILGRIM). **3.** Greek agros, field: AGRIOLOGY, AGRO-, AGROSTOL-OGY, ONAGER, STAVESACRE. [In Pok. ag- 4.]

agwesī. Ax. Germanic *akwesī, *akusjō- in Old English æx, ax: AX. [Pok. agu(e)sī 9.]

agwhno-. Lamb. Variant form *agwno- in Germanic *aun- in verb *aunōn in Old English ēanian, to bring forth young: YEAN. [Pok. aguh-no-s 9.]

ai-¹. To give, allot. **1.** Suffixed form *ai-t-ya in Greek aitia, cause, responsibility: ETIOLOGY. **2.** Suffixed form *ai-tā- in Greek diaitan (dia, DIA-), to decide, lead one's life: DIET¹. [Pok. 3. ai- 10.]

ai-². An utterance. Suffixed form *ai-no- in Greek ainos, tale: ENIGMA. [Pok. 5. ai- 11.]

aidh-. To burn. **1.** Suffixed form *aidh-sto- in: **a.** Germanic *aistaz in Old English āst, kiln: OAST; **b.** Latin aestās (stem aestāt- for earlier *aestotāt-), heat, summer: AESTIVAL. **2.** Suffixed form *aidh-lo- perhaps in Germanic *ail- in Old English āl, fire: ANNEAL. **3.** Suffixed form *aidh-i- in Latin aedēs, building, house (< "hearth"): AEDILE, EDIFICE, (EDIFY). **4.** Suffixed form *aidh-stu- in Latin aestus, heat, swell, surge, tide: ESTUARY. **5.** Suffixed form *aidh-er- in Greek aithēr, air: ETHER. [Pok. ai-dh- 11.]

aig-. Goat. Greek aigis, goatskin (shield of Athena): AEGIS. [Pok. 3. aig- 13.]

ais-. To wish, desire. Suffixed form *ais-sk- in Germanic *aiskōn in Old English āscian, ācsian, to ask, seek: ASK. [Pok. 1. ais- 16.]

aiw-. Vital force, life, long life, eternity; also, "endowed with the acme of vital force, young." **1.** Extended form in Germanic *aiwi in: **a.** Old English ā, ever: NO¹; **b.** Germanic *aiwi + *wihti, "ever a thing, anything" (*wihti-, thing; see **wekti-**), in Old English āwiht, anything, "ever a creature": AUGHT; **c.** Old English æfre (second element obscure), ever: EVER, EVERY, NEVER; **d.** Old Norse ei, ever: AYE², NAY. **2.** Suffixed form *ai-wo- in: **a.** Latin aevum, age, eternity: COEVAL, LONGEV-ITY, MEDIEVAL, PRIMEVAL; **b.** suffixed form *aiwo-tāt- in Latin aetās (stem aetāt-), age: AGE, COETANEOUS; **c.** suffixed form *aiwo-terno- in Latin aeternus, eternal: ETERNAL, SEM-PITERNAL. **3.** Suffixed form *aiw-en- in Greek aiōn, age, vital force: EON. See also *yuwen-under **yeu-²**. [Pok. aiu- 17.]

ak-. Sharp. **1.** Suffixed form *ak-yā- in: **a.** Germanic *akjō in Old English ecg, sharp side: EDGE; **b.** Germanic *akjan in Old Norse eggja, to incite, goad: EGG². **2.** Suffixed form *ak-u- in: **a.** Germanic *ahuz in Old English ēar, æhher, spike, ear of grain: EAR²; ACROSPIRE; **b.** Latin acus, needle: ACICULA, ACUITY, ACUMEN, ACUTE, AGLET, EGLANTINE; **c.** Latin acus, chaff: ACEROSE². **3.** Suffixed form *ak-men, sharp stone used as a tool, with metathetic variant *ka-men-, with variant *ka-mer- in Germanic *hamaraz in Old English hamor, hammer: HAMMER. **4.** Suffixed form *ak-onā- in Germanic *aganō in Old Norse ögn, chaff: AWN. **5.** Suffixed lengthened form *āk-ri- in Latin ācer, sharp, bitter: ACERATE, ACRID, ACRIMONY, EAGER¹, VINEGAR. **6.** Suffixed form *ak-er-bhwo- in Latin acerbus, bitter, sharp, tart: ACERB, EXACERBATE. **7.** Suffixed (stative) form *ak-ē- in Latin acēre, to be sharp: ACID. **8.** Suffixed form *ak-ēto- in Latin acētum, vinegar: ACETABULUM, ACETIC, ACETUM, ESTER. **9.** Suffixed form *ak-ā- in Greek akē, point: PARAGON. **10.** Greek akantha (second element of Mediterranean origin), thorn, thorny plant: ACANTHO-, ACANTHUS; COELACANTH, PYRACAN-THA, TRAGACANTH. **11.** Suffixed form *ak-mā- in Greek akmē, point: ACME, ACNE. **12.** Suffixed form *ak-ro- in Greek akros, topmost: ACRO-, (ACROBAT). **13.** Variant form *ok- in:

a. suffixed form *ok-ri- in Latin ocris, stony mountain: MEDIOCRE; **b.** suffixed form *ok-su- in Greek oxus, sharp, sour: AMPHIOXUS, OXA-LIS, OXY-¹, PAROXYSM. [Pok. 2. ak- 18.]

aks-. Axis. **1.** Suffixed form *aks-lo- in Old Norse ōxull, axle: AXLE. **2.** Suffixed form *aks-i- in: **a.** Latin axis, axle, pivot: AXIS; **b.** Latin diminutive axilla, armpit (< "axis point of the arm and shoulder"): AXILLA. **3.** Suffixed form *aks-lā- in Latin āla (< *axla), wing, upper arm (see axilla for semantic transition): AISLE, ALA, ALAR, ALARY, ALATE, ALIFORM, ALULA. **4.** Suffixed form *aks-on- in Greek axōn, axle: AXON. [In Pok. ag- 4.]

akwā-. Water. **1.** Germanic *ahwō in Old English ēa, water, and ē(a)gor, flood, tide (second element obscure): EAGRE, MERSEY. **2.** Germanic *ahwjo becoming *aujō, "thing on the water," in: **a.** Old English īg, īeg, ēg, island: RUNNYMEDE; **b.** compound Germanic form in Old English īgland, īegland (land, LAND), is-land: ISLAND; **c.** Germanic *Skandinaujā in Latin Scandinavia (the first element is a Germanic place name), "Island of Scandinavia": SCANDINAVIA. **3.** Latin aqua, water: AQUA, AQUARELLE, AQUARIUM, AQUATIC, AQUI-, EWER, GOUACHE, SEWER¹. [Pok. akua 23.]

al-¹. Beyond. **1.** Variant *ol-, "beyond," in: **a.** suffixed forms *ol-se-, *ol-so- in Old Latin ollus in Latin ille, "yonder," that: ALARM, ALERT, ALLIGATOR, El Dorado; **b.** suffixed forms *ol-s, *ol-tero- in Latin uls, ultrā, beyond: OUTRÉ, PENULT, ULTERIOR, ULTIMATE, ULTRA-, UTTERANCE². **2.** Suffixed form *al-tero-, "other of two," in: **a.** Latin alter, other, other of two: ALTER, ALTERCATE, ALTERNATE, ALTRUISM, SUBALTERN; **b.** Latin adulter, "one who approaches another (unlawfully), an adul-terer" (ad-, AD-), hence adulterāre, to commit adultery with, pollute: ADULTERATE. **3.** Extended form *alyo-, "other of more than two," in: **a.** Germanic *aljaz in Old English elles, else: ELSE; **b.** Latin alius, other of more than two: ALIAS, ALIBI, ALIEN, ALIQUOT, ALIUNDE, HIDALGO; **c.** Greek allos, other: AGIO, ALLE-GORY, ALLELOMORPH, ALLO-, MORPHALLAXIS, PARALLAX, PARALLEL. [Pok. 1. al- 24.]

al-². To wander. **1.** Latin ambulāre, to go about, walk (ambi-, around; see **ambhi**): AL-LEY¹, AMBULATE, FUNAMBULIST, PREAMBLE, PURLIEU. **2.** Latin exsul, exul, wanderer, exile (ex-, out, EX-): EXILE. [Pok. 3. al- 27.]

al-³. To grow, nourish. **I.** Suffixed (participial) form *al-to-, "grown," in: **1.** Germanic *alda-in: **a.** Old English eald, ald, old: ALDERMAN, OLD; **b.** Old English (comparative) ieldra, eldra, older, elder: ELDER¹; **c.** Old English (superlative) ieldesta, eldest: ELDEST; **d.** Germanic compound *werald, "life or age of man" (see **wiros**). **2.** Latin altus, high, deep: ALT, ALTIM-ETER, ALTITUDE, ALTO, ALTOCUMULUS, ALTO-STRATUS, ENHANCE, EXALT, HAUGHTY, HAUT-BOY, HAWSER. **II.** Latin alere, to nourish: ADO-LESCENT, (ADULT), ALIBLE, ALIMENT, ALIMONY, ALTRICIAL, ALUMNUS, COALESCE. **III.** Form _*al-ē-_ in Latin _abolēre,_ to retard the growth of, abolish (_ab-,_ from, AB-): ABOLISH. **IV.** Compound form _*pro-al-_ (_pro,_ forth; see **per-**[1]) in Latin _prōlēs,_ offspring: PROLAN, PROLETARIAN, PROLIFEROUS, PROLIFIC. **V.** Suffixed form _*al-mo_ in Latin _almus,_ fostering: ALMA. **VI.** Extended form _*aldh-_ in Greek _althein, althainein,_ to get well: ALTHEA. [Pok. 2. _al-_ 26.]

al-[4]. To grind, mill. Suffixed form _*al-euro-_ in Greek _aleuron,_ mill: ALEURONE. [Pok. 5. _al-_ 28.]

[al-[5]. All. Germanic root. **1.** Suffixed form _*al-na-_ in Germanic _*allaz_ in: **a.** Old English _all, eall, eal-, al-,_ all: ALL, ALSO; **b.** Frankish _*al-ōd-,_ "complete property" (_*-ōd,_ property; see **audaz**): ALLODIUM. **2.** Germanic prefix _*ala-,_ all, in _*Ala-manniz,_ "all men" (see **man-**[1]).]

albho-. White. **1.** Possibly Germanic _*albiz, *albaz,_ if meaning "white ghostlike apparitions," in: **a.** Old English _ælf,_ elf: ALFRED, ELDRITCH, ELF, OLIVER; **b.** Danish _elver,_ elf: ERLKING; **c.** Old Norse _alfr,_ elf: OAF; **d.** Middle High German _alb,_ elf: AUBREY; **e.** Old High German _Alberich,_ "elf-ruler" (_-rich,_ "ruler"; see **reg-**[1]), akin to the source of Old French _Auberon:_ OBERON. **2.** Latin _albus,_ white: ABELE, ALB, ALBEDO, ALBESCENT, ALBINO, ALBITE, ALBUM, ALBUMEN, ALBURNUM, AUBADE, AUBURN, DAUB. **3.** Greek _alphos,_ dull-white leprosy: ALPHOSIS. [Pok. _albho-_ 30.]

alek-. To ward off, protect. **1.** Suffixed zero-grade form _*alk-ā-_ in Greek _alkē,_ strength: ANALCIME. **2.** Extended form _*aleks-_ in Greek _alexein,_ to protect: ALEXIN, ALEXANDER, ALEXIS. [Pok. _aleq-_ 32.]

alu-. In words related to sorcery, magic, possession, and intoxication. **1.** Greek _aluein,_ to be distraught: HALLUCINATE. **2.** Suffixed form _*alu-t-_ in Germanic _*aluth-_ in Old English _(e)alu,_ ale: ALE. [Pok. _alu-_ 33.]

ambhi. Also **m̥bhi.** Around. **1.** Reduced form _*bhi_ in Germanic _*bi_ in: **a.** Old English _bī, bi, be,_ by: BY[1]; **b.** Old English _bī-,_ be-: BE-; **c.** Middle Dutch _bie,_ by: BILANDER; **d.** Old High German _bi,_ by, at: BIVOUAC. **2.** Germanic _*umbi_ in: **a.** Old English _ymbe,_ around: EMBER DAYS; **b.** Old Norse _um(b),_ about, around: OMBUDSMAN; **c.** Old High German _umbi,_ around: UMLAUT. **3.** Latin _ambi-,_ around, about: AMBI-. **4.** Greek _amphi,_ around, about: AMPHI-. **5.** Celtic _*ambi_ (see **ag-**). [Pok. _ambhi_ 34.]

ambhō. Both. **1.** Reduced form _*bhō_ in Germanic _*bō-, bā-_ in Old Norse _bāthir,_ both: BOTH. **2.** Latin _ambō,_ both: AMBSACE. **3.** Greek _amphō,_ both: AMPHOTERIC. [In Pok. _ambhi_ 34.]

āmer-. Day. Suffixed form _*āmer-ā_ in Greek _hēmera,_ day: EPHEMERAL, HEMERALOPIA. [Pok. _amer-_ 35.]

ames-. Blackbird. **1.** Suffixed variant form _*ams-ol-_ in Old English _ōsle,_ blackbird: OUSEL. **2.** Suffixed variant form _*mes-olā_ in Latin _merula,_ merle, blackbird: MERLE, MERLON. [Pok. _ames-_ 35.]

[amma. Various nursery words. Latin root. **1.** Latin _*amma,_ mother: AMAH. **2.** Reduced form _*am-_ in: **a.** Latin _amāre,_ to love: AMATEUR, AMATIVE, AMATORY, AMORETTO, AMOUR, ENAMOUR, INAMORATA, MABEL, PARAMOUR; **b.** Latin _amita,_ aunt: AUNT; **c.** Latin _amīcus,_ friend: AMICABLE, AMIGO, AMITY, ENEMY, INIMICAL.]

an[1]. On. Extended form _*ana._ **1.** Germanic _*ana, anō_ in: **a.** Old English _an, on, a,_ on: ON; **b.** Old Norse _ā,_ on: ALOFT; **c.** Old High German _ana,_ on: ANLAGE; **d.** Middle Dutch _aan,_ on: ONSLAUGHT. **2.** Greek _ana,_ on: ANA[2], ANA-. [Pok. 4. _an_ 39.]

an[2]. Demonstrative particle. Suffixed form _*an-tero-,_ "other (of two)" (compare _*al-tero-_ under **al-**[1]) in Germanic _*antharaz_ in Old English _ōther,_ other: OTHER. [Pok. 2. _an_ 37.]

an-. Old woman, ancestor (nursery word). Latin _anus,_ old woman: ANILE. [Pok. 1. _an-_ 36.]

andh-. Bloom. Suffixed form _*andh-os-_ in Greek _anthos,_ flower: ANTHEMION, ANTHER, ANTHESIS, ANTHO-, -ANTHOUS; AGAPANTHUS, CHRYSANTHEMUM, DIANTHUS, EXANTHEMA, HYDRANTH, MONANTHOUS, STROPHANTHIN. [Pok. _andh-_ 40.]

andho-. Blind, dark. Suffixed variant form _*ondh-ro-_ in Latin _umbra,_ shadow: UMBRA, UMBEL, UMBRELLA; ADUMBRAL, ADUMBRATE, SOMBER. [Pok. _andho-_ 41.]

anə-. To breathe. **1.** Suffixed form _*anə-mo-_ in: **a.** Latin _animus,_ reason, mind, soul, spirit, life, breath: ANIMADVERT, ANIMAL, ANIMOSITY, ANIMUS, EQUANIMITY, LONGANIMITY, MAGNANIMOUS, PUSILLANIMOUS, UNANIMOUS; **b.** Greek _anemos,_ wind: ANEMO-. **2.** Suffixed form _*anə-tyo-_ in Celtic _*anatyo-_ in Middle Welsh _eneit,_ "soul": ENID[1]. [Pok. 3. _an(ə)-_ 38.]

anət-. Duck. Germanic _*anud-_ in Old Norse _önd,_ duck: GOOSANDER, SOLAN. [Pok. _anət-_ 41.]

anətā. Doorjamb. Latin _antae_ (plural), a pair of pillars on the opposite sides of a door: ANTA. [Pok. _anəta_ 42.]

[angelos. Messenger. Greek noun, akin to Greek _angaros,_ mounted courier, both from an unknown Oriental source. **1.** Greek _angelos,_ messenger: ANGEL, ANGELIC, ARCHANGEL, EVANGEL. **2.** Greek _angaros,_ mounted courier: ANGARY.]

angh-. Tight, painfully constricted, painful. **1.** Germanic _*ang-,_ compressed, hard, painful, in Old English _angnægl,_ "painful spike (in the flesh)," corn, excrescence (_nægl,_ spike, NAIL): AGNAIL. **2.** Suffixed form _*angh-os-_ in Germanic _*angaz_ in Old Norse _angr,_ grief: ANGER. **3.** Suffixed form _*angh-os-ti-_ in Germanic _*angst_ in Old High German _angust,_ anxiety: ANGST. **4.** Latin _angere,_ to strangle, draw tight: ANXIOUS. **5.** Suffixed form _*angh-os-to-_ in Latin _angustus,_ narrow: ANGUISH. **6.** Greek _ankhein,_ to squeeze, embrace: QUINSY. **7.** Greek _ankhonē,_ a strangling: ANGINA. [Pok. _angh-_ 42.]

angwhi-. Snake, eel. **1.** Latin _anguis,_ snake: ANGUILLIFORM, ANGUINE. **2.** Taboo deformation _*ogwhi-_ in Greek _ophis,_ snake, serpent: OPHIDIAN, OPHITE, OPHIUCHUS. **3.** Taboo deformation _*eghi-_ in Greek _ekhis,_ snake, in derivatives: **a.** _ekhinos,_ hedgehog (< "snake-eater"): ECHINO-; **b.** _ekhidna,_ hedgehog: ECHIDNA. [Pok. _anghu̯i-_ 43.]

ank-. Also **ang-.** To bend. **I.** Germanic _*ank-_ in Old Norse _*ankula_ and Old English _anclēow,_ ankle: ANKLE. **II.** Suffixed form _*ank-ulo-._ **1.** Germanic _*ang-ul-_ in: **a.** Old English _angul,_ fishhook: ANGLE[1]; **b.** Old English _Engle,_ the Angles (< the shape of their original homeland, the Angul district of Schleswig): ENGLAND; **c.** probably Latin _Anglī,_ the Angles: ANGLE. **2.** Greek _ankulos,_ crooked, bent: ANCYCLOSTOMIASIS, ANKYLOSIS. **III.** Greek _ankura,_ anchor: ANCHOR. **IV.** Greek _ankōn,_ elbow: ANCON. **V.** Sanskrit _anka,_ hook, in _añcati,_ he bends: PALANQUIN. **VI.** Suffixed variant form _*onk-o-_ in Latin _uncus,_ hooked, bent: UNCINUS, UNCUS. **VII.** Suffixed form _*ang-olo-_ in Latin _angulus,_ angle, corner: ANGLE[2]. [Pok. 2. _ank-, ang-_ 45.]

āno-. Ring. **1.** Latin _ānus,_ ring, anus: ANUS. **2.** Latin diminutive _annulus,_ ring, signet ring: ANNULAR, ANNULET, ANNULUS. [Pok. _āno-_ 47.]

ans-. Loop, handle. Latin _ānsa,_ handle: ANSATE. [Pok. _ansa_ 48.]

ansu-. Spirit, demon. **1.** Germanic _*ansu-_ in: **a.** Old English _ōs,_ god: OSCAR[1], OSWALD; **b.** Old Norse _āss,_ god: AESIR. **2.** Suffixed reduced form _*n̥su-ro-_ in Avestan _ahura,_ spirit: ORMAZD. [Pok. _ansu-_ 48.]

anti. Against; with derivatives meaning in front of, before; also, end. **1.** Germanic _*andi-_ in Old English _and-,_ indicating opposition: ALONG, UN-[2]. **2.** Germanic _*andjō_ in Old English _ende,_ end: END. **3.** Latin _ante,_ before, in front of, against: ADVANCE, ANCIENT[1], ANTE, ANTE-, ANTERIOR, VANGUARD. **4.** Greek _anti,_ against: ANTI-, ENANTIOMORPH. **5.** Compound form _*anti-əkwo-,_ "appearing before, having prior aspect" (_*əkw-,_ appearance; see **okw-**), in Latin _antīquus,_ former, antique: ANTIC, ANTIQUE. **6.** Reduced form _*n̥ti-_ in Germanic _*und-_ in Old Norse _und,_ until, unto: UNTIL. **7.** Variant form _*anto-_ in Sanskrit _anta,_ end: VEDANTA. [Pok. _ant-s_ 48.]

ap-[1]. To take, reach. **1.** Latin _apere,_ to attach, join, tie to: APT, (ATTITUDE), INEPT, LARIAT. **2.** Latin _apīscī,_ to attain: ADEPT. **3.** Latin _apex,_ top, summit (< "something reached"): APEX. **4.** Prefixed form _*co-ap-_ (_co-,_ together, COM-) in Latin _cōpula,_ bond, tie, link: COPULA, COPULATE, COUPLE. **5.** Perhaps Latin _ammentum_ (< _*ap-mentum,_ "something tied"), thong, strap: AMENT[1]. [Pok. 1. _ap-_ 50.]

ap-[2]. Water, river. **1.** Sanskrit _āpah,_ waters: PUNJAB. **2.** Iranian _ap-_ in Persian _āb,_ water: JULEP. [Pok. 2. _ap-_ 51.]

āpero-. Shore. Perhaps a derivative of **ap-**[2]. Suffixed form _*āper-yo-_ in Greek _ēpeiros,_ land, mainland: EPEIROGENY. [Pok. _āpero_ 53.]

apo-. Also **ap-.** Off, away. **1.** Germanic _*af_ in: **a.** Old English _of, æf,_ off: OF, OFF; **b.** Middle Dutch _af,_ off: OFFAL; **c.** Old English _ebba,_ low tide: EBB; **d.** Old High German _aba,_ off, away from: ABLAUT; **e.** Germanic _*aftan-_ in Old English _æftan,_ behind: ABAFT. **2.** Latin _ab,_ away from: AB-[1]. **3.** Greek _apo,_ away from, from: APO-. **4.** Suffixed (comparative) form _*ap(o)-tero-_ in Germanic _*aftar-_ in Old English _æfter,_ after, behind: AFTER. **5.** Suffixed form _*ap-t-is-_ in Germanic _*aftiz_ in Old English _eft,_ again: EFTSOONS. **6.** Suffixed form _*apu-ko-_ in Germanic _afug-_ in Old Norse _ōfugr,_ turned backward: AWKWARD. **7.** Suffixed variant form _*ēp-n̥yo-_ in Germanic _*ēben-,_ "the after or later time," evening, in Old English _ǣfen,_ evening: EVEN[2], EVENING. **8.** Possibly root _*po(s),_ on, in: **a.** Russian _po,_ at, by, next to: POGROM; **b.** Latin _post,_ behind, back, afterwards: POST-, POSTERIOR, POST-MORTEM, PREPOSTEROUS, PUNY; **c.** Latin _pōnere,_ to put, place: APPOSITION, COMPOSITE, COMPOSITION, COMPOUND, DEPONE, DEPOSIT, DISPOSE, EXPOUND, IMPONE, IMPOSE, INTERPOSE, OPPOSE, POSITION, POSITIVE, POST, POSTICHE, POSTURE, PREPOSITION, PROPOSE, PROVOST, REPOSIT, SUPPOSE. [Pok. _apo-_ 53.]

apsā. Aspen. Germanic _*aspōn_ in Old English _æspe,_ aspen: ASPEN. [Pok. _apsā_ 55.]

ar-. Also **arə-.** To fit together. **I.** Basic form _arə-._ **1.** Suffixed form _*ar(ə)-mo-_ in: **a.** Germanic _armaz_ in Old English _earm,_ arm: ARM; **b.** Latin _arma,_ arms: ALARM, ARMADA, ARMADILLO, ARMATURE, ARMOIRE, ARMS, ARMY, DISARM; **c.** Latin _armus,_ upper arm: ARMILLARY SPHERE. **2.** Suffixed form _*ar(ə)-smo-_ in Greek _harmos,_ joint, shoulder: HARMONY, HARMOTOME. **3.** Suffixed form _*ar(ə)-ti-_ in: **a.** Latin _ars_ (stem _art-_), art, skill, craft: ART[1], ARTEL, ARTISAN, ARTIST; **b.** further suffixed form _*ar(ə)-ti-o-_ in Greek _artios,_ fitting: ARTIODACTYL; **c.** Latin _iners_ (stem _inert-_), unskilled (_in-,_ not, IN-): INERT, INERTIA. **4.** Suffixed form _*ar(ə)-tu-_ in Latin _artus,_ joint: ARTICLE. **5.** Suffixed form _*ar(ə)-to-_ in Latin _artus,_ tight: COARCTATE. **6.** Suffixed form _*ar(ə)-dhro-_ in Greek _arthron,_ joint: ANARTHROUS, ARTHRO-, DIARTHROSIS, ENARTHROSIS, SYNARTHROSIS. **7.** Suffixed (superlative) form _*ar(ə)-isto-_ in Greek _aristos,_ best: ARISTOCRACY. **II.** Possibly suffixed variant form _*ōr-dh-_ in: **1.** Latin _ōrdō,_ order (originally a row of threads in a loom): ORDAIN, ORDER, ORDINAL, ORDINANCE, ORDINARY, ORDINATE, ORDO; COORDINATION, INORDINATE, SUBORDINATE; **2.** Latin _ordīrī,_ to begin to weave: EXORDIUM, PRIMORDIAL; **3.** Latin _ōrnāre,_ to adorn: ORNAMENT, ORNATE; ADORN, SUBORN. **III.** Variant _*rē-_ in: **1.** Latin _rērī,_ to consider, confirm, ratify: ARRAIGN, RATE[1], RATIO, REASON; **2.** suffixed form _*rē-dh-_ in: **a.** Germanic _*rēdan_ in _(i)_ Old English _rǣdan,_ to advise: READ, REDE _(ii)_ Old English _rǣden,_ condition: HATRED, KINDRED; **b.** Germanic _*rēdaz_ in _(i)_ Old English _rǣd,_ advice: ALFRED[1], ETHELRED II _(ii)_ Old Norse _radh,_ counsel: RALPH _(iii)_ Old High German _rāt,_ counsel: BUNDESRAT _(iv)_ Old English _rǣdels,_ opinion, riddle: RIDDLE[2]. **3.** Zero-grade form _rə-_ in Germanic _*rath,_ number (see **dekm̥**). **IV.** Variant _*rī-_ in: **1.** suffixed form _*rī-tu-_ in Latin _rītus,_ rite, custom, usage: RITE; **2.** suffixed form _*(a)rī-dhmo-_ in Greek _arithmos,_ number, amount: ARITHMETIC, LOGARITHM. [Pok. 1. _ar-_ 55.]

arek-. To hold, contain, guard. Variant _*ark-_ in: **1.** Latin _arca,_ chest, box: ARCANE, ARK; **2.** Latin _arcēre,_ to enclose, confine, contain, ward off: COERCE, EXERCISE; **3.** Greek _arkein,_ to ward off, suffice: AUTARKY. [Pok. _areq-_ 65.]

arə-. To plow. Latin _arāre,_ to plow: ARABLE. [Pok. _ar(ə)-_ 62.]

arg-. To shine; white; the shining or white metal, silver. **1.** Germanic _*ark-_ in Old High German _erchan,_ genuine: ARCHIBALD. **2.** Suffixed form _*arg-ent-_ in Latin _argentum,_ silver: ARGENT, (ARGENTINA). **3.** Suffixed form _*arg-i-l(l)-_ in Greek _argillos,_ white clay: ARGIL. **4.** Suffixed form _*arg-u-ro-_ in Greek _arguros,_ silver: ARGYROL, HYDRARGYRUM, LITHARGE, PYRARGYRITE. **5.** Suffixed form _*arg-i-n-_ in Greek _arginoeis,_ brilliant, bright-shining: ARGININE. **6.** Extended form _*argu-,_ brilliance, clarity, in Latin denominative _arguere,_ to make clear, demonstrate: ARGUE. **7.** Suffixed form _*arg-ro-_ in Greek _argos_ (< _*argros_), white (see **pel-**[2]). [Pok. _ar(e)g_ 64.]

[arkhein. To begin, rule, command. Greek verb of unknown origin; with derivative _arkhē,_ rule, beginning: ARCH-, -ARCH, ARCHAEO-, ARCHAIC, ARCHIVES, ARCHON; AUTARCHY, EXARCH, MENARCHE.]

arkw-. Bow and arrow (uncertain which, perhaps both as a unit). **1.** Germanic _*arhwō_ in Old English _arwe, earh,_ and Old Norse _*arw-,_ arrow: ARROW. **2.** Latin _arcus,_ bow: ARBALEST, ARC, ARCADE, ARCH[1], ARCHER, ARCHIVOLT, ARCIFORM, ARCUATE. [Pok. _arqu-_ 67.]

aryo-. Lord, ruler; self-designation of the Indo-Iranians and perhaps even of the Indo-Europeans. **1.** Lengthened-grade form **āryo-* in: **a.** Sanskrit *ārya,* noble, Aryan: ARYAN; **b.** Old Persian *āriya,* noble: IRAN. **2.** Suffixed reduced form **ary-āko-* in Old Irish *airech,* nobleman: OIREACHTAS. [Pok. *ario-* 67.]

as-. To burn, glow. **1.** Extended form **asg-* in Germanic **askōn-* in Old English *æsce, asce,* ash: ASH[1]. **2.** Suffixed form **ās-ā-* in Latin *āra,* altar, hearth: ARA. **3.** Suffixed (stative) form **ās-ē-* in: **a.** Latin *ārēre,* to be dry, hence *āridus,* dry, parched: ARID; **b.** Latin *ardēre,* to burn, be on fire, from *āridus,* parched: ARDENT, ARDOR, ARSON. **4.** Extended form **asd-* in: **a.** Greek *azainein,* to dry: ZAMIA; **b.** Greek *azaleos,* dry: AZALEA. [Pok. *as-* 68.]

[**asinus.** Ass. Latin noun, akin to Greek *onos,* probably ultimately from the same source as Sumerian *anšu.* **1.** Latin *asinus,* ass: ASININE, ASS[1], EASEL. **2.** Greek *onos,* ass: ONAGER.]

at-. To go; with Germanic and Latin derivatives meaning a year (conceived as "the period gone through, the revolving year"). Suffixed form **at-no-* in Latin *annus,* year: ANNALS, ANNUAL, ANNUITY; ANNIVERSARY, BIENNIUM, DECENNIUM, MILLENNIUM, OCTENNIAL, PERENNIAL, QUADRENNIUM, QUINDECENNIAL, QUINQUENNIUM, SEPTENNIAL, SEXENNIAL, SUPERANNUATED, TRIENNIUM, VICENNIAL. [Pok. *at-* 69.]

āter-. Fire. **1.** Suffixed zero-grade form **ātr-o-* in Latin *āter,* black (< "blackened by fire"): ATRABILIOUS. **2.** Suffixed zero-grade form **ātr-io-* in Latin *ātrium,* forecourt, hall, atrium (perhaps originally the place where the smoke from the hearth escaped through a hole in the roof): ATRIUM. **3.** Compound shortened zero-grade form **atr-okw-* (**okw-,* looking; see **okw-**) in Latin *ătrōx,* "black-looking," frightful: ATROCIOUS. [Pok. *āt(e)r-* 69.]

[**athal-.** Race, family. Germanic root. **1.** Germanic **athal-* in: **a.** Old English *æthele, æthel,* noble: ETHELRED II; **b.** Old English *ætheling,* prince: ATHELING; **c.** Old High German *adal,* lineage: ADELA, ADELAIDE[1], ADOLPH, ALBERT. **2.** Variant Germanic **ōthel-* in Old High German *edili,* noble: EDELWEISS. [In Pok. *atos* 71.]]

atto-. Father (nursery word). Possibly Latin *atta,* father: ATAVISM. [In Pok. *atos* 71.]

au-[1]. To stay the night, dwell. Suffixed form **au-lā-* in Greek *aulē,* court, dwelling: AULIC. [Pok. 2. *au-* 72.]

au-[2]. Pronominal base appearing in particles and adverbs. Suffixed form **au-ge* in Germanic **auke* in Old English *ēac,* also: EKE[2]. [Pok. 4. *au-* 73.]

au-[3]. Off, away. **1.** Old Russian *u-,* away: UKASE, UKRAINIAN. **2.** Sanskrit *ava,* off, down: AVATAR. [Pok. 3. *au-* 72.]

[**audaz.** Property. Germanic root. **1.** Old English *ēad,* property, riches: EDGAR, EDITH, EDMUND, EDWARD[1]. **2.** Frankish **-ōd,* property (see **al-[5]**; **peku-**). [In Pok. 5. *au-* 75.]]

aug-[1]. To increase. **1.** Germanic **aukan* in: **a.** Old English *ēacan,* to increase: EKE[1]; **b.** Old English *ēaca,* an addition: NICKNAME. **2.** Variant extended forms **wogs-, *wegs-,* in Germanic **wahsan* in: **a.** Old English *weaxan,* to grow: WAX[2]; **b.** Old English **wæst,* growth, hence perhaps waist, size: WAIST. **3.** Form **aug-ē-* in: Latin *augēre,* to increase: AUCTION, AUGEND, AUGMENT, AUTHOR, OCTROI. **4.** Latin *augur,* diviner (< "he who obtains favorable presage," < "divine favor, increase"): AUGUR, INAUGURATE. **5.** Latin *augustus,* majestic, august: AUGUST. **6.** Suffixed form **aug-s-* in: **a.** Latin *auxilium,* aid, support, assistance: AUXILIARY; **b.** Greek *auxein,* to increase: AUXIN; **c.** Greek *auxanein,* to increase: AUXESIS. [Pok. *aueg-* 84.]

aug-[2]. To shine. Suffixed form **aug-ā-* in: **a.** Greek *augē,* light, ray: AUGITE; **b.** possibly Old Slavic *juga,* south: YUGOSLAVIA. [Pok. *aug-* 87.]

aukwh-. Also **aukw-.** Cooking pot. **1.** Germanic suffixed form **uhw-na-* in **ufna-* in Old English *ofen,* furnace, oven: OVEN. **2.** Suffixed form **aukw-slā-* in Latin *aulla, aula,* olla, pot, jar: OLLA. [Pok. *auqu(h)-* 88.]

aulo-. Hole, cavity. **1.** Metathetic form **alwo-* in Latin *alvus,* the belly, stomach: ALVEOLUS. **2.** Greek *aulos,* pipe, flute, hollow tube: CAROL, HYDRAULIC. [Pok. *au-lo-s* 88.]

[**aurum.** Gold. Latin noun with pre-form **aus-o-* probably from a root **aus-.* Latin *aurum,* gold: AUREATE, AUREOLE, AURIC, AURIFEROUS, AURUM, DARIOLE, DORY[2], EL DORADO, EYRIR, OR[3], ÖRE, ORIFLAMME, ORIOLE, ORMOLU, OROIDE, ORPHREY, ORPIMENT.]

aus-. To draw water. Suffixed form **aus-io-* in Latin *haurīre,* to draw up: EXHAUST, HAUSTELLUM, HAUSTORIUM. [Pok. *aus-* 90.]

aw-[1]. Also **wedh-.** To weave. **1.** Germanic **wēdiz* in Old English *wǣd, wǣde,* garment, cloth: WEED[2]. **2.** Germanic **wadlaz* in Old English *watel, watul,* wattle: WATTLE. [Pok. 5. *au-.* 75.]

aw-[2]. To perceive. Compound forms **aw-dh-, *awis-dh-,* "to place perception" (see **dhē-[1]**). **1.** Suffixed form **awisdh-io-* or **awdh-io-* in Latin *audīre,* to hear: AUDIBLE, AUDIENCE, AUDIENT, AUDILE, AUDIO-, AUDIT, AUDITOR, AUDITORIUM, AUDITORY, OBEY, OYEZ, SUBAUDITION. **2.** Greek *aisthanesthai,* to feel: AESTHETIC, ANESTHESIA. [Pok. 8. *au-* 78.]

awes-. Also **aus-.** To shine. **1.** Germanic **aust-* in: **a.** Old English *ēast,* east (< "the direction of the sunrise"): EAST; **b.** Old High German *ōstan,* east: OSTMARK. **2.** Germanic **austra-* in: **a.** Old English *ēasterne,* eastern: EASTERN; **b.** Old High German *ōstar,* eastern: AUSTRIA; **c.** Frankish **ōstra-,* eastern: AUSTRASIA; **d.** Late Latin *ostro-,* eastern: OSTROGOTH. **3.** Germanic **austrōn-,* a dawn-goddess whose holiday was celebrated at the vernal equinox, in Old English *ēastre,* Easter: EASTER. **4.** Probably suffixed form **aus-ōs-,* Indo-European goddess of the dawn, in: **a.** Latin *Aurōra,* Dawn: AURORA; **b.** Greek *ēōs,* dawn: EO-, EOS, EOSIN. [Pok. *aues-* 86.]

awi-. Bird. **I. 1.** Latin *avis,* bird: AVIAN, AVIARY, AVIATION, AVICULTURE, AVIFAUNA, BUSTARD, OCARINA, OSPREY, OSTRICH. **2.** Compound **awi-spek-,* "observer of birds" (**spek-,* to see; see **spek-**), in Latin *auspex,* augur: AUSPICE. **II.** Possible derivatives are the Indo-European words for egg, **ōwyo-, *əyo-.* **1.** Germanic **ajja(m)* in: **a.** Old English *æg,* egg: COCKNEY, KIDNEY; **b.** Old Norse *egg,* egg: EGG[1]. **2.** Latin *ōvum,* egg: OVAL, OVARY, OVATE, OVI-, OVOLO, OVULE, OVUM. **3.** Greek *ōion,* egg: OO-. [Pok. *auei-* 86.]

awo-. An adult male relative other than one's father. **1.** Latin *avus,* grandfather: ATAVISM. **2.** Latin *avunculus,* maternal uncle: AVUNCULAR, UNCLE. **3.** Latin *avia,* grandmother: AYAH. **4.** Variant **awyo-* in Old Irish *au, aue, o,* grandfather, grandson, descendant: O'. [Pok. *auo-s* 89.]

ayer-. Day, morning. **1.** Germanic **airiz* in: **a.** Old English *ǣr,* before: EARLY, ERE; **b.** Old Norse *ār,* before: OR[2]. **2.** Germanic (superlative) **airistaz* in Old English *ǣrest,* earliest: ERST. [Pok. *aier-* 12.]

ayos-. A metal, copper or bronze. **1.** Latin *aes,* bronze: AENEOUS, AERUGO, ERA. **2.** Variant **ayes-* in Germanic **aiz* in Old English *ār,* brass: ORE. [Pok. *aios-* 15.]

baba-. Root imitative of unarticulated or indistinct speech; also a child's nursery word for a baby and for various relatives. **1.** Middle English *babelen,* to babble: BABBLE. **2.** Middle English *babe, babie,* baby: BABE, BABY. **3.** Italian *bambo,* child, simpleton: BAMBINO. **4.** Polish *baba,* old woman: BABA, BABKA. **5.** Russian *baba,* old woman: BABUSHKA. **6.** Russian *balalaika,* balalaika (imitative of the sound): BALALAIKA. **7.** Latin *balbus,* stuttering, stammering: BOOBY. **8.** Old French *babine,* pendulous lip, and *baboue,* grimace (both associated with the notion of making incoherent speech sounds): BABOON. **9.** Greek *barbaros,* non-Greek, foreign, rude (< "one who speaks incomprehensibly"): BARBAROUS, (BARBARA), (BARBARIAN), (BARBARISM), BRAVE, (BRAVO[1]), (BRAVO[2]), (BRAVURA), (BRAW). **10.** Hindi *bābū,* father: BABU. [Pok. *baba-* 91.]

badyo-. Yellow, brown. A western Indo-European word. Latin *badius,* chestnut brown (used only of horses): BAY[3]. [Pok. *badios* 92.]

bak-. Staff used for support. **1.** Probably Middle Dutch *pegge,* pin, peg: PEG. **2.** Latin *baculum,* rod, walking stick: BACILLUS, BACULIFORM, BAGUETTE, DEBACLE, IMBECILE. **3.** Greek *baktron,* staff: BACTERIA. [Pok. *bak-* 93.]

bamb-. Word imitative of dull or rumbling sounds. Greek *bombos,* a booming, humming: BOMB, (BOMBARD), BOUND[1]. [Pok. *ba^{x}mb-* 93.]

band-. A drop. Possibly Middle Irish *banne,* drop: BONNYCLABBER. [Pok. *band-* 95.]

[**bassus.** Low. Late Latin adjective, possibly from Oscan: BASE[2], (BAS-RELIEF), (BASS[2]), (BASSET[1]), (BASSET[2]), BASSO; ABASE, (BOUILLABAISSE), (DEBASE).]

[**bat-.** Yawning. Latin root of unknown origin; probably imitative. **1.** Latin **batāre,* to yawn, gape: BAY[2], (BEAGLE), (BEVEL), ABASH, (ABEYANCE), BADINAGE. **2.** Possibly Vulgar Latin **abbaiāre,* to bay: BAY[4].]

[**battuere.** To beat. Latin verb of unknown origin. BAT[1], BATTER[1], (BATTER[3]), (BATTER[4]), (BATTERY), (BATTLE), (BATTLEDORE), (BATTLEMENT), (BATTUE), (BATE[3]), ABATE, COMBAT, DEBATE, RABBET, REBATE[1], (REBATO).]

bel-. Strong. **1.** Suffixed o-grade form **bol-iyo-* in Russian *bol'shoi,* large: BOLSHEVIK. **2.** Prefixed form **dē-belo-* (*dē-,* privative prefix; see **de-**), "without strength," in Latin *dēbilis,* weak: DEBILITATE, DEBILITY. [Pok. 2. *bel-* 96.]

bend-. Protruding point. **1.** Germanic **panja-,* "structure of stakes," in Old English *penn,* pen for cattle: PEN[2]. **2.** Germanic **pund-* possibly in Old English *pund-, pundfald,* enclosure for stray animals: POND, POUND[3], (PINFOLD), IMPOUND. **3.** Germanic **pin-* in Old English *pintel,* penis: PINTLE. **4.** Suffixed form **bend-no-* in Scottish Gaelic *beann,* peak: BEN[2]. [Pok. *bend-* 96.]

beu-[1]. Also **bheu-.** Appears in words loosely associated with the notion "to swell." **I.** Root form **beu-.* **1.** Germanic **puk-* in: **a.** Old English *pocc,* pustule: POCK; **b.** Frankish **pokka,* bag, pocket: POACH[1], POCKET, POKE[3], POUCH, (PUCKER). **2.** Old English *pyffan,* to blow out: PUFF. **3.** Old English *-pūte,* "fish with large head" (in *aele-pūte,* eelpout): POUT[2]. **4.** Old English **pūtian,* to blow out the cheeks: POUT[1]. **II.** Root form **bheu-* with various Germanic derivatives. **1.** Old English *bōsm,* bosom: BOSOM. **2.** Possibly Norwegian dialectal *bugge,* strong man: BIG. **3.** Old English *būc,* belly, pitcher: BUCKET, BUCKBOARD. **4.** Frankish **būk,* trunk of the body: TREBUCHET. **5.** Possibly Middle Dutch *biutelen,* to push through a sieve: BOLT[2]. **6.** Old French *boter,* to push forth: BUD[1]. **7.** Old English *b̄yle,* pustule: BOIL[2]. **8.** German dialectal *baustern,* to swell, akin to the source of Middle English *bost,* a bragging: BOAST[1]. **III.** Root form **beu-.* **1.** Latin *bulla,* bubble, round object, amulet: BILL[1], (BILLET[1]), BOLA, BOLERO, BOULE[2], BOWL[2], BULLA, (BULL[2]), BULLATE, BULLET, (BULLETIN). **2.** Latin *bullīre,* to bubble, boil: BOIL[1], (BULLY[2]), (BULLION), (BOUILLON), BUDGE[1], BOUILLABAISSE, EBULLIENT, GARBOIL, PARBOIL. **3.** Possibly Latin *bucca,* (inflated) cheek: BUCCAL, BUCKLE[1], (BUCKLE[2]), (BOUCLÉ), BOCACCIO, DEBOUCH, DISEMBOGUE, EMBOUCHURE. **4.** Greek *boubōn,* groin, swollen gland: BUBO. [Pok. 2. *beu-* 98.]

beu-[2]. Root imitative of muffled sounds. **1.** Latin *būtiō,* bittern: BITTERN[1]. **2.** Latin *būteō,* a kind of hawk: BUZZARD. [Pok. 1. *b(e)u-* 97.]

bhā-[1]. To shine. **1.** Germanic **baukna-,* beacon, signal, in: **a.** Old English *bēac(e)n,* beacon: BEACON; **b.** Old English denominative *bēcnan, biecnan,* to make a sign, beckon: BECKON; **c.** Old High German *bouhhan,* buoy (< "marker"): BUOY. **2.** Perhaps Germanic **bazja-,* berry (< "bright-colored fruit"), in Old English *berie, berige,* berry: BERRY. **3.** Germanic **bandwa-,* "identifying sign," banner, standard, sash, also "company united under a (particular) banner," in: **a.** Latin-Langobardic **bandum,* standard: BAND[2]; **b.** Spanish *banda,* sash: BANDOLEER; **c.** Late Latin *bandum,* banner, standard: BANNER, (BANNERET), (BANDEROLE). **4.** Extended form **bhawos-* in Greek *phōs* (stem *phōt-*), light: PHOS-, (PHOSPHORUS), PHOT, PHOTO-, (PHOTOGRAPH, etc.). **5.** Extended and suffixed form **bhan-yo-* in Greek *phainein,* "to bring to light," cause to appear, show, and *phainesthai* (passive), "to be brought to light," appear: FANTASY, PANT, -PHANE, PHANTASM, (PHANTOM), PHASE, PHENO-, PHENOMENON; DIAPHANOUS, EMPHASIS, EPIPHANY, HIEROPHANT, PHANEROGAM, (PHANTASMAGORIA), PHOSPHENE, SYCOPHANT, THEOPHANY, (TIFFANY). [Pok. 1. *bhā-* 104.]

bhā-[2]. To speak. **1.** Latin *fārī,* to speak: AFFABLE, FATE; EFFABLE, (INEFFABLE), INFANT, (INFANTRY), (FANTOCCINI), PREFACE. **2.** Greek *phanai,* to speak: -PHASIA, PROPHET. **3.** Suffixed form in Germanic **banwan, *bannan,* to speak publicly (used of particular kinds of proclamation in feudal or pre-feudal custom; "to proclaim under penalty, to summon to the levy, to declare outlaw"), in: **a.** Old English *bannan,* to summon, proclaim, and Old Norse *banna,* to prohibit, curse: BAN[1]; **b.** Frankish **ban,* feudal jurisdiction, summons to military service, proclamation, and Old English *gebann,* proclamation: BANNS, ABANDON, BANAL; **c.** Vulgar Latin **bannīre,* to banish: BANISH; **d.** Late Latin *bannus, bannum,* proclamation: CONTRABAND; **e.** Italian *bandire,* to muster, band together (< "to have been summoned"): BANDIT. **4.** Suffixed form **bhā-ni-* in Germanic **bōni-* in Old Norse *bōn,* prayer, request: BOON[1]. **5.** Suffixed form **bhā-ma* in: **a.** Latin *fāma,* talk, reputation, fame: FAME, (FAMOUS), (INFAMOUS), DEFAME; **b.** Greek *phēmē,* saying, speech: EUPHEMISM. **6.** Suffixed o-grade form *bhō-nā in Greek phōnē, voice, sound: PHONE[1], -PHONE, (FRANCOPHONE, TELEPHONE, etc.), PHONEME, PHONETIC, PHONO-, -PHONY; ANTHEM, (ANTIPHON), APHONIA, DIAPHONY, SYMPHONY. 7. Suffixed zero-grade form *bhə-to- in Latin fatērī, to acknowledge, admit: CONFESS, PROFESS. 8. Greek blasphēmos, evil-speaking, blasphemous (first element obscure): BLASPHEMOUS, (BLASPHEME), (BLAME). [Pok. 2. bhā- 105.]

bha-bhā-. Broad bean. 1. Latin faba, broad bean: FAVA BEAN. 2. Variant form *bha-un- in Germanic *baunō in Old English bēan, broad bean, bean of any kind: BEAN. [Pok. bhabhā 106.]

bhad-. Good. 1. Germanic (comparative) *batizō in Old English betera, better: BETTER. 2. Germanic (superlative) *batistaz in Old English bet(e)st, best: BEST. 3. Germanic noun *bōtō in Old English bōt, remedy, aid: BOOT[2]. 4. Germanic verb *batnan, to become better, in Old Norse batna, to improve: BATTEN[1]. [Pok. bhād- 106.]

bhag-[1]. To share out, apportion; also, to get a share. 1. Greek phagein, to eat (< "to have a share of food"): -PHAGE, PHAGO-, -PHAGOUS, -PHAGY. 2. Sanskrit bhajati, he apportions, and bhaga, good fortune: BHAGAVAD-GITA, PAGODA. 3. Extended form *bhags- in Avestan bakhsh- in Persian bakhshīdan, to give: BAKSHEESH, (BUCKSHEE). [Pok. 1. bhag- 107.]

bhag-[2]. Sharp. Suffixed form *bhag-ro- in Greek phagros, whetstone, also a name for the sea bream: PORGY. [Pok. 2. bhag- 107.]

bhāghu-. Elbow, shoulder. Germanic *bōguz in: a. Old English bōg, bōh, bough: BOUGH; b. Middle Low German boog, shoulder, also "bow of a ship" (an expressive nautical transference): BOW[1]. [Pok. bhāghú-s 108.]

bhāgo-. Beech tree. 1. Germanic *bōkō, beech, also "beech staff for carving runes on" (an early Germanic graphic device), in: a. Old English bōc, written document, composition: BOOK; b. Middle Dutch boek, beech: BUCKWHEAT. 2. Germanic *bōkjo in Old English bēce, beech: BEECH. [Pok. bhāgo-s 107.]

bhar-. Projection, bristle, point. 1. Suffixed o-grade form *bhor-so- in Germanic *barsaz in Old English bærs, perch, bass (a fish that has a spiny dorsal fin): BASS[1]. 2. Suffixed zero-grade form *bhr̥-sti- in Germanic *bursti- in Old English byrst, bristle: BRISTLE. 3. Extended zero-grade form *bhr̥s- in: a. Germanic *bur- in Swedish borre, bur: BUR[1]; b. suffixed form *bhr̥s-dh- in Germanic *bruzd-, point, needle, in (i) Frankish *bruzdon, to embroider: EMBROIDER (ii) Old Norse broddr, spike: BRAD; c. suffixed form *bhr̥s-ti- in Latin fastigium, summit, top: FASTIGIATE; d. possibly suffixed form *bhr̥s-tu- in Latin fastus, disdain (from the notion of prickliness): FASTIDIOUS; e. suffixed form *bhr̥s-tio- in Russian borshch, cow parsley: BORSCHT. [Pok. bhar- 108.]

bhardhā. Beard. Possibly related to **bhar-**, projection, bristle. 1. Germanic *bardaz in Old English beard, beard: BEARD. 2. Germanic *bardō, beard, also hatchet, broadax (the association of beard and ax is attested elsewhere in the Indo-European family; both were symbols of patriarchal authority), in Old High German barta, beard, and bart, ax: HALBERD. 3. Latin barba, beard: BARB[1], BARBEL, BARBELLATE, (BARBER), BARBETTE, BARBICEL, BARBULE, REBARBATIVE. [Pok. bhardhā 110.]

bhares-. Also **bhars-**. Barley. 1. Germanic *barz- in Old English bere, bære, barley: BARLEY, (BARN). 2. Latin far (stem farr-), spelt, grain: FARINA, (FARINACEOUS), FARRAGO. [Pok. bhares- 111.]

bhasko-. Band, bundle. 1. Latin fascis, bundle (as of rods, twigs, or straw), also crowd of people: FASCES, FASCICLE, FASCINE, FASCISM. 2. Latin fascia, band, fillet, bandage: FASCIA, FESS. 3. Probably Latin fascinum, fascinus, an amulet in the shape of a phallus, hence a bewitching: FASCINATE. [Pok. bhasko- 111.]

bhau-. To strike. 1. Germanic *bautan in: a. Old English bēatan, to beat: BEAT; b. Old High German bōzan, to knock: BUSHEL[2]. 2. Germanic *bautilaz, hammer, in Old English bietel, hammer, mallet: BEETLE[3]. 3. Germanic *baustjan in Old Norse beysta, to thrash, strike: BASTE[3]. 4. Germanic *būtaz in: a. Old Norse būtr, cut-off tree stump, log, block of wood: BUTT[4], (BUTT[2]), (DEBUT); b. Old English diminutive buttuc, end, strip of land: BUTTOCK. 5. Germanic *butt-, name for a flatfish (probably < "thick, heavy," < "cut-off lump"), in: a. Old Swedish but, flatfish: TURBOT; b. Middle Dutch butte, flatfish: HALIBUT. 6. Germanic *buttan in Common Romance *bottāre, to strike, push: BUTT[1], BUTTON, BUTTRESS; ABUT, (REBUT), SACKBUT. 7. Variant form *bhūt- in: a. Latin confūtāre, to check, suppress, restrain (com-, intensive prefix, COM-): CONFUTE; b. Latin refūtāre, to drive back, rebut (re-, back, RE-): REFUTE. 8. Variant form *bhū(t)- in Latin futuere, to have intercourse with (a woman): FOOTLE. [Pok. 1. bhau- 112.]

bhē-. To warm. 1. Suffixed zero-grade form *bhə-to- in Germanic *batham in Old English bæth, a bath, and its denominative bathian, to bathe: BATH[1], BATHE. 2. Suffixed zero-grade form *bhə-g- in: a. Germanic *bakan in Old English bacan, to bake: BAKE; b. Germanic *bakkan in Old High German bahhan, backan, to bake: ZWIEBACK. [Pok. bhē- 113.]

bhedh-[1]. To dig. 1. Germanic *badjam, garden plot, also sleeping place, in Old English bedd, bed: BED. 2. O-grade form *bhodh- in Latin fodere, to dig: FOSSA, (FOSSE), FOSSIL, FOSSORIAL. [Pok. 1. bhedh- 113.]

bhedh-[2]. To bend. 1. Germanic bidjan, to entreat, in Old English biddan, to ask, pray: BID. 2. Germanic *bidam, entreaty, in Old English gebed (ge-, intensive and collective prefix; see **kom**), prayer: BEAD. [Pok. 2. bhedh- 114.]

bheg-. To break. 1. Germanic nasalized form *bang- in: a. Old Norse banga, a hammering, akin to the probable Scandinavian source of English BANG[1]; b. Swedish dialectal bangla, to work inefficiently, akin to the possible Scandinavian source of English BUNGLE. 2. Possibly Germanic nasalized forms *bankiz and *bankōn-, bank of earth (probably < "feature where the contour of the ground is broken," escarpment, river bank, possibly also associated with "man-made earthwork"), later also bench, table, in: a. Old English benc, bench: BENCH; b. Old Danish banke, sandbank: BANK[1]; c. Old High German banc, bench, money-changer's table (borrowed as Italian banca): BANK[2], (BANKRUPT), BANTLING, BUNCO, MOUNTEBANK; d. Old French banc, bench: BANK[3], BANQUET; e. Provençal banca, bench: BANQUETTE. [Pok. bheg- 115.]

bhegw-. To run away. 1. Germanic *bakjaz, a stream, in Old Norse bekkr, a stream: BECK[2]. 2. Greek phebesthai, to flee in terror, forming phobos, panic, flight, fear: -PHOBE, -PHOBIA. [Pok. bhegu̯- 116.]

bhei-[1]. A bee. Germanic suffixed form *bīōn- in Old English bēo, a bee: BEE[1]. [Pok. bhei- 116.]

bhei-[2]. To strike. 1. Germanic suffixed form *bhi-li- in Old English bile, bird's beak: BILL[2]. 2. Germanic suffixed form *bhi-lio- in Old English bil, sharp weapon: BILL[3]. 3. Celtic tribal name Boii, "the fighters": BOHEMIA[1]. [Pok. bhei(ə)- 117.]

bheid-. To split; with Germanic derivatives referring to biting (hence also to eating and to hunting) and woodworking. 1. Germanic *bitiz in Old English bite, a bite, sting: BIT[2]. 2. Germanic *bītō in Old English bita, a piece bitten off, morsel: BIT[1]. 3. Germanic *bītan in: a. Old English bītan, to bite: BITE, (BEETLE[1]); b. Old English biter, "biting," sharp, bitter: BITTER. 4. Germanic *baitjan in: a. Old Norse beita (verb), to hunt with dogs, and beita (noun), pasture, food: BAIT[1]; b. Old French beter, to harass with dogs: ABET; c. prefixed form *ga-baitja- (*ga-, intensive and collective prefix; see **kom**) in Frankish *gabaiti, hunting with falcons: GIBLET. 5. Germanic *bait-, a boat (< "dugout canoe" or "split planking"), in Old English bāt, boat, and Old Norse bātr, boat: BOAT, (BOATSWAIN), BATEAU. 6. Germanic *bit- in Low German beting, bitt, akin to the source of English BITT. 7. Nasalized zero-grade form *bhi-n-d- in Latin findere (past participle fissus), to split: -FID, FISSI-, (FISSILE), FISSION, (FISSURE). [Pok. bheid- 116.]

bheidh-. To persuade, compel, confide. 1. Germanic *bīdan, to await (< "to await trustingly, expect, trust"), in Old English bīdan, to wait, stay: BIDE, ABIDE, (ABODE). 2. Germanic *baidjan in Old English bǣdan, to compel, afflict: BAD[1]. 3. Latin fīdere, to trust, confide: AFFIANCE, (AFFIANT), (AFFIDAVIT), CONFIDE, (CONFIDANT), (CONFIDENT), DEFY, (DEFIANCE), DIFFIDENT, FIANCÉ, FIDUCIAL, (FIDUCIARY). 4. O-grade form *bhoidh- in Latin foedus (stem foeder-), treaty, league: FEDERAL, FEDERATE, CONFEDERATE. 5. Zero-grade form *bhidh- in Latin fidēs, faith, trust: FAITH, (FAY[3]), FEALTY, FIDELITY, INFIDEL, PERFIDY, SOLIFIDIAN. [Pok. bheidh- 117.]

bheigw-. To shine. Greek phoibos, shining: PHOEBE, (PHOEBUS). (An uncertain but plausible root.) [Pok. bheigu̯- 118.]

bhel-[1]. To shine, flash, burn; shining white and various bright colors; fire. I. 1. Germanic *bala-, white mark, in Old English *bællede, bald (< "having a white head"): BALD. 2. Celtic *belo-, bright, in *belo-te(p)ina, "bright-fire," name of a prehistoric spring festival (*te(p)ina, fire; see **tep-**): BELTANE. 3. Russian byelii, white: BELUGA. 4. Greek phalaros, "having a white spot": PHALAROPE. II. 1. Suffixed variant form *bhlē-wo- in Germanic *blēwaz, blue, in Common Romance *blāvus: BLUE. 2. Suffixed o-grade form *bhlō-wo- in Latin flāvus, golden or reddish yellow: FLAVESCENT, FLAVIN, FLAVONE, FLAVOPROTEIN. III. Various extended Germanic forms. 1. *blaikjan, to make white, in Old English blǣcan, to bleach: BLEACH. 2. *blaikaz, shining, white, in: a. Old Norse bleikr, shining, white: BLEAK[1]; b. Old Norse bleikja, white color: BLEAK[2]. 3. *blas-, shining, white, in: a. Old English blæse, torch, bright fire: BLAZE[1]; b. Middle Low German bles, white mark: BLAZE[2]; c. Middle Dutch bles, white spot: BLESBOK; d. Old French blesmir, to make pale: BLEMISH. 4. *blend-, *bland-, to shine, dazzle, blind, confuse, in: a. Old English blind, blind: BLIND, (BLINDFOLD), (PURBLIND); b. Old High German blentan, to blind, deceive: BLENDE; c. Old Norse blanda, to mingle: BLEND; d. Old French blond, blond: BLOND. 5. *blenk-, *blank-, to shine, dazzle, blind, in: a. Old English blencan, to deceive: BLENCH[1]; b. Middle Dutch blinken, to glitter: BLINK; c. Vulgar Latin *blancus, white: BLANCH, (BLANK), (BLANKET), (BLANCMANGE). 6. *blisk-, to shine, burn, in Old English blyscan, to glow red: BLUSH. IV. Variant forms *bhleg-, *bhelg-, to shine, flash, burn. 1. Germanic *blakaz, burned, in Old English blæc, black: BLACK. 2. Germanic *blikatjan in Old High German blēcchazzen, to flash, lighten: BLITZKRIEG. 3. Zero-grade form *bhl̥g- in: a. Latin fulgēre, to flash, shine: FULGENT, FULGOR, FULGURATE, EFFULGENT, FOUDROYANT, REFULGENT; b. Latin fulmen (< *fulg-men), lightning, thunderbolt: FULMINATE. 4. a. Latin flagrāre, to blaze: FLAGRANT, CONFLAGRATION, DEFLAGRATE; b. Latin flamma (< *flag-ma), a flame: FLAME, FLAMBEAU, FLAMBOYANT, FLAMINGO, FLAMMABLE, INFLAME. 5. Greek phlegein, to burn: PHLEGM, (PHLEGMATIC), PHLEGETHON. 6. Greek phlox, a flame, also a wallflower: PHLOGISTON, PHLOGOPITE, PHLOX. [Pok. 1. bhel- 118, bheleg- 124, bhleu-(k)- 159.]

bhel-[2]. To blow, swell; with derivatives referring to various round objects and to the notion of tumescent masculinity. 1. Zero-grade form *bhl̥- in Germanic *bul- in: a. Old English bolla, pot, bowl: BOWL[1]; b. Old Norse bolr, tree trunk: BOLE[1]; c. Old Norse bulki, cargo (< "rolled-up load"): BULK[1]; d. Old High German bolla, ball: ROCAMBOLE; e. Middle High German bole, beam, plank: BULWARK, (BOULEVARD); f. Middle Dutch bolle, round object: BOLL; g. Middle Dutch bille, buttock: BILTONG; h. Swedish *buller-, "round object," in bullersten, "rounded stone," boulder, akin to the Scandinavian source of English BOULDER; i. possibly obsolete Swedish bulde, a swelling (see **wer-[1]**). 2. Suffixed zero-grade form *bhl̥-n- in: a. Germanic *bullōn, bull, in Old Norse boli, bull: BULL[1], (BULLOCK); b. Greek phallos, phallus: PHALLUS, (ITHYPHALLIC). 3. O-grade form *bhol- in Germanic *ball- in: a. Old English beallucas, testicles: BOLLIX; b. Old Norse böllr, ball: BALL[1]; c. Danish bolle, round roll: BILBERRY; d. Middle High German balle, ball: BALLOON, BALLOT, PALL-MALL; e. Frankish *balla, ball: BALLOTTEMENT; f. Old French bale, rolled-up bundle: BALE[1]. 4. Suffixed o-grade form *bhol-to- possibly in Germanic *balthaz, bold, in: a. Old English bald, beald, bold: BOLD; b. Old High German bald, bold: BAWD, ARCHIBALD, LEOPOLD. 5. Suffixed o-grade form *bhol-n- in Latin follis, bellows, inflated ball: FOLLICLE, FOOL[1], PUL. 6. Possibly Latin ballaena, whale (from its spouting?): BALEEN. 7. Conceivably (but more likely unrelated) Greek phellos, cork, cork-oak: PANTOFFLE, PHELLODERM, PHELLOGEN. (The following derivatives of this root are entered separately: **bhel-[3]**, **bhelgh-**, **bhlei-**, **bhleu-**.) [Pok. 3. bhel- 120.]

bhel-[3]. To thrive, bloom. Probably from **bhel-[2]**. I. Suffixed o-grade form *bhol-yo-, leaf. 1. Latin folium, leaf: FOIL[2], FOLIAGE, (FOLIO), FOLIUM; CINQUEFOIL, DEFOLIATE, EXFOLIATE, FEUILLETON, MILFOIL, PORTFOLIO, TREFOIL. 2. a. Greek phullon, leaf: (-PHYLL), PHYLLO-, -PHYLLOUS, CHERVIL, GILLYFLOWER, PODOPHYLLIN. b. Greek phullis, leaf (later used as a feminine name): PHYLLIS. II. Extended form *bhlē-. 1. O-grade form *bhlō- in: a. suffixed form *bhlō-w- in Germanic *blō-w- in Old English blōwan, to flower: BLOW[3]; b. Germanic suffixed form *blō-mōn in (i) Old Norse blōm, blōmi, flower, blossom: BLOOM[1] (ii) Old English blōma, a hammered ingot of iron (semantic development obscure): BLOOM[2]; c. Germanic suffixed form *blō-s- in Old English blōstm, blōstma, flower, blossom: BLOSSOM; d. Latin flōs (stem flōr-), flower: FERRET[1], FLORA, (FLORA), FLORAL, FLORENCE[2], FLORIATED, FLORID, FLORIN, FLORIST, FLORUIT, -FLOROUS, FLOSCULE, FLOUR, FLOURISH, FLOWER; CAULIFLOWER, DEFLOWER, EFFLORESCE, ENFLEURAGE. 2. Germanic suffixed form *blē-do- in Frankish *blād, produce of the land: EMBLEMENTS. 3. Suffixed zero-grade form *bhlə-to- in Germanic *bladaz in Old English blæd, leaf, blade: BLADE. [Pok. 4. bhel- 122.]

bhel-[4]. To cry out, yell. Germanic *bell- in: a. Old English bellan, to bellow, bark, roar: BELL[2]; b. Old English belle, a bell: BELL[1]; c. Old English *belgan, bylgan, to bellow: BELLOW; d. perhaps Old English bealcan, *b(i)elcan, to utter, belch forth: BELCH; e. Middle High German buldern, to make noise: POLTERGEIST; f. Icelandic baula, to low, akin to the Scandinavian source of Middle English baulen, to howl: BAWL. [Pok. 6. bhel- 123.]

bheld-. To knock, strike. Zero-grade form *bhḷd- in Germanic *bult-, missile, in Old English bolt, heavy arrow, bolt: BOLT[1]. [Pok. bheld- 124.]

bheleu-. To harm. Germanic *balwaz in Old English bealo, bealu, harm, ruin, bale: BALE[2]. [Pok. bheleu- 125.]

bhelg-. Also **bhelk-**. A plank, beam. 1. Germanic *balku- in Old Norse balkr, partition, low wall: BALK, BULK[2]. 2. Germanic *balkōn- in: a. Frankish *balk, beam: DEBAUCH; b. Old Italian balcone, scaffold: BALCONY. 3. Suffixed zero-grade form *bhḷk-io- in Latin fulcīre, to prop up, support: FULCRUM. 4. Possibly Greek phalanx, beam, finger bone, line of battle: PHALANX, (PHALANGE). [Pok. 5. bhel- 123.]

bhelgh-. To swell. An extension of **bhel-[2]**. 1. Germanic *balgiz in Old English belig, bælig, purse, bellows: BELLOWS, BELLY. 2. Germanic *bulgjan in Old Norse bylgja, a wave: BILLOW. 3. Germanic *bolgstraz in Old English bolster, cushion: BOLSTER. 4. Celtic *bolg- in Latin bulga, leather sack: BUDGET, BULGE. [Pok. bhelgh- 125.]

bhen-. To strike. Germanic *banōn in: a. Old English bana, slayer, cause of ruin or destruction: BANE; b. Middle High German ban, bane, way, road (? < "path hewn through woods"): AUTOBAHN. [Pok. bhen- 126.]

bhendh-. To bind. 1. Germanic *bindan in Old English bindan, to bind: BIND, (WOODBINE). 2. O-grade form *bhondh- in Germanic *band- in: a. Old English bend, band, ribbon: BEND[2]; b. Old English bendan, to bend: BEND[1]; c. Old Norse band, band, fetter: BAND[3], BOND; d. Middle Dutch band, band: RIBBON, (RIBAND); e. Old French bande, bond, tie, link: BAND[1]. 3. Zero-grade form *bhṇdh- in Germanic *bund- in: a. Middle High German bunt, league: BUND[2]; b. Middle Low German bunt, bundle: BUNT[2]; c. Middle Dutch bundel, sheaf of papers, bundle: BUNDLE; d. Middle Dutch bont, league: BONSPIEL. 4. Suffixed form *bhendh-nā, "tied structure" (as of wicker), in Celtic *benna, manger, in Old English binn, manger: BIN. 5. Persian band, band, bandage, also a river levee: BUND[1], CUMMERBUND. 6. Sanskrit bandhnāti, he ties: BANDANNA. [Pok. bhendh- 127.]

bhengh-. Thick, fat. Extended zero-grade form *bhṇghu- in Greek pakhus, thick, fat: PACHYDERM, PACHYSANDRA. [Pok. bhengh- 127.]

bher-[1]. To carry; also to bear children. 1. a. Germanic *beran in (i) Old English beran, to carry: BEAR[1] (ii) Old English forberan, to bear, endure (for-, FOR-): FORBEAR; b. Germanic *bērō in Old English bēr, bær, bier: BIER; c. Germanic *bēr- in Old Norse bāra, wave, billow: BORE[3]. 2. a. Germanic *barnam in Old English bearn, child: BAIRN. b. Germanic *barwōn in Old English bearwe, basket, wheelbarrow: BARROW[1]. 3. a. Germanic *bur- in Old English būrlic, exalted (< "borne up"): BURLY. b. Germanic *burthinnja in Old English byrthen, burden: BURDEN[1]. c. Germanic *burthiz in Old Norse burdh, birth: BIRTH. d. Germanic *burja- perhaps in Old Norse byrr, favorable wind: BIRR. 4. Compound root *bhrenk-, to bring (< *bher- + *enek-, to reach; see **nek-[2]**), in Germanic *brengan in Old English bringan, to bring: BRING. 5. Celtic *ber- in: a. *endo-ber-, "a carrying in" (*endo-, in; see **en**), in Old Irish in(d)ber, estuary: INVERNESS; b. Gaulish *bertā-, to shake: BERCEUSE. 6. Latin ferre, to carry: AFFERENT, CONFER, DEFER[1], DEFER[2], DIFFER, EFFERENT, -FER, FERTILE, INFER, OFFER, PREFER, PROFFER, REFER, SUFFER, TRANSFER, VOCIFERATE. 7. Latin probrum, a reproach (< *pro-bhr-o-, "something brought before one"; pro-, before, PRO-): OPPROBRIUM. 8. Possibly Latin burdus, hinny (< "beast of burden"): BORT. 9. Greek pherein, to carry: AMPHORA, (AMPOULE), (AMPULLA), ANAPHORA, DIAPHORESIS, EUPHORIA, FERETORY, METAPHOR, PERIPHERY, -PHORE, -PHORESIS, -PHOROUS, TELPHER, TOCOPHEROL. 10. Greek phernē, dowry ("that which is brought by a bride"): PARAPHERNALIA. See extension **bhreu-[1]**. [Pok. 1. bher- 128.]

bher-[2]. To cut, pierce, bore. 1. Germanic *borōn in Old English borian, to bore: BORE[1]. 2. Germanic *baru-ga-, castrated pig, in Old English bearg, barg, castrated pig: BARROW[3]. 3. Germanic *bor- in Italian burino, burin: BURIN. 4. O-grade form *bhor-ā- in Latin forāre, to pierce, bore: BIFORATE, FORAMEN, PERFORATE. 5. Suffixed form *bher-yo- in Latin ferīre, to strike, cut: INTERFERE. 6. Perhaps Greek pharunx, throat (< "a cutting, cleft, passage"): PHARYNX. 7. Slavic *bor- in Russian borot', to overcome: DUKHOBORS. [Pok. 3. bher- 133.]

bher-[3]. Bright, brown. 1. Suffixed variant form *bhrū-no- in Germanic *brūnaz in: a. Old English brūn, brown: BROWN; b. Middle Dutch bruun, brown: BRUIN; c. Old French brun, brown: BRUNET, (BURNET), BURNISH. 2. Reduplicated form *bhibhru-, *bhebhru-, "the brown animal," beaver, in Germanic *bebruz in Old English be(o)for, beaver: BEAVER[1]. 3. Germanic *berō, "the brown animal," bear, in: a. Old English bera, bear: BEAR[2]; b. Old High German bero, bear: BERNARD. 4. Germanic *bernuz in Old Norse björn (stem ber-), bear: BERSERKER. [Pok. 5. bher- 136.]

bher-[4]. To cook, bake. Extended root form *bhrīg- in Latin frīgere, to roast, fry: FRY[1]. [Pok. 6. bher- 137.]

bherdh-. To cut. 1. Zero-grade form *bhṛdh- in Germanic *burd-, plank, board, table, in: a. Old English bord, board: BOARD, STARBOARD; b. Old Norse bordh, board, table: SMORGASBORD; c. Middle Dutch bort, plank: GARBOARD; d. Frankish *bord, plank: BORDELLO, BORDER. 2. Possibly Latin forfex, a pair of scissors: FORFICATE. [Pok. bheredh- 138.]

bherəg-. To shine; bright, white. Compare the by-form **bherək-**. 1. Germanic *berhtaz, bright, in: a. Old English beorht, bright: BRIGHT; b. Old High German beraht, bright: ALBERT, BERTHA, GILBERT, HERBERT, ROBERT. 2. "The white tree," the birch (also the ash): a. Germanic *berkjōn in Old English birce, beorc(e), birch: BIRCH; b. suffixed zero-grade form *bhṛəg-s- probably in Latin fraxinus, ash tree: FRAXINELLA. [Pok. bherəg- 139.]

bherək-. To shine, glitter. A by-form of **bherəg-**. Variant form *bhrek-. 1. Germanic *bregdan, to move jerkily (< "to shimmer"), in Old English bregdan, to move quickly, weave, throw, braid: BRAID, UPBRAID. 2. Derivative West Germanic *brigdil-, bridle (referring to the movements of a horse's head), in: a. Old English brīdel, bridle: BRIDLE; b. Middle High German brīdel, bridle, rein: BRIDE[2], DÉBRIDEMENT. 3. Germanic *brēhwō, eyelid, eyelash, in Old Norse brā, eyelash: BRAE. 4. Germanic *brehwan, to shine, forming West Germanic *brehsmo, a bream, in Old French bre(s)me, a bream: BREAM[1]. [Pok. bherək- 141.]

bherg-. To buzz, growl. Germanic *berk- in Old English beorcan, to bark: BARK[1]. [Pok. bhereg- 138.]

bhergh-[1]. To hide, protect. 1. Germanic *bergan in: a. compound *h(w)als-berg-, "neck-protector," gorget (*h(w)alsaz, neck; see **kwel-[1]**); b. compound *skēr-berg-, "sword-protector," scabbard (*skēr-, sword; see **sker-[1]**). 2. Zero-grade form *bhṛgh- in: a. Germanic *burgjan in Old English byrgan, to bury: BURY; b. Germanic derivative *burgisli- in Old English byrgels, burial: BURIAL. 3. a. Germanic *borgēn, to borrow (? < "to take care of one's own interests, entrust, pledge, lend, loan"), in Old English borgian, to borrow: BORROW; b. Germanic derivative *borganjan in Old French bargaignier, to haggle: BARGAIN. [Pok. bhergh- 145.]

bhergh-[2]. High; with derivatives referring to hills and hill-forts. 1. Germanic *bergaz, hill, mountain, in: a. Old English beorg, hill: BARROW[2], BARGHEST; b. Old High German bërg, mountain: BERGSCHRUND; c. Old Norse berg, mountain: ICEBERG; d. Middle Dutch berch, hill: SPITZENBURG. 2. Compound *harja-bergaz, "army-hill," hill-fort (*harjaz, army; see **koro-**). 3. Compound *berg-frij-, "high place of safety," tower (*frij-, safety, peace; see **prī-**), in Frankish *bergfridh, in Old French berfrei, tower: BELFRY. 4. Zero-grade form *bṛgh- in Germanic *burgs, hill-fort, in: a. Old English burg, burh, byrig, (fortified) town: BURG, BOROUGH, (BURROW), CANTERBURY, (etc.); b. Old High German burg, fortress: BURGHER, BURGRAVE; c. Middle Dutch burch, town: BURGOMASTER; d. Late Latin burgus, fortified place: BOURG, BURGESS, (BOURGEOIS), BURGLAR, FAUBOURG. 5. Suffixed zero-grade form *bhṛgh-to- possibly in Latin fortis, strong (but this is also possibly from **dher-[2]**): FORCE, FORT, FORTALICE, (FORTE[1]), (FORTE[2]), FORTIS, FORTISSIMO, FORTITUDE, FORTRESS; COMFORT, DEFORCE, EFFORT, ENFORCE, FORTIFY, PIANOFORTE, REINFORCE. 6. Suffixed zero-grade form *bhṛg-ent- in Celtic *brigent- in Old Irish Brigit, name of a goddess: BRIDGET. [Pok. bheregh- 140.]

bhers-. Quick. Latin festīnāre (< *fers-tī-), to hasten: FESTINATE. [Pok. bheres- 143.]

bhes-[1]. To rub. 1. Compound root *(bh)s-amadho-, sand (*amadho-, sand, with which *bhes- has had formal and semantic interaction at various stages), in: a. Germanic *sam(a)-dam, *sandam in Old English sand, sand: SAND; b. Greek amathos, sand: see 2.b. below. 2. Suffixed form *(bh)s-abh- in: a. further suffixed form *sabh-lo- in Latin sabulum, coarse sand: SABULOUS; b. further suffixed form *bhsabh-mo- in Greek psammos, sand, contaminated with amathos, sand (see 1.b. above), to form ammos, sand: AMMOCETE. 3. Suffixed form *bhs-ā- in Greek psēn, to rub, scrape: PALIMPSEST, PSORIASIS. 4. Perhaps suffixed form *bhs-īlo- in Greek psīlos, smooth: PSILOMELANE, EPSILON, UPSILON. [Pok. bhes- 145.]

bhes-[2]. To breathe. Probably imitative. Zero-grade form *bhs- in Greek psukhein (< *bhs-ū-kh), to breathe, hence psukhē, spirit, soul: PSYCHE, (PSYCHIC), (PSYCHO-); METEMPSYCHOSIS. [Pok. 2. bhes- 146.]

bheu-. To be, exist, grow. I. 1. Extended forms *bhwiy(ō)-, *bhwī-, in: a. Germanic *biju in Old English bēon, to be: BE; b. Latin fierī, to become: FIAT. 2. Possibly suffixed form *bhwī-lyo- in Latin fīlius, son; but this is possibly from **dhēi-** (see). II. Lengthened o-grade form *bhōw- in Germanic *bōwan in: a. Old Norse būa, to live, prepare: BONDAGE, BOUND[4], HUSBAND; b. Middle Dutch bouwen, to cultivate: BOWERY; c. Old Danish bōth, dwelling, stall: BOOTH. III. Zero-grade form *bhu-. 1. Germanic *buthla in: a. Old English bold, dwelling, house, hence byldan, to build: BUILD; b. alternate Germanic form *bōthla in Middle Dutch bodel, riches, property: BOODLE. 2. Greek phuein, to bring forth, make grow, phutos, a plant, and phusis, growth, nature: PHYSIC, PHYSIQUE, PHYSIO-, -PHYTE, PHYTO-, PHYTON; DIAPHYSIS, DIPHYODONT, EPIPHYSIS, EUPHUISM, HYPOPHYSIS, IMP, MONOPHYSITE, NEOPHYTE, SYMPHYSIS. 3. Suffixed form *bhu-tā- in Welsh bod, to be: EISTEDDFOD. 4. Suffixed form *bhu-tu- in Latin futūrus, "that is to be," future: FUTURE. IV. Lengthened form *bhū-. 1. Germanic *būram, dweller, especially farmer, in: a. Old English būr, "dwelling space," bower, room: BOWER[1]; b. Old English gebūr, dweller (ge-, collective prefix; see **kom**): NEIGHBOR; c. Middle Dutch gheboer, ghebuer, peasant: BOER, BOOR. 2. Germanic *būrjam, dwelling, in: a. Old English bȳre, stall, hut: BYRE; b. Old Norse bȳr, village: BYLAW. 3. Suffixed form *bhū-lo- in Greek phulon, tribe, class, race, and phulē, tribe, clan: PHYLE, PHYLETIC, PHYLUM, PHYLOGENY. V. Suffixal forms in Latin. 1. *du-bhw-io-, "being two," in Latin dubius, doubtful, and dubitāre, to doubt (see **dwō-**). 2. *pro-bhw-o-, "growing well or straightforward" (see **per[1]**). 3. *super-bhw-o-, "being above," in Latin superbus, superior, proud (see **uper**). VI. Possibly Germanic *baumaz (and *bagmaz), tree (? < "growing thing"), in: a. Old English bēam, tree, beam: BEAM; b. Old High German boum, tree: BAUM MARTEN; c. Middle Dutch boom, tree: BOOM[2], BUMPKIN. [Pok. bheu- 146.]

bheudh-. To be aware; to make aware. 1. Germanic *(for)biudan (*for, before; see **per[1]**) in: a. Old English bēodan, to proclaim: BID; b. Old English forbēodan, to forbid: FORBID; c. Old High German farbiotan, to forbid: VERBOTEN. 2. Germanic *budōn- in Old English boda, messenger, hence bodian, to announce: BODE[1]. 3. Germanic *budilaz, herald, in Old English bydel, herald, messenger: BEADLE. 4. Germanic *budan in Old Norse bodh, command: OMBUDSMAN. 5. Extended form *bheudh- in Sanskrit bodhati, he awakes, is enlightened, becomes aware: BODHISATTVA, BO TREE, BUDDHA. [Pok. *bheudh-* 150.]

bheug-[1]. To flee. **1.** Zero-grade form **bhug-* in Latin *fugere,* to flee: FUGACIOUS, FUGIO, FUGITIVE; CENTRIFUGAL, FEVERFEW, REFUGE, SUBTERFUGE. **2.** Extended form **bhugā* in: **a.** Latin *fuga,* flight: -FUGE, FUGUE, FEBRIFUGE; **b.** Greek *phugē,* flight: APOPHYGE. [Pok. 1. *bheug-* 152.]

bheug-[2]. To enjoy. Nasalized zero-grade form **bhu-n-g-* in Latin *fungī,* to discharge, perform: FUNCTION, FUNGIBLE, DEFUNCT, PERFUNCTORY. [Pok. 4. *bheug-* 153.]

bheug-[3]. To swell; with derivatives referring to bent, pliable, or curved objects. **1.** Germanic **baugaz* in: **a.** Old English *bēag,* a ring: BEE[2]; **b.** Old Norse *bogi,* a bow: AKIMBO; **c.** Old High German *boug,* a ring: BAGEL. **2.** Germanic **bugōn-* in: **a.** Old English *boga,* a bow, arch: BOW[3]; **b.** compound **alino-bogōn-,* "forearm-bend," elbow (**alino-,* forearm; see **el-**[1]). **3.** Germanic *būgan* in Old English *būgan,* to bend: BOW[2], BUXOM. **4.** Germanic causative form **baugjan* in Old Norse *beyla,* a swelling, akin to the probable Scandinavian source of Middle English *baile,* a handle: BAIL[3]. **5.** Germanic **buhtiz* in: **a.** Old English *byht,* a bend, angle: BIGHT; **b.** Middle Low German *bucht,* a turn: BOUT. **6.** Celtic **buggo-,* "flexible, malleable," in Scottish and Irish Gaelic *bog,* soft: BOG. [Pok. 3. *bheug-* 152.]

bhilo-. Friendly, loving. Greek *philos,* dear, loving: -PHILE, -PHILIA, PHILO-, -PHILOUS, PHILTER, PAM. [Pok. *bhili-* 153.]

bhlag-. To strike. **1.** Germanic **blak-* in Old Norse *(ledhr)blaka,* "(leather-)flapper," bat: BAT[2]. **2.** Latin *flagrum,* a whip: FLAGELLATE, (FLAGELLUM), FLAIL, FLOG. **3.** Latin *flāgitāre,* to demand importunately: FLAGITIOUS. [Pok. *bhlag-* 154.]

bhlaghmen-. Priest. **1.** Latin *flāmen,* priest (of a particular deity): FLAMEN. **2.** Sanskrit *brahmán-,* priest, and *bráhman-,* prayer: (BRAHMA[1]), BRAHMAN, (BRAHMIN). [Pok. *bhlagh-men-* 154.]

bhlē-[1]. To howl. Probably imitative. **1.** Germanic suffixed form **blē-t-* in Old English *blǣtan,* to bleat: BLEAT. **2.** Germanic suffixed form **blē-r-* in Middle Dutch *bleren,* to roar: BLARE. **3.** Latin *flēre,* to weep: FEEBLE. [Pok. *bhlē-* 154.]

bhlē-[2]. Also **bhlā-**. To blow. **1.** Germanic suffixed form **blē-w-* in Old English *blāwan,* to blow: BLOW[1]. **2.** Germanic suffixed form **blē-dram,* "something blown up," in: **a.** Old English *blǣdre,* blister, bladder: BLADDER; **b.** Old Norse *bladhra,* bladder, and *bladhra,* to prattle: BLATHER. **3.** Germanic suffixed form **blē-s-* in: **a.** Old English *blǣst,* a blowing, blast: BLAST; **b.** Middle Dutch *blasen,* to blow up: BLASÉ; **c.** Middle Dutch *blas,* a bladder: ISINGLASS. **4.** Variant form **bhlā-* in: **a.** Latin *flāre,* to blow: FLABELLUM, FLATUS, FLAVOR; AFFLATUS, CONFLATION, (DEFLATE), INFLATE, SOUFFLÉ; **b.** possibly Vulgar Latin **flabeōlum,* a flute: FLAGEOLET, (FLAUTIST), (FLOUT), FLUTE. [In Pok. 3. *bhel-* 120.]

bhlei-. To blow, swell. An extended form of **bhel-**[2]. **1.** Germanic **blajinōn,* a swelling, in Old English *blegen,* a boil, blister: BLAIN. **2.** Perhaps Middle Dutch *bluyster,* a blister: BLISTER. **3.** Perhaps Old French *blostre, blotte* (from Germanic), a clod of earth: BLOT[1]. [Pok. 2. *bhlei-* 156.]

bhleu-. To swell, well up, overflow. An extended form of **bhel-**[2]. **1.** Possibly Germanic **blaut-* in: **a.** Old Norse *blautr,* soft, wet: BLOAT; **b.** Middle Dutch *bloot,* naked, exposed: BLOT[2]. **2.** Latin *fluere,* to flow, and *-fluus,* flowing: FLUCTUATE, FLUENT, FLUID, FLUME, FLUOR, (FLUORO-), (FLUORIDE), (FLUSH[2]), FLUVIAL, FLUX; AFFLUENT, CONFLUENT, EFFLUENT, (EFFLUVIUM), (EFFLUX), FLUVIOMARINE, INFLUENCE, (INFLUENZA), MELLIFLUOUS, REFLUX, SUPERFLUOUS. **3.** Suffixed zero-grade form **bhlu-g-* in Greek *phluein, phluzein,* to boil over: PHLYCTENA. **4.** Possibly Greek *phloos, phloios,* tree bark (< "swelling with growth"): PHLOEM. [Pok. *bhleu-* 158.]

bhlīg-. To strike. Latin *flīgere,* to strike: AFFLICT, CONFLICT, INFLICT, PROFLIGATE. [Pok. *bhlīg-* 160.]

bhoso-. Naked. Germanic **bazaz* in: **a.** Old English *bær,* bare: BARE[1]; **b.** Old Swedish and Old Danish *bar,* bare: BALLAST. [Pok. *bhoso-s* 163.]

bhrag-. To smell. **1.** Germanic **brak-* in Old High German *braccho,* dog that hunts game by scent: BRACH. **2.** Suffixed form **bhrag-ro-* in Latin *fragrāre,* to smell: FLAIR, FRAGRANT. [Pok. *bhrag-* 163.]

bhrāter-. Brother. **1.** Germanic **brōthar-* in Old English *brōthor,* brother: BROTHER. **2.** Latin *frāter,* brother: FRA, FRATER, (FRATERNAL), (FRATRICIDE), FRIAR, CONFRERE. **3.** Greek *phratēr,* fellow member of a clan: PHRATRY. **4.** Sanskrit *bhrātar-,* brother: PAL. [Pok. *bhrāter-* 163.]

bhreg-. To break. **1.** Germanic **brekan* in: **a.** Old English *brecan,* to break: BREAK; **b.** (Old English *brecan* and) Old High German *brehhan,* to break: BREACH, BRECCIA, BRASH[2]; **c.** Old French *breier,* to break: BRAY[2]; **d.** Old French *brier* (dialectal) and *broyer,* to knead: BRIOCHE. **2.** Germanic **brak-,* bushes (< "that which impedes motion"), in: **a.** Old English *bracu,* thicket: BRAKE[3]; **b.** Old Norse **brakni,* undergrowth, bracken: BRACKEN. **3.** Germanic **brāk-* in Middle Dutch *braeke,* crushing instrument, stopping gear: BRAKE[1]. **4.** Nasalized zero-grade form **bhr-n-g-* in Latin *frangere,* to break: FRACAS, (FRACTED), FRACTION, FRACTIOUS, FRACTURE, FRAGILE, FRAGMENT, FRANGIBLE, FRAIL[1]; ANFRACTUOUS, CHAMFER, DIFFRACTION, INFRACT, INFRANGIBLE, INFRINGE, IRREFRAGIBLE, OSSIFRAGE, REFRACT, (REFRAIN[2]), (REFRINGENT), SAXIFRAGE, SEPTIFRAGAL. **5.** Latin *suffrāgārī,* to vote for (? < "to use a broken piece of tile as a ballot"), hence *suffrāgium,* the right to vote: SUFFRAGE, (SUFFRAGAN). [Pok. 1. *bhreg-* 165.]

bhrēi-. Also **bhrī-**. To cut, break. **1.** Possibly Latin *fricāre,* to rub: FRAY[2], FRICATIVE, FRICTION, FRY[2]; AFFRICATE, DENTIFRICE. **2.** Possibly Latin *friāre,* to crumble: FRIABLE. **3.** Vulgar Latin **brīsāre,* to break (from Gaulish): BRISANCE, DEBRIS. [Pok. *bhrēi-* 166.]

bhrekw-. To cram together. **1.** Probably Latin *frequens,* frequent, crowded: FREQUENT. **2.** Suffixed zero-grade form **bhr̥kw-io-* in: **a.** Latin *farcīre,* to cram, stuff: FARCE, FARCY, INFARCT; **b.** Greek *phrassein,* to fence in, enclose, block up: DIAPHRAGM. [Pok. *bhareku̯-* 110.]

bhrem-[1]. To growl. **1.** Latin *fremere,* to growl, roar: FREMITUS. **2.** Perhaps variant **brem-* in Greek *brontē,* thunder: BRONTOSAUR, ISOBRONT. [Pok. 2. *bherem-* 142.]

bhrem-[2]. To project; a point, spike; an edge. **1.** Germanic **brēma-,* name of prickly shrubs, in: **a.** Old English *brōm,* broom: BROOM; **b.** Middle Dutch *bremme,* broom: BREAM[2]; **c.** Frankish **brām-basi-,* "bramble-berry" (**basi,* berry; see **bhā-**[1]): FRAMBESIA; **d.** Old English diminutive *bremel, brǣmbel,* bramble: BRAMBLE. **2.** Germanic **berm-, *brem-,* in: **a.** Middle English *brimme,* edge: BRIM; **b.** Middle Dutch *berme, barm,* edge of a dike: BERM. [Pok. 1. *bherem-* 142.]

bhres-. To burst. Germanic **brest-* in Old English *berstan,* to burst: BURST. [Pok. *bhres-* 169.]

bhreu-[1]. To cut, break up. An extended form of **bher-**[2]. **1.** Suffixed form **bhreu-d-* in Germanic **briutan,* to break up, in Old English **brytel,* brittle: BRITTLE. **2.** Suffixed form **bhreu-t-* in Germanic **briuthan,* to be broken up, in Old English *brēothan,* to deteriorate: BROTHEL. [Pok. 1. *bhreu-* 169.]

bhreu-[2]. To boil, bubble, effervesce, burn; with derivatives referring to cooking and brewing. **I. 1.** Germanic **breuwan,* to brew, in Old English *brēowan,* to brew: BREW. **2.** Germanic **braudam,* (cooked) food, (leavened) bread, in Old English *brēad,* piece of food, bread: BREAD. **3.** Germanic **brudam,* broth, in: **a.** Old English *broth,* broth: BROTH; **b.** Old French *breu,* broth: BREWIS, (BROIL[2]), EMBROIL, IMBRUE. **II.** Variant form **bhrē-.* **1.** Germanic **brōd-,* "a warming," hatching, rearing of young, in: **a.** Old English *brōd,* offspring, brood: BROOD; **b.** denominative **brōdjan,* to rear young, in Old English *brēdan,* to beget or cherish offspring, breed: BREED. **2.** Germanic **brēthaz,* warm air, steam, in Old English *brǣth,* odor, exhalation: BREATH, (BREATHE). **3.** Germanic **brēdōn-,* roast flesh, in: **a.** Old High German *brāt, brāto,* meat: BRATWURST, SAUERBRATEN; **b.** Old French *braon,* meat: BRAWN. **4.** Germanic **bres-,* burning, in Old French *brese,* burning coal, ember: BRAISE, BRAZE[2], BRAZIER[2], BRAZILWOOD, BREEZE[3], EMBRACER. **III.** Nasalized forms. **1.** Germanic **brenw-,* to burn, forming **brennan* (intransitive) and **brannjan* (transitive) in Old English *beornan, byrnan* (intransitive) and *bærnan* (transitive), to burn: BURN[1]. **2.** Germanic **brunja-,* burn, in Old English *brynstān,* "burning mineral" (*stān,* STONE), sulfur: BRIMSTONE. **3.** Germanic **brandaz,* a burning, a flaming torch, hence also a sword, in: **a.** Old English *brand,* piece of burning wood, sword: BRAND; **b.** Old Norse *brandr,* piece of burning wood, akin, in the sense "blackened by fire," dark-colored, to *(i)* the possible Scandinavian source of Middle English *brende,* brindled: BRINDLED, and *(ii)* Swedish *brantgas,* brant goose: BRANT; **c.** Dutch *branden,* to burn: BRANDY; **d.** Old French *brand,* sword: BRANDISH. **IV.** Reduced form **bher-,* especially in derivatives referring to fermentation. **1.** Suffixed form **bher-men-,* yeast, in: **a.** Germanic **bermōn-* in Old English *beorma,* yeast: BARM, (BARMY); **b.** further suffixed form **bhermen-to-* in Latin *fermentum,* yeast: FERMENT. **2.** Extended form **bherw-* in Latin *fervēre,* to be boiling or fermenting: FERVENT, FERVID, FERVOR; COMFREY, EFFERVESCE. **V.** As a very archaic word for a spring. **1.** Suffixed zero-grade form **bhru-n(e)n-* in Germanic **brunōn-* in Old English *burn, burna,* spring, stream: BURN[2], (BOURN[1]). **2.** Suffixed form **bhrēw-r̥* in Greek *phrear,* spring: PHREATIC. [Pok. *bh(e)reu-* 143 and 2. *bher-* 132.]

bhreus-[1]. To swell. **1.** Suffixed form **bhreus-t-* in Germanic **briustam,* "swelling," breast, in: **a.** Old English *brēost,* breast: BREAST; **b.** Old Norse *brjōst,* breast: BRISKET. **2.** Suffixed zero-grade form **bhrus-t-* in Germanic **brust-,* bud, shoot, in Old French *broust, brost,* shoot, twig: BROWSE. **3.** Suffixed zero-grade form **bhrus-nio-* in Celtic **brunnio-,* breast, rounded hill, the source of Germanic **brunjō,* breastplate, in Old Norse *brynja,* coat of mail: BYRNIE. [Pok. 1. *bhreu-s-* 170.]

bhreus-[2]. To break. **1.** Germanic **brūsjan,* to crush, in Old English *brȳsan,* to crush, pound: BRUISE. **2.** Suffixed zero-grade form **bhrus-to-,* fragment, in Latin *frustum,* piece: FRUSTUM, FRUSTULE. **3.** Suffixed zero-grade form **bhrus-k-* in Celtic **bruskia,* a possible source of Vulgar Latin **bruscia,* bundle of twigs, brushwood: BRUSH[2], (BRUSH[1]). [Pok. 2. *bhreu-s-* 171.]

bhrū-. Eyebrow. **1.** Germanic **brūs* in Old English *brū,* eyebrow, eyelid, eyelash: BROW. **2.** In the sense of a beam of wood, and perhaps a log bridge, found in Germanic **brugjō* (with cognates in Celtic and Slavic) in Old English *brycg,* bridge: BRIDGE[1]. [Pok. 1. *bhrū-* 172 and 2. *bhrū-* 173.]

bhrūg-. Agricultural produce; also to enjoy (produce, results). **1.** Germanic **brūkan* in Old English *brūcan,* to enjoy, use: BROOK[2]. **2.** Latin *frūx* (stem *frūg-*), fruit: FRUGAL, FRUGIVOROUS. **3.** Suffixed form **bhrūg-wo-* in Latin *fruī,* to enjoy, and *frūctus,* enjoyment, produce, results: FRUIT, FRUITION, FRUMENTACEOUS, FRUCTIFY. [Pok. *bhrūg-* 173.]

bhudh-. Bottom, base. (The precise pre-forms of the words listed below are obscure.) **1.** Old English *botm,* bottom: BOTTOM. **2.** Dutch *bodem,* (ship's) bottom: BOTTOMRY. **3.** Latin *fundus,* bottom, base: FOND[2], FOUND[1], FOUNDER[3], FUND, FUNDAMENT, FUNDUS; LATIFUNDIUM, PROFOUND. [Pok. *bhudh-* 174.]

bhugo-. Male animal of various kinds; stag, ram, he-goat. **1.** Germanic **bukkaz* (possibly borrowed from the Celtic form below) in: **a.** Old English *buc, bucca,* stag, he-goat: BUCK[1]; **b.** Middle Dutch *boc, bok,* buck: BLESBOK, BONTEBOK, SPRINGBOK, STEENBOK; **c.** Old High German *boc,* buck: GEMSBOK. **2.** Celtic **bukkos,* he-goat, in Old French *boc,* buck: BUTCHER. [Pok. *bhūgo-s* 174.]

[brāc-. Trousers. A northern European word, only in Celtic and Germanic. **1.** Germanic **brōks* in: **a.** Old English *brōc* (plural *brēc*), breeches: BREECH, (BREECHES), (BREEKS); **b.** Old Norse *brōk,* trousers: BROGUE[2], (BROGUE[1]). **2.** Gaulish **brāka* in Latin *brāca,* trousers: BRACKET, BRAIL.**]**

[bursa. Hide, wineskin. Greek noun of unknown origin. BOURSE, BURSA, (BOLSON), (BURSAR), (BURSE); DISBURSE, PURSE, REIMBURSE, SPORRAN.**]**

[busk-. A bush. Germanic root, possibly connected with the root **bheu-**, to grow. **1.** Middle Low German *busch,* bush: BUSH[1]. **2.** Old French *bosc,* forest: BOSCAGE, BOUQUET. **3.** Old French *bois,* wood: HAUTBOY, (OBOE). **4.** Italian *busco,* splinter: BUSK[1]. **5.** Vulgar Latin **boscus,* bush: AMBUSH, (AMBUSCADE).**]**

[carcer. Enclosure, prison, barrier. Latin noun, probably borrowed from an unidentified source. **1.** Latin *carcer* (representing reduplicated form **kar-kr-o-*): CANCEL, (CANKER), INCARCERATE. **2.** Latin *cancer* (representing a dissimilated form **kankro-*), lattice: CHANCEL, (CHANCELLOR).**]**

[caupō. Small trader. Latin noun of unknown origin. CHEAP, CHOP[2], (CHAP[2]), (CHAPMAN), COP[2].**]**

[cūra. Care. Latin noun of unknown origin. The earliest form is Old Latin *coisa-*. CURE, (CURATE), (CURATOR), (CURETTE), (CURIO), (CURIOUS); ACCURATE, MANICURE, PEDICURE, PO-

COCURANTE, PROCURE, (PROCTOR), (PROXY), SCOUR[1], SECURE, SINECURE, SURE, (ASSURE), (ENSURE), (INSURE).]

dā-. Also **dai-**. To divide. **1.** Root form *dai- in Greek daiesthai, to divide: GEODESY. **2.** Suffixed variant form *dī-ti- in Germanic *tīdiz, division of time, in: **a.** Old English tīd, time, season: TIDE[1], EVENTIDE; **b.** Old English denominative tīdan, to happen (< "to occur in time"): TIDE[2]; **c.** Old Norse tidhr, occurring: TIDINGS. **3.** Suffixed variant form *dī-mon in Germanic *tīmo in Old English tīma, time, period: TIME. **4.** Suffixed form *dā-mo-, perhaps "division of society," in Greek dēmos, people, land: DEME, DEMOS, (DEMOTIC); DEMAGOGUE, DEMIURGE, DEMOCRACY, (DEMOPHOBIA), ENDEMIC, EPIDEMIC, PANDEMIC. **5.** Suffixed form *dai-mon-, divider, provider, in Greek daimōn, divinity: DEMON, EUDEMONIA, PANDEMONIUM. [Pok. dā- 175.]

dail-. To divide. Northern Indo-European root. **1.** Germanic *dailiz in: **a.** Old English dǣl, part: DEAL[1]; **b.** Middle Dutch deel, part: FIRKIN. **2.** Germanic *dailaz in Old English dāl, portion, lot: DOLE[1]. **3.** Germanic prefixed form *uz-dailjam, "a portioning out," judgment (*uz-, out; see **ud-**), in Old English ordāl, lot, apportionment: ORDEAL. [In Pok. dā- 175.]

daiwēr. Husband's brother. Latin lēvir, husband's brother: LEVIRATE. [Pok. dāiu̯ēr 179.]

dakru-. Tear. **1.** Germanic *tahr-, *tagr- in: **a.** Old English tēar, tehher, tear: TEAR[2]; **b.** Middle Dutch traen, tear, drop: TRAIN OIL. **2.** Suffixed form *dakru-mā in Latin lacrima (Old Latin dacruma), tear: LACHRYMAL. [Pok. dakru- 179.]

[**dan-**. Low ground. Germanic root. Suffixed form *danjam in: **a.** Old English denn, lair of a wild beast: DEN; **b.** possibly Old English Dene, the Danes, and Old Norse Danr, Dane: DANE, DANISH, DANELAW. [In Pok. 2. dhen- 249.]]

dānu-. River; flowing. **1.** Old English Don (via Celtic): DON (river in Scotland). **2.** Latin Dānuvius (via Celtic): DANUBE. **3.** Russian Don (from Scythian): DON (river in Russia). [In Pok. dā- 175.]

dap-. To apportion (in exchange). Suffixed form *dap-no- in Latin damnum, damage entailing liability (for reparation), harm: DAMN, DAMAGE, DAMNIFY, CONDEMN, INDEMNITY. [In Pok. dā- 175.]

de-. Demonstrative stem, base of prepositions and adverbs. **1.** Germanic *tō in: **a.** Old English tō, to: TO, (TOO); **b.** Middle Dutch toe, to: TATTOO[1]. **2.** Perhaps Latin dē, from: DE, DE-, PEDESTAL, PEDIGREE. **3.** Latin *dēter, "deviating," bad: DETERIORATE. **4.** Latin -dem, demonstrative suffix: IDEM, TANDEM. **5.** Latin dēbilis (see **bel-**). [Pok. de-, do- 181.]

dē-. To bind. Greek dein, to bind: DESMID; ANADEM, ASYNDETON, DIADEM, PLASMODESMA, SYNDETIC, (SYNDESMOSIS). [Pok. dē- 183.]

deigh-. Insect. Germanic *tik-ō, whence expressive alteration *tikkō in Old English ticia (< *ticca), tick: TICK[2]. [Pok. deigh- 187.]

deik-. To show, pronounce solemnly; also in derivatives referring to the directing of words or objects. **I.** Variant *deig-. **1.** Germanic *taikjan, to show, in Old English tǣcan, to show, instruct: TEACH. **2.** Germanic *taiknam in: **a.** Old English tācen, tācn, sign, mark: TOKEN; **b.** Old English *bitācnian, to give as a token: BETOKEN; **c.** Gothic taikns, sign: TETCHY. **3.** Possibly Germanic *taihwō in Old English tā, tahe, toe: TOE. **4.** Latin digitus, finger (< "pointer," "indicator"): DIGIT. **II.** Basic form *deik-. **1.** Latin dīcere, to say, tell: DICTATE, DICTION, DICTUM, DITTO, DITTY; ADDICT, BENEDICTION, (BENEDICT), (BENEDICITE), CONDITION, CONTRADICT, EDICT, FATIDIC, (INDICT), INDITE, INTERDICT, JURIDICAL, JURISDICTION, MALEDICT, PREDICT, VALEDICTION, VERDICT, VERIDICAL, VOIR DIRE. **2.** Zero-grade form *dik-ā- in Latin dicāre, to proclaim: ABDICATE, DEDICATE, PREACH, PREDICATE. **3.** Agential suffix *-dik- in: **a.** Latin index, indicator, forefinger (in-, toward, IN-): INDEX, (INDICATE); **b.** Latin jūdex (< *jūs-dik-), judge, "he who pronounces the law" (jūs, law; see **yewo-**[1]): JUDGE, JUDICIAL, (PREJUDICE); **c.** Latin vindex (first element obscure), claimant, avenger: (VENDETTA), VINDICATE, AVENGE, (REVENGE). **4.** Greek deiknunai, to show: DEICTIC, APODICTIC, PARADIGM, POLICY[2]. **5.** Zero-grade form *dik- in Greek dikein, to throw (< "to direct an object"): DISK. **6.** Form *dikā in Greek dikē, justice, right: DICAST, EURYDICE, SYNDIC, THEODICY. [Pok. deik- 188.]

deiw-. To shine (and in many derivatives "sky, heaven, god"). **I.** Noun *deiwos, name of the sky god. **1.** Germanic *Tīwaz in: **a.** Old English Tīw, Tig, god of war and sky: TIU, (TUESDAY); **b.** Old Norse Týr, sky god: TYR. **2.** Latin deus, god: DEITY, (DEICIDE), (DEIFIC), (DEISM), ADIEU, JOSS. **3.** Latin dīvus, divine, god: DIVA, DIVINE[1], (DIVINE[2]). **4.** Latin dīves, rich (< "fortunate, blessed, divine"): DIVES. **5.** Suffixed form *deiw-yo-, luminous, in Latin Diāna, moon goddess: DIANA[2]. **6.** Sanskrit dēvah, dēvas, god: DEVI, DEODAR, DEVANAGARI. **7.** Avestan daēva-, demon: ASMODEUS. **II.** Variant *dyē- in Latin diēs, day: DIAL, DIARY, DIET[2], DISMAL, DIURNAL, CIRCADIAN, MERIDIAN, QUOTIDIAN, (POSTMERIDIAN), ADJOURN, JOURNAL, JOURNEY, SOJOURN. **III.** Variant *dyeu-. **1.** Latin Jovis, of Jupiter (genitive): JOVE, (JOVIAL). **2.** Derivative *jou-il- in Latin Jūlius, "descended from Jupiter" (name of a Roman gens): (JULIAN), (JULIENNE), JULIUS, (JULY). **3.** Vocative compound *dyeu-pəter- (*pəter-, father; see **pəter-**), "O father Jove" (god of the bright sky), in Latin Juppiter, head of the Pantheon: JUPITER[1]. **4.** Greek Zeus, Zeus: ZEUS, (DIOSCURI). **IV.** Variant *deiə- in Greek dēlos (< *dealos), clear: PSYCHEDELIC. [Pok. 1. dei- 183.]

dek-[1]. To take, accept. **1.** Suffixed (stative) form *dek-ē- in Latin decēre, to be fitting (< "to be acceptable"): DECENT. **2.** Suffixed (causative) o-grade form *dok-eye- in: **a.** Latin docēre, to teach (< "to cause to accept"): DOCENT, DOCILE, DOCTOR, (DOCTRINE), DOCUMENT; **b.** Greek dokein, to appear, seem, think (< "to cause to accept or be accepted"): DOGMA, (DOGMATIC), DOCETISM, DOXOLOGY, HETERODOX, ORTHODOX, PARADOX. **3.** Suffixed form *dek-os- in: **a.** Latin decus, grace, ornament: DECORATE, (DÉCOR); **b.** Latin decor, seemliness, elegance, beauty: DECOROUS. **4.** Suffixed form *dek-no- in Latin dignus, worthy, deserving, fitting: DAINTY, DEIGN, DIGNITY; CONDIGN, DISDAIN, DIGNIFY, INDIGN, INDIGNANT. **5.** Reduplicated form *di-dk-ske- in Latin discere, to learn: DISCIPLE, (DISCIPLINE). **6.** Greek dekhesthai, to accept: PANDECT, SYNECDOCHE. **7.** Greek dokos, beam, support: DIPLODOCUS. [Pok. 1. dek- 189.]

dek-[2]. Referring to a fringe, lock of hair, horsetail, etc. **1.** Suffixed o-grade form *dok-lo- in Germanic *taglaz in Old English tæg(e)l, tail: TAIL[1]. **2.** Perhaps Germanic *tag- in: **a.** Swedish tagg, prickle, akin to the Scandinavian source of Middle English tagge, pendent piece: TAG[1]; **b.** Middle High German zacke, nail: SHAKO; **c.** Old French tache, fastening, nail: TACHE, TACK[1]; **d.** probably Spanish taco, a plug: TACO. [Pok. 2. dek- 191.]

dekm̥. Ten. **I.** Basic form *dekm̥. **1.** Germanic *tehun in: **a.** Old English tien, ten: TEN; **b.** Old Norse tjan, ten (see **oktō-**). **2.** Germanic *tehan in Old English suffix -tēne, -tȳne, ten: -TEEN. **3.** Latin decem, ten: DECI-, DECIMAL, DECIMATE, DICKER, DIME, DIXIE, DECEMBER, DECEMVIR, (DECENARY), DECENNIUM, DECUPLE, DECUSSATE, DOZEN, DUODECIMAL, OCTODECIMO, SEXTODECIMO. **4.** Irregular Latin distributive dēnī, by tens, ten each (formed by analogy with nōnī, nine each): DENARIUS, DENIER[2]. **5.** Greek deka, ten: DECA-, DECADE, (DECANAL), DEAN, DODECAGON, DOYEN. **II.** Extended form *dekm̥t- in Germanic *tig- in Old English -tig, ten: -TY[2]. **III.** Ordinal number *dekm̥to- in Germanic *tehuntha- in Old English teogotha, tēotha, tenth: TENTH, (TITHE). **IV.** Suffixed zero-grade form *-dkm̥-tā, reduced to -km̥tā. **1.** Latin -gintā, ten times: NONAGENARIAN, OCTOGENARIAN, SEPTUAGINT, SEXAGENARY. **2.** Greek *-konta, ten times: PENTECOST. **V.** Suffixed zero-grade form *dkm̥-tom, hundred, reduced to km̥tom. **1.** Germanic *hundan, hundred, in Old English hundred, hundred (-red, from Germanic *rath, number; see **ar-**): HUNDRED. **2.** Germanic *thus-hundi, "swollen hundred," thousand (see **teuə-**). **3.** Latin centum, hundred: CENT, CENTAL, CENTAVO, CENTENARIAN, CENTENARY, CENTESIMAL, CENTI-, (CENTIME), (CENTNER), CENTUM, CENTURY, CENTENNIAL, CENTUPLE, CENTUPLICATE, KANTAR, PER CENT, QUATROCENTO, SEICENTO, SEXCENTENARY, TRECENTO. **4.** Greek hekaton, a hundred (he-, one; see **sem-**[1]): HECATOMB, HECTO-. **5.** Avestan satəm, hundred: SATEM. **6.** Zero-grade form *km̥t in Bulgarian sŭto, hundred: STOTINKA. See also compound root **wīkm̥tī**. [Pok. dekm̥ 191.]

deks-. Right (opposite left). Suffixed form *deks(i)-tero- in Latin dexter, right, on the right side: DEXTER, (DEXTERITY), DEXTRO-, DESTRIER, AMBIDEXTER. [In Pok. 1. dek- 189.]

del-[1]. Long. Probably extended and suffixed zero-grade form *dlon-gho-. **1.** Germanic *langaz, long, in: **a.** Old English lang, long, long: LONG[1]; **b.** Old High German lang, long: LANGLAUF; **c.** Old English denominative langian, to grow longer, yearn for: LONG[2], (BELONG); **d.** Late Latin compound Longobardus, Langobardus (with Germanic ethnic name *Bardi): LOMBARD, LUMBER[1]. **2.** Germanic abstract noun *lang-ithō in: **a.** Old English lengthu, length: LENGTH; **b.** West Germanic *langitinaz, lengthening of day, in Old English lengten, spring, Lent: LENT; **c.** Old Norse denominative lengja, to make longer, tarry: LINGER; **d.** Dutch lenghe, linghe, "long one," akin to the Low German source of Middle English lenge, ling: LING[1]. **3.** Latin longus, long: LONGI-, LONGITUDE, LONGEVITY, LONGERON; ELONGATE, ELOIGN, LUNGE[2], OBLONG, PROLONG, PURLOIN. **4.** Possibly suffixed variant *dlə-gho- in Greek dolikhos, long: DOLICHOCEPHALIC. [Pok. 5. del- 196.]

del-[2]. To recount, count. **1.** Germanic *taljan in Old English tellan, to count, recount: TELL. **2.** Germanic *talō in: **a.** Old English talu, story, and Old Norse tala, story, account: TALE; **b.** Middle Dutch tāle, speech, language: TAAL[2]. **3.** Old English denominative talian, to tell, relate: TALK. **4.** Perhaps Greek dolos, ruse, snare: DOLERITE, SEDULOUS. [Pok. 1. del- 193.]

del-[3]. To split, carve, cut. **1.** Suffixed form *del-to- in Germanic *teldam, "thing spread out," in Old English teld, awning, tent: TILT[2]. **2.** Germanic extended form *telg- in Old English telgor, telgra, twig, branch: TILLER[3]. **3.** Perhaps o-grade form *dol-ē- in Latin dolēre, to suffer (? < "to be beaten"): DOLE[2], DOLOR, CONDOLE, INDOLENT. **4.** Suffixed o-grade form *dolā-dhro- in Latin dolāre, to chisel, hew: DOLABRIFORM. [Pok. 3. del- 194.]

del-[4]. To drip. Perhaps suffixed (stative) o-grade form *dol- in Germanic *talgaz in Middle Low German talg, talch, tallow (< "dripping fat"): TALLOW. [Pok. 4. del- 196.]

demə-[1]. Also **dem-**. House, household. **1.** Suffixed reduced o-grade form *dom-o-, dom-u-, house, in: **a.** Latin domus, house: DOME, DOMESTIC, MAJOR-DOMO; **b.** Latin domicilium, dwelling (probably from *domicola, "dweller in a house"; -cola, dweller; see **kwel-**[1]): DOMICILE; **c.** suffixed form *dom-o-no- in Latin dominus, master (< "he who represents and leads the household"): DAME, DAN[3], DANGER, DOM, DOMAIN, DOMINATE, DOMINICAL, DOMINIE, DOMINION, DOMINO[1], (DOMINO[2]), DUENNA, DUNGEON, (MADAM), MADAME, MADEMOISELLE, MADONNA, (PREDOMINATE). **2.** Compound *dems-pot-, "master of the household" (*pot-, powerful; see **poti-**), in Greek despotēs, master, lord: DESPOT. **3.** Root form *dem(ə)-, to build (possibly a separate root), in: **a.** Germanic *timrum in Old English timber, building material, lumber: TIMBER; **b.** Germanic *tumftō in Old Norse topt, homestead: TOFT. [Pok. dem- 198.]

demə-[2]. To constrain, force, especially to break in (horses). **1.** Suffixed o-grade form *dom-o- in Germanic *tamaz in Old English tam, domesticated: TAME. **2.** O-grade form *domə- in Latin domāre, to tame, subdue: DAUNT, INDOMITABLE. **3.** Zero-grade form *dm̥ə- in Greek daman, to tame: ADAMANT, (DIAMOND). [Pok. (demə-), domə- 199.]

denk-. To bite. **1.** Germanic *tanhuz in Old English tōh, tenacious, sticky (< "holding fast"): TOUGH. **2.** Germanic *tanguz in Old English tang(e), pincers, tongs: TONGS. **3.** Germanic *tang- in Old Norse tangi, a point, sting: TANG[1]. **4.** Germanic *teng- in Old High German zinko, spike, prong: ZINC. [Pok. denk- 201.]

dens-[1]. Mental force. Reduplicated and suffixed zero-grade form *di-dn̥s-sko- in Greek didaskein, to teach: DIDACTIC, DIDACHE. [Pok. 1. dens- 201.]

dens-[2]. Dense, thick. **1.** Suffixed form *dens-u- in Latin dēnsus, thick: DENSE, CONDENSE. **2.** Suffixed zero-grade form *dn̥s-u- in Greek dasus, hairy, shaggy: DASYURE. [Pok. 2. dens- 202.]

dent-. Tooth. **1.** O-grade form *dont- in Germanic *tanthuz in Old English tōth, tooth: TOOTH. **2.** Zero-grade form *dn̥t- perhaps in Germanic *tunth-sk- in Old English tūsc, tūx, canine tooth: TUSK. **3.** Full-grade form *dent- in Latin dēns (stem dent-), tooth: DENTAL, DENTATE, DENTI-, DENTICLE; BIDENT, DANDELION, EDENTATE, INDENT[1], (INDENTURE), TRIDENT. **4.** O-grade variant form *(o)dont- in: **a.** Greek odōn, tooth: -ODON, -ODONT, ODONTO-; **b.** Greek odous, tooth: CERATODUS. [In Pok. ed- 287.]

deph-. To stamp. **1.** Suffixed form *deph-s-ter- in Greek diphthera, prepared hide, leather (used to write on): DIPHTHERIA. 2. Latin *littera,* letter (possibly borrowed from Greek *diphthera* in the sense of "tablet" via Etruscan): LETTER, LITERAL, LITERARY, LITERATE, LITERATIM; (ALLITERATE), (ILLITERATE), OBLITERATE, (TRANSLITERATE). [Pok. *deph-* 203.]

der-[1]. Base of roots meaning "to run, walk, step." 1. Zero-grade form **dr̥-* in Germanic **tred-* in: a. Old English *tredan,* to step: TREAD, (TREADLE); b. Middle Low German *trade,* course, track: TRADE. 2. Extended form **dreb-* in Germanic **trep-,* "something on or into which one steps," in: a. Old English *træppe, treppe,* snare: TRAP[1]; b. Middle Low German *trappe,* stair: TRAP[3]; c. Middle Dutch *trappe,* stair: WENTLETRAP; d. Old French *trape,* snare: ENTRAP; e. Medieval Latin *trappa,* trap: CALTROP; f. Middle Dutch *trippen,* to stamp, trample: TRIP. 3. Nasalized Germanic root **tramp-* in: a. Middle Low German *trampen,* to stamp, tread: TRAMP; b. Italian *trampoli,* stilts: TRAMPOLINE. 4. Germanic **trott-* (expressive derivative of **tred-*) in Frankish **trottōn,* to tread: TROT. 5. Root form **drā-* in reduplicated Germanic form **ti-trā-* in Old Norse *titra,* to tremble: TEETER. 6. Root form **drem-* in suffixed o-grade form **drom-o-* in: a. Greek *dromos,* a running, race, racecourse: -DROME, DROMOND, -DROMOUS; ANADROMOUS, LOXODROMIC, PALINDROME, PRODROME, SYNDROME; b. Greek *dromas,* runner: DROMEDARY. [Pok. 3. *(der-)* 204.]

der-[2]. To split, peel, flay; with derivatives referring to skin and leather. 1. Germanic **teran* in Old English *teran,* to tear: TEAR[1]. 2. Germanic **ter-t-* in Old English *teart,* sharp, severe: TART[1]. 3. Suffixed zero-grade form **dr̥-tom,* "something separated or discarded," in Germanic **turdam,* turd, in Old English *tord,* turd: TURD. 4. Reduplicated form **de-dr-u-* in Old English *tet(e)r,* eruption, skin disease: TETTER. 5. Greek *derris,* leather covering: DERRIS. 6. Suffixed form **der-mn̥* in Greek *derma,* skin: DERMA[1], -DERM, -DERMA, DERMATO-, EPIDERMIS. 7. Perhaps extended root **drep-* in Late Latin *drappus* (via Celtic), cloth: DRAB[1], DRAPE, TRAP[2]. [Pok. 4. *der-* 206.]

derbh-. To wind, compress. 1. Perhaps o-grade form **dorbh-* in Germanic **tarb-* in Old English **tierfan,* to roll: TOPSY-TURVY. 2. Zero-grade form **dr̥bh-* in Germanic **turb-* in: a. Old English *turf,* slab of sod or peat: TURF; b. Medieval Latin *turba,* turf: TURBARY. [Pok. *derbh-* 211.]

derə-. To work. Variant form **drā-* in Greek *dran,* to do: DRAMA, DRASTIC. [Pok. *derə-* 212.]

dergh-. To grasp. 1. Perhaps Germanic **targ-* in Frankish **targa,* shield: TARGET, (TARGE). 2. Perhaps zero-grade form **dr̥gh-* in Greek *drassesthai,* to grab: DRACHMA. [Pok. *dergh-* 212.]

derk-. To see. Suffixed zero-grade form **dr̥k-on(t)-* in Greek *drakōn,* serpent, dragon (< "monster with the evil eye"): DRAGON, (DRAGOON), (DRAKE[2]); (PENDRAGON), RANKLE, (TARRAGON). [Pok. *derk-* 213.]

deru. To be firm, solid, steadfast; hence specialized senses "wood," "tree," and derivatives referring to objects made of wood. 1. Suffixed variant form **drew-o-* in: a. Germanic **trewam* in Old English *trēow,* tree: TREE; b. Germanic **triuwō* in Old English *trēow,* pledge: TRUCE. 2. Variant form **dreu-* in Germanic **triuwaz* in: a. Old English *trēowe,* firm, true: TRUE; b. Old English *trēowian, trūwian,* to trust: TROW; c. Old Norse *tryggr,* firm, true: TRIG[1], (TRIG[2]); d. Germanic abstract noun **triuwithō* in Old English *trēowth,* faith, loyalty, truth: TRUTH, (TROTH), (BETROTH); e. Germanic abstract noun **traustyō* in Old Norse *traust,* confidence, firmness: TRUST; f. Old Norse denominative *treysta,* to trust, make firm, akin to the probable source of Old French *triste,* waiting place (< "place where one waits trustingly"): TRYST. 3. Variant form **drou-* in Germanic **traujam* in Old English *trēg, trīg,* wooden board: TRAY. 4. Suffixed zero-grade form **dru-ko-* in Germanic **trugaz* in Old English *trog,* wooden vessel, tray: TROUGH. 5. Suffixed zero-grade form **dru-mo-* in Germanic **trum-* in Old English *trum,* firm, strong: TRIM. 6. Variant form **derw-* in Germanic **terw-* in Old English *te(o)ru,* resin, pitch (obtained from the pine tree): TAR[1]. 7. Suffixed variant form **drū-ro-* in Latin *dūrus,* hard (of whose English derivatives many represent a semantic cross with Latin *dūrāre,* to last long; see **deu-**[4]): DOUR, DURAMEN, DURESS, DURO, DURUM; (DURA MATER), ENDURE, INDURATE, OBDURATE. 8. Zero-grade form **dru-* in Greek *drus,* oak: DRUPE, DRYAD, GERMANDER, HAMADRYAD. 9. Reduplicated form **der-drew-,* hence dissimilation with suffix **den-drew-on* in Greek *dendron,* tree: DENDRO-, PHILODENDRON, RHODODENDRON. 10. Compound **dru-wid-,* "knower of trees" (**wid-,* to know; see **weid-**), in Gaulish *druides,* the Celtic priestly caste, associated with a tree-cult: DRUID. 11. O-grade form **doru-* in Sanskrit *dāru,* wood, timber: DEODAR. [Pok. *deru-* 214.]

deu-[1]. To lack, be wanting. 1. Possibly suffixed form **deu-s-* in: a. Germanic **tiuzōn* in Old English *tēorian,* to fail, tire (< "to fall behind"): TIRE[1]; b. Greek *dein,* to lack, want: DEONTOLOGY. 2. Suffixed form **deu-tero-* in Greek *deuteros,* "missing," next, second: DEUTERO-, (DEUTERIUM). [Pok. 3. *deu-* 219.]

deu-[2]. To do, perform, show favor, revere. 1. Participial form **dw-enos* in Latin *bonus,* good (<"useful, efficient, working"): BONANZA, BONBON, BONITO, BONNE, BONNY, BONUS, BOON[2], BOUNTY; BONHOMIE, DEBONAIR. 2. Adverbial form **dw-enē* in Latin *bene,* well: (BENEDICT), (BENEDICITE), BENEFACTION, (BENEFACTOR), BENEFICENCE, BENEFIT, BENEVOLENT, BENIGN, (HERB BENNET). 3. Diminutive **dw-ene-lo-* in Latin *bellus,* handsome, pretty, fine: BELLE, (BELLADONNA), (BELDAM), BEAU, BEAUTY, BELVEDERE, CLARABELLA, EMBELLISH. 4. Possibly suffixed zero-grade form **dw-eye-* in Latin *beāre,* to make blessed: BEATIFIC, (BEATIFY), (BEATITUDE), (BEATRICE). 5. Suffixed zero-grade form **du-na-* in Greek *dunasthai,* to be able: DYNAMIC, (DYNAMITE), DYNAMO-, DYNAST, (DYNASTY), AERODYNE. [Pok. 2. *deu-* 218.]

deu-[3]. To burn, hurt. Germanic suffixed form **tīu-nō* in Old English *tēona,* injury: TEEN. [Pok. *dāu-* 179.]

deu-[4]. Long (in duration). Suffixed form **deu-ro-* in Latin *dūrāre,* to last: DURABLE, DURANCE, DURATION, DURING, PERDURABLE. [In Pok. 3. *deu-* 219.]

deuk-. To lead. 1. Germanic **tiuhan* in Old English *tēon,* to pull, draw, lead: TUG, WANTON. 2. Suffixed zero-grade form **duk-ā-* in Germanic **tugōn* in Old English *togian,* to draw, drag: TOW[1], TAUT. 3. Suffixed o-grade form **douk-eyo-* in Old English **tīegan, tīgan,* to bind: TIE. 4. Suffixed o-grade form **doukmo-* in Germanic **tau(h)maz* in Old English *tēam,* descendant, family, race, brood: TEAM. 5. Germanic denominative **tau(h)mjan* in Old English *tēman, tīeman,* to beget: TEEM[1]. 6. Latin *dūcere,* to lead: DOCK[1], DOGE, DOUCHE, (DUCAL), (DUCAT), (DUCHESS), (DUCHY), DUKE, (DUCT), (DUCTILE); ABDUCT, ADDUCE, CON[3], (CONDOTTIERE), CONDUCE, CONDUCT, DEDUCE, (DEDUCT), EDUCE, (ENDUE), INDUCE, INTRODUCE, PRODUCE, REDOUBT, REDUCE, SEDUCE, SUBDUE, TRADUCE, TRANSDUCER. 7. Suffixed zero-grade form **duk-a-* in Latin *ēducāre,* to lead out, bring up (*ex-,* out, EX-[1]): EDUCATE. [Pok. *deuk-* 220.]

dhabh-. To fit together. 1. Germanic **dab-,* to be fitting, in participial adjective **gadaftaz,* fitting, becoming (**ga-,* collective prefix; see **kom**), in Old English *gedæfte,* mild, gentle: DAFT. 2. Probably suffixed form **dhabh-ro-* in Latin *faber,* artisan (< "he who fits together"): FABRIC, (FABRICATE), FORGE[1]. [Pok. 2. *dhabh-* 233.]

dhal-. To bloom. 1. Suffixed form **dhal-yo-* in Greek *thallein,* to flourish, bloom, sprout (whence *thallos,* a shoot): THALIA, THALLUS, PROTHALLUS. 2. Possibly suffixed o-grade form **dol-nya-* in Old Irish *duilesc,* leaf, seaweed: DULSE. [Pok. *dhāl-* 234.]

dhē-[1]. To set, put. 1. O-grade form **dhō-* in Germanic **dōn* in Old English *dōn,* to do: DO[1], (FORDO). 2. Suffixed form **dhē-ti-,* "thing laid down or done, law, deed," in Germanic **dēdiz* in Old English *dǣd,* doing, deed: DEED. 3. Suffixed o-grade form **dhō-mo-* in Germanic **dōmaz* in: a. Old English *dōm,* judgment (< "thing set or put down"): DOOM; b. Old English *-dōm,* abstract suffix indicating state, condition, or power: -DOM; c. Old Norse *-dōmr,* condition (see **kā-**); d. Gothic *dōms,* judgment: DUMA; e. Germanic denominative **dōmian* in Old English *dēman,* to judge: DEEM. 4. Extended o-grade form **-dhōt-* in Latin agential suffix *-dōs* in Latin *sacerdōs,* priest, "performer of sacred rites" (see **sak-**). 5. Zero-grade form **dhə-* in: a. prefixed form **kom-dhə-* in Latin *condere,* to put together, establish, preserve (**kom,* together; see **kom**): CONDIMENT; ABSCOND, INCONDITE, RECONDITE, SCONCE[2]; b. compound **kred-dhə-* (see **kerd-**[1]). 6. Suffixed zero-grade form **dhə-k-* in: a. Latin *facere,* to do, make: -FACIENT, FACT, FACTION, FACTITIOUS, (FACTOR), FASHION, FAZENDA, FEASANCE, FEASIBLE, FEAT[1], FEATURE, FETISH, -FIC, -FY; AFFAIR, AFFECT[1], (AFFECT[2]), (AFFECTION), (AFFETTUOSO), AMPLIFY, ARTIFACT, BEATIFIC, BENEFACTION, (BENEFICE), BENEFICENCE, BENEFIT, CHAFE, COMFIT, CONFECT, (CONFETTI), COUNTERFEIT, (DEFEASANCE), DEFEAT, DEFECT, (DEFICIENT), (DEFICIT), DISCOMFIT, EFFECT, (EFFICIENT), (EFFICACIOUS), EDIFICE, (EDIFY), FACSIMILE, FACTOTUM, FORFEIT, HACIENDA, INFECT, JUSTIFY, MALEFACTOR, MALFEASANCE, MANUFACTURE, MISFEASANCE, MODIFY, MOLLIFY, NIDIFY, NIGRIFY, NOTIFY, NULLIFY, OFFICINAL, PERFECT, PETRIFY, (PLUPERFECT), PREFECT, (PROFICIENT), PROFIT, PUTREFY, QUALIFY, RAREFY, RECTIFY, REFECT, (REFECTORY), RUBEFACIENT, SACRIFICE, SUFFICE, (SUFFICIENT), SURFEIT, SCIRE FACIAS, TUMEFACIENT, VIVIFY; b. Latin derivative *faciēs,* shape, face (< "form imposed on something"): (FAÇADE), FACE, (FACET), (FACIAL), FACIES; (DEFACE), (EFFACE), (SURFACE), PRIMA FACIE; c. Latin compound *officium* (< **opi-fici-om*), service, duty, business, performance of work (**opi-,* work; see **op-**[1]): OFFICE; d. further suffixed form **dhə-k-oli-* in Latin *facilis* (< Old Latin *facul*), feasible, easy: FACILE, (FACILITY), FACULTY, DIFFICULTY; e. Latin suffix *-fex,* -maker: ARTIFICE, SPINIFEX, TUBIFEX. 7. Suffixed zero-grade form **dhə-s-* in Latin *fās,* divine law, right: NEFARIOUS. 8. Possibly Latin *-fārius,* -doing: MULTIFARIOUS, OMNIFARIOUS. 9. Reduplicated form **dhi-dhē-* in Greek *tithenai,* to put: THESIS, THETIC; ANATHEMA, ANTITHESIS, APOTHECARY, (APOTHECIUM), BODEGA, BOUTIQUE, DIATHESIS, EPENTHESIS, EPITHET, HYPOTHESIS, METATHESIS, PARENTHESIS, PROSTHESIS, PROTHESIS. 10. Suffixed form **dhē-k-* in Greek *thēkē,* receptacle: THECA, TICK[3]; AMPHITHECIUM, BIBLIOTHECA, ENDOTHECIUM, HYPOTHEC, PERITHECIUM. 11. Suffixed form **dhē-mn̥* in Greek *thēma,* "thing placed," proposition: THEME, (THEMATIC). 12. Suffixed zero-grade form **dhə-tlo-* in Celtic **datlos* in Old Irish *dāl,* assembly (< "a putting together"): DAIL EIREANN. 13. Reduplicated form **dhe-dhē-* in Sanskrit *dadhāti,* he places: SANDHI. 14. Reduced form **dh-* (see **aw-**[2]). [Pok. 2. *dhē-* 235.]

dhē-[2]. To vanish. 1. Possibly Old Norse *dæsa,* to languish, decay: DASTARD. 2. Possibly Old Norse **dasa,* to tire out (attested only in reflexive form *dasask,* to become exhausted): DAZE. [Pok. 3. *dhē-* 239.]

dheb-. Dense, firm, compressed. Germanic suffixed form **dap-ra-* in Middle Dutch and Middle Low German *dapper,* heavy, strong, later quick, nimble: DAPPER. [Pok. *dheb-* 239.]

dhegwh-. To burn, warm. Suffixed o-grade form **dhogwh-eyo-* in Latin *fovēre,* to warm, cherish, foment: FOMENT. [Pok. *dheguh-* 240.]

dhēi-. To suck. 1. Suffixed reduced form **dhē-mnā* in Latin *fēmina,* woman (< "she who suckles"): FEMALE, (FEME), (FEMINIE), (FEMININE), EFFEMINATE. 2. Suffixed reduced form **dhē-to-* in Latin *fētus,* pregnancy, childbearing, offspring: FAWN[2], (FETAL), (FETICIDE), FETUS, EFFETE, SUPERFETATE. 3. Suffixed reduced form **dhē-kundo-* in Latin *fēcundus,* fruitful: FECUND. 4. Suffixed reduced form **dhē-no-* in Latin *fēnum, faenum,* hay (< "produce"): FENNEL, (FENUGREEK), FINOCHIO, SAINFOIN. 5. Perhaps suffixed zero-grade form **dhī-lyo-* in Latin *fīlius,* son, and *fīlia,* daughter (but these are equally possibly from the root **bheu-**): FILIAL, FILIATE, FILICIDE, FITZHIDALGO, AFFILIATE. 6. Suffixed reduced form **dhē-lo-* in Latin *fēl(l)āre,* to suck: FELLATIO. 7. Suffixed reduced form **dhē-l-īk-* in Latin *fēlix,* fruitful, fertile, lucky, happy: (FELICITY), FELIX, FELICIFIC, (FELICITATE), INFELICITY. 8. Suffixed reduced form **dhē-lā-* in Greek *thēlē,* nipple: ENDOTHELIUM, EPITHELIUM, (MESOTHELIUM). 9. Suffixed reduced form **dhē-l-u-* in Greek *thēlus,* female: THEELIN. [Pok. *dhē(i)-* 241.]

dheigh-. To knead clay. 1. Germanic **daigjōn* in Old English *dǣge,* bread kneader: DAIRY. 2. Germanic **-dīg-* in Old English compound *hlǣfdige,* mistress of a household (< "bread kneader"; *hlǣf,* bread, LOAF[1]): LADY. 3. Extended o-grade form **dhoigho-* in Germanic **daigaz* in: a. Old English *dāg,* dough: DOUGH; b. Old High German *teic,* dough: TEIGLACH. 4. Suffixed zero-grade form **dhigh-ūrā,* in Latin *figūra,* form, shape (< "result of kneading"): FIGURE; (CONFIGURATION), (DISFIGURE), (PREFIGURE), (TRANSFIGURE). 5. Nasalized zero-grade form **dhi-n-gh-* in Latin *fingere,* to shape: (FAINT), FEIGN, (FEINT), FICTILE, FICTION, FIGMENT; EFFIGY. 6. Nasalized zero-grade form **dhi-n-g(h)-* in Greek *thinganein,* to touch: THIGMOTAXIS, THIXOTROPY. 7. Extended o-grade form **dhoigho-* in Avestan *daēza,* wall (originally made of clay or mud bricks): PARADISE. [Pok. *dheigh-* 244.]

dhel-. A hollow. **1.** Germanic **daljō* in Old English *dell,* valley: DELL. **2.** Germanic **dalam* in Old English *dæl,* valley: DALE. **3.** Germanic **del-* in Old Norse *dæla,* wooden gutter on a ship: DALLES. [Pok. 1. *dhel-* 245.]

dhelbh-. To dig, excavate. Germanic **delban* in Old English *delfan,* to dig: DELVE. [Pok. *dhelbh-* 246.]

dhelg-. To pierce; a needle. O-grade form **dholg-* in Germanic **dalk-* in German *Dolch,* dagger: DIRK. [Pok. *dhelg-* 247.]

dhembh-. To bury. Suffixed zero-grade form **dhṃbh-o-* in Greek *taphos* (<**thaphos*), tomb: CENOTAPH, EPITAPH. [Pok. *(dhembh-), dhṃbh-* 248.]

dhen-[1]. To run, flow. Suffixed o-grade form **dhon-t-* in Latin *fons* (stem *font-*), spring, fountain: FONT, FOUNTAIN. [Pok. 1. *dhen-* 249.]

dhen-[2]. Palm of the hand. Suffixed form **dhen-ṛ* in Greek *thenar,* palm of the hand: THENAR. [Pok. 2. *dhen-* 249.]

dher-[1]. To make muddy; darkness. **1.** Suffixed form **dher-g-* in Germanic **derk-* in Old English *deorc,* dark: DARK. **2.** Suffixed zero-grade form **dhr-egh-* in: **a.** Germanic suffixed form **drah-sta-* in Old English *drōs,* dregs: DROSS; **b.** Germanic **dragjō* in Old Norse *dregg,* dregs: DREGS. **3.** Suffixed extended zero-grade form **dhrə-bh-* in Germanic **drab-* in: **a.** Old English **dræf,* dregs: DRAFF; **b.** Old English *dref-lian,* to drivel: DRIVEL; **c.** probably Low German *drabbelen,* to paddle in water or mire, draggle, akin to the Low German source of Middle English *drabelen,* to draggle: DRABBLE; **d.** Middle Irish *drab,* dregs, probably akin to the Celtic source of English DRAB[2]. **4.** Suffixed extended zero-grade form **dhrə-gh-* in: **a.** Greek *tarassein* (Attic *tarattein*), to confuse, disturb: ATARACTIC; **b.** Greek *trakhus,* rough: TRACHEA, TRACHOMA, (TRACHYTE). [Pok. 1. *dher-* 251.]

dher-[2]. To hold firmly, support. **1.** Suffixed form **dher-mo-* in Latin *firmus,* firm, strong: FARM, FERMATA, FIRM, FIRMAMENT; AFFIRM, CONFIRM, (INFIRM), (INFIRMARY). **2.** Extended form **dhergh-* possibly in Latin *fortis,* strong; but this is also possibly from **bhergh-[2]** *(see).* **3.** Suffixed zero-grade form **dhr-ono-* in Greek *thronos,* seat, throne (< "support"): THRONE. **4.** Suffixed form **dher-mṇ-* in Sanskrit *dharma,* statute, law (< "that which is established firmly"): DHARMA. **5.** Old Persian *dār-,* to hold (whence Persian *-dār,* -holder): DARIUS I; JEMADAR, SIRDAR, TAHSILDAR, ZAMINDAR. [Pok. 2. *dher-* 252.]

dher-[3]. To drone, murmur, buzz. **1.** Germanic **duran-* in Old English *dora,* fly, bumblebee: DOR. **2.** Extended zero-grade form **dhrēn-* in: **a.** Germanic **dren-* in Old English *drān, dræn,* male honeybee: DRONE[1]; **b.** Greek *thrēnos,* dirge, lament: THRENODY. [Pok. 3. *dher-* 255.]

dhers-. To venture, be bold. **1.** Full-grade form **dhers-* and zero-grade form **dhṛs-* respectively in Germanic **ders-* and **durs-* in Old English *dearr* and *durst,* first and third person singular present and past indicative of *durran,* to venture: DARE, DURST. **2.** Suffixed zero-grade form **dhṛs-u-* in Greek *thrasus,* bold: THRASONICAL. **3.** Possibly Latin *-festus* in: **a.** *infestus,* hostile (? < "directed against"; *in-,* against, IN-): INFEST; **b.** *manifestus,* palpable, evident (< "caught red-handed, grasped by the hand"; *manus,* hand; see **man-[2]**): MANIFEST. [Pok. *dhers-* 259.]

dhēs-. Root of words in religious concepts. Possibly an extended form of **dhē-[1]**. **1.** Latin *fērālis,* concerning the dead: FERAL. **2.** Suffixed form **dhēs-ya* in Latin *fēriae* (Old Latin *fēsiae*), holidays: FAIR[2], FERIA, FERIAL. **3.** Suffixed form **dhēs-to-* in Latin *fēstus,* festive: FEAST, -FEST, FESTAL, FESTIVAL, FESTIVE, FESTOON, FETE, FIESTA, GABFEST. **4.** Suffixed zero-grade form **dhəs-no-* in Latin *fānum,* temple: FANE, FANATIC, PROFANE. **5.** Possibly suffixed shortened form **dhes-o-* in Greek *theos* (< **thes-os*), god: THEO-; ATHEISM, APOTHEOSIS, DOROTHY, ENTHUSIASM, PANTHEON, POLYTHEISM, TIMOTHY[1]. [Pok. *dhēs-* 259.]

dheu-[1]. The base of a wide variety of derivatives meaning "to rise in a cloud," as dust, vapor, or smoke, and related to semantic notions of breath, various color adjectives, and forms denoting defective perception or wits. **1.** Suffixed lengthened zero-grade form **dhū-mo-,* smoke, in: **a.** Latin *fūmus,* smoke: FUME, FUMARIC ACID, FUMAROLE, FUMATORIUM, FUMIGATE, FUMITORY, PERFUME; **b.** Greek *thumos,* soul, spirit: -THYMIA, ENTHYMEME; **c.** Greek *thumon, thumos,* thyme (< "plant having a strong smell"): THYME. **2.** Suffixed lengthened zero-grade form **dhū-li-* in Latin *fūligō,* soot: FULIGINOUS. **3.** Extended form **dheus-* possibly in Germanic **dus-* in: **a.** Old English *dysig,* foolish (< "stupefied," "confused"): DIZZY; **b.** Danish *døse,* to make drowsy (originally "to stupefy"): DOZE. **4.** Suffixed extended zero-grade form **dheus-o-* in Germanic **diuzam,* breathing creature, animal, in: **a.** Old English *dēor,* animal: DEER; **b.** Old Norse *dȳr,* animal, deer: REINDEER. **5.** Suffixed o-grade form **dhous-a* in Slavic **dukh-* in Russian *dukh,* breath, spirit: DUKHOBORS. **6.** Extended zero-grade form **dhwes-* in nasalized form **dhwens-* in Germanic **duns-,* dust, meal, in: **a.** Germanic suffixed form **duns-to-* in Old English *dust,* dust: DUST; **b.** Old Norse *dūnn,* bird's down (< "fine like dust"): DOWN[2], DUVETYN, EIDERDOWN. **7.** Extended zero-grade form **dhus-* in Greek *thuos,* burnt sacrifice, incense: THURIBLE, (THURIFER). **8.** Suffixed extended zero-grade form **dhus-ko-* in: **a.** Germanic *duskaz* in Old English *dox,* twilight: DUSK; **b.** Latin *fuscus,* dark, dusky: OBFUSCATE. **9.** Suffixed extended zero-grade form **dhus-no-* in: **a.** Welsh *dwn,* dull brown color, whence Old English *dun(n),* dark-brown: DUN[2]; **b.** Middle Irish *donn,* brown: DUNCAN. **10.** Suffixed zero-grade form **dhu-bh-* in Greek *tuphein* (< **thuphein*), to make smoke: TYPHUS, STEW. **11.** Suffixed form **dheu-bh-,* "beclouded in the senses," in suffixed o-grade form **dhoubh-o-* in: **a.** Germanic **daubaz* in Old English *dēaf,* deaf: DEAF; **b.** nasalized form **dhu-m-bho-* in Germanic **dumbaz* in Old English *dumb,* dumb: DUMB; **c.** Germanic **dūbōn* in Old English **dūfe,* dove (< "dark-colored bird"): DOVE[1]. **12.** Extended zero-grade form **dhwel-* in: **a.** Germanic **dwelan,* to go or lead astray, in Old English *dwellan,* to deceive (but influenced in sense by Old Norse *dvelja,* to tarry): DWELL; **b.** Germanic **dulaz* in *(i)* Old English *dol,* dull: DOLDRUMS *(ii)* Middle Low German *dul,* dull: DULL, (DOLT). **13.** Extended zero-grade form **dhwes-* in Greek suffixed form **th(w)es-os,* smoke, whence Greek *theion* (< **thweseion*), brimstone, sulfur: THIO-, (THION-). **14.** Perhaps Old English *docce,* dock (< "dark-colored plant"): DOCK[4]. **15.** Perhaps Irish *dūd,* pipe: DUDEEN. [Pok. 4. *dheu-* 261.]

dheu-[2]. To flow. Germanic **dauwaz,* dew, in: **a.** Old English *dēaw,* dew: DEW; **b.** compound **melith-dauwaz,* "honeydew" (see **melit-**). [Pok. 1. *dheu-* 259.]

dheu-[3]. To become exhausted, die. **1.** Suffixed o-grade form **dhou-to-* in Germanic **daudaz* in Old English *dēad,* dead: DEAD. **2.** Suffixed o-grade form **dhou-tu-* in Germanic **dauthuz* in Old English *dēath,* death: DEATH. **3.** Suffixed o-grade form **dhow-yo-* in Old Norse *deyja,* to die: DIE[1]. **4.** Suffixed extended zero-grade form **dhwī-no-* in Germanic **dwīnan* in Old English *dwīnan,* to diminish, languish: DWINDLE. [Pok. 2. *dheu-* 260.]

dheub-. Deep, hollow. **1.** Germanic **diupaz* in Old English *dēop,* deep: DEEP, (DEPTH). **2.** Germanic expressive denominative **duppjan* in Old English *dyppan,* to immerse, dip: DIP. **3.** Parallel root form **dheubu-* in Germanic **diub-, *dub-* in verb **dūbjan* in Old English *dȳfan,* to dip, and *dūfan,* to sink, dive: DIVE. [Pok. *dheu-b-* 267.]

dheubh-. Wedge, peg, plug. Germanic **dub-* in: **a.** Old English *dubbian,* to tap, strike (with a sword): DUB[1]; **b.** Low German *dubben,* to hit: DUB[2]; **c.** Germanic diminutive **dub-ila-* in Middle Low German *dövel,* peg: DOWEL. [Pok. *dheubh-* 268.]

dheugh-. To produce something of utility. **1.** Germanic extended form **duht-* in Old English *dyhtig,* strong (< "useful"): DOUGHTY. **2.** Suffixed form **dheugh-os-* in Greek *teukhos* (< **theukhos*), gear, anything produced, tool: HEPTATEUCH, HEXATEUCH, PENTATEUCH. [Pok. *dheugh-* 271.]

dheyə-. To see, look. Lengthened zero-grade form **dhyā-* in: **a.** suffixed form **dhyā-mṇ* in Greek *sēma,* sign (< "thing seen"): SEMANTIC, SEMAPHORE, SEMATIC, (SEMASIOLOGY), (SEMEME), SEMIOLOGY; **b.** Sanskrit *dhyāti,* he meditates (< "he observes mentally"): ZEN BUDDHISM. [Pok. *dheiə-* 243.]

dhghem-. Earth. **1.** Suffixed zero-grade form **(dh)ghṃ-on-,* "earthling," in Germanic **gumōn* in Old English *guma,* man: BRIDEGROOM. **2.** O-grade form **dhghōm-* in Greek *khthōn,* earth: CHTHONIC, AUTOCHTHON. **3.** Zero-grade form **dhghṃ-* in Greek *khamai,* on the ground: CHAMELEON, CHAMOMILE, GERMANDER. **4.** Suffixed o-grade form **dhghom-o-* in Latin *humus,* earth: HUMBLE, (HUMILIATE), (HUMILITY), HUMUS; EXHUME, INHUME, TRANSHUMANCE. **5.** Suffixed o-grade form **(dh)ghom-on-,* "earthling," in: **a.** Latin *homō,* human being, man: HOMAGE, HOMBRE[1], HOMINID, HOMO[1], HOMUNCULUS, OMBRE; BONHOMIE, HOMICIDE; **b.** Latin *hūmānus,* human, kind, humane: HUMAN, (HUMANE). **6.** Suffixed form **(dh)ghem-ya* in Russian *zemlya,* land: ZEMSTVO. **7.** Full-grade form **(dh)ghem-* in Persian *zamīn,* earth, land: ZAMINDAR. [Pok. *ghdhem-* 414.]

dhīgw-. To stick, fix. **1.** Germanic **dīk-* in: **a.** Old English *dīc,* trench, moat: DITCH, DIKE; **b.** Old French *digue,* trench: DIG. **2.** Latin *fīgere,* to fasten, fix: FIBULA, FICHU, (FIX), (FIXATE), FIXITY, (FIXTURE); AFFIX, ANTEFIX, CRUCIFY, (INFIX), MICROFICHE, PREFIX, SUFFIX, (TRANSFIGURE), TRANSFIX. [Pok. *dhēigu-* 243.]

dhragh-. To draw, drag on the ground. **1.** Germanic **dragan* in: **a.** Old English *dragan,* to draw, pull: DRAW; **b.** Old Norse *draga,* to draw, pull (or Old English *dragan*): DRAG; **c.** Old English *dræge,* dragnet: DRAY; **d.** Old Norse **drāhtr, drāttr,* act of drawing: DRAFT. **2.** Russian *droga,* beam of a wagon: DROSHKY. See also variant form **dhreg-**. [Pok. *dheragh-* 257.]

dhreg-. To draw, glide. Variant form of **dhragh-**. **1.** Nasalized Germanic form **drinkan,* to draw into the mouth, drink, in Old English *drincan,* to drink: DRINK. **2.** Nasalized Germanic form **drankjan,* "to cause to drink," in: **a.** Old English *drencan,* to soak: DRENCH; **b.** Scandinavian **drunkna, drugna,* to drown: DROWN. [Pok. *dhreg-* 273.]

dhregh-. To run. **1.** Greek *trekhein* (< **threkhein*), to run: TROCHAL, (TROCHANTER), (TROCHE), TROCHEE, (TROCHOPHORE), TRUCK[1]. **2.** O-grade form **dhrogh-* in Greek *trokhileia, trokhilia,* system of pulleys, roller of a windlass: TROCHLEA, (TRUCKLE). [Pok. 1. *dhregh-* 273.]

dhreibh-. To drive, push; snow. **1.** Germanic **drīban* in Old English *drīfan,* to drive, rush: DRIVE, DROVE[2]. **2.** Germanic noun form **driftiz* in Old Norse *drift,* snowdrift, and Middle Dutch *drift,* herd: DRIFT. [Pok. *dhreibh-* 274.]

dhreu-. To fall, flow, drip, droop. **1.** Extended form **dhreus-* in Germanic **driusan* in Old English *drēosan,* to fall: DRIZZLE. **2.** Extended o-grade form **dhrous-* in: **a.** Germanic **drauzaz* in Old English *drēor,* flowing blood: DREARY; **b.** Germanic **drūsjan* in Old English *drūsian,* to be sluggish: DROWSE. **3.** Extended zero-grade form **dhrub-* in: **a.** Germanic **drupan* in Old English *dropa,* drop: DROP; **b.** Germanic **drūpjan,* to let fall, in Old Norse *drūpa,* to hang down: DROOP; **c.** Germanic expressive form **drupp-* in Middle Danish *drippe,* to trickle: DRIP. **4.** Suffixed zero-grade form **dhrubh-yo-* in Greek *thruptein,* to crumble: LITHOTRITY. [Pok. *dhreu-* 274.]

dhreugh-. To deceive. Germanic suffixed form **drau(g)ma-* in Old English *drēam,* vision, illusion, dream (but attested only in the senses of "joy," "music"): DREAM. [Pok. 2. *dhreugh-* 276.]

dhughəter. Daughter. Germanic **dohtēr* in Old English *dohtor,* daughter: DAUGHTER. [Pok. *dhug(h)əter* 277.]

dhūno-. Fortified, enclosed place. (Only in Celtic and Germanic.) **1.** Possibly Germanic **dūnaz,* hill, in: **a.** Old English *dūn,* hill: DOWN[1], DOWN[3]; **b.** Middle Dutch *dūne,* sandy hill: DUNE. **2.** Celtic **dūn-o-,* hill, stronghold, borrowed into Germanic as **tūnaz,* fortified place, in Old English *tūn,* enclosed place, homestead, village: TOWN. [In Pok. 4. *dheu-* 261.]

dhwen-. To make noise. Germanic **duniz* in Old English *dyne,* noise: DIN. [Pok. *dhuen-* 277.]

dhwenə-. To disappear, die. Suffixed form *dhwenə-tos* in Greek *thanatos,* death: THANATOS, TANSY, EUTHANASIA. [In Pok. 4. *dheu-* 261.]

dhwer-. Door, doorway (usually in plural). Originally an apophonic noun **dhwor-, *dhur-,* in the plural, designating the entrance to the enclosure (**dhwor-o-*) surrounding the house proper. **1.** Zero-grade form **dhur-* in suffixed forms **dhur-ns* (accusative plural) and **dhur-o-* (neuter) respectively in Germanic **durunz* and **duram* in Old English *duru,* door (feminine, originally plural), and *dor,* door (neuter): DOOR. **2.** Suffixed o-grade form **dhwor-āns* (accusative plural) in Latin *forās,* (toward) out of doors, outside: FOREIGN. **3.** Suffixed o-grade form **dhwor-ois* (locative plural) in Latin *forīs,* (being) out of doors: FOREST, AFFOREST, FORECLOSE, FORFEIT, FAUBOURG,

HORS D'OEUVRE. **4.** Suffixed o-grade form **dhwor-o-* in Latin *forum,* marketplace (originally the enclosed space around a home): FORUM, FORENSIC. **5.** Zero-grade form **dhur-* in Greek *thura,* door: THYROID. **6.** Persian *dar,* door, gate: DURBAR. [Pok. *dhu̯er-* 278.]

digh-. She-goat. Germanic **tigon* (with expressive consonantism) in Old Norse *tīk,* bitch: TYKE. [Pok. *digh-* 222.]

dl̥ku-. Sweet. **1.** Suffixed form **dl̥kw-i-* in Latin *dulcis,* sweet: DULCET, DULCIFY, DULCIANA, DULCIMER, DOLCE, DOUCEUR, BILLET-DOUX. **2.** Basic form **dl̥ku-* (with **dl-* dissimilated to **gl-* in Greek because of the following *k*) in: **a.** Greek *glukus,* sweet: LICORICE; **b.** Greek *glukeros* (with suffix **-ero-*), sweet: GLYCERIN; **c.** Greek *gleukos,* must, sweet wine: GLUCOSE. [Pok. *dl̥kú-* 222.]

dn̥ghū. Tongue. **1.** Germanic **tungōn* in: **a.** Old English *tunge,* tongue: TONGUE; **b.** Middle Dutch *tonghe,* tongue: BILTONG. **2.** Latin *lingua* (< Old Latin *dingua*), tongue, language: LANGUAGE, LANGUET, LIGULE, LINGUA, LINGO, LINGUIST, BILINGUAL. [Pok. *dn̥ghū* 223.]

dō-. To give. **1.** Zero-grade form **də-* in Latin *dare,* to give: DADO, DATE, DATIVE, DATUM, DIE[2]; ADD, BETRAY, EDITION, PERDITION, (PERDU), RENDER, (RENT[1]), (SURRENDER), TRADITION, (TRAITOR), (TREASON), VEND. **2.** Suffixed form **dō-no-* in Latin *dōnum,* gift: DONATION, (DONATIVE), (DONOR); CONDONE, PARDON. **3.** Suffixed form **dō-ti-* in: **a.** Latin *dōs* (genitive *dōtis*), dowry: DOT[2], DOWAGER, DOWER, (DOWRY), ENDOW; **b.** Slavic **datia* in Russian *dacha,* gift: DACHA. **4.** Reduplicated form **di-dō-* in Greek *didonai,* to give: DOSE, ANECDOTE, ANTIDOTE, APODOSIS, EPIDOTE. **5.** Suffixed form **dō-ro-* in Greek *dōron,* gift: DOROTHY, THEODORE. [Pok. *dō-* 223.]

[dorsum. The back. Latin noun of unknown origin. DORSAL, DORSO-, DORSUM, DOSS, (DOSSAL), DOSSER, DOSSIER; ENDORSE, EXTRADOS, INTRADOS, REREDOS.**]**

drem-. To sleep. Suffixed zero-grade form **dr̥m-yo-* in Latin *dormīre,* to sleep: DORMANT, (DORMER), DORMITORY. [Pok. *drē-* 226.]

[driug-. Dry. Germanic root. **1.** Old English *drugāth,* dryness, drought: DROUGHT. **2.** Suffixed variant form **draug-iz* in Old English *drȳge,* dry: DRY. **3.** Suffixed variant form **draug-n-* in Old English *drēahnian,* to strain, drain: DRAIN.**]**

[dub-. Also **dup-**. To drop, dip. Germanic imitative root. **1.** Old English *-doppa,* dapper (<"one that dips"): DABCHICK, DIDAPPER. **2.** Middle Dutch *dōpen,* to dip: DOPE. **3.** Old English **dympel* (diminutive with nasal infix), pool, dimple: DIMPLE. **4.** Norwegian *dumpa,* to fall suddenly, akin to the Scandinavian source of Middle English *dumpen,* to dump: DUMP. [In Pok. *dheu-b-* 267.]**]**

[dud-. To shake, deceive. Germanic root. **1.** Old English *dydrian,* to deceive: DIDDLE[1]. **2.** Norwegian *dudra,* to quiver, akin to: **a.** Middle English *dadiren,* to tremble: DODDER[1]; **b.** Middle English *doder,* vine (< "that which quivers in the wind"): DODDER[2]. **3.** Middle Low German *doderen,* to tremble: DIDDLE[2]. **4.** Middle Dutch *doten,* to be silly (< "to be old and shaky"): DOTE. [In Pok. 4. *dheu-* 261.]**]**

[duellum. Later spelling *bellum.* War. Latin noun of unknown origin. BELLONA, BELLICOSE, (BELLIGERENT), DUEL; ANTEBELLUM, POSTBELLUM, REBEL, (REVEL).**]**

dus-. Bad, evil; mis- (used as prefix). Greek *dus-,* bad: DYS-. [Pok. *dus-* 227.]

dwei-. To fear. **1.** Suffixed form **dwei-ro-* in Latin *dīrus,* fearful, horrible (originally a dialectal form): DIRE. **2.** Suffixed form **dwey-eno-* in Greek *deinos,* fearful, monstrous: DINOSAUR, DINOTHERE. **3.** Suffixed form **dwei-mo-* in Greek *deimos,* fear: DEIMOS. (This root originally meant "to be in doubt, be of two minds," and is related to **dwō**.) [Pok. *du̯ei-* 227.]

dwō. Two. **I.** Full-grade form *dwō.* **1.** Germanic **twai,* two, in: **a.** Old English *twā,* two (nominative feminine of *tu*): TWO; **b.** Old English *twēgen,* two (nominative and accusative masculine of *tu*): TWAIN. **2.** Germanic compound **twa-lif-,* "two left (over from ten)," twelve (**-lif-,* left; see **leikw-**), in Old English *twelf,* twelve, and *twelfta,* twelfth: TWELVE, TWELFTH. **II.** Adverbial form **dwis* and combining form **dwi-.* **1.** Germanic **twi-* in: **a.** Old English *twi-,* two: TWILIGHT, TWIBIL; **b.** Old High German *zwi-,* two: ZWIEBACK, ZWITTERION. **2.** Latin *bis* (combining form *bi-*), twice: BI-, BIS, (BAROUCHE), (BISCUIT). **3.** Greek *dis* (combining form *di-*), twice: DI-. **4.** Germanic **twis* in Old English *-twist,* a branched or twisted object (such as a rope): TWIST. **5.** Germanic **twiyes* in Old English *twige,* twice: TWICE. **6.** Germanic compound **twēgentig,* "twice ten" (**-tig,* ten; see **dekm̥**), in Old English *twēntig,* twenty: TWENTY. **7.** Germanic **twīhna,* double thread, twisted thread, in Old English *twīn,* double thread: TWINE. **8.** Germanic compounds **bi-twīhna* and **bi-twisk,* "at the middle point of two" (**bi,* at, by; see **ambhi**), in Old English *betwēonum* and *betweohs,* between: BETWEEN, BETWIXT, (TWIXT). **9.** Germanic compound **twilic-,* "two-threaded fabric" (partial translation of Latin *bilīx:* BI- + *līcium,* thread; see **trellis**): TWILL. **10.** Suffixed form **dwis-no-* in: **a.** Germanic **twisnaz,* double, in Old English *twinn, getwinn,* two by two, twin: TWIN; **b.** Latin *bīnī,* two by two, two each: BINAL, BINARY, BINATE, (BIN-), COMBINE. **11.** Suffixed form **dwi-ko-* in Germanic **twig(g)a,* a fork, in Old English *twigge,* a branch: TWIG[1]. **12.** Compound **dwi-plo-,* twofold (**-plo-,* -fold; see **pel-**[3]), in Greek *diploos,* twofold: DIPLO-, (DIPLOE), (DIPLOMA), ANADIPLOSIS. **13.** Suffixed reduplicated form **dwi-du-mo-* in Greek *didumos,* double, the testicles: (DIDYMIUM), DIDYMOUS, EPIDIDYMIS, TETRADYMITE. **14.** Suffixed form **dwi-kha* in Greek *dikha,* in two: DICHO-, DICHASIUM. **III.** Extended form **duwō.* **1.** Latin *duo,* two: DEUCE[1], DOZEN, DUAL, DUET, DUO-, DUODECIMAL. **2.** Greek *duo, duō,* two: DUAD, DYAD, DODECAGON, HENDIADYS. **IV.** Zero-grade form **du-.* **1.** Compound **du-plo-,* twofold (**-plo-,* -fold; see **pel-**[3]), in Latin *duplus,* double: DOUBLE, (DOUBLET), (DOUBLOON), (DOUBLURE), DUPLE. **2.** Compound **du-plek-* (**-plek,* -fold; see **plek-**), twofold, in Latin *duplex,* double: DUPLEX, (DUPLICATE), (DUPLICITY), (CONDUPLICATE). **3.** Suffixed form **du-bhwio-* in Latin *dubius,* doubtful (< "hesitating between two alternatives"): DOUBT, DUBIOUS, (REDOUBTABLE). [Pok. *du̯ō(u)-* 228.]

ē. Adverbial particle. Germanic **ē* in Old English *ā-, ǣ-,* away, off: OAKUM. [Pok. *ē̆* 280.]

ed-. To eat. **1.** Germanic **itan* in: **a.** Old English *etan,* to eat: EAT; **b.** Old High German *ezzen,* to feed on, eat: ETCH; **c.** Middle Dutch *eten,* to eat: ORT; **d.** Germanic compound **fraitan,* to eat up (**fra-,* completely; see **per**[1]), in Old English *fretan,* to devour: FRET[1]. **2.** Latin *edere,* to eat: EDACIOUS, EDIBLE, ESCAROLE, ESCULENT, ESURIENT; COMEDO, COMESTIBLE, OBESE. **3.** Zero-grade form **d-* in Latin compound *prandium* (< **pram-d-ium*), "first meal," lunch (**pram-,* first; see **per**[1]): PRANDIAL. **4.** Suffixed form **ed-un-ā* in Greek *odunē,* pain (<"gnawing care"): ANODYNE. [Pok. *ed-* 287.]

eg. I (pronoun). **1.** Germanic **eg* in Old English *ic,* I: I. **2.** Extended form **egō* in Latin *ego,* I: EGO, (EGOTISM). [Pok. *eĝ-* 291.]

eg-. A lack. Suffixed (stative) form **eg-ē-* in Latin *egēre,* to lack, be in want: INDIGENT. [Pok. *eg-* 290.]

ēg-. To speak. Suffixed zero-grade form **əg-io-* in: **a.** Latin *adagium,* saying, proverb, "a speaking to" (*ad-,* to, AD-): ADAGE; **b.** Latin *prōdigium,* a portent, "a foretelling" (*prōd-,* variant of *prō-,* before, PRO-): PRODIGY. [Pok. *ēĝ-* 290.]

eghero-. Lake. Possibly a suffixed variant form **agher-ont-* in Greek *Akherōn,* a river in Hades: ACHERON. [Pok. *eĝhero-* 291.]

eghs. Out. **1.** Variant **eks* in: **a.** Latin *ex,* out of, away from: EX[1], EX-[1]; **b.** Greek *ex,* out of, from: ECTO-, EX-[2], EXO-, EXOTERIC, EXOTIC, SYNECDOCHE. **2.** Suffixed (comparative) variant form **eks-tero-* in Latin *exterus,* outward (whence ablative feminine *extera, extrā,* on the outside): EXTERIOR, EXTERNAL, EXTRA-, STRANGE. **3.** Suffixed (superlative) form in Latin *extrēmus,* outermost (**-mo-,* superlative suffix): EXTREME. **4.** Suffixed form **eghs-ko-* in Greek *eskhatos,* outermost, last: ESCHATOLOGY. [Pok. *eghs* 292.]

egnis. Fire. **1.** Latin *ignis,* fire: IGNEOUS, IGNITE, IGNITRON. **2.** Sanskrit *agniḥ,* fire: AGNI. [Pok. *egnis* 293.]

egw-. To drink. Suffixed lengthened form **ēgw-rio-* in: **a.** Latin *ēbrius,* drunk: INEBRIATE; **b.** Latin compound *sōbrius* (*se-,* without; see **seu-**[2]).

ei-[1]. To go. **1.** Full-grade form **ei-* in: **a.** Latin *īre,* to go: ADIT, AMBIENT, (AMBITION), CIRCUIT, COITUS, COMITIA, (COMMENCE), EXIT[2], INTROIT, ISSUE, OBITUARY, PERISH, PRAETOR, PRETERIT, SEDITION, SUBITO, SUDDEN, (TRANCE), TRANSIENT, (TRANSIT), (TRANSITIVE); **b.** Greek *ienai,* to go: ION, ANION, CATION, DYSPROSIUM. **2.** Suffixed zero-grade form **i-t-* in: **a.** further suffixed form **i-t-io-* in Latin *initium,* entrance, beginning (*in-,* in, IN-): INITIAL, (INITIATE); **b.** Latin *comes* (stem *comit-*), companion (< "one who goes with another"; *com-,* with, COM-): COUNT[2], CONCOMITANT, CONSTABLE, (VISCOUNT). **3.** Suffixed form **i-ter* in Latin *iter,* journey: (ERRANT), EYRE, (ITINERANT), ITINERARY. **4.** Extended form **yā-* in suffixed forms **yā-no-, yā-nu-* in: **a.** Latin *Jānus,* god of doors and of the beginning of a year: JANUS, (JANUARY), (JANITOR); **b.** Sanskrit *yāna,* way (in Buddhism, "mode of knowledge," "vehicle"): HINAYANA, MAHAYANA. [Pok. 1. *ei-* 293.]

ei-[2]. Reddish, motley; yew. Suffixed form **ei-wo-* in Germanic **īwaz,* yew, in Old English *īw,* yew: YEW. [Pok. 3. *ei-* 297.]

ēik-. To be master of, possess. **1.** Germanic **aigan,* to possess, in Old English *āgan,* to possess: OWE, OUGHT[1]. **2.** Germanic participial form **aiganaz,* possessed, owned, in Old English *agēn,* one's own: OWN. **3.** Germanic prefixed form **fra-aihtiz,* absolute possession, property (**fra-,* intensive prefix; see **per**[1]), in Middle Low German and Middle Dutch *vrecht, vracht,* "earnings," hire for a ship, freight: FRAUGHT, FREIGHT. [Pok. *ēik-* 289.]

eis-[1]. In words denoting passion. **1.** Suffixed form **eis-ā* in Latin *īra,* anger: (IRASCIBLE), (IRATE), IRE. **2.** Suffixed zero-grade form **is-əro-,* powerful, holy, in Greek *hieros,* "filled with the divine," holy: HIERATIC, HIERO-, JEROME. **3.** Germanic **isarno-,* "holy metal" (possibly from Celtic), in Old English *īse(r)n,* iron: IRON. **4.** Suffixed o-grade form **ois-tro-,* madness, in Greek *oistros,* gadfly, goad, anything causing madness: ESTRUS, (ESTRONE). **5.** Suffixed o-grade form **ois-mo-,* anger, in Avestan *aēšma-,* anger: ASMODEUS. [Pok. 1. *eis-* 299.]

eis-[2]. Ice, frost. Germanic **īs-* in Old English *īs,* ice: ICE. [Pok. 2. *ei-s-* 301.]

ekwo-. Horse. Probably originally derived from **kwon-**, dog. **1.** Latin *equus,* horse: EQUESTRIAN, EQUINE, EQUITANT, (EQUITATION), EQUISETUM, EQUULEUS. **2.** Greek *hippos,* horse: EOHIPPUS, HIPPARCH, HIPPOPOTAMUS, PHILIP. [Pok. *eku̯o-s* 301.]

el-[1]. Elbow, forearm. Extended o-grade form **olinā,* elbow, in: **a.** Germanic **alinō* in Old English *eln,* forearm, cubit: ELL[2]; **b.** Germanic compound **alino-bogōn-,* "bend of the forearm," elbow (**bogōn-,* bend, bow; see **bheug-**[3]), in Old English *elnboga,* elbow: ELBOW; **c.** Latin *ulna,* forearm: ULNA; **d.** lengthened variant form **ōlenā* in Greek *ōlenē,* elbow: OLECRANON. [Pok. 8. *el-* 307.]

el-[2]. Red, brown (forming animal and tree names). **1.** Extended form **elmo-* in Germanic **elmo-, *almo-* in Old English *elm,* elm: ELM. **2.** Germanic extended form **aliza,* alder, in Old English *alor,* alder: ALDER. **3.** Possibly Old English *ellen, ellærn,* the elder: ELDER[2]. **4.** Extended o-grade form **olki-* in Germanic **alkiz,* elk, in Old Norse *elgr,* elk: ELK. **5.** Perhaps Germanic extended form **alk-* in Old Norse *alka,* auk: AUK. **6.** Extended form **elno-* in Greek *ellos, hellos,* fawn: HELLEBORE. **7.** Extended form **eleni-* in Old Lithuanian *ellenis,* stag: ELAND. [Pok. 1. *el-* 302.]

el-[3]. To go. Suffixed extended form **ela-un-yo-* in Greek *elaunein,* to drive (< "to cause to go"): ELASTIC, ELATER, ELASMOBRANCH. [Pok. 6. *el-* 306.]

[elaia. Olive. Greek noun of Mediterranean origin. OIL, -OLE[1], OLEAGINOUS, OLEASTER, OLEO-, OLIVE; ANELE, PETROLEUM.**]**

elkos-. Wound. Latin *ulcus* (stem *ulcer-*), a sore: ULCER. [Pok. *elkos-* 310.]

em-. To take, distribute. **1.** Latin *emere,* to obtain, buy: ADEMPTION, DIRIMENT, EXAMPLE, (EXEMPLARY), (EXEMPLIFY), (EXEMPT), (IMPROMPTU), (IRREDENTIST), PEREMPTORY, PREEMPTION, PREMIUM, PROMPT, (RANSOM), REDEEM, (REDEMPTION), (SAMPLE), VINTAGE. **2.** Latin *sūmere* (< **sus(e)m-*), to take, obtain, buy (*sus-,* variant of *sub-,* up from under, SUB-): SUMPTUARY, (SUMPTUOUS); ASSUME, CONSUME, PRESUME, RESUME, SUBSUME. **3.** Polish *j(e)m-,* to take, in compound *sejm,* assembly, "a taking together" (*se,* with; see **ksun-**): SEJM. [Pok. *em-* 310.]

en. In. **1.** Germanic **in* in: **a.** Old English *in,* in: IN; **b.** Germanic (comparative) **inn(e)ra* in Old English *innera,* farther in, inner: INNER; **c.** Germanic **innan* in Old English *innan,* in, within: BEN[1]. **2.** Latin *in,* in: EN-[1], IN-[2], MOUNTEBANK. **3.** Greek *en,* in: EN-[2], PARENCHYMA, PARENTHESIS. **4.** Suffixed form **en-t(e)ro-* in: **a.** Latin *intrō,* inward, within: INTRO-; **b.** Latin *intrā,* inside, within: ENTER, INTRA-. **5.** Suffixed form **en-ter* in Latin *inter,* between, among: ENTRAILS, INTER-, INTERIM, INTERIOR, INTERNAL. 6. Latin (superlative) _intimus_ (_*-mo-_, superlative suffix), innermost: INTIMATE[2]. 7. Suffixed form _*en-tos_ in: a. Latin _intus_, within, inside: INTESTINE, INTUSSUSCEPTION, DEDANS; b. Greek _entos_, within: ENTO-. 8. Suffixed form _*en-tero-_ in Greek _enteron_, entrails: (ENTERIC), ENTERO-, ENTERON; DYSENTERY, (MESENTERY). 9. Extended form _*ens_ in: a. Greek _eis_ (< _*ens_), into: EPISODE; b. suffixed form _*ens-ō-_ in Greek _esō_ (< _*ensō_), within: ESOTERIC. 10. Extended form _*endo-_ in Celtic _*endo-_, in (see **bher-**[1]). 11. Suffixed zero-grade form _*n̥-dha_ possibly in Germanic _*anda_, _*unda_ in Old English _and_, and: AND. [Pok. 1. _en_ 311.]

en-. Year. Extended form _*eno-_ in compound _*per-no-yo-_, of last year (see **per**[1]). [Pok. 2. _en-_ 314.]

engw-. Groin, internal organ. Suffixed zero-grade form _*n̥gw-en-_ in: a. Latin _inguen_, groin: INGUINAL; b. Greek _adēn_, gut: ADENO-, LYMPHADENITIS. Derivative root **neghwro-** _(see)_. [Pok. _engu-_ 319.]

enos-. Burden. Latin _onus_, burden: ONEROUS, ONUS; EXONERATE. [Pok. _enos-_ 321.]

epi. Also **opi**. Near, at, against. 1. Latin _ob_, before, to, against: OB-. 2. Greek _epi_, on, over, at: EPI-. 3. Greek _opisthen_, behind, at the back: OPISTHOGNATHOUS. 4. Old Church Slavonic _ob_, on: OBLAST. 5. Prefix _*op-_ in _*op-wer-yo_, to cover over (see **wer-**[5]). [Pok. _epi_ 323.]

er-[1]. To set in motion. I. 1. Probably Germanic _*ar-_, _*or-_, _*art(a)_, to be, exist, in Old English _eart_ and _aron_, second person singular and plural present of _bēon_, to be: (ARE[1], ART[2]) see the verb to BE. 2. Perhaps suffixed form _*er-meno-_ in Germanic _*ermana-_, _*irmino-_, large, whole (? < "moving fast," "powerful"), in Old High German _Ermin-_, "whole," "universal": EMMA. 3. Suffixed o-grade form _*or-nio-_ in Germanic _*arnja-_ in suffixed form _*arn(ja)-ost_ in: a. Old English _eornost_, ardor in battle, seriousness: EARNEST[1]; b. Old High German _ernust_, battle, vigor: ERNEST. 4. Suffixed o-grade form _*or-io-_ in Latin _orīrī_, to arise, appear, be born: ORIENT, ORIGIN, ABORT. II. Extended root _*rei-_, to flow, run. 1. Suffixed zero-grade form _*ri-nu-_ in: a. Germanic _*ri-nw-an_, to run, in Old English _rinnan_, to run, and Old Norse _rinna_, to run: RUN, RUNNEL; b. Germanic _*ri-nu-_ in (i) Old English _ryne_, a running: EMBER DAYS (ii) Old English _*rynet_, mass of coagulated milk: RENNET. 2. Suffixed zero-grade form _*ri-l-_ in Germanic _*ril-_ in Dutch _ril_ and Low German _rille_, running stream: RILL. 3. Suffixed form _*rei-wo-_ in Latin _rīvus_, stream: RIVAL, RIVULET; DERIVE. 4. Suffixed form _*rei-no-_ in Gaulish _Rēnos_, "river": RHINE. III. Extended root _*ergh-_, to go, in suffixed o-grade form _*orgh-eyo-_ in Greek _orkheisthai_, to dance: ORCHESTRA. [Pok. 3. _er-_ 326; _ergh-_ 339.]

er-[2]. Large bird. 1. Suffixed o-grade form _*or-n-_ in Germanic _*arnuz_, eagle, in: a. Old English _earn_, eagle: ERNE; b. Old High German _arn_, eagle: ARNOLD. 2. Suffixed o-grade form _*or-n-īth-_ in Greek _ornis_ (stem _ornith-_), bird: ORNITHO-, ICHTHYORNIS, NOTORNIS. [Pok. 1. _er-_ 325.]

er-[3]. Earth, ground. Extended form _*ert-_ in Germanic _*erthō_ in: a. Old English _eorthe_, earth: EARTH; b. Middle Dutch _aerde, eerde_, earth: AARDVARK, (AARDWOLF). [Pok. 4. _er-_ 332.]

er-[4]. Base of designations of various domestic horned animals. Extended form _*eri-_ in Latin _ariēs_, ram: ARIES. [Pok. 2. _er-_ 326.]

erə-[1]. To row. Lengthened zero-grade form _*rē-_ in: a. Germanic _*rō-_ in Old English _rōwan_, to row: ROW[2]; b. extended form _*rēt-_ in Germanic _*rōthra_, rudder, in _(i)_ Old English _rōther_, steering oar: RUDDER _(ii)_ Old Norse _rōthr_, act of rowing, also to row: RUSSIA; c. suffixed form _*rē-smo-_ in Latin _rēmus_, oar: REMEX, BIREME, TRIREME. [Pok. 1. _erə_ 338.]

erə-[2]. Also **re-**. To separate. 1. Suffixed variant form _*rā-ro-_ in Latin _rārus_, "having intervals between," "full of empty spaces," rare: RARE[1]. 2. Suffixed zero-grade form _*rə-ti-_ in Latin _ratis_, raft (< "grating," "latticework"): RATITE. 3. Suffixed lengthened-grade form _*rē-ti-_ in Latin _rēte, rētis_, a net: RÉSEAU, RETE, RETIARY, RETICLE, (RETICULE), RETIFORM, RETINA. 4. Suffixed lengthened-grade form _*rē-mo-_ in Greek _erēmos_, empty, desolate, bereft: (EREMITE), HERMIT. [Pok. 5. _er-_ 332.]

erəd-. High. Suffixed zero-grade form _*rəd-wo-_ in Latin _arduus_, high, steep: ARDUOUS. [Pok. _er(ə)d-_ 339.]

erkw-. To radiate, beam, praise. Sanskrit _ṛc_, _ṛk_, "brightness," praise, poem: RIG-VEDA. [Pok. _erku-_ 340.]

ers-[1]. To be in motion. 1. Variant form _*rēs-_ in Germanic _*rēs-_ in Old Norse _rās_, rushing: RACE[2]. 2. Form _ers-ā-_ in Latin _errāre_, to wander: ERR, ERRATIC, (ERRATUM), (ERRONEOUS), (ERROR); ABERRATION. [Pok. 2. _ere-s-_ 336.]

ers-[2]. To be wet. 1. Variant form _*ros-_ in Latin _rōs_, dew: ROSEMARY. 2. Suffixed variant form _*ros-ā_ in Avestan _Ra(ṅ)hā_, name of a mystical river: RHUBARB. 3. Extended root _ersen-_, male (< "that sprinkles or ejects semen"), in Old Persian _arshan-_, man: XERXES. [Pok. 2. _ere-s-_ 336.]

ers-[3]. Variant of **ors-**.

es-. To be. 1. Athematic first person singular form _*es-mi_ in Germanic _*izm(i)_ in Old English _eam_, am: AM. 2. Athematic third person singular form _*es-ti_ in: a. Germanic _*ist(i)_ in Old English _is_, is: IS; b. Sanskrit _asti_, is: SWASTIKA. 3. Optative stem _*sī-_ in Germanic _*sijai-_ in Old English _sīe_, may it be (so): YES. 4. Participial form _*sont-_, being, existing, hence real, true, in: a. Germanic _*santhaz_ in Old English _sōth_, true: SOOTH, (SOOTHE); b. suffixed (collective) zero-grade form _*sn̥t-iā_, "that which is," in Germanic _*sun(d)jō_, sin (< "it is true," "the sin is real"), in Old English _synn_, sin: SIN[1]; c. Sanskrit _sat, sant_, existing, true, virtuous: SUTTEE, BODHISATTVA, SATYAGRAHA. 5. Latin _esse_, to be: ENTITY, ESSENCE; ABSENT, (IMPROVE), INTEREST, PRESENT[1], (PRESENT[2]), PROUD, (QUINTESSENCE), (REPRESENT). 6. Greek _einai_, to be: ONTO-; BIONT, HETEROOUSIAN, HOMOIOUSIAN, SCHIZONT. Extended root **esu-** _(see)_. [Pok. _es-_ 340.]

esen-. Harvest, fall. O-grade form _*osn-_ in Germanic _*aznōn_, to do harvest work, serve, in Old English _earnian_, to serve, gain as wages: EARN[1]. [Pok. _es-en-_ 343.]

esu-. Good. Extended form of **es-**. Greek _eus_, good, well: EU-. [Pok. _esu-s_ 342.]

eti. Above, beyond. 1. Germanic _*ith-_ in Old Norse _idh_, back: EDDY. 2. Latin _et_, and (< "furthermore"): ET CETERA. [Pok. _eti_ 344.]

ētī-. Eider duck. A probable root. Germanic _*ēthī_ in North Germanic _*āthī_ in Old Norse _ǣdhr_, eider: EIDER. [Pok. _ētī-_ 345.]

ētmen-. Breath. Sanskrit _ātman_, breath, soul: ATMAN, MAHATMA. [Pok. _ēt-men-_ 345.]

eu-[1]. To dress. 1. Latin _induere_, to don (_ind-_, variant of _in-_, in, on, IN-): ENDUE. 2. Latin _exuere_, to doff (_ex-_, off, EX-): EXUVIAE. Extended root **wes-**[4] _(see)_. [Pok. 2. _eu-_ 346.]

eu-[2]. Lacking, empty. Extended forms _*euə-, wā-, wə-_. 1. Suffixed form _*wə-no-_ in: a. Germanic _*wanēn_ in Old English _wanian_, to lessen, and _wana_, lack: WANE; b. Germanic _wanaz_ in Old English _wan-_, lacking: WANTON; c. North Germanic _*wanatōn_ in Old Norse _vanta_, to lack: WANT. 2. Suffixed form _*wā-no-_ in Latin _vānus_, empty: VAIN, VANITY, VAUNT, EVANESCE, VANISH. 3. Extended form _*wak-_ in Latin _vacāre_, to be empty: (VACANT), VACATE, (VACATION), (VACUITY), VACUUM, EVACUATE. 4. Extended form _*wok-_ (by-form of _*wak-_) in Latin _vacāre_, to be empty: VOID, AVOID, DEVOID. 5. Extended and suffixed form _*wās-to-_ in Latin _vāstus_, empty: WASTE, DEVASTATE. [Pok. 1. _eu-_ 345.]

eudh-. Udder. 1. Suffixed zero-grade form _*ūdh-r̥_ in Germanic _*ūthr-_ in Old English _ūder_, udder: UDDER. 2. Suffixed o-grade form _*oudh-r̥_ in Latin _ūber_, "breast," with derivative adjective _ūber_, fertile: EXUBERATE, (EXUBERANT). [Pok. _ēudh-_ 347.]

euk-. To become accustomed. Zero-grade form _*uk-_ in: a. suffixed (feminine) form _*uk-sor-_ in Latin _uxor_, wife (< "she who gets accustomed to the new household" after patrilocal marriage): UXORIOUS, UXORICIDE; b. nasalized form _*u-n-k-_ in Old Irish _to-ucc_, to understand, "get accustomed to" (_to-_, to, from Celtic _*to-_): TWIG[2]. [Pok. _euk-_ 347.]

eus-. To burn. 1. Latin _ūrere_, to burn: UREDO, ADUST, BUST[1], COMBUST. 2. Latin _ustus_, burned, whence Latin _ūstulāre_, to burn slightly, possibly in Vulgar Latin compound _*brustulāre_, to burn (Germanic _*brun-_, to burn; see **bhreu-**): BROIL[1]. 3. Zero-grade form _*us-_ in: Germanic _*uzjōn-_, to burn, in compound _*aim-uzjōn-_, ashes (_*aim-_, ashes, ember), in Old English _ǣmerge_, ember: EMBER. 4. Greek _hevein_, to burn, singe: EURUS. [Pok. _eus-_ 347.]

[ferrum. Iron. Latin noun, possibly borrowed (via Etruscan) from the same obscure source as Old English _bræs_, brass. 1. Latin _ferrum_: FARRIER, FERRI-, FERRO-, FERROUS, FERRUGINOUS, FER-DE-LANCE. 2. Old English _bræs_: BRASS, (BRAZEN), (BRAZIER[1]).]

[Frankon-. Frank (member of a Germanic tribe), "javelin." Germanic root. 1. Frankish _*Frank-_, Frank, borrowed into Late Latin as _Francus_: FRANCE, (FRANCHISE), (FRANCIS), FRANK[2], (FRANK[1]), (FRANK[1]). 2. Derivative adjective _*frankiskaz_, of the Franks, in Old English _frencisc_, French: FRENCH.]

[gagina. Also **gagana**. Against. Germanic root. 1. Old English _gegn-_, against: GAINSAY. 2. Germanic _*an-gagina_ (_*an-_, toward, ON), in the opposite direction, in Old English _ongeagn, ongēan_, against, back, again: AGAIN, (AGAINST). 3. Old Norse _gegn_, against, also straight, direct: GAINLY, (UNGAINLY). 4. Old High German _gegin, gagan_, against: GEGENSCHEIN.]

gal-[1]. Bald, naked. 1. Suffixed form _*gal-wo-_ in Germanic _*kalwaz_ in Old English _calu_, bare, bald: CALLOW. 2. Russian _golyĭ_, bald, naked: GALYAK. [Pok. 1. _gal-_ 349.]

gal-[2]. To call, shout. 1. Germanic expressive form _*kall-_ in Old Norse _kalla_, to call: CALL. 2. Germanic _*klat-_ in Old English _*clatrian_, to clatter (_clatrung_, a clattering): CLATTER. 3. Expressive form _*gall-_ in Latin _gallus_, cock (< "the calling bird"; but probably also associated with _Gallus_, Gallic, as if to mean "the bird of Gaul," the cock being archaeologically attested as an important symbol in the iconography of Roman and pre-Roman Gaul): GALIMATIAS, GALLINACEOUS, (GALLINULE). 4. Intensive reduplicated form _*gal-gal-_ in Old Church Slavonic _glagolŭ_, word: GLAGOLITIC. [Pok. 2. _gal-_ 350.]

gal-[3]. To be able, to have power. Gallo-Roman _*galia_, strength, power: GALLIARD. [Pok. 3. _gal-_ 351.]

gar-. To call, cry. Expressive root. 1. Germanic _*karō_, lament, hence grief, care, in: a. Old English _cearu_, care: CARE; b. adjective _*karagaz_, sorrowful, in Old English _cearig_ sorrowful: CHARY. 2. Suffixed form _*gar-m-_ in Germanic _*karm-ja-_ in Old English _cirm, cierm_, clamor, cry: CHARM[2]. 3. Celtic suffixed form _*gar-(s)mn̥_ in Old Irish _gairm_, shout, cry, call: SLOGAN. 4. Suffixed form (with expressive gemination) _*garr-yo-_ in Latin _garrīre_, to chatter: GARRULOUS. [Pok. _gar-_ 352.]

[garwian. To make, prepare, equip. Germanic verb. 1. Old Norse _gera_, to make, do: GAR[2]. 2. Form _*garwi-_, equipment, adornment, in Italian _garbo_, grace, elegance of dress: GARB. 3. Form _*garwu-_, prepared, in Old English _earu, gearu, gearo_, ready: YARE. 4. Form _*garwīn-_ in Old Norse _gervi_, equipment, gear: GEAR.]

gāu-. To rejoice; also, to have religious fear or awe. 1. Suffixed form _*gau-d-ē-_ in Latin _gaudēre_, to rejoice: GAUD, (GAUDY[1]), GAUDY[2], JOY, ENJOY, REJOICE. 2. Form (with nasal infix) _*ga-n-u-_ in Greek _ganusthai_, to rejoice: GANOID. [Pok. _gāu-_ 353.]

[gē. Also **gaia**. The earth. Greek noun of unknown origin. GAEA, GEO-; APOGEE, EPIGEAL, GEANTICLINE, GEODE, (GEORGE), (GEORGIC), HYPOGEAL, NEOGAEA, NOTOGAEA, PERIGEE.]

gēi-[1]. To sprout, split open. 1. Reduced form _*gī-_ in: a. Germanic _*kī-nan_ in Old English _cine, cinu_, cleft, ravine cut by a stream: CHINK[1]; b. Germanic _*ki-dōn_ in Frankish _*kith_, sprout, young shoot, in Old French _cion_, shoot: SCION. 2. Possibly Germanic suffixed form _*kī-l-_ in Middle Dutch _kille_, stream: KILL[2]. [Pok. _gēi-_ 355.]

gēi-[2]. To sing. Sanskrit _gītā_, song: BHAGAVAD-GITA. [Pok. _gē(i)-_ 355.]

gel-[1]. To form into a ball; with derivatives referring to a compact mass or coagulated lump, and to the qualities of viscosity and adhesiveness. I. Words meaning a mass or lump. 1. Germanic _*klamp-_ in Middle Low German _klumpe_, compact group of trees: CLUMP. 2. Germanic _*klub(b)-_ in Old Norse _klubba_, a lump of wood, club: CLUB[1]. 3. Germanic _*kliw-_ in Old English _cliewan_, a ball, ball of wool: CLEW[1], (CLUE). 4. Germanic _*klūd-_ in: a. Old English _clūd_, hill, rock: CLOUD; b. Old English _clott_, lump: CLOD, CLOT, (CLUTTER); c. Middle High German _kloz_, block, lump: KLUTZ. 5. Germanic _*klūt-_ in: a. Old English _clūt_, patch (< "lump, piece of stuff, piece of cloth"): CLOUT; b. Icelandic _klunni_, clumsy person (< "lump"), akin to the Scandinavian source of English CLOWN. 6. Germanic _*klaut-_ in Old English _*clēat_, lump, wedge: CLEAT. 7. Extended form _*glob-_ perhaps in Latin _globus_, ball, globe: GLOBE, (GLOBULE), CONGLOBATE. 8. Extended form _*glom-_ in Latin _glomus_ (stem _glomer-_), ball: GLOMERATE, GLOMERULE, AGGLOMERATE, CONGLOMERATE. 9. Extended form _*glēb-_ in Latin _glēba_, lump, clod of earth, soil, land: GLEBE.

10. Extended form *gleu- in Greek *gloutos*, buttock: GLUTEUS. 11. Reduplicated form *gal-gl- dissimilated in Greek *ganglion*, cystlike tumor, hence nerve-bundle: GANGLION. II. Words meaning to stick, cling. 1. Germanic *klupjan (< *gleb-) in Old English *clyppan*, to embrace, fasten: CLASP, CLIP[2]. 2. Germanic *klimban (< *gle-m-b-), to hold fast, hold on in climbing, in: a. Old English *climban*, to climb: CLIMB; b. Old Norse *klembra*, to grip, climb: CLAMBER. 3. Germanic *klam- in: a. Old English *clamm*, bond, fetter: CLAM[3], (CLAM[1]); b. Old English *clǣman*, to stick: CLAMMY; c. Middle Low German *klam*, stickiness: CLAM[2]. 4. Germanic *klamp- in Middle Dutch *klampe*, metal clasp: CLAMP. 5. Germanic *kleb- (< *glebh-) in: a. Old English *cleofian*, to stick, cleave: CLEAVE[2]; b. Old English *clīfe*, goosegrass (a plant with hooked prickles on the stem): CLEAVERS. 6. Germanic *kling- in: a. Old English *clingan*, to cling: CLING; b. Old English *beclencan*, to hold fast (*be-*, BE-): CLENCH, (CLINCH). 7. Germanic *kluk- in Old English *clyccan*, to clutch: CLUTCH[1]. 8. Germanic *klaw- in Old English *clawu*, a claw: CLAW. III. Words meaning "sticky material." 1. Extended form *glei- in: a. Germanic *klaijō-, clay, in Old English *clǣg*, clay: CLAY; b. probably Medieval Greek *glia*, *gloia*, glue: GLIADIN, NEUROGLIA, ZOOGLOEA; c. Russian *gleĭ*, clay: GLEY. 2. Germanic *kleg- in Danish *klagge*, mud, akin to the Scandinavian source of Middle English *claggen*, to daub with mud: CLAG. 3. Extended form *gleu- in Latin *glūten*, glue: GLUE, GLUTEN, GLUTINOUS; AGGLUTINATE, CONGLUTINATE, DEGLUTINATE. 4. Extended form *glit- possibly in Latin *glittus*, sticky: GLEET. [Pok. 1. *gel-* 357.]

gel-[2]. Bright. 1. Extended form *glei- in Germanic *klai-ni-, bright, pure, in: a. Old English *clǣne*, pure, clean: CLEAN; b. Old English *clǣnsian*, to purify, cleanse: CLEANSE. 2. Suffixed form *gel-o- in Old Irish *gel*, bright: MURIEL. 3. Extended and suffixed zero-grade form *glə-nā in Greek *glēnē*, eyeball: EUGLENA. [Pok. *gel-* 366.]

gel-[3]. Cold; to freeze. 1. Germanic *kaliz, coldness, in Old English *ciele*, chill: CHILL. 2. Germanic *kaldaz, cold, in Old English *ceald*, cold: COLD. 3. Germanic *kōl-, cool, in: a. Old English *cōl*, cold, cool: COOL; b. Germanic *koljan, to cool, in Old English *cēlan*, to cool: KEEL[3]. 4. Suffixed form *gel-ā- in Latin *gelāre*, to freeze: CONGEAL, GALANTINE, GELATIN, GELATION, JELLY. 5. Suffixed form *gel-u- in Latin *gelu*, frost, cold: GELID. 6. Probably suffixed zero-grade form *gḷ-k- in Latin *glaciēs*, ice: GLACÉ, GLACIAL, GLACIATE, GLACIER, GLACIS, GLANCE[1]. [Pok. 3. *gel(ə)-* 365.]

geli-. Also **gel-**. Small animal, especially the dormouse. Variant form *gal- in Greek *galeē*, weasel, marten: GALEA. [Pok. *geli-* 367.]

gembh-. Tooth, nail. I. Suffixed o-grade form *gombh-o-. 1. Germanic *kambaz, comb, in: a. Old English *camb*, comb: COMB, KAME; b. Old High German *kamb*, comb: CAM; c. Germanic denominative *kambjan, to comb, in Old English *cemban*, to comb: OAKUM, UNKEMPT. 2. Greek *gomphos*, tooth, peg, bolt: GOMPHOSIS. II. Perhaps Germanic *kimb- in Old English *cim-*, *cimb-*, rim (only in compounds): CHIME[2]. III. Possibly suffixed form *gembh-mā in Latin *gemma*, bud, hence gem: GEM, GEMMA, GEMMATE, GEMMULE. [Pok. *gembh-* 369.]

gemə-. To marry. Suffixed zero-grade form *gṃə-o- in Greek *gamos*, marriage: GAMETE, GAMO-, -GAMOUS, -GAMY, GAMOSEPALOUS. [Pok. *gem(e)-* 369.]

gen-. To compress into a ball. Hypothetical Indo-European base of a range of Germanic words referring to compact, knobby bodies and projections, sharp blows, etc. 1. Germanic *kn-a-pp- in: a. Old English *cnæpp*, hilltop: KNAP[2]; b. Middle Dutch *cnoppen*, to snap, and Low German *knappen*, to snap, hence "to have a bite" (akin to Middle English *knappen*, to strike sharply, snap): KNAP[1], KNAPSACK; c. Middle Dutch and Low German *knoppe*, knot in wood, knob: KNOP. 2. Germanic *kn-a-k- in: a. Low German *knak*, sharp blow: KNACK; b. Middle High German *knacken*, to crack: KNACKWURST. 3. Germanic *kn-a-r- in: a. Norwegian *knart*, knot in wood, akin to the source of Middle English *knarre*, knob: KNAR; b. Middle High German *knorre*, knob, akin to Middle English *knurre*, knob: KNUR. 4. Germanic *kn-u-b- in Middle Low German *knobbe*, knot in wood, knob: KNOB, (NUB). 5. Germanic *kn-u-d- in Old High German *knodo*, *knoto*, knob, knot: QUENELLE. 6. Germanic *kn-u-k- in: a. Old English *cnocian*, to knock: KNOCK; b. Italian *gnocco*, *nocchio*, knot in wood: GNOCCHI; c. Middle Low German *knōkel*, knuckle: KNUCKLE. 7. Germanic *kn-u-l- in: a. Old English *cnyllan*, to strike: KNELL, (KNOLL[2]); b. Old English *cnoll*, a knoll: KNOLL[1]. 8. Germanic *kn-u-p- in Middle Dutch *cnoppe*, knob, bud: KNOBKERRIE. 9. Germanic *kn-u-t- in: a. Old English *cnytten*, to tie in a knot, knit: KNIT; b. Old English *cnotta*, knot in cord: KNOT[1]; c. Old Norse *knūtr*, knot in cord: KNOUT. 10. Germanic *kn-ī-b- in Old English *cnīf*, knife: KNIFE. 11. Germanic *kn-e-th- in Old English *cnedan*, to knead: KNEAD. [Pok. *gen-* 370.]

genə-. Also **gen-**. To give birth, beget; with derivatives referring to aspects and results of procreation and to familial and tribal groups. 1. Suffixed zero-grade form *gṇ-yo- in Germanic *kunjam, family, race, in: a. Old English *cyn(n)*, race, family, kin: KIN; b. *kuningaz, king (< "son of the royal kin"), in Old English *cyning*, king: KING. 2. Suffixed zero-grade form *gṇ-ti- in: a. Germanic *kundjaz, family, race, in Old English *cynd*, *gecynd(e)*, origin, birth, race, family, kind: KIND[1], (KINDRED); b. Germanic *kundiz, natural, native, in Old English *gecynde* (*ge-*, collective prefix; see **kom**), natural, native, fitting: KIND[2]; c. Germanic variant *kinth- in Old High German *kind*, child: KINDERGARTEN, KRISS KRINGLE; d. Latin *gēns* (stem *gent-*), race, clan: GENS, (GENTILE), GENTLE, (GENTEEL); GENDARME. 3. Suffixed full-grade form *gen-es- in: a. Latin *genus* (stem *gener-*), race, kind: GENDER, GENERAL, GENERATE, (GENERATION), GENERIC, GENEROUS, GENRE, GENUS; CONGENER, (CONGENIAL), DEGENERATE, (ENGENDER), MISCEGENATION; b. Greek *genos* and *genea*, race, family: GENEALOGY, GENOCIDE, GENOTYPE, HETEROGENEOUS; c. Greek suffix *-genēs*, "-born": -GEN, -GENY. 4. Suffixed full-grade form *gen-yo- in: a. Latin *genius*, procreative divinity, inborn tutelary spirit, innate quality: GENIUS, GENIAL[1]; b. Latin *ingenium* (*in-*, IN-), inborn character: INGENIOUS, ENGINE. 5. Suffixed full-grade form *gen-ā- in Latin *indigena* (*indu-*, variant of *in-*, IN-), born in (a place), indigenous: INDIGEN, (INDIGENOUS). 6. Suffixed full-grade form *gen-wo- in Latin *ingenuus* (*in-*, IN-), born in (a place), native, natural, freeborn: INGENUOUS. 7. Suffixed full-grade form *gen-men- dissimilated in Latin *germen*, shoot, bud, embryo, germ: GERM, GERMAN[2], (GERMANE), (GERMINAL), (GERMINATE). 8. Suffixed full-grade form *genə-ti- in Greek *genesis*, birth, beginning: GENESIS, -GENESIS. 9. Reduplicated form *gi-gn- in: a. Latin *gignere* (past participle *genitus*), to beget: GENITAL, GENITIVE, GENITOR, GENT[1], GINGERLY; CONGENITAL, PRIMOGENITURE, PROGENITOR, (PROGENY); b. Greek *gignesthai*, to be born: EPIGENE. 10. Suffixed zero-grade form *-gn-o- in Latin *benignus* (*bene*, well; see **deu-[2]**), good-natured, kindly, and *malignus* (*male*, ill; see **mel-[5]**), evil-natured, malevolent: BENIGN, MALIGN. 11. Extended form *gnā- in Latin *praegnās* (*prae-*, before, PRE-), pregnant: PREGNANT[1]. 12. Suffixed zero-grade form *gṇə-sko- becoming *gnā-sko- in Latin *gnāscī*, *nāscī* (past participle *gnātus*, *nātus*), to be born: NAIVE, NASCENT, NATAL, NATION, NATIVE, NATURE, NÉE, NOËL; AGNATE, (ADNATE), COGNATE, CONNATE, ENATE, INNATE, NEONATE, PUNY, (PUISNE), RENAISSANCE. 13. Suffixed o-grade form *gon-o- in Greek *gonos* (combining form *-gonos*), child, procreation, seed: GONAD, (-GONIUM), GONO-; ARCHEGONIUM, EPIGONE. 14. Full-grade form *gen- in: a. Persian *zādan*, to be born: MIRZA; b. Persian *zāta-*, born, in *āzād-*, free: AZEDARACH. 15. Zero-grade form *gṇ- in Sanskrit *ja-* in *kṛmi-ja-*, "produced by worms" (see **kwṛmi-**). [Pok. 1. *gen-* 373.]

genu-[1]. Knee; also angle. 1. Variant form *gneu- in: a. Germanic *kniwam in Old English *cnēo*, knee: KNEE; b. Germanic *kniwljan in Old English *cnēowlian*, to kneel: KNEEL. 2. Basic form *genu- in Latin *genū*, knee: GENICULATE, GENUFLECT, GENUINE. 3. Suffixed variant form *gōn-ya- in Greek *gōnia*, angle, corner: -GON, GONION, AMBLYGONITE, GONIOMETER, GONIOMETRY, DIAGONAL, ORTHOGONAL. [Pok. 1. *genu-* 380.]

genu-[2]. Jawbone, chin. 1. Form *genw- in Germanic *kinnuz in Old English *cinn*, chin: CHIN. 2. Basic form *genu- in Greek *genus*, chin: GENIAL[2]. 3. Suffixed variant form *gnə-dho- in Greek *gnathos*, jaw: GNATHIC, -GNATHOUS, CHAETOGNATH. 4. Variant form *g(h)enu- in Sanskrit *hanu*, jaw: HANUMAN. [Pok. 2. *genu-* 381.]

geph-. Jaw, mouth. 1. Probably Germanic *kaf-, to gnaw, chew, in Old English *ceaf*, husks, chaff: CHAFF[1]. 2. Germanic *kabraz, "gnawer," in Old English *ceafor*, beetle: CHAFER, (COCKCHAFER). 3. Germanic *kabal- in Old English *ceafl*, jaw, cheek: JOLE, JOWL[2], SHIVER[1]. [Pok. *geph-* 382.]

ger-[1]. To gather. 1. Extended form *grem- in Germanic *kram- in Old English *crammian*, to stuff, cram: CRAM. 2. Reduplicated form *gre-g- in Latin *grex* (stem *greg-*), herd, flock: AGGREGATE, CONGREGATE, EGREGIOUS, GREGARIOUS, SEGREGATE. 3. Prefixed forms *(a)ger-, *(a)gor-ā, in Greek *ageirein*, to assemble, and *agora*, marketplace: AGORA[1], (AGORAPHOBIA), ALLEGORY, CATEGORY, PANEGYRIC, PAREGORIC. [Pok. 1. *ger-* 382.]

ger-[2]. To grow old. 1. Greek *gēras*, old age: AGERATUM, CALOYER, GERIATRICS. 2. Suffixed form *ger-ont- in: a. Greek *gerōn* (stem *geront-*), old man: GERONTO-; b. Avestan *zara(n)t-*, old: ZOROASTER. [Pok. *ger-* 390.]

ger-[3]. Curving, crooked; hypothetical Indo-European base for a variety of Germanic words with initial *kr-*. I. Words meaning to bend, curl; bent, crooked, hooked; something bent or hooked. 1. Germanic *krappon, a hook, especially one used in harvesting grapes, in: a. Old High German *krāpfo*, a hook: AGRAFFE; b. Old French *graper*, to harvest grapes, hence (back-formation) *grape*, vine, grape: GRAPE; c. Old French *grapon*, grapnel: GRAPNEL; d. Old Provençal *grapa*, a hook: GRAPPLE; e. Italian dialectal *grappa*, vine stem: GRAPPA. 2. Old English *crump*, *crumb*, crooked, bent, stooping: CRUMMIE, CRUMPET, (CRUMPLE). 3. Old English *gecrympan*, to curl: CRIMP[1]. 4. Middle Dutch *crampe*, hook, and Frankish *kramp, hook: CRAMP[2], CRAMPON. 5. Old High German *krampfo*, a cramp (< "a doubling over with pain"): CRAMP[1]. 6. Old English *crypel*, a cripple: CRIPPLE. 7. Old English *crēopan*, to creep: CREEP. 8. Middle Low German *krink*, a ring: CRINGLE. 9. Old English *cringan*, to yield: CRINGE. 10. Middle Dutch *crinkelen*, akin to Middle English *crynkelen*, to make kinks in: CRINKLE. 11. Old Norse *kriki*, a bend, nook: CREEK. 12. Old Norse *krōkr*, a hook: CROOK. 13. Frankish *krōk, a hook: CROCHET, (CROQUET), (CROUCH), ENCROACH. 14. Old English *crycc*, (bent) staff, crutch: CRUTCH. 15. Old French *crosse*, crook: LACROSSE, CROSIER. 16. Middle Dutch *crulle*, curly: CURL, CRULLER. 17. Old English *cranc-(stæf)*, a weaving implement: CRANK[1]. 18. Norwegian *krake*, a sickly beast, akin to the source of Middle English *crok*, an old ewe: CROCK[3]. 19. Old Norse *karpa*, to boast: CARP[1]. 20. Middle Dutch *kroes*, curled: GROSSULARITE. II. Words meaning "a rounded mass, a collection, a round object, a vessel, a container." 1. Old English *cruma*, a fragment: CRUMB. 2. Frankish *kruppa, rump: CROUP[2], (CROUPIER), (CRUPPER). 3. Old English *cropp*, cluster, bunch, ear of corn: CROP. 4. Italian *gruppo*, an assemblage: GROUP. 5. Old English *crocc*, pot: CROCK[1]. 6. Middle Dutch *cruyse*, pot: CRUSE. 7. Old English *cribb*, manger: CRIB. 8. Old English *cradel*, cradle: CRADLE. 9. Frankish *kripja, cradle: CRÈCHE. 10. Old English *cræt* and Old Norse *kartr*, wagon: CART. 11. Old English *croft*, small enclosed field: CROFT. [Pok. 3. *ger-* 385.]

ger-[4]. To cry hoarsely; also the name of the crane. I. 1. Germanic *krē- in: a. Old English *crāwe*, a crow: CROW[1]; b. Old English *crāwan*, to crow: CROW[2]; c. Old English *cracian*, to resound: CRACK; d. Middle Dutch *krāken*, to crack: CRACKNEL; e. Old Norse *krāka*, a crow: CRAKE. 2. Germanic *krō- in Middle Dutch *krōnen*, to groan, lament: CROON. 3. Germanic *kur- in Old Norse *kurra*, to growl: CUR. II. 1. Germanic *kranu-, crane, in: a. Old English *cran*, crane: CRANE; b. Middle Low German *kran*, crane: CRANBERRY. 2. Extended form *gru- in Latin *grūs*, crane: GROMWELL, GRUS, PEDIGREE. 3. Suffixed variant form *grā-k- in Latin *grāculus*, jackdaw: GRACKLE. 4. Suffixed extended form *gerə-no- in Greek *geranos*, crane: GERANIUM. [Pok. 2. *ger-* 383.]

ger-[5]. To awaken. Greek *egeirein*, to wake, in *grēgoros*, watchful: GREGORY. [Pok. 4. *ger-* 390.]

gerebh-. To scratch. 1. Variant form *grebh- in: a. Germanic *krab(b)- in Old English *crabba*, a crab: CRAB[1]; b. Germanic *krabiz- in Frankish *krabitja, crayfish: CRAYFISH; c. Germanic *kerban in Old English *ceorfan*, to cut: CARVE; d. Germanic *kurbi- in Old English *cyrf*, a cutting (off): KERF; e. perhaps Germanic *krab- in Old Norse *krafla*, to crawl: CRAWL[1]. 2. Zero-grade form *gṛbh-* in Greek *graphein*, to scratch, draw, write, and *gramma* (< *gṛbh-mṇ), a picture, written letter, piece of writing, and *grammē*, a line: GRAFFITO, GRAM[1], -GRAM[1], GRAMMAR, GRAPH, -GRAPH, -GRAPHER, GRAPHIC, GRAPHITE, -GRAPHY; AGRAPHA, AGRAPHIA, DIAGRAM, EPIGRAM, (EPIGRAPH), ICONOGRAPHY, PARAGRAPH, PROGRAM, PSEUDEPIGRAPHA, TETRAGRAMMATON, TOPOGRAPHY. [Pok. *gerebh-* 392.]

[gerere. To carry, carry on, act, do. Latin verb of unknown origin. Oldest form *ges-*, past participle *gestus*. GERENT, GERUND, GEST[1], (GEST[2]), GESTATION, (GESTICULATE), GESTURE, JEST; ARMIGER, BELLIGERENT, (CONGERIES), CONGEST, DIGEST, EGEST, INGEST, REGISTER, SUGGEST.**]**

geu-. To hasten. Possibly Germanic **kaurjan* in Old Norse *keyra*, to drive: SKIJORING. [Pok. *geu-* 399.]

gēu-. To bend. Proposed by some as the root of Greek *guros*, ring (which is more likely of unknown origin): GYRE, GYRO-; AUTOGIRO. [Pok. *gēu-* 393.]

geulo-. A glowing coal. Germanic **kolam* in: **a.** Old English *col*, a glowing coal: COAL, (COLLIE), (COLLIER), CULM[2]; **b.** probably dialectal Old French *cholle*, round lump, head: CHOLLA. [Pok. *g(e)u-lo-* 399.]

geus-. To taste, choose. **1.** Germanic **kiusan* in: **a.** Old English *cēosan, ceōsan*, to choose: CHOOSE. **b.** Gothic **kausjan*, to choose: CHOICE. **2.** Germanic **kuz-*, with variant **kur-* in Old Norse *Valkyrja*, "chooser of the slain," Valkyrie (*valr*, the slain; see **wel-**[4]). **3.** Suffixed zero-grade form **gus-tu-* in: **a.** Latin *gustus*, taste: (GUST[2]), GUSTO, DISGUST, RAGOUT; **b.** Latin *gustāre*, to taste: DEGUST. [Pok. *geus-* 399.]

ghabh-. Also **ghebh-.** To give or receive. **1.** Form **ghebh-* in Germanic **giban* in: **a.** Old English *giefan*, to give: GIVE; **b.** compound **fer-giban* (**for-*, away; see **per**[1]), to give away, in Old English *forgiefan*, to give, give up, leave off (anger), remit, forgive: FORGIVE. **2.** Suffixed form **ghebh-ti-*, something given (or received), in Germanic **giftiz* in Old Norse *gipt*, a gift: GIFT. **3.** O-grade form **ghobh-* in Germanic **gab-*, something paid (or received), in Old English *gafol*, tribute, tax, debt: GAVEL[2]. **4.** Form **ghabh-ē-* in: **a.** Latin *habēre*, to hold, possess, have, handle: ABLE, BINNACLE, HABILE, HABIT, HABITABLE, (HABITANT), (HABITAT); AVOIRDUPOIS, (BEHAVE), (COHABIT), EXHIBIT, HABEAS CORPUS, INHABIT, INHIBIT, MALADY, PREBEND, PROHIBIT, PROVENDER; **b.** Latin *dēbēre* (*dē-*, away from, DE-), to owe (< "to withhold"): DEBENTURE, (DEBIT), DEBT, DEVOIR, DUE, (DUTY), (ENDEAVOR). Compare root **kap-.** [Pok. *ghebh-* 407.]

ghabholo-. A fork, branch of a tree. Celtic **gablakko-* probably in Old French *javelot*, a throwing spear: JAVELIN. [Pok. *ghabolo-* 409.]

ghaido-. A goat. Germanic **gaitaz* in Old English *gāt*, goat: GOAT. [Pok. *ghaido-* 409.]

ghais-. To adhere, hesitate. Form **ghais-ē-* in Latin *haerēre*, to stick, cling: ADHERE, COHERE, INHERE, HESITATE. [Pok. *ghais-* 410.]

ghaiso-. A stick, spear. **1.** Germanic **gaizaz* in: **a.** Old English *gār*, spear: EDGAR, GORE[1], GARFISH, GARLIC; **b.** Compound **nabō-gaizaz*, tool for piercing wheel hubs (**nabō*, hub; see **nobh-**); **c.** Old High German *gēr* (older form **gairu*), spear, and compound name *Gērdrūd* (*drūd*, strength; see **treu-**): GERALD, GERARD, GERTRUDE, ROGER; **d.** Old Norse *geirr*, spear (in *geirfalki*, gyrfalcon): GYRFALCON. **2.** Germanic **gaizō* in: **a.** Old English *gāra*, corner, point of land: GORE[2]. [Pok. *ghaiso-* 410.]

ghait-. Curly or wavy hair. Possible root. Suffixed form **ghait-ā* in Greek *khaitē*, long hair: CHAETA, (CHAETOGNATH). [Pok. *ghait-ā-* 410.]

ghalgh-. Branch, rod. Germanic **galgōn-* in: **a.** Old English *gealga*, cross, gallows: GALLOWS; **b.** Frankish **galga*, cross, perch, windlass: GAUGE. [Pok. *ghalgh-* 411.]

ghans-. Goose. **1.** Germanic **gans-* in: **a.** Old English *gōs*, goose: GOOSE[1], (GOSHAWK); **b.** Old Norse *gās*, goose: SMORGASBORD; **c.** Old Norse diminutive *gæslingr* (*-lingr*, from Common Germanic **-linga*, -LING[1]), gosling: GOSLING. **2.** Germanic **ganr-* in Old English *ganra, gandra*, gander: GANDER. **3.** Germanic **ganōtōn* in Old English *ganot*, gannet: GANNET. **4.** Suffixed form **ghans-er-* in Latin *ānser* (< **hanser*), goose: ANSERINE, MERGANSER. **5.** Basic form **ghans-* in Greek *khēn*, goose: CHENOPOD. [Pok. *ghans-* 412.]

ghasto-. Rod, staff. **1.** Variant form **ghazdh-* in Germanic **gazdaz* in: **a.** Old English *gierd, gerd*, staff, twig, measuring rod: YARD[1]; **b.** Old Norse *gaddr*, rod, goad, spike: GAD[2]. **2.** Form **ghast-ā* in Latin *hasta*, spear: HASTATE, HASLET. [Pok. 1. *ghasto-* 412.]

ghe-. Demonstrative particle. Variant form **ghi-* in **ghi-ke*, this (see **ko-**). [Pok. *ghe-* 417.]

ghē-. To release, let go; (in the middle voice) to be released, go. **1.** Suffixed form **ghē-no-* in Germanic **gēn* in Old English *gān*, to go: GO, AGO, FOREGO. **2.** Suffixed form **ghē-ro-* in Latin *hērēs*, heir (? < "orphan" < "bereft"): HEIR, HEREDITAMENT, HEREDITY, HERES, HERITAGE, INHERIT. **3.** Suffixed o-grade form **ghō-ro-*, "empty space," in Greek *khōros*, place, country, particular spot: ANACHORISM, CHOROGRAPHY. **4.** Suffixed o-grade form **ghōr-eye-* in Greek *khōrein*, to move, go, spread about, make room for: ANCHORITE, -CHORE. **5.** Suffixed o-grade form **ghōr-ā* in Greek *khōra*, country, place: ENCHORIAL. **6.** Perhaps suffixed zero-grade form **ghə-l-* in Greek *khalan*, to slacken, let down: CALANDO, CHALONE. **7.** Suffixed zero-grade form **ghə-t(w)ā-* in Germanic **gatwōn*, a going, in Old Norse *gata*, path, street: GAIT. [Pok. *ghē-* 418.]

ghebhel-. Head. **1.** Germanic **gabl-*, top of a pitched roof, in Old Norse *gafl*, gable: GABLE. **2.** Dissimilated form **khephel-* in Greek *kephalē*, head: CEPHALIC, CEPHALO-, -CEPHALOUS, ENCEPHALO-, HYDROCEPHALUS. [Pok. *ghebh-el-* 423.]

ghedh-. To unite, join, fit. **1.** Lengthened o-grade form **ghōdh-* in Germanic **gōdaz*, "fitting, suitable," in Old English *gōd*, good: GOOD. **2.** Germanic **gaduri*, "in a body," in Old English *tōgædere* (*tō*, TO), together: TOGETHER. **3.** Germanic **gadurōn*, "to come or bring together," in: **a.** Old English *gad(e)rian*, to gather: GATHER; **b.** Middle Dutch *gaderen*, to gather: (FORGATHER), GARBOARD. **4.** Germanic **gad-* in Old English *gædeling*, companion, comrade: GAD[1]. [Pok. *ghedh-* 423.]

ghei-[1]**.** To propel, prick. **1.** Suffixed and extended o-grade form **ghoidh-ā* in Germanic **gaidō*, goad, spear, in Old English *gād*, goad: GOAD. **2.** Suffixed form **ghei-s-* perhaps in nasalized zero-grade form **ghi-n-s-* in Sanskrit *hiṁsati*, he injures: AHIMSA. (**3.** Old English *gār*, spear, which in the case of its derivative OSCAR has accidentally been referred to this root, belongs to **ghaiso-**, which itself perhaps has some connection with **ghei-**[1].) [Pok. 1. *ghei-* 424.]

ghei-[2]**.** Theoretical base of **ghiem-*, **ghyem-*, winter. **1.** Form **ghyem-* in Latin *hiems*, winter: HIEMAL. **2.** Suffixed zero-grade form **ghim-ri-no-* in Latin *hībernus*, pertaining to winter: HIBERNACULUM, HIBERNATE. **3.** Suffixed zero-grade form **ghim-ar-ya*, "female animal one year (winter) old," in Greek *khimaira*, she-goat: CHIMERA. [Pok. 2. *ghei-* 425.]

ghēi-. To yawn, gape. **1.** Variant form **ghyā-* in: **a.** nasalized form **ghi-n-ā-* in Germanic **ginōn* in Old English *ginan, ginian, geonian*, to yawn: YAWN; **b.** Latin *hiāre*, to gape, be open: HIATUS, DEHISCE. **2.** Suffixed variant form **ghə-smn̥* in Greek *khasma*, yawning gulf, chasm: CHASM. **3.** Suffixed variant form **ghə-n-* in Greek *khainein*, to gape: ACHENE. **4.** Labial extensions: **a.** Old Norse *gap*, chasm: GAP; **b.** Old Norse *gapa*, to open the mouth: GAPE; **c.** Old Norse *geispa*, to yawn: GASP. **5.** Germanic **gil-* in Old Norse *gil*, ravine, chasm: GILL[3]. **6.** Germanic **gīr-*, vulture (< "voracious or yawning bird"), in Old High German *gīr*, vulture: LAMMERGEIER. [Pok. 2. *ghē-* 419.]

gheis-. Used of the emotion of fear or amazement (original part of speech uncertain). Suffixed o-grade form **ghois-dho-* in Germanic **gaistaz*, a ghost, in: **a.** Old English *gāst*, ghost: GHOST, AGHAST, BARGHEST, GHASTLY; **b.** Old High German *geist*, ghost: POLTERGEIST; **c.** Old English denominative *gæstan*, to scare: GAST. [Pok. *gheis-* 427.]

ghel-[1]**.** To call. **1.** Germanic **gel-*, **gal-*, in: **a.** Old English *gellan, giellan*, to sound, shout: YELL; **b.** Old English *gielpan*, to boast, exult: YELP; **c.** Old English *galan*, to sing: NIGHTINGALE; **d.** Old Norse *gala*, to sing: GALE[1]. **2.** Reduplicated form **ghi-ghl-* in Greek *kikhlē*, thrush, later also the name for a kind of wrasse (a sea fish that has bright colors and jagged waving fins, reminiscent of the plumage of a bird): CICHLID. **3.** Greek **khelidwōn, khelidōn*, the swallow: CELANDINE. [Pok. *ghel-* 428.]

ghel-[2]**.** To shine; with derivatives referring to colors, to bright materials, probably "yellow metal," and to the bile or gall. **I. 1.** Suffixed form **ghel-wo-* in Germanic **gelwaz* in Old English *gealu*, yellow: YELLOW. **2.** Suffixed zero-grade form **ghl̥-wo-* in Germanic **gulwaz*, in Old Norse *gulr*, yellow: GULL[2]. **3.** Suffixed variant form **ghlō-ro-* in Greek *khlōros*, greenish yellow: CHLORO-, CHLORITE[1]. **4.** Suffixed variant form **gla-dh-ro-* in Latin *glaber*, bald: GABBRO, GLABROUS, (GLABELLA). **II. 1.** Suffixed zero-grade form **ghl̥-to-* in Germanic **gulthum*, gold, in: **a.** Old English *gold*, gold: GOLD; **b.** denominative verb **gulthjan* in Old English *gyldan*, to gild: GILD[1]; **c.** Middle Dutch *gulden*, golden: GULDEN, GUILDER; **d.** Old Norse *gulinn*, golden, akin to the possible source of Middle English *gollan*, yellow flower: GOWAN. **2.** Suffixed o-grade form **ghol-to-* in Polish *zlyoto*, gold: ZLOTY. **3.** Suffixed full-grade form **ghel-i-* in: **a.** Persian *zar*, gold: ZIRCON, JARGON[2]; **b.** the unknown Iranian source of Syriac *zarnīkā*, orpiment: ARSENIC. **4.** Suffixed form **ghel-i-* in Sanskrit *hari*, yellow: HARTAL. **III. 1.** Suffixed o-grade form **ghol-no-* in Germanic **gallōn*, bile, in Old English *gealla*, gall: GALL[1]. **2.** Suffixed o-grade form **ghol-ā* in Greek *kholē*, bile: CHOLER, (CHOLERA), CHOLE-, MELANCHOLY. **3.** Suffixed full-grade form **ghel-n-* in Latin *fel*, bile: FELON[2]. **IV.** O-grade form **ghol-* in Russian *zola*, ashes: PODZOL. **V.** A range of Germanic words (where no pre-forms are given, the words are late creations). **1.** Germanic **glaimiz* in Old English *glǣm*, bright light, gleam: GLEAM. **2.** Middle High German *glimsen*, to gleam, akin to the source of Middle English *glymsen*, to glimpse: GLIMPSE. **3.** Swedish dialectal *glinta*, to shine, akin to the source of Middle English *glinten*, to shine: GLINT. **4.** Swedish *glimra*, akin to the source of Middle English *glimeren*, to glimmer: GLIMMER. **5.** Old Norse *glitra*, to shine: GLITTER. **6.** Old English *glisnian*, to shine: GLISTEN. **7.** Middle Dutch *glisteren*, to shine: GLISTER. **8.** Germanic **glasam*, glass, in Old English *glæs*, glass: GLASS, GLAZE. **9.** Germanic **glaz-* in Middle Low German *glaren*, to glisten: GLARE[1]. **10.** Icelandic *glossi*, a spark, akin to the source of GLOSS[1]. **11.** Old High German *glanz*, bright: GLANCE[2]. **12.** Old Norse *glōggr*, clear-sighted: GLEG. **13.** Germanic **gladaz* in Old English *glæd*, shining, joyful: GLAD. **14.** Germanic **gliujam* in Old English *glēo*, sport, merriment: GLEE. **15.** Old English *glēd*, ember: GLEED. **16.** Germanic **glō-* in: **a.** Old English *glōwan*, to glow: GLOW; **b.** Norwegian dialectal *glora*, to gleam, stare, akin to the source of GLOWER; **c.** Old Norse *glotta*, to smile (scornfully), akin to the source of GLOAT. **17.** Germanic **glō-m-* in Old English *glōm*, twilight: GLOAMING. **18.** Germanic **glid-*, slippery (< "shining, smooth"), in: **a.** Old English *glīdan*, to slip, glide: GLIDE; **b.** Frankish **glīdan*, to glide: GLISSADE; **c.** Old English *glida*, kite (< "gliding, hovering bird"): GLEDE; **d.** Middle Low German *glibberich*, slippery: GLIB. [Pok. 1. *ĝhel-* 429.]

ghel-[3]**.** To cut. **1.** Germanic **galdjan*, to castrate, in Old Norse *gelda*, to castrate, and *geldingr*, a castrated animal: GELD[1], (GELDING). **2.** Germanic **gulti-* in Old Norse *gyltr*, a sow (< "castrated pig"): GILT[2]. [Pok. 2. *ĝhel-* 434.]

ghelegh-. A metal. Possible root of Greek *khalkos*, copper; which, however, is quite possibly borrowed from an unknown source: CHALCID, CHALCOCITE, CHALCOPYRITE. [Pok. *ghelegh-* 435.]

gheləd-. Hail. Zero-grade form **ghl̥əd-* in Greek *khalaza* (< **khalad-ya*), a hailstone, also a small cyst: CHALAZA. [Pok. *gheləd-* 435.]

ghelt-. To pay. Only in Germanic and Slavic. **1.** Germanic **geldjam*, payment, in: **a.** Old English *geld, gield*, payment, service: GELD[2], DANEGELD, WERGELD; **b.** Old High German *gelt*, payment, reward: GELT[1]. **2.** Germanic **geldan*, to pay, in Old English *gieldan*, to pay, yield: YIELD. **3.** Germanic **geldjōn*, payment, contribution, hence an association founded on contributions, a craftsmen's guild, in Old Norse *gildi*, guild: GUILD. [Pok. *ghel-tō* 436.]

ghelū-. Tortoise. Suffixed form **ghel-ōnā* in Greek *khelōnē*, tortoise: CHELONIAN. [Pok. *ghel-ōu-* 435.]

ghelūna. Jaw. **1.** Germanic **geliz* in Old Norse **gil*, gill of a fish: GILL[1]. **2.** Suffixed variant form **ghel-wo-* in Greek *kheilos*, lip: CHILOPOD. [Pok. *ghelunā* 436.]

ghen-. To gnaw. Germanic only. **1.** Germanic **gnag-* in: **a.** Old English *gnagan*, to gnaw: GNAW; **b.** Old Norse *gnaga*, to bite: NAG[1]. **2.** Perhaps related is Germanic **gnatt-*, "biting insect," in Old English *gnæt*, gnat: GNAT. [Pok. *ghen-* 436.]

ghend-. Also **ghed-.** To seize, take. **1.** Germanic **getan* in: **a.** Old Norse *geta*, to get: GET; **b.** compound **bigetan* (**bi-*, intensive prefix, BE-), to acquire, in Old English *begietan*, to get, beget: BEGET; **c.** compound **fer-getan* (**fer-*, prefix denoting rejection; see **per**[1]), "to lose one's hold," forget, in Old English *forgietan*, to forget: FORGET. **2.** Germanic **getisōn*, "to try to get," aim at, in Old Swedish *gissa*, to guess, akin to the Scandinavian source of Middle English *gessen*, to guess: GUESS. **3.** Basic form **ghend-* in Latin *prehendere* (*pre-*, *prae-*, before, PRE-), to get hold of, seize, grasp: PREHENSILE, PREHENSION, PRISON, PRIZE[2], (PRY[2]); APPREHEND, (APPRENTICE), (APPRISE), COMPREHEND, COMPRISE, EMPRISE, ENTERPRISE, (ENTREPRENEUR), MISPRISION, PREGNABLE, REPREHEND, (REPRISAL), (REPRISE), SURPRISE. **4.** Form **ghed-* in Latin *praeda*, booty (< **prai-heda*, "something seized before"; **prai-*, *prae-*, before, PRE-): PREDATORY, PREY, SPREE, DEPREDATE, OSPREY. [Pok. *ghend-* 437.]

ghendh-. Abscess, boil. Zero-grade form **ghn̥dh-* in Germanic **gund-* in Old English *gund*, pus: GROUNDSEL[1]. [Pok. *ghendh-* 438.]

ghengh-. To go, walk. **1.** Germanic **gang-*, a going, in: **a.** Old English *gang*, a going: GANG[1]; **b.** Old High German *gang*, a going: GANGUE. **2.** Germanic **gangan*, to go, walk, in Old English *gangan*, to go: (GANGLING), GANGREL. [Pok. *ghengh-* 438.]

gher-[1]. Gut, entrail. **1.** Suffixed form **gher-no-* in Germanic **garnō*, string, in Old English *gearn*, yarn: YARN. **2.** Suffixed form **gher-n-* in Latin *hernia*, "protruded viscus," rupture, hernia: HERNIA. **3.** Suffixed o-grade form **ghor-d-* in Greek *khordē*, gut, string: CORD, (CORDON), (CHORD[2]), HARPSICHORD, TETRACHORD. **4.** O-grade form **ghor-* in Greek *khorion*, intestinal membrane, afterbirth: CHORION. **5.** Suffixed zero-grade form **ghr̥-u-* in Latin *haruspex* (*-spex*, agential suffix, "he who sees"; see **spek-**), "he who inspects entrails," diviner: HARUSPEX. [Pok. 5. *ĝher-* 443.]

gher-[2]. To grasp, enclose; with derivatives meaning "enclosure." **1.** Suffixed zero-grade form **ghr̥-dh-* in: **a.** Germanic **gurdjan* in Old English *gyrdan*, to gird: GIRD; **b.** Old English *gyrdel*, girdle: GIRDLE; **c.** Old Norse *gjördh*, girdle, girth: GIRTH. **2.** Suffixed o-grade form **ghor-dho-* or **ghor-to-*, an enclosure, in: **a.** Germanic **gardaz* in *(i)* Old English *geard*, enclosure, garden, yard: YARD[2], ORCHARD *(ii)* Old Norse *gardhr*, garden, yard: GARTH *(iii)* Old High German *garto*, garden: KINDERGARTEN *(iv)* Frankish **gardo*, enclosure, garden: GARDEN *(v)* compound **midja-gardaz*, "middle zone," earth (see **medhyo-**); **b.** Latin *hortus*, garden: HORTICULTURE, ORCHARD, ORTOLAN. **3.** Prefixed and suffixed zero-grade form **ko-ghr̥-ti-* (**ko-*, collective prefix, "together"; see **kom**) in Latin *cohors* (stem *cohort-*), enclosed yard, company of soldiers, multitude: COHORT, CORTEGE, COURT, (COURTEOUS), (COURTESAN), (COURTESY), (COURTIER), CURTAIN, (CURTILAGE), (CURTSY). **4.** Perhaps suffixed o-grade form **ghor-o-* in Greek *khoros*, dancing ground (? perhaps originally a special enclosure for dancing), dance, dramatic chorus: CHORUS, (CHOIR), (CHORAGUS), (CHORAL), (CHORALE), (CHORIC), (CHORISTER), TERPSICHORE. [Pok. 4. *gher-* 442, *gherd-* 444.]

gher-[3]. To call out. Extended root **ghrēd-*. **1.** Germanic **grētan* in Old Norse *grāta*, to moan, sob: REGRET. **2.** Germanic **grōtjan* in Old English *grētan*, to speak to, greet: GREET. See derivative **ghrēi-**. [Pok. 1. *gher-* 439.]

gher-[4]. To shine, glow; gray. **1.** Germanic **grēwaz*, gray, in: **a.** Old English *græg*, gray: GRAY; **b.** Old Norse *grār*, gray: DAPPLE-GRAY; **c.** probably Old English *grīghund*, greyhound (*hund*, HOUND; and compare Old Norse *grey*, a bitch, perhaps originally "old gray dog"): GREYHOUND. **2.** Germanic **grīsjaz*, gray, in: **a.** Frankish **grīs*, gray: GRISAILLE, (GRILSE), (GRISETTE), (GRISON), GRIZZLE, AMBERGRIS; **b.** Medieval Latin *griseus*, gray, grayish: GRISEOUS. [Pok. 3. *ĝher-* 441.]

gher-[5]. To scrape, scratch. **1.** Suffixed zero-grade form **ghr̥(ə)-k-* in: **a.** Greek *kharax*, a pointed stake, also a kind of sea bream: CHARACIN, CHARACTER; **b.** Greek *kharassein*, to sharpen, notch, carve, cut: GASH. **2.** Extended form **ghers-* in suffixed zero-grade form **ghr̥s-to-* in Sanskrit *ghr̥ṣṭa*, rubbed: GHAT. See also extended root **ghrēu-**. [Pok. 2. *ĝher-* 439.]

gher-[6]. To like, want. **1.** Suffixed form **gher-n-* in Germanic **gernjan* in Old English *giernan*, to strive, desire, yearn: YEARN. **2.** Extended form **ghrē-* possibly in Germanic **grēduz*, hunger, forming **grēdagaz*, hungry, in Old English *grǣdig*, hungry, covetous, greedy: GREEDY. **3.** Suffixed zero-grade form **ghr̥-tā-* in Latin *hortārī*, to urge on, encourage (< "to cause to strive or desire"): HORTATIVE, EXHORT. **4.** Suffixed zero-grade form **ghr̥-i-* in Greek *kharis*, grace, favor: CHARISMA, EUCHARIST. **5.** Suffixed zero-grade form **ghr̥-yo-* in Greek *khairein*, to rejoice, delight in: CHERVIL. [Pok. 1. *ĝher-* 440.]

gher-[7]. Short, small; to become scarce, be needed. Possibly extended form **ghrē-* in Greek *khrē*, it is necessary, whence *khrēsthai*, to lack, want, use: CATACHRESIS, CHRESARD, CHRESTOMATHY. [Pok. 6. *ĝher-* 443.]

ghers-. To bristle. **1.** Extended zero-grade form **ghr̥zd-*, prickly plant, in: **a.** Germanic **gorst-* in Old English *gorst*, furze, gorse: GORSE; **b.** Latin *hordeum*, barley: ORGEAT. **2.** Lengthened-grade form **ghērs-* in Latin *hēr*, *ēr*, hedgehog: CAPRICE, URCHIN. **3.** Suffixed lengthened-grade form **ghēr(s)-ūkā* in Latin *ērūca*, caterpillar: ROCKET[2]. **4.** Suffixed full-grade form **gher-tu-*, remade to **hirsu-* in Latin *hirsūtus*, bristly, shaggy, hairy: HIRSUTE. **5.** Suffixed full-grade form **ghers-kwo-* in Latin *hispidus* (probably a dialectal borrowing), bristly, shaggy, prickly: HISPID. **6.** Suffixed o-grade form **ghors-eyo-* in Latin *horrēre*, to bristle, shudder, be terrified, look frightful: HORROR; ABHOR, ORDURE. **7.** Suffixed full-grade form **ghers-o-* in Greek *khersos*, dry land: CHERSONESE. [Pok. *ĝhers-* 445.]

gheslo-. Seen by some as a base for words meaning "thousand." **1.** Suffixed form **ghesl-yo-* in Greek *khilioi*, thousand: CHILIAD, KILO-. **(2.** Latin *mīlle*, thousand, which has been analyzed as **smī-*, "one" + a form **gzhlī-*, is of obscure origin: MIL[1], MIL[2], MILE, MILFOIL, MILLENARY, MILLENNIUM, MILLEPORE, MILLESIMAL, MILLI-, MILLIARY, MILLIEME, MILLION, MILLIPEDE, MILREIS.**)** [Pok. *ĝhéslo-* 446.]

ghesor-. Hand. Reduced form **ghesr-* in Greek *kheir*, hand: CHIRO-, (CHIRURGEON), ENCHIRIDION, SURGERY, (SURGEON). [Pok. 1. *ĝhesor-* 447.]

gheu-. To pour, pour a libation. **I.** Extended form **gheud-*. **1.** Germanic **giut-* in Old English *geotan*, to pour: INGOT. **2.** Zero-grade form **ghud-* in Germanic **gut-* in Old English *guttas*, intestines: GUT. **3.** Nasalized zero-grade form **ghu-n-d-* in Latin *fundere*, to pour: FOISON, FONDANT, FONDU, FONT[2], FOUND[2], FUNNEL, FUSE[2], FUSILE, FUSION; AFFUSION, CIRCUMFUSE, CONFOUND, CONFUSE, DIFFUSE, EFFUSE, INFUSE, PERFUSE, PROFUSE, REFUND[1], (REFUSE[1]), (REFUSE[2]), SUFFUSE, TRANSFUSE. **II.** Extended form **gheus-* in Germanic **gius-* in: **a.** Old Norse *gustr*, a cold blast of wind: GUST[1]; **b.** Old Norse *geysa*, to gush: GEYSER; **c.** Icelandic *gusa*, to gush: GUSH. **III.** Suffixed form **gheu-ti-* in Latin *fūtilis*, "(of a vessel) easily emptied, leaky," hence untrustworthy, useless: FUTILE. **IV.** Basic form **gheu-* in Greek *khein*, to pour: CHOANOCYTE, CHYLE, (CHYME), ECCHYMOSIS, PARENCHYMA. [Pok. *gheu-* 447.]

ghēu-. To yawn, gape. Compare **ghēi-**. **1.** Germanic suffixed form **gō-ma-* in Old English *gōma*, palate, jaw: GUM[2]. **2.** Variant form **ghau-* in Greek *khaos*, chasm, empty space, chaos: CHAOS, GAS. [Pok. *ĝhēu-* 449.]

gheu(ə)-. To call, invoke. Suffixed zero-grade form **ghu-to-*, "the invoked," god, in Germanic **gudam*, god, in: **a.** Old English *god*, god: GOD; **b.** Old High German *got*, god: GODFREY; **c.** Germanic **gud-igaz*, possessed by a god, in Old English *gydig*, possessed, insane: GIDDY. [Pok. *ghau-* 413.]

ghō. Behind, after. Slavic **za* in Russian *za*, by, to: SASTRUGA. [Pok. *ĝhō* 451.]

ghos-ti-. Stranger, guest, host; properly "someone with whom one has reciprocal duties of hospitality." **1.** Basic form **ghos-ti-* in: **a.** Germanic **gastiz* in Old Norse *gestr*, guest: GUEST; **b.** Latin *hostis*, enemy (< stranger): HOST[2], (HOSTILE). **2.** Compound **ghos-pot-*, **ghos-po(d)-*, "master of guests," one who symbolizes the relationship of reciprocal obligation (**pot-*, master; see **poti-**), in: **a.** Latin *hospes* (stem *hospit-*), host, guest, stranger: HOST[1], (HOSPICE), (HOSPITAL), (HOSPITALITY), (HOSTEL), (HOSTLER); **b.** Common Slavic **gospodĭ*, lord, in Russian *gospodin*, "sir, master": GOSPODIN. [Pok. *ghosti-s* 453.]

ghow-ē-. To honor, revere, worship. **1.** Germanic *gawēn* in Old Norse *gā*, to heed: GAWK. **2.** Basic form **ghow-ē-* in Latin *favēre*, to favor, be favorable: FAVOR, (FAVORITE). [Pok. *ghou(ē)-* 453.]

ghrē-. To grow, to become green. **1.** O-grade form **ghrō-* in Germanic **grō(w)an* in Old English *grōwan*, to grow: GROW. **2.** Suffixed o-grade form **ghrō-nyo-* in Germanic **grōnjaz*, green, in Old English *grēne*, green: GREEN. **3.** Suffixed zero-grade form **ghrə-so-* in Germanic **grasam*, grass, in Old English *græs*, grass: GRASS. [Pok. *ghrē-* 454.]

ghrebh-[1]. To grasp, reach. **1.** Zero-grade form **ghr̥bh-* in Sanskrit *gr̥bhṇāti*, he seizes: SATYAGRAHA. **2.** Parallel (imitative) Germanic creations with base **grab-*, **grap-* in: **a.** Old English **grapsan*, to grasp: GRASP; **b.** Middle Dutch and Middle Low German *grabben*, to seize: GRAB[1]. [Pok. 1. *ghrebh-* 455.]

ghrebh-[2]. To dig, bury, scratch. **1.** O-grade form **ghrobh-* in: **a.** Germanic **graban* in *(i)* Old English *grafan*, to dig, engrave, scratch, carve: GRAVE[3], (ENGRAVE) *(ii)* Old High German *graban*, to dig: GRABEN *(iii)* Frankish **graban*, to dig: GRAVURE, GREAVE; **b.** Germanic **graba* in Old English *græf*, trench, grave: GRAVE[1]. **2.** Germanic **grub(b)jan* in Old English **grybban*, to dig: GRUB[2]. **3.** Germanic **grōbō* in Middle Dutch *groeve*, ditch: GROOVE. **4.** Perhaps Germanic **griub-* in Low German *greven*, fibrous refuse of tallow: GREAVES. [Pok. 2. *ghrebh-* 455.]

ghredh-. To walk, go. Suffixed zero-grade form *ghr̥dh-yo-* in: **a.** Latin *gradī* (past participle *gressus*), to walk, go: AGGRESS, CONGRESS, DEGRESSION, DIGRESS, EGRESS, -GRADE, GRESSORIAL, INGRESS, PROGRESS, REGRESS, RETROGRESS, SALTIGRADE, TRANSGRESS; **b.** Latin *gradus* (< deverbative **grad-o-*), step, stage, degree, rank: GRADE, DEGRADE, DEGREE, RETROGRADE. [Pok. *ghredh-* 456.]

ghrēi-. To rub. A derivative of **gher-**[3]. **1.** Germanic **gris-*, to frighten (< "to grate on the mind"), in Old English *grislic*, terrifying: GRISLY. **2.** Germanic **grīm-*, smear, in Middle Dutch *grīme*, grime: GRIME. **3.** Extended form **ghrīs-* in Greek *khriein*, to anoint: CHRISM, CHRIST, (CHRISTEN), (CHRISTIAN), (CHRISTMAS), (CHRISTOPHER). [Pok. *ghrēi-* 457.]

ghreib-. To grip. **1.** Germanic **grip-* in Old English *gripe*, grasp, and *gripa*, handful: GRIP[1]. **2.** Germanic **grīpan* in: **a.** Old English *grīpan*, to grasp: GRIPE; **b.** Frankish **grīpan*, to grasp: GRIPPE. **3.** Suffixed o-grade form **ghroib-eyo-* in Germanic **graipjan* in Old English *grāpian*, to feel for, grope: GROPE. [Pok. *ghreib-* 457.]

ghrem-. Angry. **1.** Germanic **grimmaz* in: **a.** Old English *grim(m)*, fierce, severe: GRIM; **b.** Frankish **grīma*, mask: GRIMACE. **2.** Germanic **grum-* in Middle Dutch *grommen*, to mutter angrily: GRUMBLE. **3.** Suffixed o-grade form **ghrom-o-* in Russian *grom*, thunder: POGROM. [Pok. 2. *ghrem-* 458.]

ghren-. Also **gwhren-**. To grind. **1.** Extended form **gwhrendh-* in: **a.** Germanic **grindan* in Old English *grindan*, to grind: GRIND; **b.** Germanic **grinst-*, a grinding, in Old English *grīst*, the action of grinding: GRIST; **c.** Latin *frēnum*, horse's bit (on which his teeth grind), bridle: FRENUM; CHAMFRON, REFRAIN[1]; **d.** Latin *frendere*, to grind the teeth: FRAISE. **2.** Extended form **ghrend-* is sometimes, but improbably, regarded as the root of Greek *khondros*, granule, groats, hence cartilage: CHONDRO-, HYPOCHONDRIA, MITOCHONDRION. [Pok. *ghren-* 459.]

ghrēu-. To rub, grind. Extended root of **gher-**[5]. **1.** Germanic **griut-* in Old English *grēot*, sand, gravel: GRIT. **2.** Germanic **grut-* in Old English *grotan*, pieces of hulled grain, groats: GROATS. **3.** Germanic **grūt-* in: **a.** Old English *grūt*, coarse meal: GROUT; **b.** Old French *gruel*, porridge: GRUEL. **4.** Germanic **grautaz*, coarse, thick (< "coarsely ground"), in: **a.** Old English *grēat*, coarse, thick, bulky, large: GREAT; **b.** Middle Dutch *groot*, thick: GROAT. **5.** Germanic **grūw-*, to recoil from (< "to be offended, be grated on by"), in Middle Dutch *grūwen*, to abhor, akin to Middle English *grue*, horrible: GRUESOME. **6.** Variant form **ghrow-* in Greek *khrōs*, skin (< "rough surface" ?), hence flesh, complexion, color: -CHROOUS, RHODOCHROSITE. **7.** Suffixed variant form **ghrō-mn̥* in Greek *khrōma*, skin, complexion, color (semantic development as in **6** above): CHROMA, CHROMATIC, CHROMATO-, CHROME, -CHROME, (CHROMIUM), CHROMO-, ACHROMATIC. **8.** Probably Celtic **graw-* in Old French *grave*, *greve*, coarse sand, gravel: GRAVEL. [Pok. 2. *ghrēu-* 460.]

ghwer-. Wild beast. **1.** Suffixed form **ghwer-o-* in Latin *ferus*, wild: FERAL, FIERCE. **2.** Compound **ghwer-okw-*, "of wild aspect" (**-okw-*, "-looking"; see **okw-**), in Latin *ferōx* (stem *ferōc-*), fierce: FEROCIOUS. **3.** Lengthened-grade form **ghwēr-* in Greek *thēr*, wild beast: -THERE, THEROPOD, TREACLE. [Pok. *ĝhuer-* 493.]

gleubh-. To cut, cleave. **1.** Germanic **kliuban* in Old English *clēofan*, to split, cleave: CLEAVE[1]. **2.** Germanic **klub-*, a splitting, in: **a.**

Old English *clufu,* clove (of garlic): CLOVE[2]; **b.** Middle Dutch *clove,* a cleft: KLOOF. **3.** Germanic **klufti-* in Old English *geclyft,* fissure: CLEFT. **4.** Germanic **klaubri-* in: **a.** Old Norse *kleyfr,* easy to split, akin to Middle English *clifer,* "expert in seizing," skillful: CLEVER; **b.** Old Norse *klofi,* a cleft, akin to English *clevi,* "cleft instrument," clevis: CLEVIS. **5.** Zero-grade form **glubh-* in Greek *gluphein,* to carve: GLYPH, GLYPTIC; ANAGLYPH, HIEROGLYPHIC. **6.** Suffixed zero-grade form **glubh-mā* in Latin *glūma,* husk of grain: GLUME. [Pok. *gleubh-* 401.]

glōgh-. Thorn, point. **1.** Suffixed form **glōgh-i-* in Greek *glōkhis,* barb of an arrow: GLOCHIDIUM. **2.** Suffixed form **glōgh-ya* in Greek *glōssa, glōtta,* tongue, hence also language: GLOSS[2], (GLOSSARY), GLOSSOLALIA, GLOTTIS; BUGLOSS, ISOGLOSS, POLYGLOT, PROGLOTTID. [Pok. *glōgh-* 402.]

gnō-. To know. **1.** Extended form **gnōw-* in Germanic **knōw-, *knē(w)-* in Old English *cnāwan,* to know: KNOW. **2.** Zero-grade form **gnə-* in: **a.** Germanic **kunnan* in Old English *cunnan,* to know, know how to, be able to: CAN[1], CON[2], CUNNING; **b.** Germanic causative verb **kannjan,* to make known, in Old English *cennan,* to declare, and Old Norse *kenna,* to name (in a formal poetic metaphor): KEN, (KENNING); **c.** Germanic **kunth-* in Old English *cūth,* known, well-known, usual, excellent, familiar: COUTH, UNCOUTH; **d.** Germanic **kunthithā-* in Old English *cȳth(the), cȳththu,* knowledge, acquaintance, friendship, kinfolk: KITH. **3.** Suffixed form **gnō-sko-* in Latin *(g)nōscere,* to get to know, get acquainted with: NOTICE, NOTIFY, NOTION, NOTORIOUS; ACQUAINT, COGNITION, (COGNIZANCE), CONNOISSEUR, QUAINT, RECOGNIZE. **4.** Suffixed form **gnō-ro-* in Latin *ignōrāre,* not to know, to disregard (*ī-* for *in-,* not, IN-): IGNORE, (IGNORANT). **5.** Suffixed form **gnō-dhli-* in Latin *nōbilis,* knowable, known, famous, noble: NOBLE. **6.** Reduplicated and suffixed form **gi-gnō-sko-* in Greek *gignōskein,* to know, think, judge (and **gnō-* in *gnōmōn,* a judge, interpreter): GNOME[2], GNOMON, GNOSIS; DIAGNOSIS, PHYSIOGNOMY, PROGNOSIS. **7.** Suffixed zero-grade form **gnə-ro-* in Latin *gnārus,* knowing, expert, whence *narrāre* (< **gnarrāre*), to tell, relate: NARRATE. (**8.** Traditionally but improbably referred here are: **a.** Latin *nota,* a mark, note, sign, cipher, shorthand character: NOTE, ANNOTATE, CONNOTE, PROTHONOTARY; **b.** Latin *norma,* carpenter's square, rule, pattern, precept: NORM, NORMA[1], NORMAL; ABNORMAL, ENORMOUS.) [Pok. 2. *g̑en-* 376.]

gras-. To devour. **1.** Germanic **krasjōn-,* fodder, in Old English *cresse, cærse,* cress: CRESS. **2.** Suffixed form **gras-men* in Latin *grāmen,* "fodder," grass: GRAMA, GRAMINEOUS. **3.** Suffixed form **gras-ter-,* "the devourer," dissimilated in Greek *gastēr,* stomach: GASTRIC, GASTRO-, GASTRULA, EPIGASTRIUM. **4.** Reduplicated form **gar-gr-* dissimilated in Greek *gangraina,* gangrene: GANGRENE. [Pok. *gras-* 404.]

[**grat-.** Also **krat-.** To scratch. Germanic root. **1.** Germanic **krattōn* in Middle Dutch *cratsen,* to scrape: SCRATCH. **2.** Germanic **grat-* in Old French *grater,* to scrape: GRATE[1], REGRATE. [Pok. *gred-* 405.]]

[**gravo-, grāfo-.** A designation of rank, later corresponding with the feudal title of count. West Germanic noun. **1.** Old High German *grāvo,* count: GRAF, BURGRAVE, LANDGRAVE, WALDGRAVE. **2.** Middle Dutch *grave,* count: MARGRAVE, PALSGRAVE.]

greut-. To compress, push. Germanic **krūdan* in Old English *crūdan,* to press, hasten: CROWD[1]. [Pok. *greut-* 406.]

grə-no-. Grain. **1.** Germanic **kornam* in: **a.** Old English *corn,* grain: CORN[1]; **b.** Old English derivative noun *cyrnel,* seed, pip: KERNEL; **c.** Old High German *korn,* grain: EINKORN. **2.** Latin *grānum,* grain: GARNER, (GARNET[1]), GRAIN, (GRAM[2]), (GRANADILLA), (GRANARY), (GRANGE), (GRANITE), (GRANULE), (GRAVY), (GRENADE); (ENGRAIN), FILIGREE, POMEGRANATE. [In Pok. *g̑er-* 390.]

gru-. To grunt. Imitative. **1.** Germanic **grun-* in Old English *grunnian,* to grunt; GRUNT. **2.** Germanic intensive form **grunnatjan* in Old High German *grunnizōn,* to grunt: GRUDGE. **3.** Latin *grunnīre, grundīre,* to grunt: GRUNION, GURNARD. [Pok. *gru-* 406.]

gwā-. Also **gwem-.** To go, come. **1.** Germanic **kuman* in: **a.** Old English *cuman,* to come: COME; **b.** Germanic **kuma-,* he who comes, a guest, in compound **wil-kuma-,* a desirable guest (**wil-,* desirable; see **wel-**[2]), in Old English *wilcuma,* a welcome guest, and *wilcume,* the greeting of welcome: WELCOME; **c.** compound **bi-kuman,* to arrive, come to be (**bi-,* intensive prefix; BE-), in Old English *becuman,* to become: BECOME. **2.** Suffixed form **gw(e)m-yo-* in Latin *venīre,* to come: VENIRE, VENUE; ADVENT, (ADVENTITIOUS), (ADVENTURE), AVENUE, CIRCUMVENT, CONTRAVENE, CONVENE, (CONVENIENT), (CONVENT), (CONVENTICLE), (CONVENTION), (COVEN), (COVENANT), EVENT, INTERVENE, INVENT, MISADVENTURE, PARVENU, PREVENIENT, PREVENT, PROVENANCE, (PROVENIENCE), REVENANT, REVENUE, SOUVENIR, SUBVENTION, SUPERVENE. **3.** Suffixed zero-grade form **gwṃ-yo-* in Greek *bainein,* to go, walk, step, with *basis* (< **gwṃ-ti-*), a stepping, tread, base, and *-batēs* (< **gwə-to-*), agential suffix, "one that goes or treads, one that is based": ACROBAT, ADIABATIC, AMPHISBAENA, ANABAENA, BASE[1], BASIS, DIABASE, DIABETES, STEREOBATE, STYLOBATE. **4.** Basic form **gwā-* in Greek *bēma,* step, seat, raised platform: BEMA. **5.** Sanskrit *jigāti,* he goes: JUGGERNAUT. [Pok. *gu̯ā-* 463.]

gwadh-. To sink. Possible root. **1.** Suffixed form **gwadh-u-* in Greek *bathus,* deep: BATHOS, BATHY-. **2.** Greek *benthos,* depth, may be formed on *bathus* by analogy with *penthos,* grief, and *pathos,* passion, suffering (or it may be from an unrelated root **gw(e)ndh-*): BENTHOS. **3.** Suffixed variant form **gudh-yo-* in Greek *bussos,* bottom of the sea: ABYSS. [Pok. *gu̯ādh-* 465.]

gwēbh-[1]. To dip, sink. Suffixed zero-grade form **gwəbh-yo-* in Greek *baptein,* to dip: BAPTIST, BAPTIZE, ANABAPTIST. [Pok. *gu̯ēbh-* 465.]

gwēbh-[2]. Hypothetical base of some Germanic words associated with the notion of sliminess. **1.** Middle Dutch *quac-,* unguent, liquid: QUACKSALVER, QUAGMIRE. **2.** Low German *quabbeln,* to shake like jelly, tremble: QUAVER. [Pok. 2. *gu̯ēbh-* 466.]

gwedh-. To push, injure, destroy. Germanic **kwet-* in Middle High German *quetzen,* to push, strike: KVETCH. [Pok. *gu̯edh-* 466.]

gwei-. Also **gweiə-.** To live. **I.** Suffixed zero-grade form **gwi-wo-, *gwī-wo-,* living. **1.** Germanic **kwi(k)waz* in: **a.** Old English *cwic, cwicu,* living, alive: QUICK, (QUICKSILVER); **b.** as a name for couch grass (from its rapid growth), in Old English *cwice,* couch grass: QUITCH GRASS, (COUCH GRASS). **2. a.** Latin *vīvus,* living, alive: VIPER, VIVIFY, (VIVIPAROUS); **b.** Latin denominative *vīvere,* to live: VIAND, VICTUAL, VIVA, VIVACIOUS, VIVID; CONVIVIAL, REVIVE, SURVIVE. **3.** Further suffixed form **gwī-wo-tā* in Latin *vīta,* life: VIABLE, VITAL; LIGNUM VITAE, VITAMIN, VITASCOPE. **4.** Further suffixed form **gwī-wo-tūt-* in Celtic **bivotūt-* in Old Irish *bethu,* life: USQUEBAUGH, (WHISKEY). **II.** Suffixed variant form **gwiy-o-* in Greek *bios,* life: BIO-, BIOTA, BIOTIC; AEROBE, AMPHIBIOUS, ANABIOSIS, CENOBITE, MICROBE, RHIZOBIUM, SAPROBE, SYMBIOSIS. **III.** Extended form **gwyō-.* **1.** Greek *zoē,* life: AZO-, DIAZO. **2.** Suffixed form **gwyō-yo-* in Greek *zōon, zōion,* living being, animal: -ZOA, -ZOIC, ZOO-, ZOON, -ZOON. **IV.** Prefixed and suffixed form **su-gwiyes-ya* (**su-,* well; see **su-**[2]), "living in good condition," in Greek *hugiēs,* healthy: HYGEIA, HYGIENE. **V.** Possibly Old English *cwifer-,* nimble: QUIVER[3]. [Pok. 3. *gu̯ei-* 467.]

gwel-[1]. To throw, reach. **1.** Suffixed zero-grade form **gwḷ-no-* in: **a.** Greek *ballein,* to throw: AMPHIBOLE, BALLISTA, CATABOLISM, DEVIL, (DIABOLIC), DISCOBOLUS, (EBLIS), ECBOLIC, EMBLEM, EPIBOLY, HYPERBOLA, (HYPERBOLE), METABOLISM, (PALAVER), PARABLE, (PARABOLA), (PARLEY), (PARLIAMENT), (PARLOR), (PAROL), (PAROLE), PROBLEM, SYMBOL; **b.** Greek *ballizein,* to dance: BALL[2], (BALLAD), (BALLET), BAYADERE. **2.** Suffixed o-grade form **gwol-ā* in Greek *bolē,* beam, ray: BOLOMETER. **3.** Suffixed o-grade form **gwol-sā* in Greek *boulē,* determination, will (< "throwing forward of the mind"), council: BOULE[1]; ABULIA. **4.** Suffixed extended form **gwele-mno-* in Greek *belemnos,* dart, javelin: BELEMNITE. [Pok. 2. *gu̯el-* 471.]

gwel-[2]. To pierce. **1.** Suffixed o-grade form **gwol-eyo-* in Germanic **kwaljan* in Old English *cwellan,* to kill, destroy: QUELL. **2.** Suffixed zero-grade form **gwḷ-yo-* in Germanic **kuljan* in Old English **cyllan,* to kill: KILL[1]. [Pok. 1. *gu̯el-* 470.]

gwel-[3]. Also **gwelə-.** An acorn. **1.** Latin *glāns,* stem *gland-* (pre-form uncertain), an acorn: GLAND, (GLANDERS), (GLANDULAR), GLANS. **2.** Suffixed zero-grade form **gwḷə-no-* in Greek *balanos,* acorn, date: MYROBALAN, VALONIA. [Pok. 3. *gu̯el-* 472.]

gwel-[4]. To fly; a wing. Latin *volāre,* to fly: VOLANT, (VOLATILE), (VOLE[2]), (VOLITANT), (VOLLEY).

gwel-[5]. To swallow. **1.** Germanic **kel-* in Old English *ceolu,* throat, dewlap: JOWL[2]. **2.** Suffixed zero-grade form **gul-ā* in Latin *gula,* gullet, throat, palate: GOLIARD, GULAR, GULES, GULLET; BEAGLE. **3.** Extended (expressive) form **glutt-* in: **a.** Latin *gluttīre, glūtīre,* to swallow: GLUT, DEGLUTITION; **b.** Latin *gluttō,* a glutton: GLUTTON. [In Pok. 2. *gel-* 365.]

gwelbh-. Womb. **1.** Suffixed form **gwelbh-u-* in Greek *delphus,* womb, whence *delphis,* dolphin (referring to its shape): DOLPHIN, (DAUPHIN), (DELPHINIUM). **2.** Prefixed and suffixed form **sṃ-gwelbh-o-,* "born of one womb" (**sṃ-,* one; see **sem-**[1]), in Greek *adelphos,* brother: -ADELPHOUS, PHILADELPHIA. [Pok. *gu̯elbh-* 473.]

gwen-. Woman. **1.** Suffixed form **gwen-ā* in: **a.** Germanic **kwenōn* in Old English *cwene,* woman, prostitute, wife: QUEAN; **b.** Old Irish *ben,* woman: BANSHEE; **c.** Persian *zan,* woman: ZENANA. **2.** Suffixed lengthened-grade form **gwēn-i-* in Germanic **kwēniz,* woman, wife, queen, in Old English *cwēn,* woman, wife, queen: QUEEN. **3.** Suffixed zero-grade form **gwn-ā* in Greek *gunē,* woman: GYNO-, -GYNOUS, -GYNY; GYNAECEUM, GYNECOCRACY, GYNECOLOGY, POLYGYNY. [Pok. *gu̯enā* 473.]

gwer-[1]. Mountain. Possibly o-grade form **gwor-* in: **a.** Greek *boreios,* "coming from the north" (? < "coming from the mountains of Thrace, north of Greece"), whence *Boreas,* the north wind: BOREAS; **b.** Greek *Huper-boreioi, Huperboreoi,* name of a people living in the far north, variously explained as "they who live beyond the north wind" and "they who live beyond the mountains" (*huper-,* beyond, HYPER-): HYPERBOREAN. [Pok. 3. *gu̯er-* 477.]

gwer-[2]. Heavy. **I.** Zero-grade extended form **gwṛə-.* **1.** Suffixed form **gwṛə-u-i-* in Latin *gravis,* heavy, weighty: GRAVE[2], GRAVID, GRIEVE, (GRIEF); AGGRAVATE, AGGRIEVE. **2.** Suffixed form **gwṛə-u-* in: **a.** Greek *barus,* heavy: BARITE, (BARIUM), BARITONE, BARYON, BARYSPHERE; **b.** Sanskrit *guruḥ,* heavy, venerable: GURU. **3.** Suffixed form **gwṛə-es-* in Greek *baros,* weight: BAR[2], BARO-, CENTROBARIC, ISALLOBAR, ISOBAR. **4.** Possibly Greek *bri-* (see **gwer-**[2]). **II.** Suffixed extended form **g(w)rū-to-* in Latin *brūtus,* heavy, unwieldy, dull, stupid, brutish: BRUT, (BRUTE). **III.** Suffixed extended form **gwrī-g-o-* in: **a.** Celtic **brīg-,* strength, in *(i)* Gaulish **brigo,* strength: BRIO *(ii)* Old Italian *briga,* strife: BRIGADE; **b.** Germanic **krig-* in Old High German *krēg, chrēg,* stubbornness: BLITZKRIEG. **IV.** Suffixed form **gwerə-nā-,* millstone, in Old English *cweorn,* quern: QUERN. [Pok. 2. *gu̯er-* 476.]

gwerə-[1]. To praise (aloud). **1.** Suffixed zero-grade form **gwṛə-to-* in Latin *grātus,* pleasing, beloved, agreeable, favorable, thankful: GRACE, GRATEFUL, GRATIFY, (GRATIS), (GRATITUDE), (GRATUITY), GREE[2]; AGREE, CONGRATULATE, INGRATE, INGRATIATE. **2.** Suffixed zero-grade form **gwṛ(ə)-do-,* "he who praises," in Celtic *bardo-,* bard, in Welsh *bardd* and Scottish and Irish Gaelic *bárd,* bard: BARD[1]. [Pok. 4. *gu̯er(ə)-* 478.]

gwerə-[2]. To swallow. **1.** Possibly suffixed extended form **g(w)ro-gh-* in Germanic **krag-,* throat, in: **a.** Old English **craga,* throat: CRAW; **b.** Middle Dutch *crāghe,* throat: SCRAG. **2.** Suffixed o-grade form **gwor-ā-* in Latin *vorāre,* to swallow up: VORACIOUS, -VOROUS; DEVOUR. **3.** Suffixed zero-grade form **gwṛ-g-* in: **a.** Latin *gurges,* throat, also gulf, whirlpool: GARGET, GORGE, (GORGET), GURGITATION; INGURGITATE, REGURGITATE; **b.** Latin *gurguliō,* windpipe: GARGOYLE, (GARGLE), GURGLE. **4.** Extended form **gwrō-* in: **a.** suffixed reduplicated form **gwi-gwrō-sko-* in Greek *bibrōskein,* to eat: HELLEBORE; **b.** nasalized suffixed form **gwro-n-gh-* in Greek *bronkhos,* windpipe, throat: BRONCHUS, (BRONCHO-); **c.** suffixed form **gwrō-mṇ* in Greek *brōma,* food: THEOBROMINE. [Pok. 1. *gu̯er-* 474.]

gweru-. A spit, stick. Latin *veru,* spit: VERATRINE. [Pok. *gu̯eru-* 479.]

gwes-. To extinguish. Suffixed variant form **sgwes-nu-* in Greek *sbennunai,* to extinguish: ASBESTOS. [Pok. *gu̯es-* 479.]

gwet-[1]. Resin (?). Only in Germanic and Celtic. Extended form **gwetu-* in: **a.** Germanic **kwithu-* in Old English *cwudu, cwidu, cudu,* resin, mastic gum, "that which is chewed," cud: CUD, QUID[1]; **b.** Celtic **betu-* in Gaulish **bitū-, *bet,* pitch: BITUMEN. [Pok. 1. *gu̯et-* 480.]

gwet-[2]. To say, speak. Germanic **kwithan* in: **a.** Old English *cwethan,* to say, speak: BE-

QUEATH, QUOTH; b. suffixed form *kwith-ti- becoming *kwithiz in Old English -cwiss, "statement": BEQUEST. [Pok. 2. guet- 480.]

gwet-[3]. Intestine. Suffixed o-grade form *gwot-olo- in Latin *botulus*, intestine, sausage: BOTULIN, BOTULISM, BOWEL. [Pok. guet- 481.]

gweyə-. To press down, conquer. Sanskrit *jayati*, he conquers: JAIN. [Pok. gueiə- 469.]

gwhen-[1]. To strike, hurt. **1.** Suffixed zero-grade form *gwhn̥-tyā in Germanic *gunthjō, war, battle, in: **a.** Old English *gūth*, war, battle: EDITH; **b.** Old Norse *gunnr*, war: GUN; **c.** compound *gund-fanōn-, "battle-flag" (*fanōn-, flag; see **pan-**), in Italian *gonfalone*, standard: GONFALON. **2.** Suffixed form *gwhen-do- in: **a.** Latin *dēfendere*, to ward off (*dē-*, away, DE-): DEFEND, (DEFENSE), (FENCE); **b.** Latin *offendere*, to strike against, be offensive, offend (*ob-*, against, OB-): OFFEND, (OFFENCE). **3.** Suffixed zero-grade form *gwhn̥-tro- in Old Persian *jathra-, poison: BEZOAR. **4.** Prefixed zero-grade form *sm̥-gwhn̥-, to press together (*sm̥-, together; see **sem-[1]**), in Sanskrit *sajati*, he adheres: SANGH. [Pok. 2. guhen-(ə)- 491.]

gwhen-[2]. To swell, abound. Suffixed form *gwhen-eyo- in Greek *euthenein* (*eu-*, well; see **esu-**), to flourish: EUTHENICS. [Pok. 1. guhen- 491.]

gwher-. Warm. **1.** Suffixed form *gwher-mo- in Greek *thermos*, warm, hot: THERM, -THERM, THERMO-, -THERMY. **2.** O-grade form *ghor- in Latin *forceps*, fire tongs (< "that which holds hot things"; *-ceps*, agential suffix, "-taker"; see **kap-**): FORCEPS. **3.** Suffixed o-grade form *gwhor-no- in: **a.** Latin *fornus*, *fornāx*, oven: FORNAX, FURNACE, HORNITO; **b.** probably Latin *fornix*, arch, vault (< "vaulted brick oven"): FORNICATE[1], FORNICATE[2]. **4.** Suffixed o-grade form *gwhor-eyo- in Old Irish *guirid*, "he warms," perhaps in a Celtic compound meaning "twice-warmed," a name for a kind of cheese made with two stages of heating, in Middle High German *ziger*, whey cheese: SAPSAGO. [Pok. guher- 493.]

gwhī-. Thread, tendon. Suffixed form *gwhī-slo- in Latin *fīlum*, thread: FILAMENT, FILAR, FILARIA, FILE[1], FILET[1], FILLET, FILOSE, FILUM; DEFILE[2], ENFILADE, FILIFORM, FILIGREE, FILOPLUME, PROFILE, PURFLE. [Pok. guheiə- 489.]

gwhren-. To think. Doubtful root. Greek *phrēn*, the mind, also heart, midriff, diaphragm: FRENETIC, (FRANTIC), FRENZY, -PHRENIA, PHRENITIS, PHRENO-, EUPHRASY, EUPHROSYNE. [Pok. guhren- 496.]

gwl̥tur-. Vulture. Possible root. Latin *vultur*, vulture: VULTURE. [Pok. gultur(os) 482.]

gwou-. Ox, bull, cow. Nominative singular form *gwōu-s. **1.** Germanic *kōuz in Old English *cū*, *cȳ*, *cȳe*, cow: COW[1], (KINE), COWSLIP. **2.** Latin *bōs* (stem *bov-*), ox, bull, cow: BEEF, BOVINE, BUGLE[1], OVIBOS. **3.** Greek *bous*, ox, bull, cow: BOUSTROPHEDON, BUCEPHALUS, BUCOLIC, BUFFALO, BULIMIA, BUPRESTID, BUTTER[1], (BUTYRIC). **4.** Sanskrit *go*, *gauḥ*, cow: GAEKWAR, GAYAL. **5.** Suffixed form *gwōu-ro- in Sanskrit *gaura*, wild ox: GAUR, GORAL. **6.** Variant form *gw-ā in Greek *hekatombē*, "sacrifice of a hundred oxen" (*hekaton*, hundred; see **dekm̥**): HECATOMB. (**7.** Referred by some to this root, but improbably, is Greek *boskein*, to feed: PROBOSCIS.) [Pok. guou- 482.]

gwōu-. Dung; also disgust, annoyance. Doubtless a derivative of **gwou-**, "cow, bull." Extended zero-grade form *gwəudh- in Old Irish *buadrim*, I vex: BOTHER. [Pok. guou- 483.]

gwres-. Thick, fat. Perhaps Latin *grossus* (from an uncertain pre-form), thick: GROSS, (GROCER), (GROSCHEN), GROSZ, ENGROSS. [Pok. guretso- 485.]

gyeu-. Also **geu-**. To chew. Germanic *kewwan in Old English *cēowan*, to chew: CHEW. [Pok. g(i)eu- 400.]

gzhū-. Fish. Greek *ikhthus*, fish: ICHTHYO-. [Pok. ghdhū- 416.]

gzhyes. Yesterday. Suffixed (comparative) form *gzhyes-ter- in Germanic *ges-ter- in Old English *geostran*, "yester-": YESTER-, (YESTERDAY). [Pok. ghdhies 416.]

gzwhei-. To perish, die away. Zero-grade form *gzwhi- in Greek *phthinein*, to die away: PHTHISIS. [Pok. guhdhei(ə)- 487.]

gzwher-. To ruin. Perhaps Greek *phtheir*, louse: ICH, PHTHIRIASIS. [Pok. guhdher- 487.]

[**hulē.** Forest, timber, hence stuff, matter. Greek noun of unknown origin. HYLOZOISM, METHYLENE, -YL.]

i-. Pronominal stem. **1.** Germanic *is-līk-, same (*līk-, like; see **līk-**), in Old English *ilca*, same: ILK[1]. **2.** Germanic *jaino-, *jeno-, in Old English *geon*, that: YON. **3.** Germanic *jend- in Old English *geond*, as far as, yonder: YOND, (YONDER). **4.** Extended forms *yām, *yāi, in Germanic *ja, *je, in Old English *gea*, affirmative particle: YEA, (YES). **5.** Old English *gīet*, *gīeta* (pre-form uncertain), still: YET. **6.** Old English *gif* (pre-form uncertain), if: IF. **7.** Old Norse *idh* (pre-form uncertain), again, anew: ITHUNN. **8.** Basic form *i-, with neuter *id-em, in Latin *is*, he, and *īdem*, same: ID, IDEM, (IDENTITY). **9.** Suffixed form *i-tero- in Latin *iterum*, again: ITERATE, (REITERATE). **10.** Suffixed and extended form *it(ə)-em in Latin *item*, thus, also: ITEM. **11.** Suffixed variant form *e-tero- (see **ko-**). [Pok. 3. e- 281.]

[**Iveriū.** The prehistoric Celtic name for Ireland. **1.** Accusative form *Iverionem in Greek *Iernē*, Ireland: HIBERNIA. **2.** Old Irish *Ēriu*, Ireland: EIRE, ERIN, DAIL EIREANN. **3.** Old English *Īras*, the Irish: ERSE, IRELAND, IRISH.]

kā-. To like, desire. **1.** Suffixed form *kā-ro- in: **a.** Germanic *hōraz, "one who desires," adulterer, in (*i*) Old English *hōre*, whore: WHORE (*ii*) Old Norse compound *hōrdōmr*, whoredom (*-dōmr*, "condition"; see **dhē-[1]**): WHOREDOM; **b.** Latin *cārus*, dear: CARESS, CHARITY, CHERISH. **2.** Suffixed form *kā-mo- in Sanskrit *kāma*, love, desire: KAMASUTRA. [Pok. kā- 515.]

kad-. To fall. Latin *cadere*, to fall, die: ACCIDENT, CADAVER, CADENCE, CADENT, CADUCOUS, CASCADE, CASE[1], CHANCE, CHUTE, DECAY, DECIDUOUS, ESCHEAT, INCIDENT, OCCASION, RECIDIVISM. [Pok. 1. kad- 516.]

kād-. Sorrow, hatred. **1.** Suffixed zero-grade form *kəd-i- in: **a.** Germanic *hatiz in Old English *hete*, hate, envy: HATRED; **b.** Germanic *haton in Old English *hatian*, to hate: HATE; **c.** Germanic *hatjan in Frankish *hatjan, to hate: HEINOUS. **2.** Suffixed variant form *kēd-es- in Greek *kēdos*, care, sorrow, grief: ACCIDIE, EPICEDIUM. [Pok. kād- 517.]

kadh-. To shelter, cover. **1.** Germanic *haduz in expressive form *hattuz in Old English *hætt*, hat: HAT. **2.** Lengthened variant form *kōdh-in: **a.** Germanic *hōda in Old English *hōd*, hood: HOOD[1]; **b.** Germanic *hōdjan in Old English *hēdan*, to heed, care for, protect: HEED. [Pok. kadh- 516.]

kagh-. To catch, seize; wickerwork, fence. **1.** Germanic *hag- in: **a.** Old French *hagard*, wild hawk (< "raptor"): HAGGARD; **b.** Germanic *hagōn in Old English *haga*, hedge, hawthorn: HAW[2]; **c.** Germanic *hagiz in Old English *heg(e)*, hedge: HAYWARD; **d.** Germanic *hagjō in Old English *hecg*, hedge: HEDGE. **2.** Suffixed unaspirated form *kag-jon- in Gaulish *caio*, rampart, retaining wall: (CAY), (KEY[2]), QUAY. **3.** Variant *kogh- in: **a.** Latin *cohum*, strap from yoke to harness: INCHOATE; **b.** possibly Latin *cōlum*, sieve (< wickerwork) and its derivative *cōlāre*, to filter: COLANDER, COULEE, COULOIR, CULLIS; MACHICOLATION, PERCOLATE, PORTCULLIS. [Pok. kagh- 518.]

kaghlo-. Pebble, hail. Germanic *haglaz in Old English *hagol*, hail: HAIL[1]. [Pok. kaghlo- 518.]

kai-. Heat. Extended form *kaid- in: **a.** Germanic *haitaz in Old English *hāt*, hot: HOT; **b.** Germanic *haitī- in Old English *hǣtu*, heat: HEAT. [Pok. kăi- 519.]

kaiko-. One-eyed. Latin *caecus*, blind: CAECILIAN, CECIL, CECUM. [Pok. kai-ko 519.]

kailo-. Whole, uninjured, of good omen. **1.** Germanic *hailaz in: **a.** Old English *hāl*, hale, whole: HALE[1], WHOLE; **b.** Old English *hālsum, wholesome (*-sum*, -SOME[1]): WHOLESOME; **c.** Germanic compound *hailewīdis (*wīdaz, wide; see **wi-**) in French feminine name *Héloïse*: ELOISE; **d.** Old Norse *heill*, healthy: HAIL[2], WASSAIL. **2.** Germanic *hailithō in Old English *hǣlth*, health: HEALTH. **3.** Germanic *hailjan in Old English *hǣlan*, to heal: HEAL. **4.** Germanic *hailagaz in: **a.** Old English *hālig*, holy, sacred: HOLY; **b.** Germanic derivative verb *hailagōn in Old English *hālgian*, to consecrate, bless: HALLOW; **c.** Old Norse feminine name *Helga*, "holy": OLGA. [Pok. kailo- 622.]

kaito-. Forest, uncultivated land. **1.** Germanic *haithiz in Old English *hǣth*, heath, untilled land: HEATH. **2.** Germanic *haithinaz in: **a.** Old English *hǣthen*, heathen, "savage" (< "one inhabiting uncultivated land"): HEATHEN; **b.** Middle Dutch *heiden*, heathen: HOYDEN. [Pok. kaito- 521.]

kak-[1]. To enable, help. Sanskrit *śaknōti*, he is able, he is strong: SHAKTI, SIKH. [Pok. kak- 522.]

[**kak-[2].** A round object, disk. Germanic root. **1.** Old Norse *kaka*, cake: CAKE. **2.** Middle Dutch *koeke*, a cake: COOKY. **3.** Middle Low German *kōke*, cake: COCKAIGNE. **4.** Old High German *kuocho*, cake: KUCHEN, QUICHE. [In Pok. gag- 349.]]

kakka-. Also **kaka-**. To defecate. Imitative root. **1.** Old Norse *kūka, to defecate: CUCKING STOOL. **2.** Latin *cacāre*, to defecate: POPPYCOCK. **3.** Greek *kakos*, bad: CACO-. [Pok. kakka- 521.]

kal-[1]. Cup. **1.** Suffixed zero-grade form *kl̥-ik-in: **a.** Latin *calix*, cup, goblet: CALIX, CHALICE; **b.** Greek *kulix*, cup: KYLIX. **2.** Suffixed zero-grade form *kl̥-uk- in Greek *kalux*, seed-vessel, cup: CALYX. [Pok. 7. kel- 550.]

kal-[2]. Beautiful. **1.** Suffixed form *kal-wo- in Greek *kalos*, beautiful: CALOMEL, CALOYER, KALEIDOSCOPE. **2.** Suffixed form *kal-yo- in Greek *kallos*, beauty: CALLA, CALLI-, CALLISTO[1]. [Pok. 2. kal- 524.]

kamer-. To bend; a vault. **1.** Latin *camurus*, *camur*, bent inward: CAMBER. **2.** Greek *kamara*, a vault: BICAMERAL, (CABARET), CAMARILLA, CAMERA, CHAMBER, COMRADE. **3.** Persian *kamar*, waist, girdle, something arched: CUMMERBUND. **4.** Variant form *kem-en- in Germanic *himin- in dissimilated form *hibin-, "the vault of heaven," in Old English *heofon*, *hefn*, heaven: HEAVEN. [Pok. kam-er- 524.]

kamp-. To bend. **1.** Suffixed form *kamp-ā in Greek *kampē*, a bending, a winding: GAM[2], GAMBADO[2], GAMBIT, GAMBOL, GAMBREL, GAMMON[3], JAMB. **2.** Suffixed form *kamp-yo- in Greek *kamptein*, to bend: SCONCE[1]. [Pok. kam-p- 525.]

kan-. To sing. **1.** Germanic *han(e)nī in Old English *henn*, hen: HEN. **2.** Latin *canere*, to sing: ACCENT, CANOROUS, CANT[2], CANTABILE, CANTICLE, CANTILLATE, CANTO, CANTOR, CANZONE, CHANT, DESCANT, ENCHANT, INCANTATION, INCENTIVE, PRECENTOR, RECANT. **3.** Latin *oscen*, a singing bird used in divination (< *obs-cen, "one that sings before the augurs"; *ob-*, before, OB-): OSCINE. **4.** Suffixed form *kan-men- in Latin *carmen*, song, poem: CARMEN, CHARM[1]. [Pok. kan- 525.]

kand-. To shine. **1.** Suffixed (stative) form *kand-ē- in Latin *candēre*, to shine: CANDENT, CANDID, CANDLE, CANDOR, INCANDESCE. **2.** Latin causative *candere, to kindle, in compound *incendere*, to set fire to, kindle (*in-*, in, IN-): (INCENDIARY), INCENSE. **3.** Suffixed form *kand-ono- in Sanskrit *candanaḥ*, sandalwood (burned as incense): SANDAL[2]. **4.** Suffixed form *kand-ro- possibly in Sanskrit *candrāḥ*, shining: SANDARAC. [Pok. kand- 526.]

[**kanna.** A reed. Greek noun, akin to Greek *kanōn*, rod, of Semitic origin, akin to Babylo-Assyrian *qanū*, pipe. **1.** Greek *kanna*, reed, cane: CANAL, CANE, CANISTER, CANNELON, CANYON, CHANNEL[1], KENNEL[2]. **2.** Greek *kanōn*, rod, rule: CANON[1].]

kannabis. Hemp. Late Indo-European word borrowed from an unknown source. **1.** Germanic *hanipiz in Old English *henep*, *hænep*, hemp: HEMP. **2.** Greek *kannabis*, hemp: CANNABIS, CANVAS.

kantho-. A corner, a bending. Celtic *cantos, rim, border, in: **a.** Latin *Cantium*, Kent (a border area): KENT; **b.** Latin *cantus*, *canthus*, iron ring around a carriage wheel, a wheel, a rim: CANT[1], CANTEEN, CANTON, CHAMFER, DECANT. [Pok. kan-tho- 526.]

kap-. To grasp. **I.** Basic form *kap-. **1.** Germanic *haf- in Old English *hefeld*, thread used for weaving, heddle (a device which grasps the thread): HEDDLE. **2.** Germanic *haftjam in Old English *hæft*, handle: HAFT. **3.** Form *kap-ē- in Germanic *habēn in Old English *habban*, to have, hold: HAVE. **4.** Germanic *hafigaz, "containing something," having weight, in Old English *hefig*, heavy: HEAVY. **5.** Germanic *hafnō-, perhaps "place that holds ships," in Old English *hæfen*, a haven: HAVEN. **6.** Germanic *habukaz* in Old English *h(e)afoc*, hawk: HAWK[1]. **II.** Suffixed form *kap-yo-. **1.** Germanic *hafjan in Old English *hebban*, to lift: HEAVE. **2.** Latin *capere*, to take, seize: CABLE, CAPABLE, CAPACIOUS, CAPIAS, CAPSTAN, CAPTION, CAPTIVE, CAPTOR, CAPTURE, CATCH, CHASE[1]; ACCEPT, ANTICIPATE, CONCEIVE, DECEIVE, EXCEPT, INCEPTION, INCIPIENT, INTERCEPT, INTUSSUSCEPTION, MERCAPTAN, NUNCUPATIVE, OCCUPY, PERCEIVE, PRECEPT, RECEIVE, SUSCEPTIBLE. **3.** Latin agential suffix *-ceps*, "-taker" (as in *prīnceps*, chief, ruler; see **per[1]**): MUNICIPAL, PARTICIPATE. **4.** Suffixed form *kap-ero- in Latin *recuperāre*, to regain, recover (*re-*, again, RE-): RECUPERATE, (RECOVER). **III.** Suffixed form *kap-s- in Latin *capsa*, repository, case: CAISSON, CAPSULE, CASE[2], CHASE[2], CHASE[3], CHASSIS, CHESS[3], ENCHASE. **IV.** Lengthened-grade variant form *kōp-. **1.** Germanic *hōf- in compound

***bi-hōf,** "that which binds," requirement, obligation (**bi-,* intensive prefix; see **ambhi**), in: **a.** Old English *behōf,* use, profit, need: BEHOOF; **b.** Old English *behōfian,* to have need of: BEHOOVE. **2.** Greek *kōpē,* handle: COPEPOD. Compare the homonymous root **ghabh-.** [Pok. *kap-* 527.]

kapho-. Hoof. Lengthened-grade form **kāp(h)-o-* in Germanic **hōfaz* in Old English *hōf,* hoof: HOOF. [Pok. *kapho-* 530.]

kapro-. He-goat, buck. Latin *caper,* he-goat: CABER, CABRILLA, CABRIOLET, CAPELLA, CAPRIOLE, CHEVRON; CAPRIC ACID, CAPRICORNUS, CAPRIFIG. [Pok. *kapro-* 529.]

kaput. Head. **1.** Germanic **haubidam, *haubudam,* in: **a.** Old English *hēafod,* head: HEAD; **b.** Old High German *houbit,* head: ATAMAN. **2.** Latin *caput,* head: CABEZON, CABOTAGE, CADET, CAP, CAP-A-PIE, CAPE[1], CAPE[2], CAPITAL[1], CAPITAL[2], CAPITATE, CAPITATION, CAPITOL, CAPITULATE, CAPITULUM, CAPO, CAPORAL, CAPRICE, CAPTAIN, CAPUCHE, CATTLE, CAUDILLO, CHAPE, CHAPTER, CHIEF, CHIEFTAIN, COPE[2], HATCHMENT, KEPI; ACHIEVE, BICEPS, CHAMFRON, DECAPITATE, KERCHIEF, MISCHIEF, MUSCOVADO, OCCIPUT, PRECIPITATE, RECAPITULATE, SINCIPUT, TÊTE-BÊCHE, TRICEPS. [Pok. *kap-ut-* 529.]

kar-[1]**.** Hard. **I.** Variant form *ker-.* **1.** Suffixed o-grade form **kor-tu-* in Germanic **harduz* in: **a.** Old English *hard, heard,* hard: HARD; **b.** Old High German *hart(i),* bold, stern: BERNARD, GERARD, LEONARD; **c.** Germanic **-hart, *-hard,* bold, hardy: -ARD, RICHARD; **d.** Frankish **hard,* hard: STANDARD; **e.** Old French *hardir,* to make hard: HARDY[1]. **2.** Extended zero-grade form **kṛt-* in Greek *kratos,* strength, might, power: -CRACY. **II.** Basic form **kar-* in derivatives referring to things with hard shells. **1.** Possibly Latin *carīna,* keel of a ship, nutshell: CAREEN, CARINA. **2.** Possibly Greek *karuon,* nut: KARYO-, GILLYFLOWER, SYNKARYON. **3.** Reduplicated form **kar-kr-o* dissimilated to Latin *cancer,* crab: CANCER, CANCER, CHANCRE. **4.** Suffixed form **kar-k-ino-* in Greek *karkinos,* cancer, crab: CARCINOGEN, CARCINOMA. [Pok. 3. *kar-* 531.]

kar-[2]**.** To praise loudly, extol. **1.** Perhaps Germanic **hrōthi-* in Old High German *hrōd-,* fame: ROBERT, RODERICK, ROGER, ROLAND. **2.** Perhaps Germanic **hrōm-* in Dutch *roemen,* to praise: RUMMER. **3.** Extended lengthened-grade form **kāru-* in Greek (Doric) *karux,* (Attic) *kērux,* herald: CADUCEUS. **4.** Possibly extended form **karsā* in Russian *krasa,* beauty (< "a thing to be extolled"): CRASH[2]. [Pok. 2. *kar-* 530.]

[**karlaz.** Man. Germanic root. **1.** Old English *ceorl,* man, churl: CHURL. **2.** Old Norse *karl,* man, freeman: CARL, CARLING. **3.** Old High German *karal,* man: CARL, CHARLES[1]. [In Pok. *ĝer-* 390.]]

kars-. To card. **1.** Latin *cārere,* to card wool: CARD[2], CARMINATIVE. **2.** Perhaps Latin *carduus,* thistle, artichoke: CARDOON, CHARD. [Pok. *kars-* 532.]

kas-. Gray. **1.** Germanic **hasōn-* in Old English *hara,* hare: HARE. **2.** Suffixed form **kas-no-* in Latin *cānus,* white, gray hair: CANESCENT. [Pok. *kas-* 533.]

kat-[1]**.** Something thrown down; offspring. **1.** Greek *kata,* down: CATA-. **2.** Suffixed form **kat-olo-* in Latin *catulus,* young puppy, young of animals: CADELLE. [Pok. 2. *kat-* 534.]

kat-[2]**.** To fight. Extended form **katu-* in Old Irish *cath,* battle: KERN[1]. [Pok. *kat-* 534.]

kau-[1]**.** To howl (imitative). **1.** Reduplicated suffixed form **ka-kau-ro-* in Sanskrit *cakōra,* a partridge: CHUKAR. **2.** Reduplicated form **kū-kau-ō* in Greek *kōkuein,* to wail, lament: COCYTUS. [Pok. *kau-* 535.]

kau-[2]**.** To hew, to strike. **1.** Germanic **hawwan* in: **a.** Old English *hēawan,* to hew: HEW; **b.** Old Norse *höggva,* to cut: HAGGLE; **c.** Frankish **hauwa,* a hoe: HOE. **2.** Germanic **hawwō* in Old Norse *högg,* a gap, a cutting blow: HAG[2]. **3.** Germanic **haujam* in Old English *hīeg,* hay, cut grass: HAY[1]. **4.** Suffixed form **kau-do-* in Latin *cūdere* (< **caudere*), to strike, beat: INCUS. [Pok. *kāu-* 535.]

kaul-. Stalk, stem. Latin *caulis,* stalk, stem, cabbage-stalk, cabbage: AMPLEXICAUL, CAULESCENT, CAULICLE, CAULIFLOWER, CAULINE, COLCANNON, COLE, COLESLAW, KOHLRABI, NUDICAUL. [Pok. *kau-l-* 537.]

kē-. To sharpen, whet. Suffixed o-grade form **kō-no-,* whetstone, in: **a.** Germanic **hainō* in Old English *hān,* stone: HONE[1]; **b.** Greek *kōnos,* cone, conical object (< "a sharp-pointed object"): CONE. [Pok. *kēi-* 541.]

ked-[1]**.** To go, yield. **1.** Lengthened-grade form **kēd-* in Latin *cēdere,* to go, withdraw, yield: (CEASE), CEDE, CESSION; ABSCESS, ACCEDE, ACCESS, ANCESTOR, ANTECEDE, CONCEDE, CONCESSION, DECEASE, EXCEED, INTERCEDE, PRECEDE, PREDECESSOR, PROCEED, RECEDE, RETROCEDE, SECEDE, SUCCEED. **2.** Prefixed and suffixed form **ne-ked-ti-,* "from which one cannot draw back" (**ne-,* not; see **ne**), in Latin *necesse,* inevitable, unavoidable: NECESSARY. [In Pok. *sed-* 884.]

ked-[2]**.** To smoke. Indo-European root proposed by some as the source of Latin *citrus,* citrus, and Greek *kedros,* cedar, juniper (referring to the smoky blue berries of some varieties of each); but they are more probably borrowed from a non-Indo-European source. [Pok. *ked-* 537.]

keg-. Hook. **1.** Germanic **hakan-* in: **a.** Old Norse *haki,* hook: HAKE; **b.** Middle Low German *hake,* hook: HARQUEBUS. **2.** Germanic lengthened form **hōka-* in: **a.** Old English *hōc,* hook: HOOK; **b.** Middle Dutch *hōk, hoec,* hook: HOOKER[1]. **3.** Germanic **hakila-* in Old English **hæcel,* hatchel, a flax comb with long metal hooklike teeth: HECKLE. **4.** Germanic **hakkijan* in Old English *-haccian,* to hack to pieces as with a hooked instrument: HACK[1]. [Pok. *keg-* 537.]

kei-[1]**.** To lie; bed, couch, night's lodging, home; beloved, dear. **I.** Basic form **kei-.* **1.** Greek *keisthai,* to lie: AMMOCETE. **2.** Suffixed form **kei-wo-* in Germanic **hīwa-* in: **a.** Old English *hīwan,* members of a household: HIND[3]; **b.** Old English *higid,* a measure of land (? < "homestead"): HIDE[3]. **3.** Suffixed form **kei-wi-* in Latin *cīvis,* citizen (< "member of a household"): CITY, CIVIC, CIVIL. **II.** Suffixed o-grade form **koi-mo.* **1.** Germanic **haima,* home, in: **a.** Old English *hām,* home: HOME; **b.** Old Norse *heimr,* home: NIFLHEIM; **c.** Old High German *heim,* house: HENRY; **d.** Middle Dutch *hame,* hame (< "covering"): HAME; **e.** Old French *ham,* village, home: HAMLET; **f.** Latin *-haemum,* home: BOHEMIA[1]; **g.** Germanic **haimatjan,* to go or bring home, in Old French *hanter,* to frequent, haunt: HAUNT; **2.** Suffixed o-grade form **koi-na-* in Latin *cūnae,* a cradle: INCUNABULUM. **3.** Suffixed o-grade form **koi-mā* in Greek *koiman,* to put to sleep: CEMETERY. **III.** Suffixed zero-grade form **ki-wo-* in Sanskrit *śiva,* auspicious, dear: SHIVA. [Pok. 1. *kei-* 539.]

kei-[2]**.** Referring to various adjectives of color. **1.** Suffixed o-grade form **koi-ro-* in Germanic **hairaz,* "gray-haired," old, venerable, hence master, in: **a.** Old English *hār,* gray, hoary: HOAR; **b.** Old High German *hēr,* worthy, exalted: JUNKER; **c.** Middle Dutch *here,* master, lord: YOUNKER. **2.** Suffixed zero-grade form **ki-wo-* in Germanic **hiwan* in Old English *hīw, hēo,* color, appearance, color, form: HUE[1]. [Pok. 2. *kei-* 540.]

kei-[3]**.** To set in motion. **I.** Suffixed o-grade form **koi-d-.* **1.** Germanic **haitan* in Old English *hātan,* to call, summon, order to do something: HIGHT. **2.** Suffixed form **koi-d-tl-* in Germanic **haittiz* in: **a.** Old English *hǣs,* a command, a bidding: HEST; **b.** Old English compound *behǣs,* a vow, promise, command (*be-,* intensive prefix, BE-): BEHEST. **II.** Zero-grade form **ki-.* **1.** Form **ki-ē-* in Latin *ciēre* (past participle *citus*), with its frequentative *citāre,* to set in motion, summon: CITE, EXCITE, INCITE, OSCITANCY, RESUSCITATE, SOLICITOUS. **2.** Suffixed form **ki-neu-* in Greek *kinein,* to move: (-KINESIS), KINETIC; CINEMATOGRAPH, HYPERKINESIA, KINEMATICS, KINESTHESIA, TELEKINESIS. [Pok. *kei-* 538.]

kekw-. To excrete. Suffixed o-grade form **kokw-ro-* in Greek *kopros,* dung: COPRO-. [Pok. *kekw-* 544.]

kel-[1]**.** Warm. **1.** Extended zero-grade form **klē-* in Germanic **hlēwaz* in: **a.** Old English *hlēo, hlēow,* covering, protection (as from cold): LEE; **b.** Old English *hlēow,* warm: LUKEWARM. **2.** Suffixed zero-grade form **kḷ-ē-* in: **a.** Latin *calēre,* to be warm: CALENTURE, CHAFE; CAMOUFLAGE, DECALESCENCE, NONCHALANT, RECALESCENCE; **b.** Latin derivative adjective *calidus,* warm: CALDRON, CAUDLE, CHAUDFROID, CHOWDER, SCALD[1]. **3.** Suffixed zero-grade form **kḷ-os-* in Latin *calor,* heat: CALORIE. [Pok. 1. *kel-* 551.]

kel-[2]**.** To strike, cut; with derivatives referring to something broken or cut off; twig, piece of wood. **1.** Extended form **keldh-* in: **a.** Germanic *held-* in Old English *Hild,* "war," "combat": HILDA; **b.** Germanic feminine name **maht-hildis,* "mighty in battle" (see **magh-**[1]). **2.** Extended zero-grade form **kḷd-* in: **a.** Germanic **hulta-* in Old English *holt,* wood: HOLT; **b.** Greek *klados,* branch, shoot: CLADOCERAN, CLADOPHYLL, PHYLLOCLADE; **c.** Celtic **kaldī* in Old Irish *caill,* forest: CAPERCAILLIE; **d.** suffixed form **kḷd-yo-* in Celtic **klad-yo-* in Latin *gladius,* sword: GLADIATE, GLADIATOR, GLAIVE. **3.** Extended and suffixed o-grade form **kold-o-* in: **a.** Germanic **haltaz,* "with a broken leg," in Old English compound *lempheal*t, limping, halting (*lemp-,* hanging loosely; see **leb-**[1]): LIMP; **b.** Germanic derivative verb **haltōn* in Old English *healtian,* to limp: HALT[2]. **4.** Extended form **kḷə-* in: **a.** Greek *klan,* to break: -CLASE, -CLAST, CLASTIC; **b.** suffixed form **kḷə-ro-* in Greek *klēros,* lot, allotment (< "that which is cut off"): CLERK; **c.** suffixed form **kḷə-mṇ* in Greek *klēma,* twig: CLEMATIS; **d.** suffixed form **kḷə-mo-* in Latin *calamitās,* injury, damage, loss: CALAMITY. **5.** Extended and suffixed o-grade form **kolə-bho-* in Greek *kolaphos,* a blow: COPE[1], COUP. **6.** Extended and suffixed zero-grade form **klō-n-* in Greek *klōn,* twig: CLONE. **7.** Suffixed extended form **klad-ibo-* in Gaelic *claidheamh,* sword: CLAYMORE. See extended root **klēg-.** [Pok. 3. *kel-* 545.]

kel-[3]**.** Also **kelə-.** To shout. **I.** Extended form **klā-.* **1.** Germanic *hlō-* in Old English *hlōwan,* to roar, low: LOW[2]. **2.** Suffixed form **klā-ma-* in Latin *clāmāre,* to call, cry out: CLAIM, CLAMANT, CLAMOR; ACCLAIM, DECLAIM, EXCLAIM, PROCLAIM, RECLAIM. **II.** Variant **kal-.* **1.** Suffixed form **kal-a-* in Germanic **halōn* in: **a.** Middle Dutch *halen,* to haul, pull (? < "to call together, summon"): KEELHAUL; **b.** Middle Low German *halen,* to haul, pull: HALE[2]; **c.** Old French *haler,* to haul: HAUL. **2.** Suffixed form **kal-yo-* in Latin *concilium,* a meeting, a gathering (< "a calling together"; *con-,* together, COM-): CONCILIATE, COUNCIL. **3.** Suffixed form **kal-and-* in Latin *kalendae,* the calends, the first day of the month when it was publicly announced on which days the nones and ides of that month would fall: (CALENDAR), CALENDS. **4.** Suffixed form **kal-eyo-* in Greek *kalein,* to call: ECCLESIA, PARACLETE. **III.** Zero-grade form **klə-.* **1.** Latin *calāre,* to call, call out: INTERCALATE, NOMENCLATOR. **2.** Suffixed form **kḷə-ro-* or suffixed variant form **kḷeə-ro-* contracted to **klā-ro-* in Latin *clārus,* bright, clear: CLARA, CLEAR, GLAIR; CLAIRVOYANCE, CHIAROSCURO, DECLARE, ÉCLAIR, ÉCLAIRCISSEMENT. **IV.** Possibly extended zero-grade form **kḷd-,* becoming **klad-* in suffixed form **klad-ti-* in Latin *classis,* summons, division of citizens for military draft, hence army, fleet, also class in general: CLASS. [Pok. 6. *kel-* 548.]

kel-[4]**.** To cover, conceal, save. **1.** Germanic *haljō,* the underworld (< "concealed place"), in: **a.** Old English *hell,* hell: HELL; **b.** Old Norse *Hel,* underworld, goddess of death: HEL. **2.** Germanic **hallō,* covered place, hall, in: **a.** Old English *heall,* hall: HALL; **b.** Old Norse *hǫll,* hall: VALHALLA; **c.** Old High German *halla,* hall: TURNHALL. **3.** Zero-grade form **kḷ-* in Germanic *hul-* in: **a.** Old English *hulu,* husk, pod (< "that which covers"): HULL; **b.** Old English *hol,* a hollow: HOLE; **c.** Old English *holh,* hole, hollow: HOLLOW; **d.** Old English *healh,* secret place, small hollow: HAUGH; **e.** Dutch *holster,* holster (< "that which covers"): HOLSTER. **4.** Germanic **helmaz,* "protective covering," in: **a.** Old English *helm,* protection, covering: HELM[2]; **b.** Old High German *helm,* helmet: WILLIAM; **c.** Frankish **helm,* helmet: HEAUME, HELMET. **5.** Germanic **hulftī-* in Medieval Latin *hultia,* protective covering: HOUSING[2]. **6.** Suffixed form **kel-os-* in Latin *color,* color, hue (< "that which covers"): COLOR. **7.** Lengthened-grade form **kēl-ā-* in Latin *cēlāre,* to hide: CONCEAL. **8.** Suffixed form **kel-nā* in Latin *cella,* storeroom, chamber: CELL. **9.** Suffixed form **kel-yo-* in Latin *cilium,* lower eyelid: CILIA, SEEL, SUPERCILIOUS. **10.** Zero-grade form **kḷ-* in Latin *occulere,* to cover over (*ob-,* over, OB-): OCCULT. **11.** Extended zero-grade form **kla-* in Latin *clam,* in secret: CLANDESTINE. **12.** Suffixed variant form **kal-up-yo-* in Greek *kaluptein,* to cover, conceal: CALYPSO, CALYPTRA; APOCALYPSE, EUCALYPTUS. **13.** Suffixed o-grade form **kol-eyo-* in Greek *koleon, koleos,* sheath: COLEOPTERAN, COLEOPTILE, COLEORHIZA, COLEUS. See also **klep-.** [Pok. 4. *kel-* 553.]

kel-[5]**.** To drive, set in swift motion. **1.** Extended form **kelt-* possibly in Germanic **halthan,* to drive flocks, keep or pasture cattle, in: **a.** Old English *healdan,* to hold, retain: HOLD[1]; **b.** Old High German *haltan,* to stop, hold back: HALT[1]; **c.** Middle Dutch *houden,* to hold: AVAST. **2.** Suffixed form **kel-es-* in: **a.** Latin *celer,* swift: ACCELERATE, CELERITY; **b.** further suffixed form **kel-es-ri-* in Latin *celeber,* (of a place) much frequented, hence ta-mous: CELEBRATE, CELEBRITY. **3.** Suffixed zero-grade form **kl-on-* in Greek *klonos,* turmoil, agitation: CLONUS. [Pok. 5. *kel-* 548.]

kel-[6]. To lean, tilt. Germanic **halthjan* in Old English *hieldan,* to tilt: HEEL[2]. [Pok. 2. *k̑el-* 552.]

kel-[7]. Gray, black, dark. Suffixed form **kel-ombhā* in Latin *columba,* dove, pigeon: COLUMBA, COLUMBARIUM, COLUMBINE, CULVER. [Pok. 4. *kel-* 547.]

kel-[8]. To be prominent; hill. **1.** Suffixed zero-grade form **kḷ-ni-* in: **a.** Germanic *hulni-* in Old English *hyll,* hill: HILL; **b.** Germanic **hulm-* in Old Norse *holmr,* islet in a bay, meadow: HOLM. **2.** Suffixed form **kel-d-* in Latin *excellere,* to raise up, elevate, also to be eminent (*ex-,* up out of, EX-): EXCEL. **3.** O-grade form **kol-* in: **a.** Greek *kolophōn,* summit: COLOPHON; **b.** suffixed form **kol(u)-men-* in Latin *culmen,* top, summit: CULMINATE; **c.** extended and suffixed form **kolu-mn-ā* in Latin *columna,* a projecting object, a column: COLONEL, COLONNADE, COLUMN. [Pok. 1. *kel-* 544.]

kel-[9]. To prick. Germanic **hulin-* in Old English *holen,* holly (from its spiny leaves): HOLLY. [Pok. 2. *kel-* 545.]

kēl-. To deceive, trick. Suffixed shortened form **kel-w-,* becoming **kalu-,* in: **a.** Latin *calvī,* to deceive, trick: CALUMNY, CHALLENGE; **b.** Latin *cavilla* (< **calvilla*), a jeering: CAVIL. [Pok. *kel-* 551.]

kelb-. To help. Germanic **helpan* in Old English *helpan,* to help: HELP. [Pok. *kelb-* 554.]

kelp-. To hold, grasp. O-grade form **kolp-* in Germanic **halb-* in: **a.** Old English *hielfe,* handle: HELVE; **b.** suffixed form **halb-ma-* in *(i)* Old English *helma,* rudder, tiller: HELM[1] *(ii)* Middle High German *helm,* handle: HALBERD; **c.** suffixed form **half-tra-* in Old English *hælftre,* halter: HALTER[1]. [In Pok. 1. *(s)kel-* 923.]

kem-[1]. Hornless. **1.** Germanic **skamm-* in Old Norse *skammr,* "hornless," short: SCANT. **2.** Suffixed form **kem-tyā* in Germanic **hinthjō* in Old English *hind,* doe: HIND[2]. [Pok. 2. *kem-* 556.]

kem-[2]. To compress. Germanic **hamjan,* a compressing, hence a doubling, in Old English *hem(m),* a doubling over, a hem: HEM[1]. [Pok. 1. *kem-* 555.]

kem-[3]. To hum. Germanic **hum-* in: **a.** Middle English *hummen,* to hum: HUM; **b.** Middle Low German *hummel,* a rumble: HUMBLEBEE. [Pok. 2. *kem-* 556.]

kemə-. To be tired, to tire. Suffixed lengthened o-grade form **kōm-n̥* in Greek *kōma,* deep sleep: COMA[1]. [Pok. 4. *kem(ə)-* 557.]

ken-[1]. To be active. **1.** Suffixed o-grade form **kon-o-* in Greek *diakonos,* servant, attendant (*dia-,* thoroughly, DIA-): DEACON. **2.** Lengthened o-grade form **kōn-ā-* in Latin *cōnārī,* to endeavor: CONATION. [Pok. 4. *ken-* 564.]

ken-[2]. Hypothetical base of a number of loosely related Germanic words referring to pinching, closing the eyes, and other obscurely associated notions. **1.** Old English *hnappian,* to doze, nap: NAP[1]. **2.** Old English *nēpflōd,* neap tide (*flōd,* tide, FLOOD): NEAP TIDE. **3.** Old Norse *hnippa,* to nip: NIP[1]. **4.** Old Norse *hnøggr,* miserly: NIGGARD. **5.** Dutch *nippen,* to sip: NIP[2]. **6.** Middle Dutch *noppe,* pile: NAP[2]. **7.** Low German *nibbeln,* to nibble: NIBBLE. **8.** Middle High German *notten,* to nod: NOD. **9.** Old High German *(h)nascōn,* to nibble: NOSH. [Pok. 2. *ken-* 559.]

ken-[3]. Fresh, new, young. **1.** Suffixed form **ken-t-* in Latin *recens,* young, fresh, new (*re-,* RE-): RECENT. **2.** Suffixed zero-grade form *kn̥-yo-* in Greek *kainos,* new, fresh: -CENE, CENOGENESIS, CENOZOIC, KAINITE. [Pok. 3. *ken-* 563.]

ken-[4]. Empty. Suffixed form **ken-wo-* in Greek *kenos* (< **kenwos*), empty: CENOTAPH, KENOSIS. [Pok. *ken-* 564.]

ken-[5]. Hypothetical base of several roots associated with the notions "to compress," "something compressed." **1.** Germanic root **hnekk-,* "neck" (a narrow or compressed part), in: **a.** Old English *hnecca,* neck: NECK; **b.** Old Norse *hnakkur,* saddle, and Old Norse *hnakki,* back of the neck, akin to the unknown Scandinavian source of KNACKER. **2.** Root *knu-,* nut (< "small hard object"), in: **a.** extended form **knud-* in Old English *hnutu,* nut: NUT; **b.** extended form **knuk-* in Latin *nux,* nut: NEWEL, NOUGAT, NUCLEUS, NUCLEUS. **3.** Germanic root **hnukk-,* sharp projection, tip, in: **a.** Middle Dutch *nocke,* tip of a bow, nock: NOCK; **b.** Norwegian (dialectal) *nok,* projection, hook, akin to the Scandinavian source of Middle English *nok,* corner, nook: NOOK. [Pok. 1. *ken-* 558.]

kenəko-. Yellow, golden. Germanic **hunagam* in Old English *hunig,* honey: HONEY. [Pok. *kenəko-* 564.]

keni-. Dust, ashes. **1.** Latin *cinis,* ashes: CINERARIUM, CINEREOUS, INCINERATE. **2.** O-grade form **koni-* in Greek *konis, konia,* dust: ACONITE, CONIDIUM, KONIOLOGY. [Pok. 2. *ken-* 559.]

kenk-[1]. To gird, bind. Variant form **keng-* in Latin *cingere,* to gird: CINCH[1], CINCTURE, CINGULUM; ENCEINTE[1], ENCEINTE[2], PRECINCT, SHINGLES, SUCCINCT. [Pok. 1. *kenk-* 565.]

kenk-[2]. To suffer from hunger or thirst. Suffixed zero-grade form **kn̥k-ru-* in Germanic **hungruz* in Old English *hungor, hungur,* hunger: HUNGER. [Pok. 2. *kenk-* 565.]

kenk-[3]. Heel, bend of the knee. **1.** Germanic *hanha* in Old English *hōh,* heel: HOCK[1]. **2.** Germanic **hanhila* in Old English *hēla,* heel: HEEL[1]. [Pok. 3. *kenk-* 566.]

kens-. To proclaim, speak solemnly. **1.** Form **kens-ē-* in Latin *cēnsēre,* to judge, assess, estimate, tax: CENSOR, CENSUS, RECENSION. **2.** Probably suffixed o-grade form **kons-mo-* in Greek *kosmos,* order (see **kosmos**). [Pok. *kens-* 566.]

kent-. To prick, jab. **1.** Greek *kentein,* to prick: CENTER, DICENTRA, ECCENTRIC. **2.** Suffixed form **kent-to-* in Greek *kestos,* belt, girdle: CESTUS[1]. [Pok. *kent-* 567.]

kentho-. Also **kento-.** Cloth, rag. Latin *centō,* cento, patchwork: CENTO. [Pok. *kenth(o)-* 567.]

ker-[1]. Horn, head; with derivatives referring to horned animals, horn-shaped objects, and projecting parts. **I.** Zero-grade form **kr̥-.* **1.** Suffixed form **kr̥-n-* in: **a.** Germanic **hurnaz* in *(i)* Old English *horn,* horn: HORN, HORNBEAM *(ii)* Old High German *horn,* horn: ALTHORN, ALPENHORN, BASSET HORN, FLÜGELHORN, HORNBLENDE; **b.** Latin *cornū,* horn: CORN[2], CORNEA, CORNEOUS, CORNER, CORNET, CORNICULATE, CORNU; BICORN, CAPRICORNUS, CAVICORN, CLAVICORN, LAMELLICORN, LONGICORN, TRICORN, UNICORN. **2.** Suffixed and extended form **kr̥s-n-* in Germanic **hurznuta* in Old English *hyrnet,* hornet: HORNET. **3.** Suffixed form **kr̥-n-go-* in Sanskrit *śr̥ṅga,* ginger (from its antler-shaped root): GINGER. **4.** Suffixed form **kr-ei-* in: **a.** Germanic **hraina-* in Old Norse *hreinn,* reindeer: REINDEER; **b.** Germanic **hrinda-* in *(i)* Old High German *hrind,* ox: RINDERPEST *(ii)* Dutch *rund,* small ox: RUNT. **5.** Suffixed extended form **kr̥əs-no-* in Greek *kranion,* skull, upper part of the head: CRANIUM, (MIGRAINE), OLECRANON. **6.** Extended form **kr̥ə-* in: **a.** Greek *karē,* head: CHARIVARI, CHEER; **b.** Greek *karoun,* to stupefy, be stupefied (< "to feel heavy-headed"): CAROTID; **c.** Greek *karōton,* carrot (from its hornlike shape): CARROT. **7.** Extended form **kri-* in Greek *krios,* ram: CRIOSPHINX. **II.** Suffixed form **ker-wo-.* **1.** Latin *cervus,* deer: CERVINE, SERVAL. **2.** Latin *cervīx,* neck: CERVIX. **III.** Extended and suffixed form **keru-do-* in Germanic **herutaz* in: **a.** Old English *heorot,* hart, stag: HART; **b.** Middle Dutch *hert,* hart: HARTEBEEST. **IV.** Extended form **kerəs-.* **1.** Greek *keras,* horn: CARAT, CERASTES, CERATODUS, CERATOID, KERATIN; CHELICERA, CLADOCERAN, RHINOCEROS, TRICERATOPS. **2.** Persian *sar,* head: SIRDAR. **3.** Suffixed form **kerəs-ro-* in Latin *cerebrum,* brain: CEREBELLUM, CEREBRUM, SAVELOY. **V.** Extended o-grade form **koru-.* **1.** Greek *korumbos,* uppermost point (< "head"): CORYMB. **2.** Greek *koruphē,* head: CORYPHAEUS. **3.** Suffixed form **koru-do-* in Greek *korudos,* crested lark: CORYDALIS. [Pok. 1. *ker-* 574.]

ker-[2]. Echoic root, base of various derivatives indicating loud noises or birds. **I.** Zero-grade form **kr̥-,* becoming Germanic **hr-.* **1.** Germanic **hring-* in Old English *hringan,* to resound, clink: RING[2]. **2.** Germanic **hraik-* in Old English *hrǣcan,* to clear the throat: RETCH. **3.** Germanic **hrōkaz,* "croaking bird," crow, in Old English *hrōc,* rook: ROOK[1]. **4.** Germanic **hraban, *hrabnaz,* raven, in Old English *hræfn,* raven: RAVEN[1]. **5.** Extended form **krep-* in Latin *crepāre,* to crack, burst, creak: CRAVEN, CREPITATE, CREVICE, KESTREL; DECREPIT, DECREPITATE, QUEBRACHO. **6.** Extended form **kri-* in Germanic **krik-* in Old French *criquer,* to creak, click: CRICKET[1], CRICKET[2]. **II.** Variant form **skr̥-.* **1.** Germanic **skrīk-* in Old English *scrīc,* thrush: SHRIKE. **2.** Germanic **skrēki-* in Old Norse *skrækja,* to shriek: SCREAK, SCREECH, SHRIEK. **3.** Germanic **skrainjan,* to shout, shriek, in Old Norse *scræma,* to scream: SCREAM. **III.** O-grade form **kor-.* **1.** Latin *corvus,* raven: CORBEL, CORBINA, CORMORANT, CORVINE, CORVUS. **2.** Greek *korax,* raven: CORACOID. **IV.** Extended form *kerk-* in Greek *kerkos,* a rare word for a hawk; but Greek *kerkos,* animal's tail, is not related and is of unknown origin: CERCARIA, CERCOPITHECOID, CYSTICERCUS, HETEROCERCAL, HOMOCERCAL. (**V.** Mistakenly referred to this root is Latin *crīmen,* judgment, crime, which is a derivative of root **skeri-**.) [Pok. 1. *ker-* 567.]

ker-[3]. To grow. **1.** Suffixed form **ker-es-* in Latin *Cerēs,* goddess of agriculture, especially the growth of fruits: CERES[1], (CEREAL). **2.** Extended form **krē-* in: **a.** suffixed form **krē-yā-* in Latin *creāre,* to bring forth, create, produce (< "to cause to grow"): CREATE, CREOLE, PROCREATE; **b.** suffixed form **krē-sko-* in Latin *crēscere,* to grow, increase: CRESCENDO, CRESCENT, CREW[1]; ACCRUE, CONCRESCENCE, CONCRETE, DECREASE, EXCRESCENCE, INCREASE, RECRUIT. **3.** O-grade form **kor-* in: **a.** suffixed form **kor-wo-,* "growing," adolescent, in Greek *kouros, koros,* boy, son: DIOSCURI, HYPOCORISM; **b.** suffixed form **kor-wā* in Greek *korē,* girl, maiden, pupil of the eye: CORA. **4.** Compound **sm̥-kēro-,* "of one growth" (**sem-,* same, one; see **sem-[1]**), in Latin *sincērus,* pure, clean: SINCERE. [Pok. 2. *k̑er-* 577.]

ker-[4]. Heat, fire. **1.** Suffixed form **ker-tā* in Germanic **herthō* in Old English *heorth,* hearth: HEARTH. **2.** Zero-grade form **kr̥-* in: **a.** Latin *carbō,* charcoal, ember: CARBON, CARBONARI, CARBUNCLE; **b.** extended form **krem-* in Latin *cremāre,* to burn: CREMATE. **3.** Possibly suffixed and extended form **kerə-mo-* in Greek *keramos,* potter's clay, earthenware: CERAMIC. [Pok. 3. *ker(ə)-* 571.]

ker-[5]. Also **kerə-.** To injure. Suffixed zero-grade form **kr̥ə-yē-* in Latin *cariēs,* decay, caries: CARIES. [Pok. 4. *k̑er-* 578.]

kerd-[1]. Heart. **1.** Suffixed form **kerd-en-* in Germanic **hertōn-* in Old English *heorte,* heart: HEART. **2.** Zero-grade form **kr̥d-* in: **a.** Latin *cor* (stem *cord-*), heart: CORDATE, CORDIAL, COURAGE, QUARRY[1]; ACCORD, CORDIFORM, CONCORD, DISCORD, MISERICORD, RECORD; **b.** suffixed form **kr̥d-ya-* in Greek *kardia,* heart, stomach, orifice: CARDIA, CARDIAC, CARDIO-; DIPLOCARDIAC, ENDOCARDIUM, EPICARDIUM, MEGALOCARDIA, MYOCARDIUM, PERICARDIUM; **c.** suffixed form **kr̥d-yo-* in Old Irish *cride,* heart: MACHREE. **3.** Possibly **kred-dhə,* "to place trust" (an old religious term; **dhə-,* to do, place; see **dhē-[1]**), in Latin *crēdere,* to believe: CREDENCE, CREDENDUM, CREDIBLE, CREDIT, CREDO, CREDULOUS, GRANT; MISCREANT, RECREANT. [Pok. *k̑ered-* 579.]

kerd-[2]. Craft. Suffixed form **kerd-ā* in Old Irish *cerd,* art, artist: CAIRD. [Pok. 2. *kerd-* 579.]

kerdh-. Row, herd. Suffixed form **kerdh-ā* in Germanic **herdō* in Old English *heord,* herd: HERD. [Pok. *kerdho-* 579.]

kerem-. Also **krem-.** Wild garlic, onion. Germanic **hram-* in Old English *hramsan,* onion, garlic: RAMSON. [Pok. *kerem-* 580.]

kerə-. To mix, confuse, cook. **1.** Variant form **krō-* in Germanic **hrōr-* in: **a.** possibly Old English *hrēr,* lightly boiled, half-cooked: RARE[2]; **b.** Middle Dutch *roer,* motion: UPROAR. **2.** Zero-grade form **kr̥ə-* in: **a.** suffixed form **kr̥ə-ti-* in Greek *krasis,* a mixing: CRASIS, IDIOSYNCRACY; **b.** suffixed form **kr̥ə-ter-* in Greek *kratēr,* mixing vessel: CRATER. [Pok. *k̑erə-* 582.]

kerp-. To gather, pluck, harvest. Variant *karp-.* **1.** Germanic **harbistaz* in Old English *hærfest,* harvest: HARVEST. **2.** Latin *carpere,* to pluck: CARPET, EXCERPT, SCARCE. **3.** Greek *karpos,* fruit: -CARP, CARPEL, CARPO-, -CARPOUS. [In Pok. 4. *sker-* 938.]

kers-[1]. Dark, dirty. **1.** Suffixed form **ker(s)-no-* in Russian *chërnyĭ,* black: CHERNOZEM. **2.** Suffixed zero-grade form **kr̥s-no-* in Sanskrit *kr̥ṣṇāh,* black, dark: KRISHNA[1]. [Pok. *kers-* 583.]

kers-[2]. To run. Zero-grade form **kr̥s-.* **1.** Latin *currere* (past participle *cursus*), to run: CORRIDOR, COURANTE, COURIER, COURSE, CURRENT, CURSIVE, CURULE; CONCOURSE, CONCUR, DECURRENT, DISCOURSE, EXCURSION, HUSSAR, INCUR, INTERCOURSE, OCCUR, PERCURRENT, PRECURSOR, RECOURSE, RECUR, SUCCOR. **2.** Suffixed form **kr̥s-o-* in Gaulish *carros,* a wagon, cart, in: **a.** Latin *carrus,* a two-wheeled wagon: CAR, CAREER, CARGO, CARICATURE, CARIOLE, CAROCHE, CARRY, CHARGE, CHARIOT; **b.** Latin *carpentum,* a two-wheeled carriage: CARPENTER. [Pok. 2. *k̑ers-* 583.]

kert-. To turn, entwine. **I.** Zero-grade form **kr̥t-.* **1.** Suffixed form **kr̥t-i-* in Germanic

hurdiz*, wickerwork frame, hurdle, in: **a. Old English *hyrdel*, hurdle, frame: HURDLE; **b.** Old French *hourd*, fence, hurdle, scaffold: HOARDING[2]. **2.** Suffixed form **kṛt-sti-* in Germanic **hursti-* in Old High German *hurst*, thicket: HORST. **II.** Perhaps suffixed variant form **kṛət-i-* in Latin *crātis*, wickerwork hurdle: CRATE, GRATE[2], GRID, GRIDDLE. [Pok. *kert-* 584.]

kes-[1]. To scratch. **1.** Germanic **hezdō* in Old English *heordan*, coarse parts of flax: HARDS. **2.** Extended form **kseu-* in Greek *xuein*, to scrape: XYSTER. **3.** Nasalized form **ks-n-eu-* in: **a.** Germanic **snaww-* in Old Norse *snöggr*, "close-cropped": SNUG; **b.** Latin *novācula*, razor: NOVACULITE. [Pok. *kes-* 585.]

kes-[2]. To cut. Variant *kas-*. **1.** Suffixed form **kas-tro-* in: **a.** Latin *castrāre*, to castrate: CASTRATE; **b.** Latin *castrum*, fortified place, camp (perhaps "separated place"): CASTLE, CHESTER, ALCAZAR[1]. **2.** Suffixed form **kas-to-* in Latin *castus*, chaste, pure (< "cut off from, free from faults"): CASTE, CHASTE; CASTIGATE, INCEST. **3.** Suffixed (stative) form **kas-ē-* in Latin *carēre*, "to be cut off from," to lack: CARET. **4.** Extended geminated form **kasso-* in Latin *cassus*, empty, void: QUASH[1]. [Pok. *k̑es-* 586.]

keu-[1]. To pay attention, watch, observe, see, hear. **I.** O-grade form **kou-*. **1.** Extended form **kous-* in: **a.** Germanic **hausjan* in *(i)* Old English *hīeran*, to hear: HEAR *(ii)* Old English **heorcian*, to harken: HARK, HEARKEN; **b.** suffixed form **(a)-kous-yo-* in Greek *akouein*, to hear: ACOUSTIC. **2.** Variant **skou-* in: **a.** Germanic **skauwon* in *(i)* Old English *scēawian*, to look at: SHOW *(ii)* Flemish *scauwen*, to look at: SCAVENGER; **b.** Germanic **skaunjaz* in Middle Dutch *schoon*, beautiful, bright (< "conspicuous, attractive"): SCONE; **c.** Germanic **skauniz* in Old English *sciene*, bright, sheen: SHEEN. **II.** Variant form **kaw-ē-* in Latin *cavēre*, to beware, watch, guard against: CAUTION, CAVEAT, PRECAUTION. **III.** Perhaps suffixed zero-grade form **kū-d-os* in Greek *kudos*, glory, renown: KUDOS. [Pok. 1. *keu-* 587.]

keu-[2]. Base of various loosely related derivatives with assumed basic meaning "to bend," whence "a round or hollow object." **I.** Extended forms **keub-*, **keup-*. **1.** Germanic **haup-* in: **a.** Old English *hēap*, heap: HEAP; **b.** Dutch *hoop*, heap, troop: FORLORN HOPE; **c.** Germanic ablaut form **hūpōn-* in Old High German *hūfo*, heap, borrowed into Czech as *houf*, crowd: HOWITZER. **2.** Germanic **hupp-*, to leap (by first bending the legs), in Old English *hoppian*, to hop: HOP[1]. **3.** Germanic **hupiz* in Old English *hype*, hip: HIP[1]. **4.** Zero-grade form **kup-*, vessel, in: **a.** suffixed form **kup-s-* in Greek *kupsele*, chest, hollow vessel: CYPSELA; **b.** lengthened-grade form **kūp-* in *(i)* Germanic **hūfi-* in Old English *hȳf*, hive: HIVE *(ii)* suffixed form **kūp-a* in Latin *cūpa*, tub, vat: COP[1], CUPOLA, CUPULE; **c.** expressive form **kupp-* in Late Latin *cuppa*, drinking vessel: CUP. **5.** Zero-grade form **kub-* in: **a.** Greek *kubos*, cube: CUBE; **b.** form **kub-ā-* in *(i)* Latin *cubāre*, to lie down on (< "to bend down, prostrate"): COUVADE, COVEY, CUBICLE; CONCUBINE, INCUBATE, SUCCUBUS *(ii)* Latin *cubitum*, elbow: CUBIT; **c.** nasalized form **ku-m-b-* in Latin *-cumbere*, to lie down, recline: ACCUMBENT, DECUMBENT, INCUMBENT, PROCUMBENT, RECUMBENT, SUCCUMB; **d.** aspirated lengthened-grade form **kūbh-* in Greek *kuphos*, bent: KYPHOSIS. **II.** Extended o-grade form **kouk-*. **1.** Suffixed form **kouk-o-* in: **a.** Germanic **hauhaz*, "arched," high, in Old English *hēah*, high: HIGH; **b.** Germanic **hauhithō* in Old English *hēhthu*, height: HEIGHT. **2.** Germanic **huk-* in: **a.** Middle Low German *hūken*, to sit in a bent position, squat, akin to the Germanic source of Middle English *huck-*, *huke-*, huckle: HUCKLE; **b.** Middle Low German *hōken*, to bend, squat, bear on the back, peddle: HAWKER; **c.** Old Norse *hokra*, to crouch, akin to the Scandinavian source of HUNKER; **d.** Middle Dutch *hokester* (*-ster*, -STER), "one who squats," peddler: HUCKSTER. **III.** Reduplicated form **ka-ku-bh-* in Latin *cacūmen*, summit, point (< "arch, vault"): CACUMINAL. **IV.** Extended variant form **kauk-* in Greek *kauka*, drinking cup: QUAICH. [Pok. 2. *keu-* 588.]

keu-[3]. To swell; vault, hole. **I.** O-grade form **kou-*. **1.** Basic form **kou-* becoming **kaw-* in Latin *cavus*, hollow, and *cavea*, a hollow: CAGE, CAVE, CAVERN, CAVETTO, GABION, JAIL; CAVICORN, CONCAVE, DECOY, EXCAVATE. **2.** Suffixed form **kow-ilo-* in Greek *koilos*, hollow: -CELE[2], CELIAC, COEL-, COELOM; AMPHICOELOUS. **3.** Suffixed lengthened-grade form **kōw-o-* in Greek *kōos*, hollow place, cavity: CODEINE. **4.** Perhaps Old Breton *caubal*, a kind of boat, akin to the Celtic source of Middle English *coble*, coble: COBLE. **II.** Zero-grade form **ku-*. **1.** Suffixed form **ku-m-olo-* in Latin *cumulus*, heap, mass: CUMULATE, CUMULUS, ACCUMULATE. **2.** Lengthened-grade form **kū-* in: **a.** Germanic **hūn-* in Old Norse *hūnn*, masthead, short stick, young of an animal: HOUND[2]; **b.** suffixed form **kū-ro-*, "swollen," strong, powerful, in Greek *kurios*, master, lord: CHURCH, CYRIL, KERMISS, KIRK, KYRIE ELEISON; **c.** suffixed form **kuw-eyo-* in Greek *kuein*, to swell, and derivative *kūma* (< **kū-mṇ*), "a swelling," wave: CYMA, MAROON[1]. **III.** Suffixed and extended zero-grade form **kua-nt-*, proposed by some as the root of Greek *pas* (oblique stem *pant-*), all, which is more likely from a separate root **pant-*, "all" (cf. Tocharian *pont-*, all): PAN-, DIAPASON. [Pok. 1. *k̑eu-* 592.]

kēu-. To burn. Zero-grade form **kəu-* becoming **kaw-* in suffixed form **kaw-yo-* in Greek *kaiein*, to burn: CALM, CAUSTIC, CAUTERY; CALIBER, ENCAUSTIC, HOLOCAUST. [Pok. 2. *kēu-* 595.]

keub-. Thorn. Germanic **hiup-* in Old English *hēope*, brier, seed vessel of the wild rose: HIP[3]. [Pok. *keub-* 595.]

keuk-. To be white, be bright, shine. Suffixed zero-grade form **kuk-no-* in Greek *kuknos*, swan: CYGNET. [Pok. *keuk-* 597.]

kēwero-. North, north wind. **1.** Germanic **skūra-* in Old English *scūr*, shower, storm: SHOWER[1]. **2.** Germanic **skūrja-* in Old Norse *skūra*, "to fall like a shower," rush in: SCOUR[2]. [Pok. *k̑ēuero-* 597.]

kələwo-. Bald. Variant **kalwo-* in Latin *calvus*, bald: CALVARY, CALVIN. [Pok. *k̯ələuo-* 554.]

kīgh-. Fast, violent. Germanic **hīg-* in Old English *hīgian*, to strive, exert oneself: HIE. [Pok. *kei-gh-* 542.]

kistā. Basket. Greek *kistē*, basket: CHEST, CIST[1], CISTERN, KEISTER. [Pok. *kistā* 599.]

klā-. To spread out flat. Extended shortened form **klat-*. **1.** Germanic **hlathan* in: **a.** Old English *hladan*, to lade, lay on, load: LADE; **b.** Old Norse *hladh*, load: LATHE. **2.** Suffixed form **klat-sto-* in Germanic **hlasta-* in: **a.** Old English *hlæst*, burden, load: LAST[4]; **b.** Old Swedish and Old Danish *last*, burden: BALLAST. [Pok. *kla-* 599.]

klēg-. To cry, sound. Extended root of **kel-[2]**. Zero-grade form **kləg-* becoming **klag-*. **1.** Variant form **klak-* in: **a.** Germanic **hlahjan* in Old English *hliehhan*, to laugh: LAUGH; **b.** Germanic **hlahtraz* in Old English *hleahtor*, laughter: LAUGHTER. **2.** Nasalized form **kla-n-g-* in Latin *clangere*, to sound: CLANG. **3.** Greek *klazein* (< **klaggi-ein*), to roar: KLAXON. [Pok. *kleg-* 599.]

klei-. To lean. **I.** Full-grade form **klei-*. **1.** Suffixed form **klei-n-* in Latin *-clīnāre*, to lean, bend: DECLINE, INCLINE, RECLINE. **2.** Suffixed form **klei-tro-* in Latin **clītra*, litter, with diminutive *clītellae*, packsaddle: CLITELLUM. **3.** Suffixed form **klei-wo-* in Latin *clīvus*, a slope: ACCLIVITY, DECLIVITY, PROCLIVITY. **II.** Zero-grade form **kli-*. **1.** Germanic **hlid-*, "that which bends over," cover, in Old English *hlid*, cover: LID. **2.** Suffixed form **kli-n-* in Germanic **hlinēn*, in Old English *hlinian* and *hlænan*, to lean: LEAN[1]. **3.** Suffixed form **kli-ent-* in Latin *cliēns*, dependent, follower: CLIENT. **4.** Lengthened form **klī-* in: **a.** suffixed form **klī-n-yo-* in Greek *klinein*, to lean: CLINE, CLINO-, CLITORIS; ACLINIC, ENCLITIC, ISOCLINE, MATRICLINOUS, MONOCLINIC, PATRICLINOUS, PERICLINE, PROCLITIC, SYNCLINAL; **b.** suffixed form **klī-n-ā* in Greek *klinē*, bed: CLINIC, CLINO-, DICLINOUS, MONCLINOUS, TRICLINIUM; **c.** suffixed form **klī-m-* in Greek *klimax*, ladder: CLIMAX; **d.** suffixed form **klī-mṇ-* in Greek *klima*, sloping surface of the earth: CLIMATE. **III.** Suffixed o-grade form **kloi-tr-* in Germanic **hlaidr-* in Old English *hlǣd(d)er*, ladder: LADDER. [Pok. *k̑lei-* 600.]

kleng-. To bend, turn. **1.** Germanic **hlink-* in: **a.** Old English *hlinc*, ridge: LINKS; **b.** Old Norse **hlenkr*, loop of a chain: LINK[1]; **c.** Old French *flenchir*, to turn aside, flinch: FLINCH. **2.** Germanic **hlank-* in: **a.** Old English *hlanc*, lean, thin (< "flexible"): LANK; **b.** Frankish **hlanca*, hip, side (where the body curves): FLANK. [Pok. *kleng-* 603.]

klep-. To steal. Extension of **kel-[4]**. Suffixed form **klep-yo-* in Greek *kleptein*, to steal: CLEPSYDRA, KLEPTOMANIA. [Pok. *klep-* 604.]

kleu-[1]. To hear. **I.** Extended form **kleus-* in Germanic **hliuza-* in Old English *hlēor*, cheek (< "side of the face" < "ear"): LEER. **II.** Zero-grade form **klu-*. **1.** Germanic **hlusti* in Old English *hlystan*, to listen: LIST[4]. **2.** Germanic **hlusinōn* in Old English *hlysnan*, to listen: LISTEN. **3.** Suffixed (participial) form **klu-to-* in Germanic **hluth-*, "heard, famed," in Old High German name *Hluodowīg*, "famous in battle" (see **weik-[5]**). **4.** Suffixed lengthened form **klū-to-* in Germanic **hlūdaz*, "heard," loud, in: **a.** Old English *hlūd*, loud: LOUD; **b.** Old High German *hlūti*, sound: ABLAUT, UMLAUT. **III.** Suffixed form **klewes-yo-* in Greek *kleiein*, to praise, tell: CLIO. [Pok. 1. *k̑leu-* 605.]

kleu-[2]. To wash, clean. **1.** Latin *cloāca*, sewer, canal: CLOACA. **2.** Zero-grade form **klu-* in Greek *kluzein*, to wash out: CATACLYSM, CLYSTER, KLYSTRON. [Pok. 2. *k̑leu-* 607.]

klēu-. Hook, peg. **I.** Extended zero-grade form **klud-* possibly in Germanic **hluta-*, lot, portion (semantic development obscure). **1.** Old English *hlot*, lot: LOT. **2.** Middle Dutch *lot*, lot: LOTTERY. **3.** Frankish **lot*, lot, portion: ALLOT, LOTTO. **II.** Suffixed variant form **klau-do-* in Latin *claudere*, to close (< "to lock with a hook, bolt"): CLAUSE, CLOISONNÉ, CLOISTER, CLOSE; CONCLUDE, ECLOSION, EXCLUDE, INCLUDE, OCCLUDE, PRECLUDE, RECLUSE, SECLUDE. **III.** Variant form **klāw-*. **1.** Suffixed form **klāw-i-* in: **a.** Latin *clāvis*, key: CEMBALO, CLAVICLE, CLAVIER, CLEF, KEVEL; CLAVICHORD, CONCLAVE, ENCLAVE; **b.** Greek *kleis*, key: OPHICLEIDE. **2.** Suffixed form **klāw-o-* in: **a.** Latin *clāvus*, nail: CLOVE[1], CLOY; **b.** Latin *clāva*, club: CLAVATE, CLAVICORN, CLAVIFORM. **3.** Suffixed form **klāw-yo-* in: **a.** Greek *kleiein*, to close: CLATHRATE; **b.** Greek verbal adjective *kleistos*, closed: CLEISTOGAMOUS. [Pok. *kleu-* 604.]

klou-. To bend. Proposed by some as the root of Germanic **hlaupan*, to leap, which is more likely of unknown origin. Germanic **hlaupan* in: **a.** Old English *hlēapan*, to leap: LEAP, ELOPE; **b.** Old English *hlēapwince*, lapwing (*-wince*, perhaps "move sideways," akin to Old English *wincian*, to WINK): LAPWING; **c.** Old Norse *hlaupa*, to leap: LOPE; **d.** Middle Dutch *loopen*, to leap, run: INTERLOPE; **e.** Middle Low German *lōpen*, to run, leap: ORLOP; **f.** Middle Low German *lōp*, course, running: GANTLET[1]; **g.** Old High German *hlouf(f)an*, to leap: LANGLAUF; **h.** Frankish **hlaupan*, to jump, run: GALLOP, WALLOP.

kneigwh-. To lean on. **1.** Latin *cōnīvēre* (< **con-eniguēre; com-*, together, COM-), "to lean together" (said of eyelids), to close the eyes, be indulgent: CONNIVE. **2.** Suffixed zero-grade form **knigwh-to-* in Latin *nictāre*, to move the eyelids, wink: NICTITATE. **3.** Uncertain preform in Latin *nītī*, to lean forward, strive: NISUS, RENITENT. [Pok. *knei-guh-* 608.]

knid-. Egg of a louse. Suffixed form **knid-ā* in Germanic **hnitō* in Old English *hnitu*, egg of a louse: NIT. [Pok. *knid-* 608.]

ko-. Stem of demonstrative pronoun meaning "this." **I.** Variant form **ki-*. **1.** Germanic **hi-* in: **a.** Old English *he*, he: HE[1]; **b.** Old English *him*, him: HIM; **c.** Old English *his*, his: HIS; **d.** Old English *hire*, her: HER; **e.** Old English *hit*, it: IT; **f.** Old English *hēr*, here: HERE; **g.** Old English *heonane*, from here: HENCE. **2.** Suffixed form **ki-tro-* in Germanic **hi-thra-* in Old English *hider*, hither: HITHER. **3.** Suffixed form **ki-s* in Latin *cis*, on this side of: CIS-. **II.** Variant form **ke-*. **1.** Prefixed form **ghi-ke* (**ghi-*, demonstrative particle; see **ghe-**) in Latin *hic*, this: ENCORE. **2.** Preposed in **ke-etero-* (**e-tero-*, a second time, again; see **i-**) in Latin *cēterus*, the other part, that which remains: ET CETERA. **3.** Latin *-ce* (see **nu-**). **III.** Attributed by some to this root (but more likely of obscure origin) is Germanic root **hind-*, behind. **1.** Old English *hindan*, behind: HIND[1]. **2.** Old English *bihindan*, in the rear, behind (*bi*, at, BY): BEHIND. **3.** Old High German *hintar*, behind: HINTERLAND. **4.** Germanic derivative verb **hindrōjan*, to keep back, in Old English *hindrian*, to check, hinder: HINDER[1]. [Pok. *ko-* 609.]

kob-. To suit, fit, succeed. Germanic **hap-* in Old Norse *happ*, chance, good luck: HAP. [Pok. *kob-* 610.]

[kokkos. Kermes berry, pit. Greek noun of unknown origin: COCCID, COCCUS, COCHINEAL, COCOON, MONOCOQUE.]

koksā. Body part. Latin *coxa*, hip: COXA, CUISSE, CUSHION. [Pok. *koksā* 611.]

kolei-. Glue. Suffixed variant form **koly-a* in Greek *kolla*, glue: COLLAGE, COLLO-, COLLODION, PROTOCOL. [Pok. *kol(e)i-* 612.]

koləm-. Grass, reed. Suffixed form **koləm-o-*. **1.** Germanic **halmaz* in: **a.** Old English *healm*, straw: HAULM; **b.** Old Norse *halmr*, grass:

MARRAM. 2. Latin culmus, stalk: CULM[1]. 3. Zero-grade form *kḷəm-o- in Greek kalamos, a reed: CALAMITE, CALAMUS, CALUMET, CARAMEL, SHAWM. [Pok. k̑oləmo-s 612.]

kom. Beside, near, by, with. 1. Germanic *ga- in Old English ge-, together, with (collective and intensive prefix): Y-; HANDIWORK. 2. Latin cum, co-, with: CUM; CONQUIAN. 3. Old Latin com, with: COM-. 4. Old Welsh kom-, with: CAMBRIA, (CYMRY). 5. Suffixed form *kom-trā in Latin contrā, against, opposite: CON[1], CONTRA-, CONTRARY, COUNTER[1], COUNTRY; ENCOUNTER. 6. Suffixed form *kom-yo- in Greek koinos, common, shared: CENOBITE, COENO-, EPICENE, KOINE. 7. Reduced form *ko- (see **mei-**[1]). [Pok. kom 612.]

konəmo-. Shinbone, bone. Reduced form *kommo- perhaps in Germanic *hamma in Old English hamm, ham, thigh: HAM. [Pok. konəmo- 613.]

konk-. To hang. 1. Germanic *hanhan in: a. Old Norse hanga, Old English hon, and Old English hangian, to hang: HANG; b. Dutch (dialectal) hankeren, to long for: HANKER; c. possibly Middle English he(e)ng, hinge (ultimately from the base of Old English hangian, to hang): HINGE. 2. Suffixed form *konk-t-ā- in Latin cūnctārī, to delay: CUNCTATION. [Pok. kenk- 566, konk- 614.]

konkho-. Mussel, shellfish. 1. Greek konkhē, konkhos, mussel, conch: COCKLE[1], CONCH, CONCHO-, CONGIUS. 2. Greek kokhlos, land snail: COCHLEA. [Pok. konkho- 614.]

kormo-. Pain. Germanic *harmaz in Old English hearm, harm: HARM. [Pok. k̑ormo- 615.]

koro-. War; also war-band, host, army. I. Germanic *harjaz, army. 1. Old English here, army: HERIOT, OLIVER. 2. Old Norse herr, army: HARNESS. 3. Old High German heri, hari, army: ARRIÈRE-BAN, HERBERT, HERMAN, WALTER. 4. Compound *harja-bergaz, "army hill," hill-fort, later shelter, lodging, army quarters (*bergaz, hill; see **bhergh-**[2]), in: a. Old English herebeorg, lodging: HARBOR; b. Old Saxon heriberga, "army shelter," lodging: HARBINGER; c. Vulgar Latin *arberga, army camp: AUBERGE. 5. Compound *harja-waldaz, "army commander" (*wald-, rule, power; see **wal-**), in: a. Old Norse name Haraldr: HAROLD; b. Old French herau(l)t, herald: HERALD. II. Germanic denominative *harjōn in Old English hergian, to ravage, plunder, raid: HARRY. III. Germanic compound *harihring, assembly, "host-ring" (*hringaz, ring; see **sker-**[3]), in Medieval Latin harenga, harangue: HARANGUE. [Pok. koro-s 615.]

koselo-. Hazel. Germanic *haselaz in Old English hæsel, hazel: HAZEL. [Pok. kos(e)lo- 616.]

[kosmos. Order, universe. Greek noun, probably from *kons-mo-, a suffixed o-grade form of **kens-**. COSMOS, MACROCOSM.**]**

kost-. Bone. Probably related to root **osth-**. Latin costa, rib, side: COAST, COSTA, COSTARD, COSTREL, CUESTA, CUTLET; ACCOST, INTERCOSTAL. [Pok. kost- 616.]

krapo-. Roof. Germanic *hrōfam in Old English hrōf, roof: ROOF. [Pok. krapo- 616.]

krāu-. Also **krū-**. To conceal, hide. Suffixed extended form *krup-yo- in Greek kruptein, to hide: CRYPT, CRYPTO-, KRYPTON; APOCRYPHA. [Pok. krā(u)- 616.]

kred-. Framework, timberwork. Possible root. Germanic *hrō(d)-st- in Old English hrōst, roost: ROOST. [Pok. kred- 617.]

krek-[1]. To weave, beat. Possible root. 1. Germanic *hrehulaz in Old English hreōl, reel, spool for winding cord: REEL[1]. 2. Suffixed o-grade form *krok-u- in Greek krokus, nap of cloth: CROCIDOLITE. [Pok. 1. krek- 618.]

krek-[2]. Frog spawn, fish eggs. Germanic *hrog- in Middle Low German and Middle Dutch roge, roe: ROE[1]. [Pok. 2. krek- 619.]

krep-. Body. 1. Suffixed form *krep-es- in Germanic *hrifiz in Old English hrif, belly: MIDRIFF. 2. Suffixed zero-grade form *kṛp-es- in Latin corpus, body, substance: CORPORAL[1], CORPORAL[3], CORPUS, LEPRECHAUN. [Pok. 1. krep- 620.]

kret-[1]. To shake. O-grade form *krot- in: a. Germanic *hrathaz, swift, nimble, in Old English hræth, nimble, quick, prompt, ready: RATHE, (RATHER); b. Germanic *hra(th)skuz in Middle Dutch rasch, nimble, quick: RASH[1]. [Pok. 1. kret- 620.]

kret-[2]. To beat. O-grade form *krot- in Greek krotein, to strike, beat: DICROTISM, TRICROTIC. [Pok. 2. kret- 621.]

kreu-[1]. Raw flesh. 1. Lengthened-grade form *krēw- in Germanic *hrēwaz in Old English hrēaw, raw: RAW. 2. Suffixed form *krew-əs- in Greek kreas, flesh: CREATINE, CREODONT, PANCREAS. 3. Suffixed lengthened zero-grade form *krū-do- in: a. Latin crūdus, bloody, raw: CRUDE, ECRU, RECRUDESCE; b. Latin crūdēlis, cruel: CRUEL. [Pok. 1. kreu- 621.]

kreu-[2]. To push, strike. 1. Germanic *hrewwan in Old English hrēowan, to distress, grieve: RUE[1], RUTH. 2. O-grade form *krou- in Greek krouein, to push: ANACRUSIS. [Pok. 3. kreu- 622.]

kreup-. Scab; to become encrusted. 1. Germanic *hrub- in: a. Old Norse hrufa, scurviness, scab: DANDRUFF; b. Italian ruffia, roffia, scab, filth: RUFFIAN; c. Middle Low German ruffelen, to crumple, akin to the Germanic source of Middle English ruffelen, to ruffle: RUFFLE[1]; d. Germanic compound *ga-hrub- (*ga-, intensive prefix; see **kom**) in Middle Dutch grof, harsh: GRUFF. 2. Suffixed o-grade form *kroup-ā in Serbo-Croatian krupa, groats: GRAUPEL. [Pok. kreup- 623.]

kreut-. Reed. Germanic *hriuda- in Old English hrēod, reed: REED. [Pok. kreut- 623.]

krut-. Musical instrument. 1. Germanic *hrut- in Old French rote, a stringed instrument: ROTE[3]. 2. Geminated form *kruttā in Welsh crwth, an ancient Celtic instrument: CROWD[2]. [Pok. krut- 624.]

ksei-[1]. To settle. Zero-grade form *ksi- in Greek ktizein, to found: AMPHICTYONY. [Pok. kthei- 626.]

ksei-[2]. To rule. 1. Suffixed reduced form *kse-tro- in: a. Sanskrit ksatram, might, power, in kṣayati, he rules: KSHATRIYA; b. Old Persian khshathra-, kingdom, province: SATRAP. 2. Extended form *kseye- in: a. suffixed form *kseye-tyo- in Old Persian khshāyathiya, king, shortened to Persian shāh, king: CHECK, SHAH; b. Old Persian khshaya-, king, ruling: XERXES. [Pok. kthei(i)- 626.]

ksero-. Dry. 1. Lengthened-grade form *ksēro- in Greek xēros, dry: ELIXIR, PHYLLOXERA, XERO-. 2. Perhaps suffixed variant form *kseres-no- in Latin serēnus, serene, bright, clear: SERENE. [Pok. ksero- 625.]

ksun. Preposition and pre-verb meaning "with." 1. Greek sun, xun, with: SYN-. 2. Russian so, s-, with: SPUTNIK. 3. Polish se, with, in compound sejm, assembly (see **em-**). [In Pok. 2. sem- 902.]

ku-. Hypothetical base of a variety of conceivably related Germanic words meaning "a hollow space or place, an enclosing object, a round object, a lump," and some other derivative denotations. 1. Germanic *kubon, hut, shed, room, in: a. Old English cofa, bedchamber, closet: COVE[1]; b. Middle Dutch cubbe, "pen, stall," fish basket: CUBBY; c. Germanic compound *kubawald-, probably "house ruler," household god (wald-, power; see **wal-**), in Middle High German kobolt, an underground goblin: COBALT, GOBLIN, KOBOLD. 2. Germanic *kutam in Old English cot, cottage: COT[2]. 3. Germanic *kutōn in Old English cote, shelter: COTE[1], (COTTAGE). 4. Germanic *k(e)ud- in: a. Old English codd, bag, husk: COD[2]; b. Old English cudele, cuttlefish (from its ink bag): CUTTLE. 5. Germanic *k(e)ut- in Old English *cieter, intestines: CHITTERLINGS. 6. Germanic *kukk- in Old English *cocc, round heap, pile of straw: COCK[2]. 7. Germanic *kuk- in Old English cīcen, chicken: CHICKEN. 8. Germanic *kugg- in Swedish kugge, cog, akin to the Scandinavian source of Middle English cogge, cog: COG[1]. 9. Germanic *kuggila in Old English cycgel, rod, cudgel: CUDGEL. 10. Germanic *kubb- possibly in Swedish dialectal kubb, kubbug, block, log, akin to the Scandinavian source of CHUB. 11. Germanic *kupp- in Old English (ātor)coppe, spider (ātor, poison): COBWEB. 12. Germanic *keulaz in: a. Middle Low German kiel, ship, keel of a ship: KEELSON; b. Middle Dutch kiel, ship, keel of a ship: KEEL[2]. 13. Germanic *kelaz in Old Norse kjōlr, keel: KEEL[1]. 14. Germanic *kūp- in Middle Low German kūpe, tub, basket: COOP. 15. Germanic *kunt- in Middle Low German kunte, vulva, akin to the Low German source of Middle English cunte, vulva: CUNT. 16. Germanic *kūrā- in Icelandic kūrā, to crouch, lie in wait, akin to the Scandinavian source of Middle English couren, to cower: COWER. 17. Possibly Old Norse kūga, to oppress: COW[2]. [In Pok. gēu- 393.]

kus-. A kiss. Germanic *kussaz, a kiss, with denominative *kussjan in Old English cyssan, to kiss: KISS. [Pok. ku-, kus- 626.]

kwath-. To ferment, be sour. Suffixed variant form *kwāt-so- in Common Slavic *kwasŭ in Russian kvas, kvass: KVASS. [Pok. ku̯at(h)- 627.]

kwe. And (enclitic). Latin -que, and: SESQUI-, UBIQUITY. [Pok. ku̯e 635.]

kwed-. To sharpen. Germanic *hwatjan in Old English hwettan, to whet: WHET. [Pok. ku̯ed- 636.]

kwei-[1]. To pay, atone, compensate. 1. Suffixed o-grade form *kwoi-nā in Greek poinē, fine, penalty, borrowed into Latin as poena, penalty: IMPUNITY, PAIN, PENAL, PENOLOGY, PINE[2], PUNISH, SUBPOENA. 2. Suffixed lengthened zero-grade form *kwī-mā in Greek timē, honor, worth: TIMOCRACY, TIMOTHY[1]. [Pok. ku̯ei-t- 636.]

kwei-[2]. To pile up, build, make. O-grade form *kwoi- in: a. Sanskrit kāya, body: CHEETAH; b. suffixed form *kwoi-eyo- in Greek poiein, to make, create: POEM, POESY, POET, -POIESIS, -POIETIC; MYTHOPOEIC, ONOMATOPOEIA, PHARMACOPOEIA, PROSOPOPEIA. [Pok. 2. ku̯ei- 637.]

kwei-[4]. To hiss, whistle. Imitative root. Germanic *hwī-n- and *hwis- in: a. Old English hwīnan, to whine: WHINE; b. Old English hwisprian, to whisper: WHISPER; c. Old English hwistlian, to whistle: WHISTLE. [Pok. 2. k̑u̯ei- 628.]

kweit-. White; to shine. Suffixed form *kweit-o-. 1. Germanic *hwītaz in: a. Old English hwīt, white: WHITE; b. Middle Dutch wijting, whiting: WHITING[2]; c. Old High German hwīz, wīz, white: EDELWEISS. 2. Germanic *hwaitjaz in Old English hwǣte, wheat (from the fine white flour it yields): WHEAT. [Pok. 3. k̑u̯ei- 628.]

kwek-. To appear, see, show. Variant form *kweg- in Slavic *kaz- in Russian kazat', to show: UKASE. [Pok. ku̯ek- 638.]

kwel-[1]. To revolve, move around, sojourn, dwell. I. Basic form *kwel-. 1. Latin colere, to cultivate, inhabit: COLONY, CULTIVATE, (CULTURE), INCULT. 2. Latin inquilīnus (in-, in, IN-), tenant, dweller: INQUILINE. II. Extended form *kwelos- in Greek telos, "completion of a cycle," consummation, perfection, end, result: TELIC, TELIUM, TELO-; ENTELECHY, TALISMAN, TELEOLOGY, TELEUTOSPORE, TELSON. III. Suffixed reduplicated form *kw(e)-kwl-o-, circle. 1. Germanic *hwehula in Old English hwēol, hweogol, wheel: WHEEL. 2. Greek kuklos, circle, wheel: CYCLAMEN, CYCLE; BICYCLE, ENCYCLICAL. 3. Sanskrit cakra-, circle: CHUKKER. 4. Possibly Persian charkha, wheel: CHARKHA. IV. O-grade form *kwol-. 1. Suffixed form *kwol-so-, "that on which the head turns," neck, in: a. Germanic *h(:w)alsaz in (i) Old Norse hals, neck, ship's bow: HAWSE (ii) Middle Dutch hals, neck: RINGHALS (iii) Germanic compound *h(w)als-berg-, "neck-protector," gorget (*bergan, to protect; see **bhergh-**[1]), in Old French hauberc, hauberk: HAUBERK; b. Latin collum, neck: COL, COLLAR, COLLET, CULLET; ACCOLADE, DÉCOLLETÉ, TORTICOLLIS. 2. Suffixed form *kwol-ā in Latin -cola and incola, inhabitant (in-, in, IN-): -COLOUS, PRATINCOLE. 3. Suffixed form *kwol-o- in: a. Latin anculus, "he who bustles about," servant (an-, short for ambi-, about, around, AMBI-): ANCILLARY; b. Greek polos, axis of a sphere: POLE[1], PULLEY; c. Greek -kolos, herdsman: BUCOLIC. 4. Suffixed form *kwol-es- in Old Church Slavonic kolo, wheel: CALASH, KOLACKY. 5. Suffixed zero-grade form *kwḷ-i- in Greek palin, again (< "revolving"): PALIMPSEST, PALINDROME, PALINGENESIS, PALINODE. [Pok. 1. ku̯el- 639.]

kwel-[2]. Far (in space and time). 1. Lengthened-grade form *kwēl- in Greek tēle, far off: TELE-. 2. Suffixed zero-grade form *kwḷ-ai in Greek palai, long ago: PALEO-. [Pok. 2. ku̯el- 640.]

kweləək-. Bundle. Proposed by some as the root of Latin culcita, mattress, sack, which is more likely of unknown origin: QUILT. [Pok. ku̯elək- 630.]

kwelp-. To arch. 1. Germanic *hwalbjan in Old English *kwelfan, hwylfan, with parallel form *hwelman, to turn over: WHELM. 2. Suffixed o-grade form *kwolp-o- in Greek kolpos, bosom, womb, vagina: COLPITIS, GULF. [Pok. 2. ku̯elp- 630.]

kwen-. Holy. Suffixed zero-grade form *kwṇ-s-lo- in Germanic *hunslam in Old English hūsl, Eucharist: HOUSEL. [Pok. k̑u̯en- 630.]

kwenth-. To suffer. 1. Suffixed form *kwenth-es- in Greek penthos, grief: NEPENTHE. 2. Zero-grade form *kwṇth- in: a. Greek pathos, suffering, passion, emotion, feelings: PATHETIC, PATHO-, PATHOS, -PATHY; SYMPATHY; b. suffixed form *kwṇth-skō in Greek paskhein, to feel, suffer: PROTOPATHIC. [Pok. ku̯enth- 641.]

kwēp-. To smoke, cook, move violently, be agitated emotionally. 1. Suffixed variant form *kup-yo- in Latin cupere, to desire: COVET,

CUPID, CUPIDITY; CONCUPISCENCE. 2. Zero-grade form *kwəp-, becoming *kwap- possibly in: a. Latin *vapor*, steam, vapor: VAPOR, EVAPORATE; b. Latin *vapidus*, that has emitted steam or lost its vapor, flat, poor: VAPID. [Pok. *ku̯ēp-* 596.]

kwer-[1]. To make. 1. Sanskrit *kṛ*, to make, do: PRAKRIT, SANSKRIT. 2. Suffixed form **kwer-ōr* with dissimilated form **kwel-ōr* in Greek *pelōr*, monster (perhaps "that which does harm"): PELORIA. 3. Suffixed form **kwer-as-* in Greek *teras*, monster: TERATOID. 4. Suffixed form **kwer-mn̥-* in Sanskrit *karman*, act, deed: KARMA. [Pok. 1. *ku̯er-* 641.]

kwer-[2]. Something shaped like a dish or shell. Suffixed variant form **kwar-yo-* in Scottish Gaelic *coire*, cauldron, hollow, whirlpool: CORRIE. [Pok. 2. *ku̯er-* 642.]

kwerp-. To turn oneself. 1. Germanic **hwarb-* in Old English *hwearf*, wharf (< "place where people move about"): WHARF. 2. Germanic **hwerban* in: a. Old Norse *hverfa*, to turn: VARVE; b. Old Norse **hvirfa*, to whirl, perhaps assimilated to Danish *hvirre*, to whir, akin to the Scandinavian source of Middle English *whirren*, to whir: WHIR; c. Old Norse *hvirfla*, to whirl: WHIRL; d. Frankish **hwirbilōn*, to whirl: WARBLE[1]. 3. Suffixed zero-grade form **kwr̥p-o-* in Greek *karpos*, wrist: CARPAL, CARPUS. [Pok. *ku̯erp-* 631.]

kwes-. To pant, wheeze. 1. Germanic **hwēsjan* in Old Norse *hvæsa*, to hiss: WHEEZE. 2. Latin *querī*, to complain: QUARREL[1], QUERULOUS. 3. Suffixed zero-grade form **kus-ti-* in Greek *kustis*, bladder, bag (< "bellows"): CYST, CYSTO-. [Pok. *ku̯es-* 931.]

kwēt-. To shake. Zero-grade form **kwət-*, becoming **kwat-* in: a. Latin *quatere*, to shake, strike: CASCARA, CASHIER[2], QUASH[2], SCUTCH, SQUASH[2]; CONCUSS, DISCUSS, PERCUSS, RESCUE, SUCCUSSION; b. Greek *passein*, to sprinkle: PASTE[1]. [Pok. *ku̯ēt-* 632.]

kwetwer-. Four. I. O-grade form **kwetwor-*. 1. Probably Germanic **petwor-* in: a. Old English *fēower*, four: FOUR; b. Old English *fēowertig*, forty (*-tig*, -TY): FORTY; c. Old English *fēowertīene*, fourteen (*-tīene*, -TEEN): FOURTEEN; 2. Latin *quattuor*, four: QUATRAIN, CATER-CORNERED, QUATTROCENTO. II. Multiplicatives **kweturs*, **kwetrus*, and combining forms **kwetur-*, **kwetru-*. 1. Latin *quater*, four times: CAHIER, CARILLON, CASERN, QUATERNARY, QUIRE. 2. Latin *quadrus*, four-sided thing, square: CADRE, QUADRATE, QUARREL[2], QUARRY[2], SQUAD, SQUARE, TROCAR. 3. Latin *quadru-*, four: QUADRU-. 4. Latin *quadri-*, four: QUADRI-. 5. Latin *quadra*, square: QUADRILLE[1]. 6. Latin *quadrāns*, a fourth part: QUADRANT. 7. Latin *quadrāgintā*, forty (*-gintā*, ten times; see **dekm̥**): QUARANTINE. 8. Variant form **kwet(w)r̥-* in: a. Greek *tetra-*, four: TETRA-; b. Greek *tessares*, *tettares*, four: TESSERA; DIATESSARON; c. Greek *tetras*, group of four: TETRAD; d. Zero-grade form **kwt(w)r̥-* in Greek *tra-*, four: TRAPEZIUM. III. Ordinal adjective **kwetur-to-*. 1. Germanic **fi(th)worthon* in: a. Old English *fortha*, *fēowertha*, fourth: FOURTH; b. Middle Dutch *vierde*, fourth: FIRKIN; c. Old English *fēorthing*, fourth part of a penny: FARTHING. 2. Latin *quārtus*, fourth, quarter: QUADRILLE[2], QUADROON, QUART[1], QUARTAN, QUARTER, QUARTO. [Pok. *ku̯etu̯er-* 642.]

kweyə-. Cozy, quiet. I. Suffixed zero-grade variant form **kwī-lo-*. 1. Germanic **hwīlō* in: a. Old English *hwīl*, while: WHILE; b. Old English *hwīlum*, sometimes: WHILOM. 2. Possibly Latin *tranquillus*, tranquil (*trāns-*, TRANS-): TRANQUIL. II. Suffixed zero-grade variant form **kwyē-t-* in Latin *quiēs*, quiet: (COY), QUIET; ACQUIESCE, ACQUIT, REQUIEM, REQUIESCAT. [Pok. *ku̯ei-* 638.]

kwo-. Also **kwi-**. Stem of relative and interrogative pronouns. 1. Germanic **hwa-*, *hwi-* in: a. personal pronouns **hwas*, **hwasa*, **hwam*, in Old English *hwā*, *hwæs*, *hwæm*, who, whose, whom: WHO, WHOSE, WHOM; b. pronoun **hwat* in Old English *hwæt*, what: WHAT; c. adverb **hwī* in Old English *hwȳ*, why: WHY; d. relative pronoun **hwa-līk-* (**līk-*, body, form; see **līk-**) in Old English *hwilc*, *hwelc*, which: WHICH; e. adverb **hwō* in Old English *hū*, how: HOW[1]; f. adverb **hwan-* in *(i)* Old English *hwenne*, *hwanne*, when: WHEN *(ii)* Old English *hwanon*, whence: WHENCE; g. adverb **hwithrē* in Old English *hwider*, whither: WHITHER; h. adverb **hwar-* in Old English *hwǣr*, where: WHERE. 2. Germanic **hwatharaz* in: a. Old English *hwæther*, which of two, whether: NEITHER, WHETHER; b. Germanic phrase **aiwo gihwatharaz*, "ever each of two" (**aiwo*, **aiwi*, ever; see **aiw-**; **gi-*, from **ga-*, collective prefix; see **kom**), in Old English *ǣghwæther*, either: EITHER. 2. Latin *quī*, who: QUA, QUIBBLE, QUORUM. 3. Latin *quid*, what, something: HIDALGO, QUIDDITY, QUIDNUNC, QUIP. 4. Latin *quam*, than, how: QUASI. 5. Latin *quod*, what: QUODLIBET. 6. Latin *quot*, how many: ALIQUOT, QUOTE, QUOTIENT, QUOTIDIAN. 7. Latin *quom*, when: QUONDAM. 8. Latin *quem*, whom: CONQUIAN. 9. Latin *quantus*, how great: QUANTITY. 10. Latin *quālis*, of what kind: QUALITY. 11. Latin *ut*, that: UT. 12. Latin *uter*, either of two: NEUTER. 13. Latin *ubi*, where, and *ibi*, there: ALIBI, UBIQUITY. 14. Latin *unde*, whence: ALIUNDE. 15. Persian *chīz*, thing: CHEESE[3]. [Pok. *ku̯o-* 644.]

kwon-. Dog. 1. Greek *kuōn*, dog: CYNIC, CYNOSURE, PROCYON, QUINSY. 2. Suffixed zero-grade form **kwn̥-to-* in Germanic **hundaz* in: a. Old English *hund*, dog: HOUND[1]; b. Old High German *hunt*, dog: DACHSHUND; c. Middle Dutch *hond*, dog: KEESHOND. 3. Nominative form **kwō* in Welsh *ci*, dog: CORGI. 4. Variant **kan-i-* in Latin *canis*, dog: CANAILLE, CANICULA, CANINE, CHENILLE, KENNEL[1]; CANARY ISLANDS. [Pok. *ku̯on-* 632.]

kwr̥mi-. Mite, worm. Sanskrit *kṛmi-*, worm, in compound *kṛmi-ja-*, "(red dye) produced by worms" (*ja-*, produced; see **genə-**), borrowed into Arabic as *qirmiz*, kermes: CRIMSON, KERMES. [Pok. *ku̯r̥mi-* 649.]

lā-. Echoic root. 1. Middle Dutch *lollen*, to mutter: LOLLARD. 2. Middle Dutch *lollen*, to mutter, akin to the Low German source of Middle English *lollen*, to loll: LOLL. 3. Middle Low German *lollen*, to lull, akin to the Low German source of Middle English *lullen*, to lull: LULL. 4. Old Norse *lōmr*, loon: LOON[1]. 5. Latin *lallāre*, to sing a lullaby: LALLATION. 6. Latin *lāmentum*, expression of sorrow: LAMENT. 7. Greek *lalos*, talkative: ECHOLALIA. 8. Greek *lalein*, to talk: GLOSSOLALIA. [Pok. 1. *la-* 651.]

lab-. Lapping, smacking the lips; to lick. 1. Germanic **lapjan* in Old English *lapian*, to lap up: LAP[3]. 2. Nasalized form **la-m-b-* in: a. Germanic **lamp-* in Old French *lamper*, to gulp down: LAMPOON; b. Latin *lambere*, to lick: LAMBENT. [Pok. *lab-* 651.]

lādh-. Hidden, indirect. 1. Greek *lēthē*, forgetfulness: LETHARGY, LETHE. 2. Shortened form **ladh-*, with nasalized form *landh-*, in Greek *lanthanein* (aorist *lathein*), to escape the notice of, with middle *lanthanesthai*, to forget: ALASTOR, LANTHANUM. 3. Suffixed (stative) variant form **lat-ē-* in Latin *latēre*, to lie hidden: DELITESCENCE, LATENT. [In Pok. 2. *la-* 651.]

laiwo-. Left. Latin *laevus*, left: LEVOROTATION, LEVOROTATORY. [Pok. *laiu̯o-* 652.]

laks-. Salmon. Suffixed form **laks-o-* in Germanic **lahsaz* in Old High German *lahs*, salmon: LOX[1]. [Pok. *lak-* 653.]

laku-. Body of water, lake, sea. 1. Latin *lacus*, lake, pond, basin: LAKE[1]. 2. O-grade form **loku-* in Old Irish *loch*, lake: LOCH, LOUGH. [Pok. *laku-* 653.]

lāp-. To light, burn. Nasalized shortened form **la-m-p-* in Greek *lampein*, to shine: ECLAMPSIA, LAMP, LANTERN. [Pok. *lā(i)p-* 652.]

las-. To be eager, wanton, or unruly. 1. Suffixed form **las-tu-* in Germanic **lustuz* in: a. Old English *lust*, lust: LUST; b. Old High German *lust*, desire: WANDERLUST; c. Germanic denominative **lustjan* in Old English *lystan*, to please, to satisfy a desire: LIST[5]. 2. Suffixed form **las-ko-* in Latin *lascīvus*, wanton, lustful: LASCIVIOUS. [Pok. *las-* 654.]

lat-. Wet, moist. Latin *latex*, liquid: LATEX. [Pok. *lat-* 654.]

lāu-. Gain, profit. 1. Suffixed shortened form **lau-no-* in Germanic **launam* in Old High German *lōn*, reward: GUERDON. 2. Suffixed variant form **lu-tlo-* in Latin *lucrum*, gain, profit: LUCRATIVE, LUCRE. 3. Suffixed variant form **low-ero-* in Old Irish *lour*, sufficiency, enough: GALORE. [Pok. *lāu-* 655.]

leb-[1]. Base of loosely related derivatives meaning "hanging loosely." I. Variant form **lep-* in Germanic **lap-* in Old English *læppa*, *lappa*, flap of a garment: LAP[1]. II. Nasalized form **lemb(h)-*, with variant form **slemb(h)-*. 1. Germanic **lemp-* in Old English *limphealt*, hanging loosely (*healt*, striking; see **kel-[2]**): LIMP. 2. Germanic **lump-* in: a. Dutch *lomp*, rag, akin to the Low German source of Middle English *lump*, lump: LUMP[1]; b. Middle Dutch *lumpe*, lumpfish: LUMPFISH. 3. Germanic **slimp-* in Middle Dutch *slim(p)*, slanting, bad: SLIM. 4. Middle High German *slam*, mud: SLUMGULLION. 5. Old Norse *slambra*, to strike at, akin to the Scandinavian source of SLAM[1]. 6. Norwegian *slumpa*, to slump, akin to the Scandinavian source of SLUMP. III. Variant **(s)lab-* in Germanic **slab-*. 1. Danish *slab*, mud, akin to the Scandinavian source of SLAB[2]. 2. Swedish *slabb*, slime, mud, akin to the Scandinavian source of Irish *slab*, mud: SLOB. 3. Low German *slubberen*, to slobber: SLOBBER. IV. Variants **slap-*, **slep-*. 1. Germanic **slap-* in: a. Low German *slapp*, slap: SLAP; b. Old Norse *slafra*, to slaver: SLAVER[1]. 2. Germanic **slēpaz* in Old English *slǣp*, sleep: SLEEP. V. Variant **lab-*. 1. Germanic **lab-* in Old French *label*, ribbon, strip: LABEL. 2. Latin *lābī*, to fall, slip: LAPSE; COLLAPSE, ELAPSE, PROLAPSE, RELAPSE, SUPRALAPSARIAN. 3. Suffixed form **lab-os-* perhaps in Latin *labor*, labor, toil, exertion: LABOR, COLLABORATE, ELABORATE. VI. O-grade form **lob-* in Greek *lobos*, lobe: LOBE. [Pok. 1. *leb-* 655.]

leb-[2]. Lip. 1. Germanic **lep-* in Old English *lippa*, lip: LIP. 2. Variant form *lab-* in: a. suffixed form **lab-yo-* in Latin *labium*, lip: LABIAL, LABIUM; b. suffixed form **lab-ro-* in Latin *labrum*, lip: LABELLUM, LABRET, LABRUM. [Pok. *leb-* 655.]

leg-. To collect, with derivatives meaning "to speak." 1. Perhaps Germanic **lēkjaz*, enchanter, one who speaks magic words, in Old English *lǣce*, physician: LEECH[1]. 2. Latin *legere*, to gather, choose, pluck, read: LECTERN, LECTURE, LEGEND, LEGIBLE, LEGION, (LESSON); COIL[1], COLLECT[1], DILIGENT, ELECT, ELEGANT, INTELLIGENT, NEGLECT, PRELECT, SACRILEGE, SELECT, SORTILEGE. 3. Greek *legein*, to gather, speak: LEXICON; ALEXIA, ANALECTS, CATALOGUE, DIALECT, DIALOGUE, DYSLEXIA, ECLECTIC, EPILOGUE, PROLEGOMENON. 4. Suffixed form **leg-no-* in Latin *lignum*, wood, firewood (< "that which is gathered"): LIGNEOUS, LIGNI-. 5. Lengthened-grade form **lēg-* possibly in: a. Latin *lēx*, law (?< "collection of rules"): LEGAL, LEGISLATOR, LEGIST, LEGITIMATE, LEX, LOYAL, PRIVILEGE; b. Latin denominative *lēgāre*, to depute, commission, charge (< "to engage by contract"): LEGACY, LEGATE; ALLEGE, COLLEAGUE, DELEGATE, RELEGATE. 6. Suffixed o-grade form **log-o-* in Greek *logos*, speech, word, reason: LOGIC, LOGISTIC[1], LOGO-, LOGOS, -LOGY; ANALOGOUS, APOLOGUE, APOLOGY, DECALOGUE, HOMOLOGOUS, HOROLOGE, LOGARITHM, PARALOGISM, PROLOGUE, SYLLOGISM. [Pok. *leĝ-* 658.]

leg-[2]. To dribble, trickle. Germanic **lek-* in: a. Old English *leccan*, to moisten: LEACH; b. Old Norse *leki*, a leak: LEAK; c. Middle Dutch *lacke*, *lac*, deficiency, fault: LACK. [Pok. 1. *leg-* 657.]

legh-. Also **leg-**. To lie, lay. 1. Suffixed form **leg-yo-* in: a. Germanic **ligjan* in Old English *licgan*, to lie: LIE[1]; b. Germanic **lagjan* in *(i)* Old English *lecgan*, to lay: LAY[1], LEDGE *(ii)* Old English *belecgan*, to cover, surround (*be-*, over, BE-): BELAY *(iii)* Middle Dutch *leggen*, to lay, and *liggen* (< Germanic **ligjan*), to lie: LEDGER. 2. Suffixed form **leg-ro-* in Germanic **ligraz* in: a. Old English *leger*, lair: LAIR; b. Middle Dutch *leger*, lair, camp: LEAGUER[1], BELEAGUER; c. Old High German *legar*, bed, lair: LAAGER, LAGER[1], STALAG. 3. Celtic **leg-ya-* in Medieval Latin *lia*, sediment: LEES. 4. Lengthened-grade form **lēgh-* in Germanic **lēgaz*, "lying flat," low, in Old Norse *lāgr*, low: LOW[1]. 5. Suffixed form **legh-to-* in Latin *lectus*, bed: LITTER, WAGON-LIT. 6. Suffixed o-grade form **logh-o-* in Germanic **lagam* in: a. Old Norse **lagu*, *lag-*, law (< "that which is set down"), whence Old English *lagu*, law: LAW, DANELAW; b. Old Norse *lag*, a laying down: FELLOW; c. Old Norse *lag*, due place, layer: LAGTING; d. Old Norse *lögn*, dragnet (< "that which is laid down"): LAGAN; e. Old Norse *lög*, law: BYLAW, OUTLAW; f. Old High German *lāga*, act of laying: ANLAGE, VORLAGE. 7. Suffixed o-grade form **logh-o-* in Greek *lokhos*, place for lying in wait: LOCHIA. [Pok. *legh-* 658, 2. *lēgh-* 660.]

legwh-. Light, having little weight. 1. Suffixed form **legwh-t-* in Germanic **līht(j)az* in: a. Old English *līht*, light: LIGHT[2]; b. Middle Dutch *lichten*, to lighten: LIGHTER[2]. 2. Suffixed form **legwh-i-* in Latin *levis*, light, with its derivative *levāre*, to lighten, raise: LEAVEN, LEVER, LEVITY; ALLEVIATE, CARNIVAL, ELEVATE, LEGERDEMAIN, LEVIGATE, MEZZO-RELIEVO, RELIEVE. 3. Variant form **ləgwh-* in Old Irish *lū-*, small: LEPRECHAUN. 4. Nasalized form **l(e)ngwh-* in Germanic **lung-* in Old English *lungen*, lungs (from their lightness): LUNG. 5. Attributed by some to this root is Latin *oblīvīscī*, to forget, which is more likely from root **lei-**. [Pok. *legu̯h-* 660.]

lei-. Slimy. 1. Germanic **lī-* with various extensions in: a. Old English *slīm*, slime: SLIME; b. Old English *slipor*, slippery: SLIPPERY; c. Old

English slā, perhaps "slime": SLOWWORM; d. Old English *slice, smooth: SLICK; e. Old English līm, cement, birdlime: LIME[3]; f. Old English lām, loam: LOAM; g. Old Norse slēttr, smooth, sleek: SLIGHT; h. Middle Dutch and Middle Low German slippen, to slip, slip away: SLIP[1]; i. Middle Low German slēpen, to drag: SCHLEP. 2. Suffixed form *lei-mo- in Latin līmus, slime: LIMACINE, LIMICOLINE. 3. Suffixed form *li-n- in Latin linere, to anoint: LINIMENT. 4. Suffixed form *lei-to- in Greek litos, thin (used of soup), hence plain, simple: LITOTES. 5. Suffixed form *lei-w- in Latin oblīvīscī (ob-, away, OB-), to forget (< "to slip from the mind"): OBLIVION, OUBLIETTE. [Pok. 3. lei- 662.]

lēi-[1]. Also lē-. To get. Suffixed zero-grade form *lə-tr- in: a. Greek latreia, service (for pay), duties, worship: -LATRY; b. Greek latron, pay: LARCENY; c. Greek -latrēs, worshiper: IDOLATER. [Pok. 2. lē(i)- 665.]

lēi-[2]. Also lē-. To let go, slacken. 1. Extended form *lēd- in: a. Germanic *lētan in Old English lǣtan, to allow, leave undone: LET[1]; b. Germanic derivative *lēthigaz, freed, in Medieval Latin lētus, lītus, serf (< "free man"): LIEGE. 2. Extended zero-grade form *ləd- in: a. Germanic *lataz in Old English læt, late, with its comparative lætra, latter, and its superlative latost, last: LATE, LATTER, LAST[1]; b. Germanic *latjan in Old English lettan, to hinder, impede (< "to make late"): LET[2]; c. suffixed form *ləd-to- in Latin lassus, tired, weary: LASSITUDE, ALAS. 3. Suffixed reduced form *lē-ni- in Latin lēnis, soft, gentle: LENIENT, LENIS, LENITIVE, LENITY. [Pok. 3. lē(i)- 666.]

lēi-[3]. Also lei-. To flow. 1. Extended form *leib- in Latin lībāre, to pour out, taste: LIBATION, PRELIBATION. 2. Suffixed extended form *leit-os in Latin lītus, shore: LITTORAL. [Pok. 4. lēi- 664.]

leid-. To play, jest. Suffixed o-grade form *loid-o- in Latin lūdus, game, play, with its derivative lūdere, to play (but both words may possibly be from Etruscan): LUDICROUS; ALLUDE, COLLUDE, DELUDE, ELUDE, ILLUDE, ILLUSION, INTERLUDE, PRELUDE, PROLUSION. [Pok. leid- 666.]

leig-[1]. To bind. 1. Germanic *līk- in Middle Low German līk, leech line: LEECH[2]. 2. Zero-grade form *lig-ā- in Latin ligāre, to bind: LEAGUE[1], LEGATO, LIABLE, LIEN, LIGATE; ALLY, COLLIGATE, FURL, OBLIGE, (RALLY), RELIGION, RELY. [Pok. 4. leig- 668.]

leig-[2]. Poor. Perhaps Greek oligos, few, little: OLIGO-. [Pok. 1. leig- 667.]

leig-[3]. To leap, tremble. O-grade form *loig- in Germanic *laik- in: a. Old English -lac, suffix denoting activity: WEDLOCK; b. Old Norse leika, to play: LARK[2]. [Pok. 3. leig- 667.]

leigh-. To lick. 1. Greek leikhein, to lick: ELECTUARY, LICHEN. 2. Zero-grade form *lig- in Germanic *likkōn in: a. Old English liccian, to lick: LICK; b. Frankish *likkōn, to lick: LECHER. 3. Nasalized zero-grade form *ling- in Latin lingere, to lick: CUNNILINGUS. [Pok. leigh- 668.]

leikw-. To leave. 1. Basic form *leikw- in Greek leipein, to leave: ECLIPSE, ELLIPSIS. 2. O-grade form *loikw- in: a. Germanic *laihwnjan in Old English lǣnan, to lend, to give (< "to leave to"): LEND; b. suffixed form *loikw-nes- in Germanic *laihwniz in Old Norse lān, loan: LOAN. 3. Zero-grade form *likw- in Germanic *-lif-, left, in: a. Germanic *ainlif, "one (beyond ten)," in Old English endleofan, eleven (see **oino-**); b. Germanic *twā-lif-, "two left (beyond ten)," in Old English twelf, twelve (see **dwō**). 4. Nasalized zero-grade form *li-n-kw- in Latin linquere, to leave: DELINQUENT, DERELICT, RELINQUISH. 5. Root *wleik-, to flow, run, related by some to this root but more likely a separate Indo-European form. Zero-grade form *wlik- in: a. suffixed form *wlik-w-ā- in Latin liquāre, to dissolve: LIQUATE; b. suffixed form *wlik-w-ē- in Latin liquēre, to be liquid: DELIQUESCE, LIQUEFY, LIQUESCENT, LIQUID, LIQUOR; c. suffixed form *wlik-s- in (i) Latin lixa, lye: LIXIVIATE (ii) Latin prōlixus, poured forth, stretched out in front, extended (prō-, forth; see **per**[1]): PROLIX. [Pok. leiku̯- 669.]

leip-. To stick, adhere; fat. 1. Germanic *lībam in Old English līf, life (< "continuance"): LIFE, LIVELY. 2. Germanic *libēn in Old English lifian, libban, to live: LIVE[1]. 3. Germanic *laibjan in Old English lǣfan, to leave, have remaining: LEAVE[1]. 4. Germanic *librō in Old English lifer, liver (formerly believed to be the blood-producing organ): LIVER[1]. 5. Variant form *leip(h)- in Greek aleiphein, to anoint with oil: ALIPHATIC, SYNALEPHA. 6. Zero-grade form *lip- in Greek lipos, fat: LIPO-. [Pok. leip- 670.]

leis-. Track, furrow. 1. O-grade form *lois- in: a. Germanic *laist- in Old English lāst, sole, footprint: LAST[3]; b. Germanic *laistjan, "to follow a track," in Old English lǣstan, to continue: LAST[2]; c. suffixed o-grade form *lois-ā in Germanic *laizō in Old English lār, learning: LORE[1]; d. Germanic ablaut form *liznōn, "to follow a course (of study)," in Old English leornian, to learn: LEARN. 2. Suffixed form *leis-ā in Latin līra, a furrow: DELIRIUM. [Pok. leis- 671.]

leit-. To detest. 1. Germanic *laithaz in Old English lāth, loathsome: LOATH. 2. Germanic *laithōn in Old English lāthian, to loathe: LOATHE. [Pok. 1. leit- 672.]

leith-. To go forth, die. 1. Suffixed o-grade form *loit-eyo- in Germanic *laidjan in: a. Old English lǣdan, to lead: LEAD[1]; b. Old High German leiten, to lead: LEITMOTIF. 2. Suffixed variant o-grade form *loid-ā- in Germanic *laidō in Old English lād, course, way: LOAD, LODE; LIVELIHOOD. [Pok. leit(h)- 672.]

leizd-. Border, band. Germanic *listōn in: a. Old English līste, border, edge, strip: LIST[2]; b. Old Italian lista, border, strip of paper, list: LIST[1]. [Pok. leizd- 672.]

lek-. To leap, fly. Possibly suffixed o-grade form *lok-ost- in Latin locusta, lōcusta, a marine shellfish, lobster: LOBSTER, LOCUST[1]. [Pok. 2. lek- 673.]

lēk-. To tear. Zero-grade form *lək- becoming lak-. 1. Latin lacinia, flap of a garment: LACINIATE. 2. Suffixed form *lak-ero- in Latin lacer, torn: LACERATE. [Pok. 2. lēk- 674.]

lem-[1]. To break in pieces; broken, soft, with derivatives meaning "crippled." 1. Germanic lamōn- in: a. Old English lama, lame: LAME[1]; b. East Frisian lōm, lame: LOOM[1]. 2. Germanic *lamjan in Old Norse lemja, to flog, cripple by beating, akin to the Scandinavian source of LAM[1]. 3. Perhaps Swedish dialectal loma, to move heavily, akin to the Scandinavian source of Middle English lomeren, to lumber: LUMBER[2]. [Pok. 1. lem- 674.]

lem-[2]. Nocturnal spirits. 1. Suffixed form *lem-or- in Latin lemurēs, ghosts: LEMURES. 2. Suffixed variant form *lam-ya- in Greek lamia, monster: LAMIA. [Pok. 2. lem- 675.]

lendh-[1]. Loin. Suffixed o-grade form *londh-wo- in Latin lumbus, loin: LOIN, LUMBAGO, LUMBAR, SIRLOIN. [Pok. 2. lendh- 675.]

lendh-[2]. Open land, heath, prairie. Germanic *landam in: a. Old English land, land: LAND; b. Middle Dutch land, land: BILANDER, LANDSCAPE, UITLANDER; c. Old High German lant, land: GELÄNDESPRUNG, HINTERLAND, LANDGRAVE, LANDSMAN[2], ROLAND[1]; d. Old French launde, heath, pasture: LAWN[1]. [Pok. 3. lendh- 675.]

lengh-. To abuse. Greek elenkhein, to refute, disgrace: ELENCHUS. [Pok. lengh- 676.]

lenk-. To bend. Germanic *lengwa- in Old Norse lyng, heather: LING[2]. [Pok. lenk- 676.]

lento-. Flexible. 1. Suffixed form *lent-yo- in Germanic *linthjaz in: a. Old English līthe, flexible, mild: LITHE; b. Old English linde, linden tree (from its pliant bast): LINDEN. 2. Suffixed form *lent-o- in Latin lentus, flexible, tenacious, sluggish, slow: LENTO, RALLENTANDO, RELENT. [Pok. lento- 677.]

lep-[1]. To peel. 1. Greek lepein, to peel: LEMMA[2], LEPTO-, LEPTON[1]. 2. Suffixed form *lep-i- in Greek lepis, lepos, a scale: LEPER, LEPIDO-, LEPIDOTE. 3. Suffixed variant form *lap-aro- in Greek laparos, soft: LAPAROTOMY. 4. O-grade form *lop- in Greek elops, ellops, a fish (< *en-lopos, having scales; en-, in; see **en**): ELAPID. [Pok. 2. lep- 678.]

lep-[2]. To be flat; palm, sole, shoulder blade. Lengthened o-grade form *lōp- in Germanic *lōfō in: a. *galōfō (*ga-, collective prefix; see **kom**), "covering for the hand," in Old English glōf, glove: GLOVE; b. Middle Dutch *loef, windward side of a ship: LUFF. [Pok. 2. lēp- 679.]

lerd-. Bent, curved. Suffixed o-grade form *lord-o- in: a. Germanic *lortaz in Middle High German lurz, left, wrong: LURCH[2]; b. Greek lordos, bent backward: LORDOSIS. [Pok. lerd- 679.]

letro-. Leather. Germanic *lethram in Old English lether-, leather: LEATHER. [Pok. letro- 681.]

leu-[1]. To loosen, divide, cut apart. 1. Germanic *liusan in: a. Old English -lēosan, to lose: LORN, LOSEL; b. Germanic *fer-liusan, *for-liusan (*fer-, *for-, prefix denoting rejection or exclusion; see **per**[1]) in (i) Old English forlēosan, to forfeit, lose: FORLORN (ii) Dutch verliezen, to lose: FORLORN HOPE. 2. Germanic *lawwō in Swedish lagg, barrel stave (< "split piece of wood"): LAG[2]. 3. Germanic *lausaz in: a. Old English lēas, "loose," free from, without, untrue, lacking: LEASING, -LESS; b. Old English los, loss: LOSE, LOSS; c. Old Norse lauss, louss, loose: LOOSE; d. Swiss German lösch, loose: LOESS. 4. Zero-grade form *lu- in: a. Greek luein, to loosen, release, untie: LYSIS, -LYTE; ANALYSIS, CATALYSIS, DIALYSIS, PARALYSIS, TACHYLYTE; b. Latin luēs, plague, pestilence (< "dissolution, putrefaction"): LUES; c. prefixed form *se-lu- (se-, apart; see **seu-**[2]) in Latin solvere, to loosen, untie: SOLUBLE, SOLUTE, SOLVE; ABSOLUTE, ABSOLVE, ASSOIL, DISSOLVE, RESOLVE. [Pok. 2. leu- 681.]

leu-[2]. Dirt; make dirty. 1. Latin polluere, to pollute (< *por-luere; por-, for prō-, PRO-): POLLUTE. 2. Suffixed zero-grade form *lu-to- in Latin lutum, mud, mire, clay: LUTE[2]. [Pok. 1. leu- 681.]

lēu-[1]. Stone. 1. Welsh llech, flat stone (from an uncertain pre-form): CROMLECH. 2. Gaulish *lausa, flat stone: LOZENGE. [Pok. 2. leu- 683.]

lēu-[2]. Echoic root. 1. Extended form *leut- in Germanic *liuth- in Old High German liod, song: LIED. 2. Extended variant form *laud- in Latin laus, praise, glory, fame: LAUD. [Pok. 3. leu- 683.]

leubh-. To care, desire; love. **I.** Suffixed form *leubh-o- in Germanic *liubaz in Old English lēof, dear, beloved: LEMAN, LIEF, LIVELONG. **II.** O-grade form *loubh-. 1. Germanic *laubō in: a. Old English lēaf, permission (< "pleasure, approval"): LEAVE[2]; b. Middle Dutch verlof, leave, permission (ver-, intensive prefix; see **per**[1]): FURLOUGH; c. Germanic *galaubō (*ga-, intensive prefix; see **kom**) in Old English gelēafa, bilēafa (bi-, BE-), belief, faith: BELIEF. 2. Germanic *galaubjan (*ga-, intensive prefix; see **kom**), "to hold dear," esteem, trust, in Old English gelēfan, belēfan (be-, BE-), to believe, trust: BELIEVE. **III.** Zero-grade form *lubh-. 1. Suffixed form *lubh-ā- in Germanic lubō in Old English lufu, love: LOVE. 2. Suffixed (stative) form *lubh-ē- in Latin libēre, to be dear, be pleasing: QUODLIBET. 3. Latin libīdō, pleasure, desire: LIBIDO. [Pok. leubh- 683.]

leud-. Small. 1. Germanic *lūt- in: a. Old English lȳtel, little: LITTLE; b. Old English lūtan, to bend down: LOUT[2]; c. Old Norse lūta, to bend down (< "to make small"): LOUT[1]; d. perhaps Middle Dutch loteren, to shake, totter (< "to make smaller"): LOITER. 2. Attributed by some to this root (but more likely of obscure origin) is Greek limos, hunger, famine: BULIMIA. [Pok. leud- 684.]

leudh-[1]. To go. Zero-grade form *(e)ludh- in suffixed unextended form *elu-to- in Greek prosēlutos, "one who comes to a place," stranger (pros-, to, PROS-): PROSELYTE. [In Pok. 6. el- 306.]

leudh-[2]. To mount up, grow. 1. Germanic *leudi- in Old High German liut, people (< "mass, multitude"): LEOPOLD. 2. Suffixed form *leudh-ero- in Latin līber, free (the precise semantic development is obscure): DELIVER, LIBERAL, LIBERATE, LIBERTINE, LIBERTY, LIVERY. [Pok. 1. leudh- 684.]

leug-[1]. To bend, turn, wind. 1. Germanic *lauk-, leek (semantic transition obscure), in Old English lēac, leek: GARLIC, LEEK. 2. Zero-grade form *lug- in Germanic *luk- in: a. Old English loc, lock (perhaps < "a bending together, shutting"): LOCK[1], LOCKET; b. Old English locc, strand of hair: LOCK[2]; c. Frankish *lūk, something that closes: LUCARNE. 3. Suffixed zero-grade form *lug-so- in Latin luxus, dislocated, and luxus, excess, extravagance (originally of plants, "growing obliquely or to excess"): LUXATE, LUXURY. 4. Suffixed zero-grade form *lug-to- in Latin luctārī, to wring, wrestle, struggle: INELUCTABLE, RELUCT. [Pok. 1. leug- 685.]

leug-[2]. To break. Form leug-ē- in Latin lūgēre, to mourn (< "to break down mentally"): LUGUBRIOUS. [Pok. leug̑- 686.]

leugh-. To tell a lie. Germanic *liugan in: a. Old English lēogan, to lie: LIE[2], WARLOCK; b. Old English belēogan, to tell lies about (be-, BE-): BELIE. [Pok. leugh- 686.]

leuk-. Light, brightness. **I.** Basic form *leuk-. 1. Suffixed form *leuk-to- in Germanic *liuhtam in Old English lēoht, līht, light: LIGHT[1]. 2. Latin lūx, light: LUCIFER[1], LUCINA, LUCULENT, LUCY, LUX. 3. Suffixed form *leuk-smen- in Latin lūmen, light, opening: LIMN, LUMEN, LUMINARY, LUMINOUS; ILLUMINATE. 4. Suffixed form *leuk-snā- in Latin lūna, moon: LUNA, LUNA, LUNAR, LUNATE, LUNATIC, LUNE, LUNULA; DEMILUNE, SUBLUNARY. 5. Suffixed form *leuk-stro- in: a. Latin lūstrum, purification: LUSTER, LUSTRUM;

b. Latin lūstrāre, to purify, illuminate: ILLUSTRATE. 6. Suffixed form *leuko-dhro- in Latin lūcubrāre, to work by lamplight: LUCUBRATE. II. O-grade form *louk-. 1. Suffixed form *louk-o- in Germanic *lauhaz in Old English lēah, meadow (< "place where light shines"): LEA. 2. Suffixed (iterative) form *louk-eyo- in Latin lucere, to shine: LUCENT, LUCID; ELUCIDATE, NOCTILUCA, PELLUCID, RELUCENT, TRANSLUCENT. III. Zero-grade form *luk-. 1. Germanic *lugōn- in Old Norse logi, flame, fire: LOKI. 2. Latin lucerna, lamp: LUCERNE. 3. Suffixed form *luk-ya- in Greek lussa, rabies, madness (from the gleaming eyes characteristic of this state): ALYSSUM, LYTTA. 4. Suffixed form *luk-sno- in Greek lukhnos, lamp: LINK[2], LYCHNIS. 5. Attributed by some to this root (but more likely of obscure origin) is Greek lunx, lynx (as if from its shining eyes): LYNX, OUNCE[2]. [Pok. leuk- 687.]

leup-. To peel off, break off. 1. Germanic *laubaz in Old English lēaf, leaf: LEAF. 2. Germanic *laubja, "roof made from barks," shelter, in: a. Frankish *laubja, cloister: LODGE; b. Medieval Latin lobium, lobia, laubia, monastic cloister: LOBBY. 3. Zero-grade form *lup- in Sanskrit loptra, booty (< "that which is stripped off"): LOOT[1]. 4. Attributed by some to this root is Germanic *luftuz, sky (traditionally explained as < "roof of the world," vault of heaven), but probably a separate Germanic root, in: a. Old Norse lopt, air, attic, sky: LOFT, ALOFT; b. Germanic *luftjan, to hold up in the air, in Old Norse lypta, to lift: LIFT. [Pok. leup- 690.]

[**līk-**. Body, form; like, same. Germanic root. 1. Old English līc, form, body: ALIKE, LICH GATE. 2. Old English -līc, having the form of: LIKE[2], -LY[1]. 3. Germanic phrase *aiwo galīkaz, "ever alike" (*aiwo, *aiwi, ever; see aiw-), in Old English ǣlc, each: EACH. 4. Germanic *is-līk in Old English ilca, the same (see i-). 5. Old Norse līkr, like: LIKELY. 6. Middle Dutch -lijc, -ly: FROLIC. 7. Germanic *līkjan in Old English līcian, to please: LIKE[1]. 8. Germanic *hwa-līk-, which (see kwo-). [In Pok. 2. leig- 667.]]

lino-. Flax. 1. Greek linon, flax: LINOLEIC ACID. 2. Lengthened-grade form *līno- in Latin līnum, flax, linen: LENO, LINE[1], LINE[2], LINEN, LININ, LINGERIE, LINNET, LINOLEUM, LINT; CRINOLINE, LINSEED. [Pok. lī-no- 691.]

[**līthrā**. A scale. Mediterranean word. 1. Probably Latin lībra, a pound, balance: LEVEL, LIBRA, LIRA, LIVRE; DELIBERATE, EQUILIBRIUM. 2. Probably Greek litra, unit of weight, pound: LITER.]

lou-. To wash. 1. Suffixed form *lou-kā- in Germanic *laugō in Old English lēag, lye: LYE. 2. Suffixed form *lou-tro- in Old English lēathor, washing soda: LATHER. 3. Variant form *law- in: a. Latin lavere, to wash, with its derivative -luere, to wash: LOTION; ABLUTION, ALLUVION, COLLUVIUM, DELUGE, DILUTE, ELUVIUM; b. form *law-ā- in Latin lavāre, to wash: LAVE, LOMENT; c. Latin lavātrīna, lātrīna, a bath, privy: LATRINE. [Pok. lou- 692.]

lus-. Louse. Germanic *lus- in Old English lūs, louse: LOUSE. [Pok. lus- 692.]

mā-[1]. Good; with derivatives meaning "occurring at a good moment, timely, seasonable, early." 1. Suffixed form *mā-tu- in: a. further suffixed form *mā-tu-ro- in Latin mātūrus, seasonable, ripe, mature: MADURO, MATURE; (IMMATURE), (PREMATURE); b. further suffixed form *mā-tu-to- in Latin Mātūta, name of the goddess of dawn: MATINEE, MATINS, MATUTINAL. 2. Suffixed form *mā-ni- in: a. Latin māne, (in) the morning: MAÑANA; b. Latin mānis, good: MANES. [Pok. 2. mā- 693.]

mā-[2]. Mother. An imitative root derived from the child's cry for the breast (a linguistic universal found in many of the world's languages, often in reduplicated form). 1. Latin mamma, breast: MAMMA, MAMMALIA, MAMMILLA. 2. Probably Greek Maia, "good mother" (respectful form of address to old women), also nurse: MAIA[1], MAIEUTIC. (3. More recently formed in the same way is English MAMA.) [Pok. 3. mā- 694.]

mā-[3]. Damp. 1. Suffixed form *mā-ro- in Germanic *mōra- in Old English mōr, marsh, wilderness: MOOR[2]. 2. Suffixed form *mā-no- in Latin mānāre, to flow, trickle: EMANATE. [Pok. mā-no- 699.]

[**macula**. A spot, blemish; also, a hole in a net, mesh. Latin noun of unknown origin. MACKLE, MACLE, MACULA, MACULATE, MACULE, MAIL[2], MAILLOT, MAQUIS; IMMACULATE, TRAMMEL.]

mad-. Moist, wet; also refers to various qualities of food. 1. Latin madēre, to be wet: MAT[2]. 2. Sanskrit madati, "it bubbles, it rejoices," hence madana-, delightful, joyful, hence madana, a myna bird: MYNA. 3. Suffixed form *mad-i- in Germanic *mati- in: a. Old English mete, food: MEAT; b. Middle Low German (ge)mate (ge-, together; see kom), "he with whom one shares one's food," companion: MATE[1]; c. Middle Dutch māt, meat: MATELOTE. 4. Suffixed form *mad-sto-, becoming *mazdo-, in Germanic *masta- in Old English mæst, fodder: MAST[2]. [Pok. mad- 694.]

mag-. Also **mak-**. To knead, fashion, fit. 1. Germanic *mak- in: a. verb *makōn, to fashion, fit, in (i) Old English macian, to make: MAKE (ii) Frankish *makōn, to build: MASON; b. compound noun *ga-mak-(j)ōn (*ga-, with, together; see kom), "he who is fitted with (another)," in Old English gemæcca, mate, spouse: MATCH[1]. 2. Germanic nasalized form *mangjan, to knead together, in: a. Old English mengan, to mix: MINGLE; b. Old English gemang (ge-, together; see kom), mixture, crowd: AMONG, MONGREL. 3. Suffixed form *mak-yo- in Greek massein (aorist stem mag-), to knead, hence magma, unguent: MAGMA. 4. Suffixed lengthened-grade form *māg-ya- in Greek maza, a (kneaded) lump, barley cake: MASS, (AMASS). 5. Suffixed lengthened-grade form *māk-ero- in Latin mācerāre, to tenderize, to soften (food) by steeping: MACERATE. 6. Old Armenian matsun, fermented milk: MATZOON. [Pok. mag- 696, 2. mak- 698, men(ə)k- 730.]

magh-[1]. To be able, to have power. 1. Germanic *mag- in: a. Old English magan, to be able: MAY[1]; b. Vulgar Latin *exmagāre (ex-, out of, expressing removal, EX-), to deprive of power: DISMAY. 2. Germanic suffixed form *mah-ti-, power, in: a. Old English miht, power: MIGHT[1]; b. Germanic compound *maht-hildis, a feminine name, "mighty in battle" (held-, battle; see kel-[2]): MATILDA, (MAUD). 3. Germanic suffixed form *magena, power, in Old English mægen, power: MAIN[1]. 4. Suffixed lengthened-grade form *māgh-os-, "that which enables," in Greek (Attic) mēkhos, (Doric) mākhos, device: MACHINE, MECHANISM. 5. Possibly suffixed form *magh-u- in Old Persian maguš, member of a priestly caste (< "mighty one"): (MAGE), MAGI, MAGIC; ARCHIMAGE. [Pok. magh- 695.]

magh-[2]. To fight. 1. Old Iranian *ha-maz-an-, "the warrior" (*ha-, the; see so-), possibly borrowed into Greek as Amazōn, Amazon: AMAZON[1]. 2. Greek makhesthai, to fight: TAUROMACHY. [Pok. magh- 697.]

maghu-. Young person of either sex. Suffixed form *magho-ti- in Germanic *magadi-, with diminutive *magadin-, in Old English mægden, virgin: MAIDEN, (MAID). [Pok. maghos 696.]

mai-[1]. To cut. 1. Suffixed form *mai-d- in Germanic *mait- in: a. Germanic *ā-mait-jon, "the biter" (prefix *a-, meaning uncertain, from Indo-European ē, ō; see Pok. ē, ō 280), a small biting insect, in Old English ǣmette, ant: ANT, EMMET; b. Germanic *mitōn-, "the biter," a small biting insect, in (i) Old English mite, mite: MITE[1] (ii) Middle Dutch mite, insect, small object: MITE[2]; c. possibly Common Romance *mahagnāre, to wound: MAIM, MANGLE[1], (MAYHEM). 2. Suffixed form *mai-lo- in Old Irish máel, shorn, bald, hornless: MALCOLM, MULEY. [Pok. 1. mai- 697.]

mai-[2]. To soil, defile. 1. Suffixed form *mai-lo- in Germanic *mail- in Old English māl, spot, blemish: MOLE[1]. 2. Suffixed variant form *mi-an-yo- in Greek miainein, to pollute: MIASMA; AMIANTHUS. [Pok. 2. mai- 697.]

mak-[1]. Poppy. Lengthened-grade form *māk- in Greek mēkōn, poppy: MECONIUM. [Pok. mak(en)- 698.]

mak-[2]. (Leather) bag. Germanic form *mag-ōn, bag, stomach, in Old English maga, stomach: MAW. [Pok. mak- 698.]

māk-. Long, thin. 1. Zero-grade form *mək- becoming *mak- in suffixed form *mak-ro- in: a. Latin macer, thin: MAIGRE, MEAGER; EMACIATE; b. Greek makros, long, large: MACRO-, MACRON; AMPHIMACER. 2. Suffixed form *māk-os- in Greek mēkos, length: PARAMECIUM. 3. Possibly also from this root is Greek Makedōn, tribal name (< "Highlander"): MACEDONIA. [Pok. māk- 699.]

[**malakhē**. A mallow. Greek noun, akin to Latin malva, mallow, both probably borrowed from a pre-Indo-European Mediterranean language. 1. Greek malakhē, mallow: MALACHITE. 2. Latin malva, mallow: MALLOW, MAUVE.]

man-[1]. Also **mon-**. A man. 1. Extended forms *manu-, *manw- in Germanic *manna- (plural *manniz), in: a. Old English mann (plural menn), man: MAN, (NORMAN[1]); b. Old High German man, man: ATAMAN, FUGLEMAN, HERMAN, LANDSMAN[2]; c. Middle Dutch man, man: MANIKIN, (MANNEQUIN); d. Old Norse madhr, mannr, man: NORMAN[2], OMBUDSMAN; e. possibly Germanic *Ala-manniz, tribal name (< "all men"; *ala-, all; see al-[5]): ALEMANNI. 2. Germanic adjective *manniska-, human, in: a. Old High German mennisco, human: MENSCH; b. Low German minsk, person, hussy: MINX. 3. Slavic suffixed form *mon-gyo- in Old Church Slavonic mǫzhĭ, person: MUZHIK. [Pok. manu-s 700.]

man-[2]. Hand. 1. Latin manus, hand: MANACLE, MANAGE, (MANÈGE), MANNER, MANUAL, MANUBRIUM, MANUS; AMANUENSIS, LEGERDEMAIN, MAINTAIN, MANEUVER, MANICOTTI, MANICURE, MANIFEST, MANIPLE, (MANIPULATION), MANSUETUDE, MANUFACTURE, MANUMIT, MANUSCRIPT, MANURE, MASTIFF, MORTMAIN, QUADRUMANOUS. 2. Suffixed form *man-ko-, maimed in the hand, in Latin mancus, maimed, defective: MANQUÉ. 3. Latin compound manceps, "he who takes by the hand" (-ceps, agential suffix, "-taker"; see kap-), purchaser: EMANCIPATE. 4. Latin compound mandāre, "to give into someone's hand" (dāre, to give; see dō-), entrust, order: COMMAND, (COMMANDO), COMMEND, COUNTERMAND, DEMAND, MANDAMUS, MANDATE, (RECOMMEND), REMAND. 5. Suffixed zero-grade form *mn̥-to- in Germanic *mund-, "guarding hand," protection, in: a. Old English mund, hand, protection, protector: EDMUND; b. Dutch mond and Old Norse mund, (protecting) hand: MOUND. [Pok. mə-r- 740.]

[**mappa**. Napkin, towel, cloth. Latin noun, said by Quintilian to be of Carthaginian origin. APRON, MAP, MOP, NAPERY, NAPKIN, NAPPE.]

[**margarītēs**. Pearl. Greek noun of Oriental origin (probably immediately from Iranian). 1. Greek margaritēs, pearl: MARGARET, MARGARITE, (MAGPIE), FATA MORGANA. 2. Greek margaron, pearl (probably borrowed independently from a related source): MARGARIC, (MARGARINE).]

mari-. Young woman. Suffixed form *mari-to-, "provided with a bride," in Latin maritus, married, a husband: MARITAL, MARRY[1]. [Pok. meri̯o- 738.]

marko-. Horse. 1. Germanic *marhaz in Old High German marahscalc, "horse-servant" (Germanic *skalkaz, slave; origin unknown), hence groom, later a title for a cavalry leader: MARSHAL. 2. Germanic feminine *marhjōn in Old English mere, miere, mare: MARE[1]. [Pok. marko- 700.]

[**mas**. Male. Latin adjective of unknown origin; with derivative masculus, male, manly. MALE, MASCULINE; EMASCULATE.]

mat-. A kind of tool. 1. Vulgar Latin *mattea, club (akin to Latin mateola, rod, club, mallet): MACE[1], MACHETE, MASSACRE. 2. Old English mattuc, mattock (probably borrowed from Vulgar Latin *mattea): MATTOCK. [Pok. 2. mat- 700.]

māter-. Mother. Based ultimately on the baby-talk form mā-[2], with the kinship term suffix -ter-. 1. Germanic *mōthar- in Old English mōdor, mother: MOTHER[1]. 2. Latin māter, mother: MATER, MATERNAL, (MATERNITY), (MATRICULATE), MATRIX, MATRON; MADREPORE, MATRIMONY. 3. Greek mētēr, mother: METRO-, METROPOLIS. 4. Latin māteriēs, māteria, tree trunk (< "matrix," the tree's source of growth), hence hard timber used in carpentry, hence (by a calque on Greek hulē, wood, matter) substance, stuff, matter: MATERIAL, MATTER. 5. Greek compound Dēmētēr, name of the goddess of produce, especially cereal crops (dē-, possibly meaning "earth"): DEMETER. [Pok. māter- 700.]

math-. Worm. 1. Germanic *mathon probably in Middle English mathek, worm, grub: MAGGOT, MAWKISH. 2. With uncertain preform, but clearly related, is Old English moththe, moth: MOTH [Pok. 1. math- 700.]

[**Māwort-**. Name of an Italic deity who became the god of war at Rome (and also had agricultural attributes); hence also the name of the planet Mars (doubtless from its red color, the color of blood). 1. Latin Mārs (stem Mārt-), Mars: MARCH[1], MARS[1], MARTIAL, (MARTIAN), MARTIN, MARTLET. 2. Adjectival derivative *mārt-i-kos in Latin Marcus, a praenomen: MARCIA, MARCUS, MARK[1].]

mazdo-. Pole, rod, mast. Germanic *masta in Old English mæst, mast: MAST[1]. [Pok. mazdo-s 701.]

me-[1]. Oblique form of the personal pronoun of the first person singular (for the nominative, see eg). 1. Germanic *mē̆- in Old English mē̆ (dative and accusative): ME, MYSELF. 2. Possessive adjective *mei-no- in Germanic *mīn- in: a

Old English *mīn*, my: MINE[2], MY; **b.** Middle Dutch *mijni*, my: MYNHEER. **3.** Possessive adjective **me-yo-* in Latin *meus*, my: MADAME, MADEMOISELLE, MADONNA. **4.** Possessive adjective **me-wo-* in Old Irish *mo*, my: MACHREE, MAVOURNEEN. [Pok. 1. *me-* 702.]

me-[2]. In the middle of. **1.** Suffixed form **me-dhi-* in Germanic **mid-* in Old English *mid*, among, with: MIDWIFE. **2.** Suffixed form **me-ta-* in Greek *meta*, between, with, beside, after: META-. [Pok. 2. *me-* 702.]

mē-[1]. Expressing certain qualities of mind. **1.** Suffixed o-grade form **mō-to-* in Germanic **mōthaz* in Old English *mōd*, mind, disposition: MOOD[1]. **2.** Perhaps Latin *mōs* (< **mō-s-*), wont, humor, manner, custom: MORAL, (MORALE), MORES, MOROSE. [Pok. 5. *mē-* 704.]

mē-[2]. To measure. **I.** Basic form *mē-*. **1.** Suffixed form **mē-lo-* in Germanic **mǣlaz* in Old English *mǣl*, "measure, mark, appointed time, time for eating, meal": MEAL[2], (PIECEMEAL). **2.** Suffixed form **mē-ti-* in Latin *mētīrī*, to measure: MEASURE, (MENSURAL); (COMMENSURATE), DIMENSION, IMMENSE. **3.** Possibly Greek *metron*, measure, rule, length, proportion, poetic meter (but this is referred by some to **med-**): METER[1], METER[2], (METER[3]), -METER, METRICAL, -METRY; DIAMETER, GEOMETRY, ISOMETRIC, METROLOGY, METRONOME. **II.** Extended and suffixed forms **mēn-*, **mēn-en-*, **mēn-s-*, **mēn-ōt-*, moon, month (an ancient and universal measure of time, with the celestial body that measures it). **1.** Germanic **mǣnon* in Old English *mōna*, moon: MOON; (MONDAY). **2.** Germanic **mǣnōth-* in Old English *mōnath*, month: MONTH. **3.** Greek *mēn*, *mēnē*, month: AMENORRHEA, CATAMENIA, DYSMENORRHEA, MENARCHE, MENISCUS, MENOLOGY, MENOPAUSE. **4.** Latin *mēnsis*, month: MENSAL[2], MENSES, MENSTRUAL, (MENSTRUATE); BIMESTRIAL, SEMESTER, TRIMESTER. [Pok. 3. *mē-* 703, *mēnōt* 731.]

mē-[3]. Big. **1.** Suffixed (comparative) form **mē-is-* in Germanic **maizōn-* in Old English *māra*, greater, and *māre* (adverb), more: MORE. **2.** Suffixed (superlative) form **mē-isto-* in Germanic **maista-* in Old English *mǣst*, most: MOST. **3.** Suffixed o-grade form **mō-ro-* in Gaelic *mōr*, big: CLAYMORE. [Pok. 4. *mē-* 704.]

mē-[4]. To cut down grass or grain with a sickle or scythe. **1.** Germanic **mǣ-* in Old English *māwan*, to mow: MOW[1]. **2.** Suffixed form **mē-to-* in Germanic **mǣth-* in Old English *mǣth*, a mowing, a crop mown: AFTERMATH. **3.** Suffixed form **mē-twā-*, a mown field, in Germanic **mǣdwō* in Old English *mǣd* (oblique case *mǣdwe*), meadow: MEAD[2], (MEADOW). [Pok. 2. *mē-* 703.]

med-. To take appropriate measures. **1. a.** Germanic **metan* in Old English *metan*, to measure (out): METE[1]; **b.** Germanic derivative **mǣtō*, measure, in Old English *gemǣte* (*ge-*, with; see **kom**), "commensurate," fit: MEET[2]. **2. a.** Latin *medērī*, to look after, heal, cure: MEDICAL, MEDICATE, MEDICINE, MEDICO, (METHEGLIN), REMEDY; **b.** Latin *meditārī*, to think about, consider, reflect: MEDITATE. **3.** Suffixed form **med-es-*, replaced in Latin by **modes-* by influence of *modus* (see **4** below), in: **a.** Latin *modestus*, "keeping to the appropriate measure," moderate: MODEST, (IMMODEST); **b.** Latin *moderāre*, "to keep within measure," to moderate, control: MODERATE, (IMMODERATE). **4.** Suffixed o-grade form **mod-o-* in Latin *modus*, measure, size, limit, manner, harmony, melody: MODAL, MODE, MODEL, MODERN, MODICUM, MODIFY, MODULATE, (MODULE), MODULUS, MOLD[1], (MOOD[2]), MOULAGE; ACCOMMODATE, (COMMODE), COMMODIOUS, (COMMODITY). **5.** Suffixed o-grade form **mod-yo-* in Latin *modius*, a measure of grain: MODIOLUS, MUTCHKIN. **6.** Suffixed lengthened-grade form **mēd-tro-* in Sanskrit *mātrā*, a measure: MAHOUT. **7.** Perhaps lengthened o-grade form **mōd-* in Germanic **mōt-*, ability, leisure, in: **a.** Old English *mōtan*, to have occasion, to be permitted or obliged: MOTE[2], MUST[1]; **b.** Germanic compound **ā-mōt-itha* (prefix **a-*, meaning uncertain, from Indo-European *ē*, *ō*; see Pok. *ē*, *ō* 280) in Old English *ǣmetta*, rest, leisure: EMPTY. [Pok. 1. *med-* 705.]

medhu-. Honey; also mead. **1.** Germanic **medu* in Old English *meodu*, mead: MEAD[1]. **2.** Greek *methu*, wine: AMETHYST, METHYLENE. [Pok. *medhu* 707.]

medhyo-. Middle. **1.** Germanic **midja-* in: **a.** Old English *midd(e)*, middle: MID[1], AMID; **b.** Germanic diminutive form **middila-* in Old English *middel*, middle: MIDDLE; **c.** Germanic compound **midja-gardaz*, "middle zone" (**gardaz*, enclosure, yard; see **gher-**[2]), name of the earth conceived as an intermediate zone lying between heaven and hell, in Old Norse *Midhgardhr*, Midgard: MIDGARD. **2.** Latin *medius*, middle, half: MEAN[3], MEDIAL, MEDIAN, MEDIASTINUM, MEDIATE, MEDIUM, MITTEN, MIZZEN, MOIETY, MULLION; INTERMEDIATE, MEDIEVAL, MEDIOCRE, MEDITERRANEAN, MERIDIAN, MILIEU. **3.** Greek *mesos*, middle: MESO-. [Pok. *medhi-* 706.]

meg-. Great. **1.** Germanic suffixed form **mik-ila-* in: **a.** Old English *micel*, *mycel*, great: MUCH; **b.** Old Norse *mikill*, great: MICKLE. **2.** Suffixed form **mag-no-* in Latin *magnus*, great: MAGNANIMOUS, MAGNATE, MAGNIFIC, (MAGNIFICENT), (MAGNIFICO), (MAGNIFY), MAGNILOQUENT, MAGNITUDE, MAGNUM. **3.** Suffixed (comparative) form **mag-yos-* in: **a.** Latin *mājor*, greater: MAJOR, MAJOR-DOMO, MAJORITY, MAJUSCULE, MAYOR; **b.** Latin *mājestās*, greatness, authority: MAESTOSO, MAJESTY; **c.** Latin *magister*, master, high official (< "he who is greater"): MAESTRO, MAGISTERIAL, MAGISTERY, MAGISTRAL, MAGISTRATE, MASTER, (MISTRAL), (MISTER), (MISTRESS). **4.** Suffixed (superlative) form **mag-samo-* in Latin *maximus*, greatest: MAXIM, MAXIMUM. **5.** Suffixed form **mag-to-*, "made great," in Latin *mactus*, worshiped, blessed, sacred: MATADOR. **6.** Suffixed (feminine) form **mag-ya-*, "she who is great," in Latin *Maia*, name of a goddess: MAIA[3], MAY[1]. **7.** Suffixed form **meg-al-* in Greek *megas* (stem *megal-*), great: MEGA-, MEGALO-; ACROMEGALY, ALMAGEST, OMEGA. **8.** Variant form **megh-* in Sanskrit *mahā*, great: MAHABHARATA, MAHARAJAH, MAHARANI, MAHATMA, MAHAYANA, MAHOUT. [Pok. *meg(h)-* 708.]

mei-[1]. To change, go, move; with derivatives referring to the exchange of goods and services within a society as regulated by custom or law. **1.** Latin *meāre*, to go, pass: MEATUS; IRREMEABLE, CONGÉ, PERMEATE. **2.** Suffixed o-grade form **moi-t-* in: **a.** Germanic **ga-maid-az* (**ga-*, intensive prefix; see **kom**), "changed (for the worse)," abnormal, in Old English *gemād*, insane: MAD; **b.** Latin *mūtāre*, to change: MEW[1], (MEWS), MOLT, MUTATE; COMMUTE, PERMUTE, REMUDA, TRANSMUTE; **c.** Latin *mūtuus*, "done in exchange," borrowed, reciprocal, mutual: MUTUAL. **3.** Suffixed extended zero-grade form **mit-to-* in Germanic **missa-*, "in a changed manner," abnormally, wrongly, in: **a.** Old English *mis-*, mis-: MIS-; **b.** Old Norse *miss-*, mis-: MISTAKE; **c.** Germanic **missjan*, to go wrong, in Old English *missan*, to miss: MISS[1]; AMISS. **4.** Suffixed o-grade form **moi-n-* in: **a.** compound adjective **ko-moin-i-*, "held in common" (**ko-*, together; see **kom**), in *(i)* Germanic **gamainiz* in Old English *gemǣne*, common, public, general: MEAN[2], (DEMEAN[2]) *(ii)* Latin *commūnis*, common, public, general: COMMON, (COMMUNE), (COMMUNICATE), (COMMUNISM); **b.** Latin *mūnus*, "service performed for the community," duty, work, "public spectacle paid for by a magistrate," gift: MUNICIPAL, MUNIFICENT, REMUNERATE; **c.** Latin *immūnis* (*in-*, negative prefix, IN-), exempt from public service: IMMUNE. **5.** Extended form **meigw-* in: **a.** Greek *ameibein*, to change: AMOEBA; **b.** Latin *migrāre*, to change one's place of living: MIGRATE; EMIGRATE. [Pok. 2. *mei-*, 3. *mei* 710, *meigw-* 713, 2. *meit(h)-* 715.]

mei-[2]. Small. **1.** Greek *meiōn*, less, lesser: MEIOSIS, MIOCENE, MIOLITHIC. **2.** Latin *nimis*, too much, very (< **ne-mi-s*, "not little"; *ne-*, negative prefix; see **ne**). **3.** Suffixed zero-grade form **mi-nu-* in: **a.** Latin *minuere*, to reduce, diminish: MENU, MINCE, MINUEND, MINUTE[2]; COMMINUTE, DIMINISH; **b.** Latin *minor* (influenced by the comparative suffix *-or*), less, lesser, smaller: MINOR, MINUS, (MIS-); MINUSCULE, MUSCOVADO; **c.** further suffixed (superlative) form **minu-mo-* in Latin *minimus*, least: MINIMUM; **d.** Latin *minister*, an inferior, servant (formed after *magister*, master; see **meg-**): MINESTRONE, MINISTER, MINISTRY, MYSTERY[2]; **e.** Old Church Slavonic *mĭnĭshĭ*, less, smaller: MENSHEVIK. [Pok. 5. *mei-* 711.]

mei-[3]. To fix; to build fences or fortifications. **1.** Suffixed o-grade form **moi-ro-* in: **a.** Germanic **mair-ja-* in Old English *mǣre*, boundary, border, landmark: MERE[3], MERSEY; **b.** Latin *mūrus*, wall: MURAL, MURE; IMMURE. **2.** Suffixed o-grade form **moi-ni-* in Latin *mūnīre*, to fortify, protect, strengthen: MUNITION; (AMMUNITION), PRAEMUNIRE, PREMUNITION. **3.** Possibly suffixed lengthened-grade form **mēi-t-* in Latin *mēta*, boundary stone, limit: METE[2]. [Pok. 1. *mei-* 709.]

mei-[4]. To tie. **1.** Suffixed zero-grade form **mi-tro-*, "that which ties," in: **a.** Greek *mitra*, headband: MITER; **b.** Old Persian *Mithra-*, name of a god (< "covenant," < "bond"): MITHRAS. **2.** Possibly a suffixed zero-grade form **mi-to-* in Greek *mitos*, a warp thread: MITOSIS, DIMITY, SAMITE, MITOCHONDRION. [Pok. 4. *mei-* 710.]

mēi-. Mild. **1.** Suffixed zero-grade form **mī-lo-* in Old English *Milo*, man's name: MILES. **2.** Suffixed zero-grade form **mī-ti-* in Latin *mītis*, soft: MITIGATE. **3.** Suffixed zero-grade form **mī-ro-* in Old Church Slavonic *mirŭ*, joy, peace: MIR. [Pok. 7. *mei-* 711.]

meigh-. To urinate. **1.** Germanic suffixed form **mih-stu-*, urine, hence mist, fine rain, in: **a.** Old English *mist*, mist: MIST; **b.** Middle Dutch *mieselen*, to drizzle: MIZZLE; **c.** Germanic diminutive form **mihst-ila-*, mistletoe (which is propagated through the droppings of the missel thrush), in Old English *mistel*, mistletoe: MISTLETOE, (MISSEL THRUSH). **2.** Suffixed form **meigh-tu-* in Latin *micturīre*, to want to urinate (desiderative of *meiere*, to urinate): MICTURATE. [Pok. *meigh-* 713.]

meik-. To mix. **1.** Variant form **meig-* in Greek *mignunai*, to mix: AMPHIMIXIS, APOMICT, APOMIXIS. **2.** Suffixed zero-grade form **mik-sk-* in Latin *miscēre* (past participle *mixtus*), to mix: MEDDLE, MEDLEY, MÉLANGE, MESTIZO, MISCELLANEOUS, MISCIBLE, MIX, MIXTURE; ADMIX, COMMIX, IMMIX, MISCEGENATION, PELLMELL, PROMISCUOUS. **3.** Possibly a Germanic form **maisk-* in Old English *māsc*, mashed malt: MASH. [Pok. *meik-* 714.]

mei-no-. Opinion, intention. **1.** Germanic **main-* in Old English **mān*, opinion, complaint: MOAN. **2.** Germanic **mainjan* in Old English *mǣnan*, to signify, tell, complain of, moan: MEAN[1], BEMOAN. [Pok. *mei-no-* 714.]

mel-[1]. Soft; with derivatives referring to soft or softened materials of various kinds. **1.** Extended form **meld-* in: **a.** Germanic **meltan* in Old English *meltan*, to melt: MELT; **b.** Germanic **miltja-* in Old English *milte*, spleen, and Middle Dutch *milte*, milt: MILT; **c.** Germanic **malta-* in Old English *mealt*, malt: MALT; **d.** suffixed variant form **mled-sno-* in Greek *blennos*, slime, also a name for the blenny: BLENNY; **e.** suffixed zero-grade form **mḷd-wi-* in Latin *mollis*, soft: MOIL, MOLLIFY, MOLLUSK, MOUILLÉ, MULLEIN; EMOLLIENT; **f.** possibly extended variant form **mlədo-* in Latin *blandus*, smooth, caressing, flattering, soft-spoken: BLAND, (BLANDISH). **2.** Variant form **smeld-* in Germanic **smelt-* in: **a.** Middle Dutch and Middle Low German *smelten*, to smelt: SMELT[1]; **b.** Old High German *smalz*, animal fat: SCHMALTZ; **c.** Italian *smalto*, melted glass: SMALT; **d.** Old French *esmail*, enamel: ENAMEL; **e.** perhaps Old English *smelt*, *smylt*, a marine fish, smelt: SMELT[2]. **3.** Extended form **meldh-* in: **a.** Germanic **mildja-* in Old English *milde*, mild: MILD, (MILDRED); **b.** Greek *maltha*, a mixture of wax and pitch: MALTHA. **4.** Suffixed form **mel-sko-* in Germanic **mil-sk-* in Old English *mel(i)sc*, *mylsc*, mild, mellow: MULCH. **5.** Suffixed form **mel(ə)-k-* in Greek *malakos*, soft: MALACOLOGY, OSTEOMALACIA. **6.** Possibly Celtic **molto-*, sheep, in Medieval Latin *multō*, sheep: MUTTON. [Pok. 1. *mel-* 716.]

mel-[2]. Of a darkish color. **1.** Greek *melas*, black: MELANO-, MELANCHOLY, PSILOMELANE. **2.** Greek *mullos*, a marine fish: MULLET, (SURMULLET). **3.** Latin *mulleus*, reddish purple (used only to designate a ceremonial shoe worn by Roman magistrates): MULE[2]. **4.** Perhaps Germanic **mal-* in Middle Dutch *malen*, to paint: MAULSTICK. [Pok. 6. *mel-* 720.]

mel-[3]. A limb. Greek *melos*, limb, hence a musical member or phrase, hence music, song, melody: MELISMA; DULCIMER, MELODY, MELODRAMA. [Pok. 5. *mel-* 720.]

mel-[4]. Strong, great. **1.** Suffixed (comparative) form **mel-yos-* in Latin *melior*, better: AMELIORATE, MELIORATE, MELIORISM. **2.** Suffixed zero-grade form **mḷ-to-* in Latin *multus*, much, many: MOLTO, MULTI-, MULTITUDE. [Pok. 4. *mel-* 720.]

mel-[5]. Bad. Latin *malus*, bad, and *male*, ill: DISMAL, GRAND MAL, MAL-, MALADY, MALARIA, MALEDICT, MALEFACTOR, MALEVOLENT, MALICE, MALIGN, MALVERSATION. [Pok. *mēlo-* 724.]

mel-[6]. Wool. Suffixed zero-grade form **mḷ-no-* in Greek *mallos*, wool. [Pok. 2. *mel-* 719.]

mel-[7]. To miss, deceive. Germanic **mal-* in Middle Dutch *mal*, foolish, silly: MALLEMUCK. [Pok. 2. *mel-* 719.]

meldh-[1]. To speak words to a deity. Germanic **meld-* in Old High German *meldōn*, to proclaim, reveal: MELD[1]. [Pok. 1. *meldh-* 722.]

meldh-[2]. Lightning. Germanic **meld-unija-* in Old Norse *mjöllnir*, name of the hammer of Thor. [Pok. 2. *meldh-* 722.]

melə-. Also **mel-**. To crush, grind; with derivatives referring to various ground or crumbling substances (notably flour) and to instruments for grinding or crushing (notably millstones). **1.** O-grade form **mol-* in Germanic **mal-* in: **a.** Middle Dutch *malen,* to grind: MAELSTROM (but Middle Dutch *malen,* to paint, is a separate word; see **mel-**[2]); **b.** Germanic suffixed form **mal-mōn* in Old English *mealm-,* perhaps "crumbling, friable" (only in compounds, as *mealmstān,* sandstone): MALM. **2.** Full-grade form **mel-* in Germanic suffixed form **mel-wa-* in Old English *melu,* flour, meal: MEAL[1]. **3.** Zero-grade form **ml̥-* in Germanic **mul-* in: **a.** suffixed form **mul-dō* in *(i)* Old English *molde,* soil: MOLD[3] *(ii)* Old Norse **muldhra,* to crumble: MOLDER; **b.** Middle Dutch *mul,* dust: MULL[1], MULL[2]. **4.** Full-grade form **mel-* in: **a.** Latin *molere,* to grind (grain), and its derivative *mola,* a millstone, a mill, coarse meal customarily sprinkled on sacrificial animals: MILL[1], MOLAR[2], MOLE[4], MOULIN; EMOLUMENT, IMMOLATE, ORMOLU; **b.** suffixed form **mel-eyo-* in Latin *milium, millet:* MEALIE, MILIUM, MILLET. **5.** Suffixed variant form **mal-ni-* in Latin *malleus,* hammer, mallet: MALLEABLE, MALLET, MALLEUS, MAUL; PALL-MALL. **6.** Zero-grade form **ml̥-* in Greek *mulē,* millstone, mill: AMYLUM, MYLONITE. **7.** Extended form **mli-* in: **a.** possibly Greek *bliton,* blite (a plant that in some varieties has dusty leaves): BLITE; **b.** Old Russian *mlinŭ, blinŭ,* pancake: BLINI, BLINTZ. **8.** Prefixed extended form **n̥-mlu-,* "not ground, unsharpened" (**n̥-,* negative prefix; see **ne**), in Greek *amblus,* blunt, dull, dim: AMBLYGONITE, AMBLYOPIA. [Pok. 1. *mel-* 716.]

melg-. To rub off; to milk. **I. 1.** Zero-grade form **ml̥g-* in Latin *mulgēre,* to milk: EMULSION. **2.** Full-grade form **melg-* in Germanic **melkan,* to milk, was contaminated with an unrelated noun for milk, cognate with the Greek and Latin forms given below, to form a blend **meluk-,* in: **a.** Old English *meolc, milc,* milk: MILK; **b.** suffixed form **meluk-ja-,* giving milk, in Old English *-milce,* milch: MILCH. **II.** Included here to mark the unexplained fact that no common Indo-European noun for milk can be reconstructed is another root **g(a)lag-, *g(a)lakt-,* milk, found only in: **a.** Greek *gala* (stem *galakt-*), milk: GALACTIC, GALACTO-, GALAXY, POLYGALA; **b.** Latin *lac* (stem *lact-*), milk: LACTARY, LACTATE, LACTEAL, LACTESCENT, LACTO-, LETTUCE; **c.** the blended Germanic form cited in **I. 2.** above. [Pok. *melg-* 722, *glag-* 400.]

melit-. Honey. **1.** Greek *meli,* honey: HYDROMEL, MARMALADE, MELILOT, MELISSA, OENOMEL. **2.** Suffixed form **mel-ni-* in Latin *mel* (stem *mell-*), honey: MELLIFEROUS, MELLIFLUOUS, MOLASSES. **3.** Germanic **melith-* in compound **melith-dauwaz* (**dauwaz,* dew; see **dheu-**[2]), honeydew (a substance secreted by aphids on leaves; it was formerly imagined to be distilled from the air like dew), in Old English *mildēaw,* honeydew, nectar, later also mildew: MILDEW. [Pok. *melit-* 723.]

mēlo-. Also **smēlo-**. Small animal. Zero-grade form **smələ-* in Germanic **smal-,* small animal, hence also "small," in Old English *smæl,* small: SMALL. [Pok. *mēlo-* 724.]

melədh-. Elevation, head, tip. Suffixed zero-grade form **ml̥ədh-to-* in Greek *blastos,* shoot, bud, hence embryo, germ: -BLAST, BLASTEMA, (BLASTO-), BLASTULA. [Pok. *melōdh-* 725.]

[mēlon. An apple, or any tree-growing fruit. Attic Greek noun (Doric *mālon*), borrowed from Mediterranean. CHAMOMILE, MALIC ACID, MARMALADE, MELINITE, MELON.]

mēms-. Flesh, meat. **1.** Suffixed form **mēms-ro-* in Latin *membrum,* limb, member: MEMBRANE, MEMBER. **2.** Suffixed form **mēms-no-* in Greek *mēninx,* membrane: MENINX. [Pok. *mēmso-* 725.]

men-[1]. To think; with derivatives referring to various qualities and states of mind and thought. **I.** Zero-grade form **mn̥-.* **1.** Suffixed form **mn̥-ti-* in: **a.** Germanic **ga-mundi-* (**ga-,* intensive prefix; see **kom**), in Old English *gemynd,* memory, mind: MIND; **b.** Latin *mens* (stem *ment-*), mind: MENTAL, AMENT[2], DEMENT; **c.** Latin *mentiō,* remembrance, mention: MENTION. **2.** Suffixed form **mn̥-to-* in Greek *-matos,* "willing": AUTOMATIC. **3.** Suffixed form **mn̥-yo-* in: **a.** Greek *mainesthai,* to be mad: MAENAD; **b.** Avestan *mainyu,* spirit: AHRIMAN. **II.** Full-grade form **men-.* **1.** Suffixed form **men-ti-* in Germanic **minthjā* in: **a.** Old High German *minna,* love: MINION, MINNESINGER; **b.** Middle Dutch *minne,* love: MINIKIN. **2. a.** Reduplicated form in Latin *meminisse,* to remember: MEMENTO. **b.** Latin *comminīscī* (*com-,* intensive prefix; see **kom**), to contrive by thought: COMMENT. **c.** Latin *reminīscī* (*re-,* again, back, RE-), to recall, recollect: REMINISCENT. **d.** Possibly Latin *Minerva,* name of the goddess of wisdom: MINERVA. **3. a.** Greek *menos,* spirit: EUMENIDES. **b.** Greek *Mentōr,* man's name (probably meaning "adviser"): MENTOR. **c.** Greek *mania,* madness: MANIA, MANIAC. **d.** Greek *mantis,* seer (< "he who is mad"): -MANCY, MANTIC, MANTIS. **4.** Sanskrit *mantra,* counsel, prayer, hymn: MANDARIN, MANTRA. **III.** O-grade form **mon-.* Suffixed (causative) form **mon-eyo-* in Latin *monēre,* to remind, warn, advise: MONISH, MONITION, MONITOR, MONSTER, MONUMENT, MUSTER; ADMONISH, DEMONSTRATE, PREMONITION, SUMMON. **IV.** Extended form **mnā-.* **1.** Greek *mnasthai,* to remember: MNEMOSYNE; AMNESIA, AMNESTY. **2.** Reduplicated form in Greek *mimnēskein,* to remember: ANAMNESIS. **3.** Greek *mnēmōn,* mindful: MNEMONIC. [Pok. 3. *men-* 726.]

men-[2]. To project. **1.** Latin *minae,* projecting points, threats: MENACE, MINACIOUS; AMENABLE, DEMEAN[1], PROMENADE. **2.** Latin *-minēre,* to project, jut, threaten: EMINENT, IMMINENT, PROMINENT. **3.** Suffixed o-grade form **mon-t-* in Latin *mōns* (stem *mont-*), mountain: MONS, MONTANE, MONTE, MONTICULE, MOUNT[1], MOUNT[2], MOUNTAIN; AMOUNT, MARMOT, MOUNTEBANK, PARAMOUNT, PIEDMONT, ULTRAMONTANE. [Pok. 1. *men-* 726.]

men-[3]. To remain. Latin *manēre,* to remain: MANOR, MANSE, MANSION, MÉNAGE; IMMANENT, PERMANENT, REMAIN. [Pok. 5. *men-* 729.]

men-[4]. Small, isolated. **1.** Greek *manos,* rare, sparse: MANOMETER. **2.** Suffixed o-grade form **mon-wo-* in Greek *monos,* alone, only, single, sole: MONAD, MONASTERY, MONK, MONO-. **3.** Possibly also suffixed form **men-i-,* a small fish, in Old English *myne, mynwe,* minnow: MINNOW. [Pok. 4. *men-* 728, *meni-* 731.]

mend-. Physical defect, fault. **1.** Latin *mendum,* defect, fault: MENDICANT; AMEND, EMEND, (MEND). **2.** Latin *mendāx,* lying, liar: MENDACIOUS. [Pok. *mend(ā)* 729.]

mendh-. To learn. **1.** Greek *manthanein* (aorist stem *math-*), to learn: CHRESTOMATHY, GALIMATIAS, MATHEMATICAL, POLYMATH. **2.** Suffixed zero-grade form **mn̥dh-ta-* in Avestan *mazdā,* wise: ORMAZD. [Pok. *mendh-* 730.]

menegh-. Copious. Germanic **managa-* in Old English *manig, mænig,* many: MANY. [Pok. *men(e)gh-* 730.]

meng-. To furbish. **1.** Latin *mangō,* furbisher, gem polisher, swindler: MONGER. **2.** Greek *manganon,* magic charm, contrivance, engine of war: MANGONEL. [Pok. *meng-* 731.]

menth-. To chew; set of teeth, jaw, mouth. **1.** Extended zero-grade form **mn̥tho-* in Germanic **muntha* in Old English *mūth,* mouth: MOUTH. **2.** Latin *mandere,* to chew: MANDIBLE, MANGE, (MANGER), (BLANCMANGE). **3.** Zero-grade form **mn̥th-* in Greek *masasthai* (< **math-ya-*), to chew, with its derivatives: **a.** *mastax,* jaw, mouth: MACHICOLATION; **b.** (Doric) *mustax,* upper lip, mustache: MUSTACHE; **c.** *mastikhan,* to grind the teeth: MASTIC, MASTICATE. [Pok. 2. *menth-* 732.]

mer-[1]. To flicker; with derivatives referring to dim states of illumination. **1.** Extended form **mero-* in Latin *merus,* pure, unadulterated (< "unmixed wine," < "clear liquid"): MERE[1]. **2.** Germanic **murgana-* in: **a.** Old English *morgen,* morning: MORN, (MORNING), MORROW; **b.** Middle Dutch *morghen,* morning: MORGEN; **c.** Old High German *morgan,* morning: MORGANATIC. **3.** Possibly Germanic form **merkwia-,* twilight, in Old English *mirce,* darkness: MURK. [Pok. 2. *mer-* 733.]

mer-[2]. To rub away, harm. **I. 1.** Germanic **marōn-,* goblin, in Old English *mare, mære,* goblin, incubus: NIGHTMARE. **2.** Greek *marainein,* to waste away, wither: MARASMUS; AMARANTH. **3.** Probably suffixed zero-grade form **mr̥-to-,* "ground down," in Latin *mōrtārium,* mortar: MORTAR. **4.** Possibly suffixed form **mer-d-* in Latin *mordēre* (past participle *morsus*), to bite: MORDACIOUS, MORDANT, MORDENT, MORSEL; PREMORSE, REMORSE. **5.** Possibly suffixed form **mer-bho-* in Latin *morbus,* disease: MORBID, MORBIFIC. **II.** Possibly the same root, but more likely distinct, is **mer-,* "to die," with derivatives referring to death and to man as subject to death. **1.** Zero-grade form **mr̥-* in: **a.** suffixed form **mr̥-tro-* in Germanic suffixed form **mur-thra-* in Old English *morthor,* murder: MURDER; **b.** suffixed form **mr̥-ti-* in Latin *mors* (stem *mort-*), death: MORT[1], MORTAL, MORTUARY; AMORTIZE, IMMORTAL, MORTGAGE, MORTIFY, MORTMAIN, POST-MORTEM; **c.** suffixed form **mr̥-yo-* in Latin *morī,* to die: MORIBUND, MURRAIN; **d.** prefixed and suffixed form **n̥-mr̥-to-,* "undying, immortal" (**n̥-,* negative prefix; see **ne**), in *(i)* Greek *ambrotos,* immortal, divine (*a-* + *mbrotos, brotos,* mortal): AMBROSIA *(ii)* Sanskrit *amṛta,* immortal (*a-* + *mṛta,* death): AMRITA. **2.** Suffixed o-grade form **mor-t-yo-* in Old Persian *martīya-,* a mortal man: MANTICORE. See extended root **smerd-**. [Pok. 4. *mer-,* 5. *mer-* 735.]

mer-[3]. To tie. Possibly in: **a.** Middle Dutch *marren,* to tie: MARLINE; **b.** Middle Low German *mōren,* to tie: MOOR[1]. [Pok. 1. *mer-* 733.]

mer-[4]. To trouble. Extended form **mers-* in Germanic **marzjan* in Old English *merran, mierran,* to impede: MAR. [Pok. 6. *mer-* 737.]

mer-bh-. Also **mer-gwh-**. To gleam, sparkle. **1.** O-grade form **mor-bh-, *mor-gwh-,* in Greek *morphē,* form, beauty, outward appearance: -MORPH, MORPHEME, MORPHO-, MORPHOSIS. **2.** Possibly borrowed from Greek *morphē,* via Etruscan, is Latin *forma,* form, shape, contour, appearance, beauty: FORM, (FORMAL), (FORMULA); CONFORM, DEFORM. [Pok. 2. *mer-* 733.]

[merc-. Italic root, possibly from Etruscan, referring to aspects of commerce. **1.** Latin *merx* (stem *merc-*), merchandise: COMMERCE, MARKET, (MART), MERCER, MERCHANT. **2.** Latin *merces,* pay, reward, price: MERCEDES, MERCENARY, MERCY. **3.** Probably Latin *Mercurius,* the god of (inter alia) commerce: MERCURY. [In Pok. *merk-* 739.]]

meregh-. To murmur, trickle. Zero-grade form **mregh-* in Greek *brekhein,* to wet: EMBROCATE. [Pok. *meregh-* 738.]

merə-. To remain, delay. Latin *mora,* a delay: MORA, (MORATORIUM), MORATORY; DEMUR, (DEMURE), REMORA. [In Pok. *(s)mer-* 969.]

merg-. Boundary, border. **1.** Germanic **mark-,* boundary, border territory; also to mark out a boundary by walking around it (ceremonially "beating the bounds"); also a landmark, boundary marker, and a mark in general (and in particular a mark on a metal currency bar, hence a unit of currency); these various meanings are widely represented in Germanic descendants and in Romance borrowings: **a.** Old English *mearc,* boundary, landmark, sign, trace: MARK[1]; **b.** Middle Dutch *mark,* border: MARGRAVE; **c.** Old French *marc, marche,* border country: MARCH[2], (MARQUEE), MARQUIS; **d.** Late and Medieval Latin *marca,* boundary, border: MARCHESE, MARCHIONESS; **e.** Old Provençal *marcar,* to seize (? < "mark for seizure"): LETTERS OF MARQUE; **f.** Old Italian *marcare,* to mark out: DEMARCATION; **g.** Old English *marc* and Middle High German *marke,* a mark of weight or money: MARK[2]; **h.** Swedish *mark,* a mark of money: MARKKA. **2.** Germanic **markja-,* mark, border, in: **a.** Old English *Mierce,* "men of the border": MERCIA; **b.** Old Norse *merki,* a mark: MARQUETRY, REMARK. **3.** Germanic denominative verb **markōn* in Frankish **markōn,* to mark out: MARC, MARCH[1]. **4.** Latin *margō,* border, edge: MARGIN. **5.** Variant form **mrog-* in Old Welsh *bro,* border, region: CAMBRIA, (CYMRY). [Pok. *mereg-* 738.]

merk-. To decay. Latin *marcēre,* to decay, wither: MARCESCENT. [Pok. 1. *merk-* 739.]

meu-. Damp; with derivatives referring to swampy ground and vegetation and to figurative qualities of wetness. **1.** Extended form **meus-* in Germanic **meus-, *mus-* in: **a.** Old English *mos,* bog: MOSS; **b.** Old Norse *mosi,* bog, moss: LITMUS. **2.** Germanic suffixed form **meuz-i-* in Old Norse *mȳrr,* bog: MIRE, (QUAGMIRE). **3.** Suffixed zero-grade form **mus-to-* in Latin *mustus,* new, newborn (< "wet"): MUST[3], (MUSTARD). **4.** Possibly suffixed form **meu-ro-* in Greek *murios,* countless (< "flowing, endless"): MYRIAD. **5.** Suffixed extended zero-grade form **mud-so-* in Greek *musos,* uncleanness: MYSOPHILIA, MYSOPHOBIA. **6.** Possibly Celtic **moudo-,* "washed, pure, of pure blood," in Middle Irish *muad,* noble: MONA. [Pok. 1. *meu-* 741.]

meug-[1]. To act surreptitiously. Germanic **muk-* or Celtic **mug-* in Old French *muchier,* to skulk: MOOCH. [Pok. 1. *meug-* 743.]

meug-[2]. (Enlarged form of **meu-**, damp.) Slimy, slippery; with derivatives referring to various wet or slimy substances and conditions. **1.** Nasalized form **meu-n-g-* in Latin *mungere,* to blow the nose: EMUNCTORY. **2.** Possibly Germanic **(s)mug-,* referring to wetness and also to figurative slipperiness: **a.** Old English *smok,* shirt: SMOCK; **b.** Middle High German *smuck,* "clothing," adornment, jewel: SCHMUCK; **c.** Old Norse *mugga,* drizzle:

MUGGY; **d.** Low German *smukkelen* and Dutch *smokkelen,* to smuggle (< "to slip contraband through"): SMUGGLE; **e.** Middle Low German *smucken,* to adorn (< "to make sleek"): SMUG; **f.** Old Norse *mygla,* mold, mildew: MOLD[2]. **3.** Germanic **meuk-* in: **a.** Old Norse *myki, mykr,* muck: MIDDEN, MUCK; **b.** Old Norse *mjūkr,* soft: MEEK. **4.** Variant form **meuk-* in Latin *mūcus,* mucus: MOIST, (MUCILAGE), (MUCO-), MUCUS, (MUSTY). **5.** Zero-grade variant form **muk-* in: **a.** Greek *mukēs,* fungus, mushroom: -MYCETE, MYCO-, STREPTOMYCIN; **b.** suffixed form **muk-so-* in Greek *muxa,* mucus, lamp wick (< "nozzle of a lamp," < "nostril"): MATCH[2], MYXO-. [Pok. 2. *meug-* 744.]

mew-. Also **meu-.** To push away. Latin *movēre,* to move: (MOB), MOBILE[1], (MOMENT), (MOMENTOUS), MOMENTUM, MOSSO, (MOTIF), MOTION, MOTIVE, MOTOR, MOVE, MOVEMENT; COMMOTION, EMOTION, PROMOTE, REMOTE, REMOVE. [Pok. 2. *meu-* 743.]

mezg-[1]. To dip, plunge. **1.** Latin *mergere,* to dip, dive: MERGE; EMERGE, IMMERSE, SUBMERGE. **2.** Latin *mergus,* diver (water bird): MERGANSER. [Pok. 1. *mezg-* 745.]

mezg-[2]. To knit. Germanic **mēsk-* in Middle Dutch *masche, maesche,* knitted fabric: MESH. [Pok. 2. *mezg-* 746.]

[mimos. A mime. Greek noun of unknown origin. MIME, MIMEOGRAPH, MIMESIS, MIMIC.**]**

[Miryām. "Rebellion"; Hebrew name of Moses' sister. MARY[1], (MARIE), (MARIGOLD), (MARRY[2]), MIRIAM[1], (POLLY[1]).**]**

[miser. Wretched, unfortunate. Latin adjective of unknown origin. MISER, MISERABLE, MISERY, COMMISERATE.**]**

mizdho-. Reward. Germanic **mēda-* in Old English *mēd,* reward, compensation, meed: MEED. [Pok. *mizdho-* 746.]

mō-. To exert oneself. Suffixed form **mō-l-* in: **a.** Latin *mōlēs,* heavy bulk, mass, massive structure: MOLE[3], MOLECULE; DEMOLISH; **b.** its derivative *molestus,* labored, difficult, troublesome: MOLEST. [Pok. 1. *mō-* 746.]

mōd-. To meet, assemble. **1.** Germanic **mōt-jan* in Old English *mētan,* to meet: MEET[1]. **2.** Germanic **mōta-* in Old English *mōt, gemōt* (*ge-,* together; see **kom**), meeting, moot, assembly, council: MOOT; GEMOT, FOLKMOTE, WITENAGEMOTE. **3.** Perhaps suffixed zero-grade form **məd-tlo-* in Germanic **mathla-* in: **a.** Old English *mǣl,* conversation, council: MELVIN; **b.** Old Norse *māl,* speech, agreement: BLACKMAIL, RIKSMAL. [Pok. *mōd-* 746.]

modhro-. A color. Germanic **madraz* in Old English *mædere,* madder: MADDER[1]. [Pok. *modhro-* 747.]

molko-. Skin bag. Germanic **malhō-* in Old High German *malha,* pouch, bag: MAIL[1]. [Pok. *molko-* 747.]

mon-. Neck, nape of the neck. **1.** Germanic **manō* in Old English *manu,* mane: MANE. **2.** Latin *monīle,* necklace: MONILIFORM. [Pok. *mono-* 747.]

mori-. Body of water; lake (?), sea (?). **1.** Germanic **mari-* in: **a.** Old English *mere,* sea, lake, pond: MERE[2], (MERMAID); **b.** Old Norse *marr,* sea: MARRAM; **c.** Old High German *mari,* sea: MEERSCHAUM; **d.** Middle Low German *mare,* lake: MAAR. **2.** Germanic **mariska-,* waterlogged land, in: **a.** Old English *mersc, merisc,* marsh: MARSH; **b.** Old French *marasc,* marsh: MORASS. **3.** Latin *mare,* sea: MARE[2], MARINE, MARITIME; BÊCHE-DE-MER, (CORMORANT), ORMER, ULTRAMARINE. **4.** Old Irish *muir* (genitive *mora*), sea: MURIEL. [Pok. *mori* 748.]

mormor-. Also **murmur-.** Murmur. Imitative root. **1.** Latin *murmur,* a murmur: MURMUR. **2.** Old French *marmouser,* to murmur: MARMITE. **3.** Suffixed unreduplicated form **mur-ni-* in Old Irish *muirn,* tumult, revels, banquet: MAVOURNEEN. [Pok. *mormor-* 748.]

moro-. Blackberry, mulberry. **1.** Greek *moron,* mulberry: SYCAMORE. **2.** Latin *mōrum,* mulberry (probably from Greek): MORULA, MULBERRY, MURREY. [Pok. *moro-* 749.]

morwi-. Ant. **1.** Germanic **meur-* in Danish *myre,* ant, akin to the Scandinavian source of Middle English *mire,* ant: PISMIRE. **2.** Variant form **morm-* in: **a.** Greek *murmex,* ant: MYRMECO-; **b.** (with dissimilation) Latin *formīca,* ant: FORMIC, FORMICARY. [Pok. *moruī-* 749.]

mōulo-. Name of a plant. Greek *mōlu,* moly: MOLY. [Pok. *mō(u)-lo-* 750.]

mōuro-. Foolish. Greek *mōros,* foolish: MORON, OXYMORON. [Pok. *mō(u)ro-* 750.]

[Mousa. A Muse. Greek noun of unknown origin. MOSAIC, MUSE, MUSEUM, MUSIC.**]**

mozgo-. Marrow. Germanic **mazgā-* in Old English *mærg, mærh,* marrow: MARROW. [Pok. *moz-g-o-* 750.]

mregh-mo-. Brain. **1.** Germanic **brag-na-* in Old English *brægen,* brain: BRAIN. **2.** Greek *bregma,* the front part of the head: BREGMA. [Pok. *mregh-m(n)o-* 750.]

mreghu-. Short. **I.** Suffixed form **mregh-wi-* in Latin *brevis,* short: BRIEF, BRUMAL; ABBREVIATE, (ABRIDGE). **II.** Zero-grade form **mr̥ghu-.* **1.** Germanic **murgja-,* short, also pleasant, joyful, in: **a.** Old English *myrge, mirige,* pleasant: MERRY; **b.** Germanic **murgithō,* pleasantness, in Old English *myrgth,* pleasure, joy: MIRTH. **2.** Greek *brakhus,* short: BRACHY-, AMPHIBRACH, TRIBRACH. **3.** Greek comparative *brakhiōn,* shorter, hence also "upper arm" (as opposed to the longer forearm): BRACE, BRACERO, BRACHIUM, BRASSARD, BRASSIERE, PRETZEL; EMBRACE[1], VAMBRACE. [Pok. *mreghu-* 750.]

mu-. Imitative of inarticulate sounds. **1.** Reduplicated in Germanic **mum-* in: **a.** Middle Low German *mummen,* to be silent, akin to Middle English *mum,* silent: MUM[1], (MUMBLE); **b.** Icelandic *mumpa,* to eat greedily, akin to the probable Scandinavian source of dialectal English *mump,* to mumble, grimace: MUMPS; **c.** Low German *mops,* fool, also pug dog: MOPPET, ROLLMOPS; **d.** Middle Dutch *mopen,* to be dazed or dreamy: MOPE; **e.** Old French *momer,* to act (in dumb show): MUM[2]. **2.** Germanic **mut-* in Old Norse *mudhla,* akin to the source of Middle English *muteren,* to mutter: MUTTER. **3.** Latin *muttīre,* to mutter: MOT, MOTTO. **4.** Lengthened-grade form **mū-* in Latin *mūtus,* silent, dumb: MUTE. **5.** Greek *muein,* to close the eyes (< "to close the lips"): MIOSIS, MYOPIA, MYSTERY[1], MYSTIC. [Pok. 1. *mū-* 751.]

mū-[1]. Nominative singular *mūs.* A mouse; also a muscle (from the fancied resemblance of a flexing muscle to the movements of a mouse). **1.** Germanic **mūs-* in Old English *mūs,* mouse: MOUSE. **2.** Latin *mūs,* mouse: MURINE, MUSCLE, MUSSEL, MUSTELINE, MARMOT. **3.** Greek *mus,* mouse, muscle: MYEL-, MYO-, MYOSIN; EPIMYSIUM, MYOSOTIS, MYSTICETE, PERIMYSIUM, SYRINGOMYELIA. **4.** Sanskrit *mūṣ,* mouse: MUSK, (MUSCATEL), (NUTMEG). [Pok. *mūs* 752.]

mū-[2]. Gnat, fly. Imitative root. **1.** Germanic **mukjō-* in Old English *mycg,* midge: MIDGE. **2.** Suffixed form **mus-kā* in Latin *musca,* a fly: MOSQUITO, MUSCA, MUSCARINE, MUSH[2], MUSKET. **3.** Suffixed form **mus-ya* in Greek *muia, mua,* a fly: MYIASIS. [Pok. 2. *mū-* 752.]

muk-. A heap. Germanic **mūgōn-, *mūhōn-* in: **a.** Old English *mūga, mūha, mūwa,* heap of grain: MOW[2]; **b.** Old Norse *mūgi,* heap: MOGUL[1]; **c.** Middle Dutch *mocke,* bit, thing: MALLEMUCK. [Pok. *mūk-* 752.]

[mundus. Women's cosmetics, hence (probably by a calque on Greek *kosmos,* order, feminine adornment, world-order, universe) world. Latin noun of unknown origin; possibly from Etruscan. MUNDANE, ULTRAMUNDANE.**]**

[mūsum. Snout. Medieval Latin noun of unknown origin. MUSE, MUZZLE, (AMUSE).**]**

mut-. Cut short. Suffixed form **mut-il-* in Latin *mutilus,* maimed: MOCHILA, MOZZARELLA, MUTILATE. [Pok. *mut-o-s* 753.]

[nabja-. Bird's beak. Germanic root. **1.** Old English *neb(b),* beak: NEB, (NIPPLE). **2.** Old English *nibba,* beak (attested only in one place name): NIB.**]**

nana. Child's word for a nurse or female adult other than its mother. **1.** Greek *nanna,* aunt, whence *nannas,* uncle, whence *nan(n)os,* "little old man," dwarf: NANO-. **2.** Late and Medieval Latin *nonna,* aunt, old woman, nun: NUN[1]. **3.** English (directly from baby talk) NANA, NANNY. [Pok. *nana* 754.]

nant-. To dare. Germanic **nanthi-,* risk, in compound **Fardi-nanth-,* a masculine name, "adventurer" (**fardi-,* journey; see **per-[2]**): FERDINAND. [Pok. *nant-* 755.]

nas-. Nose. **1.** Germanic **nasō* in Old English *nosu,* nose: NOSE, (NOSTRIL). **2.** Lengthened-grade form **nās-* in: **a.** Latin *nāris,* nostril: NARES; **b.** expressive form **nāss-* in Latin *nāsus,* nose: NASAL, NASO-, NASTURTIUM, PINCE-NEZ. **3.** Expressive Indo-Aryan form **nakka-* in Prakrit *ṇakka,* nose: NARK. [Pok. *nas-* 755, *neu-ks* 768.]

nāu-[1]. Death; to be exhausted. **1.** Suffixed zero-grade form **nəu-ti-* in Germanic **naudi-* in Old English *nēod, nēd,* distress, necessity: NEED. **2.** Suffixed form **nāw-i-,* corpse, in Germanic **nawi-* in Old Norse *nār,* corpse: NARWHAL. **3.** Polish *nuda,* boredom: NUDNIK. [Pok. 2. *nāu-* 756.]

nāu-[2]. Boat. **1.** Latin *nāvis,* ship: NACELLE, NAVAL, NAVICULAR, NAVIGATE, NAVY. **2.** Greek *naus,* ship, and *nautēs,* sailor: NAUSEA, NAUTICAL, NAUTILUS, (NAUPLIUS), NOISE; AERONAUT, AQUANAUT, ARGONAUT, ASTRONAUT, COSMONAUT. [Pok. 1. *nāu-* 755.]

n̥dher-. Under. **1.** Germanic **under-* in Old English *under,* under: UNDER. **2.** Latin *īnferus,* lower: INFERIOR. **3.** Latin *īnfernus,* lower: INFERNAL, (INFERNO). **4.** Latin *īnfrā,* below: INFRA-. [Pok. *n̥dhos* 771.]

ne. Not. **1.** Germanic **ne-, *na-* in: **a.** Old English *ne,* not: (NA), (NAUGHT), (NAUGHTY), (NEITHER), NEVER, NILL, NO[1], (NO[2]), NONE, (NOR[1]), (NOT), (NOTHING); HOBNOB; **b.** Old Norse *ne,* not: NAY; **c.** Old High German *ne, ni,* not: NIX[2]. **2.** Latin *ne-,* not, and *nullus,* none (*ūllus,* any; see **oino-**): NEFARIOUS, NESCIENCE, NEUTER, NICE, NISI, NULL, NULLIFY; ANNUL. **3.** Latin *nimis,* too much, excessively, very (< **ne-mi-s,* "not little"; **mi-,* little; see **mei-[2]**): NIMIETY. **4.** Latin *nihilum,* nothing (< **ne-hīlum,* "not a whit, nothing at all"; *hīlum,* a thing, trifle; origin unknown), contracted to *nihil, nīl,* nothing: NIHIL, NIHILISM, NIHILITY, (NIL); ANNIHILATE. **5.** Latin *nōn,* not (< **ne-oinom,* "not one thing"; **oino-,* one; see **oino-**): NON-. **6.** Italic **nek,* not, in: **a.** Latin prefix *neg-,* not: NEGLECT, (NEGLIGEE), NEGOTIATE; **b.** Latin *negāre,* to deny: NEGATE; ABNEGATE, DENY, RENEGADE, (RENEGE). **7.** Greek *nē-,* not: NEPENTHE. **8.** Zero-grade combining form **n̥-* in: **a.** Germanic **un-* in Old English *un-,* not: UN-[1]; **b.** Latin *in-,* not: IN-[1]; **c.** Greek *a-, an-,* not: A-[1], AN-; **d.** Sanskrit *a-, an-,* not: AHIMSA, AMRITA. [Pok. *ne* 756.]

nebh-. Cloud. **1.** Suffixed form **nebh-lo-* in Germanic **nibla-* probably in Old Norse *nifl-,* "mist" or "dark": NIFLHEIM. **2.** Suffixed form **nebh-lā-* in Latin *nebula,* cloud: NEBULA, (NEBULOUS). **3.** Suffixed form **nebh-elā* in Greek *nephelē,* cloud: NEPHELINE, NEPHELOMETER. **4.** Basic form **nebh-* in Greek *nephos,* cloud: NEPHOLOGY. **5.** Nasalized form **ne-m-bh-* in Latin *nimbus,* rain, cloud, aura: NIMBUS. [Pok. (*enebh-*) 315.]

ned-. To bind, tie. **1.** O-grade form **nod-* in: **a.** Germanic **nati-* in Old English *net,* a net: NET[1]; **b.** Germanic **nat-ilō,* a nettle (nettles or plants of closely related genera such as hemp were used as a source of fiber), in Old English *netel(e), netle,* nettle: NETTLE; **c.** Germanic **nat-st-* in Old French *nasle,* string: LANYARD; **d.** Germanic **nat-sk-* in Old French *nouche,* brooch: OUCH[2]. **2.** Lengthened o-grade form **nōdo-* in Latin *nōdus,* a knot: NODE, (NODULE), (NODUS), DÉNOUEMENT. **3.** Reformation of the root in Latin *nectere* (past participle *nexus*), to tie, bind, connect: NEXUS, ANNEX, CONNECT. [Pok. 1. *ned-* 758.]

negwhro-. Kidney. Derivative of **engw-.** Greek *nephros,* kidney: NEPHRO-; MESONEPHROS, METANEPHROS, PERINEPHRIUM, PRONEPHROS. [In Pok. *engu-* 319.]

nei-[1]. To be excited, to shine. **1.** Suffixed form **nei-to-* in Germanic **nītha-,* animosity, in Old Norse *nīdh,* scorn: NIDDERING. **2.** Suffixed zero-grade form **ni-to-* in Latin *nitēre,* to shine: NEAT[1], NET[2]. **3.** Possibly suffixed form **nei-t-slo-* in Old Irish *Niall,* "brave," masculine name: NEIL. **4.** Possibly Persian *nīl,* indigo: ANIL, LILAC. [Pok. 2. *nei-* 760.]

nei-[2]. To lead. Sanskrit *nayati,* he leads: NAINSOOK. [Pok. 1. *nei-* 760.]

neigw-. To wash. Germanic **nikwiz, *nikuz* in Old High German *nihhus,* river monster, water spirit: NIX[1]. [Pok. *neigu-* 761.]

nek-[1]. Death. **1.** Latin *nex* (stem *nec-*), death: PERNICIOUS. **2.** Latin *necāre,* to kill: INTERNECINE. **3.** Suffixed (causative) o-grade form **nok-eyo-* in Latin *nocēre,* to injure, harm: NOCENT, NOCUOUS, NUISANCE; INNOCENT, INNOCUOUS. **4.** Suffixed o-grade form **nok-s-* in Latin *noxa,* injury, hurt, damage: NOXIOUS; OBNOXIOUS. **5.** Suffixed full-grade form **nek-ro-* in Greek *nekros,* corpse: NECRO-, NECROSIS. **6.** Greek *nektar,* the drink of the gods, "overcoming death" (**tar-,* overcoming; see **ter-[3]**): NECTAR, (NECTARINE). [Pok. *nek-* 762.]

nek-[2]. To reach, attain. **1.** O-grade form **nok-* in Germanic **ga-nah-* (**ga-,* intensive prefix; see **kom**), "satisfies," forming **ganōga-,* sufficient, in Old English *genog,* enough: ENOUGH. **2.** Variant form **enk-* reduplicated in *enenkein,* to carry, whence *onkos,* a burden, mass, hence a tumor: ONCOLOGY. **3.** Compound root **bhrenk-* (see **bher-[1]**). [Pok. *enek-* 316.]

nekwt-. Night. O-grade form **nokwt-.* **1.** Germanic **naht-* in Old English *niht, neaht,* night: NIGHT. **2.** Latin *nox* (stem *noct-*), night: NOCTI-, (NOCTURN), NOCTURNAL, NOTTURNO; EQUINOX. **3.** Latin *noctua,* night owl: NOCTUID, NOCTULE. **4.** Greek *nux* (stem *nukt-*), night: NYCTALOPIA, NYCTITROPISM. **5.** Possibly suffixed zero-grade form **n̥kt-i-* in Greek *aktis,* ray of light: ACTINO-. [Pok. *neku(t)-* 762.]

nem-[1]. Sacred grove. Latin *nemus,* grove.

[Pok. 2. nem- 764.]

nem-[2]. To assign, allot; also, to take. **1.** Germanic *nem- in: **a.** Old English niman, to take, seize: NIM, NUMB, (BENUMB); **b.** Old English nǣmel, quick to seize, and numol, quick at learning, seizing: NIMBLE. **2.** Greek nemein, to allot: NEMESIS. **3.** O-grade form *nom- in: **a.** Greek nomos, portion, usage, custom, law, division, district: NOME, NOMO-, -NOMY; ANOMIE, ANTINOMIAN, ANTINOMY, ASTRONOMER, AUTONOMOUS, BINOMIAL, DEUTERONOMY, METRONOME, NUMISMATICS, NUMMULAR; **b.** Greek nomē, pasturage, grazing, hence a spreading, a spreading ulcer: NOMA; **c.** Greek nomas, wandering in search of pasture: NOMAD. **4.** Perhaps suffixed o-grade form *nom-éso- in Latin numerus, number, division: NUMBER; ENUMERATE, SUPERNUMERARY. [Pok. 1. nem- 763.]

nepōt-. Grandson, nephew. Feminine *neptī-. Latin nepōs, grandson, nephew, and neptis, granddaughter, niece: NEPHEW, NEPOTISM, NIECE. [Pok. nepōt- 764.]

ner-[1]. Under; also, on the left; hence, with an eastward orientation, north (compare **deks-**). Suffixed zero-grade form *nr̥-t(r)o- in Germanic *north-, north, in: **a.** Old English north, north: NORTH, NORDIC, NORMAN[1]; **b.** Old English northerne, northern: NORTHERN; **c.** Old Norse nordhr, north: NORMAN[2], NORN[2], NORWAY; **d.** Middle Dutch nort, north: NORSE. [Pok. 2. ner- 765.]

ner-[2]. Man. **1.** With prothetic vowel a-, Greek anēr (stem andr-), man: ANDRO-, -ANDROUS, -ANDRY; ALEXANDER, ANDREW[1], PHILANDER. **2.** Referred by some to this root (as if "having human eyes"; ōps, eye) but more likely of unknown origin is Greek anthrōpos, man: ANTHROPIC, ANTHROPO-, -ANTHROPUS; LYCANTHROPE, MISANTHROPE, PHILANTHROPY, THEANTHROPIC. [Pok. 1. ner-(t)- 765.]

nēr-. Name of a water deity. Probably Greek Nēreus, name of a sea god: NEREUS, (NEREID[1]), (NERITIC). [Pok. 3. ner- 766.]

nes-[1]. To return safely home. O-grade form *nos- in: **a.** Germanic *nas-tja- in Old Norse nest, food for a journey: HARNESS; **b.** suffixed form *nos-to- in Greek nostos, a return home: NOSTALGIA. [Pok. nes- 766.]

nes-[2]. Oblique cases of the personal pronoun of the first person plural (for the nominative see **we-**). **1.** Zero-grade form *n̥s- in Germanic *uns in Old English ūs, us (accusative): US. **2.** Suffixed (possessive) zero-grade form *n̥s-ero- in Germanic *unsara- in Old English (ūser), ūre, our: OUR, (OURS). **3.** O-grade form *nos-, with suffixed (possessive) form *nos-t(e)ro-, in Latin nōs, we, and noster, our: NOSTRUM, PATERNOSTER. [Pok. 3. ne- 758.]

nētr-. Snake. Germanic *nēthrō- in Old English nǣdre, snake: ADDER. [Pok. nē-tr- 767.]

neu-[1]. To shout. Suffixed (participial) o-grade form *now-ent-(io)-, "shouting," in Latin nūntius, "announcing," hence a messenger, also a message, and nūntium, message: NUNCIO; ANNOUNCE, DENOUNCE, ENUNCIATE, PRONOUNCE, RENOUNCE. [Pok. 1. neu- 767.]

neu-[2]. To nod. **1.** Latin *nuere, to nod (attested only in compounds): NUTATION; INNUENDO. **2.** Suffixed form *neu-men in Latin nūmen, "a nod," hence "command," divine power, deity: NUMEN. [Pok. 2. neu- 767.]

neud-. To make use of, enjoy. Germanic *nauta-, "thing of value, possession," in: **a.** Old English nēat, bovine animal: NEAT[2]; **b.** compound form *ga-nauta- (*ga-, with, together; see **kom**), "he with whom one shares possessions," companion, fellow, in (i) Middle Dutch ghenōt, fellow: MATELOTE (ii) Old High German ginōz, companion: HUGUENOT. [Pok. neu-d- 768.]

[**nēwh-iz.** Near. Germanic root. Old English nēah, near: NEAR, NEIGHBOR, NEXT, NIGH.]

newn̥. Nine. **1.** Germanic *niwun, with variant *nigun, in Old English nigon, nine: NINE, (NINETEEN), (NINETY), (NINTH). **2.** Latin novem, nine (< *noven, with m for n by analogy with the m of septem, seven, and decem, ten): NOVEMBER, NOVENA. **3.** Ordinal form *neweno- in Latin nōnus, ninth: NONA-, NONAGENARIAN, NONES, NOON. **4.** Prothetic forms *enewn̥, *enwn̥, in Greek ennea, nine (<*ennewa, *enwa-): ENNEAD. [Pok. e-neu̯en 318.]

newo-. New. Related to **nu-**. **1.** Suffixed form *new-yo- in Germanic *neuja- in: **a.** Old English nēowe, new: NEW; **b.** Old Norse nȳr, new: SPAN-NEW. **2.** Basic form *newo- in Greek *newos, neos, new: NEO-, NEON, NEOTERIC; MISONEISM. **3.** Suffixed form *new-ero- in Greek nearos, young, fresh, contracted into nēros, fresh (used of fish and of water), hence nēron, water: ANEROID. **4.** Forms *newo- and *new-yo- in Sanskrit nava, nāvya, new: NAYA PAISA. **5.** Basic form *newo- in Latin novus, new: NOVA, NOVATION, (NOVEL[1]), NOVEL[2], (NOVELTY), NOVICE; NOVOCAIN, INNOVATE, RENOVATE. **6.** Suffixed form *new-er-ko- in Latin noverca, stepmother (< "she who is new"): NOVERCAL. [Pok. neu̯os 709.]

ni-. Down. **1.** Suffixed form *ni-t- in Germanic *nith- in Old English nithan, neothan, below: BENEATH, UNDERNEATH. **2.** Suffixed (comparative) form *ni-tero-, lower, in Germanic *nitheraz in Old English nither, lower: NETHER. **3.** Sanskrit ni, down: UPANISHAD. **4.** See compound root **nizdo-**. [In Pok. 1. en 311.]

[**niger.** Black. Latin adjective of unknown origin. NEGRO, NIELLO, NIGRESCENCE, NIGRIFY, NIGRITUDE; DENIGRATE, NECROMANCY, NIGROSINE.]

[**nikē.** Victory. Greek noun of unknown origin. EUNICE, NICHOLAS, (NICKEL), NIKE.]

[**nitron.** Sodium carbonate, natron, soda. Greek noun, probably from Egyptian ntr(j), natron, via Semitic or Hittite. **1.** Greek nitron: NITER, NITRO-, NITROUS. **2.** Probably from Greek nitron, but perhaps separately from the same source, is Arabic naṭrūn, natron: NATRON, TRONA.]

nizdo-. Bird's nest. Compound root formed from **ni-**, down + *sd-, zd-, zero-grade form of **sed-[1]**, sit; literally, "place where the bird sits down." **1.** Germanic *nist- in: **a.** Old English nest, nest: NEST; **b.** Germanic *nistilōn in Old English nestlian, to make a nest: NESTLE. **2.** Latin nīdus, nest: NICHE, NIDE, NIDUS; NIDIFY, EYAS. [In Pok. sed- 887.]

nobh-. Also **ombh-**. Navel; later also "central knob," boss of a shield, hub of a wheel. **1.** Germanic *nabō in: **a.** Old English nafu, hub of a wheel: NAVE[2]; **b.** compound *nabō-gaizaz, tool for piercing wheel hubs (*gaizaz, spear, piercing tool; see **ghaiso-**), in Old English nafōgar, auger: AUGER. **2.** Variant form *ombh- in Latin umbō, boss of a shield: UMBO. **3.** Suffixed form *nobh-alo- in Germanic *nabalō in Old English nafela, navel: NAVEL. **4.** Suffixed variant form *ombh-alo- in: **a.** Latin umbilīcus, navel: UMBILICUS; NOMBRIL; **b.** Greek omphalos, navel: OMPHALOS. [Pok. 1. (enebh-) 314.]

nogh-. Also **onogh-**, **ongh-**. Nail, claw. **1.** Suffixed (diminutive) form *nogh-ela- in Germanic *nagla- in Old English nægl, nail: NAIL. **2.** Variant form *ongh- in Latin unguis, nail, claw, hoof, with diminutive ungula, hoof, claw, talon (< *ongh-elā-): UNGUIS. **3.** Variant form *onogh- in Greek onux (stem onukh-), nail: ONYX, (SARDONYX). [Pok. onogh- 780.]

nogw-. Naked. **1.** Suffixed forms *nogw-eto-, *nogw-oto- in Germanic *nakweda-, *nakwada- in Old English nacod, naked: NAKED. **2.** Suffixed form *nogw-edo- in Latin nūdus, naked: NUDE, (NUDI-); (DENUDE). **3.** Suffixed form *nogw-no- differentiated or developed into Greek gumnos, naked: GYMNASIUM, GYMNOSOPHIST. [Pok. nogu̯- 769.]

nomen-. Also **nomn̥-**, **onomn̥-**. Name. **1.** Germanic *namōn- in Old English nama, name: NAME. **2.** Latin nōmen, name, reputation: NOMINAL, NOMINATE, NOUN; AGNOMEN, COGNOMEN, DENOMINATE, IGNOMINY, MISNOMER, NOMENCLATOR, NUNCUPATIVE, PRAENOMEN, PRONOUN, RENOWN. **3.** Greek onoma, onuma, name: ONOMASTIC, -ONYM, -ONYMY; ANONYMOUS, ANTONOMASIA, EPONYMOUS, EUONYMUS, HETERONYMOUS, HOMONYMOUS, METONYMY, METRONYMIC, ONOMATOPOEIA, PARONOMASIA, PARONYMOUS, PATRONYMIC, (PSEUDONYM), SYNONYMOUS. [Pok. en(o)mn̥- 321.]

nōt-. Buttock, back. **1.** Greek nōton, back: NOTOCHORD. **2.** Zero-grade form *nət- in Latin natis, buttock: NATES; AITCHBONE. [Pok. nōt- 770.]

[**nous.** Mind, sense, reason, intellect. Greek noun of unknown origin. NOESIS, NOUS, NOUMENON, DIANOETIC, PARANOIA.]

n̥si-. Sword. Latin ēnsis, sword: ENSIFORM. [Pok. n̥si-s 771.]

nu-. Now. Related to **newo-**, new. **1.** Germanic *neuja- in Old English nū, now: NOW. **2.** Latin nunc (< *num-ce; -ce, a particle meaning "this," "here"; see **ko-**), now: QUIDNUNC. [Pok. nu- 770.]

ō-. To announce, to hold as true. Suffixed form in Latin ōmen, a prognostic sign, omen: OMEN.

obhel-. To sweep; to pile up, increase. Greek ophelos, advantage: ANOPHELES. [Pok. obhel- 772.]

od-[1]. To smell. **1.** Suffixed form *od-es- in Latin odor, smell: ODOR. **2.** Suffixed form *od-ē- in Latin olere, to smell (with l for d representing a Sabine borrowing): OLFACTORY, REDOLENT. **3.** Suffixed form *od-yo- in Greek ozein, to smell: OZONE. **4.** Suffixed form *od-mā- in Greek osmē, smell: OSMATIC, OSMIUM; ANOSMIA. [Pok. 1. od- 772.]

od-[2]. To hate. Possibly related to **kād-**. Latin ōdī, I hate, and odium, hatred: ANNOY, ENNUI, (NOISOME), ODIUM. [Pok. 2. od- 773.]

ōg-. Fruit, berry. **1.** Zero-grade form *əg- in Germanic *ak-ran- in Old English æcern, acorn: ACORN. **2.** Latin ūva (pre-form uncertain), grape: UVEA, UVULA; PYRUVIC ACID. [Pok. ōg- 773.]

oid-. To swell. **1.** Possibly Old English āte, oat: OAT. **2.** Greek oidein, to swell: EDEMA. [Pok. oid- 774.]

oino-. One, unique. **I.** Basic form *oino-. **1.** Germanic *ainaz in: **a.** Old English ān, one: A[1], AN[1], (ALONE), ANON, (ATONE), LONE, (LONELY), (NONCE), NONE, ONCE, ONE; **b.** compound *ain-lif-, "one left (beyond ten)," eleven (*lif-, left over; see **leikw-**), in Old English endleofan, eleven: ELEVEN; **c.** Old High German ein, one: EINKORN, TURNVEREIN. **2.** Latin ūnus, one: INCH[1], ONION, OUNCE[1], UNCIAL, UNI-, UNION, UNITE, UNITY; COADUNATE, QUINCUNX, TRIUNE, UNANIMOUS, (UNICORN), (UNIVERSE). **3.** Latin nōn, not (< *ne-oinom, "not one thing"; ne, not; see **ne**). **II.** Suffixed form *oino-ko- in: **a.** Germanic *ainigaz in Old English ǣnig, one, anyone: ANY; **b.** Latin ūnicus, sole, single: UNIQUE. **III.** Suffixed form *oino-lo- in Latin ūllus, any: NULL. [In Pok. e- 281.]

oito-. An oath. Germanic *aithaz in: **a.** Old English āth, oath: OATH; **b.** Old High German eid, oath: HUGUENOT. [In Pok. 1. ei- 293.]

oktō. Eight. **1.** Germanic *ahtō in: **a.** Old English eahta, eight: EIGHT; **b.** Old Norse āttjan (tjan, ten; see **dekm̥**), eighteen: ATTO-. **2.** Latin octō, eight: OCTANT, OCTAVE, OCTET, OCTO-, OCTOBER, OCTONARY. **3.** Greek oktō, eight: OCTAD. [Pok. oktō 775.]

ōku-. Swift. Zero-grade form *əku- in Latin accipiter, hawk ("swift-flying"; *pet-ro-, flying; see **pet-[1]**): ACCIPITER. [Pok. ōku-s 775.]

okw-. To see. **1.** Germanic *augōn- (with taboo deformation), in: **a.** Old English ēage, eye: EYE, DAISY; **b.** Old Norse auge, eye: WINDOW, WALLEYED; **c.** (obsolete) Dutch oog, eye: PINK[1]; **d.** Low German oog, eye: OGLE. **2.** Suffixed form *okw-olo- in Latin oculus, eye: ANTLER, EYELET, INOCULATE, INVEIGLE, MONOCLE, OCELLUS, OCULAR, OCULIST, OCULOMOTOR, PINOCHLE, ULLAGE. **3.** Form *okw-s in: **a.** Greek ōps, eye (and stem *op-, to see): METOPIC, MYOPIA, NYCTALOPIA, PELOPS, PHLOGOPITE, PYROPE; **b.** Latin ātrox, "black-looking," frightful (*ātr-, black; see **āter-**); **c.** Latin ferōx, "wild-looking," fierce (*ghwer-, wild; see **ghwer-**). **4.** Suffixed form *okw-ti- in Greek opsis, sight, appearance: -OPSIS, -OPSY; AUTOPSY, RHODOPSIN, SYNOPSIS. **5.** Suffixed form *okw-to- in Greek optos, seen, visible: OPTIC, OPTOMETRY, CATOPTRIC, DIOPTER, PANOPTIC. **6.** Suffixed form *okw-ā in Greek opē, opening: METOPE. **7.** Suffixed form *okw-men- in Greek omma (< *opma), eye: OMMATIDIUM, OMMATOPHORE. **8.** Greek ophthalmos, eye (with taboo deformation): OPHTHALMIA, OPHTHALMIC, OPHTHALMO-, EXOPHTHALMOS. **9.** Zero-grade form *əkw- (see **anti**). [Pok. oku̯- 775.]

ol-. To destroy. Possibly suffixed zero-grade form *l-ē-to- in Latin lētum, death: LETHAL. [Pok. ol-(e)- 777.]

om-. Raw. Possibly (but doubtful both in form and meaning) Latin amārus, bitter-tasting: AMARELLE, MARASCA, (MARASCHINO), MORELLO. [Pok. om- 777.]

ombhro-. Rain. **1.** Zero-grade form *m̥bhro- in Latin imber, rain: IMBRICATE. **2.** Possibly zero-grade variant form *m̥bh- in Latin imbuere, to moisten, stain: IMBUE. [In Pok. 2. (enebh-) 315.]

omeso-. Also **omso-**. Shoulder. **1.** Form *omso- in Germanic *amsa- in Old Norse āss, a (mountain) ridge: OS[3]. **2.** Form *omeso- in Latin humerus, shoulder: HUMERUS. [Pok. om(e)so-s 778.]

omə-. To move with energy. Germanic *amal- in Old High German amal, work: MILLICENT. [Pok. omə- 778.]

oner-. Dream. Suffixed form *oner-yo- in Greek oneiros, dream: ONEIROMANCY. [Pok. oner- 779.]

ongw-. To salve, anoint. Latin unguere, to smear, anoint: ANOINT, INUNCTION, OINTMENT, PREEN, UNCTION, UNCTUOUS, UNGUENT. [Pok. ongu̯- 779.]

op-[1]. To work, produce in abundance. **1.** Possibly Germanic *oft-, frequently, in Old English oft, oft: OFT, (OFTEN). **2.** Suffixed form *op-es- in Latin opus (stem oper-), work, with its denominative verb *operārī*, to work, and secondary noun *opera*, work: OPERA[1], OPERATE, OPEROSE, OPUS; COOPERATE, ESTOVERS, INURE, MANEUVER, MANURE, OFFICINAL. **3.** Latin *officium*, service, duty, business (< **opi-fici-om*, "performance of work"; *-fici-*, doing; see **dhē-**[1]). **4.** Suffixed form **op-en-ent-* dissimilated in Latin *opulentus*, rich, wealthy: OPULENT. **5.** Suffixed form **op-ni-* in Latin *omnis*, all (< "abundant"): OMNI-, OMNIBUS, OMNIUM-GATHERUM. **6.** Suffixed (superlative) form **op-tamo-* in Latin *optimus*, best (< "wealthiest"): OPTIMUM. **7.** Prefixed form **co-op-* (*co-*, collective and intensive prefix; see **kom**) in Latin *cōpia*, profusion, plenty: COPIOUS, COPY, CORNUCOPIA. [Pok. 1. *op-* 780.]

op-[2]. To choose. **1.** Latin *optiō*, choice (from **opere*, to choose): OPTION. **2.** Latin *optāre* (frequentative of **opere*), to choose: OPT, OPTATIVE, CO-OPT, ADOPT. **3.** Possibly suffixed form **op-yen-* in Latin *opīnārī*, to be of an opinion: OPINE, OPINION. [Pok. 2. *op-* 781.]

ōr-. To pronounce a ritual formula. Latin *ōrāre*, to speak, plead, pray: ORACLE, ORATION, ORATOR, ORATORY[2]; ADORE, EXORABLE, PERORATE. [Pok. *ōr-* 781.]

orbh-. To put asunder, separate. Extended form **orbho-*, "bereft of father," also "deprived of free status," in: **a.** Greek *orphanos*, orphaned: ORPHAN; **b.** Old Slavic **orbŭ* in Old Church Slavonic *rabŭ*, slave, whence *rabota*, servitude, in Czech *robota*, compulsory labor, drudgery: ROBOT. [Pok. *orbho-* 781.]

orghi-. Testicle. Greek *orkhis*, testicle: ORCHID. [Pok. *orghi-* 782.]

ors-. Buttocks, backside. **1.** Suffixed form **ors-o-* in Germanic **arsaz* in Old English *ærs*, *ears*, backside: ASS[2]. **2.** Suffixed form **ors-ā-* in: **a.** Greek *oura*, tail: URO-[2], -UROUS; ANTHURIUM, ANURAN, CYNOSURE, SQUIRREL; **b.** probably Greek *silouros*, sheatfish (< obscure first element + *oura*): SILURID. [Pok. *ers-* 340.]

os-. Ash tree. Germanic **aski-* in Old English *æsc*, ash: ASH[2]. [Pok. *ōs-* 782.]

ōs-. Mouth. **1.** Latin *ōs* (stem *ōr-*), mouth, face, orifice, and derivative *ōstium* (< suffixed form **ōs-to-*), door: ORAL, OS[1], OSCILLATE, OSCULATE, OSCULUM, OSTIARY, OSTIUM, USHER; INOCULATE, ORIFICE, ORINASAL, OROTUND, OSCITANCY. **2.** Possibly Latin *aurīga*, charioteer (< **ōr-ig-*, "he who manages the (horse's) bit"; *-ig-*, driving, from **ag-*; see **ag-**): AURIGA. [Pok. 1. *ōus-* 784.]

osth-. Also **ost-**. Bone. **1.** Latin *os* (stem *oss-*), bone: OS[2], OSSEOUS, OSSICLE, OSSIFRAGE, OSSIFY, OSSUARY. **2.** Greek *osteon*, bone: OSTEO-; ENDOSTEUM, EXOSTOSIS, PERIOSTEM, SYNOSTOSIS, TELEOST. **3.** Suffixed form **ost-r-* in: **a.** Greek *ostrakon*, shell, potsherd: OSTRACIZE, OSTRACOD; **b.** Greek *ostreon*, oyster: OYSTER; **c.** Greek *astragalos*, vertebra, ball of the ankle joint, knucklebone, Ionic molding: ASTRAGAL, ASTRAGALUS. [Pok. *ost(h)-* 783.]

ous-. Ear. **1.** Suffixed form **ous-en-* in Germanic **auzan-* in Old English *ēare*, ear: EAR. **2.** Extended form **ausi-* in Latin *auris*, ear: AURAL[1], AURICLE, AURIFORM, ORMER. **3.** Latin *auscultāre*, to listen to (**aus-* + an obscure second element): AUSCULTATION, SCOUT[1]. **4.** Basic form **ous-* in: **a.** Greek *ous* (stem *ōt-*), ear: OTIC, OTO-, MYOSOTIS, PAROTID GLAND; **b.** Greek *lagōs*, hare (< **lag-ous-*, "with drooping ears"; **lag-*, to droop; see **slēg-**). [Pok. *ōus-* 785.]

owi-. Sheep. **1.** Germanic **awi-* in Old English *ewe*, *eowu*, ewe: EWE. **2.** Latin *ovis*, sheep: OVINE; OVIBOS. [Pok. *oui-s* 784.]

ozdo-. Branch, point. Proposed by some as the root for Germanic **uzda-* in Old Norse *oddi*, point, triangle, third, odd number: ODD.

pā-. To feed, protect. **1.** Suffixed form **pā-trom* in Germanic **fōdram* in: **a.** Old English *fōdor*, fodder: FODDER; **b.** Old French *feurre*, fodder: FORAGE; **c.** Vulgar Latin **fodrārius*, fodder: FORAY. **2.** Suffixed form **pā-dhlom* (doublet of **pā-trom*) in Latin *pābulum*, food, fodder: PABULUM. **3.** Extended form **pāt-* in: **a.** Germanic **fōd-*, food, in Old English *fōda*, food: FOOD; **b.** Germanic denominative **fōdjan*, to give food to, in Old English *fēdan*, to feed: FEED; **c.** suffixed form **pāt-tro-* in Germanic **fōstra-* in Old English *fōstor*, food, nourishment: FOSTER. **4.** Extended form **pās-* in: **a.** suffixed form **pās-k-* in Latin *pāscere*, to feed: PASTURE, (PESTER), ANTIPASTO, REPAST; **b.** Latin *pāstor*, shepherd: PASTOR; **c.** suffixed form **pās-ni-* in Latin *pānis*, bread: PANADA, PANATELA, PANNIER, PANOCHA, PANTRY, PASTILLE, PENUCHE; APPANAGE, COMPANION, (COMPANY). **5.** Suffixed form **pā-ti-* in Iranian **pāti-* in Persian *pād*, protecting against: BEZOAR. [Pok. *pā-* 787.]

pag-. Also **pak-**. To fasten. **1.** Lengthened-grade form **pāk-* in Germanic **fōgjan*, to join, fit, in Old English *fēgan*, to fit closely: FAY[1]. **2.** Nasalized form **pa-n-g-* in: **a.** Germanic **fangiz*, seizure, in (*i*) Old English *fang*, *feng*, plunder, booty: FANG (*ii*) Dutch *vang*, rope for fastening a sail: VANG; **b.** Latin *pangere*, to fasten: COMPACT[1], IMPINGE. **3.** Root form **pǎk-* in: **a.** Latin *pāx*, peace (< "a binding together by treaty or agreement"): PACE[2], PACIFIC, PACIFY, PAY[1], PEACE; APPEASE; **b.** Latin *pacīscī*, to agree: PACT. **4.** Suffixed form **pak-slo-* in: **a.** Latin *pālus*, stake (fixed in the ground): PALE[1], PALISADE, PAWL, PEEL[3], POLE[2]; IMPALE, TRAVAIL[1], (TRAVEL); **b.** probably Latin *pāla*, spade: PALETTE, PEEL[2]. **5.** Lengthened-grade form **pāg-* in: **a.** Latin *pāgus*, "boundary staked out on the ground," district, village, country: PAGAN, PEASANT; **b.** Latin *pāgina*, "trellis to which a row of vines is fixed," hence (by metaphor) column of writing, page: PAGE[2], PAGEANT, PAIL; **c.** Latin *prōpāgēs* (*prō-*, before, in front, PRO-), layer of vine, offspring (< "a fixing before"): PROPAGATE; **d.** Greek *pēgnunai*, to fasten, coagulate: PECTIN, PEGMATITE. [Pok. *pǎk-* 787.]

pan-. Fabric. **1.** Germanic **fanōn-* in: **a.** Old English *fana*, flag, banner, weathercock: VANE; **b.** Frankish **fanon*, cape: FANON; **c.** compound **gund-fanōn-*, "battle-flag" (see **gwhen-**[1]). **2.** Extended form **panno-* in Latin *pannus*, piece of cloth, rag: PANE, PANEL, PAWN[1]. **3.** Greek *pēnos*, web: PANICLE. [Pok. *pan-* 788.]

[pandoura. Three-stringed lute. Greek noun of obscure origin. BANDORE, MANDOLIN, PANDORE.**]**

pap-[1]. Teat (sound symbolism). **1.** Middle English *pappe*, nipple: PAP[1]. **2.** Latin diminutive *papula*, pimple: PAPILLA, PAPULE. **3.** Variant form **pup(p)-* in Latin *pūpus*, boy, and *pūpa*, girl: PUPA, PUPIL[1]. [In Pok. *baxb-* 91.]

pap-[2]. Food (baby-talk root). Reduplication of **pā-**. **1.** Germanic nasalized form **pamp-* in Flemish frequentative *pamperen*, to cram with food, akin to the source of Middle English *pamperen*, to pamper: PAMPER. **2.** Latin *pappa*, food: PAP[2], POPPYCOCK. **3.** Latin *pāpulum* (see **pa-**). [Pok. *pap(p)a* 789, *baxmb-* 94.]

papa. A child's word for "father," a linguistic universal found in many languages. **1.** Old French *papa*, father: PAPA. **2.** Greek *pappas*, father, and *pappos*, grandfather: PAPPUS, POPE. [Pok. *pap(p)a* 789.]

past-. Solid, firm. **1.** Germanic **fastuz*, firm, fast, in: **a.** Old English *fæst*, fixed, firm: FAST[1], (STEADFAST); **b.** Middle Dutch *vast*, firm, fast: AVAST. **2.** Germanic **fastinōn*, to make firm or fast, in Old English *fæstnian*, to fasten, establish: FASTEN. **3.** Germanic **fastēn*, to hold fast, observe abstinence, in: **a.** Old English *fæstan*, to abstain from food: FAST[2]; **b.** Old Norse *fasta*, to abstain from food: BREAKFAST. [Pok. *pasto-* 789.]

[pauein. To cease, stop. Greek noun derived from a Greek root **paus-*. PAUSE, (PESADE), POSE[1]; COMPOSE, DIAPAUSE, REPOSE[1].**]**

ped-[1]. Foot. **1.** Lengthened o-grade form **pōd-* in Germanic **fōt-* in Old English *fōt*, foot: FOOT. **2.** Suffixed form **ped-ero-* in Germanic **feterō* in Old English *fetor*, *feter*, leg iron, fetter: FETTER. **3.** Suffixed form **ped-el-* in Germanic **fetel-* in Old High German *vizzelach*, fetlock, akin to the Germanic source of Middle English *fitlock*, *fetlock* (*lock*, hair, LOCK[2]): FETLOCK. **4.** Perhaps Germanic **fet-* in Old English *fetian*, to bring back: FETCH. **5.** Basic form **ped-* in Latin *pēs* (stem *ped-*), foot: PAWN[2], -PED, PEDAL, PEDATE, PEDESTAL, PEDESTRIAN, PEDI-, PEDICEL, PEDUNCLE, PEON, PES, PIONEER; CAP-A-PIE, MILLIPEDE, PEDIGREE, PIEDMONT, SESQUIPEDALIAN, TRIPEDAL, TRIVET, VAMP[1]. **6.** Form **ped-i-* in: **a.** Latin *expedīre*, to free from a snare (*ex-*, out of, EX-): EXPEDITE; **b.** Latin *impedīre*, "to put in fetters, hobble, shackle," entangle, hinder (*in-*, in, IN-): IMPEDE. **7.** Suffixed form **ped-ikā* in Latin *pedica*, fetter, snare: DISPATCH, IMPEACH. **8.** Verbal root **ped-*, to stumble, fall, in: **a.** suffixed (comparative) form **ped-yos* in Latin *pejor*, worse (< "stumbling"): PEJORATION; IMPAIR; **b.** suffixed (superlative) form **ped-samo-* in Latin *pessimus*, worst: PESSIMISM; **c.** suffixed form **ped-ko-* in Latin *peccāre*, to stumble, sin: (PECCABLE), PECCANT; IMPECCABLE. **9.** O-grade form **pod-* in: **a.** Greek *pous* (stem *pod-*), foot: PEW, -POD, PODIUM, -PODIUM; ANTIPODES, APODAL, APPOGGIATURA, APUS, CALIBER, LYCOPODIUM, MONOPODIUM, OCTOPUS, PHALAROPE, PLATYPUS, PODAGRA, PODIATRY, PODOPHYLLIN, POLYP, POLYPOD, SYMPODIUM; **b.** Russian *pod*, bottom, ground: PODZOL. **10.** Suffixed form **ped-ya* in Greek *peza*, foot: TRAPEZIUM. **11.** Suffixed form **ped-o-* in: **a.** Greek *pedon*, ground, soil: PEDO-[1]; PARALLELEPIPED; **b.** Sanskrit *pada*, foot: PIE[3], NAYA PAISA, PUG[3]; **c.** Middle Persian *pāī*, leg, foot: PAJAMAS, TEAPOY; **d.** lengthened-grade form **pēdo-* in (*i*) Greek *pēdon*, rudder, steering oar: PILOT (*ii*) Greek *pēdan*, to leap: DIAPEDESIS. **12.** Suffixed form **ped-ī-* in Greek *pedilon*, sandal: CYPRIPEDIUM. [Pok. 2. *pĕd-* 790.]

ped-[2]. Container. **1.** Suffixed o-grade form **pod-om* in Germanic **fatam* in Old English *fæt*, cask: VAT. **2.** Suffixed o-grade form **pod-ilo-* in Germanic **fatilaz* in Old English *fetel*, girdle: FETTLE. **3.** Probably full-grade form **ped-* in Germanic **fet-* in Middle High German *vetze*, "clothes," rags, probably akin to the source of obsolete English *fitter*, to break in pieces: FRITTER[1]. [Pok. 1. *pĕd-* 790.]

peg-. Breast. **1.** Suffixed variant form **pek-tos* in Latin *pectus*, breast: PECTORAL; EXPECTORATE, PARAPET. **2.** Possibly suffixed variant form **pek-so-* in Sanskrit *pakṣa*, wing: PUNKA. [Pok. (*peg*), *pōg-* 792.]

pēi-. Also **pē-**, **pī-**. To hurt. Possible root. **1.** Suffixed (participial) form **pī-ont-* in Germanic **fījand-*, hating, hostile, in Old English *fēond*, *fīond*, enemy, devil: FIEND. **2.** Possibly **pē-* in extended zero-grade form **pət-* in Latin *patī*, to suffer: PASSIBLE, PASSION, PASSIVE, PATIENT; COMPASSION. [Pok. *pē(i)-* 792.]

peig-[1]. Also **peik-**. To cut, mark (by incision). **1.** Alternate form **peik-* in Germanic **fīhala*, cutting tool, in Old English *fīl*, file: FILE[2]. **2.** Nasalized zero-grade form **pi-n-g-* in Latin *pingere*, to embroider, tattoo, paint, picture: PAINT, PICTOR, PICTURE, PICTURESQUE, PIGMENT, (PIMENTO), PINTO; DEPICT, PICTOGRAPH. **3.** Suffixed zero-grade form **pik-ro-* in Greek *pikros*, sharp, bitter: PICRO-. **4.** O-grade form **poik-* in Greek *poikilos*, spotted, pied, various: POIKILOTHERM. [Pok. 1. *peig-* 794.]

peig-[2]. Also **peik-**. Evil-minded, hostile. **1.** Suffixed zero-grade form **pig-olo-* in Germanic **fikala-* in Old English *ficol*, treacherous, false: FICKLE. **2.** Suffixed o-grade form **poik-os* in Germanic **gafaihaz* (**ga-*; see **kom**), in Old English *gefāh*, enemy: FOE. **3.** Suffixed o-grade form **poik-yos* in Germanic **faigjaz* in Old English *fæge*, fated to die: FEY. **4.** Suffixed o-grade form **poik-itā* in Germanic **faihithō* in Old English *fēhida*, hostility, feud: FEUD[1]. **5.** Middle Dutch *fokken*: FUCK. [Pok. 2. *peiĝ-* 795.]

peis-[1]. To crush. **1.** Suffixed zero-grade form **pis-to-* in Latin *pistillum*, pestle: PESTLE, PISTIL. **2.** Nasalized zero-grade form **pi-n-s-* in Latin *pinsāre*, to pound: PISTON. **3.** Possibly suffixed form **pis-lo-* in Latin *pīlum*, javelin, pestle: PILE[2]. **4.** Perhaps Greek *ptissein* (*pt-* for *p-*), to crush, peel: PTISAN, (TISANE). [Pok. 1. (*peis-?*), *pis-* 796.]

peis-[2]. To blow. **1.** Germanic **fīs-* in Old Norse *fīsa*, to fart, akin to the Scandinavian source of Middle English *fise*, fart: FIZGIG. **2.** Germanic **fisti-* in Old English **fīstan*, to fart (attested only in the gerund *fisting*): FEIST, (FIZZLE). [Pok. 2. *peis-* 796.]

peisk-. Also **pisk-**. Fish. **1.** Germanic **fiska-* in: **a.** Old English *fisc*, fish: FISH; **b.** Middle Dutch *vische*, *vis*, fish: WEAKFISH. **2.** Extended form **piski-* in Latin *piscis*, fish: PISCARY, PISCATORIAL, PISCES, PISCI-, PISCINA, PISCINE; GRAMPUS, PORPOISE. [Pok. *peisk-* 796.]

pek-[1]. To make pretty. **1.** Possibly Germanic **fagra-* in Old English *fæger*, beautiful: FAIR[1]. **2.** Possibly Germanic **fagin-*, **fagan-*, to enjoy, in Old English *fægen*, joyful, glad: FAIN, (FAWN[1]). [Pok. 1. *pek-* 796.]

pek-[2]. To pluck the hair, fleece, comb. **1.** Extended form **pekt-* perhaps in Germanic **feht-*, to fight, in Old English *feohtan*, to fight: FIGHT. **2.** Suffixed extended form **pekt-en-* in: **a.** Latin *pecten*, a comb: PECTEN; **b.** zero-grade form **pkt-en-* in Greek *kteis* (genitive *ktenos* < **pktenos*), a comb: CTENIDIUM, CTENOID, CTENOPHORE. [Pok. 2. *pek-* 797.]

peku-. Wealth, movable property. **1.** Germanic **fehu-* in: **a.** Old Norse *fē*, property, cattle: FELLOW; **b.** Frankish **fehu*, cattle, in compound **fehu-ōd*, "cattle as property," money (**-ōd*, property; see **audaz**): FEE; **c.** Medieval Latin *feudum*, feudal estate: FEUD[2], INFEUDATION. **2.** Suffixed form **peku-n-* in Latin *pecūnia*, property, wealth: PECUNIARY; IMPECUNIOUS. **3.** Suffixed form **peku-l-* in Latin *pecūlium*, riches in cattle, private property: PECULATE, PECULIAR. [In Pok. 2. *pek-* 797.]

pekw-. To cook, ripen. **1.** Assimilated form (in Italic and Celtic) **kwekw-* in Latin *coquere*, to cook: COOK, CUISINE, (CULINARY), KILN, KITCHEN, QUITTOR; APRICOT, BISCUIT, CON-

COCT, DECOCT, PRECOCIOUS, RICOTTA. 2. Greek pepōn, ripe: PEPO. 3. Greek peptein, to cook, ripen, digest: PEPTIC; DRUPE, EUPEPTIC, PEPSIN, PEPTONE, PUMPKIN. 4. Greek -pepsia, digestion: DYSPEPSIA. 5. Sanskrit pakva, ripe: PUKKA. [Pok. peku̯- 798.]

pel-[1]. Dust, flour. 1. Latin pollen, fine flour, dust: POLLEN. 2. Latin pulvis, dust: POWDER, PULVERIZE. 3. Latin palea, chaff: PAILLASSE, PALEA. 4. Greek palunein, to sprinkle flour: PALYNOLOGY. 5. Greek poltos, porridge (made from flour), probably borrowed via Etruscan into Latin as puls, pottage: POULTICE, PULSE[2]. [Pok. 2 b. pel- 802.]

pel-[2]. Pale. 1. Suffixed variant form *pal-wo- in: a. Germanic *falwaz in Old English fealu, fealo, reddish yellow: FALLOW DEER; b. Latin pallēre, to be pale: PALE[2], PALLID, PALLOR, APPALL; c. Latin palumbēs (influenced in form by Latin columbus, dove), ringdove, "gray bird": PALOMINO. 2. Suffixed form *pel-ko- probably in Germanic *falkon, falcon (< "gray bird"), in: a. Old Norse geirfalki (geir-; see **ghaiso-**), gyrfalcon: GYRFALCON; b. Late Latin falcō, falcon (but Germanic *falkon is also possibly from the Late Latin): FALCON. 3. Suffixed extended form *peli-wo- in: a. Greek pelios, dark: PELOPS; b. o-grade form *poli-wo- in Greek polios, gray: POLIOMYELITIS. 4. Perhaps Greek pelargos (< *pelawo-argos), stork (< "black-white bird"; argos, white; see **arg-**): PELARGONIUM. 5. Suffixed extended form *plei-to- in Welsh llwyd, gray: LLOYD. [Pok. 6. pel- 804.]

pel-[3]. To fold. 1. Extended form *pelt- in Germanic *falthan in: a. Old English fealdan, faldan, to fold: FOLD[1]; b. Old High German faldan, to fold: FALTBOAT; c. Germanic compound *faldistōlaz, "folding stool" (*stōlaz, stool; see **stā-**), in (i) Medieval Latin compound faldistolium, folding chair: FALDSTOOL (ii) Old French faudestuel, faldstool: FAUTEUIL; d. Germanic combining form *-falthaz in Old English -feald, -fald, -fold: -FOLD. 2. Combining form *-plo- in: a. Latin -plus, -fold (as in triplus, threefold): CENTUPLE, DECUPLE, MULTIPLE, NONUPLE, OCTOPLE, QUADRUPLE, SEPTUPLE, (SEXTUPLE), TRIPLE; b. Greek -plos, -ploos, -fold (as in diploos, twofold, double): -PLOID. [Pok. 3 a. pel- 802.]

pel-[4]. Skin, hide. 1. Suffixed form *pel-no- in Germanic *felnam in Old English fell, skin, hide: FELL[3]. 2. Germanic suffixed form *felmen- in Old English filmen, membrane: FILM. 3. Suffixed form *pel-ni- in Latin pellis, skin: PELISSE, PELLICLE, (PELT[1]), PELTRY, PILLION; PELLAGRA, SURPLICE. 4. Greek -pelas, skin: ERYSIPELAS. 5. Suffixed form *pel-to- in Greek peltē, a shield (made of hide): PELTATE. [Pok. 3 b. pel- 803.]

pel-[5]. To sell. Lengthened o-grade form *pōl- in Greek pōlein, to sell: BIBLIOPOLE, MONOPOLY. [Pok. 5. pel 804.]

pel-[6]. To thrust, strike, drive. 1. Extended form *peld- in: a. Germanic *falt-, to beat, in Old English -fealt, beaten: ANVIL; b. Germanic *feltaz, *filtiz, compressed wool, in (i) Old English felt, felt: FELT[1] (ii) Frankish *filtir, piece of felt: FILTER; c. Latin pellere (past participle pulsus), to push, drive, strike: POUSETTE, PULSATE, PULSE[1], PUSH; COMPEL, DISPEL, EXPEL, IMPEL, PROPEL, REPEL; d. suffixed zero-grade form *pl̥d-to- in Latin pultāre, to knock, beat: PELT[2]. 2. Extended form *pelə- (present stem *pelnā-) in: a. Latin appellāre, "to drive to," address, entreat, appeal, call (ad-, to, AD-): APPEAL; b. Latin compellāre, to accost, address (com-, intensive prefix, COM-): COMPELLATION; c. Latin interpellāre, "to thrust between," interrupt (inter-, between, INTER-): INTERPELLATE. 3. Suffixed o-grade form *pol-o-, fuller of cloth, in Latin polīre, to make smooth, polish (< "to full cloth"): POLISH. 4. Suffixed extended zero-grade form *plə-tio- in Greek plēsios, near (< "pushed toward"): PLESIOSAURUS. [Pok. 2 a. pel- 801.]

pel-[7]. Dish. Suffixed lengthened-grade form *pēl-owi- in Latin pēlvis, basin: PELVIS. [Pok. 4. pel- 804.]

pel-[8]. Also **pelə-**. To fill. With derivatives referring to abundance and multitude. I. Suffixed zero-grade form *pl̥ə-no-. 1. Germanic *fulnaz, *fullaz, full, in Old English full, full: FULL[1]. 2. Derivative Germanic verb *fulljan, to fill, in Old English fyllan, to fill: FILL. 3. Latin root *plāno-, replaced by *plēno- (influenced by Latin verb plēre, to fill; see III. 1. below) in Latin plēnus, full: PLENARY, PLENITUDE, PLENTY, PLENUM; PLENIPOTENTIARY, REPLENISH, TERREPLEIN. II. Extended form *pelu-. 1. Latin palus, marsh (< "inundated"): PALUDAL, PALUDISM. 2. Variant form *pleu- in suffixed form *plew-os- in Latin plūs, more: PIÙ, PLURAL, PLUS; NONPLUS, PLUPERFECT, SURPLUS. 3. O-grade form *polu- in Greek polus, much, many: POLY-, HOI POLLOI. III. Variant form *plē-. 1. Latin plēre, to fill: ACCOMPLISH, COMPLETE, COMPLIMENT, COMPLY, EXPLETIVE, IMPLEMENT, REPLETE, SUPPLY. 2. Possibly suffixed form *plē-dhw- in Latin plēbs, plēbēs, the people, multitude: PLEBE, PLEBEIAN, PLEBS; PLEBISCITE. 3. Suffixed form *plē-dhwo- in: a. Greek plēthos (Ionic plēthus), great number: ISOPLETH; b. Greek derivative verb plēthein, to be full: PLETHORA. 4. Suffixed form *plē-ion- in Greek pleōn, pleiōn, more: PLEO-, PLEONASM; PLEIOTROPISM, PLIOCENE. 5. Suffixed (superlative) form *plē-isto- in Greek pleistos, most: PLEISTOCENE. IV. Possibly Sanskrit pūraḥ, cake (< "that which fills or satisfies"): POORI. [Pok. 1. pel- 798.]

pelə-[1]. Flat; to spread. 1. Suffixed form *pel-tus in Germanic *felthuz, flat land, in Old English feld, open field: FIELD. 2. Suffixed form *pel-tos (by-form of *pel-tus) in Germanic *felthos, flat land, in: a. Old High German feld, field: FELDSPAR; b. Middle Dutch veld, velt, field: VELDT. 3. Variant form *pleə-, contracted to *plā- in: a. suffixed form *plā-ru- in Germanic *flōruz, floor, in Old English flōr, floor: FLOOR; b. suffixed form *plā-no- in Latin plānus, flat, level, even: LLANO, PIANO[2], PLAIN, PLAN, PLANARIAN, PLANE[1], PLANE[2], PLANE[3], PLANISH, PLANO-, PLANULA; EXPLAIN. 4. Suffixed zero-grade form *pl̥ə-mā in Latin palma (< *palama), palm of the hand: PALM[1], (PALM[2]). 5. Suffixed zero-grade form *plə-n- in: a. Greek planasthai, to wander (< "to spread out"): PLANET; AIRPLANE, APLANATIC; b. possibly Germanic *flan-, *flen- in Danish flensa, to strip off the blubber or skin (of a whale): FLENSE. 6. Suffixed zero-grade form *plə-dh- in Greek plassein (< *plath-yein), to mold, "spread out": PLASMA, -PLASIA, -PLAST, PLASTER, PLASTIC, PLASTID, -PLASTY; ANAPLASTY, DYSPLASIA, METAPLASM. 7. Basic form *pelə- in: a. Russian polyĭ, open: POLYNYA; b. Polish pol-, broad flat land, field: POLACK, POLAND, POLKA. See also the extended roots **plāk-**[1] and **plat-**. [Pok. pelə 805.]

pelə-[2]. Citadel, fortified high place. 1. Greek polis, city: POLICE, POLICY[1], POLIS, POLITIC, POLITY; ACROPOLIS, COSMOPOLITE, DECAPOLIS, ISOPOLITY, MEGALOPOLIS, METROPOLIS, NECROPOLIS, POLICLINIC, PROPOLIS. 2. Sanskrit pūr, city: SINGAPORE. [In Pok. 1. pel- 798.]

pelis-. Also **pels-**. Rock, cliff. Germanic *felsam, rock, in Old Norse fjall, fell, rock, barren plateau: FJELD. [Pok. peli-s- 807.]

pen-. Swamp. Suffixed o-grade form *pon-yo- in Germanic *fanja, swamp, marsh, in Old English fenn, marsh: FEN[1]. [Pok. 2. pen- 807.]

penkwe. Five. I. Basic form *penkwe. 1. Assimilated form *pempe in Germanic *fimfi in: a. Old English fīf, five: FIVE; b. Old High German finf, funf, five: FIN[2]. 2. Germanic compound *fimftehun, fifteen (*tehun, ten; see **dekm̥**), in: a. Old English fīftēne, fifteen: FIFTEEN; b. Old Norse fimmtān, fifteen: FEMTO-. 3. Assimilated form *kwenkwe in: a. Latin quīnque, five: CINQUAIN, CINQUE, QUINQUE-; CINQUECENTO, CINQUEFOIL, QUINCUNX; b. Latin distributive quīnī, five each: KENO, QUINATE; c. Latin compound quīndecim, fifteen (decem, ten; see **dekm̥**): QUINDECENNIAL. 4. Greek pente, five: PENTA-, PENTAD, PENTECOST. 5. Sanskrit pañca, five: PUNCH[3]; PACHISI, PUNJAB. II. Compound *penkwe-konta, "five tens," fifty (*-konta, group of ten; see **dekm̥**). 1. Germanic *fimftig in Old English fīftig, fifty: FIFTY. 2. Latin quīnquāgintā, fifty: QUINQUAGENARIAN, QUINQUAGESIMA. III. Ordinal adjective *penkw-tos. 1. Germanic *fimfton in Old English fīfta, fifth: FIFTH. 2. Latin quīntus (< *quinc-tos), fifth: QUENTIN, QUINT[1], QUINTAIN, QUINTET, QUINTILE; QUINTESSENCE, QUINTILLION, QUINTUPLE. IV. Suffixed form *penkwe-ros in Germanic *fingwraz, finger (< "one of five"), in Old English finger, finger: FINGER. V. Suffixed reduced zero-grade form *pn̥k-sti- in Germanic *fū(nh)stiz in: a. Old English fȳst, fist: FIST; b. Dutch vuist, fist: FOIST. [Pok. penkue 808, pn̥ksti- 839.]

pent-. To tread, go. 1. Germanic *finthan, to come upon, discover, in Old English findan, to find: FIND, (FOUNDLING). 2. O-grade form *pont- in Latin pōns (stem pont-), bridge: PONS, PONTINE, PONTOON, PUNT[1], TRANSPONTINE. 3. Suffixed o-grade form *pont-o- in Greek pontos, "way," sea: PONTUS. 4. Zero-grade form *pn̥t- in Greek patein, to tread, walk: PERIPATETIC. 5. Iranian *path- probably borrowed (? via Scythian) into Germanic as *patha-, way, path, in: a. Old English pæth, path: PATH; b. Middle Dutch pad, way, path: FOOTPAD. 6. Extended o-grade form *ponti- in Russian put', path, way: SPUTNIK. [Pok. pent- 808.]

per[1]. Base of prepositions and preverbs with the basic meaning of "forward," "through," and a wide range of extended senses such as "in front of," "before," "early," "first," "chief," "toward," "against," "near," "at," "around." I. Basic form *per and extended form *peri. 1. Germanic *fer-, used chiefly as a prefix denoting destruction, reversal, or completion, in: a. Old High German far-: TURNVEREIN; b. Middle Dutch ver-: FRUMP; c. Middle Dutch vieren, to let out, slacken: VEER[2]; d. compound *fer-getan, "to lose one's hold," forget (see **ghend-**). 2. Suffixed (comparative) form *per-ero-, farther away, in Germanic *fer(e)ra in Old English feor(r), far: FAR. 3. Compound *per-no-yo-, of last year (*-no-, year; see **en-**), in Germanic *fernja- in Old High German firni, old: FIRN. 4. Latin per, through, for, by: PER, PER-; PARGET, PARTERRE, PARVENU, PARAMOUNT, PARAMOUR. 5. Greek peri, around, near, beyond: PERI-; PERISSODACTYL. 6. Sanskrit pari, through, around: PALANQUIN. 7. Avestan pairi, around: PARADISE. II. Zero-grade form *pr̥-. 1. Germanic *for, before, in: a. Old English for, before, instead of, on account of: FOR; b. Old English for-, prefix denoting destruction, pejoration, exclusion, or completion: FOR-. 2. Extended form *pr̥t- in Germanic *furth-, forward, in Old English forth, forth: FORTH; AFFORD. 3. Suffixed (comparative) form *pr̥-tero- in Germanic *furthera- in Old English furthra, furthor, farther away: FURTHER. 4. Suffixed (superlative) form *pr̥-mo- in: a. Germanic *fruma-, *furma- in Old English forma, first, foremost: FOREMOST, FORMER[2]; b. Latin compound prandium, "first meal," late breakfast, lunch (probably < *pram-d-ium < *pr̥mo-id-iom; second element *-id-, to eat; see **ed-**). 5. Suffixed (superlative) form *pr̥-isto- in Germanic *furista-, foremost, in Old English fyrst, fyrest, first: FIRST. 6. Compound *pr̥-sti- (or *por-sti-, with o-grade form *por-), "that which stands before," stake, post (see **stā-**). III. Extended zero-grade form *pri- in Celtic *(p)ari, are in Gaulish ari (combining form are-), before, in Latin arepennis, half-acre (second element obscure): ARPENT. IV. Extended form *p(a)rā. 1. Germanic *fora, before, in: a. Old English for(e), before: FORE, FORE-; b. Old High German fora, before: VORLAGE; c. Old Norse for-, before: FOREFATHER; d. Germanic prefixed and suffixed form *bi-fora-na, in the front (*bi-, at, by; see **ambhi**), in Old English beforan, before: BEFORE. 2. Greek para, beside, alongside of, beyond: PARA-[1]; PALFREY. V. Extended form *prō. 1. a. Germanic *fra, forward, away from, in Old Norse frā, from: FRO, FROWARD (partly from English FROM). b. Germanic *fra-, completely (see **ed-**, **eik-**). 2. Suffixed form *pro-mo- in: a. Germanic *fram, from, in Old English from, from: FROM; b. Germanic derivative verb *framjan, to come forward, in Old English framian, to avail, benefit: FRAME; c. Germanic *frum, forward, hence derivative verb *frumjan, to further, in Common Romance *fromire, *formire, *fornir, to promote, supply, provide: FURNISH, VENEER; d. Old Church Slavonic pramŭ, boat (< "a going forward," "passage"): PRAAM. 3. Suffixed form *prō-wo- in Germanic *frōwo, lady, in: a. Old High German frouwa, lady: FRAU, (FRÄULEIN); b. Germanic compound *jung-frōwo, young lady, in Middle Dutch jonefrouwe, maiden: EUPHROE. 4. Latin prō, before, for, instead of: PRO[1], PRO-[1], PURCHASE. 5. Suffixed form *prō-no- in Latin prōnus, leaning forward: PRONE. 6. Suffixed form *pro-ko- in: a. Latin compound reciprocus, alternating, "backward and forward" (*re-ko-, backward; see **re-**): RECIPROCAL; b. variant *pro-kw-, going forward, approaching, in Latin prope, near: APPROACH, RAPPROCHEMENT, REPROACH; c. suffixed form *pro-kw-inkwo- in Latin propinquus, near: PROPINQUITY; d. suffixed (superlative) form *pro-kw-samo- in Latin proximus, nearest: PROXIMATE; APPROXIMATE. 7. Compound *pro-bhwo-, growing well or straight forward (*bhw-o-, to grow; see **bheu-**), in Latin probus, upright, good, virtuous: (PROBABLE), (PROBE), PROBITY, (PROOF), PROVE; APPROVE, IMPROBITY, (IMPROVE), (REPROVE). 8. Greek pro, before, in front, forward: PRO-[2]. 9. Suffixed (comparative) form *pro-tero- in Greek proteros, before, former: PROTEROZOIC, HYSTERON PROTERON. 10. Suffixed form *prō-wo-iro- in Greek prōira, forward part of a ship: PROW. 11. Perhaps suffixed form *pro-ato- in

Greek prōtos, foremost, first: PROTEIN, PROTIST, PROTO-, PROTON. 12. Sanskrit pra, before: PRAKRIT. VI. Extended forms *prai-, *prei-. 1. Latin prae, before: PRE-, PRETERIT. 2. Suffixed (comparative) form *prei-yos- in Latin prior, former, higher: PRIOR[2]. 3. Suffixed form *prei-wo- in: a. Latin prīvus, single, alone (< "standing in front," "isolated from others"): PRIVATE, PRIVILEGE, PRIVITY, (PRIVY); DEPRIVE; b. Latin proprius, one's own, particular (< prō prīvō, in particular, from the ablative of prīvus, single): PROPER, (PROPERTY); APPROPRIATE, PROPRIOCEPTOR. 4. Extended form *preis- in: a. suffixed (superlative) form *preis-mo- in (i) Latin prīmus (< *prismus), first, foremost: PREMIER, PRIMAL, PRIMARY, PRIMATE, PRIME, PRIMITIVE, PRIMO[2], PRIMUS, IMPRIMIS, PRIMAVERA, PRIMA FACIE, PRIMEVAL, PRIMIPARA, PRIMOGENITOR, PRIMOGENITURE, PRIMORDIAL (ii) Latin compound prīnceps, "he who takes first place" (-ceps, "-taker"; see kap-), leader, chief, emperor: PRINCE, (PRINCIPAL), PRINCIPLE; b. suffixed form *preis-ko- in Latin prīscus, former, ancient: PRISCILLA; c. suffixed form *preis-tano- in Latin prīstinus, former, earlier, original: PRISTINE. VII. Extended form *pres- in compound *pres-gw-, "going before" (*gw-, to go; see gwā-), in Greek presbus, old, old man, elder: PRESBYTER, PRIEST; PRESBYOPIA. VIII. Extended form *preti-. 1. Suffixed form *preti-o- in Latin pretium, worth, value (< "that which is opposite or equivalent"): PRAISE, PRECIOUS, PRICE; APPRAISE, APPRECIATE, DEPRECIATE. 2. O-grade form *porti- in Greek pros, against, toward, near, at: PROS-. Other derivatives are grouped under per-[2], per-[3], per-[4], per-[5], per-[7], and perə-. [Pok. 2. per, Section A. 810.]

per-[2]. To lead, pass over. A verbal root belonging to the group of per[1]. I. Full-grade form *per-. 1. Suffixed form *per-tu-s in Germanic *ferthuz, place for crossing over, ford, in Old Norse fjördhr, an inlet, estuary: FIRTH, FJORD. 2. Suffixed form *per-onā in Greek peronē, pin of a brooch, buckle (< "that which pierces through"): PERONEAL. II. O-grade form *por-. 1. Germanic *faran, to go, in: a. Old English faran, to go on a journey, get along: FARE, FIELDFARE, WAYFARING, (WELFARE); b. Old High German faran, to go, travel: GABERDINE. 2. Suffixed forms *por-o-, *por-ōn-, passage, journey, in: a. Germanic *farō in Old English faru, journey: WAYFARER; b. Greek poros, journey, passage: PORE[2]; EMPORIUM. 3. Suffixed (causative) form *por-eyo-, to cause to go, lead, conduct, in: a. Germanic *fōrja- in Old English geféra, "fellow-traveler," companion (ge-, together, with; see kom): FERE; b. Germanic *fōrjan, to lead, in Old High German fuoren, to lead: FÜHRER; c. Germanic *farjōn, ferry, ferryboat, in Old Norse ferja, ferryboat: FERRY. 4. Suffixed form *por-ti- in Germanic *fardi- (see nant-). 5. Possibly suffixed form *por-no-, feather, wing (< "that which carries a bird in flight"), in: a. Germanic *farnō, feather, leaf, in Old English fearn, fern (having feathery fronds): FERN; b. Sanskrit parṇa, leaf, feather: PAN[2]. III. Zero-grade form *pr̥-. 1. Suffixed form *pr̥-tu-, passage, in: a. Germanic *furdu- in Old English ford, shallow place where one may cross a river: FORD; b. Latin portus, harbor (< "passage"): PORT[1], IMPORTUNE, OPPORTUNE; c. Avestan hupərəthwa, "good to cross over," the Euphrates (hu-, good; see su-[2]): EUPHRATES. 2. Suffixed form *pr̥-tā in Latin porta, gate: (PORCH), PORT[3], PORTAL, PORTER[2], PORTICO, PORTIÈRE, PORTCULLIS, PORTULACA. 3. Suffixed (denominative) form *pr̥-to- in Latin portāre, to carry: PORT[5], PORTABLE, PORTAGE, PORTATIVE, PORTER[1]; COMPORT, DEPORT, EXPORT, IMPORT, (IMPORTANT), PORTFOLIO, PURPORT, RAPPORT, REPORT, (SPORT), SUPPORT, TRANSPORT. [Pok. 2. per, Section B. 816.]

per-[3]. The young of an animal (< "a bringing forth," "offspring"). Derivative root belonging to the group of per[1]. Suffixed o-grade form *por-si- in Germanic *farzi-, young cow, in: a. Old English fearr, calf, and compound heahfore, calf (first element obscure): HEIFER; b. possibly Middle Dutch *varwe, *verwe-, cow past the age of bearing (perhaps originally "a young cow"): FARROW[2]. [In Pok. 2. per, Section D. 818.]

per-[4]. Also perə-. To grant, allot (reciprocally, to get in return). A verbal root belonging to the group of per[1]. Zero-grade form *pr̥ə- (becoming *par- in Latin) in: a. root form *par-ā- in Latin parāre, to try to get, prepare, equip: PARADE, PARE, PARRY, PARURE; APPARATUS, APPAREL, COMPRADOR, DISPARATE, EMPEROR, IMPERATIVE, (IMPERIAL), (PARACHUTE), PARASOL, PARFLECHE, PREPARE, RAMPART, REPAIR[1], SEPARATE, (SEVER), (SEVERAL); b. suffixed form *par-yo- in Latin parere, parīre, to get, beget, give birth: PARENT, -PAROUS, PARTURIENT, POSTPARTUM, REPERTORY, VIPER; c. suffixed form *par-os, producing, in compound *pau-paros, producing little, poor (see pōu-); d. suffixed form *par-ikā in Latin Parcae, the Fates (who assign one's destiny): PARCAE. [Pok. 2. per, Section D. 818.]

per-[5]. To try, risk (< "to lead over," "press forward"). A verbal root belonging to the group of per[1]. 1. Germanic *fēraz, danger, in Old English fær, danger, sudden calamity: FEAR. 2. Suffixed extended form *peri-tlo- in Latin perīclum, perīculum, trial, danger: (PARLOUS), PERIL. 3. Suffixed form *per-yo- in Latin experīrī, to try, learn by trying (ex-, from, EX-): EXPERIENCE, (EXPERIMENT), EXPERT. 4. Suffixed form *per-ya in Greek peira, trial, attempt: PIRATE, EMPIRIC. [Pok. 2. per, Section E. 818.]

per-[6]. To strike. Extended forms *prem-, *pres- in Latin premere (past participle pressus), to press: PREGNANT[2], PRESS[1], (PRESSURE), PRINT; APPRESSED, COMPRESS, DEPRESS, EXPRESS, IMPRESS[1], (IMPRINT), OPPRESS, REPRESS, (REPRIMAND), SUPPRESS. [Pok. 3. per- 818.]

per-[7]. To traffic in, sell (< "to hand over," "distribute"). A verbal root belonging to the group of per[1]. 1. Suffixed zero-grade form *prə-et- in Latin interpres (stem interpret-), go-between, negotiator (inter-, between, INTER-): INTERPRET. 2. Suffixed form *per-n-ē- in Greek pernēmi, I sell, whence pornē, prostitute: PORNOGRAPHY. [In Pok. 2. per, Section C. 817.]

perd-. To fart. 1. Germanic *fertan, *fartan in Old English *feortan, to fart: FART. 2. Greek perdix, partridge (which makes a sharp whirring sound when suddenly flushed): PARTRIDGE. See also variant root pezd-. [Pok. perd- 819.]

perə-. To grant, allot (reciprocally, to get in return). Extended root of per-[4]. Zero-grade form *pr̥ə- (becoming *par- in Latin) in: a. suffixed form *par-ti- in Latin pars (stem part-), a share, part: PARCEL, PARCENER, PARSE, PART; BIPARTITE, COMPART, IMPART, REPARTEE; b. possibly suffixed form *par-tiō in Latin portiō, a part (first attested in the phrase prō portiōne, in proportion, according to each part, perhaps assimilated from *prō partiōne): PORTION, PROPORTION; c. perhaps Latin pār, equal: PAIR, PAR, PARITY[2], PARLAY, PEER[2]; COMPARE, HERB PARIS, IMPARITY, NONPAREIL, PARI-MUTUEL. [Pok. 2. per, Section C. 817.]

perg-. Pole, stem. Possibly Latin pergula, a projection, balcony, outhouse: PERGOLA. [Pok. 1. perg- 819.]

perk-[1]. Speckled. Often used in names of spotted or pied animals. Greek perkē, the perch: PERCH[2]. [Pok. 2. perk̂- 820.]

perk-[2]. To ask, entreat. 1. Variant form *prek- in Latin *prex, prayer (attested only in the plural precēs), with denominative precārī, to entreat, pray: PRAY, (PRAYER[2]), PRECARIOUS; DEPRECATE, IMPRECATE. 2. Suffixed zero-grade form *pr̥k-sk- becoming *pork-sk-, contracted into *posk- in suffixed form *posk-to-, contracted into *posto-, which appears in Latin postulāre, to ask, request: POSTULATE, EXPOSTULATE. [Pok. 4. perk̂- 821.]

perk-[3]. To dig out, tear out. Zero-grade form *pr̥k- in Germanic *furh- in Old English furh, trench: FURROW. [Pok. 3. perk̂- 821.]

perkwu-. Oak. 1. Zero-grade form *pr̥kw- in Germanic *furhu- in Old English furh, fyrh, fir: FIR. 2. Assimilated form *kwerkwu- in Latin quercus, oak: (QUERCETIN), QUERCITRON. [Pok. perku̯u-s 822.]

persnā. Heel. Latin perna, ham, leg: PEARL[1]. [Pok. persnā 823.]

pes-. Penis. Suffixed form *pes-ni- in Latin pēnis (< *pesnis), penis, tail: PENCIL, PENICILLIUM, PENIS. [Pok. 3. pes- 824.]

pet-[1]. To rush, fly. 1. Suffixed form *pet-rā in Germanic *fethrō, feather, in Old English fether, feather: FEATHER. 2. Latin petere, to go toward, seek: -PETAL, PETITION, PETULANT; APPETITE, COMPETE, IMPETUS, PERPETUAL, REPEAT. 3. Suffixed form *pet-nā in Latin penna, pinna, feather, wing: PEN[1], PANACHE, PENNA, PENNATE, PENNON, PINNA, PINNACLE, PINNATE, PINNATI-, PINNULE. 4. Suffixed form *pet-ro- (see ōku-). 5. Suffixed form *pet-yo- in Latin propitius, favorable, gracious, originally a religious term meaning "falling or rushing forward," hence "eager," "well-disposed" (said of the gods; prō-, forward, PRO-): PROPITIOUS. 6. Suffixed zero-grade form *pt-ero- in Greek pteron, feather, wing: PTERO-, -PTEROUS; ACANTHOPTERYGIAN, APTERYX, ARCHAEOPTERYX, CROSSOPTERYGIAN, PERIPTERAL, PTERIDOLOGY, PTERYGOID. 7. Suffixed zero-grade form *pt-ilo- in Greek ptilon, soft feathers, down: COLEOPTILE. 8. Suffixed variant form *ptē-no- in Greek ptēnos, winged: STEAROPTENE. 9. Reduplicated form *pi-pt- in Greek piptein, to fall: PTOMAINE, PTOSIS; ASYMPTOTE, PERIPETEIA, PROPTOSIS, SYMPTOM. 10. O-grade form *pot- in Greek potamos (-amo-, Greek suffix), "rushing water," river: HIPPOPOTAMUS, MESOPOTAMIA. 11. Suffixed form *pet-tro- in Sanskrit pattra, feather, leaf: TALIPOT. [Pok. 2. pet- 826.]

pet-[2]. To spread. 1. Suffixed o-grade form *pot-mo- in Germanic *fathmaz, "length of two arms stretched out," in Old English fæthm, fathom: FATHOM. 2. Suffixed (stative) variant form *pat-ē- in Latin patēre, to be open: PATENT, PATULOUS. 3. By-form *pad- in nasalized form *pa-n-d- in Latin pandere (past participle passus), to spread out: PACE[1], PAS, PASS, PASSIM; EXPAND, REPAND. 4. Suffixed form *petalo- in Greek petalon, leaf: PETAL. 5. Suffixed form *pet-ano- in Greek patanē (< *patana), platter, "thing spread out": PAELLA, PAN[1], PATEN. [Pok. 1. pet- 824.]

[petra. Cliff. Greek noun. Collective formation from petros, rock, stone (of unknown origin). 1. Greek petros: PETER, PETROUS. 2. Greek petra: PETRO-, PETRIFY, PARSLEY, SALTPETER.]

pēu-. See peuə-[2].

peuə-[1]. To purify, cleanse. Suffixed zero-grade form *pū-ro- in Latin pūrus, pure, and pūrgāre, to purify (< *pūr-igāre; second element agere, to drive; see ag-): PURE, (PURITAN), COMPURGATION, DEPURATE, EXPURGATE, PURGE, SPURGE. [Pok. 1. peu- 827.]

peuə-[2]. To cut, strike, stamp. 1. Suffixed (participial) zero-grade form *pu-to-, cut, struck, in: a. Latin putāre, to prune, clean, settle an account, think over, reflect, consider: PUTAMEN, PUTATIVE; (ACCOUNT), AMPUTATE, COMPUTE, COUNT[1], DEPUTE, DISPUTE, IMPUTE, REPUTE; b. possibly Latin puteus, well (< "something dug"): PIT[1]. 2. Suffixed variant form *paw-yo- in: a. Latin pavīre, to beat: PAVE, (PAVÉ); b. Latin pavēre, to fear (< "to be struck"): PAVID; c. perhaps Greek paiein, to beat: ANAPEST. [Pok. 3. pēu- 827.]

peuk-. Also peug-. To prick. Zero-grade form *pug-. 1. Suffixed form *pug-no- in Latin pugnus, fist, with denominative pugnāre, to fight with the fist: PONIARD, PUGILISM, PUGNACIOUS; IMPUGN, OPPUGN, REPUGN. 2. Nasalized zero-grade form *pu-n-g- in Latin pungere, to prick: BUNG, PIVOT, POIGNANT, POINT, POINTILLISM, PONTIL, POUNCE[3], PUN, PUNCHEON[1], PUNCTUATE, PUNCTURE, PUNGENT; COMPUNCTION, COUNTERPANE, EXPUNGE, SPONTOON, TRAPUNTO. 3. Greek pugmē, fist: PYGMY. [Pok. peuk- 828.]

peyə-. Also pei-. To be fat, swell. 1. Extended o-grade form *poid- in Germanic *faitaz, plump, fat, in derivative Germanic verb *faitjan, to fatten, whence Germanic past participle *faitidaz, fattened, in Old English fǣt(t), fat: FAT. 2. Possibly suffixed zero-grade form *pī-tu- in Latin pītuīta, moisture exuded from trees, gum, phlegm: PIP[5], PITUITARY, PITUITOUS. 3. Possibly suffixed zero-grade form *pī-nu- in Latin pīnus, pine tree (yielding a resin): PINE[1], (PINEAL), PIÑON, PINNACE; PIÑA CLOTH. 4. Suffixed zero-grade form *pī-won in Greek piōn, fat: PROPIONIC ACID. 5. Latin pix, tar (see pik-). [Pok. pei(ə)- 793.]

pezd-. To fart. Variant of perd-. 1. Latin pēdere, to fart: PETARD. 2. Possibly Latin pēdis, louse (? < "foul-smelling insect"): PEDICULAR. [Pok. pezd- 829.]

pəter. Father. 1. Germanic *fadar in: a. Old English fæder, father: FATHER; b. Old Norse fadhir, father: FOREFATHER. 2. Latin pater, father: PADRE, PATER, PATERNAL, PATRI- (partly from Greek patēr), PATRICIAN, PATRIMONY, PATRON; EXPATRIATE, IMPETRATE, PERPETRATE. 3. Greek patēr, father: PATRI-, PATRIOT; ALLOPATRIC, EUPATRID, PATRIARCH, SYMPATRIC. [Pok. pətḗ(r) 829.]

phol-. To fall. Suffixed form *phol-no- in Germanic *fallan in: a. Old English feallan, to fall: FALL; b. Middle Dutch vallen, to fall: OFFAL; c. Germanic causative *falljan, "to cause to fall," strike down, in Old English fellan, fyllan, to cut down: FELL[1]; d. Germanic compound *bifallan, to fall, happen (*bi-, by, at; see ambhi), in Old English befeallan, to fall: BEFALL. [Pok. phō̆l- 851.]

[phrazein. To show, say. Greek verb of unknown origin. PHRASE; HOLOPHRASTIC, METAPHRASE, PARAPHRASE, PERIPHRASIS.]

[phulax. Watcher, guard. Greek noun of unknown origin. PHYLACTERY, PHYLAXIS; PROPHYLACTIC.]

pik-. Pitch. Latin *pix* (stem *pic-*), pitch: PAY[2], PICEOUS, PICOLINE, PITCH[1], PITCHBLENDE. [In Pok. *pei̯(ə)-* 793.]

pilo-. Hair. (A possible root.) **1.** Latin *pilus*, hair: PELAGE, PILAR, PILE[3], PILOSE, PLUCK, PLUSH, POILU; CATERPILLAR, DEPILATE. **2.** Suffixed reduced form **pil-so-* in: **a.** Latin *pilleus, pīleus*, felt cap: PILEUS, PILLAGE; **b.** Greek *pilos*, felt: PILOCARPINE. [Pok. *pi-lo-* 830.]

pipp-. To peep. Imitative root. **1.** Latin *pīpāre*, to chirp: FIFE, PIPE. **2.** Latin *pīpīre*, to chirp: PIGEON. **3.** Gaelic *pīob*, a pipe: PIBROCH. [Pok. *pīp(p)-* 830.]

[pippalī. Pepper. Sanskrit noun of unknown origin. Possibly related to *pippala*, the bo tree. **1.** Sanskrit *pippalī:* PEPPER, (PIMPERNEL). **2.** Sanskrit *pippala:* PEEPUL.]

pisk-. See **peisk-.**

[pius. Dutiful, devoted, pious. Latin word having cognates in other Italic languages. PIACULAR, (PIETÀ), (PIETY), PIOUS, PITTANCE, PITY; EXPIATE, IMPIOUS.]

plab-. To flap. Imitative root. Middle English *flappen*, to flap: FLAP. [Pok. *plab-* 831.]

plāk-[1]. Also **plak-.** To be flat. Extended form of **pelə-[1]**. **1.** Germanic **flōhō* in Old Norse *flō*, layer, coating: FLOE. **2.** Variant form **plāg-* in: **a.** Germanic **flōk-* in Old English *flōc*, flatfish: FLUKE[1]; **b.** Germanic **flakaz* in Norwegian *flak*, flat piece, flake, probably akin to the Scandinavian source of Middle English *flake*, flake: FLAKE[1]; **c.** Germanic **flaki* in Old Norse *flaki, fleki*, hurdle: FLAKE[2]. **3.** Extended form **plakā* in Germanic **flagō* in Old Norse *flaga*, layer of stone: FLAG[4], FLAW[1]. **4.** Possibly suffixed (stative) form **plak-ē-*, to be calm (as of the flat sea), in Latin *placēre*, to please, be agreeable: PLACEBO, PLACID, PLEA, (PLEAD), PLEASE, PLEASANT; COMPLACENT. **5.** Suffixed form **plak-ā-* in Latin *plācāre*, to calm (causative of *placēre*): PLACABLE, PLACATE. **6.** Nasalized form **pla-n-k-* in Latin *plancus*, flat, flat-footed, whence *planca*, board: PLANCHET, PLANK, PLANK-SHEER. **7.** Variant form **plag-* in: **a.** perhaps Latin *plaga*, net (? < "something extended"): PLAGIARY; **b.** Greek *plagos*, side: PLAGAL, PLAGIO-, PLAYA. **8.** Root form **plak-* in Greek *plax*, flat, flat land, surface: PLACENTA, PLACOID. **9.** Variant form **pelag-* in Greek *pelagos*, sea: PELAGIC; ARCHIPELAGO. [Pok. 1. *plā-k-* 831.]

plāk-[2]. To strike. **1.** Shortened form **plak-* in Germanic **flag-* in Middle Dutch *vlāghe* and Middle Low German *vlāge*, gust, blast: FLAW[2]. **2.** Nasalized variant form **pla-n-g-* in: **a.** Germanic **flang-* in Old Norse *flengja*, to flog, whip, akin to the Scandinavian source of Middle English *flingen*, to fling: FLING; **b.** Latin *plangere*, to strike (one's own breast), lament: PLAINT, PLANGENT; COMPLAIN. **3.** Variant form **plāg-* in Latin *plāga*, a blow, stroke: PLAGUE. **4.** Suffixed form **plāk-yo-* in Greek *plēssein*, to beat, strike: PLECTRUM, -PLEGIA, PLEXOR; APOPLEXY, PARAPLEGIA. **5.** Suffixed nasalized variant form **pla(-n-)g-yo-* in Greek *plazesthai*, to beat, strike, cause to wander, drift: PLANKTON. [Pok. 2. *plāk-* 832.]

plat-. To spread. Extended root of **pelə-[1]**. **1.** Variant form **plad-* in Germanic **flataz*, flat, in: **a.** Old Norse *flatr*, flat: FLAT[1]; **b.** Frankish **flat*, flat: FLATTER[1]. **2.** Suffixed variant form **plad-yo-* in Germanic **flatjam* in Old English *flett*, floor, dwelling: FLAT[2]. **3.** Basic form **plat-* in Germanic **flathō(n)*, flat cake, in Old French *flaon*, flat cheesecake, pancake: FLAN. **4.** Germanic nasalized suffixed form **flu-n-th-r-jō-* in Old Swedish *flundra*, flatfish, flounder, probably akin to the Scandinavian source of Norman French *flondre*, flounder: FLOUNDER[2]. **5.** Nasalized form **pla-n-t-* in Latin *planta*, sole of the foot, and denominative *plantāre*, to drive in with the sole of the foot, plant, whence *planta*, a plant: CLAN, PLANT, PLANTAIN[1], PLANTAR; PLANTIGRADE, SUPPLANT. **6.** Suffixed form **plat-u-* in Greek *platus*, flat, broad: PIAZZA, PLACE, PLAICE, PLATE, PLATEAU, PLATITUDE, PLATY[2], PLATY-, PLAZA, PLANE TREE. [Pok. *plat-* 833.]

[plegan. To pledge for, stake, risk, exercise oneself. West Germanic verb. **1.** Old English *plegan*, to exercise oneself, play: PLAY (verb). **2.** Old English derivative noun *plega*, exercise, sport: PLAY (noun). **3.** Frankish **plegan*, to pledge, guarantee: PLEDGE, REPLEVIN. **4.** Germanic derivative noun **plehti-* in Old English *pliht*, danger, peril: PLIGHT[2].]

plek-. To plait. **1.** Suffixed o-grade form **plok-so-* in Germanic **flahsam*, flax, in Old English *fleax*, flax: FLAX. **2.** Latin *-plex*, -fold (in compounds such as *duplex*, twofold; see **dwō**; and *supplex*, "with legs folded under one," kneeling, entreating; *sub-*, under, SUB-): COMPLICE, MULTIPLEX, QUINTUPLE, SUPPLE. **3.** Latin *plicāre*, to fold (also in compounds used as denominatives of words in *-plex*, genitive *-plicis*): PLAIT, PLIANT, PLICA, PLICATE, PLIGHT[1], PLISSÉ, PLY[1]; APPLY, COMPLICATE, DEPLOY, DISPLAY, EMPLOY, EXPLICATE, IMPLICATE, REPLICATE, SUPPLICATE. **4.** Suffixed forms **plek-t-* and **plek-so-* in Latin *plectere* (past participle *plexus*), to weave, plait, entwine: PLEXUS, PLEACH, AMPLEXICAUL, COMPLECT, COMPLEX, PERPLEX. **5.** Greek *plekein*, to plait, twine: PLECTOGNATH. [Pok. *plek̂-* 834.]

plēk-. Also **pleik-.** To tear. **1.** Zero-grade form **plək-* becoming **plak-* in Germanic **flahan* in Old English *flēan*, to strip the skin from: FLAY. **2.** Suffixed form **pleik-sko-* in Germanic **flaiskaz*, piece of flesh torn off, in Old English *flǣsc*, flesh: FLESH. **3.** Zero-grade form **plik-* in Germanic **flikkja* in: **a.** Old English *flicce*, side of a hog: FLITCH; **b.** Germanic ablaut form **flekkja* in Old Norse *flekkr*, piece of skin or flesh, spot, stain: FLECK. [Pok. *plēk̂-* 835.]

pleu-. To flow. **I.** Basic form **pleu-*. **1.** Latin *pluere*, to rain: PLOVER, PLUVIAL, PLUVIOUS. **2.** Greek *plein* (stem *pleu-*), to swim, sail: PLEUSTON. **3.** Suffixed zero-grade form **plu-elos* dissimilated into Greek *puelos*, trough, basin: PYELITIS. **4.** Suffixed form **pl(e)u-mon-*, "floater," lung(s), in: **a.** Latin *pulmō* (< **plumonēs*), lung(s): PULMONARY; **b.** Greek *pleumōn, pneumōn*, lung: PNEUMONIA, PNEUMONIC. **5.** Suffixed o-grade form **plou-to-* in Greek *ploutos*, wealth, riches (< "overflowing"): PLUTO[1], PLUTOCRACY. **II.** Extended form **pleuk-*. **1.** Germanic **fliugan*, to fly, in Old English *flēogan*, to fly: FLY[1]. **2.** Germanic **fliugjō*, flying insect, fly, in Old English *flēoge*, a fly: FLY[2]. **3.** Probably Germanic **fliuhan*, to run away, in Old English *flēon*, to flee: FLEE. **4.** Germanic causative **flauhjan* in Old English *-flȳgan* (only in *āflȳgan, āflīgan*), to put to flight: FLEY. **5.** Germanic suffixed form **fliug-ika* in Frankish **fliugika*, "feather," arrow: FLÈCHE, FLETCHER, PARFLECHE. **6.** Zero-grade form **pluk-* in: **a.** Germanic **flugja*, feather, in Old English *-flycge*, with feathers (only in *unfligge*, featherless): FLEDGE; **b.** suffixed form **flug-ti-* in Old English *flyht*, act of flying, and **flyht*, act of fleeing, escape: FLIGHT[1], FLIGHT[2]; **c.** suffixed form **flug-laz*, dissimilated into **fuglaz*, bird, in Old English *fugol*, bird: FOWL; **d.** Germanic suffixed form **flug-ila* in Middle High German *vlügel*, wing: FLÜGELHORN, FUGLEMAN. **III.** Extended form **pleud-*. **1.** Germanic **fliutan* in: **a.** Old English *flēotan*, to float, swim: FLEET[1], FLEET[2]; **b.** Old English derivative noun *fleot*, water, estuary: FLEET[3]. **2.** Zero-grade **plud-* in Germanic **flut-, *flot-* in: **a.** Germanic derivative **flotōn*, to float, in *(i)* Old English *flotian*, to float: FLOAT *(ii)* Vulgar Latin **flottāre*, to float: FLOTSAM; **b.** Old Norse *floti*, raft, fleet: FLOTILLA; **c.** Old English *floterian*, to float back and forth (*-erian*, iterative and frequentative suffix): FLUTTER; **d.** Germanic **flutjan*, to float, in Old Norse *flytja*, to further, convey: FLIT. **3.** Probably Germanic suffixed form **flaut-stā-*, contracted into **flausta-* in Icelandic *flaustr*, hurry, and *flaustra*, to bustle, probably akin to the Scandinavian source of Middle English *flostren*, to excite with drink: FLUSTER. **IV.** Alternate root form **plē-*. **1.** O-grade form **plō(u)-* in: **a.** Germanic **flōwēn*, to flow, in *(i)* Old English *flōwan*, to flow: FLOW *(ii)* perhaps Middle Dutch *vlūwe*, fishnet: FLUE[3]; **b.** suffixed form **plō-tu-* in Germanic **flōdu*, flowing water, deluge, in Old English *flōd*, flood: FLOOD. **2.** Celtic **linda*, water, in: **a.** Old Irish *linn*, pool, whence Scottish Gaelic *linn*, pool: LINN; **b.** Old Irish *linn*, liquor: METHEGLIN. [Pok. *pleu-* 835; *pl(e)u-mon-* 837.]

pleus-. To pluck; feather, fleece. **1.** Germanic **fliusaz*, fleece, in Old English *flēos*, fleece: FLEECE. **2.** Suffixed zero-grade form **plus-mā* in Latin *plūma*, a feather: PLUMATE, PLUME, PLUMOSE, PLUMULE; DEPLUME. [Pok. *pleus-* 838.]

plou-. Flea. **1.** Extended form **plouk-* in Germanic **flauhaz* in Old English *flēa(h)*, flea: FLEA. **2.** Extended zero-grade form **plus-* metathesized into **pusl-* in: **a.** Latin *pūlex* (< **puslex*), flea: PUCE; **b.** Greek *psulla*, flea: PSYLLA. [Pok. *blou-* 102.]

[plumbum. Lead. Latin noun, probably borrowed from the same unidentified source as Greek *molubdos*, lead. **1.** Latin *plumbum:* PLUMB, PLUMBAGO, PLUMBER, PLUMBISM, PLUMMET, PLUNGE, APLOMB. **2.** Greek *molubdos:* MOLYBDENUM.]

pneu-. To breathe. Imitative root. **1.** Germanic **fniu-* in Old English *fnēosan*, to sneeze: SNEEZE. **2.** Greek *pnein*, to breathe: APNEA, DIPNOAN, DYSPNEA, EUPNEA, HYPERPNEA, HYPOPNEA, POLYPNEA. **3.** Suffixed form **pneu-men-* in Greek *pneuma*, breath, wind, spirit: NEUMES, PNEUMA, PNEUMATIC, PNEUMATO-, PNEUMO-. [Pok. *pneu-* 838.]

pōi-[1]. Also **pī-.** To drink. **1.** Suffixed reduced form **pō-to-* in Latin *pōtus*, drunk, whence *pōtāre*, to drink: POISON, POTABLE, POTATION, POTATORY, POTION. **2.** Reduplicated form **pi-po-* dissimilated to **pi-bo-*, assimilated to **bi-bo-* in Latin *bibere*, to drink: BEER, BEVERAGE, BIB, BIBULOUS, IMBIBE. **3.** Suffixed variant form **po-ti-* in Greek *posis*, drink, drinking: SYMPOSIUM. **4.** Suffixed form **pī-ro-* in Old Church Slavonic *pirŭ*, feast, whence Russian *pir*, feast: PIROG. [Pok. 2. *pō(i)-* 839.]

pōi-[2]. To graze cattle, cover, protect. **1.** Suffixed reduced form **pō-tro-* in Germanic **fōthram*, sheath, case, lining, in Old French *forre*, trimming made from animal skin, fur: FUR. **2.** Suffixed reduced form **pō-wen-* has been proposed by some as the pre-form of Old Persian *-pāvan*, protector (which is more likely from **pā-wen-*, a suffixed form of root **pā-**): SATRAP. [Pok. 1. *pō(i)-* 839.]

pol-. Finger. Latin *pollex*, thumb: POLLEX. [Pok. *polo-* 840.]

pōl-. To touch, feel, shake. **1.** Germanic **fōljan*, to feel, in Old English *fēlan*, to examine by touch, feel: FEEL. **2.** Reduplicated zero-grade form **pəl-p-* in: **a.** Latin *palpus*, a touching: PALP; **b.** Latin *palpārī, palpāre*, to stroke gently, touch: PALPABLE, PALPATE[1], PALPITATE; **c.** Latin *palpebra*, eyelid (< "that which shakes or moves quickly"): PALPEBRAL. **3.** Perhaps zero-grade form **pəl-* in Greek *pallein*, to sway, brandish: CATAPULT. **4.** Perhaps zero-grade expressive form **p(s)əl-* in Greek *psallein*, to pluck, play the harp: PSALM, PSALTERY. [Pok. 1. *pel-*, Section G. 801.]

[pōmum. Apple. Latin noun of unknown origin. POMACE, POMADE, POME.]

[populus. People. Latin noun of Etruscan origin. PEOPLE, POPULACE, POPULAR, POPULATE, PUBLIC, PUEBLO, DEPOPULATE.]

porko-. Young pig. **1.** Germanic **farhaz* in: **a.** Old English *fearh*, little pig: FARROW[1]; **b.** diminutive form in Middle Dutch *varken*, small pig: AARDVARK. **2.** Latin *porcus*, pig: PORCELAIN, PORCINE, PORK, PORCUPINE, PORPOISE. **3.** Latin *porcil(l)āca, *porcillana*, purslane (< "herb for the womb"; connected to *porcus*, in vulgar senses "sow," "female pudenda"): PURSLANE. [Pok. *porko-s* 841.]

poti-. Powerful; lord. **1.** Latin *potis*, powerful, able: PODESTA. **2.** Old Latin **potere*, to be able or powerful (superseded by *posse*, to be able; see **3.** below): POTENT, POWER, (IMPOTENT), PREPOTENT. **3.** Latin compound *posse*, to be able (contracted from *potis*, able + *esse*, to be; see **es-**): POSSESS, POSSIBLE, PUISSANT. **4.** Variant form **pet-* in compound **ghos-pet-*, "guest-master," host (see **ghosti-**). **5.** Reduced form **pot-* in **dems-pot-*, "house-master," ruler (see **demə-[1]**). **6.** Old Persian *pati*, master: PADISHAH. [Pok. *poti-s* 843.]

[pott-. Pot. Celtic root. Vulgar Latin **pottus*, potter (attested in Late Latin and often in names of potters): POT, POTICHE, POTTAGE, PUDGY, PUTTY; CACHEPOT, HOTCHPOT.]

pōu-. Also **pau-.** Few, little. **I.** Variant form **pau-*, few, little. **1.** Germanic **fawaz* in Old English *fēawe*, few: FEW. **2.** Suffixed form **pau-ko-* in Latin *paucus*, little, few: PAUCITY, POCO. **3.** Suffixed form **pau-ro-* in: **a.** suffixed (diminutive) form **pau-ro-lo-* contracted into Latin *paullus, paulus*, small: PAUL; **b.** metathetical form **par-wo-* in Latin *parvus*, little, small, whence neuter *parvum*, becoming *parum*, little, rarely: PARAFFIN. **4.** Compound **pau-paros*, producing little, poor (**par-os*, producing; see **per-[4]**), in Latin *pauper*, poor: PAUPER, POOR, POVERTY. **II.** Suffixed (diminutive) variant form **pu-lo-*, young of an animal. **1.** Germanic **fulō* in Old English *fola*, young horse, colt: FOAL. **2.** Germanic derivative **fuljō* in Old Norse *fylja*, female colt: FILLY. **3.** Latin *pullus* (probably with expressive gemination), young of an animal: POLTROON, PONY, POOL[2], POULARD, PULLET; CATCHPOLE. **III.** Variant forms **pū-, *pau-*, boy, child. **1.** Suffixed form **pu-ero-* in Latin *puer*, child: PUERILE, PUERPERAL. **2.** Suffixed form **pū-so-s* in Latin *pūsos*, boy: PUSILLANIMOUS. **3.** Suffixed form **paw-id-* in Greek *pais* (stem *paid-*), child: PAGE[1], PEDO-[2], ENCYCLOPEDIA, ORTHOPEDICS. [Pok. *pōu-* 842.]

[prāk-. To make, do. Greek root. Greek *pras-*

sein (Attic *prattein*), to effect, do: BARTER, PRACTICAL, (PRACTICE), PRAGMATIC, PRAXIS; APRAXIS. [In Pok. 1. *per* 811.]]

prep-. To appear. Suffixed zero-grade form **pr̥p-yo-* in Germanic **furbjan*, to cause to have a (good) appearance, polish, in Old French *fo(u)rbir*, to polish, burnish: FURBISH. [Pok. *prep-* 845.]

preu-. To hop. **1.** Zero-grade form **pru-* in Germanic **fru-* in Old English *frogga* (with expressive suffix *-ga*), frog: FROG. **2.** Extended o-grade form **prowo-* in Germanic **frawaz* in Middle Dutch *vro*, "leaping with joy," happy: FROLIC. [Pok. *preu-* 845.]

preus-. To freeze, burn. **1.** Germanic **friusan*, to freeze, in Old English *frēosan*, to freeze: FREEZE. **2.** Suffixed zero-grade form **prus-to-* in Germanic **frustaz*, frost, in Old English *forst, frost*, frost: FROST. **3.** Suffixed form **preus-i-* in Latin **preusis, *preuris*, act of burning, whence denominative *prūrīre*, to burn, itch, yearn for: PRURIENT, PRURIGO, PRURITUS. **4.** Suffixed zero-grade form **prus-īna* in Latin *pruīna*, hoarfrost: PRUINOSE. [Pok. *preus-* 846.]

prī-. To love. **1.** Extended form **priyo-* in: **a.** Germanic **frijaz*, beloved, belonging to the loved ones, not in bondage, free, in *(i)* Old English *frēo*, free: FREE *(ii)* Dutch *vrij*, free: FILIBUSTER; **b.** Sanskrit *priya-*, dear, precious: SAPPHIRE. **2.** Suffixed (participial) form **priy-ont-*, loving, in Germanic **frijand-*, lover, friend, in Old English *frīond, frēond*, friend: FRIEND. **3.** Suffixed shortened form **pri-tu-* in Germanic **frithuz*, peace, in: **a.** Old High German *fridu*, peace: GODFREY, SIEGFRIED; **b.** Frankish **frithu, *fridu*, peace: AFFRAY; **c.** Germanic **frij-*, peace, safety, in compound **berg-frij-*, "high place of safety" (see **bhergh-**[2]); **d.** Germanic compound name **Frithu-rīc*, "peaceful ruler" (**rīkja*, ruler; see **reg-**[1]), in Old High German *Fridurīh*: FREDERICK; **e.** Germanic compound meaning peaceful region in Medieval Latin name *Galfridu, Gaufridu* (< Germanic **ga-ahwjā*; see **akwā-**): JEFFREY. **4.** Extended form **priyā*, beloved, in Germanic **frijjō*, beloved, wife, in: **a.** Old Norse *Frigg*, goddess of love, wife of Odin: FRIGG; **b.** Germanic compound **frije-dagaz*, "day of Frigg" (translation of Latin *Veneris diēs*, "Venus's day"), in Old English *frīgedæg*, Friday: FRIDAY. [Pok. *prāi-* 844.]

prōkto-. Anus. Greek *prōktos*, anus: PROCTOLOGY, PROCTOSCOPE. [Pok. *prōkto-* 846.]

pster-. Also **ster-**. To sneeze. Imitative root. **1.** Suffixed form **ster-nu-* in Latin *sternuere*, to sneeze: STERNUTATION. **2.** Suffixed form **ster-t-* in Latin *stertere*, to snore: STERTOR. [Pok. *pster-* 846.]

pteleyā. Tree name. Possible root. Possibly broken reduplicated form **pō-pel-* in Latin *pōpulus*, poplar: POPLAR, (POPPLE[2]). [Pok. *ptel(e)i̯ā* 847.]

pu-[1]. Also **p(h)ū-**. To blow, swell. Imitative root. **1.** Extended form **pus-* in Latin *pustula*, a bubble, blister: PUSTULE. **2.** Perhaps extended form **pūt-*, penis, in Latin *praepūtium*, foreskin (*prae-*, before, in front, PRE-): PREPUCE. **3.** Variant form **p(h)ū-* in Greek *phusa* (plural *phusai*), bellows: EMPHYSEMA, PHYSOSTIGMINE, PHYSOSTOMOUS. [Pok. 1. *pu-* 847.]

pu-[2]. To rot, decay. **1.** Suffixed lengthened-grade form **pū-lo-* in Germanic **fūlaz*, rotten, filthy, in: **a.** Old English *fūl*, unclean, rotten: FOUL; **b.** Old Norse *fūll*, foul: FULMAR; **c.** Germanic abstract noun **fūlithō* in Old English *fȳlth*, foulness: FILTH; **d.** Germanic denominative **fūljan*, to soil, dirty, in Old English *fȳlan*, to sully: FILE[3]; (DEFILE[1]). **2.** Extended form **pug-* in Germanic **fuk-* in Icelandic *fūki*, rotten sea grass, and Norwegian *fogg*, rank grass, probably akin to the Scandinavian source of Middle English *fog, fogge*, aftermath grass: FOG[2]. **3.** Extended variant form **pous-* in Germanic **fausa-* in Low German *fussig*, spongy: FUZZY. **4.** Suffixed form **pu-tri-* in Latin *puter* (stem *putri-*), rotten: PUTRESCENT, (PUTRID); OLLA PODRIDA, PUTREFY, POTPOURRI. **5.** Suffixed form **puw-os-* in: **a.** Latin *pus*, pus: PURULENT, PUS, SUPPURATE; **b.** Greek *puon, puos*, pus: PYO-. **6.** Greek compound *empuein*, to suppurate (*en-*, in, EN-): EMPYEMA. [Pok. 2. *pū̆-* 848.]

[**pūbēs**. Pubic hair. Latin noun of obscure origin. Related to Latin *pūber, pūbēs*, adult, grown-up. **1.** Latin *pūbēs*, pubic hair: PUBES, (PUBIC), (PUBIS). **2.** Latin *pūber, pūbēs*, adult: PUBERTY, PUBERULENT, PUBESCENT.]

puk-[1]. To make fast. Suffixed extended form **puki-no-* in Greek *pukinos*, later *puknos*, strong, fast, thick: PYCNIDIUM, PYKNIC, PYCNOMETER. [Pok. 2. *puk-* 849.]

puk-[2]. Bushy-haired. Suffixed form **puk-so-* in: **a.** Germanic **fuhsaz*, fox, in Old English *fox*, fox: FOX; **b.** Germanic feminine **fuhson* in Old English *fyxe*, she-fox: VIXEN. This root is in part a taboo deformation of **w̥l̥kwo-** and **wl̥p-**. [Pok. *pūk-* 849.]

[**pulē**. Gate. Greek noun of obscure origin. PYLON, PYLORUS; AEOLIPILE, MICROPYLE, PROPYLAEUM, PROPYLON.]

pūr-. Fire. **1.** Germanic **fūri-* in Old English *fȳr*, fire: FIRE. **2.** Greek *pur*, fire: PYRALIC, PYRE, PYRETIC, PYRITES, PYRO-, PYRRHOTITE, PYROSIS; EMPYREAL. [Pok. *peu̯ōr* 828.]

pūro-. Grain. **1.** Suffixed form (with suffix **-so-*) in Old English *fyrs*, furze: FURZE. **2.** Suffixed form in Greek *purēn* (with suffix **-ēn-*), stone of fruit: PYRENE. [Pok. *pū-ro-* 850.]

[**puxos**. Box-tree. Greek noun borrowed from an unknown source. **1.** Greek *puxos*, box-tree: BOX[3]. **2.** Derivative adjective *puxis*, (box) made of boxwood: BOX[1], (BUSH[2]).]

[**quaerere**. To seek. Latin noun of unknown origin. QUAESTOR, QUERIST, QUERY, QUEST, QUESTION; ACQUIRE, CONQUER, DISQUISITION, EXQUISITE, INQUIRE, PERQUISITE, REQUIRE.]

rabh-. Violent, impetuous. Suffixed form **rabh-yo-* in Latin *rabere*, to rave, be mad: RABID, RABIES, RAGE. [Pok. *rabh-* 852.]

rāp-. Tuber. Late Indo-European root borrowed from an unknown source. Latin *rāpa, rāpum*, turnip: RAMPION, RAPE[2], RAVIOLI; KOHLRABI. [Pok. *rāp-* 852.]

[**re-**. Also **red-**. Backward. Latin combining form conceivably from Indo-European **wret-*, metathetical variant of **wert-*, to turn (< "turned back"), an extended form of **wer-**[3]. **1.** Latin *re-, red-*, backward, again: RE-. **2.** Suffixed form **re(d)-tro-* in Latin *retrō*, backward, back, behind, with its derivative Norman French *rere*, backward: RETRAL, RETRO-; ARREAR, REAR GUARD, REARWARD[2], REREDOS. **3.** Suffixed form **re-ko-* in Latin *reciprocus*, "backward-forward" (see **per**[1]).]

rebh-. To roof over. Germanic **reb-jōn*, "covering of the chest cavity," in: **a.** Old English *ribb*, rib: RIB; **b.** Old Norse *rif*, rib, ridge: REEF[1], REEF[2]; **c.** Middle Low German *ribbe*, rib: SPARERIBS. [Pok. 2. *rebh-* 853.]

rēd-. To scrape, scratch, gnaw. **1.** O-grade form **rōd-* in: **a.** Latin *rōdere*, to gnaw: RODENT; CORRODE, ERODE; **b.** suffixed (instrumental) form **rōd-tro-* in Latin *rōstrum*, beak, ship's bow: ROSTRUM. **2.** Possibly variant form **rād-* in Latin *rādere*, to scrape: RADULA, RAIL[2], (RASCAL), RASH[2], RASORIAL; ABRADE, CORRADE, ERASE. [Pok. 2. *rēd-* 854.]

reg-[1]. To move in a straight line, with derivatives meaning "to direct in a straight line, lead, rule." **I.** Basic form **reg-* in: **1.** Suffixed form **reg-to-* in Germanic **rehtaz* in Old English *riht*, right, just, correct, straight: RIGHT; **2.** Latin *regere*, to lead straight, guide, rule (past participle *rēctus*, hence *rēctus*, right, straight): REALM, RECTO, RECTOR, RECTUM, REGENT, REGIME, REGION; CORRECT, DIRECT, ERECT, RECTANGLE, RECTIFY, RECTILINEAR, RECTITUDE, REGIMENT, RISORGIMENTO, SURGE; **3.** Greek *oregein* (with prothetic vowel), to stretch out, reach out for: ANOREXIA. **II.** Lengthened-grade form **rēg-*, Indo-European word for a tribal king. **1.** Celtic suffixed form **rīg-yo-* in Germanic **rikja* in: **a.** Old English *rīce*, realm: BISHOPRIC, ELDRITCH; **b.** Old Norse *rīki*, realm: RIKSMÅL; **c.** Old High German *rīhhi*, realm, and *rīhhi*, powerful: REICH, AUSTRIA, HENRY, RICHARD; **d.** Old English *rīce*, strong, powerful, and Frankish **rīki*, powerful: RICH; **e.** Old High German *-rich*, rule, ruler: AUBREY, RODERICK; **f.** Germanic compound **aiza-rīkja*, "honored ruler" (**aiza-*, from a root **ais-*, to honor), in Old Norse *Eirīkr*, given name: ERIC. **2.** Latin *rēx*, king: REAL[2], REGAL, REGULUS, REIGN, REX, ROYAL; INTERREX, REGICIDE, REGIUS PROFESSOR, VICEREINE, VICEROY. **3.** Suffixed form **rēg-en-* in Sanskrit *-rājā, rājan*, king, rajah, king, *rājñī*, queen, and *rājati*, he rules: RAJ, RAJAH, RANI, RYE[2]; MAHARAJAH, MAHARANI. **III.** Suffixed lengthened-grade form **rēg-olā* in Latin *rēgula*, straight piece of wood, rod: RAIL[1], REGULAR, REGULATE, REGLET, RULE. **IV.** O-grade form **rog-*. **1.** Germanic **rakō* in Old English *raca, racu*, rake (implement with straight pieces of wood): RAKE[1]. **2.** Germanic **rak-* in Middle Dutch *rec*, framework: RACK[1]. **3.** Possibly Germanic **rankaz* (with nasal infix) in Old English *ranc*, straight, strong, hence haughty, overbearing: RANK[2]. **4.** Germanic **rak-inaz*, ready, straightforward, in Old English *gerecenian*, to arrange in order, recount (*ge-*, collective prefix; see **kom**): RECKON. **5.** Form **rog-ā-* in: **a.** Latin *rogāre*, to ask (< "stretch out the hand"): ROGATION, ROGATORY, ROGUE; ABROGATE, ARROGATE, CORVÉE, DEROGATE, INTERROGATE, PREROGATIVE, PROROGUE, SUBROGATE, SUPEREROGATE; **b.** perhaps the Latin phrase **ē rogō*, "from the direction of" (*ē*, from *ex*, out of; see **eghs**), contracted into *ergō*, therefore, in consequence of: ARGAL[2], ERGO. **V.** Lengthened o-grade form **rōg-* in: **1.** Germanic **rōkjan* in Old English *rec(c)an*, to extend, stretch out, pay attention to, take care: RECK. **2.** Germanic **rōkja-* in Old English *recelēas*, careless (*-lēas*, -LESS): RECKLESS. [Pok. 1. *reg-* 854.]

reg-[2]. Moist. **1.** Suffixed variant form **rek-no-* in Germanic **regnaz*, rain, in: **a.** Old English *reg(e)n, rēn*, rain: RAIN; **b.** Old English *rēnboga*, rainbow (*boga*, bow, BOW[1]): RAINBOW. **2.** Possibly Latin *rigāre*, to wet, water: IRRIGATE. [Pok. 2. *reg-* 857.]

reg-[3]. To dye. Lengthened-grade form **rēg-*. **1.** Suffixed form **rēg-os-* in Greek *rhēgos*, blanket, rug: REGOLITH. **2.** Sanskrit *rāga*, color, red: RAGA, SANDARAC. **3.** Perhaps Sanskrit *rākshā*, earlier form of *lākshā*, red dye: LAC[1], LAC[2]. [Pok. 1. *reg-* 854.]

regwos-. Darkness. Greek *Erebos*, Erebos, a place of darkness under the earth: EREBUS. [Pok. *regu̯os-* 857.]

rei-[1]. To scratch, tear, cut. **I.** Extended form **reig-*. **1.** Germanic **rīgwa-* in Italian *riga*, line (< "something cut out"): RIGATONI. **2.** Suffixed form **rei-mā* or **reig-smā* in Latin *rīma*, crack, cleft, fissure: RIMOSE. **3.** O-grade form **roig-* in Germanic **rai(g)wa-* in Old English *rāw, rǣw*, a line, row: ROW[1]. **II.** Extended form **reipp-*. **1.** Germanic **raipaz*, rope, in: **a.** Old English *rāp*, rope: ROPE; **b.** compound **stig-raipaz*, "mount-rope," in Old English *stigrāp*, stirrup (see **steigh-**). **2.** Possibly Germanic **raip-* in Icelandic *rāfa*, to wander, loiter, akin to the Scandinavian source of Middle English *roven*, to wander: ROVE[1]. **III.** Extended form **reip-*. **1.** Germanic **rīfan*, in Old Norse *rīfa*, to tear: RIVE. **2.** Zero-grade form **rip-* in: **a.** Germanic **rifti-* in Danish *rift*, breach, akin to tne Scandinavian source of Middle English *rift*, rift: RIFT[1]; **b.** Germanic **rif-* in Old English *rȳfe*, abundant: RIFE. **3.** Suffixed form **reip-ā-* in Latin *rīpa*, bank (< "that which is cut out by a river"): RIVER[1], RAVELIN, RIPARIAN, RIVAGE; ARRIVE. **IV.** Extended form **reib-* in Germanic **rīp-* in: **1.** Germanic **rīpja-* in Old English *rīpe*, ripe, ready for reaping: RIPE; **2.** Germanic **rīpjan* in Old English *rīpan*, to reap: REAP; **3.** Middle Low German *repelen*, to remove seeds, akin to the source of Middle English *ripelen*, to remove seeds: RIPPLE[2]. [Pok. 1. *rei-* 857.]

rei-[2]. Striped in various colors, flecked. Suffixed o-grade form **roi-ko-* in Germanic **raihaz* in Old English *rā, rāha*, deer: ROE DEER. [Pok. 2. *rei-* 859.]

rei-[3]. Possession, thing. Uncertain pre-form in Latin *rēs*, thing: RE[2], REAL[1], REBUS; REIFY, REPUBLIC. [Pok. 4. *rei-* 860.]

reidh-. To ride. **I.** Basic form **reidh-*. **1.** Germanic **rīdan* in: **a.** Old English *rīdan*, to ride: RIDE; **b.** Middle Dutch *rīden*, to ride: RITTER. **2.** Celtic **vo-rēd-* in Latin *verēdus*, post horse (**vo-*, under; see **upo**): PALFREY. **II.** O-grade form **roidh-*. **1.** Germanic **raid-* in: **a.** Old English *rād*, a riding, road: RAID, ROAD; **b.** possibly Middle High German *reidel*, rod between upright stakes (< "wooden horse"): RADDLE[1]. **2.** Germanic **raid-ja-* in Old English *rǣde, gerǣde*, ready (< "prepared for a journey"): READY. **3.** Germanic **raidjan* in Vulgar Latin **rēdāre*, to provide, prepare (as for a journey): ARRAY, CURRY[1]. [Pok. *reidh-* 861.]

reig-[1]. To bind. **1.** Germanic **rigg-* (the *-gg-* is anomalous) in Norwegian *rigga*, to bind, akin to the Scandinavian source of Middle English *riggen*, to rig: RIG. **2.** Zero-grade form **rig-* in Latin *corrigia* (probably borrowed from Gaulish), thong, shoelace (*cor-*, from *com-*, COM-): SCOURGE. [Pok. *reig-* 861.]

reig-[2]. To reach, stretch out. **1.** O-grade form **roig-* in Germanic **raikjan* in Old English *rǣcan*, to stretch out, reach: REACH. **2.** Suffixed (stative) zero-grade form **rig-ē-* in Latin *rigēre*, to be stiff (< "be stretched out"): RIGID, RIGOR. [Pok. *(reig̑-)* 862.]

rēk-. To order, counsel, judge, determine. Zero-grade form **rək-* in Germanic **ragin-* in: **a.** Old English *regen*, power: REGINALD; **b.** Old Norse *regin*, decree: RONALD; **c.** Frankish name *Raginmund*, "counsel protection" (*-mund*, from Germanic **mund-*, protection; see **man-**[2]): RAYMOND. [Pok. 2. *rek-* 863.]

rendh-. To tear up. **1.** Germanic **randjan* in Old English *rendan*, to tear: REND. **2.** Germanic *rind- in Old English rind(e), rind (< "thing torn off"): RIND. [Pok. rendh- 865.]

rep-. To snatch. Latin rapere, to seize: RAPE[1], RAPACIOUS, RAPID, RAPT, RAVEN[2], RAVIN, RAVISH; EREPSIN, SURREPTITIOUS. [Pok. rep- 865.]

rēp-[1]. To creep, slink. Latin rēpere, to creep: REPENT[2], REPTANT, REPTILE, SUBREPTION. [Pok. 1. rēp- 865.]

rēp-[2]. Stake, beam. Suffixed variant form *rap-tro- in Germanic *raf-tra- in: a. Old English ræfter, rafter: RAFTER; b. Old Norse raptr, beam: RAFT[1]. [Pok. 2. rēp- 866.]

ret-. To run, roll. 1. Latin rotundus (variant of *ret-undus, by influence of rota, wheel): ROTUND, ROTUNDA, ROUND[1], PRUNE[2]. 2. Prefixed form *to-upo-ret-, "a running up to" (to-, to; upo, up, up from under; see **upo**), in Old Irish tōir, pursuit: TORY. 3. Suffixed o-grade form *rot-ā- in Latin rota, wheel: (RODEO), ROLL, ROTA, ROTARY, ROTATE, ROTE[1], ROULETTE, ROWEL; BAROUCHE, CONTROL, ROTIFORM, ROTOGRAVURE. [Pok. ret(h)- 866.]

rēt-. Post. O-grade form *rōt- in: a. Germanic *rōd- in Old English rōd, rod, cross: ROOD; b. Germanic *rodd- (geminated variant) in Old English rodd, rod: ROD. [Pok. rēt- 866.]

reu-. To bellow. 1. Extended form *reud- in Germanic *raud- in Old Norse rauta, to roar (akin to the Scandinavian source of ROTE[2]): ROUT[3]. 2. Suffixed form *reu-mos- in Latin rūmor, rumor, "common talk": RUMOR. 3. Extended form *reug- in Latin rūgīre, to roar: BRUIT, RIOT, RUT[2]. 4. Variant *rau-ko- in Latin raucus, hoarse: RAUCOUS. [Pok. 1. reu- 867.]

reudh-. Red, ruddy. I. O-grade form *roudh-. 1. Germanic *raudaz in: a. Old English rēad, red: RED[1]; b. Old Norse rauthr, red: RORQUAL. 2. Germanic *rauthnia- in Old Norse reynir, mountain ash, rowan (from its red berries), akin to the source of ROWAN. 3. Latin rōbeus, rubeus, red: ROUGE, RUBELLA, RUBEOLA, RUBY, RUBEFACIENT. 4. Latin rūfus (of dialectal Italic origin), reddish: RUFESCENT, RUFOUS, RUFUS. 5. Latin robus, red, in rōbigō, rūbigō, rust: RUBIGINOUS. 6. Latin rōbur, rōbus, red oak, hardness, and rōbustus, strong: ROBLE, ROBORANT, ROBUST; CORROBORATE, RAMBUNCTIOUS. II. Zero-grade form *rudh-. 1. Form *rudh-ā- in Germanic *rudō in: a. Old English rudu, red color: RUDDLE, RUDDY; b. Old English rudduc, robin: RUDDOCK. 2. Suffixed form *rudh-sto- in Germanic *rūst- in Old English rūst, rust: RUST. 3. Latin rubicundus, red, ruddy: RUBICUND. 4. Latin rubidus, red: RUBIDIUM. 5. Suffixed (stative) form *rudh-ē- in Latin rubēre, to be red: RUBESCENT, ERUBESCENCE. 6. Suffixed form *rudh-ro- in: a. Latin ruber, red: RUBRIC, BILIRUBIN; b. Latin rutilus, reddish: RUTILANT; c. Greek eruthros, red: ERYTHEMA, ERYTHRO-, ERYSIPELAS. 7. Suffixed form *rudh-to- in Latin russus, red: RISSOLE, ROUX, RUSSET. [Pok. reudh- 872.]

reug-. To vomit, belch, smoke, cloud. 1. Germanic *riukan in Old English rēocan, to smoke, reek: REEK. 2. Suffixed zero-grade form *rug-to- in Latin ructāre, to belch: ERUCT. [Pok. 4. reu- 871.]

reughmen-. Cream. O-grade form *roughmen- in Germanic *rau(g)ma- in Middle Low German rōm(e), cream: RAMEKIN. [Pok. reugh-m(e)n 873.]

reup-. Also **reub-**. To snatch. I. Basic form *reub- in Germanic *rupja in Flemish rippen, to rip: RIP[1]. II. O-grade form *roup-. 1. Germanic *raufjan in: a. Old English rēafian, to plunder: REAVE[1]; b. Old English berēafian, to take away (be-, BE-): BEREAVE. 2. Germanic *raubōn, to rob, in: a. Middle Dutch and Middle Low German rōven, to rob: ROVER; b. Old French rober, to rob: ROB; c. Italian rubare, to rob: RUBATO. 3. Germanic *raubō, booty, in: a. Vulgar Latin *rauba, "clothes taken as booty": ROBE; b. Norman French *robel, rubbings, spoils: RUBBLE. III. Zero-grade form *rup-. 1. Latin ūsūrpāre (< *ūsu-rup-; ūsus, use, usage, from ūtī, to USE), "to acquire by the act of using," take into use, usurp: USURP. 2. Nasalized form *ru-m-p- in Latin rumpere, to break: ROUT[1], RUPTURE; ABRUPT, BANKRUPT, CORRUPT, DISRUPT, ERUPT, INTERRUPT, IRRUPT. [Pok. 2. reu- 868.]

rewe-. To open; space. 1. Suffixed variant form *rū-mo- in Germanic *rūmaz in: a. Old English rūm, space: ROOM; b. Middle Dutch ruum, rume, rhumb line, room, space: RHUMB, RUMBA; c. Old French -rimer, ship's hold, space: RUMMAGE; d. Germanic denominative *rūmjan in Old English rȳman, to widen, open up: REAM[2]. 2. Suffixed reduced form *rew-os- in Latin rūs, "open land," the country: RURAL, RUSTIC. [Pok. reuə-, rū- 874.]

rezg-. To plait, weave, wind. Germanic *ruski- in Old English risc, rysc, rush: RUSH[2]. [Pok. rezg- 874.]

[risan. To rise. Germanic word. 1. Germanic *rīsan in: a. Old English rīsan, to rise: RISE; b. Old English ārīsan, to arise (ā-, A-): ARISE. 2. Germanic causative *raizjan in: a. Old English rǣran, to rear, raise, lift up: REAR[2]; b. Old Norse reisa, to raise: RAISE.]

r̥kso-. Perhaps originally **r̥kt(h)o-**. Bear. 1. Latin ursus, bear (< *orcsos): URSINE. 2. Greek arktos, bear: ARCTIC, ARCTURUS. 3. Celtic *arto-, bear: ARTHUR. [Pok. ŕ̥k-tho-s 875.]

ruk-[1]. Fabric, spun yarn. Celtic and Germanic root. 1. Germanic *rukkōn- in: a. Gothic *rukka, distaff: ROCKET[1]; b. Old High German rocko, distaff: ROCAMBOLE; c. Frankish *rokko, distaff: RATCHET. 2. Germanic *rukka- in Frankish *rok, coat: ROCHET. [Pok. ruk(k) 874.]

ruk-[2]. Rough; to scrape. 1. Lengthened-grade form *rūk- in Germanic *rūhwaz in Old English rūh, rough, coarse: ROUGH. 2. Suffixed variant form *rukh-yo- in Greek orussein (with prothetic vowel o-), to dig: ORC, ORYX. 3. Lengthened variant form *rūg- in Latin rūga, wrinkle: RUGA, RUGOSE, CORRUGATE. [In Pok. 2. reu- 868.]

rūno-. Mystery, secret. Germanic and Celtic technical term of magic. Germanic *runaz in: a. Old English rūn, secret council: RUNNYMEDE; b. Old English rūnian, to whisper: ROUND[2]; c. Old Norse *rūn, secret writing, and Finnish runo, song, poem: RUNE. [In Pok. 1. reu- 867.]

sā-. To satisfy. 1. Suffixed zero-grade form *sə-to- in: a. Germanic *sadaz, sated, in Old English sæd, sated, weary: SAD; b. derivative Germanic verb *sadōn, to satisfy, sate, in Old English sadian, to sate: SATE[1]. 2. Suffixed zero-grade form *sə-ti- in Latin satis, enough, sufficient: SATIATE, SATIETY, SATISFY, (ASSAI[2]), ASSETS. 3. Suffixed zero-grade form *sə-tu-ro- in Latin satur, full (of food), sated: SATIRE, SATURATE. [Pok. sā- 876.]

sab-. Juice, fluid. 1. Germanic *sapam, juice of a plant, in Old English sæp, sap: SAP[1]. 2. Illyrian sabaium, beer, probably akin to the source of Italian zabaglione, zabaione, a frothy dessert: ZABAGLIONE. [In Pok. sap- 880.]

sāg-. To seek out. 1. Suffixed form *sāg-yo- in: a. Germanic *sōkjan in Old English sǣcan, sēcan, to seek: SEEK; b. Germanic ablaut stem *sak- in derivative noun *sakō, "a seeking," accusation, strife, in Old English sacu, lawsuit, case: SAKE[1]; c. Germanic *sakjan, to lay claim to (denominative of *sakō), in Gallo-Latin *sacīre, to take possession of, seize: SEIZE, (SEIZIN); d. Germanic *sakan, to seek, accuse, quarrel, in (i) Old English forsacan, to renounce, refuse (for-, prefix denoting exclusion or rejection, FOR-): FORSAKE (ii) Old Norse -saka, to seek: RANSACK; e. Latin sāgīre, to perceive, "seek to know": PRESAGE. 2. Suffixed form *sāg-ni- in Germanic *sōkniz in Old English sōcn, attack, inquiry, right of local jurisdiction: SOKE. 3. Zero-grade form *səg- in Latin sagāx, of keen perception: SAGACIOUS. 4. Suffixed form *sāg-eyo- in Greek hēgeisthai, to lead (< "to track down"): EXEGESIS, HEGEMONY, HEGUMEN. [Pok. sāg- 876.]

sai-. Suffering. 1. Germanic *sairaz, suffering, sick, ill, in Old English sār, painful: SORE. 2. Derivative Germanic adjective *sairig-, painful, in Old English sārig, suffering mentally, sad: SORRY. [Pok. sāi- 877.]

sak-. To sanctify. 1. Suffixed form *sak-ro- in: a. Latin sacer, holy, sacred, dedicated: SACRED; CONSECRATE, EXECRATE, OBSECRATE; b. compound *sak-ro-dhōt-, "performer of sacred rites" (*-dhōt-, doer; see **dhē-[1]**), in Latin sacerdōs, priest: SACERDOTAL. 2. Nasalized form *sa-n-k- in Latin sancīre, to make sacred, consecrate: SAINT; CORPOSANT, SACROSANCT, SANCTIFY. [Pok. sak- 878.]

sal-[1]. Salt. 1. Extended form *saldo- in: a. Germanic *saltam in Old English sealt, salt: SALT; b. Germanic suffixed ablaut variant form *sult jō in (i) Old High German sulz, sulza, salt marsh: SOUSE (ii) Danish and Norwegian sylt, salt marsh, probably akin to the source of Middle English cylte, fine sand: SILT; c. Latin sallere, to salt: SAUCE. 2. Latin sāl (genitive salis), salt: SAL, SALAD, (SALAMI), SALARY, SALI-, SALINE; SALTCELLAR, SALTPETER. 3. Greek hals, salt, sea: HALO-. [Pok. 1. sal- 878.]

sal-[2]. Dirty gray. Suffixed form *sal-wo- in Germanic *salwaz in Old English salu, salo, dusky, dark: SALLOW[1]. [Pok. 2. sal- 879.]

salama. See **sim**.

salik-. Willow. 1. Variant form *salk- in Germanic suffixed form *salh-jōn- in Old English sealh, willow: SALLOW[2]. 2. Latin salix, willow: SALICIN, SARGASSO. [In Pok. 2. sal- 879.]

sānos. Healthy. Latin sānus, healthy: SANE, (SANITARY); SAINFOIN. [Pok. sāno-s 880.]

sap-. To taste, perceive. Latin sapere, to taste, have taste, be wise: SAGE[1], SAPID, SAPIENT, SAPOR, SAVANT, SAVOR, SAVVY. [Pok. sap- 880.]

saus-. Dry. 1. Extended form *sauso- in Germanic *sausaz in: a. Old English sēar, withered: SEAR[1], SERE[1]; b. Frankish *saur, dry, whence Old French saur, sor, red-brown: SORREL[2], SURMULLET. 2. Suffixed form *saus-t- in Greek austēros, harsh: AUSTERE. [Pok. saus- 880.]

sāwel-. Also **swen-**, **sun-**. The sun. 1. Variant forms *swen-, *sun- in: a. Germanic *sunnōn in Old English sunne, sun: SUN; b. Germanic compound *sunnōn-dagaz, "day of the sun" (translation of Latin diēs sōlis), in Old English sunnandæg, Sunday: SUNDAY; c. Germanic derivative *sunthaz, "sun-side," south, in Old English sūth, south, and sūtherne, southern: SOUTH, SOUTHERN. 2. Latin sōl, sun (from an uncertain root form, possibly *sāwol-, *swol-): SOL[3], SOL[5], SOL, SOLAR, SOLARIUM; GIRASOL, INSOLATE, PARASOL, SOLANINE, TURNSOLE. 3. Latin compound sōlstitium, "a standing of the sun," solstice (-stitium, a standing; see **stā-**): SOLSTICE. 4. Suffixed form *sāwel-yo- in Greek hēlios, sun: HELIACAL, HELIO-, HELIOS, HELIUM; ANTHELION, APHELION, ISOHEL, PARHELION, PERIHELION. [Pok. sāwel- 881.]

sē-[1]. To sow. 1. Suffixed form *sē-yo- in Germanic *sējan in Old English sāwan, to sow: SOW[1]. 2. Suffixed form *sē-ti-, sowing, in Germanic *sēdiz, seed, in: a. Old English sǣd, seed: SEED; b. Middle Dutch saet and Middle Low German sāt, seed: COLZA. 3. Reduplicated form *si-so- in Latin serere, to sow: SEASON, INSERT. 4. Suffixed form *sē-men-, seed, in Latin sēmen, seed: SEMÉ, SEMEN, SEMINARY, SEMINATION; DISSEMINATE. [In Pok. 2. sē(i)- 889.]

sē-[2]. Long, late. 1. Suffixed form *sē-ro- in: a. Latin sērus, late: SEROTINOUS, SOIREE; b. Middle Breton hir, long: MENHIR. 2. Possibly Germanic *sī- in: a. Germanic *sīdō, "long surface or part," in Old English sīde, side: SIDE; b. Germanic *sīth, "later," after, in Old English siththon, siththan, after that, since (< sīth tham; tham, dative singular of the, that, THE): SINCE, (SITH). [In Pok. 2. sē(i)- 891.]

sē-[3]. To sift. Suffixed form *sē-dh- in Greek ēthein, to sift: ETHMOID. [Pok. 1. sē(i)- 889.]

sed-[1]. To sit. 1. Germanic *sitan in: a. Old English sittan, to sit: SIT; b. Old High German sizzen, to sit: SITZ BATH. 2. Suffixed (causative) o-grade form *sod-eyo- in Germanic *satjan, to cause to sit, set, in: a. Old English settan, to place: SET[1]; b. Old High German sezzan, to set: ERSATZ. 3. Suffixed form *sed-lo-, seat, in Germanic *setlaz in Old English setl, seat: SETTLE. 4. O-grade form *sod- in Germanic *sadulaz, seat, saddle, in Old English sadol, saddle: SADDLE. 5. Suffixed lengthened o-grade form *sōd-o- in Germanic *sōtam in Old English sōt, soot (< "that which settles"): SOOT. 6. Suffixed lengthened-grade form *sēd-yo- in Germanic *(ge)sētjam, seat (*ge-, *ga-, collective prefix; see **kom**), in Old Norse sæti, seat: SEAT. 7. Form *sed-ē- in Latin sedēre, to sit: SÉANCE, SEDENTARY, SEDILIA, SEDIMENT, SESSILE, SESSION, SEWER[2], SIEGE; ASSESS, ASSIDUOUS, DISSIDENT, HOSTAGE, INSESSORIAL, OBSESS, PRESIDE, RESIDE, SUBSIDY, SUPERSEDE. 8. Reduplicated form *si-sd- in: a. Latin sīdere, to sit down, settle: POSSESS, SUBSIDE; b. variant form *si-zd- in Greek hizein, to sit down: SYNIZESIS. 9. Lengthened-grade form *sēd- in Latin sēdēs, seat, residence: SEE[2]. 10. Lengthened-grade form *sēd-ā- in Latin sēdāre, to settle, calm down: SEDATE[1]. 11. Suffixed form *sed-lā assimilated into Latin sella, saddle: SEDAN. 12. Suffixed o-grade form *sod-yo- in Latin solium, throne, seat: SOIL[1]. 13. Suffixed form *sed-rā- in Greek hedra, seat, chair: -HEDRON; CATHEDRA, CHAIR, EPHEDRINE, EXEDRA, SANHEDRIN, TETRAHEDRON. 14. Prefixed form *pi-sed-, to sit upon (*pi-, on; see **epi**), in Greek piezein, to press tight: PIEZO-; ISOPIESTIC. 15. Basic form *sed- in: a. Greek edaphos, ground, foundation (with Greek suffix -aphos): EDAPHIC; b. Sanskrit sad-, to sit: UPANISHAD. 16. Extended form *sedā, seat, in Welsh sedd, seat: EISTEDDFOD. See also compound root **nizdo-**. [Pok. sed- 884.]

sed-[2]. To go. Suffixed o-grade form *sod-o- in Greek hodos, way, journey: -ODE[1]; ANODE, CATHODE, EPISODE, EXODUS, HODOGRAPH, METHOD, ODOGRAPH, ODOMETER, PERIOD, STO-

MODEUM, SYNOD. [Pok. *sed-* 887.]

segh-. To hold. **1.** Suffixed form **segh-us* in Germanic **sigiz,* victory (< "a holding or conquest in battle"), in Old High German *sigu, sigo,* victory: SIEGFRIED. **2.** Greek *ekhein,* to hold, possess, be in a certain condition: HECTIC; CACHEXIA, ECHARD, ENTELECHY, EUNUCH, OPHIUCHUS. **3.** O-grade form **sogh-* in Greek *epokhē,* "a holding back," pause, cessation, position in time (*epi-,* on, at, EPI-): EPOCH. **4.** Zero-grade form **sgh-* in: **a.** Greek *skhēma,* "a holding," form, figure: SCHEME; **b.** Greek *skhedios,* "holding oneself close to," near, done extempore: SKETCH; **c.** Greek *skholē,* "a holding back," stop, rest, leisure, employment of leisure in disputation, school: (SCHOLAR), SCHOLASTIC, (SCHOLIUM), SCHOOL[1]. **5.** Perhaps suffixed form **segh-tor,* "holder back," in Greek *Hektōr,* man's name: HECTOR. **6.** Reduplicated form **si-sgh-* in Greek *iskhein,* to keep back: ISCHEMIA. [Pok. *segh-* 888.]

seikw-. To flow. Extended expressive zero-grade form **sikko-* in Latin *siccus,* dry (probably < "flowed out"): SACK[3], SECCO, SICCATIVE; DESICCATE, EXSICCATE. [Pok. *seiku-* 893.]

sek-. To cut. **1.** Germanic **segithō,* sickle, in Old English *sithe, sigthe,* sickle: SCYTHE. **2.** O-grade form **sok-* in Germanic **sagō,* a cutting tool, saw, in Old English *sagu, sage,* saw: SAW[1]. **3.** Suffixed o-grade form **sok-yo-* in Germanic **sagjaz,* "sword," plant with a cutting edge, in Old English *secg,* sedge: SEDGE. **4.** Suffixed o-grade form **sok-so-* in Germanic **sahsam,* knife, sword, traditionally (but quite doubtfully) regarded as the source of West Germanic tribal name **Saxon-,* Saxon (as if "warrior with knives"), in: **a.** Old English *Seax* (plural *Seaxan*), a Saxon: ESSEX, MIDDLESEX, SUSSEX, WESSEX; **b.** Late Latin *Saxō* (plural *Saxonēs*), a Saxon: SAXON. **5.** Extended root **skend-,* to peel off, flay, in Germanic **skinth-* in Old Norse *skinn,* skin: SKIN. **6.** Basic form **sek-* in Latin *secāre,* to cut: SECANT, -SECT, SECTILE, SECTION, SECTOR, SEGMENT; DISSECT, EXSECT, INSECT, INTERSECT, NOTCH, RESECT, RISK, TRANSECT. **7.** Lengthened-grade form **sēk-* in Latin *sēcula,* sickle: SICKLE. **8.** Suffixed variant form **sak-so-* in Latin *saxum,* stone (< "broken-off piece"): SAXATILE, SAXICOLOUS, SAXIFRAGE. See also extended roots **skei-, sker-[1], sker-[4], skeri-, skeru-, skhed-.** [Pok. 2. *sĕk-* 895, *sken-(d)-* 929.]

sēk-. Slack, calm; relax. Greek *hēka,* slowly, a little: ESSONITE. [Pok. 3. *sēk-* 896.]

sekw-[1]. To follow. **1.** Latin *sequī,* to follow: SECT, SEGUIDILLA, SEQUACIOUS, SEQUEL, SEQUENCE, SUE, SUITOR; CONSEQUENT, ENSUE, EXECUTE, OBSEQUIOUS, PERSECUTE, PROSECUTE, PURSUE, SUBSEQUENT. **2.** Latin *sequester,* "follower," mediator, depositary: SEQUESTER, SEQUESTRUM. **3.** Suffixed (participial) form **sekw-ondo-* in Latin *secundus,* following, coming next, second: SECOND[2], (SECONDO), SECUND, (SECUNDINES). **4.** Extended form **sekwos,* following, in Latin *secus,* along, alongside of: EXTRINSIC, INTRINSIC. **5.** Suffixed form **sekw-no-* in Latin *signum,* identifying mark, sign (< "object which one follows"): SCARLET, SEAL[1], SEGNO, SIGN; ASSIGN, CONSIGN, DESIGNATE, INSIGNIA, RESIGN. **6.** Suffixed o-grade form **sokw-yo-* in Latin *socius,* ally, companion (< "follower"): SOCIABLE, SOCIAL, SOCIETY, SOCIO-; ASSOCIATE, CONSOCIATE, DISSOCIATE. [Pok. 1. *seku-* 896.]

sekw-[2]. To perceive, see. **1.** Germanic **sehwan,* to see, in Old English *sēon,* to see: SEE[1]. **2.** Germanic abstract noun **sih-th* in Old English *sihth, gesiht,* vision, spectacle: SIGHT. [Pok. 2. *seku-* 872.]

sekw-[3]. To say, utter. **1.** Suffixed o-grade form **sokw-yo-* in: **a.** Germanic **sag(w)jan* in Old English *secgan,* to say: SAY; **b.** Germanic **sagō,* saying, in *(i)* Old English *sagu,* saying, speech: SAW[2] *(ii)* Old Norse *saga,* saying, narrative: SAGA. **2.** Suffixed zero-grade form **skw-et-lo-,* narration, perhaps in North Germanic **skathla* in Old Norse *skāld,* poet, "narrator": SCOLD, SKALD. [In Pok. 2. *seku-* 897.]

sel-[1]. Human settlement. **1.** O-grade form **sol-* in Germanic **sal-,* room, in Italian *sala,* hall, room: SALON, (SALOON). **2.** Suffixed form **sel-o-* in Latin *solum,* bottom, foundation, hence sole of the foot: SOLE[1], (SOLUM), ENTRESOL. [Pok. 1. *sel-* 898; 3. *(suel-)* 1046.]

sel-[2]. Of good mood; to favor. **1.** Germanic lengthened form **sēl-* in Old English *gesǣlig,* happy (*ge-,* completely; see **kom**): SILLY. **2.** Suffixed lengthened o-grade form **sōl-ā-* in Latin *sōlārī,* to comfort, console: SOLACE, CONSOLE[1]. **3.** Suffixed reduplicated form **se-sla-ro-* in Greek *hilaros* (< **helaros*), gay: HILARITY; EXHILARATE. [Pok. 6. *sel-* 900.]

sel-[3]. To take, grasp. **1.** Germanic causative verb **saljan,* to give up, sell (< "to cause to take"), in Old English *sellan,* to sell, betray: SELL. **2.** Germanic **sal-,* giving, sale, in: **a.** Old Norse *sala,* sale: SALE; **b.** compound *handsal,* giving of the hand (in closing a bargain): HANDSEL. [Pok. 3. *sel-* 899.]

sel-[4]. To jump. **1.** Suffixed variant form **sal-yo-* in: **a.** Latin *salīre,* to leap: SALACIOUS, SALIENT, SALLY, SALTANT, SAUTÉ; ASSAIL, DESULTORY, DISSILIENT, EXULT, INSULT, RESILE, RESULT, SALTIGRADE, SOMERSAULT; **b.** Greek *hallesthai,* to leap, jump: HALTER[2]. **2.** Perhaps Latin *salmō* (borrowed from Gaulish), salmon (< "the leaping fish"): SALMON. [Pok. 4. *sel-* 899.]

selg-. To release. Zero-grade form **slg-* in Germanic **sulk-* in Old English *āseolcan,* to become slack or sluggish (*ā-,* intensive prefix, A-[3]): SULKY[1]. [Pok. *selg-* 900.]

selk-. To pull, draw. **1.** Perhaps Germanic **selhos,* seal (the animal), "that which drags its body along with difficulty," in Old English *seolh,* seal: SEAL[2]. **2.** Extended o-grade form **solko-* in Latin *sulcus,* furrow, groove (< "result of drawing or plowing"): (SULCATE), SULCUS. **3.** Basic form **selk-* in Greek *helkein,* to pull, draw: HULK. [Pok. *selk-* 901.]

selp-. Fat, butter. **1.** Germanic **salb-* in Old English *sealf,* healing ointment: SALVE[1]. **2.** Germanic denominative verb **salbōn* in Middle Dutch *salven,* to anoint, salve: QUACKSALVER. [Pok. *selp-* 901.]

sem-[1]. One. **I.** Full-grade form **sem-.* **1.** Greek *heis* (< **hens,* < **hems*), one: HENDECASYLLABIC, HENDIADYS, HENOTHEISM. **2.** Suffixed form **sem-el-* in Latin *simul,* at the same time: SIMULTANEOUS; ASSEMBLE, ENSEMBLE. **3.** Suffixed form **sem-golo-* in Latin *singulus,* alone, single: SINGLE. **4.** Compound **sem-par-* (**par-,* during, for; see **per[1]**) in Latin *semper,* always, ever (< "once for all"): SEMPRE, SEMPITERNAL. **II.** O-grade form **som-.* **1.** Sanskrit *sam,* together: SAMSARA, SANDHI, SANSKRIT. **2.** Suffixed form **som-o-* in: **a.** Germanic **samaz,* same, in Old Norse *samr,* same: SAME; **b.** Greek *homos,* same: HOMEO-, HOMO-; ANOMALOUS; **c.** Greek *homou,* together: HOMILY. **3.** Lengthened-grade form **sōm-* in Germanic **sōm-* in Old Norse *sœmr,* fitting, agreeable (< "making one," "reconciling"): SEEM, SEEMLY. **4.** Suffixed form **s(o)m-alo-* in Greek *homalos,* like, even, level: HOMOLOGRAPHIC, HOMOLOSINE PROJECTION. **5.** Suffixed lengthened-grade form **sōm-o-* in Russian *samo-,* self: SAMOVAR. **III.** Zero-grade form **sm̥-.* **1.** Greek *ha-, a-,* together: ANACOLUTHON. **2.** Greek compound *haplous,* simple (*-plous, -ploos,* -fold; see **pel-[3]**): HAPLOID. **3.** Suffixed form **sm̥m-o-* in Germanic **sumaz* in: **a.** Old English *sum,* one, a certain one: SOME; **b.** Old English *-sum,* like: -SOME[1]. **4.** Suffixed form **sm̥m-alo-* in Latin *similis* (< **semelis*), of the same kind, like: SIMILAR; ASSIMILATE, RESEMBLE. **5.** Compound **sm̥-kēro-,* of one growing (see **ker-[3]**). **6.** Suffixed form **sm̥-tero-* in Greek *heteros,* one of two, other: HETERO-. **7.** Compound **sm̥-plek-,* "one-fold," simple (**plek-,* -fold; see **plek-**), in Latin *simplex,* simple: SEMPLICE, SIMPLEX, SIMPLICITY. **8.** Compound *sm̥-plo-,* "one-fold," simple (**-plo-,* -fold; see **pel-[3]**), in Latin *simplus,* simple: SIMPLE. **9.** Extended form **sm̥ma* in Greek *hama,* together with, at the same time: HAMADRYAD. **10.** Basic form *sm̥-* in Old Russian *su-,* together, in compound *suvětu,* assembly (*větu,* council; see **weit-**): SOVIET. **IV.** Compound form **sm̥-gwhn̥-,* to press together (see **gwhen-[1]**). [Pok. 2. *sem-* 902.]

sem-[2]. To pour, draw water. Suffixed zero-grade form **sm̥-tlo-* in Greek *antlos,* bilge water, bucket: ANTLIA. [Pok. 1. *sem-* 901.]

sem-[3]. Summer. Suffixed zero-grade form *sm̥m-aro-* in Germanic **sumaraz* in Old English *sumor,* summer: SUMMER[1]. [Pok. 3. *sem-* 905.]

sēmi-. Half. **1.** Germanic **sāmi-* in Old English *sām-,* half: SANDBLIND. **2.** Latin *sēmi-,* half: SEMI-. **3.** Latin *sēmis,* half: SESQUI-, SESTERCE. **4.** Greek *hēmi-,* half: HEMI-. [Pok. *sēmi-* 905.]

sen-[1]. Old. **1.** Latin *senex,* old, an elder: SEIGNIOR, SENATE, SENECTITUDE, SENESCENT, SENILE, SENIOR, SENOPIA, (SIR), SIRE, (SURLY). **2.** Suffixed form **se-no-* in: **a.** Germanic **sinaz* in compound **siniskalkaz,* old servant (Germanic **skal-kaz,* servant, slave; of unknown origin; see also **marko-**), in Medieval Latin *siniscalcus,* seneschal: SENESCHAL; **b.** Irish *sean,* old: SHANTY[1]. [Pok. *sen(o)-* 907.]

sen-[2]. Also **seni-.** Apart, separated. **1.** Suffixed zero-grade form **sn̥-ter-* in: **a.** Germanic **sundrō* in Old English *sundor,* apart: ASUNDER; **b.** Germanic denominative **sundrōn* in Old English *syndrian, sundrian,* to put apart: SUNDER; **c.** Germanic derivative adjective **sundriga-* in Old English *syndrig,* apart, separated: SUNDRY. **2.** Zero-grade form **sn̥ni-* in Latin *sine,* without (< "outside," "out of"): SANS, SINECURE. [Pok. *seni-* 907.]

sendhro-. Crystalline deposit. Germanic **sendra-,* slag, in: **a.** Old English *sinder,* iron slag, dross: CINDER; **b.** Old High German *sintar,* slag: SINTER. [Pok. *sendhro-* 906.]

sengw-. To sink. Germanic **sinkwan* in: **a.** Old English *sincan,* to sink: SINK; **b.** Scandinavian intensive form **sakk-* in Swedish *sacka,* to sink, akin to the Scandinavian source of Middle English *saggen,* to subside: SAG. [Pok. *sengu-* 906.]

sengwh-. To sing, make an incantation. **1.** Germanic **singan* in: **a.** Old English *singan,* to sing: SING; **b.** Old High German *singan,* to sing: MEISTERSINGER, MINNESINGER. **2.** Suffixed o-grade form **songwh-o-,* singing, song, in Germanic **sangwaz* in Old English *sang, song,* song: SONG. [Pok. *senguh-* 906.]

senk-. To burn. Suffixed (causative) o-grade form **sonk-eyo-* in Germanic **sangjan,* to cause to burn, in Old English *sengan,* to singe: SINGE. [Pok. *senk-* 907.]

sent-. To head for, go. **1.** Germanic **sinth-* in Old High German *sin,* way, course: WITHERSHINS. **2.** Suffixed (causative) o-grade form **sont-eyo-* in Germanic **sandjan,* to cause to go, in Old English *sendan,* to send: SEND[1]. **3.** Extended o-grade form **sonto-* in Germanic **sandaz,* that which is sent, in Old English *sand,* message, messenger: GODSEND. **4.** Perhaps suffixed form **sent-yo-* in Latin *sentīre,* to feel (< "to go mentally"): SCENT, SENSE, SENTENCE, SENTIENT, SENTIMENT, SENTINEL; ASSENT, CONSENT, DISSENT, PRESENTIMENT, RESENT. [Pok. *sent-* 908.]

sep-. To venerate (the dead). Suffixed form **sep-el-yo-* in Latin *sepelīre,* to bury: SEPULCHER, (SEPULTURE). [Pok. *sep-* 909.]

septm̥. Seven. **1.** Germanic **sibum* in Old English *seofon,* seven: SEVEN. **2.** Latin *septem,* seven: SEPTEMBER, SEPTENARY, SEPTENNIAL, SEPTET, SEPTI-, SEPTUAGINT, SEPTENTRION, SEPTUPLE. **3.** Greek *hepta,* seven: -HEBDOMAD, HEPTA-, HEPTAD. [Pok. *septm̥* 909.]

ser-[1]. To protect. **1.** Extended form **serw-* in Latin *servāre,* to keep, preserve: CONSERVE, OBSERVE, PRESERVE, RESERVE, (RESERVOIR). **2.** Suffixed lengthened-grade form **sēr-ōw-* perhaps in Greek *hērōs,* "protector," hero: HERO. [Pok. 2. *ser-* 910.]

ser-[2]. To flow. **1.** Suffixed form **ser-o-* in Latin *serum,* whey: SERAC, SERUM. **2.** Basic form **ser-* in Sanskrit *sarati, sasarti,* it flows, it runs: SAMSARA. **3.** Extended roots **sr-edh-, *sr-et-,* to whirl, bubble, in Germanic **stred-* in Old High German *stredan,* to whirl, swirl, whence ablaut formation in Middle High German *strudel,* whirlpool: STRUDEL. [Pok. 1. *ser-* 909; *sr-edh-* 1001.]

ser-[3]. To line up. **1.** Latin *serere,* to arrange, attach, join (in speech), discuss: SERIES, SERTULARIAN; ASSERT, DESERT[3], DISSERTATE, EXERT, INSERT. **2.** Suffixed form **ser-mōn-* in Latin *sermō* (stem *sermōn-*), speech, discourse: SERMON. **3.** Suffixed form **ser-ā-* perhaps in Latin *sera,* a lock, bolt, bar (< "that which joins"): SEAR[2], SERRIED. **4.** Suffixed zero-grade form **sr̥-ti-* in Latin *sors* (stem *sort-*), lot, fortune (probably from the lining up of lots before drawing): SORT, SORCERER; ASSORT, CONSORT, SORTILEGE. [Pok. 4. *ser-* 911.]

serk-. To make whole. Latin *sarcīre,* to mend, repair: SARTORIUS. [Pok. *serk-* 912.]

serp-[1]. Sickle, hook. **1.** Latin *sarpere,* to cut off, prune: SARMENTOSE. **2.** Greek *harpē,* sickle: HARPOON. [Pok. 5. *ser-* 911.]

serp-[2]. To crawl, creep. **1.** Latin *serpere,* to crawl: SERPENT, SERPIGO. **2.** Greek *herpein,* to crawl, creep: HERPES, HERPETOLOGY. [Pok. *serp-* 912.]

[servus. Slave. Latin noun of unknown origin. SERF, SERGEANT, SERVE, SERVICE, SERVILE, SERVITUDE, SIRVENTE; CONCIERGE, (DESERVE).]

seu-[1]. Also **seut-.** To seethe, boil. **1.** Germanic **siuthan* in Old English *sēothan,* to boil: SEETHE, (SODDEN). **2.** Germanic **suth-* in: **a.** Middle Dutch *sudde, sudse,* marsh, swamp: SUDS; **b.** suffixed form **suth-l-* in Middle High German *sudelen,* to soil, do sloppy work: SUTLER. [Pok. 4. *seu-* 914.]

seu-[2]. Also **se-, swe-.** Pronoun of the third person and reflexive (referring back to the subject of the sentence); further appearing in various forms referring to the social group as an entity, "(we our-)selves." **1.** Suffixed extended form **sel-bho-* in Germanic **selbaz,* self, in Old English *self, sylf,* self, same: SELF. **2.** Suffixed form **s(w)e-bh(o)-* in Germanic **sibja-,* "one's own," blood relation, relative, in Old English *sibb,* relative: SIB; GOSSIP. **3.** Suffixed form **se-ge* in Germanic **sik,* self, in Old Norse *sik,* oneself (reflexive pronoun), whence *-sk,* reflexive suffix: BASK, BUSTLE. **4.** Suffixed o-grade form **swo-ino-* in Germanic **swainaz,* "one's own (man)," attendant, servant, in Old Norse *sveinn,* herdsman, boy: SWAIN. **5.** Extended form **suwo-* in Latin *suī* (genitive), of oneself: SUICIDE. **6.** Extended lengthened-grade form **sēd* in: **a.** Latin *sēd, sē,* self, oneself (accusative): FELO DE SE, PER SE; **b.** Latin *sēd, sē,* without, apart (< "on one's own"): SECEDE, SECERN, SECLUDE, SECRET, SECURE, SEDITION, SEDUCE, SEDULOUS, SEGREGATE, SELECT, SEPARATE, SURE; **c.** Latin compound *sōbrius,* not drunk (*ēbrius,* drunk; see **egw-**): SOBER. **7.** Possibly suffixed lengthened o-grade form **sō-lo-* in Latin *sōlus,* by oneself, alone: SOLE[2], SOLITARY, SOLITUDE, SOLO; DESOLATE, SOLIFIDIAN, SOLILOQUY, SOLIPSISM, SULLEN. **8.** Extended root **swē̆dh-,* "that which is one's own," peculiarity, custom, in: **a.** Latin *sodālis,* companion (< "one's own," "relative"): SODALITY; **b.** suffixed form **swēdh-sko-* in Latin *suēscere,* to get accustomed: CONSUETUDE, CUSTOM, DESUETUDE, MANSUETUDE, MASTIFF; **c.** Greek *ēthos,* custom, disposition, trait: ETHIC, ETHOS; CACOETHES; **d.** suffixed form **swedh-no-* in Greek *ethnos,* band of people living together, nation, people (< "people of one's own kind"): ETHNIC, ETHNO-. **9.** Suffixed form **swe-t-aro-* in Greek *hetaros,* later *hetairos,* companion: HETAERA. **10.** O-grade form **swo-* in Sanskrit *sva,* one's own, whence *svāmin,* "one's own master," owner, prince: SWAMI. **11.** Variant form **swei-* in Old Irish *fēin,* selves: SINN FEIN. **12.** Possibly from this root (but via an uncertain pre-form) is Germanic **sunar-,* herd of swine, in Old French *sun(d)re,* herd of wild boars: SOUNDER[2]. [Pok. *se-* 882.]

seu-[3]. To give birth. Derivative noun **sunu-,* son, in Germanic **sunuz* in Old English *sunu,* son: SON. [Pok. 2. *seu-* 913.]

seu-[4]. To take liquid. **I.** Zero-grade form **su-* probably in Greek *huetos,* rain: HYETO-, ISOHYET. **II.** Extended zero-grade form **sūb-*. **1.** Germanic **sūp-* in: **a.** Old English *sūpan, sūpian,* to drink, sip: SUP[1]; **b.** Old French *soup(e),* soup: SOUP, SUP[2]. **2.** Germanic **sup-* in Old English *sopp,* bread dipped in liquid: SOP. **III.** Extended lengthened-grade form **sūg-*. **1.** Germanic **sūk-* in Old English *sūcan,* to suck: SUCK. **2.** Germanic shortened form **suk-* in Old English *socian,* to steep: SOAK. **3.** Latin *sūgere,* to suck: SUCTION, (SUCTORIAL). **4.** Variant form **sūk-* in Latin *sūcus, succus,* juice: SUCCULENT. [Pok. 1. *seu-* 912.]

[**sib-.** Also **sip-.** To pour out, sieve, drip, trickle. Germanic root. **1.** Basic form **sib-* in: **a.** Old English *sife,* a filter, sieve: SIEVE; **b.** Old English *siftan,* to sieve, drain: SIFT. **2.** Variant form **sip-* in: **a.** Old English *sipian, sypian,* to drip, seep: SEEP; **b.** Low German *sippen,* to sip, probably akin to the source of Middle English *sippen,* to sip: SIP. **3.** Variant form **saip-,* "dripping thing," resin, in: **a.** Old English *sāpe,* soap (originally a reddish hair dye used by Germanic warriors to give a frightening appearance): SOAP; **b.** Latin *sāpō,* soap: SAPOR, SAPONACEOUS, SAPONATED, SAPONIFY, SAPONIN, SAPONITE. [Pok. *seip-* 894.]]

silo-. Also **sil-.** Silent. Suffixed (stative) form **sil-ē-* in Latin *silēre,* to be silent: SILENT. [In Pok. 2. *sē(i)-* 889.]

skabh-. To prop up, support. Suffixed form **skabh-no-* in Latin *scamnum,* a bench: SHAMBLES. [Pok. *skabh-* 916.]

skai-. Also **kai-.** Bright, shining. **1.** Extended form **kaid-* in Germanic **haiduz,* "bright appearance," manner, quality, in: **a.** Old English *-hād,* quality, condition: -HOOD; **b.** Old High German *-heit,* quality, condition: ADELAIDE[1]. **2.** Suffixed form **ki-t-ro-* in Sanskrit *citra,* variegated, many-colored: CHEETAH, CHINTZ, CHIT[1], CHITAL. [Pok. *(s)kāi-* 916.]

skamb-. To curve, bend. Extended variant form **kambo-,* crooked, in Celtic **camb-,* an exchange (< "a turning"), in Late Latin denominative verb *cambiāre,* to exchange: CAMBIST, CAMBIUM, CHANGE. [Pok. *(s)kamb-* 918.]

skand-. Also **skend-.** To leap, climb. **1.** Latin *scandere,* to climb: SCAN, SCANDENT, SCANSION, SCANSORIAL, SCANTLING; ASCEND, CONDESCEND, DESCEND, TRANSCEND. **2.** Suffixed form **skand-alo-* in Greek *skandalon,* a snare, trap, stumbling block: SCANDAL. **3.** Suffixed form **skand-slā-* in Latin *scālae,* steps, ladder: ECHELON, ESCALADE, SCALE[2].

skei-. To cut, split. Extended root of **sek-.** **1.** Latin *scīre,* to know (< "to separate one thing from another," "discern"): SCIENCE, SCILICET, SCIOLISM, SCIRE FACIAS; ADSCITITIOUS, CONSCIENCE, CONSCIOUS, NESCIENT, NICE, OMNISCIENT, PLEBISCITE, PRESCIENT. **2.** Germanic suffixed form **ski-nōn-* in: **a.** Old English *scinu,* shin, shinbone (< "piece cut off"): SHIN[1]; **b.** Old French *eschine,* backbone, piece of meat with part of the backbone: CHINE[1]. **3.** Suffixed zero-grade form **skiy-enā* in Old Irish *scīan,* knife: SKEAN. **4.** Extended root **skeid-* in: **a.** Germanic **skītan,* to separate, defecate, in *(i)* Old English **scītan,* to defecate: SHIT *(ii)* Old Norse *skīta,* to defecate: SKATE[3]; **b.** suffixed zero-grade form **sk(h)id-yo-* in Greek *skhizein,* to split: SCHEDULE, SCHISM, SCHIST, SCHIZO-; **c.** nasalized zero-grade form **ski-n-d-* in Latin *scindere,* to split: SCISSION; EXSCIND, PRESCIND, RESCIND. **5.** Extended root **skeit-* in: **a.** Germanic **skaith-* in *(i)* Old English *scēadan,* to separate: SHED[1] *(ii)* perhaps Old English *scēath,* sheath (< "split stick"): SHEATH; **b.** Germanic **skīth-* in Old Norse *skīdh,* log, stick, snowshoe: SKI; **c.** o-grade form **skoit-* in Latin *scūtum,* shield (< "board"): ÉCU, ESCUDO, ESCUTCHEON, ESQUIRE, SCUDO, SCUTUM, SQUIRE. **6.** Extended root **skeip-* in Germanic **skif-* in: **a.** Old English **scīfe,* pulley (< "piece of wood with grooves"): SHEAVE[2]; **b.** Middle Dutch and Middle Low German *schīve,* a slice: SHIVE[1]; **c.** Old Norse *skīfa,* to slice, split: SKIVE; **d.** Middle Low German *schever,* splinter, akin to the Low German source of Middle English *scivre,* splinter: SHIVER[2]. [Pok. *skei-* 919.]

skel-[1]. To cut. **1.** Germanic **skaljō,* piece cut off, shell, scale, in: **a.** Old English *scell, sciel,* shell: SHELL; **b.** Italian *scaglia,* chip: SCAGLIOLA. **2.** Germanic **skalō* in: **a.** Old English *sc(e)alu,* husk, shell: SHALE; **b.** Old French *escale,* husk, shell: CALOTTE, CAUL, SCALE[1]. **3.** Germanic **skal-* in: **a.** Old Norse *skalli,* bald head (< "closely shaved skull"): SCALL; **b.** Old Norse *skalpr,* sheath, shell, akin to the source of Middle English *scalp,* scalp: SCALP. **4.** Germanic **skēlō* in Old Norse *skāl,* bowl, drinking vessel (made from a shell): SCALE[3], SKOAL. **5.** Germanic **skelduz* in Old English *scield,* shield (< "board"): SHIELD. **6.** Germanic **skeli-* in: **a.** Old Norse *skil,* reason, discernment, knowledge (< "incisiveness"): SKILL; **b.** Middle Dutch *schillen,* to diversify, with past participle *schillede,* separated, variegated, akin to the Low German source of Middle English *scheld,* variegated: SHELDRAKE. **7.** Germanic *skulō,* a division, in Middle Dutch *schōle,* troop: SCHOOL[2], (SHOAL[2]). **8.** Extended root **skelp-* in: **a.** Germanic **skelf-* in Middle Low German *schelf,* shelf (< "split piece of wood"): SHELF; **b.** possibly Germanic **halbaz* (< variant root **kelp-*), divided, in Old English *healf,* half: HALF; **c.** perhaps variant **skalp-* in Latin *scalpere,* to cut, scrape, with derivative *sculpere* (originally as the combining form of *scalpere*), to carve: SCALPEL, SCULPTURE. **9.** Suffixed variant form **kel-tro-* in Latin *culter,* knife: COLTER, CUTLASS, CULTRATE. [Pok. 1. *(s)kel-* 923.]

skel-[2]. To be under an obligation. O-grade form **skol-* in Germanic **skal-,* I owe, hence I ought, in Old English *sceal* (used with the first and third person singular pronouns), shall: SHALL. [Pok. 2. *(s)kel-* 927.]

skel-[3]. Crooked. With derivatives referring to a bent or curved part of the body, such as a leg, heel, knee, or hip. **1.** Suffixed form **skel-ko-* in Germanic **skelha-* in Old High German *scilihen,* to wink, blink (< "to be cross-eyed"): SCHILLER. **2.** Suffixed form **skel-os-* in Greek *skelos,* leg: ISOSCELES, TRISKELION. **3.** Suffixed o-grade form **skol-yo-* in Greek *skolios,* crooked: SCOLIOSIS. **4.** Lengthened o-grade form **skōl-* in Greek *skōlēx,* earthworm, grub (< "that which twists and turns"): SCOLEX. **5.** Zero-grade form **skl̥-* in Greek *skalēnos,* "limping," uneven: SCALENE. **6.** Suffixed lengthened-grade variant form **kōl-o-* in Greek *kōlon,* limb, member: COLON[1]. **7.** Attributed (quite doubtfully) by some to this root is Greek *kulindein,* to roll: CALENDER, CYLINDER. [Pok. 4. *skel-* 928.]

skel-[4]. To parch, wither. **1.** Greek *skellesthai,* to dry, whence *skeletos* (< suffixed extended form **skelə-to-*), dried up (body), mummy: SKELETON. **2.** Suffixed extended form **sklē-ro-* in Greek *sklēros,* hard: SCLERA, SCLERO-, SCLEROMA, SCLEROSIS, (SCLEROTIC), (SCLEROTIUM), SCLEROUS. [Pok. 3. *(s)kel-* 927.]

skeng-. Crooked. Germanic **skankō,* "that which bends," leg, in Old English *sc(e)anca,* shinbone: SHANK. [Pok. *(s)keng-* 930.]

skep-. Base of words with various technical meanings such as "to cut," "to scrape," "to hack." **1.** Germanic **skap-* in: **a.** Old English *gesceap* (*ge-,* collective prefix; see **kom**), form, creation (< "cutting"): SHAPE; **b.** Old English *-scipe,* state, condition (collective suffix): -SHIP; **c.** Middle Dutch *-scap,* condition (collective suffix): LANDSCAPE. **2.** Germanic ablaut variant **skōpō-,* "thing cut out," container, in Middle Dutch and Middle Low German *schōpe,* bucket for bailing water: SCOOP. **3.** Germanic **skaftaz* in: **a.** Old English *sceaft,* rod of a spear: SHAFT[1]; **b.** Middle Low German *schacht,* well-like excavation of a mine (original sense "something cut out"): SHAFT[2]. **4.** Germanic expressive form **skabb-* in: **a.** Old English *sceabb,* a scab, scratch: SHABBY; **b.** Old Norse *skabb,* a scab: SCAB. **5.** Germanic **skab-* in: **a.** Old English *sceafan,* to scrape, pare away: SHAVE; **b.** Old High German *skaban,* to scrape: SAPSAGO. **6.** Variant form **kop-* in Germanic **hapjō,* a cutting tool, ax, sickle, in: **a.** Old High German *hāppa, happa,* sickle, akin to the Germanic source of Old Provençal *apcha,* small ax: PIOLET; **b.** Medieval Latin *hapia,* ax, and Old French *hache,* small ax: (HASH[1]), HATCHET, NUTHATCH, QUEBRACHO. **7.** Variant form **skabh-* in: **a.** Latin *scabere,* to scrape: SCABIES; **b.** suffixed form **skabh-ro-* in Latin *scaber,* rough (< "scratched"): SCABROUS; **c.** Greek *skaphē,* boat (< "thing cut out"): SCAPHOID; BATHYSCAPH. **8.** Variant form **skap-* in Latin *scapula,* shoulder blade ("a chip"): SCAPULA. **9.** Variant form **kap-* in: **a.** Latin *capō,* castrated cock (whence Vulgar Latin **cappāre,* to castrate, cut, possibly borrowed via Germanic into Middle Low German *kappen,* to chop): CAPON, CHAP[1]; **b.** Late Latin *capulāre,* to cut: SCABBLE. **10.** Variant form **kop-* in: **a.** suffixed form **kop-yo-* in Greek *koptein,* to strike, cut: COMMA; APOCOPE, SARCOPTIC MANGE, SYNCOPE; **b.** Russian *kopat',* to hack, with derivative *kop'e,* lance: KOPECK. **11.** Possibly zero-grade form **skp-* in Greek *skuphos,* a cup: SCYPHOZOAN. [Pok. 2. *(s)kep-* 931.]

sker-[1]. Also **ker-.** To cut. Extended root of **sek-.** **I.** Basic forms **sker-, *ker-.* **1.** Germanic **skeran* in Old English *scieran, sceran,* to cut: SHEAR. **2.** Germanic **skar-* in: **a.** Old English *scēar,* plowshare: SHARE[2]; **b.** Old English *scearu, scaru,* portion, division (but recorded only in the senses of "fork of the body," "tonsure"): SHARE[1]. **3.** Germanic **skēr-* in: **a.** Old English *scēara,* scissors: SHEARS; **b.** Old High German *scār,* shears: SCABBARD. **4.** Germanic **skur-* in Old Norse *skor,* notch, tally, twenty: SCORE. **5.** Germanic suffixed form **skar-ja-* in Old Norse *sker,* low reef (< "sharp rock"): SCAR[2]. **6.** Germanic **skarduz* in Old English *sceard,* a cut, notch: SHARD. **7.** Extended form **skerd-* in Germanic **skurtaz* in: **a.** Old English *scort, sceort,* "cut," short: SHORT; **b.** Old English *scyrte,* undergarment (< "cut piece"): SHIRT; **c.** Old Norse *skyrta,* shirt: SKIRT. **8.** Germanic extended form **skerm-* in: **a.** Old High German *skirmen,* to protect, akin to the source of Old French *eskermir,* to fight with a sword, fence: SKIRMISH; **b.** Middle Dutch *scherm,* shield: SCREEN. **9.** Variant form **kar-* in Latin *carō* (stem *carn-*), flesh: CARNAGE, CARNAL, CARNASSIAL, CARNATION, CARNIVAL, CARRION, CARUNCLE, CHARNEL, CRONE; CARNIVOROUS, INCARNATE. **10.** Suffixed o-grade form **kor-yo-* in Latin *corium,* leather (originally "piece of flesh"): CORIACEOUS, CORIUM, CUIRASS, CURRIER, EXCORIATE. **11.** Suffixed zero-grade form **kr̥-to-* in Latin *curtus,* short: CURT, CURTAL, KIRTLE. **12.** Suffixed form **ker-yo-* in Greek *keirein,* to cut off, shear: CORM. **13.** Suffixed o-grade form **kor-i-* in Greek *koris,* bedbug (< "cutter"): COREOPSIS. **14.** Russian *skrest',* to scratch: SCORBUTIC. **II.** Extended roots **skert-, *kert-.* **1.** Germanic nasalized form **skrunth-* in Old High German *scrunta,* a split: BERGSCHRUND. **2.** Zero-grade form **kr̥t-* or o-grade form **kort-* in Latin *cortex,* bark (< "that which can be cut off"): CORTEX, DECORTICATE. **3.** Suffixed form **kert-snā-* in Latin *cēna,* meal (< "portion of food"): CENACLE. **III.** Extended root **skerp-* in Germanic **skerf-* in Old English *sceorf,* "scab," scurf: SCURF. **IV.** Extended root **skerb(h)-, skreb(h)-.* **1.** Germanic **skarpaz,* cutting, sharp, in: **a.** Old English *scearp,* sharp: SHARP; **b.** Gothic **skarpō,* pointed object: SCARP. **2.** Germanic **skrap-* in: **a.** Old Norse *skrap,* "pieces," remains: SCRAP[1]; **b.** Old Norse *skrapa,* to scratch: SCRAPE. **3.** Germanic **skrab-* in: **a.** Middle Dutch *schrabben,* to scrape: SCRABBLE; **b.** Middle Dutch and

Middle Low German schrobben, to scrape: SCRUB[1]. 4. Germanic *skrub- in Old English scrybb, shrub (< "rough plant"): SHRUB[1]. 5. Latin scrobis, trench, ditch: SCROBICULATE, SCREW. 6. Latin scrōfa, a sow (< "rooter, digger"): SCROFULA. [Pok. 4. sker-, Section I. 938.]

sker-[2]. To leap, jump about. Perhaps same root as sker-[3]. 1. Extended form *skerd- in Germanic *skert- in Middle High German scherzen, to leap with joy: SCHERZO. 2. Extended variant form *(s)kred- in Germanic *hrat- in Old Norse hrata, to fall, rush: RATE[2]. 3. O-grade variant form *kor- in Latin coruscāre, to vibrate, glisten, glitter: CORUSCATE. [Pok. 2. (s)ker- 933.]

sker-[3]. Also ker-. To turn, bend. Presumed base of a number of distantly related derivatives. 1. Extended form *(s)kreg- in nasalized form *(s)kre-n-g- in: a. Germanic *skrink- in Old English scrincan, to wither, shrivel up: SHRINK; b. variant *kre-n-g- in Germanic *hrunk- in (i) Old Norse hrukka, a crease, fold: RUCK[2] (ii) Frankish *hrunkjan, to wrinkle: FLOUNCE[1]. 2. Extended form *(s)kregh- in nasalized form *skre-n-gh- in Germanic *hringaz, something curved, circle, in: a. Old English hring, a ring: RING[1]; b. Frankish *hring, circle, ring, row: RANCH, RANGE, (RANK[1]), RINK; ARRANGE, DERANGE; c. Middle Dutch rinc (combining form ring-), a ring: RIBBON, RINGHALS. 3. Extended form *kreuk- in Germanic *hrugjaz in: a. Old English hrycg, spine, ridge: RIDGE; b. Old High German hrukki, back: RUCKSACK. 4. Suffixed variant form *kur-wo- in Latin curvus, bent, curved: CURB, CURVATURE, CURVE, CURVET. 5. Suffixed extended form *kris-ni- in Latin crīnis (< *crisnis), hair: CRINITE, CRINOLINE. 6. Suffixed extended form *kris-tā- in Latin crista, tuft, crest: CREST, CRISTATE. 7. Suffixed extended form *krip-so- in Latin crispus (metathesized from *cripsus), curly: CREPE, CRISP, (CRISPATE). 8. Extended expressive form *kriss- in Latin crīsāre, (of women) to wiggle the hips during copulation: CRISSUM. 9. Perhaps reduplicated form *ki-kr-o- metathesized into Greek krikos, a ring (whence Latin circus, ring, circle): CIRCA, CIRCLE, CIRCUM-, CRICOID, SEARCH. 10. Suffixed o-grade form *kor-ōno- in Greek korōnos, curved: CORNICE, CORONA, CROWN. 11. Suffixed variant form *kur-to- in Greek kurtos, bent: KURTOSIS. [Pok. 3. (s)ker- 935.]

sker-[4]. Excrement, dung. Extended form of sek-, "to cut, separate," hence "to void excrement." 1. Lengthened o-grade form *skōr- in Greek skōr (genitive skatos < *sk-n̥t-), dung: SCATO-, SCORIA, SKATOLE. 2. Extended form *skert- in taboo metathesis *sterk- in: a. Latin stercus, dung: STERCORACEOUS; b. variant forms *(s)terg-, *(s)treg- in Germanic *threkka- in Middle High German drēc, dung: DRECK. [Pok. sker-d- 947; 8. (s)ter- 1031.]

skerbh-. Also skerb-. To turn, bend. Extended root of sker-[3]. 1. Variant form *skreb- in Germanic *skrip- in Old Norse skorpna, to shrink, be shriveled: SCORCH. 2. Nasalized variant form *(s)kre-m-b- in: a. Germanic *hrimp-, *hrump- in (i) Old English hrympel, wrinkle, fold: RIMPLE (ii) Middle Dutch rompelen, to wrinkle: RUMPLE (iii) Frankish *rampōn, to contract oneself convulsively, clamber: RAMP[2]; b. Germanic *skrimp- in (i) Middle Low German schrempen, to shrink, wrinkle, perhaps akin to the Low German source of Middle English shrimp, pygmy, shrimp: SHRIMP (ii) Swedish skrympa, to shrink, perhaps akin to the Scandinavian source of SCRIMP. 3. Variant form *kramb- in Greek krambē, cabbage (having wrinkled, shrunken leaves): CRAMBO. 4. Perhaps Celtic *krumbo- in Welsh crwn, crooked, arched: CROMLECH. [Pok. (s)kerb(h)- 948.]

skeri-. To cut, separate, sift. Extended root of sker-[1]. 1. Extended form *skribh- in: a. perhaps Germanic *skrīf- in Old Norse *skrīfla, to wrinkle: SHRIVEL; b. Latin scrībere, to scratch, incise, write: SCRIBBLE, SCRIBE, SCRIPT, SCRIPTORIUM, SCRIPTURE, SERIF, SHRIVE; ASCRIBE, CIRCUMSCRIBE, CONSCRIPT, DESCRIBE, INSCRIBE, MANUSCRIPT, POSTSCRIPT, PRESCRIBE, PROSCRIBE, RESCRIPT, SUBSCRIBE, SUPERSCRIBE, TRANSCRIBE; c. Greek skariphos, scratching, sketch, pencil: SCARIFY. 2. Variant form *krei- in: a. suffixed form *krei-tro- in Germanic *hridra-, a sieve, in Old English hridder, sieve: RIDDLE[1]; b. suffixed form *krei-dhro- in Latin crībrum, a sieve: CRIBRIFORM, GARBLE; c. suffixed form *krei-men- in (i) Latin crīmen, judgment, crime: CRIME, RECRIMINATE (ii) Latin discrīmen, distinction (dis-, apart, DIS-): DISCRIMINATE; d. suffixed zero-grade form *kri-no- (participial form *kri-to-) in Latin cernere (past participle certus), to sift, separate, decide: CERTAIN; CONCERN, DECREE, DISCERN, EXCREMENT, INCERTITUDE, RECREMENT, SECERN, SECRET; e. suffixed zero-grade form *kri-n-yo- in Greek krinein, to separate, decide, judge: CRISIS, CRITIC, CRITERION; APOCRINE, DIACRITICAL, ECCRINE, ENDOCRINE, EPICRISIS[1], EXOCRINE, HEMATOCRIT, HYPOCRISY; f. Russian kraĭ, edge, brink: UKRAINIAN. [Pok. 4. sker-, Section II. 945.]

skeru-. To cut; cutting tool. Extended root of sker-[1]. 1. Variant form *skreu- in: a. Germanic *skraw- in Old English scrēawa, shrew (having a pointed snout): SHREW, (SHREWD); b. Germanic *skraud- in Old English scrēade, piece, fragment: SCREED, SHRED; c. Germanic *skrūd- in (i) Old English scrūd, garment (< "piece of cloth"): SHROUD (ii) Frankish *scrōda, *skrōda, piece, shred: SCROLL, ESCROW (iii) Middle Dutch schrode, a slice, shred: SCROD. 2. Extended variant form *skreut- in Latin scrūta, trash, frippery: SCRUTINY. 3. Extended variant form *skraut- in Latin scrōtum, scrotum (probably identified with scrautum, leather quiver for arrows): SCROTUM. [Pok. 4. (s)ker-, Section III. 947.]

skēth-. To injure. Zero-grade form *skəth- in Germanic *skathōn in Old Norse skadha, to harm: SCATHE. [Pok. skēth- 950.]

skeu-. Also keu-, (s)kū-. To cover. 1. Germanic *skūma, foam, scum (< "that which covers the water"), in: a. Old High German scūm, scum: SKIM, MEERSCHAUM; b. Middle Dutch schūm, scum: SCUM. 2. Suffixed form *skeu-lo- in Germanic *skeulam perhaps in Old Norse skjōla, vessel, basket (< "place for safekeeping"), probably akin to the Scandinavian source of Middle English skele, pail: SKILLET. 3. Extended zero-grade form *kus- in: a. Germanic *husōn- in Old English hosa, covering for the leg: HOSE[2]; b. suffixed form *kus-dho- (or suffixed extended form *kudh-to-) in Germanic *huzdam in Old English hord, stock, store, treasure (< "thing hidden away"): HOARD; c. Russian kishka, gut (< "sheath"): KISHKE. 4. Suffixed zero-grade form *kū-ti- in: a. Germanic *hūdiz in Old English hȳd, skin, hide: HIDE[2]; b. Latin cutis, skin: CUTANEOUS, CUTICLE, CUTIS, CUTIN. 5. Extended form *keud- in: a. Germanic *hūdjan in Old English hȳdan, to hide, cover up: HIDE[1]; b. Germanic *hudjōn in Old High German hutt(e)a, hut: HUT. 6. Perhaps suffixed zero-grade form *kū-lo- in Latin cūlus, the rump, backside: CULET, CULOTTES; BASCULE, RECOIL. 7. Suffixed extended zero-grade form *kut-no- in Latin cunnus, vulva (< "sheath"): CUNNILINGUS. 8. Suffixed zero-grade form *skū-ro- in Latin obscūrus, "covered," dark (ob-, away from; OB-): OBSCURE; CHIAROSCURO. 9. Suffixed zero-grade form *ku-to- in Greek kutos, a hollow, vessel: -CYTE, CYTO-. [Pok. 2. (s)keu- 951.]

skēu-. To cut. Extended form of sek-. Possibly extended form *skeur- in Germanic *skurjan, skurgan, to strike, shove, in Old High German scurigen, to push, poke: SHIRK. [Pok. skēu-(t-) 954.]

skeubh-. To shove. 1. Germanic *skiuban in Old English scūfan, to shove: SHOVE. 2. Germanic suffixed form *skub-ilōn- in: a. Old English scofl, a shovel: SHOVEL; b. Middle Dutch schoffel, schuffel, a shovel, hoe: SCUFFLE[2]. 3. Germanic *skub-, skuf- in: a. Old Norse skūfa, to push: SCUFF, SCUFFLE[1]; b. Danish skof, jest, teasing, probably akin to the Scandinavian source of Middle English scof, mocking: SCOFF; c. possibly (but quite doubtfully) Old English scop, poet (< "jester"): SCOP; d. Low German shüffeln, to walk clumsily, shuffle cards, probably akin to the source of SHUFFLE. [Pok. skeub- 955.]

skeud-. To shoot, chase, throw. 1. Germanic *skiutan, to shoot, in: a. Old English scēotan, to shoot: SHOOT; b. Old Norse skjōta, to shoot: SCOOT, SKEET, SKITTER, SKITTISH. 2. Germanic *skutaz, shooting, shot, in: a. Old English sceot, scot, shooting, a shot: SHOT[1]; b. Old High German scuz, shooting, a shot: SCHUSS; c. Old Norse skoti, shooter, akin to the possible source of SCOTER; d. Old Norse skot and Frankish skot, contribution, tax (< "money thrown down"): SCOT AND LOT; e. Middle Dutch schot, crossbar, wooden partition: WAINSCOT; f. West Flemish schote, young pig (? < "young shoot"): SHOAT. 3. Germanic *skuttjan probably in Old English scyttan, to shut (by pushing a crossbar): SHUT. 4. Germanic *skutilaz in Old English scytel, a dart, missile: SHUTTLE. 5. Germanic *skautjōn in: a. Old English scēata, corner of a sail (? < "young shoot"): SHEET[2]; b. Old English scēte, piece of cloth: SHEET[1]. 6. Germanic *skut- in Old Norse skūta, mockery (< "shooting of words"), akin to the Scandinavian source of SCOUT[2]. 7. Germanic *skaut- in Gothic skaut, seam, hem: SCUTTLE[1]. [Pok. 2. (s)keud- 956.]

skeup-. Cluster, tuft, hair of the head. 1. Germanic *skauf- in Old English scēaf, bundle, sheaf: SHEAF. 2. Germanic *skuft- in Old Norse skoft, hair of the head: SCRUFF. 3. Germanic *hupp- in Middle Dutch hoppe, the hop plant (having tuftlike inflorescence): HOP[2]. [Pok. (s)keup- 956.]

skhai-. Also k(h)ai-. To strike. 1. Latin caedere, to cut, strike: CAESARIAN SECTION, CAESURA, CEMENT, CESTUS[2], CHISEL, -CIDE, SCISSORS; ABSCISE, CIRCUMCISE, CONCISE, DECIDE, EXCISE[2], INCISE, PRECISE, RECISION. 2. Latin caelum (? < *caedlom), sculptor's chisel: CAELUM, SALLET. [Pok. (s)k(h)ai- 917.]

skhed-. Also sked-. To split, scatter. Extended root of sek-. 1. O-grade form *skod- in Germanic *skat- in Old English *sc(e)aterian, to scatter: SHATTER. 2. Variant nasalized form *ska-n-d- in Latin scandula, a shingle for roofing (< "split piece"): SHINGLE[1]. [Pok. (s)k(h)ed- 918.]

ski-. To gleam. 1. Germanic *skīnan, to gleam, shine, in: a. Old English scīnan, to shine: SHINE; b. Old High German scīnan, to shine: GEGENSCHEIN. 2. Germanic *skim- in Old English scimerian, scymrian, to shine brightly: SHIMMER. 3. Germanic *skīraz in Old English scīr, bright, shining: SHEER[2]. 4. Possibly suffixed form *ski-nto-, shining, in Latin scintilla, a spark: SCINTILLA, SCINTILLATE, STENCIL, TINSEL. 5. Suffixed form *skiy-ā in Greek skia, shadow: SKIAGRAM, SKIASCOPE, SQUIRREL. [Pok. skai- 917.]

[skipam. Ship. Germanic noun of obscure origin. 1. Old English scip, ship: SHIP. 2. Middle Dutch schip, ship: SCHIPPERKE, SKIPPER[1]. 3. Lombardic *skif, ship: SKIFF. 4. Old French eschiper, esquiper, to put to sea: EQUIP. [In Pok. skēi- 919.]]

skot-. Dark, shade 1. Germanic *skadwaz in Old English sceadu, shade: SHADE, (SHADOW). 2. Suffixed form *skot-o- in Greek skotos, darkness: SCOTOMA. [Pok. skot- 957.]

skut-. To shake. Germanic *skūd- in Middle Low German schōderen, to tremble, be afraid: SHUDDER. [Pok. (s)kūt- 957.]

skwalo-. Also kwal-. Big fish. 1. Variant form *kwal- in Germanic *hwaliz, whale, in: a. Old English hwæl, whale: WHALE; b. Old Norse hvalr, whale: NARWAL, RORQUAL; c. Old Norse compound hrosshvalr, "horse whale," walrus (hross, horse, from West Germanic *hrussa-, from Germanic *hursa-, *horsa-, HORSE), probably becoming Danish hvalros, walrus, akin to the Scandinavian source of Dutch walrus, walrus: WALRUS. 2. Latin squalus, a sea fish: SQUALENE. [Pok. (s)kualo- 958.]

slagw-. Also lagw-. To seize. 1. Suffixed form *(s)lagw-yō- in Germanic *lakkjan in Old English læccan, to seize, grasp: LATCH. 2. Variant form *lagw- becoming *lab-, with nasalized form *la-m-b- in Greek lambanein (past participle lēptos), to take, seize: LEMMA[1], -LEPSY; ANALEPTIC, ASTROLABE, CATALEPSY, EPILEPSY, NYMPHOLEPT, ORGANOLEPTIC, PROLEPSIS, SYLLABLE, SYLLEPSIS. [Pok. (s)lagu- 958.]

slak-. To strike. 1. Germanic *slahan in Old English slēan, to strike, kill: SLAY. 2. Germanic *slagja- in Old English slecg, hammer: SLEDGEHAMMER. 3. Germanic *slaht- in Old Norse slātr, butchery, "striking": SLAUGHTER. 4. Germanic *slag- in: a. Old High German slag, a blow: SCHLOCK; b. Middle Dutch schlag, a blow: ONSLAUGHT; c. probably Middle Low German slagge, metal dross (< "that which falls off in the process of striking"): SLAG; d. probably Middle Dutch slacke, dross, fragment: SLACK[2]. 5. Germanic lengthened variant form *slōg- in Old Norse slœgr, clever, cunning (< "able to strike"): SLEIGHT, SLY. [Pok. slak- 959.]

sleg-. To be slack, be languid. Zero-grade form *(s)ləg-, becoming *(s)lag-. 1. Germanic *slak- in Old English slæc, "loose," indolent, careless: SLACK[1]. 2. Suffixed form *lag-so- in Latin laxus, loose, slack: LAX, LUSH[1]; DELAY, RELAX, RELAY. 3. Suffixed nasalized form *la-n-g-u- in Latin languēre, to be languid: LANGUISH. 4. Compound *lag-ous-, "with drooping ears" (*ous-, ear; see ous-), in Greek lagōs, lagos, hare: LAGOMORPH. 5. Suffixed form *lag-no- in Greek lagnos, lustful, lascivious (< "loose in morals"): ALGOLAGNIA. 6. Variant form *lēg- in Greek lēgein, to leave off: CATALECTIC. [Pok. (s)lēg- 959.]

sleidh-. Slippery. 1. Germanic *slīdan, to slip,

slide, in Old English slīdan, to slide: SLIDE. 2. Germanic *slid- in: a. Middle Low German sledde, a sled, sledge: SLED; b. Middle Dutch slēde, a sled: SLEIGH; c. Middle Dutch sleedse, sleigh: SLEDGE. 3. Possibly nasalized variant form *(s)le-n-dh- in suffixed extended o-grade form *londhr-īko- in Latin lumbrīcus, earthworm (< "that which slides"): LUMBRICOID. [Pok. (s)leidh- 960.]

slenk-. To wind, turn. 1. Germanic *sling- in Middle Low German slinge, a strap, sling: SLING[1]. 2. Variant form *sleng- in Germanic *slinkjan, to coil, creep, in Old English slincan, to creep: SLINK. [Pok. slenk- 961.]

sleu-. Hypothetical base of a group of distantly related Germanic derivatives with various suffixes. 1. Germanic *slū-m- in Old English slūma, sleep: SLUMBER. 2. Probably Germanic *slautjan- in Old English *slēte, sleet: SLEET. 3. Germanic *slus- in Norwegian slusk, sloppy weather, probably akin to the Scandinavian source of Middle English sloche, soft mud: SLUSH. 4. Germanic *sliura- in: a. Middle High German slier, mud, slime: SCHLIEREN; b. Middle Dutch sloor, sluttish woman, "mud": SLUR. 5. Extended form *sleug- in Germanic *sluk-, *slug- in: a. Norwegian dialectal slugg and Swedish dialectal slagga, slow-moving animal or person, probably akin to the source of Middle English slugge, a sluggard, and sluggen, to be idle: SLUG[2], SLUGGARD; b. Dutch log, lazy, slack: LOGY. [Pok. (s)leu- 962.]

sleubh-. To slide, slip. I. Basic form *sleubh- in Germanic *sliub- in Old English slēf, slīf, slīef, sleeve (into which the arm slips): SLEEVE. II. Variant form *sleub-. 1. Germanic *slup- in: a. Old English slypa, slime: SLIP[1]; COWSLIP, OXLIP; b. Old English *sloppe, liquid food: SLOP[1]; c. Old English (ofer)slop, surplice (< "thing slipped into"): SLOP[2]. 2. Germanic *slaup- in: a. Old English slūpan, to slip away: SLOPE; b. Dutch sloep, sloop (< "gliding boat"): SLOOP. 3. Suffixed form *sleub-ro- in Latin lūbricus, slippery: LUBRICATE, LUBRICITY, LUBRICOUS. [Pok. sleub(h)- 963.]

slī-. Bluish. 1. O-grade form *sloi- in Germanic *slaihwōn in Old English slāh, slā, sloe (< "bluish fruit"): SLOE. 2. Suffixed form *slī-wo- in Latin līvēre, to be bluish: LIVID. 3. Suffixed form *slī-wā- in Serbo-Croatian šljiva, plum: SLIVOVITZ. [Pok. (s)lī- 965.]

[**slm.** To be whole. Semitic root. 1. Arabic salama, he was safe, and salām, peace: SALAAM; ISLAM, MUSLIM. 2. Hebrew shālōm, peace, completeness: SHALOM, SOLOMON[1]. 3. Greek Salōmē, "peace": SALOME.]

sloug-. Help, service. Celtic and Balto-Slavic. Suffixed form *sloug-o- in Old Irish slūag, slōg, army, host, whence Gaelic sluagh, army, host: SLEW[1], SLOGAN. [Pok. slougo- 965.]

smē-. To smear. 1. Extended root *smeid- in Germanic *smītan in Old English smītan, to daub, smear, pollute: SMITE. (2. Attributed by some to this root, but more likely to be of unknown origin, is the Germanic root *mas-, spot, speck, in: a. Middle Dutch masel, pustule, spot: MEASLES; b. Old French masere, knot in wood: MAZER.) 3. Attributed by some to this root, but possibly distinct, is root *smīk-, small, in: a. Latin mīca, crumb, small piece, grain: MICA; b. Greek (s)mikros, small: MICRO-, MICRON, OMICRON. [Pok. smē- 966.]

smeg-. To taste. Germanic *smak- in: a. Old English smæc, flavor, taste: SMACK[2]; b. Middle Dutch and Middle Low German smacken, to taste, make a sound with the lips while tasting food: SMACK[1]. [Pok. smeg(h)- 967.]

smei-. To laugh, smile. 1. Germanic reshaped forms *smer-, *smar- in Old English smercian (with -k- formative), to smile: SMIRK. 2. Germanic extended form *smīl- in Swedish smila, to smile, probably akin to the Scandinavian source of Middle English smilen, to smile: SMILE. 3. Suffixed form *smei-ro- in Latin mīrus, wonderful (< "causing one to smile"): MARVEL, MI, MIRACLE, MIRAGE, MIRROR, ADMIRE. 4. Prefixed zero-grade form *ko-smi-, smiling with (*ko-, *kom-, together; see **kom**), in Latin cōmis (< *cosmis), courteous: COMITY. [Pok. 1. (s)mei- 967.]

smeit-. To throw. Possibly Latin mittere, to let go, send off, throw: MASS, MESS, MESSAGE, MISSILE, MISSION, MISSIVE, MITTIMUS; ADMIT, COMMIT, COMPROMISE, DEMIT, DISMISS, EMIT, INTERMIT, INTROMIT, OMIT, PERMIT, PREMISE, PRETERMIT, PROMISE, REMIT, SUBMIT, SURMISE, TRANSMIT. [Pok. smeit- 968.]

smer-[1]. Also **mer-**. To remember. 1. Suffixed zero-grade form *mr̥-n- in Germanic *murnōn, to remember sorrowfully, in Old English murnan, to mourn: MOURN. 2. Reduplicated form *me-mor- in: a. Germanic *mi-mer- in Old Norse Mimir, a giant who guards the well of wisdom: MIMIR; b. Latin memor, mindful: MEMORABLE, MEMORANDUM, MEMORY; COMMEMORATE, REMEMBER. [Pok. (s)mer- 969.]

smer-[2]. Also **mer-**. To get a share of something. 1. Form *mer-ē- in Latin merēre, merērī, to receive a share, deserve, serve: MERETRICIOUS, MERIT, EMERITUS. 2. Suffixed form *mer-o- in Greek meros (feminine meris), a part, division: -MERE, MERISTEM, MERO-, -MEROUS; ALLOMERISM, DIMER, ISOMER, MONOMER, (TRIMER). [In Pok. (s)mer- 969.]

smer-[3]. Grease, fat. 1. Germanic *smerwjan, to spread grease on, in: a. Old English smierwan, to smear: SMEAR; b. Old High German smirwen, smerian, to apply salve, smear: SMEARCASE. 2. Germanic *smerwa-, grease, fat, in: a. Old High German smero, fat: SCHMEER; b. Old Norse smör, smjör, fat, butter: SMORGASBORD. 3. Latin medulla (< perhaps *merulla, influenced by medius, middle), marrow: MEDULLA. [Pok. smeru- 970.]

smerd-. Pain. Extended root of **mer-[2]**. Germanic *smertan in Old English smeortan, to pain, be painful: SMART. [Pok. smerd- 970.]

smeug-. To smoke; smoke. Germanic *smuk- in Old English smoca, smoke: SMOKE. [Pok. (s)meukh-, (s)meug-, (s)meugh- 971.]

smi-. Also **smī-**. To cut, work with a sharp instrument. 1. Germanic *smithaz in Old English smith, smith: SMITH. 2. Germanic *smith-ja- in Old Norse smidhja, smithy: SMITHY. [Pok. smēi- 968.]

snā-. To swim. 1. Extended form *snāgh- in Greek nēkhein, to swim: NEKTON. 2. Suffixed zero-grade form *(s)nə-to- in: a. Latin natāre, to swim: NATANT, NATATION, NATATORIAL, NATATORIUM, SUPERNATANT; b. perhaps Greek Notos, south wind (which brings wetness): NOTO-. 3. Attributed by some to this root (but more likely obscure) are: a. Greek nēsos, island: AUSTRONESIA, CHERSONESE, MELANESIA, MICRONESIA, PELOPONNESUS, POLYNESIA; b. Greek naein, to flow, whence probably Naias, fountain nymph: NAIAD. [Pok. snā- 971.]

snē-[1]. Also **nē-**. To spin, sew. 1. Suffixed form *nē-tlā in Germanic *nēthlō in Old English nǣdl, needle: NEEDLE. 2. Suffixed form *(s)nē-mn̥ in Greek nēma, thread: NEMATO-; CHROMONEMA, PROTONEMA, TREPONEME. [Pok. (s)nē- 973.]

snē-[2]. Also **sn-**. Imitative beginning of Germanic words connected with the nose. 1. Germanic *snūt-, *snut- in: a. Old English gesnott, nasal mucus (ge-, collective prefix; see **kom**): SNOT; b. Middle Dutch snut(e), snout: SNOUT; c. German Schnauze, snout: SCHNAUZER, SCHNOZZLE. 2. Germanic *snuf- in: a. Low German or Dutch snuffelen, to sniff at: SNUFFLE; b. Middle Dutch snuffen, to snuffle: SNUFF[1]; c. Old English *snyflan, to run at the nose: SNIVEL; d. Middle Swedish or Middle Danish snyfte, to sniff: SNIFTER; e. Middle English sniffen, to sniff: SNIFF. 3. Germanic *snup- in Dutch snoepen, to eat on the sly, pry: SNOOP. 4. Germanic *snip- in Low German and Dutch snippen, to snap at: SNIP. 5. Germanic *snap- in Middle Low German and Middle Dutch snappen, to snap at: SNAP. 6. Germanic *snub- in Old Norse snubba, "to snub, turn up one's nose at," scold, rebuke: SNUB. 7. Germanic *snak- in: a. Middle Dutch snac(k), a bite (< "a snapping at"): SNACK; b. Middle Dutch snakken, to snap at, akin to the Low German source of Middle English snacchen, to snatch: SNATCH. [In Pok. snā- 971.]

sneg-. To creep; creeping thing. 1. Germanic *sneggan- in Old High German snecko, snail: SCHNECKEN. 2. O-grade form *snog- in: a. Germanic *snag-ila- in Old English snæg(e)l, sneg(e)l, snail: SNAIL; b. Germanic *snakan- in Old English snaca, snake: SNAKE. [Pok. ? sneig- 974.]

sneigwh-. Snow; to snow. 1. O-grade form *snoigwh- in Germanic *snaiwaz in Old English snāw, snow: SNOW. 2. Zero-grade form *(s)nigwh- in Latin nix (stem niv-), snow: NÉVÉ, NIVAL, NIVEOUS. [Pok. sneiguh- 974.]

sneit-. To cut. 1. Germanic *snītan in Middle Dutch snīden, to cut: SNICKERSNEE. 2. Germanic *snit- in Middle High German sniz, slice: SCHNITZEL. [Pok. sneit- 974.]

sner-[1]. Expressive root of various verbs for making noises. 1. Germanic *sner- in North Frisian sneere, scornful remark: SNEER. 2. O-grade form *snor- in Germanic *(s)nor- in: a. Middle High German snurren, to hum, whirr: SCHNORRER; b. Middle High German snarchen, to snore: SNORKEL; c. Middle Low German snarren, to snarl: SNARL[1]; d. Middle English snoren, to snore: SNORE; e. Middle English snorten, to snort: SNORT; f. Old Norse Norn, goddess of fate (< "the whisperer"): NORN[1]. [Pok. 1. (s)ner- 975.]

sner-[2]. To wind, twist. 1. Extended form *snerk- in Germanic *snarh- in: a. Old Norse snara, cord, noose, trap: SNARE[1]; b. Middle Dutch snare, string: SNARE[2]. 2. Proposed by some as a derivative of this root is Germanic *narwa- in Old English nearu, narrow: NARROW. 3. Extended variant form *(s)nark- in Greek narkē, cramp, numbness: NARCEINE, NARCO-, NARCOSIS, NARCOTIC. 4. Extended zero-grade form *(s)nr̥t- in Sanskrit nṛtyati, he dances: NAUTCH. [Pok. 2. (s)ner- 975.]

sneu-. To suckle, flow. Suffixed variant form *neu-tri- in Latin nūtrix, nurse, and nūtrīre, to suckle, nourish: NOURISH, NURSE, NURTURE, NUTRIENT, NUTRIMENT, NUTRITION, NUTRITIOUS, NUTRITIVE. [In Pok. snā- 971.]

snēu-. Also **sneu-**. Tendon, sinew. 1. Variant form *senw- in Germanic *senawō in Old English sinu, seonu, tendon: SINEW. 2. Suffixed variant form *neu-ro- in: a. Greek neuron, sinew: NEURO-, NEURON, APONEUROSIS; b. metathesized form *nerwo- in Latin nervus, sinew: NERVE, ENERVATE. [Pok. snēu- 977.]

sneubh-. To marry. 1. Latin nūbere, to marry, take a husband: NUBILE, NUPTIAL; CONNUBIAL. 2. Possibly nasalized zero-grade form *nu-m-bh- in Greek numphē, nymph, bride: NYMPH. [Pok. sneubh- 977.]

sneudh-. Mist, cloud. 1. Latin nūbēs, cloud: NUANCE. 2. Attributed by some to this root (but more likely of obscure origin) is Greek nustazein, to be sleepy: NYSTAGMUS. [Pok. 1. sneud(h), 2. sneudh- 978.]

so-. This, that (nominative). For other cases see **to-**. 1. Greek ho, the: HOI POLLOI. 2. Feminine form *syā in Germanic *sō in Old English sēo, sīe, she: SHE. 3. Compound variant form *sei-ke (*-ke, "that"; see **ko-**) in Latin sīc, thus, so, in that manner: SIC[1]. 4. Old Iranian *ha-maz-an-, "the warrior" (see **magh-[2]**). [Pok. so(s), sā, sī 978.]

sōi-. To sing, proclaim. Suffixed shortened form *soi-mo- in Greek oimos, way, path, strain of a song: PROEM. [In Pok. 3. u̯ei 1123.]

sol-. Whole. I. Basic form *sol-. 1. Suffixed form *sol-ido- in Latin solidus, solid: SOLID; CONSOLIDATE. 2. Extended form *solo- in Greek holos, whole: HOLO-, CATHOLIC. 3. Extended form *sollo- in: a. Latin sollus, whole, entire, unbroken: SOLICITOUS; b. Latin sollemnis (second element obscure), celebrated at fixed dates (said of religious rites), established, religious, solemn: SOLEMN. II. Variant form *sal-. 1. Suffixed form *sal-u- in Latin salūs, health, a whole or sound condition: SALUBRIOUS, SALUTARY, SALUTE. 2. Suffixed form *sal-wo- in Latin salvus, whole, safe, uninjured: SAFE, SAGE[2], SALVAGE, SALVARSAN, SALVO[1], SAVE[1], SAVE[2]. [Pok. solo- 979.]

spei-. Sharp point. I. Basic form *spei-. 1. Germanic *spituz in Old English spitu, stake on which meat is roasted: SPIT[2]. 2. Germanic *spitja- in: a. Middle Dutch spitz, pointed: SPITZENBURG; b. Old High German spizzi, pointed: SPITZ. 3. Germanic *spī-ra- in: a. Old English spīr, slender stalk: SPIRE[1]; ACROSPIRE; b. possibly Middle Dutch spierlinc, a small, slender fish, smelt (Germanic *-ling, -LING[1]), akin to the source of Old French esperlinge, smelt: SPARLING. 4. Germanic *spīk- in Old Norse spīk, nail, and Old English spīcing, nail: SPIKE[1]. 5. Germanic *spīl- in Middle Dutch spile, bar: SPILE, SPILL[2]. 6. Suffixed form *spei-nā in Latin spīna, thorn, prickle, spine: SPINE, SPINEL, SPINNEY; PORCUPINE. 7. Suffixed form *spei-kā in Latin spīca, point, ear of grain: ASPIC[3], SPICA, SPICULUM, SPIKE[2]. II. Extended o-grade form *spoig- in Germanic *spaikōn- in Old English spāca, spoke: SPOKE[1]. [Pok. 1. sp(h)ēi- 981.]

spēi-. Also **spē-**. To thrive, prosper. 1. O-grade form *spōi- in Germanic *spōdiz in Old English spēd, success: SPEED. 2. Suffixed form *spē-s- in Latin spēs (plural spērēs), hope, with denominative spērāre, to hope: DESPAIR, ESPERANCE. 3. Suffixed zero-grade form *spə-ro- in Latin prosperus, favorable, prosperous (traditionally regarded as from pro spērē, according to one's hope; prō-, according to, PRO-): PROSPER. [Pok. 3. sp(h)ēi- 983.]

speik-. Also **peik-**. Bird's name, woodpecker, magpie. 1. Suffixed form *peik-o- in Latin pīcus, woodpecker: PICARO, PICKET, PIKE[1], PIQUE. 2. Suffixed form *peik-ā- in Latin pīca, magpie: PICA[2], PIE[2]. [Pok. (s)pīko- 999.]

spek-. To observe. I. Basic form *spek-. 1. Germanic *spehōn in: a. Frankish *spehōn, to watch: SPY; b. Germanic derivative *speha, watcher, in Italian spia, spy: ESPIONAGE,

2. Latin specere, to look at: SPECIMEN, SPECIOUS, SPECTACLE, SPECTRUM, SPECULATE, SPECULUM; ASPECT, AUSPICE, CIRCUMSPECT, CONSPICUOUS, DESPISE, EXPECT, FRONTISPIECE, INSPECT, INTROSPECT, PERSPECTIVE, PROSPECT, RESPECT, RESPITE, RETROSPECT, SUSPECT. 3. Latin speciēs, a seeing, sight, form: SPECIES; ESPECIAL. 4. Latin -spex, "he who sees," in haruspex, diviner (see **gher-[1]**). 5. Form *spek-ā- in Latin (denominative) dēspicārī, to despise, look down on (dē-, down, DE-): DESPICABLE. 6. Suffixed metathetical form *skep-yo- in Greek skeptesthai, to examine, consider: SKEPTIC. II. Extended o-grade form *spoko- metathesized in Greek skopos, one who watches, goal, and its denominative skopein (< *skop-eyo-), to see: SCOPE, -SCOPE, -SCOPY; BISHOP, EPISCOPAL, HOROSCOPE, SCOPOPHILIA, TELESCOPE. [Pok. spek̂- 984.]

spel-[1]. To split, break off. 1. Extended form *spelt- in: a. Germanic *spilt- in Middle Dutch spelte, wheat (probably from the splitting of its husk at threshing): SPELT[1]; b. Germanic *spilthjan in Old English spillan, to spill, destroy: SPILL[1]. 2. Suffixed o-grade form *spol-yo- perhaps in Latin spolium, hide torn from an animal, armor stripped from an enemy, booty: SPOIL; DESPOIL. [Pok. 1. (s)p(h)el- 985.]

spel-[2]. To shine, glow. Extended form *splend- in Latin splendēre, to shine: SPLENDID; RESPLENDENT. [Pok. 2. (s)p(h)el- 987.]

spel-[3]. To say aloud, recite. Suffixed form *spel-no-. 1. Germanic *spellam in: a. Old English spell, discourse, story: SPELL[2]; b. Old English spel, news: GOSPEL. 2. Germanic denominative *spellōn in Old French espeller, to read out: SPELL[1]. [Pok. (s)pel- 985.]

spelgh-. Spleen, milt. 1. Deformation *(p)lihēn in Latin liēn, milt, spleen: LIENAL. 2. Uncertain pre-form in: a. Greek splēn, spleen: SPLEEN; b. Greek splankhna, inward parts: SPLANCHNIC. [Pok. sp(h)elĝh(en) 987.]

spen-. Also **pen-.** To draw, stretch, spin. I. Basic form *spen-. 1. Suffixed form *spen-wo- in Germanic *spinnan, to spin, in: a. Old English spinnan, to spin, with probable derivative *spinthron, "the spinner," contracted to spīthra, spider: SPIN, SPIDER; b. Germanic derivative *spin-ilōn in Old English spinel, spindle: SPINDLE. 2. Extended form *pend- in Latin pendēre, to hang (intransitive), and pendere, to cause to hang, weigh, with its frequentative pensāre, to weigh: PAINTER[2], PANSY, PENCHANT, PENDANT, PENDENTIVE, PENDULOUS, PENSILE, PENSION[1], PENSIVE, PESO, POISE[1]; ANTEPENDIUM, APPEND, COMPENDIUM, COMPENSATE, DEPEND, DISPENSE, EXPEND, IMPEND, PENTHOUSE, PERPEND[1], PERPENDICULAR, PREPENSE, PROPEND, SUSPEND, VILIPEND. 3. Perhaps suffixed form *pen-ia in Greek penia, lack, poverty (< "a strain, exhaustion"): -PENIA. II. O-grade forms *spon-, *pon-. 1. Germanic *spannjan in: a. Middle Dutch spannen, to bind: SPAN[2]; b. Old High German spannan, to stretch: SPANNER. 2. Germanic *spanno- in Old English span(n), distance: SPAN[1]. 3. Probably Germanic *spangō in Middle Dutch spange, clasp: SPANGLE. 4. Suffixed and extended form *pond-o- in Latin pondō, by weight: POUND[1]. 5. Suffixed and extended form *pond-os- in Latin pondus (stem ponder-), weight, and its denominative ponderāre, to weigh: PONDER, PONDEROUS; EQUIPONDERATE, PREPONDERATE. 6. Perhaps suffixed form *spon-t- in Latin sponte, of one's own accord, spontaneously: SPONTANEOUS. 7. Greek ponein, to toil: GEOPONIC. [Pok. (s)pen-(d)- 988.]

spend-. To make an offering, perform a rite, hence to engage oneself by a ritual act. O-grade form *spond-. 1. Suffixed form *spond-eyo- in Latin spondēre, to make a solemn promise, pledge, betroth: SPONSOR, SPOUSE; DESPOND, ESPOUSE, RESPOND. 2. Suffixed form *spond-ā in Greek spondē, libation, offering: SPONDEE. [Pok. spend- 989.]

sper-[1]. Spear, pole. 1. Germanic *speru- in: a. Old English spere, spear: SPEAR; b. Middle Low German sper, spit: SPARERIBS. 2. Germanic *sparjōn- in Old Norse sperra, rafter, beam: SPAR[1]. [Pok. 1. (s)per- 990.]

sper-[2]. To turn, twist. 1. Suffixed form *sper-ya- in Greek speira, a winding, coil, spire: SPIRE[2]. 2. Suffixed zero-grade form *spr̥-to- in Greek sparton, rope, cable: ESPARTO. [Pok. 3. sper- 991.]

sper-[3]. Bird's name; sparrow. Suffixed o-grade form *spor-wo- in Germanic *sparwan- in Old English spearwa, sparrow: SPARROW. [Pok. sper-(g)- 997.]

sper-[4]. To strew. I. Zero-grade form *spr̥-. 1. Germanic *spr- in Old English sprēawlian, to sprawl: SPRAWL. 2. Extended form *spreut- in Germanic *sprūt- in: a. Old English sprūtan, to sprout: SPROUT; b. Old English spryttan, to sprout, come forth: SPURT; c. Old English sprēot, pole (< "sprout, stem"): SPRIT; d. Middle Low German bochspret, bogspret, bowsprit (boog, BOW[3]): BOWSPRIT. 3. Extended form *spreit- in Germanic *spraidjan in Old English sprǣdan, to spread: SPREAD. II. Basic form *sper-. 1. Suffixed form *sper-yo- in Greek speirein, to scatter: DIASPORA. 2. Suffixed form *sper-mn̥ in Greek sperma, sperm, seed (< "that which is scattered"): SPERM. III. O-grade form *spor-. 1. Suffixed form *spor-ā in Greek spora, a sowing, seed: SPORE, SPORO-. 2. Suffixed form *spor-n̥d- in Greek sporas (stem sporad-), scattered, dispersed: SPORADIC. [Pok. 2. (s)p(h)er- 993.]

spergh-. To move, hasten, spring. Nasalized root form *sprengh-. 1. Germanic *springan in: a. Old English springan, to spring: SPRING; b. Middle Dutch springen, to leap: KLIPSPRINGER, SPRINGBOK; c. Old High German springan, to jump: GELÄNDESPRUNG. 2. Germanic causative *sprangjan in: a. Old English sprengan, to sprinkle, scatter (< "to cause to jump"); BESPRENT; b. Old English *sprencg, snare used to catch game: SPRINGE. [Pok. spergh- 998.]

speud-. Also **peud-.** To push, repulse. 1. Latin pudēre, to feel shame: PUDENCY; IMPUDENT. 2. Latin repudium, a casting off (re-, off, RE-): REPUDIATE. [In Pok. pēu- 827.]

sphē-. Also **spē-.** Long, flat piece of wood. I. Basic forms *sphē-, spē-. 1. Germanic *spēnu- in: a. Old English spōn, chip of wood, splinter: SPOON; b. Old Norse spānn, shingle, chip: SPANNEW. 2. Greek sphēn, wedge: SPHENE, SPHENO-. II. Suffixed zero-grade form *spə-dh-. 1. Germanic *spadan in: a. Old English spadu, digging tool: SPADE[1]; b. Middle High German spat, spar: SPATHIC. 2. Greek spathē, broad blade: SPADE[2], SPATHE, SPATULA, SPAY. [Pok. sp(h)ē- 980.]

spher-. Ankle. Zero-grade variant form *spr̥-. 1. Germanic *spurōn in: a. Old English spura, spora, spur: SPUR; b. Germanic denominative *spurnōn in Old English spurnan, spornan, to kick, strike against: SPURN. 2. Germanic *spur- in Middle Dutch spor, spoor, track of an animal: SPOOR. [Pok. 1. sp(h)er- 992.]

sphereg-. Also **spreg-.** To jerk, scatter. 1. Germanic *spreg-, *freg- in: a. Middle Dutch sprenkelen, to sprinkle: SPRINKLE; b. Old Norse freknur, freckles (< "that which is scattered on the skin"): FRECKLE; c. Swedish dialectal spragg, twig (< "that which is jerked off a branch"), akin to the Scandinavian source of SPRAG; d. Swedish dialectal sprygg, brisk, active, akin to the Scandinavian source of SPRY. 2. Zero-grade form *spr̥g- in variant *sparg- in Latin spargere, to strew, scatter: SPARGE, SPARSE, SPURRY; ASPERSE, DISPERSE, INTERSPERSE. [Pok. (s)p(h)ereg- 996.]

sping-. Also **ping-.** Bird's name; sparrow, finch. Germanic *finki- in Old English finc, finch: FINCH. [Pok. (s)pingo- 999.]

[spīrāre. To breathe. Latin word of unknown origin, with its derivative spīritus, breath, breath of a god, inspiration: SPIRIT, SPIRACLE; ASPIRATE, CESSPOOL, CONSPIRE, EXPIRE, INSPIRE, PERSPIRE, RESPIRE, SUSPIRE, TRANSPIRE. [In Pok. peis-, speis- 796.]]

splei-. To splice, split. 1. Germanic *flī- in: a. Old English flint, flint: FLINT; b. Norwegian flindra, splinter, akin to the Scandinavian source of Middle English flenderis, bits, splinters: FLINDERS. 2. Germanic *splī- in: a. Middle Dutch splinter, splinter: SPLINTER; b. Middle Dutch splitten, to split: SPLIT; c. Middle Dutch splissen, to splice: SPLICE; d. Middle Low German and Middle Dutch splente, splinte, splint: SPLINT. [Pok. (s)plei- 1000.]

spoimo-. Foam. 1. Variant form *poimo- in Germanic *faimaz in Old English fām, foam: FOAM. 2. Variant form *spoimā in Latin spūma, foam: SPUME. 3. Suffixed reduced form *poim-ik- in Latin pūmex, pumice (from its spongelike appearance): POUNCE[2], PUMICE. [Pok. (s)poimno- 1001.]

spreg-. Also **speg-.** To speak. Germanic *sprek-, *spek- in: a. Old English specan, to speak: SPEAK; b. Germanic compound *bisprekan (*bi-, about; see **ambhi**) in Old English bisprecan, to speak about: BESPEAK; c. Old English sprǣc, spec, speech: SPEECH. [In Pok. (s)p(h)ereg- 996.]

spyeu-. Also **speu-.** To spew, spit. Expressive root. 1. Germanic *spit- in Old English spittan, to spit: SPIT[1]. 2. Germanic *spiu- in Old English spīwan, spīowan, to spew: SPEW. 3. Germanic *spāt- in Old English spātl, spittle: SPITTLE. 4. Germanic *spūt- in: a. Middle Dutch spouten, spoiten, to spout forth: SPOUT; b. Dutch sputteren, to sputter: SPUTTER. 5. Zero-grade form *spu- in Latin spuere, to spit: SPUTUM; CUSPIDOR. 6. Reduced zero-grade form *pyu- in Greek ptuein, to spit: HEMOPTYSIS, PTYALIN. [Pok. (s)p(h)ieu- 999.]

srebh-. To suck, absorb. Zero-grade form *sr̥bh- in: a. Germanic *surp- in altered form in Middle Dutch slorpen, to slurp, lap: SLURP; b. Latin sorbēre, to suck: ABSORB, ADSORB, RESORB. [Pok. srebh- 1001.]

srenk-. To snore. O-grade form *sronk- in: a. Greek rhonkos, rhonkhos, a snoring: RHONCHUS; b. Greek rhunkhos, snout, bill, beak: OXYRHYNCHUS, RHYNCHOCEPHALIAN. [Pok. srenk- 1002.]

sreu-. To flow. 1. Suffixed o-grade form *srou-mo- in Germanic *straumaz, stream, in: a. Old English strēam, stream: STREAM; b. Dutch stroom, stream: MAELSTROM. 2. Basic form *sreu- in: a. Greek rhein, to flow: RHEO-, -RRHEA; CATARRH, DIARRHEA, HEMORRHOID, RHYOLITE; b. suffixed form *sreu-mn̥ in Greek rheuma, stream, humor of the body: RHEUM. 3. Suffixed zero-grade form *sru-dhmo- in Greek rhuthmos, measure, recurring motion, rhythm: RHYME, RHYTHM. [Pok. sreu- 1003.]

srīg-. Cold. Suffixed form srīg-os- in Latin frīgus, cool, cold: FRIGID, REFRIGERATE. [Pok. srīg- 1004.]

stā-. To stand; with derivatives meaning "place or thing which is standing." I. Basic form *stā-. 1. Germanic *stōd-ja- in Old English stēda, stallion, studhorse (< "place for breeding horses"): STEED. 2. Germanic *stōdō in Old English stōd, establishment for breeding horses: STUD[2]. 3. Extended form *stāw- in Germanic *stōw- in Old English stow, place: STOW. 5. Suffixed form *stā-lo- in Germanic *stōlaz in: a. Old English stōl, stool: STOOL; b. compound *faldistōlaz (see **pel-[3]**). 6. Latin stāre, to stand, with its past participle status (from form *stə-to-) and derivatives statūra, height, stature, and statuere, to set up, erect, cause to stand: STAGE, STANCE, STANCH, STANCHION, STANZA, STATOR, STATUE, STATURE, STATUTE, STAY[1], STET; ARREST, CIRCUMSTANCE, CONSTANT, CONSTITUTE, CONTRAST, COST, DESTITUTE, DISTANT, ESTANCIA, EXTANT, INSTANT, INSTITUTE, OBSTACLE, OBSTETRIC, OUST, PROSTITUTE, REST[2], RESTITUTE, RESTIVE, STAPES, SUBSTANCE, SUBSTITUTE, SUPERSTITION. 7. Suffixed form *stā-men- in Latin stāmen, thread of the warp (a technical term): STAMEN, STAMMEL. 8. Suffixed form *stā-mon- in Greek stēmōn, thread: PENSTEMON. 9. Suffixed form *stā-ro- in Russian staryĭ, old ("long standing"): STARETS. II. Zero-grade form *stə-. 1. Suffixed variant form *sta-nd- in Germanic *standan in: a. Old English standan, to stand: STAND; b. Old English understandan, to know, stand under (under-, UNDER-): UNDERSTAND; c. Frankish *standan, to stand: STANDARD. 2. Suffixed form *stə-tyo- in Germanic *stathjon- in Old Norse stedhi, anvil: STITHY. 3. Suffixed form *stə-tlo- in Germanic *stathlaz in Old English stathol, foundation: STADDLE, STARLING[2], STALWART. 4. Suffixed form *stə-mno- in Germanic *stamniz in Old English stefn, stem, tree trunk: STEM[1]. 5. Suffixed form *stə-ti-. a. Germanic *stadiz in (i) Old English stede, place: STEAD (ii) Middle Dutch stad, stat, place: STADHOLDER. b. Latin statiō, a standing still: STATION. c. Latin -stitium, a stoppage, in solstitium, solstice (see **sāwel-**): ARMISTICE. d. Greek stasis, a standing, a standstill: STASIS, HYPOSTASIS, ICONOSTASIS, ISOSTASY. 6. Suffixed form *stə-to- in Greek statos, placed, standing: STATIC, STATO-; ASTASIA, ASTATINE. 7. Suffixed form *stə-no- in: a. Latin dēstināre, to make firm, establish (dē-, thoroughly, DE-): DESTINE; b. Latin obstināre, to set one's mind on (ob-, on, OB-): OBSTINATE. 8. Suffixed form *stə-tu- in Latin status, manner, position, condition, attitude: STATE, STATUS, STATISTICS. 9. Suffixed form *stə-dhlo- in Latin stabulum, standing place: STABLE[2]. 10. Suffixed form *stə-dhli- in Latin stabilis, standing firm: STABLE[1], ESTABLISH. 11. Suffixed form *stə-ta- in Greek -statēs, one that causes to stand, a standing: -STAT, ENSTATITE. III. Suffixed variant form *steu-ro-. 1. Germanic *stiurjō, "a steering," in Old English stēor, a steering: STARBOARD. 2. Germanic denominative *stiurjan in: a. Old English stīeran, to steer: STEER[1]; b. Old Norse stȳra, to steer, with its derivative stjōrn, a rudder, a steering: STERN[2]. IV. Suffixed variant form *stau-ro-. 1. Latin instaurāre, to restore, set upright again (in-, on, IN-): STORE; INSTAURATE, RESTORE. 2. Greek stauros, cross, post, stake: STAUROLITE. **3.** Sanskrit _sthavira,_ thick, stout: THERAVADA. **V.** Reduced form _*st-_. **1.** Reduplicated form _*si-st-_ in: **a.** Latin _sistere,_ to set, place, stop, stand: ASSIST, CONSIST, DESIST, EXIST, INSIST, INTERSTICE, PERSIST, RESIST, SUBSIST; **b.** Greek _histanai_ (aorist _stanai_), to set, place: APOSTASY, CATASTASIS, DIASTASIS, ECSTASY, EPISTASIS, EPISTEMOLOGY, METASTASIS, PROSTATE, SYSTEM; **c.** Greek _histos,_ web, tissue (< "that which is set up"): HISTO-. **2.** Compound form _*tri-st-i-,_ "third person standing by" (see **trei-**). **3.** Compound form _*por-st-i-,_ "that which stands before" (_*por-,_ before, forth; see **per**[1]), in Latin _postis,_ post: POST[1]. **VI.** Suffixed extended form _*stow-ā_ in Greek _stoa,_ porch: STOA, STOIC. **VII.** Variant _*stō-,_ standing, in _*upo-stō-,_ "one who stands under" (see **upo**). **VIII.** Extended form _*stu-_. **1.** Suffixed form _*stu-t-_ in Germanic _*stuth-_ in: **a.** Old English _stuthu,_ post, prop: STUD[1]; **b.** Germanic _*stundo-_ (with nasal infix) in Old English _stund,_ a fixed time, a while: STOUND. **2.** Suffixed lengthened-grade form _*stū-lo-_ in Greek _stulos,_ pillar: AMPHISTYLAR, ASTYLAR, EPISTYLE, HYPOSTYLE, PERISTYLE, PROSTYLE, STYLITE, STYLOBATE. See **stāk-**. [Pok. _stā-_ 1004.]

stag-. To seep, drip. Possible root. **1.** Latin _stagnum,_ pond, swamp: STAGNANT. **2.** Suffixed form _*stag-yo-_ in Greek _stazein,_ to ooze, drip: STACTE; EPISTAXIS. [Pok. _stag-_ 1010.]

stāk-. Extended root of **stā-**. To stand, place. Zero-grade form _*stək-_. **1.** Suffixed form _*stək-o-_ in Germanic _*staga-_ in: **a.** Old English _stæg,_ rope used to support a mast: STAY[3]; **b.** Middle Dutch _staeye,_ rope used to support a mast: STAY[2]. **2.** Suffixed form _*stək-lo-_ in Germanic _*stahla-_ in Old English _stēli, stȳle,_ steel (< "that which stands firm"): STEEL. [Pok. _stāk-_ 1011.]

[**stam-**. To push, stutter, stammer. Germanic root. **1.** Old English _stamerian,_ to stammer: STAMMER. **2.** Middle Dutch _stom,_ mute: STUM. **3.** Old Norse _stemma,_ to stop: STEM[2]. **4.** Old Norse _*stumla, stumra,_ to stumble: STUMBLE. [In Pok. _stem-_ 1021.]]

[**staup-**. (Cooking) vessel. Germanic root. **1.** Old Norse _staup,_ vessel: STOUP. **2.** Middle Low German and Middle Dutch _stove,_ heated chamber: STOVE[1]. **3.** Germanic denominative _*staupjan_ in Old Norse _steypa,_ to pour out: STEEP[2]. [In Pok. 1. _steu-_ 1032.]]

stebh-. Post, stem; to support, place firmly on, fasten. **I.** Basic form _*stebh-_. **1.** Germanic _*stab-_ in Old English _stæf,_ stick, rod: STAFF[1]. **2.** Greek _stephein,_ to tie around, encircle, crown, wreathe: STEMMA, STEPHEN. **II.** Unaspirated form _*steb-_. **1.** Germanic _*stap-_ in: **a.** Old English _stapol,_ post, pillar: STAPLE[2]; **b.** Old English _stæpe,_ step (< "a treading firmly on, foothold"): STEP; **c.** Middle Dutch _stapel,_ pillar, foundation: STAPLE[1]; **d.** Middle Dutch _stoep,_ stoop: STOOP[2]; **e.** Middle Low German _stope,_ a step: STOPE. **2.** Germanic nasalized form _*stamp-_ in: **a.** Old English _*stampian,_ to pound, stamp: STAMP; **b.** Middle Low German _stump,_ stump: STUMP; **c.** Old High German _stam,_ base, stem: STALAG; **d.** Spanish _estampar,_ to pound, stamp: STAMPEDE. **III.** Variant _*stabh-_ in Greek _staphulē,_ grapevine, bunch of grapes: STAPHYLO-. [Pok. _steb(h)_ 1011.]

steg-[1]. To cover. **I.** Suffixed variant o-grade form _*tog-o-_. **1.** Germanic _*thakjan_ in: **a.** Old English _theccan,_ to cover: THATCH; **b.** Middle Dutch _dekken,_ to cover: DECK[2]; **c.** Old High German _decchen,_ to cover: DECKLE. **2.** Germanic _*thakam_ in Middle Dutch _dec, decke,_ roof, covering: DECK[1]. **3.** Sanskrit _sthagati,_ he covers: THUG. **II.** Basic form _*steg-_ in Greek _stegein,_ to cover: STEGODON. **III.** Variant form _*teg-_. **1.** Latin _tegere,_ to cover, and _tegula,_ tile: TECTRIX, TEGMEN, TEGULAR, TEGUMENT, TILE, TOGA, TUILLE; DETECT, INTEGUMENT, OBTECT, PROTECT. **2.** Suffixed form _*teg-os-_ in Old Irish _tech,_ house: SHANTY[1]. **3.** Persian _tāj,_ crown: TAJ. [Pok. 1. _(s)teg-_ 1013.]

steg-[2]. Pole, stick. O-grade form _*stog-_ in Germanic _*stak-_ in: **a.** Old English _staca,_ stake: STAKE[1]; **b.** Old Norse _stakkr,_ haystack: STACK; **c.** Old Norse _staka,_ to push, cause to stumble (as with a stick): STAGGER; **d.** Gothic _*stakka,_ stake: ATTACK; **e.** Frankish _*stakka,_ stake: ATTACH; **f.** Spanish _estaca,_ stake: STOCKADE. [Pok. 2. _(s)teg-_ 1014.]

stegh-. To prick. **1.** Nasalized form _*stengh-_ in Germanic _*stengjan_ in Old English _stingan,_ to sting: STING. **2.** O-grade form _*stogh-_ in: **a.** Germanic _*stag-_ in Old English _stagga,_ stag: STAG; **b.** Greek _stokhos,_ pointed stake or pillar (used as a target for archers), goal: STOCHASTIC. [Pok. _stegh-_ 1014.]

stei-. Stone. Suffixed o-grade form _*stoi-no-_ in Germanic _*stainaz_ in: **a.** Old English _stān,_ stone: STONE; **b.** Middle Dutch _steen,_ stone: STEENBOK; **c.** Old Norse _steinn,_ stone: TUNGSTEN; **d.** Old High German _stein,_ stone: STEIN. [Pok. _stai-_ 1010.]

steig-. To stick; pointed. **I.** Zero-grade form _*stig-_. **1.** Germanic _*stik-_ in: **a.** Old English _stician,_ to pierce, stab: STICK; **b.** Old English _sticel,_ a prick, sting: STICKLEBACK; **c.** Old Norse _steikja,_ to roast on a spit: STEAK; **d.** Germanic variant _*stek-_ in Middle Dutch _steken,_ to stick, stab: ETIQUETTE, TICKET, SNICKERSNEE. **2.** Variant _*stig-_ in: **a.** Germanic expressive form _*stikkōn_ in _(i)_ Old English _sticca,_ stick: STICK _(ii)_ Old High German _stih,_ a thrust, puncture: SHTICK; **b.** suffixed form _*stig-i-_ in Germanic _*stikiz_ in Old English _stick,_ a sting, prick: STITCH; **c.** nasalized form _*sti-n-g-_ in Latin _stinguere,_ to quench, perhaps originally to prick, and its apparent derivative _distinguere,_ to separate (semantic transitions obscure): DISTINGUISH, EXTINGUISH, INSTINCT; **d.** suffixed form _*stig-yo-_ in Greek _stizein,_ to prick, tattoo: STIGMA; ASTIGMATISM; **e.** suffixed reduced form _*tig-ro-_ in Avestan _tigra,_ sharp, pointed, in Greek _tigris,_ tiger: TIGER. **II.** Basic form _*steig-_ in Latin _-stīgāre,_ to spur on, prod: INSTIGATE. [Pok. _steig-_ 1016.]

steigh-. To stride, step, rise. **I.** Basic form _*steigh-_ in Germanic _*stīgan_ in Old English _stīgan,_ to go up, rise: STY[2]. **II.** Zero-grade form _*stigh-_. **1.** Germanic _*stigila-_ in Old English _stigel,_ series of steps: STILE[1]. **2.** Suffixed form _*stigh-to-_ in Germanic _*stihtan,_ "to place on a step or base," in Old English _stihtan,_ to settle, arrange: STICKLE. **3.** Germanic compound _*stig-raipaz,_ "mount-rope" (_*raipaz,_ rope; see **rei-**[1]), in Old English _stigrāp,_ stirrup: STIRRUP. **4.** Suffixed form _*stigh-o-_ in Greek _stikhos,_ row, line, line of verse: STICH, -STICHOUS; ACROSTIC, CADASTER, DISTICH, HEMISTICH, ORTHOSTICHOUS. **III.** O-grade form _*stoigh-_. **1.** Suffixed form _*stoigh-ri-_ in Germanic _*staigrī_ in Old English _stæger,_ stair, step: STAIR. **2.** Greek _stoikheion,_ shadow line, element: STOICHIOMETRY. [Pok. _steigh-_ 1017.]

steip-. To stick, compress. **1.** Germanic _*stīfaz_ in: **a.** Old English _stīf,_ rigid, stiff: STIFF; **b.** Middle Dutch _stip,_ tip, point: STIPPLE. **2.** Latin _stīpes,_ post, tree trunk: STIPE, STIPES. **3.** Form _*steip-ā-_ in Latin _stīpāre,_ to compress, stuff, pack: CONSTIPATE, STEEVE[1], STEVEDORE. [Pok. _stēib(h)-_ 1015.]

stel-[1]. To put, stand, with derivatives referring to a standing object or place. **I.** Basic form _*stel-_. **1.** Suffixed form _*stel-ni-_ in Germanic _*stilli-_ in Old English _stille,_ quiet, fixed: STILL[1]. **2.** Suffixed form _*stel-yo-_ in Greek _stellein,_ to put in order, prepare, send, make compact: APOSTLE, DIASTOLE, EPISTLE, PERISTALSIS, SYSTALTIC. **II.** O-grade form _*stol-_. **1.** Suffixed form _*stol-no-_ in Germanic _*stalla-_ in: **a.** Old English _steall,_ standing place, stable: STALL; FORESTALL; **b.** Old High German _stal,_ stall: INSTALLMENT[1]; **c.** Frankish _*stal,_ standing place, stable: STALE[1], STALLION; **d.** Old Italian _stallo,_ stall: PEDESTAL; **e.** Medieval Latin _stallum,_ stall: INSTALL; **f.** Germanic denominative _*stalljan_ in Old High German _stellen,_ to set, place: GESTALT. **2.** Suffixed form _*stol-ōn-_ in Latin _stolō,_ branch, shoot: STOLON. **3.** Suffixed form _*stol-ido-_ in Latin _stolidus,_ "firm standing": STOLID. **4.** Suffixed form _*stol-to-_ in Latin _stultus,_ foolish (< "unmovable, uneducated"): STULTIFY. **5.** Suffixed form _*stol-ā-_ in Greek _stolē,_ garment, array, equipment: STOLE[1]. **III.** Suffixed zero-grade form _*stḷ-na-_ in Germanic _*stullōn-_ in Old High German _stollo,_ post, support: STOLLEN. **IV.** Extended form _*stelg-_ in Germanic _*stalk-_ in Norwegian dialectal _stalk,_ stalk, akin to the source of Middle English _stalke,_ stalk: STALK[1]. **V.** Extended form _*steld-_ in: **a.** Germanic _*steltjōn-_ in Low German and Flemish _stilte,_ stick, akin to the source of Middle English _stilte,_ crutch, stilt: STILT; **b.** zero-grade form _*stḷd-_ in Germanic _*stult-,_ "walking on stilts," strutting, in Old French _estout,_ stout: STOUT. **VI.** Suffixed variant form _*stal-nā-_ in Greek _stēlē,_ pillar: STELE. [Pok. 3. _stel-_ 1019.]

stel-[2]. Also **stelə-**. To extend. Zero-grade form _*stḷə-_. **1.** Suffixed form _*stḷə-to-_ in Latin _lātus,_ broad, wide: DILATE, LATITUDE. **2.** Attributed by some to this root (but more likely of obscure origin) is Latin _lāmina,_ place, layer: LAMELLA, OMELET. [Pok. 2. _stel-_ 1018.]

sten-. Narrow. Greek _stenos,_ narrow: STENO-. [Pok. 2. _sten-_ 1021.]

stenə-. To thunder. **1.** Zero-grade form _*stṇə-_ in Germanic _*thunaraz_ in: **a.** Old English _thunor,_ thunder: THUNDER; **b.** Middle Dutch _doner, donre, donder,_ thunder: BLUNDERBUSS, DUNDERHEAD; **c.** Old Norse _Thōrr_ (older form _Thunarr_), "thunder," thunder god: THOR. **2.** Basic form _*sten(ə)-_ in Greek _stenein,_ to groan, moan: STENTORIAN. **3.** Variant o-grade form _*tonə-_ in Latin _tonāre,_ to thunder: ASTONISH, DETONATE, STUN, TORNADO. [Pok. 1. _(s)ten-_ 1021.]

ster-[1]. Stiff. **I.** O-grade form _*stor-_. **1.** Suffixed form _*stor-ē-_ in Germanic _*staren_ in Old English _starian,_ to stare: STARE. **2.** Suffixed form _*stor-g-_ in: **a.** Germanic _*starkaz_ in Old English _stearc,_ hard, severe: STARK; **b.** Germanic denominative _*starkjan_ in Old English _*stercan,_ to stiffen: STARCH. **II.** Full-grade form _*ster-_. **1.** Germanic _*sternjaz_ in Old English _stierne,_ firm: STERN[1]. **2.** Suffixed form _*ster-ewo-_ in Greek _stereos,_ solid: STERE, STEREO-, CHOLESTEROL. **III.** Zero-grade form _*stṛ-_. **1.** Extended form _*stṛg-_ in Germanic _*sturkaz_ in Old English _storc,_ stork (probably from the stiff movements of the bird): STORK. **2.** Germanic _*strūt-_ in Old English _strūtian,_ to stand out stiffly: STRUT. **IV.** Extended form _*sterd-_. **1.** Germanic _*stertaz_ in Old English _steort,_ tail: REDSTART, STARK NAKED. **2.** Germanic _*stert-_ in: **a.** Old English _*styrtan,_ to leap up (< "move briskly, move stiffly"): START; **b.** Old English _steartlian,_ to kick, struggle: STARTLE. **V.** Extended form _*sterbh-_ in Germanic _*sterban_ in Old English _steorfan,_ to die (< "to become rigid"): STARVE. **VI.** Extended form _*(s)terp-_ in suffixed (stative) zero-grade form _*tṛp-ē-_ in Latin _torpēre,_ to be stiff: TORPEDO. [Pok. 1. _(s)ter-_ 1022.]

ster-[2]. To spread. **I.** Extended form _*streu-_. **1.** Germanic _*striw-_ in Old English _strēon,_ gain, offspring: STRAIN[2]. **2.** Latin _struere,_ to pile up, construct: STRUCTURE; CONSTRUCT, DESTROY, INSTRUCT, OBSTRUCT, SUBSTRUCTION. **3.** Zero-grade form _*stru-_ in Latin _industria,_ diligence, activity (_endo-,_ within; see **en**): INDUSTRY. **4.** Russian _struga,_ deep place: SASTRUGA. **5.** Germanic _*strēlō_ in Old High German _strāla,_ arrow, lightning bolt: BREMSSTRAHLUNG. **II.** Extended form _*strou-_. **1.** Suffixed form _*strou-eyo-_ in Germanic _*strawjan_ in: **a.** Old English _strēowian,_ to strew: STREW; **b.** Old High German _strouwen,_ to sprinkle, strew: STREUSEL. **2.** Lengthened form _*strōu-_ in Germanic _*strāwam,_ "that which is scattered," in Old English _strēaw,_ straw: STRAW. **III.** Basic form _*ster-_. **1.** Suffixed form _*ster-n-_ in Latin _sternere,_ to stretch, extend: STRATUS, STREET; CONSTERNATE, SUBSTRATUM. **2.** Suffixed form _*ster-no-_ in Greek _sternon,_ breast, breastbone: STERNUM. **IV.** Zero-grade form _*stṛ-_. **1.** Suffixed form _*stṛ-to-_ in: **a.** Greek _stratos,_ multitude, army, expedition: STRATAGEM, STRATOCRACY; **b.** Scottish Gaelic _srath,_ a wide river valley: STRATH. **2.** Suffixed extended form _*strə-mn-_ in Greek _strōma,_ mattress, bed: STROMA. [Pok. 5. _ster-_ 1029.]

ster-[3]. Star. **1.** Suffixed form _*ster-s-_ in Germanic _*sterrōn-_ in Old English _steorra,_ star: STAR. **2.** Suffixed form _*ster-la_ in Latin _stella,_ star: STELLA, STELLAR, STELLATE; CONSTELLATION, ESTELLE. **3.** Greek _astēr,_ star, with its derivatives _astron,_ star, and possibly compound _astrapē, asteropē,_ lightning, twinkling (< "looking like a star"; _ōps,_ stem _op-,_ eye, appearance; see **okw-**): ASTER, ASTERIATED, ASTERISK, ASTERISM, ASTEROID, ASTRAEA, ASTRAL, ASTRAPHOBIA, ASTRO-; DIASTER, DISASTER, STEROPE[1]. **4.** Persian _sitareh,_ star: ESTHER[1]. [Pok. 2. _ster-_ 1027.]

ster-[4]. To rob, steal. **1.** Dissimilated form in Germanic _*stelan_ in Old English _stelan,_ to steal: STEAL. **2.** Germanic derivative noun _*stēl-ithō_ (_-ithō,_ abstract suffix) in Old English _*stǣlth,_ stealth: STEALTH. **3.** Dissimilated form in Germanic frequentative _*stalkōjan_ in Old English _*stealcian,_ to move stealthily: STALK[2]. [Pok. 3. _ster-_ 1028.]

ster-[5]. Barren. **1.** Germanic _*sterka-_ in Old English _stirc, stierc,_ calf: STIRK. **2.** Latin _sterilis,_ unfruitful: STERILE. [Pok. 6. _ster-_ 1031.]

stern-. Extension of **ster-**[1]. Name of thorny plants. Suffixed variant zero-grade form _*tṛ-nu-_ in Germanic _*thurnu-,_ thorn, in: **a.** Old English _thorn,_ thorn: THORN; **b.** Old Swedish _törn,_ thorn: TURBOT. [Pok. 7. _(s)ter-n-_ 1031.]

steu-. To push, stick, knock, beat; with derivatives referring to projecting objects, fragments, and certain related expressive notions and qualities. **I.** Extended forms _*steup-, steub-_. **1.** Germanic _*staup-_ in Old English _stēap,_ lofty, deep, projecting: STEEP[1]. **2.** Germanic _*staupilaz_ in Old English _stȳpel,_ steeple: STEEPLE. **3.** Germanic _*stiup-,_ "bereft" (< "pushed out"), in Old English _stēop-,_ step-: STEP-. **4.** Germanic _*stūp-_ in Old English _stupian,_ to stoop: STOOP[1]. **5.** Germanic expressive form *stubb- in Old English stubb, stump: STUB. **6.** Germanic *stuf-, "fragment," small coin, in Middle Dutch stuyver, stiver: STIVER. **II.** Extended form *steud-. **1.** Nasalized form *stu-n-t- in: **a.** Germanic *stuntjan in Old English styntan, to dull: STINT[1]; **b.** Germanic *stuntaz in Old English stunt, dull: STUNT[1]. **2.** Germanic *staut- in: **a.** Old High German stōzen, to push: STOSS; **b.** Middle Low German and Middle Dutch stōten, to force (akin to the source of Middle English stutten, to stutter): STUDDINGSAIL, STUTTER. **III.** Extended form *steug-. **1.** Germanic *stukkaz in: **a.** Old English stocc, tree trunk: STOCK; **b.** Old High German stoc, staff: ALPENSTOCK; **c.** Frankish *stok, sword point: TUCK[3]. **2.** Germanic *stukkjam in Old High German stukki, crust, fragment, covering: STUCCO. **3.** Germanic *stok- in Middle Dutch stoken, to poke, thrust: STOKER. **IV.** Suffixed (stative) zero-grade extended form *stup-ē- in Latin stupēre, to be stunned: STUPEFY, STUPENDOUS, STUPID. **V.** Suffixed (stative) extended zero-grade form *stud-ē- in Latin studēre, to be diligent (< "to be pressing forward"): STUDENT, STUDY. **VI.** Extended zero-grade form *stug- in Greek Stux, the river Styx (< "hatred"): STYX. **VII.** Variant zero-grade form *tud-. **1.** Latin tudes, hammer: TOIL[1]. **2.** Suffixed form *tud-ti- in Latin tussis, cough: TUSSIS. **3.** Nasalized form *tu-n-d- in Latin tundere, to beat: CONTUSE, OBTUND, PIERCE, RETUSE. **VIII.** Variant zero-grade form *tup-. **1.** Suffixed form *tup-o- in Greek tupos, a blow, mold, die: TYPE, ANTITYPE, ARCHETYPE. **2.** Nasalized form *tu-m-p- in Greek tumpanon, drum: TYMPANUM. [Pok. 1. (s)teu- 1032.]

stewə-. To condense, cluster. **1.** Extended form *stūp- in: **a.** Greek stuppē, tuft, tow: STIFLE[1], STOP, STUFF, STUPE; **b.** Sanskrit stūpa, tuft of hair, crown of the head: STUPA, TOPE[3]. **2.** Extended form *stūbh- in Greek stuphein, to contract: STYPTIC. [Pok. stewə 1035.]

stomen-. Mouth. Greek stoma, mouth: STOMA, STOMACH, STOMATO-, STOMATOUS, -STOME; ANASTOMOSIS, ANCYLOSTOMIASIS. [Pok. stomen- 1035.]

storos. Starling. Germanic *staraz in Old English stær, starling: STARLING[1]. [Pok. storos- 1036.]

strebh-. To wind, turn. **1.** Greek strephein, to wind, turn, twist: STREPTO-, STROP, STROPHE, STROPHULUS; ANASTROPHE, APOSTROPHE[1], BOUSTROPHEDON, CATASTROPHE, DIASTROPHISM. **2.** Unaspirated o-grade form *strob- in Greek strobos, a whirling, whirlwind: STROBILE, STROBOSCOPE. **3.** Unaspirated zero-grade form *str̥b- in Greek strabos, a squinting: STRABISMUS, STRABOTOMY. [Pok. strebh- 1025.]

strei-. To hiss, to buzz. Imitative root. **1.** Extended form *strīd- in Latin strīdēre, to make a harsh sound: STRIDENT. **2.** Extended variant form *trig- in Greek trismos, trigmus, a scream: TRISMUS. [Pok. 3. streig- 1036.]

streig-. To stroke, rub, press. **I.** Basic form *streig-. **1.** Germanic *strīkan in: **a.** Old English strīcan, to stroke: STRIKE; **b.** Middle Dutch striken, to strike: TRICOT. **2.** Germanic diminutive *strik-ila- in Old English stricel, implement for smoothing corn: STRICKLE. **3.** Germanic *strikōn- in Old English strica, stroke, line: STREAK. **II.** O-grade form *stroig- in Germanic *straik- in Old English strāc, stroke: STROKE. **III.** Zero-grade form *strig-. **1.** Suffixed form *strig-ā- in Latin striga, row of grain, furrow drawn lengthwise over the field: STRIGOSE. **2.** Suffixed form *strig-yā- in Latin stria, furrow, channel: STRIA. **3.** Nasalized form *stri-n-g- in Latin stringere, to draw tight, press together: STRAIN[1], STRAIT, STRICT, STRIGIL, STRINGENDO, STRINGENT; ASTRINGE, CONSTRAIN, DISTRAIN, PRESTIGE, RESTRICT. [Pok. 1. streig- 1036; 4. ster- 1028.]

strenk-. Tight, narrow. Possible root. **1.** O-grade form *stronk- in: **a.** Germanic *strangi- in Old English streng, string: STRING; **b.** Germanic *strangaz in Old English strang, strong, powerful, strict: STRONG; **c.** Germanic *strangithō in Old English strengthu, strength, strictness: STRENGTH. **2.** Variant *strang- in: **a.** Greek strangalē, halter: STRANGULATE; **b.** Greek stranx, drop (< "that which is squeezed out"): STRANGURY. [Pok. strenk-, streng- 1036.]

strep-. To make a noise. Imitative root. Latin strepere, to make noise: OBSTREPEROUS. [Pok. (s)trep- 1037.]

su-[1]. Pig. Basic form *su-. **1.** Suffixed form *su-īno- in Germanic *swīnam in: **a.** Old English swīn, swine: SWINE; **b.** Middle Dutch swīn, swine: KEELSON. **2.** Celtic *sukko-, swine,

snout of a swine, plowshare, in: **a.** British *hukk- in Old English hogg, hog: HOG; **b.** perhaps Old French soc, plowshare: SOCKET. **II.** Lengthened-grade form *sū-. **1.** Germanic *sū- in Old English sugu, sow: SOW[2]. **2.** Latin sūs, .pig: SOIL[2]. **3.** Greek hus, swine: HYENA, HYOSCINE. [Pok. su-s 1038.]

su-[2]. Well, good. **1.** Sanskrit su-, well-being, good luck: SWASTIKA. **2.** Avestan hu-, good, in huparəthwa, "good to cross over" (see per-[2]). **3.** Compound *su-gwiyes-ya, "living in good condition" (see gwei-). [Pok. su- 1037.]

sūro-. Sour, salty, bitter. **1.** Germanic *sūraz in: **a.** Old English sūr, sour: SOUR; **b.** Old High German sūr, sour: SAUERBRATEN, SAUERKRAUT; **c.** Old French sur, sour: SORREL[1]. **2.** Perhaps Greek Surakō, name of a swamp: SYRACUSE. [Pok. sūr-o 1039.]

swād-. Sweet, pleasant. **1.** Germanic *swōtja- in Old English swēte, sweet: SWEET. **2.** Suffixed form *swād-ē- in Latin suādēre, to advise, urge (< "to recommend as good"): SUASION; ASSUASIVE, DISSUADE. **3.** Suffixed form *swad-wi- in Latin suāvis, delightful: SOAVE, SUAVE, ASSUAGE. **4.** Suffixed form *swād-es- in Greek ēdos, pleasant: AEDES. **5.** Suffixed form *swād-onā in Greek hēdonē, pleasure: HEDONIC. [Pok. swād- 1039.]

swāgh-. Also wāgh-. To resound. **1.** Germanic *swōgan in Old English swōgan, to resound: SOUGH. **2.** Suffixed form *wāgh-ā in Greek ēkhē, sound: CATECHIZE. **3.** Suffixed form *wāgh-ōi- in Greek ēkhō, noise, echo: ECHO. [Pok. uāgh- 1110.]

sward-. To laugh. Greek sardanios, sneering, scornful: SARDONIC. [Pok. suard- 1040.]

swei-[1]. To whistle, hiss. Imitative root. Latin sībilāre, to whistle at, hiss down: SIBILATE; CHUFA, PERSIFLAGE. [Pok. suei- 1040.]

swei-[2]. To bend, turn. **1.** Germanic *swīp- in: **a.** Old English swāpan, to sweep, drive, swing: SWEEP, SWOOP; **b.** Old English swift, swift, quick (< "turning quickly"): SWIFT. **2.** Germanic *swīf- in Old English swīfan, to revolve: SWIVEL. **3.** Germanic *swīg- in Old Norse sveigja, to bend, yield: SWAY. **4.** Germanic *swim- in Old English swīma, dizziness: SQUEAMISH, SWIM[2]. **5.** Possibly Germanic *swīh- in Middle Dutch swijch, bough, twig: SWITCH. **6.** German schwappen, to flap, splash, akin to the source of Middle English swappen, to splash: SWAP. [Pok. suei- 1041.]

sweid-[1]. To shine. Suffixed form *sweid-os in: **1.** Latin sīdus, constellation, star: SIDEREAL; **2.** Latin augury terms consīderāre, to examine, "to observe the stars carefully" (con-, intensive prefix; see com-), and dēsīderāre, to long for, investigate (formed on analogy with consīderāre; dē-, from, DE-): CONSIDER, DESIRE. [Pok. 1. sueid- 1042.]

sweid-[2]. Sweat; to sweat. **I.** O-grade form *swoid-. **1.** Germanic *swaidaz, sweat, with its denominative *swaidjan, to sweat, in Old English swǣtan, to sweat: SWEAT. **2.** Suffixed form *swoid-os- in Latin sūdor, sweat: SUDORIFEROUS, SUDORIFIC. **3.** O-grade form *swoid-ā- in Latin sūdāre, to sweat: SUDATORIUM, SUINT; EXUDE, TRANSUDE. **II.** Suffixed zero-grade form *swid-ro- in Greek hidrōs, sweat: HIDROSIS. [Pok. 2. sueid- 1043.]

sweks. Also seks. Six. **I.** Form *seks. **1.** Germanic *seks in Old English s(i)ex, six, six: SIX. **2.** Latin sex, six: SEX-, SEICENTO, SEMESTER, SENARY. **3.** Suffixed form *seks-to- in Latin sextus, sixth: SESTET, SESTINA, SEXT, SEXTAN, SEXTANT, SEXTILE, SEXTODECIMO. **II.** Form *sweks in Greek hex, six: HEXA-, HEXAD. [Pok. sueks 1044.]

swekwo-. Resin, juice. Variant form *sokwo- in Greek opos (< *hopos), juice: OPIUM.

swel-[1]. To eat, drink. **1.** Perhaps Germanic *swil- in Old English swilian, to wash out, gargle: SWILL. **2.** Extended form *swelk- in Germanic *swelgan, *swelhan in Old English swelgan, to swallow: SWALLOW[1]; GROUNDSEL[1]. **3.** Avestan khvar-, to eat: MANTICORE. [Pok. 1. suel(k)- 1045.]

swel-[2]. To shine, burn. **1.** Extended form *sweld- in Germanic *swiltan in Old English sweltan, to die, perish (perhaps < "be over come with heat"): SWELTER. **2.** O-grade form *swol- in Germanic *swal- in Old Norse svalr, cool (< "lukewarm," < "hot"), akin to the Scandinavian source of Middle English swale, shade, shady place: SWALE. **3.** Suffixed form *swel-enā possibly in Greek helenē, torch: HELEN. [Pok. 2. suel- 1045.]

swel-[3]. Post, board. Germanic *suljō- in Old English syll, doorsill, threshold: SILL. [Pok. 2. sel-, suel- 898.]

swem-. To move, stir, swim. Possibly an

Indo-European root, but perhaps Germanic only. **1.** Germanic *swimjan in Old English swimman, to swim: SWIM[1]. **2.** Suffixed zero-grade form *sum-d- in Germanic *sund- in Old English sund, swimming, sea: SOUND[3], SOUND[4]; RADIOSONDE, ROCKETSONDE. [Pok. suem- 1046.]

swen-. To sound. **1.** Suffixed o-grade form *swon-o- in: **a.** Germanic *swanaz, *swanon, "singer," in Old English swan, swan: SWAN; **b.** Latin sonus, a sound: SONE, SONIC, SONNET, SOUND[1], UNISON. **2.** Form *swen-ā- in Latin sonāre, to sound: SONANT, SONATA, SONOROUS; ASSONANCE, CONSONANT, DISSONANT, RESOUND. [Pok. suen- 1046.]

sweng-. To swing, turn, toss. **1.** Germanic *swingan in Old English swingan, to whip, strike, swing: SWING. **2.** Germanic *swing- in Middle Dutch swinghel, instrument for beating hemp: SWINGLETREE. **3.** O-grade form *swong- in: **a.** suffixed form *swong-eyo- in Germanic *swangjan in Old English swengan, to swing, shake: SWINGE; **b.** Germanic *swank in Middle High German swank, turn, swing: SWANK. **4.** Uncertain pre-form in Norwegian swagga, to sway, akin to the Scandinavian source of SWAG. [Pok. sueng-, suenk- 1047.]

swento-. Healthy, strong. **1.** Germanic *swinth- in Old High German swintha, strong: MILLICENT. **2.** Zero-grade form *sunto- in Germanic *sunth- in Old English gesund, healthy (ge-, intensive prefix; see kom-): SOUND[2]. [Pok. suento- 1048.]

swep-[1]. To sleep. **1.** Suffixed form *swep-os- in Latin sopor, a deep sleep: SOPOR, (SOPORIFIC). **2.** Suffixed form *swep-no- in Latin somnus, sleep: SOMNI-, SOMNOLENT, INSOMNIA. **3.** Suffixed zero-grade form *sup-no- in Greek hupnos, sleep: HYPNO-, Hypnos, HYPNOSIS, HYPNOTIC. [Pok. 1. suep- 1048.]

swep-[2]. To throw, sling, cast. **1.** O-grade form *swop- in Germanic expressive form *swabb- in Middle Dutch swabbe, mop, splash: SWAB. **2.** Suffixed zero-grade form *sup-ā- in Latin dissipāre, to disperse (dis-, apart, DIS-): DISSIPATE. [Pok. 2. suep- 1049.]

swer-[1]. To speak, talk. O-grade form *swor- in: **1.** Germanic *swarjan in Old English swerian, to swear, proclaim: SWEAR; **2.** Germanic *andswaru, "a swearing against," "rebuttal" (*and-, against; see anti), in Old English andswaru, answer: ANSWER. [Pok. 1. suer- 1049.]

swer-[2]. To buzz, whisper. Imitative root. **I.** O-grade form *swor-. **1.** Suffixed form *swor-mo- in Germanic *swarmaz in Old English swearm, swarm: SWARM. **2.** Germanic *swar- in Dutch zwirrelen, to whirl, akin to the Low German source of Middle English swyrl, eddy: SWIRL. **II.** Zero-grade form *sur-. **1.** Suffixed form *sur-do- perhaps in: **a.** Latin surdus, deaf, mute: SORDINO, SOURDINE, SURD; **b.** Latin absurdus, discordant, away from the right sound, harsh (ab-, away, AB-): ABSURD. **2.** Reduplicated expressive form *su-surr- in Latin susurrus, whisper: SUSURRATION. [Pok. 2. suer- 1049.]

swer-[3]. Post, rod. Suffixed zero-grade form *sur-o- in Latin surus, branch: SURCULOSE. [Pok. 3. suer- 1050.]

swer-[4]. To cut, pierce. Germanic *swerdam in Old English sweord, sword, sword: SWORD. [Pok. 4. suer- 1050.]

swerbh-. To turn, wipe off. **1.** Germanic *swerb- in Old English sweorfan, to file away, scour, polish: SWERVE. **2.** O-grade form *sworbh- in Germanic *swarb- in Old Norse svarf, filings, akin to the Scandinavian source of SWARF. [Pok. suerbh- 1050.]

swergh-. To worry, be sick. Germanic *sorg- in Old English sorh, sorg, anxiety, sorrow: SORROW. [Pok. suergh- 1051.]

swesor-. Sister. **1.** Zero-grade form *swesr̥- in: **a.** Germanic *swistr̥- in Old English sweostor, sister: SISTER; **b.** suffixed form *swesr-īno- in Latin sōbrīnus, maternal cousin: COUSIN. **2.** Latin soror, sister: SORORAL, SORORITY. [Pok. suesor 1051.]

swī-. To be silent. Expressive formation in Greek siōpē, silence: APOSIOPESIS. [Pok. suī- 1052.]

swo-. Pronominal stem, su. **1.** Germanic *swa- in: **a.** Old English swā, so: SO[1]; **b.** Germanic compound *swa-līk-, "so like," of the same kind (see līk-), in Old English swylc, such: SUCH. **2.** Adverbial form *swai in Latin sī, if (< "thus"): NISI, QUASI. [In Pok. 2. seu- 882.]

swombho-. Spongy. Germanic *swamba- in: **a.** Middle Low German and Middle Dutch somp, swamp: SUMP; **b.** Low German zwamp, swamp, akin to the Low German source of SWAMP. [Pok. suomb(h)o-s 1052.]

swordo-. Black, dirty. **1.** Germanic *swartaz

in Old English _sweart,_ swarthy: SWART. **2.** Reduced form _*sword-_ in Latin _sordēre,_ to be dirty: SORDID. [Pok. _su̯ordo-s_ 1052.]

syū-. To bind, sew. **I.** Basic form _*syū-_ in Germanic _*siwjan_ in Old English _seowian, siowan,_ to sew: SEW. **II.** Variant form _*sū-._ **1.** Germanic _*saumaz_ in Old English _sēam,_ seam: SEAM. **2.** Latin _suere_ (past participle _sūtus_), to sew: SUTURE, ACCOUTER, COUTURE. **3.** Suffixed form _*sū-dhlā_ in Latin _sūbula,_ awl (< "sewing instrument"): SUBULATE. **4.** Suffixed form _*sū-tro-_ in Sanskrit _sūtra,_ thread, string: SUTRA; KAMASUTRA. **5.** Suffixed shortened form _*su-men_ in Greek _humēn,_ thin skin, membrane: HYMEN. [Pok. _si̯ū-_ 915.]

tā-. To melt, dissolve. **1.** Extended form _*tāw-_ in Germanic _*thāwōn_ in Old English _thāwian,_ to thaw: THAW. **2.** Suffixed form _*tā-bh-_ in Latin _tābēs,_ a melting, wasting away, putrefaction: TABES. **3.** Suffixed form _*tā-k-_ in Greek _tēkein,_ to melt: EUTECTIC. [Pok. _tā-_ 1053.]

tag-. To touch, handle. **1.** Nasalized form _*ta-n-g-_ in Latin _tangere,_ to touch: TACT, TANGENT, TANGIBLE, TASTE, TAX; ATTAIN, CONTACT, INTACT. **2.** Compound form _*n̥-tag-ro-,_ "untouched, intact" (_*n̥-,_ negative prefix; see **ne**), in Latin _integer,_ intact, whole, complete, perfect, honest: ENTIRE, INTEGER. **3.** Suffixed form _*tag-smen-_ in Latin _contāmināre,_ to corrupt by mixing or contact (< _*con-tāmen-,_ "to bring into contact with"; _con-,_ with; see **kom**): CONTAMINATE. [Pok. _tag-_ 1054.]

tāg-. To set in order. Suffixed form _*tag-yo-_ in Greek _tassein, tattein,_ to arrange, and _taxis_ (< _*tag-ti-_), arrangement: TACTICS, (-TAXIS), TAXIS, (TAXO-); ATAXIA, EUTAXY, HYPOTAXIS, PARATAXIS, SYNTAX. [Pok. _tāg-_ 1055.]

tak-[1]. To be silent. Suffixed (stative) form _*tak-ē-_ in Latin _tacēre,_ to be silent: TACET, TACIT; RETICENT. [Pok. _tak-_ 1055.]

[**tak-[2].** To take. Germanic root. **a.** Old Norse _taka,_ to take: TAKE, WAPENTAKE. **b.** Middle Low German _taken,_ to seize: TACKLE.]

[**tap-.** Germanic base of various loosely related derivatives; "plug, wad, small compact object, projecting part; to plug, to strike lightly." Variants _*tap-, *tapp-, *topp-, *tupp-._ **1.** Old English _tæppa,_ spigot: TAP[2]. **2.** Middle Dutch _tappe,_ spigot: TATTOO[1]. **3.** Frankish _*tappo,_ plug: TAMPON. **4.** Old French _taper,_ to strike lightly: TAP[1]. **5.** Spanish _tapa,_ cover, lid: TAPADERA. **6.** Old English _top,_ summit: TOP[1]. **7.** Old English _top,_ a child's plaything, perhaps a spinning top: TOP[2]. **8.** Frankish _*topp-,_ summit: TOUPEE. **9.** Old Norse _typpi,_ end: TIP[1]. **10.** Old French _to(f)fe,_ tuft: TUFT. **11.** Old English _tæppe,_ strip of cloth: TAPE. **12.** Low German _tippen,_ to strike lightly: TIP[3].]

tauro-. Bull. **1.** Possibly Germanic _*stiuraz,_ ox, in Old English _stēor,_ steer: STEER[2]. **2.** Latin _taurus,_ bull: TAURINE[1], TAURO-, TAURUS, TOREADOR, TORERO, BITTERN[1]. **3.** Greek _tauros,_ bull: TAURO-. [In Pok. _tēu-_ 1083.]

[**taw-.** To make, manufacture. Germanic root. **1.** Germanic _*taw-_ in Old English _tow-,_ spinning (only in compounds such as _tow-hūs,_ spinning house or room): TOW[2]. **2.** Germanic _*tawjan, *tawōn,_ to fashion, in Old English _tawian,_ to prepare: TAW[1]. **3.** Germanic _*ga-tawja-_ (_*ga-,_ collective prefix; see **kom**), equipment, in Old English _geatwa,_ equipment: HERIOT. **4.** Germanic _*tōwlam,_ implement, in Old English _tōl,_ implement (possibly borrowed from the cognate Old Norse _tōl_): TOOL. [In Pok. 2. _deu-_ 218.]]

tegu-. Thick. Germanic _*thiku-_ in Old English _thicce,_ thick: THICK. [Pok. _tegu-_ 1057.]

tek-[1]. To beget, give birth to. **1.** Suffixed form _*tek-no-,_ child, in: **a.** Germanic _*thegnaz,_ boy man, servant, warrior, in Old English _thegn,_ freeman, nobleman, military vassal, warrior: THANE; **b.** possibly Germanic _*thewernō,_ girl, in Old High German _thirona, diorna,_ girl: DIRNDL. **2.** Reduplicated form _*ti-tk-,_ metathesized in Greek _tiktein,_ to beget, and suffixed o-grade form _*tok-o-_ in Greek _tokos,_ birth: TOCOLOGY, OXYTOCIC, POLYTOCOUS. [Pok. 1. _tek-_ 1057.]

tek-[2]. To reach, give. Germanic _*thig-_ in Old Swedish _thiggia,_ to beg. [Pok. 2. _tek-_ 1057.]

teks-. To weave; also to fabricate, especially with an ax, also to make wicker or wattle fabric for (mud-covered) house walls. **1.** Latin _texere,_ to weave, fabricate: TEXT, TISSUE; CONTEXT, PRETEXT. **2.** Suffixed form _*teks-lā_ in: **a.** Latin _tēla,_ web, net, warp of a fabric, also weaver's beam (to which the warp threads are tied): TELA, TILLER[2], TOIL[2]; **b.** Latin _subtīlis,_ thin, fine, precise, subtle (< _*sub-tēla,_ "thread passing under the warp," the finest thread; _sub,_ under, SUB): SUBTLE. **3.** Suffixed form _*teks-ōn,_ weaver, maker of wattle for house walls, builder, in Greek _tektōn,_ carpenter, builder: TECTONIC, ARCHITECT. **4.** Suffixed form _*teks-nā,_ craft (of weaving or fabricating), in Greek _tekhnē,_ art, craft, skill: TECHNICAL, TECHNOLOGY; PANTECHNICON, POLYTECHNIC. **5.** Possibly Germanic _*thahsu-,_ badger ("the animal that builds," referring to its burrowing skill), in Old High German _dahs,_ badger: DACHSHUND. [Pok. _tekth-_ 1058.]

tekw-. To run, flee. Suffixed o-grade form _*tokw-so-_ in Greek _toxon,_ bow, also (in the plural) bow and arrow (< "that which flies"; possibly from the cognate Iranian _taxša-,_ bow, arrow): TOXIC. [Pok. _teku̯-_ 1059.]

tel-[1]. Also **telə-.** To lift, support, weigh; with derivatives referring to measured weights and thence to money and payment. **1.** Suffixed form _*tel-os-_ in: **a.** Greek _telos,_ tax, charge: TOLL[1], PHILATELY; **b.** Latin _tolerāre,_ to bear, endure: TOLERATE. **2.** Variant form _*tal-_ in Latin _tāliō,_ reciprocal punishment in kind, "something paid out": TALION, RETALIATE. **3.** Suffixed extended variant form _*tala-nt-_ in Greek _talanton,_ balance, weight, any of several specific weights of gold or silver, hence the sum of money represented by such a weight: TALENT. **4.** Reduplicated variant form _*tan-tal-_ in Greek _Tantalos,_ name of a legendary king, "the sufferer": TANTALUS, (TANTALIZE). **5.** Variant form _*tlā-_ in Greek _Atlas_ (stem _Atlant-_), name of the Titan supporting the world: ATLAS[1] (but the _Atlas_ Mountains were probably so named by the Greeks by an alteration of Berber _ádrār,_ "mountain," so that the derivation of ATLANTIC rests on a Greek folk etymology). **6.** Suffixed form _*telə-mon-_ in Greek _telamōn,_ supporter, bearer: TELAMON. **7.** Suffixed zero-grade form _*tl̥ə-ē-_ in Germanic _*thulen_ in Old English _tholian,_ to suffer, endure: THOLE. **8.** Suffixed zero-grade form _*tl̥ə-to-_ in Latin _lātus,_ "carried, borne," used as the suppletive past participle of _ferre,_ to bear (see **bher-[1]**), with its compounds: ABLATION, COLLATE, DILATORY, ELATE, ILLATION, LEGISLATOR, OBLATE[1], PRELATE, PROLATE, RELATE, SUPERLATIVE, TRANSLATE. **9.** Suffixed zero-grade form _*tl̥ə-ā-_ in Sanskrit _tulā,_ scales, balance, weight: TAEL, TOLA. **10.** Nasalized zero-grade form _*tl̥-n-ə-_ in Latin _tollere,_ to lift: EXTOL. [Pok. 1. _tel-_ 1060.]

tel-[2]. Ground, floor, board. **1.** Germanic _*thil-_ in Middle Low German and Middle Dutch _dele,_ plank: DEAL[2]. **2.** Suffixed form _*tel-n-_ in Latin _tellūs_ (stem _tellūr-_), earth, the earth: TELLURIAN, TELLURIC, TELLURION, TELLURIUM. **3.** Possibly reduplicated form _*ti-tel-_ in Latin _titulus,_ placard, label, superscription, title: TITLE. **4.** Suffixed zero-grade form _*tl̥-m-_ becoming _*tala-m-_ in Old Irish _talam,_ earth, akin to the probable Celtic source of Latin _talūtium, talūtatium,_ a mining term, "outcrop indicating the presence of gold-bearing topsoil": TALUS[2]. [Pok. 2. _tel-_ 1061.]

tem-. To cut. **1.** Suffixed form _*tem-no-_ in Greek _temnein,_ to cut: TMESIS, TOME; ANATOMY, ATOM, DIATOM, DICHOTOMY, ENTOMO-, EPITOME. **2.** Suffixed form _*tem-do-_ in Latin _tondēre,_ to shear, shave: TONSURE. **3.** Suffixed form _*tem-lo-_ in Latin _templum,_ temple, shrine, open place for observation (augury term < "place reserved or cut out"), small piece of timber: TEMPLE[1], TEMPLE[3]; CONTEMPLATE. [Pok. 1. _tem-, tend-_ 1062.]

temə-. Dark. Extended form _*teməs-._ **1.** Latin _temerē,_ blindly, rashly: TEMERITY, (TEMERARIOUS). **2.** Suffixed form _*teməs-ra_ in Latin _tenebrae_ (plural), darkness: TENEBRAE. [Pok. _tem(ə)-_ 1063.]

temp-. To stretch. Extension of **ten-.** **1.** Possibly Latin _tempus,_ temple of the head (? where the skin is stretched from behind the eye to the ear): TEMPLE[2]. **2.** Zero-grade form _*tm̥p-_ perhaps in: **a.** Persian _tāftan,_ to weave (the warp threads are stretched on the loom): TAFFETA; **b.** Iranian _*tap-,_ "carpet," in Greek _tapēs,_ carpet: TAPESTRY. [Pok. _temp-_ 1064.]

ten-. To stretch. **I.** Derivatives in the basic meaning. **1.** Suffixed form _*ten-do-_ in: **a.** Latin _tendere,_ to stretch, extend: TEND[1], TENDER[2], TENDON, TENSE[1], TENT[1], TENTER; ATTEND, CONTEND, DETENT, DISTEND, EXTEND, INTEND, OSTENSIBLE, PRETEND, SUBTEND; **b.** Latin _portendere,_ "to stretch out before" (_por-,_ variant of _pro-,_ before, PRO-), a technical term in augury, "to indicate, presage, foretell": PORTEND. **2.** Suffixed form _*ten-yo-_ in Greek _teinein,_ to stretch: BRONCHIECTASIS, EPITASIS, HYPOTENUSE, PERITONEUM, PROTASIS, TELANGIECTASIA, TENESMUS. **3.** Suffixed zero-grade form _*tn̥-nu-_ in Sanskrit _tanōti,_ he stretches or weaves: TANTRA. **4.** Basic form _*ten-_ in Latin _tenēre,_ to hold, keep, maintain (< "to cause to endure or continue, hold on to"): TENABLE, TENACIOUS, TENACULUM, TENANT, TENEMENT, TENET, TENNIS, TENON, TENOR, TENURE, TENUTO; ABSTAIN, CONTAIN, CONTINUE, DETAIN, ENTERTAIN, LIEUTENANT, MAINTAIN, OBTAIN, PERTAIN, PERTINACIOUS, RETAIN, SUSTAIN. **II.** Derivatives meaning "stretched," hence "thin." **1.** Suffixed zero-grade form _*tn̥-u-_ in Germanic _*thunw-,_ whence _*thunniz_ in: **a.** Old English _thynne,_ thin: THIN; **b.** Middle Low German _dünne,_ thin: DUNNAGE. **2.** Suffixed full-grade form _*ten-u-_ in Latin _tenuis,_ thin, rare, fine: TENUOUS; ATTENUATE, EXTENUATE. **3.** Suffixed full-grade form _*ten-ero-_ in Latin _tener,_ tender, delicate: TENDER[1], TENDRIL. **III.** Derivatives meaning "something stretched or capable of being stretched, a string." **1.** Suffixed form _*ten-ōn-_ in Greek _tenōn,_ tendon: TENO-. **2.** Suffixed o-grade form _*ton-o-_ in Greek _tonos,_ string, hence sound, pitch: TONE. **3.** Suffixed zero-grade form _*tn̥-ya-_ in Greek _tainia,_ band, ribbon: TAENIA. **4.** Suffixed form _*ten-tro-_ in Avestan _*tąthra-,_ string: SITAR. [Pok. 1. _ten-_ 1065.]

teng-. To soak. **1.** Latin _tingere,_ to moisten, soak, dye: TAINT, TINGE, TINT; INTINCTION, STAIN. **2.** Zero-grade form _*tn̥g-_ in Germanic _*thunk-_ in Old High German _thunkōn, dunkōn,_ to soak: DUNK. [Pok. 1. _teng-_ 1067.]

tenk-[1]. To stretch. Extension of **ten-.** Perhaps Germanic _*thingam_ in: **a.** Old English _thing,_ assembly, (legal) case, thing: THING; **b.** Old Norse _thing,_ assembly: FOLKETING, HUSTINGS, LAGTING; **c.** Old High German _thing, ding,_ thing: DINGUS. [Pok. 1. _tenk-_ 1067.]

tenk-[2]. To become firm, curdle, thicken. **1.** Suffixed form _*tenk-to-,_ thickened, in Germanic _*thinhtaz_ in Old Norse _thēttr,_ dense, watertight: TIGHT. **2.** Possibly suffixed o-grade form _*tonk-lo-_ in Germanic _*thangul-_ in Old Norse _thōngull,_ seaweed (? < "thick mass"): TANGLE[2]. [Pok. 2. _tenk-_ 1068.]

tens-. To stretch, draw. Extended root of **ten-.** Suffixed zero-grade form _*tn̥s-ero-_ in Sanskrit _tasara,_ shuttle: TUSSAH. [Pok. _tens-_ 1068.]

tep-. To be warm. **1.** Suffixed (stative) form _*tep-ē-_ in Latin _tepēre,_ to be warm: TEPID. **2.** Suffixed form _*tep-n-et-_ in Celtic _*tenet-_ or _*te(p)ina,_ fire (see **bhel-[1]**). [Pok. _tep-_ 1069.]

ter-[1]. To get over, break through. **1.** Suffixed form _*ter-men-,_ "that which one gets over," boundary-marker, in Latin _terminus,_ boundary, limit: TERM, TERMINUS, (TERMINATE); DETERMINE, EXTERMINATE. **2.** Suffixed zero-grade form _*tr̥-m-_ in Germanic _*thrum-_ in Old English _thrum,_ broken-off end (attested only in _tungethrum,_ the ligament of the tongue): THRUM[2]. **3.** Referred by some to this root, but more likely from root **ter-[3]**, is extended form _*tr̥ə-_ in: **a.** Sanskrit _tirati, tarati,_ he crosses over: AVATAR; **b.** possibly Persian _sarāi,_ inn: CARAVANSARY. [Pok. 4. _ter-_ 1074.]

ter-[2]. To rub, turn; with some derivatives referring to twisting, boring, drilling, and piercing; and others referring to the rubbing of cereal grain to remove the husks, and thence to the process of threshing either by the trampling of oxen or by flailing with flails. **I.** Full-grade form _*ter-._ **1. a.** Latin _terere,_ to rub away, thresh, tread, wear out: TRITE, TRITURATE; ATTRITION, CONTRITE, DETRIMENT; **b.** Greek _terēdōn,_ a kind of biting worm: TEREDO. **2.** Suffixed form _*ter-et-_ in Latin _teres_ (stem _teret-_), rounded, smooth: TERETE. **3.** Suffixed form _*ter-sk-_ in Germanic _*thersk-,_ to thresh, tread, in: **a.** Old English _therscan,_ to thresh: THRESH, (THRASH); **b.** Old English _therscold, threscold,_ sill of a door (over which one treads; second element obscure): THRESHOLD. **II.** O-grade form _*tor-._ **1.** Greek _toreus,_ a boring tool: TOREUTICS. **2.** Suffixed form _*tor-mo-,_ hole, in Germanic _*tharma_ in Old High German _darm,_ gut: DERMA[2]. **3.** Suffixed form _*tor-no-_ in Greek _tornos,_ tool for drawing a circle, also circle, also lathe: TURN; ATTORN, CONTOUR, DETOUR, RETURN. **III.** Zero-grade form _*tr̥-_ in Germanic _*thr-_ in Middle Dutch _drillen,_ to drill: DRILL[1]. **IV.** Extended forms. **1.** Form _*trē-_ in: **a.** Germanic _*thrēw-_ in Old English _thrāwan,_ to turn, twist: THROW; **b.** Greek _trēma,_ perforation: MONOTREME, TREMATODE. **2.** Suffixed form _*trē-tu-_ in Germanic _*thrēdu-,_ twisted yarn, in Old English _thrǣd,_ thread: THREAD. **3.** Suffixed form _*trī-ōn-,_ probably in Latin _triō,_ plow ox: SEPTENTRION. **4.** Suffixed form _*trī-dhlo-_ in Latin _tribulum,_ a threshing sledge: TRIBULATION. **5.** Form _*trau-_ in Greek _trauma,_ hurt, wound: TRAUMA. **6.** Form _*tru-_ in Greek _truma, trumē,_ hole: TRYMA. **7.** Form _*trib-_ in Greek _tribein,_ to rub, thresh, pound, wear out: TRIBADE, TRYPSIN, DIATRIBE. **8.** Form _*trōg-_ in Greek _trogein,_ to gnaw: TROGON. 9. Form *trup- in Greek trupē, hole: TREPAN[1], TRYPANOSOME. 10. Form *trūg- possibly in Gaulish *trūgant-, wretched (? < "worn out"): TRUANT. [Pok. 3. ter- 1071.]

ter-[3]. Also **terə-**. Related to **ter-[1]**. To cross over, pass through, overcome. 1. Zero-grade form *tr̥- in Germanic suffixed form *thur-ila- in Old English thyr(e)l, a hole (< "a boring through"): THRILL; NOSTRIL. 2. Suffixed zero-grade form *tr̥-k- in Germanic *thurh in Old English thurh, thuruh, through: (THOROUGH), THROUGH. 3. Extended form *trā- in Latin trāns, across, over, beyond, through (perhaps originally the present participle of a verb *trāre, to cross over): TRANS-, TRANSOM, (TRESTLE). 4. Suffixed extended form *tru-k- in: a. Latin trux (stem truc-), savage, fierce, grim (< "overcoming," "powerful," "penetrating"): TRUCULENT; b. suffixed nasalized form *tru-n-k-o- in Latin truncus, deprived of branches or limbs, mutilated, hence trunk (? < "overcome, maimed"): TRENCH, (TRUNCATE), TRUNK. 5. Greek nek-tar, "overcoming death" (see **nek-[2]**). [Pok. 5. ter- 1075.]

ter-[4]. To tremble. See extended roots **trem-**, **trep-[1]**, **tres-**. [Pok. 1. ter- 1070.]

terkw-. To turn. Extended root of **ter-[2]**. 1. Variant form *t(w)erk- in Germanic *thwerh-, twisted, oblique, in: a. Old High German dwerah, twërh, oblique: QUEER; b. Old Norse thverr, transverse: THWART. 2. Zero-grade form *tr̥kw- in Latin torquēre, to twist: TART[2], TORCH, TORMENT, TORQUE[1], TORQUE[2], TORSADE, TORT, TORTUOUS, TRUSS; CONTORT, DISTORT, EXTORT, NASTURTIUM, RETORT[1], (TORTICOLLIS). [Pok. terk- 1077.]

terp-. To satisfy oneself. Greek terpein, to delight, cheer: TERPSICHORE. [Pok. terp- 1077.]

ters-. To dry. 1. Suffixed zero-grade form *tr̥s-t- in Germanic *thurs- in: a. suffixed form *thurs-tu- in Old English thurst, dryness, thirst: THIRST; b. Old Norse thorskr, cod (< "dried fish"), whence Norwegian torsk, tosk, cod, with dialectal (Norn) variant tusk, cod, stockfish: CUSK. 2. Suffixed form *ters-ā- in Latin terra, earth (< "dry land"): TERRACE, (TERRAIN), TERRAQUEOUS, TERRENE, TERRESTRIAL, TERRIER, TERRITORY, TUREEN; FUMITORY, INTER, MEDITERRANEAN, PARTERRE, SUBTERRANEAN, TERREPLEIN, TERREVERT, TERRICOLOUS, TERRIGENOUS, VERDITER. 3. Suffixed o-grade form *tors-eyo- in Latin torrēre, to dry, parch, burn: TOAST[1], TORRENT, TORRID. 4. Suffixed full-grade form *ters-o- in Greek tarsos, frame of wickerwork (originally for drying cheese), hence a flat surface, sole of the foot, ankle: TARSUS. [Pok. ters- 1078.]

teu-. To pay attention to, turn to. 1. O-grade form *tou- in Germanic *thau- in Old English thēaw, usage, custom (< "observance"): THEW. 2. Suffixed zero-grade form *tu-ē- in Latin tuērī, to look at, watch, protect: TUITION, TUTOR; INTUITION. [Pok. 2. teu- 1079.]

teuə-. Also **teu-**. To swell. 1. Extended form *teuk- in Germanic *thiuham, "the swollen or fat part of the leg," thigh, in Old English thēoh, thigh: THIGH. 2. Extended form *teus- in Germanic compound *thus-hundi-, "swollen hundred," thousand (*hundi-, hundred; see **dekm̥**), in Old English thūsend, thousand: THOUSAND. 3. Suffixed zero-grade form *tu-el- probably in Germanic *thul- in Old English thol(l), oar pin, oarlock (< "a swelling"): THOLE PIN. 4. Extended zero-grade form *tum- in: a. Germanic *thūmōn- in Old English thūma, thumb (< "the thick finger"): THUMB, (THIMBLE); b. suffixed (stative) form *tum-ē- in Latin tumēre, to swell, be swollen, be proud: TUMESCENT, TUMID, TUMOR; CONTUMACY, CONTUMELY, DETUMESCENCE, INTUMESCE, TUMEFACIENT, TUMEFY; c. suffixed form *tum-olo- in Latin tumulus, raised heap of earth, mound: TUMULUS. 5. Extended lengthened zero-grade form *tūbh- in Latin tūber, lump, swelling: TRUFFLE, TUBER; PROTUBERATE. 6. Suffixed zero-grade form *tu-ro- in Greek turos, cheese (< "a swelling," "coagulating"): BUTTER, TYROSINE, TYROTHRICIN. 7. Suffixed variant form *twō-ro- in Greek sōros, heap, pile: SOROSIS, SORUS, SORITES. 8. Suffixed variant form *twō mn̥, in Greek sōma, body (< "a swelling," "stocky form"): SOMA, SOMATO-, -SOME[2]. 9. Suffixed zero-grade form *twə-wo- in Greek saos, sōs, safe, healthy (< "swollen," "strong"), with derivative verb sōzein, to save, rescue: CREOSOTE, SOTERIOLOGY. 10. Perhaps suffixed extended form *tubh-mo- (or extended zero-grade form *tum-) in Greek tumbos, barrow, tomb: TOMB. [Pok. tēu- 1080.]

teutā-. Tribe. 1. Germanic *theudā-, people, with derivative *theudiskaz, of the people, in Middle Dutch duutsch, German, of the Germans or Teutons: DUTCH, PLATTDEUTSCH. 2. Suffixed form *teut-onōs, "they of the tribe," in Germanic tribal name *theudanōz, borrowed via Celtic into Latin as Teutonī, the Teutons: TEUTON. 3. Latin tōtus, all, whole (? < "of the whole tribe"): TEETOTUM, TOTAL, TUTTI; FACTOTUM. [In Pok. tēu- 1080.]

[**threph-.** Also **treph-**. To cause to grow, develop. Greek root. 1. Greek trephein, to feed, nourish, and trophē, nourishment: TROPHIC, TROPHO-, ATROPHY, EUTROPHIC, POLYTROPHIC. 2. Suffixed form *threph-ma in Greek thremma, creature (< "nursling"): THREMMATOLOGY. [In Pok. dherebh- 257.]]

[**thrix.** Hair. Greek word of unknown origin: TRICHINA, TRICHO-, TRICHOME, -TRICHOUS; PERITRICHA, STREPTOTHRICIN, TYROTHRICIN, ULOTRICHOUS. [In Pok. dhrigh- 276.]]

tit-. Also **tik-**, **kit-**. To tickle. Expressive root. 1. Germanic *kit- in Old Norse kitla, to tickle: KITTLE. 2. Latin titillāre, to tickle, titillate: TITILLATE. [In Pok. geid- 356.]

to-. Demonstrative pronoun. For the nominative singular see **so-**. 1. Germanic *thē- in: a. Old English thē, thȳ (instrumental case), by the: THE[1]; NATHELESS; b. Middle Dutch de, the: DAFFODIL, DECOY. 2. Germanic *thauh, "for all that," in Old Norse thō, though: THOUGH. 3. Germanic *thasi- in Old English thes, this, this: THIS, (THESE). 4. Germanic *thana- in Old English thanne, thænne, than, then: THAN, THEN. 5. Germanic *thanana- in Old English thanon, thence: THENCE. 6. Germanic *thar in Old English thǣr, thēr, there: THERE. 7. Germanic *thathro in Old English thæder, thither: THITHER. 8. Germanic nominative plural *thai in Old English thā and Old Norse their, they: THEY. 9. Germanic genitive plural *thaira in Old Norse theiṙ(r)a, theirs: THEIR. 10. Germanic dative plural *thaim in Old Norse theim and Old English thǣm, them: THEM. 11. Extended form *tod in: a. Germanic *that in Old English thæt, that: THAT, (THOSE); b. Greek to, the: TAUTO-. 12. Germanic *thus- in Old English thus, thus: THUS. 13. Adverbial (originally accusative) form *tam in Latin tam, so, so much: TANDEM, TANTAMOUNT, TAUNT[2]. 14. Suffixed reduced form *t-āli- in Latin tālis, such: TALES. [Pok. 1. to- 1086.]

tolkw-. To speak. Metathesized form *tlokw- in Latin loquī, to speak: LOCUTION, LOQUACIOUS; ALLOCUTION, CIRCUMLOCUTION, COLLOQUY, ELOCUTION, GRANDILOQUENCE, INTERLOCUTION, MAGNILOQUENT, OBLOQUY, PROLOCUTOR, SOLILOQUY, VENTRILOQUISM. [Pok. tolku- 1088.]

tong-. To think, feel. 1. Germanic *thankōn in: a. Old English thancian, to thank: THANK; b. Old English thencan, to think: THINK. 2. Germanic *(ga)thauht- (*ga-, collective prefix; see **kom**) in Old English (ge)thōht, thought: THOUGHT. 3. Germanic factitive *thunkjan in Old English thyncan, to seem: METHINKS. [Pok. 1. tong- 1088.]

tragh-. To draw, drag, move. Rhyming variant **dhragh-**. Latin trahere, to pull, draw: TRACT[1], TRACTABLE, TRACTION, TRAIL, TRAIN, TRAIT, TRAWL, TREAT; ABSTRACT, ATTRACT, CONTRACT, DETRACT, DISTRACT, EXTRACT, PORTRAY, PROTRACT, RETRACT, SUBTRACT. [Pok. tragh- 1089.]

treb-. Dwelling. 1. Zero-grade form *tr̥b- in Germanic *thurp- in Old English thorp, village, hamlet: THORP. 2. Latin trabs, beam, timber: TRABEATED, TRABECULA, TRAVE; ARCHITRAVE. [Pok. treb- 1090.]

trei-. Three. I. Nominative plural form *treyes. 1. Germanic *thrijiz in Old English thrie, thrēo, thrī, three, with its derivatives thrīga, thrīwa, thrice, and thrītig, thirty (-tig, -TY), and thrēotīne, thirteen (-tīne, -tiene, -TEEN): THREE, THRICE, THIRTY, THIRTEEN. 2. Latin trēs, three: TREY, TRIO; TRAMMEL, TRECENTO, TREPHINE, TRIUMVIR, TROCAR. II. Zero-grade form *tri-. 1. Suffixed form *tri-tyo- in: a. Germanic *thrithjaz, a third, in (i) Old English thrid(d)a, a third: THIRD (ii) Old Norse thrithi, a third: RIDING[2]; b. Latin tertius, a third: TERCEL, TERCET, TERTIAN, TERTIARY, TIERCE, SESTERCE. 2. Latin tri-, three: TRI-. 3. Greek tri-, three: TRI-, TRICLINIUM, TRICROTIC, TRIDACTYL, TRIGLYPH. 4. Sanskrit tri, three: TEAPOY, TRIMURTI. 5. Greek trias, the number three: TRIAD. 6. Greek trikha, in three parts: TRICHOTOMY. 7. Greek compound triērēs, galley with three banks of oars, trireme (-ērēs, oar; see **erə-[1]**): TRIERARCH. 8. Suffixed form *tri-to- in Greek tritos, a third: TRITANOPIA, TRITIUM. 9. Compound form *tri-pl-, "threefold" (*-pl-, from combining form *-plo-; see **pel-[3]**), in Greek triploos, triple: TRIPLOID. 10. Compound form *tri-plek-, "threefold" (*-plek-, -fold; see **plek-**), in Latin triplex, triple: TRIPLEX. 11. Compound form *tri-st-i, "third person standing by" (see **stā-**), in Latin testis, a witness: TESTAMENT, TESTIMONY, TESTIS; ATTEST, CONTEST, DETEST, OBTEST, PROTEST, TESTIFY. 12. Persian si, three: SITAR. III. Extended zero-grade form *tris-, "thrice." 1. Latin ter, thrice: TER-, TERN[2]. 2. Greek tris, thrice: TRISOCTAHEDRON. 3. Suffixed form *tris-no- in Latin trīnī, three each: TRINE, (TRINITY). IV. O-grade variant form *troy- in Russian troje, three: TROIKA. [Pok. trei- 1090.]

trem-. To tremble. Extended form of **ter-[4]**. Latin tremere, to shake, tremble: TREMENDOUS, TREMOR, TREMULOUS. [Pok. trem- 1092.]

trep-[1]. To tremble. Extended form of **ter-[4]**. Latin trepidus, agitated, alarmed: TREPID; INTREPID. [Pok. 1. trep- 1094.]

trep-[2]. To turn. 1. Greek trepein, to turn: -TROPOUS; ATROPOS, TREPONEME. 2. O-grade form *trop- in: a. suffixed form *trop-o- in Greek tropos, a turn, way, manner: TROPE, TROPO-; CONTRIVE, RETRIEVE; b. suffixed form *trop-ā- in Greek tropē, a turning, change: TROPHY, TROPIC; ENTROPY. [Pok. 2. trep- 1094.]

tres-. To tremble. Extended form of **ter-[4]**. Metathesized form *ters- in Latin terrēre, to frighten (< "to cause to tremble"): TERRIBLE, TERROR; DETER, TERRIFIC. [Pok. tres- 1095.]

treu-. To thrive. Suffixed variant form *trū-ti- in Germanic *thrūdi- in: a. Old English thrȳth, strength, power: MILDRED; b. Old High German drūd, strength: GERTRUDE. [Pok. treu- 1095.]

treud-. To squeeze. 1. Germanic *thriut- in Old English thrēat, oppression, use of force: THREAT. 2. Variant form *trūd- in Germanic *thrūstjan in Old Norse thrȳsta, to squeeze, compress: THRUST. 3. Latin trūdere, to thrust, push: ABSTRUSE, EXTRUDE, INTRUDE, OBTRUDE, PROTRUDE. [Pok. tr-eu-d 1095.]

trozdos-. Also **trosdos-**. Thrush. 1. Germanic *thrau(d)st- in Old English throstle, thrush: THROSTLE. 2. Germanic *thruskjōn- in Old English thrysce, thrush: THRUSH[1]. 3. Zero-grade reduced form *tr̥sdo- in Latin turdus, thrush: STURDY[1]. 4. Perhaps altered in Greek strouthos, sparrow, ostrich: STRUTHIOUS, (OSTRICH). [Pok. trozdos- 1096.]

tu-. Second person singular pronoun; you, thou. 1. Lengthened-grade form *tū (accusative *te, *tege) in Germanic *thū (accusative *theke) in Old English thū (accusative thec, thē), thou: THOU[1], (THEE). 2. Suffixed extended form *t(w)ei-no- in Germanic *thīnaz in Old English thīn, thine: THINE, THY. [Pok. tu- 1097.]

twei-. To agitate, shake, toss. 1. Extended form *tweid- in Germanic *thwīt- in: a. Old English thwītan, to strike, whittle down: WHITTLE; b. Middle Dutch duit, a small coin (? < "piece cut or tossed off"): DOIT. 2. Extended form *tweis- in Greek seiein, to shake: SEISM. [Pok. 2. tu̯ei- 1099.]

twengh-. To press in on. Germanic *thwang- in: a. Old English thwong, thwang, thong, band (< "constraint"): THONG; b. by-form *twangjan in Old English twengan, to pinch: TWINGE. [Pok. tu̯engh- 1099.]

twer-[1]. Also **tur-**. To turn, whirl. I. Variant form *stur-. 1. Suffixed form *stur-mo- in Germanic *sturmaz, storm (< "whirlwind"), in Old English storm, storm: STORM. 2. Germanic *sturjan in Old English styrian, to move, agitate: STIR[1]. II. Suffixed form *tur-bā in Greek turbē, tumult, disorder: TURBID, (TROUBLE), TURBINE; DISTURB, PERTURB. [Pok. 1. tu̯er-, tur- 1100.]

twer-[2]. To grasp, hold; hard. 1. Slavic *tvr̥d- altered in West Slavic kwardy, quartz: QUARTZ. 2. Suffixed form *twer-y-ēn-, she who grasps, binds, enthralls, in Greek Seirēn, Siren: SIREN. [Pok. 2. tu̯er- 1101.]

twerk-. To cut. Zero-grade form *twr̥k- in Greek sarx, flesh (< "piece of meat"): SARCASM, SARCOID, SARCOMA, SARCOUS; ANASARCA, ECTOSARC, PERISARC, SARCOCARP, SARCOPHAGUS, SARCOPTIC MANGE, SYSSARCOSIS. [Pok. tu̯erk- 1102.]

[**twik-.** To pinch off. Germanic root. 1. Old English twiccian, to pinch: TWEAK. 2. Low German twikken, to twitch, akin to the Low German source of Middle English twicchen, to twitch: TWITCH.]

ud-. Also **ūd-**. Up, out. 1. Germanic *ūt-, out, in: a. Old English ūt, OUT, UTMOST; b. Old High German ūz, out: CAROUSE; c. Old Norse ūt, out: OUTLAW; d. Middle Dutch ute, uut, out: UITLANDER; e. Middle Dutch ūteren, to drive away, speak out: UTTER[1]; f. Germanic suffixed (comparative) form *ūt-era- in Old English ūtera, outer: UTTER[2]; g. Germanic compound *bi-ūtana (*bi-, by, at; see **ambhi**), "at the outside," in Old English būtan, būte, outside (adverb): BUT, ABOUT. 2. Extended form *uds in Germanic *uz, out, and prefix *uz-, out, in: a. Old High German ir-, out: ERSATZ; b. Middle Dutch oor-, out: ORT; c. Germanic *uz-dailjan, "a portioning out," judgment (see **dail-**). 3. Suffixed (comparative) form *ud-tero- in Greek husteros, later, second, after: HYSTERESIS, HYSTERON PROTERON. 4. Greek hu- in compound hubris, violence, outrage, insolence (bri-, perhaps "heavy," "violent"; see **gwer-**[2]): HUBRIS. [Pok. ŭd- 1103.]

udero-. Abdomen, womb, stomach; with distantly similar forms (perhaps taboo deformations) in various languages. 1. Latin uterus (reshaped from *udero-), womb: UTERUS. 2. Perhaps taboo deformation *wen-tri- in Latin venter, belly: VENTER, VENTRILOQUISM. 3. Perhaps taboo deformation *wn̥s-ti- in Latin vēsīca, bladder: VESICA. 4. Variant form *ud-tero- in Greek hustera, womb: HYSTERIC, HYSTERO-. [Pok. udero- 1104.]

ul-. To howl. Imitative root. 1. Possibly Germanic *uwwalōn, owl, in Old English ūle, owl: OWL. 2. Germanic by-form *uwwilōn, owl, in Middle Dutch hūlen, to howl (like an owl): HOWL. 3. Latin ululāre, to howl: ULULATE. [Pok. 1. u- 1103, ul- 1105.]

uper. Over. 1. Extended form *uperi in Germanic *uberi in: a. Old English ofer, over: OVER; b. Middle Dutch over, over: ORLOP. 2. Extended variant form *(s)uperi in: a. Latin super, above, over: SUPER-, SOUBRETTE, SOVEREIGN, SUPERABLE, SUPERIOR, SUPREME, SIRLOIN, SUR-; b. suffixed form *(s)uper(i)-no- in Latin supernus, above, upper, top: SUPERNAL; c. suffixed form *super-bhw-o-, "being above" (*bhw-o-, being; see **bheu-**), in Latin superbus, superior, excellent, arrogant: SUPERB; d. suffixed (superlative) reduced form *sup-mo- in Latin summus, highest, topmost: SUM, SUMMIT; e. variant form *(s)uprā in Latin suprā, above, beyond: SOPRANO, SUPRA-, SOMERSAULT. 3. Basic form *uper in Greek huper, over: HYPER-. [Pok. uper 1105.]

upo. Under, up from under, over. 1. Germanic *upp-, up, in: a. Old English up, uppe, up: UP; b. Old English up-, upp-, up-: UP-; c. Middle Dutch op, up: UPROAR. 2. Germanic *upanaz, "put or set up," open, in Old English open, open: OPEN. 3. Germanic *bi-ufana, "on, above" (*bi-, by, at; see **ambhi**), in Old English būfan, above, over: ABOVE. 4. Extended form *upelo- in Germanic *ubilaz, "exceeding the proper limit," evil, in Old English yfel, evil: EVIL. 5. Extended form *upes- in Germanic *obaswa, *obizwa, vestibule, porch, eaves (< "that which is above or in front"), in: a. Old English efes, eaves: EAVES; b. Germanic *obis-drupp-, dripping water from the eaves (*drupp-, to drip; see **dhreu-**), in Old English yfesdrype, water from the eaves: EAVESDROP. 6. Variant form *(s)up- in: a. Latin sub, under: SOUTANE, SUB-; b. Latin supīnus, lying on the back (< "thrown backward or under"): SUPINE; c. suffixed form *sup-ter in Latin subter, secretly: SUBTERFUGE. 7. Basic form *upo in Greek hupo-, under: HYPO-. 8. Suffixed variant form *ups-o- in Greek hupsos, height, top: HYPSO-. 9. Basic form *upo- in Celtic *vo-, under, in Latin verēdus, post horse (see **reidh-**). 10. Compound *upo-sto- probably in Celtic *wasso-, "one who stands under," servant, young man (*sto-, standing; see **stā-**): VALET, (VARLET), VASSAL. 11. Sanskrit úpa, near to: OPAL, UPANISHAD. [Pok. upo 1106.]

[**vīnum.** Wine. Latin noun, related to Greek oinos, wine. Probably borrowed from a Mediterranean word *woin- meaning "wine." 1. Latin vīnum: (VIGNETTE), VINACEOUS, VINE, VINI-; VINEGAR, (VINEYARD), WINE. 2. Greek oinos: OENOLOGY, OENOMEL.]

[**virēre.** To be green. Latin verb of unknown origin. FARTHINGALE, VERDANT, VIREO, VIRESCENT, VIRID; BILIVERDIN, TERRE-VERTE.]

wā-[1]. To bend apart. A root suggested by some with the following possible derivatives that, however, are probably unrelated and of obscure origin. 1. Latin vārus, bent, knock-kneed: VARA, VARUS, VERANDAH; DIVARICATE, (PREVARICATE). 2. Latin varius, spotty, speckled, changeable: VARIOUS, VARY; MINIVER. 3. Latin varix, varicose vein: (VARICOSE), VARIX. [Pok. 2. u̯ā- 1108.]

wā̆-[2]. Also **wen-**. To beat, wound. 1. Suffixed zero-grade form *wn̥-to- in Germanic *wundaz in Old English wund, a wound: WOUND[1]. 2. Suffixed o-grade form *won-yo- in Germanic *wanja-, swelling, in Old English wen(n), wæn(n), wen: WEN[1]. [Pok. 1. u̯u- 1108.]

wāb-. To cry, scream. Suffixed form *wāb-eyo- in Germanic *wōpjan, to wail, in Old English wēpan, to weep: WEEP. [Pok. u̯āb- 1109.]

wadh-. A pledge; to pledge. 1. Germanic *wadi- in: a. Old English wedd, a pledge, marriage: WEDLOCK; b. Old English weddian, to pledge, bind in wedlock: WED; c. Frankish *wadi, a pledge: GAGE[1], WAGE, (WAGER); DÉGAGÉ, ENGAGE, (MORTGAGE). 2. Latin praes (for praevides), surety, pledge (< "that which is given before"; prae-, before, PRE-): PRAEDIAL. [Pok. u̯adh- 1109.]

wādh-. To go. 1. Shortened form *wadh- in Germanic *wathan, to go, in Old English wadan, to go: WADE. 2. Basic form *wādh- in Latin vādere, to go, step: VAMOOSE; EVADE, INVADE, PERVADE. [Pok. u̯ādh- 1109.]

wag-. Sheath, cover. Suffixed lengthened-grade form *wāg-inā in Latin vāgīna, sheath: VAGINA, VAGINO-, VANILLA; EVAGINATE, INVAGINATE. [Pok. 1. u̯āg- 1110.]

wai. Alas (interjection). 1. Germanic *wai in Old English wā, woe (interjection), alas: WOE, WELLAWAY. 2. Germanic *waiwalōn in Old Norse vāla, vǣla, *veila, to lament: WAIL. [Pok. u̯ai- 1110.]

wak-. Cow (perhaps "who calves for the first time"). Extended expressive form *wakkā in Latin vacca, cow: BUCKAROO, VACCINE, VAQUERO. [Pok. u̯akā 1111.]

wal-. To be strong. 1. Suffixed (stative) form *wal-ē- in Latin valēre, to be strong: VALE[2], VALENCE, VALERIAN, (VALERIE), VALETUDINARIAN, VALIANT, VALID, VALOR, VALUE; AVAIL, CONVALESCE, COUNTERVAIL, EQUIVALENT, PREVAIL. 2. Extended o-grade form *wold(h)- in: a. Germanic *walthan, *waldan, to rule, in (i) Old English wealdan (strong verb), to rule, and wieldan (weak verb), to rule, govern: WIELD (ii) Old High German waltan, to rule: GERALD, WALTER; b. Germanic derivative noun *wald-, power, rule, in (i) Old English weald, force: REGINALD (ii) Old High German wald, power: ARNOLD (iii) Old Norse valdr, ruler: RONALD (iv) Germanic compound *harja-waldaz, "army commander" (see **koro-**). 3. Suffixed extended o-grade form *wold-ti- in Old Church Slavonic vlastĭ, rule, administration: OBLAST. [Pok. u̯al- 1111.]

walso-. A post. Latin vallus, post, stake, whence vallum, a palisade, wall: VALLATION, WALL; INTERVAL. [In Pok. 7. u̯el- 1140.]

wāt-. Also **wet-**. To inspire, spiritually arouse. 1. Germanic *wōdaz in Old English wōd, insane, mad: WOOD[2]. 2. Germanic *wōd-eno-, *wōd-ono-, "raging," "mad," hence "spirit," name of the chief Teutonic god, in: a. Old English Wōden, Woden: WODEN; b. Old English Wōdnesdæg, "Woden's day": WEDNESDAY; c. Old Norse Ōdhinn, Odin: ODIN. 3. Latin vātēs, prophet, poet: VATIC. [Pok. u̯at- 1113.]

we-. We. Suffixed variant form *wei-es in Germanic *wīz in Old English wē, we, we: WE. [Pok. u̯e- 1114.]

wē-. To blow. 1. Suffixed shortened form *we-dhro in Germanic *wedram, wind, weather, in Old English weder, weather, storm, wind: WEATHER. 2. Suffixed (participial) form *wē-nt-o-, blowing, in: a. Germanic *windaz in (i) Old English wind, wind: WIND[1] (ii) Old Norse vindr, wind: WINDOW[1]; b. Latin ventus, wind: VENTAIL, VENTILATE, VENT. 3. Suffixed Germanic form *wē-ingja in Old Norse vængr, wing: WING. 4. Suffixed shortened form *we-tlo- in Germanic *we-thla- in Old High German wedil, wadal, winnowing fan, (wagging) tail: WHEEDLE. 5. Probably zero-grade form *wə- becoming *wa- in suffixed extended form *wat-no- in Latin vannus, winnowing fan: FAN[1], VAN[3]. 6. Suffixed variant form *awe-tmo- in Greek atmos (< *aetmos), breath, vapor: ATMO-. (7. Attributed by some to this root, but more likely of obscure origin, is Greek aēr, air: AERIAL, AERO-, AIR, ARIA, MALARIA. 8. Related to Greek aēr, air, is Greek aura, breath, vapor: AURA.) 9. Basic form *wē- in Sanskrit vāti (stem vā-), he blows: NIRVANA. [Pok. 10. au̯(e)- 81.]

webh-. To weave. 1. Germanic *weban in Old English wefan, to weave: WEAVE, WOOF[1]. 2. Germanic *wefta- in Old English wefta, weft, cross thread: WEFT. 3. Suffixed o-grade form *wobh-yo- in Germanic *wabjam, fabric, web, in Old English web(b), web: WEB, (WEBSTER). 4. Suffixed Germanic form *webila- in Old English wifel, weevil (< "that which moves briskly"): WEEVIL. 5. Suffixed Germanic form *wabila-, web, honeycomb, in: a. Middle Low German wāfel, honeycomb: GOFFER, WAFER; b. obsolete Dutch waefel, honeycomb: WAFFLE. 6. Possibly Germanic *wab-, to move back and forth as in weaving, in: a. Old English wafian, to move (the hand) up and down: WAVE; b. Old Norse vafra, to move unsteadily, flicker: WAVER; c. Low German wabbeln, to move from side to side, sway: WOBBLE. 7. Suffixed zero-grade form *ubh-ā- in Greek huphē, web: HYPHA. [Pok. u̯ebh- 1114.]

wed-[1]. Water; wet. 1. Suffixed o-grade form *wod-ōr in Germanic *watar- in: a. Old English wæter, water: WATER; b. Old High German wazzar, water: VASELINE. 2. Lengthened-grade form *wēd- in Germanic *wēd- in Old English wǣt, wēt, wet: WET. 3. O-grade form *wod- in Germanic suffixed form *wat-skan, to wash, in Old English wæscan, wacsan, to wash: WASH. 4. Nasalized form *we-n-d- in Germanic wintruz, winter, "wet season," in Old English winter, winter: WINTER. 5. Suffixed zero-grade form *ud-ōr in Greek hudōr, water: (HYDRANT), HYDRO-, (HYDROUS); ANHYDROUS, CLEPSYDRA, DROPSY, HYDATID, UTRICLE. 6. Suffixed nasalized zero-grade form *u-n-d-ā in Latin unda, wave: UNDINE, UNDULATE; ABOUND, INUNDATE, REDOUND, REDUNDANT, SURROUND. 7. Suffixed zero-grade form *ud-ro-, *ud-ra-, water animal, in: a. Germanic *otraz, otter, in Old English otor, otter: OTTER; b. Latin lutra, otter: NUTRIA; c. Greek hudros, a water snake: HYDRUS; d. Greek hudra, a water serpent: HYDRA[1]. 8. Suffixed zero-grade form *ud-skio- in Old Irish uisce, water: USQUEBAUGH, (WHISKEY). 9. Suffixed o-grade form *wod-ā in Russian voda, water: VODKA. [Pok. 9. au̯(e)- 78.]

wed-[2]. To speak. 1. Reduplicated form *awe-ud- dissimilated to *aweid- with suffixed o-grade form *awoid-o- respectively in Greek aeidein (Attic aidein), to sing, and aoidē (Attic ōidē), song, ode: ODE, (ODEUM); COMEDY, EPODE, HYMNODY, MELODY, MONODY, (PALINODE), PARODY, RHAPSODY, TRAGEDY. 2. Sanskrit vāda, sound, call, speech, statement: THERAVADA. [Pok. 6. au- 76.]

wedh-. To push, strike. Suffixed lengthened o-grade form *wōdh-eyo- in Greek ōthein, to push: OSMOSIS. [Pok. 1. u̯edh- 1115.]

weg-[1]. To weave a web. Related to **wokso-**. Suffixed form *weg-slo- in Latin vēlum, a sail, curtain, veil: VEIL, VELUM, VEXILLUM, VOILE; REVEAL. [Pok. u̯eg- 1117.]

weg-[2]. To be strong, be lively. 1. Suffixed o-grade form *wog-ē- in Germanic *wakēn in Old English *wacan, to wake up, arise, and wacian, to be awake: WAKE[1]. 2. Suffixed o-grade form *wog-no- in Germanic *waknan in Old English wæcnan, wæcnian, to awake: WAKEN. 3. Germanic *wakjan in Old English wæccan, to be awake: WATCH. 4. Greek *wak- in Old High German wahha, watch, vigil: BIVOUAC. 5. Germanic *waht- in: a. Frankish *wahtōn, to watch for: WAIT; b. Middle Dutch wachten, to watch, guard: WAFT. 6. Suffixed (stative) form *weg-ē- in: a. Latin vegēre, to be lively: VEGETABLE; b. Latin by-form vigēre, to be lively: VIGOR. 7. Suffixed form *weg-eli- in Latin vigil, watchful, awake: VEDETTE, VIGIL, VIGILANT; REVEILLE, SURVEILLANT. 8. Suffixed form *weg-slo- in Latin vēlōx, fast, "lively": VELOCITY. [Pok. u̯eg- 1117.]

wegh-. To go, transport in a vehicle. 1. Germanic *wigan in Old English wegan, to carry, balance in the scale: WEIGH[1]. 2. Germanic lengthened form *wǣg- in Old English wǣge, weight, unit of weight: WEE. 3. Suffixed form *wegh-ti- in Germanic *wihti- in Old English wiht, gewiht, weight: WEIGHT. 4. Germanic *wegaz, course of travel, way, in: a. Old English weg, way: WAY; (AWAY), (ALWAYS); b. Old Norse vegr, way, region: NORWAY. 5. Suffixed form *wegh-no- in Germanic *wagnaz, vehicle, in: a. Old English wæ(g)n, wagon: WAIN; b. Middle Dutch wagen, wagon: WAGON, (WAINSCOT). 6. Suffixed o-grade form *wogh-lo- in: a. Germanic *waglaz in Old Norse vagl, chicken roost, perch, beam: WALLEYED; b. Greek okhlos, populace, mob (< "moving mass"): OCHLOCRACY, OCHLOPHOBIA. 7. Distantly related to this root are: a. Germanic *wag-, "to move about," in (i) Old English wagian, to move about, sway, totter: WAG[1] (ii) Old High German waggo, wacko, boulder rolling on a river bed: GRAYWACKE; b. Germanic *wēga-, water in motion, in (i) Old English wǣg, wave: WAVE (ii) Old Low German *wogon, to float, move along in waves: VOGUE; c. Germanic *wig- in (i) Old English wicga, insect (< "thing that moves quickly"): EARWIG (ii) Middle Dutch and Middle Low German wiggelen, to move back and forth, wag: WIGGLE. 8. Basic form *wegh- in Latin vehere (past participle vectus), to carry: VECTOR, VEHICLE; ADVECTION, CONVECTION, EVECTION, INVEIGH. 9. Suffixed form *wegh-s- in Latin vexāre, to agitate (< "to set in motion"): VEX. 10. Probably suffixed form *wegh-so- in Latin convexus, "carried or drawn together (to a point)," convex (com-, together, COM-): CONVEX. [Pok. u̯egh- 1118.]

wegw-. Wet. 1. Germanic *wakw- in Old Norse vök (< *vakvō), a crack in ice (< "wet spot"): WAKE[2]. 2. Suffixed zero-grade form *ugw-sm- in: a. Latin ūmēre, hūmēre, to be wet: HUMECTANT, HUMID; b. Latin ūmor, fluid: HUMOR. 3. Suffixed zero-grade form *ugw-ro- in Greek hugros, wet, liquid: HYGRO-. 4. Regarded by some as an extended form of this root, but more likely a separate root, is *uksen-, ox, in Germanic *uhsōn- in: a. Old English oxa, ox: OX; b. Old High German ohso, ox: AUROCHS. [Pok. u̯egu̯- 1118.]

wegwh-. To preach, speak solemnly. Suffixed o-grade form *wogwh-eyo- in Latin vovēre, to pledge, vow: VOTARY, VOTE, (VOTIVE), VOW; DEVOTE, (DEVOUT). [Pok. eu̯egu̯h- 348.]

wei-[1]. To turn, twist; with derivatives referring to suppleness or binding. I. 1. Germanic suffixed form *wī-ra- in: a. Old English wīr, wire: WIRE; b. Frankish *wiara, *weara, wire, thread: GARLAND. 2. Probably suffixed Germanic form *wai-ra- in Old English wār, seaweed: SEAWARE. 3. Suffixed zero-grade form *wi-ria in Latin viriae, bracelets: FERRULE. 4. Suffixed zero-grade form *wī-ri- perhaps in Greek iris, rainbow, and Iris, rainbow goddess: IRIS. II. 1. Extended zero-grade form *wit- in Germanic *withōn in: a. Old English withig, wiry: WITHY; b. Old English withthe, supple twig: WITHE. 2. Suffixed form *wei-tā in Latin vitta (< *vīta), head band: VITTA. 3. Suffixed form *wei-ti- in Latin vītis, vine: VISE, VITICULTURE. III. Suffixed form *wei-men in Latin vīmen, osier: VIMINAL. IV. Suffixed zero-grade form *wī-n- perhaps in Greek is (genitive inos), sinew: INOSITOL. [Pok. 1. u̯ei- 1120.]

wei-[2]. To go after something. 1. Germanic *waith-, "pursuit," with denominative *waithanjan, to hunt, plunder, in Old French gaaignier, gaigner, to obtain: GAIN[1], ROWEN. 2. Attributed by some to this root, but more likely from *wegh-ya, suffixed form of root **wegh-**, is Latin via, way, road: FOY, VIA, (VIADUCT), VOYAGE; CONVEY, DEVIATE, DEVIOUS, ENVOY, OBVIOUS, PERVIOUS, PREVIOUS, (TRIVIAL), TRIVIUM. [Pok. 3. u̯ei- 1123.]

wei-[3]. To wither. Extended form *weis- in Germanic *wis- in suffixed form *wis-n-ōn in Old English wisnian, to wither, shrivel, shrink: WIZEN[1]. [Pok. 2. u̯ei- 1123.]

wei-[4]. Vice, fault, guilt. 1. Suffixed zero-grade form *wi-tio- in Latin vitium, fault, vice: VICE[1], (VICIOUS), VITIATE. 2. Suffixed form *wi-tu- in: a. Latin vitilīgō, tetter (< "blemish"): VITILIGO; b. Latin vituperāre, to abuse (perhaps formed after Latin recuperāre, to regain, RECUPERATE): VITUPERATE. [Pok. 1. u̯ī- 1175.]

wei-[5]. Vital force. Perhaps related to **wiros**. Zero-grade form *wi- in Latin vīs, force, with irregular derivatives violāre, to treat with force, and violentus, vehement: VIM, VIOLATE, VIOLENT. [In Pok. 3. u̯ei- 1123.]

weid-. To see. I. Full-grade form *weid-. 1. Germanic *wītan, to look after, guard, ascribe to, reproach, in: a. Old English wītan, to reproach: TWIT; b. Frankish *wītan, to look after, show the way, guide: GUIDE; c. Germanic derivative noun *wīti- in Old English wīte, fine, penalty: WITE[1]. 2. Suffixed form *weid-to- in Germanic *wīssaz in: a. Old English wīs, wise: WISE[1]; b. Old English wīsdōm, learning, wisdom (-dōm, abstract suffix, -DOM): WISDOM; c. Old High German wīssago, seer, prophet: WISEACRE; d. Germanic *wīssōn-, appearance, form, manner, in (i) Old English wīse, wīs, manner: WISE[2] (ii) Old French guise, manner: GUISE. 3. Suffixed form *weid-os- in Greek eidos, form, shape: EIDETIC, EIDOLON, IDOCRASE, IDOL, IDYLL, -ODE[2], -OID; KALEIDOSCOPE. 4. Perhaps Greek Haidēs (also Aidēs), the underworld, perhaps "the invisible" (a-, not, A-[1]): HADES[2]. II. Zero-grade form *wid-. 1. Germanic *wit- in: a. Old English wit, witt, knowledge, intelligence: WIT[1]; b. Old English wita, wise man, councilor: WITENAGEMOT. 2. Germanic *witan in Old English witan, to know: WIT[2]; UNWITTING. 3. Suffixed form *wid-to- in Germanic *wissaz, known, in Old English gewis, gewiss, certain, sure: IWIS. 4. Form *wid-ē- (with participial form *weid-to-) in Latin vidēre (past participle vīsus), to see, look: VIDE, VIEW, VISA, VISAGE, VISION, VISTA, VOYEUR; ADVICE, ADVISE, BELVEDERE, CLAIRVOYANCE, ENVY, EVIDENT, INTERVIEW, PREVISE, PROVIDE, REVIEW, SUPERVISE, SURVEY. 5. Suffixed form *wid-es-ya in Greek idea, appearance, form, idea: IDEA, IDEO-. 6. Suffixed form *wid-tor- in Greek histōr, wise, learned, learned man: HISTORY, STORY[1]; POLYHISTOR. 7. Suffixed nasalized zero-grade form *wi-n-d-no- in: a. Old Irish finn, white (< "clearly visible"): COLCANNON; b. Welsh gwyn, gwynn, white: GUINEVERE, PENGUIN. III. Suffixed o-grade form *woid-o- in Sanskrit veda, knowledge, and veda, I have seen, I know: VEDA; GAEKWAR, RIG-VEDA. [Pok. 2. u̯(e)di- 1125.]

weidh-. To divide, separate. 1. Suffixed zero-grade form *widh-ewo-, "woman separated (from her husband by death), bereft," in Germanic *widewaz in Old English widuwe, widow: WIDOW. 2. Zero-grade form *widh- in Latin dīvidere, to separate (dis-, DIS-): DEVISE, DIVIDE, POINT-DEVICE. [Pok. u̯eidh- 1127.]

weik-[1]. Clan (social unit above the household). 1. Suffixed form *weik-slā in Latin vīlla, country house, farm: VILLA. 2. Suffixed o-grade form *woik-o- in: a. Latin vīcus, quarter or district of a town, neighborhood: (VICINAGE), VICINITY, WICK[2]; b. Greek oikos, house, and its derivative oikia, dwelling: ANDROECIUM, AUTOECIOUS, DIOCESE, DIOECIOUS, DIOICOUS, ECESIS, ECOLOGY, ECONOMY, ECUMENICAL, HETEROECIOUS, MONOECIOUS, PARISH, TRIOECIOUS. 3. Zero-grade form *wik- in Sanskrit viś-, dwelling, house, with derivative vaiśya, settler: VAISYA. [Pok. u̯eik̑- 1131.]

weik-[2]. In words connected with magic and religious notions (in Germanic and Latin). 1. Germanic suffixed form *wih-l- in: a. Old English wigle, divination, sorcery, akin to the Germanic source of Old French guile, cunning, trickery: GUILE; b. Old Norse *wihl-, craftiness: WILE. 2. Germanic expressive form *wikk- in: a. Old English wicca, wizard, and wicce, witch: WITCH; b. Old English wiccian, to cast a spell: BEWITCH. 3. Suffixed zero-grade form *wik-tima in Latin victima, animal used as sacrifice, victim: VICTIM. [Pok. 1. u̯eik- 1128.]

weik-[3]. To be like. 1. Suffixed variant form *eik-on- in Greek eikōn, likeness, image: ICON, (ICONIC), (ICONO-); ANISEIKONIA. 2. Prefixed and suffixed zero-grade form *n̥-wik-ēs, not like (*n̥-, not; see **ne**), in Greek aikēs, unseemly: AECIUM. [Pok. 3. u̯eik- 1129.]

weik-[4]. Also **weig-**. To bend, wind. I. Form weig-. 1. Germanic *wik- in: a. Old English wice, wych elm (having pliant branches): WYCH ELM; b. Swedish viker, willow twig, wand: WICKER; c. Old Norse vikja, to bend, turn, probably akin to the Scandinavian source of Old North French wiket, wicket (< "door that turns"): WICKET. 2. Germanic *waikwaz in: a. Old Norse veikr, pliant: WEAK; b. Middle Dutch weec, weak, soft: WEAKFISH. 3. Germanic *wikōn, "a turning," series, in Old English wicu, wice, week: WEEK. II. Form *weik-. Zero-grade form *wik- in: a. Latin vicis, turn, office: VICAR, VICARIOUS, VICE[3]; VICE VERSA, VICISSITUDE; b. Latin vicia, vetch (< "twining plant"): VETCH. [Pok. 4. u̯eik- 1130.]

weik-[5]. To conquer. 1. Germanic *wīk- in: a. Old Norse vīgr, able in battle: WIGHT[2]; b. Old High German name Hluodowīg, "famous in war" (Germanic *hluth-, loud, famous; see **kleu-[1]**): LEWIS, (LOUIS). 2. Nasalized zero-grade form *wi-n-k- in Latin vincere, to conquer: VANQUISH, VICTOR, VINCENT, VINCIBLE; CONVINCE, EVICT. [Pok. 2. u̯eik- 1128.]

weip-. To turn, vacillate. 1. O-grade form *woip- in Germanic *waif- in Old Norse veif, waving thing, flag (which is probably akin to the Scandinavian source of Old North French gaif, vagabond): WAIF[1], WAIF[2]. 2. Variant form *weib- in Germanic *wīpjan, to move back and forth, in: a. Old English wīpian, to wipe: WIPE; b. Frankish *wīpan, to wipe: GUIPURE; c. Middle Dutch and Middle Low German wippen, to swing: WHIP. 3. Perhaps suffixed nasalized zero-grade form *wi-m-p-ila- in: a. Old English wimpel, covering for the neck (< "something that winds around"): WIMPLE; b. Old High German wimpal, head cloth: GIMP[1]; c. perhaps Middle Dutch wimmel, auger (< "that which turns in boring"): GIMLET, WIMBLE. 4. Suffixed zero-grade variant form *wib-ro- in Latin vibrāre, to vibrate: VIBRATE. [Pok. u̯eip- 1131.]

weis-[1]. To flow. I. 1. Germanic *wisōn, waisōn in Old English wāse, mire, mud: OOZE[2]. 2. Suffixed lengthened zero-grade form *wīs-o- in Latin vīrus, slime, poison: VIRUS. 3. Extended zero-grade form *wiks- possibly in Latin viscum, mistletoe, birdlime: VISCID, VISCOUS. II. Attributed by some to this root, but more likely of obscure origin, are some Germanic words for strong-smelling animals. 1. Germanic *wisulōn in Old English weosule, weasel: WEASEL. 2. Suffixed form *wis-onto- in Germanic *wisand-, *wisunt-, European bison (which emits a musky smell in the rutting season), in: a. Old High German wisunt, bison: WISENT; b. Latin bisōn (plural bisontēs), bison: BISON. [Pok. 3. u̯eis- 1134.]

weis-[2]. To turn, bend. Germanic *wisi- in Old English wīr, myrtle. [Pok. 2. u̯eis- 1133.]

weit-. To speak, adjudge. Extended o-grade form *woito- in Old Church Slavonic větu, council (see **sem-[1]**).

wekti-. Thing, creature. Germanic *wihti- in Old English wiht, person, thing: WIGHT[1]; (AUGHT), NAUGHT, NOT. [Pok. u̯ek-ti- 1136.]

wekw-. To speak. 1. O-grade form *wōkw- in: a. Latin vōx (stem vōc-), voice: VOCAL, VOICE, VOWEL; EQUIVOCAL, UNIVOCAL; b. Greek ops, voice: CALLIOPE. 2. O-grade form *wok(w)-ā- in Latin vocāre, to call: VOCABLE, VOCATION, VOUCH; ADVOCATE, AVOCATION, CONVOKE, EVOKE, INVOKE, PROVOKE, REVOKE. 3. Suffixed form *wekw-os- in Greek epos, song, word: EPIC, EPOS. [Pok. u̯eku̯- 1135.]

wel-[1]. To see. 1. Suffixed zero-grade form *wl̥-id- in Germanic *wlituz, appearance, in Old Norse litr, appearance, color, dye: LITMUS. 2. Suffixed form *wel-uno- perhaps in Sanskrit Varuṇa, "seer, wise one," god of the sky: VARUNA. [Pok. 1. u̯el- 1136.]

wel-[2]. To wish, will. 1. Germanic *wel- in Old English wel, well (< "according to one's wish"): WELL[2]. 2. Germanic *welōn- in Old English wela, weola, well-being, riches: WEAL[1], (WEALTH). 3. Germanic *wiljōn- in: a. Old English willa, desire, will power: WILL[1]; b. Old High German willo, will: WILLIAM. 4. Germanic *wil(l)jan in Old English wyllan, to desire: WILL[2]; NILL. 5. Germanic compound *wil-kuma- (see **gwā-**). 6. O-grade form *wol- in Germanic *wal- in Frankish *wala, well: GALA, GALLANT, GALLOP, WALLOP. 7. Basic form *wel- in Latin velle (present stem vol-), to wish, will: VELLEITY, VOLITION, VOLUNTARY; BENEVOLENT, MALEVOLENT. 8. Suffixed form *wel-up- in Latin voluptās, pleasure: (VOLUPTUARY), VOLUPTUOUS. [Pok. 2. u̯el- 1137.]

wel-[3]. To turn, roll; with derivatives referring to curved, enclosing objects. 1. Germanic *walt- in: a. Old High German walzan, to roll, waltz: WALTZ; b. Middle Dutch welteren, to roll: WELTER. 2. Germanic *weluka- in Old English weoluc, mollusk (having a spiral shell), whelk: WHELK[1]. 3. Perhaps Germanic *wel- in Old English welig, willow (with flexible twigs): WILLOW. 4. Perhaps Germanic *welk- in Old English wealcan, to roll, toss, and wealcian, to muffle up: WALK. 5. Perhaps Germanic *wōl- in Frankish *wōlōn, to tie up with cord: GALLOON. 6. O-grade form *wol- in Germanic *wall- in: a. Old English wiella, a well (< "rolling or bubbling water," "spring"): WELL[1]; b. Old High German wallōn, to roam: GABERDINE; c. Norman French walet, bag, "roll": WALLET. 7. Perhaps suffixed o-grade form *wol-ā in Germanic *walō in: a. Old English walu, streak on the skin, weal, welt: WALE; b. Old High German *-walu, a roll, round stem, in *wurzwalu, rootstock (see **wrād-**). 8. Extended form *welw- in: a. Germanic *walwōn in Old English wealwian, to roll (in mud): WALLOW; b. Latin volvere, to roll: VAULT[1], VAULT[2], VOLT[2], VOLUBLE, VOLUME, VOLUTE, VOLVOX, VOUSSOIR; CIRCUMVOLVE, CONVOLVE, DEVOLVE, EVOLVE, INVOLVE, OBVOLUTE, REVOLVE; c. suffixed o-grade form *wolw-ā in Latin vulva, volva, covering, womb: VOLVA, VULVA; d. suffixed zero-grade form *wl̥w-ā- in Latin valva, leaf of a door (< "that which turns"): VALVE; e. suffixed form *welu-tro- in Greek elutron, sheath, cover: ELYTRON. 9. Suffixed form *wel-n- in Greek eilein (< *welnein), to turn: ILEUS, NEURILEMMA. 10. Perhaps variant *wall- in Latin vallēs, vallis, valley (< "that which is surrounded by hills"): VAIL[1], VALE[1], VALLEY. 11. Suffixed form *wel-anā in: a. Greek helenē, wicker basket: INULIN; b. Greek helenion, elecampane: ELECAMPANE. 12. Suffixed form *wel-ik- in Greek helix, spiral object: HELIX. 13. Suffixed form *wel-mi-nth- in Greek helmis, helmins (stem helminth-), parasitic worm: HELMINTH; ANTHELMINTIC, PLATYHELMINTH. 14. O-grade form *wol- in Greek oulos, woolly, curly: ULOTRICHOUS. 15. Attributed by some to this root, but more likely from root **walso-**, is Greek hēlos, stud, nail: MYCELIUM. [Pok. 7. u̯el- 1140.]

wel-[4]. To tear, pull, wound. 1. Germanic *wal- in: a. Old Norse valr, the slain in battle: VALHALLA; b. Old Norse Valkyria, "chooser of the slain," name of one of the twelve war goddesses (-kyria, chooser; see **geus-**): VALKYRIE. 2. Suffixed form *wel-do- in Latin vellere, to tear, pull: AVULSE, CONVULSE, DIVULSION, EVULSION, REVULSION, SVELTE. 3. Suffixed form *wel(ə)-nes- in Latin vulnus (stem vulner-), a wound: VULNERABLE. [Pok. 8. u̯el- 1144.]

wel-[5]. Wool. Probably related to **wel-[4]**. 1. Suffixed extended zero-grade form *wl̥ə-nā in: a. Germanic *wullō in Old English wul(l), wool: WOOL; b. Latin lāna, wool, and its derivative lānūgō, down: LANATE, LANNER, LANOSE; DELAINE, LANOLIN, LANIFEROUS, LANUGO; c. Welsh gwlān, wool: FLANNEL. 2. Suffixed form *wel-nes- in Latin villus, shaggy hair, wool: VELOURS, VELVET, VILLUS. [Pok. 4. u̯el- 1139.]

welk-. Wet. Variant form *welg- in Germanic *welk- in: a. Old English wolc(e)n, cloud, sky: WELKIN; b. Middle Dutch and Middle Low German welken, to become limp (from getting wet): WILT[1]. [Pok. 2. u̯elk- 1145.]

welt-. Woods; wild. 1. Germanic *walthuz in: a. Old English weald, wald, a forest: WEALD, WOLD[1]; b. Old High German wald, a forest: WALDGRAVE; c. Old Norse vǫllr, field: VOLE[1]; d. probably Old English *weald, *wald, "?wild plant," a plant yielding a yellow dye, weld: WELD[2]. 2. Germanic *wilthigaz in: a. Old English wilde, wild: WILD; b. Old English wildēor, wilddēor, wild beast (dēor, animal, DEER): WILDERNESS; c. Middle Dutch wilt, wild: WILDEBEEST. [In Pok. 4. u̯el- 1139.]

wem-. Also **wemə-**. To vomit. 1. Germanic *wam- in Old Norse vamla, qualm, and Danish vamle, to become sick, probably akin to the Scandinavian source of Middle English wam(e)len, to feel nausea, stagger: WAMBLE. 2. Latin vomere, to vomit: VOMIT. 3. Greek emein, to vomit: EMETIC. [Pok. u̯em- 1146.]

wen-. To desire, strive for. 1. Suffixed form *wen-w- in Germanic *winn(w)an, to seek to gain, in Old English winnan, to win: WIN[1]. 2. Suffixed zero-grade form *wn̥-yā in: a. Germanic *wunjō in Old English wynsum, pleasant (-som, -SOME[1]): WINSOME; b. Germanic *wunja- in Old English wynn, pleasure, joy: WEN[2]. 3. Suffixed (stative) zero-grade form *wn̥-ē-, to be contented, in Germanic *wunēn in Old English wunian, to become accustomed to, dwell: WON[1], (WONT). 4. Germanic *wanjan in Old English wenian, to accustom, train, wean: WEAN[1]. 5. Germanic *wēniz, hope, with denominative *wēnjan, to hope, in Old English wēnan, to expect, imagine, think: WEEN. 6. Germanic *wini-, "beloved," in Old English wine, friend, protector: EDWIN, MELVIN. 7. Suffixed zero-grade form *wn̥-sko- in Germanic *wunsk- in Old English wȳscan, to desire, wish: WISH. 8. Suffixed form *wen-es- in: a. Latin venus, love: VENERATE, VENEREAL, VENERY[1], VENUS[1]; b. perhaps Old Norse Vanr, god of fertility: VANIR; c. perhaps Old Norse vana- in Vanadis, name of the goddess Freya: VANADIUM; d. suffixed form *wen-es-no- in Latin venēnum, love potion, poison: VENOM. 9. Suffixed form *wen-eto-, "beloved," possibly in: a. Germanic *Weneda-, a Slavic people, in Old High German Winida, the Wend: WEND; b. Polish Wanda, the Wend, perhaps akin to the Slavic source of the German feminine name Wanda: WANDA; c. Latin Venetī, a people in northern Italy (< "beloved," "one's own people"): VENICE. 10. Suffixed form *wen-yā in Latin venia, favor, forgiveness: VENIAL. 11. Lengthened-grade form *wēn-ā- in Latin vēnārī, to hunt: VENATIC, VENERY[2], VENISON. 12. Suffixed o-grade form *won-o- in Sanskrit vana, forest: WANDEROO. 13. Possibly Sanskrit vāṇija, merchant (? < "seeker"): BANIAN[1]. [Pok. 1. u̯en- 1146.]

wendh-. To turn, wind, weave. 1. Germanic *windan, to wind, in: a. Old English windan, to wind: WIND[2]; b. Old Norse vinda, to wind: WINDLASS. 2. Germanic causative *wandjan in: a. Old English wendan, to turn to: WEND; b. Middle Dutch wenden, to turn: WENTLETRAP. 3. Germanic *wandrōn, to roam about, in: a. Old English wandrian, to wander: WANDER; b. Old High German wandern, to wander: WANDERLUST. 4. Germanic *wand- in: a. Old Norse vǫndr, a supple twig: WAND; b. Germanic *wandliaz, "wanderer," perhaps in Latin Vandalus, a Vandal: VANDAL. 5. Germanic *wind- in Middle Dutch and Middle Low German winde, windlass: WINZE. [Pok. 1. u̯endh 1148.]

weng-. To bend, curve. 1. Germanic *wink- in Old English wincian, to close the eyes (< "to bend down the eyelids"): WINK. 2. Germanic *winkja in Old English wince, a reel, roller: WINCH. 3. Germanic *winkil- in Old English -wincel, spiral shell: PERIWINKLE[1]. 4. Germanic *wankil- in: a. Old English wencel, youth, maid (< "inconstant one"): WENCH; b. Old English wancol, inconstant, unsteady: WANGLE, WONKY. 5. Germanic *wankj- in: a. Frankish *wenkjan, to turn aside: GAUCHE; b. Norman French *wencir, to turn aside, avoid: WINCE. [Pok. u̯e-n-g- 1148.]

[**wēpnam.** Weapon. Germanic root. 1. Old English wǣp(e)n, weapon: WEAPON. 2. Old Norse vāpn, weapon: WAPENTAKE.]

wer-[1]. High, raised spot. 1. Suffixed form *wer-d- in Germanic *wartōn- in Old English wearte, wart: WART. 2. Possibly Germanic *war- in obsolete Swedish varbulde, "pus swelling" (bulde, swelling; see **bhel-[2]**), akin to the source of WARBLE[2]. 3. Suffixed and extended zero-grade form *wr̥su-ko- in Latin verrūca, a wart: VERRUCA. [Pok. 2. u̯er- 1151.]

wer-[2]. Also **swer-**. To bind, hang on the scale; heavy. 1. Suffixed lengthened-grade form *swēr-yo- in Latin sērius, serious, grave: SERIOUS. 2. Attributed by some to this root are Greek aeirein, to raise, and Greek artēria, artery, which, while related to each other, are more likely of obscure origin: AORTA, ARSIS, ARTERY, METEOR. [Pok. 1. u̯er- 1150.]

wer-[3]. Base of various Indo-European roots; to turn, bend. I. Root **wert-**, to turn, wind. 1. Germanic *werth- in: a. Germanic variant *warth- in (i) Old English -weard, toward (< "turned toward"): -WARD (ii) Germanic *inwarth, inward (*in, in; see **en**), in Old English inweard, inward: INWARD. b. perhaps Germanic derivative *werthoz, "toward, opposite," hence "equivalent, worth," in Old English weorth, worth, valuable, and derivative noun weorth, value: WORTH[1]; STALWART. 2. Germanic *werthan, "to become" (< "to turn into"), in Old English weorthan, to befall: WORTH[2]. 3. Zero-grade form *wr̥t- in Germanic *wurth- in: a. Old English wyrd, fate, destiny (< "that which befalls one"): WEIRD; b. suffixed form *wr̥t-s-ti- in Germanic *wurst- in Old High German wurst, sausage (< "rolled thing"): WURST; (LIVERWURST). 4. Latin vertere, to turn, with its frequentative versāre, to turn, and passive versārī, to stay (< "to move around a place, frequent"): VERSATILE, VERSE[1], VERSION, VERSUS, VERTEBRA, VERTEX, VERTIGO, VORTEX; ADVERSE, ANNIVERSARY, AVERT, CONTROVERSY, CONVERSE[1], CONVERT, DEXTRORSE, DIVERT, EVERT, EXTROVERSION, EXTROVERT, INTRORSE, INTROVERT, INVERT, MALVERSATION, OBVERT, PERVERT, PROSE, RETRORSE, REVERT, SINISTRORSE, SUBVERT, SUZERAIN, TERGIVERSATE, TRANSVERSE, UNIVERSE, VICE VERSA. 5. Balto-Slavic *wirstā, a turn, bend, in Russian versta, line: VERST. II. Root **wreit-**, to turn. Germanic *wrīth-, *wraith- in: a. Old English writha, band (< "that which is wound around"): WREATH; b. Old English wrīthan, to twist, torture: WRITHE; c. Old English wrāth, angry (< "tormented, twisted"): WRATH, WROTH. III. Root **wergh-**, to turn. 1. Germanic *wurgjan in Old English wyrgan, to strangle: WORRY. 2. Nasalized variant *wrengh- in: a. Germanic *wreng- in Old English wringan, to twist: WRING; b. Germanic *wrang- in (i) Old Norse *vrangr, rangr, curved, crooked, wrong: WRONG (ii) Low German wrangeln, to wrestle, akin to the Low German source of Middle English wranglen, to wrangle: WRANGLE. IV. Root **werg-**, to turn. 1. Nasalized variant form *wreng- in Germanic *wrankjan in: a. Old English wrencan, to twist: WRENCH; b. Old English gewrinclian, to wind (ge-, collective prefix; see **kom**): WRINKLE[1]. 2. Latin vergere, to turn, tend toward: VERGE[2]; CONVERGE, DIVERGE. V. Root **wreik-**, to turn. 1. Germanic *wrīg- in: a. Old English wrīgian, to turn, bend, go: WRY; b. Middle Low German wriggeln, to wriggle: WRIGGLE. 2. Germanic *wrihst- whence *wristiz in: a. Old English wrist, wrist: WRIST; b. Frankish *wrist, instep: GAITER. 3. Possibly o-grade form *wroik- in Gaulish *brūko, heather: BRIAR[1], BRUSQUE. VI. Root **wrizd-**, to turn, bend. Germanic *wraistjan in Old English wrǣstan, to twist, and its frequentative *wrǣstlian, to wrestle: WREST, WRESTLE. VII. Root **wreip-**, to turn. Germanic *wrīb- in Old High German rīban, to rub, be in heat, copulate: RIBALD. VIII. Root **werb-**, also **werbh-**, to turn, bend. 1. Germanic *werp-, *warp-, "to fling by turning the arm," in Old English weorpan, to throw away: WARP. 2. Latin verbera, whips, rods: REVERBERATE. 3. Latin verbēna, sacred foliage: VERVAIN, (VERBENA). 4. Zero-grade form *wr̥b- in Greek rhabdos, rod: RHABDOMANCY. 5. Nasalized variant form *wrembh- in Greek rhombos, magic wheel: RHOMBUS. IX. Root **werp-**, to turn, wind. 1. Metathesized form *wrep- in Germanic *wrap- in Danish dialectal vravle, to wind, akin to the source of Middle English wrappen, to wrap: WRAP. 2. Zero-grade form *wr̥p- in Greek rhaptein, to sew (< "to wind around"): RAPHE, RAPHIDE, RHAPSODY, STAPHYLORRHAPHY, TENORRHAPHY. X. Root **wermi-**, worm. 1. Germanic *wurmiz in: a. Old English wyrm, worm: WORM; b. Frankish *worm, worm: GROMMET. 2. Latin vermis, worm: VERMEIL, VERMI-, VERMICELLI, VERMICULAR, VERMIN. [Pok. 3. u̯er- 1152.]

wer-[4]. To perceive, watch out for. I. O-grade form *wor-. 1. Suffixed form *wor-o- in Germanic *waraz in: a. Old English wær, watchful: WARY; b. Old English gewær, aware (ge-, collective and intensive prefix; see **kom**): AWARE; c. Old English warian, to beware: WARE[2]; d. Norman French ware, beware (interjection): WARDER[2]. 2. Suffixed form *wor-to- in Germanic *wardaz, guard, and *wardōn, to guard, in: a. Old English weard, a watching, keeper: WARD; EDWARD[1], STEWARD; b. Norman French and Old North French warder, to guard: WARDEN, WARDROBE; AWARD, REWARD; c. Old French guarder, to guard: GUARD; d. Norman French warde, guard: REARWARD[2]. 3. Germanic *warō in Old English waru, goods, protection, guard: WARE[1]. 4. Suffixed form *wor-wo- in Greek ouros, a guard: ARCTURUS. 5. Variant *(s)wor- in Greek horan, to see: EPHOR, PANORAMA. II. Suffixed (stative) form *wer-ē- in Latin verērī, to respect, feel awe for: REVERE[1]. [Pok. 8. u̯er- 1164.]

wer-[5]. To cover. I. Basic form *wer-. 1. Germanic *werjōn- in Old English wer, dam, fish trap: WEIR. 2. Compound form *ap-wer-yo- (*ap-, off, away; see **apo-**) in Latin aperīre, to open, uncover: APERIENT, APÉRITIF, APERTURE; MALAPERT, OVERT, OVERTURE, PERT. 3. Compound form *op-wer-yo- (*op-, over; see **epi**) in Latin operīre, to cover: COVER, OPERCULUM. II. O-grade form *wor-. 1. Germanic *war-n- in Old English w(e)arnian, to take heed: WARN. 2. Germanic *-warii in Old English -ware, inhabitant (< "defender"): CANTERBURY. 3. Germanic *war- in: a. Frankish *warjan, to protect, to vouch for the truth of: GUARANTEE, WARRANT; b. Frankish *warōn, to guard, protect: GARAGE; c. Old French g(u)arir, to defend, protect: GARRET, GARRISON; d. Old North French warenne, enclosure, game preserve: WARREN; e. Old French g(u)arnir, to equip: GARMENT, GARNISH. [Pok. 5. u̯er- 1160.]

wer-[6]. To speak. 1. Suffixed zero-grade form *wr̥-dho- in Germanic *wurdam in Old English word, word: WORD. 2. Suffixed form *wer-dho- in Latin verbum, word: VERB, VERVE; ADVERB, PROVERB. 3. Suffixed form *wer-yo- in Greek eirein, to say, speak: IRONY[1]. 4. Variant form *wrē- in: a. suffixed form *wrē-mn̥ in Greek rhēma, word, verb: RHEMATIC; b. suffixed form *wrē-tor- in Greek rhētōr, public speaker: RHETOR. [Pok. 6. u̯er- 1162.]

wer-[7]. Water. 1. Suffixed variant form *eur-inā in Latin ūrīna, urine: URINE. 2. Extended o-grade form *wors- in Greek ouron, urine: URETER, URETHRA, URETIC, -URIA, URO-[1], -URONIC; DIURETIC, ENURESIS. [In Pok. 9. au̯(e)- 78.]

wer-[8]. Wide, broad. Suffixed form *wer-os in Greek eurus, wide: EURY-; ANEURYSM. [Pok. 8. u̯er- 1165.]

wer-[9]. To burn. Suffixed lengthened o-grade form *wōr-eyo- in Old Church Slavonic variti, to boil: SAMOVAR. [Pok. 12. u̯er- 1166.]

wer-[10]. Squirrel. Reduplicated expressive form *wī-wer(r)- in Latin vīverra, a ferret: VIVERRINE. [Pok. 13. u̯er- 1166.]

wer-[11]. To find. Reduplicated form *we-wr- in Greek heuriskein, to find: EUREKA, HEURISTIC. [Pok. 4. u̯er- 1160.]

werād-. Branch, root. I. Reduced form *wrād- in Germanic *wrōt- in Old Norse rōt, root: ROOT[1], RUTABAGA. II. Zero-grade form *wr̥əd-. 1. Germanic *wurtiz in: a. Old English wyrt, plant, herb: WORT; b. Old High German wurzala (< *wurzwala, rootstock; *-wala, a roll, round stem; see **wel-[3]**), root: MANGELWURZEL. 2. Latin rādix, root: RACE[3], RADICAL, RADICLE, RADISH, RADIX; DERACINATE, ERADICATE. 3. Suffixed form *wr̥əd-mo- in Latin rāmus, branch: RAMIFY, RAMOSE, RAMUS. 4. Suffixed reduced form *wr̥d-ya perhaps in Greek rhiza, root: RHIZO-, RHIZOME; COLEORHIZA, LICORICE, MYCORRHIZA. [Pok. u̯(e)rād- 1167.]

werdh-. To grow. Possibly (but more likely of obscure origin) Greek orthos, straight, correct, right: ORTHO-; ANORTHITE. [Pok. u̯erdh- 1167.]

werg-[1]. To do. I. Suffixed form *werg-o-. 1. Germanic *werkam, work, in: a. Old English weorc, werc, work: WORK; b. Old High German werc, work: BULWARK, (BOULEVARD). 2. Greek ergon, work, action: ARGON, ERG, -URGY; ADRENERGIC, ALLERGY, CHOLINERGIC, DEMIURGE, DRAMATURGE, ENERGY, ERGOGRAPH, EXERGUE, GEORGIC, LITURGY, METAL-

LURGY, SURGERY, SYNERGISM, THAUMATURGE.
II. Zero-grade form *wṛg-. **1.** Germanic
*wurg- in Old Norse *yrkja*, to work: IRK.
2. Suffixed form *wṛg-t- in Germanic *wurhtjō-
in Old English *wryhta*, maker, wright: WRIGHT.
III. O-grade form *worg- in: **a.** Greek *organon*
(with suffix *-ano-*), tool: ORGAN, ORGANON; **b.**
Greek *orgia*, secret rites, worship (< "service"): ORGY. [Pok. 2. *uerg-* 1168.]

werg-². Basic meaning uncertain. Suffixed
o-grade form *worg-ā- in Greek *organ*, to
swell: ORGASM. [Pok. 3. *uerg-* 1169.]

wēros. Stem wēro-. True. **1.** Germanic *wēra-
in: **a.** Old English *wǣr*, faith, pledge: WAR-
LOCK; **b.** Old Norse *vár*, agreement, pledge:
VARANGIAN. **2.** Latin *vērus*, true, with its derivative *vērax*, truth: VERACIOUS, VERISM, VERI-
TY, VERY; AVER, VERDICT, VERIDICAL, VERIFY,
VERISIMILAR, VERONICA, VOIR DIRE. **3.** Latin
sevērus, grave, serious (regarded by some as a
compound of *se-*, *sed*, without; see **seu-**. and
vērus, true, but the semantic difficulties make
this explanation improbable): SEVERE; AS-
SEVERATE, PERSEVERE. **4.** Russian *vjera*, faith:
VERA. [Pok. 11. *uer-* 1165.]

wers-. To confuse. **1.** Germanic *werr- in: **a.**
Old High German *werra*, confusion, strife:
WAR; **b.** Spanish *guerra*, war: GUERRILLA.
2. Germanic comparative *wersizōn- in Old
English *wyrsa*, worse: WORSE. **3.** Germanic
superlative *wersista in Old English *wyrsta*,
worst: WORST. [Pok. *uers-* 1169.]

wes-¹. To buy. **1.** Suffixed form *wes-no- in
Latin *vēnum*, sale: VENAL, VEND. **2.** Suffixed
o-grade form *wos-nā- in Greek *ōnē*, a buying:
DUOPSONY. [Pok. 8. *ues-* 1173.]

wes-². Wet. Germanic *wōs- in Old English
wōs, juice: OOZE¹. [Pok. 3. *ues-* 1171.]

wes-³. To delay, dwell, stay the night, with derivatives meaning "to be." **1.** O-grade form
*wos- in Germanic *wos- in Old English *wæs*,
wǣre, *wǣron*, was, were (singular), were (plural): WAS, WERE (for text etymologies, see **be**).
2. Germanic *wes- in Old Norse *vesa*, *vera*, to
be: WASSAIL. **3.** Suffixed form *wes-tā- perhaps in Latin *Vesta*, household goddess: VES-
TA¹. **4.** Suffixed variant form *was-tu- possibly
in Greek *astu*, town (< "place where one
dwells"), whence Latin *astus*, skill, craft (practiced in a town): ASTUTE. [Pok. 1. *ues-* 1170.]

wes-⁴. To clothe. Extensions of eu-¹ (*əw-es-
< *əeu- < *eu-). **1.** Suffixed o-grade form
*wos-eyo- in Germanic *wazjan in Old English
werian, to wear, carry: WEAR¹. **2.** Suffixed
form *wes-ti- in Latin *vestis*, garment: VEST;
DEVEST, INVEST, REVEST, TRANSVESTITE, TRAV-
ESTY. **3.** Suffixed form *wes-nu- in Greek *hennunai*, to clothe: HIMATION. [Pok. 5. *ues-*
1172.]

wespero-. Evening, night. **I.** Reduced form
*wes-. **1.** Suffixed form *wes-to- in Germanic
*west- in: **a.** Old English *west*, west: WEST; **b.**
Old English *westerne*, western: WESTERN; **c.**
Old English *westra*, more westerly: WESTERLY.
2. Possibly Germanic *wis- in Late Latin *Visigothi*, "West Goths" (*Gothi*, the GOTHS): VISI-
GOTH. **II.** Basic form *wespero-. **1.** Latin *vesper*, evening: VESPER. **2.** Greek *hesperos*, evening: HESPERIA. [Pok. *uesperos* 1173.]

wesṛ. Spring. **1.** Latin *vēr*, spring: VERNAL,
PRIMAVERA. **2.** Greek *ēr*, ear, spring: ERYNGO.
[Pok. *ues-ṛ* 1174.]

wet-. Year. **1.** Suffixed form *wet-ru- in Germanic *wethruz*, perhaps "yearling," in Old
English *wether*, wether: WETHER. **2.** Suffixed
form *wet-es- in: **a.** Latin *vetus*, old (< "having many years"): VETERAN, INVETERATE; **b.**
Latin *veterīnus*, of beasts of burden, of cattle
(perhaps chiefly old cattle): VETERINARY; **c.**
Greek *etos*, year: ETESIAN. **3.** Suffixed form
*wet-olo- in Latin *vitulus*, calf, yearling: VEAL,
VITELLUS. [Pok. *uet-* 1175.]

wi-. Apart, in half. **1.** Suffixed form *wi-itos
in Germanic *widaz in Old English *wīd*, wide
(< "far apart"): WIDE. **2.** Suffixed (comparative) form *wi-tero- in Germanic *withrō,
against, in: **a.** Old English *wither*, against, with
its derivative *with*, with, against: WITH, WITH-
ERS; **b.** Old High German *widar*, against:
GUERDON, WITHERSHINS. [Pok. 1. *uī* 1175.]

widhu-. Tree. **1.** Germanic *widu- in Old English *wudu*, wood: WOOD¹. **2.** Old Welsh *gwydd*,
wild (< "of the forest"): GAEL, GOIDELIC.
[Pok. *uidhu-* 1177.]

wikṃti. Twenty. Compound of **wi-**, in half,

hence two, and kṃt, reduced zero-grade form
of dekṃ. **1.** Latin *vigintī*, twenty: VICENARY,
VICENNAL, VIGESIMAL. **2.** Greek *eikosi*, twenty:
ICOSAHEDRON. **3.** Sanskrit *viṃśati*, twenty:
PACHISI. [Pok. *uī-kṃt-ī* 1177.]

wiros. Man. Perhaps related to wei-⁵. **1.** Germanic *weraz in: **a.** Old English *wer*, man:
WEREWOLF, WERGELD; **b.** Germanic compound
weraldh-, "life or age of man" (-aldh-, age;
see al-³), in Old English *weorold*, world:
WORLD; **c.** Frankish *werwulf, "man-wolf"
(*wulf, wolf; see wḷkwo-): LOUP-GAROU.
2. Latin *vir*, man: VIRAGO, VIRILE, VIRTUE; DE-
CEMVIR, DUUMVIR, TRIUMVIR. **3.** Possibly Latin
cūria, curia, court, if regarded as from *co-vir,
"men together" (*co-, together; see kom): CU-
RIA. [Pok. *uīro-s* 1177.]

wleik-. See leikw-.

wḷkwo-. Wolf. **1.** Taboo variant *wḷpo- in
Germanic *wulfaz in: **a.** Old English *wulf*, wolf:
WOLF; **b.** Old Norse *ulfr*, wolf: RALPH; **c.**
Middle Dutch *wolf*, *wulf*, wolf: AARDWOLF; **d.**
Old High German *wolf*, wolf: ADOLPH; WOLF-
RAM; **e.** Frankish *wulf, wolf (see wiros).
2. Taboo variant *lupo- in Latin *lupus*, wolf:
LOBO, LOUP², LUPINE; LOUP-GAROU. **3.** Taboo
variant *lukwo- in Greek *lukos*, wolf: LYCAN-
THROPE, LYCOPODIUM. [Pok. *uḷkuos* 1178.]

wḷp-. Fox, wolf. **1.** Latin *vulpes*, fox: VULPINE.
2. Greek *alōpēx*, fox: ALOPECIA. [Pok. *uḷp,
lup* 1179.]

wogwhni-. Plowshare, wedge. **1.** Perhaps
Germanic *wagjaz in Old English *wecg*, wedge:
WEDGE. **2.** Probably Latin *vōmer*, plowshare:
VOMER. [Pok. *uoguhni-s* 1179.]

wokso-. Wax. Related to weg-¹. Germanic
*wahsam in Old English *wæx*, *weax*, wax:
WAX¹. [Pok. *uokso-* 1180.]

wopsā. Wasp. Metathesized form *wospā.
1. Germanic *wosp- in Old English *wæsp*,
wasp: WASP. **2.** Latin *vespa*, wasp: VESPIARY.
[Pok. *uobhsā* 1179.]

wōs. You (plural). Latin *vōs*, you: RENDEZ-
VOUS. [In Pok. 1. *iu-* 513.]

wrāgh-. Thorn, tip. Greek *rhakhis*, ridge,
spine: RACHIS. [Pok. 1. *urāgh-* 1180.]

wreg-. To push, shove, drive, track down.
I. Basic form *wreg- in Germanic *wrekan in:
a. Old English *wrecan*, to drive, expel: WREAK;
b. Old Norse *rek* (older form *vrek*), wreckage,
akin to the Scandinavian source of Norman
French *wrec*, wreck: WRECK. **II.** O-grade form
*wrog-. **1.** Germanic *wrakjō, "pursuer, one
pursued," in: **a.** Old English *wrecca*, exile:
WRETCH; **b.** Frankish *wrakjō, "one pursued,
an exile": GASKET. **2.** Germanic *wrak- in: **a.**
Old English *wræc*, exile, punishment, and
Middle Dutch *wrak*, wreckage: WRACK¹; **b.**
Swedish *rak*, wreckage, akin to the source of
Middle English *rak*, mass of driven clouds:
RACK³. **III.** Zero-grade form *wrg-ē- in Latin
urgēre, to urge, drive: URGE. [Pok. *ureg-*
1181.]

wrēg-. To break. Suffixed form *wrēg-nu- in
Greek *rhēgnunai*, to burst forth: -RRHAGIA.
[Pok. *urēg-* 1181.]

[wrod-. Rose. A word (not common Indo-
European) of unknown origin. **1.** Suffixed
form *wrod-o- in Greek *rhodon*, rose: RHODI-
UM, RHODO-. **2.** Suffixed form *wrod-ya- (perhaps via Etruscan) in Latin *rosa*, rose: ROSE¹.
3. Zero-grade form *wṛd- in Iranian *wṛd in
Persian *gul*, rose: JULEP.]

wrōd-. To root, gnaw. Germanic *wrōt- in Old
English *wrōtan*, to dig up: ROOT². [Pok. 7.
uer- 1163.]

wrughyo-. Rye. Germanic *rugi- in Old English *ryge*, rye: RYE¹. [Pok. *urughio-* 1183.]

[xenos. Strange; stranger. Greek word (earlier
form *xenwos) of unknown origin: XENO-;
EUXENITE, PYROXENE.]

yā-. To be aroused. Suffixed form *yā-lo- in
Greek *zēlos*, zeal: JEALOUS, ZEAL. [Pok. *iā-
501.]

yag-. To worship; reverence. **1.** Suffixed form
*yag-yo- perhaps in Greek *hagios*, holy:
HAGIO-. **2.** Suffixed form *yag-no- perhaps in
Greek *hagnos*, chaste, sacred: AGNES. [Pok.
iag- 501.]

yē-. To throw. **1.** Extended zero-grade form
*yək-ē- in Latin *jacere*, to throw, lay, with its
derivative *jacēre*, to lie down (< "to be
thrown"): JACTATION, JESS, JET²; JOIST; ABJECT,
ADJACENT, ADJECTIVE, AGIST, AMICE, CON-
JECTURE, DEJECT, DISJECT, EASE, EJACULATE,

EJECT, GIST, INJECT, INTERJECT, OBJECT¹, PAR-
GET, PROJECT, REJECT, SUBJACENT, SUBJECT,
SUPERJACENT, TRAJECT. **2.** Zero-grade form
*yə- in Greek *hienai*, to send, throw: CATHE-
TER, DIESIS, ENEMA, PARESIS, SYNESIS. [Pok.
iē- 502.]

yeg-. Ice. Germanic *jakilaz, *jekilaz, in Old
English *gicel*, icicle, ice: ICICLE. [Pok. *ieg-*
503.]

yēgwā. Power, youthful strength. Greek *hēbē*,
youth, youthful vigor: HEBE; EPHEBE, HEBE-
PHRENIA. [Pok. *iēguā* 503.]

yek-. To speak. Suffixed o-grade form *yok-o-
in Latin *jocus*, joke: JEWEL, JOCOSE, JOCULAR,
JOKE, JUGGLER, JEOPARDY. [Pok. *iek-* 503.]

yēk-. To heal. Attributed by some to this root
is Greek *akos*, cure, which is more likely obscure: AUTACOID, PANACEA. [Pok. *iek-* 504.]

yekwṛ. Liver. **1.** Greek *hēpar*, liver: HEPARIN,
HEPATIC, HEPATITIS, HEPATOGENIC. **2.** Persian
jigar, liver: GIZZARD. [Pok. *ieku-ṛt* 504.]

yem-. To pair. Perhaps altered into Latin
geminus, twin: GEMINI, GIMMAL; BIGEMINAL,
TRIGEMINUS. [Pok. *iem-* 505.]

yēro-. Year, season. **1.** Basic form *yē-ro- in
Germanic *jēram in Old English *gēar*, year:
YEAR. **2.** O-grade form *yō-ro- in Greek *hōros*,
time: GHERKIN. **3.** Variant o-grade form
*yō-rā in Greek *hōrā*, season: HOUR, (HORO-
SCOPE). [In Pok. 1. *ei-* 293.]

yes-. To boil, foam, bubble. **1.** Germanic
*jest in Old English *gist*, yeast: YEAST.
2. Greek *zeein*, *zein*, to boil: ECZEMA, ZEOLITE.
[Pok. *ies-* 506.]

yeu-¹. To blend, mix food. Extended variant
form *yūs- in: **a.** Latin *jūs*, juice, broth: JUICE;
b. suffixed form *yūs-mā in Greek *zumē*, leav-
en: -ZYME, ZYMO-; ENZYME. [Pok. 1. *ieu-* 507.]

yeu-². Young. **1.** Suffixed form *yew-ṇk-. **a.**
Germanic *juwungaz in *jungaz in (i) Old
English *geong*, young: YOUNG (ii) Old High
German *jung*, young: JUNKER (iii) compound
*jung-frowa, young lady (see per¹); **b.** Ger-
manic *jugunth- in Old English *geoguth*, youth:
YOUTH. **2.** Suffixed form *yew-ṇko- in Old
Irish *ōac*, young: GALLOWGLASS. **3.** Extended
zero-grade form *yuwen- in Latin *juvenis*,
young: JUNIOR, JUVENAL, JUVENILE; REJUVE-
NATE. See also aiw-. [Pok. 3. *ieu-* 510.]

yeudh-. To move violently, fight. Zero-grade
form *yudh-ē- in Latin *jubēre*, to command (<
"to set in motion"): JUSSIVE. [Pok. *ieu-dh-
511.]

yeug-. To join. **I.** Zero-grade form *yug-.
1. Suffixed form *yug-o- in: **a.** Germanic
*yukam in Old English *geoc*, yoke: YOKE; **b.**
Latin *jugum*, yoke: JUGATE, JUGULAR, JUGUM;
CONJUGATE, SUBJUGATE; **c.** Greek *zugon*, yoke:
ZYGO-, ZYGOMA, -ZYGOUS; AZYGOUS, SYZYGY;
d. Sanskrit *yuga*, yoke: YUGA. **2.** Suffixed
(superlative) form *yug-istos in Latin *jugistā
(via), "on a nearby (road)," contracted to
*juxtā, close by: JOUST; ADJUST, JUXTAPOSITION.
3. Nasalized form *yu-n-g- in Latin *jungere*, to
join: JOIN, JUNCTION, JUNCTURE, JUNTA; AD-
JOIN, CONJOIN, CONJUGAL, CONJUNCT, ENJOIN,
INJUNCTION, SUBJOIN. **II.** Suffixed form
*yeug-mn- in Greek *zeugma*, a bond: ZEUGMA.
III. Suffixed o-grade form *youg-o- in Sanskrit
yoga, union: YOGA. [Pok. 2. *ieu-* 508.]

yewo-¹. Also **yewes-.** Law. **1.** Latin *jūs*, law,
and its derivative *jūrāre*, "to pronounce a
ritual formula," swear: JURAL, JURIST, JURY¹;
ABJURE, ADJURE, CONJURE, INJURY, JURIDICAL,
JURISCONSULT, JURISDICTION, JURISPRUDENCE,
OBJURGATE, PERJURE. **2.** Compound form
*yewes-deik-, "one who shows or pronounces
the law" (see deik-), in Latin *jūdex, judge:
JUDGE; ADJUDICATE, (PREJUDICE). **3.** Suffixed
form *yewes-to- in Latin *jūstus*, just: JUST¹.
[Pok. *ieuos* 512.]

yewo-². Grain. Suffixed reduced form *yew-ya
in Greek *zeia*, one-seeded wheat: ZEIN. [Pok.
ieuo- 512.]

yōs-. To gird. **1.** Suffixed form *yōs-ter- in
Greek *zōstēr*, girdle: ZOSTER. **2.** Suffixed form
*yōs-nā in Greek *zōnē*, girdle: ZONE, EVZONE.
[Pok. *iō(u)s-* 513.]

yu-¹. You. Second person (plural) pronoun.
Germanic *jūz (nominative) and *iwwiz (ob-
lique) in Old English *gē* and *ēow*, you: YE²,
YOU. [Pok. 1. *iu-* 513.]

yu-². Outcry (of exultation). **1.** Latin *jūbilāre*,
to raise a shout of joy: JUBILATE. **2.** Greek
iuzein, to cry, call: JINX. [Pok. 2. *iu-* 514.]

Table of Indo-European Sound Correspondences

This table shows the correspondences between initial consonants in the principal older Indo-European languages. For example, in the first row, it can be seen that Latin initial *p* corresponds to Old English initial *f*: compare Latin *piscis*, "fish," and Old English *fisc*, "fish." An alternative way of describing this situation is to say that Indo-European initial *p* remained *p* in Latin but became *f* in Germanic and thus in Old English; Indo-European ***peisk**- or ***pisk**-, "fish," became Latin *piscis* and Germanic *fiska-, Old English *fisc*. These correspondences are regular; they always occur as stated unless specific factors intervene. This table shows only the initial consonants, which are generally the simplest element involved in sound change. All other phonetic elements including stress and environment show equally regular correspondences, but often with considerable complexity.

INDO-EUROPEAN		Hittite	Tocharian	Sanskrit	Avestan	Old Persian	Old Church Slavonic	Lithuanian	Armenian	Greek	Latin	Old Irish	Common Germanic	Gothic	Old English	Old Norse	Old High German	Middle Dutch
	p	p	p	p	p	p	p	p	p	hw	p	p	*-	f	f	f	f	f	v
unvoiced	t	t	t	t	t	t	t	t	t	th	t	t	t	th	th	th	th	d	th/d
	k	k	k	ś	s	th	s	s	s	k	c	c	h	h(j)	h	h	h	h
	kw	ku	k	k/c	k/c	k	k/č/c k	kh	p/t/k	qu	c	hw	hw/w	hw	hv	hw/w	w
	b	p	p	b	b	b	b	b	p	b	b	b	p	p	p	p	p/pf	p
Stops voiced	d	t	t(c)	d	d	d	d	d	t	d	d	d	t	t	t	z	t
	g	k	k	j	z/g	g/d	z	z	c	g	g	g	k	k	k	k	k	k
	gw	ku	k	g/j	g/j	g/j	g/ž/z g	k	b/d/g	v/gu	b	kw/k	qu	cw/k	kv	qu	qu
	bh	p	p	bh	b	b	b	b	b	ph	f(b)	b	b	b	b	b	b	b
voiced aspirate	dh	t	t	dh	d	d	d	d	d	th	f(d)	d	d	d	d	d	t/d	d
	gh	k	k	h	g/z	g/d	z	z	z(j)	kh	h	g	g	g	g	g	g	g
	gwh	ku	k	gh/h	g/j	g/j	g/ž/z g	g	ph th/kh	f	g	gw/w	w	w	w	w	w
Continuant	s	s	s	s	s	h	h	s	s	h	h	s	s	s	s	s	s	s
nasals	m	m	m	m	m	m	m	m	m	m	m	m	m	m	m	m	m	m
	n	n	n	n	n	n	n	n	n	n	n	n	n	n	n	n	n	n
Sonorants liquids	r	r	r	r/l	r	r	r	r	r	r	r	r	r	r	r	r	r	r
	l	l	l	l	l/r	r	r	l	l	l	l	l	l	l	l	l	l	l
glides	i/y	y	y	y	y	y	y	y	j	j	y	h/z	j	*-	j	j	g(y)	*-	j	g
	w/u	w	w	v	v	v	v	v	v	g/v	*-	v	f	w	w	w	w	v	w

*- equals zero: w was lost in Greek.
y was lost in Old Irish, Old Norse.

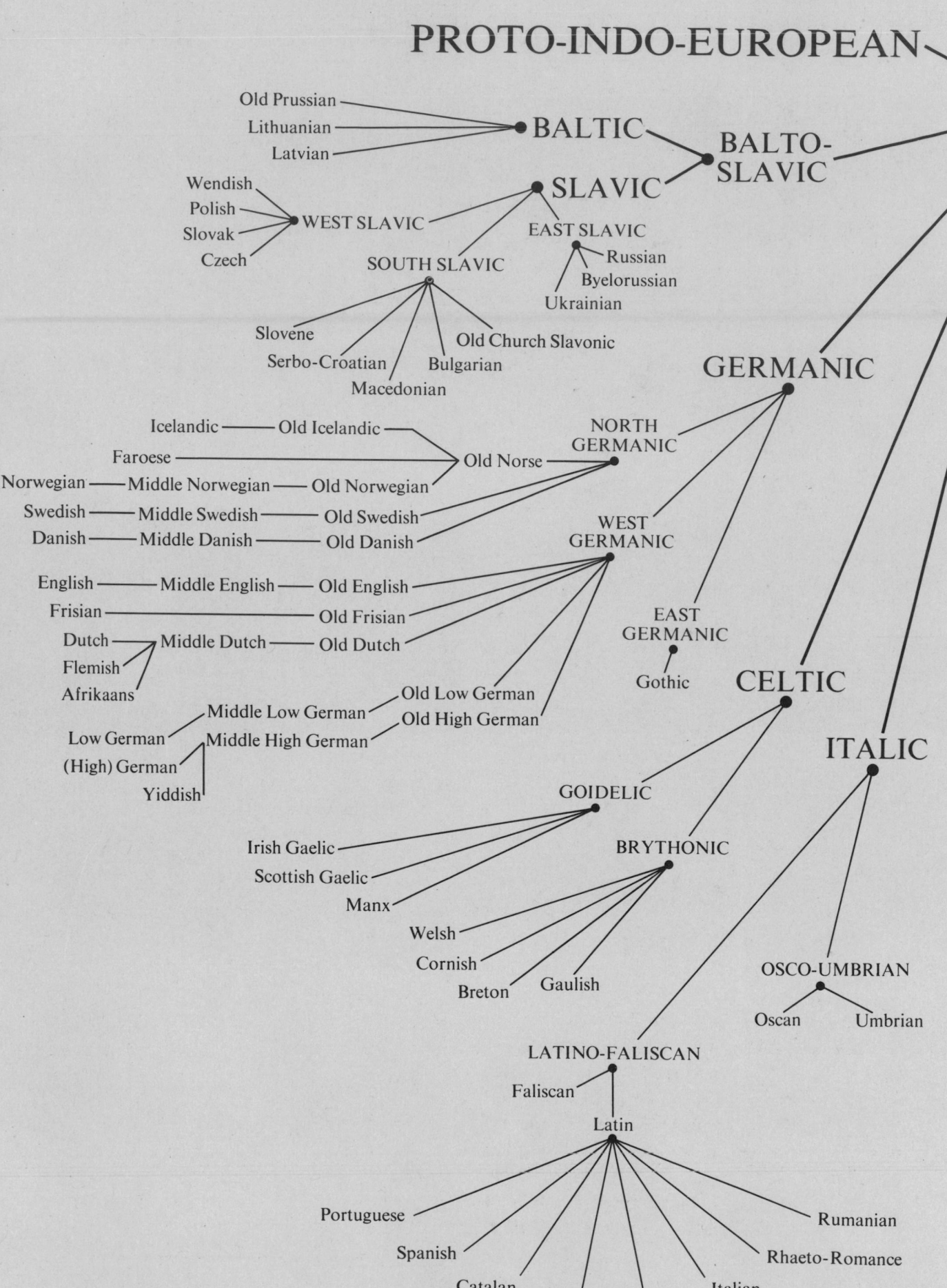